PETERSON'S®
GRADUATE PROGRAMS IN BUSINESS, EDUCATION, INFORMATION STUDIES, LAW & SOCIAL WORK

2020

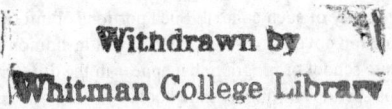

About Peterson's

Peterson's® has been your trusted educational publisher for over 50 years. It's a milestone we're quite proud of, as we continue to offer the most accurate, dependable, high-quality educational content in the field, providing you with everything you need to succeed. No matter where you are on your academic or professional path, you can rely on Peterson's for its books, online information, expert test-prep tools, the most up-to-date education exploration data, and the highest quality career success resources—everything you need to achieve your education goals. For our complete line of products, visit **www.petersons.com**.

For more information about Peterson's range of educational products, contact Peterson's, 8740 Lucent Blvd., Suite 400 Highlands Ranch, CO 80129, or find us online at **www.petersons.com**.

CONTENTS

CONTENTS

A Note from the Peterson's Editors

The six volumes of Peterson's *Graduate and Professional Programs*, the only annually updated reference work of its kind, provide wide-ranging information on the graduate and professional programs offered by accredited colleges and universities in the United States, U.S. territories, and Canada and by those institutions outside the United States that are accredited by U.S. accrediting bodies. More than 44,000 individual academic and professional programs at nearly 2,300 institutions are listed. Peterson's *Graduate and Professional Programs* have been used for more than fifty years by prospective graduate and professional students, placement counselors, faculty advisers, and all others interested in postbaccalaureate education.

Graduate & Professional Programs: An Overview contains information on institutions as a whole, while the other books in the series are devoted to specific academic and professional fields:

- *Graduate Programs in the Biological/Biomedical Sciences & Health-Related Medical Professions*

- *Graduate Programs in Business, Education, Information Studies, Law & Social Work*

- *Graduate Programs in Engineering & Applied Sciences*

- *Graduate Programs in the Humanities, Arts & Social Sciences*

- *Graduate Programs in the Physical Sciences, Mathematics, Agricultural Sciences, the Environment & Natural Resources*

The books may be used individually or as a set. For example, if you have chosen a field of study but do not know what institution you want to attend or if you have a college or university in mind but have not chosen an academic field of study, it is best to begin with the Overview guide.

Graduate & Professional Programs: An Overview presents several directories to help you identify programs of study that might interest you; you can then research those programs further in the other books in the series by using the Directory of Graduate and Professional Programs by Field, which lists 500 fields and gives the names of those institutions that offer graduate degree programs in each.

For geographical or financial reasons, you may be interested in attending a particular institution and will want to know what it has to offer. You should turn to the Directory of Institutions and Their Offerings, which lists the degree programs available at each institution. As in the Directory of Graduate and Professional Programs by Field, the level of degrees offered is also indicated.

All books in the series include advice on graduate education, including topics such as admissions tests, financial aid, and accreditation. **The Graduate Adviser** includes two essays and information about accreditation. The first essay, "The Admissions Process," discusses general admission requirements, admission tests, factors to consider when selecting a graduate school or program, when and how to apply, and how admission decisions are made. Special information for international students and tips for minority students are also included. The second essay, "Financial Support," is an overview of the broad range of support available at the graduate level. Fellowships, scholarships, and grants; assistantships and internships; federal and private loan programs, as well as Federal Work-Study; and the GI bill are detailed. This essay concludes with advice on applying for need-based financial aid. "Accreditation and Accrediting Agencies" gives information on accreditation and its purpose and lists institutional accrediting agencies first and then specialized accrediting agencies relevant to each volume's specific fields of study.

With information on more than 40,000 graduate programs in more than 500 disciplines, Peterson's *Graduate and Professional Programs* give you all the information you need about the programs that are of interest to you in three formats: **Profiles** (capsule summaries of basic information), **Displays** (information that an institution or program wants to emphasize), and **Close-Ups** (written by administrators, with more expansive information than the **Profiles**, emphasizing different aspects of the programs). By using these various formats of program information, coupled with **Appendixes** and **Indexes** covering directories and subject areas for all six books, you will find that these guides provide the most comprehensive, accurate, and up-to-date graduate study information available.

Peterson's publishes a full line of resources with information you need to guide you through the graduate admissions process. Peterson's publications can be found at college libraries and career centers and your local bookstore or library—or visit us on the Web at www.petersons.com.

Colleges and universities will be pleased to know that Peterson's helped you in your selection. Admissions staff members are more than happy to answer questions, address specific problems, and help in any way they can. The editors at Peterson's wish you great success in your graduate program search!

THE GRADUATE ADVISER

The Admissions Process

Generalizations about graduate admissions practices are not always helpful because each institution has its own set of guidelines and procedures. Nevertheless, some broad statements can be made about the admissions process that may help you plan your strategy.

Factors Involved in Selecting a Graduate School or Program

Selecting a graduate school and a specific program of study is a complex matter. Quality of the faculty; program and course offerings; the nature, size, and location of the institution; admission requirements; cost; and the availability of financial assistance are among the many factors that affect one's choice of institution. Other considerations are job placement and achievements of the program's graduates and the institution's resources, such as libraries, laboratories, and computer facilities. If you are to make the best possible choice, you need to learn as much as you can about the schools and programs you are considering before you apply.

The following steps may help you narrow your choices.

- Talk to alumni of the programs or institutions you are considering to get their impressions of how well they were prepared for work in their fields of study.
- Remember that graduate school requirements change, so be sure to get the most up-to-date information possible.
- Talk to department faculty members and the graduate adviser at your undergraduate institution. They often have information about programs of study at other institutions.
- Visit the websites of the graduate schools in which you are interested to request a graduate catalog. Contact the department chair in your chosen field of study for additional information about the department and the field.
- Visit as many campuses as possible. Call ahead for an appointment with the graduate adviser in your field of interest and be sure to check out the facilities and talk to students.

General Requirements

Graduate schools and departments have requirements that applicants for admission must meet. Typically, these requirements include undergraduate transcripts (which provide information about undergraduate grade point average and course work applied toward a major), admission test scores, and letters of recommendation. Most graduate programs also ask for an essay or personal statement that describes your personal reasons for seeking graduate study. In some fields, such as art and music, portfolios or auditions may be required in addition to other evidence of talent. Some institutions require that the applicant have an undergraduate degree in the same subject as the intended graduate major.

Most institutions evaluate each applicant on the basis of the applicant's total record, and the weight accorded any given factor varies widely from institution to institution and from program to program.

The Application Process

You should begin the application process at least one year before you expect to begin your graduate study. Find out the application deadline for each institution (many are provided in the **Profile** section of this guide). Go to the institution's website and find out if you can apply online. If not, request a paper application form. Fill out this form thoroughly and neatly. Assume that the school needs all the information it is requesting and that the admissions officer will be sensitive to the neatness and overall quality of what you submit. Do not supply more information than the school requires.

The institution may ask at least one question that will require a three- or four-paragraph answer. Compose your response on the assumption that the admissions officer is interested in both what you think and how you express yourself. Keep your statement brief and to the point, but, at the same time, include all pertinent information about your past experiences and your educational goals. Individual statements vary greatly in style and content, which helps admissions officers differentiate among applicants. Many graduate departments give considerable weight to the statement in making their admissions decisions, so be sure to take the time to prepare a thoughtful and concise statement.

If recommendations are a part of the admissions requirements, carefully choose the individuals you ask to write them. It is generally best to ask current or former professors to write the recommendations, provided they are able to attest to your intellectual ability and motivation for doing the work required of a graduate student. It is advisable to provide stamped, preaddressed envelopes to people being asked to submit recommendations on your behalf.

Completed applications, including references, transcripts, and admission test scores, should be received at the institution by the specified date.

Be advised that institutions do not usually make admissions decisions until all materials have been received. Enclose a self-addressed postcard with your application, requesting confirmation of receipt. Allow at least ten days for the return of the postcard before making further inquiries.

If you plan to apply for financial support, it is imperative that you file your application early.

ADMISSION TESTS

The major testing program used in graduate admissions is the Graduate Record Examinations (GRE®) testing program, sponsored by the GRE Board and administered by Educational Testing Service, Princeton, New Jersey.

The Graduate Record Examinations testing program consists of a General Test and six Subject Tests. The General Test measures critical thinking, verbal reasoning, quantitative reasoning, and analytical writing skills. It is offered as an Internet-based test (iBT) in the United States, Canada, and many other countries.

The GRE® revised General Test's questions were designed to reflect the kind of thinking that students need to do in graduate or business school and demonstrate that students are indeed ready for graduate-level work.

- **Verbal Reasoning**—Measures ability to analyze and evaluate written material and synthesize information obtained from it, analyze relationships among component parts of sentences, and recognize relationships among words and concepts.
- **Quantitative Reasoning**—Measures problem-solving ability, focusing on basic concepts of arithmetic, algebra, geometry, and data analysis.
- **Analytical Writing**—Measures critical thinking and analytical writing skills, specifically the ability to articulate and support complex ideas clearly and effectively.

The computer-delivered GRE® revised General Test is offered year-round at Prometric™ test centers and on specific dates at testing locations outside of the Prometric test center network. Appointments are scheduled on a first-come, first-served basis. The GRE® revised General Test is also offered as a paper-based test three times a year in areas where computer-based testing is not available.

You can take the computer-delivered GRE® revised General Test once every twenty-one days, up to five times within any continuous rolling twelve-month period (365 days)—even if you canceled your

scores on a previously taken test. You may take the paper-based GRE® revised General Test as often as it is offered.

Three scores are reported on the revised General Test:

1. A **Verbal Reasoning score** is reported on a 130–170 score scale, in 1-point increments.

2. A **Quantitative Reasoning score** is reported on a 130–170 score scale, in 1-point increments.

3. An **Analytical Writing score** is reported on a 0–6 score level, in half-point increments.

The GRE® Subject Tests measure achievement and assume undergraduate majors or extensive background in the following six disciplines:

- Biology
- Chemistry
- Literature in English
- Mathematics
- Physics
- Psychology

The Subject Tests are available three times per year as paper-based administrations around the world. Testing time is approximately 2 hours and 50 minutes. You can obtain more information about the GRE® by visiting the ETS website at **www.ets.org** or consulting the *GRE® Information Bulletin*. The *Bulletin* can be obtained at many undergraduate colleges. You can also download it from the ETS website or obtain it by contacting Graduate Record Examinations, Educational Testing Service, P.O. Box 6000, Princeton, NJ 08541-6000; phone: 609-771-7670 or 866-473-4373.

If you expect to apply for admission to a program that requires any of the GRE® tests, you should select a test date well in advance of the application deadline. Scores on the computer-based General Test are reported within ten to fifteen days; scores on the paper-based Subject Tests are reported within six weeks.

Another testing program, the Miller Analogies Test® (MAT®), is administered at more than 500 Controlled Testing Centers in the United States, Canada, and other countries. The MAT® computer-based test is now available. Testing time is 60 minutes. The test consists of 120 partial analogies. You can obtain the *Candidate Information Booklet*, which contains a list of test centers and instructions for taking the test, from **www.milleranalogies.com** or by calling 800-328-5999 (toll-free).

Check the specific requirements of the programs to which you are applying.

How Admission Decisions Are Made

The program you apply to is directly involved in the admissions process. Although the final decision is usually made by the graduate dean (or an associate) or the faculty admissions committee, recommendations from faculty members in your intended field are important. At some institutions, an interview is incorporated into the decision process.

A Special Note for International Students

In addition to the steps already described, there are some special considerations for international students who intend to apply for graduate study in the United States. All graduate schools require an indication of competence in English. The purpose of the Test of English as a Foreign Language (TOEFL®) is to evaluate the English proficiency of people who are nonnative speakers of English and want to study at colleges and universities where English is the language of instruction. The TOEFL® is administered by Educational Testing Service (ETS) under the general direction of a policy board established by the College Board and the Graduate Record Examinations Board.

The TOEFL iBT® assesses four basic language skills: listening, reading, writing, and speaking. The Internet-based test is administered at secure, official test centers. The testing time is approximately 4 hours.

The TOEFL® is also offered in a paper-based format in areas of the world where internet-based testing is not available. In 2017, ETS launched a revised TOEFL® paper-based Test, that more closely aligned to the TOEFL iBT® test. This revised paper-based test consists of three sections—listening, reading, and writing. The testing time is approximately 3 hours.

You can obtain more information for both versions of the TOEFL® by visiting the ETS website at **www.ets.org/toefl**. Information can also be obtained by contacting TOEFL® Services, Educational Testing Service, P.O. Box 6151, Princeton, NJ 08541-6151. Phone: 609-771-7100 or 877-863-3546 (toll free).

International students should apply especially early because of the number of steps required to complete the admissions process. Furthermore, many United States graduate schools have a limited number of spaces for international students, and many more students apply than the schools can accommodate.

International students may find financial assistance from institutions very limited. The U.S. government requires international applicants to submit a certification of support, which is a statement attesting to the applicant's financial resources. In addition, international students *must* have health insurance coverage.

Tips for Minority Students

Indicators of a university's values in terms of diversity are found both in its recruitment programs and its resources directed to student success. Important questions: Does the institution vigorously recruit minorities for its graduate programs? Is there funding available to help with the costs associated with visiting the school? Are minorities represented in the institution's brochures or website or on their faculty rolls? What campus-based resources or services (including assistance in locating housing or career counseling and placement) are available? Is funding available to members of underrepresented groups?

At the program level, it is particularly important for minority students to investigate the "climate" of a program under consideration. How many minority students are enrolled and how many have graduated? What opportunities are there to work with diverse faculty and mentors whose research interests match yours? How are conflicts resolved or concerns addressed? How interested are faculty in building strong and supportive relations with students? "Climate" concerns should be addressed by posing questions to various individuals, including faculty members, current students, and alumni.

Information is also available through various organizations, such as the Hispanic Association of Colleges & Universities (HACU), and publications such as *Diverse Issues in Higher Education* and *Hispanic Outlook* magazine. There are also books devoted to this topic, such as *The Multicultural Student's Guide to Colleges* by Robert Mitchell.

Financial Support

The range of financial support at the graduate level is very broad. The following descriptions will give you a general idea of what you might expect and what will be expected of you as a financial support recipient.

Fellowships, Scholarships, and Grants

These are usually outright awards of a few hundred to many thousands of dollars with no service to the institution required in return. Fellowships and scholarships are usually awarded on the basis of merit and are highly competitive. Grants are made on the basis of financial need or special talent in a field of study. Many fellowships, scholarships, and grants not only cover tuition, fees, and supplies but also include stipends for living expenses with allowances for dependents. However, the terms of each should be examined because some do not permit recipients to supplement their income with outside work. Fellowships, scholarships, and grants may vary in the number of years for which they are awarded.

In addition to the availability of these funds at the university or program level, many excellent fellowship programs are available at the national level and may be applied for before and during enrollment in a graduate program. A listing of many of these programs can be found at the Council of Graduate Schools' website, **https://cgsnet.org/**. There is a wealth of information in the "Programs" and "Awards" sections.

Assistantships and Internships

Many graduate students receive financial support through assistantships, particularly involving teaching or research duties. It is important to recognize that such appointments should not be viewed simply as employment relationships but rather should constitute an integral and important part of a student's graduate education. As such, the appointments should be accompanied by strong faculty mentoring and increasingly responsible apprenticeship experiences. The specific nature of these appointments in a given program should be considered in selecting that graduate program.

TEACHING ASSISTANTSHIPS

These usually provide a salary and full or partial tuition remission and may also provide health benefits. Unlike fellowships, scholarships, and grants, which require no service to the institution, teaching assistantships require recipients to provide the institution with a specific amount of undergraduate teaching, ideally related to the student's field of study. Some teaching assistants are limited to grading papers, compiling bibliographies, taking notes, or monitoring laboratories. At some graduate schools, teaching assistants must carry lighter course loads than regular full-time students.

RESEARCH ASSISTANTSHIPS

These are very similar to teaching assistantships in the manner in which financial assistance is provided. The difference is that recipients are given basic research assignments in their disciplines rather than teaching responsibilities. The work required is normally related to the student's field of study; in most instances, the assistantship supports the student's thesis or dissertation research.

ADMINISTRATIVE INTERNSHIPS

These are similar to assistantships in application of financial assistance funds, but the student is given an assignment on a part-time basis, usually as a special assistant with one of the university's administrative offices. The assignment may not necessarily be directly related to the recipient's discipline.

RESIDENCE HALL AND COUNSELING ASSISTANTSHIPS

These assistantships are frequently assigned to graduate students in psychology, counseling, and social work, but they may be offered to students in other disciplines, especially if the student has worked in this capacity during his or her undergraduate years. Duties can vary from being available in a dean's office for a specific number of hours for consultation with undergraduates to living in campus residences and being responsible for both counseling and administrative tasks or advising student activity groups. Residence hall assistantships often include a room and board allowance and, in some cases, tuition assistance and stipends. Contact the Housing and Student Life Office for more information.

Health Insurance

The availability and affordability of health insurance is an important issue and one that should be considered in an applicant's choice of institution and program. While often included with assistantships and fellowships, this is not always the case and, even if provided, the benefits may be limited. It is important to note that the U.S. government requires international students to have health insurance.

The GI Bill

This provides financial assistance for students who are veterans of the United States armed forces. If you are a veteran, contact your local Veterans Administration office to determine your eligibility and to get full details about benefits. There are a number of programs that offer educational benefits to current military enlistees. Some states have tuition assistance programs for members of the National Guard. Contact the VA office at the college for more information.

Federal Work-Study Program (FWS)

Employment is another way some students finance their graduate studies. The federally funded Federal Work-Study Program provides eligible students with employment opportunities, usually in public and private nonprofit organizations. Federal funds pay up to 75 percent of the wages, with the remainder paid by the employing agency. FWS is available to graduate students who demonstrate financial need. Not all schools have these funds, and some only award them to undergraduates. Each school sets its application deadline and workstudy earnings limits. Wages vary and are related to the type of work done. You must file the Free Application for Federal Student Aid (FAFSA) to be eligible for this program.

Loans

Many graduate students borrow to finance their graduate programs when other sources of assistance (which do not have to be repaid) prove insufficient. You should always read and understand the terms of any loan program before submitting your application.

FEDERAL DIRECT LOANS

Federal Direct Loans. The Federal Direct Loan Program offers a variable-fixed interest rate loan to graduate students with the Department of Education acting as the lender. Students receive a new rate with each new loan, but that rate is fixed for the life of the loan. Beginning with loans made on or after July 1, 2013, the interest rate for loans made each July 1st to June 30th period are determined based on the last 10-year Treasury note auction prior to June 1st of that year, plus an added percentage. The interest rate can be no higher than 9.5%.

Beginning July 1, 2012, the Federal Direct Loan for graduate students is an unsubsidized loan. Under the *unsubsidized* program, the grad borrower pays the interest on the loan from the day proceeds are issued and is responsible for paying interest during all periods. If the borrower chooses not to pay the interest while in school, or during the grace periods, deferment, or forbearance, the interest accrues and will be capitalized.

Graduate students may borrow up to $20,500 per year through the Direct Loan Program, up to a cumulative maximum of $138,500, including undergraduate borrowing. No more than $65,500 of the $138,500 can be from subsidized loans, including loans the grad borrower may have received for periods of enrollment that began before July 1, 2012, or for prior undergraduate borrowing. You may borrow up to the cost of attendance at the school in which you are enrolled or will attend, minus estimated financial assistance from other federal, state, and private sources, up to a maximum of $20,500. Grad borrowers who reach the aggregate loan limit over the course of their education cannot receive additional loans; however, if they repay some of their loans to bring the outstanding balance below the aggregate limit, they could be eligible to borrow again, up to that limit.

Under the *subsidized* Federal Direct Loan Program, repayment begins six months after your last date of enrollment on at least a half-time basis. Under the *unsubsidized* program, repayment of interest begins within thirty days from disbursement of the loan proceeds, and repayment of the principal begins six months after your last enrollment on at least a half-time basis. Some borrowers may choose to defer interest payments while they are in school. The accrued interest is added to the loan balance when the borrower begins repayment. There are several repayment options.

Federal Perkins Loans. The Federal Perkins Loan is available to students demonstrating financial need and is administered directly by the school. Not all schools have these funds, and some may award them to undergraduates only. Eligibility is determined from the information you provide on the FAFSA. The school will notify you of your eligibility.

Eligible graduate students may borrow up to $8,000 per year, up to a maximum of $60,000, including undergraduate borrowing (even if your previous Perkins Loans have been repaid). The interest rate for Federal Perkins Loans is 5 percent, and no interest accrues while you remain in school at least half-time. Students who are attending less than half-time need to check with their school to determine the length of their grace period. There are no guarantee, loan, or disbursement fees. Repayment begins nine months after your last date of enrollment on at least a half-time basis and may extend over a maximum of ten years with no prepayment penalty.

Federal Direct Graduate PLUS Loans. Effective July 1, 2006, graduate and professional students are eligible for Graduate PLUS loans. This program allows students to borrow up to the cost of attendance, less any other aid received. These loans have a fixed interest rate (7.08% for loans first disbursed on or after July 1, 2019, and before July 1, 2020) and interest begins to accrue at the time of disbursement. Beginning with loans made on or after July 1, 2013, the interest rate for loans made each July 1st to June 30th period are determined based on the last 10-year Treasury note auction prior to June 1st of that year. The interest rate can be no higher than 10.5%. The PLUS loans do involve a credit check; a PLUS borrower may obtain a loan with a cosigner if his or her credit is not good enough. Grad PLUS loans may be deferred while a student is in school and for the six months following a drop below half-time enrollment. For more information, you should contact a representative in your college's financial aid office.

Deferring Your Federal Loan Repayments. If you borrowed under the Federal Direct Loan Program, Federal Direct PLUS Loan Program, or the Federal Perkins Loan Program for previous undergraduate or graduate study, your payments may be deferred when you return to graduate school, depending on when you borrowed and under which program.

There are other deferment options available if you are temporarily unable to repay your loan. Information about these deferments is provided at your entrance and exit interviews. If you believe you are eligible for a deferment of your loan payments, you must contact your lender or loan servicer to request a deferment. The deferment must be filed prior to the time your payment is due, and it must be re-filed when it expires if you remain eligible for deferment at that time.

SUPPLEMENTAL (PRIVATE) LOANS

Many lending institutions offer supplemental loan programs and other financing plans, such as the ones described here, to students seeking additional assistance in meeting their education expenses. Some loan programs target all types of graduate students; others are designed specifically for business, law, or medical students. In addition, you can use private loans not specifically designed for education to help finance your graduate degree.

If you are considering borrowing through a supplemental or private loan program, you should carefully consider the terms and be sure to read the fine print. Check with the program sponsor for the most current terms that will be applicable to the amounts you intend to borrow for graduate study. Most supplemental loan programs for graduate study offer unsubsidized, credit-based loans. In general, a credit-ready borrower is one who has a satisfactory credit history or no credit history at all. A creditworthy borrower generally must pass a credit test to be eligible to borrow or act as a cosigner for the loan funds.

Many supplemental loan programs have minimum and maximum annual loan limits. Some offer amounts equal to the cost of attendance minus any other aid you will receive for graduate study. If you are planning to borrow for several years of graduate study, consider whether there is a cumulative or aggregate limit on the amount you may borrow. Often this cumulative or aggregate limit will include any amounts you borrowed and have not repaid for undergraduate or previous graduate study.

The combination of the annual interest rate, loan fees, and the repayment terms you choose will determine how much you will repay over time. Compare these features in combination before you decide which loan program to use. Some loans offer interest rates that are adjusted monthly, quarterly, or annually. Some offer interest rates that are lower during the in-school, grace, and deferment periods and then increase when you begin repayment. Some programs include a loan origination fee, which is usually deducted from the principal amount you receive when the loan is disbursed and must be repaid along with the interest and other principal when you graduate, withdraw from school, or drop below half-time study. Sometimes the loan fees are reduced if you borrow with a qualified cosigner. Some programs allow you to defer interest and/or principal payments while you are enrolled in graduate school. Many programs allow you to capitalize your interest payments; the interest due on your loan is added to the outstanding balance of your loan, so you don't have to repay immediately, but this increases the amount you owe. Other programs allow you to pay the interest as you go, which reduces the amount you later have to repay. The private loan market is very competitive, and your financial aid office can help you evaluate these programs.

Applying for Need-Based Financial Aid

Schools that award federal and institutional financial assistance based on need will require you to complete the FAFSA and, in some cases, an institutional financial aid application.

If you are applying for federal student assistance, you **must** complete the FAFSA. A service of the U.S. Department of Education, the FAFSA is free to all applicants. Most applicants apply online at **www.fafsa.ed.gov**. Paper applications are available at the financial aid office of your local college.

After your FAFSA information has been processed, you will receive a Student Aid Report (SAR). If you provided an e-mail address on the FAFSA, this will be sent to you electronically; otherwise, it will be mailed to your home address.

Follow the instructions on the SAR if you need to correct information reported on your original application. If your situation changes after you file your FAFSA, contact your financial aid officer to discuss amending

your information. You can also appeal your financial aid award if you have extenuating circumstances.

If you would like more information on federal student financial aid, visit the FAFSA website or download the most recent version of *Do You Need Money for College* at www.studentaid.ed.gov/sa/sites/default/files/2018-19-do-you-need-money.pdf. This guide is also available in Spanish.

The U.S. Department of Education also has a toll-free number for questions concerning federal student aid programs. The number is 1-800-4-FED AID (1-800-433-3243). If you are hearing impaired, call toll-free, 1-800-730-8913.

Summary

Remember that these are generalized statements about financial assistance at the graduate level. Because each institution allots its aid differently, you should communicate directly with the school and the specific department of interest to you. It is not unusual, for example, to find that an endowment vested within a specific department supports one or more fellowships. You may fit its requirements and specifications precisely.

Accreditation and Accrediting Agencies

Colleges and universities in the United States, and their individual academic and professional programs, are accredited by nongovernmental agencies concerned with monitoring the quality of education in this country. Agencies with both regional and national jurisdictions grant accreditation to institutions as a whole, while specialized bodies acting on a nationwide basis—often national professional associations—grant accreditation to departments and programs in specific fields.

Institutional and specialized accrediting agencies share the same basic concerns: the purpose an academic unit—whether university or program—has set for itself and how well it fulfills that purpose, the adequacy of its financial and other resources, the quality of its academic offerings, and the level of services it provides. Agencies that grant institutional accreditation take a broader view, of course, and examine university-wide or college-wide services with which a specialized agency may not concern itself.

Both types of agencies follow the same general procedures when considering an application for accreditation. The academic unit prepares a self-evaluation, focusing on the concerns mentioned above and usually including an assessment of both its strengths and weaknesses; a team of representatives of the accrediting body reviews this evaluation, visits the campus, and makes its own report; and finally, the accrediting body makes a decision on the application. Often, even when accreditation is granted, the agency makes a recommendation regarding how the institution or program can improve. All institutions and programs are also reviewed every few years to determine whether they continue to meet established standards; if they do not, they may lose their accreditation.

Accrediting agencies themselves are reviewed and evaluated periodically by the U.S. Department of Education and the Council for Higher Education Accreditation (CHEA). Recognized agencies adhere to certain standards and practices, and their authority in matters of accreditation is widely accepted in the educational community.

This does not mean, however, that accreditation is a simple matter, either for schools wishing to become accredited or for students deciding where to apply. Indeed, in certain fields the very meaning and methods of accreditation are the subject of a good deal of debate. For their part, those applying to graduate school should be aware of the safeguards provided by regional accreditation, especially in terms of degree acceptance and institutional longevity. Beyond this, applicants should understand the role that specialized accreditation plays in their field, as this varies considerably from one discipline to another. In certain professional fields, it is necessary to have graduated from a program that is accredited in order to be eligible for a license to practice, and in some fields the federal government also makes this a hiring requirement. In other disciplines, however, accreditation is not as essential, and there can be excellent programs that are not accredited. In fact, some programs choose not to seek accreditation, although most do.

Institutions and programs that present themselves for accreditation are sometimes granted the status of candidate for accreditation, or what is known as "preaccreditation." This may happen, for example, when an academic unit is too new to have met all the requirements for accreditation. Such status signifies initial recognition and indicates that the school or program in question is working to fulfill all requirements; it does not, however, guarantee that accreditation will be granted.

Institutional Accrediting Agencies—Regional

MIDDLE STATES COMMISSION ON HIGHER EDUCATION

Accredits institutions in Delaware, District of Columbia, Maryland, New Jersey, New York, Pennsylvania, Puerto Rico, and the Virgin Islands.

Dr. Elizabeth Sibolski, President
Middle States Commission on Higher Education
3624 Market Street, Second Floor West
Philadelphia, Pennsylvania 19104
Phone: 267-284-5000
Fax: 215-662-5501
E-mail: info@msche.org
Website: www.msche.org

NEW ENGLAND ASSOCIATION OF SCHOOLS AND COLLEGES

Accredits institutions in Connecticut, Maine, Massachusetts, New Hampshire, Rhode Island, and Vermont.

Dr. Barbara E. Brittingham, President/Director
Commission on Institutions of Higher Education
3 Burlington Woods Drive, Suite 100
Burlington, Massachusetts 01803-4531
Phone: 855-886-3272 or 781-425-7714
Fax: 781-425-1001
E-mail: cihe@neasc.org
Website: https://cihe.neasc.org

THE HIGHER LEARNING COMMISSION

Accredits institutions in Arizona, Arkansas, Colorado, Illinois, Indiana, Iowa, Kansas, Michigan, Minnesota, Missouri, Nebraska, New Mexico, North Dakota, Ohio, Oklahoma, South Dakota, West Virginia, Wisconsin, and Wyoming.

Dr. Barbara Gellman-Danley, President
The Higher Learning Commission
230 South LaSalle Street, Suite 7-500
Chicago, Illinois 60604-1413
Phone: 800-621-7440 or 312-263-0456
Fax: 312-263-7462
E-mail: info@hlcommission.org
Website: www.hlcommission.org

NORTHWEST COMMISSION ON COLLEGES AND UNIVERSITIES

Accredits institutions in Alaska, Idaho, Montana, Nevada, Oregon, Utah, and Washington.

Dr. Sandra E. Elman, President
8060 165th Avenue, NE, Suite 100
Redmond, Washington 98052
Phone: 425-558-4224
Fax: 425-376-0596
E-mail: selman@nwccu.org
Website: www.nwccu.org

SOUTHERN ASSOCIATION OF COLLEGES AND SCHOOLS

Accredits institutions in Alabama, Florida, Georgia, Kentucky, Louisiana, Mississippi, North Carolina, South Carolina, Tennessee, Texas, and Virginia.

Dr. Belle S. Wheelan, President
Commission on Colleges
1866 Southern Lane
Decatur, Georgia 30033-4097
Phone: 404-679-4500 Ext. 4504
Fax: 404-679-4558
E-mail: questions@sacscoc.org
Website: www.sacscoc.org

WESTERN ASSOCIATION OF SCHOOLS AND COLLEGES

Accredits institutions in California, Guam, and Hawaii.

Jamienne S. Studley, President
WASC Senior College and University Commission
985 Atlantic Avenue, Suite 100
Alameda, California 94501
Phone: 510-748-9001
Fax: 510-748-9797
E-mail: wasc@wscuc.org
Website: https://www.wscuc.org/

Institutional Accrediting Agencies—Other

ACCREDITING COUNCIL FOR INDEPENDENT COLLEGES AND SCHOOLS
Michelle Edwards, President
750 First Street NE, Suite 980
Washington, DC 20002-4223
Phone: 202-336-6780
Fax: 202-842-2593
E-mail: info@acics.org
Website: www.acics.org

DISTANCE EDUCATION ACCREDITING COMMISSION (DEAC)
Leah Matthews, Executive Director
1101 17th Street NW, Suite 808
Washington, DC 20036-4704
Phone: 202-234-5100
Fax: 202-332-1386
E-mail: info@deac.org
Website: www.deac.org

Specialized Accrediting Agencies

ACUPUNCTURE AND ORIENTAL MEDICINE
Mark S. McKenzie, LAc MsOM DiplOM, Executive Director
Accreditation Commission for Acupuncture and Oriental Medicine
8941 Aztec Drive, Suite 2
Eden Prairie, Minnesota 55347
Phone: 952-212-2434
Fax: 301-313-0912
E-mail: info@acaom.org
Website: www.acaom.org

ALLIED HEALTH
Kathleen Megivern, Executive Director
Commission on Accreditation of Allied Health Education Programs (CAAHEP)
25400 US Hwy 19 North, Suite 158
Clearwater, Florida 33763
Phone: 727-210-2350
Fax: 727-210-2354
E-mail: mail@caahep.org
Website: www.caahep.org

ART AND DESIGN
Karen P. Moynahan, Executive Director
National Association of Schools of Art and Design (NASAD)
Commission on Accreditation
11250 Roger Bacon Drive, Suite 21
Reston, Virginia 20190-5248
Phone: 703-437-0700
Fax: 703-437-6312
E-mail: info@arts-accredit.org
Website: http://nasad.arts-accredit.org

ATHLETIC TRAINING EDUCATION
Pamela Hansen, CAATE Director of Accreditation
Commission on Accreditation of Athletic Training Education (CAATE)
6850 Austin Center Blvd., Suite 100
Austin, Texas 78731-3184
Phone: 512-733-9700
E-mail: pamela@caate.net
Website: www.caate.net

AUDIOLOGY EDUCATION
Meggan Olek, Director
Accreditation Commission for Audiology Education (ACAE)
11480 Commerce Park Drive, Suite 220
Reston, Virginia 20191
Phone: 202-986-9500
Fax: 202-986-9550
E-mail: info@acaeaccred.org
Website: https://acaeaccred.org/

AVIATION
Dr. Gary J. Northam, President
Aviation Accreditation Board International (AABI)
3410 Skyway Drive
Auburn, Alabama 36830
Phone: 334-844-2431
Fax: 334-844-2432
E-mail: gary.northam@auburn.edu
Website: www.aabi.aero

BUSINESS
Stephanie Bryant, Executive Vice President and Chief Accreditation Officer
AACSB International—The Association to Advance Collegiate Schools of Business
777 South Harbour Island Boulevard, Suite 750
Tampa, Florida 33602
Phone: 813-769-6500
Fax: 813-769-6559
E-mail: stephanie.bryant@aacsb.edu
Website: www.aacsb.edu

BUSINESS EDUCATION
Dr. Phyllis Okrepkie, President
International Assembly for Collegiate Business Education (IACBE)
11374 Strang Line Road
Lenexa, Kansas 66215
Phone: 913-631-3009
Fax: 913-631-9154
E-mail: iacbe@iacbe.org
Website: www.iacbe.org

CHIROPRACTIC
Dr. Craig S. Little, President
Council on Chiropractic Education (CCE)
Commission on Accreditation
8049 North 85th Way
Scottsdale, Arizona 85258-4321
Phone: 480-443-8877 or 888-443-3506
Fax: 480-483-7333
E-mail: cce@cce-usa.org
Website: www.cce-usa.org

CLINICAL LABORATORY SCIENCES
Dianne M. Cearlock, Ph.D., Chief Executive Officer
National Accrediting Agency for Clinical Laboratory Sciences
5600 North River Road, Suite 720
Rosemont, Illinois 60018-5119
Phone: 773-714-8880 or 847-939-3597
Fax: 773-714-8886
E-mail: info@naacls.org
Website: www.naacls.org

CLINICAL PASTORAL EDUCATION
Trace Haythorn, Ph.D., Executive Director/CEO
Association for Clinical Pastoral Education, Inc.
One West Court Square, Suite 325
Decatur, Georgia 30030-2576
Phone: 678-363-6226
Fax: 404-320-0849
E-mail: acpe@acpe.edu
Website: www.acpe.edu

DANCE
Karen P. Moynahan, Executive Director
National Association of Schools of Dance (NASD)
Commission on Accreditation
11250 Roger Bacon Drive, Suite 21
Reston, Virginia 20190-5248
Phone: 703-437-0700
Fax: 703-437-6312
E-mail: info@arts-accredit.org
Website: http://nasd.arts-accredit.org

DENTISTRY
Dr. Kathleen T. O'Loughlin, Executive Director

Commission on Dental Accreditation
American Dental Association
211 East Chicago Avenue
Chicago, Illinois 60611
Phone: 312-440-2500
E-mail: accreditation@ada.org
Website: www.ada.org

DIETETICS AND NUTRITION
Mary B. Gregoire, Ph.D., Executive Director; RD, FADA, FAND
Academy of Nutrition and Dietetics
Accreditation Council for Education in Nutrition and Dietetics (ACEND)
120 South Riverside Plaza
Chicago, Illinois 60606-6995
Phone: 800-877-1600 or 312-899-0040
E-mail: acend@eatright.org
Website: www.eatright.org/cade

EDUCATION PREPARATION
Christopher Koch, President
Council for the Accreditation of Educator Preparation (CAEP)
1140 19th Street NW, Suite 400
Washington, DC 20036
Phone: 202-223-0077
Fax: 202-296-6620
E-mail: caep@caepnet.org
Website: www.caepnet.org

ENGINEERING
Michael Milligan, Ph.D., PE, Executive Director
Accreditation Board for Engineering and Technology, Inc. (ABET)
415 North Charles Street
Baltimore, Maryland 21201
Phone: 410-347-7700
E-mail: accreditation@abet.org
Website: www.abet.org

FORENSIC SCIENCES
Nancy J. Jackson, Director of Development and Accreditation
American Academy of Forensic Sciences (AAFS)
Forensic Science Education Program Accreditation Commission (FEPAC)
410 North 21st Street
Colorado Springs, Colorado 80904
Phone: 719-636-1100
Fax: 719-636-1993
E-mail: njackson@aafs.org
Website: www.fepac-edu.org

FORESTRY
Carol L. Redelsheimer
Director of Science and Education
Society of American Foresters
10100 Laureate Way
Bethesda, Maryland 20814-2198
Phone: 301-897-8720 or 866-897-8720
Fax: 301-897-3690
E-mail: membership@safnet.org
Website: www.eforester.com

HEALTHCARE MANAGEMENT
Commission on Accreditation of Healthcare Management Education (CAHME)
Anthony Stanowski, President and CEO
6110 Executive Boulevard, Suite 614
Rockville, Maryland 20852
Phone: 301-298-1820
E-mail: info@cahme.org
Website: www.cahme.org

HEALTH INFORMATICS AND HEALTH MANAGEMENT
Angela Kennedy, EdD, MBA, RHIA, Chief Executive Officer
Commission on Accreditation for Health Informatics and Information Management Education (CAHIIM)
233 North Michigan Avenue, 21st Floor
Chicago, Illinois 60601-5800

Phone: 312-233-1134
Fax: 312-233-1948
E-mail: info@cahiim.org
Website: www.cahiim.org

HUMAN SERVICE EDUCATION
Dr. Elaine Green, President
Council for Standards in Human Service Education (CSHSE)
3337 Duke Street
Alexandria, Virginia 22314
Phone: 571-257-3959
E-mail: info@cshse.org
Website: www.cshse.org

INTERIOR DESIGN
Holly Mattson, Executive Director
Council for Interior Design Accreditation
206 Grandview Avenue, Suite 350
Grand Rapids, Michigan 49503-4014
Phone: 616-458-0400
Fax: 616-458-0460
E-mail: info@accredit-id.org
Website: www.accredit-id.org

JOURNALISM AND MASS COMMUNICATIONS
Patricia Thompson, Executive Director
Accrediting Council on Education in Journalism and Mass Communications (ACEJMC)
201 Bishop Hall
P.O. Box 1848
University, MS 38677-1848
Phone: 662-915-5504
E-mail: pthomps1@olemiss.edu
Website: www.acejmc.org

LANDSCAPE ARCHITECTURE
Nancy Somerville, Executive Vice President, CEO
American Society of Landscape Architects (ASLA)
636 Eye Street, NW
Washington, DC 20001-3736
Phone: 202-898-2444
Fax: 202-898-1185
E-mail: info@asla.org
Website: www.asla.org

LAW
Barry Currier, Managing Director of Accreditation & Legal Education
American Bar Association
321 North Clark Street, 21st Floor
Chicago, Illinois 60654
Phone: 312-988-6738
Fax: 312-988-5681
E-mail: legaled@americanbar.org
Website: https://www.americanbar.org/groups/legal_education/accreditation.html

LIBRARY
Karen O'Brien, Director
Office for Accreditation
American Library Association
50 East Huron Street
Chicago, Illinois 60611-2795
Phone: 800-545-2433, ext. 2432 or 312-280-2432
Fax: 312-280-2433
E-mail: accred@ala.org
Website: http://www.ala.org/aboutala/offices/accreditation/

MARRIAGE AND FAMILY THERAPY
Tanya A. Tamarkin, Director of Educational Affairs
Commission on Accreditation for Marriage and Family Therapy Education (COAMFTE)
American Association for Marriage and Family Therapy
112 South Alfred Street
Alexandria, Virginia 22314-3061

Phone: 703-838-9808
Fax: 703-838-9805
E-mail: coa@aamft.org
Website: www.aamft.org

MEDICAL ILLUSTRATION

Kathleen Megivern, Executive Director
Commission on Accreditation of Allied Health Education Programs
(CAAHEP)
25400 US Highway 19 North, Suite 158
Clearwater, Florida 33756
Phone: 727-210-2350
Fax: 727-210-2354
E-mail: mail@caahep.org
Website: www.caahep.org

MEDICINE

Liaison Committee on Medical Education (LCME)
Robert B. Hash, M.D., LCME Secretary
American Medical Association
Council on Medical Education
330 North Wabash Avenue, Suite 39300
Chicago, Illinois 60611-5885
Phone: 312-464-4933
E-mail: lcme@aamc.org
Website: www.ama-assn.org

Liaison Committee on Medical Education (LCME)
Heather Lent, M.A., Director
Accreditation Services
Association of American Medical Colleges
655 K Street, NW
Washington, DC 20001-2399
Phone: 202-828-0596
E-mail: lcme@aamc.org
Website: www.lcme.org

MUSIC

Karen P. Moynahan, Executive Director
National Association of Schools of Music (NASM)
Commission on Accreditation
11250 Roger Bacon Drive, Suite 21
Reston, Virginia 20190-5248
Phone: 703-437-0700
Fax: 703-437-6312
E-mail: info@arts-accredit.org
Website: http://nasm.arts-accredit.org/

NATUROPATHIC MEDICINE

Daniel Seitz, J.D., Ed.D., Executive Director
Council on Naturopathic Medical Education
P.O. Box 178
Great Barrington, Massachusetts 01230
Phone: 413-528-8877
E-mail: https://cnme.org/contact-us/
Website: www.cnme.org

NURSE ANESTHESIA

Francis R.Gerbasi, Ph.D., CRNA, COA Executive Director
Council on Accreditation of Nurse Anesthesia Educational Programs
(CoA-NAEP)
American Association of Nurse Anesthetists
222 South Prospect Avenue
Park Ridge, Illinois 60068-4001
Phone: 847-655-1160
Fax: 847-692-7137
E-mail: accreditation@coa.us.com
Website: http://www.coacrna.org

NURSE EDUCATION

Jennifer L. Butlin, Executive Director
Commission on Collegiate Nursing Education (CCNE)
One Dupont Circle, NW, Suite 530
Washington, DC 20036-1120
Phone: 202-887-6791
Fax: 202-887-8476
E-mail: jbutlin@aacn.nche.edu
Website: www.aacn.nche.edu/accreditation

Marsal P. Stoll, Chief Executive Officer
Accreditation Commission for Education in Nursing (ACEN)
3343 Peachtree Road, NE, Suite 850
Atlanta, Georgia 30326
Phone: 404-975-5000
Fax: 404-975-5020
E-mail: mstoll@acenursing.org
Website: www.acenursing.org

NURSE MIDWIFERY

Heather L. Maurer, M.A., Executive Director
Accreditation Commission for Midwifery Education (ACME)
American College of Nurse-Midwives
8403 Colesville Road, Suite 1550
Silver Spring, Maryland 20910
Phone: 240-485-1800
Fax: 240-485-1818
E-mail: info@acnm.org
Website: www.midwife.org/Program-Accreditation

NURSE PRACTITIONER

Gay Johnson, CEO
National Association of Nurse Practitioners in Women's Health
Council on Accreditation
505 C Street, NE
Washington, DC 20002
Phone: 202-543-9693 Ext. 1
Fax: 202-543-9858
E-mail: info@npwh.org
Website: www.npwh.org

NURSING

Marsal P. Stoll, Chief Executive Director
Accreditation Commission for Education in Nursing (ACEN)
3343 Peachtree Road, NE, Suite 850
Atlanta, Georgia 30326
Phone: 404-975-5000
Fax: 404-975-5020
E-mail: info@acenursing.org
Website: www.acenursing.org

OCCUPATIONAL THERAPY

Heather Stagliano, DHSc, OTR/L, Executive Director
The American Occupational Therapy Association, Inc.
4720 Montgomery Lane, Suite 200
Bethesda, Maryland 20814-3449
Phone: 301-652-6611 Ext. 2682
TDD: 800-377-8555
Fax: 240-762-5150
E-mail: accred@aota.org
Website: www.aoteonline.org

OPTOMETRY
Joyce L. Urbeck, Administrative Director
Accreditation Council on Optometric Education (ACOE)
American Optometric Association
243 North Lindbergh Boulevard
St. Louis, Missouri 63141-7881
Phone: 314-991-4100, Ext. 4246
Fax: 314-991-4101
E-mail: accredit@aoa.org
Website: www.theacoe.org

OSTEOPATHIC MEDICINE
Director, Department of Accreditation
Commission on Osteopathic College Accreditation (COCA)
American Osteopathic Association
142 East Ontario Street
Chicago, Illinois 60611
Phone: 312-202-8048
Fax: 312-202-8202
E-mail: predoc@osteopathic.org
Website: www.aoacoca.org

PHARMACY
Peter H. Vlasses, PharmD, Executive Director
Accreditation Council for Pharmacy Education
135 South LaSalle Street, Suite 4100
Chicago, Illinois 60603-4810
Phone: 312-664-3575
Fax: 312-664-4652
E-mail: csinfo@acpe-accredit.org
Website: www.acpe-accredit.org

PHYSICAL THERAPY
Sandra Wise, Senior Director
Commission on Accreditation in Physical Therapy Education (CAPTE)
American Physical Therapy Association (APTA)
1111 North Fairfax Street
Alexandria, Virginia 22314-1488
Phone: 703-706-3245
Fax: 703-706-3387
E-mail: accreditation@apta.org
Website: www.capteonline.org

PHYSICIAN ASSISTANT STUDIES
Sharon L. Luke, Executive Director
Accredittion Review Commission on Education for the Physician
    Assistant, Inc. (ARC-PA)
12000 Findley Road, Suite 275
Johns Creek, Georgia 30097
Phone: 770-476-1224
Fax: 770-476-1738
E-mail: arc-pa@arc-pa.org
Website: www.arc-pa.org

PLANNING
Jesmarie Soto Johnson, Executive Director
American Institute of Certified Planners/Association of Collegiate
    Schools of Planning/American Planning Association
Planning Accreditation Board (PAB)
2334 West Lawrence Avenue, Suite 209
Chicago, Illinois 60625
Phone: 773-334-7200
E-mail: smerits@planningaccreditationboard.org
Website: www.planningaccreditationboard.org

PODIATRIC MEDICINE
Heather Stagliano, OTR/L, DHSc, Executive Director
Council on Podiatric Medical Education (CPME)
American Podiatric Medical Association (APMA)
9312 Old Georgetown Road
Bethesda, Maryland 20814-1621
Phone: 301-581-9200
Fax: 301-571-4903
Website: www.cpme.org

PSYCHOLOGY AND COUNSELING
Jacqueline Remondet, Associate Executive Director, CEO of the
Accrediting Unit,
Office of Program Consultation and Accreditation
American Psychological Association
750 First Street, NE
Washington, DC 20002-4202
Phone: 202-336-5979 or 800-374-2721
TDD/TTY: 202-336-6123
Fax: 202-336-5978
E-mail: apaaccred@apa.org
Website: www.apa.org/ed/accreditation

Kelly Coker, Executive Director
Council for Accreditation of Counseling and Related Educational
    Programs (CACREP)
1001 North Fairfax Street, Suite 510
Alexandria, Virginia 22314
Phone: 703-535-5990
Fax: 703-739-6209
E-mail: cacrep@cacrep.org
Website: www.cacrep.org

Richard M. McFall, Executive Director
Psychological Clinical Science Accreditation System (PCSAS)
1101 East Tenth Street
IU Psychology Building
Bloomington, Indiana 47405-7007
Phone: 812-856-2570
Fax: 812-322-5545
E-mail: rmmcfall@pcsas.org
Website: www.pcsas.org

PUBLIC HEALTH
Laura Rasar King, M.P.H., MCHES, Executive Director
Council on Education for Public Health
1010 Wayne Avenue, Suite 220
Silver Spring, Maryland 20910
Phone: 202-789-1050
Fax: 202-789-1895
E-mail: Lking@ceph.org
Website: www.ceph.org

PUBLIC POLICY, AFFAIRS AND ADMINISTRATION
Crystal Calarusse, Chief Accreditation Officer
Commission on Peer Review and Accreditation
Network of Schools of Public Policy, Affairs, and Administration
(NASPAA-COPRA)
1029 Vermont Avenue, NW, Suite 1100
Washington, DC 20005
Phone: 202-628-8965
Fax: 202-626-4978
E-mail: copra@naspaa.org
Website: accreditation.naspaa.org

RADIOLOGIC TECHNOLOGY
Leslie Winter, Chief Executive Officer Joint Review Committee on
Education in Radiologic Technology (JRCERT)
20 North Wacker Drive, Suite 2850
Chicago, Illinois 60606-3182
Phone: 312-704-5300
Fax: 312-704-5304
E-mail: mail@jrcert.org
Website: www.jrcert.org

REHABILITATION EDUCATION
Frank Lane, Ph.D., Executive Director
Council for Accreditation of Counseling and Related Educational
    Programs (CACREP)
1001 North Fairfax Street, Suite 510
Alexandria, Virginia 22314
Phone: 703-535-5990
Fax: 703-739-6209
E-mail: cacrep@cacrep.org
Website: www.cacrep.org

RESPIRATORY CARE
Thomas Smalling, Executive Director
Commission on Accreditation for Respiratory Care (CoARC)
1248 Harwood Road
Bedford, Texas 76021-4244
Phone: 817-283-2835
Fax: 817-354-8519
E-mail: tom@coarc.com
Website: www.coarc.com

SOCIAL WORK
Dr. Stacey Borasky, Director of Accreditation
Office of Social Work Accreditation
Council on Social Work Education
1701 Duke Street, Suite 200
Alexandria, Virginia 22314
Phone: 703-683-8080
Fax: 703-519-2078
E-mail: info@cswe.org
Website: www.cswe.org

SPEECH-LANGUAGE PATHOLOGY AND AUDIOLOGY
Kimberlee Moore, Accreditation Executive Director
American Speech-Language-Hearing Association
Council on Academic Accreditation in Audiology and Speech-Language Pathology
2200 Research Boulevard #310
Rockville, Maryland 20850-3289
Phone: 301-296-5700
Fax: 301-296-8750
E-mail: accreditation@asha.org
Website: http://caa.asha.org

TEACHER EDUCATION
Christopher A. Koch, President
National Council for Accreditation of Teacher Education (NCATE)
Teacher Education Accreditation Council (TEAC)
1140 19th Street, Suite 400
Washington, DC 20036
Phone: 202-223-0077
Fax: 202-296-6620
E-mail: caep@caepnet.org
Website: www.ncate.org

TECHNOLOGY
Michale S. McComis, Ed.D., Executive Director
Accrediting Commission of Career Schools and Colleges
2101 Wilson Boulevard, Suite 302
Arlington, Virginia 22201
Phone: 703-247-4212
Fax: 703-247-4533
E-mail: mccomis@accsc.org
Website: www.accsc.org

TECHNOLOGY, MANAGEMENT, AND APPLIED ENGINEERING
Kelly Schild, Director of Accreditation
The Association of Technology, Management, and Applied Engineering (ATMAE)
275 N. York Street, Suite 401
Elmhurst, Illinois 60126
Phone: 630-433-4514
Fax: 630-563-9181
E-mail: Kelly@atmae.org
Website: www.atmae.org

THEATER
Karen P. Moynahan, Executive Director
National Association of Schools of Theatre Commission on Accreditation
11250 Roger Bacon Drive, Suite 21
Reston, Virginia 20190
Phone: 703-437-0700
Fax: 703-437-6312
E-mail: info@arts-accredit.org
Website: http://nast.arts-accredit.org/

THEOLOGY
Dr. Bernard Fryshman, Executive VP
Emeritus and Interim Executive Director
Association of Advanced Rabbinical and Talmudic Schools (AARTS)
Accreditation Commission
11 Broadway, Suite 405
New York, New York 10004
Phone: 212-363-1991
Fax: 212-533-5335
E-mail: k.sharfman.aarts@gmail.com

Frank Yamada, Executive Director
Association of Theological Schools in the United States and Canada (ATS)
Commission on Accrediting
10 Summit Park Drive
Pittsburgh, Pennsylvania 15275
Phone: 412-788-6505
Fax: 412-788-6510
E-mail: ats@ats.edu
Website: www.ats.edu

Dr. Timothy Eaton, President
Transnational Association of Christian Colleges and Schools (TRACS)
Accreditation Commission
15935 Forest Road
Forest, Virginia 24551
Phone: 434-525-9539
Fax: 434-525-9538
E-mail: info@tracs.org
Website: www.tracs.org

VETERINARY MEDICINE
Dr. Karen Brandt, Director of Education and Research
American Veterinary Medical Association (AVMA)
Council on Education
1931 North Meacham Road, Suite 100
Schaumburg, Illinois 60173-4360
Phone: 847-925-8070 Ext. 6674
Fax: 847-285-5732
E-mail: info@avma.org
Website: www.avma.org

How to Use These Guides

As you identify the particular programs and institutions that interest you, you can use both the *Graduate & Professional Programs: An Overview* volume and the specialized volumes in the series to obtain detailed information.

- *Graduate Programs in the Biological/Biomedical Sciences & Health-Related Professions*
- *Graduate Programs in Business, Education, Information Studies, Law & Social Work*
- *Graduate Programs in Engineering & Applied Sciences*
- *Graduate Programs the Humanities, Arts & Social Sciences*
- *Graduate Programs in the Physical Sciences, Mathematics, Agricultural Sciences, the Environment & Natural Resources*

Each of the specialized volumes in the series is divided into sections that contain one or more directories devoted to programs in a particular field. If you do not find a directory devoted to your field of interest in a specific volume, consult "Directories and Subject Areas" (located at the end of each volume). After you have identified the correct volume, consult the "Directories and Subject Areas in This Book" index, which shows (as does the more general directory) what directories cover subjects not specifically named in a directory or section title.

Each of the specialized volumes in the series has a number of general directories. These directories have entries for the largest unit at an institution granting graduate degrees in that field. For example, the general Engineering and Applied Sciences directory in the *Graduate Programs in Engineering & Applied Sciences* volume consists of **Profiles** for colleges, schools, and departments of engineering and applied sciences.

General directories are followed by other directories, or sections, that give more detailed information about programs in particular areas of the general field that has been covered. The general Engineering and Applied Sciences directory, in the previous example, is followed by nineteen sections with directories in specific areas of engineering, such as Chemical Engineering, Industrial/Management Engineering, and Mechanical Engineering.

Because of the broad nature of many fields, any system of organization is bound to involve a certain amount of overlap. Environmental studies, for example, is a field whose various aspects are studied in several types of departments and schools. Readers interested in such studies will find information on relevant programs in the *Graduate Programs in the Biological/Biomedical Sciences & Health-Related Professions* volume under Ecology and Environmental Biology and Environmental and Occupational Health; in the *Graduate Programs in the Physical Sciences, Mathematics, Agricultural Sciences, the Environment & Natural Resources* volume under Environmental Management and Policy and Natural Resources; and in the *Graduate Programs in Engineering & Applied Sciences* volume under Energy Management and Policy and Environmental Engineering. To help you find all of the programs of interest to you, the introduction to each section within the specialized volumes includes, if applicable, a paragraph suggesting other sections and directories with information on related areas of study.

Directory of Institutions with Programs in the Physical Sciences, Mathematics, Agricultural Sciences, the Environment & Natural Resources

This directory lists institutions in alphabetical order and includes beneath each name the academic fields in which each institution offers graduate programs. The degree level in each field is also indicated, provided that the institution has supplied that information in response to

Peterson's Annual Survey of Graduate and Professional Institutions.

An M indicates that a master's degree program is offered; a D indicates that a doctoral degree program is offered; an O signifies that other advanced degrees (e.g., certificates or specialist degrees) are offered; and an * (asterisk) indicates that a **Close-Up** and/or **Display** is located in this volume. See the index, "Close-Ups and Displays," for the specific page number.

Profiles of Academic and Professional Programs in the Specialized Volumes

Each section of **Profiles** has a table of contents that lists the Program Directories, **Displays**, and **Close-Ups**. Program Directories consist of the **Profiles** of programs in the relevant fields, with **Displays** following if programs have chosen to include them. **Close-Ups,** which are more individualized statements, are also listed for those graduate schools or programs that have chosen to submit them.

The **Profiles** found in the 500 directories in the specialized volumes provide basic data about the graduate units in capsule form for quick reference. To make these directories as useful as possible, **Profiles** are generally listed for an institution's smallest academic unit within a subject area. In other words, if an institution has a College of Liberal Arts that administers many related programs, the **Profile** for the individual program (e.g., Program in History), not the entire College, appears in the directory.

There are some programs that do not fit into any current directory and are not given individual **Profiles**. The directory structure is reviewed annually in order to keep this number to a minimum and to accommodate major trends in graduate education.

The following outline describes the **Profile** information found in the guides and explains how best to use that information. Any item that does not apply to or was not provided by a graduate unit is omitted from its listing. The format of the **Profiles** is constant, making it easy to compare one institution with another and one program with another.

A ★ graphic next to the school's name indicates the institution has additional detailed information in a "Premium Profile" on Petersons.com. After reading their information here, you can learn more about the school by visiting www.petersons.com and searching for that particular college or university's graduate program.

Identifying Information. The institution's name, in boldface type, is followed by a complete listing of the administrative structure for that field of study. (For example, University of Akron, Buchtel College of Arts and Sciences, Department of Theoretical and Applied Mathematics, Program in Mathematics.) The last unit listed is the one to which all information in the **Profile** pertains. The institution's city, state, and ZIP code follow.

Offerings. Each field of study offered by the unit is listed with all postbaccalaureate degrees awarded. Degrees that are not preceded by a specific concentration are awarded in the general field listed in the unit name. Frequently, fields of study are broken down into subspecializations, and those appear following the degrees awarded; for example, "Offerings in secondary education (M.Ed.), including English education, mathematics education, science education." Students enrolled in the M.Ed. program would be able to specialize in any of the three fields mentioned.

Professional Accreditation. Some **Profiles** indicate whether a program is professionally accredited. Because it is possible for a program to receive or lose professional accreditation at any time, students entering fields in which accreditation is important to a career should verify the status of programs by contacting either the chairperson or the appropriate accrediting association.

Jointly Offered Degrees. Explanatory statements concerning programs that are offered in cooperation with other institutions are included in the list of degrees offered. This occurs most commonly on a

regional basis (for example, two state universities offering a cooperative Ph.D. in special education) or where the specialized nature of the institutions encourages joint efforts (a J.D./M.B.A. offered by a law school at an institution with no formal business programs and an institution with a business school but lacking a law school). Only programs that are truly cooperative are listed; those involving only limited course work at another institution are not. Interested students should contact the heads of such units for further information.

Program Availability. This may include the following: part-time, evening/weekend, online only, blended/hybrid learning, and/or minimal on-campus study. When information regarding the availability of part-time or evening/weekend study appears in the **Profile**, it means that students are able to earn a degree exclusively through such study. Blended/hybrid learning describes those courses in which some traditional in-class time has been replaced by online learning activities. Hybrid courses take advantage of the best features of both face-to-face and online learning.

Faculty. Figures on the number of faculty members actively involved with graduate students through teaching or research are separated into full- and part-time as well as men and women whenever the information has been supplied.

Students. Figures for the number of students enrolled in graduate and professional programs pertain to the semester of highest enrollment from the 2018–19 academic year. These figures are broken down into full- and part-time and men and women whenever the data have been supplied. Information on the number of matriculated students enrolled in the unit who are members of a minority group or are international students appears here. The average age of the matriculated students is followed by the number of applicants, the percentage accepted, and the number enrolled for fall 2018.

Degrees Awarded. The number of degrees awarded in the calendar year is listed. Many doctoral programs offer a terminal master's degree if students leave the program after completing only part of the requirements for a doctoral degree; that is indicated here. All degrees are classified into one of four types: master's, doctoral, first professional, and other advanced degrees. A unit may award one or several degrees at a given level; however, the data are only collected by type and may therefore represent several different degree programs.

Degree Requirements. The information in this section is also broken down by type of degree, and all information for a degree level pertains to all degrees of that type unless otherwise specified. Degree requirements are collected in a simplified form to provide some very basic information on the nature of the program and on foreign language, thesis or dissertation, comprehensive exam, and registration requirements. Many units also provide a short list of additional requirements, such as fieldwork or an internship. For complete information on graduation requirements, contact the graduate school or program directly.

Entrance Requirements. Entrance requirements are broken down into the four degree levels of master's, doctoral, first professional, and other advanced degrees. Within each level, information may be provided in two basic categories: entrance exams and other requirements. The entrance exams are identified by the standard acronyms used by the testing agencies, unless they are not well known. Other entrance requirements are quite varied, but they often contain an undergraduate or graduate grade point average (GPA). Unless otherwise stated, the GPA is calculated on a 4.0 scale and is listed as a minimum required for admission. Additional exam requirements/recommendations for international students may be listed here. Application deadlines for domestic and international students, the application fee, and whether electronic applications are accepted may be listed here. Note that the deadline should be used for reference only; these dates are subject to change, and students interested in applying should always contact the graduate unit directly about application procedures and deadlines.

Expenses. The typical cost of study for the 2018–2019 academic year (2017–18 if 2018–19 figures were not available) is given in two basic categories: tuition and fees. Cost of study may be quite complex at a graduate institution. There are often sliding scales for part-time study, a different cost for first-year students, and other variables that make it impossible to completely cover the cost of study for each graduate program. To provide the most usable information, figures are given for full-time study for a full year where available and for part-time study in terms of a per-unit rate (per credit, per semester hour, etc.). Occasionally, variances may be noted in tuition and fees for reasons such

as the type of program, whether courses are taken during the day or evening, whether courses are at the master's or doctoral level, or other institution-specific reasons. Respondents were also given the opportunity to provide more specific and detailed tuition and fees information at the unit level. When provided, this information will appear in place of any typical costs entered elsewhere on the university-level survey. Expenses are usually subject to change; for exact costs at any given time, contact your chosen schools and programs directly. Keep in mind that the tuition of Canadian institutions is usually given in Canadian dollars.

Financial Support. This section contains data on the number of awards administered by the institution and given to graduate students during the 2018–19 academic year. The first figure given represents the total number of students receiving financial support enrolled in that unit. If the unit has provided information on graduate appointments, these are broken down into three major categories: fellowships give money to graduate students to cover the cost of study and living expenses and are not based on a work obligation or research commitment, research assistantships provide stipends to graduate students for assistance in a formal research project with a faculty member, and teaching assistantships provide stipends to graduate students for teaching or for assisting faculty members in teaching undergraduate classes. Within each category, figures are given for the total number of awards, the average yearly amount per award, and whether full or partial tuition reimbursements are awarded. In addition to graduate appointments, the availability of several other financial aid sources is covered in this section. Tuition waivers are routinely part of a graduate appointment, but units sometimes waive part or all of a student's tuition even if a graduate appointment is not available. Federal Work Study is made available to students who demonstrate need and meet the federal guidelines; this form of aid normally includes 10 or more hours of work per week in an office of the institution. Institutionally sponsored loans are low-interest loans available to graduate students to cover both educational and living expenses. Career-related internships or fieldwork offer money to students who are participating in a formal off-campus research project or practicum. Grants, scholarships, traineeships, unspecified assistantships, and other awards may also be noted. The availability of financial support to part-time students is also indicated here.

Some programs list the financial aid application deadline and the forms that need to be completed for students to be eligible for financial awards. There are two forms: FAFSA, the Free Application for Federal Student Aid, which is required for federal aid, and the CSS PROFILE®.

Faculty Research. Each unit has the opportunity to list several keyword phrases describing the current research involving faculty members and graduate students. Space limitations prevent the unit from listing complete information on all research programs. The total expenditure for funded research from the previous academic year may also be included.

Unit Head and Application Contact. The head of the graduate program for each unit may be listed with academic title, phone and fax numbers, and e-mail address. In addition to the unit head's contact information, many graduate programs also list a separate contact for application and admission information, followed by the graduate school, program, or department's website. If no unit head or application contact is given, you should contact the overall institution for information on graduate admissions.

Displays and Close-Ups

The **Displays** and **Close-Ups** are supplementary insertions submitted by deans, chairs, and other administrators who wish to offer an additional, more individualized statement to readers. A number of graduate school and program administrators have attached a **Display** ad near the **Profile** listing. Here you will find information that an institution or program wants to emphasize. The **Close-Ups** are by their very nature more expansive and flexible than the **Profiles**, and the administrators who have written them may emphasize different aspects of their programs. All of the **Close-Ups** are organized in the same way (with the exception of a few that describe research and training opportunities instead of degree programs), and in each one you will find information on the same basic topics, such as programs of

study, research facilities, tuition and fees, financial aid, and application procedures. If an institution or program has submitted a **Close-Up**, a boldface cross-reference appears below its **Profile**. As with the **Displays**, all of the **Close-Ups** in the guides have been submitted by choice; the absence of a **Display** or **Close-Up** does not reflect any type of editorial judgment on the part of Peterson's, and their presence in the guides should not be taken as an indication of status, quality, or approval. Statements regarding a university's objectives and accomplishments are a reflection of its own beliefs and are not the opinions of the Peterson's editors.

Appendixes

This section contains two appendixes. The first, "Institutional Changes Since the 2018 Edition," lists institutions that have closed, merged, or changed their name or status since the last edition of the guides. The second, "Abbreviations Used in the Guides," gives abbreviations of degree names, along with what those abbreviations stand for. These appendixes are identical in all six volumes of *Peterson's Graduate and Professional Programs*.

Indexes

There are three indexes presented here. The first index, "Close-Ups and Displays," gives page references for all programs that have chosen to place **Close-Ups** and **Displays** in this volume. It is arranged alphabetically by institution; within institutions, the arrangement is alphabetical by subject area. It is not an index to all programs in the book's directories of **Profiles**; readers must refer to the directories themselves for **Profile** information on programs that have not submitted the additional, more individualized statements. The second index, "Directories and Subject Areas in Other Books in This Series", gives book references for the directories in the specialized volumes and also includes cross-references for subject area names not used in the directory structure, for example, "Computing Technology (see Computer Science)." The third index, "Directories and Subject Areas in This Book," gives page references for the directories in this volume and cross-references for subject area names not used in this volume's directory structure.

Data Collection Procedures

The information published in the directories and Profiles of all the books is collected through Peterson's Annual Survey of Graduate and Professional Institutions. The survey is sent each spring to nearly 2,300 institutions offering postbaccalaureate degree programs, including accredited institutions in the United States, U.S. territories, and Canada and those institutions outside the United States that are accredited by U.S. accrediting bodies. Deans and other administrators complete these surveys, providing information on programs in the 500 academic and professional fields covered in the guides as well as overall institutional information. While every effort has been made to ensure the accuracy and completeness of the data, information is sometimes unavailable or changes occur after publication deadlines. All usable information received in time for publication has been included. The omission of any particular item from a directory or Profile signifies either that the item is not applicable to the institution or program or that information was not available. Profiles of programs scheduled to begin during the 2018–19 academic year cannot, obviously, include statistics on enrollment or, in many cases, the number of faculty members. If no usable data were submitted by an institution, its name, address, and program name appear in order to indicate the availability of graduate work.

Criteria for Inclusion in This Guide

To be included in this guide, an institution must have full accreditation or be a candidate for accreditation (preaccreditation) status by an institutional or specialized accrediting body recognized by the U.S. Department of Education or the Council for Higher Education Accreditation (CHEA). Institutional accrediting bodies, which review each institution as a whole, include the six regional associations of schools and colleges (Middle States, New England, North Central, Northwest, Southern, and Western), each of which is responsible for a specified portion of the United States and its territories. Other institutional accrediting bodies are national in scope and accredit specific kinds of institutions (e.g., Bible colleges, independent colleges, and rabbinical and Talmudic schools). Program registration by the New York State Board of Regents is considered to be the equivalent of institutional accreditation, since the board requires that all programs offered by an institution meet its standards before recognition is granted. A Canadian institution must be chartered and authorized to grant degrees by the provincial government, affiliated with a chartered institution, or accredited by a recognized U.S. accrediting body. This guide also includes institutions outside the United States that are accredited by these U.S. accrediting bodies. There are recognized specialized or professional accrediting bodies in more than fifty different fields, each of which is authorized to accredit institutions or specific programs in its particular field. For specialized institutions that offer programs in one field only, we designate this to be the equivalent of institutional accreditation. A full explanation of the accrediting process and complete information on recognized institutional (regional and national) and specialized accrediting bodies can be found online at **www.chea.org** or at **www.ed.gov/admins/finaid/accred/index.html.**

DIRECTORY OF INSTITUTIONS WITH PROGRAMS IN BUSINESS, EDUCATION, INFORMATION STUDIES, LAW & SOCIAL WORK

ABILENE CHRISTIAN UNIVERSITY
Accounting — M
Business Administration and Management—General — M
Business Analytics — M
Education—General — M,O
Educational Leadership and Administration — M,D,O
Higher Education — M
Human Resources Development — M
Human Services — M,O
International Business — M
Marketing — M
Nonprofit Management — M
Reading Education — M
Social Work — M
Supply Chain Management — M

ABRAHAM LINCOLN UNIVERSITY
Law — D

ACACIA UNIVERSITY
Education—General — M
Educational Leadership and Administration — M
Elementary Education — M
English as a Second Language — M
Secondary Education — M
Special Education — M

ACADEMY OF ART UNIVERSITY
Advertising and Public Relations — M
Art Education — M

ACADIA UNIVERSITY
Counselor Education — M
Curriculum and Instruction — M
Education—General — M,D
Educational Leadership and Administration — M
Music Education — M
Recreation and Park Management — M
Special Education — M

ADAMS STATE UNIVERSITY
Business Administration and Management—General — M
Counselor Education — M,D
Curriculum and Instruction — M
Education—General — M
Educational Leadership and Administration — M
Exercise and Sports Science — M
Mathematics Education — M
Music Education — M
Physical Education — M
Science Education — M
Sports Management — M

ADELPHI UNIVERSITY
Accounting — M
Art Education — M
Business Administration and Management—General — M
Education—General — M,D,O
Educational Media/Instructional Technology — M
Elementary Education — M
English as a Second Language — M,O
Finance and Banking — M
Health Education — M,O
Human Resources Management — M,O
Management Information Systems — M
Marketing — M
Physical Education — M,O
Reading Education — M
Secondary Education — M
Social Work — M,D
Special Education — M,O
Sports Management — M
Supply Chain Management — M

ADLER GRADUATE SCHOOL
Counselor Education — M

ADLER UNIVERSITY
Counselor Education — D
Sustainability Management — M

ADRIAN COLLEGE
Accounting — M
Athletic Training and Sports Medicine — M

AIR FORCE INSTITUTE OF TECHNOLOGY
Logistics — M,D
Management Information Systems — M

ALABAMA AGRICULTURAL AND MECHANICAL UNIVERSITY
Art Education — M
Business Administration and Management—General — M
Business Education — M,O
Counselor Education — M,O
Early Childhood Education — M,D,O
Education—General — M,D,O
Educational Media/Instructional Technology — M,O
Elementary Education — M,D,O
English Education — M,O
Home Economics Education — M,O
Hospitality Management — M
Kinesiology and Movement Studies — M
Mathematics Education — M
Music Education — M
Physical Education — M
Reading Education — M,D,O
Science Education — M,O
Secondary Education — M,O
Social Sciences Education — M,O
Social Work — M,O
Special Education — M,D,O

ALABAMA STATE UNIVERSITY
Accounting — M

ALASKA PACIFIC UNIVERSITY
Business Administration and Management—General — M
Education—General — M
Elementary Education — M
Environmental Education — M
Investment Management — M,O
Middle School Education — M

ALBANY LAW SCHOOL
Law — M,D

ALBANY STATE UNIVERSITY
Accounting — M
Business Administration and Management—General — M
Counselor Education — M,O
Early Childhood Education — M,O
Education—General — M,O
Educational Leadership and Administration — M,O
English Education — M
Health Education — M,O
Human Resources Management — M
Logistics — M
Middle School Education — M,O
Physical Education — M,O
Social Work — M
Special Education — M,O
Supply Chain Management — M

ALBERTUS MAGNUS COLLEGE
Accounting — M
Business Administration and Management—General — M
Education—General — M
Human Resources Management — M
Human Services — M
Organizational Management — M
Project Management — M

ALBIZU UNIVERSITY, MIAMI CAMPUS
Business Administration and Management—General — M,D
Education of the Gifted — M,D
English as a Second Language — M,D
Entrepreneurship — M,D
Human Services — M,D
Nonprofit Management — M,D
Organizational Management — M,D
Special Education — M,D

ALBRIGHT COLLEGE
Early Childhood Education — M
Education—General — M
Elementary Education — M
English as a Second Language — M
Special Education — M

ALCORN STATE UNIVERSITY
Agricultural Education — M,O
Business Administration and Management—General — M
Counselor Education — M,O
Education—General — M,O
Elementary Education — M,O
Health Education — M,O
Physical Education — M,O
Secondary Education — M,O
Special Education — M,O
Sports Management — M,O
Vocational and Technical Education — M,O

ALFRED UNIVERSITY
Accounting — M
Business Administration and Management—General — M
Counselor Education — M,D,O
Education—General — M
Reading Education — M
Student Affairs — M

ALLEN COLLEGE
Health Education — M,D

ALLIANT INTERNATIONAL UNIVERSITY–IRVINE
Educational Psychology — M,D,O

ALLIANT INTERNATIONAL UNIVERSITY–LOS ANGELES
Business Administration and Management—General — D
Education—General — M,O
Educational Psychology — M,D,O
Student Affairs — M,D,O

ALLIANT INTERNATIONAL UNIVERSITY–SACRAMENTO
Education—General — M,O

ALLIANT INTERNATIONAL UNIVERSITY–SAN DIEGO
Business Administration and Management—General — M
Education—General — M,O
Educational Leadership and Administration — M,D,O
Educational Psychology — M,D,O

English as a Second Language — M,D,O
Higher Education — M,D,O
Student Affairs — M,D,O

ALLIANT INTERNATIONAL UNIVERSITY–SAN FRANCISCO
Counselor Education — M
Education—General — M,O
Educational Leadership and Administration — M,D,O
Educational Psychology — M,D,O
English as a Second Language — M,O
Higher Education — M,D,O
Law — D
Multilingual and Multicultural Education — M,O
Special Education — M,O

ALVERNIA UNIVERSITY
Business Administration and Management—General — M
Education—General — M
Organizational Management — D
Urban Education — M

ALVERNO COLLEGE
Adult Education — M
Business Administration and Management—General — M
Education—General — M
Educational Leadership and Administration — M
Educational Media/Instructional Technology — M
Reading Education — M
Science Education — M
Special Education — M

AMBERTON UNIVERSITY
Business Administration and Management—General — M
Counselor Education — M
Human Resources Development — M
Human Resources Management — M
International Business — M
Management Strategy and Policy — M
Project Management — M

AMERICAN BUSINESS & TECHNOLOGY UNIVERSITY
Accounting — M
Business Administration and Management—General — M
Finance and Banking — M
International Business — M
Management Information Systems — M
Marketing — M
Project Management — M

AMERICAN COLLEGE DUBLIN
Business Administration and Management—General — M
International Business — M

AMERICAN COLLEGE OF EDUCATION
Curriculum and Instruction — M
Education—General — M
Educational Leadership and Administration — M
Educational Media/Instructional Technology — M
English as a Second Language — M
Multilingual and Multicultural Education — M

THE AMERICAN COLLEGE OF FINANCIAL SERVICES
Business Administration and Management—General — M
Finance and Banking — M
Organizational Management — M

AMERICAN COLLEGE OF THESSALONIKI
Business Administration and Management—General — M,O
Entrepreneurship — M,O
Finance and Banking — M,O
Marketing — M,O

AMERICAN GRADUATE UNIVERSITY
Business Administration and Management—General — M,O
Supply Chain Management — M,O

AMERICAN INTERCONTINENTAL UNIVERSITY ATLANTA
International Business — M
Management Information Systems — M

AMERICAN INTERCONTINENTAL UNIVERSITY HOUSTON
Business Administration and Management—General — M

AMERICAN INTERCONTINENTAL UNIVERSITY ONLINE
Accounting — M
Business Administration and Management—General — M
Curriculum and Instruction — M
Education—General — M
Educational Leadership and Administration — M
Educational Measurement and Evaluation — M
Educational Media/Instructional Technology — M
Finance and Banking — M
Human Resources Management — M
Industrial and Manufacturing Management — M
International Business — M
Marketing — M
Project Management — M

AMERICAN INTERNATIONAL COLLEGE
Accounting — M,D,O

AMERICAN JEWISH UNIVERSITY
Business Administration and Management—General — M
Education—General — M
Nonprofit Management — M
Social Work — M

AMERICAN NATIONAL UNIVERSITY
Business Administration and Management—General — M

AMERICAN PUBLIC UNIVERSITY SYSTEM
Accounting — M,D
Business Administration and Management—General — M,D
Business Analytics — M,D
Educational Leadership and Administration — M,D
Logistics — M,D
Secondary Education — M,D
Sports Management — M,D
Transportation Management — M,D

AMERICAN SENTINEL UNIVERSITY
Business Administration and Management—General — M
Management Information Systems — M

AMERICAN UNIVERSITY
Accounting — M,O
Business Administration and Management—General — M,O
Education—General — M
Educational Leadership and Administration — M,O
Educational Measurement and Evaluation — M,O
Educational Media/Instructional Technology — M,O
Educational Policy — M,O
English as a Second Language — M,O
Entrepreneurship — M,D,O
Finance and Banking — M,O
Human Resources Management — M,O
International and Comparative Education — M
Law — M,D
Management Information Systems — M,D,O
Marketing — M
Nonprofit Management — M,D,O
Organizational Management — M,D,O
Project Management — M,O
Real Estate — M,O
Special Education — M,O
Sports Management — M,O
Sustainability Management — M
Taxation — M,O

AMERICAN UNIVERSITY IN BULGARIA
Business Administration and Management—General — M

THE AMERICAN UNIVERSITY IN CAIRO
Business Administration and Management—General — M,O
Education—General — M
Educational Leadership and Administration — M
English as a Second Language — M,O
Finance and Banking — M,O
International and Comparative Education — M
Law — M

THE AMERICAN UNIVERSITY IN DUBAI
Business Administration and Management—General — M
Education—General — M
Finance and Banking — M
International Business — M
Marketing — M

AMERICAN UNIVERSITY OF ARMENIA
Business Administration and Management—General — M
English as a Second Language — M
Law — M
Management Information Systems — M

AMERICAN UNIVERSITY OF BEIRUT
Business Administration and Management—General — M
Education—General — M,D
Educational Leadership and Administration — M,D
Educational Policy — M,D
Elementary Education — M,D
English as a Second Language — M,D
Finance and Banking — M,D
Human Resources Management — M
Mathematics Education — M,D
Science Education — M,D

THE AMERICAN UNIVERSITY OF PARIS
Business Administration and Management—General — M
International Business — M
Law — M

AMERICAN UNIVERSITY OF PUERTO RICO
Art Education	M
Education—General	M
Elementary Education	M
Physical Education	M
Science Education	M
Special Education	M

AMERICAN UNIVERSITY OF SHARJAH
Accounting	M,D
Business Administration and Management—General	M,D
English as a Second Language	M,D

AMRIDGE UNIVERSITY
Counselor Education	M,D
Human Services	M,D

ANAHEIM UNIVERSITY
Business Administration and Management—General	M,D,O
English as a Second Language	M,D,O
Entrepreneurship	M,D,O
International Business	M,D,O
Sustainability Management	M,D,O

ANDERSON UNIVERSITY (IN)
Accounting	M,D
Business Administration and Management—General	M,D
Education—General	M

ANDERSON UNIVERSITY (SC)
Business Administration and Management—General	M
Education—General	M
Educational Leadership and Administration	M
Elementary Education	M
Human Resources Management	M
Marketing	M
Music Education	M
Organizational Management	M
Supply Chain Management	M

ANDREWS UNIVERSITY
Accounting	M
Curriculum and Instruction	M,D,O
Education—General	M,D,O
Educational Leadership and Administration	M,D,O
Educational Psychology	M,D
Elementary Education	M,D,O
English as a Second Language	M,D,O
English Education	M,D,O
Finance and Banking	M
Foreign Languages Education	M,D,O
Higher Education	M,D,O
International and Comparative Education	M
Religious Education	M,D,O
Science Education	M,D,O
Secondary Education	M,D,O
Social Sciences Education	M,D,O
Social Work	M
Special Education	M

ANGELO STATE UNIVERSITY
Accounting	M
Business Administration and Management—General	M
Counselor Education	M
Curriculum and Instruction	M
Educational Leadership and Administration	M
English as a Second Language	M
Higher Education	M
Sports Management	M

ANNA MARIA COLLEGE
Business Administration and Management—General	M,O
Early Childhood Education	M,O
Education—General	M,O
Elementary Education	M,O
English Education	M,O
Social Work	M

ANTIOCH UNIVERSITY LOS ANGELES
Business Administration and Management—General	M
Education—General	M
Human Resources Development	M
Organizational Management	M

ANTIOCH UNIVERSITY NEW ENGLAND
Business Administration and Management—General	M
Early Childhood Education	M
Education—General	M,O
Educational Leadership and Administration	M,O
Educational Media/Instructional Technology	M,O
Elementary Education	M,O
Environmental Education	M
Foundations and Philosophy of Education	M,O
Science Education	M
Special Education	M,O
Sustainability Management	M

ANTIOCH UNIVERSITY SANTA BARBARA
Business Administration and Management—General	M
Education—General	M
Management Strategy and Policy	M
Nonprofit Management	M

ANTIOCH UNIVERSITY SEATTLE
Adult Education	M
Counselor Education	M,D
Education—General	M

APOLLOS UNIVERSITY
Business Administration and Management—General	M,D
Organizational Management	M,D

APPALACHIAN SCHOOL OF LAW
Law	D

APPALACHIAN STATE UNIVERSITY
Accounting	M
Business Administration and Management—General	M
Counselor Education	M
Curriculum and Instruction	M
Educational Leadership and Administration	M,O
Educational Media/Instructional Technology	M,O
Elementary Education	M
English Education	M
Exercise and Sports Science	M
Foreign Languages Education	M
Higher Education	M,O
Library Science	M,O
Mathematics Education	M
Middle School Education	M
Reading Education	M
Science Education	M
Social Sciences Education	M
Social Work	M
Special Education	M
Student Affairs	M
Taxation	M
Vocational and Technical Education	M

AQUINAS COLLEGE (MI)
Business Administration and Management—General	M
Education—General	M
Marketing	M
Organizational Management	M
Sustainability Management	M

AQUINAS COLLEGE (TN)
Education—General	M
Elementary Education	M
Secondary Education	M

ARCADIA UNIVERSITY
Art Education	M,D,O
Business Administration and Management—General	M
Computer Education	M,D,O
Curriculum and Instruction	M,D,O
Early Childhood Education	M,D,O
Education—General	M,D,O
Educational Leadership and Administration	M,D,O
Educational Media/Instructional Technology	M,D,O
Elementary Education	M,D,O
English Education	M,D,O
Environmental Education	M,D,O
Health Education	M
Mathematics Education	M,D,O
Music Education	M,D,O
Reading Education	M,D,O
Science Education	M,D,O
Secondary Education	M,D,O
Special Education	M,D,O

ARGOSY UNIVERSITY, ATLANTA
Accounting	M,D
Business Administration and Management—General	M,D
Counselor Education	M,D,O
Education—General	M,D,O
Educational Leadership and Administration	M,D,O
Educational Media/Instructional Technology	M,D,O
Elementary Education	M,D,O
Finance and Banking	M,D
Higher Education	M,D,O
International Business	M,D
Management Information Systems	M,D
Marketing	M,D
Secondary Education	M,D,O

ARGOSY UNIVERSITY, CHICAGO
Accounting	M,D
Adult Education	M,D,O
Business Administration and Management—General	M,D
Community College Education	M,D,O
Counselor Education	D
Education—General	M,D,O
Educational Leadership and Administration	M,D,O
Elementary Education	M,D,O
Finance and Banking	M,D
Higher Education	M,D,O
International Business	M,D
Management Information Systems	M,D
Marketing	M,D
Organizational Behavior	D
Organizational Management	D
Secondary Education	M,D,O
Sustainability Management	M,D

ARGOSY UNIVERSITY, HAWAI'I
Accounting	M,D,O
Adult Education	M,D
Business Administration and Management—General	M,D,O
Education—General	M,D
Educational Leadership and Administration	M,D
Elementary Education	M,D
Finance and Banking	M,D,O
Higher Education	M,D
International Business	M,D,O
Management Information Systems	M,D,O
Marketing	M,D,O
Organizational Management	D
Secondary Education	M,D
Sustainability Management	M,D,O

ARGOSY UNIVERSITY, LOS ANGELES
Accounting	M,D
Business Administration and Management—General	M,D
Community College Education	M,D
Education—General	M,D
Educational Leadership and Administration	M,D
Elementary Education	M,D
Finance and Banking	M,D
Higher Education	M,D
International Business	M,D
Management Information Systems	M,D
Marketing	M,D
Organizational Management	M,D
Secondary Education	M,D
Sustainability Management	M,D

ARGOSY UNIVERSITY, NORTHERN VIRGINIA
Accounting	M,D,O
Business Administration and Management—General	M,D,O
Community College Education	M,D,O
Counselor Education	M,D
Education—General	M,D,O
Educational Leadership and Administration	M,D,O
Elementary Education	M,D,O
Finance and Banking	M,D,O
Higher Education	M,D,O
International Business	M,D,O
Management Information Systems	M,D,O
Marketing	M,D,O
Organizational Management	M,D,O
Secondary Education	M,D,O
Sustainability Management	M,D,O

ARGOSY UNIVERSITY, ORANGE COUNTY
Accounting	M,D,O
Business Administration and Management—General	M,D,O
Community College Education	M,D
Education—General	M,D
Educational Leadership and Administration	M,D
Educational Media/Instructional Technology	M,D
Elementary Education	M,D
Finance and Banking	M,D,O
Higher Education	M,D
International Business	M,D,O
Management Information Systems	M,D,O
Marketing	M,D,O
Organizational Management	D
Secondary Education	M,D
Sustainability Management	M,D,O

ARGOSY UNIVERSITY, PHOENIX
Accounting	M,D
Adult Education	M,D,O
Business Administration and Management—General	M,D
Community College Education	M,D,O
Education—General	M,D,O
Educational Leadership and Administration	M,D,O
Educational Media/Instructional Technology	M,D,O
Elementary Education	M,D,O
Finance and Banking	M,D
Higher Education	M,D,O
International Business	M,D
Management Information Systems	M,D
Marketing	M,D
Secondary Education	M,D,O
Sustainability Management	M,D

ARGOSY UNIVERSITY, SEATTLE
Accounting	M,D
Adult Education	M,D
Business Administration and Management—General	M,D
Community College Education	M,D
Education—General	M,D
Educational Leadership and Administration	M,D
Educational Media/Instructional Technology	M,D
Elementary Education	M,D
Finance and Banking	M,D
Higher Education	M,D
International Business	M,D
Management Information Systems	M,D
Marketing	M,D
Organizational Management	M,D
Secondary Education	M,D
Sustainability Management	M,D

ARGOSY UNIVERSITY, TAMPA
Accounting	M,D
Business Administration and Management—General	M,D
Community College Education	M,D,O
Counselor Education	M,D,O
Education—General	M,D,O
Educational Leadership and Administration	M,D,O
Elementary Education	M,D,O
Finance and Banking	M,D
Higher Education	M,D,O
International Business	M,D
Management Information Systems	M,D
Marketing	M,D
Organizational Management	M,D
Secondary Education	M,D,O
Sustainability Management	M,D

ARGOSY UNIVERSITY, TWIN CITIES
Accounting	M,D
Business Administration and Management—General	M,D
Education—General	M,D,O
Educational Leadership and Administration	M,D,O
Educational Media/Instructional Technology	M,D,O
Elementary Education	M,D,O
Finance and Banking	M,D
Higher Education	M,D,O
International Business	M,D
Management Information Systems	M,D
Marketing	M,D
Organizational Management	M,D
Secondary Education	M,D,O
Sustainability Management	M,D

ARIZONA STATE UNIVERSITY AT THE TEMPE CAMPUS
Accounting	M,D
Art Education	M,D
Aviation Management	M
Business Administration and Management—General	M,D
Counselor Education	M
Curriculum and Instruction	M
Education—General	M,D,O
Educational Leadership and Administration	M,D
Educational Measurement and Evaluation	D
Educational Media/Instructional Technology	M,O
Educational Policy	D
Elementary Education	M
English as a Second Language	M,D,O
Entrepreneurship	M,D
Exercise and Sports Science	M,D
Finance and Banking	M,D
Foreign Languages Education	M,D
Health Education	D
Higher Education	M
International Business	M,D
Law	M,D
Legal and Justice Studies	M,D,O
Management Information Systems	M,D
Management Strategy and Policy	M,D
Marketing	M,D
Mathematics Education	M,D,O
Music Education	M,D
Nonprofit Management	M,D,O
Organizational Behavior	M,D
Physical Education	M
Real Estate	M,D
Secondary Education	M
Social Work	M,D,O
Special Education	M,O
Sports and Entertainment Law	M,D
Supply Chain Management	M,D
Travel and Tourism	M,D,O

ARKANSAS STATE UNIVERSITY
Accounting	M
Agricultural Education	M,O
Business Administration and Management—General	M
Business Education	O
Community College Education	M,D,O
Counselor Education	M,O
Early Childhood Education	M,D,O
Education of the Gifted	M,D,O
Education—General	M,D,O
Educational Leadership and Administration	M,D,O
Elementary Education	M,D,O
English Education	M,O
Exercise and Sports Science	M,O
Foundations and Philosophy of Education	M,D,O
Health Education	M,D,O
Management Information Systems	O
Mathematics Education	M
Middle School Education	M,D,O
Music Education	M,O
Physical Education	M,O
Reading Education	M,D,O
Science Education	M,O
Social Sciences Education	M,D,O
Social Work	M,O
Special Education	M,D,O
Sports Management	M,O
Student Affairs	M,O

ARKANSAS TECH UNIVERSITY
Business Administration and Management—General	M
Counselor Education	M,D,O
Education—General	M,D,O
Educational Leadership and Administration	M,D,O
Educational Media/Instructional Technology	M,D,O
Elementary Education	M,D,O
English as a Second Language	M
English Education	M
Special Education	M,D,O
Student Affairs	M,D,O

ARLINGTON BAPTIST UNIVERSITY
Curriculum and Instruction	M
Education—General	M
Educational Leadership and Administration	M

ART ACADEMY OF CINCINNATI
Art Education	M

ASBURY THEOLOGICAL SEMINARY
Religious Education	M,D,O

*M—masters degree; D—doctorate; O—other advanced degree; *—Close-Up and/or Display*

ASBURY UNIVERSITY
- Educational Leadership and Administration M
- English as a Second Language M
- Mathematics Education M
- Reading Education M
- Science Education M
- Social Sciences Education M
- Social Work M
- Special Education M

ASHLAND THEOLOGICAL SEMINARY
- Counselor Education M,D

ASHLAND UNIVERSITY
- Accounting M
- Business Administration and Management—General M
- Business Analytics M
- Education—General M,D
- Educational Leadership and Administration M,D
- Entrepreneurship M
- Exercise and Sports Science M
- Finance and Banking M
- Human Resources Management M
- International Business M
- Management Information Systems M
- Project Management M
- Sports Management M
- Supply Chain Management M

ASHWORTH COLLEGE
- Business Administration and Management—General M
- Human Resources Management M
- International Business M
- Marketing M

ASPEN UNIVERSITY
- Business Administration and Management—General M,O
- Finance and Banking M,O
- Management Information Systems M,O
- Project Management M,O

ASSUMPTION COLLEGE
- Accounting M,O
- Business Administration and Management—General M,O
- Finance and Banking M,O
- Human Resources Management M,O
- International Business M,O
- Marketing M,O
- Nonprofit Management M,O
- Special Education M,O

ATHABASCA UNIVERSITY
- Adult Education M,O
- Business Administration and Management—General M,D,O
- Counselor Education M,O
- Distance Education Development M,D,O
- Education—General M,D,O
- Organizational Management M,O
- Project Management M,D,O
- Science Education M,O

ATHENS STATE UNIVERSITY
- Logistics M
- Supply Chain Management M
- Vocational and Technical Education M

ATLANTA'S JOHN MARSHALL LAW SCHOOL
- Law M,D

ATLANTIC UNIVERSITY
- Organizational Management M,O

ATLANTIS UNIVERSITY
- Business Administration and Management—General M,D

A.T. STILL UNIVERSITY
- Athletic Training and Sports Medicine M,D,O
- Kinesiology and Movement Studies M,D,O
- Organizational Behavior M,D,O

AUBURN UNIVERSITY
- Accounting M
- Adult Education M,D,O
- Business Administration and Management—General M,D
- Curriculum and Instruction M,D,O
- Education—General M,D,O
- Educational Leadership and Administration M,D,O
- Educational Media/Instructional Technology M,D,O
- Exercise and Sports Science M,D,O
- Finance and Banking M
- Health Education M,D,O
- Higher Education M,D,O
- Physical Education M,D,O
- Real Estate M
- Social Work M
- Special Education M,D

AUBURN UNIVERSITY AT MONTGOMERY
- Accounting M
- Business Administration and Management—General M
- Counselor Education M,O
- Early Childhood Education M,O
- Education—General M,O
- Educational Leadership and Administration M,O
- Educational Media/Instructional Technology M,O
- Elementary Education M,O
- Exercise and Sports Science M,O
- Legal and Justice Studies M
- Management Information Systems M
- Physical Education M,O
- Secondary Education M,O
- Special Education M,O
- Sports Management M,O

AUGSBURG UNIVERSITY
- Business Administration and Management—General M
- Education—General M
- Organizational Management M
- Social Work M

AUGUSTANA UNIVERSITY
- Accounting M
- Education—General M
- Educational Media/Instructional Technology M
- Reading Education M
- Science Education M
- Special Education M
- Sports Management M

AUGUSTA UNIVERSITY
- Business Administration and Management—General M
- Counselor Education M,O
- Curriculum and Instruction M,O
- Education—General M,D,O
- Educational Leadership and Administration M,O
- Educational Media/Instructional Technology D
- Elementary Education M,O
- Foreign Languages Education M,O
- Middle School Education M,O
- Music Education M,O
- Secondary Education M,O
- Special Education M,O

AURORA UNIVERSITY
- Accounting M
- Adult Education M,D
- Business Administration and Management—General M
- Curriculum and Instruction M,D
- Education—General M,D
- Educational Leadership and Administration M,D
- Educational Media/Instructional Technology M,D
- English as a Second Language M,D
- Mathematics Education M
- Reading Education M,D
- Science Education M
- Social Work M,D
- Special Education M,D

AUSTIN COLLEGE
- Education—General M

AUSTIN PEAY STATE UNIVERSITY
- Business Administration and Management—General M
- Counselor Education M
- Education—General M,O
- Exercise and Sports Science M
- Health Education M
- Mathematics Education M
- Music Education M
- Organizational Management M
- Science Education M
- Social Work M
- Sports Management M

AVE MARIA SCHOOL OF LAW
- Law D

AVERETT UNIVERSITY
- Accounting M
- Business Administration and Management—General M
- Curriculum and Instruction M
- Education—General M
- Educational Leadership and Administration M
- Human Resources Management M
- Marketing M
- Special Education M

AVILA UNIVERSITY
- Business Administration and Management—General M
- Early Childhood Education M,O
- Education—General M,O
- Educational Media/Instructional Technology M
- Elementary Education M,O
- English as a Second Language M,O
- Human Resources Management M
- Middle School Education M,O
- Nonprofit Management M
- Organizational Management M
- Physical Education M,O
- Project Management M
- Secondary Education M,O

AZUSA PACIFIC UNIVERSITY
- Accounting M
- Athletic Training and Sports Medicine M
- Business Administration and Management—General M
- Counselor Education M
- Curriculum and Instruction M
- Education—General M,D
- Educational Leadership and Administration M,D
- Educational Media/Instructional Technology M
- English as a Second Language M
- Entrepreneurship M
- Finance and Banking M
- Higher Education M,D
- International Business M
- Kinesiology and Movement Studies M
- Marketing M
- Music Education M
- Organizational Management M
- Social Work M
- Special Education M
- Sports Management M

BABSON COLLEGE
- Accounting M,O
- Business Administration and Management—General M,O
- Business Analytics M,O
- Entrepreneurship M,O
- Finance and Banking M,O

BAKER COLLEGE CENTER FOR GRADUATE STUDIES–ONLINE
- Accounting M,D
- Business Administration and Management—General M,D
- Finance and Banking M,D
- Human Resources Management M,D
- Management Information Systems M,D
- Marketing M,D

BAKER UNIVERSITY
- Business Administration and Management—General M
- Education—General M,D
- Organizational Management M

BAKKE GRADUATE UNIVERSITY
- Business Administration and Management—General M,D
- Entrepreneurship M,D
- Urban Education M,D

BALDWIN WALLACE UNIVERSITY
- Accounting M
- Business Administration and Management—General M
- Business Analytics M
- Education—General M
- Educational Leadership and Administration M
- Educational Media/Instructional Technology M
- Health Education M
- Human Resources Management M
- International Business M
- Reading Education M
- Special Education M

BALL STATE UNIVERSITY
- Accounting M
- Actuarial Science M
- Adult Education M,D
- Advertising and Public Relations M
- Business Administration and Management—General M,O
- Business Education M,O
- Computer Education M,D,O
- Counselor Education M,D
- Curriculum and Instruction M,D
- Education of the Gifted M,D,O
- Education—General M,D,O
- Educational Leadership and Administration M,D,O
- Educational Measurement and Evaluation M,D,O
- Educational Media/Instructional Technology M,D
- Educational Policy D
- Educational Psychology M,D
- Elementary Education M,D,O
- English as a Second Language M
- Environmental Education M,O
- Exercise and Sports Science M,D
- Foundations and Philosophy of Education D
- Higher Education M,D
- Kinesiology and Movement Studies M,D,O
- Management Information Systems M,O
- Mathematics Education M
- Middle School Education M,O
- Music Education M,D,O
- Physical Education M
- Reading Education M,D,O
- Secondary Education M
- Special Education M,D,O
- Sports Management M

BANK STREET COLLEGE OF EDUCATION
- Early Childhood Education M
- Education—General M
- Educational Leadership and Administration M
- Elementary Education M
- Foundations and Philosophy of Education M
- Mathematics Education M
- Multilingual and Multicultural Education M
- Museum Education M
- Reading Education M
- Special Education M

BARD COLLEGE
- Education—General M
- Mathematics Education M
- Science Education M
- Secondary Education M
- Sustainability Management M,O

BARRY UNIVERSITY
- Accounting M
- Athletic Training and Sports Medicine M
- Business Administration and Management—General M,O
- Counselor Education M,D,O
- Curriculum and Instruction D,O
- Distance Education Development O
- Early Childhood Education M,D,O
- Education of the Gifted M,D,O
- Education—General M,D,O
- Educational Leadership and Administration M,D,O
- Educational Media/Instructional Technology M,D,O
- Elementary Education M,D,O
- English as a Second Language M,D,O
- Exercise and Sports Science M
- Finance and Banking O
- Higher Education M,D
- Human Resources Development M,D
- Human Resources Management O
- International Business O
- Kinesiology and Movement Studies M
- Law D
- Management Information Systems O
- Marketing O
- Reading Education M,D,O
- Social Work M,D
- Special Education M,D,O
- Sports Management M

BARTON COLLEGE
- Elementary Education M

BARUCH COLLEGE OF THE CITY UNIVERSITY OF NEW YORK
- Accounting M,D
- Business Administration and Management—General M,D,O
- Educational Leadership and Administration M,O
- Entrepreneurship M,D
- Finance and Banking M,D
- Higher Education M
- Human Resources Management M,D
- Industrial and Manufacturing Management M,D
- International Business M,D
- Management Information Systems M,D
- Marketing M,D
- Nonprofit Management M
- Organizational Behavior M,D
- Quantitative Analysis M
- Real Estate M
- Sustainability Management M,D
- Taxation M

BAYAMÓN CENTRAL UNIVERSITY
- Accounting M
- Business Administration and Management—General M
- Counselor Education M,O
- Early Childhood Education M,O
- Education—General M,O
- Educational Leadership and Administration M,O
- Elementary Education M,O
- Finance and Banking M
- Marketing M
- Special Education M,O

BAYLOR UNIVERSITY
- Accounting M
- Athletic Training and Sports Medicine M,D
- Business Administration and Management—General M
- Curriculum and Instruction M,D
- Education—General M,D,O
- Educational Leadership and Administration M,O
- Educational Psychology M,D,O
- Entrepreneurship D
- Exercise and Sports Science M,D
- Health Education M,D
- Kinesiology and Movement Studies M,D
- Law D
- Management Information Systems M,D
- Physical Education M,D
- Social Work M,D
- Special Education M,D,O

BAY PATH UNIVERSITY
- Accounting M
- Educational Leadership and Administration M
- Educational Media/Instructional Technology M
- Entrepreneurship M
- Higher Education M
- Management Information Systems M
- Management Strategy and Policy M
- Nonprofit Management M
- Special Education M

BECKER COLLEGE
- Counselor Education M

BELHAVEN UNIVERSITY (MS)
- Business Administration and Management—General M
- Education—General M,D,O
- Educational Leadership and Administration M,D,O
- Human Resources Management M
- Reading Education M,D,O
- Sports Management M

BELLARMINE UNIVERSITY
- Athletic Training and Sports Medicine M,D
- Business Administration and Management—General M
- Education—General M,D,O
- Educational Leadership and Administration M,D,O
- Elementary Education M,D,O
- Higher Education M,D,O
- Middle School Education M,D,O
- Reading Education M,D,O
- Secondary Education M,D,O

BELLEVUE UNIVERSITY
- Business Administration and Management—General M,D
- Counselor Education M
- Educational Media/Instructional Technology M
- Finance and Banking M,D
- Human Resources Management M,D
- Human Services M
- Management Information Systems M

Organizational Management — M
Project Management — M

BELMONT UNIVERSITY
Accounting — M
Business Administration and
  Management—General — M
Law — D

BEMIDJI STATE UNIVERSITY
Education—General — M
Mathematics Education — M
Special Education — M

BENEDICTINE COLLEGE
Business Administration and
  Management—General — M
Education—General — M
Educational Leadership and
  Administration — M

BENEDICTINE UNIVERSITY
Accounting — M
Business Administration and
  Management—General — M,D
Entrepreneurship — M
Exercise and Sports Science — M
Finance and Banking — M
Health Education — M
Human Resources Management — M
International Business — M
Logistics — M
Management Information Systems — M
Marketing — M
Organizational Behavior — M,D
Organizational Management — M,D

BENTLEY UNIVERSITY
Accounting — M,D
Business Administration and
  Management—General — M,D,O
Business Analytics — M,O
Finance and Banking — M
Marketing — M
Taxation — M

**BERKELEY COLLEGE–WOODLAND
PARK CAMPUS**
Business Administration and
  Management—General — M

BERKLEE COLLEGE OF MUSIC
Entertainment Management — M

BERRY COLLEGE
Business Administration and
  Management—General — M
Curriculum and Instruction — M,O
Education—General — M,O
Educational Leadership and
  Administration — O
Middle School Education — M
Reading Education — M
Secondary Education — M

BETHANY COLLEGE
Education—General — M

BETHEL UNIVERSITY (IN)
Business Administration and
  Management—General — M
Education—General — M

BETHEL UNIVERSITY (MN)
Business Administration and
  Management—General — M,D,O
Education—General — M,D,O
Educational Leadership and
  Administration — M,D,O
Elementary Education — M,D,O
Organizational Management — M,D,O
Secondary Education — M,D,O
Special Education — M,D,O

BETHEL UNIVERSITY (TN)
Business Administration and
  Management—General — M
Educational Leadership and
  Administration — M

**BINGHAMTON UNIVERSITY, STATE
UNIVERSITY OF NEW YORK**
Accounting — M
Business Administration and
  Management—General — M,D
Early Childhood Education — M
Education—General — M,D,O
Educational Leadership and
  Administration — M,D,O
English as a Second Language — M
English Education — M
Finance and Banking — D
Foreign Languages Education — M
Foundations and Philosophy of
  Education — D
Legal and Justice Studies — M,D
Management Information Systems — D
Marketing — D
Mathematics Education — M
Organizational Management — D
Reading Education — M
Science Education — M
Secondary Education — M
Social Sciences Education — M
Social Work — M
Special Education — M
Student Affairs — M
Supply Chain Management — D

BIOLA UNIVERSITY
Business Administration and
  Management—General — M
Curriculum and Instruction — M,O
Early Childhood Education — M,O
Education—General — M,O
English as a Second Language — M,D,O

Religious Education — M,D,O
Science Education — M,O
Special Education — M,O

BISHOP'S UNIVERSITY
Education—General — M,O
English as a Second Language — M,O

BLACK HILLS STATE UNIVERSITY
Business Administration and
  Management—General — M
Curriculum and Instruction — M
Management Strategy and Policy — M

BLOOMFIELD COLLEGE
Accounting — M

**BLOOMSBURG UNIVERSITY OF
PENNSYLVANIA**
Accounting — M
Athletic Training and Sports
  Medicine — M
Business Administration and
  Management—General — M,O
Business Education — M
Counselor Education — M
Curriculum and Instruction — M,O
Early Childhood Education — M
Education—General — M
Educational Leadership and
  Administration — M
Educational Media/Instructional
  Technology — M,O
English Education — M
Exercise and Sports Science — M
Mathematics Education — M
Middle School Education — M
Reading Education — M
Science Education — M
Social Sciences Education — M
Special Education — M,O
Student Affairs — M

BLUEFIELD COLLEGE
Education—General — M

BLUE MOUNTAIN COLLEGE
Elementary Education — M
Reading Education — M
Science Education — M
Secondary Education — M

BLUFFTON UNIVERSITY
Accounting — M
Business Administration and
  Management—General — M
Curriculum and Instruction — M
Education—General — M
Educational Leadership and
  Administration — M
Finance and Banking — M
Industrial and Manufacturing
  Management — M
Reading Education — M
Special Education — M
Sustainability Management — M

BOB JONES UNIVERSITY
Accounting — M,D,O
Business Administration and
  Management—General — M,D,O
Counselor Education — M,D,O
Curriculum and Instruction — M,D,O
Educational Leadership and
  Administration — M,D,O
Elementary Education — M,D,O
English Education — M,D,O
Mathematics Education — M,D,O
Music Education — M,D,O
Secondary Education — M,D,O
Social Sciences Education — M,D,O
Special Education — M,D,O
Student Affairs — M,D,O

BOISE STATE UNIVERSITY
Accounting — M
Business Administration and
  Management—General — M
Counselor Education — M,O
Curriculum and Instruction — M,D,O
Distance Education Development — M,D,O
Early Childhood Education — M
Education—General — M,D,O
Educational Leadership and
  Administration — M,D,O
Educational Media/Instructional
  Technology — M,D,O
English as a Second Language — M
English Education — M
Kinesiology and Movement Studies — M
Mathematics Education — M
Multilingual and Multicultural
  Education — M
Music Education — M
Organizational Management — M,O
Reading Education — M
Social Work — M
Special Education — M
Sports Management — M
Taxation — M

BORICUA COLLEGE
English as a Second Language — M
Human Services — M

BOSTON COLLEGE
Accounting — M
Business Administration and
  Management—General — M
Curriculum and Instruction — M,D,O
Early Childhood Education — M,D,O
Education—General — M,D,O
Educational Psychology — M,D
Elementary Education — M,D,O
English Education — M,D,O

Finance and Banking — M,D
Foreign Languages Education — M,D,O
Law — D
Mathematics Education — M,D,O
Organizational Behavior — D
Organizational Management — D
Reading Education — M,D,O
Religious Education — M,D,O
Science Education — M,D,O
Secondary Education — M,D,O
Social Sciences Education — M,D,O
Social Work — M,D
Special Education — M,D,O

BOSTON UNIVERSITY
Actuarial Science — M
Advertising and Public Relations — M
Art Education — M
Athletic Training and Sports
  Medicine — M,D
Business Administration and
  Management—General — M
Business Analytics — M,D
Education—General — M,D,O
Finance and Banking — M
Health Education — M
Health Law — M,D
Hospitality Management — M
International Business — M
Law — M,D
Management Information Systems — M,O
Management Strategy and Policy — M,O
Music Education — M,D
Organizational Management — M
Project Management — M,O
Religious Education — M,D
Risk Management — M
Social Work — M,D
Supply Chain Management — M
Travel and Tourism — M

BOWIE STATE UNIVERSITY
Business Administration and
  Management—General — M
Counselor Education — M
Education—General — M
Educational Leadership and
  Administration — M,D
Elementary Education — M
Human Resources Development — M
Management Information Systems — M,O
Reading Education — M
Secondary Education — M
Special Education — M

BOWLING GREEN STATE UNIVERSITY
Accounting — M
Art Education — M
Business Administration and
  Management—General — M
Business Education — M
Counselor Education — M
Curriculum and Instruction — M
Educational Leadership and
  Administration — M,D,O
Educational Media/Instructional
  Technology — M
Higher Education — D
International and Comparative
  Education — M
Kinesiology and Movement Studies — M
Leisure Studies — M
Mathematics Education — M,D
Music Education — M,D
Organizational Management — M
Reading Education — M,O
Recreation and Park Management — M
Science Education — M
Social Work — M
Special Education — M
Sports Management — M
Student Affairs — M
Vocational and Technical Education — M

BRADLEY UNIVERSITY
Accounting — M
Business Administration and
  Management—General — M
Counselor Education — M
Curriculum and Instruction — M
Education—General — M,D
Educational Leadership and
  Administration — M
Nonprofit Management — M

BRANDEIS UNIVERSITY
Business Administration and
  Management—General — M
Distance Education Development — M
Educational Leadership and
  Administration — M,O
Educational Measurement and
  Evaluation — O
Elementary Education — M,O
Entrepreneurship — M
Finance and Banking — M,D
Foreign Languages Education — M
Health Education — D
Human Services — M
International Business — M,D
Management Information Systems — M
Management Strategy and Policy — M
Marketing — M
Nonprofit Management — M
Project Management — M
Real Estate — M
Religious Education — M,O
Risk Management — M
Secondary Education — M,O

BRANDMAN UNIVERSITY
Accounting — M

Business Administration and
  Management—General — M
Counselor Education — M,D
Curriculum and Instruction — M,D
Early Childhood Education — M,D
Education—General — M,D
Educational Leadership and
  Administration — M,D
Educational Media/Instructional
  Technology — M,D
Elementary Education — M,D
Entrepreneurship — M
Finance and Banking — M
Human Resources Management — M
International Business — M
Marketing — M
Organizational Management — M
Secondary Education — M,D
Social Work — M,D
Special Education — M,D

BRANDON UNIVERSITY
Counselor Education — M,O
Curriculum and Instruction — M,O
Education—General — M,O
Educational Leadership and
  Administration — M,O
Music Education — M,O
Special Education — M,O

BRENAU UNIVERSITY
Accounting — M
Business Administration and
  Management—General — M,O
Early Childhood Education — M,O
Education—General — M,O
Middle School Education — M,O
Organizational Management — M
Project Management — M
Secondary Education — M,O
Special Education — M,O

BRESCIA UNIVERSITY
Business Administration and
  Management—General — M
Curriculum and Instruction — M
Social Work — M

BRIDGEWATER COLLEGE
Athletic Training and Sports
  Medicine — M

BRIDGEWATER STATE UNIVERSITY
Accounting — M
Art Education — M
Business Administration and
  Management—General — M
Counselor Education — M,O
Early Childhood Education — M
Education—General — M,O
Educational Leadership and
  Administration — M,O
Educational Media/Instructional
  Technology — M
Elementary Education — M
Finance and Banking — M
Mathematics Education — M
Physical Education — M
Reading Education — M,O
Science Education — M
Secondary Education — M
Social Sciences Education — M
Social Work — M
Special Education — M

BRIERCREST SEMINARY
Business Administration and
  Management—General — M
Organizational Management — M

BRIGHAM YOUNG UNIVERSITY
Art Education — M
Athletic Training and Sports
  Medicine — M,D
Business Administration and
  Management—General — M
Education—General — M,D,O
Educational Media/Instructional
  Technology — M
Educational Policy — M,D
English as a Second Language — M
Entrepreneurship — M
Exercise and Sports Science — M
Finance and Banking — M
Foreign Languages Education — M
Human Resources Management — M
Law — M,D
Marketing — M
Mathematics Education — M
Music Education — M
Nonprofit Management — M
Religious Education — M
Science Education — M,D
Social Work — M
Supply Chain Management — M

**BROADVIEW UNIVERSITY–WEST
JORDAN**
Business Administration and
  Management—General — M
Management Information Systems — M

BROCK UNIVERSITY
Accounting — M
Business Administration and
  Management—General — M
Education—General — M,D
English as a Second Language — M
Legal and Justice Studies — M

**BROOKLYN COLLEGE OF THE CITY
UNIVERSITY OF NEW YORK**
Accounting — M
Art Education — M

M—masters degree; D—doctorate; O—other advanced degree; *—Close-Up and/or Display

Business Administration and
   Management—General — M
Counselor Education — M
Early Childhood Education — M,O
Education—General — M,O
Educational Leadership and
   Administration — M
Elementary Education — M,O
English Education — M
Environmental Education — M
Exercise and Sports Science — M
Finance and Banking — M
Foreign Languages Education — M
International Business — M
Kinesiology and Movement Studies — M
Mathematics Education — M
Middle School Education — M,O
Multilingual and Multicultural
   Education — M
Music Education — M
Organizational Behavior — M,D
Physical Education — M
Science Education — M
Secondary Education — M
Social Sciences Education — M
Special Education — M,O
Sports Management — M

BROOKLYN LAW SCHOOL
Law — M,D

BROWN UNIVERSITY
Education—General — M
Elementary Education — M
English as a Second Language — M,D
English Education — M
Multilingual and Multicultural
   Education — M,D
Science Education — M
Secondary Education — M
Social Sciences Education — M
Urban Education — M

BRYAN COLLEGE
Business Administration and
   Management—General — M
Human Resources Management — M
Marketing — M
Sports Management — M

BRYANT UNIVERSITY
Accounting — M
Business Administration and
   Management—General — M
Taxation — M

BRYAN UNIVERSITY
Business Administration and
   Management—General — M

BRYN MAWR COLLEGE
Social Work — M,D

BUCKNELL UNIVERSITY
Education—General — M
Student Affairs — M

BUENA VISTA UNIVERSITY
Counselor Education — M
Curriculum and Instruction — M
Education—General — M
English as a Second Language — M

**BUFFALO STATE COLLEGE, STATE
UNIVERSITY OF NEW YORK**
Adult Education — M,O
Art Education — M
Business Education — M
Early Childhood Education — M
Education—General — M,O
Educational Leadership and
   Administration — O
Educational Media/Instructional
   Technology — M
English Education — M
Human Resources Management — M,O
Mathematics Education — M
Multilingual and Multicultural
   Education — O
Organizational Management — M
Reading Education — M
Science Education — M
Social Sciences Education — M
Special Education — M
Urban Education — M
Vocational and Technical Education — M

BUTLER UNIVERSITY
Business Administration and
   Management—General — M
Education—General — M,O
Educational Leadership and
   Administration — M
Music Education — M

CABRINI UNIVERSITY
Accounting — M,D
Curriculum and Instruction — M,D
Early Childhood Education — M,D
Educational Leadership and
   Administration — M,D
Elementary Education — M,D
English as a Second Language — M,D
Middle School Education — M,D
Organizational Management — M,D
Reading Education — M,D
Secondary Education — M,D
Special Education — M,D

CAIRN UNIVERSITY
Accounting — M,O
Business Administration and
   Management—General — M
Education—General — M,O
Educational Leadership and
   Administration — M,O
Entrepreneurship — M,O
Nonprofit Management — M,O

Organizational Management — M,O

CALDWELL UNIVERSITY
Business Administration and
   Management—General — M
Education—General — M,D,O
Educational Leadership and
   Administration — M,D,O
Special Education — M,D,O

CALIFORNIA BAPTIST UNIVERSITY
Accounting — M
Adult Education — M
Advertising and Public Relations — M
Athletic Training and Sports
   Medicine — M
Business Administration and
   Management—General — M
Counselor Education — M
Curriculum and Instruction — M
Distance Education Development — M
Education of Students with
   Severe/Multiple Disabilities — M
Education—General — M
Educational Leadership and
   Administration — M
Educational Media/Instructional
   Technology — M
English as a Second Language — M
English Education — M
Exercise and Sports Science — M
Health Education — M
Higher Education — M
International and Comparative
   Education — M
Music Education — M
Organizational Management — M
Physical Education — M
Reading Education — M
Science Education — M
Social Work — M
Special Education — M
Sports Management — M
Vocational and Technical Education — M

CALIFORNIA COAST UNIVERSITY
Business Administration and
   Management—General — M
Curriculum and Instruction — M,D
Education—General — M,D
Educational Leadership and
   Administration — M,D
Educational Psychology — M,D
Human Resources Management — M
Marketing — M
Organizational Management — M,D

CALIFORNIA COLLEGE OF THE ARTS
Finance and Banking — M
Organizational Management — M

**CALIFORNIA INSTITUTE OF ADVANCED
MANAGEMENT**
Business Administration and
   Management—General — M
Entrepreneurship — M

**CALIFORNIA INTERCONTINENTAL
UNIVERSITY**
Business Administration and
   Management—General — M,D
Entertainment Management — M
Entrepreneurship — M,D
Finance and Banking — M,D
Human Resources Management — M,D
International Business — M,D
Management Information Systems — M,D
Marketing — M,D
Organizational Management — M,D
Project Management — M,D
Quality Management — M,D

**CALIFORNIA INTERNATIONAL
BUSINESS UNIVERSITY**
Business Administration and
   Management—General — M,D

CALIFORNIA LUTHERAN UNIVERSITY
Business Administration and
   Management—General — M,O
Counselor Education — M,D
Education—General — M,D
Educational Leadership and
   Administration — M,D
Elementary Education — M,D
Entrepreneurship — M,O
Finance and Banking — M,O
Higher Education — M,O
International Business — M,O
Management Information Systems — M,O
Marketing — M,O
Middle School Education — M,O
Special Education — M,D

CALIFORNIA MIRAMAR UNIVERSITY
Business Administration and
   Management—General — M
Management Strategy and Policy — M
Taxation — M

**CALIFORNIA POLYTECHNIC STATE
UNIVERSITY, SAN LUIS OBISPO**
Accounting — M
Agricultural Education — M
Business Administration and
   Management—General — M
Business Analytics — M
Education—General — M
Supply Chain Management — M
Taxation — M

**CALIFORNIA STATE POLYTECHNIC
UNIVERSITY, POMONA**
Accounting — M
Business Administration and
   Management—General — M
Curriculum and Instruction — M

Educational Leadership and
   Administration — D
Hospitality Management — M
Kinesiology and Movement Studies — M
Management Information Systems — M

**CALIFORNIA STATE UNIVERSITY,
BAKERSFIELD**
Business Administration and
   Management—General — M
Counselor Education — M
Education—General — M,D
Educational Leadership and
   Administration — M,D
Science Education — M
Social Work — M
Special Education — M
Student Affairs — M

**CALIFORNIA STATE UNIVERSITY
CHANNEL ISLANDS**
Business Administration and
   Management—General — M

**CALIFORNIA STATE UNIVERSITY,
CHICO**
Agricultural Education — M
Business Administration and
   Management—General — M
Curriculum and Instruction — M
Kinesiology and Movement Studies — M
Mathematics Education — M
Recreation and Park Management — M
Social Work — M
Special Education — M
Travel and Tourism — M

**CALIFORNIA STATE UNIVERSITY,
DOMINGUEZ HILLS**
Business Administration and
   Management—General — M
Counselor Education — M
Early Childhood Education — M
Education—General — M
English as a Second Language — M,O
International and Comparative
   Education — M
Quality Management — M
Social Work — M
Special Education — M

**CALIFORNIA STATE UNIVERSITY, EAST
BAY**
Accounting — M
Actuarial Science — M
Business Administration and
   Management—General — M
Business Analytics — M
Counselor Education — M
Early Childhood Education — M
Education of Students with
   Severe/Multiple Disabilities — M
Education—General — M
Educational Leadership and
   Administration — M,D
Educational Media/Instructional
   Technology — M
English as a Second Language — M
Finance and Banking — M
Human Resources Management — M
Industrial and Manufacturing
   Management — M
Management Strategy and Policy — M
Marketing — M
Mathematics Education — M
Organizational Behavior — M
Physical Education — M
Reading Education — M
Recreation and Park Management — M
Social Sciences Education — M
Social Work — M
Special Education — M
Supply Chain Management — M
Travel and Tourism — M

**CALIFORNIA STATE UNIVERSITY,
FRESNO**
Business Administration and
   Management—General — M
Counselor Education — M
Curriculum and Instruction — M
Early Childhood Education — M
Education—General — M,D
Educational Leadership and
   Administration — M,D
English as a Second Language — M
Exercise and Sports Science — M
Kinesiology and Movement Studies — M
Mathematics Education — M
Music Education — M
Reading Education — M
Social Sciences Education — M
Social Work — M
Special Education — M
Sports Management — M
Student Affairs — M

**CALIFORNIA STATE UNIVERSITY,
FULLERTON**
Accounting — M
Business Administration and
   Management—General — M
Business Analytics — M
Counselor Education — M
Educational Leadership and
   Administration — M,D
Educational Media/Instructional
   Technology — M
Electronic Commerce — M
Elementary Education — M
Finance and Banking — M
Insurance — M
International Business — M
Management Information Systems — M
Mathematics Education — M

Multilingual and Multicultural
   Education — M
Music Education — M
Organizational Management — M
Physical Education — M
Reading Education — M
Risk Management — M
Secondary Education — M
Social Work — M
Special Education — M
Taxation — M
Travel and Tourism — M

**CALIFORNIA STATE UNIVERSITY, LONG
BEACH**
Art Education — M
Athletic Training and Sports
   Medicine — M
Business Administration and
   Management—General — M
Counselor Education — M,D
Education—General — M,D
Educational Leadership and
   Administration — M,D
Educational Psychology — M,D
Elementary Education — M
English as a Second Language — M,O
Exercise and Sports Science — M
Health Education — M
Higher Education — M,D
Kinesiology and Movement Studies — M
Leisure Studies — M
Mathematics Education — M
Physical Education — M
Recreation and Park Management — M
Science Education — M
Secondary Education — M
Social Work — M
Special Education — M,D
Sports Management — M
Student Affairs — M,D

**CALIFORNIA STATE UNIVERSITY, LOS
ANGELES**
Accounting — M
Art Education — M
Business Administration and
   Management—General — M,O
Counselor Education — M,D
Curriculum and Instruction — M
Education—General — M,D,O
Elementary Education — M
Finance and Banking — M
International Business — M
Kinesiology and Movement Studies — M,O
Management Information Systems — M
Marketing — M
Music Education — M
Physical Education — M,O
Social Work — M
Special Education — M,D

**CALIFORNIA STATE UNIVERSITY
MARITIME ACADEMY**
Transportation Management — M

**CALIFORNIA STATE UNIVERSITY,
MONTEREY BAY**
Business Administration and
   Management—General — M
Education—General — M
Management Information Systems — M
Social Work — M

**CALIFORNIA STATE UNIVERSITY,
NORTHRIDGE**
Art Education — M
Business Administration and
   Management—General — M
Counselor Education — M
Curriculum and Instruction — M
Early Childhood Education — M
Education of Students with
   Severe/Multiple Disabilities — M
Education—General — M,D
Educational Leadership and
   Administration — M,D
Educational Media/Instructional
   Technology — M
Educational Psychology — M
Elementary Education — M
English Education — M
Entertainment Management — M,O
Health Education — M,O
Hospitality Management — M,O
Kinesiology and Movement Studies — M
Mathematics Education — M
Multilingual and Multicultural
   Education — M
Music Education — M
Nonprofit Management — O
Reading Education — M
Recreation and Park Management — M,O
Science Education — M
Secondary Education — M
Social Work — M,O
Special Education — M,O
Taxation — M,O
Travel and Tourism — M

**CALIFORNIA STATE UNIVERSITY,
SACRAMENTO**
Accounting — M
Business Administration and
   Management—General — M
Counselor Education — M,D,O
Curriculum and Instruction — M,D,O
Early Childhood Education — M,D,O
Education—General — M,D,O
Educational Leadership and
   Administration — M,D,O
Educational Media/Instructional
   Technology — M,D,O
Educational Policy — M,D,O
Elementary Education — M,D,O
English as a Second Language — M

Exercise and Sports Science — M
Foreign Languages Education — M
Higher Education — M,D,O
Human Resources Development — M
Human Resources Management — M
Human Services — M
Multilingual and Multicultural Education — M,D,O
Physical Education — M
Reading Education — M,D,O
Real Estate — M
Recreation and Park Management — M
Social Work — M
Special Education — M,D,O

CALIFORNIA STATE UNIVERSITY, SAN BERNARDINO
Accounting — M
Business Administration and Management—General — M
Community College Education — M
Counselor Education — M
Education—General — M
Educational Leadership and Administration — M,D
Entrepreneurship — M
Finance and Banking — M
International Business — M
Management Information Systems — M
Marketing — M
Mathematics Education — M
Social Work — M
Supply Chain Management — M

CALIFORNIA STATE UNIVERSITY, SAN MARCOS
Education—General — M,D
Educational Leadership and Administration — M,D
Reading Education — M,D
Special Education — M,D

CALIFORNIA STATE UNIVERSITY, STANISLAUS
Business Administration and Management—General — M
Community College Education — D
Counselor Education — M
Curriculum and Instruction — M
Education—General — M,D
Educational Leadership and Administration — M,D
Educational Media/Instructional Technology — M
Elementary Education — M
English as a Second Language — M,O
Multilingual and Multicultural Education — M
Physical Education — M
Reading Education — M
Secondary Education — M
Social Work — M
Special Education — M

CALIFORNIA UNIVERSITY OF MANAGEMENT AND SCIENCES
Business Administration and Management—General — M,D
International Business — M,D
Management Information Systems — M,D
Sports Management — M,D

CALIFORNIA UNIVERSITY OF PENNSYLVANIA
Athletic Training and Sports Medicine — M
Business Administration and Management—General — M
Business Analytics — M
Counselor Education — M
Early Childhood Education — M
Education—General — M,D
Educational Leadership and Administration — M,D
Elementary Education — M
Entrepreneurship — M
Exercise and Sports Science — M
Legal and Justice Studies — M
Mathematics Education — M
Reading Education — M
Science Education — M
Secondary Education — M
Social Work — M
Special Education — M
Sports Management — M
Vocational and Technical Education — M

CALIFORNIA WESTERN SCHOOL OF LAW
Accounting — M,D
Law — M,D

CALUMET COLLEGE OF SAINT JOSEPH
Educational Leadership and Administration — M
Quality Management — M

CALVARY UNIVERSITY
Curriculum and Instruction — M
Education—General — M
Educational Leadership and Administration — M
Elementary Education — M
Organizational Management — M
Religious Education — M

CALVIN COLLEGE
Accounting — M
Curriculum and Instruction — M
Education—General — M

CALVIN THEOLOGICAL SEMINARY
Religious Education — M,D

CAMBRIDGE COLLEGE
Business Administration and Management—General — M
Counselor Education — M,O
Curriculum and Instruction — M,D,O
Early Childhood Education — M,D,O
Education—General — M,D,O
Educational Leadership and Administration — M,D,O
Educational Measurement and Evaluation — M,D,O
Educational Media/Instructional Technology — M,D,O
Elementary Education — M,D,O
English as a Second Language — M,D,O
Entrepreneurship — M
Health Education — M,D,O
Mathematics Education — M,D,O
Science Education — M,D,O
Special Education — M,D,O

CAMERON UNIVERSITY
Business Administration and Management—General — M
Education—General — M
Educational Leadership and Administration — M
Entrepreneurship — M

CAMPBELLSVILLE UNIVERSITY
Business Administration and Management—General — M,D
Education—General — M
Educational Leadership and Administration — M
English Education — M
Legal and Justice Studies — M
Music Education — M
Science Education — M
Social Work — M
Special Education — M
Sports Management — M

CAMPBELL UNIVERSITY
Athletic Training and Sports Medicine — M,D
Business Administration and Management—General — M
Counselor Education — M
Education—General — M
Educational Leadership and Administration — M
Elementary Education — M
Law — D
Middle School Education — M
Physical Education — M
Secondary Education — M

CANISIUS COLLEGE
Accounting — M
Business Administration and Management—General — M
Business Education — M,O
Counselor Education — M
Early Childhood Education — M
Education of the Gifted — M,O
Education—General — M,O
Educational Leadership and Administration — M,O
Educational Media/Instructional Technology — M,O
Elementary Education — M,O
English as a Second Language — M,O
International Business — M
Kinesiology and Movement Studies — M
Middle School Education — M
Physical Education — M
Reading Education — M,O
Secondary Education — M,O
Special Education — M,O
Sports Management — M
Student Affairs — M,O

CAPE BRETON UNIVERSITY
Business Administration and Management—General — M

CAPELLA UNIVERSITY
Accounting — M,D
Adult Education — M,D
Business Administration and Management—General — M,D
Business Education — D
Counselor Education — M,D
Curriculum and Instruction — M,D
Distance Education Development — M,D
Early Childhood Education — M
Education—General — M,D
Educational Leadership and Administration — M,D
Educational Media/Instructional Technology — M,D
Educational Psychology — M,D
Elementary Education — M,D
Entrepreneurship — M,D
Finance and Banking — M,D
Higher Education — M,D
Human Resources Management — M,D
Human Services — M,D
Management Information Systems — M,D
Management Strategy and Policy — M,D
Marketing — M,D
Middle School Education — M,D
Nonprofit Management — D
Organizational Management — M,D
Project Management — M,D
Reading Education — M,D
Social Work — D
Special Education — M,D
Supply Chain Management — M,D
Vocational and Technical Education — D

CAPITAL UNIVERSITY
Business Administration and Management—General — M
Law — M,D
Legal and Justice Studies — M
Music Education — M
Religious Education — M
Taxation — M

CAPITOL TECHNOLOGY UNIVERSITY
Business Administration and Management—General — M
Management Information Systems — M

CARDINAL STRITCH UNIVERSITY
Business Administration and Management—General — M,D
Education—General — M,D
Educational Leadership and Administration — M,D
Higher Education — M
Marketing — M
Reading Education — M,D
Special Education — M,D
Sports Management — M
Student Affairs — M,D
Urban Education — M,D

CARIBBEAN UNIVERSITY
Curriculum and Instruction — M,D
Early Childhood Education — M,D
Education—General — M,D
Educational Leadership and Administration — M,D
Educational Media/Instructional Technology — M,D
Elementary Education — M,D
English Education — M,D
Foreign Languages Education — M,D
Human Resources Management — M,D
Mathematics Education — M,D
Physical Education — M,D
Science Education — M,D
Social Sciences Education — M,D
Special Education — M,D

CARLETON UNIVERSITY
Business Administration and Management—General — M,D
Legal and Justice Studies — M,D
Social Work — M

CARLOW UNIVERSITY
Business Administration and Management—General — M
Curriculum and Instruction — M
Distance Education Development — M,O
Early Childhood Education — M,O
Education—General — M,O
Human Resources Management — M
Organizational Management — M,D,O
Project Management — M
Science Education — M
Social Work — M
Special Education — M,O
Student Affairs — M

CARNEGIE MELLON UNIVERSITY
Accounting — D
Business Administration and Management—General — M,D
Entertainment Management — M
Entrepreneurship — D
Finance and Banking — D
Industrial and Manufacturing Management — M,D
Management Information Systems — M,D
Marketing — D
Music Education — M
Organizational Behavior — D

CAROLINA CHRISTIAN COLLEGE
Religious Education — M

CARROLL UNIVERSITY
Adult Education — M
Business Administration and Management—General — M
Early Childhood Education — M
Education—General — M
Educational Leadership and Administration — M
Elementary Education — M
Exercise and Sports Science — M
Secondary Education — M

CARSON-NEWMAN UNIVERSITY
Business Administration and Management—General — M
Counselor Education — M
Curriculum and Instruction — M
Education—General — M
Educational Leadership and Administration — M
Elementary Education — M
English as a Second Language — M
Organizational Management — M
Secondary Education — M

CARTHAGE COLLEGE
Art Education — M,O
Counselor Education — M,O
Education of the Gifted — M,O
Education—General — M,O
Educational Leadership and Administration — M,O
English Education — M,O
Reading Education — M,O
Science Education — M,O
Social Sciences Education — M,O

CASE WESTERN RESERVE UNIVERSITY
Accounting — M,D
Art Education — M

Business Administration and Management—General — M,D
Business Analytics — M
Finance and Banking — M
Health Law — M,D
Industrial and Manufacturing Management — M,D
Intellectual Property Law — M,D
Law — M,D
Legal and Justice Studies — M,D
Logistics — M,D
Music Education — M,D,O
Nonprofit Management — M,D,O
Organizational Behavior — M,D
Social Work — M,D
Supply Chain Management — M,D
Sustainability Management — D

CASTLETON UNIVERSITY
Curriculum and Instruction — M
Education—General — M,O
Educational Leadership and Administration — M,O
Reading Education — M,O
Special Education — M,O

CATAWBA COLLEGE
Elementary Education — M
Science Education — M

THE CATHOLIC UNIVERSITY OF AMERICA
Accounting — M
Business Administration and Management—General — M
Early Childhood Education — M,O
Education—General — M,O
Educational Leadership and Administration — M,O
Human Resources Management — M
Information Studies — M,D
Law — M,D
Legal and Justice Studies — M,D,O
Library Science — M,O
Management Information Systems — M,O
Music Education — M,D,O
Project Management — M,O
Secondary Education — M,O
Social Work — M,D
Special Education — M,O

CEDAR CREST COLLEGE
Business Administration and Management—General — M
Education—General — M

CEDARVILLE UNIVERSITY
Business Administration and Management—General — M,D
Industrial and Manufacturing Management — M,D

CENTENARY COLLEGE OF LOUISIANA
Business Administration and Management—General — M
Education—General — M
Elementary Education — M
Secondary Education — M

CENTENARY UNIVERSITY
Accounting — M
Business Administration and Management—General — M,D
Education—General — M,D
Educational Leadership and Administration — M,D
Reading Education — M,D
Special Education — M,D

CENTRAL CONNECTICUT STATE UNIVERSITY
Accounting — M
Actuarial Science — M,O
Advertising and Public Relations — M,O
Art Education — M,O
Business Administration and Management—General — M
Counselor Education — M,O
Early Childhood Education — M,O
Education—General — M,D,O
Educational Leadership and Administration — M,D,O
Elementary Education — M,O
English Education — M,O
Exercise and Sports Science — M,O
Foreign Languages Education — M,O
Industrial and Manufacturing Management — M,O
Information Studies — M
Logistics — M,O
Music Education — M,O
Physical Education — M,O
Reading Education — M,O
Science Education — M,O
Secondary Education — M,O
Special Education — M,O
Supply Chain Management — M,O
Vocational and Technical Education — M

CENTRAL EUROPEAN UNIVERSITY
Business Administration and Management—General — M,D
Business Analytics — M,D
Finance and Banking — M,D
International Business — M,D
Law — M,D
Legal and Justice Studies — M,D

CENTRAL METHODIST UNIVERSITY
Counselor Education — M
Education—General — M
Music Education — M

M—masters degree; D—doctorate; O—other advanced degree; *—Close-Up and/or Display

CENTRAL MICHIGAN UNIVERSITY

Accounting	M,O
Business Administration and Management—General	M,O
Community College Education	M,D,O
Counselor Education	M
Curriculum and Instruction	M,D,O
Early Childhood Education	M,O
Education—General	M,D,O
Educational Leadership and Administration	M,D,O
Educational Media/Instructional Technology	M,D,O
Elementary Education	M,D,O
English as a Second Language	M
Exercise and Sports Science	M,D
Finance and Banking	M
Higher Education	M,D,O
Human Resources Management	M,O
Industrial and Manufacturing Management	M
International Business	M,O
Logistics	M,O
Management Information Systems	M,O
Marketing	M,O
Mathematics Education	M,D
Music Education	M
Nonprofit Management	M,O
Reading Education	M,D,O
Recreation and Park Management	M,O
Science Education	M
Secondary Education	M,D,O
Special Education	M,O
Sports Management	M,O
Student Affairs	M,D,O

CENTRAL PENN COLLEGE

Management Information Systems	M
Organizational Management	M

CENTRAL WASHINGTON UNIVERSITY

Curriculum and Instruction	M
Education—General	M
Educational Leadership and Administration	M
English as a Second Language	M
Health Education	M
Higher Education	M
Home Economics Education	M
Music Education	M
Physical Education	M
Reading Education	M
Sports Management	M
Vocational and Technical Education	M

CHADRON STATE COLLEGE

Business Administration and Management—General	M
Business Education	M,O
Counselor Education	M,O
Education—General	M,O
Educational Leadership and Administration	M,O
Elementary Education	M,O
English Education	M,O
Secondary Education	M,O
Social Sciences Education	M,O

CHAMINADE UNIVERSITY OF HONOLULU

Accounting	M
Business Administration and Management—General	M
Early Childhood Education	M
Education—General	M
Educational Leadership and Administration	M
Elementary Education	M
Nonprofit Management	M
Secondary Education	M
Special Education	M

CHAMPLAIN COLLEGE

Business Administration and Management—General	M
Early Childhood Education	M
Law	M

CHAPMAN UNIVERSITY

Accounting	M
Business Administration and Management—General	M
Counselor Education	M,D,O
Curriculum and Instruction	M,D,O
Education of Students with Severe/Multiple Disabilities	M,D,O
Education—General	M,D,O
Educational Leadership and Administration	M,D,O
Educational Psychology	M,D,O
Elementary Education	M,D,O
Environmental Law	M,D
Law	M,D
Secondary Education	M,D,O
Special Education	M,D,O
Sports and Entertainment Law	M,D
Taxation	M,D

CHARLESTON SCHOOL OF LAW

Law	D

CHARLESTON SOUTHERN UNIVERSITY

Accounting	M
Business Administration and Management—General	M
Education—General	M
Educational Leadership and Administration	M
Elementary Education	M
Finance and Banking	M
Human Resources Management	M
Management Information Systems	M
Organizational Management	M

CHARTER COLLEGE

Business Administration and Management—General	M

CHARTER OAK STATE COLLEGE

Organizational Management	M

CHATHAM UNIVERSITY

Accounting	M
Art Education	M
Business Administration and Management—General	M
Early Childhood Education	M
Education—General	M
Elementary Education	M
English Education	M
Environmental Education	M
Mathematics Education	M
Science Education	M
Secondary Education	M
Social Sciences Education	M
Special Education	M
Sustainability Management	M

CHESTNUT HILL COLLEGE

Early Childhood Education	M
Education—General	M
Educational Leadership and Administration	M
Educational Media/Instructional Technology	M,O
Elementary Education	M
Human Services	M,O
Middle School Education	M
Reading Education	M
Secondary Education	M
Special Education	M,O

CHEYNEY UNIVERSITY OF PENNSYLVANIA

Education—General	M,O
Educational Leadership and Administration	M,O
Elementary Education	M
Special Education	M
Urban Education	M

THE CHICAGO SCHOOL OF PROFESSIONAL PSYCHOLOGY

Organizational Management	M,D

CHICAGO STATE UNIVERSITY

Adult Education	M
Counselor Education	M
Early Childhood Education	M
Education—General	M,D
Educational Leadership and Administration	M,D
Elementary Education	M
Foundations and Philosophy of Education	M
Higher Education	M,D
Library Science	M
Middle School Education	M
Multilingual and Multicultural Education	M
Physical Education	M
Reading Education	M
Secondary Education	M
Social Work	M
Special Education	M
Vocational and Technical Education	M

CHOWAN UNIVERSITY

Education—General	M

CHRISTIAN BROTHERS UNIVERSITY

Accounting	M,O
Business Administration and Management—General	M,O
Education—General	M
Educational Leadership and Administration	M
International Business	M,O
Project Management	M,O

CHRISTOPHER NEWPORT UNIVERSITY

Education—General	M

THE CITADEL, THE MILITARY COLLEGE OF SOUTH CAROLINA

Business Administration and Management—General	M
Counselor Education	M,O
Early Childhood Education	M,O
Education—General	M,O
Educational Leadership and Administration	M,O
English Education	M,O
Exercise and Sports Science	M,O
Mathematics Education	M,O
Middle School Education	M,O
Physical Education	M,O
Project Management	M,O
Reading Education	M,O
Science Education	M,O
Secondary Education	M,O
Social Sciences Education	M,O
Sports Management	M,O
Student Affairs	M,O

CITY COLLEGE OF THE CITY UNIVERSITY OF NEW YORK

Business Administration and Management—General	M
Early Childhood Education	M
Education—General	M,O
Educational Leadership and Administration	M,O
English as a Second Language	M
English Education	M,O
Management Information Systems	M,D
Marketing	M
Mathematics Education	M,O
Middle School Education	M,O
Multilingual and Multicultural Education	M
Museum Education	M
Reading Education	M
Science Education	M
Secondary Education	M,O
Social Sciences Education	M,O
Special Education	M,O

CITY UNIVERSITY OF NEW YORK SCHOOL OF LAW

Law	D

CITY UNIVERSITY OF SEATTLE

Accounting	M,O
Business Administration and Management—General	M,O
Counselor Education	M,O
Curriculum and Instruction	M,O
Education—General	M,O
Educational Leadership and Administration	M,D,O
Elementary Education	M,O
Finance and Banking	M,O
Human Resources Management	M,O
International Business	M,O
Management Information Systems	M,O
Marketing	M,O
Organizational Management	M,O
Project Management	M,O
Reading Education	M,O
Special Education	M,O
Sustainability Management	M,O

CITY VISION UNIVERSITY

Entrepreneurship	M

CLAFLIN UNIVERSITY

Business Administration and Management—General	M

CLAREMONT GRADUATE UNIVERSITY

Archives/Archival Administration	M,D,O
Business Administration and Management—General	M,D,O
Education—General	M,D,O
Educational Leadership and Administration	M,D,O
Educational Measurement and Evaluation	M,D,O
Electronic Commerce	M,D,O
Higher Education	M,D,O
Human Resources Development	M,D,O
Human Resources Management	M
Management Information Systems	M,D,O
Management Strategy and Policy	M,D,O
Special Education	M,D,O
Student Affairs	M,D,O
Urban Education	M,D,O

CLAREMONT SCHOOL OF THEOLOGY

Religious Education	M,D

CLARION UNIVERSITY OF PENNSYLVANIA

Accounting	M
Business Administration and Management—General	M
Curriculum and Instruction	M
Early Childhood Education	M
Education—General	M
Educational Media/Instructional Technology	M
Entrepreneurship	M
Finance and Banking	M
Library Science	M
Mathematics Education	M
Reading Education	M
Science Education	M
Special Education	M
Vocational and Technical Education	M

CLARK ATLANTA UNIVERSITY

Accounting	M
Business Administration and Management—General	M
Counselor Education	M
Curriculum and Instruction	M
Education—General	M,D,O
Educational Leadership and Administration	M,D,O
Educational Psychology	M
Mathematics Education	M
Science Education	M
Social Work	M,D
Special Education	M

CLARKE UNIVERSITY

Business Administration and Management—General	M
Education—General	M
Educational Leadership and Administration	M
Social Work	M

CLARKSON UNIVERSITY

Business Administration and Management—General	M,O
Education—General	M
Human Resources Management	M,O
International Business	M,O
Supply Chain Management	M,O

CLARKS SUMMIT UNIVERSITY

Counselor Education	M
Curriculum and Instruction	M
Educational Leadership and Administration	M
Organizational Management	M,D
Religious Education	M,D

CLARK UNIVERSITY

Accounting	M
Business Administration and Management—General	M
Business Analytics	M
Education—General	M,D
Finance and Banking	M
Health Education	M
Management Information Systems	M
Marketing	M
Sustainability Management	M

CLAYTON STATE UNIVERSITY

Accounting	M
Archives/Archival Administration	M
Business Administration and Management—General	M
Education—General	M
English Education	M
Human Resources Management	M
International Business	M
Mathematics Education	M
Sports Management	M
Supply Chain Management	M

CLEARY UNIVERSITY

Business Administration and Management—General	M,O
Business Analytics	M,O
Finance and Banking	M,O
Management Strategy and Policy	M,O

CLEMSON UNIVERSITY

Accounting	M
Agricultural Education	M,D
Business Administration and Management—General	M,D
Business Analytics	M
Business Education	M,D
Counselor Education	M,D,O
Curriculum and Instruction	M,D,O
Distance Education Development	M,D,O
Early Childhood Education	M,D,O
Education—General	M,D,O
Educational Leadership and Administration	M,D,O
Educational Measurement and Evaluation	M,D,O
Elementary Education	M,D,O
Entrepreneurship	M,D
Higher Education	M,D,O
Human Resources Development	M,D,O
Management Information Systems	M,D
Marketing	M
Mathematics Education	M,D,O
Middle School Education	M,D,O
Organizational Behavior	M,D
Reading Education	M,D,O
Real Estate	M
Recreation and Park Management	M,D,O
Science Education	D,O
Secondary Education	M,D,O
Special Education	M,D,O
Sports Management	M,D,O
Student Affairs	M,D,O
Supply Chain Management	M,D
Travel and Tourism	M,D,O

CLEVELAND STATE UNIVERSITY

Accounting	M
Adult Education	M,D,O
Art Education	M
Business Administration and Management—General	M,D
Counselor Education	M,D,O
Early Childhood Education	M
Education of Students with Severe/Multiple Disabilities	M
Education—General	M,D,O
Educational Leadership and Administration	M,D,O
Educational Media/Instructional Technology	D
Educational Policy	D
English as a Second Language	M
Foreign Languages Education	M
Health Education	M
Higher Education	D
Human Resources Management	M
Law	M,D,O
Management Information Systems	D
Marketing	D
Mathematics Education	M
Music Education	M
Nonprofit Management	M,O
Physical Education	M
Real Estate	M,O
Science Education	M
Social Work	M
Special Education	M
Urban Education	D

CLEVELAND UNIVERSITY–KANSAS CITY

Health Education	M

COASTAL CAROLINA UNIVERSITY

Accounting	M,O
Business Administration and Management—General	M,O
Distance Education Development	M,O
Education—General	M,O
Educational Leadership and Administration	M,O
Educational Media/Instructional Technology	M,O
English as a Second Language	M,O
Management Information Systems	M,D,O
Reading Education	M,O
Special Education	M,O
Sports Management	M,D,O

COGSWELL POLYTECHNICAL COLLEGE

Entrepreneurship	M

COKER COLLEGE

Business Administration and Management—General	M
Curriculum and Instruction	M
Educational Media/Instructional Technology	M
Reading Education	M
Sports Management	M

COLGATE UNIVERSITY

Secondary Education	M

THE COLLEGE AT BROCKPORT, STATE UNIVERSITY OF NEW YORK
Accounting M,O
Counselor Education M,O
Curriculum and Instruction M,O
Early Childhood Education M,O
Education—General M,O
Educational Leadership and Administration M,O
English Education M,O
Health Education M
Mathematics Education M,O
Middle School Education M,O
Multilingual and Multicultural Education M,O
Nonprofit Management M,O
Physical Education M,O
Reading Education M,O
Science Education M,O
Social Sciences Education M,O
Social Work M,O
Sports Management M,O

COLLEGE FOR FINANCIAL PLANNING
Finance and Banking M

COLLEGE OF CHARLESTON
Accounting M
Business Administration and Management—General M
Early Childhood Education M
Education—General M,O
Elementary Education M
English as a Second Language O
Foreign Languages Education M
Management Information Systems M
Mathematics Education M
Music Education M
Science Education M
Special Education M

THE COLLEGE OF IDAHO
Curriculum and Instruction M
Education—General M

COLLEGE OF MOUNT SAINT VINCENT
Education—General M,O
Educational Media/Instructional Technology M,O
English as a Second Language M,O
Middle School Education M,O
Multilingual and Multicultural Education M,O
Urban Education M,O

THE COLLEGE OF NEW JERSEY
Counselor Education M
Early Childhood Education M
Education—General M,O
Educational Leadership and Administration M,O
Elementary Education M
English as a Second Language M,O
International and Comparative Education M,O
Reading Education M,O
Secondary Education M
Special Education M,O

THE COLLEGE OF NEW ROCHELLE
Art Education M
Early Childhood Education M
Education of the Gifted O
Education—General M,O
Educational Leadership and Administration M,O
Elementary Education M
English as a Second Language M,O
Human Resources Development M,O
Multilingual and Multicultural Education M,O
Reading Education M
Special Education M

COLLEGE OF SAINT ELIZABETH
Business Administration and Management—General M
Distance Education Development M,O
Early Childhood Education M,O
Education—General M,O
Educational Leadership and Administration M,D,O
Elementary Education M,O
English as a Second Language M,O
Higher Education M,D,O
Human Resources Management M
Middle School Education M,O
Organizational Management M
Special Education M,O

COLLEGE OF ST. JOSEPH
Business Administration and Management—General M
Counselor Education M
Education—General M
Elementary Education M
English Education M
Reading Education M
Secondary Education M
Social Sciences Education M
Special Education M

COLLEGE OF SAINT MARY
Education—General M
Educational Leadership and Administration M
Educational Measurement and Evaluation M
English as a Second Language M
Health Education D
Organizational Management M

THE COLLEGE OF SAINT ROSE
Accounting M
Business Administration and Management—General M
Business Analytics M
Counselor Education M,O
Curriculum and Instruction M,O
Early Childhood Education M,O
Education—General M,O
Educational Leadership and Administration M,O
Educational Psychology M,O
Finance and Banking O
Higher Education M,O
Middle School Education M,O
Organizational Management O
Reading Education M,O
Secondary Education M,O
Social Work M
Special Education M,O
Student Affairs M

THE COLLEGE OF ST. SCHOLASTICA
Athletic Training and Sports Medicine M
Business Administration and Management—General M,O
Education—General M,O
Exercise and Sports Science M
Management Information Systems M,O
Social Work M

COLLEGE OF STATEN ISLAND OF THE CITY UNIVERSITY OF NEW YORK
Accounting M
Business Administration and Management—General M
Early Childhood Education M
Education—General M,O
Educational Leadership and Administration O
Elementary Education M
English as a Second Language M,O
English Education M
Management Strategy and Policy M
Mathematics Education M
Middle School Education M
Multilingual and Multicultural Education O
Secondary Education M
Social Work M
Special Education M,O

THE COLLEGE OF WILLIAM AND MARY
Accounting M
Business Administration and Management—General M
Business Analytics M
Counselor Education M,D
Curriculum and Instruction M
Education—General M,D,O*
Educational Leadership and Administration M,D
Law M,D

COLORADO CHRISTIAN UNIVERSITY
Business Administration and Management—General M
Business Education M
Curriculum and Instruction M
Distance Education Development M
Early Childhood Education M
Education—General M
Educational Media/Instructional Technology M
Elementary Education M
Project Management M
Special Education M

THE COLORADO COLLEGE
Art Education M
Education—General M
Elementary Education M
English Education M
Foreign Languages Education M
Mathematics Education M
Music Education M
Science Education M
Secondary Education M
Social Sciences Education M

COLORADO MESA UNIVERSITY
Business Administration and Management—General M
Education of the Gifted M,O
Education—General M,O
Educational Leadership and Administration M,O
English as a Second Language M,O
Special Education M,O

COLORADO STATE UNIVERSITY
Accounting M
Adult Education M,D
Advertising and Public Relations M,D
Agricultural Education M
Business Administration and Management—General M
Counselor Education M,D
Education—General M,D
Educational Leadership and Administration M,D
Exercise and Sports Science M,D
Finance and Banking M
Higher Education M,D
Management Information Systems M
Recreation and Park Management M,D
Social Work M,D
Student Affairs M,D
Sustainability Management M
Travel and Tourism M,D

COLORADO STATE UNIVERSITY–GLOBAL CAMPUS
Accounting M
Business Administration and Management—General M
Education—General M
Educational Leadership and Administration M
Finance and Banking M
Human Resources Management M
International Business M
Management Information Systems M
Organizational Management M
Project Management M

COLORADO STATE UNIVERSITY–PUEBLO
Art Education M
Business Administration and Management—General M
Education—General M
Educational Media/Instructional Technology M
Foreign Languages Education M
Health Education M
Music Education M
Physical Education M
Special Education M

COLORADO TECHNICAL UNIVERSITY AURORA
Accounting M
Business Administration and Management—General M
Finance and Banking M
Human Resources Management M
Industrial and Manufacturing Management M
Marketing M
Project Management M

COLORADO TECHNICAL UNIVERSITY COLORADO SPRINGS
Accounting M,D
Business Administration and Management—General M,D
Finance and Banking M,D
Human Resources Management M,D
Industrial and Manufacturing Management M,D
Logistics M,D
Marketing M,D
Project Management M,D

COLUMBIA COLLEGE (MO)
Accounting M
Business Administration and Management—General M
Education—General M
Educational Leadership and Administration M
Human Resources Management M

COLUMBIA COLLEGE (SC)
Education—General M
Educational Leadership and Administration M
Elementary Education M
Higher Education M
Organizational Management M

COLUMBIA COLLEGE CHICAGO
Business Administration and Management—General M
Entertainment Management M

COLUMBIA INTERNATIONAL UNIVERSITY
Counselor Education M,D,O
Curriculum and Instruction M,D,O
Early Childhood Education M,D,O
Education—General M,D,O
Educational Leadership and Administration M,D,O
Elementary Education M,D,O
English as a Second Language M,D,O
Multilingual and Multicultural Education M,D,O
Religious Education M,D,O

COLUMBIA SOUTHERN UNIVERSITY
Business Administration and Management—General M,D
Finance and Banking M
Human Resources Management M
Marketing M
Organizational Management M

COLUMBIA UNIVERSITY
Accounting M,D
Actuarial Science M
Archives/Archival Administration M
Business Administration and Management—General M,D
Business Analytics M
Entrepreneurship M
Finance and Banking M,D
Foreign Languages Education M,D
Foundations and Philosophy of Education M,D
Human Resources Management M
Information Studies M
International Business M
Kinesiology and Movement Studies M,D
Law M,D
Legal and Justice Studies M,D
Marketing M,D
Nonprofit Management M
Quantitative Analysis M,D
Real Estate M
Science Education M,D,O
Social Work M,D
Sports Management M
Sustainability Management M

COLUMBUS STATE UNIVERSITY
Art Education M
Business Administration and Management—General M,O
Counselor Education M,D,O
Curriculum and Instruction M,D,O
Early Childhood Education M,O
Education—General M,D,O
Educational Leadership and Administration M,D,O
English as a Second Language O
English Education M,O
Exercise and Sports Science M
Health Education M
Higher Education M,D,O
Human Resources Management M,O
Mathematics Education M,O
Middle School Education M,O
Music Education M,O
Organizational Management M,O
Physical Education M
Science Education M,O
Secondary Education M,O
Social Sciences Education M,O
Special Education M,O

CONCORDIA COLLEGE
Education—General M
Foreign Languages Education M

CONCORDIA COLLEGE–NEW YORK
Organizational Management M
Special Education M

CONCORDIA UNIVERSITY (CANADA)
Adult Education M,O
Art Education M,D
Business Administration and Management—General M,D,O
Education—General M,O
Educational Media/Instructional Technology M,O
English as a Second Language M,O
Exercise and Sports Science M
Finance and Banking M,D,O
Marketing M,D,O
Mathematics Education M,D
Organizational Management M,O
Supply Chain Management M,D,O

CONCORDIA UNIVERSITY (UNITED STATES)
Art Education M,D
Business Administration and Management—General M
Curriculum and Instruction M,D
Early Childhood Education M,D
Education—General M,D
Educational Leadership and Administration M,D
Educational Media/Instructional Technology M,D
Elementary Education M,D
English as a Second Language M,D
Environmental Education M,D
Health Education M,D
Higher Education M,D
Law D
Mathematics Education M,D
Physical Education M,D
Reading Education M,D
Science Education M,D
Secondary Education M,D
Social Sciences Education M,D
Vocational and Technical Education M,D

CONCORDIA UNIVERSITY ANN ARBOR
Curriculum and Instruction M
Educational Leadership and Administration M
Organizational Management M

CONCORDIA UNIVERSITY CHICAGO
Business Administration and Management—General M,D
Counselor Education M
Curriculum and Instruction M
Early Childhood Education M
Education—General M
Educational Leadership and Administration M,D
Educational Media/Instructional Technology M
Elementary Education M
Exercise and Sports Science M
Human Services M
Reading Education M
Religious Education M
Secondary Education M

CONCORDIA UNIVERSITY IRVINE
Business Administration and Management—General M
Counselor Education M
Curriculum and Instruction M
Education—General M
Educational Leadership and Administration M
Educational Media/Instructional Technology M
Physical Education M
Sports Management M

CONCORDIA UNIVERSITY, NEBRASKA
Early Childhood Education M
Education—General M
Educational Leadership and Administration M
Elementary Education M
Reading Education M
Religious Education M
Secondary Education M

CONCORDIA UNIVERSITY, ST. PAUL
Business Administration and Management—General M

*M—masters degree; D—doctorate; O—other advanced degree; *—Close-Up and/or Display*

- Curriculum and Instruction M,D,O
- Early Childhood Education M,D,O
- Education—General M,D,O
- Educational Leadership and Administration M,D,O
- Educational Media/Instructional Technology M,D,O
- Exercise and Sports Science M,D
- Human Resources Management M
- Human Services M
- Organizational Management M
- Reading Education M,D,O
- Special Education M,D,O
- Sports Management M,D

CONCORDIA UNIVERSITY TEXAS
- Education—General M

CONCORDIA UNIVERSITY WISCONSIN
- Art Education M
- Business Administration and Management—General M
- Counselor Education M
- Early Childhood Education M
- Education—General M
- Educational Leadership and Administration M
- Environmental Education M
- Finance and Banking M
- Health Education M,D
- Human Resources Management M
- International Business M
- Management Information Systems M
- Marketing M
- Organizational Management M
- Reading Education M
- Risk Management M
- Social Work M
- Special Education M

CONCORD LAW SCHOOL
- Law D

CONCORD UNIVERSITY
- Education—General M
- Educational Leadership and Administration M
- Reading Education M
- Social Work M
- Special Education M

CONSERVATORIO DE MUSICA DE PUERTO RICO
- Music Education M

CONVERSE COLLEGE
- Art Education M
- Education of the Gifted M
- Educational Leadership and Administration M,O
- Elementary Education M
- English Education M
- Mathematics Education M
- Middle School Education M
- Music Education M
- Reading Education O
- Science Education M
- Secondary Education M
- Social Sciences Education M
- Special Education M

COPENHAGEN BUSINESS SCHOOL
- Business Administration and Management—General M,D
- International Business M,D
- Logistics M,D
- Management Information Systems M,D

COPPIN STATE UNIVERSITY
- Adult Education M
- Curriculum and Instruction M
- Education—General M
- Human Services M
- Special Education M

CORBAN UNIVERSITY
- Business Administration and Management—General M
- Education—General M
- Nonprofit Management M

CORNELL UNIVERSITY
- Accounting M,D
- Adult Education M,D
- Agricultural Education M,D
- Business Administration and Management—General M,D
- Curriculum and Instruction M,D
- Education—General M,D
- Educational Policy M,D
- Facilities Management M
- Finance and Banking D
- Foreign Languages Education M,D
- Hospitality Management M,D
- Human Resources Management M,D
- Information Studies D
- Law M,D
- Marketing D
- Mathematics Education M,D
- Organizational Behavior M,D
- Real Estate M
- Secondary Education M,D
- Social Work M,D

CORNERSTONE UNIVERSITY
- Business Administration and Management—General M,O
- Education—General M,O
- English as a Second Language M,O

COVENANT COLLEGE
- Education—General M

CRANDALL UNIVERSITY
- Education—General M
- Organizational Management M
- Reading Education M

CREIGHTON UNIVERSITY
- Accounting M,D
- Business Administration and Management—General M,D
- Business Analytics M,D
- Counselor Education M
- Education—General M
- Educational Leadership and Administration M,D
- Elementary Education M
- Finance and Banking M,D
- Investment Management M,D
- Law M,D,O
- Organizational Management M
- Secondary Education M

CULVER-STOCKTON COLLEGE
- Accounting M
- Business Administration and Management—General M
- Finance and Banking M

CUMBERLAND UNIVERSITY
- Business Administration and Management—General M
- Education—General M

CURRY COLLEGE
- Business Administration and Management—General M,O
- Education—General M,O
- Elementary Education M,O
- Finance and Banking M,O
- Foundations and Philosophy of Education M,O
- Reading Education M,O
- Special Education M,O

DAEMEN COLLEGE
- Accounting M
- Business Administration and Management—General M
- Early Childhood Education M
- Education—General M
- Health Education M
- International Business M
- Management Information Systems M
- Marketing M
- Middle School Education M
- Nonprofit Management M
- Social Work M
- Special Education M

DAKOTA STATE UNIVERSITY
- Business Administration and Management—General M,D,O
- Business Analytics M,D,O
- Education—General M
- Educational Media/Instructional Technology M
- Management Information Systems M,D,O

DAKOTA WESLEYAN UNIVERSITY
- Curriculum and Instruction M
- Education—General M
- Educational Leadership and Administration M
- Secondary Education M

DALHOUSIE UNIVERSITY
- Business Administration and Management—General M,O
- Electronic Commerce M,D
- Finance and Banking M
- Health Education M
- Information Studies M
- Kinesiology and Movement Studies M
- Law M,D
- Leisure Studies M
- Library Science M
- Management Information Systems M
- Social Work M

DALLAS BAPTIST UNIVERSITY
- Accounting M
- Business Administration and Management—General M,D
- Counselor Education M
- Curriculum and Instruction M
- Distance Education Development M
- Early Childhood Education M,D
- Education—General M
- Educational Leadership and Administration M,D
- Educational Media/Instructional Technology M
- Elementary Education M
- English as a Second Language M
- Entrepreneurship M
- Finance and Banking M
- Higher Education M,D
- Human Resources Management M
- International Business M
- Kinesiology and Movement Studies M
- Management Information Systems M
- Multilingual and Multicultural Education M
- Nonprofit Management M
- Organizational Management M,D
- Reading Education M
- Religious Education M
- Secondary Education M
- Special Education M
- Sports Management M
- Student Affairs M

DALLAS INTERNATIONAL UNIVERSITY
- Multilingual and Multicultural Education M,O

DALLAS THEOLOGICAL SEMINARY
- Adult Education M,D,O
- Educational Leadership and Administration M,D,O
- Religious Education M,D,O

DARTMOUTH COLLEGE
- Business Administration and Management—General M
- Entrepreneurship D

DAVENPORT UNIVERSITY
- Accounting M
- Business Administration and Management—General M
- Finance and Banking M
- Human Resources Management M
- Management Strategy and Policy M

DEFIANCE COLLEGE
- Business Administration and Management—General M
- Education—General M
- Management Strategy and Policy M

DELAWARE STATE UNIVERSITY
- Adult Education M
- Art Education M
- Business Administration and Management—General M
- Curriculum and Instruction M
- Education—General M,D
- Educational Leadership and Administration M,D
- Exercise and Sports Science M
- Foreign Languages Education M
- Mathematics Education M
- Reading Education M
- Science Education M,D
- Social Work M
- Special Education M

DELAWARE VALLEY UNIVERSITY
- Accounting M
- Business Administration and Management—General M
- Curriculum and Instruction M
- Educational Leadership and Administration M
- Educational Media/Instructional Technology M
- Entrepreneurship M
- Finance and Banking M
- Human Resources Management M
- International Business M
- Supply Chain Management M

DELTA STATE UNIVERSITY
- Accounting M
- Aviation Management M
- Business Administration and Management—General M
- Counselor Education M,D,O
- Education—General M,D,O
- Educational Leadership and Administration M,D,O
- Elementary Education M,D,O
- English Education M
- Exercise and Sports Science M
- Health Education M
- Higher Education D
- Physical Education M
- Recreation and Park Management M
- Secondary Education M,D,O
- Social Sciences Education M
- Special Education M

DEPAUL UNIVERSITY
- Accounting M,D
- Adult Education M
- Advertising and Public Relations M
- Business Administration and Management—General M,D
- Business Analytics M,D
- Counselor Education M,D
- Curriculum and Instruction M,D
- Early Childhood Education M,D
- Education—General M,D
- Educational Leadership and Administration M,D
- Electronic Commerce M,D
- Elementary Education M,D
- Entrepreneurship M,D
- Finance and Banking M,D
- Foreign Languages Education M,D
- Foundations and Philosophy of Education M,D
- Health Law M,D
- Higher Education M,D
- Hospitality Management M,D
- Human Resources Management M,D
- Intellectual Property Law M,D
- International Business M,D
- Law M,D
- Management Information Systems M,D
- Management Strategy and Policy M,D
- Marketing M,D
- Mathematics Education M,D
- Middle School Education M,D
- Multilingual and Multicultural Education M,D
- Music Education M,O
- Nonprofit Management M
- Physical Education M,D
- Reading Education M,D
- Real Estate M,D
- Risk Management M,D
- Science Education M,D
- Secondary Education M,D
- Social Work M
- Special Education M,D
- Student Affairs M,D
- Supply Chain Management M,D
- Sustainability Management M,D
- Taxation M,D

DEREE - THE AMERICAN COLLEGE OF GREECE
- Marketing M

DESALES UNIVERSITY
- Accounting M
- Business Administration and Management—General M
- Education—General M,O
- Educational Media/Instructional Technology M,O
- English as a Second Language M,O
- Finance and Banking M
- Human Resources Management M
- Management Information Systems M,O
- Marketing M
- Project Management M,O
- Secondary Education M,O
- Special Education M,O
- Supply Chain Management M

DEVRY COLLEGE OF NEW YORK–MIDTOWN MANHATTAN CAMPUS
- Business Administration and Management—General M

DEVRY UNIVERSITY–ALPHARETTA CAMPUS
- Business Administration and Management—General M

DEVRY UNIVERSITY–ARLINGTON CAMPUS
- Business Administration and Management—General M

DEVRY UNIVERSITY–CHARLOTTE CAMPUS
- Business Administration and Management—General M

DEVRY UNIVERSITY–CHESAPEAKE CAMPUS
- Business Administration and Management—General M

DEVRY UNIVERSITY–CHICAGO CAMPUS
- Business Administration and Management—General M

DEVRY UNIVERSITY–CHICAGO LOOP CAMPUS
- Business Administration and Management—General M

DEVRY UNIVERSITY–CINCINNATI CAMPUS
- Business Administration and Management—General M

DEVRY UNIVERSITY–COLUMBUS CAMPUS
- Business Administration and Management—General M

DEVRY UNIVERSITY–DECATUR CAMPUS
- Business Administration and Management—General M

DEVRY UNIVERSITY–FOLSOM CAMPUS
- Accounting M
- Business Administration and Management—General M
- Curriculum and Instruction M
- Educational Leadership and Administration M
- Educational Media/Instructional Technology M
- Finance and Banking M
- Higher Education M
- Human Resources Management M
- Management Information Systems M
- Project Management M

DEVRY UNIVERSITY–FREMONT CAMPUS
- Business Administration and Management—General M

DEVRY UNIVERSITY–FT. WASHINGTON CAMPUS
- Business Administration and Management—General M

DEVRY UNIVERSITY–HENDERSON CAMPUS
- Business Administration and Management—General M

DEVRY UNIVERSITY–IRVING CAMPUS
- Business Administration and Management—General M

DEVRY UNIVERSITY–JACKSONVILLE CAMPUS
- Business Administration and Management—General M

DEVRY UNIVERSITY–LONG BEACH CAMPUS
- Business Administration and Management—General M

DEVRY UNIVERSITY–MIRAMAR CAMPUS
- Business Administration and Management—General M

DEVRY UNIVERSITY–MORRISVILLE CAMPUS
- Business Administration and Management—General M

DEVRY UNIVERSITY–NASHVILLE CAMPUS
- Business Administration and Management—General M

DEVRY UNIVERSITY–NORTH BRUNSWICK CAMPUS
- Business Administration and Management—General M

DEVRY UNIVERSITY ONLINE
Business Administration and
   Management—General   M

DEVRY UNIVERSITY–ORLANDO CAMPUS
Business Administration and
   Management—General   M

DEVRY UNIVERSITY–PHOENIX CAMPUS
Business Administration and
   Management—General   M

DEVRY UNIVERSITY–POMONA CAMPUS
Business Administration and
   Management—General   M

DEVRY UNIVERSITY–SAN DIEGO CAMPUS
Business Administration and
   Management—General   M,O

DEVRY UNIVERSITY–SEVEN HILLS CAMPUS
Business Administration and
   Management—General   M,O

DEVRY UNIVERSITY–TINLEY PARK CAMPUS
Business Administration and
   Management—General   M

DICKINSON STATE UNIVERSITY
Early Childhood Education   M
Education—General   M
Entrepreneurship   M
Middle School Education   M
Reading Education   M

DOANE UNIVERSITY
Business Administration and
   Management—General   M
Counselor Education   M
Curriculum and Instruction   M,D,O
Education—General   M,D,O
Educational Leadership and
   Administration   M,D,O

DOMINICAN COLLEGE
Accounting   M
Business Administration and
   Management—General   M
Education—General   M
Elementary Education   M
Special Education   M

DOMINICAN UNIVERSITY
Accounting   M
Business Administration and
   Management—General   M
Early Childhood Education   M
Education—General   M
Elementary Education   M
English as a Second Language   M
Information Studies   M,D,O
Management Information Systems   M,D,O
Reading Education   M
Secondary Education   M
Social Work   M
Special Education   M

DOMINICAN UNIVERSITY OF CALIFORNIA
Business Administration and
   Management—General   M
Education—General   M
Special Education   M

DORDT COLLEGE
Education—General   M

DRAKE UNIVERSITY
Accounting   M
Athletic Training and Sports
   Medicine   M,D
Business Administration and
   Management—General   M
Counselor Education   M,D,O
Education—General   M,D,O
Educational Leadership and
   Administration   M,D,O
Law   M,D
Mathematics Education   M,D,O
Reading Education   M,D,O
Science Education   M,D,O
Special Education   M,D,O

DREW UNIVERSITY
Community College Education   M,D,O
Education—General   M,D,O
Elementary Education   M,D,O
Finance and Banking   M,D,O
Health Education   M,D,O
Secondary Education   M,D,O
Special Education   M,D,O

DREXEL UNIVERSITY
Accounting   M,D,O
Archives/Archival Administration   M
Business Administration and
   Management—General   M,D,O
Curriculum and Instruction   M,D
Education—General   M,D
Educational Leadership and
   Administration   M,D
Educational Media/Instructional
   Technology   M,D
Entrepreneurship   M
Finance and Banking   M,D,O
Health Law   M,D
Higher Education   M,D
Hospitality Management   M
Human Resources Development   M,D
Intellectual Property Law   M,D
International and Comparative
   Education   M,D

Law   M,D
Library Science   M,D,O
Management Information Systems   M,D,O
Management Strategy and Policy   M,D,O
Marketing   M,D,O
Organizational Behavior   M,D,O
Project Management   M
Quantitative Analysis   M,D,O
Real Estate   M
Special Education   M,D
Sports and Entertainment Law   M,D
Sports Management   M

DRURY UNIVERSITY
Business Administration and
   Management—General   M
Curriculum and Instruction   M
Education—General   M
Educational Leadership and
   Administration   M
Educational Media/Instructional
   Technology   M
Elementary Education   M
Middle School Education   M
Nonprofit Management   M
Reading Education   M
Secondary Education   M
Special Education   M

DUKE UNIVERSITY
Accounting   D
Business Administration and
   Management—General   M,D,O
Business Analytics   M
Education—General   M
Entrepreneurship   M,O
Finance and Banking   M,D,O
Industrial and Manufacturing
   Management   M,D,O
International Business   M,O
Law   M,D
Management Strategy and Policy   M,D,O
Marketing   M,D,O
Organizational Management   M,D,O
Quantitative Analysis   M,D,O

DUNLAP-STONE UNIVERSITY
Law   M

DUQUESNE UNIVERSITY
Accounting   M
Business Administration and
   Management—General   M
Counselor Education   M,D,O
Curriculum and Instruction   M,O
Early Childhood Education   M
Education—General   M
Educational Leadership and
   Administration   M,D,O
Educational Measurement and
   Evaluation   M
Educational Media/Instructional
   Technology   M,D,O
Elementary Education   M
English as a Second Language   M
English Education   M
Finance and Banking   M
Foreign Languages Education   M
Foundations and Philosophy of
   Education   M
Law   M,D
Management Information Systems   M
Marketing   M
Mathematics Education   M
Middle School Education   M
Music Education   M,O
Organizational Management   M
Reading Education   M
Science Education   M
Secondary Education   M
Social Sciences Education   M
Special Education   M,D
Sports Management   M
Supply Chain Management   M
Sustainability Management   M

D'YOUVILLE COLLEGE
Business Administration and
   Management—General   M
Education—General   M,D
Educational Leadership and
   Administration   M,D
Elementary Education   M,D
International Business   M
Secondary Education   M,D
Special Education   M,D

EARLHAM COLLEGE
Education—General   M

EAST CAROLINA UNIVERSITY
Accounting   M
Adult Education   M,O
Art Education   M
Business Administration and
   Management—General   M,D,O
Business Education   M
Community College Education   M,D,O
Counselor Education   M,D,O
Curriculum and Instruction   M,O
Distance Education Development   M,O
Early Childhood Education   M,D
Education—General   M,D,O
Educational Leadership and
   Administration   M,D,O
Educational Media/Instructional
   Technology   M,O
Elementary Education   M,O
English as a Second Language   M,O
English Education   M,O
Exercise and Sports Science   M,D,O
Health Education   M
Higher Education   M,O

Hospitality Management   M,O
Industrial and Manufacturing
   Management   M,D,O
International and Comparative
   Education   M,O
Kinesiology and Movement Studies   M,D,O
Leisure Studies   M,O
Library Science   M,O
Logistics   M,D,O
Management Information Systems   M,D,O
Mathematics Education   M,O
Middle School Education   M,O
Music Education   M,O
Physical Education   M,D,O
Reading Education   M
Recreation and Park Management   M,O
Science Education   M,O
Social Sciences Education   M,O
Social Work   M,O
Special Education   M,O
Sports Management   M,D,O
Vocational and Technical Education   M,O

EAST CENTRAL UNIVERSITY
Accounting   M
Education—General   M
Human Resources Management   M

EASTERN CONNECTICUT STATE UNIVERSITY
Accounting   M
Early Childhood Education   M
Education—General   M
Educational Media/Instructional
   Technology   M
Elementary Education   M
Organizational Management   M
Secondary Education   M

EASTERN ILLINOIS UNIVERSITY
Accounting   M
Art Education   M
Business Administration and
   Management—General   M
Counselor Education   M
Curriculum and Instruction   M
Early Childhood Education   M
Education—General   M,O
Educational Leadership and
   Administration   M,O
Elementary Education   M
Mathematics Education   M
Middle School Education   M
Music Education   M
Secondary Education   M
Special Education   M
Student Affairs   M

EASTERN KENTUCKY UNIVERSITY
Agricultural Education   M
Art Education   M
Business Administration and
   Management—General   M
Business Education   M
Counselor Education   M
Curriculum and Instruction   M
Education—General   M
Educational Leadership and
   Administration   M
Elementary Education   M
English Education   M
Exercise and Sports Science   M
Health Education   M
Higher Education   M
Home Economics Education   M
Library Science   M
Mathematics Education   M
Music Education   M
Physical Education   M
Recreation and Park Management   M
Science Education   M
Secondary Education   M
Social Sciences Education   M
Special Education   M
Sports Management   M
Vocational and Technical Education   M

EASTERN MENNONITE UNIVERSITY
Business Administration and
   Management—General   M
Counselor Education   M
Curriculum and Instruction   M
Education—General   M
Nonprofit Management   M
Organizational Management   M
Reading Education   M
Special Education   M

EASTERN MICHIGAN UNIVERSITY
Accounting   M
Art Education   M
Athletic Training and Sports
   Medicine   M,O
Business Administration and
   Management—General   M,O
Community College Education   M,D,O
Counselor Education   M,O
Curriculum and Instruction   M,O
Distance Education Development   M,O
Early Childhood Education   M
Education—General   M,D,O
Educational Leadership and
   Administration   M,D,O
Educational Measurement and
   Evaluation   M,O
Educational Media/Instructional
   Technology   M,O
Educational Policy   M
Educational Psychology   M,O
Electronic Commerce   M
English as a Second Language   M,O
English Education   M
Entrepreneurship   M,O

Exercise and Sports Science   M
Finance and Banking   M,O
Foreign Languages Education   M,O
Foundations and Philosophy of
   Education   M,O
Health Education   M,O
Higher Education   M,D,O
Hospitality Management   O
Human Resources Management   M,O
Human Services   O
International Business   M,O
Kinesiology and Movement Studies   M,O
Management Information Systems   M,O
Marketing   M,O
Middle School Education   M
Museum Education   O
Nonprofit Management   M,O
Organizational Management   M,O
Physical Education   M
Quality Management   M,O
Reading Education   M,O
Science Education   M
Secondary Education   M
Social Work   M
Special Education   M,O
Sports Management   M
Student Affairs   M,D,O
Supply Chain Management   M,O
Urban Education   M

EASTERN NAZARENE COLLEGE
Business Administration and
   Management—General   M
Early Childhood Education   M,O
Education—General   M,O
Educational Leadership and
   Administration   M,O
Elementary Education   M,O
English as a Second Language   M,O
Middle School Education   M,O
Reading Education   M,O
Secondary Education   M,O
Special Education   M,O

EASTERN NEW MEXICO UNIVERSITY
Business Administration and
   Management—General   M
Counselor Education   M
Curriculum and Instruction   M
Early Childhood Education   M
Education of the Gifted   M
Education—General   M
Educational Leadership and
   Administration   M
Educational Media/Instructional
   Technology   M
Elementary Education   M
English as a Second Language   M
Exercise and Sports Science   M
Multilingual and Multicultural
   Education   M
Physical Education   M
Reading Education   M
Secondary Education   M
Special Education   M
Sports Management   M
Vocational and Technical Education   M

EASTERN OREGON UNIVERSITY
Business Administration and
   Management—General   M
Education—General   M
Elementary Education   M
Secondary Education   M

EASTERN UNIVERSITY
Business Administration and
   Management—General   M,D,O
Early Childhood Education   M,O
Educational Leadership and
   Administration   M,D,O
Elementary Education   M,O
English as a Second Language   M,O
English Education   M,O
Foreign Languages Education   M,O
Health Education   M,O
Mathematics Education   M,O
Middle School Education   M,O
Multilingual and Multicultural
   Education   M,O
Nonprofit Management   D,O
Organizational Management   M,D,O
Physical Education   M,O
Reading Education   M,O
Science Education   M,O
Secondary Education   M,O
Social Sciences Education   M,O
Special Education   M,O

EASTERN WASHINGTON UNIVERSITY
Accounting   M
Adult Education   M
Business Administration and
   Management—General   M
Computer Education   M
Counselor Education   M
Curriculum and Instruction   M
Early Childhood Education   M
Education—General   M
Educational Leadership and
   Administration   M
Elementary Education   M
English as a Second Language   M
Exercise and Sports Science   M
Foundations and Philosophy of
   Education   M
Music Education   M
Physical Education   M
Reading Education   M
Recreation and Park Management   M
Social Work   M
Sports Management   M

---

*M—masters degree; D—doctorate; O—other advanced degree; *—Close-Up and/or Display*

EAST STROUDSBURG UNIVERSITY OF PENNSYLVANIA

Athletic Training and Sports Medicine	M
Early Childhood Education	M
Education—General	M,D
Educational Media/Instructional Technology	M
Elementary Education	M
Health Education	M
Physical Education	M
Reading Education	M
Secondary Education	M,D
Special Education	M
Sports Management	M

EAST TENNESSEE STATE UNIVERSITY

Accounting	M
Archives/Archival Administration	M,O
Business Administration and Management—General	M,O
Counselor Education	M
Curriculum and Instruction	M,O
Developmental Education	M,O
Early Childhood Education	M,D,O
Education—General	M,D,O
Educational Leadership and Administration	M,D,O
Educational Media/Instructional Technology	M,O
Elementary Education	M,O
English as a Second Language	M,O
Entrepreneurship	M,O
Exercise and Sports Science	M,D
Human Services	M
Kinesiology and Movement Studies	M,D
Library Science	M,O
Management Strategy and Policy	M,O
Marketing	M,O
Middle School Education	M,O
Nonprofit Management	M,O
Reading Education	M,O
Secondary Education	M,O
Social Work	M
Special Education	M,O
Sports Management	M,D

EAST TEXAS BAPTIST UNIVERSITY

Business Administration and Management—General	M
Education—General	M
Kinesiology and Movement Studies	M

ECOLE HÔTELIÈRE DE LAUSANNE

Hospitality Management	M

ECPI UNIVERSITY

Business Administration and Management—General	M
Management Information Systems	M

EDGEWOOD COLLEGE

Accounting	M
Business Administration and Management—General	M
Education—General	M,D,O
Sustainability Management	M

EDINBORO UNIVERSITY OF PENNSYLVANIA

Art Education	M
Counselor Education	M,O
Early Childhood Education	M,O
Educational Leadership and Administration	M
Educational Psychology	M,O
Middle School Education	M
Reading Education	M,O
Secondary Education	M
Social Work	M
Special Education	M,O

ELIZABETH CITY STATE UNIVERSITY

Community College Education	M
Education—General	M
Educational Leadership and Administration	M
Elementary Education	M
Mathematics Education	M
Science Education	M

ELMHURST COLLEGE

Business Administration and Management—General	M
Educational Leadership and Administration	M
Management Information Systems	M
Project Management	M
Special Education	M
Supply Chain Management	M

ELMS COLLEGE

Accounting	M,O
Business Administration and Management—General	M,O
Early Childhood Education	M,O
Education—General	M,O
Elementary Education	M,O
English as a Second Language	M,O
English Education	M,O
Entrepreneurship	M,O
Finance and Banking	M,O
Foreign Languages Education	M,O
Reading Education	M,O
Science Education	M,O
Secondary Education	M,O
Special Education	M,O

ELON UNIVERSITY

Business Administration and Management—General	M
Education—General	M
Elementary Education	M
Law	D

EMBRY-RIDDLE AERONAUTICAL UNIVERSITY–DAYTONA

Business Administration and Management—General	M
Finance and Banking	M
Human Resources Management	M

EMBRY-RIDDLE AERONAUTICAL UNIVERSITY–WORLDWIDE

Aviation Management	M
Business Administration and Management—General	M
Education—General	M
Entrepreneurship	M
Finance and Banking	M
Human Resources Management	M
International Business	M
Logistics	M
Management Information Systems	M
Project Management	M
Supply Chain Management	M

EMMANUEL COLLEGE (UNITED STATES)

Business Administration and Management—General	M,O
Education—General	M,O
Human Resources Management	M,O
Special Education	M,O
Urban Education	M,O

EMORY & HENRY COLLEGE

Education—General	M,D
Organizational Management	M,D
Reading Education	M,D

EMORY UNIVERSITY

Accounting	M,D
Business Administration and Management—General	M,D
Education—General	M,D
Entrepreneurship	M
Finance and Banking	M,D
Health Education	M,D
Industrial and Manufacturing Management	M
International Business	M
Law	M,D,O
Management Information Systems	M,D
Marketing	M,D
Middle School Education	M,D
Organizational Management	M,D
Real Estate	M
Secondary Education	M,D

EMPIRE COLLEGE

Law	M,D

EMPORIA STATE UNIVERSITY

Accounting	M
Business Administration and Management—General	M
Counselor Education	M
Curriculum and Instruction	M
Distance Education Development	M,O
Early Childhood Education	M
Education of the Gifted	M
Education—General	M
Educational Leadership and Administration	M
Educational Media/Instructional Technology	M,O
Elementary Education	M
English as a Second Language	M,O
Library Science	M,D,O
Physical Education	M
Reading Education	M
Special Education	M

ENDICOTT COLLEGE

Business Administration and Management—General	M
Distance Education Development	M
Early Childhood Education	M
Educational Leadership and Administration	M,D
Elementary Education	M
Management Information Systems	M
Organizational Management	M
Reading Education	M
Secondary Education	M
Special Education	M,D,O
Sports Management	M

ERIKSON INSTITUTE

Early Childhood Education	M,D
English as a Second Language	M,O
Social Work	M

ESSEC BUSINESS SCHOOL

Business Administration and Management—General	M,D
Hospitality Management	M,D
International Business	M,D

EVANGEL UNIVERSITY

Counselor Education	M
Curriculum and Instruction	M,D
Education—General	M
Educational Leadership and Administration	M,D
Organizational Management	M
Reading Education	M
Secondary Education	M

EVERGLADES UNIVERSITY

Accounting	M
Business Administration and Management—General	M
Entrepreneurship	M
Human Resources Management	M
Industrial and Manufacturing Management	M
Project Management	M

THE EVERGREEN STATE COLLEGE

Education—General	M

FAIRFIELD UNIVERSITY

Accounting	M,O
Business Administration and Management—General	M,O
Business Analytics	M,O
Counselor Education	M,O
Education—General	M,O
Educational Media/Instructional Technology	M,O
Elementary Education	M,O
English as a Second Language	M,O
Finance and Banking	M,O
Foundations and Philosophy of Education	M,O
Health Education	M,D
Management Information Systems	M,O
Marketing	M,O
Multilingual and Multicultural Education	M,O
Secondary Education	M,O
Special Education	M,O
Taxation	M,O

FAIRLEIGH DICKINSON UNIVERSITY, FLORHAM CAMPUS

Accounting	M
Business Administration and Management—General	M,O
Early Childhood Education	M,O
Education—General	M,O
Educational Leadership and Administration	M
Educational Media/Instructional Technology	M,O
Entrepreneurship	M,O
Finance and Banking	M,O
Hospitality Management	M
Human Resources Management	M
International Business	M,O
Marketing	M,O
Organizational Behavior	M,O
Organizational Management	M,O
Reading Education	M,O
Sports Management	M
Supply Chain Management	M
Sustainability Management	O
Taxation	M,O

FAIRLEIGH DICKINSON UNIVERSITY, METROPOLITAN CAMPUS

Accounting	M,O
Business Administration and Management—General	M,O
Curriculum and Instruction	M,O
Early Childhood Education	M
Education—General	M,O
Educational Leadership and Administration	M
Educational Media/Instructional Technology	M,O
Electronic Commerce	M
Entrepreneurship	M,O
Finance and Banking	M,O
Foundations and Philosophy of Education	M
Hospitality Management	M
Human Resources Management	M,O
International Business	M
Management Information Systems	M,O
Marketing	M,O
Multilingual and Multicultural Education	M
Nonprofit Management	M,O
Reading Education	M,O
Science Education	M
Special Education	M
Sports Management	M
Taxation	M

FAIRMONT STATE UNIVERSITY

Business Administration and Management—General	M
Education—General	M
Educational Media/Instructional Technology	M
Exercise and Sports Science	M
Reading Education	M
Special Education	M

FASHION INSTITUTE OF TECHNOLOGY

Business Administration and Management—General	M
Marketing	M

FAULKNER UNIVERSITY

Business Administration and Management—General	M
Counselor Education	M
Curriculum and Instruction	M
Education—General	M
Elementary Education	M
Law	D

FAYETTEVILLE STATE UNIVERSITY

Business Administration and Management—General	M
Educational Leadership and Administration	M,D
Elementary Education	M
Middle School Education	M
Secondary Education	M
Social Sciences Education	M
Social Work	M

FELICIAN UNIVERSITY

Business Administration and Management—General	M,D
Education—General	M,O
Educational Leadership and Administration	M,O
Entrepreneurship	M,D
Religious Education	M,O

FERRIS STATE UNIVERSITY

Business Administration and Management—General	M
Community College Education	D
Curriculum and Instruction	M
Developmental Education	M
Education—General	M
Educational Leadership and Administration	D
Human Services	M
Management Information Systems	M
Project Management	M
Social Work	M
Special Education	M
Supply Chain Management	M

FIELDING GRADUATE UNIVERSITY

Early Childhood Education	M,D,O
Education—General	M,D
Organizational Management	O

FISHER COLLEGE

Business Administration and Management—General	M
Management Strategy and Policy	M

FITCHBURG STATE UNIVERSITY

Accounting	M
Art Education	M,O
Business Administration and Management—General	M
Counselor Education	M,O
Curriculum and Instruction	M
Early Childhood Education	M
Educational Leadership and Administration	M,O
Elementary Education	M
English Education	M,O
Higher Education	M,O
Human Resources Management	M
Mathematics Education	M
Middle School Education	M
Reading Education	O
Science Education	M
Social Sciences Education	M
Special Education	M
Vocational and Technical Education	M

FIVE TOWNS COLLEGE

Early Childhood Education	M,D
Music Education	M,D

FLAGLER COLLEGE

Special Education	M

FLORIDA AGRICULTURAL AND MECHANICAL UNIVERSITY

Accounting	M
Adult Education	M,D
Business Administration and Management—General	M
Business Education	M
Counselor Education	M,D
Education—General	M,D
Educational Leadership and Administration	M,D
Elementary Education	M
English Education	M
Finance and Banking	M
Law	D
Management Information Systems	M
Marketing	M
Mathematics Education	M
Physical Education	M
Science Education	M
Secondary Education	M
Social Sciences Education	M
Social Work	M
Sports Management	M
Vocational and Technical Education	M

FLORIDA ATLANTIC UNIVERSITY

Accounting	M
Adult Education	M,D,O
Business Administration and Management—General	M
Counselor Education	M,D
Curriculum and Instruction	M,D,O
Early Childhood Education	M,D,O
Education—General	M,D,O
Educational Leadership and Administration	M,D,O
Educational Media/Instructional Technology	M
Elementary Education	M
English as a Second Language	M,D,O
Entrepreneurship	M
Environmental Education	M
Exercise and Sports Science	M
Higher Education	M,D,O
International Business	M
Management Information Systems	M
Multilingual and Multicultural Education	M,D,O
Nonprofit Management	M,D
Reading Education	M
Science Education	M,D
Secondary Education	M
Social Work	M,D
Special Education	M,D
Sports Management	M

FLORIDA COASTAL SCHOOL OF LAW

Law	D

FLORIDA GULF COAST UNIVERSITY

Accounting	M
Business Administration and Management—General	M
Curriculum and Instruction	M
Education of the Gifted	M
Education—General	M
Educational Leadership and Administration	M
Elementary Education	M
English as a Second Language	M
English Education	M
Management Information Systems	M
Mathematics Education	M
Middle School Education	M
Reading Education	M

Science Education — M
Social Sciences Education — M
Social Work — M
Special Education — M
Taxation — M

FLORIDA INSTITUTE OF TECHNOLOGY
Business Administration and
　Management—General — M
Human Resources Management — M
International Business — M
Logistics — M
Management Information Systems — M

FLORIDA INTERNATIONAL UNIVERSITY
Accounting — M
Adult Education — M,D,O
Art Education — M,D,O
Athletic Training and Sports
　Medicine — M
Counselor Education — M,D,O
Curriculum and Instruction — M,D,O
Early Childhood Education — M,D,O
Educational Leadership and
　Administration — M,D,O
Educational Media/Instructional
　Technology — M,D,O
Elementary Education — M,D,O
English as a Second Language — M,D,O
English Education — M,D,O
Finance and Banking — M
Foreign Languages Education — M,D,O
Higher Education — M,D,O
Hospitality Management — M
Human Resources Development — M,D,O
Human Resources Management — M,D
International and Comparative
　Education — M,D,O
International Business — M,D
Law — M,D
Management Information Systems — M,D
Marketing — M
Mathematics Education — M,D,O
Multilingual and Multicultural
　Education — M,D,O
Music Education — M
Physical Education — M,D,O
Reading Education — M,D,O
Real Estate — M
Recreation and Park Management — M,D,O
Science Education — M,D,O
Social Sciences Education — M,D,O
Social Work — M,D
Special Education — M,D,O
Sports Management — M,D,O
Urban Education — M,D,O

FLORIDA MEMORIAL UNIVERSITY
Business Administration and
　Management—General — M
Education—General — M
Elementary Education — M
Reading Education — M
Special Education — M

FLORIDA NATIONAL UNIVERSITY
Accounting — M
Business Administration and
　Management—General — M
Finance and Banking — M
Marketing — M

FLORIDA SOUTHERN COLLEGE
Accounting — M
Business Administration and
　Management—General — M
Education—General — M,D

FLORIDA STATE UNIVERSITY
Accounting — M,D
Actuarial Science — M,D
Art Education — M,D
Business Administration and
　Management—General — M,D
Curriculum and Instruction — M,D,O
Education—General — M,D,O
Educational Leadership and
　Administration — M,D,O
Educational Measurement and
　Evaluation — M,D,O
Educational Media/Instructional
　Technology — M,D,O
Educational Policy — M,D,O
Educational Psychology — M,D,O
English as a Second Language — M,D,O
English Education — M,D,O
Environmental Law — M,D
Exercise and Sports Science — M,D
Finance and Banking — M,D
Foundations and Philosophy of
　Education — M,D,O
Health Education — M,D
Health Law — M,D
Higher Education — M,D
Human Resources Management — M,D
Insurance — M
International and Comparative
　Education — M,D,O
Law — M
Management Information Systems — M,D,O
Management Strategy and Policy — M,D
Marketing — M,D
Organizational Behavior — M
Reading Education — M,D,O
Risk Management — M
Science Education — M,D
Social Work — M,D
Sports Management — M,D
Taxation — M,D

FONTBONNE UNIVERSITY
Accounting — M
Art Education — M

Business Administration and
　Management—General — M
Curriculum and Instruction — M
Early Childhood Education — M
Education—General — M
Educational Media/Instructional
　Technology — M
Elementary Education — M
Middle School Education — M
Reading Education — M
Secondary Education — M
Special Education — M
Supply Chain Management — M

FORDHAM UNIVERSITY
Accounting — M,D
Business Administration and
　Management—General — M,D
Counselor Education — M,D
Curriculum and Instruction — M,O
Early Childhood Education — M,O
Education—General — M,D,O
Educational Leadership and
　Administration — M,D,O
Educational Psychology — M,D
Electronic Commerce — M,D
Elementary Education — M,O
English as a Second Language — M,O
Entrepreneurship — M,D
Finance and Banking — M,D
Intellectual Property Law — M,D
Investment Management — M,D
Law — M,D
Management Information Systems — M,D
Marketing — M,D
Nonprofit Management — M,D
Quantitative Analysis — M,D
Religious Education — M,D,O
Social Work — M,D
Special Education — M,O
Taxation — M,D

FORT HAYS STATE UNIVERSITY
Business Administration and
　Management—General — M
Counselor Education — M
Education—General — M,O
Educational Leadership and
　Administration — M,O
Educational Media/Instructional
　Technology — M
Health Education — M
Physical Education — M
Special Education — M

FORT LEWIS COLLEGE
Educational Leadership and
　Administration — M,O

FORT VALLEY STATE UNIVERSITY
Counselor Education — M,O

FRAMINGHAM STATE UNIVERSITY
Art Education — M
Business Administration and
　Management—General — M
Curriculum and Instruction — M
Early Childhood Education — M
Educational Leadership and
　Administration — M
Educational Media/Instructional
　Technology — M
Elementary Education — M
English as a Second Language — M,O
Human Resources Management — M
Mathematics Education — M
Reading Education — M
Special Education — M

FRANCISCAN UNIVERSITY OF STEUBENVILLE
Business Administration and
　Management—General — M
Curriculum and Instruction — M
Education—General — M
Educational Leadership and
　Administration — M

FRANCIS MARION UNIVERSITY
Business Administration and
　Management—General — M
Education—General — M
Special Education — M

FRANKLIN COLLEGE
Athletic Training and Sports
　Medicine — M

FRANKLIN PIERCE UNIVERSITY
Business Administration and
　Management—General — M,D,O
Curriculum and Instruction — M,D,O
Elementary Education — M,D,O
Human Resources Management — M,D,O
Management Information Systems — M,D,O
Special Education — M,D,O
Sports Management — M,D,O
Sustainability Management — M,D,O

FRANKLIN UNIVERSITY
Accounting — M
Business Administration and
　Management—General — M
Educational Media/Instructional
　Technology — M
Marketing — M

FRANKLIN UNIVERSITY SWITZERLAND
International Business — M

FREED-HARDEMAN UNIVERSITY
Accounting — M
Business Administration and
　Management—General — M
Counselor Education — M,O

Curriculum and Instruction — M,O
Education—General — M,O
Educational Leadership and
　Administration — M,O
Management Strategy and Policy — M,O
Special Education — M,O

FRESNO PACIFIC UNIVERSITY
Business Administration and
　Management—General — M
Counselor Education — M
Curriculum and Instruction — M
Education—General — M,O
Educational Leadership and
　Administration — M
Educational Media/Instructional
　Technology — M
English as a Second Language — M,O
Kinesiology and Movement Studies — M
Mathematics Education — M
Reading Education — M,O
Science Education — M
Special Education — M
Student Affairs — M,O

FRIENDS UNIVERSITY
Accounting — M
Law — M
Logistics — M
Management Information Systems — M
Management Strategy and Policy — M
Supply Chain Management — M

FROSTBURG STATE UNIVERSITY
Business Administration and
　Management—General — M
Counselor Education — M
Curriculum and Instruction — M,D
Education—General — M,D
Educational Leadership and
　Administration — M,D
Educational Media/Instructional
　Technology — M,D
Elementary Education — M,D
Reading Education — M,D
Recreation and Park Management — M
Secondary Education — M,D
Special Education — M

FULL SAIL UNIVERSITY
Business Administration and
　Management—General — M
Educational Media/Instructional
　Technology — M
Entertainment Management — M
Marketing — M

FURMAN UNIVERSITY
Curriculum and Instruction — M,O
Early Childhood Education — M,O
Education—General — M,O
Educational Leadership and
　Administration — M,O
English as a Second Language — M,O
Reading Education — M,O
Special Education — M,O

GALLAUDET UNIVERSITY
Counselor Education — M,D,O
Early Childhood Education — M,D,O
Education—General — M,D,O
Elementary Education — M,D,O
International and Comparative
　Education — M,D,O
Multilingual and Multicultural
　Education — M,D,O
Secondary Education — M,D,O
Social Work — M,D,O
Special Education — M,D,O

GANNON UNIVERSITY
Athletic Training and Sports
　Medicine — M
Business Administration and
　Management—General — M
Curriculum and Instruction — M,O
Education—General — M,O
Educational Leadership and
　Administration — D,O
English as a Second Language — O
Exercise and Sports Science — M
Finance and Banking — M
Human Resources Management — M
Marketing — M
Organizational Management — D
Reading Education — M,O

GARDNER-WEBB UNIVERSITY
Business Administration and
　Management—General — M
Curriculum and Instruction — M,D,O
Education—General — M,D,O
Educational Leadership and
　Administration — M,D,O
English Education — M
Exercise and Sports Science — M
Organizational Management — M,D,O
Physical Education — M
Religious Education — M,D

GARRETT-EVANGELICAL THEOLOGICAL SEMINARY
Religious Education — M,D

GATEWAY SEMINARY
Early Childhood Education — M,D,O
Educational Leadership and
　Administration — M,D,O

GENEVA COLLEGE
Business Administration and
　Management—General — M
Counselor Education — M
Education—General — M

Curriculum and Instruction — M,O
Education—General — M,O
Educational Leadership and
　Administration — M,O
Management Strategy and Policy — M,O
Special Education — M,O

Educational Leadership and
　Administration — M
Finance and Banking — M
Higher Education — M
Marketing — M
Nonprofit Management — M
Organizational Management — M
Project Management — M

GEORGE FOX UNIVERSITY
Accounting — M,D
Business Administration and
　Management—General — M,D
Counselor Education — M,O
Education—General — M,D,O
Educational Leadership and
　Administration — M,D,O
Educational Media/Instructional
　Technology — M,O
English as a Second Language — M,O
Finance and Banking — M,D
Human Resources Management — M,D
Marketing — M,D
Organizational Management — M,D
Reading Education — M,O
Social Work — M,O
Special Education — M,O

GEORGE MASON UNIVERSITY
Accounting — M
Art Education — M
Athletic Training and Sports
　Medicine — M,O
Business Administration and
　Management—General — M
Counselor Education — M
Curriculum and Instruction — M
Early Childhood Education — M
Education of the Gifted — M
Education—General — M,D,O
Educational Leadership and
　Administration — M,O
Educational Media/Instructional
　Technology — M
Educational Psychology — M,O
Elementary Education — M
English as a Second Language — M
English Education — M,D,O
Exercise and Sports Science — M
Foreign Languages Education — M
Higher Education — M,D,O
Human Resources Management — M
International Business — M,O
Law — M,D
Logistics — M
Management Information Systems — M
Mathematics Education — M
Music Education — M
Organizational Management — M
Physical Education — M
Project Management — M,D
Reading Education — M
Science Education — M
Secondary Education — M
Social Sciences Education — M
Social Work — M
Special Education — M,O
Sports Management — M,O
Transportation Management — M

GEORGETOWN COLLEGE
Education—General — M
Reading Education — M
Special Education — M

GEORGETOWN UNIVERSITY
Advertising and Public Relations — M
Business Administration and
　Management—General — M
Educational Measurement and
　Evaluation — M
Environmental Law — M,D
Finance and Banking — M,D
Health Law — M,D
Hospitality Management — M,D
Human Resources Management — M,D
Industrial and Manufacturing
　Management — D
International Business — M,D
Law — M,D
Real Estate — M,D
Sports Management — M,D
Taxation — M,D

THE GEORGE WASHINGTON UNIVERSITY
Accounting — M
Adult Education — O
Art Education — M
Business Administration and
　Management—General — M,D,O
Business Analytics — M,O
Counselor Education — M,D,O
Curriculum and Instruction — M,D,O
Distance Education Development — O
Early Childhood Education — M
Education—General — M,D,O
Educational Leadership and
　Administration — M,D,O
Educational Media/Instructional
　Technology — M,D,O
Educational Policy — M,D,O
Elementary Education — M
Exercise and Sports Science — M
Finance and Banking — M
Foreign Languages Education — M
Higher Education — M,D,O
Hospitality Management — M,O
Human Resources Development — M,D,O
Human Resources Management — M,O
International and Comparative
　Education — M,D,O

International Business M,D
Investment Management M,D
Law M,D
Legal and Justice Studies M,D,O
Management Information Systems M,D
Management Strategy and Policy M,D,O
Marketing M,D
Mathematics Education M
Multilingual and Multicultural Education M,D,O
Museum Education M
Nonprofit Management M,O
Organizational Management M,O
Project Management M,D,O
Real Estate O
Science Education M
Secondary Education M
Special Education M,D,O
Sports Management M,O
Student Affairs M,D,O
Travel and Tourism M,O
Vocational and Technical Education O

GEORGIA COLLEGE & STATE UNIVERSITY
Accounting M
Business Administration and Management—General M
Curriculum and Instruction M
Early Childhood Education M
Education—General M,O
Educational Leadership and Administration M,O
Educational Media/Instructional Technology M
Exercise and Sports Science M
Health Education M
Kinesiology and Movement Studies M
Logistics M
Management Information Systems M
Middle School Education M
Music Education M
Physical Education M
Secondary Education M
Special Education M,O

GEORGIA INSTITUTE OF TECHNOLOGY
Business Administration and Management—General M,D
International Business M
Logistics M
Management Information Systems M

GEORGIAN COURT UNIVERSITY
Business Administration and Management—General M,O
Counselor Education M,O
Education—General M,O
Educational Leadership and Administration M,O
Educational Media/Instructional Technology M,O
Legal and Justice Studies M,O
Nonprofit Management M,O
Special Education M,O

GEORGIA SOUTHERN UNIVERSITY
Accounting M
Athletic Training and Sports Medicine M,O
Business Administration and Management—General M,O
Counselor Education M
Curriculum and Instruction M,D
Education—General M,D,O
Educational Leadership and Administration M,D,O
Educational Measurement and Evaluation M,D,O
Educational Media/Instructional Technology M,O
Elementary Education M,O
Foreign Languages Education M
Health Education M,D
Higher Education M,D
Kinesiology and Movement Studies M
Logistics D
Management Information Systems M,O
Middle School Education M,O
Multilingual and Multicultural Education D
Music Education M
Nonprofit Management M,O
Reading Education M,O
Secondary Education M,O
Special Education M,O
Sports Management M
Supply Chain Management D

GEORGIA SOUTHWESTERN STATE UNIVERSITY
Business Administration and Management—General M
Early Childhood Education M,O
Education—General M,O
English Education M,O
Management Information Systems M,O
Mathematics Education M,O
Middle School Education M,O
Special Education M,O

GEORGIA STATE UNIVERSITY
Accounting M
Actuarial Science M
Art Education M
Athletic Training and Sports Medicine M
Business Administration and Management—General M,D
Counselor Education M,O
Curriculum and Instruction M,D
Early Childhood Education M,D,O
Education of Students with Severe/Multiple Disabilities M,D
Education—General M,D,O
Educational Leadership and Administration M,D,O
Educational Measurement and Evaluation M,D
Educational Media/Instructional Technology M,D
Educational Policy M,D,O
Educational Psychology M,D
Elementary Education M,D,O
English Education M,D
Entrepreneurship M,D
Exercise and Sports Science M
Finance and Banking M,D,O
Foreign Languages Education M,O
Foundations and Philosophy of Education M,D
Health Education M
Human Resources Management M,D
Human Services M,O
Insurance M,D,O
International Business M
Kinesiology and Movement Studies D
Law D
Management Information Systems M,D,O
Management Strategy and Policy M,D
Marketing M,D
Mathematics Education M,D,O
Middle School Education M,D
Music Education M,D
Nonprofit Management M,D,O
Organizational Management M,D
Physical Education M
Reading Education M,D
Real Estate M,D,O
Risk Management M,D,O
Science Education M,D
Secondary Education M,D
Social Sciences Education M,D
Social Work M,O
Special Education D
Sports Management M
Taxation M
Urban Education M,D,O

GLION INSTITUTE OF HIGHER EDUCATION
Hospitality Management M

GLOBAL UNIVERSITY
Religious Education M,D

GODDARD COLLEGE
Business Administration and Management—General M
Education—General M
Sustainability Management M

GOLDEN GATE UNIVERSITY
Accounting M,D,O
Business Administration and Management—General M,D,O
Business Analytics M,D,O
Entrepreneurship M,D,O
Environmental Law M,D
Finance and Banking M,D,O
Human Resources Management M,D,O
Intellectual Property Law M,D
International Business M,D,O
Law M,D
Legal and Justice Studies M,D
Management Information Systems M,D,O
Marketing M,D,O
Project Management M,D,O
Supply Chain Management M,D,O
Taxation M,D,O

GOLDEY-BEACOM COLLEGE
Business Administration and Management—General M
Finance and Banking M
Human Resources Management M
International Business M
Management Information Systems M
Marketing M
Taxation M

GONZAGA UNIVERSITY
Accounting M
Business Administration and Management—General M
Education—General M,D
Educational Leadership and Administration M,D
Elementary Education M,D
English as a Second Language M
Law D
Organizational Management M,D
Secondary Education M,D
Special Education M,D
Sports Management M,D
Taxation M

GORDON COLLEGE
Early Childhood Education M,O
Education—General M,O
Educational Leadership and Administration M,O
Elementary Education M,O
English as a Second Language M,O
Finance and Banking M
Mathematics Education M,O
Middle School Education M,O
Music Education M
Reading Education M,O
Secondary Education M,O
Special Education M,O

GOSHEN COLLEGE
Environmental Education M

GOUCHER COLLEGE
Education—General M,O
Educational Leadership and Administration M,O
Educational Media/Instructional Technology M,O
Elementary Education M,O
Middle School Education M,O
Physical Education M,O
Reading Education M,O
Secondary Education M,O
Special Education M,O

GOVERNORS STATE UNIVERSITY
Accounting M
Actuarial Science M
Business Administration and Management—General M
Early Childhood Education M
Education—General M
Educational Leadership and Administration M,D
Human Services M,D
Legal and Justice Studies M
Management Information Systems M
Reading Education M
Social Work M
Special Education M

GRACELAND UNIVERSITY (IA)
Curriculum and Instruction M
Education—General M
Educational Leadership and Administration M
Educational Media/Instructional Technology M
Organizational Management M,D,O
Reading Education M
Special Education M

THE GRADUATE CENTER, CITY UNIVERSITY OF NEW YORK
Accounting D
Business Administration and Management—General D
Educational Psychology D
Finance and Banking D
Management Information Systems D
Organizational Behavior D
Quantitative Analysis M
Social Work D
Urban Education D

GRAMBLING STATE UNIVERSITY
Counselor Education M,D,O
Curriculum and Instruction M,D,O
Developmental Education M,D,O
Education—General M,D,O
Educational Leadership and Administration M,D,O
Educational Media/Instructional Technology M,D,O
Higher Education M,D,O
Human Resources Management M
Mathematics Education M,D,O
Reading Education M,D,O
Science Education M,D,O
Social Sciences Education M
Social Work M
Special Education M
Sports Management M
Student Affairs M,D,O

GRAND CANYON UNIVERSITY
Accounting M
Business Administration and Management—General M,D
Business Analytics M
Curriculum and Instruction M,D,O
Early Childhood Education M,D,O
Education of the Gifted M,D,O
Education—General M,D,O
Educational Leadership and Administration M,D,O
Educational Media/Instructional Technology M,D,O
Elementary Education M,D,O
English as a Second Language M,D,O
Entrepreneurship M
Finance and Banking M
Human Resources Management M
Marketing M,D
Organizational Management M,D
Project Management M
Reading Education M,D,O
Science Education M,D,O
Secondary Education M,D,O
Special Education M,D,O
Sports Management M

GRAND VALLEY STATE UNIVERSITY
Accounting M
Adult Education M
Business Administration and Management—General M
Curriculum and Instruction M
Early Childhood Education M
Education—General M
Educational Leadership and Administration M,O
Educational Media/Instructional Technology M
Elementary Education M
English as a Second Language M
English Education M
Higher Education M
Management Information Systems M
Middle School Education M
Nonprofit Management M
Reading Education M
Secondary Education M
Social Work M
Special Education M
Taxation M

GRAND VIEW UNIVERSITY
Athletic Training and Sports Medicine M,O
Educational Leadership and Administration M,O
Organizational Management M,O
Sports Management M,O
Urban Education M,O

GRANITE STATE COLLEGE
Business Administration and Management—General M
Educational Leadership and Administration M
Organizational Management M
Project Management M

GRANTHAM UNIVERSITY
Business Administration and Management—General M,O
Human Resources Development M,O
Human Resources Management M,O
Management Information Systems M,O
Management Strategy and Policy M,O
Project Management M,O

GRATZ COLLEGE
Education—General M
Educational Leadership and Administration M,D
Nonprofit Management M
Religious Education M,D
Social Work M,O

GREENSBORO COLLEGE
Education—General M
Elementary Education M
English as a Second Language M
Special Education M

GREENVILLE UNIVERSITY
Education—General M
Elementary Education M
Secondary Education M

GWYNEDD MERCY UNIVERSITY
Business Administration and Management—General M
Counselor Education M,D
Education—General M,D
Educational Leadership and Administration M,D
Management Strategy and Policy M
Special Education M,D

HALLMARK UNIVERSITY
Business Administration and Management—General M
International Business M

HAMLINE UNIVERSITY
Business Administration and Management—General M,D
Education—General M,D
English as a Second Language M,D
Environmental Education M,D
Nonprofit Management M,D
Reading Education M,D
Science Education M,D

HAMPTON UNIVERSITY
Business Administration and Management—General M,D
Counselor Education M,D,O
Education—General M,D,O
Educational Leadership and Administration M,D
English Education M
Mathematics Education M
Middle School Education M
Organizational Behavior M
Sports Management M
Student Affairs M,D,O

HANNIBAL-LAGRANGE UNIVERSITY
Education—General M
Reading Education M

HARDING UNIVERSITY
Art Education M,O
Business Administration and Management—General M
Counselor Education M,O
Early Childhood Education M,O
Education—General M,O
Educational Leadership and Administration M,O
Elementary Education M,O
English as a Second Language M,O
English Education M,O
Foreign Languages Education M,O
Health Education M,O
International Business M
Mathematics Education M,O
Organizational Management M
Reading Education M,O
Secondary Education M,O
Social Sciences Education M,O
Special Education M,O

HARDIN-SIMMONS UNIVERSITY
Business Administration and Management—General M
Counselor Education M
Education of the Gifted M
Education—General M,D
Educational Leadership and Administration D
Higher Education D
Kinesiology and Movement Studies M
Music Education M
Reading Education M
Recreation and Park Management M
Sports Management M

HARRISBURG UNIVERSITY OF SCIENCE AND TECHNOLOGY
Educational Media/Instructional Technology M
Entrepreneurship M
Management Information Systems M
Management Strategy and Policy M
Project Management M

HARRISON MIDDLETON UNIVERSITY
Education—General M,D
Legal and Justice Studies M,D

Science Education	M,D

HARVARD UNIVERSITY

Accounting	D
Art Education	M
Business Administration and Management—General	M,D,O
Curriculum and Instruction	M
Education—General	M,D
Educational Leadership and Administration	M,D
Educational Media/Instructional Technology	M,O
Educational Policy	M
Educational Psychology	M
Foundations and Philosophy of Education	M,O
Industrial and Manufacturing Management	D
International and Comparative Education	M
Law	M,D
Legal and Justice Studies	D
Management Strategy and Policy	D
Marketing	D
Mathematics Education	M,O
Organizational Behavior	D
Quantitative Analysis	M,D
Reading Education	M

HASTINGS COLLEGE

Education—General	M

HAWAI'I PACIFIC UNIVERSITY

Business Administration and Management—General	M
Educational Leadership and Administration	M
Elementary Education	M
English as a Second Language	M
Finance and Banking	M
Human Resources Management	M
International Business	M
Management Information Systems	M
Marketing	M
Organizational Management	M
Secondary Education	M
Social Work	M

HEBREW COLLEGE

Early Childhood Education	M,O
Education—General	M,O
Middle School Education	M,O
Music Education	M,O
Religious Education	M,O
Special Education	M,O

HEBREW UNION COLLEGE–JEWISH INSTITUTE OF RELIGION (NY)

Education—General	M
Nonprofit Management	M
Religious Education	M

HEC MONTREAL

Accounting	M,D,O
Business Administration and Management—General	M,D,O
Business Analytics	M
Electronic Commerce	M,O
Entrepreneurship	M,O
Finance and Banking	M,D,O
Human Resources Development	O
Human Resources Management	M,D,O
Industrial and Manufacturing Management	M
International Business	M,D
Logistics	M
Management Information Systems	M,O
Management Strategy and Policy	M
Marketing	M,D
Organizational Management	M
Supply Chain Management	M,O
Taxation	M,O

HEIDELBERG UNIVERSITY

Business Administration and Management—General	M
Education—General	M
Music Education	M

HENDERSON STATE UNIVERSITY

Business Administration and Management—General	M
Counselor Education	M,O
Curriculum and Instruction	M,O
Early Childhood Education	M,O
Education—General	M,O
Educational Leadership and Administration	M,O
English as a Second Language	M,O
Middle School Education	M,O
Physical Education	M
Special Education	M,O
Sports Management	M

HENDRIX COLLEGE

Accounting	M

HERITAGE UNIVERSITY

Counselor Education	M
Education—General	M
Educational Leadership and Administration	M
English as a Second Language	M
Multilingual and Multicultural Education	M
Reading Education	M
Science Education	M
Special Education	M

HERZING UNIVERSITY ONLINE

Accounting	M
Business Administration and Management—General	M
Human Resources Management	M
Marketing	M
Project Management	M

HIGH POINT UNIVERSITY

Athletic Training and Sports Medicine	M,D
Business Administration and Management—General	M,D
Educational Leadership and Administration	M,D
Elementary Education	M,D
Mathematics Education	M,D
Secondary Education	M,D
Special Education	M,D

HIGH TECH HIGH GRADUATE SCHOOL OF EDUCATION

Educational Leadership and Administration	M

HODGES UNIVERSITY

Accounting	M
Business Administration and Management—General	M
Legal and Justice Studies	M
Management Information Systems	M

HOFSTRA UNIVERSITY

Accounting	M,O
Advertising and Public Relations	M
Art Education	M,D,O
Business Administration and Management—General	M,O
Business Education	M,D,O
Counselor Education	M,O
Early Childhood Education	M,D,O
Education of Students with Severe/Multiple Disabilities	M,D,O
Education of the Gifted	M,D,O
Education—General	M,D,O
Educational Leadership and Administration	M,D,O
Educational Media/Instructional Technology	M,D,O
Elementary Education	M,D,O
English as a Second Language	M,D,O
English Education	M,D,O
Entertainment Management	M,O
Exercise and Sports Science	M,O
Finance and Banking	M,O
Foreign Languages Education	M,D,O
Health Education	M,D,O
Health Law	M,D,O
Higher Education	M,D,O
Human Resources Management	M,O
Intellectual Property Law	M,D,O
International Business	M,O
Investment Management	M,O
Law	M,D,O
Legal and Justice Studies	M,D,O
Management Information Systems	M,O
Management Strategy and Policy	M,O
Marketing Research	M,O
Marketing	M,O
Mathematics Education	M,D,O
Middle School Education	M,D,O
Multilingual and Multicultural Education	M,D,O
Music Education	M,D,O
Physical Education	M,D,O
Quality Management	M,O
Quantitative Analysis	M,O
Reading Education	M,D,O
Science Education	M,D,O
Secondary Education	M,D,O
Social Sciences Education	M,D,O
Special Education	M,D,O
Sports Management	M,O
Taxation	M,O

HOLLINS UNIVERSITY

Education—General	M

HOLY FAMILY UNIVERSITY

Accounting	M
Business Administration and Management—General	M
Early Childhood Education	M
Education—General	M,D
Educational Leadership and Administration	M,D
Elementary Education	M
English as a Second Language	M
Finance and Banking	M
Human Resources Management	M
Management Information Systems	M
Reading Education	M
Special Education	M

HOLY NAMES UNIVERSITY

Business Administration and Management—General	M
Education—General	M,O
Educational Psychology	M,O
Finance and Banking	M
Marketing	M
Music Education	M,O
Special Education	M,O
Urban Education	M,O

HOOD COLLEGE

Accounting	M,O
Business Administration and Management—General	M,O
Curriculum and Instruction	M,O
Education—General	M,O
Educational Leadership and Administration	M,O
Elementary Education	M,O
Management Information Systems	M,O
Mathematics Education	M,O
Middle School Education	M,O
Organizational Management	M,D,O
Reading Education	M,O
Science Education	M,O
Secondary Education	M,O
Special Education	M,O

HOPE INTERNATIONAL UNIVERSITY

Education—General	M
Educational Leadership and Administration	M
Elementary Education	M
International Business	M
Marketing	M
Nonprofit Management	M
Secondary Education	M

HOUSTON BAPTIST UNIVERSITY

Business Administration and Management—General	M,D
Counselor Education	M,D
Curriculum and Instruction	M,D
Education—General	M,D
Educational Leadership and Administration	M,D
Educational Measurement and Evaluation	M,D
Educational Media/Instructional Technology	M,D
Elementary Education	M
English as a Second Language	M,D
English Education	M
Higher Education	M,D
Human Resources Management	M
International Business	M
Kinesiology and Movement Studies	M
Middle School Education	M
Multilingual and Multicultural Education	M,D
Reading Education	M,D
Religious Education	M,D
Science Education	M,D
Special Education	M,D
Sports Management	M

HOWARD PAYNE UNIVERSITY

Business Administration and Management—General	M
Educational Leadership and Administration	M
Sports Management	M

HOWARD UNIVERSITY

Accounting	M
Business Administration and Management—General	M
Counselor Education	M
Education—General	M,D,O
Educational Leadership and Administration	M,D,O
Educational Policy	M,D,O
Educational Psychology	D
Elementary Education	M
Exercise and Sports Science	M
Finance and Banking	M
Health Education	M
Human Resources Management	M
International Business	M
Law	M,D
Leisure Studies	M
Management Information Systems	M
Marketing	M
Multilingual and Multicultural Education	M,D
Music Education	M
Physical Education	M
Secondary Education	M
Social Work	M,D
Special Education	M
Sports Management	M
Supply Chain Management	M

HULT INTERNATIONAL BUSINESS SCHOOL (UNITED STATES)

Business Administration and Management—General	M
Business Analytics	M
Entrepreneurship	M
Finance and Banking	M
International Business	M
Marketing	M
Project Management	M

HUMBOLDT STATE UNIVERSITY

Business Administration and Management—General	M
Education—General	M
English as a Second Language	M
Kinesiology and Movement Studies	M
Social Work	M

HUMPHREYS UNIVERSITY

Law	D

HUNTER COLLEGE OF THE CITY UNIVERSITY OF NEW YORK

Accounting	M
Counselor Education	M
Early Childhood Education	M,D,O
Education of Students with Severe/Multiple Disabilities	M
Education—General	M,D,O
Educational Leadership and Administration	D,O
English as a Second Language	M
English Education	M
Foreign Languages Education	M
Mathematics Education	M
Multilingual and Multicultural Education	M
Music Education	M
Science Education	M
Secondary Education	M
Social Sciences Education	M
Social Work	M
Special Education	M

HUNTINGTON UNIVERSITY

Business Administration and Management—General	M,D
Elementary Education	M,D
English as a Second Language	M,D
Middle School Education	M,D
Organizational Management	M,D

HUSSON UNIVERSITY

Business Administration and Management—General	M
Counselor Education	M
Educational Leadership and Administration	M,O
Hospitality Management	M
Organizational Management	M
Risk Management	M
Sports Management	M

HUSTON-TILLOTSON UNIVERSITY

Educational Leadership and Administration	M

IDAHO STATE UNIVERSITY

Athletic Training and Sports Medicine	M
Business Administration and Management—General	M,O
Counselor Education	M,D,O
Education—General	M,D,O
Educational Leadership and Administration	M,D,O
Educational Media/Instructional Technology	M,D
Elementary Education	M
English as a Second Language	M,D,O
Health Education	M
Human Resources Management	M,D
Management Information Systems	M,O
Mathematics Education	M,D
Music Education	M
Physical Education	M
Reading Education	M
Secondary Education	M
Special Education	M
Sports Management	M

IGLOBAL UNIVERSITY

Accounting	M
Business Administration and Management—General	M
Entrepreneurship	M
Finance and Banking	M
Hospitality Management	M
Human Resources Management	M
International Business	M
Management Information Systems	M
Project Management	M
Travel and Tourism	M

ILLINOIS COLLEGE

Education—General	M

ILLINOIS INSTITUTE OF TECHNOLOGY

Business Administration and Management—General	M,D
Computer Education	M,D
Entrepreneurship	M
Finance and Banking	M,D
Human Resources Development	M,D
Industrial and Manufacturing Management	M
Law	M,D
Legal and Justice Studies	M,D
Management Information Systems	M,D
Marketing	M
Mathematics Education	M,D
Science Education	M,D
Sustainability Management	M
Taxation	M,D

ILLINOIS STATE UNIVERSITY

Accounting	M
Business Administration and Management—General	M
Curriculum and Instruction	M,D
Educational Leadership and Administration	M,D
Educational Policy	M,D
Health Education	M
Higher Education	M,D
Management Information Systems	M
Mathematics Education	M,D
Physical Education	M
Reading Education	M
Social Work	M
Special Education	M,D,O
Student Affairs	M

IMMACULATA UNIVERSITY

Educational Leadership and Administration	M,D,O
Educational Psychology	M,D,O
English as a Second Language	M
Multilingual and Multicultural Education	M
Organizational Management	M
Secondary Education	M,D,O
Special Education	M,D,O

INDEPENDENCE UNIVERSITY

Business Administration and Management—General	M

INDIANA STATE UNIVERSITY

Athletic Training and Sports Medicine	M,D
Business Administration and Management—General	M
Counselor Education	M,D,O
Curriculum and Instruction	M,D
Education—General	M,D,O

*M—masters degree; D—doctorate; O—other advanced degree; *—Close-Up and/or Display*

Educational Leadership and
 Administration — M,D,O
Educational Media/Instructional
 Technology — M,D
English as a Second Language — M,D,O
Foreign Languages Education — M,D,O
Health Education — M,D
Higher Education — M,D,O
Human Resources Development — M
Multilingual and Multicultural
 Education — M,D,O
Music Education — M
Physical Education — M,D
Recreation and Park Management — M,D
Science Education — M,D
Social Work — M
Sports Management — M,D
Student Affairs — M,D,O
Vocational and Technical Education — M

INDIANA TECH
Accounting — M
Business Administration and
 Management—General — M
Human Resources Development — M
Human Resources Management — M
International Business — D
Marketing — M
Organizational Management — M

INDIANA UNIVERSITY BLOOMINGTON
Art Education — M,D,O
Athletic Training and Sports
 Medicine — M,D
Business Administration and
 Management—General — M,D
Counselor Education — M,D,O
Curriculum and Instruction — M,D,O
Education—General — M,D,O
Educational Leadership and
 Administration — M,D,O
Educational Measurement and
 Evaluation — M,D
Educational Media/Instructional
 Technology — M,D
Educational Policy — M,D,O
Educational Psychology — M,D,O
Elementary Education — M,D,O
English as a Second Language — M,D
Exercise and Sports Science — M,D
Finance and Banking — M,D,O
Foreign Languages Education — M,D
Foundations and Philosophy of
 Education — M,D,O
Health Education — M,D
Higher Education — M,D,O
International and Comparative
 Education — M,D,O
Kinesiology and Movement Studies — M,D
Law — M,D
Leisure Studies — M,D
Library Science — M,D,O
Management Information Systems — M,D,O
Mathematics Education — M,D,O
Multilingual and Multicultural
 Education — M,D
Nonprofit Management — M,D,O
Organizational Management — M,D,O
Physical Education — M,D,O
Reading Education — M,D,O
Recreation and Park Management — M,D
Science Education — M,D,O
Secondary Education — M,D,O
Social Sciences Education — M,D,O
Special Education — M,D,O
Sports Management — M,D
Student Affairs — M,D
Sustainability Management — M,D,O
Travel and Tourism — M,D

INDIANA UNIVERSITY EAST
Education—General — M
Social Work — M

INDIANA UNIVERSITY KOKOMO
Accounting — M,O
Business Administration and
 Management—General — M,O

INDIANA UNIVERSITY NORTHWEST
Accounting — M,O
Business Administration and
 Management—General — M,O
Education—General — M,O
Educational Leadership and
 Administration — M,O
Elementary Education — M,O
Management Information Systems — M,O
Nonprofit Management — M,O
Secondary Education — M,O
Social Work — M

INDIANA UNIVERSITY OF PENNSYLVANIA
Adult Education — M
Business Administration and
 Management—General — M
Business Education — M
Counselor Education — M
Curriculum and Instruction — D
Education—General — M,D,O
Educational Leadership and
 Administration — D,O
Educational Media/Instructional
 Technology — M,D
Educational Psychology — M,O
English as a Second Language — M,D
English Education — D
Exercise and Sports Science — M
Health Education — M
Higher Education — M
Human Resources Development — M
Mathematics Education — M
Music Education — M
Nonprofit Management — D
Physical Education — M

Reading Education — M,O
Special Education — M,O
Sports Management — M
Student Affairs — M
Vocational and Technical Education — M

INDIANA UNIVERSITY–PURDUE UNIVERSITY INDIANAPOLIS
Accounting — M
Business Administration and
 Management—General — M
Counselor Education — M,O
Curriculum and Instruction — M,O
Early Childhood Education — M,O
Education—General — M,O
Educational Leadership and
 Administration — M,O
English as a Second Language — M,O
Entrepreneurship — M
Finance and Banking — M
Foreign Languages Education — M,O
Health Education — M,D
Health Law — M
Intellectual Property Law — M,D,O
Kinesiology and Movement Studies — M
Law — M,D,O
Library Science — M,O
Marketing — M
Mathematics Education — M,D
Nonprofit Management — M,O
Organizational Management — M,O
Physical Education — M,O
Reading Education — M,O
Social Work — M,D,O
Special Education — M,O
Supply Chain Management — M

INDIANA UNIVERSITY SOUTH BEND
Accounting — M,O
Business Administration and
 Management—General — M,O
Counselor Education — M,O
Education—General — M,O
Educational Leadership and
 Administration — M,O
Educational Media/Instructional
 Technology — M,O
Elementary Education — M,O
Finance and Banking — M,O
Human Resources Management — M,O
Legal and Justice Studies — M,O
Marketing — M,O
Nonprofit Management — M,O
Secondary Education — M,O
Social Work — M,O
Special Education — M,O

INDIANA UNIVERSITY SOUTHEAST
Business Administration and
 Management—General — M
Counselor Education — M
Education—General — M
Elementary Education — M
Finance and Banking — M
Secondary Education — M

INDIANA WESLEYAN UNIVERSITY
Accounting — M,O
Athletic Training and Sports
 Medicine — M,D
Business Administration and
 Management—General — M,O
Counselor Education — M
Educational Leadership and
 Administration — M,O
Higher Education — M,O
Human Resources Management — M,O
Organizational Management — M,D,O

INSTITUTE FOR CHRISTIAN STUDIES
Education—General — M,D

INSTITUTE FOR CLINICAL SOCIAL WORK
Social Work — D

INSTITUTO CENTROAMERICANO DE ADMINISTRACIÓN DE EMPRESAS
Business Administration and
 Management—General — M
Finance and Banking — M
Real Estate — M

INSTITUTO TECNOLOGICO DE SANTO DOMINGO
Accounting — M,O
Adult Education — M,O
Business Administration and
 Management—General — M,O
Education—General — M,O
Educational Leadership and
 Administration — M,O
Educational Psychology — M,O
Environmental Education — M,D,O
Finance and Banking — M,O
Human Resources Management — M,O
Industrial and Manufacturing
 Management — M,O
International Business — M,O
Marketing — M,O
Organizational Management — M,O
Quality Management — M,O
Quantitative Analysis — M,O
Secondary Education — M,O
Social Sciences Education — M,O
Taxation — M,O
Transportation Management — M,O

INSTITUTO TECNOLÓGICO Y DE ESTUDIOS SUPERIORES DE MONTERREY, CAMPUS CENTRAL DE VERACRUZ
Business Administration and
 Management—General — M
Education—General — M
Educational Leadership and
 Administration — M

Educational Media/Instructional
 Technology — M
Electronic Commerce — M
Finance and Banking — M
International Business — M
Management Information Systems — M
Marketing — M

INSTITUTO TECNOLÓGICO Y DE ESTUDIOS SUPERIORES DE MONTERREY, CAMPUS CHIHUAHUA
International Business — M,O

INSTITUTO TECNOLÓGICO Y DE ESTUDIOS SUPERIORES DE MONTERREY, CAMPUS CIUDAD DE MÉXICO
Business Administration and
 Management—General — M,D
Education—General — M,D
Educational Media/Instructional
 Technology — M,D
Finance and Banking — M,D
International Business — M,D
Law — O
Management Information Systems — M,D
Quality Management — M

INSTITUTO TECNOLÓGICO Y DE ESTUDIOS SUPERIORES DE MONTERREY, CAMPUS CIUDAD JUÁREZ
Business Administration and
 Management—General — M
Education—General — M
Educational Leadership and
 Administration — M
Educational Media/Instructional
 Technology — M,D
Electronic Commerce — M
Management Information Systems — M
Quality Management — M

INSTITUTO TECNOLÓGICO Y DE ESTUDIOS SUPERIORES DE MONTERREY, CAMPUS CIUDAD OBREGÓN
Business Administration and
 Management—General — M
Developmental Education — M
Education—General — M
Finance and Banking — M
Management Information Systems — M
Marketing — M
Mathematics Education — M

INSTITUTO TECNOLÓGICO Y DE ESTUDIOS SUPERIORES DE MONTERREY, CAMPUS CUERNAVACA
Business Administration and
 Management—General — M
Finance and Banking — M
Human Resources Management — M
International Business — M
Marketing — M

INSTITUTO TECNOLÓGICO Y DE ESTUDIOS SUPERIORES DE MONTERREY, CAMPUS ESTADO DE MÉXICO
Business Administration and
 Management—General — M,D
Education—General — M,D
Educational Leadership and
 Administration — M,D
Educational Media/Instructional
 Technology — M,D
Electronic Commerce — M,D
Finance and Banking — M,D
Industrial and Manufacturing
 Management — M,D
Management Information Systems — M,D
Marketing — M,D
Quality Management — M,D

INSTITUTO TECNOLÓGICO Y DE ESTUDIOS SUPERIORES DE MONTERREY, CAMPUS GUADALAJARA
Business Administration and
 Management—General — M
Finance and Banking — M

INSTITUTO TECNOLÓGICO Y DE ESTUDIOS SUPERIORES DE MONTERREY, CAMPUS IRAPUATO
Business Administration and
 Management—General — M,D
Education—General — M,D
Educational Leadership and
 Administration — M,D
Educational Media/Instructional
 Technology — M,D
Electronic Commerce — M,D
Finance and Banking — M,D
Industrial and Manufacturing
 Management — M,D
International Business — M,D
Library Science — M,D
Management Information Systems — M,D
Marketing Research — M,D
Quality Management — M,D

INSTITUTO TECNOLÓGICO Y DE ESTUDIOS SUPERIORES DE MONTERREY, CAMPUS LAGUNA
Business Administration and
 Management—General — M
Management Information Systems — M

INSTITUTO TECNOLÓGICO Y DE ESTUDIOS SUPERIORES DE MONTERREY, CAMPUS LEÓN
Business Administration and
 Management—General — M

INSTITUTO TECNOLÓGICO Y DE ESTUDIOS SUPERIORES DE MONTERREY, CAMPUS MONTERREY
Business Administration and
 Management—General — M,D
Finance and Banking — M
International Business — M
Marketing — M
Science Education — M,D

INSTITUTO TECNOLÓGICO Y DE ESTUDIOS SUPERIORES DE MONTERREY, CAMPUS QUERÉTARO
Business Administration and
 Management—General — M

INSTITUTO TECNOLÓGICO Y DE ESTUDIOS SUPERIORES DE MONTERREY, CAMPUS SONORA NORTE
Business Administration and
 Management—General — M
Education—General — M

INSTITUTO TECNOLÓGICO Y DE ESTUDIOS SUPERIORES DE MONTERREY, CAMPUS TOLUCA
Business Administration and
 Management—General — M

INTER AMERICAN UNIVERSITY OF PUERTO RICO, AGUADILLA CAMPUS
Accounting — M
Business Administration and
 Management—General — M
Educational Leadership and
 Administration — M
Elementary Education — M
Finance and Banking — M
Human Resources Management — M
Management Information Systems — M
Marketing — M

INTER AMERICAN UNIVERSITY OF PUERTO RICO, ARECIBO CAMPUS
Accounting — M
Business Administration and
 Management—General — M
Counselor Education — M
Curriculum and Instruction — M
Education—General — M
Educational Leadership and
 Administration — M
Elementary Education — M
English as a Second Language — M
Finance and Banking — M
Foreign Languages Education — M
Human Resources Management — M
Mathematics Education — M
Science Education — M
Social Sciences Education — M

INTER AMERICAN UNIVERSITY OF PUERTO RICO, BARRANQUITAS CAMPUS
Accounting — M
Business Administration and
 Management—General — M
Curriculum and Instruction — M
Education—General — M
Educational Leadership and
 Administration — M
Elementary Education — M
English as a Second Language — M
Foreign Languages Education — M
Human Resources Management — M
Library Science — M
Special Education — M

INTER AMERICAN UNIVERSITY OF PUERTO RICO, BAYAMÓN CAMPUS
Human Resources Management — M

INTER AMERICAN UNIVERSITY OF PUERTO RICO, FAJARDO CAMPUS
Business Administration and
 Management—General — M
Educational Leadership and
 Administration — M
Human Resources Management — M
Management Information Systems — M
Marketing — M
Special Education — M

INTER AMERICAN UNIVERSITY OF PUERTO RICO, GUAYAMA CAMPUS
Business Administration and
 Management—General — M
Early Childhood Education — M
Elementary Education — M
Marketing — M

INTER AMERICAN UNIVERSITY OF PUERTO RICO, METROPOLITAN CAMPUS
Accounting — M
Athletic Training and Sports
 Medicine — M
Business Administration and
 Management—General — M
Business Education — M
Counselor Education — M,D
Curriculum and Instruction — M,D
Education—General — M,D
Educational Leadership and
 Administration — M,D
Educational Media/Instructional
 Technology — M
Elementary Education — M
English as a Second Language — M
Exercise and Sports Science — M
Finance and Banking — M
Foreign Languages Education — M
Health Education — M
Higher Education — M
Human Resources Development — M

Human Resources Management M
Industrial and Manufacturing
   Management M
International Business M,D
Management Information Systems M
Marketing M
Mathematics Education M
Music Education M
Physical Education M
Religious Education D
Science Education M
Social Sciences Education M
Social Work M
Special Education M
Vocational and Technical Education M

INTER AMERICAN UNIVERSITY OF PUERTO RICO, PONCE CAMPUS
Accounting M
Elementary Education M
English as a Second Language M
Finance and Banking M
Human Resources Management M
Marketing M
Mathematics Education M
Science Education M
Social Sciences Education M

INTER AMERICAN UNIVERSITY OF PUERTO RICO, SAN GERMÁN CAMPUS
Accounting M,D
Business Administration and
   Management—General M,D
Business Education M
Counselor Education M,D
Curriculum and Instruction D
Elementary Education M
English as a Second Language M
Finance and Banking M,D
Health Education M
Human Resources Development M,D
Human Resources Management M,D
Industrial and Manufacturing
   Management M,D
International Business M
Kinesiology and Movement Studies M
Library Science M,D
Management Information Systems M,D
Marketing M,D
Mathematics Education M
Music Education M
Physical Education M
Science Education M
Special Education M

INTER AMERICAN UNIVERSITY OF PUERTO RICO SCHOOL OF LAW
Law D

INTERDENOMINATIONAL THEOLOGICAL CENTER
Religious Education M,D

INTERNATIONAL BAPTIST COLLEGE AND SEMINARY
Education—General M

INTERNATIONAL INSTITUTE FOR RESTORATIVE PRACTICES
Organizational Behavior M,O

INTERNATIONAL TECHNOLOGICAL UNIVERSITY
Business Administration and
   Management—General M,D

INTERNATIONAL UNIVERSITY IN GENEVA
Business Administration and
   Management—General M,D
Entrepreneurship M,D
International Business M,D
Marketing M,D

THE INTERNATIONAL UNIVERSITY OF MONACO
Business Administration and
   Management—General M
Entrepreneurship M
Finance and Banking M
International Business M
Marketing M

IONA COLLEGE
Accounting M,O
Advertising and Public Relations M,O
Business Administration and
   Management—General M,O
Early Childhood Education M
Education—General M
Educational Leadership and
   Administration M
English Education M
Finance and Banking M,O
Foreign Languages Education M
Human Resources Management M,O
International Business M,O
Management Information Systems M,O
Marketing M,O
Mathematics Education M
Project Management M,O
Recreation and Park Management M,O
Risk Management M,O
Science Education M
Social Sciences Education M
Special Education M
Sports Management M,O

IOWA STATE UNIVERSITY OF SCIENCE AND TECHNOLOGY
Accounting M
Agricultural Education M,D
Business Administration and
   Management—General M

Business Analytics M
Counselor Education M,D
Curriculum and Instruction M,D
Education—General M,D
Educational Leadership and
   Administration M,D
Educational Measurement and
   Evaluation M,D
Educational Media/Instructional
   Technology M,D
Elementary Education M,D
English as a Second Language M
Exercise and Sports Science M
Finance and Banking M
Foundations and Philosophy of
   Education M,D
Higher Education M,D
Human Resources Development M,D
Kinesiology and Movement Studies M,D
Management Information Systems M,D
Mathematics Education M
Science Education M
Special Education M,D
Student Affairs M,D
Transportation Management M
Vocational and Technical Education M,D

IOWA WESLEYAN UNIVERSITY
Curriculum and Instruction M

ITHACA COLLEGE
Accounting M
Agricultural Education M
Business Administration and
   Management—General M
Elementary Education M
English Education M
Exercise and Sports Science M
Health Education M
Music Education M
Physical Education M
Secondary Education M
Sports Management M

JACKSON STATE UNIVERSITY
Accounting M
Business Administration and
   Management—General M,D
Counselor Education M
Early Childhood Education M,D,O
Education—General M,D,O
Educational Leadership and
   Administration M,D
Elementary Education M,D,O
English Education M
Health Education M
Higher Education M,D,O
Mathematics Education M
Music Education M
Physical Education M
Reading Education M,D,O
Science Education M,D
Social Work M,D
Special Education M
Sports Management M
Vocational and Technical Education M,D

JACKSONVILLE STATE UNIVERSITY
Business Administration and
   Management—General M
Counselor Education M
Early Childhood Education M
Education—General M,O
Educational Leadership and
   Administration M,O
Educational Media/Instructional
   Technology M
Elementary Education M
Physical Education M,O
Reading Education M
Secondary Education M
Social Work M
Special Education M

JACKSONVILLE UNIVERSITY
Accounting M
Business Administration and
   Management—General M,D
Educational Leadership and
   Administration M
Finance and Banking M
Kinesiology and Movement Studies M
Marketing M
Organizational Management M
Sports Management M

JAMES MADISON UNIVERSITY
Accounting M
Art Education M
Business Administration and
   Management—General M
Early Childhood Education M
Education of the Gifted M
Educational Leadership and
   Administration M
Educational Measurement and
   Evaluation M,D
Educational Media/Instructional
   Technology M
Elementary Education M
English as a Second Language M
Entrepreneurship M
Exercise and Sports Science M
Foreign Languages Education M
Health Education M
Higher Education M
Human Resources Management M
Kinesiology and Movement Studies M
Management Information Systems M
Management Strategy and Policy D
Mathematics Education M
Middle School Education M

Multilingual and Multicultural
   Education M
Music Education M
Nonprofit Management M,D
Organizational Management D
Physical Education M
Reading Education M
Secondary Education M
Special Education M
Sustainability Management M
Taxation M
Vocational and Technical Education M

THE JEWISH THEOLOGICAL SEMINARY
Religious Education M,D

JOHN BROWN UNIVERSITY
Business Administration and
   Management—General M
Counselor Education M,O
Curriculum and Instruction M
Education—General M
International Business M
Secondary Education M

JOHN CARROLL UNIVERSITY
Accounting M
Business Administration and
   Management—General M
Counselor Education M,O
Education—General M
Educational Psychology M,O
Nonprofit Management M

JOHN F. KENNEDY UNIVERSITY
Business Administration and
   Management—General M
Finance and Banking M
Health Education M
Human Resources Management M
Law D
Management Strategy and Policy M

JOHN JAY COLLEGE OF CRIMINAL JUSTICE OF THE CITY UNIVERSITY OF NEW YORK
Legal and Justice Studies M,D
Organizational Behavior M,D

THE JOHN MARSHALL LAW SCHOOL
Law M,D

JOHNS HOPKINS UNIVERSITY
Business Administration and
   Management—General M,O
Business Analytics M
Education—General M,D,O
Finance and Banking M,D,O
Health Education M,D
Investment Management M,O
Management Information Systems M,O
Marketing M
Nonprofit Management M,O
Real Estate M
Risk Management M

JOHNSON & WALES UNIVERSITY
Accounting M
Business Administration and
   Management—General M
Business Education M
Education—General M
Educational Leadership and
   Administration D
Elementary Education M
Finance and Banking M
Hospitality Management M
Human Resources Management M
Management Information Systems M
Nonprofit Management M
Organizational Management M
Secondary Education M
Special Education M
Sports Management M
Supply Chain Management M
Travel and Tourism M

JOHNSON C. SMITH UNIVERSITY
Social Work M

JOHNSON UNIVERSITY
Counselor Education M,D,O
Education—General M,D,O
Educational Media/Instructional
   Technology M,D,O
Higher Education M,D,O
Nonprofit Management M,D,O

JOSE MARIA VARGAS UNIVERSITY
Early Childhood Education M

THE JUDGE ADVOCATE GENERAL'S SCHOOL, U.S. ARMY
Law M

JUDSON UNIVERSITY
Business Administration and
   Management—General M
Human Services M
Organizational Management M
Reading Education M,D

JUNIATA COLLEGE
Accounting M
Business Administration and
   Management—General M
Organizational Management M

KANSAS STATE UNIVERSITY
Accounting M
Adult Education M,D,O
Advertising and Public Relations M
Agricultural Education M
Business Administration and
   Management—General M,O
Counselor Education M,D,O

Curriculum and Instruction M,D,O
Distance Education Development M,D,O
Early Childhood Education M,D,O
Education—General M,D,O
Educational Leadership and
   Administration M,D,O
Educational Media/Instructional
   Technology M,D,O
Elementary Education M,D,O
English as a Second Language M,D,O
English Education M,D,O
Entrepreneurship M,O
Finance and Banking M,D,O
Health Education M,D
Hospitality Management M,D
Human Services M
Kinesiology and Movement Studies M,D
Marketing M,O
Middle School Education M,D,O
Reading Education M,D,O
Special Education M,D,O
Student Affairs M,D,O

KANSAS WESLEYAN UNIVERSITY
Business Administration and
   Management—General M
Sports Management M

KEAN UNIVERSITY
Accounting M
Art Education M
Business Administration and
   Management—General M
Counselor Education M
Curriculum and Instruction M
Early Childhood Education M
Education—General M
Educational Leadership and
   Administration M,D
English as a Second Language M
Exercise and Sports Science M
Foreign Languages Education M
International Business M
Management Information Systems M
Multilingual and Multicultural
   Education M
Nonprofit Management M
Social Work M
Special Education M

KEISER UNIVERSITY
Accounting M
Business Administration and
   Management—General M,D
Distance Education Development M
Education—General M
Educational Leadership and
   Administration M,D,O
Educational Media/Instructional
   Technology D,O
Health Education M
International Business M,D
Management Information Systems M
Marketing M,D
Organizational Management M

KENNESAW STATE UNIVERSITY
Accounting M
Art Education M
Business Administration and
   Management—General M,D
Curriculum and Instruction O
Early Childhood Education M
Education—General M,D,O
Educational Leadership and
   Administration M,D,O
Educational Media/Instructional
   Technology M,D,O
English as a Second Language M
English Education M
Exercise and Sports Science M
Mathematics Education M
Middle School Education D,O
Reading Education M
Science Education M
Secondary Education M,D,O
Social Work M
Special Education M,D,O
Sports Management M

KENT STATE UNIVERSITY
Accounting M,D
Advertising and Public Relations M
Art Education M
Athletic Training and Sports
   Medicine M,D
Business Administration and
   Management—General M
Business Analytics M
Computer Education M,D,O
Counselor Education M,D,O
Curriculum and Instruction M,D,O
Early Childhood Education M,D,O
Education of the Gifted M,D,O
Education—General M
Educational Leadership and
   Administration M,D,O
Educational Measurement and
   Evaluation M,D
Educational Media/Instructional
   Technology M,D,O
Educational Psychology M
English as a Second Language M,D
English Education M,D
Exercise and Sports Science M,D
Finance and Banking D
Foundations and Philosophy of
   Education M,D
Health Education M,D
Higher Education M,D,O
Hospitality Management M
Human Services M,D,O

Library Science — M
Management Information Systems — D
Marketing — D
Mathematics Education — M,D
Middle School Education — M,D,O
Music Education — M
Reading Education — M
Recreation and Park Management — M
Secondary Education — M,D
Social Sciences Education — M,D
Special Education — M,D,O
Sports Management — M
Student Affairs — M
Travel and Tourism — M
Vocational and Technical Education — M

KENT STATE UNIVERSITY AT STARK
Business Administration and Management—General — M
Curriculum and Instruction — M
Education—General — M

KETTERING UNIVERSITY
Business Administration and Management—General — M

KEUKA COLLEGE
Business Administration and Management—General — M
Early Childhood Education — M
Elementary Education — M
Secondary Education — M
Social Work — M

KEYSTONE COLLEGE
Business Administration and Management—General — M
Early Childhood Education — M
Educational Leadership and Administration — M

KING'S COLLEGE
Education—General — M

KING UNIVERSITY
Accounting — M
Business Administration and Management—General — M
Finance and Banking — M
Human Resources Management — M
Marketing — M
Project Management — M

KUTZTOWN UNIVERSITY OF PENNSYLVANIA
Art Education — M
Business Administration and Management—General — M
Counselor Education — M
Curriculum and Instruction — M,D
Education—General — M,D
Educational Leadership and Administration — M
Educational Media/Instructional Technology — M
Elementary Education — M
English Education — M,D
Library Science — M
Middle School Education — M,D
Music Education — M
Reading Education — M
Secondary Education — M,D
Social Sciences Education — M,D
Social Work — M,D

LAGRANGE COLLEGE
Curriculum and Instruction — M,O
Education—General — M,O
Middle School Education — M,O
Organizational Management — M
Secondary Education — M,O

LAKE ERIE COLLEGE
Business Administration and Management—General — M
Education—General — M
Management Information Systems — M

LAKE ERIE COLLEGE OF OSTEOPATHIC MEDICINE
Health Education — M,D,O

LAKE FOREST COLLEGE
Art Education — M
Education—General — M
Elementary Education — M
English Education — M
Mathematics Education — M
Music Education — M
Science Education — M
Secondary Education — M
Social Sciences Education — M

LAKE FOREST GRADUATE SCHOOL OF MANAGEMENT
Business Administration and Management—General — M
Finance and Banking — M
International Business — M
Marketing — M
Organizational Behavior — M

LAKEHEAD UNIVERSITY
Education—General — M,D
Exercise and Sports Science — M
Kinesiology and Movement Studies — M
Social Work — M

LAKELAND UNIVERSITY
Accounting — M
Business Administration and Management—General — M
Counselor Education — M
Education—General — M
Finance and Banking — M
Project Management — M

LAMAR UNIVERSITY
Accounting — M

Business Administration and Management—General — M
Counselor Education — M
Education—General — M,D,O
Educational Leadership and Administration — M,D
Educational Media/Instructional Technology — M,D
Foreign Languages Education — M
Kinesiology and Movement Studies — M
Special Education — M,D

LANCASTER BIBLE COLLEGE
Counselor Education — M,D
Elementary Education — M,D
Secondary Education — M,D
Special Education — M,D

LANCASTER THEOLOGICAL SEMINARY
Religious Education — M,D,O

LANDER UNIVERSITY
Early Childhood Education — M
Education—General — M

LANGSTON UNIVERSITY
Education—General — M
Elementary Education — M
English as a Second Language — M
Multilingual and Multicultural Education — M
Urban Education — M

LA ROCHE UNIVERSITY
Accounting — M
Human Resources Management — M,O

LA SALLE UNIVERSITY
Accounting — M,O
Advertising and Public Relations — M,O
Business Administration and Management—General — M
Business Analytics — M,O
Early Childhood Education — M,O
Education—General — M,O
Educational Leadership and Administration — M
Educational Media/Instructional Technology — M,O
English as a Second Language — M,O
Finance and Banking — M,O
Human Resources Development — M,O
Human Resources Management — M,O
International Business — M,O
Marketing — M,O
Middle School Education — M,O
Multilingual and Multicultural Education — M
Nonprofit Management — M
Reading Education — M,O
Secondary Education — M,O
Social Sciences Education — M,O
Special Education — M,O

LASELL COLLEGE
Advertising and Public Relations — M,O
Business Administration and Management—General — M,O
Curriculum and Instruction — M,O
Education—General — M,O
Educational Leadership and Administration — M,O
Elementary Education — M,O
English as a Second Language — M,O
Hospitality Management — M,O
Human Resources Management — M,O
Marketing — M,O
Project Management — M,O
Recreation and Park Management — M,O
Special Education — M,O
Sports Management — M,O
Travel and Tourism — M,O

LA SIERRA UNIVERSITY
Accounting — M,O
Advertising and Public Relations — M
Business Administration and Management—General — M,O
Counselor Education — M,O
Curriculum and Instruction — M,D,O
Education—General — M,D,O
Educational Leadership and Administration — M,O
Educational Psychology — M,O
Finance and Banking — M,O
Human Resources Management — M,O
Marketing — M,O
Religious Education — M

LAURENTIAN UNIVERSITY
Business Administration and Management—General — M
Science Education — O
Social Work — M

LAWRENCE TECHNOLOGICAL UNIVERSITY
Business Administration and Management—General — M,D,O
Educational Media/Instructional Technology — M,O
Finance and Banking — M,D,O
Human Resources Development — M,O
Industrial and Manufacturing Management — M,D
Management Strategy and Policy — M,D,O
Marketing — M,D,O
Nonprofit Management — M,D,O
Project Management — M,D,O
Science Education — M

LEBANESE AMERICAN UNIVERSITY
Business Administration and Management—General — M

LEBANON VALLEY COLLEGE
Athletic Training and Sports Medicine — M

Business Administration and Management—General — M
Human Resources Management — M
Mathematics Education — M
Music Education — M
Project Management — M
Science Education — M,O
Social Sciences Education — M,O

LEE UNIVERSITY
Business Administration and Management—General — M
Counselor Education — M
Curriculum and Instruction — M,O
Early Childhood Education — M,O
Education—General — M,O
Educational Leadership and Administration — M,O
Elementary Education — M,O
English as a Second Language — M,O
Higher Education — M,O
Mathematics Education — M,O
Middle School Education — M,O
Music Education — M
Secondary Education — M,O
Social Sciences Education — M,O
Special Education — M,O

LEHIGH UNIVERSITY
Accounting — M
Business Administration and Management—General — M
Counselor Education — M,D,O
Curriculum and Instruction — M,D,O
Early Childhood Education — M,D,O
Education—General — M,D,O
Educational Leadership and Administration — M,D,O
Educational Media/Instructional Technology — M,D
Elementary Education — M,D
Entrepreneurship — M
Environmental Law — M,O
Finance and Banking — M
Human Services — M,D,O
Project Management — M
Quantitative Analysis — M
Special Education — M,D

LEHMAN COLLEGE OF THE CITY UNIVERSITY OF NEW YORK
Accounting — M
Art Education — M
Business Administration and Management—General — M
Counselor Education — M
Early Childhood Education — M
Education—General — M
Elementary Education — M
English as a Second Language — M
English Education — M
Health Education — M
Mathematics Education — M
Middle School Education — M
Multilingual and Multicultural Education — M
Music Education — M
Reading Education — M
Recreation and Park Management — M
Science Education — M
Secondary Education — M
Social Sciences Education — M
Social Work — M
Special Education — M

LE MOYNE COLLEGE
Business Administration and Management—General — M
Early Childhood Education — M,O
Education—General — M,O
Educational Leadership and Administration — M,O
Elementary Education — M,O
English as a Second Language — M,O
English Education — M,O
Foreign Languages Education — M,O
Management Information Systems — M
Middle School Education — M,O
Reading Education — M,O
Secondary Education — M,O
Social Sciences Education — M,O
Special Education — M,O

LENOIR-RHYNE UNIVERSITY
Accounting — M
Athletic Training and Sports Medicine — M
Business Administration and Management—General — M
Business Analytics — M
Community College Education — M
Counselor Education — M
Distance Education Development — M
Education—General — M
Educational Leadership and Administration — M
Educational Media/Instructional Technology — M
Entrepreneurship — M
Human Services — M
International Business — M
Management Information Systems — M
Management Strategy and Policy — M
Organizational Management — M
Secondary Education — M

LESLEY UNIVERSITY
Adult Education — M,D,O
Art Education — M,D,O
Computer Education — M,D,O
Curriculum and Instruction — M,D,O
Distance Education Development — M,D,O
Early Childhood Education — M,D,O
Education of Students with Severe/Multiple Disabilities — M,D,O
Education—General — M,D,O

Educational Leadership and Administration — M,D,O
Educational Media/Instructional Technology — M,D,O
Elementary Education — M,D,O
English as a Second Language — M,D,O
Mathematics Education — M,D,O
Middle School Education — M,D,O
Reading Education — M,D,O
Science Education — M,D,O
Secondary Education — M,D,O
Special Education — M,D,O

LES ROCHES INTERNATIONAL SCHOOL OF HOTEL MANAGEMENT
Hospitality Management — M

LETOURNEAU UNIVERSITY
Business Administration and Management—General — M
Curriculum and Instruction — M
Educational Leadership and Administration — M
Management Strategy and Policy — M

LEWIS & CLARK COLLEGE
Curriculum and Instruction — M
Educational Leadership and Administration — M,D,O
Elementary Education — M
Environmental Law — M,D
Law — M,D
Secondary Education — M
Special Education — M
Student Affairs — M,D,O

LEWIS UNIVERSITY
Accounting — M
Business Administration and Management—General — M
Business Analytics — M
Counselor Education — M
Curriculum and Instruction — M
Early Childhood Education — M
Education—General — M,D
Educational Leadership and Administration — M,D
Educational Media/Instructional Technology — M
Electronic Commerce — M
Elementary Education — M
English as a Second Language — M
English Education — M
Finance and Banking — M
Foreign Languages Education — M
Higher Education — M
Human Resources Management — M
International Business — M
Management Information Systems — M
Marketing — M
Middle School Education — M
Organizational Management — M
Project Management — M
Reading Education — M
Science Education — M
Secondary Education — M
Social Sciences Education — M
Social Work — M
Special Education — M
Sports Management — M
Student Affairs — M

LIBERTY UNIVERSITY
Accounting — M,D
Advertising and Public Relations — M,D
Business Administration and Management—General — M,D
Counselor Education — M,D,O
Education—General — M,D,O
Exercise and Sports Science — M,D
Facilities Management — M,D
Finance and Banking — M,D
Human Services — M,D,O
International Business — M,D
Law — M
Legal and Justice Studies — M
Marketing — M,D
Music Education — M,D
Nonprofit Management — M
Project Management — M,D
Reading Education — M,D,O
Religious Education — M,D
Taxation — M,D

LIFE UNIVERSITY
Athletic Training and Sports Medicine — M
Exercise and Sports Science — M

LIM COLLEGE
Business Administration and Management—General — M
Marketing — M

LIMESTONE COLLEGE
Business Administration and Management—General — M

LINCOLN CHRISTIAN SEMINARY
Religious Education — M,D

LINCOLN CHRISTIAN UNIVERSITY
Organizational Management — M

LINCOLN MEMORIAL UNIVERSITY
Business Administration and Management—General — M
Counselor Education — M,D,O
Curriculum and Instruction — M,D,O
Education—General — M,D,O
Educational Leadership and Administration — M,D,O
English Education — M,D,O
Higher Education — M,D,O
Human Resources Development — M,D,O
Law — D

LINCOLN UNIVERSITY (CA)
Business Administration and Management—General — M,D
Finance and Banking — M,D
Human Resources Management — M,D
International Business — M,D
Investment Management — M,D
Management Information Systems — M,D

LINCOLN UNIVERSITY (MO)
Counselor Education — M
Elementary Education — M
Higher Education — M
Middle School Education — M
Secondary Education — M

LINCOLN UNIVERSITY (PA)
Early Childhood Education — M
Educational Leadership and Administration — M
Finance and Banking — M
Human Resources Management — M
Human Services — M
Special Education — M

LINDENWOOD UNIVERSITY
Advertising and Public Relations — M
Business Administration and Management—General — M,O
Education of the Gifted — M,D,O
Education—General — M,D,O
Educational Leadership and Administration — M,D,O
Educational Media/Instructional Technology — M,D,O
English as a Second Language — M,D,O
Entrepreneurship — M
Human Resources Management — M,O
Management Information Systems — M,O
Marketing — M,O
Project Management — M,O

LINDENWOOD UNIVERSITY–BELLEVILLE
Business Administration and Management—General — M
Counselor Education — M
Education—General — M
Educational Leadership and Administration — M
Human Resources Management — M

LINDSEY WILSON COLLEGE
Counselor Education — M,D
Educational Leadership and Administration — M

LIPSCOMB UNIVERSITY
Accounting — M,O
Business Administration and Management—General — M,O
Education—General — M,D,O
Educational Leadership and Administration — M,D,O
Educational Media/Instructional Technology — M,D,O
English Education — M,D,O
Exercise and Sports Science — M
Finance and Banking — M,O
Management Information Systems — M,O
Management Strategy and Policy — M,O
Nonprofit Management — M,O
Organizational Management — M,O
Reading Education — M,D,O
Special Education — M,D,O
Taxation — M,O

LOCK HAVEN UNIVERSITY OF PENNSYLVANIA
Actuarial Science — M
Athletic Training and Sports Medicine — M
Business Education — M
Education—General — M
Educational Leadership and Administration — M
Elementary Education — M
Health Education — M
Human Services — M
Information Studies — M
Sports Management — M

LOGAN UNIVERSITY
Exercise and Sports Science — M,D
Health Education — M,D

LOMA LINDA UNIVERSITY
Counselor Education — M,D,O
Health Education — M,D
Social Work — M,D

LONDON METROPOLITAN UNIVERSITY
Athletic Training and Sports Medicine — M,D
Early Childhood Education — M,D
Education—General — M,D
English Education — M,D
Foreign Languages Education — M,D
Higher Education — M,D
Human Resources Management — M,D
Law — M,D
Management Information Systems — M,D
Social Work — M,D
Special Education — M,D
Sports and Entertainment Law — M,D

LONG ISLAND UNIVERSITY–BRENTWOOD CAMPUS
Counselor Education — M,O
Early Childhood Education — M,O
Educational Leadership and Administration — M,O
Elementary Education — M,O
Library Science —

Reading Education — M,O
Social Work — M,O
Special Education — M,O

LONG ISLAND UNIVERSITY–HUDSON
Counselor Education — M,O
Early Childhood Education — M,O
Educational Leadership and Administration — M,O
Elementary Education — M,O
English as a Second Language — M,O
Middle School Education — M,O
Multilingual and Multicultural Education — M,O
Reading Education — M,O
Special Education — M,O

LONG ISLAND UNIVERSITY–LIU BROOKLYN
Accounting — M,O
Athletic Training and Sports Medicine — M,D,O
Business Administration and Management—General — M,O
Counselor Education — M,O
Early Childhood Education — M,O
Education—General — M,O
Educational Leadership and Administration — M,O
English as a Second Language — M,O
Exercise and Sports Science — M,O
Human Resources Management — M,O
Multilingual and Multicultural Education — M,O
Nonprofit Management — M,O
Social Sciences Education — M,O
Social Work — M,O
Special Education — M,O
Taxation — M,O
Urban Education — M,O

LONG ISLAND UNIVERSITY–LIU POST
Accounting — M
Art Education — M,D,O
Business Administration and Management—General — M
Early Childhood Education — M,D,O
Education—General — M,O
Educational Leadership and Administration — M,D,O
Educational Media/Instructional Technology — M,D,O
English as a Second Language — M,D,O
Finance and Banking — M
International Business — M
Library Science — M,D,O
Management Information Systems — M
Marketing — M
Middle School Education — M,D,O
Music Education — M,D,O
Nonprofit Management — M,O
Reading Education — M,D,O
Secondary Education — M,D,O
Social Work — M,O
Special Education — M,D,O
Taxation — M

LONG ISLAND UNIVERSITY–RIVERHEAD
Early Childhood Education — M,O
Elementary Education — M,O
English as a Second Language — M,O
Reading Education — M,O
Special Education — M,O

LONGWOOD UNIVERSITY
Business Administration and Management—General — M
Counselor Education — M
Education—General — M
Educational Media/Instructional Technology — M
Elementary Education — M
Health Education — M
Mathematics Education — M
Middle School Education — M
Physical Education — M
Reading Education — M
Real Estate — M
Special Education — M

LORAS COLLEGE
Educational Leadership and Administration — M
Special Education — M

LOUISIANA COLLEGE
Education—General — M
Educational Leadership and Administration — M
Social Work — M

LOUISIANA STATE UNIVERSITY AND AGRICULTURAL & MECHANICAL COLLEGE
Accounting — M,D
Agricultural Education — M,D
Business Administration and Management—General — M,D
Business Education — M,D
Counselor Education — M,D,O
Education—General — M,D,O
Educational Leadership and Administration — M,D,O
Educational Measurement and Evaluation — M,D,O
Educational Media/Instructional Technology — M,D,O
Elementary Education — M,D,O
Finance and Banking — M,D
Higher Education — M,D,O
Home Economics Education — M,D
Human Resources Development — M,D

Information Studies — M
International and Comparative Education — M,D,O
Kinesiology and Movement Studies — M,D
Law — M,D
Library Science — M
Management Information Systems — M,D
Music Education — M,D
Secondary Education — M,D,O
Social Work — M,D
Vocational and Technical Education — M,D

LOUISIANA STATE UNIVERSITY IN SHREVEPORT
Business Administration and Management—General — M
Counselor Education — M
Curriculum and Instruction — M,D
Education—General — M,D
Educational Leadership and Administration — M,D
Nonprofit Management — M

LOUISIANA TECH UNIVERSITY
Accounting — M,D
Business Administration and Management—General — M,D,O
Curriculum and Instruction — M,D,O
Early Childhood Education — M,D,O
Education—General — M,D,O
Educational Leadership and Administration — M,D,O
Elementary Education — M,D,O
Finance and Banking — M,D
Higher Education — M,D,O
Human Services — M
Kinesiology and Movement Studies — M,D,O
Management Information Systems — M,D
Marketing — M,D
Middle School Education — M,D,O
Secondary Education — M,D,O
Special Education — M,D,O

LOURDES UNIVERSITY
Business Administration and Management—General — M
Curriculum and Instruction — M
Educational Leadership and Administration — M
Organizational Management — M
Reading Education — M

LOYOLA MARYMOUNT UNIVERSITY
Accounting — M
Business Administration and Management—General — M
Counselor Education — M
Education—General — M,D
Educational Leadership and Administration — M,D
Elementary Education — M
Higher Education — M
Law — M,D
Mathematics Education — M
Multilingual and Multicultural Education — M
Reading Education — M
Recreation and Park Management — M
Secondary Education — M
Special Education — M
Urban Education — M

LOYOLA UNIVERSITY CHICAGO
Accounting — M
Business Administration and Management—General — M,O
Business Analytics — M,O
Counselor Education — M,O
Curriculum and Instruction — M,D
Education—General — M,D,O
Educational Leadership and Administration — M,D,O
Educational Measurement and Evaluation — M,D,O
Educational Policy — M,D
Elementary Education — M
Entrepreneurship — M
Finance and Banking — M
Health Law — M,D,O
Higher Education — M,D
Human Resources Management — M
International and Comparative Education — M,D
International Business — M
Law — M,D,O
Legal and Justice Studies — M,O
Management Information Systems — M,O
Marketing — M
Religious Education — M,O
Risk Management — M
Secondary Education — M
Social Work — M,D,O
Special Education — M
Supply Chain Management — M,O
Taxation — M,D,O

LOYOLA UNIVERSITY MARYLAND
Business Administration and Management—General — M
Counselor Education — M,O
Curriculum and Instruction — M
Early Childhood Education — M,O
Education—General — M,O
Educational Leadership and Administration — M,O
Educational Media/Instructional Technology — M
Elementary Education — M,O
Finance and Banking — M
Investment Management — M
Management Information Systems — M
Marketing — M
Music Education — M

Reading Education — M
Secondary Education — M

LOYOLA UNIVERSITY NEW ORLEANS
Business Administration and Management—General — M
Education—General — M
Law — M,D
Organizational Management — M
Secondary Education — M

LYNN UNIVERSITY
Business Administration and Management—General — M
Early Childhood Education — M,D
Education of the Gifted — M,D
Education—General — M,D
Educational Leadership and Administration — M,D
Middle School Education — M,D
Special Education — M,D

MAASTRICHT SCHOOL OF MANAGEMENT
Business Administration and Management—General — M,D
Facilities Management — M,D
Sustainability Management — M,D

MADONNA UNIVERSITY
Business Administration and Management—General — M
Education—General — M
Educational Leadership and Administration — M
English as a Second Language — M
International Business — M
Quality Management — M
Reading Education — M
Social Work — M
Special Education — M

MAHARISHI UNIVERSITY OF MANAGEMENT
Accounting — M,D
Business Administration and Management—General — M,D
Sustainability Management — M,D

MAINE MARITIME ACADEMY
International Business — M
Supply Chain Management — M
Transportation Management — M

MALONE UNIVERSITY
Business Administration and Management—General — M
Counselor Education — M
Curriculum and Instruction — M
Education—General — M
Educational Leadership and Administration — M
Organizational Management — M
Special Education — M

MANCHESTER UNIVERSITY
Athletic Training and Sports Medicine — M

MANHATTAN COLLEGE
Business Administration and Management—General — M
Counselor Education — M,O
Early Childhood Education — M,O
Education—General — M,O
Educational Leadership and Administration — M,O
Educational Media/Instructional Technology — M
Elementary Education — M,O
Multilingual and Multicultural Education — M,O
Organizational Management — M
Special Education — M,O
Student Affairs — M,O

MANHATTANVILLE COLLEGE
Accounting — M,O
Art Education — M,O
Business Education — M,O
Early Childhood Education — M,O
Education—General — M,D,O
Educational Leadership and Administration — M,D,O
Elementary Education — M,O
English as a Second Language — M,O
English Education — M,O
Entrepreneurship — M
Exercise and Sports Science — M,O
Finance and Banking — M,O
Foreign Languages Education — M,O
Human Resources Management — M,O
Investment Management — M,O
Mathematics Education — M,O
Middle School Education — M,O
Multilingual and Multicultural Education — M,O
Music Education — M,O
Reading Education — M,O
Science Education — M,O
Secondary Education — M,O
Social Sciences Education — M,O
Special Education — M,O
Urban Education — M,O

MANSFIELD UNIVERSITY OF PENNSYLVANIA
Art Education — M
Education—General — M
Elementary Education — M
Information Studies — M
Library Science — M
Organizational Management — M
Secondary Education — M

---

*M—masters degree; D—doctorate; O—other advanced degree; *—Close-Up and/or Display*

Special Education — M

MAPLE SPRINGS BAPTIST BIBLE COLLEGE AND SEMINARY
Religious Education — M,D,O

MARANATHA BAPTIST UNIVERSITY
Education—General — M
Organizational Management — M

MARCONI INTERNATIONAL UNIVERSITY
Business Administration and Management—General — M,D
Educational Leadership and Administration — M,D
Educational Media/Instructional Technology — M,D
International Business — M,D

MARIAN UNIVERSITY (IN)
Counselor Education — M
Education—General — M

MARIAN UNIVERSITY (WI)
Business Administration and Management—General — M
Curriculum and Instruction — M,D
Education—General — M,D
Educational Leadership and Administration — M,D
Educational Media/Instructional Technology — M,D
Organizational Management — M
Special Education — M,D

MARIST COLLEGE
Accounting — M
Business Administration and Management—General — M,O
Business Analytics — M,O
Education—General — M,O
Management Information Systems — M,O
Marketing — M

MARLBORO COLLEGE
Business Administration and Management—General — M
Educational Media/Instructional Technology — M,O
English as a Second Language — M
Entrepreneurship — M
Legal and Justice Studies — M
Organizational Management — M
Project Management — M

MARQUETTE UNIVERSITY
Accounting — M
Advertising and Public Relations — M,O
Business Administration and Management—General — M,O
Counselor Education — M,D
Curriculum and Instruction — M,D,O
Education—General — M,D,O
Educational Leadership and Administration — M,D,O
Educational Policy — M,D,O
Elementary Education — M,D,O
Entrepreneurship — M,O
Finance and Banking — M,O
Foreign Languages Education — M
Foundations and Philosophy of Education — M,D,O
Human Resources Development — M
Human Resources Management — M,O
Industrial and Manufacturing Management — M,O
International Business — M,O
Law — D
Management Information Systems — M,O
Marketing Research — M
Marketing — M,O
Mathematics Education — M,D
Reading Education — M,D,O
Real Estate — M
Secondary Education — M,D,O
Sports Management — M,O
Student Affairs — M,D,O
Supply Chain Management — M,O

MARSHALL UNIVERSITY
Accounting — M
Adult Education — M
Advertising and Public Relations — M,O
Athletic Training and Sports Medicine — M
Business Administration and Management—General — M,O
Counselor Education — M
Education—General — M,D,O
Educational Leadership and Administration — M
Exercise and Sports Science — M
Health Education — M
Human Resources Management — M
Reading Education — M
Social Work — M
Special Education — M
Sports Management — M

MARS HILL UNIVERSITY
Elementary Education — M

MARTIN LUTHER COLLEGE
Curriculum and Instruction — M
Early Childhood Education — M
Education—General — M
Educational Leadership and Administration — M
Educational Media/Instructional Technology — M
Special Education — M

MARY BALDWIN UNIVERSITY
Education of the Gifted — M
Education—General — M
Educational Leadership and Administration — M
Elementary Education — M

English as a Second Language — M
Environmental Education — M
Higher Education — M
Middle School Education — M
Reading Education — M
Special Education — M

MARYGROVE COLLEGE
Curriculum and Instruction — M,O
Early Childhood Education — M,O
Educational Leadership and Administration — M,O
Educational Media/Instructional Technology — M,O
Elementary Education — M,O
Human Resources Management — M,O
Legal and Justice Studies — M,O
Middle School Education — M,O
Reading Education — M,O
Special Education — M,O

MARYLAND INSTITUTE COLLEGE OF ART
Art Education — M
Business Administration and Management—General — M

MARYMOUNT CALIFORNIA UNIVERSITY
Business Administration and Management—General — M

MARYMOUNT UNIVERSITY
Business Administration and Management—General — M,O
Community College Education — M,O
Counselor Education — M
Curriculum and Instruction — M
Education—General — M
Elementary Education — M
English Education — M,O
Health Education — M
Human Resources Management — O
Management Information Systems — M,O
Nonprofit Management — M,O
Project Management — M,O
Secondary Education — M
Special Education — M

MARYVILLE UNIVERSITY OF SAINT LOUIS
Accounting — M,O
Actuarial Science — M
Business Administration and Management—General — M,O
Business Education — M,O
Early Childhood Education — M,D
Education—General — M,O
Educational Leadership and Administration — M,D
Elementary Education — M,D
Finance and Banking — M,D
Higher Education — M,D
Human Resources Management — M,O
Logistics — M,O
Marketing — M,O
Middle School Education — M,D
Project Management — M,O
Reading Education — M,D
Secondary Education — M,D
Sports Management — M,O
Supply Chain Management — M,O

MARYWOOD UNIVERSITY
Art Education — M
Business Administration and Management—General — M
Counselor Education — M
Early Childhood Education — M
Education—General — M
Educational Leadership and Administration — M,D
Elementary Education — M
Exercise and Sports Science — M
Finance and Banking — M
Health Education — D
Higher Education — M,D
Investment Management — M
Management Information Systems — M
Music Education — M
Reading Education — M
Secondary Education — M
Social Work — M,D
Special Education — M

MASSACHUSETTS COLLEGE OF ART AND DESIGN
Art Education — M,O

MASSACHUSETTS COLLEGE OF LIBERAL ARTS
Business Administration and Management—General — M,O
Curriculum and Instruction — M,O
Education—General — M,O
Educational Leadership and Administration — M,O
Educational Media/Instructional Technology — M,O
Health Education — M,O
Physical Education — M,O
Reading Education — M,O
Special Education — M,O

MASSACHUSETTS INSTITUTE OF TECHNOLOGY
Business Administration and Management—General — M,D
Logistics — M
Real Estate — M

MASSACHUSETTS MARITIME ACADEMY
Facilities Management — M

MASSACHUSETTS SCHOOL OF LAW AT ANDOVER
Law — D

MCDANIEL COLLEGE
Counselor Education — M
Curriculum and Instruction — M
Educational Leadership and Administration — M
Educational Media/Instructional Technology — M
Elementary Education — M,O
English as a Second Language — M
Human Resources Development — M
Human Services — M
Kinesiology and Movement Studies — M
Library Science — M
Mathematics Education — M,O
Reading Education — M
Science Education — M,O
Secondary Education — M,O
Special Education — M

MCGILL UNIVERSITY
Accounting — M,D,O
Business Administration and Management—General — M,D,O
Curriculum and Instruction — M,D,O
Education—General — M,D,O
Educational Leadership and Administration — M,D,O
Educational Psychology — M,D,O
Entrepreneurship — M,D,O
Finance and Banking — M,D,O
Foreign Languages Education — M,D,O
Foundations and Philosophy of Education — M,D,O
Industrial and Manufacturing Management — M,D,O
Information Studies — M,D,O
International Business — M,D,O
Kinesiology and Movement Studies — M,D,O
Law — M,D,O
Library Science — M,D,O
Management Information Systems — M,D,O
Management Strategy and Policy — M,D,O
Marketing — M,D,O
Music Education — M,D
Physical Education — M,D,O
Social Work — M,D,O
Supply Chain Management — M,D,O
Transportation Management — M,D

MCKENDREE UNIVERSITY
Business Administration and Management—General — M
Curriculum and Instruction — M,D,O
Education—General — M,D,O
Educational Leadership and Administration — M,D,O
Higher Education — M,D,O
Human Resources Management — M
International Business — M
Music Education — M,D,O
Reading Education — M,D,O
Special Education — M,D,O

MCMASTER UNIVERSITY
Business Administration and Management—General — M,D
Human Resources Management — M,D
Kinesiology and Movement Studies — M,D
Management Information Systems — D
Social Work — M

MCNEESE STATE UNIVERSITY
Art Education — O
Business Administration and Management—General — M
Counselor Education — M
Curriculum and Instruction — M
Early Childhood Education — O
Education of the Gifted — M
Education—General — O
Educational Leadership and Administration — M,O
Educational Measurement and Evaluation — M,O
Educational Media/Instructional Technology — M,O
Elementary Education — M,O
Exercise and Sports Science — M
Health Education — O
Library Science — O
Mathematics Education — O
Middle School Education — O
Music Education — O
Physical Education — O
Reading Education — M
Science Education — O
Secondary Education — M,O
Special Education — M,O

MCPHERSON COLLEGE
Education—General — M

MEDAILLE COLLEGE
Business Administration and Management—General — M
Curriculum and Instruction — M
Education—General — M
Elementary Education — M
Organizational Management — M
Reading Education — M
Secondary Education — M
Special Education — M

MELBOURNE BUSINESS SCHOOL
Business Administration and Management—General — M,D,O
Marketing — M,D,O

MEMORIAL UNIVERSITY OF NEWFOUNDLAND
Adult Education — M,D,O
Business Administration and Management—General — M
Curriculum and Instruction — M,D,O
Education—General — M,D,O
Educational Leadership and Administration — M,D,O

Educational Media/Instructional Technology — M,D,O
Educational Psychology — M,D,O
Exercise and Sports Science — M
Kinesiology and Movement Studies — M
Physical Education — M
Social Work — M,D

MERCER UNIVERSITY
Accounting — M
Athletic Training and Sports Medicine — M,D
Business Administration and Management—General — M
Counselor Education — M,D
Curriculum and Instruction — M,D,O
Early Childhood Education — M,D,O
Education—General — M,D,O
Educational Leadership and Administration — M,D,O
Entrepreneurship — M
Higher Education — M,D,O
Human Services — M,D
Law — D
Middle School Education — M,D,O
Nonprofit Management — M,D
Organizational Management — M,D
Science Education — M,D,O
Secondary Education — M,D,O

MERCY COLLEGE
Accounting — M
Business Administration and Management—General — M
Counselor Education — M,O
Early Childhood Education — M,O
Education—General — M,O
Educational Leadership and Administration — M,O
Elementary Education — M
English as a Second Language — M,O
Human Resources Management — M
Middle School Education — M,O
Organizational Management — M
Reading Education — M,O
Secondary Education — M,O

MERCYHURST UNIVERSITY
Accounting — M,O
Educational Leadership and Administration — M,O
Entrepreneurship — M,O
Higher Education — M,O
Human Resources Management — M,O
Management Strategy and Policy — M,O
Organizational Management — M,O
Secondary Education — M
Special Education — M
Sports Management — M,O

MEREDITH COLLEGE
Business Administration and Management—General — M
Education of the Gifted — M,O
Education—General — M,O
Elementary Education — M,O
English as a Second Language — M,O
Health Education — M,O
Physical Education — M,O
Reading Education — M,O
Special Education — M,O

MERRIMACK COLLEGE
Accounting — M
Athletic Training and Sports Medicine — M
Business Administration and Management—General — M
Business Analytics — M
Education—General — M,O
Exercise and Sports Science — M
Health Education — M

MESSIAH COLLEGE
Business Administration and Management—General — M,O
Counselor Education — M,O
Curriculum and Instruction — M
English as a Second Language — M
Higher Education — M
Management Strategy and Policy — M,O
Organizational Management — M,O
Special Education — M
Sports Management — M
Student Affairs — M

METHODIST UNIVERSITY
Business Administration and Management—General — M

METROPOLITAN COLLEGE OF NEW YORK
Business Administration and Management—General — M
Elementary Education — M
Finance and Banking — M
Risk Management — M
Special Education — M

METROPOLITAN STATE UNIVERSITY
Business Administration and Management—General — M,D,O
Business Analytics — M,D,O
Curriculum and Instruction — M
English as a Second Language — M
English Education — M
Information Studies — M,D,O
Management Information Systems — M,D,O
Mathematics Education — M
Nonprofit Management — M
Project Management — M,D,O
Science Education — M
Secondary Education — M
Social Sciences Education — M
Special Education — M
Supply Chain Management — M,D,O
Urban Education — M

METROPOLITAN STATE UNIVERSITY OF DENVER

Accounting	M
Education—General	M
Elementary Education	M
Social Work	M
Special Education	M
Taxation	M

MGH INSTITUTE OF HEALTH PROFESSIONS

Reading Education	M,O

MIAMI UNIVERSITY

Accounting	M
Art Education	M
Business Administration and Management—General	M
Education—General	M,D,O
Educational Leadership and Administration	M,D
Educational Psychology	M,O
Exercise and Sports Science	M
Mathematics Education	M
Music Education	M
Student Affairs	M,D

MICHIGAN SCHOOL OF PSYCHOLOGY

Educational Psychology	M,D

MICHIGAN STATE UNIVERSITY

Accounting	M,D
Adult Education	M,D,O
Advertising and Public Relations	M
Business Administration and Management—General	M,D
Business Analytics	M
Counselor Education	M,D,O
Curriculum and Instruction	M,D,O
Education—General	M,D,O
Educational Leadership and Administration	M,D,O
Educational Measurement and Evaluation	M,D,O
Educational Media/Instructional Technology	M,D,O
Educational Policy	D
Educational Psychology	M,D,O
English as a Second Language	M,D
Finance and Banking	M,D
Foreign Languages Education	D
Higher Education	M,D,O
Hospitality Management	M
Human Resources Management	M,D
Kinesiology and Movement Studies	M,D
Logistics	M,D
Management Information Systems	M,D
Management Strategy and Policy	M,D
Marketing Research	M,D
Marketing	M,D
Mathematics Education	M,D
Music Education	M,D
Reading Education	M
Recreation and Park Management	M,D
Social Sciences Education	M,D
Social Work	M,D
Special Education	M,D,O
Supply Chain Management	M,D
Taxation	M,D

MICHIGAN STATE UNIVERSITY COLLEGE OF LAW

Intellectual Property Law	M,D
Law	M,D
Legal and Justice Studies	M,D

MICHIGAN TECHNOLOGICAL UNIVERSITY

Business Administration and Management—General	M
Kinesiology and Movement Studies	M,D
Science Education	M,D,O
Sustainability Management	M,D,O

MID-AMERICA CHRISTIAN UNIVERSITY

Business Administration and Management—General	M
Organizational Management	M

MIDAMERICA NAZARENE UNIVERSITY

Business Administration and Management—General	M
Education—General	M
Educational Media/Instructional Technology	M
English as a Second Language	M
Reading Education	M

MIDDLEBURY INSTITUTE OF INTERNATIONAL STUDIES AT MONTEREY

English as a Second Language	M
Foreign Languages Education	M
International and Comparative Education	M

MIDDLE GEORGIA STATE UNIVERSITY

Management Information Systems	M

MIDDLE TENNESSEE STATE UNIVERSITY

Accounting	M
Actuarial Science	M
Archives/Archival Administration	M,D,O
Aviation Management	M
Business Administration and Management—General	M
Business Education	M
Counselor Education	M
Curriculum and Instruction	M,O
Early Childhood Education	M,O
Education—General	M,D,O
Educational Leadership and Administration	M,O
Educational Media/Instructional Technology	M,O
Elementary Education	M,O
English as a Second Language	M,O
Exercise and Sports Science	M,D
Foreign Languages Education	M
Health Education	M
Human Resources Management	M
Management Information Systems	M
Management Strategy and Policy	M
Mathematics Education	M,D
Middle School Education	M,O
Physical Education	M
Reading Education	M,D
Recreation and Park Management	M
Science Education	M,D
Secondary Education	M,O
Social Work	M
Special Education	M
Vocational and Technical Education	M

MIDWAY UNIVERSITY

Business Administration and Management—General	M
Education—General	M
Organizational Management	M

MIDWESTERN BAPTIST THEOLOGICAL SEMINARY

Religious Education	M,D,O

MIDWESTERN STATE UNIVERSITY

Business Administration and Management—General	M
Counselor Education	M
Curriculum and Instruction	M
Education—General	M
Educational Leadership and Administration	M
Educational Media/Instructional Technology	M
Exercise and Sports Science	M
Human Resources Development	M
Reading Education	M
Special Education	M
Sports Management	M

MIDWEST UNIVERSITY

Aviation Management	M,D
Counselor Education	M,D
Education of the Gifted	M,D
Education—General	M,D
English as a Second Language	M,D
Entrepreneurship	M,D
International Business	M,D
Investment Management	M,D
Organizational Management	M,D
Real Estate	M,D

MILLENNIA ATLANTIC UNIVERSITY

Accounting	M
Business Administration and Management—General	M
Human Resources Management	M

MILLERSVILLE UNIVERSITY OF PENNSYLVANIA

Distance Education Development	M,D
Early Childhood Education	M
Education of the Gifted	M
Education—General	M,D,O
Educational Leadership and Administration	M,D
English Education	M
Mathematics Education	M,D
Physical Education	M,O
Reading Education	M
Science Education	M,D
Social Work	M,D
Special Education	M
Sports Management	M,O

MILLIGAN COLLEGE

Business Administration and Management—General	M,O
Counselor Education	M,O
Early Childhood Education	M,D,O
Education—General	M,D,O
Educational Leadership and Administration	M,D,O
Elementary Education	M,D,O
Industrial and Manufacturing Management	M,O
Middle School Education	M,D,O
Religious Education	M,D,O
Secondary Education	M,D,O
Special Education	M,D,O

MILLIKIN UNIVERSITY

Business Administration and Management—General	M

MILLSAPS COLLEGE

Accounting	M
Business Administration and Management—General	M

MILLS COLLEGE

Business Administration and Management—General	M
Early Childhood Education	M
Education—General	M,D,O
Educational Leadership and Administration	

MILWAUKEE SCHOOL OF ENGINEERING

Business Administration and Management—General	M
Business Education	M
Industrial and Manufacturing Management	M
International Business	M
Marketing	M

MINNESOTA STATE UNIVERSITY MANKATO

Accounting	M
Art Education	M
Business Administration and Management—General	M
Counselor Education	M,D
Education—General	M,D,O
Educational Leadership and Administration	M
English as a Second Language	M,O
Foreign Languages Education	M
Health Education	M,O
Higher Education	M
Human Services	M
Mathematics Education	M
Music Education	M
Nonprofit Management	M,O
Physical Education	M
Science Education	M
Social Sciences Education	M
Social Work	M
Special Education	M,O
Student Affairs	M,D

MINNESOTA STATE UNIVERSITY MOORHEAD

Business Administration and Management—General	M
Counselor Education	M,D,O
Education—General	M,D,O
Educational Leadership and Administration	M,D,O

MINOT STATE UNIVERSITY

Business Administration and Management—General	M
Elementary Education	M
Management Information Systems	M
Mathematics Education	M
Middle School Education	M
Science Education	M
Special Education	M

MISERICORDIA UNIVERSITY

Accounting	M
Business Administration and Management—General	M
Curriculum and Instruction	M
Education—General	M
Educational Media/Instructional Technology	M
Human Resources Management	M
Organizational Management	M
Reading Education	M
Special Education	M
Sports Management	M

MISSISSIPPI COLLEGE

Accounting	M,O
Advertising and Public Relations	M
Art Education	M,D,O
Business Administration and Management—General	M,O
Business Education	M,D,O
Computer Education	M,D,O
Counselor Education	M,O
Curriculum and Instruction	M,D,O
Education—General	M,D,O
Educational Leadership and Administration	M,D,O
Elementary Education	M,D,O
English as a Second Language	M
English Education	M,D,O
Finance and Banking	M,O
Higher Education	M,D,O
Kinesiology and Movement Studies	M
Law	D,O
Legal and Justice Studies	M,O
Mathematics Education	M,D,O
Music Education	M
Science Education	M,D,O
Secondary Education	M,D,O
Social Sciences Education	M,D,O
Special Education	M,D,O

MISSISSIPPI STATE UNIVERSITY

Accounting	M
Agricultural Education	M,D
Business Administration and Management—General	M,D
Community College Education	M,D,O
Counselor Education	M,D,O
Curriculum and Instruction	M,D,O
Early Childhood Education	M,D,O
Education—General	M,D,O
Educational Leadership and Administration	M,D,O
Educational Media/Instructional Technology	M,D,O
Educational Psychology	M,D,O
Elementary Education	M,D,O
Exercise and Sports Science	M,D
Finance and Banking	M,D
Foreign Languages Education	M
Higher Education	M,D,O
Human Resources Development	M,D,O
Industrial and Manufacturing Management	M,D
Kinesiology and Movement Studies	M,D
Management Information Systems	M,D
Marketing	D
Middle School Education	M,D,O
Physical Education	M,D
Project Management	M,D
Reading Education	M,D,O
Secondary Education	M,D,O
Special Education	M,D,O
Sports Management	M,D
Student Affairs	M,D,O
Taxation	M
Vocational and Technical Education	M,D,O

MISSISSIPPI UNIVERSITY FOR WOMEN

Curriculum and Instruction	M
Education of the Gifted	M
Education—General	M
Educational Leadership and Administration	M
Health Education	M,D,O
Reading Education	M

MISSISSIPPI VALLEY STATE UNIVERSITY

Education—General	M

MISSOURI BAPTIST UNIVERSITY

Business Administration and Management—General	M,O
Counselor Education	M,O
Education—General	M,O
Educational Leadership and Administration	M,O

MISSOURI SOUTHERN STATE UNIVERSITY

Business Administration and Management—General	M
Early Childhood Education	M
Education—General	M
Educational Media/Instructional Technology	M

MISSOURI STATE UNIVERSITY

Accounting	M
Athletic Training and Sports Medicine	M
Business Administration and Management—General	M
Counselor Education	M
Early Childhood Education	M
Educational Leadership and Administration	M,O
Educational Measurement and Evaluation	O
Educational Media/Instructional Technology	M
Elementary Education	M,O
English as a Second Language	M,O
English Education	M,O
Higher Education	M
Kinesiology and Movement Studies	M
Mathematics Education	M
Physical Education	M
Project Management	M
Reading Education	M,O
Science Education	M,O
Secondary Education	M,O
Social Sciences Education	M,O
Social Work	M
Special Education	M
Sports Management	M,O
Student Affairs	M

MISSOURI UNIVERSITY OF SCIENCE AND TECHNOLOGY

Business Administration and Management—General	M
Mathematics Education	M,D

MISSOURI WESTERN STATE UNIVERSITY

Accounting	M
Business Administration and Management—General	M
Early Childhood Education	M,O
Educational Measurement and Evaluation	M,O
English as a Second Language	M,O
Special Education	M,O
Sports Management	M

MITCHELL HAMLINE SCHOOL OF LAW

Law	M,D

MOLLOY COLLEGE

Accounting	M,O
Business Administration and Management—General	M,O
Early Childhood Education	M,O
Education—General	M,O
Educational Media/Instructional Technology	M,O
English as a Second Language	M,O
English Education	M,O
Finance and Banking	M,O
Foreign Languages Education	M,O
Marketing	M,O
Mathematics Education	M,O
Multilingual and Multicultural Education	M,O
Science Education	M,O
Social Sciences Education	M,O
Special Education	M,O

MONMOUTH UNIVERSITY

Accounting	M,O
Advertising and Public Relations	M,O
Business Administration and Management—General	M,O
Early Childhood Education	M,D,O
Education—General	M,D,O
Educational Leadership and Administration	M,D,O
Elementary Education	M,D,O
English as a Second Language	M,D,O
Finance and Banking	M,O
Information Studies	M
Marketing	M,O
Reading Education	M,D,O
Real Estate	M,O
Secondary Education	M,D,O
Social Work	M,O
Special Education	M,D,O
Student Affairs	M,D,O

*M—masters degree; D—doctorate; O—other advanced degree; *—Close-Up and/or Display*

MONROE COLLEGE
Accounting M
Business Administration and Management—General M
Entrepreneurship M
Finance and Banking M
Hospitality Management M
Human Resources Management M
Marketing M

MONTANA STATE UNIVERSITY
Accounting M
Adult Education M,D,O
Agricultural Education M
Curriculum and Instruction M,D,O
Education—General M,D,O
Educational Leadership and Administration M,D,O
Health Education M
Higher Education M,D,O
Home Economics Education M
Mathematics Education M,D
Vocational and Technical Education M,D,O

MONTANA STATE UNIVERSITY BILLINGS
Advertising and Public Relations M
Athletic Training and Sports Medicine M
Counselor Education M
Curriculum and Instruction M
Education—General M,O
Educational Media/Instructional Technology M
Elementary Education M
Reading Education M
Secondary Education M
Special Education M

MONTANA STATE UNIVERSITY–NORTHERN
Counselor Education M
Education—General M

MONTANA TECH OF THE UNIVERSITY OF MONTANA
Project Management M

MONTCLAIR STATE UNIVERSITY
Accounting M,O
Advertising and Public Relations M
Archives/Archival Administration M
Art Education M
Business Administration and Management—General M,O
Business Analytics M
Counselor Education M,D
Curriculum and Instruction M
Education—General M,D,O
Educational Leadership and Administration M,D
Educational Measurement and Evaluation O
English as a Second Language M,O
English Education M,O
Environmental Education M
Environmental Law O
Exercise and Sports Science M,O
Finance and Banking M
Health Education M
Human Resources Management M
Intellectual Property Law M,O
Law M,O
Legal and Justice Studies O
Management Information Systems M
Marketing M
Mathematics Education M,D,O
Music Education M
Physical Education M
Project Management M
Reading Education M
Science Education M
Special Education M
Sports Management M

MOODY THEOLOGICAL SEMINARY–MICHIGAN
Religious Education M,O

MOORE COLLEGE OF ART & DESIGN
Art Education M

MORAVIAN COLLEGE
Accounting M
Athletic Training and Sports Medicine M,D
Business Administration and Management—General M
Curriculum and Instruction M
Education—General M
Human Resources Management M
Supply Chain Management M

MOREHEAD STATE UNIVERSITY
Adult Education M,O
Art Education M
Business Administration and Management—General M
Business Education M,O
Counselor Education M,O
Curriculum and Instruction M,O
Education of the Gifted M,O
Education—General M,O
Educational Leadership and Administration M,O
Educational Media/Instructional Technology M,O
Elementary Education M,O
English Education M,O
Foreign Languages Education M
Health Education M
Higher Education M,O
Management Information Systems M
Mathematics Education M
Middle School Education M,O
Music Education M
Physical Education M
Reading Education M,O
Science Education M
Secondary Education M
Social Sciences Education M,O
Special Education M,O
Vocational and Technical Education M

MORGAN STATE UNIVERSITY
Accounting M,D
Business Administration and Management—General M,D
Community College Education D
Education—General M,D
Educational Leadership and Administration M,D
Elementary Education M
Higher Education M,D
Hospitality Management M
Management Information Systems D
Marketing D
Mathematics Education M,D
Project Management M
Science Education M,D
Social Work M
Student Affairs M,D
Urban Education D

MORNINGSIDE COLLEGE
Education—General M
Special Education M

MOUNT ALOYSIUS COLLEGE
Accounting M
Business Administration and Management—General M
Nonprofit Management M
Project Management M

MOUNT HOLYOKE COLLEGE
Educational Leadership and Administration M
Mathematics Education M

MOUNT MARTY COLLEGE
Business Administration and Management—General M

MOUNT MARY UNIVERSITY
Business Administration and Management—General M
Counselor Education M,O
Education—General M

MOUNT MERCY UNIVERSITY
Business Administration and Management—General M
Education—General M
Educational Leadership and Administration M
Human Resources Management M
Management Strategy and Policy M
Quality Management M
Reading Education M
Special Education M

MOUNT ST. JOSEPH UNIVERSITY
Business Administration and Management—General M
Early Childhood Education M,O
Education—General M,O
Middle School Education M,O
Multilingual and Multicultural Education M,O
Organizational Management M
Reading Education M,O
Secondary Education M,O
Special Education M,O

MOUNT SAINT MARY COLLEGE
Business Administration and Management—General M
Education—General M,O
Finance and Banking M
Middle School Education M,O
Reading Education M,O
Special Education M,O

MOUNT SAINT MARY'S UNIVERSITY (CA)
Business Administration and Management—General M,D,O
Education—General M,D,O

MOUNT ST. MARY'S UNIVERSITY (MD)
Business Administration and Management—General M
Education—General M
Sports Management M

MOUNT SAINT VINCENT UNIVERSITY
Adult Education M
Advertising and Public Relations M
Curriculum and Instruction M
Education—General M
Educational Measurement and Evaluation M
Educational Psychology M
Elementary Education M
English as a Second Language M
Foundations and Philosophy of Education M
Middle School Education M
Reading Education M
Special Education M

MOUNT VERNON NAZARENE UNIVERSITY
Business Administration and Management—General M
Education—General M

MULTNOMAH UNIVERSITY
Education—General M
English as a Second Language M

MURRAY STATE UNIVERSITY
Accounting M
Advertising and Public Relations M
Agricultural Education M,O
Business Administration and Management—General M
Counselor Education M,D,O
Early Childhood Education M,O
Education of Students with Severe/Multiple Disabilities M,O
Education—General M,D,O
Educational Leadership and Administration M,D,O
Educational Media/Instructional Technology M,D,O
Elementary Education M,O
English as a Second Language M,D,O
English Education M,D,O
Finance and Banking M
Human Resources Management M
Human Services M,D,O
Management Information Systems M
Marketing M
Mathematics Education M
Middle School Education M,D,O
Music Education M
Nonprofit Management M,O
Secondary Education M,D,O
Special Education M,O
Vocational and Technical Education M,O

MUSKINGUM UNIVERSITY
Education—General M

NAROPA UNIVERSITY
Counselor Education M
Recreation and Park Management M
Sustainability Management M

NATIONAL AMERICAN UNIVERSITY (TX)
Accounting M,D
Aviation Management M,D
Business Administration and Management—General M,D
Community College Education M,D
Educational Leadership and Administration M,D
Higher Education M,D
Human Resources Management M,D
International Business M,D
Management Information Systems M,D
Marketing M,D
Project Management M,D

NATIONAL LOUIS UNIVERSITY
Adult Education M,D,O
Business Administration and Management—General M
Counselor Education M,D,O
Curriculum and Instruction M,D,O
Developmental Education M,D,O
Early Childhood Education M,D,O
Education—General M,D,O
Educational Leadership and Administration M,D,O
Educational Media/Instructional Technology M,D,O
Educational Psychology M,D,O
Elementary Education M,D,O
English Education M,D,O
Human Resources Development M
Human Resources Management M
Human Services M,D,O
Mathematics Education M,D,O
Middle School Education M,D,O
Reading Education M,D,O
Science Education M,D,O
Secondary Education M,D,O
Special Education M,D,O

NATIONAL PARALEGAL COLLEGE
Legal and Justice Studies M
Taxation M

NATIONAL UNIVERSITY
Accounting M,O
Business Administration and Management—General M,O
Business Analytics M,O
Counselor Education M,O
Distance Education Development M,O
Education—General M,O
Educational Leadership and Administration M,O
Educational Media/Instructional Technology M,O
Higher Education M,O
Human Resources Management M,O
Human Services M,O
International Business M,O
Legal and Justice Studies M
Management Information Systems M,O
Marketing M,O
Mathematics Education M,O
Organizational Management M,O
Special Education M,O
Sustainability Management M

NATIONAL UNIVERSITY COLLEGE
Business Administration and Management—General M
Marketing M
Special Education M

NAVAL POSTGRADUATE SCHOOL
Business Administration and Management—General M
Finance and Banking M
Logistics M
Management Information Systems M,D,O
Supply Chain Management M
Transportation Management M

NAZARETH COLLEGE OF ROCHESTER
Art Education M
Business Administration and Management—General M
Early Childhood Education M
Education—General M
Educational Media/Instructional Technology M
Elementary Education M
English as a Second Language M
Human Resources Management M
Middle School Education M
Music Education M
Reading Education M
Social Work M

NEBRASKA CHRISTIAN COLLEGE OF HOPE INTERNATIONAL UNIVERSITY
Business Administration and Management—General M
Education of the Gifted M
Educational Leadership and Administration M
Elementary Education M
Entrepreneurship M
International Business M
Marketing M
Music Education M
Nonprofit Management M
Secondary Education M

NEUMANN UNIVERSITY
Accounting M
Business Administration and Management—General M
Education—General M
Educational Leadership and Administration M,D
Elementary Education M
Management Strategy and Policy M
Organizational Management M
Secondary Education M
Special Education M
Sports Management M

NEW CHARTER UNIVERSITY
Business Administration and Management—General M
Finance and Banking M

NEW ENGLAND COLLEGE
Accounting M
Business Administration and Management—General M
Education—General M,D
Educational Leadership and Administration M,D
Higher Education M,D
Human Services M
Management Strategy and Policy M
Marketing M
Nonprofit Management M
Project Management M
Recreation and Park Management M
Special Education M,D
Sports Management M

NEW ENGLAND COLLEGE OF BUSINESS AND FINANCE
Finance and Banking M
Quality Management M

NEW ENGLAND INSTITUTE OF TECHNOLOGY
Management Information Systems M

NEW ENGLAND LAW–BOSTON
Law M,D

NEW HAMPSHIRE INSTITUTE OF ART
Art Education M

NEW JERSEY CITY UNIVERSITY
Accounting M,O
Art Education M
Business Administration and Management—General M,O
Counselor Education M
Early Childhood Education M
Education—General M,D
Educational Leadership and Administration M
Educational Media/Instructional Technology M,D
Elementary Education M
English as a Second Language M
Finance and Banking M,O
Health Education M
Marketing M
Mathematics Education M
Multilingual and Multicultural Education M
Music Education M
Organizational Management M
Secondary Education M
Special Education M
Urban Education M

NEW JERSEY INSTITUTE OF TECHNOLOGY
Business Administration and Management—General M,D,O
Management Information Systems M,D,O
Transportation Management M,D

NEWMAN THEOLOGICAL COLLEGE
Religious Education M,O

NEWMAN UNIVERSITY
Business Administration and Management—General M
Curriculum and Instruction M
Education—General M
Educational Leadership and Administration M
English as a Second Language M
Finance and Banking M
International Business M
Management Information Systems M
Organizational Management M
Reading Education M
Social Work M

NEW MEXICO HIGHLANDS UNIVERSITY
Business Administration and Management—General M

Counselor Education	M
Curriculum and Instruction	M
Education—General	M
Educational Leadership and Administration	M
Exercise and Sports Science	M
Health Education	M
Human Resources Management	M
International Business	M
Social Work	M
Special Education	M
Sports Management	M

NEW MEXICO INSTITUTE OF MINING AND TECHNOLOGY

Science Education	M

NEW MEXICO STATE UNIVERSITY

Business Administration and Management—General	D
Early Childhood Education	M,D,O
Education—General	M,D,O
Educational Measurement and Evaluation	M,D,O
English as a Second Language	M,D,O
English Education	M,D
Finance and Banking	M
Higher Education	M,D
Management Information Systems	M
Multilingual and Multicultural Education	M,D,O
Music Education	M
Reading Education	M,D,O
Travel and Tourism	M

NEW ORLEANS BAPTIST THEOLOGICAL SEMINARY

Religious Education	M,D

THE NEW SCHOOL

English as a Second Language	M
Finance and Banking	M,D
Management Strategy and Policy	M,O
Nonprofit Management	M
Organizational Management	M,O
Sustainability Management	M

NEW YORK INSTITUTE OF TECHNOLOGY

Business Administration and Management—General	M
Counselor Education	M,O
Early Childhood Education	M
Educational Leadership and Administration	O
Educational Media/Instructional Technology	M,O
Elementary Education	M
English Education	M
Finance and Banking	M
Human Resources Management	M,O
Marketing	M
Mathematics Education	M,O
Middle School Education	M
Science Education	M,O
Secondary Education	M
Social Sciences Education	M
Supply Chain Management	M

NEW YORK LAW SCHOOL

Law	M,D

NEW YORK MEDICAL COLLEGE

Business Administration and Management—General	M,D,O
Health Education	M,D,O

NEW YORK UNIVERSITY

Accounting	M,D
Advertising and Public Relations	M
Archives/Archival Administration	M,D,O
Art Education	M,O
Business Administration and Management—General	M,D,O
Business Education	M,O
Counselor Education	M,D,O
Early Childhood Education	M
Education—General	M,D,O
Educational Leadership and Administration	M,D,O
Educational Media/Instructional Technology	M,D,O
Educational Policy	M,D
Educational Psychology	M,D
Elementary Education	M
English as a Second Language	M,D,O
English Education	M,D,O
Environmental Education	M
Finance and Banking	M,D
Foreign Languages Education	M,D,O
Foundations and Philosophy of Education	M,D
Higher Education	M,D
Hospitality Management	M,D
Human Resources Development	M
Human Resources Management	M
International and Comparative Education	M,D,O
International Business	M,D
Investment Management	M
Kinesiology and Movement Studies	M,D,O
Law	M,D,O
Legal and Justice Studies	M,D
Management Information Systems	M,D
Management Strategy and Policy	M,D
Marketing	M,D
Mathematics Education	M
Multilingual and Multicultural Education	M,D,O
Music Education	M,D,O
Nonprofit Management	M,D,O
Organizational Behavior	M,D
Organizational Management	M,D
Project Management	M
Reading Education	M
Real Estate	M
Risk Management	M
Science Education	M,D,O
Secondary Education	M,D,O
Social Sciences Education	M,D,O
Social Work	M,D
Special Education	M
Sports and Entertainment Law	M
Student Affairs	M,D
Taxation	M,D,O
Travel and Tourism	M

NIAGARA UNIVERSITY

Accounting	M
Business Administration and Management—General	M
Counselor Education	M,O
Early Childhood Education	M,O
Education—General	M,D,O
Educational Leadership and Administration	M,D,O
Educational Policy	M,D,O
Elementary Education	M,O
English as a Second Language	M,O
Finance and Banking	M
Human Resources Management	M
International Business	M
Management Strategy and Policy	M
Marketing	M
Middle School Education	M,O
Reading Education	M
Secondary Education	M,O
Special Education	M,O
Supply Chain Management	M

NICHOLLS STATE UNIVERSITY

Business Administration and Management—General	M
Counselor Education	M,O
Curriculum and Instruction	M
Education—General	M
Educational Leadership and Administration	M
Elementary Education	M
Health Education	M
Middle School Education	M
Secondary Education	M

NICHOLS COLLEGE

Business Administration and Management—General	M
Organizational Management	M

NIPISSING UNIVERSITY

Education—General	M,O

NORFOLK STATE UNIVERSITY

Early Childhood Education	M
Education of Students with Severe/Multiple Disabilities	M
Education—General	M
Educational Leadership and Administration	M
Music Education	M
Secondary Education	M
Social Work	M,D
Special Education	M
Urban Education	M

NORTH AMERICAN UNIVERSITY

Educational Leadership and Administration	M

NORTH CAROLINA AGRICULTURAL AND TECHNICAL STATE UNIVERSITY

Accounting	M
Adult Education	M,D
Agricultural Education	M
Business Administration and Management—General	M
Business Education	M
Counselor Education	M,D
Early Childhood Education	M
Education—General	M,D
Educational Leadership and Administration	M,D
Educational Media/Instructional Technology	M
Elementary Education	M
English Education	M
Hospitality Management	M
Human Resources Management	M
Mathematics Education	M
Reading Education	M
Science Education	M
Secondary Education	M
Social Work	M
Supply Chain Management	M

NORTH CAROLINA CENTRAL UNIVERSITY

Business Administration and Management—General	M
Counselor Education	M
Education—General	M
Educational Leadership and Administration	M
Educational Media/Instructional Technology	M
Information Studies	M
Law	D
Library Science	M
Physical Education	M
Recreation and Park Management	M
Social Work	M
Special Education	M

NORTH CAROLINA STATE UNIVERSITY

Accounting	M
Adult Education	M,D
Business Administration and Management—General	M
Business Education	M
Community College Education	M,D
Counselor Education	M,D
Curriculum and Instruction	M,D
Education—General	M,D,O
Educational Leadership and Administration	M,D
Educational Measurement and Evaluation	D
Educational Media/Instructional Technology	M,D
Elementary Education	M
Entrepreneurship	M
Human Resources Development	M
Mathematics Education	M,D
Middle School Education	M
Nonprofit Management	M,D,O
Recreation and Park Management	M,D
Science Education	M,D
Social Work	M
Special Education	M
Sports Management	M,D
Supply Chain Management	M
Travel and Tourism	M,D
Vocational and Technical Education	M,D,O

NORTH CENTRAL COLLEGE

Business Administration and Management—General	M
Education—General	M
Educational Leadership and Administration	M
Finance and Banking	M
Human Resources Management	M
Management Strategy and Policy	M

NORTHCENTRAL UNIVERSITY

Business Administration and Management—General	M,D,O
Education—General	M,D,O

NORTH DAKOTA STATE UNIVERSITY

Accounting	M
Agricultural Education	M
Athletic Training and Sports Medicine	M,D
Business Administration and Management—General	M
Counselor Education	M,D
Education—General	M,D,O
Educational Leadership and Administration	M,O
Exercise and Sports Science	M,D
Higher Education	O
Logistics	M,D
Mathematics Education	D
Music Education	M,D
Science Education	D
Transportation Management	M,D

NORTHEASTERN ILLINOIS UNIVERSITY

Accounting	M
Business Administration and Management—General	M
Counselor Education	M
Early Childhood Education	M
Education of the Gifted	M
Education—General	M
Educational Leadership and Administration	M
Elementary Education	M
English as a Second Language	M
English Education	M
Exercise and Sports Science	M
Human Resources Development	M
Mathematics Education	M
Middle School Education	M
Music Education	M
Reading Education	M
Science Education	M
Secondary Education	M
Social Sciences Education	M
Social Work	M
Special Education	M
Urban Education	M

NORTHEASTERN STATE UNIVERSITY

Accounting	M
Business Administration and Management—General	M
Early Childhood Education	M
Education—General	M
Educational Leadership and Administration	M
Educational Media/Instructional Technology	M
Finance and Banking	M
Health Education	M
Kinesiology and Movement Studies	M
Mathematics Education	M
Reading Education	M
Science Education	M
Special Education	M

NORTHEASTERN UNIVERSITY

Accounting	M
Business Administration and Management—General	M
Educational Leadership and Administration	M
Elementary Education	M
Entrepreneurship	M
Exercise and Sports Science	M,D,O
Finance and Banking	M
Higher Education	M
Human Services	M
International Business	M
Law	M,D
Legal and Justice Studies	M,D
Management Information Systems	M,D,O
Nonprofit Management	M
Project Management	M
Special Education	M
Sports Management	M
Taxation	M

NORTHERN ARIZONA UNIVERSITY

Athletic Training and Sports Medicine	M
Business Administration and Management—General	M,O
Community College Education	M,D,O
Counselor Education	M,D,O
Curriculum and Instruction	M,D
Early Childhood Education	M,D,O
Education—General	M,D,O
Educational Leadership and Administration	M,D,O
Educational Media/Instructional Technology	M,O
Educational Psychology	M,D,O
Elementary Education	M,D
English as a Second Language	M,D,O
Foreign Languages Education	M
Foundations and Philosophy of Education	M,D,O
Higher Education	M,D,O
International Business	M
Mathematics Education	M,O
Multilingual and Multicultural Education	M,O
Recreation and Park Management	M,O
Science Education	M
Secondary Education	M,D,O
Special Education	M,O
Student Affairs	M,D,O
Vocational and Technical Education	M,O

NORTHERN ILLINOIS UNIVERSITY

Accounting	M
Adult Education	M,D
Business Administration and Management—General	M
Counselor Education	M,D
Curriculum and Instruction	M,D
Early Childhood Education	M
Education—General	M,D,O
Educational Leadership and Administration	M,D,O
Educational Media/Instructional Technology	M,D
Educational Psychology	M,D,O
Elementary Education	M
Foundations and Philosophy of Education	M,D,O
Higher Education	M,D
Industrial and Manufacturing Management	M
Law	D
Management Information Systems	M
Physical Education	M
Special Education	M
Taxation	M

NORTHERN KENTUCKY UNIVERSITY

Accounting	M,O
Advertising and Public Relations	M,O
Business Administration and Management—General	M,O
Counselor Education	M
Education—General	M,D,O
Educational Leadership and Administration	M,D,O
Law	D
Nonprofit Management	M,O
Organizational Management	M
Social Work	M
Special Education	M,O
Taxation	M,O

NORTHERN MICHIGAN UNIVERSITY

Business Administration and Management—General	M
Curriculum and Instruction	M
Education—General	M
Educational Leadership and Administration	M
English as a Second Language	M,O
Exercise and Sports Science	M
Reading Education	M
Science Education	M
Special Education	M

NORTHERN STATE UNIVERSITY

Counselor Education	M
Curriculum and Instruction	M
Education—General	M
Educational Leadership and Administration	M
Educational Media/Instructional Technology	M
Finance and Banking	M
Music Education	M
Sports Management	M

NORTHERN VERMONT UNIVERSITY–JOHNSON

Counselor Education	M
Curriculum and Instruction	M
Education—General	M
Foundations and Philosophy of Education	M
Special Education	M

NORTHERN VERMONT UNIVERSITY–LYNDON

Counselor Education	M
Curriculum and Instruction	M
Education—General	M
Reading Education	M
Science Education	M
Special Education	M

NORTH GREENVILLE UNIVERSITY

Education—General	M,D
Finance and Banking	M,D

*M—masters degree; D—doctorate; O—other advanced degree; *—Close-Up and/or Display*

Human Resources Management | M,D

NORTH PARK UNIVERSITY
Business Administration and
 Management—General | M
Education—General | M
Nonprofit Management | M

NORTHWEST CHRISTIAN UNIVERSITY
Accounting | M
Business Administration and
 Management—General | M
Counselor Education | M
Education—General | M
Elementary Education | M
English as a Second Language | M
Secondary Education | M
Special Education | M

NORTHWESTERN COLLEGE
Early Childhood Education | M,O
Education—General | M,O
Educational Leadership and
 Administration | M,O

NORTHWESTERN OKLAHOMA STATE UNIVERSITY
Adult Education | M
Counselor Education | M
Curriculum and Instruction | M
Education—General | M
Educational Leadership and
 Administration | M
Elementary Education | M
Reading Education | M
Secondary Education | M

NORTHWESTERN POLYTECHNIC UNIVERSITY
Business Administration and
 Management—General | M,D

NORTHWESTERN STATE UNIVERSITY OF LOUISIANA
Adult Education | M
Counselor Education | M,O
Curriculum and Instruction | M
Early Childhood Education | M
Education—General | M,O
Educational Leadership and
 Administration | M,O
Educational Media/Instructional
 Technology | M,O
Elementary Education | M,O
Health Education | M
Middle School Education | M
Reading Education | M,O
Secondary Education | M,O
Special Education | M,O
Student Affairs | M

NORTHWESTERN UNIVERSITY
Accounting | M,D
Business Administration and
 Management—General | M,D
Business Analytics | M,D
Education—General | M,D
Educational Leadership and
 Administration | M
Educational Media/Instructional
 Technology | M,D
Electronic Commerce | M
Elementary Education | M
Entrepreneurship | M,D
Finance and Banking | M,D
Human Resources Management | M,D
Industrial and Manufacturing
 Management | M,D
International Business | M,D
Kinesiology and Movement Studies | D
Law | M,D
Management Information Systems | M
Management Strategy and Policy | M,D
Marketing | M,D
Music Education | M,D
Organizational Behavior | M
Organizational Management | M,D
Project Management | M
Quality Management | M
Real Estate | M,D
Secondary Education | M
Sports Management | M
Taxation | M,D

NORTHWEST MISSOURI STATE UNIVERSITY
Agricultural Education | M
Business Administration and
 Management—General | M
Business Analytics | M
Early Childhood Education | M,D,O
Education—General | M,D,O
Educational Leadership and
 Administration | M,D,O
Educational Media/Instructional
 Technology | M
Educational Policy | M,D,O
Elementary Education | M,D,O
English as a Second Language | M,D,O
English Education | M,O
Exercise and Sports Science | M
Health Education | M
Higher Education | M,D,O
Human Resources Management | M
Management Information Systems | M
Marketing | M
Mathematics Education | M,D,O
Middle School Education | M,D,O
Physical Education | M
Reading Education | M,D,O
Recreation and Park Management | M
Science Education | M,O
Social Sciences Education | M,O
Special Education | M,D,O

NORTHWEST NAZARENE UNIVERSITY
Business Administration and
 Management—General | M
Counselor Education | M
Curriculum and Instruction | M,D,O
Education—General | M,D,O
Educational Leadership and
 Administration | M,D,O
Social Work | M
Special Education | M,D,O

NORTHWEST UNIVERSITY
Business Administration and
 Management—General | M
Education—General | M
International Business | M
Organizational Management | M
Project Management | M

NORTHWOOD UNIVERSITY, MICHIGAN CAMPUS
Business Administration and
 Management—General | M

NORWICH UNIVERSITY
Business Administration and
 Management—General | M
Finance and Banking | M
Human Resources Management | M
International Business | M
Logistics | M
Management Strategy and Policy | M
Nonprofit Management | M
Organizational Management | M
Project Management | M
Supply Chain Management | M

NOTRE DAME COLLEGE (OH)
Reading Education | M,O
Special Education | M,O

NOTRE DAME DE NAMUR UNIVERSITY
Business Administration and
 Management—General | M
Curriculum and Instruction | M
Education—General | M
Educational Leadership and
 Administration | M
Finance and Banking | M
Special Education | M

NOTRE DAME OF MARYLAND UNIVERSITY
Business Administration and
 Management—General | M
Education—General | M
Educational Leadership and
 Administration | M,D
English as a Second Language | M
Nonprofit Management | M

NOVA SOUTHEASTERN UNIVERSITY
Accounting | M
Business Administration and
 Management—General | M
Business Analytics | M
Business Education | M
Counselor Education | M,D,O
Distance Education Development | M,D,O
Education—General | M,D,O
Educational Media/Instructional
 Technology | M,D,O
Entrepreneurship | M
Finance and Banking | M
Health Education | M,D,O
Health Law | M,D
Human Resources Management | M
International Business | M
Law | M,D
Legal and Justice Studies | M,D
Management Information Systems | M,D
Management Strategy and Policy | M
Marketing | M
Student Affairs | M,D,O
Supply Chain Management | M

NYACK COLLEGE
Business Administration and
 Management—General | M
Counselor Education | M
Elementary Education | M
English as a Second Language | M
Organizational Management | M
Social Work | M
Special Education | M

OAKLAND CITY UNIVERSITY
Business Administration and
 Management—General | M
Curriculum and Instruction | M,D
Education—General | M,D
Educational Leadership and
 Administration | M,D
Elementary Education | M,D
Management Strategy and Policy | M
Organizational Management | M,D
Secondary Education | M,D

OAKLAND UNIVERSITY
Accounting | M,O
Business Administration and
 Management—General | M,O
Early Childhood Education | M,D,O
Education—General | M,D,O
Educational Leadership and
 Administration | M,D,O
Elementary Education | M,O
English as a Second Language | M,O
Entrepreneurship | M,O
Exercise and Sports Science | M,D,O
Finance and Banking | M,O
Higher Education | M,D,O
Human Resources Management | M
Industrial and Manufacturing
 Management | M,O
International Business | M,O
Management Information Systems | M,D,O

Marketing | M,O
Music Education | M,D
Nonprofit Management | M,O
Organizational Management | M,D,O
Reading Education | M,D,O
Secondary Education | M,O
Special Education | M,O

OGLALA LAKOTA COLLEGE
Business Administration and
 Management—General | M
Educational Leadership and
 Administration | M

OHIO CHRISTIAN UNIVERSITY
Accounting | M
Business Administration and
 Management—General | M
Finance and Banking | M
Human Resources Management | M
Marketing | M
Organizational Management | M

OHIO DOMINICAN UNIVERSITY
Accounting | M
Business Administration and
 Management—General | M
Curriculum and Instruction | M
Education—General | M
Educational Leadership and
 Administration | M
English as a Second Language | M
Finance and Banking | M
Management Strategy and Policy | M
Risk Management | M
Sports Management | M

OHIO NORTHERN UNIVERSITY
Accounting | M
Law | M,D

THE OHIO STATE UNIVERSITY
Accounting | M
Actuarial Science | M,D
Agricultural Education | M,D
Art Education | M,D
Business Administration and
 Management—General | M
Education—General | M,D,O
Educational Leadership and
 Administration | M,D,O
Educational Policy | M,D,O
Finance and Banking | M
Human Resources Management | M,D
Kinesiology and Movement Studies | M,D
Law | M,D
Logistics | M
Management Information Systems | M,D
Mathematics Education | M,D
Physical Education | M,D
Social Work | M,D
Special Education | D

THE OHIO STATE UNIVERSITY AT LIMA
Social Work | M

THE OHIO STATE UNIVERSITY AT MANSFIELD
Education—General | M
Social Work | M

THE OHIO STATE UNIVERSITY AT MARION
Education—General | M

THE OHIO STATE UNIVERSITY AT NEWARK
Education—General | M
Social Work | M

OHIO UNIVERSITY
Athletic Training and Sports
 Medicine | M
Business Administration and
 Management—General | M
Computer Education | M,D
Counselor Education | M,D
Curriculum and Instruction | M,D
Education—General | M,D
Educational Leadership and
 Administration | M,D
Educational Measurement and
 Evaluation | M
Educational Media/Instructional
 Technology | M,D
Exercise and Sports Science | M,D
Finance and Banking | M
Higher Education | M,D
Middle School Education | M,O
Music Education | M,O
Physical Education | M
Reading Education | M,D
Recreation and Park Management | M
Secondary Education | M
Social Work | M
Special Education | M
Sports Management | M
Student Affairs | M,D

OHIO VALLEY UNIVERSITY
Curriculum and Instruction | M
Education—General | M

OKLAHOMA BAPTIST UNIVERSITY
Business Administration and
 Management—General | M

OKLAHOMA CHRISTIAN UNIVERSITY
Accounting | M
Business Administration and
 Management—General | M
Finance and Banking | M
Human Resources Management | M
International Business | M
Marketing | M
Nonprofit Management | M
Organizational Management | M
Project Management | M

OKLAHOMA CITY UNIVERSITY
Business Administration and
 Management—General | M
Counselor Education | M
Early Childhood Education | M
Elementary Education | M
English as a Second Language | M
Law | M,D

OKLAHOMA STATE UNIVERSITY
Accounting | M,D
Agricultural Education | M,D
Business Administration and
 Management—General | M
Curriculum and Instruction | M,D
Education—General | M,D,O
Educational Leadership and
 Administration | M,D
Educational Psychology | M,D,O
Entrepreneurship | M,D
Finance and Banking | M,D
Health Education | M,D,O
Higher Education | M,D
Hospitality Management | M
International Business | M,D
Management Information Systems | M,D
Marketing | M,D
Music Education | M
Nonprofit Management | M,D,O
Sustainability Management | M,D,O

OKLAHOMA WESLEYAN UNIVERSITY
Management Strategy and Policy | M

OLD DOMINION UNIVERSITY
Accounting | M
Athletic Training and Sports
 Medicine | M
Business Administration and
 Management—General | M,D
Business Education | M,D
Community College Education | M,D
Counselor Education | M,D,O
Curriculum and Instruction | M,D
Early Childhood Education | M,D
Education—General | M,D,O
Educational Leadership and
 Administration | M,D,O
Educational Measurement and
 Evaluation | D
Educational Media/Instructional
 Technology | M,D,O
Educational Psychology | D
Elementary Education | M,O
English as a Second Language | M
Entrepreneurship | M,O
Exercise and Sports Science | M
Finance and Banking | D
Health Education | M,D
Higher Education | M,D,O
International Business | M
Kinesiology and Movement Studies | M,D
Library Science | M,O
Management Information Systems | M,D
Marketing | M,D
Middle School Education | M,O
Music Education | M
Physical Education | M,D
Reading Education | M,D
Recreation and Park Management | M
Secondary Education | M
Special Education | M,D
Sports Management | M
Supply Chain Management | M
Travel and Tourism | M
Vocational and Technical Education | M,D

OLIVET COLLEGE
Insurance | M

OLIVET NAZARENE UNIVERSITY
Business Administration and
 Management—General | M
Curriculum and Instruction | M
Education—General | M
Educational Leadership and
 Administration | M
Elementary Education | M
Library Science | M
Organizational Management | M
Reading Education | M
Secondary Education | M

OMEGA GRADUATE SCHOOL
Organizational Management | M,D

OPEN UNIVERSITY
Business Administration and
 Management—General | M
Education—General | M

ORAL ROBERTS UNIVERSITY
Accounting | M
Business Administration and
 Management—General | M
Curriculum and Instruction | M,D
Education—General | M,D
Educational Leadership and
 Administration | M,D
Entrepreneurship | M
Finance and Banking | M
Higher Education | M,D
International Business | M
Marketing | M
Nonprofit Management | M
Religious Education | M,D

OREGON STATE UNIVERSITY
Accounting | M,D
Actuarial Science | M,D
Adult Education | M,D
Agricultural Education | M,D
Athletic Training and Sports
 Medicine | M
Business Administration and
 Management—General | M,D
Counselor Education | M,D

Education—General M,D
Educational Leadership and Administration M,D
Educational Policy M,D
Elementary Education M
English Education M
Environmental Education M,D
Finance and Banking M,D
Higher Education M,D
Kinesiology and Movement Studies M,D
Mathematics Education M,D
Music Education M
Science Education M,D
Social Sciences Education M,D
Student Affairs M
Sustainability Management M,D

OREGON STATE UNIVERSITY–CASCADES
Education—General M

OTTAWA UNIVERSITY
Business Administration and Management—General M
Counselor Education M
Curriculum and Instruction M
Early Childhood Education M
Education—General M
Educational Leadership and Administration M
Educational Media/Instructional Technology M
Elementary Education M
Finance and Banking M
Human Resources Development M
Human Resources Management M
Marketing M
Special Education M

OTTERBEIN UNIVERSITY
Business Administration and Management—General M
Education—General M

OUR LADY OF THE LAKE UNIVERSITY
Accounting M
Business Administration and Management—General M
Counselor Education M
Curriculum and Instruction M
Finance and Banking M
Management Information Systems M
Nonprofit Management M
Organizational Management M,D
Science Education M
Social Work M,D

PACE UNIVERSITY
Accounting M,O
Business Administration and Management—General M,D,O
Early Childhood Education M,O
Education—General M,O
Educational Media/Instructional Technology M,O
Electronic Commerce O
Elementary Education M,O
Entrepreneurship M
Environmental Law M,D
Finance and Banking M,D,O
Foreign Languages Education M,O
Human Resources Management M
International Business M,O
Investment Management M,O
Law M,D
Legal and Justice Studies M,D
Management Information Systems M,D,O
Management Strategy and Policy M,O
Marketing M,D,O
Nonprofit Management M
Reading Education M,O
Risk Management M
Social Sciences Education M,O
Special Education M,O
Taxation M

PACIFIC LUTHERAN UNIVERSITY
Accounting M
Business Administration and Management—General M
Curriculum and Instruction M
Education—General M
Finance and Banking M
Marketing Research M

PACIFIC OAKS COLLEGE
Early Childhood Education M
Education—General M
Special Education M

PACIFIC STATES UNIVERSITY
Accounting M,O
Business Administration and Management—General M,O
Finance and Banking M,O
International Business M,O
Management Information Systems M,O
Project Management M,O
Real Estate M,O

PACIFIC UNION COLLEGE
Education—General M
Elementary Education M
Secondary Education M

PACIFIC UNIVERSITY
Athletic Training and Sports Medicine M,D
Business Administration and Management—General M
Early Childhood Education M
Education of the Gifted M
Education—General M
Elementary Education M
English as a Second Language M
Finance and Banking M
Middle School Education M
Science Education M
Secondary Education M
Social Work M
Special Education M

PALM BEACH ATLANTIC UNIVERSITY
Business Administration and Management—General M
Counselor Education M
Education—General M
Organizational Management M
Religious Education M

PARK UNIVERSITY
Business Administration and Management—General M,O
Curriculum and Instruction M,O
Education—General M,O
Educational Leadership and Administration M,O
Finance and Banking M,O
International Business M,O
Management Information Systems M,O
Nonprofit Management M,O
Reading Education M,O
Social Work M,O

PEIRCE COLLEGE
Organizational Management M

PENN STATE ERIE, THE BEHREND COLLEGE
Accounting M
Business Administration and Management—General M
Industrial and Manufacturing Management M
Quality Management M

PENN STATE GREAT VALLEY
Business Administration and Management—General M,O
Entrepreneurship M,O
Finance and Banking M,O
Human Resources Development M,O
Human Resources Management M,O
Sustainability Management M,O

PENN STATE HARRISBURG
Accounting M,O
Adult Education M,D,O
Business Administration and Management—General M,O
Curriculum and Instruction M,D,O
Developmental Education M,D,O
Education—General M,D,O
English as a Second Language M,D,O
Finance and Banking M,D,O
Health Education M,D,O
Human Resources Management M,D,O
Management Information Systems M,O
Nonprofit Management M,D,O
Reading Education M,D,O
Supply Chain Management M,O

PENN STATE UNIVERSITY–DICKINSON LAW
Law M,D

PENN STATE UNIVERSITY PARK
Accounting M,D
Adult Education M,D,O
Agricultural Education M,D,O
Art Education M,D,O
Business Administration and Management—General M,D
Counselor Education M,D,O
Curriculum and Instruction M,D,O
Education—General M,D,O
Educational Leadership and Administration M,D,O
Educational Media/Instructional Technology M,D,O
Educational Policy M,D,O
Educational Psychology M,D,O
English as a Second Language M,D
Entrepreneurship M
Foundations and Philosophy of Education M,D,O
Higher Education M,D,O
Hospitality Management M,D
Human Resources Development M
Human Resources Management M
Kinesiology and Movement Studies M,D,O
Law M,D
Leisure Studies M,D
Management Information Systems M,D
Music Education M,D,O
Organizational Management M,D
Recreation and Park Management M,D
Special Education M,D,O
Travel and Tourism M,D
Vocational and Technical Education M,D,O

PENN STATE YORK
Curriculum and Instruction M,O
Education—General M,O
English as a Second Language M,O

PENNSYLVANIA COLLEGE OF HEALTH SCIENCES
Health Education M

PENSACOLA CHRISTIAN COLLEGE
Business Administration and Management—General M,D,O
Curriculum and Instruction M,D,O
Educational Leadership and Administration M,D,O

PEPPERDINE UNIVERSITY
Accounting M

PERU STATE COLLEGE
Curriculum and Instruction M
Education—General M
Entrepreneurship M
Organizational Management M

PFEIFFER UNIVERSITY
Business Administration and Management—General M
Elementary Education M
Organizational Management M
Religious Education M

PHILADELPHIA COLLEGE OF OSTEOPATHIC MEDICINE
Educational Psychology M,D,O

PHILLIPS GRADUATE UNIVERSITY
Counselor Education M
Organizational Behavior D

PHILLIPS THEOLOGICAL SEMINARY
Business Administration and Management—General M,D
Higher Education M,D
Religious Education M,D
Social Work M,D

PIEDMONT COLLEGE
Art Education M,D,O
Business Administration and Management—General M
Curriculum and Instruction M,D,O
Early Childhood Education M,D,O
Education—General M,D,O
Middle School Education M,D,O
Music Education M,D,O
Secondary Education M,D,O
Special Education M,D,O

PIEDMONT INTERNATIONAL UNIVERSITY
Curriculum and Instruction M,D
Educational Leadership and Administration M,D

PITTSBURG STATE UNIVERSITY
Accounting M
Business Administration and Management—General M
Counselor Education M
Education—General M,O
Educational Leadership and Administration M,O
Educational Media/Instructional Technology M
English as a Second Language M,O
Exercise and Sports Science M
Health Education M
Human Resources Development M
International Business M
Music Education M
Physical Education M
Secondary Education M,O
Special Education M,O
Sports Management M
Vocational and Technical Education M,O

PLYMOUTH STATE UNIVERSITY
Accounting M
Adult Education D
Art Education M
Athletic Training and Sports Medicine M
Business Administration and Management—General M
Counselor Education M
Curriculum and Instruction D
Education—General O
Educational Leadership and Administration M,D,O
English Education M
Health Education M
Higher Education D,O
Mathematics Education M
Music Education M
Social Sciences Education M

POINT LOMA NAZARENE UNIVERSITY
Business Administration and Management—General M
Counselor Education M
Education—General M
Educational Leadership and Administration M
Entrepreneurship M
Exercise and Sports Science M
Kinesiology and Movement Studies M
Organizational Management M
Project Management M
Special Education M
Sports Management M

POINT PARK UNIVERSITY
Adult Education M,D
Business Administration and Management—General M
Business Analytics M
Curriculum and Instruction M,D
Education—General M,D
Educational Leadership and Administration M,D
Elementary Education M,D
Entertainment Management M
International Business M
Management Information Systems M
Middle School Education M,D
Organizational Management M
Secondary Education M,D
Special Education M,D
Sports Management M

POINT UNIVERSITY
Business Administration and Management—General M

POLYTECHNIC UNIVERSITY OF PUERTO RICO
Business Administration and Management—General M
Industrial and Manufacturing Management M
International Business M
Management Information Systems M

POLYTECHNIC UNIVERSITY OF PUERTO RICO, MIAMI CAMPUS
Accounting M
Business Administration and Management—General M
Finance and Banking M
Human Resources Management M
Industrial and Manufacturing Management M
International Business M
Logistics M
Marketing M
Project Management M
Supply Chain Management M

POLYTECHNIC UNIVERSITY OF PUERTO RICO, ORLANDO CAMPUS
Accounting M
Business Administration and Management—General M
Finance and Banking M
Human Resources Management M
Industrial and Manufacturing Management M
International Business M

PONTIFICAL CATHOLIC UNIVERSITY OF PUERTO RICO
Accounting M,O
Business Administration and Management—General M,D,O
Business Education M,D
Counselor Education M
Curriculum and Instruction M,D
Education—General M,D
Educational Leadership and Administration D
Educational Psychology M
English as a Second Language M
Finance and Banking M
Human Resources Management M,O
Human Services M,D
International Business M
Law D
Logistics O
Management Information Systems M,O
Marketing M
Religious Education M
Social Work M
Transportation Management O

PONTIFICIA UNIVERSIDAD CATOLICA MADRE Y MAESTRA
Business Administration and Management—General M
Early Childhood Education M
Entrepreneurship M
Finance and Banking M
Hospitality Management M
Human Resources Management M
Insurance M
International Business M
Law M
Logistics M
Management Strategy and Policy M
Marketing M
Real Estate M
Travel and Tourism M

PORTLAND STATE UNIVERSITY
Business Administration and Management—General M,D,O
Education—General M,D
English as a Second Language M,O
Finance and Banking M
Foreign Languages Education M
Human Resources Management M,D,O
International Business M
Mathematics Education M,D,O
Middle School Education M,D,O
Nonprofit Management M,D,O
Real Estate M,D,O
Science Education M,D,O
Social Sciences Education M
Social Work M,D
Supply Chain Management M

POST UNIVERSITY
Accounting M
Business Administration and Management—General M
Curriculum and Instruction M
Distance Education Development M
Education—General M
Educational Leadership and Administration M
Educational Media/Instructional Technology M
English as a Second Language M
Finance and Banking M
Human Services M
Marketing M
Nonprofit Management M
Project Management M

PRAIRIE VIEW A&M UNIVERSITY
Accounting M
Business Administration and Management—General M
Counselor Education M,D

*M—masters degree; D—doctorate; O—other advanced degree; *—Close-Up and/or Display*

Curriculum and Instruction M
Education—General M,D
Educational Leadership and Administration M,D
Health Education M
Kinesiology and Movement Studies M
Legal and Justice Studies M,D
Management Information Systems M,D

PRATT INSTITUTE
Art Education M,O
Facilities Management M
Information Studies M,O
Library Science M,O
Real Estate M

PRESCOTT COLLEGE
Counselor Education M,D
Early Childhood Education M,D
Education—General M,D
Educational Leadership and Administration M,D
Elementary Education M,D
Environmental Education M,D
Legal and Justice Studies M
Leisure Studies M
Secondary Education M,D
Special Education M,D

PRESIDIO GRADUATE SCHOOL (CA)
Business Administration and Management—General M,O
Sustainability Management M,O

PRINCETON UNIVERSITY
Finance and Banking M

PROVIDENCE COLLEGE
Accounting M
Business Administration and Management—General M
Counselor Education M
Educational Leadership and Administration M
Elementary Education M
Finance and Banking M
International Business M
Marketing M
Mathematics Education M
Reading Education M
Secondary Education M
Special Education M
Urban Education M

PROVIDENCE UNIVERSITY COLLEGE & THEOLOGICAL SEMINARY
English as a Second Language M,D,O
Religious Education M,D,O
Student Affairs M,D,O

PURCHASE COLLEGE, STATE UNIVERSITY OF NEW YORK
Entrepreneurship M

PURDUE UNIVERSITY
Agricultural Education M,D,O
Art Education M,D,O
Aviation Management M
Business Administration and Management—General M,D
Curriculum and Instruction M,D,O
Education—General M,D,O
Educational Leadership and Administration M,D,O
Educational Media/Instructional Technology M,D,O
Elementary Education M,D,O
English Education M,D,O
Exercise and Sports Science M,D
Finance and Banking M
Foreign Languages Education M,D,O
Foundations and Philosophy of Education M,D,O
Health Education M,D
Higher Education M,D,O
Home Economics Education M,D,O
Hospitality Management M,D
Human Resources Management M,D
International Business M
Kinesiology and Movement Studies M,D
Management Information Systems M
Mathematics Education M,D,O
Organizational Behavior D
Physical Education M,D
Reading Education M,D,O
Recreation and Park Management M,D
Science Education M,D,O
Social Sciences Education M,D,O
Sports Management M,D
Travel and Tourism M,D
Vocational and Technical Education M,D,O

PURDUE UNIVERSITY FORT WAYNE
Business Administration and Management—General M
Counselor Education M,O
Education—General M,O
Educational Leadership and Administration M,O
Elementary Education M,O
English as a Second Language M,O
English Education M,O
Facilities Management M
Mathematics Education M,O
Organizational Management M,O
Secondary Education M,O
Special Education M,O

PURDUE UNIVERSITY GLOBAL
Business Administration and Management—General M
Education—General M
Educational Leadership and Administration M
Educational Media/Instructional Technology M
Entrepreneurship M
Finance and Banking M
Higher Education M
Human Resources Management M
International Business M
Law M
Legal and Justice Studies M,O
Logistics M
Management Information Systems M
Marketing M
Mathematics Education M
Organizational Management M
Project Management M
Reading Education M
Science Education M
Secondary Education M
Special Education M
Student Affairs M
Supply Chain Management M

PURDUE UNIVERSITY NORTHWEST
Accounting M
Business Administration and Management—General M
Counselor Education M
Education—General M
Educational Leadership and Administration M
Educational Media/Instructional Technology M
Human Services M
Mathematics Education M
Science Education M
Special Education M

QUEENS COLLEGE OF THE CITY UNIVERSITY OF NEW YORK
Accounting M
Archives/Archival Administration M,O
Art Education M,O
Counselor Education M,O
Early Childhood Education M,O
Education—General M,O
Educational Leadership and Administration M,O
Elementary Education M,O
English as a Second Language M,O
English Education M,O
Exercise and Sports Science M,O
Finance and Banking M
Foreign Languages Education M,O
Information Studies M,O
Library Science M,O
Mathematics Education M,O
Middle School Education M,O
Multilingual and Multicultural Education M,O
Music Education M,O
Physical Education M,O
Reading Education M,O
Risk Management M
Science Education M,O
Secondary Education M,O
Social Sciences Education M,O
Special Education M,O

QUEEN'S UNIVERSITY AT KINGSTON
Business Administration and Management—General M,D
Business Analytics M,D
Education—General M,D
Entrepreneurship M
Exercise and Sports Science M,D
Finance and Banking M,D
Information Studies M,D
International Business M
Law M,D
Legal and Justice Studies M,D
Management Information Systems M,D
Management Strategy and Policy M,D
Marketing M,D
Organizational Behavior M,D
Project Management M

QUEENS UNIVERSITY OF CHARLOTTE
Business Administration and Management—General M
Education—General M
Educational Leadership and Administration M
Elementary Education M
Organizational Management M
Reading Education M

QUINCY UNIVERSITY
Business Administration and Management—General M
Counselor Education M
Curriculum and Instruction M
Education—General M
Educational Leadership and Administration M
English as a Second Language M
Multilingual and Multicultural Education M
Reading Education M
Student Affairs M

QUINNIPIAC UNIVERSITY
Accounting M
Advertising and Public Relations M
Business Administration and Management—General M
Education—General M,O
Educational Leadership and Administration M,O
Educational Media/Instructional Technology M
Elementary Education M
English Education M
Finance and Banking M
Foreign Languages Education M
Law M,D
Mathematics Education M
Organizational Management M
Science Education M
Secondary Education M
Social Sciences Education M
Social Work M
Supply Chain Management M

RADFORD UNIVERSITY
Business Administration and Management—General M
Counselor Education M
Early Childhood Education M
Educational Leadership and Administration M
Management Information Systems M
Mathematics Education M
Reading Education M
Social Work M
Special Education M,O

RAMAPO COLLEGE OF NEW JERSEY
Accounting M
Business Administration and Management—General M
Educational Leadership and Administration M
Educational Media/Instructional Technology M
Social Work M
Special Education M

RANDOLPH COLLEGE
Curriculum and Instruction M
Education—General M
Special Education M

REFORMED THEOLOGICAL SEMINARY–JACKSON CAMPUS
Religious Education M,D,O

REFORMED UNIVERSITY
Business Administration and Management—General M

REGENT'S UNIVERSITY LONDON
Business Administration and Management—General M
Finance and Banking M
Human Resources Management M
International Business M
Management Information Systems M
Marketing M

REGENT UNIVERSITY
Accounting M,D,O
Adult Education M,D,O
Business Administration and Management—General M,D,O
Business Analytics M,D,O
Counselor Education M,D,O
Curriculum and Instruction M,D,O
Distance Education Development M,D,O
Early Childhood Education M,D,O
Education of the Gifted M,D,O
Education—General M,D,O
Educational Leadership and Administration M,D,O
Educational Media/Instructional Technology M,D,O
Educational Psychology M,D,O
Elementary Education M,D,O
English as a Second Language M,D,O
Entrepreneurship M,D,O
Finance and Banking M,D,O
Higher Education M,D,O
Human Resources Development M,D,O
Human Resources Management M,D,O
Human Services M,D,O
Investment Management M,D,O
Law M,D
Legal and Justice Studies M,D
Management Strategy and Policy M,D,O
Marketing M,D,O
Nonprofit Management M,D,O
Organizational Management M,D,O
Reading Education M,D,O
Religious Education M,D,O
Science Education M,D,O
Special Education M,D,O
Student Affairs M,D,O

REGIS COLLEGE (MA)
Education—General M,D
Educational Leadership and Administration M,D
Elementary Education M,D
Higher Education M,D
Special Education M,D

REGIS UNIVERSITY
Accounting M,O
Business Education M,O
Counselor Education M,D,O
Curriculum and Instruction M,O
Education—General M
Educational Leadership and Administration M,O
Elementary Education M,O
Finance and Banking M,O
Human Resources Management M,O
Industrial and Manufacturing Management M,O
Management Information Systems M,O
Management Strategy and Policy M,O
Marketing M,O
Nonprofit Management M,O
Organizational Management M,O
Project Management M,O
Reading Education M,O
Secondary Education M,O
Special Education M,O

REINHARDT UNIVERSITY
Business Administration and Management—General M
Early Childhood Education M
Education—General M

RELAY GRADUATE SCHOOL OF EDUCATION
Education—General M

RENSSELAER AT HARTFORD
Business Administration and Management—General M

RENSSELAER POLYTECHNIC INSTITUTE
Business Administration and Management—General M,D
Business Analytics M
Entrepreneurship M
Supply Chain Management M

RHODE ISLAND COLLEGE
Accounting M,O
Art Education M
Counselor Education M,O
Early Childhood Education M
Education of Students with Severe/Multiple Disabilities M,O
Education—General D
Educational Leadership and Administration M,O
Elementary Education M
English as a Second Language M
English Education M
Finance and Banking M,O
Foreign Languages Education M
Health Education M,O
Legal and Justice Studies M
Mathematics Education M
Music Education M
Physical Education M,O
Reading Education M
Secondary Education M
Social Sciences Education M
Social Work M
Special Education M,O

RHODE ISLAND SCHOOL OF DESIGN
Art Education M

RHODES COLLEGE
Accounting M

RICE UNIVERSITY
Business Administration and Management—General M
Education—General M
Science Education M,D

RICHMONT GRADUATE UNIVERSITY
Counselor Education M

RIDER UNIVERSITY
Accounting M,O
Business Administration and Management—General M
Counselor Education M,O
Early Childhood Education M
Education—General M,O
Elementary Education M
English as a Second Language M
Finance and Banking M
Foreign Languages Education M
Multilingual and Multicultural Education M
Music Education M
Organizational Management M
Secondary Education M
Special Education M,O

RIVIER UNIVERSITY
Business Administration and Management—General M
Counselor Education M,D,O
Curriculum and Instruction M,D,O
Early Childhood Education M,D,O
Education—General M,D,O
Educational Leadership and Administration M,D,O
Elementary Education M,D,O
Foreign Languages Education M
Management Information Systems M
Reading Education M,D,O
Social Sciences Education M
Special Education M,D,O

ROBERT MORRIS UNIVERSITY
Business Administration and Management—General M
Human Resources Management M
Management Information Systems M,D
Organizational Management M,D
Project Management M,D
Taxation M

ROBERT MORRIS UNIVERSITY ILLINOIS
Accounting M
Business Administration and Management—General M
Business Analytics M
Educational Leadership and Administration M
Finance and Banking M
Higher Education M
Human Resources Management M
Management Information Systems M
Sports Management M

ROBERTS WESLEYAN COLLEGE
Business Administration and Management—General M
Counselor Education M,D
Early Childhood Education M
Education—General M
Human Services M
Management Strategy and Policy M
Marketing M
Middle School Education M
Reading Education M
Secondary Education M
Social Work M
Special Education M

ROCHESTER COLLEGE
Religious Education M

ROCHESTER INSTITUTE OF TECHNOLOGY

Accounting	M
Art Education	M
Business Administration and Management—General	M
Entrepreneurship	M
Finance and Banking	M
Hospitality Management	M
Human Resources Development	M
Industrial and Manufacturing Management	M
International Business	M
Management Information Systems	O
Organizational Management	O
Project Management	O
Secondary Education	M
Special Education	M
Sustainability Management	M,D
Travel and Tourism	M
Vocational and Technical Education	O

ROCKFORD UNIVERSITY

Business Administration and Management—General	M
Early Childhood Education	M
Education—General	M
Educational Media/Instructional Technology	M
Elementary Education	M
Reading Education	M
Secondary Education	M
Special Education	M

ROCKHURST UNIVERSITY

Accounting	M,O
Business Administration and Management—General	M,O
Business Analytics	M,O
Education—General	M
Entrepreneurship	M,O
Finance and Banking	M,O
Human Resources Development	M,O
International Business	M,O
Management Strategy and Policy	M,O
Nonprofit Management	M,O

ROCKY MOUNTAIN COLLEGE

Accounting	M
Educational Leadership and Administration	M

ROCKY MOUNTAIN COLLEGE OF ART + DESIGN

Art Education	M

ROGERS STATE UNIVERSITY

Business Administration and Management—General	M

ROGER WILLIAMS UNIVERSITY

Business Administration and Management—General	M
Education—General	M,O
Law	M,D
Middle School Education	M,O
Reading Education	M,O

ROLLINS COLLEGE

Business Administration and Management—General	M
Counselor Education	M
Education—General	M
Elementary Education	M
Entrepreneurship	M
Finance and Banking	M
Human Resources Development	M
Human Resources Management	M
International Business	M

ROOSEVELT UNIVERSITY

Accounting	M
Actuarial Science	M
Business Administration and Management—General	M
Early Childhood Education	M
Education—General	M
Educational Leadership and Administration	M
Elementary Education	M
Hospitality Management	M
Human Resources Development	M
Human Resources Management	M
Marketing	M
Organizational Management	M
Reading Education	M
Real Estate	M
Secondary Education	M
Special Education	M

ROSALIND FRANKLIN UNIVERSITY OF MEDICINE AND SCIENCE

Health Education	M

ROSE-HULMAN INSTITUTE OF TECHNOLOGY

Management Information Systems	M

ROSEMAN UNIVERSITY OF HEALTH SCIENCES

Business Administration and Management—General	M,O

ROSEMONT COLLEGE

Business Administration and Management—General	M
Counselor Education	M
Education—General	M
Elementary Education	M
Human Services	M

ROWAN UNIVERSITY

Advertising and Public Relations	M
Business Administration and Management—General	M,O
Counselor Education	M
Education—General	M,D,O
Educational Leadership and Administration	M,D,O
Educational Media/Instructional Technology	M,O
English as a Second Language	O
English Education	O
Exercise and Sports Science	M
Higher Education	M
Library Science	M,D,O
Marketing	O
Mathematics Education	M,O
Middle School Education	O
Reading Education	M,O
Science Education	M,O
Special Education	M,O

ROYAL MILITARY COLLEGE OF CANADA

Business Administration and Management—General	M

ROYAL ROADS UNIVERSITY

Environmental Education	M,O
Legal and Justice Studies	M,O
Sustainability Management	M,O
Travel and Tourism	M,O

RUTGERS UNIVERSITY–CAMDEN

Business Administration and Management—General	M
Educational Leadership and Administration	M
Educational Policy	M
Law	D
Mathematics Education	M

RUTGERS UNIVERSITY–NEWARK

Accounting	M,D
Business Administration and Management—General	M,D
Finance and Banking	M,D
Health Education	M,D
Human Resources Management	M,D
International Business	D
Law	D
Logistics	M
Management Information Systems	M,D
Marketing	D
Organizational Management	D
Quantitative Analysis	M,O
Real Estate	M
Supply Chain Management	D

RUTGERS UNIVERSITY–NEW BRUNSWICK

Counselor Education	M
Developmental Education	M
Early Childhood Education	M,D
Education—General	M,D
Educational Leadership and Administration	M,D
Educational Measurement and Evaluation	M
Educational Policy	D
Educational Psychology	M,D
Elementary Education	M,D
English as a Second Language	M,D
English Education	M
Foreign Languages Education	M,D
Foundations and Philosophy of Education	M,D
Health Education	M,D,O
Human Resources Management	M,D
Information Studies	M,D
Legal and Justice Studies	M,D
Library Science	D
Mathematics Education	M,D
Multilingual and Multicultural Education	M,D
Music Education	M,D,O
Quality Management	M,D
Reading Education	M,D
Science Education	M,D
Social Sciences Education	M,D
Social Work	M,D
Special Education	M,D
Student Affairs	M

RYERSON UNIVERSITY

Business Administration and Management—General	M

SACRED HEART UNIVERSITY

Accounting	M,O
Business Administration and Management—General	M,O
Education—General	M,O
Educational Leadership and Administration	O
Exercise and Sports Science	M
Finance and Banking	M,D,O
Human Resources Management	M,O
Investment Management	M,D,O
Marketing	M,O
Reading Education	O
Social Work	M

SAGE GRADUATE SCHOOL

Business Administration and Management—General	M
Counselor Education	M,O
Education—General	M,D,O
Educational Leadership and Administration	D
Elementary Education	M
Health Education	M
Organizational Management	M
Reading Education	M
Special Education	M

SAGINAW VALLEY STATE UNIVERSITY

Business Administration and Management—General	M
Early Childhood Education	M
Education—General	M,O
Educational Leadership and Administration	M,O
Educational Media/Instructional Technology	M
Foreign Languages Education	M
Reading Education	M
Social Work	M
Special Education	M

ST. AMBROSE UNIVERSITY

Accounting	M
Business Administration and Management—General	M,D
Early Childhood Education	M
Education—General	M
Educational Leadership and Administration	M
Exercise and Sports Science	M
Human Resources Management	M,D
Organizational Management	M
Social Work	M

ST. AUGUSTINE'S SEMINARY OF TORONTO

Religious Education	M,O

ST. BONAVENTURE UNIVERSITY

Accounting	M
Business Administration and Management—General	M
Counselor Education	M,O
Early Childhood Education	M
Education of the Gifted	M,O
Education—General	M,O
Educational Leadership and Administration	M,O
Marketing	M
Middle School Education	M
Reading Education	M
Secondary Education	M
Special Education	M,O

ST. CATHERINE UNIVERSITY

Business Administration and Management—General	M
Curriculum and Instruction	M
Early Childhood Education	M
Education—General	M,O
Information Studies	M
Library Science	M
Marketing	M
Organizational Management	M
Social Work	M,D

ST. CLOUD STATE UNIVERSITY

Business Administration and Management—General	M
Counselor Education	M
Education—General	M,D,O
Educational Leadership and Administration	M,D
Educational Media/Instructional Technology	M,O
Higher Education	D
Human Services	M
Social Work	M
Special Education	M,O
Student Affairs	M

ST. EDWARD'S UNIVERSITY

Accounting	M
Education—General	M,O
Organizational Management	M
Student Affairs	M

ST. FRANCIS COLLEGE

Accounting	M

SAINT FRANCIS UNIVERSITY

Business Administration and Management—General	M
Education—General	M
Educational Leadership and Administration	M
Health Education	M
Human Resources Management	M
Reading Education	M

ST. FRANCIS XAVIER UNIVERSITY

Adult Education	M
Curriculum and Instruction	M
Education—General	M
Educational Leadership and Administration	M

ST. JOHN FISHER COLLEGE

Business Administration and Management—General	M
Education—General	M,D,O
Educational Leadership and Administration	M,D
Educational Media/Instructional Technology	M
Elementary Education	M,O
English Education	M
Foreign Languages Education	M
Mathematics Education	M
Middle School Education	M
Reading Education	M
Science Education	M
Social Sciences Education	M
Special Education	M,O

ST. JOHN'S UNIVERSITY (NY)

Accounting	M
Actuarial Science	M
Business Administration and Management—General	M
Business Analytics	M
Counselor Education	M,O
Curriculum and Instruction	D
Early Childhood Education	M,D,O
Education of the Gifted	D,O
Education—General	M,D,O
Educational Leadership and Administration	M,D,O
Elementary Education	M
English as a Second Language	M,O
Finance and Banking	M
Information Studies	M,O
Insurance	M
International and Comparative Education	D
International Business	M
Law	D
Legal and Justice Studies	M
Library Science	M,O
Management Information Systems	M
Management Strategy and Policy	M
Marketing	M
Mathematics Education	D
Multilingual and Multicultural Education	M,O
Reading Education	M,D,O
Risk Management	M
Science Education	D
Secondary Education	M
Special Education	M,O
Sports Management	M
Taxation	M

ST. JOSEPH'S COLLEGE, LONG ISLAND CAMPUS

Accounting	M
Business Administration and Management—General	M
Human Resources Management	M
Human Services	M
Organizational Management	M
Special Education	M

ST. JOSEPH'S COLLEGE, NEW YORK

Accounting	M
Business Administration and Management—General	M
Education—General	M
Educational Leadership and Administration	M
Human Resources Management	M
Human Services	M
Organizational Management	M
Reading Education	M
Special Education	M

SAINT JOSEPH'S COLLEGE OF MAINE

Accounting	M
Adult Education	M
Business Administration and Management—General	M
Education—General	M
Educational Leadership and Administration	M
Health Education	M

SAINT JOSEPH'S UNIVERSITY

Accounting	M,O
Business Administration and Management—General	M,O
Business Analytics	M
Curriculum and Instruction	M,D,O
Early Childhood Education	M,D,O
Education—General	M,D,O
Educational Leadership and Administration	M,D,O
Elementary Education	M,D,O
Finance and Banking	M,O
Human Resources Management	M
International Business	M,O
Law	M,O
Marketing	M,O
Middle School Education	M,D,O
Reading Education	M,D,O
Secondary Education	M,D,O
Special Education	M,D,O

SAINT LEO UNIVERSITY

Accounting	M,D
Agricultural Education	M,D
Business Administration and Management—General	M,D
Education—General	M,D,O
Educational Leadership and Administration	M,D,O
Human Resources Management	M,D
Human Services	M
Legal and Justice Studies	M,D
Marketing Research	M,D
Marketing	M,D
Social Work	M

SAINT LOUIS UNIVERSITY

Accounting	M
Athletic Training and Sports Medicine	M,D
Business Administration and Management—General	M
Curriculum and Instruction	M,D
Education—General	M,D
Educational Leadership and Administration	M,D,O
Finance and Banking	M
Foundations and Philosophy of Education	M,D
Higher Education	M,D,O
International Business	M,D
Law	M,D
Social Work	M,D
Special Education	M,D
Student Affairs	M,D,O

*M—masters degree; D—doctorate; O—other advanced degree; *—Close-Up and/or Display*

SAINT MARTIN'S UNIVERSITY
Business Administration and
  Management—General — M
Education—General — M

SAINT MARY-OF-THE-WOODS COLLEGE
Management Strategy and Policy — M
Nonprofit Management — M
Organizational Management — M

SAINT MARY'S COLLEGE OF CALIFORNIA
Accounting — M
Business Administration and
  Management—General — M
Business Analytics — M
Counselor Education — M,O
Early Childhood Education — M
Education—General — M,D,O
Educational Leadership and
  Administration — M,D,O
Exercise and Sports Science — M
Finance and Banking — M
Investment Management — M
Kinesiology and Movement Studies — M
Organizational Management — M
Special Education — M
Sports Management — M

ST. MARY'S COLLEGE OF MARYLAND
Education—General — M

SAINT MARY'S UNIVERSITY (CANADA)
Business Administration and
  Management—General — M,D

ST. MARY'S UNIVERSITY (UNITED STATES)
Business Administration and
  Management—General — M
Counselor Education — D
Education—General — M
Educational Leadership and
  Administration — M
Environmental Law — M
Health Law — M
Law — M,D
Legal and Justice Studies — M

SAINT MARY'S UNIVERSITY OF MINNESOTA
Accounting — M
Business Administration and
  Management—General — M,D
Education—General — M,O
Educational Leadership and
  Administration — M,D,O
Educational Media/Instructional
  Technology — M
Elementary Education — M
Human Resources Management — M
Organizational Management — M
Project Management — M,O
Reading Education — M
Religious Education — M
Secondary Education — M
Special Education — M,O

SAINT MICHAEL'S COLLEGE
Art Education — M,O
Education—General — M,O
Educational Leadership and
  Administration — M,O
English as a Second Language — M,O
Reading Education — M,O
Special Education — M,O

ST. NORBERT COLLEGE
Business Administration and
  Management—General — M
Supply Chain Management — M

SAINT PETER'S UNIVERSITY
Accounting — M
Business Administration and
  Management—General — M
Counselor Education — M,O
Education—General — M,D,O
Educational Leadership and
  Administration — M,D
Elementary Education — M,O
Finance and Banking — M
Higher Education — M,D
Human Resources Management — M
International Business — M
Management Information Systems — M
Marketing — M
Mathematics Education — M,D,O
Middle School Education — M,O
Reading Education — M
Risk Management — M
Secondary Education — M,O
Special Education — M,O

SAINTS CYRIL AND METHODIUS SEMINARY
Religious Education — M

ST. THOMAS AQUINAS COLLEGE
Business Administration and
  Management—General — M
Education—General — M,O
Educational Leadership and
  Administration — M,O
Elementary Education — M,O
Finance and Banking — M
Marketing — M
Middle School Education — M,O
Reading Education — M,O
Secondary Education — M,O
Special Education — M,O

ST. THOMAS UNIVERSITY
Accounting — M,O
Business Administration and
  Management—General — M,O
Counselor Education — M

Education of the Gifted — M,D,O
Education—General — M,D,O
Educational Leadership and
  Administration — M,D,O
Educational Media/Instructional
  Technology — M,D,O
Elementary Education — M,D,O
English as a Second Language — M,D,O
Human Resources Management — M,O
International Business — M,O
Law — M,D
Reading Education — M,D,O
Special Education — M,D,O
Sports Management — M,O
Taxation — M,D

SAINT VINCENT COLLEGE
Business Administration and
  Management—General — M
Curriculum and Instruction — M
Education—General — M
Educational Leadership and
  Administration — M
Educational Media/Instructional
  Technology — M
Special Education — M

SAINT XAVIER UNIVERSITY
Business Administration and
  Management—General — M,O
Counselor Education — M
Curriculum and Instruction — M
Early Childhood Education — M
Education—General — M
Educational Leadership and
  Administration — M
Educational Media/Instructional
  Technology — M
Elementary Education — M
English as a Second Language — M
Finance and Banking — M,O
Foreign Languages Education — M
Marketing — M,O
Music Education — M
Project Management — M,O
Reading Education — M
Science Education — M
Secondary Education — M
Special Education — M

SALEM COLLEGE
Art Education — M
Counselor Education — M
Education—General — M
Elementary Education — M
English as a Second Language — M
Middle School Education — M
Reading Education — M
Secondary Education — M
Special Education — M

SALEM INTERNATIONAL UNIVERSITY
Business Administration and
  Management—General — M
Curriculum and Instruction — M
Education—General — M
Educational Leadership and
  Administration — M
International Business — M

SALEM STATE UNIVERSITY
Art Education — M
Business Administration and
  Management—General — M
Counselor Education — M
Early Childhood Education — M
Educational Leadership and
  Administration — M
Educational Media/Instructional
  Technology — M
Elementary Education — M
English as a Second Language — M
Higher Education — M
Mathematics Education — M
Middle School Education — M
Physical Education — M
Reading Education — M
Science Education — M
Secondary Education — M
Social Work — M
Special Education — M

SALISBURY UNIVERSITY
Athletic Training and Sports
  Medicine — M
Business Administration and
  Management—General — M
Curriculum and Instruction — M
Educational Leadership and
  Administration — M
Mathematics Education — M
Middle School Education — M
Reading Education — M,D
Secondary Education — M
Social Work — M

SALUS UNIVERSITY
Special Education — M,O

SALVE REGINA UNIVERSITY
Business Administration and
  Management—General — M,O
Business Education — M,O
Entrepreneurship — M
Human Resources Management — M,O
Management Strategy and Policy — M,O
Nonprofit Management — M,O
Organizational Management — M,O

SAMFORD UNIVERSITY
Accounting — M
Athletic Training and Sports
  Medicine — M,D
Business Administration and
  Management—General — M
Education of the Gifted — M,D,O
Education—General — M,D,O

Educational Leadership and
  Administration — M,D,O
Educational Media/Instructional
  Technology — M,D,O
Elementary Education — M,D,O
Entrepreneurship — M
Finance and Banking — M
Law — M,D
Marketing — M
Music Education — M
Secondary Education — M,D,O
Social Work — M
Special Education — M,D,O

SAM HOUSTON STATE UNIVERSITY
Accounting — M
Business Administration and
  Management—General — M
Counselor Education — M,D
Curriculum and Instruction — M,D
Developmental Education — M,D
Education—General — M,D
Educational Leadership and
  Administration — M,D
Finance and Banking — M
Higher Education — M,D
Kinesiology and Movement Studies — M
Library Science — M
Project Management — M
Reading Education — M,D
Special Education — M
Sports Management — M

SAN DIEGO CHRISTIAN COLLEGE
Education—General — M
Organizational Management — M

SAN DIEGO STATE UNIVERSITY
Accounting — M
Advertising and Public Relations — M
Business Administration and
  Management—General — M
Counselor Education — M
Curriculum and Instruction — M
Education—General — M,D
Educational Leadership and
  Administration — M
Educational Media/Instructional
  Technology — M,D
Elementary Education — M
English as a Second Language — M,O
Entrepreneurship — M
Exercise and Sports Science — M
Finance and Banking — M
Higher Education — M
Hospitality Management — M
Human Resources Management — M
Kinesiology and Movement Studies — M
Management Information Systems — M
Marketing — M
Mathematics Education — M,D
Multilingual and Multicultural
  Education — M,D
Music Education — M
Reading Education — M
Science Education — M,D
Secondary Education — M
Social Work — M
Special Education — M
Sports Management — M
Travel and Tourism — M

SAN FRANCISCO CONSERVATORY OF MUSIC
Music Education — M,O

SAN FRANCISCO STATE UNIVERSITY
Accounting — M
Adult Education — M
Business Administration and
  Management—General — M
Early Childhood Education — M,D,O
Education—General — M,D,O
Educational Leadership and
  Administration — M,D,O
Educational Media/Instructional
  Technology — M
Elementary Education — M
English as a Second Language — M
English Education — M,O
Entrepreneurship — M
Finance and Banking — M
Health Education — M
Hospitality Management — M
Industrial and Manufacturing
  Management — M
International Business — M
Kinesiology and Movement Studies — M
Legal and Justice Studies — M
Leisure Studies — M
Management Information Systems — M
Marketing — M
Mathematics Education — M,O
Music Education — M
Nonprofit Management — M
Quantitative Analysis — M
Reading Education — M,O
Recreation and Park Management — M
Secondary Education — M,O
Social Work — M
Special Education — M,D,O
Sustainability Management — M
Travel and Tourism — M

SAN IGNACIO UNIVERSITY
Business Administration and
  Management—General — M
Early Childhood Education — M
Education—General — M
Educational Leadership and
  Administration — M
Hospitality Management — M
Human Resources Management — M
International Business — M
Marketing — M
Special Education — M

Travel and Tourism — M

SAN JOAQUIN COLLEGE OF LAW
Law — D

SAN JOSE STATE UNIVERSITY
Counselor Education — M
Curriculum and Instruction — M,O
Educational Leadership and
  Administration — M,D
Elementary Education — M,O
English as a Second Language — M,O
Higher Education — M,D
Kinesiology and Movement Studies — M
Quality Management — M
Reading Education — M,O
Special Education — M
Student Affairs — M

THE SANTA BARBARA AND VENTURA COLLEGES OF LAW–SANTA BARBARA
Law — M,D
Legal and Justice Studies — M,D

THE SANTA BARBARA AND VENTURA COLLEGES OF LAW–VENTURA
Law — M,D
Legal and Justice Studies — M,D

SANTA CLARA UNIVERSITY
Business Administration and
  Management—General — M
Business Analytics — M
Counselor Education — M,O
Education—General — M,O
Educational Leadership and
  Administration — M,O
Finance and Banking — M
Intellectual Property Law — M,D,O
Law — M,D,O
Management Information Systems — M
Supply Chain Management — M

SARAH LAWRENCE COLLEGE
Education—General — M
Kinesiology and Movement Studies — M

SAVANNAH COLLEGE OF ART AND DESIGN
Advertising and Public Relations — M
Travel and Tourism — M

SAVANNAH STATE UNIVERSITY
Business Administration and
  Management—General — M
Human Resources Management — M
Social Work — M

SAYBROOK UNIVERSITY
Organizational Behavior — M,D
Organizational Management — M,D

SCHILLER INTERNATIONAL UNIVERSITY (GERMANY)
Business Administration and
  Management—General — M
International Business — M
Management Information Systems — M

SCHILLER INTERNATIONAL UNIVERSITY
Business Administration and
  Management—General — M
International Business — M

SCHILLER INTERNATIONAL UNIVERSITY (SPAIN)
Business Administration and
  Management—General — M
International Business — M

SCHILLER INTERNATIONAL UNIVERSITY (UNITED STATES)
Business Administration and
  Management—General — M
Finance and Banking — M
Hospitality Management — M
International Business — M
Management Information Systems — M
Travel and Tourism — M

SCHOOL OF VISUAL ARTS (NY)
Art Education — M

SCHREINER UNIVERSITY
Business Administration and
  Management—General — M
Education—General — M,O
Educational Leadership and
  Administration — M,O

SEATTLE PACIFIC UNIVERSITY
Business Administration and
  Management—General — M
Counselor Education — M,D,O
Education—General — D
Educational Leadership and
  Administration — M,D,O
Educational Media/Instructional
  Technology — M
English as a Second Language — M
Human Resources Management — M
Management Information Systems — M
Mathematics Education — M
Reading Education — M
Science Education — M
Secondary Education — M
Sustainability Management — M

SEATTLE UNIVERSITY
Accounting — M
Adult Education — M,O
Business Administration and
  Management—General — M,O
Business Analytics — M
Counselor Education — M,O
Education—General — M,D,O
Educational Leadership and
  Administration — M,D,O

English as a Second Language — M,O
Finance and Banking — M,O
Health Law — M,D
Law — M,D
Organizational Management — M,O
Social Work — M
Special Education — M,O
Sports Management — M

SELMA UNIVERSITY
Religious Education — M

SETON HALL UNIVERSITY
Accounting — M,O
Advertising and Public Relations — M
Athletic Training and Sports
 Medicine — M
Business Administration and
 Management—General — M,O
Counselor Education — M,D
Education—General — M,D,O
Educational Leadership and
 Administration — D,O
Educational Measurement and
 Evaluation — M,D,O
Educational Media/Instructional
 Technology — M
Entrepreneurship — M,O
Finance and Banking — M,O
Health Law — M,D
Higher Education — D
International Business — M,O
Law — M,O
Marketing — M,D
Nonprofit Management — M,O
Social Work — M
Special Education — M
Sports Management — M,O
Student Affairs — M
Supply Chain Management — M,O

SETON HILL UNIVERSITY
Accounting — M
Business Administration and
 Management—General — M
Educational Media/Instructional
 Technology — M
Elementary Education — M
Entrepreneurship — M
Middle School Education — M
Special Education — M

SHASTA BIBLE COLLEGE
Educational Leadership and
 Administration — M
Religious Education — M

SHAWNEE STATE UNIVERSITY
Curriculum and Instruction — M
Education—General — M

SHAW UNIVERSITY
Curriculum and Instruction — M

SHENANDOAH UNIVERSITY
Athletic Training and Sports
 Medicine — M,D,O
Business Administration and
 Management—General — M,O
Early Childhood Education — M,D,O
Education—General — M,D,O

SHEPHERD UNIVERSITY (WV)
Curriculum and Instruction — M

**SHIPPENSBURG UNIVERSITY OF
PENNSYLVANIA**
Business Administration and
 Management—General — M,D,O
Business Analytics — M,D,O
Counselor Education — M,D
Curriculum and Instruction — M
Early Childhood Education — M
Education—General — M,D
Educational Leadership and
 Administration — M,D
Elementary Education — M
Finance and Banking — M,D,O
Foreign Languages Education — M
Logistics — M,D,O
Management Information Systems — M,D,O
Mathematics Education — M
Middle School Education — M
Organizational Management — M
Reading Education — M
Science Education — M
Social Work — M
Special Education — M,D
Student Affairs — M,D
Supply Chain Management — M,D,O

SHORTER UNIVERSITY
Accounting — M
Business Administration and
 Management—General — M

SIENA COLLEGE
Accounting — M
Business Administration and
 Management—General — M

SIENA HEIGHTS UNIVERSITY
Early Childhood Education — M,O
Education—General — M,O
Educational Leadership and
 Administration — M,O
Elementary Education — M,O
Higher Education — M,O
Organizational Management — M,O
Reading Education — M,O
Secondary Education — M,O
Special Education — M,O

SIERRA NEVADA COLLEGE
Education—General — M

Educational Leadership and
 Administration — M
Elementary Education — M
Secondary Education — M

**SILVER LAKE COLLEGE OF THE HOLY
FAMILY**
Business Administration and
 Management—General — M
Education—General — M
Educational Leadership and
 Administration — M

SIMMONS UNIVERSITY
Business Administration and
 Management—General — M
Education of Students with
 Severe/Multiple Disabilities — M,D,O
Elementary Education — M,D,O
Social Work — M,D
Special Education — M,D,O

SIMON FRASER UNIVERSITY
Actuarial Science — M,D
Art Education — M,D
Business Administration and
 Management—General — M,D,O
Counselor Education — M
Curriculum and Instruction — M,D
Education—General — M,D,O
Educational Leadership and
 Administration — M,D
Educational Media/Instructional
 Technology — M,D
Educational Psychology — M,D
English as a Second Language — M,D
English Education — M,D
Finance and Banking — M,D,O
Foundations and Philosophy of
 Education — M,D
Kinesiology and Movement Studies — M,D
Legal and Justice Studies — M,D
Mathematics Education — M,D
Reading Education — D

SIMPSON COLLEGE
Education—General — M
Secondary Education — M

SIMPSON UNIVERSITY
Curriculum and Instruction — M
Education—General — M
Educational Leadership and
 Administration — M
Organizational Management — M

SINTE GLESKA UNIVERSITY
Education—General — M
Elementary Education — M

SIT GRADUATE INSTITUTE
Business Administration and
 Management—General — M
Educational Leadership and
 Administration — M
English as a Second Language — M
Entrepreneurship — M
International and Comparative
 Education — M
International Business — M
Organizational Management — M
Sustainability Management — M

SITTING BULL COLLEGE
Curriculum and Instruction — M

**SLIPPERY ROCK UNIVERSITY OF
PENNSYLVANIA**
Accounting — M
Business Administration and
 Management—General — M
Counselor Education — M
Education—General — M,D
Educational Leadership and
 Administration — M,D
Educational Media/Instructional
 Technology — M,D
Elementary Education — M
English as a Second Language — M
English Education — M
Environmental Education — M
Finance and Banking — M
Marketing — M
Mathematics Education — M
Physical Education — M
Reading Education — M
Recreation and Park Management — M
Science Education — M
Secondary Education — M
Social Sciences Education — M
Special Education — M,D
Student Affairs — M

SMITH COLLEGE
Education—General — M
Elementary Education — M
English Education — M
Exercise and Sports Science — M
Mathematics Education — M
Middle School Education — M
Science Education — M
Secondary Education — M
Social Sciences Education — M
Social Work — M,D

SOKA UNIVERSITY OF AMERICA
Educational Leadership and
 Administration — M

SONOMA STATE UNIVERSITY
Business Administration and
 Management—General — M
Curriculum and Instruction — M,O
Early Childhood Education — M,O
Education—General — M,O

Educational Leadership and
 Administration — M,O
Exercise and Sports Science — M
Kinesiology and Movement Studies — M
Reading Education — M
Special Education — M,O
Sports Management — M

SOUTH CAROLINA STATE UNIVERSITY
Business Administration and
 Management—General — M
Business Education — M
Counselor Education — M
Early Childhood Education — M
Education—General — M
Elementary Education — M
English Education — M
Entrepreneurship — M
Home Economics Education — M
Human Services — M
Mathematics Education — M
Science Education — M
Secondary Education — M
Social Sciences Education — M
Special Education — M
Vocational and Technical Education — M

SOUTH DAKOTA STATE UNIVERSITY
Agricultural Education — M
Athletic Training and Sports
 Medicine — M,D
Counselor Education — M
Curriculum and Instruction — M
Education—General — M,D
Educational Leadership and
 Administration — M
Exercise and Sports Science — M,D
Human Resources Development — M
Recreation and Park Management — M,D

**SOUTHEASTERN BAPTIST
THEOLOGICAL SEMINARY**
Religious Education — M,D

**SOUTHEASTERN LOUISIANA
UNIVERSITY**
Advertising and Public Relations — M
Business Administration and
 Management—General — M
Counselor Education — M
Curriculum and Instruction — M
Education—General — M,D
Educational Leadership and
 Administration — M,D
Elementary Education — M
English Education — M
Health Education — M
Kinesiology and Movement Studies — M
Marketing — M
Reading Education — M
Special Education — M
Sustainability Management — M

**SOUTHEASTERN OKLAHOMA STATE
UNIVERSITY**
Aviation Management — M
Business Administration and
 Management—General — M
Counselor Education — M
Education—General — M
Educational Leadership and
 Administration — M
Management Information Systems — M
Mathematics Education — M
Reading Education — M

SOUTHEASTERN UNIVERSITY (FL)
Business Administration and
 Management—General — M,D
Counselor Education — M
Curriculum and Instruction — M,D
Education of the Gifted — M,D
Education—General — M,D
Educational Leadership and
 Administration — M,D
Elementary Education — M,D
English as a Second Language — M,D
Entrepreneurship — M,D
Human Services — M
International Business — M,D
Kinesiology and Movement Studies — M,D
Management Strategy and Policy — M,D
Organizational Management — M,D
Reading Education — M,D
Social Work — M
Sports Management — M,D

**SOUTHEAST MISSOURI STATE
UNIVERSITY**
Accounting — M
Business Administration and
 Management—General — M
Counselor Education — M,O
Educational Leadership and
 Administration — M,D,O
Elementary Education — M,D,O
English as a Second Language — M
Entrepreneurship — M
Exercise and Sports Science — M
Finance and Banking — M
Higher Education — M,D,O
Leisure Studies — M
Middle School Education — M
Secondary Education — M,D,O
Special Education — M
Sports Management — M

SOUTHERN ADVENTIST UNIVERSITY
Accounting — M
Business Administration and
 Management—General — M
Counselor Education — M
Education—General — M

Educational Leadership and
 Administration — M
Finance and Banking — M
Marketing — M
Reading Education — M
Religious Education — M
Social Work — M

**SOUTHERN ARKANSAS UNIVERSITY–
MAGNOLIA**
Adult Education — M
Business Administration and
 Management—General — M
Counselor Education — M
Curriculum and Instruction — M
Education of the Gifted — M
Education—General — M
Educational Leadership and
 Administration — M
Higher Education — M
Kinesiology and Movement Studies — M
Library Science — M
Organizational Management — M
Student Affairs — M
Supply Chain Management — M

**SOUTHERN CONNECTICUT STATE
UNIVERSITY**
Art Education — M
Business Administration and
 Management—General — M
Counselor Education — M,O
Education—General — M,D,O
Educational Leadership and
 Administration — M,D,O
Educational Measurement and
 Evaluation — M,D,O
Elementary Education — M,O
English as a Second Language — M
Environmental Education — M,O
Exercise and Sports Science — M
Foreign Languages Education — M
Health Education — M
Information Studies — M,O
Leisure Studies — M
Library Science — M,O
Multilingual and Multicultural
 Education — M
Physical Education — M
Reading Education — M,O
Recreation and Park Management — M
Science Education — M,O
Social Work — M
Special Education — M

SOUTHERN EVANGELICAL SEMINARY
Religious Education — M,D,O

**SOUTHERN ILLINOIS UNIVERSITY
CARBONDALE**
Accounting — M,D
Business Administration and
 Management—General — M,D
Curriculum and Instruction — M,D
Education—General — M,D
Educational Leadership and
 Administration — M,D
Educational Psychology — M,D
English as a Second Language — M
Health Education — M,D
Health Law — M
Higher Education — M
Kinesiology and Movement Studies — M
Law — M
Legal and Justice Studies — M
Physical Education — M
Recreation and Park Management — M
Social Work — M
Special Education — M,D
Vocational and Technical Education — M,D

**SOUTHERN ILLINOIS UNIVERSITY
EDWARDSVILLE**
Accounting — M
Advertising and Public Relations — M
Business Administration and
 Management—General — M
Business Analytics — M
Curriculum and Instruction — M
Education—General — M,D,O
Educational Leadership and
 Administration — M,D,O
Educational Media/Instructional
 Technology — M,O
English as a Second Language — M,O
English Education — M,O
Exercise and Sports Science — M
Finance and Banking — M
Foundations and Philosophy of
 Education — M
Health Education — M,D,O
Higher Education — M
Kinesiology and Movement Studies — M
Management Information Systems — M
Marketing Research — M
Mathematics Education — M,O
Music Education — M,O
Physical Education — M
Project Management — M
Reading Education — M,O
Social Work — M
Special Education — M,O
Student Affairs — M
Taxation — M

SOUTHERN METHODIST UNIVERSITY
Accounting — M
Advertising and Public Relations — M
Business Administration and
 Management—General — M
Business Analytics — M
Counselor Education — M,O

- Education of the Gifted M,D
- Education—General M,D
- Educational Leadership and Administration M,D
- English as a Second Language M,D
- Entrepreneurship M
- Finance and Banking M
- Higher Education M,D
- Law M,D
- Management Information Systems M
- Management Strategy and Policy M
- Marketing M
- Multilingual and Multicultural Education M,D
- Music Education M
- Reading Education M,D
- Real Estate M
- Special Education M,D
- Sports Management M,D
- Taxation M,D

SOUTHERN NAZARENE UNIVERSITY
- Business Administration and Management—General M
- Sports Management M

SOUTHERN NEW HAMPSHIRE UNIVERSITY
- Accounting M,D,O
- Advertising and Public Relations M,D,O
- Business Administration and Management—General M,D,O
- Business Analytics M,D,O
- Curriculum and Instruction M,D,O
- Early Childhood Education M,D,O
- Education—General M,D,O
- Educational Leadership and Administration M,D,O
- Educational Media/Instructional Technology M,D,O
- Elementary Education M,D,O
- English as a Second Language M,D,O
- Entertainment Management M,D,O
- Entrepreneurship M,D,O
- Finance and Banking M,D,O
- Higher Education M,D,O
- Human Resources Management M,D,O
- Industrial and Manufacturing Management M,D,O
- International Business M,D,O
- Investment Management M,D,O
- Legal and Justice Studies M,D,O
- Management Information Systems M,D,O
- Marketing M,D,O
- Nonprofit Management M,D,O
- Organizational Management M,D,O
- Project Management M,D,O
- Quality Management M,D,O
- Quantitative Analysis M,D,O
- Reading Education M,D,O
- Special Education M,D,O
- Sports Management M,D,O
- Supply Chain Management M,D,O
- Sustainability Management M,D,O
- Taxation M,D,O

SOUTHERN OREGON UNIVERSITY
- Accounting M,O
- Business Administration and Management—General M,O
- Early Childhood Education M
- Education—General M
- Educational Leadership and Administration M
- Elementary Education M
- Environmental Education M
- Foreign Languages Education M
- International Business M,O
- Reading Education M
- Secondary Education M
- Special Education M

SOUTHERN STATES UNIVERSITY
- Business Administration and Management—General M

SOUTHERN UNIVERSITY AND AGRICULTURAL AND MECHANICAL COLLEGE
- Business Administration and Management—General M
- Counselor Education M
- Education—General M,D
- Educational Leadership and Administration M
- Educational Media/Instructional Technology M
- Elementary Education M
- Law D
- Mathematics Education D
- Recreation and Park Management M
- Science Education D
- Secondary Education M

SOUTHERN UNIVERSITY AT NEW ORLEANS
- Management Information Systems M
- Social Work M

SOUTHERN UTAH UNIVERSITY
- Accounting M
- Business Administration and Management—General M
- Education—General M,O
- Exercise and Sports Science M

SOUTHERN WESLEYAN UNIVERSITY
- Business Administration and Management—General M
- Education—General M

SOUTH TEXAS COLLEGE OF LAW HOUSTON
- Law D

SOUTH UNIVERSITY (AL)
- Business Administration and Management—General M
- Management Information Systems M

SOUTH UNIVERSITY
- Business Administration and Management—General M
- Management Information Systems M

SOUTH UNIVERSITY
- Business Administration and Management—General M
- Management Information Systems M

SOUTH UNIVERSITY (GA)
- Business Administration and Management—General M
- Entrepreneurship M
- Hospitality Management M
- Organizational Management M
- Sustainability Management M

SOUTH UNIVERSITY (SC)
- Business Administration and Management—General M
- Organizational Management M

SOUTH UNIVERSITY (TX)
- Business Administration and Management—General M
- Management Information Systems M

SOUTH UNIVERSITY
- Business Administration and Management—General M

SOUTH UNIVERSITY
- Business Administration and Management—General M
- Management Information Systems M
- Organizational Management M

SOUTHWEST BAPTIST UNIVERSITY
- Business Administration and Management—General M
- Education—General M,O
- Educational Leadership and Administration M,O

SOUTHWESTERN ADVENTIST UNIVERSITY
- Accounting M
- Business Administration and Management—General M
- Curriculum and Instruction M
- Education—General M
- Educational Leadership and Administration M
- Finance and Banking M
- Reading Education M

SOUTHWESTERN ASSEMBLIES OF GOD UNIVERSITY
- Curriculum and Instruction M
- Education—General M
- Educational Leadership and Administration M
- Religious Education M
- Secondary Education M

SOUTHWESTERN BAPTIST THEOLOGICAL SEMINARY
- Religious Education M,D

SOUTHWESTERN COLLEGE (KS)
- Business Administration and Management—General M
- Curriculum and Instruction M,D
- Early Childhood Education M,D
- Education—General M,D
- Educational Leadership and Administration M,D
- Elementary Education M,D
- Higher Education M,D
- Special Education M,D

SOUTHWESTERN LAW SCHOOL
- Law M,D
- Sports and Entertainment Law M,D

SOUTHWESTERN OKLAHOMA STATE UNIVERSITY
- Art Education M
- Business Administration and Management—General M
- Counselor Education M
- Early Childhood Education M
- Education—General M,O
- Educational Leadership and Administration M
- Educational Measurement and Evaluation M
- Elementary Education M
- Health Education M
- Kinesiology and Movement Studies M
- Mathematics Education M
- Music Education M
- Physical Education M
- Recreation and Park Management M
- Science Education M
- Social Sciences Education M
- Special Education M
- Sports Management M

SOUTHWEST MINNESOTA STATE UNIVERSITY
- Business Administration and Management—General M
- Early Childhood Education M
- Education—General M
- Educational Leadership and Administration M
- English as a Second Language M
- Marketing M
- Mathematics Education M
- Reading Education M
- Special Education M

SOUTHWEST UNIVERSITY
- Business Administration and Management—General M
- Organizational Management M

SPALDING UNIVERSITY
- Art Education M
- Athletic Training and Sports Medicine M
- Business Education M
- Counselor Education M
- Education—General M,D
- Educational Leadership and Administration M,D
- Elementary Education M
- Foreign Languages Education M
- Middle School Education M
- Secondary Education M
- Social Work M
- Special Education M

SPRING ARBOR UNIVERSITY
- Business Administration and Management—General M
- Education—General M
- Reading Education M
- Social Work M
- Special Education M

SPRINGFIELD COLLEGE
- Athletic Training and Sports Medicine M
- Business Administration and Management—General M
- Counselor Education M,D,O
- Early Childhood Education M,O
- Education—General M,O
- Educational Leadership and Administration M,D,O
- Elementary Education M,O
- Exercise and Sports Science M,D,O
- Higher Education M,D,O
- Human Services M
- Organizational Management M
- Physical Education M,D,O
- Recreation and Park Management M
- Secondary Education M,O
- Social Work M,O
- Special Education M,O
- Sports Management M,D,O
- Student Affairs M,D,O

SPRING HILL COLLEGE
- Business Administration and Management—General M
- Early Childhood Education M
- Education—General M
- Elementary Education M
- Foundations and Philosophy of Education M
- Secondary Education M

STANFORD UNIVERSITY
- Business Administration and Management—General M,D
- Curriculum and Instruction M
- Education—General M,D
- Educational Leadership and Administration M
- Educational Media/Instructional Technology M
- Educational Policy M
- Elementary Education M
- Environmental Law M,D
- International and Comparative Education M,D
- Law M,D
- Legal and Justice Studies M,D
- Secondary Education M

STATE UNIVERSITY OF NEW YORK AT FREDONIA
- Curriculum and Instruction M
- Early Childhood Education M
- Education—General M
- English as a Second Language M
- English Education M,O
- Mathematics Education M,O
- Middle School Education M,O
- Music Education M
- Reading Education M
- Secondary Education M

STATE UNIVERSITY OF NEW YORK AT NEW PALTZ
- Accounting M
- Business Administration and Management—General M
- Counselor Education M,O
- Early Childhood Education M
- Education—General M,O
- Educational Leadership and Administration M,O
- Elementary Education M
- English as a Second Language M,O
- English Education M,O
- Multilingual and Multicultural Education M,O
- Reading Education M
- Science Education M,O
- Secondary Education M
- Social Sciences Education M,O
- Special Education M

STATE UNIVERSITY OF NEW YORK AT OSWEGO
- Agricultural Education M
- Art Education M
- Business Administration and Management—General M
- Business Education M
- Curriculum and Instruction M
- Early Childhood Education M
- Education—General M,O
- Educational Leadership and Administration O
- Elementary Education M
- Middle School Education M
- Reading Education M
- Secondary Education M
- Special Education M
- Vocational and Technical Education M

STATE UNIVERSITY OF NEW YORK AT PLATTSBURGH
- Counselor Education M,O
- Curriculum and Instruction M
- Early Childhood Education O
- Educational Leadership and Administration O
- Elementary Education M,O
- English Education M
- Foreign Languages Education M
- Mathematics Education M
- Reading Education M
- Science Education M
- Secondary Education M
- Social Sciences Education M
- Special Education M
- Student Affairs M,O

STATE UNIVERSITY OF NEW YORK COLLEGE AT CORTLAND
- Early Childhood Education M
- Education—General M,O
- Educational Leadership and Administration O
- English as a Second Language M
- English Education M
- Environmental Education M
- Health Education M
- Mathematics Education M
- Physical Education M
- Reading Education M
- Recreation and Park Management M
- Science Education M
- Secondary Education M
- Special Education M
- Sports Management M

STATE UNIVERSITY OF NEW YORK COLLEGE AT GENESEO
- Accounting M
- Business Administration and Management—General M
- Education—General M
- English Education M
- Multilingual and Multicultural Education M
- Reading Education M
- Secondary Education M
- Social Sciences Education M

STATE UNIVERSITY OF NEW YORK COLLEGE AT OLD WESTBURY
- Accounting M
- Business Administration and Management—General M
- Education—General M
- English Education M
- Foreign Languages Education M
- Mathematics Education M
- Science Education M
- Social Sciences Education M
- Taxation M

STATE UNIVERSITY OF NEW YORK COLLEGE AT ONEONTA
- Counselor Education M,O
- Education—General M,O
- Educational Psychology M,O
- Elementary Education M
- Reading Education M
- Special Education M,O

STATE UNIVERSITY OF NEW YORK COLLEGE AT POTSDAM
- Curriculum and Instruction M
- Early Childhood Education M
- Educational Media/Instructional Technology M
- Elementary Education M
- English Education M
- Mathematics Education M
- Middle School Education M
- Music Education M
- Reading Education M
- Science Education M
- Secondary Education M
- Social Sciences Education M
- Special Education M

STATE UNIVERSITY OF NEW YORK COLLEGE OF ENVIRONMENTAL SCIENCE AND FORESTRY
- Sustainability Management M,D,O

STATE UNIVERSITY OF NEW YORK EMPIRE STATE COLLEGE
- Adult Education M
- Business Administration and Management—General M
- Education—General M
- Educational Media/Instructional Technology M
- International Business M

STATE UNIVERSITY OF NEW YORK MARITIME COLLEGE
- Transportation Management M

STATE UNIVERSITY OF NEW YORK POLYTECHNIC INSTITUTE
- Accounting M
- Business Administration and Management—General M
- Finance and Banking M
- Human Resources Management M
- Marketing M

STEPHEN F. AUSTIN STATE UNIVERSITY
- Accounting M
- Art Education M

Athletic Training and Sports Medicine	M
Business Administration and Management—General	M
Counselor Education	M
Early Childhood Education	M
Education—General	M,D
Educational Leadership and Administration	M,D
Elementary Education	M
Kinesiology and Movement Studies	M
Marketing	M
Mathematics Education	M
Secondary Education	M,D
Social Work	M
Special Education	M

STEPHENS COLLEGE

Counselor Education	M,O

STETSON UNIVERSITY

Accounting	M
Business Administration and Management—General	M
Counselor Education	M
Education—General	M
Educational Leadership and Administration	M
Law	M,D

STEVENS INSTITUTE OF TECHNOLOGY

Business Administration and Management—General	M,O
Business Analytics	M,O
Electronic Commerce	M,O
Entrepreneurship	M,O
Finance and Banking	M,O
Human Resources Management	M
Industrial and Manufacturing Management	M
International Business	M
Management Information Systems	M,D,O
Management Strategy and Policy	M
Marketing	M,O
Project Management	M,O
Quality Management	M,O

STEVENSON UNIVERSITY

Education—General	M
Educational Leadership and Administration	M
Mathematics Education	M
Project Management	M
Quality Management	M
Science Education	M

STOCKTON UNIVERSITY

Business Administration and Management—General	M
Education—General	M
Educational Media/Instructional Technology	M
Management Strategy and Policy	M
Organizational Management	D
Quantitative Analysis	M
Social Work	M

STONEHILL COLLEGE

Special Education	M

STONY BROOK UNIVERSITY, STATE UNIVERSITY OF NEW YORK

Accounting	M,O
Business Administration and Management—General	M,O
Educational Leadership and Administration	M,O
English as a Second Language	M,O
Entrepreneurship	M,O
Finance and Banking	M,O
Foreign Languages Education	M,O
Health Education	M,O
Higher Education	M,O
Human Resources Management	M,O
Marketing	M,O
Mathematics Education	M,O
Physical Education	M,O
Science Education	M,D
Social Sciences Education	M,O
Social Work	M,D

STRATFORD UNIVERSITY (MD)

Hospitality Management	M

STRATFORD UNIVERSITY (VA)

Accounting	M,D
Business Administration and Management—General	M,D
Management Information Systems	M,D

STRAYER UNIVERSITY

Accounting	M
Business Administration and Management—General	M
Education—General	M
Educational Media/Instructional Technology	M
Finance and Banking	M
Hospitality Management	M
Human Resources Management	M
Management Information Systems	M
Marketing	M
Supply Chain Management	M
Taxation	M
Travel and Tourism	M

SUFFOLK UNIVERSITY

Accounting	M,O
Advertising and Public Relations	M
Business Administration and Management—General	M
Business Analytics	M
Counselor Education	M,D,O
Educational Leadership and Administration	M,O
Entrepreneurship	M
Finance and Banking	M
Health Law	M,D
Intellectual Property Law	M,D
International Business	M
Law	M,D
Management Information Systems	M
Management Strategy and Policy	M
Marketing	M
Nonprofit Management	M
Organizational Behavior	M
Supply Chain Management	M
Taxation	M,O

SULLIVAN UNIVERSITY

Business Administration and Management—General	M,D

SUL ROSS STATE UNIVERSITY

Art Education	M
Business Administration and Management—General	M
Counselor Education	M
Education—General	M,O
Educational Leadership and Administration	M
Educational Measurement and Evaluation	M,O
Elementary Education	M
Multilingual and Multicultural Education	M
Physical Education	M
Reading Education	M,O
Secondary Education	M

SWEET BRIAR COLLEGE

Education—General	M

SYRACUSE UNIVERSITY

Accounting	M
Advertising and Public Relations	M
Art Education	M
Business Administration and Management—General	M,D
Business Analytics	M
Counselor Education	M,D
Curriculum and Instruction	M,D,O
Early Childhood Education	M
Education of Students with Severe/Multiple Disabilities	M
Education—General	M,D,O
Educational Leadership and Administration	M,D,O
Educational Measurement and Evaluation	M,D,O
Educational Media/Instructional Technology	M,O
English as a Second Language	M,O
English Education	M
Entertainment Management	M
Entrepreneurship	M
Exercise and Sports Science	M
Finance and Banking	M,D
Foundations and Philosophy of Education	M,D,O
Higher Education	M,D
Hospitality Management	M,O
Information Studies	M
Kinesiology and Movement Studies	M,D,O
Law	M,D
Library Science	M
Management Information Systems	M,D,O
Marketing	M
Mathematics Education	M,D
Music Education	M
Organizational Management	O
Reading Education	M,D
Real Estate	M
Science Education	M,D
Social Sciences Education	M
Social Work	M
Special Education	M,D
Sports Management	M
Student Affairs	M
Supply Chain Management	M
Sustainability Management	O
Travel and Tourism	M

TABOR COLLEGE

Accounting	M
Business Administration and Management—General	M

TAFT UNIVERSITY SYSTEM

Education—General	M
Law	M,D
Legal and Justice Studies	M,D
Taxation	M,D

TARLETON STATE UNIVERSITY

Accounting	M
Athletic Training and Sports Medicine	M
Business Administration and Management—General	M
Curriculum and Instruction	M
Education—General	M,D,O
Educational Leadership and Administration	M,D,O
Educational Media/Instructional Technology	M
Elementary Education	M
Human Resources Management	M
Kinesiology and Movement Studies	M
Management Information Systems	M
Marketing	M
Music Education	M
Secondary Education	M
Social Work	M
Special Education	M

TAYLOR COLLEGE AND SEMINARY

English as a Second Language	M,O

TAYLOR UNIVERSITY

Higher Education	M

TEACHERS COLLEGE, COLUMBIA UNIVERSITY

Adult Education	M,D
Art Education	M,D,O
Computer Education	M,D
Curriculum and Instruction	M,D
Early Childhood Education	M,D
Education of Students with Severe/Multiple Disabilities	M,D,O
Education of the Gifted	M,D
Education—General	M,D
Educational Leadership and Administration	M,D
Educational Measurement and Evaluation	M,D
Educational Media/Instructional Technology	M,D
Educational Policy	M,D
Educational Psychology	M,D,O
Elementary Education	M,D
English as a Second Language	M,D,O
English Education	M,D,O
Foundations and Philosophy of Education	M,D,O
Health Education	M,D,O
Higher Education	M,D
International and Comparative Education	M,D
Kinesiology and Movement Studies	M,D
Mathematics Education	M,D
Multilingual and Multicultural Education	M,D,O
Music Education	M,D,O
Physical Education	M,D
Reading Education	M,D,O
Science Education	M,D
Secondary Education	M,D
Social Sciences Education	M,D,O
Special Education	M,D,O
Urban Education	M,D

TEACHERS COLLEGE OF SAN JOAQUIN

Early Childhood Education	M
Education—General	M
Educational Leadership and Administration	M
Educational Measurement and Evaluation	M
Mathematics Education	M
Science Education	M
Special Education	M

TÉLÉ-UNIVERSITÉ

Distance Education Development	M,D
Finance and Banking	M,D

TEMPLE UNIVERSITY

Accounting	M,D
Actuarial Science	M
Art Education	M
Athletic Training and Sports Medicine	M,D
Business Administration and Management—General	M,D
Business Education	M
Education—General	M,D,O
Educational Leadership and Administration	M,D
Educational Psychology	M,D,O
English as a Second Language	M,D
English Education	M
Entrepreneurship	M,D
Finance and Banking	M,D
Hospitality Management	M,D
Human Resources Management	M
Insurance	D
International Business	M,D
Investment Management	M,O
Kinesiology and Movement Studies	M,D
Law	M,D,O
Legal and Justice Studies	M,D
Management Information Systems	M,D
Management Strategy and Policy	D
Marketing	M,D
Mathematics Education	M
Middle School Education	M
Music Education	M,D
Physical Education	M,D
Recreation and Park Management	M,D
Risk Management	D
Science Education	M
Secondary Education	M
Social Sciences Education	M
Social Work	M
Sports Management	M,D
Taxation	M,D
Travel and Tourism	M,D
Urban Education	M
Vocational and Technical Education	M

TENNESSEE STATE UNIVERSITY

Agricultural Education	M,D
Business Administration and Management—General	M
Curriculum and Instruction	M,D
Education—General	M,D,O
Elementary Education	M,D
Exercise and Sports Science	M
Human Resources Management	M,D
Management Strategy and Policy	M,D
Physical Education	M
Social Work	M,D
Special Education	M,D
Sports Management	M

TENNESSEE TECHNOLOGICAL UNIVERSITY

Accounting	M
Business Administration and Management—General	M
Curriculum and Instruction	M,O
Early Childhood Education	M,O
Education of the Gifted	D
Education—General	M,D,O
Educational Leadership and Administration	M,O
Educational Measurement and Evaluation	D
Educational Media/Instructional Technology	M,O
Educational Psychology	M,O
Elementary Education	M,O
English as a Second Language	M
Finance and Banking	M
Health Education	M
Human Resources Management	M
International Business	M
Kinesiology and Movement Studies	M
Library Science	M,O
Management Information Systems	M
Management Strategy and Policy	M
Mathematics Education	M,O
Middle School Education	M
Music Education	M
Physical Education	M
Reading Education	D
Science Education	M,O
Secondary Education	M,O
Special Education	M,O
Sports Management	M

TENNESSEE WESLEYAN UNIVERSITY

Accounting	M
Business Administration and Management—General	M

TEXAS A&M INTERNATIONAL UNIVERSITY

Accounting	M
Business Administration and Management—General	M,D
Counselor Education	M
Curriculum and Instruction	M
Education—General	M
Educational Leadership and Administration	M
Finance and Banking	M
Foreign Languages Education	M
International Business	M,D
Management Information Systems	M,D
Special Education	M

TEXAS A&M UNIVERSITY

Accounting	M
Agricultural Education	M,D
Athletic Training and Sports Medicine	M,D
Business Administration and Management—General	M
Curriculum and Instruction	M,D
Education—General	M,D
Educational Leadership and Administration	M,D
Educational Media/Instructional Technology	M,D
Educational Psychology	M,D
Entrepreneurship	M
Finance and Banking	M
Health Education	M,D
Human Resources Development	M,D
Human Resources Management	M
Intellectual Property Law	M,D
Kinesiology and Movement Studies	M,D
Law	M,D
Management Information Systems	M
Marketing	M
Multilingual and Multicultural Education	M,D
Recreation and Park Management	M,D
Special Education	M,D
Sports Management	M,D
Transportation Management	M

TEXAS A&M UNIVERSITY–CENTRAL TEXAS

Accounting	M,O
Business Administration and Management—General	M,O
Counselor Education	M,O
Curriculum and Instruction	M,O
Educational Leadership and Administration	M,O
Educational Psychology	M,O
Human Resources Management	M,O
Management Information Systems	M,O

TEXAS A&M UNIVERSITY–COMMERCE

Accounting	M
Business Administration and Management—General	M
Business Analytics	M
Counselor Education	M,D,O
Curriculum and Instruction	M,D,O
Early Childhood Education	M,D,O
Education—General	M,D,O
Educational Leadership and Administration	M,D,O
Educational Media/Instructional Technology	M,D,O
Educational Psychology	M,D,O
Elementary Education	M,D,O
English as a Second Language	M,D,O
Exercise and Sports Science	M,D,O
Finance and Banking	M
Higher Education	M,D,O
Kinesiology and Movement Studies	M,D,O
Library Science	M,D,O
Marketing	M
Music Education	M,D,O
Reading Education	M,D,O
Secondary Education	M,D,O
Social Work	M,D,O

*M—masters degree; D—doctorate; O—other advanced degree; *—Close-Up and/or Display*

Special Education — M,D,O

TEXAS A&M UNIVERSITY–CORPUS CHRISTI

Accounting — M
Business Administration and Management—General — M
Counselor Education — M,D
Curriculum and Instruction — M,D
Early Childhood Education — M,D
Education—General — M,D
Educational Leadership and Administration — M,D
Educational Media/Instructional Technology — M,D
Elementary Education — M
Finance and Banking — M
International Business — M
Kinesiology and Movement Studies — M,D
Reading Education — M,D
Secondary Education — M
Special Education — M

TEXAS A&M UNIVERSITY–KINGSVILLE

Adult Education — M
Business Administration and Management—General — M
Counselor Education — M
Early Childhood Education — M
Education—General — M,D,O
Educational Leadership and Administration — M,D
Educational Media/Instructional Technology — M
English as a Second Language — M,D
Foreign Languages Education — M
Health Education — M
Industrial and Manufacturing Management — M
Kinesiology and Movement Studies — M
Multilingual and Multicultural Education — M,D
Music Education — M
Reading Education — M
Science Education — M
Social Work — M
Special Education — M

TEXAS A&M UNIVERSITY–SAN ANTONIO

Accounting — M
Business Administration and Management—General — M
Counselor Education — M
Early Childhood Education — M
Education—General — M
Educational Leadership and Administration — M
Educational Measurement and Evaluation — M
Kinesiology and Movement Studies — M
Multilingual and Multicultural Education — M
Reading Education — M
Special Education — M

TEXAS A&M UNIVERSITY–TEXARKANA

Accounting — M
Adult Education — M
Business Administration and Management—General — M
Curriculum and Instruction — M
Education—General — M
Educational Leadership and Administration — M
Educational Media/Instructional Technology — M
Special Education — M

TEXAS CHRISTIAN UNIVERSITY

Accounting — M
Business Administration and Management—General — M
Counselor Education — M,D
Curriculum and Instruction — M,D
Education—General — M,D
Educational Leadership and Administration — M,D
Kinesiology and Movement Studies — M
Mathematics Education — M
Music Education — M,D
Reading Education — M
Science Education — M,D
Social Work — M
Special Education — M
Taxation — M

TEXAS HEALTH AND SCIENCE UNIVERSITY

Business Administration and Management—General — M,D

TEXAS LUTHERAN UNIVERSITY

Accounting — M

TEXAS SOUTHERN UNIVERSITY

Business Administration and Management—General — M
Counselor Education — M,D
Curriculum and Instruction — M,D
Education—General — M,D
Educational Leadership and Administration — M,D
Health Education — M
Higher Education — M,D
Human Services — M
Law — D
Management Information Systems — M
Multilingual and Multicultural Education — M,D
Physical Education — M
Secondary Education — M,D
Transportation Management — M

TEXAS STATE UNIVERSITY

Accounting — M
Adult Education — M,D

Agricultural Education — M
Athletic Training and Sports Medicine — M
Business Administration and Management—General — M
Counselor Education — M
Developmental Education — M,D
Early Childhood Education — M
Education—General — M,D,O
Educational Leadership and Administration — M,D
Educational Media/Instructional Technology — M
Elementary Education — M
Health Education — M
Higher Education — M
Human Resources Management — M
Legal and Justice Studies — M
Leisure Studies — M
Management Information Systems — M
Mathematics Education — D
Multilingual and Multicultural Education — M
Music Education — M
Reading Education — M
Recreation and Park Management — M
Secondary Education — M
Social Work — M
Special Education — M
Student Affairs — M
Vocational and Technical Education — M

TEXAS TECH UNIVERSITY

Accounting — M,D
Agricultural Education — M,D
Art Education — M
Business Administration and Management—General — M,D
Counselor Education — M,D
Curriculum and Instruction — M,D
Education—General — M
Educational Leadership and Administration — M,D
Educational Media/Instructional Technology — M
Educational Psychology — M,D
Elementary Education — M,D
Exercise and Sports Science — M
Finance and Banking — M,D
Higher Education — M,D
Home Economics Education — M,D
Hospitality Management — M
Kinesiology and Movement Studies — M
Law — M,D
Legal and Justice Studies — M,D
Management Information Systems — M,D
Marketing — M,D
Multilingual and Multicultural Education — M,D
Music Education — M,D
Reading Education — M,D
Science Education — M,D
Secondary Education — M,D
Social Sciences Education — M,D
Social Work — M
Special Education — M,D
Sports Management — M
Taxation — M,D

TEXAS TECH UNIVERSITY HEALTH SCIENCES CENTER

Athletic Training and Sports Medicine — M

TEXAS WESLEYAN UNIVERSITY

Business Administration and Management—General — M
Education—General — M,D

TEXAS WOMAN'S UNIVERSITY

Accounting — M
Art Education — M
Business Administration and Management—General — M
Business Analytics — M
Counselor Education — M,D
Curriculum and Instruction — M,D
Early Childhood Education — M,D
Education—General — M,D,O
Educational Leadership and Administration — M,D
English Education — M,D
Exercise and Sports Science — M,D
Health Education — M,D
Human Resources Management — M
Library Science — M
Mathematics Education — M
Music Education — M
Reading Education — M,D,O
Special Education — M,D

THEOLOGICAL UNIVERSITY OF THE CARIBBEAN

Early Childhood Education — M,D
Middle School Education — M,D

THOMAS COLLEGE

Business Administration and Management—General — M
Business Education — M
Computer Education — M
Human Resources Management — M

THOMAS EDISON STATE UNIVERSITY

Accounting — M
Business Administration and Management—General — M
Distance Education Development — M,O
Educational Leadership and Administration — M,O
Educational Media/Instructional Technology — M,O
Finance and Banking — M
Hospitality Management — M
Human Resources Management — M
International Business — M

Nonprofit Management — M
Organizational Management — M
Project Management — M

THOMAS JEFFERSON SCHOOL OF LAW

Law — D

THOMAS JEFFERSON UNIVERSITY

Athletic Training and Sports Medicine — M
Business Administration and Management—General — M
Business Analytics — M
Health Education — M,D,O
Management Strategy and Policy — M,D
Marketing — M
Real Estate — M
Taxation — M

THOMAS MORE UNIVERSITY

Business Administration and Management—General — M
Education—General — M
Educational Leadership and Administration — M

THOMAS UNIVERSITY

Business Administration and Management—General — M
Education—General — M
Human Services — M

THOMPSON RIVERS UNIVERSITY

Business Administration and Management—General — M
Education—General — M
Social Work — M

TIFFIN UNIVERSITY

Business Administration and Management—General — M
Education—General — M
Educational Leadership and Administration — M
Educational Media/Instructional Technology — M
Finance and Banking — M
Higher Education — M
Human Resources Management — M
International Business — M
Marketing — M
Nonprofit Management — M
Sports Management — M

TOURO COLLEGE

Education—General — M
Educational Leadership and Administration — M
Educational Media/Instructional Technology — M
English as a Second Language — M
Law — M,D
Legal and Justice Studies — M,D
Management Information Systems — M
Mathematics Education — M
Reading Education — M
Social Work — M
Special Education — M

TOURO UNIVERSITY CALIFORNIA

Education—General — M,D

TOWSON UNIVERSITY

Accounting — M
Art Education — M,O
Early Childhood Education — M,O
Education—General — M
Educational Leadership and Administration — M,O
Educational Media/Instructional Technology — M
Electronic Commerce — M,O
Elementary Education — M
Human Resources Development — M
Human Resources Management — M
Marketing Research — M,O
Mathematics Education — M
Music Education — M
Reading Education — M
Secondary Education — M
Special Education — M,O
Supply Chain Management — M,O

TREVECCA NAZARENE UNIVERSITY

Business Administration and Management—General — M
Counselor Education — M,D
Curriculum and Instruction — M,O
Education—General — M,O
Educational Leadership and Administration — M,D,O
Educational Media/Instructional Technology — M
Elementary Education — M,O
English as a Second Language — M,O
Library Science — M,O
Organizational Management — M
Secondary Education — M,O
Special Education — M,O

TRIDENT UNIVERSITY INTERNATIONAL

Adult Education — M
Business Administration and Management—General — M,D
Early Childhood Education — M,D
Education—General — M,D
Educational Leadership and Administration — M,D
Educational Media/Instructional Technology — M,D
Finance and Banking — M,D
Health Education — M,D,O
Higher Education — M,D
Human Resources Management — M,D
International Business — M,D
Legal and Justice Studies — M,D,O
Logistics — M,D
Management Information Systems — M,D

Marketing — M,D
Project Management — M,D
Quality Management — M,D,O
Reading Education — M

TRINE UNIVERSITY

Business Administration and Management—General — M
Management Information Systems — M
Organizational Management — M

TRINITY BAPTIST COLLEGE

Curriculum and Instruction — M
Educational Leadership and Administration — M
Special Education — M

TRINITY CHRISTIAN COLLEGE

Special Education — M

TRINITY INTERNATIONAL UNIVERSITY

Athletic Training and Sports Medicine — M
Business Administration and Management—General — M,D,O
Education—General — M
Human Resources Management — M,D
Law — M,D
Religious Education — M,D,O

TRINITY UNIVERSITY

Accounting — M
Business Administration and Management—General — M
Education—General — M
Educational Leadership and Administration — M

TRINITY WASHINGTON UNIVERSITY

Business Administration and Management—General — M
Counselor Education — M
Curriculum and Instruction — M
Early Childhood Education — M
Education—General — M
Educational Leadership and Administration — M
Elementary Education — M
English Education — M
Human Resources Management — M
Nonprofit Management — M
Organizational Management — M
Reading Education — M
Secondary Education — M
Social Sciences Education — M
Special Education — M

TRINITY WESTERN UNIVERSITY

Business Administration and Management—General — M
Educational Leadership and Administration — M,O
English as a Second Language — M
International Business — M
Nonprofit Management — M,O
Organizational Management — M,O

TROPICAL AGRICULTURE RESEARCH AND HIGHER EDUCATION CENTER

Travel and Tourism — M,D

TROY UNIVERSITY

Accounting — M
Adult Education — M
Business Administration and Management—General — M
Counselor Education — M,O
Early Childhood Education — M,O
Education—General — M,O
Educational Leadership and Administration — M,O
Elementary Education — M,O
English as a Second Language — M
Finance and Banking — M
Human Resources Management — M
Management Information Systems — M
Secondary Education — M
Social Work — M
Sports Management — M,D

TRUETT MCCONNELL UNIVERSITY

Business Administration and Management—General — M

TRUMAN STATE UNIVERSITY

Accounting — M
Education—General — M

TUFTS UNIVERSITY

Art Education — M,D,O
Education—General — M,D,O
Elementary Education — M,D
Entrepreneurship — M
International Business — M,D
Law — M,D
Management Strategy and Policy — O
Mathematics Education — M,D
Middle School Education — M,D
Museum Education — M,D
Nonprofit Management — O
Organizational Management — M
Science Education — M,D
Secondary Education — M,D
Sustainability Management — M,D

TULANE UNIVERSITY

Accounting — M,D
Business Administration and Management—General — M,D
Business Analytics — M,D
Entrepreneurship — M,D
Finance and Banking — M,D
International Business — M,D
Law — M,D
Management Information Systems — M,D
Management Strategy and Policy — M,D
Social Work — M,D

TUSCULUM UNIVERSITY
Business Administration and
   Management—General M
Curriculum and Instruction M
Education—General M
Human Resources Development M
Special Education M

TUSKEGEE UNIVERSITY
Management Information Systems M

UNIFICATION THEOLOGICAL SEMINARY
Religious Education M,D

UNION COLLEGE (KY)
Education—General M
Educational Leadership and
   Administration M
Elementary Education M
Health Education M
Middle School Education M
Music Education M
Physical Education M
Reading Education M
Secondary Education M
Special Education M

UNION INSTITUTE & UNIVERSITY
Education—General D
Organizational Management M

UNION PRESBYTERIAN SEMINARY
Religious Education M,D

UNION UNIVERSITY
Accounting M
Business Administration and
   Management—General M
Education—General M,D,O
Educational Leadership and
   Administration M,D,O
Higher Education M,D,O
Social Work M

UNITED STATES INTERNATIONAL UNIVERSITY–AFRICA
Business Administration and
   Management—General M
Entrepreneurship M
Finance and Banking M
Human Resources Management M
International Business M
Management Information Systems M
Management Strategy and Policy M
Marketing M
Organizational Management M

UNITED STATES SPORTS ACADEMY
Exercise and Sports Science M
Physical Education M
Recreation and Park Management M
Sports Management M,D

UNIVERSIDAD ADVENTISTA DE LAS ANTILLAS
Curriculum and Instruction M
Educational Leadership and
   Administration M

UNIVERSIDAD AUTONOMA DE GUADALAJARA
Advertising and Public Relations M,D
Business Administration and
   Management—General M,D
Education—General M,D
Entertainment Management M,D
International Business M,D
Law M,D
Legal and Justice Studies M,D
Marketing Research M,D
Mathematics Education M,D

UNIVERSIDAD CENTRAL DEL ESTE
Finance and Banking M
Higher Education M
Human Resources Development M
Law D

UNIVERSIDAD DE IBEROAMERICA
Educational Psychology M,D

UNIVERSIDAD DE LAS AMERICAS, A.C.
Business Administration and
   Management—General M
Education—General M
Finance and Banking M
Marketing Research M
Organizational Behavior M
Quality Management M

UNIVERSIDAD DE LAS AMÉRICAS PUEBLA
Business Administration and
   Management—General M
Education—General M
Finance and Banking M
Industrial and Manufacturing
   Management M

UNIVERSIDAD DEL ESTE
Accounting M
Adult Education M
Business Administration and
   Management—General M
Electronic Commerce M
Elementary Education M
English as a Second Language M
Foreign Languages Education M
Human Resources Management M
Management Information Systems M
Management Strategy and Policy M
Social Work M
Special Education M

UNIVERSIDAD DEL TURABO
Accounting M
Athletic Training and Sports
   Medicine M
Business Administration and
   Management—General M,D
Counselor Education M
Curriculum and Instruction M,D
Early Childhood Education M
Education—General M,D
Educational Leadership and
   Administration M,D
English as a Second Language M
Human Resources Management M
Human Services M
Information Studies M
Library Science M
Logistics M
Management Information Systems D
Marketing M
Physical Education M
Project Management M
Quality Management M
Special Education M

UNIVERSIDAD IBEROAMERICANA
Business Administration and
   Management—General M,D
Educational Leadership and
   Administration M,D
Human Resources Development M,D
Law M,D
Marketing M,D
Real Estate M,D
Special Education M,D

UNIVERSIDAD METROPOLITANA
Accounting M
Adult Education M
Business Administration and
   Management—General M
Curriculum and Instruction M
Education—General M
Educational Leadership and
   Administration M
Elementary Education M
Finance and Banking M
Human Resources Management M
International Business M
Leisure Studies M
Management Information Systems M
Marketing M
Physical Education M
Recreation and Park Management M
Secondary Education M
Special Education M

UNIVERSIDAD NACIONAL PEDRO HENRIQUEZ URENA
Project Management M
Science Education M

UNIVERSITÉ DE MONCTON
Business Administration and
   Management—General M
Counselor Education M
Education—General M
Educational Leadership and
   Administration M
Educational Psychology M
Social Work M

UNIVERSITÉ DE MONTRÉAL
Curriculum and Instruction M,D,O
Education—General M,D,O
Educational Leadership and
   Administration M,D,O
Educational Psychology M,D
Electronic Commerce M,D
Human Services D
Information Studies M,D
Kinesiology and Movement Studies M,D,O
Law M,D,O
Library Science M,D
Physical Education M,D,O
Social Work O
Taxation M,D,O

UNIVERSITÉ DE SAINT-BONIFACE
Education—General M

UNIVERSITÉ DE SHERBROOKE
Accounting M
Business Administration and
   Management—General M,D,O
Education—General M,O
Educational Leadership and
   Administration M
Electronic Commerce M
Elementary Education M
Finance and Banking M
Health Law M,D,O
Higher Education M,O
International Business M
Kinesiology and Movement Studies M,D,O
Law M,D,O
Management Information Systems M
Marketing M
Organizational Behavior M
Physical Education M,O
Social Work M
Special Education M,O
Taxation M,O

UNIVERSITÉ DU QUÉBEC À CHICOUTIMI
Business Administration and
   Management—General M
Education—General M,D
Project Management M

UNIVERSITÉ DU QUÉBEC À MONTRÉAL
Accounting M,O
Actuarial Science O

Business Administration and
   Management—General M,D,O
Education—General M,D,O
Environmental Education M,D,O
Finance and Banking O
Kinesiology and Movement Studies M
Law O
Management Information Systems M,O
Project Management M,O
Social Work M

UNIVERSITÉ DU QUÉBEC À RIMOUSKI
Business Administration and
   Management—General M,D
Education—General M,D,O
Project Management M,O

UNIVERSITÉ DU QUÉBEC À TROIS-RIVIÈRES
Accounting M
Business Administration and
   Management—General M,D
Education—General M,D
Educational Leadership and
   Administration O
Educational Psychology M,D
Finance and Banking O
Leisure Studies M,O
Physical Education M
Travel and Tourism M

UNIVERSITÉ DU QUÉBEC, ÉCOLE NATIONALE D'ADMINISTRATION PUBLIQUE
International Business M,O

UNIVERSITÉ DU QUÉBEC EN ABITIBI-TÉMISCAMINGUE
Business Administration and
   Management—General M
Education—General M,D,O
Project Management M,O
Social Work M

UNIVERSITÉ DU QUÉBEC EN OUTAOUAIS
Accounting M,O
Education—General M,D,O
Educational Psychology M
Finance and Banking M
Foreign Languages Education O
Project Management M,O
Social Work M

UNIVERSITÉ LAVAL
Accounting M,O
Advertising and Public Relations O
Business Administration and
   Management—General M,D,O
Counselor Education M,D
Curriculum and Instruction M,D
Education—General M,D,O
Educational Leadership and
   Administration M,D,O
Educational Measurement and
   Evaluation M,D,O
Educational Media/Instructional
   Technology M,D
Educational Psychology M,D
Electronic Commerce M,O
Entrepreneurship M,O
Facilities Management M,O
Finance and Banking M,O
International Business M,O
Kinesiology and Movement Studies M,D,O
Law M,D,O
Legal and Justice Studies O
Management Information Systems M,O
Marketing M,O
Music Education M,O
Organizational Management M,O
Social Work M,D

UNIVERSITÉ SAINTE-ANNE
Education—General M

UNIVERSITY AT ALBANY, STATE UNIVERSITY OF NEW YORK
Business Administration and
   Management—General M
Business Analytics M
Curriculum and Instruction M,D,O
Education—General M,D,O
Educational Leadership and
   Administration M,D,O
Educational Media/Instructional
   Technology M,D,O
Educational Policy M,D,O
Entrepreneurship M
Finance and Banking M,D,O
Higher Education M,D,O
Human Resources Management M,D,O
International and Comparative
   Education M,D,O
Management Information Systems M,D,O
Marketing M
Nonprofit Management M,D,O
Organizational Behavior M,D,O
Reading Education M,D,O
Social Work M,D

UNIVERSITY AT BUFFALO, THE STATE UNIVERSITY OF NEW YORK
Accounting M,D
Business Administration and
   Management—General M,D
Business Analytics M,D
Counselor Education M,D,O
Curriculum and Instruction M,D,O
Distance Education Development M,D,O
Early Childhood Education M,D,O
Education of the Gifted M,D,O
Education—General M,D,O

Educational Leadership and
   Administration M,D,O
Educational Media/Instructional
   Technology M,D,O
Educational Psychology M,D,O
Electronic Commerce M,D,O
Elementary Education M,D,O
English as a Second Language M,D,O
English Education M,D,O
Environmental Law M,D
Exercise and Sports Science M,D,O
Finance and Banking M,D
Foreign Languages Education M,D,O
Foundations and Philosophy of
   Education M,D,O
Higher Education M,D,O
Human Resources Management M,O
Information Studies M,D
International Business M,D
Law M,D
Legal and Justice Studies M,D
Library Science M,O
Logistics M,D
Management Information Systems M,D,O
Marketing M
Mathematics Education M,D,O
Multilingual and Multicultural
   Education M,D,O
Music Education M,D,O
Quantitative Analysis M,D
Reading Education M,D,O
Real Estate M,D
Science Education M,D,O
Social Sciences Education M,D,O
Social Work M,D
Special Education M,D,O
Supply Chain Management M,D
Transportation Management M

THE UNIVERSITY OF AKRON
Accounting M
Art Education M
Business Administration and
   Management—General M
Counselor Education M,D
Curriculum and Instruction M
Education—General M
Educational Leadership and
   Administration M,D,O
Electronic Commerce M
Elementary Education M
English Education M
Exercise and Sports Science M
Finance and Banking M
Law M,D
Management Information Systems M
Marketing M
Mathematics Education M
Music Education M
Physical Education M
Reading Education M
Science Education M
Secondary Education M
Social Sciences Education M
Social Work M
Supply Chain Management M
Taxation M

THE UNIVERSITY OF ALABAMA
Accounting M,D
Advertising and Public Relations M
Business Administration and
   Management—General M,D
Counselor Education M,D,O
Education of the Gifted M,D,O
Educational Leadership and
   Administration M,D,O
Elementary Education M,D,O
English as a Second Language M,D
Exercise and Sports Science M,D
Finance and Banking M,D
Health Education M,D
Higher Education M,D
Hospitality Management M
Industrial and Manufacturing
   Management M,D
Information Studies M,D
Kinesiology and Movement Studies M,D
Law M,D
Library Science M,D
Marketing M,D
Music Education M,D,O
Physical Education M,D
Quality Management M
Secondary Education M,D,O
Social Work M,D
Special Education M,D,O
Sports Management M
Taxation M

THE UNIVERSITY OF ALABAMA AT BIRMINGHAM
Accounting M
Art Education M
Business Administration and
   Management—General M
Counselor Education M
Curriculum and Instruction O
Early Childhood Education M,D
Education—General M,D,O
Educational Leadership and
   Administration M,D,O
Elementary Education M
English as a Second Language M,O
Finance and Banking M
Management Information Systems M
Marketing M
Quantitative Analysis M,D
Reading Education M
Secondary Education M
Social Work M
Special Education M

M—masters degree; D—doctorate; O—other advanced degree; *—Close-Up and/or Display

THE UNIVERSITY OF ALABAMA IN HUNTSVILLE
- Accounting M,O
- Business Administration and Management—General M,O
- Business Analytics M,O
- English as a Second Language M,O
- English Education M,O
- Entrepreneurship M,O
- Finance and Banking M,O
- Human Resources Management M,O
- Logistics M,O
- Management Information Systems M,O
- Marketing M,O
- Mathematics Education M,D,O
- Project Management M,O
- Reading Education M,O
- Science Education M,D,O
- Secondary Education M,O
- Social Sciences Education M,O
- Special Education M,O
- Supply Chain Management M,O
- Taxation M

UNIVERSITY OF ALASKA ANCHORAGE
- Business Administration and Management—General M
- Early Childhood Education M,O
- Education—General M,O
- Educational Leadership and Administration M,O
- Logistics M
- Social Work M,O
- Special Education M,O

UNIVERSITY OF ALASKA FAIRBANKS
- Business Administration and Management—General M
- Counselor Education M,O
- Education—General M,O
- Finance and Banking M
- Multilingual and Multicultural Education M
- Special Education M

UNIVERSITY OF ALASKA SOUTHEAST
- Education—General M
- Educational Leadership and Administration M
- Educational Media/Instructional Technology M
- Elementary Education M
- Mathematics Education M
- Reading Education M
- Secondary Education M
- Special Education M

UNIVERSITY OF ALBERTA
- Accounting D
- Adult Education M,D,O
- Business Administration and Management—General M,D
- Counselor Education M,D
- Educational Leadership and Administration M,D,O
- Educational Media/Instructional Technology M,D
- Educational Policy M,D,O
- Educational Psychology M,D
- Elementary Education M,D
- English as a Second Language M,D
- Exercise and Sports Science M,D
- Finance and Banking M,D
- Information Studies M
- International Business M
- Kinesiology and Movement Studies M,D
- Law M,D
- Library Science M
- Marketing D
- Multilingual and Multicultural Education M
- Organizational Management D
- Physical Education M,D
- Recreation and Park Management M,D
- Secondary Education M,D
- Special Education M,D
- Sports Management M

UNIVERSITY OF ANTELOPE VALLEY
- Business Administration and Management—General M

THE UNIVERSITY OF ARIZONA
- Accounting M
- Agricultural Education M,O
- Art Education M,D
- Business Administration and Management—General M,D,O
- Counselor Education M
- Education of Students with Severe/Multiple Disabilities M,D,O
- Education—General M,D,O
- Educational Leadership and Administration M,D,O
- Educational Psychology M,D,O
- Elementary Education M,D
- English as a Second Language M,D
- English Education M,D
- Finance and Banking M
- Higher Education M,D
- Information Studies M,D
- Law M,D
- Library Science M,D
- Management Information Systems M,D
- Management Strategy and Policy M,D
- Marketing M,D
- Mathematics Education M
- Music Education M,D
- Organizational Management M,D
- Reading Education M,D,O
- Secondary Education M,D
- Special Education M,D

UNIVERSITY OF ARKANSAS
- Accounting M
- Adult Education M,D
- Agricultural Education M
- Athletic Training and Sports Medicine M
- Business Administration and Management—General M,D
- Counselor Education M,D
- Curriculum and Instruction M,D,O
- Early Childhood Education M
- Education—General M,D,O
- Educational Leadership and Administration M,D,O
- Educational Measurement and Evaluation M,D
- Educational Media/Instructional Technology M
- Educational Policy D
- Health Education M,D
- Higher Education M,D,O
- Human Resources Development M,D,O
- Industrial and Manufacturing Management M
- Kinesiology and Movement Studies M,D
- Law M,D
- Management Information Systems M
- Mathematics Education M
- Middle School Education M,D,O
- Physical Education M
- Recreation and Park Management M,D
- Secondary Education M,O
- Social Work M
- Special Education M
- Sports Management M,D
- Vocational and Technical Education M,D,O

UNIVERSITY OF ARKANSAS AT LITTLE ROCK
- Adult Education M
- Art Education M
- Business Administration and Management—General M,O
- Community College Education M,D
- Counselor Education M
- Curriculum and Instruction M
- Education of the Gifted M,O
- Education—General M,D,O
- Educational Leadership and Administration M,D,O
- Educational Media/Instructional Technology M
- English as a Second Language M
- Entrepreneurship O
- Exercise and Sports Science M
- Foreign Languages Education M
- Health Education M,D
- Higher Education M,D
- Law D
- Management Information Systems M,O
- Middle School Education M
- Nonprofit Management O
- Reading Education M,D,O
- Secondary Education M
- Social Work M
- Special Education M,O
- Sports Management M
- Student Affairs M,D

UNIVERSITY OF ARKANSAS AT MONTICELLO
- Education—General M
- Educational Leadership and Administration M

UNIVERSITY OF ARKANSAS AT PINE BLUFF
- Education—General M
- Elementary Education M
- English Education M
- Mathematics Education M
- Science Education M
- Secondary Education M
- Social Sciences Education M

UNIVERSITY OF ARKANSAS FOR MEDICAL SCIENCES
- Health Education M,D,O

UNIVERSITY OF BALTIMORE
- Accounting M,O
- Business Administration and Management—General M,O
- Entrepreneurship M
- Finance and Banking M
- Human Services M
- Intellectual Property Law M,D
- International Business M
- Law M,D
- Legal and Justice Studies M
- Management Information Systems M,O
- Marketing M
- Taxation M,D

UNIVERSITY OF BRIDGEPORT
- Accounting M
- Business Administration and Management—General M
- Computer Education M,D,O
- Early Childhood Education M,D,O
- Education—General M,D,O
- Educational Leadership and Administration M,D,O
- Elementary Education M,D,O
- Entrepreneurship M
- Finance and Banking M
- Human Resources Development M
- Human Resources Management M
- Human Services M
- Industrial and Manufacturing Management M
- International and Comparative Education M,D,O
- International Business M
- Management Information Systems M
- Marketing M
- Middle School Education M,D,O
- Music Education M,D,O
- Reading Education M,D,O
- Secondary Education M,D,O
- Student Affairs M

THE UNIVERSITY OF BRITISH COLUMBIA
- Accounting D
- Adult Education M,D
- Archives/Archival Administration M,D
- Art Education M,D
- Business Administration and Management—General M,D
- Business Analytics M
- Curriculum and Instruction M,D
- Education—General M,D,O
- Educational Leadership and Administration M,D
- Educational Measurement and Evaluation M,D,O
- Educational Policy M,D
- English as a Second Language M,D
- Finance and Banking D
- Foundations and Philosophy of Education M,D
- Higher Education M,D
- Home Economics Education M,D
- Information Studies M,D
- Kinesiology and Movement Studies M,D
- Law M,D
- Library Science M,D
- Management Information Systems D
- Management Strategy and Policy D
- Marketing D
- Mathematics Education M,D
- Music Education M,D
- Organizational Behavior D
- Physical Education M,D
- Quantitative Analysis M,D
- Reading Education M,D
- Science Education M,D
- Social Sciences Education M,D
- Social Work M,D
- Special Education M,D,O
- Sustainability Management M,D
- Taxation M,D
- Transportation Management D
- Vocational and Technical Education M,D

UNIVERSITY OF CALGARY
- Adult Education M,D
- Business Administration and Management—General M,D
- Curriculum and Instruction M,D
- Educational Leadership and Administration M,D
- Educational Measurement and Evaluation M,D
- Environmental Law M,O
- Kinesiology and Movement Studies M,D
- Law M,D,O
- Legal and Justice Studies M,O
- Management Strategy and Policy M,D
- Multilingual and Multicultural Education M,D
- Project Management M,D
- Social Work M,D,O

UNIVERSITY OF CALIFORNIA, BERKELEY
- Accounting D,O
- Business Administration and Management—General M,D,O
- Education—General M,D,O
- Educational Leadership and Administration M,D
- English as a Second Language O
- Facilities Management O
- Finance and Banking D,O
- Human Resources Management O
- Information Studies M,D
- International Business O
- Law M,D
- Legal and Justice Studies D
- Management Information Systems M,D,O
- Marketing D,O
- Mathematics Education M,D
- Organizational Behavior D
- Project Management O
- Real Estate D
- Science Education M,D
- Social Work M,D
- Special Education M,D
- Sustainability Management O

UNIVERSITY OF CALIFORNIA, DAVIS
- Accounting M
- Business Administration and Management—General M
- Business Analytics M
- Curriculum and Instruction M,D
- Education—General M,D
- Educational Psychology M,D
- Entrepreneurship M
- Exercise and Sports Science M
- Finance and Banking M
- Law M,D
- Management Strategy and Policy M
- Marketing M
- Organizational Behavior M
- Transportation Management M,D

UNIVERSITY OF CALIFORNIA, HASTINGS COLLEGE OF THE LAW
- Law M,D

UNIVERSITY OF CALIFORNIA, IRVINE
- Accounting M
- Business Administration and Management—General M,D
- Business Analytics M
- Education—General M,D
- Educational Leadership and Administration M,D
- Elementary Education M,D
- Foreign Languages Education M,D
- Law D
- Secondary Education M,D

UNIVERSITY OF CALIFORNIA, LOS ANGELES
- Accounting M,D
- Archives/Archival Administration M,D,O
- Business Administration and Management—General M,D
- Business Analytics M,D
- Education—General M,D
- Educational Leadership and Administration D
- English as a Second Language M,D,O
- Finance and Banking M,D
- Information Studies M,D,O
- Law M,D
- Library Science M,D,O
- Management Strategy and Policy M,D
- Marketing M,D
- Social Work M,D
- Special Education D

UNIVERSITY OF CALIFORNIA, MERCED
- Entrepreneurship M,D
- Sustainability Management M,D

UNIVERSITY OF CALIFORNIA, RIVERSIDE
- Accounting M,D
- Archives/Archival Administration M,D
- Business Administration and Management—General M,D
- Education—General M,D,O
- Educational Leadership and Administration M,D,O
- Educational Measurement and Evaluation M,D,O
- Educational Policy M,D,O
- Educational Psychology M,D,O
- English as a Second Language M,D,O
- Finance and Banking M,D
- Foundations and Philosophy of Education M,D,O
- Higher Education M,D,O
- Multilingual and Multicultural Education M,D,O
- Special Education M,D,O

UNIVERSITY OF CALIFORNIA, SAN DIEGO
- Business Administration and Management—General M,D
- Business Analytics M,D
- Curriculum and Instruction M,D
- Education—General M,D
- Educational Leadership and Administration M,D
- Finance and Banking M,D
- International Business M
- Mathematics Education D
- Multilingual and Multicultural Education M,D
- Nonprofit Management M
- Science Education D

UNIVERSITY OF CALIFORNIA, SAN FRANCISCO
- Health Law M

UNIVERSITY OF CALIFORNIA, SANTA BARBARA
- Education—General M,D,O
- Finance and Banking M,D
- Quantitative Analysis M,D
- Transportation Management M,D

UNIVERSITY OF CALIFORNIA, SANTA CRUZ
- Education—General M,D
- Finance and Banking M
- Social Sciences Education M

UNIVERSITY OF CENTRAL ARKANSAS
- Accounting M
- Adult Education M,O
- Business Administration and Management—General M
- Counselor Education M
- Curriculum and Instruction M,O
- Education of the Gifted M,O
- Education—General M,O
- Educational Leadership and Administration M,O
- Educational Media/Instructional Technology M
- Health Education M
- Kinesiology and Movement Studies M
- Library Science M
- Mathematics Education M
- Music Education M,O
- Organizational Management D
- Reading Education M
- Special Education M,O
- Student Affairs M

UNIVERSITY OF CENTRAL FLORIDA
- Accounting M
- Art Education M,O
- Athletic Training and Sports Medicine M
- Business Administration and Management—General M,D,O
- Community College Education M,O
- Counselor Education M,O
- Curriculum and Instruction M,O
- Educational Leadership and Administration M,O
- Educational Media/Instructional Technology M,O
- Elementary Education M
- English as a Second Language M,O
- English Education M,O
- Entrepreneurship M,O
- Exercise and Sports Science M,O
- Foreign Languages Education M,O
- Higher Education M,O
- Hospitality Management M,D,O
- Kinesiology and Movement Studies M

Mathematics Education M,O
Middle School Education M,O
Nonprofit Management M,O
Reading Education M,O
Real Estate M
Science Education M,O
Social Sciences Education M,O
Social Work M,O
Special Education M,O
Sports Management M
Student Affairs M,O
Travel and Tourism M,D,O
Vocational and Technical Education M,O

UNIVERSITY OF CENTRAL MISSOURI
Accounting M,D,O
Business Administration and
   Management—General M,D,O
Counselor Education M,D,O
Early Childhood Education M,D,O
Education—General M,D,O
Educational Leadership and
   Administration M,D,O
Educational Media/Instructional
   Technology M,D,O
Elementary Education M,D,O
English as a Second Language M,D,O
Finance and Banking M,D,O
Human Services M,D,O
Industrial and Manufacturing
   Management M,D,O
Kinesiology and Movement Studies M,D,O
Library Science M,D,O
Management Information Systems M,D,O
Marketing M,D,O
Reading Education M,D,O
Special Education M,D,O
Student Affairs M,D,O
Vocational and Technical Education M,O

UNIVERSITY OF CENTRAL OKLAHOMA
Adult Education M
Athletic Training and Sports
   Medicine M
Business Analytics M
Counselor Education M
Early Childhood Education M
Education of Students with
   Severe/Multiple Disabilities M
Education—General M
Educational Leadership and
   Administration M
Educational Media/Instructional
   Technology M
Elementary Education M
English as a Second Language M
Exercise and Sports Science M
Foundations and Philosophy of
   Education M
Library Science M
Music Education M
Nonprofit Management M
Reading Education M
Secondary Education M
Special Education M
Student Affairs M

UNIVERSITY OF CHARLESTON
Accounting M
Business Administration and
   Management—General M
Legal and Justice Studies M
Management Strategy and Policy M
Organizational Management D

UNIVERSITY OF CHICAGO
Accounting M,O
Business Administration and
   Management—General M,D,O
Entrepreneurship M,O
Finance and Banking M,O
Industrial and Manufacturing
   Management M,O
International Business M,O
Law M,D
Management Strategy and Policy M,O
Marketing M,O
Organizational Behavior M,O
Science Education D
Social Work M,D
Urban Education M

UNIVERSITY OF CINCINNATI
Accounting M,D
Art Education M
Business Administration and
   Management—General M,D
Business Analytics M,D
Counselor Education M,D,O
Curriculum and Instruction M,D
Education—General M,D,O
Educational Leadership and
   Administration M,D,O
English as a Second Language M,D
Finance and Banking M,D
Foundations and Philosophy of
   Education M,D
Health Education M,D
Human Resources Management M
Industrial and Manufacturing
   Management D
Law M,D
Management Information Systems M,D
Marketing M,D
Mathematics Education M,D
Music Education M
Organizational Management M
Reading Education M,D
Social Work M
Special Education M,D
Sports Management M
Taxation M

UNIVERSITY OF COLORADO BOULDER
Advertising and Public Relations M,D
Business Administration and
   Management—General M,D
Curriculum and Instruction M,D
Education—General M,D
Educational Measurement and
   Evaluation D
Educational Policy M,D
Educational Psychology M,D
Kinesiology and Movement Studies M,D
Law D
Multilingual and Multicultural
   Education M,D
Music Education M,D
Organizational Management M

UNIVERSITY OF COLORADO COLORADO SPRINGS
Business Administration and
   Management—General M
Counselor Education M,D
Curriculum and Instruction M,D
Education—General M,D
Educational Leadership and
   Administration M,D
English as a Second Language M,D
Human Services M,D
Special Education M,D

UNIVERSITY OF COLORADO DENVER
Accounting M
Adult Education M
Business Administration and
   Management—General M
Counselor Education M
Distance Education Development M
Early Childhood Education M,D
Education—General M,D,O
Educational Leadership and
   Administration M,D,O
Educational Measurement and
   Evaluation M,D
Educational Media/Instructional
   Technology M
Educational Policy M,D,O
Elementary Education M
English Education M
Entertainment Management M
Entrepreneurship M
Environmental Law M,D
Finance and Banking M
Health Education M
Human Resources Management M
Insurance M
International Business M
Management Information Systems M,D
Management Strategy and Policy M
Marketing M
Mathematics Education M,D
Multilingual and Multicultural
   Education M
Nonprofit Management M,D
Reading Education M
Risk Management M
Science Education M
Secondary Education M
Special Education M
Sports Management M
Sustainability Management M
Taxation M

UNIVERSITY OF CONNECTICUT
Accounting M,D
Adult Education M,O
Agricultural Education M,D
Business Administration and
   Management—General M,D
Business Analytics M,D
Counselor Education M,D
Curriculum and Instruction M,D
Education of the Gifted O
Education—General M,D
Educational Leadership and
   Administration M
Educational Media/Instructional
   Technology M,D
Educational Psychology M,D,O
Elementary Education M,D
English Education M,D
Exercise and Sports Science M,D
Finance and Banking M,D,O
Foreign Languages Education M,D
Higher Education M
Human Resources Management M
Law D
Management Information Systems M,D
Marketing M,D
Mathematics Education M,D
Multilingual and Multicultural
   Education M,D
Music Education M,D
Nonprofit Management M,O
Project Management M,O
Quantitative Analysis M,O
Reading Education M,D
Risk Management M,D
Science Education M,D
Secondary Education M,D
Social Sciences Education M,D
Social Work M,D
Sports Management M

UNIVERSITY OF DALLAS
Accounting M,D
Business Administration and
   Management—General M,D
Business Analytics M,D
Entertainment Management M,D
Finance and Banking M,D
Human Resources Management M,D
International Business M,D

Logistics M,D
Management Information Systems M,D
Management Strategy and Policy M,D
Marketing M,D
Organizational Management M,D
Project Management M,D
Sports Management M,D
Supply Chain Management M,D

UNIVERSITY OF DAYTON
Accounting M
Business Administration and
   Management—General M
Counselor Education M,O
Early Childhood Education M
Educational Leadership and
   Administration M,D,O
Educational Media/Instructional
   Technology M
Elementary Education M
English as a Second Language M
Exercise and Sports Science M
Finance and Banking M
Foreign Languages Education M
Law M,D
Marketing M
Mathematics Education M
Middle School Education M
Music Education M
Physical Education M
Reading Education M
Secondary Education M
Student Affairs M,O

UNIVERSITY OF DELAWARE
Accounting M
Agricultural Education M
Business Administration and
   Management—General M,D
Business Education M,D
Curriculum and Instruction M,D,O
Education—General M,D,O
Educational Leadership and
   Administration M,D,O
English as a Second Language M,D,O
Entrepreneurship M,D
Finance and Banking M
Foreign Languages Education M
Higher Education M,D,O
Hospitality Management M
Kinesiology and Movement Studies M,D
Management Information Systems M,D
Multilingual and Multicultural
   Education M,D,O
Music Education M

UNIVERSITY OF DENVER
Accounting M
Art Education M,O
Business Administration and
   Management—General M
Business Analytics M
Curriculum and Instruction M,D,O
Early Childhood Education M,D,O
Education—General M,D,O
Educational Leadership and
   Administration M,D,O
Educational Measurement and
   Evaluation M,D,O
Educational Policy M,D,O
Finance and Banking M
Higher Education M,D,O
Human Resources Management M,O
Law M,D,O
Legal and Justice Studies M,O
Library Science M,D,O
Marketing M
Music Education M,O
Organizational Management M
Project Management M
Real Estate M
Social Work M,D,O
Special Education M,D,O
Taxation M

UNIVERSITY OF DETROIT MERCY
Accounting M,O
Business Administration and
   Management—General M,O
Curriculum and Instruction M,D,O
Educational Leadership and
   Administration M,D,O
Finance and Banking M,D,O
Law D
Management Information Systems M,D,O
Management Strategy and Policy M,O
Mathematics Education M,D
Religious Education M,D,O
Special Education M,D,O

UNIVERSITY OF DUBUQUE
Business Administration and
   Management—General M

UNIVERSITY OF EVANSVILLE
Athletic Training and Sports
   Medicine M

UNIVERSITY OF FAIRFAX
Business Administration and
   Management—General M,D
Project Management M,D

THE UNIVERSITY OF FINDLAY
Accounting M,D
Athletic Training and Sports
   Medicine M,D
Business Administration and
   Management—General M,D
Education—General M,D
Educational Leadership and
   Administration M,D
Educational Media/Instructional
   Technology M,D

English as a Second Language M,D
Hospitality Management M,D
Reading Education M,D
Science Education M,D

UNIVERSITY OF FLORIDA
Accounting M,D
Advertising and Public Relations M,D
Agricultural Education M,D
Art Education M,D
Athletic Training and Sports
   Medicine M,D
Business Administration and
   Management—General M,D
Counselor Education M,D,O
Curriculum and Instruction M,D,O
Early Childhood Education M,D,O
Education—General M,D,O
Educational Leadership and
   Administration M,D,O
Educational Measurement and
   Evaluation M,D,O
Educational Policy M,D,O
Elementary Education M,D,O
English as a Second Language M,D,O
English Education M,D,O
Entrepreneurship M,D,O
Environmental Education M,D,O
Environmental Law M,D
Exercise and Sports Science M,D
Finance and Banking M,D,O
Foreign Languages Education M,D
Health Education M,D,O
Higher Education M,D,O
Human Resources Management M,D
Insurance M,D,O
International Business M,D
Kinesiology and Movement Studies M,D
Law M,D
Management Information Systems M,D,O
Marketing M,D,O
Mathematics Education M,D,O
Music Education M,D,O
Nonprofit Management M
Physical Education M,D
Quantitative Analysis M,D,O
Reading Education M,D,O
Real Estate M,D,O
Recreation and Park Management M,D
Science Education M,D,O
Social Sciences Education M,D,O
Special Education M,D,O
Sports Management M,D
Student Affairs M,D,O
Supply Chain Management M,D,O
Taxation M,D,O
Travel and Tourism M,D

UNIVERSITY OF GEORGIA
Accounting M
Adult Education D,O
Business Administration and
   Management—General M
Business Analytics M
Business Education M,D,O
Counselor Education M,D,O
Education—General M,D,O
Educational Leadership and
   Administration D,O
Educational Media/Instructional
   Technology M,D,O
Educational Policy D,O
Educational Psychology O
English Education M,D
Health Education M,D
Higher Education M,D
Kinesiology and Movement Studies M,D
Law M,D
Mathematics Education M,D,O
Music Education M,D
Nonprofit Management M,D,O
Physical Education M,D
Reading Education M,D
Science Education M,D,O
Social Work M,D,O
Special Education M,D,O
Student Affairs M,D,O
Vocational and Technical Education M,D,O

UNIVERSITY OF GUAM
Business Administration and
   Management—General M
Counselor Education M
Education—General M
Educational Leadership and
   Administration M
English as a Second Language M
Reading Education M
Secondary Education M
Social Work M
Special Education M

UNIVERSITY OF GUELPH
Business Administration and
   Management—General M,D
Hospitality Management M
Organizational Management M

UNIVERSITY OF HARTFORD
Accounting M,O
Business Administration and
   Management—General M
Early Childhood Education M
Education—General M,D,O
Educational Leadership and
   Administration D
Elementary Education M
Music Education M,D,O
Organizational Behavior M
Taxation M,O

UNIVERSITY OF HAWAII AT HILO
Education—General M

M—masters degree; D—doctorate; O—other advanced degree; *—Close-Up and/or Display

Foreign Languages Education	M,D

UNIVERSITY OF HAWAII AT MANOA

Accounting	M,D
Business Administration and Management—General	M
Curriculum and Instruction	M,D
Early Childhood Education	M
Education—General	M,D,O
Educational Leadership and Administration	M,D
Educational Media/Instructional Technology	M,D
Educational Policy	D
Educational Psychology	M,D
English as a Second Language	M,D,O
Entrepreneurship	M,O
Finance and Banking	M,D
Foreign Languages Education	M,D,O
Foundations and Philosophy of Education	M,D
Human Resources Management	M
Information Studies	M,O
International Business	M,D
Kinesiology and Movement Studies	M,D
Law	M,D,O
Library Science	M,O
Management Information Systems	M,D,O
Marketing	M,D
Organizational Behavior	M
Organizational Management	M,D
Real Estate	M
Social Work	M,D
Special Education	M,D
Taxation	M
Transportation Management	M,D,O
Travel and Tourism	M

UNIVERSITY OF HOLY CROSS

Business Administration and Management—General	M,D
Counselor Education	M,D
Education—General	M,D
Educational Leadership and Administration	M,D

UNIVERSITY OF HOUSTON

Accounting	M,D
Advertising and Public Relations	M
Business Administration and Management—General	M,D
Education—General	M,D
Educational Leadership and Administration	M,D
Environmental Law	M,D
Exercise and Sports Science	M,D
Finance and Banking	M
Health Education	M,D
Health Law	M,D
Higher Education	M,D
Hospitality Management	M
Human Resources Development	M
Intellectual Property Law	M,D
Kinesiology and Movement Studies	M,D
Law	M,D
Logistics	M
Marketing	D
Music Education	M,D
Physical Education	M,D
Project Management	M
Social Work	M,D
Special Education	M,D
Supply Chain Management	M
Taxation	M,D

UNIVERSITY OF HOUSTON–CLEAR LAKE

Accounting	M
Business Administration and Management—General	M
Counselor Education	M
Curriculum and Instruction	M
Early Childhood Education	M
Education—General	M,D
Educational Leadership and Administration	M,D
Educational Media/Instructional Technology	M
Exercise and Sports Science	M
Finance and Banking	M
Foundations and Philosophy of Education	M
Human Resources Management	M
Library Science	M
Management Information Systems	M
Multilingual and Multicultural Education	M
Reading Education	M

UNIVERSITY OF HOUSTON–DOWNTOWN

Accounting	M
Business Administration and Management—General	M
Curriculum and Instruction	M
Finance and Banking	M
Human Resources Management	M
International Business	M
Investment Management	M
Nonprofit Management	M
Project Management	M
Social Work	M
Supply Chain Management	M
Urban Education	M

UNIVERSITY OF HOUSTON–VICTORIA

Accounting	M
Adult Education	M,O
Business Administration and Management—General	M
Counselor Education	M,O
Curriculum and Instruction	M,O
Education—General	M,O
Educational Leadership and Administration	M,O
Educational Media/Instructional Technology	M,O
Entrepreneurship	M
Finance and Banking	M
Higher Education	M,O
International Business	M
Management Information Systems	M
Marketing	M
Reading Education	M,O
Special Education	M,O

UNIVERSITY OF IDAHO

Accounting	M
Athletic Training and Sports Medicine	M,D
Business Administration and Management—General	M
Counselor Education	M,O
Curriculum and Instruction	M,O
Education—General	M,D,O
Educational Leadership and Administration	M,O
Exercise and Sports Science	M,D
Human Services	M,O
Kinesiology and Movement Studies	M,D
Law	M,D
Physical Education	M,D
Special Education	M,O
Sports Management	M,D
Travel and Tourism	M,D
Vocational and Technical Education	M,O

UNIVERSITY OF ILLINOIS AT CHICAGO

Accounting	M
Business Administration and Management—General	M,D
Computer Education	D
Curriculum and Instruction	M,D
Early Childhood Education	M,D
Education—General	M,D
Educational Leadership and Administration	M,D
Educational Measurement and Evaluation	M,D
Educational Policy	M,D
Educational Psychology	M,D
Elementary Education	M,D
English as a Second Language	M,D
Finance and Banking	M
Foreign Languages Education	M,D
Health Education	M
Kinesiology and Movement Studies	M,D
Management Information Systems	M,D
Mathematics Education	M,D
Real Estate	M
Science Education	D
Secondary Education	M,D
Social Sciences Education	D
Social Work	M,D,O
Special Education	M,D
Urban Education	M,D

UNIVERSITY OF ILLINOIS AT SPRINGFIELD

Accounting	M
Business Administration and Management—General	M
Education—General	M,O
Educational Leadership and Administration	M,O
Health Education	M,O
Human Services	M,O
Legal and Justice Studies	M
Management Information Systems	M

UNIVERSITY OF ILLINOIS AT URBANA–CHAMPAIGN

Accounting	M,D
Actuarial Science	M,D
Advertising and Public Relations	M
Agricultural Education	M
Art Education	M,D
Business Administration and Management—General	M,D
Counselor Education	M,D,O
Curriculum and Instruction	M,D,O
Education of Students with Severe/Multiple Disabilities	M,D,O
Education—General	M,D,O
Educational Leadership and Administration	M,D,O
Educational Policy	M,D,O
Educational Psychology	M,D,O
English as a Second Language	M,D
Finance and Banking	M,D
Foreign Languages Education	M,D
Human Resources Management	M,D,O
Human Services	M,D
Information Studies	M,D,O
Kinesiology and Movement Studies	M,D
Law	M,D
Leisure Studies	M,D
Library Science	M,D,O
Management Information Systems	M,D,O
Management Strategy and Policy	M,D,O
Mathematics Education	M,D
Music Education	M,D
Science Education	M,D
Social Work	M,D
Special Education	M,D,O

UNIVERSITY OF INDIANAPOLIS

Art Education	M
Business Administration and Management—General	M,O
Curriculum and Instruction	M
Education—General	M
Educational Leadership and Administration	M
Elementary Education	M
English Education	M
Foreign Languages Education	M
Mathematics Education	M
Physical Education	M
Science Education	M
Secondary Education	M
Social Sciences Education	M
Social Work	M,D
Sports Management	M

THE UNIVERSITY OF IOWA

Accounting	M,D
Actuarial Science	M,D
Art Education	M,D
Athletic Training and Sports Medicine	M,D
Business Administration and Management—General	M,D
Business Analytics	M
Counselor Education	M,D
Developmental Education	M,D
Education—General	M,D,O
Educational Leadership and Administration	M,D,O
Educational Measurement and Evaluation	M,D,O
Educational Policy	M,D,O
Educational Psychology	M,D,O
Elementary Education	M,D
English as a Second Language	M,D
English Education	M,D
Exercise and Sports Science	M,D
Finance and Banking	M,D
Foreign Languages Education	M,D
Foundations and Philosophy of Education	M,D,O
Higher Education	M,D
Information Studies	M,D
Law	M,D
Leisure Studies	M,D
Library Science	M,D
Marketing	M,D
Mathematics Education	M,D
Music Education	M,D
Quantitative Analysis	M,D,O
Recreation and Park Management	M,D
Science Education	M,D
Secondary Education	M,D
Social Sciences Education	M,D
Social Work	M,D
Special Education	M,D
Sports Management	M,D
Student Affairs	M,D

UNIVERSITY OF JAMESTOWN

Curriculum and Instruction	M
Education—General	M

THE UNIVERSITY OF KANSAS

Accounting	M
Art Education	M
Business Administration and Management—General	M,D
Curriculum and Instruction	M,D
Early Childhood Education	M,D,O
Education—General	M,D,O
Educational Leadership and Administration	M,D
Educational Measurement and Evaluation	M,D
Educational Media/Instructional Technology	M,D
Educational Policy	M,D
Educational Psychology	M,D
Exercise and Sports Science	M,D
Finance and Banking	M,D
Health Education	M,D,O
Higher Education	M,D
Human Resources Management	M,D
Law	D
Logistics	M,D
Management Information Systems	M
Management Strategy and Policy	M,D
Marketing	M,D
Music Education	M,D
Organizational Behavior	M,D
Organizational Management	M,D,O
Physical Education	M,D
Project Management	M
Social Work	M,D
Special Education	M,D,O
Sports Management	M,D
Supply Chain Management	M,D

UNIVERSITY OF KENTUCKY

Accounting	M
Art Education	M
Athletic Training and Sports Medicine	M
Business Administration and Management—General	M,D
Curriculum and Instruction	M,D
Early Childhood Education	M,D
Education—General	M,D,O
Educational Leadership and Administration	M,D,O
Educational Measurement and Evaluation	M,D
Educational Media/Instructional Technology	M,D
Educational Policy	M,D
Educational Psychology	M,D,O
Elementary Education	M,D
Exercise and Sports Science	M,D
Foreign Languages Education	M
Higher Education	M,D
Hospitality Management	M
International Business	M
Kinesiology and Movement Studies	M,D
Law	D
Library Science	M
Middle School Education	M,D
Music Education	M,D
Physical Education	M,D
Reading Education	M,D
Secondary Education	M,D
Social Work	M,D
Special Education	M,D

UNIVERSITY OF LA VERNE

Accounting	M
Business Administration and Management—General	M,D,O
Counselor Education	M,D,O
Education—General	M,O
Educational Leadership and Administration	M,D,O
Elementary Education	M,D,O
Finance and Banking	M
Higher Education	M
Human Resources Management	M,O
International Business	M
Law	D
Management Information Systems	M
Marketing	M
Nonprofit Management	M,O
Organizational Management	M,D,O
Reading Education	M,O
Secondary Education	M,D,O
Special Education	M,D,O
Student Affairs	M
Supply Chain Management	M

UNIVERSITY OF LETHBRIDGE

Accounting	M,D
Business Administration and Management—General	M,D
Counselor Education	M,D
Education—General	M,D
Educational Leadership and Administration	M,D
Exercise and Sports Science	M,D
Finance and Banking	M,D
Human Resources Management	M,D
International Business	M,D
Kinesiology and Movement Studies	M,D
Management Information Systems	M,D
Management Strategy and Policy	M,D
Marketing	M,D

UNIVERSITY OF LOUISIANA AT LAFAYETTE

Accounting	M
Business Administration and Management—General	M
Counselor Education	M
Curriculum and Instruction	M
Early Childhood Education	M
Education of the Gifted	M
Education—General	M,D
Educational Leadership and Administration	M,D
Educational Media/Instructional Technology	M
English as a Second Language	M,D
Entrepreneurship	M
Finance and Banking	M
Hospitality Management	M
Human Resources Management	M
International Business	M
Mathematics Education	M
Music Education	M
Project Management	M
Special Education	M

UNIVERSITY OF LOUISIANA AT MONROE

Business Administration and Management—General	M,O
Counselor Education	M
Curriculum and Instruction	M,D
Education—General	M,D
Elementary Education	M
Exercise and Sports Science	M
Recreation and Park Management	M
Secondary Education	M
Special Education	M
Sports Management	M

UNIVERSITY OF LOUISVILLE

Accounting	M
Art Education	M,D,O
Business Administration and Management—General	M
Counselor Education	M,D
Curriculum and Instruction	M,D,O
Early Childhood Education	M,D,O
Education—General	M,D,O
Educational Leadership and Administration	M,D,O
Educational Measurement and Evaluation	M,D
Educational Psychology	M,D
Elementary Education	M,D,O
Entrepreneurship	M,D
Exercise and Sports Science	M,D,O
Health Education	M,D,O
Higher Education	M,D,O
Human Resources Development	M,D,O
Human Resources Management	M,D,O
International Business	M
Law	D
Logistics	M,D,O
Middle School Education	M,D,O
Music Education	M,D,O
Nonprofit Management	M,D
Physical Education	M,D,O
Secondary Education	M,D,O
Social Work	M,D,O
Special Education	M,D,O
Sports Management	M,D,O
Student Affairs	M,D
Supply Chain Management	M,D,O
Sustainability Management	M,D

UNIVERSITY OF LYNCHBURG

Athletic Training and Sports Medicine	M
Business Administration and Management—General	M
Counselor Education	M
Curriculum and Instruction	M
Educational Leadership and Administration	M,D
Higher Education	M
Nonprofit Management	M
Reading Education	M

Science Education — M
Special Education — M

UNIVERSITY OF MAINE
Business Administration and Management—General — M,O
Early Childhood Education — M,D,O
Education—General — M,D,O
Educational Leadership and Administration — M,D,O
Educational Media/Instructional Technology — M,D,O
Exercise and Sports Science — M,D,O
Finance and Banking — M
Foreign Languages Education — M
Higher Education — M
Kinesiology and Movement Studies — M,D,O
Law — D
Physical Education — M,D,O
Reading Education — M,D,O
Social Sciences Education — M,D,O
Social Work — M,O
Special Education — M,D,O

UNIVERSITY OF MAINE AT FARMINGTON
Early Childhood Education — M
Education—General — M
Educational Leadership and Administration — M
Educational Media/Instructional Technology — M

UNIVERSITY OF MANAGEMENT AND TECHNOLOGY
Business Administration and Management—General — M,D,O
Management Information Systems — M,O
Project Management — M,D,O

THE UNIVERSITY OF MANCHESTER
Accounting — M
Actuarial Science — M,D
Business Administration and Management—General — M
Business Analytics — M
Education—General — M,D
Educational Psychology — M,D
Entrepreneurship — M
Finance and Banking — M
Health Law — M,D
Human Resources Management — M
Industrial and Manufacturing Management — M,D
International Business — M
Law — M,D
Management Strategy and Policy — M
Marketing — M
Project Management — M
Social Work — M,D
Supply Chain Management — M

UNIVERSITY OF MANITOBA
Adult Education — M
Archives/Archival Administration — M,D
Business Administration and Management—General — M,D
Counselor Education — M
Curriculum and Instruction — M
Education—General — M,D
Educational Leadership and Administration — M
Educational Psychology — M
English as a Second Language — M
English Education — M
Foundations and Philosophy of Education — M
Higher Education — M
Kinesiology and Movement Studies — M
Law — M
Physical Education — M
Recreation and Park Management — M
Social Work — M,D
Special Education — M

UNIVERSITY OF MARY
Business Administration and Management—General — M
Curriculum and Instruction — M,D
Education—General — M,D
Educational Leadership and Administration — M,D
Exercise and Sports Science — M
Human Resources Management — M
Kinesiology and Movement Studies — M
Physical Education — M
Project Management — M
Reading Education — M
Special Education — M,D
Sports Management — M

UNIVERSITY OF MARY HARDIN-BAYLOR
Accounting — M
Business Administration and Management—General — M
Counselor Education — M
Curriculum and Instruction — M,D
Education—General — M,D
Educational Leadership and Administration — M,D
Elementary Education — M,D
Exercise and Sports Science — M,D
Higher Education — M,D
International Business — M
Management Information Systems — M
Secondary Education — M,D
Sports Management — M

UNIVERSITY OF MARYLAND, BALTIMORE
Law — M,D
Social Work — M,D

UNIVERSITY OF MARYLAND, BALTIMORE COUNTY
Art Education — M
Distance Education Development — M,O
Early Childhood Education — M
Education—General — M,O
Educational Media/Instructional Technology — M,O
Educational Policy — M,D
Elementary Education — M
English as a Second Language — M,O
English Education — M
Foreign Languages Education — M
Human Services — M,D
Mathematics Education — M
Multilingual and Multicultural Education — M,D
Music Education — M
Nonprofit Management — M,O
Science Education — M
Social Sciences Education — M

UNIVERSITY OF MARYLAND, COLLEGE PARK
Advertising and Public Relations — M,D
Business Administration and Management—General — M,D
Counselor Education — M,D,O
Curriculum and Instruction — M,D,O
Education—General — M,D,O
Educational Leadership and Administration — M,D,O
Educational Measurement and Evaluation — M,D
Educational Media/Instructional Technology — M,D,O
English as a Second Language — M,D,O
Foreign Languages Education — D
Foundations and Philosophy of Education — M
Health Education — M,D
Information Studies — M,D
Kinesiology and Movement Studies — M,D
Law — M,D
Library Science — M
Music Education — M,D
Quantitative Analysis — M,D
Reading Education — M,D,O
Real Estate — M
Secondary Education — M,D,O
Social Work — M
Student Affairs — M,D,O

UNIVERSITY OF MARYLAND EASTERN SHORE
Counselor Education — M
Education—General — M
Educational Leadership and Administration — D
Organizational Management — D
Special Education — M
Vocational and Technical Education — M

UNIVERSITY OF MARYLAND UNIVERSITY COLLEGE
Accounting — M,O
Business Administration and Management—General — M,D,O
Distance Education Development — M
Education—General — M
Educational Media/Instructional Technology — M
Finance and Banking — M
Management Information Systems — M,O

UNIVERSITY OF MARY WASHINGTON
Business Administration and Management—General — M
Education—General — M
Elementary Education — M

UNIVERSITY OF MASSACHUSETTS AMHERST
Accounting — M,D
Art Education — M
Business Administration and Management—General — M,D
Counselor Education — M,D,O
Early Childhood Education — M,D,O
Education—General — M,D,O
Educational Leadership and Administration — M,D,O
Educational Measurement and Evaluation — M,D,O
Educational Media/Instructional Technology — M,D,O
Educational Policy — M,D,O
Elementary Education — M,D,O
English as a Second Language — M,D,O
Entertainment Management — M,D
Entrepreneurship — M,D
Finance and Banking — M,D
Foreign Languages Education — M
Health Education — M,D
Higher Education — M,D,O
Hospitality Management — M,D
International and Comparative Education — M,D,O
Kinesiology and Movement Studies — M,D
Management Strategy and Policy — M,D
Marketing — M,D
Multilingual and Multicultural Education — M,D,O
Music Education — M,D
Organizational Management — M,D
Reading Education — M,D,O
Science Education — M,D,O
Secondary Education — M,D,O
Special Education — M,D,O
Sports Management — M,D
Travel and Tourism — M,D

UNIVERSITY OF MASSACHUSETTS BOSTON
Accounting — M
Archives/Archival Administration — M
Business Administration and Management—General — M
Business Analytics — M
Counselor Education — M
Early Childhood Education — D
Education—General — M,D,O
Educational Leadership and Administration — M,D,O
Educational Media/Instructional Technology — M,O
Educational Policy — D
Exercise and Sports Science — M
Finance and Banking — M
Higher Education — D
Human Services — M
International Business — M
Management Information Systems — M
Quality Management — M,O
Special Education — M
Urban Education — D

UNIVERSITY OF MASSACHUSETTS DARTMOUTH
Accounting — M,O
Art Education — M
Business Administration and Management—General — M,O
Education—General — M,D,O
Educational Leadership and Administration — D
Educational Policy — M,D,O
English as a Second Language — M,D,O
Finance and Banking — M,O
Law — D
Mathematics Education — M,D,O
Middle School Education — M,D,O
Science Education — M,D,O
Secondary Education — M,D,O
Special Education — M,O

UNIVERSITY OF MASSACHUSETTS LOWELL
Business Administration and Management—General — M,D
Curriculum and Instruction — M
Education—General — M
Entrepreneurship — M,D
Legal and Justice Studies — M
Music Education — M

UNIVERSITY OF MEMPHIS
Accounting — M,D
Adult Education — M,D,O
Business Administration and Management—General — M,D
Community College Education — M,D,O
Counselor Education — M,D
Curriculum and Instruction — M,D,O
Early Childhood Education — M,D
Education—General — M,D,O
Educational Leadership and Administration — M,D,O
Educational Measurement and Evaluation — M,D
Educational Media/Instructional Technology — M,D,O
Educational Psychology — M,D
Elementary Education — M,D,O
English as a Second Language — M,D,O
Exercise and Sports Science — M,O
Finance and Banking — M,D
Higher Education — M,D,O
Hospitality Management — M
Human Resources Management — M,O
Law — M
Management Information Systems — M,D,O
Management Strategy and Policy — M,O
Marketing — M,D
Mathematics Education — M,D
Music Education — M,D
Nonprofit Management — M,O
Physical Education — M,D,O
Reading Education — M,D,O
Real Estate — M,D
Science Education — M,D,O
Secondary Education — M,D,O
Social Work — M
Special Education — M,D,O
Supply Chain Management — M,D
Urban Education — M,D,O

UNIVERSITY OF MIAMI
Accounting — M,D
Advertising and Public Relations — M,D
Athletic Training and Sports Medicine — M,D
Business Administration and Management—General — M,D
Business Analytics — M,D
Counselor Education — M,O
Early Childhood Education — M,O
Education—General — M,D,O
Educational Measurement and Evaluation — M,D
Exercise and Sports Science — M,D
Finance and Banking — M,D
Higher Education — M,D,O
International Business — M,D
Law — M,D
Mathematics Education — D
Multilingual and Multicultural Education — D
Music Education — M,D,O
Reading Education — D
Real Estate — M,D
Science Education — D
Special Education — M,D,O
Sports Management — M

Taxation — M,D

UNIVERSITY OF MICHIGAN
Accounting — M,D
Business Administration and Management—General — M,D
Education—General — M,D
English Education — D
Foreign Languages Education — M,D
Health Education — M,D
Information Studies — M,D
Kinesiology and Movement Studies — M,D
Law — M,D
Music Education — M,D,O
Quantitative Analysis — M,D
Risk Management — M,D
Social Work — M
Sports Management — M,D
Supply Chain Management — M,D
Taxation — M,D

UNIVERSITY OF MICHIGAN–DEARBORN
Accounting — M
Business Administration and Management—General — M
Business Analytics — M
Curriculum and Instruction — D,O
Early Childhood Education — M
Education—General — M
Educational Leadership and Administration — M,D,O
Educational Measurement and Evaluation — M
Educational Media/Instructional Technology — M
Finance and Banking — M
Management Information Systems — M
Project Management — M
Supply Chain Management — M
Urban Education — M,D

UNIVERSITY OF MICHIGAN–FLINT
Accounting — M
Business Administration and Management—General — M,O
Curriculum and Instruction — M,D,O
Early Childhood Education — M,D,O
Education—General — M,D,O
Educational Leadership and Administration — M,D,O
Educational Media/Instructional Technology — M,D,O
Finance and Banking — M,O
Health Education — M
Industrial and Manufacturing Management — M,O
International Business — M,O
Management Information Systems — M,O
Marketing — M,O
Nonprofit Management — M
Organizational Management — M,O
Reading Education — M,D,O
Secondary Education — M,D,O

UNIVERSITY OF MINNESOTA, DULUTH
Business Administration and Management—General — M
Education—General — M,D
Music Education — M
Social Work — M

UNIVERSITY OF MINNESOTA ROCHESTER
Business Administration and Management—General — M,D

UNIVERSITY OF MINNESOTA, TWIN CITIES CAMPUS
Accounting — M,D
Adult Education — M,D,O
Art Education — M
Business Administration and Management—General — M,D
Counselor Education — M
Curriculum and Instruction — M,D
Early Childhood Education — M,D,O
Education of the Gifted — M,D,O
Education—General — M,D,O
Educational Leadership and Administration — M,D
Educational Measurement and Evaluation — M,D
Educational Media/Instructional Technology — M,D,O
Educational Policy — M,D,O
Educational Psychology — M,D,O
Elementary Education — M
English as a Second Language — M,D,O
English Education — D
Entrepreneurship — M
Exercise and Sports Science — M,D
Finance and Banking — M,D
Foreign Languages Education — M,D
Foundations and Philosophy of Education — M,D
Higher Education — M,D
Human Resources Development — M,D,O
Human Resources Management — M
International and Comparative Education — M,D
Kinesiology and Movement Studies — M,D
Law — M,D
Management Information Systems — M,D
Management Strategy and Policy — D
Marketing — M,D
Mathematics Education — M,D,O
Multilingual and Multicultural Education — M,D,O
Quantitative Analysis — M,D,O
Reading Education — M,D,O
Science Education — M
Social Sciences Education — M
Social Work — M,D

*M—masters degree; D—doctorate; O—other advanced degree; *—Close-Up and/or Display*

Peterson's Graduate Programs in Business, Education, Information Studies, Law & Social Work 2020

Special Education M,D
Sports Management M,D
Student Affairs M
Supply Chain Management M,D
Taxation M
Travel and Tourism M
Vocational and Technical Education M,D,O

UNIVERSITY OF MISSISSIPPI
Accounting M,D
Business Administration and
    Management—General M,D
Counselor Education M,D,O
Early Childhood Education M,D,O
Education—General M,D,O
Educational Leadership and
    Administration M,D,O
Elementary Education M,D,O
Exercise and Sports Science M,D
Finance and Banking M,D
Foreign Languages Education M,D
Higher Education M,D,O
Hospitality Management M,D
Kinesiology and Movement Studies M,D
Law M,D
Management Information Systems M,D
Marketing M,D
Mathematics Education M,D,O
Reading Education M,D,O
Recreation and Park Management M,D
Secondary Education M,D,O
Social Work M,D
Special Education M,D,O
Taxation M,D

UNIVERSITY OF MISSOURI
Accounting M,D,O
Adult Education M,D,O
Agricultural Education M,D,O
Art Education M,D,O
Business Administration and
    Management—General M,D
Business Education M,D,O
Curriculum and Instruction M,D,O
Early Childhood Education M,D,O
Education—General M,D,O
Educational Leadership and
    Administration M,D,O
Educational Media/Instructional
    Technology D
Educational Psychology M,D,O
Elementary Education M,D,O
English Education M,D,O
Finance and Banking M,D
Foreign Languages Education M,D,O
Health Education M,D,O
Higher Education M,D,O
Hospitality Management M,D
Information Studies D
Law M,D
Library Science D
Mathematics Education M,D,O
Music Education M,D,O
Nonprofit Management M,D,O
Organizational Management M,D,O
Reading Education M,D,O
Science Education M,D,O
Social Sciences Education M,D,O
Social Work M,D,O
Special Education D
Taxation M,D,O
Vocational and Technical Education M,D,O

UNIVERSITY OF MISSOURI–KANSAS CITY
Accounting M,D
Business Administration and
    Management—General M,D
Counselor Education M,D,O
Curriculum and Instruction M,D,O
Education—General M,D,O
Educational Leadership and
    Administration M,D,O
Finance and Banking M,D
Health Education M,D
Higher Education M,D,O
Law M,D
Music Education M,D
Reading Education M,D,O
Social Work M
Special Education M,D,O

UNIVERSITY OF MISSOURI–ST. LOUIS
Accounting M,D,O
Adult Education M,O
Business Administration and
    Management—General M
Counselor Education D
Curriculum and Instruction M
Early Childhood Education M
Education—General M,D,O
Educational Leadership and
    Administration D
Educational Measurement and
    Evaluation M,O
Educational Policy D
Educational Psychology D
Elementary Education M
English as a Second Language M
Higher Education M,O
Human Resources Management M,D,O
Logistics M,D,O
Management Information Systems M,D,O
Marketing Research M,D,O
Marketing M,D,O
Middle School Education M
Nonprofit Management M,O
Reading Education M
Secondary Education M
Social Sciences Education M,O
Social Work M
Special Education M
Supply Chain Management M,D,O

UNIVERSITY OF MOBILE
Business Administration and
    Management—General M
Education—General M
Educational Leadership and
    Administration M
Educational Policy M

UNIVERSITY OF MONTANA
Accounting M
Art Education M
Business Administration and
    Management—General M,D,O
Counselor Education M,D
Curriculum and Instruction M,D
Early Childhood Education M,D,O
Education—General M,D,O
Educational Leadership and
    Administration M,D,O
English Education M
Exercise and Sports Science M
Health Education M
Law D
Legal and Justice Studies M
Mathematics Education M,D
Physical Education M
Recreation and Park Management M,D
Social Work M

UNIVERSITY OF MONTEVALLO
Business Administration and
    Management—General M
Counselor Education M
Education—General M
Educational Leadership and
    Administration M,O
Elementary Education M
Secondary Education M

UNIVERSITY OF MOUNT OLIVE
Business Administration and
    Management—General M

UNIVERSITY OF MOUNT UNION
Educational Leadership and
    Administration M

UNIVERSITY OF NEBRASKA AT KEARNEY
Accounting M
Art Education M
Business Administration and
    Management—General M
Counselor Education M,O
Curriculum and Instruction M
Early Childhood Education M
Education of the Gifted M
Education—General M,O
Educational Leadership and
    Administration M,O
Educational Media/Instructional
    Technology M
Elementary Education M
English as a Second Language M
Exercise and Sports Science M
Foreign Languages Education M
Human Resources Management M
Human Services M
Leisure Studies M
Library Science M
Management Information Systems M
Marketing M
Mathematics Education M
Museum Education M
Music Education M
Physical Education M
Reading Education M
Recreation and Park Management M
Science Education M
Secondary Education M
Special Education M,O
Sports Management M
Student Affairs M,O

UNIVERSITY OF NEBRASKA AT OMAHA
Accounting M
Athletic Training and Sports
    Medicine M,D
Business Administration and
    Management—General M
Counselor Education M
Education—General M,D,O
Educational Leadership and
    Administration M,D,O
Elementary Education M
English as a Second Language M,O
Exercise and Sports Science M,D
Foreign Languages Education M
Health Education M,D
Human Resources Development M,D,O
Kinesiology and Movement Studies M,D
Management Information Systems M,D,O
Organizational Management M
Project Management M,D,O
Science Education M,O
Secondary Education M,O
Social Work M
Special Education M,O
Urban Education M,O

UNIVERSITY OF NEBRASKA–LINCOLN
Accounting M,D
Actuarial Science M
Adult Education M,D,O
Advertising and Public Relations M,D
Agricultural Education M
Business Administration and
    Management—General M,D
Curriculum and Instruction M,D,O
Early Childhood Education M,D
Educational Leadership and
    Administration M,D,O
Educational Measurement and
    Evaluation M,D,O
Educational Psychology M,D,O
Exercise and Sports Science M,D

Finance and Banking M,D
Home Economics Education M,D
Law M,D
Legal and Justice Studies M
Management Information Systems M
Marketing M,D
Music Education M,D
Special Education M,D,O
Vocational and Technical Education M,D,O

UNIVERSITY OF NEVADA, LAS VEGAS
Accounting M
Business Administration and
    Management—General M,O
Counselor Education M,D,O
Curriculum and Instruction M,D,O
Distance Education Development M,D,O
Early Childhood Education M,D,O
Education—General M,D,O
Educational Leadership and
    Administration M,D,O
Educational Media/Instructional
    Technology M,D,O
Elementary Education M,D,O
English as a Second Language M,D,O
Exercise and Sports Science M,D
Higher Education M,D,O
Hospitality Management M,D
Kinesiology and Movement Studies M,D
Law M,D
Management Information Systems M,O
Nonprofit Management M,D,O
Secondary Education M,D,O
Social Work M
Special Education M,D,O

UNIVERSITY OF NEVADA, RENO
Accounting M
Business Administration and
    Management—General M
Counselor Education M,D,O
Curriculum and Instruction D
Education—General M,D,O
Educational Leadership and
    Administration M,D,O
Educational Psychology M,D,O
Elementary Education M
English as a Second Language M
Finance and Banking M
Legal and Justice Studies M,D
Management Information Systems M
Mathematics Education M
Reading Education M,D
Secondary Education M
Social Work M
Special Education M,D

UNIVERSITY OF NEW BRUNSWICK FREDERICTON
Business Administration and
    Management—General M
Education—General M,D
Entrepreneurship M
Exercise and Sports Science M
Marketing M,D
Physical Education M
Recreation and Park Management M
Sports Management M

UNIVERSITY OF NEW BRUNSWICK SAINT JOHN
Business Administration and
    Management—General M
Electronic Commerce M
International Business M

UNIVERSITY OF NEW ENGLAND
Curriculum and Instruction M,D,O
Early Childhood Education M,D,O
Education—General M,D,O
Educational Leadership and
    Administration M,D,O
Reading Education M,D,O
Social Work M,D,O
Vocational and Technical Education M,D,O

UNIVERSITY OF NEW HAMPSHIRE
Accounting M
Business Administration and
    Management—General M,O
Curriculum and Instruction D,O
Early Childhood Education M
Education—General M,D,O
Educational Leadership and
    Administration M,O
Educational Media/Instructional
    Technology M,O
Elementary Education M,O
Higher Education O
Intellectual Property Law O
Kinesiology and Movement Studies M,O
Law M,D,O
Legal and Justice Studies M,D,O
Management Information Systems M,O
Mathematics Education M,D,O
Physical Education M,O
Quantitative Analysis M
Recreation and Park Management M
Science Education M,D
Secondary Education M,O
Social Work M,O
Special Education M,O
Sports and Entertainment Law M,O
Sustainability Management M,O

UNIVERSITY OF NEW HAVEN
Accounting M,O
Business Administration and
    Management—General M
Facilities Management M,O
Finance and Banking M,O
Human Resources Management M,O
Industrial and Manufacturing
    Management M,O
International Business M
Management Strategy and Policy M

Marketing M
Nonprofit Management M,O
Organizational Management M,O
Sports Management M,O
Taxation M,O

UNIVERSITY OF NEW MEXICO
Art Education M
Business Administration and
    Management—General M
Counselor Education M
Early Childhood Education D
Education of Students with
    Severe/Multiple Disabilities M,D,O
Education—General M,D,O
Educational Leadership and
    Administration M,D,O
Educational Media/Instructional
    Technology M,D,O
Educational Psychology M,D
Elementary Education M
English as a Second Language M,D
English Education M
Entrepreneurship M
Exercise and Sports Science D
Foundations and Philosophy of
    Education M,D
Health Education M
Higher Education O
Human Resources Management M
International Business M
Law M
Management Strategy and Policy M
Multilingual and Multicultural
    Education M,D
Music Education M
Organizational Behavior M
Physical Education D
Quantitative Analysis D
Reading Education M
Science Education O
Secondary Education M
Special Education M,D,O
Sports Management D
Taxation M

UNIVERSITY OF NEW ORLEANS
Accounting M
Business Administration and
    Management—General M,D
Counselor Education M,D
Curriculum and Instruction M
Educational Leadership and
    Administration M,D
Finance and Banking M,D
Higher Education M,D
Hospitality Management M
Special Education M
Taxation M
Transportation Management M
Travel and Tourism M

UNIVERSITY OF NORTH ALABAMA
Accounting M
Business Administration and
    Management—General M
Counselor Education M
Education—General M,O
Educational Leadership and
    Administration M,O
Elementary Education M,O
Exercise and Sports Science M
Finance and Banking M
Higher Education M
International Business M
Kinesiology and Movement Studies M
Law M
Management Information Systems M
Physical Education M
Project Management M
Secondary Education M
Special Education M

THE UNIVERSITY OF NORTH CAROLINA AT CHAPEL HILL
Accounting M,D
Athletic Training and Sports
    Medicine M
Business Administration and
    Management—General M,D
Counselor Education M
Curriculum and Instruction M,D
Early Childhood Education M,D
Education—General M,D
Educational Leadership and
    Administration M,D
Educational Measurement and
    Evaluation M,D
Educational Psychology M,D
English as a Second Language M
English Education M
Exercise and Sports Science D
Finance and Banking D
Foreign Languages Education M,D,O
Information Studies D
Kinesiology and Movement Studies D
Law M,D
Library Science M,D,O
Management Information Systems D
Management Strategy and Policy D
Marketing D
Mathematics Education M
Music Education D
Organizational Behavior D
Physical Education M
Reading Education M,D
Science Education M
Secondary Education M
Social Sciences Education M,D
Social Work M,D
Sports Management M

THE UNIVERSITY OF NORTH CAROLINA AT CHARLOTTE
Accounting M
Art Education M,D,O

*Peterson's Graduate Programs in Business, Education,
Information Studies, Law & Social Work 2020*

Business Administration and Management—General	M,D,O
Business Analytics	M,D,O
Business Education	D
Counselor Education	M,D,O
Curriculum and Instruction	M,D,O
Early Childhood Education	M,D,O
Education of the Gifted	M,D,O
Education—General	M,D,O
Educational Leadership and Administration	M,D,O
Educational Media/Instructional Technology	M,D,O
Elementary Education	M,O
English as a Second Language	M,D,O
Facilities Management	M,O
Finance and Banking	M,O
Foreign Languages Education	M,D,O
Industrial and Manufacturing Management	M,D,O
Kinesiology and Movement Studies	M
Logistics	M,O
Management Information Systems	M,D,O
Middle School Education	M,D,O
Nonprofit Management	M,O
Reading Education	M,O
Real Estate	M,O
Secondary Education	M,D,O
Social Work	M
Special Education	M,D,O
Supply Chain Management	M,O

THE UNIVERSITY OF NORTH CAROLINA AT GREENSBORO

Accounting	M,O
Adult Education	M,D,O
Athletic Training and Sports Medicine	M,D
Business Administration and Management—General	M,O
Counselor Education	M,D,O
Curriculum and Instruction	M,D,O
Early Childhood Education	M,D,O
Education—General	M,D,O
Educational Leadership and Administration	M,D,O
Educational Measurement and Evaluation	D
Educational Media/Instructional Technology	M,D,O
Elementary Education	D
English as a Second Language	M,D,O
English Education	M,D
Finance and Banking	M,O
Foreign Languages Education	M,D,O
Higher Education	D
Information Studies	M
Kinesiology and Movement Studies	M,D
Library Science	M
Management Information Systems	M,D,O
Marketing	M,D
Mathematics Education	M,D,O
Middle School Education	M,D,O
Multilingual and Multicultural Education	M,D,O
Music Education	M,D
Nonprofit Management	M,O
Reading Education	M,D,O
Recreation and Park Management	M
Science Education	M,D,O
Social Sciences Education	M,D,O
Social Work	M
Special Education	M,D,O
Supply Chain Management	M,D,O

THE UNIVERSITY OF NORTH CAROLINA AT PEMBROKE

Art Education	M
Business Administration and Management—General	M
Counselor Education	M
Education—General	M
Educational Leadership and Administration	M
Elementary Education	M
English Education	M
Exercise and Sports Science	M
Health Education	M
Mathematics Education	M
Physical Education	M
Reading Education	M
Science Education	M
Social Sciences Education	M
Social Work	M
Sports Management	M

THE UNIVERSITY OF NORTH CAROLINA WILMINGTON

Accounting	M
Business Administration and Management—General	M
Curriculum and Instruction	M,D
Early Childhood Education	M
Education—General	M,D
Educational Leadership and Administration	M,D
Educational Media/Instructional Technology	M
Educational Policy	M
Elementary Education	M
English as a Second Language	M
Higher Education	M,D
International Business	M
Management Information Systems	M
Middle School Education	M
Reading Education	M
Secondary Education	M
Social Work	M
Special Education	M

UNIVERSITY OF NORTH DAKOTA

Business Administration and Management—General	M
Early Childhood Education	M
Education—General	M,D,O
Educational Leadership and Administration	M,D,O
Educational Media/Instructional Technology	M
Elementary Education	M
Kinesiology and Movement Studies	M
Law	D
Music Education	M,D
Reading Education	M
Social Work	M
Special Education	M

UNIVERSITY OF NORTHERN BRITISH COLUMBIA

Education—General	M,D,O
Social Work	M,D,O

UNIVERSITY OF NORTHERN COLORADO

Accounting	M
Art Education	M
Business Administration and Management—General	M
Counselor Education	M,D
Curriculum and Instruction	M,D
Education of the Gifted	M,D
Education—General	M,D,O
Educational Leadership and Administration	M,D,O
Educational Measurement and Evaluation	M,D
Educational Policy	M,D,O
Educational Psychology	M,D
Elementary Education	M
English as a Second Language	M,D
English Education	M,D
Exercise and Sports Science	M,D
Foreign Languages Education	M,D
Health Education	M
Higher Education	M,D
Human Resources Management	M
Mathematics Education	M,D
Multilingual and Multicultural Education	M,D
Music Education	M,D
Physical Education	M,D
Reading Education	M
Science Education	M,D
Special Education	M,D
Sports Management	M,D
Student Affairs	M,D

UNIVERSITY OF NORTHERN IOWA

Accounting	M
Art Education	M
Athletic Training and Sports Medicine	M
Business Administration and Management—General	M
Community College Education	M
Counselor Education	M
Curriculum and Instruction	D
Early Childhood Education	M
Education—General	M,D,O
Educational Leadership and Administration	M,D
Educational Measurement and Evaluation	M
Educational Media/Instructional Technology	M
Educational Psychology	M
Elementary Education	M
English as a Second Language	M
English Education	M
Foreign Languages Education	M
Health Education	M
Higher Education	M
Human Services	M
Kinesiology and Movement Studies	M
Mathematics Education	M
Middle School Education	M
Music Education	M
Nonprofit Management	M
Physical Education	M
Reading Education	M
Science Education	M
Secondary Education	M
Social Work	M
Special Education	M
Sports Management	M
Student Affairs	M
Vocational and Technical Education	M,D

UNIVERSITY OF NORTH FLORIDA

Accounting	M
Adult Education	M
Business Administration and Management—General	M
Counselor Education	M,D
Education—General	M,D
Educational Leadership and Administration	M,D
Educational Media/Instructional Technology	M,D
Electronic Commerce	M
Elementary Education	M
English as a Second Language	M
Exercise and Sports Science	M,D
Finance and Banking	M
Human Resources Management	M
International Business	M
Logistics	M
Management Information Systems	M
Nonprofit Management	M,O
Reading Education	M
Secondary Education	M
Social Work	M
Special Education	M
Sports Management	M,D

UNIVERSITY OF NORTH GEORGIA

Athletic Training and Sports Medicine	M
Business Administration and Management—General	M
Curriculum and Instruction	M
Early Childhood Education	M
Education—General	M
Educational Leadership and Administration	D,O
English Education	M
Higher Education	D
Human Services	M
Kinesiology and Movement Studies	M
Mathematics Education	M
Middle School Education	M
Physical Education	M
Science Education	M
Secondary Education	M
Social Sciences Education	M

UNIVERSITY OF NORTH TEXAS

Accounting	M,D,O
Advertising and Public Relations	M,D,O
Art Education	M,D,O
Business Administration and Management—General	M,D,O
Counselor Education	M,D,O
Curriculum and Instruction	M,D,O
Early Childhood Education	M,D,O
Education of the Gifted	M,D,O
Education—General	M,D,O
Educational Leadership and Administration	M,D,O
Educational Measurement and Evaluation	M,D,O
Educational Psychology	M,D,O
English as a Second Language	M,D,O
Finance and Banking	M,D,O
Higher Education	M,D,O
Hospitality Management	M,D,O
Human Resources Management	M,D,O
Industrial and Manufacturing Management	M,D,O
Kinesiology and Movement Studies	M,D,O
Logistics	M,D,O
Management Information Systems	M,D,O
Management Strategy and Policy	M,D,O
Marketing	M,D,O
Music Education	M,D,O
Nonprofit Management	M,D,O
Quantitative Analysis	M,D,O
Special Education	M,D,O
Supply Chain Management	M,D,O
Travel and Tourism	M,D,O
Vocational and Technical Education	M,D,O

UNIVERSITY OF NORTH TEXAS AT DALLAS

Accounting	M
Business Administration and Management—General	M
Counselor Education	M
Curriculum and Instruction	M
Educational Leadership and Administration	M
Human Resources Management	M
Law	D
Management Strategy and Policy	M
Organizational Behavior	M

UNIVERSITY OF NORTHWESTERN OHIO

Business Administration and Management—General	M

UNIVERSITY OF NORTHWESTERN–ST. PAUL

Business Administration and Management—General	M
Education—General	M
Human Services	M
Organizational Management	M

UNIVERSITY OF NOTRE DAME

Accounting	M
Business Administration and Management—General	M
Business Analytics	M
Education—General	M
Entrepreneurship	M
Finance and Banking	M
Investment Management	M
Law	M,D
Marketing	M
Nonprofit Management	M
Taxation	M

UNIVERSITY OF OKLAHOMA

Accounting	M
Adult Education	M,D
Archives/Archival Administration	M,D,O
Business Administration and Management—General	M,D,O
Business Analytics	M,O
Curriculum and Instruction	M,D
Early Childhood Education	M,D
Education—General	M,D,O
Educational Leadership and Administration	M,D
Educational Media/Instructional Technology	M,D,O
Educational Psychology	M,D
Elementary Education	M,D
English Education	M,D
Entrepreneurship	M,D,O
Exercise and Sports Science	M,D
Foreign Languages Education	M,D
Higher Education	M,D
Human Resources Management	M,D,O
Human Services	M,O
Information Studies	M,D,O
Law	M,D
Library Science	M,D,O
Management Information Systems	M,D,O
Mathematics Education	M,D
Music Education	M,D,O
Nonprofit Management	M,D,O
Organizational Behavior	M,D,O
Organizational Management	M,O
Project Management	M,D,O
Reading Education	M,D
Science Education	M,D
Social Sciences Education	M,D
Social Work	M
Special Education	M,D

UNIVERSITY OF OKLAHOMA HEALTH SCIENCES CENTER

Health Education	D
Reading Education	M,D,O
Special Education	M,D,O

UNIVERSITY OF OREGON

Accounting	M,D
Business Administration and Management—General	M,D
Curriculum and Instruction	M,D
Education—General	M,D
Educational Leadership and Administration	M,D
Finance and Banking	D
Law	M,D
Management Information Systems	M
Marketing	D
Music Education	M,D
Nonprofit Management	M,O
Quantitative Analysis	M
Special Education	M,D
Sports Management	M

UNIVERSITY OF OTTAWA

Business Administration and Management—General	M
Education—General	M,D,O
Electronic Commerce	M,D,O
Finance and Banking	D,O
Kinesiology and Movement Studies	M
Law	M,D
Music Education	M,O
Project Management	M,O
Social Work	M

UNIVERSITY OF PENNSYLVANIA

Accounting	M,D
Business Administration and Management—General	M,D
Counselor Education	M
Education—General	M,D,O
Educational Leadership and Administration	M,D
Educational Measurement and Evaluation	M,D
Educational Media/Instructional Technology	M
Educational Policy	M,D
Elementary Education	M
English as a Second Language	M
English Education	M,D
Entrepreneurship	M
Finance and Banking	M,D
Foundations and Philosophy of Education	M,D
Higher Education	M,D
Insurance	M,D
International and Comparative Education	M
International Business	M
Law	M,D
Legal and Justice Studies	M,D
Management Information Systems	M,D
Marketing	M,D
Multilingual and Multicultural Education	M
Nonprofit Management	M,O
Organizational Management	M,O
Reading Education	M
Real Estate	M,D
Risk Management	M,D
Science Education	M,O
Secondary Education	M
Social Work	M,D
Urban Education	M

UNIVERSITY OF PHOENIX–BAY AREA CAMPUS

Accounting	M,D
Adult Education	M,D,O
Business Administration and Management—General	M,D
Early Childhood Education	M,D,O
Education—General	M,D,O
Educational Leadership and Administration	M,D,O
Elementary Education	M,D,O
Higher Education	M,D,O
Human Resources Management	M,D
International Business	M,D
Management Information Systems	M,D
Marketing	M,D
Organizational Management	M,D
Project Management	M,D
Secondary Education	M,D,O
Special Education	M,D,O

UNIVERSITY OF PHOENIX–CENTRAL VALLEY CAMPUS

Accounting	M
Business Administration and Management—General	M
Computer Education	M
Curriculum and Instruction	M
Education—General	M
Elementary Education	M

*M—masters degree; D—doctorate; O—other advanced degree; *—Close-Up and/or Display*

Human Resources Management M
International Business M
Management Information Systems M
Marketing M
Secondary Education M

UNIVERSITY OF PHOENIX–DALLAS CAMPUS
Accounting M
Business Administration and Management—General M
Curriculum and Instruction M
Education—General M
Electronic Commerce M
Human Resources Management M
International Business M
Management Information Systems M
Marketing M

UNIVERSITY OF PHOENIX–HAWAII CAMPUS
Accounting M
Business Administration and Management—General M
Curriculum and Instruction M
Education—General M
Educational Leadership and Administration M
Elementary Education M
Human Resources Management M
International Business M
Management Information Systems M
Marketing M
Secondary Education M
Special Education M

UNIVERSITY OF PHOENIX–HOUSTON CAMPUS
Accounting M
Business Administration and Management—General M
Curriculum and Instruction M
Education—General M
Electronic Commerce M
Human Resources Management M
International Business M
Management Information Systems M
Marketing M

UNIVERSITY OF PHOENIX–LAS VEGAS CAMPUS
Accounting M
Business Administration and Management—General M
Counselor Education M
Curriculum and Instruction M
Educational Leadership and Administration M
Elementary Education M
Human Resources Management M
International Business M
Management Information Systems M
Marketing M

UNIVERSITY OF PHOENIX–ONLINE CAMPUS
Accounting M,O
Adult Education M,O
Business Administration and Management—General M,D,O
Computer Education M,O
Curriculum and Instruction M,D,O
Early Childhood Education M,O
Education—General M,O
Educational Leadership and Administration M,D,O
Educational Media/Instructional Technology D,O
Elementary Education M,O
English as a Second Language M,O
English Education M,O
Health Education M,O
Higher Education D,O
Human Resources Management M,O
International Business M
Management Information Systems M
Marketing M,O
Mathematics Education M,O
Middle School Education M,O
Organizational Management D,O
Project Management M,O
Reading Education M,O
Science Education M,O
Secondary Education M,O
Special Education M,O

UNIVERSITY OF PHOENIX–PHOENIX CAMPUS
Accounting M,O
Adult Education M
Business Administration and Management—General M
Counselor Education M
Curriculum and Instruction M
Early Childhood Education M
Education—General M
Educational Leadership and Administration M
Elementary Education M
Human Resources Management M,O
International Business M,O
Marketing M,O
Project Management M
Reading Education M
Secondary Education M
Special Education M
Vocational and Technical Education M

UNIVERSITY OF PHOENIX–SACRAMENTO VALLEY CAMPUS
Accounting M
Adult Education M,O
Business Administration and Management—General M
Curriculum and Instruction M

Education—General M,O
Elementary Education M,O
Human Resources Management M
International Business M
Management Information Systems M
Marketing M
Secondary Education M,O

UNIVERSITY OF PHOENIX–SAN ANTONIO CAMPUS
Accounting M
Business Administration and Management—General M
Curriculum and Instruction M
Electronic Commerce M
Human Resources Management M
International Business M
Management Information Systems M
Marketing M

UNIVERSITY OF PHOENIX–SAN DIEGO CAMPUS
Accounting M
Business Administration and Management—General M
Computer Education M
Curriculum and Instruction M
Education—General M
Elementary Education M
English as a Second Language M
Human Resources Management M
International Business M
Management Information Systems M
Marketing M
Secondary Education M

UNIVERSITY OF PIKEVILLE
Business Administration and Management—General M
Education—General M
Educational Leadership and Administration M
Entrepreneurship M

UNIVERSITY OF PITTSBURGH
Accounting M,D
Athletic Training and Sports Medicine M
Business Administration and Management—General M,D
Business Analytics D
Early Childhood Education M
Education—General M,D
Educational Leadership and Administration M,D
Educational Measurement and Evaluation M
Educational Policy D
Elementary Education M
English as a Second Language D,O
English Education M,D
Environmental Law M
Exercise and Sports Science M,D
Finance and Banking M,D
Foreign Languages Education M,D
Foundations and Philosophy of Education M,D
Health Education M,D
Health Law M
Higher Education M,D
Human Resources Management M,D
Industrial and Manufacturing Management M
Intellectual Property Law M
International and Comparative Education M,D
International Business O
Law M
Legal and Justice Studies M
Library Science M,D
Management Information Systems M,D
Management Strategy and Policy M,D
Marketing M,D
Mathematics Education M,D
Nonprofit Management M
Organizational Behavior M,D
Reading Education M,D
Science Education M,D
Secondary Education M,D
Social Sciences Education M,D
Social Work M,D,O
Special Education M,D
Supply Chain Management M

UNIVERSITY OF PORTLAND
Business Administration and Management—General M
Education—General M,D
Educational Leadership and Administration M,D
English as a Second Language M,D
Entrepreneurship M
Finance and Banking M
Industrial and Manufacturing Management M
Marketing M
Nonprofit Management M
Organizational Management M,D
Reading Education M,D
Special Education M,D
Sustainability Management M

UNIVERSITY OF PRINCE EDWARD ISLAND
Education—General M,D
Educational Leadership and Administration M,D

UNIVERSITY OF PROVIDENCE
Human Services M

UNIVERSITY OF PUERTO RICO–MAYAGÜEZ
Agricultural Education M
Business Administration and Management—General M

English Education M
Exercise and Sports Science M
Finance and Banking M
Higher Education M
Human Resources Management M
Industrial and Manufacturing Management M
Kinesiology and Movement Studies M
Mathematics Education M

UNIVERSITY OF PUERTO RICO–MEDICAL SCIENCES CAMPUS
Health Education M
Special Education O

UNIVERSITY OF PUERTO RICO–RÍO PIEDRAS
Accounting M,D
Business Administration and Management—General M,D
Counselor Education M,D
Curriculum and Instruction M,D
Early Childhood Education M
Education—General M,D
Educational Leadership and Administration M,D
Educational Measurement and Evaluation M
English as a Second Language M
Exercise and Sports Science M
Finance and Banking M,D
Foreign Languages Education M,D
Human Resources Management M
Industrial and Manufacturing Management M,D
Information Studies M,O
International Business M,D
Law M,D
Library Science M,O
Marketing M,D
Mathematics Education M,D
Quantitative Analysis M,D
Science Education M,D
Social Sciences Education M,D
Social Work M,D
Special Education M

UNIVERSITY OF PUGET SOUND
Counselor Education M
Education—General M
Elementary Education M
Secondary Education M

UNIVERSITY OF REDLANDS
Business Administration and Management—General M
Education—General M,D,O
Management Information Systems M

UNIVERSITY OF REGINA
Adult Education M
Business Administration and Management—General M,O
Curriculum and Instruction M
Education—General M,D,O
Educational Leadership and Administration M
Educational Psychology M
Human Resources Development M
Human Resources Management M,O
International Business M,O
Kinesiology and Movement Studies M,O
Organizational Management M,O
Project Management M,O
Social Work M,D

UNIVERSITY OF RHODE ISLAND
Accounting M
Business Administration and Management—General M,D
Education—General M,D
Entrepreneurship M,D,O
Exercise and Sports Science M
Finance and Banking M,D
Health Education M
Human Resources Management M,O
Information Studies M
Library Science M
Management Strategy and Policy M,D,O
Marketing M,D
Music Education M
Physical Education M
Reading Education M,D
Recreation and Park Management M
Special Education M
Student Affairs M
Supply Chain Management M,D

UNIVERSITY OF RICHMOND
Business Administration and Management—General M
Law D

UNIVERSITY OF RIO GRANDE
Art Education M
Education—General M
Educational Leadership and Administration M
Physical Education M
Special Education M

UNIVERSITY OF ROCHESTER
Accounting M,D
Archives/Archival Administration M
Business Administration and Management—General M,D
Counselor Education M,D
Curriculum and Instruction M,D
Education—General M,D
Educational Leadership and Administration M,D
Educational Policy M,D
Entrepreneurship M
Finance and Banking M,D
Foundations and Philosophy of Education D
Higher Education M,D

Industrial and Manufacturing Management D
Management Information Systems M,D
Management Strategy and Policy M
Marketing Research M,D
Music Education M,D
Student Affairs M

UNIVERSITY OF ST. AUGUSTINE FOR HEALTH SCIENCES
Athletic Training and Sports Medicine M
Health Education M,D)

UNIVERSITY OF ST. FRANCIS (IL)
Accounting M
Art Education M,D,O
Business Administration and Management—General M,O
Business Analytics M,O
Curriculum and Instruction M,D,O
Education—General M,D,O
Educational Leadership and Administration M,D,O
Elementary Education M,D,O
English as a Second Language M,D,O
English Education M,D,O
Finance and Banking M,O
Human Resources Management M,O
Logistics M,O
Mathematics Education M,D,O
Reading Education M,D,O
Science Education M,D,O
Secondary Education M,D,O
Social Sciences Education M,D,O
Social Work M,O
Special Education M,D,O
Supply Chain Management M,O

UNIVERSITY OF SAINT FRANCIS (IN)
Business Administration and Management—General M
Counselor Education M,O
Education—General M
Organizational Management M
Secondary Education M
Special Education M
Sustainability Management M

UNIVERSITY OF SAINT JOSEPH
Business Administration and Management—General M
Counselor Education M
Curriculum and Instruction M
Education—General M
Educational Media/Instructional Technology M
Elementary Education M
English as a Second Language M
Reading Education M
Secondary Education M
Social Work M
Special Education M,O

UNIVERSITY OF SAINT MARY
Advertising and Public Relations M
Business Administration and Management—General M
Education—General M
Elementary Education M
Finance and Banking M
Human Resources Management M
Marketing M
Risk Management M
Special Education M

UNIVERSITY OF ST. MICHAEL'S COLLEGE
Religious Education M,D,O

UNIVERSITY OF ST. THOMAS (MN)
Accounting M
Business Administration and Management—General M
Business Analytics M
Education—General M,D,O
Educational Leadership and Administration M,D,O
Law M,D
Music Education M,D
Organizational Management D
Religious Education M
Social Work M
Special Education M,O
Student Affairs M,D,O

UNIVERSITY OF ST. THOMAS (TX)
Accounting M
Business Administration and Management—General M
Counselor Education M,D
Curriculum and Instruction M,D
Education—General M,D
Educational Leadership and Administration M,D
Educational Measurement and Evaluation M,D
Elementary Education M,D
English as a Second Language M,D
Finance and Banking M
International Business M
Multilingual and Multicultural Education M,D
Reading Education M,D
Religious Education M,D
Secondary Education M,D
Special Education M,D

UNIVERSITY OF SAN DIEGO
Business Administration and Management—General M
Counselor Education M
Curriculum and Instruction M
Education—General M,D,O
Educational Leadership and Administration M,D,O

English as a Second Language M
Higher Education M,D,O
Law M,D,O
Legal and Justice Studies M,D,O
Nonprofit Management M,D,O
Reading Education M
Real Estate M
Science Education M
Special Education M
Taxation M,D,O

UNIVERSITY OF SAN FRANCISCO
Business Administration and Management—General M
Counselor Education M
Curriculum and Instruction M,D
Education—General M,D
Educational Leadership and Administration M,D
Educational Media/Instructional Technology M,D
Entrepreneurship M
Finance and Banking M
Intellectual Property Law M
International and Comparative Education M,D
International Business M
Law D
Management Information Systems M
Marketing M
Multilingual and Multicultural Education M,D
Nonprofit Management M
Organizational Management M
Reading Education M,D
Religious Education M,D
Special Education M,D
Sports Management M
Urban Education M

UNIVERSITY OF SASKATCHEWAN
Accounting M
Business Administration and Management—General M,D
Curriculum and Instruction M,D,O
Education—General M,D,O
Educational Leadership and Administration M,D,O
Educational Measurement and Evaluation M,D
Educational Psychology M,D
English as a Second Language M
Finance and Banking M
Foundations and Philosophy of Education M,D,O
Kinesiology and Movement Studies M,D
Law M,D
Marketing M
Special Education M,D
Sustainability Management M,D

THE UNIVERSITY OF SCRANTON
Accounting M
Business Administration and Management—General M
Counselor Education M
Curriculum and Instruction M
Education—General M
Educational Leadership and Administration M
Finance and Banking M
Human Resources Development M
International Business M
Management Information Systems M
Marketing M
Reading Education M
Secondary Education M
Special Education M

UNIVERSITY OF SIOUX FALLS
Business Administration and Management—General M
Education—General M,O
Educational Leadership and Administration M,O
Educational Media/Instructional Technology M,O
Entrepreneurship M
Marketing M
Reading Education M,O

UNIVERSITY OF SOUTH AFRICA
Accounting M,D
Adult Education M,D
Business Administration and Management—General M,D
Counselor Education M,D
Curriculum and Instruction M,D
Education—General M,D
Educational Leadership and Administration M,D
Educational Media/Instructional Technology M,D
Educational Psychology M,D
English as a Second Language M,D
Environmental Education M,D
Foundations and Philosophy of Education M,D
Health Education M,D
Human Resources Development M,D
International and Comparative Education M,D
Law M,D
Logistics M,D
Management Information Systems M
Marketing M,D
Mathematics Education M,D
Quantitative Analysis M,D
Real Estate M,D
Science Education M,D
Social Work M,D
Travel and Tourism M,D

Vocational and Technical Education M,D

UNIVERSITY OF SOUTH ALABAMA
Accounting M
Art Education M,D
Business Administration and Management—General M,D
Counselor Education M,D,O
Early Childhood Education M,D
Education—General M,D,O
Educational Leadership and Administration M,D
Educational Media/Instructional Technology M,D,O
Elementary Education M,D
Exercise and Sports Science M
Health Education M
Kinesiology and Movement Studies M
Management Information Systems M,D
Marketing M,D
Music Education M
Physical Education M
Reading Education M,D
Science Education M,D
Secondary Education M,D
Special Education M,D
Sports Management M

UNIVERSITY OF SOUTH CAROLINA
Accounting M
Archives/Archival Administration M,O
Art Education M,D
Business Administration and Management—General M,D
Business Education M,D
Counselor Education D,O
Curriculum and Instruction D
Early Childhood Education M,D
Education—General M,D,O
Educational Leadership and Administration M,D,O
Educational Measurement and Evaluation M,D
Educational Media/Instructional Technology M
Educational Psychology M,D
Elementary Education M,D
English as a Second Language M,D,O
English Education M,D
Entertainment Management M
Exercise and Sports Science M,D
Foreign Languages Education M,D
Foundations and Philosophy of Education D
Health Education M,D,O
Higher Education M
Hospitality Management M
Human Resources Management M
Information Studies M,D,O
International Business M
Law D
Library Science M,D,O
Mathematics Education M,D
Music Education M,D,O
Physical Education M,D
Reading Education M,D
Science Education M,D
Secondary Education M,D
Social Sciences Education M,D
Social Work M,D
Special Education M,D
Sports Management M
Student Affairs M
Travel and Tourism M

UNIVERSITY OF SOUTH CAROLINA AIKEN
Business Administration and Management—General M
Educational Media/Instructional Technology M

UNIVERSITY OF SOUTH CAROLINA UPSTATE
Early Childhood Education M
Education—General M
Elementary Education M
Special Education M

UNIVERSITY OF SOUTH DAKOTA
Accounting M
Adult Education M,D,O
Art Education M
Business Administration and Management—General M,O
Business Analytics M,O
Counselor Education M,D,O
Curriculum and Instruction M,D,O
Early Childhood Education M,D,O
Education—General M,D,O
Educational Leadership and Administration M,D,O
Educational Media/Instructional Technology M
Educational Psychology M,D,O
Elementary Education M
English as a Second Language M
Exercise and Sports Science M
Higher Education M,D,O
Human Resources Management M
Kinesiology and Movement Studies M
Law D
Marketing M,O
Mathematics Education M
Music Education M
Organizational Management M
Reading Education M
Science Education M
Secondary Education M
Social Work M
Special Education M,D,O
Supply Chain Management M,O

UNIVERSITY OF SOUTHERN CALIFORNIA
Accounting M
Advertising and Public Relations M
Business Administration and Management—General M,D
Counselor Education M
Education—General M,D
Educational Leadership and Administration D
Educational Policy D
Educational Psychology D
English as a Second Language M
Entrepreneurship M
Health Education M
Higher Education D
Kinesiology and Movement Studies M,D
Law M,D
Multilingual and Multicultural Education D
Music Education M,D,O
Nonprofit Management M,O
Organizational Management M
Quantitative Analysis M,D
Real Estate M
Social Work M,D
Student Affairs M
Supply Chain Management M,D,O
Taxation M
Urban Education D

UNIVERSITY OF SOUTHERN INDIANA
Accounting M
Business Administration and Management—General M
Education—General M,D
Educational Leadership and Administration M,D
Elementary Education M
English as a Second Language M
Human Resources Management M
Industrial and Manufacturing Management M
Mathematics Education M
Nonprofit Management M
Secondary Education M
Social Work M
Sports Management M

UNIVERSITY OF SOUTHERN MAINE
Accounting M
Adult Education M,O
Business Administration and Management—General M,O
Counselor Education M,O
Education of the Gifted M,O
Education—General M,D,O
Educational Leadership and Administration M,O
Educational Psychology M,O
English as a Second Language M,O
Finance and Banking M
Higher Education M,O
Music Education M
Reading Education M,O
Social Work M
Special Education M,O
Sustainability Management M

UNIVERSITY OF SOUTHERN MISSISSIPPI
Accounting M
Advertising and Public Relations M,D
Business Administration and Management—General M
Counselor Education M
Curriculum and Instruction M,D
Education—General M,D,O
Educational Leadership and Administration M,D,O
Educational Measurement and Evaluation M,D,O
Educational Media/Instructional Technology M,D
Elementary Education M,D
English as a Second Language M,D
English Education M,D
Foreign Languages Education M
Higher Education M,D,O
Library Science M,O
Logistics M
Music Education M,D
Physical Education M,D
Secondary Education M,D
Social Work M
Special Education M,D
Sports Management M
Student Affairs M,D,O
Transportation Management M

UNIVERSITY OF SOUTH FLORIDA
Accounting M,D
Adult Education M,D,O
Athletic Training and Sports Medicine M,D
Business Administration and Management—General M
Community College Education M,D,O
Counselor Education M,D,O
Distance Education Development O
Early Childhood Education M,D,O
Education of Students with Severe/Multiple Disabilities O
Education—General M,D,O
Educational Leadership and Administration M,D,O
Educational Measurement and Evaluation O
Educational Media/Instructional Technology O
Educational Psychology M,D,O
Elementary Education M,D,O

English as a Second Language M,D,O
Entrepreneurship M,O
Finance and Banking M,D
Foreign Languages Education O
Health Education M,D
Higher Education M,D,O
Human Resources Development O
Human Resources Management M
Information Studies M,O
Legal and Justice Studies O
Library Science M
Management Information Systems M,D,O
Management Strategy and Policy M,D,O
Marketing M,D
Music Education M,D
Nonprofit Management O
Reading Education M,D,O
Real Estate M,D
Secondary Education O
Social Sciences Education M,D,O
Social Work M,D,O
Special Education O
Sports Management M,D
Student Affairs M,D,O
Sustainability Management M,O
Taxation M,D
Travel and Tourism M,O
Vocational and Technical Education M,D,O

UNIVERSITY OF SOUTH FLORIDA, ST. PETERSBURG
Business Administration and Management—General M
Education—General M
Educational Leadership and Administration M
Elementary Education M
English Education M
Mathematics Education M
Middle School Education M
Reading Education M
Science Education M

UNIVERSITY OF SOUTH FLORIDA SARASOTA-MANATEE
Business Administration and Management—General M
Curriculum and Instruction M
Educational Leadership and Administration M
Elementary Education M
English Education M
Hospitality Management M
Social Work M

THE UNIVERSITY OF TAMPA
Accounting M,O
Business Administration and Management—General M,O
Business Analytics M,O
Curriculum and Instruction M
Education—General M
Educational Leadership and Administration M
Educational Media/Instructional Technology M
Entrepreneurship M,O
Exercise and Sports Science M
Finance and Banking M,O
International Business M,O
Management Information Systems M,O
Marketing M,O
Nonprofit Management M,O

THE UNIVERSITY OF TENNESSEE
Accounting M,D
Adult Education M,D
Advertising and Public Relations M,D
Agricultural Education M
Art Education M,D,O
Athletic Training and Sports Medicine M,D
Business Administration and Management—General M,D
Counselor Education M,D,O
Curriculum and Instruction M,D,O
Early Childhood Education M,D,O
Education—General M,D,O
Educational Leadership and Administration M,D,O
Educational Measurement and Evaluation M,D,O
Educational Media/Instructional Technology M,D,O
Educational Psychology M,D,O
Elementary Education M,D,O
English as a Second Language M,D,O
English Education M,D,O
Exercise and Sports Science M,D,O
Finance and Banking M,D
Foreign Languages Education M,D,O
Foundations and Philosophy of Education M,D,O
Health Education M
Hospitality Management M
Human Resources Development M
Industrial and Manufacturing Management M,D
Kinesiology and Movement Studies M,D
Law D
Leisure Studies M,D
Logistics M,D
Marketing M,D
Mathematics Education M,D,O
Multilingual and Multicultural Education M,D,O
Music Education M
Reading Education M,D,O
Recreation and Park Management M,D
Science Education M,D,O
Secondary Education M,D,O
Social Sciences Education M,D,O

*M—masters degree; D—doctorate; O—other advanced degree; *—Close-Up and/or Display*

Social Work M,D
Special Education M,D,O
Sports Management M
Student Affairs M
Transportation Management M
Travel and Tourism M

THE UNIVERSITY OF TENNESSEE AT CHATTANOOGA
Accounting M
Athletic Training and Sports Medicine M
Business Administration and Management—General M
Counselor Education M,D,O
Education—General M,D,O
Educational Leadership and Administration M,D,O
Elementary Education M,D,O
Logistics M,O
Mathematics Education M
Music Education M
Nonprofit Management M,O
Physical Education M
Project Management M,O
Quality Management M,O
Secondary Education M,D,O
Social Work M
Special Education M,D,O
Supply Chain Management M,O

THE UNIVERSITY OF TENNESSEE AT MARTIN
Business Administration and Management—General M
Counselor Education M
Curriculum and Instruction M
Education—General M
Educational Leadership and Administration M
Elementary Education M
Finance and Banking M
Physical Education M
Secondary Education M
Special Education M
Student Affairs M

THE UNIVERSITY OF TEXAS AT ARLINGTON
Accounting M,D
Athletic Training and Sports Medicine M,D
Curriculum and Instruction M
Education—General M,D
Educational Leadership and Administration M,D
Educational Policy M,D
English as a Second Language M
Exercise and Sports Science M,D
Finance and Banking M,D
Higher Education M,D
Human Resources Management M
Kinesiology and Movement Studies M,D
Logistics M
Management Information Systems M,D
Marketing Research M
Marketing M
Mathematics Education M,D
Music Education M
Quantitative Analysis M,D
Reading Education M
Real Estate M,D
Science Education M,D
Social Work M,D
Taxation M

THE UNIVERSITY OF TEXAS AT AUSTIN
Accounting M,D
Actuarial Science M,D
Advertising and Public Relations M,D
Art Education M
Business Administration and Management—General M,D
Counselor Education M,D
Curriculum and Instruction M,D
Early Childhood Education M,D
Education—General M,D
Educational Leadership and Administration M,D
Educational Media/Instructional Technology M,D
Educational Psychology M,D
Entrepreneurship M
Exercise and Sports Science M,D
Finance and Banking M,D
Health Education M,D
Industrial and Manufacturing Management M,D
Information Studies M,D
Kinesiology and Movement Studies M,D
Law M,D
Management Information Systems M,D
Marketing M,D
Multilingual and Multicultural Education M,D
Music Education M,D
Organizational Behavior M
Physical Education M,D
Quantitative Analysis M,D
Reading Education M,D
Risk Management M,D
Social Work M,D
Special Education M,D
Supply Chain Management M,D

THE UNIVERSITY OF TEXAS AT DALLAS
Accounting M,D
Actuarial Science M,D
Business Administration and Management—General M,D
Entrepreneurship M,D
Finance and Banking M
Industrial and Manufacturing Management M,D
International Business M,D

Law M,D
Management Information Systems M,D
Management Strategy and Policy M
Marketing M
Mathematics Education M
Nonprofit Management M,D
Project Management M,D
Real Estate M
Science Education M
Supply Chain Management M

THE UNIVERSITY OF TEXAS AT EL PASO
Accounting M
Art Education M
Business Administration and Management—General M,D,O
Counselor Education M
Curriculum and Instruction M,D
Education—General M,D
Educational Leadership and Administration M,D
Educational Measurement and Evaluation M
Educational Psychology M
English as a Second Language M,O
English Education M,D,O
International Business M,D,O
Kinesiology and Movement Studies M
Multilingual and Multicultural Education M,D,O
Music Education M
Reading Education M,D
Social Work M
Special Education M

THE UNIVERSITY OF TEXAS AT SAN ANTONIO
Accounting M,D
Business Administration and Management—General M,D,O
Counselor Education M,D
Curriculum and Instruction M,D
Early Childhood Education M,D
Educational Leadership and Administration M,D
Educational Measurement and Evaluation M,O
Educational Media/Instructional Technology M,D
Educational Psychology M,O
English as a Second Language M,D,O
Finance and Banking M,D
Health Education M
Higher Education M,D
Kinesiology and Movement Studies M
Marketing M,D
Mathematics Education M
Multilingual and Multicultural Education M,D
Organizational Management D
Reading Education M,D
Social Work M
Special Education M,D

THE UNIVERSITY OF TEXAS AT TYLER
Accounting M
Business Administration and Management—General M
Early Childhood Education M
Health Education M
Human Resources Development M,D
Industrial and Manufacturing Management M
Kinesiology and Movement Studies M
Marketing M
Organizational Management M
Quality Management M
Reading Education M
Special Education M

THE UNIVERSITY OF TEXAS HEALTH SCIENCE CENTER AT HOUSTON
Quantitative Analysis M,D

THE UNIVERSITY OF TEXAS HEALTH SCIENCE CENTER AT SAN ANTONIO
Special Education M,D

THE UNIVERSITY OF TEXAS OF THE PERMIAN BASIN
Accounting M
Business Administration and Management—General M
Counselor Education M
Early Childhood Education M
Education—General M
Educational Leadership and Administration M
English as a Second Language M
Foundations and Philosophy of Education M
Kinesiology and Movement Studies M
Reading Education M
Special Education M

THE UNIVERSITY OF TEXAS RIO GRANDE VALLEY
Accounting M
Business Administration and Management—General M,D
Counselor Education M
Curriculum and Instruction M,D
Early Childhood Education M
Education—General M,D
Educational Leadership and Administration M,D
Educational Media/Instructional Technology M,D
Educational Psychology M
Elementary Education M,D
English as a Second Language M
Exercise and Sports Science M
Finance and Banking M,D
Kinesiology and Movement Studies M,D
Management Information Systems M

Marketing M,D
Multilingual and Multicultural Education M
Reading Education M,D
Secondary Education M,D
Special Education M

THE UNIVERSITY OF THE ARTS
Art Education M
Museum Education M
Music Education M

UNIVERSITY OF THE CUMBERLANDS
Accounting M
Business Administration and Management—General M,D
Business Education M,D,O
Counselor Education M,D,O
Education—General M,D,O
Educational Leadership and Administration M,D,O
Elementary Education M,D,O
Marketing M,D,O
Middle School Education M,D,O
Reading Education M,D,O
Secondary Education M,D,O
Special Education M,D,O
Student Affairs M,D,O

UNIVERSITY OF THE DISTRICT OF COLUMBIA
Adult Education O
Business Administration and Management—General M
Early Childhood Education M
Elementary Education M
English Education M
Law M,D
Legal and Justice Studies M,D
Mathematics Education M
Middle School Education M
Secondary Education M
Social Sciences Education M

UNIVERSITY OF THE FRASER VALLEY
Social Work M

UNIVERSITY OF THE INCARNATE WORD
Accounting M
Business Administration and Management—General M,D
Education—General M,D
Kinesiology and Movement Studies M
Mathematics Education M
Organizational Management M,D
Sports Management M,D

UNIVERSITY OF THE PACIFIC
Business Administration and Management—General M
Curriculum and Instruction M,D,O
Education—General M,D,O
Educational Leadership and Administration M,D,O
Educational Psychology M,O
Exercise and Sports Science M
Hospitality Management M
Law M,D
Music Education M
Special Education M,D,O

UNIVERSITY OF THE PEOPLE
Business Administration and Management—General M

UNIVERSITY OF THE POTOMAC
Business Administration and Management—General M

UNIVERSITY OF THE SACRED HEART
Accounting M,O
Advertising and Public Relations M
Business Administration and Management—General M,O
Early Childhood Education M,O
Education—General M,O
Educational Media/Instructional Technology M
English Education M,O
Foreign Languages Education M,O
Human Resources Management M
Legal and Justice Studies M
Management Information Systems M
Marketing M
Mathematics Education M,O
Nonprofit Management M
Taxation M

UNIVERSITY OF THE SOUTHWEST
Business Administration and Management—General M
Counselor Education M
Curriculum and Instruction M
Early Childhood Education M
Education—General M
Educational Leadership and Administration M
English as a Second Language M
Multilingual and Multicultural Education M
Special Education M
Sports Management M

UNIVERSITY OF THE VIRGIN ISLANDS
Business Administration and Management—General M
Education—General M,D,O
Educational Leadership and Administration M,D,O
Mathematics Education M
Secondary Education M

UNIVERSITY OF THE WEST
Business Administration and Management—General M
Finance and Banking M
International Business M
Management Information Systems M

Nonprofit Management M

THE UNIVERSITY OF TOLEDO
Accounting M
Art Education M,D,O
Athletic Training and Sports Medicine M,D
Business Administration and Management—General M
Business Education M,D,O
Counselor Education M,D,O
Curriculum and Instruction M,D,O
Early Childhood Education M,D,O
Education of the Gifted M,D,O
Education—General M,D,O
Educational Leadership and Administration M,D,O
Educational Measurement and Evaluation M,D,O
Educational Media/Instructional Technology M,D,O
Educational Psychology M,D,O
Elementary Education M,D,O
English as a Second Language M,D,O
English Education M,D,O
Exercise and Sports Science M,D
Finance and Banking M
Foreign Languages Education M,D,O
Foundations and Philosophy of Education M,D,O
Health Education M,D,O
Higher Education M,D,O
International Business M
Law M,D,O
Leisure Studies M,D
Marketing M
Mathematics Education M,D,O
Middle School Education M,D,O
Music Education M,O
Nonprofit Management M,O
Physical Education M
Recreation and Park Management M,D
Science Education M,D,O
Secondary Education M,D,O
Social Sciences Education M,D,O
Social Work M,O
Special Education M,D,O
Vocational and Technical Education M,D,O

UNIVERSITY OF TORONTO
Business Administration and Management—General M,D
Education—General M,D
Finance and Banking M
Human Resources Management M,D
Information Studies M,D
Kinesiology and Movement Studies M,D
Law M,D
Music Education M,D
Physical Education M,D
Social Work M,D

THE UNIVERSITY OF TULSA
Accounting M
Business Administration and Management—General M
Business Analytics M
Environmental Law M,D,O
Health Law M,D,O
Kinesiology and Movement Studies M
Law M,D,O

UNIVERSITY OF UTAH
Accounting M,D
Art Education M
Business Administration and Management—General M,D,O
Counselor Education M,D,O
Early Childhood Education M,D
Education of Students with Severe/Multiple Disabilities M,D
Education—General M,D,O
Educational Media/Instructional Technology M,D,O
Elementary Education M,D,O
Finance and Banking M,D
Health Education M,D
Higher Education M,D
Industrial and Manufacturing Management M,D,O
Kinesiology and Movement Studies M,D
Law M,D
Leisure Studies M,D
Management Information Systems M,D,O
Management Strategy and Policy M,D,O
Marketing M,D
Mathematics Education M,D
Music Education M,D
Organizational Behavior M,D
Reading Education M,D,O
Real Estate M
Recreation and Park Management M,D
Science Education M,D
Social Work M,D
Student Affairs M,D

UNIVERSITY OF VERMONT
Accounting M
Business Administration and Management—General M
Counselor Education M
Curriculum and Instruction M
Early Childhood Education M
Education—General M,D
Educational Leadership and Administration M,D
Educational Policy D
Elementary Education M
Foreign Languages Education M,O
Higher Education M
Middle School Education M
Science Education M,D
Secondary Education M
Social Work M
Special Education M
Sustainability Management M

UNIVERSITY OF VICTORIA
Art Education M,D
Business Administration and Management—General M
Counselor Education M,D
Curriculum and Instruction M,D
Early Childhood Education M,D
Education—General M,D
Educational Leadership and Administration M,D
Educational Measurement and Evaluation M,D
Educational Psychology M,D
English Education M,D
Environmental Education M,D
Foreign Languages Education M
Foundations and Philosophy of Education M,D
Kinesiology and Movement Studies M
Law M,D
Leisure Studies M
Mathematics Education M,D
Music Education M,D
Physical Education M
Reading Education M,D
Science Education M,D
Social Sciences Education M,D
Social Work M
Special Education M,D
Vocational and Technical Education M,D

UNIVERSITY OF VIRGINIA
Accounting M
Business Administration and Management—General M,D,O
Counselor Education M,D,O
Curriculum and Instruction M,D,O
Early Childhood Education M,D
Education of the Gifted M,D,O
Education—General M,D,O
Educational Leadership and Administration M,D,O
Educational Measurement and Evaluation M,D,O
Educational Media/Instructional Technology M,D,O
Educational Policy D
Educational Psychology M,D,O
Elementary Education M,D,O
English Education M,D,O
Finance and Banking M
Foreign Languages Education M,D,O
Higher Education M,D,O
International Business M,O
Kinesiology and Movement Studies M,D
Law M,D
Management Strategy and Policy M,O
Marketing M
Mathematics Education M,D,O
Physical Education M,D
Reading Education M,D
Science Education M,D,O
Social Sciences Education M,D,O
Special Education M,D,O
Student Affairs M,D,O

UNIVERSITY OF WASHINGTON
Accounting M,D
Business Administration and Management—General M,D
Curriculum and Instruction M,D
Education of Students with Severe/Multiple Disabilities M,D
Education—General M,D
Educational Leadership and Administration M,D
Educational Measurement and Evaluation M,D
Educational Media/Instructional Technology M,D
Educational Policy M,D
Educational Psychology M,D
English as a Second Language M,D
English Education M,D
Entrepreneurship M,D
Foundations and Philosophy of Education M,D
Higher Education M,D
Intellectual Property Law M,D
International Business M,D,O
Law M,D
Legal and Justice Studies M,D
Library Science M,D
Logistics O
Management Information Systems M,D
Mathematics Education M,D
Multilingual and Multicultural Education M,D
Music Education M,D
Physical Education M,D
Reading Education M,D
Science Education M,D
Social Sciences Education M,D
Social Work M,D
Special Education M,D
Supply Chain Management M,D
Taxation M,D
Transportation Management O

UNIVERSITY OF WASHINGTON, BOTHELL
Business Administration and Management—General M
Education—General M
Educational Leadership and Administration M
Middle School Education M
Secondary Education M

UNIVERSITY OF WASHINGTON, TACOMA
Accounting M
Business Administration and Management—General M
Education—General M
Educational Leadership and Administration M
Elementary Education M
Finance and Banking M
Mathematics Education M
Science Education M
Social Work M
Special Education M

UNIVERSITY OF WATERLOO
Accounting M,D
Actuarial Science M,D
Business Administration and Management—General M
Entrepreneurship M
Finance and Banking M,D
Health Education M,D
Kinesiology and Movement Studies M,D
Leisure Studies M,D
Recreation and Park Management M,D
Taxation M,D

THE UNIVERSITY OF WEST ALABAMA
Adult Education M
Business Administration and Management—General M
Counselor Education M,O
Early Childhood Education M,O
Education—General M,O
Educational Leadership and Administration M,O
Educational Media/Instructional Technology M,O
Elementary Education M,O
English Education M
Finance and Banking M
Higher Education M
Mathematics Education M
Physical Education M
Science Education M
Secondary Education M
Social Sciences Education M
Special Education M,O
Student Affairs M

THE UNIVERSITY OF WESTERN ONTARIO
Business Administration and Management—General M,D
Curriculum and Instruction M
Education—General M
Educational Policy M
Educational Psychology M
Entrepreneurship M,D
Finance and Banking M,D
Information Studies M,D
International Business M,D
Kinesiology and Movement Studies M,D
Law M,D,O
Library Science M,D
Management Strategy and Policy M,D
Marketing M,D
Special Education M

UNIVERSITY OF WEST FLORIDA
Accounting M
Business Administration and Management—General M
Curriculum and Instruction M,O
Educational Leadership and Administration M,D
Educational Media/Instructional Technology M,D
Elementary Education M
Exercise and Sports Science M
Leisure Studies M
Middle School Education M
Physical Education M,D
Reading Education M
Secondary Education M
Social Work M
Special Education M
Student Affairs M

UNIVERSITY OF WEST GEORGIA
Accounting M
Business Administration and Management—General M
Business Education M,D,O
Counselor Education M,D,O
Early Childhood Education M,D,O
Education—General M,D,O
Educational Leadership and Administration M,D,O
Educational Media/Instructional Technology M,D,O
Music Education M,O
Nonprofit Management M,D,O
Reading Education M,D,O
Secondary Education M,D,O
Special Education M,D,O

UNIVERSITY OF WEST LOS ANGELES
Business Administration and Management—General M
Entrepreneurship M
Law D
Organizational Management M

UNIVERSITY OF WINDSOR
Business Administration and Management—General M
Education—General M,D
Kinesiology and Movement Studies M
Legal and Justice Studies M
Social Work M

UNIVERSITY OF WISCONSIN–EAU CLAIRE
Business Administration and Management—General M
Education—General M
Library Science M
Reading Education M
Secondary Education M
Special Education M

UNIVERSITY OF WISCONSIN–GREEN BAY
Business Administration and Management—General M
Education—General M
Social Work M
Sustainability Management M

UNIVERSITY OF WISCONSIN–LA CROSSE
Athletic Training and Sports Medicine M
Education—General M,O
English Education M,O
Exercise and Sports Science M
Health Education M
Higher Education M,D
Physical Education M
Reading Education M,O
Recreation and Park Management M
Special Education M,O
Student Affairs M,D

UNIVERSITY OF WISCONSIN–MADISON
Accounting M,D
Actuarial Science D
Business Administration and Management—General M
Counselor Education M
Curriculum and Instruction M,D
Education—General M,D,O
Educational Leadership and Administration M,D,O
Educational Policy M,D,O
Educational Psychology M,D
English as a Second Language M,D
Finance and Banking M,D
Higher Education M,D,O
Human Resources Management M,D
Information Studies M,D
Insurance M,D
International and Comparative Education M,D,O
Investment Management D
Kinesiology and Movement Studies M,D
Law M,D
Library Science M,D
Management Information Systems D
Management Strategy and Policy M,D
Marketing Research M
Marketing D
Music Education M,D
Real Estate M,D
Risk Management M,D
Social Work M,D
Special Education M,D
Supply Chain Management M
Taxation M

UNIVERSITY OF WISCONSIN–MILWAUKEE
Actuarial Science M,D
Adult Education M,D,O
Art Education M,D,O
Athletic Training and Sports Medicine M,D
Business Administration and Management—General M,D,O
Business Analytics M,O
Curriculum and Instruction M,D,O
Early Childhood Education M
Education—General M,D,O
Educational Leadership and Administration M,D,O
Educational Measurement and Evaluation M,D,O
Educational Media/Instructional Technology M
Educational Policy M,O
Educational Psychology M,D,O
Elementary Education M
English as a Second Language M,D,O
English Education M,D
Entrepreneurship M,D,O
Exercise and Sports Science M,D
Foreign Languages Education M,O
Foundations and Philosophy of Education M,D,O
Higher Education M,O
Human Resources Management M,O
Information Studies M,D,O
Investment Management M,O
Kinesiology and Movement Studies M,D
Library Science M,D,O
Management Strategy and Policy M,D,O
Mathematics Education M,D,O
Middle School Education M
Multilingual and Multicultural Education M,D,O
Music Education M,O
Nonprofit Management M,D,O
Reading Education M
Recreation and Park Management M
Science Education M
Secondary Education M,D
Social Sciences Education M
Social Work M,D,O
Special Education M,D,O
Taxation M,O
Urban Education M,D,O

UNIVERSITY OF WISCONSIN–OSHKOSH
Business Administration and Management—General M
Counselor Education M
Curriculum and Instruction M
Early Childhood Education M
Education—General M
Educational Leadership and Administration M
International Business M
Mathematics Education M
Reading Education M
Social Work M
Special Education M

UNIVERSITY OF WISCONSIN–PARKSIDE
Business Administration and Management—General M
Sports Management M
Sustainability Management M

UNIVERSITY OF WISCONSIN–PLATTEVILLE
Adult Education M
Education—General M
Organizational Management M
Project Management M
Supply Chain Management M

UNIVERSITY OF WISCONSIN–RIVER FALLS
Agricultural Education M
Business Administration and Management—General M
Counselor Education M,O
Education—General M
Elementary Education M
English as a Second Language M
Mathematics Education M
Reading Education M
Science Education M
Social Sciences Education M

UNIVERSITY OF WISCONSIN–STEVENS POINT
Advertising and Public Relations M
Athletic Training and Sports Medicine M
Education—General M,D
Educational Leadership and Administration M,D
Elementary Education M
English Education M
Music Education M
Reading Education M
Science Education M
Secondary Education M
Social Sciences Education M
Special Education M

UNIVERSITY OF WISCONSIN–STOUT
Education—General M,D,O
Human Resources Development M
Project Management M
Quality Management M
Supply Chain Management M
Sustainability Management M
Vocational and Technical Education M,D,O

UNIVERSITY OF WISCONSIN–SUPERIOR
Art Education M
Counselor Education M
Curriculum and Instruction M
Education—General M
Educational Leadership and Administration M,O
Reading Education M
Special Education M
Sustainability Management M

UNIVERSITY OF WISCONSIN–WHITEWATER
Accounting M
Business Administration and Management—General M
Business Education M
Education—General M,O
Educational Leadership and Administration M
Finance and Banking M
Marketing M
Special Education M,O

UNIVERSITY OF WYOMING
Accounting M
Business Administration and Management—General M
Counselor Education M,D
Curriculum and Instruction M,D
Educational Leadership and Administration M,D,O
Educational Media/Instructional Technology M,D
Exercise and Sports Science M
Finance and Banking M
Health Education M
Kinesiology and Movement Studies M
Law D
Mathematics Education M,D
Music Education M
Physical Education M
Science Education M
Social Work M
Special Education M,D,O
Student Affairs M,D

UPPER IOWA UNIVERSITY
Accounting M
Business Administration and Management—General M
Early Childhood Education M
Education—General M

*M—masters degree; D—doctorate; O—other advanced degree; *—Close-Up and/or Display*

Educational Leadership and
   Administration M
English as a Second Language M
Finance and Banking M
Higher Education M
Human Resources Management M
Human Services M
Nonprofit Management M
Organizational Management M
Reading Education M
Sports Management M

URBANA UNIVERSITY–A BRANCH CAMPUS OF FRANKLIN UNIVERSITY
Business Administration and
   Management—General M
Education—General M

URSULINE COLLEGE
Accounting M
Business Administration and
   Management—General M
Educational Leadership and
   Administration M
Entrepreneurship M
Finance and Banking M
Marketing M

UTAH STATE UNIVERSITY
Accounting M
Agricultural Education M
Business Administration and
   Management—General M
Business Education D
Counselor Education M,D
Curriculum and Instruction D
Education—General M,D,O
Educational Measurement and
   Evaluation M,D
Educational Media/Instructional
   Technology M,D,O
Elementary Education M
Finance and Banking M
Health Education M,D
Home Economics Education M
Human Resources Management M
Kinesiology and Movement Studies M,D
Management Information Systems M
Multilingual and Multicultural
   Education M
Music Education M
Physical Education M,D
Recreation and Park Management M,D
Secondary Education M
Social Work M,D
Special Education M,D
Vocational and Technical Education D

UTAH VALLEY UNIVERSITY
Accounting M
Business Administration and
   Management—General M
Education—General M
Educational Leadership and
   Administration M
Educational Media/Instructional
   Technology M
Elementary Education M
English as a Second Language M
Mathematics Education M
Reading Education M
Social Work M

UTICA COLLEGE
Accounting M
Education—General M,O

VALDOSTA STATE UNIVERSITY
Accounting M
Business Administration and
   Management—General M
Counselor Education M,O
Educational Leadership and
   Administration M,D,O
Elementary Education M
English Education M
Exercise and Sports Science M
Information Studies M
Library Science M
Social Work M
Special Education M,D,O

VALLEY CITY STATE UNIVERSITY
Education—General M
Educational Media/Instructional
   Technology M
Elementary Education M
English as a Second Language M
English Education M
Library Science M
Vocational and Technical Education M

VALPARAISO UNIVERSITY
Business Administration and
   Management—General M,O
Education—General M,O
Educational Leadership and
   Administration M,O
Elementary Education M,O
English as a Second Language M,O
Entertainment Management M
Finance and Banking M
Management Information Systems M
Management Strategy and Policy M,O
Secondary Education M,O
Sports Management M

VANCOUVER ISLAND UNIVERSITY
Business Administration and
   Management—General M
Finance and Banking M
International Business M
Marketing M

VANCOUVER SCHOOL OF THEOLOGY
Religious Education M,O

VANDERBILT UNIVERSITY
Accounting M
Business Administration and
   Management—General M
Education—General M,D*
Educational Leadership and
   Administration D
Elementary Education M
English Education M
Finance and Banking M
Foreign Languages Education M,D
Law M,D
Management Strategy and Policy M
Marketing M
Multilingual and Multicultural
   Education D
Organizational Management M
Quantitative Analysis M
Reading Education M
Secondary Education M
Special Education D

VANDERCOOK COLLEGE OF MUSIC
Music Education M

VANGUARD UNIVERSITY OF SOUTHERN CALIFORNIA
Curriculum and Instruction M
Education—General M
Educational Leadership and
   Administration M
Religious Education M

VAUGHN COLLEGE OF AERONAUTICS AND TECHNOLOGY
Aviation Management M

VERMONT COLLEGE OF FINE ARTS
Art Education M

VERMONT LAW SCHOOL
Environmental Law M
Law D
Legal and Justice Studies M

VILLANOVA UNIVERSITY
Accounting M
Business Administration and
   Management—General M
Business Analytics M
Counselor Education M
Education—General M
Educational Leadership and
   Administration M
Finance and Banking M
Human Resources Development M
International Business M
Law D
Management Strategy and Policy M
Marketing M
Nonprofit Management M,O
Real Estate M
Taxation M

VIRGINIA COMMONWEALTH UNIVERSITY
Accounting M
Adult Education M
Advertising and Public Relations M
Art Education M,D
Business Administration and
   Management—General M,D
Counselor Education M,D
Curriculum and Instruction D
Early Childhood Education M
Education—General M,D,O
Educational Leadership and
   Administration M,D
Educational Measurement and
   Evaluation D
Educational Media/Instructional
   Technology M
Educational Psychology D
Elementary Education M
Exercise and Sports Science M
Finance and Banking M
Human Resources Development M
Human Resources Management M
Management Information Systems M
Music Education M
Nonprofit Management O
Reading Education M,O
Real Estate O
Recreation and Park Management M
Social Work M,D
Special Education M,D
Student Affairs M
Urban Education D

VIRGINIA INTERNATIONAL UNIVERSITY
Accounting M,O
Advertising and Public Relations M,O
Business Administration and
   Management—General M,O
Education—General M
English as a Second Language M
Entrepreneurship M,O
Finance and Banking M,O
Hospitality Management M,O
Human Resources Management M,O
International Business M,O
Logistics M,O
Management Information Systems M,O
Marketing M,O
Project Management M,O

VIRGINIA POLYTECHNIC INSTITUTE AND STATE UNIVERSITY
Accounting M,D
Business Administration and
   Management—General M,D
Business Analytics M
Counselor Education M,D,O
Curriculum and Instruction M,D,O
Distance Education Development M,O
Education—General M,O

Educational Leadership and
   Administration M,D,O
Educational Measurement and
   Evaluation M
Educational Media/Instructional
   Technology M,D,O
Educational Policy M,D,O
Exercise and Sports Science M,D
Finance and Banking M,D
Management Information Systems M,D,O
Marketing M,D
Nonprofit Management M,O
Quantitative Analysis M,O
Social Sciences Education M,D,O
Vocational and Technical Education M,D,O

VIRGINIA STATE UNIVERSITY
Counselor Education M
Education—General M,D
Educational Leadership and
   Administration M
Health Education M,D

VIRGINIA THEOLOGICAL SEMINARY
Educational Leadership and
   Administration M,D

VIRGINIA UNION UNIVERSITY
Curriculum and Instruction M
Education—General M

VIRGINIA WESLEYAN UNIVERSITY
Business Administration and
   Management—General M
Education—General M
Secondary Education M

VITERBO UNIVERSITY
Business Administration and
   Management—General M
Early Childhood Education M,O
Education of the Gifted M,O
Education—General M,O
Educational Leadership and
   Administration M,O
International Business M
Organizational Management M
Project Management M
Reading Education M
Special Education M,O

WAGNER COLLEGE
Accounting M
Business Administration and
   Management—General M
Early Childhood Education M
Education—General M
Elementary Education M
English Education M
Finance and Banking M
Foreign Languages Education M
Higher Education M
Marketing M
Mathematics Education M
Middle School Education M
Science Education M
Secondary Education M
Social Sciences Education M
Special Education M

WAKE FOREST UNIVERSITY
Accounting M
Business Administration and
   Management—General M
Business Analytics M
Counselor Education M
Education—General M
Exercise and Sports Science M
Law M,D
Secondary Education M
Taxation M

WALDEN UNIVERSITY
Accounting M,D,O
Adult Education M,D,O
Business Administration and
   Management—General M,D,O
Counselor Education M,D
Curriculum and Instruction M,D,O
Developmental Education M,D,O
Distance Education Development M,D,O
Early Childhood Education M,D,O
Education—General M,D,O
Educational Leadership and
   Administration M,D,O
Educational Measurement and
   Evaluation M,D,O
Educational Media/Instructional
   Technology M,D,O
Educational Psychology M,D,O
Elementary Education M,D,O
English as a Second Language M,D,O
Entrepreneurship M,D,O
Finance and Banking M,D,O
Health Education M,D,O
Higher Education M,D,O
Human Resources Management M,D,O
Human Services M,D
International and Comparative
   Education M,D,O
International Business M,D,O
Law M,D,O
Management Information Systems M,D,O
Marketing M,D,O
Mathematics Education M,D,O
Multilingual and Multicultural
   Education M,D,O
Nonprofit Management M,D,O
Organizational Management M,D,O
Project Management M,D,O
Reading Education M,D,O
Science Education M,D,O
Social Work M,D
Special Education M,D,O
Supply Chain Management M,D,O

WALDORF UNIVERSITY
Educational Leadership and
   Administration M
Human Resources Development M
Organizational Management M
Sports Management M

WALLA WALLA UNIVERSITY
Curriculum and Instruction M
Education—General M
Educational Leadership and
   Administration M
Reading Education M
Social Work M
Special Education M

WALSH COLLEGE OF ACCOUNTANCY AND BUSINESS ADMINISTRATION
Business Administration and
   Management—General M
Business Analytics M
Finance and Banking M
Human Resources Management M
International Business M
Investment Management M
Management Strategy and Policy M
Project Management M
Taxation M

WALSH UNIVERSITY
Business Administration and
   Management—General M
Counselor Education M
Education—General M
Higher Education M
Marketing M
Reading Education M
Religious Education M
Student Affairs M

WARNER PACIFIC UNIVERSITY
Education—General M
Human Services M
Nonprofit Management M
Organizational Management M

WARNER UNIVERSITY
Accounting M
Business Administration and
   Management—General M
Curriculum and Instruction M
Education—General M
Educational Media/Instructional
   Technology M
Elementary Education M
Human Resources Management M
International Business M
Science Education M

WASHBURN UNIVERSITY
Accounting M
Business Administration and
   Management—General M
Curriculum and Instruction M
Education—General M
Educational Leadership and
   Administration M
Health Education M
Human Services M
Law M,D
Legal and Justice Studies M,D
Reading Education M
Social Work M
Special Education M

WASHINGTON ADVENTIST UNIVERSITY
Business Administration and
   Management—General M

WASHINGTON & JEFFERSON COLLEGE
Accounting M,O

WASHINGTON AND LEE UNIVERSITY
Law D

WASHINGTON STATE UNIVERSITY
Accounting M
Business Administration and
   Management—General M,D
Business Education M,D
Curriculum and Instruction M,D
Education—General M,D
Educational Leadership and
   Administration M,D
Educational Psychology M,D
Elementary Education M,D
English as a Second Language M,D
Exercise and Sports Science M
Foreign Languages Education M,D
Mathematics Education M,D
Reading Education M,D
Secondary Education M,D
Special Education M,D
Sports Management M,D
Vocational and Technical Education M,D

WASHINGTON UNIVERSITY IN ST. LOUIS
Accounting M
Business Administration and
   Management—General M,D
Education—General M,D
Educational Measurement and
   Evaluation D
Elementary Education M
Entrepreneurship M
Finance and Banking M
Kinesiology and Movement Studies D
Law M,D
Organizational Management M
Secondary Education M
Social Work M,D
Special Education M,D
Supply Chain Management M

WAYLAND BAPTIST UNIVERSITY
Accounting M,D

Business Administration and Management—General M,D
Education—General M
Educational Leadership and Administration M
Educational Measurement and Evaluation M
Educational Media/Instructional Technology M
Elementary Education M
English as a Second Language M
English Education M
Higher Education M
Human Resources Management M,D
International Business M,D
Management Information Systems M,D
Organizational Management M,D
Project Management M,D
Science Education M
Secondary Education M
Social Sciences Education M
Special Education M
Sports Management M

WAYNESBURG UNIVERSITY
Business Administration and Management—General M,D
Counselor Education M,D
Curriculum and Instruction M,D
Distance Education Development M,D
Educational Leadership and Administration M,D
Educational Media/Instructional Technology M,D
Finance and Banking M,D
Human Resources Management M,D
Organizational Management M,D
Special Education M,D

WAYNE STATE COLLEGE
Business Administration and Management—General M
Business Education M
Counselor Education M
Curriculum and Instruction M
Early Childhood Education M
Education—General M,O
Educational Leadership and Administration M,O
Elementary Education M
English as a Second Language M
English Education M
Exercise and Sports Science M
Home Economics Education M
Mathematics Education M
Music Education M
Organizational Management M
Physical Education M
Science Education M
Social Sciences Education M
Special Education M
Sports Management M
Vocational and Technical Education M

WAYNE STATE UNIVERSITY
Accounting M,D,O
Advertising and Public Relations M,O
Archives/Archival Administration M,O
Art Education M,D,O
Athletic Training and Sports Medicine M,D
Business Administration and Management—General M,D,O
Counselor Education M,D,O
Curriculum and Instruction M,D,O
Distance Education Development M,D,O
Early Childhood Education M,D,O
Education—General M,D,O
Educational Leadership and Administration M,D,O
Educational Measurement and Evaluation M,D,O
Educational Media/Instructional Technology M,D,O
Educational Policy M,D,O
Educational Psychology M,D,O
Elementary Education M,D,O
English as a Second Language M,D,O
English Education M,D,O
Entrepreneurship M,D,O
Exercise and Sports Science M,D
Finance and Banking M,D,O
Foreign Languages Education M,D,O
Foundations and Philosophy of Education M,D,O
Health Education M,D,O
Human Resources Management M,D
Industrial and Manufacturing Management M,D
Information Studies M,O
Kinesiology and Movement Studies M,D
Law M,D
Library Science M,O
Management Information Systems M,D,O
Management Strategy and Policy M,D,O
Mathematics Education M,D,O
Multilingual and Multicultural Education M,D,O
Music Education M,O
Nonprofit Management M,D
Organizational Behavior M,D
Organizational Management M,D
Physical Education M,D
Reading Education M,D,O
Science Education M,D,O
Secondary Education M,D,O
Social Sciences Education M,D,O
Social Work M,D,O
Special Education M,D,O
Sports Management M,D
Taxation M,D,O

WEBBER INTERNATIONAL UNIVERSITY
Accounting M
Business Administration and Management—General M
International Business M
Sports Management M

WEBER STATE UNIVERSITY
Accounting M
Athletic Training and Sports Medicine M
Business Administration and Management—General M,O
Curriculum and Instruction M
Education—General M
Legal and Justice Studies M
Taxation M

WEBSTER UNIVERSITY
Accounting M
Advertising and Public Relations M
Business Administration and Management—General M,D,O
Early Childhood Education M,O
Education—General M,O
Educational Media/Instructional Technology M,O
Educational Psychology M,O
Elementary Education M,O
English as a Second Language M,O
Finance and Banking M
Human Resources Development M,D,O
Human Resources Management M,D,O
Human Services M
International Business M
Legal and Justice Studies M,O
Management Information Systems M,D,O
Marketing M,D,O
Mathematics Education M,O
Middle School Education M,O
Music Education M
Nonprofit Management M,D,O
Reading Education M,O
Secondary Education M,O
Special Education M,O

WENTWORTH INSTITUTE OF TECHNOLOGY
Facilities Management M

WESLEYAN COLLEGE
Business Administration and Management—General M
Early Childhood Education M
Education—General M

WESLEY BIBLICAL SEMINARY
Religious Education M

WESLEY COLLEGE
Business Administration and Management—General M
Education—General M

WEST CHESTER UNIVERSITY OF PENNSYLVANIA
Athletic Training and Sports Medicine M,O
Business Administration and Management—General M,O
Business Analytics M,O
Business Education M,O
Counselor Education M,O
Early Childhood Education M,O
Education—General M,D,O
Educational Leadership and Administration M,D,O
Educational Media/Instructional Technology M,D,O
Educational Policy M,D,O
English as a Second Language M,O
English Education M,O
Exercise and Sports Science M,O
Foreign Languages Education M,O
Foundations and Philosophy of Education M,O
Higher Education M,O
Human Resources Management M,O
Kinesiology and Movement Studies M,O
Management Information Systems M,O
Mathematics Education M,O
Music Education M,O
Nonprofit Management M,O
Physical Education M,O
Reading Education M,O
Science Education M,O
Social Work M,O
Special Education M,O
Sports Management M,O
Student Affairs M,O

WESTCLIFF UNIVERSITY
Business Administration and Management—General M,D
Education—General M
English as a Second Language M

WESTERN CAROLINA UNIVERSITY
Accounting M
Business Administration and Management—General M
Education—General M
English as a Second Language M,O
Entrepreneurship M
Project Management M,O
Social Work M

WESTERN CONNECTICUT STATE UNIVERSITY
Accounting M
Business Administration and Management—General M
Counselor Education M
Curriculum and Instruction M

Education—General M,D
Educational Leadership and Administration D
Educational Media/Instructional Technology M
Music Education M
Reading Education M,D
Special Education M

WESTERN GOVERNORS UNIVERSITY
Accounting M
Business Administration and Management—General M
Education—General M
Educational Leadership and Administration M,O
Educational Media/Instructional Technology M,O
Elementary Education M,O
English Education M,O
Management Information Systems M
Management Strategy and Policy M
Mathematics Education M
Science Education M,O
Special Education M,O

WESTERN ILLINOIS UNIVERSITY
Accounting M
Business Administration and Management—General M
Counselor Education M
Curriculum and Instruction M
Distance Education Development M,O
Education—General M,D,O
Educational Leadership and Administration M,D,O
Educational Media/Instructional Technology M,O
English as a Second Language M,O
Foundations and Philosophy of Education M,O
Health Education M
Higher Education M
Kinesiology and Movement Studies M
Reading Education M
Recreation and Park Management M
Social Work M
Special Education M
Sports Management M
Student Affairs M
Supply Chain Management M
Travel and Tourism M

WESTERN KENTUCKY UNIVERSITY
Adult Education M,D,O
Art Education M
Business Administration and Management—General M
Counselor Education M
Early Childhood Education M,O
Education of Students with Severe/Multiple Disabilities M,O
Educational Leadership and Administration M,D,O
Educational Media/Instructional Technology M,O
Elementary Education M,O
English as a Second Language M
English Education M
Foreign Languages Education M
Higher Education M
Middle School Education M
Music Education M
Physical Education M
Reading Education M,O
Recreation and Park Management M
Secondary Education M,O
Social Work M
Special Education M,O
Sports Management M
Student Affairs M

WESTERN MICHIGAN UNIVERSITY
Accounting M
Art Education M
Athletic Training and Sports Medicine M
Business Administration and Management—General M
Counselor Education M,D
Education—General M,D,O
Educational Leadership and Administration M,D,O
Educational Measurement and Evaluation M,D,O
Educational Media/Instructional Technology M,D,O
English Education M
Exercise and Sports Science M
Health Education D,O
Higher Education M
Human Services D,O
Mathematics Education M,D
Music Education M
Nonprofit Management M,D,O
Physical Education M
Reading Education M,D
Science Education M,D,O
Social Work M
Special Education M,D
Sports Management M
Vocational and Technical Education M

WESTERN MICHIGAN UNIVERSITY THOMAS M. COOLEY LAW SCHOOL
Environmental Law M,D
Finance and Banking M,D
Insurance M,D
Intellectual Property Law M,D
Law M,D
Legal and Justice Studies M,D
Taxation M,D

WESTERN NEW ENGLAND UNIVERSITY
Accounting M
Advertising and Public Relations M
Business Administration and Management—General M
Curriculum and Instruction M
English Education M
Law M,D
Mathematics Education M
Organizational Management M
Sports Management M

WESTERN NEW MEXICO UNIVERSITY
Business Administration and Management—General M
Education—General M
Educational Leadership and Administration M
Elementary Education M
English as a Second Language M
Multilingual and Multicultural Education M
Reading Education M
Secondary Education M
Social Work M
Special Education M

WESTERN OREGON UNIVERSITY
Early Childhood Education M
Education—General M
Educational Media/Instructional Technology M
Health Education M
Mathematics Education M
Multilingual and Multicultural Education M
Science Education M
Secondary Education M
Social Sciences Education M
Special Education M

WESTERN SEMINARY
Human Resources Development M

WESTERN STATE COLLEGE OF LAW AT ARGOSY UNIVERSITY
Law D

WESTERN STATE COLORADO UNIVERSITY
Education—General M
Educational Leadership and Administration M
Reading Education M

WESTERN UNIVERSITY OF HEALTH SCIENCES
Health Education M

WESTERN WASHINGTON UNIVERSITY
Adult Education M
Business Administration and Management—General M
Counselor Education M
Education of the Gifted M
Education—General M
Educational Leadership and Administration M
Elementary Education M
Environmental Education M
Exercise and Sports Science M
Higher Education M
Physical Education M
Science Education M
Secondary Education M

WESTFIELD STATE UNIVERSITY
Accounting M
Counselor Education M
Early Childhood Education M
Education—General M
Elementary Education M
Mathematics Education M
Nonprofit Management M
Physical Education M
Reading Education M
Science Education M
Secondary Education M
Social Sciences Education M
Social Work M
Special Education M
Vocational and Technical Education M

WEST LIBERTY UNIVERSITY
Accounting M
Business Administration and Management—General M
Education of Students with Severe/Multiple Disabilities M
Education—General M
Educational Leadership and Administration M
Organizational Management M
Physical Education M
Reading Education M
Special Education M
Sports Management M

WESTMINSTER COLLEGE (PA)
Counselor Education M
Early Childhood Education M
Educational Leadership and Administration M
Reading Education M
Special Education M

WESTMINSTER COLLEGE (UT)
Accounting M,O
Business Administration and Management—General M,O
Education—General M

WEST TEXAS A&M UNIVERSITY
Accounting M

M—masters degree; D—doctorate; O—other advanced degree; *—Close-Up and/or Display

Business Administration and
  Management—General — M
Counselor Education — M
Curriculum and Instruction — M
Education—General — M
Educational Leadership and
  Administration — M
Educational Measurement and
  Evaluation — M
Educational Media/Instructional
  Technology — M
Exercise and Sports Science — M
Finance and Banking — M
Reading Education — M
Social Work — M
Sports Management — M

WEST VIRGINIA UNIVERSITY
Accounting — M,D,O
Agricultural Education — M,D
Art Education — M,D
Athletic Training and Sports
  Medicine — M,D
Business Administration and
  Management—General — M,D,O
Business Analytics — M,D,O
Counselor Education — M,D
Curriculum and Instruction — M,D
Early Childhood Education — M,D
Education of the Gifted — M,D
Education—General — M,D
Educational Leadership and
  Administration — M,D
Educational Media/Instructional
  Technology — M,D
Educational Psychology — M,D
Elementary Education — M,D
English Education — M,D
Exercise and Sports Science — M,D
Finance and Banking — M,D,O
Higher Education — M,D
Human Services — M,D
Law — M,D
Legal and Justice Studies — M,D
Marketing — M,D,O
Music Education — M,D
Physical Education — M,D
Reading Education — M,D
Recreation and Park Management — M,D
Secondary Education — M,D
Social Work — M
Special Education — M,D
Sports Management — M,D
Travel and Tourism — M,D

WEST VIRGINIA WESLEYAN COLLEGE
Athletic Training and Sports
  Medicine — M
Business Administration and
  Management—General — M

WHEATON COLLEGE
Education—General — M
Elementary Education — M
Religious Education — M
Secondary Education — M

WHEELING JESUIT UNIVERSITY
Accounting — M
Business Administration and
  Management—General — M
Educational Leadership and
  Administration — M
Organizational Management — M

WHITTIER COLLEGE
Education—General — M
Educational Leadership and
  Administration — M
Elementary Education — M
Secondary Education — M

WHITWORTH UNIVERSITY
Business Administration and
  Management—General — M
Counselor Education — M
Education of the Gifted — M
Education—General — M
Educational Leadership and
  Administration — M
Elementary Education — M
Secondary Education — M
Special Education — M

WHU - OTTO BEISHEIM SCHOOL OF MANAGEMENT
Business Administration and
  Management—General — M

WICHITA STATE UNIVERSITY
Accounting — M
Business Administration and
  Management—General — M
Counselor Education — M,D,O
Curriculum and Instruction — M
Early Childhood Education — M
Education of the Gifted — M
Education—General — M,D,O
Educational Leadership and
  Administration — M,D,O
Educational Psychology — M,D,O
Entrepreneurship — M
Exercise and Sports Science — M
Human Services — M
Management Information Systems — M
Middle School Education — M
Music Education — M
Secondary Education — M
Social Work — M
Special Education — M
Sports Management — M
Supply Chain Management — M
Taxation — M

WIDENER UNIVERSITY
Adult Education — M,D

Business Administration and
  Management—General — M
Counselor Education — M,D
Early Childhood Education — M,D
Education—General — M
Educational Leadership and
  Administration — M,D
Educational Media/Instructional
  Technology — M,D
Educational Psychology — M,D
Elementary Education — M,D
English Education — M,D
Foundations and Philosophy of
  Education — M,D
Health Education — M,D
Health Law — M,D
Law — M,D
Mathematics Education — M,D
Middle School Education — M,D
Reading Education — M,D
Science Education — M,D
Social Sciences Education — M,D
Social Work — M,D
Special Education — M,D
Taxation — M

WILFRID LAURIER UNIVERSITY
Accounting — M,D
Business Administration and
  Management—General — M,D
Finance and Banking — M,D
Human Resources Management — M,D
Kinesiology and Movement Studies — M
Legal and Justice Studies — D
Marketing — M,D
Organizational Behavior — M,D
Organizational Management — M,D
Physical Education — M
Social Work — M,D
Supply Chain Management — M,D

WILKES UNIVERSITY
Accounting — M
Business Administration and
  Management—General — M
Distance Education Development — M,D
Education—General — M
Educational Leadership and
  Administration — M,D
Educational Measurement and
  Evaluation — M,D
Educational Media/Instructional
  Technology — M,D
English as a Second Language — M,D
Entrepreneurship — M
Finance and Banking — M
Human Resources Management — M
Industrial and Manufacturing
  Management — M
International and Comparative
  Education — M,D
International Business — M
Middle School Education — M,D
Organizational Management — M
Reading Education — M,D
Special Education — M,D

WILLAMETTE UNIVERSITY
Business Administration and
  Management—General — M
Law — M,D

WILLIAM CAREY UNIVERSITY
Art Education — M,O
Business Administration and
  Management—General — M
Education of the Gifted — M,O
Education—General — M,O
Elementary Education — M,O
English Education — M,O
Secondary Education — M,O
Social Sciences Education — M,O
Special Education — M,O

WILLIAM JAMES COLLEGE
Student Affairs — M,D,O

WILLIAM JESSUP UNIVERSITY
Education—General — M
English Education — M
Mathematics Education — M

WILLIAM JEWELL COLLEGE
Education—General — M

WILLIAM PATERSON UNIVERSITY OF NEW JERSEY
Accounting — M,O
Business Administration and
  Management—General — M,O
Business Analytics — M,O
Counselor Education — M,O
Early Childhood Education — M,O
Education—General — M,O
Educational Leadership and
  Administration — M,O
Educational Media/Instructional
  Technology — M,O
Elementary Education — M,O
English as a Second Language — M,D,O
Entertainment Management — M,O
Entrepreneurship — M,O
Exercise and Sports Science — M,D,O
Finance and Banking — M,O
Foundations and Philosophy of
  Education — M,D,O
Higher Education — M,O
Human Resources Management — M,O
Marketing — M,O
Middle School Education — M,O
Multilingual and Multicultural
  Education — M,D,O
Reading Education — M,O
Secondary Education — M,O
Special Education — M,O

WILLIAM PENN UNIVERSITY
Organizational Management — M

WILLIAMS BAPTIST COLLEGE
Education—General — M

WILLIAMSON COLLEGE
Organizational Management — M

WILLIAM WOODS UNIVERSITY
Advertising and Public Relations — M,D,O
Business Administration and
  Management—General — M,D,O
Curriculum and Instruction — M,D,O
Educational Leadership and
  Administration — M,D,O
Educational Media/Instructional
  Technology — M,D,O
Human Resources Development — M,D,O
Marketing — M,D,O
Physical Education — M,D,O

WILMINGTON COLLEGE
Education—General — M
Reading Education — M
Special Education — M

WILMINGTON UNIVERSITY
Accounting — M,D
Business Administration and
  Management—General — M,D
Counselor Education — M,D
Education of the Gifted — M,D
Education—General — M,D
Educational Leadership and
  Administration — M,D
Educational Media/Instructional
  Technology — M,D
Elementary Education — M,D
English as a Second Language — M,D
Finance and Banking — M,D
Higher Education — M,D
Human Resources Management — M,D
Human Services — M
Management Information Systems — M,D
Marketing — M,D
Organizational Management — M,D
Project Management — M
Reading Education — M,D
Secondary Education — M,D
Special Education — M,D
Vocational and Technical Education — M,D

WILSON COLLEGE
Accounting — M
Business Administration and
  Management—General — M
Education—General — M
Educational Media/Instructional
  Technology — M
Elementary Education — M
Secondary Education — M
Special Education — M

WINGATE UNIVERSITY
Accounting — M
Business Administration and
  Management—General — M
Community College Education — M,D,O
Education—General — M,D,O
Educational Leadership and
  Administration — M,D,O
Elementary Education — M,D,O
Entrepreneurship — M
Finance and Banking — M
Marketing — M
Project Management — M
Sports Management — M

WINONA STATE UNIVERSITY
Counselor Education — M,O
Education—General — O
Educational Leadership and
  Administration — M,O
English as a Second Language — M
Human Services — M,O
Multilingual and Multicultural
  Education — O
Organizational Management — M,D,O
Special Education — M
Sports Management — M,O

WINSTON-SALEM STATE UNIVERSITY
Business Administration and
  Management—General — M
Education—General — M
Management Information Systems — M
Middle School Education — M
Special Education — M

WINTHROP UNIVERSITY
Art Education — M
Business Administration and
  Management—General — M
Counselor Education — M
Education—General — M
Educational Leadership and
  Administration — M
Music Education — M
Physical Education — M
Secondary Education — M
Social Work — M
Special Education — M

WISCONSIN LUTHERAN COLLEGE
Curriculum and Instruction — M
Educational Leadership and
  Administration — M
Educational Media/Instructional
  Technology — M
Science Education — M

WITTENBERG UNIVERSITY
Education—General — M

WOODBURY UNIVERSITY
Business Administration and
  Management—General — M
Organizational Management — M

WORCESTER POLYTECHNIC INSTITUTE
Business Administration and
  Management—General — M,D,O
Educational Media/Instructional
  Technology — M,D
Management Information Systems — M,D,O
Marketing — M,D,O
Organizational Management — M,D,O
Supply Chain Management — M,D,O

WORCESTER STATE UNIVERSITY
Accounting — M
Business Administration and
  Management—General — M
Curriculum and Instruction — M,O
Early Childhood Education — M,O
Education—General — M,O
Educational Leadership and
  Administration — M,O
Elementary Education — M,O
English as a Second Language — M
English Education — M
Foreign Languages Education — M,O
Health Education — M,O
Marketing — M
Middle School Education — M,O
Nonprofit Management — M
Organizational Management — M
Reading Education — M,O
Secondary Education — M,O
Social Sciences Education — M
Special Education — M,O

WRIGHT STATE UNIVERSITY
Accounting — M
Business Administration and
  Management—General — M
Counselor Education — M
Curriculum and Instruction — O
Education—General — M,O
Educational Leadership and
  Administration — O
Elementary Education — M
Health Education — M
Logistics — M
Management Information Systems — M
Mathematics Education — D
Music Education — M
Science Education — M,D
Secondary Education — M
Special Education — M
Supply Chain Management — M

XAVIER UNIVERSITY
Accounting — M
Athletic Training and Sports
  Medicine — M
Business Administration and
  Management—General — M
Counselor Education — M
Early Childhood Education — M
Education—General — M,D
Educational Leadership and
  Administration — M,D
Elementary Education — M
Finance and Banking — M
Human Resources Development — M,D
International Business — M
Management Strategy and Policy — M
Marketing — M
Multilingual and Multicultural
  Education — M
Reading Education — M
Religious Education — M
Secondary Education — M
Special Education — M
Sports Management — M

XAVIER UNIVERSITY OF LOUISIANA
Counselor Education — M
Curriculum and Instruction — M
Educational Leadership and
  Administration — M

YALE UNIVERSITY
Accounting — D
Business Administration and
  Management—General — M,D
Finance and Banking — D
Law — M,D
Marketing — D
Organizational Management — D

YESHIVA UNIVERSITY
Accounting — M
Business Administration and
  Management—General — M
Educational Leadership and
  Administration — M,D,O
Intellectual Property Law — M,D
Law — M,D
Marketing — M
Religious Education — M,D,O
Risk Management — M
Social Work — M
Taxation — M

YORK COLLEGE OF PENNSYLVANIA
Accounting — M
Business Administration and
  Management—General — M
Education—General — M
Educational Leadership and
  Administration — M
Educational Media/Instructional
  Technology — M
Finance and Banking — M
Marketing — M
Reading Education — M

YORK UNIVERSITY
Accounting — M,D
Business Administration and
  Management—General — M,D
Business Analytics — M,D
Education—General — M,D
Finance and Banking — M,D

Human Resources Management	M,D	Actuarial Science	M	Educational Leadership and		Social Work	M
International Business	M,D	Athletic Training and Sports		Administration	M,D,O	Special Education	M
Kinesiology and Movement Studies	M,D	Medicine	M	Finance and Banking	M	Supply Chain Management	O
Law	M,D	Business Administration and		Human Services	M		
Social Work	M,D	Management—General	M	Mathematics Education	M		
		Counselor Education	M,D,O	Music Education	M		
YOUNGSTOWN STATE UNIVERSITY		Curriculum and Instruction	M	Reading Education	M		
Accounting	M	Education—General	M,D,O	Science Education	M		

M—masters degree; D—doctorate; O—other advanced degree; *—Close-Up and/or Display

ACADEMIC AND PROFESSIONAL PROGRAMS IN BUSINESS

Section 1
Business Administration and Management

This section contains a directory of institutions offering graduate work in business administration and management, followed by in-depth entries submitted by institutions that chose to prepare detailed program descriptions. Additional information about programs listed in the directory but not augmented by an in-depth entry may be obtained by writing directly to the dean of a graduate school or chair of a department at the address given in the directory.

For programs offering related work, see also in this book Sections 2–18, Education (Business Education), and Sports Management. In the other guides in this series:

Graduate Programs in the Humanities, Arts & Social Sciences

See *Art and Art History (Arts Administration), Economics, Family and Consumer Sciences (Consumer Economics), Political Science and International Affairs, Psychology (Industrial and Organizational Psychology),* and *Public, Regional, and Industrial Affairs (Industrial and Labor Relations)*

Graduate Programs in the Biological/Biomedical Sciences & Health-Related Medical Professions

See *Health Services and Nursing (Nursing and Healthcare Administration)*

Graduate Programs in the Physical Sciences, Mathematics, Agricultural Sciences, the Environment & Natural Resources

See *Environmental Sciences and Management (Environmental Management and Policy)* and *Mathematical Sciences*

Graduate Programs in Engineering & Applied Sciences

See *Computer Science and Information Technology, Civil and Environmental Engineering (Construction Engineering and Management), Industrial Engineering,* and *Management of Engineering and Technology*

CONTENTS

Program Directory

Business Administration and Management— General

Abilene Christian University, College of Graduate and Professional Studies, Program in Business Administration, Addison, TX 79699. Offers business analytics (MBA); general management (MBA); healthcare administration (MBA); international business (MBA); management: business analytics (MS); management: healthcare administration (MS); management: international business (MS); management: marketing (MS); management: operations and supply chain management (MS); marketing (MBA); nonprofit leadership (MBA). *Program availability:* Part-time, online only, 100% online. *Faculty:* 4 full-time (0 women), 7 part-time/adjunct (3 women). *Students:* 149 full-time (69 women), 53 part-time (25 women); includes 88 minority (42 Black or African American, non-Hispanic/Latino; 2 American Indian or Alaska Native, non-Hispanic/Latino; 4 Asian, non-Hispanic/Latino; 31 Hispanic/Latino; 1 Native Hawaiian or other Pacific Islander, non-Hispanic/Latino; 8 Two or more races, non-Hispanic/Latino), 4 international. 36 applicants, 100% accepted, 32 enrolled. In 2018, 24 master's awarded. *Entrance requirements:* Additional exam requirements/recommendations for international students: Required—TOEFL (minimum score 80 iBT), IELTS (minimum score 6). *Application deadline:* For fall admission, 10/7 for domestic students; for winter admission, 12/20 for domestic students; for spring admission, 2/24 for domestic students; for summer admission, 4/20 for domestic students. Applications are processed on a rolling basis. Application fee: $50. Electronic applications accepted. *Expenses:* $721 per hour. *Financial support:* In 2018–19, 16 students received support. Scholarships/grants available. Financial award application deadline: 7/1; financial award applicants required to submit FAFSA. *Faculty research:* Organizational structure, financial management, cost accounting, unit analysis management. *Unit head:* Dr. Phil Vardiman, Program Director, 325-674-2153, E-mail: pxv02b@acu.edu. *Application contact:* Graduate Advisor, 817-219-7300, E-mail: onlineadmissions@acu.edu. Website: http://www.acu.edu/online/academics/mba-business-administration.html

Adams State University, Office of Graduate Studies, School of Business, Alamosa, CO 81101. Offers MBA.

Adelphi University, Robert B. Willumstad School of Business, MBA Program, Garden City, NY 11530-0701. Offers accounting (MBA); finance (MBA); health services administration (MBA); human resource management (MBA); management (MBA); management information systems (MBA); marketing (MBA); sport management (MBA). *Accreditation:* AACSB. *Program availability:* Part-time, evening/weekend. *Students:* 343 full-time (132 women), 101 part-time (56 women); includes 75 minority (22 Black or African American, non-Hispanic/Latino; 2 American Indian or Alaska Native, non-Hispanic/Latino; 20 Asian, non-Hispanic/Latino; 23 Hispanic/Latino; 1 Native Hawaiian or other Pacific Islander, non-Hispanic/Latino; 7 Two or more races, non-Hispanic/Latino), 275 international. Average age 29. 389 applicants, 59% accepted, 187 enrolled. In 2018, 171 master's awarded. *Entrance requirements:* For master's, GMAT, official transcripts, bachelor's degree, 500 word essay, 2 letters of recommendation, resume. Additional exam requirements/recommendations for international students: Required—TOEFL (minimum score 550 paper-based; 80 iBT), IELTS (minimum score 6.5). *Application deadline:* For fall admission, 4/1 for international students; for spring admission, 11/1 for international students. Applications are processed on a rolling basis. Application fee: $50. Electronic applications accepted. *Financial support:* Research assistantships with partial tuition reimbursements, career-related internships or fieldwork, Federal Work-Study, institutionally sponsored loans, scholarships/grants, tuition waivers (partial), and unspecified assistantships available. Financial award application deadline: 3/1; financial award applicants required to submit FAFSA. *Faculty research:* Supply chain management, distribution channels, productivity benchmark analysis, data envelopment analysis, financial portfolio analysis. *Unit head:* Britt'ny Brown, Director of Graduate Programs, 516-877-4605. *Application contact:* Britt'ny Brown, Director of Graduate Programs, 516-877-4605. Website: https://business.adelphi.edu/

Alabama Agricultural and Mechanical University, School of Graduate Studies, College of Business and Public Affairs, Huntsville, AL 35811. Offers MBA. *Program availability:* Part-time, evening/weekend. *Degree requirements:* For master's, comprehensive exam. *Entrance requirements:* For master's, minimum undergraduate GPA of 2.5. Additional exam requirements/recommendations for international students: Required—TOEFL (minimum score 500 paper-based; 61 iBT). Electronic applications accepted. *Faculty research:* Consumer behavior of blacks, small business marketing, economics of education.

Alabama State University, College of Business Administration, Montgomery, AL 36101-0271. Offers M Acc. *Accreditation:* ACBSP. *Program availability:* Part-time. *Faculty:* 4 full-time (1 woman), 1 part-time/adjunct (0 women). *Students:* 16 full-time (6 women), 1 (woman) part-time; includes 14 minority (all Black or African American, non-Hispanic/Latino), 3 international. Average age 29. 14 applicants, 29% accepted, 3 enrolled. In 2018, 8 master's awarded. *Degree requirements:* For master's, comprehensive exam. *Entrance requirements:* For master's, minimum GPA of 2.75 (undergraduate), 3.0 (graduate); bachelor's degree or its equivalent from accredited college or university. Additional exam requirements/recommendations for international students: Required—TOEFL (minimum score 500 paper-based). *Application deadline:* For fall admission, 4/15 for domestic and international students; for spring admission, 11/15 for domestic students, 11/1 for international students; for summer admission, 3/15 for domestic and international students. Application fee: $25. Electronic applications accepted. *Financial support:* Fellowships, teaching assistantships, career-related internships or fieldwork, scholarships/grants, tuition waivers (partial), and unspecified assistantships available. Financial award application deadline: 6/30; financial award applicants required to submit FAFSA. *Unit head:* Dr. Dave Thompson, Director, Master of Accountancy, 334-229-6809, E-mail: dthompson@alasu.edu. *Application contact:* Dr. Ed Brown, Dean of Graduate Studies, 334-229-4274, Fax: 334-229-4928, E-mail: ebrown@alasu.edu. Website: http://www.alasu.edu/academics/colleges—departments/college-of-business-administration/index.aspx

Alaska Pacific University, Graduate Programs, Business Administration Department, Program in Business Administration, Anchorage, AK 99508-4672. Offers business administration (MBA); health services administration (MBA). *Program availability:* Part-time, evening/weekend. *Degree requirements:* For master's, capstone course. *Entrance requirements:* For master's, GMAT or GRE General Test, minimum GPA of 3.0.

Albany State University, College of Business, Albany, GA 31705-2717. Offers accounting (MBA); general business administration (MBA); healthcare (MBA); public administration (MBA); supply chain and logistics (MBA). *Accreditation:* ACBSP. *Program*

availability: Part-time, evening/weekend. *Degree requirements:* For master's, comprehensive exam, internship, 3 hours of physical education. *Entrance requirements:* For master's, GMAT (minimum score of 450)/GRE (minimum score of 800) for those without earned master's degree or higher, minimum undergraduate GPA of 2.5, 2 letters of reference, official transcript, pre-entrance medical record and certificate of immunization. Electronic applications accepted. *Faculty research:* Diversity issues, ancestry, understanding finance through use of technology.

Albertus Magnus College, Master of Business Administration Program, New Haven, CT 06511-1189. Offers accounting (MBA); general management (MBA); health care management (MBA); human resource management (MBA); leadership (MBA); project management (MBA). Program also offered in East Hartford, CT. *Program availability:* Part-time, evening/weekend, 100% online, blended/hybrid learning. *Degree requirements:* For master's, thesis, capstone project, business plan, minimum cumulative GPA of 3.0, completion of all requirements within seven years of matriculation. *Entrance requirements:* For master's, 3 years of management or related experience, minimum GPA of 2.5, 2 letters of recommendation, official transcripts. Additional exam requirements/recommendations for international students: Recommended—TOEFL (minimum score 550 paper-based; 80 iBT). Electronic applications accepted. *Expenses:* Contact institution. *Faculty research:* Finance, project management, accounting, business administration, generalist.

Albizu University, Miami Campus, Graduate Programs, Miami, FL 33172-2209. Offers clinical psychology (PhD, Psy D); entrepreneurship (MBA); exceptional student education (MS); human services (PhD); industrial/organizational psychology (MS); marriage and family therapy (MS); mental health counseling (MS); nonprofit management (MBA); organizational management (MBA); school counseling (MS); speech and language pathology (MS); teaching English for speakers of other languages (MS). *Accreditation:* APA. *Program availability:* Part-time, evening/weekend, 100% online, blended/hybrid learning. *Faculty:* 32 full-time (24 women), 27 part-time/adjunct (15 women). *Students:* 479 full-time (410 women), 146 part-time (126 women); includes 539 minority (42 Black or African American, non-Hispanic/Latino; 2 Asian, non-Hispanic/Latino; 490 Hispanic/Latino; 5 Two or more races, non-Hispanic/Latino), 22 international. Average age 33. 314 applicants, 45% accepted, 92 enrolled. In 2018, 101 master's, 64 doctorates awarded. Terminal master's awarded for partial completion of doctoral program. *Degree requirements:* For master's, comprehensive exam (for some programs), integrative project (for MBA); research project (for exceptional student education, teaching English as a second language); for doctorate, comprehensive exam, thesis/dissertation, comprehensive examinations, internship, project/dissertation. *Entrance requirements:* For master's, GRE/EXADEP, bachelor's degree from accredited institution, minimum GPA of 3.0, 3 letters of recommendation, interview, resume, statement of purpose, official transcripts; for doctorate, GRE (for Psy D), 3 letters of recommendation, resume, interview, statement of purpose, official transcripts; bachelor's degree and minimum GPA of 3.25 (for Psy D); master's degree and minimum GPA of 3.0 (for PhD). Additional exam requirements/recommendations for international students: Required—Michigan Test of English Language Proficiency. *Application deadline:* For fall admission, 4/1 priority date for domestic students, 5/1 priority date for international students; for spring admission, 11/1 priority date for domestic students, 9/1 priority date for international students. Applications are processed on a rolling basis. Application fee: $50. Electronic applications accepted. Application fee is waived when completed online. *Expenses:* Contact institution. *Financial support:* In 2018–19, 141 students received support. Federal Work-Study, scholarships/grants, unspecified assistantships, and tuition discounts available. Financial award application deadline: 6/1; financial award applicants required to submit FAFSA. *Faculty research:* Psychotherapy, forensic psychology, neuropsychology, special education, speech-language pathology, criminal justice, human services. *Unit head:* Dr. Jose Pons-Madera, PhD, President, 305-593-1223 Ext. 3120, Fax: 305-477-8983, E-mail: jpons@albizu.edu. *Application contact:* Nancy Alvarez, Director of Enrollment Management, 305-593-1223 Ext. 3136, Fax: 305-593-1854, E-mail: nalvarez@albizu.edu.

Alcorn State University, School of Graduate Studies, School of Business, Lorman, MS 39096-7500. Offers MBA. *Accreditation:* ACBSP.

Alfred University, Graduate School, School of Business, Alfred, NY 14802-1205. Offers accounting (MBA); business administration (MBA). *Accreditation:* AACSB. *Program availability:* Part-time. *Entrance requirements:* For master's, GMAT. Additional exam requirements/recommendations for international students: Required—TOEFL (minimum score 590 paper-based; 90 iBT), IELTS (minimum score 6.5). Electronic applications accepted.

Alliant International University–Los Angeles, Marshall Goldsmith School of Management, Business Division, Alhambra, CA 91803. Offers DBA.

Alliant International University–San Diego, Alliant School of Management, Business and Management Division, San Diego, CA 92131. Offers business administration (MBA); MBA/MA; MBA/PhD. *Program availability:* Part-time, evening/weekend. *Entrance requirements:* For master's, GMAT or GRE, minimum GPA of 2.75. Additional exam requirements/recommendations for international students: Required—TOEFL (minimum score 550 paper-based; 80 iBT), TWE (minimum score 5). Electronic applications accepted. *Faculty research:* Financial and commodity markets, market micro-structures, risk measurement, virtual teams, sustainable work environments.

Alvernia University, School of Graduate Studies, Department of Business, Reading, PA 19607-1799. Offers MBA. *Accreditation:* ACBSP. *Program availability:* Part-time, evening/weekend. *Degree requirements:* For master's, thesis optional. *Entrance requirements:* For master's, GMAT, GRE, or MAT. Electronic applications accepted.

Alverno College, School of Professional Studies - Business Division, Milwaukee, WI 53234-3922. Offers MBA. *Program availability:* Part-time, evening/weekend. *Entrance requirements:* For master's, 3 or more years of relevant work experience. Additional exam requirements/recommendations for international students: Required—TOEFL. Electronic applications accepted. *Expenses:* Contact institution.

Amberton University, Graduate School, Department of Business Administration, Garland, TX 75041-5595. Offers agile project management (MS); general business (MBA); international business (MBA); management (MBA); project management (MBA); strategic leadership (MBA). *Program availability:* Part-time, evening/weekend. *Entrance requirements:* For master's, minimum GPA of 3.0.

Amberton University, Graduate School, Program in Managerial Science, Garland, TX 75041-5595. Offers MS.

American Business & Technology University, Programs in Business Administration, Saint Joseph, MO 64506. Offers business administration (MBA); financial management (MBA); global business management (MBA); information systems management (MBA); marketing and social media (MBA); project and operations management (MBA); public accounting (MBA). *Program availability:* Online learning.

American College Dublin, Graduate Programs, Dublin, Ireland. Offers business administration (MBA); creative writing (MFA); international business (MBA); oil and gas management (MBA); performance (MFA).

The American College of Financial Services, Graduate Programs, Bryn Mawr, PA 19010-2105. Offers financial services (MSFS); leadership (MSM). *Program availability:* Part-time, evening/weekend, online learning. Electronic applications accepted. *Faculty research:* Retirement counseling, social security, aging, family composition, inflation.

American College of Thessaloniki, Department of Business Administration, Pylea, Greece. Offers banking and finance (MBA); entrepreneurship (MBA, Certificate); finance (Certificate); management (MBA, Certificate); marketing (MBA, Certificate). *Program availability:* Part-time, evening/weekend. *Degree requirements:* For master's, thesis. *Entrance requirements:* For master's, bachelor's degree. Additional exam requirements/recommendations for international students: Recommended—TOEFL. Electronic applications accepted.

American Graduate University, Program in Acquisition Management, Covina, CA 91724. Offers MAM, Certificate. *Program availability:* Part-time, online learning. *Degree requirements:* For master's, thesis (for some programs), comprehensive exam or project. *Entrance requirements:* For master's, undergraduate degree from institution accredited by accrediting agency recognized by the U.S. Department of Education. Additional exam requirements/recommendations for international students: Required—TOEFL. Electronic applications accepted.

American Graduate University, Program in Business Administration, Covina, CA 91724. Offers acquisition and contracting (MBA); supply chain management (MBA). *Program availability:* Part-time, online learning. *Degree requirements:* For master's, thesis. *Entrance requirements:* For master's, undergraduate degree from institution accredited by accrediting agency recognized by the U.S. Department of Education. Additional exam requirements/recommendations for international students: Required—TOEFL. Electronic applications accepted.

American Graduate University, Program in Contract Management, Covina, CA 91724. Offers MCM, Certificate. *Program availability:* Part-time, online learning. *Degree requirements:* For master's, comprehensive exam (for some programs), thesis (for some programs), comprehensive exam or project. *Entrance requirements:* For master's, undergraduate degree from institution accredited by accrediting agency recognized by the U.S. Department of Education. Additional exam requirements/recommendations for international students: Required—TOEFL. Electronic applications accepted.

American InterContinental University Houston, School of Business, Houston, TX 77042. Offers management (MBA).

American InterContinental University Online, Program in Business Administration, Schaumburg, IL 60173. Offers accounting and finance (MBA); finance (MBA); healthcare management (MBA); human resource management (MBA); international business (MBA); management (MBA); marketing (MBA); operations management (MBA); organizational psychology and development (MBA); project management (MBA). *Accreditation:* ACBSP. *Program availability:* Evening/weekend, online learning. *Entrance requirements:* Additional exam requirements/recommendations for international students: Required—TOEFL (minimum score 550 paper-based). Electronic applications accepted.

American International College, School of Business, Arts and Sciences, Springfield, MA 01109-3189. Offers accounting and taxation (MS); business administration (MBA); clinical psychology (MA); educational psychology (Ed D); forensic psychology (MS); general psychology (MA, CAGS); management (CAGS); resort and casino management (MBA, CAGS). *Program availability:* Part-time, evening/weekend. *Degree requirements:* For master's, practicum; for doctorate, comprehensive exam, thesis/dissertation, practicum. *Entrance requirements:* For master's, BS or BA, minimum undergraduate GPA of 2.75, 2 letters of recommendation, official transcripts, personal goal statement or essay; for doctorate, 3 letters of recommendation; BS or BA; minimum undergraduate GPA of 3.0 (3.25 recommended); official transcripts; personal goal statement or essay. Additional exam requirements/recommendations for international students: Required—TOEFL (minimum score 550 paper-based; 80 iBT). *Expenses:* Contact institution. *Faculty research:* Substance abuse, forensic psychology, special education.

American Jewish University, Graduate School of Nonprofit Management, Program in Business Administration, Bel Air, CA 90077-1599. Offers general nonprofit administration (MBA); Jewish nonprofit administration (MBA). *Program availability:* Part-time, evening/weekend. *Degree requirements:* For master's, thesis, internship. *Entrance requirements:* For master's, GMAT or GRE General Test, interview, minimum undergraduate GPA of 3.0. Additional exam requirements/recommendations for international students: Required—TOEFL (minimum score 550 paper-based).

American National University, Program in Business Administration, Salem, VA 24153. Offers MBA.

American Public University System, AMU/APU Graduate Programs, Charles Town, WV 25414. Offers accounting (MS); applied business analytics (MS); business administration (MBA); criminal justice (MA); cybersecurity studies (MS); educational leadership (M Ed); environmental policy and management (MS); global security (DGS); health information management (MS); history (MA), including American military history, American Revolution, civil war, war since 1945, World War II; information technology (MS); international relations and conflict resolution (MA), including American politics and government, comparative government and development, general, international relations, public policy; national security studies (MA); nursing (MSN); political science (MA); public policy (MPP); reverse logistics management (MA), including comparative and security issues, conflict resolution, international and transnational security issues, peacekeeping; space studies (MS); sports management (MS); strategic intelligence (DSI); teaching (M Ed), including secondary social studies; transportation and logistics management (MA). *Program availability:* Part-time, evening/weekend, online only, 100% online. *Students:* 406 full-time (180 women), 7,826 part-time (3,329 women); includes 2,781 minority (1,438 Black or African American, non-Hispanic/Latino; 44 American Indian or Alaska Native, non-Hispanic/Latino; 193 Asian, non-Hispanic/Latino; 747 Hispanic/Latino; 53 Native Hawaiian or other Pacific Islander, non-Hispanic/Latino; 306 Two or more races, non-Hispanic/Latino), 121 international. Average age 38. In 2018, 2,717 master's awarded. *Degree requirements:* For master's, comprehensive exam or practicum; for doctorate, practicum. *Entrance requirements:* For master's, official transcript showing earned bachelor's degree from institution accredited by recognized accrediting body. Additional exam requirements/recommendations for international students: Required—TOEFL (minimum score 550 paper-based), IELTS (minimum score 6.5). *Application deadline:* Applications are processed on a rolling basis. Application fee: $0. Electronic applications accepted. *Financial support:* Scholarships/grants available. Financial award applicants required to submit FAFSA. *Unit head:* Dr. Wallace Boston, President, 877-468-6268, Fax: 304-728-2348, E-mail: president@apus.edu. *Application*

contact: Yoci Deal, Associate Vice President, Graduate and International Admissions, 877-468-6268, Fax: 304-724-3764, E-mail: info@apus.edu. Website: http://www.apus.edu

American Sentinel University, Graduate Programs, Aurora, CO 80014. Offers business administration (MBA); business intelligence (MS); computer science (MSCS); health information management (MS); healthcare (MBA); information systems (MSIS); nursing (MSN). *Program availability:* Part-time, evening/weekend, online learning. *Entrance requirements:* Additional exam requirements/recommendations for international students: Required—TOEFL (minimum score 600 paper-based). Electronic applications accepted.

American University, Kogod School of Business, MBA Program, Washington, DC 20016-8044. Offers MBA, Certificate, MBA/JD, MBA/LL M, MBA/MA, MBA/MS. *Program availability:* Part-time, evening/weekend, 100% online. *Faculty:* 20 full-time (8 women), 52 part-time/adjunct (21 women). *Students:* 317 full-time (154 women), 232 part-time (111 women); includes 298 minority (157 Black or African American, non-Hispanic/Latino; 1 American Indian or Alaska Native, non-Hispanic/Latino; 46 Asian, non-Hispanic/Latino; 64 Hispanic/Latino; 2 Native Hawaiian or other Pacific Islander, non-Hispanic/Latino; 28 Two or more races, non-Hispanic/Latino), 19 international. Average age 31. 431 applicants, 77% accepted, 158 enrolled. In 2018, 117 master's, 1 other advanced degree awarded. *Entrance requirements:* For master's, GMAT/GRE; Please see website: https://www.american.edu/kogod/, resume, personal statement, interview, 2 letters of recommendation, transcripts. Additional exam requirements/recommendations for international students: Required—TOEFL (minimum score 100 iBT). *Application deadline:* Applications are processed on a rolling basis. Application fee: $100. *Expenses:* Contact institution. *Financial support:* Applicants required to submit FAFSA. *Faculty research:* Information technology, decision-aiding methodology, negotiation. *Unit head:* Dr. Parthiban David, Department Chair, Management, 202-885-1900, E-mail: kogodgrad@american.edu. *Application contact:* Jason Garner, Associate Director, Admissions, 202-885-1922, E-mail: jgarner@american.edu. Website: http://www.american.edu/kogod/mba/

American University in Bulgaria, Executive MBA Program, Blagoevgrad, Bulgaria. Offers EMBA. *Entrance requirements:* For master's, two essays, two professional recommendations, resume or professional curriculum vitae. Additional exam requirements/recommendations for international students: Required—TOEFL.

The American University in Cairo, School of Business, Cairo, Egypt. Offers business administration (MBA); economics (MA); economics in international development (MA, Diploma); finance (MS). *Program availability:* Part-time, evening/weekend. *Degree requirements:* For master's, comprehensive exam (for some programs), thesis (for some programs). *Entrance requirements:* For master's, GMAT, GRE. Additional exam requirements/recommendations for international students: Required—TOEFL (minimum score 450 paper-based; 45 iBT), IELTS (minimum score 5). Electronic applications accepted. *Expenses:* Contact institution. *Faculty research:* Marketing and quality management, banking operations management, economics, finance.

The American University in Dubai, Graduate Programs, Dubai, United Arab Emirates. Offers construction management (MS); education (M Ed); finance (MBA); generalist (MBA); marketing (MBA). *Program availability:* Part-time, evening/weekend. *Degree requirements:* For master's, thesis optional. *Entrance requirements:* For master's, GMAT (for MBA); GRE (for M Ed and MS), minimum undergraduate GPA of 3.0, official transcripts, two reference forms, curriculum vitae/resume, statement of career objectives, work experience. Additional exam requirements/recommendations for international students: Required—TOEFL (minimum score 550 paper-based; 79 iBT). Electronic applications accepted.

American University of Armenia, Graduate Programs, Yerevan, Armenia. Offers business administration (MBA); computer and information science (MS), including business management, design and manufacturing, energy (ME, MS), industrial engineering and systems management; economics (MS); industrial engineering and systems management (ME), including business, computer aided design/manufacturing, energy (ME, MS), information technology; law (LL M); political science and international affairs (MPSIA); public health (MPH); teaching English as a foreign language (MA). *Program availability:* Part-time, evening/weekend. *Degree requirements:* For master's, thesis (for some programs), capstone/project. *Entrance requirements:* For master's, GRE, GMAT, or LSAT. Additional exam requirements/recommendations for international students: Recommended—TOEFL (minimum score 79 iBT), IELTS (minimum score 6.5). *Faculty research:* Microfinance, finance (rural/development, international, corporate), firm life cycle theory, TESOL, language proficiency testing, public policy, administrative law, economic development, cryptography, artificial intelligence, energy efficiency/renewable energy, computer-aided design/manufacturing, health financing, tuberculosis control, mother/child health, preventive ophthalmology, post-earthquake psychopathological investigations, tobacco control, environmental health risk assessments.

American University of Beirut, Graduate Programs, Suliman S. Olayan School of Business, Executive MBA Program, 1107 2020, Lebanon. Offers EMBA. *Expenses:* Contact institution. *Faculty research:* Operations management, corporate governance, corporate finance, strategy, leadership.

American University of Beirut, Graduate Programs, Suliman S. Olayan School of Business, MBA Program, Beirut, Lebanon. Offers MBA. *Program availability:* Part-time. *Faculty:* 12 full-time (3 women), 2 part-time/adjunct (0 women). *Students:* 4 full-time (all women), 10 part-time (6 women). Average age 28. 64 applicants, 39% accepted, 14 enrolled. In 2018, 24 master's awarded. *Degree requirements:* For master's, thesis. *Entrance requirements:* Additional exam requirements/recommendations for international students: Required—TOEFL (minimum score 79 iBT), IELTS (minimum score 6). *Application deadline:* For fall admission, 6/30 for domestic and international students. Application fee: $50. *Expenses:* Tuition: Full-time $17,748; part-time $986 per credit. *Required fees:* $762. Tuition and fees vary according to course load and program. *Financial support:* In 2018–19, 4 research assistantships with partial tuition reimbursements (averaging $25,200 per year) were awarded; fellowships, teaching assistantships, scholarships/grants, tuition waivers, and unspecified assistantships also available. Financial award application deadline: 6/30. *Unit head:* Maya El-Helou, Director of Graduate Programs, 961-1-350000 Ext. 3955, E-mail: helou@aub.edu.lb. *Application contact:* Maya El-Helou, Director of Graduate Programs, 961-1-350000 Ext. 3955, E-mail: helou@aub.edu.lb. Website: http://www.aub.edu.lb/osb/MBA/Pages/default.aspx

The American University of Paris, Graduate Programs, Paris, France. Offers cross-cultural and sustainable business management (MA); cultural translation (MA); global communications (MA); global communications and civil society (MA); international affairs (MA); international affairs, conflict resolution and civil society development (MA); Middle East and Islamic studies (MA); Middle East and Islamic studies and international affairs (MA); public policy and international affairs (MA); public policy and international law (MA). *Degree requirements:* For master's, thesis (for some programs). *Entrance requirements:* For master's, minimum undergraduate GPA of 3.0. Additional exam requirements/recommendations for international students: Recommended—TOEFL, IELTS. Electronic applications accepted.

Business Administration and Management—General

American University of Sharjah, Graduate Programs, Sharjah, United Arab Emirates. Offers accounting (MS); biomedical engineering (MSBME); business administration (MBA); chemical engineering (MS Ch E); civil engineering (MSCE); computer engineering (MS); electrical engineering (MSEE); engineering systems management (MS, PhD); mathematics (MS); mechanical engineering (MSME); mechatronics engineering (MS); teaching English to speakers of other languages (MA); translation and interpreting (MA); urban planning (MUP). *Program availability:* Part-time, evening/weekend. *Degree requirements:* For master's, thesis (for some programs). *Entrance requirements:* For master's, GMAT (for MBA). Additional exam requirements/recommendations for international students: Required—TOEFL (minimum score 550 paper-based; 80 iBT), TWE (minimum score 5); Recommended—IELTS (minimum score 6.5). Electronic applications accepted. *Faculty research:* Water pollution, management and waste water treatment, energy and sustainability, air pollution, Islamic finance, family business and small and medium enterprises.

Anaheim University, Programs in Business Administration, Anaheim, CA 92806-5150. Offers entrepreneurship (ME, DBA); global sustainable management (MBA); international business (MBA, DBA, Certificate, Diploma); management (DBA); sustainable management (DBA, Certificate, Diploma). *Program availability:* Part-time, evening/weekend, online only, 100% online. In 2018, 3 master's, 4 doctorates awarded. *Application deadline:* Applications are processed on a rolling basis. Electronic applications accepted. *Unit head:* Dr. Robert Robertson, Dean, Graduate School of Business, 714-772-3330, Fax: 714-772-3331, E-mail: admissions@anaheim.edu. *Application contact:* Dr. Robert Robertson, Dean, Graduate School of Business, 714-772-3330, Fax: 714-772-3331, E-mail: admissions@anaheim.edu.

Anderson University, College of Business, Anderson, SC 29621-4035. Offers business administration (MBA); healthcare leadership (MBA); human resources (MBA); marketing (MBA); organizational leadership (MOL); supply chain management (MBA). *Accreditation:* ACBSP. *Application deadline:* Applications are processed on a rolling basis. Electronic applications accepted. *Expenses: Tuition:* Full-time $400; part-time $400 per credit. *Required fees:* $200; $200 per semester. Tuition and fees vary according to course load. *Financial support:* Scholarships/grants and tuition waivers available. Financial award application deadline: 3/1; financial award applicants required to submit FAFSA. *Unit head:* Steve Nail, Dean, 864-MBA-6000. *Application contact:* Sharon Vargo, Graduate Admission Counselor, 864-231-2000, E-mail: svargo@andersonuniversity.edu.
Website: http://www.andersonuniversity.edu/business

Anderson University, Falls School of Business, Anderson, IN 46012-3495. Offers accountancy (MA); business administration (MBA, DBA). *Accreditation:* ACBSP.

Angelo State University, College of Graduate Studies and Research, Norris-Vincent College of Business, Department of Management and Marketing, San Angelo, TX 76909. Offers business administration (MBA). *Accreditation:* ACBSP. *Program availability:* Part-time, evening/weekend. *Students:* 77 full-time (36 women), 90 part-time (37 women); includes 67 minority (11 Black or African American, non-Hispanic/Latino; 1 American Indian or Alaska Native, non-Hispanic/Latino; 1 Asian, non-Hispanic/Latino; 51 Hispanic/Latino; 1 Native Hawaiian or other Pacific Islander, non-Hispanic/Latino; 2 Two or more races, non-Hispanic/Latino), 9 international. Average age 31. *Entrance requirements:* For master's, GMAT or GRE, essay, resume. *Application deadline:* Applications are processed on a rolling basis. Application fee: $40 ($50 for international students). Electronic applications accepted. *Expenses: Tuition,* area resident: Full-time $3964; part-time $220 per credit hour. Tuition, state resident: full-time $3964; part-time $220 per credit hour. Tuition, nonresident: full-time $11,434; part-time $635 per credit hour. *International tuition:* $11,434 full-time. *Financial support:* Career-related internships or fieldwork, Federal Work-Study, and scholarships/grants available. Support available to part-time students. Financial award application deadline: 3/1; financial award applicants required to submit FAFSA. *Unit head:* Dr. Andy Tiger, Chair, 325-942-2383, Fax: 325-942-2384, E-mail: andrew.tiger@angelo.edu. *Application contact:* Christopher Houston, MBA Academic Assistant and Advisor, 325-486-6550, E-mail: christopher.houston@angelo.edu.
Website: http://www.angelo.edu/dept/management_marketing/

Anna Maria College, Graduate Division, Program in Business Administration, Paxton, MA 01612. Offers MBA, AC. *Program availability:* Part-time, evening/weekend. *Degree requirements:* For master's, capstone project. *Entrance requirements:* For master's, minimum GPA of 2.7. Additional exam requirements/recommendations for international students: Required—TOEFL (minimum score 500 paper-based). Electronic applications accepted. *Faculty research:* Management organization.

Antioch University Los Angeles, Program in Leadership, Management and Business, Culver City, CA 90230. Offers human resource development (MA); leadership (MA); organizational development (MA). *Program availability:* Part-time, evening/weekend. *Entrance requirements:* For master's, interview. Additional exam requirements/recommendations for international students: Required—TOEFL. *Faculty research:* Systems thinking and chaos theory, technology and organizational structure, nonprofit management, power and empowerment.

Antioch University New England, Graduate School, Department of Management, Program in Sustainability (Green MBA), Keene, NH 03431-3552. Offers MBA. *Program availability:* Part-time. *Entrance requirements:* For master's, GRE, resume, 3 letters of recommendation. Additional exam requirements/recommendations for international students: Required—TOEFL (minimum score 600 paper-based).

Antioch University Santa Barbara, Program in Business Administration, Santa Barbara, CA 93101-1581. Offers non-profit management (MBA); social business (MBA); strategic leadership (MBA).

Apollos University, School of Business and Management, Great Falls, MT 59401. Offers business administration (MBA, DBA); organizational management (MS).

Appalachian State University, Cratis D. Williams School of Graduate Studies, Program in Business Administration, Boone, NC 28608. Offers general management (MBA). *Accreditation:* AACSB. *Program availability:* Part-time, online learning. *Degree requirements:* For master's, comprehensive exam. *Entrance requirements:* For master's, GMAT, 3 letters of recommendation. Additional exam requirements/recommendations for international students: Required—TOEFL (minimum score 550 paper-based; 79 iBT), IELTS (minimum score 6.5). Electronic applications accepted. *Expenses: Tuition,* area resident: Full-time $4839; part-time $237 per credit hour. Tuition, state resident: full-time $4839; part-time $237 per credit hour. Tuition, nonresident: full-time $18,271; part-time $895.50 per credit hour.

Aquinas College, School of Management, Grand Rapids, MI 49506. Offers marketing management (MM); organizational leadership (MM); sustainable business (MM). *Program availability:* Part-time, evening/weekend. *Faculty:* 4 full-time (1 woman), 5 part-time/adjunct (0 women). *Students:* 12 full-time (4 women), 32 part-time (19 women); includes 3 minority (1 Black or African American, non-Hispanic/Latino; 1 Asian, non-Hispanic/Latino; 1 Hispanic/Latino), 2 international. Average age 31. In 2018, 19 master's awarded. *Entrance requirements:* For master's, GMAT, minimum undergraduate GPA of 2.75, 2 years of work experience. Additional exam requirements/recommendations for international students: Required—TOEFL (minimum score 550

paper-based). *Application deadline:* Applications are processed on a rolling basis. Application fee: $0. *Expenses: Tuition:* Part-time $593 per credit hour. *Required fees:* $120; $120. *Financial support:* Scholarships/grants available. Support available to part-time students. Financial award application deadline: 3/15; financial award applicants required to submit FAFSA. *Unit head:* Dr. Linda Hagan, Interim Dean of Business Division, 616-632-2193, Fax: 616-732-4489, E-mail: lmh010@aquinas.edu. *Application contact:* Lynn Atkins-Rykert, Program Coordinator, 616-632-2925, Fax: 616-732-4489, E-mail: atkinlyn@aquinas.edu.

Arcadia University, Program in Business Administration, Glenside, PA 19038-3295. Offers MBA. *Accreditation:* ACBSP. *Program availability:* Part-time, evening/weekend. *Faculty:* 9 full-time (5 women), 14 part-time/adjunct (5 women). *Students:* 4 full-time (3 women), 25 part-time (15 women); includes 10 minority (6 Black or African American, non-Hispanic/Latino; 1 Asian, non-Hispanic/Latino; 2 Hispanic/Latino; 1 Two or more races, non-Hispanic/Latino), 3 international. In 2018, 18 master's awarded. *Entrance requirements:* For master's, Official GMAT or GRE Scores within the last five years are strongly recommended for applicants whose undergraduate GPA is less than the recommended 3.0 or who do not have the minimum recommended work experience. [GMAT code: S82-4B-66; GRE Code 2039]. Additional exam requirements/recommendations for international students: Required—TOEFL. Application fee: $25. *Expenses:* Contact institution. *Unit head:* Dr. Thomas M. Brinker, Executive Director, 215-572-4039. *Application contact:* Office of Enrollment Management, 215-572-2910, Fax: 215-572-4049, E-mail: admiss@arcadia.edu.

Argosy University, Atlanta, College of Business, Atlanta, GA 30328. Offers accounting (DBA); corporate compliance (MBA); customized professional concentration (MBA, DBA); finance (MBA); healthcare administration (MBA); information systems (DBA); information systems management (MBA); international business (MBA, DBA); management (MBA, MSM, DBA); marketing (MBA, DBA). *Accreditation:* ACBSP.

Argosy University, Chicago, College of Business, Chicago, IL 60601. Offers accounting (DBA); customized professional concentration (MBA, DBA); finance (MBA); fraud examination (MBA); global business sustainability (DBA); healthcare administration (MBA); information systems (DBA); information systems management (MBA); international business (MBA, DBA); management (MBA, MSM, DBA); marketing (MBA, DBA); organizational leadership (Ed D); public administration (MBA); sustainable management (MBA). *Accreditation:* ACBSP. *Program availability:* Online learning.

Argosy University, Hawai`i, College of Business, Honolulu, HI 96813. Offers accounting (DBA); corporate compliance (MBA); customized professional concentration (MBA, DBA); finance (MBA, Certificate); fraud examination (MBA); global business sustainability (DBA); healthcare administration (MBA, Certificate); information systems (DBA); information systems management (MBA, Certificate); international business (MBA, DBA, Certificate); management (MBA, MSM, DBA); marketing (MBA, DBA, Certificate); organizational leadership (Ed D); public administration (MBA); sustainable management (MBA).

Argosy University, Los Angeles, College of Business, Los Angeles, CA 90045. Offers accounting (DBA); corporate compliance (MBA); customized professional concentration (MBA, DBA); finance (MBA); fraud examination (MBA); global business sustainability (DBA); healthcare administration (MBA); information systems (DBA); information systems management (MBA); international business (MBA, DBA); management (MBA, MSM, DBA); marketing (MBA, DBA); organizational leadership (Ed D); public administration (MBA); sustainable management (MBA).

Argosy University, Northern Virginia, College of Business, Arlington, VA 22209. Offers accounting (DBA); customized professional concentration (MBA, DBA); finance (MBA); fraud examination (MBA); global business sustainability (DBA); healthcare administration (MBA); information systems (DBA); information systems management (MBA); international business (MBA, DBA, Certificate); management (MBA, MSM, DBA); marketing (MBA, DBA, Certificate); organizational leadership (Ed D); public administration (MBA); sustainable management (MBA).

Argosy University, Orange County, College of Business, Orange, CA 92868. Offers accounting (DBA, Adv C); corporate compliance (MBA); customized professional concentration (MBA, DBA); finance (MBA, Certificate); fraud examination (MBA); global business sustainability (DBA); healthcare administration (MBA, Certificate); information systems (DBA, Adv C, Certificate); information systems management (MBA); international business (MBA, DBA, Adv C, Certificate); management (MBA, MSM, DBA, Adv C); marketing (MBA, DBA, Adv C, Certificate); organizational leadership (Ed D); public administration (MBA, Certificate); sustainable management (MBA).

Argosy University, Phoenix, College of Business, Phoenix, AZ 85021. Offers accounting (DBA); corporate compliance (MBA); customized professional concentration (MBA, DBA); finance (MBA); fraud examination (MBA); global business sustainability (DBA); healthcare administration (MBA); information systems (DBA); information systems management (MBA); international business (MBA, DBA); management (MBA, DBA); marketing (MBA, DBA); public administration (MBA); sustainable management (MBA).

Argosy University, Seattle, College of Business, Seattle, WA 98121. Offers accounting (DBA); corporate compliance (MBA); customized professional concentration (MBA, DBA); finance (MBA); fraud examination (MBA); global business sustainability (DBA); healthcare administration (MBA); information systems (DBA); information systems management (MBA); international business (MBA, DBA); management (MBA, MSM, DBA); marketing (MBA, DBA); organizational leadership (Ed D); public administration (MBA); sustainable management (MBA).

Argosy University, Tampa, College of Business, Tampa, FL 33607. Offers accounting (DBA); corporate compliance (MBA); customized professional concentration (MBA, DBA); finance (MBA); fraud examination (MBA); global business sustainability (DBA); healthcare administration (MBA); information systems (DBA); information systems management (MBA); international business (MBA, DBA); management (MBA, MSM, DBA); marketing (MBA, DBA); organizational leadership (Ed D); public administration (MBA); sustainable management (MBA).

Argosy University, Twin Cities, College of Business, Eagan, MN 55121. Offers accounting (DBA); customized professional concentration (MBA, DBA); finance (MBA); fraud examination (MBA); global business sustainability (DBA); healthcare administration (MBA); information systems (DBA); information systems management (MBA); international business (MBA, DBA); management (MBA, MSM, DBA); marketing (MBA, DBA); organizational leadership (Ed D); public administration (MBA); sustainable management (MBA).

Arizona State University at the Tempe campus, Thunderbird School of Global Management, Tempe, AZ 85287. Offers global affairs and management (MA); global management (MGM). *Accreditation:* AACSB. *Program availability:* Online learning. *Degree requirements:* For master's, one foreign language. *Entrance requirements:* For master's, GMAT. Additional exam requirements/recommendations for international students: Required—TOEFL.

Arizona State University at the Tempe campus, W. P. Carey School of Business, Program in Business Administration, Tempe, AZ 85287-4906. Offers entrepreneurship (MBA); finance (MBA); health sector management (MBA); international business (MBA);

leadership (MBA); marketing (MBA); organizational behavior (PhD); strategic management (PhD); supply chain management (MBA, PhD); JD/MBA; MBA/M Acc; MBA/M Arch. *Accreditation:* AACSB. *Program availability:* Part-time, evening/weekend, online learning. Terminal master's awarded for partial completion of doctoral program. *Degree requirements:* For master's, thesis or alternative, internship, interactive Program of Study (iPOS) submitted before completing 50 percent of required credit hours; for doctorate, comprehensive exam, thesis/dissertation, interactive Program of Study (iPOS) submitted before completing 50 percent of required credit hours. *Entrance requirements:* For master's, GMAT, minimum GPA of 3.0 in last 2 years of work leading to bachelor's degree, 2 letters of recommendation, professional resume, official transcripts, 3 essays; for doctorate, GMAT or GRE, minimum GPA of 3.0 in last 2 years of work leading to bachelor's degree, 3 letters of recommendation, resume, personal statement/essay. Additional exam requirements/recommendations for international students: Required—TOEFL (minimum score 550 paper-based; 80 iBT), IELTS (minimum score 6.5). Electronic applications accepted. *Expenses:* Contact institution.

Arkansas State University, Graduate School, College of Business, Department of Economics and Finance, State University, AR 72467. Offers business administration (MBA). *Accreditation:* AACSB. *Program availability:* Part-time. *Degree requirements:* For master's, comprehensive exam, thesis or alternative. *Entrance requirements:* For master's, GMAT, appropriate bachelor's degree, letters of reference, official transcripts, immunization records. Additional exam requirements/recommendations for international students: Required—TOEFL (minimum score 550 paper-based; 79 iBT), IELTS (minimum score 6), PTE (minimum score 56). Electronic applications accepted. *Expenses:* Contact institution.

Arkansas Tech University, College of Business, Russellville, AR 72801. Offers MBA. *Accreditation:* AACSB. *Program availability:* Part-time, evening/weekend, 100% online, blended/hybrid learning. *Students:* 6 full-time (1 woman), 43 part-time (29 women); includes 7 minority (3 Black or African American, non-Hispanic/Latino; 1 Asian, non-Hispanic/Latino; 1 Hispanic/Latino; 2 Two or more races, non-Hispanic/Latino). Average age 32. In 2018, 8 master's awarded. *Degree requirements:* For master's, completion of all required coursework with minimum cumulative GPA of 3.0 within six years. *Entrance requirements:* Additional exam requirements/recommendations for international students: Required—TOEFL (minimum score 550 paper-based; 79 iBT), IELTS (minimum score 6.5), PTE (minimum score 58). *Application deadline:* For fall admission, 3/1 priority date for domestic students, 5/1 priority date for international students; for spring admission, 10/1 priority date for domestic and international students. Applications are processed on a rolling basis. Application fee: $40 ($90 for international students). Electronic applications accepted. *Expenses: Tuition, area resident:* Full-time $6816; part-time $284 per credit hour. Tuition, state resident: full-time $6816; part-time $284 per credit hour. Tuition, nonresident: full-time $13,632; part-time $568 per credit hour. *International tuition:* $13,632 full-time. *Required fees:* $457.50 per semester. Tuition and fees vary according to course load and degree level. *Financial support:* In 2018–19, research assistantships with full and partial tuition reimbursements (averaging $4,800 per year), teaching assistantships with full and partial tuition reimbursements (averaging $4,800 per year) were awarded; career-related internships or fieldwork, Federal Work-Study, scholarships/grants, health care benefits, and unspecified assistantships also available. Support available to part-time students. Financial award application deadline: 4/15; financial award applicants required to submit FAFSA. *Unit head:* Dr. Kevin Mason, Interim Dean, 479-968-0498, E-mail: kmason@atu.edu. *Application contact:* Dr. Jeff Robertson, Interim Dean of Graduate College, 479-968-0398, Fax: 479-964-0542, E-mail: gradcollege@atu.edu.
Website: http://www.atu.edu/business/

Ashland University, Dauch College of Business and Economics, Ashland, OH 44805-3702. Offers accounting (MBA); business analytics (MBA); entrepreneurship (MBA); financial management (MBA); global management (MBA); health care management and leadership (MBA); human resource management (MBA); human resources (MBA); management information systems (MBA); project management (MBA); sport management (MBA); supply chain management (MBA). *Accreditation:* ACBSP. *Program availability:* Part-time, evening/weekend, 100% online, blended/hybrid learning. Terminal master's awarded for partial completion of doctoral program. *Degree requirements:* For master's, thesis optional, capstone course. *Entrance requirements:* For master's, 2 years of full-time work experience. Additional exam requirements/recommendations for international students: Required—TOEFL (minimum score 550 paper-based; 78 iBT). Electronic applications accepted. *Expenses:* Contact institution. *Faculty research:* Relationship marketing strategy, executive compensation and company performance, online marketplaces in electronic commerce, diversity training in campus recreation departments, entrepreneurship in developing and emerging economies.

Ashworth College, Graduate Programs, Norcross, GA 30092. Offers business administration (MBA); criminal justice (MS); health care administration (MBA, MS); human resource management (MBA, MS); international business (MBA); management (MS); marketing (MBA, MS).

Aspen University, Program in Business Administration, Denver, CO 80246-1930. Offers business administration (MBA); finance (MBA); information management (MBA); project management (MBA, Certificate). *Program availability:* Part-time, evening/weekend, online only, 100% online. *Faculty:* 16 full-time (15 women), 240 part-time/adjunct (120 women). *Students:* 556 part-time. Average age 37. *Degree requirements:* For master's, comprehensive exam. *Entrance requirements:* For master's and Certificate, www.aspen.edu, www.aspen.edu. *Application deadline:* Applications are processed on a rolling basis. Application fee: $0. Electronic applications accepted. *Financial support:* Applicants required to submit FAFSA. *Unit head:* Dr. Kevin Thrasher, Provost, 602-5706708, E-mail: kevin.thrasher@aspen.edu. *Application contact:* Enrollment Advisor, 800-373-7814.
Website: http://www.aspen.edu

Assumption College, Business Studies Program, Worcester, MA 01609-1296. Offers accounting (MBA); business studies (CAGS); finance/economics (MBA); human resources (MBA); international business (MBA); management (MBA); marketing (MBA); nonprofit leadership (MBA). *Program availability:* Part-time, evening/weekend. *Degree requirements:* For master's, capstone. *Entrance requirements:* For master's, bachelor's degree, three letters of recommendation, official transcripts, personal statement, current resume; for CAGS, MBA or equivalent degree in a closely related field, three letters of recommendation, official transcripts, personal statement, current resume. Additional exam requirements/recommendations for international students: Required—TOEFL (minimum score 540 paper-based; 76 iBT), IELTS (minimum score 6). Electronic applications accepted. *Faculty research:* Workplace diversity, dynamics of team interaction, utilization of leased employees, experiential learning project on due diligence market for prostheses.

Athabasca University, Faculty of Business, Edmonton, AB T5L 4W1, Canada. Offers business administration (MBA); information technology management (MBA), including policing concentration; innovative management (DBA); management (GDM); project management (MBA, GDM). *Program availability:* Part-time, evening/weekend, online learning. *Degree requirements:* For master's, thesis or alternative, applied project. *Entrance requirements:* For master's, 3-8 years of managerial experience, 3 years with undergraduate degree, 5 years' managerial experience with professional designation, 8-10 years' management experience (on exception). Electronic applications accepted. *Expenses:* Contact institution. *Faculty research:* Human resources, project management, operations research, information technology management, corporate stewardship, energy management.

Atlantis University, School of Business, Miami, FL 33132. Offers MBA, DBA.

Auburn University, Graduate School, College of Business, Department of Management, Auburn University, AL 36849. Offers management (PhD). *Accreditation:* AACSB. *Program availability:* Part-time. *Degree requirements:* For master's, thesis (for some programs); for doctorate, thesis/dissertation. *Entrance requirements:* For master's, GMAT, GRE General Test (for MS); for doctorate, GMAT, GRE General Test. Additional exam requirements/recommendations for international students: Required—TOEFL. Electronic applications accepted. *Expenses:* Tuition, state resident: full-time $11,282; part-time $535 per credit hour. Tuition, nonresident: full-time $30,542; part-time $1605 per credit hour. *Required fees:* $826 per semester. Tuition and fees vary according to degree level and program.

Auburn University, Graduate School, College of Business, Program in Business Administration, Auburn University, AL 36849. Offers MBA. *Accreditation:* AACSB. *Program availability:* Part-time. *Entrance requirements:* For master's, GMAT. Electronic applications accepted. *Expenses:* Tuition, state resident: full-time $11,282; part-time $535 per credit hour. Tuition, nonresident: full-time $30,542; part-time $1605 per credit hour. *Required fees:* $826 per semester. Tuition and fees vary according to degree level and program.

Auburn University at Montgomery, College of Business, Department of Business Administration, Montgomery, AL 36124-4023. Offers business and management (MBA). *Accreditation:* AACSB. *Students:* Average age 35. 64 applicants, 75% accepted, 34 enrolled. In 2018, 46 master's awarded. *Entrance requirements:* For master's, GMAT. Additional exam requirements/recommendations for international students: Required—TOEFL (minimum score 500 paper-based; 61 iBT), IELTS (minimum score 5.5), PTE (minimum score 44). *Application deadline:* Applications are processed on a rolling basis. Application fee: $25 ($0 for international students). Electronic applications accepted. *Expenses: Tuition, area resident:* Full-time $7146; part-time $4764 per credit hour. Tuition, state resident: full-time $7146; part-time $4764 per credit hour. Tuition, nonresident: full-time $16,056; part-time $10,704 per credit hour. *International tuition:* $16,056 full-time. *Required fees:* $766. One-time fee: $25 full-time. *Financial support:* Application deadline: 3/1; applicants required to submit FAFSA. *Unit head:* Dr. Kevin Banning, Department Head, 334-244-3485, E-mail: kbanning@aum.edu. *Application contact:* Jennifer Taylor, Assistant Director of Graduate Programs, 334-244-3587, Fax: 334-244-3137, E-mail: jtaylor5@aum.edu.
Website: http://business.aum.edu/academic-departments/business-administration

Augsburg University, Program in Business Administration, Minneapolis, MN 55454-1351. Offers MBA. *Program availability:* Evening/weekend. Electronic applications accepted.

Augusta University, Hull College of Business, Augusta, GA 30912. Offers business administration (MBA); information security management (MS). *Accreditation:* AACSB. *Program availability:* Part-time, evening/weekend. *Entrance requirements:* For master's, GMAT.

Aurora University, Dunham School of Business and Public Policy, Aurora, IL 60506-4892. Offers accountancy (MS); business (MBA). *Program availability:* Part-time, evening/weekend, 100% online, blended/hybrid learning. *Faculty:* 8 full-time (2 women), 28 part-time/adjunct (13 women). *Students:* 152 full-time (106 women), 180 part-time (112 women); includes 133 minority (51 Black or African American, non-Hispanic/Latino; 10 Asian, non-Hispanic/Latino; 63 Hispanic/Latino; 1 Native Hawaiian or other Pacific Islander, non-Hispanic/Latino; 8 Two or more races, non-Hispanic/Latino), 2 international. Average age 31. 253 applicants, 99% accepted, 156 enrolled. In 2018, 117 master's awarded. *Degree requirements:* For master's, Capstone project and internship. *Entrance requirements:* For master's, minimum GPA of 3.0, 2 years of work experience, resume. Additional exam requirements/recommendations for international students: Required—TOEFL (minimum score 550 paper-based; 79 iBT). *Application deadline:* For fall admission, 6/1 for international students; for spring admission, 10/1 for international students. Applications are processed on a rolling basis. Application fee: $0. Electronic applications accepted. *Expenses:* The listed tuition and fees is for the MBA, MS, and MPA on-ground programs. Costs vary for online and plus one programs. The Dual MBA/MSW and MPA/MSW programs are roughly double the cost of the MBA. *Financial support:* In 2018–19, 94 students received support. Federal Work-Study, scholarships/grants, and unspecified assistantships available. Financial award applicants required to submit FAFSA. *Unit head:* Dr. Toby Arquette, Dean, School of Business and Policy, 630-844-5614, E-mail: tarquett@aurora.edu. *Application contact:* Center for Graduate Studies, 630-947-8955, E-mail: AUadmission@aurora.edu.

Austin Peay State University, College of Graduate Studies, College of Business, Clarksville, TN 37044. Offers management (MS). *Program availability:* Part-time, evening/weekend, online learning. *Faculty:* 8 full-time (4 women). *Students:* 19 full-time (8 women), 47 part-time (23 women); includes 16 minority (9 Black or African American, non-Hispanic/Latino; 3 Asian, non-Hispanic/Latino; 1 Hispanic/Latino; 1 Native Hawaiian or other Pacific Islander, non-Hispanic/Latino; 2 Two or more races, non-Hispanic/Latino). Average age 35. 43 applicants, 93% accepted, 27 enrolled. In 2018, 30 master's awarded. *Degree requirements:* For master's, comprehensive exam. *Entrance requirements:* For master's, GMAT, minimum undergraduate GPA of 2.5. Additional exam requirements/recommendations for international students: Required—TOEFL (minimum score 500 paper-based). *Application deadline:* For fall admission, 8/21 priority date for domestic students. Applications are processed on a rolling basis. Application fee: $45 ($55 for international students). Electronic applications accepted. *Expenses: Tuition, area resident:* Part-time $450 per credit hour. Tuition, state resident: full-time $5987; part-time $450 per credit hour. Tuition, nonresident: full-time $8757; part-time $806 per credit hour. *Required fees:* $1583; $79.15 per credit hour. *Financial support:* Research assistantships with full tuition reimbursements, career-related internships or fieldwork, Federal Work-Study, institutionally sponsored loans, scholarships/grants, and unspecified assistantships available. Support available to part-time students. Financial award application deadline: 7/1; financial award applicants required to submit FAFSA. *Unit head:* Dr. Mickey Hepner, Dean, 931-221-7675, Fax: 931-221-7355, E-mail: hepnerm@apsu.edu. *Application contact:* Megan Mitchell, Coordinator of Graduate Admissions, 931-221-6189, Fax: 931-221-7641, E-mail: mitchellm@apsu.edu.
Website: http://www.apsu.edu/business/index.php

Averett University, Master of Business Administration Program, Danville, VA 24541-3692. Offers business administration (MBA); human resources management (MBA); leadership (MBA); marketing (MBA). *Program availability:* Part-time. *Faculty:* 7 full-time (1 woman), 10 part-time/adjunct (2 women). *Students:* 156 full-time (93 women), 2 part-time (1 woman); includes 61 minority (51 Black or African American, non-Hispanic/Latino; 2 American Indian or Alaska Native, non-Hispanic/Latino; 3 Asian, non-Hispanic/Latino; 3 Hispanic/Latino; 2 Two or more races, non-Hispanic/Latino), 2 international. Average age 35. 61 applicants, 70% accepted, 35 enrolled. In 2018, 62 master's awarded. *Degree requirements:* For master's, 41-credit core curriculum, minimum GPA of 3.0 throughout program, no more than 2 grades of C, completion of degree

requirements within six years from start of program. *Entrance requirements:* For master's, minimum cumulative GPA of 3.0 over the last 60 semester hours of undergraduate study toward a baccalaureate degree, official transcripts, three years of full-time work experience, three letters of recommendation, current resume. Additional exam requirements/recommendations for international students: Required—TOEFL (minimum score 600 paper-based; 100 iBT). *Application deadline:* Applications are processed on a rolling basis. Electronic applications accepted. *Expenses:* Contact institution. *Financial support:* Application deadline: 3/1; applicants required to submit FAFSA. *Unit head:* Dr. Peggy C. Wright, Chair, Business Department, 434-791-7118, E-mail: pwright@averett.edu. *Application contact:* Christy Davis, Assistant Director of Admissions, 434-791-7133, E-mail: cdavis@averett.edu.
Website: https://gps.averett.edu/online/business/

Avila University, School of Business, Kansas City, MO 64145-1698. Offers MBA. *Program availability:* Part-time, evening/weekend. *Faculty:* 6 full-time (2 women), 6 part-time/adjunct (2 women). *Students:* 49 full-time (28 women), 26 part-time (14 women); includes 20 minority (13 Black or African American, non-Hispanic/Latino; 1 Asian, non-Hispanic/Latino; 4 Hispanic/Latino; 2 Two or more races, non-Hispanic/Latino), 17 international. Average age 37. 51 applicants, 47% accepted, 20 enrolled. In 2018, 22 master's awarded. *Degree requirements:* For master's, comprehensive exam, capstone course. *Entrance requirements:* For master's, GMAT (minimum score 420), minimum GPA of 3.0, interview. Additional exam requirements/recommendations for international students: Required—TOEFL (minimum score 550 paper-based). *Application deadline:* For fall admission, 7/30 priority date for domestic and international students; for winter admission, 11/30 priority date for domestic and international students; for spring admission, 2/28 priority date for domestic and international students; for summer admission, 6/1 priority date for domestic and international students. Applications are processed on a rolling basis. Application fee: $0. Electronic applications accepted. *Expenses:* Contact institution. *Financial support:* In 2018–19, 15 students received support. Career-related internships or fieldwork and scholarships/grants available. Support available to part-time students. Financial award applicants required to submit FAFSA. *Faculty research:* Leadership characteristics, financial hedging, group dynamics. *Unit head:* Dr. Wendy L. Acker, Interim Dean, 816-501-3720, Fax: 816-501-2463, E-mail: wendy.acker@avila.edu. *Application contact:* Brandon Black, MBA Admission Advisor, 816-501-3601, Fax: 816-501-2463, E-mail: brandon.black@avila.edu.
Website: https://www.avila.edu/academics/graduate-studies

Avila University, School of Professional Studies, Kansas City, MO 64145-1698. Offers executive leadership (MS); fundraising (MA); instructional design and technology (MA, MS); leadership coaching (MS); project management (MA); strategic human resources (MS). *Program availability:* Part-time-only, evening/weekend, 100% online, blended/hybrid learning. *Faculty:* 14 part-time/adjunct (8 women). *Students:* 69 full-time (49 women), 48 part-time (42 women); includes 45 minority (38 Black or African American, non-Hispanic/Latino; 5 Hispanic/Latino; 2 Two or more races, non-Hispanic/Latino), 5 international. Average age 39. 63 applicants, 60% accepted, 29 enrolled. In 2018, 34 master's awarded. *Degree requirements:* For master's, thesis optional. *Entrance requirements:* For master's, 2 letters of recommendation, minimum GPA of 3.0 during last 60 hours, resume, statement of intent. Additional exam requirements/recommendations for international students: Required—TOEFL (minimum score 550 paper-based; 79 iBT). *Application deadline:* Applications are processed on a rolling basis. Application fee: $0. Electronic applications accepted. *Expenses:* Contact institution. *Financial support:* In 2018–19, 12 students received support. Unspecified assistantships available. Support available to part-time students. Financial award applicants required to submit FAFSA. *Unit head:* Sarah Sullivan, Coordinator, 816-501-0429, Fax: 816-941-4650, E-mail: advantage@avila.edu. *Application contact:* Jessica Burson, Graduate Admission Advisor, 816-501-2482, Fax: 816-941-4650, E-mail: advantage@avila.edu.
Website: https://www.avila.edu/mrk/advantage-3

Azusa Pacific University, School of Business and Management, Azusa, CA 91702-7000. Offers accounting (MBA); business administration (MBA); entrepreneurship (MBA); finance (MBA); international business (MBA); marketing (MBA); organizational science (MBA); professional accountancy (M Acc); sport management (MBA). *Program availability:* Part-time, evening/weekend. *Degree requirements:* For master's, thesis (for some programs), final project. *Entrance requirements:* For master's, GMAT, minimum GPA of 3.0. Additional exam requirements/recommendations for international students: Required—TOEFL (minimum score 600 paper-based). *Expenses:* Contact institution. *Faculty research:* Gender issues, financial risk, leadership and ethics, marketing strategy.

Babson College, F. W. Olin Graduate School of Business, Babson Park, MA 02457-0310. Offers accounting (MSA); advanced management (Certificate); business administration (MBA); business analytics (MS); finance (MS); global entrepreneurship (MS); technological entrepreneurship (MS). *Accreditation:* AACSB. *Program availability:* Part-time, evening/weekend, online learning. *Entrance requirements:* For master's, GMAT, 2 years of work experience, resume, letters of recommendation. Additional exam requirements/recommendations for international students: Required—TOEFL (minimum score 100 iBT), IELTS (minimum score 6.5). Electronic applications accepted. *Faculty research:* Entrepreneurship, sustainability, global markets, process of innovation, social media and advertising.

Baker College Center for Graduate Studies–Online, Graduate Programs, Flint, MI 48507. Offers accounting (MBA); business administration (DBA); finance (MBA); general business (MBA); health care management (MBA); human resources management (MBA); information management (MBA); leadership studies (MBA); management information systems (MSIS); marketing (MBA); occupational therapy (MOT). *Program availability:* Part-time, evening/weekend, online learning. *Degree requirements:* For master's, portfolio. *Entrance requirements:* For master's, 3 years of work experience, minimum undergraduate GPA of 2.5, writing sample, 3 letters of recommendation; for doctorate, MBA or acceptable related master's degree from accredited association, 5 years work experience, minimum graduate GPA of 3.25, writing sample, 3 professional references. Additional exam requirements/recommendations for international students: Required—TOEFL (minimum score 550 paper-based). Electronic applications accepted.

Baker University, School of Professional and Graduate Studies, Programs in Business, Baldwin City, KS 66006-0065. Offers MAOL, MBA, MSM, MSSM. Programs also offered in Overland Park, KS; Topeka, KS; and Wichita, KS. *Program availability:* Part-time, evening/weekend, online learning. *Entrance requirements:* For master's, 2 years of full-time work experience. Additional exam requirements/recommendations for international students: Required—TOEFL (minimum score 600 paper-based; 100 iBT).

Bakke Graduate University, Programs in Pastoral Ministry and Business, Dallas, TX 75243-7039. Offers business administration (MBA); church and ministry multiplication (D Min); global urban leadership (MA); leadership (D Min); ministry in complex contexts (D Min); social and civic entrepreneurship (MA); theology of work (D Min); theology reflection (D Min); transformational leadership (DTL); urban youth ministry (D Min). *Program availability:* Part-time, online learning. *Degree requirements:* For master's, thesis; for doctorate, thesis/dissertation. *Entrance requirements:* For master's, 2 years of ministry experience, BA in Biblical studies or theology; for doctorate, 3 years of ministry experience, M Div. Additional exam requirements/recommendations for international students: Required—TOEFL. Electronic applications accepted. *Faculty research:* Theological systems, church management, worship.

Baldwin Wallace University, Graduate Programs, School of Business, Master's in Management Program, Berea, OH 44017-2088. Offers MAM. *Students:* 9 full-time (5 women); includes 1 minority (Black or African American, non-Hispanic/Latino). Average age 23. 28 applicants, 68% accepted, 9 enrolled. *Degree requirements:* For master's, minimum overall GPA of 3.0. *Entrance requirements:* For master's, minimum GPA of 3.0, bachelor's degree in any field. Additional exam requirements/recommendations for international students: Required—TOEFL (minimum score 550 paper-based; 79 iBT), IELTS can be accepted in place of TOEFL. *Application deadline:* For spring admission, 4/1 for domestic students, 3/15 for international students. Applications are processed on a rolling basis. Application fee: $0. Electronic applications accepted. *Expenses:* $35,000 to complete program. *Financial support:* Scholarships/grants and tuition discounts available. Financial award application deadline: 4/1; financial award applicants required to submit FAFSA. *Unit head:* Dr. Susan Kuznik, Associate Dean, Graduate Business Programs, 440-826-2053, Fax: 440-826-3868, E-mail: skuznik@bw.edu. *Application contact:* Laura Spencer, Graduate Business Admission Specialist, 440-826-2191, Fax: 440-826-3868, E-mail: lspencer@bw.edu.
Website: http://www.bw.edu/academics/master-management/

Baldwin Wallace University, Graduate Programs, School of Business, MBA in Management - Hybrid Program, Berea, OH 44017-2088. Offers MBA. *Program availability:* Part-time-only, evening/weekend, blended/hybrid learning. *Students:* 20 full-time (9 women), 2 part-time (1 woman); includes 3 minority (2 Black or African American, non-Hispanic/Latino; 1 Two or more races, non-Hispanic/Latino). Average age 35. 18 applicants, 83% accepted, 15 enrolled. In 2018, 18 master's awarded. *Entrance requirements:* For master's, GMAT or minimum undergraduate GPA of 3.0, bachelor's degree in any field, work experience. Additional exam requirements/recommendations for international students: Required—TOEFL (minimum score 550 paper-based; 79 iBT), IELTS can be accepted in place of TOEFL. *Application deadline:* For fall admission, 7/31 for domestic students; for summer admission, 4/15 for domestic students. Applications are processed on a rolling basis. Application fee: $0. Electronic applications accepted. *Expenses:* $31,284 to complete program. *Financial support:* In 2018–19, 1 student received support. Scholarships/grants and tuition discounts available. Financial award applicants required to submit FAFSA. *Unit head:* Dr. Susan Kuznik, Associate Dean, Graduate Business Programs, 440-826-2053, Fax: 440-826-3868, E-mail: skuznik@bw.edu. *Application contact:* Laura Spencer, Graduate Business Admission Specialist, 440-826-2191, Fax: 440-826-3868, E-mail: lspencer@bw.edu.
Website: business.bw.edu

Baldwin Wallace University, Graduate Programs, School of Business, Program in Management, Berea, OH 44017-2088. Offers MBA. *Program availability:* Part-time, evening/weekend. *Students:* 51 full-time (26 women), 39 part-time (19 women); includes 21 minority (10 Black or African American, non-Hispanic/Latino; 4 Asian, non-Hispanic/Latino; 3 Hispanic/Latino; 1 Native Hawaiian or other Pacific Islander, non-Hispanic/Latino; 3 Two or more races, non-Hispanic/Latino), 1 international. Average age 33. 45 applicants, 56% accepted, 15 enrolled. In 2018, 65 master's awarded. *Degree requirements:* For master's, minimum overall GPA of 3.0. *Entrance requirements:* For master's, GMAT or minimum GPA of 3.0, bachelor's degree in any field, work experience. Additional exam requirements/recommendations for international students: Required—TOEFL (minimum score 550 paper-based; 79 iBT), IELTS can be accepted in place of TOEFL. *Application deadline:* For fall admission, 7/25 priority date for domestic students, 4/30 priority date for international students; for spring admission, 12/15 priority date for domestic students, 9/30 priority date for international students; for summer admission, 4/15 priority date for domestic students. Applications are processed on a rolling basis. Application fee: $0. Electronic applications accepted. *Expenses:* Systems Management - $31,284 to complete program. One-Year MBA - $39,900 to complete program. Executive Management - $51,368 to complete program. *Financial support:* In 2018–19, 11 students received support. Scholarships/grants and tuition discounts available. Financial award applicants required to submit FAFSA. *Unit head:* Dr. Susan Kuznik, Associate Dean, Graduate Business Programs, 440-826-2053, Fax: 440-826-3868, E-mail: skuznik@bw.edu. *Application contact:* Laura Spencer, Graduate Business Admission Specialist, 440-826-2191, Fax: 440-826-3868, E-mail: lspencer@bw.edu.
Website: business.bw.edu

Ball State University, Graduate School, Miller College of Business, Interdepartmental Program in Business Administration, Muncie, IN 47306. Offers business administration (MBA); business essentials (Graduate Certificate); community and economic development (Certificate). *Accreditation:* AACSB. *Program availability:* Part-time, 100% online, blended/hybrid learning. *Entrance requirements:* For master's, GMAT or GRE, minimum baccalaureate GPA of 2.75 or 3.0 in latter half of baccalaureate, resume or curriculum vitae, four professional letters of recommendation. Additional exam requirements/recommendations for international students: Required—TOEFL (minimum score 550 paper-based; 79 iBT), IELTS (minimum score 6.5). Electronic applications accepted. *Expenses:* Contact institution.

Barry University, Andreas School of Business, Graduate Certificate Programs, Miami Shores, FL 33161-6695. Offers finance (Certificate); health services administration (Certificate); international business (Certificate); management (Certificate); management information systems (Certificate); marketing (Certificate).

Barry University, Andreas School of Business, Program in Business Administration, Miami Shores, FL 33161-6695. Offers MBA, DPM/MBA, MBA/MS, MBA/MSN. *Accreditation:* AACSB.

Barry University, School of Adult and Continuing Education, Division of Nursing and Andreas School of Business, Program in Nursing Administration and Business Administration, Miami Shores, FL 33161-6695. Offers MSN/MBA. *Accreditation:* AACN. *Program availability:* Part-time, evening/weekend. Electronic applications accepted. *Faculty research:* Power/empowerment, health delivery systems, managed care, employee health well-being.

Barry University, School of Adult and Continuing Education, Program in Administrative Studies, Miami Shores, FL 33161-6695. Offers MA. *Program availability:* Part-time, evening/weekend. *Entrance requirements:* For master's, GMAT, GRE or MAT, recommendations. Electronic applications accepted.

Barry University, School of Human Performance and Leisure Sciences and Andreas School of Business, Program in Sport Management and Business Administration, Miami Shores, FL 33161-6695. Offers MS/MBA. *Program availability:* Part-time, evening/weekend. Electronic applications accepted. *Faculty research:* Economic impact of professional sports, sport marketing.

Barry University, School of Podiatric Medicine, Podiatric Medicine and Surgery Program and Andreas School of Business, Podiatric Medicine/Business Administration Option, Miami Shores, FL 33161-6695. Offers DPM/MBA.

Baruch College of the City University of New York, Zicklin School of Business, New York, NY 10010-5585. Offers MBA, MS, PhD, Certificate, JD/MBA. JD/MBA offered

jointly with Brooklyn Law School and New York Law School. *Accreditation:* AACSB. *Program availability:* Part-time, evening/weekend. *Degree requirements:* For doctorate, comprehensive exam, thesis/dissertation. *Entrance requirements:* For master's, GMAT or GRE, 2 letters of recommendation, resume, 2 years of work experience; for doctorate, GMAT or GRE. Additional exam requirements/recommendations for international students: Required—TOEFL (minimum iBT score of 102) or PTE. Electronic applications accepted.

Baruch College of the City University of New York, Zicklin School of Business, Zicklin Executive Programs, Executive MBA Program, New York, NY 10010-5585. Offers MBA. *Accreditation:* AACSB. *Entrance requirements:* For master's, 5 years of management-level work experience, personal interview. Additional exam requirements/recommendations for international students: Required—TOEFL. *Expenses:* Contact institution. *Faculty research:* Entrepreneurship, corporate governance, international finance, mergers and acquisitions.

Bayamón Central University, Graduate Programs, Program in Business Administration, Bayamón, PR 00960-1725. Offers accounting (MBA); finance (MBA); general business (MBA); management (MBA); marketing (MBA). *Program availability:* Part-time, evening/weekend. *Degree requirements:* For master's, comprehensive exam (for some programs). *Entrance requirements:* For master's, EXADEP, bachelor's degree in business or related field.

Baylor University, Graduate School, Hankamer School of Business, Program in Business Administration, Waco, TX 76798. Offers MBA, JD/MBA, MBA/MSIS. *Accreditation:* AACSB. *Program availability:* Part-time. *Students:* 213 full-time (76 women), 197 part-time (59 women); includes 133 minority (31 Black or African American, non-Hispanic/Latino; 1 American Indian or Alaska Native, non-Hispanic/Latino; 27 Asian, non-Hispanic/Latino; 56 Hispanic/Latino; 1 Native Hawaiian or other Pacific Islander, non-Hispanic/Latino; 17 Two or more races, non-Hispanic/Latino), 10 international. 240 applicants, 52% accepted, 83 enrolled. In 2018, 202 master's awarded. *Entrance requirements:* For master's, GMAT, minimum AACSB index of 1050. *Application deadline:* Applications are processed on a rolling basis. Application fee: $0. *Expenses:* Contact institution. *Financial support:* Research assistantships, teaching assistantships, career-related internships or fieldwork, Federal Work-Study, and institutionally sponsored loans available. *Unit head:* Dr. Gary Carini, Associate Dean, 254-710-3718, Fax: 254-710-1092, E-mail: gary_carini@baylor.edu. *Application contact:* Laurie Wilson, Director, Graduate Business Programs, 254-710-4163, Fax: 254-710-1066, E-mail: laurie_wilson@baylor.edu.

Belhaven University, School of Business, Jackson, MS 39202-1789. Offers business administration (MBA); health administration (MBA, MHA); human resources (MBA, MSL); leadership (MBA); public administration (MPA); sports administration (MBA, MSA). *Program availability:* Part-time, evening/weekend, 100% online. *Students:* Average age 35. 574 applicants, 75% accepted, 306 enrolled. In 2018, 326 master's awarded. *Degree requirements:* For master's, comprehensive exam (for some programs), thesis or alternative. *Entrance requirements:* For master's, minimum GPA of 2.8 (for MBA and MHA), 2.5 (for MSL, MPA and MSA). *Application deadline:* Applications are processed on a rolling basis. Application fee: $25. Electronic applications accepted. *Expenses:* Contact institution. *Financial support:* Applicants required to submit FAFSA. *Unit head:* Dr. Ralph Mason, Dean, 601-968-8949, Fax: 601-968-8951, E-mail: cmason@belhaven.edu. *Application contact:* Dr. Audrey Kelleher, Vice President of Adult and Graduate Marketing and Development, 407-804-1424, Fax: 407-620-5210, E-mail: akelleher@belhaven.edu.
Website: http://www.belhaven.edu/campuses/index.htm

Bellarmine University, W. Fielding Rubel School of Business, Louisville, KY 40205. Offers MBA. *Accreditation:* AACSB. *Program availability:* Part-time, evening/weekend. *Faculty:* 11 full-time (5 women), 2 part-time/adjunct (0 women). *Students:* 84 full-time (30 women), 44 part-time (13 women); includes 19 minority (6 Black or African American, non-Hispanic/Latino; 7 Asian, non-Hispanic/Latino; 3 Hispanic/Latino; 3 Two or more races, non-Hispanic/Latino), 1 international. Average age 27. 81 applicants, 70% accepted, 40 enrolled. In 2018, 65 master's awarded. *Entrance requirements:* For master's, GMAT or GRE, letters of recommendation; resume; essay. Additional exam requirements/recommendations for international students: Required—TOEFL (minimum score of 80), IELTS (minimum score 6), or Michigan English Language Assessment Battery (78). *Application deadline:* Applications are processed on a rolling basis. Application fee: $40. Electronic applications accepted. *Expenses:* Master in Business Administration, Weeknight (A)(B): $770 per credit; Master in Business Administration, Weekend (A)(B): $770 per credit; Master in Business Administration, Executive Spring 2019 (B): $1,000 per credit; $149 case fee for Weeknight and Weekend core classes; $2,500 course fee for MBA 620 - EMBA and WE/WN MBA. *Financial support:* Career-related internships or fieldwork, scholarships/grants, and unspecified assistantships available. Support available to part-time students. Financial award applicants required to submit FAFSA. *Faculty research:* Marketing, management, small business and entrepreneurship, finance, economics. *Unit head:* Dr. Frank Raymond, Interim Dean, 502-272-8487, Fax: 502-272-7443, E-mail: fraymond@bellarmine.edu. *Application contact:* Dr. Sara Pettingill, Dean of Graduate Admission, 800-274-4723 Ext. 8258, Fax: 502-272-8002, E-mail: spettingill@bellarmine.edu.
Website: http://www.bellarmine.edu/business.aspx

Bellevue University, Graduate School, College of Business, Bellevue, NE 68005-3098. Offers acquisition and contract management (MS); business administration (MBA); finance (MS); human capital management (PhD); management (MSM).

Belmont University, Jack C. Massey Graduate School of Business, Nashville, TN 37212. Offers accounting (M Acc); business (AMBA, PMBA); healthcare (MBA). *Accreditation:* AACSB. *Program availability:* Part-time, evening/weekend. *Faculty:* 29 full-time (9 women), 7 part-time/adjunct (3 women). *Students:* 163 full-time (72 women), 42 part-time (19 women); includes 36 minority (13 Black or African American, non-Hispanic/Latino; 9 Asian, non-Hispanic/Latino; 5 Hispanic/Latino; 9 Two or more races, non-Hispanic/Latino), 10 international. Average age 30. 135 applicants, 96% accepted, 102 enrolled. In 2018, 110 master's awarded. *Entrance requirements:* For master's, GMAT, 2 years of work experience (MBA). Additional exam requirements/recommendations for international students: Required—TOEFL (minimum score 550 paper-based). *Application deadline:* For fall admission, 7/1 for domestic and international students; for spring admission, 11/1 for domestic and international students. Applications are processed on a rolling basis. Application fee: $50. Electronic applications accepted. *Expenses:* Contact institution. *Financial support:* In 2018–19, 86 students received support. Scholarships/grants, tuition waivers (partial), and unspecified assistantships available. Financial award application deadline: 7/1; financial award applicants required to submit FAFSA. *Faculty research:* Music business, strategy, ethics, finance, accounting systems. *Unit head:* Dr. Patrick Raines, Dean, 615-460-6480, Fax: 615-460-6455, E-mail: pat.raines@belmont.edu. *Application contact:* Dr. Patrick Raines, Dean, 615-460-6480, Fax: 615-460-6455, E-mail: pat.raines@belmont.edu.

Benedictine College, Master of Business Administration Program, Atchison, KS 66002-1499. Offers MBA. *Program availability:* Part-time, evening/weekend. *Entrance requirements:* For master's, GMAT. Additional exam requirements/recommendations for international students: Recommended—TOEFL, IELTS. Electronic applications accepted. Application fee is waived when completed online. *Expenses:* Contact institution. *Faculty research:* Banking, strategic planning, ethics, leadership and entrepreneurship.

Benedictine University, Graduate Programs, Program in Business Administration, Lisle, IL 60532. Offers accounting (MBA); entrepreneurship and managing innovation (MBA); financial management (MBA); health administration (MBA); human resource management (MBA); information systems security (MBA); international business (MBA); management consulting (MBA); management information systems (MBA); marketing management (MBA); operations management and logistics (MBA); organizational leadership (MBA). *Program availability:* Part-time, evening/weekend, 100% online, blended/hybrid learning. *Faculty:* 7 full-time (1 woman), 36 part-time/adjunct (10 women). *Students:* 110 full-time (71 women), 500 part-time (302 women); includes 104 minority (34 Black or African American, non-Hispanic/Latino; 1 American Indian or Alaska Native, non-Hispanic/Latino; 41 Asian, non-Hispanic/Latino; 23 Hispanic/Latino; 5 Native Hawaiian or other Pacific Islander, non-Hispanic/Latino), 7 international. Average age 33. 251 applicants, 84% accepted, 202 enrolled. In 2018, 345 master's awarded. *Entrance requirements:* For master's, GMAT or GRE test scores or completed test waiver form, official transcripts; 2 letters of reference from individuals familiar with the applicant's professional or academic work, excluding family or personal friends; a 1-2 page essay addressing educational and career goals; current résumé listing chronological work history; personal interview may be required prior to an admission decision. Additional exam requirements/recommendations for international students: Required—TOEFL (minimum score 550 paper-based; 79 iBT), IELTS (minimum score 6.5). *Application deadline:* Applications are processed on a rolling basis. Application fee: $40. Electronic applications accepted. *Unit head:* Ricky Holman, Assistant Professor, 630-829-1936, E-mail: rholman@ben.edu. *Application contact:* Ricky Holman, Assistant Professor, 630-829-1936, E-mail: rholman@ben.edu.

Benedictine University, Graduate Programs, Program in Management and Organizational Behavior, Lisle, IL 60532. Offers MS, PhD, MBA/MS, MPH/MS. *Program availability:* Part-time, evening/weekend, 100% online. *Faculty:* 3 full-time (2 women), 15 part-time/adjunct (6 women). *Students:* 19 full-time (14 women), 73 part-time (53 women); includes 20 minority (11 Black or African American, non-Hispanic/Latino; 1 Asian, non-Hispanic/Latino; 7 Hispanic/Latino; 1 Native Hawaiian or other Pacific Islander, non-Hispanic/Latino), 3 international. Average age 35. 32 applicants, 81% accepted, 24 enrolled. In 2018, 35 master's awarded. *Entrance requirements:* For master's, GMAT or GRE test scores or completed test waiver form, official transcripts; 2 letters of reference from individuals familiar with the applicant's professional or academic work, excluding family or personal friends; a 1-2 page essay addressing educational and career goals; résumé; personal interview may be required prior to an admission decision. Additional exam requirements/recommendations for international students: Required—TOEFL (minimum score 550 paper-based; 79 iBT), IELTS (minimum score 6.5). *Application deadline:* Applications are processed on a rolling basis. Application fee: $40. Electronic applications accepted. *Unit head:* Dr. Peter F. Sorensen, Director, 630-829-6222, E-mail: psorensen@ben.edu. *Application contact:* Dr. Peter F. Sorensen, Director, 630-829-6222, E-mail: psorensen@ben.edu.

Bentley University, McCallum Graduate School of Business, Accelerated Online MBA Program, Waltham, MA 02452-4705. Offers MBA. *Program availability:* Evening/weekend, 100% online. *Faculty:* 118 full-time (38 women), 25 part-time/adjunct (4 women). *Students:* 24 full-time (8 women), 1 part-time; includes 7 minority (1 Black or African American, non-Hispanic/Latino; 1 American Indian or Alaska Native, non-Hispanic/Latino; 2 Asian, non-Hispanic/Latino; 2 Hispanic/Latino; 1 Two or more races, non-Hispanic/Latino), 1 international. Average age 32. 26 applicants, 85% accepted, 14 enrolled. *Entrance requirements:* For master's, GMAT or GRE Scores (may be waived for qualified students), Transcripts; Resume; Two essays; Two letters of recommendation; Interview (may be requested by Bentley). Additional exam requirements/recommendations for international students: Required—TOEFL (minimum score 100) or IELTS (minimum score 7). *Application deadline:* For fall admission, 7/31 for domestic students, 6/30 for international students; for spring admission, 1/1 for domestic students, 11/1 for international students. Applications are processed on a rolling basis. Application fee: $150. Electronic applications accepted. *Financial support:* In 2018–19, 25 students received support. Scholarships/grants and tuition waivers (partial) available. Financial award application deadline: 6/1; financial award applicants required to submit FAFSA. *Unit head:* Jill Brown, Professor and MBA Director, 781-891-2407, E-mail: jbrown@bentley.edu. *Application contact:* Office of Graduate Admissions, 781-891-2108, E-mail: applygrad@bentley.edu.
Website: https://www.bentley.edu/academics/graduate-programs/mba

Bentley University, McCallum Graduate School of Business, The Bentley MBA, Waltham, MA 02452-4705. Offers MBA. *Accreditation:* AACSB. *Program availability:* Part-time, evening/weekend. *Faculty:* 118 full-time (38 women), 25 part-time/adjunct (4 women). *Students:* 90 full-time (41 women), 247 part-time (123 women); includes 60 minority (21 Black or African American, non-Hispanic/Latino; 24 Asian, non-Hispanic/Latino; 11 Hispanic/Latino; 4 Two or more races, non-Hispanic/Latino), 52 international. Average age 30. 273 applicants, 77% accepted, 112 enrolled. In 2018, 109 master's awarded. *Entrance requirements:* For master's, GMAT or GRE General Test (may be waived for qualified students), Transcripts; Resume; Two essays; Two letters of recommendation; Interview (required for full-time applicants). Additional exam requirements/recommendations for international students: Required—TOEFL (minimum score 100) or IELTS (minimum score 7). *Application deadline:* For fall admission, 7/31 for domestic students, 6/30 for international students; for spring admission, 1/1 for domestic students, 11/1 for international students. Applications are processed on a rolling basis. Application fee: $150. Electronic applications accepted. *Financial support:* In 2018–19, 193 students received support. Scholarships/grants and tuition waivers (partial) available. Financial award application deadline: 6/1; financial award applicants required to submit FAFSA. *Faculty research:* Strategy and innovation, business process management, corporate social responsibility, organizational change and leadership, digital innovation. *Unit head:* Jill Brown, Professor and MBA Director, 781-891-2407, E-mail: jbrown@bentley.edu. *Application contact:* Office of Graduate Admissions, 781-891-2108, E-mail: applygrad@bentley.edu.
Website: https://www.bentley.edu/academics/graduate-programs/mba

Bentley University, McCallum Graduate School of Business, Graduate Business Certificate Program, Waltham, MA 02452-4705. Offers accounting (GBC); business analytics (GBC); business ethics (GBC); financial planning (GBC); fraud and forensic accounting (GBC); marketing analytics (GBC); taxation (GBC). *Accreditation:* AACSB. *Program availability:* Part-time, evening/weekend. *Faculty:* 118 full-time (38 women), 25 part-time/adjunct (4 women). *Students:* 10 part-time (6 women); includes 3 minority (all Asian, non-Hispanic/Latino), 1 international. Average age 39. 10 applicants, 90% accepted, 4 enrolled. In 2018, 73 GBCs awarded. *Entrance requirements:* For degree, GMAT or GRE General Test (may be waived for qualified applicants), Transcripts; Resume; 2 essays; Two letters of recommendation; Interview (may be requested by Bentley). Additional exam requirements/recommendations for international students: Required—TOEFL (minimum score 100) or IELTS (minimum score 7). *Application deadline:* For fall admission, 7/31 for domestic students, 6/30 for international students;

for spring admission, 1/1 for domestic students, 11/1 for international students. Applications are processed on a rolling basis. Application fee: $150. Electronic applications accepted. *Expenses:* Contact institution. *Financial support:* In 2018–19, 1 student received support. Scholarships/grants available. Financial award application deadline: 6/1; financial award applicants required to submit FAFSA. *Application contact:* Office of Graduate Admissions, 781-891-2108, E-mail: applygrad@bentley.edu.
Website: https://catalog.bentley.edu/graduate/programs/certificates

Bentley University, McCallum Graduate School of Business, PhD in Business, Waltham, MA 02452-4705. Offers PhD. *Faculty:* 76 full-time (36 women). *Students:* 17 full-time (8 women), 1 (woman) part-time, 13 international. Average age 32. In 2018, 4 doctorates awarded. *Degree requirements:* For doctorate, comprehensive exam, thesis/dissertation. *Entrance requirements:* For doctorate, GMAT or GRE General Test, master's degree; official copies of transcripts; research statement; personal statement; 3 letters of recommendation; curriculum vitae; interview. Additional exam requirements/recommendations for international students: Required—The minimum acceptable score for the TOEFL is 100 and 7 for IELTS. *Application deadline:* For fall admission, 1/6 for domestic and international students. Electronic applications accepted. *Financial support:* In 2018–19, 18 students received support. Scholarships/grants available. Financial award application deadline: 6/1; financial award applicants required to submit FAFSA. *Faculty research:* Management (including: strategy; corporate governance; organization behavior; entrepreneurship; ethics; CSR); business analytics; information systems; marketing. *Unit head:* Patricia A. Caffrey, Administrative Director of PhD Programs, 781-891-2541, E-mail: pacaffrey@bentley.edu. *Application contact:* Bentley PhD Programs, 781-891-2404, E-mail: phd@bentley.edu.
Website: https://www.bentley.edu/academics/phd-programs/programs

Berkeley College–Woodland Park Campus, MBA Program, Woodland Park, NJ 07424. Offers management (MBA).

Berry College, Graduate Programs, Campbell School of Business, Mount Berry, GA 30149. Offers MBA. *Accreditation:* AACSB. *Program availability:* Part-time, evening/weekend. *Faculty:* 4 part-time/adjunct (1 woman). *Students:* 3 full-time (2 women), 38 part-time (14 women); includes 4 minority (3 Black or African American, non-Hispanic/Latino; 1 Asian, non-Hispanic/Latino). Average age 33. In 2018, 16 master's awarded. *Degree requirements:* For master's, thesis. *Entrance requirements:* For master's, GMAT or GRE, minimum GPA of 3.0, essay/goals statement. Additional exam requirements/recommendations for international students: Required—TOEFL (minimum score 550 paper-based). *Application deadline:* For fall admission, 7/26 for domestic students; for spring admission, 12/1 for domestic students. Applications are processed on a rolling basis. Application fee: $25 ($30 for international students). Electronic applications accepted. *Expenses:* $660 per credit hour. *Financial support:* In 2018–19, 22 students received support, including 9 research assistantships with full tuition reimbursements available (averaging $8,890 per year); scholarships/grants, tuition waivers (partial), and unspecified assistantships also available. Support available to part-time students. Financial award application deadline: 3/1; financial award applicants required to submit FAFSA. *Unit head:* Dr. Joyce Heames, Dean, 706-236-2233, Fax: 706-802-6728, E-mail: jheames@berry.edu. *Application contact:* Admissions, 706-236-2215, Fax: 706-290-2178, E-mail: admissions@berry.edu.
Website: https://www.berry.edu/academics/graduate-studies/business/

Bethel University, Adult and Graduate Programs, Program in Business Administration, Mishawaka, IN 46545-5591. Offers MBA. *Program availability:* Part-time, evening/weekend, 100% online, blended/hybrid learning. *Entrance requirements:* For master's, GMAT. Additional exam requirements/recommendations for international students: Required—TOEFL (minimum score 540 paper-based). Electronic applications accepted. *Faculty research:* Marketing.

Bethel University, Graduate Programs, McKenzie, TN 38201. Offers administration and supervision (MA Ed); business administration (MBA); conflict resolution (MA); physician assistant studies (MS). *Program availability:* Part-time, evening/weekend. *Degree requirements:* For master's, thesis (for some programs). *Entrance requirements:* For master's, GRE General Test or MAT, minimum undergraduate GPA of 2.5.

Bethel University, Graduate School, St. Paul, MN 55112-6999. Offers business administration (MBA); classroom management (Certificate); counseling (MA); K-12 education (MA); leadership (Ed D); leadership foundations (Certificate); nurse educator (MS, Certificate); nurse-midwifery (MS); physician assistant (MS); special education (MA); strategic leadership (MA); teaching (MA); teaching and learning (Certificate). *Program availability:* Part-time, evening/weekend, 100% online, blended/hybrid learning. *Faculty:* 23 full-time (17 women), 73 part-time/adjunct (45 women). *Students:* 586 full-time (426 women), 372 part-time (244 women); includes 141 minority (49 Black or African American, non-Hispanic/Latino; 6 American Indian or Alaska Native, non-Hispanic/Latino; 19 Asian, non-Hispanic/Latino; 40 Hispanic/Latino; 2 Native Hawaiian or other Pacific Islander, non-Hispanic/Latino; 25 Two or more races, non-Hispanic/Latino), 25 international. Average age 35. 642 applicants, 39% accepted, 194 enrolled. In 2018, 312 master's, 28 doctorates, 134 other advanced degrees awarded. *Degree requirements:* For master's, comprehensive exam (for some programs), thesis (for some programs); for doctorate, comprehensive exam, thesis/dissertation. *Entrance requirements:* Additional exam requirements/recommendations for international students: Required—TOEFL (minimum score 550 paper-based; 80 iBT), TOEFL (minimum score 550 paper-based, 80 iBT) or IELTS. *Application deadline:* Applications are processed on a rolling basis. Application fee: $0. Electronic applications accepted. *Expenses:* Contact institution. *Financial support:* Teaching assistantships, career-related internships or fieldwork, and scholarships/grants available. Support available to part-time students. Financial award applicants required to submit FAFSA. *Unit head:* Dr. Randy Bergen, Associate Provost, 651-635-8000, Fax: 651-635-8004, E-mail: r-bergen@bethel.edu. *Application contact:* Director of Admissions, 651-635-8000, Fax: 651-635-8004, E-mail: gs@bethel.edu.
Website: https://www.bethel.edu/graduate/

Binghamton University, State University of New York, Graduate School, School of Management, Program in Business Administration, Binghamton, NY 13902-6000. Offers business administration (MBA); corporate executive (MBA); executive business administration (MBA); health care professional executive (MBA); professional business administration (MBA). Executive and Professional MBA programs offered in Manhattan. *Accreditation:* AACSB. *Program availability:* Part-time. *Entrance requirements:* For master's, GMAT. Additional exam requirements/recommendations for international students: Required—TOEFL (minimum score 96 iBT). Electronic applications accepted. *Expenses:* Contact institution.

Binghamton University, State University of New York, Graduate School, School of Management, Program in Management, Binghamton, NY 13902-6000. Offers finance (PhD); management information systems (PhD); marketing (PhD); organizational studies (PhD); supply chain management (PhD). *Degree requirements:* For doctorate, thesis/dissertation. *Entrance requirements:* For doctorate, GMAT.

Biola University, Crowell School of Business, La Mirada, CA 90639-0001. Offers MBA, MP Acc. *Accreditation:* ACBSP. *Program availability:* Part-time, evening/weekend. *Entrance requirements:* For master's, GMAT. Additional exam requirements/recommendations for international students: Required—TOEFL (minimum score 600 paper-based; 100 iBT). Electronic applications accepted. *Faculty research:* Integration of theology with business and accounting principles.

Black Hills State University, Graduate Studies, Program in Business Administration, Spearfish, SD 57799. Offers MBA. *Accreditation:* AACSB. *Program availability:* Evening/weekend. *Entrance requirements:* Additional exam requirements/recommendations for international students: Required—TOEFL (minimum score 500 paper-based; 60 iBT).

Bloomsburg University of Pennsylvania, School of Graduate Studies, Zeigler College of Business, Program in Business Administration, Bloomsburg, PA 17815-1301. Offers business administration (MBA); management (Certificate). *Accreditation:* AACSB. *Program availability:* Part-time, evening/weekend. *Degree requirements:* For master's, minimum QPA of 3.0, practicum. *Entrance requirements:* For master's, GMAT, resume, 3 letters of recommendation, personal statement. Additional exam requirements/recommendations for international students: Required—TOEFL (minimum score 550 paper-based; 79 iBT), IELTS (minimum score 7.5). Electronic applications accepted.

Bluffton University, Graduate Programs in Business, Bluffton, OH 45817. Offers accounting and financial management (MBA); health care management (MBA); leadership (MAOM, MBA); production and operations management (MBA); sustainability management (MBA). *Program availability:* Evening/weekend, blended/hybrid learning, videoconference. *Faculty:* 4 full-time (2 women), 5 part-time/adjunct (1 woman). *Students:* 38 full-time (22 women), 1 part-time (0 women); includes 11 minority (6 Black or African American, non-Hispanic/Latino; 3 Hispanic/Latino; 2 Two or more races, non-Hispanic/Latino). Average age 33. In 2018, 25 master's awarded. *Degree requirements:* For master's, integrated research project (for some programs). *Entrance requirements:* For master's, current resume, official transcript, bachelor's degree, minimum GPA of 3.0, personal essay. Additional exam requirements/recommendations for international students: Recommended—TOEFL (minimum score 550 paper-based). *Application deadline:* For fall admission, 7/31 priority date for domestic and international students. Applications are processed on a rolling basis. Electronic applications accepted. *Expenses:* Contact institution. *Financial support:* Unspecified assistantships and faculty/staff grants available. Financial award applicants required to submit FAFSA. *Unit head:* Dr. Melissa Green, Director of Graduate Programs in Business, 419-358-3447, E-mail: greenm@bluffton.edu. *Application contact:* Shelby Koenig, Enrollment Counselor for Graduate Program, 419-3583684, E-mail: koenigs@bluffton.edu.
Website: https://www.bluffton.edu/ags/index.aspx

Bob Jones University, Graduate Programs, Greenville, SC 29614. Offers accountancy (MS); Bible (MA); Bible translation (MA); Biblical studies (Certificate); business administration (MBA); church history (MA, PhD); church ministries (MA); church music (MM); cinema and video production (MA); counseling (MS); curriculum and instruction (Ed D); divinity (M Div); dramatic production (MA); educational leadership (MS, Ed D, Ed S); elementary education (M Ed, MAT); English (M Ed, MA, MAT); fine arts (MA); graphic design (MA); history (M Ed, MA); illustration (MA); interpretative speech (MA); mathematics (M Ed, MAT); medical missions (Certificate); ministry (MM, D Min); multi-categorical special education (M Ed, MAT); music (M Ed); New Testament interpretation (PhD); Old Testament interpretation (PhD); orchestral instrument performance (MM); organ performance (MM); pastoral studies (MA); personnel services (MS, Ed S); piano pedagogy (MM); piano performance (MM); platform arts (MA); rhetoric and public address (MA); secondary education (M Ed); studio art (MA); teaching Bible (MA); theology (MA, PhD); voice performance (MM); youth ministries (MA); M Div/MM.

Boise State University, College of Business and Economics, Program in Business Administration, Boise, ID 83725-0399. Offers MBA. *Accreditation:* AACSB. *Program availability:* Part-time, 100% online. *Entrance requirements:* For master's, GMAT, minimum GPA of 3.0. Additional exam requirements/recommendations for international students: Required—TOEFL (minimum score 587 paper-based; 95 iBT), IELTS (minimum score 6.5). Electronic applications accepted.

Boston College, Carroll School of Management, Business Administration Program, Chestnut Hill, MA 02467-3800. Offers MBA, JD/MBA, MBA/MA, MBA/MS, MBA/MSA, MBA/MSF, MBA/MSW, MBA/PhD. *Accreditation:* AACSB. *Program availability:* Part-time, evening/weekend. *Entrance requirements:* For master's, GMAT, GRE, 2 letters of recommendation, resume, transcript. Additional exam requirements/recommendations for international students: Required—TOEFL (minimum score 600 paper-based, 100 iBT), IELTS (minimum score 7.5), or PTE (minimum score 68). Electronic applications accepted. *Faculty research:* Investments, corporate finance, management of financial services, strategic management.

Boston University, Metropolitan College, Department of Administrative Sciences, Boston, MA 02215. Offers applied business analytics (MS); economic development and tourism management (MSAS); enterprise risk management (MS); financial management (MS); global marketing management (MS); innovation and technology (MSAS); insurance management (MS); project management (MS); supply chain management (MS). *Accreditation:* AACSB. *Program availability:* Part-time, evening/weekend, 100% online, blended/hybrid learning. *Faculty:* 27 full-time (5 women), 39 part-time/adjunct (5 women). *Students:* 617 full-time (351 women), 574 part-time (290 women); includes 196 minority (47 Black or African American, non-Hispanic/Latino; 2 American Indian or Alaska Native, non-Hispanic/Latino; 75 Asian, non-Hispanic/Latino; 60 Hispanic/Latino; 12 Two or more races, non-Hispanic/Latino), 730 international. Average age 28. 2,259 applicants, 76% accepted, 594 enrolled. In 2018, 441 master's awarded. *Degree requirements:* For master's, thesis optional. *Entrance requirements:* For master's, 1 year of work experience, minimum GPA of 3.0. Additional exam requirements/recommendations for international students: Required—TOEFL (minimum score 84 iBT). *Application deadline:* For fall admission, 8/1 priority date for domestic students, 6/1 priority date for international students; for spring admission, 12/1 priority date for domestic students, 11/15 priority date for international students; for summer admission, 4/1 priority date for domestic students, 3/1 priority date for international students. Applications are processed on a rolling basis. Application fee: $85. Electronic applications accepted. *Expenses:* Contact institution. *Financial support:* In 2018–19, 15 students received support, including 16 research assistantships (averaging $8,400 per year), 30 teaching assistantships (averaging $3,400 per year); career-related internships or fieldwork, Federal Work-Study, and unspecified assistantships also available. Financial award applicants required to submit FAFSA. *Faculty research:* International business, innovative process. *Unit head:* Dr. John Sullivan, Chair, 617-353-3016, E-mail: adminsc@bu.edu. *Application contact:* Enrollment Services, 617-358-8162, E-mail: met@bu.edu.
Website: http://www.bu.edu/met/academic-community/departments/administrative-sciences/

Boston University, Questrom School of Business, Boston, MA 02215. Offers business (EMBA, MBA); business analytics (MS); management (PhD); management studies (MSMS); mathematical finance (MS, PhD); JD/MBA; MBA/MA; MBA/MPH; MBA/MS; MD/MBA. *Accreditation:* AACSB. *Program availability:* Part-time, evening/weekend. *Faculty:* 85 full-time (23 women), 28 part-time/adjunct (10 women). *Students:* 724 full-time (322 women), 636 part-time (286 women); includes 225 minority (43 Black or African American, non-Hispanic/Latino; 1 American Indian or Alaska Native, non-Hispanic/Latino; 104 Asian, non-Hispanic/Latino; 57 Hispanic/Latino; 20 Two or more races, non-Hispanic/Latino), 451 international. Average age 28. 1,069 applicants, 40%

accepted, 164 enrolled. In 2018, 585 master's, 11 doctorates awarded. *Degree requirements:* For doctorate, comprehensive exam, thesis/dissertation. *Entrance requirements:* For master's, GMAT or GRE (for MBA and MS in mathematical finance programs), essay, resume, 2 letters of recommendation, official transcripts; for doctorate, GMAT or GRE, personal statement, resume, 3 letters of recommendation, official transcripts. Additional exam requirements/recommendations for international students: Required—TOEFL (minimum score 600 paper-based, 90 iBT), IELTS (6.5), or PTE. *Application deadline:* For fall admission, 3/18 for domestic and international students; for spring admission, 11/7 for domestic and international students. Application fee: $125. Electronic applications accepted. *Expenses:* Contact institution. *Financial support:* Career-related internships or fieldwork, Federal Work-Study, institutionally sponsored loans, scholarships/grants, and tuition waivers (partial) available. Support available to part-time students. Financial award applicants required to submit FAFSA. *Faculty research:* Digital innovation, sustainable energy, corporate social responsibility, finance, marketing. *Unit head:* Kenneth W. Freeman, Professor/Dean, 617-353-9720, Fax: 617-353-5581, E-mail: kfreeman@bu.edu. *Application contact:* Meredith C. Siegel, Assistant Dean, Graduate Admissions Office, 617-353-2670, Fax: 617-353-7368, E-mail: mba@bu.edu.
Website: http://www.bu.edu/questrom/

Bowie State University, Graduate Programs, Program in Business Administration, Bowie, MD 20715-9465. Offers MBA. *Accreditation:* ACBSP. *Program availability:* Part-time, evening/weekend. *Degree requirements:* For master's, comprehensive exam. *Entrance requirements:* For master's, GMAT, minimum undergraduate GPA of 2.5. Electronic applications accepted.

Bowling Green State University, Graduate College, College of Business, Master of Business Administration Program, Bowling Green, OH 43403. Offers MBA. *Accreditation:* AACSB. *Program availability:* Part-time, evening/weekend. *Degree requirements:* For master's, thesis or alternative, research project. *Entrance requirements:* For master's, GMAT. Additional exam requirements/recommendations for international students: Required—TOEFL. Electronic applications accepted. *Faculty research:* Management of change processes, supply chain management, impacts of money on society, corporate financing strategies, macro-marketing/management of sales staff and services.

Bradley University, The Graduate School, Foster College of Business, Business Administration Program, Peoria, IL 61625-0002. Offers MBA. *Accreditation:* AACSB. *Program availability:* Part-time, evening/weekend. *Faculty:* 28 full-time (8 women), 4 part-time/adjunct (2 women). *Students:* 21 full-time (9 women), 24 part-time (5 women); includes 5 minority (2 Black or African American, non-Hispanic/Latino; 2 Asian, non-Hispanic/Latino; 1 Two or more races, non-Hispanic/Latino), 11 international. Average age 28. 50 applicants, 98% accepted, 17 enrolled. In 2018, 22 master's awarded. *Degree requirements:* For master's, comprehensive exam. *Entrance requirements:* For master's, GMAT or GRE, minimum undergraduate GPA of 2.75 in major, 2 letters of recommendation. Additional exam requirements/recommendations for international students: Required—TOEFL (minimum score 550 paper-based; 79 iBT), IELTS (minimum score 6.5). *Application deadline:* For fall admission, 5/15 priority date for domestic and international students; for spring admission, 10/15 priority date for domestic and international students. Applications are processed on a rolling basis. Application fee: $40 ($50 for international students). Electronic applications accepted. *Expenses:* Tuition: Part-time $890 per credit. *Required fees:* $50 per unit. *Financial support:* In 2018–19, 40 students received support, including 2 fellowships with full tuition reimbursements available (averaging $17,355 per year), 7 research assistantships with full and partial tuition reimbursements available (averaging $9,917 per year); teaching assistantships with full and partial tuition reimbursements available, career-related internships or fieldwork, institutionally sponsored loans, scholarships/grants, tuition waivers (partial), and unspecified assistantships also available. Support available to part-time students. Financial award application deadline: 4/1. *Application contact:* Rachel Webb, Director of On-Campus Graduate Admissions & International Student and Scholar Services, 309-677-2375, E-mail: rkwebb@bradley.edu.
Website: http://www.bradley.edu/academic/colleges/fcba/education/grad/mba/

Bradley University, The Graduate School, Foster College of Business, Theresa S. Falcon Executive MBA Program, Peoria, IL 61625-0002. Offers MBA. *Accreditation:* AACSB. *Program availability:* Evening/weekend. *Faculty:* 11 full-time (4 women). *Students:* 9 applicants. *Entrance requirements:* For master's, company sponsorship, 7 years of managerial experience, letters of recommendation. Additional exam requirements/recommendations for international students: Required—TOEFL (minimum score 550 paper-based; 79 iBT), IELTS (minimum score 6.5). *Application deadline:* Applications are processed on a rolling basis. Application fee: $40 ($50 for international students). Electronic applications accepted. *Expenses:* Bundled cost $68000. *Application contact:* Rachel Webb, Director of On-Campus Graduate Admissions & International Student and Scholar Services, 309-677-2375, E-mail: rkwebb@bradley.edu.
Website: http://www.bradley.edu/academic/colleges/fcba/education/grad/emba/

Brandeis University, The Heller School for Social Policy and Management, Program in Nonprofit Management, Waltham, MA 02454-9110. Offers child, youth, and family management (MBA); health care management (MBA); social impact management (MBA); social policy and management (MBA); sustainable development (MBA); MBA/MA; MBA/MD. MBA/MD program offered in conjunction with Tufts University School of Medicine. *Accreditation:* AACSB. *Program availability:* Part-time. *Degree requirements:* For master's, team consulting project. *Entrance requirements:* For master's, GMAT (preferred) or GRE, 2 letters of recommendation, problem statement analysis, 3-5 years of professional experience. Additional exam requirements/recommendations for international students: Required—TOEFL (minimum score 600 paper-based; 100 iBT). Electronic applications accepted. *Expenses:* Contact institution. *Faculty research:* Health care; children and families; elder and disabled services; social impact management; organizations in the non-profit, for-profit, or public sector.

Brandman University, School of Business and Professional Studies, Irvine, CA 92618. Offers accounting (MBA); business administration (MBA); business intelligence and data analytics (MBA); e-business strategic management (MBA); entrepreneurship (MBA); finance (MBA); health administration (MBA); human resources (MBA, MS); international business (MBA); marketing (MBA); organizational leadership (MA, MBA, MPA); public administration (MPA).

Brenau University, Sydney O. Smith Graduate School, College of Business and Mass Communication, Gainesville, GA 30501. Offers accounting (MBA); business administration (MBA); healthcare management (MBA); organizational leadership (MS); project management (MBA). *Accreditation:* ACBSP. *Program availability:* Part-time, evening/weekend, online learning. *Degree requirements:* For master's, comprehensive exam (for some programs). *Entrance requirements:* For master's, resume, minimum undergraduate GPA of 2.5. Additional exam requirements/recommendations for international students: Required—TOEFL (minimum score 500 paper-based; 61 iBT); Recommended—IELTS (minimum score 5). Electronic applications accepted. *Expenses:* Contact institution.

Brescia University, Program in Business Administration, Owensboro, KY 42301-3023. Offers MBA. *Program availability:* Part-time, evening/weekend. *Entrance requirements:* For master's, minimum cumulative GPA of 2.5. Additional exam requirements/recommendations for international students: Required—TOEFL (minimum score 100 iBT). Electronic applications accepted. Application fee is waived when completed online.

Brescia University, Program in Management, Owensboro, KY 42301-3023. Offers MSM. *Program availability:* Part-time, evening/weekend. *Entrance requirements:* For master's, minimum GPA of 2.5. Additional exam requirements/recommendations for international students: Required—TOEFL (minimum score 100 iBT).

Bridgewater State University, College of Graduate Studies, Ricciardi College of Business, Department of Management, Bridgewater, MA 02325. Offers MSM. *Entrance requirements:* For master's, GMAT.

Briercrest Seminary, Graduate Programs, Program in Leadership and Management, Caronport, SK S0H 0S0, Canada. Offers organizational leadership (MA). *Program availability:* Part-time. *Degree requirements:* For master's, comprehensive exam, thesis optional. *Entrance requirements:* Additional exam requirements/recommendations for international students: Required—TOEFL (minimum score 550 paper-based).

Brigham Young University, Graduate Studies, BYU Marriott School of Business, Executive Master of Business Administration Program, Provo, UT 84602. Offers MBA. *Accreditation:* AACSB. *Program availability:* Part-time-only, evening/weekend. *Entrance requirements:* For master's, GMAT (minimum score 560) or GRE, 5 years of management experience, commitment to BYU Honor Code. Additional exam requirements/recommendations for international students: Required—TOEFL (minimum score 590 paper-based; 100 iBT), IELTS (minimum score 7). Electronic applications accepted. *Expenses:* Contact institution. *Faculty research:* Finance, marketing, supply chain management, entrepreneurship, strategic human resources.

Brigham Young University, Graduate Studies, BYU Marriott School of Business, MBA Program, Provo, UT 84602. Offers entrepreneurship (MBA); finance (MBA); global supply chain management (MBA); marketing (MBA); strategic human resources (MBA); JD/MBA; MBA/MS. *Accreditation:* AACSB. *Entrance requirements:* For master's, GMAT or GRE, commitment to BYU Honor Code, undergraduate degree. Additional exam requirements/recommendations for international students: Required—TOEFL (minimum score 590 paper-based; 100 iBT), IELTS (minimum score 7). Electronic applications accepted. *Expenses:* Contact institution. *Faculty research:* Finance, marketing, supply chain management, entrepreneurship, strategic human resources.

Broadview University–West Jordan, Graduate Programs, West Jordan, UT 84088. Offers business administration (MBA); health care management (MSM); information technology (MSM); managerial leadership (MSM).

Brock University, Faculty of Graduate Studies, Faculty of Business, Program in Business Administration, St. Catharines, ON L2S 3A1, Canada. Offers MBA. *Degree requirements:* For master's, thesis or alternative. *Entrance requirements:* For master's, honours degree. Additional exam requirements/recommendations for international students: Required—TOEFL (minimum score 575 paper-based; 89 iBT), IELTS (minimum score 7), TWE (minimum score 4.5). Electronic applications accepted.

Brock University, Faculty of Graduate Studies, Faculty of Business, Program in Management, St. Catharines, ON L2S 3A1, Canada. Offers M Sc. *Program availability:* Part-time. *Degree requirements:* For master's, thesis. *Entrance requirements:* For master's, GMAT, honors degree. Additional exam requirements/recommendations for international students: Required—TOEFL (minimum score 600 paper-based; 100 iBT), IELTS (minimum score 7), TWE (minimum score 4.5). Electronic applications accepted.

Brooklyn College of the City University of New York, School of Business, Brooklyn, NY 11210-2889. Offers accounting (MS); business administration (MS), including economic analysis, general business, global business and finance. *Program availability:* Part-time, evening/weekend. *Degree requirements:* For master's, comprehensive exam, thesis or alternative. *Entrance requirements:* For master's, GMAT, 2 letters of recommendation. Additional exam requirements/recommendations for international students: Required—TOEFL (minimum score 550 paper-based; 79 iBT). Electronic applications accepted. *Faculty research:* Econometrics, environmental economics, microeconomics, macroeconomics, taxation.

Bryan College, MBA Program, Dayton, TN 37321. Offers business administration (MBA); healthcare administration (MBA); human resources (MBA); marketing (MBA); ministry (MBA); sports management (MBA). *Program availability:* Online only, 100% online. *Entrance requirements:* For master's, resume, 2 letters of recommendation. Additional exam requirements/recommendations for international students: Required—TOEFL. Electronic applications accepted. *Expenses:* Contact institution.

Bryant University, Graduate School of Business, Smithfield, RI 02917. Offers accounting (MPAC); business administration (MBA); taxation (MST). *Program availability:* Part-time, evening/weekend, 100% online. *Faculty:* 31 full-time (8 women), 6 part-time/adjunct (2 women). *Students:* 77 full-time (31 women), 106 part-time (46 women); includes 32 minority (7 Black or African American, non-Hispanic/Latino; 1 American Indian or Alaska Native, non-Hispanic/Latino; 9 Asian, non-Hispanic/Latino; 8 Hispanic/Latino; 7 Two or more races, non-Hispanic/Latino), 8 international. Average age 28. 215 applicants, 66% accepted, 96 enrolled. In 2018, 124 master's awarded. *Degree requirements:* For master's, comprehensive exam (for some programs). *Entrance requirements:* For master's, GMAT, resume, recommendation, college transcripts. Additional exam requirements/recommendations for international students: Required—TOEFL (minimum score 580 paper-based; 95 iBT). *Application deadline:* For fall admission, 7/15 for domestic and international students; for spring admission, 11/15 for domestic and international students; for summer admission, 4/15 for domestic and international students. Applications are processed on a rolling basis. Application fee: $80. Electronic applications accepted. *Expenses:* Contact institution. *Financial support:* In 2018–19, 95 fellowships with full and partial tuition reimbursements (averaging $9,825 per year), 9 research assistantships with full and partial tuition reimbursements (averaging $7,100 per year) were awarded; scholarships/grants and unspecified assistantships also available. Support available to part-time students. Financial award application deadline: 2/15; financial award applicants required to submit FAFSA. *Faculty research:* International business, public sector auditing, taxation of partnerships, information systems security, financial markets microstructure. *Unit head:* Jamie R Grenon, Director, Graduate Programs Office, 401-232-6707, E-mail: jgrenon@bryant.edu. *Application contact:* Jeanne Creighton, Senior Admissions Assistant, 401-232-6230, Fax: 401-232-6494, E-mail: graduateprograms@bryant.edu.
Website: http://gradschool.bryant.edu/business/

Bryan University, Program in Business Administration, Springfield, MO 65804. Offers MBA. *Program availability:* Online learning.

Butler University, Lacy School of Business, Indianapolis, IN 46208-3485. Offers MBA, MP Acc. *Accreditation:* AACSB. *Program availability:* Part-time. *Faculty:* 23 full-time (8 women), 19 part-time/adjunct (5 women). *Students:* 39 full-time (14 women), 126 part-time (47 women); includes 18 minority (2 Black or African American, non-Hispanic/Latino; 5 Asian, non-Hispanic/Latino; 8 Hispanic/Latino; 3 Two or more races, non-Hispanic/Latino), 10 international. Average age 29. 144 applicants, 83% accepted, 56 enrolled. In 2018, 70 master's awarded. *Degree requirements:* For master's,

comprehensive exam, thesis optional. *Entrance requirements:* For master's, GMAT, minimum AACSB index of 950, personal statement, two letters of recommendation, official transcripts, current resume. Additional exam requirements/recommendations for international students: Required—TOEFL (minimum score 550 paper-based; 79 iBT), IELTS (minimum score 6), Michigan English Language Assessment Battery (minimum score of 80). *Application deadline:* For fall admission, 8/1 for domestic and international students; for spring admission, 12/1 for domestic and international students; for summer admission, 4/1 for domestic and international students. Applications are processed on a rolling basis. Application fee: $0. Electronic applications accepted. Application fee is waived when completed online. *Expenses:* Contact institution. *Financial support:* In 2018–19, 17 students received support. Scholarships/grants, tuition waivers (full and partial), and unspecified assistantships available. Financial award application deadline: 7/15; financial award applicants required to submit FAFSA. *Faculty research:* Higher education and pedagogy; organizational management, supply chain and logistics, domestic public policy, international finance and banking. *Unit head:* Dr. Stephen Standifird, Dean, 317-940-6307. *Application contact:* Diane Dubord, Graduate Student Service Specialist, 317-940-8107, Fax: 317-940-8250, E-mail: ddubord@butler.edu.
Website: https://www.butler.edu/lacyschool

Cairn University, School of Business, Langhorne, PA 19047-2990. Offers accounting (MBA); business administration (MBA); international entrepreneurship (MBA); nonprofit leadership (MBA); organizational leadership (MSOL, Postbaccalaureate Certificate). *Program availability:* Part-time, evening/weekend, 100% online, blended/hybrid learning. *Entrance requirements:* Additional exam requirements/recommendations for international students: Required—TOEFL (minimum score 550 paper-based). Electronic applications accepted. Application fee is waived when completed online. *Expenses:* Contact institution.

Caldwell University, School of Business and Computer Science, Caldwell, NJ 07006-6195. Offers MBA, MS. *Accreditation:* ACBSP. *Program availability:* Part-time. *Faculty:* 7 full-time (4 women), 9 part-time/adjunct (2 women). *Students:* 29 full-time (18 women), 55 part-time (35 women); includes 27 minority (7 Black or African American, non-Hispanic/Latino; 3 Asian, non-Hispanic/Latino; 15 Hispanic/Latino; 2 Two or more races, non-Hispanic/Latino), 9 international. Average age 30. 34 applicants, 85% accepted, 19 enrolled. In 2018, 23 master's awarded. *Entrance requirements:* For master's, undergraduate accounting, economics, marketing, statistics, management courses; minimum three years' relevant experience; bachelor's degree; minimum undergraduate GPA of 2.75 overall; minimum 3.0 business GPA; interview; personal statement. Additional exam requirements/recommendations for international students: Required—The TOEFL or IELTS is required of international students who were not educated at the Bachelors level in English. Recommended—TOEFL (minimum score 580 paper-based; 92 iBT), IELTS (minimum score 7.5). *Application deadline:* Applications are processed on a rolling basis. Application fee: $50. Electronic applications accepted. *Expenses:* $32,835 full MBA tuition; $22,275 full online MBA tuition; $29,850 for full MS tuition. *Financial support:* Unspecified assistantships available. *Unit head:* Virginia Rich, Associate Dean, 973-618-3516, Fax: 973-618-3355, E-mail: vrich@caldwell.edu. *Application contact:* Tom Disch, Senior Admissions Counselor, 973-618-3544, E-mail: graduate@caldwell.edu.

California Baptist University, Program in Business Administration, Riverside, CA 92504-3206. Offers accounting (MBA); construction management (MBA); healthcare management (MBA); management (MBA). *Accreditation:* ACBSP. *Program availability:* Part-time, evening/weekend, 100% online, blended/hybrid learning. *Faculty:* 22 full-time (7 women), 14 part-time/adjunct (3 women). *Students:* 124 full-time (65 women), 71 part-time (38 women); includes 108 minority (16 Black or African American, non-Hispanic/Latino; 11 Asian, non-Hispanic/Latino; 74 Hispanic/Latino; 1 Native Hawaiian or other Pacific Islander, non-Hispanic/Latino; 6 Two or more races, non-Hispanic/Latino), 21 international. Average age 36. 71 applicants, 77% accepted, 55 enrolled. In 2018, 131 master's awarded. *Degree requirements:* For master's, thesis, Interdisciplinary Capstone Project. *Entrance requirements:* For master's, GMAT, minimum GPA of 2.5; two recommendations; comprehensive essay; resume; interview. Additional exam requirements/recommendations for international students: Required—TOEFL (minimum score 80 iBT). *Application deadline:* For fall admission, 8/1 priority date for domestic students, 7/1 for international students; for spring admission, 12/1 priority date for domestic students, 11/1 for international students. Applications are processed on a rolling basis. Application fee: $45. Electronic applications accepted. *Expenses:* $662 per unit. *Financial support:* In 2018–19, 70 students received support. Federal Work-Study and scholarships/grants available. Financial award applicants required to submit CSS PROFILE or FAFSA. *Faculty research:* Behavioral economics, economic indicators, marketing ethics, international business, microfinance. *Unit head:* Dr. Andrea Scott, Dean, School of Business, 951-343-4701, E-mail: ascott@calbaptist.edu. *Application contact:* Dr. Scott Dunbar, Program Director, Online Masters in Business Administration, 951-343-2193, E-mail: sdunbar@calbaptist.edu.
Website: http://www.calbaptist.edu/mba/about/

California Coast University, School of Administration and Management, Santa Ana, CA 92701. Offers business marketing (MBA); health care management (MBA); human resource management (MBA); management (MBA, MS). *Program availability:* Online learning. Electronic applications accepted.

California Institute of Advanced Management, The MBA Program, El Monte, CA 91731. Offers executive management and entrepreneurship (MBA).

California Intercontinental University, School of Business, Irvine, CA 92614. Offers banking and finance (MBA); entrepreneurship and business management (DBA); global business leadership (DBA); international management and marketing (MBA); organizational management and human resource management (MBA).

California International Business University, Graduate Programs, San Diego, CA 92101. Offers MBA, MSIM, DBA.

California Lutheran University, Graduate Studies, School of Management, Thousand Oaks, CA 91360-2787. Offers business (IMBA); entrepreneurship (MBA, Certificate); finance (MBA, Certificate); financial planning (MBA, MS, Certificate); human capital management (MBA, Certificate); information technology (MS); information technology management (MBA, Certificate); international business (MBA, Certificate); management (MS); marketing (MBA, Certificate); public policy and administration (MPPA); quantitative economics (MS). *Program availability:* Part-time, evening/weekend, 100% online, blended/hybrid learning. *Degree requirements:* For master's, comprehensive exam (for some programs). *Entrance requirements:* For master's, GMAT, interview, minimum GPA of 3.0. Electronic applications accepted. *Expenses:* Contact institution.

California Miramar University, Program in Business Administration, San Diego, CA 92108. Offers MBA.

California Polytechnic State University, San Luis Obispo, Orfalea College of Business, Program in Business Administration, San Luis Obispo, CA 93407. Offers MBA. *Faculty:* 3 full-time (0 women). *Students:* 22 full-time (7 women), 14 part-time (6 women); includes 7 minority (2 Asian, non-Hispanic/Latino; 5 Hispanic/Latino), 2 international. Average age 27. 50 applicants, 74% accepted, 25 enrolled. In 2018, 37 master's awarded. *Degree requirements:* For master's, comprehensive exam. *Entrance requirements:* For master's, GMAT. Additional exam requirements/recommendations for international students: Required—TOEFL (minimum score 80 iBT). *Application deadline:* For fall admission, 4/1 for domestic and international students. Applications are processed on a rolling basis. Application fee: $55. Electronic applications accepted. *Expenses: Tuition, area resident:* Full-time $7176; part-time $4164 per year. Tuition, state resident: full-time $10,965. Tuition, nonresident: full-time $10,965. *Required fees:* $6336; $3711. *Financial support:* Fellowships, career-related internships or fieldwork, Federal Work-Study, institutionally sponsored loans, scholarships/grants, and unspecified assistantships available. Support available to part-time students. Financial award application deadline: 3/2; financial award applicants required to submit FAFSA. *Faculty research:* Management of high-tech firms, Pacific Rim, capital market structures, economics of environmental policy, marketing of services. *Unit head:* Dr. Scott Dawson, Dean, 805-756-2705, E-mail: scdawson@calpoly.edu. *Application contact:* Dr. Scott Dawson, Dean, 805-756-2705, E-mail: scdawson@calpoly.edu.
Website: http://www.cob.calpoly.edu/gradbusiness/degree-programs/mba/

California State Polytechnic University, Pomona, Master of Science in Business Administration Program, Pomona, CA 91768-2557. Offers business administration (MS). *Accreditation:* AACSB. *Program availability:* Part-time, evening/weekend. *Students:* 15 full-time (5 women), 9 part-time (3 women); includes 11 minority (1 Black or African American, non-Hispanic/Latino; 6 Asian, non-Hispanic/Latino; 4 Hispanic/Latino), 3 international. Average age 31. 39 applicants, 67% accepted, 18 enrolled. *Entrance requirements:* Additional exam requirements/recommendations for international students: Required—TOEFL (minimum score 550 paper-based). *Application deadline:* Applications are processed on a rolling basis. Application fee: $55. Electronic applications accepted. *Expenses:* Contact institution. *Financial support:* Application deadline: 3/2; applicants required to submit FAFSA. *Unit head:* Dr. Tarique Hossain, Associate Professor/Director of Graduate Programs, 909-869-2362, Fax: 909-869-4559, E-mail: tmhossain@cpp.edu. *Application contact:* Dr. Tarique Hossain, Associate Professor/Director of Graduate Programs, 909-869-2362, Fax: 909-869-4559, E-mail: tmhossain@cpp.edu.
Website: http://www.cpp.edu/~cba/graduate-business-programs/programs/MSBA.shtml

California State Polytechnic University, Pomona, MBA Program, Pomona, CA 91768-2557. Offers business administration (MBA). *Program availability:* Part-time, evening/weekend. *Students:* 43 full-time (14 women), 29 part-time (10 women); includes 42 minority (4 Black or African American, non-Hispanic/Latino; 1 American Indian or Alaska Native, non-Hispanic/Latino; 13 Asian, non-Hispanic/Latino; 23 Hispanic/Latino; 1 Two or more races, non-Hispanic/Latino), 4 international. Average age 31. 154 applicants, 54% accepted, 51 enrolled. In 2018, 24 master's awarded. *Entrance requirements:* Additional exam requirements/recommendations for international students: Required—TOEFL (minimum score 580 paper-based). *Application deadline:* Applications are processed on a rolling basis. Application fee: $55. Electronic applications accepted. *Expenses:* Contact institution. *Financial support:* Application deadline: 3/2; applicants required to submit FAFSA. *Unit head:* Dr. Tarique Hossain, Associate Professor/Director of Graduate Programs, 909-869-2362, Fax: 909-869-4559, E-mail: tmhossain@cpp.edu. *Application contact:* Dr. Tarique Hossain, Associate Professor/Director of Graduate Programs, 909-869-2362, Fax: 909-869-4559, E-mail: tmhossain@cpp.edu.
Website: http://www.cpp.edu/~cba/graduate-business-programs/programs/MBA.shtml

California State University, Bakersfield, Division of Graduate Studies, Program in Administration, Bakersfield, CA 93311. Offers MSA. *Program availability:* Online learning. *Degree requirements:* For master's, capstone experience. *Entrance requirements:* For master's, official transcripts, three professional references, current resume, statement of purpose. *Application deadline:* For fall admission, 5/5 priority date for domestic students; for spring admission, 10/6 priority date for domestic students; for summer admission, 3/2 priority date for domestic students. Application fee: $75. *Expenses:* Contact institution. *Financial support:* Application deadline: 3/2; applicants required to submit FAFSA. *Unit head:* Dr. Chandra Commuri, Director, 661-654-6140, E-mail: ccommuri@csub.edu. *Application contact:* Martha Manriquez, Graduate Student Center Coordinator, 661-654-2786, Fax: 661-654-2791, E-mail: gsc@csub.edu.
Website: http://www.csub.edu/eud/degrees/msa/

California State University, Bakersfield, Division of Graduate Studies, School of Business and Public Administration, Program in Business Administration, Bakersfield, CA 93311. Offers MBA. *Accreditation:* AACSB. *Faculty:* 6 full-time (0 women), 5 part-time/adjunct (0 women). *Students:* 41 full-time (24 women), 26 part-time (14 women); includes 29 minority (4 Black or African American, non-Hispanic/Latino; 4 Asian, non-Hispanic/Latino; 21 Hispanic/Latino), 2 international. Average age 35. 105 applicants, 31% accepted, 24 enrolled. In 2018, 50 master's awarded. *Entrance requirements:* For master's, GMAT or GRE, baccalaureate degree, minimum undergraduate GPA of 2.75. *Application deadline:* Applications are processed on a rolling basis. Application fee: $55. *Financial support:* In 2018–19, fellowships (averaging $1,850 per year) were awarded; Federal Work-Study, scholarships/grants, and tuition waivers (full and partial) also available. Financial award application deadline: 3/2; financial award applicants required to submit FAFSA. *Unit head:* Dr. Dan Zhou, Director, 661-654-2780, E-mail: mba@csub.edu. *Application contact:* Martha Manriquez, Graduate Student Center Coordinator, 661-654-2786, Fax: 661-654-2791, E-mail: gsc@csub.edu.
Website: http://www.csub.edu/mba/index.html

California State University Channel Islands, Extended University and International Programs, Master of Business Administration Program, Camarillo, CA 93012. Offers MBA. *Program availability:* Part-time, evening/weekend. *Students:* 81 full-time (20 women); includes 35 minority (7 Asian, non-Hispanic/Latino; 23 Hispanic/Latino; 1 Native Hawaiian or other Pacific Islander, non-Hispanic/Latino; 4 Two or more races, non-Hispanic/Latino). *Degree requirements:* For master's, thesis. *Entrance requirements:* For master's, GMAT/GRE; GRE may be waived. Additional exam requirements/recommendations for international students: Required—TOEFL (minimum score 550 paper-based; 80 iBT), IELTS (minimum score 6.5). *Application deadline:* For fall admission, 5/1 for domestic students; for spring admission, 11/1 for domestic students. Application fee: $55. Electronic applications accepted. *Expenses:* 19,800.00. *Financial support:* Applicants required to submit FAFSA. *Unit head:* Dr. John Lu, Program Director, 805-437-2058, E-mail: John.lu@csuci.edu. *Application contact:* Andrew Conley, Graduate Programs Recruiter, 805-437-2652, E-mail: andrew.conley@csuci.edu.
Website: http://ext.csuci.edu/

California State University, Chico, Office of Graduate Studies, College of Behavioral and Social Sciences, Department of Political Science and Criminal Justice, Program in Public Administration, Chico, CA 95929-0722. Offers health administration (MPA); local government management (MPA). *Accreditation:* NASPAA. *Program availability:* Part-time. *Students:* 24 full-time (15 women), 12 part-time (7 women); includes 14 minority (1 American Indian or Alaska Native, non-Hispanic/Latino; 5 Asian, non-Hispanic/Latino; 5 Hispanic/Latino; 3 Two or more races, non-Hispanic/Latino). 18 applicants, 72% accepted, 9 enrolled. *Degree requirements:* For master's, thesis or culminating practicum. *Entrance requirements:* For master's, 2 letters of recommendation and statement of purpose. Additional exam requirements/recommendations for international students: Required—TOEFL (minimum score 550 paper-based; 80 iBT), IELTS (minimum score 6.5), PTE. *Application deadline:* For fall admission, 3/1 priority date for

domestic students, 3/1 for international students; for spring admission, 9/15 priority date for domestic students, 9/15 for international students. Applications are processed on a rolling basis. Application fee: $55. Electronic applications accepted. *Expenses: Tuition, area resident:* Full-time $4622; part-time $3116 per unit. Tuition, state resident: full-time $4622; part-time $3116 per unit. Tuition, nonresident: full-time $10,634. *Required fees:* $2160; $1620 per year. Tuition and fees vary according to class time and program. *Financial support:* Fellowships, research assistantships, teaching assistantships, career-related internships or fieldwork, Federal Work-Study, scholarships/grants, traineeships, health care benefits, unspecified assistantships, and stipends available. Support available to part-time students. Financial award application deadline: 3/2; financial award applicants required to submit FAFSA. *Unit head:* Mahalley Allen, Chair, 530-898-6506, Fax: 530-898-5301, E-mail: mdallen@csuchico.edu. *Application contact:* Micah Lehner, Graduate Admissions Coordinator, 530-898-5416, Fax: 530-898-3342, E-mail: mlehner@csuchico.edu.
Website: http://catalog.csuchico.edu/viewer/12/POLS/PADMNONEMP.html

California State University, Chico, Office of Graduate Studies, College of Business, Chico, CA 95929-0722. Offers MBA. *Program availability:* Part-time. *Faculty:* 10 full-time (2 women), 1 part-time/adjunct (0 women). *Students:* 32 full-time (10 women), 27 part-time (13 women); includes 28 minority (1 American Indian or Alaska Native, non-Hispanic/Latino; 18 Asian, non-Hispanic/Latino; 8 Hispanic/Latino; 1 Two or more races, non-Hispanic/Latino). 36 applicants, 67% accepted, 16 enrolled. In 2018, 33 master's awarded. *Degree requirements:* For master's, thesis, project, or comprehensive exam. *Entrance requirements:* For master's, GMAT (desired score of 570) or GRE (desired score of 303), 2 letters of recommendation, department letter of recommendation to access waiver form, statement of purpose, resume. Additional exam requirements/recommendations for international students: Required—TOEFL (minimum score 550 paper-based; 80 iBT), IELTS, PTE (minimum score 59), PTE Academic (minimum score 59) or IELTS (6.5). *Application deadline:* For fall admission, 3/2 priority date for domestic and international students; for spring admission, 9/16 priority date for domestic and international students. Application fee: $55. Electronic applications accepted. *Expenses:* Contact institution. *Financial support:* Fellowships, research assistantships, teaching assistantships, career-related internships or fieldwork, Federal Work-Study, scholarships/grants, traineeships, health care benefits, unspecified assistantships, and stipends available. Support available to part-time students. Financial award application deadline: 3/2; financial award applicants required to submit FAFSA. *Unit head:* Dr. Terrence Lau, Dean, 530-898-6272, Fax: 530-898-4584, E-mail: tjlau@csuchico.edu. *Application contact:* Micah Lehner, Graduate Admissions Coordinator, 530-898-5416, Fax: 530-898-3342, E-mail: mlehner@csuchico.edu.
Website: http://www.csuchico.edu/cob/

California State University, Dominguez Hills, College of Business Administration and Public Policy, Program in Business Administration, Carson, CA 90747-0001. Offers MBA. *Program availability:* Part-time, evening/weekend, online learning. *Entrance requirements:* For master's, GMAT, minimum GPA of 2.75. Additional exam requirements/recommendations for international students: Required—TOEFL (minimum score 570 paper-based; 88 iBT). *Faculty research:* Management.

California State University, East Bay, Office of Graduate Studies, College of Business and Economics, MBA Program, Hayward, CA 94542-3000. Offers finance (MBA); human resources and organizational behavior (MBA); marketing management (MBA); operations and supply chain management (MBA); strategy and innovation (MBA). *Accreditation:* AACSB. *Program availability:* Part-time, evening/weekend. *Degree requirements:* For master's, comprehensive exam or thesis. *Entrance requirements:* For master's, GMAT (minimum 20th percentile verbal and quantitative section), bachelor's degree, minimum GPA of 2.75. Additional exam requirements/recommendations for international students: Required—TOEFL (minimum score 550 paper-based; 79 iBT). Electronic applications accepted. *Expenses:* Contact institution.

California State University, Fresno, Division of Research and Graduate Studies, Craig School of Business, Fresno, CA 93740-8027. Offers MBA. *Program availability:* Part-time, blended/hybrid learning. *Degree requirements:* For master's, comprehensive exam, thesis or alternative. *Entrance requirements:* For master's, GMAT, minimum GPA of 2.5, official transcripts. Additional exam requirements/recommendations for international students: Required—TOEFL (minimum score 550 paper-based; 80 iBT), IELTS (minimum score 6.5). Electronic applications accepted. *Faculty research:* Conflict resolution, business marketing, business communication.

California State University, Fullerton, Graduate Studies, College of Business and Economics, Program in Business Administration, Fullerton, CA 92831-3599. Offers business administration (MBA); business analytics (MBA); international business (MBA); organizational leadership (MBA); risk management and insurance (MBA). *Accreditation:* AACSB. *Program availability:* Part-time. *Entrance requirements:* For master's, GMAT.

California State University, Long Beach, Graduate Studies, College of Business, Long Beach, CA 90840. Offers MS. *Accreditation:* AACSB. *Program availability:* Part-time, evening/weekend. *Students:* 74 full-time (29 women), 112 part-time (53 women); includes 105 minority (9 Black or African American, non-Hispanic/Latino; 34 Asian, non-Hispanic/Latino; 53 Hispanic/Latino; 2 Native Hawaiian or other Pacific Islander, non-Hispanic/Latino; 7 Two or more races, non-Hispanic/Latino), 21 international. Average age 32. *Entrance requirements:* For master's, GMAT. Additional exam requirements/recommendations for international students: Required—TOEFL. *Application deadline:* For fall admission, 6/1 for domestic students. Applications are processed on a rolling basis. Application fee: $55. Electronic applications accepted. *Expenses: Required fees:* $2628 per term. Tuition and fees vary according to class time, course level, course load, degree level, campus/location and program. *Financial support:* Career-related internships or fieldwork and scholarships/grants available. Financial award application deadline: 3/2; financial award applicants required to submit FAFSA. *Faculty research:* Attitude formation theory, consumer motivation, gift giving, derivative and synthetic securities, financial applications of artificial intelligence. *Unit head:* Dr. Michael E. Solt, Dean, 562-985-5307, E-mail: Michael.Solt@csulb.edu. *Application contact:* Dr. Ingrid Martin, Director, Graduate Business Programs, 562-985-5565, Fax: 562-985-5742, E-mail: Ingrid.Martin@csulb.edu.
Website: http://www.csulb.edu/college-of-business

California State University, Los Angeles, Graduate Studies, College of Business and Economics, Department of Information Systems, Los Angeles, CA 90032-8530. Offers management (MS). *Program availability:* Part-time, evening/weekend. *Degree requirements:* For master's, comprehensive exam (MBA), thesis (MS). *Entrance requirements:* For master's, GMAT, minimum GPA of 2.5 during previous 2 years of course work. Additional exam requirements/recommendations for international students: Required—TOEFL (minimum score 550 paper-based). Electronic applications accepted.

California State University, Los Angeles, Graduate Studies, College of Business and Economics, Department of Management, Los Angeles, CA 90032-8530. Offers health care management (MS); management (MBA). *Accreditation:* AACSB. *Program availability:* Part-time, evening/weekend. *Entrance requirements:* For master's, GMAT, minimum GPA of 2.5 during previous 2 years of course work. Additional exam requirements/recommendations for international students: Required—TOEFL (minimum score 550 paper-based). Electronic applications accepted.

California State University, Monterey Bay, College of Business, Seaside, CA 93955-8001. Offers MBA. *Program availability:* Part-time, evening/weekend, online learning. *Entrance requirements:* For master's, recommendation, resume, work experience, bachelor's degree from accredited university. Additional exam requirements/recommendations for international students: Recommended—TOEFL (minimum score 550 paper-based; 79 iBT). Electronic applications accepted.

California State University, Northridge, Graduate Studies, David Nazarian College of Business and Economics, Northridge, CA 91330. Offers MBA. *Accreditation:* AACSB. *Program availability:* Part-time. *Degree requirements:* For master's, thesis or alternative. *Entrance requirements:* For master's, GMAT, minimum GPA of 3.0 in last 60 units. Additional exam requirements/recommendations for international students: Required—TOEFL.

California State University, Northridge, Graduate Studies, Tseng College, Program in Public Sector Management and Leadership, Northridge, CA 91330. Offers MPA. *Program availability:* Online learning.

California State University, Sacramento, College of Business Administration, Sacramento, CA 95819. Offers accountancy (MS); business administration (IMBA, MBA); human resources (MBA); urban land development (MBA). *Accreditation:* AACSB. *Program availability:* Part-time, evening/weekend, 100% online, blended/hybrid learning. *Degree requirements:* For master's, comprehensive exam, project, thesis, or writing proficiency exam. *Entrance requirements:* For master's, GMAT. Additional exam requirements/recommendations for international students: Required—TOEFL (minimum score 550 paper-based; 80 iBT). Electronic applications accepted. *Expenses:* Contact institution.

California State University, San Bernardino, Graduate Studies, College of Business and Public Administration, Program in Business Administration, San Bernardino, CA 92407. Offers accounting (MBA); entrepreneurship (MBA); finance (MBA); global business (MBA); information management (MBA); information security (MBA); management (MBA); supply chain management (MBA). *Accreditation:* AACSB. *Program availability:* Part-time, evening/weekend, online learning. *Faculty:* 5 full-time (4 women), 7 part-time/adjunct (3 women). *Students:* 40 full-time (14 women), 163 part-time (72 women); includes 99 minority (7 Black or African American, non-Hispanic/Latino; 15 Asian, non-Hispanic/Latino; 71 Hispanic/Latino; 6 Two or more races, non-Hispanic/Latino), 58 international. Average age 32. 342 applicants, 52% accepted, 91 enrolled. In 2018, 106 master's awarded. *Degree requirements:* For master's, comprehensive exam, thesis. *Entrance requirements:* Additional exam requirements/recommendations for international students: Required—TOEFL. *Application deadline:* For fall admission, 7/16 for domestic students, 7/20 for international students; for winter admission, 10/23 for domestic students, 10/20 for international students; for spring admission, 1/22 for domestic students, 1/20 for international students. Application fee: $55. *Expenses:* Contact institution. *Financial support:* Application deadline: 3/1. *Unit head:* Dr. Lawrence C. Rose, Dean, 909-537-3703, Fax: 909-537-7026, E-mail: lrose@csusb.edu. *Application contact:* Ernest Silvers, MBA Program Director, 909-537-5703, E-mail: esilvers@csusb.edu.
Website: http://mba.csusb.edu/

California State University, Stanislaus, College of Business Administration, Executive MBA Program, Turlock, CA 95382. Offers EMBA. *Accreditation:* AACSB. *Program availability:* Part-time, evening/weekend. *Degree requirements:* For master's, comprehensive exam, thesis or alternative. *Entrance requirements:* For master's, GMAT or GRE, minimum GPA of 2.5, 2 letters of reference, personal statement, interview. Additional exam requirements/recommendations for international students: Required—TOEFL (minimum score 550 paper-based). Electronic applications accepted. *Expenses:* Contact institution.

California State University, Stanislaus, College of Business Administration, Master of Business Administration Program, Turlock, CA 95382. Offers MBA. *Accreditation:* AACSB. *Program availability:* Part-time, evening/weekend. *Degree requirements:* For master's, comprehensive exam, thesis or alternative. *Entrance requirements:* For master's, GMAT or GRE, minimum GPA of 2.5, 3 letters of reference, personal statement. Additional exam requirements/recommendations for international students: Required—TOEFL (minimum score 550 paper-based). Electronic applications accepted. *Expenses:* Contact institution. *Faculty research:* Teaching creativity, graduate operations management, curricula data mining, foreign direct investment.

California University of Management and Sciences, Graduate Programs, Anaheim, CA 92801. Offers business administration (MBA, DBA); computer information systems (MS); economics (MS); international business (MS); sports management (MS).

California University of Pennsylvania, School of Graduate Studies and Research, Eberly College of Science and Technology, Program in Business Administration, California, PA 15419-1394. Offers business analytics (MBA); entrepreneurship (MBA); healthcare management (MBA). *Program availability:* Part-time, evening/weekend. *Degree requirements:* For master's, comprehensive exam. *Entrance requirements:* For master's, minimum GPA of 3.0, official transcripts. Additional exam requirements/recommendations for international students: Required—TOEFL (minimum score 550 paper-based). Electronic applications accepted. *Faculty research:* Economics, applied economics, consumer behavior, technology and business, impact of technology.

Cambridge College, School of Management, Boston, MA 02129. Offers business administration (MBA); business negotiation and conflict resolution (M Mgt); general business (M Mgt); health care (MBA); health care management (M Mgt); small business development (M Mgt); technology management (M Mgt). *Program availability:* Part-time, evening/weekend, 100% online, blended/hybrid learning. *Degree requirements:* For master's, thesis, seminars. *Entrance requirements:* For master's, resume, 2 professional references. Additional exam requirements/recommendations for international students: Required—TOEFL (minimum score 550 paper-based; 79 iBT), Michigan English Language Assessment Battery (minimum score 85); Recommended—IELTS (minimum score 6). *Application deadline:* Applications are processed on a rolling basis. Application fee: $50 ($100 for international students). Electronic applications accepted. *Expenses:* Contact institution. *Financial support:* Career-related internships or fieldwork, Federal Work-Study, and scholarships/grants available. Financial award applicants required to submit FAFSA. *Faculty research:* Negotiation, mediation and conflict resolution; leadership; management of diverse organizations; case studies and simulation methodologies for management education, digital as a second language: social networking for digital immigrants, non-profit and public management. *Unit head:* Joseph Miglio, Interim Dean, E-mail: joseph.miglio@cambridgecollege.edu. *Application contact:* Salvadore Liberto, Interim Assistant Vice President of Enrollment, 800-877-4723, E-mail: admissions@cambridgecollege.edu.
Website: https://www.cambridgecollege.edu/school/school-management

Cameron University, Office of Graduate Studies, Program in Business Administration, Lawton, OK 73505-6377. Offers MBA. *Accreditation:* ACBSP. *Program availability:* Part-time, evening/weekend, online learning. *Degree requirements:* For master's, comprehensive exam. *Entrance requirements:* Additional exam requirements/recommendations for international students: Required—TOEFL (minimum score 550 paper-based). Electronic applications accepted. *Faculty research:* Financial liberalization, right to work, recession, teaching evaluations, database management.

Business Administration and Management—General

Campbellsville University, School of Business, Economics, and Technology, Campbellsville, KY 42718-2799. Offers business administration (MBA, Professional MBA); information technology management (MS); management (PhD); management and leadership (MML). *Program availability:* Part-time, evening/weekend, 100% online, blended/hybrid learning. *Faculty:* 62 full-time (29 women), 28 part-time/adjunct (14 women). *Students:* 6,515 full-time (1,494 women), 134 part-time (35 women); includes 19 minority (16 Black or African American, non-Hispanic/Latino; 1 American Indian or Alaska Native, non-Hispanic/Latino; 1 Asian, non-Hispanic/Latino; 1 Hispanic/Latino), 6,524 international. Average age 28. 3,512 applicants, 85% accepted, 2026 enrolled. In 2018, 1,102 master's awarded. *Degree requirements:* For master's, comprehensive exam (for some programs), thesis optional; for doctorate, comprehensive exam, thesis/dissertation. *Entrance requirements:* For master's, GRE or GMAT, letters of recommendation, college transcripts; for doctorate, GMAT, resume, official transcripts, references, personal essay, interview, completion of course in statistics and research methods. Additional exam requirements/recommendations for international students: Required—TOEFL (minimum score 550 paper-based; 79 iBT); Recommended—IELTS (minimum score 6). *Application deadline:* Applications are processed on a rolling basis. Application fee: $25. Electronic applications accepted. Application fee is waived when completed online. *Expenses:* $479-$525 per credit hour (for master's); $699 per credit hour (for PhD). *Financial support:* Unspecified assistantships available. Financial award application deadline: 6/1; financial award applicants required to submit FAFSA. *Unit head:* Dr. Patricia H. Cowherd, Dean of School of Business, Economics, and Technology, 270-789-5553, Fax: 270-789-5066, E-mail: phcowherd@campbellsville.edu. *Application contact:* Monica Bamwine, Director of Graduate Admissions, 270-789-5221, Fax: 270-789-5071, E-mail: mkbamwine@campbellsville.edu.
Website: http://www.campbellsville.edu

Campbell University, Graduate and Professional Programs, Lundy-Fetterman School of Business, Buies Creek, NC 27506. Offers MBA, MTWM. *Accreditation:* ACBSP. *Program availability:* Part-time, evening/weekend. *Degree requirements:* For master's, comprehensive exam, thesis or alternative. *Entrance requirements:* For master's, GMAT or GRE, minimum GPA of 2.7, 3 letters of reference, resume. Additional exam requirements/recommendations for international students: Required—TOEFL (minimum score 550 paper-based). *Faculty research:* Agricultural economics, investments, leadership, marketing, law and economics.

Canisius College, Graduate Division, Richard J. Wehle School of Business, Department of Management, Buffalo, NY 14208-1098. Offers business administration (MBA); international business (MS). *Accreditation:* AACSB. *Program availability:* Part-time, evening/weekend. *Faculty:* 8 full-time (3 women), 4 part-time/adjunct (1 woman). *Students:* 85 full-time (38 women), 121 part-time (44 women); includes 19 minority (9 Black or African American, non-Hispanic/Latino; 1 American Indian or Alaska Native, non-Hispanic/Latino; 2 Asian, non-Hispanic/Latino; 2 Hispanic/Latino; 5 Two or more races, non-Hispanic/Latino), 19 international. Average age 28. 125 applicants, 93% accepted, 69 enrolled. In 2018, 116 master's awarded. *Entrance requirements:* For master's, GMAT, GRE, official transcript from colleges attended, current resume. Additional exam requirements/recommendations for international students: Required—TOEFL (minimum score 550 paper-based, 80 iBT), IELTS (minimum score 6.5), or CAEL (minimum score 70). *Application deadline:* For fall admission, 7/1 priority date for domestic students; for spring admission, 11/1 priority date for domestic students. Applications are processed on a rolling basis. Application fee: $0. Electronic applications accepted. *Expenses:* Tuition: Part-time $820 per credit hour. *Required fees:* $25 per semester. One-time fee: $65 part-time. Tuition and fees vary according to program. *Financial support:* In 2018–19, 35 students received support. Career-related internships or fieldwork, Federal Work-Study, scholarships/grants, tuition waivers (partial), and unspecified assistantships available. Support available to part-time students. Financial award application deadline: 4/30; financial award applicants required to submit FAFSA. *Faculty research:* Global leadership effectiveness, global supply chain management, quality management. *Unit head:* Dr. Robyn L. Brouer, Chair/Associate Professor of Management, 716-888-2226, Fax: 716-888-3215, E-mail: brouerr@canisius.edu. *Application contact:* Dr. Robyn L. Brouer, Chair/Associate Professor of Management, 716-888-2226, Fax: 716-888-3215, E-mail: brouerr@canisius.edu.
Website: http://www.canisius.edu/graduate/

Cape Breton University, Shannon School of Business, Sydney, NS B1P 6L2, Canada. Offers MBA. *Program availability:* Part-time. *Entrance requirements:* For master's, GMAT. Additional exam requirements/recommendations for international students: Required—TOEFL (minimum score 550 paper-based; 80 iBT), IELTS (minimum score 6.5). Electronic applications accepted.

Capella University, School of Business and Technology, Doctoral Programs in Business, Minneapolis, MN 55402. Offers accounting (DBA, PhD); business intelligence (DBA); finance (DBA, PhD); general business management (PhD); human resource management (DBA, PhD); leadership (DBA, PhD); management education (PhD); marketing (DBA, PhD); project management (DBA, PhD); strategy and innovation (DBA, PhD). *Accreditation:* ACBSP.

Capella University, School of Business and Technology, Master's Programs in Business, Minneapolis, MN 55402. Offers accounting (MBA); business analysis (MS); business intelligence (MBA); entrepreneurship (MBA); finance (MBA); general business administration (MBA); general human resource management (MS); general leadership (MS); health care management (MBA); human resource management (MBA); marketing (MBA); project management (MBA, MS). *Accreditation:* ACBSP.

Capital University, Law School, Program in Business Law and Taxation, Columbus, OH 43209-2394. Offers business (LL M); business and taxation (LL M); taxation (LL M); JD/LL M. *Program availability:* Part-time, evening/weekend. *Degree requirements:* For master's, thesis or alternative. *Entrance requirements:* For master's, previous course work in accounting, business law, and taxation. Additional exam requirements/recommendations for international students: Required—TOEFL (minimum score 600 paper-based). Electronic applications accepted.

Capital University, School of Management, Columbus, OH 43209-2394. Offers leadership (MBA); MBA/JD; MBA/MSN. *Accreditation:* ACBSP. *Program availability:* Part-time, evening/weekend. *Entrance requirements:* For master's, 2-3 years of professional work experience. Additional exam requirements/recommendations for international students: Required—TOEFL (minimum score 550 paper-based; 80 iBT); Recommended—IELTS (minimum score 6.5). Electronic applications accepted. Application fee is waived when completed online. *Expenses:* Contact institution. *Faculty research:* Taxation, public policy, health care, management of non-profits.

Capitol Technology University, Graduate Programs, Laurel, MD 20708-9759. Offers business administration (MBA); computer science (MS); electrical engineering (MS); information and telecommunications systems management (MS); information architecture (MS); network security (MS). *Program availability:* Part-time, evening/weekend, online learning. *Entrance requirements:* For master's, minimum GPA of 3.0. Electronic applications accepted.

Cardinal Stritch University, College of Business and Management, Milwaukee, WI 53217-3985. Offers cyber security (MBA); healthcare management (MBA); justice administration (MBA); marketing (MBA). *Accreditation:* ACBSP. *Program availability:* Part-time, evening/weekend, 100% online, blended/hybrid learning. *Degree requirements:* For master's, thesis. *Entrance requirements:* For master's, 3 years of management or related experience, minimum GPA of 2.5. Additional exam requirements/recommendations for international students: Required—TOEFL (minimum score 79 iBT), IELTS (minimum score 6.5). Electronic applications accepted. *Expenses:* Contact institution.

Carleton University, Faculty of Graduate Studies, Faculty of Business, Sprott School of Business, Ottawa, ON K1S 5B6, Canada. Offers business administration (MBA); management (PhD). *Degree requirements:* For master's, thesis optional; for doctorate, comprehensive exam, thesis/dissertation. *Entrance requirements:* For master's, GMAT, honors degree; for doctorate, GMAT. Additional exam requirements/recommendations for international students: Required—TOEFL. *Faculty research:* Business information systems, finance, international business, marketing, production and operations.

Carlow University, College of Health and Wellness, MSN-MBA Dual Degree Program, Pittsburgh, PA 15213-3165. Offers MSN/MBA. *Program availability:* Part-time, 100% online, blended/hybrid learning. *Students:* 34 full-time (28 women), 4 part-time (all women); includes 2 minority (both Black or African American, non-Hispanic/Latino). Average age 34. 8 applicants, 100% accepted, 7 enrolled. *Entrance requirements:* Additional exam requirements/recommendations for international students: Required—TOEFL (minimum score 550 paper-based). *Application deadline:* Applications are processed on a rolling basis. Application fee: $0. Electronic applications accepted. *Expenses: Tuition:* Full-time $13,090; part-time $5100 per semester. *Required fees:* $215; $84. Tuition and fees vary according to course load, degree level and program. *Financial support:* Application deadline: 4/1; applicants required to submit FAFSA. *Unit head:* Dr. Renee Ingel, Program Director, 412-578-6103, E-mail: rmingel@carlow.edu. *Application contact:* Dr. Renee Ingel, Program Director, 412-578-6103, E-mail: rmingel@carlow.edu.
Website: http://www.carlow.edu/MSN-MBA_Dual_Degree.aspx

Carlow University, College of Leadership and Social Change, MBA Program, Pittsburgh, PA 15213-3165. Offers fraud and forensics (MBA); healthcare management (MBA); human resource management (MBA); leadership and management (MBA); project management (MBA). *Program availability:* Part-time, evening/weekend, 100% online, blended/hybrid learning. *Students:* 64 full-time (47 women), 35 part-time (25 women); includes 37 minority (31 Black or African American, non-Hispanic/Latino; 1 Asian, non-Hispanic/Latino; 1 Hispanic/Latino; 4 Two or more races, non-Hispanic/Latino). Average age 33. 34 applicants, 100% accepted, 22 enrolled. In 2018, 38 master's awarded. *Entrance requirements:* For master's, minimum undergraduate GPA of 3.0 (preferred); personal essay; resume; official transcripts; two professional recommendations. Additional exam requirements/recommendations for international students: Required—TOEFL (minimum score 550 paper-based). *Application deadline:* Applications are processed on a rolling basis. Electronic applications accepted. *Expenses: Tuition:* Full-time $13,090; part-time $5100 per semester. *Required fees:* $215; $84. Tuition and fees vary according to course load, degree level and program. *Financial support:* Application deadline: 4/1; applicants required to submit FAFSA. *Unit head:* Dr. Howard Stern, Program Director, MBA Program, 412-578-8828, E-mail: hastern@carlow.edu. *Application contact:* Dr. Howard Stern, Program Director, MBA Program, 412-578-8828, E-mail: hastern@carlow.edu.
Website: http://www.carlow.edu/Business_Administration.aspx

Carnegie Mellon University, Heinz College, School of Public Policy and Management, Master of Entertainment Industry Management Program, Pittsburgh, PA 15213-3891. Offers MEIM. *Accreditation:* AACSB. *Entrance requirements:* For master's, GRE or GMAT, college-level course in advanced algebra/pre-calculus; college-level courses in economics and statistics (recommended). Additional exam requirements/recommendations for international students: Required—TOEFL or IELTS.

Carnegie Mellon University, Heinz College, School of Public Policy and Management, Master of Science Program in Biotechnology and Management, Pittsburgh, PA 15213-3891. Offers MS. *Accreditation:* AACSB. *Entrance requirements:* For master's, GRE or GMAT, college-level course in advanced algebra/pre-calculus; college-level courses in economics and statistics (recommended). Additional exam requirements/recommendations for international students: Required—TOEFL or IELTS.

Carnegie Mellon University, Tepper School of Business, Pittsburgh, PA 15213-3891. Offers accounting (PhD); business management and software engineering (MBMSE); business technologies (PhD); civil engineering and industrial management (MS); computational finance (MSCF); economics (PhD); environmental engineering and management (MEEM); financial economics (PhD); industrial administration (MBA), including administration and public management; marketing (PhD); mathematical finance (PhD); operations management (PhD); operations research (PhD); organizational behavior and theory (PhD); production and operations management (PhD); public policy and management (MS, MSED); software engineering and business management (MS); JD/MS; JD/MSIA; M Div/MS; MOM/MSIA; MSCF/MSIA. JD/MSIA offered jointly with University of Pittsburgh. *Program availability:* Part-time. Terminal master's awarded for partial completion of doctoral program. *Degree requirements:* For doctorate, thesis/dissertation. *Entrance requirements:* For master's, GMAT. Additional exam requirements/recommendations for international students: Required—TOEFL. *Expenses:* Contact institution.

Carroll University, Program in Business Administration, Waukesha, WI 53186-5593. Offers MBA. *Program availability:* Part-time. *Entrance requirements:* For master's, GRE or GMAT (waived if GPA is 2.75 or above), resume, transcripts. Additional exam requirements/recommendations for international students: Required—TOEFL. Electronic applications accepted.

Carson-Newman University, Program in Business Administration, Jefferson City, TN 37760. Offers MBA. *Program availability:* Part-time, evening/weekend, 100% online, blended/hybrid learning. *Faculty:* 4 full-time (2 women), 6 part-time/adjunct (1 woman). *Students:* 93 full-time (39 women), 39 part-time (19 women); includes 18 minority (12 Black or African American, non-Hispanic/Latino; 2 Asian, non-Hispanic/Latino; 3 Hispanic/Latino; 1 Two or more races, non-Hispanic/Latino), 20 international. Average age 31. 70 applicants, 100% accepted, 53 enrolled. In 2018, 34 master's awarded. *Entrance requirements:* Additional exam requirements/recommendations for international students: Recommended—TOEFL (minimum score 79 iBT), IELTS (minimum score 6.5), TSE (minimum score 53). *Application deadline:* For fall admission, 7/15 priority date for domestic students. Applications are processed on a rolling basis. Application fee: $50. *Expenses: Tuition:* Full-time $9036; part-time $502 per credit hour. *Required fees:* $900; $25 per credit hour. $300 per semester. One-time fee: $150. *Financial support:* Federal Work-Study and tuition waivers (full and partial) available. Financial award applicants required to submit FAFSA. *Unit head:* Dr. Kyle J. Kaplan, Director, 865-471-7124, E-mail: kkaplan@cn.edu. *Application contact:* Nilma Stewart, Graduate Admissions and Services Adviser, 865-471-3230, Fax: 865-471-3875, E-mail: adults@cn.edu.
Website: http://www.cn.edu/graduate-adult-studies/programs/business

Case Western Reserve University, Weatherhead School of Management, Executive Doctor of Management Program, Cleveland, OH 44106. Offers management (EDM).

Program availability: Part-time, evening/weekend. *Degree requirements:* For doctorate, thesis/dissertation. *Entrance requirements:* For doctorate, GMAT. Electronic applications accepted. *Expenses:* Contact institution. *Faculty research:* Information technology and design, emotional intelligence and leadership, entrepreneurship, governing of NP organizations, social ethics.

Case Western Reserve University, Weatherhead School of Management, Executive MBA Program, Cleveland, OH 44106. Offers EMBA. *Accreditation:* AACSB. *Entrance requirements:* For master's, GMAT (if candidate does not have an undergraduate degree from an accredited institution), work experience, interview. Electronic applications accepted. *Expenses:* Contact institution.

Case Western Reserve University, Weatherhead School of Management, Full Time MBA Program, Cleveland, OH 44106. Offers MBA, MBA/JD, MBA/M Acc, MBA/MD, MBA/MIM, MBA/MNO, MBA/MSM, MBA/MSN, MBA/MSSA. *Accreditation:* AACSB. *Entrance requirements:* For master's, GMAT, letters of recommendation, interview, work experience. Additional exam requirements/recommendations for international students: Required—TOEFL (minimum score 600 paper-based). Electronic applications accepted. *Expenses: Tuition:* Full-time $45,168; part-time $1939 per credit hour. *Required fees:* $36; $18 per semester. $18 per semester.

Case Western Reserve University, Weatherhead School of Management, Part-time MBA Program, Cleveland, OH 44106. Offers MBA, MBA/M Acc, MBA/MSM, MBA/MSSA. *Accreditation:* AACSB. *Program availability:* Part-time, evening/weekend. *Entrance requirements:* For master's, GMAT, interview, work experience. Additional exam requirements/recommendations for international students: Recommended—TOEFL (minimum score 600 paper-based). Electronic applications accepted. *Expenses: Tuition:* Full-time $45,168; part-time $1939 per credit hour. *Required fees:* $36; $18 per semester. $18 per semester.

The Catholic University of America, Busch School of Business and Economics, Washington, DC 20064. Offers accounting (MS); business analysis (MSBA); integral economic development management (MA); integral economic development policy (MA); management (MS), including Federal contract management, human resource management, leadership and management, project management, sales management. *Program availability:* Part-time. *Faculty:* 38 full-time (8 women), 21 part-time/adjunct (9 women). *Students:* 57 full-time (11 women), 1 (woman) part-time; includes 24 minority (3 Black or African American, non-Hispanic/Latino; 1 American Indian or Alaska Native, non-Hispanic/Latino; 8 Asian, non-Hispanic/Latino; 7 Hispanic/Latino; 5 Two or more races, non-Hispanic/Latino), 1 international. Average age 33. 96 applicants, 79% accepted, 56 enrolled. In 2018, 58 master's awarded. *Degree requirements:* For master's, comprehensive exam (for some programs). *Entrance requirements:* For master's, GRE General Test, statement of purpose, official copies of academic transcripts, three letters of recommendation. Additional exam requirements/recommendations for international students: Required—TOEFL (minimum score 550 paper-based; 80 iBT). *Application deadline:* For fall admission, 7/15 priority date for domestic students, 7/1 for international students; for spring admission, 11/15 priority date for domestic students, 11/1 for international students. Applications are processed on a rolling basis. Application fee: $55. Electronic applications accepted. *Expenses:* Contact institution. *Financial support:* Fellowships, research assistantships, teaching assistantships, Federal Work-Study, scholarships/grants, tuition waivers (full and partial), and unspecified assistantships available. Financial award application deadline: 2/1; financial award applicants required to submit FAFSA. *Faculty research:* Integrity of the marketing process, economics of energy and the environment, emerging markets, social change, international finance and economic development. *Unit head:* Dr. Andrew Abela, Dean, 202-319-6130, E-mail: DeanAbela@cua.edu. *Application contact:* Dr. Steven Brown, Director of Graduate Admissions, 202-319-5057, Fax: 202-319-6533, E-mail: cua-admissions@cua.edu.
Website: https://business.catholic.edu/

The Catholic University of America, Metropolitan School of Professional Studies, Washington, DC 20064. Offers emergency service administration (MS); health administration (MHA); social service administration (MS). *Program availability:* Part-time, evening/weekend, 100% online. *Faculty:* 40 part-time/adjunct (15 women). *Students:* 39 full-time (24 women), 62 part-time (32 women); includes 44 minority (29 Black or African American, non-Hispanic/Latino; 2 Asian, non-Hispanic/Latino; 8 Hispanic/Latino; 5 Two or more races, non-Hispanic/Latino), 26 international. Average age 34. 91 applicants, 87% accepted, 55 enrolled. In 2018, 32 master's awarded. *Degree requirements:* For master's, minimum GPA of 3.0, capstone course. *Entrance requirements:* For master's, statement of purpose, official copies of academic transcripts, three letters of recommendation, resume. Additional exam requirements/recommendations for international students: Required—TOEFL (minimum score 550 paper-based; 80 iBT). *Application deadline:* For fall admission, 7/15 priority date for domestic students, 7/1 for international students; for spring admission, 11/15 priority date for domestic students, 11/1 for international students. Applications are processed on a rolling basis. Application fee: $55. Electronic applications accepted. *Expenses:* Contact institution. *Financial support:* Scholarships/grants available. Financial award application deadline: 3/15; financial award applicants required to submit FAFSA. *Unit head:* Dr. Vince Kiernan, Dean, 202-319-5256, Fax: 202-319-6260, E-mail: kiernan@cua.edu. *Application contact:* Dr. Steven Brown, Director of Graduate Admissions, 202-319-5057, Fax: 202-319-6533, E-mail: cua-admissions@cua.edu.
Website: https://metro.catholic.edu/

Cedar Crest College, Program in Business Administration, Allentown, PA 18104-6196. Offers MBA. *Program availability:* Part-time, evening/weekend, blended/hybrid learning. *Faculty:* 2 full-time (1 woman), 10 part-time/adjunct (3 women). *Students:* 18 full-time (15 women), 24 part-time (14 women); includes 8 minority (3 Black or African American, non-Hispanic/Latino; 2 Asian, non-Hispanic/Latino; 3 Hispanic/Latino), 1 international. Average age 36. 27 applicants, 81% accepted, 20 enrolled. In 2018, 13 master's awarded. *Entrance requirements:* For master's, GRE or GMAT, two letters of recommendation, copy of current resume, official transcripts. *Application deadline:* Applications are processed on a rolling basis. Electronic applications accepted. *Expenses:* 799 per credit. *Unit head:* Michael Zalot, Program Director MBA, 610-437-4471 Ext. 4453, E-mail: michael.zalot@cedarcrest.edu. *Application contact:* Nancy Wunderly, Director of School of Adult and Graduate Education, 610-437-4471, E-mail: sage@cedarcrest.edu.
Website: http://mba.cedarcrest.edu/

Cedarville University, Graduate Programs, Cedarville, OH 45314. Offers business administration (MBA); family nurse practitioner (MSN); global ministry (M Div); global public health nursing (MSN); healthcare administration (MBA); ministry (M Min); nurse educator (MSN); operations management (MBA); pharmacy (Pharm D). *Program availability:* Part-time, evening/weekend, 100% online, blended/hybrid learning. *Faculty:* 55 full-time (19 women), 18 part-time/adjunct (8 women). *Students:* 341 full-time (201 women), 60 part-time (41 women); includes 88 minority (51 Black or African American, non-Hispanic/Latino; 2 American Indian or Alaska Native, non-Hispanic/Latino; 22 Asian, non-Hispanic/Latino; 2 Hispanic/Latino; 11 Two or more races, non-Hispanic/Latino), 3 international. Average age 26. 354 applicants, 38% accepted, 113 enrolled. In 2018, 65 master's, 34 doctorates awarded. *Degree requirements:* For master's, portfolio; for doctorate, comprehensive exam. *Entrance requirements:* For master's, GRE, 2 professional recommendations; for doctorate, PCAT, professional recommendation from a practicing pharmacist or current employer/supervisor, resume, essay, interview. Additional exam requirements/recommendations for international students: Required—TOEFL (minimum score 550 paper-based; 80 iBT). *Application deadline:* For fall admission, 5/1 priority date for domestic and international students; for spring admission, 11/1 priority date for domestic and international students. Applications are processed on a rolling basis. Application fee: $0. Electronic applications accepted. *Expenses: Tuition:* Full-time $12,594; part-time $566 per credit. One-time fee: $100 full-time. Tuition and fees vary according to degree level and program. *Financial support:* Scholarships/grants and unspecified assistantships available. Support available to part-time students. Financial award application deadline: 1/30; financial award applicants required to submit FAFSA. *Faculty research:* Establishing competencies of clinical reasoning for nursing students in Taiwan, social determinants of health in pediatric primary care, meeting needs of palliative care populations, natural product utility in cancer, monoclonal antibodies directed at angiogenesis regulation. *Unit head:* Dr. Janice Supplee, Dean of Graduate Studies, 937-766-7700, E-mail: suppleej@cedarville.edu. *Application contact:* Alexis McKay, Director of Graduate Admissions, 937-766-7878, Fax: 937-766-7700, E-mail: amckay@cedarville.edu.
Website: https://www.cedarville.edu/Admissions/Graduate/Graduate-Programs.aspx

Centenary College of Louisiana, Graduate Programs, Frost School of Business, Shreveport, LA 71104. Offers MBA. *Program availability:* Part-time, evening/weekend. *Degree requirements:* For master's, thesis. *Entrance requirements:* For master's, GMAT, minimum 5 years of professional/managerial experience. *Expenses:* Contact institution. *Faculty research:* Leadership, organizational change strategy, market behavior, executive compensation.

Centenary University, Program in Business Administration, Hackettstown, NJ 07840-2100. Offers MBA. *Program availability:* Part-time, evening/weekend, online learning. *Entrance requirements:* For master's, GMAT.

Central Connecticut State University, School of Graduate Studies, School of Business, Program in Business Administration, New Britain, CT 06050-4010. Offers MBA. *Program availability:* Part-time, evening/weekend. *Faculty:* 11 full-time (4 women), 1 (woman) part-time/adjunct. *Students:* 7 full-time (2 women), 218 part-time (96 women); includes 75 minority (32 Black or African American, non-Hispanic/Latino; 15 Asian, non-Hispanic/Latino; 24 Hispanic/Latino; 4 Two or more races, non-Hispanic/Latino), 2 international. Average age 31. 105 applicants, 77% accepted, 66 enrolled. In 2018, 60 master's awarded. *Degree requirements:* For master's, thesis or alternative. *Entrance requirements:* For master's, GMAT or GRE, minimum undergraduate GPA of 2.7, resume. Additional exam requirements/recommendations for international students: Required—TOEFL (minimum score 550 paper-based; 79 iBT); Recommended—IELTS (minimum score 6.5). *Application deadline:* For fall admission, 6/1 for domestic students, 5/1 for international students; for spring admission, 11/1 for domestic and international students. Applications are processed on a rolling basis. Application fee: $50. Electronic applications accepted. *Expenses: Tuition, area resident:* Full-time $7027; part-time $388 per credit. Tuition, state resident: full-time $9750; part-time $388 per credit. Tuition, nonresident: full-time $18,102; part-time $388 per credit. *International tuition:* $18,102 full-time. *Required fees:* $266 per semester. *Financial support:* In 2018–19, 15 students received support. Career-related internships or fieldwork, Federal Work-Study, and scholarships/grants available. Support available to part-time students. Financial award application deadline: 3/1; financial award applicants required to submit FAFSA. *Unit head:* Dr. Christopher Lee, Program Director, 860-832-3288, E-mail: christopher.lee@ccsu.edu. *Application contact:* Patricia Gardner, Associate Director of Graduate Admissions, 860-832-2350, Fax: 860-832-2362.
Website: http://www.ccsu.edu/mba/

Central European University, Department of Economics, 1051, Hungary. Offers business administration (PhD); business analytics (M Sc); economic policy in global markets (MA); economics (MA, PhD); finance (MS); global economic relations (MA); technology management and innovation (MS). *Program availability:* Part-time. *Degree requirements:* For master's, one foreign language, thesis; for doctorate, one foreign language, comprehensive exam, thesis/dissertation. *Entrance requirements:* For master's and doctorate, interview. Additional exam requirements/recommendations for international students: Required—TOEFL (minimum score 570 paper-based); Recommended—IELTS (minimum score 6.5). Electronic applications accepted. *Faculty research:* Economic theory (microeconomics and macroeconomics) and econometrics, as well as study of many applied fields, including labor economics, health economics and economics of education, industrial organization, monetary economics, international economics, law and economics, comparative institutional economics, corporate governance, and economics of transition.

Central Michigan University, Central Michigan University Global Campus, Program in Business Administration, Mount Pleasant, MI 48859. Offers enterprise resource planning (MBA, Certificate); human resource management (MBA); logistics management (MBA, Certificate); marketing (MBA); value-driven organization (MBA). *Program availability:* Part-time, evening/weekend. *Entrance requirements:* For master's, GMAT.

Central Michigan University, College of Graduate Studies, College of Business Administration, MBA Program, Mount Pleasant, MI 48859. Offers accounting (MBA); business economics (MBA); consulting (MBA); finance (MBA); general business (MBA); human resource management (MBA); information systems (MBA); international business (MBA); logistics management (MBA); marketing (MBA); value-driven organization (MBA). *Program availability:* Part-time, evening/weekend, online learning. Electronic applications accepted. *Faculty research:* Accounting, consulting, international business, marketing, information systems.

Central Michigan University, College of Graduate Studies, Interdisciplinary Administration Programs, Mount Pleasant, MI 48859. Offers acquisitions administration (MSA, Graduate Certificate); general administration (MSA, Graduate Certificate); health services administration (MSA, Graduate Certificate); human resource administration (Graduate Certificate); human resources administration (MSA); information resource management (MSA, Graduate Certificate); international administration (MSA, Graduate Certificate); leadership (MSA, Graduate Certificate); public administration (MSA, Graduate Certificate); research administration (Graduate Certificate); sport administration (MSA). *Accreditation:* AACSB. *Program availability:* Part-time, evening/weekend, online learning. *Degree requirements:* For master's, thesis or alternative. *Entrance requirements:* For master's, bachelor's degree with minimum GPA of 2.7. Electronic applications accepted. *Faculty research:* Interdisciplinary studies in acquisitions administration, health services administration, sport administration, recreation and park administration, and international administration.

Chadron State College, School of Professional and Graduate Studies, Department of Business and Economics, Chadron, NE 69337. Offers MBA. *Accreditation:* ACBSP. *Program availability:* Part-time, evening/weekend, online learning. *Degree requirements:* For master's, thesis optional. *Entrance requirements:* For master's, GMAT, minimum GPA of 2.75 or 12 graduate hours at CSC with minimum GPA of 3.25. Additional exam requirements/recommendations for international students: Required—TOEFL. Electronic applications accepted.

Business Administration and Management—General

Chaminade University of Honolulu, Graduate, Program in Business Administration, Honolulu, HI 96816-1578. Offers accounting (MBA); business (MBA); island business (MBA); not-for-profit (MBA). *Program availability:* Part-time, evening/weekend, 100% online, blended/hybrid learning. *Faculty:* 8 full-time (4 women), 6 part-time/adjunct (2 women). *Students:* 63 full-time (30 women), 45 part-time (29 women); includes 81 minority (8 Black or African American, non-Hispanic/Latino; 4 American Indian or Alaska Native, non-Hispanic/Latino; 34 Asian, non-Hispanic/Latino; 3 Hispanic/Latino; 32 Native Hawaiian or other Pacific Islander, non-Hispanic/Latino), 3 international. Average age 32. 25 applicants, 68% accepted, 15 enrolled. In 2018, 47 master's awarded. *Entrance requirements:* For master's, minimum GPA of 3.0, official transcripts, two years or more of work experience. Additional exam requirements/recommendations for international students: Required—TOEFL (minimum score 550 paper-based; 79 iBT). *Application deadline:* Applications are processed on a rolling basis. Application fee: $40. Electronic applications accepted. *Expenses:* $980 per credit; $93 fee per online course. *Financial support:* Applicants required to submit FAFSA. *Unit head:* Dr. Scott J. Schroeder, Director, 808-739-4612, Fax: 808-735-4734, E-mail: mba@chaminade.edu. *Application contact:* Dr. Scott J. Schroeder, Director, 808-739-4612, Fax: 808-735-4734, E-mail: mba@chaminade.edu.
Website: https://chaminade.edu/academic-program/mba/

Champlain College, Graduate Studies, Burlington, VT 05402-0670. Offers business (MBA); digital forensic science (MS); early childhood education (M Ed); emergent media (MFA, MS); executive leadership (MS); health care administration (MS); information security operations (MS); law (MS); mediation and applied conflict studies (MS). MS in emergent media program held in Shanghai. *Program availability:* Part-time, online learning. *Degree requirements:* For master's, capstone project. *Entrance requirements:* Additional exam requirements/recommendations for international students: Required—TOEFL (minimum score 550 paper-based; 80 iBT). Electronic applications accepted.

Chapman University, The George L. Argyros School of Business and Economics, Orange, CA 92866. Offers accounting (MS); behavioral and computational economics (MS); business administration (Exec MBA, MBA); JD/MBA. *Accreditation:* AACSB. *Program availability:* Part-time, evening/weekend. Electronic applications accepted. *Expenses:* Contact institution.

Charleston Southern University, College of Business, Charleston, SC 29423-8087. Offers accounting (MBA); finance (MBA); general management (MBA); human resource management (MS); leadership (MBA); management information systems (MBA); organizational leadership (MA). *Program availability:* Part-time, evening/weekend. *Degree requirements:* For master's, thesis optional. *Entrance requirements:* For master's, GMAT. Additional exam requirements/recommendations for international students: Required—TOEFL (minimum score 550 paper-based; 79 iBT). Electronic applications accepted.

Charter College, Program in Business Administration, Vancouver, WA 98683. Offers MBA. *Program availability:* Online learning. *Entrance requirements:* For master's, bachelor's degree in business-related field, official transcripts with minimum GPA of 2.5, three letters of recommendation, current copy of resume or curriculum vitae.

Chatham University, Program in Business Administration, Pittsburgh, PA 15232-2826. Offers business administration (MBA); healthcare management (MBA); sustainability (MBA); women's leadership (MBA). *Program availability:* Part-time, evening/weekend. *Entrance requirements:* For master's, minimum GPA of 3.0, letters of recommendation. Additional exam requirements/recommendations for international students: Required—TOEFL (minimum score 600 paper-based; 100 iBT), IELTS (minimum score 7), TWE. Electronic applications accepted. Application fee is waived when completed online. *Expenses:* Contact institution.

Christian Brothers University, School of Business, Memphis, TN 38104-5581. Offers accountancy (M Acc); business (MBA); international business (MIB); project management (Certificate); MBA/MIB. *Program availability:* Part-time, evening/weekend. *Entrance requirements:* For master's, GMAT, GRE. Additional exam requirements/recommendations for international students: Required—TOEFL.

The Citadel, The Military College of South Carolina, Citadel Graduate College, Tommy and Victoria Baker School of Business, Charleston, SC 29409. Offers MBA. *Accreditation:* AACSB. *Program availability:* Part-time, evening/weekend, 100% online, blended/hybrid learning. *Entrance requirements:* For master's, GMAT or GRE (5 years old or less), 2 letters of recommendation from professor, supervisor, military official, or someone familiar with applicant's academic or professional work; resume detailing professional work experience. Additional exam requirements/recommendations for international students: Required—TOEFL (minimum score 550 paper-based; 79 iBT). Electronic applications accepted. *Expenses:* Tuition, state resident: part-time $595 per credit hour. Tuition, nonresident: part-time $1020 per credit hour. *Required fees:* $90 per term.

City College of the City University of New York, Graduate School, Colin Powell School for Civic and Global Leadership, Department of Economics and Business, New York, NY 10031-9198. Offers economics (MA). *Program availability:* Part-time. *Degree requirements:* For master's, comprehensive exam, proficiency in a foreign language or advanced statistics. *Entrance requirements:* Additional exam requirements/recommendations for international students: Required—TOEFL (minimum score 550 paper-based; 79 iBT). Electronic applications accepted. *Faculty research:* International economics, health, banking.

City University of Seattle, Graduate Division, School of Management, Seattle, WA 98121. Offers accounting (Certificate); change leadership (MBA, Certificate); computer systems (MS); finance (Certificate); financial management (MBA); general management (MBA); general management-Europe (MBA); global marketing (MBA); human resources management (Certificate); individualized study (MBA); information security (MS); information systems (MBA); leadership (MA); marketing (MBA, Certificate); project management (MBA, MS, Certificate); sustainable business (Certificate); technology management (MBA, Certificate). *Program availability:* Part-time, evening/weekend, online learning. *Degree requirements:* For master's, comprehensive exam (for some programs), thesis (for some programs). *Entrance requirements:* For master's, baccalaureate degree or equivalent from an accredited or otherwise recognized institution. Additional exam requirements/recommendations for international students: Required—TOEFL (minimum score 567 paper-based; 87 iBT); Recommended—IELTS. Electronic applications accepted.

Claflin University, Graduate Programs, Orangeburg, SC 29115. Offers biotechnology (MS); business administration (MBA). *Program availability:* Part-time. *Degree requirements:* For master's, comprehensive exam, thesis. *Entrance requirements:* For master's, GRE, GMAT, baccalaureate degree, 3 letters of recommendation, resume, statement of purpose. Additional exam requirements/recommendations for international students: Recommended—TOEFL (minimum score 550 paper-based).

Claremont Graduate University, Graduate Programs, Peter F. Drucker and Masatoshi Ito Graduate School of Management, Claremont, CA 91711-6160. Offers EMBA, MA, MBA, MS, PhD, Certificate, MBA/MA, MBA/PhD, MS/MBA. *Program availability:* Part-time. *Entrance requirements:* For doctorate, GMAT or GRE General Test. Additional exam requirements/recommendations for international students: Required—TOEFL (minimum score 75 iBT). Electronic applications accepted. *Expenses:* Contact institution. *Faculty research:* Strategy and leadership, brand management, cost management and control, organizational transformation, general management.

Claremont Graduate University, Graduate Programs, School of Social Science, Policy and Evaluation, Program in Politics, Economics, and Business, Claremont, CA 91711-6160. Offers MA. *Program availability:* Part-time. *Entrance requirements:* For master's, GRE General Test. Additional exam requirements/recommendations for international students: Required—TOEFL (minimum score 75 iBT). Electronic applications accepted.

Clarion University of Pennsylvania, College of Business Administration and Information Sciences, Master of Business Administration Program, Clarion, PA 16214. Offers accounting (MBA); finance (MBA); health care administration (MBA); innovation and entrepreneurship (MBA); non-profit business (MBA). *Accreditation:* AACSB. *Program availability:* Part-time, evening/weekend, online only, 100% online. *Faculty:* 7 full-time (0 women), 1 part-time/adjunct (0 women). *Students:* 21 full-time (7 women), 67 part-time (34 women); includes 11 minority (5 Black or African American, non-Hispanic/Latino; 5 Hispanic/Latino; 1 Two or more races, non-Hispanic/Latino), 2 international. Average age 31. 90 applicants, 51% accepted, 38 enrolled. In 2018, 39 master's awarded. *Entrance requirements:* For master's, If GPA is below 3.0 submit the GMAT, minimum QPA of 2.75. Additional exam requirements/recommendations for international students: Required—TOEFL (minimum score 550 paper-based; 80 iBT), Or IELTS score of at least 7.0. Bachelor's degree accredited U.S. college or university is acceptable evidence of English language proficiency. *Application deadline:* For fall admission, 8/1 priority date for domestic students, 7/15 priority date for international students; for winter admission, 11/1 priority date for domestic students; for spring admission, 12/1 priority date for domestic students, 11/15 priority date for international students; for summer admission, 4/1 priority date for domestic students. Applications are processed on a rolling basis. Application fee: $40. Electronic applications accepted. *Expenses: Tuition, area resident:* Part-time $516 per credit hour. Tuition, state resident: part-time $516 per credit hour. Tuition, nonresident: part-time $774 per credit hour. *Required fees:* $159 per credit hour. One-time fee: $50 part-time. Tuition and fees vary according to degree level, campus/location and program. *Financial support:* Federal Work-Study, institutionally sponsored loans, and scholarships/grants available. Financial award application deadline: 3/1; financial award applicants required to submit FAFSA. *Unit head:* Juanice Vega, Assistant to the Dean, 814-393-2600, Fax: 814-393-1910, E-mail: mba@clarion.edu. *Application contact:* Susan Staub, Graduate Admissions Counselor, 814-393-2337, Fax: 814-393-2722, E-mail: gradstudies@clarion.edu.
Website: http://www.clarion.edu/admissions/graduate/index.html

Clark Atlanta University, School of Business Administration, Department of Business Administration, Atlanta, GA 30314. Offers MBA. *Accreditation:* AACSB. *Program availability:* Part-time. *Degree requirements:* For master's, thesis (for some programs). *Entrance requirements:* For master's, GMAT. Additional exam requirements/recommendations for international students: Required—TOEFL (minimum score 500 paper-based; 61 iBT). Electronic applications accepted.

Clarke University, Graduate Business Programs, Dubuque, IA 52001-3198. Offers MBA, MOL. *Program availability:* Part-time, evening/weekend, blended/hybrid learning. *Entrance requirements:* For master's, GMAT if GPA under 3.0, minimum GPA of 2.8, previous undergraduate course work in business, two recommendations, resume, essay, interview. Additional exam requirements/recommendations for international students: Required—TOEFL (minimum score 550 paper-based; 80 iBT), IELTS (minimum score 6.5). Electronic applications accepted. *Expenses:* Contact institution.

Clarkson University, David D. Reh School of Business, Master's Program in Business Administration, Potsdam, NY 13699. Offers business administration (MBA); business fundamentals (Advanced Certificate); global supply chain management (Advanced Certificate); human resource management (Advanced Certificate); management and leadership (Advanced Certificate). *Accreditation:* AACSB. *Program availability:* Part-time, evening/weekend, 100% online, blended/hybrid learning. *Faculty:* 36 full-time (7 women), 8 part-time/adjunct (2 women). *Students:* 68 full-time (30 women), 63 part-time (29 women); includes 17 minority (2 Black or African American, non-Hispanic/Latino; 2 American Indian or Alaska Native, non-Hispanic/Latino; 6 Asian, non-Hispanic/Latino; 4 Hispanic/Latino; 3 Two or more races, non-Hispanic/Latino), 11 international. 119 applicants, 74% accepted, 67 enrolled. In 2018, 89 master's, 2 other advanced degrees awarded. *Entrance requirements:* For master's, GRE or GMAT. Additional exam requirements/recommendations for international students: Required—TOEFL (minimum score 550 paper-based, 80 iBT) or IELTS (6.5). *Application deadline:* Applications are processed on a rolling basis. Application fee: $50. Electronic applications accepted. *Expenses: Tuition:* Full-time $24,984; part-time $1388 per credit hour. *Required fees:* $225. Tuition and fees vary according to campus/location and program. *Financial support:* Scholarships/grants available. *Unit head:* Dr. Dennis Yu, Associate Dean of Graduate Programs & Research, 315-268-2300, E-mail: dyu@clarkson.edu. *Application contact:* Dan Capogna, Director of Graduate Admissions & Recruitment, 518-631-9910, E-mail: graduate@clarkson.edu.
Website: https://www.clarkson.edu/academics/graduate

Clark University, Graduate School, Graduate School of Management, Business Administration Program, Worcester, MA 01610-1477. Offers accounting (MBA); finance (MBA); information management and business analytics (MBA); management (MBA); marketing (MBA); social change (MBA); sustainability (MBA). *Accreditation:* AACSB. *Program availability:* Part-time, evening/weekend. *Degree requirements:* For master's, thesis optional. *Entrance requirements:* For master's, GMAT or GRE, 2 references, resume or curriculum vitae, personal statement. Additional exam requirements/recommendations for international students: Required—TOEFL (minimum score 575 paper-based; 90 iBT), IELTS (minimum score 6.5). Electronic applications accepted. *Expenses:* Contact institution. *Faculty research:* Marketing, accounting, human resource management, management information systems, business finance.

Clark University, Graduate School, Graduate School of Management, Program in Management, Worcester, MA 01610-1477. Offers MSM. *Program availability:* Part-time, evening/weekend. *Entrance requirements:* For master's, GMAT or GRE, 2 references, resume or curriculum vitae, personal statement. Additional exam requirements/recommendations for international students: Required—TOEFL (minimum score 575 paper-based; 90 iBT), IELTS (minimum score 6.5). Electronic applications accepted. *Expenses:* Contact institution.

Clayton State University, School of Graduate Studies, College of Business, Program in Business Administration, Morrow, GA 30260-0285. Offers accounting (MBA); human resource leadership (MBA); international business (MBA); sports and entertainment management (MBA); supply chain management (MBA). *Accreditation:* AACSB. *Program availability:* Part-time, evening/weekend. *Degree requirements:* For master's, thesis. *Entrance requirements:* For master's, GMAT, 3 letters of recommendation; statement of purpose; 2 official transcripts. Additional exam requirements/recommendations for international students: Required—TOEFL (minimum score 550 paper-based; 80 iBT). Electronic applications accepted. *Expenses:* Contact institution.

Cleary University, Online Program in Business Administration, Howell, MI 48843. Offers analytics, technology, and innovation (MBA, Graduate Certificate); financial planning (Graduate Certificate); global leadership (MBA, Graduate Certificate); health

care leadership (MBA, Graduate Certificate). *Program availability:* Part-time, evening/weekend, online learning. *Degree requirements:* For master's, thesis. *Entrance requirements:* For master's, bachelor's degree; minimum GPA of 2.5; professional resume indicating minimum of 2 years of management or related experience; undergraduate degree from accredited college or university with at least 18 quarter hours (or 12 semester hours) of accounting study (for MBA in accounting). Additional exam requirements/recommendations for international students: Required—TOEFL (minimum score 550 paper-based; 79 iBT), Michigan English Language Assessment Battery (minimum score 75). Electronic applications accepted.

Clemson University, Graduate School, College of Business, Department of Management, Clemson, SC 29634. Offers business administration (PhD), including management information systems, strategy, entrepreneurship and organizational behavior, supply chain and operations management; management (MS). *Accreditation:* AACSB. *Faculty:* 26 full-time (9 women). *Students:* 14 full-time (5 women), 4 part-time (2 women); includes 1 minority (Asian, non-Hispanic/Latino), 10 international. Average age 30. 53 applicants, 36% accepted, 8 enrolled. In 2018, 2 master's, 4 doctorates awarded. Terminal master's awarded for partial completion of doctoral program. *Degree requirements:* For master's, comprehensive exam, thesis optional; for doctorate, comprehensive exam, thesis/dissertation. *Entrance requirements:* For master's and doctorate, GMAT or GRE General Test, unofficial transcripts, two letters of reference, curriculum vitae. Additional exam requirements/recommendations for international students: Required—TOEFL (minimum score 80 paper-based; 94 iBT); Recommended—IELTS (minimum score 7), TSE (minimum score 64). *Application deadline:* For fall admission, 4/15 priority date for international students; for spring admission, 10/15 priority date for international students. Applications are processed on a rolling basis. Application fee: $80 ($90 for international students). Electronic applications accepted. *Expenses:* $6823 per semester full-time resident, $14023 per semester full-time non-resident, $833 per credit hour part-time resident, $1731 per credit hour part-time non-resident, online $1264 per credit hour, $4938 doctoral programs resident, $10405 doctoral programs non-resident, $1144 full-time graduate assistant, other fees may apply per session. *Financial support:* In 2018–19, 10 students received support, including 1 fellowship with full and partial tuition reimbursement available (averaging $1,500 per year), 6 research assistantships with full and partial tuition reimbursements available (averaging $25,000 per year), 17 teaching assistantships with full and partial tuition reimbursements available (averaging $25,000 per year); career-related internships or fieldwork and unspecified assistantships also available. *Faculty research:* Effective use of information technology in business, manufacturing and service operations strategy, lean operations and quality management, healthcare operations, behavioral market design. *Total annual research expenditures:* $131,333. *Unit head:* Dr. Craig Wallace, Department Chair, 864-656-9963, E-mail: CW74@clemson.edu. *Application contact:* Dr. Janis Miller, Graduate Program Coordinator, 864-656-3757, E-mail: janism@clemson.edu.
Website: https://www.clemson.edu/business/departments/management/

Clemson University, Graduate School, College of Business, Master of Business Administration Program, Greenville, SC 29601. Offers business administration (MBA); business analytics (MBA); entrepreneurship and innovation (MBA). *Accreditation:* AACSB. *Program availability:* Part-time, evening/weekend, 100% online. *Faculty:* 2 full-time (1 woman), 10 part-time/adjunct (1 woman). *Students:* 113 full-time (55 women), 406 part-time (135 women); includes 88 minority (42 Black or African American, non-Hispanic/Latino; 2 American Indian or Alaska Native, non-Hispanic/Latino; 12 Asian, non-Hispanic/Latino; 22 Hispanic/Latino; 1 Native Hawaiian or other Pacific Islander, non-Hispanic/Latino; 9 Two or more races, non-Hispanic/Latino), 13 international. Average age 31. 404 applicants, 91% accepted, 261 enrolled. In 2018, 209 master's awarded. *Entrance requirements:* For master's, GMAT, resume, unofficial transcripts, personal statement, letters of recommendation. Additional exam requirements/recommendations for international students: Required—TOEFL (minimum score 80 paper-based; 80 iBT); Recommended—IELTS (minimum score 6.5), TSE (minimum score 54). *Application deadline:* For fall admission, 4/15 for international students; for spring admission, 10/15 for international students. Applications are processed on a rolling basis. Application fee: $80 ($90 for international students). Electronic applications accepted. *Expenses:* $9901 per semester full-time resident, $16051 per semester full-time non-resident, $1031 per credit hour part-time resident, $1283 per credit hour part-time non-resident, Concentration in Entrepreneurship & Innovation: $11694 full time all students. *Unit head:* Dr. Greg Pickett, Director and Associate Dean, 864-656-3975, E-mail: pgregor@clemson.edu. *Application contact:* Jane Layton, Academic Program Director, 864-656-8175, E-mail: elayton@clemson.edu.
Website: https://www.clemson.edu/business/departments/mba/

Cleveland State University, College of Graduate Studies, Monte Ahuja College of Business, Doctor of Business Administration Program, Cleveland, OH 44115. Offers information systems (DBA); marketing (DBA). *Accreditation:* AACSB. *Program availability:* Part-time, evening/weekend. *Faculty:* 50 full-time (11 women). *Students:* 8 full-time (4 women), 20 part-time (11 women); includes 7 minority (3 Black or African American, non-Hispanic/Latino; 3 Asian, non-Hispanic/Latino; 1 Hispanic/Latino), 7 international. Average age 37. In 2018, 2 doctorates awarded. *Degree requirements:* For doctorate, comprehensive exam, thesis/dissertation, oral dissertation defense. *Entrance requirements:* For doctorate, GMAT, MBA or equivalent. Additional exam requirements/recommendations for international students: Required—TOEFL (minimum score 550 paper-based; 78 iBT). *Application deadline:* For fall admission, 2/1 for domestic and international students. Application fee: $40. Electronic applications accepted. *Expenses:* Tuition, state resident: full-time $7232.55; part-time $6676 per credit hour. Tuition, nonresident: full-time $12,375. *International tuition:* $18,914 full-time. *Required fees:* $80; $80 $40. Tuition and fees vary according to program. *Financial support:* In 2018–19, 5 research assistantships with full tuition reimbursements (averaging $12,700 per year), 4 teaching assistantships with full tuition reimbursements (averaging $12,700 per year) were awarded; tuition waivers (full) and unspecified assistantships also available. Financial award applicants required to submit FAFSA. *Faculty research:* Supply chain management, international business, strategic management, risk analysis, consumer behavior. *Unit head:* Dr. Raj Shekhar G. Javalgi, Director, 216-687-3786, Fax: 216-687-9354, E-mail: r.javalgi@csuohio.edu. *Application contact:* Melinda J. Arnold, Administrative Secretary, 216-687-6952, Fax: 216-687-9257, E-mail: m.arnold@csuohio.edu.
Website: http://www.csuohio.edu/business/academics/mbajuris-doctor

Cleveland State University, College of Graduate Studies, Monte Ahuja College of Business, MBA Programs, Cleveland, OH 44115. Offers AMBA, EMBA, MBA, JD/MBA, MSN/MBA. Programs also offered at Progressive Insurance Corporation, The Cleveland Clinic, and Metro Health Medical Center. *Accreditation:* AACSB. *Program availability:* Part-time, evening/weekend, online learning. *Faculty:* 33 full-time (9 women), 16 part-time/adjunct (2 women). *Students:* 275 full-time (127 women), 371 part-time (161 women); includes 116 minority (58 Black or African American, non-Hispanic/Latino; 1 American Indian or Alaska Native, non-Hispanic/Latino; 32 Asian, non-Hispanic/Latino; 21 Hispanic/Latino; 4 Two or more races, non-Hispanic/Latino), 122 international. Average age 29. 674 applicants, 48% accepted, 126 enrolled. In 2018, 223 master's awarded. *Degree requirements:* For master's, variable foreign language requirement, comprehensive exam (for some programs), thesis (for some programs). *Entrance requirements:* For master's, GMAT or GRE, minimum cumulative GPA of 2.75 from

bachelor's degree; resume, statement of purpose and two letters of reference (for health care administration MBA). Additional exam requirements/recommendations for international students: Required—TOEFL (minimum score 550 paper-based; 78 iBT). *Application deadline:* For fall admission, 6/1 priority date for domestic students, 6/1 for international students; for spring admission, 11/1 priority date for domestic students, 11/1 for international students. Applications are processed on a rolling basis. Application fee: $40. Electronic applications accepted. *Expenses:* Tuition, state resident: full-time $7232.55; part-time $6676 per credit hour. Tuition, nonresident: full-time $12,375. *International tuition:* $18,914 full-time. *Required fees:* $80; $80 $40. Tuition and fees vary according to program. *Financial support:* In 2018–19, 594 students received support, including 45 research assistantships with tuition reimbursements available (averaging $6,960 per year), 1 teaching assistantship with tuition reimbursement available (averaging $7,800 per year); tuition waivers (full) and unspecified assistantships also available. Financial award application deadline: 5/15; financial award applicants required to submit FAFSA. *Faculty research:* Accounting and finance, management and organizational behavior, marketing, computer information systems, international business. *Total annual research expenditures:* $70,000. *Unit head:* Ronald John Mickler, Jr., Acting Assistant Director, Graduate Programs, 216-687-3730, Fax: 216-687-5311, E-mail: cbacsu@csuohio.edu. *Application contact:* Kenneth Dippong, Director, Student Services, 216-523-7545, Fax: 216-687-9354, E-mail: k.dippong@csuohio.edu.
Website: http://www.csuohio.edu/cba/

Coastal Carolina University, E. Craig Wall, Sr. College of Business Administration, Conway, SC 29528-6054. Offers accounting (M Acc); business administration (MBA); business foundations (Certificate); fraud examination (Certificate). *Accreditation:* AACSB. *Program availability:* Part-time, evening/weekend, 100% online, blended/hybrid learning. *Entrance requirements:* For master's, GMAT, official transcripts, 2 letters of recommendation, resume, baccalaureate degree, statement of purpose, minimum cumulative GPA of 3.0 overall from completed undergraduate and graduate coursework; for Certificate, GMAT, official transcripts; 2 letters of recommendation; baccalaureate degree or evidence of receiving a CPA certificate, law degree, or admittance to an accredited law school. Additional exam requirements/recommendations for international students: Required—TOEFL (minimum score 550 paper-based; 79 iBT), IELTS (minimum score 6.5). Electronic applications accepted.

Coker College, Graduate Programs, Hartsville, SC 29550. Offers college athletic administration (MS); criminal and social justice policy (MS); curriculum and instructional technology (M Ed); literacy studies (M Ed); management and leadership (MS). *Program availability:* Part-time, 100% online. *Faculty:* 15 full-time (7 women), 7 part-time/adjunct (3 women). *Students:* 144 full-time (100 women), 6 part-time (2 women); includes 42 minority (33 Black or African American, non-Hispanic/Latino; 1 Asian, non-Hispanic/Latino; 4 Hispanic/Latino; 4 Two or more races, non-Hispanic/Latino). Average age 33. 120 applicants, 61% accepted, 65 enrolled. In 2018, 92 master's awarded. *Entrance requirements:* For master's, 1. Undergraduate overall gpa of 3.0 on 4.0 scale. 2. Official transcripts from all undergraduate institutions. 3. One-page personal statement. 4. Resume. 5. Two professional references. Additionally, for MEd in Literacy Studies - 1 year of teaching in PK-12 and letter of recommendation from principal/assistant principal. *Application deadline:* Applications are processed on a rolling basis. Application fee: $0. Electronic applications accepted. *Financial support:* Unspecified assistantships available. Financial award application deadline: 6/30; financial award applicants required to submit FAFSA. *Unit head:* Dr. Kathryn Flaherty, Dean of Graduate and Professional Programs, 843-857-4227, E-mail: kflaherty@coker.edu. *Application contact:* Lacey Rice-Serafin, Director of Graduate Programs, 843-857-4128, E-mail: lriceserafin@coker.edu.

College of Charleston, Graduate School, School of Business, Program in Business Administration, Charleston, SC 29424-0001. Offers MBA. *Entrance requirements:* For master's, GMAT or GRE, transcripts, recommendations, goal statement, bachelor's degree. Additional exam requirements/recommendations for international students: Required—TOEFL (minimum score 81 iBT), IELTS. Electronic applications accepted.

College of Saint Elizabeth, Department of Business Administration and Management, Morristown, NJ 07960-6989. Offers human resource management (MS); organizational change (MS). *Program availability:* Part-time. *Degree requirements:* For master's, thesis. *Entrance requirements:* Additional exam requirements/recommendations for international students: Required—TOEFL (minimum score 550 paper-based; 79 iBT), IELTS (minimum score 6.5). Electronic applications accepted. Application fee is waived when completed online.

College of St. Joseph, Graduate Programs, Division of Business, Program in Business Administration, Rutland, VT 05701-3899. Offers MBA. *Program availability:* Part-time, evening/weekend. *Entrance requirements:* For master's, two letters of reference from academic or professional sources; official transcripts of all graduate and undergraduate study; access to computer; computer literacy. Additional exam requirements/recommendations for international students: Required—TOEFL (minimum score 550 paper-based). Electronic applications accepted. *Expenses:* Contact institution.

The College of Saint Rose, Graduate Studies, Huether School of Business, Program in Business Administration, Albany, NY 12203-1419. Offers MBA, JD/MBA. JD/MBA offered jointly with Albany Law School. *Accreditation:* ACBSP. *Program availability:* Part-time, evening/weekend. *Students:* 26 full-time (14 women), 34 part-time (20 women); includes 8 minority (3 Black or African American, non-Hispanic/Latino; 1 Asian, non-Hispanic/Latino; 1 Hispanic/Latino; 3 Two or more races, non-Hispanic/Latino), 8 international. Average age 28. 45 applicants, 78% accepted, 15 enrolled. In 2018, 55 master's awarded. *Entrance requirements:* For master's, GMAT, graduate degree, or minimum undergraduate GPA of 3.0. Additional exam requirements/recommendations for international students: Required—TOEFL (minimum score 550 paper-based; 80 iBT), IELTS (minimum score 6), PTE (minimum score 56). *Application deadline:* For fall admission, 4/1 priority date for domestic students, 4/1 for international students; for spring admission, 10/15 priority date for domestic students, 10/15 for international students; for summer admission, 3/15 priority date for domestic and international students. Applications are processed on a rolling basis. Application fee: $40. Electronic applications accepted. *Expenses:* Tuition: Full-time $14,382; part-time $799 per credit hour. *Required fees:* $924; $408 per credit. $286. *Financial support:* Career-related internships or fieldwork, scholarships/grants, tuition waivers (partial), and unspecified assistantships available. Support available to part-time students. Financial award application deadline: 4/15. *Unit head:* John F. Dion, Program Coordinator, 518-458-5488, E-mail: dionj@strose.edu. *Application contact:* Daniel Gallagher, Assistant Vice President for Graduate Recruitment and Enrollment, 518-485-3390, Fax: 518-458-5479, E-mail: grad@strose.edu.
Website: https://www.strose.edu/mba/

The College of St. Scholastica, Graduate Studies, Department of Management, Duluth, MN 55811-4199. Offers MA, Certificate. *Program availability:* Part-time, evening/weekend, online learning. *Degree requirements:* For master's, thesis. *Entrance requirements:* Additional exam requirements/recommendations for international students: Required—TOEFL (minimum score 550 paper-based; 79 iBT). Electronic applications accepted. *Expenses:* Contact institution. *Faculty research:* Violence in higher education and workplace, screening and selection procedures in law enforcement, Internet use in criminal justice, stress management in law enforcement.

Business Administration and Management—General

College of Staten Island of the City University of New York, Graduate Programs, School of Business, Program in Business Management, Staten Island, NY 10314-6600. Offers large scale data analysis (MS); strategic management (MS). *Program availability:* Part-time, evening/weekend. *Faculty:* 4. *Students:* 39. 52 applicants, 56% accepted, 26 enrolled. In 2018, 21 master's awarded. *Degree requirements:* For master's, 30 credit hours, or ten courses at three credits each. *Entrance requirements:* For master's, GMAT or the GRE. CSI graduates with a 3.2 GPA or higher in their accounting/business major may be exempt from the GMAT/GRE. The TOEFL or IELTS is required for students whose second language is English., baccalaureate degree in business or related field, overall GPA of 3.0 or higher, letter of intent, two letters of recommendation. 2 courses in accounting,1 course in communications, 1 course in computer fundamentals, 2 courses in economics, 2 courses in quantitative methods, 1 course in management, 1 course in marketing. Additional exam requirements/recommendations for international students: Required—TOEFL (minimum score 550 paper-based; 79 iBT), IELTS (minimum score 6.5). *Application deadline:* For fall admission, 6/30 priority date for domestic students, 6/30 for international students; for spring admission, 11/25 priority date for domestic students, 11/25 for international students. Applications are processed on a rolling basis. Application fee: $75. Electronic applications accepted. *Expenses: Tuition, area resident:* Full-time $10,770; part-time $455 per credit. Tuition, state resident: full-time $10,770; part-time $455 per credit. Tuition, nonresident: full-time $19,920; part-time $830 per credit. *International tuition:* $19,920 full-time. *Required fees:* $559.20; $181.10 per semester. Tuition and fees vary according to program. *Faculty research:* Knowledge integration, management innovation, organizational decision-making, Human Resource Management, Behavioral Economics. *Unit head:* Dr. Heidi Bertels, Assistant Professor, 718-982-2924, E-mail: heidi.bertels@csi.cuny.edu. *Application contact:* Sasha Spence, Associate Director for Graduate Admissions, 718-982-2019, Fax: 718-982-2500, E-mail: sasha.spence@csi.cuny.edu.
Website: https://www.csi.cuny.edu/sites/default/files/pdf/admissions/grad/pdf/Business%20Management%20Fact%20Sheet.pdf

The College of William and Mary, Raymond A. Mason School of Business, Williamsburg, VA 23185. Offers EMBA, M Acc, MBA, MS, JD/MBA, MBA/MPP. *Accreditation:* AACSB. *Program availability:* Part-time, evening/weekend, 100% online. *Faculty:* 62 full-time (22 women), 7 part-time/adjunct (3 women). *Students:* 451 full-time (163 women), 407 part-time (152 women); includes 207 minority (84 Black or African American, non-Hispanic/Latino; 3 American Indian or Alaska Native, non-Hispanic/Latino; 45 Asian, non-Hispanic/Latino; 45 Hispanic/Latino; 2 Native Hawaiian or other Pacific Islander, non-Hispanic/Latino; 28 Two or more races, non-Hispanic/Latino), 148 international. Average age 32. 1,328 applicants, 60% accepted, 406 enrolled. In 2018, 487 master's awarded. *Degree requirements:* For master's, three domestic residencies and two international trips (EMBA). *Entrance requirements:* For master's, GMAT or GRE. Additional exam requirements/recommendations for international students: Required—TOEFL (minimum score 600 paper-based; 100 iBT), IELTS (minimum score 6.5), PTE. *Application deadline:* For fall admission, 11/16 for domestic and international students; for winter admission, 1/18 for domestic and international students; for spring admission, 5/16 for domestic and international students; for summer admission, 7/15 for domestic students. Application fee: $100. Electronic applications accepted. *Expenses:* Contact institution. *Financial support:* Scholarships/grants and unspecified assistantships available. Financial award applicants required to submit FAFSA. *Faculty research:* Saving and asset allocation decisions in retirement accounts, design strategy and consumer needs, virtual and networked organizations, healthcare informatics, reporting of non-GAAP metrics in financial disclosure. *Total annual research expenditures:* $29,813. *Unit head:* Dr. Lawrence Pulley, Dean, 757-221-2891, Fax: 757-221-2937, E-mail: larry.pulley@mason.wm.edu. *Application contact:* Amanda K. Barth, Director, Full-time MBA Admissions, 757-221-2944, Fax: 757-221-2958, E-mail: amanda.barth@mason.wm.edu.
Website: http://mason.wm.edu/

Colorado Christian University, Program in Business Administration, Lakewood, CO 80226. Offers corporate training (MBA); information security (MA); leadership (MBA); project management (MBA). *Program availability:* Part-time, evening/weekend, online learning. *Degree requirements:* For master's, thesis optional. *Entrance requirements:* For master's, GMAT, 2 letters of recommendation, resume. Additional exam requirements/recommendations for international students: Required—TOEFL. Electronic applications accepted. *Expenses:* Contact institution.

Colorado Mesa University, Department of Business, Grand Junction, CO 81501-3122. Offers MBA. *Program availability:* Part-time, evening/weekend. *Degree requirements:* For master's, thesis or research practicum, written comprehensive exams. *Entrance requirements:* For master's, GMAT, MAT, or GRE, minimum GPA of 3.0 for last 60 undergraduate hours, 2 letters of recommendation. Additional exam requirements/recommendations for international students: Required—TOEFL (minimum score 550 paper-based). Electronic applications accepted. *Expenses:* Contact institution.

Colorado State University, College of Business, MBA Program, Fort Collins, CO 80523-1201. Offers MBA, MBA/DVM. *Accreditation:* AACSB. *Program availability:* Part-time, evening/weekend, 100% online, blended/hybrid learning. *Entrance requirements:* For master's, GMAT or GRE (for Global Social and Sustainable Enterprise MBA), minimum undergraduate GPA of 3.0, official transcripts, three professional recommendations, statement of purpose, resume, professional work experience. Additional exam requirements/recommendations for international students: Required—TOEFL (minimum score 86 iBT), IELTS (minimum score 6.5), PTE (minimum score 58). Electronic applications accepted. *Expenses:* Contact institution.

Colorado State University–Global Campus, Graduate Programs, Greenwood Village, CO 80111. Offers criminal justice and law enforcement administration (MS); education leadership (MS); finance (MS); healthcare administration and management (MS); human resource management (MHRM); information technology management (MITM); international management (MS); management (MS); organizational leadership (MS); professional accounting (MPA); project management (MS); teaching and learning (MS). *Accreditation:* ACBSP. *Program availability:* Online learning.

Colorado State University–Pueblo, Malik and Seeme Hasan School of Business, Pueblo, CO 81001-4901. Offers MBA. *Accreditation:* AACSB. *Program availability:* Part-time, evening/weekend. *Degree requirements:* For master's, thesis optional. *Entrance requirements:* For master's, GMAT, minimum GPA of 3.0. Additional exam requirements/recommendations for international students: Required—TOEFL (minimum score 550 paper-based). *Faculty research:* Total quality management, leadership, small business studies, case research and writing.

Colorado Technical University Aurora, Programs in Business Administration and Management, Aurora, CO 80014. Offers accounting (MBA); business administration (MBA); business administration and management (EMBA); finance (MBA); human resource management (MBA); marketing (MBA); mediation and dispute resolution (MBA); operations management (MBA); project management (MBA); technology management (MBA). *Program availability:* Part-time, evening/weekend. *Degree requirements:* For master's, thesis or alternative. *Entrance requirements:* For master's, minimum undergraduate GPA of 3.0, resume.

Colorado Technical University Colorado Springs, Graduate Studies, Program in Management, Colorado Springs, CO 80907. Offers accounting (MBA, MSA); business administration (MBA); finance (MBA); human resources management (MBA); logistics/supply chain management (MBA); management (DM); marketing (MBA); mediation and dispute resolution (MBA); operations management (MBA); project management (MBA); technology management (MBA). *Accreditation:* ACBSP. *Program availability:* Part-time, evening/weekend, online learning. *Degree requirements:* For master's, thesis or alternative; for doctorate, thesis/dissertation. *Entrance requirements:* For doctorate, minimum graduate GPA of 3.0, 5 years of related work experience. *Faculty research:* Sexual harassment, performance evaluation, critical thinking.

Columbia College, Master of Business Administration Program, Columbia, MO 65216-0002. Offers accounting (MBA); business administration (MBA); human resources (MBA). *Program availability:* Part-time, evening/weekend, 100% online, blended/hybrid learning. *Faculty:* 1 full-time (0 women), 55 part-time/adjunct (16 women). *Students:* 60 full-time (32 women), 335 part-time (201 women); includes 121 minority (67 Black or African American, non-Hispanic/Latino; 1 American Indian or Alaska Native, non-Hispanic/Latino; 6 Asian, non-Hispanic/Latino; 24 Hispanic/Latino; 1 Native Hawaiian or other Pacific Islander, non-Hispanic/Latino; 22 Two or more races, non-Hispanic/Latino), 31 international. Average age 37. 443 applicants, 92% accepted, 127 enrolled. In 2018, 195 master's awarded. *Entrance requirements:* For master's, 3 letters of recommendation, minimum cumulative undergraduate GPA of 3.0, resume, goal statement. Additional exam requirements/recommendations for international students: Required—TOEFL (minimum score 550 paper-based; 79 iBT). *Application deadline:* For fall admission, 8/9 priority date for domestic and international students; for spring admission, 12/27 priority date for domestic and international students. Applications are processed on a rolling basis. Application fee: $0. Electronic applications accepted. *Expenses:* 17640 - tuition (all fees included). *Financial support:* In 2018–19, 54 students received support. Scholarships/grants, tuition waivers (full and partial), and unspecified assistantships available. Financial award application deadline: 3/1; financial award applicants required to submit FAFSA. *Application contact:* Stephanie Johnson, Associate Vice President for Recruiting & Admissions Division, 573-875-7352, Fax: 573-875-7506, E-mail: sjohnson@ccis.edu.
Website: http://www.ccis.edu/graduate/academics/degrees.asp?MBA

Columbia College Chicago, School of Graduate Studies, Business and Entrepreneurship Department, Chicago, IL 60605-1996. Offers arts, entertainment and media management (MAM). *Entrance requirements:* For master's, self-assessment essay, resume, letters of recommendation, transcripts. Additional exam requirements/recommendations for international students: Required—TOEFL, IELTS. Electronic applications accepted. *Expenses:* Contact institution.

Columbia Southern University, DBA Program, Orange Beach, AL 36561. Offers DBA. *Program availability:* Part-time, evening/weekend, online learning. *Entrance requirements:* For doctorate, 2 years professional experience, relevant academic experience. Electronic applications accepted.

Columbia Southern University, MBA Program, Orange Beach, AL 36561. Offers finance (MBA); health care management (MBA); human resource management (MBA); marketing (MBA); project management (MBA); public administration (MBA). *Program availability:* Part-time, evening/weekend, online learning. *Entrance requirements:* For master's, bachelor's degree from accredited/approved institution. Additional exam requirements/recommendations for international students: Required—TOEFL. Electronic applications accepted.

Columbia University, Graduate School of Business, Berkeley-Columbia Executive MBA Program, New York, NY 10027. Offers EMBA. Offered jointly with University of California, Berkeley. *Program availability:* Part-time. *Entrance requirements:* For master's, GMAT, 2 letters of reference, interview, minimum 5 years of work experience, transcripts, resume, employee support, personal essays. Additional exam requirements/recommendations for international students: Required—TOEFL (minimum score 570 paper-based; 68 iBT). Electronic applications accepted. *Expenses:* Contact institution.

Columbia University, Graduate School of Business, Doctoral Program in Business, New York, NY 10027. Offers business (PhD), including accounting, decision, risk, and operations, finance and economics, management, marketing. *Accreditation:* AACSB. *Degree requirements:* For doctorate, comprehensive exam, thesis/dissertation, major field exam, research paper, thesis proposal. *Entrance requirements:* For doctorate, GMAT or GRE (finance), 2 letters of reference, resume. Additional exam requirements/recommendations for international students: Required—TOEFL. Electronic applications accepted. *Expenses:* Contact institution. *Faculty research:* Human decision making and behavioral research; real estate market and mortgage defaults; financial crisis and corporate governance; international business; security analysis and accounting.

Columbia University, Graduate School of Business, Executive MBA Global Program, New York, NY 10027. Offers EMBA. Program offered jointly with London Business School. *Entrance requirements:* For master's, GMAT, 2 letters of reference, interview, minimum 5 years of work experience, curriculum vitae or resume, employer support. Additional exam requirements/recommendations for international students: Recommended—TOEFL, IELTS. Electronic applications accepted. *Expenses:* Contact institution.

Columbia University, Graduate School of Business, Executive MBA Program, New York, NY 10027. Offers EMBA. *Entrance requirements:* For master's, GMAT, minimum 5 years of work experience, 2 letters of reference, interview, company sponsorship. Additional exam requirements/recommendations for international students: Recommended—TOEFL. Electronic applications accepted. *Expenses:* Contact institution. *Faculty research:* Human decision making and behavioral research; real estate market and mortgage defaults; financial crisis and corporate governance; international business; and security analysis and accounting.

Columbia University, Graduate School of Business, MBA Program, New York, NY 10027. Offers accounting (MBA); decision, risk, and operations (MBA); entrepreneurship (MBA); finance and economics (MBA); healthcare and pharmaceutical management (MBA); human resource management (MBA); international business (MBA); leadership and ethics (MBA); management (MBA); marketing (MBA); media (MBA); private equity (MBA); real estate (MBA); social enterprise (MBA); value investing (MBA); DDS/MBA; JD/MBA; MBA/MIA; MBA/MPH; MBA/MS; MD/MBA. *Entrance requirements:* For master's, GMAT, 2 letters of recommendation. Additional exam requirements/recommendations for international students: Required—TOEFL. Electronic applications accepted. *Expenses:* Contact institution. *Faculty research:* Human decision making and behavioral research; real estate market and mortgage defaults; financial crisis and corporate governance; international business; security analysis and accounting.

Columbus State University, Graduate Studies, Turner College of Business, Columbus, GA 31907-5645. Offers applied computer science (MS), including informational assurance, modeling and simulation, software development; business administration (MBA); cyber security (MS); human resource management (Certificate); information systems security (Certificate); modeling and simulation (Certificate); organizational leadership (MS), including human resource management, leader development, servant leadership; servant leadership (Certificate). *Accreditation:* AACSB. *Program availability:* Part-time, evening/weekend, 100% online, blended/hybrid learning. *Faculty:* 10 full-time

(3 women), 1 part-time/adjunct (0 women). *Students:* 79 full-time (24 women), 136 part-time (47 women); includes 73 minority (40 Black or African American, non-Hispanic/Latino; 1 American Indian or Alaska Native, non-Hispanic/Latino; 8 Asian, non-Hispanic/Latino; 15 Hispanic/Latino; 9 Two or more races, non-Hispanic/Latino), 27 international. Average age 31. 237 applicants, 51% accepted, 64 enrolled. In 2018, 113 master's, 10 other advanced degrees awarded. *Entrance requirements:* For master's, GMAT, GRE, minimum undergraduate GPA of 2.75, letters of recommendation. Additional exam requirements/recommendations for international students: Required—TOEFL (minimum score 550 paper-based; 79 iBT). *Application deadline:* For fall admission, 6/30 for domestic students, 5/1 for international students; for spring admission, 11/1 for domestic and international students; for summer admission, 3/1 for domestic and international students. Applications are processed on a rolling basis. Application fee: $50. Electronic applications accepted. *Expenses:* Contact institution. *Financial support:* In 2018–19, 18 students received support, including 20 research assistantships (averaging $3,000 per year); Federal Work-Study also available. Financial award application deadline: 5/1; financial award applicants required to submit FAFSA. *Unit head:* Dr. Linda U. Hadley, Dean, 706-507-8153, Fax: 706-568-2184, E-mail: hadley_linda@columbusstate.edu. *Application contact:* Catrina Smith-Edmond, Assistant Director for Graduate and Global Admission, 706-507-8824, Fax: 706-568-5091, E-mail: smithedmond_catrina@columbusstate.edu.
Website: http://turner.columbusstate.edu/

Concordia University, School of Graduate Studies, John Molson School of Business, Montreal, QC H3H 0A1, Canada. Offers administration (M Sc), including finance, management, marketing; business administration (MBA, PhD, Certificate, Diploma); executive business administration (EMBA); supply chain management (MSCM). PhD program offered jointly with HEC Montreal, McGill University, and Université du Québec à Montréal. *Program availability:* Part-time, evening/weekend. *Degree requirements:* For master's, one foreign language, thesis (for some programs), research project; for doctorate, one foreign language, thesis/dissertation; for other advanced degree, one foreign language. *Entrance requirements:* For master's, GMAT, minimum 2 years of work experience (for MBA); letters of recommendation, bachelor's degree from recognized university with minimum GPA of 3.0, curriculum vitae; for doctorate, GMAT (minimum score of 600), official transcripts, curriculum vitae, 3 letters of reference, statement of purpose; for other advanced degree, minimum GPA of 2.7, 2 letters of reference, statement of purpose, resume. Additional exam requirements/recommendations for international students: Required—TOEFL (minimum score 90 iBT), IELTS (minimum score 7). Electronic applications accepted. *Expenses:* Contact institution. *Faculty research:* General business, capital markets, international business.

Concordia University, School of Management, Portland, OR 97211-6099. Offers MBA. *Accreditation:* ACBSP. *Program availability:* Evening/weekend. *Degree requirements:* For master's, thesis optional. *Entrance requirements:* For master's, GMAT or professional portfolio, minimum GPA of 3.0, bachelor's degree, 2 years of work experience, resume. Additional exam requirements/recommendations for international students: Required—TOEFL (minimum score 550 paper-based; 80 iBT), IELTS (minimum score 6.5). *Faculty research:* Leadership characteristics in internships, marketing of MBA programs, entrepreneurship.

Concordia University Chicago, College of Graduate Studies, College of Business, River Forest, IL 60305-1499. Offers MBA, DBA. *Program availability:* Part-time, evening/weekend, online learning.

Concordia University Irvine, School of Business, Irvine, CA 92612-3299. Offers business administration (MBA). *Program availability:* Part-time, evening/weekend. *Degree requirements:* For master's, capstone project or thesis. *Entrance requirements:* For master's, official college transcript(s), signed statement of intent, resume, two references, interview (MBA); passport photo, photocopies of valid U.S. passport, and college diploma (MAIS). Additional exam requirements/recommendations for international students: Required—TOEFL. Electronic applications accepted. *Expenses:* Contact institution.

Concordia University, St. Paul, College of Business and Technology, St. Paul, MN 55104-5494. Offers business administration (MBA), including cyber-security leadership; health care management (MBA); human resource management (MA); information technology (MBA); leadership and management (MA); strategic communication management (MA). *Accreditation:* ACBSP. *Program availability:* Part-time, evening/weekend, 100% online, blended/hybrid learning. *Faculty:* 12 full-time (5 women), 28 part-time/adjunct (14 women). *Students:* 448 full-time (289 women), 30 part-time (17 women); includes 135 minority (58 Black or African American, non-Hispanic/Latino; 2 American Indian or Alaska Native, non-Hispanic/Latino; 46 Asian, non-Hispanic/Latino; 13 Hispanic/Latino; 16 Two or more races, non-Hispanic/Latino), 40 international. Average age 32. 328 applicants, 96% accepted, 149 enrolled. In 2018, 205 master's awarded. *Degree requirements:* For master's, thesis (for some programs). *Entrance requirements:* For master's, official transcripts from regionally-accredited institution stating the conferral of a bachelor's degree with minimum cumulative GPA of 3.0; personal statement; professional resume. Additional exam requirements/recommendations for international students: Recommended—TOEFL (minimum score 547 paper-based; 78 iBT), IELTS (minimum score 6). *Application deadline:* For fall admission, 8/1 for domestic and international students; for spring admission, 12/1 for domestic and international students; for summer admission, 5/1 for domestic and international students. Applications are processed on a rolling basis. Application fee: $0. Electronic applications accepted. *Expenses:* $625 a credit for 42 credits (for MBA), $475 a credit for 36 credits (for MA/MS). *Financial support:* In 2018–19, 267 students received support. Federal Work-Study, scholarships/grants, and unspecified assistantships available. Financial award applicants required to submit FAFSA. *Faculty research:* Leadership in transition and polarity, managing the evolution of a software product line, decision making and behavioral economics, strength based coaching and the relationship with student success, three-way XML merging. *Unit head:* Dr. Kevin Hall, Dean, 651-603-6165, Fax: 651-641-8807, E-mail: khall@csp.edu. *Application contact:* Amber Faletti, Director of Enrollment Management, 651-641-8838, Fax: 651-603-6320, E-mail: faletti@csp.edu.

Concordia University Wisconsin, Graduate Programs, Batterman School of Business, Mequon, WI 53097-2402. Offers MBA, MS.

Copenhagen Business School, Graduate Programs, Copenhagen, Denmark. Offers business administration (Exec MBA, MBA, PhD); business administration and information systems (M Sc); business, language and culture (M Sc); economics and business administration (M Sc); health management (MHM); international business and politics (M Sc); public administration (MPA); shipping and logistics (Exec MBA); technology, market and organization (MBA).

Corban University, Graduate School, The Corban MBA, Salem, OR 97301-9392. Offers management (MBA); non-profit management (MBA). *Program availability:* Online learning.

Cornell University, Graduate School, Graduate Field of Management, Ithaca, NY 14853. Offers accounting (PhD); finance (PhD); marketing (PhD); organizational behavior (PhD); production and operations management (PhD). *Accreditation:* AACSB. *Degree requirements:* For doctorate, comprehensive exam, thesis/dissertation. *Entrance requirements:* For doctorate, GMAT or GRE General Test. Additional exam requirements/recommendations for international students: Required—TOEFL (minimum score 600 paper-based; 77 iBT). Electronic applications accepted. *Expenses:* Contact institution. *Faculty research:* Operations and manufacturing.

Cornell University, Samuel Curtis Johnson Graduate School of Management, Ithaca, NY 14853. Offers business administration (Exec MBA); management (MBA, PhD); management - accounting (MPS); JD/MBA; M Eng/MBA; MBA/MD; MBA/MHA; MBA/MILR; MBA/MPS. *Accreditation:* AACSB. *Faculty:* 71 full-time (18 women). *Students:* 573 full-time (172 women); includes 122 minority (24 Black or African American, non-Hispanic/Latino; 2 American Indian or Alaska Native, non-Hispanic/Latino; 74 Asian, non-Hispanic/Latino; 12 Hispanic/Latino; 10 Two or more races, non-Hispanic/Latino), 168 international. Average age 28. 1,600 applicants, 33% accepted, 280 enrolled. In 2018, 283 master's awarded. *Entrance requirements:* For master's, GMAT or GRE, resume, two essays, two recommendations, interview. Additional exam requirements/recommendations for international students: Required—TOEFL, TOEFL or IELTS score report required (for applicants whose first language is not English). *Application deadline:* For fall admission, 10/8 for domestic and international students; for winter admission, 11/5 for domestic and international students; for spring admission, 1/8 for domestic and international students; for summer admission, 4/8 for domestic and international students. Application fee: $200. Electronic applications accepted. *Expenses:* Contact institution. *Financial support:* Fellowships, institutionally sponsored loans, and scholarships/grants available. Financial award applicants required to submit FAFSA. *Faculty research:* Business of food; behavioral economics and decision research; innovation, entrepreneurship and technology. *Unit head:* Dr. Mark Nelson, Dean, 607-255-6418, E-mail: dean@johnson.cornell.edu. *Application contact:* Admissions Office, 800-847-2082, Fax: 607-255-0065, E-mail: mba@johnson.cornell.edu.
Website: http://www.johnson.cornell.edu

Cornerstone University, Graduate Programs, Grand Rapids, MI 49525-5897. Offers business administration (MBA); education (MA Ed); management (MSM); teaching English to speakers of other languages (MA, Graduate Certificate). Programs also offered at Holland, Kalamazoo, and Troy, MI campuses. *Program availability:* Part-time, online learning. *Degree requirements:* For master's, comprehensive exam (for some programs), thesis (for some programs). *Entrance requirements:* For master's, minimum GPA of 2.5, 2 letters of reference. Additional exam requirements/recommendations for international students: Required—TOEFL (minimum score 575 paper-based). Electronic applications accepted.

Creighton University, Graduate School, Heider College of Business, Omaha, NE 68178-0001. Offers accounting (MAC); business administration (MBA, DBA); business intelligence and analytics (MS); finance (M Fin); investment management and financial analysis (MIMFA); JD/MBA; MBA/MIMFA; MD/MBA; Pharm D/MBA. *Accreditation:* AACSB. *Program availability:* Part-time, evening/weekend, 100% online, blended/hybrid learning. *Degree requirements:* For master's, thesis optional; for doctorate, thesis/dissertation optional. *Entrance requirements:* For master's, GMAT, resume, 2 letters of recommendation. Additional exam requirements/recommendations for international students: Required—TOEFL (minimum score 90 iBT). Electronic applications accepted. *Expenses:* Contact institution. *Faculty research:* Small business issues, economics, business analytics.

Culver-Stockton College, MBA Program, Canton, MO 63435-1299. Offers accounting and finance (MBA).

Cumberland University, Program in Business Administration, Lebanon, TN 37087. Offers MBA. *Accreditation:* ACBSP. *Program availability:* Part-time, evening/weekend. *Degree requirements:* For master's, comprehensive exam. *Entrance requirements:* For master's, GMAT or GRE General Test, 3 letters of recommendation. Additional exam requirements/recommendations for international students: Required—TOEFL (minimum score 500 paper-based). *Expenses:* Contact institution.

Curry College, Graduate Studies, Program in Business Administration, Milton, MA 02186-9984. Offers business administration (MBA); finance (Certificate). *Program availability:* Part-time, evening/weekend. *Degree requirements:* For master's, capstone applied project. *Entrance requirements:* For master's, resume, recommendations, interview, written statement. Additional exam requirements/recommendations for international students: Required—TOEFL (minimum score 550 paper-based; 80 iBT). *Expenses:* Contact institution.

Daemen College, Leadership and Innovation Programs, Amherst, NY 14226-3592. Offers business (MS); health professions (MS); not-for-profit organizations (MS). *Program availability:* Part-time-only, evening/weekend. *Faculty:* 1 (woman) full-time, 8 part-time/adjunct (4 women). *Students:* 21 part-time (15 women); includes 3 minority (2 Black or African American, non-Hispanic/Latino; 1 Hispanic/Latino). Average age 38. 10 applicants, 70% accepted, 6 enrolled. In 2018, 8 master's awarded. *Degree requirements:* For master's, thesis, A minimum cumulative grade point average (GPA) of 3.00; A student is allowed a maximum of two repeats before being dismissed. *Entrance requirements:* For master's, bachelor's degree, official transcripts, personal statement, resume, 2 letters of recommendation, interview with program director. Additional exam requirements/recommendations for international students: Required—TOEFL (minimum score 77 paper-based), IELTS (minimum score 6.5). *Application deadline:* Applications are processed on a rolling basis. Application fee: $25. Electronic applications accepted. Application fee is waived when completed online. *Expenses: Tuition:* Part-time $977 per credit hour. *Required fees:* $125; $14 per credit hour. *Financial support:* Scholarships/grants and unspecified assistantships available. Support available to part-time students. Financial award applicants required to submit FAFSA. *Unit head:* Christina Coyle-Lenz, Director, 716-839-8342, E-mail: ccoyle@daemen.edu. *Application contact:* Megan Beardi, Senior Assistant Director of Graduate Admissions, 716-566-7861, Fax: 716-839-8229, E-mail: mbeardi@daemen.edu.
Website: https://www.daemen.edu/academics/areas-study/leadership-and-innovation

Dakota State University, College of Business and Information Systems, Madison, SD 57042-1799. Offers analytics (MSA); business analytics (Graduate Certificate); general management (MBA); health informatics (MSHI); information systems (MSIS, D Sc IS); information technology (Graduate Certificate). *Accreditation:* ACBSP. *Program availability:* Part-time, evening/weekend, 100% online, blended/hybrid learning. *Faculty:* 27 full-time (10 women). *Students:* 40 full-time (11 women), 165 part-time (60 women); includes 56 minority (21 Black or African American, non-Hispanic/Latino; 4 American Indian or Alaska Native, non-Hispanic/Latino; 19 Asian, non-Hispanic/Latino; 10 Hispanic/Latino; 1 Native Hawaiian or other Pacific Islander, non-Hispanic/Latino; 1 Two or more races, non-Hispanic/Latino), 38 international. Average age 38. 246 applicants, 47% accepted, 63 enrolled. In 2018, 62 master's, 7 doctorates, 9 other advanced degrees awarded. *Degree requirements:* For master's, comprehensive exam, thesis optional, Examination, integrative project; for doctorate, comprehensive exam, thesis/dissertation, portfolio. *Entrance requirements:* For master's, GRE General Test, Demonstration of information systems skills, minimum GPA of 2.7; for doctorate, GRE General Test, Demonstration of information systems skills; for Graduate Certificate, GMAT. Additional exam requirements/recommendations for international students: Required—PTE (minimum score 53), TOEFL (minimum score 550 paper-based, 76 iBT) or IELTS (6.0). *Application deadline:* For fall admission, 6/15 for domestic students, 4/15

for international students; for spring admission, 11/15 for domestic students, 9/15 priority date for international students; for summer admission, 4/15 for domestic and international students. Applications are processed on a rolling basis. Application fee: $35. Electronic applications accepted. *Expenses:* Contact institution. *Financial support:* In 2018–19, 20 students received support. Research assistantships with partial tuition reimbursements available, teaching assistantships with partial tuition reimbursements available, career-related internships or fieldwork, Federal Work-Study, scholarships/grants, and unspecified assistantships available. Support available to part-time students. Financial award applicants required to submit FAFSA. *Faculty research:* Data mining and analytics, biometrics and information assurance, decision support systems, health informatics, STEM education for K-12 teachers/students and underrepresented populations. *Unit head:* Dr. Dorine Bennett, Dean of College of Business and Information Systems, 605-256-5176, E-mail: dorine.bennett@dsu.edu. *Application contact:* Erin Blankespoor, Senior Secretary, Office of Graduate Studies and Research, 605-256-5799, E-mail: erin.blankespoor@dsu.edu.
Website: http://dsu.edu/academics/colleges/college-of-business-and-information-systems

Dalhousie University, Faculty of Management, Centre for Advanced Management Education, Halifax, NS B3H 3J5, Canada. Offers financial services (MBA); information management (MIM); management (MPA); natural resources (MBA). *Program availability:* Part-time, online learning. *Entrance requirements:* For master's, GMAT, minimum GPA of 3.0, resume. Additional exam requirements/recommendations for international students: Required—TOEFL, IELTS, CANTEST, CAEL, or Michigan English Language Assessment Battery. Electronic applications accepted.

Dalhousie University, Faculty of Management, Rowe School of Business, Halifax, NS B3H 3J5, Canada. Offers business administration (MBA); financial services (MBA); LL B/MBA; MBA/MLIS. *Program availability:* Part-time. *Entrance requirements:* For master's, GMAT, letter of non-financial guarantee for non-Canadian students, resume, Corporate Residency Preference Form. Additional exam requirements/recommendations for international students: Required—TOEFL, IELTS, CANTEST, CAEL, or Michigan English Language Assessment Battery. Electronic applications accepted. *Faculty research:* International business, quantitative methods, operations research, MIS, marketing, finance.

Dalhousie University, Faculty of Management, School of Public Administration, Halifax, NS B3H 3J5, Canada. Offers management (MPA); public administration (MPA, GDPA); LL B/MPA; MLIS/MPA. *Program availability:* Part-time. *Entrance requirements:* For master's, GMAT. Additional exam requirements/recommendations for international students: Required—TOEFL, IELTS, CANTEST, CAEL, or Michigan English Language Assessment Battery. Electronic applications accepted. *Expenses:* Contact institution. *Faculty research:* Municipal management, policy and program management, environmental policy, economic and social policy, business and government.

Dallas Baptist University, College of Business, Management Program, Dallas, TX 75211-9299. Offers conflict resolution management (MA); general management (MA, MS); health care management (MA); human resource management (MA); professional sales and management optimization (MA). *Program availability:* Part-time, evening/weekend, online learning. *Application deadline:* Applications are processed on a rolling basis. Application fee: $25. Electronic applications accepted. Application fee is waived when completed online. *Expenses: Tuition:* Full-time $17,262; part-time $959 per credit hour. *Required fees:* $1000; $500 per semester. Tuition and fees vary according to course load and degree level. *Unit head:* Dr. Sandra Reid, Chair, Graduate School of Business, 214-333-6860, E-mail: sandra@dbu.edu. *Application contact:* Dr. Justin Gandy, Program Director, 214-333-6840, E-mail: justing@dbu.edu.
Website: https://www.dbu.edu/graduate/degree-programs/ma-management

Dallas Baptist University, College of Business, Master of Business Administration Program, Dallas, TX 75211-9299. Offers health care management (MBA); international business (MBA); management information systems (MBA). *Accreditation:* ACBSP. *Program availability:* Part-time, evening/weekend, 100% online, blended/hybrid learning. *Application deadline:* Applications are processed on a rolling basis. Application fee: $25. Electronic applications accepted. Application fee is waived when completed online. *Expenses: Tuition:* Full-time $17,262; part-time $959 per credit hour. *Required fees:* $1000; $500 per semester. Tuition and fees vary according to course load and degree level. *Unit head:* Dr. Sandra Reid, Chair of Graduate Business Programs, Program Director, 214-333-5280, E-mail: sandra@dbu.edu. *Application contact:* Dr. Sandra Reid, Chair of Graduate Business Programs, Program Director, 214-333-5280, E-mail: sandra@dbu.edu.
Website: https://www.dbu.edu/graduate/degree-programs/mba

Dallas Baptist University, Gary Cook School of Leadership, Program in Leadership Studies, Dallas, TX 75211-9299. Offers leadership studies (PhD), including business, general leadership, higher education, ministry. *Program availability:* Part-time, evening/weekend. *Degree requirements:* For doctorate, thesis/dissertation. *Application deadline:* Applications are processed on a rolling basis. Application fee: $25. Electronic applications accepted. Application fee is waived when completed online. *Expenses: Tuition:* Full-time $17,262; part-time $959 per credit hour. *Required fees:* $1000; $500 per semester. Tuition and fees vary according to course load and degree level. *Unit head:* Dr. Jack Goodyear, Director, 214-333-5595, Fax: 214-333-6809, E-mail: jackg@dbu.edu. *Application contact:* Dr. Mary Nelson, Program Director, 214-333-5396, E-mail: maryn@dbu.edu.
Website: http://www4.dbu.edu/leadership/phdleadership

Dallas Baptist University, Professional Development Program, Dallas, TX 75211-9299. Offers accounting (MA); church leadership (MA); communication (MA); counseling (MA); criminal justice (MA); English as a second language (MA); finance (MA); higher education (MA); leadership studies (MA); management (MA). *Program availability:* Part-time, evening/weekend, online learning. *Application deadline:* Applications are processed on a rolling basis. Application fee: $25. Electronic applications accepted. Application fee is waived when completed online. *Expenses: Tuition:* Full-time $17,262; part-time $959 per credit hour. *Required fees:* $1000; $500 per semester. Tuition and fees vary according to course load and degree level. *Unit head:* Jared Ingram, Program Director, 214-333-5584, E-mail: jaredi@dbu.edu. *Application contact:* Jared Ingram, Program Director, 214-333-5584, E-mail: jaredi@dbu.edu.
Website: https://www.dbu.edu/graduate/degree-programs/ma-professional-development

Dartmouth College, Tuck School of Business at Dartmouth, Hanover, NH 03755. Offers MBA. *Accreditation:* AACSB. *Faculty:* 53 full-time (11 women). *Students:* 582 full-time (259 women); includes 118 minority (27 Black or African American, non-Hispanic/Latino; 1 American Indian or Alaska Native, non-Hispanic/Latino; 52 Asian, non-Hispanic/Latino; 30 Hispanic/Latino; 1 Native Hawaiian or other Pacific Islander, non-Hispanic/Latino; 7 Two or more races, non-Hispanic/Latino), 172 international. Average age 28. 2,610 applicants, 23% accepted, 293 enrolled. In 2018, 282 master's awarded. *Entrance requirements:* For master's, GMAT or GRE, 2 letters of recommendation, 2 essays, resume/curriculum vitae. Additional exam requirements/recommendations for international students: Required—TOEFL. *Application deadline:* For fall admission, 10/1 for domestic and international students; for winter admission, 1/1 for domestic and international students; for spring admission, 4/1 for domestic and international students. Application fee: $250. Electronic applications accepted. *Financial support:* Institutionally sponsored loans and scholarships/grants available. Financial award application deadline: 4/1; financial award applicants required to submit FAFSA. *Faculty research:* Global production sourcing, customer waitlist management, origin of great strategies, effects of shopping in warehouse club stores, impact of bank credit on productivity. *Unit head:* Matthew J. Slaughter, Dean, 603-646-2460, E-mail: tuck.public.relations@tuck.dartmouth.edu. *Application contact:* Luke Anthony Pena, Executive Director of Admissions and Financial Aid, 603-646-3162, Fax: 603-646-1441, E-mail: tuck.admissions@tuck.dartmouth.edu.
Website: www.tuck.dartmouth.edu

Davenport University, Sneden Graduate School, Grand Rapids, MI 49512. Offers accounting (MBA); business administration (EMBA); finance (MBA); health care management (MBA); human resources (MBA); information assurance (MS); occupational therapy (MSOT); public health (MPH); strategic management (MBA). *Program availability:* Evening/weekend. *Entrance requirements:* For master's, GMAT, minimum undergraduate GPA of 2.75. Additional exam requirements/recommendations for international students: Required—TOEFL. Electronic applications accepted. *Faculty research:* Leadership, management, marketing, organizational culture.

Defiance College, Program in Business Administration, Defiance, OH 43512-1610. Offers leadership (MBA). *Program availability:* Part-time, evening/weekend. *Degree requirements:* For master's, thesis. *Entrance requirements:* For master's, minimum GPA of 2.75. Additional exam requirements/recommendations for international students: Recommended—TOEFL. Electronic applications accepted.

Delaware State University, Graduate Programs, College of Business, Program in Business Administration, Dover, DE 19901-2277. Offers MBA. *Accreditation:* AACSB. *Program availability:* Part-time, evening/weekend. *Degree requirements:* For master's, exit exam. *Entrance requirements:* For master's, GMAT (minimum score 400), minimum GPA of 3.0 in major, 2.75 overall. Additional exam requirements/recommendations for international students: Required—TOEFL (minimum score 550 paper-based). Electronic applications accepted. *Faculty research:* Managerial economics, strategic management, qualitative effort, finance.

Delaware Valley University, MBA Program, Doylestown, PA 18901-2697. Offers accounting (MBA); entrepreneurship (MBA); finance (MBA); food and agribusiness (MBA); general business (MBA); global executive leadership (MBA); human resource management (MBA); supply chain management (MBA). *Program availability:* Part-time, evening/weekend, online learning. *Entrance requirements:* For master's, minimum undergraduate GPA of 3.0. Electronic applications accepted. *Expenses:* Contact institution.

Delta State University, Graduate Programs, College of Business, Division of Management, Marketing, and Business Administration, Cleveland, MS 38733-0001. Offers business administration (MBA). *Accreditation:* ACBSP. *Program availability:* Part-time, evening/weekend. *Entrance requirements:* For master's, GMAT. *Expenses: Tuition, area resident:* Full-time $7076; part-time $393 per credit hour. Tuition, state resident: full-time $7076; part-time $393 per credit hour. Tuition, nonresident: full-time $7076; part-time $393 per credit hour. *International tuition:* $7076 full-time. *Required fees:* $170; $18.90 per credit hour. $9.45 per semester. Part-time tuition and fees vary according to program.

DePaul University, Kellstadt Graduate School of Business, Chicago, IL 60604. Offers accountancy (MBA, MSA); applied economics (MBA); audit and advisory services (MS); business administration (DBA); business analytics (MS); business strategy and decision-making (MBA); computational finance (MS); economics and policy analysis (MS); enterprise risk management (MS); entrepreneurship (MBA, MS); finance (MBA, MS); general business (MBA); hospitality leadership (MBA); hospitality leadership and operational performance (MS); human resources (MS); international business (MBA); management (MBA, MS); management information systems (MBA); marketing (MBA, MS); marketing analysis (MS); marketing strategy and planning (MBA); real estate (MS); real estate finance and investment (MBA); strategy, execution and valuation (MBA); supply chain management (MS); sustainable management (MS); taxation (MS); JD/MBA. *Accreditation:* AACSB. *Program availability:* Part-time, evening/weekend, online learning. *Entrance requirements:* For master's, GMAT/GRE, 2 letters of recommendation, resume, essay, official transcripts. Additional exam requirements/recommendations for international students: Required—TOEFL (minimum score 550 paper-based; 80 iBT). Electronic applications accepted. *Expenses:* Contact institution.

DeSales University, Division of Business, Center Valley, PA 18034-9568. Offers accounting (MBA); computer information systems (MBA); finance (MBA); health care systems management (MBA); human resources management (MBA); management (MBA); marketing (MBA); project management (MBA); self-design (MBA); supply chain management (MBA); DNP/MBA; MSN/MBA. *Accreditation:* ACBSP. *Program availability:* Part-time, evening/weekend, 100% online, blended/hybrid learning. *Entrance requirements:* For master's, GMAT (waived if undergraduate GPA is 3.0 or better), minimum GPA of 3.0 in undergraduate work, literacy in basic software, background or interest in the field of study, personal statement, 2 years of work experience. Additional exam requirements/recommendations for international students: Required—TOEFL. Electronic applications accepted. *Expenses:* Contact institution. *Faculty research:* Quality improvement, executive development, productivity, cross-cultural managerial differences, leadership.

DeVry College of New York–Midtown Manhattan Campus, Keller Graduate School of Management, New York, NY 10016. Offers M Acc, MAFM, MBA, MHRM, MISM, MNCM, MPA, MPM.

DeVry University–Alpharetta Campus, Keller Graduate School of Management, Alpharetta, GA 30009. Offers MAFM, MBA, MHRM, MISM, MNCM, MPA, MPM. *Accreditation:* ACBSP.

DeVry University–Arlington Campus, Keller Graduate School of Management, Arlington, VA 22202. Offers M Acc, MAFM, MBA, MHRM, MISM, MPM.

DeVry University–Charlotte Campus, Keller Graduate School of Management, Charlotte, NC 28273. Offers MAFM, MBA, MHRM, MISM, MNCM, MPA, MPM. *Accreditation:* ACBSP.

DeVry University–Chesapeake Campus, Keller Graduate School of Management, Chesapeake, VA 23320. Offers MAFM, MBA, MHRM, MISM, MNCM, MPA, MPM.

DeVry University–Chicago Campus, Keller Graduate School of Management, Chicago, IL 60618. Offers M Acc, MAFM, MBA, MHRM, MISM, MPM. *Accreditation:* ACBSP.

DeVry University–Chicago Loop Campus, Keller Graduate School of Management, Chicago, IL 60606. Offers MAFM, MBA, MHRM, MISM, MNCM, MPM. *Accreditation:* ACBSP.

DeVry University–Cincinnati Campus, Keller Graduate School of Management, Cincinnati, OH 45249. Offers MAFM, MBA, MHRM, MISM, MNCM, MPA, MPM. *Accreditation:* ACBSP.

DeVry University–Columbus Campus, Keller Graduate School of Management, Columbus, OH 43209. Offers MAFM, MBA, MHRM, MISM, MPM. *Accreditation:* ACBSP.

DeVry University–Decatur Campus, Keller Graduate School of Management, Decatur, GA 30030. Offers MAFM, MBA, MHRM, MISM, MNCM, MPA, MPM, MSA. *Accreditation:* ACBSP.

DeVry University–Folsom Campus, Graduate Programs, Folsom, CA 95630. Offers accounting (M Acc); accounting and financial management (MAFM); business administration (MBA); curriculum leadership (M Ed); educational leadership (M Ed); educational technology (M Ed); higher education leadership (M Ed); human resource management (MHRM); information systems management (MISM); network and communications management (MNCM); project management (MPM); public administration (MPA).

DeVry University–Fremont Campus, Keller Graduate School of Management, Fremont, CA 94555. Offers MAFM, MBA, MHRM, MISM, MNCM, MPA, MPM. *Accreditation:* ACBSP.

DeVry University–Ft. Washington Campus, Keller Graduate School of Management, Fort Washington, PA 19034. Offers MAFM, MBA, MHRM, MISM, MNCM, MPA, MPM. *Accreditation:* ACBSP.

DeVry University–Henderson Campus, Keller Graduate School of Management, Henderson, NV 89074. Offers MAFM, MBA, MHRM, MISM, MNCM, MPA, MPM.

DeVry University–Irving Campus, Keller Graduate School of Management, Irving, TX 75063. Offers M Acc, MAFM, MBA, MHRM, MISM, MPM.

DeVry University–Jacksonville Campus, Keller Graduate School of Management, Jacksonville, FL 32256. Offers MAFM, MBA, MHRM, MISM, MNCM, MPA, MPM. *Accreditation:* ACBSP.

DeVry University–Long Beach Campus, Keller Graduate School of Management, Long Beach, CA 90806. Offers MAFM, MBA, MHRM, MISM, MNCM, MPA, MPM. *Accreditation:* ACBSP.

DeVry University–Miramar Campus, Keller Graduate School of Management, Miramar, FL 33027. Offers MAFM, MBA, MHRM, MISM, MPM, MSA.

DeVry University–Morrisville Campus, Keller Graduate School of Management, Morrisville, NC 27560. Offers MBA, MHRM, MISM, MNCM, MPA, MPM.

DeVry University–Nashville Campus, Keller Graduate School of Management, Nashville, TN 37211. Offers MAFM, MBA, MHRM, MISM, MNCM, MPA, MPM. *Accreditation:* ACBSP.

DeVry University–North Brunswick Campus, Keller Graduate School of Management, North Brunswick, NJ 08902. Offers MBA. *Accreditation:* ACBSP.

DeVry University Online, Keller Graduate School of Management, Addison, IL 60101. Offers M Acc, MAFM, MBA, MHRM, MISM, MNCM, MPA, MPM.

DeVry University–Orlando Campus, Keller Graduate School of Management, Orlando, FL 32819. Offers MAFM, MBA, MHRM, MISM, MPA, MPM, MSA.

DeVry University–Phoenix Campus, Keller Graduate School of Management, Phoenix, AZ 85021. Offers MAFM, MBA, MISM, MPM, MSA.

DeVry University–Pomona Campus, Keller Graduate School of Management, Pomona, CA 91768. Offers MAFM, MBA, MHRM, MISM, MPM, MSA.

DeVry University–San Diego Campus, Keller Graduate School of Management, San Diego, CA 92108. Offers MAFM, MBA, MHRM, MISM, MNCM, MPA, MPM, Graduate Certificate. *Accreditation:* ACBSP.

DeVry University–Seven Hills Campus, Keller Graduate School of Management, Seven Hills, OH 44131. Offers MAFM, MBA, MHRM, MISM, MNCM, MPA, MPM, Graduate Certificate.

DeVry University–Tinley Park Campus, Keller Graduate School of Management, Tinley Park, IL 60477. Offers MAFM, MBA, MHRM, MISM, MNCM, MPA, MPM. *Accreditation:* ACBSP.

Doane University, Program in Management, Crete, NE 68333-2430. Offers MA, MBA. *Program availability:* Part-time, evening/weekend. *Faculty:* 3 full-time (2 women), 21 part-time/adjunct (9 women). *Students:* 174 full-time (105 women), 32 part-time (17 women); includes 44 minority (16 Black or African American, non-Hispanic/Latino; 7 Asian, non-Hispanic/Latino; 11 Hispanic/Latino; 10 Two or more races, non-Hispanic/ Latino), 7 international. Average age 36. In 2018, 68 master's awarded. *Degree requirements:* For master's, thesis. *Entrance requirements:* For master's, minimum GPA of 3.0. Additional exam requirements/recommendations for international students: Required—TOEFL. *Application deadline:* Applications are processed on a rolling basis. Application fee: $25. Electronic applications accepted. *Expenses:* Contact institution. *Financial support:* Application deadline: 6/1; applicants required to submit FAFSA. *Unit head:* Dr. Debora Sepich, Director of Graduate Business Program, 880-333-6263, E-mail: deb.sepich@doane.edu. *Application contact:* Cathy Dillon, Director of Academic Advising, 402-466-4774, Fax: 404-466-4228, E-mail: cathy.dillon@doane.edu.

Dominican College, MBA Program, Orangeburg, NY 10962-1210. Offers accounting (MBA); healthcare management (MBA); management (MBA). *Program availability:* Part-time, evening/weekend. *Entrance requirements:* For master's, GMAT, 2 letters of recommendation. Additional exam requirements/recommendations for international students: Required—TOEFL (minimum score 550 paper-based; 90 iBT). Electronic applications accepted. *Expenses:* Contact institution.

Dominican University, Brennan School of Business, River Forest, IL 60305-1099. Offers MBA, MSA, JD/MBA, MBA/MLIS, MBA/MSW. JD/MBA offered jointly with John Marshall Law School. *Accreditation:* AACSB. *Program availability:* Part-time, evening/ weekend, 100% online, blended/hybrid learning. *Entrance requirements:* For master's, GMAT. Additional exam requirements/recommendations for international students: Required—TOEFL (minimum score 550 paper-based; 79 iBT); Recommended—IELTS (minimum score 6). Electronic applications accepted. *Expenses:* Contact institution. *Faculty research:* Entrepreneurship, small business finance, business ethics, marketing strategy.

Dominican University of California, Barowsky School of Business, San Rafael, CA 94901-2298. Offers business (MBA); healthcare leadership (MBA). MBA in healthcare leadership offered jointly with School of Health and Natural Sciences. *Program availability:* Part-time, evening/weekend. *Degree requirements:* For master's, thesis, capstone (for MBA). *Entrance requirements:* For master's, minimum GPA of 3.0. Additional exam requirements/recommendations for international students: Required—TOEFL (minimum score 550 paper-based; 80 iBT), IELTS (minimum score 6.5). Electronic applications accepted. *Expenses:* Contact institution.

Drake University, College of Business and Public Administration, Des Moines, IA 50311-4516. Offers accounting (M Acc); business administration (MBA); public administration (MPA); JD/MBA; JD/MPA; Pharm D/MBA; Pharm D/MPA. *Program availability:* Part-time, evening/weekend, 100% online, blended/hybrid learning. *Students:* 31 full-time (15 women), 173 part-time (89 women); includes 19 minority (4 Black or African American, non-Hispanic/Latino; 1 American Indian or Alaska Native, non-Hispanic/Latino; 3 Asian, non-Hispanic/Latino; 9 Hispanic/Latino; 2 Two or more races, non-Hispanic/Latino), 11 international. Average age 31. In 2018, 121 master's awarded. *Degree requirements:* For master's, comprehensive exam (for some programs), thesis (for some programs), internships. *Entrance requirements:* For master's, GMAT, letters of recommendation, resume. Additional exam requirements/ recommendations for international students: Required—TOEFL (minimum score 550 paper-based). *Application deadline:* For fall admission, 8/15 priority date for domestic students; for winter admission, 12/20 priority date for domestic students; for spring admission, 12/1 priority date for domestic students. Applications are processed on a rolling basis. Application fee: $25. Electronic applications accepted. *Expenses:* Contact institution. *Financial support:* Fellowships with tuition reimbursements, teaching assistantships, career-related internships or fieldwork, and institutionally sponsored loans available. Support available to part-time students. Financial award application deadline: 3/1; financial award applicants required to submit FAFSA. *Faculty research:* Venture capital, online commerce, professional ethics, process improvement, project management. *Unit head:* Dr. Daniel J. Connolly, Dean, 515-271-2872, Fax: 515-271-4518, E-mail: daniel.connolly@drake.edu. *Application contact:* Danette Kenne, Assistant Dean, 515-271-2188, Fax: 515-271-4518, E-mail: cbpa.gradprograms@drake.edu.
Website: http://www.drake.edu/cbpa/

Drexel University, LeBow College of Business, Program in Business Administration, Philadelphia, PA 19104-2875. Offers business administration (MBA, PhD, APC), including accounting (MBA, PhD), decision sciences (PhD), economics (MBA, PhD), finance (MBA, PhD), legal studies (MBA), management (MBA), marketing (MBA, PhD), organizational sciences (PhD), quantitative methods (MBA), strategic management (PhD). *Accreditation:* AACSB. *Program availability:* Part-time, evening/weekend, online learning. Terminal master's awarded for partial completion of doctoral program. *Entrance requirements:* For master's, GMAT, minimum GPA of 2.75; for doctorate, GMAT. Additional exam requirements/recommendations for international students: Required—TOEFL. Electronic applications accepted. *Faculty research:* Decision support systems, individual and group behavior, operations research, techniques and strategy.

Drury University, Master in Business Administration, Springfield, MO 65802. Offers MBA. *Accreditation:* AACSB; ACBSP. *Program availability:* Part-time, evening/weekend, 100% online. *Faculty:* 5 full-time (3 women). *Students:* 28 full-time (10 women). Average age 26. 13 applicants, 100% accepted, 12 enrolled. In 2018, 29 master's awarded. *Degree requirements:* For master's, international business trip. *Entrance requirements:* For master's, GMAT, bachelor's degree; minimum GPA of 3.0; prerequisite course requirements: financial accounting, managerial accounting, microeconomics, macroeconomics, marketing, management or organizational behavior, finance, and statistics. Additional exam requirements/recommendations for international students: Recommended—TOEFL (minimum score 80 iBT), IELTS (minimum score 6.5). *Application deadline:* For fall admission, 8/4 priority date for domestic and international students; for spring admission, 1/6 priority date for domestic and international students; for summer admission, 5/26 priority date for domestic and international students. Applications are processed on a rolling basis. Application fee: $25. Electronic applications accepted. *Expenses:* Tuition is $534/credit hour. Fees are $27/credit hour + $210 for 24 of the required courses. Program is 30 credit hours. *Financial support:* In 2018–19, 1 student received support. Career-related internships or fieldwork, scholarships/grants, and unspecified assistantships available. Financial award application deadline: 6/30; financial award applicants required to submit FAFSA. *Faculty research:* Cybersecurity leadership, health care management, cross cultural management, corporate finance, social entrepreneurship. *Unit head:* Dr. Robin Soster, Director, MBA Program, 417-873-7612, E-mail: rsoster@drury.edu. *Application contact:* Dr. Robin Soster, Director, MBA Program, 417-873-7612, E-mail: rsoster@drury.edu.
Website: http://mba.drury.edu/

Duke University, The Fuqua School of Business, The Duke MBA-Daytime Program, Durham, NC 27708. Offers academic excellence in finance (Certificate); business administration (MBA); decision sciences (MBA); energy and environment (MBA); energy finance (MBA); entrepreneurship and innovation (MBA); finance (MBA); financial analysis (MBA); health sector management (Certificate); leadership and ethics (MBA); management (MBA); management science and technology management (Certificate); marketing (MBA); operations management (MBA); social entrepreneurship (MBA); strategy (MBA). *Faculty:* 100 full-time (21 women), 55 part-time/adjunct (12 women). *Students:* 875 full-time (335 women); includes 188 minority (44 Black or African American, non-Hispanic/Latino; 4 American Indian or Alaska Native, non-Hispanic/ Latino; 90 Asian, non-Hispanic/Latino; 43 Hispanic/Latino; 1 Native Hawaiian or other Pacific Islander, non-Hispanic/Latino; 6 Two or more races, non-Hispanic/Latino), 276 international. Average age 29. In 2018, 429 master's awarded. *Entrance requirements:* For master's, GMAT or GRE, transcripts, essays, resume, recommendation letters, interview. *Application deadline:* For fall admission, 9/19 for domestic and international students; for winter admission, 10/14 for domestic and international students; for spring admission, 1/6 for domestic and international students; for summer admission, 3/11 for domestic and international students. Application fee: $225. Electronic applications accepted. *Expenses:* Contact institution. *Financial support:* Scholarships/grants available. Financial award applicants required to submit FAFSA. *Unit head:* Steve Misuraca, Assistant Dean, Daytime MBA Program. *Application contact:* Shari Hubert, Associate Dean, Office of Admissions, 919-660-7705, Fax: 919-681-8026, E-mail: admissions-info@fuqua.duke.edu.
Website: https://www.fuqua.duke.edu/programs/daytime-mba

Duke University, The Fuqua School of Business, The Duke MBA-Global Executive Program, Durham, NC 27708. Offers business administration (MBA); energy and environment (MBA); entrepreneurship and innovation (MBA); finance (MBA); health sector management (Certificate); marketing (MBA); strategy (MBA). *Faculty:* 100 full-time (21 women), 55 part-time/adjunct (12 women). *Students:* 141 full-time (43 women); includes 43 minority (12 Black or African American, non-Hispanic/Latino; 25 Asian, non-Hispanic/Latino; 4 Hispanic/Latino; 1 Native Hawaiian or other Pacific Islander, non-Hispanic/Latino; 1 Two or more races, non-Hispanic/Latino), 34 international. Average age 35. In 2018, 159 master's awarded. *Entrance requirements:* For master's, Executive Assessment, GMAT, or GRE, or waived, transcripts, essays, resume, recommendation letters, letter of company support, interview. *Application deadline:* For fall admission, 10/ 16 priority date for domestic and international students; for winter admission, 12/4 priority date for domestic and international students; for spring admission, 3/11 priority date for domestic and international students; for summer admission, 5/27 for domestic and international students. Applications are processed on a rolling basis. Application fee: $225. Electronic applications accepted. *Expenses:* Contact institution. *Financial support:* Scholarships/grants available. Financial award applicants required to submit FAFSA. *Unit head:* Karen Courtney, Associate Dean, Executive Programs. *Application contact:* Shari Hubert, Associate Dean, Office of Admissions, 919-660-7705, Fax: 919-681-8026, E-mail: admissions-info@fuqua.duke.edu.
Website: https://www.fuqua.duke.edu/programs/global-executive-mba

Duke University, The Fuqua School of Business, The Duke MBA-Weekend Executive Program, Durham, NC 27708. Offers business administration (MBA); energy and

environment (MBA); entrepreneurship and innovation (MBA); finance (MBA); health sector management (Certificate); marketing (MBA); strategy (MBA). *Faculty:* 100 full-time (21 women), 55 part-time/adjunct (12 women). *Students:* 251 full-time (67 women); includes 79 minority (13 Black or African American, non-Hispanic/Latino; 2 American Indian or Alaska Native, non-Hispanic/Latino; 46 Asian, non-Hispanic/Latino; 12 Hispanic/Latino; 1 Native Hawaiian or other Pacific Islander, non-Hispanic/Latino; 5 Two or more races, non-Hispanic/Latino), 32 international. Average age 35. In 2018, 120 master's awarded. *Entrance requirements:* For master's, Executive Assessment, GMAT, or GRE, or waived, transcripts, essays, resume, recommendation letters, letter of company support, interview. *Application deadline:* For fall admission, 9/18 priority date for domestic and international students; for winter admission, 12/4 priority date for domestic and international students; for spring admission, 1/22 priority date for domestic and international students; for summer admission, 3/11 for domestic and international students. Applications are processed on a rolling basis. Application fee: $225. Electronic applications accepted. *Expenses:* Contact institution. *Financial support:* Scholarships/grants available. Financial award applicants required to submit FAFSA. *Unit head:* Karen Courtney, Associate Dean, Executive Programs. *Application contact:* Shari Hubert, Associate Dean, Office of Admissions, 919-660-7705, Fax: 919-681-8026, E-mail: admissions-info@fuqua.duke.edu.
Website: https://www.fuqua.duke.edu/programs/weekend-executive-mba

Duke University, The Fuqua School of Business, MMS: Foundations of Business Program, Durham, NC 27708. Offers MMS. *Faculty:* 100 full-time (21 women), 55 part-time/adjunct (12 women). *Students:* 132 full-time (63 women); includes 28 minority (7 Black or African American, non-Hispanic/Latino; 16 Asian, non-Hispanic/Latino; 4 Hispanic/Latino; 1 Two or more races, non-Hispanic/Latino), 76 international. Average age 23. In 2018, 125 master's awarded. *Entrance requirements:* For master's, GMAT or GRE, transcripts, essays, resume, recommendation letter, interview. *Application deadline:* For fall admission, 10/28 for domestic and international students; for winter admission, 1/22 for domestic and international students; for spring admission, 3/5 for domestic and international students; for summer admission, 4/13 for domestic and international students. Application fee: $125. Electronic applications accepted. *Expenses:* Contact institution. *Financial support:* Scholarships/grants available. Financial award applicants required to submit FAFSA. *Unit head:* Steve Misuraca, Assistant Dean, 919-660-7778. *Application contact:* Shari Hubert, Associate Dean, Office of Admissions, 919-660-7705, Fax: 919-681-8026, E-mail: mms-fob-info@fuqua.duke.edu.
Website: https://www.fuqua.duke.edu/programs/mms-foundations-business

Duke University, The Fuqua School of Business, PhD Program, Durham, NC 27708. Offers accounting (PhD); decision sciences (PhD); finance (PhD); management and organizations (PhD); marketing (PhD); operations management (PhD); strategy (PhD). *Faculty:* 100 full-time (21 women). *Students:* 84 full-time (29 women); includes 4 minority (2 Asian, non-Hispanic/Latino; 2 Hispanic/Latino), 53 international. Average age 28. In 2018, 14 doctorates awarded. *Degree requirements:* For doctorate, comprehensive exam (for some programs), thesis/dissertation, Comprehensive or Qualifying exams are required for some of the 7 areas in Business Administration. *Entrance requirements:* For doctorate, GMAT or GRE, transcripts, essays, recommendation letters, statement of purpose. Additional exam requirements/recommendations for international students: Required—TOEFL, IELTS. *Application deadline:* For fall admission, 12/31 priority date for domestic and international students. Application fee: $90. Electronic applications accepted. *Expenses:* Contact institution. *Financial support:* In 2018–19, 74 fellowships with full tuition reimbursements (averaging $33,300 per year) were awarded; research assistantships with full tuition reimbursements, teaching assistantships, institutionally sponsored loans, scholarships/grants, health care benefits, and tuition waivers (full) also available. *Unit head:* William Boulding, Dean, 919-660-7822. *Application contact:* Ravi Bansal, Director of Graduate Studies, 919-660-7753, Fax: 919-660-7971, E-mail: fuqua-phd-info@duke.edu.

Duke University, Graduate School, Department of Business Administration, Durham, NC 27708. Offers PhD. *Accreditation:* AACSB. *Degree requirements:* For doctorate, thesis/dissertation. *Entrance requirements:* For doctorate, GMAT or GRE General Test. Additional exam requirements/recommendations for international students: Required—TOEFL (minimum score 577 paper-based; 90 iBT) or IELTS (minimum score 7). Electronic applications accepted.

Duquesne University, Palumbo-Donahue School of Business, Pittsburgh, PA 15282-0001. Offers accounting (M Acc); finance (MBA); information systems management (MSISM); management (MBA, MS); marketing (MBA); sports business (MS); supply chain management (MS); sustainability (MBA); JD/MBA; MBA/M Acc; MBA/MA; MBA/MES; MBA/MHMS; MSISM/MBA; Pharm D/MBA. *Accreditation:* AACSB. *Program availability:* Part-time, evening/weekend, 100% online, blended/hybrid learning. *Faculty:* 59 full-time (23 women), 25 part-time/adjunct (6 women). *Students:* 214 full-time (74 women), 42 part-time (20 women); includes 39 minority (12 Black or African American, non-Hispanic/Latino; 13 Asian, non-Hispanic/Latino; 8 Hispanic/Latino; 6 Two or more races, non-Hispanic/Latino), 23 international. Average age 29. 228 applicants, 88% accepted, 118 enrolled. In 2018, 149 master's awarded. *Entrance requirements:* For master's, GMAT or GRE, all official transcripts, two letters of recommendation, current resume, essays. Additional exam requirements/recommendations for international students: Required—TOEFL (minimum score 90 iBT), IELTS (minimum score 7). *Application deadline:* For fall admission, 7/1 priority date for domestic and international students; for spring admission, 12/1 for domestic and international students; for summer admission, 4/1 for domestic and international students. Applications are processed on a rolling basis. Application fee: $0. Electronic applications accepted. *Expenses:* $1,284/credit hour (business), $953/credit hour (management). *Financial support:* In 2018–19, 174 students received support, including 6 fellowships with partial tuition reimbursements available (averaging $24,750 per year); career-related internships or fieldwork, scholarships/grants, and unspecified assistantships also available. Support available to part-time students. Financial award application deadline: 7/1; financial award applicants required to submit FAFSA. *Faculty research:* Investment management, business ethics, technology management, supply chain management, entrepreneurship. *Unit head:* Dr. Karen Donovan, Associate Dean of Graduate Programs and Executive Education, 412-396-5788, Fax: 412-396-1726, E-mail: donovan6@duq.edu. *Application contact:* Chris Rouhier, Director of Graduate Admissions, 412-396-6244, Fax: 412-396-1726, E-mail: rouhierc@duq.edu.
Website: http://www.duq.edu/business/grad

D'Youville College, Department of Business, Buffalo, NY 14201-1084. Offers business administration (MBA); international business (MS). *Program availability:* Part-time, evening/weekend. *Degree requirements:* For master's, one foreign language, project or thesis. *Entrance requirements:* For master's, minimum GPA of 3.0. Additional exam requirements/recommendations for international students: Required—TOEFL (minimum score 500 paper-based). Electronic applications accepted. *Faculty research:* Assessment, accreditation, supply chain, online learning, adult learning.

East Carolina University, Graduate School, College of Business, Master's of Business Administration, Greenville, NC 27858-4353. Offers MBA, MD/MBA. *Program availability:* Part-time, evening/weekend, online learning. *Entrance requirements:* For master's, GMAT or GRE. Additional exam requirements/recommendations for international students: Recommended—TOEFL, IELTS. *Expenses: Tuition, area resident:* Full-time $4749. Tuition, state resident: full-time $4749. Tuition, nonresident: full-time $17,898. *International tuition:* $17,898 full-time. *Required fees:* $2787. Part-time tuition and fees vary according to course load and program. *Unit head:* Director of Graduate Programs, E-mail: gradbus@ecu.edu. *Application contact:* Graduate School Admissions, 252-328-6012, Fax: 252-328-6071, E-mail: gradschool@ecu.edu.
Website: http://www.ecu.edu/cs-bus/grad/mba.cfm

East Carolina University, Graduate School, College of Engineering and Technology, Department of Technology Systems, Greenville, NC 27858-4353. Offers computer network professional (Certificate); cyber security professional (Certificate); information assurance (Certificate); Lean Six Sigma Black Belt (Certificate); network technology (MS), including computer networking management, digital communications technology, information security, Web technologies; occupational safety (MS); technology management (MS, PhD), including industrial distribution and logistics (MS); Website developer (Certificate). *Application deadline:* For fall admission, 6/1 priority date for domestic students. *Expenses: Tuition, area resident:* Full-time $4749. Tuition, state resident: full-time $4749. Tuition, nonresident: full-time $17,898. *International tuition:* $17,898 full-time. *Required fees:* $2787. Part-time tuition and fees vary according to course load and program. *Financial support:* Application deadline: 6/1. *Unit head:* Dr. Tijjani Mohammed, Chair, 252-328-9668, E-mail: mohammedt@ecu.edu. *Application contact:* Graduate School Admissions, 252-328-6012, Fax: 252-328-6071, E-mail: gradschool@ecu.edu.
Website: http://www.ecu.edu/cs-cet/techsystems/index.cfm

Eastern Illinois University, Graduate School, Lumpkin College of Business and Technology, Program in Business Administration, Charleston, IL 61920. Offers accountancy (MBA); applied management (MBA); geographic information systems (MBA); research (MBA). *Accreditation:* AACSB. *Program availability:* Part-time, evening/weekend. *Entrance requirements:* For master's, GMAT or GRE. Additional exam requirements/recommendations for international students: Required—TOEFL (minimum score 500 paper-based; 61 iBT), IELTS (minimum score 6). Electronic applications accepted. *Expenses:* Tuition, state resident: part-time $299 per credit hour. Tuition, nonresident: part-time $718 per credit hour. *Required fees:* $214.50 per credit hour.

Eastern Kentucky University, The Graduate School, College of Business and Technology, Program in Business Administration, Richmond, KY 40475-3102. Offers MBA. *Accreditation:* AACSB.

Eastern Mennonite University, Program in Business Administration, Harrisonburg, VA 22802-2462. Offers general management (MBA); health services administration (MBA); non-profit leadership (MBA). *Program availability:* Part-time, evening/weekend. *Degree requirements:* For master's, final capstone course. *Entrance requirements:* For master's, GMAT, minimum GPA of 2.5, 2 years of work experience, 2 letters of reference. Additional exam requirements/recommendations for international students: Required—TOEFL (minimum score 500 paper-based). Electronic applications accepted. *Expenses:* Contact institution. *Faculty research:* Information security, Anabaptist/Mennonite experiences and perspectives, limits of multi-cultural education, international development performance criteria.

Eastern Michigan University, Graduate School, College of Business, Department of Management, Ypsilanti, MI 48197. Offers entrepreneurship (Postbaccalaureate Certificate); human resources management and organizational development (MSHROD). *Program availability:* Part-time, evening/weekend, online learning. *Faculty:* 21 full-time (12 women). *Students:* 5 full-time (4 women), 68 part-time (54 women); includes 29 minority (19 Black or African American, non-Hispanic/Latino; 4 Asian, non-Hispanic/Latino; 4 Hispanic/Latino; 2 Two or more races, non-Hispanic/Latino), 3 international. Average age 32. 47 applicants, 81% accepted, 18 enrolled. In 2018, 62 master's awarded. *Entrance requirements:* For master's, GMAT. Additional exam requirements/recommendations for international students: Required—TOEFL. *Application deadline:* For fall admission, 5/15 priority date for domestic students, 2/15 priority date for international students; for winter admission, 10/15 priority date for domestic students, 9/1 priority date for international students; for summer admission, 3/15 priority date for domestic students, 3/1 priority date for international students. Applications are processed on a rolling basis. Application fee: $45. *Financial support:* Fellowships, research assistantships with full tuition reimbursements, teaching assistantships with full tuition reimbursements, career-related internships or fieldwork, Federal Work-Study, institutionally sponsored loans, scholarships/grants, tuition waivers (partial), and unspecified assistantships available. Support available to part-time students. Financial award applicants required to submit FAFSA. *Unit head:* Dr. Stephanie Newell, Interim Department Head, 734-487-0141, Fax: 734-487-4100, E-mail: snewell@emich.edu. *Application contact:* Dr. Stephanie Newell, Interim Department Head, 734-487-0141, Fax: 734-487-4100, E-mail: snewell@emich.edu.

Eastern Michigan University, Graduate School, College of Business, Programs in Business Administration, Ypsilanti, MI 48197. Offers business administration (MBA, Graduate Certificate); computer information systems (Graduate Certificate); e-business (MBA, Graduate Certificate); enterprise business intelligence (MBA); entrepreneurship (MBA, Graduate Certificate); finance (MBA, Graduate Certificate); human resources (MBA); human resources management (Graduate Certificate); information systems (MBA); internal auditing (MBA); international business (MBA, Graduate Certificate); marketing management (Graduate Certificate); nonprofit management (MBA); organizational development (Graduate Certificate); supply chain management (MBA, Graduate Certificate). *Accreditation:* AACSB. *Program availability:* Part-time, online learning. *Students:* 69 full-time (38 women), 251 part-time (140 women); includes 100 minority (63 Black or African American, non-Hispanic/Latino; 1 American Indian or Alaska Native, non-Hispanic/Latino; 12 Asian, non-Hispanic/Latino; 14 Hispanic/Latino; 10 Two or more races, non-Hispanic/Latino), 28 international. Average age 32. 199 applicants, 75% accepted, 83 enrolled. In 2018, 75 master's, 50 other advanced degrees awarded. *Entrance requirements:* For master's, GMAT (minimum score 450), minimum cumulative undergraduate GPA of 2.75. Additional exam requirements/recommendations for international students: Required—TOEFL. *Application deadline:* For fall admission, 5/15 priority date for domestic students, 2/15 priority date for international students; for winter admission, 10/15 priority date for domestic students, 9/1 priority date for international students; for summer admission, 3/15 priority date for domestic students, 3/1 priority date for international students. Applications are processed on a rolling basis. Application fee: $45. *Financial support:* Fellowships, research assistantships with full tuition reimbursements, teaching assistantships with full tuition reimbursements, career-related internships or fieldwork, Federal Work-Study, institutionally sponsored loans, scholarships/grants, tuition waivers (partial), and unspecified assistantships available. Support available to part-time students. Financial award applicants required to submit FAFSA. *Unit head:* K. Michelle Henry, Director, Graduate Business Programs, 734-487-4444, Fax: 734-483-1316, E-mail: cob.graduate@emich.edu. *Application contact:* K. Michelle Henry, Director, Graduate Business Programs, 734-487-4444, Fax: 734-483-1316, E-mail: cob.graduate@emich.edu.
Website: http://www.emich.edu/cob/mba/

Eastern Nazarene College, Adult and Graduate Studies, Program in Management, Quincy, MA 02170. Offers MSM.

Eastern New Mexico University, Graduate School, College of Business, Portales, NM 88130. Offers MBA. *Accreditation:* ACBSP. *Program availability:* Part-time, evening/weekend, online learning. *Degree requirements:* For master's, comprehensive exam, comprehensive integrative project and presentation. *Entrance requirements:* For master's, GMAT (minimum score 450), minimum undergraduate GPA of 3.0. Additional exam requirements/recommendations for international students: Required—TOEFL (minimum score 550 paper-based; 79 iBT), IELTS (minimum score 6). Electronic applications accepted. *Expenses: Tuition, area resident:* Full-time $6776. Tuition, state resident: full-time $6776; part-time $282 per credit hour. Tuition, nonresident: full-time $8986; part-time $374 per credit hour. *Required fees:* $60 per semester. One-time fee: $25.

Eastern Oregon University, Program in Business Administration, La Grande, OR 97850-2899. Offers MBA. *Program availability:* Part-time, online only, 100% online. *Faculty:* 6 full-time (2 women), 1 part-time/adjunct (0 women). *Students:* 24 full-time (9 women), 57 part-time (36 women); includes 19 minority (2 American Indian or Alaska Native, non-Hispanic/Latino; 4 Asian, non-Hispanic/Latino; 9 Hispanic/Latino; 4 Two or more races, non-Hispanic/Latino), 5 international. Average age 34. In 2018, 44 master's awarded. *Degree requirements:* For master's, thesis. *Application deadline:* For fall admission, 5/15 priority date for domestic students. Applications are processed on a rolling basis. Electronic applications accepted. *Expenses:* $377 per credit plus a $16 differential fee for each Business Credit. *Financial support:* In 2018–19, 14 students received support. Federal Work-Study, scholarships/grants, and tuition waivers (full and partial) available. Support available to part-time students. *Faculty research:* Good customer service as a global sustainable business practice; analysis and marketing of tribal business plans; market-based innovation. *Unit head:* Laura Gow-Hogge, Chair of Curriculum/Business Faculty, 541-962-3721, E-mail: lgow@eou.edu. *Application contact:* Kristin Johnson, MAT Advisor/Recruiter, 541-962-3529, Fax: 541-962-3701, E-mail: kristin.johnson@eou.edu.
Website: https://www.eou.edu/cobe/business/mba/

Eastern University, Graduate Programs in Business and Leadership, St. Davids, PA 19087-3696. Offers health administration (MBA); health services management (MS); management (MBA); organizational leadership (MA); social impact (MBA). *Program availability:* Part-time, evening/weekend, online learning. Electronic applications accepted. Application fee is waived when completed online. *Expenses:* Contact institution.

Eastern University, Program in Organizational Leadership, St. Davids, PA 19087-3696. Offers leadership studies (CAGS); organizational leadership (PhD), including business management, educational administration, public and nonprofit administration. Electronic applications accepted. *Expenses:* Contact institution.

Eastern Washington University, Graduate Studies, College of Business and Public Administration, Business Administration Program, Cheney, WA 99004-2431. Offers MBA, MBA/MPA. *Accreditation:* AACSB. *Degree requirements:* For master's, comprehensive exam, thesis optional. *Entrance requirements:* For master's, GMAT, minimum GPA of 3.0. Additional exam requirements/recommendations for international students: Required—TOEFL (minimum score 580 paper-based; 92 iBT), IELTS (minimum score 7), PTE (minimum score 63). Electronic applications accepted.

East Tennessee State University, School of Graduate Studies, College of Business and Technology, Department of Management and Marketing, Johnson City, TN 37614. Offers business administration (MBA, Postbaccalaureate Certificate); digital marketing (MS); entrepreneurial leadership (Postbaccalaureate Certificate); health care management (Postbaccalaureate Certificate). *Program availability:* Part-time, evening/weekend. *Degree requirements:* For master's, comprehensive exam, capstone. *Entrance requirements:* For master's, GMAT, minimum GPA of 2.5 (for MBA), 3.0 (for MS); current resume; three letters of recommendation; for Postbaccalaureate Certificate, minimum GPA of 2.5, undergraduate degree. Additional exam requirements/recommendations for international students: Required—TOEFL (minimum score 550 paper-based; 79 iBT). Electronic applications accepted. *Faculty research:* Sustainability, healthcare effectiveness, consumer behavior, merchandising trends, organizational management issues.

East Texas Baptist University, Master of Business Administration Program, Marshall, TX 75670-1498. Offers MBA. *Program availability:* Part-time, evening/weekend, 100% online. *Faculty:* 1 (woman) full-time, 3 part-time/adjunct (0 women). *Students:* 15 full-time (8 women), 22 part-time (10 women); includes 15 minority (13 Black or African American, non-Hispanic/Latino; 2 Hispanic/Latino). Average age 27. 34 applicants, 65% accepted, 22 enrolled. In 2018, 13 master's awarded. *Entrance requirements:* Additional exam requirements/recommendations for international students: Recommended—TOEFL (minimum score 550 paper-based; 79 iBT). *Application deadline:* For fall admission, 8/15 for domestic students; for spring admission, 1/9 for domestic students; for summer admission, 5/11 for domestic students. Applications are processed on a rolling basis. Application fee: $50. Electronic applications accepted. *Expenses:* Tuition: $725 per credit hour, graduate student fee: $150 per semester (6 or more hours enrolled)/$75 per semester (1-5 hours enrolled). *Financial support:* In 2018–19, 18 students received support. Federal Work-Study, scholarships/grants, unspecified assistantships, and staff grants available. Financial award applicants required to submit FAFSA. *Unit head:* Den Murley, Director of Graduate Admissions, 903-923-2079, Fax: 903-934-8115, E-mail: dmurley@etbu.edu. *Application contact:* Den Murley, Director of Graduate Admissions, 903-923-2079, Fax: 903-934-8115, E-mail: dmurley@etbu.edu.
Website: https://www.etbu.edu/academics/academic-schools/fred-hale-school-business/programs/business-administration-bba

ECPI University, Graduate Programs, Virginia Beach, VA 23462. Offers business administration (MBA); cybersecurity (MS); information systems (MS).

Edgewood College, Program in Business, Madison, WI 53711-1997. Offers accountancy (MS); sustainability leadership (MBA). *Accreditation:* ACBSP. *Program availability:* Part-time, evening/weekend. *Students:* 74 full-time (34 women), 47 part-time (28 women); includes 19 minority (5 Black or African American, non-Hispanic/Latino; 2 American Indian or Alaska Native, non-Hispanic/Latino; 1 Asian, non-Hispanic/Latino; 8 Hispanic/Latino; 1 Native Hawaiian or other Pacific Islander, non-Hispanic/Latino; 2 Two or more races, non-Hispanic/Latino), 5 international. Average age 28. In 2018, 43 master's awarded. *Entrance requirements:* For master's, GMAT (minimum score 430), minimum GPA of 2.75, 2 letters of recommendation. Additional exam requirements/recommendations for international students: Required—TOEFL. *Application deadline:* For fall admission, 8/15 for domestic students, 5/1 for international students; for spring admission, 1/8 for domestic students, 11/1 for international students. Applications are processed on a rolling basis. Application fee: $30. Electronic applications accepted. *Expenses: Tuition:* Part-time $963 per credit. *Financial support:* Career-related internships or fieldwork and scholarships/grants available. *Unit head:* Dean, 608-663-2224, Fax: 608-663-3291. *Application contact:* Joann Eastman, Admissions Counselor, 608-663-3250, Fax: 608-663-2214, E-mail: gps@edgewood.edu.
Website: https://www.edgewood.edu/academics/schools/school-of-business

Elmhurst College, Graduate Programs, Program in Business Administration, Elmhurst, IL 60126-3296. Offers MBA. *Program availability:* Part-time, evening/weekend, 100% online. *Faculty:* 5 full-time (2 women), 11 part-time/adjunct (2 women). *Students:* 13 full-time (6 women), 110 part-time (55 women); includes 31 minority (7 Black or African American, non-Hispanic/Latino; 6 Asian, non-Hispanic/Latino; 17 Hispanic/Latino; 1 Native Hawaiian or other Pacific Islander, non-Hispanic/Latino), 2 international. Average age 31. 116 applicants, 57% accepted, 61 enrolled. In 2018, 70 master's awarded. *Entrance requirements:* For master's, 3 recommendations, resume, statement of purpose. Additional exam requirements/recommendations for international students: Required—TOEFL (minimum score 550 paper-based; 79 iBT), IELTS (minimum score 6.5). *Application deadline:* Applications are processed on a rolling basis. Application fee: $0. Electronic applications accepted. *Expenses:* $870 per semester hour. *Financial support:* In 2018–19, 57 students received support. Fellowships, scholarships/grants, and unspecified assistantships available. Support available to part-time students. Financial award applicants required to submit FAFSA. *Unit head:* Kelly Cunningham, Associate Professor, 630-617-3223, E-mail: mcunningham@elmhurst.edu. *Application contact:* Timothy J. Panfil, Senior Director of Graduate Admission and Enrollment Management, 630-617-3300 Ext. 3256, Fax: 630-617-6471, E-mail: panfilt@elmhurst.edu.
Website: http://www.elmhurst.edu/mba

Elms College, Division of Business, Chicopee, MA 01013-2839. Offers accounting (MBA); accounting and finance (MS); financial planning (MBA, Certificate); healthcare leadership (MBA); lean entrepreneurship (MBA); management (MBA). *Program availability:* Part-time, evening/weekend. *Faculty:* 4 full-time (all women), 5 part-time/adjunct (3 women). *Students:* 36 part-time (22 women); includes 9 minority (5 Black or African American, non-Hispanic/Latino; 4 Hispanic/Latino), 1 international. Average age 35. 13 applicants, 85% accepted, 9 enrolled. In 2018, 29 master's awarded. *Entrance requirements:* For master's, minimum GPA of 3.0. *Application deadline:* Applications are processed on a rolling basis. Application fee: $30. Electronic applications accepted. *Expenses: Tuition:* Full-time $14,328; part-time $796 per credit. *Required fees:* $200. Tuition and fees vary according to degree level and program. *Unit head:* Kim Kenney-Rockwal, MBA Program Director, 413-265-2572, E-mail: kenneyrockwalk@elms.edu. *Application contact:* MBA Program Coordinator, 413-265-2592, E-mail: mba@elms.edu.

Elon University, Program in Business Administration, Elon, NC 27244-2010. Offers business (MBA); management (M Sc). *Accreditation:* AACSB. *Program availability:* Part-time, evening/weekend. *Faculty:* 19 full-time (4 women), 11 part-time/adjunct (8 women). *Students:* 55 full-time (30 women), 72 part-time (32 women); includes 25 minority (17 Black or African American, non-Hispanic/Latino; 3 Asian, non-Hispanic/Latino; 4 Hispanic/Latino; 1 Two or more races, non-Hispanic/Latino), 5 international. Average age 33. 111 applicants, 68% accepted, 57 enrolled. In 2018, 50 master's awarded. *Entrance requirements:* For master's, GMAT. Additional exam requirements/recommendations for international students: Required—TOEFL (minimum score 550 paper-based; 79 iBT). *Application deadline:* For fall admission, 8/15 priority date for domestic students; for spring admission, 2/15 priority date for domestic students. Applications are processed on a rolling basis. Application fee: $50. Electronic applications accepted. *Financial support:* Federal Work-Study and scholarships/grants available. Support available to part-time students. Financial award application deadline: 3/15; financial award applicants required to submit FAFSA. *Faculty research:* Business ethics, international business and global economics, sales force management, sustainable business practices, consumer behavior. *Unit head:* Dr. Jen Platania, Associate Dean of the Love School of Business/Associate Professor of Economics, 336-278-5938, E-mail: jplatania@elon.edu. *Application contact:* Art Fadde, Director of Graduate Admissions, 800-334-8448 Ext. 3, Fax: 336-278-7699, E-mail: afadde@elon.edu.
Website: http://www.elon.edu/mba/

Embry-Riddle Aeronautical University–Daytona, College of Business, Daytona Beach, FL 32114-3900. Offers airline management (MBA); airport management (MBA); aviation finance (MSAF); aviation human resources (MBA); aviation management (MBA-AM); aviation system management (MBA); finance (MBA). *Accreditation:* ACBSP. *Degree requirements:* For master's, thesis (for some programs). *Entrance requirements:* For master's, GRE (for some programs). Additional exam requirements/recommendations for international students: Required—TOEFL (minimum score 550 paper-based, 79 iBT) or IELTS (6). Electronic applications accepted.

Embry-Riddle Aeronautical University–Worldwide, Department of Business Administration, Daytona Beach, FL 32114-3900. Offers aviation (MBAA); MS/MBA. *Program availability:* Part-time, evening/weekend, online only, EagleVision Classroom (between classrooms), EagleVision Home (faculty and students at home), and a blend of Classroom or Home. *Degree requirements:* For master's, comprehensive exam. *Entrance requirements:* Additional exam requirements/recommendations for international students: Required—TOEFL (minimum score 550 paper-based; 79 iBT), IELTS (minimum score 6). Electronic applications accepted. *Expenses:* Contact institution.

Embry-Riddle Aeronautical University–Worldwide, Department of Decision Sciences, Daytona Beach, FL 32114-3900. Offers aviation and aerospace (MSPM); aviation/aerospace management (MSEM); financial management (MSEM, MSPM); general management (MSPM); global management (MSPM); human resources management (MSPM); information systems (MSPM); leadership (MSEM, MSPM); logistics and supply chain management (MSEM, MSLSCM, MSPM); management (MSEM, MSPM); project management (MSEM); systems engineering (MSEM, MSPM); technical management (MSPM). *Program availability:* Part-time, evening/weekend, EagleVision Classroom (between classrooms), EagleVision Home (faculty and students at home), and a blend of Classroom or Home. *Degree requirements:* For master's, comprehensive exam (for some programs), thesis (for some programs). *Entrance requirements:* Additional exam requirements/recommendations for international students: Required—TOEFL (minimum score 550 paper-based; 79 iBT), IELTS (minimum score 6). Electronic applications accepted. *Expenses:* Contact institution.

Emmanuel College, Graduate and Professional Programs, Graduate Programs in Management, Boston, MA 02115. Offers management (MSM); management and leadership (Graduate Certificate); research administration (MSM, Graduate Certificate). *Program availability:* Part-time, evening/weekend, blended/hybrid learning. *Degree requirements:* For master's, 36 credits. *Entrance requirements:* For master's and Graduate Certificate, transcripts from all regionally-accredited institutions attended (showing proof of bachelor's degree completion), 2 letters of recommendation, essay, resume. Additional exam requirements/recommendations for international students: Required—TOEFL. Electronic applications accepted. *Expenses:* Contact institution.

Emory University, Goizueta Business School, Doctoral Program in Business, Atlanta, GA 30322. Offers accounting (PhD); finance (PhD); information systems and operations management (PhD); marketing (PhD); organization and management (PhD). *Faculty:* 67 full-time (22 women). *Students:* 45 full-time (21 women); includes 5 minority (2 Black or African American, non-Hispanic/Latino; 3 Hispanic/Latino), 31 international. Average age 29. 143 applicants, 19% accepted, 10 enrolled. In 2018, 7 doctorates awarded. *Degree requirements:* For doctorate, comprehensive exam, thesis/dissertation. *Entrance requirements:* For doctorate, GMAT, interview. Additional exam requirements/recommendations for international students: Required—TOEFL (minimum score 600 paper-based; 100 iBT), IELTS, We will take either TOEFL or IELTS. *Application*

deadline: For fall admission, 1/3 priority date for domestic and international students. Applications are processed on a rolling basis. Application fee: $75. Electronic applications accepted. *Expenses:* Our students are required to pay approximately $400 in their fall and spring terms; approximately $200 in summer terms in fees. All tuition is scholarshiped 100%. *Financial support:* In 2018–19, 45 students received support, including 11 fellowships (averaging $1,000 per year); scholarships/grants, health care benefits, and Fellowships are both the Sheth Fellows and Goizueta Fellows whom are named each year based on certain milestones. also available. Financial award application deadline: 1/3. *Faculty research:* Financial and managerial accounting, asset pricing strategy and organizational behavior, information technology marketing analytics and consumer behavior. *Unit head:* Kathryn Kadous, Associate Dean, 404-727-2306, Fax: 404-727-5337, E-mail: kathryn.kadous@emory.edu. *Application contact:* Allison Gilmore, Director of Admissions and Student Services, 404-727-6353, Fax: 404-727-5337, E-mail: allison.gilmore@emory.edu.
Website: https://goizueta.emory.edu/degree/phd/index.html

Emory University, Goizueta Business School, Evening MBA Program, Atlanta, GA 30322-1100. Offers MBA. *Program availability:* Part-time-only, evening/weekend. *Faculty:* 19 full-time (3 women), 6 part-time/adjunct (2 women). *Students:* 264 part-time (96 women); includes 57 minority (13 Black or African American, non-Hispanic/Latino; 27 Asian, non-Hispanic/Latino; 14 Hispanic/Latino; 3 Two or more races, non-Hispanic/Latino), 49 international. Average age 30. 176 applicants, 65% accepted, 89 enrolled. In 2018, 80 master's awarded. *Degree requirements:* For master's, minimum 55 credit hours. *Entrance requirements:* For master's, GMAT/GRE, undergraduate degree, interview, essays, recommendation letters, resume, work experience. Additional exam requirements/recommendations for international students: Required—TOEFL (minimum score 100 iBT), IELTS (minimum score 7), PTE (minimum score 68). *Application deadline:* For fall admission, 10/24 for domestic and international students; for spring admission, 4/1 for domestic and international students; for summer admission, 6/25 for domestic and international students. Application fee: $175. Electronic applications accepted. *Expenses:* Contact institution. *Financial support:* In 2018–19, 105 students received support. Scholarships/grants available. Financial award application deadline: 6/25; financial award applicants required to submit FAFSA. *Faculty research:* Improving health care delivery systems; corporate-based valuation; marketing; finance interface, asset allocation and portfolio management; social media and network processes. *Unit head:* Corey Dortch, Associate Dean, Evening MBA Programs, 404-727-2940, E-mail: e.w.leonard@emory.edu. *Application contact:* Kathleen Edwards, Director of MBA Admissions, 404-727-8124, Fax: 404-727-4612, E-mail: kathleen.edwards@emory.edu.
Website: http://www.goizueta.emory.edu

Emory University, Goizueta Business School, Full Time MBA Program, Atlanta, GA 30322-1100. Offers accounting (MBA); alternative investments (MBA); business process consulting (MBA); business technology management (MBA); capital markets (MBA); corporate finance (MBA); customer relationship management (MBA); decision analytics (MBA); entrepreneurship (MBA); finance (MBA); global management (MBA); investment banking (MBA); management consulting (MBA); marketing (MBA); marketing analytics (MBA); marketing consulting (MBA); operations management (MBA); organization and management (MBA); product and brand management (MBA); real estate (MBA); social enterprise (MBA); strategy consulting (MBA). *Accreditation:* AACSB. *Faculty:* 74 full-time (18 women), 18 part-time/adjunct (6 women). *Students:* 349 full-time (105 women); includes 81 minority (26 Black or African American, non-Hispanic/Latino; 1 American Indian or Alaska Native, non-Hispanic/Latino; 35 Asian, non-Hispanic/Latino; 16 Hispanic/Latino; 3 Two or more races, non-Hispanic/Latino), 97 international. Average age 29. 1,380 applicants, 34% accepted, 172 enrolled. In 2018, 180 master's awarded. *Degree requirements:* For master's, 1 leadership course; 2 mid-semester module programs; 2 global components. *Entrance requirements:* For master's, GMAT/GRE, essays; recommendation letters; undergraduate degree; interview. Additional exam requirements/recommendations for international students: Required—TOEFL (minimum score 100 iBT), IELTS (minimum score 7), PTE (minimum score 68). *Application deadline:* For fall admission, 10/6 for domestic and international students; for winter admission, 11/17 for domestic and international students; for spring admission, 1/3 priority date for domestic and international students; for summer admission, 3/9 for domestic and international students. Application fee: $150. Electronic applications accepted. *Expenses:* Contact institution. *Financial support:* In 2018–19, 273 students received support. Career-related internships or fieldwork, institutionally sponsored loans, and scholarships/grants available. Financial award application deadline: 4/1; financial award applicants required to submit FAFSA. *Faculty research:* Corporate finance, information systems, digital marketing, asset pricing, sports management. *Unit head:* Brian Mitchell, Associate Dean, 404-727-4824, Fax: 404-712-9648, E-mail: brian.mitchell@emory.edu. *Application contact:* Melissa Rapp, Associate Dean, 404-727-7583, Fax: 404-727-4612, E-mail: mbaadmissions@emory.edu.
Website: http://www.goizueta.emory.edu

Emory University, Goizueta Business School, Modular MBA for Executives Program, Atlanta, GA 30322. Offers MBA. *Program availability:* Part-time-only. *Faculty:* 19 full-time (2 women), 6 part-time/adjunct (1 woman). *Students:* 42 full-time (15 women); includes 9 minority (4 Asian, non-Hispanic/Latino; 4 Hispanic/Latino; 1 Two or more races, non-Hispanic/Latino), 5 international. Average age 42. 74 applicants, 61% accepted, 21 enrolled. In 2018, 20 master's awarded. *Degree requirements:* For master's, minimum of 50 credit hours, which includes lock-step core coursework, two elective courses, experiential learning, and global business practices through week-long international colloquium. *Entrance requirements:* For master's, GMAT/GRE/GMAT Executive Assessment (or waiver), interview, essays, letters of recommendation, undergraduate degree, resume, work experience. Additional exam requirements/recommendations for international students: Required—TOEFL (minimum score 100 iBT), IELTS (minimum score 7), PTE (minimum score 68). *Application deadline:* For fall admission, 2/15 for domestic and international students; for winter admission, 4/5 for domestic and international students; for spring admission, 6/7 for domestic and international students; for summer admission, 8/2 for domestic and international students. Application fee: $175. Electronic applications accepted. *Expenses:* Contact institution. *Financial support:* Scholarships/grants available. Financial award application deadline: 8/2; financial award applicants required to submit FAFSA. *Faculty research:* Alternative investments, quality management and statistical methodology, entrepreneurial finance, effects of competition on marketing strategies, strategies for niche and specialized firms. *Unit head:* Jaclyn D. Conner, Associate Dean, Executive MBA Programs, 404-727-4370, E-mail: jaclyn.conner@emory.edu. *Application contact:* Kathleen Edwards, Director of MBA Admissions, 404-727-8124, E-mail: kathleen.edwards@emory.edu.
Website: http://goizueta.emory.edu/degree/emba/memba/

Emory University, Goizueta Business School, Weekend MBA for Executives Program, Atlanta, GA 30322-1100. Offers MBA. *Program availability:* Evening/weekend. *Faculty:* 10 full-time (0 women), 1 (woman) part-time/adjunct. *Students:* 92 full-time (33 women); includes 30 minority (9 Black or African American, non-Hispanic/Latino; 13 Asian, non-Hispanic/Latino; 6 Hispanic/Latino; 2 Two or more races, non-Hispanic/Latino), 27 international. 97 applicants, 75% accepted, 51 enrolled. In 2018, 40 master's awarded. *Degree requirements:* For master's, minimum of 51 credit hours. *Entrance requirements:* For master's, GMAT/GRE/GMAT Executive Assessment (or waiver), interview, essays, letters of recommendation, undergraduate degree, resume, work experience. Additional exam requirements/recommendations for international students: Required—TOEFL (minimum score 100 iBT), IELTS (minimum score 7), PTE (minimum score 68). *Application deadline:* For fall admission, 2/15 for domestic students, 2/1 for international students; for winter admission, 4/5 for domestic and international students; for spring admission, 6/7 for domestic and international students; for summer admission, 8/2 for domestic and international students. Application fee: $175. Electronic applications accepted. *Expenses:* Contact institution. *Financial support:* Scholarships/grants available. Financial award application deadline: 8/2; financial award applicants required to submit FAFSA. *Faculty research:* Neuro-imaging, how technology and social forces create and sustain competitive advantage, entrepreneurial finance, alternative investments, digital commerce. *Unit head:* Jaclyn Conner, Associate Dean, Executive MBA Programs, 404-727-4370, E-mail: jaclyn.conner@emory.edu. *Application contact:* Kathleen Edwards, Director of MBA Admissions, 404-727-8124, E-mail: kathleen.edwards@emory.edu.
Website: http://goizueta.emory.edu/degree/emba/wemba/

Emporia State University, Program in Business Administration, Emporia, KS 66801-5415. Offers MBA. *Accreditation:* AACSB. *Program availability:* Part-time, evening/weekend, blended/hybrid learning. *Entrance requirements:* For master's, GRE, 15 undergraduate credits in business, minimum undergraduate GPA of 2.7 in last 60 hours. Additional exam requirements/recommendations for international students: Required—TOEFL (minimum score 520 paper-based; 68 iBT). Electronic applications accepted.

Endicott College, Van Loan School of Graduate and Professional Studies, Program in Business Administration, Beverly, MA 01915-2096. Offers business administration (MBA); organizational leadership (MBA). *Program availability:* Part-time, evening/weekend, 100% online, blended/hybrid learning. *Degree requirements:* For master's, thesis, project. *Entrance requirements:* For master's, two recommendations, undergraduate transcript, essay. Additional exam requirements/recommendations for international students: Required—TOEFL. Electronic applications accepted. *Expenses:* Contact institution. *Faculty research:* Adult learning and development, supply chain management, marketing, ethics.

ESSEC Business School, Graduate Programs, Paris, France. Offers business administration (PhD); executive business administration (MBA); global business administration (MBA); hospitality management (MBA); international luxury brand management (MBA); management (MSM).

Everglades University, Graduate Programs, Program in Aviation Science, Boca Raton, FL 33431. Offers aviation operations management (MSA); aviation security (MSA); business administration (MSA). *Program availability:* Part-time, evening/weekend, 100% online. *Entrance requirements:* For master's, GMAT (minimum score of 400) or GRE (minimum score of 290), bachelor's or graduate degree from college accredited by an agency recognized by the U.S. Department of Education; minimum cumulative GPA of 2.0 at the baccalaureate level, 3.0 at the master's level. Additional exam requirements/recommendations for international students: Recommended—TOEFL (minimum score 500 paper-based). Electronic applications accepted. *Expenses:* Contact institution.

Everglades University, Graduate Programs, Program in Business Administration, Boca Raton, FL 33431. Offers accounting for managers (MBA); aviation management (MBA); human resource management (MBA); project management (MBA). *Program availability:* Part-time, evening/weekend, 100% online. *Entrance requirements:* For master's, GMAT (minimum score of 400) or GRE (minimum score of 290), bachelor's or graduate degree from college accredited by an agency recognized by the U.S. Department of Education; minimum cumulative GPA of 2.0 at the baccalaureate level, 3.0 at the master's level. Additional exam requirements/recommendations for international students: Recommended—TOEFL (minimum score 500 paper-based). Electronic applications accepted. *Expenses:* Contact institution.

Fairfield University, Dolan School of Business, Fairfield, CT 06824. Offers accounting (MBA, MS, CAS); business analytics (MS); finance (MBA, MS, CAS); information systems and business analytics (MBA); management (MBA, CAS); marketing (MBA, CAS); taxation (CAS). *Accreditation:* AACSB. *Program availability:* Part-time, evening/weekend. *Degree requirements:* For master's, capstone course. *Entrance requirements:* For master's, GMAT (minimum score 500), 2 letters of reference, resume, minimum GPA of 3.0. Additional exam requirements/recommendations for international students: Required—TOEFL (minimum score 550 paper-based; 80 iBT) or IELTS (minimum score 6.5). Electronic applications accepted. *Expenses:* Contact institution. *Faculty research:* International finance, leadership and careers, ethics in accounting, emotions in consumer behavior and organizations, data analytics.

Fairleigh Dickinson University, Florham Campus, Anthony J. Petrocelli College of Continuing Studies, School of Administrative Science, Program in Administrative Science, Madison, NJ 07940-1099. Offers MAS.

Fairleigh Dickinson University, Florham Campus, Silberman College of Business, Madison, NJ 07940-1099. Offers EMBA, MBA, MS, Certificate, MA/MBA, MBA/MA. *Accreditation:* AACSB. *Program availability:* Part-time, evening/weekend.

Fairleigh Dickinson University, Florham Campus, Silberman College of Business, Departments of Management, Marketing, and Entrepreneurial Studies, Program in Management, Madison, NJ 07940-1099. Offers evolving technology (Certificate); management (MBA); MBA/MA.

Fairleigh Dickinson University, Florham Campus, Silberman College of Business, Executive MBA Programs, Executive MBA Program in Management, Madison, NJ 07940-1099. Offers EMBA.

Fairleigh Dickinson University, Metropolitan Campus, Anthony J. Petrocelli College of Continuing Studies, School of Administrative Science, Program in Administrative Science, Teaneck, NJ 07666-1914. Offers MAS, Certificate.

Fairleigh Dickinson University, Metropolitan Campus, Silberman College of Business, Teaneck, NJ 07666-1914. Offers EMBA, MBA, MS, Certificate, MBA/MA. *Accreditation:* AACSB. *Entrance requirements:* For master's, GMAT.

Fairleigh Dickinson University, Metropolitan Campus, Silberman College of Business, Departments of Management, Marketing, and Entrepreneurial Studies, Program in Management, Teaneck, NJ 07666-1914. Offers management (MBA); management information systems (Certificate). *Accreditation:* AACSB.

Fairmont State University, Program in Business Administration, Fairmont, WV 26554. Offers MBA. *Accreditation:* ACBSP. *Program availability:* Part-time, evening/weekend. *Entrance requirements:* For master's, GRE, MAT, or GMAT, minimum overall undergraduate GPA of 2.75 or 3.0 on the last 60 hours. Additional exam requirements/recommendations for international students: Required—TOEFL (minimum score 80 iBT), IELTS (minimum score 6.5). Electronic applications accepted.

Fashion Institute of Technology, School of Graduate Studies, Program in Global Fashion Management, New York, NY 10001-5992. Offers MPS. Offered in collaboration with Hong Kong Polytechnic University and Institute Francais de la Mode. *Degree requirements:* For master's, capstone seminar. *Entrance requirements:* Additional exam requirements/recommendations for international students: Required—TOEFL (minimum score 550 paper-based). Electronic applications accepted.

Faulkner University, Harris College of Business and Executive Education, Montgomery, AL 36109-3398. Offers business administration (MBA); management (MSM). *Program availability:* Part-time, evening/weekend, 100% online, blended/hybrid learning. *Degree requirements:* For master's, comprehensive exam (for MBA only). *Entrance requirements:* For master's, GMAT (no more than two years old), bachelor's degree from regionally-accredited college or university; official transcripts from all colleges and universities attended; minimum GPA of 2.5 on undergraduate degree; resume including education and at least 4 years of relevant work experience; course in statistics, quantitative business analysis, or operations research. Additional exam requirements/recommendations for international students: Required—TOEFL (minimum score 500 paper-based). Electronic applications accepted. *Expenses:* Contact institution.

Fayetteville State University, Graduate School, Program in Business Administration, Fayetteville, NC 28301-4298. Offers MBA. *Accreditation:* AACSB. *Program availability:* Part-time, evening/weekend. *Faculty:* 14 full-time (3 women), 10 part-time/adjunct (3 women). *Students:* 193 full-time (99 women), 280 part-time (145 women); includes 251 minority (191 Black or African American, non-Hispanic/Latino; 6 American Indian or Alaska Native, non-Hispanic/Latino; 23 Asian, non-Hispanic/Latino; 29 Hispanic/Latino; 1 Native Hawaiian or other Pacific Islander, non-Hispanic/Latino; 1 Two or more races, non-Hispanic/Latino), 17 international. Average age 35. 240 applicants, 95% accepted, 153 enrolled. In 2018, 60 master's awarded. *Entrance requirements:* For master's, GMAT. Additional exam requirements/recommendations for international students: Required—TOEFL. *Application deadline:* For fall admission, 4/15 for domestic students; for spring admission, 10/15 for domestic students. Application fee: $40. *Financial support:* Application deadline: 3/1; applicants required to submit FAFSA. *Faculty research:* Business ethics, optimization and business simulation, consumer behavior, e-commerce and supply chain management, financial institutions. *Unit head:* Dr. J. Lee Brown, Interim Dean, The Broadwell College of Business and Economics, 910-672-1267, Fax: 910-672-2046, E-mail: jbrown84@uncfsu.edu. *Application contact:* John Scarsella, MBA Admission Director, 910-672-2910, Fax: 910-672-2046, E-mail: jscarse1@uncfsu.edu.

Felician University, Program in Business, Lodi, NJ 07644-2117. Offers business administration (DBA); innovation and entrepreneurial leadership (MBA). *Program availability:* Part-time-only, evening/weekend, online learning. Terminal master's awarded for partial completion of doctoral program. *Degree requirements:* For master's, comprehensive exam, thesis, presentation; for doctorate, thesis/dissertation, scholarly project. *Entrance requirements:* For master's and doctorate, GMAT, resume, personal statement, graduation from accredited baccalaureate program. Additional exam requirements/recommendations for international students: Required—TOEFL (minimum score 550 paper-based; 79 iBT), IELTS (minimum score 6.5), PTE (minimum score 56). Electronic applications accepted. Application fee is waived when completed online. *Expenses:* Contact institution. *Faculty research:* Social media, assessment, small business management, mission integration.

Ferris State University, College of Business, Big Rapids, MI 49307. Offers design and innovation management (MBA); lean systems and leadership (MBA); project management (MBA); supply chain management and lean logistics (MBA). *Accreditation:* ACBSP. *Program availability:* Part-time, evening/weekend, 100% online, blended/hybrid learning. *Faculty:* 20 full-time (7 women). *Students:* 14 full-time (9 women), 96 part-time (51 women); includes 12 minority (4 Black or African American, non-Hispanic/Latino; 1 American Indian or Alaska Native, non-Hispanic/Latino; 3 Asian, non-Hispanic/Latino; 2 Hispanic/Latino; 2 Two or more races, non-Hispanic/Latino), 8 international. Average age 33. 48 applicants, 88% accepted, 32 enrolled. In 2018, 39 master's awarded. *Degree requirements:* For master's, comprehensive exam, thesis. *Entrance requirements:* For master's, GRE or GMAT, minimum GPA of 3.0 overall and in junior-/senior-level classes; statement of purpose; 3 letters of reference; resume; transcripts. Additional exam requirements/recommendations for international students: Required—TOEFL (minimum score 500 paper-based; 70 iBT), IELTS (minimum score 6.5). *Application deadline:* For fall admission, 7/1 priority date for domestic students, 6/15 for international students; for winter admission, 11/1 priority date for domestic students, 10/15 for international students; for spring admission, 3/1 priority date for domestic students, 2/15 for international students. Applications are processed on a rolling basis. Application fee: $0 ($30 for international students). Electronic applications accepted. *Expenses:* $610 per credit hour; $12 per credit hour online fee; 33 credits for MISI $20,526; 39 credits for MBA $24,258. *Financial support:* In 2018–19, 17 students received support. Career-related internships or fieldwork, Federal Work-Study, scholarships/grants, and unspecified assistantships available. Support available to part-time students. Financial award applicants required to submit FAFSA. *Faculty research:* Digital forensics, security issues with internet of things, cybersecurity education. *Total annual research expenditures:* $130,000. *Unit head:* Dr. David Nicol, College of Business Dean, 231-591-2168, Fax: 231-591-3521, E-mail: davidnicol@ferris.edu. *Application contact:* Dr. Greg Gogolin, Professor, 231-591-3159, Fax: 231-591-3521, E-mail: greggogolin@ferris.edu. Website: http://cbgp.ferris.edu/

Fisher College, Master of Business Administration Program, Boston, MA 02116-1500. Offers strategic leadership (MBA). *Program availability:* Part-time, evening/weekend, online only, 100% online. *Degree requirements:* For master's, comprehensive exam. *Entrance requirements:* Additional exam requirements/recommendations for international students: Required—TOEFL (minimum score 80 iBT), IELTS (minimum score 6.5). Electronic applications accepted. *Faculty research:* Humanistic management, the role of human resources in employee engagement.

Fitchburg State University, Division of Graduate and Continuing Education, Program in Business Administration, Fitchburg, MA 01420-2697. Offers accounting (MBA); human resources management (MBA); management (MBA). *Program availability:* Part-time, evening/weekend, 100% online. *Entrance requirements:* Additional exam requirements/recommendations for international students: Required—TOEFL (minimum score 550 paper-based; 79 iBT). Electronic applications accepted. *Expenses:* Contact institution.

Florida Agricultural and Mechanical University, Division of Graduate Studies, Research, and Continuing Education, School of Business and Industry, Tallahassee, FL 32307-3200. Offers accounting (MBA); finance (MBA); management information systems (MBA); marketing (MBA). *Accreditation:* ACBSP. *Degree requirements:* For master's, residency. *Entrance requirements:* For master's, GMAT, minimum GPA of 3.0.

Florida Atlantic University, College of Business, Department of Management, Boca Raton, FL 33431-0991. Offers business administration (MBA); entrepreneurship (MBA); health administration (MBA); international business (MBA); sport management (MBA). *Faculty:* 8 full-time (3 women). *Students:* 109 full-time (81 women), 82 part-time (58 women); includes 106 minority (52 Black or African American, non-Hispanic/Latino; 8 Asian, non-Hispanic/Latino; 40 Hispanic/Latino; 6 Two or more races, non-Hispanic/Latino), 1 international. Average age 35. 113 applicants, 85% accepted, 72 enrolled. In 2018, 120 master's awarded. *Entrance requirements:* For master's, GMAT or GRE General Test, minimum GPA of 3.0 in last 60 hours of course work. Additional exam requirements/recommendations for international students: Required—TOEFL (minimum score 600 paper-based; 61 iBT), IELTS (minimum score 6). *Application deadline:* For fall

admission, 7/25 for domestic students, 2/15 for international students; for spring admission, 12/10 for domestic students, 7/15 for international students. Applications are processed on a rolling basis. Application fee: $30. Electronic applications accepted. *Expenses: Tuition,* area resident: Full-time $7400; part-time $369.82 per credit. Tuition, state resident: full-time $7400; part-time $369.82 per credit. Tuition, nonresident: full-time $20,496; part-time $1024.81 per credit. *Financial support:* Research assistantships with full tuition reimbursements, career-related internships or fieldwork, tuition waivers (partial), and unspecified assistantships available. *Faculty research:* Sports administration, healthcare, policy, finance, real estate, senior living. *Unit head:* Dr. Roland Kidwell, Chair, 561-297-4507, E-mail: kidwellr@fau.edu. *Application contact:* Dr. Roland Kidwell, Chair, 561-297-4507, E-mail: kidwellr@fau.edu. Website: http://business.fau.edu/departments/management/index.aspx

Florida Gulf Coast University, Lutgert College of Business, Master of Business Administration Program, Fort Myers, FL 33965-6565. Offers MBA. *Accreditation:* AACSB. *Program availability:* Part-time, evening/weekend. *Entrance requirements:* For master's, GMAT, minimum GPA of 3.0. Additional exam requirements/recommendations for international students: Required—TOEFL (minimum score 550 paper-based). Electronic applications accepted. *Faculty research:* Fraud in audits, production planning in cell manufacturing systems, collaborative learning in distance courses, characteristics of minority and women-owned businesses

Florida Institute of Technology, Hampton Roads Education Center (Virginia), Program in Public Administration, Melbourne, FL 32901-6975. Offers financial management (MPA); public administration (MPA). *Program availability:* Part-time, evening/weekend, online learning. *Application deadline:* Applications are processed on a rolling basis. Electronic applications accepted. *Expenses: Tuition:* Full-time $22,338; part-time $1241 per credit hour. Tuition and fees vary according to degree level, campus/location and program. *Financial support:* Application deadline: 3/1; applicants required to submit FAFSA. *Application contact:* Online Learning and Off-Campus Programs Admissions, 321-674-8263, E-mail: gradadm-olocp@fit.edu. Website: https://www.fit.edu/education-centers/degrees-and-programs/public-administration-mpa/

Florida Institute of Technology, Nathan M. Bisk College of Business, Melbourne, FL 32901-6975. Offers accounting and financial forensics (MS); healthcare management (MBA). *Program availability:* Part-time. *Faculty:* 22 full-time (6 women), 15 part-time/adjunct (6 women). *Students:* 62 full-time (22 women), 108 part-time (38 women); includes 47 minority (24 Black or African American, non-Hispanic/Latino; 4 Asian, non-Hispanic/Latino; 14 Hispanic/Latino; 5 Two or more races, non-Hispanic/Latino), 35 international. 85 applicants, 92% accepted, 57 enrolled. In 2018, 36 master's awarded. *Degree requirements:* For master's, comprehensive exam (for some programs), thesis optional, capstone. *Entrance requirements:* For master's, GMAT, GRE or resume showing 8 years of supervised experience, minimum GPA of 3.0 (for MBA), 2 letters of recommendation, resume, statement of objectives. Additional exam requirements/recommendations for international students: Required—TOEFL (minimum score 550 paper-based; 79 iBT). *Application deadline:* For fall admission, 4/1 for international students; for spring admission, 9/30 for international students. Applications are processed on a rolling basis. Application fee: $50. Electronic applications accepted. *Expenses: Tuition:* Full-time $22,338; part-time $1241 per credit hour. Tuition and fees vary according to degree level, campus/location and program. *Financial support:* In 2018–19, 5 students received support, including 4 research assistantships with partial tuition reimbursements available, 1 teaching assistantship with partial tuition reimbursement available; career-related internships or fieldwork, institutionally sponsored loans, and unspecified assistantships also available. Support available to part-time students. Financial award application deadline: 3/1; financial award applicants required to submit FAFSA. *Faculty research:* Investment analysis, marketing research, strategy analysis, ethics, small business. *Unit head:* Dr. Theodore R. Richardson, III, Dean, 321-674-8123, Fax: 321-674-7597, E-mail: trichardson@fit.edu. *Application contact:* Mike Perry, Executive Director of Admissions, 321-674-7127, Fax: 321-723-9468, E-mail: perrymj@fit.edu. Website: www.fit.edu/business/

Florida Memorial University, School of Business, Miami-Dade, FL 33054. Offers MBA. *Accreditation:* ACBSP. *Program availability:* Part-time. *Entrance requirements:* For master's, GMAT, 3 letters of recommendation.

Florida National University, Program in Business Administration, Hialeah, FL 33012. Offers accounting (MBA); finance (MBA); general management (MBA); health services administration (MBA); marketing (MBA); public management and leadership (MBA). *Program availability:* Part-time, blended/hybrid learning. *Faculty:* 3 full-time (1 woman), 4 part-time/adjunct (2 women). *Students:* 15 full-time (5 women), 15 part-time (6 women); all minorities (7 Black or African American, non-Hispanic/Latino; 21 Hispanic/Latino; 2 Two or more races, non-Hispanic/Latino), 1 international. Average age 35. 8 applicants, 88% accepted, 7 enrolled. In 2018, 27 master's awarded. *Degree requirements:* For master's, capstone. *Entrance requirements:* For master's, writing assessment, bachelor's degree from accredited institution; official undergraduate transcripts; minimum undergraduate GPA of 2.5, GMAT (minimum score of 400), or GRE (minimum score of 900); two letters of recommendation; resume. Additional exam requirements/recommendations for international students: Required—TOEFL (minimum score 500 paper-based; 62 iBT), IELTS (minimum score 5.5). *Application deadline:* Applications are processed on a rolling basis. Electronic applications accepted. *Expenses:* Contact institution. *Financial support:* Federal Work-Study, institutionally sponsored loans, scholarships/grants, and tuition waivers (full and partial) available. Financial award applicants required to submit FAFSA. *Unit head:* Dr. Ernesto Gonzalez, Business and Economics Department Head, 305-821-3333 Ext. 1070, Fax: 305-362-0595, E-mail: egonzalez@fnu.edu. *Application contact:* Dr. Ernesto Gonzalez, Business and Economics Department Head, 305-821-3333 Ext. 1070, Fax: 305-362-0595, E-mail: egonzalez@fnu.edu. Website: https://www.fnu.edu/prospective-students/our-programs/select-a-program/master-of-business-administration/business-administration-mba-masters/

Florida Southern College, Program in Business Administration, Lakeland, FL 33801-5698. Offers MBA. *Accreditation:* AACSB. *Program availability:* Part-time, 100% online, blended/hybrid learning. *Faculty:* 7 full-time (3 women). *Students:* 63 full-time (27 women), 6 part-time (3 women); includes 17 minority (5 Black or African American, non-Hispanic/Latino; 4 Asian, non-Hispanic/Latino; 8 Hispanic/Latino), 4 international. Average age 30. 93 applicants, 60% accepted, 50 enrolled. In 2018, 33 master's awarded. *Degree requirements:* For master's, We require all MBA candidates taking most core courses to have passed quantitative exams in Accounting, Statistics, Economics, and Finance. *Entrance requirements:* For master's, GMAT or GRE General Test, letter of reference, resume, personal statement. Additional exam requirements/recommendations for international students: Required—TOEFL (minimum score 550 paper-based; 79 iBT), IELTS (minimum score 6.5), International students from countries where English is not the standard for daily communication must submit either the TOEFL or IELTS. *Application deadline:* For fall admission, 6/1 priority date for domestic and international students; for spring admission, 11/1 priority date for domestic and international students. Applications are processed on a rolling basis. Application fee: $0. Electronic applications accepted. *Expenses:* Contact institution. *Financial support:* In

Business Administration and Management—General

2018–19, 12 students received support. Scholarships/grants, unspecified assistantships, and employee tuition grants, athletic scholarships for students still eligible available. Financial award application deadline: 8/21; financial award applicants required to submit FAFSA. *Faculty research:* Behavioral investing, Corporate governance, Marketing communications, Regional economics, Strategic leadership. *Unit head:* Krista Lewellyn, Program Director, 863-680-4285, Fax: 863-680-4355, E-mail: klewellyn@flsouthern.edu. *Application contact:* Kamalie Dodson, Associate Director of Adult and Graduate Admission, 863-680-5022, Fax: 863-680-3872, E-mail: kdodson2@flsouthern.edu.
Website: http://www.flsouthern.edu/mba

Florida State University, The Graduate School, College of Business, Tallahassee, FL 32306-1110. Offers accounting (M Acc), including assurance and advisory services, generalist, taxation; business administration (MBA, PhD), including accounting (PhD), finance (PhD), management information systems (PhD), marketing (PhD), organizational behavior and human resources (PhD), risk management and insurance (PhD), strategy (PhD); finance (MS); management information systems (MS); risk management and insurance (MS); JD/MBA; MSW/MBA. *Accreditation:* AACSB. *Program availability:* Part-time, 100% online. *Students:* Average age 31. 300 applicants, 61% accepted, 133 enrolled. In 2018, 268 master's, 9 doctorates awarded. Terminal master's awarded for partial completion of doctoral program. *Degree requirements:* For doctorate, comprehensive exam, thesis/dissertation. *Entrance requirements:* For master's, GMAT, GRE (for all except MS in finance), work experience (MBA, MS); minimum GPA of 3.0, letters of recommendation; for doctorate, GMAT, GRE (for marketing, organizational behavior, risk management and insurance, management information systems, and human resources only), minimum graduate GPA of 3.5, letters of recommendation. Additional exam requirements/recommendations for international students: Required—TOEFL (minimum score 600 paper-based; 85 iBT); Recommended—IELTS (minimum score 6). *Application deadline:* For fall admission, 6/1 for domestic and international students; for spring admission, 10/1 for domestic and international students; for summer admission, 3/1 for domestic and international students. Applications are processed on a rolling basis. Application fee: $30. Electronic applications accepted. *Expenses:* Contact institution. *Financial support:* In 2018–19, 146 students received support, including 26 fellowships (averaging $1,500 per year), 77 research assistantships with full tuition reimbursements available (averaging $20,000 per year), 43 teaching assistantships with full tuition reimbursements available (averaging $20,000 per year); career-related internships or fieldwork, scholarships/grants, health care benefits, tuition waivers (full and partial), and unspecified assistantships also available. Support available to part-time students. Financial award application deadline: 1/1; financial award applicants required to submit FAFSA. *Faculty research:* Business strategy, marketing, finance, accounting, business analytics. *Total annual research expenditures:* $1.4 million. *Unit head:* Dr. Michael Hartline, Dean, 850-644-4405, Fax: 850-644-0915, E-mail: mhartline@business.fsu.edu. *Application contact:* Jennifer Clark, Director, 850-644-6458, E-mail: gradprograms@business.fsu.edu.
Website: http://business.fsu.edu/

Fontbonne University, Graduate Programs, St. Louis, MO 63105-3098. Offers accounting (MBA, MS); art (MA); art (K-12) (MAT); business (MBA); computer science (MS); deaf education (MA); early intervention in deaf education (MA); education (MA), including autism spectrum disorders, curriculum and instruction, diverse learners, early childhood education, reading, special education; elementary education (MAT); family and consumer sciences (MA), including multidisciplinary health communication studies; fine arts (MFA); instructional design and technology (MS); management and leadership (MM); middle school education (MAT); secondary education (MAT); special education (MAT); speech-language pathology (MS); supply chain management (MS); theatre (MA). *Accreditation:* ASHA. *Program availability:* Part-time, evening/weekend, online learning. *Degree requirements:* For master's, comprehensive exam (for some programs), thesis (for some programs). *Entrance requirements:* Additional exam requirements/recommendations for international students: Required—TOEFL (minimum score 500 paper-based; 65 iBT). Electronic applications accepted.

Fordham University, Gabelli School of Business, New York, NY 10023. Offers accounting (MBA, MS); applied statistics and decision-making (MS); business economics (DPS); capital markets (DPS); communications and media management (MBA); electronic business (MBA); entrepreneurship (MBA); finance (MBA, PhD); global finance (MS); global sustainability (MBA); health administration (MS); healthcare management (MBA); information systems (MBA, MS); investor relations (MS); management (EMBA, MBA, MS, PhD); marketing (MBA); marketing intelligence (MS); media management (MS); nonprofit leadership (MS); quantitative finance (MS); strategy and decision-making (DPS); taxation (MS); JD/MBA; MS/MBA. *Accreditation:* AACSB. *Program availability:* Part-time, evening/weekend. Terminal master's awarded for partial completion of doctoral program. *Degree requirements:* For master's, internships (for some degrees); for doctorate, comprehensive exam (for some programs), thesis/dissertation. *Entrance requirements:* For master's, GMAT/GRE, 2 letters of recommendation, resume, 2 essays, transcripts, interview. Additional exam requirements/recommendations for international students: Required—TOEFL (minimum score 100 iBT), IELTS (minimum score 7). Electronic applications accepted. *Expenses:* Contact institution.

Fort Hays State University, Graduate School, W.R. and Yvonne Robbins College of Business and Entrepreneurship, Department of Management, Hays, KS 67601-4099. Offers MBA. *Degree requirements:* For master's, thesis optional. *Entrance requirements:* For master's, GMAT. Additional exam requirements/recommendations for international students: Required—TOEFL (minimum score 550 paper-based). Electronic applications accepted. *Faculty research:* Organizational behavior and performance appraisal, data processing, international marketing.

Framingham State University, Graduate Studies, Program in Business Administration, Framingham, MA 01701-9101. Offers biotechnology operations (MBA); management (MBA). *Program availability:* Part-time, evening/weekend. *Entrance requirements:* For master's, GMAT, GRE, or MAT.

Franciscan University of Steubenville, Graduate Programs, Department of Business, Steubenville, OH 43952-1763. Offers MBA. *Program availability:* Part-time, evening/weekend, 100% online, blended/hybrid learning. *Degree requirements:* For master's, research paper. *Entrance requirements:* For master's, GMAT, minimum undergraduate GPA of 2.5. Additional exam requirements/recommendations for international students: Required—TOEFL (minimum score 550 paper-based; 80 iBT). Electronic applications accepted.

Francis Marion University, Graduate Programs, School of Business, Florence, SC 29502-0547. Offers business (MBA); health executive management (MBA). *Accreditation:* AACSB. *Program availability:* Part-time, evening/weekend. *Degree requirements:* For master's, comprehensive exam. *Entrance requirements:* For master's, GMAT or GRE, official transcripts, two letters of recommendation. Additional exam requirements/recommendations for international students: Required—TOEFL (minimum score 550 paper-based; 79 iBT). *Faculty research:* Ethics, directions of MBA, international business, regional economics, environmental issues.

Franklin Pierce University, Graduate and Professional Studies, Rindge, NH 03461-0060. Offers curriculum and instruction (M Ed); elementary education (MS Ed); emerging network technologies (Graduate Certificate); energy and sustainability studies (MBA, Graduate Certificate); health administration (MBA, Graduate Certificate); human resource management (MBA, Graduate Certificate); information technology (MBA); leadership (MBA); nursing education (MS); nursing leadership (MS); physical therapy (DPT); physician assistant studies (MPAS); special education (M Ed); sports management (MBA). *Accreditation:* APTA. *Program availability:* Part-time, 100% online, blended/hybrid learning. *Degree requirements:* For master's, concentrated original research projects; student teaching; fieldwork and/or internship; leadership project; PRAXIS I and II (for M Ed); for doctorate, concentrated original research projects, clinical fieldwork and/or internship, leadership project. *Entrance requirements:* For master's, minimum GPA of 2.5, 3 letters of recommendation; competencies in accounting, economics, statistics, and computer skills through life experience or undergraduate coursework (for MBA); certification/e-portfolio, minimum C grade in all education courses (for M Ed); license to practice as RN (for MS); for doctorate, GRE, 80 hours of observation/work in PT settings; completion of anatomy, chemistry, physics, and statistics; minimum GPA of 3.0. Additional exam requirements/recommendations for international students: Required—TOEFL (minimum score 550 paper-based; 61 iBT). Electronic applications accepted. *Faculty research:* Evidence-based practice in sports physical therapy, human resource management in economic crisis, leadership in nursing, innovation in sports facility management, differentiated learning and understanding by design.

Franklin University, MBA Program, Columbus, OH 43215-5399. Offers MBA. *Program availability:* Part-time, evening/weekend, online learning. *Entrance requirements:* For master's, minimum undergraduate GPA of 2.75. Additional exam requirements/recommendations for international students: Required—TOEFL (minimum score 550 paper-based). Electronic applications accepted.

Freed-Hardeman University, Program in Business Administration, Henderson, TN 38340-2399. Offers accounting (MBA); corporate responsibility (MBA); leadership (MBA). *Accreditation:* ACBSP. *Program availability:* Part-time, evening/weekend, online learning. *Entrance requirements:* For master's, GMAT. Additional exam requirements/recommendations for international students: Required—TOEFL (minimum score 500 paper-based).

Fresno Pacific University, Graduate Programs, MBA Program, Fresno, CA 93702-4709. Offers MBA. *Entrance requirements:* For master's, GMAT, GRE, or MAT, three references; resume; official transcripts verifying BA/BS; minimum GPA of 3.0; prerequisite courses in economics, statistics, and accounting. *Expenses:* Contact institution.

Fresno Pacific University, Graduate Programs, Program in Leadership and Organizational Studies, Fresno, CA 93702-4709. Offers MA. *Program availability:* Part-time, evening/weekend. *Degree requirements:* For master's, thesis. *Entrance requirements:* For master's, MAT, GRE or GMAT, interview, three references. Additional exam requirements/recommendations for international students: Required—TOEFL (minimum score 550 paper-based). Electronic applications accepted. *Expenses:* Contact institution. *Faculty research:* Ethics, servant leadership, communication, creative problem solving.

Frostburg State University, College of Business, Frostburg, MD 21532-1099. Offers MBA. *Accreditation:* AACSB. *Program availability:* Part-time, evening/weekend. *Faculty:* 10 full-time (3 women), 3 part-time/adjunct (1 woman). *Students:* 39 full-time (19 women), 135 part-time (75 women); includes 41 minority (19 Black or African American, non-Hispanic/Latino; 9 Asian, non-Hispanic/Latino; 6 Hispanic/Latino; 7 Two or more races, non-Hispanic/Latino), 1 international. Average age 32. 86 applicants, 84% accepted, 46 enrolled. In 2018, 80 master's awarded. *Entrance requirements:* For master's, GMAT, GRE. Additional exam requirements/recommendations for international students: Required—TOEFL. *Application deadline:* For fall admission, 7/15 priority date for domestic students. Applications are processed on a rolling basis. Application fee: $45. Electronic applications accepted. *Financial support:* In 2018–19, 8 research assistantships with full tuition reimbursements (averaging $5,000 per year) were awarded; career-related internships or fieldwork and Federal Work-Study also available. Financial award application deadline: 4/1; financial award applicants required to submit FAFSA. *Faculty research:* Cooperative teaching methods, strategic change processes, political marketing. *Unit head:* Dr. Sudhir Singh, Dean, 301-687-4019, E-mail: ssingh@frostburg.edu. *Application contact:* Vickie Mazer, Director, Graduate Services, 301-687-7053, Fax: 301-687-4597, E-mail: vmmazer@frostburg.edu.
Website: http://www.frostburg.edu/colleges/cob/

Full Sail University, Entertainment Business Master of Science Program - Online, Winter Park, FL 32792-7437. Offers MS. *Program availability:* Online learning. *Entrance requirements:* Additional exam requirements/recommendations for international students: Required—TOEFL (minimum score 550 paper-based; 79 iBT).

Gannon University, School of Graduate Studies, College of Engineering and Business, Dahlkemper School of Business, Program in Business Administration, Erie, PA 16541-0001. Offers business administration (MBA); finance (MBA); human resources management (MBA); marketing (MBA). *Accreditation:* ACBSP. *Program availability:* Part-time, evening/weekend, 100% online, blended/hybrid learning. *Entrance requirements:* For master's, GMAT, bachelor's degree in any discipline from any accredited college or university, resume, transcripts, 3 letters of recommendation. Additional exam requirements/recommendations for international students: Required—TOEFL (minimum score 79 iBT). Electronic applications accepted. Application fee is waived when completed online.

Gardner-Webb University, Graduate School of Business, Boiling Springs, NC 28017. Offers IMBA, M Acc, MBA. *Accreditation:* ACBSP. *Program availability:* Part-time, evening/weekend, online learning. *Entrance requirements:* For master's, GMAT, GRE, 2 semesters of course work each in economics, statistics, and accounting. Additional exam requirements/recommendations for international students: Required—TOEFL (minimum score 500 paper-based; 61 iBT). Electronic applications accepted. *Expenses:* Contact institution.

Geneva College, Program in Business Administration, Beaver Falls, PA 15010-3599. Offers business administration (MBA); finance (MBA); marketing (MBA); operations (MBA). *Accreditation:* ACBSP. *Program availability:* Part-time, evening/weekend. *Degree requirements:* For master's, 36 credit hours of course work (30 of which are required of all students). *Entrance requirements:* For master's, GMAT (if college GPA less than 2.5), undergraduate transcript, 2 letters of recommendation, resume, goals statement. Additional exam requirements/recommendations for international students: Required—TOEFL. Electronic applications accepted. *Expenses:* Contact institution.

George Fox University, College of Business, Newberg, OR 97132-2697. Offers accounting (DBA); finance (MBA); management (DBA); management and leadership (MBA); marketing (DBA); organizational strategy (MBA); strategic human resource management (MBA). MBA offered in Newberg, OR and in Portland, OR. *Accreditation:* ACBSP. *Program availability:* Part-time, evening/weekend, online learning. *Degree requirements:* For master's, capstone project; for doctorate, credit-applied research project. *Entrance requirements:* For master's, resume (5 years of professional

experience); 3 professional references; interview; financial e-learning course; official transcripts; for doctorate, GRE or GMAT, resume; personal mission statement; academic research writing sample; official transcript from each college/university attended; three professional references. Additional exam requirements/recommendations for international students: Required—TOEFL (minimum score 577 paper-based; 90 iBT) or IELTS (minimum score 7). Electronic applications accepted. *Expenses:* Contact institution.

George Mason University, School of Business, Program in Business Administration, Fairfax, VA 22030. Offers MBA. *Accreditation:* AACSB. *Program availability:* Part-time. *Faculty:* 96 full-time (36 women), 53 part-time/adjunct (19 women). *Students:* 181 full-time (73 women), 95 part-time (37 women); includes 91 minority (36 Black or African American, non-Hispanic/Latino; 29 Asian, non-Hispanic/Latino; 20 Hispanic/Latino; 2 Native Hawaiian or other Pacific Islander, non-Hispanic/Latino; 4 Two or more races, non-Hispanic/Latino), 19 international. Average age 33. 302 applicants, 81% accepted, 146 enrolled. In 2018, 92 master's awarded. *Entrance requirements:* For master's, GMAT/GRE, resume; 2 official copies of transcripts; 2 professional letters of recommendation; personal career goals statement; professional essay; interview. Additional exam requirements/recommendations for international students: Required—TOEFL (minimum score 575 paper-based; 93 iBT), IELTS (minimum score 7), PTE (minimum score 59). *Application deadline:* For fall admission, 2/1 for domestic and international students. Application fee: $75 ($80 for international students). Electronic applications accepted. *Expenses:* $808.25 per credit in-state, $1,646.75 per credit out-of-state (for MBA); $1,504.08 per credit (for Executive MBA). *Financial support:* In 2018–19, 3 students received support, including 1 research assistantship, 2 teaching assistantships with tuition reimbursements available; career-related internships or fieldwork, Federal Work-Study, scholarships/grants, unspecified assistantships, and health care benefits (for full-time research or teaching assistantship recipients) also available. Support available to part-time students. Financial award application deadline: 3/1; financial award applicants required to submit FAFSA. *Faculty research:* Electronic commerce, marketing information systems, group decision-making, corporate governance, risk management. *Unit head:* Victoria Grady, Director, 703-993-8711, Fax: 703-993-1870, E-mail: vgrady3@gmu.edu. *Application contact:* Rebecca Diemer, Director, Graduate Academic Services, 703-993-2216, Fax: 703-993-1778, E-mail: rdiemer@gmu.edu.
Website: http://business.gmu.edu/mba-programs/

George Mason University, School of Business, Program in Management, Fairfax, VA 22030. Offers MS. *Program availability:* Evening/weekend, 100% online, blended/hybrid learning. *Faculty:* 20 full-time (8 women), 10 part-time/adjunct (5 women). *Students:* 34 full-time (20 women); includes 9 minority (2 Black or African American, non-Hispanic/Latino; 4 Asian, non-Hispanic/Latino; 1 Hispanic/Latino; 2 Two or more races, non-Hispanic/Latino), 15 international. Average age 24. 38 applicants, 84% accepted, 19 enrolled. In 2018, 37 master's awarded. *Degree requirements:* For master's, thesis optional, professional experience. *Entrance requirements:* For master's, GMAT or GRE. Additional exam requirements/recommendations for international students: Required—TOEFL (minimum score 575 paper-based; 88 iBT), IELTS (minimum score 6.5), PTE (minimum score 59). Application fee: $75 ($80 for international students). *Expenses:* $859 per credit in-state tuition, $1,709 per credit out-of-state tuition. *Unit head:* Anne Magro, Interim Dean, 703-993-1765, Fax: 703-993-2472, E-mail: amagro@gmu.edu. *Application contact:* Paige Wolf, Senior Assistant Dean of Graduate Programs, 703-993-1758, Fax: 703-993-1870, E-mail: pwolf1@gmu.edu.
Website: http://business.gmu.edu/masters-in-management/

Georgetown University, Graduate School of Arts and Sciences, McDonough School of Business, Washington, DC 20057. Offers business administration (EMBA, GEMBA, MBA); finance (MS); leadership (EML). *Accreditation:* AACSB. *Entrance requirements:* For master's, GMAT. Additional exam requirements/recommendations for international students: Required—TOEFL. *Expenses:* Contact institution.

The George Washington University, School of Business, Washington, DC 20052. Offers M Accy, MBA, MS, MSF, MSIST, MTA, PMBA, PhD, Certificate, Professional Certificate, JD/MBA, MBA/MA. PMBA also offered in Alexandria and Ashburn, VA. *Program availability:* Part-time, evening/weekend, online learning. *Students:* 822 full-time (407 women), 805 part-time (423 women); includes 492 minority (190 Black or African American, non-Hispanic/Latino; 3 American Indian or Alaska Native, non-Hispanic/Latino; 149 Asian, non-Hispanic/Latino; 107 Hispanic/Latino; 4 Native Hawaiian or other Pacific Islander, non-Hispanic/Latino; 39 Two or more races, non-Hispanic/Latino), 584 international. Average age 32. 3,792 applicants, 55% accepted, 568 enrolled. In 2018, 745 master's, 2 doctorates, 169 other advanced degrees awarded. *Entrance requirements:* For doctorate, GMAT or GRE. Additional exam requirements/recommendations for international students: Required—TOEFL. *Application deadline:* For fall admission, 4/1 priority date for domestic students; for spring admission, 10/1 for domestic students. Applications are processed on a rolling basis. Application fee: $75. Electronic applications accepted. *Financial support:* In 2018–19, 194 students received support. Fellowships, teaching assistantships, career-related internships or fieldwork, Federal Work-Study, institutionally sponsored loans, and tuition waivers (partial) available. Financial award application deadline: 4/1. *Unit head:* Dr. Vivek Choudhury, Dean, 202-994-6380, E-mail: vchoudhury@gwu.edu. *Application contact:* Christopher Storer, Executive Director, Graduate Admissions, 202-994-1212, E-mail: gwmba@gwu.edu.
Website: http://business.gwu.edu/grad

Georgia College & State University, Graduate School, The J. Whitney Bunting School of Business, Program in Business Administration, Milledgeville, GA 31061. Offers MBA. *Accreditation:* AACSB. *Program availability:* Part-time, evening/weekend, online only, 100% online. *Degree requirements:* For master's, minimum GPA of 3.0 on all business courses taken in the program, complete program within 7 years of start date. *Entrance requirements:* For master's, GRE or GMAT (not required for students who earned a business degree at an AACSB accredited business school and maintained an overall undergraduate GPA of 3.15), transcript, certificate of immunization, two years of documented related work experience. Electronic applications accepted. *Expenses:* Contact institution.

Georgia Institute of Technology, Graduate Studies, Scheller College of Business, Program in Business Administration, Atlanta, GA 30332-0001. Offers business administration (MBA); global business (MBA); management of technology (MBA). *Accreditation:* AACSB. *Program availability:* Part-time, evening/weekend. *Entrance requirements:* For master's, GMAT, two essays, three letters of recommendation, transcript from each college/university attended. Additional exam requirements/recommendations for international students: Required—TOEFL (minimum score 600 paper-based; 100 iBT). Electronic applications accepted. *Expenses:* Contact institution.

Georgia Institute of Technology, Graduate Studies, Scheller College of Business, Program in Management, Atlanta, GA 30332-0001. Offers MS, PhD. *Accreditation:* AACSB. *Program availability:* Part-time. *Degree requirements:* For doctorate, comprehensive exam, thesis/dissertation, oral exams. *Entrance requirements:* For doctorate, GMAT, two essay questions, three letters of recommendation, transcripts from each college/university attended, copy of most recent resume. Additional exam requirements/recommendations for international students: Required—TOEFL (minimum

score 600 paper-based; 100 iBT). Electronic applications accepted. *Faculty research:* Management information systems, management of technology, international business, entrepreneurship, operations management.

Georgian Court University, School of Business and Digital Media, Lakewood, NJ 08701-2697. Offers business (MBA); business essentials (Certificate); nonprofit management (Certificate). *Program availability:* Part-time, evening/weekend. *Faculty:* 5 full-time (1 woman), 6 part-time/adjunct (3 women). *Students:* 27 full-time (13 women), 26 part-time (17 women); includes 15 minority (5 Black or African American, non-Hispanic/Latino; 4 Asian, non-Hispanic/Latino; 5 Hispanic/Latino; 1 Two or more races, non-Hispanic/Latino), 3 international. Average age 30. 59 applicants, 59% accepted, 19 enrolled. In 2018, 23 master's, 3 other advanced degrees awarded. *Entrance requirements:* For master's, GMAT or CPA exam, 3 letters of recommendation. Additional exam requirements/recommendations for international students: Required—TOEFL (minimum score 550 paper-based; 79 iBT). *Application deadline:* For fall admission, 8/15 for domestic students, 5/1 for international students; for spring admission, 1/15 for domestic students, 10/1 for international students. Applications are processed on a rolling basis. Application fee: $40. Electronic applications accepted. *Expenses: Tuition:* Full-time $856; part-time $856 per credit hour. *Required fees:* $968; $496 per unit. $248 per semester. Tuition and fees vary according to campus/location and program. *Financial support:* Scholarships/grants, health care benefits, and unspecified assistantships available. Financial award application deadline: 4/15; financial award applicants required to submit FAFSA. *Unit head:* Dr. Jennifer Edmonds, Dean School of Business and Digital Media, 732-987-2662, Fax: 732-987-2024, E-mail: jedmonds@georgian.edu. *Application contact:* Patrick Givens, Director of Graduate and Professional Studies Admissions, 732-987-2736, Fax: 732-987-2000, E-mail: gps@georgian.edu.
Website: https://georgian.edu/academics/school-of-business-digital-media/

Georgia Southern University, Jack N. Averitt College of Graduate Studies, College of Arts and Humanities, Program in Professional Communication and Leadership, Statesboro, GA 30458. Offers MA, Certificate. *Program availability:* Part-time, evening/weekend. *Degree requirements:* For master's, comprehensive exam, project. *Entrance requirements:* For master's, minimum GPA of 2.5, letters of recommendation, letter of intent, resume. Additional exam requirements/recommendations for international students: Required—TOEFL (minimum score 523 paper-based; 70 iBT). Electronic applications accepted. *Expenses: Tuition,* area resident: Part-time $3324 per semester. Tuition, state resident: full-time $5814; part-time $3324 per semester. Tuition, nonresident: full-time $23,204; part-time $13,260 per semester. *Required fees:* $2092; $2092. Tuition and fees vary according to course load, degree level, campus/location and program. *Faculty research:* Organizational communication, conflict resolution and mediation, rhetoric and language identity, brand identity and marketing, communication theory.

Georgia Southern University, Jack N. Averitt College of Graduate Studies, Parker College of Business, The Georgia Web MBA, Statesboro, GA 30460. Offers MBA. *Program availability:* Part-time-only, evening/weekend, online only, 100% online. *Entrance requirements:* For master's, GMAT. Additional exam requirements/recommendations for international students: Required—TOEFL (minimum score 550 paper-based; 80 iBT), IELTS (minimum score 6). Electronic applications accepted. *Expenses:* Contact institution. *Faculty research:* International business, leadership, marketing, managerial finance, operations.

Georgia Southern University, Jack N. Averitt College of Graduate Studies, Parker College of Business, Program in Business Administration, Statesboro, GA 30458. Offers MBA. *Accreditation:* AACSB. *Program availability:* Part-time, evening/weekend, online learning. *Entrance requirements:* For master's, GMAT. Additional exam requirements/recommendations for international students: Required—TOEFL (minimum score 550 paper-based; 80 iBT), IELTS (minimum score 6). Electronic applications accepted. *Expenses: Tuition,* area resident: Part-time $3324 per semester. Tuition, state resident: full-time $5814; part-time $3324 per semester. Tuition, nonresident: full-time $23,204; part-time $13,260 per semester. *Required fees:* $2092; $2092. Tuition and fees vary according to course load, degree level, campus/location and program.

Georgia Southwestern State University, School of Business Administration, Americus, GA 31709-4693. Offers MBA. *Accreditation:* AACSB. *Program availability:* Part-time, online only, 100% online. *Degree requirements:* For master's, minimum cumulative GPA of 3.0; requirements completed within 7 years. *Entrance requirements:* For master's, GMAT or GRE, baccalaureate degree from a regionally-accredited institution; minimum undergraduate overall GPA of 2.7 as reported on official final transcripts; letters of recommendation. Electronic applications accepted. *Expenses:* Contact institution.

Georgia State University, J. Mack Robinson College of Business, Department of Managerial Sciences, Atlanta, GA 30302-3083. Offers business analysis (MBA, MS); entrepreneurship (MBA); human resources management (MBA, MS); operations management (MBA, MS); organization behavior/human resource management (PhD); organization management (MBA); organizational change (MS); strategic management (PhD). *Accreditation:* AACSB. *Program availability:* Part-time, evening/weekend. *Faculty:* 11 full-time (2 women), 1 part-time/adjunct (0 women). *Students:* 11 full-time (6 women); includes 5 minority (3 Black or African American, non-Hispanic/Latino; 1 Asian, non-Hispanic/Latino; 1 Two or more races, non-Hispanic/Latino), 3 international. Average age 29. 54 applicants, 20% accepted, 8 enrolled. In 2018, 9 master's, 3 doctorates awarded. *Entrance requirements:* For master's, GRE or GMAT, transcripts from all institutions attended, resume, essays; for doctorate, GMAT, three letters of recommendation, personal statement, transcripts from all institutions attended, resume. Additional exam requirements/recommendations for international students: Required—TOEFL (minimum score 610 paper-based; 101 iBT), IELTS (minimum score 7). *Application deadline:* For fall admission, 5/1 priority date for domestic students, 2/1 priority date for international students; for spring admission, 9/15 priority date for domestic students, 4/1 priority date for international students. Applications are processed on a rolling basis. Application fee: $50. Electronic applications accepted. *Expenses: Tuition,* area resident: Full-time $9360; part-time $390 per credit hour. Tuition, state resident: full-time $9360; part-time $390 per credit hour. Tuition, nonresident: full-time $30,024; part-time $1251 per credit hour. International tuition: $30,024 full-time. *Required fees:* $2128. *Financial support:* Research assistantships, teaching assistantships, scholarships/grants, tuition waivers, and unspecified assistantships available. Financial award applicants required to submit FAFSA. *Faculty research:* Entrepreneurship and innovation; strategy process; workplace interactions, relationships, and processes; leadership and culture; supply chain management. *Unit head:* Dr. Pamela S. Barr, Chair, 404-413-7525, Fax: 404-413-7571. *Application contact:* Toby McChesney, Assistant Dean for Graduate Recruiting and Student Services, 404-413-7167, Fax: 404-413-7162, E-mail: rcbgradadmissions@gsu.edu.
Website: http://mgmt.robinson.gsu.edu/

Georgia State University, J. Mack Robinson College of Business, Executive Doctorate in Business Program, Atlanta, GA 30302-3083. Offers EDB. *Accreditation:* AACSB. *Program availability:* Part-time, evening/weekend. *Entrance requirements:* Additional exam requirements/recommendations for international students: Required—TOEFL (minimum score 610 paper-based; 101 iBT), IELTS (minimum score 7). *Application*

deadline: Applications are processed on a rolling basis. Application fee: $100. Electronic applications accepted. *Expenses: Tuition, area resident:* Full-time $9360; part-time $390 per credit hour. Tuition, state resident: full-time $9360; part-time $390 per credit hour. Tuition, nonresident: full-time $30,024; part-time $1251 per credit hour. *International tuition:* $30,024 full-time. *Required fees:* $2128. *Financial support:* Scholarships/grants available. *Unit head:* Maury C. Kalnitz, Director of the Executive Doctorate in Business, 404-413-7178. *Application contact:* Heather Jacobs, Assistant Director of the Executive Doctorate in Business, 404-413-7178, E-mail: hjacob3@gsu.edu.
Website: https://robinson.gsu.edu/executive-doctorate-in-business/

Georgia State University, J. Mack Robinson College of Business, Program in General Business Administration, Atlanta, GA 30302-3083. Offers business administration (MBA); executive business administration (EMBA); global business administration (GMBA); professional business administration (PMBA); PMBA/MHA. *Accreditation:* AACSB. *Program availability:* Part-time, evening/weekend. *Entrance requirements:* For master's, GRE or GMAT, transcripts from all institutions attended, resume, essays. Additional exam requirements/recommendations for international students: Required—TOEFL (minimum score 610 paper-based; 101 iBT), IELTS (minimum score 7). *Application deadline:* Applications are processed on a rolling basis. Application fee: $50. Electronic applications accepted. *Expenses: Tuition, area resident:* Full-time $9360; part-time $390 per credit hour. Tuition, state resident: full-time $9360; part-time $390 per credit hour. Tuition, nonresident: full-time $30,024; part-time $1251 per credit hour. *International tuition:* $30,024 full-time. *Required fees:* $2128. *Financial support:* Research assistantships, scholarships/grants, tuition waivers, and unspecified assistantships available. Financial award application deadline: 5/1. *Unit head:* Dr. Richard D. Phillips, Associate Dean for Academic Initiatives and Innovation, 404-413-7000, Fax: 404-413-7035. *Application contact:* Toby McChesney, Assistant Dean for Graduate Recruiting and Student Services, 404-413-7167, Fax: 404-413-7162, E-mail: rcbgradadmissions@gsu.edu.

Goddard College, Graduate Division, Master of Arts in Social Innovation and Sustainability Program, Plainfield, VT 05667-9432. Offers MA. *Program availability:* Part-time, online learning. *Degree requirements:* For master's, thesis. *Entrance requirements:* For master's, 3 letters of recommendation, relevant prior training or experience, interview. Electronic applications accepted.

Golden Gate University, Ageno School of Business, San Francisco, CA 94105-2968. Offers accounting (MBA); adaptive leadership (MBA); advanced financial planning (MS); business administration (EMBA, MBA, DBA); business analytics (MBA, MS); entrepreneurship (MBA); finance (MBA, MS, Certificate); financial life planning (Certificate); financial planning (MS, Certificate); global supply chain management (MBA, Certificate); human resource management (MBA, MS, Certificate); information technology management (MBA, MS, Certificate); international business (MBA); marketing (MBA, MS, Certificate); project management (MBA, MS, Certificate); psychology (MA, Certificate); public administration (EMPA, MBA); public administration leadership (Certificate); JD/MBA. *Program availability:* Part-time, evening/weekend. *Degree requirements:* For doctorate, thesis/dissertation, qualifying examination. *Entrance requirements:* For master's, GMAT (for MBA), minimum GPA of 2.5 (MS). Additional exam requirements/recommendations for international students: Required—TOEFL (minimum score 550 paper-based; 79 iBT). Electronic applications accepted. *Expenses:* Contact institution.

Goldey-Beacom College, Graduate Program, Wilmington, DE 19808-1999. Offers business administration (MBA); finance (MS); financial management (MBA); health care management (MBA); human resource management (MBA); information technology (MBA); international business management (MBA); major finance (MBA); major taxation (MBA); management (MM); marketing management (MBA); taxation (MBA, MS). *Accreditation:* ACBSP. *Program availability:* Part-time, evening/weekend. *Entrance requirements:* For master's, GMAT, MAT, GRE, minimum GPA of 3.0. Additional exam requirements/recommendations for international students: Required—TOEFL (minimum score 65 iBT); Recommended—IELTS (minimum score 6). Electronic applications accepted.

Gonzaga University, School of Business Administration, Spokane, WA 99258. Offers accountancy (M Acc); American Indian entrepreneurship (MBA); business administration (MBA); taxation (MS); JD/M Acc; JD/MBA. *Accreditation:* AACSB. *Program availability:* Part-time, evening/weekend. *Degree requirements:* For master's, capstone course. *Entrance requirements:* For master's, GMAT or GRE, essay, two professional recommendations, resume/curriculum vitae, copy of official transcripts from all colleges attended, minimum GPA of 3.0. Additional exam requirements/recommendations for international students: Required—TOEFL (minimum score 570 paper-based, 89 iBT) or IELTS (minimum score 6.5). Electronic applications accepted. *Expenses:* Contact institution.

Governors State University, College of Business, Program in Business Administration, University Park, IL 60484. Offers MBA. *Program availability:* Part-time. *Faculty:* 11 full-time (4 women), 17 part-time/adjunct (4 women). *Students:* 18 full-time (12 women), 69 part-time (42 women); includes 51 minority (39 Black or African American, non-Hispanic/Latino; 4 Asian, non-Hispanic/Latino; 4 Hispanic/Latino; 4 Two or more races, non-Hispanic/Latino), 1 international. Average age 36. 63 applicants, 44% accepted, 19 enrolled. In 2018, 32 master's awarded. *Application deadline:* For fall admission, 4/1 for domestic students. Applications are processed on a rolling basis. Application fee: $50. Electronic applications accepted. *Expenses:* $406/credit hour; $4,872 in tuition/term; $6,002 in tuition and fees/term; $12,004/year. *Financial support:* Application deadline: 5/1; applicants required to submit FAFSA. *Unit head:* Olumide Ijose, Chair, Division of Management, Marketing and Entrepreneurship, 708-534-5000 Ext. 4932, E-mail: oijose@govst.edu. *Application contact:* Olumide Ijose, Chair, Division of Management, Marketing and Entrepreneurship, 708-534-5000 Ext. 4932, E-mail: oijose@govst.edu.

The Graduate Center, City University of New York, Graduate Studies, Program in Business, New York, NY 10016-4039. Offers accounting (PhD); behavioral science (PhD); finance (PhD); management planning systems (PhD). *Degree requirements:* For doctorate, thesis/dissertation. *Entrance requirements:* For doctorate, GMAT, writing sample (15 pages). Additional exam requirements/recommendations for international students: Required—TOEFL. Electronic applications accepted.

Grand Canyon University, Colangelo College of Business, Phoenix, AZ 85017-1097. Offers accounting (MBA, MS); business analytics (MS); disaster preparedness and executive fire service leadership (MS); finance (MBA); general management (MBA); health systems management (MBA); information technology management (MS); leadership (MBA, MS); marketing (MBA); organizational leadership and entrepreneurship (MS); project management (MBA); sports business (MBA); strategic human resource management (MBA). *Accreditation:* ACBSP. *Program availability:* Part-time, evening/weekend, online learning. *Entrance requirements:* For master's, equivalent of two years' full-time professional work experience. Additional exam requirements/recommendations for international students: Required—TOEFL (minimum score 575 paper-based; 90 iBT), IELTS (minimum score 7). Electronic applications accepted.

Grand Canyon University, College of Doctoral Studies, Phoenix, AZ 85017-1097. Offers data analytics (DBA); general psychology (PhD), including cognition and instruction, industrial and organizational psychology, integrating technology, learning, and psychology, performance psychology; management (DBA); marketing (DBA); organizational leadership (Ed D), including behavioral health, Christian ministry, health care administration, organizational development. *Degree requirements:* For doctorate, comprehensive exam, thesis/dissertation. *Entrance requirements:* For doctorate, minimum GPA of 3.4 on earned advanced degree from regionally-accredited institution; transcripts; goals statement.

Grand Valley State University, Seidman College of Business, Program in Business Administration, Allendale, MI 49401-9403. Offers MBA. *Accreditation:* AACSB. *Program availability:* Part-time, evening/weekend. *Students:* 26 full-time (9 women), 165 part-time (63 women); includes 31 minority (4 Black or African American, non-Hispanic/Latino; 1 American Indian or Alaska Native, non-Hispanic/Latino; 6 Asian, non-Hispanic/Latino; 13 Hispanic/Latino; 7 Two or more races, non-Hispanic/Latino), 9 international. Average age 32. 92 applicants, 93% accepted, 20 enrolled. In 2018, 59 master's awarded. *Entrance requirements:* For master's, GMAT, personal statement. Additional exam requirements/recommendations for international students: Required—TOEFL (minimum iBT score of 80), IELTS (6.5), or Michigan English Language Assessment Battery (77). *Application deadline:* For fall admission, 8/1 priority date for domestic students, 5/1 priority date for international students; for winter admission, 12/1 priority date for domestic students, 11/1 priority date for international students; for spring admission, 4/1 priority date for domestic students, 3/1 priority date for international students. Applications are processed on a rolling basis. Application fee: $30. Electronic applications accepted. *Expenses:* $712 per credit hour, 36 credit hours. *Financial support:* In 2018–19, 30 students received support, including 27 fellowships, 3 research assistantships with full and partial tuition reimbursements available (averaging $4,000 per year); institutionally sponsored loans and unspecified assistantships also available. Support available to part-time students. Financial award application deadline: 2/15. *Faculty research:* E-commerce, continuous improvement, currency futures, manufacturing flexibility. *Unit head:* Dr. Jaideep Motwani, Director, 616-331-7467, Fax: 616-331-7490, E-mail: motwanij@gvsu.edu. *Application contact:* Koleta Moore, Assistant Dean of Student Engagement, Graduate Program Operations, 616-331-7386, Fax: 616-331-7389, E-mail: moorekol@gvsu.edu.
Website: http://www.gvsu.edu/business/

Granite State College, MS in Management Program, Concord, NH 03301. Offers MS. *Program availability:* Part-time, 100% online, blended/hybrid learning. *Degree requirements:* For master's, capstone. *Entrance requirements:* For master's, bachelor's degree with minimum GPA of 3.0 on last 60 credit hours, 500-1000 word statement of purpose, two letters of professional or academic reference, resume, official transcripts. Additional exam requirements/recommendations for international students: Required—TOEFL (minimum score 80 iBT), IELTS (minimum score 6.5). Electronic applications accepted.

Grantham University, Mark Skousen School of Business, Lenexa, KS 66219. Offers business administration (MBA); business intelligence (MS); human resources (Certificate); information management (MBA); performance improvement (MS); project management (MBA, Certificate). *Program availability:* Part-time, evening/weekend, online only, 100% online. *Students:* 556 full-time (238 women), 301 part-time (122 women); includes 369 minority (268 Black or African American, non-Hispanic/Latino; 5 American Indian or Alaska Native, non-Hispanic/Latino; 16 Asian, non-Hispanic/Latino; 50 Hispanic/Latino; 4 Native Hawaiian or other Pacific Islander, non-Hispanic/Latino; 26 Two or more races, non-Hispanic/Latino), 1 international. Average age 40. 206 applicants, 90% accepted, 159 enrolled. In 2018, 284 master's, 16 other advanced degrees awarded. *Degree requirements:* For master's, comprehensive exam (for some programs), PMP Prep Exams throughout the term (for MBA in project management); for Certificate, comprehensive exam (for some programs), PMP Prep Exam (for project management). *Entrance requirements:* For master's, baccalaureate or master's degree with minimum cumulative GPA of 2.5 from institution accredited by agency recognized by ED or foreign equivalent; official transcripts showing proof of degree. Additional exam requirements/recommendations for international students: Required—TOEFL (minimum score 530 paper-based; 71 iBT), IELTS (minimum score 6.5), PTE (minimum score 50). *Application deadline:* Applications are processed on a rolling basis. Application fee: $0. Electronic applications accepted. *Expenses: Tuition:* Full-time $4200; part-time $350 per credit hour. *Required fees:* $50; $50 per credit hour. *Financial support:* Scholarships/grants available. Financial award applicants required to submit FAFSA. *Faculty research:* How chronic diseases contribute to the rising costs of healthcare, marketing for entrepreneurs, managers' hiring practices of workers with disability, organizational structures, organizational change, online pedagogy, impact of instructor video tips in the online classroom, decision-making techniques. *Unit head:* Dr. David Marker, Dean of the Mark Skousen School of Business, 913-309-4747, Fax: 844-260-6287, E-mail: dmarker@grantham.edu. *Application contact:* Lauren Cook, Director of Admissions, 800-955-2527 Ext. 803, Fax: 877-304-4467, E-mail: admissions@grantham.edu.
Website: https://www.grantham.edu/school-of-business/

Gwynedd Mercy University, School of Graduate and Professional Studies, Gwynedd Valley, PA 19437-0901. Offers health care administration (MBA); management (MSM); strategic management and leadership (MBA). *Program availability:* Part-time, evening/weekend. *Degree requirements:* For master's, thesis. *Entrance requirements:* For master's, minimum GPA of 3.0. *Expenses:* Contact institution.

Hallmark University, School of Business, San Antonio, TX 78230. Offers global management (MBA). *Degree requirements:* For master's, thesis (for some programs). *Entrance requirements:* For master's, bachelor's degree; minimum undergraduate GPA of 2.5; completion of one course each in college-level statistics, quantitative methods, and calculus or pre-calculus; official undergraduate transcripts; professional resume; personal statement; two letters of recommendation; two 200-word typed essays. Additional exam requirements/recommendations for international students: Required—TOEFL (minimum score 450 paper-based; 45 iBT). *Expenses:* Contact institution.

Hamline University, School of Business, St. Paul, MN 55104-1284. Offers business administration (MBA); nonprofit management (MNM); public administration (MPA, DPA); MBA/MNM; MBA/MPA; MPA/MNM. *Program availability:* Part-time, evening/weekend, blended/hybrid learning. *Degree requirements:* For master's, thesis (for some programs); for doctorate, comprehensive exam, thesis/dissertation. *Entrance requirements:* For master's and doctorate, personal statement, official transcripts, resume or curriculum vitae, letters of recommendation, writing sample. Additional exam requirements/recommendations for international students: Required—TOEFL (minimum score 550 paper-based; 80 iBT), IELTS (minimum score 6.5). Electronic applications accepted. *Expenses:* Contact institution. *Faculty research:* Experiential learning, organizational process/politics, gender differences, social equity, pyramid schemes.

Hampton University, Program in Business Administration, Hampton, VA 23668. Offers MBA, PhD. *Program availability:* Part-time, online learning. *Students:* 24 full-time (12 women), 12 part-time (4 women); includes 32 minority (31 Black or African American, non-Hispanic/Latino; 1 Hispanic/Latino), 2 international. Average age 28. 24 applicants, 42% accepted, 8 enrolled. In 2018, 21 master's, 3 doctorates awarded. *Degree requirements:* For master's, comprehensive exam (for some programs), thesis (for some programs); for doctorate, comprehensive exam (for some programs), thesis/dissertation, oral defense, qualifying exam, journal article. *Entrance requirements:* For master's,

GMAT. Additional exam requirements/recommendations for international students: Required—TOEFL, TOEFL (minimum score 525 paper-based) or IELTS (6.5). *Application deadline:* For fall admission, 6/1 priority date for domestic students, 4/1 priority date for international students; for spring admission, 11/1 priority date for domestic students, 9/1 priority date for international students; for summer admission, 4/1 priority date for domestic students, 2/1 priority date for international students. Applications are processed on a rolling basis. Application fee: $35. Electronic applications accepted. *Financial support:* Research assistantships, teaching assistantships, career-related internships or fieldwork, Federal Work-Study, institutionally sponsored loans, scholarships/grants, health care benefits, tuition waivers, unspecified assistantships, and stipends available. Support available to part-time students. Financial award application deadline: 6/30; financial award applicants required to submit FAFSA. *Faculty research:* Retirement security, transportation, workforce development, and finance research. *Unit head:* Dr. Ziette Hayes, Dean, School of Business, 757-727-5361. *Application contact:* Dr. Ziette Hayes, Dean, School of Business, 757-727-5361.
Website: http://biz.hamptonu.edu/

Harding University, Paul R. Carter College of Business Administration, Searcy, AR 72149-0001. Offers international business (MBA); leadership and organizational management (MBA). *Accreditation:* ACBSP. *Program availability:* Part-time, evening/weekend, 100% online. *Degree requirements:* For master's, portfolio. *Entrance requirements:* For master's, GMAT (minimum score of 500) or GRE (minimum score of 300), minimum GPA of 3.0, 2 letters of recommendation, resume, 3 essays, all official transcripts. Additional exam requirements/recommendations for international students: Required—TOEFL (minimum score 550 paper-based; 79 iBT).

Hardin-Simmons University, Graduate School, Kelley College of Business, Abilene, TX 79698-0001. Offers business administration (MBA); information science (MS); sports management (MBA). *Accreditation:* ACBSP. *Program availability:* Part-time. *Faculty:* 10 full-time (3 women). *Students:* 32 full-time (6 women), 55 part-time (23 women); includes 16 minority (5 Black or African American, non-Hispanic/Latino; 11 Hispanic/Latino), 2 international. Average age 29. 48 applicants, 96% accepted, 41 enrolled. In 2018, 27 master's awarded. *Degree requirements:* For master's, thesis or alternative. *Entrance requirements:* For master's, GMAT, minimum GPA of 3.0 in upper-level course work, resume, interview. Additional exam requirements/recommendations for international students: Required—TOEFL (minimum score 550 paper-based; 79 iBT). *Application deadline:* For fall admission, 8/15 priority date for domestic students, 4/1 for international students; for spring admission, 1/5 priority date for domestic students, 9/1 for international students. Applications are processed on a rolling basis. Application fee: $50. Electronic applications accepted. *Expenses: Tuition:* Full-time $750; part-time $750 per credit hour. *Required fees:* $1300; $880 per credit. Tuition and fees vary according to degree level and program. *Financial support:* Fellowships and scholarships/grants available. Support available to part-time students. Financial award application deadline: 6/30; financial award applicants required to submit FAFSA. *Unit head:* Dr. Jennifer Plantier, Program Director, 325-671-2166, Fax: 325-670-1523, E-mail: jplantier@hsutx.edu. *Application contact:* Dr. Nancy Kucinski, Dean of Graduate Studies, 325-670-1298, Fax: 325-670-1564, E-mail: gradoff@hsutx.edu.
Website: http://www.hsutx.edu/academics/kelley/graduate/

Harvard University, Extension School, Cambridge, MA 02138-3722. Offers applied sciences (CAS); biotechnology (ALM); educational technologies (ALM); educational technology (CET); English for graduate and professional studies (DGP); environmental management (ALM, CEM); information technology (ALM); journalism (ALM); liberal arts (ALM); management (ALM, CM); mathematics for teaching (ALM); museum studies (ALM); premedical studies (Diploma); publication and communication (CPC). *Program availability:* Part-time, evening/weekend. *Degree requirements:* For master's, thesis. *Entrance requirements:* For master's, 3 completed graduate courses with grade of B or higher. Additional exam requirements/recommendations for international students: Required—TOEFL (minimum score 600 paper-based), TWE (minimum score 5). *Expenses:* Contact institution.

Harvard University, Harvard Business School, Doctoral Programs in Management, Boston, MA 02163. Offers accounting and management (DBA); business economics (PhD); health policy management (PhD); management (DBA); marketing (DBA); organizational behavior (PhD); science, technology and management (PhD); strategy (DBA); technology and operations management (DBA). *Degree requirements:* For doctorate, comprehensive exam (for some programs), thesis/dissertation. *Entrance requirements:* For doctorate, GRE General Test or GMAT. Additional exam requirements/recommendations for international students: Required—TOEFL.

Harvard University, Harvard Business School, Master's Program in Business Administration, Boston, MA 02163. Offers MBA, JD/MBA. *Entrance requirements:* For master's, GMAT. Additional exam requirements/recommendations for international students: Required—TOEFL.

Hawai`i Pacific University, College of Business, Honolulu, HI 96813. Offers MA, MBA, MSIS. *Program availability:* Part-time, evening/weekend, 100% online, blended/hybrid learning. *Entrance requirements:* For master's, GMAT or GRE. Additional exam requirements/recommendations for international students: Recommended—TOEFL (minimum score 550 paper-based; 80 iBT), IELTS (minimum score 6), TWE (minimum score 5). Electronic applications accepted.

HEC Montreal, School of Business Administration, Doctoral Program in Administration, Montréal, QC H3T 2A7, Canada. Offers accounting (PhD); applied economics (PhD); data science (PhD); finance (PhD); financial engineering (PhD); information technology (PhD); international business (PhD); logistics and operations management (PhD); management science (PhD); management, strategy and organizations (PhD); marketing (PhD); organizational behaviour and human resources (PhD). Program offered jointly with Concordia University, McGill University, and Universite du Quebec a Montreal. *Accreditation:* AACSB. *Students:* 130 full-time (55 women). 114 applicants, 46% accepted, 31 enrolled. In 2018, 19 doctorates awarded. *Entrance requirements:* For doctorate, TAGE MAGE, GMAT, or GRE, master's degree in administration or related field. *Application deadline:* For fall admission, 1/15 for domestic and international students. Application fee: 91 (191 for international students). Electronic applications accepted. *Expenses: Tuition, area resident:* Full-time $3052.80 Canadian dollars; part-time $84.80 Canadian dollars per credit. Tuition, state resident: full-time $3816 Canadian dollars; part-time $264.67 Canadian dollars per credit. Tuition, nonresident: full-time $11,910 Canadian dollars. *International tuition:* $20,905.20 Canadian dollars full-time. *Required fees:* $1805.34 Canadian dollars; $43.62 Canadian dollars per credit. $71.78 Canadian dollars per term. Tuition and fees vary according to degree level and program. *Financial support:* Research assistantships, teaching assistantships, and scholarships/grants available. Financial award application deadline: 9/2. *Faculty research:* Art management, business policy, entrepreneurship, new technologies, transportation. *Unit head:* Guy Paré, Director, 514-340-6264, E-mail: guy.pare@hec.ca. *Application contact:* Julie Bilodeau, PhD Program Analyst, 514-340-6000, Fax: 514-340-6411, E-mail: analyste.phd@hec.ca.
Website: http://www.hec.ca/en/programs/phd/index.html

HEC Montreal, School of Business Administration, Graduate Diploma Programs in Administration, Program in Management, Montréal, QC H3T 2A7, Canada. Offers Graduate Diploma. All courses are given in French. *Accreditation:* AACSB. *Students:* 15 full-time (11 women), 54 part-time (37 women). 78 applicants, 58% accepted, 31 enrolled. In 2018, 15 Graduate Diplomas awarded. *Entrance requirements:* For degree, bachelor's degree. *Application deadline:* For fall admission, 4/15 for domestic and international students; for winter admission, 9/15 for domestic and international students. Applications are processed on a rolling basis. Application fee: $92 Canadian dollars ($191 Canadian dollars for international students). Electronic applications accepted. *Expenses: Tuition, area resident:* Full-time $3052.80 Canadian dollars; part-time $84.80 Canadian dollars per credit. Tuition, state resident: full-time $3816 Canadian dollars; part-time $264.67 Canadian dollars per credit. Tuition, nonresident: full-time $11,910 Canadian dollars. *International tuition:* $20,905.20 Canadian dollars full-time. *Required fees:* $1805.34 Canadian dollars; $43.62 Canadian dollars per credit. $71.78 Canadian dollars per term. Tuition and fees vary according to degree level and program. *Financial support:* Research assistantships, teaching assistantships, and scholarships/grants available. Financial award application deadline: 9/2. *Unit head:* Renaud Lachance, Director, 514-340-6428, E-mail: renaud.lachance@hec.ca. *Application contact:* Anny Caron, Administrative Director, 514-340-6000, Fax: 514-340-6411, E-mail: aide@hec.ca.
Website: http://www.hec.ca/programmes/dess/dess-gestion-management/index.html

HEC Montreal, School of Business Administration, Graduate Diploma Programs in Administration, Program in Management and Sustainable Development, Montréal, QC H3T 2A7, Canada. Offers Graduate Diploma. All courses are given in French. *Students:* 14 full-time (10 women), 27 part-time (18 women). 41 applicants, 80% accepted, 16 enrolled. In 2018, 16 Graduate Diplomas awarded. *Entrance requirements:* For degree, bachelor's degree. *Application deadline:* For fall admission, 4/15 for domestic and international students; for winter admission, 9/15 for domestic and international students. Applications are processed on a rolling basis. Application fee: $91 Canadian dollars ($191 Canadian dollars for international students). Electronic applications accepted. *Expenses: Tuition, area resident:* Full-time $3052.80 Canadian dollars; part-time $84.80 Canadian dollars per credit. Tuition, state resident: full-time $3816 Canadian dollars; part-time $264.67 Canadian dollars per credit. Tuition, nonresident: full-time $11,910 Canadian dollars. *International tuition:* $20,905.20 Canadian dollars full-time. *Required fees:* $1805.34 Canadian dollars; $43.62 Canadian dollars per credit. $71.78 Canadian dollars per term. Tuition and fees vary according to degree level and program. *Financial support:* Research assistantships, teaching assistantships, and scholarships/grants available. Financial award application deadline: 9/2. *Unit head:* Renaud Lachance, Director, 514-340-6428, E-mail: renaud.lachance@hec.ca. *Application contact:* Anny Caron, Administrative Director, 514-340-6000, Fax: 514-340-6411, E-mail: aide@hec.ca.
Website: http://www.hec.ca/programmes/dess/dess-gestion-developpement-durable/index.html

HEC Montreal, School of Business Administration, Master of Science Programs in Administration, Program on Accounting, Management, Control, and Audit, Montréal, QC H3T 2A7, Canada. Offers M Sc. Program offered in French. *Students:* 4 full-time (3 women), 6 part-time (3 women). 17 applicants, 65% accepted, 8 enrolled. In 2018, 1 master's awarded. *Entrance requirements:* For master's, short graduate program in public accounting from HEC Montreal, minimum GPA of 3.0 on 4.3 scale. Additional exam requirements/recommendations for international students: Required—TAGE MAGE (minimum recommended score of 300), GMAT (minimum recommended score of 630), or GRE. *Application deadline:* For fall admission, 3/15 for domestic and international students; for winter admission, 9/15 for domestic and international students. Application fee: $91 Canadian dollars ($191 Canadian dollars for international students). Electronic applications accepted. *Expenses: Tuition, area resident:* Full-time $3052.80 Canadian dollars; part-time $84.80 Canadian dollars per credit. Tuition, state resident: full-time $3816 Canadian dollars; part-time $264.67 Canadian dollars per credit. Tuition, nonresident: full-time $11,910 Canadian dollars. *International tuition:* $20,905.20 Canadian dollars full-time. *Required fees:* $1805.34 Canadian dollars; $43.62 Canadian dollars per credit. $71.78 Canadian dollars per term. Tuition and fees vary according to degree level and program. *Financial support:* Research assistantships, teaching assistantships, and scholarships/grants available. Financial award application deadline: 9/2. *Unit head:* Dr. Sihem Taboubi, Director, 514-340-6428, E-mail: sihem.taboubi@hec.ca. *Application contact:* Marianne de Moura, Administrative Director, 514-340-6000, Fax: 514-340-6411, E-mail: aide@hec.ca.
Website: http://www.hec.ca/programmes/maitrises/maitrise-comptabilite-controle-audit/index.html

HEC Montreal, School of Business Administration, Master's Program in Business Administration and Management, Montréal, QC H3T 2A7, Canada. Offers MBA. Program offered in French and English. *Accreditation:* AACSB. *Students:* 102 full-time (31 women), 185 part-time (49 women). 132 applicants, 57% accepted, 67 enrolled. In 2018, 142 master's awarded. *Entrance requirements:* For master's, GMAT, GRE, or TAGE MAGE, undergraduate degree. Additional exam requirements/recommendations for international students: Required—TOEFL (minimum score 94 iBT), TAGE MAGE (minimum recommended score of 300), GMAT (minimum recommended score of 630), or GRE. *Application deadline:* For fall admission, 5/15 for domestic students, 3/15 for international students; for winter admission, 9/15 for domestic students. Application fee: $91 Canadian dollars ($191 Canadian dollars for international students). Electronic applications accepted. *Expenses: Tuition, area resident:* Full-time $3052.80 Canadian dollars; part-time $84.80 Canadian dollars per credit. Tuition, state resident: full-time $3816 Canadian dollars; part-time $264.67 Canadian dollars per credit. Tuition, nonresident: full-time $11,910 Canadian dollars. *International tuition:* $20,905.20 Canadian dollars full-time. *Required fees:* $1805.34 Canadian dollars; $43.62 Canadian dollars per credit. $71.78 Canadian dollars per term. Tuition and fees vary according to degree level and program. *Financial support:* Research assistantships, teaching assistantships, and scholarships/grants available. Financial award application deadline: 9/2. *Unit head:* Louis Hebert, Director, 514-340-6294, E-mail: louis.hebert@hec.ca. *Application contact:* Anik Low, Administrative Director, 514-340-6000, Fax: 514-340-7327, E-mail: aide@hec.ca.
Website: http://www.hec.ca/en/programs/mba/index.html

Heidelberg University, Master of Business Administration Program, Tiffin, OH 44883-2462. Offers MBA. *Accreditation:* ACBSP. *Program availability:* Part-time, evening/weekend. *Students:* 38 full-time (14 women), 15 part-time (8 women). 75 applicants, 84% accepted, 37 enrolled. In 2018, 32 master's awarded. *Entrance requirements:* For master's, bachelor's degree with minimum GPA of 2.7; goal statement. Additional exam requirements/recommendations for international students: Required—TOEFL (minimum score 550 paper-based, 79 iBT) or IELTS (minimum score 6.5). *Application deadline:* For fall admission, 6/1 for domestic and international students; for spring admission, 12/3 for domestic students, 12/1 for international students; for summer admission, 5/15 for domestic students, 4/1 for international students. Applications are processed on a rolling basis. Application fee: $0. Electronic applications accepted. Application fee is waived when completed online. *Expenses:* $855 per semester hour. Program is 36 semester hours for a total cost of $30,780. *Financial support:* In 2018–19, 53 students received support. Scholarships/grants and unspecified assistantships available. Financial award

applicants required to submit FAFSA. *Unit head:* Dr. Scott Johnson, Dean of Business and Technology, 419-448-2284, E-mail: sjohnson@heidelberg.edu. *Application contact:* Katie Zeyen, Graduate Admissions Coordinator, 419-448-2602, Fax: 419-448-2565, E-mail: kzeyen@heidelberg.edu.
Website: https://www.heidelberg.edu/academics/programs/master-of-business-administration

Henderson State University, Graduate Studies, School of Business, Arkadelphia, AR 71999-0001. Offers MBA. *Accreditation:* AACSB. *Program availability:* Part-time, 100% online. *Entrance requirements:* For master's, GMAT (minimum score 400), minimum AACSB index of 1000, minimum GPA of 2.7. Additional exam requirements/recommendations for international students: Required—TOEFL (minimum score 600 paper-based); Recommended—IELTS (minimum score 6.5).

Herzing University Online, Program in Business Administration, Menomonee Falls, WI 53051. Offers accounting (MBA); business administration (MBA); business management (MBA); healthcare management (MBA); human resources (MBA); marketing (MBA); project management (MBA); technology management (MBA). *Program availability:* Online learning.

High Point University, Norcross Graduate School, High Point, NC 27268. Offers athletic training (MSAT); business administration (MBA); educational leadership (M Ed, Ed D); elementary education (M Ed, MAT); pharmacy (Pharm D); physical therapy (DPT); physician assistant studies (MPAS); secondary mathematics (M Ed, MAT); special education (M Ed); strategic communication (MA). *Accreditation:* NCATE. *Program availability:* Part-time, evening/weekend. *Degree requirements:* For master's, comprehensive exam (for some programs), thesis (for some programs). *Entrance requirements:* For master's, GMAT (MBA), GRE, MAT, minimum GPA of 3.0. Additional exam requirements/recommendations for international students: Required—TOEFL (minimum score 550 paper-based). Electronic applications accepted.

Hodges University, Graduate Programs, Naples, FL 34119. Offers accounting (M Acc); business administration (MBA); clinical mental health counseling (MS); health services administration (MS); information systems management (MIS); legal studies (MS); management (MSM). *Program availability:* Part-time, evening/weekend, 100% online, blended/hybrid learning. *Degree requirements:* For master's, comprehensive exam (for some programs), thesis (for some programs). *Entrance requirements:* For master's, essay. Additional exam requirements/recommendations for international students: Recommended—TOEFL. Electronic applications accepted.

Hofstra University, Frank G. Zarb School of Business, Executive Master's Program in Business Administration, Hempstead, NY 11549. Offers executive program in management (EMBA). *Program availability:* Evening/weekend, blended/hybrid learning. *Students:* 10 full-time (4 women), 9 part-time (4 women); includes 11 minority (6 Black or African American, non-Hispanic/Latino; 4 Asian, non-Hispanic/Latino; 1 Hispanic/Latino). Average age 38. 25 applicants, 52% accepted, 10 enrolled. In 2018, 13 master's awarded. *Entrance requirements:* For master's, 2 letters of recommendation, minimum 7 years of management experience, resume, essay, interview. Additional exam requirements/recommendations for international students: Required—TOEFL (minimum score 550 paper-based; 80 iBT); Recommended—IELTS (minimum score 6). *Application deadline:* Applications are processed on a rolling basis. Application fee: $75. Electronic applications accepted. *Expenses:* $92,000 full program costs. *Financial support:* In 2018–19, 10 students received support, including 10 fellowships with full and partial tuition reimbursements available (averaging $5,250 per year); research assistantships with full and partial tuition reimbursements available, career-related internships or fieldwork, Federal Work-Study, institutionally sponsored loans, scholarships/grants, tuition waivers (full and partial), unspecified assistantships, and scholarships and endowed scholarships also available. Support available to part-time students. Financial award applicants required to submit FAFSA. *Faculty research:* Leadership; global decision making; organizational change; marketing strategy; consumer behavior. *Unit head:* Dr. Barry Berman, Director, 516-463-5711, Fax: 516-463-5268, E-mail: barry.berman@hofstra.edu. *Application contact:* Sunil Samuel, Assistant Vice President of Admissions, 516-463-4723, Fax: 516-463-4664, E-mail: graduateadmission@hofstra.edu.
Website: http://www.hofstra.edu/business/

Hofstra University, Frank G. Zarb School of Business, Programs in Accounting and Taxation, Hempstead, NY 11549. Offers accounting (MS, Advanced Certificate); business administration (MBA), including accounting, professional accountancy, taxation; taxation (MS, Advanced Certificate). *Program availability:* Part-time, evening/weekend, blended/hybrid learning. *Students:* 121 full-time (64 women), 43 part-time (24 women); includes 29 minority (3 Black or African American, non-Hispanic/Latino; 16 Asian, non-Hispanic/Latino; 8 Hispanic/Latino; 2 Two or more races, non-Hispanic/Latino), 68 international. Average age 26. 213 applicants, 80% accepted, 63 enrolled. In 2018, 125 master's awarded. *Degree requirements:* For master's, thesis (for some programs), capstone course (for MBA), thesis (for MS), minimum GPA of 3.0. *Entrance requirements:* For master's, GMAT/GRE, 2 letters of recommendation, resume, essay. Additional exam requirements/recommendations for international students: Required—TOEFL (minimum score 550 paper-based; 80 iBT); Recommended—IELTS (minimum score 6). *Application deadline:* Applications are processed on a rolling basis. Application fee: $75. Electronic applications accepted. *Expenses:* $1,375 per credit plus fees. *Financial support:* In 2018–19, 43 students received support, including 39 fellowships with full and partial tuition reimbursements available (averaging $4,765 per year); research assistantships with full and partial tuition reimbursements available, career-related internships or fieldwork, Federal Work-Study, institutionally sponsored loans, scholarships/grants, tuition waivers (full and partial), unspecified assistantships, and scholarships and endowed scholarships also available. Support available to part-time students. Financial award applicants required to submit FAFSA. *Faculty research:* Corporate compliance, artificial intelligence, financial accounting fraud, tax reform legislation, accounting analytics. *Unit head:* Dr. Jacqueline Burke, Chairperson, 516-463-6987, E-mail: jacqueline.a.burke@hofstra.edu. *Application contact:* Sunil Samuel, Assistant Vice President of Admissions, 516-463-4723, Fax: 516-463-4664, E-mail: graduateadmission@hofstra.edu.
Website: http://www.hofstra.edu/business/

Hofstra University, Frank G. Zarb School of Business, Programs in Finance, Hempstead, NY 11549. Offers business administration (MBA), including finance; corporate finance (Advanced Certificate); finance (MS), including financial and risk management, investment analysis; investment management (Advanced Certificate); quantitative finance (MS). *Program availability:* Part-time, evening/weekend, blended/hybrid learning. *Students:* 122 full-time (36 women), 40 part-time (8 women); includes 24 minority (5 Black or African American, non-Hispanic/Latino; 1 American Indian or Alaska Native, non-Hispanic/Latino; 8 Asian, non-Hispanic/Latino; 8 Hispanic/Latino; 2 Two or more races, non-Hispanic/Latino), 90 international. Average age 25. 326 applicants, 78% accepted, 58 enrolled. In 2018, 103 master's awarded. *Degree requirements:* For master's, thesis (for some programs), capstone course (for MBA), thesis (for MS), minimum GPA of 3.0. *Entrance requirements:* For master's, GMAT/GRE, 2 letters of recommendation, resume, essay. Additional exam requirements/recommendations for international students: Required—TOEFL (minimum score 550 paper-based; 80 iBT); Recommended—IELTS (minimum score 6). *Application deadline:* Applications are processed on a rolling basis. Application fee: $75. Electronic applications accepted. *Expenses:* $1,375 per credit plus fees. *Financial support:* In 2018–19, 46 students received support, including 42 fellowships with full and partial tuition reimbursements available (averaging $5,064 per year); research assistantships with full and partial tuition reimbursements available, career-related internships or fieldwork, Federal Work-Study, institutionally sponsored loans, scholarships/grants, tuition waivers (full and partial), unspecified assistantships, and scholarships and endowed scholarships also available. Support available to part-time students. Financial award applicants required to submit FAFSA. *Faculty research:* Sustainable investing; blockchain applications in finance; machine learning in finance; text and data mining in finance; corporate inversions. *Unit head:* Dr. K.G. Viswanathan, Chairperson, 516-463-5699, Fax: 516-463-4834, E-mail: k.g.viswanathan@hofstra.edu. *Application contact:* Sunil Samuel, Assistant Vice President of Admissions, 516-463-4723, Fax: 516-463-4664, E-mail: graduateadmission@hofstra.edu.
Website: http://www.hofstra.edu/business/

Hofstra University, Frank G. Zarb School of Business, Programs in Management and General Business, Hempstead, NY 11549. Offers business administration (MBA), including health services management, management, sports and entertainment management, strategic business management, strategic healthcare management; general management (Advanced Certificate); human resource management (MS, Advanced Certificate). *Program availability:* Part-time, evening/weekend, blended/hybrid learning. *Students:* 121 full-time (48 women), 112 part-time (52 women); includes 96 minority (18 Black or African American, non-Hispanic/Latino; 1 American Indian or Alaska Native, non-Hispanic/Latino; 34 Asian, non-Hispanic/Latino; 38 Hispanic/Latino; 5 Two or more races, non-Hispanic/Latino), 16 international. Average age 33. 290 applicants, 75% accepted, 89 enrolled. In 2018, 110 master's awarded. *Degree requirements:* For master's, thesis optional, capstone course (for MBA), thesis (for MS), minimum GPA of 3.0. *Entrance requirements:* For master's, GMAT/GRE, 2 letters of recommendation, resume, essay. Additional exam requirements/recommendations for international students: Required—TOEFL (minimum score 550 paper-based; 80 iBT); Recommended—IELTS (minimum score 6). *Application deadline:* Applications are processed on a rolling basis. Application fee: $75. Electronic applications accepted. *Expenses:* $1,375 per credit plus fees. *Financial support:* In 2018–19, 91 students received support, including 84 fellowships with full and partial tuition reimbursements available (averaging $4,279 per year), 1 research assistantship with full and partial tuition reimbursement available (averaging $9,179 per year); career-related internships or fieldwork, Federal Work-Study, institutionally sponsored loans, scholarships/grants, tuition waivers (full and partial), unspecified assistantships, and scholarships and endowed scholarships also available. Support available to part-time students. Financial award applicants required to submit FAFSA. *Faculty research:* Organizational behavior; sustainability; entrepreneurial spawning; family business; global supply chain strategies. *Unit head:* Dr. Kaushik Sengupta, Chairperson, 516-463-7825, Fax: 516-463-4834, E-mail: kaushik.sengupta@hofstra.edu. *Application contact:* Sunil Samuel, Assistant Vice President of Admissions, 516-463-4723, Fax: 516-463-4664, E-mail: graduateadmission@hofstra.edu.
Website: http://www.hofstra.edu/business/

Hofstra University, Frank G. Zarb School of Business, Programs in Marketing and International Business, Hempstead, NY 11549. Offers business administration (MBA), including international business, marketing; international business (Advanced Certificate); marketing (MS, Advanced Certificate); marketing research (MS). *Program availability:* Part-time, evening/weekend, blended/hybrid learning. *Students:* 65 full-time (35 women), 19 part-time (11 women); includes 11 minority (2 Black or African American, non-Hispanic/Latino; 5 Asian, non-Hispanic/Latino; 4 Hispanic/Latino), 51 international. Average age 26. 168 applicants, 68% accepted, 35 enrolled. In 2018, 54 master's awarded. *Degree requirements:* For master's, thesis (for some programs), capstone course (for MBA), thesis (for MS), minimum GPA of 3.0. *Entrance requirements:* For master's, GMAT/GRE, 2 letters of recommendation, resume, essay. Additional exam requirements/recommendations for international students: Required—TOEFL (minimum score 550 paper-based; 80 iBT); Recommended—IELTS (minimum score 6). *Application deadline:* Applications are processed on a rolling basis. Application fee: $75. Electronic applications accepted. *Expenses:* $1,375 per credit plus fees. *Financial support:* In 2018–19, 34 students received support, including 21 fellowships with full and partial tuition reimbursements available (averaging $5,450 per year), 3 research assistantships with full and partial tuition reimbursements available (averaging $4,477 per year); career-related internships or fieldwork, Federal Work-Study, institutionally sponsored loans, scholarships/grants, tuition waivers (full and partial), unspecified assistantships, and scholarships and endowed scholarships also available. Support available to part-time students. Financial award applicants required to submit FAFSA. *Faculty research:* Cross-cultural consumer behavior; social, digital, global, and strategic issues in marketing; consumer health/well-being; ethnocentrism and animosity. *Unit head:* Dr. Anil Mathur, Chairperson, 516-463-5346, Fax: 516-463-4834, E-mail: anil.mathur@hofstra.edu. *Application contact:* Sunil Samuel, Assistant Vice President of Admissions, 516-463-4723, Fax: 516-463-4664, E-mail: graduateadmission@hofstra.edu.
Website: http://www.hofstra.edu/business/

Holy Family University, Graduate and Professional Programs, School of Business Administration, Philadelphia, PA 19114. Offers accountancy (MS); finance (MBA); health care administration (MBA); human resource management (MBA); information systems management (MBA). *Accreditation:* ACBSP. *Program availability:* Part-time, evening/weekend. *Degree requirements:* For master's, comprehensive exam, thesis optional. *Entrance requirements:* For master's, minimum GPA of 3.0, interview, essay/personal statement, current resume, official transcript of all college or university work. Additional exam requirements/recommendations for international students: Required—TOEFL (minimum score 550 paper-based; 79 iBT), IELTS (minimum score 6), PTE (minimum score 54). Electronic applications accepted.

Holy Names University, Graduate Division, Department of Business, Oakland, CA 94619-1699. Offers finance (MBA); management and leadership (MBA); marketing (MBA). *Program availability:* Part-time, evening/weekend. *Students:* 26 full-time (15 women), 16 part-time (14 women); includes 28 minority (13 Black or African American, non-Hispanic/Latino; 6 Asian, non-Hispanic/Latino; 9 Hispanic/Latino), 4 international. Average age 31. 38 applicants, 61% accepted, 17 enrolled. In 2018, 11 master's awarded. *Entrance requirements:* For master's, minimum undergraduate GPA of 2.6 overall, 3.0 in major; two recommendations (letter or form) from previous professors or current or previous work supervisors; 1-3 page personal statement; resume. Additional exam requirements/recommendations for international students: Required—TOEFL (minimum score 550 paper-based; 79 iBT). *Application deadline:* For fall admission, 8/1 priority date for domestic students, 7/15 for international students; for spring admission, 12/1 priority date for domestic students, 12/1 for international students; for summer admission, 5/1 priority date for domestic students, 5/1 for international students. Applications are processed on a rolling basis. Application fee: $65. Electronic applications accepted. Application fee is waived when completed online. *Expenses:* Contact institution. *Financial support:* Career-related internships or fieldwork, Federal Work-Study, scholarships/grants, and unspecified assistantships available. Support available to part-time students. Financial award application deadline: 3/2; financial

award applicants required to submit FAFSA. *Faculty research:* Business ethics, sustainable economics, accounting models, cross-cultural management, diversity in organizations. *Unit head:* Morris Hamm, MBA Program Director, E-mail: hamm@hnu.edu. *Application contact:* 800-430-1321, Fax: 510-436-1325, E-mail: graduateadmissions@hnu.edu.
Website: http://www.hnu.edu

Hood College, Graduate School, Department of Economics and Business Administration, Frederick, MD 21701-8575. Offers accounting (MBA); information systems (MBA); organizational management (Certificate). *Accreditation:* ACBSP. *Program availability:* Part-time, evening/weekend. *Faculty:* 3 full-time (2 women), 6 part-time/adjunct (1 woman). *Students:* 23 full-time (12 women), 176 part-time (120 women); includes 44 minority (17 Black or African American, non-Hispanic/Latino; 5 Asian, non-Hispanic/Latino; 19 Hispanic/Latino; 3 Two or more races, non-Hispanic/Latino), 13 international. Average age 35. 23 applicants, 96% accepted, 13 enrolled. In 2018, 36 master's, 2 other advanced degrees awarded. *Degree requirements:* For master's, capstone/final research project. *Entrance requirements:* For master's, minimum GPA of 3.0 (or resume and two letters of recommendation), copy of official transcripts; for Certificate, copy of official transcripts, Statement of Intent (250 words). Additional exam requirements/recommendations for international students: Required—TOEFL (minimum score 575 paper-based; 89 iBT), IELTS (minimum score 6.5). *Application deadline:* For fall admission, 8/15 for domestic students, 8/5 for international students; for spring admission, 12/1 for domestic and international students; for summer admission, 5/1 for domestic students, 4/15 for international students. Applications are processed on a rolling basis. Application fee: $50 ($100 for international students). Electronic applications accepted. *Expenses:* Business Programs: Tuition $605 per credit hour, Comprehensive Fee $115 per semester. *Financial support:* Tuition waivers (partial) and unspecified assistantships available. Financial award applicants required to submit FAFSA. *Faculty research:* Corporate strategy and sustainable competitive advantages, business ethics, entrepreneurship, investments management, economic development. *Unit head:* Dr. April M. Boulton, Dean of the Graduate School, 301-696-3600, Fax: 301-696-3597, E-mail: gofurther@hood.edu. *Application contact:* Christian DiGregorio, Director of Graduate Admissions, 301-696-3604, E-mail: gofurther@hood.edu.

Houston Baptist University, Archie W. Dunham College of Business, Program in Business Administration, Houston, TX 77074-3298. Offers MBA. *Program availability:* Part-time, evening/weekend. *Entrance requirements:* For master's, GMAT or GRE, minimum GPA of 2.5, essay/personal statement, resume, bachelor's degree conferred transcript. Additional exam requirements/recommendations for international students: Required—TOEFL (minimum score 80 iBT), IELTS (minimum score 6.5). Electronic applications accepted. Application fee is waived when completed online. *Expenses:* Contact institution.

Houston Baptist University, College of Education and Behavioral Sciences, Programs in Education, Houston, TX 77074-3298. Offers bilingual education (M Ed); counselor education (M Ed); curriculum and instruction (M Ed); curriculum and instruction (EC-6 bilingual) (M Ed); curriculum and instruction in all-level art, Spanish, music, or physical education (M Ed); curriculum and instruction in EC-6 and special education (EC-12) (M Ed); curriculum and instruction in instructional technology (M Ed); curriculum and instruction in mathematics, science, or social studies (4-8) (M Ed); curriculum and instruction with EC-6 generalist (M Ed); curriculum and instruction with English language arts and reading (4-8) (M Ed); educational administration (M Ed); educational diagnostician (M Ed); executive educational leadership (Ed D); higher education in business management (M Ed); higher education in Christian studies (M Ed); higher education in counseling (M Ed); higher education in educational technology (M Ed); reading (M Ed); special educational leadership (Ed D). *Program availability:* Part-time, evening/weekend, 100% online, blended/hybrid learning. *Degree requirements:* For master's, comprehensive exam; for doctorate, thesis/dissertation. *Entrance requirements:* For master's, minimum GPA of 2.75, two recommendations, resume, bachelor's degree conferred transcript; interview (for non-certified teachers); for doctorate, GRE, 5 letters of recommendation. Additional exam requirements/recommendations for international students: Required—TOEFL (minimum score 80 iBT), IELTS (minimum score 6.5). Electronic applications accepted. Application fee is waived when completed online. *Expenses:* Contact institution. *Faculty research:* Autism and inclusion, integrating technology into instruction, school change and leadership trust.

Howard Payne University, Program in Business Administration, Brownwood, TX 76801-2715. Offers MBA. *Program availability:* Part-time, evening/weekend. *Degree requirements:* For master's, comprehensive exam, research project. *Entrance requirements:* For master's, minimum undergraduate GPA of 3.0, 3.3 in first 9 hours of coursework; business foundation classes (for those without undergraduate business degree and no business-related coursework). Additional exam requirements/recommendations for international students: Required—TOEFL (minimum score 79 iBT). Electronic applications accepted.

Howard University, School of Business, Graduate Programs in Business, Washington, DC 20059-0002. Offers accounting (MBA); entrepreneurship (MBA); finance (MBA); general management (MBA); human resources management (MBA); information systems (MBA); international business (MBA); marketing (MBA); supply chain management (MBA); JD/MBA. *Accreditation:* AACSB. *Program availability:* Part-time, evening/weekend, online learning. *Entrance requirements:* For master's, GMAT, minimum 1 year post undergraduate work experience, resume, 3 letters of recommendation, advanced college algebra. Additional exam requirements/recommendations for international students: Required—TOEFL. *Faculty research:* Marketing research in multi-ethnic populations, U.S. trade policies and international relations, risk management (finance).

Hult International Business School, Graduate Programs, Cambridge, MA 02141. Offers business administration (EMBA); business analytics (MBA, MIB); business statistics (MBS); disruptive innovation (MDI); entrepreneurship (MBA, MIB); family business (MBA, MIB); finance (MBA, MF, MIB); international marketing (MIM); marketing (MBA, MIB); project management (MBA, MIB). MDI and MBS offered in San Francisco; MBA also offered in Boston, San Francisco, Dubai, Shanghai, and New York. *Entrance requirements:* For master's, GMAT, 3 years of work experience. Additional exam requirements/recommendations for international students: Required—TOEFL. Electronic applications accepted. *Expenses:* Contact institution.

Humboldt State University, Academic Programs, College of Professional Studies, School of Business, Arcata, CA 95521-8299. Offers MBA. *Program availability:* Part-time, evening/weekend. *Faculty:* 9 full-time (4 women), 9 part-time/adjunct (4 women). *Students:* 22 full-time (9 women), 8 part-time (4 women); includes 12 minority (1 Asian, non-Hispanic/Latino; 10 Hispanic/Latino; 1 Two or more races, non-Hispanic/Latino), 2 international. Average age 31. 50 applicants, 60% accepted, 25 enrolled. In 2018, 30 master's awarded. *Degree requirements:* For master's, thesis or alternative. *Entrance requirements:* For master's, GMAT or GRE, minimum GPA of 2.5. Additional exam requirements/recommendations for international students: Required—TOEFL (minimum score 500 paper-based). *Application deadline:* For fall admission, 6/30 for domestic and international students; for spring admission, 12/15 for domestic and international students. Applications are processed on a rolling basis. Application fee: $55. *Expenses:* Contact institution. *Financial support:* Fellowships and Federal Work-Study available. Support available to part-time students. Financial award application deadline: 3/1; financial award applicants required to submit FAFSA. *Faculty research:* International business development, small town entrepreneurship, international trade: Pacific Rim. *Unit head:* Dr. Joshua Zender, Graduate Program Coordinator, 707-826-6026, E-mail: joshua.zender@humboldt.edu. *Application contact:* Dr. Joshua Zender, Graduate Program Coordinator, 707-826-6026, E-mail: joshua.zender@humboldt.edu.
Website: http://www.humboldt.edu/biz/degrees/mba.html

Huntington University, Graduate School, Huntington, IN 46750-1299. Offers adolescent and young adult education (M Ed); business administration (MBA); counseling (MA), including licensed mental health counselor; early adolescent education (M Ed); elementary education (M Ed); global youth ministry (MA); occupational therapy (OTD); organizational leadership (MA); pastoral leadership (MA); TESOL education (M Ed). *Accreditation:* AOTA. *Program availability:* Part-time, online learning. *Degree requirements:* For master's, comprehensive exam (for some programs), thesis (for some programs). *Entrance requirements:* For master's, GRE (for counseling and education students only); for doctorate, GRE (for occupational therapy students). Additional exam requirements/recommendations for international students: Required—TOEFL (minimum score 85 iBT), IELTS (minimum score 6.5). Electronic applications accepted. *Expenses:* Contact institution. *Faculty research:* Leadership, educational technology trends, evangelism, youth ministry, mental health.

Husson University, Master of Business Administration Program, Bangor, ME 04401-2999. Offers athletic administration (MBA); biotechnology and innovation (MBA); general business administration (MBA); healthcare management (MBA); hospitality and tourism management (MBA); organizational management (MBA); risk management (MBA). *Program availability:* Part-time, evening/weekend, 100% online, blended/hybrid learning. *Degree requirements:* For master's, comprehensive exam (for some programs), thesis optional. *Entrance requirements:* For master's, minimum GPA of 3.0, letter of recommendation. Additional exam requirements/recommendations for international students: Required—TOEFL (minimum score 550 paper-based; 80 iBT), IELTS (minimum score 6.5). Electronic applications accepted. *Expenses:* Contact institution.

Idaho State University, Graduate School, College of Business, Pocatello, ID 83209-8020. Offers business administration (MBA, Postbaccalaureate Certificate); computer information systems (MS, Postbaccalaureate Certificate). *Accreditation:* AACSB. *Program availability:* Part-time. *Degree requirements:* For master's, comprehensive exam, thesis (for some programs), oral exam; for Postbaccalaureate Certificate, comprehensive exam, thesis (for some programs), 6 hours of clerkship. *Entrance requirements:* For master's, GMAT, GRE General Test, minimum GPA of 3.0, resume outlining work experience, 2 letters of reference; for Postbaccalaureate Certificate, GMAT, GRE General Test, minimum upper-level GPA of 3.0, resume of work experience. Additional exam requirements/recommendations for international students: Required—TOEFL (minimum score 550 paper-based; 80 iBT). Electronic applications accepted. *Faculty research:* Information assurance, computer information technology, finance management, marketing.

IGlobal University, Graduate Programs, Vienna, VA 22182. Offers accounting (MBA); data management and analytics (MSIT); entrepreneurship (MBA); finance (MBA); global business management (MBA); health care management (MBA); hospitality and tourism management (MBA); human resources management (MBA); information technology (MBA); information technology systems and management (MSIT); leadership and management (MBA); project management (MBA); public service and administration (MBA); software design and management (MSIT).

Illinois Institute of Technology, Stuart School of Business, Program in Business Administration, Chicago, IL 60661. Offers sustainability (MBA); JD/MBA; M Des/MBA; MBA/MS. *Accreditation:* AACSB. *Program availability:* Part-time, evening/weekend. *Entrance requirements:* For master's, GRE (minimum score 298) or GMAT (500). Additional exam requirements/recommendations for international students: Required—TOEFL (minimum score 600 paper-based; 85 iBT); Recommended—IELTS (minimum score 7). Electronic applications accepted. *Expenses:* Contact institution. *Faculty research:* Global management and marketing strategy, technological innovation, management science, financial management, knowledge management.

Illinois Institute of Technology, Stuart School of Business, Program in Management Science, Chicago, IL 60661. Offers PhD. *Accreditation:* AACSB. *Program availability:* Part-time. *Degree requirements:* For doctorate, comprehensive exam, thesis/dissertation. *Entrance requirements:* For doctorate, GRE (minimum score 316) or GMAT (minimum score 650). Additional exam requirements/recommendations for international students: Required—TOEFL (minimum score 600 paper-based; 85 iBT). Electronic applications accepted. *Expenses:* Contact institution. *Faculty research:* Scheduling systems, queuing systems, optimization, quality systems, foreign exchange, enterprise risk management, credit risk modeling.

Illinois State University, Graduate School, College of Business, Program in Business Administration, Normal, IL 61790. Offers MBA. *Accreditation:* AACSB. *Program availability:* Part-time. *Faculty:* 108 full-time (41 women), 24 part-time/adjunct (8 women). *Students:* 93 full-time (42 women), 48 part-time (24 women); includes 8 minority (1 Black or African American, non-Hispanic/Latino; 2 Asian, non-Hispanic/Latino; 1 Hispanic/Latino; 4 Two or more races, non-Hispanic/Latino), 1 international. Average age 30. 76 applicants, 95% accepted, 49 enrolled. In 2018, 54 master's awarded. *Degree requirements:* For master's, thesis optional. *Entrance requirements:* For master's, GMAT, minimum GPA of 2.75 during previous 2 years of course work. Additional exam requirements/recommendations for international students: Required—TOEFL. *Application deadline:* Applications are processed on a rolling basis. Application fee: $40. *Expenses: Tuition, area resident:* Full-time $7264.62. Tuition, state resident: full-time $9466. Tuition, nonresident: full-time $17,290. *International tuition:* $15,089.40 full-time. *Required fees:* $1481.04. *Financial support:* Research assistantships, teaching assistantships, and tuition waivers (full) available. Financial award application deadline: 4/1. *Faculty research:* McLean county small business development center. *Unit head:* Dr. Ajay Samant, Dean of the College of Business, 309-438-2251. *Application contact:* Timothy Longfellow, 309-438-8388, E-mail: longfel@ilstu.edu.
Website: http://www.lilt.ilstu.edu/mba/

Independence University, Program in Business Administration, Salt Lake City, UT 84107. Offers MBA.

Indiana State University, College of Graduate and Professional Studies, Scott College of Business, Terre Haute, IN 47809. Offers MBA. *Accreditation:* AACSB. *Program availability:* Part-time, evening/weekend. *Degree requirements:* For master's, thesis optional. *Entrance requirements:* For master's, GMAT. Electronic applications accepted. *Faculty research:* Small business and entrepreneurial sciences, production and operations management.

Indiana Tech, Program in Business Administration, Fort Wayne, IN 46803-1297. Offers accounting (MBA); health care management (MBA); human resources (MBA); management (MBA); marketing (MBA). *Program availability:* Part-time, evening/weekend, online learning. *Entrance requirements:* For master's, GMAT, bachelor's degree from regionally-accredited university; minimum undergraduate GPA of 2.5; 2 years of significant work experience; 3 letters of recommendation. Electronic applications accepted.

Business Administration and Management—General

Indiana Tech, Program in Management, Fort Wayne, IN 46803-1297. Offers MSM. *Program availability:* Part-time, evening/weekend, 100% online. *Entrance requirements:* For master's, bachelor's degree from regionally-accredited university; minimum undergraduate GPA of 2.5; 2 years of significant work experience; 3 letters of recommendation. Electronic applications accepted.

Indiana University Bloomington, Kelley School of Business, Bloomington, IN 47405-7000. Offers MBA, MPA, MS, DBA, PhD, DBA/MIS, JD/MBA, JD/MPA, MBA/MA, PhD/MIS. PhD offered through University Graduate School. *Accreditation:* AACSB. *Degree requirements:* For doctorate, comprehensive exam, thesis/dissertation. *Entrance requirements:* For master's, GMAT; for doctorate, GMAT, GRE General Test. Additional exam requirements/recommendations for international students: Required—TOEFL (minimum score 100 iBT). Electronic applications accepted. *Expenses:* Contact institution. *Faculty research:* Entrepreneurial ventures, technology-based innovation, on-line price competition, on-line shopping behavior.

Indiana University Kokomo, School of Business, Kokomo, IN 46904. Offers accounting (Postbaccalaureate Certificate); business administration (MBA); business fundamentals (Postbaccalaureate Certificate). *Accreditation:* AACSB. *Program availability:* Part-time, evening/weekend. *Degree requirements:* For master's, thesis optional, research project. *Entrance requirements:* For master's, GMAT. Additional exam requirements/recommendations for international students: Required—TOEFL (minimum score 550 paper-based; 73 iBT). Electronic applications accepted. *Expenses:* Contact institution. *Faculty research:* Investments, outsourcing, technology, adoption.

Indiana University Northwest, School of Business and Economics, Gary, IN 46408. Offers accounting (Graduate Certificate); management (Certificate); management and administrative studies (MBA). *Accreditation:* AACSB. *Program availability:* Part-time, evening/weekend. *Entrance requirements:* For master's, GMAT (not for Weekend MBA for Professionals), letter of recommendation. Electronic applications accepted. *Expenses:* Contact institution. *Faculty research:* International finance, employment law and testing, business ethics, taxation, financial institutions.

Indiana University of Pennsylvania, School of Graduate Studies and Research, Eberly College of Business and Information Technology, MBA Executive Track Program, Indiana, PA 15705. Offers MBA. *Program availability:* Part-time, evening/weekend. *Faculty:* 28 full-time (4 women), 1 part-time/adjunct (0 women). *Students:* 97 part-time (44 women); includes 17 minority (6 Black or African American, non-Hispanic/Latino; 4 Asian, non-Hispanic/Latino; 4 Hispanic/Latino; 3 Two or more races, non-Hispanic/Latino), 38 international. Average age 34. 75 applicants, 91% accepted, 58 enrolled. In 2018, 74 master's awarded. *Entrance requirements:* Additional exam requirements/recommendations for international students: Required—TOEFL (minimum score 540 paper-based). *Application deadline:* Applications are processed on a rolling basis. Application fee: $50. Electronic applications accepted. *Expenses:* Contact institution. *Financial support:* Fellowships, research assistantships, career-related internships or fieldwork, Federal Work-Study, scholarships/grants, and unspecified assistantships available. Financial award application deadline: 4/15; financial award applicants required to submit FAFSA. *Unit head:* Dr. John Lipinski, Graduate Coordinator, 724-357-2522, E-mail: John.Lipinski@iup.edu. *Application contact:* Dr. John Lipinski, Graduate Coordinator, 724-357-2522, E-mail: John.Lipinski@iup.edu.
Website: http://www.iup.edu/mba/grad/executive-mba/

Indiana University of Pennsylvania, School of Graduate Studies and Research, Eberly College of Business and Information Technology, Program in Business Administration, Indiana, PA 15705. Offers MBA. *Accreditation:* AACSB. *Program availability:* Part-time. *Faculty:* 28 full-time (4 women), 1 part-time/adjunct (0 women). *Students:* 109 full-time (44 women), 98 part-time (41 women); includes 3 minority (2 Black or African American, non-Hispanic/Latino; 1 Hispanic/Latino), 176 international. Average age 23. 169 applicants, 85% accepted, 116 enrolled. In 2018, 114 master's awarded. *Entrance requirements:* For master's, GMAT, 2 letters of recommendation. Additional exam requirements/recommendations for international students: Required—TOEFL (minimum score 540 paper-based). *Application deadline:* Applications are processed on a rolling basis. Application fee: $50. Electronic applications accepted. *Expenses:* Tuition, state resident: full-time $12,384; part-time $516 per credit hour. Tuition, nonresident: full-time $18,576; part-time $774 per credit hour. *Required fees:* $4454; $186 per credit hour. $65 per semester. Tuition and fees vary according to program and reciprocity agreements. *Financial support:* In 2018–19, 24 research assistantships (averaging $3,367 per year) were awarded; fellowships, career-related internships or fieldwork, Federal Work-Study, scholarships/grants, and unspecified assistantships also available. Support available to part-time students. Financial award application deadline: 4/15; financial award applicants required to submit FAFSA. *Unit head:* Dr. John Lipinski, Graduate Coordinator, 724-357-2522, E-mail: John.Lipinski@iup.edu. *Application contact:* Dr. John Lipinski, Graduate Coordinator, 724-357-2522, E-mail: John.Lipinski@iup.edu.
Website: http://www.iup.edu/grad/mba/default.aspx

Indiana University–Purdue University Indianapolis, Kelley School of Business, Indianapolis, IN 46202-5151. Offers MBA, MSA, MBA/JD, MBA/MD, MBA/MHA, MBA/MS, MBA/MSA, MBA/MSE. *Accreditation:* AACSB.

Indiana University South Bend, Judd Leighton School of Business and Economics, South Bend, IN 46615. Offers accounting (MSA); business (Graduate Certificate); business administration (MBA), including finance, human resource management, marketing; MBA/MSA. *Program availability:* Part-time, evening/weekend. *Entrance requirements:* For master's, GMAT. Additional exam requirements/recommendations for international students: Required—TOEFL (minimum score 550 paper-based; 79 iBT). Electronic applications accepted. *Expenses:* Contact institution. *Faculty research:* Financial accounting, consumer research, capital budgeting research, business strategy research.

Indiana University Southeast, School of Business, New Albany, IN 47150-6405. Offers business administration (MBA); strategic finance (MS). *Accreditation:* AACSB. *Program availability:* Part-time. *Degree requirements:* For master's, community service. *Entrance requirements:* For master's, GMAT, work experience. Additional exam requirements/recommendations for international students: Required—TOEFL. Electronic applications accepted. *Expenses:* Contact institution.

Indiana Wesleyan University, College of Adult and Professional Studies, Graduate Studies in Business, Marion, IN 46953. Offers accounting (MBA, Graduate Certificate); applied management (MBA); business administration (MBA); health care (MBA, Graduate Certificate); human resources (MBA, Graduate Certificate); management (MS); organizational leadership (MA). *Program availability:* Part-time, evening/weekend, online learning. *Degree requirements:* For master's, applied business or management project. *Entrance requirements:* For master's, minimum GPA of 2.5, 2 years of related work experience. Additional exam requirements/recommendations for international students: Required—TOEFL (minimum score 550 paper-based). Electronic applications accepted.

Instituto Centroamericano de Administración de Empresas, Graduate Programs, La Garita, Costa Rica. Offers agribusiness management (MIAM); business administration (EMBA); finance (MBA); real estate management (MGREM); sustainable development (MBA); technology (MBA). *Degree requirements:* For master's, comprehensive exam, essay. *Entrance requirements:* For master's, GMAT or GRE General Test, fluency in Spanish, interview, letters of recommendation, minimum 1 year of work experience. Additional exam requirements/recommendations for international students: Recommended—TOEFL. Electronic applications accepted. *Faculty research:* Competitiveness, production.

Instituto Tecnologico de Santo Domingo, Graduate School, Area of Business, Santo Domingo, Dominican Republic. Offers banking and securities markets (M Mgmt); corporate finance (M Mgmt); human resources management (M Mgmt, Certificate); international trade management (M Mgmt); marketing (M Mgmt); organizational development (M Mgmt); quality and productivity management (Certificate); tax management and planning (M Mgmt); upper management (M Mgmt).

Instituto Tecnológico y de Estudios Superiores de Monterrey, Campus Central de Veracruz, Graduate Programs, Córdoba, Mexico. Offers administration (MA); administration of information technologies (MTI); computer sciences (MCC); education (MEE); educational institution administration (MAD); educational technology (MTE); electronic commerce (MCE); finance (MAF); humanistic studies (MEH); international business for Latin America (MNL); marketing (MMT); science (MCP). *Program availability:* Part-time, evening/weekend, online learning. *Degree requirements:* For master's, thesis (for some programs). *Entrance requirements:* For master's, PAEP College Board. Electronic applications accepted.

Instituto Tecnológico y de Estudios Superiores de Monterrey, Campus Ciudad de México, School of Business Administration, Ciudad de Mexico, Mexico. Offers business administration (EMBA, MBA, PhD); economy (MBA); finance (MBA). EMBA program offered jointly with The University of Texas at Austin. *Program availability:* Part-time, evening/weekend, online learning. *Entrance requirements:* For master's and doctorate, Instituto entrance exam. Additional exam requirements/recommendations for international students: Required—TOEFL.

Instituto Tecnológico y de Estudios Superiores de Monterrey, Campus Ciudad Juárez, Program in Business Administration, Ciudad Juárez, Mexico. Offers MBA. *Program availability:* Part-time, online learning. *Entrance requirements:* Additional exam requirements/recommendations for international students: Required—TOEFL (minimum score 500 paper-based).

Instituto Tecnológico y de Estudios Superiores de Monterrey, Campus Ciudad Obregón, Program in Administration, Ciudad Obregón, Mexico. Offers MA.

Instituto Tecnológico y de Estudios Superiores de Monterrey, Campus Cuernavaca, Programs in Business Administration, Temixco, Mexico. Offers finance (MA); human resources management (MA); international business (MA); marketing (MA).

Instituto Tecnológico y de Estudios Superiores de Monterrey, Campus Estado de México, Professional and Graduate Division, Estado de Mexico, Mexico. Offers administration of information technologies (MITA); architecture (M Arch); business administration (GMBA, MBA); computer sciences (MCS, PhD); education (M Ed); educational institution administration (MAD); educational technology and innovation (PhD); electronic commerce (MEC); environmental systems (MS); finance (MAF); humanistic studies (MHS); information sciences and knowledge management (MISKM); information systems (MS); manufacturing systems (MS); marketing (MEM); quality systems and productivity (MS); science and materials engineering (PhD); telecommunications management (MTM). *Program availability:* Part-time, online learning. *Degree requirements:* For master's, one foreign language, thesis (for some programs); for doctorate, one foreign language, thesis/dissertation. *Entrance requirements:* For master's, E-PAEP 500, interview; for doctorate, E-PAEP 500, research proposal. Additional exam requirements/recommendations for international students: Required—TOEFL (minimum score 550 paper-based). *Faculty research:* Surface treatments by plasmas, mechanical properties, robotics, graphical computing, mechatronics security protocols.

Instituto Tecnológico y de Estudios Superiores de Monterrey, Campus Guadalajara, Program in Business Administration, Zapopan, Mexico. Offers IEMBA, M Ad. *Program availability:* Part-time, evening/weekend, online learning. *Degree requirements:* For master's, one foreign language. *Entrance requirements:* For master's, ITESM admission test. *Faculty research:* Strategic alliances in small business, family business practice in Mexico, competitiveness under NAFTA for Mexican firms.

Instituto Tecnológico y de Estudios Superiores de Monterrey, Campus Irapuato, Graduate Programs, Irapuato, Mexico. Offers administration (MBA); administration of information technology (MAIT); administration of telecommunications (MAT); architecture (M Arch); computer science (MCS); education (M Ed); educational administration (MEA); educational innovation and technology (DEIT); educational technology (MET); electronic commerce (MBA); environmental administration and planning (MEAP); environmental systems (MES); finances (MBA); humanistic studies (MHS); international management for Latin American executives (MIMLAE); library and information science (MLIS); manufacturing quality management (MMQM); marketing research (MBA).

Instituto Tecnológico y de Estudios Superiores de Monterrey, Campus Laguna, Graduate School, Torreón, Mexico. Offers business administration (MBA); industrial engineering (MIE); management information systems (MS). *Program availability:* Part-time. *Entrance requirements:* For master's, GMAT. *Faculty research:* Computer communications from home to the university.

Instituto Tecnológico y de Estudios Superiores de Monterrey, Campus León, Program in Business Administration, León, Mexico. Offers MBA. *Program availability:* Part-time.

Instituto Tecnológico y de Estudios Superiores de Monterrey, Campus Monterrey, Graduate School of Business Administration and Leadership, Program in Business Administration, Monterrey, Mexico. Offers business administration (MA, MBA); finance (M Sc); international business (M Sc); marketing (M Sc). *Program availability:* Part-time. *Degree requirements:* For master's, one foreign language, thesis. *Entrance requirements:* For master's, GMAT. Additional exam requirements/recommendations for international students: Required—TOEFL. *Faculty research:* Technology management, quality management, organizational theory and behavior.

Instituto Tecnológico y de Estudios Superiores de Monterrey, Campus Monterrey, Graduate School of Business Administration and Leadership, Program in Management, Monterrey, Mexico. Offers PhD. *Accreditation:* AACSB. *Program availability:* Part-time. *Degree requirements:* For doctorate, one foreign language, thesis/dissertation. *Entrance requirements:* For doctorate, GMAT. Additional exam requirements/recommendations for international students: Required—TOEFL. *Faculty research:* Quality management, manufacturing and technology management, information systems, managerial economics, business policy.

Instituto Tecnológico y de Estudios Superiores de Monterrey, Campus Querétaro, School of Business, Santiago de Querétaro, Mexico. Offers MBA. *Entrance requirements:* For master's, GRE General Test. *Faculty research:* Organizational analysis, industrial marketing, international trade.

Instituto Tecnológico y de Estudios Superiores de Monterrey, Campus Sonora Norte, Program in Business, Hermosillo, Mexico. Offers MA. *Entrance requirements:* For master's, GMAT.

Instituto Tecnológico y de Estudios Superiores de Monterrey, Campus Toluca, Graduate Programs, Toluca, Mexico. Offers MBA. *Program availability:* Part-time, evening/weekend. *Degree requirements:* For master's, one foreign language. *Faculty research:* Management in the industrial valley of Toluca.

Inter American University of Puerto Rico, Aguadilla Campus, Graduate School, Aguadilla, PR 00605. Offers accounting (MBA); counseling psychology specializing in family (MS); criminal justice (MA); educative management and leadership (MA); elementary education (M Ed); finance (MBA); human resources (MBA); industrial management (MBA); management information systems (MBA); marketing (MBA). *Program availability:* Part-time, evening/weekend. *Degree requirements:* For master's, comprehensive exam. *Entrance requirements:* For master's, EXADEP, 2 letters of recommendation, minimum GPA of 2.5. Electronic applications accepted.

Inter American University of Puerto Rico, Arecibo Campus, Program in Business Administration, Arecibo, PR 00614-4050. Offers accounting (MBA); finance (MBA); human resources (MBA).

Inter American University of Puerto Rico, Barranquitas Campus, Business Administration Program, Barranquitas, PR 00794. Offers accounting (MBA); human resources (MBA); managerial information systems (MBA). *Program availability:* Part-time, evening/weekend. *Degree requirements:* For master's, 2 foreign languages, comprehensive exam (for some programs), thesis or alternative, minimum GPA of 3.0. *Entrance requirements:* For master's, BBA or its equivalent from accredited institution, official academic transcript from institution that conferred bachelor's degree, minimum GPA of 2.5, interview (for some programs). Electronic applications accepted. *Expenses:* Contact institution.

Inter American University of Puerto Rico, Fajardo Campus, Graduate Programs, Fajardo, PR 00738-7003. Offers computer science (MS); educational management and leadership (MA Ed); general business (MBA); human resources (MBA); management information systems (MBA); marketing (MBA); special education (MA Ed). *Program availability:* Online learning.

Inter American University of Puerto Rico, Guayama Campus, Department of Business Administration, Guayama, PR 00785. Offers marketing (MBA).

Inter American University of Puerto Rico, Metropolitan Campus, Graduate Programs, Program in General Business, San Juan, PR 00919-1293. Offers MBA.

Inter American University of Puerto Rico, San Germán Campus, Graduate Studies Center, Program in Business Administration, San Germán, PR 00683-5008. Offers accounting (MBA); finance (MBA); general business administration (MBA); human resources (MBA, PhD); industrial relations (MBA); information systems (MBA); international and interregional business (PhD); management (MBA); marketing (MBA). *Program availability:* Part-time, evening/weekend. *Degree requirements:* For master's, comprehensive exam. *Entrance requirements:* For master's, GRE General Test or EXADEP, minimum GPA of 3.0. *Expenses: Tuition:* Full-time $212; part-time $212 per credit. *Required fees:* $366 per semester. One-time fee: $31. Tuition and fees vary according to degree level and program.

International Technological University, Program in Business Administration, San Jose, CA 95134. Offers MBA, DBA. *Program availability:* Part-time, evening/weekend. Terminal master's awarded for partial completion of doctoral program. *Degree requirements:* For master's, thesis or alternative, capstone project; for doctorate, comprehensive exam, thesis/dissertation. *Entrance requirements:* Additional exam requirements/recommendations for international students: Required—TOEFL, IELTS. Electronic applications accepted.

International University in Geneva, Business Programs, Geneva, Switzerland. Offers business administration (MBA, DBA); entrepreneurship (MBA); international business (MIB); international trade (MIT); sales and marketing (MBA). *Accreditation:* ACBSP. *Program availability:* Part-time, evening/weekend. *Degree requirements:* For master's, comprehensive exam. *Entrance requirements:* For master's, GMAT. Additional exam requirements/recommendations for international students: Required—TOEFL. Electronic applications accepted.

The International University of Monaco, Graduate Programs, Monte Carlo, Monaco. Offers entrepreneurship (EMBA, MBA); financial engineering (M Sc); hedge fund and private equity (M Sc); international marketing (EMBA, MBA); international wealth management (M Sc); luxury goods and services (EMBA, M Sc, MBA); wealth and asset management (EMBA, MBA). *Program availability:* Part-time. *Degree requirements:* For master's, comprehensive exam (for some programs), applied research project. *Entrance requirements:* Additional exam requirements/recommendations for international students: Required—TOEFL (minimum score 550 paper-based), IELTS. Electronic applications accepted. *Faculty research:* Gaming, leadership, disintermediation.

Iona College, School of Business, New Rochelle, NY 10801-1890. Offers MBA, MS, AC, PMC. *Accreditation:* AACSB. *Program availability:* Part-time, evening/weekend, 100% online, blended/hybrid learning. *Faculty:* 26 full-time (4 women), 6 part-time/adjunct (4 women). *Students:* 127 full-time (59 women), 190 part-time (96 women); includes 118 minority (36 Black or African American, non-Hispanic/Latino; 2 American Indian or Alaska Native, non-Hispanic/Latino; 16 Asian, non-Hispanic/Latino; 63 Hispanic/Latino; 1 Native Hawaiian or other Pacific Islander, non-Hispanic/Latino), 17 international. Average age 28. 189 applicants, 93% accepted, 89 enrolled. In 2018, 191 master's, 144 other advanced degrees awarded. *Entrance requirements:* For master's, letter of recommendation, all undergraduate and graduate transcripts, copy of current resume; for other advanced degree, copy of current resume and all official undergraduate transcripts (for AC). Additional exam requirements/recommendations for international students: Required—TOEFL (minimum score 550 paper-based; 80 iBT), IELTS (minimum score 6.5). *Application deadline:* For fall admission, 8/15 priority date for domestic students, 8/1 priority date for international students; for winter admission, 11/15 priority date for domestic students, 11/1 priority date for international students; for spring admission, 2/15 priority date for domestic students, 2/1 priority date for international students; for summer admission, 5/15 priority date for domestic students, 5/1 priority date for international students. Applications are processed on a rolling basis. Application fee: $0. Electronic applications accepted. *Expenses:* Contact institution. *Financial support:* In 2018–19, 173 students received support. Scholarships/grants, tuition waivers (partial), and unspecified assistantships available. Support available to part-time students. Financial award application deadline: 4/15; financial award applicants required to submit FAFSA. *Faculty research:* Artificial intelligence, financial services, value-based management, public policy, business ethics. *Unit head:* Richard Highfield, PhD, Interim Dean of the School of Business, 914-633-2789, Fax: 914-637-2708, E-mail: rhighfield@iona.edu. *Application contact:* Kimberly Kelly, Director of Graduate Business Admissions, 914-633-2271, Fax: 914-633-2012, E-mail: kkelly@iona.edu.
Website: https://www.iona.edu/academics/school-of-business.aspx

Iowa State University of Science and Technology, Program in Business Administration, Ames, IA 50011. Offers MBA, M Arch/MBA, MBA/MCRP, MBA/MS. *Entrance requirements:* For master's, GMAT, resume. Additional exam requirements/recommendations for international students: Recommended—TOEFL (minimum score 600 paper-based; 100 iBT), IELTS (minimum score 7). Electronic applications accepted. *Expenses:* Contact institution.

Ithaca College, School of Business, Program in Business Administration, Ithaca, NY 14850. Offers sport management (MBA). *Accreditation:* AACSB. *Program availability:* Part-time. *Faculty:* 7 full-time (2 women). *Students:* 8 full-time (5 women), 4 part-time (3 women); includes 3 minority (1 Asian, non-Hispanic/Latino; 2 Hispanic/Latino), 1 international. Average age 27. 13 applicants, 77% accepted, 8 enrolled. In 2018, 6 master's awarded. *Entrance requirements:* For master's, GMAT. Additional exam requirements/recommendations for international students: Required—TOEFL (minimum score 550 paper-based; 80 iBT). *Application deadline:* For fall admission, 5/15 for domestic and international students; for spring admission, 11/1 for domestic and international students. Applications are processed on a rolling basis. Application fee: $40. Electronic applications accepted. *Expenses:* Contact institution. *Financial support:* In 2018–19, 9 students received support, including 7 fellowships (averaging $7,857 per year); career-related internships or fieldwork, Federal Work-Study, and scholarships/grants also available. Support available to part-time students. Financial award application deadline: 3/1; financial award applicants required to submit FAFSA. *Unit head:* Dr. Rasoul Rezvanian, Associate Dean and Director, MBA Programs, 607-274-1762, Fax: 607-274-1263, E-mail: rrezvanian@ithaca.edu. *Application contact:* Nicole Eversley Bradwell, Director, Office of Admission, 607-800-429-4274, Fax: 607-274-1263, E-mail: admission@ithaca.edu.
Website: http://www.ithaca.edu/business/programs/

Jackson State University, Graduate School, College of Business, Department of Economics, Finance and General Business, Jackson, MS 39217. Offers business administration (MBA, PhD). *Accreditation:* AACSB. *Program availability:* Part-time, evening/weekend. *Degree requirements:* For master's, comprehensive exam, thesis. *Entrance requirements:* For master's, GRE General Test, GMAT. Additional exam requirements/recommendations for international students: Required—TOEFL.

Jacksonville State University, Graduate Studies, School of Business and Industry, Jacksonville, AL 36265-1602. Offers MBA. *Accreditation:* AACSB. *Program availability:* Part-time, evening/weekend, 100% online, blended/hybrid learning. *Degree requirements:* For master's, comprehensive exam, thesis (for some programs). *Entrance requirements:* For master's, GMAT. Additional exam requirements/recommendations for international students: Required—TOEFL (minimum score 500 paper-based; 61 iBT). Electronic applications accepted.

Jacksonville University, Davis College of Business, Accelerated Day-time MBA Program, Jacksonville, FL 32211. Offers accounting and finance (MBA); business administration (MBA); consumer goods and services marketing (MBA); management (MBA); management accounting (MBA). *Entrance requirements:* For master's, GMAT or GRE, bachelor's degree from regionally-accredited institution, original transcripts of academic work, statement of intent, resume, 3 letters of recommendation; 3 years of work experience (recommended); interview with program advisor. Additional exam requirements/recommendations for international students: Required—TOEFL (minimum score 550 paper-based; 79 iBT), IELTS (minimum score 6), PTE (minimum score 53). Electronic applications accepted. *Expenses:* Contact institution. *Faculty research:* Behavioral finance, game theory, regional economic integration, information sabotage, public choice and public finance.

Jacksonville University, Davis College of Business, Doctor of Business Administration Program, Jacksonville, FL 32211. Offers DBA. *Program availability:* Evening/weekend. *Degree requirements:* For doctorate, comprehensive exam, thesis/dissertation, completion of program within six years of starting. *Entrance requirements:* For doctorate, MBA or master's degree from regionally-accredited institution or comparable foreign institution with minimum GPA of 3.25; curriculum vitae or resume with minimum of 7 years' professional experience in business management or not-for-profit administration; statement of purpose; 3 letters of recommendation. Additional exam requirements/recommendations for international students: Required—TOEFL (minimum score 550 paper-based; 79 iBT), IELTS (minimum score 6), PTE (minimum score 53). Electronic applications accepted. *Expenses:* Contact institution. *Faculty research:* Leadership of organizations and ethical business practices in a contemporary world; emphasize practical application of more advanced business analytics and evidence-based decision making.

Jacksonville University, Davis College of Business, Executive Master of Business Administration Program, Jacksonville, FL 32211. Offers consumer goods and services marketing (MBA); leadership development (MBA). *Accreditation:* AACSB. *Program availability:* Evening/weekend. *Entrance requirements:* For master's, resume, 5-7 years of professional experience, 3 letters of recommendation, corporate letter of support, statement of purpose, interview. Additional exam requirements/recommendations for international students: Required—TOEFL (minimum score 550 paper-based; 79 iBT), IELTS (minimum score 6), PTE (minimum score 53). Electronic applications accepted. *Expenses:* Contact institution. *Faculty research:* Data analytics, emerging markets and economic development, high-performing teams, government deficit, learning from corporate failure.

Jacksonville University, Davis College of Business, FLEX Master of Business Administration Program, Jacksonville, FL 32211. Offers accounting and finance (MBA); business management (MBA); consumer goods and services marketing (MBA); management (MBA); management accounting (MBA); JD/MBA; MBA/MPP; MSN/MBA. MBA/JD offered jointly with Florida School of Law; MSN/MBA offered jointly with JU's Keigwin School of Nursing; MBA/MPP offered jointly with JU's Public Policy Institute. *Accreditation:* AACSB. *Program availability:* Part-time, evening/weekend, blended/hybrid learning. *Entrance requirements:* For master's, GMAT or GRE, bachelor's degree from regionally-accredited institution, 3 years of full-time work experience (recommended), resume, statement of intent, 3 letters of recommendation, interview with program advisor. Additional exam requirements/recommendations for international students: Required—TOEFL (minimum score 550 paper-based; 79 iBT), IELTS (minimum score 6), PTE (minimum score 53). Electronic applications accepted. *Expenses:* Contact institution. *Faculty research:* Downsizing with integrity; impact of YouTube videos; game theory; analysis of effective tax rates; creativity innovation and change.

James Madison University, The Graduate School, College of Business, Program in Business Administration, Harrisonburg, VA 22807. Offers business (MBA), including executive leadership, information security, innovation. *Accreditation:* AACSB. *Program availability:* Part-time, evening/weekend, blended/hybrid learning. *Students:* 37 full-time (10 women), 82 part-time (34 women); includes 28 minority (9 Black or African American, non-Hispanic/Latino; 7 Asian, non-Hispanic/Latino; 10 Hispanic/Latino; 2 Two or more races, non-Hispanic/Latino), 7 international. Average age 30. In 2018, 38 master's awarded. Application fee: $6. Electronic applications accepted. *Expenses:* Tuition, state resident: full-time $10,848. Tuition, nonresident: full-time $27,888. *Required fees:* $1128. *Financial support:* In 2018–19, 2 students received support. Federal Work-Study and 1 assistantship (averaging $7911) available. Financial award application deadline: 3/1; financial award applicants required to submit FAFSA. *Unit*

head: Dr. Matthew A. Rutherford, Department Head, 540-568-8777, E-mail: rutherma@jmu.edu. *Application contact:* Lynette D. Michael, Director of Graduate Admissions, 540-568-6131 Ext. 6395, Fax: 540-568-7860, E-mail: michaeld@jmu.edu.
Website: http://www.jmu.edu/cob/graduate/mba/index.shtml

John Brown University, Soderquist College of Business, Siloam Springs, AR 72761-2121. Offers international business (MBA); leadership and ethics (MBA, MS). *Accreditation:* ACBSP. *Program availability:* Part-time, evening/weekend, online only, 100% online, blended/hybrid learning. *Entrance requirements:* For master's, MAT, GMAT or GRE if undergraduate GPA is less than 3.0, recommendation forms from three people, 200-word essay describing professional plans and reason for seeking acceptance. Additional exam requirements/recommendations for international students: Required—TOEFL (minimum score 550 paper-based; 79 iBT). Electronic applications accepted. *Faculty research:* Ethical leadership.

John Carroll University, Graduate Studies, John M. and Mary Jo Boler College of Business, University Heights, OH 44118. Offers accountancy (MS); business (MBA); laboratory administration (MS). *Accreditation:* AACSB. *Program availability:* Part-time, evening/weekend. *Entrance requirements:* For master's, GMAT or GRE, minimum GPA of 2.8; Individual programs may have specific requirements. Additional exam requirements/recommendations for international students: Required—TOEFL. *Application deadline:* For fall admission, 8/1 priority date for domestic and international students; for spring admission, 12/1 priority date for domestic and international students; for summer admission, 4/1 priority date for domestic and international students. Applications are processed on a rolling basis. Electronic applications accepted. *Expenses:* Contact institution. *Financial support:* Fellowships, scholarships/grants, and unspecified assistantships available. Financial award applicants required to submit FAFSA. *Faculty research:* Accounting, economics and finance, management, marketing, and supply chain. *Unit head:* Dr. Alan R. Miciak, Dean, Boler College of Business, 216-397-4391, Fax: 216-397-1833. *Application contact:* Kristopher Tibbs, Assistant Dean, Graduate Business Programs, 216-397-1970, Fax: 216-397-1833, E-mail: gradbusiness@jcu.edu.
Website: https://boler.jcu.edu/graduate

John F. Kennedy University, College of Business and Professional Studies, Program in Business Administration, Pleasant Hill, CA 94523-4817. Offers business administration (MBA); finance (MBA); health care (MBA); human resources (MBA); information technology (MBA); management (MBA); sales management (MBA); strategic management (MBA). *Program availability:* Part-time, evening/weekend, online learning. *Degree requirements:* For master's, thesis or alternative. *Entrance requirements:* For master's, interview. Additional exam requirements/recommendations for international students: Required—TOEFL.

Johns Hopkins University, Carey Business School, Certificate Programs, Baltimore, MD 21218. Offers financial management (Certificate); investments (Certificate). *Program availability:* Part-time, evening/weekend. *Students:* 1 full-time, 16 part-time (3 women). 10 applicants, 80% accepted, 5 enrolled. In 2018, 18 Certificates awarded. *Degree requirements:* For Certificate, 16 credits. *Entrance requirements:* Additional exam requirements/recommendations for international students: Required—TOEFL, IELTS. *Application deadline:* Applications are processed on a rolling basis. Application fee: $100. Electronic applications accepted. *Expenses:* Contact institution. *Unit head:* Dr. Kevin Frick, Vice Dean of Education, 410-234-9272, E-mail: kfrick@jhu.edu. *Application contact:* Office of Admissions, 410-234-9220, Fax: 443-529-1554, E-mail: carey.admissions@jhu.edu.
Website: http://carey.jhu.edu/academics/certificate-programs/

Johns Hopkins University, Carey Business School, MBA Full-time Programs, Baltimore, MD 21218. Offers MBA, MBA/MA. MBA/MA offered with Maryland Institute College of Art, MBA/MPH offered through the School of Public Health within Johns Hopkins University. *Students:* 207 applicants, 61% accepted, 71 enrolled. *Degree requirements:* For master's, 54 credits. *Entrance requirements:* For master's, GMAT or GRE. Additional exam requirements/recommendations for international students: Required—TOEFL, IELTS. *Application deadline:* For fall admission, 5/1 for domestic and international students. Applications are processed on a rolling basis. Application fee: $100. Electronic applications accepted. *Expenses:* Contact institution. *Financial support:* In 2018–19, 102 students received support. Scholarships/grants available. Financial award application deadline: 4/15; financial award applicants required to submit FAFSA. *Unit head:* Dr. Kevin Frick, Vice Dean of Education, 410-234-9272, E-mail: kfrick@jhu.edu. *Application contact:* Office of Admissions, 410-234-9220, Fax: 443-529-1554, E-mail: carey.admissions@jhu.edu.
Website: http://carey.jhu.edu/academics/master-of-business-administration/

Johns Hopkins University, Carey Business School, MBA Part-time Program, Baltimore, MD 21218. Offers MBA, MBA/MA. MBA/MA offered through the Zanvyl Krieger School of Arts and Sciences. *Program availability:* Part-time, evening/weekend, blended/hybrid learning, on-site residency requirement. *Students:* 144 applicants, 77% accepted, 81 enrolled. *Degree requirements:* For master's, 54 credits. *Entrance requirements:* For master's, GMAT or GRE. Additional exam requirements/recommendations for international students: Required—TOEFL, IELTS. *Application deadline:* For fall admission, 7/15 for domestic and international students. Applications are processed on a rolling basis. Application fee: $100. Electronic applications accepted. *Expenses:* Contact institution. *Financial support:* In 2018–19, 18 students received support. Scholarships/grants available. Support available to part-time students. Financial award application deadline: 4/15; financial award applicants required to submit FAFSA. *Unit head:* Dr. Kevin Frick, Vice Dean of Education, 410-234-9272, E-mail: kfrick@jhu.edu. *Application contact:* Office of Admissions, 410-234-9220, Fax: 443-529-1554, E-mail: carey.admissions@jhu.edu.
Website: http://carey.jhu.edu/academics/master-of-business-administration/flexible-mba

Johnson & Wales University, Graduate Studies, MBA Program, Providence, RI 02903-3703. Offers accounting (MBA); business administration (MBA); finance (MBA); global fashion merchandising and management (MBA); hospitality (MBA); human resource management (MBA); information security/assurance (MBA); information technology (MBA); nonprofit management (MBA); operations and supply chain management (MBA); organizational leadership (MBA); organizational psychology (MBA); sport leadership (MBA). Program also offered on Denver campus. *Program availability:* Part-time, online learning. *Entrance requirements:* For master's, minimum GPA of 2.75. Additional exam requirements/recommendations for international students: Required—TOEFL (minimum score 550 paper-based); Recommended—IELTS, TWE. *Faculty research:* International banking, global economy, international trade, cultural differences.

Judson University, Master of Business Administration Program, Elgin, IL 60123-1498. Offers MBA. *Program availability:* Evening/weekend, 100% online. *Faculty:* 7 full-time (5 women), 100 part-time/adjunct (50 women). *Students:* 40 full-time (21 women), 20 part-time (7 women); includes 25 minority (13 Black or African American, non-Hispanic/Latino; 1 Asian, non-Hispanic/Latino; 11 Hispanic/Latino), 3 international. Average age 36. 23 applicants, 100% accepted, 23 enrolled. In 2018, 20 master's awarded. *Entrance requirements:* For master's, Bachelor's degree; minimum overall undergraduate GPA of 3.0; two years of work experience; two letters of recommendation; resume; essay. *Application deadline:* Applications are processed on a rolling basis. Application fee: $35. Electronic applications accepted. *Expenses:* Other estimated fees and expenses per semester: Living Expenses: $1,500, Books and Supplies: $500, Transportation: $300. *Financial support:* In 2018–19, 6 teaching assistantships were awarded; tuition waivers (partial) also available. Financial award applicants required to submit FAFSA. *Faculty research:* Ethics and Ethical Leadership. *Unit head:* John C. Boggs, Chair, 847-628-1041, E-mail: john.boggs@judsonu.edu. *Application contact:* Kim Surin, Enrollment Manager, 847-628-5033, E-mail: kim.surin@info.judsonu.edu.
Website: http://www.judsonu.edu/Graduate/Master_of_Business_Administration/Overview/

Juniata College, Department of Accounting, Business, and Economics, Huntingdon, PA 16652-2119. Offers accounting (M Acc); business administration (MBA); organizational leadership (MOL). *Entrance requirements:* For master's, GMAT.

Kansas State University, Graduate School, College of Business, Program in Business Administration, Manhattan, KS 66506. Offers data analytics (MBA); finance (MBA); management (MBA); marketing (MBA); technology entrepreneurship (MBA). *Accreditation:* AACSB. *Program availability:* Part-time, 100% online. *Entrance requirements:* For master's, GMAT (minimum score of 500), minimum undergraduate GPA of 3.0. Additional exam requirements/recommendations for international students: Required—TOEFL (minimum score 550 paper-based; 79 iBT); Recommended—IELTS (minimum score 7). Electronic applications accepted. *Expenses:* Contact institution. *Faculty research:* Organizational citizenship behavior, service marketing, impression management, human resources management, lean manufacturing and supply chain management, financial market behavior and investment management, data analytics, corporate responsibility, technology entrepreneurship.

Kansas Wesleyan University, Program in Business Administration, Salina, KS 67401-6196. Offers business administration (MBA); sports management (MBA). *Program availability:* Part-time, evening/weekend. *Entrance requirements:* For master's, GMAT, minimum graduate GPA of 3.0 or undergraduate GPA of 3.25.

Kean University, Nathan Weiss Graduate College, Program in Educational Administration, Union, NJ 07083. Offers school business administrator (MA); supervisor and principal (MA); supervisors, principals, and school business administrators (MA). *Accreditation:* NCATE. *Program availability:* Part-time, 100% online. *Faculty:* 4 full-time (2 women). *Students:* 5 full-time (3 women), 84 part-time (54 women); includes 33 minority (16 Black or African American, non-Hispanic/Latino; 2 Asian, non-Hispanic/Latino; 13 Hispanic/Latino; 2 Two or more races, non-Hispanic/Latino). Average age 36. 41 applicants, 88% accepted, 23 enrolled. In 2018, 24 master's awarded. *Degree requirements:* For master's, comprehensive exam (for some programs), portfolio, field experience, research component, internship, teaching experience. *Entrance requirements:* For master's, GRE General Test or MAT, minimum GPA of 3.0; New Jersey or out-of-state Standard Instructional or Educational Services Certificate; one year of experience under the appropriate certificate; official transcripts from all institutions attended; two letters of recommendation; personal statement; professional resume/curriculum vitae. Additional exam requirements/recommendations for international students: Required—TOEFL (minimum score 550 paper-based; 79 iBT), IELTS (minimum score 6.5). *Application deadline:* For fall admission, 6/30 for domestic and international students; for spring admission, 12/1 for domestic and international students; for summer admission, 5/15 for domestic and international students. Applications are processed on a rolling basis. Application fee: $75. Electronic applications accepted. *Expenses:* Tuition, state resident: full-time $15,025; part-time $733.50 per credit. Tuition, nonresident: full-time $19,890; part-time $884.50 per credit. *Required fees:* $2107.50; $89.50 per credit. Tuition and fees vary according to course level, course load, degree level and program. *Financial support:* Scholarships/grants and unspecified assistantships available. Financial award applicants required to submit FAFSA. *Unit head:* Dr. Steven Locasio, Program Coordinator, 908-737-5977, E-mail: locascst@kean.edu. *Application contact:* Brittany Gerstenhaber, Admissions Counselor, 908-737-7100, E-mail: gradadmissions@kean.edu.
Website: http://grad.kean.edu/edleadership/ma-combined

Keiser University, Doctor of Business Administration Program, Fort Lauderdale, FL 33309. Offers global business (DBA); global management (DBA); marketing (DBA).

Keiser University, Joint MS Ed/MBA Program, Fort Lauderdale, FL 33309. Offers MS Ed/MBA.

Keiser University, Master of Business Administration Program, Fort Lauderdale, FL 33309. Offers accounting (MBA); health services administration (MBA); international business (MBA); management (MBA); marketing (MBA); technology management (MBA). All concentrations except technology management also offered in Mandarin. *Program availability:* Part-time, online learning.

Kennesaw State University, Coles College of Business, Doctor of Business Administration Program, Kennesaw, GA 30144. Offers DBA. *Accreditation:* AACSB. *Program availability:* Part-time. *Students:* 5 full-time (2 women), 22 part-time (10 women); includes 9 minority (6 Black or African American, non-Hispanic/Latino; 2 Hispanic/Latino; 1 Two or more races, non-Hispanic/Latino). Average age 44. In 2018, 12 doctorates awarded. *Degree requirements:* For doctorate, thesis/dissertation. *Entrance requirements:* Additional exam requirements/recommendations for international students: Required—TOEFL (minimum score 550 paper-based; 80 iBT), IELTS (minimum score 6.5). *Application deadline:* For spring admission, 10/1 for domestic and international students. Applications are processed on a rolling basis. Application fee: $100. Electronic applications accepted. *Expenses:* Contact institution. *Financial support:* Application deadline: 4/1; applicants required to submit FAFSA. *Unit head:* Dr. Juanne Greene, Director, 470-578-4729, E-mail: jgreene@kennesaw.edu. *Application contact:* Sobia Mufti, Student Services Coordinator, 470-578-4798, Fax: 470-578-9172, E-mail: smufti@kennesaw.edu.
Website: http://coles.kennesaw.edu/dba/index.php

Kennesaw State University, Coles College of Business, Executive MBA Program, Kennesaw, GA 30144. Offers EMBA. *Accreditation:* AACSB. *Program availability:* Part-time, evening/weekend. *Students:* 44 full-time (19 women), 39 part-time (20 women); includes 37 minority (25 Black or African American, non-Hispanic/Latino; 6 Asian, non-Hispanic/Latino; 5 Hispanic/Latino; 1 Two or more races, non-Hispanic/Latino). Average age 39. 54 applicants, 83% accepted, 39 enrolled. In 2018, 27 master's awarded. *Entrance requirements:* Additional exam requirements/recommendations for international students: Required—TOEFL (minimum score 80 iBT), IELTS (minimum score 6.5). *Application deadline:* For fall admission, 7/1 priority date for domestic students. Applications are processed on a rolling basis. Application fee: $75. Electronic applications accepted. *Expenses:* Contact institution. *Financial support:* Applicants required to submit FAFSA. *Unit head:* Dr. Alison Keefe, Executive Director, 470-578-4469, E-mail: akeefe@kennesaw.edu. *Application contact:* Admission Counselor, 470-578-4377, Fax: 470-578-9172, E-mail: ksugrad@kennesaw.edu.
Website: http://coles.kennesaw.edu/emba/

Kennesaw State University, Coles College of Business, MBA Program, Kennesaw, GA 30144. Offers MBA. *Accreditation:* AACSB. *Program availability:* Part-time, evening/weekend, 100% online. *Students:* 51 full-time (18 women), 168 part-time (85 women); includes 89 minority (56 Black or African American, non-Hispanic/Latino; 14 Asian, non-

Hispanic/Latino; 15 Hispanic/Latino; 4 Two or more races, non-Hispanic/Latino), 13 international. Average age 36. 145 applicants, 43% accepted, 46 enrolled. In 2018, 56 master's awarded. *Entrance requirements:* For master's, GMAT (minimum score 530), minimum GPA of 2.8, 1 year of work experience. Additional exam requirements/ recommendations for international students: Required—TOEFL (minimum score 80 iBT), IELTS (minimum score 6.5). *Application deadline:* For fall admission, 7/1 for domestic and international students; for spring admission, 11/1 for domestic and international students; for summer admission, 4/1 for domestic and international students. Applications are processed on a rolling basis. Application fee: $60. Electronic applications accepted. *Expenses: Tuition, area resident:* Full-time $6960; part-time $290 per credit hour. Tuition, state resident: full-time $6960; part-time $290 per credit hour. Tuition, nonresident: full-time $25,080; part-time $1045 per credit hour. *International tuition:* $25,080 full-time. *Required fees:* $2006; $1706 per semester. $853 per semester. *Financial support:* Research assistantships with tuition reimbursements and unspecified assistantships available. Financial award application deadline: 4/1; financial award applicants required to submit FAFSA. *Unit head:* Sheb True, Interim Director, 470-578-6076, E-mail: strue@kennesaw.edu. *Application contact:* Daniel Audia, Assistant Director, 470-578-4470, E-mail: daudia1@kennesaw.edu.
Website: http://coles.kennesaw.edu/mba/

Kent State University, College of Business Administration, Master's Program in Business Administration, Kent, OH 44242-0001. Offers MBA. *Accreditation:* AACSB. *Program availability:* Part-time, evening/weekend, 100% online. *Faculty:* 12 full-time (5 women), 2 part-time/adjunct (0 women). *Students:* 64 full-time (26 women), 57 part-time (31 women); includes 13 minority (7 Black or African American, non-Hispanic/Latino; 1 Hispanic/Latino; 5 Two or more races, non-Hispanic/Latino), 10 international. Average age 33. 130 applicants, 76% accepted, 65 enrolled. In 2018, 61 master's awarded. *Degree requirements:* For master's, 30-37 credit hours, minimum GPA of 3.0. *Entrance requirements:* For master's, GMAT or GRE, minimum GPA of 3.0. Additional exam requirements/recommendations for international students: Required—TOEFL (minimum score 550 paper-based; 79 iBT), IELTS (minimum score 6.5). *Application deadline:* For fall admission, 6/1 for domestic students, 3/15 for international students; for spring admission, 10/15 for domestic students; for summer admission, 5/1 for domestic students. Applications are processed on a rolling basis. Application fee: $45 ($70 for international students). Electronic applications accepted. *Expenses:* Contact institution. *Financial support:* In 2018–19, 2 students received support, including 3 research assistantships with full tuition reimbursements available (averaging $8,000 per year); career-related internships or fieldwork and Federal Work-Study also available. Financial award application deadline: 3/15; financial award applicants required to submit FAFSA. *Unit head:* Louise M. Ditchey, Administrative Director, 330-672-2282, Fax: 330-672-7303, E-mail: gradbus@kent.edu. *Application contact:* Felecia A. Urbanek, Coordinator, Graduate Programs, 330-672-2282, Fax: 330-672-7303, E-mail: gradbus@kent.edu.
Website: http://www.kent.edu/business/degrees/masters-programs

Kent State University at Stark, Professional MBA Program, Canton, OH 44720-7599. Offers MBA.

Kettering University, Graduate School, Department of Business, Flint, MI 48504. Offers MBA, MS. *Accreditation:* ACBSP. *Program availability:* Part-time, evening/ weekend, online learning. *Entrance requirements:* Additional exam requirements/ recommendations for international students: Required—TOEFL (minimum score 550 paper-based; 79 iBT). Electronic applications accepted.

Keuka College, Program in Management, Keuka Park, NY 14478. Offers MS. *Program availability:* Part-time, evening/weekend, 100% online, blended/hybrid learning. *Degree requirements:* For master's, thesis, capstone/action research project. *Entrance requirements:* For master's, 2 letters of recommendation, minimum GPA of 3.0. Additional exam requirements/recommendations for international students: Required—TOEFL (minimum score 550 paper-based). *Expenses:* Contact institution. *Faculty research:* Inventory control and supply chain management; optimal order policies and supply chain coordination sustainability; using nature as an innovator and designing tool.

Keystone College, Master's in Business Administration, La Plume, PA 18440. Offers MBA. *Program availability:* Part-time, online only, 100% online. *Students:* 22. *Entrance requirements:* For master's, official college transcripts. Additional exam requirements/ recommendations for international students: Required—TOEFL (minimum score 80 iBT), IELTS (minimum score 6.5), TOEFL (minimum score 80 iBT) or IELTS (minimum score 6.5). *Application deadline:* For fall admission, 8/1 for domestic students; for spring admission, 3/1 for domestic students; for summer admission, 7/1 for domestic students. Applications are processed on a rolling basis. Application fee: $0. Electronic applications accepted. *Expenses:* Contact institution. *Financial support:* Unspecified assistantships available. Financial award applicants required to submit FAFSA. *Unit head:* Dr. Dana Harris, Associate Professor/Coordinator of MBA Program, 570-945-8421, E-mail: dana.harris@keystone.edu. *Application contact:* Sarah Louzon, Admissions Counselor, 570-945-8126, Fax: 570-945-7916, E-mail: sarah.louzon@keystone.edu.

King University, School of Business, Economics, and Technology, Bristol, TN 37620-2699. Offers accounting (MBA); finance (MBA); healthcare management (MBA); human resources management (MBA); leadership (MBA); management (MBA); marketing (MBA); project management (MBA). *Program availability:* Part-time, evening/weekend, 100% online, blended/hybrid learning. *Faculty:* 11 full-time (9 women), 10 part-time/ adjunct (7 women). *Students:* 182 full-time (107 women), 8 part-time (6 women); includes 18 minority (7 Black or African American, non-Hispanic/Latino; 4 Hispanic/ Latino; 1 Native Hawaiian or other Pacific Islander, non-Hispanic/Latino; 6 Two or more races, non-Hispanic/Latino), 2 international. Average age 32. 143 applicants, 98% accepted, 68 enrolled. In 2018, 125 master's awarded. *Degree requirements:* For master's, comprehensive exam, thesis optional. *Entrance requirements:* For master's, resume which demonstrates a minimum of 2 years of full-time work experience, minimum cumulative grade point average of 3.0 on a 4.0 scale is required. Students who do not meet this requirement may be conditionally accepted. Additional exam requirements/recommendations for international students: Required—TOEFL (minimum score 84 paper-based; 84 iBT). *Application deadline:* Applications are processed on a rolling basis. Application fee: $0 ($50 for international students). Electronic applications accepted. *Expenses: Tuition:* Full-time $13,365; part-time $495 per semester hour. *Required fees:* $900; $100 per course. One-time fee: $175. Tuition and fees vary according to class time, degree level and program. *Financial support:* Unspecified assistantships available. Financial award applicants required to submit FAFSA. *Faculty research:* International monetary policy. *Unit head:* Dr. Mark Pate, Dean, School of Business, Economics and Technology, 423-652-4814, E-mail: mjpate@king.edu. *Application contact:* Nancy Beverly, Territory Manager/Enrollment Counselor, 423-341-9495, Fax: 423-652-4727, E-mail: nmbeverly@king.edu.

Kutztown University of Pennsylvania, College of Business, Program in Business Administration, Kutztown, PA 19530-0730. Offers MBA. *Accreditation:* AACSB. *Program availability:* Part-time, evening/weekend, 100% online, blended/hybrid learning. *Faculty:* 7 full-time (5 women). *Students:* 12 full-time (4 women), 19 part-time (7 women); includes 1 minority (Hispanic/Latino), 3 international. Average age 30. 37 applicants, 86% accepted, 14 enrolled. In 2018, 12 master's awarded. *Degree requirements:* For master's, comprehensive exam, thesis (for some programs). *Entrance requirements:* For master's, GMAT or GRE, 2 letters of recommendation, resume, goal statement.

Additional exam requirements/recommendations for international students: Required—TOEFL (minimum score 550 paper-based, 79 iBT), IELTS (minimum score 6.5), or PTE (minimum score 53). *Application deadline:* For fall admission, 8/1 priority date for domestic and international students; for spring admission, 12/1 priority date for domestic and international students. Applications are processed on a rolling basis. Application fee: $35. Electronic applications accepted. *Expenses:* Tuition, state resident: part-time $516 per credit. Tuition, nonresident: part-time $774 per credit. *Required fees:* $119 per credit. One-time fee: $50 part-time. Tuition and fees vary according to degree level. *Financial support:* Career-related internships or fieldwork, Federal Work-Study, and unspecified assistantships available. Financial award application deadline: 3/1; financial award applicants required to submit FAFSA. *Unit head:* Dr. Anne Carroll, Dean, 610-683-4575, Fax: 610-683-4573, E-mail: acarroll@kutztown.edu. *Application contact:* Dr. Anne Carroll, Dean, 610-683-4575, Fax: 610-683-4573, E-mail: acarroll@kutztown.edu.
Website: http://www.kutztown.edu/MBA

Lake Erie College, School of Business, Painesville, OH 44077-3389. Offers general management (MBA); health care administration (MBA); information technology management (MBA). *Program availability:* Part-time, evening/weekend. *Entrance requirements:* For master's, GMAT or minimum GPA of 3.0, resume, personal statement. Additional exam requirements/recommendations for international students: Required—TOEFL (minimum score 550 paper-based; 79 iBT), IELTS (minimum score 6), STEP Eiken 1st and pre-1st grade level (for Japanese students). Electronic applications accepted. Application fee is waived when completed online. *Expenses:* Contact institution.

Lake Forest Graduate School of Management, The Leadership MBA Program, Lake Forest, IL 60045. Offers finance (MBA); global business (MBA); healthcare management (MBA); management (MBA); marketing (MBA); organizational behavior (MBA). *Program availability:* Part-time, evening/weekend. *Entrance requirements:* For master's, 4 years of work experience in field, interview, 2 letters of recommendation. Electronic applications accepted.

Lakeland University, Graduate Studies Division, Program in Business Administration, Plymouth, WI 53073. Offers accounting (MBA); finance (MBA); healthcare management (MBA); project management (MBA). *Entrance requirements:* For master's, GMAT. *Expenses:* Contact institution.

Lamar University, College of Graduate Studies, College of Business, Beaumont, TX 77710. Offers accounting (MBA); MSA/MBA. *Accreditation:* AACSB. *Program availability:* Part-time, evening/weekend. *Faculty:* 48 full-time (14 women), 8 part-time/ adjunct (3 women). *Students:* 38 full-time (18 women), 242 part-time (141 women); includes 113 minority (60 Black or African American, non-Hispanic/Latino; 13 Asian, non-Hispanic/Latino; 34 Hispanic/Latino; 6 Two or more races, non-Hispanic/Latino), 25 international. Average age 33. 184 applicants, 97% accepted, 48 enrolled. In 2018, 90 master's awarded. *Degree requirements:* For master's, comprehensive exam (for some programs), thesis optional. *Entrance requirements:* For master's, GMAT. Additional exam requirements/recommendations for international students: Required—TOEFL (minimum score 550 paper-based; 79 iBT), IELTS (minimum score 6.5). *Application deadline:* Applications are processed on a rolling basis. Application fee: $25 ($50 for international students). Electronic applications accepted. *Expenses:* Contact institution. *Financial support:* In 2018–19, 33 students received support. Fellowships with tuition reimbursements available, research assistantships with partial tuition reimbursements available, career-related internships or fieldwork, Federal Work-Study, institutionally sponsored loans, scholarships/grants, and tuition waivers (partial) available. Support available to part-time students. Financial award applicants required to submit FAFSA. *Faculty research:* Marketing, finance, quantitative methods, management information systems, legal, environmental. *Total annual research expenditures:* $1,430. *Unit head:* Dr. Dan French, Dean, 409-880-8603, Fax: 409-880-8088, E-mail: dan.french@lamar.edu. *Application contact:* Celeste Contreas, Director, Admissions and Academic Services, 409-880-8888, Fax: 409-880-7419, E-mail: gradmissions@lamar.edu.
Website: http://business.lamar.edu

La Salle University, School of Business, Master of Business Administration Program, Philadelphia, PA 19141-1199. Offers accounting (MBA, Post-MBA Certificate); business systems and analytics (MBA, Post-MBA Certificate); finance (MBA, Post-MBA Certificate); general business administration (MBA, Post-MBA Certificate); human resource management (MBA, Post-MBA Certificate); management (MBA, Post-MBA Certificate); marketing (Post-MBA Certificate); MBA/MSN. Program also offered in Switzerland. *Accreditation:* AACSB. *Program availability:* Part-time, evening/weekend, online learning. *Entrance requirements:* For master's, GMAT or GRE, two letters of reference; resume; for Post-MBA Certificate, MBA with minimum GPA of 3.0. Additional exam requirements/recommendations for international students: Required—TOEFL. Electronic applications accepted. Application fee is waived when completed online. *Expenses:* Contact institution.

Lasell College, Graduate and Professional Studies in Management, Newton, MA 02466-2709. Offers business administration (MBA); elder care management (MSM); hospitality and event management (MSM); human resources management (MSM, Graduate Certificate); management (MSM, Graduate Certificate); marketing (MS, Graduate Certificate); project management (MSM, Graduate Certificate). *Accreditation:* ACBSP. *Program availability:* Part-time, evening/weekend, 100% online, blended/hybrid learning. *Faculty:* 7 full-time (4 women), 14 part-time/adjunct (9 women). *Students:* 37 full-time (28 women), 76 part-time (48 women); includes 22 minority (12 Black or African American, non-Hispanic/Latino; 1 Asian, non-Hispanic/Latino; 9 Hispanic/Latino), 20 international. Average age 32. 68 applicants, 54% accepted, 20 enrolled. In 2018, 62 master's, 1 other advanced degree awarded. *Degree requirements:* For master's, minimum GPA of 3.0; internship or research paper (for MSM). *Entrance requirements:* For master's, one-page personal statement, 2 letters of recommendation, resume, bachelor's degree transcript; proof of microeconomics and statistics (for MBA); for Graduate Certificate, bachelor's degree transcript, 2 letters of recommendation, 1-page personal statement, resume. Additional exam requirements/recommendations for international students: Required—TOEFL (minimum score 550 paper-based, 79 iBT) or IELTS (minimum score 6). *Application deadline:* For fall admission, 8/31 priority date for domestic students, 6/30 priority date for international students; for spring admission, 12/31 priority date for domestic students, 10/31 priority date for international students. Applications are processed on a rolling basis. Electronic applications accepted. *Expenses: Tuition:* Part-time $600 per credit. *Required fees:* $40 per course. *Financial support:* Federal Work-Study, scholarships/grants, and tuition discounts available. Support available to part-time students. Financial award application deadline: 8/31; financial award applicants required to submit FAFSA. *Unit head:* Eric Turner, Vice President of Graduate and Professional Studies, 617-243-2071, Fax: 617-243-2450, E-mail: gradinfo@lasell.edu. *Application contact:* Adrienne Franciosi, Assistant Vice President of Graduate and Professional Studies, 617-243-2214, Fax: 617-243-2450, E-mail: gradinfo@lasell.edu.
Website: http://www.lasell.edu/academics/graduate-and-professional-studies/programs-of-study/master-of-science-in-management.html

La Sierra University, School of Business and Management, Riverside, CA 92505. Offers accounting (MBA); finance (MBA); general management (MBA); human resources management (MBA); leadership, values, and ethics for business and

management (Certificate); marketing (MBA). *Degree requirements:* For master's, research project. *Entrance requirements:* For master's, GMAT, minimum GPA of 3.0. Additional exam requirements/recommendations for international students: Required—TOEFL. *Faculty research:* Financial econometrics, institutional assessment and strategic planning, legal issues in management, behavioral finance, content of financial reports.

Laurentian University, School of Graduate Studies and Research, School of Commerce and Administration, Sudbury, ON P3E 2C6, Canada. Offers MBA. *Program availability:* Part-time, evening/weekend. *Entrance requirements:* For master's, GMAT, 2 years of work experience. *Faculty research:* Small business and entrepreneurship development, mutual fund performance, donorship behavior, stress and organizations, quality programs.

Lawrence Technological University, College of Management, Southfield, MI 48075-1058. Offers business administration (MBA, DBA), including business analytics (MBA, MS), cybersecurity (MBA, MS), finance (MBA), information systems (MBA), information technology (MBA), marketing (MBA), project management (MBA, MS); cybersecurity (Graduate Certificate); health IT management (Graduate Certificate); information assurance management (Graduate Certificate); information systems (MS), including enterprise resource planning, enterprise security management, project management (MBA, MS); information technology (MS, DM), including business analytics (MBA, MS), cybersecurity (MBA, MS), information assurance (MS), project management (MBA, MS); management (PhD); nonprofit management and leadership (Graduate Certificate); operations management (MS), including manufacturing operations, service operations; project management (Graduate Certificate). *Accreditation:* ACBSP. *Program availability:* Part-time, evening/weekend, 100% online. Terminal master's awarded for partial completion of doctoral program. *Degree requirements:* For master's, thesis (for some programs); for doctorate, comprehensive exam, thesis/dissertation. *Entrance requirements:* Additional exam requirements/recommendations for international students: Required—TOEFL (minimum score 550 paper-based; 79 iBT), IELTS (minimum score 6.5). Electronic applications accepted. *Faculty research:* Cybersecurity; risk management; IT governance; security controls and countermeasures; threat modeling cyber resilience; autonomous cars; natural language processing; text mining; machine learning; reflective leadership; emerging leadership theories and practice; motivational studies; teaching effectiveness strategies; teamwork; organization development; strategic planning; strengths-based and positive organizational scholarship; global leadership; globalization; corporate governance.

Lebanese American University, School of Business, Beirut, Lebanon. Offers MBA.

Lebanon Valley College, Program in Business Administration, Annville, PA 17003-1400. Offers business administration (MBA); healthcare management (MBA); human resources (MBA); leadership and ethics (MBA); project management (MBA). *Program availability:* Part-time, evening/weekend. *Degree requirements:* For master's, capstone course. *Entrance requirements:* For master's, GMAT, 3 years of work experience, resume, professional statement (application form, resume, personal statement, transcripts). Additional exam requirements/recommendations for international students: Required—TOEFL (minimum score 80 iBT), IELTS (minimum score 6.5) or STEP Eiken (grade 1). Electronic applications accepted. *Expenses:* Contact institution. *Faculty research:* Leadership, motivation, BI, information systems strategies, emerging market development, the role of informational business education, economic growth.

Lee University, MBA Program, Cleveland, TN 37320-3450. Offers MBA. *Program availability:* Part-time, evening/weekend, 100% online. *Faculty:* 5 full-time (1 woman). *Students:* 13 full-time (7 women), 54 part-time (26 women); includes 7 minority (4 Black or African American, non-Hispanic/Latino; 1 Asian, non-Hispanic/Latino; 1 Hispanic/Latino; 1 Two or more races, non-Hispanic/Latino), 11 international. Average age 29. 30 applicants, 80% accepted, 23 enrolled. In 2018, 27 master's awarded. *Degree requirements:* For master's, variable foreign language requirement, comprehensive exam, thesis optional, practicum. *Entrance requirements:* For master's, GMAT (taken within last 5 years), minimum undergraduate cumulative GPA of 3.0. Additional exam requirements/recommendations for international students: Required—TOEFL (minimum score 61 iBT). *Application deadline:* For fall admission, 4/1 priority date for domestic and international students; for spring admission, 10/1 priority date for domestic and international students. Applications are processed on a rolling basis. Application fee: $25. Electronic applications accepted. *Financial support:* In 2018–19, 36 students received support. Scholarships/grants available. Financial award application deadline: 3/1; financial award applicants required to submit FAFSA. *Unit head:* Dr. Shane Griffith, Director, 423-614-8694, E-mail: mba@leeuniversity.edu. *Application contact:* Jeffery McGirt, Director of Graduate Enrollment, 423-614-8691, Fax: 423-614-8317, E-mail: jmcgirt@leeuniversity.edu.
Website: http://www.leeuniversity.edu/academics/graduate/mba/

Lehigh University, College of Business, Department of Management, Bethlehem, PA 18015. Offers business administration (MBA); project management (MBA); MBA/E; MBA/M Ed. *Accreditation:* AACSB. *Program availability:* Part-time, evening/weekend, synchronous with live classroom. *Faculty:* 11 full-time (3 women), 1 part-time/adjunct (0 women). *Students:* 44 full-time (16 women), 171 part-time (45 women); includes 32 minority (4 Black or African American, non-Hispanic/Latino; 16 Asian, non-Hispanic/Latino; 8 Hispanic/Latino; 1 Native Hawaiian or other Pacific Islander, non-Hispanic/Latino; 3 Two or more races, non-Hispanic/Latino), 23 international. Average age 33. 132 applicants, 77% accepted, 68 enrolled. In 2018, 84 master's awarded. *Entrance requirements:* For master's, GMAT or GRE. Additional exam requirements/recommendations for international students: Required—TOEFL (minimum score 600 paper-based; 94 iBT), IELTS (minimum score 7). *Application deadline:* For fall admission, 7/15 for domestic students, 5/1 for international students; for spring admission, 12/1 for domestic students. Application fee: $75. Tuition and fees vary according to program. *Financial support:* In 2018–19, 33 students received support, including 10 fellowships (averaging $5,250 per year); research assistantships, scholarships/grants, health care benefits, tuition waivers, and unspecified assistantships also available. Support available to part-time students. Financial award application deadline: 1/15. *Faculty research:* Information systems, organizational behavior, supply chain management, strategic management, entrepreneurship. *Total annual research expenditures:* $26,528. *Unit head:* Dr. Corinne Post, Department Chair, 610-758-5882, Fax: 610-758-6941, E-mail: cgp208@lehigh.edu. *Application contact:* Mary Theresa Taglang, Director of Recruitment and Admissions, 610-758-4386, Fax: 610-758-5283, E-mail: mtt4@lehigh.edu.
Website: https://cbe.lehigh.edu/academics/undergraduate/management

Lehman College of the City University of New York, School of Natural and Social Sciences, Department of Economics and Business, Bronx, NY 10468-1589. Offers accounting (MS); business (MS). *Entrance requirements:* For master's, GMAT.

Le Moyne College, Madden School of Business, Syracuse, NY 13214. Offers business administration (MBA); information systems (MS). *Accreditation:* AACSB. *Program availability:* Part-time, evening/weekend. *Faculty:* 18 full-time (5 women), 5 part-time/adjunct (1 woman). *Students:* 48 full-time (21 women), 63 part-time (30 women); includes 11 minority (3 Black or African American, non-Hispanic/Latino; 1 American Indian or Alaska Native, non-Hispanic/Latino; 3 Asian, non-Hispanic/Latino; 4 Hispanic/Latino), 4 international. Average age 27. 69 applicants, 94% accepted, 61 enrolled. In 2018, 60 master's awarded. *Degree requirements:* For master's, thesis (for some programs), capstone-level course. *Entrance requirements:* For master's, GMAT or GRE General Test, bachelor's degree with minimum GPA of 3.0, resume, 2 letters of recommendation, personal statement, transcripts, interview; GMAT/GRE. Additional exam requirements/recommendations for international students: Required—TOEFL (minimum score 79 iBT); Recommended—IELTS (minimum score 6.5). *Application deadline:* For fall admission, 7/1 priority date for domestic and international students; for spring admission, 11/1 priority date for domestic and international students; for summer admission, 4/1 priority date for domestic and international students. Applications are processed on a rolling basis. Application fee: $0. Electronic applications accepted. *Expenses:* $835 per credit hour; wellness fee $70 per semester for full-time graduate students taking 9+ credit hours; technology fee $75 per semester for full-time graduate students taking 9+ credit hours, $25 per semester for part-time students. *Financial support:* In 2018–19, 35 students received support. Career-related internships or fieldwork, scholarships/grants, health care benefits, and unspecified assistantships available. Support available to part-time students. Financial award applicants required to submit FAFSA. *Faculty research:* Performance evaluation outcomes assessment, technology outsourcing, international business, systems for Web-based information-seeking, non-profit business practices, business sustainability practices, management/leadership development, operations management optimization applications. *Unit head:* James Joseph, Dean of Madden School of Business, 315-445-4280, Fax: 315-445-4787, E-mail: josepjae@lemoyne.edu. *Application contact:* Teresa M. Renn, Senior Assistant Director for Graduate Admission, 315-445-5444, Fax: 315-445-6092, E-mail: renntm@lemoyne.edu.
Website: http://www.lemoyne.edu/madden

Lenoir-Rhyne University, Graduate Programs, Charles M. Snipes School of Business, Hickory, NC 28601. Offers accounting (MBA); business analytics and information technology (MBA); entrepreneurship (MBA); global business (MBA); healthcare administration (MBA); innovation and change management (MBA); leadership development (MBA). *Accreditation:* ACBSP. *Program availability:* Part-time, evening/weekend, online learning. *Degree requirements:* For master's, capstone course. *Entrance requirements:* For master's, GMAT, GRE, MAT, minimum undergraduate GPA of 2.7, graduate 3.0. Additional exam requirements/recommendations for international students: Required—TOEFL (minimum score 600 paper-based). Electronic applications accepted. *Expenses:* Contact institution.

LeTourneau University, Graduate Programs, Longview, TX 75607-7001. Offers business administration (MBA); counseling (MA); curriculum and instruction (M Ed); educational administration (M Ed); engineering (ME, MS); engineering management (MEM); health care administration (MS); marriage and family therapy (MA); psychology (MA); strategic leadership (MSL); teacher leadership (M Ed); teaching and learning (M Ed). *Program availability:* Part-time, 100% online, blended/hybrid learning. *Students:* 61 full-time (47 women), 311 part-time (248 women); includes 184 minority (117 Black or African American, non-Hispanic/Latino; 3 American Indian or Alaska Native, non-Hispanic/Latino; 1 Asian, non-Hispanic/Latino; 35 Hispanic/Latino; 28 Two or more races, non-Hispanic/Latino), 2 international. Average age 37. In 2018, 97 master's awarded. *Entrance requirements:* Additional exam requirements/recommendations for international students: Required—TOEFL (minimum score 525 paper-based; 80 iBT), IELTS (minimum score 6), Either a TOEFL or IELTS is required for graduate students. One or the other. *Application deadline:* Applications are processed on a rolling basis. Electronic applications accepted. *Financial support:* Research assistantships, teaching assistantships, unspecified assistantships, and employee tuition waivers and institutionally sponsored loans available. Financial award applicants required to submit FAFSA.
Website: http://www.letu.edu

Lewis University, College of Nursing and Health Professions and College of Business, Program in Nursing/Business, Romeoville, IL 60446. Offers MSN/MBA. *Program availability:* Part-time, evening/weekend. *Students:* 1 (woman) full-time, 21 part-time (17 women); includes 6 minority (2 Black or African American, non-Hispanic/Latino; 1 Asian, non-Hispanic/Latino; 2 Hispanic/Latino; 1 Two or more races, non-Hispanic/Latino). Average age 35. *Entrance requirements:* Additional exam requirements/recommendations for international students: Required—TOEFL (minimum score 550 paper-based; 80 iBT). *Application deadline:* For fall admission, 4/2 priority date for domestic students, 5/1 priority date for international students; for spring admission, 11/15 priority date for international students. Applications are processed on a rolling basis. Electronic applications accepted. *Financial support:* Scholarships/grants, tuition waivers (full and partial), and unspecified assistantships available. Financial award application deadline: 5/1; financial award applicants required to submit FAFSA. *Faculty research:* Cancer prevention, phenomenological methods, public policy analysis. *Total annual research expenditures:* $1,000. *Unit head:* Dr. Stacie Elder, Program Director. *Application contact:* Nancy Wiksten, Graduate Admission Counselor, 815-838-5610, E-mail: grad@lewisu.edu.

Liberty University, School of Business, Lynchburg, VA 24515. Offers accounting (MBA, MS), including audit and financial reporting (MS), business (MS), financial services (MS), forensic accounting (MS), leadership (MS), taxation (MS); cyber security (MS); executive leadership (MA); international business (DBA); leadership (DBA); marketing (MBA, MS, DBA), including digital marketing and advertising (MS), project management (MS), public relations (MS), sports marketing and media (MS); project management (MBA, DBA); public relations (MBA). *Program availability:* Part-time, online learning. *Students:* 2,871 full-time (1,496 women), 4,437 part-time (1,969 women); includes 2,069 minority (1,424 Black or African American, non-Hispanic/Latino; 44 American Indian or Alaska Native, non-Hispanic/Latino; 133 Asian, non-Hispanic/Latino; 282 Hispanic/Latino; 16 Native Hawaiian or other Pacific Islander, non-Hispanic/Latino; 170 Two or more races, non-Hispanic/Latino), 154 international. Average age 36. 8,980 applicants, 45% accepted, 2009 enrolled. In 2018, 1,988 master's, 25 doctorates awarded. *Entrance requirements:* For master's, minimum undergraduate GPA of 3.0, 15 hours of upper-level business courses. Additional exam requirements/recommendations for international students: Required—TOEFL (minimum score 600 paper-based; 100 iBT). *Application deadline:* Applications are processed on a rolling basis. Application fee: $50. Electronic applications accepted. *Expenses:* Contact institution. *Financial support:* In 2018–19, 990 students received support. Teaching assistantships and Federal Work-Study available. Financial award applicants required to submit FAFSA. *Unit head:* Dr. Dave Bratt, Dean, 434-592-7321, E-mail: dabrat@liberty.edu. *Application contact:* Jay Bridge, Director of Graduate Admissions, 800-424-9595, Fax: 800-628-7977, E-mail: gradadmissions@liberty.edu.
Website: https://www.liberty.edu/business/

Liberty University, School of Health Sciences, Lynchburg, VA 24515. Offers anatomy and cell biology (PhD); biomedical sciences (MS); epidemiology (MPH); exercise science (MS), including clinical, community physical activity, human performance, nutrition; global health (MPH); health promotion (MPH); medical sciences (MA), including biopsychology, business management, health informatics, molecular medicine, public health; nutrition (MPH). *Program availability:* Part-time, online learning. *Students:* 729 full-time (530 women), 760 part-time (555 women); includes 505 minority (327 Black

or African American, non-Hispanic/Latino; 9 American Indian or Alaska Native, non-Hispanic/Latino; 38 Asian, non-Hispanic/Latino; 80 Hispanic/Latino; 4 Native Hawaiian or other Pacific Islander, non-Hispanic/Latino; 47 Two or more races, non-Hispanic/Latino), 71 international. Average age 31. 3,363 applicants, 32% accepted, 522 enrolled. In 2018, 373 master's awarded. *Degree requirements:* For master's, thesis (for some programs); for doctorate, thesis/dissertation. *Entrance requirements:* For doctorate, MAT or GRE, minimum GPA of 3.25 in master's program, 2-3 recommendations, writing samples (for some programs), letter of intent, professional vitae. Additional exam requirements/recommendations for international students: Required—TOEFL (minimum score 600 paper-based; 100 iBT). Application fee: $50. *Expenses: Tuition:* Full-time $10,851; part-time $562 per credit hour. *Financial support:* In 2018–19, 918 students received support. Federal Work-Study available. Financial award applicants required to submit FAFSA. *Unit head:* Dr. Ralph Linstra, Dean. *Application contact:* Jay Bridge, Director of Admissions, 800-424-9595, Fax: 800-628-7977, E-mail: gradadmissions@liberty.edu.
Website: https://www.liberty.edu/health-sciences/

LIM College, MPS Program, New York, NY 10022-5268. Offers business of fashion (MPS); fashion marketing (MPS); fashion merchandising and retail management (MPS); global fashion supply chain management (MPS). *Accreditation:* ACBSP. *Program availability:* Part-time, 100% online. *Faculty:* 2 full-time, 21 part-time/adjunct. *Students:* 125 full-time (109 women), 45 part-time (44 women); includes 64 minority (31 Black or African American, non-Hispanic/Latino; 15 Asian, non-Hispanic/Latino; 18 Hispanic/Latino), 67 international. Average age 25. 292 applicants, 67% accepted, 125 enrolled. In 2018, 146 master's awarded. *Entrance requirements:* Additional exam requirements/recommendations for international students: Required—TOEFL (minimum score 550 paper-based), IELTS (minimum score 6.5), PTE (minimum score 55). *Application deadline:* Applications are processed on a rolling basis. Application fee: $40. Electronic applications accepted. *Expenses: Tuition:* Full-time $28,500; part-time $950 per credit hour. *Required fees:* $500; $100 per semester. *Faculty research:* Marketing, Strategy, Brand Management, Entrepreneurship, Social Media. *Unit head:* John Keane, Chair of Graduate Studies, E-mail: graduatestudies@limcollege.edu. *Application contact:* George Toledo, Assistant Director of Graduate Admissions, 212-310-0634, E-mail: graduateadmissions@limcollege.edu.
Website: http://www.limcollege.edu/academics/graduate

Limestone College, MBA Program, Gaffney, SC 29340. Offers MBA. *Program availability:* Part-time, evening/weekend, 100% online, but there are three 1-hour group dynamics classes offered during weekends between semesters. *Faculty:* 10 full-time (3 women). *Students:* 43 full-time (22 women), 28 part-time (14 women); includes 30 minority (28 Black or African American, non-Hispanic/Latino; 1 Asian, non-Hispanic/Latino; 1 Two or more races, non-Hispanic/Latino), 3 international. Average age 36. 69 applicants, 39% accepted, 9 enrolled. In 2018, 30 master's awarded. *Degree requirements:* For master's, comprehensive exam, three weekend residency seminars (on campus). *Entrance requirements:* For master's, GMAT/GRE, two letters of recommendation, official transcript(s). Additional exam requirements/recommendations for international students: Required—TOEFL (minimum score 500 paper-based; 90 iBT). *Application deadline:* For fall admission, 8/1 priority date for domestic and international students; for winter admission, 12/12 priority date for domestic and international students; for spring admission, 4/1 priority date for domestic and international students. Applications are processed on a rolling basis. Application fee: $25. Electronic applications accepted. Application fee is waived when completed online. *Expenses:* Contact institution. *Financial support:* Scholarships/grants available. Financial award application deadline: 6/15; financial award applicants required to submit FAFSA. *Faculty research:* Health care management. *Unit head:* Adair Hudson, Director of Graduate Studies in Enrollment and Admissions, 864-488-4370, Fax: 864-487-8706, E-mail: ahudson@limestone.edu. *Application contact:* Adair Hudson, Director of Graduate Studies in Enrollment and Admissions, 800-795-7151 Ext. 4370, Fax: 864-467-8706, E-mail: ahaynes@limestone.edu.
Website: http://www.limestone.edu/mba-program

Lincoln Memorial University, School of Business, Harrogate, TN 37752-1901. Offers MBA. *Accreditation:* ACBSP. *Program availability:* Part-time, evening/weekend. *Degree requirements:* For master's, comprehensive exam, thesis. *Entrance requirements:* For master's, GMAT, resume, letters of recommendation, interview. Additional exam requirements/recommendations for international students: Required—TOEFL (minimum score 500 paper-based).

Lincoln University, Graduate Studies, Oakland, CA 94612. Offers finance and investments (DBA); finance management (MS); finance management and investments (MBA); general business (MBA); human resource management (MBA, DBA); international business (MBA, MS); management information systems (MBA). *Program availability:* Part-time. *Degree requirements:* For master's, research project (thesis), internship report, or comprehensive exam; for doctorate, comprehensive exam, thesis/dissertation. *Entrance requirements:* For master's, minimum GPA of 2.7; for doctorate, GMAT (minimum score: 550), GRE (minimum score: 1000), or equivalent test results (waived for master's degree with minimum cumulative GPA of 3.3). Additional exam requirements/recommendations for international students: Required—TOEFL minimum score 525 paper-based; 71 iBT or IELTS minimum score 5.5 (for MBA); TOEFL minimum score 550 paper-based; 79 iBT or IELTS minimum score 6 (for MS and DBA). Electronic applications accepted.

Lindenwood University, Graduate Programs, Plaster School of Business and Entrepreneurship, St. Charles, MO 63301-1695. Offers M Acc, MA, MBA, MS. *Accreditation:* ACBSP. *Program availability:* Part-time, evening/weekend, 100% online. *Faculty:* 14 full-time (4 women), 26 part-time/adjunct (9 women). *Students:* 234 full-time (133 women), 221 part-time (139 women); includes 121 minority (95 Black or African American, non-Hispanic/Latino; 1 American Indian or Alaska Native, non-Hispanic/Latino; 3 Asian, non-Hispanic/Latino; 12 Hispanic/Latino; 10 Two or more races, non-Hispanic/Latino), 53 international. Average age 32. 251 applicants, 38% accepted, 95 enrolled. In 2018, 210 master's awarded. *Degree requirements:* For master's, comprehensive exam (for some programs), thesis (for some programs), minimum GPA of 3.0. *Entrance requirements:* For master's, interview, minimum undergraduate cumulative GPA of 3.0, letter of recommendation. Additional exam requirements/recommendations for international students: Required—TOEFL (minimum score 553 paper-based; 81 iBT); Recommended—IELTS (minimum score 6.5). *Application deadline:* For fall admission, 8/9 priority date for domestic students, 6/1 priority date for international students; for winter admission, 12/20 priority date for domestic students, 11/1 priority date for international students; for spring admission, 2/28 priority date for domestic students, 1/3 priority date for international students; for summer admission, 5/15 priority date for domestic students, 3/27 priority date for international students. Applications are processed on a rolling basis. Application fee: $0 ($100 for international students). Electronic applications accepted. *Expenses:* Contact institution. *Financial support:* In 2018–19, 283 students received support. Career-related internships or fieldwork, Federal Work-Study, institutionally sponsored loans, scholarships/grants, tuition waivers (partial), and unspecified assistantships available. Financial award application deadline: 6/30; financial award applicants required to submit FAFSA. *Unit head:* Roger Ellis, Dean, School of Business and Entrepreneurship, 636-949-4839, E-mail: rellis@lindenwood.edu. *Application contact:* Kara Schilli, Assistant Vice President, University Admissions, 636-949-4349, Fax: 636-949-4109, E-mail: adultadmissions@lindenwood.edu.
Website: https://www.lindenwood.edu/academics/academic-schools/robert-w-plaster-school-of-business-entrepreneurship/

Lindenwood University, Graduate Programs, School of Accelerated Degree Programs, St. Charles, MO 63301-1695. Offers administration (MSA), including management, marketing, project management; business administration (MBA); communications (MA), including digital and multimedia, media management, promotions, training and development; criminal justice and administration (MS); healthcare administration (MS); human resource management (MS); information technology (Certificate); managing information security (MS); managing information technology (MS); managing virtualization and cloud computing (MS); writing (MFA). *Program availability:* Part-time, evening/weekend, 100% online. *Faculty:* 15 full-time (8 women), 62 part-time/adjunct (22 women). *Students:* 652 full-time (398 women), 66 part-time (45 women); includes 241 minority (182 Black or African American, non-Hispanic/Latino; 1 American Indian or Alaska Native, non-Hispanic/Latino; 8 Asian, non-Hispanic/Latino; 25 Hispanic/Latino; 1 Native Hawaiian or other Pacific Islander, non-Hispanic/Latino; 24 Two or more races, non-Hispanic/Latino), 81 international. Average age 36. 359 applicants, 54% accepted, 170 enrolled. In 2018, 416 master's, 2 other advanced degrees awarded. *Degree requirements:* For master's, thesis (for some programs), minimum cumulative GPA of 3.0; for Certificate, minimum cumulative GPA of 3.0. *Entrance requirements:* For master's, resume, personal statement, official undergraduate transcript, minimum undergraduate cumulative GPA of 3.0. Additional exam requirements/recommendations for international students: Required—TOEFL (minimum score 553 paper-based; 81 iBT); Recommended—IELTS (minimum score 6.5). *Application deadline:* For fall admission, 9/30 priority date for domestic and international students; for winter admission, 1/6 priority date for domestic and international students; for spring admission, 4/6 priority date for domestic and international students; for summer admission, 7/8 priority date for domestic and international students. Applications are processed on a rolling basis. Application fee: $0 ($100 for international students). Electronic applications accepted. *Expenses:* Contact institution. *Financial support:* In 2018–19, 372 students received support. Career-related internships or fieldwork, institutionally sponsored loans, scholarships/grants, tuition waivers (partial), and unspecified assistantships available. Financial award application deadline: 6/30; financial award applicants required to submit FAFSA. *Unit head:* Dr. Gina Ganahl, Dean, Accelerated Degree Programs, 636-949-4501, Fax: 636-949-4505, E-mail: gganahl@lindenwood.edu. *Application contact:* Kara Schilli, Assistant Vice President, University Admissions, 636-949-4349, Fax: 636-949-4109, E-mail: adultadmissions@lindenwood.edu.
Website: https://www.lindenwood.edu/academics/academic-schools/school-of-accelerated-degree-programs/

Lindenwood University–Belleville, Graduate Programs, Belleville, IL 62226. Offers business administration (MBA); communications (MA), including digital and multimedia, media management, promotions, training and development; counseling (MA); criminal justice administration (MS); education (MA); healthcare administration (MS); human resource management (MS); school administration (MA); teaching (MAT).

Lipscomb University, College of Business, Nashville, TN 37204-3951. Offers accounting and finance (MBA); audit/accounting (M Acc); business (Certificate); business administration (MM); healthcare management (MBA); leadership (MBA); tax (M Acc); MBA/MS; Pharm D/MM. *Accreditation:* ACBSP. *Program availability:* Part-time, evening/weekend. *Entrance requirements:* For master's, GMAT, transcripts, interview, 2 references, resume. Additional exam requirements/recommendations for international students: Required—TOEFL (minimum score 570 paper-based). Electronic applications accepted. *Expenses:* Contact institution. *Faculty research:* Impact of spirituality on organization commitment, women in corporate leadership, psychological empowerment, training.

Long Island University–LIU Brooklyn, School of Business, Public Administration and Information Sciences, Brooklyn, NY 11201-8423. Offers accounting (MBA); accounting (MS); business administration (MBA); computer science (MS); gerontology (Advanced Certificate); health administration (MPA); human resources management (MS); not-for-profit management (Advanced Certificate); public administration (MPA); taxation (MS). *Program availability:* Part-time, evening/weekend. *Entrance requirements:* Additional exam requirements/recommendations for international students: Required—TOEFL (minimum score 550 paper-based; 75 iBT). Electronic applications accepted. *Faculty research:* Tax policy; public sector budgeting and gender inequities; technology and innovation; game theory; knowledge management.

Long Island University–LIU Post, College of Management, Brookville, NY 11548-1300. Offers accountancy (MS); finance (MBA); information systems (MS); international business (MBA); management (MBA); management engineering (MS); marketing (MBA); taxation (MS); technical project management (MS); JD/MBA. *Accreditation:* AACSB. *Program availability:* Part-time, evening/weekend, blended/hybrid learning. *Entrance requirements:* For master's, GMAT, GRE, or LSAT. Additional exam requirements/recommendations for international students: Required—TOEFL (minimum score 550 paper-based, 75 iBT) or IELTS. Electronic applications accepted. *Faculty research:* Innovation and property rights, knowledge sourcing, sustainability and firm performance, China and growth markets, corporate social responsibility, workforce compensation and issues.

Longwood University, College of Graduate and Professional Studies, College of Business and Economics, Farmville, VA 23909. Offers general business (MBA); real estate (MBA); retail management (MBA). *Accreditation:* AACSB. *Program availability:* Part-time, online only, 100% online. *Degree requirements:* For master's, internship. *Entrance requirements:* For master's, GMAT or GRE, personal essay, 3 recommendations, official transcripts from all colleges and universities attended. Additional exam requirements/recommendations for international students: Required—TOEFL (minimum score 570 paper-based), IELTS (minimum score 6.5). Electronic applications accepted. *Expenses:* Contact institution.

Louisiana State University and Agricultural & Mechanical College, Graduate School, E. J. Ourso College of Business, Department of Finance, Baton Rouge, LA 70803. Offers business administration (PhD), including finance; finance (MS).

Louisiana State University and Agricultural & Mechanical College, Graduate School, E. J. Ourso College of Business, Flores MBA Program, Baton Rouge, LA 70803. Offers EMBA, MBA, PMBA, JD/IMBA. *Accreditation:* AACSB.

Louisiana State University in Shreveport, College of Business, Education, and Human Development, Program in Business Administration, Shreveport, LA 71115-2399. Offers MBA. *Accreditation:* AACSB. *Program availability:* Part-time, evening/weekend. *Degree requirements:* For master's, comprehensive exam. *Entrance requirements:* For master's, minimum undergraduate GPA of 2.5, 2.75 for last 60 credits. Additional exam requirements/recommendations for international students: Required—TOEFL (minimum score 550 paper-based; 61 iBT). Electronic applications accepted.

Louisiana Tech University, Graduate School, College of Business, Ruston, LA 71272. Offers accounting (M Acc, DBA); computer information systems (DBA); finance (MBA,

DBA); information assurance (MBA); innovation (MBA); management (DBA); marketing (MBA, DBA). *Accreditation:* AACSB. *Program availability:* Part-time, evening/weekend, 100% online, blended/hybrid learning. *Degree requirements:* For doctorate, thesis/dissertation. *Entrance requirements:* For master's and doctorate, GMAT, transcript with bachelor's degree awarded. Additional exam requirements/recommendations for international students: Required—TOEFL (minimum score 550 paper-based; 80 iBT), IELTS (minimum score 6.5). Electronic applications accepted. *Faculty research:* Consumer environmental behavior; identifying and analyzing current issues and future concerns in real estate; information assurance and related areas in business for Northwest Louisiana and the United States (business continuity, disaster recovery, accounting controls, auditing, computer forensics, and security attribution); value creation driven by the consumer and employee interface within exchange environments.

Louisiana Tech University, Graduate School, College of Education, Ruston, LA 71272. Offers counseling and guidance (MA), including clinical mental health counseling, human services, orientation and mobility; counseling psychology (PhD); curriculum and instruction (M Ed); cyber education (Graduate Certificate); dynamics of domestic and family violence (Graduate Certificate); early childhood education - PreK-3 (MAT); educational leadership (M Ed, Ed D); elementary education and special education mild/moderate grades 1-5 (MAT); higher education administration (Graduate Certificate); industrial/organizational psychology (MA, PhD); kinesiology (MS); middle school education (MAT), including mathematics; orientation and mobility (Graduate Certificate); rehabilitation teaching for the blind (Graduate Certificate); secondary education (MAT), including agriculture, biology, business, chemistry, English; special education: visually impaired (MAT); teacher leader education (Graduate Certificate); visual impairments - blind education (Graduate Certificate). *Accreditation:* NCATE. *Program availability:* Part-time. *Degree requirements:* For master's, thesis; for doctorate, thesis/dissertation. *Entrance requirements:* For master's and doctorate, GRE General Test. Additional exam requirements/recommendations for international students: Required—TOEFL (minimum score 550 paper-based; 80 iBT), IELTS (minimum score 6.5). Electronic applications accepted. *Faculty research:* Blindness and the best methods for increasing independence for individuals who are blind or visually impaired; educating and investigating factors contributing to improvements in human performance across the lifespan and a reduction in injury rates during training.

Lourdes University, Graduate School, Sylvania, OH 43560-2898. Offers business (MBA); leadership (M Ed); nurse anesthesia (MSN); nurse educator (MSN); nurse leader (MSN); organizational leadership (MOL); reading (M Ed); teaching and curriculum (M Ed); theology (MA). *Accreditation:* AANA/CANAEP. *Program availability:* Evening/weekend. *Entrance requirements:* Additional exam requirements/recommendations for international students: Required—TOEFL.

Loyola Marymount University, College of Business Administration, Los Angeles, CA 90045-2659. Offers MBA, MS, MBA/JD. *Accreditation:* AACSB. *Program availability:* Part-time. *Faculty:* 33 full-time (7 women), 12 part-time/adjunct (2 women). *Students:* 111 full-time (50 women), 4 part-time (0 women); includes 50 minority (12 Black or African American, non-Hispanic/Latino; 1 American Indian or Alaska Native, non-Hispanic/Latino; 11 Asian, non-Hispanic/Latino; 23 Hispanic/Latino; 1 Native Hawaiian or other Pacific Islander, non-Hispanic/Latino; 2 Two or more races, non-Hispanic/Latino), 24 international. Average age 31. 185 applicants, 52% accepted, 50 enrolled. In 2018, 92 master's awarded. *Entrance requirements:* For master's, official transcripts, letters of recommendation. Additional exam requirements/recommendations for international students: Required—TOEFL, IELTS. Application fee: $50. Electronic applications accepted. *Financial support:* Research assistantships, career-related internships or fieldwork, institutionally sponsored loans, scholarships/grants, and unspecified assistantships available. Support available to part-time students. Financial award application deadline: 5/1; financial award applicants required to submit FAFSA. *Unit head:* Dr. Dayle Smith, Dean, College of Business Administration, 310-338-7504, E-mail: dayle.Smith@lmu.edu. *Application contact:* Ammar Dalal, Assistant Vice Provost for Graduate Enrollment, 310-338-2721, Fax: 310-338-6086, E-mail: graduateinfo@lmu.edu.
Website: http://cba.lmu.edu

Loyola University Chicago, Quinlan School of Business, Chicago, IL 60611. Offers MBA, MS, MSA, MSF, MSHR, MSSCM, Certificate. *Accreditation:* AACSB. *Program availability:* Part-time, evening/weekend. *Entrance requirements:* For master's, GMAT or GRE, official transcripts, two letters of recommendation, statement of purpose, resume. Additional exam requirements/recommendations for international students: Required—TOEFL (minimum score 90 iBT), IELTS (minimum score 6.5). Electronic applications accepted. Application fee is waived when completed online. *Expenses:* Contact institution. *Faculty research:* Social enterprise and responsibility, emerging markets, supply chain management, risk management.

Loyola University Maryland, Graduate Programs, Sellinger School of Business, Emerging Leaders MBA Program, Baltimore, MD 21210-2699. Offers MBA. *Program availability:* Part-time. *Entrance requirements:* For master's, GMAT, essay, 2 letters of recommendation, resume, transcripts. Additional exam requirements/recommendations for international students: Required—TOEFL (minimum score 550 paper-based, 80 iBT) or IELTS (minimum score 7). Electronic applications accepted. *Expenses:* Contact institution.

Loyola University Maryland, Graduate Programs, Sellinger School of Business, Professional MBA Program, Baltimore, MD 21210-2699. Offers finance (MBA); information systems (MBA); investments and applied portfolio management (MBA); management (MBA); marketing (MBA). *Accreditation:* AACSB. *Program availability:* Part-time, evening/weekend. *Entrance requirements:* For master's, GMAT, resume, essay, official transcripts, professional letter of recommendation. Additional exam requirements/recommendations for international students: Required—TOEFL (minimum score 550 paper-based, 80 iBT) or IELTS (minimum score 7). Electronic applications accepted. *Expenses:* Contact institution.

Loyola University New Orleans, Joseph A. Butt, S.J., College of Business, Program in Business Administration, New Orleans, LA 70118-6195. Offers organizational performance excellence (MBA); JD/MBA; MBA/MPS. *Accreditation:* AACSB. *Program availability:* Part-time, evening/weekend, online learning. *Faculty:* 14 full-time (6 women), 6 part-time/adjunct (1 woman). *Students:* 48 full-time (25 women), 48 part-time (33 women); includes 34 minority (20 Black or African American, non-Hispanic/Latino; 1 Asian, non-Hispanic/Latino; 11 Hispanic/Latino; 2 Two or more races, non-Hispanic/Latino), 6 international. Average age 34. 79 applicants, 92% accepted, 43 enrolled. In 2018, 22 master's awarded. *Degree requirements:* For master's, capstone project. *Entrance requirements:* For master's, GMAT or GRE, minimum GPA of 3.0, transcript, resume, 2 letters of recommendation, work experience in field, personal statement. Additional exam requirements/recommendations for international students: Required—TOEFL (minimum score 580 paper-based; 92 iBT). *Application deadline:* For fall admission, 6/15 priority date for domestic students, 5/15 priority date for international students; for spring admission, 11/15 priority date for domestic students, 10/15 priority date for international students. Applications are processed on a rolling basis. Application fee: $50. Electronic applications accepted. *Expenses:* $1,005 per credit hour tuition, $733 per semester full-time fees, $376.50 per semester part-time fees. *Financial support:* Research assistantships, scholarships/grants, tuition waivers (partial), and unspecified assistantships available. Financial award application deadline: 5/1; financial award applicants required to submit FAFSA. *Faculty research:* Ethics, international business, entrepreneurship, quality management, risk management. *Unit head:* Dr. J. Patrick O'Brien, Interim Dean, 504-864-7979, Fax: 504-864-7970, E-mail: mba@loyno.edu. *Application contact:* Ashley Francis, Director of Graduate Programs, 504-864-7979, Fax: 504-864-7970, E-mail: mba@loyno.edu.
Website: http://www.business.loyno.edu/mba/programs

Lynn University, College of Business and Management, Boca Raton, FL 33431-5598. Offers business administration (MBA). *Program availability:* Part-time, evening/weekend, 100% online, blended/hybrid learning. *Faculty:* 34 full-time (14 women), 22 part-time/adjunct (9 women). *Students:* 283 full-time (149 women), 211 part-time (101 women); includes 132 minority (61 Black or African American, non-Hispanic/Latino; 17 Asian, non-Hispanic/Latino; 45 Hispanic/Latino; 9 Two or more races, non-Hispanic/Latino), 136 international. Average age 30. 331 applicants, 83% accepted, 205 enrolled. In 2018, 259 master's awarded. *Degree requirements:* For master's, thesis, minimum GPA of 3.0, strategic management seminar, written presentation reflecting the integration and application of theory to practice. *Entrance requirements:* For master's, bachelor's degree from accrediated institution, minimum undergraduate GPA of 2.5, official undergraduate transcripts, resume, personal statement, letter of recommendation from academic or professional sources, writing sample demonstrating capacity to perform at graduate level. Additional exam requirements/recommendations for international students: Required—TOEFL (minimum score 550 paper-based; 80 iBT), IELTS (minimum score 6.5). *Application deadline:* For fall admission, 8/18 for domestic students, 8/4 for international students; for spring admission, 12/15 for domestic students, 12/1 for international students; for summer admission, 4/17 for domestic students, 4/3 for international students. Applications are processed on a rolling basis. Application fee: $45. Electronic applications accepted. *Expenses:* 740 per credit hour. *Financial support:* In 2018–19, 137 students received support. Career-related internships or fieldwork, Federal Work-Study, scholarships/grants, tuition waivers (full and partial), and unspecified assistantships available. Support available to part-time students. Financial award application deadline: 3/1; financial award applicants required to submit FAFSA. *Faculty research:* Knowledge economy, urban economy, U.S. manufacturing industries, leadership personality, stock market reactions to terrorism, personality psychology, industrial/organizational psychology. *Unit head:* Dr. RT Good, Dean of the College of Business and Management, 561-237-7458, E-mail: rgood@lynn.edu. *Application contact:* Steven Pruitt, Director of Graduate and Undergraduate Evening Admission, 561-237-7834, Fax: 561-237-7100, E-mail: spruitt@lynn.edu.
Website: http://www.lynn.edu/academics/colleges/business-and-management

Maastricht School of Management, Graduate Programs, Maastricht, Netherlands. Offers business administration (MBA, DBA, PhD); facility management (Exec MBA); management (M Sc); sustainability (Exec MBA).

Madonna University, School of Business, Livonia, MI 48150-1173. Offers business administration (MBA); international business (MSBA); leadership studies (MSBA); leadership studies in criminal justice (MSBA); quality and operations management (MSBA). *Program availability:* Part-time, evening/weekend, online learning. *Degree requirements:* For master's, thesis (for some programs), foreign language proficiency (international business). *Entrance requirements:* For master's, GMAT, GRE General Test, minimum GPA of 3.0. Electronic applications accepted. *Expenses: Tuition:* Full-time $15,030; part-time $835 per credit hour. Tuition and fees vary according to degree level and program. *Faculty research:* Management, women in management, future studies.

Maharishi University of Management, Graduate Studies, Program in Business Administration, Fairfield, IA 52557. Offers accounting (MBA); management (PhD); sustainability (MBA). *Program availability:* Evening/weekend, online learning. *Degree requirements:* For doctorate, thesis/dissertation. *Entrance requirements:* For master's, GMAT, minimum GPA of 3.0; for doctorate, minimum GPA of 3.0. Additional exam requirements/recommendations for international students: Required—TOEFL. *Expenses: Tuition:* Full-time $29,000; part-time $4800 per credit hour. *Required fees:* $530. *Faculty research:* Leadership, effects of the group dynamics of consciousness on the economy, innovation, employee development, cooperative strategy.

Malone University, Graduate Program in Business, Canton, OH 44709. Offers MBA. *Accreditation:* ACBSP. *Program availability:* Part-time, evening/weekend, online learning. *Entrance requirements:* For master's, minimum GPA of 3.0. Additional exam requirements/recommendations for international students: Required—TOEFL (minimum score 550 paper-based; 79 iBT). *Expenses:* Contact institution. *Faculty research:* Leadership, business ethics, sustainability, globalization, non-profit financial management.

Manhattan College, Graduate Programs, School of Business, Riverdale, NY 10471. Offers MBA. *Accreditation:* AACSB. *Program availability:* Part-time, 100% online, blended/hybrid learning. *Entrance requirements:* For master's, GMAT, minimum overall GPA of 3.0, official transcripts, current resume, 2 letters of recommendation. Additional exam requirements/recommendations for international students: Required—TOEFL, IELTS. Electronic applications accepted. *Faculty research:* Supply chain networks, industrial/organizational psychology, emerging economies, financial modeling, business analytics.

Marconi International University, Graduate Programs, Miami, FL 33132. Offers business administration (DBA); education leadership (Ed D); education leadership, management and emerging technologies (M Ed); international business administration (IMBA).

Marian University, School of Business and Public Safety, Fond du Lac, WI 54935-4699. Offers organizational leadership (MS). *Program availability:* Part-time, evening/weekend. *Degree requirements:* For master's, comprehensive group project. *Entrance requirements:* For master's, 3 years of managerial experience, minimum GPA of 2.75, letters of professional reference. Additional exam requirements/recommendations for international students: Required—TOEFL (minimum score 525 paper-based; 70 iBT). Electronic applications accepted. *Expenses:* Contact institution. *Faculty research:* Organizational values, statistical decision-making, learning organization, quality planning, customer research.

Marist College, Graduate Programs, School of Management, Business Administration Program, Poughkeepsie, NY 12601-1387. Offers business administration (MBA); executive leadership (Adv C). *Accreditation:* AACSB. *Program availability:* Part-time, evening/weekend. *Entrance requirements:* For master's, GMAT, resume, 2 letters of recommendation. Additional exam requirements/recommendations for international students: Required—TOEFL (minimum score 550 paper-based; 80 iBT); Recommended—IELTS (minimum score 6.5). Electronic applications accepted. *Faculty research:* International trade law, process management, AIDS and the medical provider, mid-Hudson region economics, time quality management and organizational behavior.

Marist College, Graduate Programs, School of Management, Online MBA Program, Poughkeepsie, NY 12601-1387. Offers MBA. *Program availability:* Online learning.

Marlboro College, Graduate and Professional Studies, Program in Business Administration, Marlboro, VT 05344. Offers mission-driven organizations (MBA); project

management (MBA); social innovation (MBA). *Program availability:* Part-time, evening/weekend, blended/hybrid learning. *Degree requirements:* For master's, 45 credits including a Master Workshop. *Entrance requirements:* For master's, letter of intent, essay, transcripts, 2 letters of recommendation. Electronic applications accepted. *Expenses:* Contact institution.

Marlboro College, Graduate and Professional Studies, Program in Management, Marlboro, VT 05344. Offers mission-driven organizations (MS); project management (MS); social innovation (MS). *Program availability:* Part-time, evening/weekend, blended/hybrid learning. *Degree requirements:* For master's, capstone project. *Entrance requirements:* For master's, statement of intent, 2 letters of recommendation. Additional exam requirements/recommendations for international students: Recommended—TOEFL (minimum score 577 paper-based; 90 iBT), IELTS (minimum score 7). Electronic applications accepted. *Expenses:* Contact institution.

Marquette University, Graduate School of Management, Executive MBA Program, Milwaukee, WI 53201-1881. Offers economics (MBA); finance (MBA); human resources (MBA); international business (MBA); management information systems (MBA); marketing (MBA); operations and supply chain management (MBA); sports business (MBA). *Accreditation:* AACSB. *Degree requirements:* For master's, international trip. *Entrance requirements:* For master's, GMAT or GRE, two letters of recommendation, official transcripts from current and previous colleges/universities. Additional exam requirements/recommendations for international students: Required—TOEFL (minimum score 550 paper-based; 88 iBT), IELTS (minimum score 6.5), PTE. Electronic applications accepted. *Expenses:* Contact institution. *Faculty research:* International trade and finance, customer relationship management, consumer satisfaction, customer service.

Marquette University, Graduate School of Management, Program in Business Administration, Milwaukee, WI 53201-1881. Offers business administration (MBA); economics (MBA); entrepreneurship (Certificate); finance (MBA); human resources (MBA); international business (MBA); management information systems (MBA); marketing (MBA); operations and supply chain management (MBA); sports business (MBA); JD/MBA; MBA/MA; MBA/MSN. *Accreditation:* AACSB. *Program availability:* Part-time, evening/weekend. *Degree requirements:* For Certificate, business plan. *Entrance requirements:* For master's, GMAT or GRE, letters of recommendation. Additional exam requirements/recommendations for international students: Required—TOEFL (minimum score 550 paper-based; 88 iBT), IELTS (minimum score 6.5), PTE. Electronic applications accepted. *Faculty research:* Ethics in the professions, services marketing, technology impact on decision-making, mentoring.

Marshall University, Academic Affairs Division, College of Business, Program in Business Administration, Huntington, WV 25755. Offers business administration (MBA); management foundations (Certificate). *Accreditation:* AACSB. *Program availability:* Part-time, evening/weekend. *Degree requirements:* For master's, comprehensive assessment. *Entrance requirements:* For master's, GMAT.

Maryland Institute College of Art, Graduate Studies, Design Leadership MBA/MA Program, Baltimore, MD 21201. Offers MBA/MA. Program offered in collaboration with The Johns Hopkins University. *Entrance requirements:* Additional exam requirements/recommendations for international students: Required—TOEFL (minimum score 100 iBT) or IELTS (minimum score 7). Electronic applications accepted. *Expenses:* Contact institution.

Maryland Institute College of Art, Graduate Studies, MPS Program in Business of Art and Design, Baltimore, MD 21201. Offers MPS. *Program availability:* Part-time. *Degree requirements:* For master's, business plan presentation. *Entrance requirements:* For master's, essay, resume. Additional exam requirements/recommendations for international students: Required—TOEFL (minimum score 550 paper-based; 80 iBT), IELTS (minimum score 6.5). Electronic applications accepted. *Expenses:* Contact institution.

Marymount California University, Program in Business Administration, Rancho Palos Verdes, CA 90275-6299. Offers MBA. *Degree requirements:* For master's, field project experience.

Marymount University, School of Business and Technology, Program in Business Administration, Arlington, VA 22207-4299. Offers business administration (MBA), including data analytics, leadership; business administration with health care management (MS/MBA); business administration with human resource management (MBA/MA); MBA/MA; MS/MBA. *Accreditation:* ACBSP. *Program availability:* Part-time, evening/weekend, 100% online. *Faculty:* 10 full-time (6 women), 1 (woman) part-time/adjunct. *Students:* 27 full-time (18 women), 59 part-time (36 women); includes 42 minority (18 Black or African American, non-Hispanic/Latino; 10 Asian, non-Hispanic/Latino; 10 Hispanic/Latino; 4 Two or more races, non-Hispanic/Latino), 14 international. Average age 30. 65 applicants, 97% accepted, 28 enrolled. In 2018, 47 master's awarded. *Degree requirements:* For master's, thesis or alternative. *Entrance requirements:* For master's, GMAT or GRE General Test or qualify for test waiver, resume. Additional exam requirements/recommendations for international students: Required—TOEFL (minimum score 600 paper-based; 96 iBT), IELTS (minimum score 6.5), PTE (minimum score 58). *Application deadline:* For fall admission, 7/16 priority date for domestic and international students; for spring admission, 11/16 priority date for domestic and international students; for summer admission, 4/16 priority date for domestic and international students. Applications are processed on a rolling basis. Application fee: $40. Electronic applications accepted. *Expenses:* $1,060 per credit. *Financial support:* In 2018–19, 7 students received support. Research assistantships, teaching assistantships, career-related internships or fieldwork, scholarships/grants, and unspecified assistantships available. Support available to part-time students. Financial award application deadline: 3/1; financial award applicants required to submit FAFSA. *Unit head:* Dr. Linda Christie, MBA Director, 703-284-5925, E-mail: linda.christie@marymount.edu. *Application contact:* Rebecca Esposito, Senior Associate Director, Graduate Admissions, 703-284-5901, Fax: 703-527-3815, E-mail: grad.admissions@marymount.edu.
Website: https://www.marymount.edu/Academics/School-of-Business-and-Technology/Graduate-Programs/Business-Administration

Marymount University, School of Business and Technology, Program in Leadership and Management, Arlington, VA 22207-4299. Offers association and nonprofit management (Certificate); leadership and management (MS); management studies (Certificate). *Program availability:* Part-time, evening/weekend. *Faculty:* 1 (woman) full-time. *Students:* 14 part-time (10 women); includes 4 minority (1 Black or African American, non-Hispanic/Latino; 3 Hispanic/Latino). Average age 41. 8 applicants, 88% accepted, 5 enrolled. In 2018, 5 master's, 1 other advanced degree awarded. *Degree requirements:* For master's, thesis or alternative. *Entrance requirements:* For master's, resume, interview, at least 3 years of managerial experience, essay on a topic provided by School of Business and Technology; for Certificate, resume, at least 3 years of managerial experience. Additional exam requirements/recommendations for international students: Required—TOEFL (minimum score 600 paper-based; 96 iBT), IELTS (minimum score 6.5), PTE (minimum score 58). *Application deadline:* For fall admission, 7/16 priority date for domestic and international students; for spring admission, 11/16 priority date for domestic and international students; for summer admission, 4/16 priority date for domestic and international students. Applications are processed on a rolling basis. Application fee: $40. Electronic applications accepted. *Expenses:* $1,060 per credit. *Financial support:* Research assistantships, teaching assistantships, career-related internships or fieldwork, scholarships/grants, and unspecified assistantships available. Support available to part-time students. Financial award application deadline: 3/1; financial award applicants required to submit FAFSA. *Unit head:* Dr. Lorri Cooper, Program Director, Leadership and Management, 703-284-5950, E-mail: lorri.cooper@marymount.edu. *Application contact:* Rebecca Esposito, Senior Associate Director, Graduate Admissions, 703-284-5901, Fax: 703-527-3815, E-mail: grad.admissions@marymount.edu.
Website: https://www.marymount.edu/Academics/School-of-Business-and-Technology/Graduate-Programs/Leadership-Management-(M-S-)

Maryville University of Saint Louis, The John E. Simon School of Business, St. Louis, MO 63141-7299. Offers accounting (MBA, MS, Certificate); business studies (Certificate); cybersecurity (MBA, MS, Certificate); financial services (MBA, Certificate); health administration (MBA); healthcare administration (Certificate); human resource management (MBA); human resources management (Certificate); information technology (MBA); information technology management (Certificate); management (MBA, Certificate); management and leadership (MA); marketing (MBA, Certificate); project management (MBA, Certificate); sport business management (MBA); supply chain management (Certificate); supply chain management/logistics (MBA). *Accreditation:* ACBSP. *Program availability:* Part-time, 100% online, blended/hybrid learning. *Faculty:* 5 full-time (1 woman), 77 part-time/adjunct (19 women). *Students:* 338 full-time (166 women), 739 part-time (356 women); includes 310 minority (161 Black or African American, non-Hispanic/Latino; 6 American Indian or Alaska Native, non-Hispanic/Latino; 59 Asian, non-Hispanic/Latino; 57 Hispanic/Latino; 27 Two or more races, non-Hispanic/Latino), 30 international. Average age 33. In 2018, 143 master's awarded. *Degree requirements:* For master's, capstone course (for MBA). *Entrance requirements:* Additional exam requirements/recommendations for international students: Required—TOEFL (minimum score 563 paper-based; 85 iBT). *Application deadline:* Applications are processed on a rolling basis. Electronic applications accepted. *Expenses:* Tuition varies by program. *Financial support:* Career-related internships or fieldwork, Federal Work-Study, tuition waivers (partial), and campus employment available. Financial award application deadline: 4/1; financial award applicants required to submit FAFSA. *Unit head:* Tammy Gocial, Interim Dean, 314-529-9401, Fax: 314-529-9975, E-mail: tgocial@maryville.edu. *Application contact:* Chris Gourdine, Assistant Dean Business Administration, 314-529-6861, Fax: 314-529-9975, E-mail: cgourdine@maryville.edu.
Website: http://www.maryville.edu/bu/business-administration-masters/

Marywood University, Academic Affairs, Munley College of Liberal Arts and Sciences, School of Business and Global Innovation, Scranton, PA 18509-1598. Offers finance/investment (MBA); general management (MBA); management information systems (MBA, MS). *Accreditation:* ACBSP. *Program availability:* Part-time, online learning. Electronic applications accepted. *Faculty research:* Problem formulation in ill-structured situations, corporate tax structures.

Massachusetts College of Liberal Arts, Graduate Programs, North Adams, MA 01247-4100. Offers business (MBA); educational administration (M Ed); educational leadership (CAGS); instruction and curriculum (M Ed); instructional technology (M Ed); physical education and health (M Ed); reading (M Ed); special education (M Ed). *Program availability:* Part-time, evening/weekend. *Degree requirements:* For master's, thesis. *Entrance requirements:* For master's, writing sample.

Massachusetts Institute of Technology, MIT Sloan School of Management, Cambridge, MA 02142. Offers M Fin, MBA, MS, SM, PhD. *Accreditation:* AACSB. *Degree requirements:* For master's, thesis (for some programs); for doctorate, thesis/dissertation, exams. Electronic applications accepted. *Expenses:* Contact institution. *Financial support:* Fellowships with tuition reimbursements, research assistantships with tuition reimbursements, teaching assistantships with tuition reimbursements, Federal Work-Study, institutionally sponsored loans, scholarships/grants, health care benefits, and unspecified assistantships available. Support available to part-time students. *Unit head:* David C. Schmittlein, Dean, 617-253-2804, Fax: 617-258-6617, E-mail: dschmitt@mit.edu. *Application contact:* Rod Garcia, Director of Admissions, 617-253-5434, Fax: 617-253-6405, E-mail: mbaadmissions@sloan.mit.edu.
Website: http://mitsloan.mit.edu/

McGill University, Faculty of Graduate and Postdoctoral Studies, Desautels Faculty of Management, Montréal, QC H3A 2T5, Canada. Offers administration (PhD); entrepreneurial studies (MBA); finance (MBA); general management (Post Master's Certificate); global manufacturing and supply chain management (MMM); information systems (MBA); international business (MBA); international practicing management (MM); management (MBA); management for development (MBA); marketing (MBA); operations management (MBA); public accountancy (Diploma); strategic management (MBA); MBA/LL B; MD/MBA. MMM offered jointly with Faculty of Engineering; PhD with Concordia University, HEC Montreal, Université de Montréal, Université du Québec à Montréal.

McKendree University, Graduate Programs, Master of Business Administration Program, Lebanon, IL 62254-1299. Offers business administration (MBA); human resource management (MBA); international business (MBA). *Program availability:* Part-time, evening/weekend, online learning. *Entrance requirements:* For master's, official transcripts from all institutions attended, essay, minimum GPA of 3.0, three references, resume. Additional exam requirements/recommendations for international students: Required—TOEFL. Electronic applications accepted.

McMaster University, School of Graduate Studies, DeGroote School of Business, Hamilton, ON L8S 4M2, Canada. Offers MBA, PhD. *Program availability:* Part-time. *Degree requirements:* For doctorate, comprehensive exam, thesis/dissertation. *Entrance requirements:* For master's, GMAT; for doctorate, GMAT or GRE, master's degree. Additional exam requirements/recommendations for international students: Required—TOEFL (minimum score 580 paper-based). *Faculty research:* Mergers, acquisitions, and restructuring; business investment; capital structure and dividend policy; employee pay/reward systems; pay and employment equity.

McNeese State University, Doré School of Graduate Studies, College of Business, Master of Business Administration Program, Lake Charles, LA 70609. Offers MBA. *Accreditation:* AACSB. *Program availability:* Evening/weekend. *Entrance requirements:* For master's, GMAT. *Faculty research:* Management development, integrating technology into the work force, union/management relations, economic development.

Medaille College, Program in Business Administration - Amherst, Amherst, NY 14221. Offers business administration (MBA); organizational leadership (MA). *Program availability:* Evening/weekend. *Degree requirements:* For master's, thesis or alternative. *Entrance requirements:* For master's, GMAT, minimum undergraduate GPA of 2.7, 3 years of work experience. Additional exam requirements/recommendations for international students: Required—TOEFL (minimum score 550 paper-based). Electronic applications accepted. *Expenses:* Contact institution.

Medaille College, Program in Business Administration - Rochester, Rochester, NY 14623. Offers business administration (MBA); organizational leadership (MA). *Program*

availability: Evening/weekend. *Degree requirements:* For master's, thesis or alternative. *Entrance requirements:* For master's, GMAT, 3 years of work experience, minimum undergraduate GPA of 2.7. Additional exam requirements/recommendations for international students: Required—TOEFL (minimum score 550 paper-based). *Expenses:* Contact institution.

Melbourne Business School, Graduate Programs, Carlton, Australia. Offers business administration (Exec MBA, MBA); management (PhD); management science (PhD); marketing (PhD); social impact (Graduate Certificate); JD/MBA.

Memorial University of Newfoundland, School of Graduate Studies, Faculty of Business Administration, St. John's, NL A1C 5S7, Canada. Offers MBA. *Program availability:* Part-time. *Degree requirements:* For master's, thesis (for some programs). *Entrance requirements:* For master's, GMAT. Electronic applications accepted. *Faculty research:* International business, marketing, organizational theory and behavior, management science and information systems, small business.

Mercer University, Graduate Studies, Cecil B. Day Campus, Eugene W. Stetson School of Business and Economics (Atlanta), Atlanta, GA 30341. Offers accounting (M Acc); innovation (PMBA), including entrepreneurship; international business (MBA); DPT/MBA; M Div/MBA; MBA/M Acc; Pharm D/MBA. *Accreditation:* AACSB. *Program availability:* Part-time, evening/weekend, 100% online, blended/hybrid learning. *Entrance requirements:* For master's, GMAT or GRE. Additional exam requirements/recommendations for international students: Required—TOEFL (minimum score 550 paper-based, 80 iBT) or IELTS. Electronic applications accepted. *Expenses:* Contact institution. *Faculty research:* Entrepreneurship, market studies, international business strategy, financial analysis.

Mercer University, Graduate Studies, Macon Campus, Eugene W. Stetson School of Business and Economics (Macon), Macon, GA 31207. Offers business and economics (MBA); health care (MBA); innovation (MBA). *Accreditation:* AACSB. *Program availability:* Part-time, evening/weekend. *Entrance requirements:* For master's, GMAT/GRE. Additional exam requirements/recommendations for international students: Required—TOEFL (minimum score 550 paper-based). Electronic applications accepted. *Expenses:* Contact institution. *Faculty research:* Federal Reserve system, management of nurses, sales promotion, systems for common stock selection, interest rate premiums.

Mercy College, School of Business, Program in Business Administration, Dobbs Ferry, NY 10522-1189. Offers MBA. *Program availability:* Part-time, evening/weekend, 100% online, blended/hybrid learning. *Students:* 275 full-time (162 women), 82 part-time (52 women); includes 254 minority (117 Black or African American, non-Hispanic/Latino; 2 American Indian or Alaska Native, non-Hispanic/Latino; 22 Asian, non-Hispanic/Latino; 107 Hispanic/Latino; 1 Native Hawaiian or other Pacific Islander, non-Hispanic/Latino; 5 Two or more races, non-Hispanic/Latino), 20 international. Average age 33. 253 applicants, 70% accepted, 122 enrolled. In 2018, 204 master's awarded. *Degree requirements:* For master's, thesis or alternative, Capstone project or thesis required. *Entrance requirements:* For master's, GMAT optional, transcript(s); resume; interview may be required for some applicants. Additional exam requirements/recommendations for international students: Required—TOEFL (minimum score 80 iBT), IELTS (minimum score 6.5). *Application deadline:* Applications are processed on a rolling basis. Application fee: $40. Electronic applications accepted. *Expenses:* Contact institution. *Financial support:* Career-related internships or fieldwork, Federal Work-Study, scholarships/grants, and unspecified assistantships available. Support available to part-time students. Financial award applicants required to submit FAFSA. *Unit head:* Dr. Lloyd Gibson, Dean, School of Business, 914-674-7159, Fax: 914-674-7493, E-mail: lgibson@mercy.edu. *Application contact:* Allison Gurdineer, Executive Director of Admissions, 877-637-2946, Fax: 914-674-7382, E-mail: admissions@mercy.edu.
Website: https://www.mercy.edu/degrees-programs/mba-business-administration

Meredith College, School of Business, Raleigh, NC 27607-5298. Offers MBA. *Accreditation:* AACSB. *Program availability:* Part-time, evening/weekend. *Students:* 1 (woman) full-time, 88 part-time (69 women); includes 37 minority (28 Black or African American, non-Hispanic/Latino; 2 Asian, non-Hispanic/Latino; 6 Hispanic/Latino; 1 Two or more races, non-Hispanic/Latino), 5 international. Average age 35. In 2018, 29 master's awarded. *Degree requirements:* For master's, thesis optional. *Entrance requirements:* For master's, GMAT, interview, minimum GPA of 2.5, letters of recommendation. Additional exam requirements/recommendations for international students: Required—TOEFL. *Application deadline:* For fall admission, 7/1 priority date for domestic and international students; for spring admission, 11/1 priority date for domestic and international students. Applications are processed on a rolling basis. Application fee: $50. Electronic applications accepted. *Expenses:* Contact institution. *Financial support:* Career-related internships or fieldwork, institutionally sponsored loans, scholarships/grants, and tuition waivers (partial) available. Support available to part-time students. Financial award application deadline: 2/15; financial award applicants required to submit FAFSA. *Unit head:* Kristie Ogilvie, Dean, 919-760-8432, Fax: 919-760-8470. *Application contact:* Kristie Ogilvie, Dean, 919-760-8432, Fax: 919-760-8470.
Website: https://www.meredith.edu/school-of-business

Merrimack College, Girard School of Business, North Andover, MA 01845-5800. Offers accounting (MS); business analytics (MS); management (MS). *Program availability:* Part-time, evening/weekend, 100% online. *Faculty:* 5 full-time (1 woman), 3 part-time/adjunct (1 woman). *Students:* 81 full-time (33 women), 32 part-time (17 women); includes 11 minority (6 Black or African American, non-Hispanic/Latino; 3 Asian, non-Hispanic/Latino; 2 Two or more races, non-Hispanic/Latino), 11 international. Average age 30. 200 applicants, 75% accepted, 79 enrolled. In 2018, 78 master's awarded. *Degree requirements:* For master's, comprehensive exam (for some programs), thesis optional, capstone. *Entrance requirements:* For master's, official college transcripts, resume, personal statement, 2 recommendations. Additional exam requirements/recommendations for international students: Required—TOEFL (minimum score 84 iBT), IELTS (minimum score 6.5), PTE (minimum score 56). *Application deadline:* For fall admission, 8/24 for domestic students, 7/30 for international students; for spring admission, 1/10 for domestic and international students; for summer admission, 5/10 for domestic students, 4/10 for international students. Applications are processed on a rolling basis. Application fee: $0. Electronic applications accepted. Application fee is waived when completed online. *Expenses:* $885 per credit. *Financial support:* Career-related internships or fieldwork, scholarships/grants, health care benefits, and unspecified assistantships available. Support available to part-time students. Financial award application deadline: 5/1; financial award applicants required to submit FAFSA. *Unit head:* Dr. Catherine Usoff, Dean, 978-837-5044, E-mail: usoffc@merrimack.edu. *Application contact:* Jennifer Greenwood, Graduate Admission Counselor, 978-837-3563, E-mail: graduate@merrimack.edu.
Website: http://www.merrimack.edu/academics/graduate/

Messiah College, Program in Business and Leadership, Mechanicsburg, PA 17055. Offers leadership (MBA, Certificate); management (Certificate); strategic leadership (MA). *Program availability:* Online learning.

Methodist University, School of Graduate Studies, Professional Master of Business Administration Program, Fayetteville, NC 28311. Offers MBA. *Accreditation:* ACBSP. *Program availability:* Part-time, evening/weekend. *Degree requirements:* For master's, thesis. *Entrance requirements:* For master's, GMAT or MAT. Additional exam requirements/recommendations for international students: Required—TOEFL (minimum score 500 paper-based; 60 iBT). Electronic applications accepted. Application fee is waived when completed online. *Faculty research:* Governmental accounting, public economics, systems modeling, organizational culture.

Metropolitan College of New York, Program in Business Administration, New York, NY 10006. Offers financial services (MBA); general management (MBA); healthcare systems and risk management (MBA); media management (MBA). *Accreditation:* ACBSP. *Program availability:* Evening/weekend. *Degree requirements:* For master's, thesis, 10-day study abroad. *Entrance requirements:* For master's, GMAT. Additional exam requirements/recommendations for international students: Required—TOEFL (minimum score 600 paper-based). Electronic applications accepted. *Expenses:* Contact institution.

Metropolitan State University, College of Management, St. Paul, MN 55106-5000. Offers business administration (MBA, DBA); business analytics (Graduate Certificate); database administration (Graduate Certificate); global supply chain management (Graduate Certificate); information assurance security (Graduate Certificate); management information systems (MMIS); MIS generalist (Graduate Certificate); MIS systems analysis and design (Graduate Certificate); project management (Graduate Certificate). *Program availability:* Part-time, evening/weekend. *Degree requirements:* For master's, thesis optional, computer language (MMIS). *Entrance requirements:* For master's, GMAT (for MBA), resume. Additional exam requirements/recommendations for international students: Required—TOEFL (minimum score 550 paper-based). Electronic applications accepted. *Faculty research:* Yugoslav economic system, workers' cooperatives, participative management and job enrichment, global business systems.

Miami University, Farmer School of Business, Oxford, OH 45056. Offers M Acc, MA, MBA. *Accreditation:* AACSB. *Faculty:* 108 full-time (32 women). *Students:* 30 full-time (11 women), 107 part-time (27 women); includes 22 minority (4 Black or African American, non-Hispanic/Latino; 7 Asian, non-Hispanic/Latino; 6 Hispanic/Latino; 5 Two or more races, non-Hispanic/Latino), 9 international. Average age 32. In 2018, 131 master's awarded. *Unit head:* Dr. Marc Rubin, Dean/Chair in Business Leadership, 513-529-3381, E-mail: deanofbusiness@miamioh.edu. *Application contact:* Admission Coordinator, 513-529-3734, E-mail: applygrad@miamioh.edu.
Website: http://www.fsb.miamioh.edu/

Michigan State University, The Graduate School, Eli Broad College of Business, Department of Management, East Lansing, MI 48224. Offers management (PhD); management, strategy, and leadership (MS). *Program availability:* Part-time, online learning. *Degree requirements:* For doctorate, comprehensive exam, thesis/dissertation. *Entrance requirements:* For master's, full-time managerial experience in a supervisory role; for doctorate, GMAT or GRE, letters of recommendation, experience in teaching and conducting research, work experience in business contexts, personal essay. Additional exam requirements/recommendations for international students: Required—TOEFL (minimum score 600 paper-based). Electronic applications accepted.

Michigan State University, The Graduate School, Eli Broad College of Business, Program in Business Administration, East Lansing, MI 48224. Offers finance (MBA); human resource management (MBA); integrative management (MBA); marketing (MBA); supply chain management (MBA). MBA in integrative management is through Weekend MBA Program; other 4 concentrations are through Full-Time MBA Program. *Program availability:* Evening/weekend. *Degree requirements:* For master's, enrichment experience. *Entrance requirements:* For master's, GMAT or GRE, 4-year bachelor's degree; resume; work experience (minimum of 5 years for Weekend MBA); 2-3 personal essays; 2 letters of recommendation; personal interview. Additional exam requirements/recommendations for international students: Required—PTE (minimum score 70), TOEFL (minimum score 100 iBT) or IELTS (minimum score 7) for full-time MBA applicants. Electronic applications accepted. *Expenses:* Contact institution.

Michigan Technological University, Graduate School, School of Business and Economics, Houghton, MI 49931. Offers applied natural resource economics (MS); business administration (MBA). *Accreditation:* AACSB. *Program availability:* Part-time, evening/weekend. *Faculty:* 24 full-time (9 women), 1 part-time/adjunct. *Students:* 37 full-time (17 women), 28 part-time (16 women); includes 3 minority (1 Hispanic/Latino; 2 Two or more races, non-Hispanic/Latino), 17 international. Average age 28. 166 applicants, 25% accepted, 29 enrolled. In 2018, 26 master's awarded. *Degree requirements:* For master's, thesis (for some programs). *Entrance requirements:* For master's, GMAT/GRE (recommended minimum score in the 55th percentile), statement of purpose, personal statement, official transcripts, 2 letters of recommendation, resume/curriculum vitae. Additional exam requirements/recommendations for international students: Required—TOEFL (recommended minimum score 95 iBT) or IELTS (minimum score 7). *Application deadline:* For fall admission, 7/1 for domestic and international students; for spring admission, 12/1 for domestic and international students. Applications are processed on a rolling basis. Electronic applications accepted. *Expenses: Tuition, area resident:* Full-time $18,126; part-time $1007 per credit. Tuition, state resident: full-time $18,126; part-time $1007 per credit. Tuition, nonresident: full-time $18,126; part-time $1007 per credit. *International tuition:* $18,126 full-time. *Required fees:* $248; $124 per semester. Tuition and fees vary according to course load and program. *Financial support:* In 2018–19, 25 students received support. Health care benefits and unspecified assistantships available. Financial award application deadline: 4/1; financial award applicants required to submit FAFSA. *Faculty research:* Natural resource and mineral economics, entrepreneurship, management of technology and innovation, engineering management, management information systems. *Total annual research expenditures:* $5,834. *Unit head:* Dr. Dean Johnson, Dean, 906-487-2668, Fax: 906-487-1863, E-mail: dean@mtu.edu. *Application contact:* Carol T. Wingerson, Administrative Aide, 906-487-2328, Fax: 906-487-2284, E-mail: gradadms@mtu.edu.
Website: http://www.mtu.edu/business/

Mid-America Christian University, Program in Business Administration, Oklahoma City, OK 73170-4504. Offers MBA. *Entrance requirements:* For master's, bachelor's degree from regionally-accredited college or university, minimum overall cumulative GPA of 2.75 on undergraduate course work. Additional exam requirements/recommendations for international students: Required—TOEFL (minimum score 550 paper-based).

MidAmerica Nazarene University, School of Business, Olathe, KS 66062-1899. Offers management (MBA, MSM). *Program availability:* Part-time, evening/weekend, 100% online, blended/hybrid learning. Terminal master's awarded for partial completion of doctoral program. *Entrance requirements:* For master's, official transcript for bachelor's degree from regionally-accredited college or university; minimum GPA of 3.0 in last 60 hours of undergraduate coursework; completion of college algebra, statistics, or other higher level math with minimum grade of B-. Additional exam requirements/recommendations for international students: Required—TOEFL (minimum score 81 iBT), IELTS (minimum score 6). Electronic applications accepted. *Expenses:* Contact institution. *Faculty research:* Project management, global business, entrepreneurship, experience learning.

Middle Tennessee State University, College of Graduate Studies, Jennings A. Jones College of Business, Department of Management and Marketing, Murfreesboro, TN 37132. Offers business administration (MBA); management (MS). *Accreditation:* AACSB. *Program availability:* Part-time, evening/weekend, online learning. *Degree requirements:* For master's, comprehensive exam. *Entrance requirements:* For master's, GMAT (minimum score of 400). Additional exam requirements/recommendations for international students: Required—TOEFL (minimum score 525 paper-based; 71 iBT) or IELTS (minimum score 6). Electronic applications accepted.

Midway University, Graduate Programs, Midway, KY 40347-1120. Offers education (MAT); leadership (MBA). *Degree requirements:* For master's, capstone course. *Entrance requirements:* For master's, GMAT (for MBA); GRE or PRAXIS I (for MAT), bachelor's degree; interview; minimum GPA of 3.0 (for MBA), 2.75 (for MAT); 3 years of professional work experience (for MBA). Additional exam requirements/recommendations for international students: Required—TOEFL (minimum score 550 paper-based; 80 iBT).

Midwestern State University, Billie Doris McAda Graduate School, Dillard College of Business Administration, Wichita Falls, TX 76308. Offers MBA. *Accreditation:* AACSB. *Program availability:* Part-time, evening/weekend. *Degree requirements:* For master's, comprehensive exam, thesis optional. *Entrance requirements:* For master's, GMAT. Additional exam requirements/recommendations for international students: Required—TOEFL (minimum score 550 paper-based). Electronic applications accepted. *Faculty research:* Citizenship behavior, software solutions, mediations, sales force training, stock trading volume.

Millennia Atlantic University, Graduate Programs, Doral, FL 33178. Offers accounting (MBA); business administration (MBA); health information management (MS); human resource management (MA). *Program availability:* Online learning.

Milligan College, Area of Business Administration, Milligan College, TN 37682. Offers health sector management (MBA, Graduate Certificate); leadership (MBA, Graduate Certificate); operations management (MBA, Graduate Certificate). *Program availability:* Blended/hybrid learning. *Faculty:* 3 full-time (0 women), 5 part-time/adjunct (1 woman). *Students:* 50 full-time (17 women), 1 part-time (0 women); includes 3 minority (1 Black or African American, non-Hispanic/Latino; 1 Asian, non-Hispanic/Latino; 1 Two or more races, non-Hispanic/Latino), 2 international. Average age 36. 42 applicants, 93% accepted, 35 enrolled. In 2018, 29 master's awarded. *Degree requirements:* For master's, thesis or alternative. *Entrance requirements:* For master's, GMAT if undergraduate GPA less than 3.0, undergraduate degree and supporting transcripts, relevant full-time work experience, essay/personal statement, professional recommendations. Additional exam requirements/recommendations for international students: Required—TOEFL (minimum score 550 paper-based, 79 iBT) or IELTS (6.5). *Application deadline:* For fall admission, 8/1 for domestic students, 6/1 for international students; for spring admission, 1/15 for domestic students, 12/1 for international students. Applications are processed on a rolling basis. Application fee: $30. Electronic applications accepted. *Expenses:* Contact institution. *Financial support:* Scholarships/grants available. Financial award application deadline: 12/1; financial award applicants required to submit FAFSA. *Faculty research:* International microfinance; economic development in Appalachia; job satisfaction; business ethics; internal migration. *Unit head:* Dr. David Campbell, Area Chair of Business, 423-461-8674, Fax: 423-461-8677, E-mail: dacampbell@milligan.edu. *Application contact:* Rebecca Banton, Graduate Admissions Recruiter, Business Area, 423-461-8662, Fax: 423-461-8789, E-mail: rbbanton@milligan.edu.
Website: http://www.milligan.edu/GPS

Millikin University, Tabor School of Business, Decatur, IL 62522-2084. Offers MBA. *Accreditation:* ACBSP. *Program availability:* Evening/weekend. *Faculty:* 6 full-time (2 women), 7 part-time/adjunct (1 woman). *Students:* 33 full-time (14 women), 4 part-time (1 woman); includes 10 minority (7 Black or African American, non-Hispanic/Latino; 1 Hispanic/Latino; 2 Two or more races, non-Hispanic/Latino), 1 international. Average age 29. 69 applicants, 65% accepted, 32 enrolled. In 2018, 25 master's awarded. *Degree requirements:* For master's, comprehensive exam. *Entrance requirements:* For master's, GMAT or GRE, resume, 3 reference letters, interview, statement of purpose, transcripts. Additional exam requirements/recommendations for international students: Required—TOEFL (minimum score 550 paper-based; 79 iBT), IELTS (minimum score 6.5). *Application deadline:* For fall admission, 6/1 priority date for domestic students, 5/1 priority date for international students; for spring admission, 11/1 priority date for domestic students, 8/1 priority date for international students. Applications are processed on a rolling basis. Application fee: $0. Electronic applications accepted. *Expenses:* Both the Executive and Fast-Track formats include 40 credit hours at $861 per credit hour. *Financial support:* In 2018–19, 19 students received support, including 1 research assistantship with partial tuition reimbursement available (averaging $6,000 per year), 3 teaching assistantships with partial tuition reimbursements available (averaging $6,000 per year); tuition waivers (full) also available. Financial award applicants required to submit FAFSA. *Faculty research:* E-commerce, international marketing, pedagogy, total quality management, auditing. *Unit head:* Dr. Najiba Benabess, Dean, 217-420-6762, E-mail: nbenabess@millikin.edu. *Application contact:* Marianne Taylor, Director, Graduate Admission, 217-420-6771, Fax: 217-424-6286, E-mail: mgtaylor@millikin.edu.
Website: https://millikin.edu/mba

Millsaps College, Else School of Management, Jackson, MS 39210. Offers accounting (M Acc); business administration (MBA). *Accreditation:* AACSB. *Program availability:* Part-time. *Entrance requirements:* For master's, GMAT. Additional exam requirements/recommendations for international students: Required—TOEFL. Electronic applications accepted. *Faculty research:* Ethics, audit independence, satisfaction with assurance services, political business cycles, economic development, commercialization of new products.

Mills College, Graduate Studies, Joint MBA/MPP Program, Oakland, CA 94613-1000. Offers MBA/MPP. *Entrance requirements:* Additional exam requirements/recommendations for international students: Required—TOEFL (minimum score 550 paper-based; 80 iBT) or IELTS (minimum score 6). Electronic applications accepted. *Expenses:* Contact institution. *Faculty research:* Diversity and inclusion, applied econometrics, non-profit management, business communication and effective public speaking, social media, Internet marketing, organizational and cultural chance, economics of the family, urbanization and land conservation, gender and science, comparative race and ethnic relations.

Mills College, Graduate Studies, Lorry I. Lokey Graduate School of Business, Oakland, CA 94613-1000. Offers applied economics (MA); management (MBA, MM). *Program availability:* Part-time. *Entrance requirements:* For master's, GRE, SAT, or ACT, 3 letters of recommendation, 2 transcripts. Additional exam requirements/recommendations for international students: Required—TOEFL (minimum score 550 paper-based; 80 iBT) or IELTS (minimum score 6). *Expenses:* Contact institution. *Faculty research:* Diversity and inclusion, applied econometrics, non-profit management, business communication and effective public speaking, social media and Internet marketing.

Milwaukee School of Engineering, Program in Business Administration, Milwaukee, WI 53202-3109. Offers MBA. *Program availability:* Part-time, evening/weekend, 100% online, blended/hybrid learning. *Degree requirements:* For master's, thesis or alternative. *Entrance requirements:* For master's, GRE General Test or GMAT if undergraduate GPA less than 2.8, bachelor's degree from accredited university; 2 letters of recommendation; work experience (strongly recommended). Additional exam requirements/recommendations for international students: Required—TOEFL (minimum score 90 iBT), IELTS (minimum score 7). Electronic applications accepted.

Minnesota State University Mankato, College of Graduate Studies and Research, College of Business, Mankato, MN 56001. Offers accounting (MSA); business (MBA). *Accreditation:* AACSB. *Entrance requirements:* For master's, GMAT, 2 letters of reference, resume. Additional exam requirements/recommendations for international students: Required—TOEFL. Electronic applications accepted.

Minnesota State University Moorhead, Graduate and Extended Learning, College of Business and Innovation, Moorhead, MN 56563. Offers accounting and finance (MS); business administration (MBA). *Accreditation:* AACSB. *Program availability:* Part-time, evening/weekend, 100% online, blended/hybrid learning. *Faculty:* 13. *Students:* 19 full-time (8 women), 32 part-time (15 women); includes 1 minority (Asian, non-Hispanic/Latino), 8 international. Average age 28. 39 applicants, 44% accepted. In 2018, 26 master's awarded. *Degree requirements:* For master's, comprehensive exam (for some programs), thesis, final oral defense. *Entrance requirements:* For master's, GMAT, minimum GPA of 3.0. Additional exam requirements/recommendations for international students: Required—TOEFL (minimum score 550 paper-based); Recommended—IELTS (minimum score 6.5). *Application deadline:* For fall admission, 4/15 for domestic students; for spring admission, 11/15 for domestic students; for summer admission, 4/15 for domestic students. Applications are processed on a rolling basis. Application fee: $35. Electronic applications accepted. Tuition and fees vary according to course load, degree level, program and reciprocity agreements. *Financial support:* Federal Work-Study and unspecified assistantships available. Financial award application deadline: 10/1; financial award applicants required to submit FAFSA. *Faculty research:* Union decertification, small business development, business innovation, pedagogy, curriculum design. *Unit head:* Joshua Behl, Interim Dean, 218-477-2667, E-mail: joshua.behl@mnstate.edu. *Application contact:* Karla Wenger, Office Manager, 218-477-2344, E-mail: wengerk@mnstate.edu.
Website: http://www.mnstate.edu/cbi/

Minot State University, Graduate School, Program in Management, Minot, ND 58707-0002. Offers MSM. *Program availability:* Part-time. *Degree requirements:* For master's, comprehensive exam (for some programs), thesis optional. *Entrance requirements:* For master's, GRE, minimum GPA of 2.75. Additional exam requirements/recommendations for international students: Required—TOEFL (minimum score 79 iBT), IELTS (minimum score 6).

Misericordia University, College of Business, Master of Business Administration Program, Dallas, PA 18612-1098. Offers accounting (MBA); healthcare management (MBA); human resource management (MBA); management (MBA); sport management (MBA). *Program availability:* Part-time, evening/weekend, online learning. *Entrance requirements:* For master's, GMAT, MAT, GRE (50th percentile or higher), or minimum undergraduate GPA of 3.0, interview. Additional exam requirements/recommendations for international students: Required—TOEFL. Electronic applications accepted. Application fee is waived when completed online. *Expenses:* Contact institution.

Misericordia University, College of Business, Program in Organizational Management, Dallas, PA 18612-1098. Offers healthcare management (MS); human resource management (MS); management (MS). *Program availability:* Part-time, evening/weekend, online learning. *Entrance requirements:* For master's, GRE General Test, MAT (35th percentile or higher), or minimum undergraduate GPA of 3.0. Additional exam requirements/recommendations for international students: Required—TOEFL. Electronic applications accepted. Application fee is waived when completed online. *Expenses:* Contact institution.

Mississippi College, Graduate School, School of Business, Clinton, MS 39058. Offers accounting (Certificate); business administration (MBA), including accounting; business education (M Ed); finance (MBA, Certificate); JD/MBA. *Accreditation:* ACBSP. *Program availability:* Part-time, evening/weekend. *Degree requirements:* For master's, comprehensive exam, thesis optional. *Entrance requirements:* For master's, GMAT, minimum GPA of 2.5, 24 hours of undergraduate course work in business. Additional exam requirements/recommendations for international students: Recommended—TOEFL, IELTS. Electronic applications accepted.

Mississippi State University, College of Business, Department of Management and Information Systems, Mississippi State, MS 39762. Offers business administration (MBA); information systems (MSIS, PhD); management (PhD); project management (MBA). *Program availability:* Part-time. *Faculty:* 16 full-time (3 women), 1 part-time/adjunct (0 women). *Students:* 62 full-time (21 women), 189 part-time (50 women); includes 25 minority (13 Black or African American, non-Hispanic/Latino; 3 Asian, non-Hispanic/Latino; 9 Hispanic/Latino), 18 international. Average age 30. 136 applicants, 59% accepted, 46 enrolled. In 2018, 105 master's, 2 doctorates awarded. *Degree requirements:* For master's, comprehensive exam; for doctorate, comprehensive exam, thesis/dissertation. *Entrance requirements:* For master's, GMAT, minimum GPA of 3.0 in last 60 hours of undergraduate course work; for doctorate, GMAT (minimum score of 550), minimum GPA of 3.25 on all graduate work; BS with minimum GPA of 3.0 cumulative and last 60 hours. Additional exam requirements/recommendations for international students: Required—TOEFL (minimum score 575 paper-based; 84 iBT); Recommended—IELTS (minimum score 7). *Application deadline:* For fall admission, 7/1 for domestic students, 5/1 for international students; for spring admission, 11/1 for domestic students, 9/1 for international students. Applications are processed on a rolling basis. Application fee: $60 ($80 for international students). Electronic applications accepted. *Expenses:* Tuition, state resident: full-time $8450; part-time $360.59 per credit hour. Tuition, nonresident: full-time $23,140; part-time $969.09 per credit hour. *Required fees:* $110. One-time fee: $55 full-time. Part-time tuition and fees vary according to course load, degree level, campus/location and reciprocity agreements. *Financial support:* Career-related internships or fieldwork, Federal Work-Study, institutionally sponsored loans, scholarships/grants, and unspecified assistantships available. Financial award applicants required to submit FAFSA. *Faculty research:* Electronic commerce, management of information technology. Total annual research expenditures: $1.4 million. *Unit head:* Dr. James J. Chrisman, Professor and Head, 662-325-1991, Fax: 662-325-8651, E-mail: jchrisman@business.msstate.edu. *Application contact:* Robbie Salters, Admissions and Enrollment Assistant, 662-325-7400, E-mail: rsalters@grad.msstate.edu.
Website: http://www.business.msstate.edu/programs/mis/index.php

Missouri Baptist University, Graduate Programs, St. Louis, MO 63141-8660. Offers business administration (MBA); Christian ministries (MACM); counseling (MAC); education (MSE); education administration (MEA); educational leadership (MSE, Ed S); teaching (MAT).

Missouri Southern State University, Program in Business Administration, Joplin, MO 64801-1595. Offers MBA. Program offered jointly with Northwest Missouri State University. *Program availability:* Online learning. *Degree requirements:* For master's, capstone seminar.

Business Administration and Management—General

Missouri State University, Graduate College, College of Business, Business Administration Program, Springfield, MO 65897. Offers MBA. *Accreditation:* AACSB. *Program availability:* Part-time, evening/weekend. *Faculty:* 17 full-time (5 women). *Students:* 246 full-time (129 women), 342 part-time (128 women); includes 42 minority (9 Black or African American, non-Hispanic/Latino; 2 American Indian or Alaska Native, non-Hispanic/Latino; 9 Asian, non-Hispanic/Latino; 13 Hispanic/Latino; 1 Native Hawaiian or other Pacific Islander, non-Hispanic/Latino; 8 Two or more races, non-Hispanic/Latino), 170 international. Average age 23. 292 applicants, 63% accepted. In 2018, 262 master's awarded. *Degree requirements:* For master's, thesis optional. *Entrance requirements:* For master's, GMAT or GRE, minimum GPA of 2.75. Additional exam requirements/recommendations for international students: Required—TOEFL (minimum score 550 paper-based; 79 iBT), IELTS (minimum score 6). *Application deadline:* For fall admission, 7/20 priority date for domestic students, 5/1 for international students; for spring admission, 12/20 priority date for domestic students, 9/1 for international students; for summer admission, 5/20 priority date for domestic students. Applications are processed on a rolling basis. Application fee: $55 ($60 for international students). Electronic applications accepted. Tuition and fees vary according to class time, course level, course load, degree level, campus/location, program and student level. *Financial support:* Federal Work-Study, institutionally sponsored loans, scholarships/grants, and unspecified assistantships available. Support available to part-time students. Financial award application deadline: 1/31; financial award applicants required to submit FAFSA. *Unit head:* Dr. Elizabeth Rozell, MBA Program Director, 417-836-6040, Fax: 417-836-4407, E-mail: mbaprogram@missouristate.edu. *Application contact:* Lakan Drinker, Director, Graduate Enrollment Management, 417-836-5330, Fax: 417-836-6200, E-mail: lakandrinker@missouristate.edu.
Website: https://mba.missouristate.edu

Missouri University of Science and Technology, Department of Business and Information Technology, Rolla, MO 65401. Offers business administration (MBA); information science and technology (MS). *Degree requirements:* For master's, thesis or alternative. *Entrance requirements:* Additional exam requirements/recommendations for international students: Required—TOEFL (minimum score 600 paper-based); Recommended—IELTS. Electronic applications accepted. *Expenses:* Tuition, state resident: full-time $7545.60; part-time $419.20 per credit hour. Tuition, nonresident: full-time $22,169; part-time $1231.60 per credit hour. *International tuition:* $23,518.80 full-time. *Required fees:* $4523.05. Full-time tuition and fees vary according to course load, campus/location, program and reciprocity agreements.

Missouri Western State University, Program in Applied Science, St. Joseph, MO 64507-2294. Offers chemistry (MAS); engineering technology management (MAS); industrial life science (MAS); sport and fitness management (MAS). *Accreditation:* AACSB. *Program availability:* Part-time. *Students:* 35 full-time (11 women), 14 part-time (5 women); includes 4 minority (1 Black or African American, non-Hispanic/Latino; 1 Asian, non-Hispanic/Latino; 1 Hispanic/Latino; 1 Two or more races, non-Hispanic/Latino), 10 international. Average age 25. 31 applicants, 94% accepted, 20 enrolled. In 2018, 18 master's awarded. *Entrance requirements:* Additional exam requirements/recommendations for international students: Recommended—TOEFL (minimum score 79 iBT), IELTS (minimum score 6). *Application deadline:* For fall admission, 7/15 for domestic and international students; for spring admission, 11/1 for domestic and international students; for summer admission, 4/29 for domestic and international students. Applications are processed on a rolling basis. Application fee: $45 ($50 for international students). Electronic applications accepted. *Expenses: Tuition, area resident:* Part-time $359.39 per credit hour. Tuition, state resident: part-time $359.39 per credit hour. Tuition, nonresident: part-time $643.39 per credit hour. Tuition and fees vary according to program. *Financial support:* Scholarships/grants and unspecified assistantships available. Support available to part-time students. *Unit head:* Dr. Susan Bashinski, Dean of the Graduate School, 816-271-4394, Fax: 816-271-4525, E-mail: graduate@missouriwestern.edu. *Application contact:* Dr. Susan Bashinski, Dean of the Graduate School, 816-271-4394, Fax: 816-271-4525, E-mail: graduate@missouriwestern.edu.

Missouri Western State University, Program in Business Administration, St. Joseph, MO 64507-2294. Offers animal and life sciences (MBA); enterprise resource planning (MBA); forensic accounting (MBA); general business (MBA). *Program availability:* Part-time, 100% online. *Students:* 25 full-time (12 women), 41 part-time (17 women); includes 8 minority (3 Black or African American, non-Hispanic/Latino; 2 American Indian or Alaska Native, non-Hispanic/Latino; 2 Asian, non-Hispanic/Latino; 1 Two or more races, non-Hispanic/Latino), 1 international. Average age 32. 45 applicants, 93% accepted, 25 enrolled. In 2018, 19 master's awarded. *Entrance requirements:* Additional exam requirements/recommendations for international students: Recommended—TOEFL (minimum score 79 iBT), IELTS (minimum score 6). *Application deadline:* For fall admission, 7/15 for domestic and international students; for spring admission, 11/1 for domestic and international students; for summer admission, 4/29 for domestic and international students. Applications are processed on a rolling basis. Application fee: $45 ($50 for international students). Electronic applications accepted. *Expenses: Tuition, area resident:* Part-time $359.39 per credit hour. Tuition, state resident: part-time $359.39 per credit hour. Tuition, nonresident: part-time $643.39 per credit hour. Tuition and fees vary according to program. *Financial support:* Scholarships/grants and unspecified assistantships available. Support available to part-time students. *Unit head:* Dr. Logan Jones, Dean of Craig School of Business, 816-271-4338, E-mail: jones@missouriwestern.edu. *Application contact:* Dr. Susan Bashinski, Dean of the Graduate School, 816-271-4394, Fax: 816-271-4525, E-mail: graduate@missouriwestern.edu.
Website: https://www.missouriwestern.edu/business/mba/

Molloy College, Graduate Business Program, Rockville Centre, NY 11571-5002. Offers accounting (MBA); finance (MBA, Post-Master's Certificate, Postbaccalaureate Certificate); healthcare (MBA, Post-Master's Certificate, Postbaccalaureate Certificate); management (MBA); marketing (MBA, Post-Master's Certificate, Postbaccalaureate Certificate); personal financial planning (MBA). *Program availability:* Part-time, evening/weekend. *Faculty:* 9 full-time (2 women), 20 part-time/adjunct (8 women). *Students:* 75 full-time (45 women), 164 part-time (88 women); includes 100 minority (45 Black or African American, non-Hispanic/Latino; 21 Asian, non-Hispanic/Latino; 30 Hispanic/Latino; 1 Native Hawaiian or other Pacific Islander, non-Hispanic/Latino; 3 Two or more races, non-Hispanic/Latino), 3 international. Average age 40. 97 applicants, 78% accepted, 65 enrolled. In 2018, 91 master's, 1 other advanced degree awarded. *Entrance requirements:* Additional exam requirements/recommendations for international students: Required—TOEFL (minimum score 550 paper-based; 79 iBT). *Application deadline:* Applications are processed on a rolling basis. Application fee: $60. Electronic applications accepted. *Expenses: Tuition:* Full-time $20,790; part-time $1155 per credit. *Required fees:* $1060; $900. Tuition and fees vary according to course load and degree level. *Financial support:* Application deadline: 3/1; applicants required to submit FAFSA. *Faculty research:* Graduate education - pedagogy and the capstone experience; Freedom of Speech in the workplace; employer liability for sexual harassment in the workplace; educational economics and industrial organization; corporate governance and distressed debt analysis; social network analysis; market segmentation. *Unit head:* Dr. Maureen Mackenzie, Dean, Division of Business/Director of Graduate Programs, 516-323-3080, E-mail: mmackenzie@molloy.edu. *Application contact:* Faye Hood, Assistant Director for Admissions, 516-323-4009, E-mail: fhood@molloy.edu.
Website: http://www.molloy.edu/academics/graduate-programs/graduate-business

Monmouth University, Graduate Studies, Leon Hess Business School, West Long Branch, NJ 07764-1898. Offers accounting (MBA, Certificate); business administration (MBA); finance (MBA); management (MBA); marketing (MBA); real estate (MBA). *Accreditation:* AACSB. *Program availability:* Part-time, evening/weekend. *Faculty:* 22 full-time (5 women), 8 part-time/adjunct (1 woman). *Students:* 91 full-time (47 women), 87 part-time (35 women); includes 17 minority (2 Black or African American, non-Hispanic/Latino; 6 Asian, non-Hispanic/Latino; 7 Hispanic/Latino; 2 Two or more races, non-Hispanic/Latino), 12 international. Average age 29. In 2018, 79 master's, 1 other advanced degree awarded. *Degree requirements:* For master's, capstone course. *Entrance requirements:* For master's, GMAT or GRE, current resume; essay (500 words or less). Additional exam requirements/recommendations for international students: Required—TOEFL (minimum score 550 paper-based; 79 iBT), IELTS (minimum score 6), Michigan English Language Assessment Battery (minimum score 77) or Certificate of Advanced English (minimum score 160). *Application deadline:* For fall admission, 7/15 priority date for domestic students, 6/1 for international students; for spring admission, 12/1 priority date for domestic students, 11/1 for international students; for summer admission, 5/1 for domestic students. Applications are processed on a rolling basis. Application fee: $50. Electronic applications accepted. *Expenses: Tuition:* Part-time $1233 per credit. *Required fees:* $178 per term. *Financial support:* In 2018–19, 131 students received support. Institutionally sponsored loans, scholarships/grants, and unspecified assistantships available. Support available to part-time students. Financial award applicants required to submit FAFSA. *Faculty research:* Information technology and marketing, behavioral research in accounting, human resources, management of technology. *Unit head:* Dr. Susan Gupta, MBA Program Director, 732-571-3639, Fax: 732-263-5517, E-mail: sgupta@monmouth.edu. *Application contact:* Laurie Kuhn, Associate Director of Graduate Admission, 732-571-3452, Fax: 732-263-5123, E-mail: gradadm@monmouth.edu.
Website: https://www.monmouth.edu/business-school/leon-hess-business-school.aspx

Monroe College, King Graduate School, Bronx, NY 10468. Offers accounting (MS); business administration (MBA), including entrepreneurship, finance, general business administration, healthcare management, human resources, information technology, marketing; computer science (MS); criminal justice (MS); hospitality management (MS); public health (MPH), including biostatistics and epidemiology, community health, health administration and leadership. *Program availability:* Online learning.

Montclair State University, The Graduate School, College of Humanities and Social Sciences, MA Program in Law and Governance, Montclair, NJ 07043-1624. Offers conflict management and peace studies (MA); governance, compliance and regulation (MA); intellectual property (MA); law and governance (MA); legal management (MA). *Program availability:* Part-time, evening/weekend. *Degree requirements:* For master's, thesis or comprehensive exam. *Entrance requirements:* For master's, GRE General Test, minimum cumulative GPA of 2.75 for undergraduate work, 2 letters of recommendation, essay. Additional exam requirements/recommendations for international students: Required—TOEFL (minimum score 83 iBT) or IELTS (minimum score 6.5). Electronic applications accepted.

Montclair State University, The Graduate School, Feliciano School of Business, General MBA Program, Montclair, NJ 07043-1624. Offers accounting (MBA); business analytics (MBA); digital marketing (MBA); finance (MBA); general business administration (MBA); human resources management (MBA); management (MBA); management of information and technology (MBA); marketing (MBA); project management (MBA). *Program availability:* Part-time, evening/weekend. *Degree requirements:* For master's, culminating experience. *Entrance requirements:* For master's, GMAT or GRE General Test, 2 letters of recommendation, resume, essay. Additional exam requirements/recommendations for international students: Required—TOEFL (minimum score 83 iBT), IELTS (minimum score 6.5). Electronic applications accepted. *Faculty research:* Accounting, management, marketing.

Moravian College, Graduate and Continuing Studies, Business and Management Programs, Bethlehem, PA 18018-6650. Offers accounting (MBA); business management (MBA); health administration (MHA); HR leadership (MSHRM); supply chain management (MBA). *Program availability:* Part-time, evening/weekend. *Faculty:* 3 full-time (2 women), 13 part-time/adjunct (4 women). *Students:* 13 full-time (12 women), 70 part-time (38 women); includes 10 minority (1 Black or African American, non-Hispanic/Latino; 9 Hispanic/Latino), 1 international. Average age 30. 92 applicants, 85% accepted, 58 enrolled. In 2018, 34 master's awarded. *Entrance requirements:* For master's, current resume, official transcripts, 2 letters of recommendation. Additional exam requirements/recommendations for international students: Required—TOEFL (minimum score 577 paper-based), IELTS (minimum score 6.5). *Application deadline:* For fall admission, 8/1 priority date for domestic and international students; for spring admission, 1/1 priority date for domestic and international students; for summer admission, 5/1 priority date for domestic and international students. Applications are processed on a rolling basis. Electronic applications accepted. *Financial support:* Research assistantships available. Financial award applicants required to submit FAFSA. *Faculty research:* Leadership, change management, human resources. *Unit head:* Dr. Katie P. Desiderio, Executive Director, Graduate Business Programs, 610-861-1400, Fax: 610-861-1466, E-mail: graduate@moravian.edu. *Application contact:* Kristy Sullivan, Director of Student Recruitment Operations, 610-861-1400, Fax: 610-861-1466, E-mail: graduate@moravian.edu.
Website: https://www.moravian.edu/graduate/programs/business#/

Morehead State University, Graduate School, Elmer R. Smith College of Business and Technology, Morehead, KY 40351. Offers MA, MBA, MPA, MSIS. *Accreditation:* AACSB. *Program availability:* Part-time, evening/weekend, online learning. *Entrance requirements:* For master's, GMAT, GRE General Test, minimum GPA of 2.5 on undergraduate work. Additional exam requirements/recommendations for international students: Required—TOEFL (minimum score 525 paper-based). Electronic applications accepted. *Faculty research:* Regional economic development, accounting systems, banking market structures, macroeconomics, distance learning.

Morgan State University, School of Graduate Studies, Earl G. Graves School of Business and Management, Master of Business Administration Program, Baltimore, MD 21251. Offers MBA. *Accreditation:* AACSB. *Program availability:* Part-time, evening/weekend. *Entrance requirements:* For master's, GMAT. Additional exam requirements/recommendations for international students: Required—TOEFL (minimum score 550 paper-based). *Faculty research:* Total quality management, disaster management, impact of globalization, marketing of services.

Morgan State University, School of Graduate Studies, Earl G. Graves School of Business and Management, PhD Program in Business Administration, Baltimore, MD 21251. Offers business administration (PhD), including accounting, information systems, management and marketing. *Accreditation:* AACSB. *Entrance requirements:* For doctorate, GMAT. Additional exam requirements/recommendations for international students: Required—TOEFL (minimum score 550 paper-based).

Mount Aloysius College, Program in Business Administration, Cresson, PA 16630. Offers accounting (MBA); health and human services administration (MBA); non-profit management (MBA); project management (MBA). *Program availability:* Part-time, evening/weekend. *Entrance requirements:* Additional exam requirements/

recommendations for international students: Required—IELTS (minimum score 5.5); Recommended—TOEFL. *Application deadline:* For fall admission, 8/1 for domestic students; for spring admission, 12/1 for domestic students. Applications are processed on a rolling basis. Application fee: $30. Electronic applications accepted. Application fee is waived when completed online. *Financial support:* Unspecified assistantships available. Financial award applicants required to submit FAFSA. *Application contact:* Matthew P. Bodenschatz, Director of Graduate and Continuing Education Admissions, 814-886-6556, Fax: 814-886-6441, E-mail: mbodenschatz@mtaloy.edu.

Mount Marty College, Graduate Studies Division, Yankton, SD 57078-3724. Offers business administration (MBA); nurse anesthesia (MS); nursing (MSN); pastoral ministries (MPM). *Accreditation:* AANA/CANAEP (one or more programs are accredited). *Degree requirements:* For master's, thesis or alternative. *Entrance requirements:* For master's, GRE General Test, minimum GPA of 3.0. Electronic applications accepted. *Faculty research:* Clinical anesthesia, professional characteristics, motivations of applicants.

Mount Mary University, Graduate Programs, Program in Business Administration, Milwaukee, WI 53222-4597. Offers general management (MBA); health systems leadership (MBA). *Program availability:* Part-time, evening/weekend. *Degree requirements:* For master's, terminal project. *Entrance requirements:* For master's, minimum GPA of 2.75. Additional exam requirements/recommendations for international students: Required—TOEFL (minimum score 550 paper-based; 80 iBT); Recommended—IELTS (minimum score 6.5). Electronic applications accepted. *Expenses:* Contact institution. *Faculty research:* Economics, quantitative analysis, accounting, finance.

Mount Mercy University, Program in Business Administration, Cedar Rapids, IA 52402-4797. Offers human resource (MBA); quality management (MBA). *Program availability:* Evening/weekend. *Entrance requirements:* For master's, minimum cumulative GPA of 3.0, 2 letters of recommendation, resume. Additional exam requirements/recommendations for international students: Required—TOEFL (minimum score 570 paper-based; 88 iBT). Electronic applications accepted.

Mount St. Joseph University, Master of Business Administration Program, Cincinnati, OH 45233-1670. Offers MBA. *Program availability:* Part-time, evening/weekend. *Degree requirements:* For master's, 15 hours of foundational course work, 36 hours of MBA coursework, minimum GPA of 3.0, integrative project. *Entrance requirements:* For master's, official undergraduate transcript with minimum cumulative GPA of 3.0; MBA Required Foundational Course form; two references; one-page personal statement; interview with MBA program director or designee. Additional exam requirements/recommendations for international students: Required—TOEFL (minimum score 560 paper-based; 83 iBT). Electronic applications accepted. *Expenses:* Contact institution. *Faculty research:* Gender and cultural effects on management education, group identity formation, leadership skill development, methods for improving instructional effectiveness, technology-based productivity improvement.

Mount Saint Mary College, School of Business, Newburgh, NY 12550-3494. Offers business (MBA); financial planning (MBA); health care management (MBA). *Program availability:* Part-time, evening/weekend. *Faculty:* 6 full-time (3 women), 3 part-time/adjunct (0 women). *Students:* 37 full-time (14 women), 30 part-time (19 women); includes 14 minority (3 Black or African American, non-Hispanic/Latino; 1 Asian, non-Hispanic/Latino; 10 Hispanic/Latino). Average age 30. 16 applicants, 81% accepted, 10 enrolled. In 2018, 48 master's awarded. *Degree requirements:* For master's, thesis or alternative. *Entrance requirements:* For master's, GMAT or minimum undergraduate GPA of 2.7. Additional exam requirements/recommendations for international students: Required—TOEFL (minimum score 80 iBT). *Application deadline:* Applications are processed on a rolling basis. Application fee: $45. Electronic applications accepted. Application fee is waived when completed online. *Expenses: Tuition:* Full-time $14,454; part-time $803 per credit. *Required fees:* $172; $86 per semester. *Financial support:* In 2018–19, 13 students received support. Scholarships/grants and unspecified assistantships available. Financial award application deadline: 4/15; financial award applicants required to submit FAFSA. *Faculty research:* Financial reform, entrepreneurship and small business development, global business relations, technology's impact on business decision-making, college-assisted business education. *Unit head:* Dr. Veronica McMillian, Graduate Coordinator, 845-569-3119, Fax: 845-569-3885, E-mail: veronica.mcmillan@msmc.edu. *Application contact:* Eileen Bardney, Director of Admissions, 845-569-3254, Fax: 845-569-3438, E-mail: Eileen.Bardney@msmc.edu.
Website: http://www.msmc.edu/Academics/Graduate_Programs/master_of_business_administration.be

Mount Saint Mary's University, Graduate Division, Los Angeles, CA 90049. Offers business administration (MBA); counseling psychology (MS); creative writing (MFA); education (MS, Certificate); film and television (MFA); health policy and management (MS); humanities (MA); nursing (MSN, Certificate); physical therapy (DPT); religious studies (MA). *Program availability:* Part-time, evening/weekend. *Entrance requirements:* Additional exam requirements/recommendations for international students: Required—TOEFL. Electronic applications accepted. *Expenses: Tuition:* Full-time $45,260. *Required fees:* $170. Full-time tuition and fees vary according to course load and program.

Mount St. Mary's University, Program in Business Administration, Emmitsburg, MD 21727-7799. Offers MBA. *Program availability:* Part-time, evening/weekend. *Degree requirements:* For master's, thesis. *Entrance requirements:* For master's, minimum undergraduate GPA of 2.75, 5 years' relevant professional business experience, or GMAT (minimum score of 500). Additional exam requirements/recommendations for international students: Required—TOEFL (minimum score 550 paper-based; 83 iBT). Electronic applications accepted. *Expenses:* Contact institution.

Mount Vernon Nazarene University, Program in Management, Mount Vernon, OH 43050-9500. Offers MSM. *Accreditation:* ACBSP. *Program availability:* Part-time, evening/weekend.

Murray State University, Arthur J. Bauernfeind College of Business, MBA Program, Murray, KY 42071. Offers accounting (MBA); finance (MBA); global communications (MBA); human resource management (MBA); marketing (MBA). *Accreditation:* AACSB. *Program availability:* Part-time, evening/weekend, 100% online, blended/hybrid learning. *Entrance requirements:* For master's, GRE or GMAT, minimum university GPA of 2.75. Additional exam requirements/recommendations for international students: Required—TOEFL (minimum score 527 paper-based; 71 iBT). *Faculty research:* Human resource management, e-commerce, supply-chain management, investment management, accounting.

National American University, Roueche Graduate Center, Austin, TX 78731. Offers accounting (MBA); aviation management (MBA, MM); care coordination (MSN); community college leadership (Ed D); criminal justice (MM); e-marketing (MBA, MM); health care administration (MBA, MM); higher education (MM); human resources management (MBA, MM); information technology management (MBA, MM); international business (MBA); leadership (EMBA); management (MBA); nursing administration (MSN); nursing education (MSN); nursing informatics (MSN); operations and configuration management (MBA, MM); project and process management (MBA, MM). Master's programs offered online through the Harold D. Buckingham Graduate School. *Program availability:* Part-time, evening/weekend, online learning. *Entrance requirements:* For master's, minimum undergraduate GPA of 2.75. Additional exam requirements/recommendations for international students: Required—TOEFL, TWE. Electronic applications accepted. *Faculty research:* Tourism, finance, marketing.

National Louis University, College of Management and Business, Chicago, IL 60603. Offers business administration (MBA); human resource management and development (MS); management (MS). *Program availability:* Part-time, evening/weekend. *Entrance requirements:* For master's, college-administered critical thinking and writing skills test, minimum GPA of 3.0, resume, 3 references. Additional exam requirements/recommendations for international students: Required—TOEFL (minimum score 550 paper-based; 79 iBT).

National University, School of Business and Management, La Jolla, CA 92037-1011. Offers accountancy (M Acc, Certificate); business administration (GMBA, MBA); business analytics (MS); cause leadership (MA); global management (MGM); human resource management (MA); management information systems (MS); marketing (MS); organizational leadership (MS). GMBA offered in Spanish. *Program availability:* Part-time, evening/weekend, 100% online, blended/hybrid learning. *Degree requirements:* For master's, thesis (for some programs). *Entrance requirements:* For master's, interview, minimum GPA of 2.5. Additional exam requirements/recommendations for international students: Required—TOEFL (minimum score 550 paper-based; 79 iBT), IELTS (minimum score 6). Electronic applications accepted. *Expenses: Tuition:* Full-time $10,320; part-time $430 per unit. Tuition and fees vary according to degree level.

National University College, Graduate Programs, Bayamón, PR 00960. Offers digital marketing (MBA); general business (MBA); special education (M Ed).

Naval Postgraduate School, Departments and Academic Groups, Graduate School of Business and Public Policy, Monterey, CA 93943. Offers acquisition and contract management (MBA); business administration (EMBA, MBA); contract management (MS); defense business management (MBA); defense systems analysis (MS), including management; defense systems management (international) (MBA); financial management (MBA); information management (MBA); manpower systems analysis (MS); material logistics support management (MBA); program management (MS); resource planning and management for international defense (MBA); supply chain management (MBA); systems acquisition management (MBA); transportation management (MBA). Program only open to commissioned officers of the United States and friendly nations and selected United States federal civilian employees. *Accreditation:* AACSB; NASPAA. *Program availability:* Part-time, online learning. *Degree requirements:* For master's, thesis (for some programs), terminal project/capstone (for some programs). *Faculty research:* U.S. and European public procurement policies for small and medium-sized enterprises, examining external validity criticisms in the choice of students as subjects in accounting experiment studies, assurance of learning in contract management education, contracting for cloud computing: opportunities and risks, NPS, Apple App Store as a business model supporting U.S. Navy requirements.

Nazareth College of Rochester, Graduate Studies, Department of Business, Program in Management, Rochester, NY 14618. Offers MS. *Program availability:* Part-time, evening/weekend. *Entrance requirements:* For master's, minimum GPA of 3.0. Additional exam requirements/recommendations for international students: Required—TOEFL (minimum score 550 paper-based, 79 iBT) or IELTS (6.5).

Nebraska Christian College of Hope International University, Graduate Programs, Papillion, NE 68046. Offers biblical studies (M Div); business as mission/social entrepreneurship (MBA); children, youth, and family (M Div); church planting (M Div); counseling psychology (MS); educational administration (MA); elementary education (M Ed); general management (MBA); gifted and talented education (M Ed); intercultural studies (M Div); international development (MBA); marketing management (MBA); ministry (MA); ministry and leadership (M Div); music education (M Ed); non-profit management (MBA); pastoral care (M Div); secondary education (M Ed); spiritual formation (M Div); worship ministry (M Div).

Neumann University, Graduate Programs in Business and Information Management, Aston, PA 19014-1298. Offers accounting (MS), including forensic and fraud detection; sport business (MS). *Program availability:* Part-time, evening/weekend. *Degree requirements:* For master's, thesis (for some programs). *Entrance requirements:* For master's, official transcripts from all institutions attended, resume, letter of intent, 2-3 letters of recommendation. Additional exam requirements/recommendations for international students: Required—TOEFL (minimum score 70 iBT). Electronic applications accepted. *Expenses:* Contact institution.

New Charter University, College of Business, Salt Lake City, UT 84101. Offers finance (MBA); health care management (MBA); management (MBA). *Program availability:* Part-time, evening/weekend, online only, 100% online. *Faculty:* 13 part-time/adjunct (1 woman). *Students:* 16 part-time. Average age 40. 1 applicant, 100% accepted, 1 enrolled. In 2018, 10 master's awarded. *Entrance requirements:* For master's, course work in calculus, statistics, macroeconomics. Additional exam requirements/recommendations for international students: Required—TOEFL (minimum score 550 paper-based). *Application deadline:* Applications are processed on a rolling basis. Application fee: $50. Electronic applications accepted. *Expenses: Tuition:* Full-time $4491; part-time $1497 per term. *Required fees:* $50 per term. *Financial support:* In 2018–19, 1 student received support. Scholarships/grants available. *Unit head:* Timothy Harrington, Academic Dean, 801-8838336, E-mail: tharrington@new.edu. *Application contact:* Stephen Mann, Admissions Advisor, 801-515-3085, E-mail: smann@new.edu.
Website: https://new.edu/academics/college-of-business/

New England College, Program in Management, Henniker, NH 03242-3293. Offers accounting (MSA); healthcare administration (MS); international relations (MA); marketing management (MS); nonprofit leadership (MS); project management (MS); strategic leadership (MS). *Program availability:* Part-time, evening/weekend. *Degree requirements:* For master's, independent research project. Electronic applications accepted.

New Jersey City University, School of Business, Jersey City, NJ 07305-1597. Offers MBA, MS, Graduate Certificate. *Accreditation:* ACBSP. *Program availability:* Part-time, evening/weekend. *Entrance requirements:* Additional exam requirements/recommendations for international students: Required—TOEFL (minimum score 79 iBT).

New Jersey Institute of Technology, Martin Tuchman School of Management, Newark, NJ 07102. Offers business data science (PhD); management (MS); management of technology (MBA, Certificate). *Accreditation:* AACSB. *Program availability:* Part-time, evening/weekend. *Faculty:* 32 full-time (8 women), 22 part-time/adjunct (6 women). *Students:* 132 full-time (30 women), 128 part-time (67 women); includes 141 minority (39 Black or African American, non-Hispanic/Latino; 1 American Indian or Alaska Native, non-Hispanic/Latino; 51 Asian, non-Hispanic/Latino; 44 Hispanic/Latino; 6 Two or more races, non-Hispanic/Latino), 37 international. Average age 30. 339 applicants, 57% accepted, 88 enrolled. In 2018, 82 master's, 11 other advanced degrees awarded. Terminal master's awarded for partial completion of

doctoral program. *Degree requirements:* For doctorate, thesis/dissertation. *Entrance requirements:* For master's, GRE General Test/GMAT, minimum GPA 2.8, personal statement, 1 letter of recommendation, transcripts, resume; for doctorate, GRE General Test/GMAT, minimum GPA 3.2, personal statement, 3 letters of recommendation, transcripts, CV. Additional exam requirements/recommendations for international students: Required—TOEFL (minimum score 550 paper-based; 79 iBT), IELTS (minimum score 6.5). *Application deadline:* For fall admission, 6/1 priority date for domestic students, 5/1 priority date for international students; for spring admission, 11/15 priority date for domestic and international students. Applications are processed on a rolling basis. Application fee: $75. Electronic applications accepted. *Expenses:* $22,690 per year (in-state), $32,136 per year (out-of-state). *Financial support:* In 2018–19, 37 students received support, including 6 fellowships with full tuition reimbursements available (averaging $22,000 per year), 9 research assistantships with full tuition reimbursements available (averaging $22,000 per year), 10 teaching assistantships (averaging $22,000 per year); career-related internships or fieldwork, Federal Work-Study, scholarships/grants, and unspecified assistantships also available. Financial award application deadline: 1/15. *Faculty research:* Manufacturing systems analysis, earnings management, knowledge-based view of the firm, data envelopment analysis, human factors in human/machine systems. *Total annual research expenditures:* $687,000. *Unit head:* Dr. Oya Tukel, Dean, 973-596-3248, Fax: 973-596-3074, E-mail: oya.i.tukel@njit.edu. *Application contact:* Stephen Eck, Director of Admissions, 973-596-3300, Fax: 973-596-3461, E-mail: admissions@njit.edu.
Website: http://management.njit.edu

Newman University, MBA Program, Wichita, KS 67213-2097. Offers finance (MBA); international business (MBA); leadership (MBA); management (MBA); management information technology (MBA). *Program availability:* Part-time. *Degree requirements:* For master's, thesis optional. *Entrance requirements:* For master's, minimum GPA of 3.0; 2 letters of recommendation; course work in algebra, statistics, macroeconomics, and financial accounting. Additional exam requirements/recommendations for international students: Required—TOEFL (minimum score 600 paper-based; 100 iBT). Electronic applications accepted. *Expenses:* Contact institution.

New Mexico Highlands University, Graduate Studies, School of Business, Media and Technology, Las Vegas, NM 87701. Offers business administration (MBA), including human resource management, international business, management; media arts and technology (MA), including media arts and computer science. *Accreditation:* ACBSP. *Degree requirements:* For master's, comprehensive exam, thesis or alternative. *Entrance requirements:* For master's, minimum undergraduate GPA of 3.0. Additional exam requirements/recommendations for international students: Required—TOEFL (minimum score 540 paper-based). *Faculty research:* Real estate valuation, studying expert judgments in complex accounting, decision environments, green marketing, environmentalism, marketing research methodology.

New Mexico State University, College of Business, Department of Marketing, Las Cruces, NM 88003-8001. Offers business administration (PhD), including marketing. *Faculty:* 7 full-time (2 women). *Students:* 6 full-time (4 women), 3 part-time (1 woman); includes 2 minority (1 Hispanic/Latino; 1 Two or more races, non-Hispanic/Latino), 5 international. Average age 35. 5 applicants. In 2018, 3 doctorates awarded. *Degree requirements:* For doctorate, comprehensive exam, thesis/dissertation, 1st year paper, 2nd year paper. *Entrance requirements:* For doctorate, GMAT or GRE, graduate degree, work experience, 3 letters of recommendation, letter of motivation/statement of purpose, resume/curriculum vitae. Additional exam requirements/recommendations for international students: Required—TOEFL (minimum score 550 paper-based; 79 iBT), IELTS (minimum score 6.5). *Application deadline:* For fall admission, 2/1 for domestic and international students. Application fee: $40 ($50 for international students). Electronic applications accepted. *Expenses: Tuition, area resident:* Full-time $4216.70; part-time $252.70 per credit hour. Tuition, state resident: full-time $4216.70; part-time $252.70 per credit hour. Tuition, nonresident: full-time $12,769; part-time $881.10 per credit hour. *International tuition:* $12,769.30 full-time. *Required fees:* $878.40; $48.80 per credit hour. Full-time tuition and fees vary according to course load and reciprocity agreements. *Financial support:* In 2018–19, 8 students received support, including 1 fellowship (averaging $4,548 per year), 6 teaching assistantships (averaging $23,157 per year); career-related internships or fieldwork, Federal Work-Study, scholarships/grants, traineeships, health care benefits, and unspecified assistantships also available. Support available to part-time students. Financial award application deadline: 3/1. *Faculty research:* Consumer behavior, social media marketing, ethics in marketing, advertising, public policy. *Unit head:* Dr. David Daniel, Department Head, 575-646-3341, Fax: 575-646-1498, E-mail: ddaniel@nmsu.edu. *Application contact:* Dr. Mihai Niculescu, Coordinator, Marketing PhD Program, 575-646-2608, Fax: 575-646-1498, E-mail: niculem@nmsu.edu.
Website: http://business.nmsu.edu/departments/marketing

New York Institute of Technology, School of Management, Department of Business Administration, Old Westbury, NY 11568-8000. Offers executive management (MBA), including finance, marketing, operations and supply chain management. *Accreditation:* AACSB. *Program availability:* Part-time. *Faculty:* 25 full-time (4 women), 20 part-time/adjunct (6 women). *Students:* 296 full-time (126 women), 91 part-time (45 women); includes 42 minority (6 Black or African American, non-Hispanic/Latino; 1 American Indian or Alaska Native, non-Hispanic/Latino; 17 Asian, non-Hispanic/Latino; 12 Hispanic/Latino; 1 Native Hawaiian or other Pacific Islander, non-Hispanic/Latino; 5 Two or more races, non-Hispanic/Latino), 298 international. Average age 30. 550 applicants, 67% accepted, 111 enrolled. In 2018, 291 master's awarded. *Entrance requirements:* For master's, bachelor's degree; minimum undergraduate GPA of 3.0. Additional exam requirements/recommendations for international students: Required—TOEFL (minimum score 79 iBT), IELTS (minimum score 6), PTE (minimum score 53). *Application deadline:* Applications are processed on a rolling basis. Application fee: $50. Electronic applications accepted. *Expenses: Tuition:* Full-time $1285; part-time $1285 per credit. *Required fees:* $215; $175 per unit. Tuition and fees vary according to course load, degree level and campus/location. *Financial support:* Career-related internships or fieldwork, Federal Work-Study, scholarships/grants, tuition waivers (full and partial), and unspecified assistantships available. Support available to part-time students. Financial award application deadline: 2/15; financial award applicants required to submit FAFSA. *Faculty research:* Accounting, economics, finance, management, marketing. *Unit head:* Dr. Jess Boronico, Dean, 516-686-7838, E-mail: som@nyit.edu. *Application contact:* Alice Dolitsky, Director, Graduate Admissions, 516-686-7520, Fax: 516-686-1116, E-mail: admissions@nyit.edu.
Website: http://www.nyit.edu/degrees/management_mba

New York Medical College, School of Health Sciences and Practice, Valhalla, NY 10595. Offers behavioral sciences and health promotion (MPH); biostatistics (MS); children with special health care (Graduate Certificate); emergency preparedness (Graduate Certificate); environmental health science (MPH); epidemiology (MPH, MS); global health (Graduate Certificate); health education (Graduate Certificate); health policy and management (MPH, Dr PH); industrial hygiene (Graduate Certificate); pediatric dysphagia (Post-Graduate Certificate); physical therapy (DPT); public health (Graduate Certificate); speech-language pathology (MS). *Accreditation:* ASHA; CEPH. *Program availability:* Part-time, evening/weekend, 100% online, blended/hybrid learning. *Faculty:* 47 full-time (34 women), 239 part-time/adjunct (141 women). *Students:* 245 full-time (181 women), 233 part-time (167 women); includes 208 minority (79 Black or African American, non-Hispanic/Latino; 2 American Indian or Alaska Native, non-Hispanic/Latino; 59 Asian, non-Hispanic/Latino; 57 Hispanic/Latino; 1 Native Hawaiian or other Pacific Islander, non-Hispanic/Latino; 10 Two or more races, non-Hispanic/Latino), 13 international. Average age 27. 484 applicants, 68% accepted, 88 enrolled. In 2018, 113 master's, 47 doctorates awarded. *Degree requirements:* For master's, comprehensive exam (for some programs), thesis (for some programs); for doctorate, thesis/dissertation. *Entrance requirements:* For master's, GRE (for MS in speech-language pathology); for doctorate, GRE (for Doctor of Physical Therapy and Doctor of Public Health). Additional exam requirements/recommendations for international students: Required—TOEFL (minimum score 96 paper-based; 24 iBT), IELTS (minimum score 7). *Application deadline:* For fall admission, 8/1 for domestic students, 4/15 for international students; for spring admission, 12/1 for domestic students; for summer admission, 5/1 for domestic students, 4/15 for international students. Applications are processed on a rolling basis. Application fee: $128 ($120 for international students). Electronic applications accepted. *Expenses:* $1165 per credit, $645 fees. *Financial support:* In 2018–19, 4 students received support. Federal Work-Study, scholarships/grants, unspecified assistantships, and Federal student loans available. Financial award application deadline: 4/30; financial award applicants required to submit FAFSA. *Faculty research:* Disaster medicine, environmental health, health policy, speech-language pathology including dysphagia, biomechanics of human motion in activities of daily living and occupations. *Total annual research expenditures:* $325,000. *Unit head:* Ben Johnson, PhD, Vice Dean, 914-594-4531, E-mail: bjohnson23@nymc.edu. *Application contact:* Irene Bundziak, Assistant to Director of Admissions, 914-594-4905, E-mail: irene_bundziak@nymc.edu.
Website: http://www.nymc.edu/school-of-health-sciences-and-practice-shsp/

New York University, Leonard N. Stern School of Business, Department of Marketing, New York, NY 10012-1019. Offers entertainment, media and technology (MBA); general marketing (MBA); marketing (PhD); product management (MBA).

New York University, School of Law, New York, NY 10012-1019. Offers law (LL M, JD, JSD); law and business (Advanced Certificate); taxation (MSL, Advanced Certificate); JD/LL M; JD/MA; JD/MBA; JD/MPA; JD/MPP; JD/MSW; JD/MUP; JD/PhD. *Accreditation:* ABA. *Program availability:* Part-time, blended/hybrid learning. *Entrance requirements:* For doctorate, LSAT (for JD). Electronic applications accepted. *Expenses:* Contact institution. *Faculty research:* International law, environmental law, corporate law, globalization of law, philosophy of law.

Niagara University, Graduate Division of Business Administration, Niagara University, NY 14109. Offers accounting (MBA); business administration (MBA); finance (MBA, MS); financial planning (MBA); healthcare administration (MBA, MHA); human resources (MBA); international business (MBA); marketing (MBA); professional accountancy (MBA); strategic management (MBA); supply chain management (MBA). *Accreditation:* AACSB. *Program availability:* Part-time, evening/weekend, 100% online, blended/hybrid learning. *Students:* 224 full-time (116 women), 56 part-time (22 women); includes 36 minority (9 Black or African American, non-Hispanic/Latino; 2 American Indian or Alaska Native, non-Hispanic/Latino; 6 Asian, non-Hispanic/Latino; 12 Hispanic/Latino; 7 Two or more races, non-Hispanic/Latino), 82 international. Average age 26. In 2018, 134 master's awarded. *Entrance requirements:* For master's, GMAT. Additional exam requirements/recommendations for international students: Required—TOEFL (minimum score 550 paper-based; 79 iBT), IELTS (minimum score 6). *Application deadline:* For fall admission, 8/1 for domestic students; for spring admission, 11/1 for domestic students. Applications are processed on a rolling basis. Electronic applications accepted. *Expenses:* Contact institution. *Financial support:* Research assistantships, teaching assistantships, career-related internships or fieldwork, Federal Work-Study, scholarships/grants, and unspecified assistantships available. Support available to part-time students. Financial award application deadline: 4/15; financial award applicants required to submit FAFSA. *Faculty research:* Capital flows, Federal Reserve policy, human resource management, public policy, issues in marketing, auctions, economics of information, risk and capital markets, management strategy, consumer behavior, Internet and social media marketing. *Unit head:* Dr. Paul Richardson, MBA Director/Chair of the Marketing Department, 716-286-8169, Fax: 716-286-8206, E-mail: mba@niagara.edu. *Application contact:* Evan Pierce, Associate Director for Graduate Recruitment, 716-286-8327, Fax: 716-286-8710, E-mail: epierce@niagara.edu.
Website: http://mba.niagara.edu

Nicholls State University, Graduate Studies, College of Business Administration, Thibodaux, LA 70310. Offers MBA. *Accreditation:* AACSB. *Program availability:* Part-time, evening/weekend. *Degree requirements:* For master's, thesis optional. *Entrance requirements:* For master's, GMAT. Additional exam requirements/recommendations for international students: Required—TOEFL (minimum score 550 paper-based). Electronic applications accepted.

Nichols College, Graduate and Professional Studies, Dudley, MA 01571-5000. Offers business administration (MBA); counterterrorism (MS); organizational leadership (MSOL). *Program availability:* Part-time, evening/weekend, online learning. *Degree requirements:* For master's, project (for MOL). *Entrance requirements:* For master's, 2 letters of recommendation, current resume, official transcripts, 800-word personal statement. Additional exam requirements/recommendations for international students: Required—TOEFL (minimum score 500 paper-based). Electronic applications accepted.

North Carolina Agricultural and Technical State University, The Graduate College, College of Business and Economics, Greensboro, NC 27411. Offers accounting (MBA); business education (MAT); human resources management (MBA); supply chain systems (MBA).

North Carolina Central University, School of Business, Durham, NC 27707-3129. Offers MBA. *Accreditation:* AACSB. *Program availability:* Part-time, evening/weekend. *Entrance requirements:* For master's, GMAT. Additional exam requirements/recommendations for international students: Required—TOEFL.

North Carolina State University, Graduate School, Poole College of Management, Program in Business Administration, Raleigh, NC 27695. Offers biosciences management (MBA); entrepreneurship and technology commercialization (MBA); financial management (MBA); innovation management (MBA); marketing management (MBA); services management (MBA); supply chain management (MBA). *Accreditation:* AACSB. *Program availability:* Part-time. *Degree requirements:* For master's, thesis optional. *Entrance requirements:* For master's, GMAT, interview, 3 letters of recommendation. Additional exam requirements/recommendations for international students: Required—TOEFL (minimum score 600 paper-based; 100 iBT). Electronic applications accepted. *Faculty research:* Manufacturing strategy, information systems, technology commercialization, managing research and development, historical stock returns.

North Central College, School of Graduate and Professional Studies, Program in Business Administration, Naperville, IL 60566-7063. Offers change management (MBA); finance (MBA); human resource management (MBA); management (MBA). *Program availability:* Part-time, evening/weekend. *Degree requirements:* For master's, thesis optional, project. *Entrance requirements:* For master's, interview. Additional exam

requirements/recommendations for international students: Required—TOEFL (minimum score 550 paper-based; 80 iBT), IELTS (minimum score 6.5). Electronic applications accepted. Application fee is waived when completed online. *Expenses:* Contact institution.

North Central College, School of Graduate and Professional Studies, Program in Leadership Studies, Naperville, IL 60566-7063. Offers MLD. *Program availability:* Part-time, evening/weekend. *Degree requirements:* For master's, thesis optional, project. *Entrance requirements:* For master's, interview. Additional exam requirements/recommendations for international students: Required—TOEFL (minimum score 550 paper-based; 80 iBT), IELTS (minimum score 6.5). Electronic applications accepted. Application fee is waived when completed online. *Expenses:* Contact institution.

Northcentral University, Graduate Studies, San Diego, CA 92106. Offers business (MBA, DBA, PhD, Postbaccalaureate Certificate); education (M Ed, Ed D, PhD, Ed S, Post-Master's Certificate, Postbaccalaureate Certificate); marriage and family therapy (MA, DMFT, PhD, Post-Master's Certificate, Postbaccalaureate Certificate); psychology (MA, PhD, Post-Master's Certificate, Postbaccalaureate Certificate); technology (MS, PhD), including computer science, cybersecurity (MS), data science, technology and innovation management (PhD). *Program availability:* Part-time, evening/weekend, online only, 100% online. *Faculty:* 98 full-time (63 women), 385 part-time/adjunct (203 women). *Students:* 5,036 full-time (3,291 women), 5,747 part-time (3,977 women); includes 3,777 minority (2,550 Black or African American, non-Hispanic/Latino; 76 American Indian or Alaska Native, non-Hispanic/Latino; 192 Asian, non-Hispanic/Latino; 603 Hispanic/Latino; 39 Native Hawaiian or other Pacific Islander, non-Hispanic/Latino; 317 Two or more races, non-Hispanic/Latino). Average age 45. In 2018, 929 master's, 782 doctorates, 278 other advanced degrees awarded. *Degree requirements:* For doctorate, comprehensive exam, thesis/dissertation. *Entrance requirements:* For master's, bachelor's degree from regionally- or nationally-accredited institution, current resume or curriculum vitae, statement of intent, interview, and background check (for marriage and family therapy); for doctorate, post-baccalaureate master's degree and/or doctoral degree from nationally- or regionally-accredited academic institution; for other advanced degree, bachelor's-level or higher degree from accredited institution or university (for Post-Baccalaureate Certificate); master's and/or doctoral degree from regionally- or nationally-accredited academic institution (for Post-Master's Certificate). Additional exam requirements/recommendations for international students: Required—TOEFL (minimum score 550 paper-based; 79 iBT), IELTS (minimum score 6.5), PTE (minimum score 53). *Application deadline:* Applications are processed on a rolling basis. Application fee: $0. Electronic applications accepted. *Expenses: Tuition:* Full-time $893. *Required fees:* $95. Tuition and fees vary according to degree level and program. *Financial support:* Scholarships/grants available. *Faculty research:* Business management, curriculum and instruction, educational leadership, health psychology, organizational behavior. *Unit head:* Dr. David Harpool, Acting Provost, 888-327-2877 Ext. 8181, E-mail: provost@ncu.edu. *Application contact:* Ken Boutelle, Vice President, Enrollment Services, 888-628-4979, E-mail: enrollmentservices@ncu.edu.

North Dakota State University, College of Graduate and Interdisciplinary Studies, College of Business, Fargo, ND 58102. Offers accountancy (M Acc); business administration (MBA). *Accreditation:* AACSB. *Program availability:* Part-time, evening/weekend. *Entrance requirements:* For master's, GMAT. Additional exam requirements/recommendations for international students: Required—TOEFL (minimum score 550 paper-based; 79 iBT). Electronic applications accepted. *Faculty research:* Labor management, operations, international finance, agency, Internet marketing.

Northeastern Illinois University, College of Graduate Studies and Research, College of Business and Management, MBA Program, Chicago, IL 60625. Offers MBA.

Northeastern State University, College of Business and Technology, Master of Business Administration Program, Tahlequah, OK 74464-2399. Offers MBA. *Accreditation:* ACBSP. *Program availability:* Part-time, evening/weekend. *Faculty:* 9 full-time (1 woman), 1 part-time/adjunct (0 women). *Students:* 29 full-time (11 women), 46 part-time (30 women); includes 40 minority (5 Black or African American, non-Hispanic/Latino; 8 American Indian or Alaska Native, non-Hispanic/Latino; 6 Asian, non-Hispanic/Latino; 5 Hispanic/Latino; 16 Two or more races, non-Hispanic/Latino), 2 international. Average age 32. In 2018, 11 master's awarded. *Degree requirements:* For master's, comprehensive exam, thesis, business plan, oral exam. *Entrance requirements:* For master's, GMAT, minimum GPA of 2.5. Additional exam requirements/recommendations for international students: Required—TOEFL. *Application deadline:* For fall admission, 6/1 priority date for domestic students. Applications are processed on a rolling basis. Application fee: $25. Electronic applications accepted. *Expenses: Tuition, area resident:* Full-time $4500; part-time $250 per credit hour. Tuition, state resident: full-time $4500; part-time $250 per credit hour. Tuition, nonresident: full-time $9999; part-time $555.50 per credit hour. *International tuition:* $9999 full-time. *Required fees:* $601.20; $33.40 per credit hour. *Financial support:* Teaching assistantships and Federal Work-Study available. Financial award application deadline: 3/1. *Unit head:* Dr. Sandra Edwards, Director, Business and Technology Graduate Studies, 918-449-6542, E-mail: edwar001@nsuok.edu. *Application contact:* Josh McCollum, Graduate Coordinator, 918-444-2093, E-mail: mccolluj@nsuok.edu.
Website: http://academics.nsuok.edu/businesstechnology/Graduate/MBA.aspx

Northeastern State University, College of Business and Technology, Professional Master of Business Administration Program, Tahlequah, OK 74464-2399. Offers PMBA. *Program availability:* Part-time. *Faculty:* 9 full-time (1 woman), 1 part-time/adjunct (0 women). *Students:* 3 full-time (1 woman), 26 part-time (15 women); includes 15 minority (4 Black or African American, non-Hispanic/Latino; 6 American Indian or Alaska Native, non-Hispanic/Latino; 3 Hispanic/Latino; 2 Two or more races, non-Hispanic/Latino), 1 international. Average age 38. In 2018, 11 master's awarded. *Degree requirements:* For master's, integrative project or research. *Application deadline:* Applications are processed on a rolling basis. Application fee: $25. Electronic applications accepted. *Expenses: Tuition, area resident:* Full-time $4500; part-time $250 per credit hour. Tuition, state resident: full-time $4500; part-time $250 per credit hour. Tuition, nonresident: full-time $9999; part-time $555.50 per credit hour. *International tuition:* $9999 full-time. *Required fees:* $601.20; $33.40 per credit hour. *Unit head:* Dr. Sandra Edwards, Director, Business and Technology Graduate Studies, 918-449-6542, E-mail: edwar001@nsuok.edu. *Application contact:* Josh McCollum, Graduate Coordinator, 918-444-2093, E-mail: mccolluj@nsuok.edu.
Website: http://academics.nsuok.edu/businesstechnology/Graduate/PMBA.aspx

Northeastern University, D'Amore-McKim School of Business, Boston, MA 02115-5096. Offers accounting (MS); business administration (EMBA, MBA); finance (MS); innovation (MS); international business (MS); international management (MS); taxation (MS); technological entrepreneurship (MS); JD/MBA; LL M/MBA; MBA/MSN; MS/MBA. *Accreditation:* AACSB. *Program availability:* Part-time, evening/weekend, online learning. *Entrance requirements:* For master's, GMAT or GRE. Electronic applications accepted. *Expenses:* Contact institution.

Northern Arizona University, The W. A. Franke College of Business, Flagstaff, AZ 86011. Offers business administration (MBA); business foundations (Graduate Certificate). *Accreditation:* AACSB. *Program availability:* Part-time, 100% online, blended/hybrid learning. *Degree requirements:* For master's, variable foreign language

requirement, comprehensive exam (for some programs), thesis (for some programs); for Graduate Certificate, comprehensive exam (for some programs). *Entrance requirements:* For master's, GMAT/GRE. Additional exam requirements/recommendations for international students: Required—TOEFL (minimum score 83 iBT). Electronic applications accepted. *Expenses:* Contact institution. *Faculty research:* Data processing applications for business situations and problems, accounting fraud, effects of sales tactics, self-efficacy and performance.

Northern Illinois University, Graduate School, College of Business, MBA Program, De Kalb, IL 60115-2854. Offers MBA. *Accreditation:* AACSB. *Program availability:* Part-time, evening/weekend. *Faculty:* 53 full-time (17 women), 3 part-time/adjunct (0 women). *Students:* 102 full-time (39 women), 250 part-time (67 women); includes 121 minority (22 Black or African American, non-Hispanic/Latino; 1 American Indian or Alaska Native, non-Hispanic/Latino; 48 Asian, non-Hispanic/Latino; 41 Hispanic/Latino; 9 Two or more races, non-Hispanic/Latino), 21 international. Average age 33. 126 applicants, 81% accepted, 73 enrolled. In 2018, 243 master's awarded. *Degree requirements:* For master's, thesis optional, seminar. *Entrance requirements:* For master's, GMAT, minimum GPA of 2.75. Additional exam requirements/recommendations for international students: Required—TOEFL (minimum score 550 paper-based). *Application deadline:* For fall admission, 6/1 for domestic students, 5/1 for international students; for spring admission, 11/1 for domestic students, 10/1 for international students. Applications are processed on a rolling basis. Application fee: $40. Electronic applications accepted. *Financial support:* In 2018–19, 8 research assistantships with full tuition reimbursements, 3 teaching assistantships with full tuition reimbursements were awarded; fellowships with full tuition reimbursements, career-related internships or fieldwork, Federal Work-Study, scholarships/grants, tuition waivers (full), and unspecified assistantships also available. Support available to part-time students. Financial award applicants required to submit FAFSA. *Unit head:* Mona Salmon, Director, 815-753-1245, E-mail: mba@niu.edu. *Application contact:* Office of Graduate Studies in Business, 815-753-6301.
Website: http://www.cob.niu.edu/mbaprograms/

Northern Kentucky University, Office of Graduate Programs, College of Business, Program in Business Administration, Highland Heights, KY 41099. Offers MBA, Certificate, JD/MBA. *Accreditation:* AACSB. *Program availability:* Part-time, evening/weekend. *Degree requirements:* For master's, thesis optional, capstone course. *Entrance requirements:* For master's, GMAT, 3 years of work experience; undergraduate transcripts; 3 letters of recommendation; resume; essay explaining how MBA will benefit student in life and career. Additional exam requirements/recommendations for international students: Required—TOEFL (minimum score 79 iBT); Recommended—IELTS (minimum score 6.5). Electronic applications accepted. *Expenses:* Contact institution. *Faculty research:* Influence, diversity, organizational culture, ethics, corporate governance, corporate scandals, market research methods, consumer privacy, mergers and acquisitions of financial institutions, sustainability.

Northern Kentucky University, Office of Graduate Programs, College of Business, Program in Executive Leadership and Organizational Change, Highland Heights, KY 41099. Offers MS. *Program availability:* Part-time, evening/weekend. *Entrance requirements:* For master's, resume, current career essay, future career objectives essay, personal statement, 3 letters of recommendation with cover forms, transcripts. Additional exam requirements/recommendations for international students: Required—TOEFL (minimum score 79 iBT); Recommended—IELTS (minimum score 6.5). Electronic applications accepted. *Expenses:* Contact institution. *Faculty research:* Leadership assessment and development, teams and conflict management, organizational strategy development and systems thinking, organizational consultation.

Northern Michigan University, Office of Graduate Education and Research, College of Business, Marquette, MI 49855-5301. Offers MBA. *Accreditation:* AACSB. *Program availability:* Part-time. *Degree requirements:* For master's, strategic analysis research project and report in capstone course. *Entrance requirements:* For master's, GMAT, bachelor's degree; minimum undergraduate GPA of 3.0; statement of purpose; resume. Additional exam requirements/recommendations for international students: Required—TOEFL (minimum score 550 paper-based; 79 iBT), IELTS (minimum score 6.5). Electronic applications accepted.

North Park University, School of Business and Nonprofit Management, Chicago, IL 60625-4895. Offers MBA, MHEA, MHRM, MM, MNA. *Program availability:* Part-time, evening/weekend, online learning. *Entrance requirements:* For master's, GMAT, GRE. Additional exam requirements/recommendations for international students: Required—TOEFL. *Expenses:* Contact institution.

Northwest Christian University, School of Business and Management, Eugene, OR 97401-3745. Offers accounting (MBA); management (MBA). *Program availability:* Part-time, evening/weekend, online only, 100% online. *Entrance requirements:* For master's, GMAT, GRE, MAT, minimum undergraduate GPA of 3.0, 500-word essay, resume. Additional exam requirements/recommendations for international students: Required—TOEFL (minimum score 550 paper-based; 80 iBT). Electronic applications accepted. *Expenses:* Contact institution.

Northwestern Polytechnic University, School of Business and Information Technology, Fremont, CA 94539-7482. Offers MBA, DBA. *Program availability:* Part-time, evening/weekend. *Degree requirements:* For master's, thesis optional; for doctorate, thesis/dissertation. *Entrance requirements:* For master's, GMAT, minimum GPA of 3.0. Additional exam requirements/recommendations for international students: Required—TOEFL (minimum score 550 paper-based; 79 iBT). *Expenses:* Contact institution. *Faculty research:* Entrepreneurship, accounting, information technology.

Northwestern University, The Graduate School, Kellogg School of Management, Management Programs, Evanston, IL 60208. Offers accounting information and management (MBA, PhD); analytical finance (MBA); business administration (MBA); decision sciences (MBA); entrepreneurship and innovation (MBA); finance (MBA, PhD); health enterprise management (MBA); human resources management (MBA); international business (MBA); management and organizations (MBA, PhD); management and organizations and sociology (PhD); management and strategy (MBA); management studies (MS); managerial analytics (MBA); managerial economics (MBA); managerial economics and strategy (PhD); marketing (MBA, PhD); marketing management (MBA); media management (MBA); operations management (MBA, PhD); real estate (MBA); social enterprise at Kellogg (MBA); JD/MBA. *Program availability:* Part-time, evening/weekend. Terminal master's awarded for partial completion of doctoral program. *Degree requirements:* For doctorate, thesis/dissertation, 2 years of coursework, qualifying (field) exam and candidacy, summer research papers and presentations to faculty, proposal defense, final exam/defense. *Entrance requirements:* For master's, GMAT, GRE, interview, 2 letters of recommendation, college transcripts, resume, essays, Kellogg honor code; for doctorate, GMAT, GRE, statement of purpose, transcripts, 2 letters of recommendation, resume, interview. Additional exam requirements/recommendations for international students: Required—TOEFL, IELTS. Electronic applications accepted. *Expenses:* Contact institution. *Faculty research:* Business cycles and international finance, health policy, networks, non-market strategy, consumer psychology.

Business Administration and Management—General

Northwestern University, McCormick School of Engineering and Applied Science, MMM Program, Evanston, IL 60208. Offers design innovation (MBA, MS). *Entrance requirements:* For master's, GMAT or GRE, transcripts, two letters of recommendation, resume, evaluative interview report, work experience, two core essays, interest essay, video essay. Additional exam requirements/recommendations for international students: Required—TOEFL, IELTS. *Expenses:* Contact institution.

Northwest Missouri State University, Graduate School, Melvin and Valorie Booth College of Business and Professional Studies, Maryville, MO 64468-6001. Offers agricultural economics (MBA); business decision and analytics (MBA); general management (MBA); human resource management (MBA); marketing (MBA). *Program availability:* Part-time. *Faculty:* 24 full-time (12 women). *Students:* 56 full-time (31 women), 220 part-time (126 women); includes 47 minority (23 Black or African American, non-Hispanic/Latino; 6 Asian, non-Hispanic/Latino; 10 Hispanic/Latino; 8 Two or more races, non-Hispanic/Latino), 15 international. Average age 32. 154 applicants, 75% accepted, 104 enrolled. In 2018, 53 master's awarded. *Degree requirements:* For master's, comprehensive exam. *Entrance requirements:* For master's, GMAT, GRE, minimum GPA of 2.5. Additional exam requirements/recommendations for international students: Required—TOEFL (minimum score 550 paper-based). *Application deadline:* For fall admission, 7/1 for domestic and international students; for spring admission, 11/15 for domestic and international students; for summer admission, 4/1 for domestic and international students. Applications are processed on a rolling basis. Application fee: $0 ($50 for international students). Electronic applications accepted. *Expenses:* $13,530 to complete degree (online MBA program); 401.06/credit hour in-state& 653.92/credit hour out-of-state. *Financial support:* Research assistantships with full tuition reimbursements, teaching assistantships with full tuition reimbursements, career-related internships or fieldwork, unspecified assistantships, and administrative assistantships, tutorial assistantships available. Financial award application deadline: 4/1; financial award applicants required to submit FAFSA. *Unit head:* Dr. Steve Ludwig, Director of the Melvin And Valorie Booth School of Business, 660-562-1749, Fax: 660-562-1096, E-mail: sludwig@nwmissouri.edu. *Application contact:* Dr. Steve Ludwig, Director of the Melvin And Valorie Booth School of Business, 660-562-1749, Fax: 660-562-1096, E-mail: sludwig@nwmissouri.edu.
Website: https://www.nwmissouri.edu/business/index.htm

Northwest Nazarene University, Graduate Business Programs, Nampa, ID 83686-5897. Offers MBA. *Accreditation:* ACBSP. *Program availability:* Part-time, evening/weekend, 100% online, blended/hybrid learning, 100% Face-to-face. *Faculty:* 7 full-time (2 women), 8 part-time/adjunct (3 women). *Students:* 45 full-time (24 women), 26 part-time (15 women). Average age 34. 26 applicants, 62% accepted, 11 enrolled. In 2018, 32 master's awarded. *Degree requirements:* For master's, comprehensive exam, thesis or alternative. *Entrance requirements:* For master's, minimum GPA of 3.0; undergraduate degree from a regionally-accredited institution. Additional exam requirements/recommendations for international students: Required—TOEFL (minimum score 82 iBT). *Application deadline:* Applications are processed on a rolling basis. Application fee: $50. Electronic applications accepted. *Expenses:* Tuition: Cost per credit for 2018-2019 $595. Core program is 33 credits; other fees include technology fee and graduation application fee. If student needs business foundation courses, then there is an additional 9 credits for a total of 42 credits. *Financial support:* In 2018–19, 129,205 students received support. Scholarships/grants available. Financial award applicants required to submit FAFSA. *Faculty research:* Leadership, international business, organizational development, economic sustainability, human resource management. *Unit head:* Dr. Joshua Jensen, Director of Graduate Studies, 208-467-8852, Fax: 208-467-8440, E-mail: mba@nnu.edu. *Application contact:* Melinda Siems, Program Coordinator, 208-467-8100, Fax: 208-467-8440, E-mail: mba@nnu.edu.
Website: http://nnu.edu/mba

Northwest University, College of Business, Kirkland, WA 98033. Offers business administration (MBA); international business (MBA); project management (MBA); social entrepreneurship (MBA). *Accreditation:* ACBSP. *Program availability:* Part-time, evening/weekend. *Degree requirements:* For master's, formalized research. *Entrance requirements:* For master's, GMAT. Additional exam requirements/recommendations for international students: Required—TOEFL (minimum score 550 paper-based; 75 iBT). Electronic applications accepted. *Expenses:* Contact institution.

Northwood University, Michigan Campus, DeVos Graduate School, Midland, MI 48640-2398. Offers MBA, MSOL. MBA also offered on Florida and Texas campuses; MSOL offered online only. *Program availability:* Part-time, evening/weekend, online learning. *Faculty:* 6 full-time (1 woman), 8 part-time/adjunct (2 women). *Students:* 44 full-time (21 women), 267 part-time (98 women); includes 34 minority (22 Black or African American, non-Hispanic/Latino; 1 American Indian or Alaska Native, non-Hispanic/Latino; 7 Asian, non-Hispanic/Latino; 4 Hispanic/Latino), 53 international. Average age 32. 127 applicants, 71% accepted, 84 enrolled. In 2018, 127 master's awarded. *Degree requirements:* For master's, capstone project. *Entrance requirements:* For master's, interview, letters of recommendation, resume. Additional exam requirements/recommendations for international students: Required—TOEFL (minimum score 550 paper-based). *Application deadline:* For fall admission, 7/1 priority date for domestic and international students; for winter admission, 12/1 priority date for domestic students. Applications are processed on a rolling basis. Application fee: $50. Electronic applications accepted. *Expenses:* *Tuition:* Full-time $37,080; part-time $18,540 per year. Tuition and fees vary according to course load and program. *Financial support:* In 2018–19, 130 students received support. Federal Work-Study and scholarships/grants available. Support available to part-time students. Financial award application deadline: 6/30; financial award applicants required to submit FAFSA. *Unit head:* Dr. William T Busby, Dean and Chief Operating Officer, 989-837-4488, Fax: 989-837-4800, E-mail: busby@northwood.edu. *Application contact:* Matt Bennett, Director of Enrollment, 989-837-4178, Fax: 989-837-4800, E-mail: mba@northwood.edu.
Website: http://www.northwood.edu/graduate

Norwich University, College of Graduate and Continuing Studies, Master of Business Administration Program, Northfield, VT 05663. Offers construction management (MBA); energy management (MBA); finance (MBA); logistics (MBA); organizational leadership (MBA); project management (MBA); supply chain management (MBA). *Accreditation:* ACBSP. *Program availability:* Evening/weekend, online only, mostly all online with a week-long residency requirement. *Degree requirements:* For master's, comprehensive exam. *Entrance requirements:* For master's, minimum undergraduate GPA of 2.75. Additional exam requirements/recommendations for international students: Required—TOEFL (minimum score 550 paper-based; 80 iBT), IELTS (minimum score 6.5). Electronic applications accepted. *Expenses:* Contact institution.

Notre Dame de Namur University, Division of Academic Affairs, School of Business and Management, Program in Business Administration, Belmont, CA 94002-1908. Offers finance (MBA). *Accreditation:* ACBSP. *Program availability:* Part-time, evening/weekend. *Students:* 31 full-time (21 women), 76 part-time (44 women); includes 61 minority (8 Black or African American, non-Hispanic/Latino; 2 American Indian or Alaska Native, non-Hispanic/Latino; 26 Asian, non-Hispanic/Latino; 18 Hispanic/Latino; 4 Native Hawaiian or other Pacific Islander, non-Hispanic/Latino; 3 Two or more races, non-Hispanic/Latino), 12 international. Average age 34. *Entrance requirements:* For master's, minimum GPA of 2.5. Additional exam requirements/recommendations for international students: Required—TOEFL (minimum score 550 paper-based; 79 iBT). *Application deadline:* For fall admission, 8/1 priority date for domestic students; for spring admission, 12/1 priority date for domestic students. Applications are processed on a rolling basis. Application fee: $60. Electronic applications accepted. *Expenses:* *Tuition:* Full-time $16,596; part-time $11,064 per semester. *Required fees:* $130; $130 per unit. $65 per semester. Tuition and fees vary according to program. *Financial support:* Applicants required to submit FAFSA. *Unit head:* Jordan Holtzman, Program Director, Graduate Business Programs, 510-375-1348, E-mail: jholtzman@ndnu.edu. *Application contact:* Jordan Holtzman, Program Director, Graduate Business Programs, 510-375-1348, E-mail: jholtzman@ndnu.edu.
Website: http://www.ndnu.edu/academics/schools-programs/school-business/

Notre Dame of Maryland University, Graduate Studies, Program in Management, Baltimore, MD 21210-2476. Offers MA. *Program availability:* Part-time, evening/weekend. *Degree requirements:* For master's, thesis optional. *Entrance requirements:* For master's, minimum GPA of 3.0. Additional exam requirements/recommendations for international students: Required—TOEFL (minimum score 500 paper-based; 61 iBT). Electronic applications accepted.

Nova Southeastern University, H. Wayne Huizenga College of Business and Entrepreneurship, Fort Lauderdale, FL 33314-7796. Offers accounting (M Acc); business (MBA); business intelligence/analytics (MBA); complex health systems (MBA); enterprise informatics (MBA); entrepreneurship (MBA); finance (MBA); human resource management (MBA); international business (MBA); management (MBA); marketing (MBA); process improvement (MBA); public administration (MPA); real estate development (MS); sport revenue generation (MBA); supply chain management (MBA). *Accreditation:* NASPAA. *Program availability:* Part-time, evening/weekend, 100% online, blended/hybrid learning. *Entrance requirements:* For master's, GMAT or GRE (depending on undergraduate GPA), official transcripts from all schools attended while in pursuit of bachelor's degree; minimum GPA of 2.5 from regionally-accredited institution. Additional exam requirements/recommendations for international students: Required—TOEFL (minimum score 550 paper-based; 79 iBT), IELTS (minimum score 6), PTE (minimum score 54). Electronic applications accepted. *Expenses:* Contact institution. *Faculty research:* Entrepreneurship and venture capital, ethics and social responsibility, global commerce and cultures, business process management.

Nyack College, School of Business and Leadership, Nyack, NY 10960. Offers business administration (MBA); organizational leadership (MS). *Program availability:* Part-time, evening/weekend, 100% online, blended/hybrid learning. *Students:* 31 full-time (18 women), 10 part-time (6 women); includes 32 minority (20 Black or African American, non-Hispanic/Latino; 1 Asian, non-Hispanic/Latino; 10 Hispanic/Latino; 1 Two or more races, non-Hispanic/Latino), 4 international. Average age 37. In 2018, 26 master's awarded. *Degree requirements:* For master's, thesis (for some programs), capstone project (for MBA). *Entrance requirements:* For master's, transcripts, personal goals statement, recommendations, resume, interview. Additional exam requirements/recommendations for international students: Required—TOEFL (minimum score 550 paper-based; 80 iBT), IELTS (minimum score 6.5). *Application deadline:* Applications are processed on a rolling basis. Application fee: $50. Electronic applications accepted. *Expenses:* MS in Org Ldrshp - $725/credit; MBA - $800/credit. *Financial support:* Scholarships/grants available. Financial award applicants required to submit FAFSA. *Unit head:* Dr. Anita Underwood, Dean, 845-675-4511. *Application contact:* Dr. Anita Underwood, Dean, 845-675-4511.
Website: http://www.nyack.edu/sbl

Oakland City University, School of Business, Oakland City, IN 47660-1099. Offers business administration (MBA); strategic management (MS). *Program availability:* Part-time, evening/weekend. *Degree requirements:* For master's, thesis or alternative. *Entrance requirements:* For master's, GMAT, GRE, or MAT, appropriate bachelor's degree, computer literacy. Additional exam requirements/recommendations for international students: Required—TOEFL. *Faculty research:* Leadership and management styles, international business, new technologies.

Oakland University, Graduate Study and Lifelong Learning, School of Business Administration, Rochester, MI 48309-4401. Offers EMBA, M Acc, MBA, MS, Certificate. *Accreditation:* AACSB. *Program availability:* Part-time, evening/weekend. *Entrance requirements:* For master's, GMAT, minimum GPA of 3.0. Additional exam requirements/recommendations for international students: Required—TOEFL (minimum score 550 paper-based). Electronic applications accepted. *Expenses:* Contact institution.

Oglala Lakota College, Graduate Studies, Program in Lakota Leadership and Management, Kyle, SD 57752-0490. Offers MA. *Program availability:* Part-time, evening/weekend. *Degree requirements:* For master's, thesis. *Entrance requirements:* For master's, minimum GPA of 2.5. *Faculty research:* Curriculum, values, retention of administrators, behavior, graduate follow-up.

Ohio Christian University, Graduate Programs, Circleville, OH 43113. Offers accounting (MBA); business administration (MBA); digital marketing (MBA); finance (MBA); healthcare management (MBA); human resources (MBA); management (MM); organizational leadership (MBA); pastoral care and counseling (MAM); practical theology (MAM).

Ohio Dominican University, Division of Business, Columbus, OH 43219-2099. Offers business administration (MBA), including accounting, data analytics, finance, leadership, risk management, sport management; healthcare administration (MS); sport management (MS). *Accreditation:* ACBSP. *Program availability:* Part-time, evening/weekend, 100% online, blended/hybrid learning. *Faculty:* 13 full-time (4 women), 17 part-time/adjunct (3 women). *Students:* 60 full-time (24 women), 100 part-time (48 women); includes 38 minority (24 Black or African American, non-Hispanic/Latino; 1 American Indian or Alaska Native, non-Hispanic/Latino; 4 Asian, non-Hispanic/Latino; 5 Hispanic/Latino; 4 Two or more races, non-Hispanic/Latino), 22 international. Average age 30. 141 applicants, 43% accepted, 38 enrolled. In 2018, 70 master's awarded. *Degree requirements:* For master's, thesis or alternative. *Entrance requirements:* Additional exam requirements/recommendations for international students: Required—TOEFL (minimum score 550 paper-based), IELTS (minimum score 6.5). *Application deadline:* For fall admission, 8/15 for domestic students, 6/10 for international students; for spring admission, 1/4 for domestic students, 11/2 for international students. Applications are processed on a rolling basis. Application fee: $25. Electronic applications accepted. *Expenses:* *Tuition:* Full-time $10,800; part-time $600 per credit hour. *Required fees:* $450; $225 per semester. Tuition and fees vary according to program. *Financial support:* Applicants required to submit FAFSA. *Unit head:* Dr. Kenneth C. Fah, Chair, 614-251-4566, E-mail: fahk@ohiodominican.edu. *Application contact:* John W. Naughton, Vice President for Enrollment & Student Success, 614-251-4721, Fax: 614-251-6654, E-mail: grad@ohiodominican.edu.
Website: http://www.ohiodominican.edu/academics/graduate/mba

The Ohio State University, Graduate School, Max M. Fisher College of Business, Program in Business Administration, Columbus, OH 43210. Offers MA, MBA, PhD. *Accreditation:* AACSB. *Students:* 289 full-time (90 women), 316 part-time (121 women). Average age 31. In 2018, 270 master's, 9 doctorates awarded. *Degree requirements:* For doctorate, thesis/dissertation. *Entrance requirements:* For master's and doctorate,

GMAT. Additional exam requirements/recommendations for international students: Required—TOEFL (minimum score 600 paper-based; 100 iBT), Michigan English Language Assessment Battery (minimum score 86); Recommended—IELTS (minimum score 7). *Application deadline:* For fall admission, 11/15 priority date for domestic and international students. Applications are processed on a rolling basis. Application fee: $60 ($70 for international students). Electronic applications accepted. *Financial support:* Fellowships, research assistantships, teaching assistantships, Federal Work-Study, institutionally sponsored loans, and unspecified assistantships available. Support available to part-time students. *Unit head:* Dr. Walter Zinn, Associate Dean for Students and Programs, 614-292-0797, E-mail: zinn.13@osu.edu. *Application contact:* Graduate and Professional Admissions, 614-292-9444, Fax: 614-292-3895, E-mail: gpadmissions@osu.edu.
Website: http://fisher.osu.edu/

The Ohio State University, Graduate School, Max M. Fisher College of Business, Program in Business Logistics Engineering, Columbus, OH 43210. Offers MBLE. *Students:* 47 (26 women). Average age 24. In 2018, 20 master's awarded. *Entrance requirements:* For master's, GRE or GMAT. Additional exam requirements/recommendations for international students: Required—TOEFL (minimum score 550 paper-based; 79 iBT), Michigan English Language Assessment Battery (minimum score 82); Recommended—IELTS (minimum score 7). *Application deadline:* For fall admission, 12/13 priority date for domestic students, 11/30 priority date for international students. Applications are processed on a rolling basis. Application fee: $60 ($70 for international students). Electronic applications accepted. *Financial support:* Scholarships/grants available. *Unit head:* Steve DeNunzio, Program Director, 614-769-3155, E-mail: dununzio.4@osu.edu. *Application contact:* Graduate and Professional Admissions, 614-292-9444, Fax: 614-292-3895, E-mail: gpadmissions@osu.edu.
Website: http://fisher.osu.edu/mble

Ohio University, Graduate College, College of Business, Program in Business Administration, Athens, OH 45701-2979. Offers executive management (MBA); MBA/MSA. *Accreditation:* AACSB. *Program availability:* Part-time, evening/weekend, online learning. *Entrance requirements:* For master's, minimum GPA of 3.0. Additional exam requirements/recommendations for international students: Required—TOEFL (minimum score 600 paper-based). Electronic applications accepted. *Expenses:* Contact institution.

Oklahoma Baptist University, Master of Business Administration in Transformational Leadership, Shawnee, OK 74804. Offers energy management (MBA); transformational leadership (MBA). *Accreditation:* ACBSP. *Program availability:* Part-time, evening/weekend, 100% online, blended/hybrid learning. *Students:* 18 full-time (8 women), 33 part-time (15 women); includes 14 minority (1 Black or African American, non-Hispanic/Latino; 11 American Indian or Alaska Native, non-Hispanic/Latino; 1 Hispanic/Latino; 1 Two or more races, non-Hispanic/Latino), 5 international. Average age 32. *Degree requirements:* For master's, comprehensive exam. *Entrance requirements:* Additional exam requirements/recommendations for international students: Recommended—TOEFL, IELTS. *Application deadline:* Applications are processed on a rolling basis. Application fee: $0. Electronic applications accepted. *Expenses: Tuition:* Full-time $9900; part-time $6600 per credit hour. *Financial support:* Applicants required to submit FAFSA. *Unit head:* Will Brantley, Director of Recruitment, 405-5854607, Fax: 405-5854646, E-mail: will.brantley@okbu.edu. *Application contact:* Will Brantley, Director of Recruitment, 405-5854607, Fax: 405-5854646, E-mail: will.brantley@okbu.edu.
Website: http://www.okbu.edu/graduate/mba/

Oklahoma Christian University, Graduate School of Business, Oklahoma City, OK 73136-1100. Offers accounting (M Acc, MBA); financial services (MBA); general business (MBA); health services management (MBA); human resources (MBA); international business (MBA); leadership and organizational development (MBA); marketing (MBA); nonprofit management (MBA); project management (MBA). *Accreditation:* ACBSP. *Program availability:* Part-time, 100% online. *Entrance requirements:* For master's, bachelor's degree. Additional exam requirements/recommendations for international students: Required—TOEFL (minimum score 550 paper-based). Electronic applications accepted. *Expenses:* Contact institution.

Oklahoma City University, Meinders School of Business, Oklahoma City, OK 73106-1402. Offers business (MBA, MSA); computer science (MS); energy legal studies (MS); energy management (MS); JD/MBA. *Program availability:* Part-time, evening/weekend, 100% online. *Degree requirements:* For master's, practicum/capstone. *Entrance requirements:* For master's, undergraduate degree from accredited institution, minimum GPA of 3.0, essay, letters of recommendation. Additional exam requirements/recommendations for international students: Required—TOEFL (minimum score 550 paper-based; 80 iBT). Electronic applications accepted. *Expenses:* Contact institution. *Faculty research:* Group support systems, leadership, decision models in accounting.

Oklahoma City University, Petree College of Arts and Sciences, Oklahoma City, OK 73106-1402. Offers applied behavioral studies (M Ed); applied sociology: nonprofit leadership (MA); creative writing (MFA); criminology (MS); early childhood education (M Ed); elementary education (M Ed); general studies (MLA); leadership/management (MLA); moving image arts (MFA); professional counseling (M Ed); teaching (MA); teaching English to speakers of other languages (MA). *Program availability:* Part-time, evening/weekend. *Degree requirements:* For master's, capstone/practicum. *Entrance requirements:* For master's, bachelor's degree from accredited institution with minimum GPA of 3.0, essay, recommendation letters. Additional exam requirements/recommendations for international students: Required—TOEFL (minimum score 550 paper-based; 80 iBT). Electronic applications accepted. *Expenses:* Contact institution.

Oklahoma State University, Spears School of Business, Department of Management, Stillwater, OK 74078. Offers MBA, MS, PhD. *Program availability:* Part-time. *Faculty:* 27 full-time (10 women), 15 part-time/adjunct (5 women). *Students:* 6 full-time (4 women), 3 part-time (all women); includes 3 minority (1 Black or African American, non-Hispanic/Latino; 1 Asian, non-Hispanic/Latino; 1 Hispanic/Latino), 3 international. Average age 33. 2 applicants, 100% accepted, 2 enrolled. In 2018, 3 doctorates awarded. *Entrance requirements:* For master's and doctorate, GRE or GMAT. Additional exam requirements/recommendations for international students: Required—TOEFL (minimum score 550 paper-based; 79 iBT). *Application deadline:* For fall admission, 3/1 priority date for international students; for spring admission, 8/1 priority date for international students. Applications are processed on a rolling basis. Application fee: $40 ($75 for international students). Electronic applications accepted. *Expenses: Tuition, area resident:* Full-time $4148. Tuition, state resident: full-time $4148. Tuition, nonresident: full-time $10,517. *International tuition:* $10,517 full-time. *Required fees:* $4394; $2929 per credit hour. Tuition and fees vary according to course load and program. *Financial support:* Research assistantships, teaching assistantships, career-related internships or fieldwork, Federal Work-Study, scholarships/grants, health care benefits, tuition waivers (partial), and unspecified assistantships available. Support available to part-time students. Financial award application deadline: 3/1; financial award applicants required to submit FAFSA. *Faculty research:* Telecommunications management, innovative decision support techniques, knowledge networking, organizational research methods, strategic planning. *Unit head:* Dr. James Pappas, Department Head, 405-744-5201, Fax: 405-744-5180, E-mail: james.pappas@okstate.edu. *Application contact:* Dr. Toby Joplin, PhD Coordinator, 405-744-5115, Fax: 405-744-5180, E-mail: toby.joplin@okstate.edu.
Website: https://business.okstate.edu/management/

Old Dominion University, Strome College of Business, Doctoral Program in Business Administration, Norfolk, VA 23529. Offers business administration (PhD), including finance, IT and supply chain management, marketing, strategic management. *Accreditation:* AACSB. *Degree requirements:* For doctorate, comprehensive exam, thesis/dissertation. *Entrance requirements:* For doctorate, GMAT or GRE. Additional exam requirements/recommendations for international students: Required—TOEFL (minimum score 550 paper-based; 79 iBT). Electronic applications accepted. *Faculty research:* International business, buyer behavior, financial markets, strategy, operations research.

Old Dominion University, Strome College of Business, MBA Program, Norfolk, VA 23529. Offers MBA. *Accreditation:* AACSB. *Program availability:* Part-time, evening/weekend, 100% online, blended/hybrid learning. *Entrance requirements:* For master's, GMAT or GRE, letter of reference, resume, essay, official transcripts from all previously attended institutions. Additional exam requirements/recommendations for international students: Required—TOEFL or IELTS. Electronic applications accepted. *Faculty research:* International business, buyer behavior, financial markets, strategy, operations research, maritime and transportation economics.

Olivet Nazarene University, Graduate School, Department of Business, Bourbonnais, IL 60914. Offers business administration (MBA). *Program availability:* Evening/weekend. *Degree requirements:* For master's, thesis or alternative. *Expenses:* Contact institution.

Open University, Graduate Programs, Milton Keynes, United Kingdom. Offers business (MBA); education (M Ed); engineering (M Eng); history (MA); music (MA); philosophy (MA).

Oral Roberts University, School of Business, Tulsa, OK 74171. Offers accounting (MBA); entrepreneurship (MBA); finance (MBA); international business (MBA); management (MBA); marketing (MBA); not for profit management (MNM). *Accreditation:* ACBSP. *Program availability:* Part-time, online learning. *Degree requirements:* For master's, thesis optional. *Entrance requirements:* For master's, minimum cumulative GPA of 3.0 from regionally-accredited institution. Electronic applications accepted. Application fee is waived when completed online. *Faculty research:* Social media, international business and marketing.

Oregon State University, College of Business, Program in Business Administration, Corvallis, OR 97331. Offers business administration (PhD), including accounting; corporate finance (MBA). *Program availability:* Part-time, blended/hybrid learning. *Entrance requirements:* For master's, GMAT. Additional exam requirements/recommendations for international students: Required—TOEFL (minimum score 91 iBT), IELTS (minimum score 7). *Expenses:* Contact institution.

Ottawa University, Graduate Studies-Arizona, Programs in Business, Ottawa, KS 66067-3399. Offers business administration (MBA); finance (MBA); human resources (MA, MBA); leadership (MBA); marketing (MBA). Programs offered in Mesa, Phoenix, Tempe and West Valley, AZ. *Program availability:* Part-time, evening/weekend, online learning. *Degree requirements:* For master's, thesis or alternative. *Entrance requirements:* For master's, minimum undergraduate GPA of 3.0. Additional exam requirements/recommendations for international students: Required—TOEFL (minimum score 550 paper-based). Electronic applications accepted.

Ottawa University, Graduate Studies-International, Ottawa, KS 66067-3399. Offers business administration (MBA). *Program availability:* Online learning. *Degree requirements:* For master's, thesis or alternative. *Entrance requirements:* For master's, minimum undergraduate GPA of 3.0. Additional exam requirements/recommendations for international students: Required—TOEFL (minimum score 550 paper-based). Electronic applications accepted. *Expenses:* Contact institution.

Ottawa University, Graduate Studies-Kansas City, Overland Park, KS 66211. Offers business administration (MBA); human resources (MA). *Program availability:* Part-time, evening/weekend, online learning. *Degree requirements:* For master's, thesis or alternative. *Entrance requirements:* For master's, resume, 3 letters of recommendation. Additional exam requirements/recommendations for international students: Required—TOEFL (minimum score 550 paper-based). Electronic applications accepted. *Expenses:* Contact institution.

Ottawa University, Graduate Studies-Wisconsin, Brookfield, WI 53005. Offers business administration (MBA). *Program availability:* Part-time, evening/weekend, online learning. *Degree requirements:* For master's, thesis or alternative. *Entrance requirements:* For master's, resume, 3 letters of recommendation. Additional exam requirements/recommendations for international students: Required—TOEFL (minimum score 550 paper-based). Electronic applications accepted.

Otterbein University, Department of Business, Accounting and Economics, Westerville, OH 43081. Offers MBA. *Program availability:* Part-time, evening/weekend. *Degree requirements:* For master's, consulting project team. *Entrance requirements:* For master's, GMAT, 2 reference forms, resume. Additional exam requirements/recommendations for international students: Required—TOEFL (minimum score 550 paper-based; 79 iBT). *Expenses:* Contact institution. *Faculty research:* Organizational design, dispute resolution international trade, developing economies, marketing consumer goods, human resources development.

Our Lady of the Lake University, School of Business and Leadership, Program in Management, San Antonio, TX 78207-4689. Offers MBA. *Program availability:* Part-time, evening/weekend, 100% online, blended/hybrid learning. *Faculty:* 4 full-time (2 women), 6 part-time/adjunct (1 woman). *Students:* 56 full-time (32 women), 15 part-time (12 women); includes 54 minority (2 Black or African American, non-Hispanic/Latino; 2 Asian, non-Hispanic/Latino; 49 Hispanic/Latino; 1 Native Hawaiian or other Pacific Islander, non-Hispanic/Latino). Average age 33. 25 applicants, 92% accepted, 11 enrolled. In 2018, 40 master's awarded. *Entrance requirements:* For master's, official transcripts showing 6 hours of coursework in economics and 3 hours of coursework in each of the following ares: statistics, management, business law, and finance; resume including detailed work history describing managerial or professional work experience. Additional exam requirements/recommendations for international students: Required—TOEFL. *Application deadline:* For fall admission, 6/15 for domestic and international students; for spring admission, 11/15 for domestic and international students; for summer admission, 4/15 for domestic and international students. Applications are processed on a rolling basis. Application fee: $40 ($50 for international students). Electronic applications accepted. Application fee is waived when completed online. *Expenses: Tuition:* Full-time $16,326; part-time $907 per credit. *Financial support:* In 2018–19, 25 students received support. Federal Work-Study, scholarships/grants, unspecified assistantships, and tuition discounts available. Support available to part-time students. Financial award application deadline: 5/1; financial award applicants required to submit FAFSA. *Unit head:* Dr. Ronald Crowe, E-mail: rcrowe@ollusa.edu. *Application contact:* Office of Graduate Admissions, 210-431-3995, Fax: 210-431-3945, E-mail: gradadm@ollusa.edu.
Website: http://www.ollusa.edu/s/1190/hybrid/default-hybrid-ollu.aspx?sid-1190&gid-1&pgid-7873

Pace University, Lubin School of Business, New York, NY 10038. Offers MBA, MS, DPS, APC. *Accreditation:* AACSB. *Program availability:* Part-time, evening/weekend, blended/hybrid learning. *Students:* 397 full-time (229 women), 330 part-time (182

women); includes 185 minority (56 Black or African American, non-Hispanic/Latino; 70 Asian, non-Hispanic/Latino; 46 Hispanic/Latino; 1 Native Hawaiian or other Pacific Islander, non-Hispanic/Latino; 12 Two or more races, non-Hispanic/Latino), 311 international. Average age 30. 765 applicants, 74% accepted, 246 enrolled. In 2018, 366 master's, 8 doctorates awarded. *Degree requirements:* For doctorate, thesis/dissertation, oral and written exam. *Entrance requirements:* For master's, GMAT, GRE. If accumulative GPA is 3.20 or above for all undergraduate work, and bachelors degree from accredited institution, may be considered from admission to any MBA or MS program without submitting GMAT or GRE score. MBA applicant with business related masters or doctoral degree, could request GMAT/GRE waiver., undergraduate degree, transcripts from all accredited colleges/universities attended, two letters of recommendation, resume, personal statement; for doctorate and APC, MBA or similar master's degree, 10 years of experience in business, transcripts from all accredited colleges/universities attended, 4 letters of recommendation, interview. Additional exam requirements/recommendations for international students: Required—TOEFL (minimum score 90 iBT), IELTS (minimum score 7) or PTE (minimum score 61). *Application deadline:* For fall admission, 8/1 priority date for domestic students, 6/1 for international students; for spring admission, 12/1 priority date for domestic students, 10/1 for international students; for summer admission, 5/1 priority date for domestic students, 3/1 for international students. Applications are processed on a rolling basis. Application fee: $70. Electronic applications accepted. *Expenses:* Contact institution. *Financial support:* Research assistantships, career-related internships or fieldwork, Federal Work-Study, tuition waivers (full and partial), and unspecified assistantships available. Support available to part-time students. Financial award application deadline: 2/15; financial award applicants required to submit FAFSA. *Faculty research:* Accounting standards and reporting, financial markets and instruments, strategy and entrepreneurship, management learning, marketing and customers. *Unit head:* Neil S. Braun, Dean, Lubin School of Business, 212-618-6600, Fax: 212-618-6603, E-mail: nbraun@pace.edu. *Application contact:* Susan Ford-Goldschein, Director of Graduate Admissions, 212-346-1531, Fax: 212-346-1585, E-mail: graduateadmission@pace.edu.
Website: http://www.pace.edu/lubin

Pacific Lutheran University, School of Business, MBA Program, Tacoma, WA 98447. Offers MBA. *Program availability:* Part-time, evening/weekend. *Entrance requirements:* For master's, GMAT or GRE, statement of professional goals, resume, two letters of recommendation. Additional exam requirements/recommendations for international students: Required—TOEFL (minimum score 88 iBT), IELTS (minimum score 6.5). Electronic applications accepted. *Expenses:* Contact institution.

Pacific States University, College of Business, Los Angeles, CA 90010. Offers accounting (MBA, Certificate); beauty management (MBA); finance (MBA); international business (MBA); management of information technology (MBA); project management (Certificate); real estate management (MBA). *Program availability:* Part-time, evening/weekend, online learning. *Entrance requirements:* For master's, minimum undergraduate GPA of 2.5 during last 90 quarter units of course work, bachelor's degree in business administration or economics. Additional exam requirements/recommendations for international students: Required—TOEFL (minimum score 500 paper-based; 61 iBT), IELTS (minimum score 5.5).

Pacific University, College of Business, Forest Grove, OR 97116-1797. Offers business administration (MBA); finance (MSF).

Palm Beach Atlantic University, Rinker School of Business, West Palm Beach, FL 33416-4708. Offers MACC, MBA. *Program availability:* Part-time, evening/weekend. *Faculty:* 2 full-time (1 woman), 3 part-time/adjunct (1 woman). *Students:* 36 full-time (19 women), 40 part-time (20 women); includes 26 minority (8 Black or African American, non-Hispanic/Latino; 2 Asian, non-Hispanic/Latino; 16 Hispanic/Latino), 20 international. Average age 31. In 2018, 17 master's awarded. *Degree requirements:* For master's, Capstone course. *Entrance requirements:* For master's, minimum GPA of 3.0. Additional exam requirements/recommendations for international students: Required—TOEFL (minimum score 550 paper-based; 79 iBT). *Application deadline:* Applications are processed on a rolling basis. Application fee: $50. Electronic applications accepted. *Expenses: Tuition:* Part-time $767 per credit. Tuition and fees vary according to program. *Financial support:* In 2018–19, 46 students received support. Scholarships/grants and employee education grants available. Financial award application deadline: 5/1; financial award applicants required to submit FAFSA. *Faculty research:* International business, finance, banking. *Unit head:* Dr. David Smith, MBA Program Director, 561-803-2473, E-mail: david_smith@pba.edu. *Application contact:* Graduate Admissions, 888-468-6722, Fax: 561-803-2115, E-mail: grad@pba.edu.
Website: http://learn-well.pba.edu/academics/mba/index.html

Park University, School of Graduate and Professional Studies, Kansas City, MO 54105. Offers adult education (M Ed); business and government leadership (Graduate Certificate); business, government, and global society (MPA); communication and leadership (MA); creative and life writing (Graduate Certificate); disaster and emergency management (MPA, Graduate Certificate); educational leadership (M Ed); finance (MBA, Graduate Certificate); general business (MBA); global business (Graduate Certificate); healthcare administration (MHA); healthcare services management and leadership (Graduate Certificate); international business (MBA); language and literacy (M Ed), including English for speakers of other languages, special reading teacher/literacy coach; leadership of international healthcare organizations (Graduate Certificate); management information systems (MBA, Graduate Certificate); music performance (ADP, Graduate Certificate), including cello (MM, ADP), piano (MM, ADP), viola (MM, ADP), violin (MM, ADP); nonprofit and community services management (MPA); nonprofit leadership (Graduate Certificate); performance (MM), including cello (MM, ADP), piano (MM, ADP), viola (MM, ADP), violin (MM, ADP); public management (MPA); social work (MSW); teacher leadership (M Ed), including curriculum and assessment, instructional leader. *Program availability:* Part-time, evening/weekend, online learning. *Degree requirements:* For master's, comprehensive exam (for some programs), thesis (for some programs), internship (for some programs); exam (for some programs). *Entrance requirements:* For master's, GRE or GMAT (for some programs), teacher certification (for some M Ed programs), letters of recommendation, essay, resume (for some programs). Additional exam requirements/recommendations for international students: Required—TOEFL (minimum score 550 paper-based; 79 iBT), IELTS (minimum score 6). Electronic applications accepted.

Penn State Erie, The Behrend College, Graduate School, Erie, PA 16563. Offers accounting (MPAC); applied clinical psychology (MA); business administration (MBA); quality and manufacturing management (MMM). *Accreditation:* AACSB. *Program availability:* Part-time. *Entrance requirements:* Additional exam requirements/recommendations for international students: Required—TOEFL (minimum score 550 paper-based; 80 iBT), IELTS. Electronic applications accepted.

Penn State Great Valley, Graduate Studies, Management Division, Malvern, PA 19355-1488. Offers business administration (MBA); cyber security (Certificate); data analytics (MPS, MS, Certificate); distributed energy and grid modernization (Certificate); finance (M Fin); health sector management (Certificate); human resource management (Certificate); information science (MSIS); leadership development (MLD); new ventures and entrepreneurship (Certificate); sustainable management practices (Certificate). *Accreditation:* AACSB.

Penn State Harrisburg, Graduate School, School of Business Administration, Middletown, PA 17057. Offers accounting (MPAC, Certificate); business administration (MBA); information systems (MS); operations and supply chain management (Certificate). *Program availability:* Part-time, evening/weekend.

Penn State University Park, Graduate School, Smeal College of Business, University Park, PA 16802. Offers accounting (M Acc); business administration (MBA, MS, PhD); management and organizational leadership (MPS). *Accreditation:* AACSB. *Program availability:* Part-time, evening/weekend. *Entrance requirements:* Additional exam requirements/recommendations for international students: Required—TOEFL (minimum score 550 paper-based; 80 iBT), IELTS. Electronic applications accepted. *Expenses:* Contact institution.

Pensacola Christian College, Graduate Studies, Pensacola, FL 32503-2267. Offers business administration (MBA); curriculum and instruction (MS, Ed D, Ed S); dramatics (MFA); educational leadership (MS, Ed D, Ed S); graphic design (MA, MFA); music (MA); nursing (MSN); performance studies (MA); studio art (MA, MFA).

Pfeiffer University, Program in Business Administration, Misenheimer, NC 28109-0960. Offers MBA, MBA/MHA. *Program availability:* Part-time, evening/weekend, online learning. *Entrance requirements:* For master's, GMAT, minimum GPA of 3.0.

Phillips Theological Seminary, Programs in Theology, Tulsa, OK 74116. Offers administration of church agencies (M Div); campus ministry (M Div); church-related social work (M Div); college and seminary teaching (M Div); global mission work (M Div); institutional chaplaincy (M Div); ministerial vocations in Christian education (M Div); ministry (D Min), including parish ministry, pastoral counseling, practices of ministry; ministry and culture (MAMC), including Christian education, congregational leadership, history and practice of Christian spirituality, theology, ethics, and culture; ministry of music (M Div); pastoral care and counseling (M Div); pastoral ministry (M Div); theological studies (MTS). *Accreditation:* ATS. *Program availability:* Part-time, online learning. *Degree requirements:* For master's, thesis (for some programs); for doctorate, thesis/dissertation. *Entrance requirements:* For master's, minimum GPA of 2.5; for doctorate, M Div, minimum GPA of 3.0. *Faculty research:* Biblical studies, historical studies, theology and culture, practical theology, theology and film.

Piedmont College, School of Business, Demorest, GA 30535. Offers MBA. *Accreditation:* ACBSP. *Program availability:* Part-time, evening/weekend. *Students:* 27 full-time (11 women), 13 part-time (7 women); includes 13 minority (6 Black or African American, non-Hispanic/Latino; 1 Asian, non-Hispanic/Latino; 4 Hispanic/Latino; 2 Native Hawaiian or other Pacific Islander, non-Hispanic/Latino). Average age 29. 10 applicants, 70% accepted, 7 enrolled. In 2018, 23 master's awarded. *Degree requirements:* For master's, capstone. *Entrance requirements:* For master's, GMAT, GRE. Additional exam requirements/recommendations for international students: Required—TOEFL (minimum score 550 paper-based). *Application deadline:* For fall admission, 7/15 for domestic students; for spring admission, 12/1 for domestic students. Applications are processed on a rolling basis. Electronic applications accepted. *Expenses: Tuition:* Full-time $9738; part-time $541 per credit. *Required fees:* $200 per semester. *Financial support:* Federal Work-Study and unspecified assistantships available. Financial award applicants required to submit FAFSA. *Unit head:* Dr. Edward Taylor, Dean, 706-778-3000, E-mail: etaylor@piedmont.edu. *Application contact:* Kathleen Carter, Director of Graduate Enrollment Management, 706-778-3000, E-mail: kcarter@piedmont.edu.
Website: http://www.piedmont.edu

Pittsburg State University, Graduate School, Kelce College of Business, Department of Management and Marketing, Pittsburg, KS 66762. Offers general administration (MBA); international business (MBA). *Accreditation:* AACSB. *Program availability:* Part-time. *Degree requirements:* For master's, thesis or alternative. *Entrance requirements:* For master's, GMAT or GRE. Additional exam requirements/recommendations for international students: Required—TOEFL (minimum score 550 paper-based; 79 iBT), IELTS (minimum score 6.5), PTE (minimum score 53). Electronic applications accepted. *Expenses:* Contact institution. *Faculty research:* Consumer behavior, productions management, forecasting interest rate swaps, strategy management.

Plymouth State University, College of Graduate Studies, Graduate Studies in Business, Plymouth, NH 03264-1595. Offers accounting (MS); general management (MBA). *Accreditation:* ACBSP. *Program availability:* Part-time, evening/weekend, online learning. *Entrance requirements:* For master's, minimum GPA of 2.5. Additional exam requirements/recommendations for international students: Required—TOEFL (minimum score 550 paper-based). *Expenses:* Contact institution.

Point Loma Nazarene University, Fermanian School of Business, San Diego, CA 92106-2899. Offers general business (MBA); healthcare management (MBA); innovation and entrepreneurship (MBA); organizational leadership (MBA); project management (MBA). *Accreditation:* ACBSP. *Program availability:* Part-time, evening/weekend. *Entrance requirements:* For master's, GMAT, letters of recommendation, essay, interview. Additional exam requirements/recommendations for international students: Required—TOEFL. Electronic applications accepted. *Expenses:* Contact institution.

Point Park University, Rowland School of Business, Pittsburgh, PA 15222-1984. Offers MA, MBA, MS. *Program availability:* Part-time, evening/weekend, 100% online. *Degree requirements:* For master's, comprehensive exam (for some programs), thesis or alternative. *Entrance requirements:* For master's, minimum QPA of 2.75; 2 letters of recommendation; resume (MA). Additional exam requirements/recommendations for international students: Required—TOEFL (minimum score 550 paper-based; 79 iBT). Electronic applications accepted. *Faculty research:* Technology issues, foreign direct investment, multinational corporate issues, cross-cultural international organizations/administrations, regional integration issues.

Point University, Graduate Programs, West Point, GA 31833. Offers business transformation (MBA); transformative ministry (MTM). *Program availability:* Part-time, online only, 100% online. *Faculty:* 2 full-time (both women), 8 part-time/adjunct (3 women). *Students:* 8 full-time (1 woman), 27 part-time (19 women); includes 19 minority (15 Black or African American, non-Hispanic/Latino; 2 Hispanic/Latino; 2 Two or more races, non-Hispanic/Latino), 1 international. Average age 40. *Entrance requirements:* Additional exam requirements/recommendations for international students: Required—TOEFL (minimum score 550 paper-based; 80 iBT). *Application deadline:* Applications are processed on a rolling basis. Application fee: $0. Electronic applications accepted. *Expenses: Tuition:* Full-time $515; part-time $515 per credit hour. *Required fees:* $250 per term. Tuition and fees vary according to program. *Application contact:* Rusty Hassell, Executive Director of Enrollment, 706-385-1503, E-mail: rhassell@point.edu.

Polytechnic University of Puerto Rico, Graduate School, Hato Rey, PR 00918. Offers business administration (MBA), including computer information systems, general management, management of information systems, management of international enterprises; civil engineering (ME, MS); computer engineering (ME, MS); computer science (MCS, MS); electrical engineering (ME, MS); engineering management (MEM); environmental management (MEM); landscape architecture (M Land Arch); manufacturing competitiveness (MMC, MS); manufacturing engineering (ME, MS); mechanical engineering (M Mech E). *Accreditation:* ASLA. *Program availability:* Part-time, evening/weekend. *Entrance requirements:* For master's, 3 letters of recommendation.

Polytechnic University of Puerto Rico, Miami Campus, Graduate School, Miami, FL 33166. Offers accounting (MBA); business administration (MBA); construction management (MEM); environmental management (MEM); finance (MBA); human resources management (MBA); logistics and supply chain management (MBA); management of international enterprises (MBA); manufacturing management (MEM); marketing management (MBA); project management (MBA). *Program availability:* Part-time, evening/weekend, online learning. *Entrance requirements:* For master's, minimum GPA of 3.0. Electronic applications accepted.

Polytechnic University of Puerto Rico, Orlando Campus, Graduate School, Orlando, FL 32825. Offers accounting (MBA); business administration (MBA); construction management (MEM); engineering management (MEM); environmental management (MEM); finance (MBA); human resources management (MBA); management of international enterprises (MBA); management of technology (MBA); manufacturing management (MEM). *Program availability:* Part-time, evening/weekend, online learning. *Entrance requirements:* For master's, minimum GPA of 3.0. Additional exam requirements/recommendations for international students: Recommended—TOEFL. Electronic applications accepted.

Pontifical Catholic University of Puerto Rico, College of Business Administration, Ponce, PR 00717-0777. Offers MBA, DBA, PhD, Professional Certificate. *Program availability:* Part-time, evening/weekend. *Degree requirements:* For master's, thesis; for doctorate, comprehensive exam, thesis/dissertation. *Entrance requirements:* For master's, GRE, interview, minimum GPA of 2.75; for doctorate, 2 letters of recommendation, 2 years experience in a related field, interview.

Pontificia Universidad Catolica Madre y Maestra, Graduate School, Faculty of Social and Administrative Sciences, Santiago, Dominican Republic. Offers business administration (MBA), including business development, finance, international business, management skills (M Mgmt, MBA), marketing, operations, strategic cost management, strategy, tourist destination planning and management; law (LL M), including civil law, corporate business law, criminal law, international relations, real estate law; management (M Mgmt), including higher financial management, insurance program administration, management skills (M Mgmt, MBA); psychology (MA), including clinical child and adolescent psychology, forensic psychology; strategic human resources (EMBA).

Portland State University, Graduate Studies, College of Liberal Arts and Sciences, Systems Science Program, Portland, OR 97207-0751. Offers computational intelligence (Certificate); computer modeling and simulation (Certificate); systems science (MS); systems science/anthropology (PhD); systems science/business administration (PhD); systems science/civil engineering (PhD); systems science/economics (PhD); systems science/engineering management (PhD); systems science/general (PhD); systems science/mathematical sciences (PhD); systems science/mechanical engineering (PhD); systems science/psychology (PhD); systems science/sociology (PhD). *Degree requirements:* For master's, comprehensive exam (for some programs), thesis optional; for doctorate, variable foreign language requirement, comprehensive exam (for some programs), thesis/dissertation. *Entrance requirements:* For master's, GRE/GMAT (recommended), minimum GPA of 3.0 on undergraduate or graduate work, 2 letters of recommendation, statement of interest; for doctorate, GMAT, GRE General Test, minimum GPA of 3.0 undergraduate, 3.25 graduate; 3 letters of recommendation; statement of interest. Additional exam requirements/recommendations for international students: Required—TOEFL (minimum score 550 paper-based; 80 iBT). Electronic applications accepted. *Faculty research:* Systems theory and methodology, artificial intelligence neural networks, information theory, nonlinear dynamics/chaos, modeling and simulation.

Portland State University, Graduate Studies, The School of Business, Program in Business Administration, Portland, OR 97207-0751. Offers MBA. *Accreditation:* AACSB. *Program availability:* Part-time, evening/weekend. *Degree requirements:* For master's, one foreign language, project. *Entrance requirements:* For master's, GMAT or GRE, minimum GPA of 3.0 in upper-division course work, 2 recommendations, resume, interview. Additional exam requirements/recommendations for international students: Required—TOEFL (minimum score 550 paper-based). Electronic applications accepted. *Expenses:* Contact institution. *Faculty research:* Quality management and organizational excellence, performance measurement, customer satisfaction, values, technology management and technology transfer.

Post University, Program in Business Administration, Waterbury, CT 06723-2540. Offers accounting (MSA); business administration (MBA); corporate finance (MBA); corporate innovation (MBA); healthcare systems leadership (MBA); leadership (MBA); marketing (MBA); project management (MBA, MS). *Accreditation:* ACBSP. *Program availability:* Online learning. *Entrance requirements:* For master's, resume. *Expenses:* Tuition: Full-time $8300; part-time $570 per credit. *Required fees:* $140 per term. Tuition and fees vary according to course level, campus/location and program.

Prairie View A&M University, College of Business, Prairie View, TX 77446. Offers accounting (MS); business administration (MBA). *Accreditation:* AACSB. *Program availability:* Part-time, evening/weekend. *Faculty:* 18 full-time (2 women), 1 part-time/adjunct (0 women). *Students:* 57 full-time (33 women), 132 part-time (85 women); includes 174 minority (148 Black or African American, non-Hispanic/Latino; 1 American Indian or Alaska Native, non-Hispanic/Latino; 13 Asian, non-Hispanic/Latino; 10 Hispanic/Latino; 1 Native Hawaiian or other Pacific Islander, non-Hispanic/Latino; 1 Two or more races, non-Hispanic/Latino), 9 international. Average age 29. 90 applicants, 86% accepted, 59 enrolled. In 2018, 98 master's awarded. *Degree requirements:* For master's, comprehensive exam, thesis optional. *Entrance requirements:* For master's, GMAT, GRE, minimum GPA of 2.45, essay. Additional exam requirements/recommendations for international students: Required—TOEFL (minimum score 550 paper-based; 79 iBT). *Application deadline:* For fall admission, 5/1 for domestic students, 5/1 priority date for international students; for spring admission, 10/1 for domestic students, 9/1 priority date for international students; for summer admission, 3/1 for domestic students, 2/1 for international students. Applications are processed on a rolling basis. Application fee: $50. Electronic applications accepted. *Expenses:* $8,019 per year in-state, $17,417 per year out-of-state. *Financial support:* In 2018–19, 3 research assistantships (averaging $1,600 per year) were awarded; scholarships/grants and unspecified assistantships also available. Financial award application deadline: 4/1; financial award applicants required to submit FAFSA. *Faculty research:* Accounting (energy, oil and gas); finance (international finance, personal finance, real estate markets and institutions); marketing management (supply chain, human resources, entrepreneurship, small business ownership, ethics); management information systems (cyber-security, managing social media during crises). *Unit head:* Dr. Munir Quddus, Dean, 936-261-9200, Fax: 936-261-9241, E-mail: cob@pvamu.edu. *Application contact:* Gabriel Crosby, Director, Graduate Programs in Business, 936-261-9217, Fax: 936-261-9232, E-mail: mba@pvamu.edu.
Website: http://www.pvamu.edu/business/

Presidio Graduate School, MBA Programs - Seattle, San Francisco, CA 94129. Offers cooperative management (Certificate); sustainable business (MBA); sustainable systems (MBA). *Program availability:* Part-time, evening/weekend, blended/hybrid learning. *Entrance requirements:* For master's and Certificate, Quantitative Assessment Summary, GRE, or GMAT, resume, two letters of recommendation, essay, transcripts. Additional exam requirements/recommendations for international students: Required—TOEFL (minimum score 90 iBT), IELTS (minimum score 6.5). Electronic applications accepted.

Providence College, School of Business, Providence, RI 02918. Offers accounting (MBA); finance (MBA); international business (MBA); management (MBA); marketing (MBA). *Accreditation:* AACSB. *Program availability:* Part-time, evening/weekend. *Entrance requirements:* For master's, GMAT. Additional exam requirements/recommendations for international students: Required—TOEFL (minimum score 577 paper-based; 90 iBT). *Expenses:* Contact institution.

Purdue University, Graduate School, Krannert School of Management, Doctoral Program in Management, West Lafayette, IN 47907-2056. Offers PhD. *Degree requirements:* For doctorate, comprehensive exam, thesis/dissertation, first-year summer paper, dissertation proposal, dissertation defense. *Entrance requirements:* For doctorate, GMAT or GRE. Additional exam requirements/recommendations for international students: Required—TOEFL (minimum score 575 paper-based); Recommended—TWE. Electronic applications accepted. *Faculty research:* Accounting, finance, marketing, management information systems, supply chain and operations management, organizational behavior and human resource management, quantitative methods/management science, strategic management.

Purdue University, Graduate School, Krannert School of Management, Executive MBA Programs, West Lafayette, IN 47907. Offers MBA. *Entrance requirements:* For master's, GMAT or GRE, two professional recommendations; essays; official transcripts and, in some instances, copy of diploma; current professional resume; in-person or virtual interview. Additional exam requirements/recommendations for international students: Required—TOEFL, IELTS. Electronic applications accepted. *Expenses:* Contact institution. *Faculty research:* Trust in organizations, alliances, organizational change, negotiations, risk management.

Purdue University, Graduate School, Krannert School of Management, Master of Business Administration Program, West Lafayette, IN 47907. Offers MBA. *Accreditation:* AACSB. *Entrance requirements:* For master's, GMAT, four-year baccalaureate degree, minimum GPA of 3.0, essays, recommendation letters, work/internship experience. Additional exam requirements/recommendations for international students: Required—TOEFL (minimum score 600 paper-based; 93 iBT), IELTS (minimum score 7.5), or PTE (minimum score 70). Electronic applications accepted. *Expenses:* Contact institution. *Faculty research:* Capital market imperfections and the sensitivity of investment to stock prices, identifying beneficial collaboration in decentralized logistics systems, performance periods and the dynamics of the performance-risk relationship, applications of global optimization to process and molecular design.

Purdue University, Graduate School, Krannert School of Management, Weekend Master of Business Administration Program, West Lafayette, IN 47907. Offers MBA. *Program availability:* Part-time-only, evening/weekend. *Entrance requirements:* For master's, GMAT, minimum GPA of 3.0, four-year baccalaureate degree, essays, letters of recommendation. Additional exam requirements/recommendations for international students: Required—TOEFL (minimum score 600 paper-based; 93 iBT), IELTS (minimum score 7.5), PTE (minimum score 70). Electronic applications accepted. *Expenses:* Contact institution.

Purdue University Fort Wayne, Doermer School of Business, Fort Wayne, IN 46805-1499. Offers MBA. *Accreditation:* AACSB. *Program availability:* Part-time. *Entrance requirements:* For master's, GMAT, minimum GPA of 3.0, two letters of recommendation, essay, interview. Additional exam requirements/recommendations for international students: Required—TOEFL (minimum score 600 paper-based; 100 iBT). *Faculty research:* Buddhist ethics education framework, earth orbit pollution, information technology and business school graduates.

Purdue University Global, School of Business, Davenport, IA 52807. Offers business administration (MBA); change leadership (MS); entrepreneurship (MBA); finance (MBA); health care management (MBA, MS); human resource (MBA); international business (MBA); management (MS); marketing (MBA); project management (MBA, MS); supply chain management and logistics (MBA, MS). *Accreditation:* ACBSP. *Program availability:* Part-time, evening/weekend, online learning. *Entrance requirements:* Additional exam requirements/recommendations for international students: Required—TOEFL (minimum score 550 paper-based; 80 iBT). Electronic applications accepted.

Purdue University Northwest, Graduate Studies Office, School of Management, Hammond, IN 46323-2094. Offers accountancy (M Acc); business administration (MBA); business administration for executives (EMBA). *Accreditation:* AACSB. *Program availability:* Part-time, evening/weekend. *Entrance requirements:* For master's, GMAT. Additional exam requirements/recommendations for international students: Required—TOEFL. Electronic applications accepted.

Queen's University at Kingston, Smith School of Business, Doctoral Program in Management, Kingston, ON K7L 3N6, Canada. Offers analytics (PhD); business economics (PhD); finance (PhD); management information systems (PhD); marketing (PhD); organizational behavior (PhD); strategy (PhD).

Queen's University at Kingston, Smith School of Business, Master of Science in Management Program, Kingston, ON K7L 3N6, Canada. Offers analytics (M Sc); business economics (M Sc); finance (M Sc); management information systems (M Sc); marketing (M Sc); organizational behavior (M Sc); strategy (M Sc).

Queen's University at Kingston, Smith School of Business, Program in Business Administration, Kingston, ON K7L 3N6, Canada. Offers consulting and project management (MBA); finance (MBA); innovation and entrepreneurship (MBA); marketing (MBA). *Degree requirements:* For master's, thesis optional, research project. *Entrance requirements:* For master's, GMAT, minimum B+ average. Additional exam requirements/recommendations for international students: Required—TOEFL. Electronic applications accepted. *Faculty research:* Management fundamentals, strategic thinking, global business, innovation and change, leadership.

Queens University of Charlotte, McColl School of Business, Charlotte, NC 28274-0002. Offers business administration (EMBA, MBA, PMBA); organization development (MSOD). *Accreditation:* AACSB. *Program availability:* Part-time, evening/weekend, online learning. *Degree requirements:* For master's, capstone course. *Entrance requirements:* For master's, GMAT, minimum GPA of 2.5. Additional exam requirements/recommendations for international students: Required—TOEFL. Electronic applications accepted. *Expenses:* Contact institution.

Quincy University, MBA Program, Quincy, IL 62301-2699. Offers MBA. *Program availability:* Part-time, evening/weekend, online learning. *Entrance requirements:* For master's, GMAT (if GPA less than 3.0), previous course work in accounting, economics, finance, management or marketing, and statistics. Additional exam requirements/recommendations for international students: Required—TOEFL (minimum score 550 paper-based; 79 iBT). Electronic applications accepted. *Expenses:* Contact institution. *Faculty research:* Macroeconomic forecasting.

Quinnipiac University, School of Business, Program in Business Administration, Hamden, CT 06518-1940. Offers finance (MBA); health care management (MBA);

supply chain management (MBA); JD/MBA. *Accreditation:* AACSB. *Program availability:* Part-time, evening/weekend, 100% online, blended/hybrid learning. *Entrance requirements:* For master's, GMAT or GRE, minimum GPA of 3.0. Additional exam requirements/recommendations for international students: Required—TOEFL (minimum score 575 paper-based; 90 iBT), IELTS (minimum score 6.5). Electronic applications accepted. *Expenses:* Contact institution. *Faculty research:* Financial markets and investments, international business, supply chain management, health care management, corporate governance.

Radford University, College of Graduate Studies and Research, Program in Business Administration, Radford, VA 24142. Offers MBA. *Accreditation:* AACSB. *Program availability:* Part-time, evening/weekend, online learning. *Faculty:* 5 full-time (2 women). *Students:* 10 full-time (4 women), 28 part-time (11 women); includes 1 minority (Black or African American, non-Hispanic/Latino), 3 international. Average age 31. 23 applicants, 87% accepted, 10 enrolled. In 2018, 10 master's awarded. *Entrance requirements:* For master's, GMAT or GRE (waiver may be submitted based on work experience), minimum GPA of 2.75, 2 letters of reference, letter of intent, resume, official transcripts. Additional exam requirements/recommendations for international students: Required—TOEFL (minimum score 550 paper-based; 79 iBT), IELTS (minimum score 6.5). *Application deadline:* For fall admission, 7/15 priority date for domestic students, 12/1 for international students; for spring admission, 11/1 priority date for domestic students, 7/1 for international students. Applications are processed on a rolling basis. Application fee: $50. Electronic applications accepted. *Expenses: Tuition, area resident:* Full-time $8915; part-time $371 per credit hour. Tuition, state resident: full-time $8915; part-time $371 per credit hour. Tuition, nonresident: full-time $17,441. *Required fees:* $3288; $138 per credit hour. *Financial support:* In 2018–19, 9 students received support, including 4 teaching assistantships (averaging $10,000 per year); scholarships/grants and unspecified assistantships also available. Support available to part-time students. Financial award application deadline: 12/1; financial award applicants required to submit FAFSA. *Unit head:* Dr. Gary Schirr, MBA Program Director, 540-831-6905, E-mail: radfordmba@radford.edu. *Application contact:* Dr. Gary Schirr, MBA Program Director, 540-831-6905, E-mail: radfordmba@radford.edu.
Website: http://www.radford.edu/content/cobe/home/programs/mba.html

Ramapo College of New Jersey, Master of Business Administration Program, Mahwah, NJ 07430-1680. Offers leadership (MBA). *Accreditation:* AACSB. *Program availability:* Part-time-only, evening/weekend. *Faculty:* 3 full-time (all women). *Students:* 66 part-time (35 women); includes 18 minority (1 Black or African American, non-Hispanic/Latino; 4 Asian, non-Hispanic/Latino; 13 Hispanic/Latino). Average age 31. 90 applicants, 53% accepted, 34 enrolled. In 2018, 30 master's awarded. *Degree requirements:* For master's, capstone course. *Entrance requirements:* For master's, official transcript of baccalaureate degree from accredited institution with minimum recommended GPA of 3.0; personal statement; 2 letters of recommendation; resume; interview. Additional exam requirements/recommendations for international students: Required—TOEFL (minimum score 550 paper-based; 79 iBT), TOEFL minimum required scores: 550 paper-based score for tests taken prior to July 2017 and 79 iBT score for tests taken after July 2017; Recommended—IELTS (minimum score 6). *Application deadline:* For fall admission, 5/1 for domestic and international students. Applications are processed on a rolling basis. Application fee: $65. Electronic applications accepted. *Expenses:* $983 per credit tuition for academic year 2018-2019, $57.50 per credit tuition-related fees for academic year 2018-2019, $70.10 per credit Immersion Trip fees for academic year 2018-2019; MBA is a 42 credit program. *Financial support:* In 2018–19, 5 students received support. Career-related internships or fieldwork and scholarships/grants available. Financial award application deadline: 3/1; financial award applicants required to submit FAFSA. *Faculty research:* Ethical implications of taxation on society, organizational governance, applied labor economics, empirical market microstructure, foreign direct investment. *Unit head:* Dr. Edward Petkus, Dean of the Anisfield School of Business, 201-684-7377, E-mail: epetkus@ramapo.edu. *Application contact:* Timothy Landers, Assistant Dean/Director of the MBA Program, 201-684-7771, E-mail: tlanders@ramapo.edu.
Website: http://www.ramapo.edu/mba/

Reformed University, Graduate Programs, Lawrenceville, GA 30043. Offers management (MBA); theology (M Div).

Regent's University London, Webster Graduate School, London, United Kingdom. Offers business (MBA); finance (MS); human resources (MA); information technology management (MA); international business (MA); international non-governmental organizations (MA); international relations (MA); management and leadership (MA); marketing (MA). *Program availability:* Part-time.

Regent University, Graduate School, School of Business and Leadership, Virginia Beach, VA 23464-9800. Offers business administration (MBA), including accounting, economics, entrepreneurship, finance and investing, general management, healthcare management (MA, MBA), human resource management (MA, MBA), innovation management, leadership, marketing, not-for-profit management (MA, MBA); business analytics (MS); business and design management (MA); church leadership (MA); leadership (Certificate); organizational leadership (MA, PhD), including ecclesial leadership (DSL, PhD), entrepreneurial leadership (PhD), healthcare management (MA, MBA), human resource development (PhD), human resource management (MA, MBA), individualized studies (DSL, PhD), interdisciplinary studies (MA), leadership coaching and mentoring (MA), not-for-profit management (MA, MBA), organizational development consulting (MA), servant leadership (MA, DSL); strategic leadership (DSL), including ecclesial leadership (DSL, PhD), global consulting, healthcare leadership, individualized studies (DSL, PhD), leadership coaching, servant leadership (MA, DSL), strategic foresight. *Program availability:* Part-time, evening/weekend, 100% online, blended/hybrid learning. *Degree requirements:* For master's, thesis or alternative, 3-credit hour culminating experience; for doctorate, thesis/dissertation. *Entrance requirements:* For master's, college transcripts, resume, essay; for doctorate, college transcripts, resume, essay, writing sample; for Certificate, writing sample, resume, transcripts. Additional exam requirements/recommendations for international students: Required—TOEFL (minimum score 577 paper-based). Electronic applications accepted. *Expenses:* Contact institution. *Faculty research:* Servant leadership, global business, team effectiveness, technology utilization, leadership development.

Reinhardt University, McCamish School of Business & Sport Studies, Waleska, GA 30183-2981. Offers MBA. *Program availability:* Part-time, evening/weekend, 100% online. *Faculty:* 5 full-time (3 women). *Students:* 7 full-time (1 woman), 37 part-time (12 women); includes 13 minority (10 Black or African American, non-Hispanic/Latino; 2 Hispanic/Latino; 1 Two or more races, non-Hispanic/Latino), 2 international. Average age 44. In 2018, 12 master's awarded. *Entrance requirements:* For master's, GMAT score of 500 or higher, or a GRE score in the upper 50th percentile. Applicants may request a waiver. Additional exam requirements/recommendations for international students: Required—TOEFL (minimum score 500 paper-based). *Application deadline:* Applications are processed on a rolling basis. Application fee: $50. Electronic applications accepted. Application fee is waived when completed online. *Expenses:* Contact institution. *Financial support:* Application deadline: 7/1; applicants required to submit FAFSA. *Unit head:* Jacob Harney, Interim Dean, 770-720-9102, E-mail: jph@reinhardt.edu. *Application contact:* Dr. Dana L. Hall, Program Coordinator, 770-720-5756, Fax: 770-720-9236, E-mail: dlh@reinhardt.edu.
Website: https://www.reinhardt.edu/academics/graduate-programs/

Rensselaer at Hartford, Lally School of Management and Technology, Hartford, CT 06120-2991. Offers MBA, MS. *Program availability:* Part-time, evening/weekend, online learning. *Degree requirements:* For master's, capstone course. *Entrance requirements:* For master's, GMAT (MBA). Additional exam requirements/recommendations for international students: Required—TOEFL (minimum score 600 paper-based; 100 iBT). Electronic applications accepted.

Rensselaer Polytechnic Institute, Graduate School, Lally School of Management, Troy, NY 12180-3590. Offers MBA, MS, PhD, MS/MBA. *Accreditation:* AACSB. *Program availability:* Part-time. *Faculty:* 36 full-time (9 women), 5 part-time/adjunct (0 women). *Students:* 201 full-time (97 women), 32 part-time (11 women); includes 27 minority (5 Black or African American, non-Hispanic/Latino; 8 Asian, non-Hispanic/Latino; 9 Hispanic/Latino; 5 Two or more races, non-Hispanic/Latino), 158 international. Average age 24. 1,198 applicants, 40% accepted, 142 enrolled. In 2018, 124 master's, 6 doctorates awarded. *Degree requirements:* For doctorate, thesis/dissertation. *Entrance requirements:* For master's and doctorate, GMAT or GRE. Additional exam requirements/recommendations for international students: Required—TOEFL (minimum score 570 paper-based; 88 iBT), IELTS (minimum score 6.5), PTE (minimum score 60). *Application deadline:* For fall admission, 1/1 priority date for domestic and international students. Applications are processed on a rolling basis. Application fee: $75. Electronic applications accepted. *Expenses:* Contact institution. *Financial support:* In 2018–19, 64 students received support. Scholarships/grants available. Financial award application deadline: 1/1; financial award applicants required to submit FAFSA. *Faculty research:* Business analytics, quantitative finance and risk analytics, management, supply chain management, technology commercialization and entrepreneurship. *Total annual research expenditures:* $314,757. *Unit head:* Dr. Chanaka Edirisinghe, Associate Dean, Lally School of Management, 518-276-3336, E-mail: edirin@rpi.edu. *Application contact:* Jarron Decker, Director of Graduate Admissions, 518-276-6216, Fax: 518-276-4072, E-mail: gradadmissions@rpi.edu.
Website: http://lallyschool.rpi.edu/

Rice University, Graduate Programs, Jesse H. Jones Graduate School of Business, Houston, TX 77251-1892. Offers business administration (EMBA, MBA, PMBA); MBA/M Eng; MD/MBA. *Accreditation:* AACSB. *Program availability:* Evening/weekend. *Degree requirements:* For master's, one foreign language, comprehensive exam. *Entrance requirements:* For master's, GMAT or GRE. Additional exam requirements/recommendations for international students: Required—TOEFL (minimum score 600 paper-based). Electronic applications accepted. *Expenses:* Contact institution. *Faculty research:* Marketing strategy, technology transfer initiatives, management accounting, leadership and change management, financial management.

Rider University, College of Business Administration, Executive MBA Program, Lawrenceville, NJ 08648-3001. Offers EMBA. *Program availability:* Evening/weekend. *Students:* 6 full-time (2 women); includes 1 minority (Asian, non-Hispanic/Latino). Average age 42. 11 applicants, 36% accepted. In 2018, 7 master's awarded. *Application deadline:* For fall admission, 8/1 for domestic students. Applications are processed on a rolling basis. Application fee: $50. Electronic applications accepted. *Expenses: Tuition:* Full-time $850; part-time $850 per credit hour. *Required fees:* $50; $50 per course. Tuition and fees vary according to program. *Financial support:* Applicants required to submit FAFSA. *Unit head:* John Donovan, EMBA Program Director, 609-895-5541, E-mail: jdonovan@rider.edu. *Application contact:* Jamie L. Mitchell, Director of Graduate Admissions, 609-896-5036, Fax: 609-895-5680, E-mail: jmitchell@rider.edu.
Website: https://www.rider.edu/emba

Rider University, College of Business Administration, MBA Program, Lawrenceville, NJ 08648-3001. Offers MBA. *Program availability:* Part-time-only, 100% online, blended/hybrid learning. *Students:* 33 full-time (14 women), 117 part-time (45 women); includes 34 minority (16 Black or African American, non-Hispanic/Latino; 1 American Indian or Alaska Native, non-Hispanic/Latino; 5 Asian, non-Hispanic/Latino; 8 Hispanic/Latino; 4 Two or more races, non-Hispanic/Latino), 17 international. Average age 31. 67 applicants, 75% accepted, 26 enrolled. In 2018, 47 master's awarded. *Entrance requirements:* For master's, GMAT, application fee, statement of aims and objectives, official prior college transcripts, resume. Additional exam requirements/recommendations for international students: Required—TOEFL (minimum score 540 paper-based; 79 iBT). *Application deadline:* For fall admission, 8/1 for domestic students; for spring admission, 12/1 for domestic students; for summer admission, 5/1 for domestic students. Application fee: $50. Electronic applications accepted. *Expenses: Tuition:* Full-time $850; part-time $850 per credit hour. *Required fees:* $50; $50 per course. Tuition and fees vary according to program. *Financial support:* Applicants required to submit FAFSA. *Unit head:* Jean Cherney, Academic Coordinator/Graduate Programs, 609-895-5557, E-mail: jcherney@rider.edu. *Application contact:* Jamie L. Mitchell, Director of Graduate Admissions, 609-896-5036, Fax: 609-895-5680, E-mail: jmitchell@rider.edu.

Rivier University, School of Graduate Studies, Department of Business Administration, Nashua, NH 03060. Offers MBA. *Program availability:* Part-time, evening/weekend. *Entrance requirements:* Additional exam requirements/recommendations for international students: Recommended—TOEFL.

Robert Morris University, School of Business, Moon Township, PA 15108-1189. Offers business administration (MBA); human resource management (MS); taxation (MS); MBA/MS. *Accreditation:* AACSB. *Program availability:* Part-time-only, evening/weekend, 100% online. *Faculty:* 18 full-time (7 women), 1 (woman) part-time/adjunct. *Students:* 214 part-time (84 women); includes 12 minority (6 Black or African American, non-Hispanic/Latino; 5 Asian, non-Hispanic/Latino; 1 Two or more races, non-Hispanic/Latino), 7 international. Average age 30. 77 applicants, 97% accepted, 71 enrolled. In 2018, 83 master's awarded. *Degree requirements:* For master's, Completion of 36 or 30 credit hours depending upon program. *Entrance requirements:* For master's, GMAT, GRE, letters of recommendation, work experience. Additional exam requirements/recommendations for international students: Required—TOEFL (minimum score 550 paper-based; 79 iBT). *Application deadline:* For fall admission, 7/1 priority date for domestic and international students; for spring admission, 11/1 priority date for domestic and international students. Applications are processed on a rolling basis. Application fee: $35. Electronic applications accepted. Application fee is waived when completed online. *Expenses: Tuition:* Part-time $925 per credit hour. *Required fees:* $80 per credit hour. Tuition and fees vary according to degree level. *Financial support:* Institutionally sponsored loans available. Support available to part-time students. Financial award application deadline: 5/1; financial award applicants required to submit FAFSA. *Unit head:* Dr. Michelle L. Patrick, Dean, 412-397-5445, Fax: 412-397-2585, E-mail: patrick@rmu.edu. *Application contact:* Dr. Jodi Potter, Director, MBA Program, 412-397-6387, E-mail: potterj@rmu.edu.
Website: http://sbus.rmu.edu

Robert Morris University Illinois, Morris Graduate School of Management, Chicago, IL 60605. Offers accounting (MBA); accounting/finance (MBA); business analytics (MIS); health care administration (MM); higher education administration (MM); human performance (MS); human resource management (MBA); information security (MIS);

information systems management (MIS); law enforcement administration (MM); management (MBA); management/finance (MBA); management/human resource management (MBA); sports administration (MM). *Program availability:* Part-time, evening/weekend. *Entrance requirements:* For master's, official transcripts and letters of recommendation (for some programs); written personal statement. *Additional exam requirements/recommendations for international students:* Required—TOEFL (minimum score 550 paper-based). Electronic applications accepted.

Roberts Wesleyan College, Graduate Business Programs, Rochester, NY 14624-1997. Offers strategic leadership (MS); strategic marketing (MS). *Program availability:* Evening/weekend. *Degree requirements:* For master's, thesis or alternative. *Entrance requirements:* For master's, GMAT, minimum GPA of 2.75, verifiable work experience. *Expenses:* Contact institution.

Rochester Institute of Technology, Graduate Enrollment Services, Saunders College of Business, Rochester, NY 14623-5608. Offers Exec MBA, MBA, MS. *Program availability:* Part-time, evening/weekend, 100% online, blended/hybrid learning. *Students:* 221 full-time (102 women), 150 part-time (73 women); includes 38 minority (11 Black or African American, non-Hispanic/Latino; 13 Asian, non-Hispanic/Latino; 8 Hispanic/Latino; 6 Two or more races, non-Hispanic/Latino), 101 international. Average age 30. 588 applicants, 49% accepted, 138 enrolled. In 2018, 145 master's awarded. *Entrance requirements:* For master's, GMAT or GRE, minimum GPA of 3.0 (recommended). *Additional exam requirements/recommendations for international students:* Required—PTE (minimum score 58). *Application deadline:* Applications are processed on a rolling basis. Application fee: $65. Electronic applications accepted. *Expenses:* Contact institution. *Financial support:* In 2018–19, 221 students received support. Research assistantships with partial tuition reimbursements available, teaching assistantships with partial tuition reimbursements available, career-related internships or fieldwork, Federal Work-Study, scholarships/grants, and unspecified assistantships available. Support available to part-time students. Financial award applicants required to submit FAFSA. *Faculty research:* Corporate environmental strategy and sustainability, lean manufacturing and environmental performance, entrepreneurship, data analytics, computational finance, technology and information management, marketing and digital marketing. *Unit head:* Dr. Jacqueline Mozrall, Dean, 585-475-6025, E-mail: gradbus@saunders.rit.edu. *Application contact:* Diane Ellison, Senior Associate Vice President, Graduate Enrollment Services, 585-475-2229, Fax: 585-475-7164, E-mail: gradinfo@rit.edu.
Website: http://saunders.rit.edu/

Rochester Institute of Technology, Graduate Enrollment Services, Saunders College of Business, Marketing and Management Department, MBA Executive Program - Online, Rochester, NY 14623-5603. Offers MBA. *Program availability:* Part-time, evening/weekend, online only, 100% online. *Students:* 30 full-time (10 women), 28 part-time (6 women); includes 6 minority (3 Black or African American, non-Hispanic/Latino; 3 Hispanic/Latino), 1 international. Average age 36. 60 applicants, 90% accepted, 51 enrolled. In 2018, 24 master's awarded. *Entrance requirements:* For master's, minimum GPA of 3.0 (recommended), six years of work experience, participate in an interview, personal statement, resume, three letters of recommendation. *Additional exam requirements/recommendations for international students:* Required—TOEFL (minimum score 88 iBT), IELTS (minimum score 6.5), PTE (minimum score 58). *Application deadline:* For fall admission, 6/1 priority date for domestic and international students. Applications are processed on a rolling basis. Application fee: $65. Electronic applications accepted. *Expenses:* Contact institution. *Financial support:* In 2018–19, 28 students received support. Scholarships/grants available. Support available to part-time students. Financial award applicants required to submit FAFSA. *Faculty research:* Active learning pedagogy; consumer experience; relationship marketing; virtual ethnography; online learning; globalization of manufacturing R&D and engineering; competitive dynamics and internal vs. external network idea sourcing new products; creativity, cognitive learning style and innovation outcomes; R&D project management in resource-constrained business conditions; crowd sourcing vs. mergers and acquisitions as open innovation strategies; cultural impacts on technology adoption. *Unit head:* Amanda Williams, Admissions Officer, 585-475-2729, E-mail: awilliams@saunders.rit.edu. *Application contact:* Diane Ellison, Senior Associate Vice President, Graduate Enrollment Services, 585-475-2229, Fax: 585-475-7164, E-mail: gradinfo@rit.edu.
Website: https://www.rit.edu/study/business-administration-online-executive-mba

Rochester Institute of Technology, Graduate Enrollment Services, Saunders College of Business, Marketing and Management Department, MBA Program, Rochester, NY 14623-5603. Offers MBA. *Accreditation:* AACSB. *Program availability:* Part-time, evening/weekend. *Students:* 84 full-time (35 women), 37 part-time (12 women); includes 13 minority (5 Black or African American, non-Hispanic/Latino; 4 Asian, non-Hispanic/Latino; 2 Hispanic/Latino; 2 Two or more races, non-Hispanic/Latino), 44 international. Average age 28. 107 applicants, 71% accepted, 30 enrolled. In 2018, 55 master's awarded. *Entrance requirements:* For master's, GMAT or GRE, minimum GPA of 3.0 (recommended), personal statement, resume. *Additional exam requirements/recommendations for international students:* Required—TOEFL (minimum score 580 paper-based; 92 iBT), IELTS (minimum score 7), PTE (minimum score 63). *Application deadline:* Applications are processed on a rolling basis. Application fee: $65. Electronic applications accepted. *Financial support:* In 2018–19, 82 students received support. Research assistantships with partial tuition reimbursements available, teaching assistantships with partial tuition reimbursements available, career-related internships or fieldwork, scholarships/grants, and unspecified assistantships available. Support available to part-time students. Financial award applicants required to submit FAFSA. *Faculty research:* Health IT adoption; technology management, creativity, and innovation; social media and entrepreneurship; leadership; cybersecurity; and corporate social responsibility and business ethics. *Unit head:* Matt Cornwell, Assistant Director of Student Services and Outreach, 585-475-6916, E-mail: mcornwell@saunders.rit.edu. *Application contact:* Diane Ellison, Senior Associate Vice President, Graduate Enrollment Services, 585-475-2229, Fax: 585-475-7164, E-mail: gradinfo@rit.edu.
Website: https://www.rit.edu/study/business-administration-mba

Rochester Institute of Technology, Graduate Enrollment Services, Saunders College of Business, Marketing and Management Department, MBA Program–Executive Option, Rochester, NY 14623-5603. Offers Exec MBA. *Accreditation:* AACSB. *Program availability:* Part-time-only, evening/weekend. *Students:* 31 full-time (17 women), 11 part-time (8 women); includes 3 minority (2 Asian, non-Hispanic/Latino; 1 Hispanic/Latino), 1 international. Average age 37. 26 applicants, 85% accepted, 19 enrolled. In 2018, 18 master's awarded. *Entrance requirements:* For master's, minimum of 6 years of work experience, minimum GPA of 3.0 (recommended), participate in an interview, personal statement, resume, three letters of recommendation from a current employer. *Additional exam requirements/recommendations for international students:* Required—TOEFL (minimum score 88 iBT), IELTS (minimum score 6.5), PTE (minimum score 58). *Application deadline:* For fall admission, 6/30 priority date for domestic and international students. Applications are processed on a rolling basis. Application fee: $65. Electronic applications accepted. *Financial support:* In 2018–19, 35 students received support. Scholarships/grants available. Support available to part-time students. Financial award applicants required to submit FAFSA. *Faculty research:* Active learning pedagogy; consumer experience; relationship marketing; virtual ethnography; online learning;

globalization of manufacturing R&D and engineering; competitive dynamics and internal vs. external network idea sourcing new products; creativity, cognitive learning style and innovation outcomes; R&D project management in resource-constrained business conditions; crowd sourcing vs. mergers and acquisitions as open innovation strategies; cultural impacts on technology adoption. *Unit head:* Amanda Williams, Admissions Officer, 585-475-2729, E-mail: awilliams@saunders.rit.edu. *Application contact:* Diane Ellison, Senior Associate Vice President, Graduate Enrollment Services, 585-475-2229, Fax: 585-475-7164, E-mail: gradinfo@rit.edu.
Website: https://www.rit.edu/study/business-administration-executive-mba

Rockford University, Graduate Studies, Program in Business Administration, Rockford, IL 61108-2393. Offers MBA. *Program availability:* Part-time, evening/weekend. *Entrance requirements:* For master's, GMAT, 3 letters of recommendation. *Additional exam requirements/recommendations for international students:* Required—TOEFL (minimum score 550 paper-based; 79 iBT). Electronic applications accepted. *Faculty research:* Entrepreneurship, leadership, international business, services marketing, project management.

Rockhurst University, Helzberg School of Management, Kansas City, MO 64110-2561. Offers accounting (MBA); business intelligence (MBA, Certificate); business intelligence and analytics (MS); data science (MBA, Certificate); entrepreneurship (MBA); finance (MBA); fundraising leadership (MBA, Certificate); healthcare management (MBA, Certificate); human capital (Certificate); international business (Certificate); management (MA, MBA, Certificate); nonprofit administration (Certificate); organizational development (Certificate); science leadership (Certificate). *Accreditation:* AACSB. *Program availability:* Part-time, evening/weekend. *Entrance requirements:* For master's, GMAT or GRE. *Additional exam requirements/recommendations for international students:* Required—TOEFL (minimum score 550 paper-based; 79 iBT). Electronic applications accepted. *Faculty research:* Offshoring/outsourcing, systems analysis/synthesis, work teams, multilateral trade, path dependencies/creation.

Rogers State University, Program in Business Administration, Claremore, OK 74017-3252. Offers MBA.

Roger Williams University, Mario J. Gabelli School of Business, Bristol, RI 02809. Offers MBA. *Faculty:* 5 full-time (2 women), 1 part-time/adjunct. *Students:* 19 full-time (10 women); includes 3 minority (2 Hispanic/Latino; 1 Two or more races, non-Hispanic/Latino). Average age 24. 39 applicants, 72% accepted, 19 enrolled. In 2018, 6 master's awarded. *Degree requirements:* For master's, internship, international experience. *Entrance requirements:* For master's, GRE or GMAT, 2 letters of recommendation, letter of intent, official college transcripts. *Additional exam requirements/recommendations for international students:* Required—TOEFL (minimum score 85 iBT), IELTS (minimum score 6.5). *Application deadline:* For fall admission, 4/1 priority date for domestic students. Application fee: $50. Electronic applications accepted. *Financial support:* In 2018–19, 9 students received support. Scholarships/grants available. Financial award application deadline: 3/15; financial award applicants required to submit FAFSA. *Unit head:* Dr. Susan McTiernan, Dean, 401-254-3444, E-mail: smctiernan@rwu.edu. *Application contact:* Marcus Hanscom, Director of Graduate Admissions, 401-254-3345, Fax: 401-254-3557, E-mail: mhanscom@rwu.edu.
Website: https://www.rwu.edu/academics/schools-and-colleges/gsb

Rollins College, Crummer Graduate School of Business, Winter Park, FL 32789-4499. Offers entrepreneurship (MBA); finance (MBA); international business (MBA); management (MBA). *Accreditation:* AACSB. *Program availability:* Part-time, evening/weekend, online learning. *Degree requirements:* For master's, minimum GPA of 2.85. *Entrance requirements:* For master's, GMAT or GRE, official transcripts, two letters of recommendation, essay, current resume/curriculum vitae, interview. *Additional exam requirements/recommendations for international students:* Required—TOEFL (minimum score 100 iBT) or IELTS (minimum score 7). Electronic applications accepted. *Expenses:* Contact institution. *Faculty research:* Sustainability, world financial markets, international business, market research, strategic marketing.

Roosevelt University, Graduate Division, Walter E. Heller College of Business, Program in Business Administration, Chicago, IL 60605. Offers MBA. *Accreditation:* ACBSP. *Program availability:* Part-time, evening/weekend. Electronic applications accepted.

Roseman University of Health Sciences, College of Dental Medicine - Henderson Campus, Henderson, NV 89014. Offers business administration (MBA); dental medicine (Post-Doctoral Certificate). *Degree requirements:* For master's, comprehensive exam, thesis or alternative. *Entrance requirements:* For master's, National Board Dental Examination 1 and 2, graduation from U.S. or Canadian dental school, Nevada dental license. *Expenses:* Contact institution. *Faculty research:* Oral cancer; CBCT (Cone Beam Computed Tomography) 3D scan data related projects; in-vitro biomaterial testing such as orthodontic bond strength studies using Instron; nanotechnology and orthodontic practice management research.

Roseman University of Health Sciences, MBA Program, Henderson, NV 89014. Offers MBA. *Program availability:* Part-time, evening/weekend. *Degree requirements:* For master's, comprehensive exam, entrepreneurial project, summative assessment and capstone. *Entrance requirements:* For master's, GMAT or leveling course (for applicants whose overall GPA is below 3.0), bachelor's degree. *Additional exam requirements/recommendations for international students:* Required—TOEFL (minimum score 550 paper-based; 79 iBT). *Faculty research:* Using a cash flow-based Z-score to access the progressive solvency of the U.S. commercial banking system; identifying the causes and consequences associated with; groups and retirement preparedness; evaluating the performance of individual stocks relative to indexes.

Rosemont College, Schools of Graduate and Professional Studies, Business Administration and Leadership Programs, Rosemont, PA 19010-1699. Offers business administration (MBA); leadership (MS); management (MS). *Program availability:* Part-time, evening/weekend, online learning. *Degree requirements:* For master's, thesis (for some programs). *Entrance requirements:* For master's, minimum college GPA of 3.0, 3 letters of recommendation. Application fee is waived when completed online. *Expenses:* Contact institution.

Rowan University, Graduate School, Rohrer College of Business, Department of Business Administration, Glassboro, NJ 08028-1701. Offers MBA. *Accreditation:* AACSB. *Program availability:* Part-time, evening/weekend. *Degree requirements:* For master's, comprehensive exam, thesis. *Entrance requirements:* For master's, GRE General Test. *Additional exam requirements/recommendations for international students:* Required—TOEFL. Electronic applications accepted.

Rowan University, Graduate School, Rohrer College of Business, Department of Marketing and Business Information Systems, Program in Business, Glassboro, NJ 08028-1701. Offers CGS. *Program availability:* Part-time, evening/weekend. *Entrance requirements:* Additional exam requirements/recommendations for international students: Required—TOEFL. Electronic applications accepted.

Royal Military College of Canada, Division of Graduate Studies, Continuing Studies, Department of Business Administration, Kingston, ON K7K 7B4, Canada. Offers MBA. *Degree requirements:* For master's, thesis. *Entrance requirements:* For master's, GMAT, honours degree with second-class standing. Electronic applications accepted.

Business Administration and Management—General

Rutgers University–Camden, School of Business, Camden, NJ 08102-1401. Offers MBA, JD/MBA. *Accreditation:* AACSB. *Program availability:* Part-time, evening/weekend. *Entrance requirements:* For master's, GMAT, 2 letters of recommendation. Additional exam requirements/recommendations for international students: Required—TOEFL (minimum score 89 iBT). Electronic applications accepted. *Expenses:* Contact institution. *Faculty research:* Efficiency in utility industry, management information systems development, management/labor relations.

Rutgers University–Newark, Graduate School, Program in Management, Newark, NJ 07102. Offers accounting (PhD); accounting information systems (PhD); computer information systems (PhD); finance (PhD); information technology (PhD); international business (PhD); management science (PhD); marketing (PhD); organization management (PhD). Program offered jointly with New Jersey Institute of Technology. *Accreditation:* AACSB. *Degree requirements:* For doctorate, thesis/dissertation, cumulative exams. *Entrance requirements:* For doctorate, GMAT or GRE General Test, minimum undergraduate B average. Additional exam requirements/recommendations for international students: Required—TOEFL. Electronic applications accepted. *Faculty research:* Technology management, leadership and teams, consumer behavior, financial and markets, logistics.

Rutgers University–Newark, Rutgers Business School–Newark and New Brunswick, Program in Business Administration, Newark, NJ 07102. Offers MBA. *Entrance requirements:* For master's, GMAT. Additional exam requirements/recommendations for international students: Required—TOEFL.

Ryerson University, School of Graduate Studies, Ted Rogers School of Management, Toronto, ON M5B 2K3, Canada. Offers global business administration (MBA); management (MSM); management of technology and innovation (MBA).

Sacred Heart University, Graduate Programs, Jack Welch College of Business, Department of Management, Fairfield, CT 06825. Offers administration (MBA); human resource management (MS, Graduate Certificate); management (Graduate Certificate). *Program availability:* Part-time, evening/weekend. *Degree requirements:* For master's, capstone project. *Entrance requirements:* For master's, GMAT/GRE, bachelor's degree. Additional exam requirements/recommendations for international students: Required—TOEFL (minimum score 570 paper-based, 80 iBT), TWE, or IELTS (6.5). Electronic applications accepted. *Expenses:* Contact institution.

Sage Graduate School, School of Management, Program in Business Administration, Troy, NY 12180-4115. Offers MBA. *Program availability:* Part-time, evening/weekend, 100% online, blended/hybrid learning. *Faculty:* 5 full-time (3 women), 4 part-time/adjunct (1 woman). *Students:* 20 full-time (9 women), 45 part-time (35 women); includes 16 minority (6 Black or African American, non-Hispanic/Latino; 2 American Indian or Alaska Native, non-Hispanic/Latino; 2 Asian, non-Hispanic/Latino; 5 Hispanic/Latino; 1 Two or more races, non-Hispanic/Latino), 1 international. Average age 31. 51 applicants, 47% accepted, 12 enrolled. In 2018, 26 master's awarded. *Entrance requirements:* For master's, completed application, minimum GPA 2.75, current resume, 2 letters of recommendation, career goals essay, official transcripts from each previous colleges attended. Additional exam requirements/recommendations for international students: Required—TOEFL (minimum score 550 paper-based). *Application deadline:* Applications are processed on a rolling basis. Application fee: $30. Electronic applications accepted. *Financial support:* Fellowships, research assistantships, and unspecified assistantships available. Financial award application deadline: 3/1; financial award applicants required to submit FAFSA. *Unit head:* Dr. Kimberly Fredericks, Dean, School of Management, 518-292-1782, Fax: 518-292-1964, E-mail: fredek1@sage.edu. *Application contact:* Michael Jones, SR Associate Director of Graduate Enrollment Management, 518-292-8615, Fax: 518-292-1912, E-mail: jonesm4@sage.edu.

Saginaw Valley State University, College of Business and Management, Program in Business Administration, University Center, MI 48710. Offers MBA. *Accreditation:* AACSB. *Program availability:* Part-time, evening/weekend, online only, 100% online, blended/hybrid learning. *Faculty:* 9 full-time (2 women), 1 part-time/adjunct (0 women). *Students:* 16 full-time (7 women), 44 part-time (16 women); includes 12 minority (3 Black or African American, non-Hispanic/Latino; 2 Asian, non-Hispanic/Latino; 4 Hispanic/Latino; 3 Two or more races, non-Hispanic/Latino), 14 international. Average age 30. 58 applicants, 62% accepted, 21 enrolled. In 2018, 10 master's awarded. *Degree requirements:* For master's, thesis optional. *Entrance requirements:* For master's, GMAT. Additional exam requirements/recommendations for international students: Required—TOEFL (minimum score 550 paper-based; 79 iBT). *Application deadline:* For fall admission, 7/15 for international students; for winter admission, 11/15 for international students; for spring admission, 4/15 for international students. Applications are processed on a rolling basis. Application fee: $30 ($90 for international students). Electronic applications accepted. *Expenses: Tuition, area resident:* Full-time $6225; part-time $623 per credit hour. Tuition, state resident: full-time $6225; part-time $623 per credit hour. Tuition, nonresident: full-time $14,215; part-time $1185 per credit hour. *International tuition:* $14,215 full-time. *Required fees:* $263; $14.60 per credit hour. Tuition and fees vary according to degree level. *Financial support:* Federal Work-Study and scholarships/grants available. Support available to part-time students. Financial award application deadline: 4/15; financial award applicants required to submit FAFSA. *Unit head:* Dr. Mark McCartney, MBA Program Coordinator, 989-964-4064. *Application contact:* Jenna Briggs, Director, Graduate and International Admissions, 989-964-6096, Fax: 989-964-2788, E-mail: gradadm@svsu.edu.
Website: http://www.svsu.edu/mba/

St. Ambrose University, College of Business, Program in Business Administration, Davenport, IA 52803-2898. Offers business administration (DBA); health care (MBA); human resources (MBA). *Accreditation:* ACBSP. *Program availability:* Part-time, evening/weekend. *Degree requirements:* For master's, comprehensive exam (for some programs), thesis or alternative, capstone seminar; for doctorate, comprehensive exam, thesis/dissertation, oral and written exams. *Entrance requirements:* For master's, GMAT; for doctorate, GMAT, master's degree. Additional exam requirements/recommendations for international students: Required—TOEFL. Electronic applications accepted. *Expenses:* Contact institution.

St. Bonaventure University, School of Graduate School, School of Business, St. Bonaventure, NY 14778-2284. Offers general business (MBA); professional accountancy (MBA). *Accreditation:* AACSB. *Program availability:* Part-time, evening/weekend, 100% online. *Faculty:* 15 full-time (4 women), 6 part-time/adjunct (3 women). *Students:* 86 full-time (44 women), 108 part-time (52 women); includes 16 minority (7 Black or African American, non-Hispanic/Latino; 1 Asian, non-Hispanic/Latino; 5 Hispanic/Latino; 3 Two or more races, non-Hispanic/Latino), 8 international. Average age 28. 88 applicants, 98% accepted, 71 enrolled. In 2018, 125 master's awarded. *Entrance requirements:* For master's, GMAT or GRE, undergraduate degree, official transcripts, current resume. Additional exam requirements/recommendations for international students: Required—TOEFL (minimum score 550 paper-based; 79 iBT). *Application deadline:* For fall admission, 3/15 priority date for domestic students, 2/1 priority date for international students; for spring admission, 10/15 priority date for domestic students, 7/1 priority date for international students. Applications are processed on a rolling basis. Application fee: $0. Electronic applications accepted. *Financial support:* In 2018–19, 9 students received support. Career-related internships or fieldwork, scholarships/grants, health care benefits, and unspecified assistantships available. Financial award application deadline: 4/15; financial award applicants required to submit FAFSA. *Faculty research:* Serial entrepreneurship and venture performance, supply chain relationship, customer/employee relationships/interactions, nonparametric applications to financial markets. *Unit head:* Dr. Matrecia James, Dean, 716-375-2200, Fax: 716-372-2191, E-mail: mjames@sbu.edu. *Application contact:* Matthew Retchless, Director of Graduate Admissions, 716-375-2021, Fax: 716-375-4015, E-mail: gradsch@sbu.edu.
Website: http://www.sbu.edu/academics/schools/business/graduate-degrees/master-of-business-administration-(mba)

St. Catherine University, Graduate Programs, Program in Business Administration, St. Paul, MN 55105. Offers healthcare (MBA); integrated marketing communications (MBA); management (MBA). *Program availability:* Part-time, evening/weekend. *Entrance requirements:* For master's, GMAT (if undergraduate GPA is less than 3.0), 2+ years' work or volunteer experience in professional setting(s). Additional exam requirements/recommendations for international students: Required—TOEFL. *Expenses:* Contact institution.

St. Cloud State University, School of Graduate Studies, Herberger Business School, St. Cloud, MN 56301-4498. Offers business administration (MBA); information assurance (MS). *Accreditation:* AACSB. *Program availability:* Part-time, evening/weekend. *Degree requirements:* For master's, thesis or alternative. *Entrance requirements:* For master's, GMAT, minimum GPA of 2.75. Additional exam requirements/recommendations for international students: Required—Michigan English Language Assessment Battery; Recommended—TOEFL (minimum score 550 paper-based), IELTS (minimum score 6.5). Electronic applications accepted. *Expenses:* Contact institution.

Saint Francis University, School of Business, Loretto, PA 15940-0600. Offers business administration (MBA); human resource management (MHRM). *Program availability:* Part-time, evening/weekend. *Degree requirements:* For master's, comprehensive exam (for some programs), thesis (for some programs). *Entrance requirements:* For master's, GMAT (waived if undergraduate QPA is 3.3 or above), 2 letters of recommendation, minimum GPA of 2.75, two essays. Additional exam requirements/recommendations for international students: Required—TOEFL (minimum score 550 paper-based; 57 iBT). Electronic applications accepted. *Expenses:* Contact institution.

St. John Fisher College, School of Business, MBA Program, Rochester, NY 14618-3597. Offers MBA. *Accreditation:* AACSB. *Program availability:* Part-time, evening/weekend. *Faculty:* 6 full-time (0 women), 7 part-time/adjunct (2 women). *Students:* 53 full-time (29 women), 70 part-time (28 women); includes 18 minority (5 Black or African American, non-Hispanic/Latino; 7 Asian, non-Hispanic/Latino; 5 Hispanic/Latino; 1 Two or more races, non-Hispanic/Latino), 2 international. Average age 27. 97 applicants, 89% accepted, 52 enrolled. In 2018, 67 master's awarded. *Degree requirements:* For master's, capstone project. *Entrance requirements:* For master's, 2 letters of recommendation, personal statement, current resume, interview. Additional exam requirements/recommendations for international students: Required—TOEFL (minimum score 575 paper-based; 80 iBT). *Application deadline:* Applications are processed on a rolling basis. Application fee: $30. Electronic applications accepted. *Expenses:* Contact institution. *Financial support:* Scholarships/grants available. Financial award applicants required to submit FAFSA. *Faculty research:* Business strategy, consumer behavior, cross-cultural management practices, international finance, organizational trust. *Unit head:* Carol Wittmeyer, Program Director, 585-385-8238, E-mail: cwittmeyer@sjfc.edu. *Application contact:* Michelle Gosier, Director of Transfer and Graduate Admissions, 585-385-8064, E-mail: mgosier@sjfc.edu.
Website: https://www.sjfc.edu/graduate-programs/master-of-business-administration-mba/

St. John's University, The Peter J. Tobin College of Business, Department of Management, Queens, NY 11439. Offers business administration (MBA), including strategic management. *Entrance requirements:* For master's, GMAT or GRE, 2 letters of recommendation, essay, resume, unofficial transcripts. Additional exam requirements/recommendations for international students: Required—TOEFL (minimum score 80 iBT), IELTS (minimum score 6.5). Electronic applications accepted. *Expenses:* Contact institution.

St. John's University, The Peter J. Tobin College of Business, Department of Marketing, Queens, NY 11439. Offers business administration (MBA), including marketing management. *Entrance requirements:* For master's, GMAT or GRE, 2 letters of recommendation, essay, resume, unofficial transcripts. Additional exam requirements/recommendations for international students: Required—TOEFL (minimum score 80 iBT), IELTS (minimum score 6.5). Electronic applications accepted. *Expenses:* Contact institution.

St. John's University, The Peter J. Tobin College of Business, Program in International Business, Queens, NY 11439. Offers business administration (MBA), including international business. *Entrance requirements:* For master's, GMAT or GRE, 2 letters of recommendation, essay, resume, unofficial transcripts. Additional exam requirements/recommendations for international students: Required—TOEFL (minimum score 80 iBT), IELTS (minimum score 6.5). Electronic applications accepted. *Expenses:* Contact institution.

St. John's University, The Peter J. Tobin College of Business, School of Risk Management, Insurance and Actuarial Science, Queens, NY 11439. Offers actuarial science (MS); business administration (MBA), including risk management and insurance; enterprise risk management (MBA, MS), including enterprise risk management (MS); risk management and insurance (MS). *Entrance requirements:* For master's, GMAT or GRE, 2 letters of recommendation, essay, resume, unofficial transcripts. Additional exam requirements/recommendations for international students: Required—TOEFL (minimum score 80 iBT), IELTS (minimum score 6.5). Electronic applications accepted. *Expenses:* Contact institution. *Faculty research:* Insurance company operations and financial analysis, enterprise risk management, risk theory and modeling, credibility theory and actuarial price modeling, international insurance.

St. Joseph's College, Long Island Campus, Programs in Business Management and Administration, Field in Business Administration, Patchogue, NY 11772-2399. Offers MBA. *Program availability:* Part-time, evening/weekend, 100% online, blended/hybrid learning. *Faculty:* 13 full-time (5 women), 23 part-time/adjunct (8 women). *Entrance requirements:* For master's, Application, $25 application fee, two letters of reference forms, verification of employment form, current resume, 250 word written statement, official transcripts. Additional exam requirements/recommendations for international students: Required—TOEFL (minimum score 80 iBT). Application fee: $25. *Expenses: Tuition:* Full-time $18,450; part-time $1025 per credit. *Required fees:* $414. *Unit head:* Mary A. Chance, Assistant Professor/Interim Director of Graduate Management Studies, 631-687-1297, E-mail: mchance@sjcny.edu. *Application contact:* Mary A. Chance, Assistant Professor/Interim Director of Graduate Management Studies, 631-687-1297, E-mail: mchance@sjcny.edu.

St. Joseph's College, Long Island Campus, Programs in Business Management and Administration, Field of Executive Business Administration, Patchogue, NY 11772-2399.

Offers EMBA. *Program availability:* Part-time, evening/weekend, 100% online, blended/hybrid learning. *Faculty:* 13 full-time (5 women), 23 part-time/adjunct (8 women). *Students:* 25 full-time (15 women), 94 part-time (50 women); includes 33 minority (10 Black or African American, non-Hispanic/Latino; 4 Asian, non-Hispanic/Latino; 17 Hispanic/Latino; 1 Native Hawaiian or other Pacific Islander, non-Hispanic/Latino; 1 Two or more races, non-Hispanic/Latino). Average age 34. 85 applicants, 62% accepted, 33 enrolled. In 2018, 23 master's awarded. *Entrance requirements:* For master's, Application, $25 application fee, two letters of reference forms, verification of employment form, current resume, 250 word written statement, official transcripts. Additional exam requirements/recommendations for international students: Required—TOEFL (minimum score 80 iBT). *Application deadline:* Applications are processed on a rolling basis. Application fee: $25. Electronic applications accepted. *Expenses: Tuition:* Full-time $18,450; part-time $1025 per credit. *Required fees:* $414. *Financial support:* In 2018–19, 23 students received support. *Unit head:* Mary A. Chance, Assistant Professor/Interim Director of Graduate Management Studies, 631-687-1297, E-mail: mchance@sjcny.edu. *Application contact:* Mary A. Chance, Assistant Professor/Interim Director of Graduate Management Studies, 631-687-1297, E-mail: mchance@sjcny.edu.
Website: http://www.sjcny.edu

St. Joseph's College, Long Island Campus, Programs in Management, Patchogue, NY 11772-2399. Offers health care management (MS); human resources management (MS); human services leadership (MS); organizational management (MS). *Program availability:* Part-time, evening/weekend, 100% online, blended/hybrid learning. *Faculty:* 13 full-time (5 women), 23 part-time/adjunct (8 women). *Students:* 35 full-time (29 women), 151 part-time (116 women); includes 64 minority (30 Black or African American, non-Hispanic/Latino; 3 Asian, non-Hispanic/Latino; 26 Hispanic/Latino; 5 Two or more races, non-Hispanic/Latino). Average age 35. 165 applicants, 62% accepted, 77 enrolled. In 2018, 38 master's awarded. *Entrance requirements:* For master's, Application, $25 application fee, official transcripts, two letters of recommendation, current resume, 250 word written statement. Additional exam requirements/recommendations for international students: Required—TOEFL (minimum score 80 iBT). *Application deadline:* Applications are processed on a rolling basis. Application fee: $25. Electronic applications accepted. *Expenses: Tuition:* Full-time $18,450; part-time $1025 per credit. *Required fees:* $414. *Financial support:* In 2018–19, 31 students received support. *Unit head:* Mary A. Chance, Assistant Professor/Interim Director of Graduate Management Studies, 631-687-1297, E-mail: mchance@sjcny.edu. *Application contact:* Mary A. Chance, Assistant Professor/Interim Director of Graduate Management Studies, 631-687-1297, E-mail: mchance@sjcny.edu.

St. Joseph's College, New York, Programs in Business Management and Administration, Field of Business Administration, Brooklyn, NY 11205-3688. Offers MBA. *Program availability:* Part-time, evening/weekend, 100% online, blended/hybrid learning. *Faculty:* 5 part-time/adjunct (4 women). In 2018, 1 master's awarded. *Entrance requirements:* For master's, Application, $25 application fee, two letters of recommendation, current resume, 250 word essay, official transcripts. Additional exam requirements/recommendations for international students: Required—TOEFL (minimum score 80 iBT). Application fee: $25. *Expenses: Tuition:* Full-time $18,450; part-time $1025 per credit. *Required fees:* $414. *Unit head:* John Capela, Associate Chair, 718-940-5843, E-mail: jcapela@sjcny.edu. *Application contact:* John Capela, Associate Chair, 718-940-5843, E-mail: jcapela@sjcny.edu.
Website: https://www.sjcny.edu/brooklyn/academics/graduate/graduate-degrees/executive-mba

Saint Joseph's College of Maine, Master of Business Administration in Leadership Program, Standish, ME 04084. Offers MBA. *Program availability:* Part-time, online learning. *Entrance requirements:* For master's, two years of work experience.

Saint Joseph's University, Erivan K. Haub School of Business, Philadelphia, PA 19131-1395. Offers MBA, MS, Post Master's Certificate, Postbaccalaureate Certificate, DO/MBA. *Accreditation:* AACSB. *Program availability:* Part-time-only, evening/weekend, 100% online. *Degree requirements:* For master's and other advanced degree, minimum GPA of 3.0. *Entrance requirements:* For master's, GMAT, MAT, GRE, letters of recommendation, resume, personal statement, official undergraduate and graduate transcripts; structured interview (for some programs); for other advanced degree, official master's-level transcripts. Additional exam requirements/recommendations for international students: Required—PTE, TOEFL, IELTS, or PTE. Electronic applications accepted.

Saint Leo University, Graduate Studies in Business, Saint Leo, FL 33574-6665. Offers accounting (M Acc); cybersecurity management (MBA); health care management (MBA); human resource management (MBA); marketing (MBA); marketing research and social media analytics (MBA); software engineering (MS). *Accreditation:* ACBSP. *Program availability:* Part-time, evening/weekend, 100% online, blended/hybrid learning. *Faculty:* 51 full-time (16 women), 54 part-time/adjunct (22 women). *Students:* 8 full-time (3 women), 2,209 part-time (1,288 women); includes 1,046 minority (691 Black or African American, non-Hispanic/Latino; 10 American Indian or Alaska Native, non-Hispanic/Latino; 47 Asian, non-Hispanic/Latino; 249 Hispanic/Latino; 5 Native Hawaiian or other Pacific Islander, non-Hispanic/Latino; 44 Two or more races, non-Hispanic/Latino), 71 international. Average age 37. 760 applicants, 83% accepted, 498 enrolled. In 2018, 763 master's, 14 doctorates awarded. *Degree requirements:* For doctorate, comprehensive exam, thesis/dissertation. *Entrance requirements:* For master's, GMAT with minimum score 500 (for M Acc), official transcripts, current resume, 2 professional recommendations, personal statement, bachelor's degree from regionally-accredited university; undergraduate degree in accounting and minimum undergraduate GPA of 3.0 (for M Acc); minimum undergraduate GPA of 3.0 in final 2 years of undergraduate study and 2 years' work experience (for MBA); for doctorate, GMAT (minimum score of 550) if master's GPA is under 3.25, official transcripts, current resume, 2 professional recommendations, personal statement, master's degree from regionally-accredited university with minimum GPA of 3.25, 3 years' work experience, interview. Additional exam requirements/recommendations for international students: Required—TOEFL (minimum score 550 paper-based; 78 iBT). *Application deadline:* For fall admission, 7/1 priority date for domestic and international students; for spring admission, 11/12 priority date for domestic students, 11/1 for international students. Applications are processed on a rolling basis. Application fee: $80. Electronic applications accepted. *Expenses:* Onground Master of Accounting $555 per credit, Online Master of Accounting $720 per credit, Onground MBA $555 per credit, Onground MBA Intl/Experiential $720 per credit, Online MBA/Cybersecurity military rate $555 per credit, Online MBA civilian rate $720, MS Cybersecurity civilian rate $770, DBA $900 per credit. *Financial support:* In 2018–19, 213 students received support. Scholarships/grants, unspecified assistantships, and tuition remission for Saint Leo employees and their dependents available. Financial award application deadline: 3/1; financial award applicants required to submit FAFSA. *Faculty research:* Servant leadership, work/life balance, emotional intelligence, pricing, marketing. *Unit head:* Dr. Robyn Parker, Dean, School of Business, 352-588-8599, Fax: 352-588-8912, E-mail: mbaslu@saintleo.edu. *Application contact:* Mark Russum, Assistant Vice President, Enrollment, 800-707-8846, Fax: 352-588-7873, E-mail: grad.admissions@saintleo.edu.
Website: https://www.saintleo.edu/college-of-business

Saint Louis University, Graduate Programs, John Cook School of Business, Program in Business Administration, St. Louis, MO 63103. Offers MBA. *Accreditation:* AACSB. *Program availability:* Part-time, evening/weekend. *Entrance requirements:* For master's, GMAT, letter of recommendation, resume. Additional exam requirements/recommendations for international students: Required—TOEFL (minimum score 570 paper-based; 88 iBT). Electronic applications accepted. *Expenses:* Contact institution.

Saint Martin's University, Office of Graduate Studies, School of Business, Lacey, WA 98503. Offers MBA. *Accreditation:* ACBSP. *Program availability:* Part-time, evening/weekend. *Faculty:* 5 full-time (3 women), 12 part-time/adjunct (2 women). *Students:* 36 full-time (15 women), 25 part-time (9 women); includes 28 minority (8 Black or African American, non-Hispanic/Latino; 9 Asian, non-Hispanic/Latino; 8 Hispanic/Latino; 3 Two or more races, non-Hispanic/Latino), 8 international. Average age 33. 64 applicants, 61% accepted, 29 enrolled. In 2018, 32 master's awarded. *Entrance requirements:* For master's, personal essay. Additional exam requirements/recommendations for international students: Required—TOEFL (minimum score 550 paper-based; 79 iBT); Recommended—IELTS (minimum score 6.5). *Application deadline:* For fall admission, 7/1 priority date for domestic and international students; for spring admission, 12/1 for domestic students, 12/1 priority date for international students. Applications are processed on a rolling basis. Application fee: $50. Electronic applications accepted. *Expenses: Tuition:* Full-time $22,950; part-time $1275 per credit. Tuition and fees vary according to course load, campus/location and program. *Financial support:* Career-related internships or fieldwork and scholarships/grants available. Support available to part-time students. Financial award application deadline: 3/1; financial award applicants required to submit FAFSA. *Unit head:* Dr. Jeff Crane, Interim Dean, School of Business, 360-438-4564, E-mail: jcrane@stmartin.edu. *Application contact:* Chantelle Petron Marker, Senior Recruiter, 360-412-6128, E-mail: cmarker@stmartin.edu.
Website: https://www.stmartin.edu

Saint Mary's College of California, School of Economics and Business Administration, Executive MBA Program, Moraga, CA 94556. Offers MBA. *Accreditation:* AACSB. *Program availability:* Part-time, evening/weekend, blended/hybrid learning. *Entrance requirements:* For master's, 5 years of management experience. Additional exam requirements/recommendations for international students: Required—TOEFL. *Expenses:* Contact institution.

Saint Mary's College of California, School of Economics and Business Administration, MS in Management Program, Moraga, CA 94575. Offers MS.

Saint Mary's College of California, School of Economics and Business Administration, Professional MBA Program, Moraga, CA 94556. Offers MBA. *Accreditation:* AACSB. *Program availability:* Part-time, evening/weekend. *Degree requirements:* For master's, 4 half-day management practica. *Entrance requirements:* For master's, GMAT. Additional exam requirements/recommendations for international students: Required—TOEFL. *Expenses:* Contact institution.

St. Mary's University, Graduate Studies, Greehey School of Business, San Antonio, TX 78228. Offers business administration (MBA); JD/MBA. *Accreditation:* AACSB. *Program availability:* Part-time, evening/weekend. *Students:* 34 full-time (18 women), 52 part-time (25 women); includes 44 minority (7 Black or African American, non-Hispanic/Latino; 1 Asian, non-Hispanic/Latino; 34 Hispanic/Latino; 1 Native Hawaiian or other Pacific Islander, non-Hispanic/Latino; 1 Two or more races, non-Hispanic/Latino), 13 international. Average age 33. 84 applicants, 55% accepted, 29 enrolled. In 2018, 67 master's awarded. *Degree requirements:* For master's, comprehensive exam. *Entrance requirements:* For master's, GMAT (minimum score of 525) or GRE (minimum score of 306), undergraduate degree from accredited institution, letters of reference, current resume. Additional exam requirements/recommendations for international students: Required—TOEFL (minimum score 570 paper-based; 87 iBT); Recommended—IELTS (minimum score 6.5), TSE. *Application deadline:* For fall admission, 7/1 for domestic students; for spring admission, 11/15 for domestic students; for summer admission, 4/1 for domestic students. Application fee: $0. Electronic applications accepted. *Expenses: Tuition:* Full-time $16,830; part-time $935 per credit hour. *Required fees:* $1055. Tuition and fees vary according to program. *Financial support:* Research assistantships, institutionally sponsored loans, scholarships/grants, and unspecified assistantships available. Financial award application deadline: 3/31; financial award applicants required to submit FAFSA. *Faculty research:* Investment strategies, cross-culture marketing, organizational culture, supply chain management, small-firm internalization. *Unit head:* Jeremy Grace, Director, Master of Business Administration Programs, 210-431-2027, E-mail: jmgrace@stmarytx.edu. *Application contact:* Jeremy Grace, Director, Master of Business Administration Programs, 210-431-2027, E-mail: jmgrace@stmarytx.edu.
Website: https://www.stmarytx.edu/academics/business/

Saint Mary's University, Sobey School of Business, Halifax, NS B3H 3C3, Canada. Offers MBA, MF, PhD. *Program availability:* Part-time, evening/weekend. *Degree requirements:* For master's, research project; for doctorate, thesis/dissertation. *Entrance requirements:* For master's, GMAT, minimum B average; for doctorate, GMAT or GRE, MBA or other master's-level degree, minimum B+ average. *Expenses:* Contact institution.

Saint Mary's University of Minnesota, Schools of Graduate and Professional Programs, Graduate School of Business and Technology, Business Administration Program, Winona, MN 55987-1399. Offers MBA, DBA. *Unit head:* Holly Tapper, Director, 612-238-4547, Fax: 612-728-5121, E-mail: htapper@smumn.edu. *Application contact:* Laurie Roy, Director of Admission of Schools of Graduate and Professional Programs, 507-457-8606, Fax: 612-728-5121, E-mail: lroy@smumn.edu.
Website: https://www.smumn.edu/academics/graduate/business-technology/master-of-business-administration-mba

Saint Mary's University of Minnesota, Schools of Graduate and Professional Programs, Graduate School of Business and Technology, Doctor of Business Administration Program, Winona, MN 55987-1399. Offers DBA. *Unit head:* Dr. Matt Nowakowski, Director, 612-728-5142, E-mail: mnowakow@smumn.edu. *Application contact:* Laurie Roy, Director of Admission of Schools of Graduate and Professional Programs, 507-457-8606, Fax: 612-728-5121, E-mail: lroy@smumn.edu.
Website: http://www.smumn.edu/academics/graduate/business-technology/programs/doctor-of-business-administration-dba

Saint Mary's University of Minnesota, Schools of Graduate and Professional Programs, Graduate School of Business and Technology, Management Program, Winona, MN 55987-1399. Offers MA. *Entrance requirements:* For master's, undergraduate degree from regionally-accredited institution with minimum overall GPA of 2.75, official transcripts, personal statement, two letters of recommendation, resume. Application fee: $25. Electronic applications accepted. *Unit head:* Paula Justich, Director, 612-728-5165, E-mail: pjustich@smumn.edu. *Application contact:* Laurie Roy, Director of Admission of Schools of Graduate and Professional Programs, 507-457-8606, Fax: 612-728-5121, E-mail: lroy@smumn.edu.
Website: http://www.smumn.edu/graduate-home/areas-of-study/graduate-school-of-business-technology/ma-in-management

St. Norbert College, Master of Business Administration Program, De Pere, WI 54115-2099. Offers business (MBA); health care (MBA); supply chain and manufacturing (MBA). *Program availability:* Part-time-only, evening/weekend. *Faculty:* 11 full-time (3

women), 10 part-time/adjunct (3 women). *Students:* 66 part-time (38 women); includes 6 minority (1 American Indian or Alaska Native, non-Hispanic/Latino; 2 Asian, non-Hispanic/Latino; 2 Hispanic/Latino; 1 Two or more races, non-Hispanic/Latino). Average age 33. 15 applicants, 100% accepted, 14 enrolled. In 2018, 31 master's awarded. *Entrance requirements:* For master's, official transcripts, letters of recommendation, professional resume, essay. *Application deadline:* For fall admission, 8/4 for domestic students; for winter admission, 12/15 for domestic students; for spring admission, 3/2 for domestic students; for summer admission, 4/20 for domestic students. Applications are processed on a rolling basis. Application fee: $50. Electronic applications accepted. *Expenses:* Tuition per credit $725; estimated total cost to complete 39 credits $28,275; technology fee per course $37.50; estimated cost of textbooks for entire program $1,500; application for graduation fee $100; audit-only course, per credit $375. *Financial support:* Federal Work-Study available. Financial award application deadline: 1/1; financial award applicants required to submit FAFSA. *Faculty research:* Urban segregation, religious identity, crisis decision-making, normative ethics, psychological effects of change on individuals and organizations. *Unit head:* Lisa Gray, Coordinator of MBA Program, 920-403-3449, E-mail: lisa.gray@snc.edu. *Application contact:* Brenda Busch, Associate Director of Graduate Recruitment, 920-403-3942, Fax: 920-403-4072, E-mail: brenda.busch@snc.edu.
Website: https://schneiderschool.snc.edu/mba/

Saint Peter's University, Graduate Business Programs, MBA Program, Jersey City, NJ 07306-5997. Offers finance (MBA); health care administration (MBA); human resource management (MBA); international business (MBA); management (MBA); management information systems (MBA); marketing (MBA); risk management (MBA); MBA/MS. *Program availability:* Part-time, evening/weekend. *Entrance requirements:* Additional exam requirements/recommendations for international students: Required—TOEFL. Electronic applications accepted. *Faculty research:* Finance, health care management, human resource management, international business, management, management information systems, marketing, risk management.

St. Thomas Aquinas College, Division of Business Administration, Sparkill, NY 10976. Offers business administration (MBA); finance (MBA); management (MBA); marketing (MBA). *Program availability:* Part-time, evening/weekend. *Entrance requirements:* For master's, GMAT. Additional exam requirements/recommendations for international students: Required—TOEFL. Electronic applications accepted.

St. Thomas University, School of Business, Department of Business Administration, Miami Gardens, FL 33054-6459. Offers M Acc, MBA, Certificate. *Program availability:* Part-time, evening/weekend. *Degree requirements:* For master's, comprehensive exam. *Entrance requirements:* Additional exam requirements/recommendations for international students: Required—TOEFL (minimum score 550 paper-based; 79 iBT). Electronic applications accepted.

St. Thomas University, School of Business, Department of Management, Miami Gardens, FL 33054-6459. Offers accounting (MBA); general management (MSM, Certificate); health management (MBA, MSM, Certificate); human resource management (MBA, MSM, Certificate); international business (MBA, MIB, MSM, Certificate); justice administration (MSM, Certificate); management accounting (MSM, Certificate); public management (MSM, Certificate); sports administration (MS). *Program availability:* Part-time, evening/weekend. *Degree requirements:* For master's, comprehensive exam. *Entrance requirements:* For master's, interview, minimum GPA of 3.0 or GMAT. Additional exam requirements/recommendations for international students: Required—TOEFL (minimum score 550 paper-based; 79 iBT). Electronic applications accepted.

St. Thomas University, School of Leadership Studies, Program in Professional Studies, Miami Gardens, FL 33054-6459. Offers executive management (MPS). *Entrance requirements:* Additional exam requirements/recommendations for international students: Required—TOEFL (minimum score 550 paper-based; 79 iBT).

Saint Vincent College, Program in Business, Latrobe, PA 15650-2690. Offers MS. *Entrance requirements:* For master's, bachelor's degree, minimum overall GPA of 3.0, three recommendations, personal statement, curriculum vitae or resume. Additional exam requirements/recommendations for international students: Required—TOEFL (minimum score 91 iBT), IELTS (minimum score 6.5).

Saint Xavier University, Graduate Studies, Graham School of Management, Chicago, IL 60655-3105. Offers employee health benefits (Certificate); finance (MBA); financial fraud examination and management (MBA, Certificate); financial planning (MBA, Certificate); generalist/individualized (MBA); health administration (MBA); managed care (Certificate); management (MBA); marketing (MBA); project management (MBA, Certificate); MBA/MS. *Accreditation:* AACSB. *Program availability:* Part-time, evening/weekend. *Entrance requirements:* For master's, GMAT, minimum GPA of 3.0, 2 years of work experience. Electronic applications accepted. *Expenses:* Contact institution.

Salem International University, School of Business, Salem, WV 26426-0500. Offers information security (MBA); international business (MBA). *Program availability:* Part-time, online learning. *Entrance requirements:* For master's, minimum undergraduate GPA of 2.5, course work in business, resume. Additional exam requirements/recommendations for international students: Recommended—TOEFL (minimum score 550 paper-based), IELTS (minimum score 6.5). Electronic applications accepted. *Expenses:* Contact institution. *Faculty research:* Organizational behavior strategy, marketing services.

Salem State University, School of Graduate Studies, Program in Business Administration, Salem, MA 01970-5353. Offers MBA. *Program availability:* Part-time, evening/weekend. *Entrance requirements:* For master's, GMAT. Additional exam requirements/recommendations for international students: Required—TOEFL (minimum score 550 paper-based; 80 iBT) or IELTS (minimum score 5.5).

Salisbury University, Perdue School of Business, Salisbury, MD 21801-6837. Offers business administration (MBA). *Accreditation:* AACSB. *Program availability:* Part-time, evening/weekend, 100% online, blended/hybrid learning. *Faculty:* 6 full-time (1 woman). *Students:* 39 full-time (23 women), 30 part-time (14 women); includes 14 minority (9 Black or African American, non-Hispanic/Latino; 1 Asian, non-Hispanic/Latino; 4 Two or more races, non-Hispanic/Latino), 1 international. Average age 29. 77 applicants, 75% accepted, 45 enrolled. In 2018, 38 master's awarded. *Entrance requirements:* For master's, GMAT, transcripts from all colleges or universities attended; three letters of recommendation; resume; essay. Additional exam requirements/recommendations for international students: Required—TOEFL (minimum score 550 paper-based; 79 iBT), IELTS (minimum score 6.5). *Application deadline:* For fall admission, 3/1 priority date for domestic and international students. Applications are processed on a rolling basis. Application fee: $65. Electronic applications accepted. *Expenses:* Residents - $412 per credit hour; Non-Residents - $746 per credit hour; Fees - $108; Online - $765 per credit hour & no fees. *Financial support:* In 2018–19, 18 students received support, including 10 research assistantships with full tuition reimbursements available (averaging $8,000 per year), 8 teaching assistantships with full tuition reimbursements available (averaging $8,500 per year); career-related internships or fieldwork and scholarships/grants also available. Support available to part-time students. Financial award application deadline: 3/1; financial award applicants required to submit FAFSA. *Faculty research:* Shared entrepreneurship; analytical CRM; collective efficacy, visualization, usability; health marketing; machine learning, econometrics, poverty/inequality, economics of regulation. *Unit head:* Yvonne Hanley, Graduate Program Director, 410-548-3983, E-mail: yxdownie@salisbury.edu. *Application contact:* Yvonne Hanley, Graduate Program Director, 410-548-3983, E-mail: yxdownie@salisbury.edu.
Website: https://www.salisbury.edu/explore-academics/programs/graduate-degree-programs/business-admin-master/

Salve Regina University, Program in Business Administration, Newport, RI 02840-4192. Offers cybersecurity issues in business (MBA); entrepreneurial enterprise (MBA); health care administration and management (MBA); nonprofit management (MBA); social ventures (MBA). *Program availability:* Part-time, evening/weekend, online learning. *Entrance requirements:* For master's, GMAT, GRE General Test, or MAT, 6 undergraduate credits each in accounting, economics, quantitative analysis and calculus or statistics. Additional exam requirements/recommendations for international students: Required—TOEFL (minimum score 600 paper-based; 100 iBT) or IELTS. Electronic applications accepted. *Expenses: Tuition:* Full-time $10,530; part-time $585 per credit. *Required fees:* $60 per term. Tuition and fees vary according to course level, course load, degree level and program.

Salve Regina University, Program in Management, Newport, RI 02840-4192. Offers business studies (CGS); human resource management (CGS); innovation and strategic management (MS); management (CGS); nonprofit management (CGS); social entrepreneurship (CGS). *Program availability:* Part-time, evening/weekend, online learning. *Entrance requirements:* For master's, GMAT, GRE General Test, or MAT. Additional exam requirements/recommendations for international students: Required—TOEFL (minimum score 600 paper-based; 100 iBT). Electronic applications accepted. *Expenses: Tuition:* Full-time $10,530; part-time $585 per credit. *Required fees:* $60 per term. Tuition and fees vary according to course level, course load, degree level and program.

Samford University, Brock School of Business, Birmingham, AL 35229. Offers accountancy (M Acc); entrepreneurship (MBA); finance (MBA); marketing (MBA); JD/M Acc; JD/MBA; MBA/M Acc; MBA/M Div; MBA/MSEM; MBA/Pharm D. Programs offered jointly with Cumberland School of Law, Beeson School of Divinity, Howard College of Arts and Sciences, and McWhorter School of Pharmacy. *Accreditation:* AACSB. *Program availability:* Part-time, 100% online, blended/hybrid learning. *Faculty:* 7 full-time (1 woman), 4 part-time/adjunct (0 women). *Students:* 76 full-time (30 women), 20 part-time (11 women); includes 8 minority (4 Black or African American, non-Hispanic/Latino; 1 Asian, non-Hispanic/Latino; 1 Hispanic/Latino; 2 Two or more races, non-Hispanic/Latino), 7 international. Average age 28. 41 applicants, 88% accepted, 26 enrolled. In 2018, 74 master's awarded. *Degree requirements:* For master's, capstone course. *Entrance requirements:* For master's, GMAT or GRE, resume, transcripts, WES or ECE Evaluation (international applicants only), essay (international applicants only). Additional exam requirements/recommendations for international students: Required—TOEFL (minimum score 90 iBT), IELTS (minimum score 6.5). *Application deadline:* For fall admission, 8/1 for domestic and international students; for spring admission, 1/1 for domestic and international students. Applications are processed on a rolling basis. Application fee: $35. Electronic applications accepted. Application fee is waived when completed online. *Expenses: Tuition:* Full-time $17,255; part-time $837 per credit. *Required fees:* $610; $305 per term. Tuition and fees vary according to course load, degree level, program and student level. *Financial support:* In 2018–19, 46 students received support. Scholarships/grants available. Financial award application deadline: 2/15; financial award applicants required to submit FAFSA. *Unit head:* Dr. Barbara Cartledge, Assistant Dean, 205-726-2935, Fax: 205-726-2540, E-mail: bhcartle@samford.edu. *Application contact:* Elizabeth Gambrell, Associate Director, 205-726-2040, Fax: 205-726-2540, E-mail: eagambre@samford.edu.
Website: http://www.samford.edu/business

Sam Houston State University, College of Business Administration, Department of General Business and Finance, Huntsville, TX 77341. Offers banking and financial institutions (EMBA); business administration (MBA). *Accreditation:* AACSB. *Program availability:* Part-time, evening/weekend, online learning. *Degree requirements:* For master's, comprehensive exam (for some programs). *Entrance requirements:* For master's, GMAT, interview (for EMBA); resume, transcript(s). Additional exam requirements/recommendations for international students: Required—TOEFL (minimum score 550 paper-based; 79 iBT), IELTS (minimum score 6.5). Electronic applications accepted.

San Diego State University, Graduate and Research Affairs, Fowler College of Business, Department of Management, San Diego, CA 92182. Offers entrepreneurship (MS); human resources management (MS); management science (MS). *Program availability:* Part-time, evening/weekend. *Degree requirements:* For master's, thesis or alternative. *Entrance requirements:* For master's, GMAT, resume, letters of reference. Additional exam requirements/recommendations for international students: Required—TOEFL. Electronic applications accepted.

San Diego State University, Graduate and Research Affairs, Fowler College of Business, Program in Business Administration, San Diego, CA 92182. Offers MBA. *Accreditation:* AACSB. *Program availability:* Part-time. *Degree requirements:* For master's, thesis or alternative. *Entrance requirements:* For master's, GMAT, resume, letters of reference. Additional exam requirements/recommendations for international students: Required—TOEFL. Electronic applications accepted.

San Francisco State University, Division of Graduate Studies, College of Business, San Francisco, CA 94132-1722. Offers EMBA, MA, MBA, MSA.

San Ignacio University, Graduate Programs, Doral, FL 33178. Offers business administration (MBA), including human resources management, international business, marketing management; education (M Ed), including early childhood education, educational leadership, special education; hospitality management (MA), including gastronomy and restaurant management, tourism management.

Santa Clara University, Leavey School of Business, Santa Clara, CA 95053. Offers business administration (MBA); business analytics (MS); finance (MS); information systems (MS); supply chain management and analytics (MS); JD/MBA. *Accreditation:* AACSB. *Program availability:* Part-time, online learning. *Faculty:* 101 full-time (32 women), 47 part-time/adjunct (15 women). *Students:* 487 full-time (278 women), 326 part-time (139 women); includes 295 minority (14 Black or African American, non-Hispanic/Latino; 207 Asian, non-Hispanic/Latino; 39 Hispanic/Latino; 35 Two or more races, non-Hispanic/Latino), 294 international. Average age 31. 694 applicants, 65% accepted, 281 enrolled. In 2018, 195 master's awarded. *Entrance requirements:* For master's, Varies based on program. Additional exam requirements/recommendations for international students: Required—TOEFL (minimum score 90 iBT). Application fee: $100 ($150 for international students). Electronic applications accepted. *Financial support:* In 2018–19, 192 students received support. Fellowships, Federal Work-Study, and scholarships/grants available. Support available to part-time students. Financial award applicants required to submit FAFSA. *Unit head:* Caryn Beck-Dudley, Dean, 408-554-4523, E-mail: cbeckdudley@scu.edu. *Application contact:* Caryn Beck-Dudley, Dean, 408-554-4523, E-mail: cbeckdudley@scu.edu.
Website: http://www.scu.edu/business/

Savannah State University, Master of Business Administration Program, Savannah, GA 31404. Offers MBA. *Accreditation:* AACSB. *Program availability:* Part-time, evening/weekend. *Entrance requirements:* For master's, GMAT, GRE, or successful completion of pre-MBA program, BA/BS from an accredited institution, official transcripts, essay, 3 letters of recommendation, immunization certificate, current resume. Additional exam requirements/recommendations for international students: Required—TOEFL. Electronic applications accepted. *Expenses:* Contact institution.

Schiller International University, MBA Program, Madrid, Spain, Madrid, Spain. Offers international business (MBA). *Program availability:* Part-time. *Degree requirements:* For master's, comprehensive exam, thesis optional. *Entrance requirements:* Additional exam requirements/recommendations for international students: Required—TOEFL (minimum score 550 paper-based).

Schiller International University, MBA Program Paris, France, Paris, France. Offers international business (MBA). Bilingual French/English MBA available for native French speakers. *Program availability:* Part-time, evening/weekend, online learning. *Degree requirements:* For master's, comprehensive exam, thesis or alternative. *Entrance requirements:* Additional exam requirements/recommendations for international students: Required—TOEFL (minimum score 550 paper-based).

Schiller International University, MBA Programs, Florida, Largo, FL 33771. Offers financial planning (MBA); information technology (MBA); international business (MBA); international hotel and tourism management (MBA). *Program availability:* Part-time, evening/weekend, online learning. *Degree requirements:* For master's, thesis optional. *Entrance requirements:* Additional exam requirements/recommendations for international students: Required—TOEFL (minimum score 550 paper-based).

Schiller International University, MBA Programs, Heidelberg, Germany, Heidelberg, Germany. Offers international business (MBA, MIM); management of information technology (MBA). *Program availability:* Part-time, evening/weekend. *Degree requirements:* For master's, thesis optional. *Entrance requirements:* Additional exam requirements/recommendations for international students: Required—TOEFL (minimum score 550 paper-based). *Faculty research:* Leadership, international economy, foreign direct investment.

Schreiner University, MBA Program, Kerrville, TX 78028-5697. Offers ethical leadership (MBA). *Program availability:* Part-time, online learning. *Entrance requirements:* For master's, 3 recommendations; personal essay; transcripts; resume. Additional exam requirements/recommendations for international students: Required—TOEFL. Electronic applications accepted. *Expenses:* Contact institution.

Seattle Pacific University, Master of Arts in Management Program, Seattle, WA 98119-1997. Offers business intelligence and data analytics (MA); cybersecurity (MA); faith and business (MA); human resources (MA); social and sustainable management (MA). *Students:* 12 part-time (9 women); includes 3 minority (2 Black or African American, non-Hispanic/Latino; 1 Asian, non-Hispanic/Latino), 4 international. Average age 31. 11 applicants, 45% accepted, 2 enrolled. *Entrance requirements:* For master's, GMAT scores above 500 (25 verbal; 30 quantitative; 4.4 analytical writing) are preferred. https://spu.edu/academics/school-of-business-and-economics/graduate-programs/mba#application, bachelor's degree from accredited college or university, resume, essay, official transcript. *Application deadline:* For fall admission, 8/1 for domestic students, 6/1 for international students; for winter admission, 11/1 for domestic students, 9/1 for international students; for spring admission, 2/1 for domestic students, 12/1 for international students; for summer admission, 5/1 for domestic students. Application fee: $50.
Website: http://spu.edu/academics/school-of-business-and-economics/graduate-programs/ma-management

Seattle Pacific University, Master of Business Administration Program, Seattle, WA 98119-1997. Offers business administration (MBA); social and sustainable enterprise (MBA). *Accreditation:* AACSB. *Program availability:* Part-time. *Students:* 2 full-time (1 woman), 40 part-time (25 women); includes 13 minority (4 Black or African American, non-Hispanic/Latino; 5 Asian, non-Hispanic/Latino; 2 Hispanic/Latino; 2 Two or more races, non-Hispanic/Latino), 9 international. Average age 32. 36 applicants, 53% accepted, 7 enrolled. In 2018, 14 master's awarded. *Entrance requirements:* For master's, GMAT (minimum preferred scores of 500; 25 verbal; 30 quantitative; 4.4 analytical writing), BA, resume as evidence of substantive work experience. Additional exam requirements/recommendations for international students: Required—TOEFL (minimum score 90 iBT), IELTS (minimum score 7). *Application deadline:* For fall admission, 8/1 for domestic and international students; for winter admission, 11/1 for domestic and international students; for spring admission, 2/1 for domestic and international students. Applications are processed on a rolling basis. Application fee: $50. Electronic applications accepted. *Financial support:* Scholarships/grants available. Financial award applicants required to submit FAFSA. *Unit head:* Gary Karns, Associate Dean for Graduate Studies, 206-281-2948, Fax: 206-281-2733. *Application contact:* Gary Karns, Associate Dean for Graduate Studies, 206-281-2948, Fax: 206-281-2733.
Website: http://spu.edu/academics/school-of-business-and-economics/graduate-programs/mba

Seattle University, Albers School of Business and Economics, Bridge MBA Program, Seattle, WA 98122-1090. Offers MBA. *Faculty:* 134 full-time (48 women), 34 part-time/adjunct (16 women). *Students:* 13 full-time (7 women); includes 3 minority (all Hispanic/Latino), 4 international. Average age 25. 49 applicants, 41% accepted, 14 enrolled. In 2018, 27 master's awarded. *Entrance requirements:* For master's, GMAT. Additional exam requirements/recommendations for international students: Required—TOEFL or IELTS. *Application deadline:* For fall admission, 7/1 for domestic students. Applications are processed on a rolling basis. Application fee: $55. Electronic applications accepted. *Expenses:* Contact institution. *Financial support:* In 2018–19, 6 students received support. Scholarships/grants available. Financial award application deadline: 6/1. *Unit head:* John Merle, Director, 206-398-4628, E-mail: merlej@seattleu.edu. *Application contact:* Jeff Millard, Assistant Dean of Graduate Programs, 206-296-5700, E-mail: albersgrad@seattleu.edu.
Website: http://www.seattleu.edu/albers/bridgemba/

Seattle University, Albers School of Business and Economics, Master of Business Administration Program, Seattle, WA 98122-1090. Offers MBA, Certificate, JD/MBA, MBA/MSBA, MBA/MSF. *Accreditation:* AACSB. *Program availability:* Part-time, evening/weekend. *Faculty:* 67 full-time (24 women), 17 part-time/adjunct (8 women). *Students:* 67 full-time (30 women), 223 part-time (98 women); includes 72 minority (4 Black or African American, non-Hispanic/Latino; 1 American Indian or Alaska Native, non-Hispanic/Latino; 34 Asian, non-Hispanic/Latino; 24 Hispanic/Latino; 1 Native Hawaiian or other Pacific Islander, non-Hispanic/Latino; 8 Two or more races, non-Hispanic/Latino), 36 international. Average age 31. 89 applicants, 71% accepted, 45 enrolled. In 2018, 107 master's awarded. *Entrance requirements:* For master's, GMAT, minimum GPA of 3.0, 2 years of related work experience. Additional exam requirements/recommendations for international students: Required—TOEFL (minimum score 580 paper-based; 92 iBT). *Application deadline:* For fall admission, 8/20 priority date for domestic students, 4/1 priority date for international students; for winter admission, 11/20 priority date for domestic students, 9/1 priority date for international students; for spring admission, 2/20 priority date for domestic students, 12/1 priority date for

international students. Applications are processed on a rolling basis. Application fee: $55. Electronic applications accepted. *Expenses:* Contact institution. *Financial support:* In 2018–19, 104 students received support. Career-related internships or fieldwork and Federal Work-Study available. Support available to part-time students. Financial award applicants required to submit FAFSA. *Unit head:* Dr. Greg Magnan, Director, 206-296-5700, Fax: 206-296-5795, E-mail: gmagnan@seattleu.edu. *Application contact:* Janet Shandley, Director of Graduate Admissions, 206-296-5900, Fax: 206-298-5656, E-mail: grad_admissions@seattleu.edu.
Website: http://www.seattleu.edu/albers/mba/

Seton Hall University, Stillman School of Business, South Orange, NJ 07079-2697. Offers accounting (MS). *Accreditation:* AACSB. *Program availability:* Part-time, evening/weekend. *Faculty:* 27 full-time (5 women), 18 part-time/adjunct (2 women). *Students:* 87 full-time (39 women), 491 part-time (198 women); includes 81 minority (30 Black or African American, non-Hispanic/Latino; 14 Asian, non-Hispanic/Latino; 28 Hispanic/Latino; 9 Two or more races, non-Hispanic/Latino), 294 international. Average age 33. 449 applicants, 86% accepted, 230 enrolled. In 2018, 135 master's awarded. *Degree requirements:* For master's, 20 hours of community service (Social Responsibility Project). *Entrance requirements:* For master's, GMAT or GRE, MS in business discipline, professional degree or designation (MD, JD, PhD, DVM, DDS, CPA, etc.), minimum undergraduate GPA of 3.0. Additional exam requirements/recommendations for international students: Required—TOEFL (minimum score 607 paper-based; 80 iBT), IELTS (minimum score 6), PTE. *Application deadline:* For fall admission, 5/31 priority date for domestic students, 3/31 priority date for international students; for spring admission, 10/31 priority date for domestic students, 9/30 priority date for international students; for summer admission, 4/30 priority date for domestic students, 3/31 priority date for international students. Applications are processed on a rolling basis. Application fee: $75. Electronic applications accepted. Application fee is waived when completed online. *Expenses:* $1,305 per credit hour (for graduate business programs); degree programs range from 40 to 30 credit hours in length; certificate programs range from 16-12 credit hours in length; university fee for full-time graduate students is $135 per semester and $110 per semester for part-time students; technology fee for full-time students is $25 per semester and $12 per semester for part-time students. *Financial support:* Research assistantships with full tuition reimbursements, career-related internships or fieldwork, scholarships/grants, and unspecified assistantships available. Financial award application deadline: 6/30; financial award applicants required to submit FAFSA. *Faculty research:* Sport, hedge funds, executive compensation, social media, and legal issues. *Unit head:* Dr. Joyce Strawser, Dean, 973-761-9013, Fax: 973-275-2465, E-mail: joyce.strawser@shu.edu. *Application contact:* Alfred Ayoub, Director of Graduate Admissions, 973-761-9262, Fax: 973-761-9208, E-mail: alfred.ayoub@shu.edu.
Website: http://www.shu.edu/academics/business/

Seton Hill University, MBA Program, Greensburg, PA 15601. Offers entrepreneurship (MBA); forensic accounting and fraud examination (MBA); healthcare administration (MBA); management (MBA). *Program availability:* Part-time, evening/weekend. *Entrance requirements:* For master's, resume, 3 letters of recommendation, personal statement, transcripts. Additional exam requirements/recommendations for international students: Required—TOEFL (minimum score 600 paper-based; 100 iBT), IELTS (minimum score 6.5). *Application deadline:* Applications are processed on a rolling basis. Application fee: $0. Electronic applications accepted. *Financial support:* Federal Work-Study, scholarships/grants, and tuition discounts available. Financial award application deadline: 8/15; financial award applicants required to submit FAFSA. *Unit head:* Dr. Douglas Nelson, Associate Professor, Business/MBA Program Director, E-mail: dnelson@setonhill.edu. *Application contact:* Dr. Douglas Nelson, Associate Professor, Business/MBA Program Director, E-mail: dnelson@setonhill.edu.
Website: http://www.setonhill.edu/academics/graduate_programs/mba

Shenandoah University, Harry F. Byrd, Jr. School of Business, Winchester, VA 22601. Offers MBA, Certificate. *Accreditation:* AACSB. *Program availability:* Part-time, evening/weekend. *Faculty:* 9 full-time (3 women), 4 part-time/adjunct (0 women). *Students:* 45 full-time (12 women), 34 part-time (18 women); includes 11 minority (3 Black or African American, non-Hispanic/Latino; 1 American Indian or Alaska Native, non-Hispanic/Latino; 2 Asian, non-Hispanic/Latino; 4 Hispanic/Latino; 1 Two or more races, non-Hispanic/Latino), 22 international. Average age 29. 73 applicants, 93% accepted, 44 enrolled. In 2018, 47 master's, 12 other advanced degrees awarded. *Degree requirements:* For master's, 36-48 credit hours completed, depending on transcript. *Entrance requirements:* For master's, transcripts from all institutions of higher learning; minimum GPA of 3.0 in appropriate undergraduate course work; 2 letters of recommendation; resume; interview; brief narrative essay (2-3 pages) of career, professional development and goals, as they relate to the completion of an MBA. Additional exam requirements/recommendations for international students: Required—TOEFL (minimum score 550 paper-based; 79 iBT), IELTS (minimum score 6.5), TOEFL (minimum score 550 paper-based, 79 iBT) OR IELTS (6.5). *Application deadline:* For fall admission, 6/15 for domestic students, 5/15 for international students; for spring admission, 11/15 for domestic students, 10/15 for international students; for summer admission, 3/1 for domestic and international students. Application fee: $30. Electronic applications accepted. *Expenses:* $875 per credit hour (36), student service fee, technology fee. *Financial support:* In 2018–19, 27 students received support. Scholarships/grants and unspecified assistantships available. Financial award application deadline: 1/15; financial award applicants required to submit FAFSA. *Faculty research:* Entrepreneurship, sports ethics, healthcare economics, leaderships, sustainability. *Unit head:* Astrid Sheil, PhD, Dean of Harry F. Byrd, Jr. School of Business, 540-545-7253, Fax: 540-665-5437, E-mail: asheil@su.edu. *Application contact:* Andrew Woodall, Assistant Vice President for Admissions and Recruitment, 540-665-4581, Fax: 540-665-4627, E-mail: admit@su.edu.
Website: http://www.su.edu/business/

Shippensburg University of Pennsylvania, School of Graduate Studies, John L. Grove College of Business, Shippensburg, PA 17257-2299. Offers advanced studies in business (Certificate); advanced supply chain and logistics management (Certificate); business administration (MBA, DBA), including business administration (MBA), business analytics (MBA), finance (MBA), healthcare management (MBA), management information systems (MBA), supply chain management (MBA); finance (Certificate); health care management (Certificate); management information systems (Certificate). *Accreditation:* AACSB. *Program availability:* Part-time, evening/weekend, 100% online, blended/hybrid learning. *Faculty:* 20 full-time (4 women), 2 part-time/adjunct (0 women). *Students:* 31 full-time (14 women), 174 part-time (67 women); includes 33 minority (17 Black or African American, non-Hispanic/Latino; 6 Asian, non-Hispanic/Latino; 7 Hispanic/Latino; 3 Two or more races, non-Hispanic/Latino), 13 international. Average age 33. 149 applicants, 61% accepted, 60 enrolled. In 2018, 104 master's, 1 other advanced degree awarded. *Degree requirements:* For master's, comprehensive exam (for some programs), thesis optional, practicum capstone course; for doctorate, comprehensive exam, thesis/dissertation, comprehensive exam dissertation. *Entrance requirements:* For master's, GMAT (minimum score 450 if less than 5 years of mid-level experience, including management experience), current resume; relevant work/classroom experience; 500-word statement of purpose; prerequisites of quantitative analysis, computer usage, and oral and written communications; laptop computer; for

doctorate, GMAT (minimum score of 600 if less than 5 years of substantive professional or teaching experience), 2 letters of recommendation from professionals in academia or industry; 2-3 page personal and professional statement; interview; resume. Additional exam requirements/recommendations for international students: Required—TOEFL (minimum score 550 paper-based; 68 iBT), IELTS (minimum score 6), TOEFL (minimum score 550 paper-based, 68 iBT) or IELTS (minimum score 6). *Application deadline:* For fall admission, 4/30 for international students; for spring admission, 9/30 for international students. Applications are processed on a rolling basis. Application fee: $45. Electronic applications accepted. *Expenses:* Tuition, state resident: part-time $516 per credit. Tuition, nonresident: part-time $750 per credit. *Required fees:* $149 per credit. *Financial support:* In 2018–19, 15 students received support. Career-related internships or fieldwork, scholarships/grants, unspecified assistantships, and resident hall director and student payroll positions available. Support available to part-time students. Financial award application deadline: 3/1; financial award applicants required to submit FAFSA. *Unit head:* Dr. John G. Kooti, Dean of the College of Business, 717-477-1435, Fax: 717-477-4003, E-mail: jgkooti@ship.edu. *Application contact:* Maya T. Mapp, Director of Admissions, 717-477-1231, Fax: 717-477-4016, E-mail: mtmapp@ship.edu.
Website: http://www.ship.edu/business

Shorter University, Professional Studies, Rome, GA 30165. Offers accountancy (MAC); business administration (MBA); management (MM). *Program availability:* Evening/weekend. *Degree requirements:* For master's, project. *Entrance requirements:* For master's, minimum undergraduate GPA of 2.75 in last 60 hours, 3 years of work experience. Additional exam requirements/recommendations for international students: Required—TOEFL (minimum score 550 paper-based; 79 iBT). Electronic applications accepted.

Siena College, School of Business, Loudonville, NY 12211-1462. Offers accounting (MS). *Program availability:* Evening/weekend. *Degree requirements:* For master's, internship.

Silver Lake College of the Holy Family, Graduate School, Graduate Business Program, Manitowoc, WI 54220-9319. Offers leadership and organizational development (MS). *Program availability:* Part-time, evening/weekend. *Degree requirements:* For master's, comprehensive exam (for some programs), thesis optional, capstone culminating project, thesis research, comprehensive portfolio, or public presentation of project. *Entrance requirements:* For master's, ACT (preferred) or SAT, minimum undergraduate GPA of 3.0. Additional exam requirements/recommendations for international students: Required—TOEFL (minimum score 550 paper-based; 89 iBT). Electronic applications accepted. *Expenses:* Contact institution. *Faculty research:* Leadership development; organizational change; organizational behavior.

Simmons University, College of Organizational, Computational, and Information Sciences, Boston, MA 02115. Offers business administration (MBA); health care (MBA); MBA/MSW. *Accreditation:* AACSB. *Program availability:* Part-time, 100% online, blended/hybrid learning. *Faculty:* 32 full-time (22 women), 38 part-time/adjunct (30 women). *Students:* 315 full-time (263 women), 473 part-time (406 women); includes 102 minority (12 Black or African American, non-Hispanic/Latino; 20 Asian, non-Hispanic/Latino; 42 Hispanic/Latino; 28 Two or more races, non-Hispanic/Latino), 12 international. Average age 31. 493 applicants, 87% accepted, 240 enrolled. In 2018, 740 master's awarded. *Degree requirements:* For master's, thesis (for some programs). *Entrance requirements:* For master's, GMAT or GRE. Additional exam requirements/recommendations for international students: Required—TOEFL. *Application deadline:* For fall admission, 7/18 priority date for domestic students; for summer admission, 4/24 priority date for domestic students. Applications are processed on a rolling basis. Application fee: $75. Electronic applications accepted. *Expenses:* $1,270 per credit hour plus fees. *Financial support:* In 2018–19, 16 students received support, including 5 fellowships (averaging $22,000 per year), 11 teaching assistantships (averaging $19,500 per year); scholarships/grants also available. Financial award applicants required to submit FAFSA. *Faculty research:* Library science, information science, gender and organizations, leadership. *Unit head:* Dr. Marie desJardins, Dean, E-mail: marie.desjardins@simmons.edu. *Application contact:* Kate Benson, Director, Library Science Admission Office, 617-5212801, E-mail: kate.benson@simmons.edu.
Website: https://www.simmons.edu/academics/colleges-schools-departments/cocis

Simon Fraser University, Office of Graduate Studies and Postdoctoral Fellows, Faculty of Business Administration, Vancouver, BC V6B 5K3, Canada. Offers business administration (EMBA, PhD, Graduate Diploma); finance (M Sc); management of technology (MBA); management of technology/biotechnology (MBA). *Program availability:* Online learning. *Degree requirements:* For master's, thesis (for some programs); for doctorate, comprehensive exam, thesis/dissertation. *Entrance requirements:* For master's, GMAT, minimum GPA of 3.0 (on scale of 4.33) or 3.33 based on last 60 credits of undergraduate courses; for doctorate, minimum GPA of 3.5 (on scale of 4.33); for Graduate Diploma, minimum GPA of 2.5 (on scale of 4.33) or 2.67 based on last 60 credits of undergraduate courses. Additional exam requirements/recommendations for international students: Recommended—TOEFL (minimum score 580 paper-based; 93 iBT), IELTS (minimum score 7), TWE (minimum score 5). *Expenses:* Contact institution. *Faculty research:* Accounting, management and organizational studies, technology and operations management, finance, international business.

SIT Graduate Institute, Graduate Programs, Master's Programs in Intercultural Service, Leadership, and Management, Brattleboro, VT 05302-0676. Offers intercultural service, leadership, and management (self-designed) (MA); international education (MA); peace and justice leadership (MA); sustainable development (MA). *Program availability:* Online learning. *Degree requirements:* For master's, one foreign language, thesis. *Entrance requirements:* For master's, 3 letters of reference. Additional exam requirements/recommendations for international students: Required—TOEFL, IELTS. *Faculty research:* Intercultural communication, conflict resolution, international education, world issues, international affairs.

Slippery Rock University of Pennsylvania, Graduate Studies (Recruitment), College of Business, School of Business, Slippery Rock, PA 16057-1383. Offers accounting/finance (MBA); general (MBA); marketing/management (MBA). *Program availability:* Part-time, evening/weekend. *Faculty:* 12 full-time (7 women), 1 part-time/adjunct (0 women). *Students:* 21 full-time (8 women), 22 part-time (15 women); includes 3 minority (1 Black or African American, non-Hispanic/Latino; 1 Asian, non-Hispanic/Latino; 1 Hispanic/Latino). Average age 29. 53 applicants, 62% accepted, 23 enrolled. In 2018, 23 master's awarded. *Degree requirements:* For master's, comprehensive exam (for some programs), thesis (for some programs). *Entrance requirements:* For master's, minimum cumulative GPA of 3.0, official transcripts, three references. Additional exam requirements/recommendations for international students: Required—TOEFL (minimum score 550 paper-based; 80 iBT). *Application deadline:* For fall admission, 3/1 priority date for domestic students, 5/1 priority date for international students; for spring admission, 10/1 priority date for domestic students, 9/1 priority date for international students. Applications are processed on a rolling basis. Application fee: $25 ($30 for international students). Electronic applications accepted. *Expenses:* Contact institution. *Financial support:* In 2018–19, 9 students received support. Career-related internships or fieldwork, Federal Work-Study, institutionally sponsored loans, scholarships/grants, tuition waivers (partial), and unspecified assistantships available. Support available to part-time students. Financial award application deadline: 5/1; financial award applicants required to submit FAFSA. *Unit head:* Dr. Larry McCarthy, Graduate Coordinator, 724-738-2552, Fax: 724-738-2959, E-mail: larry.mccarthy@sru.edu. *Application contact:* Brandi Weber-Mortimer, Director of Graduate Admissions, 724-738-2051, Fax: 724-738-2146, E-mail: graduate.admissions@sru.edu.
Website: http://www.sru.edu/academics/graduate-programs/mba-master-of-business-administration

Sonoma State University, School of Business and Economics, Rohnert Park, CA 94928. Offers wine business (Exec MBA, MBA). *Accreditation:* AACSB. *Program availability:* Part-time, evening/weekend. *Degree requirements:* For master's, thesis or alternative. *Entrance requirements:* For master's, GMAT. Additional exam requirements/recommendations for international students: Required—TOEFL (minimum score 500 paper-based).

South Carolina State University, College of Graduate and Professional Studies, Department of Business Administration, Orangeburg, SC 29117-0001. Offers agribusiness (MBA); entrepreneurship (MBA); general business administration (MBA); healthcare management (MBA). *Program availability:* Part-time, evening/weekend. *Faculty:* 7 full-time (2 women). *Students:* 20 full-time (9 women), 6 part-time (2 women); all minorities (all Black or African American, non-Hispanic/Latino). Average age 28. 12 applicants, 92% accepted, 9 enrolled. In 2018, 14 master's awarded. *Degree requirements:* For master's, comprehensive exam, business plan. *Entrance requirements:* For master's, GMAT, minimum GPA of 2.8. Additional exam requirements/recommendations for international students: Required—TOEFL. *Application deadline:* For fall admission, 6/15 for domestic and international students; for spring admission, 11/1 for domestic and international students. Application fee: $25. Electronic applications accepted. *Expenses: Tuition, area resident:* Full-time $9928; part-time $552 per credit hour. Tuition, state resident: full-time $9928. Tuition, nonresident: full-time $21,038; part-time $1169 per credit hour. *Required fees:* $1532; $85 per credit hour. *Financial support:* Fellowships, research assistantships, career-related internships or fieldwork, Federal Work-Study, scholarships/grants, and unspecified assistantships available. Financial award application deadline: 6/1. *Unit head:* Dr. David Jamison, Interim Chair, 803-536-8443, Fax: 803-536-8078, E-mail: djamison@scsu.edu. *Application contact:* Ellen R. Ricoma, MBA Program Director, 803-533-3777, Fax: 803-516-4651, E-mail: ericoma1@scsu.edu.

Southeastern Louisiana University, College of Business, Hammond, LA 70402. Offers MBA. *Accreditation:* AACSB. *Program availability:* Part-time. *Faculty:* 17 full-time (3 women). *Students:* 89 full-time (39 women), 18 part-time (12 women); includes 14 minority (5 Black or African American, non-Hispanic/Latino; 7 Hispanic/Latino; 2 Two or more races, non-Hispanic/Latino), 13 international. Average age 27. 72 applicants, 44% accepted, 24 enrolled. In 2018, 60 master's awarded. *Entrance requirements:* For master's, GRE/GMAT, minimum cumulative GPA of 2.75 for all undergraduate work attempted or 3.0 on all upper-division undergraduate course work attempted. Additional exam requirements/recommendations for international students: Required—TOEFL (minimum score 500 paper-based; 61 iBT). *Application deadline:* For fall admission, 7/15 priority date for domestic students, 6/1 priority date for international students; for spring admission, 12/1 priority date for domestic students, 10/1 priority date for international students. Applications are processed on a rolling basis. Application fee: $20 ($30 for international students). Electronic applications accepted. *Expenses: Tuition, area resident:* Full-time $6684. Tuition, state resident: full-time $6684. Tuition, nonresident: full-time $19,162. *Required fees:* $2097. *Financial support:* In 2018–19, 62 students received support, including 1 fellowship with tuition reimbursement available (averaging $3,500 per year); career-related internships or fieldwork, Federal Work-Study, institutionally sponsored loans, scholarships/grants, and unspecified assistantships also available. Support available to part-time students. Financial award application deadline: 5/1; financial award applicants required to submit FAFSA. *Faculty research:* Human Resources - Employment Discrimination; Organizational behavior/strategy; Cultural Difference; Taxomonifies in International Contexts; Healthcare Administration Strategy. *Unit head:* Dr. Antoinette Phillips, Dean, 985-549-2258, Fax: 985-549-5038, E-mail: business@southeastern.edu. *Application contact:* Dr. Antoinette Phillips, Dean, 985-549-2258, Fax: 985-549-5038, E-mail: business@southeastern.edu.
Website: http://www.selu.edu/acad_research/colleges/bus/index.html

Southeastern Oklahoma State University, John Massey School of Business, Durant, OK 74701-0609. Offers MBA. *Accreditation:* AACSB. *Program availability:* Part-time, evening/weekend. *Degree requirements:* For master's, thesis optional. *Entrance requirements:* For master's, GMAT, minimum GPA of 3.0 in last 60 hours or 2.75 overall. Additional exam requirements/recommendations for international students: Required—TOEFL (minimum score 550 paper-based; 79 iBT). Electronic applications accepted.

Southeastern University, Jannetides College of Business and Entrepreneurial Leadership, Lakeland, FL 33801-6099. Offers executive leadership (MBA); global business administration (MBA); healthcare administration (MBA); missional leadership (MBA); organizational leadership (PhD); sport management (MBA); strategic leadership (DSL). *Accreditation:* ACBSP. *Program availability:* Evening/weekend, online learning. *Entrance requirements:* For master's, GMAT, minimum cumulative GPA of 3.0, writing sample. Electronic applications accepted.

Southeast Missouri State University, School of Graduate Studies, Harrison College of Business and Computing, Cape Girardeau, MO 63701-4799. Offers accounting (MBA); entrepreneurship (MBA); financial management (MBA); sport management (MBA). *Accreditation:* AACSB. *Program availability:* Part-time, evening/weekend, 100% online. *Faculty:* 27 full-time (7 women), 1 (woman) part-time/adjunct. *Students:* 94 full-time (50 women), 88 part-time (39 women); includes 18 minority (9 Black or African American, non-Hispanic/Latino; 4 Asian, non-Hispanic/Latino; 5 Hispanic/Latino), 79 international. Average age 29. 80 applicants, 100% accepted, 80 enrolled. In 2018, 62 master's awarded. *Degree requirements:* For master's, variable foreign language requirement, comprehensive exam (for some programs), thesis or alternative. *Entrance requirements:* For master's, GMAT or GRE, minimum undergraduate GPA of 2.5, minimum grade of C in prerequisite courses. Additional exam requirements/recommendations for international students: Required—TOEFL (minimum score 550 paper-based; 79 iBT), IELTS (minimum score 6), PTE (minimum score 53). *Application deadline:* For fall admission, 8/1 for domestic students, 6/1 for international students; for spring admission, 11/21 for domestic students, 10/1 for international students; for summer admission, 5/15 for domestic students. Applications are processed on a rolling basis. Application fee: $30 ($40 for international students). Electronic applications accepted. *Expenses:* Contact institution. *Financial support:* In 2018–19, 16 students received support. Career-related internships or fieldwork, Federal Work-Study, scholarships/grants, traineeships, tuition waivers (full), and unspecified assistantships available. Financial award application deadline: 6/30; financial award applicants required to submit FAFSA. *Faculty research:* Organizational justice, ethics, leadership, corporate finance, generational differences. *Unit head:* Dr. Alberto Davila, Dean, 573-651-2112, E-mail: adavila@semo.edu. *Application contact:* Dr. Alberto Davila, Dean, 573-651-2112, E-mail: adavila@semo.edu.
Website: http://www.semo.edu/mba

Southern Adventist University, School of Business, Collegedale, TN 37315-0370. Offers accounting (MBA); computer information systems (MBA); finance (MBA);

healthcare administration (MBA); management (MBA). *Program availability:* Part-time, evening/weekend, 100% online. *Faculty:* 7 full-time (2 women). *Students:* 23 applicants, 48% accepted, 8 enrolled. In 2018, 8 master's awarded. *Entrance requirements:* For master's, GMAT, minimum cumulative undergraduate GPA of 3.0. Additional exam requirements/recommendations for international students: Required—TOEFL (minimum score 100 iBT). *Application deadline:* For fall admission, 7/1 for domestic students, 5/1 for international students; for winter admission, 11/1 for domestic students, 9/1 for international students; for summer admission, 4/1 for domestic students, 2/1 for international students. Applications are processed on a rolling basis. Application fee: $40. Electronic applications accepted. *Financial support:* Scholarships/grants and unspecified assistantships available. Financial award application deadline: 9/1; financial award applicants required to submit FAFSA. *Unit head:* Dr. Stephanie Sheehan, Dean, 423-236-2659, Fax: 423-236-1527, E-mail: ssheehan@southern.edu. *Application contact:* Teshia Price, Graduate Studies Coordinator, 423-236-2751, Fax: 423-236-1527, E-mail: tprice@southern.edu.
Website: https://www.southern.edu/academics/business.html

Southern Arkansas University–Magnolia, School of Graduate Studies, Magnolia, AR 71753. Offers agriculture (MS); business administration (MBA), including agribusiness, social entrepreneurship, supply chain management; clinical and mental health counseling (MS); computer and information sciences (MS), including cyber security and privacy, data science, information technology; gifted and talented (M Ed), including curriculum and instruction, educational administration and supervision, gifted and talented P-8/7-12, instructional specialist P-4; higher, adult and lifelong education (M Ed); kinesiology (M Ed), including coaching; library media and information specialist (M Ed); public administration (MPA); school counseling K-12 (M Ed); student affairs and college counseling (M Ed); teaching (MAT). *Accreditation:* NCATE. *Program availability:* Part-time, 100% online, blended/hybrid learning. *Faculty:* 36 full-time (21 women), 32 part-time/adjunct (15 women). *Students:* 164 full-time (77 women), 762 part-time (510 women); includes 192 minority (163 Black or African American, non-Hispanic/Latino; 7 American Indian or Alaska Native, non-Hispanic/Latino; 13 Asian, non-Hispanic/Latino; 1 Hispanic/Latino; 8 Two or more races, non-Hispanic/Latino), 213 international. Average age 28. 363 applicants, 100% accepted, 237 enrolled. In 2018, 716 master's awarded. *Degree requirements:* For master's, comprehensive exam (for some programs), thesis optional. *Entrance requirements:* For master's, GRE, MAT or GMAT, minimum GPA of 2.5. Additional exam requirements/recommendations for international students: Required—TOEFL (minimum score 550 paper-based), IELTS (minimum score 6). *Application deadline:* For fall admission, 8/1 for domestic and international students; for spring admission, 12/1 for domestic students, 11/15 for international students; for summer admission, 4/1 for domestic students, 5/10 for international students. Applications are processed on a rolling basis. Application fee: $25 ($90 for international students). Electronic applications accepted. *Expenses: Tuition, area resident:* Full-time $5130; part-time $3420 per year. Tuition, state resident: full-time $5130; part-time $3420 per year. Tuition, nonresident: full-time $7866; part-time $5244 per year. *International tuition:* $7866 full-time. *Required fees:* $1052; $710 per unit. Tuition and fees vary according to course load. *Financial support:* Career-related internships or fieldwork, Federal Work-Study, scholarships/grants, tuition waivers (full), and unspecified assistantships available. Financial award applicants required to submit FAFSA. *Faculty research:* Alternative certification for teachers, supervision of instruction, instructional leadership, counseling. *Unit head:* Dr. Kim Bloss, Dean, School of Graduate Studies, 870-235-4150, Fax: 870-235-5227, E-mail: kkbloss@saumag.edu. *Application contact:* Talia Jett, Admissions Coordinator, 870-2355450, Fax: 870-235-5227, E-mail: taliajett@saumag.edu.
Website: http://www.saumag.edu/graduate

Southern Connecticut State University, School of Graduate Studies, School of Business, Program in Business Administration, New Haven, CT 06515-1355. Offers MBA. *Program availability:* Part-time, evening/weekend. *Entrance requirements:* For master's, GMAT, interview. Electronic applications accepted.

Southern Illinois University Carbondale, Graduate School, College of Business and Administration, Department of Business Administration, Carbondale, IL 62901-4701. Offers MBA, PhD, JD/MBA, MBA/MA, MBA/MS. *Accreditation:* AACSB. *Degree requirements:* For doctorate, thesis/dissertation. *Entrance requirements:* For master's, GMAT, minimum GPA of 2.7; for doctorate, GMAT, minimum graduate GPA of 3.25. Additional exam requirements/recommendations for international students: Required—TOEFL (minimum score 550 paper-based; 80 iBT). Electronic applications accepted. *Faculty research:* Marketing, corporate finance, organizational behavior, accounting, management information systems, international business.

Southern Illinois University Edwardsville, Graduate School, School of Business, Program in Business Administration, Edwardsville, IL 62026. Offers business analytics (MBA); management information systems (MBA); project management (MBA). *Accreditation:* AACSB. *Program availability:* Part-time, evening/weekend. *Degree requirements:* For master's, comprehensive exam. *Entrance requirements:* For master's, GMAT. Additional exam requirements/recommendations for international students: Required—TOEFL (minimum score 550 paper-based; 79 iBT), IELTS (minimum score 6.5). Electronic applications accepted.

Southern Methodist University, Cox School of Business, Dallas, TX 75275. Offers EMBA, MBA, MS, MSA, MSF, MSM, JD/MBA. *Accreditation:* AACSB. *Program availability:* Part-time, evening/weekend. *Entrance requirements:* For master's, GMAT. Additional exam requirements/recommendations for international students: Required—TOEFL, PTE. Electronic applications accepted. *Expenses:* Contact institution. *Faculty research:* Financial markets structure, international finance, accounting disclosure, corporate finance, leadership, change management, organizational behavior, entrepreneurship, strategic marketing, corporate strategy, product innovation, information systems, knowledge management, energy markets, customer relationship management.

Southern Nazarene University, College of Professional and Graduate Studies, School of Business, Bethany, OK 73008. Offers business administration (MBA); health care management (MBA); management (MS Mgt). *Accreditation:* ACBSP. *Program availability:* Part-time, evening/weekend, online learning. *Degree requirements:* For master's, thesis optional. *Entrance requirements:* For master's, resume. Additional exam requirements/recommendations for international students: Required—TOEFL (minimum score 550 paper-based; 80 iBT), IELTS (minimum score 7). Electronic applications accepted.

Southern New Hampshire University, School of Business, Manchester, NH 03106-1045. Offers accounting (MBA, Graduate Certificate); accounting finance (MS); accounting/auditing (MS); accounting/forensic accounting (MS); accounting/management accounting (MS); accounting/taxation (MS); applied economics (MS); athletic administration (MBA, Graduate Certificate); business administration (IMBA, Certificate), including business information systems (Certificate), human resource management (Certificate); business analytics (MBA); business intelligence (MBA); communication (MA), including new media and marketing, public relations; community economic development (MBA); criminal justice (MBA); data analytics (MS); economics (MBA); engineering management (MBA); entrepreneurship (MBA); finance (MBA, MS, Graduate Certificate); finance/corporate finance (MS); finance/investments (MS); forensic accounting (MBA); forensic accounting and fraud examination (Graduate Certificate); healthcare informatics (MBA); healthcare management (MBA); human resource management (MS); human resources (MBA); information technology (MS); information technology management (MBA); international business (PhD); Internet marketing (MBA); leadership (MBA); leadership of nonprofit organizations (Graduate Certificate); management (MS); marketing (MBA, MS, Graduate Certificate); music business (MBA); operations and project management (MS); operations and supply chain management (MBA, Graduate Certificate); organizational leadership (MS); project management (MBA, Graduate Certificate); public administration (MBA, Graduate Certificate); quantitative analysis (MBA); Six Sigma (Graduate Certificate); Six Sigma quality (MBA); social media marketing (MBA, Graduate Certificate); sport management (MBA, MS, Graduate Certificate); sustainability and environmental compliance (MBA); MBA/Certificate. *Accreditation:* ACBSP. *Program availability:* Part-time, evening/weekend, online learning. Terminal master's awarded for partial completion of doctoral program. *Degree requirements:* For master's, one foreign language, comprehensive exam (for some programs), thesis or alternative; for doctorate, one foreign language, comprehensive exam, thesis/dissertation. *Entrance requirements:* For master's, minimum GPA of 2.5; for doctorate, GMAT. Additional exam requirements/recommendations for international students: Required—TOEFL (minimum score 500 paper-based). Electronic applications accepted.

Southern Oregon University, Graduate Studies, School of Business, Ashland, OR 97520. Offers accounting (Postbaccalaureate Certificate); business administration (MBA); international management (MIM). *Accreditation:* ACBSP. *Program availability:* Part-time, evening/weekend, online learning. *Degree requirements:* For master's, comprehensive exam. *Entrance requirements:* For master's, GMAT, minimum cumulative GPA of 3.0 in the last 90 quarter credits (60 semester credits) of undergraduate coursework. Additional exam requirements/recommendations for international students: Required—TOEFL (minimum score 540 paper-based; 76 iBT), IELTS (minimum score 6), ELPT (minimum score 964) or ELS (minimum score 112). Electronic applications accepted.

Southern States University, Graduate Programs, San Diego, CA 92110. Offers business administration (MBA); information technology (MSIT).

Southern University and Agricultural and Mechanical College, College of Business, Baton Rouge, LA 70813. Offers MBA. *Accreditation:* AACSB. *Degree requirements:* For master's, comprehensive exam. *Entrance requirements:* For master's, GMAT. Additional exam requirements/recommendations for international students: Required—TOEFL (minimum score 525 paper-based). *Faculty research:* Accounting theory, auditing, governmental and non-profit accounting.

Southern Utah University, Master of Accountancy/MBA Dual Degree Program, Cedar City, UT 84720-2498. Offers MBA/M Acc. *Program availability:* Part-time, online only, 100% online. *Students:* 1. 9 applicants, 100% accepted. *Entrance requirements:* Additional exam requirements/recommendations for international students: Required—TOEFL (minimum score 550 paper-based; 79 iBT), TOEFL (minimum score 550 paper-based, 79 iBT) or IELTS (minimum score 6). *Application deadline:* For fall admission, 7/15 for domestic and international students; for spring admission, 12/1 for domestic and international students; for summer admission, 5/1 for domestic and international students. Applications are processed on a rolling basis. Application fee: $60 ($65 for international students). Electronic applications accepted. *Expenses:* Contact institution. *Financial support:* Unspecified assistantships available.
Website: https://www.suu.edu/business/graduate/

Southern Utah University, Program in Business Administration, Cedar City, UT 84720-2498. Offers MBA. *Accreditation:* AACSB. *Program availability:* Part-time, 100% online. *Faculty:* 7 full-time (0 women), 2 part-time/adjunct (0 women). *Students:* 35 full-time (12 women), 49 part-time (16 women); includes 10 minority (2 Black or African American, non-Hispanic/Latino; 2 American Indian or Alaska Native, non-Hispanic/Latino; 2 Asian, non-Hispanic/Latino; 4 Hispanic/Latino), 8 international. Average age 31. 56 applicants, 52% accepted, 29 enrolled. In 2018, 31 master's awarded. *Entrance requirements:* For master's, GMAT or GRE. Additional exam requirements/recommendations for international students: Required—TOEFL (minimum score 550 paper-based; 79 iBT), TOEFL (minimum score 550 paper-based, 79 iBT) or IELTS (minimum score 6); Recommended—IELTS (minimum score 6). *Application deadline:* For fall admission, 7/15 for domestic and international students; for spring admission, 12/1 for domestic and international students; for summer admission, 5/1 for domestic and international students. Applications are processed on a rolling basis. Application fee: $60 ($65 for international students). Electronic applications accepted. *Expenses:* Contact institution. *Financial support:* Scholarships/grants available. *Unit head:* Kenneth Hall, MBA Program Director, 435-865-8541, Fax: 435-586-5493, E-mail: kennethhall2@suu.edu. *Application contact:* Kenneth Hall, MBA Program Director, 435-865-8541, Fax: 435-586-5493, E-mail: kennethhall2@suu.edu.
Website: https://www.suu.edu/business/mba/

Southern Wesleyan University, Program in Business Administration, Central, SC 29630-1020. Offers MBA. *Program availability:* Evening/weekend. *Degree requirements:* For master's, comprehensive exam. *Entrance requirements:* For master's, GMAT, GRE, or MAT, minimum of 3 undergraduate semester credit hours each in accounting, economics, and statistics; minimum of 18 undergraduate semester credit hours in business administration; minimum of 2 years' significant work experience. Additional exam requirements/recommendations for international students: Required—TOEFL (minimum score 500 paper-based).

Southern Wesleyan University, Program in Management, Central, SC 29630-1020. Offers MSM. *Program availability:* Evening/weekend. *Entrance requirements:* For master's, GMAT, GRE, or MAT, minimum of 18 undergraduate semester credit hours in business administration; minimum of 2 years significant work experience. Additional exam requirements/recommendations for international students: Required—TOEFL (minimum score 500 paper-based). *Expenses:* Contact institution.

South University, Graduate Programs, College of Business, Savannah, GA 31406. Offers corrections (MBA); entrepreneurship and small business (MBA); healthcare administration (MBA); hospitality management (MBA); leadership (MS); public administration (MPA); sustainability (MBA).

South University, Program in Business Administration, Royal Palm Beach, FL 33411. Offers business administration (MBA); healthcare administration (MBA).

South University, Program in Business Administration, Montgomery, AL 36116-1120. Offers MBA.

South University, Program in Business Administration, Columbia, SC 29203. Offers MBA.

South University, Program in Business Administration, Glen Allen, VA 23060. Offers MBA.

South University, Program in Business Administration, Virginia Beach, VA 23452. Offers MBA.

South University, Program in Business Administration, Round Rock, TX 78681. Offers MBA.

Business Administration and Management—General

South University, Program in Business Administration, Tampa, FL 33614. Offers MBA.

Southwest Baptist University, Program in Business, Bolivar, MO 65613-2597. Offers business administration (MBA); health administration (MBA). *Accreditation:* ACBSP. *Program availability:* Part-time, online learning. *Degree requirements:* For master's, comprehensive exam. *Entrance requirements:* For master's, interviews, minimum GPA of 2.75. Additional exam requirements/recommendations for international students: Required—TOEFL (minimum score 550 paper-based).

Southwestern Adventist University, Business Administration Department, Keene, TX 76059. Offers accounting (MBA); finance (MBA); management/leadership (MBA). *Program availability:* Part-time, evening/weekend. *Degree requirements:* For master's, capstone course. *Entrance requirements:* For master's, GMAT, GRE General Test.

Southwestern College, Fifth-Year Graduate Programs, Winfield, KS 67156-2499. Offers management (MBA). *Program availability:* Part-time. *Faculty:* 5 full-time (2 women). *Students:* 18 full-time (5 women), 2 part-time (both women); includes 7 minority (6 Black or African American, non-Hispanic/Latino; 1 Hispanic/Latino), 5 international. Average age 25. 25 applicants, 52% accepted, 10 enrolled. In 2018, 9 master's awarded. *Entrance requirements:* For master's, baccalaureate degree, minimum GPA of 3.0. Additional exam requirements/recommendations for international students: Required—TOEFL (minimum score 60 paper-based; 70 iBT), IELTS (minimum score 5.5). *Application deadline:* For fall admission, 8/26 for domestic students; for spring admission, 1/21 for domestic students. Applications are processed on a rolling basis. Application fee: $25. Electronic applications accepted. *Expenses:* $733 per credit hour. *Financial support:* In 2018–19, 14 students received support. Fellowships, unspecified assistantships, and employee tuition waivers available. Financial award applicants required to submit FAFSA. *Unit head:* Dr. Kurt Keiser, Professor/Division Chair, 620-229-6361, E-mail: kurt.keiser@sckans.edu. *Application contact:* Adam Jenkins, Vice President for Enrollment Management, 620-229-6091, E-mail: adam.jenkins@sckans.edu.
Website: http://www.sckans.edu/graduate

Southwestern College, Professional Studies Programs, Wichita, KS 67207. Offers business administration (MBA); leadership (MS); management (MS); security administration (MS); specialized ministries (MA). *Program availability:* Part-time, evening/weekend, online only, 100% online. *Faculty:* 19 part-time/adjunct (4 women). *Students:* 20 full-time (5 women), 43 part-time (18 women); includes 16 minority (8 Black or African American, non-Hispanic/Latino; 1 Asian, non-Hispanic/Latino; 5 Hispanic/Latino; 2 Two or more races, non-Hispanic/Latino). Average age 37. 24 applicants, 100% accepted, 17 enrolled. In 2018, 37 master's awarded. *Degree requirements:* For master's, thesis (for some programs), practicum/capstone project. *Entrance requirements:* For master's, baccalaureate degree; minimum GPA of 3.0. Additional exam requirements/recommendations for international students: Required—TOEFL (minimum score 60 paper-based; 70 iBT), IELTS (minimum score 5.5). *Application deadline:* Applications are processed on a rolling basis. Application fee: $40. Electronic applications accepted. *Expenses:* MBA is $695 per credit hour; MSL, MSSA, MSM and graduate certificates are $629 per credit hour; MASM and MATS are $500 per credit hour. *Financial support:* In 2018–19, 11 students received support. Unspecified assistantships and employee tuition waivers available. Financial award applicants required to submit FAFSA. *Unit head:* Jen Caughron, Director of Enrollment Services & Marketing, 888-684-5335 Ext. 3312, Fax: 316-688-5218, E-mail: jennifer.caughron@sckans.edu. *Application contact:* Jen Caughron, Director of Enrollment Services & Marketing, 888-684-5335 Ext. 3312, Fax: 316-688-5218, E-mail: jennifer.caughron@sckans.edu.
Website: https://ps.sckans.edu/

Southwestern Oklahoma State University, College of Professional and Graduate Studies, Everett Dobson School of Business and Technology, Weatherford, OK 73096-3098. Offers MBA, MSM. MBA distance learning degree program offered to Oklahoma residents only. *Program availability:* Part-time, evening/weekend, online learning. *Degree requirements:* For master's, comprehensive exam. *Entrance requirements:* For master's, GMAT, minimum GPA of 2.5. Additional exam requirements/recommendations for international students: Required—TOEFL (minimum score 550 paper-based), IELTS (minimum score 6.5).

Southwest Minnesota State University, Department of Business and Public Affairs, Marshall, MN 56258. Offers leadership (MBA); management (MBA); marketing (MBA). *Program availability:* Part-time, evening/weekend, online learning. *Degree requirements:* For master's, thesis. *Entrance requirements:* For master's, GMAT (minimum score: 450). Additional exam requirements/recommendations for international students: Recommended—TOEFL (minimum score 550 paper-based; 79 iBT), IELTS. Electronic applications accepted.

Southwest University, MBA Program, Kenner, LA 70062. Offers business administration (MBA); management (MBA); organizational management (MBA).

Southwest University, Program in Management, Kenner, LA 70062. Offers MA.

Spring Arbor University, Gainey School of Business, Spring Arbor, MI 49283-9799. Offers MBA. *Program availability:* Part-time, evening/weekend, online learning. *Degree requirements:* For master's, thesis. *Entrance requirements:* For master's, minimum overall GPA of 3.0 for all undergraduate coursework, bachelor's degree from regionally-accredited college or university, two recommendation forms from professional/academic individuals. Additional exam requirements/recommendations for international students: Required—TOEFL (minimum score 600 paper-based).

Springfield College, Graduate Programs, Program in Business Administration, Springfield, MA 01109-3797. Offers MBA. *Program availability:* Part-time, evening/weekend. *Entrance requirements:* Additional exam requirements/recommendations for international students: Required—TOEFL (minimum score 90 iBT); Recommended—IELTS (minimum score 7). Electronic applications accepted. *Faculty research:* Marketing theory and practice, measurement of attribution of leadership to entrepreneurial output, brand management.

Spring Hill College, Graduate Programs, Program in Business Administration, Mobile, AL 36608-1791. Offers MBA. *Program availability:* Part-time. *Faculty:* 4 full-time (1 woman), 3 part-time/adjunct (2 women). *Students:* 4 full-time (all women), 45 part-time (8 women); includes 7 minority (6 Black or African American, non-Hispanic/Latino; 1 Two or more races, non-Hispanic/Latino). Average age 32. In 2018, 1 master's awarded. *Degree requirements:* For master's, comprehensive exam, capstone course, completion of program within 6 calendar years. *Entrance requirements:* For master's, GMAT, bachelor's degree. Additional exam requirements/recommendations for international students: Required—TOEFL (minimum score 550 paper-based; 80 iBT), IELTS (minimum score 6.5), CPE or CAE (minimum score C), Michigan English Language Assessment Battery (minimum score 90). *Application deadline:* For fall admission, 8/1 priority date for domestic and international students; for spring admission, 12/1 priority date for domestic and international students. Applications are processed on a rolling basis. Application fee: $25 ($35 for international students). Electronic applications accepted. *Expenses:* Contact institution. *Financial support:* Fellowships, research assistantships, teaching assistantships, and tuition waivers available. Financial award applicants required to submit FAFSA. *Unit head:* Dr. James Larriviere, Division Chair, 251-380-4453, Fax: 251-460-2178, E-mail: jlarriviere@shc.edu. *Application contact:* Gary Bracken, Vice President of Enrollment Management, 251-380-3038, Fax: 251-460-2186, E-mail: gbracken@shc.edu.
Website: http://ug.shc.edu/graduate-degrees/master-business-administration/

Stanford University, Graduate School of Business, Stanford, CA 94305-2004. Offers MBA, PhD, JD/MBA, MBA/MS. *Accreditation:* AACSB. *Expenses: Tuition:* Full-time $50,703; part-time $32,970 per year. *Required fees:* $651.
Website: http://www.gsb.stanford.edu/

State University of New York at New Paltz, Graduate and Extended Learning School, School of Business, New Paltz, NY 12561. Offers business administration (MBA); public accountancy (MBA). *Accreditation:* AACSB. *Program availability:* Part-time, evening/weekend. *Faculty:* 14 full-time (2 women), 4 part-time/adjunct (1 woman). *Students:* 61 full-time (33 women), 48 part-time (24 women); includes 24 minority (6 Black or African American, non-Hispanic/Latino; 6 Asian, non-Hispanic/Latino; 11 Hispanic/Latino; 1 Two or more races, non-Hispanic/Latino), 8 international. 49 applicants, 96% accepted, 38 enrolled. In 2018, 42 master's awarded. *Entrance requirements:* For master's, GMAT or GRE, minimum GPA of 3.0. Additional exam requirements/recommendations for international students: Required—TOEFL (minimum score 550 paper-based; 80 iBT), IELTS (minimum score 6.5). *Application deadline:* Applications are processed on a rolling basis. Application fee: $50. Electronic applications accepted. *Expenses:* Contact institution. *Financial support:* In 2018–19, 6 research assistantships with partial tuition reimbursements (averaging $5,000 per year), 1 teaching assistantship with partial tuition reimbursement (averaging $5,000 per year) were awarded; scholarships/grants, traineeships, and unspecified assistantships also available. Financial award application deadline: 8/1. *Faculty research:* Cognitive styles in management education, supporting SME e-commerce migration through e-learning, earnings management and board activity, trading future spread portfolio, global equity market correlation and volatility. *Unit head:* Dr. Kristin Backhaus, Dean, 845-257-2930, E-mail: mba@newpaltz.edu. *Application contact:* Aaron Hines, Director of MBA Program, 845-257-2968, E-mail: mba@newpaltz.edu.
Website: http://mba.newpaltz.edu

State University of New York at Oswego, Graduate Studies, School of Business, Oswego, NY 13126. Offers MBA. *Program availability:* Part-time, evening/weekend. *Entrance requirements:* For master's, GMAT, minimum GPA of 2.6. Additional exam requirements/recommendations for international students: Required—TOEFL (minimum score 560 paper-based).

State University of New York College at Geneseo, Graduate Studies, School of Business, Geneseo, NY 14454. Offers accounting (MS). *Accreditation:* AACSB. *Degree requirements:* For master's, thesis. *Entrance requirements:* For master's, GMAT, bachelor's degree in accounting. Additional exam requirements/recommendations for international students: Required—TOEFL (minimum score 525 paper-based; 71 iBT), IELTS (minimum score 6.5), PTE, iTEP. Electronic applications accepted. *Expenses:* Contact institution.

State University of New York College at Old Westbury, School of Business, Old Westbury, NY 11568-0210. Offers accounting (MS); taxation (MS). *Program availability:* Part-time, evening/weekend. *Entrance requirements:* For master's, GMAT, 2 letters of recommendation. Additional exam requirements/recommendations for international students: Required—TOEFL (minimum score 550 paper-based). Electronic applications accepted. *Faculty research:* Corporate governance, asset pricing, corporate finance, hedge funds, taxation.

State University of New York Empire State College, School for Graduate Studies, Program in Business Administration, Saratoga Springs, NY 12866-4391. Offers global leadership (MBA); management (MBA). *Program availability:* Part-time, online learning. *Degree requirements:* For master's, thesis or alternative. *Entrance requirements:* For master's, previous course work in statistics, macroeconomics, microeconomics, and accounting. Additional exam requirements/recommendations for international students: Required—TOEFL (minimum score 600 paper-based). Electronic applications accepted. *Expenses:* Contact institution. *Faculty research:* Corporate strategy, managerial competencies, decision analysis, economics in transition, organizational communication.

State University of New York Polytechnic Institute, MBA Program in Technology Management, Utica, NY 13502. Offers accounting and finance (MBA); business management (MBA); health informatics (MBA); human resource management (MBA); marketing management (MBA). *Program availability:* Part-time, 100% online. *Students:* 29 full-time (13 women), 85 part-time (41 women); includes 18 minority (4 Black or African American, non-Hispanic/Latino; 8 Asian, non-Hispanic/Latino; 6 Hispanic/Latino). Average age 32. 54 applicants, 54% accepted, 26 enrolled. In 2018, 29 master's awarded. *Degree requirements:* For master's, comprehensive exam, capstone project. *Entrance requirements:* For master's, GMAT or approved GMAT waiver, resume, letter of reference. Additional exam requirements/recommendations for international students: Required—TOEFL (minimum score 79 iBT), IELTS (minimum score 6.5), PTE (minimum score 53), TOEFL, IELTS, or PTE; GMAT or approved GMAT waiver. *Application deadline:* For fall admission, 7/1 priority date for domestic students, 7/1 for international students; for spring admission, 12/1 for domestic students, 11/1 for international students. Applications are processed on a rolling basis. Application fee: $60. Electronic applications accepted. *Expenses:* Contact institution. *Financial support:* Fellowships, research assistantships, and unspecified assistantships available. Financial award application deadline: 6/1; financial award applicants required to submit FAFSA. *Faculty research:* Entrepreneurial capacity development. *Unit head:* Dr. Rafael Romero, Coordinator, 315-792-7207, E-mail: rafael.romero@sunypoly.edu. *Application contact:* Alicia Foster, Director of Graduate Admissions, 315-792-7347, E-mail: fostera3@sunypoly.edu.
Website: https://sunypoly.edu/academics/majors-and-programs/technology-management.html

Stephen F. Austin State University, Graduate School, Nelson Rusche College of Business, Program in Business Administration, Nacogdoches, TX 75962. Offers business (MBA); management and marketing (MBA). *Accreditation:* AACSB. *Program availability:* Part-time, evening/weekend. *Degree requirements:* For master's, comprehensive exam. *Entrance requirements:* For master's, GMAT, minimum AACSB index of 1000. Additional exam requirements/recommendations for international students: Required—TOEFL (minimum score 550 paper-based). *Faculty research:* Strategic implications, information search, multinational firms, philosophical guidance.

Stetson University, School of Business Administration, Program in Business Administration, DeLand, FL 32723. Offers EMBA, MBA, JD/MBA, MBA/MS. *Accreditation:* AACSB. *Program availability:* Part-time, evening/weekend, online learning. *Faculty:* 14 full-time (3 women), 1 (woman) part-time/adjunct. *Students:* 77 full-time (46 women), 25 part-time (14 women); includes 41 minority (11 Black or African American, non-Hispanic/Latino; 5 Asian, non-Hispanic/Latino; 15 Hispanic/Latino; 10 Two or more races, non-Hispanic/Latino), 6 international. Average age 32. 65 applicants, 69% accepted, 38 enrolled. In 2018, 60 master's awarded. *Entrance requirements:* For master's, GMAT, GRE, transcripts, resume, two letters of recommendation, personal statement. Additional exam requirements/recommendations

for international students: Required—TOEFL (minimum score 90 iBT), IELTS (minimum score 7.5). *Application deadline:* For fall admission, 8/1 for domestic students; for spring admission, 1/1 for domestic students; for summer admission, 5/1 for domestic students. Applications are processed on a rolling basis. Application fee: $50. Electronic applications accepted. *Expenses:* $1020 per credit hour (for MBA, JD/MBA,MBA/MS), $1205 per credit hour (EMBA). *Financial support:* In 2018–19, 19 students received support. Career-related internships or fieldwork, Federal Work-Study, scholarships/grants, unspecified assistantships, and tuition waivers (for staff and dependents) available. Support available to part-time students. Financial award applicants required to submit FAFSA. *Faculty research:* Leadership Development, Global Business, Corporate Finance, Venture Capital, Investments. *Unit head:* Giovanni Fernandez, Director, 386-822-7410, E-mail: gfernan1@stetson.edu. *Application contact:* Jamie Vanderlip, Director of Admissions for Graduate, Transfer and Adult Programs, 386-822-7100, Fax: 386-822-7112, E-mail: jlvander@stetson.edu.

Stevens Institute of Technology, Graduate School, School of Business, Program in Business Administration, Hoboken, NJ 07030. Offers business intelligence and analytics (MBA); engineering management (MBA); finance (MBA); information systems (MBA); innovation and entrepreneurship (MBA); marketing (MBA); pharmaceutical management (MBA); project management (MBA, Certificate); technology management (MBA); telecommunications management (MBA). *Accreditation:* AACSB. *Program availability:* Part-time, evening/weekend. *Faculty:* 58 full-time (8 women), 18 part-time/adjunct (3 women). *Students:* 44 full-time (23 women), 202 part-time (90 women); includes 56 minority (12 Black or African American, non-Hispanic/Latino; 2 American Indian or Alaska Native, non-Hispanic/Latino; 40 Asian, non-Hispanic/Latino; 2 Hispanic/Latino), 28 international. Average age 37. In 2018, 45 master's awarded. Terminal master's awarded for partial completion of doctoral program. *Degree requirements:* For master's, thesis optional, minimum B average in major field and overall; for Certificate, minimum B average. *Entrance requirements:* For master's, GRE/GMAT scores: GRE scores are required for all applicants applying to a full-time graduate program in the Schaefer School of Engineering and Science (SES). International applicants must submit TOEFL/IELTS scores and fulfill the English Language Proficiency Requirements in order to be considered. Additional exam requirements/recommendations for international students: Required—TOEFL (minimum score 74 iBT), IELTS (minimum score 6). *Application deadline:* For fall admission, 4/1 for domestic and international students; for spring admission, 11/1 for domestic and international students; for summer admission, 5/1 for domestic students. Applications are processed on a rolling basis. Application fee: $60. Electronic applications accepted. *Expenses: Tuition:* Full-time $35,960; part-time $1620 per credit. *Required fees:* $1290; $600 per semester. Tuition and fees vary according to course load. *Financial support:* Fellowships, research assistantships, teaching assistantships, career-related internships or fieldwork, Federal Work-Study, scholarships/grants, and unspecified assistantships available. Financial award application deadline: 2/15; financial award applicants required to submit FAFSA. *Unit head:* Dr. Gregory Prastacos, Dean, 201-216-8366, E-mail: gprastac@stevens.edu. *Application contact:* Graduate Admissions, 888-783-8367, Fax: 888-511-1306, E-mail: graduate@stevens.edu.
Website: https://www.stevens.edu/school-business/masters-programs/mbaemba

Stevens Institute of Technology, Graduate School, School of Business, Program in Management, Hoboken, NJ 07030. Offers general management (MS); global innovation management (MS); human resource management (MS); information management (MS); project management (MS); technology commercialization (MS); technology management (MS). *Program availability:* Part-time, evening/weekend. *Faculty:* 58 full-time (8 women), 18 part-time/adjunct (3 women). *Students:* 101 full-time (41 women), 66 part-time (34 women); includes 14 minority (4 Black or African American, non-Hispanic/Latino; 9 Asian, non-Hispanic/Latino; 1 Hispanic/Latino), 115 international. Average age 28. In 2018, 70 master's awarded. Terminal master's awarded for partial completion of doctoral program. *Degree requirements:* For master's, thesis optional, minimum B average in major field and overall. *Entrance requirements:* For master's, GRE/GMAT scores: GRE scores are required for all applicants applying to a full-time graduate program in the Schaefer School of Engineering and Science (SES). International applicants must submit TOEFL/IELTS scores and fulfill the English Language Proficiency Requirements in order to be considered. Additional exam requirements/recommendations for international students: Required—TOEFL (minimum score 74 iBT), IELTS (minimum score 6). *Application deadline:* For fall admission, 4/1 for domestic and international students; for spring admission, 11/1 for domestic and international students; for summer admission, 5/1 for domestic students. Applications are processed on a rolling basis. Application fee: $60. Electronic applications accepted. *Expenses: Tuition:* Full-time $35,960; part-time $1620 per credit. *Required fees:* $1290; $600 per semester. Tuition and fees vary according to course load. *Financial support:* Fellowships, research assistantships, teaching assistantships, career-related internships or fieldwork, Federal Work-Study, scholarships/grants, and unspecified assistantships available. Financial award application deadline: 2/15; financial award applicants required to submit FAFSA. *Unit head:* Dr. Gregory Prascatos, Dean of SB, 201-216 8366, E-mail: gprastac@stevens.edu. *Application contact:* Graduate Admissions, 888-783-8367, Fax: 888-511-1306, E-mail: graduate@stevens.edu.
Website: https://www.stevens.edu/school-business/masters-programs/management

Stockton University, Office of Graduate Studies, Program in Business Administration, Galloway, NJ 08205-9441. Offers MBA. *Accreditation:* AACSB. *Program availability:* Part-time, evening/weekend. *Faculty:* 16 full-time (4 women), 3 part-time/adjunct (1 woman). *Students:* 23 full-time (11 women), 72 part-time (41 women); includes 23 minority (5 Black or African American, non-Hispanic/Latino; 1 American Indian or Alaska Native, non-Hispanic/Latino; 6 Asian, non-Hispanic/Latino; 9 Hispanic/Latino; 2 Two or more races, non-Hispanic/Latino). Average age 31. 67 applicants, 81% accepted, 43 enrolled. In 2018, 45 master's awarded. *Degree requirements:* For master's, project. *Entrance requirements:* For master's, GMAT. Additional exam requirements/recommendations for international students: Required—TOEFL (minimum score 550 paper-based; 80 iBT). *Application deadline:* For fall admission, 7/1 for domestic and international students; for spring admission, 12/1 for domestic students, 11/1 for international students. Applications are processed on a rolling basis. Application fee: $50. Electronic applications accepted. *Expenses:* Contact institution. *Financial support:* Fellowships, research assistantships with partial tuition reimbursements, career-related internships or fieldwork, Federal Work-Study, scholarships/grants, and unspecified assistantships available. Support available to part-time students. Financial award application deadline: 3/1; financial award applicants required to submit FAFSA. *Faculty research:* Business ethics, marketing channels development, event studies, total quality management. *Unit head:* Dr. Diane Holtzman, Graduate Program Director, 609-626-3640, E-mail: mba@stockton.edu. *Application contact:* Tara Williams, Assistant Director of Graduate Enrollment Management, 609-626-3640, Fax: 609-626-6050, E-mail: gradschool@stockton.edu.

Stony Brook University, State University of New York, Graduate School, College of Business, Program in Business Administration, Stony Brook, NY 11794. Offers accounting (MBA); business administration (MBA); finance (MBA, Certificate); health care management (MBA); human resources (MBA); innovation (MBA); management (MBA); marketing (MBA); operations management (MBA). *Faculty:* 38 full-time (13 women), 8 part-time/adjunct (3 women). *Students:* 153 full-time (74 women), 148 part-time (76 women); includes 76 minority (16 Black or African American, non-Hispanic/Latino; 29 Asian, non-Hispanic/Latino; 27 Hispanic/Latino; 4 Two or more races, non-Hispanic/Latino), 36 international. Average age 28. 128 applicants, 78% accepted, 75 enrolled. In 2018, 76 master's awarded. *Entrance requirements:* For master's, GMAT, 3 letters of recommendation from current or former employers or professors, transcripts, personal statement, resume. Additional exam requirements/recommendations for international students: Required—TOEFL (minimum score 550 paper-based; 80 iBT), IELTS (minimum score 6.5). *Application deadline:* For fall admission, 5/15 for domestic students, 3/15 for international students; for spring admission, 12/1 for domestic students, 10/15 for international students. Application fee: $100. *Expenses:* Contact institution. *Financial support:* Teaching assistantships available. *Total annual research expenditures:* $2,070. *Unit head:* Dr. Manuel London, Dean, 631-632-7159, E-mail: manuel.london@stonybrook.edu. *Application contact:* Dr. Dmytro Holod, Associate Dean for Academic Programs/Graduate Director, 631-632-7183, Fax: 631-632-8181, E-mail: dmytro.holod@stonybrook.edu.
Website: https://www.stonybrook.edu/commcms/business/

Stratford University, School of Graduate Studies, Falls Church, VA 22043. Offers accounting (MS); business administration (MBA, DBA); cyber security (MS); cyber security leadership and policy (MS); digital forensics (MS); healthcare administration (MS); information systems (MS); information technology (DIT); networking and telecommunications (MS); software engineering (MS). *Program availability:* Part-time, evening/weekend, 100% online, blended/hybrid learning. *Degree requirements:* For master's, comprehensive exam, capstone project. *Entrance requirements:* For master's, GRE or GMAT, baccalaureate degree. Additional exam requirements/recommendations for international students: Required—TOEFL (minimum score 79 iBT), IELTS (minimum score 6.5), PTE (minimum score 5). Electronic applications accepted. *Expenses: Tuition:* Full-time $22,275; part-time $11,137 per year. One-time fee: $385.

Strayer University, Graduate Studies, Washington, DC 20005-2603. Offers accounting (MS); acquisition (MBA); business administration (MBA); communications technology (MS); educational management (M Ed); finance (MBA); health services administration (MHSA); hospitality and tourism management (MBA); human resource management (MBA); information systems (MS), including computer security management, decision support system management, enterprise resource management, network management, software engineering management, systems development management; management (MBA); management information systems (MS); marketing (MBA); professional accounting (MS), including accounting information systems, controllership, taxation; public administration (MPA); supply chain management (MBA); technology in education (M Ed). Programs also offered at campus locations in Birmingham, AL; Chamblee, GA; Cobb County, GA; Morrow, GA; White Marsh, MD; Charleston, SC; Columbia, SC; Greensboro, NC; Greenville, SC; Lexington, KY; Louisville, KY; Nashville, TN; North Raleigh, NC; Washington, DC. *Accreditation:* ACBSP. *Program availability:* Part-time, evening/weekend, online learning. *Degree requirements:* For master's, thesis. *Entrance requirements:* For master's, GMAT, GRE General Test, bachelor's degree from an accredited college or university, minimum undergraduate GPA of 2.75. Electronic applications accepted.

Suffolk University, Sawyer Business School, Master of Business Administration Program, Boston, MA 02108-2770. Offers accounting (MBA); entrepreneurship (MBA); executive business administration (EMBA); finance (MBA); global business administration (GMBA); health administration (MBA); international business (MBA); marketing (MBA); nonprofit management (MBA); organizational behavior (MBA); strategic management (MBA); supply chain management (MBA); taxation (MBA); JD/MBA; MBA/MHA; MBA/MSA; MBA/MSF; MBA/MST. *Accreditation:* AACSB. *Program availability:* Part-time, evening/weekend, 100% online. *Faculty:* 18 full-time (5 women), 5 part-time/adjunct (0 women). *Students:* 79 full-time (46 women), 193 part-time (107 women); includes 69 minority (17 Black or African American, non-Hispanic/Latino; 18 Asian, non-Hispanic/Latino; 28 Hispanic/Latino; 6 Two or more races, non-Hispanic/Latino), 40 international. Average age 30. 274 applicants, 67% accepted, 83 enrolled. In 2018, 125 master's awarded. *Entrance requirements:* For master's, GMAT, minimum undergraduate GPA of 2.75 (MBA), 5 years of managerial experience (EMBA). Additional exam requirements/recommendations for international students: Required—TOEFL (minimum score 550 paper-based; 80 iBT). *Application deadline:* For fall admission, 3/15 priority date for domestic students, 10/15 priority date for international students; for spring admission, 10/15 priority date for domestic and international students. Applications are processed on a rolling basis. Application fee: $50. Electronic applications accepted. *Expenses:* Contact institution. *Financial support:* In 2018–19, 170 students received support, including 4 fellowships (averaging $2,906 per year); career-related internships or fieldwork, Federal Work-Study, institutionally sponsored loans, and scholarships/grants also available. Support available to part-time students. Financial award application deadline: 4/1; financial award applicants required to submit FAFSA. *Faculty research:* Foreign investments; career strategies and boundaryless careers; corporate ethics codes; interest rates, inflation, and growth options; innovation and product development performance. *Unit head:* Jodi Detjen, Director of MBA Programs, 617-573-8306, E-mail: jdetjen@suffolk.edu. *Application contact:* Mara Marzocchi, Associate Director of Graduate Admissions, 617-573-8302, Fax: 617-305-1733, E-mail: grad.admission@suffolk.edu.
Website: http://www.suffolk.edu/mba

Sullivan University, School of Business, Louisville, KY 40205. Offers EMBA, MBA, MPM, MSCM, MSCS, MSHRL, MSM, MSMIT, PhD, Pharm D. *Program availability:* Part-time, online learning. *Degree requirements:* For doctorate, comprehensive exam, thesis/dissertation. *Entrance requirements:* Additional exam requirements/recommendations for international students: Required—TOEFL.

Sul Ross State University, College of Professional Studies, Department of Business Administration, Alpine, TX 79832. Offers EMBA, MBA. Two-year Executive MBA program in cooperation with La Universidad de Chihuahua, Mexico (UACH). *Program availability:* Part-time, evening/weekend. *Degree requirements:* For master's, thesis optional. *Entrance requirements:* For master's, GMAT or GRE General Test, minimum GPA of 2.5 in last 60 hours of undergraduate work. *Faculty research:* Cross-cultural comparisons, U.S.-Mexico management relations.

Sul Ross State University, Rio Grande College of Sul Ross State University, Alpine, TX 79832. Offers business administration (MBA); teacher education (M Ed), including bilingual education, counseling, educational diagnostics, elementary education, general education, reading, school administration, secondary education. *Program availability:* Part-time, evening/weekend, online learning. *Degree requirements:* For master's, comprehensive exam, thesis optional, minimum GPA of 3.0. *Entrance requirements:* For master's, GMAT or GRE General Test, minimum GPA of 2.5 in last 60 hours of undergraduate work. Additional exam requirements/recommendations for international students: Required—TOEFL.

Syracuse University, Martin J. Whitman School of Management, Syracuse, NY 13244. Offers MBA, MS, PhD, JD/MBA. *Accreditation:* AACSB. *Program availability:* Part-time, 100% online. *Faculty:* 73 full-time (28 women), 66 part-time/adjunct (15 women). *Students:* 336 full-time (159 women), 1,113 part-time (360 women); includes 461 minority (171 Black or African American, non-Hispanic/Latino; 3 American Indian or Alaska Native, non-Hispanic/Latino; 102 Asian, non-Hispanic/Latino; 136 Hispanic/

Latino; 6 Native Hawaiian or other Pacific Islander, non-Hispanic/Latino; 43 Two or more races, non-Hispanic/Latino), 220 international. Average age 33. 1,327 applicants, 66% accepted, 326 enrolled. In 2018, 475 master's, 4 doctorates awarded. *Degree requirements:* For master's, comprehensive exam (for MS in business analytics); for doctorate, comprehensive exam, thesis/dissertation, summer research paper. *Entrance requirements:* For master's and doctorate, GMAT or GRE. Additional exam requirements/recommendations for international students: Required—PTE (minimum score 68), TOEFL (minimum iBT score of 100) or IELTS (7); GMAT; GRE. *Application deadline:* For fall admission, 11/30 for domestic and international students; for winter admission, 1/1 for domestic and international students; for spring admission, 2/15 for domestic and international students; for summer admission, 4/19 for domestic students. Application fee: $75. Electronic applications accepted. *Financial support:* In 2018–19, 45 students received support. Fellowships with full tuition reimbursements available, research assistantships, teaching assistantships, career-related internships or fieldwork, and scholarships/grants available. Financial award application deadline: 2/15. *Faculty research:* Marketing, supply chain management, management, finance, entrepreneurship. *Unit head:* Eugene Anderson, Dean, 315-443-9494, Fax: 315-443-9517, E-mail: genea@syr.edu. *Application contact:* Shri Ramakrishnan, Assistant Director, Graduate Recruitment, 315-443-3497, Fax: 315-443-9517, E-mail: sramak01@syr.edu.
Website: http://whitman.syr.edu

Tabor College, Graduate Program, Hillsboro, KS 67063. Offers accounting (MBA). Program offered at the Wichita campus only.

Tarleton State University, College of Graduate Studies, College of Business Administration, Master of Business Administration Program, Stephenville, TX 76402. Offers MBA. *Program availability:* Part-time, evening/weekend, 100% online, blended/hybrid learning. *Faculty:* 30 full-time (5 women), 6 part-time/adjunct (2 women). *Students:* 32 full-time (20 women), 264 part-time (144 women). Average age 32. 150 applicants, 87% accepted, 109 enrolled. In 2018, 79 master's awarded. *Degree requirements:* For master's, comprehensive exam, thesis (for some programs). *Entrance requirements:* For master's, GRE, minimum GPA of 3.0. Additional exam requirements/recommendations for international students: Required—TOEFL (minimum score 520 paper-based; 69 iBT); Recommended—IELTS (minimum score 6), TSE (minimum score 50). *Application deadline:* For fall admission, 8/15 for domestic students; for spring admission, 1/1 for domestic students. Applications are processed on a rolling basis. Application fee: $50 ($130 for international students). Electronic applications accepted. *Expenses:* Contact institution. *Financial support:* Application deadline: 5/1; applicants required to submit FAFSA. *Unit head:* Dr. Chris Shao, Dean, 254-968-9350, Fax: 254-968-9328, E-mail: shao@tarleton.edu. *Application contact:* Information Contact, 254-968-9104, Fax: 254-968-9670, E-mail: gradoffice@tarleton.edu.

Temple University, Fox School of Business, Doctoral Programs in Business, Philadelphia, PA 19122-6096. Offers accounting (PhD); entrepreneurship (PhD); finance (PhD); international business (PhD); management information systems (PhD); marketing (PhD); risk management and insurance (PhD); statistics (PhD); strategic management (PhD); tourism and sport (PhD). *Accreditation:* AACSB. *Degree requirements:* For doctorate, thesis/dissertation. *Entrance requirements:* For doctorate, GRE General Test, GMAT, minimum GPA of 3.0, master's degree. Additional exam requirements/recommendations for international students: Required—TOEFL (minimum score 600 paper-based; 100 iBT), IELTS (minimum score 7.5). Electronic applications accepted.

Temple University, Fox School of Business, MBA Programs, Philadelphia, PA 19122-6096. Offers accounting (MBA); business management (MBA); financial management (MBA); healthcare and life sciences innovation (MBA); human resource management (MBA); international business (IMBA); IT management (MBA); marketing management (MBA); pharmaceutical management (MBA); strategic management (EMBA, MBA). EMBA offered in Philadelphia, PA and Tokyo, Japan. *Accreditation:* AACSB. *Program availability:* Part-time, evening/weekend, online learning. *Entrance requirements:* For master's, GMAT, minimum undergraduate GPA of 3.0. Additional exam requirements/recommendations for international students: Required—TOEFL (minimum score 600 paper-based; 100 iBT), IELTS (minimum score 7.5).

Temple University, Fox School of Business, Specialized Master's Programs, Philadelphia, PA 19122-6096. Offers accountancy (MS); actuarial science (MS); finance (MS); financial engineering (MS); human resource management (MS); innovation management and entrepreneurship (MS); marketing (MS); statistics (MS). MS in innovation management and entrepreneurship delivered jointly with College of Engineering. *Accreditation:* AACSB. *Program availability:* Part-time. *Entrance requirements:* For master's, GRE General Test or GMAT, minimum undergraduate GPA of 3.0. Additional exam requirements/recommendations for international students: Required—TOEFL (minimum score 600 paper-based; 100 iBT), IELTS (minimum score 7.5).

Tennessee State University, The School of Graduate Studies and Research, College of Business, Nashville, TN 37209-1561. Offers MBA. *Accreditation:* AACSB. *Program availability:* Part-time, evening/weekend, online learning. *Entrance requirements:* For master's, GMAT. Additional exam requirements/recommendations for international students: Required—TOEFL (minimum score 500 paper-based). Electronic applications accepted. *Faculty research:* Supply chain management, health economics, accounting, e-commerce, international business.

Tennessee Technological University, College of Graduate Studies, College of Business, MBA Program, Cookeville, TN 38505. Offers finance (MBA); human resource management (MBA); international business (MBA); management information systems (MBA). *Program availability:* Part-time, evening/weekend. *Students:* 32 full-time (10 women), 156 part-time (66 women); includes 16 minority (7 Black or African American, non-Hispanic/Latino; 1 Asian, non-Hispanic/Latino; 5 Hispanic/Latino; 3 Two or more races, non-Hispanic/Latino), 5 international. 115 applicants, 68% accepted, 57 enrolled. In 2018, 88 master's awarded. *Entrance requirements:* For master's, GMAT or GRE. *Financial support:* In 2018–19, 2 research assistantships, 3 teaching assistantships were awarded; fellowships and unspecified assistantships also available. Financial award application deadline: 4/1; financial award applicants required to submit FAFSA. *Unit head:* Kate Nicewicz, Director, 931-372-3600, E-mail: knicewicz@tntech.edu. *Application contact:* Shelia K. Kendrick, Coordinator of Graduate Studies, 931-372-3808, Fax: 931-372-3497, E-mail: skendrick@tntech.edu.
Website: https://www.tntech.edu/cob/mba/

Tennessee Wesleyan University, Graduate Programs, Athens, TN 37303. Offers accounting (MBA); management (MBA). *Program availability:* Part-time. *Faculty:* 4 full-time (1 woman), 2 part-time/adjunct (1 woman). *Students:* 12 full-time (8 women), 19 part-time (13 women). Average age 28. 29 applicants, 83% accepted, 16 enrolled. In 2018, 9 master's awarded. *Degree requirements:* For master's, comprehensive exam, Capstone. *Entrance requirements:* For master's, GMAT, official transcripts, three letters of recommendation, current curriculum vitae or resume. *Application deadline:* For fall admission, 8/19 for domestic students; for spring admission, 1/14 for domestic students; for summer admission, 5/6 for domestic students. Electronic applications accepted. *Expenses: Tuition:* Full-time $9000; part-time $500 per credit hour. *Financial support:* Application deadline: 4/30; applicants required to submit FAFSA. *Application contact:* Makhaila Woodlief, Adult and Graduate Admissions Counselor, 423-746-5285, Fax: 423-745-9335, E-mail: mwoodlief@tnwesleyan.edu.
Website: http://www.tnwesleyan.edu/academics/graduate-programs/

Texas A&M International University, Office of Graduate Studies and Research, A.R. Sanchez, Jr. School of Business, Laredo, TX 78041. Offers MBA, MP Acc, MSIS, PhD. *Accreditation:* AACSB. *Program availability:* Part-time, evening/weekend. *Degree requirements:* For master's, thesis (for some programs). *Entrance requirements:* For master's, GMAT or GRE General Test. Additional exam requirements/recommendations for international students: Required—TOEFL (minimum score 550 paper-based; 79 iBT), IELTS (minimum score 6.5).

Texas A&M University, Mays Business School, Department of Management, College Station, TX 77843. Offers entrepreneurial leadership (MS); human resource management (MS). *Faculty:* 30. *Students:* 103 full-time (79 women), 1 part-time (0 women); includes 20 minority (2 Black or African American, non-Hispanic/Latino; 5 Asian, non-Hispanic/Latino; 13 Hispanic/Latino), 6 international. Average age 26. 131 applicants, 39% accepted, 40 enrolled. In 2018, 48 master's awarded. Terminal master's awarded for partial completion of doctoral program. *Degree requirements:* For master's, comprehensive exam. *Entrance requirements:* For master's, GMAT or GRE. Additional exam requirements/recommendations for international students: Required—TOEFL (minimum score 550 paper-based; 80 iBT), IELTS (minimum score 6), PTE (minimum score 53). *Application deadline:* For fall admission, 5/26 for domestic and international students. Applications are processed on a rolling basis. Application fee: $50 ($90 for international students). Electronic applications accepted. *Expenses:* Contact institution. *Financial support:* In 2018–19, 86 students received support, including 30 research assistantships with tuition reimbursements available (averaging $10,805 per year), 19 teaching assistantships with tuition reimbursements available (averaging $7,111 per year); career-related internships or fieldwork, institutionally sponsored loans, scholarships/grants, traineeships, health care benefits, tuition waivers (full and partial), and unspecified assistantships also available. Support available to part-time students. Financial award application deadline: 3/15; financial award applicants required to submit FAFSA. *Faculty research:* Strategic and human resource management, business and public policy, organizational behavior, organizational theory. *Unit head:* Dr. Wendy R. Boswell, Head, 979-845-4045, Fax: 979-845-9641, E-mail: wboswell@mays.tamu.edu. *Application contact:* Kristi R. Mora, Senior Academic Advisor II, 979-845-6127, Fax: 979-845-9641, E-mail: kmora@mays.tamu.edu.
Website: http://mays.tamu.edu/mgmt/

Texas A&M University–Central Texas, Graduate Studies and Research, Killeen, TX 76549. Offers accounting (MS); business administration (MBA); clinical mental health counseling (MS); criminal justice (MCJ); curriculum and instruction (M Ed); educational administration (M Ed); educational psychology - experimental psychology (MS); history (MA); human resource management (MS); information systems (MS); liberal studies (MS); management and leadership (MS); marriage and family therapy (MS); mathematics (MS); political science (MA); school counseling (M Ed); school psychology (Ed S).

Texas A&M University–Commerce, College of Business, Commerce, TX 75429. Offers accounting (MSA); business administration (MBA); business analytics (MS); finance (MSF); management (MS); marketing (MS). *Accreditation:* AACSB. *Program availability:* Part-time, evening/weekend, 100% online, blended/hybrid learning. *Faculty:* 48 full-time (15 women), 2 part-time/adjunct (1 woman). *Students:* 391 full-time (209 women), 948 part-time (511 women); includes 583 minority (249 Black or African American, non-Hispanic/Latino; 4 American Indian or Alaska Native, non-Hispanic/Latino; 89 Asian, non-Hispanic/Latino; 205 Hispanic/Latino; 1 Native Hawaiian or other Pacific Islander, non-Hispanic/Latino; 35 Two or more races, non-Hispanic/Latino), 156 international. Average age 33. 930 applicants, 58% accepted, 355 enrolled. In 2018, 628 master's awarded. *Degree requirements:* For master's, comprehensive exam. *Entrance requirements:* For master's, GRE General Test, GMAT, letter of recommendation. Additional exam requirements/recommendations for international students: Required—TOEFL (minimum score 550 paper-based; 79 iBT), IELTS (minimum score 6), PTE (minimum score 53). *Application deadline:* For fall admission, 6/1 priority date for international students; for spring admission, 10/15 priority date for international students; for summer admission, 3/15 priority date for international students. Applications are processed on a rolling basis. Application fee: $50 ($75 for international students). Electronic applications accepted. *Expenses: Tuition, area resident:* Full-time $3630. Tuition, state resident: full-time $3630. Tuition, nonresident: full-time $11,100. *International tuition:* $11,100 full-time. *Required fees:* $2794. Tuition and fees vary according to course load, degree level and program. *Financial support:* In 2018–19, 61 students received support, including 57 research assistantships with partial tuition reimbursements available (averaging $3,286 per year); Federal Work-Study, institutionally sponsored loans, scholarships/grants, health care benefits, and unspecified assistantships also available. Financial award application deadline: 5/1; financial award applicants required to submit FAFSA. *Faculty research:* Strategic management and organizational behavior phenomena; marketing and big data decisions of product choice behavior and channel behavior of consumers; international accounting in governmental sectors; finance research on banking, investments, financial institutions and risk management; applied economics with emphasis on industries that are important to the region including health and energy. *Unit head:* Dr. Shanan Gwaltney Gibson, Dean of College of Business, 903-886-5191, Fax: 903-886-5650, E-mail: shanan.gibson@tamuc.edu. *Application contact:* Shanna Hoskison, Director, Graduate Advising, 903-886-5190, E-mail: shanna.hoskison@tamuc.edu.
Website: https://new.tamuc.edu/business/

Texas A&M University–Corpus Christi, College of Graduate Studies, College of Business, Corpus Christi, TX 78412. Offers accounting (M Acc); business (MBA); finance (MBA); health care administration (MBA); international business (MBA). *Accreditation:* AACSB. *Program availability:* Part-time, evening/weekend, 100% online, blended/hybrid learning. *Degree requirements:* For master's, 30 to 42 hours (for MBA; varies by concentration area, delivery format, and necessity for foundational courses for students with nonbusiness degrees). *Entrance requirements:* For master's, GMAT, GRE. Additional exam requirements/recommendations for international students: Required—TOEFL (minimum score 550 paper-based; 79 iBT), IELTS (minimum score 6.5). Electronic applications accepted.

Texas A&M University–Kingsville, College of Graduate Studies, College of Business Administration, Kingsville, TX 78363. Offers MBA. *Program availability:* Online only, 100% online, blended/hybrid learning. *Entrance requirements:* Additional exam requirements/recommendations for international students: Required—TOEFL (minimum score 550 paper-based; 79 iBT); Recommended—IELTS. Electronic applications accepted.

Texas A&M University–San Antonio, School of Business, San Antonio, TX 78224. Offers business administration (MBA); professional accounting (MPA). *Program availability:* Part-time, evening/weekend, online learning. *Degree requirements:* For master's, comprehensive exam. *Entrance requirements:* For master's, GMAT. Additional exam requirements/recommendations for international students: Required—TOEFL (minimum score 550 paper-based; 79 iBT), IELTS (minimum score 6). Electronic applications accepted. *Faculty research:* Culture and its effect on organizational processes; diversity and teams.

Texas A&M University–Texarkana, Graduate Studies and Research, College of Business, Texarkana, TX 75503. Offers accounting (MSA); business administration (MBA, MS). *Program availability:* Part-time, evening/weekend. *Degree requirements:* For master's, thesis or alternative. *Entrance requirements:* For master's, minimum GPA of 2.5 in last 60 hours of bachelor's degree. Additional exam requirements/ recommendations for international students: Required—TOEFL. Electronic applications accepted.

Texas Christian University, Neeley School of Business, Executive MBA Program, Fort Worth, TX 76129-0002. Offers MBA. *Program availability:* Evening/weekend. *Faculty:* 83 full-time (26 women), 14 part-time/adjunct (5 women). *Students:* 50 full-time (13 women); includes 10 minority (4 Black or African American, non-Hispanic/Latino; 1 Asian, non-Hispanic/Latino; 4 Hispanic/Latino; 1 Two or more races, non-Hispanic/ Latino), 1 international. Average age 39. 38 applicants, 95% accepted, 29 enrolled. In 2018, 30 master's awarded. *Entrance requirements:* Additional exam requirements/ recommendations for international students: Recommended—TOEFL. *Application deadline:* For winter admission, 2/1 for domestic and international students; for summer admission, 7/19 for domestic and international students. Applications are processed on a rolling basis. Application fee: $100. Electronic applications accepted. *Expenses:* Contact institution. *Financial support:* In 2018–19, 13 students received support. Scholarships/grants and tuition waivers (partial) available. Financial award application deadline: 2/1; financial award applicants required to submit FAFSA. *Unit head:* Dr. Suzanne M. Carter, EMBA Executive Director/Professor of Strategy Practice, 817-257-7543, E-mail: s.carter@tcu.edu. *Application contact:* Kevin T. Davis, Director, Executive MBA Recruiting and External Relations, 817-257-4681, Fax: 817-257-7719, E-mail: kevin.davis@tcu.edu.
Website: http://emba.tcu.edu

Texas Christian University, Neeley School of Business, Full-time Master's Program in Business Administration and Accelerated MBA, Fort Worth, TX 76129-0002. Offers MBA. *Accreditation:* AACSB. *Program availability:* Part-time, evening/weekend. *Faculty:* 83 full-time (26 women), 14 part-time/adjunct (5 women). *Students:* 93 full-time (26 women); includes 11 minority (3 Black or African American, non-Hispanic/Latino; 1 American Indian or Alaska Native, non-Hispanic/Latino; 1 Asian, non-Hispanic/Latino; 5 Hispanic/Latino; 1 Two or more races, non-Hispanic/Latino), 25 international. Average age 28. 170 applicants, 54% accepted, 48 enrolled. In 2018, 47 master's awarded. *Entrance requirements:* For master's, GMAT (preferred); GRE. Additional exam requirements/recommendations for international students: Required—TOEFL; Recommended—IELTS. *Application deadline:* For fall admission, 10/15 priority date for domestic and international students; for winter admission, 1/5 for domestic and international students; for spring admission, 3/1 for domestic and international students; for summer admission, 4/5 for domestic and international students. Applications are processed on a rolling basis. Application fee: $100. Electronic applications accepted. Application fee is waived when completed online. *Financial support:* In 2018–19, 99 students received support. Career-related internships or fieldwork, scholarships/grants, and unspecified assistantships available. Financial award application deadline: 4/5; financial award applicants required to submit FAFSA. *Unit head:* Anne Rooney, Executive Director, Graduate Programs, 817-257-7991, Fax: 817-257-6431, E-mail: mbainfo@tcu.edu. *Application contact:* Hoai Nguyen, Assistant Director, Graduate Programs Recruiting & Admissions, 817-257-7531, E-mail: mbainfo@tcu.edu.
Website: http://www.neeley.tcu.edu/mba

Texas Christian University, Neeley School of Business, Professional MBA Program, Fort Worth, TX 76129-0002. Offers general, energy, healthcare (MBA). *Program availability:* Part-time-only, evening/weekend. *Faculty:* 83 full-time (26 women), 14 part-time/adjunct (5 women). *Students:* 124 full-time (35 women), 23 part-time (6 women); includes 18 minority (4 Black or African American, non-Hispanic/Latino; 1 American Indian or Alaska Native, non-Hispanic/Latino; 5 Asian, non-Hispanic/Latino; 8 Hispanic/ Latino), 1 international. Average age 30. 97 applicants, 97% accepted, 66 enrolled. In 2018, 59 master's awarded. *Entrance requirements:* For master's, GMAT (preferred) or GRE. *Application deadline:* For fall admission, 11/1 priority date for domestic and international students; for winter admission, 1/15 for domestic and international students; for spring admission, 3/1 for domestic and international students; for summer admission, 4/15 for domestic and international students. Applications are processed on a rolling basis. Application fee: $100. Electronic applications accepted. Application fee is waived when completed online. *Expenses:* 1710 per semester hour. *Unit head:* Anne Rooney, Executive Director, Graduate Programs, 817-257-7991, E-mail: mbainfo@ tcu.edu. *Application contact:* Christina Rangel-Bautista, Assistant Director of Graduate Recruiting & Admission, 817-257-7531.
Website: http://www.neeley.tcu.edu/Professional_MBA.aspx

Texas Health and Science University, Graduate Programs, Austin, TX 78704. Offers acupuncture and Oriental medicine (MS, DAOM); business administration (MBA); healthcare management (MBA). *Accreditation:* ACAOM. *Entrance requirements:* For master's, 60 hours applicable to bachelor's degree. Additional exam requirements/ recommendations for international students: Required—TOEFL (minimum score 500 paper-based), TWE. Electronic applications accepted.

Texas Southern University, Jesse H. Jones School of Business, Program in Business Administration, Houston, TX 77004-4584. Offers MBA. *Accreditation:* AACSB. *Program availability:* Part-time, evening/weekend. *Degree requirements:* For master's, comprehensive exam. *Entrance requirements:* For master's, GMAT, minimum GPA of 2.5. Electronic applications accepted.

Texas State University, The Graduate College, Emmett and Miriam McCoy College of Business Administration, Program in Business Administration, San Marcos, TX 78666. Offers MBA. *Accreditation:* AACSB. *Program availability:* Part-time. *Faculty:* 34 full-time (16 women), 2 part-time/adjunct (0 women). *Students:* 69 full-time (26 women), 143 part-time (50 women); includes 64 minority (8 Black or African American, non-Hispanic/ Latino; 2 American Indian or Alaska Native, non-Hispanic/Latino; 18 Asian, non-Hispanic/Latino; 34 Hispanic/Latino; 2 Two or more races, non-Hispanic/Latino), 12 international. Average age 31. 208 applicants, 39% accepted, 49 enrolled. In 2018, 87 master's awarded. *Degree requirements:* For master's, comprehensive exam, thesis optional. *Entrance requirements:* For master's, official GMAT or GRE (general test only) required with competitive scores, baccalaureate degree from regionally-accredited university; a competitive GPA in your last 60 hours of undergraduate course work (plus any completed graduate courses); two letters or forms of recommendation;; essay; detailed resume. Additional exam requirements/recommendations for international students: Required—TOEFL (minimum score 550 paper-based; 78 iBT), IELTS (minimum score 6.5). *Application deadline:* For fall admission, 1/15 priority date for domestic and international students; for spring admission, 10/1 for domestic and international students. Application fee: $55 ($90 for international students). Electronic applications accepted. *Expenses:* Tuition, state resident: full-time $8102; part-time $4051 per semester. Tuition, nonresident: full-time $18,229; part-time $9115 per semester. *International tuition:* $18,229 full-time. *Required fees:* $2116; $120 per credit hour. Tuition and fees vary according to course load. *Financial support:* In 2018–19, 68 students received support, including 8 teaching assistantships (averaging $13,685 per year); research assistantships, Federal Work-Study, institutionally sponsored loans, scholarships/grants, health care benefits, and unspecified assistantships also available. Support available to part-time students. Financial award application deadline: 1/15; financial award applicants required to submit FAFSA. *Unit head:* Dr. William Chittenden, Associate Dean, 512-245-3591, Fax: 512-245-7973, E-mail: businessgraduate@ txstate.edu. *Application contact:* Dr. Andrea Golato, Dean of Graduate School, 512-245-2581, Fax: 512-245-8365, E-mail: gradcollege@txstate.edu.
Website: http://graduate.mccoy.txstate.edu/

Texas Tech University, Rawls College of Business Administration, Lubbock, TX 79409-2101. Offers accounting (MSA, PhD), including audit/financial reporting (MSA), taxation (MSA); data science (MS); finance (PhD); general business (MBA); healthcare management (MS); information systems and operations management (PhD); management (PhD); marketing (PhD); STEM (MBA); JD/MBA; JD/MSA; MBA/M Arch; MBA/MD; MBA/MS; MBA/Pharm D. *Accreditation:* AACSB. *Program availability:* Evening/weekend, 100% online, blended/hybrid learning. *Degree requirements:* For master's, thesis (for MS); capstone course; for doctorate, comprehensive exam, thesis/ dissertation, qualifying exams. *Entrance requirements:* For master's, GMAT, GRE, MCAT, PCAT, LSAT, or DAT, holistic review of academic credentials, resume, essay, letters of recommendation; for doctorate, GMAT, GRE, holistic review of academic credentials, resume, statement of purpose, letters of recommendation. Additional exam requirements/recommendations for international students: Required—TOEFL (minimum score 550 paper-based; 79 iBT), IELTS (minimum score 6.5), PTE (minimum score 60). Electronic applications accepted. *Expenses:* Contact institution. *Faculty research:* Governmental and nonprofit accounting, securities and options futures, statistical analysis and design, leadership, consumer behavior.

Texas Wesleyan University, Graduate Programs, Graduate Business Programs, Fort Worth, TX 76105. Offers MBA. *Accreditation:* AACSB; ACBSP. *Program availability:* Part-time, online only, 100% online. *Degree requirements:* For master's, capstone course. *Entrance requirements:* For master's, GMAT or GRE, bachelor's degree, minimum overall undergraduate GPA of 2.6, three letters of recommendation, written essay that shows objectives in pursuing an MBA. Additional exam requirements/ recommendations for international students: Required—TOEFL (minimum score 550 paper-based; 79 iBT), IELTS (minimum score 6.5). Electronic applications accepted. *Expenses:* Contact institution.

Texas Woman's University, Graduate School, College of Business, Denton, TX 76204. Offers business administration (MBA), including accounting, business analytics, healthcare administration (MBA, MHA), human resources management, management; health systems management (MHSM); healthcare administration (MHA), including healthcare administration (MBA, MHA). *Accreditation:* ACBSP. *Program availability:* Part-time, 100% online, blended/hybrid learning. *Faculty:* 26 full-time (9 women), 14 part-time/adjunct (7 women). *Students:* 483 full-time (429 women), 445 part-time (373 women); includes 643 minority (325 Black or African American, non-Hispanic/Latino; 4 American Indian or Alaska Native, non-Hispanic/Latino; 134 Asian, non-Hispanic/Latino; 152 Hispanic/Latino; 1 Native Hawaiian or other Pacific Islander, non-Hispanic/Latino; 27 Two or more races, non-Hispanic/Latino), 38 international. Average age 33. 401 applicants, 84% accepted, 251 enrolled. In 2018, 471 master's awarded. *Degree requirements:* For master's, thesis or alternative, capstone. *Entrance requirements:* For master's, minimum GPA of 3.0 in last 60 hours of undergraduate coursework and prior graduate coursework, resume. Additional exam requirements/recommendations for international students: Required—TOEFL (minimum score 550 paper-based; 79 iBT); Recommended—IELTS (minimum score 6.5), TSE (minimum score 53). *Application deadline:* Applications are processed on a rolling basis. Application fee: $50 ($75 for international students). Electronic applications accepted. *Expenses: Tuition, area resident:* Full-time $4852; part-time $270 per semester hour. Tuition, state resident: full-time $4852; part-time $270 per semester hour. Tuition, nonresident: full-time $12,322; part-time $685 per semester hour. *International tuition:* $12,322 full-time. *Required fees:* $2714; $113 per semester hour. $296 per semester. Tuition and fees vary according to course level, course load, degree level, campus/location and program. *Financial support:* In 2018–19, 138 students received support, including 12 teaching assistantships (averaging $10,666 per year); career-related internships or fieldwork, Federal Work-Study, institutionally sponsored loans, scholarships/grants, traineeships, health care benefits, and unspecified assistantships also available. Support available to part-time students. Financial award application deadline: 3/1; financial award applicants required to submit FAFSA. *Faculty research:* Marketing and market research, economics, accounting, logistics and supply chain management, health systems. *Unit head:* Dr. James R. Lumpkin, Dean, 940-898-2458, Fax: 940-898-2120, E-mail: mba@ twu.edu. *Application contact:* Korie Hawkins, Associate Director of Admissions, Graduate Recruitment, 940-898-3188, Fax: 940-898-3081, E-mail: admissions@ twu.edu.
Website: http://www.twu.edu/business/

Thomas College, Graduate School, Programs in Business, Waterville, ME 04901-5097. Offers business (MBA); computer technology education (MS); education (MS); human resource management (MBA). *Program availability:* Part-time, evening/weekend. *Entrance requirements:* For master's, GMAT, GRE, MAT or minimum GPA of 3.3 in first 3 graduate-level courses. Additional exam requirements/recommendations for international students: Recommended—TOEFL.

Thomas Edison State University, School of Business and Management, MBA Program, Trenton, NJ 08608. Offers MBA. *Program availability:* Online learning. *Expenses:* Contact institution.

Thomas Edison State University, School of Business and Management, Program in Management, Trenton, NJ 08608. Offers accounting (MSM); organizational leadership (MSM); project management (MSM). *Program availability:* Part-time, 100% online. *Degree requirements:* For master's, final capstone project. *Entrance requirements:* For master's, bachelor's degree from a regionally-accredited college or university; minimum 2 letters of recommendation; 3-5 years of related working experience; current resume. Additional exam requirements/recommendations for international students: Required—TOEFL (minimum score 550 paper-based; 79 iBT). Electronic applications accepted.

Thomas Jefferson University, Kanbar College of Design, Engineering and Commerce, Innovation MBA Program, Philadelphia, PA 19107. Offers business analytics (MBA); general business (MBA); management (MBA); marketing (MBA); strategy and design thinking (MBA); MBA/MS. *Program availability:* Part-time, evening/weekend, online learning. *Entrance requirements:* For master's, GMAT. Additional exam requirements/ recommendations for international students: Required—TOEFL (minimum score 550 paper-based; 79 iBT).

Thomas More University, Program in Business Administration, Crestview Hills, KY 41017-3495. Offers MBA. *Accreditation:* ACBSP. *Program availability:* Evening/ weekend, 100% online. *Degree requirements:* For master's, comprehensive exam, final project. *Entrance requirements:* For master's, GMAT, minimum GPA of 2.7. Additional exam requirements/recommendations for international students: Required—TOEFL (minimum score 600 paper-based; 100 iBT). Electronic applications accepted. *Expenses:* Contact institution. *Faculty research:* Leadership, elder abuse and neglect, community health asset mapping, critical thinking in higher education, business communication, corporate social responsibility.

Business Administration and Management—General

Thomas University, Department of Business Administration, Thomasville, GA 31792-7499. Offers MBA. *Program availability:* Part-time. *Entrance requirements:* For master's, resume, 3 professional or academic references. Additional exam requirements/recommendations for international students: Required—TOEFL (minimum score 600 paper-based). Electronic applications accepted.

Thompson Rivers University, Program in Business Administration, Kamloops, BC V2C 0C8, Canada. Offers MBA. *Program availability:* Part-time. *Entrance requirements:* For master's, GMAT, undergraduate degree with minimum B- average in last 60 credits, personal resume. Additional exam requirements/recommendations for international students: Required—TOEFL (570 paper-based, 88 iBT), IELTS (6.5), or CAEL (70).

Tiffin University, Program in Business Administration, Tiffin, OH 44883-2161. Offers finance (MBA); general management (MBA); healthcare administration (MBA); human resource management (MBA); international business (MBA); leadership (MBA); marketing (MBA); non-profit management (MBA); sports management (MBA). *Accreditation:* ACBSP. *Program availability:* Part-time, evening/weekend, online learning. *Entrance requirements:* For master's, minimum undergraduate GPA of 2.5, work experience. Additional exam requirements/recommendations for international students: Required—TOEFL (minimum score 550 paper-based; 79 iBT), IELTS. Electronic applications accepted. Application fee is waived when completed online. *Faculty research:* Small business, executive development operations, research and statistical analysis, market research, management information systems.

Trevecca Nazarene University, Graduate Business Programs, Nashville, TN 37210-2877. Offers business administration (MBA); health care leadership and innovation (MS); management (MSM). *Program availability:* Evening/weekend, online learning. *Entrance requirements:* For master's, minimum GPA of 2.75, resume, official transcript from regionally accredited institution, minimum math grade of C, minimum English composition grade of C. Additional exam requirements/recommendations for international students: Required—TOEFL (minimum score 550 paper-based; 80 iBT). Electronic applications accepted. *Expenses:* Contact institution.

Trident University International, College of Business Administration, Program in Business Administration, Cypress, CA 90630. Offers business administration (PhD); conflict and negotiation management (MBA); criminal justice administration (MBA); entrepreneurship (MBA); finance (MBA); general management (MBA); government accounting (MBA); human resource management (MBA); information security and digital assurance management (MBA); information technology management (MBA); international business (MBA); logistics management (MBA); marketing (MBA); project management (MBA); public management (MBA); quality management (MBA); strategic leadership (MBA). *Program availability:* Part-time, evening/weekend, online learning. *Degree requirements:* For doctorate, comprehensive exam, thesis/dissertation, defense of dissertation. *Entrance requirements:* For master's, minimum GPA of 2.5 (students with GPA 3.0 or greater may transfer up to 30% of graduate level credits); for doctorate, minimum GPA of 3.4, curriculum vitae, course work in research methods or statistics. Additional exam requirements/recommendations for international students: Required—TOEFL. Electronic applications accepted.

Trine University, Program in Business Administration, Angola, IN 46703-1764. Offers MBA.

Trinity International University, Trinity Evangelical Divinity School, Deerfield, IL 60015-1284. Offers academic ministry (M Div); Biblical and Near Eastern archaeology and languages (MA); chaplaincy and ministry care (MA); Christian studies (Certificate); church and parachurch ministry (M Div); church history (MA, Th M); counseling (Th M); educational ministries (MA); educational ministry (Th M); educational studies (PhD); intercultural studies (MA, PhD); leadership and management (D Min); mental health counseling (MA); military chaplaincy (D Min); ministry (MA); missions (Th M); missions and evangelism (D Min); New Testament (MA, Th M); Old Testament (Th M); Old Testament and Semitic languages (MA); pastoral ministry and care (D Min); pastoral theology (Th M); preaching and teaching (D Min); spiritual formation and education (D Min); systematic theology (MA, Th M); theological studies (MA, PhD); urban ministry (MA). *Program availability:* Part-time, online learning. *Degree requirements:* For master's, comprehensive exam, thesis, fieldwork; for doctorate, comprehensive exam (for some programs), thesis/dissertation; for Certificate, comprehensive exam, integrative papers. *Entrance requirements:* For master's, GRE, MAT, minimum cumulative undergraduate GPA of 3.0; for doctorate, GRE, minimum cumulative graduate GPA of 3.2; for Certificate, GRE, MAT, minimum undergraduate GPA of 2.5. Additional exam requirements/recommendations for international students: Required—TOEFL (minimum score 580 paper-based), TWE (minimum score 4). Electronic applications accepted.

Trinity University, School of Business, San Antonio, TX 78212-7200. Offers accounting (MS). *Accreditation:* AACSB. *Faculty:* 2 full-time (both women), 3 part-time/adjunct (0 women). *Students:* 17 full-time (5 women); includes 4 minority (1 Black or African American, non-Hispanic/Latino; 1 Asian, non-Hispanic/Latino; 1 Hispanic/Latino; 1 Two or more races, non-Hispanic/Latino), 3 international. Average age 22. In 2018, 16 master's awarded. *Entrance requirements:* For master's, GMAT, minimum GPA of 3.0, course work in accounting and business law, letters of recommendation. *Application deadline:* For fall admission, 2/1 for domestic and international students. Electronic applications accepted. Tuition and fees vary according to program and student level. *Financial support:* Institutionally sponsored loans and scholarships/grants available. Financial award application deadline: 5/1; financial award applicants required to submit FAFSA. *Unit head:* Dr. Julie Persellin, Chair, Department of Accounting, 210-999-7230, E-mail: jpersell@trinity.edu. *Application contact:* Dr. Julie Persellin, Chair, Department of Accounting, 210-999-7230, E-mail: jpersell@trinity.edu.
Website: https://new.trinity.edu/academics/departments/school-business/graduate-accounting-program

Trinity Washington University, School of Business and Graduate Studies, Washington, DC 20017-1094. Offers business administration (MBA); communication (MA); international security studies (MA); organizational management (MSA), including federal program management, human resource management, nonprofit management, organizational development, public and community health. *Program availability:* Part-time, evening/weekend. *Degree requirements:* For master's, thesis (for some programs), capstone project (MSA). *Entrance requirements:* For master's, minimum GPA of 2.5. Additional exam requirements/recommendations for international students: Required—TOEFL (minimum score 550 paper-based).

Trinity Western University, School of Graduate Studies, Program in Business Administration, Langley, BC V2Y 1Y1, Canada. Offers international business (MBA); management of the growing enterprise (MBA); non-profit and charitable organization management (MBA). *Program availability:* Part-time, online learning. *Degree requirements:* For master's, thesis or alternative, applied project. *Entrance requirements:* For master's, GMAT (minimum score of 550 recommended). Additional exam requirements/recommendations for international students: Required—TOEFL (minimum score 600 paper-based; 100 iBT), IELTS (minimum score 7). *Application deadline:* For spring admission, 4/30 for domestic and international students. Applications are processed on a rolling basis. Electronic applications accepted. *Financial support:* Scholarships/grants available. *Unit head:* Dr. Mark A. Lee, Director,

MBA Program, 604-888-7511 Ext. 3474, Fax: 604-513-2042, E-mail: mark.lee@twu.ca. *Application contact:* Phil Kay, Director of Graduate and International Admissions, 604-513-2121 Ext. 3444, E-mail: phil.kay@twu.edu.
Website: http://www.twu.ca/mba

Troy University, Graduate School, College of Business, Program in Business Administration, Troy, AL 36082. Offers accounting (EMBA, MBA); criminal justice (EMBA); finance (MBA); general management (EMBA, MBA); healthcare management (EMBA); information systems (EMBA, MBA); international economic development (MBA). *Accreditation:* ACBSP. *Program availability:* Part-time, evening/weekend. *Faculty:* 12 full-time (1 woman), 1 part-time/adjunct (0 women). *Students:* 27 full-time (16 women), 93 part-time (44 women); includes 31 minority (27 Black or African American, non-Hispanic/Latino; 1 Asian, non-Hispanic/Latino; 3 Hispanic/Latino), 29 international. Average age 30. 108 applicants, 37% accepted, 22 enrolled. In 2018, 74 master's awarded. *Degree requirements:* For master's, minimum GPA of 3.0, capstone course, research course. *Entrance requirements:* For master's, GMAT (minimum score 500) or GRE (minimum score 900 on old exam or 294 on new exam), bachelor's degree; minimum undergraduate GPA of 2.5 or 3.0 on last 30 semester hours, letter of recommendation. Additional exam requirements/recommendations for international students: Required—TOEFL (minimum score 523 paper-based; 70 iBT), IELTS (minimum score 6). *Application deadline:* Applications are processed on a rolling basis. Application fee: $50. Electronic applications accepted. *Expenses: Tuition, area resident:* Full-time $425; part-time $425 per credit hour. Tuition, state resident: full-time $425; part-time $425 per credit hour. Tuition, nonresident: full-time $850; part-time $850 per credit hour. *International tuition:* $850 full-time. *Required fees:* $50 per semester. Tuition and fees vary according to campus/location and program. *Financial support:* Fellowships, career-related internships or fieldwork, and scholarships/grants available. Support available to part-time students. Financial award applicants required to submit FAFSA. *Unit head:* Dr. Robert Wheatley, Professor, Director of Graduate Business Programs, 334-670-3194, Fax: 334-670-3708, E-mail: rwheat@troy.edu. *Application contact:* Jessica A. Kimbro, Assistant Director of Graduate Programs, 334-670-3189, E-mail: jacord@troy.edu.
Website: https://www.troy.edu/academics/academic-programs/sorrell-college-business-programs.php

Troy University, Graduate School, College of Business, Program in Management, Troy, AL 36082. Offers MS, MSM. *Accreditation:* ACBSP. *Program availability:* Part-time, evening/weekend. *Faculty:* 12 full-time (5 women). *Students:* 50 full-time (26 women), 379 part-time (156 women); includes 90 minority (75 Black or African American, non-Hispanic/Latino; 3 American Indian or Alaska Native, non-Hispanic/Latino; 8 Hispanic/Latino; 4 Two or more races, non-Hispanic/Latino). Average age 37. 225 applicants, 97% accepted, 148 enrolled. In 2018, 73 master's awarded. *Degree requirements:* For master's, Graduate Educational Testing Service Major Field Test, capstone exam, minimum GPA of 3.0. *Entrance requirements:* For master's, GRE (minimum score of 900 on old exam or 294 on new exam) or GMAT (minimum score of 500), bachelor's degree; minimum undergraduate GPA of 2.5 or 3.0 on last 30 semester hours, letter of recommendation. Additional exam requirements/recommendations for international students: Required—TOEFL (minimum score 523 paper-based; 70 iBT), IELTS (minimum score 6). *Application deadline:* Applications are processed on a rolling basis. Application fee: $50. Electronic applications accepted. *Expenses:* Contact institution. *Financial support:* Fellowships, career-related internships or fieldwork, and scholarships/grants available. Support available to part-time students. *Unit head:* Dr. Bob Wheatley, Director, Graduate Business Programs, 334-670-3299, Fax: 334-670-3599, E-mail: rwheat@troy.edu. *Application contact:* Jessica A. Kimbro, Assistant Director of Graduate Programs, 334-670-3189, E-mail: jacord@troy.edu.
Website: https://www.troy.edu/academics/academic-programs/sorrell-college-business-programs.php

Truett McConnell University, Hans Hut School of Business, Cleveland, GA 30528. Offers MBA. *Program availability:* Part-time, evening/weekend, 100% online. *Entrance requirements:* For master's, bachelor's degree from accredited institution, minimum GPA of 2.75. Electronic applications accepted.

Tulane University, A. B. Freeman School of Business, New Orleans, LA 70118-5669. Offers accounting (M Acct); analytics (MBA); banking and financial services (M Fin); energy (M Fin, MBA); entrepreneurship (MBA); finance (MBA, PhD); financial accounting (PhD); international business (MBA); international management (MBA); strategic management and leadership (MBA); JD/M Acct; JD/MBA; MBA/M Acc; MBA/MA; MBA/MD; MBA/ME; MBA/MPH. *Accreditation:* AACSB. *Program availability:* Part-time, evening/weekend. *Faculty:* 43 full-time (11 women), 45 part-time/adjunct (8 women). *Students:* 432 full-time (218 women), 533 part-time (262 women); includes 99 minority (32 Black or African American, non-Hispanic/Latino; 1 American Indian or Alaska Native, non-Hispanic/Latino; 26 Asian, non-Hispanic/Latino; 35 Hispanic/Latino; 5 Two or more races, non-Hispanic/Latino), 644 international. Average age 28. 1,911 applicants, 77% accepted, 411 enrolled. In 2018, 728 master's, 4 doctorates awarded. Terminal master's awarded for partial completion of doctoral program. *Degree requirements:* For master's, one foreign language, comprehensive exam (for some programs); for doctorate, one foreign language, comprehensive exam, thesis/dissertation. *Entrance requirements:* For master's and doctorate, GMAT or GRE, interview. Additional exam requirements/recommendations for international students: Required—TOEFL or IELTS. *Application deadline:* For fall admission, 11/1 priority date for domestic students, 11/1 for international students; for winter admission, 1/6 for domestic and international students; for spring admission, 3/1 priority date for domestic students, 3/1 for international students; for summer admission, 5/5 for domestic students. Applications are processed on a rolling basis. Application fee: $125. Electronic applications accepted. *Expenses:* Contact institution. *Financial support:* In 2018–19, 153 students received support. Fellowships with tuition reimbursements available, research assistantships, teaching assistantships, career-related internships or fieldwork, Federal Work-Study, tuition waivers (full and partial), and unspecified assistantships available. Support available to part-time students. Financial award application deadline: 4/15; financial award applicants required to submit FAFSA. *Faculty research:* Corporate finance, managerial accounting and financial reporting, strategic management and leadership, consumer behavior and decision making, organizational behavior and human resource management. *Unit head:* Ira Solomon, PhD, Dean, 504-865-5407, Fax: 504-865-5491, E-mail: businessdean@tulane.edu. *Application contact:* Melissa Booth, Assistant Dean for Graduate Admissions, 800-223-5402, E-mail: freeman.admissions@tulane.edu.
Website: http://www.freeman.tulane.edu

Tusculum University, Program in Business Administration, Greeneville, TN 37743-9997. Offers general management (MBA). *Program availability:* Evening/weekend. *Entrance requirements:* For master's, GMAT, GRE, 3 years of work experience, minimum GPA of 2.75.

Union University, McAfee School of Business Administration, Jackson, TN 38305-3697. Offers accountancy (M Acc). Program also available at Germantown campus. *Program availability:* Evening/weekend, online learning. *Entrance requirements:* For master's, GMAT, minimum GPA of 2.5. Electronic applications accepted. *Expenses:* Contact institution. *Faculty research:* Personal financial management, strategy, accounting, marketing, economics.

United States International University–Africa, School of Business Administration, Nairobi, Kenya. Offers business administration (GEMBA); entrepreneurship (MBA); finance (MBA); human resource management (MBA); information technology management (MBA); integrated studies (MBA); international business administration (MBA); management and organizational development (MS); marketing (MBA); organizational development (EMS); strategic management (MBA). *Program availability:* Part-time, evening/weekend. *Degree requirements:* For master's, thesis. *Entrance requirements:* For master's, GMAT, 2 letters of reference, resume. Additional exam requirements/recommendations for international students: Required—TOEFL (minimum score 550 paper-based). *Faculty research:* Marketing in small business enterprises, total quality management in Kenya.

Universidad Autonoma de Guadalajara, Graduate Programs, Guadalajara, Mexico. Offers administrative law and justice (LL M); advertising and corporate communications (MA); architecture (M Arch); business (MBA); computational science (MCC); education (Ed M, Ed D); English-Spanish translation (MA); entrepreneurship and management (MBA); integrated management of digital animation (MA); international business (MIB); international corporate law (LL M); Internet technologies (MS); manufacturing systems (MMS); occupational health (MS); philosophy (MA, PhD); power electronics (MS); quality systems (MQS); renewable energy (MS); social evaluation of projects (MBA); strategic market research (MBA); tax law (MA); teaching mathematics (MA).

Universidad de las Americas, A.C., Program in Business Administration, Mexico City, Mexico. Offers finance (MBA); marketing research (MBA); production and quality (MBA).

Universidad de las Américas Puebla, Division of Graduate Studies, School of Business and Economics, Puebla, Mexico. Offers business administration (MBA); finance (M Adm). *Program availability:* Part-time, evening/weekend. *Degree requirements:* For master's, one foreign language, thesis. *Entrance requirements:* Additional exam requirements/recommendations for international students: Required—TOEFL. *Faculty research:* System dynamics, information technology, marketing, international business, strategic planning, quality.

Universidad del Este, Graduate School, Carolina, PR 00984. Offers accounting (MBA); adult education (M Ed); agribusiness (MBA); criminal justice and criminology (MA); curriculum and instruction - early education (M Ed); curriculum and instruction - elementary (M Ed); curriculum and instruction - English (M Ed); curriculum and instruction - Spanish (M Ed); human resources (MBA); information security management (MBA); information technology and Web business development (MBA); management (MBA); public policy (MPA); social work (MA), including clinical social work; special education (M Ed); strategic leadership (MBA).

Universidad del Turabo, Graduate Programs, School of Business and Entrepreneurship, Program in Management, Gurabo, PR 00778-3030. Offers MBA, DBA. *Program availability:* Part-time, evening/weekend. *Entrance requirements:* For master's, GRE, EXADEP or GMAT, interview, essay, official transcript, recommendation letters; for doctorate, GRE, EXADEP or GMAT, official transcript, recommendation letters, essay, curriculum vitae, interview. Electronic applications accepted.

Universidad Iberoamericana, Graduate School, Santo Domingo D.N., Dominican Republic. Offers business administration (MBA, PMBA); constitutional law (LL M); dentistry (DMD); educational management (MA); integrated marketing communication (MA); psychopedagogical intervention (M Ed); real estate law (LL M); strategic management of human talent (MM).

Universidad Metropolitana, School of Business Administration, San Juan, PR 00928-1150. Offers accounting (MBA); finance (MBA); human resources management (MBA); international business (MBA); management (MBA); management information systems (MBA); marketing (MBA). *Program availability:* Part-time, evening/weekend. *Degree requirements:* For master's, thesis or alternative. Electronic applications accepted. *Faculty research:* Latin American trade, international investments, central city business development, Hispanic consumer research, Caribbean and Asian trade cooperation.

Université de Moncton, Faculty of Administration, Moncton, NB E1A 3E9, Canada. Offers MBA, JD/MBA. *Program availability:* Part-time, evening/weekend, 100% online. *Degree requirements:* For master's, one foreign language, thesis. *Entrance requirements:* For master's, minimum undergraduate GPA of 3.0. Electronic applications accepted. *Expenses:* Contact institution. *Faculty research:* Service management, corporate reputation, financial management, accounting, supply chain.

Université de Sherbrooke, Faculty of Administration, Doctoral Program in Business Administration, Sherbrooke, QC J1K 2R1, Canada. Offers DBA. *Degree requirements:* For doctorate, one foreign language, comprehensive exam, thesis/dissertation. *Entrance requirements:* For doctorate, 3 years of related work experience, interview, fluency in French, advanced English, good oral and written French comprehension (tested with an interview). Electronic applications accepted. *Faculty research:* Change management, international business and finance, work organization, information technology implementation and impact on organizations, strategic management.

Université de Sherbrooke, Faculty of Administration, Master of Business Administration Program, Sherbrooke, QC J1K 2R1, Canada. Offers executive business administration (EMBA); general management (MBA). *Program availability:* Part-time, evening/weekend. *Entrance requirements:* For master's, bachelor's degree, minimum GPA of 2.7 (on 4.3 scale), minimum of two years of work experience, letters of recommendation. Electronic applications accepted.

Université de Sherbrooke, Faculty of Law, Sherbrooke, QC J1K 2R1, Canada. Offers alternative dispute resolution (LL M, Diploma); business law (Diploma); common law (JD); criminal and penal law (Diploma); health law (LL M, Diploma); international law (LL M); law (LL D); legal management (Diploma); notarial law (Diploma); transnational law (Diploma). *Program availability:* Part-time, evening/weekend. *Degree requirements:* For master's, thesis; for Diploma, one foreign language. *Entrance requirements:* For master's and Diploma, LL B. Electronic applications accepted.

Université du Québec à Chicoutimi, Graduate Programs, Program in Small and Medium-Sized Organization Management, Chicoutimi, QC G7H 2B1, Canada. Offers M Sc. *Program availability:* Part-time. *Degree requirements:* For master's, thesis. *Entrance requirements:* For master's, appropriate bachelor's degree, proficiency in French.

Université du Québec à Montréal, Graduate Programs, PhD Program in Business Administration, Montréal, QC H3C 3P8, Canada. Offers PhD. *Program availability:* Part-time. *Degree requirements:* For doctorate, thesis/dissertation. *Entrance requirements:* For doctorate, appropriate master's degree or equivalent, proficiency in French.

Université du Québec à Montréal, Graduate Programs, Program in Business Administration (Professional), Montréal, QC H3C 3P8, Canada. Offers business administration (MBA); management consultant (Diploma). *Program availability:* Part-time. *Entrance requirements:* For master's and Diploma, appropriate bachelor's degree or equivalent, proficiency in French.

Université du Québec à Montréal, Graduate Programs, Program in Business Administration (Research), Montréal, QC H3C 3P8, Canada. Offers MBA. *Program availability:* Part-time. *Entrance requirements:* For master's, appropriate bachelor's degree or equivalent and proficiency in French.

Université du Québec à Rimouski, Graduate Programs, Program in Business Administration, Rimouski, QC G5L 3A1, Canada. Offers MBA.

Université du Québec à Rimouski, Graduate Programs, Program in Management of People in Working Situation, Rimouski, QC G5L 3A1, Canada. Offers M Sc, Diploma.

Université du Québec à Trois-Rivières, Graduate Programs, Program in Business Administration, Trois-Rivières, QC G9A 5H7, Canada. Offers MBA, DBA. DBA offered jointly with Université de Sherbrooke. *Degree requirements:* For doctorate, thesis/dissertation.

Université du Québec en Abitibi-Témiscamingue, Graduate Programs, Program in Business Administration, Rouyn-Noranda, QC J9X 5E4, Canada. Offers MBA.

Université du Québec en Abitibi-Témiscamingue, Graduate Programs, Program in Organization Management, Rouyn-Noranda, QC J9X 5E4, Canada. Offers M Sc. *Program availability:* Part-time. *Degree requirements:* For master's, thesis. *Entrance requirements:* For master's, appropriate bachelor's degree, proficiency in French.

Université Laval, Faculty of Administrative Sciences, Program in Organizations Management and Development, Québec, QC G1K 7P4, Canada. Offers Diploma. *Program availability:* Part-time. *Entrance requirements:* For degree, knowledge of French. Electronic applications accepted.

Université Laval, Faculty of Administrative Sciences, Programs in Administrative Studies, Québec, QC G1K 7P4, Canada. Offers administrative studies (M Sc, PhD); financial engineering (M Sc). *Accreditation:* AACSB. Terminal master's awarded for partial completion of doctoral program. *Degree requirements:* For master's, thesis (for some programs); for doctorate, comprehensive exam, thesis/dissertation. *Entrance requirements:* For master's and doctorate, knowledge of French and English. Electronic applications accepted.

Université Laval, Faculty of Administrative Sciences, Programs in Business Administration, Québec, QC G1K 7P4, Canada. Offers accounting (MBA); agri-food management (MBA); electronic business (MBA, Diploma); factory management and logistics (MBA); finance (MBA); firm management (MBA); geomatic management (MBA); information technology management (MBA); international management (MBA); management (MBA); management accounting (MBA, Diploma); marketing (MBA); modeling and organizational decision (MBA); occupational health and safety management (MBA); pharmacy management (MBA); social and environmental responsibility (MBA); technological entrepreneurship (Diploma). *Accreditation:* AACSB. *Program availability:* Part-time, evening/weekend, online learning. *Entrance requirements:* For master's and Diploma, knowledge of French and English. Electronic applications accepted.

University at Albany, State University of New York, School of Business, Albany, NY 12222-0001. Offers MBA, MS. *Accreditation:* AACSB. *Program availability:* Part-time, evening/weekend. *Faculty:* 34 full-time (11 women), 21 part-time/adjunct (3 women). *Students:* 277 full-time (94 women), 192 part-time (74 women); includes 127 minority (44 Black or African American, non-Hispanic/Latino; 2 American Indian or Alaska Native, non-Hispanic/Latino; 36 Asian, non-Hispanic/Latino; 34 Hispanic/Latino; 11 Two or more races, non-Hispanic/Latino), 37 international. 485 applicants, 63% accepted, 236 enrolled. In 2018, 221 master's awarded. Terminal master's awarded for partial completion of doctoral program. *Degree requirements:* For master's, project. *Entrance requirements:* For master's, GMAT. Additional exam requirements/recommendations for international students: Required—TOEFL (minimum score 550 paper-based). *Application deadline:* For fall admission, 3/1 for domestic students, 5/1 for international students. Applications are processed on a rolling basis. Application fee: $75. Electronic applications accepted. *Expenses:* Contact institution. *Financial support:* Fellowships, research assistantships, career-related internships or fieldwork, and Federal Work-Study available. *Unit head:* Nilanjan Sen, Dean, 518-956-8370, E-mail: nsen@albany.edu. *Application contact:* Michael DeRensis, Director, Graduate Admissions, 518-442-3980, Fax: 518-442-3922, E-mail: graduate@albany.edu. Website: http://www.albany.edu/business

University at Buffalo, the State University of New York, Graduate School, School of Management, Buffalo, NY 14260. Offers accounting (MS); analytics (MBA); business administration (PMBA); consulting (MBA); finance (MBA, MS), including financial risk management (MS), quantitative finance (MS); healthcare (MBA); information assurance (MBA); information systems (MBA); international management (MBA); management (EMBA, PhD); management information systems (MS); marketing (MBA); supply chain and operations (MBA); supply chains and operations management (MS); Au D/MBA; DDS/MBA; JD/MBA; M Arch/MBA; MD/MBA; MPH/MBA; MSW/MBA; Pharm D/MBA. *Accreditation:* AACSB. *Program availability:* Part-time, evening/weekend. *Degree requirements:* For master's, capstone courses or projects; for doctorate, comprehensive exam, thesis/dissertation. *Entrance requirements:* For master's, GMAT (for MS in accounting, finance); GRE or GMAT (for MBA, MS in management information systems, supply chains and operations management), essays, letters of recommendation; for doctorate, GMAT or GRE, essays, writing sample, letters of recommendation. Additional exam requirements/recommendations for international students: Required—TOEFL (minimum score 95 iBT) or IELTS (minimum score 6.5); Recommended—TSE (minimum score 73). Electronic applications accepted. *Expenses:* Contact institution. *Faculty research:* Data analytics, accounting and law, rate finance, consumer behavior, supply chain logistics, leadership and team effectiveness.

The University of Akron, Graduate School, College of Business Administration, Department of Management, Program in Management, Akron, OH 44325. Offers MBA. *Entrance requirements:* For master's, GMAT, GRE, MCAT, LSAT, PCAT, or CAT, minimum GPA of 3.0 (preferred), two letters of recommendation, resume, statement of purpose. Additional exam requirements/recommendations for international students: Required—TOEFL (minimum score 79 iBT), IELTS (minimum score 6.5). Electronic applications accepted.

The University of Alabama, Graduate School, Manderson Graduate School of Business, Department of Management, Tuscaloosa, AL 35487. Offers MA, MS, PhD. *Accreditation:* AACSB. *Program availability:* Part-time, evening/weekend, online learning. Terminal master's awarded for partial completion of doctoral program. *Degree requirements:* For master's, comprehensive exam (for some programs), thesis (for some programs), formal project paper; for doctorate, comprehensive exam, thesis/dissertation. *Entrance requirements:* For master's and doctorate, GMAT or GRE, minimum GPA of 3.0. *Faculty research:* Leadership, entrepreneurship, health care management, organizational behavior, strategy.

The University of Alabama, Graduate School, Manderson Graduate School of Business, Program in General Commerce and Business, Tuscaloosa, AL 35487. Offers EMBA, MBA. *Accreditation:* AACSB. *Entrance requirements:* For master's, GMAT or GRE. Additional exam requirements/recommendations for international students: Required—TOEFL (minimum score 550 paper-based). Electronic applications accepted.

The University of Alabama at Birmingham, Collat School of Business, Birmingham, AL 35294. Offers M Acct, MBA, MS, MD/MBA. MD/MBA program offered in partnership with the School of Medicine. *Accreditation:* AACSB. *Program availability:* Part-time, evening/weekend, blended/hybrid learning. *Entrance requirements:* For master's, GMAT. Additional exam requirements/recommendations for international students:

Business Administration and Management—General

Required—TOEFL (minimum score 80 iBT), IELTS (minimum score 6.5). Electronic applications accepted. *Expenses: Tuition, area resident:* Full-time $8100; part-time $8100 per year. Tuition, state resident: full-time $8100. Tuition, nonresident: full-time $19,188; part-time $19,188 per year. Tuition and fees vary according to program. *Faculty research:* Open innovation, capital markets, business to business sales and marketing, healthcare management, workplace issues, global supply chain.

The University of Alabama in Huntsville, School of Graduate Studies, College of Business Administration, Programs in Business and Management, Huntsville, AL 35899. Offers business analytics (MSMS); federal contracting and procurement management (Certificate); human resource management (MSM); management (MBA), including acquisition management, entrepreneurship, federal contract accounting, finance, human resource management, logistics and supply chain management, marketing, project management; supply chain management (Certificate); technology and innovation management (Certificate). *Accreditation:* AACSB. *Program availability:* Part-time. *Faculty:* 8 full-time (3 women). *Students:* 57 full-time (25 women), 152 part-time (76 women); includes 37 minority (20 Black or African American, non-Hispanic/Latino; 2 American Indian or Alaska Native, non-Hispanic/Latino; 6 Asian, non-Hispanic/Latino; 8 Hispanic/Latino; 1 Two or more races, non-Hispanic/Latino), 24 international. Average age 33. 178 applicants, 80% accepted, 84 enrolled. In 2018, 96 master's, 1 other advanced degree awarded. *Degree requirements:* For master's, comprehensive exam, thesis or alternative. *Entrance requirements:* For master's, GMAT (minimum score 500), minimum AACSB index of 1080. Additional exam requirements/recommendations for international students: Required—TOEFL (minimum score 550 paper-based; 80 iBT), IELTS (minimum score 6.5). *Application deadline:* For fall admission, 7/15 priority date for domestic students, 4/1 priority date for international students; for spring admission, 11/30 priority date for domestic students, 9/1 priority date for international students. Applications are processed on a rolling basis. Application fee: $50. Electronic applications accepted. *Expenses: Tuition, area resident:* Full-time $10,632; part-time $412 per credit hour. Tuition, state resident: full-time $10,632. Tuition, nonresident: full-time $23,604; part-time $412 per credit hour. *Required fees:* $582; $582. Tuition and fees vary according to course load and program. *Financial support:* In 2018–19, 15 students received support, including 15 teaching assistantships with full tuition reimbursements available (averaging $4,871 per year); research assistantships with full tuition reimbursements available, career-related internships or fieldwork, Federal Work-Study, institutionally sponsored loans, scholarships/grants, health care benefits, tuition waivers (full and partial), and unspecified assistantships also available. Support available to part-time students. Financial award application deadline: 4/1; financial award applicants required to submit FAFSA. *Faculty research:* Supply chain management, management of research and development, international marketing and branding, organizational behavior and human resource management, social networks and computational economics. *Unit head:* Dr. Fan Tseng, Chair, 256-824-6804, Fax: 256-824-6328, E-mail: fan.tseng@uah.edu. *Application contact:* Jennifer Pettitt, Director of Advising, 256-824-6681, Fax: 256-824-7571, E-mail: jennifer.pettitt@uah.edu.

University of Alaska Anchorage, College of Business and Public Policy, Program in Business Administration, Anchorage, AK 99508. Offers MBA. *Accreditation:* AACSB. *Program availability:* Part-time. *Degree requirements:* For master's, comprehensive exam, thesis (for some programs), capstone projects. *Entrance requirements:* Additional exam requirements/recommendations for international students: Required—TOEFL (minimum score 550 paper-based). *Faculty research:* Complex global environments.

University of Alaska Fairbanks, School of Management, Department of Business Administration, Fairbanks, AK 99775-6080. Offers capital markets (MBA); general management (MBA). *Accreditation:* AACSB. *Program availability:* Part-time, online only, 100% online. *Faculty:* 9 full-time (4 women). *Students:* 24 full-time (12 women), 70 part-time (42 women); includes 25 minority (2 Black or African American, non-Hispanic/Latino; 4 American Indian or Alaska Native, non-Hispanic/Latino; 5 Asian, non-Hispanic/Latino; 6 Hispanic/Latino; 8 Two or more races, non-Hispanic/Latino), 2 international. Average age 32. 50 applicants, 56% accepted, 19 enrolled. In 2018, 34 master's awarded. *Degree requirements:* For master's, comprehensive exam, thesis or alternative. *Entrance requirements:* For master's, GRE General Test, GMAT, bachelor's degree from accredited institution with minimum cumulative undergraduate and major GPA of 2.75; GRE, GMAT or alternate entrance exam (Watson Glaser) may be required depending on undergraduate GPA. Additional exam requirements/recommendations for international students: Required—TOEFL (minimum score 550 paper-based; 79 iBT), IELTS (minimum score 6.5). *Application deadline:* For fall admission, 3/1 priority date for domestic students, 2/1 for international students; for spring admission, 9/1 priority date for domestic students, 9/1 for international students. Applications are processed on a rolling basis. Application fee: $60. Electronic applications accepted. *Expenses:* School of Management (SOM) tuition has a 20% surcharge per credit hour over that for credits of most other UAF colleges. Assuming 60 credits for PhD and 32 for Master's, this augments costs by $6,180 for in-state PhD, $3,296 for in-state Master's, $12,948 for non-resident PhD and $6,912 for non-resident Masters students, respectively. *Financial support:* In 2018–19, 4 teaching assistantships with full tuition reimbursements (averaging $12,967 per year) were awarded; fellowships with full tuition reimbursements, research assistantships with full tuition reimbursements, career-related internships or fieldwork, Federal Work-Study, scholarships/grants, health care benefits, and unspecified assistantships also available. Support available to part-time students. Financial award application deadline: 2/15; financial award applicants required to submit FAFSA. *Faculty research:* Consumer behavior, marketing, international finance and business, strategic risk, organization theory. *Unit head:* Dr. Nicole Cundiff, Program Director, 907-474-7461, E-mail: uaf-som@alaska.edu. *Application contact:* Samara Taber, Director of Admissions, 907-474-7500, E-mail: uaf-admissions@alaska.edu. Website: http://www.uaf.edu/som/degrees/graduate/mba/

University of Alberta, Faculty of Graduate Studies and Research, Doctoral Program in Business, Edmonton, AB T6G 2E1, Canada. Offers accounting (PhD); finance (PhD); human resources/industrial relations (PhD); management science (PhD); marketing (PhD); organizational analysis (PhD); MBA/PhD. *Accreditation:* AACSB. *Program availability:* Part-time. *Degree requirements:* For doctorate, comprehensive exam, thesis/dissertation. *Entrance requirements:* For doctorate, GMAT. Additional exam requirements/recommendations for international students: Required—TOEFL (minimum score 550 paper-based). Electronic applications accepted. *Faculty research:* Accounting, capital markets and corporate finance, organizational change and human resource management, marketing, strategic management.

University of Alberta, Faculty of Graduate Studies and Research, Executive MBA Program, Edmonton, AB T6G 2E1, Canada. Offers Exec MBA. Program offered jointly with University of Calgary. *Accreditation:* AACSB. *Entrance requirements:* For master's, GMAT. Additional exam requirements/recommendations for international students: Required—TOEFL. Electronic applications accepted. *Expenses:* Contact institution.

University of Alberta, Faculty of Graduate Studies and Research, Program in Business Administration, Edmonton, AB T6G 2E1, Canada. Offers international business (MBA); leisure and sport management (MBA); natural resources and energy (MBA); technology commercialization (MBA); MBA/LL B; MBA/M Ag; MBA/M Eng; MBA/MF; MBA/PhD. *Accreditation:* AACSB. *Program availability:* Part-time, evening/weekend. *Degree*

requirements: For master's, thesis or alternative. *Entrance requirements:* For master's, GMAT. Additional exam requirements/recommendations for international students: Required—TOEFL (minimum score 600 paper-based). Electronic applications accepted. *Faculty research:* Natural resources and energy/management and policy/family enterprise/international business/healthcare research management.

University of Antelope Valley, Program in Business Management, Lancaster, CA 93534. Offers MS. *Degree requirements:* For master's, capstone. *Entrance requirements:* For master's, official transcripts documenting earned bachelor's degree from nationally- or regionally-accredited institution with minimum cumulative GPA of 2.0.

The University of Arizona, Eller College of Management, Tucson, AZ 85721. Offers M Ac, MA, MBA, MS, PhD, Graduate Certificate, JD/MBA. *Accreditation:* AACSB. *Program availability:* Evening/weekend. *Degree requirements:* For doctorate, thesis/dissertation. *Entrance requirements:* Additional exam requirements/recommendations for international students: Required—TOEFL (minimum score 550 paper-based; 79 iBT). Electronic applications accepted. *Expenses:* Contact institution.

University of Arkansas, Graduate School, Sam M. Walton College of Business Administration, Program in Business Administration, Fayetteville, AR 72701. Offers MBA, PhD. *Accreditation:* AACSB. *Program availability:* Part-time, evening/weekend, online learning. In 2018, 128 master's awarded. *Entrance requirements:* For master's and doctorate, GMAT. *Application deadline:* For fall admission, 8/1 for domestic students, 4/1 for international students; for spring admission, 12/1 for domestic students, 10/1 for international students; for summer admission, 4/15 for domestic students, 3/1 for international students. Application fee: $60. Electronic applications accepted. *Financial support:* In 2018–19, 23 research assistantships were awarded; fellowships with tuition reimbursements, teaching assistantships, career-related internships or fieldwork, and Federal Work-Study also available. Support available to part-time students. Financial award application deadline: 4/1; financial award applicants required to submit FAFSA. *Unit head:* Dr. Alan Ellstrand, Associate Dean for Programs and Research, 479-575-7105, E-mail: aellstra@uark.edu. *Application contact:* Mike Waldie, Director, 479-575-2851, E-mail: mwaldie@walton.uark.edu. Website: https://gsb.uark.edu/executive-mba/

University of Arkansas at Little Rock, Graduate School, College of Business, Little Rock, AR 72204-1099. Offers business administration (MBA); business information systems (MS, Graduate Certificate); management (Graduate Certificate). *Accreditation:* AACSB. *Program availability:* Part-time, evening/weekend. *Entrance requirements:* For master's, GMAT, minimum undergraduate GPA of 2.7. Additional exam requirements/recommendations for international students: Required—TOEFL (minimum score 525 paper-based).

University of Baltimore, Graduate School, Merrick School of Business, Baltimore, MD 21201-5779. Offers MBA, MS, Graduate Certificate, JD/MBA, MBA/MSN, MBA/Pharm D. *Accreditation:* AACSB. *Program availability:* Part-time, evening/weekend, online learning. *Entrance requirements:* For master's, GMAT. Additional exam requirements/recommendations for international students: Required—TOEFL (minimum score 550 paper-based). Electronic applications accepted. *Faculty research:* Finance, economics, accounting, health care, management information systems.

University of Baltimore, Joint University of Baltimore/Towson University (UB/Towson) MBA Program, Baltimore, MD 21201-5779. Offers MBA, JD/MBA, MBA/MSN, MBA/Pharm D. MBA/MSN, MBA/Pharm D offered jointly with University of Maryland, Baltimore. *Accreditation:* AACSB. *Program availability:* Part-time, evening/weekend, online learning. *Entrance requirements:* For master's, GMAT. Additional exam requirements/recommendations for international students: Required—TOEFL (minimum score 550 paper-based).

University of Bridgeport, School of Business, Bridgeport, CT 06604. Offers accounting (MBA); finance (MBA); general business (MBA); global financial services (MBA); human resource management (MBA); information systems and knowledge management (MBA); international business (MBA); management (MBA); marketing (MBA); operations management (MBA); small business and entrepreneurship (MBA); specialized business (MBA). *Accreditation:* ACBSP. *Program availability:* Part-time, evening/weekend. *Degree requirements:* For master's, thesis optional. *Entrance requirements:* For master's, GMAT. Additional exam requirements/recommendations for international students: Recommended—TOEFL (minimum score 550 paper-based; 80 iBT), IELTS (minimum score 6.5). Electronic applications accepted. *Expenses:* Contact institution.

The University of British Columbia, Sauder School of Business, Doctoral Program in Business Administration, Vancouver, BC V6T 1Z2, Canada. Offers accounting (PhD); finance (PhD); management information systems (PhD); management science (PhD); marketing (PhD); organizational behavior (PhD); strategy and business economics (PhD); transportation and logistics (PhD); urban land economics (PhD). *Degree requirements:* For doctorate, comprehensive exam, thesis/dissertation. *Entrance requirements:* For doctorate, GMAT or GRE. Additional exam requirements/recommendations for international students: Required—TOEFL (minimum score 600 paper-based; 100 iBT). Electronic applications accepted. *Expenses:* Contact institution.

The University of British Columbia, Sauder School of Business, MBA Program, Vancouver, BC V6T 1Z2, Canada. Offers IMBA, MBA. *Expenses:* Contact institution.

University of Calgary, Faculty of Graduate Studies, Haskayne School of Business, EMBA Program, Calgary, AB T2N 1N4, Canada. Offers EMBA. Program offered with School of Business at University of Alberta. *Accreditation:* AACSB. *Program availability:* Part-time. *Entrance requirements:* For master's, GMAT, minimum GPA of 3.0, minimum 7 years of work experience, 3 letters of reference. Additional exam requirements/recommendations for international students: Required—TOEFL (minimum score 600 paper-based; 100 iBT). *Expenses:* Contact institution. *Faculty research:* Accounting, data analysis and modeling, strategy, entrepreneurship, negotiations.

University of Calgary, Faculty of Graduate Studies, Haskayne School of Business, MBA Program, Calgary, AB T2N 1N4, Canada. Offers MBA, MBA/LL B, MBA/MBT, MBA/MD, MBA/MSW. *Accreditation:* AACSB. *Program availability:* Part-time, evening/weekend. *Degree requirements:* For master's, comprehensive exam, thesis optional. *Entrance requirements:* For master's, GMAT (minimum score 550), minimum GPA of 3.0, resume, 3 years of work experience, 3 letters of reference, 4 year bachelor degree. Additional exam requirements/recommendations for international students: Required—TOEFL (minimum score 600 paper-based). Electronic applications accepted. *Expenses:* Contact institution. *Faculty research:* Entrepreneurship, ethics, strategy, finance energy management and sustainability.

University of Calgary, Faculty of Graduate Studies, Haskayne School of Business, Program in Management, Calgary, AB T2N 1N4, Canada. Offers MBA, PhD. *Accreditation:* AACSB. Terminal master's awarded for partial completion of doctoral program. *Degree requirements:* For master's, one foreign language, comprehensive exam, thesis; for doctorate, one foreign language, comprehensive exam, thesis/dissertation, written and oral exams. *Entrance requirements:* For master's, GMAT, GRE, minimum GPA of 3.3 in last 2 years of course work, 2 letters of reference; for doctorate, GMAT, GRE, minimum GPA of 3.5 in last 2 years of course work, 2 letters of reference. Additional exam requirements/recommendations for international students: Required—TOEFL (minimum score 600 paper-based; 100 iBT), IELTS (minimum score 7).

Electronic applications accepted. *Faculty research:* Operations management, international business, management information systems, accounting, finance, sustainable development.

University of California, Berkeley, Graduate Division, Haas School of Business, The Berkeley MBA for Executives Program, Berkeley, CA 94720. Offers EMBA. *Accreditation:* AACSB. *Program availability:* Part-time. *Entrance requirements:* For master's, GMAT or GRE, BA or BS. Additional exam requirements/recommendations for international students: Required—TOEFL (minimum score 570 paper-based, 90 iBT) or IELTS (minimum score 7). Electronic applications accepted. *Expenses:* Contact institution.

University of California, Berkeley, Graduate Division, Haas School of Business and School of Law, Concurrent JD/MBA Program, Berkeley, CA 94720. Offers JD/MBA. *Accreditation:* AACSB; ABA. *Entrance requirements:* Additional exam requirements/ recommendations for international students: Required—TOEFL (minimum score 570 paper-based; 90 iBT). Electronic applications accepted. *Expenses:* Contact institution. *Faculty research:* Accounting, business and public policy, economic analysis and public policy, entrepreneurship, finance, management of organizations, marketing, operations and information technology management, real estate.

University of California, Berkeley, Graduate Division, Haas School of Business and School of Public Health, Concurrent MBA/MPH Program, Berkeley, CA 94720. Offers MBA/MPH. *Accreditation:* AACSB. *Entrance requirements:* Additional exam requirements/recommendations for international students: Required—TOEFL (minimum score 570 paper-based; 90 iBT); Recommended—IELTS (minimum score 7). Electronic applications accepted. *Expenses:* Contact institution. *Faculty research:* Accounting, business and public policy, economic analysis and public policy, entrepreneurship, finance, management of organizations, marketing, operations and information technology management, real estate.

University of California, Berkeley, Graduate Division, Haas School of Business, Evening and Weekend MBA Program, Berkeley, CA 94720. Offers MBA. *Accreditation:* AACSB. *Program availability:* Part-time, evening/weekend. *Degree requirements:* For master's, comprehensive exam, orientation, academic retreat, experiential learning course, 42 units of coursework. *Entrance requirements:* For master's, GMAT or GRE, BA or BS. Additional exam requirements/recommendations for international students: Required—TOEFL (minimum score 570 paper-based; 90 iBT); Recommended—IELTS (minimum score 7). Electronic applications accepted. *Expenses:* Contact institution. *Faculty research:* Accounting, business and public policy, economic analysis and public policy, finance, management of organizations, marketing, operations and information technology management, real estate.

University of California, Berkeley, Graduate Division, Haas School of Business, Full-Time MBA Program, Berkeley, CA 94720-1902. Offers MBA. *Accreditation:* AACSB. *Degree requirements:* For master's, 51 units, one experiential learning course. *Entrance requirements:* For master's, GMAT or GRE, four-year degree (BA/BS). Additional exam requirements/recommendations for international students: Required—TOEFL (minimum score 570 paper-based, 90 iBT) or IELTS (minimum score 7). Electronic applications accepted. *Expenses:* Contact institution.

University of California, Berkeley, Graduate Division, Haas School of Business, PhD in Business Administration Program, Berkeley, CA 94720. Offers accounting (PhD); business and public policy (PhD); finance (PhD); management of organizations (PhD); marketing (PhD); real estate (PhD). *Accreditation:* AACSB. *Degree requirements:* For doctorate, comprehensive exam, thesis/dissertation, written preliminary exams, oral qualifying exam. *Entrance requirements:* For doctorate, GMAT or GRE, minimum GPA of 3.0 in undergraduate and graduate coursework. Additional exam requirements/ recommendations for international students: Required—TOEFL (minimum score 570 paper-based, 70 iBT), IELTS (minimum score 7). Electronic applications accepted. *Expenses:* Contact institution. *Faculty research:* Accounting, business and public policy, entrepreneurship, finance, management of organizations, marketing, operations and information technology management, real estate.

University of California, Berkeley, UC Berkeley Extension, Certificate Programs in Business, Berkeley, CA 94720. Offers accounting (Certificate); business administration (Certificate); finance (Certificate); human resource management (Certificate); management (Certificate); marketing (Certificate); project management (Certificate). *Accreditation:* AACSB. *Program availability:* Online learning.

University of California, Berkeley, UC Berkeley Extension, International Diploma Programs, Berkeley, CA 94720. Offers business administration (Certificate); finance (Certificate); global business management (Certificate); marketing (Certificate); project management (Certificate). *Accreditation:* AACSB.

University of California, Davis, Graduate School of Management, Full-Time MBA Program, Davis, CA 95616. Offers business analytics and technologies (MBA); entrepreneurship and innovation (MBA); finance and accounting (MBA); general management (MBA); marketing (MBA); organizational behavior (MBA); public health management (MBA); strategy (MBA); technology management (MBA); DVM/MBA; JD/MBA; M Engr/MBA; MBA/MPH; MBA/MS; MD/MBA; MSN/MBA; PhD/MBA. *Faculty:* 31 full-time (10 women). *Students:* 89 full-time (35 women); includes 21 minority (1 Black or African American, non-Hispanic/Latino; 14 Asian, non-Hispanic/Latino; 6 Hispanic/Latino) 43 international. Average age 28. 290 applicants, 39% accepted, 44 enrolled. In 2018, 45 master's awarded. *Degree requirements:* For master's, comprehensive exam, integrated management project. *Entrance requirements:* For master's, GMAT or GRE, letters of recommendation, resume, essays, equivalent of a 4-year U.S. undergraduate degree, transcript. Additional exam requirements/recommendations for international students: Required—TOEFL (minimum score 600 paper-based; 100 iBT), IELTS (minimum score 7). *Application deadline:* For fall admission, 9/15 priority date for domestic and international students. Applications are processed on a rolling basis. Application fee: $125. Electronic applications accepted. *Expenses:* Contact institution. *Financial support:* In 2018–19, 85 students received support. Fellowships with full and partial tuition reimbursements available, research assistantships with partial tuition reimbursements available, teaching assistantships with partial tuition reimbursements available, institutionally sponsored loans, scholarships/grants, health care benefits, tuition waivers (partial), and unspecified assistantships available. Financial award application deadline: 3/1; financial award applicants required to submit FAFSA. *Faculty research:* Finance, marketing, management, business analytics, accounting. *Unit head:* Amanda Opperman, Assistant Dean of Student Affairs, 530-752-7658, Fax: 530-754-9355, E-mail: admissions@gsm.ucdavis.edu. *Application contact:* Andrea Shaw, Senior Director of Admissions, 530-754-5476, Fax: 530-754-9355, E-mail: admissions@gsm.ucdavis.edu.
Website: http://gsm.ucdavis.edu/daytime-mba-program

University of California, Davis, Graduate School of Management, MBA Programs in Sacramento and San Francisco Bay Area, Davis, CA 95616. Offers business analytics and technologies (MBA); entrepreneurship and innovation (MBA); finance and accounting (MBA); general management (MBA); marketing (MBA); organizational behavior (MBA); public health management (MBA); strategy (MBA); technology management (MBA). *Program availability:* Part-time-only, evening/weekend. *Faculty:* 17 full-time (7 women), 42 part-time/adjunct (11 women). *Students:* 279 part-time (107

women); includes 146 minority (12 Black or African American, non-Hispanic/Latino; 3 American Indian or Alaska Native, non-Hispanic/Latino; 102 Asian, non-Hispanic/Latino; 29 Hispanic/Latino), 24 international. Average age 30. 158 applicants, 83% accepted, 91 enrolled. In 2018, 91 master's awarded. *Degree requirements:* For master's, integrated management project. *Entrance requirements:* For master's, GMAT or GRE, letters of recommendation, resume, equivalent of a 4-year undergraduate degree. Additional exam requirements/recommendations for international students: Required—TOEFL (minimum score 600 paper-based; 100 iBT), IELTS (minimum score 7). *Application deadline:* For fall admission, 9/15 priority date for domestic and international students. Applications are processed on a rolling basis. Application fee: $125. Electronic applications accepted. *Expenses:* Contact institution. *Financial support:* In 2018–19, 89 students received support. Fellowships, teaching assistantships with partial tuition reimbursements available, scholarships/grants, and unspecified assistantships available. Support available to part-time students. Financial award application deadline: 3/1; financial award applicants required to submit FAFSA. *Faculty research:* Accounting, finance, marketing, management, business analytics. *Unit head:* Amanda Opperman, Assistant Dean of Student Affairs, 530-752-7658, Fax: 530-754-9355, E-mail: admissions@gsm.ucdavis.edu. *Application contact:* Andrea Shaw, Senior Director of Admissions, 530-754-5476, Fax: 530-754-9355, E-mail: admissions@gsm.ucdavis.edu.
Website: http://gsm.ucdavis.edu/mba-programs

University of California, Irvine, The Paul Merage School of Business, Doctoral Program in Management, Irvine, CA 92697. Offers PhD. *Students:* 54 full-time (27 women), 1 (woman) part-time; includes 10 minority (1 Black or African American, non-Hispanic/Latino; 1 American Indian or Alaska Native, non-Hispanic/Latino; 5 Asian, non-Hispanic/Latino; 2 Hispanic/Latino; 1 Native Hawaiian or other Pacific Islander, non-Hispanic/Latino), 36 international. Average age 31. 269 applicants, 4% accepted, 8 enrolled. In 2018, 7 doctorates awarded. Application fee: $105 ($125 for international students). *Unit head:* Dr. Terry Shevlin, Director, 949-824-6149, E-mail: tshevlin@uci.edu. *Application contact:* Noel Negrete, Associate Director, 949-824-8318, Fax: 949-824-1592, E-mail: nnegrete@uci.edu.
Website: http://merage.uci.edu/PhD/Default.aspx

University of California, Irvine, The Paul Merage School of Business, Executive MBA Program, Irvine, CA 92697. Offers EMBA. *Students:* 79 full-time (23 women), 5 part-time (1 woman); includes 53 minority (3 Black or African American, non-Hispanic/Latino; 3 American Indian or Alaska Native, non-Hispanic/Latino; 37 Asian, non-Hispanic/Latino; 9 Hispanic/Latino; 1 Native Hawaiian or other Pacific Islander, non-Hispanic/Latino), 3 international. Average age 41. 88 applicants, 78% accepted, 50 enrolled. In 2018, 31 master's awarded. Application fee: $105 ($125 for international students). *Unit head:* Anthony Hansford, Senior Assistant Dean, 949-824-3801, E-mail: hansfora@uci.edu. *Application contact:* Jon Masciana, Senior Director, 949-824-8595, E-mail: jmascian@uci.edu.
Website: http://merage.uci.edu/ExecutiveMBA/

University of California, Irvine, The Paul Merage School of Business, Full-Time MBA Program, Irvine, CA 92697. Offers MBA. *Students:* 140 full-time (46 women), 19 part-time (6 women); includes 65 minority (3 Black or African American, non-Hispanic/Latino; 53 Asian, non-Hispanic/Latino; 9 Hispanic/Latino), 61 international. Average age 30. 595 applicants, 25% accepted, 73 enrolled. In 2018, 86 master's awarded. Application fee: $105 ($125 for international students). *Unit head:* Jon Kaplan, Assistant Dean, 949-824-9654, E-mail: jbkaplan@uci.edu. *Application contact:* Courtney Watts, Director of Recruitment and Admissions, 949-824-0462, Fax: 949-824-2235, E-mail: courtney.elmes@uci.edu.
Website: http://merage.uci.edu/FullTimeMBA/default.aspx

University of California, Irvine, The Paul Merage School of Business, Fully Employed MBA Program, Irvine, CA 92697. Offers MBA. *Program availability:* Part-time. *Students:* 140 full-time (54 women), 199 part-time (77 women); includes 227 minority (5 Black or African American, non-Hispanic/Latino; 14 American Indian or Alaska Native, non-Hispanic/Latino; 178 Asian, non-Hispanic/Latino; 29 Hispanic/Latino; 1 Native Hawaiian or other Pacific Islander, non-Hispanic/Latino), 10 international. Average age 30. 190 applicants, 81% accepted, 96 enrolled. In 2018, 124 master's awarded. *Application deadline:* For fall admission, 7/11 for domestic students. Application fee: $105 ($125 for international students). *Unit head:* Anthony Hansford, Senior Assistant Dean, 949-824-3801, Fax: 949-824-2944, E-mail: hansfora@uci.edu. *Application contact:* Melanie Coburn, Senior Associate Director, Admissions, 949-824-7505, E-mail: mcoburn@uci.edu.
Website: http://merage.uci.edu/FullyEmployedMBA/default.aspx

University of California, Los Angeles, Graduate Division, UCLA Anderson School of Management, Los Angeles, CA 90095-1481. Offers accounting (PhD); behavioral decision making (PhD); business administration (EMBA, MBA); business administration/computer science (MBA/MSCS); business administration/latin american studies (MBA/MLAS); business administration/law (MBA/JD); business administration/library science (MBA/MLIS); business administration/medicine (MBA/MD); business administration/nursing (MBA/MN); business administration/public health (MBA/MPH); business administration/public policy (MBA/MPP); business administration/urban and regional planning (MBA/MURP); business analytics (MSBA); decisions, operations, and technology management (PhD); finance (PhD); financial engineering (MFE); global economics and management (PhD); management and organizations (PhD); marketing (PhD); strategy and policy (PhD); DDS/MBA; MBA/JD; MBA/MD; MBA/MLAS; MBA/MLIS; MBA/MN; MBA/MPH; MBA/MPP; MBA/MSCS; MBA/MURP. UCLA-NUS EMBA: UCLA Anderson and the National University of Singapore. *Accreditation:* AACSB. *Program availability:* Part-time, evening/weekend. *Faculty:* 86 full-time (19 women), 102 part-time/adjunct (16 women). *Students:* 1,040 full-time (378 women), 1,262 part-time (391 women); includes 784 minority (47 Black or African American, non-Hispanic/Latino; 1 American Indian or Alaska Native, non-Hispanic/Latino; 539 Asian, non-Hispanic/Latino; 116 Hispanic/Latino; 5 Native Hawaiian or other Pacific Islander, non-Hispanic/Latino; 76 Two or more races, non-Hispanic/Latino), 609 international. Average age 31. 6,708 applicants, 27% accepted, 949 enrolled. In 2018, 885 master's, 13 doctorates awarded. Terminal master's awarded for partial completion of doctoral program. *Degree requirements:* For master's, comprehensive exam, field consulting project (for MBA, FEMBA, EMBA, UCLA-NUS EMBA, MFE, and MSBA); internship (for MBA only); for doctorate, comprehensive exam, thesis/dissertation, oral and written qualifying exams. *Entrance requirements:* For master's, GMAT or GRE (for MBA, MFE, MSBA); Executive Assessment (EA) for candidates with 10+ years of work experience (FEMBA); Executive Assessment (EA) or STEM Master's degree or JD, MBA, CPA (EMBA), 4-year bachelor's degree or equivalent; 2 letters of recommendation; interview (invitation only); 2 essays; average 4-8 years of full-time work experience (for FEMBA); minimum 8 years of work experience with at least 3 years at management level (for EMBA); 10 years of full-time high managerial responsibility work experience (UCLA-NUS EMBA); for doctorate, GMAT or GRE, bachelor's degree from college or university of fully-recognized standing, minimum B average during junior and senior undergraduate years, 3 letters of recommendation, statement of purpose. Additional exam requirements/recommendations for international students: Required—TOEFL (minimum score 560 paper-based; 87 iBT), IELTS (minimum score 7), TOEFL with minimum iBT score of 100 (for MSBA). *Application deadline:* For fall admission, 10/2 for domestic and international

students; for winter admission, 1/8 for domestic and international students; for spring admission, 4/16 for domestic and international students. Applications are processed on a rolling basis. Application fee: $200. Electronic applications accepted. *Expenses:* Per Year - MBA: $64,292, FEMBA: $42,420, EMBA: $81,120, UCLA-NUS EMBA (UC Portion only): $57,500, MFE: $75,816, MSBA: $64,1,43, PhD: $32,049. *Financial support:* Fellowships, research assistantships with partial tuition reimbursements, teaching assistantships with partial tuition reimbursements, career-related internships or fieldwork, institutionally sponsored loans, and scholarships/grants available. Support available to part-time students. *Faculty research:* Finance/global economics, entrepreneurship, accounting, human resources/organizational behavior, marketing and behavioral decision making. *Total annual research expenditures:* $2 million. *Unit head:* Dr. Antonio Bernardo, Dean & John E. Anderson Chair in Management, 310-825-7982, Fax: 310-206-2073, E-mail: a.bernardo@anderson.ucla.edu. *Application contact:* Alex Lawrence, Assistant Dean and Director of MBA Admissions, 310-825-6944, Fax: 310-825-8582, E-mail: mba.admissions@anderson.ucla.edu.
Website: http://www.anderson.ucla.edu/

University of California, Riverside, Graduate Division, The A. Gary Anderson Graduate School of Management, Riverside, CA 92521-0102. Offers accounting (MPAC); business administration (MBA, PhD); finance (M Fin). *Accreditation:* AACSB. *Program availability:* Part-time, evening/weekend. Terminal master's awarded for partial completion of doctoral program. *Degree requirements:* For master's, thesis optional; for doctorate, comprehensive exam, thesis/dissertation. *Entrance requirements:* For master's and doctorate, GMAT or GRE. Additional exam requirements/recommendations for international students: Required—TOEFL (minimum score 550 paper-based; 80 iBT), IELTS (minimum score 7). Electronic applications accepted. *Expenses:* Contact institution. *Faculty research:* Finance, management, marketing, operations and supply chain management, accounting and information systems.

University of California, San Diego, Graduate Division, Rady School of Management, La Jolla, CA 92093. Offers business administration (MBA); business analytics (MS); finance (MF); management (PhD). *Accreditation:* AACSB. *Program availability:* Part-time, evening/weekend. *Faculty:* 28 full-time (5 women), 5 part-time/adjunct (1 woman). *Students:* 452 full-time (206 women), 158 part-time (91 women). 2,403 applicants, 34% accepted, 336 enrolled. In 2018, 297 master's, 3 doctorates awarded. *Degree requirements:* For master's, capstone project; for doctorate, comprehensive exam, thesis/dissertation. *Entrance requirements:* For master's, GMAT (for MBA); GMAT or GRE General Test (for MF and MPAC); for doctorate, GMAT or GRE General Test. Additional exam requirements/recommendations for international students: Required—TOEFL (minimum score 550 paper-based; 80 iBT), IELTS (minimum score 7). *Application deadline:* Applications are processed on a rolling basis. Application fee: $200. Electronic applications accepted. *Expenses:* Contact institution. *Financial support:* Fellowships, teaching assistantships, and scholarships/grants available. Financial award applicants required to submit FAFSA. *Faculty research:* Innovation technology, operations management, finance, behavioral economics, organizational strategy, marketing, business analytics. *Unit head:* Robert Sullivan, Dean, 858-822-0830, E-mail: rssullivan@ucsd.edu. *Application contact:* Jay Bryant, Director of Graduate Recruitment and Admissions, 858-534-0864, E-mail: radygradadmissions@ucsd.edu.
Website: http://rady.ucsd.edu/

University of Central Arkansas, Graduate School, College of Business Administration, Program in Business Administration, Conway, AR 72035-0001. Offers MBA. *Accreditation:* AACSB. *Program availability:* Part-time, evening/weekend. *Entrance requirements:* For master's, GMAT or GRE, minimum GPA of 2.7. Additional exam requirements/recommendations for international students: Required—TOEFL (minimum score 550 paper-based).

University of Central Florida, College of Business Administration, Department of Management, Orlando, FL 32816. Offers entrepreneurship (Graduate Certificate); management (MSM); technology ventures (Graduate Certificate). *Accreditation:* AACSB. *Program availability:* Part-time. *Students:* 95 part-time (45 women); includes 43 minority (11 Black or African American, non-Hispanic/Latino; 10 Asian, non-Hispanic/Latino; 17 Hispanic/Latino; 5 Two or more races, non-Hispanic/Latino). Average age 30. 66 applicants, 79% accepted, 41 enrolled. In 2018, 15 master's, 16 other advanced degrees awarded. *Entrance requirements:* For master's, GMAT, minimum GPA of 3.0 in last 60 hours, letters of recommendation, resume, goal statement. Additional exam requirements/recommendations for international students: Required—TOEFL. *Application deadline:* For fall admission, 6/15 for domestic students; for spring admission, 11/15 for domestic students. Application fee: $30. Electronic applications accepted. *Financial support:* Fellowships available. Financial award application deadline: 3/1; financial award applicants required to submit FAFSA. *Unit head:* Dr. Stephen Goodman, Chair, 407-823-2675, Fax: 407-823-3725, E-mail: sgoodman@ucf.edu. *Application contact:* Associate Director, Graduate Admissions, 407-823-2766, Fax: 407-823-6442, E-mail: gradadmissions@ucf.edu.
Website: http://business.ucf.edu/departments-schools/management/

University of Central Florida, College of Business Administration, Program in Business Administration, Orlando, FL 32816. Offers MBA, PhD. *Accreditation:* AACSB. *Program availability:* Part-time, evening/weekend. *Students:* 136 full-time (65 women), 533 part-time (254 women); includes 287 minority (70 Black or African American, non-Hispanic/Latino; 47 Asian, non-Hispanic/Latino; 161 Hispanic/Latino; 9 Two or more races, non-Hispanic/Latino), 35 international. Average age 31. 645 applicants, 51% accepted, 269 enrolled. In 2018, 269 master's, 5 doctorates awarded. *Degree requirements:* For master's, capstone course; for doctorate, comprehensive exam, thesis/dissertation, departmental candidacy exam. *Entrance requirements:* For master's and doctorate, GMAT, minimum GPA of 3.0 in last 60 hours, letters of recommendation, goal statement, resume. Additional exam requirements/recommendations for international students: Required—TOEFL. *Application deadline:* For fall admission, 7/1 for domestic students. Application fee: $30. Electronic applications accepted. *Financial support:* In 2018–19, 42 students received support, including 6 fellowships with partial tuition reimbursements available (averaging $8,167 per year), 58 teaching assistantships with partial tuition reimbursements available (averaging $12,411 per year); career-related internships or fieldwork, Federal Work-Study, institutionally sponsored loans, health care benefits, tuition waivers (partial), and unspecified assistantships also available. Financial award application deadline: 3/1; financial award applicants required to submit FAFSA. *Unit head:* Dr. Paul Jarley, Dean, 407-823-5113, E-mail: pjarley@bus.ucf.edu. *Application contact:* Associate Director, Graduate Admissions, 407-823-2766, Fax: 407-823-6442, E-mail: gradadmissions@ucf.edu.
Website: http://www.bus.ucf.edu

University of Central Missouri, The Graduate School, Warrensburg, MO 64093. Offers accountancy (MA); accounting (MBA); applied mathematics (MS); aviation safety (MA); biology (MS); business administration (MBA); career and technical education leadership (MS); college student personnel administration (MS); communication (MA); computer science (MS); counseling (MS); criminal justice (MS); educational leadership (Ed D); educational technology (MS); elementary and early childhood education (MSE); English (MA); environmental studies (MA); finance (MBA); history (MA); human services/educational technology (Ed S); human services/learning resources (Ed S); human services/professional counseling (Ed S); industrial hygiene (MS); industrial management (MS); information systems (MBA); information technology (MS); kinesiology (MS); library science and information services (MS); literacy education (MSE); marketing (MBA); mathematics (MS); music (MA); occupational safety management (MS); psychology (MS); rural family nursing (MS); school administration (MSE); social gerontology (MS); sociology (MA); special education (MSE); speech language pathology (MS); superintendency (Ed S); teaching (MAT); teaching English as a second language (MA); technology (MS); technology management (PhD); theatre (MA). *Accreditation:* ASHA. *Program availability:* Part-time, 100% online, blended/hybrid learning. *Degree requirements:* For master's and Ed S, comprehensive exam (for some programs), thesis (for some programs). *Entrance requirements:* Additional exam requirements/recommendations for international students: Required—TOEFL (minimum score 550 paper-based; 79 iBT). Electronic applications accepted.

University of Charleston, Master of Business Administration Program, Charleston, WV 25304-1099. Offers MBA. *Program availability:* Part-time, evening/weekend. *Entrance requirements:* Additional exam requirements/recommendations for international students: Required—TOEFL, IELTS. Electronic applications accepted.

University of Chicago, Booth School of Business, Doctoral Program in Business, Chicago, IL 60637-1513. Offers PhD. *Accreditation:* AACSB. *Entrance requirements:* For doctorate, GMAT or GRE (for most areas of study), transcripts, resume, two letters of reference, essays. Additional exam requirements/recommendations for international students: Required—TOEFL or IELTS. Electronic applications accepted. *Expenses:* Contact institution.

University of Chicago, Booth School of Business, Full-Time MBA Program, Chicago, IL 60637. Offers accounting (MBA); analytic finance (MBA); analytic management (MBA); econometrics and statistics (MBA); economics (MBA); entrepreneurship (MBA); finance (MBA); general management (MBA); health administration and policy (Certificate); international business (MBA); managerial and organizational behavior (MBA); marketing analytics (MBA); marketing management (MBA); operations management (MBA); strategic management (MBA); MBA/AM; MBA/JD; MBA/MA; MBA/MD; MBA/MPP. *Accreditation:* AACSB. *Entrance requirements:* For master's, GMAT or GRE, transcripts, resume, 2 letters of recommendation, essays, interview. Additional exam requirements/recommendations for international students: Required—TOEFL, IELTS, or PTE. Electronic applications accepted. *Expenses:* Contact institution.

University of Chicago, Booth School of Business, Part-Time Evening and Weekend MBA Programs, Chicago, IL 60611. Offers MBA. *Accreditation:* AACSB. *Program availability:* Part-time-only, evening/weekend. *Entrance requirements:* For master's, GMAT or GRE, transcripts, resume, 2 letters of recommendation, essay, interview. Additional exam requirements/recommendations for international students: Required—TOEFL or IELTS. Electronic applications accepted. *Expenses:* Contact institution.

University of Cincinnati, Carl H. Lindner College of Business, MBA Program, Cincinnati, OH 45221. Offers MBA. *Accreditation:* AACSB. *Program availability:* Part-time, evening/weekend, 100% online, blended/hybrid learning. *Faculty:* 117 full-time (37 women), 32 part-time/adjunct (4 women). *Students:* 42 full-time (19 women), 104 part-time (54 women); includes 27 minority (14 Black or African American, non-Hispanic/Latino; 8 Asian, non-Hispanic/Latino; 3 Hispanic/Latino; 1 Native Hawaiian or other Pacific Islander, non-Hispanic/Latino; 1 Two or more races, non-Hispanic/Latino), 14 international. Average age 31. 427 applicants, 50% accepted, 146 enrolled. In 2018, 217 master's awarded. *Degree requirements:* For master's, capstone project. *Entrance requirements:* For master's, GMAT or GRE, resume, letters of recommendation, essays, official transcripts. Additional exam requirements/recommendations for international students: Required—TOEFL (minimum score 577 paper-based; 90 iBT), IELTS (minimum score 6.5). *Application deadline:* For fall admission, 6/30 priority date for domestic students, 3/15 for international students; for spring admission, 12/15 for domestic students, 9/15 for international students; for summer admission, 4/15 for domestic and international students. Applications are processed on a rolling basis. Application fee: $65 ($70 for international students). Electronic applications accepted. *Expenses:* Full-time resident $10,479 per term, full-time non resident $14,398 per term, part-time $890 per credit hour. *Financial support:* In 2018–19, 61 students received support. Scholarships/grants, tuition waivers (full and partial), and unspecified assistantships available. Financial award application deadline: 3/15; financial award applicants required to submit FAFSA. *Faculty research:* Business analytics, financial management, organizational behavior, financial accounting, consumer insights. *Total annual research expenditures:* $39,943. *Unit head:* Dr. Marianne Lewis, Dean, 513-556-7001, Fax: 513-556-4891, E-mail: marianne.lewis@uc.edu. *Application contact:* Dona Clary, Executive Director, Graduate Programs, 513-556-3546, Fax: 513-558-7006, E-mail: dona.clary@uc.edu.
Website: http://business.uc.edu/graduate/mba.html

University of Cincinnati, Carl H. Lindner College of Business, PhD Programs, Cincinnati, OH 45221. Offers accounting (PhD); business analytics (PhD); economics (PhD); finance (PhD); information systems (PhD); management (PhD); marketing (PhD); operations and business analytics (PhD); operations research (PhD). *Faculty:* 101 full-time (37 women). *Students:* 15 full-time (5 women), 10 part-time (4 women); includes 4 minority (1 Black or African American, non-Hispanic/Latino; 3 Asian, non-Hispanic/Latino), 20 international. Average age 31. 125 applicants, 12% accepted, 4 enrolled. In 2018, 7 doctorates awarded. *Degree requirements:* For doctorate, comprehensive exam, thesis/dissertation. *Entrance requirements:* For doctorate, GMAT, GRE, transcripts, essays, resume, letters of recommendation. Additional exam requirements/recommendations for international students: Required—TOEFL (minimum score 600 paper-based; 100 iBT), IELTS (minimum score 7). *Application deadline:* For fall admission, 1/15 for domestic and international students. Application fee: $65 ($70 for international students). Electronic applications accepted. *Expenses:* Contact institution. *Financial support:* In 2018–19, 35 students received support, including 25 research assistantships with full tuition reimbursements available (averaging $23,250 per year); scholarships/grants, health care benefits, tuition waivers (full), and unspecified assistantships also available. Financial award application deadline: 1/15; financial award applicants required to submit FAFSA. *Faculty research:* Bayesian Prediction Theory, organizational fairness, consumer insight and market research, consumer insight and market research, density estimation from correlated data. *Unit head:* Dr. Olivier Parent, Director, 513-556-3941, Fax: 513-556-5499, E-mail: olivier.parent@uc.edu. *Application contact:* Angel Elvin, Assistant Director, 513-556-7190, Fax: 513-558-7006, E-mail: angel.elvin@uc.edu.
Website: http://business.uc.edu/graduate/phd.html

University of Colorado Boulder, Leeds School of Business, MBA Program, Boulder, CO 80309. Offers MBA. *Accreditation:* AACSB. *Entrance requirements:* For master's, GMAT, minimum undergraduate GPA of 2.75. Electronic applications accepted. Application fee is waived when completed online.

University of Colorado Boulder, Leeds School of Business, MS and PhD Programs, Boulder, CO 80309. Offers MS, PhD. *Entrance requirements:* For master's, GMAT, minimum undergraduate GPA of 3.0. Electronic applications accepted. Application fee is waived when completed online.

University of Colorado Colorado Springs, College of Business, Colorado Springs, CO 80918. Offers MBA, MSA. *Accreditation:* AACSB. *Program availability:* Part-time,

evening/weekend, 100% online, blended/hybrid learning. *Faculty:* 43 full-time (14 women), 85 part-time/adjunct (29 women). *Students:* 63 full-time (28 women), 304 part-time (140 women); includes 94 minority (12 Black or African American, non-Hispanic/Latino; 1 American Indian or Alaska Native, non-Hispanic/Latino; 16 Asian, non-Hispanic/Latino; 46 Hispanic/Latino; 19 Two or more races, non-Hispanic/Latino), 9 international. Average age 34. 161 applicants, 77% accepted, 92 enrolled. In 2018, 83 master's awarded. *Entrance requirements:* For master's, GRE or GMAT is recommended but may be waived in certain instances related to prior work experience, military experience, or prior educational experience., A goal statement addressing your interest in the program is required for all applicants. Additional exam requirements/recommendations for international students: Recommended—TOEFL (minimum score 85 iBT). *Application deadline:* For fall admission, 6/1 priority date for domestic students, 6/1 for international students; for spring admission, 11/1 priority date for domestic students, 11/1 for international students; for summer admission, 4/1 priority date for domestic students, 4/1 for international students. Applications are processed on a rolling basis. Application fee: $60 ($100 for international students). Electronic applications accepted. *Expenses:* Program tuition and fees vary by course load and residency classification. Please visit the University of Colorado Colorado Springs Student Financial Services website to see current program costs: https://www.uccs.edu/bursar/index.php/estimate-your-bill. *Financial support:* In 2018–19, 6 students received support. Career-related internships or fieldwork, Federal Work-Study, scholarships/grants, and unspecified assistantships available. Support available to part-time students. Financial award application deadline: 3/1; financial award applicants required to submit FAFSA. *Faculty research:* Management information systems, marketing science, organizational behavior and human decision processes, accounting. *Total annual research expenditures:* $50,873. *Unit head:* Dr. Eric Olson, Interim Dean, 719-255-3113, Fax: 719-255-3100, E-mail: eolson@uccs.edu. *Application contact:* Janice Dowsett, Director of Graduate Programs, 719-255-3070, E-mail: cobgrad@uccs.edu.
Website: https://www.uccs.edu/business/programs/masters

University of Colorado Denver, Business School, Master of Business Administration Program, Denver, CO 80217. Offers business administration (MBA); health administration (MBA). *Accreditation:* AACSB. *Program availability:* Part-time, evening/weekend, 100% online, blended/hybrid learning. *Degree requirements:* For master's, 48 semester hours, including 30 of core courses, 3 in international business, and 15 in electives from over 50 other business courses. *Entrance requirements:* For master's, GMAT, resume, official transcripts, essay, two letters of recommendation, financial statements (for international applicants). Additional exam requirements/recommendations for international students: Required—TOEFL (minimum score 560 paper-based; 83 iBT); Recommended—IELTS (minimum score 6.5). Electronic applications accepted. *Expenses:* Contact institution. *Faculty research:* Marketing, management, entrepreneurship, finance, health administration.

University of Colorado Denver, Business School, Program in Management and Organization, Denver, CO 80217. Offers business strategy (MS); change and innovation (MS); enterprise technology management (MS); entrepreneurship and innovation (MS); global management (MS); leadership (MS); managing for sustainability (MS); managing human resources (MS); sports and entertainment (MS); strategic management (MS). *Accreditation:* AACSB. *Program availability:* Part-time, evening/weekend, online learning. *Degree requirements:* For master's, 30 semester hours (12 of required courses, 12 of management electives, and 6 of free electives). *Entrance requirements:* For master's, GMAT, resume, two letters of recommendation, essay, financial statements (for international applicants). Additional exam requirements/recommendations for international students: Required—TOEFL (minimum score 525 paper-based; 71 iBT); Recommended—IELTS (minimum score 6.5). Electronic applications accepted. *Expenses:* Contact institution. *Faculty research:* Human resource management, management of catastrophe, turnaround strategies.

University of Connecticut, Graduate School, School of Business, Storrs, CT 06269. Offers accounting (MS, PhD); business (PhD); business administration (MBA); business analytics and project management (MS); finance (PhD); financial risk management (MS); health care management and insurance studies (MBA); human resource management (MS); management (PhD); management consulting (MBA); marketing (PhD); marketing intelligence (MBA); operations and information management (PhD). *Accreditation:* AACSB. *Degree requirements:* For master's, comprehensive exam; for doctorate, thesis/dissertation. *Entrance requirements:* For master's and doctorate, GMAT. Additional exam requirements/recommendations for international students: Required—TOEFL (minimum score 550 paper-based). Electronic applications accepted.

University of Dallas, Satish and Yasmin Gupta College of Business, Irving, TX 75062. Offers accounting (MBA, MS); business administration (DBA); business analytics (MS); business management (MBA); corporate finance (MBA); cybersecurity (MS); finance (MS); financial services (MBA); global business (MBA, MS); health services management (MBA); human resource management (MBA); information and technology management (MS); information assurance (MBA); information technology (MBA); information technology service management (MBA); marketing management (MBA); organization development (MBA); project management (MBA); sports and entertainment management (MBA); strategic leadership (MBA); supply chain management (MBA). *Accreditation:* AACSB. *Program availability:* Part-time, evening/weekend, 100% online. *Students:* 147 full-time (56 women), 584 part-time (232 women); includes 402 minority (204 Black or African American, non-Hispanic/Latino; 95 Asian, non-Hispanic/Latino; 92 Hispanic/Latino; 2 Native Hawaiian or other Pacific Islander, non-Hispanic/Latino; 9 Two or more races, non-Hispanic/Latino), 113 international. Average age 34, 992 applicants, 30% accepted, 157 enrolled. In 2018, 336 master's, 5 doctorates awarded. *Degree requirements:* For doctorate, thesis/dissertation. *Entrance requirements:* For master's and doctorate, U.S. bachelor's degree with a minimum cumulative GPA of 2.0 from a regionally accredited college or university (or comparable foreign degree); minimum 3.0 GPA in any graduate-level coursework completed; good academic standing with all colleges attended. Additional exam requirements/recommendations for international students: Required—TOEFL (minimum score 80 iBT), IELTS (minimum score 6.5), PTE (minimum score 67). *Application deadline:* Applications are processed on a rolling basis. Application fee: $50. Electronic applications accepted. *Expenses:* $1250 per credit hour. *Financial support:* In 2018–19, 291 students received support. Research assistantships, teaching assistantships, scholarships/grants, and unspecified assistantships available. Support available to part-time students. Financial award application deadline: 2/15; financial award applicants required to submit FAFSA. *Unit head:* Brett J.L. Landry, Dean, 972-721-5356, E-mail: blandry@udallas.edu. *Application contact:* Breonna Collins, Director, Graduate Admissions, 972-7215304, E-mail: bcollins@udallas.edu. Website: http://www.udallas.edu/cob/

University of Dayton, School of Business Administration, Dayton, OH 45469. Offers accounting (MBA); cyber security (MBA); finance (MBA); marketing (MBA); JD/MBA. *Accreditation:* AACSB. *Program availability:* Part-time, evening/weekend, blended/hybrid learning. *Entrance requirements:* For master's, GMAT (minimum score of 500 total, 19 verbal); GRE (minimum score of 149 verbal, 146 quantitative), minimum GPA of 3.0, current resume. Additional exam requirements/recommendations for international students: Required—TOEFL (minimum score 550 paper-based; 80 iBT); Recommended—IELTS (minimum score 6.5). Electronic applications accepted.

Expenses: Contact institution. *Faculty research:* Management information systems, economics, finance, marketing, entrepreneurship, accounting, cyber security, analytics.

University of Delaware, Alfred Lerner College of Business and Economics, Program in Business Administration, Newark, DE 19716. Offers MBA, MA/MBA, MBA/MIB, MBA/MS. *Accreditation:* AACSB. *Program availability:* Part-time, evening/weekend. *Entrance requirements:* For master's, GMAT, 2 letters of recommendation, resume. Additional exam requirements/recommendations for international students: Required—TOEFL (minimum score 600 paper-based; 79 iBT). Electronic applications accepted. *Expenses:* Contact institution. *Faculty research:* Finance, corporate governance, information systems, leadership, marketing.

University of Delaware, College of Agriculture and Natural Resources, Department of Entomology and Wildlife Ecology, Newark, DE 19716. Offers entomology and applied ecology (MS, PhD), including avian ecology, evolution and taxonomy, insect biological control, insect ecology and behavior (MS), insect genetics, pest management, plant-insect interactions, wildlife ecology and management. *Program availability:* Part-time. *Degree requirements:* For master's, comprehensive exam, thesis, oral exam, seminar; for doctorate, comprehensive exam, thesis/dissertation, qualifying exam, seminar. *Entrance requirements:* For master's, GRE General Test, minimum GPA of 3.0 in field, 2.8 overall; for doctorate, GRE General Test, GRE Subject Test (biology), minimum GPA of 3.0 in field, 2.8 overall. Additional exam requirements/recommendations for international students: Required—TOEFL. Electronic applications accepted. *Faculty research:* Ecology and evolution of plant-insect interactions, ecology of wildlife conservation management, habitat restoration, biological control, applied ecosystem management.

University of Denver, Daniels College of Business, Denver, CO 80208. Offers M Acc, MBA, MS. *Accreditation:* AACSB. *Program availability:* Part-time, evening/weekend, online learning. *Faculty:* 107 full-time (40 women), 36 part-time/adjunct (9 women). *Students:* 305 full-time (125 women), 460 part-time (197 women); includes 130 minority (12 Black or African American, non-Hispanic/Latino; 1 American Indian or Alaska Native, non-Hispanic/Latino; 20 Asian, non-Hispanic/Latino; 73 Hispanic/Latino; 2 Native Hawaiian or other Pacific Islander, non-Hispanic/Latino; 22 Two or more races, non-Hispanic/Latino), 98 international. Average age 32. 1,185 applicants, 63% accepted, 376 enrolled. In 2018, 406 master's awarded. *Entrance requirements:* For master's, GRE General Test or GMAT, bachelor's degree, transcripts, essays, resume, interview. Additional exam requirements/recommendations for international students: Required—TOEFL (minimum score 575 paper-based; 94 iBT). *Application deadline:* For fall admission, 10/15 priority date for domestic and international students; for spring admission, 9/15 priority date for domestic and international students. Applications are processed on a rolling basis. Application fee: $100. Electronic applications accepted. *Expenses:* $49,695 per year full-time; $1,372 per credit. *Financial support:* In 2018–19, 412 students received support. Teaching assistantships, career-related internships or fieldwork, Federal Work-Study, institutionally sponsored loans, scholarships/grants, and unspecified assistantships available. Support available to part-time students. Financial award application deadline: 2/15; financial award applicants required to submit FAFSA. *Faculty research:* Corporate governance, decision making, emerging economies, ethics, leadership. *Unit head:* Dr. Vivek Choudhury, Dean, 303-871-3411, E-mail: vivek.choudhury@du.edu. *Application contact:* Information Contact, 303-732-6186, E-mail: daniels@du.edu.
Website: http://daniels.du.edu/

University of Detroit Mercy, College of Business Administration, Detroit, MI 48221. Offers business administration (MBA); business fundamentals (Certificate); business turnaround management (Certificate); ethical leadership and change management (Certificate); finance (Certificate); forensic accounting (Certificate); JD/MBA; MBA/MHSA. *Program availability:* Part-time, evening/weekend, 100% online, blended/hybrid learning. *Entrance requirements:* For master's, GMAT, resume, letter of recommendation, transcripts; for Certificate, resume, letter of recommendation, transcripts. Electronic applications accepted. Application fee is waived when completed online. *Expenses:* Contact institution. *Faculty research:* Ethics, international finance, trade policy, leadership, information technology.

University of Dubuque, Program in Business Administration, Dubuque, IA 52001-5099. Offers MBA. *Program availability:* Part-time, evening/weekend. *Entrance requirements:* For master's, 2 letters of recommendation. Electronic applications accepted.

University of Fairfax, Graduate Programs, Vienna, VA 22182. Offers business administration (DBA); computer science (MCS); cybersecurity (MBA, MS); general business administration (MBA); information technology (MBA); project management (MBA).

The University of Findlay, Office of Graduate Admissions, Findlay, OH 45840-3653. Offers applied security and analytics (MSAS); athletic training (MAT); business (MBA), including certified management accountant, certified public accountant, health care management, hospitality management; education (MA Ed, Ed D), including children's literature (MA Ed), curriculum and teaching (MA Ed), education (MA Ed), educational administration (MA Ed), human resource development (MA Ed), mathematics (MA Ed), reading (MA Ed), science education (MA Ed), superintendent (Ed D), teaching (Ed D), technology (MA Ed); environmental, safety, and health management (MSEM); health informatics (MS); occupational therapy (MOT); pharmacy (Pharm D); physical therapy (DPT); physician assistant (MPA); rhetoric and writing (MA); teaching English to speakers of other languages (TESOL) and applied linguistics (MA). *Program availability:* Part-time, evening/weekend, 100% online, blended/hybrid learning. *Degree requirements:* For master's, comprehensive exam (for some programs), thesis (for some programs), cumulative project, capstone project; for doctorate, thesis/dissertation (for some programs). *Entrance requirements:* For master's, GRE/GMAT, bachelor's degree from accredited institution, minimum undergraduate GPA of 2.5 in last 64 hours of course work; for doctorate, GRE, MAT, minimum cumulative GPA of 3.0. Additional exam requirements/recommendations for international students: Required—TOEFL (minimum score 79 iBT), IELTS (minimum score 7), PTE (minimum score 61). Electronic applications accepted.

University of Florida, Graduate School, Warrington College of Business Administration, Hough Graduate School of Business, Department of Management, Gainesville, FL 32611. Offers health care risk management (MS); international business (MA); management (MS, PhD). *Accreditation:* AACSB. *Program availability:* Online learning. *Degree requirements:* For master's, comprehensive exam, thesis. *Entrance requirements:* For master's, GMAT (minimum score of 465) or GRE General Test, minimum GPA of 3.0. Additional exam requirements/recommendations for international students: Required—TOEFL (minimum score 550 paper-based; 80 iBT), IELTS (minimum score 6). Electronic applications accepted. *Faculty research:* Job attitudes, personality and individual differences, organizational entry and exit, knowledge management, competitive dynamics.

University of Florida, Graduate School, Warrington College of Business Administration, Hough Graduate School of Business, Programs in Business Administration, Gainesville, FL 32611. Offers business administration (MA, MS, PhD); competitive strategy (MBA); finance (MBA); global management (MBA); Graham-Buffett security analysis (MBA); human resource management (MBA); information systems and

operations management (MBA); international studies (MBA); management (MBA); real estate (MBA); JD/MBA; MBA/MS; MBA/PhD; MBA/Pharm D; MD/MBA. *Accreditation:* AACSB. *Program availability:* Part-time, evening/weekend, online learning. *Degree requirements:* For master's, capstone course. *Entrance requirements:* For master's and doctorate, GMAT (minimum score 465), minimum GPA of 3.0, interview. Additional exam requirements/recommendations for international students: Required—TOEFL (minimum score 550 paper-based; 80 iBT), IELTS (minimum score 6). Electronic applications accepted. *Faculty research:* Accounting, finance, insurance, management, real estate, urban analysis marketing.

University of Georgia, Terry College of Business, Program in Business Administration, Athens, GA 30602. Offers Exec MBA, MBA. *Accreditation:* AACSB. *Degree requirements:* For master's, thesis (MA). *Entrance requirements:* For master's, GMAT (for MBA), GRE General Test (for MA). Electronic applications accepted.

University of Guam, Office of Graduate Studies, School of Business and Public Administration, Business Administration Program, Mangilao, GU 96923. Offers PMBA. *Entrance requirements:* For master's, GMAT. Additional exam requirements/recommendations for international students: Required—TOEFL.

University of Guelph, Office of Graduate and Postdoctoral Studies, College of Management and Economics, Guelph, ON N1G 2W1, Canada. Offers M Sc, MA, MBA, PhD.

University of Hartford, Barney School of Business, Program in Business Administration, West Hartford, CT 06117-1599. Offers MBA, MBA/M Eng. *Accreditation:* AACSB. *Program availability:* Part-time, evening/weekend. *Entrance requirements:* For master's, GMAT, 2 letters of recommendation, resume. Additional exam requirements/recommendations for international students: Required—TOEFL (minimum score 550 paper-based). Electronic applications accepted.

University of Hartford, College of Education, Nursing, and Health Professions, Program in Nursing, West Hartford, CT 06117-1599. Offers community/public health nursing (MSN); nursing education (MSN); nursing management (MSN). *Accreditation:* AACN. *Program availability:* Part-time, evening/weekend. *Degree requirements:* For master's, research project. *Entrance requirements:* For master's, BSN, Connecticut RN license. Additional exam requirements/recommendations for international students: Required—TOEFL (minimum score 550 paper-based). Electronic applications accepted. *Expenses:* Contact institution. *Faculty research:* Child development, women in doctoral study, applying feminist theory in teaching methods, near death experience, grandmothers as primary care providers.

University of Hawaii at Manoa, Office of Graduate Education, Shidler College of Business, Executive MBA Programs, Honolulu, HI 96822. Offers executive business administration (EMBA); Vietnam focused business administration (EMBA). *Accreditation:* AACSB. *Program availability:* Part-time. *Entrance requirements:* For master's, GMAT, minimum GPA of 3.0.

University of Hawaii at Manoa, Office of Graduate Education, Shidler College of Business, Program in Business Administration, Honolulu, HI 96822. Offers Asian business studies (MBA); Chinese business studies (MBA); decision sciences (MBA); entrepreneurship (MBA); finance (MBA); finance and banking (MBA); human resources management (MBA); information management (MBA); information technology (MBA); international business (MBA); Japanese business studies (MBA); marketing (MBA); organizational behavior (MBA); organizational management (MBA); real estate (MBA); student-designed track (MBA). *Accreditation:* AACSB. *Program availability:* Part-time, evening/weekend. *Degree requirements:* For master's, thesis optional. *Entrance requirements:* For master's, GMAT, minimum GPA of 3.0. Additional exam requirements/recommendations for international students: Required—TOEFL (minimum score 600 paper-based; 100 iBT), IELTS (minimum score 7). *Expenses:* Contact institution.

University of Holy Cross, Graduate Programs, New Orleans, LA 70131-7399. Offers biomedical sciences (MS); Catholic theology (MA); counseling (MA, PhD), including community counseling (MA), marriage and family counseling (MA), school counseling (MA); educational leadership (M Ed); executive leadership (Ed D); management (MS), including healthcare management, operations management; teaching and learning (M Ed). *Accreditation:* ACA; NCATE. *Program availability:* Part-time, evening/weekend, online learning. *Degree requirements:* For master's, thesis. *Entrance requirements:* For master's, GRE General Test, minimum GPA of 2.7.

University of Houston, Bauer College of Business, Houston, TX 77204. Offers MBA, MS, MS Accy, PhD. *Accreditation:* AACSB. *Program availability:* Part-time, evening/weekend. *Degree requirements:* For master's, 30 hours completed in residence, minimum cumulative GPA of 3.0 at UH, no more than 11 semester hours of 'C' grades or below in graduate courses taken at UH; for doctorate, comprehensive exam, thesis/dissertation, minimum GPA of 3.25, continuous full time enrollment, dissertation defense within 6 years of entering the program. *Entrance requirements:* For master's, GMAT or GRE (MBA), official transcripts from all higher education institutions attended, resume, letters of recommendation, self appraisal and goal statement (MBA); for doctorate, GMAT or GRE, letter of financial backing, statement of understanding, reference letters, statement of academic and research interests. Additional exam requirements/recommendations for international students: Required—TOEFL (minimum score 603 paper-based; 100 iBT), IELTS (minimum score 6.5), PTE (minimum score 70). Electronic applications accepted. *Faculty research:* Accountancy and taxation, finance, international business, management.

University of Houston–Clear Lake, School of Business, Program in Business Administration, Houston, TX 77058-1002. Offers MBA. *Accreditation:* AACSB. *Program availability:* Part-time, evening/weekend. *Degree requirements:* For master's, thesis optional. *Entrance requirements:* For master's, GMAT. Additional exam requirements/recommendations for international students: Required—TOEFL (minimum score 550 paper-based). Electronic applications accepted.

University of Houston–Downtown, Marilyn Davies College of Business, MBA Program, Houston, TX 77002. Offers accounting (MBA); finance (MBA); human resource management (MBA); international business (MBA); investment management (MBA); leadership (MBA); project management and process improvement (MBA); sales management and business development (MBA); supply chain management (MBA). *Accreditation:* AACSB. *Program availability:* Part-time, evening/weekend. *Entrance requirements:* For master's, GMAT, two letters of recommendation from professional references, personal statement, resume. Additional exam requirements/recommendations for international students: Required—TOEFL (minimum score 81 iBT). Electronic applications accepted. *Expenses:* Contact institution.

University of Houston–Victoria, School of Business Administration, Victoria, TX 77901-4450. Offers accounting (MBA); economic development and entrepreneurship (MS); finance (GMBA, MBA); general business (MBA); international business (MBA); management (GMBA, MBA); marketing (MBA). *Accreditation:* AACSB. *Program availability:* Part-time, evening/weekend, online learning. *Entrance requirements:* For master's, GMAT. Additional exam requirements/recommendations for international students: Required—TOEFL (minimum score 550 paper-based). Electronic applications accepted. *Expenses: Tuition, area resident:* Full-time $6154; part-time $3077 per semester. Tuition, state resident: full-time $6154; part-time $3077 per semester. Tuition, nonresident: full-time $13,624; part-time $6812 per semester. *International tuition:* $13,624 full-time. *Required fees:* $1405; $847 per semester. $423 per semester. Tuition and fees vary according to program. *Faculty research:* Economic development, marketing, finance.

University of Idaho, College of Graduate Studies, College of Business and Economics, Department of Business and Economics, Moscow, ID 83844-2282. Offers general management (MBA). *Faculty:* 6 full-time. *Students:* 16 full-time (8 women). Average age 41. *Entrance requirements:* For master's, minimum GPA of 3.0. Additional exam requirements/recommendations for international students: Required—TOEFL (minimum score 100 iBT). *Application deadline:* For fall admission, 8/1 for domestic students. Applications are processed on a rolling basis. Application fee: $60. Electronic applications accepted. *Expenses:* Tuition, state resident: full-time $7266.44; part-time $474.50 per credit hour. Tuition, nonresident: full-time $24,902; part-time $1453.50 per credit hour. *Required fees:* $2085.56; $45.50 per credit hour. *Financial support:* Applicants required to submit FAFSA. *Unit head:* Dr. John Lawrence, EMBA Academic Director, 208-885-0555, E-mail: emba@uidaho.edu. *Application contact:* Dr. John Lawrence, EMBA Academic Director, 208-885-0555, E-mail: emba@uidaho.edu.
Website: http://www.uidaho.edu/cbe

University of Illinois at Chicago, Liautaud Graduate School of Business, Program in Business Administration, Chicago, IL 60607-7128. Offers MBA, PhD, MBA/MA, MBA/MD, MBA/MPH, MBA/MS. *Accreditation:* AACSB. *Program availability:* Part-time. *Entrance requirements:* For master's, GMAT, minimum GPA of 2.75; for doctorate, GMAT. Additional exam requirements/recommendations for international students: Required—TOEFL. Electronic applications accepted. *Expenses:* Contact institution.

University of Illinois at Springfield, Graduate Programs, College of Business and Management, Program in Business Administration, Springfield, IL 62703-5407. Offers MBA. *Accreditation:* AACSB. *Program availability:* Part-time, evening/weekend. *Faculty:* 15 full-time (5 women), 2 part-time/adjunct (1 woman). *Students:* 45 full-time (19 women), 37 part-time (16 women); includes 12 minority (4 Black or African American, non-Hispanic/Latino; 4 Asian, non-Hispanic/Latino; 2 Hispanic/Latino; 2 Two or more races, non-Hispanic/Latino), 15 international. Average age 32. 96 applicants, 42% accepted, 24 enrolled. In 2018, 45 master's awarded. *Degree requirements:* For master's, closure course with minimum grade of B. *Entrance requirements:* For master's, GMAT or substantial supervisory experience and managerial responsibility, minimum cumulative GPA of 2.0 (2.5 preferred); current resume; 3 letters of reference; statement of purpose with reasons for pursuing the MBA. Additional exam requirements/recommendations for international students: Required—TOEFL (minimum score 550 paper-based; 61 iBT). *Application deadline:* Applications are processed on a rolling basis. Application fee: $60 ($75 for international students). Electronic applications accepted. *Expenses:* Contact institution. *Financial support:* In 2018–19, research assistantships with full tuition reimbursements (averaging $10,384 per year), teaching assistantships with full tuition reimbursements (averaging $10,303 per year) were awarded; fellowships, career-related internships or fieldwork, Federal Work-Study, scholarships/grants, health care benefits, and unspecified assistantships also available. Support available to part-time students. Financial award application deadline: 11/15; financial award applicants required to submit FAFSA. *Unit head:* Dr. William Kline, Program Administrator, 217-206-6780, Fax: 217-206-7541, E-mail: wklin2@uis.edu. *Application contact:* Dr. William Kline, Program Administrator, 217-206-6780, Fax: 217-206-7541, E-mail: wklin2@uis.edu.
Website: http://www.uis.edu/mba/

University of Illinois at Urbana–Champaign, Graduate College, Gies College of Business, Department of Business Administration, Champaign, IL 61820. Offers business administration (MS, PhD); technology management (MS). *Accreditation:* AACSB. *Expenses:* Contact institution.

University of Illinois at Urbana–Champaign, Graduate College, Gies College of Business, MBA Program, Champaign, IL 61820. Offers MBA, Ed M/MBA, JD/MBA, M Arch/MBA, MCS/MBA, MHRIR/MBA, MS/MBA. *Accreditation:* AACSB.

University of Indianapolis, Graduate Programs, School of Business, Indianapolis, IN 46227-3697. Offers EMBA, MBA, Graduate Certificate. *Program availability:* Part-time, evening/weekend. *Entrance requirements:* For master's, GMAT, interview, minimum GPA of 2.8, 2 letters of recommendation, resume. Additional exam requirements/recommendations for international students: Required—TOEFL (minimum score 550 paper-based).

The University of Iowa, Tippie College of Business, Department of Management and Organizations, Iowa City, IA 52242-1316. Offers PhD. *Accreditation:* AACSB. *Degree requirements:* For doctorate, comprehensive exam, thesis/dissertation. *Entrance requirements:* For doctorate, GMAT or GRE. Additional exam requirements/recommendations for international students: Required—TOEFL (minimum score 100 iBT), IELTS (minimum score 7). Electronic applications accepted. *Faculty research:* Decision-making, human resources, personal selection, organizational behavior, training.

The University of Iowa, Tippie College of Business, Department of Management Sciences, Iowa City, IA 52242-1316. Offers PhD. *Accreditation:* AACSB. *Degree requirements:* For doctorate, comprehensive exam, thesis/dissertation. *Entrance requirements:* For doctorate, GRE General Test or GMAT. Additional exam requirements/recommendations for international students: Required—TOEFL (minimum score 100 iBT) or IELTS (minimum score 7.0). Electronic applications accepted. *Faculty research:* Optimization, supply chain management, data mining, logistics, database management.

The University of Iowa, Tippie College of Business, Executive MBA Program, Iowa City, IA 52242. Offers EMBA. *Program availability:* Part-time-only, evening/weekend. Electronic applications accepted. *Expenses:* Contact institution.

The University of Iowa, Tippie College of Business, Professional MBA Program, Iowa City, IA 52242-1316. Offers business administration (MBA); business analytics (MBA); finance (MBA); leadership (MBA); marketing (MBA). *Program availability:* Part-time-only, evening/weekend. *Degree requirements:* For master's, successful completion of nine required courses and six electives totaling 45 credits, minimum GPA of 2.75. *Entrance requirements:* For master's, GMAT or GRE. Additional exam requirements/recommendations for international students: Required—TOEFL (minimum score 600 paper-based; 100 iBT), IELTS (minimum score 7). Electronic applications accepted. *Expenses:* Contact institution. *Faculty research:* Capital markets; analytics techniques and applications; organizational and market systems analysis; applied econometrics; talent effectiveness.

The University of Kansas, Graduate Studies, School of Business, Program in Business, Lawrence, KS 66045. Offers business and organizational leadership (MS); decision sciences and supply chain management (PhD); finance (PhD); human resources management (PhD); marketing (PhD); organizational behavior (PhD); strategic management (PhD); supply chain management and logistics (MS). *Accreditation:* AACSB. *Program availability:* Part-time. *Students:* 69 full-time (20 women), 150 part-time (62 women); includes 42 minority (14 Black or African American,

non-Hispanic/Latino; 2 American Indian or Alaska Native, non-Hispanic/Latino; 6 Asian, non-Hispanic/Latino; 7 Hispanic/Latino; 13 Two or more races, non-Hispanic/Latino), 24 international. Average age 32. 306 applicants, 51% accepted, 132 enrolled. In 2018, 22 master's, 1 doctorate awarded. *Entrance requirements:* For master's, GMAT, official transcript, three letters of recommendation, resume, statement of purpose; for doctorate, GMAT or GRE, official transcript, three letters of recommendation, resume, statement of purpose. Additional exam requirements/recommendations for international students: Required—TOEFL, IELTS. *Application deadline:* For fall admission, 1/10 for domestic and international students. Application fee: $65 ($85 for international students). Electronic applications accepted. *Financial support:* Fellowships, research assistantships, teaching assistantships, scholarships/grants, health care benefits, tuition waivers (full), and unspecified assistantships available. Financial award application deadline: 1/10. *Faculty research:* Strategic human resource management, business ethics, organizational theory/behavior, corporate strategy, international business, supply chain management, Bayesian networks, game theory, decision analysis and time/series analysis, pricing, consumer effects, advertising and emotion. *Unit head:* Charly Edmonds, Director, 785-864-3841, E-mail: cedmonds@ku.edu. *Application contact:* Andrea Noltner, Graduate Admission Contact, 785-864-7556, E-mail: anoltner@ku.edu.
Website: http://www.business.ku.edu/

The University of Kansas, Graduate Studies, School of Business, Program in Business Administration and Management, Lawrence, KS 66045. Offers MBA, JD/MBA, MBA/MA, MBA/MM, MBA/MS, MBA/Pharm D. *Accreditation:* AACSB. *Program availability:* Part-time, online learning. *Students:* 71 full-time (27 women), 293 part-time (103 women); includes 71 minority (16 Black or African American, non-Hispanic/Latino; 2 American Indian or Alaska Native, non-Hispanic/Latino; 14 Asian, non-Hispanic/Latino; 14 Hispanic/Latino; 1 Native Hawaiian or other Pacific Islander, non-Hispanic/Latino; 24 Two or more races, non-Hispanic/Latino), 13 international. Average age 32. 202 applicants, 76% accepted, 133 enrolled. In 2018, 140 master's awarded. *Entrance requirements:* For master's, GMAT, official transcript; two recommendation forms; current resume; three essays; acknowledge the University Honor Code. Additional exam requirements/recommendations for international students: Required—TOEFL, IELTS. *Application deadline:* For fall admission, 8/6 for domestic and international students; for spring admission, 1/2 for domestic and international students; for summer admission, 4/23 for domestic and international students. Application fee: $65 ($85 for international students). Electronic applications accepted. *Financial support:* Research assistantships, career-related internships or fieldwork, Federal Work-Study, institutionally sponsored loans, scholarships/grants, and unspecified assistantships available. Financial award application deadline: 1/15; financial award applicants required to submit FAFSA. *Unit head:* Charly Edmonds, Director, 785-864-3841, E-mail: cedmonds@ku.edu. *Application contact:* Andrea Noltner, Graduate Admissions Contact, 785-864-7556, E-mail: anoltner@ku.edu.
Website: http://www.business.ku.edu/

University of Kentucky, Graduate School, Gatton College of Business and Economics, Program in Business Administration, Lexington, KY 40506-0032. Offers MBA, PhD. *Accreditation:* AACSB. *Degree requirements:* For master's, comprehensive exam; for doctorate, comprehensive exam, thesis/dissertation. *Entrance requirements:* For master's, GMAT, minimum undergraduate GPA of 2.75; for doctorate, GMAT, minimum undergraduate GPA of 3.0. Additional exam requirements/recommendations for international students: Required—TOEFL (minimum score 550 paper-based). Electronic applications accepted. *Faculty research:* Expert systems in manufacturing, knowledge acquisition and management, financial institutions, market in service organizations, strategic planning.

University of La Verne, College of Business and Public Management, Graduate Programs in Business Administration, La Verne, CA 91750-4443. Offers accounting (MBA, MBA-EP); finance (MBA, MBA-EP); health services management (MBA); information technology (MBA, MBA-EP); international business (MBA, MBA-EP); management and leadership (MBA, MBA-EP); marketing (MBA, MBA-EP); supply chain management (MBA, MBA-EP). *Program availability:* Part-time, evening/weekend. *Entrance requirements:* For master's, GMAT, MAT, or GRE, minimum undergraduate GPA of 3.0, 2 letters of recommendation, resume, statement of purpose. Additional exam requirements/recommendations for international students: Required—TOEFL (minimum score 550 paper-based; 85 iBT).

University of La Verne, College of Business and Public Management, Program in Health Administration, La Verne, CA 91750-4443. Offers financial management (MHA); management and leadership (MHA); marketing and business development (MHA). *Program availability:* Part-time. *Entrance requirements:* For master's, bachelor's degree, experience in health services industry (preferred). Additional exam requirements/recommendations for international students: Required—TOEFL (minimum score 550 paper-based). *Expenses:* Contact institution.

University of La Verne, College of Business and Public Management, Program in Leadership and Management, La Verne, CA 91750-4443. Offers human resource management (Certificate); leadership and management (MS), including human resource management, nonprofit management, organizational development; nonprofit management (Certificate); organizational leadership (Certificate). *Program availability:* Part-time. *Entrance requirements:* For master's, bachelor's degree, minimum undergraduate GPA of 2.75, 2 letters of recommendation, interview, resume. Additional exam requirements/recommendations for international students: Required—TOEFL (minimum score 550 paper-based).

University of La Verne, Regional and Online Campuses, Graduate Programs, Central Coast/Vandenberg Air Force Base Campuses, La Verne, CA 91750-4443. Offers business administration for experienced professionals (MBA), including health services management, information technology; leadership and management (MS). *Program availability:* Part-time. *Expenses:* Contact institution.

University of La Verne, Regional and Online Campuses, Graduate Programs, High Desert Campus, Victorville, CA 92392. Offers business administration for experienced professionals (MBA); educational (special emphasis) (M Ed); educational counseling (MS); leadership and management (MS); multiple subject (elementary) (Credential); preliminary administrative services (Credential); pupil personnel services (Credential); single subject (secondary) (Credential). *Expenses:* Contact institution.

University of La Verne, Regional and Online Campuses, Graduate Programs, Inland Empire Campus, Ontario, CA 91730. Offers business administration (MBA, MBA-EP), including accounting (MBA), finance (MBA), health services management (MBA-EP), information technology (MBA-EP), international business (MBA), managed care (MBA), management and leadership (MBA-EP), marketing (MBA-EP), supply chain management (MBA); leadership and management (MS), including human resource management, nonprofit management, organizational development. *Program availability:* Part-time, evening/weekend. *Expenses:* Contact institution.

University of La Verne, Regional and Online Campuses, Graduate Programs, Kern County Campus, Bakersfield, CA 93301. Offers business administration for experienced professionals (MBA-EP); education (special emphasis) (M Ed); educational counseling (MS); educational leadership (M Ed); health administration (MHA); leadership and management (MS); mild/moderate education specialist (Credential); multiple subject (elementary) (Credential); organizational leadership (Ed D); preliminary administrative services (Credential); single subject (secondary) (Credential); special education studies (MS). *Program availability:* Part-time, evening/weekend. *Expenses:* Contact institution.

University of La Verne, Regional and Online Campuses, Graduate Programs, Orange County Campus, Irvine, CA 92840. Offers business administration for experienced professionals (MBA); educational counseling (MS); educational leadership (M Ed); health administration (MHA); leadership and management (MS); preliminary administrative services (Credential); pupil personnel services (Credential). *Program availability:* Part-time. *Expenses:* Contact institution.

University of La Verne, Regional and Online Campuses, Graduate Programs, San Fernando Valley Campus, Burbank, CA 91505. Offers business administration for experienced professionals (MBA-EP); educational counseling (MS); educational leadership (M Ed); leadership and management (MS); preliminary administrative services (Credential); pupil personnel services (Credential). *Program availability:* Part-time, evening/weekend. *Expenses:* Contact institution.

University of La Verne, Regional and Online Campuses, Graduate Programs, Ventura County/Point Mugu Naval Air Station Campuses, Oxnard, CA 93036. Offers business administration for experienced professionals (MS); educational counseling (MS); educational leadership (M Ed); leadership and management (MS); multiple subject (elementary) (Credential); pupil personnel services (Credential); single subject (secondary) (Credential). *Program availability:* Part-time, evening/weekend. *Expenses:* Contact institution.

University of La Verne, Regional and Online Campuses, Graduate Program, ULV Online, La Verne, CA 91750-4443. Offers business administration for experienced professionals (MBA); child development (MS); leadership and management (MS). *Program availability:* Part-time, evening/weekend, online learning. *Entrance requirements:* For master's, GMAT, MAT, or GRE, minimum undergraduate GPA of 3.0, 2 letters of recommendation, resume, statement of purpose.

University of Lethbridge, School of Graduate Studies, Lethbridge, AB T1K 3M4, Canada. Offers addictions counseling (M Sc); agricultural biotechnology (M Sc); agricultural studies (M Sc, MA); anthropology (MA); archaeology (M Sc, MA); art (MA, MFA); biochemistry (M Sc); biological sciences (M Sc); biomolecular science (PhD); biosystems and biodiversity (PhD); Canadian studies (MA); chemistry (M Sc); computer science (M Sc); computer science and geographical information science (M Sc); counseling (MC); counseling psychology (M Ed); dramatic arts (MA); earth, space, and physical science (PhD); economics (MA); education (MA, PhD); educational leadership (M Ed); English (MA); environmental science (M Sc); evolution and behavior (PhD); exercise science (M Sc); French (MA); French/German (MA); French/Spanish (MA); general education (M Ed); geography (M Sc, MA); German (MA); health sciences (M Sc); individualized multidisciplinary (M Sc, MA); kinesiology (M Sc, MA); management (M Sc), including accounting, finance, human resource management and labor relations, information systems, international management, marketing, policy and strategy; mathematics (M Sc); music (M Mus, MA); Native American studies (MA); neuroscience (M Sc, PhD); new media (MA, MFA); nursing (M Sc, MN); philosophy (MA); physics (M Sc); political science (MA); psychology (M Sc, MA); religious studies (MA); sociology (MA); theatre and dramatic arts (MFA); theoretical and computational science (PhD); urban and regional studies (MA); women and gender studies (MA). *Program availability:* Part-time, evening/weekend. *Degree requirements:* For master's, thesis (for some programs); for doctorate, comprehensive exam, thesis/dissertation. *Entrance requirements:* For master's, GMAT (for M Sc in management), bachelor's degree in related field, minimum GPA of 3.0 during previous 20 graded semester courses, 2 years' teaching or related experience (M Ed); for doctorate, master's degree, minimum graduate GPA of 3.5. Additional exam requirements/recommendations for international students: Required—TOEFL (minimum score 580 paper-based; 93 iBT). Electronic applications accepted. *Faculty research:* Movement and brain plasticity, gibberellin physiology, photosynthesis, carbon cycling, molecular properties of main-group ring components.

University of Louisiana at Lafayette, BI Moody III College of Business Administration, Lafayette, LA 70504. Offers accounting (MS); business administration (MBA); entrepreneurship (MBA); finance (MBA); global management (MBA); health care administration (MBA); hospitality management (MBA); human resource management (MBA); project management (MBA); sales leadership (MBA). *Accreditation:* AACSB. *Program availability:* Part-time, evening/weekend. *Entrance requirements:* For master's, GRE General Test. Additional exam requirements/recommendations for international students: Required—TOEFL (minimum score 550 paper-based).

University of Louisiana at Monroe, Graduate School, College of Business and Social Sciences, MBA Program, Monroe, LA 71209-0001. Offers MBA. Program also offered at Shue Yan University in Hong Kong. *Program availability:* Evening/weekend. *Faculty:* 11 full-time (4 women). *Students:* 27 full-time (14 women), 38 part-time (21 women); includes 14 minority (6 Black or African American, non-Hispanic/Latino; 2 Asian, non-Hispanic/Latino; 3 Hispanic/Latino; 3 Two or more races, non-Hispanic/Latino), 12 international. Average age 29. 36 applicants, 89% accepted, 17 enrolled. In 2018, 28 master's awarded. *Expenses:* Contact institution. *Financial support:* In 2018–19, 23 students received support. Teaching assistantships and unspecified assistantships available. *Unit head:* Dr. Ronald Berry, Dean, 318-342-1103, E-mail: rberry@ulm.edu. *Application contact:* Dr. Ronald Berry, Dean, 318-342-1103, E-mail: rberry@ulm.edu.
Website: http://www.ulm.edu/cbss/mba/

University of Louisiana at Monroe, Graduate School, College of Business and Social Sciences, Program in Gerontology, Monroe, LA 71209-0001. Offers aging studies (MA); gerontology (CGS); grief care management (MA); long-term care administration (MA); mental health (MA); program administration (MA); small business management (MA). *Program availability:* Part-time. *Faculty:* 1 (woman) full-time, 5 part-time/adjunct (3 women). *Students:* 7 full-time (all women), 10 part-time (all women); includes 11 minority (all Black or African American, non-Hispanic/Latino). Average age 30. 4 applicants, 75% accepted, 2 enrolled. In 2018, 3 master's awarded. *Degree requirements:* For master's, thesis (for some programs), internship. *Entrance requirements:* For master's, GRE General Test (waived for students with a 2.5 GPA or above); for CGS, GRE General Test. Additional exam requirements/recommendations for international students: Required—TOEFL (minimum score 500 paper-based; 61 iBT). *Application deadline:* For fall admission, 8/24 priority date for domestic students, 7/1 for international students; for winter admission, 12/14 priority date for domestic students; for spring admission, 1/19 for domestic students, 11/1 for international students. Applications are processed on a rolling basis. Application fee: $20 ($30 for international students). Electronic applications accepted. *Financial support:* In 2018–19, 2 students received support. Career-related internships or fieldwork, Federal Work-Study, and unspecified assistantships available. Financial award application deadline: 4/1; financial award applicants required to submit FAFSA. *Unit head:* Dr. Anita Sharma, Director, 318-342-1467, E-mail: sharma@ulm.edu. *Application contact:* Dr. Anita Sharma, Director, 318-342-1467, E-mail: sharma@ulm.edu.
Website: http://www.ulm.edu/gerontology/

University of Louisville, Graduate School, College of Business, MBA Programs, Louisville, KY 40292-0001. Offers entrepreneurship (MBA); global business (MBA);

health sector management (MBA). *Accreditation:* AACSB. *Program availability:* Part-time, evening/weekend, 100% online, blended/hybrid learning. *Students:* 227 full-time (82 women), 28 part-time (13 women); includes 58 minority (32 Black or African American, non-Hispanic/Latino; 1 American Indian or Alaska Native, non-Hispanic/Latino; 13 Asian, non-Hispanic/Latino; 9 Hispanic/Latino; 3 Two or more races, non-Hispanic/Latino), 34 international. Average age 32. 236 applicants, 69% accepted, 126 enrolled. In 2018, 102 master's awarded. *Degree requirements:* For master's, international learning experience. *Entrance requirements:* For master's, GMAT, 2 letters of reference, personal interview, resume, personal statement, college transcript(s). Additional exam requirements/recommendations for international students: Required—TOEFL (minimum score 83 iBT). *Application deadline:* For fall admission, 7/1 for domestic students; for spring admission, 12/1 for domestic students. Applications are processed on a rolling basis. Application fee: $65. *Expenses: Tuition, area resident:* Full-time $6500; part-time $723 per credit hour. Tuition, state resident: full-time $6500. Tuition, nonresident: full-time $13,557; part-time $1507 per credit hour. Tuition and fees vary according to course load and program. *Financial support:* In 2018–19, 105 students received support. Fellowships with full tuition reimbursements available, research assistantships with full tuition reimbursements available, health care benefits, and unspecified assistantships available. Financial award application deadline: 3/31; financial award applicants required to submit FAFSA. *Faculty research:* Entrepreneurship, venture capital, retailing/franchising, corporate governance and leadership, supply chain management. *Total annual research expenditures:* $859,000. *Unit head:* Dr. Todd Mooradian, Dean, 502-852-6443, Fax: 502-852-7557, E-mail: todd.mooradian@louisville.edu. *Application contact:* Susan E. Hildebrand, Program Director, 502-852-7257, Fax: 502-852-4901, E-mail: s.hildebrand@louisville.edu.
Website: http://business.louisville.edu/mba

University of Lynchburg, Graduate Studies, MBA Program, Lynchburg, VA 24501-3199. Offers MBA. *Accreditation:* ACBSP. *Program availability:* Part-time, evening/weekend, 100% online, blended/hybrid learning. *Degree requirements:* For master's, capstone course. *Entrance requirements:* For master's, GMAT (minimum score of 400) or GRE, personal essay, 3 letters of recommendation, official transcripts (bachelor's, others as relevant), career goals statement. Additional exam requirements/recommendations for international students: Required—TOEFL (minimum score 550 paper-based; 80 iBT), IELTS (minimum score 6). Electronic applications accepted. Application fee is waived when completed online. *Expenses:* Contact institution.

University of Maine, Graduate School, The Maine Business School, Orono, ME 04469. Offers MBA, CGS. *Accreditation:* AACSB. *Program availability:* Part-time, evening/weekend, online learning. *Faculty:* 14 full-time (4 women), 6 part-time/adjunct (1 woman). *Students:* 44 full-time (13 women), 53 part-time (25 women); includes 10 minority (1 Black or African American, non-Hispanic/Latino; 2 American Indian or Alaska Native, non-Hispanic/Latino; 4 Asian, non-Hispanic/Latino; 1 Hispanic/Latino; 2 Two or more races, non-Hispanic/Latino), 5 international. Average age 32. 70 applicants, 93% accepted, 40 enrolled. In 2018, 28 master's, 9 other advanced degrees awarded. *Entrance requirements:* For master's, GMAT. Additional exam requirements/recommendations for international students: Required—TOEFL (minimum score 550 paper-based; 80 iBT), IELTS (minimum score 6.5). *Application deadline:* For fall admission, 7/1 priority date for domestic and international students; for spring admission, 12/1 priority date for domestic and international students; for summer admission, 4/1 priority date for domestic and international students. Applications are processed on a rolling basis. Application fee: $65. Electronic applications accepted. *Expenses:* Contact institution. *Financial support:* In 2018–19, 15 students received support, including 1 fellowship with full tuition reimbursement available (averaging $10,000 per year), 3 teaching assistantships with full tuition reimbursements available (averaging $15,600 per year); career-related internships or fieldwork, Federal Work-Study, institutionally sponsored loans, scholarships/grants, tuition waivers (full and partial), and unspecified assistantships also available. Financial award application deadline: 3/1. *Faculty research:* Audit, socially responsible investing, capital acquisition, international management, corporate social responsibility. *Total annual research expenditures:* $36,170. *Unit head:* Scott Spolan, MBA Director and Lecturer in Management, 207-581-1973, E-mail: scott.spolan@maine.edu. *Application contact:* Scott G. Delcourt, Assistant Vice President for Graduate Studies and Senior Associate Dean, 207-581-3291, Fax: 207-581-3232, E-mail: graduate@maine.edu.
Website: http://www.umaine.edu/business/

University of Management and Technology, Program in Business Administration, Arlington, VA 22209-1609. Offers general management (MBA, DBA); project management (MBA). *Program availability:* Part-time, 100% online. *Degree requirements:* For master's, comprehensive exam; for doctorate, thesis/dissertation. *Entrance requirements:* For master's, 3 recommendations, resume. Additional exam requirements/recommendations for international students: Required—TOEFL (minimum score 530 paper-based; 71 iBT). Electronic applications accepted. *Expenses: Tuition:* Full-time $7020; part-time $1170 per course.

University of Management and Technology, Program in Management, Arlington, VA 22209-1609. Offers acquisition management (MS, AC); criminal justice administration (MS); general management (MS); project management (MS, AC). *Program availability:* Part-time, evening/weekend, online learning. *Entrance requirements:* For master's, 3 recommendations, resume. Additional exam requirements/recommendations for international students: Required—TOEFL (minimum score 530 paper-based; 71 iBT). Electronic applications accepted. *Expenses: Tuition:* Full-time $7020; part-time $1170 per course.

The University of Manchester, Alliance Manchester Business School, M15 6PB, United Kingdom. Offers accounting and finance (M Sc); business (M Ent); business analysis and strategic management (M Sc); business analytics: operational research and risk analysis (M Sc); business psychology (M Sc); corporate communications and reputation management (M Sc); finance (M Sc); finance and business economics (M Sc); human resource management and industrial relations (M Sc); innovation management and entrepreneurship (M Sc); international business and management (M Sc); international human resource management and comparative industrial relations (M Sc); management (M Sc); marketing (M Sc); operations, project and supply chain management (M Sc); organizational psychology (M Sc); quantitative finance (M Sc). *Entrance requirements:* For master's, UK 2:1 honours degree or overseas equivalent. Additional exam requirements/recommendations for international students: Required—TOEFL (minimum score 100 iBT), IELTS (minimum score 7), PTE. Electronic applications accepted. *Faculty research:* Accounting and finance, management sciences and marketing, people management and organization, innovation management and policy, decision sciences.

University of Manitoba, Faculty of Graduate Studies, Asper School of Business, Winnipeg, MB R3T 2N2, Canada. Offers M Sc, MBA, PhD. *Accreditation:* AACSB.

University of Mary, Gary Tharaldson School of Business, Bismarck, ND 58504-9652. Offers business administration (MBA); energy management (MBA, MS); executive (MBA, MS); health care (MBA, MS); human resource management (MBA); project management (MBA, MPM); virtuous leadership (MBA, MPM, MS). *Program availability:* Part-time, evening/weekend. *Entrance requirements:* For master's, minimum GPA of 2.5. Additional exam requirements/recommendations for international students: Required—TOEFL (minimum score 550 paper-based; 80 iBT). Electronic applications accepted.

University of Mary Hardin-Baylor, Graduate Studies in Business Administration, Belton, TX 76513. Offers accounting (MBA); information systems management (MBA); international business (MBA); management (MBA). *Program availability:* Part-time, evening/weekend. *Degree requirements:* For master's, comprehensive exam. *Entrance requirements:* For master's, minimum GPA of 3.0, interview. Additional exam requirements/recommendations for international students: Required—TOEFL (minimum score 60 iBT), IELTS (minimum score 4.5). Electronic applications accepted. *Faculty research:* Financial management, financial markets, supply chain management.

University of Maryland, College Park, Academic Affairs, Joint Program in Business and Management/Public Policy, College Park, MD 20742. Offers MBA/MPM. *Accreditation:* AACSB. Electronic applications accepted.

University of Maryland, College Park, Academic Affairs, Robert H. Smith School of Business, Combined MSW/MBA Program, College Park, MD 20742. Offers MSW/MBA. *Accreditation:* AACSB. *Entrance requirements:* Additional exam requirements/recommendations for international students: Required—TOEFL.

University of Maryland, College Park, Academic Affairs, Robert H. Smith School of Business, Executive MBA Program, College Park, MD 20742. Offers EMBA. *Accreditation:* AACSB. *Entrance requirements:* For master's, minimum GPA of 3.0, 7-12 years of professional experience. Additional exam requirements/recommendations for international students: Required—TOEFL.

University of Maryland, College Park, Academic Affairs, Robert H. Smith School of Business, Joint Program in Business and Management, College Park, MD 20742. Offers MBA/MS. *Accreditation:* AACSB. *Entrance requirements:* Additional exam requirements/recommendations for international students: Required—TOEFL. Electronic applications accepted.

University of Maryland, College Park, Academic Affairs, Robert H. Smith School of Business, Program in Business Administration, College Park, MD 20742. Offers MBA. *Accreditation:* AACSB. *Program availability:* Part-time, evening/weekend, online learning. *Entrance requirements:* For master's, GMAT, minimum GPA of 3.0, resume, 3 letters of recommendation. Additional exam requirements/recommendations for international students: Required—TOEFL. Electronic applications accepted. *Faculty research:* Accounting, entrepreneurship, finance management and organization, management server and statistical information systems.

University of Maryland, College Park, Academic Affairs, Robert H. Smith School of Business, Program in Business and Management, College Park, MD 20742. Offers MS, PhD. *Accreditation:* AACSB. *Program availability:* Part-time. *Degree requirements:* For master's, thesis optional; for doctorate, comprehensive exam, thesis/dissertation. *Entrance requirements:* For master's, GMAT, minimum GPA of 3.0, resume, 2 letters of recommendation; for doctorate, GMAT or GRE General Test, minimum GPA of 3.0, resume, 2 letters of recommendation. Additional exam requirements/recommendations for international students: Required—TOEFL. Electronic applications accepted.

University of Maryland, College Park, Academic Affairs, Robert H. Smith School of Business, Program in Business Management/Law, College Park, MD 20742. Offers JD/MBA. *Accreditation:* AACSB. *Entrance requirements:* Additional exam requirements/recommendations for international students: Required—TOEFL.

University of Maryland University College, The Graduate School, Doctoral Program in Management, Adelphi, MD 20783. Offers DM. *Accreditation:* AACSB. *Program availability:* Part-time. *Students:* 185 part-time (97 women); includes 105 minority (69 Black or African American, non-Hispanic/Latino; 12 Asian, non-Hispanic/Latino; 17 Hispanic/Latino; 7 Two or more races, non-Hispanic/Latino), 3 international. Average age 45. 140 applicants, 100% accepted, 3 enrolled. In 2018, 46 doctorates awarded. *Degree requirements:* For doctorate, comprehensive exam, thesis/dissertation. *Application deadline:* Applications are processed on a rolling basis. Application fee: $100. Electronic applications accepted. *Financial support:* Scholarships/grants available. Support available to part-time students. Financial award application deadline: 6/1; financial award applicants required to submit FAFSA. *Unit head:* Leslie Dinauer, Program Director, 240-684-2400, E-mail: leslie.dinauer@umuc.edu. *Application contact:* Admissions, 800-888-8682, E-mail: studentsfirst@umuc.edu.
Website: http://www.umuc.edu/academic-programs/doctor-of-management.cfm

University of Maryland University College, The Graduate School, Program in Business Administration, Adelphi, MD 20783. Offers MBA. *Accreditation:* AACSB. *Program availability:* Part-time, evening/weekend, online learning. *Students:* 2,632 part-time (1,408 women); includes 1,472 minority (949 Black or African American, non-Hispanic/Latino; 5 American Indian or Alaska Native, non-Hispanic/Latino; 194 Asian, non-Hispanic/Latino; 214 Hispanic/Latino; 11 Native Hawaiian or other Pacific Islander, non-Hispanic/Latino; 99 Two or more races, non-Hispanic/Latino), 52 international. Average age 36. 1,143 applicants, 100% accepted, 505 enrolled. In 2018, 1,375 master's awarded. *Degree requirements:* For master's, thesis or alternative. *Application deadline:* Applications are processed on a rolling basis. Application fee: $50. Electronic applications accepted. *Financial support:* Scholarships/grants available. Support available to part-time students. Financial award application deadline: 6/1; financial award applicants required to submit FAFSA. *Unit head:* Ravi Mittal, Professor, 240-684-2143, E-mail: ravi.mittal@umuc.edu. *Application contact:* Admissions, 800-888-8682, E-mail: studentsfirst@umuc.edu.
Website: https://www.umuc.edu/academic-programs/masters-degrees/master-of-business-administration-mba.cfm

University of Maryland University College, The Graduate School, Program in Management, Adelphi, MD 20783. Offers MS, Certificate. *Program availability:* Part-time, online learning. *Students:* 31 full-time (22 women), 3,072 part-time (2,048 women); includes 1,886 minority (1,451 Black or African American, non-Hispanic/Latino; 10 American Indian or Alaska Native, non-Hispanic/Latino; 111 Asian, non-Hispanic/Latino; 225 Hispanic/Latino; 9 Native Hawaiian or other Pacific Islander, non-Hispanic/Latino; 80 Two or more races, non-Hispanic/Latino), 41 international. Average age 36. 759 applicants, 100% accepted, 554 enrolled. In 2018, 840 master's, 188 other advanced degrees awarded. *Degree requirements:* For master's, thesis or alternative. *Application deadline:* Applications are processed on a rolling basis. Application fee: $50. Electronic applications accepted. *Financial support:* Scholarships/grants available. Support available to part-time students. Financial award application deadline: 6/1; financial award applicants required to submit FAFSA. *Unit head:* Monica Sava Bruenn, Program Director, 203-304-9724, E-mail: Monica.Sava@umuc.edu. *Application contact:* Admissions, 888-888-8682, E-mail: Studentsfirst@umuc.edu.
Website: https://www.umuc.edu/academic-programs/masters-degrees/management/index.cfm

University of Mary Washington, College of Business, Fredericksburg, VA 22401-5300. Offers MBA. *Program availability:* Part-time-only, evening/weekend. *Entrance requirements:* For master's, GMAT or GRE, minimum GPA of 3.0. Additional exam requirements/recommendations for international students: Required—TOEFL (minimum score 570 paper-based; 80 iBT), IELTS (minimum score 6.5). Electronic applications accepted. Application fee is waived when completed online. *Expenses:* Contact

institution. *Faculty research:* Power laws/CEO compensation, sustainable competitive advantage, resistance to security implementation, profiling sustainable curriculums, perceived customer value.

University of Massachusetts Amherst, Graduate School, Interdisciplinary Programs, Dual Degree Program in Management and Public Policy and Administration, Amherst, MA 01003. Offers MPPA/MBA. *Accreditation:* AACSB. *Program availability:* Part-time. *Entrance requirements:* Additional exam requirements/recommendations for international students: Required—TOEFL (minimum score 600 paper-based; 100 iBT), IELTS (minimum score 7). Electronic applications accepted.

University of Massachusetts Amherst, Graduate School, Interdisciplinary Programs, Dual Degree Program in Management and Sport Management, Amherst, MA 01003. Offers MBA/MS. *Program availability:* Part-time. *Entrance requirements:* Additional exam requirements/recommendations for international students: Required—TOEFL (minimum score 600 paper-based; 100 iBT), IELTS (minimum score 7). Electronic applications accepted.

University of Massachusetts Amherst, Graduate School, Interdisciplinary Programs, Dual Degree Programs in Management and Engineering, Amherst, MA 01003. Offers MBA/MIE, MBA/MSEWRE, MSCE/MBA, MSME/MBA. *Program availability:* Part-time. *Entrance requirements:* Additional exam requirements/recommendations for international students: Required—TOEFL (minimum score 600 paper-based; 100 iBT), IELTS (minimum score 7). Electronic applications accepted.

University of Massachusetts Amherst, Graduate School, Isenberg School of Management, Program in Management, Amherst, MA 01003. Offers accounting (PhD); business administration (MBA); entrepreneurship (MBA); finance (MBA, PhD); healthcare administration (MBA); hospitality and tourism management (PhD); management science (PhD); marketing (MBA, PhD); organization studies (PhD); sport management (PhD); strategic management (PhD); MBA/MS. *Accreditation:* AACSB. *Program availability:* Part-time, evening/weekend, online learning. Terminal master's awarded for partial completion of doctoral program. *Degree requirements:* For doctorate, comprehensive exam, thesis/dissertation. *Entrance requirements:* For master's and doctorate, GMAT or GRE General Test. Additional exam requirements/recommendations for international students: Required—TOEFL (minimum score 550 paper-based; 80 iBT), IELTS (minimum score 6.5). Electronic applications accepted.

University of Massachusetts Boston, College of Management, Program in Business Administration, Boston, MA 02125-3393. Offers MBA. *Accreditation:* AACSB. *Program availability:* Part-time, evening/weekend. *Students:* 113 full-time (56 women), 176 part-time (90 women); includes 67 minority (22 Black or African American, non-Hispanic/Latino; 25 Asian, non-Hispanic/Latino; 16 Hispanic/Latino; 4 Two or more races, non-Hispanic/Latino), 74 international. Average age 32. 197 applicants, 66% accepted, 96 enrolled. In 2018, 132 master's awarded. *Entrance requirements:* For master's, GMAT, minimum GPA of 3.0. *Application deadline:* For fall admission, 2/1 for domestic students; for spring admission, 11/1 for domestic students; for summer admission, 5/1 for domestic students. *Expenses: Tuition, area resident:* Full-time $17,896. Tuition, state resident: full-time $17,896. Tuition, nonresident: full-time $34,932. *International tuition:* $34,932 full-time. *Required fees:* $355. *Financial support:* Research assistantships, teaching assistantships, career-related internships or fieldwork, Federal Work-Study, and unspecified assistantships available. Support available to part-time students. Financial award application deadline: 3/1; financial award applicants required to submit FAFSA. *Faculty research:* International finance, human resource management, management information systems, investment and corporate finance, international marketing. *Unit head:* Vesela Veleva, Director, 617-287.6293, E-mail: Vesela.Veleva@umb.edu. *Application contact:* Graduate Admissions Coordinator, 617-287-6400, Fax: 617-287-6236, E-mail: graduate.admissions@umb.edu.

University of Massachusetts Dartmouth, Graduate School, Charlton College of Business, North Dartmouth, MA 02747-2300. Offers accounting and finance (MS, Postbaccalaureate Certificate), including accounting, finance (Postbaccalaureate Certificate); business administration (MBA), including business administration; decision and information sciences (MS), including healthcare management, technology management. *Program availability:* Part-time, 100% online, blended/hybrid learning. *Students:* Average age 32. 233 applicants, 86% accepted, 145 enrolled. In 2018, 190 master's, 21 other advanced degrees awarded. *Degree requirements:* For master's, thesis (for some programs), thesis or project (for healthcare management); e-portfolio (for business administration). *Entrance requirements:* For master's, GMAT (or waiver), statement of purpose (minimum of 300 words), resume, official transcripts, 2 letters of recommendation; for Postbaccalaureate Certificate, statement of purpose (minimum of 300 words), resume, official transcripts. Additional exam requirements/recommendations for international students: Required—TOEFL (minimum score 533 paper-based; 72 iBT), IELTS (minimum score 6). *Application deadline:* For fall admission, 8/1 priority date for domestic students, 7/1 priority date for international students; for spring admission, 11/15 priority date for domestic students, 10/15 priority date for international students. Application fee: $60. Electronic applications accepted. *Financial support:* In 2018–19, 2 research assistantships (averaging $8,000 per year) were awarded; teaching assistantships, tuition waivers (full and partial), and unspecified assistantships also available. Support available to part-time students. Financial award application deadline: 3/1; financial award applicants required to submit FAFSA. *Faculty research:* Effects of managerial behaviors and personality on strategic decision making, asset pricing, applications in multivariate diagnosis/pattern recognition and data mining, sustainable development, social media marketing. *Total annual research expenditures:* $233,000. *Unit head:* Melissa Pacheco, Assistant Dean of Graduate Programs, 508-999-8543, Fax: 508-999-8646, E-mail: mpacheco@umassd.edu. *Application contact:* Steven Briggs, Director of Recruitment and Marketing for Graduate Studies, 508-999-8604, Fax: 508-999-8183, E-mail: graduate@umassd.edu.
Website: http://www.umassd.edu/charlton

University of Massachusetts Lowell, Manning School of Business, Lowell, MA 01854. Offers business administration (MBA, PhD); healthcare innovation and entrepreneurship (MS). *Accreditation:* AACSB. *Program availability:* Part-time, evening/weekend. *Entrance requirements:* For master's, GMAT.

University of Memphis, Graduate School, Fogelman College of Business and Economics, Program in Business Administration, Memphis, TN 38152. Offers accounting (MBA, PhD); business administration (IMBA); economics (PhD); executive business administration (MBA); finance (PhD); management (PhD); marketing (MS); marketing and supply chain management (PhD); real estate development (MS); JD/MBA. *Accreditation:* AACSB. *Students:* 189 full-time (96 women), 364 part-time (151 women); includes 178 minority (89 Black or African American, non-Hispanic/Latino; 1 American Indian or Alaska Native, non-Hispanic/Latino; 68 Asian, non-Hispanic/Latino; 12 Hispanic/Latino; 8 Two or more races, non-Hispanic/Latino), 102 international. Average age 32. 298 applicants, 72% accepted, 139 enrolled. In 2018, 200 master's, 3 doctorates awarded. *Degree requirements:* For master's, comprehensive exam; for doctorate, comprehensive exam, thesis/dissertation. *Entrance requirements:* For master's, GMAT, resume; for doctorate, GMAT, interview, minimum GPA of 3.4, resume, letter of recommendation. Additional exam requirements/recommendations for international students: Required—TOEFL (minimum score 550 paper-based). *Application deadline:* For fall admission, 8/1 for domestic students; for spring admission, 12/1 for domestic students. Application fee: $35 ($60 for international students). *Expenses: Tuition, area resident:* Full-time $10,240; part-time $503 per credit hour. Tuition, state resident: full-time $10,464. Tuition, nonresident: full-time $20,224; part-time $991 per credit hour. *Required fees:* $850; $106 per credit hour. *Financial support:* Research assistantships with full tuition reimbursements, teaching assistantships with full tuition reimbursements, career-related internships or fieldwork, Federal Work-Study, scholarships/grants, and unspecified assistantships available. Financial award application deadline: 2/15; financial award applicants required to submit FAFSA. *Faculty research:* Competitive business strategy, finance microstructures, supply chain management innovations, health care economics, litigation risks and corporate audits. *Unit head:* Dr. Balaji Krishnan, Director, MBA Programs, 901-678-2786, E-mail: krishnan@memphis.edu. *Application contact:* Dr. Balaji Krishnan, Director, MBA Programs, 901-678-2786, E-mail: krishnan@memphis.edu.
Website: https://www.memphis.edu/mba/index.php

University of Miami, Miami Business School, Coral Gables, FL 33146. Offers accounting (M Acc); business (PhD); business administration (MBA); business analytics (MSBA); economics (PhD); finance (MSF); health administration (MHA); international business (MIBS); real estate (MBA); taxation (MS Tax); JD/MBA; MD/MBA. *Accreditation:* AACSB; CAHME (one or more programs are accredited). *Program availability:* Part-time, evening/weekend, 100% online, blended/hybrid learning. *Faculty:* 155 full-time (47 women), 14 part-time/adjunct (5 women). *Students:* 1,083 full-time (469 women); includes 422 minority (79 Black or African American, non-Hispanic/Latino; 1 American Indian or Alaska Native, non-Hispanic/Latino; 43 Asian, non-Hispanic/Latino; 274 Hispanic/Latino; 3 Native Hawaiian or other Pacific Islander, non-Hispanic/Latino; 22 Two or more races, non-Hispanic/Latino), 282 international. Average age 30. 2,564 applicants, 38% accepted, 450 enrolled. In 2018, 558 master's, 5 doctorates awarded. Terminal master's awarded for partial completion of doctoral program. *Degree requirements:* For master's, comprehensive exam; for doctorate, comprehensive exam, thesis/dissertation. *Entrance requirements:* For master's, GMAT or GRE; for doctorate, GRE General Test. Additional exam requirements/recommendations for international students: Required—TOEFL (minimum score 94 iBT), IELTS (minimum score 7), TOEFL (minimum score 587 paper-based, 94 iBT) or IELTS (7). *Application deadline:* For fall admission, 6/30 priority date for domestic students, 5/30 priority date for international students; for spring admission, 10/31 priority date for domestic students, 9/30 priority date for international students. Applications are processed on a rolling basis. Application fee: $48. Electronic applications accepted. *Expenses:* Contact institution. *Financial support:* In 2018–19, 643 students received support, including 1 fellowship with full tuition reimbursement available (averaging $20,000 per year), 47 research assistantships with full and partial tuition reimbursements available (averaging $28,826 per year), 6 teaching assistantships with full and partial tuition reimbursements available (averaging $2,183 per year); career-related internships or fieldwork, Federal Work-Study, institutionally sponsored loans, scholarships/grants, and unspecified assistantships also available. Support available to part-time students. Financial award application deadline: 3/26; financial award applicants required to submit FAFSA. *Faculty research:* Behavioral finance; computational economics; consumer research; risk perception; consumer behavior; consumer choice research; behavioral decision theory; business analytics; point processes; longitudinal data analyses; international business; global business strategy, joint ventures, and alliances; emerging economies; global economic growth and development, money and financial markets, and computed dynamic models; health policy; innovative payment mechanisms. *Total annual research expenditures:* $703,773. *Unit head:* Dr. John Quelch, Dean, 305-284-6515, Fax: 305-284-6526, E-mail: jquelch@miami.edu. *Application contact:* Loubna Bouamane, Director of Graduate Business Recruiting and Admissions, 305-284-2510, Fax: 305-284-5905, E-mail: loubna@miami.edu.
Website: www.mbs.miami.edu

University of Michigan, Ross School of Business, Ann Arbor, MI 48109-1234. Offers accounting (M Acc); business (MBA); business administration (PhD); supply chain management (MSCM); JD/MBA; MBA/M Arch; MBA/M Eng; MBA/MA; MBA/MEM; MBA/MHSA; MBA/MM; MBA/MPP; MBA/MS; MBA/MSE; MBA/MSI; MBA/MSW; MBA/MUP; MD/MBA; MHSA/MBA. *Accreditation:* AACSB. *Program availability:* Part-time, evening/weekend. *Degree requirements:* For doctorate, comprehensive exam, thesis/dissertation, oral defense of dissertation, preliminary exam. *Entrance requirements:* For master's, GMAT or GRE, completion of equivalent of four-year U.S. bachelor's degree, two letters of recommendation, essays, resume; for doctorate, GMAT or GRE. Additional exam requirements/recommendations for international students: Required—TOEFL (minimum score 600 paper-based; 100 iBT). Electronic applications accepted. *Faculty research:* Finance and accounting, marketing, technology and operations management, corporate strategy, management and organizations.

University of Michigan–Dearborn, College of Business, MBA Program, Dearborn, MI 48126. Offers MBA. *Accreditation:* AACSB. *Program availability:* Part-time, evening/weekend, 100% online. *Faculty:* 41 full-time (17 women), 9 part-time/adjunct (6 women). *Students:* 31 full-time (12 women), 264 part-time (102 women); includes 66 minority (11 Black or African American, non-Hispanic/Latino; 1 American Indian or Alaska Native, non-Hispanic/Latino; 34 Asian, non-Hispanic/Latino; 12 Hispanic/Latino; 8 Two or more races, non-Hispanic/Latino), 14 international. Average age 30. 181 applicants, 63% accepted, 80 enrolled. In 2018, 45 master's awarded. *Entrance requirements:* For master's, GMAT or GRE, equivalent of four-year U.S. bachelor's degree from regionally-accredited institution, undergraduate course in finite math, pre-calculus, or calculus. Additional exam requirements/recommendations for international students: Required—TOEFL (minimum score 560 paper-based; 84 iBT), IELTS (minimum score 6.5). *Application deadline:* For fall admission, 8/1 for domestic students, 5/1 for international students; for winter admission, 12/1 for domestic students, 9/1 for international students; for spring admission, 4/1 for domestic students, 1/1 for international students. Applications are processed on a rolling basis. Application fee: $60. Electronic applications accepted. *Expenses:* $15,740 per academic year (typical full-time in-state); $24,308 per academic year (typical full-time out-of-state). *Financial support:* In 2018–19, 49 students received support. Scholarships/grants and non-resident tuition scholarships available. Financial award application deadline: 3/1; financial award applicants required to submit FAFSA. *Faculty research:* Business intelligence, behavioral finance, brand management and new media, management education, operations strategy. *Unit head:* Dr. Michael Kamen, Director, College of Business Graduate Programs, 313-593-5460, E-mail: mkamen@umich.edu. *Application contact:* Joan Doherty, Academic Advisor/Counselor, 313-593-5460, Fax: 313-271-9838, E-mail: umd-gradbusiness@umich.edu.
Website: http://umdearborn.edu/cob/mba-program/

University of Michigan–Flint, School of Management, Flint, MI 48502-1950. Offers MBA, MS, MSA, Graduate Certificate, Post-Master's Certificate. *Accreditation:* AACSB. *Program availability:* Part-time, evening/weekend, mixed mode format. *Faculty:* 30 full-time (4 women), 10 part-time/adjunct (2 women). *Students:* 28 full-time (16 women), 193 part-time (77 women); includes 56 minority (27 Black or African American, non-Hispanic/Latino; 4 American Indian or Alaska Native, non-Hispanic/Latino; 10 Asian, non-Hispanic/Latino; 9 Hispanic/Latino; 6 Two or more races, non-Hispanic/Latino), 27 international. Average age 35. 182 applicants, 78% accepted, 73 enrolled. In 2018, 75

master's, 1 other advanced degree awarded. *Degree requirements:* For master's, thesis or alternative. *Entrance requirements:* For master's, bachelor's degree in arts, sciences, and engineering, or business administration from regionally-accredited college or university; overall UG GPA all schools combined with their GMAT or GRE score; student's statement of purpose, resume and recommendations; quantitative formula index for standard admission 1100 or greater probationary 1000-1099; for other advanced degree, bachelor's degree from regionally-accredited college with minimum GPA of 3.0 and completion of college-level math, statistics, or quantitative course (for Graduate Certificate); MBA or equivalent from accredited college or university (for Post-Master's Certificate). Additional exam requirements/recommendations for international students: Required—TOEFL (minimum score 84 iBT), IELTS (minimum score 6.5). *Application deadline:* For fall admission, 8/1 for domestic students, 5/1 for international students; for winter admission, 11/15 for domestic students, 9/1 for international students; for spring admission, 3/15 for domestic students, 1/1 for international students; for summer admission, 5/15 for domestic students. Applications are processed on a rolling basis. Application fee: $55. Electronic applications accepted. *Expenses:* Contact institution. *Financial support:* Federal Work-Study, scholarships/grants, and unspecified assistantships available. Support available to part-time students. Financial award application deadline: 3/1; financial award applicants required to submit FAFSA. *Unit head:* Dr. Scott Johnson, Dean, School of Management, 810-762-6579, Fax: 810-237-6685, E-mail: scotjohn@umflint.edu. *Application contact:* Matt Bohlen, Director of Graduate Admissions, 810-762-3171, Fax: 810-766-6789, E-mail: mbohlen@umflint.edu.
Website: https://www.umflint.edu/som/graduate-business-programs

University of Minnesota, Duluth, Graduate School, Labovitz School of Business and Economics, Program in Business Administration, Duluth, MN 55812-2496. Offers MBA. *Accreditation:* AACSB. *Program availability:* Part-time, evening/weekend. *Entrance requirements:* For master's, GMAT, minimum GPA of 3.0; course work in accounting, business administration, and economics. Additional exam requirements/recommendations for international students: Required—TOEFL (minimum score 550 paper-based; 79 iBT). *Expenses:* Contact institution. *Faculty research:* Regional economic analysis, marketing, management, human resources, organizational behavior.

University of Minnesota Rochester, Graduate Programs, Rochester, MN 55904. Offers bioinformatics and computational biology (MS, PhD); business administration (MBA); occupational therapy (MOT). *Accreditation:* AOTA.

University of Minnesota, Twin Cities Campus, Carlson School of Management, Minneapolis, MN 55455. Offers EMBA, M Acc, MA, MBA, MBT, MS, PhD, JD/MBA, MBA/MPP, MBA/MSBA, MD/MBA, MHA/MBA, Pharm D/MBA. *Accreditation:* AACSB. *Program availability:* Part-time, evening/weekend, 100% online, blended/hybrid learning. *Faculty:* 150 full-time (43 women), 57 part-time/adjunct (18 women). *Students:* 537 full-time (232 women), 949 part-time (326 women); includes 210 minority (33 Black or African American, non-Hispanic/Latino; 18 American Indian or Alaska Native, non-Hispanic/Latino; 116 Asian, non-Hispanic/Latino; 41 Hispanic/Latino; 2 Native Hawaiian or other Pacific Islander, non-Hispanic/Latino), 305 international. Average age 28. 1,956 applicants, 45% accepted, 498 enrolled. In 2018, 565 master's, 14 doctorates awarded. Terminal master's awarded for partial completion of doctoral program. *Degree requirements:* For doctorate, comprehensive exam, thesis/dissertation. *Entrance requirements:* For master's, GMAT or GRE. Additional exam requirements/recommendations for international students: Required—TOEFL, IELTS, PTE. Application fee: $75 ($95 for international students). Electronic applications accepted. *Expenses:* Contact institution. *Financial support:* Fellowships with full and partial tuition reimbursements, research assistantships with full tuition reimbursements, teaching assistantships with full and partial tuition reimbursements, career-related internships or fieldwork, Federal Work-Study, institutionally sponsored loans, scholarships/grants, health care benefits, tuition waivers (full and partial), and unspecified assistantships available. Support available to part-time students. Financial award application deadline: 4/1; financial award applicants required to submit FAFSA. *Faculty research:* Finance and accounting: financial reporting, asset pricing models and corporate finance; information and decision sciences: on-line auctions, information transparency and recommender systems; marketing: psychological influences on consumer behavior, brand equity, pricing and marketing channels; operations: lean manufacturing, quality management and global supply chains; strategic management and organization: global strategy, networks, entrepreneurship and innovation, sustainability. *Unit head:* Prof. Alok Gupta, Associate Dean of Faculty and Research, 612-626-0276, Fax: 612-624-6374, E-mail: gupta037@umn.edu. *Application contact:* Graduate School Admissions, 612-625-3014, Fax: 612-625-6002, E-mail: gsquest@umn.edu.
Website: http://www.carlsonschool.umn.edu

University of Mississippi, Graduate School, School of Business Administration, University, MS 38677. Offers business administration (MBA, PhD); finance (PhD); management (PhD); management information systems (PhD); marketing (PhD); JD/MBA. *Accreditation:* AACSB. *Faculty:* 60 full-time (18 women), 7 part-time/adjunct (1 woman). *Students:* 62 full-time (18 women), 83 part-time (20 women); includes 13 minority (4 Black or African American, non-Hispanic/Latino; 3 Asian, non-Hispanic/Latino; 4 Hispanic/Latino; 2 Two or more races, non-Hispanic/Latino), 14 international. Average age 30. In 2018, 83 master's, 11 doctorates awarded. *Entrance requirements:* For master's, GMAT, minimum GPA of 3.0; for doctorate, GMAT. Additional exam requirements/recommendations for international students: Required—TOEFL. *Application deadline:* Applications are processed on a rolling basis. Application fee: $50. Electronic applications accepted. *Financial support:* Fellowships, career-related internships or fieldwork, scholarships/grants, tuition waivers (full), and unspecified assistantships available. Financial award application deadline: 3/1; financial award applicants required to submit FAFSA. *Unit head:* Dr. Ken Cyree, Dean, 662-915-5820, Fax: 662-915-5821, E-mail: info@bus.olemiss.edu. *Application contact:* Temeka Smith, Graduate Activities Specialist for Admissions, 662-915-7474, Fax: 662-915-7577, E-mail: gschool@olemiss.edu.
Website: http://www.olemissbusiness.com/

University of Missouri, Office of Research and Graduate Studies, Robert J. Trulaske, Sr. College of Business, Program in Business Administration, Columbia, MO 65211. Offers business administration (MBA); finance (PhD); MBA/MHA. *Accreditation:* AACSB. *Degree requirements:* For doctorate, thesis/dissertation. *Entrance requirements:* For master's and doctorate, GMAT, minimum GPA of 3.0. Additional exam requirements/recommendations for international students: Required—TOEFL (minimum score 500 paper-based; 61 iBT). Electronic applications accepted.

University of Missouri–Kansas City, Henry W. Bloch School of Management, Kansas City, MO 64110-2499. Offers accounting (MS); finance (MS); public affairs (MPA, PhD); JD/MBA; LL M/MPA. PhD (interdisciplinary) offered through the School of Graduate Studies. *Accreditation:* AACSB; NASPAA. *Program availability:* Part-time, evening/weekend. Terminal master's awarded for partial completion of doctoral program. *Entrance requirements:* For master's, GMAT, GRE, 2 essays, 2 references, support of employer; for doctorate, GRE, minimum GPA of 3.0. Additional exam requirements/recommendations for international students: Required—TOEFL (minimum score 550 paper-based; 80 iBT). Electronic applications accepted. *Faculty research:* Entrepreneurship, finance, non-profit, risk management.

University of Missouri–St. Louis, College of Business Administration, St. Louis, MO 63121. Offers accounting (M Acc); business administration (MBA, DBA, PhD, Certificate), including logistics and supply chain management (PhD); business intelligence (Certificate); cybersecurity (Certificate); digital and social media marketing (Certificate); human resources management (Certificate); information systems (MS); logistics and supply chain management (Certificate); marketing management (Certificate). *Program availability:* Part-time, evening/weekend. *Degree requirements:* For doctorate, thesis/dissertation. *Entrance requirements:* For master's, GMAT, 2 letters of recommendation; for doctorate, GMAT or GRE, 3 letters of recommendation. Additional exam requirements/recommendations for international students: Recommended—TOEFL (minimum score 550 paper-based; 79 iBT), IELTS (minimum score 6.5). Electronic applications accepted. *Faculty research:* Statistical decision aids, commercial banking, corporate finance, operations management, information systems.

University of Missouri–St. Louis, Graduate School, Program in Public Policy Administration, St. Louis, MO 63121. Offers local government management (MPPA, Certificate); nonprofit management and leadership (MPPA, Certificate); policy and program evaluation (MPPA, Certificate). *Accreditation:* NASPAA. *Program availability:* Part-time, evening/weekend. *Degree requirements:* For master's, exit project. *Entrance requirements:* For master's, 3 letters of recommendation, personal statement. Additional exam requirements/recommendations for international students: Recommended—TOEFL (minimum score 550 paper-based), IELTS (minimum score 6.5). Electronic applications accepted. *Faculty research:* Urban policy, public finance, evaluation.

University of Mobile, Graduate Studies, Program in Business Administration, Mobile, AL 36613. Offers MBA. *Accreditation:* ACBSP. *Program availability:* Part-time, evening/weekend, blended/hybrid learning. *Students:* 34 full-time (20 women), 1 part-time; includes 19 minority (16 Black or African American, non-Hispanic/Latino; 1 Asian, non-Hispanic/Latino; 1 Hispanic/Latino; 1 Two or more races, non-Hispanic/Latino), 6 international. In 2018, 7 master's awarded. *Degree requirements:* For master's, comprehensive exam. *Entrance requirements:* For master's, GMAT, if overall undergraduate gpa is below 2.50. Additional exam requirements/recommendations for international students: Required—TOEFL (minimum score 550 paper-based; 80 iBT). *Application deadline:* For fall admission, 8/3 priority date for domestic and international students; for spring admission, 12/23 priority date for domestic and international students. Applications are processed on a rolling basis. Application fee: $40 ($50 for international students). Electronic applications accepted. *Expenses:* Contact institution. *Financial support:* Application deadline: 8/1; applicants required to submit FAFSA. *Faculty research:* Management, personnel management, small business, diversity. *Unit head:* Dr. Todd Greer, Dean, School of Business, 251-442-2701, Fax: 251-442-2523, E-mail: tgreer@umobile.edu. *Application contact:* Brian Boyle, Director of Recruitment, 251-442-2727, Fax: 251-442-2523.
Website: https://umobile.edu/academics/school-of-business/mba/

University of Montana, Graduate School, School of Business Administration, MBA Program, Missoula, MT 59812. Offers MBA, JD/MBA, MBA/Pharm D. *Accreditation:* AACSB. *Program availability:* Part-time, evening/weekend, online learning. *Degree requirements:* For master's, thesis optional. *Entrance requirements:* For master's, GMAT. Additional exam requirements/recommendations for international students: Required—TOEFL. *Faculty research:* Information systems, research methods, international business, human resource management, marketing.

University of Montevallo, Stephens College of Business, Montevallo, AL 35115. Offers MBA. *Accreditation:* AACSB. *Program availability:* Part-time, evening/weekend. *Students:* 10 full-time (7 women), 25 part-time (18 women); includes 10 minority (6 Black or African American, non-Hispanic/Latino; 2 Asian, non-Hispanic/Latino; 2 Hispanic/Latino), 2 international. In 2018, 19 master's awarded. *Degree requirements:* For master's, comprehensive exam. *Entrance requirements:* Additional exam requirements/recommendations for international students: Required—TOEFL (minimum score 550 paper-based). *Application deadline:* For fall admission, 7/15 for domestic students; for spring admission, 11/15 for domestic students. Application fee: $30. *Expenses: Tuition, area resident:* Full-time $10,512. Tuition, state resident: full-time $10,512. Tuition, nonresident: full-time $22,464. *International tuition:* $22,464 full-time. *Unit head:* Dr. Stephen H. Craft, Dean, 205-665-6540, E-mail: scob@montevallo.edu. *Application contact:* Dr. Stephen H. Craft, Dean, 205-665-6540, E-mail: scob@montevallo.edu.
Website: https://www.montevallo.edu/academics/colleges/college-of-business/mba/

University of Mount Olive, Graduate Programs, Mount Olive, NC 28365. Offers business (MBA); education (M Ed); nursing (MSN). *Program availability:* Online learning.

University of Nebraska at Kearney, College of Business and Technology, Department of Business, Kearney, NE 68849-0001. Offers accounting (MBA); generalist (MBA); human resources (MBA); human services (MBA); marketing (MBA). *Accreditation:* AACSB. *Program availability:* Part-time, evening/weekend. *Degree requirements:* For master's, thesis optional, capstone course. *Entrance requirements:* For master's, GRE or GMAT (if no significant managerial experience), letters of recommendation, essay, resume. Additional exam requirements/recommendations for international students: Recommended—TOEFL (minimum score 550 paper-based; 79 iBT), IELTS (minimum score 6.5). Electronic applications accepted. *Faculty research:* Small business financial management, employment law, expert systems, international trade and marketing, environmental economics.

University of Nebraska at Omaha, Graduate Studies, College of Business Administration, Program in Business Administration, Omaha, NE 68182. Offers business administration (MBA); business for bioscientists (Certificate); executive business administration (EMBA); human resources and training (Certificate). *Accreditation:* AACSB. *Program availability:* Part-time, evening/weekend. *Degree requirements:* For master's, thesis (for some programs), capstone course. *Entrance requirements:* For master's, GMAT or GRE, minimum GPA of 3.0, official transcripts, resume; for Certificate, minimum GPA of 3.0, official transcripts, resume, letter of recommendation, statement of purpose. Additional exam requirements/recommendations for international students: Required—TOEFL, IELTS, PTE. Electronic applications accepted.

University of Nebraska–Lincoln, Graduate College, College of Business Administration, Interdepartmental Area of Business, Lincoln, NE 68588. Offers accountancy (PhD); business (MBA); finance (MA, PhD), including business; management (MA, PhD), including business; marketing (MA, PhD), including business; JD/MBA; M Arch/MBA. *Accreditation:* AACSB. *Program availability:* Part-time, online learning. *Degree requirements:* For doctorate, comprehensive exam, thesis/dissertation. *Entrance requirements:* For master's and doctorate, GMAT. Additional exam requirements/recommendations for international students: Required—TOEFL (minimum score 550 paper-based). Electronic applications accepted.

University of Nevada, Las Vegas, Graduate College, Lee Business School, Program in Business Administration, Las Vegas, NV 89154-6031. Offers business administration (Certificate); business administration/dental (DMD/MBA); business administration/law (MBA/JD); business administration/management information system (MBA/MS); DMD/MBA; MBA/JD; MBA/MS. *Accreditation:* AACSB. *Program availability:* Part-time, evening/weekend. *Faculty:* 1 full-time (0 women), 4 part-time/adjunct (1 woman). *Students:* 116 full-time (48 women), 76 part-time (34 women); includes 70 minority (7 Black or African American, non-Hispanic/Latino; 1 American Indian or Alaska Native,

non-Hispanic/Latino; 23 Asian, non-Hispanic/Latino; 26 Hispanic/Latino; 13 Two or more races, non-Hispanic/Latino), 18 international. Average age 33. 100 applicants, 50% accepted, 37 enrolled. In 2018, 81 master's awarded. *Degree requirements:* For master's, capstone course. *Entrance requirements:* For master's, GMAT, 2 letters of recommendation; statement of purpose. Additional exam requirements/recommendations for international students: Required—TOEFL (minimum score 550 paper-based; 80 iBT), IELTS (minimum score 7). *Application deadline:* For fall admission, 7/15 for domestic students, 5/1 for international students; for spring admission, 11/15 for domestic students, 10/1 for international students; for summer admission, 4/1 for domestic students, 3/1 for international students. Application fee: $60 ($95 for international students). Electronic applications accepted. *Expenses:* Contact institution. *Financial support:* In 2018–19, 13 students received support, including 10 research assistantships with full tuition reimbursements available (averaging $11,625 per year), 3 teaching assistantships with full tuition reimbursements available (averaging $13,250 per year); institutionally sponsored loans, scholarships/grants, health care benefits, and unspecified assistantships also available. Financial award application deadline: 3/15; financial award applicants required to submit FAFSA. *Faculty research:* Economic effects on wages; benefits and economic effects of risk, uncertainty; asymmetric information: adverse selection, moral hazard; business processes. *Unit head:* Dr. Stoney Alder, Vice Dean, 702-895-2052, Fax: 702-895-4090, E-mail: business.assoc.dean@unlv.edu. *Application contact:* Dr. Vincent Hsu, Director MBA Programs/Professor, 702-895-3842, Fax: 702-895-3632, E-mail: mba.director@unlv.edu.
Website: http://business.unlv.edu/mba/

University of Nevada, Reno, Graduate School, College of Business, Department of Business Administration, Reno, NV 89557. Offers MBA. *Accreditation:* AACSB. *Program availability:* Part-time, evening/weekend, online learning. *Entrance requirements:* For master's, GMAT, minimum GPA of 2.75. Additional exam requirements/recommendations for international students: Required—TOEFL (minimum score 500 paper-based; 61 iBT), IELTS (minimum score 6). Electronic applications accepted.

University of New Brunswick Fredericton, School of Graduate Studies, Faculty of Business Administration, Fredericton, NB E3B 5A3, Canada. Offers business administration (MBA); engineering management (MBA); entrepreneurship (MBA); sports and recreation management (MBA); MBA/LL B. *Program availability:* Part-time. *Degree requirements:* For master's, thesis optional. *Entrance requirements:* For master's, GMAT (minimum score 550), minimum GPA of 3.0; 3-5 years of work experience; 3 letters of reference with at least one academic reference. Additional exam requirements/recommendations for international students: Required—TOEFL (minimum score 580 paper-based; 92 iBT) or IELTS (minimum score 7). Electronic applications accepted. *Faculty research:* Entrepreneurship, finance, law, sport and recreation management, engineering management.

University of New Brunswick Saint John, Faculty of Business, Saint John, NB E2L 4L5, Canada. Offers administration (MBA); electronic commerce (MBA); international business (MBA); natural resource management (MBA). *Program availability:* Part-time. *Entrance requirements:* For master's, GMAT (minimum score of 550) or GRE (minimum 54th percentile), minimum GPA of 3.0. Additional exam requirements/recommendations for international students: Required—TOEFL (minimum score 580 paper-based; 93 iBT), TWE (minimum score 4.5). Electronic applications accepted. *Expenses:* Contact institution. *Faculty research:* International business, project management, innovation and technology management; business use of Weblogs and podcasts to communicate; corporate governance; high-involvement work systems; international competitiveness; supply chain management and logistics.

University of New Hampshire, Graduate School Manchester Campus, Manchester, NH 03101. Offers business administration (MBA); cybersecurity policy and risk management (MS); educational administration and supervision (Ed S); educational studies (M Ed); elementary education (M Ed); information technology (MS); public administration (MPA); public health (MPH, Certificate); secondary education (M Ed, MAT); social work (MSW); substance use disorders (Certificate). *Program availability:* Part-time, evening/weekend. *Entrance requirements:* Additional exam requirements/recommendations for international students: Required—TOEFL (minimum score 550 paper-based; 80 iBT). Electronic applications accepted.

University of New Hampshire, Graduate School, Peter T. Paul College of Business and Economics, Program in Business Administration, Durham, NH 03824. Offers MBA, MBA/JD. *Accreditation:* AACSB. *Program availability:* Part-time, evening/weekend, online learning. *Entrance requirements:* For master's, GMAT. Additional exam requirements/recommendations for international students: Required—TOEFL (minimum score 550 paper-based; 80 iBT). Electronic applications accepted. *Expenses:* Contact institution.

University of New Haven, Graduate School, College of Business, Executive Program in Business Administration, West Haven, CT 06516. Offers EMBA. *Accreditation:* AACSB. *Program availability:* Part-time, evening/weekend. *Students:* 25 full-time (7 women); includes 10 minority (4 Black or African American, non-Hispanic/Latino; 4 Asian, non-Hispanic/Latino; 2 Hispanic/Latino), 1 international. Average age 37. 12 applicants, 100% accepted, 11 enrolled. In 2018, 11 master's awarded. *Entrance requirements:* Additional exam requirements/recommendations for international students: Required—TOEFL (minimum score 80 iBT), IELTS, PTE. *Application deadline:* Applications are processed on a rolling basis. Application fee: $50. Electronic applications accepted. Application fee is waived when completed online. *Expenses:* Contact institution. *Financial support:* Application deadline: 5/1. *Unit head:* Michael Davis, Program Director, 203-932-7433, E-mail: MDavis@newhaven.edu. *Application contact:* Selina O'Toole, Senior Associate Director of Graduate Admissions, 203-932-7337, E-mail: SOToole@newhaven.edu.
Website: https://www.newhaven.edu/business/graduate-programs/emba/

University of New Haven, Graduate School, College of Business, Program in Business Administration, West Haven, CT 06516. Offers accounting (MBA); business administration (MBA); business intelligence (MBA); business policy and strategic leadership (MBA); finance (MBA), including chartered financial analyst; global marketing (MBA); human resources management (MBA); sport management (MBA). *Accreditation:* AACSB. *Program availability:* Part-time, evening/weekend. *Students:* 151 full-time (73 women), 70 part-time (30 women); includes 51 minority (23 Black or African American, non-Hispanic/Latino; 13 Asian, non-Hispanic/Latino; 14 Hispanic/Latino; 1 Two or more races, non-Hispanic/Latino), 74 international. Average age 28. 197 applicants, 91% accepted, 82 enrolled. In 2018, 70 master's awarded. *Entrance requirements:* For master's, GMAT. Additional exam requirements/recommendations for international students: Required—TOEFL (minimum score 80 iBT), IELTS, PTE. *Application deadline:* Applications are processed on a rolling basis. Application fee: $50. Electronic applications accepted. Application fee is waived when completed online. *Expenses:* Tuition: Full-time $16,470; part-time $915 per credit hour. *Required fees:* $230; $95 per term. *Financial support:* Research assistantships with partial tuition reimbursements, teaching assistantships with partial tuition reimbursements, career-related internships or fieldwork, Federal Work-Study, scholarships/grants, and unspecified assistantships available. Support available to part-time students. Financial award applicants required to submit FAFSA. *Unit head:* Darell Singleterry, Director, 203-932-7386, E-mail: dsingleterry@newhaven.edu. *Application contact:* Selina O'Toole, Senior Associate Director of Graduate Admissions, 203-932-7337, E-mail: SOToole@newhaven.edu.
Website: http://www.newhaven.edu/business/graduate-programs/mba/index.php

University of New Mexico, Anderson School of Management, Albuquerque, NM 87131. Offers information systems and assurance (MS); JD/M Acct; JD/MBA; MBA/MA; MBA/MEME; MBA/Pharm D. *Accreditation:* AACSB. *Program availability:* Part-time, evening/weekend. *Faculty:* 62 full-time (27 women), 41 part-time/adjunct (17 women). *Students:* 392 part-time (201 women); includes 186 minority (5 Black or African American, non-Hispanic/Latino; 9 American Indian or Alaska Native, non-Hispanic/Latino; 18 Asian, non-Hispanic/Latino; 145 Hispanic/Latino; 9 Two or more races, non-Hispanic/Latino), 38 international. Average age 28. 329 applicants, 53% accepted, 141 enrolled. In 2018, 330 master's awarded. *Degree requirements:* For master's, minimum of 33 credit hours, capstone course, minimum GPA of 3.0. *Entrance requirements:* For master's, GMAT or GRE (minimum score of 500), minimum GPA of 3.0 on last 60 hours of college coursework including any post baccalaureate work. Additional exam requirements/recommendations for international students: Required—TOEFL (minimum score 550 paper-based; 79 iBT), IELTS (minimum score 6.5). *Application deadline:* For fall admission, 3/1 priority date for domestic students, 5/1 priority date for international students; for spring admission, 9/1 priority date for domestic students, 10/1 priority date for international students. Applications are processed on a rolling basis. Application fee: $50 ($70 for international students). Electronic applications accepted. *Expenses:* $542.36 per credit resident part-time and full-time, $1229.36 per credit non-resident part-time and full-time. *Financial support:* In 2018–19, 79 students received support, including 50 fellowships (averaging $15,746 per year), 52 research assistantships with partial tuition reimbursements available (averaging $15,400 per year); career-related internships or fieldwork, Federal Work-Study, scholarships/grants, and unspecified assistantships also available. Support available to part-time students. Financial award application deadline: 6/1; financial award applicants required to submit FAFSA. *Faculty research:* Organizational and social aspects of accounting, international management of technology and entrepreneurship, business ethics and corporate social responsibility, marketing, information assurance and fraud. *Unit head:* Dr. Shawn Berman, Interim Dean, 505-277-1792, E-mail: sberman@unm.edu. *Application contact:* Lisa Beauchene-Lawson, Supervisor, Graduate Admissions & Advisement, 505-277-3290, E-mail: andersongrad@unm.edu.
Website: http://www.mgt.unm.edu

University of New Orleans, Graduate School, College of Business Administration, Program in Business Administration, New Orleans, LA 70148. Offers MBA. *Accreditation:* AACSB. *Degree requirements:* For master's, thesis optional. *Entrance requirements:* For master's, GMAT. Additional exam requirements/recommendations for international students: Required—TOEFL (minimum score 550 paper-based; 79 iBT). Electronic applications accepted.

University of North Alabama, College of Business, Florence, AL 35632-0001. Offers business administration (MBA), including accounting, enterprise resource planning systems, executive, finance, health care management, information systems, international business, project management. *Accreditation:* AACSB; ACBSP. *Program availability:* Part-time, 100% online, blended/hybrid learning. *Entrance requirements:* For master's, GMAT, GRE, minimum GPA of 2.75 in last 60 hours, 2.5 overall (on a 3.0 scale); 27 hours of course work in business and economics. Additional exam requirements/recommendations for international students: Required—TOEFL (minimum score 79 iBT), IELTS (minimum score 6), PTE (minimum score 54). Electronic applications accepted.

The University of North Carolina at Chapel Hill, Kenan-Flagler Business School, Doctoral Program in Business Administration, Chapel Hill, NC 27599. Offers accounting (PhD); finance (PhD); marketing (PhD); operations management (PhD); organizational behavior (PhD); strategy (PhD). *Accreditation:* AACSB. *Degree requirements:* For doctorate, thesis/dissertation. *Entrance requirements:* For doctorate, GMAT or GRE General Test. Electronic applications accepted. *Expenses:* Contact institution.

The University of North Carolina at Chapel Hill, Kenan-Flagler Business School, Executive MBA Programs, Chapel Hill, NC 27599. Offers MBA. *Accreditation:* AACSB. *Program availability:* Evening/weekend, online learning. *Degree requirements:* For master's, exams, project. *Entrance requirements:* For master's, GMAT, 5 years of full-time work experience, interview. Electronic applications accepted. *Expenses:* Contact institution.

The University of North Carolina at Chapel Hill, Kenan-Flagler Business School, MBA Program, Chapel Hill, NC 27599. Offers MBA, MBA/JD, MBA/MHA, MBA/MRP, MBA/MSIS. *Accreditation:* AACSB. *Degree requirements:* For master's, exams, practicum. *Entrance requirements:* For master's, GMAT, interview, minimum 2 years of work experience. Additional exam requirements/recommendations for international students: Required—TOEFL. Electronic applications accepted.

The University of North Carolina at Charlotte, Belk College of Business, Department of Management, Charlotte, NC 28223-0001. Offers business administration (MBA, DBA, PhD); business analytics (Graduate Certificate); management (MS). *Program availability:* Part-time, evening/weekend. *Students:* 135 full-time (67 women), 266 part-time (86 women); includes 115 minority (45 Black or African American, non-Hispanic/Latino; 1 American Indian or Alaska Native, non-Hispanic/Latino; 35 Asian, non-Hispanic/Latino; 22 Hispanic/Latino; 12 Two or more races, non-Hispanic/Latino), 103 international. Average age 29. 314 applicants, 70% accepted, 147 enrolled. In 2018, 98 master's, 3 doctorates, 5 other advanced degrees awarded. *Degree requirements:* For doctorate, comprehensive exam (for some programs), thesis/dissertation. *Entrance requirements:* For master's, GMAT or GRE, bachelor's degree from regionally-accredited college or university; at least three evaluations from persons familiar with applicant's personal and professional qualifications; essay describing applicant's experience and objectives; resume; for doctorate, GMAT (minimum score of 650) or GRE (minimum 700 on quantitative section, 500 on verbal), baccalaureate or master's degree in business, economics, or related field such as mathematical finance, mathematics, or physics with minimum undergraduate GPA of 3.5 (3.25 graduate); three letters of recommendation; statement of purpose; for Graduate Certificate, transcripts, minimum undergraduate GPA of 2.75, essay describing experience and objectives. Additional exam requirements/recommendations for international students: Required—TOEFL (minimum score 523 paper-based; 70 iBT), IELTS (minimum score 6), TOEFL (minimum score 523 paper-based, 70 iBT) or IELTS (6.0). *Application deadline:* Applications are processed on a rolling basis. Application fee: $75. Electronic applications accepted. *Expenses:* Contact institution. *Financial support:* Research assistantships, teaching assistantships, career-related internships or fieldwork, institutionally sponsored loans, scholarships/grants, and unspecified assistantships available. Support available to part-time students. Financial award application deadline: 3/1; financial award applicants required to submit FAFSA. *Total annual research expenditures:* $167,166. *Unit head:* Dr. David J. Woehr, Department Chair, 704-687-7684, Fax: 704-687-1380, E-mail: dwoehr@uncc.edu. *Application contact:* Kathy B. Giddings, Director of Graduate Admissions, 704-687-5503, Fax: 704-687-1668, E-mail: gradadm@uncc.edu.
Website: https://belkcollege.uncc.edu/departments/management

Business Administration and Management—General

The University of North Carolina at Greensboro, Graduate School, Bryan School of Business and Economics, Department of Business Administration, Greensboro, NC 27412-5001. Offers MBA, PMC, Postbaccalaureate Certificate, MS/MBA, MSN/MBA. *Accreditation:* AACSB. *Entrance requirements:* For master's, GMAT, GRE General Test, managerial experience. Additional exam requirements/recommendations for international students: Required—TOEFL. Electronic applications accepted.

The University of North Carolina at Pembroke, The Graduate School, School of Business, Pembroke, NC 28372-1510. Offers MBA. *Accreditation:* AACSB. *Program availability:* Part-time, evening/weekend. *Entrance requirements:* For master's, GMAT, minimum GPA of 3.0 in major or 2.5 overall. Additional exam requirements/recommendations for international students: Required—TOEFL.

The University of North Carolina Wilmington, Cameron School of Business, Business Administration Program, Wilmington, NC 28403-3297. Offers business administration (MBA); business administration - international (MBA); business administration - professional (MBA). *Accreditation:* AACSB. *Program availability:* Part-time-only. *Degree requirements:* For master's, thesis (for some programs), written case analysis and oral presentation (for professional), oral competency (for international). *Entrance requirements:* For master's, GMAT (for some programs), 2 years of appropriate work experience (for professional option), baccalaureate degree in the area of business and/or economics or six business prerequisite courses (for international option), resume, 3 letters of recommendation. Additional exam requirements/recommendations for international students: Required—TOEFL (minimum score 550 paper-based; 79 iBT), IELTS (minimum score 6.5). Electronic applications accepted. *Expenses:* Contact institution.

University of North Dakota, Graduate School, College of Business and Public Administration, Business Administration Program, Grand Forks, ND 58202. Offers MBA, MBA/JD. *Accreditation:* AACSB. *Program availability:* Part-time, evening/weekend, online learning. *Degree requirements:* For master's, comprehensive exam, thesis or alternative, project. *Entrance requirements:* For master's, GMAT, minimum GPA of 3.25. Additional exam requirements/recommendations for international students: Required—TOEFL (minimum score 550 paper-based; 79 iBT), IELTS (minimum score 6.5). Electronic applications accepted.

University of Northern Colorado, Graduate School, Monfort College of Business, Greeley, CO 80639. Offers accounting (MA); general business management (MBA); healthcare administration (MBA); human resources management (MBA). *Accreditation:* AACSB.

University of Northern Iowa, Graduate College, College of Business Administration, MBA Program, Cedar Falls, IA 50614. Offers MBA. *Accreditation:* AACSB. *Program availability:* Part-time, evening/weekend. *Entrance requirements:* For master's, GMAT (minimum score 500), minimum GPA of 3.0. Additional exam requirements/recommendations for international students: Required—TOEFL (minimum score 500 paper-based; 61 iBT). Electronic applications accepted.

University of North Florida, Coggin College of Business, MBA Program, Jacksonville, FL 32224. Offers accounting (MBA); construction management (MBA); e-commerce (MBA); economics (MBA); finance (MBA); human resource management (MBA); international business (MBA); logistics (MBA); management applications (MBA). *Accreditation:* AACSB. *Program availability:* Part-time, evening/weekend. *Faculty:* 40 full-time (14 women). *Students:* 368 part-time (158 women); includes 83 minority (30 Black or African American, non-Hispanic/Latino; 20 Asian, non-Hispanic/Latino; 16 Hispanic/Latino; 17 Two or more races, non-Hispanic/Latino), 28 international. Average age 30. 311 applicants, 51% accepted, 99 enrolled. In 2018, 151 master's awarded. *Entrance requirements:* For master's, GMAT or GRE, U.S. bachelor's degree from regionally-accredited university or equivalent foreign degree. Additional exam requirements/recommendations for international students: Required—TOEFL (minimum score 550 paper-based; 79 iBT). *Application deadline:* For fall admission, 8/1 priority date for domestic students, 5/1 for international students; for spring admission, 12/1 priority date for domestic students, 10/1 for international students; for summer admission, 4/29 priority date for domestic students, 2/1 for international students. Application fee: $30. *Expenses: Tuition, area resident:* Part-time $408.10 per credit hour. Tuition, state resident: part-time $408.10 per credit hour. Tuition, nonresident: part-time $932.61 per credit hour. *Required fees:* $111.81 per credit hour. Tuition and fees vary according to course load, campus/location and program. *Financial support:* In 2018–19, 41 students received support, including 1 research assistantship (averaging $2,143 per year); teaching assistantships, Federal Work-Study, and tuition waivers (partial) also available. Support available to part-time students. Financial award application deadline: 4/1; financial award applicants required to submit FAFSA. *Faculty research:* Performance measures, costing, and inventory issues in logistics and supply chain management; inter-organizational systems; international management and marketing practices; e-commerce; organizational learning and socialization processes. *Unit head:* Dr. Parvez Ahmed, Graduate Program Director, 904-620-1678, E-mail: pahmed@unf.edu. *Application contact:* Amy Bishop, MSM Advisor, 904-620-2575, Fax: 904-620-2832, E-mail: coggin.students@unf.edu.
Website: http://www.unf.edu/graduateschool/academics/programs/MBA.aspx

University of North Georgia, Mike Cottrell College of Business, Dahlonega, GA 30597. Offers MBA. *Accreditation:* AACSB. *Program availability:* Part-time-only, evening/weekend. *Degree requirements:* For master's, capstone leadership experience. *Entrance requirements:* For master's, GRE or GMAT, 2 references, resume. Additional exam requirements/recommendations for international students: Required—TOEFL (minimum score 550 paper-based; 79 iBT), IELTS (minimum score 6.5). Electronic applications accepted. Application fee is waived when completed online. *Expenses:* Contact institution.

University of North Texas, Toulouse Graduate School, Denton, TX 76203-5459. Offers accounting (MS); applied anthropology (MA, MS); applied behavior analysis (Certificate); applied geography (MA); applied technology and performance improvement (M Ed, MS); art education (MA); art history (MA); arts leadership (Certificate); audiology (Au D); behavior analysis (MS); behavioral science (PhD); biochemistry and molecular biology (MS); biology (MA, MS); biomedical engineering (MS); business analysis (MS); chemistry (MS); clinical health psychology (PhD); communication studies (MA, MS); computer engineering (MS); computer science (MS); counseling (M Ed, MS), including clinical mental health counseling (MS), college and university counseling, elementary school counseling, secondary school counseling; creative writing (MA); criminal justice (MS); curriculum and instruction (M Ed); decision sciences (MBA); design (MA, MFA), including fashion design (MFA), innovation studies, interior design (MFA); early childhood studies (MS); economics (MS); educational leadership (M Ed, Ed D); educational psychology (MS, PhD), including family studies (MS), gifted and talented (MS), human development (MS), learning and cognition (MS), research, measurement and evaluation (MS); electrical engineering (MS); emergency management (MPA); engineering technology (MS); English (MA); English as a second language (MA); environmental science (MS); finance (MBA, MS); financial management (MPA); French (MA); health services management (MBA); higher education (M Ed, Ed D); history (MA, MS); hospitality management (MS); human resources management (MPA); information science (MS); information systems (PhD); information technologies (MBA); interdisciplinary studies (MA, MS); international studies (MA); international sustainable tourism (MS); jazz studies (MM); journalism (MA, MJ, Graduate Certificate), including interactive and virtual digital communication (Graduate Certificate), narrative journalism (Graduate Certificate), public relations (Graduate Certificate); kinesiology (MS); linguistics (MA); local government management (MPA); logistics (PhD); logistics and supply chain management (MBA); long-term care, senior housing, and aging services (MA); management (PhD); marketing (MBA); mathematics (MA, MS); mechanical and energy engineering (MS, PhD); music (MA), including ethnomusicology, music theory, musicology, performance; music composition (PhD); music education (MM Ed, PhD); nonprofit management (MPA); operations and supply chain management (MBA); performance (MM, DMA); philosophy (MA); political science (MA); professional and technical communication (MA); radio, television and film (MA, MFA); rehabilitation counseling (Certificate); sociology (MA); Spanish (MA); special education (M Ed); speech-language pathology (MA); strategic management (MBA); studio art (MFA); teaching (M Ed); MBA/MS. *Program availability:* Part-time, evening/weekend, online learning. Terminal master's awarded for partial completion of doctoral program. *Degree requirements:* For master's, variable foreign language requirement, comprehensive exam (for some programs), thesis (for some programs); for doctorate, variable foreign language requirement, comprehensive exam (for some programs), thesis/dissertation; for other advanced degree, variable foreign language requirement, comprehensive exam (for some programs). *Entrance requirements:* For master's and doctorate, GRE, GMAT. Additional exam requirements/recommendations for international students: Required—TOEFL (minimum score 550 paper-based; 79 iBT). Electronic applications accepted.

University of North Texas at Dallas, Graduate School, Dallas, TX 75241. Offers accounting (MBA); counseling (M Ed, MS); criminal justice (MS); curriculum and instruction (M Ed); educational administration (M Ed); human resources and organizational behavior (MBA); public leadership (MS); strategic management (MBA).

University of Northwestern Ohio, Graduate College, Lima, OH 45805-1498. Offers business administration (MBA). *Program availability:* Evening/weekend, online learning.

University of Northwestern–St. Paul, Master of Business Administration Program, St. Paul, MN 55113-1598. Offers MBA. *Program availability:* Part-time, evening/weekend, online learning. Electronic applications accepted.

University of Notre Dame, Mendoza College of Business, Executive Master of Business Administration Program, Notre Dame, IN 46556. Offers MBA. Program offered at the Stayer Center for Executive Education in Notre Dame, Indiana and also at Notre Dame Chicago Commons in Chicago, Illinois on Michigan Avenue. *Accreditation:* AACSB. *Entrance requirements:* For master's, five or more years of significant experience managing people, projects or business units. Additional exam requirements/recommendations for international students: Required—TOEFL, IELTS. Electronic applications accepted. Application fee is waived when completed online. *Expenses:* Contact institution. *Faculty research:* Economic determinants of multinational firm behavior and foreign direct investment; psychology of ethical decision making - examining why individuals behave unethically; role of corporate governance on voluntary financial statement disclosures; proactive personality and behavior at work; strategy design and implementation.

University of Notre Dame, Mendoza College of Business, Master of Business Administration Program, Notre Dame, IN 46556. Offers business analytics (MBA); business leadership (MBA); consulting (MBA); corporate finance (MBA); innovation and entrepreneurship (MBA); investments (MBA); marketing (MBA); MBA/MSBA. *Accreditation:* AACSB. *Entrance requirements:* For master's, GMAT or GRE, work experience, essay, four-slide presentation, two recommendations, transcripts from all colleges and/or universities attended, interview. Additional exam requirements/recommendations for international students: Required—PTE (minimum score 68), TOEFL (minimum iBT score of 109), IELTS (7.5), or documentation of at least six semesters of full-time university education in English. Electronic applications accepted. *Expenses:* Contact institution. *Faculty research:* Market micro-structure; marketing and public policy; corporate finance and accounting; corporate governance and ethical behavior; high performing organizations.

University of Notre Dame, Mendoza College of Business, Master of Science in Management Program, Notre Dame, IN 46556. Offers MSM. *Entrance requirements:* For master's, GMAT or GRE, essay, two recommendations, transcript from all colleges or universities attended, resume, interview. Additional exam requirements/recommendations for international students: Required—PTE (minimum score 68), TOEFL (minimum iBT score of 109), IELTS (7.5), or documentation of at least six semesters of full-time university education in English. Electronic applications accepted. *Expenses:* Contact institution.

University of Oklahoma, Price College of Business, Norman, OK 73019. Offers accounting (M Acc); business administration (MBA, PMBA, PhD), including business administration (EMBA, MBA, PMBA, PhD); business entrepreneurship (Graduate Certificate); digital technologies (Graduate Certificate), including digital technologies; energy (EMBA), including business administration (EMBA, MBA, PMBA, PhD); foundations of business (Graduate Certificate); management information technology (MS), including management of information technology; the business of energy (Graduate Certificate); JD/MBA; MBA/MA; MBA/MLIS; MBA/MPH; MBA/MS. *Program availability:* Part-time, evening/weekend, 100% online. *Faculty:* 58 full-time (16 women), 6 part-time/adjunct (0 women). *Students:* 108 full-time (31 women), 267 part-time (84 women); includes 92 minority (16 Black or African American, non-Hispanic/Latino; 9 American Indian or Alaska Native, non-Hispanic/Latino; 16 Asian, non-Hispanic/Latino; 33 Hispanic/Latino; 1 Native Hawaiian or other Pacific Islander, non-Hispanic/Latino; 17 Two or more races, non-Hispanic/Latino), 38 international. Average age 33. 265 applicants, 44% accepted, 83 enrolled. In 2018, 132 master's, 5 doctorates, 41 other advanced degrees awarded. *Degree requirements:* For doctorate, comprehensive exam, thesis/dissertation. *Entrance requirements:* For master's, GMAT/GRE; for doctorate, GMAT. Additional exam requirements/recommendations for international students: Required—TOEFL (minimum score 100 iBT) or IELTS (minimum score 7.0). *Application deadline:* Applications are processed on a rolling basis. Application fee: $50 ($100 for international students). Electronic applications accepted. *Expenses:* Contact institution. *Financial support:* Fellowships, research assistantships, teaching assistantships, career-related internships or fieldwork, scholarships/grants, health care benefits, and unspecified assistantships available. Support available to part-time students. Financial award application deadline: 6/1; financial award applicants required to submit FAFSA. *Unit head:* Wayne Thomas, Interim Dean, 405-325-0100, Fax: 405-325-3421, E-mail: wthomas@ou.edu. *Application contact:* Amber Hasbrook, Academic Counselor, 405-325-5815, Fax: 405-325-7753, E-mail: ahasbrook@ou.edu.
Website: http://www.ou.edu/price

University of Oregon, Graduate School, Charles H. Lundquist College of Business, Department of Management, Eugene, OR 97403. Offers PhD. *Accreditation:* AACSB. *Program availability:* Part-time. Terminal master's awarded for partial completion of doctoral program. *Degree requirements:* For doctorate, thesis/dissertation, 2 comprehensive exams. *Entrance requirements:* For doctorate, GMAT. Additional exam requirements/recommendations for international students: Required—TOEFL.

University of Oregon, Graduate School, Charles H. Lundquist College of Business, Department of Management: General Business, Eugene, OR 97403. Offers MBA. *Accreditation:* AACSB. *Entrance requirements:* For master's, GMAT. Additional exam requirements/recommendations for international students: Required—TOEFL.

University of Ottawa, Faculty of Graduate and Postdoctoral Studies, Telfer School of Management, Executive Business Administration Program, Ottawa, ON K1N 6N5, Canada. Offers EMBA. *Accreditation:* AACSB. *Program availability:* Evening/weekend. *Entrance requirements:* For master's, bachelor's degree or equivalent, minimum B average, business experience. Additional exam requirements/recommendations for international students: Recommended—TOEFL. Electronic applications accepted. *Expenses:* Contact institution.

University of Ottawa, Faculty of Graduate and Postdoctoral Studies, Telfer School of Management, MBA Program, Ottawa, ON K1N 6N5, Canada. Offers MBA. *Accreditation:* AACSB. *Program availability:* Part-time, evening/weekend. *Degree requirements:* For master's, thesis optional. *Entrance requirements:* For master's, GMAT, bachelor's degree or equivalent, minimum B average, minimum 2 years of work experience. Additional exam requirements/recommendations for international students: Recommended—TOEFL. Electronic applications accepted.

University of Pennsylvania, Wharton School, Management Department, Philadelphia, PA 19104. Offers MBA, PhD. *Accreditation:* AACSB. *Entrance requirements:* For master's, GMAT; for doctorate, GMAT or GRE. *Faculty research:* Cross-cultural leadership, international technology transfers, human resource management, financial services.

University of Pennsylvania, Wharton School, Wharton Doctoral Programs, Philadelphia, PA 19104. Offers accounting (PhD); applied economics (PhD); ethics and legal studies (PhD); finance (PhD); health care management and economics (PhD); management (PhD); marketing (PhD); operations and information management (PhD); statistics (PhD). *Accreditation:* AACSB. *Degree requirements:* For doctorate, thesis/dissertation. *Entrance requirements:* For doctorate, GMAT or GRE, letters of recommendation. Additional exam requirements/recommendations for international students: Required—TOEFL, TWE. Electronic applications accepted.

University of Pennsylvania, Wharton School, The Wharton MBA Program, Philadelphia, PA 19104. Offers MBA, DMD/MBA, JD/MBA, MBA/MA, MBA/MS, MBA/MSN, MBA/MSW, MBA/PhD, MD/MBA, VMD/MBA. *Accreditation:* AACSB. *Entrance requirements:* For master's, GMAT, interview, 2 letters of recommendation, resume/curriculum vitae. Additional exam requirements/recommendations for international students: Required—TOEFL. Electronic applications accepted. *Faculty research:* Entrepreneurial studies, finance, management of technology.

University of Pennsylvania, Wharton School, The Wharton MBA Program for Executives, Wharton Executive MBA East, Philadelphia, PA 19104. Offers MBA. *Accreditation:* AACSB. *Program availability:* Evening/weekend. *Entrance requirements:* For master's, GMAT. Additional exam requirements/recommendations for international students: Recommended—TOEFL.

University of Pennsylvania, Wharton School, The Wharton MBA Program for Executives, Wharton Executive MBA West, Philadelphia, PA 19104. Offers MBA. *Accreditation:* AACSB. *Program availability:* Evening/weekend. *Entrance requirements:* For master's, GMAT. Additional exam requirements/recommendations for international students: Recommended—TOEFL.

University of Phoenix–Bay Area Campus, School of Business, San Jose, CA 95134-1805. Offers accountancy (MS); accounting (MBA); business administration (MBA, DBA); energy management (MBA); global management (MBA); health care management (MBA); human resource management (MBA); human resources management (MM); management (MM); marketing (MBA); organizational leadership (DM); project management (MBA); public administration (MPA); technology management (MBA). *Accreditation:* ACBSP. *Program availability:* Evening/weekend, online learning. *Degree requirements:* For master's, thesis (for some programs). *Entrance requirements:* For master's, minimum undergraduate GPA of 3.0, 3 years of work experience. Additional exam requirements/recommendations for international students: Required—TOEFL (minimum score 550 paper-based; 79 iBT). Electronic applications accepted.

University of Phoenix–Central Valley Campus, School of Business, Fresno, CA 93720-1552. Offers accounting (MBA); business administration (MBA); global management (MBA); human resources management (MBA, MM); management (MM); marketing (MBA); public administration (MBA, MM). *Accreditation:* ACBSP.

University of Phoenix–Dallas Campus, School of Business, Dallas, TX 75251. Offers accounting (MBA); business administration (MBA); global management (MBA); human resources management (MBA, MM); management (MM); marketing (MBA); public administration (MBA, MM). *Accreditation:* ACBSP. *Program availability:* Evening/weekend, online learning. *Degree requirements:* For master's, thesis (for some programs). *Entrance requirements:* For master's, 3 years of work experience, minimum undergraduate GPA of 3.0. Additional exam requirements/recommendations for international students: Required—TOEFL (minimum score 550 paper-based; 79 iBT). Electronic applications accepted.

University of Phoenix–Hawaii Campus, School of Business, Honolulu, HI 96813-3800. Offers accounting (MBA); business administration (MBA); global management (MBA); human resources management (MBA, MM); management (MM); marketing (MBA); public administration (MBA, MM). *Accreditation:* ACBSP. *Program availability:* Evening/weekend. *Degree requirements:* For master's, thesis (for some programs). *Entrance requirements:* For master's, minimum undergraduate GPA of 3.0, 3 years of work experience. Additional exam requirements/recommendations for international students: Required—TOEFL (minimum score 550 paper-based; 79 iBT). Electronic applications accepted.

University of Phoenix–Houston Campus, School of Business, Houston, TX 77079-2004. Offers accounting (MBA); business administration (MBA); global management (MBA); human resources management (MBA, MM); management (MM); marketing (MBA); public administration (MBA, MM). *Accreditation:* ACBSP. *Program availability:* Evening/weekend, online learning. *Degree requirements:* For master's, thesis (for some programs). *Entrance requirements:* For master's, 3 years of work experience, minimum undergraduate GPA of 3.0. Additional exam requirements/recommendations for international students: Required—TOEFL (minimum score 550 paper-based; 79 iBT). Electronic applications accepted.

University of Phoenix–Las Vegas Campus, School of Business, Las Vegas, NV 89135. Offers accounting (MBA); business administration (MBA); global management (MBA); human resources management (MBA, MM); management (MM); marketing (MBA); public administration (MM). *Accreditation:* ACBSP. *Program availability:* Evening/weekend, online learning. *Degree requirements:* For master's, thesis (for some programs). *Entrance requirements:* For master's, minimum undergraduate GPA of 3.0, 3 years of work experience. Additional exam requirements/recommendations for international students: Required—TOEFL (minimum score 550 paper-based; 79 iBT). Electronic applications accepted.

University of Phoenix–Online Campus, School of Advanced Studies, Phoenix, AZ 85034-7209. Offers business administration (DBA); education (Ed S); educational leadership (Ed D), including curriculum and instruction, education technology, educational leadership; health administration (DHA); higher education administration (PhD); industrial/organizational psychology (PhD); nursing (PhD); organizational leadership (DM), including information systems and technology, organizational leadership. *Program availability:* Evening/weekend, online learning. *Degree requirements:* For doctorate, thesis/dissertation. *Entrance requirements:* Additional exam requirements/recommendations for international students: Required—TOEFL, TOEIC (Test of English as an International Communication), Berlitz Online English Proficiency Exam, PTE, or IELTS. Electronic applications accepted. *Expenses:* Contact institution.

University of Phoenix–Online Campus, School of Business, Phoenix, AZ 85034-7209. Offers accountancy (MS); accounting (MBA, Certificate); business administration (MBA); energy management (MBA); global management (MBA); health care management (MBA); human resource management (MBA, Certificate); human resources management (MM); management (MM); marketing (MBA, Certificate); project management (MBA, Certificate); public administration (MBA, MM); technology management (MBA). *Program availability:* Evening/weekend, online learning. *Entrance requirements:* Additional exam requirements/recommendations for international students: Required—TOEFL, TOEIC (Test of English as an International Communication), Berlitz Online English Proficiency Exam, PTE, or IELTS. Electronic applications accepted. *Expenses:* Contact institution.

University of Phoenix–Phoenix Campus, School of Business, Tempe, AZ 85282-2371. Offers accounting (MBA, MS, Certificate); business administration (MBA); energy management (MBA); global management (MBA); health care management (MBA); human resource management (MBA, Certificate); management (MM); marketing (MBA); project management (MBA); technology management (MBA). *Program availability:* Evening/weekend, online learning. *Entrance requirements:* Additional exam requirements/recommendations for international students: Required—TOEFL, TOEIC (Test of English as an International Communication), Berlitz Online English Proficiency Exam, PTE, or IELTS. Electronic applications accepted. *Expenses:* Contact institution.

University of Phoenix–Sacramento Valley Campus, College of Information Systems and Technology, Sacramento, CA 95833-4334. Offers management (MIS); technology management (MBA). *Program availability:* Evening/weekend. *Degree requirements:* For master's, thesis (for some programs). *Entrance requirements:* For master's, minimum undergraduate GPA of 3.0, 3 years work experience. Additional exam requirements/recommendations for international students: Required—TOEFL (minimum score 550 paper-based; 79 iBT). Electronic applications accepted.

University of Phoenix–Sacramento Valley Campus, School of Business, Sacramento, CA 95833-4334. Offers accounting (MBA); business administration (MBA); global management (MBA); human resources management (MBA, MM); management (MM); marketing (MBA); public administration (MBA, MM). *Accreditation:* ACBSP. *Program availability:* Evening/weekend. *Degree requirements:* For master's, thesis (for some programs). *Entrance requirements:* For master's, minimum undergraduate GPA of 3.0, 3 years work experience. Additional exam requirements/recommendations for international students: Required—TOEFL (minimum score 550 paper-based; 79 iBT). Electronic applications accepted.

University of Phoenix–San Antonio Campus, School of Business, San Antonio, TX 78230. Offers accounting (MBA); business administration (MBA); e-business (MBA); global management (MBA); human resources management (MBA, MM); management (MM); marketing (MBA); public administration (MBA, MM). *Accreditation:* ACBSP.

University of Phoenix–San Diego Campus, College of Information Systems and Technology, San Diego, CA 92123. Offers management (MIS); technology management (MBA). *Program availability:* Evening/weekend. *Degree requirements:* For master's, thesis (for some programs). *Entrance requirements:* For master's, minimum undergraduate GPA of 3.0, 3 years work experience. Additional exam requirements/recommendations for international students: Required—TOEFL (minimum score 550 paper-based; 79 iBT). Electronic applications accepted.

University of Phoenix–San Diego Campus, School of Business, San Diego, CA 92123. Offers accounting (MBA); business administration (MBA); global management (MBA); human resources management (MBA, MM); management (MM); marketing (MBA); public administration (MBA). *Accreditation:* ACBSP. *Program availability:* Evening/weekend. *Degree requirements:* For master's, thesis (for some programs). *Entrance requirements:* For master's, 3 years of work experience, minimum undergraduate GPA of 3.0. Additional exam requirements/recommendations for international students: Required—TOEFL (minimum score 550 paper-based; 79 iBT). Electronic applications accepted.

University of Pikeville, Coleman College of Business, Pikeville, KY 41501. Offers business (MBA); entrepreneurship (MBA); healthcare (MBA). *Program availability:* Part-time, evening/weekend. *Degree requirements:* For master's, comprehensive exam (for some programs). *Entrance requirements:* For master's, official transcripts, two professional letters of recommendation, three years of work experience. *Expenses:* Contact institution.

University of Pittsburgh, Katz Graduate School of Business, Doctoral Program in Business Administration, Pittsburgh, PA 15260. Offers accounting (PhD); business analytics and operations (PhD); finance (PhD); information systems and technology management (PhD); marketing (PhD); organizational behavior and human resources (PhD); strategic management (PhD). *Accreditation:* AACSB. *Program availability:* Evening/weekend. *Degree requirements:* For doctorate, comprehensive exam, thesis/dissertation, student teaching. *Entrance requirements:* For doctorate, GMAT or GRE, 3 recommendations, statement of purpose, transcripts of all previous course work and degrees. Additional exam requirements/recommendations for international students: Required—TOEFL (minimum score 100 iBT) or IELTS (minimum score 7.0). Electronic applications accepted. *Faculty research:* Accounting systems/financial reporting, corporate finance, shopper marketing/consumer behavior, management information systems, organizational behavior and entrepreneurship.

University of Pittsburgh, Katz Graduate School of Business, Executive MBA Program, Pittsburgh, PA 15260. Offers EMBA. *Accreditation:* AACSB. *Entrance requirements:* For master's, GMAT (for candidates with less than 10 years experience, GPA less than 3.0, or limited quantitative background), minimum 5 years of management experience, resume, 2 letters of recommendation, essay, interview. Additional exam requirements/recommendations for international students: Required—TOEFL (minimum score 100 iBT) or IELTS (minimum score 7.0). Electronic applications accepted. *Expenses:* Contact institution. *Faculty research:* Accounting systems/financial reporting, corporate finance, shopper marketing/consumer behavior, management information systems, organizational behavior and entrepreneurship.

University of Pittsburgh, Katz Graduate School of Business, Master of Business Administration Programs, Pittsburgh, PA 15260. Offers finance (MBA); information systems (MBA); marketing (MBA); operations (MBA); organizational behavior and human resources (MBA); strategy, environment and organizations (MBA); MBA/JD;

Business Administration and Management—General

MBA/MID; MBA/MIS; MBA/MSE. *Accreditation:* AACSB. *Program availability:* Part-time, evening/weekend, blended/hybrid learning. *Degree requirements:* For master's, minimum GPA of 3.0. *Entrance requirements:* For master's, GMAT, GRE. Additional exam requirements/recommendations for international students: Required—TOEFL (minimum score 100 iBT) or IELTS (minimum score 7.0). Electronic applications accepted. *Faculty research:* Accounting systems/financial reporting, corporate finance, shopper marketing/consumer behavior, management information systems, organizational behavior and entrepreneurship.

University of Pittsburgh, Katz Graduate School of Business, MBA/Juris Doctor Program, Pittsburgh, PA 15260. Offers MBA/JD. *Entrance requirements:* Additional exam requirements/recommendations for international students: Required—TOEFL (minimum score 100 iBT) or IELTS (minimum score 7.0). Electronic applications accepted. *Faculty research:* Accounting systems/financial reporting, corporate finance, shopper marketing/consumer behavior, management information systems, organizational behavior and entrepreneurship.

University of Pittsburgh, Katz Graduate School of Business, MBA/Master of Health Administration in Health Policy and Management Program, Pittsburgh, PA 15260. Offers MBA/MHA. *Program availability:* Part-time, evening/weekend. *Entrance requirements:* Additional exam requirements/recommendations for international students: Required—TOEFL (minimum score 100 iBT), IELTS (minimum score 7). Electronic applications accepted. *Faculty research:* Accounting systems/financial reporting, corporate finance, shopper marketing/consumer behavior, management information systems, organizational behavior and entrepreneurship.

University of Pittsburgh, Katz Graduate School of Business, MBA/Master of International Business Dual Degree Program, Pittsburgh, PA 15260. Offers MBA/MIB. *Program availability:* Part-time, evening/weekend. *Entrance requirements:* Additional exam requirements/recommendations for international students: Required—TOEFL (minimum score 100 iBT) or IELTS (minimum score 7.0). Electronic applications accepted. *Faculty research:* Accounting systems/financial reporting, corporate finance, shopper marketing/consumer behavior, management information systems, organizational behavior and entrepreneurship.

University of Pittsburgh, Katz Graduate School of Business, MBA/Master of International Development Joint Degree Program, Pittsburgh, PA 15260. Offers MID/MBA. *Accreditation:* AACSB. *Program availability:* Part-time, evening/weekend. *Entrance requirements:* Additional exam requirements/recommendations for international students: Required—TOEFL (minimum score 100 iBT) or IELTS (minimum score 7.0). Electronic applications accepted. *Faculty research:* Accounting systems/financial reporting, corporate finance, shopper marketing/consumer behavior, management information systems, organizational behavior and entrepreneurship.

University of Pittsburgh, Katz Graduate School of Business, MBA/Master of Public and International Affairs Dual-Degree Program, Pittsburgh, PA 15260. Offers MBA/MPIA. *Accreditation:* AACSB. *Program availability:* Part-time, evening/weekend. *Entrance requirements:* Additional exam requirements/recommendations for international students: Required—TOEFL (minimum score 100 iBT) or IELTS (minimum score 7.0). Electronic applications accepted. *Faculty research:* Accounting systems/financial reporting, corporate finance, shopper marketing/consumer behavior, management information systems, organizational behavior and entrepreneurship.

University of Pittsburgh, Katz Graduate School of Business, MBA/Master of Science in Engineering Joint Degree Program, Pittsburgh, PA 15260. Offers MBA/MSE. *Accreditation:* AACSB. *Program availability:* Part-time, evening/weekend. *Entrance requirements:* Additional exam requirements/recommendations for international students: Required—TOEFL (minimum score 100 iBT) or IELTS (minimum score 7.0). Electronic applications accepted. *Faculty research:* Accounting systems/financial reporting, corporate finance, shopper marketing/consumer behavior, management information systems, organizational behavior and entrepreneurship.

University of Portland, Dr. Robert B. Pamplin, Jr. School of Business, Portland, OR 97203-5798. Offers entrepreneurship (MBA); finance (MBA, MS); health care management (MBA); marketing (MBA); nonprofit management (EMBA); operations and technology management (MBA, MS); sustainability (MBA). *Accreditation:* AACSB. *Program availability:* Part-time, evening/weekend. *Faculty:* 26 full-time (5 women), 8 part-time/adjunct (1 woman). *Students:* 35 full-time (16 women), 114 part-time (47 women); includes 21 minority (3 Black or African American, non-Hispanic/Latino; 2 American Indian or Alaska Native, non-Hispanic/Latino; 8 Asian, non-Hispanic/Latino; 8 Hispanic/Latino), 24 international. Average age 32. In 2018, 55 master's awarded. *Entrance requirements:* For master's, GMAT or GRE, minimum GPA of 3.0, resume, statement of goals, 2 letters of recommendation. Additional exam requirements/recommendations for international students: Required—TOEFL (minimum score 88 iBT), IELTS (minimum score 7). *Application deadline:* For fall admission, 7/19 priority date for domestic and international students; for spring admission, 12/7 priority date for domestic and international students; for summer admission, 4/12 priority date for domestic and international students. Applications are processed on a rolling basis. Application fee: $0. Electronic applications accepted. *Expenses:* Contact institution. *Financial support:* Application deadline: 3/1; applicants required to submit FAFSA. *Unit head:* Melissa McCarthy, Director, 503-943-7224, E-mail: mba-up@up.edu. *Application contact:* Melissa McCarthy, Director, 503-943-7224, E-mail: mba-up@up.edu.

University of Puerto Rico–Mayagüez, Graduate Studies, College of Business Administration, Mayagüez, PR 00681-9000. Offers business administration (MBA); finance (MBA); human resources (MBA); industrial management (MBA). *Program availability:* Part-time, evening/weekend. *Degree requirements:* For master's, one foreign language, comprehensive exam, thesis (for some programs). *Entrance requirements:* For master's, GMAT or EXADEP, bachelor's degree with courses in calculus, microeconomics, accounting and statistics. Additional exam requirements/recommendations for international students: Required—TOEFL (minimum score 500 paper-based), GMAT or EXADEP. Electronic applications accepted. *Faculty research:* Organizational studies, management, accounting, entrepreneurship, leadership and motivation.

University of Puerto Rico–Río Piedras, College of Business Administration, San Juan, PR 00931-3300. Offers accounting (MBA); finance (MBA, PhD); general business (MBA); human resources management (MBA); international trade and business (MBA, PhD); marketing (MBA); operations management (MBA); quantitative methods (MBA). *Accreditation:* AACSB. *Program availability:* Part-time. *Degree requirements:* For master's, comprehensive exam, thesis or alternative, research project. *Entrance requirements:* For master's, GMAT or PAEG, minimum GPA of 3.0, letter of recommendation; for doctorate, GMAT, PAEG, minimum GPA of 3.0, master degree. *Faculty research:* Management.

University of Redlands, School of Business, Redlands, CA 92373-0999. Offers business (MBA); information technology (MS); management (MA). *Program availability:* Evening/weekend. *Entrance requirements:* For master's, minimum GPA of 3.0, 2 letters of recommendation. *Faculty research:* Human resources management, educational leadership, humanities, teacher education.

University of Regina, Faculty of Graduate Studies and Research, Kenneth Levene Graduate School of Business, Regina, SK S4S 0A2, Canada. Offers EMBA, M Admin, MBA, MHRM, Master's Certificate, PGD. *Program availability:* Part-time. *Faculty:* 41 full-time (15 women), 7 part-time/adjunct (3 women). *Students:* 72 full-time (52 women), 47 part-time (34 women). Average age 30. 271 applicants, 31% accepted, 36 enrolled. In 2018, 62 master's, 9 other advanced degrees awarded. *Degree requirements:* For master's, project (for some programs), research paper for EMBA. *Entrance requirements:* For master's, MBA and Post grad Diploma mandatory requires GMAT, two years of relevant work experience (MHRM, M Admin); two years of relevant work experience (MBA); at least 8 years full time work experience (EMBA). See www.uregina.ca/gradstudies/future-students/programs/Business for full admission requirements; for other advanced degree, two years of relevant work experience (Master's Certificate); three years' relevant work experience (PGD). Additional exam requirements/recommendations for international students: Required—TOEFL (minimum score 580 paper-based; 80 iBT), IELTS (minimum score 6.5), PTE (minimum score 59), other options are MELAb, CANTEST, CAEl or UR ESL; GMAT is mandatory required. *Application deadline:* For fall admission, 3/1 for domestic and international students; for winter admission, 7/1 for domestic and international students; for spring admission, 10/1 for domestic and international students; for summer admission, 10/1 for domestic and international students. Application fee: $100. Electronic applications accepted. *Expenses:* Tuition and fees varies depends on your choice major in Kenneth Levene Garduate School Faculty. To see the fees for each major visit www.uregina.ca/levene/programs/ select the major you wish to apply and go to tuition information. *Financial support:* In 2018–19, 58 students received support, including 37 fellowships, 9 teaching assistantships (averaging $2,552 per year); research assistantships, career-related internships or fieldwork, Federal Work-Study, scholarships/grants, unspecified assistantships, and travel award and Graduate Scholarship Base funds also available. Support available to part-time students. Financial award application deadline: 9/30. *Faculty research:* Management of public and private sector organizations. *Unit head:* Dr. Gina Grandy, Dean, 306-585-4435, Fax: 306-585-5361, E-mail: business.levene@uregina.ca. *Application contact:* Dr. Adrian Pitariu, Associate Dean, Research and Graduate Programs, 306-585-6294, Fax: 306-585-5361, E-mail: business.AD.levene@uregina.ca.
Website: http://www.uregina.ca/business/levene/

University of Rhode Island, Graduate School, College of Business, Program in Business Administration, Kingston, RI 02881. Offers finance (MBA); general business (MBA); management (MBA); marketing (MBA, PhD); operations and supply chain management (PhD); supply chain management (MBA); Pharm D/MBA. *Faculty:* 33 full-time (17 women). *Students:* 54 full-time (21 women), 161 part-time (64 women); includes 30 minority (11 Black or African American, non-Hispanic/Latino; 11 Asian, non-Hispanic/Latino; 6 Hispanic/Latino; 1 Native Hawaiian or other Pacific Islander, non-Hispanic/Latino; 1 Two or more races, non-Hispanic/Latino), 17 international. 92 applicants, 87% accepted, 74 enrolled. In 2018, 90 master's, 5 doctorates awarded. *Entrance requirements:* Additional exam requirements/recommendations for international students: Required—TOEFL. *Application deadline:* For fall admission, 6/30 for domestic students; for spring admission, 10/31 for domestic students; for summer admission, 3/31 for domestic students. Electronic applications accepted. *Expenses: Tuition, area resident:* Full-time $13,226; part-time $735 per credit. Tuition, state resident: full-time $13,226; part-time $735 per credit. Tuition, nonresident: full-time $25,854; part-time $1436 per credit. *International tuition:* $25,854 full-time. *Required fees:* $1698; $50 per credit. $35 per semester. One-time fee: $165. *Financial support:* In 2018–19, 15 teaching assistantships (averaging $17,739 per year) were awarded. Financial award application deadline: 2/1. *Unit head:* Lisa Lancellotta, Coordinator, MBA Programs, 401-874-4241, E-mail: mba@uri.edu. *Application contact:* Lisa Lancellotta, Coordinator, MBA Programs, 401-874-4241, E-mail: mba@uri.edu.

University of Richmond, Robins School of Business, University of Richmond, VA 23173. Offers MBA, JD/MBA. *Accreditation:* AACSB. *Program availability:* Part-time, evening/weekend. *Degree requirements:* For master's, capstone project. *Entrance requirements:* For master's, GMAT or GRE, minimum of two years' professional work experience. Additional exam requirements/recommendations for international students: Required—TOEFL (minimum score 600 paper-based; 100 iBT). Electronic applications accepted. *Faculty research:* Entrepreneurship, investments, auditing, consumer behavior, strategic management.

University of Rochester, Simon Business School, Doctoral Program in Business Administration, Rochester, NY 14627. Offers accounting (PhD); computer information systems (PhD); finance (PhD); marketing (PhD); operations management (PhD). *Accreditation:* AACSB. *Degree requirements:* For doctorate, comprehensive exam, thesis/dissertation, qualifying exam. *Entrance requirements:* For doctorate, GMAT or GRE. Additional exam requirements/recommendations for international students: Required—TOEFL. Electronic applications accepted. *Expenses:* Contact institution. *Faculty research:* Empirical industrial organization, risk management, financial disclosure and regulation, social media, health care management.

University of Rochester, Simon Business School, Executive MBA Program, Rochester, NY 14627. Offers MBA. *Program availability:* Part-time-only, evening/weekend. Electronic applications accepted. *Expenses:* Contact institution. *Faculty research:* Empirical industrial organization, risk management, financial disclosure and regulation, social media, health care management.

University of Rochester, Simon Business School, Full-Time Master's Program in Business Administration, Rochester, NY 14627. Offers business systems consulting (MBA); competitive and organizational strategy (MBA); computers and information systems (MBA); corporate accounting (MBA); entrepreneurship (MBA); finance (MBA); health sciences management (MBA); marketing (MBA); operations management (MBA); public accounting (MBA); strategy and organizations (MBA). *Accreditation:* AACSB. *Entrance requirements:* For master's, GMAT or GRE. *Expenses: Tuition:* Full-time $52,974; part-time $1654 per credit hour. *Required fees:* $612. One-time fee: $30 part-time. Tuition and fees vary according to campus/location and program. *Faculty research:* Empirical industrial organization, risk management, financial disclosure and regulation, social media, health care management.

University of Rochester, Simon Business School, Part-Time MBA Program, Rochester, NY 14627. Offers business systems consulting (MBA); competitive and organizational strategy (MBA); computers and information systems (MBA); corporate accounting (MBA); entrepreneurship (MBA); finance (MBA); health sciences management (MBA); marketing (MBA), including brand management, marketing strategy, pricing; operations management (MBA); public accounting (MBA). *Program availability:* Part-time-only, evening/weekend. *Entrance requirements:* For master's, GRE or GMAT. Electronic applications accepted. *Expenses:* Contact institution.

University of St. Francis, College of Business and Health Administration, Joliet, IL 60435-6169. Offers accounting (MBA, Certificate); business analytics (MBA, Certificate); e-learning (Certificate); finance (MBA, Certificate); health administration (MBA, MS); human resource management (MBA, Certificate); logistics (Certificate); management (MBA, MSM); management of training and development (Certificate); supply chain management (MBA); training and development (MBA); training specialist (Certificate). *Program availability:* Part-time, evening/weekend, 100% online, blended/hybrid learning.

Faculty: 13 full-time (6 women), 20 part-time/adjunct (7 women). *Students:* 139 full-time (94 women), 206 part-time (159 women); includes 86 minority (51 Black or African American, non-Hispanic/Latino; 1 American Indian or Alaska Native, non-Hispanic/Latino; 11 Asian, non-Hispanic/Latino; 21 Hispanic/Latino; 2 Two or more races, non-Hispanic/Latino), 24 international. Average age 37. 261 applicants, 63% accepted, 98 enrolled. In 2018, 129 master's, 3 other advanced degrees awarded. *Degree requirements:* For master's, comprehensive exam (for some programs). *Entrance requirements:* Additional exam requirements/recommendations for international students: Required—TOEFL (minimum score 550 paper-based; 79 iBT), IELTS (minimum score 6). *Application deadline:* Applications are processed on a rolling basis. Electronic applications accepted. Application fee is waived when completed online. *Expenses:* Contact institution. *Financial support:* In 2018–19, 126 students received support. Scholarships/grants and tuition waivers (partial) available. Support available to part-time students. Financial award applicants required to submit FAFSA. *Unit head:* Dr. Orlando Griego, Dean, 815-740-3395, Fax: 815-740-3452, E-mail: ogriego@stfrancis.edu. *Application contact:* Sandee Sloka, Director Adult & Graduate Admissions, 800-735-7500, E-mail: ssloka@stfrancis.edu.
Website: https://www.stfrancis.edu/business-health-administration/

University of Saint Francis, Graduate School, Keith Busse School of Business and Entrepreneurial Leadership, Fort Wayne, IN 46808-3994. Offers business administration (MBA), including sustainability; environmental health (MEH); healthcare administration (MHA); organizational leadership (MOL). *Accreditation:* ACBSP. *Program availability:* Part-time, evening/weekend, online only, 100% online. *Faculty:* 4 full-time (3 women), 11 part-time/adjunct (1 woman). *Students:* 62 full-time (33 women), 94 part-time (53 women); includes 40 minority (23 Black or African American, non-Hispanic/Latino; 1 American Indian or Alaska Native, non-Hispanic/Latino; 10 Hispanic/Latino; 1 Native Hawaiian or other Pacific Islander, non-Hispanic/Latino; 5 Two or more races, non-Hispanic/Latino). Average age 33. 72 applicants, 96% accepted, 51 enrolled. In 2018, 112 master's awarded. *Application deadline:* For fall admission, 7/1 for international students; for spring admission, 11/1 for international students; for summer admission, 3/1 for international students. Applications are processed on a rolling basis. Application fee: $0. Electronic applications accepted. *Expenses:* Tuition: Full-time $22,440; part-time $935 per credit hour. *Required fees:* $330 per semester. Tuition and fees vary according to degree level, campus/location and program. *Unit head:* Dr. Robert W. Lee, Dean, 260-399-7700 Ext. 8304, Fax: 260-399-8174, E-mail: rlee@sf.edu. *Application contact:* Kyle Richardson, Associate Director of Enrollment Services for Adult Learning, 260-399-7700 Ext. 6310, Fax: 260-399-8152, E-mail: krichardson@sf.edu.
Website: https://admissions.sf.edu/graduate/

University of Saint Joseph, Department of Business Administration, West Hartford, CT 06117-2700. Offers management (MS). *Program availability:* Part-time, evening/weekend. *Entrance requirements:* For master's, 2 letters of recommendation. Electronic applications accepted. Application fee is waived when completed online.

University of Saint Mary, Graduate Programs, Program in Business Administration, Leavenworth, KS 66048-5082. Offers enterprise risk management (MBA); finance (MBA); general management (MBA); health care management (MBA); human resources management (MBA); marketing and advertising management (MBA). *Program availability:* Part-time, evening/weekend, 100% online, blended/hybrid learning. *Faculty:* 1 full-time, 23 part-time/adjunct (7 women). *Students:* 177 full-time (116 women), 50 part-time (29 women); includes 73 minority (30 Black or African American, non-Hispanic/Latino; 3 American Indian or Alaska Native, non-Hispanic/Latino; 12 Asian, non-Hispanic/Latino; 18 Hispanic/Latino; 1 Native Hawaiian or other Pacific Islander, non-Hispanic/Latino; 9 Two or more races, non-Hispanic/Latino), 2 international. Average age 33. *Degree requirements:* For master's, thesis. *Entrance requirements:* For master's, Minimum undergraduate GPA of 2.75, official transcripts. *Application deadline:* Applications are processed on a rolling basis. Application fee: $25. Electronic applications accepted. *Expenses:* Contact institution. *Financial support:* Applicants required to submit FAFSA. *Unit head:* Mark Harvey, Director of Graduate Business Programs, 913-319-3011, E-mail: mark.harvey@stmary.edu. *Application contact:* Mark Harvey, Director of Graduate Business Programs, 913-319-3011, E-mail: mark.harvey@stmary.edu.
Website: https://www.stmary.edu/mba

University of St. Thomas, Cameron School of Business, Houston, TX 77006-4696. Offers MBA, MCTM, MIB, MSA, MSF. *Program availability:* Part-time, evening/weekend. *Degree requirements:* For master's, capstone (for some programs), additional course requirements for those sitting for state accountancy exam. *Entrance requirements:* For master's, minimum GPA of 2.5, 3 letters of recommendation. Additional exam requirements/recommendations for international students: Required—TOEFL (minimum score 550 paper-based; 79 iBT), IELTS (minimum score 6.5), PTE (minimum score 53). Electronic applications accepted.

University of St. Thomas, Opus College of Business, Executive MBA Program, Minneapolis, MN 55403. Offers MBA. *Program availability:* Part-time. *Entrance requirements:* For master's, five years of significant management or leadership experience. *Application deadline:* For fall admission, 7/15 for domestic and international students. Applications are processed on a rolling basis. Application fee: $100. Electronic applications accepted. *Expenses:* Contact institution. *Financial support:* Scholarships/grants available. Financial award applicants required to submit FAFSA. *Unit head:* Melissa Lammers, Assistant Director, 651-962-4114, Fax: 651-962-4235, E-mail: melissa.lammers@stthomas.edu. *Application contact:* Tiffany Cork, Director of Recruiting and Admissions, 651-962-8801, Fax: 651-962-4129, E-mail: ustmba@stthomas.edu.
Website: https://business.stthomas.edu/degrees-programs/mba/executive/

University of St. Thomas, Opus College of Business, Full-time UST MBA Program, Minneapolis, MN 55403. Offers MBA. *Entrance requirements:* For master's, GMAT, GRE. Additional exam requirements/recommendations for international students: Required—TOEFL (minimum score 90 iBT), IELTS (minimum score 7), or Michigan English Language Assessment Battery. *Application deadline:* For fall admission, 12/15 priority date for domestic and international students. Applications are processed on a rolling basis. Application fee: $60. Electronic applications accepted. Tuition and fees vary according to course load, degree level and program. *Financial support:* Scholarships/grants, tuition waivers (full and partial), and unspecified assistantships available. Financial award application deadline: 4/15. *Unit head:* Hannah Hedegard, Program Director, 651-962-8819. *Application contact:* Josie Visser, Associate Director of Recruiting and Admissions, 651-962-8825, Fax: 651-962-4129, E-mail: jtvisser@stthomas.edu.
Website: http://www.stthomas.edu/mba

University of St. Thomas, Opus College of Business, Part-time MBA Program, Minneapolis, MN 55403. Offers MBA. *Program availability:* Part-time, evening/weekend, 100% online, blended/hybrid learning. *Entrance requirements:* For master's, GMAT. *Application deadline:* For fall admission, 5/1 priority date for domestic students; for spring admission, 11/1 priority date for domestic students; for summer admission, 4/1 priority date for domestic students. Applications are processed on a rolling basis. Application fee: $60. Electronic applications accepted. Tuition and fees vary according to course load, degree level and program. *Financial support:* Scholarships/grants

available. Financial award application deadline: 6/1. *Unit head:* Corey Eakins, Senior Program Director, 651-962-4228, Fax: 651-962-4129. *Application contact:* Susan Haun, Associate Director of Recruiting and Admissions, 651-962-4312, Fax: 651-962-4129.
Website: https://www.stthomas.edu/business/part-time-mba/

University of San Diego, School of Business, Masters of Business Administration Programs, San Diego, CA 92110-2492. Offers MBA, JD/MBA. *Program availability:* Part-time, evening/weekend. *Students:* 127 full-time (45 women), 61 part-time (24 women); includes 45 minority (2 Black or African American, non-Hispanic/Latino; 12 Asian, non-Hispanic/Latino; 26 Hispanic/Latino; 1 Native Hawaiian or other Pacific Islander, non-Hispanic/Latino; 4 Two or more races, non-Hispanic/Latino), 35 international. Average age 30. In 2018, 75 master's awarded. *Degree requirements:* For master's, community service, capstone project. *Entrance requirements:* For master's, GMAT (minimum score 600 for full-time, 550 for part-time), minimum GPA of 3.0, minimum 2 years of full-time professional experience. Additional exam requirements/recommendations for international students: Required—TOEFL (minimum score 580 paper-based; 92 iBT), TWE. *Application deadline:* For fall admission, 11/1 priority date for domestic students; for spring admission, 10/1 priority date for domestic students. Applications are processed on a rolling basis. Application fee: $80. Electronic applications accepted. *Financial support:* In 2018–19, 125 students received support. Career-related internships or fieldwork, Federal Work-Study, institutionally sponsored loans, scholarships/grants, and unspecified assistantships available. Support available to part-time students. Financial award application deadline: 4/1; financial award applicants required to submit FAFSA. *Faculty research:* Exchange rate forecasting, corporate governance, performance of private equity funds, economic geography, food banking. *Unit head:* Dr. Manzur Rahman, Academic Director, MBA Programs, 619-260-2388, E-mail: mba@sandiego.edu. *Application contact:* Erika Garwood, Associate Director of Graduate Admissions, 619-260-, E-mail: grads@sandiego.edu.
Website: http://www.sandiego.edu/business/graduate/mba/

University of San Francisco, School of Management, Executive Master of Business Administration Program, San Francisco, CA 94117. Offers MBA. *Accreditation:* AACSB. *Program availability:* Part-time, evening/weekend. *Students:* 42 full-time (17 women); includes 24 minority (4 Black or African American, non-Hispanic/Latino; 8 Asian, non-Hispanic/Latino; 8 Hispanic/Latino; 4 Two or more races, non-Hispanic/Latino), 1 international. Average age 40. 44 applicants, 82% accepted, 26 enrolled. In 2018, 25 master's awarded. *Entrance requirements:* For master's, GMAT (for applicants with less than eight years of post-undergraduate professional experience), resume demonstrating minimum of eight years of professional work experience, transcripts from each college or university attended, two letters of recommendation, essays, interview. Additional exam requirements/recommendations for international students: Required—TOEFL (minimum score 600 paper-based, 100 iBT), IELTS (minimum score 7) or PTE (minimum score 68). *Application deadline:* Applications are processed on a rolling basis. Application fee: $55. Electronic applications accepted. *Expenses:* Contact institution. *Financial support:* Scholarships/grants available. Financial award application deadline: 3/2; financial award applicants required to submit FAFSA. *Unit head:* Dr. Richard Stackman, Chair, 415-422-6939, E-mail: emba@usfca.edu. *Application contact:* Office of Graduate Recruiting and Admissions, 415-422-2221, E-mail: management@usfca.edu.
Website: http://www.usfca.edu/emba

University of San Francisco, School of Management, Master of Business Administration Program, San Francisco, CA 94117. Offers entrepreneurship and innovation (MBA); finance (MBA); marketing (MBA); organization development (MBA); DDS/MBA; JD/MBA; MBA/MAPS. *Accreditation:* AACSB. *Program availability:* Part-time, evening/weekend. *Students:* 136 full-time (67 women), 7 part-time (2 women); includes 57 minority (5 Black or African American, non-Hispanic/Latino; 29 Asian, non-Hispanic/Latino; 14 Hispanic/Latino; 1 Native Hawaiian or other Pacific Islander, non-Hispanic/Latino; 8 Two or more races, non-Hispanic/Latino), 27 international. Average age 29. 226 applicants, 61% accepted, 56 enrolled. In 2018, 76 master's awarded. *Entrance requirements:* For master's, GMAT or GRE, resume (two years of professional work experience required for part-time students, preferred for full-time), transcripts from each college or university attended, two letters of recommendation, personal statement, interview. Additional exam requirements/recommendations for international students: Required—TOEFL (minimum score 600 paper-based, 100 iBT), IELTS (minimum score 7) or PTE (minimum score 68). *Application deadline:* For fall admission, 6/5 for domestic students, 5/15 for international students; for spring admission, 11/30 for domestic students. Application fee: $55. Electronic applications accepted. *Expenses:* Contact institution. *Financial support:* Fellowships and scholarships/grants available. Financial award application deadline: 3/2; financial award applicants required to submit FAFSA. *Faculty research:* International financial markets, technology transfer licensing, international marketing, strategic planning. *Total annual research expenditures:* $50,000. *Unit head:* Dr. Frank Fletcher, Director, 415-422-2221, E-mail: management@usfca.edu. *Application contact:* Office of Graduate Recruiting and Admissions, 415-422-2221, E-mail: management@usfca.edu.
Website: http://www.usfca.edu/mba

University of Saskatchewan, College of Graduate and Postdoctoral Studies, Edwards School of Business, Saskatoon, SK S7N 5A2, Canada. Offers M Sc, MBA, MP Acc, PhD. *Program availability:* Part-time. *Degree requirements:* For master's, thesis (for some programs). *Entrance requirements:* For master's, GMAT. Additional exam requirements/recommendations for international students: Required—TOEFL.

The University of Scranton, Kania School of Management, Program in Business Administration, Scranton, PA 18510. Offers accounting (MBA); finance (MBA); general business administration (MBA); health care management (MBA); international business (MBA); management information systems (MBA); marketing (MBA); operations management (MBA). *Accreditation:* AACSB. *Program availability:* Part-time, evening/weekend, 100% online. *Entrance requirements:* For master's, GMAT (for MBA). *Faculty research:* Financial markets, strategic impact of total quality management, internal accounting controls, consumer preference, information systems and the Internet.

University of Sioux Falls, Vucurevich School of Business, Sioux Falls, SD 57105-1699. Offers entrepreneurial leadership (MBA); general management (MBA); health care management (MBA); marketing (MBA). *Program availability:* Part-time, evening/weekend. *Degree requirements:* For master's, project. *Entrance requirements:* For master's, minimum GPA of 3.0. Additional exam requirements/recommendations for international students: Required—TOEFL. *Expenses:* Contact institution.

University of South Africa, College of Economic and Management Sciences, Pretoria, South Africa. Offers accounting (D Admin, D Com); accounting science (DA); auditing (D Admin, D Com); business administration (M Tech); business economics (D Admin); business leadership (DBL); business management (D Admin, D Com); economic management analysis (M Tech); economics (D Admin, D Com, PhD); human resource development (M Tech); industrial psychology (D Admin, D Com, PhD); logistics (D Com); marketing (M Tech); public administration (D Admin, D Com, DPA, PhD); public management (M Tech); quantitative management (D Admin, D Com); real estate (M Tech); statistics (D Admin, PhD); tourism management (D Admin, D Com); transport economics (D Admin, D Com).

Business Administration and Management—General

University of South Africa, Graduate School of Business Leadership, Pretoria, South Africa. Offers MBA, MBL, DBL.

University of South Alabama, Mitchell College of Business, Program in Business Administration, Mobile, AL 36688. Offers business administration (MBA); management (DBA); marketing (DBA). *Accreditation:* AACSB. *Program availability:* Part-time, evening/weekend. *Degree requirements:* For master's, comprehensive exam; for doctorate, comprehensive exam, thesis/dissertation. *Entrance requirements:* For master's, GMAT (minimum score of 450, 3.0 in Analytical Writing section), minimum undergraduate GPA of 3.0; for doctorate, MBA/specialized master's degree, 5 years of professional experience, 3 letters of reference, curriculum vitae, interview. Additional exam requirements/recommendations for international students: Required—TOEFL (minimum score 525 paper-based; 71 iBT). Electronic applications accepted. *Expenses:* Contact institution.

University of South Carolina, The Graduate School, Darla Moore School of Business, Columbia, SC 29208. Offers accountancy (M Acc), including business measurement and assurance; business administration (MBA, PhD), including business administration (PhD), economics (PhD); economics (MA); human resources (MHR); international business administration (IMBA); JD/M Acc; JD/MA; JD/MHR. *Accreditation:* AACSB. *Program availability:* Part-time, evening/weekend, online learning. *Degree requirements:* For doctorate, one foreign language, thesis/dissertation. *Entrance requirements:* For master's, GMAT, GRE, minimum GPA of 3.0; for doctorate, GMAT or GRE. Additional exam requirements/recommendations for international students: Required—TOEFL (minimum score 600 paper-based). Electronic applications accepted. *Expenses:* Contact institution. *Faculty research:* Finance, marketing, strategic management, international management, operations.

University of South Carolina Aiken, Program in Business Administration, Aiken, SC 29801. Offers MBA. *Program availability:* Part-time, evening/weekend, online only, 100% online. *Faculty:* 6 full-time (4 women), 5 part-time/adjunct (1 woman). *Students:* 26 full-time (15 women), 86 part-time (38 women); includes 34 minority (25 Black or African American, non-Hispanic/Latino; 2 Asian, non-Hispanic/Latino; 4 Hispanic/Latino; 3 Two or more races, non-Hispanic/Latino), 4 international. Average age 36. 198 applicants, 55% accepted, 76 enrolled. In 2018, 14 master's awarded. *Degree requirements:* For master's, capstone course(s). *Entrance requirements:* For master's, GMAT or GRE. Additional exam requirements/recommendations for international students: Required—TOEFL (minimum score 551 paper-based; 80 iBT), IELTS (minimum score 6), PTE (minimum score 53), USC Aiken accepts the TOEFL, IELTS, or PTE exams to demonstrate English proficiency. *Application deadline:* For fall admission, 7/31 for domestic and international students; for spring admission, 12/16 for domestic and international students. Applications are processed on a rolling basis. Application fee: $45 ($100 for international students). Electronic applications accepted. *Expenses:* $450 per credit hour tuition in-state and out-of-state. *Financial support:* In 2018–19, 7 students received support. Scholarships/grants and tuition waivers (partial) available. Support available to part-time students. Financial award application deadline: 3/1; financial award applicants required to submit FAFSA. *Faculty research:* Accounting, economics, finance, management, marketing. *Unit head:* Dr. Michael J. Fekula, Dean for School of Business Administration, 803-641-3340, E-mail: mickf@usca.edu. *Application contact:* Dan Robb, Associate Vice Chancellor for Enrollment Management, 803-641-3487, Fax: 803-641-3727, E-mail: danr@usca.edu.
Website: https://online.usca.edu/programs/business-programs.aspx

University of South Dakota, Graduate School, Beacom School of Business, Department of Business Administration, Vermillion, SD 57069. Offers business administration (MBA); business analytics (MBA, Graduate Certificate); health services administration (MBA); long term care management (Graduate Certificate); marketing (MBA, Graduate Certificate); operations and supply chain management (MBA, Graduate Certificate); JD/MBA. *Accreditation:* AACSB. *Program availability:* Part-time, blended/hybrid learning. *Degree requirements:* For master's, thesis or alternative. *Entrance requirements:* For master's, GMAT, minimum GPA of 2.7, resume. Additional exam requirements/recommendations for international students: Required—TOEFL (minimum score 550 paper-based; 79 iBT), IELTS (minimum score 6). Electronic applications accepted. *Expenses:* Contact institution.

University of South Dakota, Graduate School, College of Arts and Sciences, Program in Administrative Studies, Vermillion, SD 57069. Offers addiction studies (MSA); criminal justice studies (MSA); health services administration (MSA); human resources (MSA); interdisciplinary studies (MSA); long term care administration (MSA); organizational leadership (MSA). *Program availability:* Part-time, evening/weekend, 100% online. *Degree requirements:* For master's, thesis or alternative. *Entrance requirements:* For master's, 3 years of work or experience, minimum GPA of 2.7, resume. Additional exam requirements/recommendations for international students: Required—TOEFL (minimum score 550 paper-based; 79 iBT). Electronic applications accepted.

University of Southern California, Graduate School, Marshall School of Business, Los Angeles, CA 90089. Offers M Acc, MBA, MBT, MBV, MMM, MS, PhD, DDS/MBA, JD/MBT, MBA/Ed D, MBA/M Pl, MBA/MD, MBA/MRED, MBA/MS, MBA/MSW, MBA/Pharm D. *Accreditation:* AACSB. *Degree requirements:* For doctorate, thesis/dissertation. *Entrance requirements:* For master's, GMAT and/or CPA Exam; for doctorate, GMAT or GRE. Additional exam requirements/recommendations for international students: Required—TOEFL. Electronic applications accepted.

University of Southern Indiana, Graduate Studies, Romain College of Business, Program in Business Administration, Evansville, IN 47712-3590. Offers accounting (MBA); data analytics (MBA); engineering management (MBA); general business administration (MBA); healthcare administration (MBA); human resource management (MBA). *Accreditation:* AACSB. *Program availability:* Part-time, evening/weekend, 100% online, blended/hybrid learning. *Entrance requirements:* For master's, GMAT or GRE, minimum GPA of 2.5, resume, 3 professional references. Additional exam requirements/recommendations for international students: Required—TOEFL (minimum score 550 paper-based; 79 iBT), IELTS (minimum score 6). Electronic applications accepted.

University of Southern Maine, College of Management and Human Service, School of Business, Portland, ME 04104-9300. Offers accounting (MBA); business administration (MBA); finance (MBA); health management and policy (MBA); sustainability (MBA); JD/MBA; MBA/MSA; MBA/MSN; MS/MBA. *Accreditation:* AACSB. *Program availability:* Part-time, evening/weekend. *Entrance requirements:* For master's, GMAT or GRE, minimum AACSB index of 1100. Additional exam requirements/recommendations for international students: Required—TOEFL (minimum score 550 paper-based; 79 iBT). Electronic applications accepted. *Faculty research:* Economic development, management information systems, real options, system dynamics, simulation.

University of Southern Maine, Lewiston-Auburn College, Program in Leadership Studies, Portland, ME 04103. Offers creative leadership/global strategies (CGS); leadership studies (MA). *Program availability:* Part-time, online learning.

University of Southern Mississippi, College of Business and Economic Development, Program in Business Administration, Hattiesburg, MS 39406-0001. Offers business administration (MBA); sport security management (MBA). *Accreditation:* AACSB. *Program availability:* Part-time, evening/weekend. *Degree requirements:* For master's, comprehensive exam. *Entrance requirements:* For master's, GMAT, minimum GPA of 2.75 on last 60 hours. Additional exam requirements/recommendations for international students: Required—TOEFL, IELTS. Electronic applications accepted. *Faculty research:* Inflation accounting, self-esteem training, international trade policy, health care marketing, ethics in strategic planning.

University of South Florida, Muma College of Business, Department of Management, Tampa, FL 33620-9951. Offers management (MS), including human resources, management information systems. *Accreditation:* AACSB. *Program availability:* Part-time, online learning. *Faculty:* 4 full-time (2 women). *Students:* 22 full-time (10 women), 36 part-time (23 women); includes 21 minority (6 Black or African American, non-Hispanic/Latino; 1 Asian, non-Hispanic/Latino; 14 Hispanic/Latino), 14 international. Average age 31. 81 applicants, 63% accepted, 27 enrolled. In 2018, 43 master's awarded. Terminal master's awarded for partial completion of doctoral program. *Degree requirements:* For master's, comprehensive exam, thesis (for some programs). *Entrance requirements:* For master's, GMAT, letters of recommendation, resume, statement of purpose, relevant work experience. Additional exam requirements/recommendations for international students: Required—TOEFL (minimum score 550 paper-based; 79 iBT) or IELTS (minimum score 6.5). *Application deadline:* For fall admission, 6/1 for domestic students, 2/1 for international students; for spring admission, 10/15 for domestic students, 7/1 for international students. Application fee: $30. Electronic applications accepted. *Expenses:* Tuition, state resident: full-time $6350. Tuition, nonresident: full-time $19,048. *International tuition:* $19,048 full-time. *Required fees:* $2079. *Financial support:* In 2018–19, 6 students received support, including 1 research assistantship with tuition reimbursement available (averaging $9,002 per year), 3 teaching assistantships with tuition reimbursements available (averaging $9,002 per year); tuition waivers also available. Financial award applicants required to submit FAFSA. *Faculty research:* Leadership and employment relations, time management, personal motivation, crew resource management in aviation, psychology of gambling, organizational culture, issues of fairness, employment law, marketing strategy/implementation, organizational diversity, ethics, environmentally-friendly business practices, green business, sustainable business plans, institutional theory, social movement theory, diffusion of innovations, stakeholder human resources management, social responsibility. *Total annual research expenditures:* $24,235. *Unit head:* Dr. Sally Fuller, Interim Department Chair/Associate Professor, 813-974-1766, Fax: 813-905-9964, E-mail: sfuller@usf.edu. *Application contact:* Stacee Bender, Academic Services Administrator, 813-974-4516, Fax: 813-974-9964, E-mail: staceebender@usf.edu.
Website: http://www.usf.edu/business/graduate/masters/management/

University of South Florida, St. Petersburg, Kate Tiedemann College of Business, St. Petersburg, FL 33701. Offers MBA. *Accreditation:* AACSB. *Program availability:* Part-time. *Entrance requirements:* For master's, GMAT (minimum score of 500), bachelor's degree with minimum GPA of 3.0 overall or in upper two years from regionally-accredited institution; resume. Additional exam requirements/recommendations for international students: Required—TOEFL (minimum score 550 paper-based; 79 iBT); Recommended—IELTS. Electronic applications accepted.

University of South Florida Sarasota-Manatee, College of Business, Sarasota, FL 34243. Offers MBA. *Accreditation:* AACSB. *Program availability:* Part-time, evening/weekend. *Faculty:* 8 full-time (1 woman). *Students:* 24 full-time (9 women), 47 part-time (20 women); includes 26 minority (5 Black or African American, non-Hispanic/Latino; 4 Asian, non-Hispanic/Latino; 16 Hispanic/Latino; 1 Two or more races, non-Hispanic/Latino). Average age 33. 41 applicants, 34% accepted, 10 enrolled. In 2018, 25 master's awarded. *Degree requirements:* For master's, capstone project. *Entrance requirements:* For master's, GMAT (min score 500) or GRE (min score 1050 if taken before 8/1/2011 or 300 if taken after 8/1/2011). An applicant who has not taken the GMAT/GRE may be conditionally admitted provided s/he has at least 1 year FT work experience, a UG GPA of at least a 3.00, and a UG degree from an AACSB-accredited business school or membership in Beta Gamma Sigma., two years of full-time work experience (preferred, but not required); resume; two letters of recommendation; statement of purpose. Additional exam requirements/recommendations for international students: Required—TOEFL (minimum score 550 paper-based; 79 iBT), IELTS (minimum score 6.5). *Application deadline:* For fall admission, 6/1 priority date for domestic students, 6/1 for international students; for spring admission, 10/1 priority date for domestic students, 10/1 for international students; for summer admission, 3/1 for domestic and international students. Applications are processed on a rolling basis. Application fee: $30. Electronic applications accepted. *Expenses:* $453 tuition & fees per credit hour plus six semesters of $5 flat fee ($30). 40 credit hour program. *Financial support:* Federal Work-Study, scholarships/grants, health care benefits, and unspecified assistantships available. Support available to part-time students. Financial award application deadline: 6/30; financial award applicants required to submit FAFSA. *Faculty research:* Mergers and acquisitions, customer loyalty, employment discrimination, measurement of quality, efficiency of markets. *Unit head:* Dr. Thomas Becker, Interim Dean, 941-359-4245, E-mail: teb1@sar.usf.edu. *Application contact:* Brandon Avery, Interim Director, Admissions, 941-359-4331, E-mail: bavery@sar.usf.edu.
Website: http://usfsm.edu/college-of-business/

The University of Tampa, Sykes College of Business, Tampa, FL 33606-1490. Offers accounting (MS); business analytics (MBA); cybersecurity (MBA, MS); entrepreneurship (MBA, MS); finance (MBA, MS); information systems management (MBA); innovation management (MBA); international business (MBA); marketing (MBA, MS); nonprofit management (MBA, Certificate). *Accreditation:* AACSB. *Program availability:* Part-time, evening/weekend. *Faculty:* 61 full-time (13 women), 11 part-time/adjunct (3 women). *Students:* 361 full-time (153 women), 122 part-time (52 women); includes 101 minority (31 Black or African American, non-Hispanic/Latino; 5 Asian, non-Hispanic/Latino; 57 Hispanic/Latino; 1 Native Hawaiian or other Pacific Islander, non-Hispanic/Latino; 7 Two or more races, non-Hispanic/Latino), 144 international. Average age 29. 1,079 applicants, 57% accepted, 263 enrolled. In 2018, 281 master's, 12 other advanced degrees awarded. *Degree requirements:* For master's, capstone. *Entrance requirements:* For master's, GMAT or GRE, official transcripts from all colleges and/or universities previously attended, resume, personal statement, letters of recommendation. Additional exam requirements/recommendations for international students: Required—TOEFL (minimum score 577 paper-based; 90 iBT), IELTS (minimum score 7.5). *Application deadline:* Applications are processed on a rolling basis. Application fee: $40. Electronic applications accepted. *Expenses:* Contact institution. *Financial support:* In 2018–19, 123 students received support. Career-related internships or fieldwork, scholarships/grants, and unspecified assistantships available. Financial award applicants required to submit FAFSA. *Faculty research:* Job market signaling, on-line shopping behaviors and social media, the Tampa Bay economy, digital literacy, entrepreneurship in small businesses. *Unit head:* Dr. Natasha F. Veltri, Associate Dean, 813-253-6289, E-mail: nveltri@ut.edu. *Application contact:* Ashley Russell, Staff Assistant, Admissions for Graduate and Continuing Studies, 813-253-6249, E-mail: arussell@ut.edu.
Website: http://www.ut.edu/business/

The University of Tennessee, Graduate School, College of Business Administration, Program in Business Administration, Knoxville, TN 37996. Offers accounting (PhD); finance (MBA, PhD); logistics and transportation (MBA, PhD); management (PhD); marketing (MBA, PhD); operations management (MBA); professional business

administration (MBA); statistics (PhD); JD/MBA; MS/MBA; Pharm D/MBA. Pharm D/MBA offered jointly with The University of Tennessee Health Science Center. *Accreditation:* AACSB. *Program availability:* Online learning. *Degree requirements:* For master's, thesis or alternative; for doctorate, thesis/dissertation. *Entrance requirements:* For master's and doctorate, GMAT, minimum GPA of 2.7. Additional exam requirements/recommendations for international students: Required—TOEFL. Electronic applications accepted.

The University of Tennessee, Graduate School, College of Business Administration, Program in Management Science, Knoxville, TN 37996. Offers MS, PhD. *Accreditation:* AACSB. *Degree requirements:* For master's, thesis or alternative; for doctorate, thesis/dissertation. *Entrance requirements:* For master's and doctorate, GMAT or GRE General Test, minimum GPA of 2.7. Additional exam requirements/recommendations for international students: Required—TOEFL. Electronic applications accepted.

The University of Tennessee at Chattanooga, Program in Business Administration, Chattanooga, TN 37403. Offers EMBA, MBA, PMBA. *Accreditation:* AACSB. *Program availability:* Part-time, evening/weekend. *Entrance requirements:* For master's, GMAT (minimum score 450) or GRE General Test (minimum score 146 on verbal and 144 on quantitative), minimum overall undergraduate GPA of 2.7 or 3.0 in final two years. Additional exam requirements/recommendations for international students: Required—TOEFL (minimum score 550 paper-based; 79 iBT), IELTS (minimum score 6). Electronic applications accepted. *Expenses:* Contact institution. *Faculty research:* Diversity, operations/production management, entrepreneurial processes, customer satisfaction and retention, branding.

The University of Tennessee at Martin, Graduate Programs, College of Business and Global Affairs, Program in Business, Martin, TN 38238. Offers agricultural business (MBA); financial services (MBA); general business (MBA). *Accreditation:* AACSB. *Program availability:* Part-time, online only, 100% online, blended/hybrid learning. *Faculty:* 33. *Students:* 8 full-time (2 women), 58 part-time (32 women); includes 5 minority (3 Black or African American, non-Hispanic/Latino; 1 Hispanic/Latino; 1 Two or more races, non-Hispanic/Latino). Average age 36. 65 applicants, 28% accepted, 13 enrolled. In 2018, 39 master's awarded. *Degree requirements:* For master's, comprehensive exam. *Entrance requirements:* For master's, GMAT, GRE, minimum GPA of 2.5, resume. Additional exam requirements/recommendations for international students: Required—TOEFL (minimum score 525 paper-based; 71 iBT). *Application deadline:* For fall admission, 7/27 priority date for domestic students, 7/27 for international students; for spring admission, 12/17 priority date for domestic students, 12/17 for international students; for summer admission, 5/10 priority date for domestic and international students. Applications are processed on a rolling basis. Application fee: $30 ($130 for international students). Electronic applications accepted. *Expenses: Tuition, area resident:* Full-time $8918; part-time $495 per credit hour. Tuition, state resident: full-time $8918; part-time $485 per credit hour. Tuition, nonresident: full-time $14,958; part-time $831 per credit hour. *International tuition:* $22,862 full-time. *Required fees:* $1446; $81 per credit hour. Part-time tuition and fees vary according to course load. *Financial support:* In 2018–19, 30 students received support, including 5 research assistantships with full tuition reimbursements available (averaging $7,289 per year), 4 teaching assistantships with full tuition reimbursements available (averaging $8,187 per year); scholarships/grants and tuition waivers (full and partial) also available. Financial award application deadline: 2/1; financial award applicants required to submit FAFSA. *Unit head:* Dr. Tommy Cates, Coordinator, 731-881-7208, Fax: 731-881-7231, E-mail: mba@utm.edu. *Application contact:* Jolene L. Cunningham, Student Services Specialist, 731-881-7012, Fax: 731-881-7499, E-mail: jcunningham@utm.edu.

The University of Texas at Austin, Graduate School, McCombs School of Business, Department of Management, Austin, TX 78712-1111. Offers PhD. *Accreditation:* AACSB. *Degree requirements:* For doctorate, thesis/dissertation. *Entrance requirements:* For doctorate, GMAT or GRE. Electronic applications accepted.

The University of Texas at Austin, Graduate School, McCombs School of Business, Executive MBA Program at Mexico City, Austin, TX 78712-1111. Offers MBA. Program offered jointly with Instituto Tecnológico y de Estudios Superiores de Monterrey, Campus Ciudad de México. *Accreditation:* AACSB. *Entrance requirements:* For master's, GMAT, 5 years of work experience. Additional exam requirements/recommendations for international students: Required—TOEFL.

The University of Texas at Austin, Graduate School, McCombs School of Business, MBA Programs, Austin, TX 78712-1111. Offers MBA, JD/MBA, MBA/MA, MBA/MP Aff, MBA/MSN. *Accreditation:* AACSB. *Program availability:* Part-time. *Entrance requirements:* For master's, GMAT, minimum 2 years of full-time work experience. Additional exam requirements/recommendations for international students: Required—TOEFL. Electronic applications accepted.

The University of Texas at Dallas, Naveen Jindal School of Management, Richardson, TX 75080. Offers EMBA, MBA, MS, PhD, MS/MBA, MSEE/MBA. *Program availability:* Part-time, evening/weekend, online learning. *Faculty:* 108 full-time (22 women), 132 part-time/adjunct (38 women). *Students:* 2,848 full-time (1,224 women), 1,723 part-time (789 women); includes 952 minority (129 Black or African American, non-Hispanic/Latino; 4 American Indian or Alaska Native, non-Hispanic/Latino; 524 Asian, non-Hispanic/Latino; 224 Hispanic/Latino; 71 Two or more races, non-Hispanic/Latino), 2,614 international. Average age 30. 5,382 applicants, 64% accepted, 1575 enrolled. In 2018, 2,300 master's, 23 doctorates awarded. *Degree requirements:* For doctorate, thesis/dissertation. *Entrance requirements:* For master's and doctorate, GMAT. Additional exam requirements/recommendations for international students: Required—TOEFL (minimum score 550 paper-based). *Application deadline:* For fall admission, 7/15 for domestic students, 5/1 priority date for international students; for spring admission, 11/15 for domestic students, 9/1 priority date for international students. Applications are processed on a rolling basis. Application fee: $50 ($100 for international students). Electronic applications accepted. *Expenses: Tuition, area resident:* Full-time $13,458. Tuition, state resident: full-time $13,458. Tuition, nonresident: full-time $26,852. *International tuition:* $26,852 full-time. Tuition and fees vary according to course load. *Financial support:* In 2018–19, 104 students received support, including 25 research assistantships with partial tuition reimbursements available (averaging $36,440 per year), 149 teaching assistantships with partial tuition reimbursements available (averaging $18,444 per year); fellowships, career-related internships or fieldwork, Federal Work-Study, institutionally sponsored loans, scholarships/grants, and unspecified assistantships also available. Support available to part-time students. Financial award application deadline: 4/30; financial award applicants required to submit FAFSA. *Faculty research:* Finance, marketing and organization, strategy, management education for physicians. *Total annual research expenditures:* $7.6 million. *Unit head:* Dr. Hasan Pirkul, Dean, 972-883-2705, Fax: 972-883-2799, E-mail: hpirkul@utdallas.edu. *Application contact:* Dr. Hasan Pirkul, Dean, 972-883-2705, Fax: 972-883-2799, E-mail: hpirkul@utdallas.edu. Website: http://jindal.utdallas.edu/

The University of Texas at El Paso, Graduate School, College of Business Administration, Programs in Business Administration, El Paso, TX 79968-0001. Offers business administration (MBA, Certificate); international business (PhD). *Accreditation:* AACSB. *Program availability:* Part-time, evening/weekend, online learning. *Degree*

requirements: For master's, comprehensive exam. *Entrance requirements:* For master's and doctorate, GMAT. Additional exam requirements/recommendations for international students: Required—TOEFL. Electronic applications accepted. *Faculty research:* Cross-border modeling, human resources, and outsourcing and manufacturing; global information technology transfer; international investments and risk management.

The University of Texas at San Antonio, College of Business, Department of Information Systems and Cyber Security, San Antonio, TX 78249-0617. Offers cyber security (MSIT); information technology (MS, PhD); management of technology (MBA); technology entrepreneurship and management (Certificate). *Program availability:* Part-time, evening/weekend. *Degree requirements:* For master's, comprehensive exam (for some programs), thesis optional; for doctorate, comprehensive exam, thesis/dissertation. *Entrance requirements:* For master's and doctorate, GMAT/GRE, official transcripts, statement of purpose, letters of recommendation. Additional exam requirements/recommendations for international students: Required—TOEFL (minimum score 550 paper-based; 79 iBT), IELTS (minimum score 6.5). Electronic applications accepted. *Expenses:* Contact institution. *Faculty research:* Cyber security, digital forensics, economics of information systems, information systems privacy, information technology adoption.

The University of Texas at San Antonio, College of Business, Department of Management, San Antonio, TX 78249-0617. Offers management and organization studies (PhD). Terminal master's awarded for partial completion of doctoral program. *Degree requirements:* For doctorate, comprehensive exam, thesis/dissertation. *Entrance requirements:* For doctorate, GMAT, GRE. Additional exam requirements/recommendations for international students: Required—TOEFL (minimum score 550 paper-based; 79 iBT), IELTS (minimum score 6.5). Electronic applications accepted.

The University of Texas at San Antonio, College of Business, Department of Management Science and Statistics, San Antonio, TX 78249-0617. Offers applied statistics (MS, PhD); management science (MBA). *Accreditation:* AACSB. *Program availability:* Part-time, evening/weekend. *Degree requirements:* For master's, comprehensive exam (for some programs), thesis or alternative; for doctorate, comprehensive exam, thesis/dissertation. *Entrance requirements:* For master's, GMAT, minimum of 36 semester credit hours of coursework beyond any hours acquired in the MBA-leveling courses; statement of purpose; for doctorate, GRE, minimum cumulative GPA of 3.3 in the last 60 hours of coursework; transcripts from all colleges and universities attended; curriculum vitae; statement of academic work experiences, interests, and goals; three letters of recommendation; BA, BS, or MS in mathematics, statistics, or closely-related field. Additional exam requirements/recommendations for international students: Required—TOEFL (minimum score 550 paper-based; 79 iBT), IELTS (minimum score 6.5). Electronic applications accepted. *Faculty research:* Statistical signal processing, reliability and life-testing experiments, modeling decompression sickness using survival analysis.

The University of Texas at Tyler, Soules College of Business, Department of Management and Marketing, Tyler, TX 75799-0001. Offers cyber security (MBA); engineering management (MBA); general management (MBA); healthcare management (MBA); internal assurance and consulting (MBA); marketing (MBA); oil, gas and energy (MBA); organizational development (MBA); quality management (MBA). *Accreditation:* AACSB. *Program availability:* Part-time, online learning. *Students:* Average age 29. 73 applicants, 96% accepted, 35 enrolled. In 2018, 37 master's awarded. *Entrance requirements:* Additional exam requirements/recommendations for international students: Required—TOEFL (minimum score 550 paper-based). *Application deadline:* For fall admission, 8/17 priority date for domestic students, 7/1 priority date for international students; for spring admission, 12/21 priority date for domestic students, 11/1 priority date for international students. Application fee: $25 ($50 for international students). *Faculty research:* General business, inventory control, institutional markets, service marketing, product distribution, accounting fraud, financial reporting and recognition. *Unit head:* Dr. Krist Swimberghe, Chair, 903-565-5803, E-mail: kswimberghe@uttyler.edu. *Application contact:* Dr. Krist Swimberghe, Chair, 903-565-5803, E-mail: kswimberghe@uttyler.edu. Website: https://www.uttyler.edu/cbt/manamark/

The University of Texas of the Permian Basin, Office of Graduate Studies, College of Business, Program in Management, Odessa, TX 79762-0001. Offers MBA. *Accreditation:* AACSB. *Entrance requirements:* For master's, GMAT. Additional exam requirements/recommendations for international students: Required—TOEFL (minimum score 550 paper-based).

The University of Texas Rio Grande Valley, Robert C. Vackar College of Business and Entrepreneurship, Edinburg, TX 78539. Offers M Acc, MBA, MS, PhD. *Accreditation:* AACSB. *Program availability:* Part-time, evening/weekend. *Degree requirements:* For master's, thesis optional; for doctorate, one foreign language, thesis/dissertation, internship. *Entrance requirements:* For master's, GMAT, minimum AACSB index of 1000 (based on last 60 semester hours); for doctorate, GMAT. Additional exam requirements/recommendations for international students: Required—TOEFL. *Expenses: Tuition, area resident:* Full-time $6888. Tuition, state resident: full-time $6888. Tuition, nonresident: full-time $14,484. *International tuition:* $14,484 full-time. *Required fees:* $1468.

University of the Cumberlands, Hutton School of Business, Williamsburg, KY 40769-1372. Offers accounting (MBA); business (MBA). *Program availability:* Part-time, online learning. *Entrance requirements:* For master's, GMAT, GRE. Additional exam requirements/recommendations for international students: Required—TOEFL. Electronic applications accepted.

University of the District of Columbia, School of Business and Public Administration, Program in Business Administration, Washington, DC 20008-1175. Offers MBA. *Accreditation:* ACBSP. *Degree requirements:* For master's, comprehensive exam, thesis optional. *Entrance requirements:* For master's, GMAT, writing proficiency exam.

University of the Incarnate Word, H-E-B School of Business and Administration, San Antonio, TX 78209-6397. Offers accounting (MS); business administration (MBA); health administration (MHA). *Program availability:* Part-time, evening/weekend. *Faculty:* 22 full-time (12 women), 13 part-time/adjunct (5 women). *Students:* 249 full-time (120 women), 27 part-time (12 women); includes 162 minority (24 Black or African American, non-Hispanic/Latino; 1 American Indian or Alaska Native, non-Hispanic/Latino; 8 Asian, non-Hispanic/Latino; 124 Hispanic/Latino; 1 Native Hawaiian or other Pacific Islander, non-Hispanic/Latino; 4 Two or more races, non-Hispanic/Latino), 40 international. 202 applicants, 98% accepted, 108 enrolled. In 2018, 142 master's awarded. *Degree requirements:* For master's, capstone. *Entrance requirements:* For master's, GMAT, GRE, writing sample, interview. Additional exam requirements/recommendations for international students: Required—TOEFL (minimum score 560 paper-based; 83 iBT). *Application deadline:* Applications are processed on a rolling basis. Application fee: $20. Electronic applications accepted. *Expenses: Tuition:* Full-time $22,560; part-time $940 per credit hour. *Required fees:* $2484; $94 per credit hour. Tuition and fees vary according to degree level, program and student level. *Financial support:* Research assistantships, Federal Work-Study, scholarships/grants, tuition waivers (partial), and unspecified assistantships available. Financial award applicants required to submit FAFSA. *Faculty research:* Importance of business sustainability, comparison of tax/legal

research services, fair trade branding as a tool for the marketing of developing society crafts, ethnocentrism and country of origin effects among immigrant consumers, international trade and investment. *Unit head:* Dr. Forrest Aven, Dean, 210-805-5884, Fax: 210-805-3564, E-mail: aven@uiwtx.edu. *Application contact:* Jessica Delarosa, Associate Director of Admissions, 210-8296005, Fax: 210-829-3921, E-mail: admis@uiwtx.edu.
Website: https://www.uiw.edu/hebsba/index.html

University of the Incarnate Word, School of Professional Studies, San Antonio, TX 78209-6397. Offers communication arts (MAA), including applied administration, communication arts, healthcare administration, industrial and organizational psychology, organizational development; organizational development and leadership (MS); professional studies (DBA). *Program availability:* Part-time, evening/weekend, 100% online, blended/hybrid learning. *Faculty:* 9 full-time (3 women), 26 part-time/adjunct (10 women). *Students:* 475 full-time (229 women), 358 part-time (151 women); includes 536 minority (122 Black or African American, non-Hispanic/Latino; 5 American Indian or Alaska Native, non-Hispanic/Latino; 19 Asian, non-Hispanic/Latino; 366 Hispanic/Latino; 3 Native Hawaiian or other Pacific Islander, non-Hispanic/Latino; 21 Two or more races, non-Hispanic/Latino). 593 applicants, 91% accepted, 287 enrolled. In 2018, 488 master's, 11 doctorates awarded. *Degree requirements:* For master's, comprehensive exam (for some programs), thesis or alternative. *Entrance requirements:* For master's, GMAT, GRE, official transcripts from all other colleges attended. Additional exam requirements/recommendations for international students: Required—TOEFL (minimum score 560 paper-based; 83 iBT). *Application deadline:* Applications are processed on a rolling basis. Electronic applications accepted. *Expenses:* Tuition: Full-time $22,560; part-time $940 per credit hour. *Required fees:* $2484; $94 per credit hour. Tuition and fees vary according to degree level, program and student level. *Financial support:* Scholarships/grants and unspecified assistantships available. Financial award applicants required to submit FAFSA. *Unit head:* Vincent Porter, Dean, 210-8292770, E-mail: porterv@uiwtx.edu. *Application contact:* Julie Weber, Director of Marketing and Recruitment, 210-318-1876, Fax: 210-829-2756, E-mail: eapadmission@uiwtx.edu.
Website: https://sps.uiw.edu/

University of the Pacific, Eberhardt School of Business, Stockton, CA 95211-0197. Offers M Acc, MBA, JD/MBA, Pharm D/MBA. *Accreditation:* AACSB. *Program availability:* Part-time. *Entrance requirements:* For master's, GMAT. Additional exam requirements/recommendations for international students: Required—TOEFL.

University of the People, Master of Business Administration Program, Pasadena, CA 91101. Offers MBA. *Program availability:* Online learning.

University of the Potomac, Program in Business Administration, Washington, DC 20005. Offers MBA. Program also offered at Vienna, VA campus. *Program availability:* Online learning.

University of the Sacred Heart, Graduate Programs, Department of Business Administration, San Juan, PR 00914-0383. Offers human resource management (MBA); information systems auditing (MS); information technology (Certificate); international marketing (MBA); management information systems (MBA); production and marketing of special events (Certificate); taxation (MBA). *Program availability:* Part-time, evening/weekend. *Degree requirements:* For master's, thesis. *Entrance requirements:* For master's, EXADEP, minimum undergraduate GPA of 2.75, interview.

University of the Southwest, Graduate Programs, Hobbs, NM 88240-9129. Offers business administration (MBA); curriculum and instruction (MSE); curriculum and instruction: bilingual (MSE); curriculum and instruction: TESOL (MSE); early childhood education (MSE); educational administration (MSE); mental health counseling (MSE); school counseling (MSE); special education (MSE); sports management (MBA). *Program availability:* Part-time, evening/weekend, online learning. *Degree requirements:* For master's, comprehensive exam, thesis (for some programs). *Entrance requirements:* Additional exam requirements/recommendations for international students: Recommended—TOEFL. Electronic applications accepted.

University of the Virgin Islands, School of Business, St. Thomas, VI 00802. Offers EMBA, MBA. *Program availability:* Part-time, evening/weekend. *Students:* 5 full-time (4 women), 29 part-time (18 women); includes 27 minority (23 Black or African American, non-Hispanic/Latino; 1 Asian, non-Hispanic/Latino; 3 Hispanic/Latino), 5 international. Average age 31. In 2018, 5 master's awarded. *Degree requirements:* For master's, comprehensive exam, thesis, comprehensive exam or thesis. *Entrance requirements:* For master's, GMAT, minimum GPA of 2.5. Additional exam requirements/recommendations for international students: Required—TOEFL (minimum score 550 paper-based). *Application deadline:* For fall admission, 4/30 for domestic and international students; for spring admission, 10/30 for domestic and international students. Applications are processed on a rolling basis. Application fee: $30. Electronic applications accepted. *Expenses:* Contact institution. *Financial support:* Application deadline: 4/15; applicants required to submit FAFSA. *Unit head:* Dr. Kendra Harris, Dean, 340-693-1301, Fax: 340-693-1305, E-mail: kendra.harris@uvi.edu. *Application contact:* Charmaine M Smith, Director of Admissions, 340-692-4070, E-mail: csmith@uvi.edu.
Website: http://www.uvi.edu/academics/school-business/

University of the West, Department of Business Administration, Rosemead, CA 91770. Offers business administration (EMBA); computer information systems (MBA); finance (MBA); international business (MBA); nonprofit organization management (MBA). *Program availability:* Part-time, evening/weekend. *Entrance requirements:* Additional exam requirements/recommendations for international students: Required—TOEFL.

The University of Toledo, College of Graduate Studies, College of Business and Innovation, Department of Management, Toledo, OH 43606-3390. Offers MBA. *Program availability:* Part-time, evening/weekend. *Entrance requirements:* For master's, GMAT, GRE, or LSAT, minimum GPA of 2.7 for all prior academic work, three letters of recommendation, statement of purpose, transcripts from all prior institutions attended. Additional exam requirements/recommendations for international students: Required—TOEFL (minimum score 550 paper-based; 80 iBT). Electronic applications accepted. *Faculty research:* Stress, deviation, workplace, globalization, recruitment.

University of Toronto, School of Graduate Studies, Rotman School of Management, Toronto, ON M5S 1A1, Canada. Offers MBA, MF, PhD, JD/MBA. *Accreditation:* AACSB. *Program availability:* Part-time, evening/weekend. *Degree requirements:* For doctorate, thesis/dissertation. *Entrance requirements:* For master's, GMAT (MBA), minimum mid-B average in final undergraduate year; minimum 2 years of full-time work experience; 2-3 letters of reference; for doctorate, GMAT or GRE, minimum B+ average, master's degree in business administration, 2-3 letters of reference. *Expenses:* Contact institution. *Faculty research:* Natural resources, organizational behavior, finance, marketing, strategic management.

The University of Tulsa, Graduate School, Collins College of Business, Master of Business Administration Program, Tulsa, OK 74104-3189. Offers MBA, JD/MBA, MBA/MSCS, MBA/MSF. *Accreditation:* AACSB. *Program availability:* Part-time, evening/weekend. *Faculty:* 32 full-time (6 women). *Students:* 41 full-time (16 women), 44 part-time (14 women); includes 15 minority (2 Black or African American, non-Hispanic/Latino; 4 American Indian or Alaska Native, non-Hispanic/Latino; 3 Asian, non-Hispanic/

Latino; 4 Hispanic/Latino; 2 Two or more races, non-Hispanic/Latino), 9 international. Average age 29. 50 applicants, 82% accepted, 28 enrolled. In 2018, 34 master's awarded. *Entrance requirements:* For master's, GMAT. Additional exam requirements/recommendations for international students: Required—TOEFL (minimum score 577 paper-based; 91 iBT), IELTS (minimum score 6.5). *Application deadline:* Applications are processed on a rolling basis. Application fee: $55. Electronic applications accepted. *Expenses:* Tuition: Full-time $22,230; part-time $1235 per credit hour. *Required fees:* $2100; $6 per credit hour. One-time fee: $400 full-time. Tuition and fees vary according to course level, course load and program. *Financial support:* In 2018–19, 9 students received support, including 9 teaching assistantships with full tuition reimbursements available (averaging $8,468 per year); fellowships, research assistantships with full tuition reimbursements available, career-related internships or fieldwork, institutionally sponsored loans, scholarships/grants, health care benefits, tuition waivers (full and partial), and unspecified assistantships also available. Support available to part-time students. Financial award application deadline: 2/1; financial award applicants required to submit FAFSA. *Faculty research:* Accounting, energy management, finance, international business, management information systems, taxation. *Unit head:* Dr. Ralph Jackson, Associate Dean of the Collins College of Business, 918-631-2242, Fax: 918-631-2142, E-mail: ralph-jackson@utulsa.edu. *Application contact:* Information Contact, 918-631-2242, E-mail: graduate-business@utulsa.edu.

University of Utah, Graduate School, David Eccles School of Business, Salt Lake City, UT 84112-8939. Offers EMBA, M Acc, MBA, MHA, MRED, MS, MSF, PMBA, PhD, Graduate Certificate, MBA/JD, MBA/MHA, MBA/MS, MHA/MPA, MPH/MHA, MRED/JD, MRED/M Arch, MRED/MCMP, MSF/MSBA, MSF/PMBA, PMBA/MHA. *Accreditation:* AACSB. *Program availability:* Part-time, evening/weekend. *Degree requirements:* For master's, comprehensive exam (for some programs), thesis (for some programs); for doctorate, comprehensive exam (for some programs), thesis/dissertation. *Entrance requirements:* Additional exam requirements/recommendations for international students: Required—TOEFL. Electronic applications accepted. *Expenses:* Contact institution. *Faculty research:* Information systems, investment, financial accounting, international strategy.

University of Vermont, Graduate College, Grossman School of Business, Burlington, VT 05405. Offers M Acc, MBA, MBA/JD. *Accreditation:* AACSB. *Program availability:* Part-time. *Entrance requirements:* For master's, GMAT or GRE, resume. Additional exam requirements/recommendations for international students: Required—TOEFL (minimum iBT score of 90) or IELTS (6.5). Electronic applications accepted.

University of Victoria, Faculty of Graduate Studies, Peter B. Gustavson School of Business, Victoria, BC V8W 2Y2, Canada. Offers MBA, MBA/LL B. *Accreditation:* AACSB. *Program availability:* Part-time. *Entrance requirements:* For master's, GMAT, minimum B average. Additional exam requirements/recommendations for international students: Required—TOEFL (minimum score 575 paper-based), IELTS (minimum score 7). Electronic applications accepted. *Expenses:* Contact institution. *Faculty research:* Organizational design and analysis, negotiation and conflict management, human resources management, entrepreneurship, international marketing and tourism.

University of Virginia, Darden School of Business, Charlottesville, VA 22903. Offers MBA, MSBA, PhD, MBA/JD, MBA/M Ed, MBA/MA, MBA/MD, MBA/ME, MBA/MPP, MBA/MS, MBA/MSDS, MBA/MSN. *Accreditation:* AACSB. *Degree requirements:* For doctorate, thesis/dissertation. *Entrance requirements:* For master's, GMAT, resume; 2 letters of recommendation; interview; for doctorate, GMAT, resume; essay; 2 letters of recommendation; interview. Additional exam requirements/recommendations for international students: Required—TOEFL. Electronic applications accepted. *Expenses:* Contact institution.

University of Virginia, McIntire School of Commerce, Charlottesville, VA 22904. Offers MS, MSC, Certificate, JD/MS. *Accreditation:* AACSB. *Faculty:* 76 full-time (23 women), 1 (woman) part-time/adjunct. *Students:* 342 full-time (134 women); includes 59 minority (16 Black or African American, non-Hispanic/Latino; 31 Asian, non-Hispanic/Latino; 12 Hispanic/Latino), 77 international. Average age 23. *Entrance requirements:* For master's, GMAT or GRE, 2 letters of recommendation. Additional exam requirements/recommendations for international students: Required—TOEFL (minimum score 100 iBT), IELTS (minimum score 7.5), TOEFL (minimum score 100 iBT) or IELTS (minimum score 7.5). *Application deadline:* Applications are processed on a rolling basis. Application fee: $75. Electronic applications accepted. *Expenses:* Contact institution. *Financial support:* Federal Work-Study, scholarships/grants, and unspecified assistantships available. Financial award application deadline: 2/1; financial award applicants required to submit FAFSA. *Unit head:* Carl Zeithaml, Dean, 877-349-2620, Fax: 434-924-7074, E-mail: mcintiregrad@virginia.edu. *Application contact:* Emma Candelier, Assistant Dean of Graduate Recruiting, 434-243-4992, Fax: 434-924-4511, E-mail: ecandelier@virginia.edu.
Website: http://www.commerce.virginia.edu

University of Washington, Graduate School, Michael G. Foster School of Business, Seattle, WA 98195-3200. Offers auditing and assurance (MP Acc); business administration (MBA, PhD); entrepreneurship (MS); executive business administration (MBA); global executive business administration (MBA); information systems (MSIS); supply chain management (MSSCM); taxation (MP Acc); technology management (MBA); JD/MBA; MBA/MAIS; MBA/MHA. *Accreditation:* AACSB. *Program availability:* Part-time, evening/weekend, blended/hybrid learning. Terminal master's awarded for partial completion of doctoral program. *Degree requirements:* For doctorate, comprehensive exam, thesis/dissertation. *Entrance requirements:* For master's and doctorate, GMAT, GRE. Additional exam requirements/recommendations for international students: Required—TOEFL (minimum score 600 paper-based; 100 iBT). Electronic applications accepted. *Expenses:* Contact institution. *Faculty research:* Finance, consumer behavior, marketing analytics, technology management, supply chain.

University of Washington, Bothell, School of Business, Bothell, WA 98011. Offers leadership (MBA); technology (MBA). *Accreditation:* AACSB. *Program availability:* Part-time, evening/weekend. *Degree requirements:* For master's, 72 credits, minimum cumulative GPA of 3.0. *Entrance requirements:* For master's, GMAT or GRE General Test. Additional exam requirements/recommendations for international students: Required—TOEFL (minimum score 580 paper-based; 92 iBT), IELTS (minimum score 7). Electronic applications accepted. *Expenses:* Contact institution. *Faculty research:* Leadership, supply chain management, entrepreneurship, game theory, corporate finance, marketing innovation.

University of Washington, Tacoma, Graduate Programs, MBA Programs, Tacoma, WA 98402-3100. Offers accounting (MBA); business administration (MBA); certified financial analyst (MBA). *Accreditation:* AACSB. *Program availability:* Part-time, evening/weekend. *Entrance requirements:* For master's, GMAT, minimum GPA of 3.0 in final graded 90 quarter credits or 60 graded semester credits; at least 2 years of professional/management work experience. Additional exam requirements/recommendations for international students: Required—TOEFL (minimum score 580 paper-based; 92 iBT). Electronic applications accepted. *Expenses:* Contact institution. *Faculty research:* International accounting, marketing, change management, investments, corporate social responsibility.

University of Waterloo, Graduate Studies and Postdoctoral Affairs, Faculty of Engineering, Conrad School of Entrepreneurship and Business, Waterloo, ON N2L 3G1, Canada. Offers MBET. *Entrance requirements:* For master's, honors degree. Additional exam requirements/recommendations for international students: Required—TOEFL (minimum score 90 iBT), IELTS (minimum score 7), PTE (minimum score 63). *Application deadline:* Applications are processed on a rolling basis. Application fee: $125. Electronic applications accepted. *Application contact:* Tracie Wilkinson, Administrative Liaison and Support, 519-888-4567 Ext. 37167, Fax: 519-747-7287, E-mail: twilkins@uwaterloo.ca.
Website: https://uwaterloo.ca/conrad-business-entrepreneurship-technology/

The University of West Alabama, School of Graduate Studies, College of Business and Technology, Livingston, AL 35470. Offers finance (MBA); general business (MBA). *Program availability:* Part-time, evening/weekend, 100% online. *Faculty:* 1 full-time (0 women), 15 part-time/adjunct (11 women). *Students:* 169 full-time (124 women), 8 part-time (0 women); includes 97 minority (87 Black or African American, non-Hispanic/Latino; 1 American Indian or Alaska Native, non-Hispanic/Latino; 2 Asian, non-Hispanic/Latino; 1 Hispanic/Latino; 6 Two or more races, non-Hispanic/Latino). Average age 30. 110 applicants, 95% accepted, 78 enrolled. In 2018, 16 master's awarded. *Degree requirements:* For master's, nine hours completed for emphasis area. *Entrance requirements:* For master's, bachelor's degree with minimum GPA of 2.75. Additional exam requirements/recommendations for international students: Required—TOEFL (minimum score 500 paper-based; 61 iBT). *Application deadline:* Applications are processed on a rolling basis. Application fee: $40. Electronic applications accepted. *Expenses: Tuition, area resident:* Full-time $9100. Tuition, state resident: full-time $9100. Tuition, nonresident: full-time $19,200. *Required fees:* $1890; $130. *Financial support:* Federal Work-Study and scholarships/grants available. Support available to part-time students. Financial award application deadline: 3/1; financial award applicants required to submit FAFSA. *Unit head:* Dr. Aliquippa Allen, Dean of College of Business and Technology, 205-652-3564, Fax: 205-652-3776, E-mail: aallen@uwa.edu. *Application contact:* Dr. Aliquippa Allen, Dean of College of Business and Technology, 205-652-3564, Fax: 205-652-3776, E-mail: aallen@uwa.edu.
Website: http://www.uwa.edu/academics/collegeofbusinessandtechnology

The University of Western Ontario, Ivey Business School, London, ON N6A 3K7, Canada. Offers business (EMBA, PhD); corporate strategy and leadership elective (MBA); entrepreneurship elective (MBA); finance elective (MBA); health sector stream (MBA); international management elective (MBA); marketing elective (MBA); JD/MBA. *Degree requirements:* For master's, thesis (for some programs); for doctorate, thesis/dissertation. *Entrance requirements:* For master's, GMAT, 2 years of full-time work experience, interview. Additional exam requirements/recommendations for international students: Required—TOEFL (minimum score 100 iBT) or IELTS (minimum score 6). Electronic applications accepted. *Faculty research:* Strategy, organizational behavior, international business, finance, operations management.

University of West Florida, College of Business, Program in Business Administration, Pensacola, FL 32514-5750. Offers MBA. *Accreditation:* AACSB. *Program availability:* Part-time, evening/weekend. *Degree requirements:* For master's, industry portfolio project based on information from five of the core MBA courses. *Entrance requirements:* For master's, GMAT or GRE, official transcripts; minimum undergraduate GPA of 3.0; bachelor's degree; business course academic preparation; graduate-level motivation and writing abilities as noted in essay responses; two letters of recommendation; appropriate employment at increasing levels of responsibility via resume. Additional exam requirements/recommendations for international students: Required—TOEFL (minimum score 550 paper-based). *Faculty research:* Robotics, corporate behavior, international trade, franchising, counterfeiting.

University of West Georgia, Richards College of Business, Carrollton, GA 30118. Offers accounting (MP Acc); business administration (MBA). *Program availability:* Part-time, evening/weekend, 100% online, blended/hybrid learning. *Faculty:* 38 full-time (15 women). *Students:* 57 full-time (34 women), 118 part-time (68 women); includes 60 minority (45 Black or African American, non-Hispanic/Latino; 3 Asian, non-Hispanic/Latino; 10 Hispanic/Latino; 2 Two or more races, non-Hispanic/Latino), 9 international. Average age 30. 123 applicants, 96% accepted, 73 enrolled. In 2018, 112 master's awarded. *Entrance requirements:* Additional exam requirements/recommendations for international students: Required—TOEFL (minimum score 550 paper-based; 79 iBT); Recommended—IELTS (minimum score 6.5). *Application deadline:* For fall admission, 7/15 for domestic students, 6/1 for international students; for spring admission, 11/15 for domestic students, 10/15 for international students; for summer admission, 5/15 for domestic students, 3/30 for international students. Applications are processed on a rolling basis. Application fee: $40. Electronic applications accepted. Tuition and fees vary according to course load, degree level, campus/location and program. *Financial support:* Fellowships, research assistantships, teaching assistantships, career-related internships or fieldwork, Federal Work-Study, institutionally sponsored loans, scholarships/grants, and unspecified assistantships available. Support available to part-time students. Financial award application deadline: 4/1; financial award applicants required to submit FAFSA. *Unit head:* Dr. Faye S. McIntyre, Dean of Richards College of Business, 678-839-6467, Fax: 678-839-5040, E-mail: fmcintyr@westga.edu. *Application contact:* Dr. Toby Ziglar, Assistant Dean of the Graduate School, 678-839-1394, Fax: 678-839-1395, E-mail: graduate@westga.edu.
Website: https://www.westga.edu/business

University of West Los Angeles, School of Business, Inglewood, CA 90301. Offers organizational leadership and business innovation (MS).

University of Windsor, Faculty of Graduate Studies, Odette School of Business, Windsor, ON N9B 3P4, Canada. Offers MBA, MM, MBA/LL B. *Program availability:* Evening/weekend. *Degree requirements:* For master's, thesis or alternative. *Entrance requirements:* For master's, GMAT, minimum B average. Additional exam requirements/recommendations for international students: Required—TOEFL (minimum score 600 paper-based). Electronic applications accepted. *Faculty research:* Accounting, administrative studies, finance, marketing, business policy and strategy.

University of Wisconsin–Eau Claire, College of Business, Program in Business Administration, Eau Claire, WI 54702-4004. Offers MBA. *Accreditation:* AACSB. *Program availability:* Part-time, evening/weekend, online learning. Terminal master's awarded for partial completion of doctoral program. *Degree requirements:* For master's, thesis optional, applied field project. *Entrance requirements:* For master's, GMAT or GRE, minimum GPA of 2.75 overall. Additional exam requirements/recommendations for international students: Required—TOEFL (minimum score 79 iBT). *Expenses:* Contact institution.

University of Wisconsin–Green Bay, Graduate Studies, Program in Management, Green Bay, WI 54311-7001. Offers MS. *Program availability:* Part-time, evening/weekend. *Degree requirements:* For master's, thesis or alternative. *Entrance requirements:* For master's, GMAT or GRE General Test, minimum GPA of 3.0. Electronic applications accepted. *Faculty research:* Planning methods, budgeting, decision-making, organizational behavior and theory, management.

University of Wisconsin–Madison, Graduate School, Wisconsin School of Business, Wisconsin Evening MBA Program, Madison, WI 53706-1380. Offers general management (MBA). *Program availability:* Part-time-only, evening/weekend. *Faculty:* 15 full-time (1 woman), 5 part-time/adjunct (2 women). *Students:* 142 part-time (42 women); includes 16 minority (1 Black or African American, non-Hispanic/Latino; 1 American Indian or Alaska Native, non-Hispanic/Latino; 11 Asian, non-Hispanic/Latino; 2 Hispanic/Latino; 1 Two or more races, non-Hispanic/Latino), 6 international. Average age 29. 76 applicants, 72% accepted, 44 enrolled. In 2018, 57 master's awarded. *Entrance requirements:* For master's, GMAT or GRE, essay, resume, 1 professional recommendations, official college transcripts, two years of professional experience. Additional exam requirements/recommendations for international students: Required—TOEFL (minimum score 600 paper-based; 106 iBT). *Application deadline:* For fall admission, 7/1 priority date for domestic and international students. Applications are processed on a rolling basis. Application fee: $75 ($81 for international students). Electronic applications accepted. *Expenses:* Contact institution. *Financial support:* In 2018–19, 21 students received support. Scholarships/grants available. Support available to part-time students. Financial award application deadline: 7/1. *Faculty research:* Creativity, leadership, healthcare operations, financial accounting, compensation. *Unit head:* Dr. Leslie Petty, Assistant Dean, 608-890-2499, E-mail: emba@wsb.wisc.edu. *Application contact:* Betsy Kacisak, Director of Admissions, 608-262-8948, E-mail: emba@wsb.wisc.edu.
Website: https://wsb.wisc.edu/programs-degrees/mba/evening

University of Wisconsin–Madison, Graduate School, Wisconsin School of Business, Wisconsin Executive MBA Program, Madison, WI 53706-1380. Offers general management (MBA). *Program availability:* Part-time-only, evening/weekend. *Faculty:* 14 full-time (1 woman), 5 part-time/adjunct (3 women). *Students:* 87 full-time (31 women); includes 20 minority (3 Black or African American, non-Hispanic/Latino; 10 Asian, non-Hispanic/Latino; 7 Hispanic/Latino), 1 international. Average age 41. 72 applicants, 86% accepted, 52 enrolled. In 2018, 40 master's awarded. *Entrance requirements:* For master's, essay, two professional recommendations, official college transcripts, resume, interview, eight years of professional work experience, five years of leadership experience, employer authorization form. Additional exam requirements/recommendations for international students: Required—TOEFL (minimum score 600 paper-based; 106 iBT). *Application deadline:* For fall admission, 7/1 priority date for domestic and international students. Applications are processed on a rolling basis. Application fee: $75 ($81 for international students). Electronic applications accepted. *Expenses:* Contact institution. *Financial support:* In 2018–19, 24 students received support. Scholarships/grants available. Support available to part-time students. Financial award application deadline: 7/1. *Faculty research:* Entrepreneurship, environmental issues in supply chain, leadership, marketing channels, strategic leadership. *Unit head:* Dr. Leslie Petty, Assistant Dean, 608-262-2499, E-mail: emba@wsb.wisc.edu. *Application contact:* Betsy Kacizak, Director of Admissions, 608-262-8948, E-mail: emba@wsb.wisc.edu.
Website: https://wsb.wisc.edu/programs-degrees/mba/executive

University of Wisconsin–Madison, Graduate School, Wisconsin School of Business, Wisconsin Full-Time MBA Program, Madison, WI 53706-1380. Offers applied security analysis (MBA); arts administration (MBA); brand and product management (MBA); corporate finance and investment banking (MBA); marketing research (MBA); operations and technology management (MBA); real estate (MBA); risk management and insurance (MBA); strategic human resource management (MBA); supply chain management (MBA). *Faculty:* 137 full-time (36 women), 39 part-time/adjunct (11 women). *Students:* 183 full-time (59 women); includes 31 minority (5 Black or African American, non-Hispanic/Latino; 1 American Indian or Alaska Native, non-Hispanic/Latino; 6 Asian, non-Hispanic/Latino; 13 Hispanic/Latino; 6 Two or more races, non-Hispanic/Latino), 40 international. Average age 28. 465 applicants, 33% accepted, 79 enrolled. In 2018, 104 master's awarded. *Entrance requirements:* For master's, GMAT or GRE, bachelor's or equivalent degree, essay, letter of recommendation, resume. Additional exam requirements/recommendations for international students: Required—TOEFL (minimum score 100 iBT), IELTS (minimum score 7.5), TOEFL is not required for international students whose undergraduate training was in English. *Application deadline:* For fall admission, 11/1 for domestic and international students; for winter admission, 1/10 for domestic and international students; for spring admission, 3/1 for domestic and international students; for summer admission, 4/10 for domestic students, 4/10 priority date for international students. Applications are processed on a rolling basis. Application fee: $75 ($81 for international students). Electronic applications accepted. *Expenses:* Wisconsin Resident tuition and fees - $39,156; Nonresident tuition and fees - $76,635. *Financial support:* In 2018–19, 148 students received support, including 7 fellowships with full tuition reimbursements available (averaging $25,871 per year), 7 research assistantships with full tuition reimbursements available (averaging $14,832 per year), 47 teaching assistantships with full tuition reimbursements available (averaging $14,832 per year); scholarships/grants, health care benefits, tuition waivers (full and partial), and unspecified assistantships also available. Financial award application deadline: 6/1. *Faculty research:* Ecology, environmental studies, and business; decision making; tax policy; diversity and inclusion in governance boards; marketing and social media. *Unit head:* Dr. Enno Siemsen, Associate Dean of the MBA and Masters Programs, 608-890-3130, E-mail: esiemsen@wisc.edu. *Application contact:* Betsy Kacizak, Director of Admissions and Recruiting, Full-time MBA Program, 608-262-4000, E-mail: betsy.kacizak@wisc.edu.
Website: https://wsb.wisc.edu/

University of Wisconsin–Milwaukee, Graduate School, Lubar School of Business, Milwaukee, WI 53201. Offers business administration (MBA); executive business administration (EMBA); management science (MS, PhD, Graduate Certificate), including business analytics (Graduate Certificate), enterprise resource planning (Graduate Certificate), information technology management (MS), investment management (Graduate Certificate), nonprofit management (Graduate Certificate), nonprofit management and leadership (MS), state and local taxation (Graduate Certificate); technology entrepreneurship (Graduate Certificate). *Accreditation:* AACSB. *Program availability:* Part-time, evening/weekend. *Students:* 282 full-time (122 women), 280 part-time (115 women); includes 95 minority (19 Black or African American, non-Hispanic/Latino; 2 American Indian or Alaska Native, non-Hispanic/Latino; 35 Asian, non-Hispanic/Latino; 7 Hispanic/Latino; 32 Two or more races, non-Hispanic/Latino), 65 international. Average age 32. 389 applicants, 66% accepted, 191 enrolled. In 2018, 212 master's, 2 doctorates, 18 other advanced degrees awarded. *Degree requirements:* For master's, comprehensive exam (for some programs); for doctorate, comprehensive exam, thesis/dissertation. *Entrance requirements:* For master's and doctorate, GMAT or GRE General Test. Additional exam requirements/recommendations for international students: Required—TOEFL (minimum score 550 paper-based; 79 iBT), IELTS (minimum score 6.5). *Application deadline:* For fall admission, 1/1 priority date for domestic students; for spring admission, 9/1 for domestic students. Application fee: $56 ($96 for international students). Electronic applications accepted. *Expenses:* Contact institution. *Financial support:* Fellowships with full tuition reimbursements, research assistantships with full tuition reimbursements, teaching assistantships with full tuition reimbursements, career-related internships or fieldwork, Federal Work-Study, health care benefits, unspecified assistantships, and project assistantships available. Support available to part-time students. Financial award application deadline: 4/15; financial award applicants required to submit FAFSA. *Faculty research:* Applied management

research in finance, management information systems, marketing, operations research, organizational sciences. *Unit head:* V. Kanti Prasad, Dean, 414-229-6256, E-mail: dean-prasad@uwm.edu. *Application contact:* Business Graduate Student Services, 414-229-5403, E-mail: mba-ms@uwm.edu.
Website: https://uwm.edu/business/

University of Wisconsin–Oshkosh, Graduate Studies, College of Business, Program in Business Administration, Oshkosh, WI 54901. Offers MBA. *Accreditation:* AACSB. *Program availability:* Part-time. *Degree requirements:* For master's, integrative seminar. *Entrance requirements:* For master's, GMAT, GRE, minimum undergraduate GPA of 2.75. Additional exam requirements/recommendations for international students: Required—TOEFL (minimum score 550 paper-based; 79 iBT). Electronic applications accepted.

University of Wisconsin–Parkside, College of Business, Economics, and Computing, Kenosha, WI 53141-2000. Offers MBA, MSCIS. *Accreditation:* AACSB. *Program availability:* Part-time, evening/weekend. *Entrance requirements:* For master's, GMAT. Additional exam requirements/recommendations for international students: Required—TOEFL (minimum score 550 paper-based; 79 iBT). Electronic applications accepted. *Expenses:* Contact institution. *Faculty research:* Business strategy, ethics in accounting and finance, mutual funds, decision analysis and neural networks, management skills.

University of Wisconsin–River Falls, Outreach and Graduate Studies, College of Business and Economics, River Falls, WI 54022. Offers MBA, MM. *Accreditation:* AACSB. *Degree requirements:* For master's, thesis or alternative. *Entrance requirements:* Additional exam requirements/recommendations for international students: Required—TOEFL (minimum score 550 paper-based; 79 iBT). Electronic applications accepted.

University of Wisconsin–Whitewater, School of Graduate Studies, College of Business and Economics, Program in Business Administration, Whitewater, WI 53190-1790. Offers finance (MBA). *Accreditation:* AACSB. *Program availability:* Part-time, evening/weekend, online learning. *Entrance requirements:* For master's, GMAT or GRE, minimum AACSB index of 1000, minimum GPA of 2.75. Additional exam requirements/recommendations for international students: Required—TOEFL (minimum score 550 paper-based; 80 iBT), IELTS (minimum score 6). Electronic applications accepted. *Faculty research:* Interface between social institutions and individual behavior, technology and innovation management, occupational mental health, workplace deviance and workplace romance.

University of Wyoming, College of Business, Program in Business Administration, Laramie, WY 82071. Offers MBA. *Accreditation:* AACSB. *Program availability:* Part-time, evening/weekend, online learning. *Degree requirements:* For master's, comprehensive exam, thesis or alternative. *Entrance requirements:* For master's, GMAT, GRE General Test, minimum GPA of 3.0. Additional exam requirements/recommendations for international students: Required—TOEFL (minimum score 550 paper-based; 80 iBT). Electronic applications accepted. *Expenses: Tuition, area resident:* Full-time $6504; part-time $271 per credit hour. Tuition, state resident: full-time $6504; part-time $271 per credit hour. Tuition, nonresident: full-time $19,464; part-time $811 per credit hour. *International tuition:* $19,464 full-time. *Required fees:* $1410.94; $343.82 per semester. $343.82 per semester. Tuition and fees vary according to course load, program and reciprocity agreements. *Faculty research:* Natural resource marketing and product development, work place violence.

Upper Iowa University, Online Master's Programs, Fayette, IA 52142-1857. Offers accounting (MBA); corporate financial management (MBA); emergency management and homeland security (MPA); general management (MBA); general studies (MPA); government administration (MPA); health and human services (MPA); human resources management (MBA); nonprofit organizational management (MPA); organizational development (MPA); public management (MPA); sport administration (MSA). MBA also available at Madison, WI campus. *Program availability:* Part-time, online learning. *Degree requirements:* For master's, research project. *Entrance requirements:* For master's, GMAT, GRE, or minimum GPA of 2.7 during last 60 hours. Additional exam requirements/recommendations for international students: Required—TOEFL (minimum score 570 paper-based). Electronic applications accepted. *Faculty research:* Total quality management, teams, organization culture and climate, management.

Urbana University–A Branch Campus of Franklin University, Division of Business Administration, Urbana, OH 43078-2091. Offers MBA. *Program availability:* Part-time, evening/weekend. *Degree requirements:* For master's, comprehensive exam, thesis or alternative. *Entrance requirements:* For master's, GMAT, minimum GPA of 2.7, BS in business, 3 letters of recommendation, work experience. Additional exam requirements/recommendations for international students: Required—TOEFL (minimum score 550 paper-based). *Faculty research:* Organizational behavior, taxation, segmentation, information systems, retail gravitation.

Ursuline College, School of Graduate and Professional Studies, Program in Business Administration, Pepper Pike, OH 44124-4398. Offers ethical and entrepreneurial leadership (MBA); financial planning and accounting (MBA); health services management (MBA); management (MBA); management and leadership (MBA); marketing and communications management (MBA). *Program availability:* Part-time, evening/weekend. *Faculty:* 2 full-time (both women), 2 part-time/adjunct (1 woman). *Students:* 17 full-time (all women), 5 part-time (3 women); includes 10 minority (9 Black or African American, non-Hispanic/Latino; 1 Two or more races, non-Hispanic/Latino). Average age 40. 33 applicants, 100% accepted, 6 enrolled. In 2018, 16 master's awarded. *Degree requirements:* For master's, comprehensive exam (for some programs). *Entrance requirements:* For master's, GRE. Additional exam requirements/recommendations for international students: Required—TOEFL (minimum score 500 paper-based) or GRE. *Application deadline:* For fall admission, 8/1 for domestic students. Applications are processed on a rolling basis. Application fee: $25. Electronic applications accepted. *Expenses:* 36 hours at $903/per. *Financial support:* In 2018–19, 2 students received support. Campus work-study available. Financial award application deadline: 8/1; financial award applicants required to submit FAFSA. *Faculty research:* Gift economy; sharing economy; cooperative business models; collaborative leadership; corporate social responsibility and the triple bottom line, defined as the three P's: people, planet and profit. *Unit head:* Dr. Debra Fleming, Professor, 440-440-720-3864, Fax: 440-684-6088, E-mail: dfleming@ursuline.edu. *Application contact:* Melanie Steele, Director of Graduate Admission, 440-646-8146, Fax: 440-684-6138, E-mail: graduateadmissions@ursuline.edu.

Utah State University, School of Graduate Studies, Jon M. Huntsman School of Business, Program in Business Administration, Logan, UT 84322. Offers MBA. *Accreditation:* AACSB. *Program availability:* Part-time, evening/weekend, online learning. *Degree requirements:* For master's, comprehensive exam. *Entrance requirements:* For master's, GMAT or GRE, minimum GPA of 3.0. Additional exam requirements/recommendations for international students: Required—TOEFL. Electronic applications accepted. *Faculty research:* Marketing strategy, technology and innovation, public utility finance, international competitiveness.

Utah Valley University, MBA Program, Orem, UT 84058-5999. Offers accounting (MBA); management (MBA). *Accreditation:* AACSB. *Program availability:* Part-time, evening/weekend. *Entrance requirements:* For master's, GMAT, official transcripts, current resume, three letters of recommendation, essay. Additional exam requirements/recommendations for international students: Required—TOEFL (minimum score 79 iBT). Electronic applications accepted. *Expenses:* Contact institution.

Valdosta State University, Langdale College of Business, Valdosta, GA 31698. Offers accountancy (M Acc); business administration (MBA); healthcare administration (MBA). MBA program is a member of the Georgia WebMBA. *Accreditation:* AACSB. *Program availability:* Part-time, evening/weekend, 100% online, blended/hybrid learning. *Degree requirements:* For master's, comprehensive written and/or oral exams. *Entrance requirements:* For master's, GMAT or GRE, minimum GPA of 2.75. Additional exam requirements/recommendations for international students: Required—TOEFL (minimum score 523 paper-based); Recommended—IELTS. Electronic applications accepted. *Expenses:* Contact institution.

Valparaiso University, Graduate School and Continuing Education, College of Business, Valparaiso, IN 46383. Offers business administration (MBA); business decision-making (Certificate); business intelligence (Certificate); engineering management (Certificate); finance (Certificate); general business (Certificate); leading the global enterprise (Certificate); management (Certificate); JD/MBA; MSN/MBA. *Accreditation:* AACSB. *Program availability:* Part-time, evening/weekend, online learning. *Students:* 7 full-time (5 women), 43 part-time (16 women); includes 5 minority (4 Black or African American, non-Hispanic/Latino; 1 Two or more races, non-Hispanic/Latino). Average age 31. *Entrance requirements:* For master's, GMAT, GRE, minimum GPA of 3.0. Additional exam requirements/recommendations for international students: Required—TOEFL (minimum score 550 paper-based; 80 iBT), IELTS (minimum score 6). *Application deadline:* Applications are processed on a rolling basis. Application fee: $30 ($50 for international students). Electronic applications accepted. *Expenses:* Contact institution. *Financial support:* Available to part-time students. Applicants required to submit FAFSA. *Unit head:* Jim Brodzinski, Dean, 219-464-5035, E-mail: jim.brodzinski@valpo.edu. *Application contact:* Cindy Scanlan, Director of Graduate Programs in Management, 219-465-7952, Fax: 219-464-5789, E-mail: cindy.scanlan@valpo.edu.
Website: http://www.valpo.edu/college-of-business/

Vancouver Island University, Master of Business Administration Program, Nanaimo, BC V9R 5S5, Canada. Offers international business (MBA), including finance, marketing. Program offered jointly with University of Hertfordshire. *Accreditation:* ACBSP. *Program availability:* Part-time. *Degree requirements:* For master's, thesis. *Entrance requirements:* Additional exam requirements/recommendations for international students: Required—TOEFL (minimum score 88 iBT), IELTS (minimum score 6.5). Electronic applications accepted. *Expenses:* Contact institution. *Faculty research:* Tourism development, entrepreneurship, organizational development, strategic planning, international business strategy, intercultural team work.

Vanderbilt University, Vanderbilt University Owen Graduate School of Management, Vanderbilt Executive MBA Programs, Nashville, TN 37203. Offers EMBA, MBA. *Accreditation:* AACSB. *Program availability:* Evening/weekend. *Entrance requirements:* For master's, GMAT, minimum of 5 years of professional work experience. Electronic applications accepted. *Expenses:* Contact institution.

Vanderbilt University, Vanderbilt University Owen Graduate School of Management, Vanderbilt MBA Program, Nashville, TN 37203. Offers accounting (MBA); finance (MBA); general management (MBA); health care (MBA); human and organizational performance (MBA); marketing (MBA); operations (MBA); strategy (MBA); MBA/JD; MBA/M Div; MBA/MD; MBA/MSN; MBA/MTS; MBA/PhD. *Accreditation:* AACSB. *Degree requirements:* For master's, 62 credit hours of coursework; completion of ethics course; minimum GPA of 3.0. *Entrance requirements:* For master's, GMAT (preferred) or GRE, 2 years of work experience (recommended). Additional exam requirements/recommendations for international students: Required—TOEFL (minimum score 100 iBT). Electronic applications accepted. *Expenses:* Contact institution. *Faculty research:* Accounting and finance, business strategy and economics, marketing, operations management, organization studies.

Villanova University, Villanova School of Business, Executive MBA Program, Radnor, PA 19087. Offers EMBA. *Accreditation:* AACSB. *Program availability:* Part-time-only, evening/weekend. *Faculty:* 101 full-time (38 women), 36 part-time/adjunct (9 women). *Students:* 62 part-time (15 women); includes 8 minority (4 Black or African American, non-Hispanic/Latino; 2 Asian, non-Hispanic/Latino; 1 Hispanic/Latino; 1 Two or more races, non-Hispanic/Latino), 2 international. Average age 38. 43 applicants, 95% accepted, 27 enrolled. In 2018, 34 master's awarded. *Degree requirements:* For master's, minimum cumulative GPA of 3.0. *Entrance requirements:* For master's, Application, official transcripts, 2 letters of recommendation, resume, essay, interview. Additional exam requirements/recommendations for international students: Required—TOEFL (minimum score 550 paper-based; 100 iBT). *Application deadline:* For fall admission, 7/31 for domestic and international students. Applications are processed on a rolling basis. Application fee: $65. Electronic applications accepted. *Expenses:* Contact institution. *Financial support:* Scholarships/grants available. Financial award application deadline: 6/30; financial award applicants required to submit FAFSA. *Faculty research:* Real Estate, Business Analytics, Global Leadership, Marketing and Consumer Insights, Church management. *Unit head:* Dr. Joyce E. A. Russell, Dean of Villanova School of Business, 610-519-6082, E-mail: joyce.russell@villanova.edu. *Application contact:* Anthony Penna, Recruiting Manager, Executive Programs, 610-5196570, E-mail: anthony.penna@villanova.edu.
Website: http://www.emba.villanova.edu/

Villanova University, Villanova School of Business, MBA - The Fast Track Program, Villanova, PA 19085. Offers finance (MBA); healthcare (MBA); international business (MBA); strategic management (MBA). *Accreditation:* AACSB. *Program availability:* Part-time, evening/weekend. *Faculty:* 101 full-time (38 women), 36 part-time/adjunct (9 women). *Students:* 111 part-time (47 women); includes 20 minority (3 Black or African American, non-Hispanic/Latino; 7 Asian, non-Hispanic/Latino; 9 Hispanic/Latino; 1 Two or more races, non-Hispanic/Latino), 4 international. Average age 30. 45 applicants, 80% accepted, 26 enrolled. In 2018, 55 master's awarded. *Degree requirements:* For master's, minimum GPA of 3.0. *Entrance requirements:* For master's, GMAT or GRE, Application, official transcripts, 2 letters of recommendation, resume, 2 essays. Additional exam requirements/recommendations for international students: Required—TOEFL (minimum score 550 paper-based; 100 iBT). *Application deadline:* For fall admission, 7/31 for domestic and international students. Applications are processed on a rolling basis. Application fee: $65. Electronic applications accepted. *Expenses:* Contact institution. *Financial support:* Scholarships/grants available. Financial award application deadline: 6/30; financial award applicants required to submit FAFSA. *Faculty research:* Real Estate, Business Analytics, Global Leadership, Marketing and Consumer Insights, Church management. *Unit head:* Dr. Joyce E. A. Russell, Dean of Villanova School of Business, 610-519-6082, Fax: 610-519-6273, E-mail: joyce.russell@villanova.edu. *Application contact:* Daniel Guertin, Assistant Director, Recruitment, 610-519-8031, Fax: 610-519-6273, E-mail: daniel.guertin@villanova.edu.
Website: http://www1.villanova.edu/villanova/business/graduate/mba.html

Villanova University, Villanova School of Business, MBA - The Flex Track Program, Villanova, PA 19085. Offers healthcare (MBA); international business (MBA); marketing

(MBA); real estate (MBA); strategic management (MBA); JD/MBA. *Accreditation:* AACSB. *Program availability:* Part-time, evening/weekend, online learning. *Faculty:* 101 full-time (38 women), 36 part-time/adjunct (9 women). *Students:* 13 full-time (5 women), 427 part-time (157 women); includes 74 minority (12 Black or African American, non-Hispanic/Latino; 29 Asian, non-Hispanic/Latino; 23 Hispanic/Latino; 10 Two or more races, non-Hispanic/Latino), 12 international. Average age 32. 156 applicants, 92% accepted, 139 enrolled. In 2018, 124 master's awarded. *Degree requirements:* For master's, minimum GPA of 3.0. *Entrance requirements:* For master's, GMAT or GRE, Application, official transcripts, 2 letters of recommendation, resume, 2 essays. Additional exam requirements/recommendations for international students: Required—TOEFL (minimum score 550 paper-based; 100 iBT). *Application deadline:* For fall admission, 7/31 for domestic and international students; for spring admission, 11/30 for domestic and international students; for summer admission, 4/30 for domestic and international students. Applications are processed on a rolling basis. Application fee: $65. Electronic applications accepted. *Expenses:* Contact institution. *Financial support:* Research assistantships and scholarships/grants available. Financial award application deadline: 6/30; financial award applicants required to submit FAFSA. *Faculty research:* Real Estate, Business Analytics, Global Leadership, Marketing and Consumer Insights, Church management. *Unit head:* Dr. Joyce E. A. Russell, Dean of Villanova School of Business, 610-519-6082, Fax: 610-519-6273, E-mail: joyce.russell@villanova.edu. *Application contact:* Daniel Guertin, Assistant Director, Recruitment, 610-519-8031, Fax: 610-519-6273, E-mail: daniel.guertin@villanova.edu.
Website: http://www1.villanova.edu/villanova/business/graduate/mba.html

Villanova University, Villanova School of Business, Online MBA Program, Villanova, PA 19085-1699. Offers MBA. *Program availability:* Part-time-only, evening/weekend, 100% online, blended/hybrid learning. *Faculty:* 101 full-time (38 women), 36 part-time/adjunct (9 women). *Students:* 220 part-time (91 women); includes 49 minority (16 Black or African American, non-Hispanic/Latino; 1 American Indian or Alaska Native, non-Hispanic/Latino; 19 Asian, non-Hispanic/Latino; 7 Hispanic/Latino; 6 Two or more races, non-Hispanic/Latino), 3 international. Average age 32. 172 applicants, 80% accepted, 106 enrolled. In 2018, 78 master's awarded. *Degree requirements:* For master's, minimum cumulative GPA of 3.0. *Entrance requirements:* For master's, GMAT or GRE, Application, official transcripts, 3 letters of recommendation, resume, 2 essays. Additional exam requirements/recommendations for international students: Required—TOEFL (minimum score 550 paper-based; 100 iBT). *Application deadline:* For fall admission, 7/31 for domestic and international students; for spring admission, 11/30 for domestic and international students; for summer admission, 4/30 for domestic and international students. Applications are processed on a rolling basis. Application fee: $65. Electronic applications accepted. *Expenses:* Contact institution. *Financial support:* Scholarships/grants available. Financial award application deadline: 6/30; financial award applicants required to submit FAFSA. *Faculty research:* Real Estate, Business Analytics, Global Leadership, Marketing and Consumer Insights, Church management. *Unit head:* Dr. Joyce E. A. Russell, Dean of Villanova School of Business, 610-519-6082, Fax: 610-519-6273, E-mail: joyce.russell@villanova.edu. *Application contact:* Claire Bruno, Director of Recruitment and Enrollment Management, 610-519-4336, Fax: 610-519-6273, E-mail: claire.bruno@villanova.edu.

Virginia Commonwealth University, Graduate School, School of Business, Program in Business Administration, Richmond, VA 23284-9005. Offers MBA, PhD. *Degree requirements:* For doctorate, thesis/dissertation. *Entrance requirements:* For master's and doctorate, GMAT. Additional exam requirements/recommendations for international students: Required—TOEFL (minimum score 600 paper-based; 100 iBT). Electronic applications accepted.

Virginia International University, School of Business, Fairfax, VA 22030. Offers accounting (MBA, MS); entrepreneurship (MBA); executive management (Graduate Certificate); global logistics (MBA); health care management (MBA); hospitality and tourism management (MBA); human resources management (MBA); international business management (MBA); international finance (MBA); marketing management (MBA); mass media and public relations (MBA); project management (MBA, MS). *Program availability:* Part-time, online learning. *Entrance requirements:* For master's and Graduate Certificate, bachelor's degree. Additional exam requirements/recommendations for international students: Required—TOEFL (minimum score 550 paper-based; 80 iBT), IELTS (minimum score 6). Electronic applications accepted.

Virginia Polytechnic Institute and State University, Graduate School, Pamplin College of Business, Blacksburg, VA 24061. Offers accounting and information systems (MACIS, PhD); business administration (MS), including business analytics, hospitality and tourism management; business information technology (PhD); executive business research (PhD); finance (PhD); marketing (PhD), including marketing; MS/MBA. *Faculty:* 141 full-time (42 women), 2 part-time/adjunct (1 woman). *Students:* 227 full-time (89 women), 217 part-time (75 women); includes 131 minority (30 Black or African American, non-Hispanic/Latino; 58 Asian, non-Hispanic/Latino; 25 Hispanic/Latino; 18 Two or more races, non-Hispanic/Latino), 81 international. Average age 32. 361 applicants, 55% accepted, 152 enrolled. In 2018, 181 master's, 8 doctorates awarded. *Degree requirements:* For master's, comprehensive exam (for some programs), thesis (for some programs); for doctorate, comprehensive exam (for some programs), thesis/dissertation (for some programs). *Entrance requirements:* For master's and doctorate, GRE/GMAT. Additional exam requirements/recommendations for international students: Required—TOEFL (minimum score 90 iBT). *Application deadline:* For fall admission, 8/1 for domestic students, 4/1 for international students; for spring admission, 1/1 for domestic students, 9/1 for international students. Applications are processed on a rolling basis. Application fee: $75. Electronic applications accepted. *Expenses:* Tuition, state resident: full-time $15,510; part-time $739.50 per credit hour. Tuition, nonresident: full-time $29,629; part-time $1490.25 per credit hour. *Required fees:* $2804; $550 per semester. Tuition and fees vary according to course load, campus/location and program. *Financial support:* In 2018–19, 1 fellowship with full tuition reimbursement (averaging $3,999 per year), 4 research assistantships with full tuition reimbursements (averaging $20,163 per year), 66 teaching assistantships with full tuition reimbursements (averaging $19,822 per year) were awarded; scholarships/grants and unspecified assistantships also available. Financial award application deadline: 3/1; financial award applicants required to submit FAFSA. *Total annual research expenditures:* $3.1 million. *Unit head:* Dr. Robert T. Sumichrast, Dean, 540-231-6601, Fax: 540-231-4487, E-mail: busdean@vt.edu. *Application contact:* Kimberly Ridpath, Executive Assistant, 540-231-9647, Fax: 540-231-4487, E-mail: ridpathk@vt.edu.
Website: http://www.pamplin.vt.edu/

Virginia Wesleyan University, Graduate Studies, Virginia Beach, VA 23455. Offers business administration (MBA); secondary and PreK-12 education (MA Ed). *Program availability:* Online learning.

Viterbo University, Master of Business Administration Program, La Crosse, WI 54601-4797. Offers general business administration (MBA); health care management (MBA); international business (MBA); leadership (MBA); project management (MBA). *Accreditation:* ACBSP. *Program availability:* Part-time, evening/weekend. *Degree requirements:* For master's, 34 semester credits. *Entrance requirements:* For master's, bachelor's degree, transcripts, minimum undergraduate cumulative GPA of 3.0, 2 letters of reference, 3-5 page essay. Additional exam requirements/recommendations for

international students: Recommended—TOEFL (minimum score 550 paper-based). Electronic applications accepted. *Expenses:* Contact institution.

Wagner College, Division of Graduate Studies, Nicolais School of Business, Staten Island, NY 10301-4495. Offers accounting (MS); business administration (MBA); finance (MBA); management (Exec MBA); marketing (MBA); media management (MS). *Accreditation:* ACBSP. *Program availability:* Part-time, evening/weekend. *Degree requirements:* For master's, thesis optional. *Entrance requirements:* For master's, minimum GPA of 2.75, proficiency in computers and math. Additional exam requirements/recommendations for international students: Required—TOEFL (minimum score 550 paper-based; 79 iBT), IELTS (minimum score 6.5).

Wake Forest University, School of Business, Master in Management Program, Winston-Salem, NC 27106. Offers MA. *Degree requirements:* For master's, 41.5 credit hours. *Entrance requirements:* For master's, GMAT or GRE, letters of recommendation, official transcripts, current resume or curriculum vitae, interview. Additional exam requirements/recommendations for international students: Required—TOEFL (minimum score 600 paper-based; 100 iBT). Electronic applications accepted. *Expenses:* Contact institution. *Faculty research:* Influence of personal relationships on business decision-making and management of change; drivers of perceived value and consumer behavior; impact of accounting on auditing, financial, managerial, systems and taxation stakeholders; corporate governance and executive compensation; impact of operations strategies on competitiveness.

Wake Forest University, School of Business, Working Professionals MBA Program, Winston-Salem, NC 27106. Offers MBA, PhD/MBA. *Accreditation:* AACSB. *Program availability:* Part-time-only, evening/weekend. *Degree requirements:* For master's, 54 total credit hours. *Entrance requirements:* For master's, GMAT or GRE, letters of recommendation, official transcripts, current resume or curriculum vitae, two years of work experience, interview. Additional exam requirements/recommendations for international students: Required—TOEFL (minimum score 600 paper-based; 100 iBT). Electronic applications accepted. *Expenses:* Contact institution. *Faculty research:* Influence of personal relationships on business decision-making and management of change; drivers of perceived value and consumer behavior; impact of accounting on auditing, financial, managerial, systems and taxation stakeholders; corporate governance and executive compensation; impact of operations strategies on competitiveness.

Walden University, Graduate Programs, School of Management, Minneapolis, MN 55401. Offers accounting (MBA, MS, DBA), including accounting for the professional (MS), accounting with CPA emphasis (MS), self-designed (MS); advanced project management (Graduate Certificate); applied project management (Graduate Certificate); auditing (Graduate Certificate); bridge to business administration (Post-Doctoral Certificate); bridge to management (Post-Doctoral Certificate); business management (Graduate Certificate); communication (MBA); corporate finance (MBA); digital marketing (Graduate Certificate); entrepreneurship (DBA); entrepreneurship and small business (MBA); finance (MS, DBA), including finance for the professional (MS), finance with CFA/investment (MS), finance with CPA emphasis (MS); global supply chain management (DBA); healthcare management (MBA, DBA); human resource management (MBA, MS, Graduate Certificate), including functional human resource management (MS), general program (MS), integrating functional and strategic human resource management (MS), organizational strategy (MS); human resources management (DBA); information systems management (DBA); international business (MBA, DBA); leadership (MBA, MS, DBA, Graduate Certificate), including general program (MS); human resource leadership (MS), leader development (MS), self-designed (MS); management (MS, PhD), including communications (MS), finance (PhD), general program (MS), healthcare management (MS), human resource management (MS), human resources management (PhD), information systems management (PhD), international business (MS), leadership (MS), leadership and organizational change (PhD), marketing (MS), project management (MS), strategy and operations (MS); managerial accounting (Graduate Certificate); marketing (MBA, MS, DBA); project management (MBA, MS, DBA); self-designed (MBA, DBA); social impact management (DBA); technology entrepreneurship (DBA). *Accreditation:* ACBSP. *Program availability:* Part-time, evening/weekend, online only, 100% online. *Degree requirements:* For master's, thesis (for some programs), residency (for EMBA); for doctorate, thesis/dissertation (for some programs), residency. *Entrance requirements:* For master's, bachelor's degree or higher; minimum GPA of 2.5; official transcripts; goal statement (for some programs); access to computer and Internet; for doctorate, master's degree or higher; three years of related professional or academic experience (preferred); minimum GPA of 3.0; goal statement and current resume (for select programs); official transcripts; access to computer and Internet; for other advanced degree, relevant work experience; access to computer and Internet. Additional exam requirements/recommendations for international students: Required—TOEFL (minimum score 550 paper-based, 79 iBT), IELTS (minimum score 6.5), Michigan English Language Assessment Battery (minimum score 82), or PTE (minimum score 53). Electronic applications accepted.

Walden University, Graduate Programs, School of Public Policy and Administration, Minneapolis, MN 55401. Offers criminal justice (MPA, MPP, MS, Graduate Certificate), including emergency management (MS, PhD); general program (MS); global leadership (MS, PhD), homeland security and policy coordination (MS, PhD), law and public policy (MS, PhD), policy analysis (MS, PhD), public management and leadership (MS, PhD), self-designed (MS), terrorism, mediation, and peace (MS, PhD); criminal justice and executive management (MS), including global leadership (MS, PhD); criminal justice leadership and executive management (MS), including emergency management (MS, PhD), general program, homeland security and policy coordination (MS, PhD), law and public policy (MS, PhD), policy analysis (MS, PhD), public management and leadership (MS, PhD), self-designed, terrorism, mediation, and peace (MS, PhD); emergency management (MPA, MPP, MS), including criminal justice (MS, PhD), general program (MS), homeland security (MS), public management and leadership (MS, PhD), terrorism and emergency management (MS); general program (MPA, MPP); global leadership (MPA, MPP); government management (Graduate Certificate); health policy (MPA, MPP); homeland security (Graduate Certificate); homeland security and policy coordination (MPA, MPP); international nongovernmental organizations (MPA, MPP); law and public policy (MPA, MPP); local government management for sustainable communities (MPA, MPP); nonprofit management (Graduate Certificate); nonprofit management and leadership (MPA, MPP, MS), including global leadership (MS, PhD), international nongovernmental organization (MS), local government for sustainable communities (MS), self-designed (MS); online teaching in higher education (Post-Master's Certificate); policy analysis (MPA); public management and leadership (MPA, MPP, Graduate Certificate); public policy (Graduate Certificate); public policy and administration (PhD), including criminal justice (MS, PhD), emergency management (MS, PhD), global leadership (MS, PhD), health policy, homeland security and policy coordination (MS, PhD), international nongovernmental organizations, law and public policy (MS, PhD), local government management for sustainable communities, nonprofit management and leadership, policy analysis (MS, PhD), public management and leadership (MS, PhD), terrorism, mediation, and peace (MS, PhD); strategic planning and public policy (Graduate Certificate); terrorism, mediation, and peace (MPA, MPP).

Business Administration and Management—General

Program availability: Part-time, evening/weekend, online only, 100% online. *Degree requirements:* For doctorate, thesis/dissertation, residency. *Entrance requirements:* For master's, bachelor's degree or higher; minimum GPA of 2.5; official transcripts; goal statement (for some programs); access to computer and Internet; for doctorate, master's degree or higher; three years of related professional or academic experience (preferred); minimum GPA of 3.0; goal statement and current resume (for select programs); official transcripts; access to computer and Internet; for other advanced degree, relevant work experience; access to computer and Internet. Additional exam requirements/recommendations for international students: Required—TOEFL (minimum score 550 paper-based, 79 iBT), IELTS (minimum score 6.5), Michigan English Language Assessment Battery (minimum score 82), or PTE (minimum score 53). Electronic applications accepted.

Walsh College of Accountancy and Business Administration, Graduate Programs, Program in Business Administration, Troy, MI 48083. Offers MBA, MBA/MSF, MBA/MSITL, MBA/MSM, MBA/MSMKT. *Accreditation:* ACBSP. *Program availability:* Part-time, evening/weekend, 100% online, blended/hybrid learning. *Faculty:* 15 full-time (6 women), 12 part-time/adjunct (4 women). *Students:* 6 full-time (5 women), 451 part-time (195 women); includes 93 minority (46 Black or African American, non-Hispanic/Latino; 2 American Indian or Alaska Native, non-Hispanic/Latino; 29 Asian, non-Hispanic/Latino; 8 Hispanic/Latino; 8 Two or more races, non-Hispanic/Latino), 13 international. Average age 33. 115 applicants, 88% accepted, 64 enrolled. In 2018, 148 master's awarded. *Entrance requirements:* For master's, minimum overall cumulative GPA of 2.750 from all colleges previously attended. Additional exam requirements/recommendations for international students: Required—TOEFL (minimum score 550 paper-based, 79-80 internet based), IELTS (6.5), Michigan Test of English Language Proficiency, or MTELP (80). *Application deadline:* Applications are processed on a rolling basis. Application fee: $35. Electronic applications accepted. *Expenses:* $785 per credit hour plus $175 student support fee per semester. International students pay $785 per credit hour plus $175 student support fee and $275 international student fee per semester. *Financial support:* In 2018–19, 18 students received support. Fellowships, scholarships/grants, and Tuition Exchange Program available. Financial award application deadline: 6/30; financial award applicants required to submit FAFSA. *Faculty research:* Strategy practice and process, management learning and decision making, consumer behavior, data and decision making. *Unit head:* Dr. Michael Rinkus, Executive Vice President/Chief Academic Officer, 248-823-1269, Fax: 248-689-0920, E-mail: mrinkus@walshcollege.edu. *Application contact:* Karen Mahaffy, Executive Director, Admissions and Enrollment Services, 248-823-1600, Fax: 248-823-1611, E-mail: kmahaffy@walshcollege.edu.

Walsh University, Graduate Programs, MBA Program, North Canton, OH 44720-3396. Offers healthcare management (MBA); management (MBA); marketing (MBA). *Program availability:* Part-time, evening/weekend, online only, 100% online. *Degree requirements:* For master's, capstone course in strategic management. *Entrance requirements:* For master's, GMAT (minimum score of 490), minimum GPA of 3.0. Additional exam requirements/recommendations for international students: Required—TOEFL (minimum score 500 paper-based; 61 iBT). Electronic applications accepted. Application fee is waived when completed online. *Expenses:* Contact institution. *Faculty research:* Medical tourism, familial influence in financial fitness, pedagogy in finance courses, sociocultural aspects of women entrepreneurs, patient satisfaction.

Warner University, School of Business, Lake Wales, FL 33859. Offers accounting (MBA); business administration (MBA); human resource management (MBA); international business (MBA); management (MSMC). *Program availability:* Part-time, evening/weekend, online learning. *Degree requirements:* For master's, comprehensive exam, thesis. *Entrance requirements:* For master's, minimum GPA of 3.0, 2 letters of recommendation. Additional exam requirements/recommendations for international students: Required—TOEFL. Electronic applications accepted.

Washburn University, School of Business, Topeka, KS 66621. Offers accountancy (M Acc). *Accreditation:* AACSB. *Program availability:* Part-time, evening/weekend. *Entrance requirements:* For master's, GMAT, minimum GPA of 2.75. Additional exam requirements/recommendations for international students: Required—TOEFL (minimum score 550 paper-based; 80 iBT); Recommended—IELTS (minimum score 6.5). Electronic applications accepted. *Faculty research:* Ethics in information technology, forecasting for shareholder value creation, model for measuring expected losses from litigation contingencies, business vs. family commitment in family businesses, calculated intangible value and brand recognition.

Washington Adventist University, MBA Program, Takoma Park, MD 20912. Offers MBA. *Program availability:* Part-time, evening/weekend, online learning. *Entrance requirements:* For master's, minimum undergraduate GPA of 2.75, curriculum vitae, interview, essay, personal statement. Additional exam requirements/recommendations for international students: Required—TOEFL (minimum score 550 paper-based), IELTS (minimum score 5).

Washington State University, Carson College of Business, Pullman, WA 99164-4750. Offers M Acc, MBA, PhD. Programs also offered at the Tri-Cities, Vancouver, and Global (online) campuses. *Program availability:* Online learning. *Degree requirements:* For master's, comprehensive exam (for some programs), thesis (for some programs); for doctorate, comprehensive exam, thesis/dissertation. *Entrance requirements:* For master's and doctorate, GMAT (minimum score of 600), resume; statement of purpose identifying area of interest, experiences, and intended research focus; minimum GPA of 3.25. Additional exam requirements/recommendations for international students: Required—TOEFL (minimum score 580 paper-based), IELTS.

Washington University in St. Louis, Olin Business School, Executive MBA Program, St. Louis, MO 63130-4899. Offers EMBA. *Program availability:* Part-time, evening/weekend. *Faculty:* 85 full-time (16 women), 46 part-time/adjunct (13 women). *Students:* 141 part-time (50 women); includes 27 minority (7 Black or African American, non-Hispanic/Latino; 11 Asian, non-Hispanic/Latino; 6 Hispanic/Latino; 1 Native Hawaiian or other Pacific Islander, non-Hispanic/Latino; 2 Two or more races, non-Hispanic/Latino), 6 international. Average age 41. 57 applicants, 96% accepted, 44 enrolled. In 2018, 76 master's awarded. *Degree requirements:* For master's, 60 credit hours. *Entrance requirements:* For master's, two letters of recommendation, letter of commitment/sponsorship, transcripts. Additional exam requirements/recommendations for international students: Required—TOEFL, IELTS. *Application deadline:* For fall admission, 10/10 for domestic and international students; for winter admission, 1/7 for domestic and international students; for spring admission, 3/18 for domestic and international students; for summer admission, 7/15 for domestic and international students. Applications are processed on a rolling basis. Application fee: $0. Electronic applications accepted. *Expenses:* 128,000. *Financial support:* Applicants required to submit FAFSA. *Unit head:* Dr. Steve Malter, Senior Associate Dean, Undergraduate and Graduate Programs, 314-935-6315, E-mail: malter@wustl.edu. *Application contact:* Ruthie Pyles, Assistant Dean of Admissions, Recruiting and Financial Aid, 314-935-9009, Fax: 314-935-7161, E-mail: ruthie.pyles@wustl.edu.
Website: http://www.olin.wustl.edu/execed/emba.cfm

Washington University in St. Louis, Olin Business School, Full-time MBA Program, St. Louis, MO 63130-4899. Offers MBA, JD/MBA, M Arch/MBA, M Eng/MBA, MBA/MA, MBA/MPH, MBA/MSW. *Faculty:* 161 full-time (0 women), 112 part-time/adjunct (0 women). *Students:* 273 full-time (111 women); includes 68 minority (21 Black or African American, non-Hispanic/Latino; 19 Asian, non-Hispanic/Latino; 12 Hispanic/Latino; 1 Native Hawaiian or other Pacific Islander, non-Hispanic/Latino; 15 Two or more races, non-Hispanic/Latino), 94 international. Average age 29. 1,175 applicants, 40% accepted, 145 enrolled. In 2018, 127 master's awarded. *Degree requirements:* For master's, 67 credit hours. *Entrance requirements:* For master's, GMAT or GRE, U.S. bachelor's degree or equivalent, one letter of recommendation. Additional exam requirements/recommendations for international students: Required—TOEFL, IELTS. *Application deadline:* For fall admission, 10/10 for domestic and international students; for winter admission, 1/15 for domestic students, 1/15 priority date for international students; for spring admission, 3/18 for domestic and international students. Applications are processed on a rolling basis. Application fee: $0. Electronic applications accepted. *Expenses:* 127031.5. *Financial support:* Institutionally sponsored loans and scholarships/grants available. Financial award application deadline: 4/19; financial award applicants required to submit CSS PROFILE or FAFSA. *Unit head:* Dr. Steve Malter, Senior Associate Dean, Undergrad and Graduate Programs, 314-935-6315, Fax: 314-935-9095, E-mail: Malter@wustl.edu. *Application contact:* Ruthie Pyles, Assistant Dean and Director of Graduate Admissions, 314-935-7301, Fax: 314-935-4464, E-mail: OlinGradAdmissions@wustl.edu.
Website: http://www.olin.wustl.edu/mba/

Washington University in St. Louis, Olin Business School, IIT Bombay-Washington University Executive MBA Program, Mumbai, MO 63130-4899. Offers EMBA. Program offered in partnership with Shailesh J. Mehta School of Management at the Indian Institute of Technology in Bombay. *Program availability:* Part-time-only. *Faculty:* 85 full-time (16 women), 46 part-time/adjunct (13 women). *Students:* 2 full-time (both women), 22 part-time (5 women); includes 21 minority (all Asian, non-Hispanic/Latino), 1 international. Average age 40. 29 applicants, 100% accepted, 23 enrolled. In 2018, 21 master's awarded. *Degree requirements:* For master's, 60 credit hours. *Entrance requirements:* For master's, bachelor's degree with 7 years of work experience and 5 years of managerial experience. *Application deadline:* Applications are processed on a rolling basis. Application fee: $0. Electronic applications accepted. *Expenses:* Contact institution. *Unit head:* Dr. Steve Malter, Senior Associate Dean, Undergraduate and Graduate Programs, 314-9356344, E-mail: malter@wustl.edu. *Application contact:* Dr. Steve Malter, Senior Associate Dean, Undergraduate and Graduate Programs, 314-9356344, E-mail: malter@wustl.edu.

Washington University in St. Louis, Olin Business School, PhD Program in Business Administration, St. Louis, MO 63130-4899. Offers PhD. *Faculty:* 85 full-time (16 women), 46 part-time/adjunct (13 women). *Students:* 65 full-time (26 women); includes 8 minority (all Asian, non-Hispanic/Latino), 49 international. 412 applicants, 10% accepted, 16 enrolled. In 2018, 13 doctorates awarded. *Degree requirements:* For doctorate, comprehensive exam, thesis/dissertation, field exam, 2nd-year paper presentation, thesis proposal defense. *Entrance requirements:* For doctorate, GMAT or GRE. Additional exam requirements/recommendations for international students: Required—TOEFL, IELTS, TOEFL or IELTS. *Application deadline:* For fall admission, 12/31 for domestic and international students. Application fee: $100. Electronic applications accepted. *Expenses:* Contact institution. *Financial support:* In 2018–19, fellowships with full tuition reimbursements (averaging $25,000 per year) were awarded; health care benefits and travel support for conferences also available. *Unit head:* Prof. Anjan Thakor, Professor/Director, 314-935-7197, Fax: 314-935-6359, E-mail: thakor@wust.edu. *Application contact:* Jessica Hatch, Assoc Dir of Doc Admissions & Student Affairs, 314-935-6340, Fax: 314-935-9484, E-mail: jessica.hatch@wustl.edu.
Website: http://www.olin.wustl.edu/prospective/phd.cfm

Washington University in St. Louis, Olin Business School, Professional MBA Program, St. Louis, MO 63130-4899. Offers MBA. *Program availability:* Part-time, evening/weekend. *Faculty:* 85 full-time (16 women), 46 part-time/adjunct (13 women). *Students:* 246 part-time (83 women); includes 54 minority (10 Black or African American, non-Hispanic/Latino; 26 Asian, non-Hispanic/Latino; 7 Hispanic/Latino; 1 Native Hawaiian or other Pacific Islander, non-Hispanic/Latino; 10 Two or more races, non-Hispanic/Latino), 14 international. Average age 31. 106 applicants, 85% accepted, 65 enrolled. In 2018, 103 master's awarded. *Degree requirements:* For master's, 54 credits. *Entrance requirements:* For master's, GMAT or GRE, U.S. bachelor's degree or equivalent, one letter of recommendation. Additional exam requirements/recommendations for international students: Required—TOEFL, IELTS. *Application deadline:* For fall admission, 10/10 for domestic and international students; for winter admission, 1/7 for domestic and international students; for spring admission, 3/18 for domestic and international students; for summer admission, 7/15 for domestic and international students. Applications are processed on a rolling basis. Application fee: $100. Electronic applications accepted. *Expenses:* 90504. *Financial support:* Applicants required to submit CSS PROFILE or FAFSA. *Unit head:* Dr. Steve Malter, Senior Associate Dean, Programs, 314-935-6315, Fax: 314-935-9095, E-mail: malter@wustl.edu. *Application contact:* Ruthie Pyles, Assistant Dean and Director of Graduate Admissions, 314-935-7301, Fax: 314-935-4464, E-mail: olingradadmissions@wustl.edu.
Website: http://www.olin.wustl.edu/prospective/pmba.cfm

Washington University in St. Louis, Olin Business School, Washington University-Fudan University Executive MBA Program, Shanghai, MO 63130-4899. Offers EMBA. *Program availability:* Part-time. *Faculty:* 85 full-time (16 women), 46 part-time/adjunct (13 women). *Students:* 66 part-time (30 women); includes 65 minority (all Asian, non-Hispanic/Latino). Average age 39. 248 applicants, 28% accepted, 66 enrolled. In 2018, 50 master's awarded. *Degree requirements:* For master's, 60 credit hours. *Entrance requirements:* For master's, bachelor's degree or above. Additional exam requirements/recommendations for international students: Required—TOEFL. *Application deadline:* For fall admission, 9/8 for domestic and international students; for winter admission, 1/26 for domestic and international students; for spring admission, 3/13 for domestic and international students; for summer admission, 6/20 for domestic and international students. Applications are processed on a rolling basis. Application fee: 1,200 Chinese yuans. Electronic applications accepted. *Expenses:* 98000. *Unit head:* Dr. Steve Malter, Senior Associate Dean, Undergrad and Graduate Programs, 314-935-6315, E-mail: malter@wustl.edu. *Application contact:* Chen Zhang, Recruiting Director, 314-935-3622, E-mail: EMBA-Shanghai@olin.wustl.edu.
Website: http://www.olin.wustl.edu/EN-US/executive-programs/executive-mba-shanghai/Pages/default.aspx

Wayland Baptist University, Graduate Programs, Programs in Business Administration/Management, Plainview, TX 79072-6998. Offers accounting (MBA); general business (MBA); health care administration (MAM, MBA); human resource management (MAM, MBA); international management (MBA); management (MBA, D Mgt); management information systems (MBA); organization management (MAM); project management (MBA). *Program availability:* Part-time, evening/weekend, online learning. *Degree requirements:* For master's, capstone course. *Entrance requirements:* For master's, GMAT, GRE or MAT. Additional exam requirements/recommendations for international students: Required—TOEFL (minimum score 500 paper-based; 61 iBT). Electronic applications accepted.

Waynesburg University, Graduate and Professional Studies, Canonsburg, PA 15370. Offers business (MBA), including energy management, finance, health systems, human resources, leadership, market development; counseling (MA), including addictions counseling, clinical mental health; counselor education and supervision (PhD); criminal investigation (MA); education (M Ed), including autism, curriculum and instruction, educational leadership, online teaching; nursing (MSN), including administration, education, informatics; nursing practice (DNP); special education (M Ed); technology (M Ed); MSN/MBA. *Accreditation:* AACN. *Program availability:* Part-time, evening/weekend. *Degree requirements:* For doctorate, thesis/dissertation. *Entrance requirements:* Additional exam requirements/recommendations for international students: Required—TOEFL. Electronic applications accepted.

Wayne State College, School of Business and Technology, Wayne, NE 68787. Offers MBA. *Program availability:* Part-time, evening/weekend, online learning. *Entrance requirements:* For master's, GMAT, minimum overall GPA of 3.0. Additional exam requirements/recommendations for international students: Required—TOEFL (minimum score 550 paper-based).

Wayne State University, Mike Ilitch School of Business, Detroit, MI 48202. Offers accounting (MS, MSA, Postbaccalaureate Certificate); business (EMS, Graduate Certificate); business administration (MBA, PhD); data science (MS), including business analytics; entrepreneurship and innovation (Postbaccalaureate Certificate); finance (MS); information systems management (Postbaccalaureate Certificate); taxation (MST); JD/MBA. Application deadline for PhD is February 15. *Accreditation:* AACSB. *Program availability:* Part-time, evening/weekend. *Faculty:* 31. *Students:* 286 full-time (152 women), 1,166 part-time (533 women); includes 409 minority (236 Black or African American, non-Hispanic/Latino; 83 Asian, non-Hispanic/Latino; 53 Hispanic/Latino; 37 Two or more races, non-Hispanic/Latino), 74 international. Average age 30. 1,212 applicants, 38% accepted, 294 enrolled. In 2018, 285 master's, 6 doctorates, 7 other advanced degrees awarded. *Degree requirements:* For doctorate, thesis/dissertation. *Entrance requirements:* For master's, GMAT, GRE, LSAT, MCAT, at least three years of relevant work experience that shows increased responsibility, or minimum GPA of 3.0 from AACSB-accredited program or 3.2 from regionally-accredited program, undergraduate degree from accredited institution; undergraduate degree in accounting, business administration, or area of business administration (for MS and MST); for doctorate, GMAT (minimum score of 600), minimum undergraduate GPA of 3.0, 3.5 upper-division or graduate; three letters of recommendation; brief essay; undergraduate degree from accredited institution; personal statement; for other advanced degree, bachelor's degree from accredited institution. Additional exam requirements/recommendations for international students: Required—TOEFL (minimum score 550 paper-based; 79 iBT), Michigan English Language Assessment Battery (minimum score 85); Recommended—IELTS (minimum score 6.5), TWE (minimum score 5.5). *Application deadline:* For fall admission, 7/1 for domestic students, 5/1 priority date for international students; for winter admission, 11/1 for domestic students, 9/1 priority date for international students; for spring admission, 3/1 for domestic students, 1/1 priority date for international students. Applications are processed on a rolling basis. Application fee: $50. Electronic applications accepted. *Expenses:* Contact institution. *Financial support:* In 2018–19, 175 students received support, including 1 fellowship with tuition reimbursement available (averaging $20,000 per year), 5 research assistantships with tuition reimbursements available (averaging $21,393 per year); teaching assistantships with tuition reimbursements available, scholarships/grants, health care benefits, and unspecified assistantships also available. Support available to part-time students. Financial award applicants required to submit FAFSA. *Faculty research:* Executive compensation and stock performance, consumer reactions to pricing strategies, communication across the automotive supply chain, performance of firms in sub-Saharan Africa, implementation issues with ERP software. *Unit head:* Dr. Robert Forsythe, Dean, School of Business Administration, 313-577-4501, E-mail: robert.forsythe@wayne.edu. *Application contact:* Kiantee N. Rupert-Jones, Director, 313-577-4511, Fax: 313-577-9442, E-mail: gradbusiness@wayne.edu. Website: http://ilitchbusiness.wayne.edu/

Webber International University, Graduate School of Business, Babson Park, FL 33827. Offers accounting (MBA); business (MBA); criminal justice management (MBA); international business (MBA); sport business management (MBA). *Program availability:* Part-time, evening/weekend, 100% online, blended/hybrid learning. *Faculty:* 11 full-time (5 women), 1 part-time/adjunct (0 women). *Students:* 69 full-time (34 women), 11 part-time (5 women); includes 26 minority (17 Black or African American, non-Hispanic/Latino; 1 Asian, non-Hispanic/Latino; 8 Hispanic/Latino), 10 international. Average age 24. 64 applicants, 61% accepted, 32 enrolled. In 2018, 17 master's awarded. *Degree requirements:* For master's, International Learning Experience required for the master in International Business, other majors have a practicum project. *Entrance requirements:* For master's, three recommendation letters, resume, essay, official transcripts from all colleges and universities attended. Additional exam requirements/recommendations for international students: Recommended—TOEFL (minimum score 500 paper-based; 61 iBT), IELTS (minimum score 6). *Application deadline:* For fall admission, 8/1 for domestic students, 6/1 for international students; for spring admission, 1/1 for domestic students. Applications are processed on a rolling basis. Application fee: $0. Electronic applications accepted. *Financial support:* In 2018–19, 11 students received support. Scholarships/grants and unspecified assistantships available. Financial award application deadline: 8/1; financial award applicants required to submit FAFSA. *Unit head:* Dr. Nikos Orphanoudakis, Dean, 863-638-2910, Fax: 863-638-1591, E-mail: orphanoudakisn@webber.edu. *Application contact:* Lacy Edwards, Admissions Counselor and MBA Coordinator, 863-638-2910, Fax: 863-638-1591, E-mail: admissions@webber.edu. Website: www.webber.edu

Weber State University, Goddard School of Business and Economics, Program in Business Administration, Ogden, UT 84408-1001. Offers MBA, Graduate Certificate. *Accreditation:* AACSB. *Program availability:* Part-time, evening/weekend. *Faculty:* 11 full-time (3 women), 1 part-time/adjunct (0 women). *Students:* 58 full-time (20 women), 142 part-time (46 women); includes 10 minority (1 Black or African American, non-Hispanic/Latino; 1 American Indian or Alaska Native, non-Hispanic/Latino; 1 Asian, non-Hispanic/Latino; 5 Hispanic/Latino; 2 Two or more races, non-Hispanic/Latino), 6 international. Average age 36. In 2018, 88 master's, 38 other advanced degrees awarded. *Entrance requirements:* For master's, GMAT or GRE, resume, letters of recommendation. Additional exam requirements/recommendations for international students: Required—TOEFL (minimum score 550 paper-based). *Application deadline:* For fall admission, 5/1 for domestic and international students; for spring admission, 11/1 for domestic and international students. Application fee: $60 ($90 for international students). Electronic applications accepted. *Financial support:* In 2018–19, 16 students received support. Scholarships/grants available. Financial award application deadline: 4/1; financial award applicants required to submit FAFSA. *Unit head:* Dr. Matt Mouritsen, MBA Program Director/Associate Professor of Accounting, 801-626-8151, Fax: 801-626-7423, E-mail: mmouritsen@weber.edu. *Application contact:* Dr. Mark A. Stevenson, MBA Enrollment Director, 801-395-3528, Fax: 801-395-3525, E-mail: mba@weber.edu. Website: http://www.weber.edu/mba/

Webster University, George Herbert Walker School of Business and Technology, Department of Business, St. Louis, MO 63119-3194. Offers business and organizational security management (MBA); decision support systems (MBA); environmental management (MBA); finance (MBA, MS); forensic accounting (MS); gerontology (MBA); human resources development (MBA); human resources management (MBA); information technology management (MBA); international business (MA, MBA); international relations (MBA); management and leadership (MBA); marketing (MBA); media communications (MBA); procurement and acquisitions management (MBA); Web services (MBA). *Accreditation:* ACBSP. *Program availability:* Part-time, evening/weekend, online learning. *Degree requirements:* For master's, comprehensive exam (for some programs), thesis (for some programs). *Entrance requirements:* Additional exam requirements/recommendations for international students: Required—TOEFL. *Expenses: Tuition:* Full-time $22,500; part-time $750 per credit hour. Tuition and fees vary according to degree level, campus/location and program.

Webster University, George Herbert Walker School of Business and Technology, Department of Management, St. Louis, MO 63119-3194. Offers business and organizational security management (MA); digital marketing management (Graduate Certificate); government contracting (Graduate Certificate); health administration (MHA); health care management (MA); health services management (MA); human resources development (MA); human resources management (MA); information technology management (MA, MS); management (D Mgt); management and leadership (MA); marketing (MA); nonprofit leadership (MA); nonprofit revenue development (Graduate Certificate); organizational development (Graduate Certificate); procurement and acquisitions management (MA); public administration (MPA); space systems operations management (MS). *Program availability:* Part-time, evening/weekend, online learning. *Degree requirements:* For master's, thesis (for some programs); for doctorate, thesis/dissertation, written exam. *Entrance requirements:* For doctorate, GMAT, 3 years of work experience, MBA. Additional exam requirements/recommendations for international students: Required—TOEFL. *Expenses: Tuition:* Full-time $22,500; part-time $750 per credit hour. Tuition and fees vary according to degree level, campus/location and program.

Wesleyan College, Department of Business and Economics, EMBA Program, Macon, GA 31210-4462. Offers EMBA. *Program availability:* Evening/weekend. *Entrance requirements:* For master's, GMAT, LSAT, GRE or MAT, 5 years of work experience, 5 years of management experience. Additional exam requirements/recommendations for international students: Required—TOEFL (minimum score 550 paper-based). Electronic applications accepted. *Expenses:* Contact institution. *Unit head:* Dr. Dwight Hines, EMBA Program Director, 478-757-5184, E-mail: dhines@wesleyancollege.edu. *Application contact:* Mariana Furlin, Program Assistant to the EMBA, 478-7572801, E-mail: mfurlin@wesleyancollege.edu.

Wesley College, Business Program, Dover, DE 19901-3875. Offers environmental management (MBA); executive leadership (MBA); management (MBA). Executive leadership concentration also offered at New Castle, DE location. *Program availability:* Part-time, evening/weekend. *Entrance requirements:* For master's, GMAT or GRE, minimum undergraduate GPA of 2.75.

West Chester University of Pennsylvania, College of Business and Public Management, School of Business, West Chester, PA 19383. Offers business analytics (Certificate); business education (MBA). *Accreditation:* AACSB. *Program availability:* Part-time, evening/weekend, online only, 100% online. *Degree requirements:* For master's, minimum GPA of 3.0. *Entrance requirements:* For master's, GMAT or GRE, statement of professional goals, resume, three letters of recommendation, transcripts. Additional exam requirements/recommendations for international students: Required—TOEFL or IELTS. Electronic applications accepted.

Westcliff University, College of Business, Irvine, CA 92606. Offers MBA, DBA.

Western Carolina University, Graduate School, College of Business, Program in Business Administration, Cullowhee, NC 28723. Offers MBA. *Accreditation:* AACSB. *Program availability:* Part-time, evening/weekend. *Entrance requirements:* For master's, GMAT, appropriate undergraduate degree, 3 letters of recommendation. Additional exam requirements/recommendations for international students: Required—TOEFL (minimum score 550 paper-based; 79 iBT). *Expenses: Tuition, area resident:* Full-time $4435. Tuition, state resident: full-time $4435. Tuition, nonresident: full-time $14,842. *International tuition:* $14,842 full-time. *Required fees:* $2979. Part-time tuition and fees vary according to course load, degree level and program. *Faculty research:* Marketing strategy, biotechnology, executive education, business statistics, supply chain management, innovation.

Western Connecticut State University, Division of Graduate Studies, Ancell School of Business, Program in Business Administration, Danbury, CT 06810-6885. Offers accounting (MBA); business administration (MBA). *Program availability:* Part-time. *Degree requirements:* For master's, comprehensive exam, completion of program within 8 years. *Entrance requirements:* For master's, GMAT. Additional exam requirements/recommendations for international students: Recommended—TOEFL (minimum score 550 paper-based; 79 iBT), IELTS (minimum score 6). *Application deadline:* For fall admission, 8/5 priority date for domestic students; for spring admission, 1/5 priority date for domestic students. Applications are processed on a rolling basis. Application fee: $50. *Financial support:* Application deadline: 5/1; applicants required to submit FAFSA. *Faculty research:* Global strategic marketing planning, project management and team coordination; email, discussion boards that act as blogs and videoconferencing. *Unit head:* Dr. Karen Koza, MBA Coordinator, 203-837-9036, Fax: 203-837-8527, E-mail: kozak@wcsu.edu. *Application contact:* Chris Shankle, Associate Director of Graduate Studies, 203-837-9005, Fax: 203-837-8326, E-mail: shanklec@wcsu.edu.

Western Governors University, College of Business, Salt Lake City, UT 84107. Offers accounting (MS); information technology management (MBA); management and leadership (MS); management and strategy (MBA); strategic leadership (MBA). *Program availability:* Evening/weekend, online learning. *Degree requirements:* For master's, capstone project. *Entrance requirements:* For master's, transcripts. Additional exam requirements/recommendations for international students: Required—TOEFL (minimum score 450 paper-based; 80 iBT). Electronic applications accepted. Application fee is waived when completed online.

Western Illinois University, School of Graduate Studies, College of Business and Technology, Program in Business Administration, Macomb, IL 61455-1390. Offers business administration (MBA, Certificate); supply chain management (Certificate). *Accreditation:* AACSB. *Program availability:* Part-time. *Students:* 32 full-time (15 women), 73 part-time (21 women); includes 14 minority (3 Black or African American, non-Hispanic/Latino; 1 American Indian or Alaska Native, non-Hispanic/Latino; 5 Asian, non-Hispanic/Latino; 3 Hispanic/Latino; 2 Two or more races, non-Hispanic/Latino), 6 international. Average age 33. 76 applicants, 72% accepted, 30 enrolled. In 2018, 38 master's, 3 other advanced degrees awarded. *Entrance requirements:* For master's, GMAT. Additional exam requirements/recommendations for international students: Required—TOEFL (minimum score 550 paper-based; 80 iBT). *Application deadline:* Applications are processed on a rolling basis. Application fee: $30. Electronic applications accepted. *Financial support:* Research assistantships with full tuition reimbursements and unspecified assistantships available. Financial award applicants

required to submit FAFSA. *Unit head:* Dr. Tara Feld, Associate Dean, 309-298-2442. *Application contact:* Dr. Mark Mossman, Associate Provost and Director of Graduate Studies, 309-298-1806, Fax: 309-298-2345, E-mail: grad-office@wiu.edu.
Website: http://wiu.edu/cbt

Western Kentucky University, Graduate School, Gordon Ford College of Business, MBA Program, Bowling Green, KY 42101. Offers MBA. *Accreditation:* AACSB. *Program availability:* Part-time, evening/weekend. *Degree requirements:* For master's, comprehensive exam, thesis optional. *Entrance requirements:* For master's, GMAT, minimum GPA of 2.5. Additional exam requirements/recommendations for international students: Required—TOEFL (minimum score 555 paper-based; 79 iBT). *Faculty research:* Business and international education, web page development, management training, international studies, globalization.

Western Michigan University, Graduate College, Haworth College of Business, Department of Interdisciplinary Business, Kalamazoo, MI 49008. Offers business administration (MBA). *Accreditation:* AACSB.

Western New England University, College of Business, Program in Business Administration, Springfield, MA 01119. Offers MBA, JD/MBA, MS/MBA, Pharm D/MBA. *Accreditation:* AACSB. *Program availability:* Part-time, evening/weekend, online learning. *Faculty:* 6 full-time (4 women). *Students:* 81 part-time (42 women); includes 10 minority (3 Black or African American, non-Hispanic/Latino; 4 Asian, non-Hispanic/Latino; 3 Hispanic/Latino), 1 international. Average age 31. 61 applicants, 82% accepted, 36 enrolled. In 2018, 45 master's awarded. *Entrance requirements:* For master's, GMAT or GRE, official transcript, two letters of recommendation, essay, resume. Additional exam requirements/recommendations for international students: Required—TOEFL (minimum score 79 iBT). *Application deadline:* Applications are processed on a rolling basis. Application fee: $30. Electronic applications accepted. *Expenses:* Contact institution. *Financial support:* Application deadline: 4/15; applicants required to submit FAFSA. *Unit head:* Dr. Sharianne Walker, Dean, 413-782-1389. *Application contact:* Matthew Fox, Executive Director of Graduate Admissions, 413-782-1410, Fax: 413-782-1777, E-mail: study@wne.edu.
Website: http://www1.wne.edu/academics/graduate/mba.cfm

Western New Mexico University, Graduate Division, School of Business, Silver City, NM 88062-0680. Offers business administration (MBA). *Accreditation:* ACBSP. *Program availability:* Part-time, online learning. *Entrance requirements:* For master's, GMAT. Additional exam requirements/recommendations for international students: Required—TOEFL (minimum score 550 paper-based). Electronic applications accepted. *Faculty research:* Migration: an analysis of Puerto Rican interest to migrate to the United States using Internet search trends, entrepreneurship management in rural U.S. areas, exports and maritime ports: Puerto Rico and the port of Las Americas, female labor force participation in the border states.

Western Washington University, Graduate School, College of Business and Economics, Bellingham, WA 98225-5996. Offers MBA, MP Acc. *Accreditation:* AACSB. *Program availability:* Part-time, evening/weekend. *Degree requirements:* For master's, comprehensive exam. *Entrance requirements:* For master's, GMAT, minimum GPA of 3.0 in last 60 semester hours or last 90 quarter hours. Additional exam requirements/recommendations for international students: Required—TOEFL (minimum score 567 paper-based). Electronic applications accepted. *Faculty research:* Enterprise strategy/corporate social performance, sustainability/environmental management/nonprofit marketing, managerial/environmental accounting, organizational applications of collaborative technology, environmental and resource economics.

West Liberty University, Gary E. West College of Business, West Liberty, WV 26074. Offers accounting (MBA); management (MBA).

Westminster College, The Bill and Vieve Gore School of Business, Salt Lake City, UT 84105-3697. Offers accountancy (M Acc); business administration (MBA, Certificate); technology commercialization (MBA). *Program availability:* Part-time, evening/weekend, blended/hybrid learning. *Degree requirements:* For master's, International Context Tour (for MBA). *Entrance requirements:* For master's, GMAT (waived on a case-by-case basis), 2 professional recommendations, employer letter of support, personal resume, essay, official transcripts. Additional exam requirements/recommendations for international students: Required—TOEFL (minimum score 84 iBT), IELTS (minimum score 7). Electronic applications accepted. *Expenses:* Contact institution. *Faculty research:* Innovation and entrepreneurship, business strategy and change, financial analysis and capital budgeting, leadership development, knowledge management.

West Texas A&M University, College of Business, Department of Management, Marketing and General Business, Canyon, TX 79015. Offers business administration (MBA). *Accreditation:* AACSB. *Program availability:* Part-time, evening/weekend, 100% online. *Entrance requirements:* For master's, GMAT. Additional exam requirements/recommendations for international students: Required—TOEFL (minimum score 550 paper-based). Electronic applications accepted. *Faculty research:* Human resources, international business, southern Asian markets, global strategies, international trade composition.

West Virginia University, College of Business and Economics, Morgantown, WV 26506. Offers accountancy (M Acc); accounting (PhD); business administration (MBA); business cyber security management (MS); business data analytics (MS); economics (MA, PhD); finance (MS, PhD); forensic and fraud examination (MS); industrial relations (MS); management (PhD); marketing (PhD). *Program availability:* Part-time, online learning. *Students:* 341 full-time (139 women), 44 part-time (13 women); includes 39 minority (10 Black or African American, non-Hispanic/Latino; 12 Asian, non-Hispanic/Latino; 7 Hispanic/Latino; 10 Two or more races, non-Hispanic/Latino), 40 international. In 2018, 208 master's, 20 doctorates awarded. Terminal master's awarded for partial completion of doctoral program. *Degree requirements:* For master's, thesis optional; for doctorate, comprehensive exam, thesis/dissertation. *Entrance requirements:* For doctorate, GRE General Test, minimum GPA of 3.0. Additional exam requirements/recommendations for international students: Required—TOEFL (minimum score 550 paper-based; 92 iBT). *Application deadline:* For fall admission, 10/15 priority date for domestic and international students; for spring admission, 3/1 priority date for domestic and international students. Applications are processed on a rolling basis. Application fee: $60. Electronic applications accepted. *Expenses:* Contact institution. *Financial support:* Fellowships, research assistantships, teaching assistantships, career-related internships or fieldwork, Federal Work-Study, institutionally sponsored loans, scholarships/grants, health care benefits, tuition waivers (full and partial), unspecified assistantships, and administrative assistantships available. Financial award application deadline: 2/1; financial award applicants required to submit FAFSA. *Faculty research:* Regional labor market studies, economic development, market research, economic forecasting, energy analysis. *Unit head:* Dr. Javier Reyes, Dean, 304-293-7800, Fax: 304-293-4056, E-mail: javier.reyes@mail.wvu.edu. *Application contact:* Dr. Virginia F Kleist, Associate Dean for Graduate Programs, 304-293-7939, Fax: 304-293-7188, E-mail: Virginia.Kleist@mail.wvu.edu.
Website: http://www.be.wvu.edu

West Virginia Wesleyan College, MBA Program, Buckhannon, WV 26201. Offers MBA. *Program availability:* Part-time, evening/weekend. *Degree requirements:* For master's, exit evaluation. *Entrance requirements:* For master's, GMAT. Additional exam requirements/recommendations for international students: Required—TOEFL.

Wheeling Jesuit University, Department of Business, Wheeling, WV 26003-6295. Offers accounting (MSA); business administration (MBA). *Accreditation:* ACBSP. *Program availability:* Part-time, evening/weekend. *Entrance requirements:* For master's, minimum undergraduate GPA of 2.8. Additional exam requirements/recommendations for international students: Required—TOEFL (minimum score 600 paper-based; 100 iBT). Electronic applications accepted. *Faculty research:* Forensic economics, consumer behavior, economic development, capitalism, leadership.

Whitworth University, School of Business, Spokane, WA 99251-0001. Offers MBA. *Program availability:* Part-time, evening/weekend. *Degree requirements:* For master's, variable foreign language requirement. *Entrance requirements:* For master's, GMAT or GRE, minimum undergraduate GPA of 3.25, or alternate exam, two letters of recommendation; resume; completion of prerequisite courses in micro-economics, macro-economics, financial accounting, finance, and marketing; interview with director. Additional exam requirements/recommendations for international students: Required—TOEFL (minimum score 88 iBT), TWE. Electronic applications accepted. *Faculty research:* International business (European, Central America and Asian topics), entrepreneurship and business plan development.

WHU - Otto Beisheim School of Management, Graduate Programs, Vallendar, Germany. Offers EMBA, MBA, MS. EMBA offered jointly with Kellogg School of Management.

Wichita State University, Graduate School, W. Frank Barton School of Business, Department of Business, Wichita, KS 67260. Offers EMBA, MBA. *Accreditation:* AACSB. *Program availability:* Part-time, evening/weekend. *Unit head:* Nedra Henry, Graduate Advisor, 316-978-3230, E-mail: Nedra.Henry@wichita.edu. *Application contact:* Jordan Oleson, Admissions Coordinator, 316-978-3095, Fax: 316-978-3253, E-mail: jordan.oleson@wichita.edu.
Website: http://www.wichita.edu/mba

Widener University, School of Business Administration, Chester, PA 19013-5792. Offers MBA, MHA, MS, JD/MBA, MD/MBA, MD/MHA, ME/MBA, Psy D/MBA, Psy D/MHA. *Accreditation:* AACSB. *Program availability:* Part-time, evening/weekend, 100% online, blended/hybrid learning. *Entrance requirements:* For master's, minimum GPA of 2.5. Electronic applications accepted. *Expenses:* Contact institution. *Faculty research:* Cost containment in health care, human resource management, productivity, globalization.

Wilfrid Laurier University, Faculty of Graduate and Postdoctoral Studies, Lazaridis School of Business and Economics, Business Administration Program, Waterloo, ON N2L 3C5, Canada. Offers co-op (MBA); full-time (MBA); part-time (MBA). *Accreditation:* AACSB. *Program availability:* Part-time, evening/weekend. *Degree requirements:* For master's, thesis. *Entrance requirements:* For master's, GMAT, minimum 2 years of business experience (for 12-month or part-time MBA formats), minimum B average in 4-year BA program. Additional exam requirements/recommendations for international students: Required—TOEFL (minimum score 89 iBT). Electronic applications accepted.

Wilfrid Laurier University, Faculty of Graduate and Postdoctoral Studies, Lazaridis School of Business and Economics, Department of Business, Waterloo, ON N2L 3C5, Canada. Offers accounting (PhD); finance (M Fin); financial economics (PhD); marketing (PhD); operations and supply chain management (PhD); organizational behavior and human resource management (M Sc); organizational behaviour and human resource management (PhD); supply chain management (M Sc); technology management (EMTM). *Accreditation:* AACSB. *Program availability:* Part-time, evening/weekend. *Degree requirements:* For master's, thesis optional; for doctorate, comprehensive exam, thesis/dissertation. *Entrance requirements:* For master's, GMAT, 4-year honors degree with minimum B+ average; for doctorate, GMAT, master's degree, minimum B+ average. Additional exam requirements/recommendations for international students: Required—TOEFL (minimum score 89 iBT). Electronic applications accepted. *Faculty research:* Financial economics, management and organizational behavior, operations and supply chain management.

Wilkes University, College of Graduate and Professional Studies, Jay S. Sidhu School of Business and Leadership, Wilkes-Barre, PA 18766-0002. Offers accounting (MBA); global business (MBA); human resource management (MBA); international business (MBA); leadership (MBA); management (MBA); operations management (MBA); organizational leadership and development (MBA). *Accreditation:* ACBSP. *Program availability:* Part-time, evening/weekend. *Students:* 16 full-time (9 women), 64 part-time (33 women); includes 11 minority (3 Black or African American, non-Hispanic/Latino; 3 Asian, non-Hispanic/Latino; 3 Hispanic/Latino; 2 Two or more races, non-Hispanic/Latino), 7 international. Average age 30. In 2018, 49 master's awarded. *Entrance requirements:* For master's, GMAT. Additional exam requirements/recommendations for international students: Required—TOEFL (minimum score 550 paper-based; 79 iBT). *Application deadline:* Applications are processed on a rolling basis. Application fee: $45 ($65 for international students). Electronic applications accepted. *Expenses:* Contact institution. *Financial support:* Unspecified assistantships available. Financial award application deadline: 3/1; financial award applicants required to submit FAFSA. *Unit head:* Dr. Abel Adekola, Dean, 570-408-4701, Fax: 570-408-7846, E-mail: abel.adekola@wilkes.edu. *Application contact:* Kristin Donati, Associate Director of Graduate Admissions, 570-408-3338, Fax: 570-408-7846, E-mail: kristin.donati@wilkes.edu.
Website: http://www.wilkes.edu/academics/colleges/sidhu-school-of-business-leadership/index.aspx

Willamette University, Atkinson Graduate School of Management, Salem, OR 97301-3931. Offers accounting, entrepreneurship, finance, global management, human resources, management science and quantitative methods (stem), marketing, operations (MBA); JD/MBA. JD/MBA offered jointly with Willamette University College of Law. *Accreditation:* AACSB; NASPAA. *Program availability:* Part-time, evening/weekend. *Faculty:* 18 full-time (5 women), 19 part-time/adjunct (7 women). *Students:* 126 full-time (52 women), 111 part-time (55 women); includes 67 minority (16 Black or African American, non-Hispanic/Latino; 12 Asian, non-Hispanic/Latino; 26 Hispanic/Latino; 1 Native Hawaiian or other Pacific Islander, non-Hispanic/Latino; 12 Two or more races, non-Hispanic/Latino), 17 international. Average age 28. 261 applicants, 67% accepted, 105 enrolled. In 2018, 118 master's awarded. *Degree requirements:* For master's, minimum cumulative GPA of 3.0 and 60 semester credits for full time MBA; or 3.0 and 48 semester credits for MBA for Professionals. *Entrance requirements:* For master's, GMAT or GRE, essays, transcripts, references, resume, interview. Additional exam requirements/recommendations for international students: Required—TOEFL (minimum score 570 paper-based; 88 iBT), IELTS (minimum score 6.5). *Application deadline:* 5/1 priority date for domestic and international students. Applications are processed on a rolling basis. Application fee: $0. Electronic applications accepted. *Expenses:* Early Career full-time: for the year 2018-2019 $41,900 tuition plus $390 fees, $86,065 for entire program; MBA for Professionals: for the year 2018-2019 $37,075 (no fees), $74,150 for entire program. *Financial support:* In 2018–19, 232 students received support. Federal Work-Study, scholarships/grants, and unspecified assistantships available. Financial award application deadline: 5/1; financial award applicants required

to submit FAFSA. *Faculty research:* Entrepreneurship and angel investing, corporate finance and investment, political economy and public management, sustainability and corporate responsibility, marketing, operations, social networks for managers, managing interorganizational interactions, employer duty of care, values and leadership, statistical methods and computing, employee well being and conflict management. *Unit head:* Dr. Michael L. Hand, Interim Dean, Professor of Applied Statistics and Information Systems, 503-370-6790, Fax: 503-370-3011, E-mail: mhand@willamette.edu. *Application contact:* Juliet Valdez, Director of Recruitment, 503-370-6792, Fax: 503-370-3011, E-mail: jvaldez@willamette.edu.
Website: http://willamette.edu/mba/index.html

William Carey University, School of Business, Hattiesburg, MS 39401. Offers MBA. *Program availability:* Part-time. *Entrance requirements:* For master's, GMAT. Additional exam requirements/recommendations for international students: Required—TOEFL (minimum score 500 paper-based).

William Paterson University of New Jersey, Cotsakos College of Business, Wayne, NJ 07470-8420. Offers applied business analytics (MS); business administration (MBA), including accounting, entrepreneurship, finance, general business administration, human resource management, marketing, music and entertainment management; MBA pathways (Certificate); sales leadership (MS). *Accreditation:* AACSB. *Program availability:* Part-time, evening/weekend. *Faculty:* 21 full-time (6 women), 5 part-time/adjunct (1 woman). *Students:* 78 full-time (40 women), 250 part-time (113 women); includes 161 minority (39 Black or African American, non-Hispanic/Latino; 1 American Indian or Alaska Native, non-Hispanic/Latino; 23 Asian, non-Hispanic/Latino; 82 Hispanic/Latino; 16 Two or more races, non-Hispanic/Latino), 14 international. Average age 31. 222 applicants, 86% accepted, 136 enrolled. In 2018, 95 master's awarded. *Degree requirements:* For master's, Programs Differ see: https://academiccatalog.wpunj.edu/content.php?catoid=1&navoid=68. *Entrance requirements:* For master's, program details: https://www.wpunj.edu/admissions/graduate/admission-deadlines-and-requirements/. Additional exam requirements/recommendations for international students: Required—TOEFL (minimum score 550 paper-based; 79 iBT), IELTS (minimum score 6). *Application deadline:* For fall admission, 6/1 for domestic students, 3/1 for international students; for spring admission, 11/1 for domestic students, 10/1 for international students. Applications are processed on a rolling basis. Application fee: $50. Electronic applications accepted. *Expenses:* Tuition, area resident: Full-time $14,714; part-time $727 per credit. Tuition, state resident: full-time $14,714; part-time $727 per credit. Tuition, nonresident: full-time $22,952; part-time $727 per credit. International tuition: $22,952 full-time. *Required fees:* $4 per semester. Tuition and fees vary according to course load, degree level and program. *Financial support:* In 2018–19, 18 students received support. Career-related internships or fieldwork, Federal Work-Study, scholarships/grants, tuition waivers, and unspecified assistantships available. Support available to part-time students. Financial award application deadline: 3/15; financial award applicants required to submit FAFSA. *Faculty research:* Labor markets, job characteristics and ethical behavior, institutional trading of stocks and bonds, education funding, pricing strategies in business-to-business markets. *Unit head:* Dr. Siamack Shojai, Dean, 973-720-2964, Fax: 973-720-2809, E-mail: shojais@wpunj.edu. *Application contact:* Tinu Adeniran, Assistant Director, Graduate Admissions, 973-720-2764, Fax: 973-720-2035, E-mail: adenirant@wpunj.edu.
Website: http://www.wpunj.edu/ccob

William Woods University, Graduate and Adult Studies, Fulton, MO 65251-1098. Offers administration (M Ed, Ed S); athletic/activities administration (M Ed); curriculum and instruction (M Ed, Ed S); educational leadership (Ed D); equestrian education (M Ed); health management (MBA); human resources (MBA); leadership (MBA); marketing, advertising, and public relations (MBA); teaching and technology (M Ed). *Program availability:* Part-time, evening/weekend. *Degree requirements:* For master's, capstone course (MBA), action research (M Ed); for Ed S, field experience. *Entrance requirements:* Additional exam requirements/recommendations for international students: Required—TOEFL (minimum score 550 paper-based). Electronic applications accepted. *Expenses:* Contact institution.

Wilmington University, College of Business, New Castle, DE 19720-6491. Offers accounting (MBA, MS); business administration (MBA, DBA); environmental stewardship (MBA); finance (MBA); health care administration (MBA, MSM); homeland security (MBA, MSM); human resource management (MSM); management information systems (MBA, MSN); marketing (MSM); marketing management (MBA); military leadership (MSM); organizational leadership (MBA, MSM); public administration (MSM). *Program availability:* Part-time, evening/weekend. *Entrance requirements:* Additional exam requirements/recommendations for international students: Required—TOEFL (minimum score 500 paper-based). Electronic applications accepted.

Wilson College, Graduate Programs, Chambersburg, PA 17201-1285. Offers accounting (M Acc); choreography and visual art (MFA); education (M Ed); educational technology (MET); healthcare administration (MHA); humanities (MA), including art and culture, critical/cultural theory, English language and literature, women's studies; management (MSM); nursing (MSN), including nursing education, nursing leadership and management; special education (MSE). *Program availability:* Evening/weekend. *Degree requirements:* For master's, project. *Entrance requirements:* For master's, PRAXIS, minimum undergraduate cumulative GPA of 3.0, 2 letters of recommendation, current certification for eligibility to teach in grades K-12, resume, personal interview. Electronic applications accepted.

Wingate University, Porter B. Byrum School of Business, Wingate, NC 28174. Offers accounting (MAC); corporate innovation (MBA); finance (MBA); general management (MBA); healthcare management (MBA); marketing (MBA); project management (MBA). *Accreditation:* ACBSP. *Program availability:* Part-time, evening/weekend. *Entrance requirements:* For master's, GMAT, work experience, 2 letters of recommendation. Electronic applications accepted. *Expenses:* Contact institution. *Faculty research:* Stochastic processes, business ethics, regional economic development, municipal finance, consumer behavior.

Winston-Salem State University, Program in Business Administration, Winston-Salem, NC 27110-0003. Offers MBA. *Accreditation:* AACSB. *Program availability:* Part-time, evening/weekend, online learning. *Entrance requirements:* For master's, GMAT, resume, 3 letters of recommendation. Electronic applications accepted. *Faculty research:* Innovative entrepreneurship and customer service, econometrics and operations research.

Winthrop University, College of Business Administration, Program in Business Administration, Rock Hill, SC 29733. Offers MBA. *Accreditation:* AACSB. *Program availability:* Part-time. *Students:* 28 full-time (16 women), 100 part-time (53 women); includes 28 minority (23 Black or African American, non-Hispanic/Latino; 2 Asian, non-Hispanic/Latino; 3 Hispanic/Latino), 29 international. Average age 29. In 2018, 36 master's awarded. *Entrance requirements:* For master's, GMAT. Additional exam requirements/recommendations for international students: Required—TOEFL (minimum score 550 paper-based; 79 iBT), IELTS (minimum score 6). Application fee: $50. *Expenses:* Tuition, state resident: full-time $15,166; part-time $635 per credit hour. Tuition, nonresident: full-time $29,214. *Required fees:* $500; $180 per semester. *Unit head:* Keith Benson, Director of Graduate Studies, 803-323-2409, E-mail: bensonk@

winthrop.edu. *Application contact:* 800-411-7041, Fax: 803-323-2292, E-mail: gradschool@winthrop.edu.
Website: http://www.winthrop.edu/cba/mba/

Woodbury University, School of Business, Burbank, CA 91504-1052. Offers business administration (MBA); organizational leadership (MA). *Accreditation:* AACSB; ACBSP. *Program availability:* Part-time, evening/weekend. *Entrance requirements:* For master's, GMAT, transcripts, resume. Additional exam requirements/recommendations for international students: Required—TOEFL (minimum score 550 paper-based; 83 iBT), IELTS (minimum score 6.5). *Faculty research:* Total quality management, leadership.

Worcester Polytechnic Institute, Graduate Admissions, Foisie Business School, Worcester, MA 01609-2280. Offers business administration (PhD); information technology (MS), including information security management; management (MS, Graduate Certificate); marketing and innovation (MS); operations analytics and management (MS); supply chain management (MS). *Accreditation:* AACSB. *Program availability:* Part-time, evening/weekend, 100% online, blended/hybrid learning. *Students:* 136 full-time (74 women), 214 part-time (85 women); includes 29 minority (4 Black or African American, non-Hispanic/Latino; 11 Asian, non-Hispanic/Latino; 9 Hispanic/Latino; 5 Two or more races, non-Hispanic/Latino), 189 international. Average age 29. 636 applicants, 64% accepted, 104 enrolled. In 2018, 165 master's, 1 doctorate, 10 other advanced degrees awarded. *Degree requirements:* For master's, thesis optional. *Entrance requirements:* For master's and Graduate Certificate, GMAT or GRE General Test, 3 letters of recommendation, statement of purpose, resume. Additional exam requirements/recommendations for international students: Required—TOEFL (minimum score 563 paper-based; 84 iBT), IELTS (minimum score 7). *Application deadline:* For fall admission, 6/1 priority date for domestic and international students; for spring admission, 11/1 priority date for domestic students, 10/1 priority date for international students. Applications are processed on a rolling basis. Application fee: $70. Electronic applications accepted. *Financial support:* Career-related internships or fieldwork, institutionally sponsored loans, scholarships/grants, and unspecified assistantships available. Financial award application deadline: 6/1. *Unit head:* Melissa Terrio, Director of Graduate Recruitment & Admissions, 508-831-4665, Fax: 508-831-5866, E-mail: biz@wpi.edu. *Application contact:* Amy Trakimas, Associate Director of Graduate Recruitment & Admissions, 508-831-4665, Fax: 508-831-5866, E-mail: atrakimas@wpi.edu.
Website: https://www.wpi.edu/academics/business

Worcester State University, Graduate School, Program in Management, Worcester, MA 01602-2597. Offers accounting (MS); leadership (MS); marketing (MS). *Program availability:* Part-time, evening/weekend. *Faculty:* 6 full-time (3 women), 1 part-time/adjunct (0 women). *Students:* 15 full-time (6 women), 43 part-time (24 women); includes 14 minority (4 Black or African American, non-Hispanic/Latino; 5 Asian, non-Hispanic/Latino; 5 Hispanic/Latino), 7 international. Average age 38. 32 applicants, 100% accepted, 24 enrolled. In 2018, 24 master's awarded. *Degree requirements:* For master's, comprehensive exam (for some programs), thesis (for some programs), For a detail list in Degree Completion requirements please see the graduate catalog at catalog.worcester.edu. *Entrance requirements:* For master's, GMAT, For a detail list of entrance requirements please see the graduate catalog at catalog.worcester.edu. Additional exam requirements/recommendations for international students: Required—TOEFL (minimum score 550 paper-based; 79 iBT), IELTS (minimum score 6). *Application deadline:* For fall admission, 3/1 for domestic and international students; for spring admission, 11/1 for domestic and international students; for summer admission, 3/1 for domestic and international students. Applications are processed on a rolling basis. Application fee: $50. Electronic applications accepted. *Expenses:* Tuition, area resident: Full-time $3042; part-time $169 per credit hour. Tuition, state resident: full-time $3042; part-time $169 per credit hour. Tuition, nonresident: full-time $3042; part-time $169 per credit hour. International tuition: $3042 full-time. *Required fees:* $2754; $153 per credit hour. *Financial support:* Career-related internships or fieldwork, scholarships/grants, and unspecified assistantships available. Financial award application deadline: 3/1; financial award applicants required to submit FAFSA. *Unit head:* Dr. Elizabeth Wark, Program Coordinator, 508-929-8743, Fax: 508-929-8048, E-mail: ewark@worcester.edu. *Application contact:* Sara Grady, Associate Dean, Graduate Studies and Professional Development, 508-929-8130, Fax: 508-929-8100, E-mail: sara.grady@worcester.edu.

Wright State University, Graduate School, Raj Soin College of Business, Program in Business Administration, Dayton, OH 45435. Offers MBA.

Xavier University, Williams College of Business, Master of Business Administration Program, Cincinnati, OH 45207. Offers business administration (Exec MBA, MBA); business intelligence (MBA); finance (MBA); health industry (MBA); international business (MBA); marketing (MBA); values-based leadership (MBA); MBA/MHSA; MSN/MBA. *Accreditation:* AACSB. *Program availability:* Part-time, evening/weekend. *Degree requirements:* For master's, capstone course. *Entrance requirements:* For master's, GMAT or GRE, official transcript; resume. Additional exam requirements/recommendations for international students: Required—TOEFL (minimum score 550 paper-based; 79 iBT). Electronic applications accepted. Application fee is waived when completed online. *Expenses:* Contact institution.

Yale University, Yale School of Management, Doctoral Program in Management, New Haven, CT 06520. Offers accounting (PhD); financial economics (PhD); marketing (PhD); organizations and management (PhD). *Accreditation:* AACSB. *Degree requirements:* For doctorate, comprehensive exam, thesis/dissertation. *Entrance requirements:* For doctorate, GMAT or GRE General Test. Additional exam requirements/recommendations for international students: Required—TOEFL or IELTS. Electronic applications accepted. *Expenses:* Contact institution. *Faculty research:* Pricing of options and futures, term structure of interest rates, use of accounting numbers in debt contracts, product differentiation, e-commerce and marketing, behavioral finance.

Yale University, Yale School of Management, Program in Business Administration, New Haven, CT 06520. Offers MBA, MBA/JD, MBA/M Arch, MBA/M Div, MBA/MA, MBA/MEM, MBA/MF, MBA/MFA, MBA/MPH, MBA/PhD, MD/MBA. *Accreditation:* AACSB. Terminal master's awarded for partial completion of doctoral program. *Degree requirements:* For master's, international experience. *Entrance requirements:* For master's, GMAT or GRE. Additional exam requirements/recommendations for international students: Required—TOEFL, PTE, or IELTS. Electronic applications accepted. *Expenses:* Contact institution. *Faculty research:* Finance, strategy, marketing, leadership, operations.

Yeshiva University, Sy Syms School of Business, New York, NY 10016. Offers accounting (MS); business (EMBA); marketing (MS); taxation (MS). *Program availability:* Part-time. *Entrance requirements:* For master's, minimum GPA of 3.5 or GMAT.

York College of Pennsylvania, Graham School of Business, York, PA 17403-3651. Offers accounting (M Acc); business (MBA); continuous improvement (MBA); financial management (MBA); health care management (MBA); management (MBA); marketing (MBA); self-designed (MBA). *Accreditation:* ACBSP. *Program availability:* Part-time, evening/weekend. *Faculty:* 11 full-time (5 women), 3 part-time/adjunct (1 woman). *Students:* 13 full-time (4 women), 73 part-time (32 women); includes 11 minority (5 Black

Business Administration and Management—General

or African American, non-Hispanic/Latino; 2 Asian, non-Hispanic/Latino; 2 Hispanic/Latino; 2 Two or more races, non-Hispanic/Latino), 1 international. Average age 35. 57 applicants, 65% accepted, 25 enrolled. In 2018, 8 master's awarded. *Degree requirements:* For master's, directed study. *Entrance requirements:* For master's, GMAT. Additional exam requirements/recommendations for international students: Required—TOEFL (minimum score 530 paper-based; 72 iBT), IELTS (minimum score 6). *Application deadline:* For fall admission, 7/15 priority date for domestic students, 5/1 for international students; for spring admission, 11/15 priority date for domestic students, 9/1 for international students; for summer admission, 4/15 priority date for domestic students. Applications are processed on a rolling basis. Application fee: $0. Electronic applications accepted. *Expenses:* Contact institution. *Financial support:* In 2018–19, 3 students received support. Scholarships/grants available. Financial award applicants required to submit FAFSA. *Unit head:* Nicole Cornell Sadowski, MBA Director, 717-815-1491, Fax: 717-600-3999, E-mail: ncornell@ycp.edu. *Application contact:* MBA Office, 717-815-1491, Fax: 717-600-3999, E-mail: mba@ycp.edu. Website: http://www.ycp.edu/mba

York University, Faculty of Graduate Studies, Schulich School of Business, Toronto, ON M3J 1P3, Canada. Offers accounting (M Acc); administration (PhD); business (MBA); business analytics (MBA); finance (MF); international business (IMBA); MBA/JD; MBA/MA; MBA/MFA. *Program availability:* Part-time, evening/weekend. *Degree requirements:* For master's, advanced proficiency in a second language, work term (IMBA); for doctorate, comprehensive exam, thesis/dissertation. *Entrance requirements:* For master's, GMAT or GRE, minimum GPA of 3.0 (3.3 for MF, MBA in business analytics, and IMBA); for doctorate, GMAT or GRE, minimum GPA of 3.3. Additional exam requirements/recommendations for international students: Required—TOEFL (minimum score 600 paper-based; 100 iBT), IELTS (minimum score 7), York English Language Test (minimum score 1); PearsonVUE (minimum score 64). Electronic applications accepted. *Faculty research:* Accounting, finance, marketing, operations management and information systems, organizational studies, strategic management.

Youngstown State University, College of Graduate Studies, Williamson College of Business Administration, Program in Business Administration, Youngstown, OH 44555-0001. Offers MBA. *Program availability:* Part-time, evening/weekend. *Degree requirements:* For master's, thesis optional. *Entrance requirements:* For master's, GMAT, minimum GPA of 2.7. Additional exam requirements/recommendations for international students: Required—TOEFL. *Faculty research:* Media, international marketing, advanced marketing simulations, ethics in business.

Section 2
Accounting and Finance

This section contains a directory of institutions offering graduate work in accounting and finance. Additional information about programs listed in the directory but not augmented by an in-depth entry may be obtained by writing directly to the dean of a graduate school or chair of a department at the address given in the directory.

For programs offering related work, see also in this book *Business Administration and Management, International Business,* and *Nonprofit Management.* In the other guides in this series:

Graduate Programs in the Humanities, Arts & Social Sciences

See *Economics* and *Family and Consumer Sciences (Consumer Economics)*

Graduate Programs in the Physical Sciences, Mathematics, Agricultural Sciences, the Environment & Natural Resources

See *Mathematical Sciences*

Graduate Programs in Engineering & Applied Sciences

See *Computer Science and Information Technology*

CONTENTS

Program Directories

Accounting

Abilene Christian University, Graduate Programs, College of Business Administration, Program in Accountancy, Abilene, TX 79699. Offers M Acc. *Program availability:* Part-time. *Faculty:* 7 part-time/adjunct (0 women). *Students:* 14 full-time (2 women), 3 part-time (2 women); includes 2 minority (both Hispanic/Latino), 1 international. 35 applicants, 26% accepted, 9 enrolled. In 2018, 33 master's awarded. *Entrance requirements:* For master's, GMAT. Additional exam requirements/recommendations for international students: Required—TOEFL (minimum score 80 iBT), IELTS (minimum score 6). *Application deadline:* For fall admission, 8/10 for domestic students; for spring admission, 11/1 for domestic students. Applications are processed on a rolling basis. Application fee: $65. Electronic applications accepted. *Financial support:* In 2018–19, 15 students received support. Federal Work-Study and scholarships/grants available. Support available to part-time students. Financial award application deadline: 4/1; financial award applicants required to submit FAFSA. *Unit head:* John Neill, Graduate Director, 325-674-2053, Fax: 325-674-2507, E-mail: john.neill@acu.edu. *Application contact:* Graduate Admissions, 325-674-6911, E-mail: gradinfo@acu.edu.
Website: http://www.acu.edu/graduate/academics/accounting.html

Adelphi University, Robert B. Willumstad School of Business, MBA Program, Garden City, NY 11530-0701. Offers accounting (MBA); finance (MBA); health services administration (MBA); human resource management (MBA); management (MBA); management information systems (MBA); marketing (MBA); sport management (MBA). *Accreditation:* AACSB. *Program availability:* Part-time, evening/weekend. *Students:* 343 full-time (132 women), 101 part-time (56 women); includes 75 minority (22 Black or African American, non-Hispanic/Latino; 2 American Indian or Alaska Native, non-Hispanic/Latino; 20 Asian, non-Hispanic/Latino; 23 Hispanic/Latino; 1 Native Hawaiian or other Pacific Islander, non-Hispanic/Latino; 7 Two or more races, non-Hispanic/Latino; 275 international. Average age 29. 389 applicants, 59% accepted, 187 enrolled. In 2018, 171 master's awarded. *Entrance requirements:* For master's, GMAT, official transcripts, bachelor's degree, 500 word essay, 2 letters of recommendation, resume. Additional exam requirements/recommendations for international students: Required—TOEFL (minimum score 550 paper-based; 80 iBT), IELTS (minimum score 6.5). *Application deadline:* For fall admission, 4/1 for international students; for spring admission, 11/1 for international students. Applications are processed on a rolling basis. Application fee: $50. Electronic applications accepted. *Financial support:* Research assistantships with partial tuition reimbursements, career-related internships or fieldwork, Federal Work-Study, institutionally sponsored loans, scholarships/grants, tuition waivers (partial), and unspecified assistantships available. Financial award application deadline: 3/1; financial award applicants required to submit FAFSA. *Faculty research:* Supply chain management, distribution channels, productivity benchmark analysis, data envelopment analysis, financial portfolio analysis. *Unit head:* Britt'ny Brown, Director of Graduate Programs, 516-877-4605. *Application contact:* Britt'ny Brown, Director of Graduate Programs, 516-877-4605.
Website: https://business.adelphi.edu/

Adrian College, Graduate Programs, Adrian, MI 49221-2575. Offers accounting (MS); athletic training (MS); criminal justice (MA). *Degree requirements:* For master's, comprehensive exam (for some programs), thesis (for some programs), thesis, internship or practicum with corresponding in-depth paper and/or presentation. *Entrance requirements:* For master's, appropriate undergraduate degree, minimum cumulative and major GPA of 3.0, personal statement.

Alabama State University, College of Business Administration, Department of Accounting and Finance, Montgomery, AL 36101-0271. Offers accountancy (M Acc). *Students:* Average age 22. 16 applicants, 63% accepted, 8 enrolled. In 2018, 8 master's awarded. *Entrance requirements:* For master's, minimum GPA of 2.75 (undergraduate), 3.0 (graduate). Additional exam requirements/recommendations for international students: Required—TOEFL (minimum score 500 paper-based). *Application deadline:* For fall admission, 4/15 for domestic and international students; for spring admission, 11/15 for domestic and international students; for summer admission, 3/15 for domestic and international students. Applications are processed on a rolling basis. Application fee: $25. Electronic applications accepted. *Expenses:* Contact institution. *Financial support:* In 2018–19, 11 students received support. Fellowships, teaching assistantships, career-related internships or fieldwork, institutionally sponsored loans, tuition waivers (partial), and unspecified assistantships available. Financial award applicants required to submit FAFSA. *Unit head:* Dr. Dave Thompson, Chair, 334-229-4134, Fax: 334-229-4870, E-mail: dthompson@asunet.alasu.edu. *Application contact:* Dr. William Person, Dean of Graduate Studies, 334-229-4274, Fax: 334-229-4928, E-mail: wperson@alasu.edu.
Website: http://www.alasu.edu/academics/colleges—departments/college-of-business-administration/college-of-business-academics/accounting—finance/index.aspx

Albany State University, College of Business, Albany, GA 31705-2717. Offers accounting (MBA); general business administration (MBA); healthcare (MBA); public administration (MBA); supply chain and logistics (MBA). *Accreditation:* ACBSP. *Program availability:* Part-time, evening/weekend. *Degree requirements:* For master's, comprehensive exam, internship, 3 hours of physical education. *Entrance requirements:* For master's, GMAT (minimum score of 450)/GRE (minimum score of 800) for those without earned master's degree or higher, minimum undergraduate GPA of 2.5, 2 letters of reference, official transcript, pre-entrance medical record and certificate of immunization. Electronic applications accepted. *Faculty research:* Diversity issues, ancestry, understanding finance through use of technology.

Albertus Magnus College, Master of Business Administration Program, New Haven, CT 06511-1189. Offers accounting (MBA); general management (MBA); health care management (MBA); human resource management (MBA); leadership (MBA); project management (MBA). Program also offered in East Hartford, CT. *Program availability:* Part-time, evening/weekend, 100% online, blended/hybrid learning. *Degree requirements:* For master's, thesis, capstone project, business plan, minimum cumulative GPA of 3.0, completion of all requirements within seven years of matriculation. *Entrance requirements:* For master's, 3 years of management or related experience, minimum GPA of 2.5, 2 letters of recommendation, official transcripts. Additional exam requirements/recommendations for international students: Recommended—TOEFL (minimum score 550 paper-based; 80 iBT). Electronic applications accepted. *Expenses:* Contact institution. *Faculty research:* Finance, project management, accounting, business administration, generalist.

Albertus Magnus College, Master of Science in Accounting Program, New Haven, CT 06511-1189. Offers MSA. *Program availability:* Part-time, evening/weekend, 100% online, blended/hybrid learning. *Degree requirements:* For master's, project. *Entrance requirements:* For master's, bachelor's degree; minimum cumulative GPA of 3.0; 24 undergraduate credits in accounting, 22 in business (separate from accounting); 2 letters of recommendation; essay. Additional exam requirements/recommendations for

international students: Recommended—TOEFL (minimum score 575 paper-based). Electronic applications accepted. *Expenses:* Contact institution.

Alfred University, Graduate School, School of Business, Alfred, NY 14802-1205. Offers accounting (MBA); business administration (MBA). *Accreditation:* AACSB. *Program availability:* Part-time. *Entrance requirements:* For master's, GMAT. Additional exam requirements/recommendations for international students: Required—TOEFL (minimum score 590 paper-based; 90 iBT), IELTS (minimum score 6.5). Electronic applications accepted.

American Business & Technology University, Programs in Business Administration, Saint Joseph, MO 64506. Offers business administration (MBA); financial management (MBA); global business management (MBA); information systems management (MBA); marketing and social media (MBA); project and operations management (MBA); public accounting (MBA). *Program availability:* Online learning.

American InterContinental University Online, Program in Business Administration, Schaumburg, IL 60173. Offers accounting and finance (MBA); finance (MBA); healthcare management (MBA); human resource management (MBA); international business (MBA); management (MBA); marketing (MBA); operations management (MBA); organizational psychology and development (MBA); project management (MBA). *Accreditation:* ACBSP. *Program availability:* Evening/weekend, online learning. *Entrance requirements:* Additional exam requirements/recommendations for international students: Required—TOEFL (minimum score 550 paper-based). Electronic applications accepted.

American International College, School of Business, Arts and Sciences, Springfield, MA 01109-3189. Offers accounting and taxation (MS); business administration (MBA); clinical psychology (MA); educational psychology (Ed D); forensic psychology (MS); general psychology (MA, CAGS); management (CAGS); resort and casino management (MBA, CAGS). *Program availability:* Part-time, evening/weekend. *Degree requirements:* For master's, practicum; for doctorate, comprehensive exam, thesis/dissertation, practicum. *Entrance requirements:* For master's, BS or BA, minimum undergraduate GPA of 2.75, 2 letters of recommendation, official transcripts, personal goal statement or essay; for doctorate, 3 letters of recommendation; BS or BA; minimum undergraduate GPA of 3.0 (3.25 recommended); official transcripts; personal goal statement or essay. Additional exam requirements/recommendations for international students: Required—TOEFL (minimum score 550 paper-based; 80 iBT). *Expenses:* Contact institution. *Faculty research:* Substance abuse, forensic psychology, special education.

American Public University System, AMU/APU Graduate Programs, Charles Town, WV 25414. Offers accounting (MS); applied business analytics (MS); business administration (MBA); criminal justice (MA); cybersecurity studies (MS); educational leadership (M Ed); environmental policy and management (MS); global security (DGS); health information management (MS); history (MA), including American military history, American Revolution, civil war, war since 1945, World War II; information technology (MS); international relations and conflict resolution (MA), including American politics and government, comparative government and development, general, international relations, public policy; national security studies (MA); nursing (MSN); political science (MA); public policy (MPP); reverse logistics management (MA), including comparative and security issues, conflict resolution, international and transnational security issues, peacekeeping; space studies (MS); sports management (MS); strategic intelligence (DSI); teaching (M Ed), including secondary social studies; transportation and logistics management (MA). *Program availability:* Part-time, evening/weekend, online only, 100% online. *Students:* 406 full-time (180 women), 7,826 part-time (3,329 women); includes 2,781 minority (1,438 Black or African American, non-Hispanic/Latino; 44 American Indian or Alaska Native, non-Hispanic/Latino; 193 Asian, non-Hispanic/Latino; 747 Hispanic/Latino; 53 Native Hawaiian or other Pacific Islander, non-Hispanic/Latino; 306 Two or more races, non-Hispanic/Latino; 121 international. Average age 38. In 2018, 2,717 master's awarded. *Degree requirements:* For master's, comprehensive exam or practicum; for doctorate, practicum. *Entrance requirements:* For master's, official transcript showing earned bachelor's degree from institution accredited by recognized accrediting body. Additional exam requirements/recommendations for international students: Required—TOEFL (minimum score 550 paper-based), IELTS (minimum score 6.5). *Application deadline:* Applications are processed on a rolling basis. Application fee: $0. Electronic applications accepted. *Financial support:* Scholarships/grants available. Financial award applicants required to submit FAFSA. *Unit head:* Dr. Wallace Boston, President, 877-468-6268, Fax: 304-728-2348, E-mail: president@apus.edu. *Application contact:* Yoci Deal, Associate Vice President, Graduate and International Admissions, 877-468-6268, Fax: 304-724-3764, E-mail: info@apus.edu.
Website: http://www.apus.edu

American University, Kogod School of Business, Department of Accounting, Washington, DC 20016-8044. Offers accounting (MS, Certificate), including accounting (MS), forensic accounting (Certificate); taxation (MS, Certificate), including tax (Certificate), taxation (MS). *Program availability:* Part-time, evening/weekend. *Faculty:* 14 full-time (6 women), 11 part-time/adjunct (5 women). *Students:* 76 full-time (51 women), 57 part-time (26 women); includes 45 minority (21 Black or African American, non-Hispanic/Latino; 9 Asian, non-Hispanic/Latino; 12 Hispanic/Latino; 3 Two or more races, non-Hispanic/Latino), 52 international. Average age 29. 129 applicants, 77% accepted, 30 enrolled. In 2018, 49 master's, 15 other advanced degrees awarded. *Entrance requirements:* For master's, GMAT/GRE, resume, interview, personal statement, 2 letters of recommendation, transcripts; for Certificate, bachelor's degree. Additional exam requirements/recommendations for international students: Required—TOEFL (minimum score 100 iBT). *Application deadline:* Applications are processed on a rolling basis. Application fee: $100. *Expenses:* Contact institution. *Financial support:* Applicants required to submit FAFSA. *Faculty research:* Harmonization of international accounting standards, federal accounting and financial reporting, taxation of U.S. corporations doing business abroad, tax planning for real estate transactions. *Unit head:* Dr. Donald T. Williamson, Chair, Department of Accounting, 202-885-1900, E-mail: kogodgrad@american.edu. *Application contact:* Jason Garner, Director of Admissions, 202-885-1926, E-mail: jgarner@american.edu.
Website: http://www.american.edu/kogod/

American University of Sharjah, Graduate Programs, Sharjah, United Arab Emirates. Offers accounting (MS); biomedical engineering (MSBME); business administration (MBA); chemical engineering (MS Ch E); civil engineering (MSCE); computer engineering (MS); electrical engineering (MSEE); engineering systems management (MS, PhD); mathematics (MS); mechanical engineering (MSME); mechatronics engineering (MS); teaching English to speakers of other languages (MA); translation and interpreting (MA); urban planning (MUP). *Program availability:* Part-time, evening/weekend. *Degree requirements:* For master's, thesis (for some programs). *Entrance requirements:* For master's, GMAT (for MBA). Additional exam requirements/

recommendations for international students: Required—TOEFL (minimum score 550 paper-based; 80 iBT), TWE (minimum score 5); Recommended—IELTS (minimum score 6.5). Electronic applications accepted. *Faculty research:* Water pollution, management and waste water treatment, energy and sustainability, air pollution, Islamic finance, family business and small and medium enterprises.

Anderson University, Falls School of Business, Anderson, IN 46012-3495. Offers accountancy (MA); business administration (MBA, DBA). *Accreditation:* ACBSP.

Andrews University, School of Graduate Studies, School of Business, Graduate Programs in Business, Berrien Springs, MI 49104. Offers MBA, MSA. *Entrance requirements:* For master's, GMAT. Additional exam requirements/recommendations for international students: Required—TOEFL (minimum score 550 paper-based).

Angelo State University, College of Graduate Studies and Research, Norris-Vincent College of Business, Department of Accounting, Economics and Finance, San Angelo, TX 76909. Offers professional accountancy (MPAC). *Program availability:* Part-time, evening/weekend. *Students:* 18 full-time (12 women), 5 part-time (2 women); includes 7 minority (6 Hispanic/Latino; 1 Two or more races, non-Hispanic/Latino), 2 international. Average age 24. *Entrance requirements:* For master's, GMAT, essay. Additional exam requirements/recommendations for international students: Required—TOEFL or IELTS. *Application deadline:* For fall admission, 7/15 priority date for domestic students, 6/10 for international students; for spring admission, 12/1 priority date for domestic students, 11/1 for international students. Applications are processed on a rolling basis. Application fee: $40 ($50 for international students). Electronic applications accepted. *Expenses: Tuition, area resident:* Full-time $3964; part-time $220 per credit hour. Tuition, state resident: full-time $3964; part-time $220 per credit hour. Tuition, nonresident: full-time $11,434; part-time $635 per credit hour. *International tuition:* $11,434 full-time. *Financial support:* Career-related internships or fieldwork, Federal Work-Study, and scholarships/grants available. Support available to part-time students. Financial award application deadline: 3/1; financial award applicants required to submit FAFSA. *Unit head:* Dr. Charles Aaron Pier, Chair, 325-942-2046, Fax: 325-942-2285, E-mail: chuck.pier@angelo.edu. *Application contact:* Cathryn Golden, Graduate Advisor, 325-942-2046, E-mail: cathryn.golden@angelo.edu.
Website: http://www.angelo.edu/dept/aef/

Appalachian State University, Cratis D. Williams School of Graduate Studies, Department of Accounting, Boone, NC 28608. Offers taxation (MS). *Program availability:* Part-time. *Degree requirements:* For master's, comprehensive exam, thesis optional. *Entrance requirements:* For master's, GMAT, 3 letters of recommendation. Additional exam requirements/recommendations for international students: Required—TOEFL (minimum score 550 paper-based; 79 iBT), IELTS (minimum score 6.5). Electronic applications accepted. *Expenses: Tuition, area resident:* Full-time $4839; part-time $237 per credit hour. Tuition, state resident: full-time $4839; part-time $237 per credit hour. Tuition, nonresident: full-time $18,271; part-time $895.50 per credit hour. *Faculty research:* Audit assurance risk, state taxation, financial accounting inconsistencies, management information systems, charitable contribution taxation.

Argosy University, Atlanta, College of Business, Atlanta, GA 30328. Offers accounting (DBA); corporate compliance (MBA); customized professional concentration (MBA, DBA); finance (MBA); healthcare administration (MBA); information systems (DBA); information systems management (MBA); international business (MBA, DBA); management (MBA, MSM, DBA); marketing (MBA, DBA). *Accreditation:* ACBSP.

Argosy University, Chicago, College of Business, Chicago, IL 60601. Offers accounting (DBA); customized professional concentration (MBA, DBA); finance (MBA); fraud examination (MBA); global business sustainability (DBA); healthcare administration (MBA); information systems (DBA); information systems management (MBA); international business (MBA, DBA); management (MBA, MSM, DBA); marketing (MBA, DBA); organizational leadership (Ed D); public administration (MBA); sustainable management (MBA). *Accreditation:* ACBSP. *Program availability:* Online learning.

Argosy University, Hawai`i, College of Business, Honolulu, HI 96813. Offers accounting (DBA); corporate compliance (MBA); customized professional concentration (MBA, DBA); finance (MBA, Certificate); fraud examination (MBA); global business sustainability (DBA); healthcare administration (MBA, Certificate); information systems (DBA); information systems management (MBA, Certificate); international business (MBA, DBA, Certificate); management (MBA, MSM, DBA); marketing (MBA, DBA, Certificate); organizational leadership (Ed D); public administration (MBA); sustainable management (MBA).

Argosy University, Los Angeles, College of Business, Los Angeles, CA 90045. Offers accounting (DBA); corporate compliance (MBA); customized professional concentration (MBA, DBA); finance (MBA); fraud examination (MBA); global business sustainability (DBA); healthcare administration (MBA); information systems (DBA); information systems management (MBA); international business (MBA, DBA); management (MBA, MSM, DBA); marketing (MBA, DBA); organizational leadership (Ed D); public administration (MBA); sustainable management (MBA).

Argosy University, Northern Virginia, College of Business, Arlington, VA 22209. Offers accounting (DBA); customized professional concentration (MBA, DBA); finance (MBA); fraud examination (MBA); global business sustainability (DBA); healthcare administration (MBA); information systems (DBA); information systems management (MBA); international business (MBA, DBA, Certificate); management (MBA, MSM, DBA); marketing (MBA, DBA, Certificate); organizational leadership (Ed D); public administration (MBA); sustainable management (MBA).

Argosy University, Orange County, College of Business, Orange, CA 92868. Offers accounting (DBA, Adv C); corporate compliance (MBA); customized professional concentration (MBA, DBA); finance (MBA, Certificate); fraud examination (MBA); global business sustainability (DBA); healthcare administration (MBA, Certificate); information systems (DBA, Adv C, Certificate); information systems management (MBA); international business (MBA, DBA, Adv C, Certificate); management (MBA, MSM, DBA, Adv C); marketing (MBA, DBA, Adv C, Certificate); organizational leadership (Ed D); public administration (MBA, Certificate); sustainable management (MBA).

Argosy University, Phoenix, College of Business, Phoenix, AZ 85021. Offers accounting (DBA); corporate compliance (MBA); customized professional concentration (MBA, DBA); finance (MBA); fraud examination (MBA); global business sustainability (DBA); healthcare administration (MBA); information systems (DBA); information systems management (MBA); international business (MBA, DBA); management (MBA, DBA); marketing (MBA, DBA); public administration (MBA); sustainable management (MBA).

Argosy University, Seattle, College of Business, Seattle, WA 98121. Offers accounting (DBA); corporate compliance (MBA); customized professional concentration (MBA, DBA); finance (MBA); fraud examination (MBA); global business sustainability (DBA); healthcare administration (MBA); information systems (DBA); information systems management (MBA); international business (MBA, DBA); management (MBA, MSM, DBA); marketing (MBA, DBA); organizational leadership (Ed D); public administration (MBA); sustainable management (MBA).

Argosy University, Tampa, College of Business, Tampa, FL 33607. Offers accounting (DBA); corporate compliance (MBA); customized professional concentration (MBA, DBA); finance (MBA); fraud examination (MBA); global business sustainability (DBA); healthcare administration (MBA); information systems (DBA); information systems management (MBA); international business (MBA, DBA); management (MBA, MSM, DBA); marketing (MBA, DBA); organizational leadership (Ed D); public administration (MBA); sustainable management (MBA).

Argosy University, Twin Cities, College of Business, Eagan, MN 55121. Offers accounting (DBA); customized professional concentration (MBA, DBA); finance (MBA); fraud examination (MBA); global business sustainability (DBA); healthcare administration (MBA); information systems (DBA); information systems management (MBA); international business (MBA, DBA); management (MBA, MSM, DBA); marketing (MBA, DBA); organizational leadership (Ed D); public administration (MBA); sustainable management (MBA).

Arizona State University at the Tempe campus, W. P. Carey School of Business, School of Accountancy, Tempe, AZ 85287-3606. Offers accountancy (M Acc, M Tax); business administration (PhD), including accountancy. *Accreditation:* AACSB. *Program availability:* Part-time, evening/weekend. *Degree requirements:* For master's, thesis optional, interactive Program of Study (iPOS) submitted before completing 50 percent of required credit hours. *Entrance requirements:* For master's, GMAT (waivers may apply for ASU accountancy undergraduates), minimum GPA of 3.0 in last 2 years of work leading to bachelor's degree, 2 letters of recommendation, professional resume, official transcripts, responses to 3 essay questions. Additional exam requirements/recommendations for international students: Required—TOEFL (minimum score 550 paper-based; 80 iBT), IELTS (minimum score 6.5). Electronic applications accepted. *Expenses:* Contact institution.

Arkansas State University, Graduate School, College of Business, Department of Accounting, State University, AR 72467. Offers accountancy (M Acc). *Program availability:* Part-time. *Degree requirements:* For master's, comprehensive exam, thesis or alternative. *Entrance requirements:* For master's, GMAT, appropriate bachelor's degree, letters of reference, official transcript, immunization records. Additional exam requirements/recommendations for international students: Required—TOEFL (minimum score 550 paper-based; 79 iBT), IELTS (minimum score 6), PTE (minimum score 56). Electronic applications accepted. *Expenses:* Contact institution.

Ashland University, Dauch College of Business and Economics, Ashland, OH 44805-3702. Offers accounting (MBA); business analytics (MBA); entrepreneurship (MBA); financial management (MBA); global management (MBA); health care management and leadership (MBA); human resource management (MBA); human resources (MBA); management information systems (MBA); project management (MBA); sport management (MBA); supply chain management (MBA). *Accreditation:* ACBSP. *Program availability:* Part-time, evening/weekend, 100% online, blended/hybrid learning. Terminal master's awarded for partial completion of doctoral program. *Degree requirements:* For master's, thesis optional, capstone course. *Entrance requirements:* For master's, 2 years of full-time work experience. Additional exam requirements/recommendations for international students: Required—TOEFL (minimum score 550 paper-based; 78 iBT). Electronic applications accepted. *Expenses:* Contact institution. *Faculty research:* Relationship marketing strategy, executive compensation and company performance, online marketplaces in electronic commerce, diversity training in campus recreation departments, entrepreneurship in developing and emerging economies.

Assumption College, Business Studies Program, Worcester, MA 01609-1296. Offers accounting (MBA); business studies (CAGS); finance/economics (MBA); human resources (MBA); international business (MBA); management (MBA); marketing (MBA); nonprofit leadership (MBA). *Program availability:* Part-time, evening/weekend. *Degree requirements:* For master's, capstone. *Entrance requirements:* For master's, bachelor's degree, three letters of recommendation, official transcripts, personal statement, current resume; for CAGS, MBA or equivalent degree in a closely related field, three letters of recommendation, official transcripts, personal statement, current resume. Additional exam requirements/recommendations for international students: Required—TOEFL (minimum score 540 paper-based; 76 iBT), IELTS (minimum score 6). Electronic applications accepted. *Faculty research:* Workplace diversity, dynamics of team interaction, utilization of leased employees, experiential learning project on due diligence market for prostheses.

Auburn University, Graduate School, College of Business, School of Accountancy, Auburn University, AL 36849. Offers M Acc. *Accreditation:* AACSB. *Program availability:* Part-time. *Entrance requirements:* For master's, GMAT, GRE General Test. Additional exam requirements/recommendations for international students: Required—TOEFL. Electronic applications accepted. *Expenses:* Tuition, state resident: full-time $11,282; part-time $535 per credit hour. Tuition, nonresident: full-time $30,542; part-time $1605 per credit hour. *Required fees:* $826 per semester. Tuition and fees vary according to degree level and program.

Auburn University at Montgomery, College of Business, School of Accountancy, Montgomery, AL 36124-4023. Offers M Acc. *Program availability:* Part-time. *Students:* Average age 28. 34 applicants, 85% accepted, 23 enrolled. In 2018, 10 master's awarded. *Entrance requirements:* For master's, GMAT. Additional exam requirements/recommendations for international students: Required—TOEFL (minimum score 500 paper-based; 61 iBT), IELTS (minimum score 5.5), PTE (minimum score 44). *Application deadline:* Applications are processed on a rolling basis. Application fee: $25 ($0 for international students). Electronic applications accepted. *Expenses: Tuition, area resident:* Full-time $7146; part-time $4764 per credit hour. Tuition, state resident: full-time $7146; part-time $4764 per credit hour. Tuition, nonresident: full-time $16,056; part-time $10,704 per credit hour. *International tuition:* $16,056 full-time. *Required fees:* $766. One-time fee: $25 full-time. *Financial support:* Scholarships/grants available. Financial award applicants required to submit FAFSA. *Application contact:* Rhonda Seay, Graduate Advisor, 334-244-3115, E-mail: rseay@aum.edu.
Website: http://business.aum.edu/academic-departments/accounting

Augustana University, Master of Professional Accountancy Program, Sioux Falls, SD 57197. Offers MPA. *Program availability:* Part-time. *Entrance requirements:* For master's, GRE or GMAT, essay. Additional exam requirements/recommendations for international students: Required—TOEFL. Electronic applications accepted. *Expenses:* Contact institution.

Aurora University, Dunham School of Business and Public Policy, Aurora, IL 60506-4892. Offers accountancy (MS); business (MBA). *Program availability:* Part-time, evening/weekend, 100% online, blended/hybrid learning. *Faculty:* 8 full-time (2 women), 28 part-time/adjunct (13 women). *Students:* 152 full-time (106 women), 180 part-time (112 women); includes 133 minority (51 Black or African American, non-Hispanic/Latino; 10 Asian, non-Hispanic/Latino; 63 Hispanic/Latino; 1 Native Hawaiian or other Pacific Islander, non-Hispanic/Latino; 8 Two or more races, non-Hispanic/Latino), 2 international. Average age 31. 253 applicants, 99% accepted, 156 enrolled. In 2018, 117 master's awarded. *Degree requirements:* For master's, Capstone project and internship. *Entrance requirements:* For master's, minimum GPA of 3.0, 2 years of work experience, resume. Additional exam requirements/recommendations for international students: Required—TOEFL (minimum score 550 paper-based; 79 iBT). *Application deadline:* For fall admission, 6/1 for international students; for spring admission, 10/1 for international students. Applications are processed on a rolling basis. Application fee: $0. Electronic

applications accepted. *Expenses:* The listed tuition and fees is for the MBA, MS, and MPA on-ground programs. Costs vary for online and plus one programs. The Dual MBA/MSW and MPA/MSW programs are roughly double the cost of the MBA. *Financial support:* In 2018–19, 94 students received support. Federal Work-Study, scholarships/grants, and unspecified assistantships available. Financial award applicants required to submit FAFSA. *Unit head:* Dr. Toby Arquette, Dean, School of Business and Policy, 630-844-5614, E-mail: tarquett@aurora.edu. *Application contact:* Center for Graduate Studies, 630-947-8955, E-mail: AUadmission@aurora.edu.

Averett University, Master of Accountancy Program, Danville, VA 24541-3692. Offers M Acc. *Program availability:* Part-time. *Faculty:* 2 full-time (1 woman). *Students:* 6 full-time (5 women), 2 part-time (both women). Average age 31. 5 applicants, 80% accepted, 4 enrolled. In 2018, 2 master's awarded. *Degree requirements:* For master's, 30 credit hours, minimum GPA of 3.0 throughout program, completion of degree requirements within six years from start of program. *Entrance requirements:* For master's, GMAT, minimum cumulative GPA of 3.0, undergraduate degree in accounting, work experience. minimum of 15 credit hours in accounting (above principles of accounting). Additional exam requirements/recommendations for international students: Required—TOEFL. *Application deadline:* Applications are processed on a rolling basis. Electronic applications accepted. *Expenses:* Contact institution. *Financial support:* In 2018–19, 1 student received support. Application deadline: 3/1; applicants required to submit FAFSA. *Unit head:* Dr. Peggy C. Wright, Director of the Master in Accountancy Program, 434-791-7118, E-mail: pwright@averett.edu. *Application contact:* Christy Davis, Assistant Director of Admissions, 434-791-7133, E-mail: cdavis@averett.edu.

Azusa Pacific University, School of Business and Management, Azusa, CA 91702-7000. Offers accounting (MBA); business administration (MBA); entrepreneurship (MBA); finance (MBA); international business (MBA); marketing (MBA); organizational science (MBA); professional accountancy (M Acc); sport management (MBA). *Program availability:* Part-time, evening/weekend. *Degree requirements:* For master's, thesis (for some programs), final project. *Entrance requirements:* For master's, GMAT, minimum GPA of 3.0. Additional exam requirements/recommendations for international students: Required—TOEFL (minimum score 600 paper-based). *Expenses:* Contact institution. *Faculty research:* Gender issues, financial risk, leadership and ethics, marketing strategy.

Babson College, F. W. Olin Graduate School of Business, Babson Park, MA 02457-0310. Offers accounting (MSA); advanced management (Certificate); business administration (MBA); business analytics (MS); finance (MS); global entrepreneurship (MS); technological entrepreneurship (MS). *Accreditation:* AACSB. *Program availability:* Part-time, evening/weekend, online learning. *Entrance requirements:* For master's, GMAT, 2 years of work experience, resume, letters of recommendation. Additional exam requirements/recommendations for international students: Required—TOEFL (minimum score 100 iBT), IELTS (minimum score 6.5). Electronic applications accepted. *Faculty research:* Entrepreneurship, sustainability, global markets, process of innovation, social media and advertising.

Baker College Center for Graduate Studies–Online, Graduate Programs, Flint, MI 48507. Offers accounting (MBA); business administration (DBA); finance (MBA); general business (MBA); health care management (MBA); human resources management (MBA); information management (MBA); leadership studies (MBA); management information systems (MSIS); marketing (MBA); occupational therapy (MOT). *Program availability:* Part-time, evening/weekend, online learning. *Degree requirements:* For master's, portfolio. *Entrance requirements:* For master's, 3 years of work experience, minimum undergraduate GPA of 2.5, writing sample, 3 letters of recommendation; for doctorate, MBA or acceptable related master's degree from accredited association, 5 years work experience, minimum graduate GPA of 3.25, writing sample, 3 professional references. Additional exam requirements/recommendations for international students: Required—TOEFL (minimum score 550 paper-based). Electronic applications accepted.

Baldwin Wallace University, Graduate Programs, School of Business, Program in Accounting, Berea, OH 44017-2088. Offers MBA. *Program availability:* Part-time, evening/weekend. *Students:* 1 full-time (0 women), 5 part-time (3 women); includes 1 minority (Hispanic/Latino). Average age 36. 2 applicants, 50% accepted. In 2018, 26 master's awarded. *Degree requirements:* For master's, minimum overall GPA of 3.0. *Entrance requirements:* For master's, GMAT or minimum undergraduate GPA of 3.0, minimum GPA of 3.0, work experience, bachelor's degree in any field, undergraduate accounting coursework. Additional exam requirements/recommendations for international students: Required—TOEFL (minimum score 550 paper-based; 79 iBT). *Expenses:* Contact institution. *Financial support:* Applicants required to submit FAFSA. *Unit head:* Linda Chase, Professor/Chair, Accounting and Finance, 440-826-3039, Fax: 440-826-3868, E-mail: lichase@bw.edu. *Application contact:* Laura Spencer, Graduate Business Admission Specialist, 440-826-2191, Fax: 440-826-3868, E-mail: lspencer@bw.edu.

Ball State University, Graduate School, Miller College of Business, Department of Accounting, Muncie, IN 47306. Offers MS. *Accreditation:* AACSB. *Program availability:* Part-time. *Entrance requirements:* For master's, GMAT, minimum baccalaureate GPA of 2.75 or 3.0 in latter half of baccalaureate. Additional exam requirements/recommendations for international students: Required—TOEFL (minimum score 550 paper-based; 79 iBT), IELTS (minimum score 6.5). Electronic applications accepted. *Expenses:* Contact institution.

Barry University, Andreas School of Business, Program in Accounting, Miami Shores, FL 33161-6695. Offers MSA.

Baruch College of the City University of New York, Zicklin School of Business, Department of Accounting, Program in Accounting, New York, NY 10010-5585. Offers MBA, MS, PhD. PhD offered jointly with Graduate School and University Center of the City University of New York. *Accreditation:* AACSB. *Program availability:* Part-time, evening/weekend. *Degree requirements:* For doctorate, comprehensive exam, thesis/dissertation. *Entrance requirements:* For master's, GMAT, 2 letters of recommendation, resume, 2 years of work experience; for doctorate, GMAT. Additional exam requirements/recommendations for international students: Required—TOEFL (minimum score 590 paper-based), TWE (minimum score 5).

Bayamón Central University, Graduate Programs, Program in Business Administration, Bayamón, PR 00960-1725. Offers accounting (MBA); finance (MBA); general business (MBA); management (MBA); marketing (MBA). *Program availability:* Part-time, evening/weekend. *Degree requirements:* For master's, comprehensive exam (for some programs). *Entrance requirements:* For master's, EXADEP, bachelor's degree in business or related field.

Baylor University, Graduate School, Hankamer School of Business, Department of Accounting and Business Law, Waco, TX 76798. Offers M Acc, MT, JD/MT. *Accreditation:* AACSB. *Program availability:* Part-time. *Students:* 114 full-time (56 women), 16 part-time (12 women); includes 27 minority (2 Black or African American, non-Hispanic/Latino; 5 Asian, non-Hispanic/Latino; 11 Hispanic/Latino; 9 Two or more races, non-Hispanic/Latino), 5 international. In 2018, 104 master's awarded. *Entrance requirements:* For master's, GMAT. Additional exam requirements/recommendations for international students: Required—TOEFL (minimum score 100 iBT). Application fee: $50. Electronic applications accepted. *Financial support:* Research assistantships, career-related internships or fieldwork, Federal Work-Study, and institutionally sponsored loans available. *Faculty research:* Financial reporting, auditing, professional skepticism, tax policy, international financial reporting. *Unit head:* Dr. Gia Chevis, Adviser, 254-710-1328, Fax: 254-710-1067, E-mail: gia_chevis@baylor.edu. *Application contact:* Drew Snyder, Assistant Director of Admissions, 254-710-6281, E-mail: drew_snyder@baylor.edu.

Bay Path University, Program in Accounting, Longmeadow, MA 01106-2292. Offers forensic accounting (MS); private accounting (MS); public accounting (tax and audit) (MS). *Program availability:* Part-time, online only, 100% online. *Students:* 1 (woman) full-time, 16 part-time (all women); includes 2 minority (1 Black or African American, non-Hispanic/Latino; 1 Asian, non-Hispanic/Latino). Average age 34. In 2018, 3 master's awarded. *Entrance requirements:* For master's, Completed application, official copies of undergraduate and graduate transcripts (a GPA of 3.0 or higher is preferred); current resume; two recommendations, interview via phone or in person. *Application deadline:* Applications are processed on a rolling basis. Electronic applications accepted. Application fee is waived when completed online. *Expenses:* Contact institution. *Financial support:* In 2018–19, 2 students received support. Scholarships/grants and unspecified assistantships available. Financial award applicants required to submit FAFSA. *Unit head:* Kara Stevens, Director of Finance and Accounting Programs, 413-565-1344, E-mail: kastevens@baypath.edu. *Application contact:* Sheryl Kosakowski, Executive Director of Graduate Admissions, 413-565-1075, Fax: 413-565-1250, E-mail: skosakowski@baypath.edu.
Website: https://www.baypath.edu/academics/graduate-programs/accounting-ms/

Belmont University, Jack C. Massey Graduate School of Business, Nashville, TN 37212. Offers accounting (M Acc); business (AMBA, PMBA); healthcare (MBA). *Accreditation:* AACSB. *Program availability:* Part-time, evening/weekend. *Faculty:* 29 full-time (9 women), 7 part-time/adjunct (3 women). *Students:* 163 full-time (72 women), 42 part-time (19 women); includes 36 minority (13 Black or African American, non-Hispanic/Latino; 9 Asian, non-Hispanic/Latino; 5 Hispanic/Latino; 9 Two or more races, non-Hispanic/Latino), 10 international. Average age 30. 135 applicants, 96% accepted, 102 enrolled. In 2018, 110 master's awarded. *Entrance requirements:* For master's, GMAT, 2 years of work experience (MBA). Additional exam requirements/recommendations for international students: Required—TOEFL (minimum score 550 paper-based). *Application deadline:* For fall admission, 7/1 for domestic and international students; for spring admission, 11/1 for domestic and international students. Applications are processed on a rolling basis. Application fee: $50. Electronic applications accepted. *Expenses:* Contact institution. *Financial support:* In 2018–19, 86 students received support. Scholarships/grants, tuition waivers (partial), and unspecified assistantships available. Financial award application deadline: 7/1; financial award applicants required to submit FAFSA. *Faculty research:* Music business, strategy, ethics, finance, accounting systems. *Unit head:* Dr. Patrick Raines, Dean, 615-460-6480, Fax: 615-460-6455, E-mail: pat.raines@belmont.edu. *Application contact:* Dr. Patrick Raines, Dean, 615-460-6480, Fax: 615-460-6455, E-mail: pat.raines@belmont.edu.

Benedictine University, Graduate Programs, Program in Accountancy, Lisle, IL 60532. Offers MS. *Program availability:* Part-time, evening/weekend. *Faculty:* 2 full-time (0 women), 5 part-time/adjunct (1 woman). *Students:* 18 part-time (10 women); includes 10 minority (6 Asian, non-Hispanic/Latino; 4 Hispanic/Latino). Average age 31. 9 applicants, 89% accepted, 7 enrolled. In 2018, 8 master's awarded. *Entrance requirements:* For master's, GRE or GMAT or completed test waiver form, official transcripts; 2 letters of reference from individuals familiar with the applicant's professional or academic work, excluding family or personal friends; current résumé listing chronological work history; a 1-2 page essay addressing educational and career goals; personal interview may be required prior to an admission decision. Additional exam requirements/recommendations for international students: Required—TOEFL (minimum score 550 paper-based; 79 iBT), IELTS (minimum score 6.5). *Application deadline:* Applications are processed on a rolling basis. Application fee: $40. Electronic applications accepted. *Unit head:* John Draut, Director, 630-829-1937, E-mail: jdraut@ben.edu. *Application contact:* John Draut, Director, 630-829-1937, E-mail: jdraut@ben.edu.

Benedictine University, Graduate Programs, Program in Business Administration, Lisle, IL 60532. Offers accounting (MBA); entrepreneurship and managing innovation (MBA); financial management (MBA); health administration (MBA); human resource management (MBA); information systems security (MBA); international business (MBA); management consulting (MBA); management information systems (MBA); marketing management (MBA); operations management and logistics (MBA); organizational leadership (MBA). *Program availability:* Part-time, evening/weekend, 100% online, blended/hybrid learning. *Faculty:* 7 full-time (1 woman), 36 part-time/adjunct (10 women). *Students:* 110 full-time (71 women), 500 part-time (302 women); includes 104 minority (34 Black or African American, non-Hispanic/Latino; 1 American Indian or Alaska Native, non-Hispanic/Latino; 41 Asian, non-Hispanic/Latino; 23 Hispanic/Latino; 5 Native Hawaiian or other Pacific Islander, non-Hispanic/Latino), 7 international. Average age 33. 251 applicants, 84% accepted, 202 enrolled. In 2018, 345 master's awarded. *Entrance requirements:* For master's, GMAT or GRE test scores or completed test waiver form, official transcripts; 2 letters of reference from individuals familiar with the applicant's professional or academic work, excluding family or personal friends; a 1-2 page essay addressing educational and career goals; current résumé listing chronological work history; personal interview may be required prior to an admission decision. Additional exam requirements/recommendations for international students: Required—TOEFL (minimum score 550 paper-based; 79 iBT), IELTS (minimum score 6.5). *Application deadline:* Applications are processed on a rolling basis. Application fee: $40. Electronic applications accepted. *Unit head:* Ricky Holman, Assistant Professor, 630-829-1936, E-mail: rholman@ben.edu. *Application contact:* Ricky Holman, Assistant Professor, 630-829-1936, E-mail: rholman@ben.edu.

Bentley University, McCallum Graduate School of Business, Masters in Accountancy, Waltham, MA 02452-4705. Offers MSA. *Accreditation:* AACSB. *Program availability:* Part-time, evening/weekend. *Faculty:* 118 full-time (38 women), 25 part-time/adjunct (4 women). *Students:* 139 full-time (87 women), 44 part-time (30 women); includes 30 minority (4 Black or African American, non-Hispanic/Latino; 20 Asian, non-Hispanic/Latino; 5 Hispanic/Latino; 1 Two or more races, non-Hispanic/Latino), 82 international. Average age 26. 243 applicants, 91% accepted, 95 enrolled. In 2018, 158 master's awarded. *Entrance requirements:* For master's, GMAT or GRE General Test (may be waived for qualified applicants), Transcripts; Resume; Two essays; Two letters of recommendation; Interview (may be requested by Bentley). Additional exam requirements/recommendations for international students: Required—TOEFL (minimum score 100) or IELTS (minimum score 7). *Application deadline:* For fall admission, 7/31 for domestic students, 6/30 for international students; for spring admission, 1/1 for domestic students, 11/1 for international students. Applications are processed on a rolling basis. Application fee: $150. Electronic applications accepted. *Financial support:* In 2018–19, 80 students received support. Scholarships/grants and unspecified assistantships available. Financial award application deadline: 6/1; financial award applicants required to submit FAFSA. *Faculty research:* Audit risk assessment; ethics in accounting; corporate governance; accounting information systems and management

control; tax policy, forensic accounting. *Unit head:* Leonard Pepe, Lecturer and MSA/MSAA Program Director, 781-891-2470, E-mail: lpepe@bentley.edu. *Application contact:* Office of Graduate Admissions, 781-891-2108, E-mail: applygrad@bentley.edu.
Website: https://www.bentley.edu/academics/graduate-programs/masters-accounting

Bentley University, McCallum Graduate School of Business, PhD in Accountancy, Waltham, MA 02452-4705. Offers PhD. *Faculty:* 20 full-time (6 women). *Students:* 6 full-time (all women), 2 international. Average age 29. *Degree requirements:* For doctorate, comprehensive exam, thesis/dissertation. *Entrance requirements:* For doctorate, GMAT or GRE General Test, master's degree; official copies of transcripts; research statement; personal statement; 3 letters of recommendation; curriculum vitae; interview. Additional exam requirements/recommendations for international students: Required—The minimum acceptable score for the TOEFL is 100 and 7 for IELTS. *Application deadline:* For fall admission, 1/6 for domestic and international students. Electronic applications accepted. *Financial support:* In 2018–19, 6 students received support. Scholarships/grants available. Financial award application deadline: 6/1; financial award applicants required to submit FAFSA. *Faculty research:* Auditing; accounting information systems; capital markets; governance and control; judgment and decision-making. *Unit head:* Patricia A. Caffrey, Administrative Director of PhD Programs, 781-891-2541, E-mail: pacaffrey@bentley.edu. *Application contact:* Bentley PhD Programs, 781-891-2404, E-mail: phd@bentley.edu.
Website: https://www.bentley.edu/academics/phd-programs/programs

Binghamton University, State University of New York, Graduate School, School of Management, Program in Accounting, Binghamton, NY 13902-6000. Offers MS. *Program availability:* Part-time, evening/weekend. *Entrance requirements:* For master's, GMAT. Additional exam requirements/recommendations for international students: Required—TOEFL (minimum score 90 iBT). Electronic applications accepted.

Bloomfield College, Program in Accounting, Bloomfield, NJ 07003-9981. Offers MS.

Bloomsburg University of Pennsylvania, School of Graduate Studies, Zeigler College of Business, Program in Accounting, Bloomsburg, PA 17815-1301. Offers M Acc. *Program availability:* Part-time, evening/weekend. *Degree requirements:* For master's, minimum QPA of 3.0. *Entrance requirements:* For master's, GRE/GMAT (waived for BU accounting majors with minimum GPA of 3.0 in accounting classes and overall), 2 letters of recommendation, resume. Additional exam requirements/recommendations for international students: Required—TOEFL, IELTS. Electronic applications accepted.

Bluffton University, Graduate Programs in Business, Bluffton, OH 45817. Offers accounting and financial management (MBA); health care management (MBA); leadership (MAOM, MBA); production and operations management (MBA); sustainability management (MBA). *Program availability:* Evening/weekend, blended/hybrid learning, videoconference. *Faculty:* 4 full-time (2 women), 5 part-time/adjunct (1 woman). *Students:* 38 full-time (22 women), 1 part-time (0 women); includes 11 minority (6 Black or African American, non-Hispanic/Latino; 3 Hispanic/Latino; 2 Two or more races, non-Hispanic/Latino). Average age 33. In 2018, 25 master's awarded. *Degree requirements:* For master's, integrated research project (for some programs). *Entrance requirements:* For master's, current resume, official transcript, bachelor's degree, minimum GPA of 3.0, personal essay. Additional exam requirements/recommendations for international students: Recommended—TOEFL (minimum score 550 paper-based). *Application deadline:* For fall admission, 7/31 priority date for domestic and international students. Applications are processed on a rolling basis. Electronic applications accepted. *Expenses:* Contact institution. *Financial support:* Unspecified assistantships and faculty/staff grants available. Financial award applicants required to submit FAFSA. *Unit head:* Dr. Melissa Green, Director of Graduate Programs in Business, 419-358-3447, E-mail: greenm@bluffton.edu. *Application contact:* Shelby Koenig, Enrollment Counselor for Graduate Program, 419-3583684, E-mail: koenigs@bluffton.edu.
Website: https://www.bluffton.edu/ags/index.aspx

Bob Jones University, Graduate Programs, Greenville, SC 29614. Offers accountancy (MS); Bible (MA); Bible translation (MA); Biblical studies (Certificate); business administration (MBA); church history (MA, PhD); church ministries (MA); church music (MM); cinema and video production (MA); counseling (MS); curriculum and instruction (Ed D); divinity (M Div); dramatic production (MA); educational leadership (MS, Ed D, Ed S); elementary education (M Ed, MAT); English (M Ed, MA, MAT); fine arts (MA); graphic design (MA); history (M Ed, MA); illustration (MA); interpretative speech (MA); mathematics (M Ed, MAT); medical missions (Certificate); ministry (MM, D Min); multi-categorical special education (M Ed, MAT); music (M Ed); New Testament interpretation (PhD); Old Testament interpretation (PhD); orchestral instrument performance (MM); organ performance (MM); pastoral studies (MA); personnel services (MS, Ed S); piano pedagogy (MM); piano performance (MM); platform arts (MA); rhetoric and public address (MA); secondary education (M Ed); studio art (MA); teaching Bible (MA); theology (MA, PhD); voice performance (MM); youth ministries (MA); M Div/MM.

Boise State University, College of Business and Economics, Department of Accountancy, Boise, ID 83725-0399. Offers accountancy (MSA); accountancy taxation (MSAT). *Accreditation:* AACSB. *Program availability:* Part-time. *Entrance requirements:* For master's, GMAT, minimum GPA of 3.0. Additional exam requirements/recommendations for international students: Required—TOEFL (minimum score 587 paper-based; 95 iBT), IELTS (minimum score 6.5). Electronic applications accepted.

Boston College, Carroll School of Management, Programs in Accounting, Chestnut Hill, MA 02467-3800. Offers MSA. *Entrance requirements:* For master's, GMAT, GRE, recommendations, resume, transcript. Additional exam requirements/recommendations for international students: Required—TOEFL (minimum score 600 paper-based, 100 iBT), IELTS (minimum score 7.5), or PTE (minimum score 68). Electronic applications accepted. *Faculty research:* Financial reporting, auditing, tax planning, financial statement analysis.

Bowling Green State University, Graduate College, College of Business, Program in Accountancy, Bowling Green, OH 43403. Offers M Acc. *Accreditation:* AACSB. *Program availability:* Part-time. *Degree requirements:* For master's, thesis or alternative. *Entrance requirements:* For master's, GMAT. Additional exam requirements/recommendations for international students: Required—TOEFL. Electronic applications accepted. *Faculty research:* Financial reporting and auditing, accounting information systems, taxation.

Bradley University, The Graduate School, Foster College of Business, Program in Accounting, Peoria, IL 61625-0002. Offers MSA. *Accreditation:* AACSB. *Program availability:* Part-time, evening/weekend. *Faculty:* 6 full-time (2 women). *Students:* 2 full-time (1 woman), 2 part-time (0 women). Average age 34. In 2018, 23 master's awarded. *Degree requirements:* For master's, comprehensive exam. *Entrance requirements:* For master's, GMAT, 2 letters of recommendation. Additional exam requirements/recommendations for international students: Required—TOEFL (minimum score 550 paper-based; 79 iBT), IELTS (minimum score 6.5). *Application deadline:* For fall admission, 5/15 priority date for domestic and international students; for spring admission, 10/15 priority date for domestic and international students. Applications are processed on a rolling basis. Application fee: $40 ($50 for international students). Electronic applications accepted. *Expenses: Tuition:* Part-time $890 per credit. *Required fees:* $50 per unit. *Financial support:* In 2018–19, 3 students received support, including 1 research assistantship with full and partial tuition reimbursement available (averaging $8,010 per year); career-related internships or fieldwork, institutionally sponsored loans, scholarships/grants, tuition waivers (partial), and unspecified assistantships also available. Support available to part-time students. Financial award application deadline: 4/1. *Unit head:* Stephen Kerr, Chairperson, 309-677-2283, E-mail: skerr@bradley.edu. *Application contact:* Rachel Webb, Director of On-Campus Graduate Admissions & International Student and Scholar Services, 309-677-2375, E-mail: rkwebb@bradley.edu.
Website: http://www.bradley.edu/academic/colleges/fcba/education/grad/msa/

Brandman University, School of Business and Professional Studies, Irvine, CA 92618. Offers accounting (MBA); business administration (MBA); business intelligence and data analytics (MBA); e-business strategic management (MBA); entrepreneurship (MBA); finance (MBA); health administration (MBA); human resources (MBA, MS); international business (MBA); marketing (MBA); organizational leadership (MA, MBA, MPA); public administration (MPA).

Brenau University, Sydney O. Smith Graduate School, College of Business and Mass Communication, Gainesville, GA 30501. Offers accounting (MBA); business administration (MBA); healthcare management (MBA); organizational leadership (MS); project management (MBA). *Accreditation:* ACBSP. *Program availability:* Part-time, evening/weekend, online learning. *Degree requirements:* For master's, comprehensive exam (for some programs). *Entrance requirements:* For master's, resume, minimum undergraduate GPA of 2.5. Additional exam requirements/recommendations for international students: Required—TOEFL (minimum score 500 paper-based; 61 iBT); Recommended—IELTS (minimum score 5). Electronic applications accepted. *Expenses:* Contact institution.

Bridgewater State University, College of Graduate Studies, Ricciardi College of Business, Department of Accounting and Finance, Bridgewater, MA 02325. Offers MSM. *Program availability:* Part-time, evening/weekend. *Entrance requirements:* For master's, GMAT.

Brock University, Faculty of Graduate Studies, Faculty of Business, Program in Accountancy, St. Catharines, ON L2S 3A1, Canada. Offers M Acc. *Degree requirements:* For master's, thesis or alternative. *Entrance requirements:* For master's, honours degree. Additional exam requirements/recommendations for international students: Required—TOEFL (minimum score 550 paper-based; 80 iBT), IELTS (minimum score 6.5), TWE (minimum score 4.5). Electronic applications accepted.

Brooklyn College of the City University of New York, School of Business, Brooklyn, NY 11210-2889. Offers accounting (MS); business administration (MS), including economic analysis, general business, global business and finance. *Program availability:* Part-time, evening/weekend. *Degree requirements:* For master's, comprehensive exam, thesis or alternative. *Entrance requirements:* For master's, GMAT, 2 letters of recommendation. Additional exam requirements/recommendations for international students: Required—TOEFL (minimum score 550 paper-based; 79 iBT). Electronic applications accepted. *Faculty research:* Econometrics, environmental economics, microeconomics, macroeconomics, taxation.

Bryant University, Graduate School of Business, Smithfield, RI 02917. Offers accounting (MPAC); business administration (MBA); taxation (MST). *Program availability:* Part-time, evening/weekend, 100% online. *Faculty:* 31 full-time (8 women), 6 part-time/adjunct (2 women). *Students:* 77 full-time (31 women), 106 part-time (46 women); includes 32 minority (7 Black or African American, non-Hispanic/Latino; 1 American Indian or Alaska Native, non-Hispanic/Latino; 9 Asian, non-Hispanic/Latino; 8 Hispanic/Latino; 7 Two or more races, non-Hispanic/Latino), 8 international. Average age 28. 215 applicants, 66% accepted, 96 enrolled. In 2018, 124 master's awarded. *Degree requirements:* For master's, comprehensive exam (for some programs). *Entrance requirements:* For master's, GMAT, resume, recommendation, college transcripts. Additional exam requirements/recommendations for international students: Required—TOEFL (minimum score 580 paper-based; 95 iBT). *Application deadline:* For fall admission, 7/15 for domestic and international students; for spring admission, 11/15 for domestic and international students; for summer admission, 4/15 for domestic and international students. Applications are processed on a rolling basis. Application fee: $80. Electronic applications accepted. *Expenses:* Contact institution. *Financial support:* In 2018–19, 95 fellowships with full and partial tuition reimbursements (averaging $9,825 per year), 9 research assistantships with full and partial tuition reimbursements (averaging $7,100 per year) were awarded; scholarships/grants and unspecified assistantships also available. Support available to part-time students. Financial award application deadline: 2/15; financial award applicants required to submit FAFSA. *Faculty research:* International business, public sector auditing, taxation of partnerships, information systems security, financial markets microstructure. *Unit head:* Jamie R Grenon, Director, Graduate Programs Office, 401-232-6707, E-mail: jgrenon@bryant.edu. *Application contact:* Jeanne Creighton, Senior Admissions Assistant, 401-232-6230, Fax: 401-232-6494, E-mail: graduateprograms@bryant.edu.
Website: http://gradschool.bryant.edu/business/

Cabrini University, Academic Affairs, Radnor, PA 19087. Offers accounting (M Acc); autism spectrum disorder (M Ed); biological sciences (MS), including civic leadership; criminology and criminal justice (MA); curriculum, instruction, and assessment (M Ed); educational leadership (M Ed, Ed D), including curriculum and instructional leadership (Ed D), preK-12 leadership (Ed D); English as a second language (M Ed); organizational leadership (DBA, PhD); preK to 4 (M Ed); reading specialist (M Ed); secondary education (M Ed), including biology, chemistry, English, English/communication, mathematics, social studies; special education grades 7-12 (M Ed); special education preK-8 (M Ed); teaching and learning (M Ed). *Program availability:* Part-time, evening/weekend. *Degree requirements:* For master's, comprehensive exam (for some programs), thesis (for some programs); for doctorate, comprehensive exam (for some programs), thesis/dissertation. *Entrance requirements:* For master's, professional resume, personal statement, two recommendations, official transcripts; for doctorate, official transcripts, minimum master's GPA of 3.0, two recommendations, interview with admissions committee. Additional exam requirements/recommendations for international students: Required—TOEFL (minimum score 80 iBT). Electronic applications accepted. Application fee is waived when completed online. *Expenses:* Contact institution.

Cairn University, School of Business, Langhorne, PA 19047-2990. Offers accounting (MBA); business administration (MBA); international entrepreneurship (MBA); nonprofit leadership (MBA); organizational leadership (MSOL, Postbaccalaureate Certificate). *Program availability:* Part-time, evening/weekend, 100% online, blended/hybrid learning. *Entrance requirements:* Additional exam requirements/recommendations for international students: Required—TOEFL (minimum score 550 paper-based). Electronic applications accepted. Application fee is waived when completed online. *Expenses:* Contact institution.

California Baptist University, Program in Accounting, Riverside, CA 92504-3206. Offers MS. *Program availability:* Part-time, evening/weekend, online only, 100% online. *Faculty:* 4 full-time (2 women), 1 part-time/adjunct (0 women). *Students:* 12 full-time (5 women), 15 part-time (8 women); includes 11 minority (2 Black or African American, non-Hispanic/Latino; 2 Asian, non-Hispanic/Latino; 5 Hispanic/Latino; 1 Native Hawaiian or other Pacific Islander, non-Hispanic/Latino; 1 Two or more races, non-Hispanic/Latino). Average age 32. 25 applicants, 44% accepted, 10 enrolled. In 2018, 10 master's

awarded. *Degree requirements:* For master's, Interdisciplinary Capstone Project. *Entrance requirements:* For master's, minimum cumulative GPA of 2.5, prerequisite courses completed with minimum C grade, two letters of recommendation, 500-word essay, current resume. Additional exam requirements/recommendations for international students: Required—TOEFL (minimum score 80 iBT). *Application deadline:* For fall admission, 8/1 priority date for domestic students, 7/1 priority date for international students; for spring admission, 12/1 priority date for domestic students, 11/1 priority date for international students. Applications are processed on a rolling basis. Application fee: $45. Electronic applications accepted. Application fee is waived when completed online. *Expenses:* $662 per unit. *Financial support:* In 2018–19, 9 students received support. Federal Work-Study and scholarships/grants available. Financial award applicants required to submit CSS PROFILE or FAFSA. *Faculty research:* Financial stability, social entrepreneurship, cross-sector collaboration, business and government relations. *Unit head:* Pamela Daly, Vice President, Online and Professional Studies, 951-343-3901, E-mail: pdaly@calbaptist.edu. *Application contact:* Dr. Julianna Browning, Program Director, Accounting, 951-343-3972, E-mail: jbrowning@calbaptist.edu.
Website: http://www.cbuonline.edu/programs/program/master-of-science-in-accounting

California Baptist University, Program in Business Administration, Riverside, CA 92504-3206. Offers accounting (MBA); construction management (MBA); healthcare management (MBA); management (MBA). *Accreditation:* ACBSP. *Program availability:* Part-time, evening/weekend, 100% online, blended/hybrid learning. *Faculty:* 22 full-time (7 women), 14 part-time/adjunct (3 women). *Students:* 124 full-time (65 women), 71 part-time (38 women); includes 108 minority (16 Black or African American, non-Hispanic/Latino; 11 Asian, non-Hispanic/Latino; 74 Hispanic/Latino; 1 Native Hawaiian or other Pacific Islander, non-Hispanic/Latino; 6 Two or more races, non-Hispanic/Latino), 21 international. Average age 36. 71 applicants, 77% accepted, 55 enrolled. In 2018, 131 master's awarded. *Degree requirements:* For master's, thesis, Interdisciplinary Capstone Project. *Entrance requirements:* For master's, GMAT, minimum GPA of 2.5; two recommendations; comprehensive essay; resume; interview. Additional exam requirements/recommendations for international students: Required—TOEFL (minimum score 80 iBT). *Application deadline:* For fall admission, 8/1 priority date for domestic students, 7/1 for international students; for spring admission, 12/1 priority date for domestic students, 11/1 for international students. Applications are processed on a rolling basis. Application fee: $45. Electronic applications accepted. *Expenses:* $662 per unit. *Financial support:* In 2018–19, 70 students received support. Federal Work-Study and scholarships/grants available. Financial award applicants required to submit CSS PROFILE or FAFSA. *Faculty research:* Behavioral economics, economic indicators, marketing ethics, international business, microfinance. *Unit head:* Dr. Andrea Scott, Dean, School of Business, 951-343-4701, E-mail: ascott@calbaptist.edu. *Application contact:* Dr. Scott Dunbar, Program Director, Online Masters in Business Administration, 951-343-2193, E-mail: sdunbar@calbaptist.edu.
Website: http://www.calbaptist.edu/mba/about/

California Polytechnic State University, San Luis Obispo, Orfalea College of Business, Program in Accounting, San Luis Obispo, CA 93407. Offers MS. *Students:* 23 full-time (16 women); includes 9 minority (2 Asian, non-Hispanic/Latino; 5 Hispanic/Latino; 1 Native Hawaiian or other Pacific Islander, non-Hispanic/Latino; 1 Two or more races, non-Hispanic/Latino). Average age 23. In 2018, 25 master's awarded. *Degree requirements:* For master's, comprehensive exam. *Entrance requirements:* For master's, GMAT. Additional exam requirements/recommendations for international students: Required—TOEFL (minimum score 80 iBT). *Application deadline:* For fall admission, 4/1 for domestic and international students. Applications are processed on a rolling basis. Electronic applications accepted. *Expenses: Tuition, area resident:* Full-time $7176; part-time $4164 per year. Tuition, state resident: full-time $10,965. Tuition, nonresident: full-time $10,965. *Required fees:* $6336; $3711. *Financial support:* Fellowships, career-related internships or fieldwork, Federal Work-Study, institutionally sponsored loans, scholarships/grants, and unspecified assistantships available. Support available to part-time students. Financial award application deadline: 3/2; financial award applicants required to submit FAFSA. *Faculty research:* Management of high-tech firms, Pacific Rim, capital market structures, economics of environmental policy, marketing of services. *Unit head:* Dr. Scott Dawson, Dean, 805-756-2705, E-mail: scdawson@calpoly.edu. *Application contact:* Dr. Scott Dawson, Dean, 805-756-2705, E-mail: scdawson@calpoly.edu.
Website: http://www.cob.calpoly.edu/gradbusiness/degree-programs/ms-accounting/

California State Polytechnic University, Pomona, Master of Science in Business Administration Program, Pomona, CA 91768-2557. Offers business administration (MS). *Accreditation:* AACSB. *Program availability:* Part-time, evening/weekend. *Students:* 15 full-time (5 women), 9 part-time (3 women); includes 11 minority (1 Black or African American, non-Hispanic/Latino; 6 Asian, non-Hispanic/Latino; 4 Hispanic/Latino), 3 international. Average age 31. 39 applicants, 67% accepted, 18 enrolled. *Entrance requirements:* Additional exam requirements/recommendations for international students: Required—TOEFL (minimum score 550 paper-based). *Application deadline:* Applications are processed on a rolling basis. Application fee: $55. Electronic applications accepted. *Expenses:* Contact institution. *Financial support:* Application deadline: 3/2; applicants required to submit FAFSA. *Unit head:* Dr. Tarique Hossain, Associate Professor/Director of Graduate Programs, 909-869-2362, Fax: 909-869-4559, E-mail: tmhossain@cpp.edu. *Application contact:* Dr. Tarique Hossain, Associate Professor/Director of Graduate Programs, 909-869-2362, Fax: 909-869-4559, E-mail: tmhossain@cpp.edu.
Website: http://www.cpp.edu/~cba/graduate-business-programs/programs/MSBA.shtml

California State Polytechnic University, Pomona, Program in Accountancy, Pomona, CA 91768-2557. Offers MS. *Program availability:* Part-time, evening/weekend. *Students:* 18 full-time (7 women), 7 part-time (4 women); includes 13 minority (7 Asian, non-Hispanic/Latino; 6 Hispanic/Latino), 5 international. Average age 26. 65 applicants, 55% accepted, 21 enrolled. In 2018, 12 master's awarded. *Entrance requirements:* Additional exam requirements/recommendations for international students: Required—TOEFL (minimum score 550 paper-based). *Application deadline:* Applications are processed on a rolling basis. Application fee: $55. Electronic applications accepted. *Expenses:* Contact institution. *Financial support:* Application deadline: 3/2; applicants required to submit FAFSA. *Faculty research:* International accounting, accounting in not-for-profit organizations, auditing. *Unit head:* Dr. Meihua Koo, Assistant Professor/MSA Coordinator, 909-869-4531, Fax: 909-869-4511, E-mail: mkoo@cpp.edu. *Application contact:* Dr. Meihua Koo, Assistant Professor/MSA Coordinator, 909-869-4531, Fax: 909-869-4511, E-mail: mkoo@cpp.edu.
Website: http://www.cpp.edu/~ceu/degree-programs/accountancy/index.shtml

California State University, East Bay, Office of Graduate Studies, College of Business and Economics, Department of Accounting and Finance, Hayward, CA 94542-3000. Offers accountancy (MS). *Program availability:* Part-time, evening/weekend. *Degree requirements:* For master's, comprehensive exam or thesis. *Entrance requirements:* For master's, GMAT, minimum GPA of 2.75. Additional exam requirements/recommendations for international students: Required—TOEFL (minimum score 550 paper-based). Electronic applications accepted.

California State University, Fullerton, Graduate Studies, College of Business and Economics, Department of Accounting, Fullerton, CA 92831-3599. Offers accounting (MBA, MS). *Accreditation:* AACSB. *Program availability:* Part-time. *Degree requirements:* For master's, thesis or alternative, project. *Entrance requirements:* For master's, GMAT, minimum AACSB index of 950. Electronic applications accepted.

California State University, Los Angeles, Graduate Studies, College of Business and Economics, Department of Accounting, Los Angeles, CA 90032-8530. Offers MBA. *Program availability:* Part-time, evening/weekend. *Degree requirements:* For master's, comprehensive exam (MBA), thesis (MS). *Entrance requirements:* For master's, GMAT, minimum GPA of 2.5 during previous 2 years of course work. Additional exam requirements/recommendations for international students: Required—TOEFL (minimum score 550 paper-based). Electronic applications accepted.

California State University, Sacramento, College of Business Administration, Sacramento, CA 95819. Offers accountancy (MS); business administration (IMBA, MBA); human resources (MBA); urban land development (MBA). *Accreditation:* AACSB. *Program availability:* Part-time, evening/weekend, 100% online, blended/hybrid learning. *Degree requirements:* For master's, comprehensive exam, project, thesis, or writing proficiency exam. *Entrance requirements:* For master's, GMAT. Additional exam requirements/recommendations for international students: Required—TOEFL (minimum score 550 paper-based; 80 iBT). Electronic applications accepted. *Expenses:* Contact institution.

California State University, San Bernardino, Graduate Studies, College of Business and Public Administration, Program in Accountancy, San Bernardino, CA 92407. Offers MSA. *Faculty:* 6 full-time (0 women), 1 part-time/adjunct (0 women). *Students:* 34 full-time (16 women), 45 part-time (22 women); includes 47 minority (3 Black or African American, non-Hispanic/Latino; 8 Asian, non-Hispanic/Latino; 34 Hispanic/Latino; 1 Native Hawaiian or other Pacific Islander, non-Hispanic/Latino; 1 Two or more races, non-Hispanic/Latino), 17 international. Average age 29. 38 applicants, 58% accepted, 14 enrolled. In 2018, 55 master's awarded. *Application deadline:* For fall admission, 7/16 for domestic students. Application fee: $55. *Unit head:* Dr. Lawrence C. Rose, Dean, 909-537-3703, E-mail: lrose@csusb.edu. *Application contact:* Dr. Dorota Huizinga, Dean of Graduate Studies, 909-537-3064, Fax: 909-537-5078, E-mail: dorota.huizinga@csusb.edu.

California State University, San Bernardino, Graduate Studies, College of Business and Public Administration, Program in Business Administration, San Bernardino, CA 92407. Offers accounting (MBA); entrepreneurship (MBA); finance (MBA); global business (MBA); information management (MBA); information security (MBA); management (MBA); supply chain management (MBA). *Accreditation:* AACSB. *Program availability:* Part-time, evening/weekend, online learning. *Faculty:* 5 full-time (4 women), 7 part-time/adjunct (3 women). *Students:* 40 full-time (14 women), 163 part-time (72 women); includes 99 minority (7 Black or African American, non-Hispanic/Latino; 15 Asian, non-Hispanic/Latino; 71 Hispanic/Latino; 6 Two or more races, non-Hispanic/Latino), 58 international. Average age 32. 342 applicants, 52% accepted, 91 enrolled. In 2018, 106 master's awarded. *Degree requirements:* For master's, comprehensive exam, thesis. *Entrance requirements:* Additional exam requirements/recommendations for international students: Required—TOEFL. *Application deadline:* For fall admission, 7/16 for domestic students, 7/20 for international students; for winter admission, 10/23 for domestic students, 10/20 for international students; for spring admission, 1/22 for domestic students, 1/20 for international students. Application fee: $55. *Expenses:* Contact institution. *Financial support:* Application deadline: 3/1. *Unit head:* Dr. Lawrence C. Rose, Dean, 909-537-3703, Fax: 909-537-7026, E-mail: lrose@csusb.edu. *Application contact:* Ernest Silvers, MBA Program Director, 909-537-5703, E-mail: esilvers@csusb.edu.
Website: http://mba.csusb.edu/

California Western School of Law, Graduate and Professional Programs, San Diego, CA 92101-3090. Offers law (JD); Spanish language in trial advocacy (LL M); JD/MBA; JD/MSW; MCL/LL M. JD/MSW and JD/MBA offered jointly with San Diego State University. *Accreditation:* ABA. *Program availability:* Part-time. *Entrance requirements:* For doctorate, LSAT. Additional exam requirements/recommendations for international students: Required—TOEFL. Electronic applications accepted. *Faculty research:* Biotechnology, health law, international law, labor and employment law, business law.

Calvin College, Program in Accounting, Grand Rapids, MI 49546-4388. Offers M Acc. *Program availability:* Part-time.

Canisius College, Graduate Division, Richard J. Wehle School of Business, Department of Accounting, Buffalo, NY 14208-1098. Offers accounting (MBA); forensic accounting (MS); professional accounting (MBA). *Program availability:* Part-time, evening/weekend. *Students:* Average age 27. 47 applicants, 81% accepted, 24 enrolled. In 2018, 49 master's awarded. *Entrance requirements:* For master's, GMAT, GRE, official transcript from colleges attended, current resume. Additional exam requirements/recommendations for international students: Required—TOEFL (minimum score 550 paper-based, 80 iBT), IELTS (minimum score 6.5), or CAEL (minimum score 70). *Application deadline:* For fall admission, 7/1 priority date for domestic students; for spring admission, 11/1 priority date for domestic students. Applications are processed on a rolling basis. Application fee: $0. Electronic applications accepted. *Expenses: Tuition:* Part-time $820 per credit hour. *Required fees:* $25 per semester. One-time fee: $65 part-time. Tuition and fees vary according to program. *Financial support:* Career-related internships or fieldwork, Federal Work-Study, scholarships/grants, and unspecified assistantships available. Financial award application deadline: 4/30; financial award applicants required to submit FAFSA. *Faculty research:* Auditing (process and operational factors), fraud from a global perspective, managing risk in software development, valuation of intellectual property. *Unit head:* Dr. Ian J. Redpath, Chair/Professor, 716-888-2880, E-mail: redpathi@canisius.edu. *Application contact:* Dr. Ian J. Redpath, Chair/Professor, 716-888-2880, E-mail: redpathi@canisius.edu.
Website: http://www.canisius.edu/graduate/

Capella University, School of Business and Technology, Doctoral Programs in Business, Minneapolis, MN 55402. Offers accounting (DBA, PhD); business intelligence (DBA); finance (DBA, PhD); general business management (PhD); human resource management (DBA, PhD); leadership (DBA, PhD); management education (PhD); marketing (DBA, PhD); project management (DBA, PhD); strategy and innovation (DBA, PhD). *Accreditation:* ACBSP.

Capella University, School of Business and Technology, Master's Programs in Business, Minneapolis, MN 55402. Offers accounting (MBA); business analysis (MS); business intelligence (MBA); entrepreneurship (MBA); finance (MBA); general business administration (MBA); general human resource management (MS); general leadership (MS); health care management (MBA); human resource management (MBA); marketing (MBA); project management (MBA, MS). *Accreditation:* ACBSP.

Carnegie Mellon University, Tepper School of Business, Program in Accounting, Pittsburgh, PA 15213-3891. Offers PhD. *Accreditation:* AACSB. *Degree requirements:* For doctorate, thesis/dissertation. *Entrance requirements:* For doctorate, GRE.

Case Western Reserve University, Weatherhead School of Management, Department of Accountancy, Cleveland, OH 44106. Offers M Acc, PhD, MBA/M Acc. *Accreditation:*

AACSB. *Program availability:* Evening/weekend. *Degree requirements:* For doctorate, thesis/dissertation. *Entrance requirements:* For master's and doctorate, GMAT. *Expenses: Tuition:* Full-time $45,168; part-time $1939 per credit hour. *Required fees:* $36; $18 per semester. $18 per semester. *Faculty research:* Auditing, regulation, financial reporting, public interest, efficient markets.

The Catholic University of America, Busch School of Business and Economics, Washington, DC 20064. Offers accounting (MS); business analysis (MSBA); integral economic development management (MA); integral economic development policy (MA); management (MS), including Federal contract management, human resource management, leadership and management, project management, sales management. *Program availability:* Part-time. *Faculty:* 38 full-time (8 women), 21 part-time/adjunct (9 women). *Students:* 57 full-time (11 women), 1 (woman) part-time; includes 24 minority (3 Black or African American, non-Hispanic/Latino; 1 American Indian or Alaska Native, non-Hispanic/Latino; 8 Asian, non-Hispanic/Latino; 7 Hispanic/Latino; 5 Two or more races, non-Hispanic/Latino; 1 international. Average age 33. 96 applicants, 79% accepted, 56 enrolled. In 2018, 58 master's awarded. *Degree requirements:* For master's, comprehensive exam (for some programs). *Entrance requirements:* For master's, GRE General Test, statement of purpose, official copies of academic transcripts, three letters of recommendation. Additional exam requirements/recommendations for international students: Required—TOEFL (minimum score 550 paper-based; 80 iBT). *Application deadline:* For fall admission, 7/15 priority date for domestic students, 7/1 for international students; for spring admission, 11/15 priority date for domestic students, 11/1 for international students. Applications are processed on a rolling basis. Application fee: $55. Electronic applications accepted. *Expenses:* Contact institution. *Financial support:* Fellowships, research assistantships, teaching assistantships, Federal Work-Study, scholarships/grants, tuition waivers (full and partial), and unspecified assistantships available. Financial award application deadline: 2/1; financial award applicants required to submit FAFSA. *Faculty research:* Integrity of the marketing process, economics of energy and the environment, emerging markets, social change, international finance and economic development. *Unit head:* Dr. Andrew Abela, Dean, 202-319-6130, E-mail: DeanAbela@cua.edu. *Application contact:* Dr. Steven Brown, Director of Graduate Admissions, 202-319-5057, Fax: 202-319-6533, E-mail: cua-admissions@cua.edu. Website: https://business.catholic.edu/

Centenary University, Program in Professional Accounting, Hackettstown, NJ 07840-2100. Offers MS. *Program availability:* Part-time, evening/weekend, online learning.

Central Connecticut State University, School of Graduate Studies, School of Business, Department of Accounting, New Britain, CT 06050-4010. Offers MSA. *Program availability:* Part-time, evening/weekend. *Faculty:* 7 full-time (4 women), 4 part-time/adjunct (0 women). *Students:* 35 full-time (18 women), 46 part-time (28 women); includes 26 minority (2 Black or African American, non-Hispanic/Latino; 10 Asian, non-Hispanic/Latino; 12 Hispanic/Latino; 2 Two or more races, non-Hispanic/Latino). Average age 29. 60 applicants, 83% accepted, 32 enrolled. In 2018, 15 master's awarded. *Degree requirements:* For master's, thesis or alternative. *Entrance requirements:* For master's, GMAT or GRE, minimum undergraduate GPA of 2.7, resume. Additional exam requirements/recommendations for international students: Required—TOEFL (minimum score 550 paper-based; 79 iBT); Recommended—IELTS (minimum score 6.5). *Application deadline:* For fall admission, 6/1 for domestic students, 5/1 for international students; for spring admission, 11/1 for domestic and international students. Applications are processed on a rolling basis. Application fee: $50. Electronic applications accepted. *Expenses: Tuition, area resident:* Full-time $7027; part-time $388 per credit. Tuition, state resident: full-time $9750; part-time $388 per credit. Tuition, nonresident: full-time $18,102; part-time $388 per credit. *International tuition:* $18,102 full-time. *Required fees:* $266 per semester. *Financial support:* In 2018–19, 14 students received support. Career-related internships or fieldwork, Federal Work-Study, scholarships/grants, and unspecified assistantships available. Support available to part-time students. Financial award application deadline: 3/1; financial award applicants required to submit FAFSA. *Unit head:* Monique Durant, Chair, 860-832-3220, E-mail: durantmon@ccsu.edu. *Application contact:* Patricia Gardner, Associate Director of Graduate Admissions, 860-832-2350, Fax: 860-832-2362. Website: http://www.ccsu.edu/accounting/

Central Michigan University, College of Graduate Studies, College of Business Administration, Department of Business Information Systems, Mount Pleasant, MI 48859. Offers business computing (Graduate Certificate); information systems (MS), including accounting information systems, business informatics, enterprise systems using SAP software, information systems. *Program availability:* Part-time, evening/weekend. *Degree requirements:* For master's, thesis or alternative. Electronic applications accepted. *Faculty research:* Enterprise software, electronic commerce, decision support systems, ethical issues in information systems, information technology management and teaching issues.

Central Michigan University, College of Graduate Studies, College of Business Administration, MBA Program, Mount Pleasant, MI 48859. Offers accounting (MBA); business economics (MBA); consulting (MBA); finance (MBA); general business (MBA); human resource management (MBA); information systems (MBA); international business (MBA); logistics management (MBA); marketing (MBA); value-driven organization (MBA). *Program availability:* Part-time, evening/weekend, online learning. Electronic applications accepted. *Faculty research:* Accounting, consulting, international business, marketing, information systems.

Chaminade University of Honolulu, Graduate, Program in Business Administration, Honolulu, HI 96816-1578. Offers accounting (MBA); business (MBA); island business (MBA); not-for-profit (MBA). *Program availability:* Part-time, evening/weekend, 100% online, blended/hybrid learning. *Faculty:* 8 full-time (4 women), 6 part-time/adjunct (2 women). *Students:* 63 full-time (30 women), 45 part-time (29 women); includes 81 minority (8 Black or African American, non-Hispanic/Latino; 4 American Indian or Alaska Native, non-Hispanic/Latino; 34 Asian, non-Hispanic/Latino; 3 Hispanic/Latino; 32 Native Hawaiian or other Pacific Islander, non-Hispanic/Latino), 3 international. Average age 32. 25 applicants, 68% accepted, 15 enrolled. In 2018, 47 master's awarded. *Entrance requirements:* For master's, minimum GPA of 3.0, official transcripts, two years or more of work experience. Additional exam requirements/recommendations for international students: Required—TOEFL (minimum score 550 paper-based; 79 iBT). *Application deadline:* Applications are processed on a rolling basis. Application fee: $40. Electronic applications accepted. *Expenses:* $980 per credit; $93 fee per online course. *Financial support:* Applicants required to submit FAFSA. *Unit head:* Dr. Scott J. Schroeder, Director, 808-739-4612, Fax: 808-735-4734, E-mail: mba@chaminade.edu. *Application contact:* Dr. Scott J. Schroeder, Director, 808-739-4612, Fax: 808-735-4734, E-mail: mba@chaminade.edu. Website: https://chaminade.edu/academic-program/mba/

Chapman University, The George L. Argyros School of Business and Economics, Orange, CA 92866. Offers accounting (MS); behavioral and computational economics (MS); business administration (Exec MBA, MBA); JD/MBA. *Accreditation:* AACSB. *Program availability:* Part-time, evening/weekend. Electronic applications accepted. *Expenses:* Contact institution.

Charleston Southern University, College of Business, Charleston, SC 29423-8087. Offers accounting (MBA); finance (MBA); general management (MBA); human resource

management (MS); leadership (MBA); management information systems (MBA); organizational leadership (MA). *Program availability:* Part-time, evening/weekend. *Degree requirements:* For master's, thesis optional. *Entrance requirements:* For master's, GMAT. Additional exam requirements/recommendations for international students: Required—TOEFL (minimum score 550 paper-based; 79 iBT). Electronic applications accepted.

Chatham University, Program in Accounting, Pittsburgh, PA 15232-2826. Offers M Acc, MAC. *Program availability:* Part-time, evening/weekend. *Entrance requirements:* Additional exam requirements/recommendations for international students: Required—TOEFL (minimum score 600 paper-based; 100 iBT), IELTS (minimum score 7), TWE. Electronic applications accepted. Application fee is waived when completed online. *Expenses:* Contact institution.

Christian Brothers University, School of Business, Memphis, TN 38104-5581. Offers accountancy (M Acc); business (MBA); international business (MIB); project management (Certificate); MBA/MIB. *Program availability:* Part-time, evening/weekend. *Entrance requirements:* For master's, GMAT, GRE. Additional exam requirements/recommendations for international students: Required—TOEFL.

City University of Seattle, Graduate Division, School of Management, Seattle, WA 98121. Offers accounting (Certificate); change leadership (MBA, Certificate); computer systems (MS); finance (Certificate); financial management (MBA); general management (MBA); general management-Europe (MBA); global marketing (MBA); human resources management (Certificate); individualized study (MBA); information security (MS); information systems (MBA); leadership (MA); marketing (MBA, Certificate); project management (MBA, MS, Certificate); sustainable business (Certificate); technology management (MBA, Certificate). *Program availability:* Part-time, evening/weekend, online learning. *Degree requirements:* For master's, comprehensive exam (for some programs), thesis (for some programs). *Entrance requirements:* For master's, baccalaureate degree or equivalent from an accredited or otherwise recognized institution. Additional exam requirements/recommendations for international students: Required—TOEFL (minimum score 567 paper-based; 87 iBT); Recommended—IELTS. Electronic applications accepted.

Clarion University of Pennsylvania, College of Business Administration and Information Sciences, Master of Business Administration Program, Clarion, PA 16214. Offers accounting (MBA); finance (MBA); health care administration (MBA); innovation and entrepreneurship (MBA); non-profit business (MBA). *Accreditation:* AACSB. *Program availability:* Part-time, evening/weekend, online only, 100% online. *Faculty:* 7 full-time (0 women), 1 part-time/adjunct (0 women). *Students:* 21 full-time (7 women), 67 part-time (34 women); includes 11 minority (5 Black or African American, non-Hispanic/Latino; 5 Hispanic/Latino; 1 Two or more races, non-Hispanic/Latino), 2 international. Average age 31. 90 applicants, 51% accepted, 38 enrolled. In 2018, 39 master's awarded. *Entrance requirements:* For master's, If GPA is below 3.0 submit the GMAT, minimum QPA of 2.75. Additional exam requirements/recommendations for international students: Required—TOEFL (minimum score 550 paper-based; 80 iBT), Or IELTS score of at least 7.0. Bachelor's degree accredited U.S. college or university is acceptable evidence of English language proficiency. *Application deadline:* For fall admission, 8/1 priority date for domestic students, 7/15 priority date for international students; for winter admission, 11/1 priority date for domestic students; for spring admission, 12/1 priority date for domestic students, 11/15 priority date for international students; for summer admission, 4/1 priority date for domestic students. Applications are processed on a rolling basis. Application fee: $40. Electronic applications accepted. *Expenses: Tuition, area resident:* Part-time $516 per credit hour. Tuition, state resident: part-time $516 per credit hour. Tuition, nonresident: part-time $774 per credit hour. *Required fees:* $159 per credit hour. One-time fee: $50 part-time. Tuition and fees vary according to degree level, campus/location and program. *Financial support:* Federal Work-Study, institutionally sponsored loans, and scholarships/grants available. Financial award application deadline: 3/1; financial award applicants required to submit FAFSA. *Unit head:* Juanice Vega, Assistant to the Dean, 814-393-2600, Fax: 814-393-1910, E-mail: mba@clarion.edu. *Application contact:* Susan Staub, Graduate Admissions Counselor, 814-393-2337, Fax: 814-393-2722, E-mail: gradstudies@clarion.edu. Website: http://www.clarion.edu/admissions/graduate/index.html

Clarion University of Pennsylvania, College of Business Administration and Information Sciences, MS Program in Accounting, Clarion, PA 16214. Offers MS. *Program availability:* Part-time, evening/weekend, online only, 100% online. *Faculty:* 3 full-time (0 women). *Students:* 10 full-time (8 women), 25 part-time (14 women); includes 7 minority (2 Black or African American, non-Hispanic/Latino; 1 American Indian or Alaska Native, non-Hispanic/Latino; 3 Asian, non-Hispanic/Latino; 1 Hispanic/Latino). Average age 32. 44 applicants, 59% accepted, 21 enrolled. In 2018, 10 master's awarded. *Entrance requirements:* For master's, minimum undergraduate GPA of 3.0. Additional exam requirements/recommendations for international students: Required—TOEFL (minimum score 550 paper-based; 80 iBT), Or IELTS score of at least 7.0. Bachelor's degree accredited U.S. college or university is acceptable evidence of English language proficiency. *Application deadline:* For fall admission, 8/1 priority date for domestic students, 7/15 priority date for international students; for winter admission, 11/1 priority date for domestic students; for spring admission, 12/1 priority date for domestic students, 11/15 priority date for international students; for summer admission, 4/1 priority date for domestic students. Applications are processed on a rolling basis. Application fee: $40. Electronic applications accepted. *Expenses: Tuition, area resident:* Part-time $516 per credit hour. Tuition, state resident: part-time $516 per credit hour. Tuition, nonresident: part-time $774 per credit hour. *Required fees:* $159 per credit hour. One-time fee: $50 part-time. Tuition and fees vary according to degree level, campus/location and program. *Financial support:* Federal Work-Study, institutionally sponsored loans, and scholarships/grants available. Financial award application deadline: 3/1; financial award applicants required to submit FAFSA. *Unit head:* Dr. Anthony Grenci, Department Chair, 814-393-2628, E-mail: agrenci@clarion.edu. *Application contact:* Susan Staub, Graduate Admissions Counselor, 814-393-2337, Fax: 814-393-2722, E-mail: gradstudies@clarion.edu.

Clark Atlanta University, School of Business Administration, Department of Accounting, Atlanta, GA 30314. Offers MA. *Program availability:* Part-time. *Entrance requirements:* For master's, GMAT, minimum undergraduate GPA of 2.5. Additional exam requirements/recommendations for international students: Required—TOEFL (minimum score 500 paper-based; 61 iBT). Electronic applications accepted.

Clark University, Graduate School, Graduate School of Management, Business Administration Program, Worcester, MA 01610-1477. Offers accounting (MBA); finance (MBA); information management and business analytics (MBA); management (MBA); marketing (MBA); social change (MBA); sustainability (MBA). *Accreditation:* AACSB. *Program availability:* Part-time, evening/weekend. *Degree requirements:* For master's, thesis optional. *Entrance requirements:* For master's, GMAT or GRE, 2 references, resume or curriculum vitae, personal statement. Additional exam requirements/recommendations for international students: Required—TOEFL (minimum score 575 paper-based; 90 iBT), IELTS (minimum score 6.5). Electronic applications accepted. *Expenses:* Contact institution. *Faculty research:* Marketing, accounting, human resource management, management information systems, business finance.

Accounting

Clark University, Graduate School, Graduate School of Management, Program in Accounting, Worcester, MA 01610-1477. Offers MSA. *Program availability:* Part-time, evening/weekend. *Entrance requirements:* For master's, GMAT or GRE, statement of purpose, resume, two letters of recommendation. Additional exam requirements/recommendations for international students: Required—TOEFL (minimum score 575 paper-based; 90 iBT), IELTS (minimum score 6.5). Electronic applications accepted. *Expenses:* Contact institution.

Clayton State University, School of Graduate Studies, College of Business, Program in Business Administration, Morrow, GA 30260-0285. Offers accounting (MBA); human resource leadership (MBA); international business (MBA); sports and entertainment management (MBA); supply chain management (MBA). *Accreditation:* AACSB. *Program availability:* Part-time, evening/weekend. *Degree requirements:* For master's, thesis. *Entrance requirements:* For master's, GMAT, 3 letters of recommendation; statement of purpose; 2 official transcripts. Additional exam requirements/recommendations for international students: Required—TOEFL (minimum score 550 paper-based; 80 iBT). Electronic applications accepted. *Expenses:* Contact institution.

Clemson University, Graduate School, College of Business, School of Accountancy, Clemson, SC 29634. Offers accounting (MP Acc). *Accreditation:* AACSB. *Program availability:* Part-time. *Faculty:* 24 full-time (8 women), 1 part-time/adjunct (0 women). *Students:* 91 full-time (51 women), 9 part-time (4 women); includes 11 minority (1 Black or African American, non-Hispanic/Latino; 1 American Indian or Alaska Native, non-Hispanic/Latino; 4 Asian, non-Hispanic/Latino; 4 Hispanic/Latino; 1 Two or more races, non-Hispanic/Latino), 2 international. Average age 24. 189 applicants, 80% accepted, 105 enrolled. In 2018, 108 master's awarded. *Entrance requirements:* For master's, GMAT, unofficial transcripts, letters of recommendation. Additional exam requirements/recommendations for international students: Required—TOEFL (minimum score 80 paper-based; 80 iBT); Recommended—IELTS (minimum score 6.5), TSE (minimum score 54). *Application deadline:* For fall admission, 4/15 priority date for international students; for spring admission, 10/15 priority date for international students. Applications are processed on a rolling basis. Application fee: $80 ($90 for international students). Electronic applications accepted. *Expenses:* $6823 per semester full-time resident, $14023 per semester full-time non-resident, $833 per credit hour part-time resident, $1731 per credit hour part-time non-resident, online $1264 per credit hour, $4938 doctoral programs resident, $10405 doctoral programs non-resident, $1144 full-time graduate assistant, other fees may apply per session. *Financial support:* In 2018–19, 20 students received support, including 3 fellowships with full and partial tuition reimbursements available (averaging $1,500 per year); career-related internships or fieldwork and unspecified assistantships also available. Financial award application deadline: 12/31. *Faculty research:* Financial accounting, auditing, managerial accounting. *Unit head:* Dr. Sally Widener, Director, 864-656-1275, E-mail: kwidene@clemson.edu. *Application contact:* Suzanne Pearse, Graduate Program Coordinator, 864-656-0131, E-mail: spearse@clemson.edu.
Website: https://www.clemson.edu/business/departments/accountancy/index.html

Cleveland State University, College of Graduate Studies, Monte Ahuja College of Business, Department of Accounting, Cleveland, OH 44115. Offers financial accounting/audit (M Acc). *Accreditation:* AACSB. *Program availability:* Part-time, evening/weekend. *Faculty:* 13 full-time (3 women), 11 part-time/adjunct (3 women). *Students:* 40 full-time (20 women), 88 part-time (48 women); includes 29 minority (14 Black or African American, non-Hispanic/Latino; 7 Asian, non-Hispanic/Latino; 7 Hispanic/Latino; 1 Two or more races, non-Hispanic/Latino), 15 international. Average age 31. 89 applicants, 85% accepted, 36 enrolled. In 2018, 51 master's awarded. *Entrance requirements:* For master's, GMAT, minimum GPA of 2.75. Additional exam requirements/recommendations for international students: Required—TOEFL (minimum score 550 paper-based; 78 iBT). *Application deadline:* For fall admission, 7/1 priority date for domestic students, 5/15 for international students; for spring admission, 11/15 priority date for domestic students, 11/1 for international students; for summer admission, 4/1 for domestic students, 3/15 for international students. Applications are processed on a rolling basis. Application fee: $40. Electronic applications accepted. *Expenses:* Tuition, state resident: full-time $7232.55; part-time $6676 per credit hour. Tuition, nonresident: full-time $12,375. International tuition: $18,914 full-time. *Required fees:* $80; $80 $40. Tuition and fees vary according to program. *Financial support:* In 2018–19, 3 research assistantships with tuition reimbursements (averaging $6,960 per year) were awarded; career-related internships or fieldwork, Federal Work-Study, scholarships/grants, and unspecified assistantships also available. Financial award applicants required to submit FAFSA. *Faculty research:* Internal auditing, computer auditing, accounting education, managerial accounting. *Unit head:* Dr. Heidi Meier, Chair/Professor, 216-687-3671, Fax: 216-687-9212, E-mail: h.meier@csuohio.edu. *Application contact:* Marilyn Leadbetter, Administrative Secretary, 216-687-4721, Fax: 216-687-5311, E-mail: m.leadbetter@csuohio.edu.
Website: http://www.csuohio.edu/business/academics/master-accountancy

Coastal Carolina University, E. Craig Wall, Sr. College of Business Administration, Conway, SC 29528-6054. Offers accounting (M Acc); business administration (MBA); business foundations (Certificate); fraud examination (Certificate). *Accreditation:* AACSB. *Program availability:* Part-time, evening/weekend, 100% online, blended/hybrid learning. *Entrance requirements:* For master's, GMAT, official transcripts, 2 letters of recommendation, resume, baccalaureate degree, statement of purpose, minimum cumulative GPA of 3.0 overall from completed undergraduate and graduate coursework; for Certificate, GMAT, official transcripts; 2 letters of recommendation; baccalaureate degree or evidence of receiving a CPA certificate, law degree, or admittance to an accredited law school. Additional exam requirements/recommendations for international students: Required—TOEFL (minimum score 550 paper-based; 79 iBT), IELTS (minimum score 6.5). Electronic applications accepted.

The College at Brockport, State University of New York, School of Business and Management, Brockport, NY 14420-2997. Offers accounting (MS); public administration (MPA, AGC), including arts administration (AGC), nonprofit management (AGC), public administration (MPA). *Program availability:* Part-time. *Faculty:* 9 full-time (5 women), 8 part-time/adjunct (2 women). *Students:* 64 full-time (39 women), 164 part-time (99 women); includes 24 minority (18 Black or African American, non-Hispanic/Latino; 2 Asian, non-Hispanic/Latino; 4 Hispanic/Latino). 160 applicants, 79% accepted, 96 enrolled. In 2018, 124 master's, 15 other advanced degrees awarded. *Entrance requirements:* For master's, GMAT or GRE General Test. Additional exam requirements/recommendations for international students: Required—TOEFL (minimum score 550 paper-based; 79 iBT), IELTS (minimum score 6.5). *Application deadline:* For fall admission, 7/1 priority date for domestic and international students; for spring admission, 12/1 priority date for domestic and international students. Application fee: $50. Electronic applications accepted. *Expenses:* Tuition, state resident: part-time $471 per credit. Tuition, nonresident: part-time $963 per credit. *Financial support:* Career-related internships or fieldwork, Federal Work-Study, scholarships/grants, and unspecified assistantships available. Financial award application deadline: 3/15; financial award applicants required to submit FAFSA. *Unit head:* Dr. Lerong He, Interim Associate Dean, 585-395-5781, Fax: 585-395-2542, E-mail: lhe@brockport.edu. *Application contact:* Danielle A. Welch, Graduate Counselor, 585-395-5430, Fax: 585-395-2515, E-mail: dwelch@brockport.edu.
Website: http://www.brockport.edu/academics/school_business_management/

College of Charleston, Graduate School, School of Business, Program in Accountancy, Charleston, SC 29424-0001. Offers MS. *Accreditation:* AACSB. *Program availability:* Evening/weekend. *Entrance requirements:* For master's, GMAT, minimum GPA of 3.0 in last 60 hours of undergraduate course work, 24 hours of course work in accounting, 2 letters of reference. Additional exam requirements/recommendations for international students: Required—TOEFL (minimum score 81 iBT). Electronic applications accepted.

The College of Saint Rose, Graduate Studies, Huether School of Business, Program in Accounting, Albany, NY 12203-1419. Offers MS. *Program availability:* Part-time, evening/weekend. *Students:* 26 full-time (10 women), 8 part-time (7 women); includes 10 minority (6 Black or African American, non-Hispanic/Latino; 1 American Indian or Alaska Native, non-Hispanic/Latino; 1 Asian, non-Hispanic/Latino; 1 Hispanic/Latino; 1 Two or more races, non-Hispanic/Latino), 1 international. Average age 32. 9 applicants, 67% accepted, 6 enrolled. In 2018, 21 master's awarded. *Entrance requirements:* For master's, GMAT, graduate degree, or minimum undergraduate GPA of 3.0. Additional exam requirements/recommendations for international students: Required—TOEFL (minimum score 550 paper-based; 80 iBT), IELTS (minimum score 6), PTE (minimum score 56). *Application deadline:* For fall admission, 4/1 priority date for domestic and international students; for spring admission, 10/15 priority date for domestic and international students; for summer admission, 3/15 priority date for domestic and international students. Applications are processed on a rolling basis. Application fee: $40. Electronic applications accepted. *Expenses: Tuition:* Full-time $14,382; part-time $799 per credit hour. *Required fees:* $924; $408 per credit. $286. *Financial support:* Career-related internships or fieldwork, scholarships/grants, tuition waivers (partial), and unspecified assistantships available. Support available to part-time students. Financial award application deadline: 4/15; financial award applicants required to submit FAFSA. *Unit head:* Rajarshi Aroskar, Interim Dean, 518-454-5272, Fax: 518-458-5449, E-mail: aroskarr@strose.edu. *Application contact:* Daniel Gallgher, Assistant Vice President for Graduate Recruitment and Enrollment, 518-485-3390, Fax: 518-458-5479, E-mail: grad@strose.edu.
Website: https://www.strose.edu/accounting-ms/

College of Staten Island of the City University of New York, Graduate Programs, School of Business, Program in Accounting, Staten Island, NY 10314-6600. Offers MS. *Program availability:* Part-time, evening/weekend. *Students:* 29. 23 applicants, 39% accepted, 8 enrolled. In 2018, 16 master's awarded. *Degree requirements:* For master's, 30 credits or 10 courses worth 3 credits each; significant written assignment in capstone course. *Entrance requirements:* For master's, GMAT or College of Staten Island degree with minimum GPA of 3.2 in accounting or business pre-major and major. TOEFL or IETLS is a requirement of students whom English is a second language, Baccalaureate degree in accounting or related field; letter of intent; minimum GPA of 3.0; two letters of recommendation from instructors or employers; proficiency in business fundamentals and in depth knowledge of accounting through undergrad coursework, passing CLEP score may substitute for proficiency requirements. Additional exam requirements/recommendations for international students: Required—TOEFL (minimum score 550 paper-based; 79 iBT), IELTS (minimum score 6.5). *Application deadline:* For fall admission, 6/30 priority date for domestic students, 6/30 for international students; for spring admission, 11/25 priority date for domestic students, 11/25 for international students. Applications are processed on a rolling basis. Application fee: $75. Electronic applications accepted. *Expenses: Tuition,* area resident: Full-time $10,770; part-time $455 per credit. Tuition, state resident: full-time $10,770; part-time $455 per credit. Tuition, nonresident: full-time $19,920; part-time $830 per credit. *International tuition:* $19,920 full-time. *Required fees:* $559.20; $181.10 per semester. Tuition and fees vary according to program. *Faculty research:* Fair value reporting, forensic accounting, pension asset allocation, archival empirical analysis. *Unit head:* Prof. John Sandler, Graduate Program Coordinator, 718-982-2963, E-mail: john.sandler@csi.cuny.edu. *Application contact:* Sasha Spence, Associate Director for Graduate Admissions, 718-982-2019, Fax: 718-982-2500, E-mail: sasha.spence@csi.cuny.edu.
Website: http://www.csi.cuny.edu/schoolofbusiness/programs_graduate.php

The College of William and Mary, Raymond A. Mason School of Business, Master of Accounting Program, Williamsburg, VA 23185. Offers M Acc. *Accreditation:* AACSB. *Faculty:* 13 full-time (6 women), 3 part-time/adjunct (0 women). *Students:* 83 full-time (46 women); includes 28 minority (11 Black or African American, non-Hispanic/Latino; 9 Asian, non-Hispanic/Latino; 3 Hispanic/Latino; 5 Two or more races, non-Hispanic/Latino), 15 international. Average age 25. 314 applicants, 60% accepted, 69 enrolled. In 2018, 102 master's awarded. *Degree requirements:* For master's, 30 credit hours. *Entrance requirements:* For master's, GRE or GMAT (recommended), 2 written recommendations, interview, transcripts. Additional exam requirements/recommendations for international students: Required—TOEFL (minimum iBT score of 100), IELTS (7), or 4 years of studies in the U.S. *Application deadline:* For fall admission, 12/1 priority date for domestic and international students; for winter admission, 2/1 for domestic and international students; for spring admission, 4/1 for domestic and international students; for summer admission, 6/1 for domestic and international students. Application fee: $100. Electronic applications accepted. *Expenses:* Contact institution. *Financial support:* Fellowships, research assistantships, scholarships/grants, and unspecified assistantships available. Financial award application deadline: 8/1; financial award applicants required to submit FAFSA. *Faculty research:* Valuation, voluntary disclosure, auditing, taxation, Non-Gaap Disclosures. *Unit head:* Denise Jones, Accounting Department Chair, 757-221-2876, Fax: 757-221-7862, E-mail: denise.jones@mason.wm.edu. *Application contact:* Midori Juarez, Associate Director, 757-221-2934, Fax: 757-221-7862, E-mail: midori.juarez@mason.wm.edu.
Website: http://mason.wm.edu/programs/macc/index.php

Colorado State University, College of Business, Department of Accounting, Fort Collins, CO 80523-1271. Offers accounting (M Acc). *Entrance requirements:* For master's, GMAT (minimum score of 550), minimum GPA of 3.25, BA/BS, 3 letters of reference, official transcripts, statement of purpose, resume. Additional exam requirements/recommendations for international students: Required—TOEFL (minimum score 95 iBT), IELTS (minimum score 7), PTE (minimum score 70). Electronic applications accepted. *Expenses:* Contact institution. *Faculty research:* Theoretical application of economics and psychology; internal and external auditing issues; taxation; accounting choices and social dynamics; managerial accounting; accounting practice and tax policy.

Colorado State University–Global Campus, Graduate Programs, Greenwood Village, CO 80111. Offers criminal justice and law enforcement administration (MS); education leadership (MS); finance (MS); healthcare administration and management (MS); human resource management (MHRM); information technology management (MITM); international management (MS); management (MS); organizational leadership (MS); professional accounting (MPA); project management (MS); teaching and learning (MS). *Accreditation:* ACBSP. *Program availability:* Online learning.

Colorado Technical University Aurora, Programs in Business Administration and Management, Aurora, CO 80014. Offers accounting (MBA); business administration (MBA); business administration and management (EMBA); finance (MBA); human resource management (MBA); marketing (MBA); mediation and dispute resolution (MBA); operations management (MBA); project management (MBA); technology

management (MBA). *Program availability:* Part-time, evening/weekend. *Degree requirements:* For master's, thesis or alternative. *Entrance requirements:* For master's, minimum undergraduate GPA of 3.0, resume.

Colorado Technical University Colorado Springs, Graduate Studies, Program in Management, Colorado Springs, CO 80907. Offers accounting (MBA, MSA); business administration (MBA); finance (MBA); human resources management (MBA); logistics/supply chain management (MBA); management (DM); marketing (MBA); mediation and dispute resolution (MBA); operations management (MBA); project management (MBA); technology management (MBA). *Accreditation:* ACBSP. *Program availability:* Part-time, evening/weekend, online learning. *Degree requirements:* For master's, thesis or alternative; for doctorate, thesis/dissertation. *Entrance requirements:* For doctorate, minimum graduate GPA of 3.0, 5 years of related work experience. *Faculty research:* Sexual harassment, performance evaluation, critical thinking.

Columbia College, Master of Business Administration Program, Columbia, MO 65216-0002. Offers accounting (MBA); business administration (MBA); human resources (MBA). *Program availability:* Part-time, evening/weekend, 100% online, blended/hybrid learning. *Faculty:* 1 full-time (0 women), 55 part-time/adjunct (16 women). *Students:* 60 full-time (32 women), 335 part-time (201 women); includes 121 minority (67 Black or African American, non-Hispanic/Latino; 1 American Indian or Alaska Native, non-Hispanic/Latino; 6 Asian, non-Hispanic/Latino; 24 Hispanic/Latino; 1 Native Hawaiian or other Pacific Islander, non-Hispanic/Latino; 22 Two or more races, non-Hispanic/Latino), 31 international. Average age 37. 443 applicants, 92% accepted, 127 enrolled. In 2018, 195 master's awarded. *Entrance requirements:* For master's, 3 letters of recommendation, minimum cumulative undergraduate GPA of 3.0, resume, goal statement. Additional exam requirements/recommendations for international students: Required—TOEFL (minimum score 550 paper-based; 79 iBT). *Application deadline:* For fall admission, 8/9 priority date for domestic and international students; for spring admission, 12/27 priority date for domestic and international students. Applications are processed on a rolling basis. Application fee: $0. Electronic applications accepted. *Expenses:* 17640 - tuition (all fees included). *Financial support:* In 2018–19, 54 students received support. Scholarships/grants, tuition waivers (full and partial), and unspecified assistantships available. Financial award application deadline: 3/1; financial award applicants required to submit FAFSA. *Application contact:* Stephanie Johnson, Associate Vice President for Recruiting & Admissions Division, 573-875-7352, Fax: 573-875-7506, E-mail: sjohnson@ccis.edu.
Website: http://www.ccis.edu/graduate/academics/degrees.asp?MBA

Columbia University, Graduate School of Business, Doctoral Program in Business, New York, NY 10027. Offers business (PhD), including accounting, decision, risk, and operations, finance and economics, management, marketing. *Accreditation:* AACSB. *Degree requirements:* For doctorate, comprehensive exam, thesis/dissertation, major field exam, research paper, thesis proposal. *Entrance requirements:* For doctorate, GMAT or GRE (finance), 2 letters of reference, resume. Additional exam requirements/recommendations for international students: Required—TOEFL. Electronic applications accepted. *Expenses:* Contact institution. *Faculty research:* Human decision making and behavioral research; real estate market and mortgage defaults; financial crisis and corporate governance; international business; security analysis and accounting.

Columbia University, Graduate School of Business, MBA Program, New York, NY 10027. Offers accounting (MBA); decision, risk, and operations (MBA); entrepreneurship (MBA); finance and economics (MBA); healthcare and pharmaceutical management (MBA); human resource management (MBA); international business (MBA); leadership and ethics (MBA); management (MBA); marketing (MBA); media (MBA); private equity (MBA); real estate (MBA); social enterprise (MBA); value investing (MBA); DDS/MBA; JD/MBA; MBA/MIA; MBA/MPH; MBA/MS; MD/MBA. *Entrance requirements:* For master's, GMAT, 2 letters of recommendation. Additional exam requirements/recommendations for international students: Required—TOEFL. Electronic applications accepted. *Expenses:* Contact institution. *Faculty research:* Human decision making and behavioral research; real estate market and mortgage defaults; financial crisis and corporate governance; international business; security analysis and accounting.

Cornell University, Graduate School, Graduate Field of Management, Ithaca, NY 14853. Offers accounting (PhD); finance (PhD); marketing (PhD); organizational behavior (PhD); production and operations management (PhD). *Accreditation:* AACSB. *Degree requirements:* For doctorate, comprehensive exam, thesis/dissertation. *Entrance requirements:* For doctorate, GMAT or GRE General Test. Additional exam requirements/recommendations for international students: Required—TOEFL (minimum score 600 paper-based; 77 iBT). Electronic applications accepted. *Expenses:* Contact institution. *Faculty research:* Operations and manufacturing.

Cornell University, Samuel Curtis Johnson Graduate School of Management, Ithaca, NY 14853. Offers business administration (Exec MBA); management (MBA, PhD); management - accounting (MPS); JD/MBA; M Eng/MBA; MBA/MD; MBA/MHA; MBA/MILR; MBA/MPS. *Accreditation:* AACSB. *Faculty:* 71 full-time (18 women). *Students:* 573 full-time (172 women); includes 122 minority (24 Black or African American, non-Hispanic/Latino; 2 American Indian or Alaska Native, non-Hispanic/Latino; 74 Asian, non-Hispanic/Latino; 12 Hispanic/Latino; 10 Two or more races, non-Hispanic/Latino), 168 international. Average age 28. 1,600 applicants, 33% accepted, 280 enrolled. In 2018, 283 master's awarded. *Entrance requirements:* For master's, GMAT or GRE, resume, two essays, two recommendations, interview. Additional exam requirements/recommendations for international students: Required—TOEFL, TOEFL or IELTS score report required (for applicants whose first language is not English) *Application deadline:* For fall admission, 10/8 for domestic and international students; for winter admission, 11/5 for domestic and international students; for spring admission, 1/8 for domestic and international students; for summer admission, 4/8 for domestic and international students. Application fee: $200. Electronic applications accepted. *Expenses:* Contact institution. *Financial support:* Fellowships, institutionally sponsored loans, and scholarships/grants available. Financial award applicants required to submit FAFSA. *Faculty research:* Business of food; behavioral economics and decision research; innovation, entrepreneurship and technology. *Unit head:* Dr. Mark Nelson, Dean, 607-255-6418, E-mail: dean@johnson.cornell.edu. *Application contact:* Admissions Office, 800-847-2082, Fax: 607-255-0065, E-mail: mba@johnson.cornell.edu.
Website: http://www.johnson.cornell.edu

Creighton University, Graduate School, Heider College of Business, Omaha, NE 68178-0001. Offers accounting (MAC); business administration (MBA, DBA); business intelligence and analytics (MS); finance (M Fin); investment management and financial analysis (MIMFA); JD/MBA; MBA/MIMFA; MD/MBA; Pharm D/MBA. *Accreditation:* AACSB. *Program availability:* Part-time, evening/weekend, 100% online, blended/hybrid learning. *Degree requirements:* For master's, thesis optional; for doctorate, thesis/dissertation optional. *Entrance requirements:* For master's, GMAT, resume, 2 letters of recommendation. Additional exam requirements/recommendations for international students: Required—TOEFL (minimum score 90 iBT). Electronic applications accepted. *Expenses:* Contact institution. *Faculty research:* Small business issues, economics, business analytics.

Culver-Stockton College, MBA Program, Canton, MO 63435-1299. Offers accounting and finance (MBA).

Daemen College, International Business Program, Amherst, NY 14226-3592. Offers global business (MS), including accounting, global business, management information systems, marketing. *Program availability:* Part-time, evening/weekend. *Faculty:* 3 full-time (2 women), 3 part-time/adjunct (1 woman). *Students:* 4 full-time (2 women), 5 part-time (3 women); includes 1 minority (Black or African American, non-Hispanic/Latino), 2 international. Average age 34. 7 applicants, 57% accepted, 2 enrolled. In 2018, 4 master's awarded. *Degree requirements:* For master's, minimum GPA of 3.0. *Entrance requirements:* For master's, GMAT if undergraduate GPA is less than 3.0, baccalaureate degree from an accredited college or university with a major concentration in a business related field, such as accounting, business administration, economics, management, or marketing; official transcripts; undergrad GPA 3.0 higher or needs to take the GMAT; resume; 2 letters of recommendation; personal statement. Additional exam requirements/recommendations for international students: Required—TOEFL (minimum score 77 paper-based), IELTS (minimum score 6.5). *Application deadline:* Applications are processed on a rolling basis. Application fee: $25. Electronic applications accepted. Application fee is waived when completed online. *Expenses: Tuition:* Part-time $977 per credit hour. *Required fees:* $125; $14 per credit hour. *Financial support:* Scholarships/grants and unspecified assistantships available. Support available to part-time students. Financial award applicants required to submit FAFSA. *Unit head:* Dr. Torsten Doering, Director of International Business Program, 716-839-8239, E-mail: tdoering@daemen.edu. *Application contact:* Megan Beardi, Senior Assistant Director of Graduate Admissions, 716-566-7861, Fax: 716-839-8229, E-mail: mbeardi@daemen.edu.
Website: https://www.daemen.edu/academics/areas-study/international-business

Dallas Baptist University, Professional Development Program, Dallas, TX 75211-9299. Offers accounting (MA); church leadership (MA); communication (MA); counseling (MA); criminal justice (MA); English as a second language (MA); finance (MA); higher education (MA); leadership studies (MA); management (MA). *Program availability:* Part-time, evening/weekend, online learning. *Application deadline:* Applications are processed on a rolling basis. Application fee: $25. Electronic applications accepted. Application fee is waived when completed online. *Expenses: Tuition:* Full-time $17,262; part-time $959 per credit hour. *Required fees:* $1000; $500 per semester. Tuition and fees vary according to course load and degree level. *Unit head:* Jared Ingram, Program Director, 214-333-5584, E-mail: jaredi@dbu.edu. *Application contact:* Jared Ingram, Program Director, 214-333-5584, E-mail: jaredi@dbu.edu.
Website: https://www.dbu.edu/graduate/degree-programs/ma-professional-development

Davenport University, Sneden Graduate School, Grand Rapids, MI 49512. Offers accounting (MBA); business administration (EMBA); finance (MBA); health care management (MBA); human resources (MBA); information assurance (MS); occupational therapy (MSOT); public health (MPH); strategic management (MBA). *Program availability:* Evening/weekend. *Entrance requirements:* For master's, GMAT, minimum undergraduate GPA of 2.75. Additional exam requirements/recommendations for international students: Required—TOEFL. Electronic applications accepted. *Faculty research:* Leadership, management, marketing, organizational culture.

Delaware Valley University, MBA Program, Doylestown, PA 18901-2697. Offers accounting (MBA); entrepreneurship (MBA); finance (MBA); food and agribusiness (MBA); general business (MBA); global executive leadership (MBA); human resource management (MBA); supply chain management (MBA). *Program availability:* Part-time, evening/weekend, online learning. *Entrance requirements:* For master's, minimum undergraduate GPA of 3.0. Electronic applications accepted. *Expenses:* Contact institution.

Delta State University, Graduate Programs, College of Business, Division of Accounting, Computer Information Systems, and Finance, Cleveland, MS 38733-0001. Offers accountancy (MPA). *Expenses: Tuition, area resident:* Full-time $7076; part-time $393 per credit hour. Tuition, state resident: full-time $7076; part-time $393 per credit hour. Tuition, nonresident: full-time $7076; part-time $393 per credit hour. International tuition: $7076 full-time. *Required fees:* $170; $18.90 per credit hour. $9.45 per semester. Part-time tuition and fees vary according to program.

DePaul University, Kellstadt Graduate School of Business, Chicago, IL 60604. Offers accountancy (MBA, MSA); applied economics (MBA); audit and advisory services (MS); business administration (DBA); business analytics (MS); business strategy and decision-making (MBA); computational finance (MS); economics and policy analysis (MS); enterprise risk management (MS); entrepreneurship (MBA, MS); finance (MBA, MS); general business (MBA); hospitality leadership (MBA); hospitality leadership and operational performance (MS); human resources (MS); international business (MBA); management (MBA, MS); management information systems (MBA); marketing (MBA, MS); marketing analysis (MS); marketing strategy and planning (MBA); real estate (MS); real estate finance and investment (MBA); strategy, execution and valuation (MBA); supply chain management (MS); sustainable management (MS); taxation (MS); JD/MBA. *Accreditation:* AACSB. *Program availability:* Part-time, evening/weekend, online learning. *Entrance requirements:* For master's, GMAT/GRE, 2 letters of recommendation, resume, essay, official transcripts. Additional exam requirements/recommendations for international students: Required—TOEFL (minimum score 550 paper-based; 80 iBT). Electronic applications accepted. *Expenses:* Contact institution.

DeSales University, Division of Business, Center Valley, PA 18034-9568. Offers accounting (MBA); computer information systems (MBA); finance (MBA); health care systems management (MBA); human resources management (MBA); management (MBA); marketing (MBA); project management (MBA); self-design (MBA); supply chain management (MBA); DNP/MBA; MSN/MBA. *Accreditation:* ACBSP. *Program availability:* Part-time, evening/weekend, 100% online, blended/hybrid learning. *Entrance requirements:* For master's, GMAT (waived if undergraduate GPA is 3.0 or better), minimum GPA of 3.0 in undergraduate work, literacy in basic software, background or interest in the field of study, personal statement, 2 years of work experience. Additional exam requirements/recommendations for international students: Required—TOEFL. Electronic applications accepted. *Expenses:* Contact institution. *Faculty research:* Quality improvement, executive development, productivity, cross-cultural managerial differences, leadership.

DeVry University–Folsom Campus, Graduate Programs, Folsom, CA 95630. Offers accounting (M Acc); accounting and financial management (MAFM); business administration (MBA); curriculum leadership (M Ed); educational leadership (M Ed); educational technology (M Ed); higher education leadership (M Ed); human resource management (MHRM); information systems management (MISM); network and communications management (MNCM); project management (MPM); public administration (MPA).

Dominican College, MBA Program, Orangeburg, NY 10962-1210. Offers accounting (MBA); healthcare management (MBA); management (MBA). *Program availability:* Part-time, evening/weekend. *Entrance requirements:* For master's, GMAT, 2 letters of recommendation. Additional exam requirements/recommendations for international students: Required—TOEFL (minimum score 550 paper-based; 90 iBT). Electronic applications accepted. *Expenses:* Contact institution.

Dominican University, Brennan School of Business, River Forest, IL 60305-1099. Offers MBA, MSA, JD/MBA, MBA/MLIS, MBA/MSW. JD/MBA offered jointly with John

Marshall Law School. *Accreditation:* AACSB. *Program availability:* Part-time, evening/weekend, 100% online, blended/hybrid learning. *Entrance requirements:* For master's, GMAT. Additional exam requirements/recommendations for international students: Required—TOEFL (minimum score 550 paper-based; 79 iBT); Recommended—IELTS (minimum score 6). Electronic applications accepted. *Expenses:* Contact institution. *Faculty research:* Entrepreneurship, small business finance, business ethics, marketing strategy.

Drake University, College of Business and Public Administration, Des Moines, IA 50311-4516. Offers accounting (M Acc); business administration (MBA); public administration (MPA); JD/MBA; JD/MPA; Pharm D/MBA; Pharm D/MPA. *Program availability:* Part-time, evening/weekend, 100% online, blended/hybrid learning. *Students:* 31 full-time (15 women), 173 part-time (89 women); includes 19 minority (4 Black or African American, non-Hispanic/Latino; 1 American Indian or Alaska Native, non-Hispanic/Latino; 3 Asian, non-Hispanic/Latino; 9 Hispanic/Latino; 2 Two or more races, non-Hispanic/Latino), 11 international. Average age 31. In 2018, 121 master's awarded. *Degree requirements:* For master's, comprehensive exam (for some programs), thesis (for some programs), internships. *Entrance requirements:* For master's, GMAT, letters of recommendation, resume. Additional exam requirements/recommendations for international students: Required—TOEFL (minimum score 550 paper-based). *Application deadline:* For fall admission, 8/15 priority date for domestic students; for winter admission, 12/20 priority date for domestic students; for spring admission, 12/1 priority date for domestic students. Applications are processed on a rolling basis. Application fee: $25. Electronic applications accepted. *Expenses:* Contact institution. *Financial support:* Fellowships with tuition reimbursements, teaching assistantships, career-related internships or fieldwork, and institutionally sponsored loans available. Support available to part-time students. Financial award application deadline: 3/1; financial award applicants required to submit FAFSA. *Faculty research:* Venture capital, online commerce, professional ethics, process improvement, project management. *Unit head:* Dr. Daniel J. Connolly, Dean, 515-271-2872, Fax: 515-271-4518, E-mail: daniel.connolly@drake.edu. *Application contact:* Danette Kenne, Assistant Dean, 515-271-2188, Fax: 515-271-4518, E-mail: cbpa.gradprograms@drake.edu.
Website: http://www.drake.edu/cbpa/

Drexel University, LeBow College of Business, Department of Accounting, Program in Accounting, Philadelphia, PA 19104-2875. Offers MS. *Entrance requirements:* For master's, GMAT, minimum GPA of 2.75. Additional exam requirements/recommendations for international students: Required—TOEFL. Electronic applications accepted.

Drexel University, LeBow College of Business, Program in Business Administration, Philadelphia, PA 19104-2875. Offers business administration (MBA, PhD, APC), including accounting (MBA, PhD), decision sciences (PhD), economics (MBA, PhD), finance (MBA, PhD), legal studies (MBA), management (MBA), marketing (MBA, PhD), organizational sciences (PhD), quantitative methods (MBA), strategic management (PhD). *Accreditation:* AACSB. *Program availability:* Part-time, evening/weekend, online learning. Terminal master's awarded for partial completion of doctoral program. *Entrance requirements:* For master's, GMAT, minimum GPA of 2.75; for doctorate, GMAT. Additional exam requirements/recommendations for international students: Required—TOEFL. Electronic applications accepted. *Faculty research:* Decision support systems, individual and group behavior, operations research, techniques and strategy.

Duke University, The Fuqua School of Business, PhD Program, Durham, NC 27708. Offers accounting (PhD); decision sciences (PhD); finance (PhD); management and organizations (PhD); marketing (PhD); operations management (PhD); strategy (PhD). *Faculty:* 100 full-time (21 women). *Students:* 84 full-time (29 women); includes 4 minority (2 Asian, non-Hispanic/Latino; 2 Hispanic/Latino), 53 international. Average age 28. In 2018, 14 doctorates awarded. *Degree requirements:* For doctorate, comprehensive exam (for some programs), thesis/dissertation, Comprehensive or Qualifying exams are required for some of the 7 areas in Business Administration. *Entrance requirements:* For doctorate, GMAT or GRE, transcripts, essays, recommendation letters, statement of purpose. Additional exam requirements/recommendations for international students: Required—TOEFL, IELTS. *Application deadline:* For fall admission, 12/31 priority date for domestic and international students. Application fee: $90. Electronic applications accepted. *Expenses:* Contact institution. *Financial support:* In 2018–19, 74 fellowships with full tuition reimbursements (averaging $33,300 per year) were awarded; research assistantships with full tuition reimbursements, teaching assistantships, institutionally sponsored loans, scholarships/grants, health care benefits, and tuition waivers (full) also available. *Unit head:* William Boulding, Dean, 919-660-7822. *Application contact:* Ravi Bansal, Director of Graduate Studies, 919-660-7753, Fax: 919-660-7971, E-mail: fuqua-phd-info@duke.edu.

Duquesne University, Palumbo-Donahue School of Business, Pittsburgh, PA 15282-0001. Offers accounting (M Acc); finance (MBA); information systems management (MSISM); management (MBA, MS); marketing (MBA); sports business (MS); supply chain management (MS); sustainability (MBA); JD/MBA; MBA/M Acc; MBA/MA; MBA/MES; MBA/MHMS; MSISM/MBA; Pharm D/MBA. *Accreditation:* AACSB. *Program availability:* Part-time, evening/weekend, 100% online, blended/hybrid learning. *Faculty:* 59 full-time (23 women), 25 part-time/adjunct (6 women). *Students:* 214 full-time (74 women), 42 part-time (20 women); includes 39 minority (12 Black or African American, non-Hispanic/Latino; 13 Asian, non-Hispanic/Latino; 8 Hispanic/Latino; 6 Two or more races, non-Hispanic/Latino), 23 international. Average age 29. 228 applicants, 88% accepted, 118 enrolled. In 2018, 149 master's awarded. *Entrance requirements:* For master's, GMAT or GRE, all official transcripts, two letters of recommendation, current resume, essays. Additional exam requirements/recommendations for international students: Required—TOEFL (minimum score 90 iBT), IELTS (minimum score 7). *Application deadline:* For fall admission, 7/1 priority date for domestic and international students; for spring admission, 12/1 for domestic and international students; for summer admission, 4/1 for domestic and international students. Applications are processed on a rolling basis. Application fee: $0. Electronic applications accepted. *Expenses:* $1,284/credit hour (business), $953/credit hour (management). *Financial support:* In 2018–19, 174 students received support, including 6 fellowships with partial tuition reimbursements available (averaging $24,750 per year); career-related internships or fieldwork, scholarships/grants, and unspecified assistantships also available. Support available to part-time students. Financial award application deadline: 7/1; financial award applicants required to submit FAFSA. *Faculty research:* Investment management, business ethics, technology management, supply chain management, entrepreneurship. *Unit head:* Dr. Karen Donovan, Associate Dean of Graduate Programs and Executive Education, 412-396-5788, Fax: 412-396-1726, E-mail: donovan6@duq.edu. *Application contact:* Chris Rouhier, Director of Graduate Admissions, 412-396-6244, Fax: 412-396-1726, E-mail: rouhierc@duq.edu.
Website: http://www.duq.edu/business/grad

East Carolina University, Graduate School, College of Business, Department of Accounting, Greenville, NC 27858-4353. Offers MSA. *Program availability:* Part-time. *Expenses: Tuition, area resident:* Full-time $4749. Tuition, state resident: full-time $4749. Tuition, nonresident: full-time $17,898. *International tuition:* $17,898 full-time. *Required fees:* $2787. Part-time tuition and fees vary according to course load and program. *Unit head:* Dr. Dan L. Schisler, Interim Chair, 252-328-6622, E-mail: schislerd@ecu.edu. *Application contact:* Graduate School Admissions, 252-328-6012, Fax: 252-328-6071, E-mail: gradschool@ecu.edu.
Website: https://business.ecu.edu/grad/msa/

East Central University, School of Graduate Studies, Department of Accounting, Ada, OK 74820. Offers MS.

Eastern Connecticut State University, School of Education and Professional Studies/Graduate Division, Program in Accounting, Willimantic, CT 06226-2295. Offers MS. *Accreditation:* NCATE. *Program availability:* Part-time, evening/weekend. *Entrance requirements:* For master's, minimum GPA of 2.7, bachelor's degree from accredited institution. Additional exam requirements/recommendations for international students: Required—TOEFL (minimum score 550 paper-based; 79 iBT); Recommended—IELTS (minimum score 6). Electronic applications accepted.

Eastern Illinois University, Graduate School, Lumpkin College of Business and Technology, Program in Business Administration, Charleston, IL 61920. Offers accountancy (MBA); applied management (MBA); geographic information systems (MBA); research (MBA). *Accreditation:* AACSB. *Program availability:* Part-time, evening/weekend. *Entrance requirements:* For master's, GMAT or GRE. Additional exam requirements/recommendations for international students: Required—TOEFL (minimum score 500 paper-based; 61 iBT), IELTS (minimum score 6). Electronic applications accepted. *Expenses:* Tuition, state resident: part-time $299 per credit hour. Tuition, nonresident: part-time $718 per credit hour. *Required fees:* $214.50 per credit hour.

Eastern Michigan University, Graduate School, College of Business, Department of Accounting and Finance, Ypsilanti, MI 48197. Offers accounting (MS); accounting information systems (MS). *Program availability:* Part-time, evening/weekend, online learning. *Faculty:* 25 full-time (11 women). *Students:* 45 full-time (27 women), 53 part-time (22 women); includes 27 minority (8 Black or African American, non-Hispanic/Latino; 1 American Indian or Alaska Native, non-Hispanic/Latino; 12 Asian, non-Hispanic/Latino; 5 Hispanic/Latino; 1 Two or more races, non-Hispanic/Latino), 4 international. Average age 28. 55 applicants, 82% accepted, 30 enrolled. In 2018, 55 master's awarded. *Entrance requirements:* For master's, GMAT. Additional exam requirements/recommendations for international students: Required—TOEFL. *Application deadline:* Applications are processed on a rolling basis. Application fee: $45. *Financial support:* Fellowships, research assistantships with full tuition reimbursements, teaching assistantships with full tuition reimbursements, career-related internships or fieldwork, Federal Work-Study, institutionally sponsored loans, scholarships/grants, tuition waivers (partial), and unspecified assistantships available. Support available to part-time students. Financial award applicants required to submit FAFSA. *Unit head:* Dr. Phil Lewis, Interim Department Head, 734-487-3320, Fax: 734-487-0806, E-mail: plewis4@emich.edu. *Application contact:* Dr. Phil Lewis, Interim Department Head, 734-487-3320, Fax: 734-487-0806, E-mail: plewis4@emich.edu.
Website: http://www.accfin.emich.edu

Eastern Washington University, Graduate Studies, College of Business and Public Administration, Program in Professional Accounting, Cheney, WA 99004-2431. Offers MP Acc. Admissions temporarily suspended. *Accreditation:* NCATE. *Degree requirements:* For master's, comprehensive exam, thesis optional.

East Tennessee State University, School of Graduate Studies, College of Business and Technology, Department of Accountancy, Johnson City, TN 37614. Offers M Acc. *Accreditation:* AACSB. *Program availability:* Part-time, evening/weekend. *Degree requirements:* For master's, comprehensive exam, capstone, professional accounting experience. *Entrance requirements:* For master's, GMAT, minimum GPA of 2.5. Additional exam requirements/recommendations for international students: Required—TOEFL (minimum score 550 paper-based; 79 iBT). Electronic applications accepted. *Faculty research:* Smaller firm practice management, personal financial planning, accounting education, taxation issues.

Edgewood College, Program in Business, Madison, WI 53711-1997. Offers accountancy (MS); sustainability leadership (MBA). *Accreditation:* ACBSP. *Program availability:* Part-time, evening/weekend. *Students:* 74 full-time (34 women), 47 part-time (28 women); includes 19 minority (5 Black or African American, non-Hispanic/Latino; 2 American Indian or Alaska Native, non-Hispanic/Latino; 1 Asian, non-Hispanic/Latino; 8 Hispanic/Latino; 1 Native Hawaiian or other Pacific Islander, non-Hispanic/Latino; 2 Two or more races, non-Hispanic/Latino), 5 international. Average age 28. In 2018, 43 master's awarded. *Entrance requirements:* For master's, GMAT (minimum score 430), minimum GPA of 2.75, 2 letters of recommendation. Additional exam requirements/recommendations for international students: Required—TOEFL. *Application deadline:* For fall admission, 8/15 for domestic students, 5/1 for international students; for spring admission, 1/8 for domestic students, 11/1 for international students. Applications are processed on a rolling basis. Application fee: $30. Electronic applications accepted. *Expenses: Tuition:* Part-time $963 per credit. *Financial support:* Career-related internships or fieldwork and scholarships/grants available. *Unit head:* Dean, 608-663-2224, Fax: 608-663-3291. *Application contact:* Joann Eastman, Admissions Counselor, 608-663-3250, Fax: 608-663-2214, E-mail: gps@edgewood.edu.
Website: https://www.edgewood.edu/academics/schools/school-of-business

Elms College, Division of Business, Chicopee, MA 01013-2839. Offers accounting (MBA); accounting and finance (MS); financial planning (MBA, Certificate); healthcare leadership (MBA); lean entrepreneurship (MBA); management (MBA). *Program availability:* Part-time, evening/weekend. *Faculty:* 4 full-time (all women), 5 part-time/adjunct (3 women). *Students:* 36 part-time (22 women); includes 9 minority (5 Black or African American, non-Hispanic/Latino; 4 Hispanic/Latino), 1 international. Average age 35. 13 applicants, 85% accepted, 9 enrolled. In 2018, 29 master's awarded. *Entrance requirements:* For master's, minimum GPA of 3.0. *Application deadline:* Applications are processed on a rolling basis. Application fee: $30. Electronic applications accepted. *Expenses: Tuition:* Full-time $14,328; part-time $796 per credit. *Required fees:* $200. Tuition and fees vary according to degree level and program. *Unit head:* Kim Kenney-Rockwal, MBA Program Director, 413-265-2572, E-mail: kenneyrockwalk@elms.edu. *Application contact:* MBA Program Coordinator, 413-265-2592, E-mail: mba@elms.edu.

Emory University, Goizueta Business School, Doctoral Program in Business, Atlanta, GA 30322. Offers accounting (PhD); finance (PhD); information systems and operations management (PhD); marketing (PhD); organization and management (PhD). *Faculty:* 67 full-time (22 women). *Students:* 45 full-time (21 women); includes 5 minority (2 Black or African American, non-Hispanic/Latino; 3 Hispanic/Latino), 31 international. Average age 29. 143 applicants, 19% accepted, 10 enrolled. In 2018, 7 doctorates awarded. *Degree requirements:* For doctorate, comprehensive exam, thesis/dissertation. *Entrance requirements:* For doctorate, GMAT, interview. Additional exam requirements/recommendations for international students: Required—TOEFL (minimum score 600 paper-based; 100 iBT), IELTS, We will take either TOEFL or IELTS. *Application deadline:* For fall admission, 1/3 priority date for domestic and international students. Applications are processed on a rolling basis. Application fee: $75. Electronic applications accepted. *Expenses:* Our students are required to pay approximately $400 in their fall and spring terms; approximately $200 in summer terms in fees. All tuition is scholarshiped 100%. *Financial support:* In 2018–19, 45 students received support, including 11 fellowships (averaging $1,000 per year); scholarships/grants, health care

benefits, and Fellowships are both the Sheth Fellows and Goizueta Fellows whom are named each year based on certain milestones. also available. Financial award application deadline: 1/3. *Faculty research:* Financial and managerial accounting, asset pricing strategy and organizational behavior, information technology marketing analytics and consumer behavior. *Unit head:* Kathryn Kadous, Associate Dean, 404-727-2306, Fax: 404-727-5337, E-mail: kathryn.kadous@emory.edu. *Application contact:* Allison Gilmore, Director of Admissions and Student Services, 404-727-6353, Fax: 404-727-5337, E-mail: allison.gilmore@emory.edu.
Website: https://goizueta.emory.edu/degree/phd/index.html

Emory University, Goizueta Business School, Full Time MBA Program, Atlanta, GA 30322-1100. Offers accounting (MBA); alternative investments (MBA); business process consulting (MBA); business technology management (MBA); capital markets (MBA); corporate finance (MBA); customer relationship management (MBA); decision analytics (MBA); entrepreneurship (MBA); finance (MBA); global management (MBA); investment banking (MBA); management consulting (MBA); marketing (MBA); marketing analytics (MBA); marketing consulting (MBA); operations management (MBA); organization and management (MBA); product and brand management (MBA); real estate (MBA); social enterprise (MBA); strategy consulting (MBA). *Accreditation:* AACSB. *Faculty:* 74 full-time (18 women), 18 part-time/adjunct (6 women). *Students:* 349 full-time (105 women); includes 81 minority (26 Black or African American, non-Hispanic/Latino; 1 American Indian or Alaska Native, non-Hispanic/Latino; 35 Asian, non-Hispanic/Latino; 16 Hispanic/Latino; 3 Two or more races, non-Hispanic/Latino), 97 international. Average age 29. 1,380 applicants, 34% accepted, 172 enrolled. In 2018, 180 master's awarded. *Degree requirements:* For master's, 1 leadership course; 2 mid-semester module programs; 2 global components. *Entrance requirements:* For master's, GMAT/GRE, essays; recommendation letters; undergraduate degree; interview. Additional exam requirements/recommendations for international students: Required—TOEFL (minimum score 100 iBT), IELTS (minimum score 7), PTE (minimum score 68). *Application deadline:* For fall admission, 10/6 for domestic and international students; for winter admission, 11/17 for domestic and international students; for spring admission, 1/3 priority date for domestic and international students; for summer admission, 3/9 for domestic and international students. Application fee: $150. Electronic applications accepted. *Expenses:* Contact institution. *Financial support:* In 2018–19, 273 students received support. Career-related internships or fieldwork, institutionally sponsored loans, and scholarships/grants available. Financial award application deadline: 4/1; financial award applicants required to submit FAFSA. *Faculty research:* Corporate finance, information systems, digital marketing, asset pricing, sports management. *Unit head:* Brian Mitchell, Associate Dean, 404-727-4824, Fax: 404-712-9648, E-mail: brian.mitchell@emory.edu. *Application contact:* Melissa Rapp, Associate Dean, 404-727-7583, Fax: 404-727-4612, E-mail: mbaadmissions@emory.edu.
Website: http://www.goizueta.emory.edu

Emporia State University, Program in Accountancy, Emporia, KS 66801-5415. Offers M Acc. *Program availability:* Part-time, 100% online, blended/hybrid learning. *Entrance requirements:* For master's, bachelor's degree in accounting. Additional exam requirements/recommendations for international students: Required—TOEFL (minimum score 550 paper-based). Electronic applications accepted.

Everglades University, Graduate Programs, Program in Business Administration, Boca Raton, FL 33431. Offers accounting for managers (MBA); aviation management (MBA); human resource management (MBA); project management (MBA). *Program availability:* Part-time, evening/weekend, 100% online. *Entrance requirements:* For master's, GMAT (minimum score of 400) or GRE (minimum score of 290), bachelor's or graduate degree from college accredited by an agency recognized by the U.S. Department of Education; minimum cumulative GPA of 2.0 at the baccalaureate level, 3.0 at the master's level. Additional exam requirements/recommendations for international students: Recommended—TOEFL (minimum score 500 paper-based). Electronic applications accepted. *Expenses:* Contact institution.

Fairfield University, Dolan School of Business, Fairfield, CT 06824. Offers accounting (MBA, MS, CAS); business analytics (MS); finance (MBA, MS, CAS); information systems and business analytics (MBA); management (MBA, CAS); marketing (MBA, CAS); taxation (CAS). *Accreditation:* AACSB. *Program availability:* Part-time, evening/weekend. *Degree requirements:* For master's, capstone course. *Entrance requirements:* For master's, GMAT (minimum score 500), 2 letters of reference, resume, minimum GPA of 3.0. Additional exam requirements/recommendations for international students: Required—TOEFL (minimum score 550 paper-based; 80 iBT) or IELTS (minimum score 6.5). Electronic applications accepted. *Expenses:* Contact institution. *Faculty research:* International finance, leadership and careers, ethics in accounting, emotions in consumer behavior and organizations, data analytics.

Fairleigh Dickinson University, Florham Campus, Silberman College of Business, Department of Accounting, Law, and Tax, Program in Accounting, Madison, NJ 07940-1099. Offers MS. *Entrance requirements:* For master's, GMAT.

Fairleigh Dickinson University, Metropolitan Campus, Silberman College of Business, Department of Accounting, Law, and Tax, Program in Accounting, Teaneck, NJ 07666-1914. Offers MBA, MS, Certificate. *Faculty research:* Corporate accounting, legal issues.

Fitchburg State University, Division of Graduate and Continuing Education, Program in Business Administration, Fitchburg, MA 01420-2697. Offers accounting (MBA); human resources management (MBA); management (MBA). *Program availability:* Part-time, evening/weekend, 100% online. *Entrance requirements:* Additional exam requirements/recommendations for international students: Required—TOEFL (minimum score 550 paper-based; 79 iBT). Electronic applications accepted. *Expenses:* Contact institution.

Florida Agricultural and Mechanical University, Division of Graduate Studies, Research, and Continuing Education, School of Business and Industry, Tallahassee, FL 32307-3200. Offers accounting (MBA); finance (MBA); management information systems (MBA); marketing (MBA). *Accreditation:* ACBSP. *Degree requirements:* For master's, residency. *Entrance requirements:* For master's, GMAT, minimum GPA of 3.0.

Florida Atlantic University, College of Business, School of Accounting, Boca Raton, FL 33431-0991. Offers MAC. *Accreditation:* AACSB. *Program availability:* Part-time, evening/weekend, online learning. *Faculty:* 15 full-time (5 women), 2 part-time/adjunct (1 woman). *Students:* 88 full-time (51 women), 472 part-time (261 women); includes 276 minority (54 Black or African American, non-Hispanic/Latino; 1 American Indian or Alaska Native, non-Hispanic/Latino; 31 Asian, non-Hispanic/Latino; 169 Hispanic/Latino; 21 Two or more races, non-Hispanic/Latino), 12 international. Average age 32. 408 applicants, 59% accepted, 203 enrolled. In 2018, 227 master's awarded. *Degree requirements:* For master's, comprehensive exam, thesis optional. *Entrance requirements:* For master's, GMAT with minimum score 500 (preferred) or GRE (minimum score 1000 old test, 153 Verbal, 144 Quantitative, 4 Writing) taken within last 5 years, BS in accounting or equivalent, minimum GPA of 3.0 in last 60 hours of undergraduate study. Additional exam requirements/recommendations for international students: Required—TOEFL (minimum score 600 paper-based; 61 iBT), IELTS (minimum score 6). *Application deadline:* For fall admission, 7/1 priority date for domestic students, 2/15 priority date for international students; for spring admission, 11/1 priority date for domestic students, 7/15 priority date for international students. Applications are processed on a rolling basis. Application fee: $30. *Expenses: Tuition, area resident:* Full-time $7400; part-time $369.82 per credit. Tuition, state resident: full-time $7400; part-time $369.82 per credit. Tuition, nonresident: full-time $20,496; part-time $1024.81 per credit. *Financial support:* Fellowships, research assistantships with partial tuition reimbursements, teaching assistantships, career-related internships or fieldwork, Federal Work-Study, institutionally sponsored loans, scholarships/grants, and tuition waivers (partial) available. Support available to part-time students. Financial award application deadline: 3/1. *Faculty research:* Systems and computer applications, accounting theory, information systems. *Unit head:* George Young, Director, 561-297-3638, E-mail: soa@fau.edu. *Application contact:* George Young, Director, 561-297-3638, E-mail: soa@fau.edu.
Website: http://business.fau.edu/departments/accounting/index.aspx

Florida Gulf Coast University, Lutgert College of Business, Program in Accounting and Taxation, Fort Myers, FL 33965-6565. Offers MS. *Program availability:* Part-time, evening/weekend. *Degree requirements:* For master's, thesis or alternative. *Entrance requirements:* For master's, GMAT, minimum GPA of 3.0. Additional exam requirements/recommendations for international students: Required—TOEFL (minimum score 550 paper-based). Electronic applications accepted. *Faculty research:* Stock petitions, mergers and acquisitions, deferred taxes, fraud and accounting regulations, graphical reporting practices.

Florida International University, Chapman Graduate School of Business, School of Accounting, Miami, FL 33199. Offers M Acc. *Program availability:* Part-time, evening/weekend. *Faculty:* 24 full-time (11 women), 11 part-time/adjunct (1 woman). *Students:* 94 full-time (53 women), 18 part-time (8 women); includes 101 minority (6 Black or African American, non-Hispanic/Latino; 4 Asian, non-Hispanic/Latino; 89 Hispanic/Latino; 2 Two or more races, non-Hispanic/Latino), 2 international. Average age 27. 200 applicants, 53% accepted, 90 enrolled. In 2018, 115 master's awarded. *Entrance requirements:* For master's, GMAT or GRE, minimum GPA of 3.0 in upper-level coursework. Additional exam requirements/recommendations for international students: Required—TOEFL (minimum score 550 paper-based; 80 iBT) or IELTS (minimum score 6.5). *Application deadline:* For fall admission, 6/1 for domestic students, 4/1 for international students; for spring admission, 10/1 for domestic students, 9/1 for international students. Applications are processed on a rolling basis. Application fee: $30. Electronic applications accepted. *Expenses:* Contact institution. *Financial support:* Institutionally sponsored loans and scholarships/grants available. Financial award application deadline: 3/1; financial award applicants required to submit FAFSA. *Faculty research:* Financial and managerial accounting. *Unit head:* Clark Wheatley, Director, 305-348-4209, Fax: 305-348-2914, E-mail: Clark.Wheatley@fiu.edu. *Application contact:* Nanett Rojas, Manager, Admissions Operations, 305-348-7464, Fax: 305-348-7441, E-mail: gradadm@fiu.edu.

Florida National University, Program in Business Administration, Hialeah, FL 33012. Offers accounting (MBA); finance (MBA); general management (MBA); health services administration (MBA); marketing (MBA); public management and leadership (MBA). *Program availability:* Part-time, blended/hybrid learning. *Faculty:* 3 full-time (1 woman), 4 part-time/adjunct (2 women). *Students:* 15 full-time (5 women), 15 part-time (6 women); all minorities (7 Black or African American, non-Hispanic/Latino; 21 Hispanic/Latino; 2 Two or more races, non-Hispanic/Latino), 1 international. Average age 35. 8 applicants, 88% accepted, 7 enrolled. In 2018, 27 master's awarded. *Degree requirements:* For master's, capstone. *Entrance requirements:* For master's, writing assessment, bachelor's degree from accredited institution; official undergraduate transcripts; minimum undergraduate GPA of 2.5, GMAT (minimum score of 400), or GRE (minimum score of 900); two letters of recommendation; resume. Additional exam requirements/recommendations for international students: Required—TOEFL (minimum score 500 paper-based; 62 iBT), IELTS (minimum score 5.5). *Application deadline:* Applications are processed on a rolling basis. Electronic applications accepted. *Expenses:* Contact institution. *Financial support:* Federal Work-Study, institutionally sponsored loans, scholarships/grants, and tuition waivers (full and partial) available. Financial award applicants required to submit FAFSA. *Unit head:* Dr. Ernesto Gonzalez, Business and Economics Department Head, 305-821-3333 Ext. 1070, Fax: 305-362-0595, E-mail: egonzalez@fnu.edu. *Application contact:* Dr. Ernesto Gonzalez, Business and Economics Department Head, 305-821-3333 Ext. 1070, Fax: 305-362-0595, E-mail: egonzalez@fnu.edu.
Website: https://www.fnu.edu/prospective-students/our-programs/select-a-program/master-of-business-administration/business-administration-mba-masters/

Florida Southern College, Program in Accounting, Lakeland, FL 33801-5698. Offers M Acc. *Program availability:* Part-time, evening/weekend, blended/hybrid learning. *Faculty:* 5 full-time (2 women). *Students:* 10 full-time (6 women), 9 part-time (4 women); includes 7 minority (2 Black or African American, non-Hispanic/Latino; 1 Asian, non-Hispanic/Latino; 4 Hispanic/Latino), 1 international. Average age 32. 23 applicants, 74% accepted, 15 enrolled. In 2018, 10 master's awarded. *Entrance requirements:* For master's, GMAT or GRE General Test, letter of reference, resume, personal statement. Additional exam requirements/recommendations for international students: Required—TOEFL (minimum score 550 paper-based; 79 iBT), IELTS (minimum score 6.5), International students from countries where English is not the standard for daily communication must submit either the TOEFL or IELTS. *Application deadline:* For fall admission, 6/1 priority date for domestic and international students; for spring admission, 11/1 priority date for domestic and international students. Applications are processed on a rolling basis. Application fee: $30. Electronic applications accepted. *Expenses:* Contact institution. *Financial support:* In 2018–19, 1 student received support. Federal Work-Study, unspecified assistantships, and employee tuition grants, athletic scholarships for students still eligible available. Financial award application deadline: 8/21; financial award applicants required to submit FAFSA. *Faculty research:* Auditing, financial accounting, data analytics, taxation, and internal control. *Unit head:* Dr. William Quilliam, MAcc Director, 863-680-4279, E-mail: wquilliam@flsouthern.edu. *Application contact:* Kamalie Dodson, Associate Director, Adult and Graduate Admission (MBA MAcc), 863-680-5022, Fax: 863-680-3872, E-mail: kdodson2@flsouthern.edu.
Website: http://www.flsouthern.edu/sage/graduate/programs/master-of-accountancy.aspx

Florida State University, The Graduate School, College of Business, Tallahassee, FL 32306-1110. Offers accounting (M Acc), including assurance and advisory services, generalist, taxation; business administration (MBA, PhD), including accounting (PhD), finance (PhD), management information systems (PhD), marketing (PhD), organizational behavior and human resources (PhD), risk management and insurance (PhD), strategy (PhD); finance (MS); management information systems (MS); risk management and insurance (MS); JD/MBA; MSW/MBA. *Accreditation:* AACSB. *Program availability:* Part-time, 100% online. *Students:* Average age 31. 300 applicants, 61% accepted, 133 enrolled. In 2018, 268 master's, 9 doctorates awarded. Terminal master's awarded for partial completion of doctoral program. *Degree requirements:* For doctorate, comprehensive exam, thesis/dissertation. *Entrance requirements:* For master's, GMAT, GRE (for all except MS in finance), work experience (MBA, MS); minimum GPA of 3.0, letters of recommendation; for doctorate, GMAT, GRE (for marketing, organizational behavior, risk management and insurance, management

information systems, and human resources only), minimum graduate GPA of 3.5, letters of recommendation. Additional exam requirements/recommendations for international students: Required—TOEFL (minimum score 600 paper-based; 85 iBT); Recommended—IELTS (minimum score 6). *Application deadline:* For fall admission, 6/1 for domestic and international students; for spring admission, 10/1 for domestic and international students; for summer admission, 3/1 for domestic and international students. Applications are processed on a rolling basis. Application fee: $30. Electronic applications accepted. *Expenses:* Contact institution. *Financial support:* In 2018–19, 146 students received support, including 26 fellowships (averaging $1,500 per year), 77 research assistantships with full tuition reimbursements available (averaging $20,000 per year), 43 teaching assistantships with full tuition reimbursements available (averaging $20,000 per year); career-related internships or fieldwork, scholarships/grants, health care benefits, tuition waivers (full and partial), and unspecified assistantships also available. Support available to part-time students. Financial award application deadline: 1/1; financial award applicants required to submit FAFSA. *Faculty research:* Business strategy, marketing, finance, accounting, business analytics. *Total annual research expenditures:* $1.4 million. *Unit head:* Dr. Michael Hartline, Dean, 850-644-4405, Fax: 850-644-0915, E-mail: mhartline@business.fsu.edu. *Application contact:* Jennifer Clark, Director, 850-644-6458, E-mail: gradprograms@business.fsu.edu.
Website: http://business.fsu.edu/

Fontbonne University, Graduate Programs, St. Louis, MO 63105-3098. Offers accounting (MBA, MS); art (MA); art (K-12) (MAT); business (MBA); computer science (MS); deaf education (MA); early intervention in deaf education (MA); education (MA), including autism spectrum disorders, curriculum and instruction, diverse learners, early childhood education, reading, special education; elementary education (MAT); family and consumer sciences (MA), including multidisciplinary health communication studies; fine arts (MFA); instructional design and technology (MS); management and leadership (MM); middle school education (MAT); secondary education (MAT); special education (MAT); speech-language pathology (MS); supply chain management (MS); theatre (MA). *Accreditation:* ASHA. *Program availability:* Part-time, evening/weekend, online learning. *Degree requirements:* For master's, comprehensive exam (for some programs), thesis (for some programs). *Entrance requirements:* Additional exam requirements/recommendations for international students: Required—TOEFL (minimum score 500 paper-based; 65 iBT). Electronic applications accepted.

Fordham University, Gabelli School of Business, New York, NY 10023. Offers accounting (MBA, MS); applied statistics and decision-making (MS); business economics (DPS); capital markets (DPS); communications and media management (MBA); electronic business (MBA); entrepreneurship (MBA); finance (MBA, PhD); global finance (MS); global sustainability (MBA); health administration (MS); healthcare management (MBA); information systems (MBA, MS); investor relations (MS); management (EMBA, MBA, MS, PhD); marketing (MBA); marketing intelligence (MS); media management (MS); nonprofit leadership (MS); quantitative finance (MS); strategy and decision-making (DPS); taxation (MS); JD/MBA; MS/MBA. *Accreditation:* AACSB. *Program availability:* Part-time, evening/weekend. Terminal master's awarded for partial completion of doctoral program. *Degree requirements:* For master's, internships (for some degrees); for doctorate, comprehensive exam (for some programs), thesis/dissertation. *Entrance requirements:* For master's, GMAT/GRE, 2 letters of recommendation, resume, 2 essays, transcripts, interview. Additional exam requirements/recommendations for international students: Required—TOEFL (minimum score 100 iBT), IELTS (minimum score 7). Electronic applications accepted. *Expenses:* Contact institution.

Franklin University, Accounting Program, Columbus, OH 43215-5399. Offers MSA. *Program availability:* Online learning.

Freed-Hardeman University, Program in Business Administration, Henderson, TN 38340-2399. Offers accounting (MBA); corporate responsibility (MBA); leadership (MBA). *Accreditation:* ACBSP. *Program availability:* Part-time, evening/weekend, online learning. *Entrance requirements:* For master's, GMAT. Additional exam requirements/recommendations for international students: Required—TOEFL (minimum score 500 paper-based).

Friends University, Graduate School, Wichita, KS 67213. Offers family therapy (MSFT); global business administration (MBA), including accounting, business law, change management, health care leadership, management information systems, supply chain management and logistics; health care leadership (MHCL); management information systems (MMIS); professional business administration (MBA), including accounting, business law, change management, health care leadership, management information systems, supply chain management and logistics. *Program availability:* Part-time, evening/weekend, online learning. *Degree requirements:* For master's, research project. *Entrance requirements:* For master's, bachelor's degree from accredited institution, official transcripts, interview with program director, letter(s) of recommendation. Additional exam requirements/recommendations for international students: Required—TOEFL (minimum score 560 paper-based). Electronic applications accepted.

George Fox University, College of Business, Newberg, OR 97132-2697. Offers accounting (DBA); finance (MBA); management (DBA); management and leadership (MBA); marketing (DBA); organizational strategy (MBA); strategic human resource management (MBA). MBA offered in Newberg, OR and in Portland, OR. *Accreditation:* ACBSP. *Program availability:* Part-time, evening/weekend, online learning. *Degree requirements:* For master's, capstone project; for doctorate, credit-applied research project. *Entrance requirements:* For master's, resume (5 years of professional experience); 3 professional references; interview; financial e-learning course; official transcripts; for doctorate, GRE or GMAT, resume; personal mission statement; academic research writing sample; official transcript from each college/university attended; three professional references. Additional exam requirements/recommendations for international students: Required—TOEFL (minimum score 577 paper-based; 90 iBT) or IELTS (minimum score 7). Electronic applications accepted. *Expenses:* Contact institution.

George Mason University, School of Business, Program in Accounting, Fairfax, VA 22030. Offers MS. *Accreditation:* AACSB. *Program availability:* Evening/weekend, 100% online. *Faculty:* 21 full-time (9 women), 14 part-time/adjunct (6 women). *Students:* 54 full-time (35 women), 60 part-time (39 women); includes 37 minority (13 Black or African American, non-Hispanic/Latino; 14 Asian, non-Hispanic/Latino; 9 Hispanic/Latino; 1 Two or more races, non-Hispanic/Latino), 33 international. Average age 29. 98 applicants, 90% accepted, 50 enrolled. In 2018, 68 master's awarded. *Entrance requirements:* For master's, GMAT/GRE, resume; official transcripts; 2 letters of recommendation; personal statement; professional essay; interview. Additional exam requirements/recommendations for international students: Required—TOEFL (minimum score 575 paper-based; 93 iBT), IELTS (minimum score 7), PTE (minimum score 59). *Application deadline:* For fall admission, 2/1 for domestic and international students. Application fee: $75 ($80 for international students). Electronic applications accepted. *Expenses:* $859 per credit in-state tuition, $1,709 per credit out-of-state tuition. *Financial support:* In 2018–19, 11 students received support, including 7 research assistantships with tuition reimbursements available (averaging $5,547 per year), 5 teaching assistantships with tuition reimbursements available (averaging $8,364 per year); career-related internships or fieldwork, Federal Work-Study, scholarships/grants, unspecified assistantships, and health care benefits (for full-time research or teaching assistantship recipients) also available. Support available to part-time students. Financial award application deadline: 3/1; financial award applicants required to submit FAFSA. *Faculty research:* Current leading global business issues, including offshore outsourcing, international financial risk, and comparative systems of innovation; business management/practices; emerging technology and generating new business. *Unit head:* JK Aier, Chair, 703-993-4546, Fax: 703-993-1809, E-mail: jaier@gmu.edu. *Application contact:* Mary Hayes Colllins, Program Manager, 703-993-9093, E-mail: mhayesco@gmu.edu.
Website: http://business.gmu.edu/masters-in-accounting/

The George Washington University, School of Business, Department of Accountancy, Washington, DC 20052. Offers M Accy. *Accreditation:* AACSB. *Program availability:* Part-time, evening/weekend. *Students:* 137 full-time (93 women), 43 part-time (27 women); includes 36 minority (11 Black or African American, non-Hispanic/Latino; 14 Asian, non-Hispanic/Latino; 9 Hispanic/Latino; 2 Native Hawaiian or other Pacific Islander, non-Hispanic/Latino), 66 international. Average age 28. 446 applicants, 63% accepted, 81 enrolled. In 2018, 111 master's awarded. *Entrance requirements:* For master's, GMAT. Additional exam requirements/recommendations for international students: Required—TOEFL. *Application deadline:* For fall admission, 4/1 priority date for domestic students; for spring admission, 10/1 for domestic students. Applications are processed on a rolling basis. Application fee: $75. *Financial support:* In 2018–19, 50 students received support. Fellowships, teaching assistantships, career-related internships or fieldwork, Federal Work-Study, and institutionally sponsored loans available. Financial award application deadline: 4/1. *Faculty research:* Management accounting and capital markets, financial accounting and the analytic hierarchy process, ethics and accounting, accounting information systems. *Unit head:* Dr. Angela Gore, Chair, 202-994-6195, E-mail: agore@gwu.edu. *Application contact:* Tatyana I. Kuzina, Administrative Manager, 202-994-4181, Fax: 202-994-5164, E-mail: tkuzina@gwu.edu.
Website: http://business.gwu.edu/about-us/departments/department-of-accountancy/

Georgia College & State University, Graduate School, The J. Whitney Bunting School of Business, Program in Accounting, Milledgeville, GA 31061. Offers M Acc. *Program availability:* Part-time, evening/weekend. *Degree requirements:* For master's, minimum GPA of 3.0 on all business courses taken at Georgia College, complete program within 7 years of start date. *Entrance requirements:* For master's, GRE or GMAT (not required if graduated from AASCB-accredited business school with accounting degree, overall GPA of 3.25, and major GPA of 3.0), transcript, certification of immunization. Electronic applications accepted. *Expenses:* Contact institution.

Georgia Southern University, Jack N. Averitt College of Graduate Studies, Parker College of Business, Program in Accounting, Statesboro, GA 30460. Offers forensic accounting (M Acc). *Accreditation:* AACSB. *Program availability:* Part-time, 100% online. *Entrance requirements:* For master's, GMAT. Additional exam requirements/recommendations for international students: Required—TOEFL (minimum score 550 paper-based; 80 iBT), IELTS (minimum score 6). Electronic applications accepted. *Expenses:* Contact institution. *Faculty research:* Financial fraud in financial statements, determinants of firms switching auditors, whistle-blowing, impact of new tax code on firms, pedagogy issues in accounting and law courses.

Georgia State University, J. Mack Robinson College of Business, School of Accountancy, Program in Professional Accountancy, Atlanta, GA 30303. Offers MPA. *Accreditation:* AACSB. *Program availability:* Part-time, evening/weekend. *Entrance requirements:* For master's, GRE or GMAT, transcripts from all institutions attended, resume, essays. Additional exam requirements/recommendations for international students: Required—TOEFL (minimum score 610 paper-based; 101 iBT), IELTS (minimum score 7). *Application deadline:* Applications are processed on a rolling basis. Application fee: $50. Electronic applications accepted. *Expenses: Tuition, area resident:* Full-time $9360; part-time $390 per credit hour. Tuition, state resident: full-time $9360; part-time $390 per credit hour. Tuition, nonresident: full-time $30,024; part-time $1251 per credit hour. *International tuition:* $30,024 full-time. *Required fees:* $2128. *Financial support:* Research assistantships, scholarships/grants, tuition waivers, and unspecified assistantships available. *Unit head:* Dr. Galen R. Sevcik, Director of the School of Accountancy, 404-413-7200, Fax: 404-413-7203. *Application contact:* Toby McChesney, Assistant Dean for Graduate Recruiting and Student Services, 404-413-7167, Fax: 404-413-7162, E-mail: rcbgradadmissions@gsu.edu.
Website: https://robinson.gsu.edu/academic-departments/accountancy/

Golden Gate University, Ageno School of Business, San Francisco, CA 94105-2968. Offers accounting (MBA); adaptive leadership (MBA); advanced financial planning (MS); business administration (EMBA, MBA, DBA); business analytics (MBA, MS); entrepreneurship (MBA); finance (MBA, MS, Certificate); financial life planning (Certificate); financial planning (MS, Certificate); global supply chain management (MBA, Certificate); human resource management (MBA, MS, Certificate); information technology management (MBA, MS, Certificate); international business (MBA); marketing (MBA, MS, Certificate); project management (MBA, MS, Certificate); psychology (MA, Certificate); public administration (EMPA, MBA); public administration leadership (Certificate); JD/MBA. *Program availability:* Part-time, evening/weekend. *Degree requirements:* For doctorate, thesis/dissertation, qualifying examination. *Entrance requirements:* For master's, GMAT (for MBA), minimum GPA of 2.5 (MS). Additional exam requirements/recommendations for international students: Required—TOEFL (minimum score 550 paper-based; 79 iBT). Electronic applications accepted. *Expenses:* Contact institution.

Golden Gate University, School of Accounting, San Francisco, CA 94105-2968. Offers financial accounting and reporting (M Ac, MSA, Graduate Certificate); forensic accounting (M Ac, MSA, Graduate Certificate); internal auditing (M Ac, MSA, Certificate); management accounting (M Ac, MSA); taxation (M Ac, MSA). *Program availability:* Part-time, evening/weekend. *Entrance requirements:* For master's, minimum GPA of 3.0. Additional exam requirements/recommendations for international students: Required—TOEFL (minimum score 550 paper-based), IELTS (minimum score 6.5). Electronic applications accepted. *Expenses:* Contact institution. *Faculty research:* Forensic accounting, audit, tax, CPA exam.

Gonzaga University, School of Business Administration, Spokane, WA 99258. Offers accountancy (M Acc); American Indian entrepreneurship (MBA); business administration (MBA); taxation (MS); JD/M Acc; JD/MBA. *Accreditation:* AACSB. *Program availability:* Part-time, evening/weekend. *Degree requirements:* For master's, capstone course. *Entrance requirements:* For master's, GMAT or GRE, essay, two professional recommendations, resume/curriculum vitae, copy of official transcripts from all colleges attended, minimum GPA of 3.0. Additional exam requirements/recommendations for international students: Required—TOEFL (minimum score 570 paper-based, 89 iBT) or IELTS (minimum score 6.5). Electronic applications accepted. *Expenses:* Contact institution.

Governors State University, College of Business, Program in Accounting, University Park, IL 60484. Offers MS. *Program availability:* Part-time. *Faculty:* 14 full-time (4 women), 17 part-time/adjunct (7 women). *Students:* 11 full-time (6 women), 24 part-time (13 women); includes 17 minority (10 Black or African American, non-Hispanic/Latino; 1

Asian, non-Hispanic/Latino; 6 Hispanic/Latino), 1 international. Average age 34. 21 applicants, 62% accepted, 11 enrolled. In 2018, 11 master's awarded. *Application deadline:* For fall admission, 4/1 for domestic students. Applications are processed on a rolling basis. Application fee: $50. Electronic applications accepted. *Expenses:* $406/ credit hour; $4,872 in tuition/term; $6,002 in tuition and fees/term; $12,004/year. *Financial support:* Application deadline: 5/1; applicants required to submit FAFSA. *Unit head:* David Green, Chair, Division of Accounting, Finance, Management Information Systems, and Economics, 708-534-5000 Ext. 4967, E-mail: dgreen@govst.edu. *Application contact:* David Green, Chair, Division of Accounting, Finance, Management Information Systems, and Economics, 708-534-5000 Ext. 4967, E-mail: dgreen@govst.edu.

The Graduate Center, City University of New York, Graduate Studies, Program in Business, New York, NY 10016-4039. Offers accounting (PhD); behavioral science (PhD); finance (PhD); management planning systems (PhD). *Degree requirements:* For doctorate, thesis/dissertation. *Entrance requirements:* For doctorate, GMAT, writing sample (15 pages). Additional exam requirements/recommendations for international students: Required—TOEFL. Electronic applications accepted.

Grand Canyon University, Colangelo College of Business, Phoenix, AZ 85017-1097. Offers accounting (MBA, MS); business analytics (MS); disaster preparedness and executive fire service leadership (MS); finance (MBA); general management (MBA); health systems management (MBA); information technology management (MS); leadership (MBA, MS); marketing (MBA); organizational leadership and entrepreneurship (MS); project management (MBA); sports business (MBA); strategic human resource management (MBA). *Accreditation:* ACBSP. *Program availability:* Part-time, evening/weekend, online learning. *Entrance requirements:* For master's, equivalent of two years' full-time professional work experience. Additional exam requirements/recommendations for international students: Required—TOEFL (minimum score 575 paper-based; 90 iBT), IELTS (minimum score 7). Electronic applications accepted.

Grand Valley State University, Seidman College of Business, Program in Accounting, Allendale, MI 49401-9403. Offers MSA. *Accreditation:* AACSB. *Program availability:* Part-time, evening/weekend. *Faculty:* 9 full-time (3 women), 3 part-time/adjunct (1 woman). *Students:* 50 full-time (24 women), 20 part-time (12 women); includes 6 minority (5 Asian, non-Hispanic/Latino; 1 Hispanic/Latino), 2 international. Average age 26. 35 applicants, 97% accepted, 19 enrolled. In 2018, 44 master's awarded. *Entrance requirements:* For master's, GMAT, personal statement. Additional exam requirements/ recommendations for international students: Required—TOEFL (minimum iBT score of 80), IELTS (6.5), or Michigan English Language Assessment Battery (77). *Application deadline:* For fall admission, 8/1 priority date for domestic students, 5/1 priority date for international students; for winter admission, 11/1 priority date for domestic and international students; for spring admission, 4/1 priority date for domestic students, 3/1 priority date for international students. Applications are processed on a rolling basis. Application fee: $30. *Expenses:* $712 per credit hour, 33 credit hours. *Financial support:* In 2018–19, 18 students received support, including 9 fellowships, 8 research assistantships with full and partial tuition reimbursements available (averaging $4,000 per year); Federal Work-Study, scholarships/grants, and unspecified assistantships also available. Support available to part-time students. Financial award application deadline: 2/15; financial award applicants required to submit FAFSA. *Faculty research:* Public trust, capacity measurement, theoretical capacity, economic order quantity. *Unit head:* Dr. Aaron Lowen, Director, 616-331-7441, Fax: 616-331-7412, E-mail: lowena@gvsu.edu. *Application contact:* Koleta Moore, Assistant Dean of Student Engagement, Graduate Program Operations, 616-331-7386, Fax: 616-331-7389, E-mail: moorekol@gvsu.edu.
Website: http://www.gvsu.edu/business/

Harvard University, Harvard Business School, Doctoral Programs in Management, Boston, MA 02163. Offers accounting and management (DBA); business economics (PhD); health policy management (PhD); management (DBA); marketing (DBA); organizational behavior (PhD); science, technology and management (PhD); strategy (DBA); technology and operations management (DBA). *Degree requirements:* For doctorate, comprehensive exam (for some programs), thesis/dissertation. *Entrance requirements:* For doctorate, GRE General Test or GMAT. Additional exam requirements/recommendations for international students: Required—TOEFL.

HEC Montreal, School of Business Administration, Doctoral Program in Administration, Montréal, QC H3T 2A7, Canada. Offers accounting (PhD); applied economics (PhD); data science (PhD); finance (PhD); financial engineering (PhD); information technology (PhD); international business (PhD); logistics and operations management (PhD); management science (PhD); management, strategy and organizations (PhD); marketing (PhD); organizational behaviour and human resources (PhD). Program offered jointly with Concordia University, McGill University, and Universite du Quebec a Montreal. *Accreditation:* AACSB. *Students:* 130 full-time (55 women). 114 applicants, 46% accepted, 31 enrolled. In 2018, 19 doctorates awarded. *Entrance requirements:* For doctorate, TAGE MAGE, GMAT, or GRE, master's degree in administration or related field. *Application deadline:* For fall admission, 1/15 for domestic and international students. Application fee: 91 (191 for international students). Electronic applications accepted. *Expenses: Tuition, area resident:* Full-time $3052.80 Canadian dollars; part-time $84.80 Canadian dollars per credit. Tuition, state resident: full-time $3816 Canadian dollars; part-time $264.67 Canadian dollars per credit. Tuition, nonresident: full-time $11,910 Canadian dollars. *International tuition:* $20,905.20 Canadian dollars full-time. *Required fees:* $1805.34 Canadian dollars; $43.62 Canadian dollars per credit. $71.78 Canadian dollars per term. Tuition and fees vary according to degree level and program. *Financial support:* Research assistantships, teaching assistantships, and scholarships/grants available. Financial award application deadline: 9/2. *Faculty research:* Art management, business policy, entrepreneurship, new technologies, transportation. *Unit head:* Guy Paré, Director, 514-340-6264, E-mail: guy.pare@hec.ca. *Application contact:* Julie Bilodeau, PhD Program Analyst, 514-340-6000, Fax: 514-340-6411, E-mail: analyste.phd@hec.ca.
Website: http://www.hec.ca/en/programs/phd/index.html

HEC Montreal, School of Business Administration, Graduate Diploma Programs in Administration, Program in Professional Accounting, Montréal, QC H3T 2A7, Canada. Offers Graduate Diploma. All courses are given in French. *Students:* 181 full-time (101 women), 78 part-time (41 women). 301 applicants, 87% accepted, 191 enrolled. In 2018, 217 Graduate Diplomas awarded. *Entrance requirements:* For degree, bachelor's degree in accounting. *Application deadline:* For winter admission, 9/15 for domestic and international students; for spring admission, 2/10 for domestic and international students. Application fee: $91 Canadian dollars ($191 Canadian dollars for international students). Electronic applications accepted. *Expenses: Tuition, area resident:* Full-time $3052.80 Canadian dollars; part-time $84.80 Canadian dollars per credit. Tuition, state resident: full-time $3816 Canadian dollars; part-time $264.67 Canadian dollars per credit. Tuition, nonresident: full-time $11,910 Canadian dollars. *International tuition:* $20,905.20 Canadian dollars full-time. *Required fees:* $1805.34 Canadian dollars; $43.62 Canadian dollars per credit. $71.78 Canadian dollars per term. Tuition and fees vary according to degree level and program. *Financial support:* Research assistantships, teaching assistantships, and scholarships/grants available. Financial award application deadline: 9/2. *Unit head:* Renaud Lachance, Director, 514-340-6428, E-mail: renaud.lachance@hec.ca. *Application contact:* Anny Caron, Administrative Director, 514-340-6000, Fax: 514-340-6411, E-mail: aide@hec.ca.
Website: http://www.hec.ca/programmes/dess/dess-comptabilite-professionnelle-cpa/index.html

HEC Montreal, School of Business Administration, Master of Science Programs in Administration, Program on Accounting, Management, Control, and Audit, Montréal, QC H3T 2A7, Canada. Offers M Sc. Program offered in French. *Students:* 4 full-time (3 women), 6 part-time (3 women). 17 applicants, 65% accepted, 8 enrolled. In 2018, 1 master's awarded. *Entrance requirements:* For master's, short graduate program in public accounting from HEC Montreal, minimum GPA of 3.0 on 4.3 scale. Additional exam requirements/recommendations for international students: Required—TAGE MAGE (minimum recommended score of 300), GMAT (minimum recommended score of 630), or GRE. *Application deadline:* For fall admission, 3/15 for domestic and international students; for winter admission, 9/15 for domestic and international students. Application fee: $91 Canadian dollars ($191 Canadian dollars for international students). Electronic applications accepted. *Expenses: Tuition, area resident:* Full-time $3052.80 Canadian dollars; part-time $84.80 Canadian dollars per credit. Tuition, state resident: full-time $3816 Canadian dollars; part-time $264.67 Canadian dollars per credit. Tuition, nonresident: full-time $11,910 Canadian dollars. *International tuition:* $20,905.20 Canadian dollars full-time. *Required fees:* $1805.34 Canadian dollars; $43.62 Canadian dollars per credit. $71.78 Canadian dollars per term. Tuition and fees vary according to degree level and program. *Financial support:* Research assistantships, teaching assistantships, and scholarships/grants available. Financial award application deadline: 9/2. *Unit head:* Dr. Sihem Taboubi, Director, 514-340-6428, E-mail: sihem.taboubi@hec.ca. *Application contact:* Marianne de Moura, Administrative Director, 514-340-6000, Fax: 514-340-6411, E-mail: aide@hec.ca.
Website: http://www.hec.ca/programmes/maitrises/maitrise-comptabilite-controle-audit/index.html

Hendrix College, Program in Accounting, Conway, AR 72032. Offers MA. *Program availability:* Part-time. *Entrance requirements:* For master's, GMAT. Additional exam requirements/recommendations for international students: Required—TOEFL. *Faculty research:* Meta-analysis, utility regulatory entities.

Herzing University Online, Program in Business Administration, Menomonee Falls, WI 53051. Offers accounting (MBA); business administration (MBA); business management (MBA); healthcare management (MBA); human resources (MBA); marketing (MBA); project management (MBA); technology management (MBA). *Program availability:* Online learning.

Hodges University, Graduate Programs, Naples, FL 34119. Offers accounting (M Acc); business administration (MBA); clinical mental health counseling (MS); health services administration (MS); information systems management (MIS); legal studies (MS); management (MSM). *Program availability:* Part-time, evening/weekend, 100% online, blended/hybrid learning. *Degree requirements:* For master's, comprehensive exam (for some programs), thesis (for some programs). *Entrance requirements:* For master's, essay. Additional exam requirements/recommendations for international students: Recommended—TOEFL. Electronic applications accepted.

Hofstra University, Frank G. Zarb School of Business, Programs in Accounting and Taxation, Hempstead, NY 11549. Offers accounting (MS, Advanced Certificate); business administration (MBA), including accounting, professional accountancy, taxation; taxation (MS, Advanced Certificate). *Program availability:* Part-time, evening/ weekend, blended/hybrid learning. *Students:* 121 full-time (64 women), 43 part-time (24 women); includes 29 minority (3 Black or African American, non-Hispanic/Latino; 16 Asian, non-Hispanic/Latino; 8 Hispanic/Latino; 2 Two or more races, non-Hispanic/ Latino), 68 international. Average age 26. 213 applicants, 80% accepted, 63 enrolled. In 2018, 125 master's awarded. *Degree requirements:* For master's, thesis (for some programs), capstone course (for MBA), thesis (for MS), minimum GPA of 3.0. *Entrance requirements:* For master's, GMAT/GRE, 2 letters of recommendation, resume, essay. Additional exam requirements/recommendations for international students: Required—TOEFL (minimum score 550 paper-based; 80 iBT); Recommended—IELTS (minimum score 6). *Application deadline:* Applications are processed on a rolling basis. Application fee: $75. Electronic applications accepted. *Expenses:* $1,375 per credit plus fees. *Financial support:* In 2018–19, 43 students received support, including 39 fellowships with full and partial tuition reimbursements available (averaging $4,765 per year); research assistantships with full and partial tuition reimbursements available, career-related internships or fieldwork, Federal Work-Study, institutionally sponsored loans, scholarships/grants, tuition waivers (full and partial), unspecified assistantships, and scholarships and endowed scholarships also available. Support available to part-time students. Financial award applicants required to submit FAFSA. *Faculty research:* Corporate compliance, artificial intelligence, financial accounting fraud, tax reform legislation, accounting analytics. *Unit head:* Dr. Jacqueline Burke, Chairperson, 516-463-6987, E-mail: jacqueline.a.burke@hofstra.edu. *Application contact:* Sunil Samuel, Assistant Vice President of Admissions, 516-463-4723, Fax: 516-463-4664, E-mail: graduateadmission@hofstra.edu.
Website: http://www.hofstra.edu/business/

Holy Family University, Graduate and Professional Programs, School of Business Administration, Philadelphia, PA 19114. Offers accountancy (MS); finance (MBA); health care administration (MBA); human resource management (MBA); information systems management (MBA). *Accreditation:* ACBSP. *Program availability:* Part-time, evening/ weekend. *Degree requirements:* For master's, comprehensive exam, thesis optional. *Entrance requirements:* For master's, minimum GPA of 3.0, interview, essay/personal statement, current resume, official transcript of all college or university work. Additional exam requirements/recommendations for international students: Required—TOEFL (minimum score 550 paper-based; 79 iBT), IELTS (minimum score 6), PTE (minimum score 54). Electronic applications accepted.

Hood College, Graduate School, Department of Economics and Business Administration, Frederick, MD 21701-8575. Offers accounting (MBA); information systems (MBA); organizational management (Certificate). *Accreditation:* ACBSP. *Program availability:* Part-time, evening/weekend. *Faculty:* 3 full-time (2 women), 6 part-time/adjunct (1 woman). *Students:* 23 full-time (12 women), 176 part-time (120 women); includes 44 minority (17 Black or African American, non-Hispanic/Latino; 5 Asian, non-Hispanic/Latino; 19 Hispanic/Latino; 3 Two or more races, non-Hispanic/Latino), 13 international. Average age 35. 23 applicants, 96% accepted, 13 enrolled. In 2018, 36 master's, 2 other advanced degrees awarded. *Degree requirements:* For master's, capstone/final research project. *Entrance requirements:* For master's, minimum GPA of 3.0 (or resume and two letters of recommendation), copy of official transcripts; for Certificate, copy of official transcripts, Statement of Intent (250 words). Additional exam requirements/recommendations for international students: Required—TOEFL (minimum score 575 paper-based; 89 iBT), IELTS (minimum score 6.5). *Application deadline:* For fall admission, 8/15 for domestic students, 8/5 for international students; for spring admission, 12/1 for domestic and international students; for summer admission, 5/1 for domestic students, 4/15 for international students. Applications are processed on a rolling basis. Application fee: $50 ($100 for international students). Electronic applications accepted. *Expenses:* Business Programs: Tuition $605 per credit hour,

Comprehensive Fee $115 per semester. *Financial support:* Tuition waivers (partial) and unspecified assistantships available. Financial award applicants required to submit FAFSA. *Faculty research:* Corporate strategy and sustainable competitive advantages, business ethics, entrepreneurship, investments management, economic development. *Unit head:* Dr. April M. Boulton, Dean of the Graduate School, 301-696-3600, Fax: 301-696-3597, E-mail: gofurther@hood.edu. *Application contact:* Christian DiGregorio, Director of Graduate Admissions, 301-696-3604, E-mail: gofurther@hood.edu.

Howard University, School of Business, Graduate Programs in Business, Washington, DC 20059-0002. Offers accounting (MBA); entrepreneurship (MBA); finance (MBA); general management (MBA); human resources management (MBA); information systems (MBA); international business (MBA); marketing (MBA); supply chain management (MBA); JD/MBA. *Accreditation:* AACSB. *Program availability:* Part-time, evening/weekend, online learning. *Entrance requirements:* For master's, GMAT, minimum 1 year post undergraduate work experience, resume, 3 letters of recommendation, advanced college algebra. Additional exam requirements/recommendations for international students: Required—TOEFL. *Faculty research:* Marketing research in multi-ethnic populations, U.S. trade policies and international relations, risk management (finance).

Hunter College of the City University of New York, Graduate School, School of Arts and Sciences, Department of Economics, Program in Accounting, New York, NY 10065-5085. Offers MS. *Entrance requirements:* For master's, GMAT, statement of purpose, bachelor's degree, official transcripts, two letters of recommendation. Additional exam requirements/recommendations for international students: Required—TOEFL (minimum score 550 paper-based; 60 iBT). Electronic applications accepted.

IGlobal University, Graduate Programs, Vienna, VA 22182. Offers accounting (MBA); data management and analytics (MSIT); entrepreneurship (MBA); finance (MBA); global business management (MBA); health care management (MBA); hospitality and tourism management (MBA); human resources management (MBA); information technology (MBA); information technology systems and management (MSIT); leadership and management (MBA); project management (MBA); public service and administration (MBA); software design and management (MSIT).

Illinois State University, Graduate School, College of Business, Department of Accounting, Normal, IL 61790. Offers MPA, MS. *Accreditation:* AACSB. *Faculty:* 29 full-time (14 women), 7 part-time/adjunct (3 women). *Students:* 92 full-time (39 women); includes 8 minority (1 Black or African American, non-Hispanic/Latino; 2 Asian, non-Hispanic/Latino; 1 Hispanic/Latino; 4 Two or more races, non-Hispanic/Latino), 1 international. Average age 23. 61 applicants, 87% accepted, 35 enrolled. In 2018, 45 master's awarded. *Degree requirements:* For master's, comprehensive exam. *Entrance requirements:* For master's, GMAT, minimum GPA of 2.75 in last 60 hours of course work. *Application deadline:* Applications are processed on a rolling basis. Application fee: $40. *Expenses: Tuition, area resident:* Full-time $7264.62. Tuition, state resident: full-time $9466. Tuition, nonresident: full-time $17,290. *International tuition:* $15,089.40 full-time. *Required fees:* $1481.04. *Financial support:* In 2018–19, 13 research assistantships were awarded; Federal Work-Study, institutionally sponsored loans, and tuition waivers (full) also available. Financial award application deadline: 4/1. *Unit head:* Dr. Deborah Seifert, Department Chair, 309-438-7651, E-mail: dseifer@illinoisstate.edu. *Application contact:* Jay Rich, Director of AAC Graduate Program, 309-438-7040, E-mail: jsrich@ilstu.edu.
Website: http://www.acc.ilstu.edu/

Indiana Tech, Program in Business Administration, Fort Wayne, IN 46803-1297. Offers accounting (MBA); health care management (MBA); human resources (MBA); management (MBA); marketing (MBA). *Program availability:* Part-time, evening/weekend, online learning. *Entrance requirements:* For master's, GMAT, bachelor's degree from regionally-accredited university; minimum undergraduate GPA of 2.5; 2 years of significant work experience; 3 letters of recommendation. Electronic applications accepted.

Indiana University Kokomo, School of Business, Kokomo, IN 46904. Offers accounting (Postbaccalaureate Certificate); business administration (MBA); business fundamentals (Postbaccalaureate Certificate). *Accreditation:* AACSB. *Program availability:* Part-time, evening/weekend. *Degree requirements:* For master's, thesis optional, research project. *Entrance requirements:* For master's, GMAT. Additional exam requirements/recommendations for international students: Required—TOEFL (minimum score 550 paper-based; 73 iBT). Electronic applications accepted. *Expenses:* Contact institution. *Faculty research:* Investments, outsourcing, technology, adoption.

Indiana University Northwest, School of Business and Economics, Gary, IN 46408. Offers accounting (Graduate Certificate); management (Certificate); management and administrative studies (MBA). *Accreditation:* AACSB. *Program availability:* Part-time, evening/weekend. *Entrance requirements:* For master's, GMAT (not for Weekend MBA for Professionals), letter of recommendation. Electronic applications accepted. *Expenses:* Contact institution. *Faculty research:* International finance, employment law and testing, business ethics, taxation, financial institutions.

Indiana University–Purdue University Indianapolis, Kelley School of Business, Evening MBA Program, Indianapolis, IN 46202-5151. Offers accounting (MBA); entrepreneurship (MBA); finance (MBA); general administration (MBA); marketing (MBA); supply chain management (MBA); MBA/JD; MBA/MD; MBA/MHA; MBA/MS; MBA/MSA; MBA/MSE. *Program availability:* Part-time-only, evening/weekend, online learning. *Entrance requirements:* For master's, GMAT or GRE, 2 years of professional work experience. Additional exam requirements/recommendations for international students: Required—TOEFL or IELTS. Electronic applications accepted. *Expenses:* Contact institution. *Faculty research:* Entrepreneurship; corporate finance; international business; consumer behavior; supply chain; business law.

Indiana University–Purdue University Indianapolis, Kelley School of Business, Graduate Accounting Program, Indianapolis, IN 46202-5151. Offers MBA, MSA. *Entrance requirements:* For master's, GMAT, previous coursework in accounting and statistics. *Faculty research:* Auditing analytics; international accounting; taxation; financial accounting; corporate finance.

Indiana University South Bend, Judd Leighton School of Business and Economics, South Bend, IN 46615. Offers accounting (MSA); business (Graduate Certificate); business administration (MBA), including finance, human resource management, marketing; MBA/MSA. *Program availability:* Part-time, evening/weekend. *Entrance requirements:* For master's, GMAT. Additional exam requirements/recommendations for international students: Required—TOEFL (minimum score 550 paper-based; 79 iBT). Electronic applications accepted. *Expenses:* Contact institution. *Faculty research:* Financial accounting, consumer research, capital budgeting research, business strategy research.

Indiana Wesleyan University, College of Adult and Professional Studies, Graduate Studies in Business, Marion, IN 46953. Offers accounting (MBA, Graduate Certificate); applied management (MBA); business administration (MBA); health care (MBA, Graduate Certificate); human resources (MBA, Graduate Certificate); management (MS); organizational leadership (MA). *Program availability:* Part-time, evening/weekend, online learning. *Degree requirements:* For master's, applied business or management project. *Entrance requirements:* For master's, minimum GPA of 2.5, 2 years of related work experience. Additional exam requirements/recommendations for international students: Required—TOEFL (minimum score 550 paper-based). Electronic applications accepted.

Instituto Tecnologico de Santo Domingo, Graduate School, Area of Humanities and Social Sciences, Santo Domingo, Dominican Republic. Offers accounting (Certificate); adult education (Certificate); applied linguistics (MA); economics (MA); education (M Ed); educational psychology (MA, Certificate); gender and development (MA, Certificate); humanistic studies (MA); international marketing management (Certificate); international relations in the Caribbean basin (Certificate); intervention systems in family therapy (MA); linguistic and literary communication (Certificate); pedagogical support (MA); social science education (M Ed); sustainable human development (MA); terminal illness and death psychology (Certificate); youth and adult education (M Ed).

Inter American University of Puerto Rico, Aguadilla Campus, Graduate School, Aguadilla, PR 00605. Offers accounting (MBA); counseling psychology specializing in family (MS); criminal justice (MA); educative management and leadership (MA); elementary education (M Ed); finance (MBA); human resources (MBA); industrial management (MBA); management information systems (MBA); marketing (MBA). *Program availability:* Part-time, evening/weekend. *Degree requirements:* For master's, comprehensive exam. *Entrance requirements:* For master's, EXADEP, 2 letters of recommendation, minimum GPA of 2.5. Electronic applications accepted.

Inter American University of Puerto Rico, Arecibo Campus, Program in Business Administration, Arecibo, PR 00614-4050. Offers accounting (MBA); finance (MBA); human resources (MBA).

Inter American University of Puerto Rico, Barranquitas Campus, Business Administration Program, Barranquitas, PR 00794. Offers accounting (MBA); human resources (MBA); managerial information systems (MBA). *Program availability:* Part-time, evening/weekend. *Degree requirements:* For master's, 2 foreign languages, comprehensive exam (for some programs), thesis or alternative, minimum GPA of 3.0. *Entrance requirements:* For master's, BBA or its equivalent from accredited institution, official academic transcript from institution that conferred bachelor's degree, minimum GPA of 2.5, interview (for some programs). Electronic applications accepted. *Expenses:* Contact institution.

Inter American University of Puerto Rico, Metropolitan Campus, Graduate Programs, Program in Accounting, San Juan, PR 00919-1293. Offers MBA. *Degree requirements:* For master's, comprehensive exam. *Entrance requirements:* For master's, GRE or EXADEP, interview. Electronic applications accepted.

Inter American University of Puerto Rico, Ponce Campus, Graduate School, Mercedita, PR 00715-1602. Offers accounting (MBA); biology (M Ed); chemistry (M Ed); criminal justice (MA); elementary education (M Ed); English as a Second Language (M Ed); finance (MBA); history (M Ed); human resources (MBA); marketing (MBA); mathematics (M Ed); Spanish (M Ed). *Entrance requirements:* For master's, minimum GPA of 2.5.

Inter American University of Puerto Rico, San Germán Campus, Graduate Studies Center, Program in Business Administration, San Germán, PR 00683-5008. Offers accounting (MBA); finance (MBA); general business administration (MBA); human resources (MBA, PhD); industrial relations (MBA); information systems (MBA); international and interregional business (PhD); management (MBA); marketing (MBA). *Program availability:* Part-time, evening/weekend. *Degree requirements:* For master's, comprehensive exam. *Entrance requirements:* For master's, GRE General Test or EXADEP, minimum GPA of 3.0. *Expenses: Tuition:* Full-time $212; part-time $212 per credit. *Required fees:* $366 per semester. One-time fee: $31. Tuition and fees vary according to degree level and program.

Iona College, School of Business, Department of Accounting, New Rochelle, NY 10801-1890. Offers accounting and information systems (MS); general accounting (MBA, AC); public accounting (MBA, MS, AC). *Program availability:* Part-time, evening/weekend. *Faculty:* 6 full-time (2 women), 2 part-time/adjunct (both women). *Students:* 25 full-time (10 women), 43 part-time (20 women); includes 23 minority (1 Black or African American, non-Hispanic/Latino; 2 American Indian or Alaska Native, non-Hispanic/Latino; 5 Asian, non-Hispanic/Latino; 14 Hispanic/Latino; 1 Two or more races, non-Hispanic/Latino), 3 international. Average age 29. 32 applicants, 94% accepted, 19 enrolled. In 2018, 55 master's awarded. *Entrance requirements:* For master's and AC, minimum GPA of 3.0. Additional exam requirements/recommendations for international students: Required—TOEFL (minimum score 550 paper-based; 80 iBT), IELTS (minimum score 6.5). *Application deadline:* For fall admission, 8/15 priority date for domestic students, 8/1 priority date for international students; for winter admission, 11/15 priority date for domestic students, 11/1 priority date for international students; for spring admission, 2/15 priority date for domestic students, 2/1 priority date for international students; for summer admission, 5/15 priority date for domestic students, 5/1 priority date for international students. Applications are processed on a rolling basis. Application fee: $0. Electronic applications accepted. *Expenses: Tuition:* Full-time $14,064; part-time $7032 per credit. *Required fees:* $245 per semester. One-time fee: $250. Tuition and fees vary according to program. *Financial support:* In 2018–19, 38 students received support. Scholarships/grants, tuition waivers (partial), and unspecified assistantships available. Support available to part-time students. Financial award application deadline: 4/15; financial award applicants required to submit FAFSA. *Faculty research:* Tax policy, investment returns, international accounting standards. *Unit head:* Katherine Kinkela, LLM, Chair, Accounting Department, 914-633-2267, E-mail: kkinkela@iona.edu. *Application contact:* Kimberly Kelly, Director of Graduate Business Admissions, 914-633-2271, Fax: 914-633-2012, E-mail: kkelly@iona.edu.
Website: https://www.iona.edu/academics/school-of-business/departments/accounting.aspx

Iona College, School of Business, Department of Information Systems, New Rochelle, NY 10801-1890. Offers accounting and information systems (MS); business continuity and risk management (AC); information systems (MBA, MS, PMC); project management (MS). *Program availability:* Part-time, evening/weekend. *Faculty:* 5 full-time (0 women). *Students:* 12 full-time (7 women), 9 part-time (4 women); includes 7 minority (3 Black or African American, non-Hispanic/Latino; 2 Asian, non-Hispanic/Latino; 2 Hispanic/Latino), 1 international. Average age 28. 9 applicants, 89% accepted, 2 enrolled. In 2018, 12 master's awarded. *Entrance requirements:* For master's, GMAT, 2 letters of recommendation, minimum GPA of 3.0; for other advanced degree, GMAT, minimum GPA of 3.0. Additional exam requirements/recommendations for international students: Required—TOEFL (minimum score 550 paper-based; 80 iBT), IELTS (minimum score 6.5). *Application deadline:* For fall admission, 8/15 priority date for domestic students, 8/1 priority date for international students; for winter admission, 11/15 priority date for domestic students, 11/1 priority date for international students; for spring admission, 2/15 priority date for domestic students, 2/1 priority date for international students; for summer admission, 5/15 priority date for domestic students, 5/1 priority date for international students. Applications are processed on a rolling basis. Application fee: $50. Electronic applications accepted. *Expenses:* Contact institution. *Financial support:* In 2018–19, 12 students received support. Scholarships/grants, tuition waivers (partial), and unspecified assistantships available. Support available to part-time students.

Financial award application deadline: 4/15; financial award applicants required to submit FAFSA. *Faculty research:* Fuzzy sets, risk management, computer security, competence set analysis, investment strategies. *Unit head:* Dr. Shoshana Altschuller, Department Chair, 914-637-7726, E-mail: saltschuller@iona.edu. *Application contact:* Kimberly Kelly, Director of Graduate Business Admissions, 914-633-2271, Fax: 914-633-2012, E-mail: kkelly@iona.edu.
Website: http://www.iona.edu/Academics/Hagan-School-of-Business/Departments/Information-Systems/Graduate-Programs.aspx

Iowa State University of Science and Technology, Department of Accounting, Ames, IA 50011. Offers M Acc. *Accreditation:* AACSB. *Degree requirements:* For master's, thesis or alternative. *Entrance requirements:* For master's, GMAT, resume. Additional exam requirements/recommendations for international students: Recommended—TOEFL (minimum score 600 paper-based; 100 iBT), IELTS (minimum score 7). Electronic applications accepted.

Ithaca College, School of Business, Program in Accounting, Ithaca, NY 14850. Offers MS. *Program availability:* Part-time. *Faculty:* 5 full-time (3 women). *Students:* 16 full-time (7 women), 1 part-time (0 women); includes 6 minority (2 Asian, non-Hispanic/Latino; 2 Hispanic/Latino; 2 Two or more races, non-Hispanic/Latino), 2 international. Average age 22. 22 applicants, 95% accepted, 15 enrolled. In 2018, 27 master's awarded. *Entrance requirements:* For master's, GMAT. Additional exam requirements/recommendations for international students: Required—TOEFL (minimum score 550 paper-based; 80 iBT). *Application deadline:* For fall admission, 5/15 for domestic and international students; for spring admission, 11/1 for domestic and international students. Applications are processed on a rolling basis. Application fee: $40. Electronic applications accepted. *Expenses:* Contact institution. *Financial support:* In 2018–19, 16 students received support, including 16 fellowships (averaging $9,906 per year); career-related internships or fieldwork, Federal Work-Study, and scholarships/grants also available. Support available to part-time students. Financial award application deadline: 3/1; financial award applicants required to submit FAFSA. *Unit head:* Dr. Rasoul Rezvanian, Associate Dean and Director, MBA Programs, 607-274-1762, Fax: 607-274-1263, E-mail: rrezvanian@ithaca.edu. *Application contact:* Nicole Eversley Bradwell, Director, Office of Admission, 800-429-4274, Fax: 607-274-1263, E-mail: admission@ithaca.edu.
Website: https://www.ithaca.edu/business/programs/accounting

Jackson State University, Graduate School, College of Business, Department of Accounting, Jackson, MS 39217. Offers MPA. *Accreditation:* AACSB. *Program availability:* Part-time, evening/weekend. *Degree requirements:* For master's, comprehensive exam. *Entrance requirements:* For master's, GRE General Test, GMAT. Additional exam requirements/recommendations for international students: Required—TOEFL (minimum score 520 paper-based; 67 iBT).

Jacksonville University, Davis College of Business, Accelerated Day-time MBA Program, Jacksonville, FL 32211. Offers accounting and finance (MBA); business administration (MBA); consumer goods and services marketing (MBA); management (MBA); management accounting (MBA). *Entrance requirements:* For master's, GMAT or GRE, bachelor's degree from regionally-accredited institution, original transcripts of academic work, statement of intent, resume, 3 letters of recommendation; 3 years of work experience (recommended); interview with program advisor. Additional exam requirements/recommendations for international students: Required—TOEFL (minimum score 550 paper-based; 79 iBT), IELTS (minimum score 6), PTE (minimum score 53). Electronic applications accepted. *Expenses:* Contact institution. *Faculty research:* Behavioral finance, game theory, regional economic integration, information sabotage, public choice and public finance.

Jacksonville University, Davis College of Business, FLEX Master of Business Administration Program, Jacksonville, FL 32211. Offers accounting and finance (MBA); business management (MBA); consumer goods and services marketing (MBA); management (MBA); management accounting (MBA); JD/MBA; MBA/MPP; MSN/MBA. MBA/JD offered jointly with Florida School of Law; MSN/MBA offered jointly with JU's Keigwin School of Nursing; MBA/MPP offered jointly with JU's Public Policy Institute. *Accreditation:* AACSB. *Program availability:* Part-time, evening/weekend, blended/hybrid learning. *Entrance requirements:* For master's, GMAT or GRE, bachelor's degree from regionally-accredited institution, 3 years of full-time work experience (recommended), resume, statement of intent, 3 letters of recommendation, interview with program advisor. Additional exam requirements/recommendations for international students: Required—TOEFL (minimum score 550 paper-based; 79 iBT), IELTS (minimum score 6), PTE (minimum score 53). Electronic applications accepted. *Expenses:* Contact institution. *Faculty research:* Downsizing with integrity; impact of YouTube videos; game theory; analysis of effective tax rates; creativity innovation and change.

James Madison University, The Graduate School, College of Business, Program in Accounting, Harrisonburg, VA 22807. Offers accounting information systems (MS); taxation (MS). *Accreditation:* AACSB. *Program availability:* Part-time, evening/weekend. *Students:* 64 full-time (25 women), 1 part-time (0 women); includes 11 minority (2 Asian, non-Hispanic/Latino; 6 Hispanic/Latino; 3 Two or more races, non-Hispanic/Latino), 1 international. Average age 30. In 2018, 114 master's awarded. Application fee: $60. Electronic applications accepted. *Expenses:* Tuition, state resident: full-time $10,848. Tuition, nonresident: full-time $27,888. *Required fees:* $1128. *Financial support:* In 2018–19, 28 students received support, including 23 fellowships; Federal Work-Study and assistantships (averaging $6911), also available. Financial award application deadline: 3/1; financial award applicants required to submit FAFSA. *Unit head:* Dr. Tim J. Louwers, Director of the School of Accounting, 540-568-3027, E-mail: louwertj@jmu.edu. *Application contact:* Lynette D. Michael, Director of Graduate Admissions, 540-568-6131 Ext. 6395, Fax: 540-568-7860, E-mail: michaeld@jmu.edu.
Website: https://www.jmu.edu/cob/accounting/masters/index.shtml

John Carroll University, Graduate Studies, John M. and Mary Jo Boler College of Business, University Heights, OH 44118. Offers accountancy (MS); business (MBA); laboratory administration (MS). *Accreditation:* AACSB. *Program availability:* Part-time, evening/weekend. *Entrance requirements:* For master's, GMAT or GRE, minimum GPA of 2.8; Individual programs may have specific requirements. Additional exam requirements/recommendations for international students: Required—TOEFL. *Application deadline:* For fall admission, 8/1 priority date for domestic and international students; for spring admission, 12/1 priority date for domestic and international students; for summer admission, 4/1 priority date for domestic and international students. Applications are processed on a rolling basis. Electronic applications accepted. *Expenses:* Contact institution. *Financial support:* Fellowships, scholarships/grants, and unspecified assistantships available. Financial award applicants required to submit FAFSA. *Faculty research:* Accounting, economics and finance, management, marketing, and supply chain. *Unit head:* Dr. Alan R. Miciak, Dean, Boler College of Business, 216-397-4391, Fax: 216-397-1833. *Application contact:* Kristopher Tibbs, Assistant Dean, Graduate Business Programs, 216-397-1970, Fax: 216-397-1833, E-mail: gradbusiness@jcu.edu.
Website: https://boler.jcu.edu/graduate

Johnson & Wales University, Graduate Studies, MBA Program, Providence, RI 02903-3703. Offers accounting (MBA); business administration (MBA); finance (MBA); global fashion merchandising and management (MBA); hospitality (MBA); human resource management (MBA); information security/assurance (MBA); information technology (MBA); nonprofit management (MBA); operations and supply chain management (MBA); organizational leadership (MBA); organizational psychology (MBA); sport leadership (MBA). Program also offered on Denver campus. *Program availability:* Part-time, online learning. *Entrance requirements:* For master's, minimum GPA of 2.75. Additional exam requirements/recommendations for international students: Required—TOEFL (minimum score 550 paper-based); Recommended—IELTS, TWE. *Faculty research:* International banking, global economy, international trade, cultural differences.

Juniata College, Department of Accounting, Business, and Economics, Huntingdon, PA 16652-2119. Offers accounting (M Acc); business administration (MBA); organizational leadership (MOL). *Entrance requirements:* For master's, GMAT.

Kansas State University, Graduate School, College of Business, Department of Accounting, Manhattan, KS 66506. Offers M Acc. *Accreditation:* AACSB. *Program availability:* Part-time. *Entrance requirements:* For master's, GMAT (minimum score of 500), minimum undergraduate GPA of 3.0. Additional exam requirements/recommendations for international students: Required—TOEFL (minimum score 550 paper-based; 79 iBT); Recommended—IELTS (minimum score 7). Electronic applications accepted. *Faculty research:* Accounting education, accounting ethics, capital markets (empirical/archival), research in tax and financial reporting, behavioral research in accounting.

Kean University, College of Business and Public Management, Program in Accounting, Union, NJ 07083. Offers MS. *Program availability:* Part-time, evening/weekend. *Faculty:* 10 full-time (1 woman). *Students:* 22 full-time (11 women), 21 part-time (11 women); includes 21 minority (9 Black or African American, non-Hispanic/Latino; 3 Asian, non-Hispanic/Latino; 7 Hispanic/Latino; 1 Native Hawaiian or other Pacific Islander, non-Hispanic/Latino; 1 Two or more races, non-Hispanic/Latino), 6 international. Average age 31. 23 applicants, 100% accepted, 18 enrolled. In 2018, 25 master's awarded. *Entrance requirements:* For master's, GMAT/GRE, two letters of recommendation; professional resume/curriculum vitae; personal statement; minimum cumulative GPA of 3.0; official transcripts from all institutions attended. Additional exam requirements/recommendations for international students: Required—TOEFL (minimum score 550 paper-based; 79 iBT), IELTS (minimum score 6.5). *Application deadline:* For fall admission, 6/1 for domestic and international students; for spring admission, 12/1 for domestic and international students. Applications are processed on a rolling basis. Application fee: $75. Electronic applications accepted. *Expenses:* Tuition, state resident: full-time $15,025; part-time $733.50 per credit. Tuition, nonresident: full-time $19,890; part-time $884.50 per credit. *Required fees:* $2107.50; $89.50 per credit. Tuition and fees vary according to course level, course load, degree level and program. *Financial support:* Scholarships/grants and unspecified assistantships available. Financial award applicants required to submit FAFSA. *Unit head:* Dr. Veysel Yucetepe, Program Coordinator, 908-737-4762, E-mail: vyucetep@kean.edu. *Application contact:* Pedro Lopes, Office of Graduate Admissions, 908-737-7100, E-mail: gradadmissions@kean.edu.
Website: http://grad.kean.edu/masters-programs/accounting

Keiser University, Master of Accountancy Program, Fort Lauderdale, FL 33309. Offers forensic accounting (M Acc). *Entrance requirements:* For master's, baccalaureate degree from accredited institution in accounting, business or a related discipline.

Keiser University, Master of Business Administration Program, Fort Lauderdale, FL 33309. Offers accounting (MBA); health services administration (MBA); international business (MBA); management (MBA); marketing (MBA); technology management (MBA). All concentrations except technology management also offered in Mandarin. *Program availability:* Part-time, online learning.

Kennesaw State University, Coles College of Business, Program in Accounting, Kennesaw, GA 30144. Offers M Acc. *Accreditation:* AACSB. *Program availability:* Part-time, evening/weekend. *Students:* 35 full-time (22 women); includes 12 minority (2 Black or African American, non-Hispanic/Latino; 3 Asian, non-Hispanic/Latino; 5 Hispanic/Latino; 2 Two or more races, non-Hispanic/Latino), 2 international. Average age 24. 75 applicants, 64% accepted, 35 enrolled. In 2018, 54 master's awarded. *Entrance requirements:* For master's, GMAT, minimum GPA of 2.8. Additional exam requirements/recommendations for international students: Required—TOEFL (minimum score 550 paper-based; 80 iBT), IELTS (minimum score 6.5). *Application deadline:* For fall admission, 4/1 for domestic and international students. Applications are processed on a rolling basis. Application fee: $60. Electronic applications accepted. *Expenses:* Contact institution. *Financial support:* Research assistantships with tuition reimbursements, career-related internships or fieldwork, scholarships/grants, and unspecified assistantships available. Financial award application deadline: 4/1; financial award applicants required to submit FAFSA. *Unit head:* Heather Hermanson, Director, 470-578-6041, E-mail: hhermans@kennesaw.edu. *Application contact:* Cynthia True, Program Coordinator, 470-578-7628, E-mail: ctrue2@kennesaw.edu.
Website: http://coles.kennesaw.edu/macc/

Kent State University, College of Business Administration, Doctoral Program in Accounting, Kent, OH 44242. Offers PhD. *Faculty:* 3 full-time (2 women). *Students:* 12 full-time (4 women); includes 1 minority (Asian, non-Hispanic/Latino), 10 international. Average age 33. 22 applicants, 27% accepted, 2 enrolled. In 2018, 3 doctorates awarded. *Degree requirements:* For doctorate, comprehensive exam, thesis/dissertation, oral defense. *Entrance requirements:* For doctorate, GMAT. Additional exam requirements/recommendations for international students: Required—TOEFL (minimum score 600 paper-based; 100 iBT), IELTS (minimum score 7). *Application deadline:* For fall admission, 1/1 for domestic students, 2/1 for international students. Application fee: $45 ($70 for international students). Electronic applications accepted. *Expenses:* Contact institution. *Financial support:* In 2018–19, 11 students received support, including 11 teaching assistantships with full tuition reimbursements available (averaging $23,000 per year). Financial award application deadline: 2/1; financial award applicants required to submit FAFSA. *Faculty research:* Information economics, capital management, use of accounting information, curriculum design. *Unit head:* Dr. Wei Li, Interim Chair, Department of Accounting, 330-672-2545, Fax: 330-672-2548, E-mail: gradbus@kent.edu. *Application contact:* Felecia A. Urbanek, Assistant Director, 330-672-2282, Fax: 330-672-7303, E-mail: gradbus@kent.edu.
Website: http://www.kent.edu/business/phd

Kent State University, College of Business Administration, Master of Science Program in Accounting, Kent, OH 44242. Offers MS. *Program availability:* Part-time, evening/weekend. *Faculty:* 4 full-time (2 women), 2 part-time/adjunct (1 woman). *Students:* 26 full-time (11 women), 2 part-time (1 woman); includes 1 minority (Two or more races, non-Hispanic/Latino), 5 international. Average age 24. 40 applicants, 85% accepted, 17 enrolled. In 2018, 15 master's awarded. *Degree requirements:* For master's, internship. *Entrance requirements:* For master's, GMAT, minimum GPA of 3.0. Additional exam requirements/recommendations for international students: Required—TOEFL (minimum score 550 paper-based; 79 iBT), IELTS (minimum score 6.5). *Application deadline:* For

fall admission, 3/15 priority date for domestic students, 3/15 for international students; for spring admission, 10/15 for domestic and international students; for summer admission, 5/1 for domestic and international students. Applications are processed on a rolling basis. Application fee: $45 ($70 for international students). Electronic applications accepted. *Expenses:* Contact institution. *Financial support:* In 2018–19, 5 students received support, including 5 research assistantships with full tuition reimbursements available (averaging $4,000 per year); Federal Work-Study also available. Financial award application deadline: 3/15; financial award applicants required to submit FAFSA. *Faculty research:* Financial accounting, managerial accounting, auditing, accounting systems. *Unit head:* Wei Lei, Interim Chair, Department of Accounting, 330-672-2545, Fax: 330-672-2548, E-mail: gradbus@kent.edu. *Application contact:* Louise M. Ditchey, Administrative Director, 330-672-2282, Fax: 330-672-7303, E-mail: gradbus@kent.edu.
Website: http://www.kent.edu/business/ms-accounting

King University, School of Business, Economics, and Technology, Bristol, TN 37620-2699. Offers accounting (MBA); finance (MBA); healthcare management (MBA); human resources management (MBA); leadership (MBA); management (MBA); marketing (MBA); project management (MBA). *Program availability:* Part-time, evening/weekend, 100% online, blended/hybrid learning. *Faculty:* 11 full-time (9 women), 10 part-time/adjunct (7 women). *Students:* 182 full-time (107 women), 8 part-time (6 women); includes 18 minority (7 Black or African American, non-Hispanic/Latino; 4 Hispanic/Latino; 1 Native Hawaiian or other Pacific Islander, non-Hispanic/Latino; 6 Two or more races, non-Hispanic/Latino), 2 international. Average age 32. 143 applicants, 98% accepted, 68 enrolled. In 2018, 125 master's awarded. *Degree requirements:* For master's, comprehensive exam, thesis optional. *Entrance requirements:* For master's, resume which demonstrates a minimum of 2 years of full-time work experience, minimum cumulative grade point average of 3.0 on a 4.0 scale is required. Students who do not meet this requirement may be conditionally accepted. Additional exam requirements/recommendations for international students: Required—TOEFL (minimum score 84 paper-based; 84 iBT). *Application deadline:* Applications are processed on a rolling basis. Application fee: $0 ($50 for international students). Electronic applications accepted. *Expenses: Tuition:* Full-time $13,365; part-time $495 per semester hour. *Required fees:* $900; $100 per course. One-time fee: $175. Tuition and fees vary according to class time, degree level and program. *Financial support:* Unspecified assistantships available. Financial award applicants required to submit FAFSA. *Faculty research:* International monetary policy. *Unit head:* Dr. Mark Pate, Dean, School of Business, Economics and Technology, 423-652-4814, E-mail: mjpate@king.edu. *Application contact:* Nancy Beverly, Territory Manager/Enrollment Counselor, 423-341-9495, Fax: 423-652-4727, E-mail: nmbeverly@king.edu.

Lakeland University, Graduate Studies Division, Program in Business Administration, Plymouth, WI 53073. Offers accounting (MBA); finance (MBA); healthcare management (MBA); project management (MBA). *Entrance requirements:* For master's, GMAT. *Expenses:* Contact institution.

Lamar University, College of Graduate Studies, College of Business, Beaumont, TX 77710. Offers accounting (MBA); MSA/MBA. *Accreditation:* AACSB. *Program availability:* Part-time, evening/weekend. *Faculty:* 48 full-time (14 women), 8 part-time/adjunct (3 women). *Students:* 38 full-time (18 women), 242 part-time (141 women); includes 113 minority (60 Black or African American, non-Hispanic/Latino; 13 Asian, non-Hispanic/Latino; 34 Hispanic/Latino; 6 Two or more races, non-Hispanic/Latino), 25 international. Average age 33. 184 applicants, 97% accepted, 48 enrolled. In 2018, 90 master's awarded. *Degree requirements:* For master's, comprehensive exam (for some programs), thesis optional. *Entrance requirements:* For master's, GMAT. Additional exam requirements/recommendations for international students: Required—TOEFL (minimum score 550 paper-based; 79 iBT), IELTS (minimum score 6.5). *Application deadline:* Applications are processed on a rolling basis. Application fee: $25 ($50 for international students). Electronic applications accepted. *Expenses:* Contact institution. *Financial support:* In 2018–19, 33 students received support. Fellowships with tuition reimbursements available, research assistantships with partial tuition reimbursements available, career-related internships or fieldwork, Federal Work-Study, institutionally sponsored loans, scholarships/grants, and tuition waivers (partial) available. Support available to part-time students. Financial award applicants required to submit FAFSA. *Faculty research:* Marketing, finance, quantitative methods, management information systems, legal, environmental. *Total annual research expenditures:* $1,430. *Unit head:* Dr. Dan French, Dean, 409-880-8603, Fax: 409-880-8088, E-mail: dan.french@lamar.edu. *Application contact:* Celeste Contreas, Director, Admissions and Academic Services, 409-880-8888, Fax: 409-880-7419, E-mail: gradmissions@lamar.edu.
Website: http://business.lamar.edu

La Roche University, School of Graduate Studies and Adult Education, Program in Accounting, Pittsburgh, PA 15237-5898. Offers MS. *Program availability:* Part-time, evening/weekend. *Faculty:* 1 (woman) full-time, 2 part-time/adjunct (0 women). *Students:* 4 full-time (2 women), 9 part-time (7 women); includes 1 minority (Hispanic/Latino), 5 international. Average age 31. 21 applicants, 71% accepted, 3 enrolled. In 2018, 6 master's awarded. *Entrance requirements:* For master's, baccalaureate degree in business, accounting or finance from accredited college or university; two letters of recommendation; resume; personal essay. *Application deadline:* For fall admission, 8/15 for domestic and international students; for spring admission, 12/15 for domestic and international students. Applications are processed on a rolling basis. Application fee: $50. Electronic applications accepted. *Expenses: Tuition:* Part-time $735 per credit. *Required fees:* $80; $80 per unit. *Unit head:* Sheila Mueller, Professor/Department Chair of Accounting and Finance, 412-536-1180, Fax: 412-536-1179, E-mail: sheila.mueller@laroche.edu. *Application contact:* Erin Pottgen, Assistant Director, Graduate Admissions, 412-847-2509, Fax: 412-536-1283, E-mail: erin.pottgen@laroche.edu.

La Salle University, School of Business, Master of Business Administration Program, Philadelphia, PA 19141-1199. Offers accounting (MBA, Post-MBA Certificate); business systems and analytics (MBA, Post-MBA Certificate); finance (MBA, Post-MBA Certificate); general business administration (MBA, Post-MBA Certificate); human resource management (MBA, Post-MBA Certificate); management (MBA, Post-MBA Certificate); marketing (Post-MBA Certificate); MBA/MSN. Program also offered in Switzerland. *Accreditation:* AACSB. *Program availability:* Part-time, evening/weekend, online learning. *Entrance requirements:* For master's, GMAT or GRE, two letters of reference; resume; for Post-MBA Certificate, MBA with minimum GPA of 3.0. Additional exam requirements/recommendations for international students: Required—TOEFL. Electronic applications accepted. Application fee is waived when completed online. *Expenses:* Contact institution.

La Sierra University, School of Business and Management, Riverside, CA 92505. Offers accounting (MBA); finance (MBA); general management (MBA); human resources management (MBA); leadership, values, and ethics for business and management (Certificate); marketing (MBA). *Degree requirements:* For master's, research project. *Entrance requirements:* For master's, GMAT, minimum GPA of 3.0. Additional exam requirements/recommendations for international students: Required—TOEFL. *Faculty research:* Financial econometrics, institutional assessment and strategic planning, legal issues in management, behavioral finance, content of financial reports.

Lehigh University, College of Business, Department of Accounting, Bethlehem, PA 18015. Offers accounting and information analysis (MS). *Accreditation:* AACSB. *Program availability:* Part-time. *Faculty:* 6 full-time (0 women), 1 (woman) part-time/adjunct. *Students:* 30 full-time (25 women), 1 part-time (0 women); includes 2 minority (both Asian, non-Hispanic/Latino), 24 international. Average age 24. 68 applicants, 65% accepted, 13 enrolled. In 2018, 24 master's awarded. *Entrance requirements:* For master's, GMAT. Additional exam requirements/recommendations for international students: Required—TOEFL (minimum score 105 iBT). *Application deadline:* For fall admission, 4/15 for domestic and international students. Application fee: $75. *Expenses:* $1280 per credit hour; 30 credits required for degree. *Financial support:* In 2018–19, 19 students received support. Fellowships and scholarships/grants available. Financial award application deadline: 1/15. *Faculty research:* Behavioral accounting, internal control, information systems, supply chain management, financial accounting. *Unit head:* Dr. C. Bryan Cloyd, Chairman, 610-758-2816, Fax: 610-758-6429, E-mail: cbc215@lehigh.edu. *Application contact:* Mary Theresa Taglang, Director of Recruitment and Admissions, 610-758-4386, Fax: 610-758-5283, E-mail: mtt4@lehigh.edu.
Website: https://cbe.lehigh.edu/academics/graduate/master-accounting-and-information-analysis

Lehman College of the City University of New York, School of Natural and Social Sciences, Department of Economics and Business, Bronx, NY 10468-1589. Offers accounting (MS); business (MS). *Entrance requirements:* For master's, GMAT.

Lenoir-Rhyne University, Graduate Programs, Charles M. Snipes School of Business, Hickory, NC 28601. Offers accounting (MBA); business analytics and information technology (MBA); entrepreneurship (MBA); global business (MBA); healthcare administration (MBA); innovation and change management (MBA); leadership development (MBA). *Accreditation:* ACBSP. *Program availability:* Part-time, evening/weekend, online learning. *Degree requirements:* For master's, capstone course. *Entrance requirements:* For master's, GMAT, GRE, MAT, minimum undergraduate GPA of 2.7, graduate 3.0. Additional exam requirements/recommendations for international students: Required—TOEFL (minimum score 600 paper-based). Electronic applications accepted. *Expenses:* Contact institution.

Lewis University, College of Business, Program in Business Administration, Romeoville, IL 60446. Offers accounting (MBA); custom elective option (MBA); e-business (MBA); finance (MBA); healthcare management (MBA); human resources management (MBA); international business (MBA); management information systems (MBA); marketing (MBA); project management (MBA); technology and operations management (MBA). *Program availability:* Part-time, evening/weekend. *Students:* 114 full-time (72 women), 143 part-time (87 women); includes 84 minority (21 Black or African American, non-Hispanic/Latino; 2 American Indian or Alaska Native, non-Hispanic/Latino; 11 Asian, non-Hispanic/Latino; 45 Hispanic/Latino; 5 Two or more races, non-Hispanic/Latino), 17 international. Average age 31. In 2018, 99 master's awarded. *Entrance requirements:* For master's, interview, bachelor's degree, resume, two recommendations. Additional exam requirements/recommendations for international students: Required—TOEFL (minimum score 550 paper-based), IELTS. *Application deadline:* For fall admission, 8/15 priority date for domestic students, 5/1 priority date for international students; for spring admission, 11/15 priority date for international students. Applications are processed on a rolling basis. Application fee: $40. Electronic applications accepted. *Financial support:* Career-related internships or fieldwork, Federal Work-Study, scholarships/grants, and unspecified assistantships available. Financial award application deadline: 5/1; financial award applicants required to submit FAFSA. *Unit head:* Dr. Maureen Culleeney, Academic Program Director, 815-838-0500 Ext. 5631, E-mail: culleema@lewisu.edu. *Application contact:* Michele Ryan, Director of Admission, 815-838-0500 Ext. 5384, E-mail: ryanml@lewisu.edu.

Liberty University, School of Business, Lynchburg, VA 24515. Offers accounting (MBA, MS), including audit and financial reporting (MS), business (MS), financial services (MS), forensic accounting (MS), leadership (MS), taxation (MS); cyber security (MS); executive leadership (MA); international business (DBA); leadership (DBA); marketing (MBA, MS, DBA), including digital marketing and advertising (MS), project management (MS), public relations (MS), sports marketing and media (MS); project management (MBA, DBA); public relations (MBA). *Program availability:* Part-time, online learning. *Students:* 2,871 full-time (1,496 women), 4,437 part-time (1,969 women); includes 2,069 minority (1,424 Black or African American, non-Hispanic/Latino; 44 American Indian or Alaska Native, non-Hispanic/Latino; 133 Asian, non-Hispanic/Latino; 282 Hispanic/Latino; 16 Native Hawaiian or other Pacific Islander, non-Hispanic/Latino; 170 Two or more races, non-Hispanic/Latino), 154 international. Average age 36. 8,980 applicants, 45% accepted, 2009 enrolled. In 2018, 1,988 master's, 25 doctorates awarded. *Entrance requirements:* For master's, minimum undergraduate GPA of 3.0, 15 hours of upper-level business courses. Additional exam requirements/recommendations for international students: Required—TOEFL (minimum score 600 paper-based; 100 iBT). *Application deadline:* Applications are processed on a rolling basis. Application fee: $50. Electronic applications accepted. *Expenses:* Contact institution. *Financial support:* In 2018–19, 990 students received support. Teaching assistantships and Federal Work-Study available. Financial award applicants required to submit FAFSA. *Unit head:* Dr. Dave Bratt, Dean, 434-592-7321, E-mail: dabrat@liberty.edu. *Application contact:* Jay Bridge, Director of Graduate Admissions, 800-424-9595, Fax: 800-628-7977, E-mail: gradadmissions@liberty.edu.
Website: https://www.liberty.edu/business/

Lipscomb University, College of Business, Nashville, TN 37204-3951. Offers accounting and finance (MBA); audit/accounting (M Acc); business (Certificate); business administration (MM); healthcare management (MBA); leadership (MBA); tax (M Acc); MBA/MS; Pharm D/MM. *Accreditation:* ACBSP. *Program availability:* Part-time, evening/weekend. *Entrance requirements:* For master's, GMAT, transcripts, interview, 2 references, resume. Additional exam requirements/recommendations for international students: Required—TOEFL (minimum score 570 paper-based). Electronic applications accepted. *Expenses:* Contact institution. *Faculty research:* Impact of spirituality on organization commitment, women in corporate leadership, psychological empowerment, training.

Long Island University–LIU Brooklyn, School of Business, Public Administration and Information Sciences, Brooklyn, NY 11201-8423. Offers accounting (MBA); accounting (MS); business administration (MBA); computer science (MS); gerontology (Advanced Certificate); health administration (MPA); human resources management (MS); not-for-profit management (Advanced Certificate); public administration (MPA); taxation (MS). *Program availability:* Part-time, evening/weekend. *Entrance requirements:* Additional exam requirements/recommendations for international students: Required—TOEFL (minimum score 550 paper-based; 75 iBT). Electronic applications accepted. *Faculty research:* Tax policy; public sector budgeting and gender inequities; technology and innovation; game theory; knowledge management.

Long Island University–LIU Post, College of Management, Brookville, NY 11548-1300. Offers accountancy (MS); finance (MBA); information systems (MS); international business (MBA); management (MBA); management engineering (MS); marketing (MBA); taxation (MS); technical project management (MS); JD/MBA. *Accreditation:* AACSB. *Program availability:* Part-time, evening/weekend, blended/hybrid learning.

Entrance requirements: For master's, GMAT, GRE, or LSAT. Additional exam requirements/recommendations for international students: Required—TOEFL (minimum score 550 paper-based, 75 iBT) or IELTS. Electronic applications accepted. *Faculty research:* Innovation and property rights, knowledge sourcing, sustainability and firm performance, China and growth markets, corporate social responsibility, workforce compensation and issues.

Louisiana State University and Agricultural & Mechanical College, Graduate School, E. J. Ourso College of Business, Department of Accounting, Baton Rouge, LA 70803. Offers MS, PhD.

Louisiana Tech University, Graduate School, College of Business, Ruston, LA 71272. Offers accounting (M Acc, DBA); computer information systems (DBA); finance (MBA, DBA); information assurance (MBA); innovation (MBA); management (DBA); marketing (MBA, DBA). *Accreditation:* AACSB. *Program availability:* Part-time, evening/weekend, 100% online, blended/hybrid learning. *Degree requirements:* For doctorate, thesis/dissertation. *Entrance requirements:* For master's and doctorate, GMAT, transcript with bachelor's degree awarded. Additional exam requirements/recommendations for international students: Required—TOEFL (minimum score 550 paper-based; 80 iBT), IELTS (minimum score 6.5). Electronic applications accepted. *Faculty research:* Consumer environmental behavior; identifying and analyzing current issues and future concerns in real estate; information assurance and related areas in business for Northwest Louisiana and the United States (business continuity, disaster recovery, accounting controls, auditing, computer forensics, and security attribution); value creation driven by the consumer and employee interface within exchange environments.

Loyola Marymount University, College of Business Administration, Master of Science in Accounting Program, Los Angeles, CA 90045. Offers MS. *Unit head:* Dr. Terry Wang, Director, Master of Science in Accounting Program, 310-338-7792, E-mail: YingYing.Wang@lmu.edu. *Application contact:* Ammar Dalal, Assistant Vice Provost for Graduate Enrollment, 310-338-2721, Fax: 310-338-6086, E-mail: graduateinfo@lmu.edu.
Website: http://cba.lmu.edu/academics/msinaccounting

Loyola University Chicago, Quinlan School of Business, Master of Science in Accountancy Program, Chicago, IL 60611. Offers MSA. *Accreditation:* AACSB. *Program availability:* Part-time, evening/weekend. *Entrance requirements:* For master's, GMAT or GRE, official transcripts, two letters of recommendation, statement of purpose, resume. Additional exam requirements/recommendations for international students: Required—TOEFL (minimum score 90 iBT) or IELTS (minimum score 6.5). Electronic applications accepted. Application fee is waived when completed online. *Expenses:* Contact institution. *Faculty research:* Investigate taxonomy of financial ratios across industries and financial reporting standards, federal transfer taxation, federal fiduciary taxation, estate planning, fraud in local governments, multi-disciplinary instructional cases for class use, impact of changes in accounting standards and business practices on the use of financial ratios, employment attributes for college graduates, credit relevance of litigation materiality disclosures.

Loyola University Chicago, Quinlan School of Business, MBA Programs, Chicago, IL 60611. Offers accounting (MBA); business ethics (MBA); derivative markets (MBA); economics (MBA); entrepreneurship (MBA); finance (MBA); healthcare management (MBA); human resources management (MBA); information systems management (MBA); international business (MBA); management (MBA); marketing (MBA); risk management (MBA); supply chain management (MBA). *Program availability:* Part-time, evening/weekend. *Entrance requirements:* For master's, GMAT or GRE, official transcripts, two letters of recommendation, statement of purpose, resume. Additional exam requirements/recommendations for international students: Required—TOEFL (minimum score 90 iBT) or IELTS (minimum score 6.5). Electronic applications accepted. Application fee is waived when completed online. *Expenses:* Contact institution. *Faculty research:* Social enterprise and responsibility, emerging markets, supply chain management, risk management.

Maharishi University of Management, Graduate Studies, Program in Business Administration, Fairfield, IA 52557. Offers accounting (MBA); management (PhD); sustainability (MBA). *Program availability:* Evening/weekend, online learning. *Degree requirements:* For doctorate, thesis/dissertation. *Entrance requirements:* For master's, GMAT, minimum GPA of 3.0; for doctorate, minimum GPA of 3.0. Additional exam requirements/recommendations for international students: Required—TOEFL. *Expenses:* Tuition: Full-time $29,000; part-time $4800 per credit hour. *Required fees:* $530. *Faculty research:* Leadership, effects of the group dynamics of consciousness on the economy, innovation, employee development, cooperative strategy.

Manhattanville College, School of Professional Studies, Master of Science in Finance, Purchase, NY 10577-2132. Offers finance (MS, Advanced Certificate), including accounting (MS), corporate finance (MS), investment management (MS). *Program availability:* Part-time, evening/weekend. *Faculty:* 6 part-time/adjunct (2 women). *Students:* 12 full-time (5 women), 8 part-time (3 women); includes 8 minority (2 Black or African American, non-Hispanic/Latino; 6 Hispanic/Latino), 1 international. Average age 32. 19 applicants, 16% accepted, 2 enrolled. In 2018, 13 master's awarded. *Degree requirements:* For master's, thesis (for some programs), final project. *Entrance requirements:* For master's, scores of GRE and GMAT are optional, personal essay, transcripts, 2 letters of recommendation (academic or professional), resume, health form with proof of immunization (for those born after 1957). Additional exam requirements/recommendations for international students: Required—TOEFL (minimum score 563 paper-based; 85 iBT), TOEFL (minimum score 563 paper-based, 85 iBT), IELTS (7), or iTEP (B2); Recommended—IELTS (minimum score 7). *Application deadline:* Applications are processed on a rolling basis. Application fee: $75. Electronic applications accepted. *Expenses:* 935 per credit. *Financial support:* Federal Work-Study, institutionally sponsored loans, scholarships/grants, and unspecified assistantships available. Financial award application deadline: 3/15; financial award applicants required to submit FAFSA. *Unit head:* Laura Persky, Associate Dean, 914-323-5188, E-mail: Laura.Persky@mville.edu. *Application contact:* Monika Pottgen, Assistant Director of Recruitment and Admissions, 914-323-5150, E-mail: sps@mville.edu.
Website: https://www.mville.edu/programs/ms-finance

Marist College, Graduate Programs, School of Management, Program in Professional Accountancy, Poughkeepsie, NY 12601-1387. Offers MS.

Marquette University, Graduate School of Management, Program in Accounting, Milwaukee, WI 53201-1881. Offers MSA. *Accreditation:* AACSB. *Program availability:* Part-time, evening/weekend. *Entrance requirements:* For master's, GMAT or GRE, letters of recommendation (if applying for financial aid). Additional exam requirements/recommendations for international students: Required—TOEFL (minimum score 550 paper-based; 88 iBT), IELTS (minimum score 6.5), PTE. Electronic applications accepted. *Faculty research:* Financial (accounting) literacy, international perception of corruption, effect of carbon credits on accounting and tax transactions, targeted tax breaks.

Marshall University, Academic Affairs Division, College of Business, Program in Accountancy, Huntington, WV 25755. Offers MS. *Entrance requirements:* For master's, undergraduate degree in accounting with minimum GPA of 3.0 or GMAT.

Maryville University of Saint Louis, The John E. Simon School of Business, St. Louis, MO 63141-7299. Offers accounting (MBA, MS, Certificate); business studies (Certificate); cybersecurity (MBA, MS, Certificate); financial services (MBA, Certificate); health administration (MBA); healthcare administration (Certificate); human resource management (MBA); human resources management (Certificate); information technology (MBA); information technology management (Certificate); management (MBA, Certificate); management and leadership (MA); marketing (MBA, Certificate); project management (MBA, Certificate); sport business management (MBA); supply chain management (Certificate); supply chain management/logistics (MBA). *Accreditation:* ACBSP. *Program availability:* Part-time, 100% online, blended/hybrid learning. *Faculty:* 5 full-time (1 woman), 77 part-time/adjunct (19 women). *Students:* 338 full-time (166 women), 739 part-time (356 women); includes 310 minority (161 Black or African American, non-Hispanic/Latino; 6 American Indian or Alaska Native, non-Hispanic/Latino; 59 Asian, non-Hispanic/Latino; 57 Hispanic/Latino; 27 Two or more races, non-Hispanic/Latino), 30 international. Average age 33. In 2018, 143 master's awarded. *Degree requirements:* For master's, capstone course (for MBA). *Entrance requirements:* Additional exam requirements/recommendations for international students: Required—TOEFL (minimum score 563 paper-based; 85 iBT). *Application deadline:* Applications are processed on a rolling basis. Electronic applications accepted. *Expenses:* Tuition varies by program. *Financial support:* Career-related internships or fieldwork, Federal Work-Study, tuition waivers (partial), and campus employment available. Financial award application deadline: 4/1; financial award applicants required to submit FAFSA. *Unit head:* Tammy Gocial, Interim Dean, 314-529-9401, Fax: 314-529-9975, E-mail: tgocial@maryville.edu. *Application contact:* Chris Gourdine, Assistant Dean Business Administration, 314-529-6861, Fax: 314-529-9975, E-mail: cgourdine@maryville.edu.
Website: http://www.maryville.edu/bu/business-administration-masters/

McGill University, Faculty of Graduate and Postdoctoral Studies, Desautels Faculty of Management, Montréal, QC H3A 2T5, Canada. Offers administration (PhD); entrepreneurial studies (MBA); finance (MBA); general management (Post Master's Certificate); global manufacturing and supply chain management (MMM); information systems (MBA); international business (MBA); international practicing management (MM); management (MBA); management for development (MBA); marketing (MBA); operations management (MBA); public accountancy (Diploma); strategic management (MBA); MBA/LL B; MD/MBA. MMM offered jointly with Faculty of Engineering; PhD with Concordia University, HEC Montreal, Université de Montréal, Université du Québec à Montréal.

Mercer University, Graduate Studies, Cecil B. Day Campus, Eugene W. Stetson School of Business and Economics (Atlanta), Atlanta, GA 30341. Offers accounting (M Acc); innovation (PMBA), including entrepreneurship; international business (MBA); DPT/MBA; M Div/MBA; MBA/M Acc; Pharm D/MBA. *Accreditation:* AACSB. *Program availability:* Part-time, evening/weekend, 100% online, blended/hybrid learning. *Entrance requirements:* For master's, GMAT or GRE. Additional exam requirements/recommendations for international students: Required—TOEFL (minimum score 550 paper-based, 80 iBT) or IELTS. Electronic applications accepted. *Expenses:* Contact institution. *Faculty research:* Entrepreneurship, market studies, international business strategy, financial analysis.

Mercy College, School of Business, Program in Public Accounting, Dobbs Ferry, NY 10522-1189. Offers accounting (MS). *Program availability:* Part-time, evening/weekend. *Students:* 24 full-time (12 women), 4 part-time (2 women); includes 13 minority (2 Black or African American, non-Hispanic/Latino; 4 Asian, non-Hispanic/Latino; 6 Hispanic/Latino; 1 Two or more races, non-Hispanic/Latino). Average age 26. 20 applicants, 45% accepted, 8 enrolled. In 2018, 15 master's awarded. *Degree requirements:* For master's, thesis or alternative, Capstone project required. *Entrance requirements:* For master's, GMAT or equivalent may be required for some applicants, transcript(s); personal statement; interview. Additional exam requirements/recommendations for international students: Required—TOEFL (minimum score 80 iBT), IELTS (minimum score 6.5). *Application deadline:* Applications are processed on a rolling basis. Application fee: $40. Electronic applications accepted. *Expenses:* Contact institution. *Financial support:* Career-related internships or fieldwork, Federal Work-Study, scholarships/grants, and unspecified assistantships available. Support available to part-time students. Financial award applicants required to submit FAFSA. *Unit head:* Dr. Lloyd Gibson, Dean, School of Business, 914-674-7159, E-mail: lgibson@mercy.edu. *Application contact:* Allison Gurdineer, Executive Director of Admissions, 877-637-2946, Fax: 914-674-7382, E-mail: admissions@mercy.edu.
Website: https://www.mercy.edu/degrees-programs/ms-public-accounting

Mercyhurst University, Graduate Studies, Program in Organizational Leadership, Erie, PA 16546. Offers accounting (MS); higher education administration (MS); human resources (MS); organizational leadership (MS, Certificate); sports leadership (MS); strategy and innovation (MS). *Program availability:* Part-time, evening/weekend. *Degree requirements:* For master's, thesis. *Entrance requirements:* For master's, GRE General Test or MAT, interview, resume, essay, three professional references, transcripts. Additional exam requirements/recommendations for international students: Required—TOEFL (minimum score 80 iBT), IELTS (minimum score 6.5). Electronic applications accepted. *Faculty research:* Leadership training, organizational communication, leadership pedagogy.

Merrimack College, Girard School of Business, North Andover, MA 01845-5800. Offers accounting (MS); business analytics (MS); management (MS). *Program availability:* Part-time, evening/weekend, 100% online. *Faculty:* 5 full-time (1 woman), 3 part-time/adjunct (1 woman). *Students:* 81 full-time (33 women), 32 part-time (17 women); includes 11 minority (6 Black or African American, non-Hispanic/Latino; 3 Asian, non-Hispanic/Latino; 2 Two or more races, non-Hispanic/Latino), 11 international. Average age 30. 200 applicants, 75% accepted, 79 enrolled. In 2018, 78 master's awarded. *Degree requirements:* For master's, comprehensive exam (for some programs), thesis optional, capstone. *Entrance requirements:* For master's, official college transcripts, resume, personal statement, 2 recommendations. Additional exam requirements/recommendations for international students: Required—TOEFL (minimum score 84 iBT), IELTS (minimum score 6.5), PTE (minimum score 56). *Application deadline:* For fall admission, 8/24 for domestic students, 7/30 for international students; for spring admission, 1/10 for domestic and international students; for summer admission, 5/10 for domestic students, 4/10 for international students. Applications are processed on a rolling basis. Application fee: $0. Electronic applications accepted. Application fee is waived when completed online. *Expenses:* $885 per credit. *Financial support:* Career-related internships or fieldwork, scholarships/grants, health care benefits, and unspecified assistantships available. Support available to part-time students. Financial award application deadline: 5/1; financial award applicants required to submit FAFSA. *Unit head:* Dr. Catherine Usoff, Dean, 978-837-5044, E-mail: usoffc@merrimack.edu. *Application contact:* Jennifer Greenwood, Graduate Admission Counselor, 978-837-3563, E-mail: graduate@merrimack.edu.
Website: http://www.merrimack.edu/academics/graduate/

Metropolitan State University of Denver, School of Business, Denver, CO 80204. Offers accounting (MP Acc); fraud exam and forensic auditing (MP Acc); internal audit (MP Acc); public accounting (MP Acc); taxation (MP Acc). *Accreditation:* AACSB. *Entrance requirements:* For master's, GMAT. *Expenses:* Contact institution.

Accounting

Miami University, Farmer School of Business, Department of Accountancy, Oxford, OH 45056. Offers M Acc. *Accreditation:* AACSB. *Faculty:* 20 full-time (6 women). *Students:* 18 full-time (6 women); includes 4 minority (2 Asian, non-Hispanic/Latino; 1 Hispanic/Latino; 1 Two or more races, non-Hispanic/Latino), 1 international. Average age 22. In 2018, 53 master's awarded. *Unit head:* Andrew Reffett, Chair and Professor, 513-529-6212, E-mail: reffeta@miamioh.edu. *Application contact:* Amanda Pyzoha, Academic Program Coordinator, 513-529-3372, E-mail: shickar@miamioh.edu.
Website: http://www.MiamiOH.edu/accountancy

Michigan State University, The Graduate School, Eli Broad College of Business, Department of Accounting and Information Systems, East Lansing, MI 48224. Offers accounting (MS, PhD), including information systems (MS), public and corporate accounting (MS), taxation (MS); business information systems (PhD). *Accreditation:* AACSB. *Degree requirements:* For doctorate, comprehensive exam, thesis/dissertation. *Entrance requirements:* For master's, GMAT (minimum score 550), bachelor's degree in accounting; minimum cumulative GPA of 3.0 at any institution attended and in any junior-/senior-level accounting courses taken; 3 letters of recommendation (at least 1 from faculty); working knowledge of computers including word processing, spreadsheets, networking, and database management system; for doctorate, GMAT (minimum score 600), bachelor's degree; transcripts; 3 letters of recommendation; statement of purpose; resume; on-campus interview; personal qualifications of sound character, perseverance, intellectual curiosity, and interest in scholarly research. Additional exam requirements/recommendations for international students: Required—TOEFL (minimum score 600 paper-based; 100 iBT), IELTS (minimum score 7) accepted for MS only. Electronic applications accepted.

Middle Tennessee State University, College of Graduate Studies, Jennings A. Jones College of Business, Department of Accounting, Murfreesboro, TN 37132. Offers M Acc. *Accreditation:* AACSB. *Program availability:* Part-time, evening/weekend, online learning. *Entrance requirements:* For master's, GMAT (minimum score of 400). Additional exam requirements/recommendations for international students: Required—TOEFL (minimum score 525 paper-based; 71 iBT) or IELTS (minimum score 6). Electronic applications accepted.

Millennia Atlantic University, Graduate Programs, Doral, FL 33178. Offers accounting (MBA); business administration (MBA); health information management (MS); human resource management (MA). *Program availability:* Online learning.

Millsaps College, Else School of Management, Jackson, MS 39210. Offers accounting (M Acc); business administration (MBA). *Accreditation:* AACSB. *Program availability:* Part-time. *Entrance requirements:* For master's, GMAT. Additional exam requirements/recommendations for international students: Required—TOEFL. Electronic applications accepted. *Faculty research:* Ethics, audit independence, satisfaction with assurance services, political business cycles, economic development, commercialization of new products.

Minnesota State University Mankato, College of Graduate Studies and Research, College of Business, Mankato, MN 56001. Offers accounting (MSA); business (MBA). *Accreditation:* AACSB. *Entrance requirements:* For master's, GMAT, 2 letters of reference, resume. Additional exam requirements/recommendations for international students: Required—TOEFL. Electronic applications accepted.

Misericordia University, College of Business, Master of Business Administration Program, Dallas, PA 18612-1098. Offers accounting (MBA); healthcare management (MBA); human resource management (MBA); management (MBA); sport management (MBA). *Program availability:* Part-time, evening/weekend, online learning. *Entrance requirements:* For master's, GMAT, MAT, GRE (50th percentile or higher), or minimum undergraduate GPA of 3.0, interview. Additional exam requirements/recommendations for international students: Required—TOEFL. Electronic applications accepted. Application fee is waived when completed online. *Expenses:* Contact institution.

Mississippi College, Graduate School, School of Business, Clinton, MS 39058. Offers accounting (Certificate); business administration (MBA), including accounting; business education (M Ed); finance (MBA, Certificate); JD/MBA. *Accreditation:* ACBSP. *Program availability:* Part-time, evening/weekend. *Degree requirements:* For master's, comprehensive exam, thesis optional. *Entrance requirements:* For master's, GMAT, minimum GPA of 2.5, 24 hours of undergraduate course work in business. Additional exam requirements/recommendations for international students: Recommended—TOEFL, IELTS. Electronic applications accepted.

Mississippi State University, College of Business, Adkerson School of Accountancy, Mississippi State, MS 39762. Offers accountancy (MPA); systems (MPA). *Accreditation:* AACSB. *Faculty:* 10 full-time (0 women). *Students:* 63 full-time (43 women), 1 part-time (0 women); includes 2 minority (1 Asian, non-Hispanic/Latino; 1 Hispanic/Latino), 1 international. Average age 24. 32 applicants, 78% accepted, 20 enrolled. In 2018, 59 master's awarded. *Degree requirements:* For master's, comprehensive exam. *Entrance requirements:* For master's, GMAT (minimum score of 510), minimum GPA of 3.0 over last 60 hours of undergraduate course work. Additional exam requirements/recommendations for international students: Required—TOEFL (minimum score 575 paper-based; 84 iBT); Recommended—IELTS (minimum score 7). *Application deadline:* For fall admission, 7/1 for domestic students, 5/1 for international students; for spring admission, 11/1 for domestic students, 9/1 for international students. Applications are processed on a rolling basis. Application fee: $60 ($80 for international students). Electronic applications accepted. *Expenses:* Tuition, state resident: full-time $8450; part-time $360.59 per credit hour. Tuition, nonresident: full-time $23,140; part-time $969.09 per credit hour. *Required fees:* $110. One-time fee: $55 full-time. Part-time tuition and fees vary according to course load, degree level, campus/location and reciprocity agreements. *Financial support:* Career-related internships or fieldwork, Federal Work-Study, institutionally sponsored loans, scholarships/grants, and unspecified assistantships available. Support available to part-time students. Financial award application deadline: 4/1; financial award applicants required to submit FAFSA. *Faculty research:* Income tax, financial accounting system, managerial accounting, auditing. *Unit head:* Dr. Shawn Mauldin, Professor and Director, 662-325-3710, Fax: 662-325-1646, E-mail: smauldin@business.msstate.edu. *Application contact:* Robbie Salters, Admissions and Enrollment Assistant, 662-325-7400, E-mail: rsalters@grad.msstate.edu.
Website: http://www.business.msstate.edu/programs/adkerson

Missouri State University, Graduate College, College of Business, School of Accountancy, Springfield, MO 65897. Offers M Acc. *Accreditation:* AACSB. *Program availability:* Part-time, evening/weekend. *Faculty:* 13 full-time (3 women). *Students:* 42 full-time (23 women), 16 part-time (11 women); includes 8 minority (5 Asian, non-Hispanic/Latino; 2 Hispanic/Latino; 1 Two or more races, non-Hispanic/Latino), 7 international. Average age 22. 39 applicants, 38% accepted. In 2018, 27 master's awarded. *Entrance requirements:* For master's, GMAT (minimum composite score of 500), minimum GPA of 3.2 in last 60 hours of coursework. Additional exam requirements/recommendations for international students: Required—TOEFL (minimum score 90 iBT). *Application deadline:* For fall admission, 7/20 priority date for domestic students, 5/1 for international students; for spring admission, 12/20 priority date for domestic students, 9/1 for international students; for summer admission, 5/20 priority date for domestic students. Applications are processed on a rolling basis. Application fee: $55 ($60 for international students). Electronic applications accepted. Tuition and fees vary according to class time, course level, course load, degree level, campus/location, program and student level. *Financial support:* Career-related internships or fieldwork, Federal Work-Study, institutionally sponsored loans, scholarships/grants, tuition waivers (partial), and unspecified assistantships available. Support available to part-time students. Financial award application deadline: 1/31; financial award applicants required to submit FAFSA. *Faculty research:* Forensic accounting, accounting information systems, accounting education, tax compliance. *Unit head:* Dr. John R. Williams, Director, 417-836-5414, Fax: 417-836-6337, E-mail: accountancy@missouristate.edu. *Application contact:* Lakan Drinker, Director, Graduate Enrollment Management, 417-836-5330, Fax: 417-836-6200, E-mail: lakandrinker@missouristate.edu.
Website: http://www.missouristate.edu/soa/

Missouri Western State University, Program in Business Administration, St. Joseph, MO 64507-2294. Offers animal and life sciences (MBA); enterprise resource planning (MBA); forensic accounting (MBA); general business (MBA). *Program availability:* Part-time, 100% online. *Students:* 25 full-time (12 women), 41 part-time (17 women); includes 8 minority (3 Black or African American, non-Hispanic/Latino; 2 American Indian or Alaska Native, non-Hispanic/Latino; 2 Asian, non-Hispanic/Latino; 1 Two or more races, non-Hispanic/Latino), 1 international. Average age 32. 45 applicants, 93% accepted, 25 enrolled. In 2018, 19 master's awarded. *Entrance requirements:* Additional exam requirements/recommendations for international students: Recommended—TOEFL (minimum score 79 iBT), IELTS (minimum score 6). *Application deadline:* For fall admission, 7/15 for domestic and international students; for spring admission, 11/1 for domestic and international students; for summer admission, 4/29 for domestic and international students. Applications are processed on a rolling basis. Application fee: $45 ($50 for international students). Electronic applications accepted. *Expenses: Tuition, area resident:* Part-time $359.39 per credit hour. Tuition, state resident: part-time $359.39 per credit hour. Tuition, nonresident: part-time $643.39 per credit hour. Tuition and fees vary according to program. *Financial support:* Scholarships/grants and unspecified assistantships available. Support available to part-time students. *Unit head:* Dr. Logan Jones, Dean of Craig School of Business, 816-271-4338, E-mail: jones@missouriwestern.edu. *Application contact:* Dr. Susan Bashinski, Dean of the Graduate School, 816-271-4394, Fax: 816-271-4525, E-mail: graduate@missouriwestern.edu.
Website: https://www.missouriwestern.edu/business/mba/

Molloy College, Graduate Business Program, Rockville Centre, NY 11571-5002. Offers accounting (MBA); finance (MBA, Post-Master's Certificate, Postbaccalaureate Certificate); healthcare (MBA, Post-Master's Certificate, Postbaccalaureate Certificate); management (MBA); marketing (MBA, Post-Master's Certificate, Postbaccalaureate Certificate); personal financial planning (MBA). *Program availability:* Part-time, evening/weekend. *Faculty:* 9 full-time (2 women), 20 part-time/adjunct (8 women). *Students:* 75 full-time (45 women), 164 part-time (88 women); includes 100 minority (45 Black or African American, non-Hispanic/Latino; 21 Asian, non-Hispanic/Latino; 30 Hispanic/Latino; 1 Native Hawaiian or other Pacific Islander, non-Hispanic/Latino; 3 Two or more races, non-Hispanic/Latino), 3 international. Average age 40. 97 applicants, 78% accepted, 65 enrolled. In 2018, 91 master's, 1 other advanced degree awarded. *Entrance requirements:* Additional exam requirements/recommendations for international students: Required—TOEFL (minimum score 550 paper-based; 79 iBT). *Application deadline:* Applications are processed on a rolling basis. Application fee: $60. Electronic applications accepted. *Expenses: Tuition:* Full-time $20,790; part-time $1155 per credit. *Required fees:* $1060; $900. Tuition and fees vary according to course load and degree level. *Financial support:* Application deadline: 3/1; applicants required to submit FAFSA. *Faculty research:* Graduate education - pedagogy and the capstone experience; Freedom of Speech in the workplace; employer liability for sexual harassment in the workplace; educational economics and industrial organization; corporate governance and distressed debt analysis; social network analysis; market segmentation. *Unit head:* Dr. Maureen Mackenzie, Dean, Division of Business/Director of Graduate Programs, 516-323-3080, E-mail: mmackenzie@molloy.edu. *Application contact:* Faye Hood, Assistant Director for Admissions, 516-323-4009, E-mail: fhood@molloy.edu.
Website: http://www.molloy.edu/academics/graduate-programs/graduate-business

Monmouth University, Graduate Studies, Leon Hess Business School, West Long Branch, NJ 07764-1898. Offers accounting (MBA, Certificate); business administration (MBA); finance (MBA); management (MBA); marketing (MBA); real estate (MBA). *Accreditation:* AACSB. *Program availability:* Part-time, evening/weekend. *Faculty:* 22 full-time (5 women), 8 part-time/adjunct (1 woman). *Students:* 91 full-time (47 women), 87 part-time (35 women); includes 17 minority (2 Black or African American, non-Hispanic/Latino; 6 Asian, non-Hispanic/Latino; 7 Hispanic/Latino; 2 Two or more races, non-Hispanic/Latino), 12 international. Average age 29. In 2018, 79 master's, 1 other advanced degree awarded. *Degree requirements:* For master's, capstone course. *Entrance requirements:* For master's, GMAT or GRE, current resume; essay (500 words or less). Additional exam requirements/recommendations for international students: Required—TOEFL (minimum score 550 paper-based; 79 iBT), IELTS (minimum score 6), Michigan English Language Assessment Battery (minimum score 77) or Certificate of Advanced English (minimum score 160). *Application deadline:* For fall admission, 7/15 priority date for domestic students, 6/1 for international students; for spring admission, 12/1 priority date for domestic students, 11/1 for international students; for summer admission, 5/1 for domestic students. Applications are processed on a rolling basis. Application fee: $50. Electronic applications accepted. *Expenses: Tuition:* Part-time $1233 per credit. *Required fees:* $178 per term. *Financial support:* In 2018–19, 131 students received support. Institutionally sponsored loans, scholarships/grants, and unspecified assistantships available. Support available to part-time students. Financial award applicants required to submit FAFSA. *Faculty research:* Information technology and marketing, behavioral research in accounting, human resources, management of technology. *Unit head:* Dr. Susan Gupta, MBA Program Director, 732-571-3639, Fax: 732-263-5517, E-mail: sgupta@monmouth.edu. *Application contact:* Laurie Kuhn, Associate Director of Graduate Admission, 732-571-3452, Fax: 732-263-5123, E-mail: gradadm@monmouth.edu.
Website: https://www.monmouth.edu/business-school/leon-hess-business-school.aspx

Monroe College, King Graduate School, Bronx, NY 10468. Offers accounting (MS); business administration (MBA), including entrepreneurship, finance, general business administration, healthcare management, human resources, information technology, marketing; computer science (MS); criminal justice (MS); hospitality management (MS); public health (MPH), including biostatistics and epidemiology, community health, health administration and leadership. *Program availability:* Online learning.

Montana State University, The Graduate School, College of Business, Bozeman, MT 59717. Offers professional accountancy (MP Ac). *Accreditation:* AACSB. *Program availability:* Part-time. *Degree requirements:* For master's, comprehensive exam. *Entrance requirements:* For master's, GRE General Test, GMAT, minimum undergraduate GPA of 3.1 (preferred). Additional exam requirements/recommendations for international students: Required—TOEFL (minimum score 550 paper-based). Electronic applications accepted. *Faculty research:* Tax research, accounting education, fraud issues, CPA exams.

Montclair State University, The Graduate School, Feliciano School of Business, General MBA Program, Montclair, NJ 07043-1624. Offers accounting (MBA); business analytics (MBA); digital marketing (MBA); finance (MBA); general business administration (MBA); human resources management (MBA); management (MBA); management of information and technology (MBA); marketing (MBA); project management (MBA). *Program availability:* Part-time, evening/weekend. *Degree requirements:* For master's, culminating experience. *Entrance requirements:* For master's, GMAT or GRE General Test, 2 letters of recommendation, resume, essay. Additional exam requirements/recommendations for international students: Required—TOEFL (minimum score 83 iBT), IELTS (minimum score 6.5). Electronic applications accepted. *Faculty research:* Accounting, management, marketing.

Montclair State University, The Graduate School, Feliciano School of Business, Post Master's Certificate Program in Accounting, Montclair, NJ 07043-1624. Offers Post Master's Certificate. *Program availability:* Part-time, evening/weekend. *Entrance requirements:* For degree, 2 letters of recommendation, essay. Additional exam requirements/recommendations for international students: Required—TOEFL (minimum score 83 iBT), IELTS (minimum score 6.5). Electronic applications accepted. *Faculty research:* Economic costs and benefits of tax incentive programs, sustainability and financial accounting, auditors' expanded role post-Great Recession, revising rules for restructuring charges, aggressive accounting and ethical behavior.

Montclair State University, The Graduate School, Feliciano School of Business, Program in Accounting, Montclair, NJ 07043-1624. Offers MS. *Program availability:* Part-time, evening/weekend. *Degree requirements:* For master's, culminating experience. *Entrance requirements:* For master's, GMAT, 2 letters of recommendation, resume, essay. Additional exam requirements/recommendations for international students: Required—TOEFL (minimum score 83 iBT), IELTS (minimum score 6.5). Electronic applications accepted. *Faculty research:* Economic costs and benefits of tax incentive programs, sustainability and financial accounting, auditors' expanded role post-Great Recession, revising rules for restructuring charges, aggressive accounting and ethical behavior.

Montclair State University, The Graduate School, Feliciano School of Business, Program in Forensic Accounting, Montclair, NJ 07043-1624. Offers Graduate Certificate.

Moravian College, Graduate and Continuing Studies, Business and Management Programs, Bethlehem, PA 18018-6650. Offers accounting (MBA); business management (MBA); health administration (MHA); HR leadership (MSHRM); supply chain management (MBA). *Program availability:* Part-time, evening/weekend. *Faculty:* 3 full-time (2 women), 13 part-time/adjunct (4 women). *Students:* 13 full-time (12 women), 70 part-time (38 women); includes 10 minority (1 Black or African American, non-Hispanic/Latino; 9 Hispanic/Latino), 1 international. Average age 30. 92 applicants, 85% accepted, 58 enrolled. In 2018, 34 master's awarded. *Entrance requirements:* For master's, current resume, official transcripts, 2 letters of recommendation. Additional exam requirements/recommendations for international students: Required—TOEFL (minimum score 577 paper-based), IELTS (minimum score 6.5). *Application deadline:* For fall admission, 8/1 priority date for domestic and international students; for spring admission, 1/1 priority date for domestic and international students; for summer admission, 5/1 priority date for domestic and international students. Applications are processed on a rolling basis. Electronic applications accepted. *Financial support:* Research assistantships available. Financial award applicants required to submit FAFSA. *Faculty research:* Leadership, change management, human resources. *Unit head:* Dr. Katie P. Desiderio, Executive Director, Graduate Business Programs, 610-861-1400, Fax: 610-861-1466, E-mail: graduate@moravian.edu. *Application contact:* Kristy Sullivan, Director of Student Recruitment Operations, 610-861-1400, Fax: 610-861-1466, E-mail: graduate@moravian.edu.
Website: https://www.moravian.edu/graduate/programs/business#/

Morgan State University, School of Graduate Studies, Earl G. Graves School of Business and Management, PhD Program in Business Administration, Baltimore, MD 21251. Offers business administration (PhD), including accounting, information systems, management and marketing. *Accreditation:* AACSB. *Entrance requirements:* For doctorate, GMAT. Additional exam requirements/recommendations for international students: Required—TOEFL (minimum score 550 paper-based).

Morgan State University, School of Graduate Studies, Earl G. Graves School of Business and Management, Program in Accounting, Baltimore, MD 21251. Offers MS.

Mount Aloysius College, Program in Business Administration, Cresson, PA 16630. Offers accounting (MBA); health and human services administration (MBA); non-profit management (MBA); project management (MBA). *Program availability:* Part-time, evening/weekend. *Entrance requirements:* Additional exam requirements/recommendations for international students: Required—IELTS (minimum score 5.5); Recommended—TOEFL. *Application deadline:* For fall admission, 8/1 for domestic students; for spring admission, 12/1 for domestic students. Applications are processed on a rolling basis. Application fee: $30. Electronic applications accepted. Application fee is waived when completed online. *Financial support:* Unspecified assistantships available. Financial award applicants required to submit FAFSA. *Application contact:* Matthew P. Bodenschatz, Director of Graduate and Continuing Education Admissions, 814-886-6556, Fax: 814-886-6441, E-mail: mbodenschatz@mtaloy.edu.

Murray State University, Arthur J. Bauernfeind College of Business, MBA Program, Murray, KY 42071. Offers accounting (MBA); finance (MBA); global communications (MBA); human resource management (MBA); marketing (MBA). *Accreditation:* AACSB. *Program availability:* Part-time, evening/weekend, 100% online, blended/hybrid learning. *Entrance requirements:* For master's, GRE or GMAT, minimum university GPA of 2.75. Additional exam requirements/recommendations for international students: Required—TOEFL (minimum score 527 paper-based; 71 iBT). *Faculty research:* Human resource management, e-commerce, supply-chain management, investment management, accounting.

National American University, Roueche Graduate Center, Austin, TX 78731. Offers accounting (MBA); aviation management (MBA, MM); care coordination (MSN); community college leadership (Ed D); criminal justice (MM); e-marketing (MBA, MM); health care administration (MBA, MM); higher education (MM); human resources management (MBA, MM); information technology management (MBA, MM); international business (MBA); leadership (EMBA); management (MBA); nursing administration (MSN); nursing education (MSN); nursing informatics (MSN); operations and configuration management (MBA, MM); project and process management (MBA, MM). Master's programs offered online through the Harold D. Buckingham Graduate School. *Program availability:* Part-time, evening/weekend, online learning. *Entrance requirements:* For master's, minimum undergraduate GPA of 2.75. Additional exam requirements/recommendations for international students: Required—TOEFL, TWE. Electronic applications accepted. *Faculty research:* Tourism, finance, marketing.

National University, School of Business and Management, La Jolla, CA 92037-1011. Offers accountancy (M Acc, Certificate); business administration (GMBA, MBA); business analytics (MS); cause leadership (MA); global management (MGM); human resource management (MA); management information systems (MS); marketing (MS); organizational leadership (MS). GMBA offered in Spanish. *Program availability:* Part-time, evening/weekend, 100% online, blended/hybrid learning. *Degree requirements:*

For master's, thesis (for some programs). *Entrance requirements:* For master's, interview, minimum GPA of 2.5. Additional exam requirements/recommendations for international students: Required—TOEFL (minimum score 550 paper-based; 79 iBT), IELTS (minimum score 6). Electronic applications accepted. *Expenses: Tuition:* Full-time $10,320; part-time $430 per unit. Tuition and fees vary according to degree level.

Neumann University, Graduate Programs in Business and Information Management, Aston, PA 19014-1298. Offers accounting (MS), including forensic and fraud detection; sport business (MS). *Program availability:* Part-time, evening/weekend. *Degree requirements:* For master's, thesis (for some programs). *Entrance requirements:* For master's, official transcripts from all institutions attended, resume, letter of intent, 2-3 letters of recommendation. Additional exam requirements/recommendations for international students: Required—TOEFL (minimum score 70 iBT). Electronic applications accepted. *Expenses:* Contact institution.

New England College, Program in Management, Henniker, NH 03242-3293. Offers accounting (MSA); healthcare administration (MS); international relations (MA); marketing management (MS); nonprofit leadership (MS); project management (MS); strategic leadership (MS). *Program availability:* Part-time, evening/weekend. *Degree requirements:* For master's, independent research project. Electronic applications accepted.

New Jersey City University, School of Business, Program in Accounting, Jersey City, NJ 07305-1597. Offers MS, Graduate Certificate. *Program availability:* Part-time, evening/weekend. *Entrance requirements:* Additional exam requirements/recommendations for international students: Required—TOEFL (minimum score 79 iBT).

New York University, Leonard N. Stern School of Business, Department of Accounting, New York, NY 10012-1019. Offers MBA, PhD. *Accreditation:* AACSB. *Faculty research:* Earnings management and financial analysis effectiveness and accounting policy, value-relevance of financial reporting, intangibles-related reporting and analysis, equity.

Niagara University, Graduate Division of Business Administration, Niagara University, NY 14109. Offers accounting (MBA); business administration (MBA); finance (MBA, MS); financial planning (MBA); healthcare administration (MBA, MHA); human resources (MBA); international business (MBA); marketing (MBA); professional accountancy (MBA); strategic management (MBA); supply chain management (MBA). *Accreditation:* AACSB. *Program availability:* Part-time, evening/weekend, 100% online, blended/hybrid learning. *Students:* 224 full-time (116 women), 56 part-time (22 women); includes 36 minority (9 Black or African American, non-Hispanic/Latino; 2 American Indian or Alaska Native, non-Hispanic/Latino; 6 Asian, non-Hispanic/Latino; 12 Hispanic/Latino; 7 Two or more races, non-Hispanic/Latino), 82 international. Average age 26. In 2018, 134 master's awarded. *Entrance requirements:* For master's, GMAT. Additional exam requirements/recommendations for international students: Required—TOEFL (minimum score 550 paper-based; 79 iBT), IELTS (minimum score 6). *Application deadline:* For fall admission, 8/1 for domestic students; for spring admission, 11/1 for domestic students. Applications are processed on a rolling basis. Electronic applications accepted. *Expenses:* Contact institution. *Financial support:* Research assistantships, teaching assistantships, career-related internships or fieldwork, Federal Work-Study, scholarships/grants, and unspecified assistantships available. Support available to part-time students. Financial award application deadline: 4/15; financial award applicants required to submit FAFSA. *Faculty research:* Capital flows, Federal Reserve policy, human resource management, public policy, issues in marketing, auctions, economics of information, risk and capital markets, management strategy, consumer behavior, Internet and social media marketing. *Unit head:* Dr. Paul Richardson, MBA Director/Chair of the Marketing Department, 716-286-8169, Fax: 716-286-8206, E-mail: mba@niagara.edu. *Application contact:* Evan Pierce, Associate Director for Graduate Recruitment, 716-286-8327, Fax: 716-286-8710, E-mail: epierce@niagara.edu. Website: http://mba.niagara.edu

North Carolina Agricultural and Technical State University, The Graduate College, College of Business and Economics, Greensboro, NC 27411. Offers accounting (MBA); business education (MAT); human resources management (MBA); supply chain systems (MBA).

North Carolina State University, Graduate School, Poole College of Management, Program in Accounting, Raleigh, NC 27695. Offers MAC. *Program availability:* Part-time. *Degree requirements:* For master's, thesis optional. *Entrance requirements:* For master's, GMAT, interview. Additional exam requirements/recommendations for international students: Required—TOEFL. Electronic applications accepted. *Faculty research:* Financial reporting issues using positive economic models and empirical studies of human behavior related to accounting decisions.

North Dakota State University, College of Graduate and Interdisciplinary Studies, College of Business, Fargo, ND 58102. Offers accountancy (M Acc); business administration (MBA). *Accreditation:* AACSB. *Program availability:* Part-time, evening/weekend. *Entrance requirements:* For master's, GMAT. Additional exam requirements/recommendations for international students: Required—TOEFL (minimum score 550 paper-based; 79 iBT). Electronic applications accepted. *Faculty research:* Labor management, operations, international finance, agency, Internet marketing.

Northeastern Illinois University, College of Graduate Studies and Research, College of Business and Management, Master of Science in Accounting Program, Chicago, IL 60625. Offers MSA.

Northeastern State University, College of Business and Technology, Program in Accounting and Financial Analysis, Tahlequah, OK 74464-2399. Offers MS. *Program availability:* Part-time, evening/weekend. *Faculty:* 5 full-time (1 woman). *Students:* 12 full-time (7 women), 43 part-time (23 women); includes 22 minority (4 Black or African American, non-Hispanic/Latino; 4 American Indian or Alaska Native, non-Hispanic/Latino; 1 Asian, non-Hispanic/Latino; 2 Hispanic/Latino; 11 Two or more races, non-Hispanic/Latino). Average age 33. In 2018, 12 master's awarded. *Entrance requirements:* For master's, GMAT. Additional exam requirements/recommendations for international students: Required—TOEFL. *Application deadline:* For fall admission, 6/1 priority date for domestic students. Applications are processed on a rolling basis. Application fee: $25. Electronic applications accepted. *Expenses: Tuition, area resident:* Full-time $4500; part-time $250 per credit hour. Tuition, state resident: full-time $4500; part-time $250 per credit hour. Tuition, nonresident: full-time $9999; part-time $555.50 per credit hour. International tuition: $9999 full-time. Required fees: $601.20; $33.40 per credit hour. *Faculty research:* Information systems and organizational performance, capital markets, sustainability. *Unit head:* Dr. Gary Freeman, Director, Master of Accounting and Financial Analysis, 918-449-6524, E-mail: freemadg@nsuok.edu. *Application contact:* Josh McCollum, Graduate Coordinator, 918-444-2093, E-mail: mccolluj@nsuok.edu.
Website: http://academics.nsuok.edu/businesstechnology/Graduate/MAFA.aspx

Northeastern University, D'Amore-McKim School of Business, Boston, MA 02115-5096. Offers accounting (MS); business administration (EMBA, MBA); finance (MS); innovation (MS); international business (MS); international management (MS); taxation (MS); technological entrepreneurship (MS); JD/MBA; LL M/MBA; MBA/MSN; MS/MBA. *Accreditation:* AACSB. *Program availability:* Part-time, evening/weekend, online learning. *Entrance requirements:* For master's, GMAT or GRE. Electronic applications accepted. *Expenses:* Contact institution.

Accounting

Northern Illinois University, Graduate School, College of Business, Department of Accountancy, De Kalb, IL 60115-2854. Offers MAC, MAS, MST. *Accreditation:* AACSB. *Program availability:* Part-time, evening/weekend. *Faculty:* 14 full-time (4 women). *Students:* 117 full-time (50 women), 83 part-time (51 women); includes 70 minority (13 Black or African American, non-Hispanic/Latino; 21 Asian, non-Hispanic/Latino; 32 Hispanic/Latino; 4 Two or more races, non-Hispanic/Latino), 18 international. Average age 28. 89 applicants, 76% accepted, 41 enrolled. In 2018, 138 master's awarded. *Degree requirements:* For master's, thesis optional. *Entrance requirements:* For master's, GMAT, minimum GPA of 2.75. Additional exam requirements/recommendations for international students: Required—TOEFL (minimum score 550 paper-based). *Application deadline:* For fall admission, 4/1 priority date for domestic students, 5/1 for international students; for spring admission, 9/15 priority date for domestic students, 10/1 for international students. Applications are processed on a rolling basis. Application fee: $40. Electronic applications accepted. *Financial support:* In 2018–19, 5 research assistantships with full tuition reimbursements, 31 teaching assistantships with full tuition reimbursements were awarded; fellowships with full tuition reimbursements, career-related internships or fieldwork, Federal Work-Study, scholarships/grants, tuition waivers (full), and unspecified assistantships also available. Support available to part-time students. Financial award applicants required to submit FAFSA. *Faculty research:* Accounting fraud, governmental accounting, corporate income tax planning, auditing, ethics. *Unit head:* Sarah Marsh, Chair, 815-753-1250, Fax: 815-753-8515. *Application contact:* Graduate Advising, 815-753-1325, E-mail: cobadvising@niu.edu.
Website: http://www.cob.niu.edu/accy/

Northern Kentucky University, Office of Graduate Programs, College of Business, Program in Accountancy, Highland Heights, KY 41099. Offers accountancy (M Acc); advanced taxation (Certificate). *Program availability:* Part-time, evening/weekend. *Degree requirements:* For master's, capstone course. *Entrance requirements:* For master's, GMAT, master's degree, MD, or PhD, official transcripts, current resume, 3 years of work experience (strongly suggested), statement of purpose. Additional exam requirements/recommendations for international students: Required—TOEFL (minimum score 79 iBT); Recommended—IELTS (minimum score 6.5). Electronic applications accepted. *Faculty research:* Ethics, accounting history, financial reporting.

Northwest Christian University, School of Business and Management, Eugene, OR 97401-3745. Offers accounting (MBA); management (MBA). *Program availability:* Part-time, evening/weekend, online only, 100% online. *Entrance requirements:* For master's, GMAT, GRE, MAT, minimum undergraduate GPA of 3.0, 500-word essay, resume. Additional exam requirements/recommendations for international students: Required—TOEFL (minimum score 550 paper-based; 80 iBT). Electronic applications accepted. *Expenses:* Contact institution.

Northwestern University, The Graduate School, Kellogg School of Management, Department of Accounting Information and Management, Evanston, IL 60208. Offers PhD. Admissions and degree offered through The Graduate School. *Accreditation:* AACSB. *Degree requirements:* For doctorate, comprehensive exam, thesis/dissertation. *Entrance requirements:* For doctorate, GMAT or GRE General Test. Additional exam requirements/recommendations for international students: Required—TOEFL. Electronic applications accepted. *Faculty research:* Managerial and financial accounting theory, financial accounting/theory, managerial accounting and performance measurement, international accounting, joint cost allocation.

Northwestern University, The Graduate School, Kellogg School of Management, Management Programs, Evanston, IL 60208. Offers accounting information and management (MBA, PhD); analytical finance (MBA); business administration (MBA); decision sciences (MBA); entrepreneurship and innovation (MBA); finance (MBA, PhD); health enterprise management (MBA); human resources management (MBA); international business (MBA); management and organizations (MBA, PhD); management and organizations and sociology (PhD); management and strategy (MBA); management studies (MS); managerial analytics (MBA); managerial economics (MBA); managerial economics and strategy (PhD); marketing (MBA, PhD); marketing management (MBA); media management (MBA); operations management (MBA, PhD); real estate (MBA); social enterprise at Kellogg (MBA); JD/MBA. *Program availability:* Part-time, evening/weekend. Terminal master's awarded for partial completion of doctoral program. *Degree requirements:* For doctorate, thesis/dissertation, 2 years of coursework, qualifying (field) exam and candidacy, summer research papers and presentations to faculty, proposal defense, final exam/defense. *Entrance requirements:* For master's, GMAT, GRE, interview, 2 letters of recommendation, college transcripts, resume, essays, Kellogg honor code; for doctorate, GMAT, GRE, statement of purpose, transcripts, 2 letters of recommendation, resume, interview. Additional exam requirements/recommendations for international students: Required—TOEFL, IELTS. Electronic applications accepted. *Expenses:* Contact institution. *Faculty research:* Business cycles and international finance, health policy, networks, non-market strategy, consumer psychology.

Nova Southeastern University, H. Wayne Huizenga College of Business and Entrepreneurship, Fort Lauderdale, FL 33314-7796. Offers accounting (M Acc); business (MBA); business intelligence/analytics (MBA); complex health systems (MBA); enterprise informatics (MBA); entrepreneurship (MBA); finance (MBA); human resource management (MBA); international business (MBA); management (MBA); marketing (MBA); process improvement (MBA); public administration (MPA); real estate development (MS); sport revenue generation (MBA); supply chain management (MBA). *Accreditation:* NASPAA. *Program availability:* Part-time, evening/weekend, 100% online, blended/hybrid learning. *Entrance requirements:* For master's, GMAT or GRE (depending on undergraduate GPA), official transcripts from all schools attended while in pursuit of bachelor's degree; minimum GPA of 2.5 from regionally-accredited institution. Additional exam requirements/recommendations for international students: Required—TOEFL (minimum score 550 paper-based; 79 iBT), IELTS (minimum score 6), PTE (minimum score 54). Electronic applications accepted. *Expenses:* Contact institution. *Faculty research:* Entrepreneurship and venture capital, ethics and social responsibility, global commerce and cultures, business process management.

Oakland University, Graduate Study and Lifelong Learning, School of Business Administration, Department of Accounting and Finance, Rochester, MI 48309-4401. Offers accounting (M Acc, Certificate); finance (Certificate).

Ohio Christian University, Graduate Programs, Circleville, OH 43113. Offers accounting (MBA); business administration (MBA); digital marketing (MBA); finance (MBA); healthcare management (MBA); human resources (MBA); management (MM); organizational leadership (MBA); pastoral care and counseling (MAM); practical theology (MAM)

Ohio Dominican University, Division of Business, Program in Business Administration, Columbus, OH 43219-2099. Offers accounting (MBA); data analytics (MBA); finance (MBA); leadership (MBA); risk management (MBA); sport management (MBA). *Program availability:* Part-time, evening/weekend, 100% online, blended/hybrid learning. *Faculty:* 10 full-time (4 women), 12 part-time/adjunct (1 woman). *Students:* 42 full-time (17 women), 88 part-time (43 women); includes 29 minority (16 Black or African American, non-Hispanic/Latino; 1 American Indian or Alaska Native, non-Hispanic/Latino; 3 Asian,

non-Hispanic/Latino; 5 Hispanic/Latino; 4 Two or more races, non-Hispanic/Latino), 14 international. Average age 31. 97 applicants, 44% accepted, 26 enrolled. In 2018, 56 master's awarded. *Entrance requirements:* For master's, minimum overall GPA of 3.0 in undergraduate degree from regionally-accredited institution or 2.75 in last 60 semester hours of bachelor's degree. Additional exam requirements/recommendations for international students: Required—TOEFL (minimum score 550 paper-based), IELTS (minimum score 6.5). *Application deadline:* For fall admission, 8/15 for domestic students, 6/10 for international students; for spring admission, 1/4 for domestic students, 11/2 for international students; for summer admission, 5/30 for domestic students. Applications are processed on a rolling basis. Application fee: $25. Electronic applications accepted. *Expenses: Tuition:* Full-time $10,800; part-time $600 per credit hour. *Required fees:* $450; $225 per semester. Tuition and fees vary according to program. *Financial support:* Applicants required to submit FAFSA. *Unit head:* Dr. Thomas Eveland, Director of Graduate Programs in Business, 614-251-4569, E-mail: evelandt@ohiodominican.edu. *Application contact:* John W. Naughton, Vice President for Enrollment and Student Success, 614-251-4721, Fax: 614-251-6654, E-mail: grad@ohiodominican.edu.
Website: http://www.ohiodominican.edu/academics/graduate/mba

Ohio Northern University, College of Business, Ada, OH 45810-1599. Offers MSA.

The Ohio State University, Graduate School, Max M. Fisher College of Business, Department of Accounting and Management Information Systems, Program in Accounting, Columbus, OH 43210. Offers M Acc. *Faculty:* 21. *Students:* 96 full-time (51 women). Average age 23. In 2018, 64 master's awarded. *Entrance requirements:* For master's, GMAT. Additional exam requirements/recommendations for international students: Required—TOEFL (minimum score 600 paper-based; 100 iBT), Michigan English Language Assessment Battery (minimum score 86); Recommended—IELTS (minimum score 7). *Application deadline:* For fall admission, 11/18 priority date for domestic and international students. Applications are processed on a rolling basis. Application fee: $60 ($70 for international students). Electronic applications accepted. *Financial support:* Fellowships with tuition reimbursements available. *Unit head:* Dr. Brian Mittendorf, Professor and Chair, 614-292-1720, E-mail: mittendorf.3@osu.edu. *Application contact:* Dr. Brian Mittendorf, Professor and Chair, 614-292-1720, E-mail: mittendorf.3@osu.edu.
Website: http://fisher.osu.edu/macc

Oklahoma Christian University, Graduate School of Business, Oklahoma City, OK 73136-1100. Offers accounting (M Acc, MBA); financial services (MBA); general business (MBA); health services management (MBA); human resources (MBA); international business (MBA); leadership and organizational development (MBA); marketing (MBA); nonprofit management (MBA); project management (MBA). *Accreditation:* ACBSP. *Program availability:* Part-time, 100% online. *Entrance requirements:* For master's, bachelor's degree. Additional exam requirements/recommendations for international students: Required—TOEFL (minimum score 550 paper-based). Electronic applications accepted. *Expenses:* Contact institution.

Oklahoma State University, Spears School of Business, School of Accounting, Stillwater, OK 74078. Offers MS, PhD. *Accreditation:* AACSB. *Program availability:* Part-time. *Faculty:* 16 full-time (8 women), 4 part-time/adjunct (3 women). *Students:* 43 full-time (27 women), 18 part-time (13 women); includes 16 minority (2 Black or African American, non-Hispanic/Latino; 2 American Indian or Alaska Native, non-Hispanic/Latino; 4 Asian, non-Hispanic/Latino; 1 Hispanic/Latino; 7 Two or more races, non-Hispanic/Latino), 5 international. Average age 23. 34 applicants, 50% accepted, 12 enrolled. In 2018, 38 master's awarded. *Entrance requirements:* For master's and doctorate, GRE or GMAT. Additional exam requirements/recommendations for international students: Required—TOEFL (minimum score 550 paper-based; 79 iBT). *Application deadline:* For fall admission, 3/1 priority date for international students; for spring admission, 8/1 priority date for international students. Applications are processed on a rolling basis. Application fee: $40 ($75 for international students). Electronic applications accepted. *Expenses: Tuition, area resident:* Full-time $4148. Tuition, state resident: full-time $4148. Tuition, nonresident: full-time $10,517. *International tuition:* $10,517 full-time. *Required fees:* $4394; $2929 per credit hour. Tuition and fees vary according to course load and program. *Financial support:* Research assistantships, teaching assistantships, career-related internships or fieldwork, Federal Work-Study, scholarships/grants, health care benefits, tuition waivers (partial), and unspecified assistantships available. Support available to part-time students. Financial award application deadline: 3/1; financial award applicants required to submit FAFSA. *Faculty research:* International accounting, accounting education, cost-management, taxation, oil and gas. *Unit head:* Dr. Audrey Gramling, Department Head, 405-744-1245, Fax: 405-744-1680, E-mail: audrey.gramling@okstate.edu. *Application contact:* Dr. Alyssa Vowell, Graduate Coordinator, 405-744-6635, Fax: 405-744-1680, E-mail: alyssa.vowell@okstate.edu.
Website: https://business.okstate.edu/accounting/

Old Dominion University, Strome College of Business, Program in Accounting, Norfolk, VA 23529. Offers MS. *Accreditation:* AACSB. *Program availability:* Part-time, evening/weekend. *Degree requirements:* For master's, comprehensive exam. *Entrance requirements:* For master's, GMAT, minimum GPA of 3.0. Additional exam requirements/recommendations for international students: Required—TOEFL (minimum score 550 paper-based). Electronic applications accepted. *Expenses:* Contact institution. *Faculty research:* Assurance services, auditing, managerial accounting, financial accounting, accounting history.

Oral Roberts University, School of Business, Tulsa, OK 74171. Offers accounting (MBA); entrepreneurship (MBA); finance (MBA); international business (MBA); management (MBA); marketing (MBA); not for profit management (MNM). *Accreditation:* ACBSP. *Program availability:* Part-time, online learning. *Degree requirements:* For master's, thesis optional. *Entrance requirements:* For master's, minimum cumulative GPA of 3.0 from regionally-accredited institution. Electronic applications accepted. Application fee is waived when completed online. *Faculty research:* Social media, international business and marketing.

Oregon State University, College of Business, Program in Business Administration, Corvallis, OR 97331. Offers business administration (PhD), including accounting; corporate finance (MBA). *Program availability:* Part-time, blended/hybrid learning. *Entrance requirements:* For master's, GMAT. Additional exam requirements/recommendations for international students: Required—TOEFL (minimum score 91 iBT), IELTS (minimum score 7). *Expenses:* Contact institution.

Our Lady of the Lake University, School of Business and Leadership, Program in Accounting, San Antonio, TX 78207-4689. Offers MS. *Program availability:* Part-time, evening/weekend. *Faculty:* 2 full-time (both women), 1 part-time/adjunct (0 women). *Students:* 8 full-time (5 women), 5 part-time (4 women); includes 9 minority (all Hispanic/Latino). Average age 32. 6 applicants, 83% accepted, 4 enrolled. In 2018, 7 master's awarded. *Entrance requirements:* For master's, GMAT, GRE General Test, or MAT, official transcripts showing undergraduate degree in accounting or 30 hours of accounting courses previously taken with minimum cumulative GPA of 2.5; 2 letters of recommendation; resume highlighting managerial or professional work experience. Additional exam requirements/recommendations for international students: Required—

TOEFL. *Application deadline:* For fall admission, 6/15 for domestic and international students; for spring admission, 11/15 for domestic and international students; for summer admission, 4/15 for domestic and international students. Applications are processed on a rolling basis. Application fee: $40 ($50 for international students). Electronic applications accepted. Application fee is waived when completed online. *Expenses: Tuition:* Full-time $16,326; part-time $907 per credit. *Financial support:* In 2018–19, 2 students received support. Federal Work-Study, scholarships/grants, unspecified assistantships, and tuition discounts available. Support available to part-time students. Financial award application deadline: 5/1; financial award applicants required to submit FAFSA. *Unit head:* Kathryn Winney, Associate Dean, 210-434-6711 Ext. 2297, E-mail: kmwinney@ollusa.edu. *Application contact:* Graduate Admission, 210-431-3995, Fax: 210-431-3945, E-mail: gradadm@ollusa.edu. Website: http://www.ollusa.edu/s/1190/hybrid/default-hybrid-ollu.aspx?sid-1190&gid-1&pgid-7870

Pace University, Lubin School of Business, Accounting Program, New York, NY 10038. Offers public accounting (MBA, MS). *Accreditation:* AACSB. *Program availability:* Part-time, evening/weekend. *Students:* 96 full-time (60 women), 65 part-time (39 women); includes 38 minority (6 Black or African American, non-Hispanic/Latino; 17 Asian, non-Hispanic/Latino; 11 Hispanic/Latino; 4 Two or more races, non-Hispanic/Latino), 80 international. Average age 27. 134 applicants, 82% accepted, 55 enrolled. In 2018, 122 master's awarded. *Entrance requirements:* For master's, GMAT, GRE, undergraduate degree, transcripts from all accredited colleges/universities attended, two letters of recommendation, resume, personal statement. Additional exam requirements/recommendations for international students: Required—TOEFL (minimum score 90 iBT), IELTS (minimum score 7) or PTE (minimum score 61). *Application deadline:* For fall admission, 8/1 priority date for domestic students, 6/1 for international students; for spring admission, 12/1 priority date for domestic students, 10/1 for international students. Applications are processed on a rolling basis. Application fee: $70. Electronic applications accepted. *Expenses:* Contact institution. *Financial support:* Research assistantships, career-related internships or fieldwork, Federal Work-Study, and unspecified assistantships available. Support available to part-time students. Financial award application deadline: 2/15; financial award applicants required to submit FAFSA. *Unit head:* Dr. Charles Tang, Chairperson, Accounting Department, 212-618-6430, E-mail: ytang@pace.edu. *Application contact:* Susan Ford-Goldschein, Director of Graduate Admissions, 212-346-1531, Fax: 212-346-1585, E-mail: graduateadmission@pace.edu.
Website: http://www.pace.edu/lubin/sections/explore-program/graduate-programs

Pace University, Lubin School of Business, Advanced Professional Certificate Program, New York, NY 10038. Offers business economics (APC); e-business (APC); financial management (APC); international business (APC); international economics (APC); investment management (APC); marketing (APC); public accounting (APC). *Program availability:* Part-time, evening/weekend. *Entrance requirements:* For degree, MBA or MS in business discipline, relevant professional experience. Additional exam requirements/recommendations for international students: Required—TOEFL (minimum score 90 iBT), IELTS (minimum score 7) or PTE (minimum score 61). *Application deadline:* For fall admission, 8/1 priority date for domestic students, 6/1 for international students; for spring admission, 12/1 for domestic students, 10/1 for international students. Applications are processed on a rolling basis. Application fee: $70. Electronic applications accepted. *Unit head:* Dr. Ibraiz Tarique, Chairperson, 212-618-6583, E-mail: itarique@pace.edu. *Application contact:* Susan Ford-Goldschein, Director of Graduate Admissions, 212-346-1531, Fax: 212-346-1585, E-mail: graduateadmission@pace.edu.
Website: http://www.pace.edu/lubin/agc

Pacific Lutheran University, School of Business, Master of Science in Accounting Program, Tacoma, WA 98447. Offers MSA. *Program availability:* Part-time. *Entrance requirements:* For master's, GMAT or GRE. Additional exam requirements/recommendations for international students: Required—TOEFL (minimum score 550 paper-based; 88 iBT). *Expenses:* Contact institution.

Pacific States University, College of Business, Los Angeles, CA 90010. Offers accounting (MBA, Certificate); beauty management (MBA); finance (MBA); international business (MBA); management of information technology (MBA); project management (Certificate); real estate management (MBA). *Program availability:* Part-time, evening/weekend, online learning. *Entrance requirements:* For master's, minimum undergraduate GPA of 2.5 during last 90 quarter units of course work, bachelor's degree in business administration or economics. Additional exam requirements/recommendations for international students: Required—TOEFL (minimum score 500 paper-based; 61 iBT), IELTS (minimum score 5.5).

Penn State Erie, The Behrend College, Graduate School, Erie, PA 16563. Offers accounting (MPAC); applied clinical psychology (MA); business administration (MBA); quality and manufacturing management (MMM). *Accreditation:* AACSB. *Program availability:* Part-time. *Entrance requirements:* Additional exam requirements/recommendations for international students: Required—TOEFL (minimum score 550 paper-based; 80 iBT), IELTS. Electronic applications accepted.

Penn State Harrisburg, Graduate School, School of Business Administration, Middletown, PA 17057. Offers accounting (MPAC, Certificate); business administration (MBA); information systems (MS); operations and supply chain management (Certificate). *Program availability:* Part-time, evening/weekend.

Penn State University Park, Graduate School, Smeal College of Business, University Park, PA 16802. Offers accounting (M Acc); business administration (MBA, MS, PhD); management and organizational leadership (MPS). *Accreditation:* AACSB. *Program availability:* Part-time, evening/weekend. *Entrance requirements:* Additional exam requirements/recommendations for international students: Required—TOEFL (minimum score 550 paper-based; 80 iBT), IELTS. Electronic applications accepted. *Expenses:* Contact institution.

Pepperdine University, Seaver College, Malibu, CA 90263. Offers business (MS), including accounting; communication (MFA), including cinematic media production; humanities (MA, MFA), including American studies (MA), writing for screen and television (MFA); religion (M Div, MA, MS), including ministry (MS), religion (M Div, MA); JD/M Div. *Students:* 6 full-time (1 woman), 70 part-time (42 women); includes 19 minority (6 Black or African American, non-Hispanic/Latino; 1 American Indian or Alaska Native, non-Hispanic/Latino; 2 Asian, non-Hispanic/Latino; 5 Hispanic/Latino; 1 Native Hawaiian or other Pacific Islander, non-Hispanic/Latino; 4 Two or more races, non-Hispanic/Latino), 11 international. Average age 30. 54 applicants, 65% accepted, 29 enrolled. In 2018, 27 master's awarded. *Entrance requirements:* For master's, GRE General Test. Additional exam requirements/recommendations for international students: Required—TOEFL. *Application deadline:* For fall admission, 2/1 priority date for domestic students. Applications are processed on a rolling basis. Application fee: $65. *Expenses:* Contact institution. *Financial support:* Fellowships, research assistantships, teaching assistantships, career-related internships or fieldwork, Federal Work-Study, institutionally sponsored loans, scholarships/grants, and tuition waivers (partial) available. Support available to part-time students. Financial award application deadline: 2/15; financial award applicants required to submit FAFSA. *Unit head:* Dr.

Dana Dudley, Assistant Dean, Special Academic and Graduate Programs for Seaver College, 310-506-6047, Fax: 310-506-4816, E-mail: dana.dudley@pepperdine.edu. *Application contact:* Joy Brown, Admission Counselor, 310-506-4392, E-mail: joy.brown@pepperdine.edu.
Website: http://seaver.pepperdine.edu/

Pittsburg State University, Graduate School, Kelce College of Business, Department of Accounting, Pittsburg, KS 66762. Offers MBA. *Program availability:* Part-time. *Degree requirements:* For master's, thesis or alternative. *Entrance requirements:* For master's, GMAT or GRE. Additional exam requirements/recommendations for international students: Required—TOEFL (minimum score 550 paper-based; 79 iBT), IELTS (minimum score 6.5), PTE (minimum score 53). Electronic applications accepted. *Expenses:* Contact institution. *Faculty research:* Accountant's legal liability, computer audit.

Plymouth State University, College of Graduate Studies, Graduate Studies in Business, Plymouth, NH 03264-1595. Offers accounting (MS); general management (MBA). *Accreditation:* ACBSP. *Program availability:* Part-time, evening/weekend, online learning. *Entrance requirements:* For master's, minimum GPA of 2.5. Additional exam requirements/recommendations for international students: Required—TOEFL (minimum score 550 paper-based). *Expenses:* Contact institution.

Polytechnic University of Puerto Rico, Miami Campus, Graduate School, Miami, FL 33166. Offers accounting (MBA); business administration (MBA); construction management (MEM); environmental management (MEM); finance (MBA); human resources management (MBA); logistics and supply chain management (MBA); management of international enterprises (MBA); manufacturing management (MEM); marketing management (MBA); project management (MBA). *Program availability:* Part-time, evening/weekend, online learning. *Entrance requirements:* For master's, minimum GPA of 3.0. Electronic applications accepted.

Polytechnic University of Puerto Rico, Orlando Campus, Graduate School, Orlando, FL 32825. Offers accounting (MBA); business administration (MBA); construction management (MEM); engineering management (MEM); environmental management (MEM); finance (MBA); human resources management (MBA); management of international enterprises (MBA); management of technology (MBA); manufacturing management (MEM). *Program availability:* Part-time, evening/weekend, online learning. *Entrance requirements:* For master's, minimum GPA of 3.0. Additional exam requirements/recommendations for international students: Recommended—TOEFL. Electronic applications accepted.

Pontifical Catholic University of Puerto Rico, College of Business Administration, Program in Accounting, Ponce, PR 00717-0777. Offers MBA. *Program availability:* Part-time, evening/weekend. *Degree requirements:* For master's, thesis. *Entrance requirements:* For master's, GRE, interview, minimum GPA of 2.75.

Pontifical Catholic University of Puerto Rico, College of Business Administration, Program in Management and Accounting, Ponce, PR 00717-0777. Offers Professional Certificate.

Post University, Program in Business Administration, Waterbury, CT 06723-2540. Offers accounting (MSA); business administration (MBA); corporate finance (MBA); corporate innovation (MBA); healthcare systems leadership (MBA); leadership (MBA); marketing (MBA); project management (MBA, MS). *Accreditation:* ACBSP. *Program availability:* Online learning. *Entrance requirements:* For master's, resume. *Expenses: Tuition:* Full-time $8300; part-time $570 per credit. *Required fees:* $140 per term. Tuition and fees vary according to course level, campus/location and program.

Prairie View A&M University, College of Business, Prairie View, TX 77446. Offers accounting (MS); business administration (MBA). *Accreditation:* AACSB. *Program availability:* Part-time, evening/weekend. *Faculty:* 18 full-time (2 women), 1 part-time/adjunct (0 women). *Students:* 57 full-time (33 women), 132 part-time (85 women); includes 174 minority (148 Black or African American, non-Hispanic/Latino; 1 American Indian or Alaska Native, non-Hispanic/Latino; 13 Asian, non-Hispanic/Latino; 10 Hispanic/Latino; 1 Native Hawaiian or other Pacific Islander, non-Hispanic/Latino; 1 Two or more races, non-Hispanic/Latino), 9 international. Average age 29. 90 applicants, 86% accepted, 59 enrolled. In 2018, 98 master's awarded. *Degree requirements:* For master's, comprehensive exam, thesis optional. *Entrance requirements:* For master's, GMAT, GRE, minimum GPA of 2.45, essay. Additional exam requirements/recommendations for international students: Required—TOEFL (minimum score 550 paper-based; 79 iBT). *Application deadline:* For fall admission, 5/1 for domestic students, 5/1 priority date for international students; for spring admission, 10/1 for domestic students, 9/1 priority date for international students; for summer admission, 3/1 for domestic students, 2/1 for international students. Applications are processed on a rolling basis. Application fee: $50. Electronic applications accepted. *Expenses:* $8,019 per year in-state, $17,417 per year out-of-state. *Financial support:* In 2018–19, 3 research assistantships (averaging $1,600 per year) were awarded; scholarships/grants and unspecified assistantships also available. Financial award application deadline: 4/1; financial award applicants required to submit FAFSA. *Faculty research:* Accounting (energy, oil and gas); finance (international finance, personal finance, real estate markets and institutions); marketing management (supply chain, human resources, entrepreneurship, small business ownership, ethics); management information systems (cyber-security, managing social media during crises). *Unit head:* Dr. Munir Quddus, Dean, 936-261-9200, Fax: 936-261-9241, E-mail: cob@pvamu.edu. *Application contact:* Gabriel Crosby, Director, Graduate Programs in Business, 936-261-9217, Fax: 936-261-9232, E-mail: mba@pvamu.edu.
Website: http://www.pvamu.edu/business/

Providence College, School of Business, Providence, RI 02918. Offers accounting (MBA); finance (MBA); international business (MBA); management (MBA); marketing (MBA). *Accreditation:* AACSB. *Program availability:* Part-time, evening/weekend. *Entrance requirements:* For master's, GMAT. Additional exam requirements/recommendations for international students: Required—TOEFL (minimum score 577 paper-based; 90 iBT). *Expenses:* Contact institution.

Purdue University Northwest, Graduate Studies Office, School of Management, Hammond, IN 46323-2094. Offers accountancy (M Acc); business administration (MBA); business administration for executives (EMBA). *Accreditation:* AACSB. *Program availability:* Part-time, evening/weekend. *Entrance requirements:* For master's, GMAT. Additional exam requirements/recommendations for international students: Required—TOEFL. Electronic applications accepted.

Queens College of the City University of New York, Division of Social Sciences, Department of Accounting and Information Systems, Queens, NY 11367-1597. Offers accounting (MS). *Program availability:* Part-time. *Faculty:* 22 full-time (4 women), 38 part-time/adjunct (9 women). *Students:* 22 full-time (14 women), 188 part-time (108 women); includes 145 minority (11 Black or African American, non-Hispanic/Latino; 92 Asian, non-Hispanic/Latino; 36 Hispanic/Latino; 1 Native Hawaiian or other Pacific Islander, non-Hispanic/Latino; 5 Two or more races, non-Hispanic/Latino), 21 international. Average age 30. In 2018, 78 master's awarded. *Entrance requirements:* For master's, minimum GPA of 3.0. Additional exam requirements/recommendations for international students: Required—TOEFL (minimum score 100 iBT), IELTS (minimum

score 7). *Application deadline:* For fall admission, 4/1 for domestic students; for spring admission, 11/1 for domestic students. Application fee: $125. Electronic applications accepted. *Financial support:* Career-related internships or fieldwork and unspecified assistantships available. *Unit head:* Dr. Israel Blumenfrucht, Chair, 718-997-5070, E-mail: israel.blumenfrucht@qc.cuny.edu. *Application contact:* Elizabeth D'Amico-Ramirez, Assistant Director of Graduate Admissions, 718-997-5203, E-mail: elizabeth.damicoramirez@qc.cuny.edu.

Queens College of the City University of New York, Division of Social Sciences, Department of Economics, Queens, NY 11367-1597. Offers risk management: accounting (MS); risk management: dynamic financial analysis (MS); risk management: finance (MS). Risk Management is a graduate program offered jointly by the Departments of Economics and Accounting & Information Systems. *Faculty:* 23 full-time (8 women), 42 part-time/adjunct (9 women). *Students:* 3 full-time (2 women), 26 part-time (15 women); includes 24 minority (4 Black or African American, non-Hispanic/Latino; 10 Asian, non-Hispanic/Latino; 7 Hispanic/Latino; 3 Two or more races, non-Hispanic/Latino), 5 international. Average age 30. 24 applicants, 79% accepted, 12 enrolled. In 2018, 20 master's awarded. *Degree requirements:* For master's, thesis, Capstone Class/Thesis Project. *Entrance requirements:* For master's, minimum GPA of 3.0. Additional exam requirements/recommendations for international students: Required—TOEFL (minimum score 100 iBT), IELTS (minimum score 7). *Application deadline:* For fall admission, 6/30 for domestic and international students; for spring admission, 11/30 for domestic and international students. Applications are processed on a rolling basis. Application fee: $75. Electronic applications accepted. *Financial support:* In 2018–19, 1 student received support. Federal Work-Study, institutionally sponsored loans, and scholarships/grants available. Financial award application deadline: 4/1; financial award applicants required to submit FAFSA. *Faculty research:* Business economics, urban economic problems, international economics, economics of nonprofit sector. *Unit head:* Cara Marshall, Program Director, 718-997-5387, E-mail: cara.marshall@qc.cuny.edu. *Application contact:* Elvira Casper, Program Coordinator, 718-997-5507, E-mail: elvira.casper@qc.cuny.edu.

Quinnipiac University, School of Business, Program in Accounting, Hamden, CT 06518-1940. Offers MS. *Entrance requirements:* For master's, GMAT/GRE, BS in accounting or prerequisite course work in accounting. Additional exam requirements/recommendations for international students: Required—TOEFL (minimum score 575 paper-based; 90 iBT), IELTS (minimum score 6.5). Electronic applications accepted.

Ramapo College of New Jersey, Master of Science in Accounting Program, Mahwah, NJ 07430-1680. Offers MS. *Program availability:* Part-time. *Faculty:* 3 full-time (1 woman). *Students:* 24 full-time (9 women), 17 part-time (12 women); includes 8 minority (4 Asian, non-Hispanic/Latino; 4 Hispanic/Latino), 1 international. Average age 28. 52 applicants, 77% accepted, 28 enrolled. In 2018, 8 master's awarded. *Degree requirements:* For master's, capstone course, including research project. *Entrance requirements:* For master's, undergraduate degree in business with accounting or finance major or accounting minor from accredited institution with minimum GPA of 3.0; personal statement; letter of recommendation. Additional exam requirements/recommendations for international students: Required—TOEFL (minimum score 550 paper-based; 79 iBT); Recommended—IELTS (minimum score 6). *Application deadline:* For fall admission, 5/1 for domestic and international students; for spring admission, 12/1 for domestic and international students; for summer admission, 5/1 for domestic and international students. Applications are processed on a rolling basis. Application fee: $65. Electronic applications accepted. *Expenses:* $803.65 per credit tuition for academic year 2018-2019, $57.50 per credit fees for academic year 2018-2019; MSAC is a 30 credit program. *Financial support:* Career-related internships or fieldwork available. Financial award application deadline: 3/1; financial award applicants required to submit FAFSA. *Faculty research:* Leadership, accountability and ethics; tax strategy and regulatory compliance; accounting pedagogy and curriculum development; earnings, forecasting and financial statement analysis; fraud detection and audit implications; cyber security threats and audit planning. *Unit head:* Dr. Edward Petkus, Dean of the Anisfield School of Business, 201-684-7377, E-mail: epetkus@ramapo.edu. *Application contact:* Dr. Constance Crawford, Director of the Master of Science in Accounting Program, 201-684-7396, E-mail: ccrawfor@ramapo.edu.
Website: http://www.ramapo.edu/ms-accounting/

Regent University, Graduate School, School of Business and Leadership, Virginia Beach, VA 23464-9800. Offers business administration (MBA), including accounting, economics, entrepreneurship, finance and investing, general management, healthcare management (MA, MBA), human resource management (MA, MBA), innovation management, leadership, marketing, not-for-profit management (MA, MBA); business analytics (MS); business and design management (MA); church leadership (MA); leadership (Certificate); organizational leadership (MA, PhD), including ecclesial leadership (DSL, PhD), entrepreneurial leadership (PhD), healthcare management (MA, MBA), human resource development (PhD), human resource management (MA, MBA), individualized studies (DSL, PhD), interdisciplinary studies (MA), leadership coaching and mentoring (MA), not-for-profit management (MA, MBA), organizational development consulting (MA), servant leadership (MA, DSL); strategic leadership (DSL), including ecclesial leadership (DSL, PhD), global consulting, healthcare leadership, individualized studies (DSL, PhD), leadership coaching, servant leadership (MA, DSL), strategic foresight. *Program availability:* Part-time, evening/weekend, 100% online, blended/hybrid learning. *Degree requirements:* For master's, thesis or alternative, 3-credit hour culminating experience; for doctorate, thesis/dissertation. *Entrance requirements:* For master's, college transcripts, resume, essay; for doctorate, college transcripts, resume, essay, writing sample; for Certificate, writing sample, resume, transcripts. Additional exam requirements/recommendations for international students: Required—TOEFL (minimum score 577 paper-based). Electronic applications accepted. *Expenses:* Contact institution. *Faculty research:* Servant leadership, global business, team effectiveness, technology utilization, leadership development.

Regis University, College of Business and Economics, Denver, CO 80221-1099. Offers accounting (MS); executive leadership (Certificate); finance (MS); finance and accounting (MBA); health industry leadership (MBA); human resource management and leadership (MSOL); management (MBA); marketing (MBA); nonprofit leadership (Post-Graduate Certificate); nonprofit management (MNM); nonprofit organizational capacity building (Certificate); operations management (MBA); organizational leadership and management (MSOL); project leadership and management (MS, MSOL); strategic business management (Certificate); strategic human resource integration (Certificate); strategic management (MBA). Programs offered at Colorado Springs Campus, Northwest Denver Campus, Southeast Denver Campus, Fort Collins Campus, Broomfield Campus, Henderson (Nevada) Campus, and Summerlin (Nevada) Campus. *Program availability:* Part-time, evening/weekend, 100% online, blended/hybrid learning. *Degree requirements:* For master's, thesis (for some programs), capstone or final research project. *Entrance requirements:* For master's, official transcript reflecting baccalaureate degree awarded from regionally-accredited college or university, interview, 2 years of full-time related work experience, resume, letters of recommendation. Additional exam requirements/recommendations for international students: Required—TOEFL (minimum score 550 paper-based; 82 iBT). Electronic applications accepted. *Expenses:* Contact institution. *Faculty research:* Impact of information technology on small business regulation of accounting, international project financing, mineral development, delivery of healthcare to rural indigenous communities.

Rhode Island College, School of Graduate Studies, School of Business, Department of Accounting and Computer Information Systems, Providence, RI 02908-1991. Offers accounting (MP Ac); financial planning (CGS). *Program availability:* Part-time, evening/weekend. *Faculty:* 1 (woman) full-time, 2 part-time/adjunct (1 woman). *Students:* 1 (woman) full-time, 10 part-time (4 women); includes 6 minority (4 Black or African American, non-Hispanic/Latino; 2 Hispanic/Latino). Average age 29. In 2018, 2 master's awarded. *Entrance requirements:* For master's, GMAT (unless applicant is a CPA or has passed a state bar exam); for CGS, GMAT, bachelor's degree from an accredited college or university, official transcripts of all undergraduate and graduate records. Additional exam requirements/recommendations for international students: Required—TOEFL (minimum score 550 paper-based; 80 iBT). *Application deadline:* For fall admission, 3/1 for domestic students. Applications are processed on a rolling basis. Application fee: $50. Electronic applications accepted. *Expenses: Tuition, area resident:* Part-time $407 per credit. Tuition, nonresident: part-time $792 per credit. *Required fees:* $29 per credit. $100 per semester. *Financial support:* Teaching assistantships with full tuition reimbursements, Federal Work-Study, scholarships/grants, and health care benefits available. Support available to part-time students. Financial award application deadline: 5/15; financial award applicants required to submit FAFSA. *Unit head:* Dr. Lisa Bain, Chair, 401-456-9829, E-mail: lbain@ric.edu. *Application contact:* Dr. Lisa Bain, Chair, 401-456-9829, E-mail: lbain@ric.edu.
Website: http://www.ric.edu/accountingcomputerinformationsystems/Pages/Accounting-Program.aspx

Rhodes College, Department of Business, Memphis, TN 38112-1690. Offers accounting (MS). *Program availability:* Part-time. *Faculty:* 2 full-time (both women), 2 part-time/adjunct (0 women). *Students:* 18 full-time (4 women); includes 2 minority (1 American Indian or Alaska Native, non-Hispanic/Latino; 1 Two or more races, non-Hispanic/Latino). Average age 22. In 2018, 21 master's awarded. *Entrance requirements:* For master's, GMAT. Additional exam requirements/recommendations for international students: Required—TOEFL (minimum score 550 paper-based). *Application deadline:* For fall admission, 3/1 for domestic students. Electronic applications accepted. *Expenses: Tuition:* Full-time $47,580. *Required fees:* $310. *Financial support:* Career-related internships or fieldwork and scholarships/grants available. Financial award application deadline: 3/1; financial award applicants required to submit FAFSA. *Application contact:* Dr. Pamela H. Church, Program Director, 901-843-3863, Fax: 901-843-3798, E-mail: church@rhodes.edu.
Website: http://www.rhodes.edu

Rider University, College of Business Administration, Program in Accountancy, Lawrenceville, NJ 08648-3001. Offers M Acc, Certificate. *Accreditation:* AACSB. *Program availability:* Part-time, 100% online, blended/hybrid learning. *Students:* 30 full-time (17 women), 33 part-time (21 women); includes 14 minority (2 Black or African American, non-Hispanic/Latino; 6 Asian, non-Hispanic/Latino; 5 Hispanic/Latino; 1 Two or more races, non-Hispanic/Latino), 11 international. Average age 27. 53 applicants, 79% accepted, 28 enrolled. In 2018, 28 master's awarded. *Entrance requirements:* For master's, GMAT, resume, application fee, statement of aims and objectives, official prior college transcripts. Additional exam requirements/recommendations for international students: Required—TOEFL (minimum score 540 paper-based; 79 iBT). *Application deadline:* For fall admission, 8/1 priority date for domestic students, 3/15 priority date for international students; for spring admission, 12/1 priority date for domestic students, 11/1 priority date for international students. Applications are processed on a rolling basis. Application fee: $50. Electronic applications accepted. *Expenses: Tuition:* Full-time $850; part-time $850 per credit hour. *Required fees:* $50; $50 per course. Tuition and fees vary according to program. *Financial support:* Applicants required to submit FAFSA. *Faculty research:* Financial reporting, corporate governance, information technology, ethics, pedagogy. *Unit head:* Dr. Margaret O'Reilly-Allen, Associate Professor and Chairperson, 609-895-5505, Fax: 609-896-5304, E-mail: oreillyallen@rider.edu. *Application contact:* Jamie L. Mitchell, Director of Graduate Admissions, 609-896-5036, Fax: 609-895-5680, E-mail: jmitchell@rider.edu.

Robert Morris University Illinois, Morris Graduate School of Management, Chicago, IL 60605. Offers accounting (MBA); accounting/finance (MBA); business analytics (MIS); health care administration (MM); higher education administration (MM); human performance (MS); human resource management (MBA); information security (MIS); information systems management (MIS); law enforcement administration (MM); management (MBA); management/finance (MBA); management/human resource management (MBA); sports administration (MM). *Program availability:* Part-time, evening/weekend. *Entrance requirements:* For master's, official transcripts and letters of recommendation (for some programs); written personal statement. Additional exam requirements/recommendations for international students: Required—TOEFL (minimum score 550 paper-based). Electronic applications accepted.

Rochester Institute of Technology, Graduate Enrollment Services, Saunders College of Business, Accounting and Finance Department, MBA Program in Accounting, Rochester, NY 14623-5603. Offers MBA. *Program availability:* Part-time, evening/weekend. *Students:* 5 full-time (3 women); includes 2 minority (both Asian, non-Hispanic/Latino), 1 international. Average age 26. 11 applicants, 73% accepted, 3 enrolled. In 2018, 5 master's awarded. *Entrance requirements:* For master's, GRE or GMAT, minimum GPA of 3.0 (recommended), working knowledge of algebra and statistics, personal statement, resume. Additional exam requirements/recommendations for international students: Required—TOEFL (minimum score 580 paper-based; 92 iBT), IELTS (minimum score 7), PTE (minimum score 63). *Application deadline:* Applications are processed on a rolling basis. Application fee: $65. Electronic applications accepted. *Financial support:* In 2018–19, 6 students received support. Research assistantships with partial tuition reimbursements available, teaching assistantships with partial tuition reimbursements available, career-related internships or fieldwork, scholarships/grants, and unspecified assistantships available. Support available to part-time students. Financial award applicants required to submit FAFSA. *Faculty research:* Corporate financial reporting disclosure and quality, fraud and litigation risk, audit quality, opinion, and pricing decision, financial regulations, information technology performance. *Unit head:* Matt Cornwell, Assistant Director of Student Services and Outreach, 585-475-6916, E-mail: gradbus@saunders.rit.edu. *Application contact:* Diane Ellison, Senior Associate Vice President, Graduate Enrollment Services, 585-475-2229, Fax: 585-475-7164, E-mail: gradinfo@rit.edu.
Website: https://www.rit.edu/study/accounting-mba

Rochester Institute of Technology, Graduate Enrollment Services, Saunders College of Business, Accounting and Finance Department, MS Program in Accounting, Rochester, NY 14623-5603. Offers MS. *Program availability:* Part-time, evening/weekend. *Students:* 3 full-time (2 women), 1 international. Average age 23. 12 applicants, 67% accepted, 3 enrolled. In 2018, 7 master's awarded. *Degree requirements:* For master's, comprehensive exam. *Entrance requirements:* For master's, GMAT or GRE, minimum GPA of 3.0 (recommended), personal statement, resume. Additional exam requirements/recommendations for international students: Required—TOEFL (minimum score 92 iBT), IELTS (minimum score 7), PTE (minimum score 63). *Application deadline:* Applications are processed on a rolling basis.

Application fee: $65. Electronic applications accepted. *Financial support:* In 2018–19, 1 student received support. Research assistantships with partial tuition reimbursements available, teaching assistantships with partial tuition reimbursements available, career-related internships or fieldwork, and unspecified assistantships available. Support available to part-time students. Financial award applicants required to submit FAFSA. *Faculty research:* Corporate financial reporting disclosure and quality, fraud and litigation risk, audit quality, opinion, and pricing decision, financial regulations, information technology performance. *Unit head:* Matt Cornwell, Assistant Director of Student Services and Outreach, 585-475-6916, E-mail: mcornwell@saunders.rit.edu. *Application contact:* Diane Ellison, Senior Associate Vice President, Graduate Enrollment Services, 585-475-2229, Fax: 585-475-7164, E-mail: gradinfo@rit.edu.
Website: https://www.rit.edu/study/accounting-ms

Rockhurst University, Helzberg School of Management, Kansas City, MO 64110-2561. Offers accounting (MBA); business intelligence (MBA, Certificate); business intelligence and analytics (MS); data science (MBA, Certificate); entrepreneurship (MBA); finance (MBA); fundraising leadership (MBA, Certificate); healthcare management (MBA, Certificate); human capital (Certificate); international business (Certificate); management (MA, MBA, Certificate); nonprofit administration (Certificate); organizational development (Certificate); science leadership (Certificate). *Accreditation:* AACSB. *Program availability:* Part-time, evening/weekend. *Entrance requirements:* For master's, GMAT or GRE. Additional exam requirements/recommendations for international students: Required—TOEFL (minimum score 550 paper-based; 79 iBT). Electronic applications accepted. *Faculty research:* Offshoring/outsourcing, systems analysis/synthesis, work teams, multilateral trade, path dependencies/creation.

Rocky Mountain College, Program in Accountancy, Billings, MT 59102-1796. Offers M Acc. *Program availability:* Part-time-only. *Faculty:* 2 full-time (0 women). *Students:* 2 part-time (0 women); includes 1 minority (American Indian or Alaska Native, non-Hispanic/Latino). Average age 34. In 2018, 6 master's awarded. *Entrance requirements:* Additional exam requirements/recommendations for international students: Required—TOEFL (minimum score 570 paper-based; 88 iBT), IELTS (minimum score 6.5). *Application deadline:* Applications are processed on a rolling basis. Application fee: $35 ($40 for international students). Electronic applications accepted. Application fee is waived when completed online. *Expenses:* Contact institution. *Financial support:* In 2018–19, 1 student received support. Campus work-study available. Financial award applicants required to submit FAFSA. *Unit head:* Anthony Piltz, Professor of Business Administration and Economics, 406-657-1069, E-mail: piltza@rocky.edu. *Application contact:* Austin Mapston, Dean of Enrollment Services, 406-657-1026, Fax: 406-657-1189, E-mail: admissions@rocky.edu.
Website: https://www.rocky.edu/academics/academic-programs/graduate/master-accountancy

Roosevelt University, Graduate Division, Walter E. Heller College of Business, Program in Accounting, Chicago, IL 60605. Offers accounting (MSA); accounting forensics (MSAF). *Program availability:* Part-time, evening/weekend. Electronic applications accepted.

Rutgers University–Newark, Graduate School, Program in Management, Newark, NJ 07102. Offers accounting (PhD); accounting information systems (PhD); computer information systems (PhD); finance (PhD); information technology (PhD); international business (PhD); management science (PhD); marketing (PhD); organization management (PhD). Program offered jointly with New Jersey Institute of Technology. *Accreditation:* AACSB. *Degree requirements:* For doctorate, thesis/dissertation, cumulative exams. *Entrance requirements:* For doctorate, GMAT or GRE General Test, minimum undergraduate B average. Additional exam requirements/recommendations for international students: Required—TOEFL. Electronic applications accepted. *Faculty research:* Technology management, leadership and teams, consumer behavior, financial and markets, logistics.

Rutgers University–Newark, Rutgers Business School–Newark and New Brunswick, Doctoral Programs in Management, Newark, NJ 07102. Offers accounting (PhD); accounting information systems (PhD); economics (PhD); finance (PhD); individualized study (PhD); information technology (PhD); international business (PhD); management science (PhD); marketing science (PhD); organizational management (PhD); science, technology and management (PhD); supply chain management (PhD). *Degree requirements:* For doctorate, comprehensive exam, thesis/dissertation. *Entrance requirements:* For doctorate, GRE or GMAT. Additional exam requirements/recommendations for international students: Required—TOEFL (minimum score 550 paper-based; 79 iBT). Electronic applications accepted.

Rutgers University–Newark, Rutgers Business School–Newark and New Brunswick, Program in Accountancy, Newark, NJ 07102. Offers M Accy. *Accreditation:* AACSB. *Program availability:* Online learning.

Rutgers University–Newark, Rutgers Business School–Newark and New Brunswick, Program in Professional Accounting, Newark, NJ 07102. Offers MBA. *Accreditation:* AACSB. *Entrance requirements:* For master's, GMAT. Additional exam requirements/recommendations for international students: Required—TOEFL. Electronic applications accepted.

Sacred Heart University, Graduate Programs, Jack Welch College of Business, Department of Accounting, Fairfield, CT 06825. Offers MBA, MS, Graduate Certificate. *Program availability:* Part-time, evening/weekend. *Entrance requirements:* For master's, bachelor's degree with minimum GPA of 3.0. Additional exam requirements/recommendations for international students: Required—TOEFL (minimum score 570 paper-based, 80 iBT), TWE, or IELTS (6.5). Electronic applications accepted. *Expenses:* Contact institution.

St. Ambrose University, College of Business, Program in Accounting, Davenport, IA 52803-2898. Offers MAC. *Program availability:* Part-time, evening/weekend. *Degree requirements:* For master's, comprehensive exam (for some programs), thesis or alternative, capstone seminar. *Entrance requirements:* For master's, GMAT. Electronic applications accepted.

St. Bonaventure University, School of Graduate School, School of Business, St. Bonaventure, NY 14778-2284. Offers general business (MBA); professional accountancy (MBA). *Accreditation:* AACSB. *Program availability:* Part-time, evening/weekend, 100% online. *Faculty:* 15 full-time (4 women), 6 part-time/adjunct (3 women). *Students:* 86 full-time (44 women), 108 part-time (52 women); includes 16 minority (7 Black or African American, non-Hispanic/Latino; 1 Asian, non-Hispanic/Latino; 5 Hispanic/Latino; 3 Two or more races, non-Hispanic/Latino), 8 international. Average age 28. 88 applicants, 98% accepted, 71 enrolled. In 2018, 125 master's awarded. *Entrance requirements:* For master's, GMAT or GRE, undergraduate degree, official transcripts, current resume. Additional exam requirements/recommendations for international students: Required—TOEFL (minimum score 550 paper-based; 79 iBT). *Application deadline:* For fall admission, 3/15 priority date for domestic students, 2/1 priority date for international students; for spring admission, 10/15 priority date for domestic students, 7/1 priority date for international students. Applications are processed on a rolling basis. Application fee: $0. Electronic applications accepted. *Financial support:* In 2018–19, 9 students received support. Career-related internships or fieldwork, scholarships/grants, health care benefits, and unspecified assistantships available. Financial award application deadline: 4/15; financial award applicants required to submit FAFSA. *Faculty research:* Serial entrepreneurship and venture performance, supply chain relationship, customer/employee relationships/interactions, nonparametric applications to financial markets. *Unit head:* Dr. Matrecia James, Dean, 716-375-2200, Fax: 716-372-2191, E-mail: mjames@sbu.edu. *Application contact:* Matthew Retchless, Director of Graduate Admissions, 716-375-2021, Fax: 716-375-4015, E-mail: gradsch@sbu.edu.
Website: http://www.sbu.edu/academics/schools/business/graduate-degrees/master-of-business-administration-(mba)

St. Edward's University, Bill Munday School of Business, Master of Accounting Program, Austin, TX 78704. Offers M Ac. *Program availability:* Part-time, evening/weekend. *Entrance requirements:* Additional exam requirements/recommendations for international students: Required—TOEFL, IELTS. Electronic applications accepted.

St. Edward's University, Bill Munday School of Business, Master of Business Administration Program, Austin, TX 78704. Offers accounting (MBA); digital management (MBA). *Program availability:* Part-time, evening/weekend. *Entrance requirements:* Additional exam requirements/recommendations for international students: Required—TOEFL, IELTS. Electronic applications accepted.

St. Francis College, Program in Professional Accountancy, Brooklyn Heights, NY 11201-4398. Offers MS.

St. John's University, The Peter J. Tobin College of Business, Department of Accountancy, Program in Accounting, Queens, NY 11439. Offers MS. *Accreditation:* AACSB. *Program availability:* Part-time, evening/weekend, 100% online, blended/hybrid learning. *Degree requirements:* For master's, thesis (for some programs). *Entrance requirements:* For master's, GMAT or GRE, 2 letters of recommendation, essay, resume, unofficial transcripts. Additional exam requirements/recommendations for international students: Required—TOEFL (minimum score 80 iBT), IELTS (minimum score 6.5). Electronic applications accepted. *Expenses:* Contact institution. *Faculty research:* Accounting theory, auditing, managerial accounting, accounting information systems, accounting education.

St. Joseph's College, Long Island Campus, Programs in Business Management and Administration, Program in Accounting, Patchogue, NY 11772-2399. Offers MBA. *Program availability:* Part-time, evening/weekend. *Faculty:* 13 full-time (5 women), 23 part-time/adjunct (8 women). *Students:* 27 full-time (13 women), 50 part-time (22 women); includes 15 minority (2 Black or African American, non-Hispanic/Latino; 5 Asian, non-Hispanic/Latino; 8 Hispanic/Latino). Average age 29. 49 applicants, 71% accepted, 24 enrolled. In 2018, 24 master's awarded. *Entrance requirements:* For master's, Application, $25 application fee, two letters of reference forms, verification of employment form, current resume, 250 word written statement, official transcripts. Additional exam requirements/recommendations for international students: Required—TOEFL (minimum score 80 iBT). *Application deadline:* Applications are processed on a rolling basis. Application fee: $25. Electronic applications accepted. *Expenses: Tuition:* Full-time $18,450; part-time $1025 per credit. *Required fees:* $414. *Financial support:* In 2018–19, 23 students received support. Federal Work-Study available. *Unit head:* Mary A. Chance, Assistant Professor/Interim Director of Graduate Management Studies, 631-687-1297, E-mail: mchance@sjcny.edu. *Application contact:* Mary A. Chance, Assistant Professor/Interim Director of Graduate Management Studies, 631-687-1297, E-mail: mchance@sjcny.edu.
Website: http://www.sjcny.edu

St. Joseph's College, New York, Programs in Business Management and Administration, Program in Accounting, Brooklyn, NY 11205-3688. Offers MBA. *Program availability:* Part-time, evening/weekend. *Faculty:* 5 part-time/adjunct (4 women). *Students:* 1 full-time (0 women), 8 part-time (4 women); includes 7 minority (6 Black or African American, non-Hispanic/Latino; 1 Hispanic/Latino). Average age 28. 8 applicants, 63% accepted, 2 enrolled. In 2018, 1 master's awarded. *Entrance requirements:* For master's, Application, $25 application fee, two letters of recommendation, current resume, 250 word essay, official transcripts. Additional exam requirements/recommendations for international students: Required—TOEFL (minimum score 80 iBT). *Application deadline:* Applications are processed on a rolling basis. Application fee: $25. Electronic applications accepted. *Expenses: Tuition:* Full-time $18,450; part-time $1025 per credit. *Required fees:* $414. *Financial support:* In 2018–19, 1 student received support. *Unit head:* Christopher Smith, Assistant Professor/Associate Chair, 718-940-5786, E-mail: csmith2@sjcny.edu. *Application contact:* Christopher Smith, Assistant Professor/Associate Chair, 718-940-5786, E-mail: csmith2@sjcny.edu.
Website: https://www.sjcny.edu/brooklyn/academics/graduate/graduate-degrees/accounting

Saint Joseph's College of Maine, Master of Accountancy Program, Standish, ME 04084. Offers M Acc. *Program availability:* Part-time, online learning. *Entrance requirements:* For master's, baccalaureate degree with minimum cumulative GPA of 2.5; successful completion of each of the following prior to program enrollment: financial accounting, managerial accounting, introduction of finance/business finance and macroeconomics. Electronic applications accepted.

Saint Joseph's University, Erivan K. Haub School of Business, MBA Program, Philadelphia, PA 19131-1395. Offers accounting (MBA); business intelligence analytics (MBA); finance (MBA); financial analysis reporting (Postbaccalaureate Certificate); general business (MBA); health and medical services administration (MBA); international business (MBA); international marketing (MBA); leading (MBA); marketing (MBA); DO/MBA. DO/MBA offered jointly with Philadelphia College of Osteopathic Medicine. *Program availability:* Part-time-only, evening/weekend, 100% online. *Degree requirements:* For master's, minimum GPA of 3.0. *Entrance requirements:* For master's, GMAT or GRE, 2 letters of recommendation, resume, personal statement, official undergraduate and graduate transcripts. Additional exam requirements/recommendations for international students: Required—PTE, TOEFL, IELTS, or PTE. Electronic applications accepted. *Expenses:* Contact institution.

Saint Leo University, Graduate Studies in Business, Saint Leo, FL 33574-6665. Offers accounting (M Acc); cybersecurity management (MBA); health care management (MBA); human resource management (MBA); marketing (MBA); marketing research and social media analytics (MBA); software engineering (MS). *Accreditation:* ACBSP. *Program availability:* Part-time, evening/weekend, 100% online, blended/hybrid learning. *Faculty:* 51 full-time (16 women), 54 part-time/adjunct (22 women). *Students:* 8 full-time (3 women), 2,209 part-time (1,288 women); includes 1,046 minority (691 Black or African American, non-Hispanic/Latino; 10 American Indian or Alaska Native, non-Hispanic/Latino; 47 Asian, non-Hispanic/Latino; 249 Hispanic/Latino; 5 Native Hawaiian or other Pacific Islander, non-Hispanic/Latino; 44 Two or more races, non-Hispanic/Latino), 71 international. Average age 37. 760 applicants, 83% accepted, 498 enrolled. In 2018, 763 master's, 14 doctorates awarded. *Degree requirements:* For doctorate, comprehensive exam, thesis/dissertation. *Entrance requirements:* For master's, GMAT with minimum score 500 (for M Acc), official transcripts, current resume, 2 professional recommendations, personal statement, bachelor's degree from regionally-accredited university; undergraduate degree in accounting and minimum undergraduate GPA of 3.0 (for M Acc); minimum undergraduate GPA of 3.0 in final 2 years of undergraduate study

and 2 years' work experience (for MBA); for doctorate, GMAT (minimum score of 550) if master's GPA is under 3.25, official transcripts, current resume, 2 professional recommendations, personal statement, master's degree from regionally-accredited university with minimum GPA of 3.25, 3 years' work experience, interview. Additional exam requirements/recommendations for international students: Required—TOEFL (minimum score 550 paper-based; 78 iBT). *Application deadline:* For fall admission, 7/1 priority date for domestic and international students; for spring admission, 11/12 priority date for domestic students, 11/1 for international students. Applications are processed on a rolling basis. Application fee: $80. Electronic applications accepted. *Expenses:* Onground Master of Accounting $555 per credit, Online Master of Accounting $720 per credit, Onground MBA $555 per credit, Onground MBA Intl/Experiential $720 per credit, Online MBA/Cybersecurity military rate $555 per credit, Online MBA civilian rate $720, MS Cybersecurity civilian rate $770, DBA $900 per credit. *Financial support:* In 2018–19, 213 students received support. Scholarships/grants, unspecified assistantships, and tuition remission for Saint Leo employees and their dependents available. Financial award application deadline: 3/1; financial award applicants required to submit FAFSA. *Faculty research:* Servant leadership, work/life balance, emotional intelligence, pricing, marketing. *Unit head:* Dr. Robyn Parker, Dean, School of Business, 352-588-8599, Fax: 352-588-8912, E-mail: mbaslu@saintleo.edu. *Application contact:* Mark Russum, Assistant Vice President, Enrollment, 800-707-8846, Fax: 352-588-7873, E-mail: grad.admissions@saintleo.edu.
Website: https://www.saintleo.edu/college-of-business

Saint Louis University, Graduate Programs, John Cook School of Business, Department of Accounting, St. Louis, MO 63103. Offers M Acct, MBA. *Program availability:* Part-time, evening/weekend. *Entrance requirements:* For master's, GMAT. Additional exam requirements/recommendations for international students: Required—TOEFL (minimum score 570 paper-based; 88 iBT). Electronic applications accepted. *Expenses:* Contact institution. *Faculty research:* Tax policy, market valuation/corporate governance, foreign currency translation, accounting for income taxes, earnings quality.

Saint Mary's College of California, School of Economics and Business Administration, MS in Accounting Program, Moraga, CA 94575. Offers MS.

Saint Mary's University of Minnesota, Schools of Graduate and Professional Programs, Graduate School of Business and Technology, Accounting Program, Winona, MN 55987-1399. Offers MS. *Program availability:* Online learning. *Unit head:* Melanie Torborg, Program Director, 612-238-4525, E-mail: mtorborg@smumn.edu. *Application contact:* Laurie Roy, Director of Admission of Schools of Graduate and Professional Programs, 507-457-8606, Fax: 612-728-5121, E-mail: lroy@smumn.edu.
Website: http://www.smumn.edu/graduate-home/areas-of-study/graduate-school-of-business-technology/ms-in-accountancy

Saint Peter's University, Graduate Business Programs, Program in Accountancy, Jersey City, NJ 07306-5997. Offers MS, MBA/MS. *Program availability:* Part-time, evening/weekend. *Entrance requirements:* Additional exam requirements/recommendations for international students: Required—TOEFL. Electronic applications accepted.

St. Thomas University, School of Business, Department of Management, Miami Gardens, FL 33054-6459. Offers accounting (MBA); general management (MSM, Certificate); health management (MBA, MSM, Certificate); human resource management (MBA, MSM, Certificate); international business (MBA, MIB, MSM, Certificate); justice administration (MSM, Certificate); management accounting (MSM, Certificate); public management (MSM, Certificate); sports administration (MS). *Program availability:* Part-time, evening/weekend. *Degree requirements:* For master's, comprehensive exam. *Entrance requirements:* For master's, interview, minimum GPA of 3.0 or GMAT. Additional exam requirements/recommendations for international students: Required—TOEFL (minimum score 550 paper-based; 79 iBT). Electronic applications accepted.

Samford University, Brock School of Business, Birmingham, AL 35229. Offers accountancy (M Acc); entrepreneurship (MBA); finance (MBA); marketing (MBA); JD/M Acc; JD/MBA; MBA/M Acc; MBA/M Div; MBA/MSEM; MBA/Pharm D. Programs offered jointly with Cumberland School of Law, Beeson School of Divinity, Howard College of Arts and Sciences, and McWhorter School of Pharmacy. *Accreditation:* AACSB. *Program availability:* Part-time, 100% online, blended/hybrid learning. *Faculty:* 7 full-time (1 woman), 4 part-time/adjunct (0 women). *Students:* 76 full-time (30 women), 20 part-time (11 women); includes 8 minority (4 Black or African American, non-Hispanic/Latino; 1 Asian, non-Hispanic/Latino; 1 Hispanic/Latino; 2 Two or more races, non-Hispanic/Latino), 7 international. Average age 28. 41 applicants, 88% accepted, 26 enrolled. In 2018, 74 master's awarded. *Degree requirements:* For master's, capstone course. *Entrance requirements:* For master's, GMAT or GRE, resume, transcripts, WES or ECE Evaluation (international applicants only), essay (international applicants only). Additional exam requirements/recommendations for international students: Required—TOEFL (minimum score 90 iBT), IELTS (minimum score 6.5). *Application deadline:* For fall admission, 8/1 for domestic and international students; for spring admission, 1/1 for domestic and international students. Applications are processed on a rolling basis. Application fee: $35. Electronic applications accepted. Application fee is waived when completed online. *Expenses: Tuition:* Full-time $17,255; part-time $837 per credit. *Required fees:* $610; $305 per term. Tuition and fees vary according to course load, degree level, program and student level. *Financial support:* In 2018–19, 46 students received support. Scholarships/grants available. Financial award application deadline: 2/15; financial award applicants required to submit FAFSA. *Unit head:* Dr. Barbara Cartledge, Assistant Dean, 205-726-2935, Fax: 205-726-2540, E-mail: bhcartle@samford.edu. *Application contact:* Elizabeth Gambrell, Associate Director, 205-726-2040, Fax: 205-726-2540, E-mail: eagambre@samford.edu.
Website: http://www.samford.edu/business

Sam Houston State University, College of Business Administration, Department of Accounting, Huntsville, TX 77341. Offers MS. *Program availability:* Part-time. *Degree requirements:* For master's, comprehensive exam. *Entrance requirements:* For master's, GMAT. Additional exam requirements/recommendations for international students: Required—TOEFL (minimum score 550 paper-based; 79 iBT), IELTS (minimum score 6.5). Electronic applications accepted.

San Diego State University, Graduate and Research Affairs, Fowler College of Business, Charles W. Lamden School of Accountancy, San Diego, CA 92182. Offers MS. *Accreditation:* AACSB. *Degree requirements:* For master's, thesis or alternative. *Entrance requirements:* For master's, GMAT, resume, letters of reference. Additional exam requirements/recommendations for international students: Required—TOEFL. Electronic applications accepted.

San Francisco State University, Division of Graduate Studies, College of Business, Department of Accounting, San Francisco, CA 94132-1722. Offers MSA. *Program availability:* Part-time. *Entrance requirements:* For master's, GMAT, copy of transcripts, written statement of purpose, resume, two letters of reference. Additional exam requirements/recommendations for international students: Required—TOEFL or IELTS. Electronic applications accepted. *Unit head:* Dr. Sanjit Sengupta, Faculty Director, 415-817-4366, Fax: 415-817-4340, E-mail: sengupta@sfsu.edu. *Application contact:* Dr. Theresa Hammond, Graduate Coordinator, 415-338-6283, Fax: 415-817-4340, E-mail: thammond@sfsu.edu.
Website: http://cob.sfsu.edu/graduate-programs/MSA

Seattle University, Albers School of Business and Economics, Master of Professional Accounting Program, Seattle, WA 98122-1090. Offers MPAC, JD/MPAC, MBA/MPAC, MPAC/MSF. *Program availability:* Part-time, evening/weekend. *Faculty:* 11 full-time (4 women). *Students:* 41 full-time (29 women), 23 part-time (16 women); includes 17 minority (15 Asian, non-Hispanic/Latino; 2 Two or more races, non-Hispanic/Latino), 38 international. Average age 26. 74 applicants, 69% accepted, 22 enrolled. In 2018, 50 master's awarded. *Entrance requirements:* For master's, GMAT, minimum GPA of 3.0. Additional exam requirements/recommendations for international students: Required—TOEFL (minimum score 580 paper-based; 92 iBT). *Application deadline:* For fall admission, 5/1 priority date for domestic students, 4/1 priority date for international students; for winter admission, 11/20 priority date for domestic students, 9/1 priority date for international students; for spring admission, 2/20 priority date for domestic students, 12/1 priority date for international students. Applications are processed on a rolling basis. Application fee: $55. Electronic applications accepted. *Expenses:* Contact institution. *Financial support:* In 2018–19, 20 students received support. Career-related internships or fieldwork and Federal Work-Study available. Support available to part-time students. Financial award applicants required to submit FAFSA. *Unit head:* Dr. Bruce Koch, Program Director, 206-296-5700, Fax: 206-296-5795, E-mail: kochb@seattleu.edu. *Application contact:* Janet Shandley, Director of Graduate Admissions, 206-296-5900, Fax: 206-298-5656, E-mail: grad_admissions@seattleu.edu.
Website: http://www.seattleu.edu/albers/mpac/

Seton Hall University, Stillman School of Business, Programs in Business Administration, South Orange, NJ 07079-2697. Offers accounting (MBA); entrepreneurial studies (Certificate); finance (MBA); financial decision making (Certificate); information technology management (MBA); international business (MBA); management (MBA); marketing (MBA); sport management (MBA); supply chain management (MBA, Certificate). *Program availability:* Part-time, evening/weekend. *Faculty:* 27 full-time (5 women), 18 part-time/adjunct (2 women). *Students:* 85 full-time (40 women), 363 part-time (147 women); includes 78 minority (22 Black or African American, non-Hispanic/Latino; 4 Asian, non-Hispanic/Latino; 18 Hispanic/Latino; 29 Native Hawaiian or other Pacific Islander, non-Hispanic/Latino; 5 Two or more races, non-Hispanic/Latino), 282 international. Average age 34. 483 applicants, 85% accepted, 302 enrolled. In 2018, 96 master's awarded. *Degree requirements:* For master's, 20 hours of community service (Social Responsibility Project). *Entrance requirements:* For master's, GMAT or CPA, GRE (waived based on work experience or advanced degree from AACSB institution), MS in business discipline, professional degree or designation (MD, JD, PhD, DVM, DDS, CPA, etc.), minimum undergraduate GPA of 3.0. Additional exam requirements/recommendations for international students: Required—TOEFL (minimum score 607 paper-based; 80 iBT), IELTS (minimum score 6), PTE. *Application deadline:* For fall admission, 5/31 priority date for domestic students, 4/30 priority date for international students; for spring admission, 10/31 priority date for domestic students, 9/30 priority date for international students; for summer admission, 3/31 priority date for domestic students. Applications are processed on a rolling basis. Application fee: $75. Electronic applications accepted. Application fee is waived when completed online. *Expenses:* Tuition is $1,305 per credit hour and the overall MBA is a 40 credit hour program. University fees are $115 per semester. The university also has a technology that is $125 per semester. *Financial support:* In 2018–19, 44 students received support, including 25 research assistantships with partial tuition reimbursements available (averaging $3,644 per year); career-related internships or fieldwork, scholarships/grants, and unspecified assistantships also available. Financial award application deadline: 6/30; financial award applicants required to submit FAFSA. *Faculty research:* Sport, hedge funds, executive compensation, social media, legal studies. *Unit head:* Dr. Joyce Strawser, Dean, 973-761-9013, Fax: 973-761-9217, E-mail: joyce.strawser@shu.edu. *Application contact:* Alfred Ayoub, Director of Graduate Admissions, 973-761-9262, Fax: 973-761-9208, E-mail: alfred.ayoub@shu.edu.
Website: http://www.shu.edu/business/mba-programs.cfm

Seton Hill University, MBA Program, Greensburg, PA 15601. Offers entrepreneurship (MBA); forensic accounting and fraud examination (MBA); healthcare administration (MBA); management (MBA). *Program availability:* Part-time, evening/weekend. *Entrance requirements:* For master's, resume, 3 letters of recommendation, personal statement, transcripts. Additional exam requirements/recommendations for international students: Required—TOEFL (minimum score 600 paper-based; 100 iBT), IELTS (minimum score 6.5). *Application deadline:* Applications are processed on a rolling basis. Application fee: $0. Electronic applications accepted. *Financial support:* Federal Work-Study, scholarships/grants, and tuition discounts available. Financial award application deadline: 8/15; financial award applicants required to submit FAFSA. *Unit head:* Dr. Douglas Nelson, Associate Professor, Business/MBA Program Director, E-mail: dnelson@setonhill.edu. *Application contact:* Dr. Douglas Nelson, Associate Professor, Business/MBA Program Director, E-mail: dnelson@setonhill.edu.
Website: http://www.setonhill.edu/academics/graduate_programs/mba

Shorter University, Professional Studies, Rome, GA 30165. Offers accountancy (MAC); business administration (MBA); management (MM). *Program availability:* Evening/weekend. *Degree requirements:* For master's, project. *Entrance requirements:* For master's, minimum undergraduate GPA of 2.75 in last 60 hours, 3 years of work experience. Additional exam requirements/recommendations for international students: Required—TOEFL (minimum score 550 paper-based; 79 iBT). Electronic applications accepted.

Siena College, School of Business, Loudonville, NY 12211-1462. Offers accounting (MS). *Program availability:* Evening/weekend. *Degree requirements:* For master's, internship.

Slippery Rock University of Pennsylvania, Graduate Studies (Recruitment), College of Business, School of Business, Slippery Rock, PA 16057-1383. Offers accounting/finance (MBA); general (MBA); marketing/management (MBA). *Program availability:* Part-time, evening/weekend. *Faculty:* 12 full-time (7 women), 1 part-time/adjunct (0 women). *Students:* 21 full-time (8 women), 22 part-time (15 women); includes 3 minority (1 Black or African American, non-Hispanic/Latino; 1 Asian, non-Hispanic/Latino; 1 Hispanic/Latino). Average age 29. 53 applicants, 62% accepted, 23 enrolled. In 2018, 23 master's awarded. *Degree requirements:* For master's, comprehensive exam (for some programs), thesis (for some programs). *Entrance requirements:* For master's, minimum cumulative GPA of 3.0, official transcripts, three references. Additional exam requirements/recommendations for international students: Required—TOEFL (minimum score 550 paper-based; 80 iBT). *Application deadline:* For fall admission, 3/1 priority date for domestic students, 5/1 priority date for international students; for spring admission, 10/1 priority date for domestic students, 9/1 priority date for international students. Applications are processed on a rolling basis. Application fee: $25 ($30 for international students). Electronic applications accepted. *Expenses:* Contact institution. *Financial support:* In 2018–19, 9 students received support. Career-related internships or fieldwork, Federal Work-Study, institutionally sponsored loans, scholarships/grants, tuition waivers (partial), and unspecified assistantships available. Support available to part-time students. Financial award application deadline: 5/1; financial award applicants required to submit FAFSA. *Unit head:* Dr. Larry McCarthy, Graduate Coordinator, 724-738-2552, Fax: 724-738-2959, E-mail: larry.mccarthy@sru.edu. *Application contact:* Brandi Weber-Mortimer, Director of Graduate Admissions, 724-738-2051, Fax: 724-738-

2146, E-mail: graduate.admissions@sru.edu.
Website: http://www.sru.edu/academics/graduate-programs/mba-master-of-business-administration

Southeast Missouri State University, School of Graduate Studies, Harrison College of Business and Computing, Cape Girardeau, MO 63701-4799. Offers accounting (MBA); entrepreneurship (MBA); financial management (MBA); sport management (MBA). *Accreditation:* AACSB. *Program availability:* Part-time, evening/weekend, 100% online. *Faculty:* 27 full-time (7 women), 1 (woman) part-time/adjunct. *Students:* 94 full-time (50 women), 88 part-time (39 women); includes 18 minority (9 Black or African American, non-Hispanic/Latino; 4 Asian, non-Hispanic/Latino; 5 Hispanic/Latino), 79 international. Average age 29. 80 applicants, 100% accepted, 80 enrolled. In 2018, 62 master's awarded. *Degree requirements:* For master's, variable foreign language requirement, comprehensive exam (for some programs), thesis or alternative. *Entrance requirements:* For master's, GMAT or GRE, minimum undergraduate GPA of 2.5, minimum grade of C in prerequisite courses. Additional exam requirements/recommendations for international students: Required—TOEFL (minimum score 550 paper-based; 79 iBT), IELTS (minimum score 6), PTE (minimum score 53). *Application deadline:* For fall admission, 8/1 for domestic students, 6/1 for international students; for spring admission, 11/21 for domestic students, 10/1 for international students; for summer admission, 5/15 for domestic students. Applications are processed on a rolling basis. Application fee: $30 ($40 for international students). Electronic applications accepted. *Expenses:* Contact institution. *Financial support:* In 2018–19, 16 students received support. Career-related internships or fieldwork, Federal Work-Study, scholarships/grants, traineeships, tuition waivers (full), and unspecified assistantships available. Financial award application deadline: 6/30; financial award applicants required to submit FAFSA. *Faculty research:* Organizational justice, ethics, leadership, corporate finance, generational differences. *Unit head:* Dr. Alberto Davila, Dean, 573-651-2112, E-mail: adavila@semo.edu. *Application contact:* Dr. Alberto Davila, Dean, 573-651-2112, E-mail: adavila@semo.edu.
Website: http://www.semo.edu/mba

Southern Adventist University, School of Business, Collegedale, TN 37315-0370. Offers accounting (MBA); computer information systems (MBA); finance (MBA); healthcare administration (MBA); management (MBA). *Program availability:* Part-time, evening/weekend, 100% online. *Faculty:* 7 full-time (2 women). *Students:* 23 applicants, 48% accepted, 8 enrolled. In 2018, 8 master's awarded. *Entrance requirements:* For master's, GMAT, minimum cumulative undergraduate GPA of 3.0. Additional exam requirements/recommendations for international students: Required—TOEFL (minimum score 100 iBT). *Application deadline:* For fall admission, 7/1 for domestic students, 5/1 for international students; for winter admission, 11/1 for domestic students, 9/1 for international students; for summer admission, 4/1 for domestic students, 2/1 for international students. Applications are processed on a rolling basis. Application fee: $40. Electronic applications accepted. *Financial support:* Scholarships/grants and unspecified assistantships available. Financial award application deadline: 9/1; financial award applicants required to submit FAFSA. *Unit head:* Dr. Stephanie Sheehan, Dean, 423-236-2659, Fax: 423-236-1527, E-mail: ssheehan@southern.edu. *Application contact:* Teshia Price, Graduate Studies Coordinator, 423-236-2751, Fax: 423-236-1527, E-mail: tprice@southern.edu.
Website: https://www.southern.edu/academics/business.html

Southern Illinois University Carbondale, Graduate School, College of Business and Administration, School of Accountancy, Carbondale, IL 62901-4701. Offers M Acc, PhD, JD/M Acc. *Accreditation:* AACSB. *Program availability:* Part-time. *Degree requirements:* For doctorate, thesis/dissertation. *Entrance requirements:* For master's, GMAT, minimum GPA of 2.7; for doctorate, GMAT, minimum graduate GPA of 3.25. Additional exam requirements/recommendations for international students: Required—TOEFL (minimum score 550 paper-based; 80 iBT). Electronic applications accepted. *Faculty research:* Not-for-profit accounting, SEC regulations, computers and accounting education, taxation.

Southern Illinois University Edwardsville, Graduate School, School of Business, Department of Accounting, Edwardsville, IL 62026. Offers accountancy (MSA); taxation (MSA). *Accreditation:* AACSB. *Program availability:* Part-time, evening/weekend. *Degree requirements:* For master's, thesis or alternative, final exam. *Entrance requirements:* For master's, GMAT. Additional exam requirements/recommendations for international students: Required—TOEFL (minimum score 550 paper-based; 79 iBT), IELTS (minimum score 6.5). Electronic applications accepted.

Southern Methodist University, Cox School of Business, MBA Program, Dallas, TX 75275. Offers accounting (MBA, PMBA); business (EMBA); business analytics (PMBA); finance (MBA, PMBA); information technology and operations management (MBA, PMBA), including business analytics (MBA), information and operations (MBA); management (MBA, PMBA); marketing (MBA, PMBA); real estate (MBA, PMBA); strategy and entrepreneurship (MBA, PMBA); JD/MBA; MA/MBA. *Program availability:* Part-time, evening/weekend. *Entrance requirements:* For master's, GMAT. Additional exam requirements/recommendations for international students: Required—TOEFL. Electronic applications accepted. *Expenses:* Contact institution. *Faculty research:* Corporate finance, financial reporting, modeling consumer decision-making, competition between national brands and store brands, institutional determinants of firms' strategy.

Southern Methodist University, Cox School of Business, Program in Accounting, Dallas, TX 75275. Offers MSA. *Program availability:* Part-time, evening/weekend. *Entrance requirements:* For master's, GMAT. Additional exam requirements/recommendations for international students: Required—TOEFL. *Expenses:* Contact institution. *Faculty research:* Capital markets, taxation, business combinations, intangibles accounting, accounting history.

Southern New Hampshire University, School of Business, Manchester, NH 03106-1045. Offers accounting (MBA, Graduate Certificate); accounting finance (MS); accounting/auditing (MS); accounting/forensic accounting (MS); accounting/management accounting (MS); accounting/taxation (MS); applied economics (MS); athletic administration (MBA, Graduate Certificate); business administration (IMBA, Certificate), including business information systems (Certificate), human resource management (Certificate); business analytics (MBA); business intelligence (MBA); communication (MA), including new media and marketing, public relations; community economic development (MBA); criminal justice (MBA); data analytics (MS); economics (MBA); engineering management (MBA); entrepreneurship (MBA); finance (MBA, MS, Graduate Certificate); finance/corporate finance (MS); finance/investments (MS); forensic accounting (MBA); forensic accounting and fraud examination (Graduate Certificate); healthcare informatics (MBA); healthcare management (MBA); human resource management (MS); human resources (MBA); information technology (MS); information technology management (MBA); international business (PhD); Internet marketing (MBA); leadership (MBA); leadership of nonprofit organizations (Graduate Certificate); management (MS); marketing (MBA, MS, Graduate Certificate); music business (MBA); operations and project management (MS); operations and supply chain management (MBA, Graduate Certificate); organizational leadership (MS); project management (MBA, Graduate Certificate); public administration (MBA, Graduate Certificate); quantitative analysis (MBA); Six Sigma (Graduate Certificate); Six Sigma quality (MBA); social media marketing (MBA, Graduate Certificate); sport management (MBA, MS, Graduate Certificate); sustainability and environmental compliance (MBA); MBA/Certificate. *Accreditation:* ACBSP. *Program availability:* Part-time, evening/weekend, online learning. Terminal master's awarded for partial completion of doctoral program. *Degree requirements:* For master's, one foreign language, comprehensive exam (for some programs), thesis or alternative; for doctorate, one foreign language, comprehensive exam, thesis/dissertation. *Entrance requirements:* For master's, minimum GPA of 2.5; for doctorate, GMAT. Additional exam requirements/recommendations for international students: Required—TOEFL (minimum score 500 paper-based). Electronic applications accepted.

Southern Oregon University, Graduate Studies, School of Business, Ashland, OR 97520. Offers accounting (Postbaccalaureate Certificate); business administration (MBA); international management (MIM). *Accreditation:* ACBSP. *Program availability:* Part-time, evening/weekend, online learning. *Degree requirements:* For master's, comprehensive exam. *Entrance requirements:* For master's, GMAT, minimum cumulative GPA of 3.0 in the last 90 quarter credits (60 semester credits) of undergraduate coursework. Additional exam requirements/recommendations for international students: Required—TOEFL (minimum score 540 paper-based; 76 iBT), IELTS (minimum score 6), ELPT (minimum score 964) or ELS (minimum score 112). Electronic applications accepted.

Southern Utah University, Master of Accountancy/MBA Dual Degree Program, Cedar City, UT 84720-2498. Offers MBA/M Acc. *Program availability:* Part-time, online only, 100% online. *Students:* 1. 9 applicants, 100% accepted. *Entrance requirements:* Additional exam requirements/recommendations for international students: Required—TOEFL (minimum score 550 paper-based; 79 iBT), TOEFL (minimum score 550 paper-based, 79 iBT) or IELTS (minimum score 6). *Application deadline:* For fall admission, 7/15 for domestic and international students; for spring admission, 12/1 for domestic and international students; for summer admission, 5/1 for domestic and international students. Applications are processed on a rolling basis. Application fee: $60 ($65 for international students). Electronic applications accepted. *Expenses:* Contact institution. *Financial support:* Unspecified assistantships available.
Website: https://www.suu.edu/business/graduate/

Southern Utah University, Program in Accounting, Cedar City, UT 84720-2498. Offers M Acc. *Program availability:* Part-time, 100% online. *Faculty:* 7 full-time (0 women), 1 part-time/adjunct (0 women). *Students:* 43 full-time (12 women), 48 part-time (16 women); includes 11 minority (2 Black or African American, non-Hispanic/Latino; 2 American Indian or Alaska Native, non-Hispanic/Latino; 1 Asian, non-Hispanic/Latino; 6 Hispanic/Latino), 2 international. Average age 29. 40 applicants, 95% accepted, 31 enrolled. In 2018, 62 master's awarded. *Entrance requirements:* For master's, GMAT or GRE, official transcripts of all academic work prior to admission with transcripts verifying minimum GPA of 3.0 for all work completed; three letters of recommendation from former/current college professors, assigned mentors, supervisors or associates (for non-SUU business majors). Additional exam requirements/recommendations for international students: Required—TOEFL (minimum score 550 paper-based; 79 iBT), TOEFL (minimum scores: 550 paper-based, 79 iBT) or IELTS (minimum score 6). *Application deadline:* For fall admission, 7/15 for domestic and international students; for spring admission, 12/1 for domestic and international students; for summer admission, 5/1 for domestic and international students. Applications are processed on a rolling basis. Application fee: $60 ($65 for international students). Electronic applications accepted. *Expenses:* Contact institution. *Financial support:* Unspecified assistantships available. *Faculty research:* Cost accounting, intermediate accounting text, GAAP policy, Statements on Standards for Accounting and Review Services (SSARS). *Unit head:* Dr. Robin Boneck, Department Chair, 435-586-7773, Fax: 435-586-5493, E-mail: boneck@suu.edu. *Application contact:* Dr. Robin Boneck, Department Chair, 435-586-7773, Fax: 435-586-5493, E-mail: boneck@suu.edu.
Website: https://www.suu.edu/business/macc/

Southwestern Adventist University, Business Administration Department, Keene, TX 76059. Offers accounting (MBA); finance (MBA); management/leadership (MBA). *Program availability:* Part-time, evening/weekend. *Degree requirements:* For master's, capstone course. *Entrance requirements:* For master's, GMAT, GRE General Test.

State University of New York at New Paltz, Graduate and Extended Learning School, School of Business, New Paltz, NY 12561. Offers business administration (MBA); public accountancy (MBA). *Accreditation:* AACSB. *Program availability:* Part-time, evening/weekend. *Faculty:* 14 full-time (2 women), 4 part-time/adjunct (1 woman). *Students:* 61 full-time (33 women), 48 part-time (24 women); includes 24 minority (6 Black or African American, non-Hispanic/Latino; 6 Asian, non-Hispanic/Latino; 11 Hispanic/Latino; 1 Two or more races, non-Hispanic/Latino), 8 international. 49 applicants, 96% accepted, 38 enrolled. In 2018, 42 master's awarded. *Entrance requirements:* For master's, GMAT or GRE, minimum GPA of 3.0. Additional exam requirements/recommendations for international students: Required—TOEFL (minimum score 550 paper-based; 80 iBT), IELTS (minimum score 6.5). *Application deadline:* Applications are processed on a rolling basis. Application fee: $50. Electronic applications accepted. *Expenses:* Contact institution. *Financial support:* In 2018–19, 6 research assistantships with partial tuition reimbursements (averaging $5,000 per year), 1 teaching assistantship with partial tuition reimbursement (averaging $5,000 per year) were awarded; scholarships/grants, traineeships, and unspecified assistantships also available. Financial award application deadline: 8/1. *Faculty research:* Cognitive styles in management education, supporting SME e-commerce migration through e-learning, earnings management and board activity, trading future spread portfolio, global equity market correlation and volatility. *Unit head:* Dr. Kristin Backhaus, Dean, 845-257-2930, E-mail: mba@newpaltz.edu. *Application contact:* Aaron Hines, Director of MBA Program, 845-257-2968, E-mail: mba@newpaltz.edu.
Website: http://mba.newpaltz.edu

State University of New York College at Geneseo, Graduate Studies, School of Business, Geneseo, NY 14454. Offers accounting (MS). *Accreditation:* AACSB. *Degree requirements:* For master's, thesis. *Entrance requirements:* For master's, GMAT, bachelor's degree in accounting. Additional exam requirements/recommendations for international students: Required—TOEFL (minimum score 525 paper-based; 71 iBT), IELTS (minimum score 6.5), PTE, iTEP. Electronic applications accepted. *Expenses:* Contact institution.

State University of New York College at Old Westbury, School of Business, Old Westbury, NY 11568-0210. Offers accounting (MS); taxation (MS). *Program availability:* Part-time, evening/weekend. *Entrance requirements:* For master's, GMAT, 2 letters of recommendation. Additional exam requirements/recommendations for international students: Required—TOEFL (minimum score 550 paper-based). Electronic applications accepted. *Faculty research:* Corporate governance, asset pricing, corporate finance, hedge funds, taxation.

State University of New York Polytechnic Institute, MBA Program in Technology Management, Utica, NY 13502. Offers accounting and finance (MBA); business management (MBA); health informatics (MBA); human resource management (MBA); marketing management (MBA). *Program availability:* Part-time, 100% online. *Students:* 29 full-time (13 women), 85 part-time (41 women); includes 18 minority (4 Black or African American, non-Hispanic/Latino; 8 Asian, non-Hispanic/Latino; 6 Hispanic/

Latino). Average age 32. 54 applicants, 54% accepted, 26 enrolled. In 2018, 29 master's awarded. *Degree requirements:* For master's, comprehensive exam, capstone project. *Entrance requirements:* For master's, GMAT or approved GMAT waiver, resume, letter of reference. Additional exam requirements/recommendations for international students: Required—TOEFL (minimum score 79 iBT), IELTS (minimum score 6.5), PTE (minimum score 53), TOEFL, IELTS, or PTE; GMAT or approved GMAT waiver. *Application deadline:* For fall admission, 7/1 priority date for domestic students, 7/1 for international students; for spring admission, 12/1 for domestic students, 11/1 for international students. Applications are processed on a rolling basis. Application fee: $60. Electronic applications accepted. *Expenses:* Contact institution. *Financial support:* Fellowships, research assistantships, and unspecified assistantships available. Financial award application deadline: 6/1; financial award applicants required to submit FAFSA. *Faculty research:* Entrepreneurial capacity development. *Unit head:* Dr. Rafael Romero, Coordinator, 315-792-7207, E-mail: rafael.romero@sunypoly.edu. *Application contact:* Alicia Foster, Director of Graduate Admissions, 315-792-7347, E-mail: fostera3@sunypoly.edu.
Website: https://sunypoly.edu/academics/majors-and-programs/technology-management.html

State University of New York Polytechnic Institute, State University of New York Polytechnic Institute, Utica, NY 13502. Offers MS. *Accreditation:* AACSB. *Program availability:* Part-time, 100% online. *Students:* 24 full-time (15 women), 77 part-time (40 women); includes 32 minority (5 Black or African American, non-Hispanic/Latino; 1 American Indian or Alaska Native, non-Hispanic/Latino; 10 Asian, non-Hispanic/Latino; 12 Hispanic/Latino; 1 Native Hawaiian or other Pacific Islander, non-Hispanic/Latino; 3 Two or more races, non-Hispanic/Latino). Average age 31. 76 applicants, 53% accepted, 28 enrolled. In 2018, 19 master's awarded. *Entrance requirements:* For master's, GMAT or approved GMAT waiver, undergraduate accounting prerequisites required for completion of program. *Application deadline:* For fall admission, 7/1 for domestic and international students; for spring admission, 11/1 for domestic and international students. Applications are processed on a rolling basis. Application fee: $60. Electronic applications accepted. *Expenses: Tuition, area resident:* Full-time $8316; part-time $462 per credit hour. Tuition, nonresident: full-time $16,992; part-time $944 per credit hour. *International tuition:* $16,992 full-time. *Required fees:* $1023; $56.87 per credit hour. Tuition and fees vary according to course load, campus/location and program. *Financial support:* Fellowships, research assistantships, and unspecified assistantships available. Financial award application deadline: 6/1; financial award applicants required to submit FAFSA. *Faculty research:* Business interruption insurance claims, social security and income planning, income equality and pay ratio disclosure, medicaid and the nursing home dilemma, fake news. *Unit head:* Peter Karl, Program Coordinator, 315-792-7120, E-mail: pak3rd@sunypoly.edu. *Application contact:* Alicia Foster, Director of Graduate Admissions, 315-792-7347, E-mail: fostera3@sunypoly.edu.
Website: https://sunypoly.edu/academics/majors-and-programs/ms-accountancy.html

Stephen F. Austin State University, Graduate School, Nelson Rusche College of Business, Program in Professional Accountancy, Nacogdoches, TX 75962. Offers MPA. *Degree requirements:* For master's, comprehensive exam. *Entrance requirements:* For master's, GMAT. Additional exam requirements/recommendations for international students: Required—TOEFL.

Stetson University, School of Business Administration, Program in Accounting, DeLand, FL 32723. Offers M Acc. *Accreditation:* AACSB. *Program availability:* Part-time, online learning. *Faculty:* 14 full-time (3 women), 1 (woman) part-time/adjunct. *Students:* 25 full-time (14 women); includes 2 minority (both Hispanic/Latino), 2 international. Average age 28. 31 applicants, 68% accepted, 19 enrolled. In 2018, 17 master's awarded. *Entrance requirements:* For master's, GMAT, GRE, transcripts, resume, two letters of recommendation, personal statement. Additional exam requirements/recommendations for international students: Required—TOEFL (minimum score 90 iBT), IELTS (minimum score 7.5). *Application deadline:* For fall admission, 8/1 for domestic students; for spring admission, 1/1 for domestic students; for summer admission, 5/1 for domestic students. Applications are processed on a rolling basis. Application fee: $50. Electronic applications accepted. *Expenses:* $1020 per credit hour (for MAcc), $900 per credit hour (for Online MAcc). *Financial support:* In 2018–19, 11 students received support. Career-related internships or fieldwork, Federal Work-Study, institutionally sponsored loans, unspecified assistantships, and tuition waivers (for staff and dependents) available. Support available to part-time students. Financial award application deadline: 3/15; financial award applicants required to submit FAFSA. *Faculty research:* Scholarship of teaching and learning, behavioral accounting and legal tax research, corporate governance and financial reporting quality, and auditor conservatism and going concern decisions. *Unit head:* Dr. Michael E. Bitter, Director, 386-822-7410. *Application contact:* Jamie Vanderlip, Director of Admissions for Graduate, Transfer and Adult Programs, 386-822-7100, Fax: 386-822-7112, E-mail: jlvander@stetson.edu.

Stony Brook University, State University of New York, Graduate School, College of Business, Program in Accounting, Stony Brook, NY 11794. Offers MS. *Program availability:* Part-time. *Students:* 27 full-time (12 women), 15 part-time (9 women); includes 12 minority (1 Black or African American, non-Hispanic/Latino; 8 Asian, non-Hispanic/Latino; 3 Hispanic/Latino), 5 international. 76 applicants, 55% accepted, 27 enrolled. In 2018, 34 master's awarded. *Degree requirements:* For master's, capstone. *Entrance requirements:* For master's, GMAT or GRE. Additional exam requirements/recommendations for international students: Required—TOEFL (minimum score 80 iBT). *Application deadline:* For fall admission, 5/15 for domestic students, 3/15 for international students; for spring admission, 12/15 for domestic students, 10/15 for international students. *Expenses:* Contact institution. *Unit head:* Dr. Manuel London, Dean, 631-632-7159, E-mail: manuel.london@stonybrook.edu. *Application contact:* Erica Robey, Graduate Coordinator, 631-632-7171, Fax: 631-632-8181, E-mail: oss@stonybrook.edu.
Website: https://www.stonybrook.edu/commcms/business/academics/_graduate-program/ms-accounting.php

Stony Brook University, State University of New York, Graduate School, College of Business, Program in Business Administration, Stony Brook, NY 11794. Offers accounting (MBA); business administration (MBA); finance (MBA, Certificate); health care management (MBA); human resources (MBA); innovation (MBA); management (MBA); marketing (MBA); operations management (MBA). *Faculty:* 38 full-time (13 women), 8 part-time/adjunct (3 women). *Students:* 153 full-time (74 women), 148 part-time (76 women); includes 76 minority (16 Black or African American, non-Hispanic/Latino; 29 Asian, non-Hispanic/Latino; 27 Hispanic/Latino; 4 Two or more races, non-Hispanic/Latino), 36 international. Average age 28. 128 applicants, 78% accepted, 75 enrolled. In 2018, 76 master's awarded. *Entrance requirements:* For master's, GMAT, 3 letters of recommendation from current or former employers or professors, transcripts, personal statement, resume. Additional exam requirements/recommendations for international students: Required—TOEFL (minimum score 550 paper-based; 80 iBT), IELTS (minimum score 6.5). *Application deadline:* For fall admission, 5/15 for domestic students, 3/15 for international students; for spring admission, 12/1 for domestic students, 10/15 for international students. Application fee: $100. *Expenses:* Contact institution. *Financial support:* Teaching assistantships available. *Total annual research expenditures:* $2,070. *Unit head:* Dr. Manuel London, Dean, 631-632-7159, E-mail: manuel.london@stonybrook.edu. *Application contact:* Dr. Dmytro Holod, Associate Dean for Academic Programs/Graduate Director, 631-632-7183, Fax: 631-632-8181, E-mail: dmytro.holod@stonybrook.edu.
Website: https://www.stonybrook.edu/commcms/business/

Stratford University, School of Graduate Studies, Falls Church, VA 22043. Offers accounting (MS); business administration (MBA, DBA); cyber security (MS); cyber security leadership and policy (MS); digital forensics (MS); healthcare administration (MS); information systems (MS); information technology (DIT); networking and telecommunications (MS); software engineering (MS). *Program availability:* Part-time, evening/weekend, 100% online, blended/hybrid learning. *Degree requirements:* For master's, comprehensive exam, capstone project. *Entrance requirements:* For master's, GRE or GMAT, baccalaureate degree. Additional exam requirements/recommendations for international students: Required—TOEFL (minimum score 79 iBT), IELTS (minimum score 6.5), PTE (minimum score 5). Electronic applications accepted. *Expenses: Tuition:* Full-time $22,275; part-time $11,137 per year. One-time fee: $385.

Strayer University, Graduate Studies, Washington, DC 20005-2603. Offers accounting (MS); acquisition (MBA); business administration (MBA); communications technology (MS); educational management (M Ed); finance (MBA); health services administration (MHSA); hospitality and tourism management (MBA); human resource management (MBA); information systems (MS), including computer security management, decision support system management, enterprise resource management, network management, software engineering management, systems development management; management (MBA); management information systems (MS); marketing (MBA); professional accounting (MS), including accounting information systems, controllership, taxation; public administration (MPA); supply chain management (MBA); technology in education (M Ed). Programs also offered at campus locations in Birmingham, AL; Chamblee, GA; Cobb County, GA; Morrow, GA; White Marsh, MD; Charleston, SC; Columbia, SC; Greensboro, NC; Greenville, SC; Lexington, KY; Louisville, KY; Nashville, TN; North Raleigh, NC; Washington, DC. *Accreditation:* ACBSP. *Program availability:* Part-time, evening/weekend, online learning. *Degree requirements:* For master's, thesis. *Entrance requirements:* For master's, GMAT, GRE General Test, bachelor's degree from an accredited college or university, minimum undergraduate GPA of 2.75. Electronic applications accepted.

Suffolk University, Sawyer Business School, Department of Accounting, Boston, MA 02108-2770. Offers accounting (MSA, Graduate Certificate); taxation (MST); MBA/MSA; MBA/MST. *Accreditation:* AACSB. *Program availability:* Part-time, evening/weekend, 100% online. *Faculty:* 5 full-time (1 woman), 4 part-time/adjunct (1 woman). *Students:* 56 full-time (43 women), 80 part-time (51 women); includes 43 minority (12 Black or African American, non-Hispanic/Latino; 21 Asian, non-Hispanic/Latino; 8 Hispanic/Latino; 2 Two or more races, non-Hispanic/Latino), 27 international. Average age 29. 119 applicants, 75% accepted, 52 enrolled. In 2018, 85 master's awarded. *Entrance requirements:* For master's, GMAT. Additional exam requirements/recommendations for international students: Required—TOEFL (minimum score 550 paper-based; 80 iBT). *Application deadline:* For fall admission, 3/15 priority date for domestic and international students; for spring admission, 10/15 priority date for domestic and international students. Applications are processed on a rolling basis. Application fee: $50. Electronic applications accepted. *Expenses:* Contact institution. *Financial support:* In 2018–19, 85 students received support, including 3 fellowships (averaging $6,975 per year); career-related internships or fieldwork, Federal Work-Study, institutionally sponsored loans, and scholarships/grants also available. Support available to part-time students. Financial award application deadline: 4/1; financial award applicants required to submit FAFSA. *Faculty research:* Tax policy, tax research, decision-making in accounting, accounting information systems, capital markets and strategic planning. *Unit head:* Tracy Riley, Chair, 617-994-4276, E-mail: triley@suffolk.edu. *Application contact:* Mara Marzocchi, Associate Director of Graduate Admissions, 617-573-8302, Fax: 617-305-1733, E-mail: grad.admission@suffolk.edu.
Website: http://www.suffolk.edu/msa

Suffolk University, Sawyer Business School, Master of Business Administration Program, Boston, MA 02108-2770. Offers accounting (MBA); entrepreneurship (MBA); executive business administration (EMBA); finance (MBA); global business administration (GMBA); health administration (MBA); international business (MBA); marketing (MBA); nonprofit management (MBA); organizational behavior (MBA); strategic management (MBA); supply chain management (MBA); taxation (MBA); JD/MBA; MBA/MHA; MBA/MSA; MBA/MSF; MBA/MST. *Accreditation:* AACSB. *Program availability:* Part-time, evening/weekend, 100% online. *Faculty:* 18 full-time (5 women), 5 part-time/adjunct (0 women). *Students:* 79 full-time (46 women), 193 part-time (107 women); includes 69 minority (17 Black or African American, non-Hispanic/Latino; 18 Asian, non-Hispanic/Latino; 28 Hispanic/Latino; 6 Two or more races, non-Hispanic/Latino), 40 international. Average age 30. 274 applicants, 67% accepted, 83 enrolled. In 2018, 125 master's awarded. *Entrance requirements:* For master's, GMAT, minimum undergraduate GPA of 2.75 (MBA), 5 years of managerial experience (EMBA). Additional exam requirements/recommendations for international students: Required—TOEFL (minimum score 550 paper-based; 80 iBT). *Application deadline:* For fall admission, 3/15 priority date for domestic students, 10/15 priority date for international students; for spring admission, 10/15 priority date for domestic and international students. Applications are processed on a rolling basis. Application fee: $50. Electronic applications accepted. *Expenses:* Contact institution. *Financial support:* In 2018–19, 170 students received support, including 4 fellowships (averaging $2,906 per year); career-related internships or fieldwork, Federal Work-Study, institutionally sponsored loans, and scholarships/grants also available. Support available to part-time students. Financial award application deadline: 4/1; financial award applicants required to submit FAFSA. *Faculty research:* Foreign investments; career strategies and boundaryless careers; corporate ethics codes; interest rates, inflation, and growth options; innovation and product development performance. *Unit head:* Jodi Detjen, Director of MBA Programs, 617-573-8306, E-mail: jdetjen@suffolk.edu. *Application contact:* Mara Marzocchi, Associate Director of Graduate Admissions, 617-573-8302, Fax: 617-305-1733, E-mail: grad.admission@suffolk.edu.
Website: http://www.suffolk.edu/mba

Syracuse University, Martin J. Whitman School of Management, Master of Business Administration Program, Syracuse, NY 13244. Offers accounting (MBA); business analytics (MBA); entrepreneurship (MBA); marketing management (MBA); real estate (MBA); supply chain management (MBA); JD/MBA. *Program availability:* Part-time, 100% online. *Students:* Average age 32. 1,086 applicants, 73% accepted, 516 enrolled. In 2018, 84 master's awarded. *Entrance requirements:* For master's, GMAT or GRE, resume, essay, 5-minute video interview, two letters of recommendation, transcripts (unofficial). Additional exam requirements/recommendations for international students: Required—TOEFL (minimum score 100 iBT), IELTS (minimum score 7), PTE (minimum score 68). *Application deadline:* For fall admission, 11/30 for domestic students, 11/30 priority date for international students; for winter admission, 1/1 for domestic students, 1/1 priority date for international students; for spring admission, 2/15 for domestic and international students; for summer admission, 4/19 for domestic students. Application

fee: $75. Electronic applications accepted. *Expenses:* Contact institution. *Financial support:* In 2018–19, 22 students received support. Merit scholarships available. Financial award application deadline: 2/15. *Faculty research:* Data analysis, economics of international business, financial markets and institutions, operations management, supply chain management. *Unit head:* Dr. Alexander McKelvie, Associate Dean for Undergraduate and Full-time Master's Education, 315-443-7252, E-mail: mckelvie@syr.edu. *Application contact:* Shri Ramakrishnan, Assistant Director, Graduate Recruitment, 315-443-3497, Fax: 315-443-9517, E-mail: busgrad@syr.edu. Website: http://whitman.syr.edu/ftmba/

Syracuse University, Martin J. Whitman School of Management, MS Program in Professional Accounting, Syracuse, NY 13244. Offers MS. *Program availability:* Part-time, evening/weekend, 100% online. *Students:* Average age 23. 429 applicants, 55% accepted, 103 enrolled. In 2018, 76 master's awarded. *Entrance requirements:* For master's, GMAT or GRE, resume, essay, 5-minute video interview, two letters of recommendation, transcripts (unofficial). Additional exam requirements/recommendations for international students: Required—TOEFL (minimum score 100 iBT), IELTS (minimum score 7), PTE (minimum score 68). *Application deadline:* For fall admission, 11/30 for domestic students, 11/30 priority date for international students; for winter admission, 1/1 for domestic students, 1/1 priority date for international students; for spring admission, 2/15 for domestic and international students; for summer admission, 4/19 for domestic students. Application fee: $75. Electronic applications accepted. *Expenses:* Contact institution. *Financial support:* In 2018–19, 41 students received support. Merit-based scholarships available. Financial award application deadline: 2/15. *Faculty research:* Financial statement analysis, international reporting and analysis, advanced auditing, taxes and business strategy, principles of fraud examination. *Unit head:* Dr. Joseph Comprix, Chair/Associate Professor, 315-443-3674, E-mail: jjcompri@syr.edu. *Application contact:* Shri Ramakrishnan, Assistant Director, Graduate Recruitment, 315-443-3497, Fax: 315-443-9517, E-mail: busgrad@syr.edu. Website: http://whitman.syr.edu/msacc/

Tabor College, Graduate Program, Hillsboro, KS 67063. Offers accounting (MBA). Program offered at the Wichita campus only.

Tarleton State University, College of Graduate Studies, College of Business Administration, Department of Accounting, Finance and Economics, Stephenville, TX 76402. Offers accounting (M Acc). *Program availability:* Part-time, evening/weekend. *Faculty:* 13 full-time (3 women), 2 part-time/adjunct (1 woman). *Students:* 15 full-time (12 women), 31 part-time (23 women). Average age 30. 27 applicants, 81% accepted, 19 enrolled. In 2018, 13 master's awarded. *Degree requirements:* For master's, comprehensive exam, thesis (for some programs). *Entrance requirements:* For master's, GRE or GMAT, minimum GPA of 3.0. Additional exam requirements/recommendations for international students: Required—TOEFL (minimum score 520 paper-based; 69 iBT); Recommended—IELTS (minimum score 6), TSE (minimum score 50). *Application deadline:* For fall admission, 8/5 priority date for domestic students; for spring admission, 12/1 for domestic students. Applications are processed on a rolling basis. Application fee: $50 ($130 for international students). Electronic applications accepted. *Expenses:* Contact institution. *Financial support:* Research assistantships and teaching assistantships available. Financial award application deadline: 5/1; financial award applicants required to submit FAFSA. *Unit head:* Dr. Keldon Bauer, Department Head, 254-968-9909, Fax: 254-968-9665, E-mail: kbauer@tarleton.edu. *Application contact:* Information Contact, 254-968-9104, Fax: 254-968-9670, E-mail: gradoffice@tarleton.edu. Website: http://www.tarleton.edu/afe/

Temple University, Fox School of Business, Doctoral Programs in Business, Philadelphia, PA 19122-6096. Offers accounting (PhD); entrepreneurship (PhD); finance (PhD); international business (PhD); management information systems (PhD); marketing (PhD); risk management and insurance (PhD); statistics (PhD); strategic management (PhD); tourism and sport (PhD). *Accreditation:* AACSB. *Degree requirements:* For doctorate, thesis/dissertation. *Entrance requirements:* For doctorate, GRE General Test, GMAT, minimum GPA of 3.0, master's degree. Additional exam requirements/recommendations for international students: Required—TOEFL (minimum score 600 paper-based; 100 iBT), IELTS (minimum score 7.5). Electronic applications accepted.

Temple University, Fox School of Business, MBA Programs, Philadelphia, PA 19122-6096. Offers accounting (MBA); business management (MBA); financial management (MBA); healthcare and life sciences innovation (MBA); human resource management (MBA); international business (IMBA); IT management (MBA); marketing management (MBA); pharmaceutical management (MBA); strategic management (EMBA, MBA). EMBA offered in Philadelphia, PA and Tokyo, Japan. *Accreditation:* AACSB. *Program availability:* Part-time, evening/weekend, online learning. *Entrance requirements:* For master's, GMAT, minimum undergraduate GPA of 3.0. Additional exam requirements/recommendations for international students: Required—TOEFL (minimum score 600 paper-based; 100 iBT), IELTS (minimum score 7.5).

Temple University, Fox School of Business, Specialized Master's Programs, Philadelphia, PA 19122-6096. Offers accountancy (MS); actuarial science (MS); finance (MS); financial engineering (MS); human resource management (MS); innovation management and entrepreneurship (MS); marketing (MS); statistics (MS). MS in innovation management and entrepreneurship delivered jointly with College of Engineering. *Accreditation:* AACSB. *Program availability:* Part-time. *Entrance requirements:* For master's, GRE General Test or GMAT, minimum undergraduate GPA of 3.0. Additional exam requirements/recommendations for international students: Required—TOEFL (minimum score 600 paper-based; 100 iBT), IELTS (minimum score 7.5).

Tennessee Technological University, College of Graduate Studies, College of Business, Master of Accountancy Program, Cookeville, TN 38505. Offers M Acc. *Program availability:* Part-time, evening/weekend. *Students:* 7 full-time (4 women), 23 part-time (17 women); includes 1 minority (Asian, non-Hispanic/Latino). 46 applicants, 65% accepted, 21 enrolled. *Entrance requirements:* For master's, GMAT or GRE. *Application deadline:* For fall admission, 7/1 for domestic students, 5/1 for international students; for spring admission, 12/1 for domestic students, 10/1 for international students; for summer admission, 5/1 for domestic students, 2/1 for international students. Applications are processed on a rolling basis. Application fee: $35 ($40 for international students). Electronic applications accepted. *Financial support:* In 2018–19, 1 teaching assistantship (averaging $7,500 per year) was awarded; fellowships, research assistantships, and unspecified assistantships also available. Financial award application deadline: 4/1; financial award applicants required to submit FAFSA. *Unit head:* Kate Nicewicz, Director, 931-372-3600, E-mail: knicewicz@tntech.edu. *Application contact:* Shelia K. Kendrick, Coordinator of Graduate Studies, 931-372-3808, Fax: 931-372-3497, E-mail: skendrick@tntech.edu. Website: https://www.tntech.edu/cob/macc/

Tennessee Wesleyan University, Graduate Programs, Athens, TN 37303. Offers accounting (MBA); management (MBA). *Program availability:* Part-time. *Faculty:* 4 full-time (1 woman), 2 part-time/adjunct (1 woman). *Students:* 12 full-time (8 women), 19 part-time (13 women). Average age 28. 29 applicants, 83% accepted, 16 enrolled. In

2018, 9 master's awarded. *Degree requirements:* For master's, comprehensive exam, Capstone. *Entrance requirements:* For master's, GMAT, official transcripts, three letters of recommendation, current curriculum vitae or resume. *Application deadline:* For fall admission, 8/19 for domestic students; for spring admission, 1/14 for domestic students; for summer admission, 5/6 for domestic students. Electronic applications accepted. *Expenses: Tuition:* Full-time $9000; part-time $500 per credit hour. *Financial support:* Application deadline: 4/30; applicants required to submit FAFSA. *Application contact:* Makhaila Woodlief, Adult and Graduate Admissions Counselor, 423-746-5285, Fax: 423-745-9335, E-mail: mwoodlief@tnwesleyan.edu. Website: http://www.tnwesleyan.edu/academics/graduate-programs/

Texas A&M International University, Office of Graduate Studies and Research, A.R. Sanchez, Jr. School of Business, Division of International Banking and Finance Studies, Laredo, TX 78041. Offers accounting (MP Acc); international banking and finance (MBA). *Entrance requirements:* For master's, GMAT or GRE General Test. Additional exam requirements/recommendations for international students: Required—TOEFL (minimum score 550 paper-based; 79 iBT).

Texas A&M University, Mays Business School, Department of Accounting, College Station, TX 77843. Offers MS. *Accreditation:* AACSB. *Faculty:* 30. *Students:* 158 full-time (99 women), 3 part-time (2 women); includes 38 minority (2 Black or African American, non-Hispanic/Latino; 12 Asian, non-Hispanic/Latino; 22 Hispanic/Latino; 2 Two or more races, non-Hispanic/Latino), 10 international. Average age 24. 171 applicants, 21% accepted, 25 enrolled. In 2018, 129 master's awarded. Terminal master's awarded for partial completion of doctoral program. *Degree requirements:* For master's, comprehensive exam. *Entrance requirements:* For master's, GMAT or GRE. Additional exam requirements/recommendations for international students: Required—TOEFL (minimum score 550 paper-based; 80 iBT), IELTS (minimum score 6), PTE (minimum score 53). *Application deadline:* For fall admission, 3/15 for domestic students, 2/15 for international students; for spring admission, 10/15 for domestic and international students. Applications are processed on a rolling basis. Application fee: $50 ($90 for international students). *Expenses:* Contact institution. *Financial support:* In 2018–19, 83 students received support, including 1 fellowship with tuition reimbursement available (averaging $6,800 per year), 16 research assistantships with tuition reimbursements available (averaging $20,198 per year); career-related internships or fieldwork, institutionally sponsored loans, scholarships/grants, traineeships, health care benefits, tuition waivers (full and partial), and unspecified assistantships also available. Support available to part-time students. Financial award application deadline: 3/15; financial award applicants required to submit FAFSA. *Faculty research:* Financial reporting, taxation management, decision-making, accounting information systems, government accounting. *Unit head:* Dr. James J. Benjamin, Head, 979-845-0356, Fax: 979-845-0028, E-mail: jbenjamin@mays.tamu.edu. *Application contact:* Dr. Bala Shetty, Interim Associate Dean for Graduate Programs, 979-845-7024, Fax: 979-845-0028, E-mail: bshetty@mays.tamu.edu. Website: http://mays.tamu.edu/acct/

Texas A&M University–Central Texas, Graduate Studies and Research, Killeen, TX 76549. Offers accounting (MS); business administration (MBA); clinical mental health counseling (MS); criminal justice (MCJ); curriculum and instruction (M Ed); educational administration (M Ed); educational psychology - experimental psychology (MS); history (MA); human resource management (MS); information systems (MS); liberal studies (MS); management and leadership (MS); marriage and family therapy (MS); mathematics (MS); political science (MA); school counseling (M Ed); school psychology (Ed S).

Texas A&M University–Commerce, College of Business, Commerce, TX 75429. Offers accounting (MSA); business administration (MBA); business analytics (MS); finance (MSF); management (MS); marketing (MS). *Accreditation:* AACSB. *Program availability:* Part-time, evening/weekend, 100% online, blended/hybrid learning. *Faculty:* 48 full-time (15 women), 2 part-time/adjunct (1 woman). *Students:* 391 full-time (209 women), 948 part-time (511 women); includes 583 minority (249 Black or African American, non-Hispanic/Latino; 4 American Indian or Alaska Native, non-Hispanic/Latino; 89 Asian, non-Hispanic/Latino; 205 Hispanic/Latino; 1 Native Hawaiian or other Pacific Islander, non-Hispanic/Latino; 35 Two or more races, non-Hispanic/Latino), 156 international. Average age 33. 930 applicants, 58% accepted, 355 enrolled. In 2018, 628 master's awarded. *Degree requirements:* For master's, comprehensive exam. *Entrance requirements:* For master's, GRE General Test, GMAT, letter of recommendation. Additional exam requirements/recommendations for international students: Required—TOEFL (minimum score 550 paper-based; 79 iBT), IELTS (minimum score 6), PTE (minimum score 53). *Application deadline:* For fall admission, 6/1 priority date for international students; for spring admission, 10/15 priority date for international students; for summer admission, 3/15 priority date for international students. Applications are processed on a rolling basis. Application fee: $50 ($75 for international students). Electronic applications accepted. *Expenses: Tuition, area resident:* Full-time $3630. *Tuition, state resident:* full-time $3630. *Tuition, nonresident:* full-time $11,100. *International tuition:* $11,100 full-time. *Required fees:* $2794. Tuition and fees vary according to course load, degree level and program. *Financial support:* In 2018–19, 61 students received support, including 57 research assistantships with partial tuition reimbursements available (averaging $3,286 per year); Federal Work-Study, institutionally sponsored loans, scholarships/grants, health care benefits, and unspecified assistantships also available. Financial award application deadline: 5/1; financial award applicants required to submit FAFSA. *Faculty research:* Strategic management and organizational behavior phenomena; marketing and big data decisions of product choice behavior and channel behavior of consumers; international accounting in governmental sectors; finance research on banking, investments, financial institutions and risk management; applied economics with emphasis on industries that are important to the region including health and energy. *Unit head:* Dr. Shanan Gwaltney Gibson, Dean of College of Business, 903-886-5191, Fax: 903-886-5650, E-mail: shanan.gibson@tamuc.edu. *Application contact:* Shanna Hoskison, Director, Graduate Advising, 903-886-5190, E-mail: shanna.hoskison@tamuc.edu. Website: https://new.tamuc.edu/business/

Texas A&M University–Corpus Christi, College of Graduate Studies, College of Business, Corpus Christi, TX 78412. Offers accounting (M Acc); business (MBA); finance (MBA); health care administration (MBA); international business (MBA). *Accreditation:* AACSB. *Program availability:* Part-time, evening/weekend, 100% online, blended/hybrid learning. *Degree requirements:* For master's, 30 to 42 hours (for MBA; varies by concentration area, delivery format, and necessity for foundational courses for students with nonbusiness degrees). *Entrance requirements:* For master's, GMAT, GRE. Additional exam requirements/recommendations for international students: Required—TOEFL (minimum score 550 paper-based; 79 iBT), IELTS (minimum score 6.5). Electronic applications accepted.

Texas A&M University–San Antonio, School of Business, San Antonio, TX 78224. Offers business administration (MBA); professional accounting (MPA). *Program availability:* Part-time, evening/weekend, online learning. *Degree requirements:* For master's, comprehensive exam. *Entrance requirements:* For master's, GMAT. Additional exam requirements/recommendations for international students: Required—TOEFL (minimum score 550 paper-based; 79 iBT), IELTS (minimum score 6). Electronic applications accepted. *Faculty research:* Culture and its effect on organizational processes; diversity and teams.

Accounting

Texas A&M University–Texarkana, Graduate Studies and Research, College of Business, Texarkana, TX 75503. Offers accounting (MSA); business administration (MBA, MS). *Program availability:* Part-time, evening/weekend. *Degree requirements:* For master's, thesis or alternative. *Entrance requirements:* For master's, minimum GPA of 2.5 in last 60 hours of bachelor's degree. Additional exam requirements/recommendations for international students: Required—TOEFL. Electronic applications accepted.

Texas Christian University, Neeley School of Business, Master of Accounting Program, Fort Worth, TX 76129. Offers advisory and valuation (M Ac); audit & assurance services (M Ac); taxation (M Ac). *Accreditation:* AACSB. *Faculty:* 17 full-time (8 women). *Students:* 52 full-time (42 women). Average age 22. 81 applicants, 99% accepted, 65 enrolled. In 2018, 52 master's awarded. *Entrance requirements:* Additional exam requirements/recommendations for international students: Recommended—TOEFL. *Application deadline:* For fall admission, 2/15 for domestic and international students; for spring admission, 9/15 for domestic and international students. Application fee: $0. Electronic applications accepted. *Expenses:* Graduate student fee, $1,450 per semester. *Financial support:* Unspecified assistantships available. Financial award application deadline: 1/31. *Faculty research:* Financial accounting, market valuation of accounting information, corporate governance, managerial compensation and incentives, taxation. *Unit head:* Dr. Mary A. Stanford, Department Chair, 817-257-7483, Fax: 817-257-7227, E-mail: m.stanford@tcu.edu. *Application contact:* Dr. Renee Olvera, Director, 817-257-7578, Fax: 817-257-7227, E-mail: renee.olvera@tcu.edu.
Website: http://www.neeley.tcu.edu/Academics/Master_of_Accounting/MAc.aspx

Texas Lutheran University, Program in Accounting, Seguin, TX 78155-5999. Offers M Acy.

Texas State University, The Graduate College, Emmett and Miriam McCoy College of Business Administration, Program in Accounting, San Marcos, TX 78666. Offers M Acy. *Program availability:* Part-time. *Faculty:* 14 full-time (7 women), 1 part-time/adjunct (0 women). *Students:* 41 full-time (23 women), 11 part-time (3 women); includes 20 minority (7 Asian, non-Hispanic/Latino; 13 Hispanic/Latino), 1 international. Average age 25. 60 applicants, 47% accepted, 20 enrolled. In 2018, 67 master's awarded. *Degree requirements:* For master's, comprehensive exam. *Entrance requirements:* For master's, official GMAT or GRE (general test only) required with competitive scores, baccalaureate degree from regionally-accredited university; a minimum of a 3.2 GPA or higher in the last 60 hours of undergrad work; two forms of recommendation; essays; resume; a minimum of a 3.4 GPA or higher in upper-level accounting courses. Additional exam requirements/recommendations for international students: Required—TOEFL (minimum score 550 paper-based; 78 iBT); Recommended—IELTS (minimum score 6.5). *Application deadline:* For fall admission, 1/15 priority date for domestic and international students; for spring admission, 10/1 for domestic and international students; for summer admission, 4/1 for domestic students, 3/15 for international students. Application fee: $55 ($90 for international students). Electronic applications accepted. *Expenses:* Tuition, state resident: full-time $8102; part-time $4051 per semester. Tuition, nonresident: full-time $18,229; part-time $9115 per semester. *International tuition:* $18,229 full-time. *Required fees:* $2116; $120 per credit hour. Tuition and fees vary according to course load. *Financial support:* In 2018–19, 24 students received support, including 1 research assistantship (averaging $13,009 per year), 7 teaching assistantships (averaging $13,216 per year); Federal Work-Study, institutionally sponsored loans, scholarships/grants, health care benefits, and unspecified assistantships also available. Support available to part-time students. Financial award application deadline: 1/15; financial award applicants required to submit FAFSA. *Unit head:* Dr. William Chittenden, Graduate Advisor, 512-245-3591, Fax: 512-245-8365, E-mail: businessgraduate@txstate.edu. *Application contact:* Dr. Andrea Golato, Dean of Graduate School, 512-245-2581, Fax: 512-245-8365, E-mail: gradcollege@txstate.edu.
Website: http://accounting.mccoy.txstate.edu/

Texas State University, The Graduate College, Emmett and Miriam McCoy College of Business Administration, Program in Accounting and Information Technology, San Marcos, TX 78666. Offers MS. *Program availability:* Part-time. *Faculty:* 8 full-time (2 women). *Students:* 9 full-time (4 women), 9 part-time (6 women); includes 11 minority (1 Black or African American, non-Hispanic/Latino; 2 Asian, non-Hispanic/Latino; 7 Hispanic/Latino; 1 Native Hawaiian or other Pacific Islander, non-Hispanic/Latino), 2 international. Average age 36. 8 applicants, 50% accepted, 3 enrolled. In 2018, 5 master's awarded. *Degree requirements:* For master's, comprehensive exam. *Entrance requirements:* For master's, official GMAT or GRE (general test only) required with competitive scores, baccalaureate degree from regionally-accredited university; a competitive GPA in your last 60 hours of undergraduate course work; two letters or forms of recommendation; essay; resume showing work experience, extracurricular and community activities, and honors and achievements. Additional exam requirements/recommendations for international students: Required—TOEFL (minimum score 550 paper-based; 78 iBT), IELTS (minimum score 6.5). *Application deadline:* For fall admission, 1/15 priority date for domestic and international students; for spring admission, 10/1 for domestic and international students. Application fee: $55 ($90 for international students). Electronic applications accepted. *Expenses:* Tuition, state resident: full-time $8102; part-time $4051 per semester. Tuition, nonresident: full-time $18,229; part-time $9115 per semester. *International tuition:* $18,229 full-time. *Required fees:* $2116; $120 per credit hour. Tuition and fees vary according to course load. *Financial support:* In 2018–19, 10 students received support, including 5 teaching assistantships (averaging $11,981 per year); research assistantships, Federal Work-Study, institutionally sponsored loans, scholarships/grants, health care benefits, and unspecified assistantships also available. Support available to part-time students. Financial award application deadline: 1/15; financial award applicants required to submit FAFSA. *Unit head:* Dr. William Chittenden, Associate Dean, 512-245-3591, Fax: 512-245-8365, E-mail: wc10@txstate.edu. *Application contact:* Dr. Andrea Golato, Dean of Graduate School, 512-245-2581, Fax: 512-245-8365, E-mail: gradcollege@txstate.edu.
Website: https://www.cis.txstate.edu/prospective/msait.html

Texas Tech University, Rawls College of Business Administration, Lubbock, TX 79409-2101. Offers accounting (MSA, PhD), including audit/financial reporting (MSA), taxation (MSA); data science (MS); finance (PhD); general business (MBA); healthcare management (MS); information systems and operations management (PhD); management (PhD); marketing (PhD); STEM (MBA); JD/MBA; JD/MSA; MBA/M Arch; MBA/MD; MBA/MS; MBA/Pharm D. *Accreditation:* AACSB. *Program availability:* Evening/weekend, 100% online, blended/hybrid learning. *Degree requirements:* For master's, thesis (for MS); capstone course; for doctorate, comprehensive exam, thesis/dissertation, qualifying exams. *Entrance requirements:* For master's, GMAT, GRE, MCAT, PCAT, LSAT, or DAT, holistic review of academic credentials, resume, essay, letters of recommendation; for doctorate, GMAT, GRE, holistic review of academic credentials, resume, statement of purpose, letters of recommendation. Additional exam requirements/recommendations for international students: Required—TOEFL (minimum score 550 paper-based; 79 iBT), IELTS (minimum score 6.5), PTE (minimum score 60). Electronic applications accepted. *Expenses:* Contact institution. *Faculty research:* Governmental and nonprofit accounting, securities and options futures, statistical analysis and design, leadership, consumer behavior.

Texas Woman's University, Graduate School, College of Business, Denton, TX 76204. Offers business administration (MBA), including accounting, business analytics, healthcare administration (MBA, MHA), human resources management, management; health systems management (MHSM); healthcare administration (MHA), including healthcare administration (MBA, MHA). *Accreditation:* ACBSP. *Program availability:* Part-time, 100% online, blended/hybrid learning. *Faculty:* 26 full-time (9 women), 14 part-time/adjunct (7 women). *Students:* 483 full-time (429 women), 445 part-time (373 women); includes 643 minority (325 Black or African American, non-Hispanic/Latino; 4 American Indian or Alaska Native, non-Hispanic/Latino; 134 Asian, non-Hispanic/Latino; 152 Hispanic/Latino; 1 Native Hawaiian or other Pacific Islander, non-Hispanic/Latino; 27 Two or more races, non-Hispanic/Latino), 38 international. Average age 33. 401 applicants, 84% accepted, 251 enrolled. In 2018, 471 master's awarded. *Degree requirements:* For master's, thesis or alternative, capstone. *Entrance requirements:* For master's, minimum GPA of 3.0 in last 60 hours of undergraduate coursework and prior graduate coursework, resume. Additional exam requirements/recommendations for international students: Required—TOEFL (minimum score 550 paper-based; 79 iBT); Recommended—IELTS (minimum score 6.5), TSE (minimum score 53). *Application deadline:* Applications are processed on a rolling basis. Application fee: $50 ($75 for international students). Electronic applications accepted. *Expenses: Tuition, area resident:* Full-time $4852; part-time $270 per semester hour. Tuition, state resident: full-time $4852; part-time $270 per semester hour. Tuition, nonresident: full-time $12,322; part-time $685 per semester hour. *International tuition:* $12,322 full-time. *Required fees:* $2714; $113 per semester hour. $296 per semester. Tuition and fees vary according to course level, course load, degree level, campus/location and program. *Financial support:* In 2018–19, 138 students received support, including 12 teaching assistantships (averaging $10,666 per year); career-related internships or fieldwork, Federal Work-Study, institutionally sponsored loans, scholarships/grants, traineeships, health care benefits, and unspecified assistantships also available. Support available to part-time students. Financial award application deadline: 3/1; financial award applicants required to submit FAFSA. *Faculty research:* Marketing and market research, economics, accounting, logistics and supply chain management, health systems. *Unit head:* Dr. James R. Lumpkin, Dean, 940-898-2458, Fax: 940-898-2120, E-mail: mba@twu.edu. *Application contact:* Korie Hawkins, Associate Director of Admissions, Graduate Recruitment, 940-898-3188, Fax: 940-898-3081, E-mail: admissions@twu.edu.
Website: http://www.twu.edu/business/

Thomas Edison State University, School of Business and Management, Program in Management, Trenton, NJ 08608. Offers accounting (MSM); organizational leadership (MSM); project management (MSM). *Program availability:* Part-time, 100% online. *Degree requirements:* For master's, final capstone project. *Entrance requirements:* For master's, bachelor's degree from a regionally-accredited college or university; minimum 2 letters of recommendation; 3-5 years of related working experience; current resume. Additional exam requirements/recommendations for international students: Required—TOEFL (minimum score 550 paper-based; 79 iBT). Electronic applications accepted.

Towson University, College of Business and Economics, Program in Accounting, Towson, MD 21252-0001. Offers MS. *Accreditation:* AACSB. *Program availability:* Part-time, evening/weekend. *Entrance requirements:* For master's, GMAT, GRE General Test, minimum GPA of 3.0; prerequisite courses in accounting, economics, communications, math, marketing, finance, business law, and business ethics. Electronic applications accepted. *Expenses: Tuition, area resident:* Full-time $9196; part-time $418 per unit. Tuition, state resident: full-time $9196; part-time $418 per unit. Tuition, nonresident: full-time $19,030; part-time $865 per unit. *International tuition:* $19,030 full-time. *Required fees:* $3102; $141 per year. $423 per term. Tuition and fees vary according to campus/location and program.

Trinity University, School of Business, San Antonio, TX 78212-7200. Offers accounting (MS). *Accreditation:* AACSB. *Faculty:* 2 full-time (both women), 3 part-time/adjunct (0 women). *Students:* 17 full-time (5 women); includes 4 minority (1 Black or African American, non-Hispanic/Latino; 1 Asian, non-Hispanic/Latino; 1 Hispanic/Latino; 1 Two or more races, non-Hispanic/Latino), 3 international. Average age 22. In 2018, 16 master's awarded. *Entrance requirements:* For master's, GMAT, minimum GPA of 3.0, course work in accounting and business law, letters of recommendation. *Application deadline:* For fall admission, 2/1 for domestic and international students. Electronic applications accepted. Tuition and fees vary according to program and student level. *Financial support:* Institutionally sponsored loans and scholarships/grants available. Financial award application deadline: 5/1; financial award applicants required to submit FAFSA. *Unit head:* Dr. Julie Persellin, Chair, Department of Accounting, 210-999-7230, E-mail: jpersell@trinity.edu. *Application contact:* Dr. Julie Persellin, Chair, Department of Accounting, 210-999-7230, E-mail: jpersell@trinity.edu.
Website: https://new.trinity.edu/academics/departments/school-business/graduate-accounting-program

Troy University, Graduate School, College of Business, Program in Accountancy, Troy, AL 36082. Offers M Acc. *Program availability:* Part-time, evening/weekend. *Faculty:* 2 full-time (both women), 1 part-time/adjunct (0 women). *Students:* 32 full-time (17 women), 8 part-time (4 women); includes 4 minority (2 Black or African American, non-Hispanic/Latino; 1 Asian, non-Hispanic/Latino; 1 Hispanic/Latino), 7 international. Average age 24. 39 applicants, 95% accepted, 27 enrolled. In 2018, 27 master's awarded. *Degree requirements:* For master's, minimum GPA of 3.0, research course. *Entrance requirements:* For master's, GMAT (minimum score of 500), bachelor's degree; minimum undergraduate GPA of 2.5 or 3.0 on last 30 semester hours, letter of recommendation. Additional exam requirements/recommendations for international students: Required—TOEFL (minimum score 523 paper-based; 70 iBT), IELTS (minimum score 6). *Application deadline:* Applications are processed on a rolling basis. Application fee: $50. Electronic applications accepted. *Expenses: Tuition, area resident:* Full-time $425; part-time $425 per credit hour. Tuition, state resident: full-time $425; part-time $425 per credit hour. Tuition, nonresident: full-time $850; part-time $850 per credit hour. *International tuition:* $850 full-time. *Required fees:* $50 per semester. Tuition and fees vary according to campus/location and program. *Financial support:* Fellowships, career-related internships or fieldwork, and scholarships/grants available. Support available to part-time students. Financial award applicants required to submit FAFSA. *Unit head:* Dr. Steve Grice, Professor, Chair, Master of Accountancy, 334-670-3149, Fax: 334-670-3592, E-mail: sgrice@troy.edu. *Application contact:* Jessica A. Kimbro, Assistant Director of Graduate Programs, 334-670-3189, E-mail: jacord@troy.edu.
Website: https://www.troy.edu/academics/academic-programs/accounting-public-accounting.html

Troy University, Graduate School, College of Business, Program in Business Administration, Troy, AL 36082. Offers accounting (EMBA, MBA); criminal justice (EMBA); finance (MBA); general management (EMBA, MBA); healthcare management (EMBA); information systems (EMBA, MBA); international economic development (MBA). *Accreditation:* ACBSP. *Program availability:* Part-time, evening/weekend. *Faculty:* 12 full-time (1 woman), 1 part-time/adjunct (0 women). *Students:* 27 full-time

(16 women), 93 part-time (44 women); includes 31 minority (27 Black or African American, non-Hispanic/Latino; 1 Asian, non-Hispanic/Latino; 3 Hispanic/Latino), 29 international. Average age 30. 108 applicants, 37% accepted, 22 enrolled. In 2018, 74 master's awarded. *Degree requirements:* For master's, minimum GPA of 3.0, capstone course, research course. *Entrance requirements:* For master's, GMAT (minimum score 500) or GRE (minimum score 900 on old exam or 294 on new exam), bachelor's degree; minimum undergraduate GPA of 2.5 or 3.0 on last 30 semester hours, letter of recommendation. Additional exam requirements/recommendations for international students: Required—TOEFL (minimum score 523 paper-based; 70 iBT), IELTS (minimum score 6). *Application deadline:* Applications are processed on a rolling basis. Application fee: $50. Electronic applications accepted. *Expenses:* Tuition, area resident: Full-time $425; part-time $425 per credit hour. Tuition, state resident: full-time $425; part-time $425 per credit hour. Tuition, nonresident: full-time $850; part-time $850 per credit hour. *International tuition:* $850 full-time. *Required fees:* $50 per semester. Tuition and fees vary according to campus/location and program. *Financial support:* Fellowships, career-related internships or fieldwork, and scholarships/grants available. Support available to part-time students. Financial award applicants required to submit FAFSA. *Unit head:* Dr. Robert Wheatley, Professor, Director of Graduate Business Programs, 334-670-3194, Fax: 334-670-3708, E-mail: rwheat@troy.edu. *Application contact:* Jessica A. Kimbro, Assistant Director of Graduate Programs, 334-670-3189, E-mail: jacord@troy.edu.
Website: https://www.troy.edu/academics/academic-programs/sorrell-college-business-programs.php

Truman State University, Graduate School, School of Business, Program in Accounting, Kirksville, MO 63501-4221. Offers M Ac. *Accreditation:* AACSB. *Faculty:* 11 full-time (4 women). *Students:* 27 full-time (7 women), 1 part-time; includes 4 minority (3 Asian, non-Hispanic/Latino; 1 Two or more races, non-Hispanic/Latino). Average age 23. 27 applicants, 93% accepted, 23 enrolled. In 2018, 38 master's awarded. *Degree requirements:* For master's, comprehensive exam. *Entrance requirements:* For master's, GMAT, minimum GPA of 3.0. Additional exam requirements/recommendations for international students: Required—TOEFL (minimum score 550 paper-based). *Application deadline:* For fall admission, 6/1 for domestic and international students; for spring admission, 11/1 for domestic and international students; for summer admission, 4/1 for domestic and international students. Applications are processed on a rolling basis. Application fee: $40. Electronic applications accepted. *Expenses:* Tuition, state resident: full-time $385.50; part-time $385.50 per credit hour. Tuition, nonresident: full-time $668; part-time $668 per credit hour. *International tuition:* $668 full-time. *Required fees:* $648. *Financial support:* In 2018–19, 6 research assistantships with full and partial tuition reimbursements (averaging $5,000 per year), 4 teaching assistantships with full and partial tuition reimbursements (averaging $5,000 per year) were awarded. Financial award application deadline: 5/1; financial award applicants required to submit FAFSA. *Unit head:* Dr. Alan Davis, Director, 660-785-5550, Fax: 660-785-7471, E-mail: abdavis@truman.edu. *Application contact:* Bethany Gibson, Graduate Office Secretary, 660-785-4109, Fax: 660-785-7460, E-mail: gradinfo@truman.edu.

Tulane University, A. B. Freeman School of Business, New Orleans, LA 70118-5669. Offers accounting (M Acct); analytics (MBA); banking and financial services (M Fin); energy (M Fin, MBA); entrepreneurship (MBA); finance (MBA, PhD); financial accounting (PhD); international business (MBA); international management (MBA); strategic management and leadership (MBA); JD/M Acct; JD/MBA; MBA/M Acc; MBA/MA; MBA/MD; MBA/ME; MBA/MPH. *Accreditation:* AACSB. *Program availability:* Part-time, evening/weekend. *Faculty:* 43 full-time (11 women), 45 part-time/adjunct (8 women). *Students:* 432 full-time (218 women), 533 part-time (262 women); includes 99 minority (32 Black or African American, non-Hispanic/Latino; 1 American Indian or Alaska Native, non-Hispanic/Latino; 26 Asian, non-Hispanic/Latino; 35 Hispanic/Latino; 5 Two or more races, non-Hispanic/Latino), 644 international. Average age 28. 1,911 applicants, 77% accepted, 411 enrolled. In 2018, 728 master's, 4 doctorates awarded. Terminal master's awarded for partial completion of doctoral program. *Degree requirements:* For master's, one foreign language, comprehensive exam (for some programs); for doctorate, one foreign language, comprehensive exam, thesis/dissertation. *Entrance requirements:* For master's and doctorate, GMAT or GRE, interview. Additional exam requirements/recommendations for international students: Required—TOEFL or IELTS. *Application deadline:* For fall admission, 11/1 priority date for domestic students, 11/1 for international students; for winter admission, 1/6 for domestic and international students; for spring admission, 3/1 priority date for domestic students, 3/1 for international students; for summer admission, 5/5 for domestic students. Applications are processed on a rolling basis. Application fee: $125. Electronic applications accepted. *Expenses:* Contact institution. *Financial support:* In 2018–19, 153 students received support. Fellowships with tuition reimbursements available, research assistantships, teaching assistantships, career-related internships or fieldwork, Federal Work-Study, tuition waivers (full and partial), and unspecified assistantships available. Support available to part-time students. Financial award application deadline: 4/15; financial award applicants required to submit FAFSA. *Faculty research:* Corporate finance, managerial accounting and financial reporting, strategic management and leadership, consumer behavior and decision making, organizational behavior and human resource management. *Unit head:* Ira Solomon, PhD, Dean, 504-865-5407, Fax: 504-865-5491, E-mail: businessdean@tulane.edu. *Application contact:* Melissa Booth, Assistant Dean for Graduate Admissions, 800-223-5402, E-mail: freeman.admissions@tulane.edu.
Website: http://www.freeman.tulane.edu

Union University, McAfee School of Business Administration, Jackson, TN 38305-3697. Offers accountancy (M Acc). Program also available at Germantown campus. *Program availability:* Evening/weekend, online learning. *Entrance requirements:* For master's, GMAT, minimum GPA of 2.5. Electronic applications accepted. *Expenses:* Contact institution. *Faculty research:* Personal financial management, strategy, accounting, marketing, economics.

Universidad del Este, Graduate School, Carolina, PR 00984. Offers accounting (MBA); adult education (M Ed); agribusiness (MBA); criminal justice and criminology (MA); curriculum and instruction - early education (M Ed); curriculum and instruction - elementary (M Ed); curriculum and instruction - English (M Ed); curriculum and instruction - Spanish (M Ed); human resources (MBA); information security management (MBA); information technology and Web business development (MBA); management (MBA); public policy (MPA); social work (MA), including clinical social work; special education (M Ed); strategic leadership (MBA).

Universidad del Turabo, Graduate Programs, School of Business and Entrepreneurship, Program in Accounting, Gurabo, PR 00778-3030. Offers MBA. *Program availability:* Part-time, evening/weekend. *Entrance requirements:* For master's, GRE, EXADEP, GMAT, interview, essay, official transcript, recommendation letters. Electronic applications accepted.

Universidad Metropolitana, School of Business Administration, Program in Accounting, San Juan, PR 00928-1150. Offers MBA. *Program availability:* Part-time. *Degree requirements:* For master's, thesis or alternative. *Entrance requirements:* For master's, GMAT, PAEG, interview. Electronic applications accepted.

Université de Sherbrooke, Faculty of Administration, Program in Accounting, Sherbrooke, QC J1K 2R1, Canada. Offers M Sc. *Degree requirements:* For master's, one foreign language, thesis. *Entrance requirements:* For master's, bachelor's degree in related field, minimum GPA of 3.0 (on 4.3 scale). Electronic applications accepted. *Faculty research:* Financial analysis, management accounting, certification, system and control.

Université du Québec à Montréal, Graduate Programs, Program in Accounting, Montréal, QC H3C 3P8, Canada. Offers M Sc, MPA, Diploma. *Program availability:* Part-time. *Degree requirements:* For master's, thesis (for some programs). *Entrance requirements:* For master's, appropriate bachelor's degree or equivalent and proficiency in French.

Université du Québec à Trois-Rivières, Graduate Programs, Program in Accounting Science, Trois-Rivières, QC G9A 5H7, Canada. Offers MBA.

Université du Québec en Outaouais, Graduate Programs, Program in Accounting, Gatineau, QC J8X 3X7, Canada. Offers MA, DESS, Diploma. *Program availability:* Part-time, evening/weekend.

Université du Québec en Outaouais, Graduate Programs, Program in Executive Certified Management Accounting, Gatineau, QC J8X 3X7, Canada. Offers MA, MBA, DESS. *Program availability:* Part-time, evening/weekend. *Degree requirements:* For master's, thesis (for some programs).

Université Laval, Faculty of Administrative Sciences, Programs in Business Administration, Québec, QC G1K 7P4, Canada. Offers accounting (MBA); agri-food management (MBA); electronic business (MBA, Diploma); factory management and logistics (MBA); finance (MBA); firm management (MBA); geomatic management (MBA); information technology management (MBA); international management (MBA); management (MBA); management accounting (MBA, Diploma); marketing (MBA); modeling and organizational decision (MBA); occupational health and safety management (MBA); pharmacy management (MBA); social and environmental responsibility (MBA); technological entrepreneurship (Diploma). *Accreditation:* AACSB. *Program availability:* Part-time, evening/weekend, online learning. *Entrance requirements:* For master's and Diploma, knowledge of French and English. Electronic applications accepted.

Université Laval, Faculty of Administrative Sciences, Programs in Public Accountancy, Québec, QC G1K 7P4, Canada. Offers MBA, Diploma. *Program availability:* Part-time. *Entrance requirements:* For master's and Diploma, knowledge of French and English. Electronic applications accepted.

University at Buffalo, the State University of New York, Graduate School, School of Management, Buffalo, NY 14260. Offers accounting (MS); analytics (MBA); business administration (PMBA); consulting (MBA); finance (MBA, MS), including financial risk management (MS), quantitative finance (MS); healthcare (MBA); information assurance (MBA); information systems (MBA); international management (MBA); management (EMBA, PhD); management information systems (MS); marketing (MBA); supply chain and operations (MBA); supply chains and operations management (MS); Au D/MBA; DDS/MBA; JD/MBA; M Arch/MBA; MD/MBA; MPH/MBA; MSW/MBA; Pharm D/MBA. *Accreditation:* AACSB. *Program availability:* Part-time, evening/weekend. *Degree requirements:* For master's, capstone courses or projects; for doctorate, comprehensive exam, thesis/dissertation. *Entrance requirements:* For master's, GMAT (for MS in accounting, finance); GRE or GMAT (for MBA, MS in management information systems, supply chains and operations management), essays, letters of recommendation; for doctorate, GMAT or GRE, essays, writing sample, letters of recommendation. Additional exam requirements/recommendations for international students: Required—TOEFL (minimum score 95 iBT) or IELTS (minimum score 6.5); Recommended—TSE (minimum score 73). Electronic applications accepted. *Expenses:* Contact institution. *Faculty research:* Data analytics, accounting and law, rate finance, consumer behavior, supply chain logistics, leadership and team effectiveness.

The University of Akron, Graduate School, College of Business Administration, The George W. Daverio School of Accountancy, Program in Accounting, Akron, OH 44325. Offers MSA. *Entrance requirements:* For master's, GMAT, GRE, MCAT, LSAT, PCAT, or CAT, minimum GPA of 3.0 (preferred), two letters of recommendation, resume, statement of purpose. Additional exam requirements/recommendations for international students: Required—TOEFL (minimum score 79 iBT), IELTS (minimum score 6.5).

The University of Alabama, Graduate School, Manderson Graduate School of Business, Culverhouse School of Accountancy, Tuscaloosa, AL 35487. Offers accounting (M Acc, PhD); tax accounting (MTA). *Accreditation:* AACSB. *Degree requirements:* For doctorate, thesis/dissertation. *Entrance requirements:* For master's, GMAT, minimum GPA of 3.0 overall or on last 60 hours; for doctorate, GMAT, minimum GPA of 3.0. Additional exam requirements/recommendations for international students: Required—TOEFL. Electronic applications accepted. *Faculty research:* Corporate governance, audit decision-making, earning management, valuation, executive compensation.

The University of Alabama at Birmingham, Collat School of Business, Program in Accounting, Birmingham, AL 35294. Offers accounting (M Acct), including internal auditing. *Accreditation:* AACSB. *Program availability:* Part-time, evening/weekend, 100% online, blended/hybrid learning. *Entrance requirements:* For master's, GMAT (minimum score of 500). Additional exam requirements/recommendations for international students: Required—TOEFL (minimum score 80 iBT). Electronic applications accepted. *Expenses:* Tuition, area resident: Full-time $8100; part-time $8100 per year. Tuition, state resident: full-time $8100. Tuition, nonresident: full-time $19,188; part-time $19,188 per year. Tuition and fees vary according to program. *Faculty research:* Capital markets, accounting information systems, international accounting, regulatory oversight, earnings forecasts.

The University of Alabama in Huntsville, School of Graduate Studies, College of Business Administration, Program in Accounting, Huntsville, AL 35899. Offers accounting (M Acc), including CPA preparatory with an emphasis in taxation, CPA preparatory with emphasis in assurance and financial reporting, general accounting, information systems audit and control (ISAC). *Accreditation:* AACSB. *Program availability:* Part-time. *Faculty:* 3 full-time (1 woman). *Students:* 14 full-time (6 women), 25 part-time (18 women); includes 5 minority (2 Black or African American, non-Hispanic/Latino; 2 Asian, non-Hispanic/Latino; 1 Hispanic/Latino), 3 international. Average age 29. 40 applicants, 73% accepted, 17 enrolled. In 2018, 12 master's awarded. *Degree requirements:* For master's, comprehensive exam, thesis or alternative. *Entrance requirements:* For master's, GMAT (minimum score 500), minimum AACSB index of 1080. Additional exam requirements/recommendations for international students: Required—TOEFL (minimum score 550 paper-based; 80 iBT), IELTS (minimum score 6.5). *Application deadline:* For fall admission, 7/15 priority date for domestic students, 4/1 priority date for international students; for spring admission, 11/30 priority date for domestic students, 9/1 priority date for international students. Applications are processed on a rolling basis. Application fee: $50. Electronic applications accepted. *Expenses:* Tuition, area resident: Full-time $10,632; part-time $412 per credit hour. Tuition, state resident: full-time $10,632. Tuition, nonresident: full-time $23,604; part-time $412 per credit hour. *Required fees:* $582; $582. Tuition and

fees vary according to course load and program. *Financial support:* In 2018–19, 4 students received support, including 3 teaching assistantships with full tuition reimbursements available (averaging $5,100 per year); career-related internships or fieldwork, Federal Work-Study, institutionally sponsored loans, scholarships/grants, health care benefits, and unspecified assistantships also available. Support available to part-time students. Financial award application deadline: 4/1; financial award applicants required to submit FAFSA. *Faculty research:* Accounting information systems, managerial accounting, behavioral accounting, state and local taxation, financial accounting. *Unit head:* Dr. Allen Wilhite, Interim Chair, 256-824-6591, Fax: 256-824-2929, E-mail: allen.wilhite@uah.edu. *Application contact:* Jennifer Pettitt, Director of Graduate Programs, 256-824-6681, Fax: 256-824-7571, E-mail: jennifer.pettitt@uah.edu.

The University of Alabama in Huntsville, School of Graduate Studies, College of Business Administration, Programs in Business and Management, Huntsville, AL 35899. Offers business analytics (MSMS); federal contracting and procurement management (Certificate); human resource management (MSM); management (MBA), including acquisition management, entrepreneurship, federal contract accounting, finance, human resource management, logistics and supply chain management, marketing, project management; supply chain management (Certificate); technology and innovation management (Certificate). *Accreditation:* AACSB. *Program availability:* Part-time. *Faculty:* 8 full-time (3 women). *Students:* 57 full-time (25 women), 152 part-time (76 women); includes 37 minority (20 Black or African American, non-Hispanic/Latino; 2 American Indian or Alaska Native, non-Hispanic/Latino; 6 Asian, non-Hispanic/Latino; 8 Hispanic/Latino; 1 Two or more races, non-Hispanic/Latino), 24 international. Average age 33. 178 applicants, 80% accepted, 84 enrolled. In 2018, 96 master's, 1 other advanced degree awarded. *Degree requirements:* For master's, comprehensive exam, thesis or alternative. *Entrance requirements:* For master's, GMAT (minimum score 500), minimum AACSB index of 1080. Additional exam requirements/recommendations for international students: Required—TOEFL (minimum score 550 paper-based; 80 iBT), IELTS (minimum score 6.5). *Application deadline:* For fall admission, 7/15 priority date for domestic students, 4/1 priority date for international students; for spring admission, 11/30 priority date for domestic students, 9/1 priority date for international students. Applications are processed on a rolling basis. Application fee: $50. Electronic applications accepted. *Expenses: Tuition, area resident:* Full-time $10,632; part-time $412 per credit hour. Tuition, state resident: full-time $10,632. Tuition, nonresident: full-time $23,604; part-time $412 per credit hour. *Required fees:* $582; $582. Tuition and fees vary according to course load and program. *Financial support:* In 2018–19, 15 students received support, including 15 teaching assistantships with full tuition reimbursements available (averaging $4,871 per year); research assistantships with full tuition reimbursements available, career-related internships or fieldwork, Federal Work-Study, institutionally sponsored loans, scholarships/grants, health care benefits, tuition waivers (full and partial), and unspecified assistantships also available. Support available to part-time students. Financial award application deadline: 4/1; financial award applicants required to submit FAFSA. *Faculty research:* Supply chain management, management of research and development, international marketing and branding, organizational behavior and human resource management, social networks and computational economics. *Unit head:* Dr. Fan Tseng, Chair, 256-824-6804, Fax: 256-824-6328, E-mail: fan.tseng@uah.edu. *Application contact:* Jennifer Pettitt, Director of Advising, 256-824-6681, Fax: 256-824-7571, E-mail: jennifer.pettitt@uah.edu.

University of Alberta, Faculty of Graduate Studies and Research, Doctoral Program in Business, Edmonton, AB T6G 2E1, Canada. Offers accounting (PhD); finance (PhD); human resources/industrial relations (PhD); management science (PhD); marketing (PhD); organizational analysis (PhD); MBA/PhD. *Accreditation:* AACSB. *Program availability:* Part-time. *Degree requirements:* For doctorate, comprehensive exam, thesis/dissertation. *Entrance requirements:* For doctorate, GMAT. Additional exam requirements/recommendations for international students: Required—TOEFL (minimum score 550 paper-based). Electronic applications accepted. *Faculty research:* Accounting, capital markets and corporate finance, organizational change and human resource management, marketing, strategic management.

The University of Arizona, Eller College of Management, Department of Accounting, Tucson, AZ 85721. Offers M Ac, MS. *Accreditation:* AACSB. *Program availability:* Part-time. *Degree requirements:* For master's, comprehensive exam, 1-year residency. *Entrance requirements:* For master's, GMAT (minimum score 550), 2 letters of recommendation, 3 writing samples, resume. Additional exam requirements/recommendations for international students: Required—TOEFL (minimum score 600 paper-based; 100 iBT). Electronic applications accepted. *Expenses:* Contact institution. *Faculty research:* Auditing, financial reporting and financial markets, taxation policy and markets, behavioral research in accounting.

University of Arkansas, Graduate School, Sam M. Walton College of Business Administration, Department of Accounting, Fayetteville, AR 72701. Offers M Acc. *Accreditation:* AACSB. In 2018, 53 master's awarded. *Entrance requirements:* For master's, GMAT. *Application deadline:* For fall admission, 8/1 for domestic students, 4/1 for international students; for spring admission, 12/1 for domestic students, 10/1 for international students; for summer admission, 4/15 for domestic students, 3/1 for international students. Application fee: $60. Electronic applications accepted. *Financial support:* In 2018–19, 18 research assistantships, 2 teaching assistantships were awarded; fellowships with tuition reimbursements, career-related internships or fieldwork, and Federal Work-Study also available. Support available to part-time students. Financial award application deadline: 4/1; financial award applicants required to submit FAFSA. *Unit head:* Dr. Gary Peters, Department Chair, 479-575-4117, Fax: 479-575-2863, E-mail: peters@uark.edu. *Application contact:* Cory Cassell, Assistant Professor - WCOB, 479-575-6126, Fax: 479-575-2863, E-mail: cacassel@uark.edu. Website: https://accounting.uark.edu/

University of Baltimore, Graduate School, Merrick School of Business, Department of Accounting, Baltimore, MD 21201-5779. Offers accounting and business advisory services (MS); accounting fundamentals (Graduate Certificate); forensic accounting (Graduate Certificate); taxation (MS). *Program availability:* Part-time, evening/weekend. *Entrance requirements:* For master's, GMAT. Additional exam requirements/recommendations for international students: Required—TOEFL (minimum score 550 paper-based). Electronic applications accepted. *Faculty research:* Health care, accounting and administration, managerial accounting, financial accounting theory, accounting information.

University of Baltimore, Graduate School, Merrick School of Business, Department of Information Systems and Decision Science, Baltimore, MD 21201-5779. Offers accounting and business advisory services (MS).

University of Bridgeport, School of Business, Bridgeport, CT 06604. Offers accounting (MBA); finance (MBA); general business (MBA); global financial services (MBA); human resource management (MBA); information systems and knowledge management (MBA); international business (MBA); management (MBA); marketing (MBA); operations management (MBA); small business and entrepreneurship (MBA); specialized business (MBA). *Accreditation:* ACBSP. *Program availability:* Part-time, evening/weekend. *Degree requirements:* For master's, thesis optional. *Entrance requirements:* For master's, GMAT. Additional exam requirements/recommendations for international students: Recommended—TOEFL (minimum score 550 paper-based; 80 iBT), IELTS (minimum score 6.5). Electronic applications accepted. *Expenses:* Contact institution.

The University of British Columbia, Sauder School of Business, Doctoral Program in Business Administration, Vancouver, BC V6T 1Z2, Canada. Offers accounting (PhD); finance (PhD); management information systems (PhD); management science (PhD); marketing (PhD); organizational behavior (PhD); strategy and business economics (PhD); transportation and logistics (PhD); urban land economics (PhD). *Degree requirements:* For doctorate, comprehensive exam, thesis/dissertation. *Entrance requirements:* For doctorate, GMAT or GRE. Additional exam requirements/recommendations for international students: Required—TOEFL (minimum score 600 paper-based; 100 iBT). Electronic applications accepted. *Expenses:* Contact institution.

University of California, Berkeley, Graduate Division, Haas School of Business, PhD in Business Administration Program, Berkeley, CA 94720. Offers accounting (PhD); business and public policy (PhD); finance (PhD); management of organizations (PhD); marketing (PhD); real estate (PhD). *Accreditation:* AACSB. *Degree requirements:* For doctorate, comprehensive exam, thesis/dissertation, written preliminary exams, oral qualifying exam. *Entrance requirements:* For doctorate, GMAT or GRE, minimum GPA of 3.0 in undergraduate and graduate coursework. Additional exam requirements/recommendations for international students: Required—TOEFL (minimum score 570 paper-based; 70 iBT), IELTS (minimum score 7). Electronic applications accepted. *Expenses:* Contact institution. *Faculty research:* Accounting, business and public policy, entrepreneurship, finance, management of organizations, marketing, operations and information technology management, real estate.

University of California, Berkeley, UC Berkeley Extension, Certificate Programs in Business, Berkeley, CA 94720. Offers accounting (Certificate); business administration (Certificate); finance (Certificate); human resource management (Certificate); management (Certificate); marketing (Certificate); project management (Certificate). *Accreditation:* AACSB. *Program availability:* Online learning.

University of California, Davis, Graduate School of Management, Full-Time MBA Program, Davis, CA 95616. Offers business analytics and technologies (MBA); entrepreneurship and innovation (MBA); finance and accounting (MBA); general management (MBA); marketing (MBA); organizational behavior (MBA); public health management (MBA); strategy (MBA); technology management (MBA); DVM/MBA; JD/MBA; M Engr/MBA; MBA/MPH; MBA/MS; MD/MBA; MSN/MBA; PhD/MBA. *Faculty:* 31 full-time (10 women). *Students:* 89 full-time (35 women); includes 21 minority (1 Black or African American, non-Hispanic/Latino; 14 Asian, non-Hispanic/Latino; 6 Hispanic/Latino), 43 international. Average age 28. 290 applicants, 39% accepted, 44 enrolled. In 2018, 45 master's awarded. *Degree requirements:* For master's, comprehensive exam, integrated management project. *Entrance requirements:* For master's, GMAT or GRE, letters of recommendation, resume, essays, equivalent of a 4-year U.S. undergraduate degree, transcript. Additional exam requirements/recommendations for international students: Required—TOEFL (minimum score 600 paper-based; 100 iBT), IELTS (minimum score 7). *Application deadline:* For fall admission, 9/15 priority date for domestic and international students. Applications are processed on a rolling basis. Application fee: $125. Electronic applications accepted. *Expenses:* Contact institution. *Financial support:* In 2018–19, 85 students received support. Fellowships with full and partial tuition reimbursements available, research assistantships with partial tuition reimbursements available, teaching assistantships with partial tuition reimbursements available, institutionally sponsored loans, scholarships/grants, health care benefits, tuition waivers (partial), and unspecified assistantships available. Financial award application deadline: 3/1; financial award applicants required to submit FAFSA. *Faculty research:* Finance, marketing, management, business analytics, accounting. *Unit head:* Amanda Opperman, Assistant Dean of Student Affairs, 530-752-7658, Fax: 530-754-9355, E-mail: admissions@gsm.ucdavis.edu. *Application contact:* Andrea Shaw, Senior Director of Admissions, 530-754-5476, Fax: 530-754-9355, E-mail: admissions@gsm.ucdavis.edu.
Website: http://gsm.ucdavis.edu/daytime-mba-program

University of California, Davis, Graduate School of Management, Master of Professional Accountancy Program, Davis, CA 95616. Offers audit analytics (MP Ac); financial accounting (MP Ac). *Faculty:* 5 full-time (2 women), 8 part-time/adjunct (3 women). *Students:* 71 full-time (45 women); includes 35 minority (1 Black or African American, non-Hispanic/Latino; 20 Asian, non-Hispanic/Latino; 14 Hispanic/Latino), 20 international. Average age 24. 360 applicants, 30% accepted, 59 enrolled. In 2018, 64 master's awarded. *Entrance requirements:* For master's, GMAT or GRE, letters of recommendation, resume, essays, equivalent of a 4-year U.S. undergraduate degree. Additional exam requirements/recommendations for international students: Required—TOEFL (minimum score 600 paper-based; 100 iBT), IELTS (minimum score 7). *Application deadline:* For fall admission, 9/15 priority date for domestic and international students. Applications are processed on a rolling basis. Application fee: $125. Electronic applications accepted. *Expenses:* Contact institution. *Financial support:* In 2018–19, 52 students received support. Fellowships, research assistantships, teaching assistantships with partial tuition reimbursements available, scholarships/grants, and tuition waivers (partial) available. Financial award application deadline: 3/1; financial award applicants required to submit FAFSA. *Faculty research:* Financial accounting, audit, audit analytics, business ethics, taxation. *Unit head:* Amanda Opperman, Assistant Dean of Student Affairs, 530-752-7658, Fax: 530-754-9355, E-mail: admissions@gsm.ucdavis.edu. *Application contact:* Andrea Shaw, Senior Director of Admissions, 530-754-5476, Fax: 530-754-9355, E-mail: admissions@gsm.ucdavis.edu.
Website: http://gsm.ucdavis.edu/master-professional-accountancy

University of California, Davis, Graduate School of Management, MBA Programs in Sacramento and San Francisco Bay Area, Davis, CA 95616. Offers business analytics and technologies (MBA); entrepreneurship and innovation (MBA); finance and accounting (MBA); general management (MBA); marketing (MBA); organizational behavior (MBA); public health management (MBA); strategy (MBA); technology management (MBA). *Program availability:* Part-time-only, evening/weekend. *Faculty:* 17 full-time (7 women), 42 part-time/adjunct (11 women). *Students:* 279 part-time (107 women); includes 146 minority (12 Black or African American, non-Hispanic/Latino; 3 American Indian or Alaska Native, non-Hispanic/Latino; 102 Asian, non-Hispanic/Latino; 29 Hispanic/Latino), 24 international. Average age 30. 158 applicants, 83% accepted, 91 enrolled. In 2018, 91 master's awarded. *Degree requirements:* For master's, integrated management project. *Entrance requirements:* For master's, GMAT or GRE, letters of recommendation, resume, equivalent of a 4-year undergraduate degree. Additional exam requirements/recommendations for international students: Required—TOEFL (minimum score 600 paper-based; 100 iBT), IELTS (minimum score 7). *Application deadline:* For fall admission, 9/15 priority date for domestic and international students. Applications are processed on a rolling basis. Application fee: $125. Electronic applications accepted. *Expenses:* Contact institution. *Financial support:* In 2018–19, 89 students received support. Fellowships, teaching assistantships with partial tuition reimbursements available, scholarships/grants, and unspecified assistantships available. Support available to part-time students. Financial award application deadline: 3/1; financial award applicants required to submit FAFSA. *Faculty research:* Accounting, finance, marketing, management, business analytics. *Unit head:* Amanda Opperman, Assistant Dean of Student Affairs, 530-752-7658, Fax: 530-754-9355, E-mail:

admissions@gsm.ucdavis.edu. *Application contact:* Andrea Shaw, Senior Director of Admissions, 530-754-5476, Fax: 530-754-9355, E-mail: admissions@gsm.ucdavis.edu.
Website: http://gsm.ucdavis.edu/mba-programs

University of California, Irvine, The Paul Merage School of Business, Program in Professional Accountancy, Irvine, CA 92697. Offers MPA. *Students:* 135 full-time (93 women), 18 part-time (11 women); includes 72 minority (3 Black or African American, non-Hispanic/Latino; 60 Asian, non-Hispanic/Latino; 9 Hispanic/Latino), 46 international. Average age 26. 663 applicants, 44% accepted, 134 enrolled. In 2018, 136 master's awarded. Application fee: $105 ($125 for international students). *Unit head:* Morton Pincus, Director, 949-824-4062, E-mail: mpincus@uci.edu. *Application contact:* Burt Slusher, Senior Associate Director, Recruitment and Admissions, 949-824-1609, E-mail: bslusher@uci.edu.
Website: http://merage.uci.edu/MPAc/

University of California, Los Angeles, Graduate Division, UCLA Anderson School of Management, Los Angeles, CA 90095-1481. Offers accounting (PhD); behavioral decision making (PhD); business administration (EMBA, MBA); business administration/computer science (MBA/MSCS); business administration/latin american studies (MBA/MLAS); business administration/law (MBA/JD); business administration/library science (MBA/MLIS); business administration/medicine (MBA/MD); business administration/nursing (MBA/MN); business administration/public health (MBA/MPH); business administration/public policy (MBA/MPP); business administration/urban and regional planning (MBA/MURP); business analytics (MSBA); decisions, operations, and technology management (PhD); finance (PhD); financial engineering (MFE); global economics and management (PhD); management and organizations (PhD); marketing (PhD); strategy and policy (PhD); DDS/MBA; MBA/JD; MBA/MD; MBA/MLAS; MBA/MLIS; MBA/MN; MBA/MPH; MBA/MPP; MBA/MSCS; MBA/MURP. UCLA-NUS EMBA: UCLA Anderson and the National University of Singapore. *Accreditation:* AACSB. *Program availability:* Part-time, evening/weekend. *Faculty:* 86 full-time (19 women), 102 part-time/adjunct (16 women). *Students:* 1,040 full-time (378 women), 1,262 part-time (391 women); includes 784 minority (47 Black or African American, non-Hispanic/Latino; 1 American Indian or Alaska Native, non-Hispanic/Latino; 539 Asian, non-Hispanic/Latino; 116 Hispanic/Latino; 5 Native Hawaiian or other Pacific Islander, non-Hispanic/Latino; 76 Two or more races, non-Hispanic/Latino), 609 international. Average age 31. 6,708 applicants, 27% accepted, 949 enrolled. In 2018, 885 master's, 13 doctorates awarded. Terminal master's awarded for partial completion of doctoral program. *Degree requirements:* For master's, comprehensive exam, field consulting project (for MBA, FEMBA, EMBA, UCLA-NUS EMBA, MFE, and MSBA); internship (for MBA only); for doctorate, comprehensive exam, thesis/dissertation, oral and written qualifying exams. *Entrance requirements:* For master's, GMAT or GRE (for MBA, MFE, MSBA); Executive Assessment (EA) for candidates with 10+ years of work experience (FEMBA); Executive Assessment (EA) or STEM Master's degree or JD, MBA, CPA (EMBA), 4-year bachelor's degree or equivalent; 2 letters of recommendation; interview (invitation only); 2 essays; average 4-8 years of full-time work experience (for FEMBA); minimum 8 years of work experience with at least 3 years at management level (for EMBA); 10 years of full-time high managerial responsibility work experience (UCLA-NUS EMBA); for doctorate, GMAT or GRE, bachelor's degree from college or university of fully-recognized standing, minimum B average during junior and senior undergraduate years, 3 letters of recommendation, statement of purpose. Additional exam requirements/recommendations for international students: Required—TOEFL (minimum score 560 paper-based; 87 iBT), IELTS (minimum score 7), TOEFL with minimum iBT score of 100 (for MSBA). *Application deadline:* For fall admission, 10/2 for domestic and international students; for winter admission, 1/8 for domestic and international students; for spring admission, 4/16 for domestic and international students. Applications are processed on a rolling basis. Application fee: $200. Electronic applications accepted. *Expenses:* Per Year - MBA: $64,292, FEMBA: $42,420, EMBA: $81,120, UCLA-NUS EMBA (UC Portion only): $57,500, MFE: $75,816, MSBA: $64,1,43, PhD: $32,049. *Financial support:* Fellowships, research assistantships with partial tuition reimbursements, teaching assistantships with partial tuition reimbursements, career-related internships or fieldwork, institutionally sponsored loans, and scholarships/grants available. Support available to part-time students. *Faculty research:* Finance/global economics, entrepreneurship, accounting, human resources/organizational behavior, marketing and behavioral decision making. *Total annual research expenditures:* $2 million. *Unit head:* Dr. Antonio Bernardo, Dean & John E. Anderson Chair in Management, 310-825-7982, Fax: 310-206-2073, E-mail: a.bernardo@anderson.ucla.edu. *Application contact:* Alex Lawrence, Assistant Dean and Director of MBA Admissions, 310-825-6944, Fax: 310-825-8582, E-mail: mba.admissions@anderson.ucla.edu.
Website: http://www.anderson.ucla.edu/

University of California, Riverside, Graduate Division, The A. Gary Anderson Graduate School of Management, Riverside, CA 92521-0102. Offers accounting (MPAC); business administration (MBA, PhD); finance (M Fin). *Accreditation:* AACSB. *Program availability:* Part-time, evening/weekend. Terminal master's awarded for partial completion of doctoral program. *Degree requirements:* For master's, thesis optional; for doctorate, comprehensive exam, thesis/dissertation. *Entrance requirements:* For master's and doctorate, GMAT or GRE. Additional exam requirements/recommendations for international students: Required—TOEFL (minimum score 550 paper-based; 80 iBT), IELTS (minimum score 7). Electronic applications accepted. *Expenses:* Contact institution. *Faculty research:* Finance, management, marketing, operations and supply chain management, accounting and information systems.

University of Central Arkansas, Graduate School, College of Business Administration, Program in Accounting, Conway, AR 72035-0001. Offers M Acc. *Program availability:* Part-time. *Degree requirements:* For master's, capstone course. *Entrance requirements:* For master's, GMAT or GRE, minimum GPA of 2.7. Additional exam requirements/recommendations for international students: Required—TOEFL (minimum score 550 paper-based; 80 iBT).

University of Central Florida, College of Business Administration, Kenneth G. Dixon School of Accounting, Orlando, FL 32816. Offers MSA. *Accreditation:* AACSB. *Program availability:* Part-time, evening/weekend. *Students:* 89 full-time (42 women), 47 part-time (27 women); includes 51 minority (7 Black or African American, non-Hispanic/Latino; 16 Asian, non-Hispanic/Latino; 24 Hispanic/Latino; 4 Two or more races, non-Hispanic/Latino), 5 international. Average age 27. 91 applicants, 53% accepted, 37 enrolled. In 2018, 89 master's awarded. *Entrance requirements:* For master's, GMAT, minimum GPA of 3.0 in last 60 hours, resume. Additional exam requirements/recommendations for international students: Required—TOEFL. *Application deadline:* For fall admission, 7/15 for domestic students; for spring admission, 12/1 for domestic students; for summer admission, 4/15 for domestic students. Application fee: $30. Electronic applications accepted. *Financial support:* In 2018–19, 21 students received support, including 21 teaching assistantships with partial tuition reimbursements available (averaging $8,625 per year); career-related internships or fieldwork, Federal Work-Study, institutionally sponsored loans, health care benefits, tuition waivers (partial), and unspecified assistantships also available. Financial award application deadline: 3/1; financial award applicants required to submit FAFSA. *Unit head:* Dr. Gregory Trompeter, Director, 407-823-2876, Fax: 407-823-3881, E-mail: trompete@ucf.edu. *Application contact:* Associate Director, Graduate Admissions, 407-823-2766, Fax: 407-823-6442, E-mail: gradadmissions@ucf.edu.
Website: https://business.ucf.edu/departments-schools/kenneth-g-dixon-school-of-accounting/

University of Central Missouri, The Graduate School, Warrensburg, MO 64093. Offers accountancy (MA); accounting (MBA); applied mathematics (MS); aviation safety (MA); biology (MS); business administration (MBA); career and technical education leadership (MS); college student personnel administration (MS); communication (MA); computer science (MS); counseling (MS); criminal justice (MS); educational leadership (Ed D); educational technology (MS); elementary and early childhood education (MSE); English (MA); environmental studies (MA); finance (MBA); history (MA); human services/educational technology (Ed S); human services/learning resources (Ed S); human services/professional counseling (Ed S); industrial hygiene (MS); industrial management (MS); information systems (MBA); information technology (MS); kinesiology (MS); library science and information services (MS); literacy education (MSE); marketing (MBA); mathematics (MS); music (MA); occupational safety management (MS); psychology (MS); rural family nursing (MS); school administration (MSE); social gerontology (MS); sociology (MA); special education (MSE); speech language pathology (MS); superintendency (Ed S); teaching (MAT); teaching English as a second language (MA); technology (MS); technology management (PhD); theatre (MA). *Accreditation:* ASHA. *Program availability:* Part-time, 100% online, blended/hybrid learning. *Degree requirements:* For master's and Ed S, comprehensive exam (for some programs), thesis (for some programs). *Entrance requirements:* Additional exam requirements/recommendations for international students: Required—TOEFL (minimum score 550 paper-based; 79 iBT). Electronic applications accepted.

University of Charleston, Master of Forensic Accounting Program, Charleston, WV 25304-1099. Offers EMFA. *Program availability:* Part-time, blended/hybrid learning. *Entrance requirements:* Additional exam requirements/recommendations for international students: Required—TOEFL. Electronic applications accepted.

University of Chicago, Booth School of Business, Full-Time MBA Program, Chicago, IL 60637. Offers accounting (MBA); analytic finance (MBA); analytic management (MBA); econometrics and statistics (MBA); economics (MBA); entrepreneurship (MBA); finance (MBA); general management (MBA); health administration and policy (Certificate); international business (MBA); managerial and organizational behavior (MBA); marketing analytics (MBA); marketing management (MBA); operations management (MBA); strategic management (MBA); MBA/AM; MBA/JD; MBA/MA; MBA/MD; MBA/MPP. *Accreditation:* AACSB. *Entrance requirements:* For master's, GMAT or GRE, transcripts, resume, 2 letters of recommendation, essays, interview. Additional exam requirements/recommendations for international students: Required—TOEFL, IELTS, or PTE. Electronic applications accepted. *Expenses:* Contact institution.

University of Cincinnati, Carl H. Lindner College of Business, MS Program, Cincinnati, OH 45221. Offers accounting (MS); applied economics (MS); business analytics (MS); finance (MS); information systems (MS); marketing (MS); taxation (MS). *Program availability:* Part-time, evening/weekend. *Faculty:* 98 full-time (27 women), 28 part-time/adjunct (4 women). *Students:* 305 full-time (123 women), 190 part-time (83 women); includes 35 minority (13 Black or African American, non-Hispanic/Latino; 1 American Indian or Alaska Native, non-Hispanic/Latino; 10 Asian, non-Hispanic/Latino; 6 Hispanic/Latino; 5 Two or more races, non-Hispanic/Latino), 309 international. Average age 29. 1,219 applicants, 55% accepted, 495 enrolled. In 2018, 355 master's awarded. *Degree requirements:* For master's, thesis (for some programs), capstone. *Entrance requirements:* For master's, GMAT, GRE, resume, transcripts, essays, letters of recommendation. Additional exam requirements/recommendations for international students: Required—TOEFL (minimum score 577 paper-based; 90 iBT), IELTS (minimum score 6.5). *Application deadline:* For fall admission, 6/30 priority date for domestic students, 3/15 for international students; for spring admission, 12/15 for domestic students, 9/15 for international students; for summer admission, 4/15 for domestic and international students. Applications are processed on a rolling basis. Application fee: $65 ($70 for international students). Electronic applications accepted. *Expenses:* Full-time resident $10,479 per term, full-time nonresident $14,398 per term, part-time $890 per credit hour. *Financial support:* In 2018–19, 251 students received support, including 12 teaching assistantships with full and partial tuition reimbursements available (averaging $3,500 per year); scholarships/grants, tuition waivers (full and partial), and unspecified assistantships also available. Financial award application deadline: 2/1; financial award applicants required to submit FAFSA. *Faculty research:* Business analytics, financial management, organizational behavior, financial accounting, consumer insights. *Total annual research expenditures:* $39,943. *Unit head:* Dr. Marianne Lewis, Dean, 513-556-7001, Fax: 513-556-4891, E-mail: marianne.lewis@uc.edu. *Application contact:* Dona Clary, Executive Director, Graduate Programs, 513-556-3546, Fax: 513-558-7006, E-mail: dona.clary@uc.edu.
Website: http://business.uc.edu/graduate/masters.html

University of Cincinnati, Carl H. Lindner College of Business, PhD Programs, Cincinnati, OH 45221. Offers accounting (PhD); business analytics (PhD); economics (PhD); finance (PhD); information systems (PhD); management (PhD); marketing (PhD); operations and business analytics (PhD); operations research (PhD). *Faculty:* 101 full-time (37 women). *Students:* 15 full-time (5 women), 10 part-time (4 women); includes 4 minority (1 Black or African American, non-Hispanic/Latino; 3 Asian, non-Hispanic/Latino), 20 international. Average age 31. 125 applicants, 12% accepted, 4 enrolled. In 2018, 7 doctorates awarded. *Degree requirements:* For doctorate, comprehensive exam, thesis/dissertation. *Entrance requirements:* For doctorate, GMAT, GRE, transcripts, essays, resume, letters of recommendation. Additional exam requirements/recommendations for international students: Required—TOEFL (minimum score 600 paper-based; 100 iBT), IELTS (minimum score 7). *Application deadline:* For fall admission, 1/15 for domestic and international students. Application fee: $65 ($70 for international students). Electronic applications accepted. *Expenses:* Contact institution. *Financial support:* In 2018–19, 35 students received support, including 25 research assistantships with full tuition reimbursements available (averaging $23,250 per year); scholarships/grants, health care benefits, tuition waivers (full), and unspecified assistantships also available. Financial award application deadline: 1/15; financial award applicants required to submit FAFSA. *Faculty research:* Bayesian Prediction Theory, organizational fairness, consumer insight and market research, consumer insight and market research, density estimation from correlated data. *Unit head:* Dr. Olivier Parent, Director, 513-556-3941, Fax: 513-556-5499, E-mail: olivier.parent@uc.edu. *Application contact:* Angel Elvin, Assistant Director, 513-556-7190, Fax: 513-558-7006, E-mail: angel.elvin@uc.edu.
Website: http://business.uc.edu/graduate/phd.html

University of Colorado Denver, Business School, Program in Accounting, Denver, CO 80217. Offers accounting and information systems audit control (MS); auditing (MS); controllership and financial leadership (MS). *Accreditation:* AACSB. *Program availability:* Part-time, evening/weekend. *Degree requirements:* For master's, 30 semester hours. *Entrance requirements:* For master's, GMAT (waived for students who already hold a graduate degree, or an undergraduate degree from CU Denver), essay, resume, two letters of recommendation; financial statements (for international students). Additional exam requirements/recommendations for international students: Required—TOEFL (minimum score 537 paper-based; 75 iBT); Recommended—IELTS (minimum score 6.5). Electronic applications accepted. *Expenses:* Contact institution.

Accounting

University of Colorado Denver, Business School, Program in Information Systems, Denver, CO 80217. Offers accounting and information systems audit and control (MS); business intelligence systems (MS); digital health entrepreneurship (MS); enterprise risk management (MS); enterprise technology management (MS); geographic information systems (MS); health information technology (MS); technology innovation and entrepreneurship (MS); Web and mobile computing (MS). *Program availability:* Part-time, evening/weekend, online learning. *Degree requirements:* For master's, 30 credit hours. *Entrance requirements:* For master's, GMAT, resume, essay, two letters of recommendation, financial statements (for international applicants). Additional exam requirements/recommendations for international students: Required—TOEFL (minimum score 525 paper-based; 71 iBT); Recommended—IELTS (minimum score 6.5). Electronic applications accepted. *Expenses:* Contact institution. *Faculty research:* Human-computer interaction, expert systems, database management, electronic commerce, object-oriented software development.

University of Connecticut, Graduate School, School of Business, Storrs, CT 06269. Offers accounting (MS, PhD); business (PhD); business administration (MBA); business analytics and project management (MS); finance (PhD); financial risk management (MS); health care management and insurance studies (MBA); human resource management (MS); management (PhD); management consulting (MBA); marketing (PhD); marketing intelligence (MBA); operations and information management (PhD). *Accreditation:* AACSB. *Degree requirements:* For master's, comprehensive exam; for doctorate, thesis/dissertation. *Entrance requirements:* For master's and doctorate, GMAT. Additional exam requirements/recommendations for international students: Required—TOEFL (minimum score 550 paper-based). Electronic applications accepted.

University of Dallas, Satish and Yasmin Gupta College of Business, Irving, TX 75062. Offers accounting (MBA, MS); business administration (DBA); business analytics (MS); business management (MBA); corporate finance (MBA); cybersecurity (MS); finance (MS); financial services (MBA); global business (MBA, MS); health services management (MBA); human resource management (MBA); information and technology management (MS); information assurance (MBA); information technology (MBA); information technology service management (MBA); marketing management (MBA); organization development (MBA); project management (MBA); sports and entertainment management (MBA); strategic leadership (MBA); supply chain management (MBA). *Accreditation:* AACSB. *Program availability:* Part-time, evening/weekend, 100% online. *Students:* 147 full-time (56 women), 584 part-time (232 women); includes 402 minority (204 Black or African American, non-Hispanic/Latino; 95 Asian, non-Hispanic/Latino; 92 Hispanic/Latino; 2 Native Hawaiian or other Pacific Islander, non-Hispanic/Latino; 9 Two or more races, non-Hispanic/Latino), 113 international. Average age 34. 992 applicants, 30% accepted, 157 enrolled. In 2018, 336 master's, 5 doctorates awarded. *Degree requirements:* For doctorate, thesis/dissertation. *Entrance requirements:* For master's and doctorate, U.S. bachelor's degree with a minimum cumulative GPA of 2.0 from a regionally accredited college or university (or comparable foreign degree); minimum 3.0 GPA in any graduate-level coursework completed; good academic standing with all colleges attended. Additional exam requirements/recommendations for international students: Required—TOEFL (minimum score 80 iBT), IELTS (minimum score 6.5), PTE (minimum score 67). *Application deadline:* Applications are processed on a rolling basis. Application fee: $50. Electronic applications accepted. *Expenses:* $1250 per credit hour. *Financial support:* In 2018–19, 291 students received support. Research assistantships, teaching assistantships, scholarships/grants, and unspecified assistantships available. Support available to part-time students. Financial award application deadline: 2/15; financial award applicants required to submit FAFSA. *Unit head:* Brett J.L. Landry, Dean, 972-721-5356, E-mail: blandry@udallas.edu. *Application contact:* Breonna Collins, Director, Graduate Admissions, 972-7215304, E-mail: bcollins@udallas.edu.
Website: http://www.udallas.edu/cob/

University of Dayton, School of Business Administration, Dayton, OH 45469. Offers accounting (MBA); cyber security (MBA); finance (MBA); marketing (MBA); JD/MBA. *Accreditation:* AACSB. *Program availability:* Part-time, evening/weekend, blended/hybrid learning. *Entrance requirements:* For master's, GMAT (minimum score of 500 total, 19 verbal); GRE (minimum score of 149 verbal, 146 quantitative), minimum GPA of 3.0, current resume. Additional exam requirements/recommendations for international students: Required—TOEFL (minimum score 550 paper-based; 80 iBT); Recommended—IELTS (minimum score 6.5). Electronic applications accepted. *Expenses:* Contact institution. *Faculty research:* Management information systems, economics, finance, marketing, entrepreneurship, accounting, cyber security, analytics.

University of Delaware, Alfred Lerner College of Business and Economics, Department of Accounting and Management Information Systems, Newark, DE 19716. Offers accounting (MS); information systems and technology management (MS). *Accreditation:* AACSB. *Program availability:* Part-time, evening/weekend. *Degree requirements:* For master's, thesis optional. *Entrance requirements:* For master's, GMAT. Additional exam requirements/recommendations for international students: Required—TOEFL (minimum score 550 paper-based). Electronic applications accepted. *Faculty research:* External reporting, managerial accounting, auditing information systems, taxation.

University of Denver, Daniels College of Business, School of Accountancy, Denver, CO 80208. Offers accounting (M Acc, MBA). *Accreditation:* AACSB. *Program availability:* Part-time, evening/weekend. *Faculty:* 17 full-time (8 women), 2 part-time/adjunct (1 woman). *Students:* 48 full-time (21 women), 26 part-time (15 women); includes 11 minority (1 Black or African American, non-Hispanic/Latino; 1 Asian, non-Hispanic/Latino; 8 Hispanic/Latino; 1 Two or more races, non-Hispanic/Latino), 27 international. Average age 26. 138 applicants, 56% accepted, 35 enrolled. In 2018, 75 master's awarded. *Entrance requirements:* For master's, GRE General Test or GMAT, bachelor's degree, transcripts, resume, essays, interview. Additional exam requirements/recommendations for international students: Required—TOEFL (minimum score 575 paper-based; 94 iBT). *Application deadline:* For fall admission, 10/15 priority date for domestic and international students; for spring admission, 9/15 priority date for domestic and international students. Applications are processed on a rolling basis. Application fee: $100. Electronic applications accepted. *Expenses:* $49,695 per year full-time; $1,372 per credit. *Financial support:* In 2018–19, 56 students received support. Teaching assistantships with tuition reimbursements available, career-related internships or fieldwork, Federal Work-Study, institutionally sponsored loans, scholarships/grants, and unspecified assistantships available. Support available to part-time students. Financial award application deadline: 2/15; financial award applicants required to submit FAFSA. *Faculty research:* Privacy and security, autonomous systems, software testing, robotics and human computer interaction, machine learning. *Unit head:* Dr. Sharon Lassar, Professor/Director, School of Accountancy, 303-871-2032, E-mail: slassar@du.edu. *Application contact:* Jacquelyn Villa, Assistant to the Director, 303-871-2032, E-mail: jacquelyn.villa@du.edu.
Website: https://daniels.du.edu/accountancy

University of Detroit Mercy, College of Business Administration, Detroit, MI 48221. Offers business administration (MBA); business fundamentals (Certificate); business turnaround management (Certificate); ethical leadership and change management (Certificate); finance (Certificate); forensic accounting (Certificate); JD/MBA; MBA/MHSA. *Program availability:* Part-time, evening/weekend, 100% online, blended/hybrid learning. *Entrance requirements:* For master's, GMAT, resume, letter of recommendation, transcripts; for Certificate, resume, letter of recommendation, transcripts. Electronic applications accepted. Application fee is waived when completed online. *Expenses:* Contact institution. *Faculty research:* Ethics, international finance, trade policy, leadership, information technology.

The University of Findlay, Office of Graduate Admissions, Findlay, OH 45840-3653. Offers applied security and analytics (MSAS); athletic training (MAT); business (MBA), including certified management accountant, certified public accountant, health care management, hospitality management; education (MA Ed, Ed D), including children's literature (MA Ed), curriculum and teaching (MA Ed), education (MA Ed), educational administration (MA Ed), human resource development (MA Ed), mathematics (MA Ed), reading (MA Ed), science education (MA Ed), superintendent (Ed D), teaching (Ed D), technology (MA Ed); environmental, safety, and health management (MSEM); health informatics (MS); occupational therapy (MOT); pharmacy (Pharm D); physical therapy (DPT); physician assistant (MPA); rhetoric and writing (MA); teaching English to speakers of other languages (TESOL) and applied linguistics (MA). *Program availability:* Part-time, evening/weekend, 100% online, blended/hybrid learning. *Degree requirements:* For master's, comprehensive exam (for some programs), thesis (for some programs), cumulative project, capstone project; for doctorate, thesis/dissertation (for some programs). *Entrance requirements:* For master's, GRE/GMAT, bachelor's degree from accredited institution, minimum undergraduate GPA of 2.5 in last 64 hours of course work; for doctorate, GRE, MAT, minimum cumulative GPA of 3.0. Additional exam requirements/recommendations for international students: Required—TOEFL (minimum score 79 iBT), IELTS (minimum score 7), PTE (minimum score 61). Electronic applications accepted.

University of Florida, Graduate School, Warrington College of Business Administration, Fisher School of Accounting, Gainesville, FL 32611. Offers M Acc, PhD, JD/M Acc. *Accreditation:* AACSB. *Program availability:* Part-time. *Degree requirements:* For master's, comprehensive exam, thesis optional; for doctorate, comprehensive exam, thesis/dissertation. *Entrance requirements:* For master's, GMAT (minimum score of 465) or GRE General Test, minimum GPA of 3.0. Additional exam requirements/recommendations for international students: Required—TOEFL (minimum score 550 paper-based; 80 iBT), IELTS (minimum score 6). Electronic applications accepted. *Faculty research:* Financial reporting, managerial accounting, auditing, taxation.

University of Georgia, Terry College of Business, J.M. Tull School of Accounting, Athens, GA 30602. Offers M Acc. *Accreditation:* AACSB. *Entrance requirements:* For master's, GMAT. Electronic applications accepted.

University of Hartford, Barney School of Business, Department of Accounting and Taxation, West Hartford, CT 06117-1599. Offers professional accounting (Certificate); taxation (MSAT). *Program availability:* Part-time, evening/weekend. *Entrance requirements:* For master's, GMAT, 2 letters of recommendation, resume. Additional exam requirements/recommendations for international students: Required—TOEFL (minimum score 550 paper-based). Electronic applications accepted.

University of Hawaii at Manoa, Office of Graduate Education, Shidler College of Business, Program in Accounting, Honolulu, HI 96822. Offers accounting (M Acc); accounting law (M Acc); information systems (M Acc); taxation (M Acc). *Program availability:* Part-time. *Entrance requirements:* For master's, GMAT, bachelor's degree in accounting, minimum GPA of 3.0. Additional exam requirements/recommendations for international students: Required—TOEFL (minimum score 550 paper-based; 79 iBT), IELTS (minimum score 5). *Faculty research:* International accounting, current tax topics, insurance industry financial reporting, behavioral accounting, auditing.

University of Hawaii at Manoa, Office of Graduate Education, Shidler College of Business, Program in International Management, Honolulu, HI 96822. Offers Asian finance (PhD); global information technology management (PhD); international accounting (PhD); international marketing (PhD); international organization and strategy (PhD). *Program availability:* Part-time. *Degree requirements:* For doctorate, comprehensive exam, thesis/dissertation. *Entrance requirements:* For doctorate, GMAT or GRE General Test, minimum GPA of 3.0. Additional exam requirements/recommendations for international students: Required—TOEFL (minimum score 600 paper-based; 100 iBT), IELTS (minimum score 7). *Expenses:* Contact institution.

University of Houston, Bauer College of Business, Accountancy and Taxation Program, Houston, TX 77204. Offers accountancy (MS Accy); accountancy and taxation (PhD). *Accreditation:* AACSB. *Program availability:* Part-time, evening/weekend. *Degree requirements:* For master's, 30 hours completed in residence, minimum cumulative GPA of 3.0 at UH, no more than 11 semester hours of 'C' grades or below in graduate courses taken at UH; for doctorate, continuous full time enrollment, dissertation defense within 6 years of entering the program. *Entrance requirements:* For master's, GMAT, official transcripts from all higher education institutions attended, letters of recommendation, resume, goals statement; for doctorate, GMAT or GRE, letter of financial backing, statement of understanding, reference letters, statement of academic and research interests. Additional exam requirements/recommendations for international students: Required—TOEFL (minimum score 550 paper-based; 79 iBT), IELTS (minimum score 6.5), PTE (minimum score 70). Electronic applications accepted. *Faculty research:* Accountancy and taxation, finance, international business, management.

University of Houston–Clear Lake, School of Business, Program in Accounting, Houston, TX 77058-1002. Offers accounting (MS); professional accounting (MS). *Accreditation:* AACSB. *Program availability:* Part-time, evening/weekend. *Degree requirements:* For master's, thesis optional. *Entrance requirements:* For master's, GMAT. Additional exam requirements/recommendations for international students: Required—TOEFL (minimum score 550 paper-based). Electronic applications accepted.

University of Houston–Downtown, Marilyn Davies College of Business, MBA Program, Houston, TX 77002. Offers accounting (MBA); finance (MBA); human resource management (MBA); international business (MBA); investment management (MBA); leadership (MBA); project management and process improvement (MBA); sales management and business development (MBA); supply chain management (MBA). *Accreditation:* AACSB. *Program availability:* Part-time, evening/weekend. *Entrance requirements:* For master's, GMAT, two letters of recommendation from professional references, personal statement, resume. Additional exam requirements/recommendations for international students: Required—TOEFL (minimum score 81 iBT). Electronic applications accepted. *Expenses:* Contact institution.

University of Houston–Victoria, School of Business Administration, Victoria, TX 77901-4450. Offers accounting (MBA); economic development and entrepreneurship (MS); finance (GMBA, MBA); general business (MBA); international business (MBA); management (GMBA, MBA); marketing (MBA). *Accreditation:* AACSB. *Program availability:* Part-time, evening/weekend, online learning. *Entrance requirements:* For master's, GMAT. Additional exam requirements/recommendations for international students: Required—TOEFL (minimum score 550 paper-based). Electronic applications accepted. *Expenses: Tuition, area resident:* Full-time $6154; part-time $3077 per semester. Tuition, state resident: full-time $6154; part-time $3077 per semester. Tuition, nonresident: full-time $13,624; part-time $6812 per semester. *International tuition:* $13,624 full-time. *Required fees:* $1405; $847 per semester. $423 per semester. Tuition and fees vary according to program. *Faculty research:* Economic development, marketing, finance.

University of Idaho, College of Graduate Studies, College of Business and Economics, Department of Accounting, Moscow, ID 83844-2282. Offers accountancy (M Acct). *Accreditation:* AACSB. *Faculty:* 6 full-time. *Students:* 32. Average age 26. In 2018, 33 master's awarded. *Entrance requirements:* For master's, minimum GPA of 3.0. Additional exam requirements/recommendations for international students: Required—TOEFL (minimum score 88 iBT). *Application deadline:* For fall admission, 7/1 for domestic students; for spring admission, 11/1 for domestic students. Applications are processed on a rolling basis. Application fee: $60. Electronic applications accepted. *Expenses:* Tuition, state resident: full-time $7266.44; part-time $474.50 per credit hour. Tuition, nonresident: full-time $24,902; part-time $1453.50 per credit hour. *Required fees:* $2085.56; $45.50 per credit hour. *Financial support:* Research assistantships and teaching assistantships available. Financial award applicants required to submit FAFSA. *Unit head:* Dr. Marla Kraut, Head, 208-885-6478, Fax: 208-885-5087, E-mail: cbe@uidaho.edu. *Application contact:* Dr. Marla Kraut, Head, 208-885-6478, Fax: 208-885-5087, E-mail: cbe@uidaho.edu.
Website: https://www.uidaho.edu/cbe/accounting-department

University of Illinois at Chicago, Liautaud Graduate School of Business, Department of Accounting, Chicago, IL 60607-7128. Offers MS, MBA/MS. *Accreditation:* AACSB. *Program availability:* Part-time. *Entrance requirements:* For master's, GMAT, minimum GPA of 2.75. Additional exam requirements/recommendations for international students: Required—TOEFL. Electronic applications accepted. *Expenses:* Contact institution. *Faculty research:* Governmental accounting, managerial accounting, auditing.

University of Illinois at Springfield, Graduate Programs, College of Business and Management, Program in Accountancy, Springfield, IL 62703-5407. Offers MA. *Program availability:* Part-time, evening/weekend. *Faculty:* 10 full-time (1 woman), 2 part-time/adjunct (0 women). *Students:* 69 full-time (33 women), 27 part-time (16 women); includes 12 minority (4 Black or African American, non-Hispanic/Latino; 4 Asian, non-Hispanic/Latino; 1 Hispanic/Latino; 3 Two or more races, non-Hispanic/Latino), 32 international. Average age 27. 94 applicants, 60% accepted, 41 enrolled. In 2018, 32 master's awarded. *Degree requirements:* For master's, closure exercise including capstone courses. *Entrance requirements:* For master's, minimum undergraduate GPA of 2.7 in prerequisite coursework; introductory course in financial and managerial accounting, college math through business calculus, principles of economics (micro and macro), and statistics. Additional exam requirements/recommendations for international students: Required—TOEFL (minimum score 550 paper-based). *Application deadline:* Applications are processed on a rolling basis. Application fee: $60 ($75 for international students). Electronic applications accepted. *Financial support:* In 2018–19, research assistantships with full tuition reimbursements (averaging $10,384 per year), teaching assistantships with full tuition reimbursements (averaging $10,303 per year) were awarded; fellowships, career-related internships or fieldwork, Federal Work-Study, scholarships/grants, health care benefits, and unspecified assistantships also available. Support available to part-time students. Financial award application deadline: 11/15; financial award applicants required to submit FAFSA. *Unit head:* Dr. Mark Buxton, Program Administrator, 217-206-6299, Fax: 217-206-7914, E-mail: mbuxt2@uis.edu. *Application contact:* Dr. Mark Buxton, Program Administrator, 217-206-6299, Fax: 217-206-7914, E-mail: mbuxt2@uis.edu.
Website: http://www.uis.edu/accountancy

University of Illinois at Urbana–Champaign, Graduate College, Gies College of Business, Department of Accountancy, Champaign, IL 61820. Offers accountancy (MS, PhD); accounting science (MAS). *Accreditation:* AACSB.

The University of Iowa, Tippie College of Business, M Ac Program in Accounting, Iowa City, IA 52242-1316. Offers M Ac, JD/M Ac. *Entrance requirements:* Additional exam requirements/recommendations for international students: Required—TOEFL (minimum score 100 iBT). Electronic applications accepted. *Expenses:* Contact institution.

The University of Iowa, Tippie College of Business, PhD Program in Accounting, Iowa City, IA 52242-1316. Offers PhD. *Accreditation:* AACSB. *Degree requirements:* For doctorate, comprehensive exam, thesis/dissertation. *Entrance requirements:* For doctorate, GMAT. Additional exam requirements/recommendations for international students: Required—TOEFL (minimum score 100 iBT), IELTS (minimum score 7). Electronic applications accepted. *Faculty research:* Corporate financial reporting issues; financial statement information and capital markets; cost structure: analysis, estimation, and management; experimental and prediction economics; income taxes and interaction of financial and tax reporting systems.

The University of Kansas, Graduate Studies, School of Business, Master of Accounting Program, Lawrence, KS 66045. Offers M Acc. *Accreditation:* AACSB. *Program availability:* Part-time. *Students:* 110 full-time (57 women), 32 part-time (20 women); includes 17 minority (1 Black or African American, non-Hispanic/Latino; 10 Asian, non-Hispanic/Latino; 4 Hispanic/Latino; 2 Two or more races, non-Hispanic/Latino), 12 international. Average age 26. 84 applicants, 77% accepted, 71 enrolled. In 2018, 136 master's awarded. *Entrance requirements:* For master's, GMAT, official transcript, two letters of recommendation, pledge to support Honor System of School of Business, current resume, three essays. Additional exam requirements/recommendations for international students: Required—TOEFL, IELTS. *Application deadline:* For fall admission, 12/15 for domestic and international students; for spring admission, 8/1 for domestic and international students; for summer admission, 12/15 for domestic and international students. Application fee: $65 ($85 for international students). Electronic applications accepted. *Financial support:* Fellowships, research assistantships, teaching assistantships, career-related internships or fieldwork, Federal Work-Study, institutionally sponsored loans, and scholarships/grants available. Financial award application deadline: 2/15; financial award applicants required to submit FAFSA. *Faculty research:* Earnings quality, financial reporting conservatism, internal control systems, auditing and corporate governance, financial reporting restatements. *Unit head:* Keith Jones, Director, 785-864-6997, E-mail: keithjones@ku.edu. *Application contact:* Rachel Green, Graduate Admissions Contact, 785-864-7558, E-mail: ragreen@ku.edu.
Website: https://business.ku.edu/degrees/accounting/macc/

University of Kentucky, Graduate School, Gatton College of Business and Economics, Program in Accounting, Lexington, KY 40506-0032. Offers MSACC. *Accreditation:* AACSB. *Degree requirements:* For master's, comprehensive exam. *Entrance requirements:* For master's, GRE General Test, minimum undergraduate GPA of 2.75. Additional exam requirements/recommendations for international students: Required—TOEFL (minimum score 550 paper-based). Electronic applications accepted. *Faculty research:* Taxation, financial accounting and auditing, managerial accounting, not-for-profit accounting.

University of La Verne, College of Business and Public Management, Graduate Programs in Business Administration, La Verne, CA 91750-4443. Offers accounting (MBA, MBA-EP); finance (MBA, MBA-EP); health services management (MBA); information technology (MBA, MBA-EP); international business (MBA, MBA-EP); management and leadership (MBA, MBA-EP); marketing (MBA, MBA-EP); supply chain management (MBA, MBA-EP). *Program availability:* Part-time, evening/weekend. *Entrance requirements:* For master's, GMAT, MAT, or GRE, minimum undergraduate GPA of 3.0, 2 letters of recommendation, resume, statement of purpose. Additional exam requirements/recommendations for international students: Required—TOEFL (minimum score 550 paper-based; 85 iBT).

University of La Verne, College of Business and Public Management, Program in Accounting, La Verne, CA 91750-4443. Offers MS. *Program availability:* Part-time. *Entrance requirements:* For master's, GMAT, MAT, or GRE, minimum undergraduate GPA of 3.0, 2 letters of recommendation, resume, statement of purpose. Additional exam requirements/recommendations for international students: Required—TOEFL (minimum score 550 paper-based; 85 iBT). *Expenses:* Contact institution.

University of La Verne, Regional and Online Campuses, Graduate Programs, Inland Empire Campus, Ontario, CA 91730. Offers business administration (MBA, MBA-EP), including accounting (MBA), finance (MBA), health services management (MBA-EP), information technology (MBA-EP), international business (MBA), managed care (MBA), management and leadership (MBA-EP), marketing (MBA-EP), supply chain management (MBA); leadership and management (MS), including human resource management, nonprofit management, organizational development. *Program availability:* Part-time, evening/weekend. *Expenses:* Contact institution.

University of Lethbridge, School of Graduate Studies, Lethbridge, AB T1K 3M4, Canada. Offers addictions counseling (M Sc); agricultural biotechnology (M Sc); agricultural studies (M Sc, MA); anthropology (MA); archaeology (M Sc, MA); art (MA, MFA); biochemistry (M Sc); biological sciences (M Sc); biomolecular science (PhD); biosystems and biodiversity (PhD); Canadian studies (MA); chemistry (M Sc); computer science (M Sc); computer science and geographical information science (M Sc); counseling (MC); counseling psychology (M Ed); dramatic arts (MA); earth, space, and physical science (PhD); economics (MA); education (MA, PhD); educational leadership (M Ed); English (MA); environmental science (M Sc); evolution and behavior (PhD); exercise science (M Sc); French (MA); French/German (MA); French/Spanish (MA); general education (M Ed); geography (M Sc, MA); German (MA); health sciences (M Sc); individualized multidisciplinary (M Sc, MA); kinesiology (M Sc, MA); management (M Sc), including accounting, finance, human resource management and labor relations, information systems, international management, marketing, policy and strategy; mathematics (M Sc); music (M Mus, MA); Native American studies (MA); neuroscience (M Sc, PhD); new media (MA, MFA); nursing (M Sc, MN); philosophy (MA); physics (M Sc); political science (MA); psychology (M Sc, MA); religious studies (MA); sociology (MA); theatre and dramatic arts (MFA); theoretical and computational science (PhD); urban and regional studies (MA); women and gender studies (MA). *Program availability:* Part-time, evening/weekend. *Degree requirements:* For master's, thesis (for some programs); for doctorate, comprehensive exam, thesis/dissertation. *Entrance requirements:* For master's, GMAT (for M Sc in management), bachelor's degree in related field, minimum GPA of 3.0 during previous 20 graded semester courses, 2 years' teaching or related experience (M Ed); for doctorate, master's degree, minimum graduate GPA of 3.5. Additional exam requirements/recommendations for international students: Required—TOEFL (minimum score 580 paper-based; 93 iBT). Electronic applications accepted. *Faculty research:* Movement and brain plasticity, gibberellin physiology, photosynthesis, carbon cycling, molecular properties of main-group ring components.

University of Louisiana at Lafayette, BI Moody III College of Business Administration, Lafayette, LA 70504. Offers accounting (MS); business administration (MBA); entrepreneurship (MBA); finance (MBA); global management (MBA); health care administration (MBA); hospitality management (MBA); human resource management (MBA); project management (MBA); sales leadership (MBA). *Accreditation:* AACSB. *Program availability:* Part-time, evening/weekend. *Entrance requirements:* For master's, GRE General Test. Additional exam requirements/recommendations for international students: Required—TOEFL (minimum score 550 paper-based).

University of Louisville, Graduate School, College of Business, School of Accountancy, Louisville, KY 40292-0001. Offers MAC, MBA/MAC. *Accreditation:* AACSB. *Program availability:* Part-time, evening/weekend. *Faculty:* 10 full-time (5 women), 4 part-time/adjunct (2 women). *Students:* 5 full-time (1 woman), 52 part-time (37 women); includes 9 minority (2 Black or African American, non-Hispanic/Latino; 2 Asian, non-Hispanic/Latino; 1 Hispanic/Latino; 4 Two or more races, non-Hispanic/Latino). Average age 35. 7 applicants, 14% accepted, 1 enrolled. *Entrance requirements:* For master's, GMAT, 2 letters of reference, resume, personal statement, personal interview, transcript. Additional exam requirements/recommendations for international students: Required—TOEFL (minimum score 83 iBT). *Application deadline:* For fall admission, 5/15 priority date for domestic students. Applications are processed on a rolling basis. Application fee: $65. *Expenses:* Tuition, area resident: Full-time $6500; part-time $723 per credit hour. Tuition, state resident: full-time $6500. Tuition, nonresident: full-time $13,557; part-time $1507 per credit hour. Tuition and fees vary according to course load and program. *Financial support:* In 2018–19, 17 students received support, including research assistantships with full tuition reimbursements available (averaging $1,200 per year); health care benefits and unspecified assistantships also available. Financial award application deadline: 3/15; financial award applicants required to submit FAFSA. *Faculty research:* Audit judgment and decision-making, information systems, taxation, cost and managerial accounting. *Total annual research expenditures:* $19,347. *Unit head:* Dr. Todd Mooradian, Dean, 502-852-6443, Fax: 502-852-7557, E-mail: todd.mooradian@louisville.edu. *Application contact:* Susan E. Hildebrand, Director of IT and Master's Programs Admissions/Recruiting Manager, 502-852-7257, Fax: 502-852-4901, E-mail: s.hildebrand@louisville.edu.
Website: http://business.louisville.edu/graduate-programs

The University of Manchester, Alliance Manchester Business School, M15 6PB, United Kingdom. Offers accounting and finance (M Sc); business (M Ent); business analysis and strategic management (M Sc); business analytics: operational research and risk analysis (M Sc); business psychology (M Sc); corporate communications and reputation management (M Sc); finance (M Sc); finance and business economics (M Sc); human resource management and industrial relations (M Sc); innovation management and entrepreneurship (M Sc); international business and management (M Sc); international human resource management and comparative industrial relations (M Sc); management (M Sc); marketing (M Sc); operations, project and supply chain management (M Sc); organizational psychology (M Sc); quantitative finance (M Sc). *Entrance requirements:* For master's, UK 2:1 honours degree or overseas equivalent. Additional exam requirements/recommendations for international students: Required—TOEFL (minimum score 100 iBT), IELTS (minimum score 7), PTE. Electronic applications accepted. *Faculty research:* Accounting and finance, management sciences and marketing, people management and organization, innovation management and policy, decision sciences.

University of Mary Hardin-Baylor, Graduate Studies in Business Administration, Belton, TX 76513. Offers accounting (MBA); information systems management (MBA); international business (MBA); management (MBA). *Program availability:* Part-time, evening/weekend. *Degree requirements:* For master's, comprehensive exam. *Entrance requirements:* For master's, minimum GPA of 3.0, interview. Additional exam requirements/recommendations for international students: Required—TOEFL (minimum score 60 iBT), IELTS (minimum score 4.5). Electronic applications accepted. *Faculty research:* Financial management, financial markets, supply chain management.

Accounting

University of Maryland University College, The Graduate School, Program in Accounting and Financial Management, Adelphi, MD 20783. Offers MS. *Accreditation:* AACSB. *Program availability:* Part-time, evening/weekend, online learning. *Students:* 12 full-time (7 women), 497 part-time (313 women); includes 291 minority (196 Black or African American, non-Hispanic/Latino; 4 American Indian or Alaska Native, non-Hispanic/Latino; 34 Asian, non-Hispanic/Latino; 39 Hispanic/Latino; 1 Native Hawaiian or other Pacific Islander, non-Hispanic/Latino; 17 Two or more races, non-Hispanic/Latino), 17 international. Average age 36. 169 applicants, 100% accepted, 127 enrolled. In 2018, 84 master's awarded. *Degree requirements:* For master's, thesis or alternative, capstone course. *Application deadline:* Applications are processed on a rolling basis. Application fee: $50. Electronic applications accepted. *Financial support:* Scholarships/grants available. Support available to part-time students. Financial award application deadline: 6/1; financial award applicants required to submit FAFSA. *Unit head:* Kirby Cundiff, Program Chair, 240-684-2400, E-mail: kirby.cundiff@umuc.edu. *Application contact:* Admissions, 800-888-8682, E-mail: studentsfirst@umuc.edu. Website: https://www.umuc.edu/academic-programs/masters-degrees/accounting-and-financial-management.cfm

University of Maryland University College, The Graduate School, Program in Accounting and Information Systems, Adelphi, MD 20783. Offers MS, Certificate. *Accreditation:* AACSB. *Program availability:* Part-time, evening/weekend, online learning. *Degree requirements:* For master's, thesis or alternative, capstone course. Electronic applications accepted.

University of Massachusetts Amherst, Graduate School, Isenberg School of Management, Department of Accounting, Amherst, MA 01003. Offers MSA. *Accreditation:* AACSB. *Program availability:* Part-time. *Entrance requirements:* For master's, GMAT. Additional exam requirements/recommendations for international students: Required—TOEFL (minimum score 550 paper-based; 80 iBT), IELTS (minimum score 6.5). Electronic applications accepted.

University of Massachusetts Amherst, Graduate School, Isenberg School of Management, Program in Management, Amherst, MA 01003. Offers accounting (PhD); business administration (MBA); entrepreneurship (MBA); finance (MBA, PhD); healthcare administration (MBA); hospitality and tourism management (PhD); management science (PhD); marketing (MBA, PhD); organization studies (PhD); sport management (PhD); strategic management (PhD); MBA/MS. *Accreditation:* AACSB. *Program availability:* Part-time, evening/weekend, online learning. Terminal master's awarded for partial completion of doctoral program. *Degree requirements:* For doctorate, comprehensive exam, thesis/dissertation. *Entrance requirements:* For master's and doctorate, GMAT or GRE General Test. Additional exam requirements/recommendations for international students: Required—TOEFL (minimum score 550 paper-based; 80 iBT), IELTS (minimum score 6.5). Electronic applications accepted.

University of Massachusetts Boston, College of Management, Program in Accounting, Boston, MA 02125-3393. Offers MS. *Expenses: Tuition, area resident:* Full-time $17,896. Tuition, state resident: full-time $17,896. Tuition, nonresident: full-time $34,932. *International tuition:* $34,932 full-time. *Required fees:* $355.

University of Massachusetts Dartmouth, Graduate School, Charlton College of Business, Department of Accounting and Finance, North Dartmouth, MA 02747-2300. Offers accounting (MS, Postbaccalaureate Certificate); finance (Postbaccalaureate Certificate). *Program availability:* Part-time, 100% online, blended/hybrid learning. *Faculty:* 15 full-time (5 women), 3 part-time/adjunct (1 woman). *Students:* 22 full-time (12 women), 18 part-time (9 women); includes 10 minority (4 Asian, non-Hispanic/Latino; 3 Hispanic/Latino; 3 Two or more races, non-Hispanic/Latino), 7 international. Average age 30. 30 applicants, 87% accepted, 14 enrolled. In 2018, 31 master's awarded. *Entrance requirements:* For master's, GMAT or waiver, statement of purpose (minimum 300 words), resume, official transcript, 2 letters of recommendation; for Postbaccalaureate Certificate, statement of purpose (minimum 300 words), resume, official transcript. Additional exam requirements/recommendations for international students: Required—TOEFL (minimum score 550 paper-based; 79 iBT), IELTS (minimum score 6.5). *Application deadline:* For fall admission, 7/1 priority date for domestic students, 6/1 priority date for international students; for spring admission, 12/1 priority date for domestic students, 11/1 for international students. Application fee: $60. Electronic applications accepted. *Financial support:* Tuition waivers available. Financial award application deadline: 3/1; financial award applicants required to submit FAFSA. *Faculty research:* Accounting information systems, analytical controls in continuous auditing, accounting education, managerial accounting, e-commerce. *Unit head:* Dr. Jia Wu, Program Coordinator, Accounting, 508-999-8428, E-mail: jwu@umassd.edu. *Application contact:* Scott Webster, Director of Graduate Studies & Admissions, 508-999-8604, Fax: 508-999-8183, E-mail: graduate@umassd.edu. Website: http://www.umassd.edu/charlton/programs/graduate/msaccounting/

University of Memphis, Graduate School, Fogelman College of Business and Economics, Program in Business Administration, Memphis, TN 38152. Offers accounting (MBA, PhD); business administration (IMBA); economics (PhD); executive business administration (MBA); finance (PhD); management (PhD); marketing (MS); marketing and supply chain management (PhD); real estate development (MS); JD/MBA. *Accreditation:* AACSB. *Students:* 189 full-time (96 women), 364 part-time (151 women); includes 178 minority (89 Black or African American, non-Hispanic/Latino; 1 American Indian or Alaska Native, non-Hispanic/Latino; 68 Asian, non-Hispanic/Latino; 12 Hispanic/Latino; 8 Two or more races, non-Hispanic/Latino), 102 international. Average age 32. 298 applicants, 72% accepted, 139 enrolled. In 2018, 200 master's, 3 doctorates awarded. *Degree requirements:* For master's, comprehensive exam; for doctorate, comprehensive exam, thesis/dissertation. *Entrance requirements:* For master's, GMAT, resume; for doctorate, GMAT, interview, minimum GPA of 3.4, resume, letter of recommendation. Additional exam requirements/recommendations for international students: Required—TOEFL (minimum score 550 paper-based). *Application deadline:* For fall admission, 8/1 for domestic students; for spring admission, 12/1 for domestic students. Application fee: $35 ($60 for international students). *Expenses: Tuition, area resident:* Full-time $10,240; part-time $503 per credit hour. Tuition, state resident: full-time $10,464. Tuition, nonresident: full-time $20,224; part-time $991 per credit hour. *Required fees:* $850; $106 per credit hour. *Financial support:* Research assistantships with full tuition reimbursements, teaching assistantships with full tuition reimbursements, career-related internships or fieldwork, Federal Work-Study, scholarships/grants, and unspecified assistantships available. Financial award application deadline: 2/15; financial award applicants required to submit FAFSA. *Faculty research:* Competitive business strategy, finance microstructures, supply chain management innovations, health care economics, litigation risks and corporate audits. *Unit head:* Dr. Balaji Krishnan, Director, MBA Programs, 901-678-2786, E-mail: krishnan@memphis.edu. *Application contact:* Dr. Balaji Krishnan, Director, MBA Programs, 901-678-2786, E-mail: krishnan@memphis.edu. Website: https://www.memphis.edu/mba/index.php

University of Memphis, Graduate School, Fogelman College of Business and Economics, School of Accountancy, Memphis, TN 38152. Offers accounting (MS). *Accreditation:* AACSB. *Students:* 37 full-time (19 women), 36 part-time (16 women); includes 22 minority (14 Black or African American, non-Hispanic/Latino; 5 Asian, non-Hispanic/Latino; 1 Hispanic/Latino; 2 Two or more races, non-Hispanic/Latino), 6

international. Average age 29. 45 applicants, 93% accepted, 17 enrolled. In 2018, 42 master's awarded. *Degree requirements:* For master's, comprehensive exam. *Entrance requirements:* For master's, GMAT. Additional exam requirements/recommendations for international students: Required—TOEFL (minimum score 550 paper-based; 79 iBT). *Application deadline:* For fall admission, 8/1 for domestic students; for spring admission, 12/1 for domestic students. Application fee: $35 ($60 for international students). Electronic applications accepted. *Expenses: Tuition, area resident:* Full-time $10,240; part-time $503 per credit hour. Tuition, state resident: full-time $10,464. Tuition, nonresident: full-time $20,224; part-time $991 per credit hour. *Required fees:* $850; $106 per credit hour. *Financial support:* Research assistantships with full tuition reimbursements, teaching assistantships with full tuition reimbursements, Federal Work-Study, scholarships/grants, and unspecified assistantships available. Financial award application deadline: 2/1; financial award applicants required to submit FAFSA. *Faculty research:* Financial accounting, corporate governance, EDP auditing, evolution of system analysis, investor behavior and investment decisions. *Unit head:* Dr. Kenton Walker, Director, 901-678-4569, E-mail: kbwalker@memphis.edu. *Application contact:* Dr. Jim Lukawitz, Master's Program Advisor, 901-678-3030, E-mail: jlukawtz@memphis.edu. Website: http://www.memphis.edu/accountancy/

University of Miami, Miami Business School, Coral Gables, FL 33146. Offers accounting (M Acc); business (PhD); business administration (MBA); business analytics (MSBA); economics (PhD); finance (MSF); health administration (MHA); international business (MIBS); real estate (MBA); taxation (MS Tax); JD/MBA; MD/MBA. *Accreditation:* AACSB; CAHME (one or more programs are accredited). *Program availability:* Part-time, evening/weekend, 100% online, blended/hybrid learning. *Faculty:* 155 full-time (47 women), 14 part-time/adjunct (5 women). *Students:* 1,083 full-time (469 women); includes 422 minority (79 Black or African American, non-Hispanic/Latino; 1 American Indian or Alaska Native, non-Hispanic/Latino; 43 Asian, non-Hispanic/Latino; 274 Hispanic/Latino; 3 Native Hawaiian or other Pacific Islander, non-Hispanic/Latino; 22 Two or more races, non-Hispanic/Latino), 282 international. Average age 30. 2,564 applicants, 38% accepted, 450 enrolled. In 2018, 558 master's, 5 doctorates awarded. Terminal master's awarded for partial completion of doctoral program. *Degree requirements:* For master's, comprehensive exam; for doctorate, comprehensive exam, thesis/dissertation. *Entrance requirements:* For master's, GMAT or GRE; for doctorate, GRE General Test. Additional exam requirements/recommendations for international students: Required—TOEFL (minimum score 94 iBT), IELTS (minimum score 7), TOEFL (minimum score 587 paper-based, 94 iBT) or IELTS (7). *Application deadline:* For fall admission, 6/30 priority date for domestic students, 5/30 priority date for international students; for spring admission, 10/31 priority date for domestic students, 9/30 priority date for international students. Applications are processed on a rolling basis. Application fee: $48. Electronic applications accepted. *Expenses:* Contact institution. *Financial support:* In 2018–19, 643 students received support, including 1 fellowship with full tuition reimbursement available (averaging $20,000 per year), 47 research assistantships with full and partial tuition reimbursements available (averaging $28,826 per year), 6 teaching assistantships with full and partial tuition reimbursements available (averaging $2,183 per year); career-related internships or fieldwork, Federal Work-Study, institutionally sponsored loans, scholarships/grants, and unspecified assistantships also available. Support available to part-time students. Financial award application deadline: 3/26; financial award applicants required to submit FAFSA. *Faculty research:* Behavioral finance; computational economics; consumer research; risk perception; consumer behavior; consumer choice research; behavioral decision theory; business analytics; point processes; longitudinal data analyses; international business; global business strategy, joint ventures, and alliances; emerging economies; global economic growth and development, money and financial markets, and computed dynamic models; health policy; innovative payment mechanisms. *Total annual research expenditures:* $703,773. *Unit head:* Dr. John Quelch, Dean, 305-284-6515, Fax: 305-284-6526, E-mail: jquelch@miami.edu. *Application contact:* Loubna Bouamane, Director of Graduate Business Recruiting and Admissions, 305-284-2510, Fax: 305-284-5905, E-mail: loubna@miami.edu. Website: www.mbs.miami.edu.

University of Michigan, Ross School of Business, Ann Arbor, MI 48109-1234. Offers accounting (M Acc); business (MBA); business administration (PhD); supply chain management (MSCM); JD/MBA; MBA/M Arch; MBA/M Eng; MBA/MA; MBA/MEM; MBA/MHSA; MBA/MM; MBA/MPP; MBA/MS; MBA/MSE; MBA/MSI; MBA/MSW; MBA/MUP; MD/MBA; MHSA/MBA. *Accreditation:* AACSB. *Program availability:* Part-time, evening/weekend. *Degree requirements:* For doctorate, comprehensive exam, thesis/dissertation, oral defense of dissertation, preliminary exam. *Entrance requirements:* For master's, GMAT or GRE, completion of equivalent of four-year U.S. bachelor's degree, two letters of recommendation, essays, resume; for doctorate, GMAT or GRE. Additional exam requirements/recommendations for international students: Required—TOEFL (minimum score 600 paper-based; 100 iBT). Electronic applications accepted. *Faculty research:* Finance and accounting, marketing, technology and operations management, corporate strategy, management and organizations.

University of Michigan–Dearborn, College of Business, MS Program in Accounting, Dearborn, MI 48126. Offers MS. *Program availability:* Part-time, evening/weekend. *Faculty:* 41 full-time (17 women), 9 part-time/adjunct (6 women). *Students:* 14 full-time (9 women), 25 part-time (16 women); includes 8 minority (1 Black or African American, non-Hispanic/Latino; 4 Asian, non-Hispanic/Latino; 2 Hispanic/Latino; 1 Two or more races, non-Hispanic/Latino), 4 international. Average age 30. 25 applicants, 76% accepted, 12 enrolled. In 2018, 11 master's awarded. *Entrance requirements:* For master's, GMAT or GRE, equivalent of four-year U.S. bachelor's degree from regionally-accredited institution, undergraduate course in finite math, pre-calculus, or calculus. Additional exam requirements/recommendations for international students: Required—TOEFL (minimum score 560 paper-based; 84 iBT), IELTS (minimum score 6.5). *Application deadline:* For fall admission, 8/1 for domestic students, 5/1 for international students; for winter admission, 12/1 for domestic students, 9/1 for international students; for spring admission, 4/1 for domestic students, 1/1 for international students. Applications are processed on a rolling basis. Application fee: $60. Electronic applications accepted. *Expenses:* $15,740 (typical full-time in-state); $24,308 (typical full-time out-of-state). *Financial support:* In 2018–19, 15 students received support. Scholarships/grants and non-resident tuition scholarships available. Financial award application deadline: 3/1; financial award applicants required to submit FAFSA. *Faculty research:* Business intelligence, behavioral finance, brand management and new media, management education, operations strategy. *Unit head:* Dr. Michael Kamen, Director, College of Business Graduate Programs, 313-593-5460, E-mail: mkamen@umich.edu. *Application contact:* Joan Doherty, Academic Advisor/Counselor, 313-593-5460, Fax: 313-271-9838, E-mail: umd-gradbusiness@umich.edu. Website: http://umdearborn.edu/cob/ms-accounting/

University of Michigan–Flint, School of Management, Program in Accounting, Flint, MI 48502-1950. Offers MSA, Post-Master's Certificate. *Program availability:* Part-time, evening/weekend, mixed mode format. *Faculty:* 30 full-time (4 women), 10 part-time/adjunct (2 women). *Students:* 4 full-time (2 women), 28 part-time (11 women); includes 10 minority (4 Black or African American, non-Hispanic/Latino; 1 American Indian or Alaska Native, non-Hispanic/Latino; 3 Asian, non-Hispanic/Latino; 2 Two or more races, non-

Hispanic/Latino), 6 international. Average age 33. 22 applicants, 59% accepted, 7 enrolled. In 2018, 25 master's awarded. *Entrance requirements:* For master's, bachelor's degree in arts, sciences, engineering, or business administration from regionally-accredited college or university; for Post-Master's Certificate, MBA or equivalent degree from accredited college or university (for Post-Master's Certificate). Additional exam requirements/recommendations for international students: Required—TOEFL (minimum score 84 iBT), IELTS (minimum score 3.5). *Application deadline:* For fall admission, 8/1 for domestic students, 5/1 for international students; for winter admission, 11/15 for domestic students, 9/1 for international students; for spring admission, 3/15 for domestic students, 1/1 for international students; for summer admission, 5/15 for domestic students. Applications are processed on a rolling basis. Application fee: $55. Electronic applications accepted. *Expenses:* Contact institution. *Financial support:* Federal Work-Study, scholarships/grants, and unspecified assistantships available. Support available to part-time students. Financial award application deadline: 3/1; financial award applicants required to submit FAFSA. *Unit head:* Dr. Scott Johnson, Dean, School of Management, 810-762-3164, Fax: 810-237-6685, E-mail: scotjohn@umflint.edu. *Application contact:* Matt Bohlen, Director of Graduate Admissions, 810-762-3171, Fax: 810-766-6789, E-mail: mbohlen@umflint.edu.
Website: http://www.umflint.edu/graduateprograms/accounting-msa

University of Michigan–Flint, School of Management, Program in Business Administration, Flint, MI 48502-1950. Offers accounting (MBA); computer information systems (MBA); finance (MBA, Post-Master's Certificate); general business (Graduate Certificate); general business administration (MBA); health care management (MBA); international business (MBA, Post-Master's Certificate); lean manufacturing (MBA); marketing (Post-Master's Certificate); marketing and innovation management (MBA); organizational leadership (MBA). *Program availability:* Part-time, evening/weekend, mixed mode format. *Faculty:* 30 full-time (4 women), 10 part-time/adjunct (2 women). *Students:* 24 full-time (14 women), 151 part-time (60 women); includes 45 minority (22 Black or African American, non-Hispanic/Latino; 3 American Indian or Alaska Native, non-Hispanic/Latino; 7 Asian, non-Hispanic/Latino; 9 Hispanic/Latino; 4 Two or more races, non-Hispanic/Latino), 19 international. Average age 36. 160 applicants, 75% accepted, 62 enrolled. In 2018, 50 master's, 1 other advanced degree awarded. *Entrance requirements:* For master's, bachelor's degree in arts, sciences, engineering, or business administration from regionally-accredited college or university; for other advanced degree, bachelor's degree in arts, sciences, engineering, or business administration from regionally-accredited college or university. college-level math, statistics, or quantitative course (for Graduate Certificate); MBA or equivalent degree from regionally-accredited college or university (for Post Master's Certificate). Additional exam requirements/recommendations for international students: Required—TOEFL (minimum score 84 iBT), IELTS (minimum score 6.5). *Application deadline:* For fall admission, 8/1 for domestic students, 5/1 for international students; for winter admission, 11/15 for domestic students, 9/1 for international students; for spring admission, 3/15 for domestic students, 1/1 for international students; for summer admission, 5/15 for domestic students. Applications are processed on a rolling basis. Application fee: $55. Electronic applications accepted. *Expenses:* Contact institution. *Financial support:* Federal Work-Study, scholarships/grants, and unspecified assistantships available. Support available to part-time students. Financial award application deadline: 3/1; financial award applicants required to submit FAFSA. *Unit head:* Dr. Scott Johnson, Dean, School of Management, 810-762-3164, Fax: 810-237-6685, E-mail: scotjohn@umflint.edu. *Application contact:* Matt Bohlen, Director of Graduate Admissions, 810-762-3171, E-mail: mbohlen@umflint.edu.
Website: http://www.umflint.edu/graduateprograms/business-administration-mba

University of Minnesota, Twin Cities Campus, Carlson School of Management, Doctoral Program in Business Administration, Minneapolis, MN 55455-0213. Offers accounting (PhD); finance (PhD); information and decision sciences (PhD); marketing (PhD); strategic management and entrepreneurship (PhD); supply chain and operations (PhD); work and organizations (PhD). *Faculty:* 106 full-time (33 women). *Students:* 88 full-time (34 women); includes 9 minority (2 Black or African American, non-Hispanic/Latino; 6 Asian, non-Hispanic/Latino; 1 Hispanic/Latino), 66 international. Average age 30. 306 applicants, 8% accepted, 15 enrolled. In 2018, 14 doctorates awarded. *Degree requirements:* For doctorate, comprehensive exam, thesis/dissertation, written and oral preliminary exams, proposal defense, final defense. *Entrance requirements:* For doctorate, GMAT or GRE, minimum undergraduate GPA of 3.0, graduate 3.5 (recommended). Additional exam requirements/recommendations for international students: Required—Either or: TOEFL or IELTS; Recommended—TOEFL, IELTS. *Application deadline:* For fall admission, 12/15 for domestic students, 12/15 priority date for international students. Applications are processed on a rolling basis. Application fee: $75 ($95 for international students). Electronic applications accepted. *Financial support:* In 2018–19, 80 students received support, including 80 fellowships with full tuition reimbursements available (averaging $12,500 per year), 72 research assistantships with full tuition reimbursements available (averaging $7,800 per year), 72 teaching assistantships with full tuition reimbursements available (averaging $7,800 per year); health care benefits, unspecified assistantships, and full student service fee waivers also available. Financial award application deadline: 12/15. *Faculty research:* Finance, strategy and entrepreneurship, marketing, information and decision science, operations, accounting, supply chain, human resources and industrial relations, organizational behavior. *Unit head:* Dr. Shawn P. Curley, Director, 612-624-6546, Fax: 612-624-8221, E-mail: curley@umn.edu. *Application contact:* Sandy Herzan, Associate Director, 612-624-0875, Fax: 612-624-8221, E-mail: herza002@umn.edu.
Website: http://carlsonschool.umn.edu/degrees/phd

University of Minnesota, Twin Cities Campus, Carlson School of Management, Master's Program in Accountancy, Minneapolis, MN 55455-0213. Offers M Acc. *Accreditation:* AACSB. *Program availability:* Part-time. *Faculty:* 23 full-time (5 women), 1 part-time/adjunct (0 women). *Students:* 50 full-time (23 women), 4 part-time (2 women); includes 4 minority (all Asian, non-Hispanic/Latino), 18 international. Average age 26. 124 applicants, 50% accepted, 43 enrolled. In 2018, 34 master's awarded. *Entrance requirements:* For master's, GMAT, letters of recommendation. Additional exam requirements/recommendations for international students: Required—TOEFL (minimum score 550 paper-based; 79 iBT), IELTS (minimum score 6.5). *Application deadline:* For fall admission, 2/1 priority date for domestic and international students; for spring admission, 10/1 priority date for domestic and international students. Applications are processed on a rolling basis. Application fee: $75 ($95 for international students). Electronic applications accepted. *Expenses:* $21,100 resident tuition for 2 semesters, $580 semester Carlson School fee, $436.60 semester student service fee, $24 transportation fee, $75 capital enhancement fee, $16.23 professional student government fee, $6 stadium fee. *Financial support:* In 2018–19, 35 students received support, including 6 teaching assistantships with partial tuition reimbursements available (averaging $9,000 per year); scholarships/grants also available. Financial award application deadline: 7/15. *Faculty research:* Capital market-based accounting, cognitive skill acquisition in auditing, incentives and control in organizations, economic consequences of securities regulation, earnings management. *Unit head:* Clayton Forester, Director of Graduate Studies, 612-626-7532, E-mail: claytonf@umn.edu. *Application contact:* Rhonda Bjurlin, Information Contact, 612-625-6516, E-mail: macct@umn.edu.
Website: http://carlsonschool.umn.edu/degrees/master-accountancy

University of Mississippi, Graduate School, School of Accountancy, University, MS 38677. Offers accountancy (M Acc, PhD); accounting and data analytics (MA); taxation accounting (M Tax). *Accreditation:* AACSB. *Faculty:* 20 full-time (6 women), 2 part-time/adjunct (both women). *Students:* 228 full-time (102 women), 4 part-time (2 women); includes 32 minority (16 Black or African American, non-Hispanic/Latino; 4 Asian, non-Hispanic/Latino; 5 Hispanic/Latino; 1 Native Hawaiian or other Pacific Islander, non-Hispanic/Latino; 6 Two or more races, non-Hispanic/Latino), 7 international. Average age 24. In 2018, 131 master's, 2 doctorates awarded. *Entrance requirements:* For master's, GMAT, minimum GPA of 3.0; for doctorate, GMAT. Additional exam requirements/recommendations for international students: Required—TOEFL. *Application deadline:* Applications are processed on a rolling basis. Application fee: $50. Electronic applications accepted. *Financial support:* Scholarships/grants available. Financial award application deadline: 3/1; financial award applicants required to submit FAFSA. *Unit head:* Dr. W. Mark Wilder, Dean, School of Accountancy, 662-915-7468, Fax: 662-915-7483, E-mail: umaccy@olemiss.edu. *Application contact:* Tameka Smith, Graduate Activities Specialist for Admissions, 662-915-7474, Fax: 662-915-7577, E-mail: gschool@olemiss.edu.
Website: https://www.olemiss.edu

University of Missouri, Office of Research and Graduate Studies, Robert J. Trulaske, Sr. College of Business, School of Accountancy, Columbia, MO 65211. Offers accountancy (M Acc, PhD); taxation (Certificate). *Accreditation:* AACSB. *Program availability:* Part-time. *Degree requirements:* For master's, thesis or alternative; for doctorate, thesis/dissertation. *Entrance requirements:* For master's and doctorate, GMAT, minimum GPA of 3.0. Additional exam requirements/recommendations for international students: Required—TOEFL (minimum score 600 paper-based; 100 iBT). Electronic applications accepted.

University of Missouri–Kansas City, Henry W. Bloch School of Management, Kansas City, MO 64110-2499. Offers accounting (MS); finance (MS); public affairs (MPA, PhD); JD/MBA; LL M/MPA. PhD (interdisciplinary) offered through the School of Graduate Studies. *Accreditation:* AACSB; NASPAA. *Program availability:* Part-time, evening/weekend. Terminal master's awarded for partial completion of doctoral program. *Entrance requirements:* For master's, GMAT, GRE, 2 essays, 2 references, support of employer; for doctorate, GRE, minimum GPA of 3.0. Additional exam requirements/recommendations for international students: Required—TOEFL (minimum score 550 paper-based; 80 iBT). Electronic applications accepted. *Faculty research:* Entrepreneurship, finance, non-profit, risk management.

University of Missouri–St. Louis, College of Business Administration, St. Louis, MO 63121. Offers accounting (M Acc); business administration (MBA, DBA, PhD, Certificate), including logistics and supply chain management (PhD); business intelligence (Certificate); cybersecurity (Certificate); digital and social media marketing (Certificate); human resources management (Certificate); information systems (MS); logistics and supply chain management (Certificate); marketing management (Certificate). *Program availability:* Part-time, evening/weekend. *Degree requirements:* For doctorate, thesis/dissertation. *Entrance requirements:* For master's, GMAT, 2 letters of recommendation; for doctorate, GMAT or GRE, 3 letters of recommendation. Additional exam requirements/recommendations for international students: Recommended—TOEFL (minimum score 550 paper-based; 79 iBT), IELTS (minimum score 6.5). Electronic applications accepted. *Faculty research:* Statistical decision aids, commercial banking, corporate finance, operations management, information systems.

University of Montana, Graduate School, School of Business Administration, Department of Accounting and Finance, Missoula, MT 59812. Offers accounting (M Acct). *Accreditation:* AACSB. *Degree requirements:* For master's, thesis optional. *Entrance requirements:* For master's, GMAT. Additional exam requirements/recommendations for international students: Required—TOEFL (minimum score 580 paper-based). *Faculty research:* Income tax, financial markets, nonprofit accounting, accounting information systems, auditing.

University of Nebraska at Kearney, College of Business and Technology, Department of Business, Kearney, NE 68849-0001. Offers accounting (MBA); generalist (MBA); human resources (MBA); human services (MBA); marketing (MBA). *Accreditation:* AACSB. *Program availability:* Part-time, evening/weekend. *Degree requirements:* For master's, thesis optional, capstone course. *Entrance requirements:* For master's, GRE or GMAT (if no significant managerial experience), letters of recommendation, essay, resume. Additional exam requirements/recommendations for international students: Recommended—TOEFL (minimum score 550 paper-based; 79 iBT), IELTS (minimum score 6.5). Electronic applications accepted. *Faculty research:* Small business financial management, employment law, expert systems, international trade and marketing, environmental economics.

University of Nebraska at Omaha, Graduate Studies, College of Business Administration, Department of Accounting, Omaha, NE 68182. Offers M Acc. *Program availability:* Part-time, evening/weekend. *Degree requirements:* For master's, comprehensive exam (for some programs), thesis (for some programs). *Entrance requirements:* For master's, GMAT, minimum GPA of 3.0 in undergraduate courses related to accounting, official transcript. Additional exam requirements/recommendations for international students: Required—TOEFL, IELTS, PTE. Electronic applications accepted.

University of Nebraska–Lincoln, Graduate College, College of Business Administration, Interdepartmental Area of Business, Lincoln, NE 68588. Offers accountancy (PhD); business (MBA); finance (MA, PhD), including business; management (MA, PhD), including business; marketing (MA, PhD), including business; JD/MBA; M Arch/MBA. *Accreditation:* AACSB. *Program availability:* Part-time, online learning. *Degree requirements:* For doctorate, comprehensive exam, thesis/dissertation. *Entrance requirements:* For master's and doctorate, GMAT. Additional exam requirements/recommendations for international students: Required—TOEFL (minimum score 550 paper-based). Electronic applications accepted.

University of Nebraska–Lincoln, Graduate College, College of Business Administration, School of Accountancy, Lincoln, NE 68588. Offers MPA, PhD, JD/MPA. *Accreditation:* AACSB. *Entrance requirements:* For master's, GMAT. Additional exam requirements/recommendations for international students: Required—TOEFL (minimum score 550 paper-based). Electronic applications accepted. *Faculty research:* Auditing, financial accounting, managerial accounting, capital markets, tax accounting.

University of Nevada, Las Vegas, Graduate College, Lee Business School, Department of Accounting, Las Vegas, NV 89154-6003. Offers accountancy (MS); accounting (Advanced Certificate, Certificate). *Accreditation:* AACSB. *Program availability:* Part-time. *Faculty:* 10 full-time (5 women), 5 part-time/adjunct (2 women). *Students:* 64 full-time (32 women), 42 part-time (20 women); includes 44 minority (2 Black or African American, non-Hispanic/Latino; 27 Asian, non-Hispanic/Latino; 13 Hispanic/Latino; 2 Two or more races, non-Hispanic/Latino), 16 international. Average age 29. 52 applicants, 58% accepted, 20 enrolled. In 2018, 61 master's awarded. *Entrance requirements:* For master's, GMAT, bachelor's degree with minimum GPA 3.0. Additional exam requirements/recommendations for international students: Required—TOEFL (minimum score 550 paper-based; 80 iBT), IELTS (minimum score 7). *Application deadline:* For fall admission, 8/1 for domestic students, 5/1 for international

students; for spring admission, 12/1 for domestic students, 10/1 for international students; for summer admission, 5/15 for domestic students, 3/1 for international students. Application fee: $60 ($95 for international students). Electronic applications accepted. *Expenses:* Contact institution. *Financial support:* In 2018–19, 15 students received support, including 4 research assistantships with full tuition reimbursements available (averaging $11,688 per year), 11 teaching assistantships with full tuition reimbursements available (averaging $11,250 per year); institutionally sponsored loans, scholarships/grants, health care benefits, and unspecified assistantships also available. Financial award application deadline: 3/15; financial award applicants required to submit FAFSA. *Faculty research:* Audit judgments and decision-making, fraud, corporate governance, information systems technology and decision-making, internal audit. *Total annual research expenditures:* $200. *Unit head:* Dr. Bob Cornell, Chair/Associate Professor, 702-895-4323, E-mail: accounting.chair@unlv.edu. *Application contact:* Dr. Kim Charron, Graduate Coordinator, 702-895-3975, E-mail: accounting.gradcoord@unlv.edu.
Website: http://business.unlv.edu/accounting/

University of Nevada, Reno, Graduate School, College of Business, Department of Accounting, Reno, NV 89557. Offers M Acc. *Accreditation:* AACSB. *Entrance requirements:* For master's, GMAT or GRE (if undergraduate degree is not from an AACSB-accredited business school with minimum GPA of 3.5), minimum GPA of 2.75. Additional exam requirements/recommendations for international students: Required—TOEFL (minimum score 500 paper-based; 61 iBT), IELTS (minimum score 6). Electronic applications accepted. *Faculty research:* Financial reporting/auditing, taxation.

University of New Hampshire, Graduate School, Peter T. Paul College of Business and Economics, Department of Accounting and Finance, Durham, NH 03824. Offers accounting (MS). *Program availability:* Part-time. *Entrance requirements:* For master's, GMAT. Additional exam requirements/recommendations for international students: Required—TOEFL (minimum score 550 paper-based; 80 iBT). Electronic applications accepted.

University of New Haven, Graduate School, College of Business, Program in Accounting, West Haven, CT 06516. Offers MS, Graduate Certificate. *Accreditation:* AACSB. *Students:* 26 full-time (11 women), 3 part-time (1 woman); includes 13 minority (6 Black or African American, non-Hispanic/Latino; 5 Asian, non-Hispanic/Latino; 2 Hispanic/Latino), 5 international. Average age 29. 33 applicants, 100% accepted, 18 enrolled. In 2018, 2 master's, 1 other advanced degree awarded. *Application deadline:* Applications are processed on a rolling basis. Application fee: $50. *Expenses: Tuition:* Full-time $16,470; part-time $915 per credit hour. *Required fees:* $230; $95 per term. *Financial support:* Research assistantships with partial tuition reimbursements, teaching assistantships with partial tuition reimbursements, and Federal Work-Study available. Support available to part-time students. Financial award application deadline: 5/1; financial award applicants required to submit FAFSA. *Unit head:* Michael Rolleri, Associate Professor, 203-932-7092, E-mail: mrolleri@newhaven.edu. *Application contact:* Selina O'Toole, Senior Associate Director of Graduate Admissions, 203-932-7337, E-mail: SOToole@newhaven.edu.
Website: https://www.newhaven.edu/business/graduate-programs/accounting/

University of New Haven, Graduate School, College of Business, Program in Business Administration, West Haven, CT 06516. Offers accounting (MBA); business administration (MBA); business intelligence (MBA); business policy and strategic leadership (MBA); finance (MBA), including chartered financial analyst; global marketing (MBA); human resources management (MBA); sport management (MBA). *Accreditation:* AACSB. *Program availability:* Part-time, evening/weekend. *Students:* 151 full-time (73 women), 70 part-time (30 women); includes 51 minority (23 Black or African American, non-Hispanic/Latino; 13 Asian, non-Hispanic/Latino; 14 Hispanic/Latino; 1 Two or more races, non-Hispanic/Latino), 74 international. Average age 28. 197 applicants, 91% accepted, 82 enrolled. In 2018, 70 master's awarded. *Entrance requirements:* For master's, GMAT. Additional exam requirements/recommendations for international students: Required—TOEFL (minimum score 80 iBT), IELTS, PTE. *Application deadline:* Applications are processed on a rolling basis. Application fee: $50. Electronic applications accepted. Application fee is waived when completed online. *Expenses: Tuition:* Full-time $16,470; part-time $915 per credit hour. *Required fees:* $230; $95 per term. *Financial support:* Research assistantships with partial tuition reimbursements, teaching assistantships with partial tuition reimbursements, career-related internships or fieldwork, Federal Work-Study, scholarships/grants, and unspecified assistantships available. Support available to part-time students. Financial award applicants required to submit FAFSA. *Unit head:* Darell Singleterry, Director, 203-932-7386, E-mail: dsingleterry@newhaven.edu. *Application contact:* Selina O'Toole, Senior Associate Director of Graduate Admissions, 203-932-7337, E-mail: SOToole@newhaven.edu.
Website: http://www.newhaven.edu/business/graduate-programs/mba/index.php

University of New Orleans, Graduate School, College of Business Administration, Department of Accounting, Program in Accounting, New Orleans, LA 70148. Offers MS. *Accreditation:* AACSB. *Program availability:* Part-time, evening/weekend. *Degree requirements:* For master's, thesis optional. *Entrance requirements:* For master's, GMAT. Additional exam requirements/recommendations for international students: Required—TOEFL (minimum score 550 paper-based; 79 iBT). Electronic applications accepted.

University of North Alabama, College of Business, Florence, AL 35632-0001. Offers business administration (MBA), including accounting, enterprise resource planning systems, executive, finance, health care management, information systems, international business, project management. *Accreditation:* AACSB; ACBSP. *Program availability:* Part-time, 100% online, blended/hybrid learning. *Entrance requirements:* For master's, GMAT, GRE, minimum GPA of 2.75 in last 60 hours, 2.5 overall (on a 3.0 scale); 27 hours of course work in business and economics. Additional exam requirements/recommendations for international students: Required—TOEFL (minimum score 79 iBT), IELTS (minimum score 6), PTE (minimum score 54). Electronic applications accepted.

The University of North Carolina at Chapel Hill, Kenan-Flagler Business School, Accounting Program, Chapel Hill, NC 27599. Offers MAC. *Entrance requirements:* For master's, GMAT. Additional exam requirements/recommendations for international students: Required—TOEFL. *Expenses:* Contact institution. *Faculty research:* Corporate taxation, international taxation, financial accounting, corporate governance, strategy.

The University of North Carolina at Chapel Hill, Kenan-Flagler Business School, Doctoral Program in Business Administration, Chapel Hill, NC 27599. Offers accounting (PhD); finance (PhD); marketing (PhD); operations management (PhD); organizational behavior (PhD); strategy (PhD). *Accreditation:* AACSB. *Degree requirements:* For doctorate, thesis/dissertation. *Entrance requirements:* For doctorate, GMAT or GRE General Test. Electronic applications accepted. *Expenses:* Contact institution.

The University of North Carolina at Charlotte, Belk College of Business, Turner School of Accountancy, Charlotte, NC 28223-0001. Offers M Acct. *Accreditation:* AACSB. *Program availability:* Part-time, evening/weekend. *Students:* 65 full-time (35 women), 30 part-time (12 women); includes 24 minority (3 Black or African American, non-Hispanic/Latino; 8 Asian, non-Hispanic/Latino; 11 Hispanic/Latino; 2 Two or more races, non-Hispanic/Latino), 6 international. Average age 26. 101 applicants, 76% accepted, 60 enrolled. In 2018, 68 master's awarded. *Entrance requirements:* For master's, GMAT or GRE, bachelor's degree from accredited college or university; official transcript of all previous academic work; minimum overall GPA of 3.0 on previous work beyond high school; completion of a principles of financial accounting course with minimum B grade; at least three evaluations; essay. Additional exam requirements/recommendations for international students: Required—TOEFL (minimum score 523 paper-based; 70 iBT), IELTS (minimum score 6), TOEFL (minimum score 523 paper-based, 70 iBT) or IELTS (6.0). *Application deadline:* Applications are processed on a rolling basis. Application fee: $75. Electronic applications accepted. *Expenses:* Contact institution. *Financial support:* Research assistantships, teaching assistantships, career-related internships or fieldwork, institutionally sponsored loans, scholarships/grants, and unspecified assistantships available. Support available to part-time students. Financial award application deadline: 3/1; financial award applicants required to submit FAFSA. *Faculty research:* Corporate financial reporting trends, use of latest software for accounting and business applications, latest developments in federal and international taxation. *Unit head:* Dr. Hughlene Burton, Chair, 704-687-7701, Fax: 704-687-1382, E-mail: haburton@uncc.edu. *Application contact:* Kathy B. Giddings, Director of Graduate Admissions, 704-687-5503, Fax: 704-687-1668, E-mail: gradadm@uncc.edu.
Website: http://belkcollege.uncc.edu/departments/accounting

The University of North Carolina at Greensboro, Graduate School, Bryan School of Business and Economics, Department of Accounting and Finance, Greensboro, NC 27412-5001. Offers accounting (MS); financial analysis (PMC). *Accreditation:* AACSB. *Entrance requirements:* For master's, GMAT, GRE General Test, previous course work in accounting and business. Additional exam requirements/recommendations for international students: Required—TOEFL. Electronic applications accepted.

The University of North Carolina Wilmington, Cameron School of Business, Accountancy Program, Wilmington, NC 28403-3297. Offers MSA. *Degree requirements:* For master's, written and oral comprehensive case analysis. *Entrance requirements:* For master's, GMAT, 3 letters of recommendation, resume. Additional exam requirements/recommendations for international students: Required—TOEFL (minimum score 550 paper-based; 79 iBT), IELTS (minimum score 6.5). Electronic applications accepted. *Expenses:* Contact institution.

University of Northern Colorado, Graduate School, Monfort College of Business, Greeley, CO 80639. Offers accounting (MA); general business management (MBA); healthcare administration (MBA); human resources management (MBA). *Accreditation:* AACSB.

University of Northern Iowa, Graduate College, College of Business Administration, M Acc Program in Accounting, Cedar Falls, IA 50614. Offers M Acc. *Degree requirements:* For master's, thesis or alternative. *Entrance requirements:* For master's, GMAT. Additional exam requirements/recommendations for international students: Required—TOEFL (minimum score 575 paper-based; 89 iBT).

University of North Florida, Coggin College of Business, M Acc Program, Jacksonville, FL 32224. Offers M Acc. *Accreditation:* AACSB. *Program availability:* Part-time, evening/weekend. *Faculty:* 16 full-time (3 women), 1 part-time/adjunct (0 women). *Students:* 39 full-time (20 women), 30 part-time (17 women); includes 14 minority (4 Black or African American, non-Hispanic/Latino; 3 Asian, non-Hispanic/Latino; 2 Hispanic/Latino; 5 Two or more races, non-Hispanic/Latino), 3 international. Average age 27. 63 applicants, 60% accepted, 24 enrolled. In 2018, 29 master's awarded. *Entrance requirements:* For master's, GMAT or GRE, U.S. bachelor's degree from regionally-accredited university or equivalent foreign degree. Additional exam requirements/recommendations for international students: Required—TOEFL (minimum score 550 paper-based; 79 iBT). *Application deadline:* For fall admission, 8/1 priority date for domestic students, 5/1 for international students; for spring admission, 12/1 priority date for domestic students, 10/1 for international students; for summer admission, 3/15 priority date for domestic students, 2/1 for international students. Application fee: $30. Electronic applications accepted. *Expenses: Tuition, area resident:* Part-time $408.10 per credit hour. Tuition, state resident: part-time $408.10 per credit hour. Tuition, nonresident: part-time $932.61 per credit hour. *Required fees:* $111.81 per credit hour. Tuition and fees vary according to course load, campus/location and program. *Financial support:* Career-related internships or fieldwork, Federal Work-Study, and tuition waivers (partial) available. Financial award application deadline: 4/1; financial award applicants required to submit FAFSA. *Faculty research:* Enterprise-wide risk management, accounting input in the strategic planning process, accounting information systems, taxation issues in lawsuits and damage awards, database design. *Unit head:* Dr. David Jaeger, Chair, 904-620-2630, E-mail: djaeger@unf.edu. *Application contact:* Dr. Amanda Pascale, Director, The Graduate School, 904-620-1360, Fax: 904-620-1362, E-mail: graduateschool@unf.edu.
Website: http://www.unf.edu/coggin/academics/graduate/macc.aspx

University of North Florida, Coggin College of Business, MBA Program, Jacksonville, FL 32224. Offers accounting (MBA); construction management (MBA); e-commerce (MBA); economics (MBA); finance (MBA); human resource management (MBA); international business (MBA); logistics (MBA); management applications (MBA). *Accreditation:* AACSB. *Program availability:* Part-time, evening/weekend. *Faculty:* 40 full-time (14 women). *Students:* 368 part-time (158 women); includes 83 minority (30 Black or African American, non-Hispanic/Latino; 20 Asian, non-Hispanic/Latino; 16 Hispanic/Latino; 17 Two or more races, non-Hispanic/Latino), 28 international. Average age 30. 311 applicants, 51% accepted, 99 enrolled. In 2018, 151 master's awarded. *Entrance requirements:* For master's, GMAT or GRE, U.S. bachelor's degree from regionally-accredited university or equivalent foreign degree. Additional exam requirements/recommendations for international students: Required—TOEFL (minimum score 550 paper-based; 79 iBT). *Application deadline:* For fall admission, 8/1 priority date for domestic students, 5/1 for international students; for spring admission, 12/1 priority date for domestic students, 10/1 for international students; for summer admission, 4/29 priority date for domestic students, 2/1 for international students. Application fee: $30. *Expenses: Tuition, area resident:* Part-time $408.10 per credit hour. Tuition, state resident: part-time $408.10 per credit hour. Tuition, nonresident: part-time $932.61 per credit hour. *Required fees:* $111.81 per credit hour. Tuition and fees vary according to course load, campus/location and program. *Financial support:* In 2018–19, 41 students received support, including 1 research assistantship (averaging $2,143 per year); teaching assistantships, Federal Work-Study, and tuition waivers (partial) also available. Support available to part-time students. Financial award application deadline: 4/1; financial award applicants required to submit FAFSA. *Faculty research:* Performance measures, costing, and inventory issues in logistics and supply chain management; inter-organizational systems; international management and marketing practices; e-commerce; organizational learning and socialization processes. *Unit head:* Dr. Parvez Ahmed, Graduate Program Director, 904-620-1678, E-mail: pahmed@unf.edu. *Application contact:* Amy Bishop, MSM Advisor, 904-620-2575, Fax: 904-620-2832, E-mail: coggin.students@unf.edu.
Website: http://www.unf.edu/graduateschool/academics/programs/MBA.aspx

University of North Texas, Toulouse Graduate School, Denton, TX 76203-5459. Offers accounting (MS); applied anthropology (MA, MS); applied behavior analysis (Certificate); applied geography (MA); applied technology and performance improvement (M Ed, MS); art education (MA); art history (MA); arts leadership (Certificate); audiology (Au D); behavior analysis (MS); behavioral science (PhD); biochemistry and molecular biology

(MS); biology (MA, MS); biomedical engineering (MS); business analysis (MS); chemistry (MS); clinical health psychology (PhD); communication studies (MA, MS); computer engineering (MS); computer science (MS); counseling (M Ed, MS), including clinical mental health counseling (MS), college and university counseling, elementary school counseling, secondary school counseling; creative writing (MA); criminal justice (MS); curriculum and instruction (M Ed); decision sciences (MBA); design (MA, MFA), including fashion design (MFA), innovation studies, interior design (MFA); early childhood studies (MS); economics (MS); educational leadership (M Ed, Ed D); educational psychology (MS, PhD), including family studies (MS), gifted and talented (MS), human development (MS), learning and cognition (MS), research, measurement and evaluation (MS); electrical engineering (MS); emergency management (MPA); engineering technology (MS); English (MA); English as a second language (MA); environmental science (MS); finance (MBA, MS); financial management (MPA); French (MA); health services management (MBA); higher education (M Ed, Ed D); history (MA, MS); hospitality management (MS); human resources management (MPA); information science (MS); information systems (PhD); information technologies (MBA); interdisciplinary studies (MA, MS); international studies (MA); international sustainable tourism (MS); jazz studies (MM); journalism (MA, MJ, Graduate Certificate), including interactive and virtual digital communication (Graduate Certificate), narrative journalism (Graduate Certificate), public relations (Graduate Certificate); kinesiology (MS); linguistics (MA); local government management (MPA); logistics (PhD); logistics and supply chain management (MBA); long-term care, senior housing, and aging services (MA); management (PhD); marketing (MBA); mathematics (MA, MS); mechanical and energy engineering (MS, PhD); music (MA), including ethnomusicology, music theory, musicology, performance; music composition (PhD); music education (MM Ed, PhD); nonprofit management (MPA); operations and supply chain management (MBA); performance (MM, DMA); philosophy (MA); political science (MA); professional and technical communication (MA); radio, television and film (MA, MFA); rehabilitation counseling (Certificate); sociology (MA); Spanish (MA); special education (M Ed); speech-language pathology (MA); strategic management (MBA); studio art (MFA); teaching (M Ed); MBA/MS. *Program availability:* Part-time, evening/weekend, online learning. Terminal master's awarded for partial completion of doctoral program. *Degree requirements:* For master's, variable foreign language requirement, comprehensive exam (for some programs), thesis (for some programs); for doctorate, variable foreign language requirement, comprehensive exam (for some programs), thesis/dissertation; for other advanced degree, variable foreign language requirement, comprehensive exam (for some programs). *Entrance requirements:* For master's and doctorate, GRE, GMAT. Additional exam requirements/recommendations for international students: Required—TOEFL (minimum score 550 paper-based; 79 iBT). Electronic applications accepted.

University of North Texas at Dallas, Graduate School, Dallas, TX 75241. Offers accounting (MBA); counseling (M Ed, MS); criminal justice (MS); curriculum and instruction (M Ed); educational administration (M Ed); human resources and organizational behavior (MBA); public leadership (MS); strategic management (MBA).

University of Notre Dame, Mendoza College of Business, Master of Science in Accountancy Program, Notre Dame, IN 46556. Offers assurance and advisory services (MSA); tax services (MSA). *Accreditation:* AACSB. *Entrance requirements:* For master's, GMAT, essay, two recommendations, transcripts from all colleges or universities attended, resume, interview, course descriptions for accounting prerequisites. Additional exam requirements/recommendations for international students: Required—PTE (minimum score 68), TOEFL (minimum iBT score of 109), IELTS (7.5), or documentation of at least six semesters of full-time university education in English. Electronic applications accepted. *Expenses:* Contact institution. *Faculty research:* Stock valuation, accounting information in decision-making, choice of accounting method, taxes cost on capital.

University of Oklahoma, Price College of Business, John T. Steed School of Accounting, Norman, OK 73019. Offers M Acc. *Accreditation:* AACSB. *Program availability:* Part-time, 100% online. *Faculty:* 13 full-time (4 women). *Students:* 10 full-time (7 women), 76 part-time (39 women); includes 33 minority (12 Black or African American, non-Hispanic/Latino; 1 American Indian or Alaska Native, non-Hispanic/Latino; 4 Asian, non-Hispanic/Latino; 12 Hispanic/Latino; 1 Native Hawaiian or other Pacific Islander, non-Hispanic/Latino; 3 Two or more races, non-Hispanic/Latino), 2 international. Average age 35. 71 applicants, 73% accepted, 33 enrolled. In 2018, 19 master's awarded. *Entrance requirements:* For master's, GMAT or GRE, resume, statement of goals, 3 letters of recommendation. Additional exam requirements/recommendations for international students: Required—TOEFL (minimum score 100 iBT) or IELTS (minimum score 7). *Application deadline:* For fall admission, 6/15 for domestic students, 3/1 for international students; for spring admission, 11/15 for domestic students, 8/1 for international students; for summer admission, 3/15 for domestic students, 1/1 for international students. Applications are processed on a rolling basis. Application fee: $50 ($100 for international students). Electronic applications accepted. *Expenses:* Contact institution. *Financial support:* In 2018–19, 15 students received support, including 1 fellowship (averaging $5,000 per year), 5 research assistantships (averaging $14,940 per year), 9 teaching assistantships (averaging $13,701 per year); career-related internships or fieldwork, scholarships/grants, and unspecified assistantships also available. Support available to part-time students. Financial award application deadline: 6/1; financial award applicants required to submit FAFSA. *Faculty research:* Tax professional judgment and taxpayer compliance; financial disclosure and reporting decisions; regulation and auditing profession; behavioral issues of auditor-client dyad; market based accounting research. *Unit head:* Wayne Thomas, Director/Chair, 405-325-5799, Fax: 405-325-7348, E-mail: wthomas@ou.edu. *Application contact:* Jennifer Aragon, Academic Advisor, 405-325-2074, Fax: 405-325-7118, E-mail: jhardman@ou.edu.
Website: http://www.ou.edu/content/price/accounting.html

University of Oregon, Graduate School, Charles H. Lundquist College of Business, Department of Accounting, Eugene, OR 97403. Offers M Actg, PhD. *Accreditation:* AACSB. *Program availability:* Part-time. *Degree requirements:* For doctorate, thesis/dissertation, 2 comprehensive exams. *Entrance requirements:* For master's, GMAT, minimum GPA of 3.0, bachelor's degree in accounting or equivalent; for doctorate, GMAT. Additional exam requirements/recommendations for international students: Required—TOEFL. *Faculty research:* Empirical financial accounting, effects of regulation on accounting standards, use of protocol analysis as a research methodology in accounting.

University of Pennsylvania, Wharton School, Accounting Department, Philadelphia, PA 19104. Offers MBA, PhD. *Accreditation:* AACSB. Terminal master's awarded for partial completion of doctoral program. *Degree requirements:* For doctorate, thesis/dissertation. *Entrance requirements:* For master's, GMAT; for doctorate, GMAT or GRE. *Faculty research:* Financial reporting, information disclosure, performance measurement, executive compensation, corporate governance.

University of Phoenix–Bay Area Campus, School of Business, San Jose, CA 95134-1805. Offers accountancy (MS); accounting (MBA); business administration (MBA, DBA); energy management (MBA); global management (MBA); health care management (MBA); human resource management (MBA); human resources management (MM); management (MM); marketing (MBA); organizational leadership (DM); project management (MBA); public administration (MPA); technology management (MBA). *Accreditation:* ACBSP. *Program availability:* Evening/weekend, online learning. *Degree requirements:* For master's, thesis (for some programs). *Entrance requirements:* For master's, minimum undergraduate GPA of 3.0, 3 years of work experience. Additional exam requirements/recommendations for international students: Required—TOEFL (minimum score 550 paper-based; 79 iBT). Electronic applications accepted.

University of Phoenix–Central Valley Campus, School of Business, Fresno, CA 93720-1552. Offers accounting (MBA); business administration (MBA); global management (MBA); human resources management (MBA, MM); management (MM); marketing (MBA); public administration (MBA, MM). *Accreditation:* ACBSP.

University of Phoenix–Dallas Campus, School of Business, Dallas, TX 75251. Offers accounting (MBA); business administration (MBA); global management (MBA); human resources management (MBA, MM); management (MM); marketing (MBA); public administration (MBA, MM). *Accreditation:* ACBSP. *Program availability:* Evening/weekend, online learning. *Degree requirements:* For master's, thesis (for some programs). *Entrance requirements:* For master's, 3 years of work experience, minimum undergraduate GPA of 3.0. Additional exam requirements/recommendations for international students: Required—TOEFL (minimum score 550 paper-based; 79 iBT). Electronic applications accepted.

University of Phoenix–Hawaii Campus, School of Business, Honolulu, HI 96813-3800. Offers accounting (MBA); business administration (MBA); global management (MBA); human resources management (MBA, MM); management (MM); marketing (MBA); public administration (MBA, MM). *Accreditation:* ACBSP. *Program availability:* Evening/weekend. *Degree requirements:* For master's, thesis (for some programs). *Entrance requirements:* For master's, minimum undergraduate GPA of 3.0, 3 years of work experience. Additional exam requirements/recommendations for international students: Required—TOEFL (minimum score 550 paper-based; 79 iBT). Electronic applications accepted.

University of Phoenix–Houston Campus, School of Business, Houston, TX 77079-2004. Offers accounting (MBA); business administration (MBA); global management (MBA); human resources management (MBA, MM); management (MM); marketing (MBA); public administration (MBA, MM). *Accreditation:* ACBSP. *Program availability:* Evening/weekend, online learning. *Degree requirements:* For master's, thesis (for some programs). *Entrance requirements:* For master's, 3 years of work experience, minimum undergraduate GPA of 3.0. Additional exam requirements/recommendations for international students: Required—TOEFL (minimum score 550 paper-based; 79 iBT). Electronic applications accepted.

University of Phoenix–Las Vegas Campus, School of Business, Las Vegas, NV 89135. Offers accounting (MBA); business administration (MBA); global management (MBA); human resources management (MBA, MM); management (MM); marketing (MBA); public administration (MM). *Accreditation:* ACBSP. *Program availability:* Evening/weekend, online learning. *Degree requirements:* For master's, thesis (for some programs). *Entrance requirements:* For master's, minimum undergraduate GPA of 3.0, 3 years of work experience. Additional exam requirements/recommendations for international students: Required—TOEFL (minimum score 550 paper-based; 79 iBT). Electronic applications accepted.

University of Phoenix–Online Campus, School of Business, Phoenix, AZ 85034-7209. Offers accountancy (MS); accounting (MBA, Certificate); business administration (MBA); energy management (MBA); global management (MBA); health care management (MBA); human resource management (MBA, Certificate); human resources management (MM); management (MM); marketing (MBA, Certificate); project management (MBA, Certificate); public administration (MBA, MM); technology management (MBA). *Program availability:* Evening/weekend, online learning. *Entrance requirements:* Additional exam requirements/recommendations for international students: Required—TOEFL, TOEIC (Test of English as an International Communication), Berlitz Online English Proficiency Exam, PTE, or IELTS. Electronic applications accepted. *Expenses:* Contact institution.

University of Phoenix–Phoenix Campus, School of Business, Tempe, AZ 85282-2371. Offers accounting (MBA, MS, Certificate); business administration (MBA); energy management (MBA); global management (MBA); health care management (MBA); human resource management (MBA, Certificate); management (MM); marketing (MBA); project management (MBA); technology management (MBA). *Program availability:* Evening/weekend, online learning. *Entrance requirements:* Additional exam requirements/recommendations for international students: Required—TOEFL, TOEIC (Test of English as an International Communication), Berlitz Online English Proficiency Exam, PTE, or IELTS. Electronic applications accepted. *Expenses:* Contact institution.

University of Phoenix–Sacramento Valley Campus, School of Business, Sacramento, CA 95833-4334. Offers accounting (MBA); business administration (MBA); global management (MBA); human resources management (MBA, MM); management (MM); marketing (MBA); public administration (MBA, MM). *Accreditation:* ACBSP. *Program availability:* Evening/weekend. *Degree requirements:* For master's, thesis (for some programs). *Entrance requirements:* For master's, minimum undergraduate GPA of 3.0, 3 years work experience. Additional exam requirements/recommendations for international students: Required—TOEFL (minimum score 550 paper-based; 79 iBT). Electronic applications accepted.

University of Phoenix–San Antonio Campus, School of Business, San Antonio, TX 78230. Offers accounting (MBA); business administration (MBA); e-business (MBA); global management (MBA); human resources management (MBA, MM); management (MM); marketing (MBA); public administration (MBA, MM). *Accreditation:* ACBSP.

University of Phoenix–San Diego Campus, School of Business, San Diego, CA 92123. Offers accounting (MBA); business administration (MBA); global management (MBA); human resources management (MBA, MM); management (MM); marketing (MBA); public administration (MBA). *Accreditation:* ACBSP. *Program availability:* Evening/weekend. *Degree requirements:* For master's, thesis (for some programs). *Entrance requirements:* For master's, 3 years of work experience, minimum undergraduate GPA of 3.0. Additional exam requirements/recommendations for international students: Required—TOEFL (minimum score 550 paper-based; 79 iBT). Electronic applications accepted.

University of Pittsburgh, Katz Graduate School of Business, Doctoral Program in Business Administration, Pittsburgh, PA 15260. Offers accounting (PhD); business analytics and operations (PhD); finance (PhD); information systems and technology management (PhD); marketing (PhD); organizational behavior and human resources (PhD); strategic management (PhD). *Accreditation:* AACSB. *Program availability:* Evening/weekend. *Degree requirements:* For doctorate, comprehensive exam, thesis/dissertation, student teaching. *Entrance requirements:* For doctorate, GMAT or GRE, 3 recommendations, statement of purpose, transcripts of all previous course work and degrees. Additional exam requirements/recommendations for international students: Required—TOEFL (minimum score 100 iBT) or IELTS (minimum score 7.0). Electronic applications accepted. *Faculty research:* Accounting systems/financial reporting, corporate finance, shopper marketing/consumer behavior, management information systems, organizational behavior and entrepreneurship.

Accounting

University of Pittsburgh, Katz Graduate School of Business, Master of Science in Accounting Program, Pittsburgh, PA 15260. Offers MS. *Program availability:* Part-time, blended/hybrid learning. *Degree requirements:* For master's, 30 credits; minimum cumulative GPA of 3.0. *Entrance requirements:* For master's, GMAT, GRE. Additional exam requirements/recommendations for international students: Required—TOEFL (minimum score 100 iBT) or IELTS (minimum score 7.0). Electronic applications accepted. *Faculty research:* Accounting systems/financial reporting, corporate finance, shopper marketing/consumer behavior, management information systems, organizational behavior and entrepreneurship.

University of Puerto Rico–Río Piedras, College of Business Administration, San Juan, PR 00931-3300. Offers accounting (MBA); finance (MBA, PhD); general business (MBA); human resources management (MBA); international trade and business (MBA, PhD); marketing (MBA); operations management (MBA); quantitative methods (MBA). *Accreditation:* AACSB. *Program availability:* Part-time. *Degree requirements:* For master's, comprehensive exam, thesis or alternative, research project. *Entrance requirements:* For master's, GMAT or PAEG, minimum GPA of 3.0, letter of recommendation; for doctorate, GMAT, PAEG, minimum GPA of 3.0, master degree. *Faculty research:* Management.

University of Rhode Island, Graduate School, College of Business, Program in Accounting, Kingston, RI 02881. Offers MS. *Accreditation:* AACSB. *Faculty:* 12 full-time (7 women). *Students:* 18 full-time (5 women), 9 part-time (8 women); includes 4 minority (2 Asian, non-Hispanic/Latino; 1 Hispanic/Latino; 1 Two or more races, non-Hispanic/Latino). 22 applicants, 77% accepted, 16 enrolled. In 2018, 28 master's awarded. *Entrance requirements:* Additional exam requirements/recommendations for international students: Required—TOEFL. *Application deadline:* For fall admission, 7/15 for domestic students, 2/15 for international students. Application fee: $35. Electronic applications accepted. *Expenses: Tuition, area resident:* Full-time $13,226; part-time $735 per credit. Tuition, state resident: full-time $13,226; part-time $735 per credit. Tuition, nonresident: full-time $25,854; part-time $1436 per credit. *International tuition:* $25,854 full-time. *Required fees:* $1698; $50 per credit. $35 per semester. One-time fee: $165. *Financial support:* Application deadline: 2/1. *Unit head:* Prof. Alejandro (Alex) Hazera, Area Coordinator, 401-874-4332, E-mail: sofborder@uri.edu. *Application contact:* Prof. Alejandro (Alex) Hazera, Area Coordinator, 401-874-4332, E-mail: sofborder@uri.edu.
Website: https://web.uri.edu/business/m-s-in-accounting/

University of Rochester, Simon Business School, Doctoral Program in Business Administration, Rochester, NY 14627. Offers accounting (PhD); computer information systems (PhD); finance (PhD); marketing (PhD); operations management (PhD). *Accreditation:* AACSB. *Degree requirements:* For doctorate, comprehensive exam, thesis/dissertation, qualifying exam. *Entrance requirements:* For doctorate, GMAT or GRE. Additional exam requirements/recommendations for international students: Required—TOEFL. Electronic applications accepted. *Expenses:* Contact institution. *Faculty research:* Empirical industrial organization, risk management, financial disclosure and regulation, social media, health care management.

University of Rochester, Simon Business School, Full-Time Master's Program in Business Administration, Rochester, NY 14627. Offers business systems consulting (MBA); competitive and organizational strategy (MBA); computers and information systems (MBA); corporate accounting (MBA); entrepreneurship (MBA); finance (MBA); health sciences management (MBA); marketing (MBA); operations management (MBA); public accounting (MBA); strategy and organizations (MBA). *Accreditation:* AACSB. *Entrance requirements:* For master's, GMAT or GRE. *Expenses: Tuition:* Full-time $52,974; part-time $1654 per credit hour. *Required fees:* $612. One-time fee: $30 part-time. Tuition and fees vary according to campus/location and program. *Faculty research:* Empirical industrial organization, risk management, financial disclosure and regulation, social media, health care management.

University of Rochester, Simon Business School, Master of Science Program in Accountancy, Rochester, NY 14627. Offers MS. *Entrance requirements:* For master's, GMAT or GRE. *Expenses: Tuition:* Full-time $52,974; part-time $1654 per credit hour. *Required fees:* $612. One-time fee: $30 part-time. Tuition and fees vary according to campus/location and program. *Faculty research:* Empirical industrial organization, risk management, financial disclosure and regulation, social media, health care management.

University of Rochester, Simon Business School, Part-Time MBA Program, Rochester, NY 14627. Offers business systems consulting (MBA); competitive and organizational strategy (MBA); computers and information systems (MBA); corporate accounting (MBA); entrepreneurship (MBA); finance (MBA); health sciences management (MBA); marketing (MBA), including brand management, marketing strategy, pricing; operations management (MBA); public accounting (MBA). *Program availability:* Part-time-only, evening/weekend. *Entrance requirements:* For master's, GRE or GMAT. Electronic applications accepted. *Expenses:* Contact institution.

University of St. Francis, College of Business and Health Administration, Joliet, IL 60435-6169. Offers accounting (MBA, Certificate); business analytics (MBA, Certificate); e-learning (Certificate); finance (MBA, Certificate); health administration (MBA, MS); human resource management (MBA, Certificate); logistics (Certificate); management (MBA, MSM); management of training and development (Certificate); supply chain management (MBA); training and development (MBA); training specialist (Certificate). *Program availability:* Part-time, evening/weekend, 100% online, blended/hybrid learning. *Faculty:* 13 full-time (6 women), 20 part-time/adjunct (7 women). *Students:* 139 full-time (94 women), 206 part-time (159 women); includes 86 minority (51 Black or African American, non-Hispanic/Latino; 1 American Indian or Alaska Native, non-Hispanic/Latino; 11 Asian, non-Hispanic/Latino; 21 Hispanic/Latino; 2 Two or more races, non-Hispanic/Latino), 24 international. Average age 37. 261 applicants, 63% accepted, 98 enrolled. In 2018, 129 master's, 3 other advanced degrees awarded. *Degree requirements:* For master's, comprehensive exam (for some programs). *Entrance requirements:* Additional exam requirements/recommendations for international students: Required—TOEFL (minimum score 550 paper-based; 79 iBT), IELTS (minimum score 6). *Application deadline:* Applications are processed on a rolling basis. Electronic applications accepted. Application fee is waived when completed online. *Expenses:* Contact institution. *Financial support:* In 2018–19, 126 students received support. Scholarships/grants and tuition waivers (partial) available. Support available to part-time students. Financial award applicants required to submit FAFSA. *Unit head:* Dr. Orlando Griego, Dean, 815-740-3395, Fax: 815-740-3452, E-mail: ogriego@stfrancis.edu. *Application contact:* Sandee Sloka, Director Adult & Graduate Admissions, 800-735-7500, E-mail: ssloka@stfrancis.edu.
Website: https://www.stfrancis.edu/business-health-administration/

University of St. Thomas, Cameron School of Business, Houston, TX 77006-4696. Offers MBA, MCTM, MIB, MSA, MSF. *Program availability:* Part-time, evening/weekend. *Degree requirements:* For master's, capstone (for some programs), additional course requirements for those sitting for state accountancy exam. *Entrance requirements:* For master's, minimum GPA of 2.5, 3 letters of recommendation. Additional exam requirements/recommendations for international students: Required—TOEFL (minimum score 550 paper-based; 79 iBT), IELTS (minimum score 6.5), PTE (minimum score 53). Electronic applications accepted.

University of St. Thomas, Opus College of Business, Master of Science in Accountancy Program, Minneapolis, MN 55403. Offers MS. *Entrance requirements:* For master's, GMAT. Additional exam requirements/recommendations for international students: Required—TOEFL (minimum score 94 iBT), IELTS (minimum score 7). *Application deadline:* For spring admission, 5/4 for domestic students, 1/13 for international students. Applications are processed on a rolling basis. Application fee: $60. Electronic applications accepted. Tuition and fees vary according to course load, degree level and program. *Financial support:* Career-related internships or fieldwork and scholarships/grants available. *Unit head:* Kristine Sharockman DeVinck, Director, 651-962-4124, Fax: 651-962-4141, E-mail: msacct@stthomas.edu. *Application contact:* Eric Wilkinson, Outreach Coordinator, 651-962-4222, Fax: 651-962-4141, E-mail: eric.wilkinson@stthomas.edu.
Website: http://www.stthomas.edu/accountancy

University of Saskatchewan, College of Graduate and Postdoctoral Studies, Edwards School of Business, Department of Accounting, Saskatoon, SK S7N 5A2, Canada. Offers MP Acc. *Program availability:* Part-time. *Degree requirements:* For master's, thesis (for some programs). *Entrance requirements:* For master's, GMAT. Additional exam requirements/recommendations for international students: Required—TOEFL.

The University of Scranton, Kania School of Management, Program in Accountancy, Scranton, PA 18510. Offers M Acc.

The University of Scranton, Kania School of Management, Program in Business Administration, Scranton, PA 18510. Offers accounting (MBA); finance (MBA); general business administration (MBA); health care management (MBA); international business (MBA); management information systems (MBA); marketing (MBA); operations management (MBA). *Accreditation:* AACSB. *Program availability:* Part-time, evening/weekend, 100% online. *Entrance requirements:* For master's, GMAT (for MBA). *Faculty research:* Financial markets, strategic impact of total quality management, internal accounting controls, consumer preference, information systems and the Internet.

University of South Africa, College of Economic and Management Sciences, Pretoria, South Africa. Offers accounting (D Admin, D Com); accounting science (DA); auditing (D Admin, D Com); business administration (M Tech); business economics (D Admin); business leadership (DBL); business management (D Admin, D Com); economic management analysis (M Tech); economics (D Admin, D Com, PhD); human resource development (M Tech); industrial psychology (D Admin, D Com, PhD); logistics (D Com); marketing (M Tech); public administration (D Admin, D Com, DPA, PhD); public management (M Tech); quantitative management (D Admin, D Com); real estate (M Tech); statistics (D Admin, PhD); tourism management (D Admin, D Com); transport economics (D Admin, D Com).

University of South Alabama, Mitchell College of Business, Department of Accounting, Mobile, AL 36688. Offers M Acc. *Program availability:* Part-time, evening/weekend. *Degree requirements:* For master's, comprehensive exam. *Entrance requirements:* For master's, GMAT (minimum score of 450, 3.0 in Analytical Writing section), minimum undergraduate GPA of 3.0. Additional exam requirements/recommendations for international students: Required—TOEFL (minimum score 525 paper-based; 71 iBT), IELTS (minimum score 6). Electronic applications accepted. *Expenses:* Contact institution.

University of South Carolina, The Graduate School, Darla Moore School of Business, Master of Accountancy Program, Columbia, SC 29208. Offers business measurement and assurance (M Acc); JD/M Acc. *Accreditation:* AACSB. *Program availability:* Part-time. *Degree requirements:* For master's, comprehensive exam. *Entrance requirements:* For master's, GMAT. Additional exam requirements/recommendations for international students: Required—TOEFL (minimum score 100 iBT); Recommended—IELTS. Electronic applications accepted. *Faculty research:* Judgment modeling, international accounting, accounting information systems, behavioral accounting, cost/management accounting.

University of South Dakota, Graduate School, Beacom School of Business, Department of Accounting, Vermillion, SD 57069. Offers professional accountancy (MP Acc); JD/MP Acc. *Program availability:* Part-time, evening/weekend, online learning. *Degree requirements:* For master's, comprehensive exam. *Entrance requirements:* For master's, GMAT, minimum GPA of 2.7, resume. Additional exam requirements/recommendations for international students: Required—TOEFL (minimum score 550 paper-based; 79 iBT), IELTS (minimum score 6). Electronic applications accepted.

University of Southern California, Graduate School, Marshall School of Business, Leventhal School of Accounting, Los Angeles, CA 90089. Offers accounting (M Acc); business taxation (MBT); JD/MBT. *Program availability:* Part-time. *Degree requirements:* For master's, 30-48 units of study. *Entrance requirements:* For master's, GMAT, undergraduate degree, communication skills. Additional exam requirements/recommendations for international students: Required—TOEFL. Electronic applications accepted. *Faculty research:* State and local taxation, Securities and Exchange Commission, governance, auditing fees, financial accounting, enterprise zones, women in business.

University of Southern Indiana, Graduate Studies, Romain College of Business, Program in Business Administration, Evansville, IN 47712-3590. Offers accounting (MBA); data analytics (MBA); engineering management (MBA); general business administration (MBA); healthcare administration (MBA); human resource management (MBA). *Accreditation:* AACSB. *Program availability:* Part-time, evening/weekend, 100% online, blended/hybrid learning. *Entrance requirements:* For master's, GMAT or GRE, minimum GPA of 2.5, resume, 3 professional references. Additional exam requirements/recommendations for international students: Required—TOEFL (minimum score 550 paper-based; 79 iBT), IELTS (minimum score 6). Electronic applications accepted.

University of Southern Maine, College of Management and Human Service, School of Business, Portland, ME 04104-9300. Offers accounting (MBA); business administration (MBA); finance (MBA); health management and policy (MBA); sustainability (MBA); JD/MBA; MBA/MSA; MBA/MSN; MS/MBA. *Accreditation:* AACSB. *Program availability:* Part-time, evening/weekend. *Entrance requirements:* For master's, GMAT or GRE, minimum AACSB index of 1100. Additional exam requirements/recommendations for international students: Required—TOEFL (minimum score 550 paper-based; 79 iBT). Electronic applications accepted. *Faculty research:* Economic development, management information systems, real options, system dynamics, simulation.

University of Southern Mississippi, College of Business and Economic Development, School of Accountancy, Hattiesburg, MS 39406-0001. Offers accountancy (MPA). *Accreditation:* AACSB. *Program availability:* Part-time, evening/weekend. *Degree requirements:* For master's, comprehensive exam. *Entrance requirements:* For master's, GMAT, minimum GPA of 2.75 on last 60 hours. Additional exam requirements/recommendations for international students: Required—TOEFL, IELTS. Electronic applications accepted. *Faculty research:* Bank liquidity, subchapter S corporations, internal auditing, governmental accounting, inflation accounting.

University of South Florida, Muma College of Business, Lynn Pippenger School of Accountancy, Tampa, FL 33620-9951. Offers accountancy (M Acc, PhD), including assurance (M Acc), corporate accounting (M Acc), tax (M Acc). *Accreditation:* AACSB. *Program availability:* Part-time, evening/weekend. *Faculty:* 11 full-time (5 women). *Students:* 69 full-time (31 women), 28 part-time (14 women); includes 34 minority (2 Black or African American, non-Hispanic/Latino; 1 American Indian or Alaska Native, non-Hispanic/Latino; 7 Asian, non-Hispanic/Latino; 18 Hispanic/Latino; 6 Two or more races, non-Hispanic/Latino), 8 international. Average age 24. 104 applicants, 59% accepted, 49 enrolled. In 2018, 50 master's awarded. Terminal master's awarded for partial completion of doctoral program. *Degree requirements:* For master's, comprehensive exam, thesis or alternative; for doctorate, comprehensive exam, thesis/dissertation. *Entrance requirements:* For master's, GMAT or GRE, minimum overall GPA of 3.0 in general upper-level coursework and in upper-level accounting coursework (minimum of 21 hours at a U.S. accredited program within past 5 years); for doctorate, GMAT or GRE, personal statement, recommendations, interview. Additional exam requirements/recommendations for international students: Required—TOEFL, TOEFL (minimum score 550 paper-based; 79 iBT) or IELTS (minimum score 6.5). *Application deadline:* For fall admission, 3/1 priority date for domestic students, 3/1 for international students; for spring admission, 10/1 for domestic students, 9/15 for international students; for summer admission, 2/15 for domestic and international students. Application fee: $30. Electronic applications accepted. *Expenses:* Tuition, state resident: full-time $6350. Tuition, nonresident: full-time $19,048. International tuition: $19,048 full-time. *Required fees:* $2079. *Financial support:* In 2018–19, 55 students received support, including 18 teaching assistantships with tuition reimbursements available (averaging $12,273 per year); scholarships/grants, health care benefits, and unspecified assistantships also available. Financial award applicants required to submit FAFSA. *Faculty research:* Auditing, auditor independence, audit committee decisions, fraud detection and reporting, disclosure effects, effects of information technology on accounting, governmental accounting/auditing, accounting information systems, data modeling and design methodologies for accounting systems, auditing computer-based systems, expert systems, group support systems in accounting, fair value accounting issues, corporate governance, financial accounting, financial reporting quality. *Unit head:* Dr. Uday Murthy, Interim Director, School of Accountancy, 813-974-6516, Fax: 813-974-6528, E-mail: umurthy@usf.edu. *Application contact:* Stacee Bender, Academic Services Administrator, 813-974-4516, E-mail: staceebender@usf.edu. Website: http://business.usf.edu/departments/accountancy/

The University of Tampa, Sykes College of Business, Tampa, FL 33606-1490. Offers accounting (MS); business analytics (MBA); cybersecurity (MBA, MS); entrepreneurship (MBA, MS); finance (MBA, MS); information systems management (MBA); innovation management (MBA); international business (MBA); marketing (MBA, MS); nonprofit management (MBA, Certificate). *Accreditation:* AACSB. *Program availability:* Part-time, evening/weekend. *Faculty:* 61 full-time (13 women), 11 part-time/adjunct (3 women). *Students:* 361 full-time (153 women), 122 part-time (52 women); includes 101 minority (31 Black or African American, non-Hispanic/Latino; 5 Asian, non-Hispanic/Latino; 57 Hispanic/Latino; 1 Native Hawaiian or other Pacific Islander, non-Hispanic/Latino; 7 Two or more races, non-Hispanic/Latino), 144 international. Average age 29. 1,079 applicants, 57% accepted, 263 enrolled. In 2018, 281 master's, 12 other advanced degrees awarded. *Degree requirements:* For master's, capstone. *Entrance requirements:* For master's, GMAT or GRE, official transcripts from all colleges and/or universities previously attended, resume, personal statement, letters of recommendation. Additional exam requirements/recommendations for international students: Required—TOEFL (minimum score 577 paper-based; 90 iBT), IELTS (minimum score 7.5). *Application deadline:* Applications are processed on a rolling basis. Application fee: $40. Electronic applications accepted. *Expenses:* Contact institution. *Financial support:* In 2018–19, 123 students received support. Career-related internships or fieldwork, scholarships/grants, and unspecified assistantships available. Financial award applicants required to submit FAFSA. *Faculty research:* Job market signaling, on-line shopping behaviors and social media, the Tampa Bay economy, digital literacy, entrepreneurship in small businesses. *Unit head:* Dr. Natasha F. Veltri, Associate Dean, 813-253-6289, E-mail: nveltri@ut.edu. *Application contact:* Ashley Russell, Staff Assistant, Admissions for Graduate and Continuing Studies, 813-253-6249, E-mail: arussell@ut.edu. Website: http://www.ut.edu/business/

The University of Tennessee, Graduate School, College of Business Administration, Department of Accounting, Knoxville, TN 37996. Offers accounting (M Acc), including assurance; systems (M Acc); taxation (M Acc). *Accreditation:* AACSB. *Degree requirements:* For master's, thesis or alternative. *Entrance requirements:* For master's, GMAT, minimum GPA of 2.7. Additional exam requirements/recommendations for international students: Required—TOEFL. Electronic applications accepted.

The University of Tennessee, Graduate School, College of Business Administration, Program in Business Administration, Knoxville, TN 37996. Offers accounting (PhD); finance (MBA, PhD); logistics and transportation (MBA, PhD); management (PhD); marketing (MBA, PhD); operations management (MBA); professional business administration (MBA); statistics (PhD); JD/MBA; MS/MBA; Pharm D/MBA. Pharm D/MBA offered jointly with The University of Tennessee Health Science Center. *Accreditation:* AACSB. *Program availability:* Online learning. *Degree requirements:* For master's, thesis or alternative; for doctorate, thesis/dissertation. *Entrance requirements:* For master's and doctorate, GMAT, minimum GPA of 2.7. Additional exam requirements/recommendations for international students: Required—TOEFL. Electronic applications accepted.

The University of Tennessee at Chattanooga, Program in Accountancy, Chattanooga, TN 37403. Offers M Acc. *Accreditation:* AACSB. *Program availability:* Part-time, evening/weekend. *Entrance requirements:* For master's, GMAT (minimum score 450). Additional exam requirements/recommendations for international students: Required—TOEFL (minimum score 550 paper-based; 79 iBT), IELTS (minimum score 6). Electronic applications accepted. *Expenses:* Contact institution. *Faculty research:* Performance measurement, auditing, income taxation, corporate efficiency, portfolio management and performance..

The University of Texas at Arlington, Graduate School, College of Business, Accounting Department, Arlington, TX 76019. Offers accounting (MP Acc, MS, PhD); taxation (MS). *Accreditation:* AACSB. *Program availability:* Part-time, evening/weekend. *Degree requirements:* For master's, thesis optional; for doctorate, comprehensive exam, thesis/dissertation. *Entrance requirements:* For master's and doctorate, GMAT. Additional exam requirements/recommendations for international students: Required—TOEFL (minimum score 550 paper-based; 79 iBT).

The University of Texas at Austin, Graduate School, McCombs School of Business, Department of Accounting, Austin, TX 78712-1111. Offers MPA, PhD. *Accreditation:* AACSB. *Degree requirements:* For doctorate, comprehensive exam, thesis/dissertation. *Entrance requirements:* For master's and doctorate, GMAT. Additional exam requirements/recommendations for international students: Required—TOEFL. Electronic applications accepted.

The University of Texas at Dallas, Naveen Jindal School of Management, Program in Accounting, Richardson, TX 75080. Offers MS. *Accreditation:* AACSB. *Faculty:* 20 full-time (8 women), 22 part-time/adjunct (6 women). *Students:* 358 full-time (217 women), 200 part-time (115 women); includes 179 minority (17 Black or African American, non-Hispanic/Latino; 2 American Indian or Alaska Native, non-Hispanic/Latino; 100 Asian, non-Hispanic/Latino; 45 Hispanic/Latino; 15 Two or more races, non-Hispanic/Latino), 236 international. Average age 28. 344 applicants, 65% accepted, 124 enrolled. In 2018, 333 master's awarded. *Entrance requirements:* For master's, GMAT, minimum GPA of 3.0 in upper-level course work in field. Additional exam requirements/recommendations for international students: Required—TOEFL (minimum score 550 paper-based). *Application deadline:* For fall admission, 7/15 for domestic students, 5/1 priority date for international students; for spring admission, 11/15 for domestic students, 9/1 priority date for international students. Applications are processed on a rolling basis. Application fee: $50 ($100 for international students). Electronic applications accepted. *Expenses:* Tuition, area resident: Full-time $13,458. Tuition, state resident: full-time $13,458. Tuition, nonresident: full-time $26,852. International tuition: $26,852 full-time. Tuition and fees vary according to course load. *Financial support:* In 2018–19, 2 students received support, including 9 teaching assistantships with partial tuition reimbursements available (averaging $10,050 per year); research assistantships with partial tuition reimbursements available, career-related internships or fieldwork, Federal Work-Study, institutionally sponsored loans, scholarships/grants, and unspecified assistantships also available. Support available to part-time students. Financial award application deadline: 4/30; financial award applicants required to submit FAFSA. *Faculty research:* Privatization and accounting/auditing, corporate performance and executive compensation, risk management, information technology in accounting. *Unit head:* Dr. William Cready, Area Coordinator, 972-883-4185, Fax: 972-883-6823, E-mail: cready@utdallas.edu. *Application contact:* Mary Guan, Program Director, 972-883-5031, Fax: 972-883-6823, E-mail: mary.guan@utdallas.edu. Website: http://jindal.utdallas.edu/accounting

The University of Texas at El Paso, Graduate School, College of Business Administration, Department of Accounting, El Paso, TX 79968-0001. Offers M Acc. *Accreditation:* AACSB. *Program availability:* Part-time, evening/weekend. *Entrance requirements:* For master's, GMAT, minimum GPA of 3.0. Additional exam requirements/recommendations for international students: Required—TOEFL; Recommended—IELTS. Electronic applications accepted. *Faculty research:* Financial and managerial accounting, auditing and accounting information systems.

The University of Texas at San Antonio, College of Business, Department of Accounting, San Antonio, TX 78249-0617. Offers M Acy, PhD. *Accreditation:* AACSB. *Program availability:* Part-time, evening/weekend. *Degree requirements:* For master's, thesis or alternative. *Entrance requirements:* For master's, GMAT, bachelor's degree, transcripts, statement of purpose. Additional exam requirements/recommendations for international students: Required—TOEFL (minimum score 550 paper-based; 79 iBT), IELTS (minimum score 6.5). Electronic applications accepted. *Expenses:* Contact institution. *Faculty research:* Capital markets, corporate governance, auditing, health care accounting, fraud.

The University of Texas at Tyler, Soules College of Business, Department of Accounting, Finance, and Business Law, Tyler, TX 75799-0001. Offers M Acc. *Entrance requirements:* For master's, GMAT, official transcripts, current resume. *Unit head:* Dr. Roger Lirely, Chair, 903-566-7346. *Application contact:* Dr. Roger Lirely, Chair, 903-566-7346. Website: https://www.uttyler.edu/cbt/fabl/

The University of Texas of the Permian Basin, Office of Graduate Studies, College of Business, Program in Accountancy, Odessa, TX 79762-0001. Offers MPA. *Entrance requirements:* For master's, GMAT. Additional exam requirements/recommendations for international students: Required—TOEFL (minimum score 550 paper-based).

The University of Texas Rio Grande Valley, Robert C. Vackar College of Business and Entrepreneurship, Program in Accounting, Edinburg, TX 78539. Offers M Acc, MS. *Program availability:* Part-time, evening/weekend. *Entrance requirements:* For master's, GMAT. Additional exam requirements/recommendations for international students: Required—TOEFL (minimum score 500 paper-based). Electronic applications accepted. *Expenses:* Tuition, area resident: Full-time $6888. Tuition, state resident: full-time $6888. Tuition, nonresident: full-time $14,484. International tuition: $14,484 full-time. *Required fees:* $1468. *Faculty research:* Financial and managerial accounting, international accounting, taxation, ethics.

University of the Cumberlands, Hutton School of Business, Williamsburg, KY 40769-1372. Offers accounting (MBA); business (MBA). *Program availability:* Part-time, online learning. *Entrance requirements:* For master's, GMAT, GRE. Additional exam requirements/recommendations for international students: Required—TOEFL. Electronic applications accepted.

University of the Incarnate Word, H-E-B School of Business and Administration, San Antonio, TX 78209-6397. Offers accounting (MS); business administration (MBA); health administration (MHA). *Program availability:* Part-time, evening/weekend. *Faculty:* 22 full-time (12 women), 13 part-time/adjunct (5 women). *Students:* 249 full-time (120 women), 27 part-time (12 women); includes 162 minority (24 Black or African American, non-Hispanic/Latino; 1 American Indian or Alaska Native, non-Hispanic/Latino; 8 Asian, non-Hispanic/Latino; 124 Hispanic/Latino; 1 Native Hawaiian or other Pacific Islander, non-Hispanic/Latino; 4 Two or more races, non-Hispanic/Latino), 40 international. 202 applicants, 98% accepted, 108 enrolled. In 2018, 142 master's awarded. *Degree requirements:* For master's, capstone. *Entrance requirements:* For master's, GMAT, GRE, writing sample, interview. Additional exam requirements/recommendations for international students: Required—TOEFL (minimum score 560 paper-based; 83 iBT). *Application deadline:* Applications are processed on a rolling basis. Application fee: $20. Electronic applications accepted. *Expenses:* Tuition: Full-time $22,560; part-time $940 per credit hour. *Required fees:* $2484; $94 per credit hour. Tuition and fees vary according to degree level, program and student level. *Financial support:* Research assistantships, Federal Work-Study, scholarships/grants, tuition waivers (partial), and unspecified assistantships available. Financial award applicants required to submit FAFSA. *Faculty research:* Importance of business sustainability, comparison of tax/legal research services, fair trade branding as a tool for the marketing of developing society crafts, ethnocentrism and country of origin effects among immigrant consumers, international trade and investment. *Unit head:* Dr. Forrest Aven, Dean, 210-805-5884, Fax: 210-805-3564, E-mail: aven@uiwtx.edu. *Application contact:* Jessica Delarosa, Associate Director of Admissions, 210-8296005, Fax: 210-829-3921, E-mail: admis@uiwtx.edu. Website: https://www.uiw.edu/hebsba/index.html

University of the Sacred Heart, Graduate Programs, Department of Business Administration, San Juan, PR 00914-0383. Offers human resource management (MBA); information systems auditing (MS); information technology (Certificate); international marketing (MBA); management information systems (MBA); production and marketing of special events (Certificate); taxation (MBA). *Program availability:* Part-time, evening/weekend. *Degree requirements:* For master's, thesis. *Entrance requirements:* For master's, EXADEP, minimum undergraduate GPA of 2.75, interview.

The University of Toledo, College of Graduate Studies, College of Business and Innovation, Department of Accounting, Toledo, OH 43606-3390. Offers MBA, MSA.

Accreditation: AACSB. *Program availability:* Part-time, evening/weekend. *Entrance requirements:* For master's, GMAT, GRE, or LSAT, minimum GPA of 2.7 for all prior academic work, three letters of recommendation, statement of purpose, transcripts from all prior institutions attended. Additional exam requirements/recommendations for international students: Required—TOEFL (minimum score 550 paper-based; 80 iBT). Electronic applications accepted. *Faculty research:* Estate gift tax, audit and legal liability, corporate tax, accounting information systems.

The University of Tulsa, Graduate School, Collins College of Business, Program in Accounting, Tulsa, OK 74104-3189. Offers M Acc. *Program availability:* Part-time. *Faculty:* 10 full-time (4 women). *Students:* 18 full-time (8 women), 7 part-time (2 women); includes 3 minority (1 Hispanic/Latino; 2 Two or more races, non-Hispanic/Latino), 2 international. Average age 25. 10 applicants, 80% accepted, 3 enrolled. In 2018, 14 master's awarded. *Entrance requirements:* For master's, GMAT. Additional exam requirements/recommendations for international students: Required—TOEFL (minimum score 577 paper-based; 91 iBT). *Application deadline:* Applications are processed on a rolling basis. Application fee: $55. Electronic applications accepted. *Expenses: Tuition:* Full-time $22,230; part-time $1235 per credit hour. *Required fees:* $2100; $6 per credit hour. One-time fee: $400 full-time. Tuition and fees vary according to course level, course load and program. *Financial support:* In 2018–19, 6 students received support, including 6 teaching assistantships with full tuition reimbursements available (averaging $12,292 per year); fellowships, research assistantships, career-related internships or fieldwork, Federal Work-Study, scholarships/grants, health care benefits, tuition waivers (full and partial), and unspecified assistantships also available. Support available to part-time students. Financial award application deadline: 2/1; financial award applicants required to submit FAFSA. *Faculty research:* Capital markets, financial reporting, innovation in accounting. *Unit head:* Dr. Ralph Jackson, Associate Dean, 918-631-2242, Fax: 918-631-2142, E-mail: ralph-jackson@utulsa.edu. *Application contact:* Information Contact, 918-631-2242, E-mail: graduate-business@utulsa.edu.

University of Utah, Graduate School, David Eccles School of Business, Business Administration Program, Salt Lake City, UT 84112. Offers accounting (PhD); business administration (EMBA, MBA, PMBA); finance (PhD); information systems (PhD); marketing (PhD); operations management (PhD); organizational behavior (PhD); strategic management (PhD); MBA/JD; MBA/MHA; MBA/MS. *Program availability:* Part-time, evening/weekend, online learning. *Students:* 112 full-time (26 women), 7 part-time (2 women); includes 12 minority (1 Asian, non-Hispanic/Latino; 7 Hispanic/Latino; 4 Two or more races, non-Hispanic/Latino), 13 international. Average age 29. 182 applicants, 51% accepted, 58 enrolled. In 2018, 58 master's awarded. *Entrance requirements:* For master's, GMAT or GRE; for doctorate, GMAT. Additional exam requirements/recommendations for international students: Required—TOEFL (minimum score 100 iBT), IELTS (minimum score 7). *Application deadline:* For fall admission, 5/1 for domestic students, 3/1 for international students. Application fee: $55 ($65 for international students). Electronic applications accepted. *Expenses:* Contact institution. *Financial support:* In 2018–19, 57 students received support. Scholarships/grants available. Financial award application deadline: 5/1; financial award applicants required to submit FAFSA. *Faculty research:* Corporate finance, strategy services, consumer behavior, financial disclosures, operations. *Unit head:* Brad Vierig, Associate Dean, MBA Programs & Executive Education. *Application contact:* Stephanie Geisler, Director, Full-Time MBA, 801-585-6291, E-mail: ftmba@utah.edu.
Website: http://www.business.utah.edu/

University of Utah, Graduate School, David Eccles School of Business, School of Accounting, Salt Lake City, UT 84112. Offers accounting (PhD); accounting information systems (M Acc); financial/audit (M Acc); tax (M Acc). *Accreditation:* AACSB. *Program availability:* Part-time, evening/weekend. *Degree requirements:* For doctorate, comprehensive exam, thesis/dissertation, oral qualifying exams, written qualifying exams. *Entrance requirements:* For master's, minimum undergraduate GPA of 3.0. Additional exam requirements/recommendations for international students: Required—TOEFL (minimum score 600 paper-based; 100 iBT), IELTS (minimum score 7). Electronic applications accepted. *Expenses:* Contact institution. *Faculty research:* Auditing, taxation, information systems, financial accounting, accounting theory, international accounting.

University of Vermont, Graduate College, Grossman School of Business, Program in Accountancy, Burlington, VT 05405. Offers M Acc. *Entrance requirements:* For master's, GMAT (500 minimum) or GRE, resume. Additional exam requirements/recommendations for international students: Required—TOEFL (minimum score 550 paper-based, 90 iBT) or IELTS (6.5). Electronic applications accepted.

University of Virginia, McIntire School of Commerce, M.S. in Accounting, Charlottesville, VA 22903. Offers MS, JD/MS. *Accreditation:* AACSB. *Faculty:* 12 full-time (6 women). *Students:* 50 full-time (27 women); includes 6 minority (1 Black or African American, non-Hispanic/Latino; 3 Asian, non-Hispanic/Latino; 2 Hispanic/Latino), 12 international. Average age 22. 185 applicants, 39% accepted, 50 enrolled. In 2018, 56 master's awarded. *Entrance requirements:* For master's, GMAT, 2 letters of recommendation, 12 hours of accounting courses. Additional exam requirements/recommendations for international students: Required—TOEFL (minimum score 600 paper-based; 100 iBT), IELTS (minimum score 7.5). *Application deadline:* For fall admission, 9/15 for domestic students, 11/15 for international students; for winter admission, 1/15 for domestic students; for spring admission, 3/15 for domestic students. Applications are processed on a rolling basis. Application fee: $75. Electronic applications accepted. *Expenses:* Contact institution. *Financial support:* Federal Work-Study, scholarships/grants, and unspecified assistantships available. Financial award application deadline: 12/16; financial award applicants required to submit FAFSA. *Faculty research:* Accounting, analytics, forensics, tax, communication. *Unit head:* Andrea Roberts, Program Director, 434-243-1561, Fax: 434-924-4511, E-mail: msaccounting@virginia.edu. *Application contact:* Emma Candelier, Assistant Dean of Graduate Recruiting, 434-243-4992, Fax: 434-924-4511, E-mail: ecandelier@virginia.edu.
Website: http://www.commerce.virginia.edu/msaccounting/Pages/default.aspx

University of Washington, Graduate School, Michael G. Foster School of Business, Seattle, WA 98195-3200. Offers auditing and assurance (MP Acc); business administration (MBA, PhD); entrepreneurship (MS); executive business administration (MBA); global executive business administration (MBA); information systems (MSIS); supply chain management (MSSCM); taxation (MP Acc); technology management (MBA); JD/MBA; MBA/MAIS; MBA/MHA. *Accreditation:* AACSB. *Program availability:* Part-time, evening/weekend, blended/hybrid learning. Terminal master's awarded for partial completion of doctoral program. *Degree requirements:* For doctorate, comprehensive exam, thesis/dissertation. *Entrance requirements:* For master's and doctorate, GMAT, GRE. Additional exam requirements/recommendations for international students: Required—TOEFL (minimum score 600 paper-based; 100 iBT). Electronic applications accepted. *Expenses:* Contact institution. *Faculty research:* Finance, consumer behavior, marketing analytics, technology management, supply chain.

University of Washington, Tacoma, Graduate Programs, MBA Programs, Tacoma, WA 98402-3100. Offers accounting (MBA); business administration (MBA); certified financial analyst (MBA). *Accreditation:* AACSB. *Program availability:* Part-time, evening/weekend. *Entrance requirements:* For master's, GMAT, minimum GPA of 3.0 in final graded 90 quarter credits or 60 graded semester credits; at least 2 years of professional/management work experience. Additional exam requirements/recommendations for international students: Required—TOEFL (minimum score 580 paper-based; 92 iBT). Electronic applications accepted. *Expenses:* Contact institution. *Faculty research:* International accounting, marketing, change management, investments, corporate social responsibility.

University of Waterloo, Graduate Studies and Postdoctoral Affairs, Faculty of Arts, School of Accounting and Finance, Waterloo, ON N2L 3G1, Canada. Offers accounting (M Acc, PhD); finance (M Acc); taxation (M Tax). *Degree requirements:* For master's, thesis or alternative; for doctorate, thesis/dissertation. *Entrance requirements:* For master's, honors degree, minimum B average, resume; for doctorate, GMAT, master's degree, minimum A- average, resume. Additional exam requirements/recommendations for international students: Required—TOEFL, IELTS, PTE. Application fee: $125 Canadian dollars. Electronic applications accepted. *Expenses:* Contact institution. *Financial support:* Fellowships and research assistantships available. *Faculty research:* Auditing, management accounting.
Website: https://uwaterloo.ca/school-of-accounting-and-finance/

University of West Florida, College of Business, Program in Accounting, Pensacola, FL 32514-5750. Offers M Acc. *Program availability:* Part-time, evening/weekend. *Entrance requirements:* For master's, GMAT (minimum score 450) or equivalent GRE score, official transcripts; bachelor's degree; two letters of recommendation; letter of intent. Additional exam requirements/recommendations for international students: Required—TOEFL (minimum score 550 paper-based). *Faculty research:* Audit risk, tax legislation, product costing, bank core deposit intangibles, financial reporting.

University of West Georgia, Richards College of Business, Carrollton, GA 30118. Offers accounting (MP Acc); business administration (MBA). *Program availability:* Part-time, evening/weekend, 100% online, blended/hybrid learning. *Faculty:* 38 full-time (15 women). *Students:* 57 full-time (34 women), 118 part-time (68 women); includes 60 minority (45 Black or African American, non-Hispanic/Latino; 3 Asian, non-Hispanic/Latino; 10 Hispanic/Latino; 2 Two or more races, non-Hispanic/Latino), 9 international. Average age 30. 123 applicants, 96% accepted, 73 enrolled. In 2018, 112 master's awarded. *Entrance requirements:* Additional exam requirements/recommendations for international students: Required—TOEFL (minimum score 550 paper-based; 79 iBT); Recommended—IELTS (minimum score 6.5). *Application deadline:* For fall admission, 7/15 for domestic students, 6/1 for international students; for spring admission, 11/15 for domestic students, 10/15 for international students; for summer admission, 5/15 for domestic students, 3/30 for international students. Applications are processed on a rolling basis. Application fee: $40. Electronic applications accepted. Tuition and fees vary according to course load, degree level, campus/location and program. *Financial support:* Fellowships, research assistantships, teaching assistantships, career-related internships or fieldwork, Federal Work-Study, institutionally sponsored loans, scholarships/grants, and unspecified assistantships available. Support available to part-time students. Financial award application deadline: 4/1; financial award applicants required to submit FAFSA. *Unit head:* Dr. Faye S. McIntyre, Dean of Richards College of Business, 678-839-6467, Fax: 678-839-5040, E-mail: fmcintyr@westga.edu. *Application contact:* Dr. Toby Ziglar, Assistant Dean of the Graduate School, 678-839-1394, Fax: 678-839-1395, E-mail: graduate@westga.edu.
Website: https://www.westga.edu/business

University of Wisconsin–Madison, Graduate School, Wisconsin School of Business, Doctoral Program in Accounting and Information Systems, Madison, WI 53706-1380. Offers PhD. *Accreditation:* AACSB. *Degree requirements:* For doctorate, comprehensive exam, thesis/dissertation. *Entrance requirements:* For doctorate, GMAT or GRE. Additional exam requirements/recommendations for international students: Recommended—TOEFL (minimum score 623 paper-based; 106 iBT), IELTS (minimum score 7.5). Electronic applications accepted. *Expenses:* Contact institution. *Faculty research:* Auditing, financial reporting, economic theory, strategy, computer models, internal audit and fraud, health care fiscal management, tax reporting, incentives used in nonprofit hospitals, CFO compensation, state and local taxation, audit quality, FASB pronouncements, financial statement analysis.

University of Wisconsin–Madison, Graduate School, Wisconsin School of Business, Master of Accountancy Program, Madison, WI 53706-1380. Offers accountancy (M Acc); taxation (M Acc). *Degree requirements:* For master's, minimum GPA of 3.0. *Entrance requirements:* For master's, GMAT, essays. Additional exam requirements/recommendations for international students: Required—TOEFL (minimum score 104 iBT), IELTS (minimum score 8), GMAT. Electronic applications accepted. *Faculty research:* Tax reserves, audit committee incentives, internal audit, accounting report's impact on management decisions.

University of Wisconsin–Whitewater, School of Graduate Studies, College of Business and Economics, Department of Accounting, Whitewater, WI 53190-1790. Offers MPA. *Program availability:* Part-time, evening/weekend, online learning. *Degree requirements:* For master's, thesis or alternative. *Entrance requirements:* For master's, GMAT or GRE, minimum AACSB index of 1000, minimum GPA of 2.75. Additional exam requirements/recommendations for international students: Required—TOEFL (minimum score 550 paper-based; 80 iBT), IELTS (minimum score 6). Electronic applications accepted. *Faculty research:* Laws/economy/quality of life; tax, accounting and public policy.

University of Wyoming, College of Business, Department of Accounting and Finance, Program in Accounting, Laramie, WY 82071. Offers MS. *Degree requirements:* For master's, thesis optional. *Entrance requirements:* For master's, GMAT or GRE, minimum GPA of 3.0. Additional exam requirements/recommendations for international students: Required—TOEFL (minimum score 540 paper-based; 76 iBT). Electronic applications accepted. *Expenses: Tuition, area resident:* Full-time $6504; part-time $271 per credit hour. Tuition, state resident: full-time $6504; part-time $271 per credit hour. Tuition, nonresident: full-time $19,464; part-time $811 per credit hour. *International tuition:* $19,464 full-time. *Required fees:* $1410.94; $343.82 per semester. $343.82 per semester. Tuition and fees vary according to course load, program and reciprocity agreements. *Faculty research:* Taxation, accounting education, assessment, not-for-profit accounting, fraud examination, ethics, management accounting.

Upper Iowa University, Online Master's Programs, Fayette, IA 52142-1857. Offers accounting (MBA); corporate financial management (MBA); emergency management and homeland security (MPA); general management (MBA); general studies (MPA); government administration (MPA); health and human services (MPA); human resources management (MBA); nonprofit organizational management (MPA); organizational development (MBA); public management (MPA); sport administration (MSA). MBA also available at Madison, WI campus. *Program availability:* Part-time, online learning. *Degree requirements:* For master's, research project. *Entrance requirements:* For master's, GMAT, GRE, or minimum GPA of 2.7 during last 60 hours. Additional exam requirements/recommendations for international students: Required—TOEFL (minimum score 570 paper-based). Electronic applications accepted. *Faculty research:* Total quality management, teams, organization culture and climate, management.

Ursuline College, School of Graduate and Professional Studies, Program in Business Administration, Pepper Pike, OH 44124-4398. Offers ethical and entrepreneurial leadership (MBA); financial planning and accounting (MBA); health services management (MBA); management (MBA); management and leadership (MBA); marketing and communications management (MBA). *Program availability:* Part-time, evening/weekend. *Faculty:* 2 full-time (both women), 2 part-time/adjunct (1 woman). *Students:* 17 full-time (all women), 5 part-time (3 women); includes 10 minority (9 Black or African American, non-Hispanic/Latino; 1 Two or more races, non-Hispanic/Latino). Average age 40. 33 applicants, 100% accepted, 6 enrolled. In 2018, 16 master's awarded. *Degree requirements:* For master's, comprehensive exam (for some programs). *Entrance requirements:* For master's, GRE. Additional exam requirements/recommendations for international students: Required—TOEFL (minimum score 500 paper-based) or GRE. *Application deadline:* For fall admission, 8/1 for domestic students. Applications are processed on a rolling basis. Application fee: $25. Electronic applications accepted. *Expenses:* 36 hours at $903/per. *Financial support:* In 2018–19, 2 students received support. Campus work-study available. Financial award application deadline: 8/1; financial award applicants required to submit FAFSA. *Faculty research:* Gift economy; sharing economy; cooperative business models; collaborative leadership; corporate social responsibility and the triple bottom line, defined as the three P's: people, planet and profit. *Unit head:* Dr. Debra Fleming, Professor, 440-440-720-3864, Fax: 440-684-6088, E-mail: dfleming@ursuline.edu. *Application contact:* Melanie Steele, Director of Graduate Admission, 440-646-8146, Fax: 440-684-6138, E-mail: graduateadmissions@ursuline.edu.

Utah State University, School of Graduate Studies, Jon M. Huntsman School of Business, School of Accountancy, Logan, UT 84322. Offers M Acc. *Accreditation:* AACSB. *Program availability:* Part-time. *Entrance requirements:* For master's, GMAT, minimum GPA of 3.0, 3 recommendation letters. Additional exam requirements/recommendations for international students: Required—TOEFL. *Faculty research:* Relationship theory, enterprise systems, just in time/loan, reported earnings measures, accounting education.

Utah Valley University, MBA Program, Orem, UT 84058-5999. Offers accounting (MBA); management (MBA). *Accreditation:* AACSB. *Program availability:* Part-time, evening/weekend. *Entrance requirements:* For master's, GMAT, official transcripts, current resume, three letters of recommendation, essay. Additional exam requirements/recommendations for international students: Required—TOEFL (minimum score 79 iBT). Electronic applications accepted. *Expenses:* Contact institution.

Utica College, Program in Accountancy, Utica, NY 13502-4892. Offers MBA. *Program availability:* Part-time, evening/weekend. *Faculty:* 3 full-time (1 woman). *Students:* 9 full-time (6 women), 3 part-time (2 women); includes 5 minority (1 Black or African American, non-Hispanic/Latino; 1 Asian, non-Hispanic/Latino; 3 Hispanic/Latino). Average age 25. 11 applicants, 64% accepted, 6 enrolled. In 2018, 13 master's awarded. *Entrance requirements:* For master's, BS, minimum GPA of 3.0. Additional exam requirements/recommendations for international students: Required—TOEFL (minimum score 525 paper-based). *Application deadline:* Applications are processed on a rolling basis. Application fee: $50. Electronic applications accepted. *Expenses:* Contact institution. *Financial support:* Career-related internships or fieldwork, scholarships/grants, tuition waivers (partial), and unspecified assistantships available. Support available to part-time students. Financial award application deadline: 3/15; financial award applicants required to submit FAFSA. *Unit head:* Dr. Zhaodan Huang, MBA Director, 315-792-3247, E-mail: zhuang@utica.edu. *Application contact:* John D. Rowe, Director of Graduate Admissions, 315-792-3824, Fax: 315-792-3003, E-mail: jrowe@utica.edu.
Website: http://www.utica.edu/academic/ssm/accounting/mba/

Valdosta State University, Langdale College of Business, Valdosta, GA 31698. Offers accountancy (M Acc); business administration (MBA); healthcare administration (MBA). MBA program is a member of the Georgia WebMBA. *Accreditation:* AACSB. *Program availability:* Part-time, evening/weekend, 100% online, blended/hybrid learning. *Degree requirements:* For master's, comprehensive written and/or oral exams. *Entrance requirements:* For master's, GMAT or GRE, minimum GPA of 2.75. Additional exam requirements/recommendations for international students: Required—TOEFL (minimum score 523 paper-based); Recommended—IELTS. Electronic applications accepted. *Expenses:* Contact institution.

Vanderbilt University, Vanderbilt University Owen Graduate School of Management, Master of Accountancy in Valuation Program, Nashville, TN 37203. Offers M Acc. *Entrance requirements:* For master's, GMAT or GRE. Additional exam requirements/recommendations for international students: Required—TOEFL, IELTS. Electronic applications accepted. *Expenses: Tuition:* Full-time $47,208; part-time $2026 per credit hour. *Required fees:* $478.

Vanderbilt University, Vanderbilt University Owen Graduate School of Management, Master of Accountancy Program, Nashville, TN 37240-1001. Offers M Acc. *Accreditation:* AACSB. *Entrance requirements:* For master's, GMAT or GRE. Additional exam requirements/recommendations for international students: Required—TOEFL, IELTS. Electronic applications accepted. *Expenses:* Contact institution.

Vanderbilt University, Vanderbilt University Owen Graduate School of Management, Vanderbilt MBA Program, Nashville, TN 37203. Offers accounting (MBA); finance (MBA); general management (MBA); health care (MBA); human and organizational performance (MBA); marketing (MBA); operations (MBA); strategy (MBA); MBA/JD; MBA/M Div; MBA/MD; MBA/MSN; MBA/MTS; MBA/PhD. *Accreditation:* AACSB. *Degree requirements:* For master's, 62 credit hours of coursework; completion of ethics course; minimum GPA of 3.0. *Entrance requirements:* For master's, GMAT (preferred) or GRE, 2 years of work experience (recommended). Additional exam requirements/recommendations for international students: Required—TOEFL (minimum score 100 iBT). Electronic applications accepted. *Expenses:* Contact institution. *Faculty research:* Accounting and finance, business strategy and economics, marketing, operations management, organization studies.

Villanova University, Villanova School of Business, Master of Accounting with Data Analytics, Villanova, PA 19085. Offers MAC. *Accreditation:* AACSB. *Faculty:* 101 full-time (38 women), 36 part-time/adjunct (9 women). *Students:* 50 part-time (24 women); includes 15 minority (3 Black or African American, non-Hispanic/Latino; 3 Asian, non-Hispanic/Latino; 6 Hispanic/Latino; 3 Two or more races, non-Hispanic/Latino). Average age 23. 110 applicants, 65% accepted, 52 enrolled. In 2018, 24 master's awarded. *Degree requirements:* For master's, minimum cumulative GPA of 3.0. *Entrance requirements:* For master's, Application, official transcripts, 2 letters of recommendation, resume, 2 essays, interview. Additional exam requirements/recommendations for international students: Required—TOEFL (minimum score 550 paper-based; 100 iBT). *Application deadline:* For fall admission, 6/30 for domestic and international students. Applications are processed on a rolling basis. Application fee: $65. Electronic applications accepted. *Expenses:* Contact institution. *Financial support:* Scholarships/grants available. Financial award application deadline: 6/30; financial award applicants required to submit FAFSA. *Faculty research:* Real Estate, Business Analytics, Global Leadership, Marketing and Consumer Insights, Church management. *Unit head:* Dr. Joyce E. A. Russell, Dean of Villanova School of Business, 610-519-5424, Fax: 610-519-6273, E-mail: joyce.russell@villanova.edu. *Application contact:* Daniel Guertin, Assistant Director, Recruitment, 610-519-8031, Fax: 610-519-6273, E-mail: daniel.guertin@villanova.edu.
Website: http://www1.villanova.edu/villanova/business/graduate/specializedprograms/mac.html

Virginia Commonwealth University, Graduate School, School of Business, Program in Accounting, Richmond, VA 23284-9005. Offers M Acc. *Accreditation:* AACSB. *Entrance requirements:* For master's, GMAT. Additional exam requirements/recommendations for international students: Required—TOEFL (minimum score 600 paper-based; 100 iBT). Electronic applications accepted.

Virginia International University, School of Business, Fairfax, VA 22030. Offers accounting (MBA, MS); entrepreneurship (MBA); executive management (Graduate Certificate); global logistics (MBA); health care management (MBA); hospitality and tourism management (MBA); human resources management (MBA); international business management (MBA); international finance (MBA); marketing management (MBA); mass media and public relations (MBA); project management (MBA, MS). *Program availability:* Part-time, online learning. *Entrance requirements:* For master's and Graduate Certificate, bachelor's degree. Additional exam requirements/recommendations for international students: Required—TOEFL (minimum score 550 paper-based; 80 iBT), IELTS (minimum score 6). Electronic applications accepted.

Virginia Polytechnic Institute and State University, Graduate School, Pamplin College of Business, Blacksburg, VA 24061. Offers accounting and information systems (MACIS, PhD); business administration (MS), including business analytics, hospitality and tourism management; business information technology (PhD); executive business research (PhD); finance (PhD); marketing (PhD), including marketing; MS/MBA. *Faculty:* 141 full-time (42 women), 2 part-time/adjunct (1 woman). *Students:* 227 full-time (89 women), 217 part-time (75 women); includes 131 minority (30 Black or African American, non-Hispanic/Latino; 58 Asian, non-Hispanic/Latino; 25 Hispanic/Latino; 18 Two or more races, non-Hispanic/Latino), 81 international. Average age 32. 361 applicants, 55% accepted, 152 enrolled. In 2018, 181 master's, 8 doctorates awarded. *Degree requirements:* For master's, comprehensive exam (for some programs), thesis (for some programs); for doctorate, comprehensive exam (for some programs), thesis/dissertation (for some programs). *Entrance requirements:* For master's and doctorate, GRE/GMAT. Additional exam requirements/recommendations for international students: Required—TOEFL (minimum score 90 iBT). *Application deadline:* For fall admission, 8/1 for domestic students, 4/1 for international students; for spring admission, 1/1 for domestic students, 9/1 for international students. Applications are processed on a rolling basis. Application fee: $75. Electronic applications accepted. *Expenses:* Tuition, state resident: full-time $15,510; part-time $739.50 per credit hour. Tuition, nonresident: full-time $29,629; part-time $1490.25 per credit hour. *Required fees:* $2804; $550 per semester. Tuition and fees vary according to course load, campus/location and program. *Financial support:* In 2018–19, 1 fellowship with full tuition reimbursement (averaging $3,999 per year), 4 research assistantships with full tuition reimbursements (averaging $20,163 per year), 66 teaching assistantships with full tuition reimbursements (averaging $19,822 per year) were awarded; scholarships/grants and unspecified assistantships also available. Financial award application deadline: 3/1; financial award applicants required to submit FAFSA. *Total annual research expenditures:* $3.1 million. *Unit head:* Dr. Robert T. Sumichrast, Dean, 540-231-6601, Fax: 540-231-4487, E-mail: busdean@vt.edu. *Application contact:* Kimberly Ridpath, Executive Assistant, 540-231-9647, Fax: 540-231-4487, E-mail: ridpathk@vt.edu.
Website: http://www.pamplin.vt.edu/

Wagner College, Division of Graduate Studies, Nicolais School of Business, Staten Island, NY 10301-4495. Offers accounting (MS); business administration (MBA); finance (MBA); management (Exec MBA); marketing (MBA); media management (MS). *Accreditation:* ACBSP. *Program availability:* Part-time, evening/weekend. *Degree requirements:* For master's, thesis optional. *Entrance requirements:* For master's, minimum GPA of 2.75, proficiency in computers and math. Additional exam requirements/recommendations for international students: Required—TOEFL (minimum score 550 paper-based; 79 iBT), IELTS (minimum score 6.5).

Wake Forest University, School of Business, MS in Accountancy Program, Winston-Salem, NC 27106. Offers assurance services (MSA); tax consulting (MSA); transaction services (MSA). *Degree requirements:* For master's, 30 credit hours. *Entrance requirements:* For master's, GMAT/GRE, letters of recommendation, official transcripts, current resume or curriculum vitae, interview. Additional exam requirements/recommendations for international students: Required—TOEFL (minimum score 600 paper-based; 100 iBT). Electronic applications accepted. *Expenses:* Contact institution. *Faculty research:* Influence of personal relationships on business decision-making and management of change; drivers of perceived value and consumer behavior; impact of accounting on auditing, financial, managerial, systems and taxation stakeholders; corporate governance and executive compensation; impact of operations strategies on competitiveness.

Walden University, Graduate Programs, School of Management, Minneapolis, MN 55401. Offers accounting (MBA, MS, DBA), including accounting for the professional (MS), accounting with CPA emphasis (MS), self-designed (MS); advanced project management (Graduate Certificate); applied project management (Graduate Certificate); auditing (Graduate Certificate); bridge to business administration (Post-Doctoral Certificate); bridge to management (Post-Doctoral Certificate); business management (Graduate Certificate); communication (MBA); corporate finance (MBA); digital marketing (Graduate Certificate); entrepreneurship (DBA); entrepreneurship and small business (MBA); finance (MS, DBA), including finance for the professional (MS), finance with CFA/investment (MS), finance with CPA emphasis (MS); global supply chain management (DBA); healthcare management (MBA, DBA); human resource management (MBA, MS, Graduate Certificate), including functional human resource management (MS), general program (MS), integrating functional and strategic human resource management (MS), organizational strategy (MS); human resources management (DBA); information systems management (DBA); international business (MBA, DBA); leadership (MBA, MS, DBA, Graduate Certificate), including general program (MS), human resource leadership (MS), leader development (MS), self-designed (MS); management (MS, PhD), including communications (MS), finance (PhD), general program (MS), healthcare management (MS), human resource management (MS), human resources management (PhD), information systems management (PhD), international business (MS), leadership (MS), leadership and organizational change (PhD), marketing (MS), project management (MS), strategy and operations (MS); managerial accounting (Graduate Certificate); marketing (MBA, MS, DBA); project management (MBA, MS, DBA); self-designed (MBA, DBA); social impact management (DBA); technology entrepreneurship (DBA). *Accreditation:* ACBSP. *Program availability:* Part-time, evening/weekend, online only, 100% online. *Degree requirements:* For master's, thesis (for some programs), residency (for EMBA); for doctorate, thesis/dissertation (for some programs), residency. *Entrance requirements:* For master's, bachelor's degree or higher; minimum GPA of 2.5; official transcripts; goal statement (for some programs); access to computer and Internet; for doctorate, master's degree or higher; three years of related professional or academic experience (preferred); minimum GPA of 3.0; goal statement and current resume (for select

programs); official transcripts; access to computer and Internet; for other advanced degree, relevant work experience; access to computer and Internet. Additional exam requirements/recommendations for international students: Required—TOEFL (minimum score 550 paper-based, 79 iBT), IELTS (minimum score 6.5), Michigan English Language Assessment Battery (minimum score 82), or PTE (minimum score 53). Electronic applications accepted.

Warner University, School of Business, Lake Wales, FL 33859. Offers accounting (MBA); business administration (MBA); human resource management (MBA); international business (MBA); management (MSMC). *Program availability:* Part-time, evening/weekend, online learning. *Degree requirements:* For master's, comprehensive exam, thesis. *Entrance requirements:* For master's, minimum GPA of 3.0, 2 letters of recommendation. Additional exam requirements/recommendations for international students: Required—TOEFL. Electronic applications accepted.

Washburn University, School of Business, Topeka, KS 66621. Offers accountancy (M Acc). *Accreditation:* AACSB. *Program availability:* Part-time, evening/weekend. *Entrance requirements:* For master's, GMAT, minimum GPA of 2.75. Additional exam requirements/recommendations for international students: Required—TOEFL (minimum score 550 paper-based; 80 iBT); Recommended—IELTS (minimum score 6.5). Electronic applications accepted. *Faculty research:* Ethics in information technology, forecasting for shareholder value creation, model for measuring expected losses from litigation contingencies, business vs. family commitment in family businesses, calculated intangible value and brand recognition.

Washington & Jefferson College, Graduate and Continuing Studies, Washington, PA 15301. Offers applied health care economics and outcomes management (MS); professional accounting (MAC); professional writing (Graduate Certificate); thanatology (Graduate Certificate).

Washington State University, Carson College of Business, Department of Accounting, Pullman, WA 99164-4729. Offers M Acc. Program also offered at the Vancouver campus. *Accreditation:* AACSB. *Program availability:* Part-time. *Degree requirements:* For master's, comprehensive exam, thesis or alternative. *Entrance requirements:* For master's, GMAT (minimum score of 500), minimum GPA of 3.0, statement of purpose. Additional exam requirements/recommendations for international students: Required—TOEFL (minimum score 580 paper-based; 93 iBT), IELTS (minimum score 7.5). Electronic applications accepted. *Faculty research:* Ethics, taxation, auditing, finance.

Washington University in St. Louis, Olin Business School, Program in Accounting, St. Louis, MO 63130-4899. Offers MS. *Program availability:* Part-time. *Faculty:* 85 full-time (16 women), 46 part-time/adjunct (13 women). *Students:* 137 full-time (114 women); includes 3 minority (all Asian, non-Hispanic/Latino), 129 international. Average age 23. 395 applicants, 41% accepted, 75 enrolled. In 2018, 50 master's awarded. *Degree requirements:* For master's, 33 credit hours. *Entrance requirements:* For master's, GMAT or GRE, U.S. bachelor's degree or equivalent, one letter of recommendation. Additional exam requirements/recommendations for international students: Required—TOEFL, IELTS. *Application deadline:* For fall admission, 10/10 for domestic and international students; for winter admission, 1/15 for domestic students, 1/15 priority date for international students; for spring admission, 3/18 for domestic and international students. Applications are processed on a rolling basis. Application fee: $100. Electronic applications accepted. *Financial support:* Institutionally sponsored loans and scholarships/grants available. Financial award applicants required to submit FAFSA. *Unit head:* Dr. Steve Malter, Senior Associate Dean, Undergrad and Graduate Programs, 314-935-6315, Fax: 314-935-9095, E-mail: malter@wustl.edu. *Application contact:* Ruthie Pyles, Asst Dean & Dir of Grad Admissions & Fin Aid, 314-935-7301, E-mail: olingradadmissions@wustl.edu.
Website: http://www.olin.wustl.edu

Wayland Baptist University, Graduate Programs, Programs in Business Administration/Management, Plainview, TX 79072-6998. Offers accounting (MBA); general business (MBA); health care administration (MAM, MBA); human resource management (MAM, MBA); international management (MBA); management (MBA, D Mgt); management information systems (MBA); organization management (MAM); project management (MBA). *Program availability:* Part-time, evening/weekend, online learning. *Degree requirements:* For master's, capstone course. *Entrance requirements:* For master's, GMAT, GRE or MAT. Additional exam requirements/recommendations for international students: Required—TOEFL (minimum score 500 paper-based; 61 iBT). Electronic applications accepted.

Wayne State University, Mike Ilitch School of Business, Detroit, MI 48202. Offers accounting (MS, MSA, Postbaccalaureate Certificate); business (EMS, Graduate Certificate); business administration (MBA, PhD); data science (MS), including business analytics; entrepreneurship and innovation (Postbaccalaureate Certificate); finance (MS); information systems management (Postbaccalaureate Certificate); taxation (MST); JD/MBA. Application deadline for PhD is February 15. *Accreditation:* AACSB. *Program availability:* Part-time, evening/weekend. *Faculty:* 31. *Students:* 286 full-time (152 women), 1,166 part-time (533 women); includes 409 minority (236 Black or African American, non-Hispanic/Latino; 83 Asian, non-Hispanic/Latino; 53 Hispanic/Latino; 37 Two or more races, non-Hispanic/Latino), 74 international. Average age 30. 1,212 applicants, 38% accepted, 294 enrolled. In 2018, 285 master's, 6 doctorates, 7 other advanced degrees awarded. *Degree requirements:* For doctorate, thesis/dissertation. *Entrance requirements:* For master's, GMAT, GRE, LSAT, MCAT, at least three years of relevant work experience that shows increased responsibility, or minimum GPA of 3.0 from AACSB-accredited program or 3.2 from regionally-accredited program, undergraduate degree from accredited institution; undergraduate degree in accounting, business administration, or area of business administration (for MS and MST); for doctorate, GMAT (minimum score of 600), minimum undergraduate GPA of 3.0, 3.5 upper-division or graduate; three letters of recommendation; brief essay; undergraduate degree from accredited institution; personal statement; for other advanced degree, bachelor's degree from accredited institution. Additional exam requirements/recommendations for international students: Required—TOEFL (minimum score 550 paper-based; 79 iBT), Michigan English Language Assessment Battery (minimum score 85); Recommended—IELTS (minimum score 6.5), TWE (minimum score 5.5). *Application deadline:* For fall admission, 7/1 for domestic students, 5/1 priority date for international students; for winter admission, 11/1 for domestic students, 9/1 priority date for international students; for spring admission, 3/1 for domestic students, 1/1 priority date for international students. Applications are processed on a rolling basis. Application fee: $50. Electronic applications accepted. *Expenses:* Contact institution. *Financial support:* In 2018–19, 175 students received support, including 1 fellowship with tuition reimbursement available (averaging $20,000 per year), 5 research assistantships with tuition reimbursements available (averaging $21,393 per year); teaching assistantships with tuition reimbursements available, scholarships/grants, health care benefits, and unspecified assistantships also available. Support available to part-time students. Financial award applicants required to submit FAFSA. *Faculty research:* Executive compensation and stock performance, consumer reactions to pricing strategies, communication across the automotive supply chain, performance of firms in sub-Saharan Africa, implementation issues with ERP software. *Unit head:* Dr. Robert Forsythe, Dean, School of Business Administration, 313-577-4501, E-mail: robert.forsythe@wayne.edu. *Application contact:* Kiantee N. Rupert-Jones, Director, 313-577-4511, Fax: 313-577-9442, E-mail: gradbusiness@wayne.edu.
Website: http://ilitchbusiness.wayne.edu/

Webber International University, Graduate School of Business, Babson Park, FL 33827. Offers accounting (MBA); business (MBA); criminal justice management (MBA); international business (MBA); sport business management (MBA). *Program availability:* Part-time, evening/weekend, 100% online, blended/hybrid learning. *Faculty:* 11 full-time (5 women), 1 part-time/adjunct (0 women). *Students:* 69 full-time (34 women), 11 part-time (5 women); includes 26 minority (17 Black or African American, non-Hispanic/Latino; 1 Asian, non-Hispanic/Latino; 8 Hispanic/Latino), 10 international. Average age 24. 64 applicants, 61% accepted, 32 enrolled. In 2018, 17 master's awarded. *Degree requirements:* For master's, International Learning Experience required for the master in International Business, other majors have a practicum project. *Entrance requirements:* For master's, three recommendation letters, resume, essay, official transcripts from all colleges and universities attended. Additional exam requirements/recommendations for international students: Recommended—TOEFL (minimum score 500 paper-based; 61 iBT), IELTS (minimum score 6). *Application deadline:* For fall admission, 8/1 for domestic students, 6/1 for international students; for spring admission, 1/1 for domestic students. Applications are processed on a rolling basis. Application fee: $0. Electronic applications accepted. *Financial support:* In 2018–19, 11 students received support. Scholarships/grants and unspecified assistantships available. Financial award application deadline: 8/1; financial award applicants required to submit FAFSA. *Unit head:* Dr. Nikos Orphanoudakis, Dean, 863-638-2910, Fax: 863-638-1591, E-mail: orphanoudakisn@webber.edu. *Application contact:* Lacy Edwards, Admissions Counselor and MBA Coordinator, 863-638-2910, Fax: 863-638-1591, E-mail: admissions@webber.edu.
Website: www.webber.edu

Weber State University, Goddard School of Business and Economics, School of Accounting and Taxation, Ogden, UT 84408-1001. Offers accounting (M Acc); taxation (M Tax). *Accreditation:* AACSB. *Program availability:* Part-time, evening/weekend. *Faculty:* 7 full-time (3 women), 1 part-time/adjunct (0 women). *Students:* 29 full-time (16 women), 25 part-time (10 women); includes 5 minority (2 Asian, non-Hispanic/Latino; 3 Hispanic/Latino), 1 international. Average age 32. In 2018, 44 master's awarded. *Entrance requirements:* For master's, GMAT. Additional exam requirements/recommendations for international students: Required—TOEFL (minimum score 80 iBT). *Application deadline:* For fall admission, 8/1 for domestic students; for spring admission, 12/1 for domestic students; for summer admission, 4/1 for domestic students. Application fee: $60 ($90 for international students). Electronic applications accepted. *Financial support:* In 2018–19, 20 students received support. Scholarships/grants available. Financial award application deadline: 4/1; financial award applicants required to submit FAFSA. *Unit head:* Dr. Ryan Pace, Program Director, 801-626-7562, Fax: 801-626-7423, E-mail: rpace@weber.edu. *Application contact:* Dr. Larry A. Deppe, Graduate Coordinator, 801-626-7838, Fax: 801-626-7423, E-mail: ldeppe1@weber.edu.
Website: http://www.weber.edu/goddard/accounting-taxation.html

Webster University, George Herbert Walker School of Business and Technology, Department of Business, St. Louis, MO 63119-3194. Offers business and organizational security management (MBA); decision support systems (MBA); environmental management (MBA); finance (MBA, MS); forensic accounting (MS); gerontology (MBA); human resources development (MBA); human resources management (MBA); information technology management (MBA); international business (MA, MBA); international relations (MBA); management and leadership (MBA); marketing (MBA); media communications (MBA); procurement and acquisitions management (MBA); Web services (MBA). *Accreditation:* ACBSP. *Program availability:* Part-time, evening/weekend, online learning. *Degree requirements:* For master's, comprehensive exam (for some programs), thesis (for some programs). *Entrance requirements:* Additional exam requirements/recommendations for international students: Required—TOEFL. *Expenses: Tuition:* Full-time $22,500; part-time $750 per credit hour. Tuition and fees vary according to degree level, campus/location and program.

Western Carolina University, Graduate School, College of Business, Program in Accountancy, Cullowhee, NC 28723. Offers M Ac. *Program availability:* Part-time, evening/weekend. *Entrance requirements:* For master's, GMAT, appropriate undergraduate degree, 3 letters of recommendation. Additional exam requirements/recommendations for international students: Required—TOEFL (minimum score 550 paper-based; 79 iBT). *Expenses: Tuition, area resident:* Full-time $4435. Tuition, state resident: full-time $4435. Tuition, nonresident: full-time $14,842. *International tuition:* $14,842 full-time. *Required fees:* $2979. Part-time tuition and fees vary according to course load, degree level and program.

Western Connecticut State University, Division of Graduate Studies, Ancell School of Business, Program in Business Administration, Danbury, CT 06810-6885. Offers accounting (MBA); business administration (MBA). *Program availability:* Part-time. *Degree requirements:* For master's, comprehensive exam, completion of program within 8 years. *Entrance requirements:* For master's, GMAT. Additional exam requirements/recommendations for international students: Recommended—TOEFL (minimum score 550 paper-based; 79 iBT), IELTS (minimum score 6). *Application deadline:* For fall admission, 8/5 priority date for domestic students; for spring admission, 1/5 priority date for domestic students. Applications are processed on a rolling basis. Application fee: $50. *Financial support:* Application deadline: 5/1; applicants required to submit FAFSA. *Faculty research:* Global strategic marketing planning, project management and team coordination; email, discussion boards that act as blogs and videoconferencing. *Unit head:* Dr. Karen Koza, MBA Coordinator, 203-837-9036, Fax: 203-837-8527, E-mail: kozak@wcsu.edu. *Application contact:* Chris Shankle, Associate Director of Graduate Studies, 203-837-9005, Fax: 203-837-8326, E-mail: shanklec@wcsu.edu.

Western Governors University, College of Business, Salt Lake City, UT 84107. Offers accounting (MS); information technology management (MBA); management and leadership (MS); management and strategy (MBA); strategic leadership (MBA). *Program availability:* Evening/weekend, online learning. *Degree requirements:* For master's, capstone project. *Entrance requirements:* For master's, transcripts. Additional exam requirements/recommendations for international students: Required—TOEFL (minimum score 450 paper-based; 80 iBT). Electronic applications accepted. Application fee is waived when completed online.

Western Illinois University, School of Graduate Studies, College of Business and Technology, Department of Accountancy, Macomb, IL 61455-1390. Offers M Acct. *Accreditation:* AACSB. *Program availability:* Part-time. *Students:* 16 full-time (8 women), 4 part-time (3 women); includes 4 minority (1 Black or African American, non-Hispanic/Latino; 2 Hispanic/Latino; 1 Two or more races, non-Hispanic/Latino), 4 international. Average age 26. 15 applicants, 80% accepted, 7 enrolled. In 2018, 17 master's awarded. *Entrance requirements:* For master's, GMAT. Additional exam requirements/recommendations for international students: Required—TOEFL (minimum score 550 paper-based; 80 iBT). *Application deadline:* Applications are processed on a rolling basis. Application fee: $30. Electronic applications accepted. *Financial support:* Unspecified assistantships available. Financial award applicants required to submit FAFSA. *Unit head:* Dr. Gregg Woodruff, Chairperson, 309-298-1152. *Application contact:* Dr. Mark Mossman, Assistant Director of Graduate Studies, 309-298-1806, Fax: 309-298-2345, E-mail: grad-office@wiu.edu.
Website: http://wiu.edu/accountancy

Western Michigan University, Graduate College, Haworth College of Business, Department of Accountancy, Kalamazoo, MI 49008. Offers MSA. *Accreditation:* AACSB.

Western New England University, College of Business, Program in Accounting, Springfield, MA 01119. Offers MSA, JD/MSA. *Program availability:* Part-time, evening/weekend. *Faculty:* 9 full-time (3 women). *Students:* 21 part-time (9 women); includes 2 minority (1 Asian, non-Hispanic/Latino; 1 Hispanic/Latino). Average age 27. 19 applicants, 84% accepted, 12 enrolled. In 2018, 17 master's awarded. *Entrance requirements:* For master's, GMAT or GRE, official transcript, two letters of recommendation, essay, resume. Additional exam requirements/recommendations for international students: Required—TOEFL (minimum score 79 iBT). *Application deadline:* Applications are processed on a rolling basis. Application fee: $30. Electronic applications accepted. *Expenses:* Contact institution. *Financial support:* Application deadline: 4/15; applicants required to submit FAFSA. *Unit head:* Dr. William Bosworth, Chair, Accounting and Finance, 413-782-1738, E-mail: william.bosworth@wne.edu. *Application contact:* Matthew Fox, Executive Director of Graduate Admissions, 413-782-1410, Fax: 413-782-1779, E-mail: study@wne.edu.
Website: http://www1.wne.edu/academics/graduate/msa.cfm

Westfield State University, College of Graduate and Continuing Education, Department of Economics and Business Management, Westfield, MA 01086. Offers accounting (MS). *Program availability:* Part-time, evening/weekend. *Degree requirements:* For master's, comprehensive exam, thesis (for some programs). *Entrance requirements:* For master's, GRE General Test or MAT, minimum undergraduate GPA of 2.8. Additional exam requirements/recommendations for international students: Recommended—TOEFL (minimum score 550 paper-based; 79 iBT).

West Liberty University, Gary E. West College of Business, West Liberty, WV 26074. Offers accounting (MBA); management (MBA).

Westminster College, The Bill and Vieve Gore School of Business, Salt Lake City, UT 84105-3697. Offers accountancy (M Acc); business administration (MBA, Certificate); technology commercialization (MBA). *Program availability:* Part-time, evening/weekend, blended/hybrid learning. *Degree requirements:* For master's, International Context Tour (for MBA). *Entrance requirements:* For master's, GMAT (waived on a case-by-case basis), 2 professional recommendations, employer letter of support, personal resume, essay, official transcripts. Additional exam requirements/recommendations for international students: Required—TOEFL (minimum score 84 iBT), IELTS (minimum score 7). Electronic applications accepted. *Expenses:* Contact institution. *Faculty research:* Innovation and entrepreneurship, business strategy and change, financial analysis and capital budgeting, leadership development, knowledge management.

West Texas A&M University, College of Business, Department of Accounting, Economics and Finance, Canyon, TX 79015. Offers accounting (MPA); finance and economics (MS). *Program availability:* Part-time, evening/weekend, online learning. *Degree requirements:* For master's, comprehensive exam, thesis optional. *Entrance requirements:* For master's, GMAT. Additional exam requirements/recommendations for international students: Required—TOEFL (minimum score 550 paper-based). Electronic applications accepted. *Faculty research:* Texas economy, decision report service learning and entrepreneurship, small business, trade effects of financial flow.

West Virginia University, College of Business and Economics, Morgantown, WV 26506. Offers accountancy (M Acc); accounting (PhD); business administration (MBA); business cyber security management (MS); business data analytics (MS); economics (MA, PhD); finance (MS, PhD); forensic and fraud examination (MS); industrial relations (MS); management (PhD); marketing (PhD). *Program availability:* Part-time, online learning. *Students:* 341 full-time (139 women), 44 part-time (13 women); includes 39 minority (10 Black or African American, non-Hispanic/Latino; 12 Asian, non-Hispanic/Latino; 7 Hispanic/Latino; 10 Two or more races, non-Hispanic/Latino), 40 international. In 2018, 208 master's, 20 doctorates awarded. Terminal master's awarded for partial completion of doctoral program. *Degree requirements:* For master's, thesis optional; for doctorate, comprehensive exam, thesis/dissertation. *Entrance requirements:* For doctorate, GRE General Test, minimum GPA of 3.0. Additional exam requirements/recommendations for international students: Required—TOEFL (minimum score 550 paper-based; 92 iBT). *Application deadline:* For fall admission, 10/15 priority date for domestic and international students; for spring admission, 3/1 priority date for domestic and international students. Applications are processed on a rolling basis. Application fee: $60. Electronic applications accepted. *Expenses:* Contact institution. *Financial support:* Fellowships, research assistantships, teaching assistantships, career-related internships or fieldwork, Federal Work-Study, institutionally sponsored loans, scholarships/grants, health care benefits, tuition waivers (full and partial), unspecified assistantships, and administrative assistantships available. Financial award application deadline: 2/1; financial award applicants required to submit FAFSA. *Faculty research:* Regional labor market studies, economic development, market research, economic forecasting, energy analysis. *Unit head:* Dr. Javier Reyes, Dean, 304-293-7800, Fax: 304-293-4056, E-mail: javier.reyes@mail.wvu.edu. *Application contact:* Dr. Virginia F Kleist, Associate Dean for Graduate Programs, 304-293-7939, Fax: 304-293-7188, E-mail: Virginia.Kleist@mail.wvu.edu.
Website: http://www.be.wvu.edu

Wheeling Jesuit University, Department of Business, Wheeling, WV 26003-6295. Offers accounting (MSA); business administration (MBA). *Accreditation:* ACBSP. *Program availability:* Part-time, evening/weekend. *Entrance requirements:* For master's, minimum undergraduate GPA of 2.8. Additional exam requirements/recommendations for international students: Required—TOEFL (minimum score 600 paper-based; 100 iBT). Electronic applications accepted. *Faculty research:* Forensic economics, consumer behavior, economic development, capitalism, leadership.

Wichita State University, Graduate School, W. Frank Barton School of Business, School of Accountancy, Wichita, KS 67260. Offers accounting information systems (M Acc); taxation (M Acc). *Accreditation:* AACSB. *Program availability:* Part-time, evening/weekend. *Unit head:* Dr. Jeffrey Bryant, Director, 316-978-3215, Fax: 316-978-3660, E-mail: jeffrey.bryant@wichita.edu. *Application contact:* Jordan Oleson, Admissions Coordinator, 316-978-3095, Fax: 316-978-3253, E-mail: jordan.oleson@wichita.edu.
Website: http://www.wichita.edu/acct

Wilfrid Laurier University, Faculty of Graduate and Postdoctoral Studies, Lazaridis School of Business and Economics, Department of Business, Waterloo, ON N2L 3C5, Canada. Offers accounting (PhD); finance (M Fin); financial economics (PhD); marketing (PhD); operations and supply chain management (PhD); organizational behavior and human resource management (M Sc); organizational behaviour and human resource management (PhD); supply chain management (M Sc); technology management (EMTM). *Accreditation:* AACSB. *Program availability:* Part-time, evening/weekend. *Degree requirements:* For master's, thesis optional; for doctorate, comprehensive exam, thesis/dissertation. *Entrance requirements:* For master's, GMAT, 4-year honors degree with minimum B+ average; for doctorate, GMAT, master's degree, minimum B+ average. Additional exam requirements/recommendations for international students: Required—TOEFL (minimum score 89 iBT). Electronic applications accepted. *Faculty research:* Financial economics, management and organizational behavior, operations and supply chain management.

Wilkes University, College of Graduate and Professional Studies, Jay S. Sidhu School of Business and Leadership, Wilkes-Barre, PA 18766-0002. Offers accounting (MBA); global business (MBA); human resource management (MBA); international business (MBA); leadership (MBA); management (MBA); operations management (MBA); organizational leadership and development (MBA). *Accreditation:* ACBSP. *Program availability:* Part-time, evening/weekend. *Students:* 16 full-time (9 women), 64 part-time (33 women); includes 11 minority (3 Black or African American, non-Hispanic/Latino; 3 Asian, non-Hispanic/Latino; 3 Hispanic/Latino; 2 Two or more races, non-Hispanic/Latino), 7 international. Average age 30. In 2018, 49 master's awarded. *Entrance requirements:* For master's, GMAT. Additional exam requirements/recommendations for international students: Required—TOEFL (minimum score 550 paper-based; 79 iBT). *Application deadline:* Applications are processed on a rolling basis. Application fee: $45 ($65 for international students). Electronic applications accepted. *Expenses:* Contact institution. *Financial support:* Unspecified assistantships available. Financial award application deadline: 3/1; financial award applicants required to submit FAFSA. *Unit head:* Dr. Abel Adekola, Dean, 570-408-4701, Fax: 570-408-7846, E-mail: abel.adekola@wilkes.edu. *Application contact:* Kristin Donati, Associate Director of Graduate Admissions, 570-408-3338, Fax: 570-408-7846, E-mail: kristin.donati@wilkes.edu.
Website: http://www.wilkes.edu/academics/colleges/sidhu-school-of-business-leadership/index.aspx

William Paterson University of New Jersey, Cotsakos College of Business, Wayne, NJ 07470-8420. Offers applied business analytics (MS); business administration (MBA), including accounting, entrepreneurship, finance, general business administration, human resource management, marketing, music and entertainment management; MBA pathways (Certificate); sales leadership (MS). *Accreditation:* AACSB. *Program availability:* Part-time, evening/weekend. *Faculty:* 21 full-time (6 women), 5 part-time/adjunct (1 woman). *Students:* 78 full-time (40 women), 250 part-time (113 women); includes 161 minority (39 Black or African American, non-Hispanic/Latino; 1 American Indian or Alaska Native, non-Hispanic/Latino; 23 Asian, non-Hispanic/Latino; 82 Hispanic/Latino; 16 Two or more races, non-Hispanic/Latino), 14 international. Average age 31. 222 applicants, 86% accepted, 136 enrolled. In 2018, 95 master's awarded. *Degree requirements:* For master's, Programs Differ see: https://academiccatalog.wpunj.edu/content.php?catoid=1&navoid=68. *Entrance requirements:* For master's, program details: https://www.wpunj.edu/admissions/graduate/admission-deadlines-and-requirements/. Additional exam requirements/recommendations for international students: Required—TOEFL (minimum score 550 paper-based; 79 iBT), IELTS (minimum score 6). *Application deadline:* For fall admission, 6/1 for domestic students, 3/1 for international students; for spring admission, 11/1 for domestic students, 10/1 for international students. Applications are processed on a rolling basis. Application fee: $50. Electronic applications accepted. *Expenses: Tuition, area resident:* Full-time $14,714; part-time $727 per credit. *Tuition, state resident:* full-time $14,714; part-time $727 per credit. *Tuition, nonresident:* full-time $22,952; part-time $727 per credit. *International tuition:* $22,952 full-time. *Required fees:* $4 per semester. Tuition and fees vary according to course load, degree level and program. *Financial support:* In 2018-19, 18 students received support. Career-related internships or fieldwork, Federal Work-Study, scholarships/grants, tuition waivers, and unspecified assistantships available. Support available to part-time students. Financial award application deadline: 3/15; financial award applicants required to submit FAFSA. *Faculty research:* Labor markets, job characteristics and ethical behavior, institutional trading of stocks and bonds, education funding, pricing strategies in business-to-business markets. *Unit head:* Dr. Siamack Shojai, Dean, 973-720-2964, Fax: 973-720-2809, E-mail: shojais@wpunj.edu. *Application contact:* Tinu Adeniran, Assistant Director, Graduate Admissions, 973-720-2764, Fax: 973-720-2035, E-mail: adenirant@wpunj.edu.
Website: http://www.wpunj.edu/ccob

Wilmington University, College of Business, New Castle, DE 19720-6491. Offers accounting (MBA, MS); business administration (MBA, DBA); environmental stewardship (MBA); finance (MBA); health care administration (MBA, MSM); homeland security (MBA, MSM); human resource management (MSM); management information systems (MBA, MSN); marketing (MSM); marketing management (MBA); military leadership (MSM); organizational leadership (MBA, MSM); public administration (MSM). *Program availability:* Part-time, evening/weekend. *Entrance requirements:* Additional exam requirements/recommendations for international students: Required—TOEFL (minimum score 500 paper-based). Electronic applications accepted.

Wilson College, Graduate Programs, Chambersburg, PA 17201-1285. Offers accounting (M Acc); choreography and visual art (MFA); education (M Ed); educational technology (MET); healthcare administration (MHA); humanities (MA), including art and culture, critical/cultural theory, English language and literature, women's studies; management (MSM); nursing (MSN), including nursing education, nursing leadership and management; special education (MSE). *Program availability:* Evening/weekend. *Degree requirements:* For master's, project. *Entrance requirements:* For master's, PRAXIS, minimum undergraduate cumulative GPA of 3.0, 2 letters of recommendation, current certification for eligibility to teach in grades K-12, resume, personal interview. Electronic applications accepted.

Wingate University, Porter B. Byrum School of Business, Wingate, NC 28174. Offers accounting (MAC); corporate innovation (MBA); finance (MBA); general management (MBA); healthcare management (MBA); marketing (MBA); project management (MBA). *Accreditation:* ACBSP. *Program availability:* Part-time, evening/weekend. *Entrance requirements:* For master's, GMAT, work experience, 2 letters of recommendation. Electronic applications accepted. *Expenses:* Contact institution. *Faculty research:* Stochastic processes, business ethics, regional economic development, municipal finance, consumer behavior.

Worcester State University, Graduate School, Program in Management, Worcester, MA 01602-2597. Offers accounting (MS); leadership (MS); marketing (MS). *Program availability:* Part-time, evening/weekend. *Faculty:* 6 full-time (3 women), 1 part-time/adjunct (0 women). *Students:* 15 full-time (6 women), 43 part-time (24 women); includes 14 minority (4 Black or African American, non-Hispanic/Latino; 5 Asian, non-Hispanic/Latino; 5 Hispanic/Latino), 7 international. Average age 38. 32 applicants, 100% accepted, 24 enrolled. In 2018, 24 master's awarded. *Degree requirements:* For master's, comprehensive exam (for some programs), thesis (for some programs), For a detail list in Degree Completion requirements please see the graduate catalog at catalog.worcester.edu. *Entrance requirements:* For master's, GMAT, For a detail list of entrance requirements please see the graduate catalog at catalog.worcester.edu. Additional exam requirements/recommendations for international students: Required—TOEFL (minimum score 550 paper-based; 79 iBT), IELTS (minimum score 6). *Application deadline:* For fall admission, 3/1 for domestic and international students; for spring admission, 11/1 for domestic and international students; for summer admission, 3/1 for domestic and international students. Applications are processed on a rolling basis. Application fee: $50. Electronic applications accepted. *Expenses: Tuition, area resident:* Full-time $3042; part-time $169 per credit hour. *Tuition, state resident:* full-time $3042; part-time $169 per credit hour. *Tuition, nonresident:* full-time $3042; part-time $169 per credit hour. *International tuition:* $3042 full-time. *Required fees:* $2754; $153 per credit hour. *Financial support:* Career-related internships or fieldwork,

scholarships/grants, and unspecified assistantships available. Financial award application deadline: 3/1; financial award applicants required to submit FAFSA. *Unit head:* Dr. Elizabeth Wark, Program Coordinator, 508-929-8743, Fax: 508-929-8048, E-mail: ewark@worcester.edu. *Application contact:* Sara Grady, Associate Dean, Graduate Studies and Professional Development, 508-929-8130, Fax: 508-929-8100, E-mail: sara.grady@worcester.edu.

Wright State University, Graduate School, Raj Soin College of Business, Department of Accountancy, Accountancy Program, Dayton, OH 45435. Offers M Acc.

Xavier University, Williams College of Business, Master of Science in Accountancy Program, Cincinnati, OH 45207. Offers MS. *Entrance requirements:* For master's, GMAT, official transcript; resume; 3 letters of recommendation. Additional exam requirements/recommendations for international students: Required—TOEFL (minimum score 550 paper-based; 70 iBT) or IELTS. Electronic applications accepted. Application fee is waived when completed online. *Expenses:* Contact institution.

Yale University, Yale School of Management, Doctoral Program in Management, New Haven, CT 06520. Offers accounting (PhD); financial economics (PhD); marketing (PhD); organizations and management (PhD). *Accreditation:* AACSB. *Degree requirements:* For doctorate, comprehensive exam, thesis/dissertation. *Entrance requirements:* For doctorate, GMAT or GRE General Test. Additional exam requirements/recommendations for international students: Required—TOEFL or IELTS. Electronic applications accepted. *Expenses:* Contact institution. *Faculty research:* Pricing of options and futures, term structure of interest rates, use of accounting numbers in debt contracts, product differentiation, e-commerce and marketing, behavioral finance.

Yeshiva University, Sy Syms School of Business, New York, NY 10016. Offers accounting (MS); business (EMBA); marketing (MS); taxation (MS). *Program availability:* Part-time. *Entrance requirements:* For master's, minimum GPA of 3.5 or GMAT.

York College of Pennsylvania, Graham School of Business, York, PA 17403-3651. Offers accounting (M Acc); business (MBA); continuous improvement (MBA); financial management (MBA); health care management (MBA); management (MBA); marketing (MBA); self-designed (MBA). *Accreditation:* ACBSP. *Program availability:* Part-time, evening/weekend. *Faculty:* 11 full-time (5 women), 3 part-time/adjunct (1 woman). *Students:* 13 full-time (4 women), 73 part-time (32 women); includes 11 minority (5 Black or African American, non-Hispanic/Latino; 2 Asian, non-Hispanic/Latino; 2 Hispanic/Latino; 2 Two or more races, non-Hispanic/Latino), 1 international. Average age 35. 57 applicants, 65% accepted, 25 enrolled. In 2018, 8 master's awarded. *Degree requirements:* For master's, directed study. *Entrance requirements:* For master's, GMAT. Additional exam requirements/recommendations for international students: Required—TOEFL (minimum score 530 paper-based; 72 iBT), IELTS (minimum score 6). *Application deadline:* For fall admission, 7/15 priority date for domestic students, 5/1 for international students; for spring admission, 11/15 priority date for domestic students, 9/1 for international students; for summer admission, 4/15 priority date for domestic students. Applications are processed on a rolling basis. Application fee: $0. Electronic applications accepted. *Expenses:* Contact institution. *Financial support:* In 2018–19, 3 students received support. Scholarships/grants available. Financial award applicants required to submit FAFSA. *Unit head:* Nicole Cornell Sadowski, MBA Director, 717-815-1491, Fax: 717-600-3999, E-mail: ncornell@ycp.edu. *Application contact:* MBA Office, 717-815-1491, Fax: 717-600-3999, E-mail: mba@ycp.edu.
Website: http://www.ycp.edu/mba

York University, Faculty of Graduate Studies, Schulich School of Business, Toronto, ON M3J 1P3, Canada. Offers accounting (M Acc); administration (PhD); business (MBA); business analytics (MBA); finance (MF); international business (IMBA); MBA/JD; MBA/MA; MBA/MFA. *Program availability:* Part-time, evening/weekend. *Degree requirements:* For master's, advanced proficiency in a second language, work term (IMBA); for doctorate, comprehensive exam, thesis/dissertation. *Entrance requirements:* For master's, GMAT or GRE, minimum GPA of 3.0 (3.3 for MF, MBA in business analytics, and IMBA); for doctorate, GMAT or GRE, minimum GPA of 3.3. Additional exam requirements/recommendations for international students: Required—TOEFL (minimum score 600 paper-based; 100 iBT), IELTS (minimum score 7), York English Language Test (minimum score 1); PearsonVUE (minimum score 64). Electronic applications accepted. *Faculty research:* Accounting, finance, marketing, operations management and information systems, organizational studies, strategic management.

Youngstown State University, College of Graduate Studies, Williamson College of Business Administration, Department of Accounting and Finance, Youngstown, OH 44555-0001. Offers accountancy (M Acc). *Accreditation:* AACSB. *Program availability:* Part-time, evening/weekend. *Degree requirements:* For master's, thesis optional. *Entrance requirements:* For master's, GMAT, minimum GPA of 2.7. Additional exam requirements/recommendations for international students: Required—TOEFL. *Faculty research:* Taxation and compliance, capital markets, accounting information systems, accounting theory, tax and government accounting.

Finance and Banking

Adelphi University, Robert B. Willumstad School of Business, MBA Program, Garden City, NY 11530-0701. Offers accounting (MBA); finance (MBA); health services administration (MBA); human resource management (MBA); management (MBA); management information systems (MBA); marketing (MBA); sport management (MBA). *Accreditation:* AACSB. *Program availability:* Part-time, evening/weekend. *Students:* 343 full-time (132 women), 101 part-time (56 women); includes 75 minority (22 Black or African American, non-Hispanic/Latino; 2 American Indian or Alaska Native, non-Hispanic/Latino; 20 Asian, non-Hispanic/Latino; 23 Hispanic/Latino; 1 Native Hawaiian or other Pacific Islander, non-Hispanic/Latino; 7 Two or more races, non-Hispanic/Latino), 275 international. Average age 29. 389 applicants, 59% accepted, 187 enrolled. In 2018, 171 master's awarded. *Entrance requirements:* For master's, GMAT, official transcripts, bachelor's degree, 500 word essay, 2 letters of recommendation, resume. Additional exam requirements/recommendations for international students: Required—TOEFL (minimum score 550 paper-based; 80 iBT), IELTS (minimum score 6.5). *Application deadline:* For fall admission, 4/1 for international students; for spring admission, 11/1 for international students. Applications are processed on a rolling basis. Application fee: $50. Electronic applications accepted. *Financial support:* Research assistantships with partial tuition reimbursements, career-related internships or fieldwork, Federal Work-Study, institutionally sponsored loans, scholarships/grants, tuition waivers (partial), and unspecified assistantships available. Financial award application deadline: 3/1; financial award applicants required to submit FAFSA. *Faculty research:* Supply chain management, distribution channels, productivity benchmark analysis, data envelopment analysis, financial portfolio analysis. *Unit head:* Britt'ny Brown, Director of Graduate Programs, 516-877-4605. *Application contact:* Britt'ny Brown, Director of Graduate Programs, 516-877-4605.
Website: https://business.adelphi.edu/

American Business & Technology University, Programs in Business Administration, Saint Joseph, MO 64506. Offers business administration (MBA); financial management (MBA); global business management (MBA); information systems management (MBA); marketing and social media (MBA); project and operations management (MBA); public accounting (MBA). *Program availability:* Online learning.

The American College of Financial Services, Graduate Programs, Bryn Mawr, PA 19010-2105. Offers financial services (MSFS); leadership (MSM). *Program availability:* Part-time, evening/weekend, online learning. Electronic applications accepted. *Faculty research:* Retirement counseling, social security, aging, family composition, inflation.

American College of Thessaloniki, Department of Business Administration, Pylea, Greece. Offers banking and finance (MBA); entrepreneurship (MBA, Certificate); finance (Certificate); management (MBA, Certificate); marketing (MBA, Certificate). *Program availability:* Part-time, evening/weekend. *Degree requirements:* For master's, thesis. *Entrance requirements:* For master's, bachelor's degree. Additional exam requirements/recommendations for international students: Recommended—TOEFL. Electronic applications accepted.

American InterContinental University Online, Program in Business Administration, Schaumburg, IL 60173. Offers accounting and finance (MBA); finance (MBA); healthcare management (MBA); human resource management (MBA); international business (MBA); management (MBA); marketing (MBA); operations management (MBA); organizational psychology and development (MBA); project management (MBA). *Accreditation:* ACBSP. *Program availability:* Evening/weekend, online learning. *Entrance requirements:* Additional exam requirements/recommendations for international students: Required—TOEFL (minimum score 550 paper-based). Electronic applications accepted.

American University, Kogod School of Business, Department of Finance, Washington, DC 20016-8044. Offers finance (MS, Certificate); real estate (MS, Certificate). *Program availability:* Part-time, evening/weekend. *Faculty:* 13 full-time (4 women), 5 part-time/adjunct (2 women). *Students:* 61 full-time (33 women), 26 part-time (10 women); includes 12 minority (5 Black or African American, non-Hispanic/Latino; 4 Asian, non-Hispanic/Latino; 3 Hispanic/Latino), 56 international. Average age 26. 176 applicants, 69% accepted, 40 enrolled. In 2018, 3,349 master's, 4 other advanced degrees awarded. *Degree requirements:* For master's, comprehensive exam (for some programs). *Entrance requirements:* For master's, GMAT/GRE; Please see website: https://www.american.edu/kogod/, resume, personal statement, interview, 2 letters of recommendation, transcripts. Additional exam requirements/recommendations for international students: Required—TOEFL (minimum score 100 iBT). *Application deadline:* Applications are processed on a rolling basis. Application fee: $100. *Expenses:* Contact institution. *Financial support:* Applicants required to submit FAFSA. *Unit head:* Dr. Jeffrey Harris, Department Chair, Finance and Real Estate, 202-885-1900, E-mail: kogodgrad@american.edu. *Application contact:* Jason Garner, Director of Admissions, 202-885-1926, E-mail: jgarner@american.edu.
Website: http://www.american.edu/kogod/

The American University in Cairo, School of Business, Cairo, Egypt. Offers business administration (MBA); economics (MA); economics in international development (MA, Diploma); finance (MS). *Program availability:* Part-time, evening/weekend. *Degree requirements:* For master's, comprehensive exam (for some programs), thesis (for some programs). *Entrance requirements:* For master's, GMAT, GRE. Additional exam requirements/recommendations for international students: Required—TOEFL (minimum score 450 paper-based; 45 iBT), IELTS (minimum score 5). Electronic applications accepted. *Expenses:* Contact institution. *Faculty research:* Marketing and quality management, banking operations management, economics, finance.

The American University in Dubai, Graduate Programs, Dubai, United Arab Emirates. Offers construction management (MS); education (M Ed); finance (MBA); generalist (MBA); marketing (MBA). *Program availability:* Part-time, evening/weekend. *Degree requirements:* For master's, thesis optional. *Entrance requirements:* For master's, GMAT (for MBA); GRE (for M Ed and MS), minimum undergraduate GPA of 3.0, official transcripts, two reference forms, curriculum vitae/resume, statement of career objectives, work experience. Additional exam requirements/recommendations for international students: Required—TOEFL (minimum score 550 paper-based; 79 iBT). Electronic applications accepted.

American University of Beirut, Graduate Programs, Faculty of Arts and Sciences, Beirut 1107 2020, Lebanon. Offers anthropology (MA); Arab and Middle Eastern history (PhD); Arabic language and literature (MA, PhD); archaeology (MA); art history and curating (MA); biology (MS); cell and molecular biology (PhD); chemistry (MS); clinical psychology (MA); computational sciences (MS); computer science (MS); economics (MA); education (MA), including administration and policy studies, elementary education, mathematics education, psychology school guidance, psychology test and measurements, science education, teaching English as a foreign language; English language (MA); English literature (MA); environmental policy planning (MS); financial economics (MAFE); general psychology (MA); geology (MS); history (MA); Islamic studies (MA); mathematics (MS); media studies (MA); Middle East studies (MA); philosophy (MA); physics (MS); political studies (MA); public administration (MA); public policy and international affairs (MA); sociology (MA); theoretical physics (PhD). *Program availability:* Part-time. *Faculty:* 187 full-time (64 women), 27 part-time/adjunct (15 women). *Students:* 292 full-time (215 women), 216 part-time (148 women). Average age 27. 422 applicants, 64% accepted, 124 enrolled. In 2018, 90 master's, 3 doctorates awarded. *Degree requirements:* For master's, comprehensive exam, thesis (for some programs), project; for doctorate, comprehensive exam, thesis/dissertation (for some programs). *Entrance requirements:* For master's, GRE General Test (for archaeology, clinical psychology, general psychology, economics, financial economics and biology); for doctorate, GRE General Test for all PhD programs, GRE Subject Test for theoretical physics. Additional exam requirements/recommendations for international students: Required—TOEFL (minimum score 583 paper-based; 97 iBT), IELTS (minimum score 7). *Application deadline:* For fall admission, 3/18 for domestic students; for spring admission, 11/5 for domestic students. Application fee: $50. Electronic applications accepted. *Expenses:* MA/MS: Humanities and social sciences=$912/credit.

Sciences=$943/credit. Financial economics=$986/credit. Thesis: Humanities/social sciences=$6565 and sciences=$6865. *Financial support:* In 2018–19, 227 fellowships with full tuition reimbursements, 17 research assistantships with full tuition reimbursements, 83 teaching assistantships with full tuition reimbursements were awarded; scholarships/grants, tuition waivers (full and partial), and unspecified assistantships also available. Financial award application deadline: 3/18. *Faculty research:* Sciences: Physics: High energy, Particle, Polymer and Soft Matter, Thermal, Plasma; String Theory, Mathematical physics, Astrophysics (stellar evolution, planet and galaxy formation and evolution, astrophysical dynamics), Solid State physics/thin films, Spintronics, Magnetic properties of materials, Mineralogy, Petrology, and Geochemistry of Hard Rocks, Geophysics and Petrophysics, Hydrogeology, Micropaleontology, Sedimentology, and Stratigraphy, Structural Geology and Geotectonics, Renewable en. *Total annual research expenditures:* $4.3 million. *Unit head:* Dr. Nadia Maria El Cheikh, Dean, Faculty of Arts and Sciences, 961-1-350000 Ext. 3800, Fax: 961-1-744461, E-mail: nmcheikh@aub.edu.lb. *Application contact:* Adriana Michelle Zanaty, Curriculum and Graduate Studies Officer, 961-1-350000 Ext. 3833, Fax: 961-1-744461, E-mail: az48@aub.edu.lb.
Website: https://www.aub.edu.lb/fas/Pages/default.aspx

American University of Beirut, Graduate Programs, Suliman S. Olayan School of Business, Master's in Finance Program, Beirut, Lebanon. Offers M Fin. *Program availability:* Part-time. *Faculty:* 7 full-time (0 women), 4 part-time/adjunct (0 women). *Students:* 27 full-time (17 women), 10 part-time (4 women). Average age 23. 116 applicants, 68% accepted, 37 enrolled. In 2018, 39 master's awarded. *Entrance requirements:* Additional exam requirements/recommendations for international students: Required—TOEFL (minimum score 79 iBT), IELTS (minimum score 6), AUB-EN. *Application deadline:* For fall admission, 6/30 for domestic and international students. Applications are processed on a rolling basis. Application fee: $50. Electronic applications accepted. *Expenses: Tuition:* Full-time $17,748; part-time $986 per credit. *Required fees:* $762. Tuition and fees vary according to course load and program. *Financial support:* In 2018–19, 22 students received support, including 21 research assistantships with partial tuition reimbursements available (averaging $21,000 per year); fellowships, teaching assistantships, scholarships/grants, tuition waivers, and unspecified assistantships also available. Financial award application deadline: 6/30. *Unit head:* Maya El Helou, Director of Graduate Programs, 961-1-350000 Ext. 3955, E-mail: helou@aub.edu.lb. *Application contact:* Maya El-Helou, Director of Graduate Programs, 1-350000 Ext. 3955, E-mail: helou@aub.edu.lb.
Website: http://www.aub.edu.lb/osb/MFIN/Pages/default.aspx

Andrews University, School of Graduate Studies, School of Business, Graduate Programs in Business, Berrien Springs, MI 49104. Offers MBA, MSA. *Entrance requirements:* For master's, GMAT. Additional exam requirements/recommendations for international students: Required—TOEFL (minimum score 550 paper-based).

Argosy University, Atlanta, College of Business, Atlanta, GA 30328. Offers accounting (DBA); corporate compliance (MBA); customized professional concentration (MBA, DBA); finance (MBA); healthcare administration (MBA); information systems (DBA); information systems management (MBA); international business (MBA, DBA); management (MBA, MSM, DBA); marketing (MBA, DBA). *Accreditation:* ACBSP.

Argosy University, Chicago, College of Business, Chicago, IL 60601. Offers accounting (DBA); customized professional concentration (MBA, DBA); finance (MBA); fraud examination (MBA); global business sustainability (DBA); healthcare administration (MBA); information systems (DBA); information systems management (MBA); international business (MBA, DBA); management (MBA, MSM, DBA); marketing (MBA, DBA); organizational leadership (Ed D); public administration (MBA); sustainable management (MBA). *Accreditation:* ACBSP. *Program availability:* Online learning.

Argosy University, Hawai`i, College of Business, Honolulu, HI 96813. Offers accounting (DBA); corporate compliance (MBA); customized professional concentration (MBA, DBA); finance (MBA, Certificate); fraud examination (MBA); global business sustainability (DBA); healthcare administration (MBA, Certificate); information systems (DBA); information systems management (MBA, Certificate); international business (MBA, DBA, Certificate); management (MBA, MSM, DBA); marketing (MBA, DBA, Certificate); organizational leadership (Ed D); public administration (MBA); sustainable management (MBA).

Argosy University, Los Angeles, College of Business, Los Angeles, CA 90045. Offers accounting (DBA); corporate compliance (MBA); customized professional concentration (MBA, DBA); finance (MBA); fraud examination (MBA); global business sustainability (DBA); healthcare administration (MBA); information systems (DBA); information systems management (MBA); international business (MBA, DBA); management (MBA, MSM, DBA); marketing (MBA, DBA); organizational leadership (Ed D); public administration (MBA); sustainable management (MBA).

Argosy University, Northern Virginia, College of Business, Arlington, VA 22209. Offers accounting (DBA); customized professional concentration (MBA, DBA); finance (MBA); fraud examination (MBA); global business sustainability (DBA); healthcare administration (MBA); information systems (DBA); information systems management (MBA); international business (MBA, DBA, Certificate); management (MBA, MSM, DBA); marketing (MBA, DBA, Certificate); organizational leadership (Ed D); public administration (MBA); sustainable management (MBA).

Argosy University, Orange County, College of Business, Orange, CA 92868. Offers accounting (DBA, Adv C); corporate compliance (MBA); customized professional concentration (MBA, DBA); finance (MBA, Certificate); fraud examination (MBA); global business sustainability (DBA); healthcare administration (MBA, Certificate); information systems (DBA, Adv C, Certificate); information systems management (MBA); international business (MBA, DBA, Adv C, Certificate); management (MBA, MSM, DBA, Adv C); marketing (MBA, DBA, Adv C, Certificate); organizational leadership (Ed D); public administration (MBA, Certificate); sustainable management (MBA).

Argosy University, Phoenix, College of Business, Phoenix, AZ 85021. Offers accounting (DBA); corporate compliance (MBA); customized professional concentration (MBA, DBA); finance (MBA); fraud examination (MBA); global business sustainability (DBA); healthcare administration (MBA); information systems (DBA); information systems management (MBA); international business (MBA, DBA); management (MBA, DBA); marketing (MBA, DBA); public administration (MBA); sustainable management (MBA).

Argosy University, Seattle, College of Business, Seattle, WA 98121. Offers accounting (DBA); corporate compliance (MBA); customized professional concentration (MBA, DBA); finance (MBA); fraud examination (MBA); global business sustainability (DBA); healthcare administration (MBA); information systems (DBA); information systems management (MBA); international business (MBA, DBA); management (MBA, MSM, DBA); marketing (MBA, DBA); organizational leadership (Ed D); public administration (MBA); sustainable management (MBA).

Argosy University, Tampa, College of Business, Tampa, FL 33607. Offers accounting (DBA); corporate compliance (MBA); customized professional concentration (MBA, DBA); finance (MBA); fraud examination (MBA); global business sustainability (DBA); healthcare administration (MBA); information systems (DBA); information systems management (MBA); international business (MBA, DBA); management (MBA, MSM, DBA); marketing (MBA, DBA); organizational leadership (Ed D); public administration (MBA); sustainable management (MBA).

Argosy University, Twin Cities, College of Business, Eagan, MN 55121. Offers accounting (DBA); customized professional concentration (MBA, DBA); finance (MBA); fraud examination (MBA); global business sustainability (DBA); healthcare administration (MBA); information systems (DBA); information systems management (MBA); international business (MBA, DBA); management (MBA, MSM, DBA); marketing (MBA, DBA); organizational leadership (Ed D); public administration (MBA); sustainable management (MBA).

Arizona State University at the Tempe campus, W. P. Carey School of Business, Program in Business Administration, Tempe, AZ 85287-4906. Offers entrepreneurship (MBA); finance (MBA); health sector management (MBA); international business (MBA); leadership (MBA); marketing (MBA); organizational behavior (PhD); strategic management (PhD); supply chain management (MBA, PhD); JD/MBA; MBA/M Acc; MBA/M Arch. *Accreditation:* AACSB. *Program availability:* Part-time, evening/weekend, online learning. Terminal master's awarded for partial completion of doctoral program. *Degree requirements:* For master's, thesis or alternative, internship, interactive Program of Study (iPOS) submitted before completing 50 percent of required credit hours; for doctorate, comprehensive exam, thesis/dissertation, interactive Program of Study (iPOS) submitted before completing 50 percent of required credit hours. *Entrance requirements:* For master's, GMAT, minimum GPA of 3.0 in last 2 years of work leading to bachelor's degree, 2 letters of recommendation, professional resume, official transcripts, 3 essays; for doctorate, GMAT or GRE, minimum GPA of 3.0 in last 2 years of work leading to bachelor's degree, 3 letters of recommendation, resume, personal statement/essay. Additional exam requirements/recommendations for international students: Required—TOEFL (minimum score 550 paper-based; 80 iBT), IELTS (minimum score 6.5). Electronic applications accepted. *Expenses:* Contact institution.

Ashland University, Dauch College of Business and Economics, Ashland, OH 44805-3702. Offers accounting (MBA); business analytics (MBA); entrepreneurship (MBA); financial management (MBA); global management (MBA); health care management and leadership (MBA); human resource management (MBA); human resources (MBA); management information systems (MBA); project management (MBA); sport management (MBA); supply chain management (MBA). *Accreditation:* ACBSP. *Program availability:* Part-time, evening/weekend, 100% online, blended/hybrid learning. Terminal master's awarded for partial completion of doctoral program. *Degree requirements:* For master's, thesis optional, capstone course. *Entrance requirements:* For master's, 2 years of full-time work experience. Additional exam requirements/recommendations for international students: Required—TOEFL (minimum score 550 paper-based; 78 iBT). Electronic applications accepted. *Expenses:* Contact institution. *Faculty research:* Relationship marketing strategy, executive compensation and company performance, online marketplaces in electronic commerce, diversity training in campus recreation departments, entrepreneurship in developing and emerging economies.

Aspen University, Program in Business Administration, Denver, CO 80246-1930. Offers business administration (MBA); finance (MBA); information management (MBA); project management (MBA, Certificate). *Program availability:* Part-time, evening/weekend, online only, 100% online. *Faculty:* 16 full-time (15 women), 240 part-time/adjunct (120 women). *Students:* 556 part-time. Average age 37. *Degree requirements:* For master's, comprehensive exam. *Entrance requirements:* For master's and Certificate, www.aspen.edu, www.aspen.edu. *Application deadline:* Applications are processed on a rolling basis. Application fee: $0. Electronic applications accepted. *Financial support:* Applicants required to submit FAFSA. *Unit head:* Dr. Kevin Thrasher, Provost, 602-5706708, E-mail: kevin.thrasher@aspen.edu. *Application contact:* Enrollment Advisor, 800-373-7814.
Website: http://www.aspen.edu

Assumption College, Business Studies Program, Worcester, MA 01609-1296. Offers accounting (MBA); business studies (CAGS); finance/economics (MBA); human resources (MBA); international business (MBA); management (MBA); marketing (MBA); nonprofit leadership (MBA). *Program availability:* Part-time, evening/weekend. *Degree requirements:* For master's, capstone. *Entrance requirements:* For master's, bachelor's degree, three letters of recommendation, official transcripts, personal statement, current resume; for CAGS, MBA or equivalent degree in a closely related field, three letters of recommendation, official transcripts, personal statement, current resume. Additional exam requirements/recommendations for international students: Required—TOEFL (minimum score 540 paper-based; 76 iBT), IELTS (minimum score 6). Electronic applications accepted. *Faculty research:* Workplace diversity, dynamics of team interaction, utilization of leased employees, experiential learning project on due diligence market for prostheses.

Auburn University, Graduate School, College of Business, Department of Finance, Auburn University, AL 36849. Offers MS. *Expenses:* Tuition, state resident: full-time $11,282; part-time $535 per credit hour. Tuition, nonresident: full-time $30,542; part-time $1605 per credit hour. *Required fees:* $826 per semester. Tuition and fees vary according to degree level and program.

Azusa Pacific University, School of Business and Management, Azusa, CA 91702-7000. Offers accounting (MBA); business administration (MBA); entrepreneurship (MBA); finance (MBA); international business (MBA); marketing (MBA); organizational science (MBA); professional accountancy (M Acc); sport management (MBA). *Program availability:* Part-time, evening/weekend. *Degree requirements:* For master's, thesis (for some programs), final project. *Entrance requirements:* For master's, GMAT, minimum GPA of 3.0. Additional exam requirements/recommendations for international students: Required—TOEFL (minimum score 600 paper-based). *Expenses:* Contact institution. *Faculty research:* Gender issues, financial risk, leadership and ethics, marketing strategy.

Babson College, F. W. Olin Graduate School of Business, Babson Park, MA 02457-0310. Offers accounting (MSA); advanced management (Certificate); business administration (MBA); business analytics (MS); finance (MS); global entrepreneurship (MS); technological entrepreneurship (MS). *Accreditation:* AACSB. *Program availability:* Part-time, evening/weekend, online learning. *Entrance requirements:* For master's, GMAT, 2 years of work experience, resume, letters of recommendation. Additional exam requirements/recommendations for international students: Required—TOEFL (minimum score 100 iBT), IELTS (minimum score 6.5). Electronic applications accepted. *Faculty research:* Entrepreneurship, sustainability, global markets, process of innovation, social media and advertising.

Baker College Center for Graduate Studies–Online, Graduate Programs, Flint, MI 48507. Offers accounting (MBA); business administration (DBA); finance (MBA); general business (MBA); health care management (MBA); human resources management (MBA); information management (MBA); leadership studies (MBA); management information systems (MSIS); marketing (MBA); occupational therapy (MOT). *Program availability:* Part-time, evening/weekend, online learning. *Degree requirements:* For master's, portfolio. *Entrance requirements:* For master's, 3 years of work experience, minimum undergraduate GPA of 2.5, writing sample, 3 letters of recommendation; for doctorate, MBA or acceptable related master's degree from accredited association, 5

years work experience, minimum graduate GPA of 3.25, writing sample, 3 professional references. Additional exam requirements/recommendations for international students: Required—TOEFL (minimum score 550 paper-based). Electronic applications accepted.

Barry University, Andreas School of Business, Graduate Certificate Programs, Miami Shores, FL 33161-6695. Offers finance (Certificate); health services administration (Certificate); international business (Certificate); management (Certificate); management information systems (Certificate); marketing (Certificate).

Baruch College of the City University of New York, Zicklin School of Business, Department of Economics and Finance, Program in Finance, New York, NY 10010-5585. Offers MBA, MS, PhD. PhD offered jointly with Graduate School and University Center of the City University of New York. *Program availability:* Part-time, evening/weekend. *Degree requirements:* For doctorate, comprehensive exam, thesis/dissertation. *Entrance requirements:* For master's, GMAT, 2 letters of recommendation, resume, 2 years of work experience; for doctorate, GMAT. Additional exam requirements/recommendations for international students: Required—TOEFL (minimum score 590 paper-based), TWE (minimum score 5).

Baruch College of the City University of New York, Zicklin School of Business, Zicklin Executive Programs, Executive Program in Finance, New York, NY 10010-5585. Offers MS. *Program availability:* Evening/weekend. *Entrance requirements:* For master's, personal interview, work experience. *Expenses:* Contact institution. *Faculty research:* Corporate finance, investments, options, securities, system risk.

Bayamón Central University, Graduate Programs, Program in Business Administration, Bayamón, PR 00960-1725. Offers accounting (MBA); finance (MBA); general business (MBA); management (MBA); marketing (MBA). *Program availability:* Part-time, evening/weekend. *Degree requirements:* For master's, comprehensive exam (for some programs). *Entrance requirements:* For master's, EXADEP, bachelor's degree in business or related field.

Bellevue University, Graduate School, College of Business, Bellevue, NE 68005-3098. Offers acquisition and contract management (MS); business administration (MBA); finance (MS); human capital management (PhD); management (MSM).

Benedictine University, Graduate Programs, Program in Business Administration, Lisle, IL 60532. Offers accounting (MBA); entrepreneurship and managing innovation (MBA); financial management (MBA); health administration (MBA); human resource management (MBA); information systems security (MBA); international business (MBA); management consulting (MBA); management information systems (MBA); marketing management (MBA); operations management and logistics (MBA); organizational leadership (MBA). *Program availability:* Part-time, evening/weekend, 100% online, blended/hybrid learning. *Faculty:* 7 full-time (1 woman), 36 part-time/adjunct (10 women). *Students:* 110 full-time (71 women), 500 part-time (302 women); includes 104 minority (34 Black or African American, non-Hispanic/Latino; 1 American Indian or Alaska Native, non-Hispanic/Latino; 41 Asian, non-Hispanic/Latino; 23 Hispanic/Latino; 5 Native Hawaiian or other Pacific Islander, non-Hispanic/Latino), 7 international. Average age 33. 251 applicants, 84% accepted, 202 enrolled. In 2018, 345 master's awarded. *Entrance requirements:* For master's, GMAT or GRE test scores or completed test waiver form, official transcripts; 2 letters of reference from individuals familiar with the applicant's professional or academic work, excluding family or personal friends; a 1-2 page essay addressing educational and career goals; current résumé listing chronological work history; personal interview may be required prior to an admission decision. Additional exam requirements/recommendations for international students: Required—TOEFL (minimum score 550 paper-based; 79 iBT), IELTS (minimum score 6.5). *Application deadline:* Applications are processed on a rolling basis. Application fee: $40. Electronic applications accepted. *Unit head:* Ricky Holman, Assistant Professor, 630-829-1936, E-mail: rholman@ben.edu. *Application contact:* Ricky Holman, Assistant Professor, 630-829-1936, E-mail: rholman@ben.edu.

Bentley University, McCallum Graduate School of Business, Masters in Finance, Waltham, MA 02452-4705. Offers MSF. *Program availability:* Part-time, evening/weekend. *Faculty:* 118 full-time (38 women), 25 part-time/adjunct (4 women). *Students:* 65 full-time (27 women), 16 part-time (9 women); includes 5 minority (4 Asian, non-Hispanic/Latino; 1 Hispanic/Latino), 58 international. Average age 24. 191 applicants, 79% accepted, 37 enrolled. In 2018, 51 master's awarded. *Entrance requirements:* For master's, GMAT or GRE General Test (may be waived for qualified applicants), Transcripts; Resume; Two essays; Two letters of recommendation; Interview (may be requested by Bentley). Additional exam requirements/recommendations for international students: Required—TOEFL (minimum score 100) or IELTS (minimum score 7). *Application deadline:* For fall admission, 7/31 for domestic students, 6/30 for international students; for spring admission, 1/1 for domestic students, 11/1 for international students. Applications are processed on a rolling basis. Application fee: $150. Electronic applications accepted. *Financial support:* In 2018–19, 39 students received support. Scholarships/grants and unspecified assistantships available. Financial award application deadline: 6/1; financial award applicants required to submit FAFSA. *Faculty research:* Management of financial institutions; corporate governance and executive compensation; asset valuation; international mergers and acquisitions; hedging, risk management and derivatives. *Unit head:* Claude Cicchetti, Senior Lecturer and MSF Director, 781-891-2511, E-mail: ccicchetti@bentley.edu. *Application contact:* Office of Graduate Admissions, 781-891-2108, E-mail: applygrad@bentley.edu.
Website: https://www.bentley.edu/academics/graduate-programs/masters-finance

Binghamton University, State University of New York, Graduate School, School of Management, Program in Management, Binghamton, NY 13902-6000. Offers finance (PhD); management information systems (PhD); marketing (PhD); organizational studies (PhD); supply chain management (PhD). *Degree requirements:* For doctorate, thesis/dissertation. *Entrance requirements:* For doctorate, GMAT.

Bluffton University, Graduate Programs in Business, Bluffton, OH 45817. Offers accounting and financial management (MBA); health care management (MBA); leadership (MAOM, MBA); production and operations management (MBA); sustainability management (MBA). *Program availability:* Evening/weekend, blended/hybrid learning, videoconference. *Faculty:* 4 full-time (2 women), 5 part-time/adjunct (1 woman). *Students:* 38 full-time (22 women), 1 part-time (0 women); includes 11 minority (6 Black or African American, non-Hispanic/Latino; 3 Hispanic/Latino; 2 Two or more races, non-Hispanic/Latino). Average age 33. In 2018, 25 master's awarded. *Degree requirements:* For master's, integrated research project (for some programs). *Entrance requirements:* For master's, current resume, official transcript, bachelor's degree, minimum GPA of 3.0, personal essay. Additional exam requirements/recommendations for international students: Recommended—TOEFL (minimum score 550 paper-based). *Application deadline:* For fall admission, 7/31 priority date for domestic and international students. Applications are processed on a rolling basis. Electronic applications accepted. *Expenses:* Contact institution. *Financial support:* Unspecified assistantships and faculty/staff grants available. Financial award applicants required to submit FAFSA. *Unit head:* Dr. Melissa Green, Director of Graduate Programs in Business, 419-358-3447, E-mail: greenm@bluffton.edu. *Application contact:* Shelby Koenig, Enrollment Counselor for Graduate Program, 419-3583684, E-mail: koenigs@bluffton.edu.
Website: https://www.bluffton.edu/ags/index.aspx

Boston College, Carroll School of Management, Graduate Finance Programs, Chestnut Hill, MA 02467-3800. Offers MSF, PhD, MBA/MSF. *Program availability:* Part-time. *Degree requirements:* For doctorate, thesis/dissertation. *Entrance requirements:* For master's, GMAT or GRE, resume, recommendations; for doctorate, GMAT or GRE, curriculum vitae, recommendations. Additional exam requirements/recommendations for international students: Required—TOEFL (minimum score 600 paper-based, 100 iBT), IELTS (minimum score 7.5), or PTE (minimum score 68). Electronic applications accepted. *Faculty research:* Security and derivative markets, financial institutions, corporate finance and capital markets, market macrostructure, investments, portfolio analysis.

Boston University, Metropolitan College, Department of Administrative Sciences, Boston, MA 02215. Offers applied business analytics (MS); economic development and tourism management (MSAS); enterprise risk management (MS); financial management (MS); global marketing management (MS); innovation and technology (MSAS); insurance management (MS); project management (MS); supply chain management (MS). *Accreditation:* AACSB. *Program availability:* Part-time, evening/weekend, 100% online, blended/hybrid learning. *Faculty:* 27 full-time (5 women), 39 part-time/adjunct (5 women). *Students:* 617 full-time (351 women), 574 part-time (290 women); includes 196 minority (47 Black or African American, non-Hispanic/Latino; 2 American Indian or Alaska Native, non-Hispanic/Latino; 75 Asian, non-Hispanic/Latino; 60 Hispanic/Latino; 12 Two or more races, non-Hispanic/Latino), 730 international. Average age 28. 2,259 applicants, 76% accepted, 594 enrolled. In 2018, 441 master's awarded. *Degree requirements:* For master's, thesis optional. *Entrance requirements:* For master's, 1 year of work experience, minimum GPA of 3.0. Additional exam requirements/recommendations for international students: Required—TOEFL (minimum score 84 iBT). *Application deadline:* For fall admission, 8/1 priority date for domestic students, 6/1 priority date for international students; for spring admission, 12/1 priority date for domestic students, 11/15 priority date for international students; for summer admission, 4/1 priority date for domestic students, 3/1 priority date for international students. Applications are processed on a rolling basis. Application fee: $85. Electronic applications accepted. *Expenses:* Contact institution. *Financial support:* In 2018–19, 15 students received support, including 16 research assistantships (averaging $8,400 per year), 30 teaching assistantships (averaging $3,400 per year); career-related internships or fieldwork, Federal Work-Study, and unspecified assistantships also available. Financial award applicants required to submit FAFSA. *Faculty research:* International business, innovative process. *Unit head:* Dr. John Sullivan, Chair, 617-353-3016, E-mail: adminsc@bu.edu. *Application contact:* Enrollment Services, 617-358-8162, E-mail: met@bu.edu.
Website: http://www.bu.edu/met/academic-community/departments/administrative-sciences/

Brandeis University, International Business School (IBS), Master of Arts in International Economics and Finance Program, Waltham, MA 02454-9110. Offers applied economic analysis (MA). *Entrance requirements:* For master's, GMAT or GRE. Additional exam requirements/recommendations for international students: Required—TOEFL (minimum score 600 paper-based; 100 iBT), IELTS (minimum score 7), PTE (minimum score 68). Electronic applications accepted. *Expenses:* Contact institution. *Faculty research:* International economic policy analysis, macroeconomics, econometrics, business economics, economic development.

Brandeis University, International Business School (IBS), Master of Business Administration Program, Waltham, MA 02454-9110. Offers data analytics (MBA); finance (MBA); marketing (MBA); real estate (MBA). *Entrance requirements:* For master's, GMAT or GRE, minimum two years of full-time work experience. Additional exam requirements/recommendations for international students: Required—TOEFL (minimum score 600 paper-based; 100 iBT), IELTS (minimum score 7), PTE (minimum score 68). Electronic applications accepted. *Expenses:* Contact institution. *Faculty research:* Strategic alliances, IPO and venture capital financing, real estate, risk management, data analytics.

Brandeis University, International Business School (IBS), Master of Science in Finance Program, Waltham, MA 02454-9110. Offers asset management (MSF); corporate finance (MSF); risk management (MSF). *Entrance requirements:* For master's, GMAT or GRE. Additional exam requirements/recommendations for international students: Required—TOEFL (minimum score 600 paper-based; 100 iBT), IELTS (minimum score 7), PTE (minimum score 68). Electronic applications accepted. *Expenses:* Contact institution. *Faculty research:* Asset management, municipal finance, corporate finance, venture capital, international trade.

Brandeis University, International Business School (IBS), PhD in International Economics and Finance Program, Waltham, MA 02454-9110. Offers advanced macroeconomics (PhD); applied microeconomics (PhD). *Degree requirements:* For doctorate, thesis/dissertation. *Entrance requirements:* Additional exam requirements/recommendations for international students: Required—TOEFL (minimum score 600 paper-based; 100 iBT), IELTS (minimum score 7), PTE (minimum score 68). *Expenses:* Contact institution. *Faculty research:* Global business, global trade, global finance, macroeconomics, development and institutions.

Brandman University, School of Business and Professional Studies, Irvine, CA 92618. Offers accounting (MBA); business administration (MBA); business intelligence and data analytics (MBA); e-business strategic management (MBA); entrepreneurship (MBA); finance (MBA); health administration (MBA); human resources (MBA, MS); international business (MBA); marketing (MBA); organizational leadership (MA, MBA, MPA); public administration (MPA).

Bridgewater State University, College of Graduate Studies, Ricciardi College of Business, Department of Accounting and Finance, Bridgewater, MA 02325. Offers MSM. *Program availability:* Part-time, evening/weekend. *Entrance requirements:* For master's, GMAT.

Brigham Young University, Graduate Studies, BYU Marriott School of Business, MBA Program, Provo, UT 84602. Offers entrepreneurship (MBA); finance (MBA); global supply chain management (MBA); marketing (MBA); strategic human resources (MBA); JD/MBA; MBA/MS. *Accreditation:* AACSB. *Entrance requirements:* For master's, GMAT or GRE, commitment to BYU Honor Code, undergraduate degree. Additional exam requirements/recommendations for international students: Required—TOEFL (minimum score 590 paper-based; 100 iBT), IELTS (minimum score 7). Electronic applications accepted. *Expenses:* Contact institution. *Faculty research:* Finance, marketing, supply chain management, entrepreneurship, strategic human resources.

Brooklyn College of the City University of New York, School of Business, Brooklyn, NY 11210-2889. Offers accounting (MS); business administration (MS), including economic analysis, general business, global business and finance. *Program availability:* Part-time, evening/weekend. *Degree requirements:* For master's, comprehensive exam, thesis or alternative. *Entrance requirements:* For master's, GMAT, 2 letters of recommendation. Additional exam requirements/recommendations for international students: Required—TOEFL (minimum score 550 paper-based; 79 iBT). Electronic applications accepted. *Faculty research:* Econometrics, environmental economics, microeconomics, macroeconomics, taxation.

California College of the Arts, Graduate Programs, MBA in Design Strategy Program, San Francisco, CA 94107. Offers MBA. *Accreditation:* NASAD. *Faculty:* 1 (woman) full-time, 14 part-time/adjunct (4 women). *Students:* 79 full-time (54 women); includes 24 minority (3 Black or African American, non-Hispanic/Latino; 10 Asian, non-Hispanic/Latino; 10 Hispanic/Latino; 1 Native Hawaiian or other Pacific Islander, non-Hispanic/Latino), 18 international. Average age 31. In 2018, 39 master's awarded. *Degree requirements:* For master's, thesis. *Entrance requirements:* Additional exam requirements/recommendations for international students: Required—TOEFL, IELTS, or PTE. *Application deadline:* For fall admission, 1/31 priority date for domestic and international students. Applications are processed on a rolling basis. Application fee: $70. Electronic applications accepted. *Expenses:* $51,210 per year for full-time students. *Financial support:* Federal Work-Study and scholarships/grants available. Financial award application deadline: 7/31; financial award applicants required to submit FAFSA. *Unit head:* Andy Dong, Program Chair, 800-447-1ART, E-mail: andy@cca.edu. *Application contact:* David Murray, Director of Graduate Admissions, 415-703-9533, Fax: 415-703-9539, E-mail: dmurray@cca.edu.

California Intercontinental University, School of Business, Irvine, CA 92614. Offers banking and finance (MBA); entrepreneurship and business management (DBA); global business leadership (DBA); international management and marketing (MBA); organizational management and human resource management (MBA).

California Lutheran University, Graduate Studies, School of Management, Thousand Oaks, CA 91360-2787. Offers business (IMBA); entrepreneurship (MBA, Certificate); finance (MBA, Certificate); financial planning (MBA, MS, Certificate); human capital management (MBA, Certificate); information technology (MS); information technology management (MBA, Certificate); international business (MBA, Certificate); management (MS); marketing (MBA, Certificate); public policy and administration (MPPA); quantitative economics (MS). *Program availability:* Part-time, evening/weekend, 100% online, blended/hybrid learning. *Degree requirements:* For master's, comprehensive exam (for some programs). *Entrance requirements:* For master's, GMAT, interview, minimum GPA of 3.0. Electronic applications accepted. *Expenses:* Contact institution.

California State University, East Bay, Office of Graduate Studies, College of Business and Economics, MBA Program, Option in Finance, Hayward, CA 94542-3000. Offers MBA. *Degree requirements:* For master's, comprehensive exam or thesis. *Entrance requirements:* For master's, GMAT, minimum GPA of 2.75. Additional exam requirements/recommendations for international students: Required—TOEFL (minimum score 550 paper-based). Electronic applications accepted.

California State University, Fullerton, Graduate Studies, College of Business and Economics, Department of Finance, Fullerton, CA 92831-3599. Offers MBA. *Program availability:* Part-time. *Entrance requirements:* For master's, GMAT, minimum AACSB index of 950.

California State University, Los Angeles, Graduate Studies, College of Business and Economics, Department of Finance and Law, Los Angeles, CA 90032-8530. Offers finance and banking (MBA, MS). *Program availability:* Part-time, evening/weekend. *Degree requirements:* For master's, comprehensive exam (MBA), thesis (MS). *Entrance requirements:* For master's, GMAT, minimum GPA of 2.5 during previous 2 years of course work. Additional exam requirements/recommendations for international students: Required—TOEFL (minimum score 550 paper-based). Electronic applications accepted.

California State University, San Bernardino, Graduate Studies, College of Business and Public Administration, Program in Business Administration, San Bernardino, CA 92407. Offers accounting (MBA); entrepreneurship (MBA); finance (MBA); global business (MBA); information management (MBA); information security (MBA); management (MBA); supply chain management (MBA). *Accreditation:* AACSB. *Program availability:* Part-time, evening/weekend, online learning. *Faculty:* 5 full-time (4 women), 7 part-time/adjunct (3 women). *Students:* 40 full-time (14 women), 163 part-time (72 women); includes 99 minority (7 Black or African American, non-Hispanic/Latino; 15 Asian, non-Hispanic/Latino; 71 Hispanic/Latino; 6 Two or more races, non-Hispanic/Latino), 58 international. Average age 32. 342 applicants, 52% accepted, 91 enrolled. In 2018, 106 master's awarded. *Degree requirements:* For master's, comprehensive exam, thesis. *Entrance requirements:* Additional exam requirements/recommendations for international students: Required—TOEFL. *Application deadline:* For fall admission, 7/16 for domestic students, 7/20 for international students; for winter admission, 10/23 for domestic students, 10/20 for international students; for spring admission, 1/22 for domestic students, 1/20 for international students. Application fee: $55. *Expenses:* Contact institution. *Financial support:* Application deadline: 3/1. *Unit head:* Dr. Lawrence C. Rose, Dean, 909-537-3703, Fax: 909-537-7026, E-mail: lrose@csusb.edu. *Application contact:* Ernest Silvers, MBA Program Director, 909-537-5703, E-mail: esilvers@csusb.edu.
Website: http://mba.csusb.edu/

Capella University, School of Business and Technology, Doctoral Programs in Business, Minneapolis, MN 55402. Offers accounting (DBA, PhD); business intelligence (DBA); finance (DBA, PhD); general business management (PhD); human resource management (DBA, PhD); leadership (DBA, PhD); management education (PhD); marketing (DBA, PhD); project management (DBA, PhD); strategy and innovation (DBA, PhD). *Accreditation:* ACBSP.

Capella University, School of Business and Technology, Master's Programs in Business, Minneapolis, MN 55402. Offers accounting (MBA); business analysis (MS); business intelligence (MBA); entrepreneurship (MBA); finance (MBA); general business administration (MBA); general human resource management (MS); general leadership (MS); health care management (MBA); human resource management (MBA); marketing (MBA); project management (MBA, MS). *Accreditation:* ACBSP.

Carnegie Mellon University, Tepper School of Business, Program in Financial Economics, Pittsburgh, PA 15213-3891. Offers PhD. *Degree requirements:* For doctorate, thesis/dissertation. *Entrance requirements:* For doctorate, GRE General Test.

Case Western Reserve University, Weatherhead School of Management, Department of Banking and Finance, Cleveland, OH 44106. Offers finance (MSM). *Entrance requirements:* For master's, GMAT. *Expenses:* Tuition: Full-time $45,168; part-time $1939 per credit hour. *Required fees:* $36; $18 per semester. $18 per semester. *Faculty research:* Monetary and fiscal policy, corporate finance, future markets, derivative pricing, capital market efficiency.

Central European University, Department of Economics, 1051, Hungary. Offers business administration (PhD); business analytics (M Sc); economic policy in global markets (MA); economics (MA, PhD); finance (MS); global economic relations (MA); technology management and innovation (MS). *Program availability:* Part-time. *Degree requirements:* For master's, one foreign language, thesis; for doctorate, one foreign language, comprehensive exam, thesis/dissertation. *Entrance requirements:* For master's and doctorate, interview. Additional exam requirements/recommendations for international students: Required—TOEFL (minimum score 570 paper-based); Recommended—IELTS (minimum score 6.5). Electronic applications accepted. *Faculty research:* Economic theory (microeconomics and macroeconomics) and econometrics, as well as study of many applied fields, including labor economics, health economics and economics of education, industrial organization, monetary economics, international

economics, law and economics, comparative institutional economics, corporate governance, and economics of transition.

Central Michigan University, College of Graduate Studies, College of Business Administration, MBA Program, Mount Pleasant, MI 48859. Offers accounting (MBA); business economics (MBA); consulting (MBA); finance (MBA); general business (MBA); human resource management (MBA); information systems (MBA); international business (MBA); logistics management (MBA); marketing (MBA); value-driven organization (MBA). *Program availability:* Part-time, evening/weekend, online learning. Electronic applications accepted. *Faculty research:* Accounting, consulting, international business, marketing, information systems.

Charleston Southern University, College of Business, Charleston, SC 29423-8087. Offers accounting (MBA); finance (MBA); general management (MBA); human resource management (MS); leadership (MBA); management information systems (MBA); organizational leadership (MA). *Program availability:* Part-time, evening/weekend. *Degree requirements:* For master's, thesis optional. *Entrance requirements:* For master's, GMAT. Additional exam requirements/recommendations for international students: Required—TOEFL (minimum score 550 paper-based; 79 iBT). Electronic applications accepted.

City University of Seattle, Graduate Division, School of Management, Seattle, WA 98121. Offers accounting (Certificate); change leadership (MBA, Certificate); computer systems (MS); finance (Certificate); financial management (MBA); general management (MBA); general management-Europe (MBA); global marketing (MBA); human resources management (Certificate); individualized study (MBA); information security (MS); information systems (MBA); leadership (MA); marketing (MBA, Certificate); project management (MBA, MS, Certificate); sustainable business (Certificate); technology management (MBA, Certificate). *Program availability:* Part-time, evening/weekend, online learning. *Degree requirements:* For master's, comprehensive exam (for some programs), thesis (for some programs). *Entrance requirements:* For master's, baccalaureate degree or equivalent from an accredited or otherwise recognized institution. Additional exam requirements/recommendations for international students: Required—TOEFL (minimum score 567 paper-based; 87 iBT); Recommended—IELTS. Electronic applications accepted.

Clarion University of Pennsylvania, College of Business Administration and Information Sciences, Master of Business Administration Program, Clarion, PA 16214. Offers accounting (MBA); finance (MBA); health care administration (MBA); innovation and entrepreneurship (MBA); non-profit business (MBA). *Accreditation:* AACSB. *Program availability:* Part-time, evening/weekend, online only, 100% online. *Faculty:* 7 full-time (0 women), 1 part-time/adjunct (0 women). *Students:* 21 full-time (7 women), 67 part-time (34 women); includes 11 minority (5 Black or African American, non-Hispanic/Latino; 5 Hispanic/Latino; 1 Two or more races, non-Hispanic/Latino), 2 international. Average age 31. 90 applicants, 51% accepted, 38 enrolled. In 2018, 39 master's awarded. *Entrance requirements:* For master's, If GPA is below 3.0 submit the GMAT, minimum QPA of 2.75. Additional exam requirements/recommendations for international students: Required—TOEFL (minimum score 550 paper-based; 80 iBT), Or IELTS score of at least 7.0. Bachelor's degree accredited U.S. college or university is acceptable evidence of English language proficiency. *Application deadline:* For fall admission, 8/1 priority date for domestic students, 7/15 priority date for international students; for winter admission, 11/1 priority date for domestic students; for spring admission, 12/1 priority date for domestic students, 11/15 priority date for international students; for summer admission, 4/1 priority date for domestic students. Applications are processed on a rolling basis. Application fee: $40. Electronic applications accepted. *Expenses:* Tuition, area resident: Part-time $516 per credit hour. Tuition, state resident: part-time $516 per credit hour. Tuition, nonresident: part-time $774 per credit hour. *Required fees:* $159 per credit hour. One-time fee: $50 part-time. Tuition and fees vary according to degree level, campus/location and program. *Financial support:* Federal Work-Study, institutionally sponsored loans, and scholarships/grants available. Financial award application deadline: 3/1; financial award applicants required to submit FAFSA. *Unit head:* Juanice Vega, Assistant to the Dean, 814-393-2600, Fax: 814-393-1910, E-mail: mba@clarion.edu. *Application contact:* Susan Staub, Graduate Admissions Counselor, 814-393-2337, Fax: 814-393-2722, E-mail: gradstudies@clarion.edu. Website: http://www.clarion.edu/admissions/graduate/index.html

Clark University, Graduate School, Graduate School of Management, Business Administration Program, Worcester, MA 01610-1477. Offers accounting (MBA); finance (MBA); information management and business analytics (MBA); management (MBA); marketing (MBA); social change (MBA); sustainability (MBA). *Accreditation:* AACSB. *Program availability:* Part-time, evening/weekend. *Degree requirements:* For master's, thesis optional. *Entrance requirements:* For master's, GMAT or GRE, 2 references, resume or curriculum vitae, personal statement. Additional exam requirements/recommendations for international students: Required—TOEFL (minimum score 575 paper-based; 90 iBT), IELTS (minimum score 6.5). Electronic applications accepted. *Expenses:* Contact institution. *Faculty research:* Marketing, accounting, human resource management, management information systems, business finance.

Clark University, Graduate School, Graduate School of Management, Program in Finance, Worcester, MA 01610-1477. Offers MSF. *Degree requirements:* For master's, thesis optional. *Entrance requirements:* For master's, GMAT or GRE, 2 references, resume or curriculum vitae, personal statement. Additional exam requirements/recommendations for international students: Required—TOEFL (minimum score 575 paper-based; 90 iBT), IELTS (minimum score 6.5). Electronic applications accepted. *Expenses:* Contact institution. *Faculty research:* Marketing, accounting, human resource management, management information systems, business finance.

Cleary University, Online Program in Business Administration, Howell, MI 48843. Offers analytics, technology, and innovation (MBA, Graduate Certificate); financial planning (Graduate Certificate); global leadership (MBA, Graduate Certificate); health care leadership (MBA, Graduate Certificate). *Program availability:* Part-time, evening/weekend, online learning. *Degree requirements:* For master's, thesis. *Entrance requirements:* For master's, bachelor's degree; minimum GPA of 2.5; professional resume indicating minimum of 2 years of management or related experience; undergraduate degree from accredited college or university with at least 18 quarter hours (or 12 semester hours) of accounting study (for MBA in accounting). Additional exam requirements/recommendations for international students: Required—TOEFL (minimum score 550 paper-based; 79 iBT), Michigan English Language Assessment Battery (minimum score 75). Electronic applications accepted.

College for Financial Planning, Graduate Programs, Centennial, CO 80112. Offers finance (MSF); personal financial planning (MS). *Program availability:* Part-time, evening/weekend, online only, 100% online. *Degree requirements:* For master's, capstone course or thesis. *Entrance requirements:* Additional exam requirements/recommendations for international students: Required—TOEFL (minimum score 550 paper-based). Electronic applications accepted.

The College of Saint Rose, Graduate Studies, Huether School of Business, Program in Financial Planning, Albany, NY 12203-1419. Offers Advanced Certificate. *Program availability:* Part-time, evening/weekend. *Students:* 1 (woman) full-time, 4 part-time (0 women); includes 1 minority (Hispanic/Latino). Average age 36. 4 applicants, 50%

accepted, 2 enrolled. In 2018, 3 Advanced Certificates awarded. *Degree requirements:* For Advanced Certificate, comprehensive exam. *Entrance requirements:* Additional exam requirements/recommendations for international students: Required—TOEFL (minimum score 550 paper-based; 80 iBT), IELTS (minimum score 6), PTE (minimum score 56). *Application deadline:* For fall admission, 4/1 priority date for domestic and international students; for spring admission, 10/15 priority date for domestic students, 10/15 for international students; for summer admission, 3/15 priority date for domestic and international students. Applications are processed on a rolling basis. Application fee: $40. Electronic applications accepted. *Expenses: Tuition:* Full-time $14,382; part-time $799 per credit hour. *Required fees:* $924; $408 per credit. $286. *Financial support:* Career-related internships or fieldwork and scholarships/grants available. Support available to part-time students. Financial award application deadline: 4/15. *Unit head:* John F. Dion, Program Coordinator, 518-458-5488, E-mail: dionj@strose.edu. *Application contact:* Daniel Gallagher, Assistant Vice President for Graduate Recruitment and Enrollment, 518-485-3390, Fax: 518-458-5479, E-mail: grad@strose.edu.
Website: https://www.strose.edu/academics/graduate-programs/graduate-studies/financial-planning/

Colorado State University, College of Business, Program in Finance, Fort Collins, CO 80523-1201. Offers M Fin. *Program availability:* Part-time. *Entrance requirements:* For master's, GMAT (minimum score 620) or GRE (minimum score 315), undergraduate degree with minimum GPA of 3.0; current resume; 3 letters of recommendation; official transcripts; statement of purpose. Additional exam requirements/recommendations for international students: Required—TOEFL (minimum score 86 iBT), IELTS (minimum score 6.5), PTE (minimum score 58). Electronic applications accepted. *Expenses:* Contact institution. *Faculty research:* Individual risk management and insurance decision-making; corporate finance; quantitative and empirical finance; equity offerings; equity creation and preservation including taxation.

Colorado State University–Global Campus, Graduate Programs, Greenwood Village, CO 80111. Offers criminal justice and law enforcement administration (MS); education leadership (MS); finance (MS); healthcare administration and management (MS); human resource management (MHRM); information technology management (MITM); international management (MS); management (MS); organizational leadership (MS); professional accounting (MPA); project management (MS); teaching and learning (MS). *Accreditation:* ACBSP. *Program availability:* Online learning.

Colorado Technical University Aurora, Programs in Business Administration and Management, Aurora, CO 80014. Offers accounting (MBA); business administration (MBA); business administration and management (EMBA); finance (MBA); human resource management (MBA); marketing (MBA); mediation and dispute resolution (MBA); operations management (MBA); project management (MBA); technology management (MBA). *Program availability:* Part-time, evening/weekend. *Degree requirements:* For master's, thesis or alternative. *Entrance requirements:* For master's, minimum undergraduate GPA of 3.0, resume.

Colorado Technical University Colorado Springs, Graduate Studies, Program in Management, Colorado Springs, CO 80907. Offers accounting (MBA, MSA); business administration (MBA); finance (MBA); human resources management (MBA); logistics/supply chain management (MBA); management (DM); marketing (MBA); mediation and dispute resolution (MBA); operations management (MBA); project management (MBA); technology management (MBA). *Accreditation:* ACBSP. *Program availability:* Part-time, evening/weekend, online learning. *Degree requirements:* For master's, thesis or alternative; for doctorate, thesis/dissertation. *Entrance requirements:* For doctorate, minimum graduate GPA of 3.0, 5 years of related work experience. *Faculty research:* Sexual harassment, performance evaluation, critical thinking.

Columbia Southern University, MBA Program, Orange Beach, AL 36561. Offers finance (MBA); health care management (MBA); human resource management (MBA); marketing (MBA); project management (MBA); public administration (MBA). *Program availability:* Part-time, evening/weekend, online learning. *Entrance requirements:* For master's, bachelor's degree from accredited/approved institution. Additional exam requirements/recommendations for international students: Required—TOEFL. Electronic applications accepted.

Columbia University, Graduate School of Arts and Sciences, New York, NY 10027. Offers African-American studies (MA); American studies (MA); anthropology (MA, PhD); art history and archaeology (MA, PhD); astronomy (PhD); biological sciences (PhD); biotechnology (MA); chemical physics (PhD); chemistry (PhD); classical studies (MA, PhD); classics (MA, PhD); climate and society (MA); conservation biology (MA); earth and environmental sciences (PhD); East Asia: regional studies (MA); East Asian languages and cultures (MA, PhD); ecology, evolution and environmental biology (MA), including conservation biology; ecology, evolution, and environmental biology (PhD), including ecology and evolutionary biology, evolutionary primatology; economics (MA, PhD); English and comparative literature (MA, PhD); French and Romance philology (MA, PhD); Germanic languages (MA, PhD); global French studies (MA); global thought (MA); Hispanic cultural studies (MA); history (PhD); history and literature (MA); human rights studies (MA); Islamic studies (MA); Italian (MA, PhD); Japanese pedagogy (MA); Jewish studies (MA); Latin America and the Caribbean: regional studies (MA); Latin American and Iberian cultures (PhD); mathematics (MA, PhD), including finance (MA); medieval and Renaissance studies (MA); Middle Eastern, South Asian, and African studies (MA, PhD); modern art: critical and curatorial studies (MA); modern European studies (MA); museum anthropology (MA); music (DMA, PhD); oral history (MA); philosophical foundations of physics (MA); philosophy (MA, PhD); physics (PhD); political science (MA, PhD); psychology (PhD); quantitative methods in the social sciences (MA); religion (MA, PhD); Russia, Eurasia and East Europe: regional studies (MA); Russian translation (MA); Slavic cultures (MA); Slavic languages (MA, PhD); sociology (MA, PhD); South Asian studies (MA); statistics (MA, PhD); theatre (PhD). Dual-degree programs require admission to both Graduate School of Arts and Sciences and another Columbia school. *Program availability:* Part-time. Terminal master's awarded for partial completion of doctoral program. *Degree requirements:* For master's, variable foreign language requirement, comprehensive exam (for some programs), thesis (for some programs); for doctorate, variable foreign language requirement, comprehensive exam (for some programs), thesis/dissertation. *Entrance requirements:* For master's and doctorate, GRE General Test, GRE Subject Test (for some programs). Additional exam requirements/recommendations for international students: Required—TOEFL, IELTS. Electronic applications accepted.

Columbia University, Graduate School of Business, Doctoral Program in Business, New York, NY 10027. Offers business (PhD), including accounting, decision, risk, and operations, finance and economics, management, marketing. *Accreditation:* AACSB. *Degree requirements:* For doctorate, comprehensive exam, thesis/dissertation, major field exam, research paper, thesis proposal. *Entrance requirements:* For doctorate, GMAT or GRE (finance), 2 letters of reference, resume. Additional exam requirements/recommendations for international students: Required—TOEFL. Electronic applications accepted. *Expenses:* Contact institution. *Faculty research:* Human decision making and behavioral research; real estate market and mortgage defaults; financial crisis and corporate governance; international business; security analysis and accounting.

Columbia University, Graduate School of Business, MBA Program, New York, NY 10027. Offers accounting (MBA); decision, risk, and operations (MBA); entrepreneurship (MBA); finance and economics (MBA); healthcare and pharmaceutical management (MBA); human resource management (MBA); international business (MBA); leadership and ethics (MBA); management (MBA); marketing (MBA); media (MBA); private equity (MBA); real estate (MBA); social enterprise (MBA); value investing (MBA); DDS/MBA; JD/MBA; MBA/MIA; MBA/MPH; MBA/MS; MD/MBA. *Entrance requirements:* For master's, GMAT, 2 letters of recommendation. Additional exam requirements/recommendations for international students: Required—TOEFL. Electronic applications accepted. *Expenses:* Contact institution. *Faculty research:* Human decision making and behavioral research; real estate market and mortgage defaults; financial crisis and corporate governance; international business; security analysis and accounting.

Concordia University, School of Graduate Studies, John Molson School of Business, Montreal, QC H3H 0A1, Canada. Offers administration (M Sc), including finance, management, marketing; business administration (MBA, PhD, Certificate, Diploma); executive business administration (EMBA); supply chain management (MSCM). PhD program offered jointly with HEC Montreal, McGill University, and Université du Québec à Montréal. *Program availability:* Part-time, evening/weekend. *Degree requirements:* For master's, one foreign language, thesis (for some programs), research project; for doctorate, one foreign language, thesis/dissertation; for other advanced degree, one foreign language. *Entrance requirements:* For master's, GMAT, minimum 2 years of work experience (for MBA); letters of recommendation, bachelor's degree from recognized university with minimum GPA of 3.0, curriculum vitae; for doctorate, GMAT (minimum score of 600), official transcripts, curriculum vitae, 3 letters of reference, statement of purpose; for other advanced degree, minimum GPA of 2.7, 2 letters of reference, statement of purpose, resume. Additional exam requirements/recommendations for international students: Required—TOEFL (minimum score 90 iBT), IELTS (minimum score 7). Electronic applications accepted. *Expenses:* Contact institution. *Faculty research:* General business, capital markets, international business.

Concordia University Wisconsin, Graduate Programs, Batterman School of Business, MBA Program, Mequon, WI 53097-2402. Offers finance (MBA); health care administration (MBA); human resource management (MBA); international business (MBA); international business-bilingual English/Chinese (MBA); management (MBA); management information systems (MBA); managerial communications (MBA); marketing (MBA); public administration (MBA); risk management (MBA). *Program availability:* Online learning. *Degree requirements:* For master's, comprehensive exam, thesis or alternative. *Entrance requirements:* Additional exam requirements/recommendations for international students: Required—TOEFL. *Expenses:* Contact institution.

Cornell University, Graduate School, Graduate Field of Management, Ithaca, NY 14853. Offers accounting (PhD); finance (PhD); marketing (PhD); organizational behavior (PhD); production and operations management (PhD). *Accreditation:* AACSB. *Degree requirements:* For doctorate, comprehensive exam, thesis/dissertation. *Entrance requirements:* For doctorate, GMAT or GRE General Test. Additional exam requirements/recommendations for international students: Required—TOEFL (minimum score 600 paper-based; 77 iBT). Electronic applications accepted. *Expenses:* Contact institution. *Faculty research:* Operations and manufacturing.

Cornell University, Graduate School, Graduate Fields of Arts and Sciences, Field of Economics, Ithaca, NY 14853. Offers applied economics (PhD); basic analytical economics (PhD); econometrics and economic statistics (PhD); economic development and planning (PhD); economic theory (PhD); industrial organization and control (PhD); international economics (PhD); labor economics (PhD); monetary and macro economics (PhD); public finance (PhD). *Degree requirements:* For doctorate, comprehensive exam, thesis/dissertation. *Entrance requirements:* For doctorate, GRE General Test, 3 letters of recommendation. Additional exam requirements/recommendations for international students: Required—TOEFL (minimum score 550 paper-based; 77 iBT). Electronic applications accepted. *Faculty research:* Learning and games, economics of education, political economy, transfer payments, time series and nonparametrics.

Creighton University, Graduate School, Heider College of Business, Omaha, NE 68178-0001. Offers accounting (MAC); business administration (MBA, DBA); business intelligence and analytics (MS); finance (M Fin); investment management and financial analysis (MIMFA); JD/MBA; MBA/MIMFA; MD/MBA; Pharm D/MBA. *Accreditation:* AACSB. *Program availability:* Part-time, evening/weekend, 100% online, blended/hybrid learning. *Degree requirements:* For master's, thesis optional; for doctorate, thesis/dissertation optional. *Entrance requirements:* For master's, GMAT, resume, 2 letters of recommendation. Additional exam requirements/recommendations for international students: Required—TOEFL (minimum score 90 iBT). Electronic applications accepted. *Expenses:* Contact institution. *Faculty research:* Small business issues, economics, business analytics.

Culver-Stockton College, MBA Program, Canton, MO 63435-1299. Offers accounting and finance (MBA).

Curry College, Graduate Studies, Program in Business Administration, Milton, MA 02186-9984. Offers business administration (MBA); finance (Certificate). *Program availability:* Part-time, evening/weekend. *Degree requirements:* For master's, capstone applied project. *Entrance requirements:* For master's, resume, recommendations, interview, written statement. Additional exam requirements/recommendations for international students: Required—TOEFL (minimum score 550 paper-based; 80 iBT). *Expenses:* Contact institution.

Dalhousie University, Faculty of Management, Centre for Advanced Management Education, Halifax, NS B3H 3J5, Canada. Offers financial services (MBA); information management (MIM); management (MPA); natural resources (MBA). *Program availability:* Part-time, online learning. *Entrance requirements:* For master's, GMAT, minimum GPA of 3.0, resume. Additional exam requirements/recommendations for international students: Required—TOEFL, IELTS, CANTEST, CAEL, or Michigan English Language Assessment Battery. Electronic applications accepted.

Dalhousie University, Faculty of Management, Rowe School of Business, Halifax, NS B3H 3J5, Canada. Offers business administration (MBA); financial services (MBA); LL B/MBA; MBA/MLIS. *Program availability:* Part-time. *Entrance requirements:* For master's, GMAT, letter of non-financial guarantee for non-Canadian students, resume, Corporate Residency Preference Form. Additional exam requirements/recommendations for international students: Required—TOEFL, IELTS, CANTEST, CAEL, or Michigan English Language Assessment Battery. Electronic applications accepted. *Faculty research:* International business, quantitative methods, operations research, MIS, marketing, finance.

Dallas Baptist University, Professional Development Program, Dallas, TX 75211-9299. Offers accounting (MA); church leadership (MA); communication (MA); counseling (MA); criminal justice (MA); English as a second language (MA); finance (MA); higher education (MA); leadership studies (MA); management (MA). *Program availability:* Part-time, evening/weekend, online learning. *Application deadline:* Applications are processed on a rolling basis. Application fee: $25. Electronic applications accepted. Application fee is waived when completed online. *Expenses: Tuition:* Full-time $17,262; part-time $959 per credit hour. *Required fees:* $1000; $500 per semester. Tuition and

fees vary according to course load and degree level. *Unit head:* Jared Ingram, Program Director, 214-333-5584, E-mail: jaredi@dbu.edu. *Application contact:* Jared Ingram, Program Director, 214-333-5584, E-mail: jaredi@dbu.edu.
Website: https://www.dbu.edu/graduate/degree-programs/ma-professional-development

Davenport University, Sneden Graduate School, Grand Rapids, MI 49512. Offers accounting (MBA); business administration (EMBA); finance (MBA); health care management (MBA); human resources (MBA); information assurance (MS); occupational therapy (MSOT); public health (MPH); strategic management (MBA). *Program availability:* Evening/weekend. *Entrance requirements:* For master's, GMAT, minimum undergraduate GPA of 2.75. Additional exam requirements/recommendations for international students: Required—TOEFL. Electronic applications accepted. *Faculty research:* Leadership, management, marketing, organizational culture.

Delaware Valley University, MBA Program, Doylestown, PA 18901-2697. Offers accounting (MBA); entrepreneurship (MBA); finance (MBA); food and agribusiness (MBA); general business (MBA); global executive leadership (MBA); human resource management (MBA); supply chain management (MBA). *Program availability:* Part-time, evening/weekend, online learning. *Entrance requirements:* For master's, minimum undergraduate GPA of 3.0. Electronic applications accepted. *Expenses:* Contact institution.

DePaul University, Kellstadt Graduate School of Business, Chicago, IL 60604. Offers accountancy (MBA, MSA); applied economics (MBA); audit and advisory services (MS); business administration (DBA); business analytics (MS); business strategy and decision-making (MBA); computational finance (MS); economics and policy analysis (MS); enterprise risk management (MS); entrepreneurship (MBA, MS); finance (MBA, MS); general business (MBA); hospitality leadership (MBA); hospitality leadership and operational performance (MS); human resources (MS); international business (MBA); management (MBA, MS); management information systems (MBA); marketing (MBA, MS); marketing analysis (MS); marketing strategy and planning (MBA); real estate (MS); real estate finance and investment (MBA); strategy, execution and valuation (MBA); supply chain management (MS); sustainable management (MS); taxation (MS); JD/MBA. *Accreditation:* AACSB. *Program availability:* Part-time, evening/weekend, online learning. *Entrance requirements:* For master's, GMAT/GRE, 2 letters of recommendation, resume, essay, official transcripts. Additional exam requirements/recommendations for international students: Required—TOEFL (minimum score 550 paper-based; 80 iBT). Electronic applications accepted. *Expenses:* Contact institution.

DeSales University, Division of Business, Center Valley, PA 18034-9568. Offers accounting (MBA); computer information systems (MBA); finance (MBA); health care systems management (MBA); human resources management (MBA); management (MBA); marketing (MBA); project management (MBA); self-design (MBA); supply chain management (MBA); DNP/MBA; MSN/MBA. *Accreditation:* ACBSP. *Program availability:* Part-time, evening/weekend, 100% online, blended/hybrid learning. *Entrance requirements:* For master's, GMAT (waived if undergraduate GPA is 3.0 or better), minimum GPA of 3.0 in undergraduate work, literacy in basic software, background or interest in the field of study, personal statement, 2 years of work experience. Additional exam requirements/recommendations for international students: Required—TOEFL. Electronic applications accepted. *Expenses:* Contact institution. *Faculty research:* Quality improvement, executive development, productivity, cross-cultural managerial differences, leadership.

DeVry University–Folsom Campus, Graduate Programs, Folsom, CA 95630. Offers accounting (M Acc); accounting and financial management (MAFM); business administration (MBA); curriculum leadership (M Ed); educational leadership (M Ed); educational technology (M Ed); higher education leadership (M Ed); human resource management (MHRM); information systems management (MISM); network and communications management (MNCM); project management (MPM); public administration (MPA).

Drew University, Caspersen School of Graduate Studies, Madison, NJ 07940-1493. Offers conflict resolution and leadership (Certificate), including community leadership, moderation, peace building; education (M Ed); finance (MA); history and culture (MA, PhD), including American history, book history, British history, European history, intellectual history, Irish history, print culture, public history; K-12 education (MAT), including art, biology, chemistry, elementary education, English, French, Italian, math, secondary education, special education, teacher of students with disabilities; liberal studies (M Litt, D Litt), including history, Irish/Irish-American studies, literature (M Litt, MMH, D Litt, DMH, CMH), religion, spirituality, teaching in the two-year college, writing; medical humanities (MMH, DMH, CMH), including arts, health, healthcare, literature (M Litt, MMH, D Litt, DMH, CMH), scientific research; poetry (MFA). *Program availability:* Part-time, evening/weekend. *Faculty:* 3 full-time (2 women), 27 part-time/adjunct (13 women). *Students:* 66 full-time (38 women), 179 part-time (117 women); includes 37 minority (15 Black or African American, non-Hispanic/Latino; 2 Asian, non-Hispanic/Latino; 15 Hispanic/Latino; 5 Two or more races, non-Hispanic/Latino), 14 international. Average age 42. 157 applicants, 82% accepted, 57 enrolled. In 2018, 34 master's, 24 doctorates, 17 other advanced degrees awarded. Terminal master's awarded for partial completion of doctoral program. *Degree requirements:* For master's and other advanced degree, thesis (for some programs); for doctorate, one foreign language, comprehensive exam (for some programs), thesis/dissertation. *Entrance requirements:* For master's, PRAXIS Core and Subject Area tests (for MAT), GRE/GMAT (for MFin MS in Data Analytics), resume, transcripts, writing sample, personal statement, letters of recommendation; for doctorate, GRE (PhD in history and culture), resume, transcripts, writing sample, personal statement, letters of recommendation; for other advanced degree, resume, transcripts, personal statement. Additional exam requirements/recommendations for international students: Required—TOEFL (minimum score 587 paper-based; 80 iBT), IELTS (minimum score 6), TWE (minimum score 4). *Application deadline:* For fall admission, 8/1 for domestic students, 6/1 for international students; for spring admission, 12/1 for domestic students, 10/1 for international students. Applications are processed on a rolling basis. Application fee: $35. Electronic applications accepted. *Financial support:* Fellowships, research assistantships, teaching assistantships, career-related internships or fieldwork, Federal Work-Study, scholarships/grants, and unspecified assistantships available. Support available to part-time students. Financial award applicants required to submit FAFSA. *Unit head:* Dr. Debra Liebowitz, Provost and Dean of the College of Liberal Arts & Caspersen School of Graduate Studies, 973-4083139, E-mail: dliebowi@drew.edu. *Application contact:* Amo-Augustus Kubeyinje, Associate Vice President for Graduate Enrollment, 973-408-3111, E-mail: akubeyinje@drew.edu.
Website: http://www.drew.edu/caspersen

Drexel University, LeBow College of Business, Department of Finance, Philadelphia, PA 19104-2875. Offers MS. *Degree requirements:* For master's, seminar paper. *Entrance requirements:* For master's, GMAT, minimum GPA of 2.75. Additional exam requirements/recommendations for international students: Required—TOEFL. Electronic applications accepted. *Faculty research:* Investment analysis, portfolio mix, capital budgeting, banking and financial institutions, international finance.

Drexel University, LeBow College of Business, Program in Business Administration, Philadelphia, PA 19104-2875. Offers business administration (MBA, PhD, APC), including accounting (MBA, PhD), decision sciences (PhD), economics (MBA, PhD), finance (MBA, PhD), legal studies (MBA), management (MBA), marketing (MBA, PhD), organizational sciences (PhD), quantitative methods (MBA), strategic management (PhD). *Accreditation:* AACSB. *Program availability:* Part-time, evening/weekend, online learning. Terminal master's awarded for partial completion of doctoral program. *Entrance requirements:* For master's, GMAT, minimum GPA of 2.75; for doctorate, GMAT. Additional exam requirements/recommendations for international students: Required—TOEFL. Electronic applications accepted. *Faculty research:* Decision support systems, individual and group behavior, operations research, techniques and strategy.

Duke University, The Fuqua School of Business, The Duke MBA-Daytime Program, Durham, NC 27708. Offers academic excellence in finance (Certificate); business administration (MBA); decision sciences (MBA); energy and environment (MBA); energy finance (MBA); entrepreneurship and innovation (MBA); finance (MBA); financial analysis (MBA); health sector management (Certificate); leadership and ethics (MBA); management (MBA); management science and technology management (Certificate); marketing (MBA); operations management (MBA); social entrepreneurship (MBA); strategy (MBA). *Faculty:* 100 full-time (21 women), 55 part-time/adjunct (12 women). *Students:* 875 full-time (335 women); includes 188 minority (44 Black or African American, non-Hispanic/Latino; 4 American Indian or Alaska Native, non-Hispanic/Latino; 90 Asian, non-Hispanic/Latino; 43 Hispanic/Latino; 1 Native Hawaiian or other Pacific Islander, non-Hispanic/Latino; 6 Two or more races, non-Hispanic/Latino), 276 international. Average age 29. In 2018, 429 master's awarded. *Entrance requirements:* For master's, GMAT or GRE, transcripts, essays, resume, recommendation letters, interview. *Application deadline:* For fall admission, 9/19 for domestic and international students; for winter admission, 10/14 for domestic and international students; for spring admission, 1/6 for domestic and international students; for summer admission, 3/11 for domestic and international students. Application fee: $225. Electronic applications accepted. *Expenses:* Contact institution. *Financial support:* Scholarships/grants available. Financial award applicants required to submit FAFSA. *Unit head:* Steve Misuraca, Assistant Dean, Daytime MBA Program. *Application contact:* Shari Hubert, Associate Dean, Office of Admissions, 919-660-7705, Fax: 919-681-8026, E-mail: admissions-info@fuqua.duke.edu.
Website: https://www.fuqua.duke.edu/programs/daytime-mba

Duke University, The Fuqua School of Business, The Duke MBA-Global Executive Program, Durham, NC 27708. Offers business administration (MBA); energy and environment (MBA); entrepreneurship and innovation (MBA); finance (MBA); health sector management (Certificate); marketing (MBA); strategy (MBA). *Faculty:* 100 full-time (21 women), 55 part-time/adjunct (12 women). *Students:* 141 full-time (43 women); includes 43 minority (12 Black or African American, non-Hispanic/Latino; 25 Asian, non-Hispanic/Latino; 4 Hispanic/Latino; 1 Native Hawaiian or other Pacific Islander, non-Hispanic/Latino; 1 Two or more races, non-Hispanic/Latino), 34 international. Average age 35. In 2018, 159 master's awarded. *Entrance requirements:* For master's, Executive Assessment, GMAT, or GRE, or waived, transcripts, essays, resume, recommendation letters, letter of company support, interview. *Application deadline:* For fall admission, 10/16 priority date for domestic and international students; for winter admission, 12/4 priority date for domestic and international students; for spring admission, 3/11 priority date for domestic and international students; for summer admission, 5/27 for domestic and international students. Applications are processed on a rolling basis. Application fee: $225. Electronic applications accepted. *Expenses:* Contact institution. *Financial support:* Scholarships/grants available. Financial award applicants required to submit FAFSA. *Unit head:* Karen Courtney, Associate Dean, Executive Programs. *Application contact:* Shari Hubert, Associate Dean, Office of Admissions, 919-660-7705, Fax: 919-681-8026, E-mail: admissions-info@fuqua.duke.edu.
Website: https://www.fuqua.duke.edu/programs/global-executive-mba

Duke University, The Fuqua School of Business, The Duke MBA-Weekend Executive Program, Durham, NC 27708. Offers business administration (MBA); energy and environment (MBA); entrepreneurship and innovation (MBA); finance (MBA); health sector management (Certificate); marketing (MBA); strategy (MBA). *Faculty:* 100 full-time (21 women), 55 part-time/adjunct (12 women). *Students:* 251 full-time (67 women); includes 79 minority (13 Black or African American, non-Hispanic/Latino; 2 American Indian or Alaska Native, non-Hispanic/Latino; 46 Asian, non-Hispanic/Latino; 12 Hispanic/Latino; 1 Native Hawaiian or other Pacific Islander, non-Hispanic/Latino; 5 Two or more races, non-Hispanic/Latino), 32 international. Average age 35. In 2018, 120 master's awarded. *Entrance requirements:* For master's, Executive Assessment, GMAT, or GRE, or waived, transcripts, essays, resume, recommendation letters, letter of company support, interview. *Application deadline:* For fall admission, 9/18 priority date for domestic and international students; for winter admission, 12/4 priority date for domestic and international students; for spring admission, 1/22 priority date for domestic and international students; for summer admission, 3/11 for domestic and international students. Applications are processed on a rolling basis. Application fee: $225. Electronic applications accepted. *Expenses:* Contact institution. *Financial support:* Scholarships/grants available. Financial award applicants required to submit FAFSA. *Unit head:* Karen Courtney, Associate Dean, Executive Programs. *Application contact:* Shari Hubert, Associate Dean, Office of Admissions, 919-660-7705, Fax: 919-681-8026, E-mail: admissions-info@fuqua.duke.edu.
Website: https://www.fuqua.duke.edu/programs/weekend-executive-mba

Duke University, The Fuqua School of Business, Master of Quantitative Management Program: Business Analytics, Durham, NC 27708. Offers finance (MQM); forensics (MQM); marketing (MQM); strategy (MQM). *Faculty:* 100 full-time (21 women), 55 part-time/adjunct (12 women). *Students:* 136 full-time (56 women); includes 15 minority (1 Black or African American, non-Hispanic/Latino; 14 Asian, non-Hispanic/Latino), 99 international. Average age 23. In 2018, 136 master's awarded. *Entrance requirements:* For master's, GMAT/GRE, transcripts, essays, resume, recommendation letter, interview. *Application deadline:* For fall admission, 10/21 for domestic and international students; for winter admission, 1/15 for domestic and international students; for spring admission, 2/27 for domestic and international students; for summer admission, 4/6 for domestic and international students. Application fee: $125. Electronic applications accepted. *Expenses:* Contact institution. *Financial support:* Scholarships/grants available. Financial award applicants required to submit FAFSA. *Unit head:* Jeremy Petranka, Associate Dean, 919-660-7778. *Application contact:* Shari Hubert, Associate Dean, Office of Admissions, 919-660-7705, Fax: 919-681-8026, E-mail: mqmbusinessanalytics@fuqua.duke.edu.
Website: https://www.fuqua.duke.edu/programs/mqm-business-analytics

Duke University, The Fuqua School of Business, PhD Program, Durham, NC 27708. Offers accounting (PhD); decision sciences (PhD); finance (PhD); management and organizations (PhD); marketing (PhD); operations management (PhD); strategy (PhD). *Faculty:* 100 full-time (21 women). *Students:* 84 full-time (29 women); includes 4 minority (2 Asian, non-Hispanic/Latino; 2 Hispanic/Latino), 53 international. Average age 28. In 2018, 14 doctorates awarded. *Degree requirements:* For doctorate, comprehensive exam (for some programs), thesis/dissertation, Comprehensive or Qualifying exams are

required for some of the 7 areas in Business Administration. *Entrance requirements:* For doctorate, GMAT or GRE, transcripts, essays, recommendation letters, statement of purpose. Additional exam requirements/recommendations for international students: Required—TOEFL, IELTS. *Application deadline:* For fall admission, 12/31 priority date for domestic and international students. Application fee: $90. Electronic applications accepted. *Expenses:* Contact institution. *Financial support:* In 2018–19, 74 fellowships with full tuition reimbursements (averaging $33,300 per year) were awarded; research assistantships with full tuition reimbursements, teaching assistantships, institutionally sponsored loans, scholarships/grants, health care benefits, and tuition waivers (full) also available. *Unit head:* William Boulding, Dean, 919-660-7822. *Application contact:* Ravi Bansal, Director of Graduate Studies, 919-660-7753, Fax: 919-660-7971, E-mail: fuqua-phd-info@duke.edu.

Duquesne University, Palumbo-Donahue School of Business, Pittsburgh, PA 15282-0001. Offers accounting (M Acc); finance (MBA); information systems management (MSISM); management (MBA, MS); marketing (MBA); sports business (MS); supply chain management (MS); sustainability (MBA); JD/MBA; MBA/M Acc; MBA/MA; MBA/MES; MBA/MHMS; MSISM/MBA; Pharm D/MBA. *Accreditation:* AACSB. *Program availability:* Part-time, evening/weekend, 100% online, blended/hybrid learning. *Faculty:* 59 full-time (23 women), 25 part-time/adjunct (6 women). *Students:* 214 full-time (74 women), 42 part-time (20 women); includes 39 minority (12 Black or African American, non-Hispanic/Latino; 13 Asian, non-Hispanic/Latino; 8 Hispanic/Latino; 6 Two or more races, non-Hispanic/Latino), 23 international. Average age 29. 228 applicants, 88% accepted, 118 enrolled. In 2018, 149 master's awarded. *Entrance requirements:* For master's, GMAT or GRE, all official transcripts, two letters of recommendation, current resume, essays. Additional exam requirements/recommendations for international students: Required—TOEFL (minimum score 90 iBT), IELTS (minimum score 7). *Application deadline:* For fall admission, 7/1 priority date for domestic and international students; for spring admission, 12/1 for domestic and international students; for summer admission, 4/1 for domestic and international students. Applications are processed on a rolling basis. Application fee: $0. Electronic applications accepted. *Expenses:* $1,284/credit hour (business), $953/credit hour (management). *Financial support:* In 2018–19, 174 students received support, including 6 fellowships with partial tuition reimbursements available (averaging $24,750 per year); career-related internships or fieldwork, scholarships/grants, and unspecified assistantships also available. Support available to part-time students. Financial award application deadline: 7/1; financial award applicants required to submit FAFSA. *Faculty research:* Investment management, business ethics, technology management, supply chain management, entrepreneurship. *Unit head:* Dr. Karen Donovan, Associate Dean of Graduate Programs and Executive Education, 412-396-5788, Fax: 412-396-1726, E-mail: donovan6@duq.edu. *Application contact:* Chris Rouhier, Director of Graduate Admissions, 412-396-6244, Fax: 412-396-1726, E-mail: rouhierc@duq.edu.
Website: http://www.duq.edu/business/grad

Eastern Michigan University, Graduate School, College of Business, Programs in Business Administration, Ypsilanti, MI 48197. Offers business administration (MBA, Graduate Certificate); computer information systems (Graduate Certificate); e-business (MBA, Graduate Certificate); enterprise business intelligence (MBA); entrepreneurship (MBA, Graduate Certificate); finance (MBA, Graduate Certificate); human resources (MBA); human resources management (Graduate Certificate); information systems (MBA); internal auditing (MBA); international business (MBA, Graduate Certificate); marketing management (Graduate Certificate); nonprofit management (MBA); organizational development (Graduate Certificate); supply chain management (MBA, Graduate Certificate). *Accreditation:* AACSB. *Program availability:* Part-time, online learning. *Students:* 69 full-time (38 women), 251 part-time (140 women); includes 100 minority (63 Black or African American, non-Hispanic/Latino; 1 American Indian or Alaska Native, non-Hispanic/Latino; 12 Asian, non-Hispanic/Latino; 14 Hispanic/Latino; 10 Two or more races, non-Hispanic/Latino), 28 international. Average age 32. 199 applicants, 75% accepted, 83 enrolled. In 2018, 75 master's, 50 other advanced degrees awarded. *Entrance requirements:* For master's, GMAT (minimum score 450), minimum cumulative undergraduate GPA of 2.75. Additional exam requirements/recommendations for international students: Required—TOEFL. *Application deadline:* For fall admission, 5/15 priority date for domestic students, 2/15 priority date for international students; for winter admission, 10/15 priority date for domestic students, 9/1 priority date for international students; for summer admission, 3/15 priority date for domestic students, 3/1 priority date for international students. Applications are processed on a rolling basis. Application fee: $45. *Financial support:* Fellowships, research assistantships with full tuition reimbursements, teaching assistantships with full tuition reimbursements, career-related internships or fieldwork, Federal Work-Study, institutionally sponsored loans, scholarships/grants, tuition waivers (partial), and unspecified assistantships available. Support available to part-time students. Financial award applicants required to submit FAFSA. *Unit head:* K. Michelle Henry, Director, Graduate Business Programs, 734-487-4444, Fax: 734-483-1316, E-mail: cob.graduate@emich.edu. *Application contact:* K. Michelle Henry, Director, Graduate Business Programs, 734-487-4444, Fax: 734-483-1316, E-mail: cob.graduate@emich.edu.
Website: http://www.emich.edu/cob/mba/

Elms College, Division of Business, Chicopee, MA 01013-2839. Offers accounting (MBA); accounting and finance (MS); financial planning (MBA, Certificate); healthcare leadership (MBA); lean entrepreneurship (MBA); management (MBA). *Program availability:* Part-time, evening/weekend. *Faculty:* 4 full-time (all women), 5 part-time/adjunct (3 women). *Students:* 36 part-time (22 women); includes 9 minority (5 Black or African American, non-Hispanic/Latino; 4 Hispanic/Latino), 1 international. Average age 35. 13 applicants, 85% accepted, 9 enrolled. In 2018, 29 master's awarded. *Entrance requirements:* For master's, minimum GPA of 3.0. *Application deadline:* Applications are processed on a rolling basis. Application fee: $30. Electronic applications accepted. *Expenses: Tuition:* Full-time $14,328; part-time $796 per credit. *Required fees:* $200. Tuition and fees vary according to degree level and program. *Unit head:* Kim Kenney-Rockwal, MBA Program Director, 413-265-2572, E-mail: kenneyrockwalk@elms.edu. *Application contact:* MBA Program Coordinator, 413-265-2592, E-mail: mba@elms.edu.

Embry-Riddle Aeronautical University–Daytona, College of Business, Daytona Beach, FL 32114-3900. Offers airline management (MBA); airport management (MBA); aviation finance (MSAF); aviation human resources (MBA); aviation management (MBA-AM); aviation system management (MBA); finance (MBA). *Accreditation:* ACBSP. *Degree requirements:* For master's, thesis (for some programs). *Entrance requirements:* For master's, GRE (for some programs). Additional exam requirements/recommendations for international students: Required—TOEFL (minimum score 550 paper-based, 79 iBT) or IELTS (6). Electronic applications accepted.

Embry-Riddle Aeronautical University–Worldwide, Department of Decision Sciences, Daytona Beach, FL 32114-3900. Offers aviation and aerospace (MSPM); aviation/aerospace management (MSEM); financial management (MSEM, MSPM); general management (MSPM); global management (MSPM); human resources management (MSPM); information systems (MSPM); leadership (MSEM, MSPM); logistics and supply chain management (MSEM, MSLSCM, MSPM); management (MSEM, MSPM); project management (MSEM); systems engineering (MSEM, MSPM); technical management (MSPM). *Program availability:* Part-time, evening/weekend, EagleVision Classroom (between classrooms), EagleVision Home (faculty and students at home), and a blend of Classroom or Home. *Degree requirements:* For master's, comprehensive exam (for some programs), thesis (for some programs). *Entrance requirements:* Additional exam requirements/recommendations for international students: Required—TOEFL (minimum score 550 paper-based; 79 iBT), IELTS (minimum score 6). Electronic applications accepted. *Expenses:* Contact institution.

Emory University, Goizueta Business School, Doctoral Program in Business, Atlanta, GA 30322. Offers accounting (PhD); finance (PhD); information systems and operations management (PhD); marketing (PhD); organization and management (PhD). *Faculty:* 67 full-time (22 women). *Students:* 45 full-time (21 women); includes 5 minority (2 Black or African American, non-Hispanic/Latino; 3 Hispanic/Latino), 31 international. Average age 29. 143 applicants, 19% accepted, 10 enrolled. In 2018, 7 doctorates awarded. *Degree requirements:* For doctorate, comprehensive exam, thesis/dissertation. *Entrance requirements:* For doctorate, GMAT, interview. Additional exam requirements/recommendations for international students: Required—TOEFL (minimum score 600 paper-based; 100 iBT), IELTS, We will take either TOEFL or IELTS. *Application deadline:* For fall admission, 1/3 priority date for domestic and international students. Applications are processed on a rolling basis. Application fee: $75. Electronic applications accepted. *Expenses:* Our students are required to pay approximately $400 in their fall and spring terms; approximately $200 in summer terms in fees. All tuition is scholarshiped 100%. *Financial support:* In 2018–19, 45 students received support, including 11 fellowships (averaging $1,000 per year); scholarships/grants, health care benefits, and Fellowships are both the Sheth Fellows and Goizueta Fellows whom are named each year based on certain milestones. also available. Financial award application deadline: 1/3. *Faculty research:* Financial and managerial accounting, asset pricing strategy and organizational behavior, information technology marketing analytics and consumer behavior. *Unit head:* Kathryn Kadous, Associate Dean, 404-727-2306, Fax: 404-727-5337, E-mail: kathryn.kadous@emory.edu. *Application contact:* Allison Gilmore, Director of Admissions and Student Services, 404-727-6353, Fax: 404-727-5337, E-mail: allison.gilmore@emory.edu.
Website: https://goizueta.emory.edu/degree/phd/index.html

Emory University, Goizueta Business School, Full Time MBA Program, Atlanta, GA 30322-1100. Offers accounting (MBA); alternative investments (MBA); business process consulting (MBA); business technology management (MBA); capital markets (MBA); corporate finance (MBA); customer relationship management (MBA); decision analytics (MBA); entrepreneurship (MBA); finance (MBA); global management (MBA); investment banking (MBA); management consulting (MBA); marketing (MBA); marketing analytics (MBA); marketing consulting (MBA); operations management (MBA); organization and management (MBA); product and brand management (MBA); real estate (MBA); social enterprise (MBA); strategy consulting (MBA). *Accreditation:* AACSB. *Faculty:* 74 full-time (18 women), 18 part-time/adjunct (6 women). *Students:* 349 full-time (105 women); includes 81 minority (26 Black or African American, non-Hispanic/Latino; 1 American Indian or Alaska Native, non-Hispanic/Latino; 35 Asian, non-Hispanic/Latino; 16 Hispanic/Latino; 3 Two or more races, non-Hispanic/Latino), 97 international. Average age 29. 1,380 applicants, 34% accepted, 172 enrolled. In 2018, 180 master's awarded. *Degree requirements:* For master's, 1 leadership course; 2 mid-semester module programs; 2 global components. *Entrance requirements:* For master's, GMAT/GRE, essays; recommendation letters; undergraduate degree; interview. Additional exam requirements/recommendations for international students: Required—TOEFL (minimum score 100 iBT), IELTS (minimum score 7), PTE (minimum score 68). *Application deadline:* For fall admission, 10/6 for domestic and international students; for winter admission, 11/17 for domestic and international students; for spring admission, 1/3 priority date for domestic and international students; for summer admission, 3/9 for domestic and international students. Application fee: $150. Electronic applications accepted. *Expenses:* Contact institution. *Financial support:* In 2018–19, 273 students received support. Career-related internships or fieldwork, institutionally sponsored loans, and scholarships/grants available. Financial award application deadline: 4/1; financial award applicants required to submit FAFSA. *Faculty research:* Corporate finance, information systems, digital marketing, asset pricing, sports management. *Unit head:* Brian Mitchell, Associate Dean, 404-727-4824, Fax: 404-712-9648, E-mail: brian.mitchell@emory.edu. *Application contact:* Melissa Rapp, Associate Dean, 404-727-7583, Fax: 404-727-4612, E-mail: mbaadmissions@emory.edu.
Website: http://www.goizueta.emory.edu

Fairfield University, Dolan School of Business, Fairfield, CT 06824. Offers accounting (MBA, MS, CAS); business analytics (MS); finance (MBA, MS, CAS); information systems and business analytics (MBA); management (MBA, CAS); marketing (MBA, CAS); taxation (CAS). *Accreditation:* AACSB. *Program availability:* Part-time, evening/weekend. *Degree requirements:* For master's, capstone course. *Entrance requirements:* For master's, GMAT (minimum score 500), 2 letters of reference, resume, minimum GPA of 3.0. Additional exam requirements/recommendations for international students: Required—TOEFL (minimum score 550 paper-based; 80 iBT) or IELTS (minimum score 6.5). Electronic applications accepted. *Expenses:* Contact institution. *Faculty research:* International finance, leadership and careers, ethics in accounting, emotions in consumer behavior and organizations, data analytics.

Fairleigh Dickinson University, Florham Campus, Silberman College of Business, Department of Economics, Finance, and International Business, Program in Finance, Madison, NJ 07940-1099. Offers MBA, Certificate.

Fairleigh Dickinson University, Metropolitan Campus, Silberman College of Business, Department of Economics, Finance and International Business, Program in Finance, Teaneck, NJ 07666-1914. Offers MBA, Certificate.

Florida Agricultural and Mechanical University, Division of Graduate Studies, Research, and Continuing Education, School of Business and Industry, Tallahassee, FL 32307-3200. Offers accounting (MBA); finance (MBA); management information systems (MBA); marketing (MBA). *Accreditation:* ACBSP. *Degree requirements:* For master's, residency. *Entrance requirements:* For master's, GMAT, minimum GPA of 3.0.

Florida International University, Chapman Graduate School of Business, Department of Finance, Miami, FL 33199. Offers MSF. *Program availability:* Part-time, evening/weekend. *Faculty:* 24 full-time (5 women), 9 part-time/adjunct (1 woman). *Students:* 86 full-time (29 women), 16 part-time (7 women); includes 73 minority (6 Black or African American, non-Hispanic/Latino; 2 Asian, non-Hispanic/Latino; 64 Hispanic/Latino; 1 Two or more races, non-Hispanic/Latino), 24 international. Average age 29. 213 applicants, 48% accepted, 72 enrolled. In 2018, 76 master's awarded. *Entrance requirements:* For master's, GMAT or GRE, minimum GPA of 3.0 in upper-level coursework; letter of intent; resume. Additional exam requirements/recommendations for international students: Required—TOEFL (minimum score 550 paper-based; 80 iBT) or IELTS (minimum score 6.5). *Application deadline:* For fall admission, 6/1 for domestic students, 4/1 for international students; for spring admission, 10/1 for domestic students, 9/1 for international students. Applications are processed on a rolling basis. Application fee: $30. Electronic applications accepted. *Expenses:* Contact institution. *Financial support:* Institutionally sponsored loans and scholarships/grants available. Financial award application deadline: 3/1; financial award applicants required to submit FAFSA. *Faculty research:* Investment, corporate and international finance. *Unit head:* Dr. Shahid Hamid,

Chair, 305-348-2727, Fax: 305-348-4245, E-mail: hamids@fiu.edu. *Application contact:* Nanett Rojas, Manager, Admissions Operations, 305-348-7464, Fax: 305-348-7441, E-mail: gradadm@fiu.edu.

Florida National University, Program in Business Administration, Hialeah, FL 33012. Offers accounting (MBA); finance (MBA); general management (MBA); health services administration (MBA); marketing (MBA); public management and leadership (MBA). *Program availability:* Part-time, blended/hybrid learning. *Faculty:* 3 full-time (1 woman), 4 part-time/adjunct (2 women). *Students:* 15 full-time (5 women), 15 part-time (6 women); all minorities (7 Black or African American, non-Hispanic/Latino; 21 Hispanic/Latino; 2 Two or more races, non-Hispanic/Latino), 1 international. Average age 35. 8 applicants, 88% accepted, 7 enrolled. In 2018, 27 master's awarded. *Degree requirements:* For master's, capstone. *Entrance requirements:* For master's, writing assessment, bachelor's degree from accredited institution; official undergraduate transcripts; minimum undergraduate GPA of 2.5, GMAT (minimum score of 400), or GRE (minimum score of 900); two letters of recommendation; resume. Additional exam requirements/recommendations for international students: Required—TOEFL (minimum score 500 paper-based; 62 iBT), IELTS (minimum score 5.5). *Application deadline:* Applications are processed on a rolling basis. Electronic applications accepted. *Expenses:* Contact institution. *Financial support:* Federal Work-Study, institutionally sponsored loans, scholarships/grants, and tuition waivers (full and partial) available. Financial award applicants required to submit FAFSA. *Unit head:* Dr. Ernesto Gonzalez, Business and Economics Department Head, 305-821-3333 Ext. 1070, Fax: 305-362-0595, E-mail: egonzalez@fnu.edu. *Application contact:* Dr. Ernesto Gonzalez, Business and Economics Department Head, 305-821-3333 Ext. 1070, Fax: 305-362-0595, E-mail: egonzalez@fnu.edu.
Website: https://www.fnu.edu/prospective-students/our-programs/select-a-program/master-of-business-administration/business-administration-mba-masters/

Florida State University, The Graduate School, College of Business, Tallahassee, FL 32306-1110. Offers accounting (M Acc), including assurance and advisory services, generalist, taxation; business administration (MBA, PhD), including accounting (PhD), finance (PhD), management information systems (PhD), marketing (PhD), organizational behavior and human resources (PhD), risk management and insurance (PhD), strategy (PhD); finance (MS); management information systems (MS); risk management and insurance (MS); JD/MBA; MSW/MBA. *Accreditation:* AACSB. *Program availability:* Part-time, 100% online. *Students:* Average age 31. 300 applicants, 61% accepted, 133 enrolled. In 2018, 268 master's, 9 doctorates awarded. Terminal master's awarded for partial completion of doctoral program. *Degree requirements:* For doctorate, comprehensive exam, thesis/dissertation. *Entrance requirements:* For master's, GMAT, GRE (for all except MS in finance), work experience (MBA, MS); minimum GPA of 3.0, letters of recommendation; for doctorate, GMAT, GRE (for marketing, organizational behavior, risk management and insurance, management information systems, and human resources only), minimum graduate GPA of 3.5, letters of recommendation. Additional exam requirements/recommendations for international students: Required—TOEFL (minimum score 600 paper-based; 85 iBT); Recommended—IELTS (minimum score 6). *Application deadline:* For fall admission, 6/1 for domestic and international students; for spring admission, 10/1 for domestic and international students; for summer admission, 3/1 for domestic and international students. Applications are processed on a rolling basis. Application fee: $30. Electronic applications accepted. *Expenses:* Contact institution. *Financial support:* In 2018–19, 146 students received support, including 26 fellowships (averaging $1,500 per year), 77 research assistantships with full tuition reimbursements available (averaging $20,000 per year), 43 teaching assistantships with full tuition reimbursements available (averaging $20,000 per year); career-related internships or fieldwork, scholarships/grants, health care benefits, tuition waivers (full and partial), and unspecified assistantships also available. Support available to part-time students. Financial award application deadline: 1/1; financial award applicants required to submit FAFSA. *Faculty research:* Business strategy, marketing, finance, accounting, business analytics. *Total annual research expenditures:* $1.4 million. *Unit head:* Dr. Michael Hartline, Dean, 850-644-4405, Fax: 850-644-0915, E-mail: mhartline@business.fsu.edu. *Application contact:* Jennifer Clark, Director, 850-644-6458, E-mail: gradprograms@business.fsu.edu.
Website: http://business.fsu.edu/

Fordham University, Gabelli School of Business, New York, NY 10023. Offers accounting (MBA, MS); applied statistics and decision-making (MS); business economics (DPS); capital markets (DPS); communications and media management (MBA); electronic business (MBA); entrepreneurship (MBA); finance (MBA, PhD); global finance (MS); global sustainability (MBA); health administration (MS); healthcare management (MBA); information systems (MBA, MS); investor relations (MS); management (EMBA, MBA, MS, PhD); marketing (MBA); marketing intelligence (MS); media management (MS); nonprofit leadership (MS); quantitative finance (MS); strategy and decision-making (DPS); taxation (MS); JD/MBA; MS/MBA. *Accreditation:* AACSB. *Program availability:* Part-time, evening/weekend. Terminal master's awarded for partial completion of doctoral program. *Degree requirements:* For master's, internships (for some degrees); for doctorate, comprehensive exam (for some programs), thesis/dissertation. *Entrance requirements:* For master's, GMAT/GRE, 2 letters of recommendation, resume, 2 essays, transcripts, interview. Additional exam requirements/recommendations for international students: Required—TOEFL (minimum score 100 iBT), IELTS (minimum score 7). Electronic applications accepted. *Expenses:* Contact institution.

Gannon University, School of Graduate Studies, College of Engineering and Business, Dahlkemper School of Business, Program in Business Administration, Erie, PA 16541-0001. Offers business administration (MBA); finance (MBA); human resources management (MBA); marketing (MBA). *Accreditation:* ACBSP. *Program availability:* Part-time, evening/weekend, 100% online, blended/hybrid learning. *Entrance requirements:* For master's, GMAT, bachelor's degree in any discipline from any accredited college or university, resume, transcripts, 3 letters of recommendation. Additional exam requirements/recommendations for international students: Required—TOEFL (minimum score 79 iBT). Electronic applications accepted. Application fee is waived when completed online.

Geneva College, Program in Business Administration, Beaver Falls, PA 15010-3599. Offers business administration (MBA); finance (MBA); marketing (MBA); operations (MBA). *Accreditation:* ACBSP. *Program availability:* Part-time, evening/weekend. *Degree requirements:* For master's, 36 credit hours of course work (30 of which are required of all students). *Entrance requirements:* For master's, GMAT (if college GPA less than 2.5), undergraduate transcript, 2 letters of recommendation, resume, goals statement. Additional exam requirements/recommendations for international students: Required—TOEFL. Electronic applications accepted. *Expenses:* Contact institution.

George Fox University, College of Business, Newberg, OR 97132-2697. Offers accounting (DBA); finance (MBA); management (DBA); management and leadership (MBA); marketing (DBA); organizational strategy (MBA); strategic human resource management (MBA). MBA offered in Newberg, OR and in Portland, OR. *Accreditation:* ACBSP. *Program availability:* Part-time, evening/weekend, online learning. *Degree requirements:* For master's, capstone project; for doctorate, credit-applied research project. *Entrance requirements:* For master's, resume (5 years of professional experience); 3 professional references; interview; financial e-learning course; official transcripts; for doctorate, GRE or GMAT, resume; personal mission statement; academic research writing sample; official transcript from each college/university attended; three professional references. Additional exam requirements/recommendations for international students: Required—TOEFL (minimum score 577 paper-based; 90 iBT) or IELTS (minimum score 7). Electronic applications accepted. *Expenses:* Contact institution.

Georgetown University, Graduate School of Arts and Sciences, Department of Economics, Washington, DC 20057. Offers econometrics (PhD); economic development (PhD); economic theory (PhD); industrial organization (PhD); international macro and finance (PhD); international trade (PhD); labor economics (PhD); macroeconomics (PhD); public economics and political economy (PhD); MA/PhD; MS/MA. *Degree requirements:* For doctorate, comprehensive exam, thesis/dissertation. *Entrance requirements:* For doctorate, GRE General Test. Additional exam requirements/recommendations for international students: Required—TOEFL. *Faculty research:* International economics, economic development.

Georgetown University, Graduate School of Arts and Sciences, McDonough School of Business, Washington, DC 20057. Offers business administration (EMBA, GEMBA, MBA); finance (MS); leadership (EML). *Accreditation:* AACSB. *Entrance requirements:* For master's, GMAT. Additional exam requirements/recommendations for international students: Required—TOEFL. *Expenses:* Contact institution.

The George Washington University, School of Business, Department of Finance, Washington, DC 20052. Offers finance (MSF, PhD); finance and investments (MBA). *Program availability:* Part-time, evening/weekend. *Students:* 151 full-time (72 women), 1 (woman) part-time; includes 12 minority (1 Black or African American, non-Hispanic/Latino; 1 American Indian or Alaska Native, non-Hispanic/Latino; 7 Asian, non-Hispanic/Latino; 2 Hispanic/Latino; 1 Two or more races, non-Hispanic/Latino), 133 international. Average age 27. 754 applicants, 53% accepted, 44 enrolled. In 2018, 143 master's awarded. *Entrance requirements:* For master's, GMAT; for doctorate, GMAT or GRE. Additional exam requirements/recommendations for international students: Required—TOEFL. *Application deadline:* For fall admission, 4/1 priority date for domestic students; for spring admission, 10/1 for domestic students. Applications are processed on a rolling basis. Application fee: $75. *Financial support:* In 2018–19, 38 students received support. Fellowships, teaching assistantships, career-related internships or fieldwork, Federal Work-Study, and institutionally sponsored loans available. Financial award application deadline: 4/1. *Unit head:* Robert Van Order, Chair, 202-994-3427, E-mail: rvo@gwu.edu. *Application contact:* Christopher Storer, Executive Director, Graduate Admissions, 202-994-1212, E-mail: gwmba@gwu.edu.

The George Washington University, School of Business, Program in Government Contracts, Washington, DC 20052. Offers MS. *Program availability:* Part-time, evening/weekend. *Students:* 5 full-time (1 woman), 54 part-time (30 women); includes 30 minority (19 Black or African American, non-Hispanic/Latino; 3 Asian, non-Hispanic/Latino; 5 Hispanic/Latino; 3 Two or more races, non-Hispanic/Latino), 2 international. Average age 41. 34 applicants, 62% accepted, 13 enrolled. In 2018, 23 master's awarded. *Entrance requirements:* For master's, GMAT/GRE or seven years of full-time, relevant professional work experience. *Application deadline:* For fall admission, 7/31 for domestic students. *Unit head:* Dr. George Jabbour, Associate Dean, 202-994-3879, E-mail: wemba@gwu.edu. *Application contact:* Neal Couture, Director, 202-994-2693, E-mail: ncouture@gwu.edu.
Website: http://gwsbwebsite.com/programs/specialized-masters/m-s-in-government-contracts/

Georgia State University, Andrew Young School of Policy Studies, Department of Economics, Atlanta, GA 30302-3083. Offers economics (MA); environmental economics (PhD); experimental economics (PhD); labor economics (PhD); policy (MA); public finance (PhD); urban and regional economics (PhD). MA offered through the College of Arts and Sciences. *Program availability:* Part-time. *Faculty:* 19 full-time (4 women). *Students:* 116 full-time (47 women), 10 part-time (5 women); includes 33 minority (14 Black or African American, non-Hispanic/Latino; 9 Asian, non-Hispanic/Latino; 7 Hispanic/Latino; 3 Two or more races, non-Hispanic/Latino), 57 international. Average age 28. 263 applicants, 43% accepted, 38 enrolled. In 2018, 21 master's, 11 doctorates awarded. Terminal master's awarded for partial completion of doctoral program. *Degree requirements:* For master's, thesis optional; for doctorate, comprehensive exam, thesis/dissertation. *Entrance requirements:* For master's and doctorate, GRE. Additional exam requirements/recommendations for international students: Required—TOEFL (minimum score 603 paper-based; 100 iBT) or IELTS (minimum score 7). *Application deadline:* For fall admission, 1/15 for domestic and international students. Application fee: $50. Electronic applications accepted. *Expenses: Tuition, area resident:* Full-time $9360; part-time $390 per credit hour. Tuition, state resident: full-time $9360; part-time $390 per credit hour. Tuition, nonresident: full-time $30,024; part-time $1251 per credit hour. *International tuition:* $30,024 full-time. *Required fees:* $2128. *Financial support:* In 2018–19, fellowships with full tuition reimbursements (averaging $11,333 per year), research assistantships with full tuition reimbursements (averaging $9,788 per year), teaching assistantships with full tuition reimbursements (averaging $3,000 per year) were awarded; career-related internships or fieldwork also available. Financial award application deadline: 2/15; financial award applicants required to submit FAFSA. *Faculty research:* Public, experimental, urban/environmental, labor, and health economics. *Unit head:* Dr. Rusty Tchernis, Director of the Doctoral Program, 404-413-0154, Fax: 404-413-0145, E-mail: rtchernis@gsu.edu. *Application contact:* Dr. Rusty Tchernis, Director of the Doctoral Program, 404-413-0154, Fax: 404-413-0145, E-mail: rtchernis@gsu.edu.
Website: http://economics.gsu.edu/

Georgia State University, Andrew Young School of Policy Studies, Department of Public Management and Policy, Atlanta, GA 30303. Offers criminal justice (MPA); disaster management (Certificate); disaster policy (MPA); environmental policy (PhD); health policy (PhD); management and finance (MPA); nonprofit management (MPA, Certificate); nonprofit policy (MPA); planning and economic development (MPP, Certificate); policy analysis and evaluation (MPA), including planning and economic development; public and nonprofit management (PhD); public finance and budgeting (PhD), including science and technology policy, urban and regional economic development; public finance policy (MPA), including social policy; public health (MPA). *Accreditation:* NASPAA (one or more programs are accredited). *Program availability:* Part-time. *Faculty:* 13 full-time (6 women), 2 part-time/adjunct (0 women). *Students:* 126 full-time (77 women), 96 part-time (65 women); includes 104 minority (80 Black or African American, non-Hispanic/Latino; 4 Asian, non-Hispanic/Latino; 10 Hispanic/Latino; 10 Two or more races, non-Hispanic/Latino), 32 international. Average age 32. 304 applicants, 59% accepted, 99 enrolled. In 2018, 57 master's, 7 doctorates, 8 other advanced degrees awarded. Terminal master's awarded for partial completion of doctoral program. *Degree requirements:* For master's, thesis optional; for doctorate, comprehensive exam, thesis/dissertation. *Entrance requirements:* For master's and doctorate, GRE. Additional exam requirements/recommendations for international students: Required—TOEFL (minimum score 603 paper-based; 100 iBT) or IELTS (minimum score 7). *Application deadline:* For fall admission, 1/15 for domestic and international students. Application fee: $50. Electronic applications accepted. *Expenses:*

Tuition, area resident: Full-time $9360; part-time $390 per credit hour. Tuition, state resident: full-time $9360; part-time $390 per credit hour. Tuition, nonresident: full-time $30,024; part-time $1251 per credit hour. *International tuition:* $30,024 full-time. *Required fees:* $2128. *Financial support:* In 2018–19, fellowships (averaging $8,194 per year), research assistantships (averaging $8,068 per year), teaching assistantships (averaging $3,600 per year) were awarded; institutionally sponsored loans, scholarships/grants, health care benefits, and unspecified assistantships also available. Financial award application deadline: 2/1. *Faculty research:* Public budgeting and finance, public management, nonprofit management, performance measurement and management, urban development. *Unit head:* Dr. Greg Lewis, Chair and Professor, 404-413-0014, Fax: 404-413-0104, E-mail: glewis@gsu.edu. *Application contact:* Dr. Greg Lewis, Chair and Professor, 404-413-0014, Fax: 404-413-0104, E-mail: glewis@gsu.edu.
Website: https://aysps.gsu.edu/public-management-policy/

Georgia State University, J. Mack Robinson College of Business, Department of Finance, Atlanta, GA 30302-3083. Offers MBA, MS, PhD. *Program availability:* Part-time, evening/weekend. *Faculty:* 7 full-time (1 woman), 1 part-time/adjunct (0 women). *Students:* 45 full-time (15 women), 8 part-time (2 women); includes 15 minority (8 Black or African American, non-Hispanic/Latino; 3 Asian, non-Hispanic/Latino; 3 Hispanic/Latino; 1 Two or more races, non-Hispanic/Latino), 30 international. Average age 28. 155 applicants, 40% accepted, 27 enrolled. In 2018, 18 master's, 1 doctorate awarded. *Entrance requirements:* For master's, GRE or GMAT, transcripts from all institutions attended, resume, essays; for doctorate, GRE or GMAT, three letters of recommendation, personal statement, transcripts from all institutions attended, resume. Additional exam requirements/recommendations for international students: Required—TOEFL (minimum score 610 paper-based; 101 iBT), IELTS (minimum score 7). *Application deadline:* For fall admission, 5/1 priority date for domestic students, 2/1 priority date for international students; for spring admission, 9/15 priority date for domestic students, 4/1 priority date for international students. Applications are processed on a rolling basis. Application fee: $50. Electronic applications accepted. *Expenses: Tuition, area resident:* Full-time $9360; part-time $390 per credit hour. Tuition, state resident: full-time $9360; part-time $390 per credit hour. Tuition, nonresident: full-time $30,024; part-time $1251 per credit hour. *International tuition:* $30,024 full-time. *Required fees:* $2128. *Financial support:* Research assistantships, teaching assistantships, scholarships/grants, tuition waivers, and unspecified assistantships available. *Faculty research:* Mergers and acquisitions, asset pricing, mutual and hedge funds, derivatives, corporate governance. *Unit head:* Dr. Gerald D. Gay, Professor/Chair, 404-413-7310, Fax: 404-413-7312. *Application contact:* Toby McChesney, Assistant Dean for Graduate Recruiting and Student Services, 404-413-7167, Fax: 404-413-7162, E-mail: rcbgradadmissions@gsu.edu.
Website: http://www.robinson.gsu.edu/finance/

Georgia State University, J. Mack Robinson College of Business, Department of Risk Management and Insurance, Program in Risk Management and Insurance, Atlanta, GA 30302-3083. Offers enterprise risk management (MBA, Certificate); financial risk management (MBA); mathematical risk management (MS); risk and insurance (MS); risk management and insurance (MBA, PhD); MAS/MRM. *Program availability:* Part-time, evening/weekend. *Entrance requirements:* For master's, GRE or GMAT, transcripts from all institutions attended, resume, essays. Additional exam requirements/recommendations for international students: Required—TOEFL (minimum score 610 paper-based; 101 iBT), IELTS (minimum score 7). *Application deadline:* Applications are processed on a rolling basis. Application fee: $50. Electronic applications accepted. *Expenses: Tuition, area resident:* Full-time $9360; part-time $390 per credit hour. Tuition, state resident: full-time $9360; part-time $390 per credit hour. Tuition, nonresident: full-time $30,024; part-time $1251 per credit hour. *International tuition:* $30,024 full-time. *Required fees:* $2128. *Financial support:* Research assistantships, scholarships/grants, tuition waivers, and unspecified assistantships available. *Faculty research:* Insurance economics, structure and performance of insurance markets, regulation and policy in insurance markets, asset pricing theory, financial econometrics. *Unit head:* Dr. Haci Akin, Director, 404-413-7467, Fax: 404-413-7467, E-mail: hakcin1@gsu.edu. *Application contact:* Toby McChesney, Graduate Recruiting Contact, 404-413-7167, Fax: 404-413-7162, E-mail: rcbgradadmissions@gsu.edu.
Website: http://rmi.robinson.gsu.edu/academic-programs/ms-rmi/

Golden Gate University, Ageno School of Business, San Francisco, CA 94105-2968. Offers accounting (MBA); adaptive leadership (MBA); advanced financial planning (MS); business administration (EMBA, MBA, DBA); business analytics (MBA, MS); entrepreneurship (MBA); finance (MBA, MS, Certificate); financial life planning (Certificate); financial planning (MS, Certificate); global supply chain management (MBA, Certificate); human resource management (MBA, MS, Certificate); information technology management (MBA, MS, Certificate); international business (MBA); marketing (MBA, MS, Certificate); project management (MBA, MS, Certificate); psychology (MA, Certificate); public administration (EMPA, MBA); public administration leadership (Certificate); JD/MBA. *Program availability:* Part-time, evening/weekend. *Degree requirements:* For doctorate, thesis/dissertation, qualifying examination. *Entrance requirements:* For master's, GMAT (for MBA), minimum GPA of 2.5 (MS). Additional exam requirements/recommendations for international students: Required—TOEFL (minimum score 550 paper-based; 79 iBT). Electronic applications accepted. *Expenses:* Contact institution.

Golden Gate University, School of Taxation, San Francisco, CA 94105-2968. Offers advanced studies in taxation (Certificate); estate planning (Certificate); financial planning and taxation (MS); international taxation (Certificate); state and local taxation (Certificate); taxation (MS, Certificate). *Program availability:* Part-time, evening/weekend. *Entrance requirements:* For master's, minimum GPA of 3.0. Additional exam requirements/recommendations for international students: Required—TOEFL (minimum score 550 paper-based), IELTS (minimum score 6.5). Electronic applications accepted. *Expenses:* Contact institution.

Goldey-Beacom College, Graduate Program, Wilmington, DE 19808-1999. Offers business administration (MBA); finance (MS); financial management (MBA); health care management (MBA); human resource management (MBA); information technology (MBA); international business management (MBA); major finance (MBA); major taxation (MBA); management (MM); marketing management (MBA); taxation (MBA, MS). *Accreditation:* ACBSP. *Program availability:* Part-time, evening/weekend. *Entrance requirements:* For master's, GMAT, MAT, GRE, minimum GPA of 3.0. Additional exam requirements/recommendations for international students: Required—TOEFL (minimum score 65 iBT); Recommended—IELTS (minimum score 6). Electronic applications accepted.

Gordon College, Graduate Financial Analysis Program, Wenham, MA 01984-1899. Offers MS. *Program availability:* Part-time, evening/weekend. *Entrance requirements:* For master's, two academic references; one personal reference; resume; academic transcript(s). Additional exam requirements/recommendations for international students: Required—TOEFL, IELTS, or PTE. Electronic applications accepted. *Expenses:* Contact institution. *Faculty research:* International trade, international monetary, security analysis, accounting, financial analysis.

The Graduate Center, City University of New York, Graduate Studies, Program in Business, New York, NY 10016-4039. Offers accounting (PhD); behavioral science (PhD); finance (PhD); management planning systems (PhD). *Degree requirements:* For doctorate, thesis/dissertation. *Entrance requirements:* For doctorate, GMAT, writing sample (15 pages). Additional exam requirements/recommendations for international students: Required—TOEFL. Electronic applications accepted.

Grand Canyon University, Colangelo College of Business, Phoenix, AZ 85017-1097. Offers accounting (MBA, MS); business analytics (MS); disaster preparedness and executive fire service leadership (MS); finance (MBA); general management (MBA); health systems management (MBA); information technology management (MS); leadership (MBA, MS); marketing (MBA); organizational leadership and entrepreneurship (MS); project management (MBA); sports business (MBA); strategic human resource management (MBA). *Accreditation:* ACBSP. *Program availability:* Part-time, evening/weekend, online learning. *Entrance requirements:* For master's, equivalent of two years' full-time professional work experience. Additional exam requirements/recommendations for international students: Required—TOEFL (minimum score 575 paper-based; 90 iBT), IELTS (minimum score 7). Electronic applications accepted.

Hawai`i Pacific University, College of Business, Program in Business Administration, Honolulu, HI 96813. Offers finance (MBA); human resource management (MBA); information systems (MBA); international business (MBA); management (MBA); marketing (MBA); organizational change and development (MBA). *Program availability:* Part-time, evening/weekend, 100% online, blended/hybrid learning. *Entrance requirements:* For master's, GMAT or GRE. Additional exam requirements/recommendations for international students: Recommended—TOEFL (minimum score 550 paper-based; 80 iBT), IELTS (minimum score 6), TWE (minimum score 5). Electronic applications accepted.

HEC Montreal, School of Business Administration, Doctoral Program in Administration, Montréal, QC H3T 2A7, Canada. Offers accounting (PhD); applied economics (PhD); data science (PhD); finance (PhD); financial engineering (PhD); information technology (PhD); international business (PhD); logistics and operations management (PhD); management science (PhD); management, strategy and organizations (PhD); marketing (PhD); organizational behaviour and human resources (PhD). Program offered jointly with Concordia University, McGill University, and Universite du Quebec a Montreal. *Accreditation:* AACSB. *Students:* 130 full-time (55 women). 114 applicants, 46% accepted, 31 enrolled. In 2018, 19 doctorates awarded. *Entrance requirements:* For doctorate, TAGE MAGE, GMAT, or GRE, master's degree in administration or related field. *Application deadline:* For fall admission, 1/15 for domestic and international students. Application fee: 91 (191 for international students). Electronic applications accepted. *Expenses: Tuition, area resident:* Full-time $3052.80 Canadian dollars; part-time $84.80 Canadian dollars per credit. Tuition, state resident: full-time $3816 Canadian dollars; part-time $264.67 Canadian dollars per credit. Tuition, nonresident: full-time $11,910 Canadian dollars. *International tuition:* $20,905.20 Canadian dollars full-time. *Required fees:* $1805.34 Canadian dollars; $43.62 Canadian dollars per credit. $71.78 Canadian dollars per term. Tuition and fees vary according to degree level and program. *Financial support:* Research assistantships, teaching assistantships, and scholarships/grants available. Financial award application deadline: 9/2. *Faculty research:* Art management, business policy, entrepreneurship, new technologies, transportation. *Unit head:* Guy Paré, Director, 514-340-6264, E-mail: guy.pare@hec.ca. *Application contact:* Julie Bilodeau, PhD Program Analyst, 514-340-6000, Fax: 514-340-6411, E-mail: analyste.phd@hec.ca.
Website: http://www.hec.ca/en/programs/phd/index.html

HEC Montreal, School of Business Administration, Graduate Diploma Programs in Administration, Program in Financial Professions, Montréal, QC H3T 2A7, Canada. Offers Graduate Diploma. All courses are given in French. *Students:* 13 full-time (2 women), 11 part-time (4 women). 48 applicants, 54% accepted, 11 enrolled. In 2018, 11 Graduate Diplomas awarded. *Entrance requirements:* For degree, bachelor's degree in administration (finance option). *Application deadline:* For fall admission, 4/15 for domestic and international students. Application fee: $91 Canadian dollars ($191 Canadian dollars for international students). Electronic applications accepted. *Expenses: Tuition, area resident:* Full-time $3052.80 Canadian dollars; part-time $84.80 Canadian dollars per credit. Tuition, state resident: full-time $3816 Canadian dollars; part-time $264.67 Canadian dollars per credit. Tuition, nonresident: full-time $11,910 Canadian dollars. *International tuition:* $20,905.20 Canadian dollars full-time. *Required fees:* $1805.34 Canadian dollars; $43.62 Canadian dollars per credit. $71.78 Canadian dollars per term. Tuition and fees vary according to degree level and program. *Financial support:* Research assistantships, teaching assistantships, and scholarships/grants available. Financial award application deadline: 9/2. *Unit head:* Renaud Lachance, Academic Supervisor, 514-340-3428, E-mail: renaud.lachance@hec.ca. *Application contact:* Anny Caron, Administrative Director, 514-340-6000, Fax: 514-340-6411, E-mail: aide@hec.ca.
Website: http://www.hec.ca/programmes/dess/dess-professions-financieres/index.html

HEC Montreal, School of Business Administration, Master of Science Programs in Administration, Program in Applied Financial Economics, Montréal, QC H3T 2A7, Canada. Offers M Sc. Program offered in French (Thesis stream, Supervised project Stream) and also in English (Thesis Stream). *Students:* 34 full-time (17 women), 11 part-time (5 women). 37 applicants, 70% accepted, 14 enrolled. In 2018, 12 master's awarded. *Entrance requirements:* For master's, BBA, undergraduate degree in another field, degree deemed equivalent by program director and minimum GPA of 3.0 on 4.3 scale. Additional exam requirements/recommendations for international students: Required—TAGE MAGE (minimum recommended score of 300), GMAT (minimum recommended score of 630), or GRE. *Application deadline:* For fall admission, 3/15 for domestic and international students; for winter admission, 9/15 for domestic and international students. Application fee: $91 Canadian dollars ($191 Canadian dollars for international students). Electronic applications accepted. *Expenses: Tuition, area resident:* Full-time $3052.80 Canadian dollars; part-time $84.80 Canadian dollars per credit. Tuition, state resident: full-time $3816 Canadian dollars; part-time $264.67 Canadian dollars per credit. Tuition, nonresident: full-time $11,910 Canadian dollars. *International tuition:* $20,905.20 Canadian dollars full-time. *Required fees:* $1805.34 Canadian dollars; $43.62 Canadian dollars per credit. $71.78 Canadian dollars per term. Tuition and fees vary according to degree level and program. *Financial support:* Research assistantships, teaching assistantships, and scholarships/grants available. Financial award application deadline: 9/2. *Unit head:* Dr. Sihem Taboubi, Director, 514-340-6428, E-mail: sihem.taboubi@hec.ca. *Application contact:* Marianne de Moura, Administrative Director, 514-340-6000, Fax: 514-340-6411, E-mail: aide@hec.ca.
Website: http://www.hec.ca/en/programs/masters/master-applied-financial-economics/index.html

HEC Montreal, School of Business Administration, Master of Science Programs in Administration, Program in Finance, Montréal, QC H3T 2A7, Canada. Offers M Sc. Program offered in French (Thesis stream, Supervised project Stream) and also in English (Thesis Stream). *Students:* 106 full-time (27 women), 24 part-time (5 women). 76 applicants, 70% accepted, 34 enrolled. In 2018, 30 master's awarded. *Entrance requirements:* For master's, BBA, undergraduate degree in another field, degree

deemed equivalent by program director and minimum GPA of 3.0 on 4.3 scale. Additional exam requirements/recommendations for international students: Required—TAGE MAGE (minimum recommended score of 300), GMAT (minimum recommended score of 630), or GRE. *Application deadline:* For fall admission, 3/15 for domestic and international students; for winter admission, 9/15 for domestic and international students. Application fee: $91 Canadian dollars ($191 Canadian dollars for international students). Electronic applications accepted. *Expenses: Tuition, area resident:* Full-time $3052.80 Canadian dollars; part-time $84.80 Canadian dollars per credit. Tuition, state resident: full-time $3816 Canadian dollars; part-time $264.67 Canadian dollars per credit. Tuition, nonresident: full-time $11,910 Canadian dollars. *International tuition:* $20,905.20 Canadian dollars full-time. *Required fees:* $1805.34 Canadian dollars; $43.62 Canadian dollars per credit. $71.78 Canadian dollars per term. Tuition and fees vary according to degree level and program. *Financial support:* Research assistantships, teaching assistantships, and scholarships/grants available. Financial award application deadline: 9/2. *Unit head:* Dr. Sihem Taboubi, Director, 514-340-6428, E-mail: sihem.taboubi@hec.ca. *Application contact:* Marianne de Moura, Administrative Director, 514-340-6000, Fax: 514-340-6411, E-mail: aide@hec.ca.
Website: http://www.hec.ca/en/programs/masters/master-finance/index.html

Hofstra University, Frank G. Zarb School of Business, Programs in Finance, Hempstead, NY 11549. Offers business administration (MBA), including finance; corporate finance (Advanced Certificate); finance (MS), including financial and risk management, investment analysis; investment management (Advanced Certificate); quantitative finance (MS). *Program availability:* Part-time, evening/weekend, blended/hybrid learning. *Students:* 122 full-time (36 women), 40 part-time (8 women); includes 24 minority (5 Black or African American, non-Hispanic/Latino; 1 American Indian or Alaska Native, non-Hispanic/Latino; 8 Asian, non-Hispanic/Latino; 8 Hispanic/Latino; 2 Two or more races, non-Hispanic/Latino), 90 international. Average age 25. 326 applicants, 78% accepted, 58 enrolled. In 2018, 103 master's awarded. *Degree requirements:* For master's, thesis (for some programs), capstone course (for MBA), thesis (for MS), minimum GPA of 3.0. *Entrance requirements:* For master's, GMAT/GRE, 2 letters of recommendation, resume, essay. Additional exam requirements/recommendations for international students: Required—TOEFL (minimum score 550 paper-based; 80 iBT); Recommended—IELTS (minimum score 6). *Application deadline:* Applications are processed on a rolling basis. Application fee: $75. Electronic applications accepted. *Expenses:* $1,375 per credit plus fees. *Financial support:* In 2018–19, 46 students received support, including 42 fellowships with full and partial tuition reimbursements available (averaging $5,064 per year); research assistantships with full and partial tuition reimbursements available, career-related internships or fieldwork, Federal Work-Study, institutionally sponsored loans, scholarships/grants, tuition waivers (full and partial), unspecified assistantships, and scholarships and endowed scholarships also available. Support available to part-time students. Financial award applicants required to submit FAFSA. *Faculty research:* Sustainable investing; blockchain applications in finance; machine learning in finance; text and data mining in finance; corporate inversions. *Unit head:* Dr. K.G. Viswanathan, Chairperson, 516-463-5699, Fax: 516-463-4834, E-mail: k.g.viswanathan@hofstra.edu. *Application contact:* Sunil Samuel, Assistant Vice President of Admissions, 516-463-4723, Fax: 516-463-4664, E-mail: graduateadmission@hofstra.edu.
Website: http://www.hofstra.edu/business/

Holy Family University, Graduate and Professional Programs, School of Business Administration, Philadelphia, PA 19114. Offers accountancy (MS); finance (MBA); health care administration (MBA); human resources management (MBA); information systems management (MBA). *Accreditation:* ACBSP. *Program availability:* Part-time, evening/weekend. *Degree requirements:* For master's, comprehensive exam, thesis optional. *Entrance requirements:* For master's, minimum GPA of 3.0, interview, essay/personal statement, current resume, official transcript of all college or university work. Additional exam requirements/recommendations for international students: Required—TOEFL (minimum score 550 paper-based; 79 iBT), IELTS (minimum score 6), PTE (minimum score 54). Electronic applications accepted.

Holy Names University, Graduate Division, Department of Business, Oakland, CA 94619-1699. Offers finance (MBA); management and leadership (MBA); marketing (MBA). *Program availability:* Part-time, evening/weekend. *Students:* 26 full-time (15 women), 16 part-time (14 women); includes 28 minority (13 Black or African American, non-Hispanic/Latino; 6 Asian, non-Hispanic/Latino; 9 Hispanic/Latino), 4 international. Average age 31. 38 applicants, 61% accepted, 17 enrolled. In 2018, 11 master's awarded. *Entrance requirements:* For master's, minimum undergraduate GPA of 2.6 overall, 3.0 in major; two recommendations (letter or form) from previous professors or current or previous work supervisors; 1-3 page personal statement; resume. Additional exam requirements/recommendations for international students: Required—TOEFL (minimum score 550 paper-based; 79 iBT). *Application deadline:* For fall admission, 8/1 priority date for domestic students, 7/15 for international students; for spring admission, 12/1 priority date for domestic students, 12/1 for international students; for summer admission, 5/1 priority date for domestic students, 5/1 for international students. Applications are processed on a rolling basis. Application fee: $65. Electronic applications accepted. Application fee is waived when completed online. *Expenses:* Contact institution. *Financial support:* Career-related internships or fieldwork, Federal Work-Study, scholarships/grants, and unspecified assistantships available. Support available to part-time students. Financial award application deadline: 3/2; financial award applicants required to submit FAFSA. *Faculty research:* Business ethics, sustainable economics, accounting models, cross-cultural management, diversity in organizations. *Unit head:* Morris Hamm, MBA Program Director, E-mail: hamm@hnu.edu. *Application contact:* 800-430-1321, Fax: 510-436-1325, E-mail: graduateadmissions@hnu.edu.
Website: http://www.hnu.edu

Howard University, School of Business, Graduate Programs in Business, Washington, DC 20059-0002. Offers accounting (MBA); entrepreneurship (MBA); finance (MBA); general management (MBA); human resources management (MBA); information systems (MBA); international business (MBA); marketing (MBA); supply chain management (MBA); JD/MBA. *Accreditation:* AACSB. *Program availability:* Part-time, evening/weekend, online learning. *Entrance requirements:* For master's, GMAT, minimum 1 year post undergraduate work experience, resume, 3 letters of recommendation, advanced college algebra. Additional exam requirements/recommendations for international students: Required—TOEFL. *Faculty research:* Marketing research in multi-ethnic populations, U.S. trade policies and international relations, risk management (finance).

Hult International Business School, Graduate Programs, Cambridge, MA 02141. Offers business administration (EMBA); business analytics (MBA, MIB); business statistics (MBS); disruptive innovation (MDI); entrepreneurship (MBA, MIB); family business (MBA, MIB); finance (MBA, MF, MIB); international marketing (MIM); marketing (MBA, MIB); project management (MBA, MIB). MDI and MBS offered in San Francisco; MBA also offered in Boston, San Francisco, Dubai, Shanghai, and New York. *Entrance requirements:* For master's, GMAT, 3 years of work experience. Additional exam requirements/recommendations for international students: Required—TOEFL. Electronic applications accepted. *Expenses:* Contact institution.

IGlobal University, Graduate Programs, Vienna, VA 22182. Offers accounting (MBA); data management and analytics (MSIT); entrepreneurship (MBA); finance (MBA); global business management (MBA); health care management (MBA); hospitality and tourism management (MBA); human resources management (MBA); information technology (MBA); information technology systems and management (MSIT); leadership and management (MBA); project management (MBA); public service and administration (MBA); software design and management (MSIT).

Illinois Institute of Technology, Chicago-Kent College of Law, Chicago, IL 60661-3691. Offers family law (LL M); financial services law (LL M); international intellectual property law (LL M); law (JD); legal studies (JSD); taxation (LL M); U.S., international, and transnational law (LL M); JD/LL M; JD/MBA; JD/MPA; JD/MPH; JD/MS. *Accreditation:* ABA. *Program availability:* Part-time, evening/weekend. Terminal master's awarded for partial completion of doctoral program. *Entrance requirements:* For master's, 1st degree in law or certified license to practice law; for doctorate, LSAT. Additional exam requirements/recommendations for international students: Required—TOEFL (minimum score 600 paper-based; 100 iBT); Recommended—IELTS (minimum score 7). Electronic applications accepted. *Expenses:* Contact institution. *Faculty research:* Constitutional law, bioethics, environmental law, intellectual property.

Illinois Institute of Technology, Graduate College, College of Science, Department of Computer Science, Chicago, IL 60616. Offers business (MCS); computational intelligence (MCS); computer science (MCS, MS, PhD); cyber-physical systems (MCS); data analytics (MCS); data science (MAS); database systems (MCS); distributed and cloud computing (MCS); education (MCS); finance (MCS); information security and assurance (MCS); networking and communications (MCS); software engineering (MCS); telecommunications and software engineering (MAS); MS/MAS. *Program availability:* Part-time, evening/weekend, online learning. Terminal master's awarded for partial completion of doctoral program. *Degree requirements:* For master's, thesis optional; for doctorate, comprehensive exam, thesis/dissertation. *Entrance requirements:* For master's, GRE General Test with minimum scores of 298 Quantitative and Verbal, 3.0 Analytical Writing (for MS); GRE General Test with minimum scores of 292 Quantitative and Verbal, 2.5 Analytical Writing (for MAS), minimum undergraduate GPA of 3.0; for doctorate, GRE General Test (minimum scores: 304 Quantitative and Verbal, 3.5 Analytical Writing), minimum undergraduate GPA of 3.0. Additional exam requirements/recommendations for international students: Required—TOEFL (minimum score 523 paper-based; 70 iBT). Electronic applications accepted. *Faculty research:* Parallel and distributed processing, high-performance computing, computational linguistics, information retrieval, data mining, grid computing.

Illinois Institute of Technology, Stuart School of Business, Program in Finance, Chicago, IL 60661. Offers MS, JD/MS, MBA/MS. *Program availability:* Part-time, evening/weekend. *Entrance requirements:* For master's, GRE (minimum score 1200) or GMAT (600). Additional exam requirements/recommendations for international students: Required—TOEFL (minimum score 600 paper-based; 85 iBT); Recommended—IELTS (minimum score 7). Electronic applications accepted. *Expenses:* Contact institution. *Faculty research:* Factor models for investment management, credit rating and credit risk management, hedge fund performance analysis, option trading and risk management, global asset allocation strategies.

Indiana University Bloomington, School of Public and Environmental Affairs, Public Affairs Programs, Bloomington, IN 47405. Offers economic development (MPA); energy (MPA); environmental policy (PhD); environmental policy and natural resource management (MPA); information systems (MPA); international development (MPA); local government management (MPA); nonprofit management (MPA, Certificate); policy analysis (MPA); public budgeting and financial management (Certificate); public finance (PhD); public financial administration (MPA); public management (MPA, PhD, Certificate); public policy analysis (PhD); social entrepreneurship (Certificate); specialized public affairs (MPA); sustainability and sustainable development (MPA); JD/MPA; MPA/MA; MPA/MIS; MPA/MLS; MSES/MPA. *Accreditation:* NASPAA (one or more programs are accredited). *Program availability:* Part-time. *Degree requirements:* For master's, capstone, internship; for doctorate, comprehensive exam, thesis/dissertation. *Entrance requirements:* For master's, GRE General Test or GMAT, official transcripts, 3 letters of recommendation, resume, personal statement; for doctorate, GRE General Test, official transcripts, 3 letters of recommendation, statement of purpose. Additional exam requirements/recommendations for international students: Required—TOEFL (minimum score 600 paper-based; 96 iBT); Recommended—IELTS (minimum score 7). Electronic applications accepted. *Faculty research:* International development, environmental policy and resource management, policy analysis, public finance, public management, urban management, nonprofit management, energy policy, social policy, public finance.

Indiana University–Purdue University Indianapolis, Kelley School of Business, Evening MBA Program, Indianapolis, IN 46202-5151. Offers accounting (MBA); entrepreneurship (MBA); finance (MBA); general administration (MBA); marketing (MBA); supply chain management (MBA); MBA/JD; MBA/MD; MBA/MHA; MBA/MS; MBA/MSA; MBA/MSE. *Program availability:* Part-time-only, evening/weekend, online learning. *Entrance requirements:* For master's, GMAT or GRE, 2 years of professional work experience. Additional exam requirements/recommendations for international students: Required—TOEFL or IELTS. Electronic applications accepted. *Expenses:* Contact institution. *Faculty research:* Entrepreneurship; corporate finance; international business; consumer behavior; supply chain; business law.

Indiana University South Bend, Judd Leighton School of Business and Economics, South Bend, IN 46615. Offers accounting (MSA); business (Graduate Certificate); business administration (MBA), including finance, human resource management, marketing; MBA/MSA. *Program availability:* Part-time, evening/weekend. *Entrance requirements:* For master's, GMAT. Additional exam requirements/recommendations for international students: Required—TOEFL (minimum score 550 paper-based; 79 iBT). Electronic applications accepted. *Expenses:* Contact institution. *Faculty research:* Financial accounting, consumer research, capital budgeting research, business strategy research.

Indiana University Southeast, School of Business, New Albany, IN 47150-6405. Offers business administration (MBA); strategic finance (MS). *Accreditation:* AACSB. *Program availability:* Part-time. *Degree requirements:* For master's, community service. *Entrance requirements:* For master's, GMAT, work experience. Additional exam requirements/recommendations for international students: Required—TOEFL. Electronic applications accepted. *Expenses:* Contact institution.

Instituto Centroamericano de Administración de Empresas, Graduate Programs, La Garita, Costa Rica. Offers agribusiness management (MIAM); business administration (EMBA); finance (MBA); real estate management (MGREM); sustainable development (MBA); technology (MBA). *Degree requirements:* For master's, comprehensive exam, essay. *Entrance requirements:* For master's, GMAT or GRE General Test, fluency in Spanish, interview, letters of recommendation, minimum 1 year of work experience. Additional exam requirements/recommendations for international students: Recommended—TOEFL. Electronic applications accepted. *Faculty research:* Competitiveness, production.

Finance and Banking

Instituto Tecnologico de Santo Domingo, Graduate School, Area of Business, Santo Domingo, Dominican Republic. Offers banking and securities markets (M Mgmt); corporate finance (M Mgmt); human resources management (M Mgmt, Certificate); international trade management (M Mgmt); marketing (M Mgmt); organizational development (M Mgmt); quality and productivity management (Certificate); tax management and planning (M Mgmt); upper management (M Mgmt).

Instituto Tecnológico y de Estudios Superiores de Monterrey, Campus Central de Veracruz, Graduate Programs, Córdoba, Mexico. Offers administration (MA); administration of information technologies (MTI); computer sciences (MCC); education (MEE); educational institution administration (MAD); educational technology (MTE); electronic commerce (MCE); finance (MAF); humanistic studies (MEH); international business for Latin America (MNL); marketing (MMT); science (MCP). *Program availability:* Part-time, evening/weekend, online learning. *Degree requirements:* For master's, thesis (for some programs). *Entrance requirements:* For master's, PAEP College Board. Electronic applications accepted.

Instituto Tecnológico y de Estudios Superiores de Monterrey, Campus Ciudad de México, School of Business Administration, Ciudad de Mexico, Mexico. Offers business administration (EMBA, MBA, PhD); economy (MBA); finance (MBA). EMBA program offered jointly with The University of Texas at Austin. *Program availability:* Part-time, evening/weekend, online learning. *Entrance requirements:* For master's and doctorate, Instituto entrance exam. Additional exam requirements/recommendations for international students: Required—TOEFL.

Instituto Tecnológico y de Estudios Superiores de Monterrey, Campus Ciudad Obregón, Program in Finance, Ciudad Obregón, Mexico. Offers MF.

Instituto Tecnológico y de Estudios Superiores de Monterrey, Campus Cuernavaca, Programs in Business Administration, Temixco, Mexico. Offers finance (MA); human resources management (MA); international business (MA); marketing (MA).

Instituto Tecnológico y de Estudios Superiores de Monterrey, Campus Estado de México, Professional and Graduate Division, Estado de Mexico, Mexico. Offers administration of information technologies (MITA); architecture (M Arch); business administration (GMBA, MBA); computer sciences (MCS, PhD); education (M Ed); educational institution administration (MAD); educational technology and innovation (PhD); electronic commerce (MEC); environmental systems (MS); finance (MAF); humanistic studies (MHS); information sciences and knowledge management (MISKM); information systems (MS); manufacturing systems (MS); marketing (MEM); quality systems and productivity (MS); science and materials engineering (PhD); telecommunications management (MTM). *Program availability:* Part-time, online learning. *Degree requirements:* For master's, one foreign language, thesis (for some programs); for doctorate, one foreign language, thesis/dissertation. *Entrance requirements:* For master's, E-PAEP 500, interview; for doctorate, E-PAEP 500, research proposal. Additional exam requirements/recommendations for international students: Required—TOEFL (minimum score 550 paper-based). *Faculty research:* Surface treatments by plasmas, mechanical properties, robotics, graphical computing, mechatronics security protocols.

Instituto Tecnológico y de Estudios Superiores de Monterrey, Campus Guadalajara, Program in Finance, Zapopan, Mexico. Offers MF. *Degree requirements:* For master's, one foreign language, thesis. *Entrance requirements:* For master's, ITESM admission test.

Instituto Tecnológico y de Estudios Superiores de Monterrey, Campus Irapuato, Graduate Programs, Irapuato, Mexico. Offers administration (MBA); administration of information technology (MAIT); administration of telecommunications (MAT); architecture (M Arch); computer science (MCS); education (M Ed); educational administration (MEA); educational innovation and technology (DEIT); educational technology (MET); electronic commerce (MBA); environmental administration and planning (MEAP); environmental systems (MES); finances (MBA); humanistic studies (MHS); international management for Latin American executives (MIMLAE); library and information science (MLIS); manufacturing quality management (MMQM); marketing research (MBA).

Instituto Tecnológico y de Estudios Superiores de Monterrey, Campus Monterrey, Graduate School of Business Administration and Leadership, Program in Business Administration, Monterrey, Mexico. Offers business administration (MA, MBA); finance (M Sc); international business (M Sc); marketing (M Sc). *Program availability:* Part-time. *Degree requirements:* For master's, one foreign language, thesis. *Entrance requirements:* For master's, GMAT. Additional exam requirements/recommendations for international students: Required—TOEFL. *Faculty research:* Technology management, quality management, organizational theory and behavior.

Inter American University of Puerto Rico, Aguadilla Campus, Graduate School, Aguadilla, PR 00605. Offers accounting (MBA); counseling psychology specializing in family (MS); criminal justice (MA); educative management and leadership (MA); elementary education (M Ed); finance (MBA); human resources (MBA); industrial management (MBA); management information systems (MBA); marketing (MBA). *Program availability:* Part-time, evening/weekend. *Degree requirements:* For master's, comprehensive exam. *Entrance requirements:* For master's, EXADEP, 2 letters of recommendation, minimum GPA of 2.5. Electronic applications accepted.

Inter American University of Puerto Rico, Arecibo Campus, Program in Business Administration, Arecibo, PR 00614-4050. Offers accounting (MBA); finance (MBA); human resources (MBA).

Inter American University of Puerto Rico, Metropolitan Campus, Graduate Programs, Program in Finance, San Juan, PR 00919-1293. Offers MBA. *Degree requirements:* For master's, comprehensive exam. *Entrance requirements:* For master's, GRE or EXADEP, interview. Electronic applications accepted.

Inter American University of Puerto Rico, Ponce Campus, Graduate School, Mercedita, PR 00715-1602. Offers accounting (MBA); biology (M Ed); chemistry (M Ed); criminal justice (MA); elementary education (M Ed); English as a Second Language (M Ed); finance (MBA); history (M Ed); human resources (MBA); marketing (MBA); mathematics (M Ed); Spanish (M Ed). *Entrance requirements:* For master's, minimum GPA of 2.5.

Inter American University of Puerto Rico, San Germán Campus, Graduate Studies Center, Program in Business Administration, San Germán, PR 00683-5008. Offers accounting (MBA); finance (MBA); general business administration (MBA); human resources (MBA, PhD); industrial relations (MBA); information systems (MBA); international and interregional business (PhD); management (MBA); marketing (MBA). *Program availability:* Part-time, evening/weekend. *Degree requirements:* For master's, comprehensive exam. *Entrance requirements:* For master's, GRE General Test or EXADEP, minimum GPA of 3.0. *Expenses: Tuition:* Full-time $212; part-time $212 per credit. *Required fees:* $366 per semester. One-time fee: $31. Tuition and fees vary according to degree level and program.

The International University of Monaco, Graduate Programs, Monte Carlo, Monaco. Offers entrepreneurship (EMBA, MBA); financial engineering (M Sc); hedge fund and private equity (M Sc); international marketing (EMBA, MBA); international wealth management (M Sc); luxury goods and services (EMBA, M Sc, MBA); wealth and asset management (EMBA, MBA). *Program availability:* Part-time. *Degree requirements:* For master's, comprehensive exam (for some programs), applied research project. *Entrance requirements:* Additional exam requirements/recommendations for international students: Required—TOEFL (minimum score 550 paper-based), IELTS. Electronic applications accepted. *Faculty research:* Gaming, leadership, disintermediation.

Iona College, School of Business, Department of Finance, Business Economics and Legal Studies, New Rochelle, NY 10801-1890. Offers finance (MS); financial management (MBA, PMC); financial services (MS); international finance (MS). *Program availability:* Part-time, evening/weekend. *Faculty:* 5 full-time (1 woman). *Students:* 38 full-time (10 women), 34 part-time (12 women); includes 24 minority (11 Black or African American, non-Hispanic/Latino; 2 Asian, non-Hispanic/Latino; 11 Hispanic/Latino), 7 international. Average age 26. 52 applicants, 96% accepted, 27 enrolled. In 2018, 52 master's awarded. *Entrance requirements:* For master's, GMAT, 2 letters of recommendation, minimum GPA of 3.0; for PMC, minimum GPA of 3.0. Additional exam requirements/recommendations for international students: Required—TOEFL (minimum score 550 paper-based; 80 iBT), IELTS (minimum score 6.5). *Application deadline:* For fall admission, 8/15 priority date for domestic students, 8/1 priority date for international students; for winter admission, 11/15 priority date for domestic students, 11/1 priority date for international students; for spring admission, 2/15 priority date for domestic students, 2/1 priority date for international students; for summer admission, 5/15 priority date for domestic students, 5/1 priority date for international students. Applications are processed on a rolling basis. Application fee: $50. Electronic applications accepted. *Expenses:* Contact institution. *Financial support:* In 2018–19, 45 students received support. Scholarships/grants, tuition waivers (partial), and unspecified assistantships available. Support available to part-time students. Financial award application deadline: 4/15; financial award applicants required to submit FAFSA. *Faculty research:* Options, insurance financing, asset depreciation ranges, international finance, emerging markets. *Unit head:* Dr. John F. Manley, Department Chair, 914-633-2284, E-mail: jmanley@iona.edu. *Application contact:* Kimberly Kelly, Director of Graduate Business Admissions, 914-633-2271, Fax: 914-633-2012, E-mail: kkelly@iona.edu.
Website: http://www.iona.edu/Academics/Hagan-School-of-Business/Departments/Finance-Business-Economics-Legal-Studies/Graduate-Programs.aspx

Iowa State University of Science and Technology, Program in Finance, Ames, IA 50011. Offers M Fin. *Entrance requirements:* For master's, GMAT, GRE Writing Test, minimum undergraduate GPA of 3.25, resume, three letters of recommendation, personal essay. Additional exam requirements/recommendations for international students: Required—TOEFL (minimum score 600 paper-based; 100 iBT), IELTS (minimum score 7). *Expenses:* Contact institution.

Jacksonville University, Davis College of Business, Accelerated Day-time MBA Program, Jacksonville, FL 32211. Offers accounting and finance (MBA); business administration (MBA); consumer goods and services marketing (MBA); management (MBA); management accounting (MBA). *Entrance requirements:* For master's, GMAT or GRE, bachelor's degree from regionally-accredited institution, original transcripts of academic work, statement of intent, resume, 3 letters of recommendation; 3 years of work experience (recommended); interview with program advisor. Additional exam requirements/recommendations for international students: Required—TOEFL (minimum score 550 paper-based; 79 iBT), IELTS (minimum score 6), PTE (minimum score 53). Electronic applications accepted. *Expenses:* Contact institution. *Faculty research:* Behavioral finance, game theory, regional economic integration, information sabotage, public choice and public finance.

Jacksonville University, Davis College of Business, FLEX Master of Business Administration Program, Jacksonville, FL 32211. Offers accounting and finance (MBA); business management (MBA); consumer goods and services marketing (MBA); management (MBA); management accounting (MBA); JD/MBA; MBA/MPP; MSN/MBA. MBA/JD offered jointly with Florida School of Law; MSN/MBA offered jointly with JU's Keigwin School of Nursing; MBA/MPP offered jointly with JU's Public Policy Institute. *Accreditation:* AACSB. *Program availability:* Part-time, evening/weekend, blended/hybrid learning. *Entrance requirements:* For master's, GMAT or GRE, bachelor's degree from regionally-accredited institution, 3 years of full-time work experience (recommended), resume, statement of intent, 3 letters of recommendation, interview with program advisor. Additional exam requirements/recommendations for international students: Required—TOEFL (minimum score 550 paper-based; 79 iBT), IELTS (minimum score 6), PTE (minimum score 53). Electronic applications accepted. *Expenses:* Contact institution. *Faculty research:* Downsizing with integrity; impact of YouTube videos; game theory; analysis of effective tax rates; creativity innovation and change.

John F. Kennedy University, College of Business and Professional Studies, Program in Business Administration, Pleasant Hill, CA 94523-4817. Offers business administration (MBA); finance (MBA); health care (MBA); human resources (MBA); information technology (MBA); management (MBA); sales management (MBA); strategic management (MBA). *Program availability:* Part-time, evening/weekend, online learning. *Degree requirements:* For master's, thesis or alternative. *Entrance requirements:* For master's, interview. Additional exam requirements/recommendations for international students: Required—TOEFL.

Johns Hopkins University, Carey Business School, Certificate Programs, Baltimore, MD 21218. Offers financial management (Certificate); investments (Certificate). *Program availability:* Part-time, evening/weekend. *Students:* 1 full-time, 16 part-time (3 women). 10 applicants, 80% accepted, 5 enrolled. In 2018, 18 Certificates awarded. *Degree requirements:* For Certificate, 16 credits. *Entrance requirements:* Additional exam requirements/recommendations for international students: Required—TOEFL, IELTS. *Application deadline:* Applications are processed on a rolling basis. Application fee: $100. Electronic applications accepted. *Expenses:* Contact institution. *Unit head:* Dr. Kevin Frick, Vice Dean of Education, 410-234-9272, E-mail: kfrick@jhu.edu. *Application contact:* Office of Admissions, 410-234-9220, Fax: 443-529-1554, E-mail: carey.admissions@jhu.edu.
Website: http://carey.jhu.edu/academics/certificate-programs/

Johns Hopkins University, Carey Business School, MS in Finance Program, Baltimore, MD 21218. Offers finance (MS). *Program availability:* Part-time, evening/weekend, blended/hybrid learning, on-site residency requirement. *Students:* 514 full-time (296 women), 153 part-time (48 women). 2,306 applicants, 69% accepted, 590 enrolled. In 2018, 511 master's awarded. *Degree requirements:* For master's, 36 credits. *Entrance requirements:* For master's, GMAT or GRE. Additional exam requirements/recommendations for international students: Required—TOEFL, IELTS. *Application deadline:* For fall admission, 4/3 for domestic and international students. Applications are processed on a rolling basis. Application fee: $100. Electronic applications accepted. *Expenses:* Contact institution. *Financial support:* In 2018–19, 91 students received support. Scholarships/grants available. Support available to part-time students. Financial award application deadline: 4/15; financial award applicants required to submit FAFSA. *Faculty research:* Derivatives, financial institutions, fixed income securities, international finance, investments. *Unit head:* Dr. Kevin Frick, Vice Dean of Education, 410-234-9272, E-mail: kfrick@jhu.edu. *Application contact:* Office of Admissions, 410-234-9220, Fax: 443-529-1554, E-mail: carey.admissions@jhu.edu.
Website: http://carey.jhu.edu/academics/master-of-science/ms-in-finance

Johns Hopkins University, School of Advanced International Studies, Washington, DC 20036. Offers global risk (MA); international development (MA, Certificate), including international economics (MA); international economics (Certificate); international economics and finance (MA); international public policy (MIPP); international relations (PhD); international studies (Certificate); Japan studies (MA), including international economics; Korea studies (MA), including international economics; South Asia studies (MA), including international economics; Southeast Asia studies (MA), including international economics; JD/MA; MBA/MA; MHS/MA. Dual-degree with Nanjing University (MAIS); other dual degree programs offered with Johns Hopkins, University of Pennsylvania; INSEAD, and others. *Program availability:* Evening/weekend. *Faculty:* 103 full-time (37 women). *Students:* 857 full-time (435 women), 32 part-time (17 women). 1,302 applicants, 89% accepted, 471 enrolled. In 2018, 592 master's, 6 doctorates, 38 other advanced degrees awarded. *Degree requirements:* For master's, 4-6 international economics courses, 5-6 functional or regional concentration courses, 2 core examinations, proficiency in language other than native language, capstone project; for doctorate, 2 foreign languages, thesis/dissertation, 3 comprehensive exams, economics, quantitative and qualitative course, dissertation prospectus and defense. *Entrance requirements:* For master's, GMAT or GRE General Test, previous course work in economics, foreign language, undergraduate degree; for doctorate, GRE General Test, Master's degree. Additional exam requirements/recommendations for international students: Required—TOEFL (minimum score 600 paper-based; 100 iBT), IELTS (minimum score 7), TOEFL (minimum score 600 paper-based; 100 iBT) or IELTS (minimum score 7). *Application deadline:* For fall admission, 1/7 for domestic and international students; for spring admission, 10/15 for domestic and international students. Application fee: $85. Electronic applications accepted. *Expenses:* Https://sais.jhu.edu/admissions/tuition-and-aid/tuition-and-costs. *Financial support:* In 2018–19, 431 students received support, including 431 fellowships (averaging $20,358 per year); research assistantships, teaching assistantships, Federal Work-Study, institutionally sponsored loans, and scholarships/grants also available. Support available to part-time students. Financial award application deadline: 2/15; financial award applicants required to submit FAFSA. *Faculty research:* International economics; international relations/regional studies; international development; energy, resources, and environment; international security/strategic studies. *Unit head:* Eliot Cohen, Dean, 202-663-5781, E-mail: ecohen1@jhu.edu. *Application contact:* Karen Ohen, Director of Admissions, 202-663-5700, Fax: 202-663-7788, E-mail: sais.dc.admissions@jhu.edu. Website: http://www.sais-jhu.edu/

Johnson & Wales University, Graduate Studies, MBA Program, Providence, RI 02903-3703. Offers accounting (MBA); business administration (MBA); finance (MBA); global fashion merchandising and management (MBA); hospitality (MBA); human resource management (MBA); information security/assurance (MBA); information technology (MBA); nonprofit management (MBA); operations and supply chain management (MBA); organizational leadership (MBA); organizational psychology (MBA); sport leadership (MBA). Program also offered on Denver campus. *Program availability:* Part-time, online learning. *Entrance requirements:* For master's, minimum GPA of 2.75. Additional exam requirements/recommendations for international students: Required—TOEFL (minimum score 550 paper-based); Recommended—IELTS, TWE. *Faculty research:* International banking, global economy, international trade, cultural differences.

Johnson & Wales University, Graduate Studies, MS Program in Finance, Providence, RI 02903-3703. Offers MS. *Program availability:* Online learning.

Kansas State University, Graduate School, College of Business, Program in Business Administration, Manhattan, KS 66506. Offers data analytics (MBA); finance (MBA); management (MBA); marketing (MBA); technology entrepreneurship (MBA). *Accreditation:* AACSB. *Program availability:* Part-time, 100% online. *Entrance requirements:* For master's, GMAT (minimum score of 500), minimum undergraduate GPA of 3.0. Additional exam requirements/recommendations for international students: Required—TOEFL (minimum score 550 paper-based; 79 iBT); Recommended—IELTS (minimum score 7). Electronic applications accepted. *Expenses:* Contact institution. *Faculty research:* Organizational citizenship behavior, service marketing, impression management, human resources management, lean manufacturing and supply chain management, financial market behavior and investment management, data analytics, corporate responsibility, technology entrepreneurship.

Kansas State University, Graduate School, College of Human Ecology, School of Family Studies and Human Services, Manhattan, KS 66506-1403. Offers applied family sciences (MS); communication sciences and disorders (MS); conflict resolution (Graduate Certificate); couple and family therapy (MS); early childhood education (MS); family and community service (MS); life-span human development (MS); personal financial planning (MS, PhD, Graduate Certificate); youth development (MS, Graduate Certificate). *Accreditation:* AAMFT/COAMFTE; ASHA. *Program availability:* Part-time, online learning. *Degree requirements:* For master's, comprehensive exam (for some programs), thesis optional. *Entrance requirements:* For master's, GRE, minimum GPA of 3.0 in last 2 years (60 semester hours) of undergraduate study; for doctorate, GRE. Additional exam requirements/recommendations for international students: Required—TOEFL (minimum score 600 paper-based). Electronic applications accepted. *Faculty research:* Health and security of military families, training in and evaluation of professional human services (marriage and couple therapy, family life education, treatment of speech and swallowing disorders, financial therapy), disorders of communication and swallowing, family and relationship development and health, financial decision-making.

Kent State University, College of Business Administration, Doctoral Program in Finance, Kent, OH 44242-0001. Offers PhD. *Faculty:* 4 full-time (1 woman). *Students:* 12 full-time (5 women), all international. Average age 31. 20 applicants, 25% accepted, 2 enrolled. In 2018, 3 doctorates awarded. *Degree requirements:* For doctorate, comprehensive exam, thesis/dissertation, oral defense. *Entrance requirements:* For doctorate, GMAT or GRE. Additional exam requirements/recommendations for international students: Required—TOEFL (minimum score 600 paper-based; 100 iBT), IELTS (minimum score 7). *Application deadline:* For fall admission, 1/1 for domestic students, 2/1 for international students. Application fee: $45 ($70 for international students). Electronic applications accepted. *Expenses:* Contact institution. *Financial support:* In 2018–19, 9 students received support, including 9 teaching assistantships with full tuition reimbursements available (averaging $23,000 per year). Financial award application deadline: 2/1; financial award applicants required to submit FAFSA. *Faculty research:* Corporate finance, investments, international finance, futures and options, risk and insurance. *Unit head:* Steven Dennis, Chair and Associate Professor, 330-672-2426, Fax: 330-672-9806, E-mail: sdenni14@kent.edu. *Application contact:* Felecia A. Urbanek, Assistant Director, 330-672-2282, Fax: 330-672-7303, E-mail: gradbus@kent.edu.
Website: http://www.kent.edu/business/phd

King University, School of Business, Economics, and Technology, Bristol, TN 37620-2699. Offers accounting (MBA); finance (MBA); healthcare management (MBA); human resources management (MBA); leadership (MBA); management (MBA); marketing (MBA); project management (MBA). *Program availability:* Part-time, evening/weekend, 100% online, blended/hybrid learning. *Faculty:* 11 full-time (9 women), 10 part-time/

adjunct (7 women). *Students:* 182 full-time (107 women), 8 part-time (6 women); includes 18 minority (7 Black or African American, non-Hispanic/Latino; 4 Hispanic/Latino; 1 Native Hawaiian or other Pacific Islander, non-Hispanic/Latino; 6 Two or more races, non-Hispanic/Latino), 2 international. Average age 32. 143 applicants, 98% accepted, 68 enrolled. In 2018, 125 master's awarded. *Degree requirements:* For master's, comprehensive exam, thesis optional. *Entrance requirements:* For master's, resume which demonstrates a minimum of 2 years of full-time work experience, minimum cumulative grade point average of 3.0 on a 4.0 scale is required. Students who do not meet this requirement may be conditionally accepted. Additional exam requirements/recommendations for international students: Required—TOEFL (minimum score 84 paper-based; 84 iBT). *Application deadline:* Applications are processed on a rolling basis. Application fee: $0 ($50 for international students). Electronic applications accepted. *Expenses: Tuition:* Full-time $13,365; part-time $495 per semester hour. *Required fees:* $900; $100 per course. One-time fee: $175. Tuition and fees vary according to class time, degree level and program. *Financial support:* Unspecified assistantships available. Financial award applicants required to submit FAFSA. *Faculty research:* International monetary policy. *Unit head:* Dr. Mark Pate, Dean, School of Business, Economics and Technology, 423-652-4814, E-mail: mjpate@king.edu. *Application contact:* Nancy Beverly, Territory Manager/Enrollment Counselor, 423-341-9495, Fax: 423-652-4727, E-mail: nmbeverly@king.edu.

Lake Forest Graduate School of Management, The Leadership MBA Program, Lake Forest, IL 60045. Offers finance (MBA); global business (MBA); healthcare management (MBA); management (MBA); marketing (MBA); organizational behavior (MBA). *Program availability:* Part-time, evening/weekend. *Entrance requirements:* For master's, 4 years of work experience in field, interview, 2 letters of recommendation. Electronic applications accepted.

Lakeland University, Graduate Studies Division, Program in Business Administration, Plymouth, WI 53073. Offers accounting (MBA); finance (MBA); healthcare management (MBA); project management (MBA). *Entrance requirements:* For master's, GMAT. *Expenses:* Contact institution.

La Salle University, School of Business, Master of Business Administration Program, Philadelphia, PA 19141-1199. Offers accounting (MBA, Post-MBA Certificate); business systems and analytics (MBA, Post-MBA Certificate); finance (MBA, Post-MBA Certificate); general business administration (MBA, Post-MBA Certificate); human resource management (MBA, Post-MBA Certificate); management (MBA, Post-MBA Certificate); marketing (Post-MBA Certificate); MBA/MSN. Program also offered in Switzerland. *Accreditation:* AACSB. *Program availability:* Part-time, evening/weekend, online learning. *Entrance requirements:* For master's, GMAT or GRE, two letters of reference; resume; for Post-MBA Certificate, MBA with minimum GPA of 3.0. Additional exam requirements/recommendations for international students: Required—TOEFL. Electronic applications accepted. Application fee is waived when completed online. *Expenses:* Contact institution.

La Sierra University, School of Business and Management, Riverside, CA 92505. Offers accounting (MBA); finance (MBA); general management (MBA); human resources management (MBA); leadership, values, and ethics for business and management (Certificate); marketing (MBA). *Degree requirements:* For master's, research project. *Entrance requirements:* For master's, GMAT, minimum GPA of 3.0. Additional exam requirements/recommendations for international students: Required—TOEFL. *Faculty research:* Financial econometrics, institutional assessment and strategic planning, legal issues in management, behavioral finance, content of financial reports.

Lawrence Technological University, College of Management, Southfield, MI 48075-1058. Offers business administration (MBA, DBA), including business analytics (MBA, MS), cybersecurity (MBA, MS), finance (MBA), information systems (MBA), information technology (MBA), marketing (MBA), project management (MBA, MS); cybersecurity (Graduate Certificate); health IT management (Graduate Certificate); information assurance management (Graduate Certificate); information systems (MS), including enterprise resource planning, enterprise security management, project management (MBA, MS); information technology (MS, DM), including business analytics (MBA, MS), cybersecurity (MBA, MS), information assurance (MS), project management (MBA, MS); management (PhD); nonprofit management and leadership (Graduate Certificate); operations management (MS), including manufacturing operations, service operations; project management (Graduate Certificate). *Accreditation:* ACBSP. *Program availability:* Part-time, evening/weekend, 100% online. Terminal master's awarded for partial completion of doctoral program. *Degree requirements:* For master's, thesis (for some programs); for doctorate, comprehensive exam, thesis/dissertation. *Entrance requirements:* Additional exam requirements/recommendations for international students: Required—TOEFL (minimum score 550 paper-based; 79 iBT), IELTS (minimum score 6.5). Electronic applications accepted. *Faculty research:* Cybersecurity; risk management; IT governance; security controls and countermeasures; threat modeling cyber resilience; autonomous cars; natural language processing; text mining; machine learning; reflective leadership; emerging leadership theories and practice; motivational studies; teaching effectiveness strategies; teamwork; organization development; strategic planning; strengths-based and positive organizational scholarship; global leadership; globalization; corporate governance.

Lehigh University, College of Business, Department of Finance, Bethlehem, PA 18015. Offers analytical finance (MS). *Faculty:* 4 full-time (0 women), 1 (woman) part-time/adjunct. *Students:* 40 full-time (23 women), 1 part-time (0 women), 37 international. Average age 23. 192 applicants, 49% accepted, 22 enrolled. In 2018, 38 master's awarded. *Degree requirements:* For master's, capstone project. *Entrance requirements:* For master's, GMAT or GRE, bachelor's degree from a mathematically rigorous program, minimum GPA of 3.0. Additional exam requirements/recommendations for international students: Required—TOEFL (minimum score 600 paper-based; 94 iBT), IELTS (minimum score 7). *Application deadline:* For fall admission, 7/15 for domestic students, 4/15 for international students. Application fee: $75. Tuition and fees vary according to program. *Financial support:* Fellowships, research assistantships, teaching assistantships, and health care benefits available. *Unit head:* Nandu Nayar, Department Chair, 610-758-4161, E-mail: nan2@lehigh.edu. *Application contact:* Mary Theresa Taglang, Director of Recruitment and Admissions, 610-758-4386, Fax: 610-758-5283, E-mail: mtt4@lehigh.edu.
Website: https://cbe.lehigh.edu/academics/graduate/master-analytical-finance

Lewis University, College of Business, Program in Business Administration, Romeoville, IL 60446. Offers accounting (MBA); custom elective option (MBA); e-business (MBA); finance (MBA); healthcare management (MBA); human resources management (MBA); international business (MBA); management information systems (MBA); marketing (MBA); project management (MBA); technology and operations management (MBA). *Program availability:* Part-time, evening/weekend. *Students:* 114 full-time (72 women), 143 part-time (87 women); includes 84 minority (21 Black or African American, non-Hispanic/Latino; 2 American Indian or Alaska Native, non-Hispanic/Latino; 11 Asian, non-Hispanic/Latino; 45 Hispanic/Latino; 5 Two or more races, non-Hispanic/Latino), 17 international. Average age 31. In 2018, 99 master's awarded. *Entrance requirements:* For master's, interview, bachelor's degree, resume, two recommendations. Additional exam requirements/recommendations for international

students: Required—TOEFL (minimum score 550 paper-based), IELTS. *Application deadline:* For fall admission, 8/15 priority date for domestic students, 5/1 priority date for international students; for spring admission, 11/15 priority date for international students. Applications are processed on a rolling basis. Application fee: $40. Electronic applications accepted. *Financial support:* Career-related internships or fieldwork, Federal Work-Study, scholarships/grants, and unspecified assistantships available. Financial award application deadline: 5/1; financial award applicants required to submit FAFSA. *Unit head:* Dr. Maureen Culleeney, Academic Program Director, 815-838-0500 Ext. 5631, E-mail: culleema@lewisu.edu. *Application contact:* Michele Ryan, Director of Admission, 815-838-0500 Ext. 5384, E-mail: ryanml@lewisu.edu.

Lewis University, College of Business, Program in Finance, Romeoville, IL 60446. Offers MS. *Program availability:* Part-time, evening/weekend. *Students:* 8 full-time (4 women), 6 part-time (3 women); includes 4 minority (3 Black or African American, non-Hispanic/Latino; 1 Hispanic/Latino), 5 international. Average age 30. *Entrance requirements:* For master's, bachelor's degree, interview, resume, two letters of recommendation, minimum GPA of 2.75. Additional exam requirements/recommendations for international students: Required—TOEFL (minimum score 550 paper-based; 80 iBT), IELTS. *Application deadline:* For fall admission, 5/1 priority date for international students; for spring admission, 11/15 priority date for international students. Applications are processed on a rolling basis. Application fee: $40. Electronic applications accepted. *Financial support:* Career-related internships or fieldwork, Federal Work-Study, scholarships/grants, and unspecified assistantships available. Financial award application deadline: 5/1; financial award applicants required to submit FAFSA. *Unit head:* Dr. Ryan Butt, Dean. *Application contact:* Office of Graduate Admission, 815-836-5610, E-mail: grad@lewisu.edu.

Liberty University, School of Business, Lynchburg, VA 24515. Offers accounting (MBA, MS), including audit and financial reporting (MS), business (MS), financial services (MS), forensic accounting (MS), leadership (MS), taxation (MS); cyber security (MS); executive leadership (MA); international business (DBA); leadership (DBA); marketing (MBA, MS, DBA), including digital marketing and advertising (MS), project management (MS), public relations (MS), sports marketing and media (MS); project management (MBA, DBA); public relations (MBA). *Program availability:* Part-time, online learning. *Students:* 2,871 full-time (1,496 women), 4,437 part-time (1,969 women); includes 2,069 minority (1,424 Black or African American, non-Hispanic/Latino; 44 American Indian or Alaska Native, non-Hispanic/Latino; 133 Asian, non-Hispanic/Latino; 282 Hispanic/Latino; 16 Native Hawaiian or other Pacific Islander, non-Hispanic/Latino; 170 Two or more races, non-Hispanic/Latino), 154 international. Average age 36. 8,980 applicants, 45% accepted, 2009 enrolled. In 2018, 1,988 master's, 25 doctorates awarded. *Entrance requirements:* For master's, minimum undergraduate GPA of 3.0, 15 hours of upper-level business courses. Additional exam requirements/recommendations for international students: Required—TOEFL (minimum score 600 paper-based; 100 iBT). *Application deadline:* Applications are processed on a rolling basis. Application fee: $50. Electronic applications accepted. *Expenses:* Contact institution. *Financial support:* In 2018–19, 990 students received support. Teaching assistantships and Federal Work-Study available. Financial award applicants required to submit FAFSA. *Unit head:* Dr. Dave Bratt, Dean, 434-592-7321, E-mail: dabrat@liberty.edu. *Application contact:* Jay Bridge, Director of Graduate Admissions, 800-424-9595, Fax: 800-628-7977, E-mail: gradadmissions@liberty.edu.
Website: https://www.liberty.edu/business/

Lincoln University, Graduate Studies, Oakland, CA 94612. Offers finance and investments (DBA); finance management (MS); finance management and investments (MBA); general business (MBA); human resource management (MBA, DBA); international business (MBA, MS); management information systems (MBA). *Program availability:* Part-time. *Degree requirements:* For master's, research project (thesis), internship report, or comprehensive exam; for doctorate, comprehensive exam, thesis/dissertation. *Entrance requirements:* For master's, minimum GPA of 2.7; for doctorate, GMAT (minimum score: 550), GRE (minimum score: 1000), or equivalent test results (waived for master's degree with minimum cumulative GPA of 3.3). Additional exam requirements/recommendations for international students: Required—TOEFL minimum score 525 paper-based; 71 iBT or IELTS minimum score 5.5 (for MBA); TOEFL minimum score 550 paper-based; 79 iBT or IELTS minimum score 6 (for MS and DBA). Electronic applications accepted.

Lincoln University, The School of Adult & Continuing Education, Philadelphia, PA 19104. Offers counseling (MSC); early childhood education (M Ed), including PreK-4; early childhood education and special education (M Ed); educational leadership (M Ed), including principal certification; finance (MBA); human resources management (MBA); human services delivery (MAHS). *Program availability:* Part-time, evening/weekend. *Faculty:* 8 full-time (3 women), 22 part-time/adjunct (12 women). *Students:* 192 full-time (154 women), 62 part-time (40 women); includes 230 minority (218 Black or African American, non-Hispanic/Latino; 9 Hispanic/Latino; 3 Two or more races, non-Hispanic/Latino), 3 international. Average age 33. 278 applicants, 58% accepted, 94 enrolled. In 2018, 105 master's awarded. *Degree requirements:* For master's, comprehensive exam, thesis or alternative, capstone, grant proposal. *Entrance requirements:* For master's, GRE/GMAT (Optional), Official academic transcript(s), letters of recommendation, personal statement, resume, supervisor's evaluation form, Application fee. Additional exam requirements/recommendations for international students: Required—TOEFL (minimum score 500 paper-based; 71 iBT); Recommended—IELTS (minimum score 6.5). *Application deadline:* For fall admission, 8/19 for domestic and international students; for spring admission, 12/30 for domestic and international students. Applications are processed on a rolling basis. Application fee: $50. Electronic applications accepted. *Financial support:* Scholarships/grants available. Financial award application deadline: 4/1; financial award applicants required to submit FAFSA. *Unit head:* Dr. Patricia Joseph, Dean of Faculty, 484-365-7659, E-mail: joseph@lincoln.edu. *Application contact:* Jernice Lea, Director, Student Services and Admissions, 215-590-8231, Fax: 215-387-3859, E-mail: jlea@lincoln.edu.
Website: http://www.lincoln.edu/admissions/graduate-admissions

Lipscomb University, College of Business, Nashville, TN 37204-3951. Offers accounting and finance (MBA); audit/accounting (M Acc); business (Certificate); business administration (MM); healthcare management (MBA); leadership (MBA); tax (M Acc); MBA/MS; Pharm D/MM. *Accreditation:* ACBSP. *Program availability:* Part-time, evening/weekend. *Entrance requirements:* For master's, GMAT, transcripts, interview, 2 references, resume. Additional exam requirements/recommendations for international students: Required—TOEFL (minimum score 570 paper-based). Electronic applications accepted. *Expenses:* Contact institution. *Faculty research:* Impact of spirituality on organization commitment, women in corporate leadership, psychological empowerment, training.

Long Island University–LIU Post, College of Management, Brookville, NY 11548-1300. Offers accountancy (MS); finance (MBA); information systems (MS); international business (MBA); management (MBA); management engineering (MS); marketing (MBA); taxation (MS); technical project management (MS); JD/MBA. *Accreditation:* AACSB. *Program availability:* Part-time, evening/weekend, blended/hybrid learning. *Entrance requirements:* For master's, GMAT, GRE, or LSAT. Additional exam requirements/recommendations for international students: Required—TOEFL (minimum score 550 paper-based, 75 iBT) or IELTS. Electronic applications accepted. *Faculty research:* Innovation and property rights, knowledge sourcing, sustainability and firm performance, China and growth markets, corporate social responsibility, workforce compensation and issues.

Louisiana State University and Agricultural & Mechanical College, Graduate School, E. J. Ourso College of Business, Department of Finance, Baton Rouge, LA 70803. Offers business administration (PhD), including finance; finance (MS).

Louisiana Tech University, Graduate School, College of Business, Ruston, LA 71272. Offers accounting (M Acc, DBA); computer information systems (DBA); finance (MBA, DBA); information assurance (MBA); innovation (MBA); management (DBA); marketing (MBA, DBA). *Accreditation:* AACSB. *Program availability:* Part-time, evening/weekend, 100% online, blended/hybrid learning. *Degree requirements:* For doctorate, thesis/dissertation. *Entrance requirements:* For master's and doctorate, GMAT, transcript with bachelor's degree awarded. Additional exam requirements/recommendations for international students: Required—TOEFL (minimum score 550 paper-based; 80 iBT), IELTS (minimum score 6.5). Electronic applications accepted. *Faculty research:* Consumer environmental behavior; identifying and analyzing current issues and future concerns in real estate; information assurance and related areas in business for Northwest Louisiana and the United States (business continuity, disaster recovery, accounting controls, auditing, computer forensics, and security attribution); value creation driven by the consumer and employee interface within exchange environments.

Loyola University Chicago, Quinlan School of Business, Master of Science in Finance Program, Chicago, IL 60611. Offers asset management (MSF). *Program availability:* Part-time, evening/weekend. *Entrance requirements:* For master's, GMAT or GRE, official transcripts, letters of recommendation, statement of purpose, resume. Additional exam requirements/recommendations for international students: Required—TOEFL (minimum score 90 iBT) or IELTS (minimum score 6.5). Electronic applications accepted. Application fee is waived when completed online. *Expenses:* Contact institution. *Faculty research:* Corporate finance, banking, risk management and derivatives, investment, theoretical finance.

Loyola University Chicago, Quinlan School of Business, MBA Programs, Chicago, IL 60611. Offers accounting (MBA); business ethics (MBA); derivative markets (MBA); economics (MBA); entrepreneurship (MBA); finance (MBA); healthcare management (MBA); human resources management (MBA); information systems management (MBA); international business (MBA); management (MBA); marketing (MBA); risk management (MBA); supply chain management (MBA). *Program availability:* Part-time, evening/weekend. *Entrance requirements:* For master's, GMAT or GRE, official transcripts, two letters of recommendation, statement of purpose, resume. Additional exam requirements/recommendations for international students: Required—TOEFL (minimum score 90 iBT) or IELTS (minimum score 6.5). Electronic applications accepted. Application fee is waived when completed online. *Expenses:* Contact institution. *Faculty research:* Social enterprise and responsibility, emerging markets, supply chain management, risk management.

Loyola University Maryland, Graduate Programs, Sellinger School of Business, Professional MBA Program, Baltimore, MD 21210-2699. Offers finance (MBA); information systems (MBA); investments and applied portfolio management (MBA); management (MBA); marketing (MBA). *Accreditation:* AACSB. *Program availability:* Part-time, evening/weekend. *Entrance requirements:* For master's, GMAT, resume, essay, official transcripts, professional letter of recommendation. Additional exam requirements/recommendations for international students: Required—TOEFL (minimum score 550 paper-based, 80 iBT) or IELTS (minimum score 7). Electronic applications accepted. *Expenses:* Contact institution.

Manhattanville College, School of Professional Studies, Master of Science in International Management Program, Purchase, NY 10577-2132. Offers international management (MS, Advanced Certificate), including business leadership (MS), finance (MS), human resource management (MS), marketing communication management (MS). *Program availability:* Part-time, evening/weekend. *Faculty:* 6 part-time/adjunct (3 women). *Students:* 2 full-time (1 woman), 1 part-time (0 women); includes 1 minority (Hispanic/Latino). Average age 24. 9 applicants, 44% accepted, 2 enrolled. In 2018, 5 master's awarded. *Degree requirements:* For master's, thesis (for some programs), final project. *Entrance requirements:* For master's, scores of GRE and GMAT are optional, personal essay, transcripts, 2 letters of recommendation (academic or professional), resume, health form with proof of immunization (for those born after 1957). Additional exam requirements/recommendations for international students: Required—TOEFL (minimum score 563 paper-based; 85 iBT), TOEFL (minimum score 563 paper-based, 85 iBT), IELTS (7), or iTEP (B2); Recommended—IELTS (minimum score 7). *Application deadline:* Applications are processed on a rolling basis. Application fee: $75. Electronic applications accepted. *Expenses:* 935 per credit. *Financial support:* Federal Work-Study, institutionally sponsored loans, scholarships/grants, and unspecified assistantships available. Financial award application deadline: 3/15; financial award applicants required to submit FAFSA. *Unit head:* Laura Persky, Associate Dean, 914-323-5188, E-mail: Laura.Persky@mville.edu. *Application contact:* Monika Pottgen, Assistant Director, Recruitment and Admissions, 914-323-5150, E-mail: business@mville.edu.
Website: https://www.mville.edu/programs/ms-international-management

Marquette University, Graduate School of Management, Executive MBA Program, Milwaukee, WI 53201-1881. Offers economics (MBA); finance (MBA); human resources (MBA); international business (MBA); management information systems (MBA); marketing (MBA); operations and supply chain management (MBA); sports business (MBA). *Accreditation:* AACSB. *Degree requirements:* For master's, international trip. *Entrance requirements:* For master's, GMAT or GRE, two letters of recommendation, official transcripts from current and previous colleges/universities. Additional exam requirements/recommendations for international students: Required—TOEFL (minimum score 550 paper-based; 88 iBT), IELTS (minimum score 6.5), PTE. Electronic applications accepted. *Expenses:* Contact institution. *Faculty research:* International trade and finance, customer relationship management, consumer satisfaction, customer service.

Marquette University, Graduate School of Management, Program in Business Administration, Milwaukee, WI 53201-1881. Offers business administration (MBA); economics (MBA); entrepreneurship (Certificate); finance (MBA); human resources (MBA); international business (MBA); management information systems (MBA); marketing (MBA); operations and supply chain management (MBA); sports business (MBA); JD/MBA; MBA/MA; MBA/MSN. *Accreditation:* AACSB. *Program availability:* Part-time, evening/weekend. *Degree requirements:* For Certificate, business plan. *Entrance requirements:* For master's, GMAT or GRE, letters of recommendation. Additional exam requirements/recommendations for international students: Required—TOEFL (minimum score 550 paper-based; 88 iBT), IELTS (minimum score 6.5), PTE. Electronic applications accepted. *Faculty research:* Ethics in the professions, services marketing, technology impact on decision-making, mentoring.

Maryville University of Saint Louis, The John E. Simon School of Business, St. Louis, MO 63141-7299. Offers accounting (MBA, MS, Certificate); business studies (Certificate); cybersecurity (MBA, MS, Certificate); financial services (MBA, Certificate);

health administration (MBA); healthcare administration (Certificate); human resource management (MBA); human resources management (Certificate); information technology (MBA); information technology management (Certificate); management (MBA, Certificate); management and leadership (MA); marketing (MBA, Certificate); project management (MBA, Certificate); sport business management (MBA); supply chain management (Certificate); supply chain management/logistics (MBA). *Accreditation:* ACBSP. *Program availability:* Part-time, 100% online, blended/hybrid learning. *Faculty:* 5 full-time (1 woman), 77 part-time/adjunct (19 women). *Students:* 338 full-time (166 women), 739 part-time (356 women); includes 310 minority (161 Black or African American, non-Hispanic/Latino; 6 American Indian or Alaska Native, non-Hispanic/Latino; 59 Asian, non-Hispanic/Latino; 57 Hispanic/Latino; 27 Two or more races, non-Hispanic/Latino), 30 international. Average age 33. In 2018, 143 master's awarded. *Degree requirements:* For master's, capstone course (for MBA). *Entrance requirements:* Additional exam requirements/recommendations for international students: Required—TOEFL (minimum score 563 paper-based; 85 iBT). *Application deadline:* Applications are processed on a rolling basis. Electronic applications accepted. *Expenses:* Tuition varies by program. *Financial support:* Career-related internships or fieldwork, Federal Work-Study, tuition waivers (partial), and campus employment available. Financial award application deadline: 4/1; financial award applicants required to submit FAFSA. *Unit head:* Tammy Gocial, Interim Dean, 314-529-9401, Fax: 314-529-9975, E-mail: tgocial@maryville.edu. *Application contact:* Chris Gourdine, Assistant Dean Business Administration, 314-529-6861, Fax: 314-529-9975, E-mail: cgourdine@maryville.edu.
Website: http://www.maryville.edu/bu/business-administration-masters/

Marywood University, Academic Affairs, Munley College of Liberal Arts and Sciences, School of Business and Global Innovation, Emphasis in Finance/Investment, Scranton, PA 18509-1598. Offers MBA. *Entrance requirements:* For master's, GMAT. Electronic applications accepted.

McGill University, Faculty of Graduate and Postdoctoral Studies, Desautels Faculty of Management, Montréal, QC H3A 2T5, Canada. Offers administration (PhD); entrepreneurial studies (MBA); finance (MBA); general management (Post Master's Certificate); global manufacturing and supply chain management (MMM); information systems (MBA); international business (MBA); international practicing management (MM); management (MBA); management for development (MBA); marketing (MBA); operations management (MBA); public accountancy (Diploma); strategic management (MBA); MBA/LL B; MD/MBA. MMM offered jointly with Faculty of Engineering; PhD with Concordia University, HEC Montreal, Université de Montréal, Université du Québec à Montréal.

Metropolitan College of New York, Program in Business Administration, New York, NY 10006. Offers financial services (MBA); general management (MBA); healthcare systems and risk management (MBA); media management (MBA). *Accreditation:* ACBSP. *Program availability:* Evening/weekend. *Degree requirements:* For master's, thesis, 10-day study abroad. *Entrance requirements:* For master's, GMAT. Additional exam requirements/recommendations for international students: Required—TOEFL (minimum score 600 paper-based). Electronic applications accepted. *Expenses:* Contact institution.

Michigan State University, The Graduate School, Eli Broad College of Business, Department of Finance, East Lansing, MI 48224. Offers MS, PhD. PhD program admits students only in odd-numbered years. *Degree requirements:* For doctorate, comprehensive exam, thesis/dissertation. *Entrance requirements:* For master's, GMAT (minimum score 550) or GRE (minimum score 1050 verbal and quantitative taken within 5 years), 4-year bachelor's degree or equivalent with minimum cumulative GPA of 3.0, transcripts, at least 2 years' work experience, 2 letters of recommendation, working knowledge of computers, laptop computer; for doctorate, GMAT or GRE, transcripts from all colleges/universities attended, 3 letters of recommendation, statement of purpose. Additional exam requirements/recommendations for international students: Required—TOEFL (minimum score 600 paper-based; 100 iBT), IELTS (minimum score 7) accepted for MS only. Electronic applications accepted.

Michigan State University, The Graduate School, Eli Broad College of Business, Program in Business Administration, East Lansing, MI 48224. Offers finance (MBA); human resource management (MBA); integrative management (MBA); marketing (MBA); supply chain management (MBA). MBA in integrative management is through Weekend MBA Program; other 4 concentrations are through Full-Time MBA Program. *Program availability:* Evening/weekend. *Degree requirements:* For master's, enrichment experience. *Entrance requirements:* For master's, GMAT or GRE, 4-year bachelor's degree; resume; work experience (minimum of 5 years for Weekend MBA); 2-3 personal essays; 2 letters of recommendation; personal interview. Additional exam requirements/recommendations for international students: Required—PTE (minimum score 70), TOEFL (minimum score 100 iBT) or IELTS (minimum score 7) for full-time MBA applicants. Electronic applications accepted. *Expenses:* Contact institution.

Mississippi College, Graduate School, School of Business, Clinton, MS 39058. Offers accounting (Certificate); business administration (MBA), including accounting; business education (M Ed); finance (MBA, Certificate); JD/MBA. *Accreditation:* ACBSP. *Program availability:* Part-time, evening/weekend. *Degree requirements:* For master's, comprehensive exam, thesis optional. *Entrance requirements:* For master's, GMAT, minimum GPA of 2.5, 24 hours of undergraduate course work in business. Additional exam requirements/recommendations for international students: Recommended—TOEFL, IELTS. Electronic applications accepted.

Mississippi State University, College of Business, Department of Finance and Economics, Mississippi State, MS 39762. Offers applied economics (PhD); economics (MA). PhD in applied economics offered jointly with Department of Agricultural Economics. *Program availability:* Part-time. *Faculty:* 17 full-time (4 women), 1 part-time/adjunct (0 women). *Students:* 7 full-time (2 women), 6 international. Average age 30. In 2018, 3 doctorates awarded. Terminal master's awarded for partial completion of doctoral program. *Degree requirements:* For master's, comprehensive exam, thesis optional; for doctorate, comprehensive exam, thesis/dissertation, written and oral exams. *Entrance requirements:* For master's, GRE, previously-completed intermediate microeconomics and macroeconomics; for doctorate, GRE, BS with minimum GPA of 3.0 cumulative and over last 60 hours of undergraduate work, 3.25 on all graduate work. Additional exam requirements/recommendations for international students: Required—TOEFL (minimum score 575 paper-based; 84 iBT); Recommended—IELTS (minimum score 6.5). *Application deadline:* For fall admission, 7/1 for domestic students, 5/1 for international students; for spring admission, 11/1 for domestic students, 10/1 for international students. Applications are processed on a rolling basis. Application fee: $60 ($80 for international students). Electronic applications accepted. *Expenses:* Tuition, state resident: full-time $8450; part-time $360.59 per credit hour. Tuition, nonresident: full-time $23,140; part-time $969.09 per credit hour. *Required fees:* $110. One-time fee: $55 full-time. Part-time tuition and fees vary according to course load, degree level, campus/location and reciprocity agreements. *Financial support:* Federal Work-Study, scholarships/grants, health care benefits, and unspecified assistantships available. Financial award application deadline: 4/1; financial award applicants required to submit FAFSA. *Faculty research:* Economics development, mergers, event studies, economic education, bank performance. *Total annual research expenditures:* $1.3 million. *Unit head:* Dr. Kathleen Thomas, Professor/Head, 662-325-2561, Fax: 662-325-1977, E-mail: mkt27@msstate.edu. *Application contact:* Robbie Salters, Admissions and Enrollment Assistant, 662-325-7400, E-mail: rsalters@grad.msstate.edu.
Website: http://www.business.msstate.edu/programs/fe/index.php

Molloy College, Graduate Business Program, Rockville Centre, NY 11571-5002. Offers accounting (MBA); finance (MBA, Post-Master's Certificate, Postbaccalaureate Certificate); healthcare (MBA, Post-Master's Certificate, Postbaccalaureate Certificate); management (MBA); marketing (MBA, Post-Master's Certificate, Postbaccalaureate Certificate); personal financial planning (MBA). *Program availability:* Part-time, evening/weekend. *Faculty:* 9 full-time (2 women), 20 part-time/adjunct (8 women). *Students:* 75 full-time (45 women), 164 part-time (88 women); includes 100 minority (45 Black or African American, non-Hispanic/Latino; 21 Asian, non-Hispanic/Latino; 30 Hispanic/Latino; 1 Native Hawaiian or other Pacific Islander, non-Hispanic/Latino; 3 Two or more races, non-Hispanic/Latino), 3 international. Average age 40. 97 applicants, 78% accepted, 65 enrolled. In 2018, 91 master's, 1 other advanced degree awarded. *Entrance requirements:* Additional exam requirements/recommendations for international students: Required—TOEFL (minimum score 550 paper-based; 79 iBT). *Application deadline:* Applications are processed on a rolling basis. Application fee: $60. Electronic applications accepted. *Expenses: Tuition:* Full-time $20,790; part-time $1155 per credit. *Required fees:* $1060; $900. Tuition and fees vary according to course load and degree level. *Financial support:* Application deadline: 3/1; applicants required to submit FAFSA. *Faculty research:* Graduate education - pedagogy and the capstone experience; Freedom of Speech in the workplace; employer liability for sexual harassment in the workplace; educational economics and industrial organization; corporate governance and distressed debt analysis; social network analysis; market segmentation. *Unit head:* Dr. Maureen Mackenzie, Dean, Division of Business/Director of Graduate Programs, 516-323-3080, E-mail: mmackenzie@molloy.edu. *Application contact:* Faye Hood, Assistant Director for Admissions, 516-323-4009, E-mail: fhood@molloy.edu.
Website: http://www.molloy.edu/academics/graduate-programs/graduate-business

Monmouth University, Graduate Studies, Leon Hess Business School, West Long Branch, NJ 07764-1898. Offers accounting (MBA, Certificate); business administration (MBA); finance (MBA); management (MBA); marketing (MBA); real estate (MBA). *Accreditation:* AACSB. *Program availability:* Part-time, evening/weekend. *Faculty:* 22 full-time (5 women), 8 part-time/adjunct (1 woman). *Students:* 91 full-time (47 women), 87 part-time (35 women); includes 17 minority (2 Black or African American, non-Hispanic/Latino; 6 Asian, non-Hispanic/Latino; 7 Hispanic/Latino; 2 Two or more races, non-Hispanic/Latino), 12 international. Average age 29. In 2018, 79 master's, 1 other advanced degree awarded. *Degree requirements:* For master's, capstone course. *Entrance requirements:* For master's, GMAT or GRE, current resume; essay (500 words or less). Additional exam requirements/recommendations for international students: Required—TOEFL (minimum score 550 paper-based; 79 iBT), IELTS (minimum score 6), Michigan English Language Assessment Battery (minimum score 77) or Certificate of Advanced English (minimum score 160). *Application deadline:* For fall admission, 7/15 priority date for domestic students, 6/1 for international students; for spring admission, 12/1 priority date for domestic students, 11/1 for international students; for summer admission, 5/1 for domestic students. Applications are processed on a rolling basis. Application fee: $50. Electronic applications accepted. *Expenses: Tuition:* Part-time $1233 per credit. *Required fees:* $178 per term. *Financial support:* In 2018–19, 131 students received support. Institutionally sponsored loans, scholarships/grants, and unspecified assistantships available. Support available to part-time students. Financial award applicants required to submit FAFSA. *Faculty research:* Information technology and marketing, behavioral research in accounting, human resources, management of technology. *Unit head:* Dr. Susan Gupta, MBA Program Director, 732-571-3639, Fax: 732-263-5517, E-mail: sgupta@monmouth.edu. *Application contact:* Laurie Kuhn, Associate Director of Graduate Admission, 732-571-3452, Fax: 732-263-5123, E-mail: gradadm@monmouth.edu.
Website: https://www.monmouth.edu/business-school/leon-hess-business-school.aspx

Monroe College, King Graduate School, Bronx, NY 10468. Offers accounting (MS); business administration (MBA), including entrepreneurship, finance, general business administration, healthcare management, human resources, information technology, marketing; computer science (MS); criminal justice (MS); hospitality management (MS); public health (MPH), including biostatistics and epidemiology, community health, health administration and leadership. *Program availability:* Online learning.

Montclair State University, The Graduate School, Feliciano School of Business, General MBA Program, Montclair, NJ 07043-1624. Offers accounting (MBA); business analytics (MBA); digital marketing (MBA); finance (MBA); general business administration (MBA); human resources management (MBA); management (MBA); management of information and technology (MBA); marketing (MBA); project management (MBA). *Program availability:* Part-time, evening/weekend. *Degree requirements:* For master's, culminating experience. *Entrance requirements:* For master's, GMAT or GRE General Test, 2 letters of recommendation, resume, essay. Additional exam requirements/recommendations for international students: Required—TOEFL (minimum score 83 iBT), IELTS (minimum score 6.5). Electronic applications accepted. *Faculty research:* Accounting, management, marketing.

Mount Saint Mary College, School of Business, Newburgh, NY 12550-3494. Offers business (MBA); financial planning (MBA); health care management (MBA). *Program availability:* Part-time, evening/weekend. *Faculty:* 6 full-time (3 women), 3 part-time/adjunct (0 women). *Students:* 37 full-time (14 women), 30 part-time (19 women); includes 14 minority (3 Black or African American, non-Hispanic/Latino; 1 Asian, non-Hispanic/Latino; 10 Hispanic/Latino). Average age 30. 16 applicants, 81% accepted, 10 enrolled. In 2018, 48 master's awarded. *Degree requirements:* For master's, thesis or alternative. *Entrance requirements:* For master's, GMAT or minimum undergraduate GPA of 2.7. Additional exam requirements/recommendations for international students: Required—TOEFL (minimum score 80 iBT). *Application deadline:* Applications are processed on a rolling basis. Application fee: $45. Electronic applications accepted. Application fee is waived when completed online. *Expenses: Tuition:* Full-time $14,454; part-time $803 per credit. *Required fees:* $172; $86 per semester. *Financial support:* In 2018–19, 13 students received support. Scholarships/grants and unspecified assistantships available. Financial award application deadline: 4/15; financial award applicants required to submit FAFSA. *Faculty research:* Financial reform, entrepreneurship and small business development, global business relations, technology's impact on business decision-making, college-assisted business education. *Unit head:* Dr. Veronica McMillian, Graduate Coordinator, 845-569-3119, Fax: 845-569-3885, E-mail: veronica.mcmillan@msmc.edu. *Application contact:* Eileen Bardney, Director of Admissions, 845-569-3254, Fax: 845-569-3438, E-mail: Eileen.Bardney@msmc.edu.
Website: http://www.msmc.edu/Academics/Graduate_Programs/master_of_business_administration.be

Murray State University, Arthur J. Bauernfeind College of Business, Department of Economics and Finance, Murray, KY 42071. Offers economic development (MS); economics (MS), including finance. *Program availability:* Part-time. *Entrance requirements:* For master's, GRE General Test or GMAT, minimum university GPA of 2.75. Additional exam requirements/recommendations for international students: Required—TOEFL (minimum score 527 paper-based; 71 iBT). Electronic applications accepted.

Finance and Banking

Murray State University, Arthur J. Bauernfeind College of Business, MBA Program, Murray, KY 42071. Offers accounting (MBA); finance (MBA); global communications (MBA); human resource management (MBA); marketing (MBA). *Accreditation:* AACSB. *Program availability:* Part-time, evening/weekend, 100% online, blended/hybrid learning. *Entrance requirements:* For master's, GRE or GMAT, minimum university GPA of 2.75. Additional exam requirements/recommendations for international students: Required—TOEFL (minimum score 527 paper-based; 71 iBT). *Faculty research:* Human resource management, e-commerce, supply-chain management, investment management, accounting.

Naval Postgraduate School, Departments and Academic Groups, Department of Defense Analysis, Monterey, CA 93943. Offers command and control (MS); communications (MS); defense analysis (MS), including astronautics; financial management (MS); information operations (MS); irregular warfare (MS); national security affairs (MS); operations analysis (MS); special operations (MA, MS), including command and control (MS), communications (MS), financial management (MS), information operations (MS), irregular warfare (MS), national security affairs, operations analysis (MS), tactile missiles (MS), terrorist operations and financing (MS); tactile missiles (MS); terrorist operations and financing (MS). Program only open to commissioned officers of the United States and friendly nations and selected United States federal civilian employees. *Program availability:* Part-time. *Degree requirements:* For master's, thesis. *Faculty research:* CTF Global Ecco Project, Afghanistan endgames, core lab Philippines project, Defense Manpower Data Center (DMDC) data vulnerability.

Naval Postgraduate School, Departments and Academic Groups, Graduate School of Business and Public Policy, Monterey, CA 93943. Offers acquisition and contract management (MBA); business administration (EMBA, MBA); contract management (MS); defense business management (MBA); defense systems analysis (MS), including management; defense systems management (international) (MBA); financial management (MBA); information management (MBA); manpower systems analysis (MS); material logistics support management (MBA); program management (MS); resource planning and management for international defense (MBA); supply chain management (MBA); systems acquisition management (MBA); transportation management (MBA). Program only open to commissioned officers of the United States and friendly nations and selected United States federal civilian employees. *Accreditation:* AACSB; NASPAA. *Program availability:* Part-time, online learning. *Degree requirements:* For master's, thesis (for some programs), terminal project/capstone (for some programs). *Faculty research:* U.S. and European public procurement policies for small and medium-sized enterprises, examining external validity criticisms in the choice of students as subjects in accounting experiment studies, assurance of learning in contract management education, contracting for cloud computing: opportunities and risks, NPS, Apple App Store as a business model supporting U.S. Navy requirements.

New Charter University, College of Business, Salt Lake City, UT 84101. Offers finance (MBA); health care management (MBA); management (MBA). *Program availability:* Part-time, evening/weekend, online only, 100% online. *Faculty:* 13 part-time/adjunct (1 woman). *Students:* 16 part-time. Average age 40. 1 applicant, 100% accepted, 1 enrolled. In 2018, 10 master's awarded. *Entrance requirements:* For master's, course work in calculus, statistics, macroeconomics. Additional exam requirements/recommendations for international students: Required—TOEFL (minimum score 550 paper-based). *Application deadline:* Applications are processed on a rolling basis. Application fee: $50. Electronic applications accepted. *Expenses: Tuition:* Full-time $4491; part-time $1497 per term. *Required fees:* $50 per term. *Financial support:* In 2018–19, 1 student received support. Scholarships/grants available. *Unit head:* Timothy Harrington, Academic Dean, 801-8838336, E-mail: tharrington@new.edu. *Application contact:* Stephen Mann, Admissions Advisor, 801-515-3085, E-mail: smann@new.edu. Website: https://new.edu/academics/college-of-business/

New England College of Business and Finance, Program in Finance, Boston, MA 02111-2645. Offers MSF. *Program availability:* Online learning.

New Jersey City University, School of Business, Program in Finance, Jersey City, NJ 07305-1597. Offers MBA, MS, Graduate Certificate. *Program availability:* Part-time, evening/weekend. *Degree requirements:* For master's, thesis. *Entrance requirements:* Additional exam requirements/recommendations for international students: Required—TOEFL (minimum score 79 iBT).

Newman University, MBA Program, Wichita, KS 67213-2097. Offers finance (MBA); international business (MBA); leadership (MBA); management (MBA); management information technology (MBA). *Program availability:* Part-time. *Degree requirements:* For master's, thesis optional. *Entrance requirements:* For master's, minimum GPA of 3.0; 2 letters of recommendation; course work in algebra, statistics, macroeconomics, and financial accounting. Additional exam requirements/recommendations for international students: Required—TOEFL (minimum score 600 paper-based; 100 iBT). Electronic applications accepted. *Expenses:* Contact institution.

New Mexico State University, College of Business, MBA Program, Las Cruces, NM 88003-8001. Offers agribusiness (MBA); finance (MBA); information systems (MBA). *Accreditation:* AACSB. *Program availability:* Part-time-only, evening/weekend, online with required 2-3 day orientation and 2-3 day concluding session in Las Cruces. *Students:* Average age 33. 166 applicants, 82% accepted, 19 enrolled. In 2018, 79 master's awarded. *Entrance requirements:* For master's, GMAT or GRE (depending upon undergraduate or graduate degree institution and GPA), minimum GPA of 3.5 from AACSB international or ACBSP-accredited institution or graduate degree from regionally-accredited U.S. university (without GMAT or GRE). Additional exam requirements/recommendations for international students: Required—TOEFL (minimum score 550 paper-based; 79 iBT), IELTS (minimum score 6.5). *Application deadline:* For fall admission, 7/15 priority date for domestic students, 4/15 priority date for international students; for spring admission, 4/15 priority date for domestic students, 9/15 priority date for international students; for summer admission, 4/15 for domestic students, 1/15 for international students. Applications are processed on a rolling basis. Application fee: $40 ($50 for international students). Electronic applications accepted. *Expenses: Tuition, area resident:* Full-time $4216.70; part-time $252.70 per credit hour. *Tuition, state resident:* full-time $4216.70; part-time $252.70 per credit hour. *Tuition, nonresident:* full-time $12,769; part-time $881.10 per credit hour. *International tuition:* $12,769.30 full-time. *Required fees:* $878.40; $48.80 per credit hour. Full-time tuition and fees vary according to course load and reciprocity agreements. *Financial support:* In 2018–19, 29 students received support. Fellowships, Federal Work-Study, institutionally sponsored loans, scholarships/grants, health care benefits, and unspecified assistantships available. Financial award application deadline: 3/1. *Unit head:* Dr. Kathy Brook, Associate Dean, 575-646-8003, Fax: 575-646-7977, E-mail: kbrook@nmsu.edu. *Application contact:* John Shonk, MBA Advisor, 575-646-8003, Fax: 575-646-7977, E-mail: mbaprog@nmsu.edu. Website: http://business.nmsu.edu/mba

The New School, The New School for Social Research, Department of Economics, New York, NY 10003. Offers economics (MA, MS, PhD); global political economy and finance (MA). *Program availability:* Part-time. Terminal master's awarded for partial completion of doctoral program. *Degree requirements:* For master's, comprehensive exam (for some programs), mentored research/internship; for doctorate, one foreign language, comprehensive exam, thesis/dissertation. *Entrance requirements:* For master's, GRE, letters of recommendation, writing sample, essays, transcript; for doctorate, letters of recommendation, writing sample, essays, transcript. Additional exam requirements/recommendations for international students: Required—TOEFL (minimum score 100 iBT), IELTS (minimum score 7), PTE (minimum score 68). Electronic applications accepted. *Expenses:* Contact institution.

New York Institute of Technology, School of Management, Department of Business Administration, Old Westbury, NY 11568-8000. Offers executive management (MBA), including finance, marketing, operations and supply chain management. *Accreditation:* AACSB. *Program availability:* Part-time. *Faculty:* 25 full-time (4 women), 20 part-time/adjunct (6 women). *Students:* 296 full-time (126 women), 91 part-time (45 women); includes 42 minority (6 Black or African American, non-Hispanic/Latino; 1 American Indian or Alaska Native, non-Hispanic/Latino; 17 Asian, non-Hispanic/Latino; 12 Hispanic/Latino; 1 Native Hawaiian or other Pacific Islander, non-Hispanic/Latino; 5 Two or more races, non-Hispanic/Latino), 298 international. Average age 30. 550 applicants, 67% accepted, 111 enrolled. In 2018, 291 master's awarded. *Entrance requirements:* For master's, bachelor's degree; minimum undergraduate GPA of 3.0. Additional exam requirements/recommendations for international students: Required—TOEFL (minimum score 79 iBT), IELTS (minimum score 6), PTE (minimum score 53). *Application deadline:* Applications are processed on a rolling basis. Application fee: $50. Electronic applications accepted. *Expenses: Tuition:* Full-time $1285; part-time $1285 per credit. *Required fees:* $215; $175 per unit. Tuition and fees vary according to course load, degree level and campus/location. *Financial support:* Career-related internships or fieldwork, Federal Work-Study, scholarships/grants, tuition waivers (full and partial), and unspecified assistantships available. Support available to part-time students. Financial award application deadline: 2/15; financial award applicants required to submit FAFSA. *Faculty research:* Accounting, economics, finance, management, marketing. *Unit head:* Dr. Jess Boronico, Dean, 516-686-7838, E-mail: som@nyit.edu. *Application contact:* Alice Dolitsky, Director, Graduate Admissions, 516-686-7520, Fax: 516-686-1116, E-mail: admissions@nyit.edu. Website: http://www.nyit.edu/degrees/management_mba

New York University, Leonard N. Stern School of Business, Department of Finance, New York, NY 10012-1019. Offers MBA, PhD. *Faculty research:* Derivative securities, pricing of assets, credit risk, portfolio management, international finance.

New York University, School of Professional Studies, Jonathan M. Tisch Center of Hospitality, Program in Hospitality Industry Studies, New York, NY 10012-1019. Offers hospitality industry studies (MS), including brand strategy, hotel finance, lodging operations, revenue management. *Program availability:* Part-time, evening/weekend. *Degree requirements:* For master's, thesis. *Entrance requirements:* For master's, GRE or GMAT (only upon request), bachelor's degree, resume with relevant professional work, internship or volunteer experience, two letters of recommendation, statement of purpose. Additional exam requirements/recommendations for international students: Required—TOEFL (minimum score 600 paper-based; 100 iBT), IELTS (minimum score 7). Electronic applications accepted. *Expenses:* Contact institution.

New York University, School of Professional Studies, Schack Institute of Real Estate, Program in Real Estate, New York, NY 10012-1019. Offers real estate (MS), including finance and investment, real estate asset management. *Program availability:* Part-time, evening/weekend. *Degree requirements:* For master's, thesis, capstone project. *Entrance requirements:* For master's, GRE or GMAT (only upon request), bachelor's degree, resume with relevant professional work, internship or volunteer experience, two letters of recommendation, statement of purpose. Additional exam requirements/recommendations for international students: Required—TOEFL (minimum score 600 paper-based; 100 iBT), IELTS (minimum score 7). Electronic applications accepted. *Expenses:* Contact institution.

New York University, Tandon School of Engineering, Department of Finance and Risk Engineering, New York, NY 10012-1019. Offers financial engineering (MS), including capital markets, computational finance, financial technology. *Program availability:* Part-time, evening/weekend. *Faculty:* 8 full-time (2 women), 42 part-time/adjunct (5 women). *Students:* 271 full-time (124 women), 5 part-time (1 woman); includes 132 minority (9 Asian, non-Hispanic/Latino; 123 Two or more races, non-Hispanic/Latino), 259 international. Average age 25. 1,905 applicants, 20% accepted, 110 enrolled. In 2018, 146 master's awarded. *Degree requirements:* For master's, comprehensive exam (for some programs), thesis (for some programs). *Entrance requirements:* For master's, GMAT, minimum B average in undergraduate course work. Additional exam requirements/recommendations for international students: Required—TOEFL (minimum score 550 paper-based; 90 iBT); Recommended—IELTS (minimum score 7). *Application deadline:* For fall admission, 2/15 priority date for domestic and international students; for spring admission, 11/1 priority date for domestic and international students. Applications are processed on a rolling basis. Application fee: $75. Electronic applications accepted. *Expenses:* Contact institution. *Financial support:* In 2018–19, 253 students received support. Fellowships, research assistantships, teaching assistantships, career-related internships or fieldwork, scholarships/grants, tuition waivers, and unspecified assistantships available. Support available to part-time students. Financial award application deadline: 2/15. *Faculty research:* Optimal control theory, general modeling and analysis, risk parity optimality, a new algorithmic approach to entangled political economy. Total annual research expenditures: $775,200. *Unit head:* Dr. Peter Paul Carr, Department Chair, 646-997-3539, E-mail: petercarr@nyu.edu. *Application contact:* Elizabeth Ensweiler, Senior Director of Graduate Enrollment and Graduate Admissions, 646-997-3182, E-mail: elizabeth.ensweiler@nyu.edu.

Niagara University, Graduate Division of Business Administration, Niagara University, NY 14109. Offers accounting (MBA); business administration (MBA); finance (MBA, MS); financial planning (MBA); healthcare administration (MBA, MHA); human resources (MBA); international business (MBA); marketing (MBA); professional accountancy (MBA); strategic management (MBA); supply chain management (MBA). *Accreditation:* AACSB. *Program availability:* Part-time, evening/weekend, 100% online, blended/hybrid learning. *Students:* 224 full-time (116 women), 56 part-time (22 women); includes 36 minority (9 Black or African American, non-Hispanic/Latino; 2 American Indian or Alaska Native, non-Hispanic/Latino; 6 Asian, non-Hispanic/Latino; 12 Hispanic/Latino; 7 Two or more races, non-Hispanic/Latino), 82 international. Average age 26. In 2018, 134 master's awarded. *Entrance requirements:* For master's, GMAT. Additional exam requirements/recommendations for international students: Required—TOEFL (minimum score 550 paper-based; 79 iBT), IELTS (minimum score 6). *Application deadline:* For fall admission, 8/1 for domestic students; for spring admission, 11/1 for domestic students. Applications are processed on a rolling basis. Electronic applications accepted. *Expenses:* Contact institution. *Financial support:* Research assistantships, teaching assistantships, career-related internships or fieldwork, Federal Work-Study, scholarships/grants, and unspecified assistantships available. Support available to part-time students. Financial award application deadline: 4/15; financial award applicants required to submit FAFSA. *Faculty research:* Capital flows, Federal Reserve policy, human resource management, public policy, issues in marketing, auctions, economics

of information, risk and capital markets, management strategy, consumer behavior, Internet and social media marketing. *Unit head:* Dr. Paul Richardson, MBA Director/ Chair of the Marketing Department, 716-286-8169, Fax: 716-286-8206, E-mail: mba@niagara.edu. *Application contact:* Evan Pierce, Associate Director for Graduate Recruitment, 716-286-8327, Fax: 716-286-8710, E-mail: epierce@niagara.edu.
Website: http://mba.niagara.edu

North Central College, School of Graduate and Professional Studies, Program in Business Administration, Naperville, IL 60566-7063. Offers change management (MBA); finance (MBA); human resource management (MBA); management (MBA). *Program availability:* Part-time, evening/weekend. *Degree requirements:* For master's, thesis optional, project. *Entrance requirements:* For master's, interview. Additional exam requirements/recommendations for international students: Required—TOEFL (minimum score 550 paper-based; 80 iBT), IELTS (minimum score 6.5). Electronic applications accepted. Application fee is waived when completed online. *Expenses:* Contact institution.

Northeastern State University, College of Business and Technology, Program in Accounting and Financial Analysis, Tahlequah, OK 74464-2399. Offers MS. *Program availability:* Part-time, evening/weekend. *Faculty:* 5 full-time (1 woman). *Students:* 12 full-time (7 women), 43 part-time (23 women); includes 22 minority (4 Black or African American, non-Hispanic/Latino; 4 American Indian or Alaska Native, non-Hispanic/ Latino; 1 Asian, non-Hispanic/Latino; 2 Hispanic/Latino; 11 Two or more races, non-Hispanic/Latino). Average age 33. In 2018, 12 master's awarded. *Entrance requirements:* For master's, GMAT. Additional exam requirements/recommendations for international students: Required—TOEFL. *Application deadline:* For fall admission, 6/1 priority date for domestic students. Applications are processed on a rolling basis. Application fee: $25. Electronic applications accepted. *Expenses: Tuition, area resident:* Full-time $4500; part-time $250 per credit hour. Tuition, state resident: full-time $4500; part-time $250 per credit hour. Tuition, nonresident: full-time $9999; part-time $555.50 per credit hour. *International tuition:* $9999 full-time. *Required fees:* $601.20; $33.40 per credit hour. *Faculty research:* Information systems and organizational performance, capital markets, sustainability. *Unit head:* Dr. Gary Freeman, Director, Master of Accounting and Financial Analysis, 918-449-6524, E-mail: freemadg@nsuok.edu. *Application contact:* Josh McCollum, Graduate Coordinator, 918-444-2093, E-mail: mccolluj@nsuok.edu.
Website: http://academics.nsuok.edu/businesstechnology/Graduate/MAFA.aspx

Northeastern University, D'Amore-McKim School of Business, Boston, MA 02115-5096. Offers accounting (MS); business administration (EMBA, MBA); finance (MS); innovation (MS); international business (MS); international management (MS); taxation (MS); technological entrepreneurship (MS); JD/MBA; LL M/MBA; MBA/MSN; MS/MBA. *Accreditation:* AACSB. *Program availability:* Part-time, evening/weekend, online learning. *Entrance requirements:* For master's, GMAT or GRE. Electronic applications accepted. *Expenses:* Contact institution.

Northern State University, MS Program in Banking and Financial Services, Aberdeen, SD 57401-7198. Offers MS. *Program availability:* Part-time, online learning. *Degree requirements:* For master's, capstone course. *Entrance requirements:* For master's, GMAT or GRE, minimum GPA of 2.75. Additional exam requirements/recommendations for international students: Required—TOEFL (minimum score 550 paper-based; 78 iBT), IELTS (minimum score 6). Electronic applications accepted.

North Greenville University, T. Walter Brashier Graduate School, Greer, SC 29651. Offers Christian ministry (MCM, D Min); education (M Ed, MAT); financial planning (MBA); human resources (MBA). *Program availability:* Part-time, evening/weekend, online learning. *Degree requirements:* For master's, comprehensive exam (for some programs), thesis or alternative, capstone course. *Entrance requirements:* For master's, minimum GPA of 2.25 overall, 2.5 in major; for doctorate, MAT. Additional exam requirements/recommendations for international students: Required—TOEFL (minimum score 550 paper-based). Electronic applications accepted. *Faculty research:* Organizational behavior, church growth, homiletics, human resources, business strategy.

Northwestern University, The Graduate School, Kellogg School of Management, Department of Finance, Evanston, IL 60208. Offers PhD. Admissions and degree offered through The Graduate School. *Degree requirements:* For doctorate, comprehensive exam, thesis/dissertation. *Entrance requirements:* For doctorate, GMAT or GRE General Test, 2 years of undergraduate course work in mathematics. Additional exam requirements/recommendations for international students: Required—TOEFL. Electronic applications accepted. *Faculty research:* Corporate finance, asset pricing, international finance, micro-structure, empirical finance.

Northwestern University, The Graduate School, Kellogg School of Management, Management Programs, Evanston, IL 60208. Offers accounting information and management (MBA, PhD); analytical finance (MBA); business administration (MBA); decision sciences (MBA); entrepreneurship and innovation (MBA); finance (MBA, PhD); health enterprise management (MBA); human resources management (MBA); international business (MBA); management and organizations (MBA, PhD); management and organizations and sociology (PhD); management and strategy (MBA); management studies (MS); managerial analytics (MBA); managerial economics (MBA); managerial economics and strategy (PhD); marketing (MBA, PhD); marketing management (MBA); media management (MBA); operations management (MBA, PhD); real estate (MBA); social enterprise at Kellogg (MBA); JD/MBA. *Program availability:* Part-time, evening/weekend. Terminal master's awarded for partial completion of doctoral program. *Degree requirements:* For doctorate, thesis/dissertation, 2 years of coursework, qualifying (field) exam and candidacy, summer research papers and presentations to faculty, proposal defense, final exam/defense. *Entrance requirements:* For master's, GMAT, GRE, interview, 2 letters of recommendation, college transcripts, resume, essays, Kellogg honor code; for doctorate, GMAT, GRE, statement of purpose, transcripts, 2 letters of recommendation, resume, interview. Additional exam requirements/recommendations for international students: Required—TOEFL, IELTS. Electronic applications accepted. *Expenses:* Contact institution. *Faculty research:* Business cycles and international finance, health policy, networks, non-market strategy, consumer psychology.

Norwich University, College of Graduate and Continuing Studies, Master of Business Administration Program, Northfield, VT 05663. Offers construction management (MBA); energy management (MBA); finance (MBA); logistics (MBA); organizational leadership (MBA); project management (MBA); supply chain management (MBA). *Accreditation:* ACBSP. *Program availability:* Evening/weekend, online only, mostly all online with a week-long residency requirement. *Degree requirements:* For master's, comprehensive exam. *Entrance requirements:* For master's, minimum undergraduate GPA of 2.75. Additional exam requirements/recommendations for international students: Required—TOEFL (minimum score 550 paper-based; 80 iBT), IELTS (minimum score 6.5). Electronic applications accepted. *Expenses:* Contact institution.

Notre Dame de Namur University, Division of Academic Affairs, School of Business and Management, Program in Business Administration, Belmont, CA 94002-1908. Offers finance (MBA). *Accreditation:* ACBSP. *Program availability:* Part-time, evening/ weekend. *Students:* 31 full-time (21 women), 76 part-time (44 women); includes 61 minority (8 Black or African American, non-Hispanic/Latino; 2 American Indian or Alaska Native, non-Hispanic/Latino; 26 Asian, non-Hispanic/Latino; 18 Hispanic/Latino; 4 Native Hawaiian or other Pacific Islander, non-Hispanic/Latino; 3 Two or more races, non-Hispanic/Latino), 12 international. Average age 34. *Entrance requirements:* For master's, minimum GPA of 2.5. Additional exam requirements/recommendations for international students: Required—TOEFL (minimum score 550 paper-based; 79 iBT). *Application deadline:* For fall admission, 8/1 priority date for domestic students; for spring admission, 12/1 priority date for domestic students. Applications are processed on a rolling basis. Application fee: $60. Electronic applications accepted. *Expenses: Tuition:* Full-time $16,596; part-time $11,064 per semester. *Required fees:* $130; $130 per unit. $65 per semester. Tuition and fees vary according to program. *Financial support:* Applicants required to submit FAFSA. *Unit head:* Jordan Holtzman, Program Director, Graduate Business Programs, 510-375-1348, E-mail: jholtzman@ndnu.edu. *Application contact:* Jordan Holtzman, Program Director, Graduate Business Programs, 510-375-1348, E-mail: jholtzman@ndnu.edu.
Website: http://www.ndnu.edu/academics/schools-programs/school-business/

Nova Southeastern University, H. Wayne Huizenga College of Business and Entrepreneurship, Fort Lauderdale, FL 33314-7796. Offers accounting (M Acc); business (MBA); business intelligence/analytics (MBA); complex health systems (MBA); enterprise informatics (MBA); entrepreneurship (MBA); finance (MBA); human resource management (MBA); international business (MBA); management (MBA); marketing (MBA); process improvement (MBA); public administration (MPA); real estate development (MS); sport revenue generation (MBA); supply chain management (MBA). *Accreditation:* NASPAA. *Program availability:* Part-time, evening/weekend, 100% online, blended/hybrid learning. *Entrance requirements:* For master's, GMAT or GRE (depending on undergraduate GPA), official transcripts from all schools attended while in pursuit of bachelor's degree; minimum GPA of 2.5 from regionally-accredited institution. Additional exam requirements/recommendations for international students: Required—TOEFL (minimum score 550 paper-based; 79 iBT), IELTS (minimum score 6), PTE (minimum score 54). Electronic applications accepted. *Expenses:* Contact institution. *Faculty research:* Entrepreneurship and venture capital, ethics and social responsibility, global commerce and cultures, business process management.

Oakland University, Graduate Study and Lifelong Learning, School of Business Administration, Department of Accounting and Finance, Rochester, MI 48309-4401. Offers accounting (M Acc, Certificate); finance (Certificate).

Ohio Christian University, Graduate Programs, Circleville, OH 43113. Offers accounting (MBA); business administration (MBA); digital marketing (MBA); finance (MBA); healthcare management (MBA); human resources (MBA); management (MM); organizational leadership (MBA); pastoral care and counseling (MAM); practical theology (MAM).

Ohio Dominican University, Division of Business, Program in Business Administration, Columbus, OH 43219-2099. Offers accounting (MBA); data analytics (MBA); finance (MBA); leadership (MBA); risk management (MBA); sport management (MBA). *Program availability:* Part-time, evening/weekend, 100% online, blended/hybrid learning. *Faculty:* 10 full-time (4 women), 12 part-time/adjunct (1 woman). *Students:* 42 full-time (17 women), 88 part-time (43 women); includes 29 minority (16 Black or African American, non-Hispanic/Latino; 1 American Indian or Alaska Native, non-Hispanic/Latino; 3 Asian, non-Hispanic/Latino; 5 Hispanic/Latino; 4 Two or more races, non-Hispanic/Latino), 14 international. Average age 31. 97 applicants, 44% accepted, 26 enrolled. In 2018, 56 master's awarded. *Entrance requirements:* For master's, minimum overall GPA of 3.0 in undergraduate degree from regionally-accredited institution or 2.75 in last 60 semester hours of bachelor's degree. Additional exam requirements/recommendations for international students: Required—TOEFL (minimum score 550 paper-based), IELTS (minimum score 6.5). *Application deadline:* For fall admission, 8/15 for domestic students, 6/10 for international students; for spring admission, 1/4 for domestic students, 11/2 for international students; for summer admission, 5/30 for domestic students. Applications are processed on a rolling basis. Application fee: $25. Electronic applications accepted. *Expenses: Tuition:* Full-time $10,800; part-time $600 per credit hour. *Required fees:* $450; $225 per semester. Tuition and fees vary according to program. *Financial support:* Applicants required to submit FAFSA. *Unit head:* Dr. Thomas Eveland, Director of Graduate Programs in Business, 614-251-4569, E-mail: evelandt@ohiodominican.edu. *Application contact:* John W. Naughton, Vice President for Enrollment and Student Success, 614-251-4721, Fax: 614-251-6654, E-mail: grad@ohiodominican.edu.
Website: http://www.ohiodominican.edu/academics/graduate/mba

The Ohio State University, Graduate School, Max M. Fisher College of Business, Program in Finance, Columbus, OH 43210. Offers MF. *Students:* 60 full-time (29 women). Average age 23. In 2018, 52 master's awarded. *Entrance requirements:* For master's, GMAT (preferred with minimum score of 550 recommended, 600 preferred) or GRE. Additional exam requirements/recommendations for international students: Required—TOEFL (minimum score 600 paper-based; 100 iBT). *Application deadline:* For fall admission, 11/15 priority date for domestic and international students; for spring admission, 10/1 for domestic students. Applications are processed on a rolling basis. Application fee: $60 ($70 for international students). Electronic applications accepted. *Financial support:* Fellowships with tuition reimbursements available. *Unit head:* George Pinteris, Graduate Studies Chair, 614-292-4334, E-mail: pinteris.1@osu.edu. *Application contact:* Graduate and Professional Admissions, 614-292-9444, Fax: 614-292-3895, E-mail: gpadmissions@osu.edu.
Website: http://fisher.osu.edu/smf

Ohio University, Graduate College, College of Arts and Sciences, Department of Economics, Athens, OH 45701-2979. Offers applied economics (MA); financial economics (MFE). *Program availability:* Part-time, evening/weekend. *Degree requirements:* For master's, thesis or alternative. *Entrance requirements:* For master's, GRE or GMAT (recommended), minimum GPA of 3.0. Additional exam requirements/ recommendations for international students: Required—TOEFL (minimum score 550 paper-based; 80 iBT) or IELTS (minimum score 6.5). Electronic applications accepted. *Faculty research:* Macroeconomics, public finance, international economics and finance, monetary theory, healthcare economics.

Oklahoma Christian University, Graduate School of Business, Oklahoma City, OK 73136-1100. Offers accounting (M Acc, MBA); financial services (MBA); general business (MBA); health services management (MBA); human resources (MBA); international business (MBA); leadership and organizational development (MBA); marketing (MBA); nonprofit management (MBA); project management (MBA). *Accreditation:* ACBSP. *Program availability:* Part-time, 100% online. *Entrance requirements:* For master's, bachelor's degree. Additional exam requirements/ recommendations for international students: Required—TOEFL (minimum score 550 paper-based). Electronic applications accepted. *Expenses:* Contact institution.

Oklahoma State University, Spears School of Business, Department of Finance, Stillwater, OK 74078. Offers MS, PhD. *Program availability:* Part-time. *Faculty:* 13 full-time (3 women), 2 part-time/adjunct (0 women). *Students:* 11 full-time (5 women), 7 part-time (0 women); includes 1 minority (Hispanic/Latino), 13 international. Average age 26. 31 applicants, 35% accepted, 10 enrolled. In 2018, 7 master's, 15 doctorates awarded.

Entrance requirements: For master's and doctorate, GRE or GMAT. Additional exam requirements/recommendations for international students: Required—TOEFL (minimum score 550 paper-based; 79 iBT). *Application deadline:* For fall admission, 3/1 priority date for international students; for spring admission, 8/1 priority date for international students. Applications are processed on a rolling basis. Application fee: $40 ($75 for international students). Electronic applications accepted. *Expenses: Tuition, area resident:* Full-time $4148. Tuition, state resident: full-time $4148. Tuition, nonresident: full-time $10,517. *International tuition:* $10,517 full-time. *Required fees:* $4394; $2929 per credit hour. Tuition and fees vary according to course load and program. *Financial support:* Research assistantships, teaching assistantships, career-related internships or fieldwork, Federal Work-Study, scholarships/grants, health care benefits, tuition waivers (partial), and unspecified assistantships available. Support available to part-time students. Financial award application deadline: 3/1; financial award applicants required to submit FAFSA. *Faculty research:* Corporate risk management, derivatives banking, investments and securities issuance, corporate governance, banking. *Unit head:* Dr. Betty Simkins, Interim Department Head, 405-744-8625, Fax: 405-744-5180, E-mail: betty.simkins@okstate.edu. *Application contact:* Dr. Sheryl Tucker, Dean, 405-744-6368, Fax: 405-744-0355, E-mail: gradi@okstate.edu.
Website: https://business.okstate.edu/finance/

Old Dominion University, Strome College of Business, Doctoral Program in Business Administration, Norfolk, VA 23529. Offers business administration (PhD), including finance, IT and supply chain management, marketing, strategic management. *Accreditation:* AACSB. *Degree requirements:* For doctorate, comprehensive exam, thesis/dissertation. *Entrance requirements:* For doctorate, GMAT or GRE. Additional exam requirements/recommendations for international students: Required—TOEFL (minimum score 550 paper-based; 79 iBT). Electronic applications accepted. *Faculty research:* International business, buyer behavior, financial markets, strategy, operations research.

Oral Roberts University, School of Business, Tulsa, OK 74171. Offers accounting (MBA); entrepreneurship (MBA); finance (MBA); international business (MBA); management (MBA); marketing (MBA); not for profit management (MNM). *Accreditation:* ACBSP. *Program availability:* Part-time, online learning. *Degree requirements:* For master's, thesis optional. *Entrance requirements:* For master's, minimum cumulative GPA of 3.0 from regionally-accredited institution. Electronic applications accepted. Application fee is waived when completed online. *Faculty research:* Social media, international business and marketing.

Oregon State University, College of Business, Program in Business Administration, Corvallis, OR 97331. Offers business administration (PhD), including accounting; corporate finance (MBA). *Program availability:* Part-time, blended/hybrid learning. *Entrance requirements:* For master's, GMAT. Additional exam requirements/recommendations for international students: Required—TOEFL (minimum score 91 iBT), IELTS (minimum score 7). *Expenses:* Contact institution.

Ottawa University, Graduate Studies-Arizona, Programs in Business, Ottawa, KS 66067-3399. Offers business administration (MBA); finance (MBA); human resources (MA, MBA); leadership (MBA); marketing (MBA). Programs offered in Mesa, Phoenix, Tempe and West Valley, AZ. *Program availability:* Part-time, evening/weekend, online learning. *Degree requirements:* For master's, thesis or alternative. *Entrance requirements:* For master's, minimum undergraduate GPA of 3.0. Additional exam requirements/recommendations for international students: Required—TOEFL (minimum score 550 paper-based). Electronic applications accepted.

Our Lady of the Lake University, School of Business and Leadership, Program in Finance, San Antonio, TX 78207-4689. Offers MBA. *Program availability:* Part-time, evening/weekend. *Faculty:* 1 full-time (0 women). *Students:* 5 full-time (4 women), 7 part-time (3 women); includes 7 minority (1 Black or African American, non-Hispanic/Latino; 6 Hispanic/Latino). Average age 36. In 2018, 4 master's awarded. *Entrance requirements:* For master's, official transcripts showing 6 hours of coursework in economics and 3 hours of coursework in each of the following ares: statistics, management, business law, and finance; resume including detailed work history describing managerial or professional work experience. Additional exam requirements/recommendations for international students: Required—TOEFL. *Application deadline:* For fall admission, 6/15 for domestic students, 7/15 for international students; for spring admission, 11/15 for domestic and international students; for summer admission, 4/15 for domestic and international students. Applications are processed on a rolling basis. Application fee: $40 ($50 for international students). Electronic applications accepted. Application fee is waived when completed online. *Expenses: Tuition:* Full-time $16,326; part-time $907 per credit. *Financial support:* In 2018–19, 5 students received support. Federal Work-Study, unspecified assistantships, and tuition discounts available. Support available to part-time students. Financial award application deadline: 5/1; financial award applicants required to submit FAFSA. *Unit head:* Dr. Ronald Crowe, Business Programs Chair, E-mail: rcrowe@ollusa.edu. *Application contact:* Office of Graduate Admissions, 210-431-3995, Fax: 210-431-3945, E-mail: gradadm@ollusa.edu.

Pace University, Lubin School of Business, Advanced Professional Certificate Program, New York, NY 10038. Offers business economics (APC); e-business (APC); financial management (APC); international business (APC); international economics (APC); investment management (APC); marketing (APC); public accounting (APC). *Program availability:* Part-time, evening/weekend. *Entrance requirements:* For degree, MBA or MS in business discipline, relevant professional experience. Additional exam requirements/recommendations for international students: Required—TOEFL (minimum score 90 iBT), IELTS (minimum score 7) or PTE (minimum score 61). *Application deadline:* For fall admission, 8/1 priority date for domestic students, 6/1 for international students; for spring admission, 12/1 for domestic students, 10/1 for international students. Applications are processed on a rolling basis. Application fee: $70. Electronic applications accepted. *Unit head:* Dr. Ibraiz Tarique, Chairperson, 212-618-6583, E-mail: itarique@pace.edu. *Application contact:* Susan Ford-Goldschein, Director of Graduate Admissions, 212-346-1531, Fax: 212-346-1585, E-mail: graduateadmission@pace.edu.
Website: http://www.pace.edu/lubin/agc

Pace University, Lubin School of Business, Doctor of Professional Studies Program, New York, NY 10038. Offers finance (DPS); management (DPS); marketing (DPS). *Program availability:* Part-time, blended/hybrid learning. *Students:* 9 full-time (3 women), 63 part-time (31 women); includes 20 minority (11 Black or African American, non-Hispanic/Latino; 4 Asian, non-Hispanic/Latino; 4 Hispanic/Latino; 1 Two or more races, non-Hispanic/Latino), 4 international. Average age 50. 29 applicants, 79% accepted, 12 enrolled. In 2018, 8 doctorates awarded. *Degree requirements:* For doctorate, thesis/dissertation, oral and written exam. *Entrance requirements:* For doctorate, MBA or similar master's degree, 10 years of experience in business, transcripts from all accredited colleges/universities attended, 4 letters of recommendation, interview. Additional exam requirements/recommendations for international students: Required—TOEFL (minimum score 90 iBT), IELTS (minimum score 7) or PTE (minimum score 61). *Application deadline:* For fall admission, 6/1 priority date for domestic students, 6/1 for international students. Applications are processed on a rolling basis. Application fee: $70. Electronic applications accepted. *Unit head:* Dr. Noushi Rahman, Director, Doctoral Program in Business, 212-618-6661, E-mail: nrahman@pace.edu. *Application contact:* Margaret Hanson, Program Coordinator for Doctoral Programs, 212-618-6660, E-mail: dps.bus@pace.edu.
Website: http://www.pace.edu/lubin/dps/

Pace University, Lubin School of Business, Finance Program, New York, NY 10038. Offers financial management (MBA, MS); financial risk management (MS); international finance (MBA); investment management (MBA, MS). *Program availability:* Part-time, evening/weekend. *Students:* 120 full-time (52 women), 79 part-time (30 women); includes 33 minority (10 Black or African American, non-Hispanic/Latino; 14 Asian, non-Hispanic/Latino; 8 Hispanic/Latino; 1 Two or more races, non-Hispanic/Latino), 119 international. Average age 26. 236 applicants, 77% accepted, 64 enrolled. In 2018, 132 master's awarded. *Entrance requirements:* For master's, GMAT, GRE (GMAT not required for MS with passing of Level 1 of Chartered Financial Analyst exam or Level 1 of Financial Risk Manager Exam), Undergrad degree, transcripts from all accredited colleges/universities attended, 2 letters of recommendation, resume, personal statement. If applying to the 1 year fast track MBA in Financial Management, must have a cumulative GPA of 3.30 or above, a grade of B or better for all business core courses from an AACSB-accredited U.S. business school. Additional exam requirements/recommendations for international students: Required—TOEFL (minimum score 90 iBT), IELTS (minimum score 7) or PTE (minimum score 61). *Application deadline:* For fall admission, 8/1 priority date for domestic students, 6/1 for international students; for spring admission, 12/1 for domestic students, 10/1 for international students. Applications are processed on a rolling basis. Application fee: $70. Electronic applications accepted. *Financial support:* Research assistantships, career-related internships or fieldwork, Federal Work-Study, tuition waivers (full and partial), and unspecified assistantships available. Support available to part-time students. Financial award application deadline: 2/15; financial award applicants required to submit FAFSA. *Unit head:* Dr. Aron Gottesman, Chairperson, Finance Department, 212-618-6525, E-mail: agottesman@pace.edu. *Application contact:* Susan Ford-Goldschein, Director of Graduate Admissions, 212-346-1531, Fax: 212-346-1585, E-mail: graduateadmissions@pace.edu.
Website: http://www.pace.edu/lubin/sections/explore-programs/graduate-programs

Pacific Lutheran University, School of Business, Master of Science in Finance Program, Tacoma, WA 98447. Offers MSF. *Entrance requirements:* For master's, GRE or GMAT. Additional exam requirements/recommendations for international students: Required—TOEFL (minimum score 550 paper-based; 88 iBT). Electronic applications accepted. *Expenses:* Contact institution.

Pacific States University, College of Business, Los Angeles, CA 90010. Offers accounting (MBA, Certificate); beauty management (MBA); finance (MBA); international business (MBA); management of information technology (MBA); project management (Certificate); real estate management (MBA). *Program availability:* Part-time, evening/weekend, online learning. *Entrance requirements:* For master's, minimum undergraduate GPA of 2.5 during last 90 quarter units of course work, bachelor's degree in business administration or economics. Additional exam requirements/recommendations for international students: Required—TOEFL (minimum score 500 paper-based; 61 iBT), IELTS (minimum score 5.5).

Pacific University, College of Business, Forest Grove, OR 97116-1797. Offers business administration (MBA); finance (MSF).

Park University, School of Graduate and Professional Studies, Kansas City, MO 54105. Offers adult education (M Ed); business and government leadership (Graduate Certificate); business, government, and global society (MPA); communication and leadership (MA); creative and life writing (Graduate Certificate); disaster and emergency management (MPA, Graduate Certificate); educational leadership (M Ed); finance (MBA, Graduate Certificate); general business (MBA); global business (Graduate Certificate); healthcare administration (MHA); healthcare services management and leadership (Graduate Certificate); international business (MBA); language and literacy (M Ed), including English for speakers of other languages, special reading teacher/literacy coach; leadership of international healthcare organizations (Graduate Certificate); management information systems (MBA, Graduate Certificate); music performance (ADP, Graduate Certificate), including cello (MM, ADP), piano (MM, ADP), viola (MM, ADP), violin (MM, ADP); nonprofit and community services management (MPA); nonprofit leadership (Graduate Certificate); performance (MM), including cello (MM, ADP), piano (MM, ADP), viola (MM, ADP), violin (MM, ADP); public management (MPA); social work (MSW); teacher leadership (M Ed), including curriculum and assessment, instructional leader. *Program availability:* Part-time, evening/weekend, online learning. *Degree requirements:* For master's, comprehensive exam (for some programs), thesis (for some programs), internship (for some programs); exam (for some programs). *Entrance requirements:* For master's, GRE or GMAT (for some programs), teacher certification (for some M Ed programs), letters of recommendation, essay, resume (for some programs). Additional exam requirements/recommendations for international students: Required—TOEFL (minimum score 550 paper-based; 79 iBT), IELTS (minimum score 6). Electronic applications accepted.

Penn State Great Valley, Graduate Studies, Management Division, Malvern, PA 19355-1488. Offers business administration (MBA); cyber security (Certificate); data analytics (MPS, MS, Certificate); distributed energy and grid modernization (Certificate); finance (M Fin); health sector management (Certificate); human resource management (Certificate); information science (MSIS); leadership development (MLD); new ventures and entrepreneurship (Certificate); sustainable management practices (Certificate). *Accreditation:* AACSB.

Penn State Harrisburg, Graduate School, School of Public Affairs, Middletown, PA 17057. Offers criminal justice (MA); health administration (MHA); health administration: long term care (Certificate); homeland security (MPS, Certificate); public administration (MPA, PhD); public administration: non-profit administration (Certificate); public budgeting and financial management (Certificate); public sector human resource management (Certificate). *Accreditation:* NASPAA.

Polytechnic University of Puerto Rico, Miami Campus, Graduate School, Miami, FL 33166. Offers accounting (MBA); business administration (MBA); construction management (MEM); environmental management (MEM); finance (MBA); human resources management (MBA); logistics and supply chain management (MBA); management of international enterprises (MBA); manufacturing management (MEM); marketing management (MBA); project management (MBA). *Program availability:* Part-time, evening/weekend, online learning. *Entrance requirements:* For master's, minimum GPA of 3.0. Electronic applications accepted.

Polytechnic University of Puerto Rico, Orlando Campus, Graduate School, Orlando, FL 32825. Offers accounting (MBA); business administration (MBA); construction management (MEM); engineering management (MEM); environmental management (MEM); finance (MBA); human resources management (MBA); management of international enterprises (MBA); management of technology (MBA); manufacturing management (MEM). *Program availability:* Part-time, evening/weekend, online learning. *Entrance requirements:* For master's, minimum GPA of 3.0. Additional exam requirements/recommendations for international students: Recommended—TOEFL. Electronic applications accepted.

Pontifical Catholic University of Puerto Rico, College of Business Administration, Program in Finance, Ponce, PR 00717-0777. Offers MBA. *Program availability:* Part-time, evening/weekend. *Degree requirements:* For master's, thesis. *Entrance requirements:* For master's, GRE, interview, minimum GPA of 2.75.

Pontificia Universidad Catolica Madre y Maestra, Graduate School, Faculty of Social and Administrative Sciences, Santiago, Dominican Republic. Offers business administration (MBA), including business development, finance, international business, management skills (M Mgmt, MBA), marketing, operations, strategic cost management, strategy, tourist destination planning and management; law (LL M), including civil law, corporate business law, criminal law, international relations, real estate law; management (M Mgmt), including higher financial management, insurance program administration, management skills (M Mgmt, MBA); psychology (MA), including clinical child and adolescent psychology, forensic psychology; strategic human resources (EMBA).

Portland State University, Graduate Studies, The School of Business, Master of Science in Financial Analysis Program, Portland, OR 97207-0751. Offers MSF. *Program availability:* Part-time, evening/weekend. *Entrance requirements:* For master's, GMAT or GRE, minimum GPA of 2.75, 2 recommendations, statement of purpose, resume, interview. Additional exam requirements/recommendations for international students: Required—TOEFL (minimum score 550 paper-based; 80 iBT). Electronic applications accepted. *Expenses:* Contact institution.

Post University, Program in Business Administration, Waterbury, CT 06723-2540. Offers accounting (MSA); business administration (MBA); corporate finance (MBA); corporate innovation (MBA); healthcare systems leadership (MBA); leadership (MBA); marketing (MBA); project management (MBA, MS). *Accreditation:* ACBSP. *Program availability:* Online learning. *Entrance requirements:* For master's, resume. *Expenses: Tuition:* Full-time $8300; part-time $570 per credit. *Required fees:* $140 per term. Tuition and fees vary according to course level, campus/location and program.

Princeton University, Graduate School, Bendheim Center for Finance, Princeton, NJ 08544. Offers M Fin. *Faculty:* 9 full-time (1 woman), 7 part-time/adjunct. *Students:* 49 full-time (23 women); includes 3 minority (2 Asian, non-Hispanic/Latino; 1 Two or more races, non-Hispanic/Latino), 43 international. Average age 23. 565 applicants, 7% accepted, 29 enrolled. In 2018, 27 master's awarded. *Degree requirements:* For master's, 5 core courses, 11 approved electives unless a student completes program in one year in which case 5 approved electives. *Entrance requirements:* For master's, GRE General Test or GMAT. Additional exam requirements/recommendations for international students: Required—TOEFL, IF not TOEFL, IELTS. *Application deadline:* For fall admission, 12/31 for domestic and international students. Application fee: $0. Electronic applications accepted. *Financial support:* In 2018–19, 9 students received support, including 10 teaching assistantships (averaging $10,000 per year); scholarships/grants also available. *Faculty research:* Corporate finance, financial econometrics, machine learning and artificial intelligence, financial frictions and institutional finance, commodities markets. *Unit head:* Rene Carmona, Director of Graduate Studies, 609-258-2310, Fax: 609-258-3791, E-mail: rcarmona@princeton.edu. *Application contact:* Graduate Admissions Office, 609-258-3034, Fax: 609-258-7262, E-mail: gsadmit@princeton.edu.
Website: http://www.princeton.edu/bcf/

Providence College, School of Business, Providence, RI 02918. Offers accounting (MBA); finance (MBA); international business (MBA); management (MBA); marketing (MBA). *Accreditation:* AACSB. *Program availability:* Part-time, evening/weekend. *Entrance requirements:* For master's, GMAT. Additional exam requirements/recommendations for international students: Required—TOEFL (minimum score 577 paper-based; 90 iBT). *Expenses:* Contact institution.

Purdue University, Graduate School, Krannert School of Management, Master of Science in Finance Program, West Lafayette, IN 47907. Offers MSF. *Entrance requirements:* For master's, GMAT or GRE, minimum GPA of 3.0, four-year baccalaureate degree, essays, letters of recommendation. Additional exam requirements/recommendations for international students: Required—TOEFL (minimum score 600 paper-based; 93 iBT), IELTS (minimum score 7.5). Electronic applications accepted. *Expenses:* Contact institution. *Faculty research:* Capital market imperfections and sensitivity of investment to stock prices, identifying beneficial collaboration in decentralized logistics systems, performance periods and the dynamics of the performance-risk relationship, applications of global optimization to process and molecular design.

Purdue University Global, School of Business, Davenport, IA 52807. Offers business administration (MBA); change leadership (MS); entrepreneurship (MBA); finance (MBA); health care management (MBA, MS); human resource (MBA); international business (MBA); management (MS); marketing (MBA); project management (MBA, MS); supply chain management and logistics (MBA, MS). *Accreditation:* ACBSP. *Program availability:* Part-time, evening/weekend, online learning. *Entrance requirements:* Additional exam requirements/recommendations for international students: Required—TOEFL (minimum score 550 paper-based; 80 iBT). Electronic applications accepted.

Queens College of the City University of New York, Division of Social Sciences, Department of Economics, Queens, NY 11367-1597. Offers risk management: accounting (MS); risk management: dynamic financial analysis (MS); risk management: finance (MS). Risk Management is a graduate program offered jointly by the Departments of Economics and Accounting & Information Systems. *Faculty:* 23 full-time (8 women), 42 part-time/adjunct (9 women). *Students:* 3 full-time (2 women), 26 part-time (15 women); includes 24 minority (4 Black or African American, non-Hispanic/Latino; 10 Asian, non-Hispanic/Latino; 7 Hispanic/Latino; 3 Two or more races, non-Hispanic/Latino), 5 international. Average age 30. 24 applicants, 79% accepted, 12 enrolled. In 2018, 20 master's awarded. *Degree requirements:* For master's, thesis, Capstone Class/Thesis Project. *Entrance requirements:* For master's, minimum GPA of 3.0. Additional exam requirements/recommendations for international students: Required—TOEFL (minimum score 100 iBT), IELTS (minimum score 7). *Application deadline:* For fall admission, 6/30 for domestic and international students; for spring admission, 11/30 for domestic and international students. Applications are processed on a rolling basis. Application fee: $75. Electronic applications accepted. *Financial support:* In 2018–19, 1 student received support. Federal Work-Study, institutionally sponsored loans, and scholarships/grants available. Financial award application deadline: 4/1; financial award applicants required to submit FAFSA. *Faculty research:* Business economics, urban economic problems, international economics, economics of nonprofit sector. *Unit head:* Cara Marshall, Program Director, 718-997-5387, E-mail: cara.marshall@qc.cuny.edu. *Application contact:* Elvira Casper, Program Coordinator, 718-997-5507, E-mail: elvira.casper@qc.cuny.edu.

Queen's University at Kingston, Smith School of Business, Doctoral Program in Management, Kingston, ON K7L 3N6, Canada. Offers analytics (PhD); business economics (PhD); finance (PhD); management information systems (PhD); marketing (PhD); organizational behavior (PhD); strategy (PhD).

Queen's University at Kingston, Smith School of Business, Master of Science in Management Program, Kingston, ON K7L 3N6, Canada. Offers analytics (M Sc); business economics (M Sc); finance (M Sc); management information systems (M Sc); marketing (M Sc); organizational behavior (M Sc); strategy (M Sc).

Queen's University at Kingston, Smith School of Business, Program in Business Administration, Kingston, ON K7L 3N6, Canada. Offers consulting and project management (MBA); finance (MBA); innovation and entrepreneurship (MBA); marketing (MBA). *Degree requirements:* For master's, thesis optional, research project. *Entrance requirements:* For master's, GMAT, minimum B+ average. Additional exam requirements/recommendations for international students: Required—TOEFL. Electronic applications accepted. *Faculty research:* Management fundamentals, strategic thinking, global business, innovation and change, leadership.

Quinnipiac University, School of Business, Program in Business Administration, Hamden, CT 06518-1940. Offers finance (MBA); health care management (MBA); supply chain management (MBA); JD/MBA. *Accreditation:* AACSB. *Program availability:* Part-time, evening/weekend, 100% online, blended/hybrid learning. *Entrance requirements:* For master's, GMAT or GRE, minimum GPA of 3.0. Additional exam requirements/recommendations for international students: Required—TOEFL (minimum score 575 paper-based; 90 iBT), IELTS (minimum score 6.5). Electronic applications accepted. *Expenses:* Contact institution. *Faculty research:* Financial markets and investments, international business, supply chain management, health care management, corporate governance.

Regent's University London, Webster Graduate School, London, United Kingdom. Offers business (MBA); finance (MS); human resources (MA); information technology management (MA); international business (MA); international non-governmental organizations (MA); international relations (MA); management and leadership (MA); marketing (MA). *Program availability:* Part-time.

Regent University, Graduate School, School of Business and Leadership, Virginia Beach, VA 23464-9800. Offers business administration (MBA), including accounting, economics, entrepreneurship, finance and investing, general management, healthcare management (MA, MBA), human resource management (MA, MBA), innovation management, leadership, marketing, not-for-profit management (MA, MBA); business analytics (MS); business and design management (MA); church leadership (MA); leadership (Certificate); organizational leadership (MA, PhD), including ecclesial leadership (DSL, PhD), entrepreneurial leadership (PhD), healthcare management (MA, MBA), human resource development (PhD), human resource management (MA, MBA), individualized studies (DSL, PhD), interdisciplinary studies (MA), leadership coaching and mentoring (MA), not-for-profit management (MA, MBA), organizational development consulting (MA), servant leadership (MA, DSL); strategic leadership (DSL), including ecclesial leadership (DSL, PhD), global consulting, healthcare leadership, individualized studies (DSL, PhD), leadership coaching, servant leadership (MA, DSL), strategic foresight. *Program availability:* Part-time, evening/weekend, 100% online, blended/hybrid learning. *Degree requirements:* For master's, thesis or alternative, 3-credit hour culminating experience; for doctorate, thesis/dissertation. *Entrance requirements:* For master's, college transcripts, resume, essay; for doctorate, college transcripts, resume, essay, writing sample; for Certificate, writing sample, resume, transcripts. Additional exam requirements/recommendations for international students: Required—TOEFL (minimum score 577 paper-based). Electronic applications accepted. *Expenses:* Contact institution. *Faculty research:* Servant leadership, global business, team effectiveness, technology utilization, leadership development.

Regis University, College of Business and Economics, Denver, CO 80221-1099. Offers accounting (MS); executive leadership (Certificate); finance (MS); finance and accounting (MBA); health industry leadership (MBA); human resource management and leadership (MSOL); management (MBA); marketing (MBA); nonprofit leadership (Post-Graduate Certificate); nonprofit management (MNM); nonprofit organizational capacity building (Certificate); operations management (MBA); organizational leadership and management (MSOL); project leadership and management (MS, MSOL); strategic business management (Certificate); strategic human resource integration (Certificate); strategic management (MBA). Programs offered at Colorado Springs Campus, Northwest Denver Campus, Southeast Denver Campus, Fort Collins Campus, Broomfield Campus, Henderson (Nevada) Campus, and Summerlin (Nevada) Campus. *Program availability:* Part-time, evening/weekend, 100% online, blended/hybrid learning. *Degree requirements:* For master's, thesis (for some programs), capstone or final research project. *Entrance requirements:* For master's, official transcript reflecting baccalaureate degree awarded from regionally-accredited college or university, interview, 2 years of full-time related work experience, resume, letters of recommendation. Additional exam requirements/recommendations for international students: Required—TOEFL (minimum score 550 paper-based; 82 iBT). Electronic applications accepted. *Expenses:* Contact institution. *Faculty research:* Impact of information technology on small business regulation of accounting, international project financing, mineral development, delivery of healthcare to rural indigenous communities.

Rhode Island College, School of Graduate Studies, School of Business, Department of Accounting and Computer Information Systems, Providence, RI 02908-1991. Offers accounting (MP Ac); financial planning (CGS). *Program availability:* Part-time, evening/weekend. *Faculty:* 1 (woman) full-time, 2 part-time/adjunct (1 woman). *Students:* 1 (woman) full-time, 10 part-time (4 women); includes 6 minority (4 Black or African American, non-Hispanic/Latino; 2 Hispanic/Latino). Average age 29. In 2018, 2 master's awarded. *Entrance requirements:* For master's, GMAT (unless applicant is a CPA or has passed a state bar exam); for CGS, GMAT, bachelor's degree from an accredited college or university, official transcripts of all undergraduate and graduate records. Additional exam requirements/recommendations for international students: Required—TOEFL (minimum score 550 paper-based; 80 iBT). *Application deadline:* For fall admission, 3/1 for domestic students. Applications are processed on a rolling basis. Application fee: $50. Electronic applications accepted. *Expenses: Tuition, area resident:* Part-time $407 per credit. Tuition, nonresident: part-time $792 per credit. *Required fees:* $29 per credit. $100 per semester. *Financial support:* Teaching assistantships with full tuition reimbursements, Federal Work-Study, scholarships/grants, and health care benefits available. Support available to part-time students. Financial award application deadline: 5/15; financial award applicants required to submit FAFSA. *Unit head:* Dr. Lisa Bain, Chair, 401-456-9829, E-mail: lbain@ric.edu. *Application contact:* Dr. Lisa Bain, Chair, 401-456-9829, E-mail: lbain@ric.edu.
Website: http://www.ric.edu/accountingcomputerinformationsystems/Pages/Accounting-Program.aspx

Rider University, College of Business Administration, Program in Corporate Finance, Lawrenceville, NJ 08648-3001. Offers MS. *Program availability:* Evening/weekend, online learning. *Students:* 2 full-time (0 women), 1 (woman) part-time; includes 1 minority (Hispanic/Latino). Average age 29. In 2018, 2 master's awarded. *Entrance requirements:* For master's, GMAT, application fee, statement of aims and objectives, official prior college transcripts, resume. Additional exam requirements/recommendations for international students: Required—TOEFL (minimum score 540 paper-based; 79 iBT). *Application deadline:* For fall admission, 8/1 for domestic students; for spring admission, 12/1 for domestic students; for summer admission, 5/1 for domestic students. Application fee: $50. Electronic applications accepted. *Expenses: Tuition:* Full-time $850; part-time $850 per credit hour. *Required fees:* $50; $50 per course. Tuition and fees vary according to program. *Financial support:* Applicants

required to submit FAFSA. *Unit head:* Jean Cherney, Academic Coordinator/Graduate Programs, 609-895-5557, E-mail: jcherney@rider.edu. *Application contact:* Jamie L. Mitchell, Director of Graduate Admissions, 609-896-5036, Fax: 609-895-5680, E-mail: jmitchell@rider.edu.
Website: https://www.rider.edu/academics/colleges-schools/college-business-administration/graduate-programs/ms-corporate-finance

Robert Morris University Illinois, Morris Graduate School of Management, Chicago, IL 60605. Offers accounting (MBA); accounting/finance (MBA); business analytics (MIS); health care administration (MM); higher education administration (MM); human performance (MS); human resource management (MBA); information security (MIS); information systems management (MIS); law enforcement administration (MM); management (MBA); management/finance (MBA); management/human resource management (MBA); sports administration (MM). *Program availability:* Part-time, evening/weekend. *Entrance requirements:* For master's, official transcripts and letters of recommendation (for some programs); written personal statement. Additional exam requirements/recommendations for international students: Required—TOEFL (minimum score 550 paper-based). Electronic applications accepted.

Rochester Institute of Technology, Graduate Enrollment Services, Saunders College of Business, Accounting and Finance Department, MS Program in Finance, Rochester, NY 14623-5603. Offers MS. *Program availability:* Part-time, evening/weekend. *Students:* 9 full-time (3 women), 7 part-time (2 women), 8 international. Average age 27. 71 applicants, 56% accepted, 7 enrolled. In 2018, 5 master's awarded. *Degree requirements:* For master's, comprehensive exam. *Entrance requirements:* For master's, GMAT or GRE, minimum GPA of 3.0 (recommended), personal statement, resume. Additional exam requirements/recommendations for international students: Required—TOEFL (minimum score 580 paper-based; 92 iBT), IELTS (minimum score 7), PTE (minimum score 63). *Application deadline:* Applications are processed on a rolling basis. Application fee: $65. Electronic applications accepted. *Financial support:* In 2018–19, 14 students received support. Research assistantships with partial tuition reimbursements available, teaching assistantships with partial tuition reimbursements available, career-related internships or fieldwork, scholarships/grants, and unspecified assistantships available. Support available to part-time students. Financial award applicants required to submit FAFSA. *Faculty research:* Trading algorithms, short selling effects, corporate governance effects, optimal incentive compensation contracts, debt contract parameters, tax policy. *Unit head:* Matt Cornwell, Assistant Director of Student Services and Outreach, 585-475-6916, E-mail: mcornwell@saunders.rit.edu. *Application contact:* Diane Ellison, Senior Associate Vice President, Graduate Enrollment Services, 585-475-2229, Fax: 585-475-7164, E-mail: gradinfo@rit.edu.
Website: https://www.rit.edu/study/finance-ms

Rockhurst University, Helzberg School of Management, Kansas City, MO 64110-2561. Offers accounting (MBA); business intelligence (MBA, Certificate); business intelligence and analytics (MS); data science (MBA, Certificate); entrepreneurship (MBA); finance (MBA); fundraising leadership (MBA, Certificate); healthcare management (MBA, Certificate); human capital (Certificate); international business (Certificate); management (MA, MBA, Certificate); nonprofit administration (Certificate); organizational development (Certificate); science leadership (Certificate). *Accreditation:* AACSB. *Program availability:* Part-time, evening/weekend. *Entrance requirements:* For master's, GMAT or GRE. Additional exam requirements/recommendations for international students: Required—TOEFL (minimum score 550 paper-based; 79 iBT). Electronic applications accepted. *Faculty research:* Offshoring/outsourcing, systems analysis/synthesis, work teams, multilateral trade, path dependencies/creation.

Rollins College, Crummer Graduate School of Business, Winter Park, FL 32789-4499. Offers entrepreneurship (MBA); finance (MBA); international business (MBA); management (MBA). *Accreditation:* AACSB. *Program availability:* Part-time, evening/weekend, online learning. *Degree requirements:* For master's, minimum GPA of 2.85. *Entrance requirements:* For master's, GMAT or GRE, official transcripts, two letters of recommendation, essay, current resume/curriculum vitae, interview. Additional exam requirements/recommendations for international students: Required—TOEFL (minimum score 100 iBT) or IELTS (minimum score 7). Electronic applications accepted. *Expenses:* Contact institution. *Faculty research:* Sustainability, world financial markets, international business, market research, strategic marketing.

Rutgers University–Newark, Graduate School, Program in Management, Newark, NJ 07102. Offers accounting (PhD); accounting information systems (PhD); computer information systems (PhD); finance (PhD); information technology (PhD); international business (PhD); management science (PhD); marketing (PhD); organization management (PhD). Program offered jointly with New Jersey Institute of Technology. *Accreditation:* AACSB. *Degree requirements:* For doctorate, thesis/dissertation, cumulative exams. *Entrance requirements:* For doctorate, GMAT or GRE General Test, minimum undergraduate B average. Additional exam requirements/recommendations for international students: Required—TOEFL. Electronic applications accepted. *Faculty research:* Technology management, leadership and teams, consumer behavior, financial and markets, logistics.

Rutgers University–Newark, Rutgers Business School–Newark and New Brunswick, Doctoral Programs in Management, Newark, NJ 07102. Offers accounting (PhD); accounting information systems (PhD); economics (PhD); finance (PhD); individualized study (PhD); information technology (PhD); international business (PhD); management science (PhD); marketing science (PhD); organizational management (PhD); science, technology and management (PhD); supply chain management (PhD). *Degree requirements:* For doctorate, comprehensive exam, thesis/dissertation. *Entrance requirements:* For doctorate, GRE or GMAT. Additional exam requirements/recommendations for international students: Required—TOEFL (minimum score 550 paper-based; 79 iBT). Electronic applications accepted.

Rutgers University–Newark, Rutgers Business School–Newark and New Brunswick, Program in Financial Analysis, Newark, NJ 07102. Offers MFA. *Entrance requirements:* For master's, GMAT. Additional exam requirements/recommendations for international students: Required—TOEFL.

Rutgers University–Newark, Rutgers Business School–Newark and New Brunswick, Program in Quantitative Finance, Newark, NJ 07102. Offers MQF. *Entrance requirements:* For master's, GMAT (MBA), GRE General Test (MQF). Additional exam requirements/recommendations for international students: Required—TOEFL.

Sacred Heart University, Graduate Programs, Jack Welch College of Business, Department of Finance, Fairfield, CT 06825. Offers administration (DBA); finance (MBA, Graduate Certificate); finance and investment management (MS). *Program availability:* Part-time, evening/weekend. *Degree requirements:* For doctorate, comprehensive exam. *Entrance requirements:* For master's, GMAT or GRE, official transcripts from all institutions attended; for doctorate, GMAT or GRE with master's degree and 5 years' experience. Additional exam requirements/recommendations for international students: Required—TOEFL (minimum score 570 paper-based, 80 iBT), TWE, or IELTS (6.5). Electronic applications accepted. *Expenses:* Contact institution.

St. John's University, The Peter J. Tobin College of Business, Department of Economics and Finance, Queens, NY 11439. Offers finance (MBA, MS). *Program availability:* Part-time, evening/weekend, 100% online, blended/hybrid learning. *Degree requirements:* For master's, 36 credit hours. *Entrance requirements:* For master's, GMAT or GRE, 2 letters of recommendation, essay, resume, unofficial transcripts. Additional exam requirements/recommendations for international students: Required—TOEFL (minimum score 80 iBT), IELTS (minimum score 6.5). Electronic applications accepted. *Expenses:* Contact institution. *Faculty research:* Exchange rate exposure, corporate default likelihood, credit derivatives, emerging markets, stock returns predictability.

Saint Joseph's University, Erivan K. Haub School of Business, MBA Program, Philadelphia, PA 19131-1395. Offers accounting (MBA); business intelligence analytics (MBA); finance (MBA); financial analysis reporting (Postbaccalaureate Certificate); general business (MBA); health and medical services administration (MBA); international business (MBA); international marketing (MBA); leading (MBA); marketing (MBA); DO/MBA. DO/MBA offered jointly with Philadelphia College of Osteopathic Medicine. *Program availability:* Part-time-only, evening/weekend, 100% online. *Degree requirements:* For master's, minimum GPA of 3.0. *Entrance requirements:* For master's, GMAT or GRE, 2 letters of recommendation, resume, personal statement, official undergraduate and graduate transcripts. Additional exam requirements/recommendations for international students: Required—PTE, TOEFL, IELTS, or PTE. Electronic applications accepted. *Expenses:* Contact institution.

Saint Joseph's University, Erivan K. Haub School of Business, MS in Financial Services Program, Philadelphia, PA 19131-1395. Offers MS. *Program availability:* Part-time, evening/weekend, online learning. *Degree requirements:* For master's, minimum GPA of 3.0. *Entrance requirements:* For master's, GMAT or GRE, 2 letters of recommendation, resume, personal statement, official undergraduate and graduate transcripts. Additional exam requirements/recommendations for international students: Required—PTE, TOEFL, IELTS, or PTE. Electronic applications accepted. *Expenses:* Contact institution.

Saint Louis University, Graduate Programs, John Cook School of Business, Department of Finance, St. Louis, MO 63103. Offers MBA, MSF. *Program availability:* Part-time, evening/weekend. *Degree requirements:* For master's, thesis. *Entrance requirements:* For master's, GMAT or GRE General Test, letters of recommendation, resume. Additional exam requirements/recommendations for international students: Required—TOEFL (minimum score 570 paper-based; 88 iBT). Electronic applications accepted. *Expenses:* Contact institution. *Faculty research:* Market microstructure, corporate governance, banking, portfolio performance and asset allocation.

Saint Mary's College of California, School of Economics and Business Administration, MS in Financial Analysis and Investment Management Program, Moraga, CA 94556. Offers MS. *Expenses:* Contact institution.

Saint Peter's University, Graduate Business Programs, MBA Program, Jersey City, NJ 07306-5997. Offers finance (MBA); health care administration (MBA); human resource management (MBA); international business (MBA); management (MBA); management information systems (MBA); marketing (MBA); risk management (MBA); MBA/MS. *Program availability:* Part-time, evening/weekend. *Entrance requirements:* Additional exam requirements/recommendations for international students: Required—TOEFL. Electronic applications accepted. *Faculty research:* Finance, health care management, human resource management, international business, management, management information systems, marketing, risk management.

St. Thomas Aquinas College, Division of Business Administration, Sparkill, NY 10976. Offers business administration (MBA); finance (MBA); management (MBA); marketing (MBA). *Program availability:* Part-time, evening/weekend. *Entrance requirements:* For master's, GMAT. Additional exam requirements/recommendations for international students: Required—TOEFL. Electronic applications accepted.

Saint Xavier University, Graduate Studies, Graham School of Management, Chicago, IL 60655-3105. Offers employee health benefits (Certificate); finance (MBA); financial fraud examination and management (MBA, Certificate); financial planning (MBA, Certificate); generalist/individualized (MBA); health administration (MBA); managed care (Certificate); management (MBA); marketing (MBA); project management (MBA, Certificate); MBA/MS. *Accreditation:* AACSB. *Program availability:* Part-time, evening/weekend. *Entrance requirements:* For master's, GMAT, minimum GPA of 3.0, 2 years of work experience. Electronic applications accepted. *Expenses:* Contact institution.

Samford University, Brock School of Business, Birmingham, AL 35229. Offers accountancy (M Acc); entrepreneurship (MBA); finance (MBA); marketing (MBA); JD/M Acc; JD/MBA; MBA/M Acc; MBA/M Div; MBA/MSEM; MBA/Pharm D. Programs offered jointly with Cumberland School of Law, Beeson School of Divinity, Howard College of Arts and Sciences, and McWhorter School of Pharmacy. *Accreditation:* AACSB. *Program availability:* Part-time, 100% online, blended/hybrid learning. *Faculty:* 7 full-time (1 woman), 4 part-time/adjunct (0 women). *Students:* 76 full-time (30 women), 20 part-time (11 women); includes 8 minority (4 Black or African American, non-Hispanic/Latino; 1 Asian, non-Hispanic/Latino; 1 Hispanic/Latino; 2 Two or more races, non-Hispanic/Latino), 7 international. Average age 28. 41 applicants, 88% accepted, 26 enrolled. In 2018, 74 master's awarded. *Degree requirements:* For master's, capstone course. *Entrance requirements:* For master's, GMAT or GRE, resume, transcripts, WES or ECE Evaluation (international applicants only), essay (international applicants only). Additional exam requirements/recommendations for international students: Required—TOEFL (minimum score 90 iBT), IELTS (minimum score 6.5). *Application deadline:* For fall admission, 8/1 for domestic and international students; for spring admission, 1/1 for domestic and international students. Applications are processed on a rolling basis. Application fee: $35. Electronic applications accepted. Application fee is waived when completed online. *Expenses: Tuition:* Full-time $17,255; part-time $837 per credit. *Required fees:* $610; $305 per term. Tuition and fees vary according to course load, degree level, program and student level. *Financial support:* In 2018–19, 46 students received support. Scholarships/grants available. Financial award application deadline: 2/15; financial award applicants required to submit FAFSA. *Unit head:* Dr. Barbara Cartledge, Assistant Dean, 205-726-2935, Fax: 205-726-2540, E-mail: bhcartle@samford.edu. *Application contact:* Elizabeth Gambrell, Associate Director, 205-726-2040, Fax: 205-726-2540, E-mail: eagambre@samford.edu.
Website: http://www.samford.edu/business

Sam Houston State University, College of Business Administration, Department of General Business and Finance, Huntsville, TX 77341. Offers banking and financial institutions (EMBA); business administration (MBA). *Accreditation:* AACSB. *Program availability:* Part-time, evening/weekend, online learning. *Degree requirements:* For master's, comprehensive exam (for some programs). *Entrance requirements:* For master's, GMAT, interview (for EMBA); resume, transcript(s). Additional exam requirements/recommendations for international students: Required—TOEFL (minimum score 550 paper-based; 79 iBT), IELTS (minimum score 6.5). Electronic applications accepted.

San Diego State University, Graduate and Research Affairs, Fowler College of Business, Department of Finance, San Diego, CA 92182. Offers MS. *Program availability:* Part-time, evening/weekend. *Degree requirements:* For master's, thesis or alternative. *Entrance requirements:* For master's, GMAT, resume, letters of reference. Additional exam requirements/recommendations for international students: Required—TOEFL. Electronic applications accepted.

San Francisco State University, Division of Graduate Studies, College of Business, Program in Business Administration, San Francisco, CA 94132-1722. Offers decision sciences/operations research (MBA); ethics and compliance (MBA); finance (MBA); global business and innovation (MBA); healthcare administration (MBA); hospitality and tourism management (MBA); information systems (MBA); leadership (MBA); marketing (MBA); nonprofit and social enterprise leadership (MBA); sustainable business (MBA). *Accreditation:* AACSB. *Program availability:* Part-time, evening/weekend. *Degree requirements:* For master's, thesis, essay test. *Entrance requirements:* For master's, GMAT, minimum GPA of 2.7 in last 60 units. Additional exam requirements/recommendations for international students: Required—TOEFL (minimum score 550 paper-based).

Santa Clara University, Leavey School of Business, Santa Clara, CA 95053. Offers business administration (MBA); business analytics (MS); finance (MS); information systems (MS); supply chain management and analytics (MS); JD/MBA. *Accreditation:* AACSB. *Program availability:* Part-time, online learning. *Faculty:* 101 full-time (32 women), 47 part-time/adjunct (15 women). *Students:* 487 full-time (278 women), 326 part-time (139 women); includes 295 minority (14 Black or African American, non-Hispanic/Latino; 207 Asian, non-Hispanic/Latino; 39 Hispanic/Latino; 35 Two or more races, non-Hispanic/Latino), 294 international. Average age 31. 694 applicants, 65% accepted, 281 enrolled. In 2018, 195 master's awarded. *Entrance requirements:* For master's, Varies based on program. Additional exam requirements/recommendations for international students: Required—TOEFL (minimum score 90 iBT). Application fee: $100 ($150 for international students). Electronic applications accepted. *Financial support:* In 2018–19, 192 students received support. Fellowships, Federal Work-Study, and scholarships/grants available. Support available to part-time students. Financial award applicants required to submit FAFSA. *Unit head:* Caryn Beck-Dudley, Dean, 408-554-4523, E-mail: cbeckdudley@scu.edu. *Application contact:* Caryn Beck-Dudley, Dean, 408-554-4523, E-mail: cbeckdudley@scu.edu.
Website: http://www.scu.edu/business/

Schiller International University, MBA Programs, Florida, Largo, FL 33771. Offers financial planning (MBA); information technology (MBA); international business (MBA); international hotel and tourism management (MBA). *Program availability:* Part-time, evening/weekend, online learning. *Degree requirements:* For master's, thesis optional. *Entrance requirements:* Additional exam requirements/recommendations for international students: Required—TOEFL (minimum score 550 paper-based).

Seattle University, Albers School of Business and Economics, Master of Science in Finance Program, Seattle, WA 98122-1090. Offers MSF, Certificate, JD/MSF, MPAC/MSF, MSF/MSBA. *Program availability:* Part-time, evening/weekend. *Faculty:* 9 full-time (3 women), 1 (woman) part-time/adjunct. *Students:* 50 full-time (26 women), 38 part-time (8 women); includes 17 minority (2 Black or African American, non-Hispanic/Latino; 1 American Indian or Alaska Native, non-Hispanic/Latino; 10 Asian, non-Hispanic/Latino; 2 Hispanic/Latino; 2 Two or more races, non-Hispanic/Latino), 40 international. Average age 27. 64 applicants, 63% accepted, 23 enrolled. In 2018, 29 master's, 9 Certificates awarded. *Entrance requirements:* For master's, GMAT, minimum GPA of 3.0, 2 years of related work experience. Additional exam requirements/recommendations for international students: Required—TOEFL (minimum score 580 paper-based; 92 iBT). *Application deadline:* For fall admission, 8/20 priority date for domestic students, 4/1 priority date for international students; for winter admission, 11/20 priority date for domestic students, 9/1 priority date for international students; for spring admission, 2/20 priority date for domestic students, 12/1 priority date for international students. Applications are processed on a rolling basis. Application fee: $55. Electronic applications accepted. *Expenses:* Contact institution. *Financial support:* In 2018–19, 16 students received support. Career-related internships or fieldwork and Federal Work-Study available. Support available to part-time students. Financial award applicants required to submit FAFSA. *Unit head:* Dr. Fiona Robertson, Chair, 206-296-5791, Fax: 206-296-5795, E-mail: robertsf@seattleu.edu. *Application contact:* Janet Shandley, Director of Graduate Admissions, 206-296-5900, Fax: 206-298-5656, E-mail: grad_admissions@seattleu.edu.
Website: http://www.seattleu.edu/albers/msf/

Seton Hall University, Stillman School of Business, Programs in Business Administration, South Orange, NJ 07079-2697. Offers accounting (MBA); entrepreneurial studies (Certificate); finance (MBA); financial decision making (Certificate); information technology management (MBA); international business (MBA); management (MBA); marketing (MBA); sport management (MBA); supply chain management (MBA, Certificate). *Program availability:* Part-time, evening/weekend. *Faculty:* 27 full-time (5 women), 18 part-time/adjunct (2 women). *Students:* 85 full-time (40 women), 363 part-time (147 women); includes 78 minority (22 Black or African American, non-Hispanic/Latino; 4 Asian, non-Hispanic/Latino; 18 Hispanic/Latino; 29 Native Hawaiian or other Pacific Islander, non-Hispanic/Latino; 5 Two or more races, non-Hispanic/Latino), 282 international. Average age 34. 483 applicants, 85% accepted, 302 enrolled. In 2018, 96 master's awarded. *Degree requirements:* For master's, 20 hours of community service (Social Responsibility Project). *Entrance requirements:* For master's, GMAT or CPA, GRE (waived based on work experience or advanced degree from AACSB institution), MS in business discipline, professional degree or designation (MD, JD, PhD, DVM, DDS, CPA, etc.), minimum undergraduate GPA of 3.0. Additional exam requirements/recommendations for international students: Required—TOEFL (minimum score 607 paper-based; 80 iBT), IELTS (minimum score 6), PTE. *Application deadline:* For fall admission, 5/31 priority date for domestic students, 4/30 priority date for international students; for spring admission, 10/31 priority date for domestic students, 9/30 priority date for international students; for summer admission, 3/31 priority date for domestic students. Applications are processed on a rolling basis. Application fee: $75. Electronic applications accepted. Application fee is waived when completed online. *Expenses:* Tuition is $1,305 per credit hour and the overall MBA is a 40 credit hour program. University fees are $115 per semester. The university also has a technology that is $125 per semester. *Financial support:* In 2018–19, 44 students received support, including 25 research assistantships with partial tuition reimbursements available (averaging $3,644 per year); career-related internships or fieldwork, scholarships/grants, and unspecified assistantships also available. Financial award application deadline: 6/30; financial award applicants required to submit FAFSA. *Faculty research:* Sport, hedge funds, executive compensation, social media, legal studies. *Unit head:* Dr. Joyce Strawser, Dean, 973-761-9013, Fax: 973-761-9217, E-mail: joyce.strawser@shu.edu. *Application contact:* Alfred Ayoub, Director of Graduate Admissions, 973-761-9262, Fax: 973-761-9208, E-mail: alfred.ayoub@shu.edu.
Website: http://www.shu.edu/business/mba-programs.cfm

Shippensburg University of Pennsylvania, School of Graduate Studies, John L. Grove College of Business, Shippensburg, PA 17257-2299. Offers advanced studies in business (Certificate); advanced supply chain and logistics management (Certificate); business administration (MBA, DBA), including business administration (MBA), business analytics (MBA), finance (MBA), healthcare management (MBA), management information systems (MBA), supply chain management (MBA); finance (Certificate); health care management (Certificate); management information systems (Certificate). *Accreditation:* AACSB. *Program availability:* Part-time, evening/weekend, 100% online, blended/hybrid learning. *Faculty:* 20 full-time (4 women), 2 part-time/adjunct (0 women).

Students: 31 full-time (14 women), 174 part-time (67 women); includes 33 minority (17 Black or African American, non-Hispanic/Latino; 6 Asian, non-Hispanic/Latino; 7 Hispanic/Latino; 3 Two or more races, non-Hispanic/Latino), 13 international. Average age 33. 149 applicants, 61% accepted, 60 enrolled. In 2018, 104 master's, 1 other advanced degree awarded. *Degree requirements:* For master's, comprehensive exam (for some programs), thesis optional, practicum capstone course; for doctorate, comprehensive exam, thesis/dissertation, comprehensive exam dissertation. *Entrance requirements:* For master's, GMAT (minimum score 450 if less than 5 years of mid-level experience, including management experience), current resume; relevant work/classroom experience; 500-word statement of purpose; prerequisites of quantitative analysis, computer usage, and oral and written communications; laptop computer; for doctorate, GMAT (minimum score of 600 if less than 5 years of substantive professional or teaching experience), 2 letters of recommendation from professionals in academia or industry; 2-3 page personal and professional statement; interview; resume. Additional exam requirements/recommendations for international students: Required—TOEFL (minimum score 550 paper-based; 68 iBT), IELTS (minimum score 6), TOEFL (minimum score 550 paper-based, 68 iBT) or IELTS (minimum score 6). *Application deadline:* For fall admission, 4/30 for international students; for spring admission, 9/30 for international students. Applications are processed on a rolling basis. Application fee: $45. Electronic applications accepted. *Expenses:* Tuition, state resident: part-time $516 per credit. Tuition, nonresident: part-time $750 per credit. *Required fees:* $149 per credit. *Financial support:* In 2018–19, 15 students received support. Career-related internships or fieldwork, scholarships/grants, unspecified assistantships, and resident hall director and student payroll positions available. Support available to part-time students. Financial award application deadline: 3/1; financial award applicants required to submit FAFSA. *Unit head:* Dr. John G. Kooti, Dean of the College of Business, 717-477-1435, Fax: 717-477-4003, E-mail: jgkooti@ship.edu. *Application contact:* Maya T. Mapp, Director of Admissions, 717-477-1231, Fax: 717-477-4016, E-mail: mtmapp@ship.edu.
Website: http://www.ship.edu/business

Simon Fraser University, Office of Graduate Studies and Postdoctoral Fellows, Faculty of Business Administration, Vancouver, BC V6B 5K3, Canada. Offers business administration (EMBA, PhD, Graduate Diploma); finance (M Sc); management of technology (MBA); management of technology/biotechnology (MBA). *Program availability:* Online learning. *Degree requirements:* For master's, thesis (for some programs); for doctorate, comprehensive exam, thesis/dissertation. *Entrance requirements:* For master's, GMAT, minimum GPA of 3.0 (on scale of 4.33) or 3.33 based on last 60 credits of undergraduate courses; for doctorate, minimum GPA of 3.5 (on scale of 4.33); for Graduate Diploma, minimum GPA of 2.5 (on scale of 4.33) or 2.67 based on last 60 credits of undergraduate courses. Additional exam requirements/recommendations for international students: Recommended—TOEFL (minimum score 580 paper-based; 93 iBT), IELTS (minimum score 7), TWE (minimum score 5). *Expenses:* Contact institution. *Faculty research:* Accounting, management and organizational studies, technology and operations management, finance, international business.

Slippery Rock University of Pennsylvania, Graduate Studies (Recruitment), College of Business, School of Business, Slippery Rock, PA 16057-1383. Offers accounting/finance (MBA); general (MBA); marketing/management (MBA). *Program availability:* Part-time, evening/weekend. *Faculty:* 12 full-time (7 women), 1 part-time/adjunct (0 women). *Students:* 21 full-time (8 women), 22 part-time (15 women); includes 3 minority (1 Black or African American, non-Hispanic/Latino; 1 Asian, non-Hispanic/Latino; 1 Hispanic/Latino). Average age 29. 53 applicants, 62% accepted, 23 enrolled. In 2018, 23 master's awarded. *Degree requirements:* For master's, comprehensive exam (for some programs), thesis (for some programs). *Entrance requirements:* For master's, minimum cumulative GPA of 3.0, official transcripts, three references. Additional exam requirements/recommendations for international students: Required—TOEFL (minimum score 550 paper-based; 80 iBT). *Application deadline:* For fall admission, 3/1 priority date for domestic students, 5/1 priority date for international students; for spring admission, 10/1 priority date for domestic students, 9/1 priority date for international students. Applications are processed on a rolling basis. Application fee: $25 ($30 for international students). Electronic applications accepted. *Expenses:* Contact institution. *Financial support:* In 2018–19, 9 students received support. Career-related internships or fieldwork, Federal Work-Study, institutionally sponsored loans, scholarships/grants, tuition waivers (partial), and unspecified assistantships available. Support available to part-time students. Financial award application deadline: 5/1; financial award applicants required to submit FAFSA. *Unit head:* Dr. Larry McCarthy, Graduate Coordinator, 724-738-2552, Fax: 724-738-2959, E-mail: larry.mccarthy@sru.edu. *Application contact:* Brandi Weber-Mortimer, Director of Graduate Admissions, 724-738-2051, Fax: 724-738-2146, E-mail: graduate.admissions@sru.edu.
Website: http://www.sru.edu/academics/graduate-programs/mba-master-of-business-administration

Southeast Missouri State University, School of Graduate Studies, Harrison College of Business and Computing, Cape Girardeau, MO 63701-4799. Offers accounting (MBA); entrepreneurship (MBA); financial management (MBA); sport management (MBA). *Accreditation:* AACSB. *Program availability:* Part-time, evening/weekend, 100% online. *Faculty:* 27 full-time (7 women), 1 (woman) part-time/adjunct. *Students:* 94 full-time (50 women), 88 part-time (39 women); includes 18 minority (9 Black or African American, non-Hispanic/Latino; 4 Asian, non-Hispanic/Latino; 5 Hispanic/Latino), 79 international. Average age 29. 80 applicants, 100% accepted, 80 enrolled. In 2018, 62 master's awarded. *Degree requirements:* For master's, variable foreign language requirement, comprehensive exam (for some programs), thesis or alternative. *Entrance requirements:* For master's, GMAT or GRE, minimum undergraduate GPA of 2.5, minimum grade of C in prerequisite courses. Additional exam requirements/recommendations for international students: Required—TOEFL (minimum score 550 paper-based; 79 iBT), IELTS (minimum score 6), PTE (minimum score 53). *Application deadline:* For fall admission, 8/1 for domestic students, 6/1 for international students; for spring admission, 11/21 for domestic students, 10/1 for international students; for summer admission, 5/15 for domestic students. Applications are processed on a rolling basis. Application fee: $30 ($40 for international students). Electronic applications accepted. *Expenses:* Contact institution. *Financial support:* In 2018–19, 16 students received support. Career-related internships or fieldwork, Federal Work-Study, scholarships/grants, traineeships, tuition waivers (full), and unspecified assistantships available. Financial award application deadline: 6/30; financial award applicants required to submit FAFSA. *Faculty research:* Organizational justice, ethics, leadership, corporate finance, generational differences. *Unit head:* Dr. Alberto Davila, Dean, 573-651-2112, E-mail: adavila@semo.edu. *Application contact:* Dr. Alberto Davila, Dean, 573-651-2112, E-mail: adavila@semo.edu.
Website: http://www.semo.edu/mba

Southern Adventist University, School of Business, Collegedale, TN 37315-0370. Offers accounting (MBA); computer information systems (MBA); finance (MBA); healthcare administration (MBA); management (MBA). *Program availability:* Part-time, evening/weekend, 100% online. *Faculty:* 7 full-time (2 women). *Students:* 23 applicants, 48% accepted, 8 enrolled. In 2018, 8 master's awarded. *Entrance requirements:* For master's, GMAT, minimum cumulative undergraduate GPA of 3.0. Additional exam requirements/recommendations for international students: Required—TOEFL (minimum

score 100 iBT). *Application deadline:* For fall admission, 7/1 for domestic students, 5/1 for international students; for winter admission, 11/1 for domestic students, 9/1 for international students; for summer admission, 4/1 for domestic students, 2/1 for international students. Applications are processed on a rolling basis. Application fee: $40. Electronic applications accepted. *Financial support:* Scholarships/grants and unspecified assistantships available. Financial award application deadline: 9/1; financial award applicants required to submit FAFSA. *Unit head:* Dr. Stephanie Sheehan, Dean, 423-236-2659, Fax: 423-236-1527, E-mail: ssheehan@southern.edu. *Application contact:* Teshia Price, Graduate Studies Coordinator, 423-236-2751, Fax: 423-236-1527, E-mail: tprice@southern.edu.
Website: https://www.southern.edu/academics/business.html

Southern Illinois University Edwardsville, Graduate School, School of Business, Department of Economics and Finance, Edwardsville, IL 62026. Offers MA, MS. *Program availability:* Part-time, evening/weekend. *Degree requirements:* For master's, thesis or alternative, final exam, portfolio. *Entrance requirements:* For master's, GMAT or GRE. Additional exam requirements/recommendations for international students: Required—TOEFL (minimum score 550 paper-based; 79 iBT), IELTS (minimum score 6.5). Electronic applications accepted.

Southern Methodist University, Cox School of Business, MBA Program, Dallas, TX 75275. Offers accounting (MBA, PMBA); business (EMBA); business analytics (PMBA); finance (MBA, PMBA); information technology and operations management (MBA, PMBA), including business analytics (MBA), information and operations (MBA); management (MBA, PMBA); marketing (MBA, PMBA); real estate (MBA, PMBA); strategy and entrepreneurship (MBA, PMBA); JD/MBA; MA/MBA. *Program availability:* Part-time, evening/weekend. *Entrance requirements:* For master's, GMAT. Additional exam requirements/recommendations for international students: Required—TOEFL. Electronic applications accepted. *Expenses:* Contact institution. *Faculty research:* Corporate finance, financial reporting, modeling consumer decision-making, competition between national brands and store brands, institutional determinants of firms' strategy.

Southern Methodist University, Cox School of Business, Program in Finance, Dallas, TX 75275. Offers MS.

Southern New Hampshire University, School of Business, Manchester, NH 03106-1045. Offers accounting (MBA, Graduate Certificate); accounting finance (MS); accounting/auditing (MS); accounting/forensic accounting (MS); accounting/management accounting (MS); accounting/taxation (MS); applied economics (MS); athletic administration (MBA, Graduate Certificate); business administration (IMBA, Certificate), including business information systems (Certificate), human resource management (Certificate); business analytics (MBA); business intelligence (MBA); communication (MA), including new media and marketing, public relations; community economic development (MBA); criminal justice (MBA); data analytics (MS); economics (MBA); engineering management (MBA); entrepreneurship (MBA); finance (MBA, MS, Graduate Certificate); finance/corporate finance (MS); finance/investments (MS); forensic accounting (MBA); forensic accounting and fraud examination (Graduate Certificate); healthcare informatics (MBA); healthcare management (MBA); human resource management (MS); human resources (MBA); information technology (MS); information technology management (MBA); international business (PhD); Internet marketing (MBA); leadership (MBA); leadership of nonprofit organizations (Graduate Certificate); management (MS); marketing (MBA, MS, Graduate Certificate); music business (MBA); operations and project management (MS); operations and supply chain management (MBA, Graduate Certificate); organizational leadership (MS); project management (MBA, Graduate Certificate); public administration (MBA, Graduate Certificate); quantitative analysis (MBA); Six Sigma (Graduate Certificate); Six Sigma quality (MBA); social media marketing (MBA, Graduate Certificate); sport management (MBA, MS, Graduate Certificate); sustainability and environmental compliance (MBA); MBA/Certificate. *Accreditation:* ACBSP. *Program availability:* Part-time, evening/weekend, online learning. Terminal master's awarded for partial completion of doctoral program. *Degree requirements:* For master's, one foreign language, comprehensive exam (for some programs), thesis or alternative; for doctorate, one foreign language, comprehensive exam, thesis/dissertation. *Entrance requirements:* For master's, minimum GPA of 2.5; for doctorate, GMAT. Additional exam requirements/recommendations for international students: Required—TOEFL (minimum score 500 paper-based). Electronic applications accepted.

Southwestern Adventist University, Business Administration Department, Keene, TX 76059. Offers accounting (MBA); finance (MBA); management/leadership (MBA). *Program availability:* Part-time, evening/weekend. *Degree requirements:* For master's, capstone course. *Entrance requirements:* For master's, GMAT, GRE General Test.

State University of New York Polytechnic Institute, MBA Program in Technology Management, Utica, NY 13502. Offers accounting and finance (MBA); business management (MBA); health informatics (MBA); human resource management (MBA); marketing management (MBA). *Program availability:* Part-time, 100% online. *Students:* 29 full-time (13 women), 85 part-time (41 women); includes 18 minority (4 Black or African American, non-Hispanic/Latino; 8 Asian, non-Hispanic/Latino; 6 Hispanic/Latino). Average age 32. 54 applicants, 54% accepted, 26 enrolled. In 2018, 29 master's awarded. *Degree requirements:* For master's, comprehensive exam, capstone project. *Entrance requirements:* For master's, GMAT or approved GMAT waiver, resume, letter of reference. Additional exam requirements/recommendations for international students: Required—TOEFL (minimum score 79 iBT), IELTS (minimum score 6.5), PTE (minimum score 53), TOEFL, IELTS, or PTE; GMAT or approved GMAT waiver. *Application deadline:* For fall admission, 7/1 priority date for domestic students, 7/1 for international students; for spring admission, 12/1 for domestic students, 11/1 for international students. Applications are processed on a rolling basis. Application fee: $60. Electronic applications accepted. *Expenses:* Contact institution. *Financial support:* Fellowships, research assistantships, and unspecified assistantships available. Financial award application deadline: 6/1; financial award applicants required to submit FAFSA. *Faculty research:* Entrepreneurial capacity development. *Unit head:* Dr. Rafael Romero, Coordinator, 315-792-7207, E-mail: rafael.romero@sunypoly.edu. *Application contact:* Alicia Foster, Director of Graduate Admissions, 315-792-7347, E-mail: fostera3@sunypoly.edu.
Website: https://sunypoly.edu/academics/majors-and-programs/technology-management.html

Stevens Institute of Technology, Graduate School, School of Business, Program in Business Administration, Hoboken, NJ 07030. Offers business intelligence and analytics (MBA); engineering management (MBA); finance (MBA); information systems (MBA); innovation and entrepreneurship (MBA); marketing (MBA); pharmaceutical management (MBA); project management (MBA, Certificate); technology management (MBA); telecommunications management (MBA). *Accreditation:* AACSB. *Program availability:* Part-time, evening/weekend. *Faculty:* 58 full-time (8 women), 18 part-time/adjunct (3 women). *Students:* 44 full-time (23 women), 202 part-time (90 women); includes 56 minority (12 Black or African American, non-Hispanic/Latino; 2 American Indian or Alaska Native, non-Hispanic/Latino; 40 Asian, non-Hispanic/Latino; 2 Hispanic/Latino), 28 international. Average age 37. In 2018, 45 master's awarded. Terminal master's awarded for partial completion of doctoral program. *Degree requirements:* For master's, thesis optional, minimum B average in major field and overall; for Certificate, minimum B average. *Entrance requirements:* For master's, GRE/GMAT scores: GRE scores are required for all applicants applying to a full-time graduate program in the Schaefer School of Engineering and Science (SES). International applicants must submit TOEFL/IELTS scores and fulfill the English Language Proficiency Requirements in order to be considered. Additional exam requirements/recommendations for international students: Required—TOEFL (minimum score 74 iBT), IELTS (minimum score 6). *Application deadline:* For fall admission, 4/1 for domestic and international students; for spring admission, 11/1 for domestic and international students; for summer admission, 5/1 for domestic students. Applications are processed on a rolling basis. Application fee: $60. Electronic applications accepted. *Expenses: Tuition:* Full-time $35,960; part-time $1620 per credit. *Required fees:* $1290; $600 per semester. Tuition and fees vary according to course load. *Financial support:* Fellowships, research assistantships, teaching assistantships, career-related internships or fieldwork, Federal Work-Study, scholarships/grants, and unspecified assistantships available. Financial award application deadline: 2/15; financial award applicants required to submit FAFSA. *Unit head:* Dr. Gregory Prastacos, Dean, 201-216-8366, E-mail: gprastac@stevens.edu. *Application contact:* Graduate Admissions, 888-783-8367, Fax: 888-511-1306, E-mail: graduate@stevens.edu.
Website: https://www.stevens.edu/school-business/masters-programs/mbaemba

Stevens Institute of Technology, Graduate School, School of Business, Program in Finance, Hoboken, NJ 07030. Offers MS. *Program availability:* Part-time, evening/weekend. *Faculty:* 58 full-time (8 women), 18 part-time/adjunct (3 women). *Students:* 57 full-time (21 women), 6 part-time (3 women); includes 3 minority (all Asian, non-Hispanic/Latino), 50 international. Average age 24. In 2018, 21 master's awarded. *Degree requirements:* For master's, thesis optional, minimum B average in major field and overall. *Entrance requirements:* For master's, GRE/GMAT scores: GRE scores are required for all applicants applying to a full-time graduate program in the Schaefer School of Engineering and Science (SES). International applicants must submit TOEFL/IELTS scores and fulfill the English Language Proficiency Requirements in order to be considered. Additional exam requirements/recommendations for international students: Required—TOEFL (minimum score 74 iBT), IELTS (minimum score 6). *Application deadline:* For fall admission, 4/1 for domestic and international students; for spring admission, 11/1 for domestic and international students; for summer admission, 5/1 for domestic students. Applications are processed on a rolling basis. Application fee: $60. Electronic applications accepted. *Expenses: Tuition:* Full-time $35,960; part-time $1620 per credit. *Required fees:* $1290; $600 per semester. Tuition and fees vary according to course load. *Financial support:* Fellowships, research assistantships, teaching assistantships, career-related internships or fieldwork, Federal Work-Study, scholarships/grants, and unspecified assistantships available. Financial award application deadline: 2/15; financial award applicants required to submit FAFSA. *Unit head:* Dr. Gregory Prascatos, Dean of SB, 201-216 8366, E-mail: gprastac@stevens.edu. *Application contact:* Graduate Admissions, 888-793-8367, Fax: 888-511-1306, E-mail: graduate@stevens.edu.
Website: http://www.stevens.edu/school-business/masters-programs/finance

Stony Brook University, State University of New York, Graduate School, College of Business, Program in Business Administration, Stony Brook, NY 11794. Offers accounting (MBA); business administration (MBA); finance (MBA, Certificate); health care management (MBA); human resources (MBA); innovation (MBA); management (MBA); marketing (MBA); operations management (MBA). *Faculty:* 38 full-time (13 women), 8 part-time/adjunct (3 women). *Students:* 153 full-time (74 women), 148 part-time (76 women); includes 76 minority (16 Black or African American, non-Hispanic/Latino; 29 Asian, non-Hispanic/Latino; 27 Hispanic/Latino; 4 Two or more races, non-Hispanic/Latino), 36 international. Average age 28. 128 applicants, 78% accepted, 75 enrolled. In 2018, 76 master's awarded. *Entrance requirements:* For master's, GMAT, 3 letters of recommendation from current or former employers or professors, transcripts, personal statement, resume. Additional exam requirements/recommendations for international students: Required—TOEFL (minimum score 550 paper-based; 80 iBT), IELTS (minimum score 6.5). *Application deadline:* For fall admission, 5/15 for domestic students, 3/15 for international students; for spring admission, 12/1 for domestic students, 10/15 for international students. Application fee: $100. *Expenses:* Contact institution. *Financial support:* Teaching assistantships available. *Total annual research expenditures:* $2,070. *Unit head:* Dr. Manuel London, Dean, 631-632-7159, E-mail: manuel.london@stonybrook.edu. *Application contact:* Dr. Dmytro Holod, Associate Dean for Academic Programs/Graduate Director, 631-632-7183, Fax: 631-632-8181, E-mail: dmytro.holod@stonybrook.edu.
Website: https://www.stonybrook.edu/commcms/business/

Stony Brook University, State University of New York, Graduate School, College of Business, Program in Finance, Stony Brook, NY 11794. Offers MS, AGC. *Program availability:* Part-time. *Students:* 8 full-time (2 women), 5 part-time (2 women), 7 international. 156 applicants, 63% accepted, 28 enrolled. In 2018, 53 master's, 2 other advanced degrees awarded. *Degree requirements:* For master's, capstone course. *Entrance requirements:* For master's, GMAT or GRE, letters of recommendation, minimum GPA of 3.0 in prior academic work. Additional exam requirements/recommendations for international students: Required—TOEFL (minimum score 80 iBT). *Application deadline:* For fall admission, 5/15 for domestic students, 3/15 for international students; for spring admission, 12/1 for domestic students, 10/15 for international students; for summer admission, 3/15 for domestic students. *Expenses:* Contact institution. *Unit head:* Dr. Manuel London, Dean, 631-632-7159, E-mail: manuel.london@stonybrook.edu. *Application contact:* Erica Robey, Graduate Coordinator, 631-632-7171, Fax: 631-632-8181, E-mail: oss@stonybrook.edu.
Website: https://www.stonybrook.edu/commcms/business/academics/graduate-programs.php

Strayer University, Graduate Studies, Washington, DC 20005-2603. Offers accounting (MS); acquisition (MBA); business administration (MBA); communications technology (MS); educational management (M Ed); finance (MBA); health services administration (MHSA); hospitality and tourism management (MBA); human resource management (MBA); information systems (MS), including computer security management, decision support system management, enterprise resource management, network management, software engineering management, systems development management; management (MBA); management information systems (MS); marketing (MBA); professional accounting (MS), including accounting information systems, controllership, taxation; public administration (MPA); supply chain management (MBA); technology in education (M Ed). Programs also offered at campus locations in Birmingham, AL; Chamblee, GA; Cobb County, GA; Morrow, GA; White Marsh, MD; Charleston, SC; Columbia, SC; Greensboro, NC; Greenville, SC; Lexington, KY; Louisville, KY; Nashville, TN; North Raleigh, NC; Washington, DC. *Accreditation:* ACBSP. *Program availability:* Part-time, evening/weekend, online learning. *Degree requirements:* For master's, thesis. *Entrance requirements:* For master's, GMAT, GRE General Test, bachelor's degree from an accredited college or university, minimum undergraduate GPA of 2.75. Electronic applications accepted.

Suffolk University, Sawyer Business School, Master of Business Administration Program, Boston, MA 02108-2770. Offers accounting (MBA); entrepreneurship (MBA); executive business administration (EMBA); finance (MBA); global business

administration (GMBA); health administration (MBA); international business (MBA); marketing (MBA); nonprofit management (MBA); organizational behavior (MBA); strategic management (MBA); supply chain management (MBA); taxation (MBA); JD/MBA; MBA/MHA; MBA/MSA; MBA/MSF; MBA/MST. *Accreditation:* AACSB. *Program availability:* Part-time, evening/weekend, 100% online. *Faculty:* 18 full-time (5 women), 5 part-time/adjunct (0 women). *Students:* 79 full-time (46 women), 193 part-time (107 women); includes 69 minority (17 Black or African American, non-Hispanic/Latino; 18 Asian, non-Hispanic/Latino; 28 Hispanic/Latino; 6 Two or more races, non-Hispanic/Latino), 40 international. Average age 30. 274 applicants, 67% accepted, 83 enrolled. In 2018, 125 master's awarded. *Entrance requirements:* For master's, GMAT, minimum undergraduate GPA of 2.75 (MBA), 5 years of managerial experience (EMBA). Additional exam requirements/recommendations for international students: Required—TOEFL (minimum score 550 paper-based; 80 iBT). *Application deadline:* For fall admission, 3/15 priority date for domestic students, 10/15 priority date for international students; for spring admission, 10/15 priority date for domestic and international students. Applications are processed on a rolling basis. Application fee: $50. Electronic applications accepted. *Expenses:* Contact institution. *Financial support:* In 2018–19, 170 students received support, including 4 fellowships (averaging $2,906 per year); career-related internships or fieldwork, Federal Work-Study, institutionally sponsored loans, and scholarships/grants also available. Support available to part-time students. Financial award application deadline: 4/1; financial award applicants required to submit FAFSA. *Faculty research:* Foreign investments; career strategies and boundaryless careers; corporate ethics codes; interest rates, inflation, and growth options; innovation and product development performance. *Unit head:* Jodi Detjen, Director of MBA Programs, 617-573-8306, E-mail: jdetjen@suffolk.edu. *Application contact:* Mara Marzocchi, Associate Director of Graduate Admissions, 617-573-8302, Fax: 617-305-1733, E-mail: grad.admission@suffolk.edu.
Website: http://www.suffolk.edu/mba

Suffolk University, Sawyer Business School, Programs in Finance, Boston, MA 02108-2770. Offers MSF, MSFSB, JD/MSF, MBA/MSF, MSF/MSA. *Accreditation:* AACSB. *Program availability:* Part-time, evening/weekend. *Faculty:* 6 full-time (4 women), 4 part-time/adjunct (0 women). *Students:* 34 full-time (18 women), 28 part-time (12 women); includes 13 minority (4 Black or African American, non-Hispanic/Latino; 7 Asian, non-Hispanic/Latino; 2 Hispanic/Latino), 37 international. Average age 27. 126 applicants, 58% accepted, 27 enrolled. In 2018, 38 master's awarded. *Entrance requirements:* For master's, GMAT, interview. Additional exam requirements/recommendations for international students: Required—TOEFL (minimum score 550 paper-based; 80 iBT). *Application deadline:* For fall admission, 3/15 priority date for domestic and international students; for spring admission, 10/15 priority date for domestic and international students. Applications are processed on a rolling basis. Application fee: $50. Electronic applications accepted. *Expenses:* Contact institution. *Financial support:* In 2018–19, 45 students received support, including 2 fellowships (averaging $3,100 per year); career-related internships or fieldwork, Federal Work-Study, institutionally sponsored loans, and scholarships/grants also available. Support available to part-time students. Financial award application deadline: 4/1; financial award applicants required to submit FAFSA. *Faculty research:* Financial institutions, corporate finance, ownership structure, dividend policy, corporate restructuring. *Unit head:* Dr. Shahriar Khaksari, Chairperson/Professor of Finance, 617-573-8366, E-mail: skhaksari@suffolk.edu. *Application contact:* Mara Marzocchi, Associate Director of Graduate Admissions, 617-573-8302, Fax: 617-305-1733, E-mail: grad.admission@suffolk.edu.
Website: http://www.suffolk.edu/msf

Syracuse University, Martin J. Whitman School of Management, MS in Finance Program, Syracuse, NY 13244. Offers MS. *Students:* Average age 23. 454 applicants, 42% accepted, 26 enrolled. In 2018, 43 master's awarded. *Entrance requirements:* For master's, GMAT or GRE, resume, essay, 5-minute video interview, two letters of recommendation, transcripts (unofficial). Additional exam requirements/recommendations for international students: Required—TOEFL (minimum score 100 iBT), IELTS (minimum score 7), PTE (minimum score 68). *Application deadline:* For fall admission, 11/30 for domestic students, 11/30 priority date for international students; for winter admission, 1/1 for domestic students, 1/1 priority date for international students; for spring admission, 2/15 for domestic and international students; for summer admission, 4/19 for domestic students. Application fee: $75. Electronic applications accepted. *Expenses:* Contact institution. *Financial support:* Merit scholarships available. Financial award application deadline: 2/15. *Faculty research:* Financial accounting, investment analysis, corporate financial policy and strategy, data analysis/business statistics, managerial finance. *Unit head:* Tom Barkley, Director, MS in Finance Program/Professor of Finance Practice, 315-443-8107, E-mail: tbarkley@syr.edu. *Application contact:* Shri Ramakrishnan, Assistant Director, Graduate Recruitment, 315-443-3497, Fax: 315-443-9517, E-mail: sramak01@syr.edu.
Website: http://whitman.syr.edu/msfin/

Syracuse University, Martin J. Whitman School of Management, PhD Programs, Syracuse, NY 13244. Offers finance (PhD); management information systems (PhD). In 2018, 2 doctorates awarded. *Degree requirements:* For doctorate, comprehensive exam, thesis/dissertation, summer research paper. *Entrance requirements:* For doctorate, GMAT (preferred) or GRE, master's degree (preferred), transcripts, three recommendation letters, personal statement. Additional exam requirements/recommendations for international students: Required—TOEFL (minimum score 600 paper-based; 100 iBT). *Application deadline:* For fall admission, 1/15 for domestic and international students. Application fee: $75. Electronic applications accepted. *Financial support:* Fellowships with full tuition reimbursements, research assistantships with full tuition reimbursements, teaching assistantships with full tuition reimbursements, and scholarships/grants available. *Faculty research:* Marketing models, market microstructure, supply chain, auditing, corporate governance. *Unit head:* Dr. Michel Benaroch, Associate Dean for Research and PhD Programs, 315-443-3492, E-mail: mbenaroc@syr.edu. *Application contact:* Lisa Svegl, Executive Assistant for Development and PhD Programs, 315-443-9141, E-mail: lmsvegl@syr.edu.

Télé-université, Graduate Programs, Québec, QC G1K 9H5, Canada. Offers computer science (PhD); corporate finance (MS); distance learning (MS). *Program availability:* Part-time.

Temple University, Fox School of Business, Doctoral Programs in Business, Philadelphia, PA 19122-6096. Offers accounting (PhD); entrepreneurship (PhD); finance (PhD); international business (PhD); management information systems (PhD); marketing (PhD); risk management and insurance (PhD); statistics (PhD); strategic management (PhD); tourism and sport (PhD). *Accreditation:* AACSB. *Degree requirements:* For doctorate, thesis/dissertation. *Entrance requirements:* For doctorate, GRE General Test, GMAT, minimum GPA of 3.0, master's degree. Additional exam requirements/recommendations for international students: Required—TOEFL (minimum score 600 paper-based; 100 iBT), IELTS (minimum score 7.5). Electronic applications accepted.

Temple University, Fox School of Business, Specialized Master's Programs, Philadelphia, PA 19122-6096. Offers accountancy (MS); actuarial science (MS); finance (MS); financial engineering (MS); human resource management (MS); innovation management and entrepreneurship (MS); marketing (MS); statistics (MS). MS in

innovation management and entrepreneurship delivered jointly with College of Engineering. *Accreditation:* AACSB. *Program availability:* Part-time. *Entrance requirements:* For master's, GRE General Test or GMAT, minimum undergraduate GPA of 3.0. Additional exam requirements/recommendations for international students: Required—TOEFL (minimum score 600 paper-based; 100 iBT), IELTS (minimum score 7.5).

Tennessee Technological University, College of Graduate Studies, College of Business, MBA Program, Cookeville, TN 38505. Offers finance (MBA); human resource management (MBA); international business (MBA); management information systems (MBA). *Program availability:* Part-time, evening/weekend. *Students:* 32 full-time (10 women), 156 part-time (66 women); includes 16 minority (7 Black or African American, non-Hispanic/Latino; 1 Asian, non-Hispanic/Latino; 5 Hispanic/Latino; 3 Two or more races, non-Hispanic/Latino), 5 international. 115 applicants, 68% accepted, 57 enrolled. In 2018, 88 master's awarded. *Entrance requirements:* For master's, GMAT or GRE. *Financial support:* In 2018–19, 2 research assistantships, 3 teaching assistantships were awarded; fellowships and unspecified assistantships also available. Financial award application deadline: 4/1; financial award applicants required to submit FAFSA. *Unit head:* Kate Nicewicz, Director, 931-372-3600, E-mail: knicewicz@tntech.edu. *Application contact:* Shelia K. Kendrick, Coordinator of Graduate Studies, 931-372-3808, Fax: 931-372-3497, E-mail: skendrick@tntech.edu.
Website: https://www.tntech.edu/cob/mba/

Texas A&M International University, Office of Graduate Studies and Research, A.R. Sanchez, Jr. School of Business, Division of International Banking and Finance Studies, Laredo, TX 78041. Offers accounting (MP Acc); international banking and finance (MBA). *Entrance requirements:* For master's, GMAT or GRE General Test. Additional exam requirements/recommendations for international students: Required—TOEFL (minimum score 550 paper-based; 79 iBT).

Texas A&M University, Mays Business School, Department of Finance, College Station, TX 77843. Offers finance (MS); financial management (MFM); land economics and real estate (MRE). *Faculty:* 20. *Students:* 256 full-time (72 women), 11 part-time (3 women); includes 55 minority (3 Black or African American, non-Hispanic/Latino; 1 American Indian or Alaska Native, non-Hispanic/Latino; 15 Asian, non-Hispanic/Latino; 34 Hispanic/Latino; 2 Two or more races, non-Hispanic/Latino), 16 international. Average age 24. 250 applicants, 42% accepted, 87 enrolled. In 2018, 187 master's awarded. Terminal master's awarded for partial completion of doctoral program. *Degree requirements:* For master's, comprehensive exam. *Entrance requirements:* For master's, GMAT or GRE. Additional exam requirements/recommendations for international students: Required—TOEFL (minimum score 550 paper-based; 80 iBT), IELTS (minimum score 6), PTE (minimum score 53). *Application deadline:* For fall admission, 4/7 for domestic students. Applications are processed on a rolling basis. Application fee: $50 ($90 for international students). Electronic applications accepted. *Expenses:* Contact institution. *Financial support:* In 2018–19, 194 students received support, including 32 fellowships with tuition reimbursements available (averaging $1,250 per year), 22 research assistantships with tuition reimbursements available (averaging $15,842 per year), 8 teaching assistantships with tuition reimbursements available (averaging $5,534 per year); career-related internships or fieldwork, institutionally sponsored loans, scholarships/grants, traineeships, health care benefits, tuition waivers (full and partial), and unspecified assistantships also available. Support available to part-time students. Financial award application deadline: 3/15; financial award applicants required to submit FAFSA. *Unit head:* Dr. Sorin Sorescu, Head, 979-458-0380, Fax: 979-845-3884, E-mail: smsorescu@mays.tamu.edu. *Application contact:* Angela G. Degelman, Program Coordinator/Graduate Academic Advisor, 979-845-4858, Fax: 979-845-3884, E-mail: adegelman@mays.tamu.edu.
Website: http://mays.tamu.edu/finc/

Texas A&M University–Commerce, College of Business, Commerce, TX 75429. Offers accounting (MSA); business administration (MBA); business analytics (MS); finance (MSF); management (MS); marketing (MS). *Accreditation:* AACSB. *Program availability:* Part-time, evening/weekend, 100% online, blended/hybrid learning. *Faculty:* 48 full-time (15 women), 2 part-time/adjunct (1 woman). *Students:* 391 full-time (209 women), 948 part-time (511 women); includes 583 minority (249 Black or African American, non-Hispanic/Latino; 4 American Indian or Alaska Native, non-Hispanic/Latino; 89 Asian, non-Hispanic/Latino; 205 Hispanic/Latino; 1 Native Hawaiian or other Pacific Islander, non-Hispanic/Latino; 35 Two or more races, non-Hispanic/Latino), 156 international. Average age 33. 930 applicants, 58% accepted, 355 enrolled. In 2018, 628 master's awarded. *Degree requirements:* For master's, comprehensive exam. *Entrance requirements:* For master's, GRE General Test, GMAT, letter of recommendation. Additional exam requirements/recommendations for international students: Required—TOEFL (minimum score 550 paper-based; 79 iBT), IELTS (minimum score 6), PTE (minimum score 53). *Application deadline:* For fall admission, 6/1 priority date for international students; for spring admission, 10/15 priority date for international students; for summer admission, 3/15 priority date for international students. Applications are processed on a rolling basis. Application fee: $50 ($75 for international students). Electronic applications accepted. *Expenses:* Tuition, area resident: Full-time $3630. Tuition, state resident: full-time $3630. Tuition, nonresident: full-time $11,100. *International tuition:* $11,100 full-time. *Required fees:* $2794. Tuition and fees vary according to course load, degree level and program. *Financial support:* In 2018–19, 61 students received support, including 57 research assistantships with partial tuition reimbursements available (averaging $3,286 per year); Federal Work-Study, institutionally sponsored loans, scholarships/grants, health care benefits, and unspecified assistantships also available. Financial award application deadline: 5/1; financial award applicants required to submit FAFSA. *Faculty research:* Strategic management and organizational behavior phenomena; marketing and big data decisions of product choice behavior and channel behavior of consumers; international accounting in governmental sectors; finance research on banking, investments, financial institutions and risk management; applied economics with emphasis on industries that are important to the region including health and energy. *Unit head:* Dr. Shanan Gwaltney Gibson, Dean of College of Business, 903-886-5191, Fax: 903-886-5650, E-mail: shanan.gibson@tamuc.edu. *Application contact:* Shanna Hoskison, Director, Graduate Advising, 903-886-5190, E-mail: shanna.hoskison@tamuc.edu.
Website: https://new.tamuc.edu/business/

Texas A&M University–Corpus Christi, College of Graduate Studies, College of Business, Corpus Christi, TX 78412. Offers accounting (M Acc); business (MBA); finance (MBA); health care administration (MBA); international business (MBA). *Accreditation:* AACSB. *Program availability:* Part-time, evening/weekend, 100% online, blended/hybrid learning. *Degree requirements:* For master's, 30 to 42 hours (for MBA; varies by concentration area, delivery format, and necessity for foundational courses for students with nonbusiness degrees). *Entrance requirements:* For master's, GMAT, GRE. Additional exam requirements/recommendations for international students: Required—TOEFL (minimum score 550 paper-based; 79 iBT), IELTS (minimum score 6.5). Electronic applications accepted.

Texas Tech University, Rawls College of Business Administration, Lubbock, TX 79409-2101. Offers accounting (MSA, PhD), including audit/financial reporting (MSA), taxation (MSA); data science (MS); finance (PhD); general business (MBA); healthcare

management (MS); information systems and operations management (PhD); management (PhD); marketing (PhD); STEM (MBA); JD/MBA; JD/MSA; MBA/M Arch; MBA/MD; MBA/MS; MBA/Pharm D. *Accreditation:* AACSB. *Program availability:* Evening/weekend, 100% online, blended/hybrid learning. *Degree requirements:* For master's, thesis (for MS); capstone course; for doctorate, comprehensive exam, thesis/dissertation, qualifying exams. *Entrance requirements:* For master's, GMAT, GRE, MCAT, PCAT, LSAT, or DAT, holistic review of academic credentials, resume, essay, letters of recommendation; for doctorate, GMAT, GRE, holistic review of academic credentials, resume, statement of purpose, letters of recommendation. Additional exam requirements/recommendations for international students: Required—TOEFL (minimum score 550 paper-based; 79 iBT), IELTS (minimum score 6.5), PTE (minimum score 60). Electronic applications accepted. *Expenses:* Contact institution. *Faculty research:* Governmental and nonprofit accounting, securities and options futures, statistical analysis and design, leadership, consumer behavior.

Thomas Edison State University, School of Business and Management, Program in International Business Finance, Trenton, NJ 08608. Offers MS. *Program availability:* Online learning. *Entrance requirements:* For master's, undergraduate coursework in financial accounting, microeconomics, finance and statistics.

Tiffin University, Program in Business Administration, Tiffin, OH 44883-2161. Offers finance (MBA); general management (MBA); healthcare administration (MBA); human resource management (MBA); international business (MBA); leadership (MBA); marketing (MBA); non-profit management (MBA); sports management (MBA). *Accreditation:* ACBSP. *Program availability:* Part-time, evening/weekend, online learning. *Entrance requirements:* For master's, minimum undergraduate GPA of 2.5, work experience. Additional exam requirements/recommendations for international students: Required—TOEFL (minimum score 550 paper-based; 79 iBT), IELTS. Electronic applications accepted. Application fee is waived when completed online. *Faculty research:* Small business, executive development operations, research and statistical analysis, market research, management information systems.

Trident University International, College of Business Administration, Program in Business Administration, Cypress, CA 90630. Offers business administration (PhD); conflict and negotiation management (MBA); criminal justice administration (MBA); entrepreneurship (MBA); finance (MBA); general management (MBA); government accounting (MBA); human resource management (MBA); information security and digital assurance management (MBA); information technology management (MBA); international business (MBA); logistics management (MBA); marketing (MBA); project management (MBA); public management (MBA); quality management (MBA); strategic leadership (MBA). *Program availability:* Part-time, evening/weekend, online learning. *Degree requirements:* For doctorate, comprehensive exam, thesis/dissertation, defense of dissertation. *Entrance requirements:* For master's, minimum GPA of 2.5 (students with GPA 3.0 or greater may transfer up to 30% of graduate level credits); for doctorate, minimum GPA of 3.4, curriculum vitae, course work in research methods or statistics. Additional exam requirements/recommendations for international students: Required—TOEFL. Electronic applications accepted.

Troy University, Graduate School, College of Business, Program in Business Administration, Troy, AL 36082. Offers accounting (EMBA, MBA); criminal justice (EMBA); finance (MBA); general management (EMBA, MBA); healthcare management (EMBA); information systems (EMBA, MBA); international economic development (MBA). *Accreditation:* ACBSP. *Program availability:* Part-time, evening/weekend. *Faculty:* 12 full-time (1 woman), 1 part-time/adjunct (0 women). *Students:* 27 full-time (16 women), 93 part-time (44 women); includes 31 minority (27 Black or African American, non-Hispanic/Latino; 1 Asian, non-Hispanic/Latino; 3 Hispanic/Latino), 29 international. Average age 30. 108 applicants, 37% accepted, 22 enrolled. In 2018, 74 master's awarded. *Degree requirements:* For master's, minimum GPA of 3.0, capstone course, research course. *Entrance requirements:* For master's, GMAT (minimum score 500) or GRE (minimum score 900 on old exam or 294 on new exam), bachelor's degree; minimum undergraduate GPA of 2.5 or 3.0 on last 30 semester hours, letter of recommendation. Additional exam requirements/recommendations for international students: Required—TOEFL (minimum score 523 paper-based; 70 iBT), IELTS (minimum score 6). *Application deadline:* Applications are processed on a rolling basis. Application fee: $50. Electronic applications accepted. *Expenses: Tuition, area resident:* Full-time $425; part-time $425 per credit hour. Tuition, state resident: full-time $425; part-time $425 per credit hour. Tuition, nonresident: full-time $850; part-time $850 per credit hour. *International tuition:* $850 full-time. *Required fees:* $50 per semester. Tuition and fees vary according to campus/location and program. *Financial support:* Fellowships, career-related internships or fieldwork, and scholarships/grants available. Support available to part-time students. Financial award applicants required to submit FAFSA. *Unit head:* Dr. Robert Wheatley, Professor, Director of Graduate Business Programs, 334-670-3194, Fax: 334-670-3708, E-mail: rwheat@troy.edu. *Application contact:* Jessica A. Kimbro, Assistant Director of Graduate Programs, 334-670-3189, E-mail: jacord@troy.edu.
Website: https://www.troy.edu/academics/academic-programs/sorrell-college-business-programs.php

Tulane University, A. B. Freeman School of Business, New Orleans, LA 70118-5669. Offers accounting (M Acct); analytics (MBA); banking and financial services (M Fin); energy (M Fin , MBA); entrepreneurship (MBA); finance (MBA, PhD); financial accounting (PhD); international business (MBA); international management (MBA); strategic management and leadership (MBA); JD/M Acct; JD/MBA; MBA/M Acc; MBA/MA; MBA/MD; MBA/ME; MBA/MPH. *Accreditation:* AACSB. *Program availability:* Part-time, evening/weekend. *Faculty:* 43 full-time (11 women), 45 part-time/adjunct (8 women). *Students:* 432 full-time (218 women), 533 part-time (262 women); includes 99 minority (32 Black or African American, non-Hispanic/Latino; 1 American Indian or Alaska Native, non-Hispanic/Latino; 26 Asian, non-Hispanic/Latino; 35 Hispanic/Latino; 5 Two or more races, non-Hispanic/Latino), 644 international. Average age 28. 1,911 applicants, 77% accepted, 411 enrolled. In 2018, 728 master's, 4 doctorates awarded. Terminal master's awarded for partial completion of doctoral program. *Degree requirements:* For master's, one foreign language, comprehensive exam (for some programs); for doctorate, one foreign language, comprehensive exam, thesis/dissertation. *Entrance requirements:* For master's and doctorate, GMAT or GRE, interview. Additional exam requirements/recommendations for international students: Required—TOEFL or IELTS. *Application deadline:* For fall admission, 11/1 priority date for domestic students, 11/1 for international students; for winter admission, 1/6 for domestic and international students; for spring admission, 3/1 priority date for domestic students, 3/1 for international students; for summer admission, 5/5 for domestic students. Applications are processed on a rolling basis. Application fee: $125. Electronic applications accepted. *Expenses:* Contact institution. *Financial support:* In 2018–19, 153 students received support. Fellowships with tuition reimbursements available, research assistantships, teaching assistantships, career-related internships or fieldwork, Federal Work-Study, tuition waivers (full and partial), and unspecified assistantships available. Support available to part-time students. Financial award application deadline: 4/15; financial award applicants required to submit FAFSA. *Faculty research:* Corporate finance, managerial accounting and financial reporting, strategic management and leadership, consumer behavior and decision making, organizational behavior and

human resource management. *Unit head:* Ira Solomon, PhD, Dean, 504-865-5407, Fax: 504-865-5491, E-mail: businessdean@tulane.edu. *Application contact:* Melissa Booth, Assistant Dean for Graduate Admissions, 800-223-5402, E-mail: freeman.admissions@tulane.edu.
Website: http://www.freeman.tulane.edu

United States International University–Africa, School of Business Administration, Nairobi, Kenya. Offers business administration (GEMBA); entrepreneurship (MBA); finance (MBA); human resource management (MBA); information technology management (MBA); integrated studies (MBA); international business administration (MBA); management and organizational development (MS); marketing (MBA); organizational development (EMS); strategic management (MBA). *Program availability:* Part-time, evening/weekend. *Degree requirements:* For master's, thesis. *Entrance requirements:* For master's, GMAT, 2 letters of reference, resume. Additional exam requirements/recommendations for international students: Required—TOEFL (minimum score 550 paper-based). *Faculty research:* Marketing in small business enterprises, total quality management in Kenya.

Universidad Central del Este, Graduate School, San Pedro de Macoris, Dominican Republic. Offers environmental engineering (ME); financial management (M Ad); higher education (M Ed), including higher education management, higher education pedagogy; human resources (M Ad). *Entrance requirements:* For master's, letters of recommendation.

Universidad de las Americas, A.C., Program in Business Administration, Mexico City, Mexico. Offers finance (MBA); marketing research (MBA); production and quality (MBA).

Universidad de las Américas Puebla, Division of Graduate Studies, School of Business and Economics, Puebla, Mexico. Offers business administration (MBA); finance (M Adm). *Program availability:* Part-time, evening/weekend. *Degree requirements:* For master's, one foreign language, thesis. *Entrance requirements:* Additional exam requirements/recommendations for international students: Required—TOEFL. *Faculty research:* System dynamics, information technology, marketing, international business, strategic planning, quality.

Universidad de las Américas Puebla, Division of Graduate Studies, School of Social Sciences, Program in Economics, Puebla, Mexico. Offers economics (MA); finance (M Adm). *Program availability:* Part-time, evening/weekend. *Degree requirements:* For master's, one foreign language, thesis. *Faculty research:* Economic models (mathematics), industrial organization, assets and values market.

Universidad Metropolitana, School of Business Administration, Program in Finance, San Juan, PR 00928-1150. Offers MBA.

Université de Sherbrooke, Faculty of Administration, Program in Finance, Sherbrooke, QC J1K 2R1, Canada. Offers M Sc. *Degree requirements:* For master's, one foreign language, thesis. *Entrance requirements:* For master's, bachelor's degree in related field, minimum GPA of 3.0 (on 4.3 scale). Electronic applications accepted. *Faculty research:* Public projects analysis, financial econometrics, risk management, portfolio management.

Université du Québec à Montréal, Graduate Programs, Program in Finance, Montréal, QC H3C 3P8, Canada. Offers Diploma. *Program availability:* Part-time. *Entrance requirements:* For degree, appropriate bachelor's degree or equivalent, proficiency in French.

Université du Québec à Trois-Rivières, Graduate Programs, Program in Finance, Trois-Rivières, QC G9A 5H7, Canada. Offers DESS.

Université du Québec en Outaouais, Graduate Programs, Program in Financial Services, Gatineau, QC J8X 3X7, Canada. Offers MBA, DESS, Diploma. *Program availability:* Part-time, evening/weekend. *Degree requirements:* For master's, thesis (for some programs).

Université Laval, Faculty of Administrative Sciences, Programs in Business Administration, Québec, QC G1K 7P4, Canada. Offers accounting (MBA); agri-food management (MBA); electronic business (MBA, Diploma); factory management and logistics (MBA); finance (MBA); firm management (MBA); geomatic management (MBA); information technology management (MBA); international management (MBA); management (MBA); management accounting (MBA, Diploma); marketing (MBA); modeling and organizational decision (MBA); occupational health and safety management (MBA); pharmacy management (MBA); social and environmental responsibility (MBA); technological entrepreneurship (Diploma). *Accreditation:* AACSB. *Program availability:* Part-time, evening/weekend, online learning. *Entrance requirements:* For master's and Diploma, knowledge of French and English. Electronic applications accepted.

University at Albany, State University of New York, Nelson A. Rockefeller College of Public Affairs and Policy, Department of Public Administration and Policy, Albany, NY 12222-0001. Offers financial management and public economics (MPA); financial market regulation (MPA); health policy (MPA); healthcare management (MPA); homeland security (MPA); human resources management (MPA); information strategy and management (MPA); local government management (MPA); nonprofit management (MPA); nonprofit management and leadership (Certificate); organizational behavior and theory (MPA, PhD); planning and policy analysis (CAS); policy analysis (MPA); politics and administration (PhD); public finance (PhD); public management (PhD); public policy (PhD); public sector management (Certificate); women and public policy (Certificate); JD/MPA. JD/MPA offered jointly with Albany Law School. *Accreditation:* NASPAA (one or more programs are accredited). *Faculty:* 24 full-time (10 women), 19 part-time/adjunct (10 women). *Students:* 117 full-time (62 women), 101 part-time (58 women); includes 56 minority (20 Black or African American, non-Hispanic/Latino; 8 Asian, non-Hispanic/Latino; 20 Hispanic/Latino; 8 Two or more races, non-Hispanic/Latino), 28 international. 236 applicants, 69% accepted, 86 enrolled. In 2018, 57 master's, 1 doctorate, 14 other advanced degrees awarded. *Degree requirements:* For doctorate, one foreign language, thesis/dissertation. *Entrance requirements:* For doctorate, GRE General Test. Additional exam requirements/recommendations for international students: Required—TOEFL (minimum score 550 paper-based). *Application deadline:* For fall admission, 2/1 priority date for domestic students, 5/1 for international students; for spring admission, 12/1 for domestic students. Applications are processed on a rolling basis. Application fee: $75. Electronic applications accepted. *Financial support:* Application deadline: 2/1. *Unit head:* Victor Asal, Chair, 518-591-8729, E-mail: vasal@albany.edu. *Application contact:* Victor Asal, Chair, 518-591-8729, E-mail: vasal@albany.edu.
Website: http://www.albany.edu/rockefeller/pad.shtml

University at Albany, State University of New York, School of Business, MBA Programs, Albany, NY 12222-0001. Offers business administration (MBA); cyber security (MBA); entrepreneurship (MBA); finance (MBA); human resource information systems (MBA); information systems and business analytics (MBA); marketing (MBA); JD/MBA. JD/MBA offered jointly with Albany Law School. *Program availability:* Part-time, evening/weekend. *Faculty:* 29 full-time (13 women), 9 part-time/adjunct (2 women). *Students:* 103 full-time (36 women), 188 part-time (69 women); includes 76 minority (27 Black or African American, non-Hispanic/Latino; 33 Asian, non-Hispanic/Latino; 16 Hispanic/Latino), 16 international. Average age 25. 181 applicants, 80% accepted, 114 enrolled. In 2018, 103 master's awarded. *Degree requirements:* For

master's, thesis (for some programs), field or research project. *Entrance requirements:* For master's, GMAT, minimum undergraduate GPA of 3.0; 3 letters of recommendation; resume; statement of goals. Additional exam requirements/recommendations for international students: Required—TOEFL (minimum score 100 iBT); Recommended—IELTS (minimum score 7). *Application deadline:* For fall admission, 4/1 priority date for domestic students, 2/15 for international students; for spring admission, 12/1 for domestic students; for summer admission, 5/1 for domestic students. Applications are processed on a rolling basis. Application fee: $75. Electronic applications accepted. *Expenses:* 16818. *Financial support:* In 2018–19, 25 students received support, including 7 fellowships with partial tuition reimbursements available (averaging $6,000 per year), 4 research assistantships with partial tuition reimbursements available, 21 teaching assistantships with partial tuition reimbursements available; unspecified assistantships also available. Financial award application deadline: 4/1; financial award applicants required to submit FAFSA. *Faculty research:* Social goods, information assurance, social computing, corporate entrepreneurship, asset pricing. *Total annual research expenditures:* $136,000. *Unit head:* Dr. Nilanjan Sen, Dean, 518-956-8370, Fax: 518-442-3273, E-mail: nsen@albany.edu. *Application contact:* Zina Mega Lawrence, Assistant Dean of Graduate Student Services, 518-956-8320, Fax: 518-442-4042, E-mail: zlawrence@albany.edu.
Website: https://graduatebusiness.albany.edu/

University at Buffalo, the State University of New York, Graduate School, School of Management, Buffalo, NY 14260. Offers accounting (MS); analytics (MBA); business administration (PMBA); consulting (MBA); finance (MBA, MS), including financial risk management (MS), quantitative finance (MS); healthcare (MBA); information assurance (MBA); information systems (MBA); international management (MBA); management (EMBA, PhD); management information systems (MS); marketing (MBA); supply chain and operations (MBA); supply chains and operations management (MS); Au D/MBA; DDS/MBA; JD/MBA; M Arch/MBA; MD/MBA; MPH/MBA; MSW/MBA; Pharm D/MBA. *Accreditation:* AACSB. *Program availability:* Part-time, evening/weekend. *Degree requirements:* For master's, capstone courses or projects; for doctorate, comprehensive exam, thesis/dissertation. *Entrance requirements:* For master's, GMAT (for MS in accounting, finance); GRE or GMAT (for MBA, MS in management information systems, supply chains and operations management), essays, letters of recommendation; for doctorate, GMAT or GRE, essays, writing sample, letters of recommendation. Additional exam requirements/recommendations for international students: Required—TOEFL (minimum score 95 iBT) or IELTS (minimum score 6.5); Recommended—TSE (minimum score 73). Electronic applications accepted. *Expenses:* Contact institution. *Faculty research:* Data analytics, accounting and law, rate finance, consumer behavior, supply chain logistics, leadership and team effectiveness.

The University of Akron, Graduate School, College of Business Administration, Department of Finance, Akron, OH 44325. Offers MBA. *Program availability:* Part-time, evening/weekend. *Entrance requirements:* For master's, GMAT, GRE, MCAT, LSAT, PCAT, or CAT, minimum GPA of 3.0 (preferred), two letters of recommendation, statement of purpose, resume. Additional exam requirements/recommendations for international students: Required—TOEFL (minimum score 79 iBT), IELTS (minimum score 6.5). Electronic applications accepted. *Faculty research:* Corporate finance, financial markets and institutions, investment and equity market analysis, personal financial planning, real estate.

The University of Alabama, Graduate School, Manderson Graduate School of Business, Economics, Finance and Legal Studies Department, Tuscaloosa, AL 35487. Offers economics (MA, PhD); finance (MS, PhD). Terminal master's awarded for partial completion of doctoral program. *Degree requirements:* For master's, comprehensive exam (MA), thesis (MS); for doctorate, comprehensive exam, thesis/dissertation. *Entrance requirements:* For master's, GMAT, GRE; for doctorate, GRE or GMAT. Additional exam requirements/recommendations for international students: Required—TOEFL (minimum score 550 paper-based; 79 iBT). Electronic applications accepted. *Faculty research:* Taxation, futures market, monetary theory and policy, income distribution.

The University of Alabama at Birmingham, Collat School of Business, Program in Business Administration, Birmingham, AL 35294. Offers business administration (MBA), including finance, health care management, information technology management, marketing; MD/MBA. *Program availability:* Part-time, evening/weekend, 100% online, blended/hybrid learning. *Entrance requirements:* For master's, GMAT. Additional exam requirements/recommendations for international students: Required—TOEFL (minimum score 80 iBT), IELTS (minimum score 6.5). Electronic applications accepted. *Expenses: Tuition, area resident:* Full-time $8100; part-time $8100 per year. *Tuition, state resident:* full-time $8100. *Tuition, nonresident:* full-time $19,188; part-time $19,188 per year. Tuition and fees vary according to program. *Faculty research:* Open innovation, workplace issues, leadership, supply chain management, capital markets.

The University of Alabama in Huntsville, School of Graduate Studies, College of Business Administration, Program in Accounting, Huntsville, AL 35899. Offers accounting (M Acc), including CPA preparatory with an emphasis in taxation, CPA preparatory with emphasis in assurance and financial reporting, general accounting, information systems audit and control (ISAC). *Accreditation:* AACSB. *Program availability:* Part-time. *Faculty:* 3 full-time (1 woman). *Students:* 14 full-time (6 women), 25 part-time (18 women); includes 5 minority (2 Black or African American, non-Hispanic/Latino; 2 Asian, non-Hispanic/Latino; 1 Hispanic/Latino), 3 international. Average age 29. 40 applicants, 73% accepted, 17 enrolled. In 2018, 12 master's awarded. *Degree requirements:* For master's, comprehensive exam, thesis or alternative. *Entrance requirements:* For master's, GMAT (minimum score 500), minimum AACSB index of 1080. Additional exam requirements/recommendations for international students: Required—TOEFL (minimum score 550 paper-based; 80 iBT), IELTS (minimum score 6.5). *Application deadline:* For fall admission, 7/15 priority date for domestic students, 4/1 priority date for international students; for spring admission, 11/30 priority date for domestic students, 9/1 priority date for international students. Applications are processed on a rolling basis. Application fee: $50. Electronic applications accepted. *Expenses: Tuition, area resident:* Full-time $10,632; part-time $412 per credit hour. *Tuition, state resident:* full-time $10,632. *Tuition, nonresident:* full-time $23,604; part-time $412 per credit hour. *Required fees:* $582; $582. Tuition and fees vary according to course load and program. *Financial support:* In 2018–19, 4 students received support, including 3 teaching assistantships with full tuition reimbursements available (averaging $5,100 per year); career-related internships or fieldwork, Federal Work-Study, institutionally sponsored loans, scholarships/grants, health care benefits, and unspecified assistantships also available. Support available to part-time students. Financial award application deadline: 4/1; financial award applicants required to submit FAFSA. *Faculty research:* Accounting information systems, managerial accounting, behavioral accounting, state and local taxation, financial accounting. *Unit head:* Dr. Allen Wilhite, Interim Chair, 256-824-6591, Fax: 256-824-2929, E-mail: allen.wilhite@uah.edu. *Application contact:* Jennifer Pettitt, Director of Graduate Programs, 256-824-6681, Fax: 256-824-7571, E-mail: jennifer.pettitt@uah.edu.

The University of Alabama in Huntsville, School of Graduate Studies, College of Business Administration, Programs in Business and Management, Huntsville, AL 35899.

Offers business analytics (MSMS); federal contracting and procurement management (Certificate); human resource management (MSM); management (MBA), including acquisition management, entrepreneurship, federal contract accounting, finance, human resource management, logistics and supply chain management, marketing, project management; supply chain management (Certificate); technology and innovation management (Certificate). *Accreditation:* AACSB. *Program availability:* Part-time. *Faculty:* 8 full-time (3 women). *Students:* 57 full-time (25 women), 152 part-time (76 women); includes 37 minority (20 Black or African American, non-Hispanic/Latino; 2 American Indian or Alaska Native, non-Hispanic/Latino; 6 Asian, non-Hispanic/Latino; 8 Hispanic/Latino; 1 Two or more races, non-Hispanic/Latino), 24 international. Average age 33. 178 applicants, 80% accepted, 84 enrolled. In 2018, 96 master's, 1 other advanced degree awarded. *Degree requirements:* For master's, comprehensive exam, thesis or alternative. *Entrance requirements:* For master's, GMAT (minimum score 500), minimum AACSB index of 1080. Additional exam requirements/recommendations for international students: Required—TOEFL (minimum score 550 paper-based; 80 iBT), IELTS (minimum score 6.5). *Application deadline:* For fall admission, 7/15 priority date for domestic students, 4/1 priority date for international students; for spring admission, 11/30 priority date for domestic students, 9/1 priority date for international students. Applications are processed on a rolling basis. Application fee: $50. Electronic applications accepted. *Expenses: Tuition, area resident:* Full-time $10,632; part-time $412 per credit hour. *Tuition, state resident:* full-time $10,632. *Tuition, nonresident:* full-time $23,604; part-time $412 per credit hour. *Required fees:* $582; $582. Tuition and fees vary according to course load and program. *Financial support:* In 2018–19, 15 students received support, including 15 teaching assistantships with full tuition reimbursements available (averaging $4,871 per year); research assistantships with full tuition reimbursements available, career-related internships or fieldwork, Federal Work-Study, institutionally sponsored loans, scholarships/grants, health care benefits, tuition waivers (full and partial), and unspecified assistantships also available. Support available to part-time students. Financial award application deadline: 4/1; financial award applicants required to submit FAFSA. *Faculty research:* Supply chain management, management of research and development, international marketing and branding, organizational behavior and human resource management, social networks and computational economics. *Unit head:* Dr. Fan Tseng, Chair, 256-824-6804, Fax: 256-824-6328, E-mail: fan.tseng@uah.edu. *Application contact:* Jennifer Pettitt, Director of Advising, 256-824-6681, Fax: 256-824-7571, E-mail: jennifer.pettitt@uah.edu.

University of Alaska Fairbanks, School of Management, Department of Business Administration, Fairbanks, AK 99775-6080. Offers capital markets (MBA); general management (MBA). *Accreditation:* AACSB. *Program availability:* Part-time, online only, 100% online. *Faculty:* 9 full-time (4 women). *Students:* 24 full-time (12 women), 70 part-time (42 women); includes 25 minority (2 Black or African American, non-Hispanic/Latino; 4 American Indian or Alaska Native, non-Hispanic/Latino; 5 Asian, non-Hispanic/Latino; 6 Hispanic/Latino; 8 Two or more races, non-Hispanic/Latino), 2 international. Average age 32. 50 applicants, 56% accepted, 19 enrolled. In 2018, 34 master's awarded. *Degree requirements:* For master's, comprehensive exam, thesis or alternative. *Entrance requirements:* For master's, GRE General Test, GMAT, bachelor's degree from accredited institution with minimum cumulative undergraduate and major GPA of 2.75; GRE, GMAT or alternate entrance exam (Watson Glaser) may be required depending on undergraduate GPA. Additional exam requirements/recommendations for international students: Required—TOEFL (minimum score 550 paper-based; 79 iBT), IELTS (minimum score 6.5). *Application deadline:* For fall admission, 3/1 priority date for domestic students, 2/1 for international students; for spring admission, 9/1 priority date for domestic students, 9/1 for international students. Applications are processed on a rolling basis. Application fee: $60. Electronic applications accepted. *Expenses:* School of Management (SOM) tuition has a 20% surcharge per credit hour over that for credits of most other UAF colleges. Assuming 60 credits for PhD and 32 for Master's, this augments costs by $6,180 for in-state PhD, $3,296 for in-state Master's, $12,948 for non-resident PhD and $6,912 for non-resident Masters students, respectively. *Financial support:* In 2018–19, 4 teaching assistantships with full tuition reimbursements (averaging $12,967 per year) were awarded; fellowships with full tuition reimbursements, research assistantships with full tuition reimbursements, career-related internships or fieldwork, Federal Work-Study, scholarships/grants, health care benefits, and unspecified assistantships also available. Support available to part-time students. Financial award application deadline: 2/15; financial award applicants required to submit FAFSA. *Faculty research:* Consumer behavior, marketing, international finance and business, strategic risk, organization theory. *Unit head:* Dr. Nicole Cundiff, Program Director, 907-474-7461, E-mail: uaf-som@alaska.edu. *Application contact:* Samara Taber, Director of Admissions, 907-474-7500, E-mail: uaf-admissions@alaska.edu. Website: http://www.uaf.edu/som/degrees/graduate/mba

University of Alberta, Faculty of Graduate Studies and Research, Department of Economics, Edmonton, AB T6G 2E1, Canada. Offers economics (MA, PhD); economics and finance (MA); environmental and natural resource economics (PhD). *Program availability:* Part-time. *Degree requirements:* For doctorate, thesis/dissertation. *Entrance requirements:* For master's and doctorate, GRE. Additional exam requirements/recommendations for international students: Required—TOEFL. *Faculty research:* Public finance, international trade, industrial organization, Pacific Rim economics, monetary economics.

University of Alberta, Faculty of Graduate Studies and Research, Doctoral Program in Business, Edmonton, AB T6G 2E1, Canada. Offers accounting (PhD); finance (PhD); human resources/industrial relations (PhD); management science (PhD); marketing (PhD); organizational analysis (PhD); MBA/PhD. *Accreditation:* AACSB. *Program availability:* Part-time. *Degree requirements:* For doctorate, comprehensive exam, thesis/dissertation. *Entrance requirements:* For doctorate, GMAT. Additional exam requirements/recommendations for international students: Required—TOEFL (minimum score 550 paper-based). Electronic applications accepted. *Faculty research:* Accounting, capital markets and corporate finance, organizational change and human resource management, marketing, strategic management.

The University of Arizona, Eller College of Management, Department of Finance, Tucson, AZ 85721. Offers MS. *Program availability:* Part-time. Terminal master's awarded for partial completion of doctoral program. *Degree requirements:* For master's, project. *Entrance requirements:* Additional exam requirements/recommendations for international students: Required—TOEFL (minimum score 550 paper-based; 79 iBT). Electronic applications accepted. *Expenses:* Contact institution. *Faculty research:* Corporate finance, banking, investments, stock market.

University of Baltimore, Graduate School, Merrick School of Business, Department of Finance and Economics, Baltimore, MD 21201-5779. Offers business/finance (MS). *Program availability:* Part-time, evening/weekend. *Entrance requirements:* For master's, GMAT. Additional exam requirements/recommendations for international students: Required—TOEFL (minimum score 550 paper-based). Electronic applications accepted. *Faculty research:* International finance, corporate finance, health care, regional economics, small business.

University of Bridgeport, School of Business, Bridgeport, CT 06604. Offers accounting (MBA); finance (MBA); general business (MBA); global financial services (MBA); human resource management (MBA); information systems and knowledge management

(MBA); international business (MBA); management (MBA); marketing (MBA); operations management (MBA); small business and entrepreneurship (MBA); specialized business (MBA). *Accreditation:* ACBSP. *Program availability:* Part-time, evening/weekend. *Degree requirements:* For master's, thesis optional. *Entrance requirements:* For master's, GMAT. Additional exam requirements/recommendations for international students: Recommended—TOEFL (minimum score 550 paper-based; 80 iBT), IELTS (minimum score 6.5). Electronic applications accepted. *Expenses:* Contact institution.

The University of British Columbia, Sauder School of Business, Doctoral Program in Business Administration, Vancouver, BC V6T 1Z2, Canada. Offers accounting (PhD); finance (PhD); management information systems (PhD); management science (PhD); marketing (PhD); organizational behavior (PhD); strategy and business economics (PhD); transportation and logistics (PhD); urban land economics (PhD). *Degree requirements:* For doctorate, comprehensive exam, thesis/dissertation. *Entrance requirements:* For doctorate, GMAT or GRE. Additional exam requirements/recommendations for international students: Required—TOEFL (minimum score 600 paper-based; 100 iBT). Electronic applications accepted. *Expenses:* Contact institution.

University of California, Berkeley, Graduate Division, Haas School of Business, PhD in Business Administration Program, Berkeley, CA 94720. Offers accounting (PhD); business and public policy (PhD); finance (PhD); management of organizations (PhD); marketing (PhD); real estate (PhD). *Accreditation:* AACSB. *Degree requirements:* For doctorate, comprehensive exam, thesis/dissertation, written preliminary exams, oral qualifying exam. *Entrance requirements:* For doctorate, GMAT or GRE, minimum GPA of 3.0 in undergraduate and graduate coursework. Additional exam requirements/recommendations for international students: Required—TOEFL (minimum score 570 paper-based; 70 iBT), IELTS (minimum score 7). Electronic applications accepted. *Expenses:* Contact institution. *Faculty research:* Accounting, business and public policy, entrepreneurship, finance, management of organizations, marketing, operations and information technology management, real estate.

University of California, Berkeley, UC Berkeley Extension, Certificate Programs in Business, Berkeley, CA 94720. Offers accounting (Certificate); business administration (Certificate); finance (Certificate); human resource management (Certificate); management (Certificate); marketing (Certificate); project management (Certificate). *Accreditation:* AACSB. *Program availability:* Online learning.

University of California, Berkeley, UC Berkeley Extension, International Diploma Programs, Berkeley, CA 94720. Offers business administration (Certificate); finance (Certificate); global business management (Certificate); marketing (Certificate); project management (Certificate). *Accreditation:* AACSB.

University of California, Davis, Graduate School of Management, Full-Time MBA Program, Davis, CA 95616. Offers business analytics and technologies (MBA); entrepreneurship and innovation (MBA); finance and accounting (MBA); general management (MBA); marketing (MBA); organizational behavior (MBA); public health management (MBA); strategy (MBA); technology management (MBA); DVM/MBA; JD/MBA; M Engr/MBA; MBA/MPH; MBA/MS; MD/MBA; MSN/MBA; PhD/MBA. *Faculty:* 31 full-time (10 women). *Students:* 89 full-time (35 women); includes 21 minority (1 Black or African American, non-Hispanic/Latino; 14 Asian, non-Hispanic/Latino; 6 Hispanic/Latino), 43 international. Average age 28. 290 applicants, 39% accepted, 44 enrolled. In 2018, 45 master's awarded. *Degree requirements:* For master's, comprehensive exam, integrated management project. *Entrance requirements:* For master's, GMAT or GRE, letters of recommendation, resume, essays, equivalent of a 4-year U.S. undergraduate degree, transcript. Additional exam requirements/recommendations for international students: Required—TOEFL (minimum score 600 paper-based; 100 iBT), IELTS (minimum score 7). *Application deadline:* For fall admission, 9/15 priority date for domestic and international students. Applications are processed on a rolling basis. Application fee: $125. Electronic applications accepted. *Expenses:* Contact institution. *Financial support:* In 2018–19, 85 students received support. Fellowships with full and partial tuition reimbursements available, research assistantships with partial tuition reimbursements available, teaching assistantships with partial tuition reimbursements available, institutionally sponsored loans, scholarships/grants, health care benefits, tuition waivers (partial), and unspecified assistantships available. Financial award application deadline: 3/1; financial award applicants required to submit FAFSA. *Faculty research:* Finance, marketing, management, business analytics, accounting. *Unit head:* Amanda Opperman, Assistant Dean of Student Affairs, 530-752-7658, Fax: 530-754-9355, E-mail: admissions@gsm.ucdavis.edu. *Application contact:* Andrea Shaw, Senior Director of Admissions, 530-754-5476, Fax: 530-754-9355, E-mail: admissions@gsm.ucdavis.edu.
Website: http://gsm.ucdavis.edu/daytime-mba-program

University of California, Davis, Graduate School of Management, MBA Programs in Sacramento and San Francisco Bay Area, Davis, CA 95616. Offers business analytics and technologies (MBA); entrepreneurship and innovation (MBA); finance and accounting (MBA); general management (MBA); marketing (MBA); organizational behavior (MBA); public health management (MBA); strategy (MBA); technology management (MBA). *Program availability:* Part-time-only, evening/weekend. *Faculty:* 17 full-time (7 women), 42 part-time/adjunct (11 women). *Students:* 279 part-time (107 women); includes 146 minority (12 Black or African American, non-Hispanic/Latino; 3 American Indian or Alaska Native, non-Hispanic/Latino; 102 Asian, non-Hispanic/Latino; 29 Hispanic/Latino), 24 international. Average age 30. 158 applicants, 83% accepted, 91 enrolled. In 2018, 91 master's awarded. *Degree requirements:* For master's, integrated management project. *Entrance requirements:* For master's, GMAT or GRE, letters of recommendation, resume, equivalent of a 4-year undergraduate degree. Additional exam requirements/recommendations for international students: Required—TOEFL (minimum score 600 paper-based; 100 iBT), IELTS (minimum score 7). *Application deadline:* For fall admission, 9/15 priority date for domestic and international students. Applications are processed on a rolling basis. Application fee: $125. Electronic applications accepted. *Expenses:* Contact institution. *Financial support:* In 2018–19, 89 students received support. Fellowships, teaching assistantships with partial tuition reimbursements available, scholarships/grants, and unspecified assistantships available. Support available to part-time students. Financial award application deadline: 3/1; financial award applicants required to submit FAFSA. *Faculty research:* Accounting, finance, marketing, management, business analytics. *Unit head:* Amanda Opperman, Assistant Dean of Student Affairs, 530-752-7658, Fax: 530-754-9355, E-mail: admissions@gsm.ucdavis.edu. *Application contact:* Andrea Shaw, Senior Director of Admissions, 530-754-5476, Fax: 530-754-9355, E-mail: admissions@gsm.ucdavis.edu.
Website: http://gsm.ucdavis.edu/mba-programs

University of California, Los Angeles, Graduate Division, UCLA Anderson School of Management, Los Angeles, CA 90095-1481. Offers accounting (PhD); behavioral decision making (PhD); business administration (EMBA, MBA); business administration/computer science (MBA/MSCS); business administration/latin american studies (MBA/MLAS); business administration/law (MBA/JD); business administration/library science (MBA/MLIS); business administration/medicine (MBA/MD); business administration/nursing (MBA/MN); business administration/public health (MBA/MPH); business administration/public policy (MBA/MPP); business administration/urban and regional planning (MBA/MURP); business analytics (MSBA); decisions, operations, and technology management (PhD); finance (PhD); financial engineering (MFE); global economics and management (PhD); management and organizations (PhD); marketing (PhD); strategy and policy (PhD); DDS/MBA; MBA/JD; MBA/MD; MBA/MLAS; MBA/MLIS; MBA/MN; MBA/MPH; MBA/MPP; MBA/MSCS; MBA/MURP. UCLA-NUS EMBA: UCLA Anderson and the National University of Singapore. *Accreditation:* AACSB. *Program availability:* Part-time, evening/weekend. *Faculty:* 86 full-time (19 women), 102 part-time/adjunct (16 women). *Students:* 1,040 full-time (378 women), 1,262 part-time (391 women); includes 784 minority (47 Black or African American, non-Hispanic/Latino; 1 American Indian or Alaska Native, non-Hispanic/Latino; 539 Asian, non-Hispanic/Latino; 116 Hispanic/Latino; 5 Native Hawaiian or other Pacific Islander, non-Hispanic/Latino; 76 Two or more races, non-Hispanic/Latino), 609 international. Average age 31. 6,708 applicants, 27% accepted, 949 enrolled. In 2018, 885 master's, 13 doctorates awarded. Terminal master's awarded for partial completion of doctoral program. *Degree requirements:* For master's, comprehensive exam, field consulting project (for MBA, FEMBA, EMBA, UCLA-NUS EMBA, MFE, and MSBA); internship (for MBA only); for doctorate, comprehensive exam, thesis/dissertation, oral and written qualifying exams. *Entrance requirements:* For master's, GMAT or GRE (for MBA, MFE, MSBA); Executive Assessment (EA) for candidates with 10+ years of work experience (FEMBA); Executive Assessment (EA) or STEM Master's degree or JD, MBA, CPA (EMBA), 4-year bachelor's degree or equivalent; 2 letters of recommendation; interview (invitation only); 2 essays; average 4-8 years of full-time work experience (for FEMBA); minimum 8 years of work experience with at least 3 years at management level (for EMBA); 10 years of full-time high managerial responsibility work experience (UCLA-NUS EMBA); for doctorate, GMAT or GRE, bachelor's degree from college or university of fully-recognized standing, minimum B average during junior and senior undergraduate years, 3 letters of recommendation, statement of purpose. Additional exam requirements/recommendations for international students: Required—TOEFL (minimum score 560 paper-based; 87 iBT), IELTS (minimum score 7), TOEFL with minimum iBT score of 100 (for MSBA). *Application deadline:* For fall admission, 10/2 for domestic and international students; for winter admission, 1/8 for domestic and international students; for spring admission, 4/16 for domestic and international students. Applications are processed on a rolling basis. Application fee: $200. Electronic applications accepted. *Expenses:* Per Year - MBA: $64,292, FEMBA: $42,420, EMBA: $81,120, UCLA-NUS EMBA (UC Portion only): $57,500, MFE: $75,816, MSBA: $64,1,43, PhD: $32,049. *Financial support:* Fellowships, research assistantships with partial tuition reimbursements, teaching assistantships with partial tuition reimbursements, career-related internships or fieldwork, institutionally sponsored loans, and scholarships/grants available. Support available to part-time students. *Faculty research:* Finance/global economics, entrepreneurship, accounting, human resources/organizational behavior, marketing and behavioral decision making. *Total annual research expenditures:* $2 million. *Unit head:* Dr. Antonio Bernardo, Dean & John E. Anderson Chair in Management, 310-825-7982, Fax: 310-206-2073, E-mail: a.bernardo@anderson.ucla.edu. *Application contact:* Alex Lawrence, Assistant Dean and Director of MBA Admissions, 310-825-6944, Fax: 310-825-8582, E-mail: mba.admissions@anderson.ucla.edu.
Website: http://www.anderson.ucla.edu/

University of California, Riverside, Graduate Division, The A. Gary Anderson Graduate School of Management, Riverside, CA 92521-0102. Offers accounting (MPAC); business administration (MBA, PhD); finance (M Fin). *Accreditation:* AACSB. *Program availability:* Part-time, evening/weekend. Terminal master's awarded for partial completion of doctoral program. *Degree requirements:* For master's, thesis optional; for doctorate, comprehensive exam, thesis/dissertation. *Entrance requirements:* For master's and doctorate, GMAT or GRE. Additional exam requirements/recommendations for international students: Required—TOEFL (minimum score 550 paper-based; 80 iBT), IELTS (minimum score 7). Electronic applications accepted. *Expenses:* Contact institution. *Faculty research:* Finance, management, marketing, operations and supply chain management, accounting and information systems.

University of California, San Diego, Graduate Division, Rady School of Management, La Jolla, CA 92093. Offers business administration (MBA); business analytics (MS); finance (MF); management (PhD). *Accreditation:* AACSB. *Program availability:* Part-time, evening/weekend. *Faculty:* 28 full-time (5 women), 5 part-time/adjunct (1 woman). *Students:* 452 full-time (206 women), 158 part-time (91 women). 2,403 applicants, 34% accepted, 336 enrolled. In 2018, 297 master's, 3 doctorates awarded. *Degree requirements:* For master's, capstone project; for doctorate, comprehensive exam, thesis/dissertation. *Entrance requirements:* For master's, GMAT (for MBA); GMAT or GRE General Test (for MF and MPAC); for doctorate, GMAT or GRE General Test. Additional exam requirements/recommendations for international students: Required—TOEFL (minimum score 550 paper-based; 80 iBT), IELTS (minimum score 7). *Application deadline:* Applications are processed on a rolling basis. Application fee: $200. Electronic applications accepted. *Expenses:* Contact institution. *Financial support:* Fellowships, teaching assistantships, and scholarships/grants available. Financial award applicants required to submit FAFSA. *Faculty research:* Innovation technology, operations management, finance, behavioral economics, organizational strategy, marketing, business analytics. *Unit head:* Robert Sullivan, Dean, 858-822-0830, E-mail: rssullivan@ucsd.edu. *Application contact:* Jay Bryant, Director of Graduate Recruitment and Admissions, 858-534-0864, E-mail: radygradadmissions@ucsd.edu.
Website: http://rady.ucsd.edu/

University of California, Santa Barbara, Graduate Division, College of Letters and Sciences, Division of Social Sciences, Department of Economics, Santa Barbara, CA 93106-9210. Offers economics (MA); mathematical economics (PhD); public finance (PhD); MA/PhD. Terminal master's awarded for partial completion of doctoral program. *Degree requirements:* For master's, comprehensive exam; for doctorate, comprehensive exam, thesis/dissertation. *Entrance requirements:* For master's and doctorate, GRE General Test, 3 letters of recommendation, statement of purpose, personal achievements/contributions statement, resume/curriculum vitae, transcripts for post-secondary institutions attended. Additional exam requirements/recommendations for international students: Required—TOEFL (minimum score 550 paper-based; 80 iBT), IELTS (minimum score 7), TOEFL (minimum score 600 paper-based or 100 iBT) for PhD. Electronic applications accepted. *Faculty research:* Labor economics, econometrics, macroeconomic theory and policy, environmental and natural resources economics, experimental and behavioral economics.

University of California, Santa Cruz, Division of Graduate Studies, Division of Social Sciences, Program in Applied Economics and Finance, Santa Cruz, CA 95064. Offers MS. *Degree requirements:* For master's, thesis or alternative, project. *Entrance requirements:* For master's, GRE General Test, GRE Subject Test. Additional exam requirements/recommendations for international students: Required—TOEFL (minimum score 550 paper-based; 83 iBT); Recommended—IELTS (minimum score 8). Electronic applications accepted. *Faculty research:* Economic decision-making skills for the design and operation of complex institutional systems.

University of Central Missouri, The Graduate School, Warrensburg, MO 64093. Offers accountancy (MA); accounting (MBA); applied mathematics (MS); aviation safety (MA); biology (MS); business administration (MBA); career and technical education leadership (MS); college student personnel administration (MS); communication (MA); computer science (MS); counseling (MS); criminal justice (MS); educational leadership (Ed D); educational technology (MS); elementary and early childhood education (MSE); English

(MA); environmental studies (MA); finance (MBA); history (MA); human services/educational technology (Ed S); human services/learning resources (Ed S); human services/professional counseling (Ed S); industrial hygiene (MS); industrial management (MS); information systems (MBA); information technology (MS); kinesiology (MS); library science and information services (MS); literacy education (MSE); marketing (MBA); mathematics (MS); music (MA); occupational safety management (MS); psychology (MS); rural family nursing (MS); school administration (MSE); social gerontology (MS); sociology (MA); special education (MSE); speech language pathology (MS); superintendency (Ed S); teaching (MAT); teaching English as a second language (MA); technology (MS); technology management (PhD); theatre (MA). *Accreditation:* ASHA. *Program availability:* Part-time, 100% online, blended/hybrid learning. *Degree requirements:* For master's and Ed S, comprehensive exam (for some programs), thesis (for some programs). *Entrance requirements:* Additional exam requirements/recommendations for international students: Required—TOEFL (minimum score 550 paper-based; 79 iBT). Electronic applications accepted.

University of Chicago, Booth School of Business, Full-Time MBA Program, Chicago, IL 60637. Offers accounting (MBA); analytic finance (MBA); analytic management (MBA); econometrics and statistics (MBA); economics (MBA); entrepreneurship (MBA); finance (MBA); general management (MBA); health administration and policy (Certificate); international business (MBA); managerial and organizational behavior (MBA); marketing analytics (MBA); marketing management (MBA); operations management (MBA); strategic management (MBA); MBA/AM; MBA/JD; MBA/MA; MBA/MD; MBA/MPP. *Accreditation:* AACSB. *Entrance requirements:* For master's, GMAT or GRE, transcripts, resume, 2 letters of recommendation, essays, interview. Additional exam requirements/recommendations for international students: Required—TOEFL, IELTS, or PTE. Electronic applications accepted. *Expenses:* Contact institution.

University of Cincinnati, Carl H. Lindner College of Business, MS Program, Cincinnati, OH 45221. Offers accounting (MS); applied economics (MS); business analytics (MS); finance (MS); information systems (MS); marketing (MS); taxation (MS). *Program availability:* Part-time, evening/weekend. *Faculty:* 98 full-time (27 women), 28 part-time/adjunct (4 women). *Students:* 305 full-time (123 women), 190 part-time (83 women); includes 35 minority (13 Black or African American, non-Hispanic/Latino; 1 American Indian or Alaska Native, non-Hispanic/Latino; 10 Asian, non-Hispanic/Latino; 6 Hispanic/Latino; 5 Two or more races, non-Hispanic/Latino), 309 international. Average age 29. 1,219 applicants, 55% accepted, 495 enrolled. In 2018, 355 master's awarded. *Degree requirements:* For master's, thesis (for some programs), capstone. *Entrance requirements:* For master's, GMAT, GRE, resume, transcripts, essays, letters of recommendation. Additional exam requirements/recommendations for international students: Required—TOEFL (minimum score 577 paper-based; 90 iBT), IELTS (minimum score 6.5). *Application deadline:* For fall admission, 6/30 priority date for domestic students, 3/15 for international students; for spring admission, 12/15 for domestic students, 9/15 for international students; for summer admission, 4/15 for domestic and international students. Applications are processed on a rolling basis. Application fee: $65 ($70 for international students). Electronic applications accepted. *Expenses:* Full-time resident $10,479 per term, full-time nonresident $14,398 per term, part-time $890 per credit hour. *Financial support:* In 2018–19, 251 students received support, including 12 teaching assistantships with full and partial tuition reimbursements available (averaging $3,500 per year); scholarships/grants, tuition waivers (full and partial), and unspecified assistantships also available. Financial award application deadline: 2/1; financial award applicants required to submit FAFSA. *Faculty research:* Business analytics, financial management, organizational behavior, financial accounting, consumer insights. *Total annual research expenditures:* $39,943. *Unit head:* Dr. Marianne Lewis, Dean, 513-556-7001; Fax: 513-556-4891, E-mail: marianne.lewis@uc.edu. *Application contact:* Dona Clary, Executive Director, Graduate Programs, 513-556-3546, Fax: 513-558-7006, E-mail: dona.clary@uc.edu.
Website: http://business.uc.edu/graduate/masters.html

University of Cincinnati, Carl H. Lindner College of Business, PhD Programs, Cincinnati, OH 45221. Offers accounting (PhD); business analytics (PhD); economics (PhD); finance (PhD); information systems (PhD); management (PhD); marketing (PhD); operations and business analytics (PhD); operations research (PhD). *Faculty:* 101 full-time (37 women). *Students:* 15 full-time (5 women), 10 part-time (4 women); includes 4 minority (1 Black or African American, non-Hispanic/Latino; 3 Asian, non-Hispanic/Latino), 20 international. Average age 31. 125 applicants, 12% accepted, 4 enrolled. In 2018, 7 doctorates awarded. *Degree requirements:* For doctorate, comprehensive exam, thesis/dissertation. *Entrance requirements:* For doctorate, GMAT, GRE, transcripts, essays, resume, letters of recommendation. Additional exam requirements/recommendations for international students: Required—TOEFL (minimum score 600 paper-based; 100 iBT), IELTS (minimum score 7). *Application deadline:* For fall admission, 1/15 for domestic and international students. Application fee: $65 ($70 for international students). Electronic applications accepted. *Expenses:* Contact institution. *Financial support:* In 2018–19, 35 students received support, including 25 research assistantships with full tuition reimbursements available (averaging $23,250 per year); scholarships/grants, health care benefits, tuition waivers (full), and unspecified assistantships also available. Financial award application deadline: 1/15; financial award applicants required to submit FAFSA. *Faculty research:* Bayesian Prediction Theory, organizational fairness, consumer insight and market research, consumer insight and market research, density estimation from correlated data. *Unit head:* Dr. Olivier Parent, Director, 513-556-3941, Fax: 513-556-5499, E-mail: olivier.parent@uc.edu. *Application contact:* Angel Elvin, Assistant Director, 513-556-7190, Fax: 513-558-7006, E-mail: angel.elvin@uc.edu.
Website: http://business.uc.edu/graduate/phd.html

University of Colorado Denver, Business School, Program in Finance, Denver, CO 80217. Offers economics (MS); finance (MS); financial analysis and management (MS); financial and commodities risk management (MS); risk management and insurance (MS). *Program availability:* Part-time, evening/weekend. *Degree requirements:* For master's, 30 semester hours (18 of required core courses, 9 of finance electives, and 3 of free elective). *Entrance requirements:* For master's, GMAT, essay, resume, two letters of recommendation; financial statements (for international students). Additional exam requirements/recommendations for international students: Required—TOEFL (minimum score 537 paper-based; 75 iBT); Recommended—IELTS (minimum score 6.5). Electronic applications accepted. *Expenses:* Contact institution. *Faculty research:* Corporate governance, debt maturity policies, regulation and financial markets, option management strategies.

University of Connecticut, Graduate School, College of Liberal Arts and Sciences, Department of Public Policy, Storrs, CT 06269. Offers public administration (MPA, Graduate Certificate), including nonprofit management (Graduate Certificate), public financial management (Graduate Certificate); survey research (MA, Graduate Certificate), including quantitative research methods (Graduate Certificate), survey research (MA); JD/MPA; MPA/MSW. *Degree requirements:* For master's, comprehensive exam. *Entrance requirements:* For master's, GRE General Test. Additional exam requirements/recommendations for international students: Required—TOEFL (minimum score 550 paper-based). Electronic applications accepted.

University of Connecticut, Graduate School, School of Business, Storrs, CT 06269. Offers accounting (MS, PhD); business (PhD); business administration (MBA); business analytics and project management (MS); finance (PhD); financial risk management (MS); health care management and insurance studies (MBA); human resource management (MS); management (PhD); management consulting (MBA); marketing (PhD); marketing intelligence (MBA); operations and information management (PhD). *Accreditation:* AACSB. *Degree requirements:* For master's, comprehensive exam; for doctorate, thesis/dissertation. *Entrance requirements:* For master's and doctorate, GMAT. Additional exam requirements/recommendations for international students: Required—TOEFL (minimum score 550 paper-based). Electronic applications accepted.

University of Dallas, Satish and Yasmin Gupta College of Business, Irving, TX 75062. Offers accounting (MBA, MS); business administration (DBA); business analytics (MS); business management (MBA); corporate finance (MBA); cybersecurity (MS); finance (MS); financial services (MBA); global business (MBA, MS); health services management (MBA); human resource management (MBA); information and technology management (MS); information assurance (MBA); information technology (MBA); information technology service management (MBA); marketing management (MBA); organization development (MBA); project management (MBA); sports and entertainment management (MBA); strategic leadership (MBA); supply chain management (MBA). *Accreditation:* AACSB. *Program availability:* Part-time, evening/weekend, 100% online. *Students:* 147 full-time (56 women), 584 part-time (232 women); includes 402 minority (204 Black or African American, non-Hispanic/Latino; 95 Asian, non-Hispanic/Latino; 92 Hispanic/Latino; 2 Native Hawaiian or other Pacific Islander, non-Hispanic/Latino; 9 Two or more races, non-Hispanic/Latino), 113 international. Average age 34. 992 applicants, 30% accepted, 157 enrolled. In 2018, 336 master's, 5 doctorates awarded. *Degree requirements:* For doctorate, thesis/dissertation. *Entrance requirements:* For master's and doctorate, U.S. bachelor's degree with a minimum cumulative GPA of 2.0 from a regionally accredited college or university (or comparable foreign degree); minimum 3.0 GPA in any graduate-level coursework completed; good academic standing with all colleges attended. Additional exam requirements/recommendations for international students: Required—TOEFL (minimum score 80 iBT), IELTS (minimum score 6.5), PTE (minimum score 67). *Application deadline:* Applications are processed on a rolling basis. Application fee: $50. Electronic applications accepted. *Expenses:* $1250 per credit hour. *Financial support:* In 2018–19, 291 students received support. Research assistantships, teaching assistantships, scholarships/grants, and unspecified assistantships available. Support available to part-time students. Financial award application deadline: 2/15; financial award applicants required to submit FAFSA. *Unit head:* Brett J.L. Landry, Dean, 972-721-5356, E-mail: blandry@udallas.edu. *Application contact:* Breonna Collins, Director, Graduate Admissions, 972-7215304, E-mail: bcollins@udallas.edu. Website: http://www.udallas.edu/cob/

University of Dayton, School of Business Administration, Dayton, OH 45469. Offers accounting (MBA); cyber security (MBA); finance (MBA); marketing (MBA); JD/MBA. *Accreditation:* AACSB. *Program availability:* Part-time, evening/weekend, blended/hybrid learning. *Entrance requirements:* For master's, GMAT (minimum score of 500 total, 19 verbal); GRE (minimum score of 149 verbal, 146 quantitative), minimum GPA of 3.0, current resume. Additional exam requirements/recommendations for international students: Required—TOEFL (minimum score 550 paper-based; 80 iBT); Recommended—IELTS (minimum score 6.5). Electronic applications accepted. *Expenses:* Contact institution. *Faculty research:* Management information systems, economics, finance, marketing, entrepreneurship, accounting, cyber security, analytics.

University of Delaware, Alfred Lerner College of Business and Economics, Department of Finance, Newark, DE 19716. Offers MS.

University of Denver, Daniels College of Business, Reiman School of Finance, Denver, CO 80208. Offers applied quantitative finance (MS); finance (MBA). *Program availability:* Part-time, evening/weekend. *Faculty:* 16 full-time (4 women). *Students:* 35 full-time (14 women), 26 part-time (12 women); includes 11 minority (1 American Indian or Alaska Native, non-Hispanic/Latino; 3 Asian, non-Hispanic/Latino; 4 Hispanic/Latino; 1 Native Hawaiian or other Pacific Islander, non-Hispanic/Latino; 2 Two or more races, non-Hispanic/Latino), 28 international. Average age 26. 144 applicants, 53% accepted, 32 enrolled. In 2018, 33 master's awarded. *Entrance requirements:* For master's, GRE General Test or GMAT, bachelor's degree, transcripts, resume, essays, interview. Additional exam requirements/recommendations for international students: Required—TOEFL (minimum score 575 paper-based; 94 iBT). *Application deadline:* For fall admission, 10/15 priority date for domestic and international students; for spring admission, 9/15 priority date for domestic and international students. Applications are processed on a rolling basis. Application fee: $100. Electronic applications accepted. *Expenses:* $49,695 per year full-time; $1,372 per credit. *Financial support:* In 2018–19, 50 students received support. Teaching assistantships with tuition reimbursements available, career-related internships or fieldwork, Federal Work-Study, institutionally sponsored loans, scholarships/grants, tuition waivers, and unspecified assistantships available. Support available to part-time students. Financial award application deadline: 2/15; financial award applicants required to submit FAFSA. *Faculty research:* Sector forecasting, analysts estimates and guidance, derivatives, SEC comment letters, corporate governance. *Unit head:* Dr. Conrad Ciccotello, Director, 303-871-2282, E-mail: conrad.ciccotello@du.edu. *Application contact:* Claudia Walinder, Office Manager, 303-871-3322, E-mail: claudia.walinder@du.edu.
Website: https://daniels.du.edu/finance

University of Detroit Mercy, College of Business Administration, Detroit, MI 48221. Offers business administration (MBA); business fundamentals (Certificate); business turnaround management (Certificate); ethical leadership and change management (Certificate); finance (Certificate); forensic accounting (Certificate); JD/MBA; MBA/MHSA. *Program availability:* Part-time, evening/weekend, 100% online, blended/hybrid learning. *Entrance requirements:* For master's, GMAT, resume, letter of recommendation, transcripts; for Certificate, resume, letter of recommendation, transcripts. Electronic applications accepted. Application fee is waived when completed online. *Expenses:* Contact institution. *Faculty research:* Ethics, international finance, trade policy, leadership, information technology.

University of Detroit Mercy, College of Liberal Arts and Education, Detroit, MI 48221. Offers addiction counseling (MA); addiction studies (Certificate); clinical mental health counseling (MA); clinical psychology (MA, PhD); computer and information systems (MS); criminal justice (MA); curriculum and instruction (MA); economics (MA); educational administration (MA); financial economics (MA); industrial/organizational psychology (MA); information assurance (MS); intelligence analysis (MA); liberal studies (MALS); religious studies (MA); school counseling (MA, Certificate); school psychology (Spec); security administration (MS); special education: emotionally impaired/behaviorally disordered (MA); special education: learning disabilities (MA). *Program availability:* Part-time, evening/weekend. *Degree requirements:* For doctorate, departmental qualifying exam. *Faculty research:* Psychology of aging, history of technology, Renaissance humanism, U.S. and Japanese economic relations.

University of Florida, Graduate School, Warrington College of Business Administration, Hough Graduate School of Business, Department of Finance, Insurance and Real Estate, Gainesville, FL 32611. Offers entrepreneurship (MS); finance (MS, PhD); financial services (Certificate); insurance (PhD); quantitative finance (PhD); real

estate (MS); real estate and urban analysis (PhD); JD/MBA; JD/MS. Terminal master's awarded for partial completion of doctoral program. *Degree requirements:* For master's, comprehensive exam, thesis; for doctorate, comprehensive exam, thesis/dissertation. *Entrance requirements:* For master's, GMAT (minimum score of 465) or GRE General Test, minimum GPA of 3.0 for last 60 hours of undergraduate degree, work experience (preferred); for doctorate, GMAT (minimum score of 465) or GRE General Test, minimum GPA of 3.0. Additional exam requirements/recommendations for international students: Required—TOEFL (minimum score 550 paper-based; 80 iBT), IELTS (minimum score 6). Electronic applications accepted. *Faculty research:* Banking, empirical corporate finance, hedge funds.

University of Florida, Graduate School, Warrington College of Business Administration, Hough Graduate School of Business, Programs in Business Administration, Gainesville, FL 32611. Offers business administration (MA, MS, PhD); competitive strategy (MBA); finance (MBA); global management (MBA); Graham-Buffett security analysis (MBA); human resource management (MBA); information systems and operations management (MBA); international studies (MBA); management (MBA); real estate (MBA); JD/MBA; MBA/MS; MBA/PhD; MBA/Pharm D; MD/MBA. *Accreditation:* AACSB. *Program availability:* Part-time, evening/weekend, online learning. *Degree requirements:* For master's, capstone course. *Entrance requirements:* For master's and doctorate, GMAT (minimum score 465), minimum GPA of 3.0, interview. Additional exam requirements/recommendations for international students: Required—TOEFL (minimum score 550 paper-based; 80 iBT), IELTS (minimum score 6). Electronic applications accepted. *Faculty research:* Accounting, finance, insurance, management, real estate, urban analysis marketing.

University of Hawaii at Manoa, Office of Graduate Education, Shidler College of Business, Program in Business Administration, Honolulu, HI 96822. Offers Asian business studies (MBA); Chinese business studies (MBA); decision sciences (MBA); entrepreneurship (MBA); finance (MBA); finance and banking (MBA); human resources management (MBA); information management (MBA); information technology (MBA); international business (MBA); Japanese business studies (MBA); marketing (MBA); organizational behavior (MBA); organizational management (MBA); real estate (MBA); student-designed track (MBA). *Accreditation:* AACSB. *Program availability:* Part-time, evening/weekend. *Degree requirements:* For master's, thesis optional. *Entrance requirements:* For master's, GMAT, minimum GPA of 3.0. Additional exam requirements/recommendations for international students: Required—TOEFL (minimum score 600 paper-based; 100 iBT), IELTS (minimum score 7). *Expenses:* Contact institution.

University of Hawaii at Manoa, Office of Graduate Education, Shidler College of Business, Program in International Management, Honolulu, HI 96822. Offers Asian finance (PhD); global information technology management (PhD); international accounting (PhD); international marketing (PhD); international organization and strategy (PhD). *Program availability:* Part-time. *Degree requirements:* For doctorate, comprehensive exam, thesis/dissertation. *Entrance requirements:* For doctorate, GMAT or GRE General Test, minimum GPA of 3.0. Additional exam requirements/recommendations for international students: Required—TOEFL (minimum score 600 paper-based; 100 iBT), IELTS (minimum score 7). *Expenses:* Contact institution.

University of Houston, Bauer College of Business, Finance Program, Houston, TX 77204. Offers MS. *Program availability:* Part-time, evening/weekend. *Degree requirements:* For master's, 30 hours completed in residence, minimum cumulative GPA of 3.0 at UH, no more than 11 semester hours of 'C' grades or below in graduate courses taken at UH. *Entrance requirements:* For master's, GMAT or GRE, official transcripts from all higher education institutions attended, resume, goal statement, letters of recommendation. Additional exam requirements/recommendations for international students: Required—TOEFL (minimum score 620 paper-based; 105 iBT), IELTS (minimum score 7.5). Electronic applications accepted. *Faculty research:* Accountancy and taxation, finance, international business, management.

University of Houston–Clear Lake, School of Business, Program in Finance, Houston, TX 77058-1002. Offers MS. *Program availability:* Part-time, evening/weekend. *Degree requirements:* For master's, thesis optional. *Entrance requirements:* For master's, GMAT. Additional exam requirements/recommendations for international students: Required—TOEFL (minimum score 550 paper-based). Electronic applications accepted.

University of Houston–Downtown, Marilyn Davies College of Business, MBA Program, Houston, TX 77002. Offers accounting (MBA); finance (MBA); human resource management (MBA); international business (MBA); investment management (MBA); leadership (MBA); project management and process improvement (MBA); sales management and business development (MBA); supply chain management (MBA). *Accreditation:* AACSB. *Program availability:* Part-time, evening/weekend. *Entrance requirements:* For master's, GMAT, two letters of recommendation from professional references, personal statement, resume. Additional exam requirements/recommendations for international students: Required—TOEFL (minimum score 81 iBT). Electronic applications accepted. *Expenses:* Contact institution.

University of Houston–Victoria, School of Business Administration, Victoria, TX 77901-4450. Offers accounting (MBA); economic development and entrepreneurship (MS); finance (GMBA, MBA); general business (MBA); international business (MBA); management (GMBA, MBA); marketing (MBA). *Accreditation:* AACSB. *Program availability:* Part-time, evening/weekend, online learning. *Entrance requirements:* For master's, GMAT. Additional exam requirements/recommendations for international students: Required—TOEFL (minimum score 550 paper-based). Electronic applications accepted. *Expenses: Tuition, area resident:* Full-time $6154; part-time $3077 per semester. Tuition, state resident: full-time $6154; part-time $3077 per semester. Tuition, nonresident: full-time $13,624; part-time $6812 per semester. *International tuition:* $13,624 full-time. *Required fees:* $1405; $847 per semester. $423 per semester. Tuition and fees vary according to program. *Faculty research:* Economic development, marketing, finance.

University of Illinois at Chicago, Liautaud Graduate School of Business, Department of Finance, Chicago, IL 60607-7128. Offers MS. *Entrance requirements:* Additional exam requirements/recommendations for international students: Required—TOEFL. Electronic applications accepted. *Expenses:* Contact institution. *Faculty research:* Global financial markets.

University of Illinois at Urbana–Champaign, Graduate College, Gies College of Business, Department of Finance, Champaign, IL 61820. Offers MS, PhD.

The University of Iowa, Tippie College of Business, Department of Finance, Iowa City, IA 52242-1316. Offers PhD. *Degree requirements:* For doctorate, comprehensive exam, thesis/dissertation. *Entrance requirements:* For doctorate, GMAT or GRE. Additional exam requirements/recommendations for international students: Required—TOEFL (minimum score 100 iBT) or IELTS (minimum score 7.0). Electronic applications accepted. *Faculty research:* International finance, real estate finance, theoretical and empirical corporate finance, theoretical and empirical asset pricing, bond pricing and derivatives.

The University of Iowa, Tippie College of Business, MS Program in Finance, Iowa City, IA 52242-1316. Offers MS. *Expenses:* Contact institution.

The University of Iowa, Tippie College of Business, Professional MBA Program, Iowa City, IA 52242-1316. Offers business administration (MBA); business analytics (MBA); finance (MBA); leadership (MBA); marketing (MBA). *Program availability:* Part-time-only, evening/weekend. *Degree requirements:* For master's, successful completion of nine required courses and six electives totaling 45 credits, minimum GPA of 2.75. *Entrance requirements:* For master's, GMAT or GRE. Additional exam requirements/recommendations for international students: Required—TOEFL (minimum score 600 paper-based; 100 iBT), IELTS (minimum score 7). Electronic applications accepted. *Expenses:* Contact institution. *Faculty research:* Capital markets; analytics techniques and applications; organizational and market systems analysis; applied econometrics; talent effectiveness.

The University of Kansas, Graduate Studies, School of Business, Program in Business, Lawrence, KS 66045. Offers business and organizational leadership (MS); decision sciences and supply chain management (PhD); finance (PhD); human resources management (PhD); marketing (PhD); organizational behavior (PhD); strategic management (PhD); supply chain management and logistics (MS). *Accreditation:* AACSB. *Program availability:* Part-time. *Students:* 69 full-time (20 women), 150 part-time (62 women); includes 42 minority (14 Black or African American, non-Hispanic/Latino; 2 American Indian or Alaska Native, non-Hispanic/Latino; 6 Asian, non-Hispanic/Latino; 7 Hispanic/Latino; 13 Two or more races, non-Hispanic/Latino), 24 international. Average age 32. 306 applicants, 51% accepted, 132 enrolled. In 2018, 22 master's, 1 doctorate awarded. *Entrance requirements:* For master's, GMAT, official transcript, three letters of recommendation, resume, statement of purpose; for doctorate, GMAT or GRE, official transcript, three letters of recommendation, resume, statement of purpose. Additional exam requirements/recommendations for international students: Required—TOEFL, IELTS. *Application deadline:* For fall admission, 1/10 for domestic and international students. Application fee: $65 ($85 for international students). Electronic applications accepted. *Financial support:* Fellowships, research assistantships, teaching assistantships, scholarships/grants, health care benefits, tuition waivers (full), and unspecified assistantships available. Financial award application deadline: 1/10. *Faculty research:* Strategic human resource management, business ethics, organizational theory/behavior, corporate strategy, international business, supply chain management, Bayesian networks, game theory, decision analysis and time/series analysis, pricing, consumer effects, advertising and emotion. *Unit head:* Charly Edmonds, Director, 785-864-3841, E-mail: cedmonds@ku.edu. *Application contact:* Andrea Noltner, Graduate Admission Contact, 785-864-7556, E-mail: anoltner@ku.edu. Website: http://www.business.ku.edu/

University of La Verne, College of Business and Public Management, Graduate Programs in Business Administration, La Verne, CA 91750-4443. Offers accounting (MBA, MBA-EP); finance (MBA, MBA-EP); health services management (MBA); information technology (MBA, MBA-EP); international business (MBA, MBA-EP); management and leadership (MBA, MBA-EP); marketing (MBA, MBA-EP); supply chain management (MBA, MBA-EP). *Program availability:* Part-time, evening/weekend. *Entrance requirements:* For master's, GMAT, MAT, or GRE, minimum undergraduate GPA of 3.0, 2 letters of recommendation, resume, statement of purpose. Additional exam requirements/recommendations for international students: Required—TOEFL (minimum score 550 paper-based; 85 iBT).

University of La Verne, College of Business and Public Management, Program in Finance, La Verne, CA 91750-4443. Offers MS. *Program availability:* Part-time. *Entrance requirements:* For master's, bachelor's degree, minimum preferred GPA of 3.0, 2 recommendations, resume, personal statement. Additional exam requirements/recommendations for international students: Required—TOEFL (minimum score 550 paper-based; 79 iBT). *Expenses:* Contact institution.

University of La Verne, Regional and Online Campuses, Graduate Programs, Inland Empire Campus, Ontario, CA 91730. Offers business administration (MBA, MBA-EP), including accounting (MBA), finance (MBA), health services management (MBA-EP), information technology (MBA-EP), international business (MBA), managed care (MBA), management and leadership (MBA-EP), marketing (MBA-EP), supply chain management (MBA); leadership and management (MS), including human resource management, nonprofit management, organizational development. *Program availability:* Part-time, evening/weekend. *Expenses:* Contact institution.

University of Lethbridge, School of Graduate Studies, Lethbridge, AB T1K 3M4, Canada. Offers addictions counseling (M Sc); agricultural biotechnology (M Sc); agricultural studies (M Sc, MA); anthropology (MA); archaeology (M Sc, MA); art (MA, MFA); biochemistry (M Sc); biological sciences (M Sc); biomolecular science (PhD); biosystems and biodiversity (PhD); Canadian studies (MA); chemistry (M Sc); computer science (M Sc); computer science and geographical information science (M Sc); counseling (MC); counseling psychology (M Ed); dramatic arts (MA); earth, space, and physical science (PhD); economics (MA); education (MA, PhD); educational leadership (M Ed); English (MA); environmental science (M Sc); evolution and behavior (PhD); exercise science (M Sc); French (MA); French/German (MA); French/Spanish (MA); general education (M Ed); geography (M Sc, MA); German (MA); health sciences (M Sc); individualized multidisciplinary (M Sc, MA); kinesiology (M Sc, MA); management (M Sc), including accounting, finance, human resource management and labor relations, information systems, international management, marketing, policy and strategy; mathematics (M Sc); music (M Mus, MA); Native American studies (MA); neuroscience (M Sc, PhD); new media (MA, MFA); nursing (M Sc, MN); philosophy (MA); physics (M Sc); political science (MA); psychology (M Sc, MA); religious studies (MA); sociology (MA); theatre and dramatic arts (MFA); theoretical and computational science (PhD); urban and regional studies (MA); women and gender studies (MA). *Program availability:* Part-time, evening/weekend. *Degree requirements:* For master's, thesis (for some programs); for doctorate, comprehensive exam, thesis/dissertation. *Entrance requirements:* For master's, GMAT (for M Sc in management), bachelor's degree in related field, minimum GPA of 3.0 during previous 20 graded semester courses, 2 years' teaching or related experience (M Ed); for doctorate, master's degree, minimum graduate GPA of 3.5. Additional exam requirements/recommendations for international students: Required—TOEFL (minimum score 580 paper-based; 93 iBT). Electronic applications accepted. *Faculty research:* Movement and brain plasticity, gibberellin physiology, photosynthesis, carbon cycling, molecular properties of main-group ring components.

University of Louisiana at Lafayette, BI Moody III College of Business Administration, Lafayette, LA 70504. Offers accounting (MS); business administration (MBA); entrepreneurship (MBA); finance (MBA); global management (MBA); health care administration (MBA); hospitality management (MBA); human resource management (MBA); project management (MBA); sales leadership (MBA). *Accreditation:* AACSB. *Program availability:* Part-time, evening/weekend. *Entrance requirements:* For master's, GRE General Test. Additional exam requirements/recommendations for international students: Required—TOEFL (minimum score 550 paper-based).

University of Maine, Graduate School, College of Natural Sciences, Forestry, and Agriculture, School of Economics, Orono, ME 04469. Offers economics (MA); financial economics (MA); resource economics and policy (MS). *Program availability:* Part-time. *Faculty:* 12 full-time (4 women), 2 part-time/adjunct (0 women). *Students:* 25 full-time (13 women); includes 1 minority (Asian, non-Hispanic/Latino), 5 international. Average

age 25. 20 applicants, 90% accepted, 11 enrolled. In 2018, 12 master's awarded. *Degree requirements:* For master's, thesis (for some programs). *Entrance requirements:* For master's, GRE General Test. Additional exam requirements/recommendations for international students: Required—TOEFL (minimum score 580 paper-based; 92 iBT), IELTS (minimum score 6.9). *Application deadline:* For spring admission, 1/30 for domestic and international students. Applications are processed on a rolling basis. Application fee: $65. Electronic applications accepted. *Financial support:* In 2018–19, 14 students received support, including 8 research assistantships with full tuition reimbursements available (averaging $16,000 per year), 5 teaching assistantships with full tuition reimbursements available (averaging $15,600 per year); career-related internships or fieldwork, Federal Work-Study, institutionally sponsored loans, scholarships/grants, and tuition waivers (full and partial) also available. Support available to part-time students. Financial award application deadline: 3/1. *Faculty research:* Environmental and resource economics, environmental behavior, sustainability science. *Total annual research expenditures:* $780,303. *Unit head:* Dr. Mario Teisl, Director, 207-581-3151, Fax: 207-581-4278. *Application contact:* Scott G. Delcourt, Assistant Vice President for Graduate Studies and Senior Associate Dean, 207-581-3291, Fax: 207-581-3232, E-mail: graduate@maine.edu.
Website: http://umaine.edu/soe/

The University of Manchester, Alliance Manchester Business School, M15 6PB, United Kingdom. Offers accounting and finance (M Sc); business (M Ent); business analysis and strategic management (M Sc); business analytics: operational research and risk analysis (M Sc); business psychology (M Sc); corporate communications and reputation management (M Sc); finance (M Sc); finance and business economics (M Sc); human resource management and industrial relations (M Sc); innovation management and entrepreneurship (M Sc); international business and management (M Sc); international human resource management and comparative industrial relations (M Sc); management (M Sc); marketing (M Sc); operations, project and supply chain management (M Sc); organizational psychology (M Sc); quantitative finance (M Sc). *Entrance requirements:* For master's, UK 2:1 honours degree or overseas equivalent. Additional exam requirements/recommendations for international students: Required—TOEFL (minimum score 100 iBT), IELTS (minimum score 7), PTE. Electronic applications accepted. *Faculty research:* Accounting and finance, management sciences and marketing, people management and organization, innovation management and policy, decision sciences.

University of Maryland University College, The Graduate School, Program in Accounting and Financial Management, Adelphi, MD 20783. Offers MS. *Accreditation:* AACSB. *Program availability:* Part-time, evening/weekend, online learning. *Students:* 12 full-time (7 women), 497 part-time (313 women); includes 291 minority (196 Black or African American, non-Hispanic/Latino; 4 American Indian or Alaska Native, non-Hispanic/Latino; 34 Asian, non-Hispanic/Latino; 39 Hispanic/Latino; 1 Native Hawaiian or other Pacific Islander, non-Hispanic/Latino; 17 Two or more races, non-Hispanic/Latino), 17 international. Average age 36. 169 applicants, 100% accepted, 127 enrolled. In 2018, 84 master's awarded. *Degree requirements:* For master's, thesis or alternative, capstone course. *Application deadline:* Applications are processed on a rolling basis. Application fee: $50. Electronic applications accepted. *Financial support:* Scholarships/grants available. Support available to part-time students. Financial award application deadline: 6/1; financial award applicants required to submit FAFSA. *Unit head:* Kirby Cundiff, Program Chair, 240-684-2400, E-mail: kirby.cundiff@umuc.edu. *Application contact:* Admissions, 800-888-8682, E-mail: studentsfirst@umuc.edu.
Website: https://www.umuc.edu/academic-programs/masters-degrees/accounting-and-financial-management.cfm

University of Massachusetts Amherst, Graduate School, Isenberg School of Management, Program in Management, Amherst, MA 01003. Offers accounting (PhD); business administration (MBA); entrepreneurship (MBA); finance (MBA, PhD); healthcare administration (MBA); hospitality and tourism management (PhD); management science (PhD); marketing (MBA, PhD); organization studies (PhD); sport management (PhD); strategic management (PhD); MBA/MS. *Accreditation:* AACSB. *Program availability:* Part-time, evening/weekend, online learning. Terminal master's awarded for partial completion of doctoral program. *Degree requirements:* For doctorate, comprehensive exam, thesis/dissertation. *Entrance requirements:* For master's and doctorate, GMAT or GRE General Test. Additional exam requirements/recommendations for international students: Required—TOEFL (minimum score 550 paper-based; 80 iBT), IELTS (minimum score 6.5). Electronic applications accepted.

University of Massachusetts Boston, College of Management, Program in Finance, Boston, MA 02125-3393. Offers MS. *Faculty:* 24 full-time (9 women), 7 part-time/adjunct (1 woman). *Students:* 34 full-time (14 women), 13 part-time (6 women); includes 9 minority (2 Black or African American, non-Hispanic/Latino; 6 Asian, non-Hispanic/Latino; 1 Hispanic/Latino), 27 international. Average age 29. 40 applicants, 73% accepted, 19 enrolled. In 2018, 33 master's awarded. *Application deadline:* For fall admission, 7/1 for domestic students; for spring admission, 11/15 for domestic students. *Expenses: Tuition, area resident:* Full-time $17,896. Tuition, state resident: full-time $17,896. Tuition, nonresident: full-time $34,932. *International tuition:* $34,932 full-time. *Required fees:* $355. *Unit head:* Dr. Kun Yun, Associate Professor of Accounting, 617-287.7715, E-mail: Kun.Yu@umb.edu. *Application contact:* Graduate Admissions Coordinator, 617-287-6400, Fax: 617-287-6236, E-mail: graduate.admissions@umb.edu.

University of Massachusetts Dartmouth, Graduate School, Charlton College of Business, Department of Accounting and Finance, North Dartmouth, MA 02747-2300. Offers accounting (MS, Postbaccalaureate Certificate); finance (Postbaccalaureate Certificate). *Program availability:* Part-time, 100% online, blended/hybrid learning. *Faculty:* 15 full-time (5 women), 3 part-time/adjunct (1 woman). *Students:* 22 full-time (12 women), 18 part-time (9 women); includes 10 minority (4 Asian, non-Hispanic/Latino; 3 Hispanic/Latino; 3 Two or more races, non-Hispanic/Latino), 7 international. Average age 30. 30 applicants, 87% accepted, 14 enrolled. In 2018, 31 master's awarded. *Entrance requirements:* For master's, GMAT or waiver, statement of purpose (minimum 300 words), resume, official transcript, 2 letters of recommendation; for Postbaccalaureate Certificate, statement of purpose (minimum 300 words), resume, official transcript. Additional exam requirements/recommendations for international students: Required—TOEFL (minimum score 550 paper-based; 79 iBT), IELTS (minimum score 6.5). *Application deadline:* For fall admission, 7/1 priority date for domestic students, 6/1 priority date for international students; for spring admission, 12/1 priority date for domestic students, 11/1 for international students. Application fee: $60. Electronic applications accepted. *Financial support:* Tuition waivers available. Financial award application deadline: 3/1; financial award applicants required to submit FAFSA. *Faculty research:* Accounting information systems, analytical controls in continuous auditing, accounting education, managerial accounting, e-commerce. *Unit head:* Dr. Jia Wu, Program Coordinator, Accounting, 508-999-8428, E-mail: jwu@umassd.edu. *Application contact:* Scott Webster, Director of Graduate Studies & Admissions, 508-999-8604, Fax: 508-999-8183, E-mail: graduate@umassd.edu.
Website: http://www.umassd.edu/charlton/programs/graduate/msaccounting/

University of Memphis, Graduate School, Fogelman College of Business and Economics, Program in Business Administration, Memphis, TN 38152. Offers accounting (MBA, PhD); business administration (IMBA); economics (PhD); executive business administration (MBA); finance (PhD); management (PhD); marketing (MS); marketing and supply chain management (PhD); real estate development (MS); JD/MBA. *Accreditation:* AACSB. *Students:* 189 full-time (96 women), 364 part-time (151 women); includes 178 minority (89 Black or African American, non-Hispanic/Latino; 1 American Indian or Alaska Native, non-Hispanic/Latino; 68 Asian, non-Hispanic/Latino; 12 Hispanic/Latino; 8 Two or more races, non-Hispanic/Latino), 102 international. Average age 32. 298 applicants, 72% accepted, 139 enrolled. In 2018, 200 master's, 3 doctorates awarded. *Degree requirements:* For master's, comprehensive exam; for doctorate, comprehensive exam, thesis/dissertation. *Entrance requirements:* For master's, GMAT, resume; for doctorate, GMAT, interview, minimum GPA of 3.4, resume, letter of recommendation. Additional exam requirements/recommendations for international students: Required—TOEFL (minimum score 550 paper-based). *Application deadline:* For fall admission, 8/1 for domestic students; for spring admission, 12/1 for domestic students. Application fee: $35 ($60 for international students). *Expenses: Tuition, area resident:* Full-time $10,240; part-time $503 per credit hour. Tuition, state resident: full-time $10,464. Tuition, nonresident: full-time $20,224; part-time $991 per credit hour. *Required fees:* $850; $106 per credit hour. *Financial support:* Research assistantships with full tuition reimbursements, teaching assistantships with full tuition reimbursements, career-related internships or fieldwork, Federal Work-Study, scholarships/grants, and unspecified assistantships available. Financial award application deadline: 2/15; financial award applicants required to submit FAFSA. *Faculty research:* Competitive business strategy, finance microstructures, supply chain management innovations, health care economics, litigation risks and corporate audits. *Unit head:* Dr. Balaji Krishnan, Director, MBA Programs, 901-678-2786, E-mail: krishnan@memphis.edu. *Application contact:* Dr. Balaji Krishnan, Director, MBA Programs, 901-678-2786, E-mail: krishnan@memphis.edu.
Website: https://www.memphis.edu/mba/index.php

University of Miami, Miami Business School, Coral Gables, FL 33146. Offers accounting (M Acc); business (PhD); business administration (MBA); business analytics (MSBA); economics (PhD); finance (MSF); health administration (MHA); international business (MIBS); real estate (MBA); taxation (MS Tax); JD/MBA; MD/MBA. *Accreditation:* AACSB; CAHME (one or more programs are accredited). *Program availability:* Part-time, evening/weekend, 100% online, blended/hybrid learning. *Faculty:* 155 full-time (47 women), 14 part-time/adjunct (5 women). *Students:* 1,083 full-time (469 women); includes 422 minority (79 Black or African American, non-Hispanic/Latino; 1 American Indian or Alaska Native, non-Hispanic/Latino; 43 Asian, non-Hispanic/Latino; 274 Hispanic/Latino; 3 Native Hawaiian or other Pacific Islander, non-Hispanic/Latino; 22 Two or more races, non-Hispanic/Latino), 282 international. Average age 30. 2,564 applicants, 38% accepted, 450 enrolled. In 2018, 558 master's, 5 doctorates awarded. Terminal master's awarded for partial completion of doctoral program. *Degree requirements:* For master's, comprehensive exam; for doctorate, comprehensive exam, thesis/dissertation. *Entrance requirements:* For master's, GMAT or GRE; for doctorate, GRE General Test. Additional exam requirements/recommendations for international students: Required—TOEFL (minimum score 94 iBT), IELTS (minimum score 7), TOEFL (minimum score 587 paper-based, 94 iBT) or IELTS (7). *Application deadline:* For fall admission, 6/30 priority date for domestic students, 5/30 priority date for international students; for spring admission, 10/31 priority date for domestic students, 9/30 priority date for international students. Applications are processed on a rolling basis. Application fee: $48. Electronic applications accepted. *Expenses:* Contact institution. *Financial support:* In 2018–19, 643 students received support, including 1 fellowship with full tuition reimbursement available (averaging $20,000 per year), 47 research assistantships with full and partial tuition reimbursements available (averaging $28,826 per year), 6 teaching assistantships with full and partial tuition reimbursements available (averaging $2,183 per year); career-related internships or fieldwork, Federal Work-Study, institutionally sponsored loans, scholarships/grants, and unspecified assistantships also available. Support available to part-time students. Financial award application deadline: 3/26; financial award applicants required to submit FAFSA. *Faculty research:* Behavioral finance; computational economics; consumer research; risk perception; consumer behavior; consumer choice research; behavioral decision theory; business analytics; point processes; longitudinal data analyses; international business; global business strategy, joint ventures, and alliances; emerging economies; global economic growth and development, money and financial markets, and computed dynamic models; health policy; innovative payment mechanisms. *Total annual research expenditures:* $703,773. *Unit head:* Dr. John Quelch, Dean, 305-284-6515, Fax: 305-284-6526, E-mail: jquelch@miami.edu. *Application contact:* Loubna Bouamane, Director of Graduate Business Recruiting and Admissions, 305-284-2510, Fax: 305-284-5905, E-mail: loubna@miami.edu.
Website: www.mbs.miami.edu

University of Michigan–Dearborn, College of Business, MS Program in Finance, Dearborn, MI 48126. Offers MS. *Program availability:* Part-time, evening/weekend, 100% online. *Faculty:* 41 full-time (17 women), 9 part-time/adjunct (6 women). *Students:* 2 full-time (0 women), 33 part-time (13 women); includes 8 minority (1 American Indian or Alaska Native, non-Hispanic/Latino; 6 Asian, non-Hispanic/Latino; 1 Two or more races, non-Hispanic/Latino), 2 international. Average age 32. 46 applicants, 41% accepted, 9 enrolled. In 2018, 19 master's awarded. *Entrance requirements:* For master's, GRE or GMAT, equivalent of four-year U.S. bachelor's degree from regionally-accredited institution, undergraduate course in finite math, pre-calculus, or calculus. Additional exam requirements/recommendations for international students: Required—TOEFL (minimum score 560 paper-based; 84 iBT), IELTS (minimum score 6.5). *Application deadline:* For fall admission, 8/1 for domestic students, 5/1 for international students; for winter admission, 12/1 for domestic students, 9/1 for international students; for spring admission, 4/1 for domestic students, 1/1 for international students. Applications are processed on a rolling basis. Application fee: $60. Electronic applications accepted. *Expenses:* $15,740 (typical full-time in-state); $24,308 (typical full-time out-of-state). *Financial support:* In 2018–19, 5 students received support. Scholarships/grants and non-resident tuition scholarships available. Financial award application deadline: 3/1; financial award applicants required to submit FAFSA. *Faculty research:* Business intelligence, behavioral finance, brand management and new media, management education, operations strategy. *Unit head:* Dr. Michael Kamen, Director, Graduate Programs, 313-593-5460, E-mail: mkamen@umich.edu. *Application contact:* Joan Doherty, Academic Advisor/Counselor, 313-593-5460, Fax: 313-271-9838, E-mail: umd-gradbusiness@umich.edu.
Website: http://umdearborn.edu/cob/ms-finance/

University of Michigan–Flint, School of Management, Program in Business Administration, Flint, MI 48502-1950. Offers accounting (MBA); computer information systems (MBA); finance (MBA, Post-Master's Certificate); general business (Graduate Certificate); general business administration (MBA); health care management (MBA); international business (MBA, Post-Master's Certificate); lean manufacturing (MBA); marketing (Post-Master's Certificate); marketing and innovation management (MBA); organizational leadership (MBA). *Program availability:* Part-time, evening/weekend, mixed mode format. *Faculty:* 30 full-time (4 women), 10 part-time/adjunct (2 women). *Students:* 24 full-time (14 women), 151 part-time (60 women); includes 45 minority (22 Black or African American, non-Hispanic/Latino; 3 American Indian or Alaska Native,

non-Hispanic/Latino; 7 Asian, non-Hispanic/Latino; 9 Hispanic/Latino; 4 Two or more races, non-Hispanic/Latino), 19 international. Average age 36. 160 applicants, 75% accepted, 62 enrolled. In 2018, 50 master's, 1 other advanced degree awarded. *Entrance requirements:* For master's, bachelor's degree in arts, sciences, engineering, or business administration from regionally-accredited college or university; for other advanced degree, bachelor's degree in arts, sciences, engineering, or business administration from regionally-accredited college or university. college-level math, statistics, or quantitative course (for Graduate Certificate); MBA or equivalent degree from regionally-accredited college or university (for Post Master's Certificate). Additional exam requirements/recommendations for international students: Required—TOEFL (minimum score 84 iBT), IELTS (minimum score 6.5). *Application deadline:* For fall admission, 8/1 for domestic students, 5/1 for international students; for winter admission, 11/15 for domestic students, 9/1 for international students; for spring admission, 3/15 for domestic students, 1/1 for international students; for summer admission, 5/15 for domestic students. Applications are processed on a rolling basis. Application fee: $55. Electronic applications accepted. *Expenses:* Contact institution. *Financial support:* Federal Work-Study, scholarships/grants, and unspecified assistantships available. Support available to part-time students. Financial award application deadline: 3/1; financial award applicants required to submit FAFSA. *Unit head:* Dr. Scott Johnson, Dean, School of Management, 810-762-3164, Fax: 810-237-6685, E-mail: scotjohn@umflint.edu. *Application contact:* Matt Bohlen, Director of Graduate Admissions, 810-762-3171, E-mail: mbohlen@umflint.edu.
Website: http://www.umflint.edu/graduateprograms/business-administration-mba

University of Minnesota, Twin Cities Campus, Carlson School of Management, Carlson Full-Time MBA Program, Minneapolis, MN 55455. Offers finance (MBA); information technology (MBA); management (MBA); marketing (MBA); medical industry orientation (MBA); supply chain and operations (MBA); JD/MBA; MBA/MPP; MBA/MSBA; MD/MBA; MHA/MBA; Pharm D/MBA. *Accreditation:* AACSB. *Faculty:* 150 full-time (43 women), 21 part-time/adjunct (5 women). *Students:* 169 full-time (57 women); includes 32 minority (6 Black or African American, non-Hispanic/Latino; 4 American Indian or Alaska Native, non-Hispanic/Latino; 14 Asian, non-Hispanic/Latino; 8 Hispanic/Latino), 36 international. Average age 29. 529 applicants, 39% accepted, 92 enrolled. In 2018, 76 master's awarded. *Degree requirements:* For master's, None are required for MBA. *Entrance requirements:* For master's, GMAT or GRE, 2 recommendations, personal statement, resume. Additional exam requirements/recommendations for international students: Required—TOEFL (minimum score 580 paper-based; 84 iBT), IELTS (minimum score 7), PTE. *Application deadline:* For fall admission, 4/1 for domestic students, 2/1 for international students. Application fee: $75. Electronic applications accepted. *Expenses:* FTMBA Tuition; Collegiate fee; Student Services fee; Hospitalization. *Financial support:* In 2018–19, 139 students received support. Teaching assistantships with partial tuition reimbursements available, scholarships/grants, and unspecified assistantships available. Financial award application deadline: 4/1. *Faculty research:* Market regulation and asset pricing, social networks and data analytics, consumer behavior, innovation and entrepreneurship, workplace wellbeing and labor relationships. *Total annual research expenditures:* $577,440. *Unit head:* Philip J. Miller, Assistant Dean, MBA and MS Programs, 612-625-5555, Fax: 612-625-1012, E-mail: mba@umn.edu. *Application contact:* Linh Gilles, Director of Admissions and Recruiting, 612-625-5555, Fax: 612-625-1012, E-mail: ftmba@umn.edu.
Website: http://www.csom.umn.edu/MBA/full-time/

University of Minnesota, Twin Cities Campus, Carlson School of Management, Carlson Part-Time MBA Program, Minneapolis, MN 55455. Offers finance (MBA); information technology (MBA); management (MBA); marketing (MBA); medical industry orientation (MBA); supply chain and operations (MBA). *Program availability:* Part-time-only, evening/weekend, 100% online, blended/hybrid learning. *Faculty:* 150 full-time (43 women), 23 part-time/adjunct (6 women). *Students:* 822 part-time (260 women); includes 122 minority (18 Black or African American, non-Hispanic/Latino; 11 American Indian or Alaska Native, non-Hispanic/Latino; 67 Asian, non-Hispanic/Latino; 24 Hispanic/Latino; 2 Native Hawaiian or other Pacific Islander, non-Hispanic/Latino), 41 international. Average age 29. 204 applicants, 83% accepted, 141 enrolled. In 2018, 257 master's awarded. *Degree requirements:* For master's, None for MBA. *Entrance requirements:* For master's, GMAT or GRE, 2 recommendations, personal statement, current resume. Additional exam requirements/recommendations for international students: Required—TOEFL (minimum score 580 paper-based; 84 iBT), IELTS (minimum score 7), PTE. *Application deadline:* For fall admission, 5/15 priority date for domestic and international students; for spring admission, 10/15 priority date for domestic and international students. Applications are processed on a rolling basis. Application fee: $75. Electronic applications accepted. *Expenses:* PTMBA tuition; Collegiate fee. *Financial support:* Applicants required to submit FAFSA. *Faculty research:* Market regulation and asset pricing, social networks and data analytics, consumer behavior, innovation and entrepreneurship, workplace wellbeing and labor relationships. *Total annual research expenditures:* $577,440. *Unit head:* Philip J. Miller, Assistant Dean, MBA and MS Programs, 612-624-2039, Fax: 612-625-1012, E-mail: mba@umn.edu. *Application contact:* Linh Gilles, Director of Admissions and Recruiting, 612-625-5555, Fax: 612-625-1012, E-mail: ptmba@umn.edu.
Website: http://www.carlsonschool.umn.edu/ptmba

University of Minnesota, Twin Cities Campus, Carlson School of Management, Doctoral Program in Business Administration, Minneapolis, MN 55455-0213. Offers accounting (PhD); finance (PhD); information and decision sciences (PhD); marketing (PhD); strategic management and entrepreneurship (PhD); supply chain and operations (PhD); work and organizations (PhD). *Faculty:* 106 full-time (33 women). *Students:* 88 full-time (34 women); includes 9 minority (2 Black or African American, non-Hispanic/Latino; 6 Asian, non-Hispanic/Latino; 1 Hispanic/Latino), 66 international. Average age 30. 306 applicants, 8% accepted, 15 enrolled. In 2018, 14 doctorates awarded. *Degree requirements:* For doctorate, comprehensive exam, thesis/dissertation, written and oral preliminary exams, proposal defense, final defense. *Entrance requirements:* For doctorate, GMAT or GRE, minimum undergraduate GPA of 3.0, graduate 3.5 (recommended). Additional exam requirements/recommendations for international students: Required—Either or: TOEFL or IELTS; Recommended—TOEFL, IELTS. *Application deadline:* For fall admission, 12/15 for domestic students, 12/15 priority date for international students. Applications are processed on a rolling basis. Application fee: $75 ($95 for international students). Electronic applications accepted. *Financial support:* In 2018–19, 80 students received support, including 80 fellowships with full tuition reimbursements available (averaging $12,500 per year), 72 research assistantships with full tuition reimbursements available (averaging $7,800 per year), 72 teaching assistantships with full tuition reimbursements available (averaging $7,800 per year); health care benefits, unspecified assistantships, and full student service fee waivers also available. Financial award application deadline: 12/15. *Faculty research:* Finance, strategy and entrepreneurship, marketing, information and decision science, operations, accounting, supply chain, human resources and industrial relations, organizational behavior. *Unit head:* Dr. Shawn P. Curley, Director, 612-624-6546, Fax: 612-624-8221, E-mail: curley@umn.edu. *Application contact:* Sandy Herzan, Associate Director, 612-624-0875, Fax: 612-624-8221, E-mail: herza002@umn.edu.
Website: http://carlsonschool.umn.edu/degrees/phd

University of Mississippi, Graduate School, School of Business Administration, University, MS 38677. Offers business administration (MBA, PhD); finance (PhD); management (PhD); management information systems (PhD); marketing (PhD); JD/MBA. *Accreditation:* AACSB. *Faculty:* 60 full-time (18 women), 7 part-time/adjunct (1 woman). *Students:* 62 full-time (18 women), 83 part-time (20 women); includes 13 minority (4 Black or African American, non-Hispanic/Latino; 3 Asian, non-Hispanic/Latino; 4 Hispanic/Latino; 2 Two or more races, non-Hispanic/Latino), 14 international. Average age 30. In 2018, 83 master's, 11 doctorates awarded. *Entrance requirements:* For master's, GMAT, minimum GPA of 3.0; for doctorate, GMAT. Additional exam requirements/recommendations for international students: Required—TOEFL. *Application deadline:* Applications are processed on a rolling basis. Application fee: $50. Electronic applications accepted. *Financial support:* Fellowships, career-related internships or fieldwork, scholarships/grants, tuition waivers (full), and unspecified assistantships available. Financial award application deadline: 3/1; financial award applicants required to submit FAFSA. *Unit head:* Dr. Ken Cyree, Dean, 662-915-5820, Fax: 662-915-5821, E-mail: info@bus.olemiss.edu. *Application contact:* Temeka Smith, Graduate Activities Specialist for Admissions, 662-915-7474, Fax: 662-915-7577, E-mail: gschool@olemiss.edu.
Website: http://www.olemissbusiness.com/

University of Missouri, Office of Research and Graduate Studies, Robert J. Trulaske, Sr. College of Business, Program in Business Administration, Columbia, MO 65211. Offers business administration (MBA); finance (PhD); MBA/MHA. *Accreditation:* AACSB. *Degree requirements:* For doctorate, thesis/dissertation. *Entrance requirements:* For master's and doctorate, GMAT, minimum GPA of 3.0. Additional exam requirements/recommendations for international students: Required—TOEFL (minimum score 500 paper-based; 61 iBT). Electronic applications accepted.

University of Missouri–Kansas City, Henry W. Bloch School of Management, Kansas City, MO 64110-2499. Offers accounting (MS); finance (MS); public affairs (MPA, PhD); JD/MBA; LL M/MPA. PhD (interdisciplinary) offered through the School of Graduate Studies. *Accreditation:* AACSB; NASPAA. *Program availability:* Part-time, evening/weekend. Terminal master's awarded for partial completion of doctoral program. *Entrance requirements:* For master's, GMAT, GRE, 2 essays, 2 references, support of employer; for doctorate, GRE, minimum GPA of 3.0. Additional exam requirements/recommendations for international students: Required—TOEFL (minimum score 550 paper-based; 80 iBT). Electronic applications accepted. *Faculty research:* Entrepreneurship, finance, non-profit, risk management.

University of Nebraska–Lincoln, Graduate College, College of Business Administration, Interdepartmental Area of Business, Department of Finance, Lincoln, NE 68588. Offers business (MA, PhD). *Degree requirements:* For doctorate, comprehensive exam, thesis/dissertation. *Entrance requirements:* For master's and doctorate, GMAT. Additional exam requirements/recommendations for international students: Required—TOEFL (minimum score 100 iBT). Electronic applications accepted. *Faculty research:* Banking, investments, international finance, insurance, corporate finance.

University of Nevada, Reno, Graduate School, College of Business, Department of Finance, Reno, NV 89557. Offers MS. *Program availability:* Part-time. *Degree requirements:* For master's, thesis optional. *Entrance requirements:* For master's, GMAT or GRE, minimum GPA of 2.75. Additional exam requirements/recommendations for international students: Required—TOEFL (minimum score 500 paper-based; 61 iBT), IELTS (minimum score 6). Electronic applications accepted. *Faculty research:* Financial business problems, economic theory, financial concepts theory.

University of New Haven, Graduate School, College of Business, Program in Business Administration, West Haven, CT 06516. Offers accounting (MBA); business administration (MBA); business intelligence (MBA); business policy and strategic leadership (MBA); finance (MBA), including chartered financial analyst; global marketing (MBA); human resources management (MBA); sport management (MBA). *Accreditation:* AACSB. *Program availability:* Part-time, evening/weekend. *Students:* 151 full-time (73 women), 70 part-time (30 women); includes 51 minority (23 Black or African American, non-Hispanic/Latino; 13 Asian, non-Hispanic/Latino; 14 Hispanic/Latino; 1 Two or more races, non-Hispanic/Latino), 74 international. Average age 28. 197 applicants, 91% accepted, 82 enrolled. In 2018, 70 master's awarded. *Entrance requirements:* For master's, GMAT. Additional exam requirements/recommendations for international students: Required—TOEFL (minimum score 80 iBT), IELTS, PTE. *Application deadline:* Applications are processed on a rolling basis. Application fee: $50. Electronic applications accepted. Application fee is waived when completed online. *Expenses: Tuition:* Full-time $16,470; part-time $915 per credit hour. *Required fees:* $230; $95 per term. *Financial support:* Research assistantships with partial tuition reimbursements, teaching assistantships with partial tuition reimbursements, career-related internships or fieldwork, Federal Work-Study, scholarships/grants, and unspecified assistantships available. Support available to part-time students. Financial award applicants required to submit FAFSA. *Unit head:* Darell Singleterry, Director, 203-932-7386, E-mail: dsingleterry@newhaven.edu. *Application contact:* Selina O'Toole, Senior Associate Director of Graduate Admissions, 203-932-7337, E-mail: SOToole@newhaven.edu.
Website: http://www.newhaven.edu/business/graduate-programs/mba/index.php

University of New Haven, Graduate School, College of Business, Program in Finance, West Haven, CT 06516. Offers MS. *Students:* 29 full-time (12 women), 5 part-time (0 women); includes 6 minority (1 Black or African American, non-Hispanic/Latino; 3 Asian, non-Hispanic/Latino; 2 Hispanic/Latino), 24 international. Average age 26. 56 applicants, 86% accepted, 13 enrolled. In 2018, 10 master's awarded. *Application deadline:* Applications are processed on a rolling basis. Application fee: $50. *Expenses: Tuition:* Full-time $16,470; part-time $915 per credit hour. *Required fees:* $230; $95 per term. *Financial support:* Research assistantships with partial tuition reimbursements, teaching assistantships with partial tuition reimbursements, and Federal Work-Study available. Financial award application deadline: 5/1; financial award applicants required to submit FAFSA. *Unit head:* Dr. Charlie Boynton, Associate Professor, 203-932-7356, E-mail: cboynton@newhaven.edu. *Application contact:* Selina O'Toole, Senior Associate Director of Graduate Admissions, 203-932-7337, E-mail: SOToole@newhaven.edu.
Website: https://www.newhaven.edu/business/graduate-programs/finance

University of New Haven, Graduate School, Henry C. Lee College of Criminal Justice and Forensic Sciences, Program in Public Administration, West Haven, CT 06516. Offers fire and emergency medical services (MPA); municipal management (MPA); nonprofit organization management (MPA); public administration (MPA, Graduate Certificate); public finance (MPA); public safety (MPA). *Program availability:* Part-time, evening/weekend. *Students:* 20 full-time (10 women), 34 part-time (10 women); includes 14 minority (9 Black or African American, non-Hispanic/Latino; 1 Asian, non-Hispanic/Latino; 4 Hispanic/Latino), 5 international. Average age 33. 53 applicants, 85% accepted, 21 enrolled. In 2018, 21 master's, 1 other advanced degree awarded. *Entrance requirements:* Additional exam requirements/recommendations for international students: Required—TOEFL (minimum score 80 iBT), IELTS, PTE. *Application deadline:* Applications are processed on a rolling basis. Application fee: $50. Electronic applications accepted. Application fee is waived when completed online. *Expenses: Tuition:* Full-time $16,470; part-time $915 per credit hour. *Required fees:* $230; $95 per term. *Financial support:* Research assistantships with partial tuition

reimbursements, teaching assistantships with partial tuition reimbursements, career-related internships or fieldwork, Federal Work-Study, scholarships/grants, and unspecified assistantships available. Support available to part-time students. Financial award application deadline: 5/1; financial award applicants required to submit FAFSA. *Unit head:* Dr. Christy Smith, Assistant Professor, 203-479-4193, E-mail: cdsmith@newhaven.edu. *Application contact:* Selina O'Toole, Senior Associate Director of Graduate Admissions, 203-932-7337, E-mail: SOToole@newhaven.edu.
Website: http://www.newhaven.edu/lee-college/graduate-programs/public-administration/

University of New Orleans, Graduate School, College of Business Administration, Department of Economics and Finance, Program in Finance, New Orleans, LA 70148. Offers MS.

University of North Alabama, College of Business, Florence, AL 35632-0001. Offers business administration (MBA), including accounting, enterprise resource planning systems, executive, finance, health care management, information systems, international business, project management. *Accreditation:* AACSB; ACBSP. *Program availability:* Part-time, 100% online, blended/hybrid learning. *Entrance requirements:* For master's, GMAT, GRE, minimum GPA of 2.75 in last 60 hours, 2.5 overall (on a 3.0 scale); 27 hours of course work in business and economics. Additional exam requirements/recommendations for international students: Required—TOEFL (minimum score 79 iBT), IELTS (minimum score 6), PTE (minimum score 54). Electronic applications accepted.

The University of North Carolina at Chapel Hill, Kenan-Flagler Business School, Doctoral Program in Business Administration, Chapel Hill, NC 27599. Offers accounting (PhD); finance (PhD); marketing (PhD); operations management (PhD); organizational behavior (PhD); strategy (PhD). *Accreditation:* AACSB. *Degree requirements:* For doctorate, thesis/dissertation. *Entrance requirements:* For doctorate, GMAT or GRE General Test. Electronic applications accepted. *Expenses:* Contact institution.

The University of North Carolina at Charlotte, College of Liberal Arts and Sciences, Department of Political Science and Public Administration, Charlotte, NC 28223-0001. Offers emergency management (Graduate Certificate); non-profit management (Graduate Certificate); public administration (MPA), including arts administration, emergency management, non-profit management, public budgeting and finance, urban management and policy; public budgeting and finance (Graduate Certificate); urban management and policy (Graduate Certificate). *Accreditation:* NASPAA. *Program availability:* Part-time, evening/weekend. *Students:* 25 full-time (16 women), 55 part-time (39 women); includes 27 minority (18 Black or African American, non-Hispanic/Latino; 1 American Indian or Alaska Native, non-Hispanic/Latino; 7 Hispanic/Latino; 1 Two or more races, non-Hispanic/Latino), 1 international. Average age 29. 45 applicants, 78% accepted, 25 enrolled. In 2018, 26 master's, 13 other advanced degrees awarded. *Entrance requirements:* For master's, GRE General Test, bachelor's degree, or its equivalent, from accredited college or university; minimum undergraduate GPA of 3.0; 3 letters of recommendation; statement of purpose; for Graduate Certificate, statement of purpose (1-2 pages in length) explaining applicant's career goals, how the Graduate Certificate fits into achieving those goals, and any relevant work experience; official transcripts; letters of recommendation. Additional exam requirements/recommendations for international students: Required—TOEFL (minimum score 523 paper-based; 70 iBT), IELTS (minimum score 6), TOEFL (minimum score 523 paper-based, 70 iBT) or IELTS (6). *Application deadline:* Applications are processed on a rolling basis. Application fee: $75. Electronic applications accepted. Tuition and fees vary according to course load and program. *Financial support:* Research assistantships, teaching assistantships, career-related internships or fieldwork, Federal Work-Study, institutionally sponsored loans, scholarships/grants, and unspecified assistantships available. Support available to part-time students. Financial award application deadline: 3/1; financial award applicants required to submit FAFSA. *Total annual research expenditures:* $660,034. *Unit head:* Dr. Greg Weeks, Chair, 704-687-7574, E-mail: gbweeks@uncc.edu. *Application contact:* Kathy B. Giddings, Director of Graduate Admissions, 704-687-5503, Fax: 704-687-1668, E-mail: gradadm@uncc.edu.
Website: http://politicalscience.uncc.edu/

The University of North Carolina at Greensboro, Graduate School, Bryan School of Business and Economics, Department of Accounting and Finance, Greensboro, NC 27412-5001. Offers accounting (MS); financial analysis (PMC). *Accreditation:* AACSB. *Entrance requirements:* For master's, GMAT, GRE General Test, previous course work in accounting and business. Additional exam requirements/recommendations for international students: Required—TOEFL. Electronic applications accepted.

University of North Florida, Coggin College of Business, MBA Program, Jacksonville, FL 32224. Offers accounting (MBA); construction management (MBA); e-commerce (MBA); economics (MBA); finance (MBA); human resource management (MBA); international business (MBA); logistics (MBA); management applications (MBA). *Accreditation:* AACSB. *Program availability:* Part-time, evening/weekend. *Faculty:* 40 full-time (14 women). *Students:* 368 part-time (158 women); includes 83 minority (30 Black or African American, non-Hispanic/Latino; 20 Asian, non-Hispanic/Latino; 16 Hispanic/Latino; 17 Two or more races, non-Hispanic/Latino), 28 international. Average age 30. 311 applicants, 51% accepted, 99 enrolled. In 2018, 151 master's awarded. *Entrance requirements:* For master's, GMAT or GRE, U.S. bachelor's degree from regionally-accredited university or equivalent foreign degree. Additional exam requirements/recommendations for international students: Required—TOEFL (minimum score 550 paper-based; 79 iBT). *Application deadline:* For fall admission, 8/1 priority date for domestic students, 5/1 for international students; for spring admission, 12/1 priority date for domestic students, 10/1 for international students; for summer admission, 4/29 priority date for domestic students, 2/1 for international students. Application fee: $30. *Expenses: Tuition, area resident:* Part-time $408.10 per credit hour. Tuition, state resident: part-time $408.10 per credit hour. Tuition, nonresident: part-time $932.61 per credit hour. *Required fees:* $111.81 per credit hour. Tuition and fees vary according to course load, campus/location and program. *Financial support:* In 2018–19, 41 students received support, including 1 research assistantship (averaging $2,143 per year); teaching assistantships, Federal Work-Study, and tuition waivers (partial) also available. Support available to part-time students. Financial award application deadline: 4/1; financial award applicants required to submit FAFSA. *Faculty research:* Performance measures, costing, and inventory issues in logistics and supply chain management; inter-organizational systems; international management and marketing practices; e-commerce; organizational learning and socialization processes. *Unit head:* Dr. Parvez Ahmed, Graduate Program Director, 904-620-1678, E-mail: pahmed@unf.edu. *Application contact:* Amy Bishop, MSM Advisor, 904-620-2575, Fax: 904-620-2832, E-mail: coggin.students@unf.edu.
Website: http://www.unf.edu/graduateschool/academics/programs/MBA.aspx

University of North Texas, Toulouse Graduate School, Denton, TX 76203-5459. Offers accounting (MS); applied anthropology (MA, MS); applied behavior analysis (Certificate); applied geography (MA); applied technology and performance improvement (M Ed, MS); art education (MA); art history (MA); arts leadership (Certificate); audiology (Au D); behavior analysis (MS); behavioral science (PhD); biochemistry and molecular biology (MS); biology (MA, MS); biomedical engineering (MS); business analysis (MS); chemistry (MS); clinical health psychology (PhD); communication studies (MA, MS); computer engineering (MS); computer science (MS); counseling (M Ed, MS), including clinical mental health counseling (MS), college and university counseling, elementary school counseling, secondary school counseling; creative writing (MA); criminal justice (MS); curriculum and instruction (M Ed); decision sciences (MBA); design (MA, MFA), including fashion design (MFA), innovation studies, interior design (MFA); early childhood studies (MS); economics (MS); educational leadership (M Ed, Ed D); educational psychology (MS, PhD), including family studies (MS), gifted and talented (MS), human development (MS), learning and cognition (MS), research, measurement and evaluation (MS); electrical engineering (MS); emergency management (MPA); engineering technology (MS); English (MA); English as a second language (MA); environmental science (MS); finance (MBA, MS); financial management (MPA); French (MA); health services management (MBA); higher education (M Ed, Ed D); history (MA, MS); hospitality management (MS); human resources management (MPA); information science (MS); information systems (PhD); information technologies (MBA); interdisciplinary studies (MA, MS); international studies (MA); international sustainable tourism (MS); jazz studies (MM); journalism (MA, MJ, Graduate Certificate), including interactive and virtual digital communication (Graduate Certificate), narrative journalism (Graduate Certificate), public relations (Graduate Certificate); kinesiology (MS); linguistics (MA); local government management (MPA); logistics (PhD); logistics and supply chain management (MBA); long-term care, senior housing, and aging services (MA); management (PhD); marketing (MBA); mathematics (MA, MS); mechanical and energy engineering (MS, PhD); music (MA), including ethnomusicology, music theory, musicology, performance; music composition (PhD); music education (MM Ed, PhD); nonprofit management (MPA); operations and supply chain management (MBA); performance (MM, DMA); philosophy (MA); political science (MA); professional and technical communication (MA); radio, television and film (MA, MFA); rehabilitation counseling (Certificate); sociology (MA); Spanish (MA); special education (M Ed); speech-language pathology (MA); strategic management (MBA); studio art (MFA); teaching (M Ed); MBA/MS. *Program availability:* Part-time, evening/weekend, online learning. Terminal master's awarded for partial completion of doctoral program. *Degree requirements:* For master's, variable foreign language requirement, comprehensive exam (for some programs), thesis (for some programs); for doctorate, variable foreign language requirement, comprehensive exam (for some programs), thesis/dissertation; for other advanced degree, variable foreign language requirement, comprehensive exam (for some programs). *Entrance requirements:* For master's and doctorate, GRE, GMAT. Additional exam requirements/recommendations for international students: Required—TOEFL (minimum score 550 paper-based; 79 iBT). Electronic applications accepted.

University of Notre Dame, Mendoza College of Business, Master of Business Administration Program, Notre Dame, IN 46556. Offers business analytics (MBA); business leadership (MBA); consulting (MBA); corporate finance (MBA); innovation and entrepreneurship (MBA); investments (MBA); marketing (MBA); MBA/MSBA. *Accreditation:* AACSB. *Entrance requirements:* For master's, GMAT or GRE, work experience, essay, four-slide presentation, two recommendations, transcripts from all colleges and/or universities attended, interview. Additional exam requirements/recommendations for international students: Required—PTE (minimum score 68), TOEFL (minimum iBT score of 109), IELTS (7.5), or documentation of at least six semesters of full-time university education in English. Electronic applications accepted. *Expenses:* Contact institution. *Faculty research:* Market micro-structure; marketing and public policy; corporate finance and accounting; corporate governance and ethical behavior; high performing organizations.

University of Notre Dame, Mendoza College of Business, Master of Science in Finance Program, Notre Dame, IN 46556. Offers MSF. *Entrance requirements:* For master's, minimum of two years' work experience and active employment. Additional exam requirements/recommendations for international students: Required—TOEFL, IELTS. Electronic applications accepted. *Expenses:* Contact institution.

University of Oregon, Graduate School, Charles H. Lundquist College of Business, Department of Finance, Eugene, OR 97403. Offers PhD. *Program availability:* Part-time. Terminal master's awarded for partial completion of doctoral program. *Degree requirements:* For doctorate, thesis/dissertation, 2 comprehensive exams. *Entrance requirements:* For doctorate, GMAT. Additional exam requirements/recommendations for international students: Required—TOEFL. *Faculty research:* Changes in firm value in response to corporate takeovers and defenses, capital structure, regulatory changes, financial intermediaries.

University of Ottawa, Faculty of Graduate and Postdoctoral Studies, Interdisciplinary Programs, Ottawa, ON K1N 6N5, Canada. Offers e-business (Certificate); e-commerce (Certificate); finance (Certificate); health services and policies research (Diploma); population health (PhD); population health risk assessment and management (Certificate); public management and governance (Certificate); systems science (Certificate).

University of Pennsylvania, Wharton School, Finance Department, Philadelphia, PA 19104. Offers MBA, PhD. *Degree requirements:* For doctorate, thesis/dissertation. *Entrance requirements:* For doctorate, GMAT or GRE. *Faculty research:* Corporate finance, investments, macroeconomics, international finance.

University of Pittsburgh, Katz Graduate School of Business, Doctoral Program in Business Administration, Pittsburgh, PA 15260. Offers accounting (PhD); business analytics and operations (PhD); finance (PhD); information systems and technology management (PhD); marketing (PhD); organizational behavior and human resources (PhD); strategic management (PhD). *Accreditation:* AACSB. *Program availability:* Evening/weekend. *Degree requirements:* For doctorate, comprehensive exam, thesis/dissertation, student teaching. *Entrance requirements:* For doctorate, GMAT or GRE, 3 recommendations, statement of purpose, transcripts of all previous course work and degrees. Additional exam requirements/recommendations for international students: Required—TOEFL (minimum score 100 iBT) or IELTS (minimum score 7.0). Electronic applications accepted. *Faculty research:* Accounting systems/financial reporting, corporate finance, shopper marketing/consumer behavior, management information systems, organizational behavior and entrepreneurship.

University of Pittsburgh, Katz Graduate School of Business, Master of Business Administration Programs, Pittsburgh, PA 15260. Offers finance (MBA); information systems (MBA); marketing (MBA); operations (MBA); organizational behavior and human resources (MBA); strategy, environment and organizations (MBA); MBA/JD; MBA/MID; MBA/MIS; MBA/MSE. *Accreditation:* AACSB. *Program availability:* Part-time, evening/weekend, blended/hybrid learning. *Degree requirements:* For master's, minimum GPA of 3.0. *Entrance requirements:* For master's, GMAT, GRE. Additional exam requirements/recommendations for international students: Required—TOEFL (minimum score 100 iBT) or IELTS (minimum score 7.0). Electronic applications accepted. *Faculty research:* Accounting systems/financial reporting, corporate finance, shopper marketing/consumer behavior, management information systems, organizational behavior and entrepreneurship.

University of Pittsburgh, Katz Graduate School of Business, Master of Science in Finance Program, Pittsburgh, PA 15260. Offers MS. *Degree requirements:* For master's, minimum GPA of 3.0. *Entrance requirements:* For master's, GMAT, GRE. Additional

exam requirements/recommendations for international students: Required—TOEFL (minimum score 100 iBT), IELTS (minimum score 7). Electronic applications accepted. *Expenses:* Contact institution. *Faculty research:* Accounting systems/financial reporting, corporate finance, shopper marketing/consumer behavior, management information systems, organizational behavior and entrepreneurship.

University of Portland, Dr. Robert B. Pamplin, Jr. School of Business, Portland, OR 97203-5798. Offers entrepreneurship (MBA); finance (MBA, MS); health care management (MBA); marketing (MBA); nonprofit management (EMBA); operations and technology management (MBA, MS); sustainability (MBA). *Accreditation:* AACSB. *Program availability:* Part-time, evening/weekend. *Faculty:* 26 full-time (5 women), 8 part-time/adjunct (1 woman). *Students:* 35 full-time (16 women), 114 part-time (47 women); includes 21 minority (3 Black or African American, non-Hispanic/Latino; 2 American Indian or Alaska Native, non-Hispanic/Latino; 8 Asian, non-Hispanic/Latino; 8 Hispanic/Latino), 24 international. Average age 32. In 2018, 55 master's awarded. *Entrance requirements:* For master's, GMAT or GRE, minimum GPA of 3.0, resume, statement of goals, 2 letters of recommendation. Additional exam requirements/recommendations for international students: Required—TOEFL (minimum score 88 iBT), IELTS (minimum score 7). *Application deadline:* For fall admission, 7/19 priority date for domestic and international students; for spring admission, 12/7 priority date for domestic and international students; for summer admission, 4/12 priority date for domestic and international students. Applications are processed on a rolling basis. Application fee: $0. Electronic applications accepted. *Expenses:* Contact institution. *Financial support:* Application deadline: 3/1; applicants required to submit FAFSA. *Unit head:* Melissa McCarthy, Director, 503-943-7224, E-mail: mba-up@up.edu. *Application contact:* Melissa McCarthy, Director, 503-943-7224, E-mail: mba-up@up.edu.

University of Puerto Rico–Mayagüez, Graduate Studies, College of Business Administration, Mayagüez, PR 00681-9000. Offers business administration (MBA); finance (MBA); human resources (MBA); industrial management (MBA). *Program availability:* Part-time, evening/weekend. *Degree requirements:* For master's, one foreign language, comprehensive exam, thesis (for some programs). *Entrance requirements:* For master's, GMAT or EXADEP, bachelor's degree with courses in calculus, microeconomics, accounting and statistics. Additional exam requirements/recommendations for international students: Required—TOEFL (minimum score 500 paper-based), GMAT or EXADEP. Electronic applications accepted. *Faculty research:* Organizational studies, management, accounting, entrepreneurship, leadership and motivation.

University of Puerto Rico–Río Piedras, College of Business Administration, San Juan, PR 00931-3300. Offers accounting (MBA); finance (MBA, PhD); general business (MBA); human resources management (MBA); international trade and business (MBA, PhD); marketing (MBA); operations management (MBA); quantitative methods (MBA). *Accreditation:* AACSB. *Program availability:* Part-time. *Degree requirements:* For master's, comprehensive exam, thesis or alternative, research project. *Entrance requirements:* For master's, GMAT or PAEG, minimum GPA of 3.0, letter of recommendation; for doctorate, GMAT, PAEG, minimum GPA of 3.0, master degree. *Faculty research:* Management.

University of Rhode Island, Graduate School, College of Business, Program in Business Administration, Kingston, RI 02881. Offers finance (MBA); general business (MBA); management (MBA); marketing (MBA, PhD); operations and supply chain management (PhD); supply chain management (MBA); Pharm D/MBA. *Faculty:* 33 full-time (17 women). *Students:*. 54 full-time (21 women), 161 part-time (64 women); includes 30 minority (11 Black or African American, non-Hispanic/Latino; 11 Asian, non-Hispanic/Latino; 6 Hispanic/Latino; 1 Native Hawaiian or other Pacific Islander, non-Hispanic/Latino; 1 Two or more races, non-Hispanic/Latino), 17 international. 92 applicants, 87% accepted, 74 enrolled. In 2018, 90 master's, 5 doctorates awarded. *Entrance requirements:* Additional exam requirements/recommendations for international students: Required—TOEFL. *Application deadline:* For fall admission, 6/30 for domestic students; for spring admission, 10/31 for domestic students; for summer admission, 3/31 for domestic students. Electronic applications accepted. *Expenses: Tuition, area resident:* Full-time $13,226; part-time $735 per credit. Tuition, state resident: full-time $13,226; part-time $735 per credit. Tuition, nonresident: full-time $25,854; part-time $1436 per credit. *International tuition:* $25,854 full-time. *Required fees:* $1698; $50 per credit. $35 per semester. One-time fee: $165. *Financial support:* In 2018–19, 15 teaching assistantships (averaging $17,739 per year) were awarded. Financial award application deadline: 2/1. *Unit head:* Lisa Lancellotta, Coordinator, MBA Programs, 401-874-4241, E-mail: mba@uri.edu. *Application contact:* Lisa Lancellotta, Coordinator, MBA Programs, 401-874-4241, E-mail: mba@uri.edu.

University of Rhode Island, Graduate School, College of Business, Program in Finance, Kingston, RI 02881. Offers MS, PhD. *Program availability:* Part-time, evening/weekend, blended/hybrid learning. *Faculty:* 9 full-time (1 woman). *Students:* 2 full-time (0 women), 4 part-time (0 women); includes 1 minority (Asian, non-Hispanic/Latino), 2 international. 9 applicants, 67% accepted, 3 enrolled. *Entrance requirements:* Additional exam requirements/recommendations for international students: Required—TOEFL. *Application deadline:* For fall admission, 2/1 for domestic and international students. Electronic applications accepted. *Expenses: Tuition, area resident:* Full-time $13,226; part-time $735 per credit. Tuition, state resident: full-time $13,226; part-time $735 per credit. Tuition, nonresident: full-time $25,854; part-time $1436 per credit. *International tuition:* $25,854 full-time. *Required fees:* $1698; $50 per credit. $35 per semester. One-time fee: $165. *Financial support:* Application deadline: 2/1. *Unit head:* Dr. Bingxuan Lin, Professor/Area Coordinator for Finance, 401-874-4895, E-mail: bingxuan@uri.edu. *Application contact:* Dr. Shingo Goto, Graduate Program Director, E-mail: shingo_goto@uri.edu.
Website: https://web.uri.edu/business/academics/graduate/finance/

University of Rochester, Simon Business School, Doctoral Program in Business Administration, Rochester, NY 14627. Offers accounting (PhD); computer information systems (PhD); finance (PhD); marketing (PhD); operations management (PhD). *Accreditation:* AACSB. *Degree requirements:* For doctorate, comprehensive exam, thesis/dissertation, qualifying exam. *Entrance requirements:* For doctorate, GMAT or GRE. Additional exam requirements/recommendations for international students: Required—TOEFL. Electronic applications accepted. *Expenses:* Contact institution. *Faculty research:* Empirical industrial organization, risk management, financial disclosure and regulation, social media, health care management.

University of Rochester, Simon Business School, Full-Time Master's Program in Business Administration, Rochester, NY 14627. Offers business systems consulting (MBA); competitive and organizational strategy (MBA); computers and information systems (MBA); corporate accounting (MBA); entrepreneurship (MBA); finance (MBA); health sciences management (MBA); marketing (MBA); operations management (MBA); public accounting (MBA); strategy and organizations (MBA). *Accreditation:* AACSB. *Entrance requirements:* For master's, GMAT or GRE. *Expenses: Tuition:* Full-time $52,974; part-time $1654 per credit hour. *Required fees:* $612. One-time fee: $30 part-time. Tuition and fees vary according to campus/location and program. *Faculty research:* Empirical industrial organization, risk management, financial disclosure and regulation, social media, health care management.

University of Rochester, Simon Business School, Master of Science Program in Finance, Rochester, NY 14627. Offers MS. *Entrance requirements:* For master's, GMAT or GRE. *Expenses: Tuition:* Full-time $52,974; part-time $1654 per credit hour. *Required fees:* $612. One-time fee: $30 part-time. Tuition and fees vary according to campus/location and program.

University of Rochester, Simon Business School, Part-Time MBA Program, Rochester, NY 14627. Offers business systems consulting (MBA); competitive and organizational strategy (MBA); computers and information systems (MBA); corporate accounting (MBA); entrepreneurship (MBA); finance (MBA); health sciences management (MBA); marketing (MBA), including brand management, marketing strategy, pricing; operations management (MBA); public accounting (MBA). *Program availability:* Part-time-only, evening/weekend. *Entrance requirements:* For master's, GRE or GMAT. Electronic applications accepted. *Expenses:* Contact institution.

University of St. Francis, College of Business and Health Administration, Joliet, IL 60435-6169. Offers accounting (MBA, Certificate); business analytics (MBA, Certificate); e-learning (Certificate); finance (MBA, Certificate); health administration (MBA, MS); human resource management (MBA, Certificate); logistics (Certificate); management (MBA, MSM); management of training and development (Certificate); supply chain management (MBA); training and development (MBA); training specialist (Certificate). *Program availability:* Part-time, evening/weekend, 100% online, blended/hybrid learning. *Faculty:* 13 full-time (6 women), 20 part-time/adjunct (7 women). *Students:* 139 full-time (94 women), 206 part-time (159 women); includes 86 minority (51 Black or African American, non-Hispanic/Latino; 1 American Indian or Alaska Native, non-Hispanic/Latino; 11 Asian, non-Hispanic/Latino; 21 Hispanic/Latino; 2 Two or more races, non-Hispanic/Latino), 24 international. Average age 37. 261 applicants, 63% accepted, 98 enrolled. In 2018, 129 master's, 3 other advanced degrees awarded. *Degree requirements:* For master's, comprehensive exam (for some programs). *Entrance requirements:* Additional exam requirements/recommendations for international students: Required—TOEFL (minimum score 550 paper-based; 79 iBT), IELTS (minimum score 6). *Application deadline:* Applications are processed on a rolling basis. Electronic applications accepted. Application fee is waived when completed online. *Expenses:* Contact institution. *Financial support:* In 2018–19, 126 students received support. Scholarships/grants and tuition waivers (partial) available. Support available to part-time students. Financial award applicants required to submit FAFSA. *Unit head:* Dr. Orlando Griego, Dean, 815-740-3395, Fax: 815-740-3452, E-mail: ogriego@stfrancis.edu. *Application contact:* Sandee Sloka, Director Adult & Graduate Admissions, 800-735-7500, E-mail: ssloka@stfrancis.edu.
Website: https://www.stfrancis.edu/business-health-administration/

University of Saint Mary, Graduate Programs, Program in Business Administration, Leavenworth, KS 66048-5082. Offers enterprise risk management (MBA); finance (MBA); general management (MBA); health care management (MBA); human resources management (MBA); marketing and advertising management (MBA). *Program availability:* Part-time, evening/weekend, 100% online, blended/hybrid learning. *Faculty:* 1 full-time, 23 part-time/adjunct (7 women). *Students:* 177 full-time (116 women), 50 part-time (29 women); includes 73 minority (30 Black or African American, non-Hispanic/Latino; 3 American Indian or Alaska Native, non-Hispanic/Latino; 12 Asian, non-Hispanic/Latino; 18 Hispanic/Latino; 1 Native Hawaiian or other Pacific Islander, non-Hispanic/Latino; 9 Two or more races, non-Hispanic/Latino), 2 international. Average age 33. *Degree requirements:* For master's, thesis. *Entrance requirements:* For master's, Minimum undergraduate GPA of 2.75, official transcripts. *Application deadline:* Applications are processed on a rolling basis. Application fee: $25. Electronic applications accepted. *Expenses:* Contact institution. *Financial support:* Applicants required to submit FAFSA. *Unit head:* Mark Harvey, Director of Graduate Business Programs, 913-319-3011, E-mail: mark.harvey@stmary.edu. *Application contact:* Mark Harvey, Director of Graduate Business Programs, 913-319-3011, E-mail: mark.harvey@stmary.edu.
Website: https://www.stmary.edu/mba

University of St. Thomas, Cameron School of Business, Houston, TX 77006-4696. Offers MBA, MCTM, MIB, MSA, MSF. *Program availability:* Part-time, evening/weekend. *Degree requirements:* For master's, capstone (for some programs), additional course requirements for those sitting for state accountancy exam. *Entrance requirements:* For master's, minimum GPA of 2.5, 3 letters of recommendation. Additional exam requirements/recommendations for international students: Required—TOEFL (minimum score 550 paper-based; 79 iBT), IELTS (minimum score 6.5), PTE (minimum score 53). Electronic applications accepted.

University of San Francisco, School of Management, Master of Business Administration Program, San Francisco, CA 94117. Offers entrepreneurship and innovation (MBA); finance (MBA); marketing (MBA); organization development (MBA); DDS/MBA; JD/MBA; MBA/MAPS. *Accreditation:* AACSB. *Program availability:* Part-time, evening/weekend. *Students:* 136 full-time (67 women), 7 part-time (2 women); includes 57 minority (5 Black or African American, non-Hispanic/Latino; 29 Asian, non-Hispanic/Latino; 14 Hispanic/Latino; 1 Native Hawaiian or other Pacific Islander, non-Hispanic/Latino; 8 Two or more races, non-Hispanic/Latino), 27 international. Average age 29. 226 applicants, 61% accepted, 56 enrolled. In 2018, 76 master's awarded. *Entrance requirements:* For master's, GMAT or GRE, resume (two years of professional work experience required for part-time students, preferred for full-time), transcripts from each college or university attended, two letters of recommendation, personal statement, interview. Additional exam requirements/recommendations for international students: Required—TOEFL (minimum score 600 paper-based, 100 iBT), IELTS (minimum score 7) or PTE (minimum score 68). *Application deadline:* For fall admission, 6/5 for domestic students, 5/15 for international students; for spring admission, 11/30 for domestic students. Application fee: $55. Electronic applications accepted. *Expenses:* Contact institution. *Financial support:* Fellowships and scholarships/grants available. Financial award application deadline: 3/2; financial award applicants required to submit FAFSA. *Faculty research:* International financial markets, technology transfer licensing, international marketing, strategic planning. *Total annual research expenditures:* $50,000. *Unit head:* Dr. Frank Fletcher, Director, 415-422-2221, E-mail: management@usfca.edu. *Application contact:* Office of Graduate Recruiting and Admissions, 415-422-2221, E-mail: management@usfca.edu.
Website: http://www.usfca.edu/mba

University of San Francisco, School of Management, Master of Science in Financial Analysis Program, San Francisco, CA 94117. Offers MSFA, MS/MBA. *Program availability:* Part-time, evening/weekend. *Students:* 93 full-time (43 women); includes 27 minority (3 Black or African American, non-Hispanic/Latino; 13 Asian, non-Hispanic/Latino; 8 Hispanic/Latino; 3 Two or more races, non-Hispanic/Latino), 57 international. Average age 25. 180 applicants, 76% accepted, 40 enrolled. In 2018, 70 master's awarded. *Entrance requirements:* For master's, GMAT or GRE, resume (minimum of two years of professional work experience for working professionals format), transcripts from each college or university attended showing completion of required foundation courses, two letters of recommendation, personal statement. Additional exam requirements/recommendations for international students: Required—TOEFL (minimum score 600 paper-based, 100 iBT), IELTS (minimum score 7) or PTE (minimum score 68). *Application deadline:* For fall admission, 6/15 for domestic students, 5/15 for

international students; for spring admission, 11/15 for domestic students, 10/15 for international students. Application fee: $55. Electronic applications accepted. *Expenses:* Contact institution. *Financial support:* Scholarships/grants available. Financial award applicants required to submit FAFSA. *Unit head:* Dr. John Veitch, Director, 415-422-2221, E-mail: management@usfca.edu. *Application contact:* Office of Graduate Recruiting and Admission, 415-422-2221, E-mail: management@usfca.edu.
Website: http://www.usfca.edu/msfa

University of Saskatchewan, College of Graduate and Postdoctoral Studies, Edwards School of Business, Department of Finance and Management Science, Saskatoon, SK S7N 5A2, Canada. Offers finance (M Sc). *Program availability:* Part-time. *Degree requirements:* For master's, thesis. *Entrance requirements:* For master's, GMAT. Additional exam requirements/recommendations for international students: Required—TOEFL.

The University of Scranton, Kania School of Management, Program in Business Administration, Scranton, PA 18510. Offers accounting (MBA); finance (MBA); general business administration (MBA); health care management (MBA); international business (MBA); management information systems (MBA); marketing (MBA); operations management (MBA). *Accreditation:* AACSB. *Program availability:* Part-time, evening/weekend, 100% online. *Entrance requirements:* For master's, GMAT (for MBA). *Faculty research:* Financial markets, strategic impact of total quality management, internal accounting controls, consumer preference, information systems and the Internet.

University of Southern Maine, College of Management and Human Service, School of Business, Portland, ME 04104-9300. Offers accounting (MBA); business administration (MBA); finance (MBA); health management and policy (MBA); sustainability (MBA); JD/MBA; MBA/MSA; MBA/MSN; MS/MBA. *Accreditation:* AACSB. *Program availability:* Part-time, evening/weekend. *Entrance requirements:* For master's, GMAT or GRE, minimum AACSB index of 1100. Additional exam requirements/recommendations for international students: Required—TOEFL (minimum score 550 paper-based; 79 iBT). Electronic applications accepted. *Faculty research:* Economic development, management information systems, real options, system dynamics, simulation.

University of South Florida, Muma College of Business, Department of Finance, Tampa, FL 33620-9951. Offers business administration (PhD), including finance; finance (MS); real estate (MSRE). *Program availability:* Part-time, evening/weekend. *Faculty:* 13 full-time (3 women), 1 part-time/adjunct (0 women). *Students:* 83 full-time (33 women), 22 part-time (7 women); includes 7 minority (1 Black or African American, non-Hispanic/Latino; 2 Asian, non-Hispanic/Latino; 4 Hispanic/Latino), 8,594 international. Average age 25. 119 applicants, 55% accepted, 37 enrolled. In 2018, 71 master's awarded. Terminal master's awarded for partial completion of doctoral program. *Degree requirements:* For master's, comprehensive exam, thesis or alternative; for doctorate, comprehensive exam, thesis/dissertation. *Entrance requirements:* For master's, GMAT score of 550 or higher (or equivalent GRE score). Applicants with lower GMAT (GRE) scores may be admitted if the application as a whole convinces the committee that the applicant warrants an admission to the major., minimum undergraduate GPA of 3.0; for doctorate, GMAT or GRE, minimum undergraduate GPA of 3.0 in upper-division coursework, personal statement, recommendations, interview. Additional exam requirements/recommendations for international students: Required—TOEFL, TOEFL (minimum score 550 paper-based; 79 iBT) or IELTS (minimum score 6.5). *Application deadline:* For fall admission, 6/1 for domestic students, 1/2 for international students; for spring admission, 10/15 for domestic students, 7/1 for international students; for summer admission, 2/15 for domestic students, 1/1 for international students. Application fee: $30. Electronic applications accepted. *Expenses:* Tuition, state resident: full-time $6350. Tuition, nonresident: full-time $19,048. *International tuition:* $19,048 full-time. *Required fees:* $2079. *Financial support:* In 2018–19, 12 students received support, including 8 research assistantships (averaging $14,357 per year), 9 teaching assistantships with tuition reimbursements available (averaging $11,972 per year); scholarships/grants, health care benefits, and unspecified assistantships also available. Financial award application deadline: 6/30. *Faculty research:* International corporate finance, corporate finance, market efficiency, mergers and acquisitions, agency theory, corporate governance, investments, mutual fund industry, mergers and acquisitions, corporate creditworthiness, credit risk issues, empirical asset pricing, financial intermediation, corporate finance theory, public offerings, business strategy. *Total annual research expenditures:* $30,000. *Unit head:* Dr. Scott Besley, Chairperson and Associate Professor, 813-974-6341, Fax: 813-974-3084, E-mail: sbesley@usf.edu. *Application contact:* Yuting DiGiovanni, 813-974-6358, Fax: 813-974-3084, E-mail: yuting2@usf.edu.
Website: http://business.usf.edu/departments/finance/

The University of Tampa, Sykes College of Business, Tampa, FL 33606-1490. Offers accounting (MS); business analytics (MBA); cybersecurity (MBA, MS); entrepreneurship (MBA, MS); finance (MBA, MS); information systems management (MBA); innovation management (MBA); international business (MBA); marketing (MBA, MS); nonprofit management (MBA, Certificate). *Accreditation:* AACSB. *Program availability:* Part-time, evening/weekend. *Faculty:* 61 full-time (13 women), 11 part-time/adjunct (3 women). *Students:* 361 full-time (153 women), 122 part-time (52 women); includes 101 minority (31 Black or African American, non-Hispanic/Latino; 5 Asian, non-Hispanic/Latino; 57 Hispanic/Latino; 1 Native Hawaiian or other Pacific Islander, non-Hispanic/Latino; 7 Two or more races, non-Hispanic/Latino), 144 international. Average age 29. 1,079 applicants, 57% accepted, 263 enrolled. In 2018, 281 master's, 12 other advanced degrees awarded. *Degree requirements:* For master's, capstone. *Entrance requirements:* For master's, GMAT or GRE, official transcripts from all colleges and/or universities previously attended, resume, personal statement, letters of recommendation. Additional exam requirements/recommendations for international students: Required—TOEFL (minimum score 577 paper-based; 90 iBT), IELTS (minimum score 7.5). *Application deadline:* Applications are processed on a rolling basis. Application fee: $40. Electronic applications accepted. *Expenses:* Contact institution. *Financial support:* In 2018–19, 123 students received support. Career-related internships or fieldwork, scholarships/grants, and unspecified assistantships available. Financial award applicants required to submit FAFSA. *Faculty research:* Job market signaling, on-line shopping behaviors and social media, the Tampa Bay economy, digital literacy, entrepreneurship in small businesses. *Unit head:* Dr. Natasha F. Veltri, Associate Dean, 813-253-6289, E-mail: nveltri@ut.edu. *Application contact:* Ashley Russell, Staff Assistant, Admissions for Graduate and Continuing Studies, 813-253-6249, E-mail: arussell@ut.edu.
Website: http://www.ut.edu/business/

The University of Tennessee, Graduate School, College of Business Administration, Program in Business Administration, Knoxville, TN 37996. Offers accounting (PhD); finance (MBA, PhD); logistics and transportation (MBA, PhD); management (PhD); marketing (MBA, PhD); operations management (MBA); professional business administration (MBA); statistics (PhD); JD/MBA; MS/MBA; Pharm D/MBA. Pharm D/MBA offered jointly with The University of Tennessee Health Science Center. *Accreditation:* AACSB. *Program availability:* Online learning. *Degree requirements:* For master's, thesis or alternative; for doctorate, thesis/dissertation. *Entrance requirements:* For master's and doctorate, GMAT, minimum GPA of 2.7. Additional exam requirements/recommendations for international students: Required—TOEFL. Electronic applications accepted.

The University of Tennessee at Martin, Graduate Programs, College of Business and Global Affairs, Program in Business, Martin, TN 38238. Offers agricultural business (MBA); financial services (MBA); general business (MBA). *Accreditation:* AACSB. *Program availability:* Part-time, online only, 100% online, blended/hybrid learning. *Faculty:* 33. *Students:* 8 full-time (2 women), 58 part-time (32 women); includes 5 minority (3 Black or African American, non-Hispanic/Latino; 1 Hispanic/Latino; 1 Two or more races, non-Hispanic/Latino). Average age 36. 65 applicants, 28% accepted, 13 enrolled. In 2018, 39 master's awarded. *Degree requirements:* For master's, comprehensive exam. *Entrance requirements:* For master's, GMAT, GRE, minimum GPA of 2.5, resume. Additional exam requirements/recommendations for international students: Required—TOEFL (minimum score 525 paper-based; 71 iBT). *Application deadline:* For fall admission, 7/27 priority date for domestic students, 7/27 for international students; for spring admission, 12/17 priority date for domestic students, 12/17 for international students; for summer admission, 5/10 priority date for domestic and international students. Applications are processed on a rolling basis. Application fee: $30 ($130 for international students). Electronic applications accepted. *Expenses: Tuition, area resident:* Full-time $8918; part-time $495 per credit hour. Tuition, state resident: full-time $8918; part-time $485 per credit hour. Tuition, nonresident: full-time $14,958; part-time $831 per credit hour. *International tuition:* $22,862 full-time. *Required fees:* $1446; $81 per credit hour. Part-time tuition and fees vary according to course load. *Financial support:* In 2018–19, 30 students received support, including 5 research assistantships with full tuition reimbursements available (averaging $7,289 per year), 4 teaching assistantships with full tuition reimbursements available (averaging $8,187 per year); scholarships/grants and tuition waivers (full and partial) also available. Financial award application deadline: 2/1; financial award applicants required to submit FAFSA. *Unit head:* Dr. Tommy Cates, Coordinator, 731-881-7208, Fax: 731-881-7231, E-mail: mba@utm.edu. *Application contact:* Jolene L. Cunningham, Student Services Specialist, 731-881-7012, Fax: 731-881-7499, E-mail: jcunningham@utm.edu.

The University of Texas at Arlington, Graduate School, College of Business, Department of Finance and Real Estate, Arlington, TX 76019. Offers finance (PhD); quantitative finance (MS); real estate (MS). *Program availability:* Part-time, evening/weekend. *Degree requirements:* For master's, thesis optional; for doctorate, comprehensive exam, thesis/dissertation. *Entrance requirements:* For master's, GMAT/GRE, minimum GPA of 3.0; for doctorate, GMAT/GRE. Additional exam requirements/recommendations for international students: Required—TOEFL (minimum score 550 paper-based; 79 iBT).

The University of Texas at Austin, Graduate School, McCombs School of Business, Department of Finance, Austin, TX 78712-1111. Offers MSF, PhD. *Entrance requirements:* For doctorate, GMAT or GRE. Electronic applications accepted.

The University of Texas at Dallas, Naveen Jindal School of Management, Program in Finance and Managerial Economics, Richardson, TX 75080. Offers finance (MS), including energy risk management, enterprise risk management, real estate, risk management insurance. *Program availability:* Part-time, evening/weekend. *Faculty:* 27 full-time (2 women), 19 part-time/adjunct (6 women). *Students:* 244 full-time (87 women), 93 part-time (30 women); includes 57 minority (5 Black or African American, non-Hispanic/Latino; 29 Asian, non-Hispanic/Latino; 15 Hispanic/Latino; 8 Two or more races, non-Hispanic/Latino), 211 international. Average age 27. 452 applicants, 53% accepted, 122 enrolled. In 2018, 181 master's awarded. *Entrance requirements:* For master's, GMAT or GRE. Additional exam requirements/recommendations for international students: Required—TOEFL (minimum score 550 paper-based). *Application deadline:* For fall admission, 7/15 for domestic students, 5/1 priority date for international students; for spring admission, 11/15 for domestic students, 9/1 priority date for international students. Applications are processed on a rolling basis. Application fee: $50 ($100 for international students). Electronic applications accepted. *Expenses: Tuition, area resident:* Full-time $13,458. Tuition, state resident: full-time $13,458. Tuition, nonresident: full-time $26,852. *International tuition:* $26,852 full-time. Tuition and fees vary according to course load. *Financial support:* In 2018–19, 10 teaching assistantships with partial tuition reimbursements (averaging $10,050 per year) were awarded; research assistantships with partial tuition reimbursements, career-related internships or fieldwork, Federal Work-Study, institutionally sponsored loans, scholarships/grants, and unspecified assistantships also available. Support available to part-time students. Financial award application deadline: 4/30; financial award applicants required to submit FAFSA. *Faculty research:* Econometrics, industrial organization, auction theory, file-sharing copyrights and bundling, international financial management, entrepreneurial finance. *Unit head:* Dr. Harold Zhang, Area Coordinator, 972-883-4777, E-mail: harold.zhang@utdallas.edu. *Application contact:* Dr. Harold Zhang, Area Coordinator, 972-883-4777, E-mail: harold.zhang@utdallas.edu.
Website: http://jindal.utdallas.edu/finance

The University of Texas at San Antonio, College of Business, Department of Finance, San Antonio, TX 78249-0617. Offers MBA, MS, PhD. *Program availability:* Part-time, evening/weekend. *Degree requirements:* For master's, comprehensive exam, thesis or alternative, 33 semester credit hours to be taken from a specified list of courses; for doctorate, comprehensive exam, thesis/dissertation. *Entrance requirements:* For master's and doctorate, GMAT or GRE, statement of purpose; 3 letters of recommendation. Additional exam requirements/recommendations for international students: Required—TOEFL (minimum score 550 paper-based; 79 iBT), IELTS (minimum score 6.5). Electronic applications accepted. *Faculty research:* Corporate finance, international finance, options and futures, market microstructure, financial institutions.

The University of Texas Rio Grande Valley, Robert C. Vackar College of Business and Entrepreneurship, Program in Business Administration, Edinburg, TX 78539. Offers business administration (MBA); finance (PhD); management (PhD); marketing (PhD). *Program availability:* Part-time, evening/weekend, online learning. *Degree requirements:* For master's, thesis optional. *Entrance requirements:* For master's, GMAT, minimum GPA of 3.0. Additional exam requirements/recommendations for international students: Required—TOEFL (minimum score 500 paper-based). Electronic applications accepted. *Expenses: Tuition, area resident:* Full-time $6888. Tuition, state resident: full-time $6888. Tuition, nonresident: full-time $14,484. *International tuition:* $14,484 full-time. *Required fees:* $1468. *Faculty research:* Human resources, border region, entrepreneurship, marketing.

University of the West, Department of Business Administration, Rosemead, CA 91770. Offers business administration (EMBA); computer information systems (MBA); finance (MBA); international business (MBA); nonprofit organization management (MBA). *Program availability:* Part-time, evening/weekend. *Entrance requirements:* Additional exam requirements/recommendations for international students: Required—TOEFL.

The University of Toledo, College of Graduate Studies, College of Business and Innovation, Department of Finance, Toledo, OH 43606-3390. Offers MBA. *Program availability:* Part-time, evening/weekend. *Entrance requirements:* For master's, GMAT, GRE, or LSAT, minimum GPA of 2.7 for all prior academic work, three letters of recommendation, statement of purpose, transcripts from all prior institutions attended.

Finance and Banking

Additional exam requirements/recommendations for international students: Required—TOEFL (minimum score 550 paper-based; 80 iBT). Electronic applications accepted. *Faculty research:* Financial management, banking, international finance, investments.

University of Toronto, School of Graduate Studies, Faculty of Arts and Science, Department of Economics, Program in Financial Economics, Toronto, ON M5S 1A1, Canada. Offers MFE. *Entrance requirements:* Additional exam requirements/recommendations for international students: Required—TOEFL (minimum score 102 iBT), TWE. Electronic applications accepted.

University of Utah, Graduate School, David Eccles School of Business, Business Administration Program, Salt Lake City, UT 84112. Offers accounting (PhD); business administration (EMBA, MBA, PMBA); finance (PhD); information systems (PhD); marketing (PhD); operations management (PhD); organizational behavior (PhD); strategic management (PhD); MBA/JD; MBA/MHA; MBA/MS. *Program availability:* Part-time, evening/weekend, online learning. *Students:* 112 full-time (26 women), 7 part-time (2 women); includes 12 minority (1 Asian, non-Hispanic/Latino; 7 Hispanic/Latino; 4 Two or more races, non-Hispanic/Latino), 13 international. Average age 29. 182 applicants, 51% accepted, 58 enrolled. In 2018, 58 master's awarded. *Entrance requirements:* For master's, GMAT or GRE; for doctorate, GMAT. Additional exam requirements/recommendations for international students: Required—TOEFL (minimum score 100 iBT), IELTS (minimum score 7). *Application deadline:* For fall admission, 5/1 for domestic students, 3/1 for international students. Application fee: $55 ($65 for international students). Electronic applications accepted. *Expenses:* Contact institution. *Financial support:* In 2018–19, 57 students received support. Scholarships/grants available. Financial award application deadline: 5/1; financial award applicants required to submit FAFSA. *Faculty research:* Corporate finance, strategy services, consumer behavior, financial disclosures, operations. *Unit head:* Brad Vierig, Associate Dean, MBA Programs & Executive Education. *Application contact:* Stephanie Geisler, Director, Full-Time MBA, 801-585-6291, E-mail: ftmba@utah.edu.
Website: http://www.business.utah.edu/

University of Utah, Graduate School, David Eccles School of Business, Master of Science in Finance Program, Salt Lake City, UT 84112. Offers MSF, MSF/MSBA, MSF/PMBA. *Program availability:* Part-time. *Degree requirements:* For master's, comprehensive exam. *Entrance requirements:* For master's, GMAT or GRE, minimum undergraduate GPA of 3.0. Additional exam requirements/recommendations for international students: Required—TOEFL (minimum score 90 iBT), IELTS (minimum score 6.5). Electronic applications accepted. *Expenses:* Contact institution. *Faculty research:* Investment, corporate finance, risk management, financial analysis, venture capital.

University of Virginia, McIntire School of Commerce, M.S. in Commerce, Charlottesville, VA 22903. Offers business analytics (MSC); finance (MSC); marketing and management (MSC). *Faculty:* 24 full-time (5 women). *Students:* 123 full-time (50 women). Average age 22. 448 applicants, 40% accepted, 123 enrolled. In 2018, 120 master's awarded. *Entrance requirements:* For master's, GMAT or GRE, 2 letters of recommendation; prerequisite course work in financial accounting, microeconomics, and introduction to statistics. Additional exam requirements/recommendations for international students: Required—TOEFL (minimum score 600 paper-based; 100 iBT), IELTS (minimum score 7.5). *Application deadline:* For fall admission, 11/1 priority date for domestic students, 1/1 priority date for international students; for winter admission, 2/1 for domestic students; for spring admission, 3/15 for domestic students; for summer admission, 6/1 for domestic students. Applications are processed on a rolling basis. Application fee: $75. Electronic applications accepted. *Expenses:* Contact institution. *Financial support:* In 2018–19, 30 students received support. Scholarships/grants available. Financial award application deadline: 2/1; financial award applicants required to submit FAFSA. *Faculty research:* Management, marketing, finance, analytics, and communication. *Unit head:* Ira C. Harris, Program Director, 434-924-8816, Fax: 434-924-7074, E-mail: ich3x@comm.virginia.edu. *Application contact:* Emma Candelier, Assistant Dean of Graduate Recruiting, 434-243-4992, Fax: 434-924-4511, E-mail: ecandelier@virginia.edu.
Website: https://www.commerce.virginia.edu/ms-commerce

University of Washington, Tacoma, Graduate Programs, MBA Programs, Tacoma, WA 98402-3100. Offers accounting (MBA); business administration (MBA); certified financial analyst (MBA). *Accreditation:* AACSB. *Program availability:* Part-time, evening/weekend. *Entrance requirements:* For master's, GMAT, minimum GPA of 3.0 in final graded 90 quarter credits or 60 graded semester credits; at least 2 years of professional/management work experience. Additional exam requirements/recommendations for international students: Required—TOEFL (minimum score 580 paper-based; 92 iBT). Electronic applications accepted. *Expenses:* Contact institution. *Faculty research:* International accounting, marketing, change management, investments, corporate social responsibility.

University of Waterloo, Graduate Studies and Postdoctoral Affairs, Faculty of Arts, School of Accounting and Finance, Waterloo, ON N2L 3G1, Canada. Offers accounting (M Acc, PhD); finance (M Acc); taxation (M Tax). *Degree requirements:* For master's, thesis or alternative; for doctorate, thesis/dissertation. *Entrance requirements:* For master's, honors degree, minimum B average, resume; for doctorate, GMAT, master's degree, minimum A- average, resume. Additional exam requirements/recommendations for international students: Required—TOEFL, IELTS, PTE. Application fee: $125 Canadian dollars. Electronic applications accepted. *Expenses:* Contact institution. *Financial support:* Fellowships and research assistantships available. *Faculty research:* Auditing, management accounting.
Website: https://uwaterloo.ca/school-of-accounting-and-finance/

The University of West Alabama, School of Graduate Studies, College of Business and Technology, Livingston, AL 35470. Offers finance (MBA); general business (MBA). *Program availability:* Part-time, evening/weekend, 100% online. *Faculty:* 1 full-time (0 women), 15 part-time/adjunct (11 women). *Students:* 169 full-time (124 women), 8 part-time (0 women); includes 97 minority (87 Black or African American, non-Hispanic/Latino; 1 American Indian or Alaska Native, non-Hispanic/Latino; 2 Asian, non-Hispanic/Latino; 1 Hispanic/Latino; 6 Two or more races, non-Hispanic/Latino). Average age 30. 110 applicants, 95% accepted, 78 enrolled. In 2018, 16 master's awarded. *Degree requirements:* For master's, nine hours completed for emphasis area. *Entrance requirements:* For master's, bachelor's degree with minimum GPA of 2.75. Additional exam requirements/recommendations for international students: Required—TOEFL (minimum score 500 paper-based; 61 iBT). *Application deadline:* Applications are processed on a rolling basis. Application fee: $40. Electronic applications accepted. *Expenses: Tuition, area resident:* Full-time $9100. Tuition, state resident: full-time $9100. Tuition, nonresident: full-time $19,200. *Required fees:* $1890; $130. *Financial support:* Federal Work-Study and scholarships/grants available. Support available to part-time students. Financial award application deadline: 3/1; financial award applicants required to submit FAFSA. *Unit head:* Dr. Aliquippa Allen, Dean of College of Business and Technology, 205-652-3564, Fax: 205-652-3776, E-mail: aallen@uwa.edu. *Application contact:* Dr. Aliquippa Allen, Dean of College of Business and Technology, 205-652-3564, Fax: 205-652-3776, E-mail: aallen@uwa.edu.
Website: http://www.uwa.edu/academics/collegeofbusinessandtechnology

The University of Western Ontario, Ivey Business School, London, ON N6A 3K7, Canada. Offers business (EMBA, PhD); corporate strategy and leadership elective (MBA); entrepreneurship elective (MBA); finance elective (MBA); health sector stream (MBA); international management elective (MBA); marketing elective (MBA); JD/MBA. *Degree requirements:* For master's, thesis (for some programs); for doctorate, thesis/dissertation. *Entrance requirements:* For master's, GMAT, 2 years of full-time work experience, interview. Additional exam requirements/recommendations for international students: Required—TOEFL (minimum score 100 iBT) or IELTS (minimium score 6). Electronic applications accepted. *Faculty research:* Strategy, organizational behavior, international business, finance, operations management.

University of Wisconsin–Madison, Graduate School, Wisconsin School of Business, Doctoral Program in Finance, Investment and Banking, Madison, WI 53706-1380. Offers PhD. *Degree requirements:* For doctorate, comprehensive exam, thesis/dissertation. *Entrance requirements:* For doctorate, GMAT or GRE. Additional exam requirements/recommendations for international students: Recommended—TOEFL (minimum score 623 paper-based; 106 iBT), IELTS (minimum score 7.5), TSE (minimum score 73). Electronic applications accepted. *Expenses:* Contact institution. *Faculty research:* Banking and financial institutions, business cycles, investments, derivatives, corporate finance, economics, bankruptcy, foreclosures, mergers and acquisitions, portfolio theory.

University of Wisconsin–Madison, Graduate School, Wisconsin School of Business, Wisconsin Full-Time MBA Program, Madison, WI 53706-1380. Offers applied security analysis (MBA); arts administration (MBA); brand and product management (MBA); corporate finance and investment banking (MBA); marketing research (MBA); operations and technology management (MBA); real estate (MBA); risk management and insurance (MBA); strategic human resource management (MBA); supply chain management (MBA). *Faculty:* 137 full-time (36 women), 39 part-time/adjunct (11 women). *Students:* 183 full-time (59 women); includes 31 minority (5 Black or African American, non-Hispanic/Latino; 1 American Indian or Alaska Native, non-Hispanic/Latino; 6 Asian, non-Hispanic/Latino; 13 Hispanic/Latino; 6 Two or more races, non-Hispanic/Latino), 40 international. Average age 28. 465 applicants, 33% accepted, 79 enrolled. In 2018, 104 master's awarded. *Entrance requirements:* For master's, GMAT or GRE, bachelor's or equivalent degree, essay, letter of recommendation, resume. Additional exam requirements/recommendations for international students: Required—TOEFL (minimum score 100 iBT), IELTS (minimum score 7.5), TOEFL is not required for international students whose undergraduate training was in English. *Application deadline:* For fall admission, 11/1 for domestic and international students; for winter admission, 1/10 for domestic and international students; for spring admission, 3/1 for domestic and international students; for summer admission, 4/10 for domestic students, 4/10 priority date for international students. Applications are processed on a rolling basis. Application fee: $75 ($81 for international students). Electronic applications accepted. *Expenses:* Wisconsin Resident tuition and fees - $39,156; Nonresident tuition and fees - $76,635. *Financial support:* In 2018–19, 148 students received support, including 7 fellowships with full tuition reimbursements available (averaging $25,871 per year), 7 research assistantships with full tuition reimbursements available (averaging $14,832 per year), 47 teaching assistantships with full tuition reimbursements available (averaging $14,832 per year); scholarships/grants, health care benefits, tuition waivers (full and partial), and unspecified assistantships also available. Financial award application deadline: 6/1. *Faculty research:* Ecology, environmental studies, and business; decision making; tax policy; diversity and inclusion in governance boards; marketing and social media. *Unit head:* Dr. Enno Siemsen, Associate Dean of the MBA and Masters Programs, 608-890-3130, E-mail: esiemsen@wisc.edu. *Application contact:* Betsy Kacizak, Director of Admissions and Recruiting, Full-time MBA Program, 608-262-4000, E-mail: betsy.kacizak@wisc.edu.
Website: https://wsb.wisc.edu/

University of Wisconsin–Whitewater, School of Graduate Studies, College of Business and Economics, Program in Business Administration, Whitewater, WI 53190-1790. Offers finance (MBA). *Accreditation:* AACSB. *Program availability:* Part-time, evening/weekend, online learning. *Entrance requirements:* For master's, GMAT or GRE, minimum AACSB index of 1000, minimum GPA of 2.75. Additional exam requirements/recommendations for international students: Required—TOEFL (minimum score 550 paper-based; 80 iBT), IELTS (minimum score 6). Electronic applications accepted. *Faculty research:* Interface between social institutions and individual behavior, technology and innovation management, occupational mental health, workplace deviance and workplace romance.

University of Wyoming, College of Business, Department of Accounting and Finance, Program in Finance, Laramie, WY 82071. Offers MS. *Program availability:* Part-time. *Degree requirements:* For master's, thesis. *Entrance requirements:* For master's, GMAT, GRE, minimum GPA of 3.0. Additional exam requirements/recommendations for international students: Required—TOEFL (minimum score 540 paper-based; 76 iBT). *Expenses: Tuition, area resident:* Full-time $6504; part-time $271 per credit hour. Tuition, state resident: full-time $6504; part-time $271 per credit hour. Tuition, nonresident: full-time $19,464; part-time $811 per credit hour. International tuition: $19,464 full-time. *Required fees:* $1410.94; $343.82 per semester. $343.82 per semester. Tuition and fees vary according to course load, program and reciprocity agreements. *Faculty research:* Banking.

Upper Iowa University, Online Master's Programs, Fayette, IA 52142-1857. Offers accounting (MBA); corporate financial management (MBA); emergency management and homeland security (MPA); general management (MBA); general studies (MPA); government administration (MPA); health and human services (MPA); human resources management (MBA); nonprofit organizational management (MPA); organizational development (MBA); public management (MPA); sport administration (MSA). MBA also available at Madison, WI campus. *Program availability:* Part-time, online learning. *Degree requirements:* For master's, research project. *Entrance requirements:* For master's, GMAT, GRE, or minimum GPA of 2.7 during last 60 hours. Additional exam requirements/recommendations for international students: Required—TOEFL (minimum score 570 paper-based). Electronic applications accepted. *Faculty research:* Total quality management, teams, organization culture and climate, management.

Ursuline College, School of Graduate and Professional Studies, Program in Business Administration, Pepper Pike, OH 44124-4398. Offers ethical and entrepreneurial leadership (MBA); financial planning and accounting (MBA); health services management (MBA); management (MBA); management and leadership (MBA); marketing and communications management (MBA). *Program availability:* Part-time, evening/weekend. *Faculty:* 2 full-time (both women), 2 part-time/adjunct (1 woman). *Students:* 17 full-time (all women), 5 part-time (3 women); includes 10 minority (9 Black or African American, non-Hispanic/Latino; 1 Two or more races, non-Hispanic/Latino). Average age 40. 33 applicants, 100% accepted, 6 enrolled. In 2018, 16 master's awarded. *Degree requirements:* For master's, comprehensive exam (for some programs). *Entrance requirements:* For master's, GRE. Additional exam requirements/recommendations for international students: Required—TOEFL (minimum score 500 paper-based) or GRE. *Application deadline:* For fall admission, 8/1 for domestic students. Applications are processed on a rolling basis. Application fee: $25. Electronic applications accepted. *Expenses:* 36 hours at $903/per. *Financial support:* In 2018–19,

2 students received support. Campus work-study available. Financial award application deadline: 8/1; financial award applicants required to submit FAFSA. *Faculty research:* Gift economy; sharing economy; cooperative business models; collaborative leadership; corporate social responsibility and the triple bottom line, defined as the three P's: people, planet and profit. *Unit head:* Dr. Debra Fleming, Professor, 440-440-720-3864, Fax: 440-684-6088, E-mail: dfleming@ursuline.edu. *Application contact:* Melanie Steele, Director of Graduate Admission, 440-646-8146, Fax: 440-684-6138, E-mail: graduateadmissions@ursuline.edu.

Utah State University, School of Graduate Studies, Jon M. Huntsman School of Business, Department of Economics and Finance, Logan, UT 84322. Offers economics (MS); financial economics (MS). *Degree requirements:* For master's, thesis (for some programs). *Entrance requirements:* For master's, GRE General Test, GMAT, minimum GPA of 3.0. Additional exam requirements/recommendations for international students: Required—TOEFL. Electronic applications accepted. *Faculty research:* Resource economics, economic theory, international trade, industrial organization, development.

Valparaiso University, Graduate School and Continuing Education, College of Business, Valparaiso, IN 46383. Offers business administration (MBA); business decision-making (Certificate); business intelligence (Certificate); engineering management (Certificate); finance (Certificate); general business (Certificate); leading the global enterprise (Certificate); management (Certificate); JD/MBA; MSN/MBA. *Accreditation:* AACSB. *Program availability:* Part-time, evening/weekend, online learning. *Students:* 7 full-time (5 women), 43 part-time (16 women); includes 5 minority (4 Black or African American, non-Hispanic/Latino; 1 Two or more races, non-Hispanic/Latino). Average age 31. *Entrance requirements:* For master's, GMAT, GRE, minimum GPA of 3.0. Additional exam requirements/recommendations for international students: Required—TOEFL (minimum score 550 paper-based; 80 iBT), IELTS (minimum score 6). *Application deadline:* Applications are processed on a rolling basis. Application fee: $30 ($50 for international students). Electronic applications accepted. *Expenses:* Contact institution. *Financial support:* Available to part-time students. Applicants required to submit FAFSA. *Unit head:* Jim Brodzinski, Dean, 219-464-5035, E-mail: jim.brodzinski@valpo.edu. *Application contact:* Cindy Scanlan, Director of Graduate Programs in Management, 219-465-7952, Fax: 219-464-5789, E-mail: cindy.scanlan@valpo.edu.
Website: http://www.valpo.edu/college-of-business/

Valparaiso University, Graduate School and Continuing Education, Program in International Economics and Finance, Valparaiso, IN 46383. Offers MS. *Program availability:* Part-time, evening/weekend. *Entrance requirements:* For master's, 1 semester of college-level calculus; 1 statistics or quantitative methods class; 2 semesters of introductory economics (course content in introductory economics must include both introductory microeconomics and macroeconomics); 1 introductory accounting course; minimum undergraduate GPA of 3.0; 2 letters of recommendation. Additional exam requirements/recommendations for international students: Required—TOEFL (minimum score 550 paper-based; 80 iBT), IELTS (minimum score 6).

Vancouver Island University, Master of Business Administration Program, Nanaimo, BC V9R 5S5, Canada. Offers international business (MBA), including finance, marketing. Program offered jointly with University of Hertfordshire. *Accreditation:* ACBSP. *Program availability:* Part-time. *Degree requirements:* For master's, thesis. *Entrance requirements:* Additional exam requirements/recommendations for international students: Required—TOEFL (minimum score 88 iBT), IELTS (minimum score 6.5). Electronic applications accepted. *Expenses:* Contact institution. *Faculty research:* Tourism development, entrepreneurship, organizational development, strategic planning, international business strategy, intercultural team work.

Vanderbilt University, Vanderbilt University Owen Graduate School of Management, MS in Finance Program, Nashville, TN 37203. Offers MS. *Entrance requirements:* For master's, GMAT and/or GRE. Additional exam requirements/recommendations for international students: Required—TOEFL (minimum score 105 iBT). Electronic applications accepted. *Expenses:* Contact institution.

Vanderbilt University, Vanderbilt University Owen Graduate School of Management, Vanderbilt MBA Program, Nashville, TN 37203. Offers accounting (MBA); finance (MBA); general management (MBA); health care (MBA); human and organizational performance (MBA); marketing (MBA); operations (MBA); strategy (MBA); MBA/JD; MBA/M Div; MBA/MD; MBA/MSN; MBA/MTS; MBA/PhD. *Accreditation:* AACSB. *Degree requirements:* For master's, 62 credit hours of coursework; completion of ethics course; minimum GPA of 3.0. *Entrance requirements:* For master's, GMAT (preferred) or GRE, 2 years of work experience (recommended). Additional exam requirements/recommendations for international students: Required—TOEFL (minimum score 100 iBT). Electronic applications accepted. *Expenses:* Contact institution. *Faculty research:* Accounting and finance, business strategy and economics, marketing, operations management, organization studies.

Villanova University, Villanova School of Business, Master of Science in Finance Program, Villanova, PA 19085-1699. Offers MSF. *Faculty:* 101 full-time (38 women), 36 part-time/adjunct (9 women). *Students:* 23 full-time (5 women); includes 1 minority (Black or African American, non-Hispanic/Latino), 6 international. Average age 23. 94 applicants, 56% accepted, 23 enrolled. In 2018, 22 master's awarded. *Degree requirements:* For master's, minimum cumulative GPA of 3.0. *Entrance requirements:* For master's, GMAT, Application, official transcripts, 2 letters of recommendation, resume, essay, interview. Additional exam requirements/recommendations for international students: Required—TOEFL (minimum score 550 paper-based; 100 iBT). *Application deadline:* For summer admission, 3/15 for domestic and international students. Applications are processed on a rolling basis. Application fee: $65. Electronic applications accepted. *Expenses:* Contact institution. *Financial support:* In 2018–19, 4 research assistantships (averaging $6,550 per year) were awarded; scholarships/grants also available. Financial award application deadline: 6/30; financial award applicants required to submit FAFSA. *Faculty research:* Real Estate, Business Analytics, Global Leadership, Marketing and Consumer Insights, Church management. *Unit head:* Dr. Joyce E. A. Russell, Dean of Villanova School of Business, 610-519-6082, Fax: 610-519-6273, E-mail: joyce.russell@villanova.edu. *Application contact:* Kimberly Kane, Manager, Recruitment, 610-519-3701, Fax: 610-519-6273, E-mail: kimberly.kane@villanova.edu.
Website: http://www1.villanova.edu/villanova/business/graduate/specializedprograms/msf.html

Villanova University, Villanova School of Business, MBA - The Fast Track Program, Villanova, PA 19085. Offers finance (MBA); healthcare (MBA); international business (MBA); strategic management (MBA). *Accreditation:* AACSB. *Program availability:* Part-time, evening/weekend. *Faculty:* 101 full-time (38 women), 36 part-time/adjunct (9 women). *Students:* 111 part-time (47 women); includes 20 minority (3 Black or African American, non-Hispanic/Latino; 7 Asian, non-Hispanic/Latino; 9 Hispanic/Latino; 1 Two or more races, non-Hispanic/Latino), 4 international. Average age 30. 45 applicants, 80% accepted, 26 enrolled. In 2018, 55 master's awarded. *Degree requirements:* For master's, minimum GPA of 3.0. *Entrance requirements:* For master's, GMAT or GRE, Application, official transcripts, 2 letters of recommendation, resume, 2 essays. Additional exam requirements/recommendations for international students: Required—TOEFL (minimum score 550 paper-based; 100 iBT). *Application deadline:* For fall admission, 7/31 for domestic and international students. Applications are processed on a rolling basis. Application fee: $65. Electronic applications accepted. *Expenses:* Contact institution. *Financial support:* Scholarships/grants available. Financial award application deadline: 6/30; financial award applicants required to submit FAFSA. *Faculty research:* Real Estate, Business Analytics, Global Leadership, Marketing and Consumer Insights, Church management. *Unit head:* Dr. Joyce E. A. Russell, Dean of Villanova School of Business, 610-519-6082, Fax: 610-519-6273, E-mail: joyce.russell@villanova.edu. *Application contact:* Daniel Guertin, Assistant Director, Recruitment, 610-519-8031, Fax: 610-519-6273, E-mail: daniel.guertin@villanova.edu.
Website: http://www1.villanova.edu/villanova/business/graduate/mba.html

Virginia Commonwealth University, Graduate School, L. Douglas Wilder School of Government and Public Affairs, Program in Public Administration, Richmond, VA 23284-9005. Offers financial management (MPA); human resource management (MPA); state and local government management (MPA). *Accreditation:* NASPAA. *Program availability:* Part-time. *Entrance requirements:* For master's, GRE, GMAT or LSAT. Additional exam requirements/recommendations for international students: Required—TOEFL (minimum score 600 paper-based; 100 iBT); Recommended—IELTS (minimum score 6.5). Electronic applications accepted. *Faculty research:* Environmental policy, executive leadership, human resource management, local government management, nonprofit management, public financial management, public policy analysis and evaluation.

Virginia International University, School of Business, Fairfax, VA 22030. Offers accounting (MBA, MS); entrepreneurship (MBA); executive management (Graduate Certificate); global logistics (MBA); health care management (MBA); hospitality and tourism management (MBA); human resources management (MBA); international business management (MBA); international finance (MBA); marketing management (MBA); mass media and public relations (MBA); project management (MBA, MS). *Program availability:* Part-time, online learning. *Entrance requirements:* For master's and Graduate Certificate, bachelor's degree. Additional exam requirements/recommendations for international students: Required—TOEFL (minimum score 550 paper-based; 80 iBT), IELTS (minimum score 6). Electronic applications accepted.

Virginia Polytechnic Institute and State University, Graduate School, Pamplin College of Business, Blacksburg, VA 24061. Offers accounting and information systems (MACIS, PhD); business administration (MS), including business analytics, hospitality and tourism management; business information technology (PhD); executive business research (PhD); finance (PhD); marketing (PhD), including marketing; MS/MBA. *Faculty:* 141 full-time (42 women), 2 part-time/adjunct (1 woman). *Students:* 227 full-time (89 women), 217 part-time (75 women); includes 131 minority (30 Black or African American, non-Hispanic/Latino; 58 Asian, non-Hispanic/Latino; 25 Hispanic/Latino; 18 Two or more races, non-Hispanic/Latino), 81 international. Average age 32. 361 applicants, 55% accepted, 152 enrolled. In 2018, 181 master's, 8 doctorates awarded. *Degree requirements:* For master's, comprehensive exam (for some programs), thesis (for some programs); for doctorate, comprehensive exam (for some programs), thesis/dissertation (for some programs). *Entrance requirements:* For master's and doctorate, GRE/GMAT. Additional exam requirements/recommendations for international students: Required—TOEFL (minimum score 90 iBT). *Application deadline:* For fall admission, 8/1 for domestic students, 4/1 for international students; for spring admission, 1/1 for domestic students, 9/1 for international students. Applications are processed on a rolling basis. Application fee: $75. Electronic applications accepted. *Expenses:* Tuition, state resident: full-time $15,510; part-time $739.50 per credit hour. Tuition, nonresident: full-time $29,629; part-time $1490.25 per credit hour. *Required fees:* $2804; $550 per semester. Tuition and fees vary according to course load, campus/location and program. *Financial support:* In 2018–19, 1 fellowship with full tuition reimbursement (averaging $3,999 per year), 4 research assistantships with full tuition reimbursements (averaging $20,163 per year), 66 teaching assistantships with full tuition reimbursements (averaging $19,822 per year) were awarded; scholarships/grants and unspecified assistantships also available. Financial award application deadline: 3/1; financial award applicants required to submit FAFSA. *Total annual research expenditures:* $3.1 million. *Unit head:* Dr. Robert T. Sumichrast, Dean, 540-231-6601, Fax: 540-231-4487, E-mail: busdean@vt.edu. *Application contact:* Kimberly Ridpath, Executive Assistant, 540-231-9647, Fax: 540-231-4487, E-mail: ridpathk@vt.edu.
Website: http://www.pamplin.vt.edu/

Wagner College, Division of Graduate Studies, Nicolais School of Business, Staten Island, NY 10301-4495. Offers accounting (MS); business administration (MBA); finance (MBA); management (Exec MBA); marketing (MBA); media management (MS). *Accreditation:* ACBSP. *Program availability:* Part-time, evening/weekend. *Degree requirements:* For master's, thesis optional. *Entrance requirements:* For master's, minimum GPA of 2.75, proficiency in computers and math. Additional exam requirements/recommendations for international students: Required—TOEFL (minimum score 550 paper-based; 79 iBT), IELTS (minimum score 6.5).

Walden University, Graduate Programs, School of Management, Minneapolis, MN 55401. Offers accounting (MBA, MS, DBA), including accounting for the professional (MS), accounting with CPA emphasis (MS), self-designed (MS); advanced project management (Graduate Certificate); applied project management (Graduate Certificate); auditing (Graduate Certificate); bridge to business administration (Post-Doctoral Certificate); bridge to management (Post-Doctoral Certificate); business management (Graduate Certificate); communication (MBA); corporate finance (MBA); digital marketing (Graduate Certificate); entrepreneurship (DBA); entrepreneurship and small business (MBA); finance (MS, DBA), including finance for the professional (MS), finance with CFA/investment (MS), finance with CPA emphasis (MS); global supply chain management (DBA); healthcare management (MBA, DBA); human resource management (MBA, MS, Graduate Certificate), including functional human resource management (MS), general program (MS), integrating functional and strategic human resource management (MS), organizational strategy (MS); human resources management (DBA); information systems management (DBA); international business (MBA, DBA); leadership (MBA, MS, DBA, Graduate Certificate), including general program (MS), human resource leadership (MS), leader development (MS), self-designed (MS); management (MS, PhD), including communications (MS), finance (PhD), general program (MS), healthcare management (MS), human resource management (MS), human resources management (PhD), information systems management (PhD), international business (MS), leadership (MS), leadership and organizational change (PhD), marketing (MS), project management (MS), strategy and operations (MS); managerial accounting (Graduate Certificate); marketing (MBA, MS, DBA); project management (MBA, MS, DBA); self-designed (MBA, DBA); social impact management (DBA); technology entrepreneurship (DBA). *Accreditation:* ACBSP. *Program availability:* Part-time, evening/weekend, online only, 100% online. *Degree requirements:* For master's, thesis (for some programs), residency (for EMBA); for doctorate, thesis/dissertation (for some programs), residency. *Entrance requirements:* For master's, bachelor's degree or higher; minimum GPA of 2.5; official transcripts; goal statement (for some programs); access to computer and Internet; for doctorate, master's degree or higher; three years of related professional or academic experience (preferred); minimum GPA of 3.0; goal statement and current resume (for select

programs); official transcripts; access to computer and Internet; for other advanced degree, relevant work experience; access to computer and Internet. Additional exam requirements/recommendations for international students: Required—TOEFL (minimum score 550 paper-based, 79 iBT), IELTS (minimum score 6.5), Michigan English Language Assessment Battery (minimum score 82), or PTE (minimum score 53). Electronic applications accepted.

Walsh College of Accountancy and Business Administration, Graduate Programs, Program in Accountancy, Troy, MI 48083. Offers data analytics (MAC); finance (MAC); taxation (MAC). *Program availability:* Part-time, evening/weekend. *Faculty:* 6 full-time (2 women), 14 part-time/adjunct (7 women). *Students:* 14 full-time (3 women), 209 part-time (127 women); includes 51 minority (19 Black or African American, non-Hispanic/Latino; 21 Asian, non-Hispanic/Latino; 10 Hispanic/Latino; 1 Two or more races, non-Hispanic/Latino), 14 international. Average age 33. 67 applicants, 91% accepted, 39 enrolled. In 2018, 84 master's awarded. *Degree requirements:* For master's, thesis optional. *Entrance requirements:* For master's, minimum overall cumulative GPA of 2.75 from all colleges previously attended. Additional exam requirements/recommendations for international students: Required—TOEFL (minimum score 550 paper-based, 79-80 internet based), IELTS (6.5), Michigan Test of English Language Proficiency or MTELP (80). *Application deadline:* Applications are processed on a rolling basis. Application fee: $35. Electronic applications accepted. *Expenses:* Tuition: Full-time $21,195; part-time $14,130 per credit hour. *Required fees:* $525; $525 per semester. $175 per semester. *Financial support:* In 2018–19, 22 students received support. Scholarships/grants available. Financial award application deadline: 6/30; financial award applicants required to submit FAFSA. *Unit head:* John Black, Chair, Accounting, 248-823-1635, Fax: 248-689-0920, E-mail: jblack@walshcollege.edu. *Application contact:* Karen Mahaffy, Executive Director, Admissions and Enrollment Services, 248-823-1600, Fax: 248-823-1611, E-mail: kmahafyy@walshcollege.edu.
Website: https:www.walshcollege.edu/masters-ms-degree-accounting

Washington University in St. Louis, Olin Business School, DBA Program, St. Louis, MO 63130-4899. Offers marketing (DBA). *Program availability:* Part-time. *Faculty:* 85 full-time (16 women), 46 part-time/adjunct (13 women). *Students:* 10 full-time (4 women), 6 part-time (2 women); includes 2 minority (1 Black or African American, non-Hispanic/Latino; 1 Hispanic/Latino), 11 international. 27 applicants, 48% accepted, 4 enrolled. In 2018, 2 doctorates awarded. *Degree requirements:* For doctorate, comprehensive exam, thesis/dissertation, 72 credit- hour, 2nd-year paper presentation, thesis proposal defense. *Entrance requirements:* For doctorate, GRE or GMAT. Additional exam requirements/recommendations for international students: Required—TOEFL or IELTS. *Application deadline:* For fall admission, 6/1 for domestic and international students. Applications are processed on a rolling basis. Application fee: $99. Electronic applications accepted. *Financial support:* Fellowships, health care benefits, and Travel support for conference available. *Unit head:* Prof. Anjan Thakor, Director, 314-935-7197, E-mail: thakor@wustl.edu. *Application contact:* Erin Murdock, Associate Director of Doctoral Admissions and Student Affairs, 314-935-6340, Fax: 314-935-9484, E-mail: murdockel@wustl.edu.
Website: http://www.olin.wustl.edu/EN-US/academic-programs/dba-in-finance/

Washington University in St. Louis, Olin Business School, Program in Finance, St. Louis, MO 63130-4899. Offers corporate finance and investments (MS); quantitative finance (MS). *Program availability:* Part-time. *Faculty:* 98 full-time (25 women), 54 part-time/adjunct (12 women). *Students:* 85 full-time (16 women), 46 part-time (13 women); includes 26 minority (16 Asian, non-Hispanic/Latino; 9 Hispanic/Latino; 1 Two or more races, non-Hispanic/Latino), 125 international. Average age 25. 1,468 applicants, 20% accepted, 124 enrolled. In 2018, 113 master's awarded. *Degree requirements:* For master's, 11-18 months. *Entrance requirements:* For master's, GMAT or GRE, U.S. bachelor's degree or equivalent, one letter of recommendation. Additional exam requirements/recommendations for international students: Required—TOEFL, IELTS. *Application deadline:* For fall admission, 10/10 for domestic and international students; for winter admission, 1/15 for domestic students, 1/15 priority date for international students; for spring admission, 3/18 for domestic and international students. Applications are processed on a rolling basis. Application fee: $100. Electronic applications accepted. *Expenses:* Contact institution. *Financial support:* Institutionally sponsored loans and scholarships/grants available. Financial award applicants required to submit FAFSA. *Unit head:* Dr. Steve Malter, Senior Associate Dean, Undergrad and Graduate Programs, 314-935-6315, Fax: 314-935-9095, E-mail: malter@wustl.edu. *Application contact:* Ruthie Pyles, Asst Dean & Dir of Grad Admissions & Fin Aid, 314-935-7301, Fax: 314-935-4464, E-mail: olingradadmissions@wustl.edu.
Website: http://www.olin.wustl.edu/prospective/

Waynesburg University, Graduate and Professional Studies, Canonsburg, PA 15370. Offers business (MBA), including energy management, finance, health systems, human resources, leadership, market development; counseling (MA), including addictions counseling, clinical mental health; counselor education and supervision (PhD); criminal investigation (MA); education (M Ed), including autism, curriculum and instruction, educational leadership, online teaching; nursing (MSN), including administration, education, informatics; nursing practice (DNP); special education (M Ed); technology (M Ed); MSN/MBA. *Accreditation:* AACN. *Program availability:* Part-time, evening/weekend. *Degree requirements:* For doctorate, thesis/dissertation. *Entrance requirements:* Additional exam requirements/recommendations for international students: Required—TOEFL. Electronic applications accepted.

Wayne State University, Law School, Detroit, MI 48202. Offers corporate and finance law (LL M); labor and employment law (LL M); law (JD); taxation (LL M); United States law (LL M); JD/MA; JD/MADR; JD/MBA; JD/MS. *Accreditation:* ABA. *Program availability:* Part-time, evening/weekend. *Faculty:* 43 full-time (18 women), 17 part-time/adjunct (9 women). *Students:* 406 full-time (198 women), 38 part-time (9 women); includes 51 minority (35 Black or African American, non-Hispanic/Latino; 3 American Indian or Alaska Native, non-Hispanic/Latino; 7 Asian, non-Hispanic/Latino; 1 Hispanic/Latino; 5 Two or more races, non-Hispanic/Latino), 15 international. Average age 26. 859 applicants, 49% accepted, 137 enrolled. In 2018, 6 master's awarded. *Degree requirements:* For master's, thesis (for some programs). *Entrance requirements:* For master's, JD or LL B from ABA-accredited institution and member institution of the AALS; for doctorate, LSAT, LDAS report, bachelor's degree from accredited institution, personal statement, transcripts from all U.S. undergraduate schools attended and an analysis and summary of the transcripts; letter of recommendation (up to two are accepted). Additional exam requirements/recommendations for international students: Required—TOEFL, Michigan English Language Assessment Battery (minimum score 85); Recommended—IELTS. *Application deadline:* For fall admission, 7/1 for domestic students. Applications are processed on a rolling basis. Application fee: $0. Electronic applications accepted. *Expenses:* Resident tuition: $1,055.56 per credit hour, $315.70 per semester registration fee, $54.56 per credit hour student service fee. Non-resident tuition: $1,158 per credit hour, $315.70 per semester registration fee, $54.56 per credit hour student service fee. *Financial support:* In 2018–19, 365 students received support. Fellowships, Federal Work-Study, and scholarships/grants available. Support available to part-time students. Financial award application deadline: 6/30; financial award applicants required to submit FAFSA. *Unit head:* Richard A. Bierschbach, Dean and Professor of Law, 313-577-3933, E-mail: rbierschbach@wayne.edu. *Application contact:*

Kathy Fox, Assistant Dean of Admissions, 313-577-3937, Fax: 313-993-8129, E-mail: lawinquire@wayne.edu.
Website: http://law.wayne.edu/

Wayne State University, Mike Ilitch School of Business, Detroit, MI 48202. Offers accounting (MS, MSA, Postbaccalaureate Certificate); business (EMS, Graduate Certificate); business administration (MBA, PhD); data science (MS), including business analytics; entrepreneurship and innovation (Postbaccalaureate Certificate); finance (MS); information systems management (Postbaccalaureate Certificate); taxation (MST); JD/MBA. Application deadline for PhD is February 15. *Accreditation:* AACSB. *Program availability:* Part-time, evening/weekend. *Faculty:* 31. *Students:* 286 full-time (152 women), 1,166 part-time (533 women); includes 409 minority (236 Black or African American, non-Hispanic/Latino; 83 Asian, non-Hispanic/Latino; 53 Hispanic/Latino; 37 Two or more races, non-Hispanic/Latino), 74 international. Average age 30. 1,212 applicants, 38% accepted, 294 enrolled. In 2018, 285 master's, 6 doctorates, 7 other advanced degrees awarded. *Degree requirements:* For doctorate, thesis/dissertation. *Entrance requirements:* For master's, GMAT, GRE, LSAT, MCAT, at least three years of relevant work experience that shows increased responsibility, or minimum GPA of 3.0 from AACSB-accredited program or 3.2 from regionally-accredited program, undergraduate degree from accredited institution; undergraduate degree in accounting, business administration, or area of business administration (for MS and MST); for doctorate, GMAT (minimum score of 600), minimum undergraduate GPA of 3.0, 3.5 upper-division or graduate; three letters of recommendation; brief essay; undergraduate degree from accredited institution; personal statement; for other advanced degree, bachelor's degree from accredited institution. Additional exam requirements/ recommendations for international students: Required—TOEFL (minimum score 550 paper-based; 79 iBT), Michigan English Language Assessment Battery (minimum score 85); Recommended—IELTS (minimum score 6.5), TWE (minimum score 5.5). *Application deadline:* For fall admission, 7/1 for domestic students, 5/1 priority date for international students; for winter admission, 11/1 for domestic students, 9/1 priority date for international students; for spring admission, 3/1 for domestic students, 1/1 priority date for international students. Applications are processed on a rolling basis. Application fee: $50. Electronic applications accepted. *Expenses:* Contact institution. *Financial support:* In 2018–19, 175 students received support, including 1 fellowship with tuition reimbursement available (averaging $20,000 per year), 5 research assistantships with tuition reimbursements available (averaging $21,393 per year); teaching assistantships with tuition reimbursements available, scholarships/grants, health care benefits, and unspecified assistantships also available. Support available to part-time students. Financial award applicants required to submit FAFSA. *Faculty research:* Executive compensation and stock performance, consumer reactions to pricing strategies, communication across the automotive supply chain, performance of firms in sub-Saharan Africa, implementation issues with ERP software. *Unit head:* Dr. Robert Forsythe, Dean, School of Business Administration, 313-577-4501, E-mail: robert.forsythe@wayne.edu. *Application contact:* Kiantee N. Rupert-Jones, Director, 313-577-4511, Fax: 313-577-9442, E-mail: gradbusiness@wayne.edu.
Website: http://ilitchbusiness.wayne.edu/

Webster University, George Herbert Walker School of Business and Technology, Department of Business, St. Louis, MO 63119-3194. Offers business and organizational security management (MBA); decision support systems (MBA); environmental management (MBA); finance (MBA, MS); forensic accounting (MS); gerontology (MBA); human resources development (MBA); human resources management (MBA); information technology management (MBA); international business (MA, MBA); international relations (MBA); management and leadership (MBA); marketing (MBA); media communications (MBA); procurement and acquisitions management (MBA); Web services (MBA). *Accreditation:* ACBSP. *Program availability:* Part-time, evening/weekend, online learning. *Degree requirements:* For master's, comprehensive exam (for some programs), thesis (for some programs). *Entrance requirements:* Additional exam requirements/recommendations for international students: Required—TOEFL. *Expenses:* Tuition: Full-time $22,500; part-time $750 per credit hour. Tuition and fees vary according to degree level, campus/location and program.

Western Michigan University Thomas M. Cooley Law School, Graduate Programs, Lansing, MI 48901-3038. Offers administrative law (public law) (JD); business transactions (JD); Canadian law practice (JD); corporate law and finance (LL M); environmental law (public law) (JD); general practice (JD), including solo and small firm; general studies (LL M); homeland and national security law (LL M); insurance law (LL M); intellectual property (JD); intellectual property law (LL M); international law (JD); litigation (JD); taxation (LL M); U.S. legal studies for foreign attorneys (LL M); JD/LL M; JD/MBA; JD/MHA; JD/MPA; JD/MSW. *Accreditation:* ABA. *Program availability:* Part-time, evening/weekend, 100% online, blended/hybrid learning. *Degree requirements:* For master's, thesis (for some programs); for doctorate, minimum of 3 credits of clinical experience. *Entrance requirements:* For master's, JD or LL B; for doctorate, LSAT. Additional exam requirements/recommendations for international students: Required—TOEFL (for U.S. legal studies for foreign attorneys LL M program); Recommended—TOEFL. Electronic applications accepted. *Expenses:* Contact institution. *Faculty research:* Wrongful convictions, civil rights, environmental law, litigation techniques, data mining, intellectual property, practical and skills-based legal education.

West Texas A&M University, College of Business, Department of Accounting, Economics and Finance, Canyon, TX 79015. Offers accounting (MPA); finance and economics (MS). *Program availability:* Part-time, evening/weekend, online learning. *Degree requirements:* For master's, comprehensive exam, thesis optional. *Entrance requirements:* For master's, GMAT. Additional exam requirements/recommendations for international students: Required—TOEFL (minimum score 550 paper-based). Electronic applications accepted. *Faculty research:* Texas economy, decision report service learning and entrepreneurship, small business, trade effects of financial flow.

West Virginia University, College of Business and Economics, Morgantown, WV 26506. Offers accountancy (M Acc); accounting (PhD); business administration (MBA); business cyber security management (MS); business data analytics (MS); economics (MA, PhD); finance (MS, PhD); forensic and fraud examination (MS); industrial relations (MS); management (PhD); marketing (PhD). *Program availability:* Part-time, online learning. *Students:* 341 full-time (139 women), 44 part-time (13 women); includes 39 minority (10 Black or African American, non-Hispanic/Latino; 12 Asian, non-Hispanic/Latino; 7 Hispanic/Latino; 10 Two or more races, non-Hispanic/Latino), 40 international. In 2018, 208 master's, 20 doctorates awarded. Terminal master's awarded for partial completion of doctoral program. *Degree requirements:* For master's, thesis optional; for doctorate, comprehensive exam, thesis/dissertation. *Entrance requirements:* For doctorate, GRE General Test, minimum GPA of 3.0. Additional exam requirements/ recommendations for international students: Required—TOEFL (minimum score 550 paper-based; 92 iBT). *Application deadline:* For fall admission, 10/15 priority date for domestic and international students; for spring admission, 3/1 priority date for domestic and international students. Applications are processed on a rolling basis. Application fee: $60. Electronic applications accepted. *Expenses:* Contact institution. *Financial support:* Fellowships, research assistantships, teaching assistantships, career-related internships or fieldwork, Federal Work-Study, institutionally sponsored loans, scholarships/grants, health care benefits, tuition waivers (full and partial), unspecified

assistantships, and administrative assistantships available. Financial award application deadline: 2/1; financial award applicants required to submit FAFSA. *Faculty research:* Regional labor market studies, economic development, market research, economic forecasting, energy analysis. *Unit head:* Dr. Javier Reyes, Dean, 304-293-7800, Fax: 304-293-4056, E-mail: javier.reyes@mail.wvu.edu. *Application contact:* Dr. Virginia F Kleist, Associate Dean for Graduate Programs, 304-293-7939, Fax: 304-293-7188, E-mail: Virginia.Kleist@mail.wvu.edu.
Website: http://www.be.wvu.edu

Wilfrid Laurier University, Faculty of Graduate and Postdoctoral Studies, Lazaridis School of Business and Economics, Department of Business, Waterloo, ON N2L 3C5, Canada. Offers accounting (PhD); finance (M Fin); financial economics (PhD); marketing (PhD); operations and supply chain management (PhD); organizational behavior and human resource management (M Sc); organizational behaviour and human resource management (PhD); supply chain management (M Sc); technology management (EMTM). *Accreditation:* AACSB. *Program availability:* Part-time, evening/weekend. *Degree requirements:* For master's, thesis optional; for doctorate, comprehensive exam, thesis/dissertation. *Entrance requirements:* For master's, GMAT, 4-year honors degree with minimum B+ average; for doctorate, GMAT, master's degree, minimum B+ average. Additional exam requirements/recommendations for international students: Required—TOEFL (minimum score 89 iBT). Electronic applications accepted. *Faculty research:* Financial economics, management and organizational behavior, operations and supply chain management.

Wilkes University, College of Graduate and Professional Studies, Jay S. Sidhu School of Business and Leadership, Wilkes-Barre, PA 18766-0002. Offers accounting (MBA); global business (MBA); human resource management (MBA); international business (MBA); leadership (MBA); management (MBA); operations management (MBA); organizational leadership and development (MBA). *Accreditation:* ACBSP. *Program availability:* Part-time, evening/weekend. *Students:* 16 full-time (9 women), 64 part-time (33 women); includes 11 minority (3 Black or African American, non-Hispanic/Latino; 3 Asian, non-Hispanic/Latino; 3 Hispanic/Latino; 2 Two or more races, non-Hispanic/Latino), 7 international. Average age 30. In 2018, 49 master's awarded. *Entrance requirements:* For master's, GMAT. Additional exam requirements/recommendations for international students: Required—TOEFL (minimum score 550 paper-based; 79 iBT). *Application deadline:* Applications are processed on a rolling basis. Application fee: $45 ($65 for international students). Electronic applications accepted. *Expenses:* Contact institution. *Financial support:* Unspecified assistantships available. Financial award application deadline: 3/1; financial award applicants required to submit FAFSA. *Unit head:* Dr. Abel Adekola, Dean, 570-408-4701, Fax: 570-408-7846, E-mail: abel.adekola@wilkes.edu. *Application contact:* Kristin Donati, Associate Director of Graduate Admissions, 570-408-3338, Fax: 570-408-7846, E-mail: kristin.donati@wilkes.edu.
Website: http://www.wilkes.edu/academics/colleges/sidhu-school-of-business-leadership/index.aspx

William Paterson University of New Jersey, Cotsakos College of Business, Wayne, NJ 07470-8420. Offers applied business analytics (MS); business administration (MBA), including accounting, entrepreneurship, finance, general business administration, human resource management, marketing, music and entertainment management; MBA pathways (Certificate); sales leadership (MS). *Accreditation:* AACSB. *Program availability:* Part-time, evening/weekend. *Faculty:* 21 full-time (6 women), 5 part-time/adjunct (1 woman). *Students:* 78 full-time (40 women), 250 part-time (113 women); includes 161 minority (39 Black or African American, non-Hispanic/Latino; 1 American Indian or Alaska Native, non-Hispanic/Latino; 23 Asian, non-Hispanic/Latino; 82 Hispanic/Latino; 16 Two or more races, non-Hispanic/Latino), 14 international. Average age 31. 222 applicants, 86% accepted, 136 enrolled. In 2018, 95 master's awarded. *Degree requirements:* For master's, Programs Differ see: https://academiccatalog.wpunj.edu/content.php?catoid=1&navoid=68. *Entrance requirements:* For master's, program details: https://www.wpunj.edu/admissions/graduate/admission-deadlines-and-requirements/. Additional exam requirements/recommendations for international students: Required—TOEFL (minimum score 550 paper-based; 79 iBT), IELTS (minimum score 6). *Application deadline:* For fall admission, 6/1 for domestic students, 3/1 for international students; for spring admission, 11/1 for domestic students, 10/1 for international students. Applications are processed on a rolling basis. Application fee: $50. Electronic applications accepted. *Expenses: Tuition, area resident:* Full-time $14,714; part-time $727 per credit. Tuition, state resident: full-time $14,714; part-time $727 per credit. Tuition, nonresident: full-time $22,952; part-time $727 per credit. *International tuition:* $22,952 full-time. *Required fees:* $4 per semester. Tuition and fees vary according to course load, degree level and program. *Financial support:* In 2018–19, 18 students received support. Career-related internships or fieldwork, Federal Work-Study, scholarships/grants, tuition waivers, and unspecified assistantships available. Support available to part-time students. Financial award application deadline: 3/15; financial award applicants required to submit FAFSA. *Faculty research:* Labor markets, job characteristics and ethical behavior, institutional trading of stocks and bonds, education funding, pricing strategies in business-to-business markets. *Unit head:* Dr. Siamack Shojai, Dean, 973-720-2964, Fax: 973-720-2809, E-mail: shojais@wpunj.edu. *Application contact:* Tinu Adeniran, Assistant Director, Graduate Admissions, 973-720-2764, Fax: 973-720-2035, E-mail: adenirant@wpunj.edu.
Website: http://www.wpunj.edu/ccob

Wilmington University, College of Business, New Castle, DE 19720-6491. Offers accounting (MBA, MS); business administration (MBA, DBA); environmental stewardship (MBA); finance (MBA); health care administration (MBA, MSM); homeland security (MBA, MSM); human resource management (MSM); management information systems (MBA, MSN); marketing (MSM); marketing management (MBA); military leadership (MSM); organizational leadership (MBA, MSM); public administration (MSM). *Program availability:* Part-time, evening/weekend. *Entrance requirements:* Additional exam requirements/recommendations for international students: Required—TOEFL (minimum score 500 paper-based). Electronic applications accepted.

Wingate University, Porter B. Byrum School of Business, Wingate, NC 28174. Offers accounting (MAC); corporate innovation (MBA); finance (MBA); general management (MBA); healthcare management (MBA); marketing (MBA); project management (MBA). *Accreditation:* ACBSP. *Program availability:* Part-time, evening/weekend. *Entrance requirements:* For master's, GMAT, work experience, 2 letters of recommendation. Electronic applications accepted. *Expenses:* Contact institution. *Faculty research:* Stochastic processes, business ethics, regional economic development, municipal finance, consumer behavior.

Xavier University, Williams College of Business, Master of Business Administration Program, Cincinnati, OH 45207. Offers business administration (Exec MBA, MBA); business intelligence (MBA); finance (MBA); health industry (MBA); international business (MBA); marketing (MBA); values-based leadership (MBA); MBA/MHSA; MSN/MBA. *Accreditation:* AACSB. *Program availability:* Part-time, evening/weekend. *Degree requirements:* For master's, capstone course. *Entrance requirements:* For master's, GMAT or GRE, official transcript; resume. Additional exam requirements/recommendations for international students: Required—TOEFL (minimum score 550 paper-based; 79 iBT). Electronic applications accepted. Application fee is waived when completed online. *Expenses:* Contact institution.

Yale University, Yale School of Management, Doctoral Program in Management, New Haven, CT 06520. Offers accounting (PhD); financial economics (PhD); marketing (PhD); organizations and management (PhD). *Accreditation:* AACSB. *Degree requirements:* For doctorate, comprehensive exam, thesis/dissertation. *Entrance requirements:* For doctorate, GMAT or GRE General Test. Additional exam requirements/recommendations for international students: Required—TOEFL or IELTS. Electronic applications accepted. *Expenses:* Contact institution. *Faculty research:* Pricing of options and futures, term structure of interest rates, use of accounting numbers in debt contracts, product differentiation, e-commerce and marketing, behavioral finance.

York College of Pennsylvania, Graham School of Business, York, PA 17403-3651. Offers accounting (M Acc); business (MBA); continuous improvement (MBA); financial management (MBA); health care management (MBA); management (MBA); marketing (MBA); self-designed (MBA). *Accreditation:* ACBSP. *Program availability:* Part-time, evening/weekend. *Faculty:* 11 full-time (5 women), 3 part-time/adjunct (1 woman). *Students:* 13 full-time (4 women), 73 part-time (32 women); includes 11 minority (5 Black or African American, non-Hispanic/Latino; 2 Asian, non-Hispanic/Latino; 2 Hispanic/Latino; 2 Two or more races, non-Hispanic/Latino), 1 international. Average age 35. 57 applicants, 65% accepted, 25 enrolled. In 2018, 8 master's awarded. *Degree requirements:* For master's, directed study. *Entrance requirements:* For master's, GMAT. Additional exam requirements/recommendations for international students: Required—TOEFL (minimum score 530 paper-based; 72 iBT), IELTS (minimum score 6). *Application deadline:* For fall admission, 7/15 priority date for domestic students, 5/1 for international students; for spring admission, 11/15 priority date for domestic students, 9/1 for international students; for summer admission, 4/15 priority date for domestic students. Applications are processed on a rolling basis. Application fee: $0. Electronic applications accepted. *Expenses:* Contact institution. *Financial support:* In 2018–19, 3 students received support. Scholarships/grants available. Financial award applicants required to submit FAFSA. *Unit head:* Nicole Cornell Sadowski, MBA Director, 717-815-1491, Fax: 717-600-3999, E-mail: ncornell@ycp.edu. *Application contact:* MBA Office, 717-815-1491, Fax: 717-600-3999, E-mail: mba@ycp.edu.
Website: http://www.ycp.edu/mba

York University, Faculty of Graduate Studies, Schulich School of Business, Toronto, ON M3J 1P3, Canada. Offers accounting (M Acc); administration (PhD); business (MBA); business analytics (MBA); finance (MF); international business (IMBA); MBA/JD; MBA/MA; MBA/MFA. *Program availability:* Part-time, evening/weekend. *Degree requirements:* For master's, advanced proficiency in a second language, work term (IMBA); for doctorate, comprehensive exam, thesis/dissertation. *Entrance requirements:* For master's, GMAT or GRE, minimum GPA of 3.0 (3.3 for MF, MBA in business analytics, and IMBA); for doctorate, GMAT or GRE, minimum GPA of 3.3. Additional exam requirements/recommendations for international students: Required—TOEFL (minimum score 600 paper-based; 100 iBT), IELTS (minimum score 7), York English Language Test (minimum score 1); PearsonVUE (minimum score 64). Electronic applications accepted. *Faculty research:* Accounting, finance, marketing, operations management and information systems, organizational studies, strategic management.

Youngstown State University, College of Graduate Studies, College of Liberal Arts and Social Sciences, Department of Economics, Youngstown, OH 44555-0001. Offers economics (MA); financial economics (MA). *Program availability:* Part-time. *Degree requirements:* For master's, comprehensive exam, thesis optional. *Entrance requirements:* For master's, minimum GPA of 2.7, 21 hours in economics. Additional exam requirements/recommendations for international students: Required—TOEFL. *Faculty research:* Forecasting, applied econometrics, labor economics, applied macroeconomics, industrial organization.

Investment Management

Alaska Pacific University, Graduate Programs, Business Administration Department, Anchorage, AK 99508-4672. Offers business administration (MBA), including business administration, health services administration; information and communication technology (MBAICT); investment (CGS). *Program availability:* Part-time, evening/weekend. *Degree requirements:* For master's, capstone course. *Entrance requirements:* For master's, GMAT or GRE General Test, minimum GPA of 3.0. Additional exam requirements/recommendations for international students: Required—TOEFL (minimum score 550 paper-based).

Creighton University, Graduate School, Heider College of Business, Omaha, NE 68178-0001. Offers accounting (MAC); business administration (MBA, DBA); business intelligence and analytics (MS); finance (M Fin); investment management and financial analysis (MIMFA); JD/MBA; MBA/MIMFA; MD/MBA; Pharm D/MBA. *Accreditation:* AACSB. *Program availability:* Part-time, evening/weekend, 100% online, blended/hybrid learning. *Degree requirements:* For master's, thesis optional; for doctorate, thesis/dissertation optional. *Entrance requirements:* For master's, GMAT, resume, 2 letters of recommendation. Additional exam requirements/recommendations for international students: Required—TOEFL (minimum score 90 iBT). Electronic applications accepted. *Expenses:* Contact institution. *Faculty research:* Small business issues, economics, business analytics.

Fordham University, Gabelli School of Business, New York, NY 10023. Offers accounting (MBA, MS); applied statistics and decision-making (MS); business economics (DPS); capital markets (DPS); communications and media management (MBA); electronic business (MBA); entrepreneurship (MBA); finance (MBA, PhD); global finance (MS); global sustainability (MBA); health administration (MS); healthcare management (MBA); information systems (MBA, MS); investor relations (MS); management (EMBA, MBA, MS, PhD); marketing (MBA); marketing intelligence (MS); media management (MS); nonprofit leadership (MS); quantitative finance (MS); strategy and decision-making (DPS); taxation (MS); JD/MBA; MS/MBA. *Accreditation:* AACSB.

Investment Management

Program availability: Part-time, evening/weekend. Terminal master's awarded for partial completion of doctoral program. *Degree requirements:* For master's, internships (for some degrees); for doctorate, comprehensive exam (for some programs), thesis/dissertation. *Entrance requirements:* For master's, GMAT/GRE, 2 letters of recommendation, resume, 2 essays, transcripts, interview. Additional exam requirements/recommendations for international students: Required—TOEFL (minimum score 100 iBT), IELTS (minimum score 7). Electronic applications accepted. *Expenses:* Contact institution.

The George Washington University, School of Business, Department of Finance, Washington, DC 20052. Offers finance (MSF, PhD); finance and investments (MBA). *Program availability:* Part-time, evening/weekend. *Students:* 151 full-time (72 women), 1 (woman) part-time; includes 12 minority (1 Black or African American, non-Hispanic/Latino; 1 American Indian or Alaska Native, non-Hispanic/Latino; 7 Asian, non-Hispanic/Latino; 2 Hispanic/Latino; 1 Two or more races, non-Hispanic/Latino), 133 international. Average age 27. 754 applicants, 53% accepted, 44 enrolled. In 2018, 143 master's awarded. *Entrance requirements:* For master's, GMAT; for doctorate, GMAT or GRE. Additional exam requirements/recommendations for international students: Required—TOEFL. *Application deadline:* For fall admission, 4/1 priority date for domestic students; for spring admission, 10/1 for domestic students. Applications are processed on a rolling basis. Application fee: $75. *Financial support:* In 2018–19, 38 students received support. Fellowships, teaching assistantships, career-related internships or fieldwork, Federal Work-Study, and institutionally sponsored loans available. Financial award application deadline: 4/1. *Unit head:* Robert Van Order, Chair, 202-994-3427, E-mail: rvo@gwu.edu. *Application contact:* Christopher Storer, Executive Director, Graduate Admissions, 202-994-1212, E-mail: gwmba@gwu.edu.

Hofstra University, Frank G. Zarb School of Business, Programs in Finance, Hempstead, NY 11549. Offers business administration (MBA), including finance; corporate finance (Advanced Certificate); finance (MS), including financial and risk management, investment analysis; investment management (Advanced Certificate); quantitative finance (MS). *Program availability:* Part-time, evening/weekend, blended/hybrid learning. *Students:* 122 full-time (36 women), 40 part-time (8 women); includes 24 minority (5 Black or African American, non-Hispanic/Latino; 1 American Indian or Alaska Native, non-Hispanic/Latino; 8 Asian, non-Hispanic/Latino; 8 Hispanic/Latino; 2 Two or more races, non-Hispanic/Latino), 90 international. Average age 25. 326 applicants, 78% accepted, 58 enrolled. In 2018, 103 master's awarded. *Degree requirements:* For master's, thesis (for some programs), capstone course (for MBA), thesis (for MS), minimum GPA of 3.0. *Entrance requirements:* For master's, GMAT/GRE, 2 letters of recommendation, resume, essay. Additional exam requirements/recommendations for international students: Required—TOEFL (minimum score 550 paper-based; 80 iBT); Recommended—IELTS (minimum score 6). *Application deadline:* Applications are processed on a rolling basis. Application fee: $75. Electronic applications accepted. *Expenses:* $1,375 per credit plus fees. *Financial support:* In 2018–19, 46 students received support, including 42 fellowships with full and partial tuition reimbursements available (averaging $5,064 per year); research assistantships with full and partial tuition reimbursements available, career-related internships or fieldwork, Federal Work-Study, institutionally sponsored loans, scholarships/grants, tuition waivers (full and partial), unspecified assistantships, and scholarships and endowed scholarships also available. Support available to part-time students. Financial award applicants required to submit FAFSA. *Faculty research:* Sustainable investing; blockchain applications in finance; machine learning in finance; text and data mining in finance; corporate inversions. *Unit head:* Dr. K.G. Viswanathan, Chairperson, 516-463-5699, Fax: 516-463-4834, E-mail: k.g.viswanathan@hofstra.edu. *Application contact:* Sunil Samuel, Assistant Vice President of Admissions, 516-463-4723, Fax: 516-463-4664, E-mail: graduateadmission@hofstra.edu.
Website: http://www.hofstra.edu/business/

Johns Hopkins University, Carey Business School, Certificate Programs, Baltimore, MD 21218. Offers financial management (Certificate); investments (Certificate). *Program availability:* Part-time, evening/weekend. *Students:* 1 full-time, 16 part-time (3 women). 10 applicants, 80% accepted, 5 enrolled. In 2018, 18 Certificates awarded. *Degree requirements:* For Certificate, 16 credits. *Entrance requirements:* Additional exam requirements/recommendations for international students: Required—TOEFL, IELTS. *Application deadline:* Applications are processed on a rolling basis. Application fee: $100. Electronic applications accepted. *Expenses:* Contact institution. *Unit head:* Dr. Kevin Frick, Vice Dean of Education, 410-234-9272, E-mail: kfrick@jhu.edu. *Application contact:* Office of Admissions, 410-234-9220, Fax: 443-529-1554, E-mail: carey.admissions@jhu.edu.
Website: http://carey.jhu.edu/academics/certificate-programs/

Johns Hopkins University, Carey Business School, MS in Business Analytics and Risk Management Program, Baltimore, MD 21218. Offers MS. *Students:* 73 full-time (42 women), 9 part-time (3 women). 156 applicants, 70% accepted, 50 enrolled. In 2018, 13 master's awarded. *Degree requirements:* For master's, 36 credits. *Entrance requirements:* For master's, GMAT or GRE. Additional exam requirements/recommendations for international students: Required—TOEFL, IELTS. *Application deadline:* For fall admission, 4/3 for domestic and international students. Applications are processed on a rolling basis. Application fee: $100. Electronic applications accepted. *Expenses:* Contact institution. *Financial support:* In 2018–19, 20 students received support. Scholarships/grants available. Financial award application deadline: 4/15; financial award applicants required to submit FAFSA. *Faculty research:* Emerging issues in business analytics and risk management. *Unit head:* Dr. Kevin Frick, Vice Dean of Education, 410-234-9272, E-mail: kfrick@jhu.edu. *Application contact:* Office of Admissions, 410-234-9220, Fax: 443-529-1554, E-mail: carey.admissions@jhu.edu.

Lincoln University, Graduate Studies, Oakland, CA 94612. Offers finance and investments (DBA); finance management (MS); finance management and investments (MBA); general business (MBA); human resource management (MBA, DBA); international business (MBA, MS); management information systems (MBA). *Program availability:* Part-time. *Degree requirements:* For master's, research project (thesis), internship report, or comprehensive exam; for doctorate, comprehensive exam, thesis/dissertation. *Entrance requirements:* For master's, minimum GPA of 2.7; for doctorate, GMAT (minimum score: 550), GRE (minimum score: 1000), or equivalent test results (waived for master's degree with minimum cumulative GPA of 3.3). Additional exam requirements/recommendations for international students: Required—TOEFL minimum score 525 paper-based; 71 iBT or IELTS minimum score 5.5 (for MBA); TOEFL minimum score 550 paper-based; 79 iBT or IELTS minimum score 6 (for MS and DBA). Electronic applications accepted.

Loyola University Maryland, Graduate Programs, Sellinger School of Business, Professional MBA Program, Baltimore, MD 21210-2699. Offers finance (MBA); information systems (MBA); investments and applied portfolio management (MBA); management (MBA); marketing (MBA). *Accreditation:* AACSB. *Program availability:* Part-time, evening/weekend. *Entrance requirements:* For master's, GMAT, resume, essay, official transcripts, professional letter of recommendation. Additional exam requirements/recommendations for international students: Required—TOEFL (minimum score 550 paper-based, 80 iBT) or IELTS (minimum score 7). Electronic applications accepted. *Expenses:* Contact institution.

Manhattanville College, School of Professional Studies, Master of Science in Finance, Purchase, NY 10577-2132. Offers finance (MS, Advanced Certificate), including accounting (MS); corporate finance (MS); investment management (MS). *Program availability:* Part-time, evening/weekend. *Faculty:* 6 part-time/adjunct (2 women). *Students:* 12 full-time (5 women), 8 part-time (3 women); includes 8 minority (2 Black or African American, non-Hispanic/Latino; 6 Hispanic/Latino), 1 international. Average age 32. 19 applicants, 16% accepted, 2 enrolled. In 2018, 13 master's awarded. *Degree requirements:* For master's, thesis (for some programs), final project. *Entrance requirements:* For master's, scores of GRE and GMAT are optional, personal essay, transcripts, 2 letters of recommendation (academic or professional), resume, health form with proof of immunization (for those born after 1957). Additional exam requirements/recommendations for international students: Required—TOEFL (minimum score 563 paper-based; 85 iBT), TOEFL (minimum score 563 paper-based, 85 iBT), IELTS (7), or iTEP (B2); Recommended—IELTS (minimum score 7). *Application deadline:* Applications are processed on a rolling basis. Application fee: $75. Electronic applications accepted. *Expenses:* 935 per credit. *Financial support:* Federal Work-Study, institutionally sponsored loans, scholarships/grants, and unspecified assistantships available. Financial award application deadline: 3/15; financial award applicants required to submit FAFSA. *Unit head:* Laura Persky, Associate Dean, 914-323-5188, E-mail: Laura.Persky@mville.edu. *Application contact:* Monika Pottgen, Assistant Director of Recruitment and Admissions, 914-323-5150, E-mail: sps@mville.edu.
Website: https://www.mville.edu/programs/ms-finance

Marywood University, Academic Affairs, Munley College of Liberal Arts and Sciences, School of Business and Global Innovation, Emphasis in Finance/Investment, Scranton, PA 18509-1598. Offers MBA. *Entrance requirements:* For master's, GMAT. Electronic applications accepted.

Midwest University, Graduate Programs, Wentzville, MO 63385. Offers asset management/investment/real estate (MBA); Christian counseling (D Min); Christian education (D Min); counseling (MA), including marriage and family counseling, school counseling; divinity (M Div); education (MA), including brain and gifted education, Christian education; global business management (MBA); global leadership (MBA); leadership (PhD), including brain and gifted educational leadership, entrepreneurial leadership, international aviation leadership, organizational leadership, political leadership; mission studies (D Min); music (MM, DMA); pastoral theology (D Min); public policy/administration (MBA); teaching English to speakers of other languages (MA). *Program availability:* Part-time, online learning. *Degree requirements:* For master's, thesis (for some programs); for doctorate, thesis/dissertation. *Entrance requirements:* Additional exam requirements/recommendations for international students: Recommended—TOEFL (minimum score 550 paper-based).

New York University, School of Professional Studies, Schack Institute of Real Estate, Program in Real Estate, New York, NY 10012-1019. Offers real estate (MS), including finance and investment, real estate asset management. *Program availability:* Part-time, evening/weekend. *Degree requirements:* For master's, thesis, capstone project. *Entrance requirements:* For master's, GRE or GMAT (only upon request), bachelor's degree, resume with relevant professional work, internship or volunteer experience, two letters of recommendation, statement of purpose. Additional exam requirements/recommendations for international students: Required—TOEFL (minimum score 600 paper-based; 100 iBT), IELTS (minimum score 7). Electronic applications accepted. *Expenses:* Contact institution.

Pace University, Lubin School of Business, Advanced Professional Certificate Program, New York, NY 10038. Offers business economics (APC); e-business (APC); financial management (APC); international business (APC); international economics (APC); investment management (APC); marketing (APC); public accounting (APC). *Program availability:* Part-time, evening/weekend. *Entrance requirements:* For degree, MBA or MS in business discipline, relevant professional experience. Additional exam requirements/recommendations for international students: Required—TOEFL (minimum score 90 iBT), IELTS (minimum score 7) or PTE (minimum score 61). *Application deadline:* For fall admission, 8/1 priority date for domestic students, 6/1 for international students; for spring admission, 12/1 for domestic students, 10/1 for international students. Applications are processed on a rolling basis. Application fee: $70. Electronic applications accepted. *Unit head:* Dr. Ibraiz Tarique, Chairperson, 212-618-6583, E-mail: itarique@pace.edu. *Application contact:* Susan Ford-Goldschein, Director of Graduate Admissions, 212-346-1531, Fax: 212-346-1585, E-mail: graduateadmission@pace.edu.
Website: http://www.pace.edu/lubin/agc

Pace University, Lubin School of Business, Finance Program, New York, NY 10038. Offers financial management (MBA, MS); financial risk management (MS); international finance (MBA); investment management (MBA, MS). *Program availability:* Part-time, evening/weekend. *Students:* 120 full-time (52 women), 79 part-time (30 women); includes 33 minority (10 Black or African American, non-Hispanic/Latino; 14 Asian, non-Hispanic/Latino; 8 Hispanic/Latino; 1 Two or more races, non-Hispanic/Latino), 119 international. Average age 26. 236 applicants, 77% accepted, 64 enrolled. In 2018, 132 master's awarded. *Entrance requirements:* For master's, GMAT, GRE (GMAT not required for MS with passing of Level 1 of Chartered Financial Analyst exam or Level 1 of Financial Risk Manager Exam), Undergrad degree, transcripts from all accredited colleges/universities attended, 2 letters of recommendation, resume, personal statement. If applying to the 1 year fast track MBA in Financial Management, must have a cumulative GPA of 3.30 or above, a grade of B or better for all business core courses from an AACSB-accredited U.S. business school. Additional exam requirements/recommendations for international students: Required—TOEFL (minimum score 90 iBT), IELTS (minimum score 7) or PTE (minimum score 61). *Application deadline:* For fall admission, 8/1 priority date for domestic students, 6/1 for international students; for spring admission, 12/1 for domestic students, 10/1 for international students. Applications are processed on a rolling basis. Application fee: $70. Electronic applications accepted. *Financial support:* Research assistantships, career-related internships or fieldwork, Federal Work-Study, tuition waivers (full and partial), and unspecified assistantships available. Support available to part-time students. Financial award application deadline: 2/15; financial award applicants required to submit FAFSA. *Unit head:* Dr. Aron Gottesman, Chairperson, Finance Department, 212-618-6525, E-mail: agottesman@pace.edu. *Application contact:* Susan Ford-Goldschein, Director of Graduate Admissions, 212-346-1531, Fax: 212-346-1585, E-mail: graduateadmissions@pace.edu.
Website: http://www.pace.edu/lubin/sections/explore-programs/graduate-programs

Regent University, Graduate School, School of Business and Leadership, Virginia Beach, VA 23464-9800. Offers business administration (MBA), including accounting, economics, entrepreneurship, finance and investing, general management, healthcare management (MA, MBA), human resource management (MA, MBA), innovation management, leadership, marketing, not-for-profit management (MA, MBA); business analytics (MS); business and design management (MA); church leadership (MA); leadership (Certificate); organizational leadership (MA, PhD), including ecclesial leadership (DSL, PhD), entrepreneurial leadership (PhD), healthcare management (MA, MBA), human resource development (PhD), human resource management (MA, MBA),

individualized studies (DSL, PhD), interdisciplinary studies (MA), leadership coaching and mentoring (MA), not-for-profit management (MA, MBA), organizational development consulting (MA), servant leadership (MA, DSL); strategic leadership (DSL), including ecclesial leadership (DSL, PhD), global consulting, healthcare leadership, individualized studies (DSL, PhD), leadership coaching, servant leadership (MA, DSL), strategic foresight. *Program availability:* Part-time, evening/weekend, 100% online, blended/hybrid learning. *Degree requirements:* For master's, thesis or alternative, 3-credit hour culminating experience; for doctorate, thesis/dissertation. *Entrance requirements:* For master's, college transcripts, resume, essay; for doctorate, college transcripts, resume, essay, writing sample; for Certificate, writing sample, resume, transcripts. Additional exam requirements/recommendations for international students: Required—TOEFL (minimum score 577 paper-based). Electronic applications accepted. *Expenses:* Contact institution. *Faculty research:* Servant leadership, global business, team effectiveness, technology utilization, leadership development.

Sacred Heart University, Graduate Programs, Jack Welch College of Business, Department of Finance, Fairfield, CT 06825. Offers administration (DBA); finance (MBA, Graduate Certificate); finance and investment management (MS). *Program availability:* Part-time, evening/weekend. *Degree requirements:* For doctorate, comprehensive exam. *Entrance requirements:* For master's, GMAT or GRE, official transcripts from all institutions attended; for doctorate, GMAT or GRE with master's degree and 5 years' experience. Additional exam requirements/recommendations for international students: Required—TOEFL (minimum score 570 paper-based, 80 iBT), TWE, or IELTS (6.5). Electronic applications accepted. *Expenses:* Contact institution.

Saint Mary's College of California, School of Economics and Business Administration, MS in Financial Analysis and Investment Management Program, Moraga, CA 94556. Offers MS. *Expenses:* Contact institution.

Southern New Hampshire University, School of Business, Manchester, NH 03106-1045. Offers accounting (MBA, Graduate Certificate); accounting finance (MS); accounting/auditing (MS); accounting/forensic accounting (MS); accounting/management accounting (MS); accounting/taxation (MS); applied economics (MS); athletic administration (MBA, Graduate Certificate); business administration (IMBA, Certificate), including business information systems (Certificate), human resource management (Certificate); business analytics (MBA); business intelligence (MBA); communication (MA), including new media and marketing, public relations; community economic development (MBA); criminal justice (MBA); data analytics (MS); economics (MBA); engineering management (MBA); entrepreneurship (MBA); finance (MBA, MS, Graduate Certificate); finance/corporate finance (MS); finance/investments (MS); forensic accounting (MBA); forensic accounting and fraud examination (Graduate Certificate); healthcare informatics (MBA); healthcare management (MBA); human resource management (MS); human resources (MBA); information technology (MS); information technology management (MBA); international business (PhD); Internet marketing (MBA); leadership (MBA); leadership of nonprofit organizations (Graduate Certificate); management (MS); marketing (MBA, MS, Graduate Certificate); music business (MBA); operations and project management (MS); operations and supply chain management (MBA, Graduate Certificate); organizational leadership (MS); project management (MBA, Graduate Certificate); public administration (MBA, Graduate Certificate); quantitative analysis (MBA); Six Sigma (Graduate Certificate); Six Sigma quality (MBA); social media marketing (MBA, Graduate Certificate); sport management (MBA, MS, Graduate Certificate); sustainability and environmental compliance (MBA); MBA/Certificate. *Accreditation:* ACBSP. *Program availability:* Part-time, evening/weekend, online learning. Terminal master's awarded for partial completion of doctoral program. *Degree requirements:* For master's, one foreign language, comprehensive exam (for some programs), thesis or alternative; for doctorate, one foreign language, comprehensive exam, thesis/dissertation. *Entrance requirements:* For master's, minimum GPA of 2.5; for doctorate, GMAT. Additional exam requirements/recommendations for international students: Required—TOEFL (minimum score 500 paper-based). Electronic applications accepted.

Temple University, Beasley School of Law, Master's and Certificate Programs, Philadelphia, PA 19122-6096. Offers Asian law (LL M); business law (Certificate); employee benefits (Certificate); estate planning (Certificate); trial advocacy (LL M); trial advocacy and litigation (Certificate).

University of Houston–Downtown, Marilyn Davies College of Business, MBA Program, Houston, TX 77002. Offers accounting (MBA); finance (MBA); human resource management (MBA); international business (MBA); investment management (MBA); leadership (MBA); project management and process improvement (MBA); sales management and business development (MBA); supply chain management (MBA). *Accreditation:* AACSB. *Program availability:* Part-time, evening/weekend. *Entrance requirements:* For master's, GMAT, two letters of recommendation from professional references, personal statement, resume. Additional exam requirements/recommendations for international students: Required—TOEFL (minimum score 81 iBT). Electronic applications accepted. *Expenses:* Contact institution.

University of Notre Dame, Mendoza College of Business, Master of Business Administration Program, Notre Dame, IN 46556. Offers business analytics (MBA); business leadership (MBA); consulting (MBA); corporate finance (MBA); innovation and entrepreneurship (MBA); investments (MBA); marketing (MBA); MBA/MSBA. *Accreditation:* AACSB. *Entrance requirements:* For master's, GMAT or GRE, work experience, essay, four-slide presentation, two recommendations, transcripts from all colleges and/or universities attended, interview. Additional exam requirements/recommendations for international students: Required—PTE (minimum score 68), TOEFL (minimum iBT score of 109), IELTS (7.5), or documentation of at least six semesters of full-time university education in English. Electronic applications accepted. *Expenses:* Contact institution. *Faculty research:* Market micro-structure; marketing and public policy; corporate finance and accounting; corporate governance and ethical behavior; high performing organizations.

University of Wisconsin–Madison, Graduate School, Wisconsin School of Business, Doctoral Program in Finance, Investment and Banking, Madison, WI 53706-1380. Offers PhD. *Degree requirements:* For doctorate, comprehensive exam, thesis/dissertation. *Entrance requirements:* For doctorate, GMAT or GRE. Additional exam requirements/recommendations for international students: Recommended—TOEFL (minimum score 623 paper-based; 106 iBT), IELTS (minimum score 7.5), TSE (minimum score 73). Electronic applications accepted. *Expenses:* Contact institution. *Faculty research:* Banking and financial institutions, business cycles, investments, derivatives, corporate finance, economics, bankruptcy, foreclosures, mergers and acquisitions, portfolio theory.

University of Wisconsin–Milwaukee, Graduate School, Lubar School of Business, Other Business Programs, Milwaukee, WI 53201-0413. Offers business analytics (Graduate Certificate); enterprise resource planning (Graduate Certificate); information technology management (MS); investment management (Graduate Certificate); nonprofit management (Graduate Certificate); nonprofit management and leadership (MS); state and local taxation (Graduate Certificate). *Students:* 132 full-time (63 women), 120 part-time (58 women); includes 45 minority (11 Black or African American, non-Hispanic/Latino; 15 Asian, non-Hispanic/Latino; 4 Hispanic/Latino; 15 Two or more races, non-Hispanic/Latino), 52 international. Average age 31. 196 applicants, 63% accepted, 80 enrolled. In 2018, 108 master's, 18 other advanced degrees awarded. *Entrance requirements:* Additional exam requirements/recommendations for international students: Required—TOEFL (minimum score 550 paper-based; 79 iBT), IELTS (minimum score 6.5). Application fee: $56 ($96 for international students). Electronic applications accepted. *Financial support:* Fellowships, research assistantships, teaching assistantships, health care benefits, unspecified assistantships, and project assistantships available. Financial award applicants required to submit FAFSA. *Application contact:* General Information Contact, 414-229-4982, Fax: 414-229-6967, E-mail: gradschool@uwm.edu.

Walsh College of Accountancy and Business Administration, Graduate Programs, Program in Finance, Troy, MI 48083. Offers financial investments (MSF); financial management (MSF); financial services (MSF). *Program availability:* Part-time, evening/weekend, 100% online, blended/hybrid learning. *Faculty:* 9 full-time (4 women), 7 part-time/adjunct (3 women). *Students:* 3 full-time (0 women), 80 part-time (33 women); includes 18 minority (16 Black or African American, non-Hispanic/Latino; 2 Asian, non-Hispanic/Latino), 3 international. Average age 32. 33 applicants, 94% accepted, 14 enrolled. In 2018, 34 master's awarded. *Entrance requirements:* For master's, minimum overall cumulative GPA of 2.750 from all colleges previously attended. Additional exam requirements/recommendations for international students: Required—TOEFL (minimum score 550 paper-based, 79-80 internet based), IELTS (6.5), Michigan Test of English Language Proficiency, or MTELP (80). *Application deadline:* Applications are processed on a rolling basis. Application fee: $35. Electronic applications accepted. *Expenses:* $785 per credit hour plus $175 student support fee per semester. International students pay $785 per credit hour plus $175 student support fee and $275 international student fee per semester. *Financial support:* In 2018–19, 3 students received support. Scholarships/grants available. Financial award application deadline: 6/30; financial award applicants required to submit FAFSA. *Unit head:* Dr. John Moore, Chair, Finance and Economics, 248-823-1635, Fax: 248-689-0920, E-mail: jmoore1@walshcollege.edu. *Application contact:* Karen Mahaffy, Executive Director, Admissions and Enrollment Services, 248-823-1600, Fax: 248-823-1611, E-mail: kmahaffy@walshcollege.edu.

Taxation

American International College, School of Business, Arts and Sciences, Springfield, MA 01109-3189. Offers accounting and taxation (MS); business administration (MBA); clinical psychology (MA); educational psychology (Ed D); forensic psychology (MS); general psychology (MA, CAGS); management (CAGS); resort and casino management (MBA, CAGS). *Program availability:* Part-time, evening/weekend. *Degree requirements:* For master's, practicum; for doctorate, comprehensive exam, thesis/dissertation, practicum. *Entrance requirements:* For master's, BS or BA, minimum undergraduate GPA of 2.75, 2 letters of recommendation, official transcripts, personal goal statement or essay; for doctorate, 3 letters of recommendation; BS or BA; minimum undergraduate GPA of 3.0 (3.25 recommended); official transcripts; personal goal statement or essay. Additional exam requirements/recommendations for international students: Required—TOEFL (minimum score 550 paper-based; 80 iBT). *Expenses:* Contact institution. *Faculty research:* Substance abuse, forensic psychology, special education.

American University, Kogod School of Business, Department of Accounting, Washington, DC 20016-8044. Offers accounting (MS, Certificate), including accounting (MS), forensic accounting (Certificate); taxation (MS, Certificate), including tax (Certificate), taxation (MS). *Program availability:* Part-time, evening/weekend. *Faculty:* 14 full-time (6 women), 11 part-time/adjunct (5 women). *Students:* 76 full-time (51 women), 57 part-time (26 women); includes 45 minority (21 Black or African American, non-Hispanic/Latino; 9 Asian, non-Hispanic/Latino; 12 Hispanic/Latino; 3 Two or more races, non-Hispanic/Latino), 52 international. Average age 29. 129 applicants, 77% accepted, 30 enrolled. In 2018, 49 master's, 15 other advanced degrees awarded. *Entrance requirements:* For master's, GMAT/GRE, resume, interview, personal statement, 2 letters of recommendation, transcripts; for Certificate, bachelor's degree. Additional exam requirements/recommendations for international students: Required—TOEFL (minimum score 100 iBT). *Application deadline:* Applications are processed on a rolling basis. Application fee: $100. *Expenses:* Contact institution. *Financial support:* Applicants required to submit FAFSA. *Faculty research:* Harmonization of international accounting standards, federal accounting and financial reporting, taxation of U.S. corporations doing business abroad, tax planning for real estate transactions. *Unit head:* Dr. Donald T. Williamson, Chair, Department of Accounting, 202-885-1900, E-mail: kogodgrad@american.edu. *Application contact:* Jason Garner, Director of Admissions, 202-885-1926, E-mail: jgarner@american.edu.
Website: http://www.american.edu/kogod/

Appalachian State University, Cratis D. Williams School of Graduate Studies, Department of Accounting, Boone, NC 28608. Offers taxation (MS). *Program availability:* Part-time. *Degree requirements:* For master's, comprehensive exam, thesis optional. *Entrance requirements:* For master's, GMAT, 3 letters of recommendation. Additional exam requirements/recommendations for international students: Required—TOEFL (minimum score 550 paper-based; 79 iBT), IELTS (minimum score 6.5). Electronic applications accepted. *Expenses: Tuition, area resident:* Full-time $4839; part-time $237 per credit hour. Tuition, state resident: full-time $4839; part-time $237 per credit hour. Tuition, nonresident: full-time $18,271; part-time $895.50 per credit hour. *Faculty research:* Audit assurance risk, state taxation, financial accounting inconsistencies, management information systems, charitable contribution taxation.

Baruch College of the City University of New York, Zicklin School of Business, Department of Accounting, Program in Taxation, New York, NY 10010-5585. Offers MBA, MS. *Program availability:* Part-time, evening/weekend. *Entrance requirements:* For master's, GMAT, 2 letters of recommendation, resume, 2 years of work experience. Additional exam requirements/recommendations for international students: Required—TOEFL (minimum score 590 paper-based), TWE.

Taxation

Bentley University, McCallum Graduate School of Business, Masters in Accounting Analytics, Waltham, MA 02452-4705. Offers MS. *Program availability:* Part-time, evening/weekend. *Faculty:* 118 full-time (38 women), 25 part-time/adjunct (4 women). *Students:* 25 full-time (19 women), 1 part-time; includes 1 minority (Asian, non-Hispanic/Latino), 19 international. Average age 23. 25 applicants, 92% accepted, 16 enrolled. *Entrance requirements:* For master's, GMAT or GRE General Test (may be waived for qualified applicants), Transcripts; Resume; Two essays; Two letters of recommendation; Interview (may be requested by Bentley). Additional exam requirements/recommendations for international students: Required—TOEFL (minimum score 100) or IELTS (minimum score 7). *Application deadline:* For fall admission, 7/31 for domestic students, 6/30 for international students; for spring admission, 1/1 for domestic students, 11/1 for international students. Applications are processed on a rolling basis. Application fee: $150. Electronic applications accepted. *Financial support:* In 2018–19, 24 students received support. Scholarships/grants and unspecified assistantships available. Financial award application deadline: 6/1; financial award applicants required to submit FAFSA. *Unit head:* Leonard Pepe, Lecturer and MSA/MSAA Program Director, 781-891-2470, E-mail: lpepe@bentley.edu. *Application contact:* Office of Graduate Admissions, 781-891-2108, E-mail: applygrad@bentley.edu. Website: https://www.bentley.edu/academics/graduate-programs/masters-accounting-analytics

Bentley University, McCallum Graduate School of Business, Masters in Taxation, Waltham, MA 02452-4705. Offers MST. *Program availability:* Part-time, evening/weekend, 100% online, blended/hybrid learning. *Faculty:* 118 full-time (38 women), 25 part-time/adjunct (4 women). *Students:* 29 full-time (15 women), 40 part-time (16 women); includes 10 minority (9 Asian, non-Hispanic/Latino; 1 Two or more races, non-Hispanic/Latino), 11 international. Average age 29. 46 applicants, 89% accepted, 30 enrolled. In 2018, 71 master's awarded. *Entrance requirements:* For master's, GMAT or GRE General Test (may be waived for qualified applicants), Transcripts; Resume; Two essays; Two letters of recommendation; Interview (may be requested by Bentley). Additional exam requirements/recommendations for international students: Required—TOEFL (minimum score 100) or IELTS (minimum score 7). *Application deadline:* For fall admission, 7/31 for domestic students, 6/30 for international students; for spring admission, 1/1 for domestic students, 11/1 for international students. Applications are processed on a rolling basis. Application fee: $150. Electronic applications accepted. *Financial support:* In 2018–19, 28 students received support. Scholarships/grants and unspecified assistantships available. Financial award application deadline: 6/1; financial award applicants required to submit FAFSA. *Faculty research:* Taxation of intellectual property, tax dispute resolution, corporate tax planning and advocacy, estate and financial planning. *Unit head:* Scott Thomas, Assistant Professor and MSFP/MST Director, 781-891-2979, E-mail: sthoma1@bentley.edu. *Application contact:* Office of Graduate Admissions, 781-891-2108, E-mail: applygrad@bentley.edu. Website: https://www.bentley.edu/academics/graduate-programs/masters-taxation

Boise State University, College of Business and Economics, Department of Accountancy, Boise, ID 83725-0399. Offers accountancy (MSA); accountancy taxation (MSAT). *Accreditation:* AACSB. *Program availability:* Part-time. *Entrance requirements:* For master's, GMAT, minimum GPA of 3.0. Additional exam requirements/recommendations for international students: Required—TOEFL (minimum score 587 paper-based; 95 iBT), IELTS (minimum score 6.5). Electronic applications accepted.

Bryant University, Graduate School of Business, Smithfield, RI 02917. Offers accounting (MPAC); business administration (MBA); taxation (MST). *Program availability:* Part-time, evening/weekend, 100% online. *Faculty:* 31 full-time (8 women), 6 part-time/adjunct (2 women). *Students:* 77 full-time (31 women), 106 part-time (46 women); includes 32 minority (7 Black or African American, non-Hispanic/Latino; 1 American Indian or Alaska Native, non-Hispanic/Latino; 9 Asian, non-Hispanic/Latino; 8 Hispanic/Latino; 7 Two or more races, non-Hispanic/Latino), 8 international. Average age 28. 215 applicants, 66% accepted, 96 enrolled. In 2018, 124 master's awarded. *Degree requirements:* For master's, comprehensive exam (for some programs). *Entrance requirements:* For master's, GMAT, resume, recommendation, college transcripts. Additional exam requirements/recommendations for international students: Required—TOEFL (minimum score 580 paper-based; 95 iBT). *Application deadline:* For fall admission, 7/15 for domestic and international students; for spring admission, 11/15 for domestic and international students; for summer admission, 4/15 for domestic and international students. Applications are processed on a rolling basis. Application fee: $80. Electronic applications accepted. *Expenses:* Contact institution. *Financial support:* In 2018–19, 95 fellowships with full and partial tuition reimbursements (averaging $9,825 per year), 9 research assistantships with full and partial tuition reimbursements (averaging $7,100 per year) were awarded; scholarships/grants and unspecified assistantships also available. Support available to part-time students. Financial award application deadline: 2/15; financial award applicants required to submit FAFSA. *Faculty research:* International business, public sector auditing, taxation of partnerships, information systems security, financial markets microstructure. *Unit head:* Jamie R Grenon, Director, Graduate Programs Office, 401-232-6707, E-mail: jgrenon@bryant.edu. *Application contact:* Jeanne Creighton, Senior Admissions Assistant, 401-232-6230, Fax: 401-232-6494, E-mail: graduateprograms@bryant.edu. Website: http://gradschool.bryant.edu/business/

California Miramar University, Program in Taxation and Trade for Executives, San Diego, CA 92108. Offers MT.

California Polytechnic State University, San Luis Obispo, Orfalea College of Business, Program in Taxation, San Luis Obispo, CA 93407. Offers MS. *Students:* 14 full-time (10 women); includes 10 minority (5 Asian, non-Hispanic/Latino; 4 Hispanic/Latino; 1 Two or more races, non-Hispanic/Latino). Average age 23. In 2018, 16 master's awarded. *Degree requirements:* For master's, comprehensive exam. *Entrance requirements:* For master's, GMAT. Additional exam requirements/recommendations for international students: Required—TOEFL (minimum score 80 iBT). *Application deadline:* Applications are processed on a rolling basis. Application fee: $55. Electronic applications accepted. *Expenses: Tuition, area resident:* Full-time $7176; part-time $4164 per year. Tuition, state resident: full-time $10,965. Tuition, nonresident: full-time $10,965. *Required fees:* $6336; $3711. *Financial support:* Fellowships, career-related internships or fieldwork, Federal Work-Study, institutionally sponsored loans, scholarships/grants and unspecified assistantships available. Support available to part-time students. Financial award application deadline: 3/2; financial award applicants required to submit FAFSA. *Unit head:* Dr. Scott Dawson, Dean, 805-756-2705, E-mail: scdawson@calpoly.edu. *Application contact:* Dr. Scott Dawson, Dean, 805-756-2705, E-mail: scdawson@calpoly.edu. Website: http://www.cob.calpoly.edu/gradbusiness/degree-programs/ms-tax/

California State University, Fullerton, Graduate Studies, College of Business and Economics, Department of Accounting, Fullerton, CA 92831-3599. Offers accounting (MBA, MS). *Accreditation:* AACSB. *Program availability:* Part-time. *Degree requirements:* For master's, thesis or alternative, project. *Entrance requirements:* For master's, GMAT, minimum AACSB index of 950. Electronic applications accepted.

California State University, Northridge, Graduate Studies, Tseng College, Northridge, CA 91330. Offers business administration (Graduate Certificate); health administration (MPA); health education (MPH); knowledge management (MKM); music industry administration (MA); nonprofit-sector management (Graduate Certificate); public administration (MPA); public sector management and leadership (MPA); social work (MSW); taxation (MS); tourism, hospitality and recreation management (MS). *Entrance requirements:* For master's, GRE (if cumulative undergraduate GPA less than 3.0).

Capital University, Law School, Program in Business Law and Taxation, Columbus, OH 43209-2394. Offers business (LL M); business and taxation (LL M); taxation (LL M); JD/LL M. *Program availability:* Part-time, evening/weekend. *Degree requirements:* For master's, thesis or alternative. *Entrance requirements:* For master's, previous course work in accounting, business law, and taxation. Additional exam requirements/recommendations for international students: Required—TOEFL (minimum score 600 paper-based). Electronic applications accepted.

Capital University, Law School, Program in Taxation, Columbus, OH 43209-2394. Offers taxation (MT). *Program availability:* Part-time, evening/weekend. *Degree requirements:* For master's, thesis or alternative. *Entrance requirements:* For master's, previous course work in accounting, business law, and taxation. Additional exam requirements/recommendations for international students: Required—TOEFL (minimum score 600 paper-based). Electronic applications accepted. *Expenses:* Contact institution.

Chapman University, Dale E. Fowler School of Law, Orange, CA 92866. Offers advocacy and dispute resolution (JD); business law (LL M, JD); criminal law (JD); entertainment and media law (LL M); entertainment law (JD); environmental, land use, and real estate law (JD); international and comparative law (LL M); international law (JD); law (JD); prosecutorial science (LL M); tax law (JD); taxation (LL M); trial advocacy (LL M); JD/MBA; JD/MFA. *Accreditation:* ABA. *Program availability:* Part-time. *Entrance requirements:* For doctorate, LSAT. Additional exam requirements/recommendations for international students: Required—TOEFL (minimum score 600 paper-based; 100 iBT). Electronic applications accepted. *Expenses:* Contact institution.

DePaul University, College of Law, Chicago, IL 60604. Offers business law and taxation (MJ); criminal law (MJ); health and intellectual property law (MJ); health care compliance (MJ); health law (LL M, MJ); intellectual property law (LL M); international and comparative law (MJ); international law (LL M); law (JD); public interest law (MJ); taxation (LL M); U.S. legal studies (LL M); JD/LL M; JD/MA; JD/MBA; JD/MS. *Accreditation:* ABA. *Program availability:* Part-time, evening/weekend. *Entrance requirements:* For doctorate, LSAT, LSAC applicant evaluation/letter of recommendation, personal statement, resume. Additional exam requirements/recommendations for international students: Required—TOEFL (minimum score 577 paper-based; 90 iBT), IELTS (minimum score 6.5). Electronic applications accepted. *Expenses:* Contact institution.

DePaul University, Kellstadt Graduate School of Business, Chicago, IL 60604. Offers accountancy (MBA, MSA); applied economics (MBA); audit and advisory services (MS); business administration (DBA); business analytics (MS); business strategy and decision-making (MBA); computational finance (MS); economics and policy analysis (MS); enterprise risk management (MS); entrepreneurship (MBA, MS); finance (MBA, MS); general business (MBA); hospitality leadership (MBA); hospitality leadership and operational performance (MS); human resources (MS); international business (MBA); management (MBA, MS); management information systems (MBA); marketing (MBA, MS); marketing analysis (MS); marketing strategy and planning (MBA); real estate (MS); real estate finance and investment (MBA); strategy, execution and valuation (MBA); supply chain management (MS); sustainable management (MS); taxation (MS); JD/MBA. *Accreditation:* AACSB. *Program availability:* Part-time, evening/weekend, online learning. *Entrance requirements:* For master's, GMAT/GRE, 2 letters of recommendation, resume, essay, official transcripts. Additional exam requirements/recommendations for international students: Required—TOEFL (minimum score 550 paper-based; 80 iBT). Electronic applications accepted. *Expenses:* Contact institution.

Fairfield University, Dolan School of Business, Fairfield, CT 06824. Offers accounting (MBA, MS, CAS); business analytics (MS); finance (MBA, MS, CAS); information systems and business analytics (MBA); management (MBA, CAS); marketing (MBA, CAS); taxation (CAS). *Accreditation:* AACSB. *Program availability:* Part-time, evening/weekend. *Degree requirements:* For master's, capstone course. *Entrance requirements:* For master's, GMAT (minimum score 500), 2 letters of reference, resume, minimum GPA of 3.0. Additional exam requirements/recommendations for international students: Required—TOEFL (minimum score 550 paper-based; 80 iBT) or IELTS (minimum score 6.5). Electronic applications accepted. *Expenses:* Contact institution. *Faculty research:* International finance, leadership and careers, ethics in accounting, emotions in consumer behavior and organizations, data analytics.

Fairleigh Dickinson University, Florham Campus, Silberman College of Business, Department of Accounting, Law, and Tax, Program in Taxation, Madison, NJ 07940-1099. Offers MS, Certificate.

Fairleigh Dickinson University, Metropolitan Campus, Silberman College of Business, Department of Accounting, Law, and Tax, Program in Taxation, Teaneck, NJ 07666-1914. Offers MS.

Florida Gulf Coast University, Lutgert College of Business, Program in Accounting and Taxation, Fort Myers, FL 33965-6565. Offers MS. *Program availability:* Part-time, evening/weekend. *Degree requirements:* For master's, thesis or alternative. *Entrance requirements:* For master's, GMAT, minimum GPA of 3.0. Additional exam requirements/recommendations for international students: Required—TOEFL (minimum score 550 paper-based). Electronic applications accepted. *Faculty research:* Stock petitions, mergers and acquisitions, deferred taxes, fraud and accounting regulations, graphical reporting practices.

Florida State University, The Graduate School, College of Business, Tallahassee, FL 32306-1110. Offers accounting (M Acc), including assurance and advisory services, generalist, taxation; business administration (MBA, PhD), including accounting (PhD), finance (PhD), management information systems (PhD), marketing (PhD), organizational behavior and human resources (PhD), risk management and insurance (PhD), strategy (PhD); finance (MS); management information systems (MS); risk management and insurance (MS); JD/MBA; MSW/MBA. *Accreditation:* AACSB. *Program availability:* Part-time, 100% online. *Students:* Average age 31. 300 applicants, 61% accepted, 133 enrolled. In 2018, 268 master's, 9 doctorates awarded. Terminal master's awarded for partial completion of doctoral program. *Degree requirements:* For doctorate, comprehensive exam, thesis/dissertation. *Entrance requirements:* For master's, GMAT, GRE (for all except MS in finance), work experience (MBA, MS), minimum GPA of 3.0, letters of recommendation; for doctorate, GMAT, GRE (for marketing, organizational behavior, risk management and insurance, management information systems, and human resources only), minimum graduate GPA of 3.5, letters of recommendation. Additional exam requirements/recommendations for international students: Required—TOEFL (minimum score 600 paper-based; 85 iBT); Recommended—IELTS (minimum score 6). *Application deadline:* For fall admission, 6/1 for domestic and international students; for spring admission, 10/1 for domestic and international students; for summer admission, 3/1 for domestic and international students. Applications are processed on a rolling basis. Application fee: $30. Electronic applications accepted. *Expenses:* Contact institution. *Financial support:* In 2018–19, 146 students received support, including 26 fellowships (averaging $1,500 per year), 77

research assistantships with full tuition reimbursements available (averaging $20,000 per year), 43 teaching assistantships with full tuition reimbursements available (averaging $20,000 per year); career-related internships or fieldwork, scholarships/grants, health care benefits, tuition waivers (full and partial), and unspecified assistantships also available. Support available to part-time students. Financial award application deadline: 1/1; financial award applicants required to submit FAFSA. *Faculty research:* Business strategy, marketing, finance, accounting, business analytics. *Total annual research expenditures:* $1.4 million. *Unit head:* Dr. Michael Hartline, Dean, 850-644-4405, Fax: 850-644-0915, E-mail: mhartline@business.fsu.edu. *Application contact:* Jennifer Clark, Director, 850-644-6458, E-mail: gradprograms@business.fsu.edu.
Website: http://business.fsu.edu/

Fordham University, Gabelli School of Business, New York, NY 10023. Offers accounting (MBA, MS); applied statistics and decision-making (MS); business economics (DPS); capital markets (DPS); communications and media management (MBA); electronic business (MBA); entrepreneurship (MBA); finance (MBA, PhD); global finance (MS); global sustainability (MBA); health administration (MS); healthcare management (MBA); information systems (MBA, MS); investor relations (MS); management (EMBA, MBA, MS, PhD); marketing (MBA); marketing intelligence (MS); media management (MS); nonprofit leadership (MS); quantitative finance (MS); strategy and decision-making (DPS); taxation (MS); JD/MBA; MS/MBA. *Accreditation:* AACSB. *Program availability:* Part-time, evening/weekend. Terminal master's awarded for partial completion of doctoral program. *Degree requirements:* For master's, internships (for some degrees); for doctorate, comprehensive exam (for some programs), thesis/dissertation. *Entrance requirements:* For master's, GMAT/GRE, 2 letters of recommendation, resume, 2 essays, transcripts, interview. Additional exam requirements/recommendations for international students: Required—TOEFL (minimum score 100 iBT), IELTS (minimum score 7). Electronic applications accepted. *Expenses:* Contact institution.

Georgetown University, Law Center, Washington, DC 20001. Offers environmental law (LL M); global health law (LL M); global health law and international institutions (LL M); individualized study (LL M); international business and economic law (LL M); law (JD, SJD); national security law (LL M); securities and financial regulation (LL M); taxation (LL M); JD/LL M; JD/MA; JD/MBA; JD/MPH; JD/PhD. *Accreditation:* ABA. *Program availability:* Part-time, evening/weekend. *Degree requirements:* For master's, thesis; for doctorate, thesis/dissertation (for some programs). *Entrance requirements:* For master's, JD, LL B, or first law degree earned in country of origin; for doctorate, LSAT (for JD). Additional exam requirements/recommendations for international students: Required—TOEFL. *Expenses:* Contact institution. *Faculty research:* Constitutional law, legal history, jurisprudence.

Georgia State University, J. Mack Robinson College of Business, School of Accountancy, Program in Taxation, Atlanta, GA 30303. Offers M Tax, JD/M Tax. *Program availability:* Part-time, evening/weekend. *Entrance requirements:* For master's, GRE or GMAT, transcripts from all institutions attended, resume, essays. Additional exam requirements/recommendations for international students: Required—TOEFL (minimum score 610 paper-based; 101 iBT), IELTS (minimum score 7). *Application deadline:* Applications are processed on a rolling basis. Application fee: $50. Electronic applications accepted. *Expenses: Tuition, area resident:* Full-time $9360; part-time $390 per credit hour. Tuition, state resident: full-time $9360; part-time $390 per credit hour. Tuition, nonresident: full-time $30,024; part-time $1251 per credit hour. *International tuition:* $30,024 full-time. *Required fees:* $2128. *Financial support:* Research assistantships, career-related internships or fieldwork, scholarships/grants, tuition waivers, and unspecified assistantships available. Financial award application deadline: 5/1. *Application contact:* Toby McChesney, Assistant Dean for Graduate Recruiting and Student Services, 404-413-7167, Fax: 404-413-7162, E-mail: rcbgradadmissions@gsu.edu.
Website: https://robinson.gsu.edu/academic-departments/accountancy/

Golden Gate University, School of Accounting, San Francisco, CA 94105-2968. Offers financial accounting and reporting (M Ac, MSA, Graduate Certificate); forensic accounting (M Ac, MSA, Graduate Certificate); internal auditing (M Ac, MSA, Certificate); management accounting (M Ac, MSA); taxation (M Ac, MSA). *Program availability:* Part-time, evening/weekend. *Entrance requirements:* For master's, minimum GPA of 3.0. Additional exam requirements/recommendations for international students: Required—TOEFL (minimum score 550 paper-based), IELTS (minimum score 6.5). Electronic applications accepted. *Expenses:* Contact institution. *Faculty research:* Forensic accounting, audit, tax, CPA exam.

Golden Gate University, School of Law, San Francisco, CA 94105-2968. Offers environmental law (LL M); estate planning (LL M); intellectual property law (LL M); international legal studies (LL M, SJD); law (JD); taxation law (LL M); U.S. legal studies (LL M); JD/MBA. *Accreditation:* ABA. *Program availability:* Part-time, evening/weekend. *Degree requirements:* For doctorate, thesis/dissertation (for some programs). *Entrance requirements:* For doctorate, LSAT (for JD). Additional exam requirements/recommendations for international students: Required—TOEFL (minimum score 600 paper-based). Electronic applications accepted. *Expenses:* Contact institution. *Faculty research:* International law, intellectual property law, environmental law, real estate, civil rights.

Golden Gate University, School of Taxation, San Francisco, CA 94105-2968. Offers advanced studies in taxation (Certificate); estate planning (Certificate); financial planning and taxation (MS); international taxation (Certificate); state and local taxation (Certificate); taxation (MS, Certificate). *Program availability:* Part-time, evening/weekend. *Entrance requirements:* For master's, minimum GPA of 3.0. Additional exam requirements/recommendations for international students: Required—TOEFL (minimum score 550 paper-based), IELTS (minimum score 6.5). Electronic applications accepted. *Expenses:* Contact institution.

Goldey-Beacom College, Graduate Program, Wilmington, DE 19808-1999. Offers business administration (MBA); finance (MS); financial management (MBA); health care management (MBA); human resource management (MBA); information technology (MBA); international business management (MBA); major finance (MBA); major taxation (MBA); management (MM); marketing management (MBA); taxation (MBA, MS). *Accreditation:* ACBSP. *Program availability:* Part-time, evening/weekend. *Entrance requirements:* For master's, GMAT, MAT, GRE, minimum GPA of 3.0. Additional exam requirements/recommendations for international students: Required—TOEFL (minimum score 65 iBT); Recommended—IELTS (minimum score 6). Electronic applications accepted.

Gonzaga University, School of Business Administration, Spokane, WA 99258. Offers accountancy (M Acc); American Indian entrepreneurship (MBA); business administration (MBA); taxation (MS); JD/M Acc; JD/MBA. *Accreditation:* AACSB. *Program availability:* Part-time, evening/weekend. *Degree requirements:* For master's, capstone course. *Entrance requirements:* For master's, GMAT or GRE, essay, two professional recommendations, resume/curriculum vitae, copy of official transcripts from all colleges attended, minimum GPA of 3.0. Additional exam requirements/recommendations for international students: Required—TOEFL (minimum score 570

paper-based, 89 iBT) or IELTS (minimum score 6.5). Electronic applications accepted. *Expenses:* Contact institution.

Grand Valley State University, Seidman College of Business, Program in Taxation, Allendale, MI 49401-9403. Offers MST. *Program availability:* Part-time, evening/weekend. *Students:* 12 part-time (7 women); includes 1 minority (Two or more races, non-Hispanic/Latino), 2 international. Average age 32. 3 applicants, 100% accepted, 3 enrolled. In 2018, 6 master's awarded. *Entrance requirements:* For master's, GMAT, personal statement. Additional exam requirements/recommendations for international students: Required—TOEFL (minimum iBT score of 80), IELTS (6.5), or Michigan English Language Assessment Battery (77). *Application deadline:* For fall admission, 8/1 priority date for domestic students, 5/1 priority date for international students; for winter admission, 12/1 priority date for domestic students, 11/1 priority date for international students; for spring admission, 4/1 priority date for domestic students, 3/1 priority date for international students. Applications are processed on a rolling basis. Application fee: $30. Electronic applications accepted. *Expenses:* $712 per credit hour, 33 credit hours. *Financial support:* In 2018–19, 2 students received support, including 2 research assistantships; fellowships, Federal Work-Study, institutionally sponsored loans, and unspecified assistantships also available. Financial award application deadline: 2/15. *Faculty research:* Individual income taxation, state taxation, pass-through entities, estate and gift taxation, sale-leasebacks. *Unit head:* Dr. Aaron Lowen, Director, 616-331-7441, Fax: 616-331-7412, E-mail: lowena@gvsu.edu. *Application contact:* Koleta Moore, Assistant Dean of Student Engagement, Graduate Program Operations, 616-331-7386, Fax: 616-331-7389, E-mail: moorekol@gvsu.edu.
Website: http://www.gvsu.edu/business/

HEC Montreal, School of Business Administration, Graduate Diploma Programs in Administration, Program in Taxation, Montréal, QC H3T 2A7, Canada. Offers Graduate Diploma. All courses are given in French. *Students:* 34 full-time (23 women), 61 part-time (27 women). 83 applicants, 51% accepted, 22 enrolled. In 2018, 25 Graduate Diplomas awarded. *Entrance requirements:* For degree, bachelor's diploma in law, accounting, or economics. *Application deadline:* For fall admission, 3/15 for domestic and international students; for winter admission, 9/15 for domestic and international students. Application fee: $91 Canadian dollars ($191 Canadian dollars for international students). Electronic applications accepted. *Expenses: Tuition, area resident:* Full-time $3052.80 Canadian dollars; part-time $84.80 Canadian dollars per credit. Tuition, state resident: full-time $3816 Canadian dollars; part-time $264.67 Canadian dollars per credit. Tuition, nonresident: full-time $11,910 Canadian dollars. *International tuition:* $20,905.20 Canadian dollars full-time. *Required fees:* $1805.34 Canadian dollars; $43.62 Canadian dollars per credit. $71.78 Canadian dollars per term. Tuition and fees vary according to degree level and program. *Financial support:* Research assistantships, teaching assistantships, and scholarships/grants available. Financial award application deadline: 9/2. *Unit head:* Renaud Lachance, Director, 514-340-6428, E-mail: renaud.lachance@hec.ca. *Application contact:* Anny Caron, Administrative Director, 514-340-6000, Fax: 514-340-6411, E-mail: aide@hec.ca.
Website: http://www.hec.ca/programmes/dess/dess-fiscalite/index.html

HEC Montreal, School of Business Administration, Master of Laws in Taxation Program, Montréal, QC H3T 2A7, Canada. Offers LL M. All courses are given in French. *Students:* 6 full-time (4 women), 13 part-time (10 women). 6 applicants, 100% accepted, 4 enrolled. In 2018, 11 master's awarded. *Entrance requirements:* For master's, bachelor's degree in taxation, accounting, law or economics. *Application deadline:* For fall admission, 8/1 for domestic and international students; for winter admission, 11/15 for domestic and international students; for summer admission, 3/15 for domestic and international students. Application fee: $91 Canadian dollars ($191 Canadian dollars for international students). Electronic applications accepted. *Expenses: Tuition, area resident:* Full-time $3052.80 Canadian dollars; part-time $84.80 Canadian dollars per credit. Tuition, state resident: full-time $3816 Canadian dollars; part-time $264.67 Canadian dollars per credit. Tuition, nonresident: full-time $11,910 Canadian dollars. *International tuition:* $20,905.20 Canadian dollars full-time. *Required fees:* $1805.34 Canadian dollars; $43.62 Canadian dollars per credit. $71.78 Canadian dollars per term. Tuition and fees vary according to degree level and program. *Financial support:* Research assistantships, teaching assistantships, and scholarships/grants available. Financial award application deadline: 9/2. *Unit head:* Renaud Lachance, Director, 514-340-6428, E-mail: renaud.lachance@hec.ca. *Application contact:* Anny Caron, Administrative Director, 514-340-6000, Fax: 514-340-6411, E-mail: aide@hec.ca.
Website: http://www.hec.ca/programmes/maitrises/maitrise-droit-llm-fiscalite/index.html

Hofstra University, Frank G. Zarb School of Business, Programs in Accounting and Taxation, Hempstead, NY 11549. Offers accounting (MS, Advanced Certificate); business administration (MBA), including accounting, professional accountancy, taxation; taxation (MS, Advanced Certificate). *Program availability:* Part-time, evening/weekend, blended/hybrid learning. *Students:* 121 full-time (64 women), 43 part-time (24 women); includes 29 minority (3 Black or African American, non-Hispanic/Latino; 16 Asian, non-Hispanic/Latino; 8 Hispanic/Latino; 2 Two or more races, non-Hispanic/Latino), 68 international. Average age 26. 213 applicants, 80% accepted, 63 enrolled. In 2018, 125 master's awarded. *Degree requirements:* For master's, thesis (for some programs), capstone course (for MBA), thesis (for MS), minimum GPA of 3.0. *Entrance requirements:* For master's, GMAT/GRE, 2 letters of recommendation, resume, essay. Additional exam requirements/recommendations for international students: Required—TOEFL (minimum score 550 paper-based; 80 iBT); Recommended—IELTS (minimum score 6). *Application deadline:* Applications are processed on a rolling basis. Application fee: $75. Electronic applications accepted. *Expenses:* $1,375 per credit plus fees. *Financial support:* In 2018–19, 43 students received support, including 39 fellowships with full and partial tuition reimbursements available (averaging $4,765 per year); research assistantships with full and partial tuition reimbursements available, career-related internships or fieldwork, Federal Work-Study, institutionally sponsored loans, scholarships/grants, tuition waivers (full and partial), unspecified assistantships, and scholarships and endowed scholarships also available. Support available to part-time students. Financial award applicants required to submit FAFSA. *Faculty research:* Corporate compliance, artificial intelligence, financial accounting fraud, tax reform legislation, accounting analytics. *Unit head:* Dr. Jacqueline Burke, Chairperson, 516-463-6987, E-mail: jacqueline.a.burke@hofstra.edu. *Application contact:* Sunil Samuel, Assistant Vice President of Admissions, 516-463-4723, Fax: 516-463-4664, E-mail: graduateadmission@hofstra.edu.
Website: http://www.hofstra.edu/business/

Illinois Institute of Technology, Chicago-Kent College of Law, Chicago, IL 60661-3691. Offers family law (LL M); financial services law (LL M); international intellectual property law (LL M); law (JD); legal studies (JSD); taxation (LL M); U.S., international, and transnational law (LL M); JD/LL M; JD/MBA; JD/MPA; JD/MPH; JD/MS. *Accreditation:* ABA. *Program availability:* Part-time, evening/weekend. Terminal master's awarded for partial completion of doctoral program. *Entrance requirements:* For master's, 1st degree in law or certified license to practice law; for doctorate, LSAT. Additional exam requirements/recommendations for international students: Required—TOEFL (minimum score 600 paper-based; 100 iBT); Recommended—IELTS (minimum score 7). Electronic applications accepted. *Expenses:* Contact institution. *Faculty research:* Constitutional law, bioethics, environmental law, intellectual property.

Taxation

Instituto Tecnologico de Santo Domingo, Graduate School, Area of Business, Santo Domingo, Dominican Republic. Offers banking and securities markets (M Mgmt); corporate finance (M Mgmt); human resources management (M Mgmt, Certificate); international trade management (M Mgmt); marketing (M Mgmt); organizational development (M Mgmt); quality and productivity management (Certificate); tax management and planning (M Mgmt); upper management (M Mgmt).

James Madison University, The Graduate School, College of Business, Program in Accounting, Harrisonburg, VA 22807. Offers accounting information systems (MS); taxation (MS). *Accreditation:* AACSB. *Program availability:* Part-time, evening/weekend. *Students:* 64 full-time (25 women), 1 part-time (0 women); includes 11 minority (2 Asian, non-Hispanic/Latino; 6 Hispanic/Latino; 3 Two or more races, non-Hispanic/Latino), 1 international. Average age 30. In 2018, 114 master's awarded. Application fee: $60. Electronic applications accepted. *Expenses:* Tuition, state resident: full-time $10,848. Tuition, nonresident: full-time $27,888. *Required fees:* $1128. *Financial support:* In 2018–19, 28 students received support, including 23 fellowships; Federal Work-Study and assistantships (averaging $6911), also available. Financial award application deadline: 3/1; financial award applicants required to submit FAFSA. *Unit head:* Dr. Tim J. Louwers, Director of the School of Accounting, 540-568-3027, E-mail: louwertj@jmu.edu. *Application contact:* Lynette D. Michael, Director of Graduate Admissions, 540-568-6131 Ext. 6395, Fax: 540-568-7860, E-mail: michaeld@jmu.edu.
Website: https://www.jmu.edu/cob/accounting/masters/index.shtml

Liberty University, School of Business, Lynchburg, VA 24515. Offers accounting (MBA, MS), including audit and financial reporting (MS), business (MS), financial services (MS), forensic accounting (MS), leadership (MS), taxation (MS); cyber security (MS); executive leadership (MA); international business (DBA); leadership (DBA); marketing (MBA, MS, DBA), including digital marketing and advertising (MS), project management (MS), public relations (MS), sports marketing and media (MS); project management (MBA, DBA); public relations (MBA). *Program availability:* Part-time, online learning. *Students:* 2,871 full-time (1,496 women), 4,437 part-time (1,969 women); includes 2,069 minority (1,424 Black or African American, non-Hispanic/Latino; 44 American Indian or Alaska Native, non-Hispanic/Latino; 133 Asian, non-Hispanic/Latino; 282 Hispanic/Latino; 16 Native Hawaiian or other Pacific Islander, non-Hispanic/Latino; 170 Two or more races, non-Hispanic/Latino), 154 international. Average age 36. 8,980 applicants, 45% accepted, 2009 enrolled. In 2018, 1,988 master's, 25 doctorates awarded. *Entrance requirements:* For master's, minimum undergraduate GPA of 3.0, 15 hours of upper-level business courses. Additional exam requirements/recommendations for international students: Required—TOEFL (minimum score 600 paper-based; 100 iBT). *Application deadline:* Applications are processed on a rolling basis. Application fee: $50. Electronic applications accepted. *Expenses:* Contact institution. *Financial support:* In 2018–19, 990 students received support. Teaching assistantships and Federal Work-Study available. Financial award applicants required to submit FAFSA. *Unit head:* Dr. Dave Bratt, Dean, 434-592-7321, E-mail: dabrat@liberty.edu. *Application contact:* Jay Bridge, Director of Graduate Admissions, 800-424-9595, Fax: 800-628-7977, E-mail: gradadmissions@liberty.edu.
Website: https://www.liberty.edu/business/

Lipscomb University, College of Business, Nashville, TN 37204-3951. Offers accounting and finance (MBA); audit/accounting (M Acc); business (Certificate); business administration (MM); healthcare management (MBA); leadership (MBA); tax (M Acc); MBA/MS; Pharm D/MM. *Accreditation:* ACBSP. *Program availability:* Part-time, evening/weekend. *Entrance requirements:* For master's, GMAT, transcripts, interview, 2 references, resume. Additional exam requirements/recommendations for international students: Required—TOEFL (minimum score 570 paper-based). Electronic applications accepted. *Expenses:* Contact institution. *Faculty research:* Impact of spirituality on organization commitment, women in corporate leadership, psychological empowerment, training.

Long Island University–LIU Brooklyn, School of Business, Public Administration and Information Sciences, Brooklyn, NY 11201-8423. Offers accounting (MBA); accounting (MS); business administration (MBA); computer science (MS); gerontology (Advanced Certificate); health administration (MPA); human resources management (MS); not-for-profit management (Advanced Certificate); public administration (MPA); taxation (MS). *Program availability:* Part-time, evening/weekend. *Entrance requirements:* Additional exam requirements/recommendations for international students: Required—TOEFL (minimum score 550 paper-based; 75 iBT). Electronic applications accepted. *Faculty research:* Tax policy; public sector budgeting and gender inequities; technology and innovation; game theory; knowledge management.

Long Island University–LIU Post, College of Management, Brookville, NY 11548-1300. Offers accountancy (MS); finance (MBA); information systems (MS); international business (MBA); management (MBA); management engineering (MS); marketing (MBA); taxation (MS); technical project management (MS); JD/MBA. *Accreditation:* AACSB. *Program availability:* Part-time, evening/weekend, blended/hybrid learning. *Entrance requirements:* For master's, GMAT, GRE, or LSAT. Additional exam requirements/recommendations for international students: Required—TOEFL (minimum score 550 paper-based, 75 iBT) or IELTS. Electronic applications accepted. *Faculty research:* Innovation and property rights, knowledge sourcing, sustainability and firm performance, China and growth markets, corporate social responsibility, workforce compensation and issues.

Loyola University Chicago, School of Law, Chicago, IL 60611. Offers advocacy (LL M); business and compliance (MJ); business law (LL M); child and family (LL M); child and family law (MJ, Certificate); global competition (LL M, MJ); health law (LL M, MJ, Certificate); international law (LL M); law (JD); public interest law (Certificate); rule of law for development (LL M, MJ); tax (LL M); tax law (Certificate); transactional law (Certificate); trial advocacy (Certificate); JD/MA; JD/MBA; JD/MPP; JD/MSW; MJ/MSW; MS/MJ. *Accreditation:* ABA. *Program availability:* Part-time, evening/weekend, 100% online, blended/hybrid learning. *Faculty:* 69 full-time (36 women), 306 part-time/adjunct (148 women). *Students:* 870 full-time (530 women), 239 part-time (185 women); includes 380 minority (134 Black or African American, non-Hispanic/Latino; 64 Asian, non-Hispanic/Latino; 142 Hispanic/Latino; 40 Two or more races, non-Hispanic/Latino), 34 international. Average age 31. 2,711 applicants, 46% accepted, 387 enrolled. In 2018, 151 master's, 193 doctorates, 152 Certificates awarded. *Entrance requirements:* For doctorate, LSAT. Additional exam requirements/recommendations for international students: Required—TOEFL (minimum score 100 iBT); Recommended—IELTS (minimum score 7). *Application deadline:* For fall admission, 4/1 for domestic and international students. Applications are processed on a rolling basis. Application fee: $0. Electronic applications accepted. *Expenses:* Contact institution. *Financial support:* In 2018–19, 598 students received support, including 67 fellowships; research assistantships, Federal Work-Study, scholarships/grants, and health care benefits also available. Financial award application deadline: 3/1; financial award applicants required to submit FAFSA. *Faculty research:* Constitutional law including hate speech and supreme court advocacy; early childhood education including law policy and pedagogy; hedonic psychology - legal and social determinants of happiness; racial inequality; intersection of law, science, and technology. *Unit head:* Dr. James Faught, JD, Associate Dean for Administration, Law School, 312-915-7131, Fax: 312-915-6911, E-mail: law-admissions@luc.edu. *Application contact:* Jill Schur, Director, Graduate Enrollment Management, 312-915-8902, E-mail: gradinfo@luc.edu.
Website: http://www.luc.edu/law/

Metropolitan State University of Denver, School of Business, Denver, CO 80204. Offers accounting (MP Acc); fraud exam and forensic auditing (MP Acc); internal audit (MP Acc); public accounting (MP Acc); taxation (MP Acc). *Accreditation:* AACSB. *Entrance requirements:* For master's, GMAT. *Expenses:* Contact institution.

Michigan State University, The Graduate School, Eli Broad College of Business, Department of Accounting and Information Systems, East Lansing, MI 48224. Offers accounting (MS, PhD), including information systems (MS), public and corporate accounting (MS), taxation (MS); business information systems (PhD). *Accreditation:* AACSB. *Degree requirements:* For doctorate, comprehensive exam, thesis/dissertation. *Entrance requirements:* For master's, GMAT (minimum score 550), bachelor's degree in accounting; minimum cumulative GPA of 3.0 at any institution attended and in any junior-/senior-level accounting courses taken; 3 letters of recommendation (at least 1 from faculty); working knowledge of computers including word processing, spreadsheets, networking, and database management system; for doctorate, GMAT (minimum score 600), bachelor's degree; transcripts; 3 letters of recommendation; statement of purpose; resume; on-campus interview; personal qualifications of sound character, perseverance, intellectual curiosity, and interest in scholarly research. Additional exam requirements/recommendations for international students: Required—TOEFL (minimum score 600 paper-based; 100 iBT), IELTS (minimum score 7) accepted for MS only. Electronic applications accepted.

Mississippi State University, College of Business, Adkerson School of Accountancy, Mississippi State, MS 39762. Offers accountancy (MPA); systems (MPA). *Accreditation:* AACSB. *Faculty:* 10 full-time (0 women). *Students:* 63 full-time (43 women), 1 part-time (0 women); includes 2 minority (1 Asian, non-Hispanic/Latino; 1 Hispanic/Latino), 1 international. Average age 24. 32 applicants, 78% accepted, 20 enrolled. In 2018, 59 master's awarded. *Degree requirements:* For master's, comprehensive exam. *Entrance requirements:* For master's, GMAT (minimum score of 510), minimum GPA of 3.0 over last 60 hours of undergraduate course work. Additional exam requirements/recommendations for international students: Required—TOEFL (minimum score 575 paper-based; 84 iBT); Recommended—IELTS (minimum score 7). *Application deadline:* For fall admission, 7/1 for domestic students, 5/1 for international students; for spring admission, 11/1 for domestic students, 9/1 for international students. Applications are processed on a rolling basis. Application fee: $60 ($80 for international students). Electronic applications accepted. *Expenses:* Tuition, state resident: full-time $8450; part-time $360.59 per credit hour. Tuition, nonresident: full-time $23,140; part-time $969.09 per credit hour. *Required fees:* $110. One-time fee: $55 full-time. Part-time tuition and fees vary according to course load, degree level, campus/location and reciprocity agreements. *Financial support:* Career-related internships or fieldwork, Federal Work-Study, institutionally sponsored loans, scholarships/grants, and unspecified assistantships available. Support available to part-time students. Financial award application deadline: 4/1; financial award applicants required to submit FAFSA. *Faculty research:* Income tax, financial accounting system, managerial accounting, auditing. *Unit head:* Dr. Shawn Mauldin, Professor and Director, 662-325-3710, Fax: 662-325-1646, E-mail: smauldin@business.msstate.edu. *Application contact:* Robbie Salters, Admissions and Enrollment Assistant, 662-325-7400, E-mail: rsalters@grad.msstate.edu.
Website: http://www.business.msstate.edu/programs/adkerson

National Paralegal College, Graduate Programs, Phoenix, AZ 85014. Offers compliance law (MS); legal studies (MS); taxation (MS). *Program availability:* Part-time. Electronic applications accepted.

New York University, School of Law, New York, NY 10012-1019. Offers law (LL M, JD, JSD); law and business (Advanced Certificate); taxation (MSL, Advanced Certificate); JD/LL M; JD/MA; JD/MBA; JD/MPA; JD/MPP; JD/MSW; JD/MUP; JD/PhD. *Accreditation:* ABA. *Program availability:* Part-time, blended/hybrid learning. *Entrance requirements:* For doctorate, LSAT (for JD). Electronic applications accepted. *Expenses:* Contact institution. *Faculty research:* International law, environmental law, corporate law, globalization of law, philosophy of law.

Northeastern University, D'Amore-McKim School of Business, Boston, MA 02115-5096. Offers accounting (MS); business administration (EMBA, MBA); finance (MS); innovation (MS); international business (MS); international management (MS); taxation (MS); technological entrepreneurship (MS); JD/MBA; LL M/MBA; MBA/MSN; MS/MBA. *Accreditation:* AACSB. *Program availability:* Part-time, evening/weekend, online learning. *Entrance requirements:* For master's, GMAT or GRE. Electronic applications accepted. *Expenses:* Contact institution.

Northern Illinois University, Graduate School, College of Business, Department of Accountancy, De Kalb, IL 60115-2854. Offers MAC, MAS, MST. *Accreditation:* AACSB. *Program availability:* Part-time, evening/weekend. *Faculty:* 14 full-time (4 women). *Students:* 117 full-time (50 women), 83 part-time (51 women); includes 70 minority (13 Black or African American, non-Hispanic/Latino; 21 Asian, non-Hispanic/Latino; 32 Hispanic/Latino; 4 Two or more races, non-Hispanic/Latino), 18 international. Average age 28. 89 applicants, 76% accepted, 41 enrolled. In 2018, 138 master's awarded. *Degree requirements:* For master's, thesis optional. *Entrance requirements:* For master's, GMAT, minimum GPA of 2.75. Additional exam requirements/recommendations for international students: Required—TOEFL (minimum score 550 paper-based). *Application deadline:* For fall admission, 4/1 priority date for domestic students, 5/1 for international students; for spring admission, 9/15 priority date for domestic students, 10/1 for international students. Applications are processed on a rolling basis. Application fee: $40. Electronic applications accepted. *Financial support:* In 2018–19, 5 research assistantships with full tuition reimbursements, 31 teaching assistantships with full tuition reimbursements were awarded; fellowships with full tuition reimbursements, career-related internships or fieldwork, Federal Work-Study, scholarships/grants, tuition waivers (full), and unspecified assistantships also available. Support available to part-time students. Financial award applicants required to submit FAFSA. *Faculty research:* Accounting fraud, governmental accounting, corporate income tax planning, auditing, ethics. *Unit head:* Sarah Marsh, Chair, 815-753-1250, Fax: 815-753-8515. *Application contact:* Graduate Advising, 815-753-1325, E-mail: cobadvising@niu.edu.
Website: http://www.cob.niu.edu/accy/

Northern Kentucky University, Office of Graduate Programs, College of Business, Program in Accountancy, Highland Heights, KY 41099. Offers accountancy (M Acc); advanced taxation (Certificate). *Program availability:* Part-time, evening/weekend. *Degree requirements:* For master's, capstone course. *Entrance requirements:* For master's, GMAT, master's degree, MD, or PhD, official transcripts, current resume, 3 years of work experience (strongly suggested), statement of purpose. Additional exam requirements/recommendations for international students: Required—TOEFL (minimum score 79 iBT); Recommended—IELTS (minimum score 6.5). Electronic applications accepted. *Faculty research:* Ethics, accounting history, financial reporting.

Northwestern University, Pritzker School of Law, Chicago, IL 60611-3069. Offers international human rights (LL M); law (MSL, JD); tax (LL M in Tax); JD/LL M; JD/MBA; JD/PhD; LL M/Certificate. Executive LL M programs offered in Madrid (Spain), Seoul

(South Korea), and Tel Aviv (Israel). *Accreditation:* ABA. *Program availability:* Part-time, online learning. *Entrance requirements:* For master's, law degree or equivalent, letter of recommendation, resume; for doctorate, LSAT, 1 letter of recommendation, resume. Additional exam requirements/recommendations for international students: Required—TOEFL. Electronic applications accepted. *Expenses:* Contact institution. *Faculty research:* Constitutional law, corporate law, international law, law and social policy, ethical studies.

Pace University, Lubin School of Business, Taxation Program, New York, NY 10038. Offers taxation (MBA, MS). *Program availability:* Part-time, evening/weekend. *Students:* 21 full-time (13 women), 26 part-time (13 women); includes 29 minority (5 Black or African American, non-Hispanic/Latino; 19 Asian, non-Hispanic/Latino; 4 Hispanic/Latino; 1 Two or more races, non-Hispanic/Latino), 6 international. Average age 30. 26 applicants, 92% accepted, 17 enrolled. In 2018, 22 master's awarded. *Entrance requirements:* For master's, GMAT or GRE (MS Taxation applicants can request waiver if currently a CPA, CMA, or have been admitted to the bar), undergraduate degree, transcripts from all accredited colleges/universities attended, two letters of recommendation, resume, personal statement. Additional exam requirements/recommendations for international students: Required—TOEFL (minimum score 90 iBT), IELTS (minimum score 7) or PTE (minimum score 61). *Application deadline:* For fall admission, 8/1 priority date for domestic students, 6/1 for international students; for spring admission, 12/1 for domestic students, 10/1 for international students. Applications are processed on a rolling basis. Application fee: $70. Electronic applications accepted. *Financial support:* Research assistantships, career-related internships or fieldwork, Federal Work-Study, and unspecified assistantships available. Support available to part-time students. Financial award application deadline: 2/15; financial award applicants required to submit FAFSA. *Unit head:* Dr. Vincent Barrella, Chairperson, Legal Studies and Taxation Department, 212-618-6479, E-mail: vbarrella@pace.edu. *Application contact:* Susan Ford-Goldschein, Director of Graduate Admissions, 212-346-1531, Fax: 212-346-1585, E-mail: graduateadmission@pace.edu.
Website: http://www.pace.edu/lubin/sections/explore-programs/graduate-programs

Robert Morris University, School of Business, Moon Township, PA 15108-1189. Offers business administration (MBA); human resource management (MS); taxation (MS); MBA/MS. *Accreditation:* AACSB. *Program availability:* Part-time-only, evening/weekend, 100% online. *Faculty:* 18 full-time (7 women), 1 (woman) part-time/adjunct. *Students:* 214 part-time (84 women); includes 12 minority (6 Black or African American, non-Hispanic/Latino; 5 Asian, non-Hispanic/Latino; 1 Two or more races, non-Hispanic/Latino), 7 international. Average age 30. 77 applicants, 97% accepted, 71 enrolled. In 2018, 83 master's awarded. *Degree requirements:* For master's, Completion of 36 or 30 credit hours depending upon program. *Entrance requirements:* For master's, GMAT, GRE, letters of recommendation, work experience. Additional exam requirements/recommendations for international students: Required—TOEFL (minimum score 550 paper-based; 79 iBT). *Application deadline:* For fall admission, 7/1 priority date for domestic and international students; for spring admission, 11/1 priority date for domestic and international students. Applications are processed on a rolling basis. Application fee: $35. Electronic applications accepted. Application fee is waived when completed online. *Expenses: Tuition:* Part-time $925 per credit hour. *Required fees:* $80 per credit hour. Tuition and fees vary according to degree level. *Financial support:* Institutionally sponsored loans available. Support available to part-time students. Financial award application deadline: 5/1; financial award applicants required to submit FAFSA. *Unit head:* Dr. Michelle L. Patrick, Dean, 412-397-5445, Fax: 412-397-2585, E-mail: patrick@rmu.edu. *Application contact:* Dr. Jodi Potter, Director, MBA Program, 412-397-6387, E-mail: potterj@rmu.edu.
Website: http://sbus.rmu.edu

St. John's University, The Peter J. Tobin College of Business, Department of Accountancy, Program in Taxation, Queens, NY 11439. Offers MBA, MS. *Program availability:* Part-time, evening/weekend, 100% online, blended/hybrid learning. *Degree requirements:* For master's, thesis. *Entrance requirements:* For master's, GMAT or GRE, 2 letters of recommendation, essay, resume, unofficial transcripts. Additional exam requirements/recommendations for international students: Required—TOEFL (minimum score 80 iBT), IELTS (minimum score 6.5). Electronic applications accepted. *Expenses:* Contact institution. *Faculty research:* Tax policy, taxation systems.

St. Thomas University, School of Law, Miami Gardens, FL 33054-6459. Offers international human rights (LL M); international taxation (LL M); law (JD); JD/MBA; JD/MS. *Accreditation:* ABA. *Program availability:* Online learning. *Degree requirements:* For master's, thesis (international taxation). *Entrance requirements:* For doctorate, LSAT. Electronic applications accepted. *Expenses:* Contact institution.

Southern Illinois University Edwardsville, Graduate School, School of Business, Department of Accounting, Edwardsville, IL 62026. Offers accountancy (MSA); taxation (MSA). *Accreditation:* AACSB. *Program availability:* Part-time, evening/weekend. *Degree requirements:* For master's, thesis or alternative, final exam. *Entrance requirements:* For master's, GMAT. Additional exam requirements/recommendations for international students: Required—TOEFL (minimum score 550 paper-based; 79 iBT), IELTS (minimum score 6.5). Electronic applications accepted.

Southern Methodist University, Dedman School of Law, Dallas, TX 75275-0110. Offers general law (LL M); international and comparative law (LL M); law (JD, SJD); taxation (LL M); JD/MA; JD/MBA. *Accreditation:* ABA. *Program availability:* Part-time, evening/weekend. *Degree requirements:* For master's, thesis optional; for doctorate, thesis/dissertation (for some programs), 30 hours of public service (for JD). *Entrance requirements:* For master's, JD; for doctorate, LSAT (for JD). Additional exam requirements/recommendations for international students: Required—TOEFL (minimum score 575 paper-based; 91 iBT). Electronic applications accepted. *Expenses:* Contact institution. *Faculty research:* Corporate law, intellectual property, international law, commercial law, dispute resolution.

Southern New Hampshire University, School of Business, Manchester, NH 03106-1045. Offers accounting (MBA, Graduate Certificate); accounting finance (MS); accounting/auditing (MS); accounting/forensic accounting (MS); accounting/management accounting (MS); accounting/taxation (MS); applied economics (MS); athletic administration (MBA, Graduate Certificate); business administration (IMBA, Certificate), including business information systems (Certificate), human resource management (Certificate); business analytics (MBA); business intelligence (MBA); communication (MA), including new media and marketing, public relations; community economic development (MBA); criminal justice (MBA); data analytics (MS); economics (MBA); engineering management (MBA); entrepreneurship (MBA); finance (MBA, MS, Graduate Certificate); finance/corporate finance (MS); finance/investments (MS); forensic accounting (MBA); forensic accounting and fraud examination (Graduate Certificate); healthcare informatics (MBA); healthcare management (MBA); human resource management (MS); human resources (MBA); information technology (MS); information technology management (MBA); international business (PhD); Internet marketing (MBA); leadership (MBA); leadership of nonprofit organizations (Graduate Certificate); management (MS); marketing (MBA, MS, Graduate Certificate); music business (MBA); operations and project management (MS); operations and supply chain management (MBA, Graduate Certificate); organizational leadership (MS); project management (MBA, Graduate Certificate); public administration (MBA, Graduate Certificate); quantitative analysis (MBA); Six Sigma (Graduate Certificate); Six Sigma quality (MBA); social media marketing (MBA, Graduate Certificate); sport management (MBA, MS, Graduate Certificate); sustainability and environmental compliance (MBA); MBA/Certificate. *Accreditation:* ACBSP. *Program availability:* Part-time, evening/weekend, online learning. Terminal master's awarded for partial completion of doctoral program. *Degree requirements:* For master's, one foreign language, comprehensive exam (for some programs), thesis or alternative; for doctorate, one foreign language, comprehensive exam, thesis/dissertation. *Entrance requirements:* For master's, minimum GPA of 2.5; for doctorate, GMAT. Additional exam requirements/recommendations for international students: Required—TOEFL (minimum score 500 paper-based). Electronic applications accepted.

State University of New York College at Old Westbury, School of Business, Old Westbury, NY 11568-0210. Offers accounting (MS); taxation (MS). *Program availability:* Part-time, evening/weekend. *Entrance requirements:* For master's, GMAT, 2 letters of recommendation. Additional exam requirements/recommendations for international students: Required—TOEFL (minimum score 550 paper-based). Electronic applications accepted. *Faculty research:* Corporate governance, asset pricing, corporate finance, hedge funds, taxation.

Strayer University, Graduate Studies, Washington, DC 20005-2603. Offers accounting (MS); acquisition (MBA); business administration (MBA); communications technology (MS); educational management (M Ed); finance (MBA); health services administration (MHSA); hospitality and tourism management (MBA); human resource management (MBA); information systems (MS), including computer security management, decision support system management, enterprise resource management, network management, software engineering management, systems development management; management (MBA); management information systems (MS); marketing (MBA); professional accounting (MS), including accounting information systems, controllership, taxation; public administration (MPA); supply chain management (MBA); technology in education (M Ed). Programs also offered at campus locations in Birmingham, AL; Chamblee, GA; Cobb County, GA; Morrow, GA; White Marsh, MD; Charleston, SC; Columbia, SC; Greensboro, NC; Greenville, SC; Lexington, KY; Louisville, KY; Nashville, TN; North Raleigh, NC; Washington, DC. *Accreditation:* ACBSP. *Program availability:* Part-time, evening/weekend, online learning. *Degree requirements:* For master's, thesis. *Entrance requirements:* For master's, GMAT, GRE General Test, bachelor's degree from an accredited college or university, minimum undergraduate GPA of 2.75. Electronic applications accepted.

Suffolk University, Sawyer Business School, Department of Accounting, Boston, MA 02108-2770. Offers accounting (MSA, Graduate Certificate); taxation (MST); MBA/MSA; MBA/MST. *Accreditation:* AACSB. *Program availability:* Part-time, evening/weekend, 100% online. *Faculty:* 5 full-time (1 woman), 4 part-time/adjunct (1 woman). *Students:* 56 full-time (43 women), 80 part-time (51 women); includes 43 minority (12 Black or African American, non-Hispanic/Latino; 21 Asian, non-Hispanic/Latino; 8 Hispanic/Latino; 2 Two or more races, non-Hispanic/Latino), 27 international. Average age 29. 119 applicants, 75% accepted, 52 enrolled. In 2018, 85 master's awarded. *Entrance requirements:* For master's, GMAT. Additional exam requirements/recommendations for international students: Required—TOEFL (minimum score 550 paper-based; 80 iBT). *Application deadline:* For fall admission, 3/15 priority date for domestic and international students; for spring admission, 10/15 priority date for domestic and international students. Applications are processed on a rolling basis. Application fee: $50. Electronic applications accepted. *Expenses:* Contact institution. *Financial support:* In 2018–19, 85 students received support, including 3 fellowships (averaging $6,975 per year); career-related internships or fieldwork, Federal Work-Study, institutionally sponsored loans, and scholarships/grants also available. Support available to part-time students. Financial award application deadline: 4/1; financial award applicants required to submit FAFSA. *Faculty research:* Tax policy, tax research, decision-making in accounting, accounting information systems, capital markets and strategic planning. *Unit head:* Tracy Riley, Chair, 617-994-4276, E-mail: triley@suffolk.edu. *Application contact:* Mara Marzocchi, Associate Director of Graduate Admissions, 617-573-8302, Fax: 617-305-1733, E-mail: grad.admission@suffolk.edu.
Website: http://www.suffolk.edu/msa

Suffolk University, Sawyer Business School, Master of Business Administration Program, Boston, MA 02108-2770. Offers accounting (MBA); entrepreneurship (MBA); executive business administration (EMBA); finance (MBA); global business administration (GMBA); health administration (MBA); international business (MBA); marketing (MBA); nonprofit management (MBA); organizational behavior (MBA); strategic management (MBA); supply chain management (MBA); taxation (MBA); JD/MBA; MBA/MHA; MBA/MSA; MBA/MSF; MBA/MST. *Accreditation:* AACSB. *Program availability:* Part-time, evening/weekend, 100% online. *Faculty:* 18 full-time (5 women), 5 part-time/adjunct (0 women). *Students:* 79 full-time (46 women), 193 part-time (107 women); includes 69 minority (17 Black or African American, non-Hispanic/Latino; 18 Asian, non-Hispanic/Latino; 28 Hispanic/Latino; 6 Two or more races, non-Hispanic/Latino), 40 international. Average age 30. 274 applicants, 67% accepted, 83 enrolled. In 2018, 125 master's awarded. *Entrance requirements:* For master's, GMAT, minimum undergraduate GPA of 2.75 (MBA), 5 years of managerial experience (EMBA). Additional exam requirements/recommendations for international students: Required—TOEFL (minimum score 550 paper-based; 80 iBT). *Application deadline:* For fall admission, 3/15 priority date for domestic students, 10/15 priority date for international students; for spring admission, 10/15 priority date for domestic and international students. Applications are processed on a rolling basis. Application fee: $50. Electronic applications accepted. *Expenses:* Contact institution. *Financial support:* In 2018–19, 170 students received support, including 4 fellowships (averaging $2,906 per year); career-related internships or fieldwork, Federal Work-Study, institutionally sponsored loans, and scholarships/grants also available. Support available to part-time students. Financial award application deadline: 4/1; financial award applicants required to submit FAFSA. *Faculty research:* Foreign investments; career strategies and boundaryless careers; corporate ethics codes; interest rates, inflation, and growth options; innovation and product development performance. *Unit head:* Jodi Detjen, Director of MBA Programs, 617-573-8306, E-mail: jdetjen@suffolk.edu. *Application contact:* Mara Marzocchi, Associate Director of Graduate Admissions, 617-573-8302, Fax: 617-305-1733, E-mail: grad.admission@suffolk.edu.
Website: http://www.suffolk.edu/mba

Taft University System, Taft Law School, Denver, CO 80246. Offers American jurisprudence (LL M); law (JD); taxation (LL M).

Taft University System, W. Edwards Deming School of Business, Denver, CO 80246. Offers taxation (MS).

Temple University, Beasley School of Law, Philadelphia, PA 19122. Offers Asian law (LL M); law (JD); legal education (SJD); taxation (LL M); transnational law (LL M); trial advocacy (LL M); JD/LL M; JD/MBA; JD/MPH. *Accreditation:* ABA. *Program availability:* Part-time, evening/weekend. *Entrance requirements:* For doctorate, LSAT (for JD). Additional exam requirements/recommendations for international students: Recommended—TOEFL. Electronic applications accepted. *Expenses:* Contact institution. *Faculty research:* Cybersecurity, gender issues, health care law, immigration law, intellectual property law.

Taxation

Texas Christian University, Neeley School of Business, Master of Accounting Program, Fort Worth, TX 76129. Offers advisory and valuation (M Ac); audit & assurance services (M Ac); taxation (M Ac). *Accreditation:* AACSB. *Faculty:* 17 full-time (8 women). *Students:* 52 full-time (42 women). Average age 22. 81 applicants, 99% accepted, 65 enrolled. In 2018, 52 master's awarded. *Entrance requirements:* Additional exam requirements/recommendations for international students: Recommended—TOEFL. *Application deadline:* For fall admission, 2/15 for domestic and international students; for spring admission, 9/15 for domestic and international students. Application fee: $0. Electronic applications accepted. *Expenses:* Graduate student fee, $1,450 per semester. *Financial support:* Unspecified assistantships available. Financial award application deadline: 1/31. *Faculty research:* Financial accounting, market valuation of accounting information, corporate governance, managerial compensation and incentives, taxation. *Unit head:* Dr. Mary A. Stanford, Department Chair, 817-257-7483, Fax: 817-257-7227, E-mail: m.stanford@tcu.edu. *Application contact:* Dr. Renee Olvera, Director, 817-257-7578, Fax: 817-257-7227, E-mail: renee.olvera@tcu.edu.
Website: http://www.neeley.tcu.edu/Academics/Master_of_Accounting/MAc.aspx

Texas Tech University, Rawls College of Business Administration, Lubbock, TX 79409-2101. Offers accounting (MSA, PhD), including audit/financial reporting (MSA), taxation (MSA); data science (MS); finance (PhD); general business (MBA); healthcare management (MS); information systems and operations management (PhD); management (PhD); marketing (PhD); STEM (MBA); JD/MBA; JD/MSA; MBA/M Arch; MBA/MD; MBA/MS; MBA/Pharm D. *Accreditation:* AACSB. *Program availability:* Evening/weekend, 100% online, blended/hybrid learning. *Degree requirements:* For master's, thesis (for MS); capstone course; for doctorate, comprehensive exam, thesis/dissertation, qualifying exams. *Entrance requirements:* For master's, GMAT, GRE, MCAT, PCAT, LSAT, or DAT, holistic review of academic credentials, resume, essay, letters of recommendation; for doctorate, GMAT, GRE, holistic review of academic credentials, resume, statement of purpose, letters of recommendation. Additional exam requirements/recommendations for international students: Required—TOEFL (minimum score 550 paper-based; 79 iBT), IELTS (minimum score 6.5), PTE (minimum score 60). Electronic applications accepted. *Expenses:* Contact institution. *Faculty research:* Governmental and nonprofit accounting, securities and options futures, statistical analysis and design, leadership, consumer behavior.

Thomas Jefferson University, Kanbar College of Design, Engineering and Commerce, Program in Taxation, Philadelphia, PA 19107. Offers MS. *Program availability:* Part-time, evening/weekend. *Entrance requirements:* For master's, GMAT. Additional exam requirements/recommendations for international students: Required—TOEFL (minimum score 550 paper-based; 79 iBT). Electronic applications accepted.

Université de Montréal, Faculty of Law, Montréal, QC H3C 3J7, Canada. Offers business law (DESS); common law (North America) (JD); international law (DESS); law (LL M, LL D, DDN, DESS, LL B); tax law (LL M). *Program availability:* Part-time. *Degree requirements:* For master's, thesis; for doctorate, thesis/dissertation, project; for other advanced degree, thesis (for some programs). Electronic applications accepted. *Faculty research:* Legal theory; constitutional, private, and public law.

Université de Sherbrooke, Faculty of Administration, Program in Taxation, Sherbrooke, QC J1K 2R1, Canada. Offers M Tax, Diploma. *Program availability:* Part-time, evening/weekend. *Degree requirements:* For master's, one foreign language, thesis. *Entrance requirements:* For master's, bachelor's degree in business, law or economics; basic knowledge of Canadian taxation (2 courses). Electronic applications accepted. *Faculty research:* Taxation research, public finances.

The University of Akron, Graduate School, College of Business Administration, The George W. Daverio School of Accountancy, Program in Taxation, Akron, OH 44325. Offers MT, JD/MT. *Entrance requirements:* For master's, GMAT, GRE, MCAT, LSAT, PCAT, or CAT, minimum GPA of 3.0 (preferred), two letters of recommendation, resume, statement of purpose. Additional exam requirements/recommendations for international students: Required—TOEFL (minimum score 79 iBT), IELTS (minimum score 6.5). Electronic applications accepted.

The University of Alabama, Graduate School, Manderson Graduate School of Business, Culverhouse School of Accountancy, Tuscaloosa, AL 35487. Offers accounting (M Acc, PhD); tax accounting (MTA). *Accreditation:* AACSB. *Degree requirements:* For doctorate, thesis/dissertation. *Entrance requirements:* For master's, GMAT, minimum GPA of 3.0 overall or on last 60 hours; for doctorate, GMAT, minimum GPA of 3.0. Additional exam requirements/recommendations for international students: Required—TOEFL. Electronic applications accepted. *Faculty research:* Corporate governance, audit decision-making, earning management, valuation, executive compensation.

The University of Alabama, Hugh F. Culverhouse Jr. School of Law, Tuscaloosa, AL 35487. Offers business transactions (LL M); comparative law (LL M, JSD); law (JD, JSD); taxation (LL M); JD/MBA. *Accreditation:* ABA. *Degree requirements:* For master's, 24 hours, exams; for doctorate, 90 hours, including 6 hours of experiential learning, 1 seminar, and 34 required hours. *Entrance requirements:* For master's, LSAT, JD (for business transactions and taxation); undergraduate degree in law, letters of recommendation, personal statement, resume, and official transcripts (for comparative law); for doctorate, LSAT (for JD), undergraduate degree, letter of recommendation, resume, personal statement, and CAS report (for JD). Additional exam requirements/recommendations for international students: Required—TOEFL, IELTS. Electronic applications accepted. *Expenses:* Contact institution. *Faculty research:* Public interest law, Constitutional law, civil rights, international law, tax law.

The University of Alabama in Huntsville, School of Graduate Studies, College of Business Administration, Program in Accounting, Huntsville, AL 35899. Offers accounting (M Acc), including CPA preparatory with an emphasis in taxation, CPA preparatory with emphasis in assurance and financial reporting, general accounting, information systems audit and control (ISAC). *Accreditation:* AACSB. *Program availability:* Part-time. *Faculty:* 3 full-time (1 woman). *Students:* 14 full-time (6 women), 25 part-time (18 women); includes 5 minority (2 Black or African American, non-Hispanic/Latino; 2 Asian, non-Hispanic/Latino; 1 Hispanic/Latino), 3 international. Average age 29. 40 applicants, 73% accepted, 17 enrolled. In 2018, 12 master's awarded. *Degree requirements:* For master's, comprehensive exam, thesis or alternative. *Entrance requirements:* For master's, GMAT (minimum score 500), minimum AACSB index of 1080. Additional exam requirements/recommendations for international students: Required—TOEFL (minimum score 550 paper-based; 80 iBT), IELTS (minimum score 6.5). *Application deadline:* For fall admission, 7/15 priority date for domestic students, 4/1 priority date for international students; for spring admission, 11/30 priority date for domestic students, 9/1 priority date for international students. Applications are processed on a rolling basis. Application fee: $50. Electronic applications accepted. *Expenses:* Tuition, area resident: Full-time $10,632; part-time $412 per credit hour. Tuition, state resident: full-time $10,632. Tuition, nonresident: full-time $23,604; part-time $412 per credit hour. *Required fees:* $582; $582. Tuition and fees vary according to course load and program. *Financial support:* In 2018–19, 4 students received support, including 3 teaching assistantships with full tuition reimbursements available (averaging $5,100 per year); career-related internships or fieldwork, Federal Work-Study, institutionally sponsored loans, scholarships/grants, health care benefits, and unspecified assistantships also available. Support available to part-time students. Financial award application deadline: 4/1; financial award applicants required to submit FAFSA. *Faculty research:* Accounting information systems, managerial accounting, behavioral accounting, state and local taxation, financial accounting. *Unit head:* Dr. Allen Wilhite, Interim Chair, 256-824-6591, Fax: 256-824-2929, E-mail: allen.wilhite@uah.edu. *Application contact:* Jennifer Pettitt, Director of Graduate Programs, 256-824-6681, Fax: 256-824-7571, E-mail: jennifer.pettitt@uah.edu.

University of Baltimore, Graduate School, Merrick School of Business, Department of Accounting, Program in Taxation, Baltimore, MD 21201-5779. Offers MS. *Program availability:* Part-time, evening/weekend. *Entrance requirements:* For master's, GMAT, minimum GPA of 3.0. Additional exam requirements/recommendations for international students: Required—TOEFL (minimum score 550 paper-based). *Expenses:* Contact institution. *Faculty research:* Taxation of not-for-profit entities.

University of Baltimore, School of Law, Baltimore, MD 21201. Offers business law (JD); criminal practice (JD); estate planning (JD); family law (JD); intellectual property (JD); international law (JD); law (JD); law of the United States (LL M); litigation and advocacy (JD); public service (JD); real estate practice (JD); taxation (LL M); JD/LL M; JD/MBA; JD/MPA; JD/MS; JD/PhD. JD/MS offered jointly with Division of Criminology, Criminal Justice, and Social Policy; JD/PhD with University of Maryland, Baltimore. *Accreditation:* ABA. *Program availability:* Part-time, evening/weekend. *Entrance requirements:* For doctorate, LSAT. Additional exam requirements/recommendations for international students: Required—TOEFL (for LL M in law of the United States). Electronic applications accepted. *Expenses:* Contact institution. *Faculty research:* Plain view doctrine, statute of limitations, bankruptcy, family law, international and comparative law, Constitutional law.

The University of British Columbia, Peter A. Allard School of Law, Vancouver, BC V6T 1Z1, Canada. Offers common law (LL M CL); law (LL M, PhD); taxation (LL M). *Program availability:* Part-time. *Degree requirements:* For master's, variable foreign language requirement, thesis, seminar; for doctorate, variable foreign language requirement, comprehensive exam, thesis/dissertation, seminar. *Entrance requirements:* For master's, LL B or JD, thesis proposal, 3 letters of reference; for doctorate, LL B or JD, LL M, thesis proposal, 3 letters of reference. Additional exam requirements/recommendations for international students: Required—TOEFL, IELTS. Electronic applications accepted. *Expenses:* Contact institution. *Faculty research:* Aboriginal rights/native law, Asian legal studies, criminal law, environmental law, international law, corporate, human rights, intellectual property, dispute resolution, entertainment.

University of Cincinnati, Carl H. Lindner College of Business, MS Program, Cincinnati, OH 45221. Offers accounting (MS); applied economics (MS); business analytics (MS); finance (MS); information systems (MS); marketing (MS); taxation (MS). *Program availability:* Part-time, evening/weekend. *Faculty:* 98 full-time (27 women), 28 part-time/adjunct (4 women). *Students:* 305 full-time (123 women), 190 part-time (83 women); includes 35 minority (13 Black or African American, non-Hispanic/Latino; 1 American Indian or Alaska Native, non-Hispanic/Latino; 10 Asian, non-Hispanic/Latino; 6 Hispanic/Latino; 5 Two or more races, non-Hispanic/Latino), 309 international. Average age 29. 1,219 applicants, 55% accepted, 495 enrolled. In 2018, 355 master's awarded. *Degree requirements:* For master's, thesis (for some programs), capstone. *Entrance requirements:* For master's, GMAT, GRE, resume, transcripts, essays, letters of recommendation. Additional exam requirements/recommendations for international students: Required—TOEFL (minimum score 577 paper-based; 90 iBT), IELTS (minimum score 6.5). *Application deadline:* For fall admission, 6/30 priority date for domestic students, 3/15 for international students; for spring admission, 12/15 for domestic students, 9/15 for international students; for summer admission, 4/15 for domestic and international students. Applications are processed on a rolling basis. Application fee: $65 ($70 for international students). Electronic applications accepted. *Expenses:* Full-time resident $10,479 per term, full-time nonresident $14,398 per term, part-time $890 per credit hour. *Financial support:* In 2018–19, 251 students received support, including 12 teaching assistantships with full and partial tuition reimbursements available (averaging $3,500 per year); scholarships/grants, tuition waivers (full and partial), and unspecified assistantships also available. Financial award application deadline: 2/1; financial award applicants required to submit FAFSA. *Faculty research:* Business analytics, financial management, organizational behavior, financial accounting, consumer insights. *Total annual research expenditures:* $39,943. *Unit head:* Dr. Marianne Lewis, Dean, 513-556-7001, Fax: 513-556-4891, E-mail: marianne.lewis@uc.edu. *Application contact:* Dona Clary, Executive Director, Graduate Programs, 513-556-3546, Fax: 513-558-7006, E-mail: dona.clary@uc.edu.
Website: http://business.uc.edu/graduate/masters.html

University of Colorado Denver, Business School, Program in Taxation, Denver, CO 80217. Offers MS. *Degree requirements:* For master's, 30 semester hours of course work. *Entrance requirements:* For master's, GMAT, resume, essay, transcripts from all universities or colleges attended, letters of recommendation (strongly encouraged). Additional exam requirements/recommendations for international students: Required—TOEFL (minimum score 525 paper-based; 71 iBT); Recommended—IELTS (minimum score 6.5). Electronic applications accepted. *Expenses:* Tuition, state resident: full-time $6786; part-time $337 per credit hour. Tuition, nonresident: full-time $22,590; part-time $1255 per credit hour. *Required fees:* $1231; $137 per credit hour. Tuition and fees vary according to program and reciprocity agreements.

University of Denver, Sturm College of Law, Graduate Tax Program, Denver, CO 80208. Offers LL M, MT. *Program availability:* Part-time, evening/weekend. *Faculty:* 4 full-time (2 women), 4 part-time/adjunct (0 women). *Students:* 14 full-time (7 women), 68 part-time (36 women); includes 19 minority (2 Black or African American, non-Hispanic/Latino; 10 Asian, non-Hispanic/Latino; 6 Hispanic/Latino; 1 Two or more races, non-Hispanic/Latino), 7 international. Average age 33. 56 applicants, 89% accepted, 25 enrolled. In 2018, 46 master's awarded. *Entrance requirements:* For master's, GMAT or GRE for MT; bachelor's degree in accounting or business for MT; transcripts; JD from ABA-approved institution (for LLM); 1 letter of recommendation; personal statement; resume. Additional exam requirements/recommendations for international students: Required—TOEFL (minimum score 550 paper-based; 80 iBT). *Application deadline:* For fall admission, 7/29 priority date for domestic and international students. Applications are processed on a rolling basis. Application fee: $65. Electronic applications accepted. *Expenses:* $49,764 per year full-time; $16,588 per year part-time. *Financial support:* In 2018–19, 69 students received support. Federal Work-Study, institutionally sponsored loans, and scholarships/grants available. Support available to part-time students. Financial award application deadline: 6/30; financial award applicants required to submit FAFSA. *Faculty research:* Individual, estate and gift, and state and local tax; qualified plans; partnerships; c corporations and s corporations; procedural and ethical aspects of the practice of tax. *Unit head:* John Wilson, Professor of the Practice of Taxation and Department Chair, 303-871-6000, E-mail: john.r.wilson@du.edu. *Application contact:* Information Contact, 303-871-6239, E-mail: gtp@du.edu.
Website: http://www.du.edu/tax

University of Florida, Levin College of Law, Gainesville, FL 32611. Offers comparative law (LL M), including tropical conservation and development; environmental and land use law (LL M); international taxation (LL M); law (JD); taxation (LL M, SJD). *Accreditation:* ABA. *Entrance requirements:* For doctorate, LSAT (for JD). Electronic applications accepted. *Faculty research:* Environmental and land use law, taxation, dispute resolution, family law, Constitutional law.

University of Hartford, Barney School of Business, Department of Accounting and Taxation, West Hartford, CT 06117-1599. Offers professional accounting (Certificate); taxation (MSAT). *Program availability:* Part-time, evening/weekend. *Entrance requirements:* For master's, GMAT, 2 letters of recommendation, resume. Additional exam requirements/recommendations for international students: Required—TOEFL (minimum score 550 paper-based). Electronic applications accepted.

University of Hawaii at Manoa, Office of Graduate Education, Shidler College of Business, Program in Accounting, Honolulu, HI 96822. Offers accounting (M Acc); accounting law (M Acc); information systems (M Acc); taxation (M Acc). *Program availability:* Part-time. *Entrance requirements:* For master's, GMAT, bachelor's degree in accounting, minimum GPA of 3.0. Additional exam requirements/recommendations for international students: Required—TOEFL (minimum score 550 paper-based; 79 iBT), IELTS (minimum score 5). *Faculty research:* International accounting, current tax topics, insurance industry financial reporting, behavioral accounting, auditing.

University of Houston, University of Houston Law Center, Houston, TX 77204-6060. Offers energy, environment, and natural resources (LL M); health law (LL M); intellectual property and information law (LL M); international law (LL M); law (JD); tax law (LL M); U.S. law (LL M). *Accreditation:* ABA. *Program availability:* Part-time, evening/weekend. *Faculty:* 58 full-time (22 women), 148 part-time/adjunct (45 women). *Students:* 606 full-time (303 women), 98 part-time (41 women); includes 260 minority (43 Black or African American, non-Hispanic/Latino; 6 American Indian or Alaska Native, non-Hispanic/Latino; 72 Asian, non-Hispanic/Latino; 137 Hispanic/Latino; 2 Native Hawaiian or other Pacific Islander, non-Hispanic/Latino), 14 international. Average age 26. 2,596 applicants, 33% accepted, 202 enrolled. In 2018, 75 master's awarded. *Degree requirements:* For master's, thesis optional. *Entrance requirements:* For doctorate, LSAT. Additional exam requirements/recommendations for international students: Required—TOEFL (minimum score 600 paper-based; 100 iBT), IELTS (minimum score 7). *Application deadline:* For fall admission, 2/15 for domestic and international students. Applications are processed on a rolling basis. Application fee: $0. Electronic applications accepted. Application fee is waived when completed online. *Expenses:* Texas Resident $31,090/year; Non Texas Resident $45,640/year. *Financial support:* In 2018–19, 573 students received support, including 47 fellowships (averaging $3,768 per year); research assistantships, career-related internships or fieldwork, Federal Work-Study, scholarships/grants, and tuition waivers (full and partial) also available. Support available to part-time students. Financial award application deadline: 3/15; financial award applicants required to submit FAFSA. *Faculty research:* Health law, international law, tax, environmental law/energy, information law/intellectual property. *Total annual research expenditures:* $336,944. *Unit head:* Leonard M. Baynes, Dean and Professor of Law, 713-743-2100, Fax: 713-743-2122, E-mail: lbaynes@central.uh.edu. *Application contact:* Pilar Mensah, Assistant Dean for Admissions, 713-743-2280, Fax: 713-743-2194, E-mail: lpmensah@central.uh.edu.
Website: http://www.law.uh.edu/

University of Miami, Miami Business School, Coral Gables, FL 33146. Offers accounting (M Acc); business (PhD); business administration (MBA); business analytics (MSBA); economics (PhD); finance (MSF); health administration (MHA); international business (MIBS); real estate (MBA); taxation (MS Tax); JD/MBA; MD/MBA. *Accreditation:* AACSB; CAHME (one or more programs are accredited). *Program availability:* Part-time, evening/weekend, 100% online, blended/hybrid learning. *Faculty:* 155 full-time (47 women), 14 part-time/adjunct (5 women). *Students:* 1,083 full-time (469 women); includes 422 minority (79 Black or African American, non-Hispanic/Latino; 1 American Indian or Alaska Native, non-Hispanic/Latino; 43 Asian, non-Hispanic/Latino; 274 Hispanic/Latino; 3 Native Hawaiian or other Pacific Islander, non-Hispanic/Latino; 22 Two or more races, non-Hispanic/Latino), 282 international. Average age 30. 2,564 applicants, 38% accepted, 450 enrolled. In 2018, 558 master's, 5 doctorates awarded. Terminal master's awarded for partial completion of doctoral program. *Degree requirements:* For master's, comprehensive exam; for doctorate, comprehensive exam, thesis/dissertation. *Entrance requirements:* For master's, GMAT or GRE; for doctorate, GRE General Test. Additional exam requirements/recommendations for international students: Required—TOEFL (minimum score 94 iBT), IELTS (minimum score 7), TOEFL (minimum score 587 paper-based, 94 iBT) or IELTS (7). *Application deadline:* For fall admission, 6/30 priority date for domestic students, 5/30 priority date for international students; for spring admission, 10/31 priority date for domestic students, 9/30 priority date for international students. Applications are processed on a rolling basis. Application fee: $48. Electronic applications accepted. *Expenses:* Contact institution. *Financial support:* In 2018–19, 643 students received support, including 1 fellowship with full tuition reimbursement available (averaging $20,000 per year), 47 research assistantships with full and partial tuition reimbursements available (averaging $28,826 per year), 6 teaching assistantships with full and partial tuition reimbursements available (averaging $2,183 per year); career-related internships or fieldwork, Federal Work-Study, institutionally sponsored loans, scholarships/grants, and unspecified assistantships also available. Support available to part-time students. Financial award application deadline: 3/26; financial award applicants required to submit FAFSA. *Faculty research:* Behavioral finance; computational economics; consumer research; risk perception; consumer behavior; consumer choice research; behavioral decision theory; business analytics; point processes; longitudinal data analyses; international business; global business strategy, joint ventures, and alliances; emerging economies; global economic growth and development, money and financial markets, and computed dynamic models; health policy; innovative payment mechanisms. *Total annual research expenditures:* $703,773. *Unit head:* Dr. John Quelch, Dean, 305-284-6515, Fax: 305-284-6526, E-mail: jquelch@miami.edu. *Application contact:* Loubna Bouamane, Director of Graduate Business Recruiting and Admissions, 305-284-2510, Fax: 305-284-5905, E-mail: loubna@miami.edu.
Website: www.mbs.miami.edu

University of Michigan, Law School, Ann Arbor, MI 48109-1215. Offers comparative law (MCL); international tax (LL M); law (LL M, JD, SJD); JD/MA; JD/MBA; JD/MHSA; JD/MPH; JD/MPP; JD/MS; JD/MSI; JD/MSW; JD/MUP; JD/PhD. *Accreditation:* ABA. *Faculty:* 106 full-time (37 women), 89 part-time/adjunct (23 women). *Students:* 1,012 full-time (490 women); includes 238 minority (45 Black or African American, non-Hispanic/Latino; 6 American Indian or Alaska Native, non-Hispanic/Latino; 77 Asian, non-Hispanic/Latino; 63 Hispanic/Latino; 47 Two or more races, non-Hispanic/Latino), 39 international. 5,698 applicants, 20% accepted, 362 enrolled. In 2018, 37 master's, 291 doctorates awarded. *Entrance requirements:* For doctorate, LSAT. *Application deadline:* For fall admission, 2/15 for domestic students. Applications are processed on a rolling basis. Application fee: $75. Electronic applications accepted. *Expenses:* Contact institution. *Financial support:* In 2018–19, 876 students received support. Career-related internships or fieldwork, Federal Work-Study, institutionally sponsored loans, and scholarships/grants available. Financial award applicants required to submit FAFSA. *Unit head:* Mark D. West, Dean, 734-764-1358. *Application contact:* Sarah C. Zearfoss, Assistant Dean and Director of Admissions, 734-764-0537, Fax: 734-647-3218, E-mail: law.jd.admissions@umich.edu.
Website: http://www.law.umich.edu/

University of Minnesota, Twin Cities Campus, Carlson School of Management, Master of Business Taxation Program, Minneapolis, MN 55455-0213. Offers MBT. *Program availability:* Part-time, evening/weekend, 100% online, blended/hybrid learning. *Faculty:* 3 full-time (1 woman), 17 part-time/adjunct (4 women). *Students:* 13 full-time (3 women), 57 part-time (28 women); includes 10 minority (1 American Indian or Alaska Native, non-Hispanic/Latino; 7 Asian, non-Hispanic/Latino; 2 Hispanic/Latino), 9 international. Average age 31. 36 applicants, 94% accepted, 28 enrolled. In 2018, 30 master's awarded. *Entrance requirements:* For master's, GMAT or LSAT. Additional exam requirements/recommendations for international students: Required—TOEFL (minimum score 550 paper-based; 79 iBT), IELTS (minimum score 6.5). *Application deadline:* For fall admission, 6/15 priority date for domestic and international students; for spring admission, 10/15 priority date for domestic and international students; for summer admission, 3/15 priority date for domestic and international students. Applications are processed on a rolling basis. Application fee: $75 ($95 for international students). Electronic applications accepted. *Financial support:* In 2018–19, 19 students received support, including 2 teaching assistantships with partial tuition reimbursements available (averaging $7,500 per year); scholarships/grants also available. Financial award application deadline: 8/1. *Unit head:* Paul Gutterman, Director of Graduate Studies, 612-624-8515, Fax: 612-626-7795, E-mail: pgutterm@umn.edu. *Application contact:* Rhonda Bjurlin, Information Contact, 612-625-6516, E-mail: mbt@umn.edu.
Website: http://carlsonschool.umn.edu/degrees/master-business-taxation

University of Mississippi, Graduate School, School of Accountancy, University, MS 38677. Offers accountancy (M Acc, PhD); accounting and data analytics (MA); taxation accounting (M Tax). *Accreditation:* AACSB. *Faculty:* 20 full-time (6 women), 2 part-time/adjunct (both women). *Students:* 228 full-time (102 women), 4 part-time (2 women); includes 32 minority (16 Black or African American, non-Hispanic/Latino; 4 Asian, non-Hispanic/Latino; 5 Hispanic/Latino; 1 Native Hawaiian or other Pacific Islander, non-Hispanic/Latino; 6 Two or more races, non-Hispanic/Latino), 7 international. Average age 24. In 2018, 131 master's, 2 doctorates awarded. *Entrance requirements:* For master's, GMAT, minimum GPA of 3.0; for doctorate, GMAT. Additional exam requirements/recommendations for international students: Required—TOEFL. *Application deadline:* Applications are processed on a rolling basis. Application fee: $50. Electronic applications accepted. *Financial support:* Scholarships/grants available. Financial award application deadline: 3/1; financial award applicants required to submit FAFSA. *Unit head:* Dr. W. Mark Wilder, Dean, School of Accountancy, 662-915-7468, Fax: 662-915-7483, E-mail: umaccy@olemiss.edu. *Application contact:* Tameka Smith, Graduate Activities Specialist for Admissions, 662-915-7474, Fax: 662-915-7577, E-mail: gschool@olemiss.edu.
Website: https://www.olemiss.edu

University of Missouri, Office of Research and Graduate Studies, Robert J. Trulaske, Sr. College of Business, School of Accountancy, Columbia, MO 65211. Offers accountancy (M Acc, PhD); taxation (Certificate). *Accreditation:* AACSB. *Program availability:* Part-time. *Degree requirements:* For master's, thesis or alternative; for doctorate, thesis/dissertation. *Entrance requirements:* For master's and doctorate, GMAT, minimum GPA of 3.0. Additional exam requirements/recommendations for international students: Required—TOEFL (minimum score 600 paper-based; 100 iBT). Electronic applications accepted.

University of New Haven, Graduate School, College of Business, Program in Taxation, West Haven, CT 06516. Offers MS, Graduate Certificate. *Program availability:* Part-time, evening/weekend. *Students:* 5 full-time (1 woman), 7 part-time (4 women); includes 5 minority (2 Black or African American, non-Hispanic/Latino; 2 Asian, non-Hispanic/Latino; 1 Hispanic/Latino). Average age 33. 6 applicants, 100% accepted, 4 enrolled. In 2018, 19 master's awarded. *Degree requirements:* For master's, thesis or alternative. *Entrance requirements:* For master's, GMAT. Additional exam requirements/recommendations for international students: Required—TOEFL (minimum score 80 iBT), IELTS, PTE. *Application deadline:* Applications are processed on a rolling basis. Application fee: $50. Electronic applications accepted. Application fee is waived when completed online. *Expenses:* Contact institution. *Financial support:* Research assistantships with partial tuition reimbursements, teaching assistantships with partial tuition reimbursements, career-related internships or fieldwork, Federal Work-Study, scholarships/grants, and unspecified assistantships available. Support available to part-time students. Financial award application deadline: 5/1; financial award applicants required to submit FAFSA. *Unit head:* Robert Wnek, Professor, 203-932-7111, E-mail: rwnek@newhaven.edu. *Application contact:* Selina O'Toole, Senior Associate Director of Graduate Admissions, 203-932-7337, E-mail: SOToole@newhaven.edu.
Website: https://www.newhaven.edu/business/graduate-programs/taxation/

University of New Mexico, Anderson School of Management, Department of Accounting, Albuquerque, NM 87131. Offers accounting (MBA); advanced accounting (M Acct); information assurance (M Acct); professional accounting (M Acct); tax accounting (M Acct); JD/M Acct. *Accreditation:* AACSB. *Program availability:* Part-time, evening/weekend. *Faculty:* 15 full-time (9 women), 5 part-time/adjunct (2 women). *Students:* 69 applicants, 70% accepted, 36 enrolled. In 2018, 52 master's awarded. *Entrance requirements:* For master's, GMAT/GRE (minimum score of 500), minimum GPA of 3.25, 3.0 on last 60 hours of coursework (for M Acct in professional accounting). Additional exam requirements/recommendations for international students: Required—TOEFL (minimum score 550 paper-based; 79 iBT), IELTS (minimum score 6.5). *Application deadline:* For fall admission, 4/1 priority date for domestic and international students; for spring admission, 10/1 priority date for domestic and international students. Applications are processed on a rolling basis. Application fee: $50. Electronic applications accepted. *Expenses:* $531.34 per credit hour resident, $1197.99 per credit hour non-resident. *Financial support:* In 2018–19, 20 students received support, including 5 fellowships (averaging $16,744 per year), 14 research assistantships with partial tuition reimbursements available (averaging $15,345 per year); career-related internships or fieldwork, Federal Work-Study, scholarships/grants, and unspecified assistantships also available. Support available to part-time students. Financial award application deadline: 6/1; financial award applicants required to submit FAFSA. *Faculty research:* Critical accounting, accounting pedagogy, theory, taxation, information fraud. *Unit head:* Dr. Richard Brody, Interim Chair, 505-277-6471, E-mail: tmarmijo@unm.edu. *Application contact:* Dr. Richard Brody, Interim Chair, 505-277-6471, E-mail: tmarmijo@unm.edu.
Website: https://www.mgt.unm.edu/acct/default.asp?mm-faculty

University of New Orleans, Graduate School, College of Business Administration, Department of Accounting, Program in Taxation, New Orleans, LA 70148. Offers MS. *Program availability:* Part-time, evening/weekend. *Degree requirements:* For master's, thesis optional. *Entrance requirements:* For master's, GMAT. Additional exam requirements/recommendations for international students: Required—TOEFL (minimum score 550 paper-based; 79 iBT). Electronic applications accepted.

University of Notre Dame, Mendoza College of Business, Master of Science in Accountancy Program, Notre Dame, IN 46556. Offers assurance and advisory services

(MSA); tax services (MSA). *Accreditation:* AACSB. *Entrance requirements:* For master's, GMAT, essay, two recommendations, transcripts from all colleges or universities attended, resume, interview, course descriptions for accounting prerequisites. Additional exam requirements/recommendations for international students: Required—PTE (minimum score 68), TOEFL (minimum iBT score of 109), IELTS (7.5), or documentation of at least six semesters of full-time university education in English. Electronic applications accepted. *Expenses:* Contact institution. *Faculty research:* Stock valuation, accounting information in decision-making, choice of accounting method, taxes cost on capital.

University of San Diego, School of Business, Programs in Accountancy and Taxation, San Diego, CA 92110-2492. Offers accountancy (MS); taxation (MS). *Program availability:* Part-time, evening/weekend. *Students:* 11 full-time (5 women), 12 part-time (8 women); includes 7 minority (1 Asian, non-Hispanic/Latino; 5 Hispanic/Latino; 1 Two or more races, non-Hispanic/Latino), 9 international. Average age 25. In 2018, 27 master's awarded. *Entrance requirements:* For master's, GMAT (minimum score of 550), minimum GPA of 3.0. Additional exam requirements/recommendations for international students: Required—TOEFL (minimum score 580 paper-based; 92 iBT), TWE. *Application deadline:* For fall admission, 5/1 for domestic and international students; for spring admission, 11/1 for domestic and international students. Applications are processed on a rolling basis. Application fee: $125. Electronic applications accepted. *Financial support:* In 2018–19, 15 students received support. Career-related internships or fieldwork, Federal Work-Study, institutionally sponsored loans, scholarships/grants, and unspecified assistantships available. Support available to part-time students. Financial award application deadline: 4/1; financial award applicants required to submit FAFSA. *Faculty research:* Accounting, financial report, taxation, Sarbanes-Oxley. *Unit head:* Dr. Diane Pattison, Academic Director, Accountancy Programs, 619-260-4850, E-mail: pattison@sandiego.edu. *Application contact:* Erika Garwood, Associate Director of Graduate Admissions, 619-260-4524, Fax: 619-260-4158, E-mail: grads@sandiego.edu.
Website: http://www.sandiego.edu/business/graduate/accounting-tax/

University of San Diego, School of Law, San Diego, CA 92110. Offers business and corporate law (LL M); comparative law (LL M); general studies (LL M); international law (LL M); law (JD); legal studies (MS); peace and law (JD/MA); taxation (LL M, Diploma); JD/IMBA; JD/MA; JD/MBA. *Accreditation:* ABA. *Program availability:* Part-time, evening/weekend. *Faculty:* 45 full-time (16 women), 72 part-time/adjunct (21 women). *Students:* 661 full-time (363 women), 92 part-time (49 women); includes 244 minority (31 Black or African American, non-Hispanic/Latino; 12 American Indian or Alaska Native, non-Hispanic/Latino; 75 Asian, non-Hispanic/Latino; 110 Hispanic/Latino; 4 Native Hawaiian or other Pacific Islander, non-Hispanic/Latino; 12 Two or more races, non-Hispanic/Latino), 31 international. Average age 27. 3,511 applicants, 240 enrolled. In 2018, 59 master's, 264 doctorates awarded. *Entrance requirements:* For master's, JD, LL B or equivalent from an ABA-accredited law school; for doctorate, LSAT (less than 5 years old), bachelor's degree, registration with the Credential Assemble Service (CAS). Additional exam requirements/recommendations for international students: Required—TOEFL (minimum score 600 paper-based; 100 iBT), IELTS (minimum score 7). *Application deadline:* For fall admission, 2/1 priority date for domestic students. Applications are processed on a rolling basis. Application fee: $0. Electronic applications accepted. *Expenses:* Contact institution. *Financial support:* In 2018–19, 640 students received support. Career-related internships or fieldwork, Federal Work-Study, institutionally sponsored loans, and scholarships/grants available. Support available to part-time students. Financial award application deadline: 3/1; financial award applicants required to submit FAFSA. *Faculty research:* Corporate law, children's advocacy, Constitutional and criminal law, international and comparative law, public interest law, intellectual property and tax law. *Unit head:* Dr. Stephen C. Ferruolo, Dean, 619-260-4527, E-mail: lawdean@sandiego.edu. *Application contact:* Jorge Garcia, Assistant Dean, JD Admissions, 619-260-4528, Fax: 619-260-2218, E-mail: jdinfo@sandiego.edu.
Website: http://www.sandiego.edu/law/

University of Southern California, Graduate School, Marshall School of Business, Leventhal School of Accounting, Los Angeles, CA 90089. Offers accounting (M Acc); business taxation (MBT); JD/MBT. *Program availability:* Part-time. *Degree requirements:* For master's, 30-48 units of study. *Entrance requirements:* For master's, GMAT, undergraduate degree, communication skills. Additional exam requirements/recommendations for international students: Required—TOEFL. Electronic applications accepted. *Faculty research:* State and local taxation, Securities and Exchange Commission, governance, auditing fees, financial accounting, enterprise zones, women in business.

University of South Florida, Muma College of Business, Lynn Pippenger School of Accountancy, Tampa, FL 33620-9951. Offers accountancy (M Acc, PhD), including assurance (M Acc); corporate accounting (M Acc); tax (M Acc). *Accreditation:* AACSB. *Program availability:* Part-time, evening/weekend. *Faculty:* 11 full-time (5 women). *Students:* 69 full-time (31 women), 28 part-time (14 women); includes 34 minority (2 Black or African American, non-Hispanic/Latino; 1 American Indian or Alaska Native, non-Hispanic/Latino; 7 Asian, non-Hispanic/Latino; 18 Hispanic/Latino; 6 Two or more races, non-Hispanic/Latino), 8 international. Average age 24. 104 applicants, 59% accepted, 49 enrolled. In 2018, 50 master's awarded. Terminal master's awarded for partial completion of doctoral program. *Degree requirements:* For master's, comprehensive exam, thesis or alternative; for doctorate, comprehensive exam, thesis/dissertation. *Entrance requirements:* For master's, GMAT or GRE, minimum overall GPA of 3.0 in general upper-level coursework and in upper-level accounting coursework (minimum of 21 hours at a U.S. accredited program within past 5 years); for doctorate, GMAT or GRE, personal statement, recommendations, interview. Additional exam requirements/recommendations for international students: Required—TOEFL, TOEFL (minimum score 550 paper-based; 79 iBT) or IELTS (minimum score 6.5). *Application deadline:* For fall admission, 3/1 priority date for domestic students, 3/1 for international students; for spring admission, 10/1 for domestic students, 9/15 for international students; for summer admission, 2/15 for domestic and international students. Application fee: $30. Electronic applications accepted. *Expenses:* Tuition, state resident: full-time $6350. Tuition, nonresident: full-time $19,048. *International tuition:* $19,048 full-time. *Required fees:* $2079. *Financial support:* In 2018–19, 55 students received support, including 18 teaching assistantships with tuition reimbursements available (averaging $12,273 per year); scholarships/grants, health care benefits, and unspecified assistantships also available. Financial award applicants required to submit FAFSA. *Faculty research:* Auditing, auditor independence, audit committee decisions, fraud detection and reporting, disclosure effects, effects of information technology on accounting, governmental accounting/auditing, accounting information systems, data modeling and design methodologies for accounting systems, auditing computer-based systems, expert systems, group support systems in accounting, fair value accounting issues, corporate governance, financial accounting, financial reporting quality. *Unit head:* Dr. Uday Murthy, Interim Director, School of Accountancy, 813-974-6516, Fax: 813-974-6528, E-mail: umurthy@usf.edu. *Application contact:* Stacee Bender, Academic Services Administrator, 813-974-4516, E-mail: staceebender@usf.edu.
Website: http://business.usf.edu/departments/accountancy/

The University of Texas at Arlington, Graduate School, College of Business, Accounting Department, Arlington, TX 76019. Offers accounting (MP Acc, MS, PhD); taxation (MS). *Accreditation:* AACSB. *Program availability:* Part-time, evening/weekend. *Degree requirements:* For master's, thesis optional; for doctorate, comprehensive exam, thesis/dissertation. *Entrance requirements:* For master's and doctorate, GMAT. Additional exam requirements/recommendations for international students: Required—TOEFL (minimum score 550 paper-based; 79 iBT).

University of the Sacred Heart, Graduate Programs, Department of Business Administration, Program in Taxation, San Juan, PR 00914-0383. Offers MBA. *Program availability:* Part-time, evening/weekend. *Degree requirements:* For master's, thesis. *Entrance requirements:* For master's, EXADEP, minimum undergraduate GPA of 2.75, interview.

University of Washington, Graduate School, Michael G. Foster School of Business, Seattle, WA 98195-3200. Offers auditing and assurance (MP Acc); business administration (MBA, PhD); entrepreneurship (MS); executive business administration (MBA); global executive business administration (MBA); information systems (MSIS); supply chain management (MSSCM); taxation (MP Acc); technology management (MBA); JD/MBA; MBA/MAIS; MBA/MHA. *Accreditation:* AACSB. *Program availability:* Part-time, evening/weekend, blended/hybrid learning. Terminal master's awarded for partial completion of doctoral program. *Degree requirements:* For doctorate, comprehensive exam, thesis/dissertation. *Entrance requirements:* For master's and doctorate, GMAT, GRE. Additional exam requirements/recommendations for international students: Required—TOEFL (minimum score 600 paper-based; 100 iBT). Electronic applications accepted. *Expenses:* Contact institution. *Faculty research:* Finance, consumer behavior, marketing analytics, technology management, supply chain.

University of Washington, Graduate School, School of Law, Seattle, WA 98195-3020. Offers Asian law (LL M, PhD); intellectual property law and policy (LL M); law (JD); law of sustainable international development (LL M); taxation (LL M); JD/LL M; JD/MA; JD/MAIS; JD/MBA; JD/MPA; JD/MS; JD/PhD. *Accreditation:* ABA. *Degree requirements:* For master's, thesis; for doctorate, thesis/dissertation (for some programs). *Entrance requirements:* For master's, language proficiency (LL M in Asian law); for doctorate, LSAT (for JD). Additional exam requirements/recommendations for international students: Required—TOEFL. *Expenses:* Contact institution. *Faculty research:* Asian, international and comparative law, intellectual property law, health law, environmental law, taxation.

University of Waterloo, Graduate Studies and Postdoctoral Affairs, Faculty of Arts, School of Accounting and Finance, Waterloo, ON N2L 3G1, Canada. Offers accounting (M Acc, PhD); finance (M Acc); taxation (M Tax). *Degree requirements:* For master's, thesis or alternative; for doctorate, thesis/dissertation. *Entrance requirements:* For master's, honors degree, minimum B average, resume; for doctorate, GMAT, master's degree, minimum A- average, resume. Additional exam requirements/recommendations for international students: Required—TOEFL, IELTS, PTE. Application fee: $125 Canadian dollars. Electronic applications accepted. *Expenses:* Contact institution. *Financial support:* Fellowships and research assistantships available. *Faculty research:* Auditing, management accounting.
Website: https://uwaterloo.ca/school-of-accounting-and-finance/

University of Wisconsin–Madison, Graduate School, Wisconsin School of Business, Master of Accountancy Program, Madison, WI 53706-1380. Offers accountancy (M Acc); taxation (M Acc). *Degree requirements:* For master's, minimum GPA of 3.0. *Entrance requirements:* For master's, GMAT, essays. Additional exam requirements/recommendations for international students: Required—TOEFL (minimum score 104 iBT), IELTS (minimum score 8), GMAT. Electronic applications accepted. *Faculty research:* Tax reserves, audit committee incentives, internal audit, accounting report's impact on management decisions.

University of Wisconsin–Milwaukee, Graduate School, Lubar School of Business, Other Business Programs, Milwaukee, WI 53201-0413. Offers business analytics (Graduate Certificate); enterprise resource planning (Graduate Certificate); information technology management (MS); investment management (Graduate Certificate); nonprofit management (Graduate Certificate); nonprofit management and leadership (MS); state and local taxation (Graduate Certificate). *Students:* 132 full-time (63 women), 120 part-time (58 women); includes 45 minority (11 Black or African American, non-Hispanic/Latino; 15 Asian, non-Hispanic/Latino; 4 Hispanic/Latino; 15 Two or more races, non-Hispanic/Latino), 52 international. Average age 31. 196 applicants, 63% accepted, 80 enrolled. In 2018, 108 master's, 18 other advanced degrees awarded. *Entrance requirements:* Additional exam requirements/recommendations for international students: Required—TOEFL (minimum score 550 paper-based; 79 iBT), IELTS (minimum score 6.5). Application fee: $56 ($96 for international students). Electronic applications accepted. *Financial support:* Fellowships, research assistantships, teaching assistantships, health care benefits, unspecified assistantships, and project assistantships available. Financial award applicants required to submit FAFSA. *Application contact:* General Information Contact, 414-229-4982, Fax: 414-229-6967, E-mail: gradschool@uwm.edu.

Villanova University, Charles Widger School of Law and Villanova School of Business, Tax Program, Villanova, PA 19085-1699. Offers LL M, JD/LL M. *Program availability:* Part-time, evening/weekend. *Entrance requirements:* For master's, LSAT, JD (for LL M). Additional exam requirements/recommendations for international students: Required—TOEFL (minimum score 600 paper-based). Electronic applications accepted. *Expenses:* Contact institution. *Faculty research:* Taxation and estate planning, corporate tax planning, international taxation, state taxation.

Wake Forest University, School of Business, MS in Accountancy Program, Winston-Salem, NC 27106. Offers assurance services (MSA); tax consulting (MSA); transaction services (MSA). *Degree requirements:* For master's, 30 credit hours. *Entrance requirements:* For master's, GMAT/GRE, letters of recommendation, official transcripts, current resume or curriculum vitae, interview. Additional exam requirements/recommendations for international students: Required—TOEFL (minimum score 600 paper-based; 100 iBT). Electronic applications accepted. *Expenses:* Contact institution. *Faculty research:* Influence of personal relationships on business decision-making and management of change; drivers of perceived value and consumer behavior; impact of accounting on auditing, financial, managerial, systems and taxation stakeholders; corporate governance and executive compensation; impact of operations strategies on competitiveness.

Walsh College of Accountancy and Business Administration, Graduate Programs, Program in Accountancy, Troy, MI 48083. Offers data analytics (MAC); finance (MAC); taxation (MAC). *Program availability:* Part-time, evening/weekend. *Faculty:* 6 full-time (2 women), 14 part-time/adjunct (7 women). *Students:* 14 full-time (3 women), 209 part-time (127 women); includes 51 minority (19 Black or African American, non-Hispanic/Latino; 21 Asian, non-Hispanic/Latino; 10 Hispanic/Latino; 1 Two or more races, non-Hispanic/Latino), 14 international. Average age 33. 67 applicants, 91% accepted, 39 enrolled. In 2018, 84 master's awarded. *Degree requirements:* For master's, thesis optional. *Entrance requirements:* For master's, minimum overall cumulative GPA of 2.75 from all colleges previously attended. Additional exam requirements/recommendations

for international students: Required—TOEFL (minimum score 550 paper-based, 79-80 internet based), IELTS (6.5), Michigan Test of English Language Proficiency or MTELP (80). *Application deadline:* Applications are processed on a rolling basis. Application fee: $35. Electronic applications accepted. *Expenses: Tuition:* Full-time $21,195; part-time $14,130 per credit hour. *Required fees:* $525; $525 per semester. $175 per semester. *Financial support:* In 2018–19, 22 students received support. Scholarships/grants available. Financial award application deadline: 6/30; financial award applicants required to submit FAFSA. *Unit head:* John Black, Chair, Accounting, 248-823-1635, Fax: 248-689-0920, E-mail: jblack@walshcollege.edu. *Application contact:* Karen Mahaffy, Executive Director, Admissions and Enrollment Services, 248-823-1600, Fax: 248-823-1611, E-mail: kmahaffy@walshcollege.edu.
Website: https:www.walshcollege.edu/masters-ms-degree-accounting

Wayne State University, Law School, Detroit, MI 48202. Offers corporate and finance law (LL M); labor and employment law (LL M); law (JD); taxation (LL M); United States law (LL M); JD/MA; JD/MADR; JD/MBA; JD/MS. *Accreditation:* ABA. *Program availability:* Part-time, evening/weekend. *Faculty:* 43 full-time (18 women), 17 part-time/adjunct (9 women). *Students:* 406 full-time (198 women), 38 part-time (9 women); includes 51 minority (35 Black or African American, non-Hispanic/Latino; 3 American Indian or Alaska Native, non-Hispanic/Latino; 7 Asian, non-Hispanic/Latino; 1 Hispanic/Latino; 5 Two or more races, non-Hispanic/Latino), 15 international. Average age 26. 859 applicants, 49% accepted, 137 enrolled. In 2018, 6 master's awarded. *Degree requirements:* For master's, thesis (for some programs). *Entrance requirements:* For master's, JD or LL B from ABA-accredited institution and member institution of the AALS; for doctorate, LSAT, LDAS report, bachelor's degree from accredited institution, personal statement, transcripts from all U.S. undergraduate schools attended and an analysis and summary of the transcripts; letter of recommendation (up to two are accepted). Additional exam requirements/recommendations for international students: Required—TOEFL, Michigan English Language Assessment Battery (minimum score 85); Recommended—IELTS. *Application deadline:* For fall admission, 7/1 for domestic students. Applications are processed on a rolling basis. Application fee: $0. Electronic applications accepted. *Expenses:* Resident tuition: $1,055.56 per credit hour, $315.70 per semester registration fee, $54.56 per credit hour student service fee. Non-resident tuition: $1,158 per credit hour, $315.70 per semester registration fee, $54.56 per credit hour student service fee. *Financial support:* In 2018–19, 365 students received support. Fellowships, Federal Work-Study, and scholarships/grants available. Support available to part-time students. Financial award application deadline: 6/30; financial award applicants required to submit FAFSA. *Unit head:* Richard A. Bierschbach, Dean and Professor of Law, 313-577-3933, E-mail: rbierschbach@wayne.edu. *Application contact:* Kathy Fox, Assistant Dean of Admissions, 313-577-3937, Fax: 313-993-8129, E-mail: lawinquire@wayne.edu.
Website: http://law.wayne.edu/

Wayne State University, Mike Ilitch School of Business, Detroit, MI 48202. Offers accounting (MS, MSA, Postbaccalaureate Certificate); business (EMS, Graduate Certificate); business administration (MBA, PhD); data science (MS), including business analytics; entrepreneurship and innovation (Postbaccalaureate Certificate); finance (MS); information systems management (Postbaccalaureate Certificate); taxation (MST); JD/MBA. Application deadline for PhD is February 15. *Accreditation:* AACSB. *Program availability:* Part-time, evening/weekend. *Faculty:* 31. *Students:* 286 full-time (152 women), 1,166 part-time (533 women); includes 409 minority (236 Black or African American, non-Hispanic/Latino; 83 Asian, non-Hispanic/Latino; 53 Hispanic/Latino; 37 Two or more races, non-Hispanic/Latino), 74 international. Average age 30. 1,212 applicants, 38% accepted, 294 enrolled. In 2018, 285 master's, 6 doctorates, 7 other advanced degrees awarded. *Degree requirements:* For doctorate, thesis/dissertation. *Entrance requirements:* For master's, GMAT, GRE, LSAT, MCAT, at least three years of relevant work experience that shows increased responsibility, or minimum GPA of 3.0 from AACSB-accredited program or 3.2 from regionally-accredited program, undergraduate degree from accredited institution; undergraduate degree in accounting, business administration, or area of business administration (for MS and MST); for doctorate, GMAT (minimum score of 600), minimum undergraduate GPA of 3.0, 3.5 upper-division or graduate; three letters of recommendation; brief essay; undergraduate degree from accredited institution; personal statement; for other advanced degree, bachelor's degree from accredited institution. Additional exam requirements/recommendations for international students: Required—TOEFL (minimum score 550 paper-based; 79 iBT), Michigan English Language Assessment Battery (minimum score 85); Recommended—IELTS (minimum score 6.5), TWE (minimum score 5.5). *Application deadline:* For fall admission, 7/1 for domestic students, 5/1 priority date for

international students; for winter admission, 11/1 for domestic students, 9/1 priority date for international students; for spring admission, 3/1 for domestic students, 1/1 priority date for international students. Applications are processed on a rolling basis. Application fee: $50. Electronic applications accepted. *Expenses:* Contact institution. *Financial support:* In 2018–19, 175 students received support, including 1 fellowship with tuition reimbursement available (averaging $20,000 per year), 5 research assistantships with tuition reimbursements available (averaging $21,393 per year); teaching assistantships with tuition reimbursements available, scholarships/grants, health care benefits, and unspecified assistantships also available. Support available to part-time students. Financial award applicants required to submit FAFSA. *Faculty research:* Executive compensation and stock performance, consumer reactions to pricing strategies, communication across the automotive supply chain, performance of firms in sub-Saharan Africa, implementation issues with ERP software. *Unit head:* Dr. Robert Forsythe, Dean, School of Business Administration, 313-577-4501, E-mail: robert.forsythe@wayne.edu. *Application contact:* Kiantee N. Rupert-Jones, Director, 313-577-4511, Fax: 313-577-9442, E-mail: gradbusiness@wayne.edu.
Website: http://ilitchbusiness.wayne.edu/

Weber State University, Goddard School of Business and Economics, School of Accounting and Taxation, Ogden, UT 84408-1001. Offers accounting (M Acc); taxation (M Tax). *Accreditation:* AACSB. *Program availability:* Part-time, evening/weekend. *Faculty:* 7 full-time (3 women), 1 part-time/adjunct (0 women). *Students:* 29 full-time (16 women), 25 part-time (10 women); includes 5 minority (2 Asian, non-Hispanic/Latino; 3 Hispanic/Latino), 1 international. Average age 32. In 2018, 44 master's awarded. *Entrance requirements:* For master's, GMAT. Additional exam requirements/recommendations for international students: Required—TOEFL (minimum score 80 iBT). *Application deadline:* For fall admission, 8/1 for domestic students; for spring admission, 12/1 for domestic students; for summer admission, 4/1 for domestic students. Application fee: $60 ($90 for international students). Electronic applications accepted. *Financial support:* In 2018–19, 20 students received support. Scholarships/grants available. Financial award application deadline: 4/1; financial award applicants required to submit FAFSA. *Unit head:* Dr. Ryan Pace, Program Director, 801-626-7562, Fax: 801-626-7423, E-mail: rpace@weber.edu. *Application contact:* Dr. Larry A. Deppe, Graduate Coordinator, 801-626-7838, Fax: 801-626-7423, E-mail: ldeppe1@weber.edu.
Website: http://www.weber.edu/goddard/accounting-taxation.html

Western Michigan University Thomas M. Cooley Law School, Graduate Programs, Lansing, MI 48901-3038. Offers administrative law (public law) (JD); business transactions (JD); Canadian law practice (JD); corporate law and finance (LL M); environmental law (public law) (JD); general practice (JD), including solo and small firm; general studies (LL M); homeland and national security law (LL M); insurance law (LL M); intellectual property (JD); intellectual property law (LL M); international law (JD); litigation (JD); taxation (LL M); U.S. legal studies for foreign attorneys (LL M); JD/LL M; JD/MBA; JD/MHA; JD/MPA; JD/MSW. *Accreditation:* ABA. *Program availability:* Part-time, evening/weekend, 100% online, blended/hybrid learning. *Degree requirements:* For master's, thesis (for some programs); for doctorate, minimum of 3 credits of clinical experience. *Entrance requirements:* For master's, JD or LL B; for doctorate, LSAT. Additional exam requirements/recommendations for international students: Required—TOEFL (for U.S. legal studies for foreign attorneys LL M program); Recommended—TOEFL. Electronic applications accepted. *Expenses:* Contact institution. *Faculty research:* Wrongful convictions, civil rights, environmental law, litigation techniques, data mining, intellectual property, practical and skills-based legal education.

Wichita State University, Graduate School, W. Frank Barton School of Business, School of Accountancy, Wichita, KS 67260. Offers accounting information systems (M Acc); taxation (M Acc). *Accreditation:* AACSB. *Program availability:* Part-time, evening/weekend. *Unit head:* Dr. Jeffrey Bryant, Director, 316-978-3215, Fax: 316-978-3660, E-mail: jeffrey.bryant@wichita.edu. *Application contact:* Jordan Oleson, Admissions Coordinator, 316-978-3095, Fax: 316-978-3253, E-mail: jordan.oleson@wichita.edu.
Website: http://www.wichita.edu/acct

Widener University, School of Business Administration, Program in Taxation, Chester, PA 19013-5792. Offers MS. *Program availability:* Part-time, evening/weekend. *Entrance requirements:* For master's, Certified Public Accountant Exam or GMAT. Electronic applications accepted. *Faculty research:* Financial planning, taxation fraud.

Yeshiva University, Sy Syms School of Business, New York, NY 10016. Offers accounting (MS); business (EMBA); marketing (MS); taxation (MS). *Program availability:* Part-time. *Entrance requirements:* For master's, minimum GPA of 3.5 or GMAT.

Section 3
Advertising and Public Relations

This section contains a directory of institutions offering graduate work in electronic commerce. Additional information about programs listed in the directory but not augmented by an in-depth entry may be obtained by writing directly to the dean of a graduate school or chair of a department at the address given in the directory.

For programs offering related work, see also in this book *Business Administration* and *Management and Marketing*. In another guide in this series:

Graduate Programs in the Humanities, Arts & Social Sciences
See *Communication and Media*

CONTENTS

Program Directory

Advertising and Public Relations

Academy of Art University, Graduate Programs, School of Advertising, San Francisco, CA 94105-3410. Offers advertising (MFA); advertising and branded media technology (MA). *Program availability:* Part-time, 100% online. *Degree requirements:* For master's, final review. *Entrance requirements:* For master's, statement of intent; resume; portfolio/reel; official college transcripts. Electronic applications accepted.

Ball State University, Graduate School, College of Communication, Information, and Media, Department of Journalism, Program in Public Relations, Muncie, IN 47306. Offers MA. *Program availability:* Part-time, 100% online, blended/hybrid learning. *Entrance requirements:* For master's, GRE General Test (minimum score 150 verbal), minimum baccalaureate GPA of 2.75 or 3.0 in latter half of baccalaureate, transcripts of all prior course work, current resume or curriculum vitae, statement of purpose, writing sample. Additional exam requirements/recommendations for international students: Required—TOEFL (minimum score 550 paper-based; 79 iBT), IELTS (minimum score 6.5). Electronic applications accepted.

Boston University, College of Communication, Department of Mass Communication, Advertising, and Public Relations, Boston, MA 02215. Offers advertising (MS); mass communication (MS), including communication studies, marketing communication research; public relations (MS); JD/MS. *Program availability:* Part-time. *Faculty:* 26 full-time, 33 part-time/adjunct. *Students:* 217 full-time (193 women), 10 part-time (9 women); includes 13 minority (6 Black or African American, non-Hispanic/Latino; 2 Asian, non-Hispanic/Latino; 2 Hispanic/Latino; 3 Two or more races, non-Hispanic/Latino), 183 international. Average age 23. 563 applicants, 64% accepted, 120 enrolled. In 2018, 131 master's awarded. *Degree requirements:* For master's, comprehensive exam (for some programs), thesis (for some programs). *Entrance requirements:* For master's, GRE General Test for some programs only, transcript(s), resume/CV, 3 letters of recommendation, personal statement/essay. Additional exam requirements/recommendations for international students: Required—TOEFL (minimum score 600 paper-based; 100 iBT), Either TOEFL or IELTS is required, but not both.; Recommended—IELTS (minimum score 7). *Application deadline:* For fall admission, 5/1 for domestic and international students. Applications are processed on a rolling basis. Application fee: $95. Electronic applications accepted. *Financial support:* Research assistantships, teaching assistantships with partial tuition reimbursements, career-related internships or fieldwork, Federal Work-Study, scholarships/grants, and unspecified assistantships available. Support available to part-time students. Financial award application deadline: 5/1; financial award applicants required to submit FAFSA. *Unit head:* Donald Wright, Chairperson, 617-353-3482, E-mail: mcadvpr@bu.edu. *Application contact:* Jackie Cummings, Admission and Financial Aid Counselor, 617-353-3481, E-mail: comgrad@bu.edu.
Website: http://www.bu.edu/com/academics/masscomm-ad-pr/

Boston University, Metropolitan College, Program in Advertising, Boston, MA 02215. Offers MS. *Program availability:* Part-time, evening/weekend. *Faculty:* 1 full-time (0 women), 8 part-time/adjunct (3 women). *Students:* 11 part-time (6 women); includes 5 minority (1 Black or African American, non-Hispanic/Latino; 2 Hispanic/Latino; 2 Two or more races, non-Hispanic/Latino). Average age 29. In 2018, 9 master's awarded. *Entrance requirements:* For master's, undergraduate degree in appropriate field of study. *Application deadline:* Applications are processed on a rolling basis. Application fee: $85. Electronic applications accepted. *Expenses:* Contact institution. *Financial support:* Unspecified assistantships available. Support available to part-time students. Financial award applicants required to submit FAFSA. *Faculty research:* Communication and advertising. *Unit head:* Dr. Christopher Cakebread, Associate Professor, 617-353-3476, E-mail: ccakebr@bu.edu. *Application contact:* Nadine Hyacinthe, Program Administrator, 617-358-6643.
Website: http://www.bu.edu/met/advertising

California Baptist University, Program in Public Relations, Riverside, CA 92504-3206. Offers MA. *Program availability:* Part-time, evening/weekend, online only, 100% online, blended/hybrid learning. *Faculty:* 1 (woman) full-time, 2 part-time/adjunct (both women). *Students:* 11 full-time (7 women), 9 part-time (all women); includes 12 minority (2 Black or African American, non-Hispanic/Latino; 1 Asian, non-Hispanic/Latino; 9 Hispanic/Latino). Average age 34. 17 applicants, 47% accepted, 8 enrolled. In 2018, 15 master's awarded. *Degree requirements:* For master's, comprehensive capstone. *Entrance requirements:* For master's, minimum undergraduate GPA of 2.5, 2 recommendations, current resume, 500-word essay. Additional exam requirements/recommendations for international students: Required—TOEFL (minimum score 80 iBT). *Application deadline:* For fall admission, 8/1 priority date for domestic students, 7/1 for international students; for spring admission, 12/1 priority date for domestic students, 11/1 priority date for international students. Applications are processed on a rolling basis. Application fee: $45. Electronic applications accepted. *Expenses:* $580 per unit. *Financial support:* In 2018–19, 5 students received support. Federal Work-Study and scholarships/grants available. Financial award applicants required to submit CSS PROFILE or FAFSA. *Faculty research:* New media technologies, media relations, journalism, media effects. *Unit head:* Pamela Daly, Vice President, Online and Professional Studies, 951-343-3901, E-mail: pdaly@calbaptist.edu. *Application contact:* Dr. Cammy Purper, Assistant Dean, Arts and Sciences, 951-343-3935, E-mail: cpurper@calbaptist.edu.
Website: http://www.cbuonline.edu/programs/program/master-of-arts-in-public-relations

Central Connecticut State University, School of Graduate Studies, College of Liberal Arts and Social Sciences, Department of Communication, New Britain, CT 06050-4010. Offers communication (MS); public relations/promotions (Certificate). *Program availability:* Part-time, evening/weekend. *Faculty:* 6 full-time (1 woman), 1 (woman) part-time/adjunct. *Students:* 12 full-time (5 women), 23 part-time (18 women); includes 13 minority (6 Black or African American, non-Hispanic/Latino; 1 Asian, non-Hispanic/Latino; 5 Hispanic/Latino; 1 Two or more races, non-Hispanic/Latino). Average age 28. 23 applicants, 83% accepted, 14 enrolled. In 2018, 12 master's, 2 other advanced degrees awarded. *Degree requirements:* For master's, comprehensive exam, thesis or alternative, special project; for Certificate, qualifying exam. *Entrance requirements:* For master's, minimum undergraduate GPA of 3.0, resume, references, essay. Additional exam requirements/recommendations for international students: Required—TOEFL (minimum score 550 paper-based; 79 iBT); Recommended—IELTS (minimum score 6.5). *Application deadline:* For fall admission, 6/1 for domestic students, 5/1 for international students; for spring admission, 11/1 for domestic and international students. Applications are processed on a rolling basis. Application fee: $50. Electronic applications accepted. *Expenses: Tuition, area resident:* Full-time $7027; part-time $388 per credit. Tuition, state resident: full-time $9750; part-time $388 per credit. Tuition, nonresident: full-time $18,102; part-time $388 per credit. *International tuition:* $18,102 full-time. *Required fees:* $266 per semester. *Financial support:* In 2018–19, 12 students received support. Career-related internships or fieldwork, Federal Work-Study, scholarships/grants, and unspecified assistantships available. Support available to part-time students. Financial award application deadline: 3/1; financial award applicants required to submit FAFSA. *Faculty research:* Organizational communication, mass communication, intercultural communication, political communication, information management. *Unit head:* Dr. Christopher Pudlinski, Chair, 860-832-2690, E-mail: pudlinskic@ccsu.edu. *Application contact:* Patricia Gardner, Associate Director of Graduate Studies, 860-832-2350, Fax: 860-832-2362.
Website: http://comm.ccsu.edu/

Colorado State University, College of Liberal Arts, Department of Journalism and Media Communication, Fort Collins, CO 80523-1785. Offers communications and media management (MCMM); public communication and technology (MS, PhD). *Program availability:* Part-time, blended/hybrid learning. Terminal master's awarded for partial completion of doctoral program. *Degree requirements:* For master's, thesis (for some programs), research project; for doctorate, comprehensive exam, thesis/dissertation. *Entrance requirements:* For master's, GRE General Test (for MS program only), minimum GPA of 3.0; transcripts; letters of recommendation; writing sample, curriculum vitae/resume; statement of purpose; for doctorate, GRE General Test, minimum GPA of 3.0; transcripts; letters of recommendation; writing sample, curriculum vitae/resume; statement of purpose. Additional exam requirements/recommendations for international students: Required—TOEFL (minimum score 550 paper-based; 80 iBT), IELTS (minimum score 6.5); Recommended—TWE. Electronic applications accepted. *Expenses:* Contact institution. *Faculty research:* Food marketing communication models of influence; sports media and journalism; health and science communication; social interaction in online contexts; public discourse and media sociology.

DePaul University, College of Communication, Chicago, IL 60604. Offers digital communication and media arts (MA); health communication (MA); journalism (MA); media and cinema studies (MA); multicultural communication (MA); organizational communication (MA); public relations and advertising (MA); relational communication (MA). *Program availability:* Part-time, evening/weekend. *Entrance requirements:* Additional exam requirements/recommendations for international students: Required—TOEFL (minimum score 590 paper-based; 96 iBT), IELTS (minimum score 7.5) or PTE. Electronic applications accepted.

Georgetown University, Graduate School of Arts and Sciences, School of Continuing Studies, Program in Public Relations and Corporate Communications, Washington, DC 20057. Offers MPS. *Degree requirements:* For master's, capstone course.

Hofstra University, Lawrence Herbert School of Communication, Programs in Journalism and Public Relations, Hempstead, NY 11549. Offers journalism (MA); public relations (MA). *Program availability:* Part-time, evening/weekend. *Students:* 47 full-time (24 women), 18 part-time (14 women); includes 34 minority (21 Black or African American, non-Hispanic/Latino; 2 Asian, non-Hispanic/Latino; 10 Hispanic/Latino; 1 Native Hawaiian or other Pacific Islander, non-Hispanic/Latino), 3 international. Average age 27. 76 applicants, 79% accepted, 30 enrolled. In 2018, 27 master's awarded. *Degree requirements:* For master's, thesis. *Entrance requirements:* For master's, bachelor's degree. Additional exam requirements/recommendations for international students: Required—TOEFL (minimum score 550 paper-based; 95 iBT). *Application deadline:* Applications are processed on a rolling basis. Application fee: $75. Electronic applications accepted. *Financial support:* In 2018–19, 34 students received support, including 33 fellowships with full and partial tuition reimbursements available (averaging $3,488 per year), 1 research assistantship with full and partial tuition reimbursement available (averaging $6,180 per year); career-related internships or fieldwork, Federal Work-Study, institutionally sponsored loans, scholarships/grants, tuition waivers (full and partial), unspecified assistantships, and scholarships and endowed scholarships also available. Support available to part-time students. Financial award applicants required to submit FAFSA. *Faculty research:* Global public relations and use of social media; use of digital graphics and design during the 2016 presidential campaign; framing and representation of bi-racial individuals in the media; data visualizations and storytelling in news media; using social media in journalism and in classroom settings. *Unit head:* Dr. Cliff Jernigan, Chairperson, 516-463-4873, E-mail: cliff.jernigan@hofstra.edu. *Application contact:* Sunil Samuel, Assistant Vice President of Admissions, 516-463-4723, Fax: 516-463-4664, E-mail: graduateadmission@hofstra.edu.
Website: http://www.hofstra.edu/academics/colleges/soc/

Iona College, School of Arts and Science, Department of Mass Communication, New Rochelle, NY 10801-1890. Offers public relations (MA); sports communication and media (MA). *Accreditation:* ACEJMC (one or more programs are accredited). *Program availability:* Part-time, evening/weekend. *Faculty:* 2 full-time (1 woman), 2 part-time/adjunct (0 women). *Students:* 15 full-time (7 women), 17 part-time (10 women); includes 12 minority (10 Black or African American, non-Hispanic/Latino; 1 Asian, non-Hispanic/Latino; 1 Hispanic/Latino), 2 international. Average age 25. 16 applicants, 94% accepted, 11 enrolled. In 2018, 9 master's, 1 other advanced degree awarded. *Degree requirements:* For master's, comprehensive exam (for some programs), thesis or alternative. *Entrance requirements:* For master's, GRE General Test if undergraduate GPA is below 3.0. Additional exam requirements/recommendations for international students: Required—TOEFL (minimum score 550 paper-based; 80 iBT), IELTS (minimum score 6). *Application deadline:* For fall admission, 8/1 for domestic students, 5/1 for international students; for spring admission, 1/1 for domestic students, 9/1 for international students. Applications are processed on a rolling basis. Electronic applications accepted. *Expenses:* Contact institution. *Financial support:* In 2018–19, 1 student received support. Scholarships/grants, tuition waivers (partial), and unspecified assistantships available. Support available to part-time students. Financial award application deadline: 4/15; financial award applicants required to submit FAFSA. *Faculty research:* Media ecology, new media, corporate communication, media images, organizational learning in public relations, media law, medicine ethics. *Unit head:* Anthony Kelso, PhD, Chair, 914-633-7795, E-mail: akelso@iona.edu. *Application contact:* RoseDeline Martinez, Director of Graduate Admissions, School of Arts & Sciences, 914-633-2427, Fax: 914-633-2277, E-mail: rmartinez@iona.edu.
Website: http://www.iona.edu/Academics/School-of-Arts-Science/Departments/Mass-Communication/Graduate-Programs.aspx

Kansas State University, Graduate School, College of Arts and Sciences, A.Q. Miller School of Journalism and Mass Communications, Manhattan, KS 66506. Offers advertising (MS); community journalism (MS); global communication (MS); health communication (MS); media management (MS); public relations (MS). *Program availability:* Part-time, evening/weekend. *Degree requirements:* For master's, comprehensive exam, thesis. *Entrance requirements:* For master's, GRE General Test, minimum GPA of 3.0. Additional exam requirements/recommendations for international students: Required—TOEFL (minimum score 79 iBT). Electronic applications accepted. *Faculty research:* Health communication, risk communication, strategic communications, community journalism, global communication.

Kent State University, College of Communication and Information, School of Journalism and Mass Communication, Kent, OH 44242-0001. Offers journalism and mass communication (MA), including media management, public relations, reporting and editing-broadcast, reporting and editing-convergence, reporting and editing-journalism educators, reporting and editing-magazine, reporting and editing-newspaper. *Program availability:* Part-time, 100% online. *Faculty:* 14 full-time (9 women), 4 part-time/adjunct (2 women). *Students:* 12 full-time (8 women), 44 part-time (29 women); includes 7 minority (5 Black or African American, non-Hispanic/Latino; 1 Hispanic/Latino; 1 Two or more races, non-Hispanic/Latino), 3 international. Average age 36. 23 applicants, 78% accepted, 12 enrolled. In 2018, 41 master's awarded. *Degree requirements:* For master's, thesis or project. *Entrance requirements:* For master's, GRE, minimum GPA of 3.0, statement of purpose, 3 online recommendations, resume. Additional exam requirements/recommendations for international students: Required—TOEFL (minimum score 587 paper-based, 94 iBT), Michigan English Language Assessment Battery (minimum score 82), IELTS (minimum score 7.0) or PTE (minimum score 65). *Application deadline:* For fall admission, 7/1 for domestic and international students. Applications are processed on a rolling basis. Application fee: $45 ($70 for international students). Electronic applications accepted. *Expenses:* Tuition, state resident: full-time $11,766; part-time $536 per credit. Tuition, nonresident: full-time $21,952; part-time $999 per credit. *International tuition:* $21,952 full-time. Tuition and fees vary according to course load. *Financial support:* Research assistantships with full tuition reimbursements, teaching assistantships with full tuition reimbursements, scholarships/grants, and unspecified assistantships available. Financial award application deadline: 3/1. *Unit head:* Jeff Fruit, Interim Director and Professor, 330-672-2572, E-mail: jmc@kent.edu. *Application contact:* Mark Goodman, Graduate Coordinator/Professor, 330-672-6239, E-mail: mgoodm10@kent.edu. Website: http://www.kent.edu/jmc

La Salle University, School of Arts and Sciences, Program in Strategic Communication, Philadelphia, PA 19141-1199. Offers communication consulting and development (MA); communication management (MA); general professional communication (MA); professional and business communication (Certificate); public relations (MA); social and new media (Certificate). *Program availability:* Part-time, evening/weekend, online learning. *Degree requirements:* For master's, practicum. *Entrance requirements:* For master's, writing assessment, professional resume; minimum overall B average; two letters of recommendation (if GPA below 3.25); brief personal statement (about 500 words); interview; for Certificate, writing assessment, minimum GPA of 2.75 in undergraduate studies; brief personal statement (about 500 words); interview. Additional exam requirements/recommendations for international students: Required—TOEFL. Electronic applications accepted. Application fee is waived when completed online. *Expenses:* Contact institution.

Lasell College, Graduate and Professional Studies in Communication, Newton, MA 02466-2709. Offers health communication (MSC, Graduate Certificate); integrated marketing communication (MSC, Graduate Certificate); public relations (MSC, Graduate Certificate). *Program availability:* Part-time, evening/weekend, 100% online, blended/hybrid learning. *Faculty:* 5 full-time (4 women), 8 part-time/adjunct (4 women). *Students:* 27 full-time (18 women), 28 part-time (23 women); includes 12 minority (5 Black or African American, non-Hispanic/Latino; 6 Hispanic/Latino; 1 Two or more races, non-Hispanic/Latino), 17 international. Average age 30. 55 applicants, 44% accepted, 21 enrolled. In 2018, 34 master's, 2 other advanced degrees awarded. *Degree requirements:* For master's, comprehensive exam, thesis or alternative, minimum GPA of 3.0; special project or internship. *Entrance requirements:* For master's, one-page personal statement, 2 letters of recommendation, resume, bachelor's degree transcript; for Graduate Certificate, bachelor's degree transcript, 2 letters of recommendation, 1-page personal statement, resume. Additional exam requirements/recommendations for international students: Required—TOEFL (minimum score 550 paper-based, 79 iBT) or IELTS (minimum score 6). *Application deadline:* For fall admission, 8/31 priority date for domestic students, 6/30 priority date for international students; for spring admission, 12/31 priority date for domestic students, 10/31 priority date for international students. Applications are processed on a rolling basis. Electronic applications accepted. *Expenses: Tuition:* Part-time $600 per credit. *Required fees:* $40 per course. *Financial support:* Federal Work-Study, scholarships/grants, and tuition discounts available. Support available to part-time students. Financial award application deadline: 8/31; financial award applicants required to submit FAFSA. *Faculty research:* Terrorists' use of the Internet; refugees' use of cell phones as means of communication in Jordan and Germany; political communication; analysis of the media coverage of the conflict and peace process in northern Ireland; interpersonal communication; strategies to address bullying in online communities, in schools and in the workplace. *Unit head:* Eric Turner, Vice President of Graduate and Professional Studies, 617-243-2071, Fax: 617-243-2450, E-mail: gradinfo@lasell.edu. *Application contact:* Adrienne Franciosi, Assistant Vice President of Graduate and Professional Studies, 617-243-2214, Fax: 617-243-2450, E-mail: gradinfo@lasell.edu. Website: http://www.lasell.edu/academics/graduate-and-professional-studies/programs-of-study/master-of-science-in-communication.html

La Sierra University, College of Arts and Sciences, Department of English and Communication, Riverside, CA 92505. Offers communication (MA), including public relations/advertising, theory emphasis; English (MA), including literary emphasis, writing emphasis. *Program availability:* Part-time. *Degree requirements:* For master's, one foreign language. *Entrance requirements:* For master's, GRE General Test.

Liberty University, School of Business, Lynchburg, VA 24515. Offers accounting (MBA, MS), including audit and financial reporting (MS), business (MS), financial services (MS), forensic accounting (MS), leadership (MS), taxation (MS); cyber security (MS); executive leadership (MA); international business (DBA); leadership (DBA); marketing (MBA, MS, DBA), including digital marketing and advertising (MS), project management (MS), public relations (MS), sports marketing and media (MS); project management (MBA, DBA), public relations (MBA). *Program availability:* Part-time, online learning. *Students:* 2,871 full-time (1,496 women), 4,437 part-time (1,969 women); includes 2,069 minority (1,424 Black or African American, non-Hispanic/Latino; 44 American Indian or Alaska Native, non-Hispanic/Latino; 133 Asian, non-Hispanic/Latino; 282 Hispanic/Latino; 16 Native Hawaiian or other Pacific Islander, non-Hispanic/Latino; 170 Two or more races, non-Hispanic/Latino), 154 international. Average age 36. 8,980 applicants, 45% accepted, 2009 enrolled. In 2018, 1,988 master's, 25 doctorates awarded. *Entrance requirements:* For master's, minimum undergraduate GPA of 3.0, 15 hours of upper-level business courses. Additional exam requirements/recommendations for international students: Required—TOEFL (minimum score 600 paper-based; 100 iBT). *Application deadline:* Applications are processed on a rolling basis. Application fee: $50. Electronic applications accepted. *Expenses:* Contact institution. *Financial support:* In 2018–19, 990 students received support. Teaching assistantships and Federal Work-Study available. Financial award applicants required to submit FAFSA. *Unit head:* Dr. Dave Bratt, Dean, 434-592-7321, E-mail: dabrat@liberty.edu. *Application contact:* Jay Bridge, Director of Graduate Admissions, 800-424-9595, Fax: 800-628-7977, E-mail: gradadmissions@liberty.edu. Website: https://www.liberty.edu/business/

Lindenwood University, Graduate Programs, School of Arts, Media, and Communications, St. Charles, MO 63301-1695. Offers advertising (MA); art history (MA); cinema and media arts (MFA); communications (MA); digital and Web design (MA); fashion and business design (MS); journalism (MA); mass communications (MA); social media and digital content (MS). *Program availability:* Part-time, 100% online. *Faculty:* 15 full-time (2 women), 7 part-time/adjunct (6 women). *Students:* 40 full-time (23 women), 26 part-time (21 women); includes 18 minority (7 Black or African American, non-Hispanic/Latino; 1 American Indian or Alaska Native, non-Hispanic/Latino; 8 Hispanic/Latino; 2 Two or more races, non-Hispanic/Latino), 7 international. Average age 33. 98 applicants, 65% accepted, 23 enrolled. In 2018, 12 master's awarded. *Degree requirements:* For master's, thesis (for some programs), minimum cumulative GPA of 3.0. *Entrance requirements:* For master's, audition or interview, minimum GPA of 3.0, portfolio, letter of recommendation. Additional exam requirements/recommendations for international students: Required—TOEFL (minimum score 553 paper-based; 81 iBT); Recommended—IELTS (minimum score 6.5). *Application deadline:* For fall admission, 8/9 priority date for domestic students, 6/1 priority date for international students; for spring admission, 12/20 for domestic students, 11/1 priority date for international students; for summer admission, 5/15 priority date for domestic students, 3/27 priority date for international students. Applications are processed on a rolling basis. Application fee: $0 ($100 for international students). Electronic applications accepted. *Expenses: Tuition:* Full-time $16,900; part-time $480 per credit hour. *Required fees:* $700; $350 per unit. Tuition and fees vary according to degree level. *Financial support:* In 2018–19, 29 students received support. Career-related internships or fieldwork, institutionally sponsored loans, scholarships/grants, tuition waivers (partial), and unspecified assistantships available. Financial award application deadline: 6/30; financial award applicants required to submit FAFSA. *Unit head:* Dr. Jason Lively, Dean, School of Arts, Media, and Communications, 636-949-4164, Fax: 636-949-4910, E-mail: JLively@lindenwood.edu. *Application contact:* Kara Schilli, Assistant Vice President, University Admissions, 636-949-4349, Fax: 636-949-4109, E-mail: adultadmissions@lindenwood.edu. Website: https://www.lindenwood.edu/academics/academic-schools/school-of-arts-media-and-communications/

Marquette University, Graduate School, College of Communication, Milwaukee, WI 53201-1881. Offers advertising and public relations (MA); communication studies (MA); digital storytelling (Certificate); journalism (MA); mass communication (MA); science, health and environmental communication (MA). *Accreditation:* ACEJMC (one or more programs are accredited). *Program availability:* Part-time, evening/weekend. *Degree requirements:* For master's, comprehensive exam, thesis or alternative. *Entrance requirements:* For master's, GRE, official transcripts from all current and previous colleges/universities except Marquette, three letters of recommendation, statement of academic and professional goals. Additional exam requirements/recommendations for international students: Required—TOEFL (minimum score 530 paper-based). Electronic applications accepted. *Faculty research:* Urban journalism, gender and communication, intercultural communication, religious communication.

Marshall University, Academic Affairs Division, College of Arts and Media, Program in Journalism, Huntington, WV 25755. Offers journalism (MAJ, Certificate), including health care public relations (MAJ). *Degree requirements:* For master's, thesis optional. *Entrance requirements:* For master's, GRE General Test.

Michigan State University, The Graduate School, College of Communication Arts and Sciences, Department of Advertising and Public Relations, East Lansing, MI 48824. Offers advertising (MA); public relations (MA). *Entrance requirements:* Additional exam requirements/recommendations for international students: Required—TOEFL. Electronic applications accepted.

Mississippi College, Graduate School, College of Arts and Sciences, School of Christian Studies and the Arts, Department of Communication, Clinton, MS 39058. Offers applied communication (MSC); public relations and corporate communication (MSC). *Program availability:* Part-time. *Degree requirements:* For master's, comprehensive exam, thesis optional. *Entrance requirements:* For master's, GRE or NTE, minimum GPA of 2.5. Additional exam requirements/recommendations for international students: Recommended—TOEFL, IELTS. Electronic applications accepted.

Monmouth University, Graduate Studies, Department of Communication, West Long Branch, NJ 07764-1898. Offers public service communication specialist (Certificate); strategic public relations and new media (Certificate). *Program availability:* Part-time, evening/weekend, online learning. *Faculty:* 7 full-time (5 women). *Students:* 11 full-time (7 women), 15 part-time (12 women); includes 4 minority (1 Black or African American, non-Hispanic/Latino; 1 Asian, non-Hispanic/Latino; 2 Hispanic/Latino). Average age 27. In 2018, 10 master's awarded. Terminal master's awarded for partial completion of doctoral program. *Degree requirements:* For master's, comprehensive exam (for some programs), thesis (for some programs), project. *Entrance requirements:* For master's, GRE, baccalaureate degree with minimum GPA of 3.0 in major, 2.75 overall; two letters of recommendation; personal essay (750 words or less describing preparation for study and personal objectives); digital or hard copy portfolio of select samples of work including writing sample; resume. Additional exam requirements/recommendations for international students: Required—TOEFL (minimum score 550 paper-based; 79 iBT), IELTS (minimum score 6), Michigan English Language Assessment Battery (minimum score 77). *Application deadline:* For fall admission, 7/15 priority date for domestic students, 6/1 for international students; for spring admission, 12/1 priority date for domestic students, 11/1 for international students; for summer admission, 5/1 for domestic students. Applications are processed on a rolling basis. Application fee: $50. Electronic applications accepted. *Expenses: Tuition:* Part-time $1233 per credit. *Required fees:* $178 per term. *Financial support:* In 2018–19, 26 students received support. Institutionally sponsored loans, scholarships/grants, and unspecified assistantships available. Support available to part-time students. Financial award applicants required to submit FAFSA. *Faculty research:* Service-learning, history of television, feminism and the media, executive communication, public relations pedagogy. *Unit head:* Dr. Deanna Shoemaker, Program Director, 732-571-3449, Fax: 732-571-3609, E-mail: dshoemak@monmouth.edu. *Application contact:* Kevin New, Graduate Admission Counselor, 732-571-3452, Fax: 732-263-5123, E-mail: gradadm@monmouth.edu. Website: http://www.monmouth.edu/cpc

Montana State University Billings, College of Arts and Sciences, Department of Communication and Theatre, Billings, MT 59101. Offers public relations (MS). *Program availability:* Part-time, 100% online, blended/hybrid learning. *Degree requirements:* For master's, comprehensive exam, thesis optional. *Entrance requirements:* For master's, GRE General Test, minimum undergraduate GPA of 3.0, letters of recommendation, letter of intent, resume. Additional exam requirements/recommendations for international students: Required—TOEFL (minimum score 79 iBT), IELTS (minimum score 6.5). Electronic applications accepted.

Montclair State University, The Graduate School, College of the Arts, MA Program in Public and Organizational Relations, Montclair, NJ 07043-1624. Offers MA. *Program availability:* Part-time, evening/weekend. *Degree requirements:* For master's, comprehensive exam. *Entrance requirements:* For master's, GRE General Test, 2

letters of recommendation. Additional exam requirements/recommendations for international students: Required—TOEFL (minimum score 83 iBT) or IELTS (minimum score 6.5). Electronic applications accepted. *Faculty research:* Organizational problem solving and innovation, social media, health communication, globalization, organizational change management.

Mount Saint Vincent University, Graduate Programs, Department of Communication Studies, Halifax, NS B3M 2J6, Canada. Offers communication (MA); public relations (MPR).

Murray State University, Arthur J. Bauernfeind College of Business, Department of Journalism and Mass Communications, Murray, KY 42071. Offers mass communications (MA, MS), including public relations. *Program availability:* Part-time. *Entrance requirements:* For master's, GRE or GMAT, minimum university GPA of 2.75. Additional exam requirements/recommendations for international students: Required—TOEFL (minimum score 527 paper-based; 51 iBT). Electronic applications accepted. *Faculty research:* Mass media, audience analysis, press and politics, government open records laws, public relations.

New York University, School of Professional Studies, Division of Programs in Business, Programs in Marketing and Public Relations, New York, NY 10012-1019. Offers public relations and corporate communication (MS), including corporate and organizational communication, public relations management. *Program availability:* Part-time, evening/weekend. *Degree requirements:* For master's, thesis. *Entrance requirements:* For master's, GRE or GMAT (only upon request), bachelor's degree, resume with relevant professional work, internship or volunteer experience, two letters of recommendation, statement of purpose. Additional exam requirements/recommendations for international students: Required—TOEFL (minimum score 600 paper-based; 100 iBT), IELTS (minimum score 7). Electronic applications accepted. *Expenses:* Contact institution.

Northern Kentucky University, Office of Graduate Programs, College of Informatics, Program in Communication, Highland Heights, KY 41099. Offers communication (MA); communication teaching (Certificate); documentary studies (Certificate); public relations (Certificate); relationships (Certificate). *Program availability:* Part-time, evening/ weekend. Terminal master's awarded for partial completion of doctoral program. *Degree requirements:* For master's, comprehensive exams, thesis or applied capstone project. *Entrance requirements:* For master's, GRE, minimum GPA of 3.0, 3 letters of recommendation, letter of intent. Additional exam requirements/recommendations for international students: Required—TOEFL (minimum score 79 iBT); Recommended—IELTS (minimum score 6.5). Electronic applications accepted. *Faculty research:* Mediating effect of health communication, organizational communication, quantitative and qualitative research methods, family and interpersonal communication.

Quinnipiac University, School of Communications, Program in Public Relations, Hamden, CT 06518-1940. Offers public relations (MS), including social media. *Program availability:* Part-time, evening/weekend. *Entrance requirements:* Additional exam requirements/recommendations for international students: Required—TOEFL (minimum score 575 paper-based; 90 iBT), IELTS (minimum score 6.5). Electronic applications accepted. *Faculty research:* Social media, corporate social responsibility, ethics, international communications and international public relations, public diplomacy, non-profit management, crisis management, investor relations.

Rowan University, Graduate School, College of Communication and Creative Arts, Program in Public Relations/Advertising, Glassboro, NJ 08028-1701. Offers MA. *Program availability:* Part-time, evening/weekend. *Degree requirements:* For master's, thesis. *Entrance requirements:* For master's, GRE General Test. Additional exam requirements/recommendations for international students: Required—TOEFL. Electronic applications accepted.

San Diego State University, Graduate and Research Affairs, College of Professional Studies and Fine Arts, School of Communication, San Diego, CA 92182. Offers advertising and public relations (MA); critical-cultural studies (MA); interaction studies (MA); intercultural and international studies (MA); new media studies (MA); news and information studies (MA); telecommunications and media management (MA). *Degree requirements:* For master's, thesis. *Entrance requirements:* For master's, GRE General Test, 3 letters of recommendation. Additional exam requirements/recommendations for international students: Required—TOEFL. Electronic applications accepted.

Savannah College of Art and Design, Program in Advertising, Savannah, GA 31402-3146. Offers MA, MFA. *Program availability:* Part-time. *Faculty:* 9 full-time (4 women), 6 part-time/adjunct (2 women). *Students:* 26 full-time (19 women), 5 part-time (3 women); includes 9 minority (6 Black or African American, non-Hispanic/Latino; 1 American Indian or Alaska Native, non-Hispanic/Latino; 1 Asian, non-Hispanic/Latino; 1 Hispanic/Latino), 17 international. Average age 27. 69 applicants, 25% accepted, 10 enrolled. In 2018, 14 master's awarded. *Degree requirements:* For master's, final project (for MA); thesis (for MFA). *Entrance requirements:* For master's, GRE (recommended), portfolio (submitted in digital format), audition or writing submission, resume, statement of purpose, two letters of recommendation. Additional exam requirements/recommendations for international students: Recommended—TOEFL (minimum score 550 paper-based; 85 iBT), IELTS (minimum score 6.5). *Application deadline:* For fall admission, 4/1 for domestic and international students. Applications are processed on a rolling basis. Application fee: $40. Electronic applications accepted. *Expenses: Tuition:* Full-time $37,530; part-time $4170 per course. One-time fee: $500. *Financial support:* Career-related internships or fieldwork, Federal Work-Study, and scholarships/grants available. Financial award application deadline: 4/1; financial award applicants required to submit FAFSA. *Unit head:* Duke Greenhill, Chair of Advertising Design. *Application contact:* Jenny Jaquillard, Executive Director of Admission Recruitment, 912-525-5100, Fax: 912-525-5985, E-mail: admission@scad.edu.
Website: http://www.scad.edu/academics/programs/advertising

Seton Hall University, College of Communication and the Arts, Program in Public Relations, South Orange, NJ 07079-2697. Offers MA. *Program availability:* Part-time, evening/weekend, online learning. *Degree requirements:* For master's, thesis (for some programs). *Entrance requirements:* For master's, GRE or MAT, official transcripts, resume, personal statement, 3 letters of recommendation. Additional exam requirements/recommendations for international students: Required—TOEFL (minimum iBT score 80) or IELTS (6.5). Electronic applications accepted. *Faculty research:* Leadership, art history, reputation management, image management, public relations.

Southeastern Louisiana University, College of Arts, Humanities and Social Sciences, Department of Communication and Media Studies, Hammond, LA 70402. Offers health communications (MA); journalism (MA); marketing (MA); public relations (MA); sociology (MA). *Program availability:* Part-time, evening/weekend. *Faculty:* 8 full-time (6 women). *Students:* 3 full-time (2 women), 15 part-time (11 women); includes 9 minority (6 Black or African American, non-Hispanic/Latino; 2 Hispanic/Latino; 1 Two or more races, non-Hispanic/Latino). Average age 30. 12 applicants, 75% accepted, 4 enrolled. In 2018, 6 master's awarded. *Degree requirements:* For master's, comprehensive exam. *Entrance requirements:* For master's, GRE (minimum score 148 on Verbal section, 3.5 Written). Additional exam requirements/recommendations for international students: Required—TOEFL (minimum score 525 paper-based; 75 iBT). *Application deadline:* For fall admission, 7/15 priority date for domestic students, 6/1 priority date for international

students; for spring admission, 12/1 priority date for domestic students, 10/1 priority date for international students. Applications are processed on a rolling basis. Application fee: $20 ($30 for international students). Electronic applications accepted. *Expenses: Tuition, area resident:* Full-time $6684. Tuition, state resident: full-time $6684. Tuition, nonresident: full-time $19,162. *Required fees:* $2097. *Financial support:* In 2018–19, 13 students received support, including 4 research assistantships with tuition reimbursements available (averaging $8,963 per year); career-related internships or fieldwork, Federal Work-Study, institutionally sponsored loans, scholarships/grants, traineeships, health care benefits, tuition waivers (full), and unspecified assistantships also available. Financial award application deadline: 5/1; financial award applicants required to submit FAFSA. *Faculty research:* Communicate with the millennial generation to enhance organizational effectiveness, conflict resolution and mediation among nations, journalism history, media law, media writing, media convergence, external compliances accreditation and strategic planning. *Unit head:* Dr. James O'Connor, Department Head, 985-549-5310, Fax: 985-549-3088, E-mail: james.oconnor@selu.edu. *Application contact:* Office of Admissions, 985-549-5637, Fax: 985-549-5632, E-mail: admissions@southeastern.edu.
Website: http://www.southeastern.edu/acad_research/depts/comm/index.html

Southern Illinois University Edwardsville, Graduate School, College of Arts and Sciences, Department of Applied Communication Studies, Program in Public Relations, Edwardsville, IL 62026. Offers MA. *Program availability:* Part-time, evening/weekend. *Degree requirements:* For master's, comprehensive exam (for some programs), thesis (for some programs). *Entrance requirements:* Additional exam requirements/recommendations for international students: Required—TOEFL (minimum score 550 paper-based, 79 iBT), IELTS (minimum score 6.5), Michigan Test of English Language Proficiency or PTE. Electronic applications accepted.

Southern Methodist University, Meadows School of the Arts, Temerlin Advertising Institute, Dallas, TX 75275. Offers MA. *Entrance requirements:* For master's, GRE, GMAT. Additional exam requirements/recommendations for international students: Required—TOEFL (minimum score 550 paper-based; 80 iBT). Electronic applications accepted.

Southern New Hampshire University, School of Business, Manchester, NH 03106-1045. Offers accounting (MBA, Graduate Certificate); accounting finance (MS); accounting/auditing (MS); accounting/forensic accounting (MS); accounting/management accounting (MS); accounting/taxation (MS); applied economics (MS); athletic administration (MBA, Graduate Certificate); business administration (IMBA, Certificate), including business information systems (Certificate), human resource management (Certificate); business analytics (MBA); business intelligence (MBA); communication (MA), including new media and marketing, public relations; community economic development (MBA); criminal justice (MBA); data analytics (MS); economics (MBA); engineering management (MBA); entrepreneurship (MBA); finance (MBA, MS, Graduate Certificate); finance/corporate finance (MS); finance/investments (MS); forensic accounting (MBA); forensic accounting and fraud examination (Graduate Certificate); healthcare informatics (MBA); healthcare management (MBA); human resource management (MS); human resources (MBA); information technology (MS); information technology management (MBA); international business (PhD); Internet marketing (MBA); leadership (MBA); leadership of nonprofit organizations (Graduate Certificate); management (MS); marketing (MBA, MS, Graduate Certificate); music business (MBA); operations and project management (MS); operations and supply chain management (MBA, Graduate Certificate); organizational leadership (MS); project management (MBA, Graduate Certificate); public administration (MBA, Graduate Certificate); quantitative analysis (MBA); Six Sigma (Graduate Certificate); Six Sigma quality (MBA); social media marketing (MBA, Graduate Certificate); sport management (MBA, MS, Graduate Certificate); sustainability and environmental compliance (MBA); MBA/Certificate. *Accreditation:* ACBSP. *Program availability:* Part-time, evening/weekend, online learning. Terminal master's awarded for partial completion of doctoral program. *Degree requirements:* For master's, one foreign language, comprehensive exam (for some programs), thesis or alternative; for doctorate, one foreign language, comprehensive exam, thesis/dissertation. *Entrance requirements:* For master's, minimum GPA of 2.5; for doctorate, GMAT. Additional exam requirements/recommendations for international students: Required—TOEFL (minimum score 500 paper-based). Electronic applications accepted.

Suffolk University, College of Arts and Sciences, Advertising and Public Relations Department, Boston, MA 02108-2770. Offers communication studies (MAC); integrated marketing communication (MAC); public relations and advertising (MAC). *Program availability:* Part-time, evening/weekend. *Faculty:* 9 full-time (8 women). *Students:* 19 full-time (16 women), 9 part-time (6 women); includes 5 minority (1 Black or African American, non-Hispanic/Latino; 1 Asian, non-Hispanic/Latino; 2 Hispanic/Latino; 1 Two or more races, non-Hispanic/Latino), 9 international. Average age 26. 54 applicants, 69% accepted, 10 enrolled. In 2018, 20 master's awarded. *Degree requirements:* For master's, thesis optional. *Entrance requirements:* For master's, GRE General Test, MAT, or GMAT, 2 letters of recommendation, resume. Additional exam requirements/recommendations for international students: Required—TOEFL (minimum score 550 paper-based; 80 iBT). *Application deadline:* For fall admission, 3/15 priority date for domestic and international students; for spring admission, 10/15 priority date for domestic and international students. Applications are processed on a rolling basis. Application fee: $50. Electronic applications accepted. *Expenses:* Contact institution. *Financial support:* In 2018–19, 31 students received support. Fellowships, career-related internships or fieldwork, Federal Work-Study, institutionally sponsored loans, and scholarships/grants available. Support available to part-time students. Financial award application deadline: 4/1; financial award applicants required to submit FAFSA. *Faculty research:* Branding law and management, health care communication, gender roles and violence in video games, new media, political communication. *Unit head:* Robert Rosenthal, Chair, 617-573-8502, E-mail: rrosenthal@suffolk.edu. *Application contact:* Mara Marzocchi, Associate Director of Graduate Admissions, 617-573-8302, Fax: 617-305-1733, E-mail: grad.admission@suffolk.edu.
Website: http://www.suffolk.edu/college/graduate/69298.php

Syracuse University, S. I. Newhouse School of Public Communications, MA Program in Advertising, Syracuse, NY 13244. Offers MA. *Students:* Average age 24. *Entrance requirements:* For master's, GRE General Test, resume, official transcripts, personal statement, three letters of recommendation. Additional exam requirements/recommendations for international students: Required—TOEFL (minimum score 600 paper-based; 100 iBT). *Application deadline:* For summer admission, 1/15 for domestic and international students. Application fee: $45. Electronic applications accepted. *Financial support:* Fellowships with full tuition reimbursements, research assistantships with partial tuition reimbursements, and teaching assistantships with full tuition reimbursements available. Financial award application deadline: 1/1. *Faculty research:* Advertising management, digital advertising and branding, marketing communication, strategic media planning, advertising campaigns. *Unit head:* Prof. James Tsao, Chair, 315-443-7362, E-mail: jctsao@syr.edu. *Application contact:* Martha Coria, Graduate Records Office, 315-443-4039, Fax: 315-443-1834, E-mail: pcgrad@syr.edu.
Website: http://newhouse.syr.edu/academics/degrees/masters/advertising

Syracuse University, S. I. Newhouse School of Public Communications, MS in Public Relations Program, Syracuse, NY 13244. Offers MS. *Students:* Average age 24. *Entrance requirements:* For master's, GRE General Test, resume, official transcripts, personal statement, three letters of recommendation. Additional exam requirements/recommendations for international students: Required—TOEFL (minimum score 600 paper-based; 100 iBT). *Application deadline:* For summer admission, 1/15 priority date for domestic and international students. Application fee: $45. Electronic applications accepted. *Financial support:* Fellowships with full tuition reimbursements, research assistantships with partial tuition reimbursements, and teaching assistantships with partial tuition reimbursements available. Financial award application deadline: 2/1. *Faculty research:* Media law, visual communication, public relations, financial markets and institutions. *Unit head:* Prof. Rochelle Ford, Chair, 315-443-9347, E-mail: pcgrad@syr.edu. *Application contact:* Martha Coria, Graduate Records Office, 315-443-4039, Fax: 315-443-1834, E-mail: pcgrad@syr.edu.
Website: http://newhouse.syr.edu/academics/degrees/masters/public-relations

Universidad Autonoma de Guadalajara, Graduate Programs, Guadalajara, Mexico. Offers administrative law and justice (LL M); advertising and corporate communications (MA); architecture (M Arch); business (MBA); computational science (MCC); education (Ed M, Ed D); English-Spanish translation (MA); entrepreneurship and management (MBA); integrated management of digital animation (MA); international business (MIB); international corporate law (LL M); Internet technologies (MS); manufacturing systems (MMS); occupational health (MS); philosophy (MA, PhD); power electronics (MS); quality systems (MQS); renewable energy (MS); social evaluation of projects (MBA); strategic market research (MBA); tax law (MA); teaching mathematics (MA).

Université Laval, Faculty of Letters, Program in Public Relations, Québec, QC G1K 7P4, Canada. Offers Diploma. *Program availability:* Part-time, evening/weekend. *Entrance requirements:* For degree, knowledge of French, comprehension of written English. Electronic applications accepted.

The University of Alabama, Graduate School, College of Communication and Information Sciences, Department of Advertising and Public Relations, Tuscaloosa, AL 35487-0172. Offers MA. *Program availability:* Part-time. *Degree requirements:* For master's, comprehensive exam, thesis or alternative. *Entrance requirements:* For master's, GRE (minimum score: 300 verbal plus quantitative; 4.0 in writing), minimum undergraduate GPA of 3.0 for last 60 hours. Additional exam requirements/recommendations for international students: Required—TOEFL (minimum score 600 paper-based; 100 iBT); Recommended—IELTS (minimum score 7). Electronic applications accepted. *Faculty research:* Advertising and public relations management, leadership, ethics, public opinion, political communication, advertising media, social and digital media, international communication, creativity, consumer privacy, crisis communication, disaster communication, sports communication, advertising and public relations history.

University of Colorado Boulder, Graduate School, College of Media, Communication and Information, Department of Advertising, Public Relations and Media Design, Boulder, CO 80309. Offers media research and practice (PhD); strategic communication design (MA). Electronic applications accepted. *Faculty research:* Advertising; mass communication/media; electronic media; communications; consumer behavior.

University of Florida, Graduate School, College of Journalism and Communications, Program in Advertising, Gainesville, FL 32611. Offers M Adv. *Degree requirements:* For master's, thesis or terminal project. *Entrance requirements:* For master's, GRE General Test, minimum GPA of 3.0. Additional exam requirements/recommendations for international students: Required—TOEFL (minimum score 550 paper-based; 80 iBT), IELTS (minimum score 6). Electronic applications accepted. *Faculty research:* Branding, information flow between clients and suppliers, message and media strategies, emotional response.

University of Florida, Graduate School, College of Journalism and Communications, Program in Mass Communication, Gainesville, FL 32611. Offers international/intercultural communication (MAMC); journalism (MAMC); mass communication (MAMC, PhD), including clinical translational science (MAMC); public relations (MAMC); science/health communication (MAMC); telecommunication (MAMC). *Entrance requirements:* For master's and doctorate, GRE General Test, minimum GPA of 3.0.

University of Houston, College of Liberal Arts and Social Sciences, Jack J. Valenti School of Communication, Houston, TX 77204. Offers health communication (MA); mass communication studies (MA); public relations studies (MA); speech communication (MA). *Program availability:* Part-time. *Degree requirements:* For master's, comprehensive exam (for some programs), thesis (for some programs), 30-33 hours. *Entrance requirements:* For master's, GRE. Additional exam requirements/recommendations for international students: Required—TOEFL. Electronic applications accepted.

University of Illinois at Urbana–Champaign, Graduate College, College of Media, Charles H. Sandage Department of Advertising, Champaign, IL 61820. Offers MS.

University of Maryland, College Park, Academic Affairs, College of Arts and Humanities, Department of Communication, College Park, MD 20742. Offers MA, PhD. *Degree requirements:* For master's, thesis optional; for doctorate, comprehensive exam, thesis/dissertation. *Entrance requirements:* For master's, GRE General Test, minimum GPA of 3.0, sample of scholarly writing, 3 letters of recommendation, statement of goals and experiences; for doctorate, GRE General Test. Additional exam requirements/recommendations for international students: Required—TOEFL. Electronic applications accepted. *Faculty research:* Health communication, interpersonal communication, persuasion, intercultural communication, contemporary rhetoric theory.

University of Miami, Graduate School, School of Communication, Coral Gables, FL 33124. Offers communication (PhD); communication studies (MA); film studies (MA, PhD); motion pictures (MFA), including production, producing, and screenwriting; print journalism (MA); public relations (MA); Spanish language journalism (MA); television broadcast journalism (MA). *Program availability:* Part-time. *Degree requirements:* For master's, comprehensive exam (for some programs), thesis (for some programs); for doctorate, comprehensive exam, thesis/dissertation. *Entrance requirements:* For master's, GRE General Test; for doctorate, GRE General Test, master's thesis or scholarly research. Additional exam requirements/recommendations for international students: Required—TOEFL (minimum score 600 paper-based; 100 iBT). Electronic applications accepted. *Faculty research:* Communication studies, mass communication, international/interpersonal communication, film studies, journalism.

University of Nebraska–Lincoln, Graduate College, College of Arts and Sciences, Department of Communication Studies, Lincoln, NE 68588. Offers instructional communication (MA, PhD); interpersonal communication (MA, PhD); marketing, communication studies, and advertising (MA, PhD); organizational communication (MA, PhD); rhetoric and culture (MA, PhD). *Degree requirements:* For master's, thesis optional; for doctorate, comprehensive exam, thesis/dissertation. *Entrance requirements:* For master's and doctorate, GRE General Test, writing sample. Additional exam requirements/recommendations for international students: Required—TOEFL (minimum score 600 paper-based). Electronic applications accepted. *Faculty research:*

Message strategies, gender communication, political communication, organizational communication, instructional communication.

University of Nebraska–Lincoln, Graduate College, College of Journalism and Mass Communications, Lincoln, NE 68588. Offers marketing, communication and advertising (MA); professional journalism (MA). *Program availability:* Online learning. *Degree requirements:* For master's, thesis. *Entrance requirements:* For master's, samples of work. Additional exam requirements/recommendations for international students: Required—TOEFL (minimum score 600 paper-based). Electronic applications accepted. *Faculty research:* Interactive media and the Internet, community newspapers, children's radio, advertising involvement, telecommunications policy.

University of North Texas, Toulouse Graduate School, Denton, TX 76203-5459. Offers accounting (MS); applied anthropology (MA, MS); applied behavior analysis (Certificate); applied geography (MA); applied technology and performance improvement (M Ed, MS); art education (MA); art history (MA); arts leadership (Certificate); audiology (Au D); behavior analysis (MS); behavioral science (PhD); biochemistry and molecular biology (MS); biology (MA, MS); biomedical engineering (MS); business analysis (MS); chemistry (MS); clinical health psychology (PhD); communication studies (MA, MS); computer engineering (MS); computer science (MS); counseling (M Ed, MS), including clinical mental health counseling (MS), college and university counseling, elementary school counseling, secondary school counseling; creative writing (MA); criminal justice (MS); curriculum and instruction (M Ed); decision sciences (MBA); design (MA, MFA), including fashion design (MFA), innovation studies, interior design (MFA); early childhood studies (MS); economics (MS); educational leadership (M Ed, Ed D); educational psychology (MS, PhD), including family studies (MS), gifted and talented (MS), human development (MS), learning and cognition (MS), research, measurement and evaluation (MS); electrical engineering (MS); emergency management (MPA); engineering technology (MS); English (MA); English as a second language (MA); environmental science (MS); finance (MBA, MS); financial management (MPA); French (MA); health services management (MBA); higher education (M Ed, Ed D); history (MA, MS); hospitality management (MS); human resources management (MPA); information science (MS); information systems (PhD); information technologies (MBA); interdisciplinary studies (MA, MS); international studies (MA); international sustainable tourism (MS); jazz studies (MM); journalism (MA, MJ, Graduate Certificate), including interactive and virtual digital communication (Graduate Certificate), narrative journalism (Graduate Certificate), public relations (Graduate Certificate); kinesiology (MS); linguistics (MA); local government management (MPA); logistics (PhD); logistics and supply chain management (MBA); long-term care, senior housing, and aging services (MA); management (PhD); marketing (MBA); mathematics (MA, MS); mechanical and energy engineering (MS, PhD); music (MA), including ethnomusicology, music theory, musicology, performance; music composition (PhD); music education (MM Ed, PhD); nonprofit management (MPA); operations and supply chain management (MBA); performance (MM, DMA); philosophy (MA); political science (MA); professional and technical communication (MA); radio, television and film (MA, MFA); rehabilitation counseling (Certificate); sociology (MA); Spanish (MA); special education (M Ed); speech-language pathology (MA); strategic management (MBA); studio art (MFA); teaching (M Ed); MBA/MS. *Program availability:* Part-time, evening/weekend, online learning. Terminal master's awarded for partial completion of doctoral program. *Degree requirements:* For master's, variable foreign language requirement, comprehensive exam (for some programs), thesis (for some programs); for doctorate, variable foreign language requirement, comprehensive exam (for some programs), thesis/dissertation; for other advanced degree, variable foreign language requirement, comprehensive exam (for some programs). *Entrance requirements:* For master's and doctorate, GRE, GMAT. Additional exam requirements/recommendations for international students: Required—TOEFL (minimum score 550 paper-based; 79 iBT). Electronic applications accepted.

University of Saint Mary, Graduate Programs, Program in Business Administration, Leavenworth, KS 66048-5082. Offers enterprise risk management (MBA); finance (MBA); general management (MBA); health care management (MBA); human resources management (MBA); marketing and advertising management (MBA). *Program availability:* Part-time, evening/weekend, 100% online, blended/hybrid learning. *Faculty:* 1 full-time, 23 part-time/adjunct (7 women). *Students:* 177 full-time (116 women), 50 part-time (29 women); includes 73 minority (30 Black or African American, non-Hispanic/Latino; 3 American Indian or Alaska Native, non-Hispanic/Latino; 12 Asian, non-Hispanic/Latino; 18 Hispanic/Latino; 1 Native Hawaiian or other Pacific Islander, non-Hispanic/Latino; 9 Two or more races, non-Hispanic/Latino), 2 international. Average age 33. *Degree requirements:* For master's, thesis. *Entrance requirements:* For master's, Minimum undergraduate GPA of 2.75, official transcripts. *Application deadline:* Applications are processed on a rolling basis. Application fee: $25. Electronic applications accepted. *Expenses:* Contact institution. *Financial support:* Applicants required to submit FAFSA. *Unit head:* Mark Harvey, Director of Graduate Business Programs, 913-319-3011, E-mail: mark.harvey@stmary.edu. *Application contact:* Mark Harvey, Director of Graduate Business Programs, 913-319-3011, E-mail: mark.harvey@stmary.edu.
Website: https://www.stmary.edu/mba

University of Southern California, Graduate School, Annenberg School for Communication and Journalism, School of Journalism, Program in Strategic Public Relations, Los Angeles, CA 90089. Offers MA. *Accreditation:* ACEJMC. *Program availability:* Part-time, evening/weekend. *Students:* 106 full-time, 7 part-time; includes 53 minority (17 Black or African American, non-Hispanic/Latino; 14 Asian, non-Hispanic/Latino; 18 Hispanic/Latino; 4 Two or more races, non-Hispanic/Latino), 33 international. Average age 24. 199 applicants, 41% accepted, 51 enrolled. In 2018, 36 master's awarded. *Degree requirements:* For master's, comprehensive exam (for some programs), thesis optional. *Entrance requirements:* For master's, GRE General Test, resume, writing samples, letters of recommendation, statement of purpose. Additional exam requirements/recommendations for international students: Required—TOEFL (minimum score 114 iBT), IELTS (minimum score 8). *Application deadline:* For fall admission, 1/1 priority date for domestic students. Application fee: $90. Electronic applications accepted. *Financial support:* In 2018–19, 4 fellowships with full and partial tuition reimbursements (averaging $22,000 per year), 2 teaching assistantships with full and partial tuition reimbursements (averaging $22,000 per year) were awarded; career-related internships or fieldwork, Federal Work-Study, scholarships/grants, and health care benefits also available. Support available to part-time students. Financial award application deadline: 1/1; financial award applicants required to submit FAFSA. *Unit head:* Dr. Burghardt Tenderich, Director of Journalism School, 213-740-0446, E-mail: tenderic@usc.edu. *Application contact:* Allyson Hill, Associate Dean for Admissions, 213-821-0770, Fax: 213-740-1933, E-mail: ascadm@usc.edu.
Website: http://www.annenberg.usc.edu/

University of Southern Mississippi, College of Arts and Sciences, School of Communication, Hattiesburg, MS 39406-0001. Offers communication (MA, MS, PhD); public relations (MS). *Program availability:* Part-time. *Degree requirements:* For master's, comprehensive exam, thesis optional; for doctorate, comprehensive exam, thesis/dissertation. *Entrance requirements:* For master's, GRE General Test, minimum GPA of 3.0 in last 60 hours and in major; for doctorate, GRE General Test, minimum

Advertising and Public Relations

GPA of 3.5. Additional exam requirements/recommendations for international students: Required—TOEFL, IELTS. Electronic applications accepted. *Faculty research:* Persuasion and social influence, interpersonal communication, organizational communication, political communication, crisis communication, public advocacy.

The University of Tennessee, Graduate School, College of Communication and Information, Knoxville, TN 37996. Offers advertising (MS, PhD); communications (MS, PhD); information sciences (MS, PhD); journalism and electronic media (MS, PhD); public relations (MS, PhD). *Program availability:* Part-time, evening/weekend, online learning. *Degree requirements:* For master's, thesis or alternative; for doctorate, thesis/dissertation. *Entrance requirements:* For master's and doctorate, GRE General Test, minimum GPA of 2.7. Additional exam requirements/recommendations for international students: Required—TOEFL. Electronic applications accepted.

The University of Texas at Austin, Graduate School, College of Communication, Department of Advertising, Austin, TX 78712-1111. Offers MA, PhD. *Entrance requirements:* For master's and doctorate, GRE General Test. Electronic applications accepted. *Faculty research:* Interactive advertising, advertising laws and ethics, advertising creativity, media planning and modeling, international advertising.

University of the Sacred Heart, Graduate Programs, Department of Communication, Program in Public Relations, San Juan, PR 00914-0383. Offers MA. *Program availability:* Part-time, evening/weekend. *Degree requirements:* For master's, thesis. *Entrance requirements:* For master's, EXADEP, minimum undergraduate GPA of 2.75, interview.

University of Wisconsin–Stevens Point, College of Fine Arts and Communication, Division of Communication, Stevens Point, WI 54481-3897. Offers interpersonal communication (MA); media studies (MA); organizational communication (MA); public relations (MA). *Program availability:* Part-time. *Degree requirements:* For master's, thesis or alternative. *Entrance requirements:* For master's, GRE. Additional exam requirements/recommendations for international students: Required—TOEFL (minimum score 575 paper-based). *Faculty research:* Communication theory and research, film history.

Virginia Commonwealth University, Graduate School, College of Humanities and Sciences, Richard T. Robertson School of Media and Culture, Program in Mass Communications, Richmond, VA 23284-9005. Offers multimedia journalism (MS); strategic public relations (MS). *Degree requirements:* For master's, comprehensive exam, thesis optional. *Entrance requirements:* For master's, GRE General Test. Additional exam requirements/recommendations for international students: Required—TOEFL (minimum score 600 paper-based; 100 iBT); Recommended—IELTS (minimum score 6.5). Electronic applications accepted. *Faculty research:* Multimedia journalism, strategic public relations.

Virginia International University, School of Business, Fairfax, VA 22030. Offers accounting (MBA, MS); entrepreneurship (MBA); executive management (Graduate Certificate); global logistics (MBA); health care management (MBA); hospitality and tourism management (MBA); human resources management (MBA); international business management (MBA); international finance (MBA); marketing management (MBA); mass media and public relations (MBA); project management (MBA, MS). *Program availability:* Part-time, online learning. *Entrance requirements:* For master's and Graduate Certificate, bachelor's degree. Additional exam requirements/recommendations for international students: Required—TOEFL (minimum score 550 paper-based; 80 iBT), IELTS (minimum score 6). Electronic applications accepted.

Wayne State University, College of Fine, Performing and Communication Arts, Department of Communication, Detroit, MI 48202. Offers communication (PhD), including democratic participation and culture, identity and representation, media, society and culture, risk, crisis and conflict, wellness, work life and relationships; communication and new media (Graduate Certificate); communication studies (MA); dispute resolution (MADR, Graduate Certificate), including community and urban studies (MADR), conflict area studies (MADR), health and family (MADR), international conflict and cooperation (MADR), professional practice (MADR), theory of conflict (MADR), workplace (MADR); health communication (Graduate Certificate); journalism (MA); media arts (MA); media studies (MA); public relations and organizational communication (MA); JD/MADR. Doctoral program admits for fall only. *Program availability:* Online learning. *Faculty:* 20. *Students:* 65 full-time (38 women), 73 part-time (48 women); includes 49 minority (40 Black or African American, non-Hispanic/Latino; 1 Asian, non-Hispanic/Latino; 3 Hispanic/Latino; 5 Two or more races, non-Hispanic/Latino), 10 international. Average age 33. 141 applicants, 38% accepted, 31 enrolled. In 2018, 37 master's, 8 doctorates, 3 other advanced degrees awarded. *Degree requirements:* For master's, thesis (for some programs), thesis or essay; for doctorate, thesis/dissertation. *Entrance requirements:* For master's, GRE (for MA if undergraduate GPA less than 3.2), personal statement; BA or BS in communication or related field with minimum upper-division GPA of 3.2 and minimum upper-division undergraduate GPA of 3.0, and sample of academic writing (for MA); undergraduate degree with minimum upper-division GPA of 3.0 and three letters of recommendation (for MADR); for doctorate, GRE, undergraduate degree in communication or related field; master's degree in communication or related field with minimum GPA of 3.5; letters of recommendation; personal statement; sample of written scholarship. Additional exam requirements/recommendations for international students: Required—TOEFL (minimum score 100 iBT), IELTS, TWE. Application fee: $50. Electronic applications accepted. *Expenses:* Contact institution. *Financial support:* In 2018–19, 55 students received support, including 5 fellowships with tuition reimbursements available (averaging $21,500 per year), 2 research assistantships with tuition reimbursements available (averaging $18,901 per year), 21 teaching assistantships with tuition reimbursements available (averaging $19,358 per year); scholarships/grants and unspecified assistantships also available. Financial award applicants required to submit FAFSA. *Faculty research:* Democratic participation and culture; identity and representation; media, society and culture; risk, crisis and conflict; wellness, work life, and relationships. *Unit head:* Dr. Lee Wilkins, Professor and Chair, 313-577-2943, E-mail: eh8899@wayne.edu. *Application contact:* Dr. Lee Wilkins, Professor and Chair, 313-577-2943, E-mail: eh8899@wayne.edu.
Website: http://comm.wayne.edu/

Webster University, School of Communications, Program in Advertising and Marketing Communications, St. Louis, MO 63119-3194. Offers MA. *Program availability:* Online learning. *Expenses: Tuition:* Full-time $22,500; part-time $750 per credit hour. Tuition and fees vary according to degree level, campus/location and program.

Webster University, School of Communications, Program in Public Relations, St. Louis, MO 63119-3194. Offers MA. *Expenses: Tuition:* Full-time $22,500; part-time $750 per credit hour. Tuition and fees vary according to degree level, campus/location and program.

Western New England University, College of Arts and Sciences, Program in Communication, Springfield, MA 01119. Offers public relations (MA). *Program availability:* Part-time, evening/weekend. *Faculty:* 6 full-time (5 women). *Students:* 9 part-time (4 women); includes 2 minority (1 Asian, non-Hispanic/Latino; 1 Hispanic/Latino). Average age 32. 7 applicants, 100% accepted, 6 enrolled. In 2018, 6 master's awarded. *Degree requirements:* For master's, independent study or thesis. *Entrance requirements:* For master's, official transcript, personal statement, resume, three letters of recommendation. Additional exam requirements/recommendations for international students: Required—TOEFL (minimum score 79 iBT). *Application deadline:* Applications are processed on a rolling basis. Application fee: $30. Electronic applications accepted. *Expenses:* Contact institution. *Financial support:* Application deadline: 4/15; applicants required to submit FAFSA. *Unit head:* Dr. Saeed Ghahramani, Dean, 413-782-1218, Fax: 413-796-2118, E-mail: sghahram@wne.edu. *Application contact:* Matthew Fox, Executive Director of Graduate Admissions, Admissions, 413-782-1410, Fax: 413-782-1777, E-mail: study@wne.edu.
Website: http://www1.wne.edu/academics/graduate/ma-communication.cfm

William Woods University, Graduate and Adult Studies, Fulton, MO 65251-1098. Offers administration (M Ed, Ed S); athletic/activities administration (M Ed); curriculum and instruction (M Ed, Ed S); educational leadership (Ed D); equestrian education (M Ed); health management (MBA); human resources (MBA); leadership (MBA); marketing, advertising, and public relations (MBA); teaching and technology (M Ed). *Program availability:* Part-time, evening/weekend. *Degree requirements:* For master's, capstone course (MBA), action research (M Ed); for Ed S, field experience. *Entrance requirements:* Additional exam requirements/recommendations for international students: Required—TOEFL (minimum score 550 paper-based). Electronic applications accepted. *Expenses:* Contact institution.

Section 4
Electronic Commerce

This section contains a directory of institutions offering graduate work in electronic commerce. Additional information about programs listed in the directory but not augmented by an in-depth entry may be obtained by writing directly to the dean of a graduate school or chair of a department at the address given in the directory.

CONTENTS

Program Directory

Electronic Commerce

California State University, Fullerton, Graduate Studies, College of Business and Economics, Department of Information Systems and Decision Sciences, Fullerton, CA 92831-3599. Offers decision science (MBA); information systems (MBA, MS); information systems and decision sciences (MS); information systems and e-commerce (MS); information technology (MS). *Program availability:* Part-time. *Entrance requirements:* For master's, GMAT, minimum AACSB index of 950.

Claremont Graduate University, Graduate Programs, Center for Information Systems and Technology, Claremont, CA 91711-6160. Offers cybersecurity and networking (MS); data science and analytics (MS); electronic commerce (PhD); geographic information systems (MS); health informatics (MS); information systems (Certificate); IT strategy and innovation (MS); knowledge management (PhD); systems development (PhD); telecommunications and networking (PhD); MBA/MS. *Program availability:* Part-time. *Degree requirements:* For doctorate, comprehensive exam, thesis/dissertation, portfolio. *Entrance requirements:* For master's and doctorate, GMAT, GRE General Test. Additional exam requirements/recommendations for international students: Required—TOEFL (minimum score 75 iBT). Electronic applications accepted. *Faculty research:* Man-machine interaction, organizational aspects of computing, implementation of information systems, information systems practice.

Dalhousie University, Faculty of Computer Science, Halifax, NS B3H 1W5, Canada. Offers computational biology and bioinformatics (M Sc); computer science (MA Sc, MC Sc, PhD); electronic commerce (MEC); health informatics (MHI). *Degree requirements:* For master's, thesis (for some programs); for doctorate, thesis/dissertation. *Entrance requirements:* Additional exam requirements/recommendations for international students: Required—1 of 5 approved tests: TOEFL, IELTS, CANTEST, CAEL, Michigan English Language Assessment Battery. Electronic applications accepted.

DePaul University, College of Computing and Digital Media, Chicago, IL 60604. Offers animation (MA, MFA); applied technology (MS); business information technology (MS); computational finance (MS); computer and information sciences (PhD); computer science (MS); creative producing (MFA); cybersecurity (MS); data science (MS); digital communication and media arts (MA); documentary (MFA); e-commerce technology (MS); experience design (MA); film and television (MS); film and television directing (MFA); game design (MFA); game programming (MS); health informatics (MS); human centered design (PhD); human-computer interaction (MS); information systems (MS); network engineering and security (MS); product innovation and computing (MS); screenwriting (MFA); software engineering (MS); JD/MS. *Program availability:* Part-time, evening/weekend, online learning. *Degree requirements:* For master's, thesis (for some programs); for doctorate, comprehensive exam, thesis/dissertation. *Entrance requirements:* For master's, GRE or GMAT (for MS in computational finance only), bachelor's degree, resume (MS in predictive analytics only), IT experience (MS in information technology project management only), portfolio review (all MFA programs and MA in animation); for doctorate, GRE, master's degree in computer science. Additional exam requirements/recommendations for international students: Required—TOEFL (minimum score 590 paper-based; 80 iBT), IELTS (minimum score 6.5), PTE (minimum score 53). Electronic applications accepted. *Expenses:* Contact institution. *Faculty research:* Data mining, computer science, human-computer interaction, security, animation and film.

Eastern Michigan University, Graduate School, College of Business, Department of Marketing, Ypsilanti, MI 48197. Offers e-business (MBA); integrated marketing communications (MS, Postbaccalaureate Certificate); international business (MBA); marketing management (MBA); supply chain management (MBA). *Program availability:* Part-time, evening/weekend, online learning. *Faculty:* 22 full-time (7 women). *Students:* 31 full-time (25 women), 33 part-time (22 women); includes 25 minority (15 Black or African American, non-Hispanic/Latino; 1 Asian, non-Hispanic/Latino; 9 Hispanic/Latino). Average age 30. 32 applicants, 84% accepted, 16 enrolled. In 2018, 23 master's awarded. *Entrance requirements:* For master's, GMAT. Additional exam requirements/recommendations for international students: Required—TOEFL. *Application deadline:* For fall admission, 5/15 priority date for domestic students, 2/15 priority date for international students; for winter admission, 10/15 priority date for domestic students, 9/1 priority date for international students; for summer admission, 3/15 priority date for domestic students, 3/1 priority date for international students. Applications are processed on a rolling basis. Application fee: $45. *Financial support:* Fellowships, research assistantships with full tuition reimbursements, teaching assistantships with full tuition reimbursements, career-related internships or fieldwork, Federal Work-Study, institutionally sponsored loans, scholarships/grants, tuition waivers (partial), and unspecified assistantships available. Support available to part-time students. Financial award applicants required to submit FAFSA. *Unit head:* Dr. Lewis Hershey, Department Head, 734-487-3323, Fax: 734-487-7099, E-mail: lhershe1@emich.edu. *Application contact:* K. Michelle Henry, Director, Graduate Business Programs, 734-487-4444, Fax: 734-483-1316, E-mail: cob.graduate@emich.edu.
Website: http://www.mkt.emich.edu/index.html

Eastern Michigan University, Graduate School, College of Business, Programs in Business Administration, Ypsilanti, MI 48197. Offers business administration (MBA, Graduate Certificate); computer information systems (Graduate Certificate); e-business (MBA, Graduate Certificate); enterprise business intelligence (MBA); entrepreneurship (MBA, Graduate Certificate); finance (MBA, Graduate Certificate); human resources (MBA); human resources management (Graduate Certificate); information systems (MBA); internal auditing (MBA); international business (MBA, Graduate Certificate); marketing management (Graduate Certificate); nonprofit management (MBA); organizational development (Graduate Certificate); supply chain management (MBA, Graduate Certificate). *Accreditation:* AACSB. *Program availability:* Part-time, online learning. *Students:* 69 full-time (38 women), 251 part-time (140 women); includes 100 minority (63 Black or African American, non-Hispanic/Latino; 1 American Indian or Alaska Native, non-Hispanic/Latino; 12 Asian, non-Hispanic/Latino; 14 Hispanic/Latino; 10 Two or more races, non-Hispanic/Latino), 28 international. Average age 32. 199 applicants, 75% accepted, 83 enrolled. In 2018, 75 master's, 50 other advanced degrees awarded. *Entrance requirements:* For master's, GMAT (minimum score 450), minimum cumulative undergraduate GPA of 2.75. Additional exam requirements/recommendations for international students: Required—TOEFL. *Application deadline:* For fall admission, 5/15 priority date for domestic students, 2/15 priority date for international students; for winter admission, 10/15 priority date for domestic students, 9/1 priority date for international students; for summer admission, 3/15 priority date for domestic students, 3/1 priority date for international students. Applications are processed on a rolling basis. Application fee: $45. *Financial support:* Fellowships, research assistantships with full tuition reimbursements, teaching assistantships with full tuition reimbursements, career-related internships or fieldwork, Federal Work-Study, institutionally sponsored loans, scholarships/grants, tuition waivers (partial), and unspecified assistantships available. Support available to part-time students. Financial award applicants required to submit FAFSA. *Unit head:* K. Michelle Henry, Director, Graduate Business Programs, 734-487-4444, Fax: 734-483-1316, E-mail: cob.graduate@emich.edu. *Application contact:* K. Michelle Henry, Director, Graduate Business Programs, 734-487-4444, Fax: 734-483-1316, E-mail: cob.graduate@emich.edu.
Website: http://www.emich.edu/cob/mba/

Fairleigh Dickinson University, Metropolitan Campus, University College: Arts, Sciences, and Professional Studies, School of Computer Sciences and Engineering, Program in E-Commerce, Teaneck, NJ 07666-1914. Offers MS.

Fordham University, Gabelli School of Business, New York, NY 10023. Offers accounting (MBA, MS); applied statistics and decision-making (MS); business economics (DPS); capital markets (DPS); communications and media management (MBA); electronic business (MBA); entrepreneurship (MBA); finance (MBA, PhD); global finance (MS); global sustainability (MBA); health administration (MS); healthcare management (MBA); information systems (MBA, MS); investor relations (MS); management (EMBA, MBA, MS, PhD); marketing (MBA); marketing intelligence (MS); media management (MS); nonprofit leadership (MS); quantitative finance (MS); strategy and decision-making (DPS); taxation (MS); JD/MBA; MS/MBA. *Accreditation:* AACSB. *Program availability:* Part-time, evening/weekend. Terminal master's awarded for partial completion of doctoral program. *Degree requirements:* For master's, internships (for some degrees); for doctorate, comprehensive exam (for some programs), thesis/dissertation. *Entrance requirements:* For master's, GMAT/GRE, 2 letters of recommendation, resume, 2 essays, transcripts, interview. Additional exam requirements/recommendations for international students: Required—TOEFL (minimum score 100 iBT), IELTS (minimum score 7). Electronic applications accepted. *Expenses:* Contact institution.

HEC Montreal, School of Business Administration, Graduate Diploma Programs in Administration, Program in E-Business, Montréal, QC H3T 2A7, Canada. Offers Graduate Diploma. All courses are given in French. *Students:* 23 full-time (14 women), 61 part-time (43 women). 91 applicants, 55% accepted, 36 enrolled. In 2018, 17 Graduate Diplomas awarded. *Entrance requirements:* For degree, bachelor's degree in administration or equivalent. *Application deadline:* For fall admission, 4/15 for domestic and international students; for winter admission, 9/15 for domestic and international students. Application fee: $91 Canadian dollars ($191 Canadian dollars for international students). Electronic applications accepted. *Expenses: Tuition, area resident:* Full-time $3052.80 Canadian dollars; part-time $84.80 Canadian dollars per credit. Tuition, state resident: full-time $3816 Canadian dollars; part-time $264.67 Canadian dollars per credit. Tuition, nonresident: full-time $11,910 Canadian dollars. *International tuition:* $20,905.20 Canadian dollars full-time. *Required fees:* $1805.34 Canadian dollars; $43.62 Canadian dollars per credit. $71.78 Canadian dollars per term. Tuition and fees vary according to degree level and program. *Financial support:* Research assistantships, teaching assistantships, and scholarships/grants available. Financial award application deadline: 9/2. *Unit head:* Renaud Lachance, Director, 514-340-6428, E-mail: renaud.lachance@hec.ca. *Application contact:* Anny Caron, Administrative Director, 514-340-6000, Fax: 514-340-6411, E-mail: aide@hec.ca.
Website: http://www.hec.ca/programmes/dess/dess-gestion-commerce-electronique/index.html

HEC Montreal, School of Business Administration, Master of Science Programs in Administration, Program in Electronic Commerce, Montréal, QC H3T 2A7, Canada. Offers M Sc. Program offered in French (only Supervised project Stream). *Students:* 41 full-time (26 women), 16 part-time (11 women). 43 applicants, 58% accepted, 18 enrolled. In 2018, 15 master's awarded. *Entrance requirements:* For master's, bachelor's degree in law, management, information systems or related field with minimum GPA of 3.0 out of 4.3. Additional exam requirements/recommendations for international students: Required—TAGE MAGE (minimum recommended score of 300), GMAT (minimum recommended score of 630), or GRE. *Application deadline:* For fall admission, 3/1 for domestic and international students; for winter admission, 9/15 for domestic and international students. Application fee: $91 Canadian dollars ($191 Canadian dollars for international students). Electronic applications accepted. *Expenses: Tuition, area resident:* Full-time $3052.80 Canadian dollars; part-time $84.80 Canadian dollars per credit. Tuition, state resident: full-time $3816 Canadian dollars; part-time $264.67 Canadian dollars per credit. Tuition, nonresident: full-time $11,910 Canadian dollars. *International tuition:* $20,905.20 Canadian dollars full-time. *Required fees:* $1805.34 Canadian dollars; $43.62 Canadian dollars per credit. $71.78 Canadian dollars per term. Tuition and fees vary according to degree level and program. *Financial support:* Research assistantships, teaching assistantships, and scholarships/grants available. Financial award application deadline: 9/2. *Unit head:* Dr. Sihem Taboubi, Director, 514-340-6428, E-mail: sihem.taboubi@hec.ca. *Application contact:* Marianne de Moura, Administrative Director, 514-340-6000, Fax: 514-340-6411, E-mail: aide@hec.ca.
Website: http://www.hec.ca/programmes/maitrises/maitrise-commerce-electronique/index.html

Instituto Tecnológico y de Estudios Superiores de Monterrey, Campus Central de Veracruz, Graduate Programs, Córdoba, Mexico. Offers administration (MA); administration of information technologies (MTI); computer sciences (MCC); education (MEE); educational institution administration (MAD); educational technology (MTE); electronic commerce (MCE); finance (MAF); humanistic studies (MEH); international business for Latin America (MNL); marketing (MMT); science (MCP). *Program availability:* Part-time, evening/weekend, online learning. *Degree requirements:* For master's, thesis (for some programs). *Entrance requirements:* For master's, PAEP College Board. Electronic applications accepted.

Instituto Tecnológico y de Estudios Superiores de Monterrey, Campus Ciudad Juárez, Program in Electronic Commerce, Ciudad Juárez, Mexico. Offers MEC.

Instituto Tecnológico y de Estudios Superiores de Monterrey, Campus Estado de México, Professional and Graduate Division, Estado de Mexico, Mexico. Offers administration of information technologies (MITA); architecture (M Arch); business administration (GMBA, MBA); computer sciences (MCS, PhD); education (M Ed); educational institution administration (MAD); educational technology and innovation (PhD); electronic commerce (MEC); environmental systems (MS); finance (MAF); humanistic studies (MHS); information sciences and knowledge management (MISKM); information systems (MS); manufacturing systems (MS); marketing (MEM); quality systems and productivity (MS); science and materials engineering (PhD); telecommunications management (MTM). *Program availability:* Part-time, online learning. *Degree requirements:* For master's, one foreign language, thesis (for some programs); for doctorate, one foreign language, thesis/dissertation. *Entrance*

requirements: For master's, E-PAEP 500, interview; for doctorate, E-PAEP 500, research proposal. Additional exam requirements/recommendations for international students: Required—TOEFL (minimum score 550 paper-based). *Faculty research:* Surface treatments by plasmas, mechanical properties, robotics, graphical computing, mechatronics security protocols.

Instituto Tecnológico y de Estudios Superiores de Monterrey, Campus Irapuato, Graduate Programs, Irapuato, Mexico. Offers administration (MBA); administration of information technology (MAIT); administration of telecommunications (MAT); architecture (M Arch); computer science (MCS); education (M Ed); educational administration (MEA); educational innovation and technology (DEIT); educational technology (MET); electronic commerce (MBA); environmental administration and planning (MEAP); environmental systems (MES); finances (MBA); humanistic studies (MHS); international management for Latin American executives (MIMLAE); library and information science (MLIS); manufacturing quality management (MMQM); marketing research (MBA).

Lewis University, College of Business, Program in Business Administration, Romeoville, IL 60446. Offers accounting (MBA); custom elective option (MBA); e-business (MBA); finance (MBA); healthcare management (MBA); human resources management (MBA); international business (MBA); management information systems (MBA); marketing (MBA); project management (MBA); technology and operations management (MBA). *Program availability:* Part-time, evening/weekend. *Students:* 114 full-time (72 women), 143 part-time (87 women); includes 84 minority (21 Black or African American, non-Hispanic/Latino; 2 American Indian or Alaska Native, non-Hispanic/Latino; 11 Asian, non-Hispanic/Latino; 45 Hispanic/Latino; 5 Two or more races, non-Hispanic/Latino), 17 international. Average age 31. In 2018, 99 master's awarded. *Entrance requirements:* For master's, interview, bachelor's degree, resume, two recommendations. Additional exam requirements/recommendations for international students: Required—TOEFL (minimum score 550 paper-based), IELTS. *Application deadline:* For fall admission, 8/15 priority date for domestic students, 5/1 priority date for international students; for spring admission, 11/15 priority date for international students. Applications are processed on a rolling basis. Application fee: $40. Electronic applications accepted. *Financial support:* Career-related internships or fieldwork, Federal Work-Study, scholarships/grants, and unspecified assistantships available. Financial award application deadline: 5/1; financial award applicants required to submit FAFSA. *Unit head:* Dr. Maureen Culleeney, Academic Program Director, 815-838-0500 Ext. 5631, E-mail: culleema@lewisu.edu. *Application contact:* Michele Ryan, Director of Admission, 815-838-0500 Ext. 5384, E-mail: ryanml@lewisu.edu.

Northwestern University, Medill School of Journalism, Media, and Integrated Marketing Communications, Integrated Marketing Communications Program, Evanston, IL 60208. Offers brand strategy (MSIMC); content marketing (MSIMC); direct and interactive marketing (MSIMC); marketing analytics (MSIMC); strategic communications (MSIMC). *Program availability:* Part-time. *Entrance requirements:* For master's, GRE General Test or GMAT, full-time work experience (preferred). Additional exam requirements/recommendations for international students: Required—TOEFL. Electronic applications accepted. *Faculty research:* Data mining, business to business marketing, values in advertising, political advertising.

Northwestern University, School of Professional Studies, Program in Data Science, Evanston, IL 60208. Offers computer-based data mining (MS); marketing analytics (MS); predictive modeling (MS); risk analytics (MS); Web analytics (MS). *Program availability:* Online learning. *Entrance requirements:* For master's, official transcripts, two letters of recommendation, statement of purpose, current resume or curriculum vitae. Additional exam requirements/recommendations for international students: Required—TOEFL (minimum score 600 paper-based; 100 iBT) or IELTS (minimum score 7).

Pace University, Lubin School of Business, Advanced Professional Certificate Program, New York, NY 10038. Offers business economics (APC); e-business (APC); financial management (APC); international business (APC); international economics (APC); investment management (APC); marketing (APC); public accounting (APC). *Program availability:* Part-time, evening/weekend. *Entrance requirements:* For degree, MBA or MS in business discipline, relevant professional experience. Additional exam requirements/recommendations for international students: Required—TOEFL (minimum score 90 iBT), IELTS (minimum score 7) or PTE (minimum score 61). *Application deadline:* For fall admission, 8/1 priority date for domestic students, 6/1 for international students; for spring admission, 12/1 for domestic students, 10/1 for international students. Applications are processed on a rolling basis. Application fee: $70. Electronic applications accepted. *Unit head:* Dr. Ibraiz Tarique, Chairperson, 212-618-6583, E-mail: itarique@pace.edu. *Application contact:* Susan Ford-Goldschein, Director of Graduate Admissions, 212-346-1531, Fax: 212-346-1585, E-mail: graduateadmission@pace.edu.
Website: http://www.pace.edu/lubin/agc

Stevens Institute of Technology, Graduate School, School of Business, Program in Information Systems, Hoboken, NJ 07030. Offers computer science (MS); e-commerce (MS); enterprise systems (MS); entrepreneurial information technology (MS); information architecture (MS); information management (MS, Certificate); information security (MS); information technology in financial services industry (MS); information technology in the pharmaceutical industry (MS); information technology outsourcing management (MS); project management (MS, Certificate); software engineering (MS); telecommunications (MS). *Program availability:* Part-time, evening/weekend. *Students:* 248 full-time (87 women), 54 part-time (20 women); includes 25 minority (8 Black or African American, non-Hispanic/Latino; 17 Asian, non-Hispanic/Latino), 245 international. Average age 27. In 2018, 202 master's, 16 other advanced degrees awarded. Terminal master's awarded for partial completion of doctoral program. *Degree requirements:* For master's, thesis optional, minimum B average in major field and overall; for Certificate, minimum B average. *Entrance requirements:* For master's, GRE/GMAT scores: GRE scores are required for all applicants applying to a full-time graduate program in the Schaefer School of Engineering and Science (SES). International applicants must submit TOEFL/IELTS scores and fulfill the English Language Proficiency Requirements in order to be considered. Additional exam requirements/recommendations for international students: Required—TOEFL (minimum score 74 iBT), IELTS (minimum score 6). *Application deadline:* For fall admission, 4/1 for domestic and international students; for spring admission, 11/1 for domestic and international students; for summer admission, 5/1 for domestic students. Applications are processed on a rolling basis. Application fee: $60. Electronic applications accepted. *Expenses: Tuition:* Full-time $35,960; part-time $1620 per credit. *Required fees:* $1290; $600 per semester. Tuition and fees vary according to course load. *Financial support:* Fellowships, research assistantships, teaching assistantships, career-related internships or fieldwork, Federal Work-Study, scholarships/grants, and unspecified assistantships available. Financial award application deadline: 2/15; financial award applicants required to submit FAFSA. *Unit head:* Dr. Gregory Prastacos, Dean of SB, 201-216-8366, E-mail: gprastac@stevens.edu. *Application contact:* Graduate Admissions, 888-783-8367, Fax: 888-511-1306, E-mail: graduate@stevens.edu.
Website: https://www.stevens.edu/school-business/masters-programs/information-systems

Towson University, College of Business and Economics, Program in e-Business and Technology Management, Towson, MD 21252-0001. Offers project, program and portfolio management (Postbaccalaureate Certificate); supply chain management (MS). *Entrance requirements:* For master's and Postbaccalaureate Certificate, GRE or GMAT, bachelor's degree in relevant field and/or three years of post-bachelor's experience working in supply chain related areas; minimum cumulative GPA of 3.0; resume; 2 reference letters. Additional exam requirements/recommendations for international students: Required—TOEFL (minimum score 550 paper-based). Electronic applications accepted. *Expenses: Tuition, area resident:* Full-time $9196; part-time $418 per unit. Tuition, state resident: full-time $9196; part-time $418 per unit. Tuition, nonresident: full-time $19,030; part-time $865 per unit. *International tuition:* $19,030 full-time. *Required fees:* $3102; $141 per year. $423 per term. Tuition and fees vary according to campus/location and program.

Universidad del Este, Graduate School, Carolina, PR 00984. Offers accounting (MBA); adult education (M Ed); agribusiness (MBA); criminal justice and criminology (MA); curriculum and instruction - early education (M Ed); curriculum and instruction - elementary (M Ed); curriculum and instruction - English (M Ed); curriculum and instruction - Spanish (M Ed); human resources (MBA); information security management (MBA); information technology and Web business development (MBA); management (MBA); public policy (MPA); social work (MA), including clinical social work; special education (M Ed); strategic leadership (MBA).

Université de Montréal, Faculty of Arts and Sciences, Department of Computer Science and Operational Research, Montréal, QC H3C 3J7, Canada. Offers computer systems (M Sc, PhD); electronic commerce (M Sc). *Program availability:* Part-time. Terminal master's awarded for partial completion of doctoral program. *Degree requirements:* For master's, one foreign language, thesis; for doctorate, one foreign language, thesis/dissertation, general exam. *Entrance requirements:* For master's, B Sc in related field; for doctorate, MA or M Sc in related field. Electronic applications accepted. *Faculty research:* Optimization statistics, programming languages, telecommunications, theoretical computer science, artificial intelligence.

Université de Sherbrooke, Faculty of Administration, Program in E-Commerce, Sherbrooke, QC J1K 2R1, Canada. Offers M Sc. *Degree requirements:* For master's, one foreign language, thesis. *Entrance requirements:* For master's, bachelor's degree in related field, minimum GPA of 3.0 (on 4.3 scale), letters of reference, fluency in French. Electronic applications accepted. *Faculty research:* Radio frequency identification (RFID), Web value concept.

Université Laval, Faculty of Administrative Sciences, Programs in Business Administration, Québec, QC G1K 7P4, Canada. Offers accounting (MBA); agri-food management (MBA); electronic business (MBA, Diploma); factory management and logistics (MBA); finance (MBA); firm management (MBA); geomatic management (MBA); information technology management (MBA); international management (MBA); management (MBA); management accounting (MBA, Diploma); marketing (MBA); modeling and organizational decision (MBA); occupational health and safety management (MBA); pharmacy management (MBA); social and environmental responsibility (MBA); technological entrepreneurship (Diploma). *Accreditation:* AACSB. *Program availability:* Part-time, evening/weekend, online learning. *Entrance requirements:* For master's and Diploma, knowledge of French and English. Electronic applications accepted.

University at Buffalo, the State University of New York, Graduate School, College of Arts and Sciences, Department of Economics, Buffalo, NY 14260. Offers econometrics and quantitative economics (MS); economics (MA, PhD); financial economics (Certificate); health services (Certificate); information and Internet economics (Certificate); international economics (Certificate); law and regulation (Certificate); urban and regional economics (Certificate). *Program availability:* Part-time. Terminal master's awarded for partial completion of doctoral program. *Degree requirements:* For master's, comprehensive exam; for doctorate, comprehensive exam, thesis/dissertation, field and theory exams. *Entrance requirements:* For master's, GRE General Test or GMAT; for doctorate, GRE General Test. Additional exam requirements/recommendations for international students: Required—TOEFL (minimum score 550 paper-based; 79 iBT), TWE. Electronic applications accepted. *Faculty research:* Human capital, international economics, econometrics, applied economics, urban economics, economic growth and development.

The University of Akron, Graduate School, College of Business Administration, Department of Management, Program in Global Technological Innovation, Akron, OH 44325. Offers MBA. *Entrance requirements:* For master's, GMAT, minimum GPA of 2.75, two letters of recommendation, statement of purpose, resume. Additional exam requirements/recommendations for international students: Required—TOEFL (minimum score 550 paper-based; 79 iBT). Electronic applications accepted.

University of New Brunswick Saint John, Faculty of Business, Saint John, NB E2L 4L5, Canada. Offers administration (MBA); electronic commerce (MBA); international business (MBA); natural resource management (MBA). *Program availability:* Part-time. *Entrance requirements:* For master's, GMAT (minimum score of 550) or GRE (minimum 54th percentile), minimum GPA of 3.0. Additional exam requirements/recommendations for international students: Required—TOEFL (minimum score 580 paper-based; 93 iBT), TWE (minimum score 4.5). Electronic applications accepted. *Expenses:* Contact institution. *Faculty research:* International business, project management, innovation and technology management; business use of Weblogs and podcasts to communicate; corporate governance; high-involvement work systems; international competitiveness; supply chain management and logistics.

University of North Florida, Coggin College of Business, MBA Program, Jacksonville, FL 32224. Offers accounting (MBA); construction management (MBA); e-commerce (MBA); economics (MBA); finance (MBA); human resource management (MBA); international business (MBA); logistics (MBA); management applications (MBA). *Accreditation:* AACSB. *Program availability:* Part-time, evening/weekend. *Faculty:* 40 full-time (14 women). *Students:* 368 part-time (158 women); includes 83 minority (30 Black or African American, non-Hispanic/Latino; 20 Asian, non-Hispanic/Latino; 16 Hispanic/Latino; 17 Two or more races, non-Hispanic/Latino), 28 international. Average age 30. 311 applicants, 51% accepted, 99 enrolled. In 2018, 151 master's awarded. *Entrance requirements:* For master's, GMAT or GRE, U.S. bachelor's degree from regionally-accredited university or equivalent foreign degree. Additional exam requirements/recommendations for international students: Required—TOEFL (minimum score 550 paper-based; 79 iBT). *Application deadline:* For fall admission, 8/1 priority date for domestic students, 5/1 for international students; for spring admission, 12/1 priority date for domestic students, 10/1 for international students; for summer admission, 4/29 priority date for domestic students, 2/1 for international students. Application fee: $30. *Expenses: Tuition, area resident:* Part-time $408.10 per credit hour. Tuition, state resident: part-time $408.10 per credit hour. Tuition, nonresident: part-time $932.61 per credit hour. *Required fees:* $111.81 per credit hour. Tuition and fees vary according to course load, campus/location and program. *Financial support:* In 2018–19, 41 students received support, including 1 research assistantship (averaging $2,143 per year); teaching assistantships, Federal Work-Study, and tuition waivers (partial) also available. Support available to part-time students. Financial award

Electronic Commerce

application deadline: 4/1; financial award applicants required to submit FAFSA. *Faculty research:* Performance measures, costing, and inventory issues in logistics and supply chain management; inter-organizational systems; international management and marketing practices; e-commerce; organizational learning and socialization processes. *Unit head:* Dr. Parvez Ahmed, Graduate Program Director, 904-620-1678, E-mail: pahmed@unf.edu. *Application contact:* Amy Bishop, MSM Advisor, 904-620-2575, Fax: 904-620-2832, E-mail: coggin.students@unf.edu.
Website: http://www.unf.edu/graduateschool/academics/programs/MBA.aspx

University of Ottawa, Faculty of Graduate and Postdoctoral Studies, Interdisciplinary Programs, Ottawa, ON K1N 6N5, Canada. Offers e-business (Certificate); e-commerce (Certificate); finance (Certificate); health services and policies research (Diploma); population health (PhD); population health risk assessment and management (Certificate); public management and governance (Certificate); systems science (Certificate).

University of Ottawa, Faculty of Graduate and Postdoctoral Studies, Program in E-Business Technologies, Ottawa, ON K1N 6N5, Canada. Offers M Sc, MEBT. *Degree requirements:* For master's, thesis or alternative, project. *Entrance requirements:* For master's, honours degree or equivalent, minimum B average.

University of Phoenix–Dallas Campus, College of Information Systems and Technology, Dallas, TX 75251. Offers e-business (MBA); information systems (MIS); technology management (MBA). *Program availability:* Evening/weekend. *Degree requirements:* For master's, thesis (for some programs). *Entrance requirements:* For master's, minimum undergraduate GPA of 3.0, 3 years of work experience. Additional exam requirements/recommendations for international students: Required—TOEFL (minimum score 550 paper-based; 79 iBT). Electronic applications accepted.

University of Phoenix–Houston Campus, College of Information Systems and Technology, Houston, TX 77079-2004. Offers e-business (MBA); information systems (MIS); technology management (MBA). *Program availability:* Evening/weekend, online learning. *Degree requirements:* For master's, comprehensive exam (for some programs), thesis. *Entrance requirements:* For master's, minimum undergraduate GPA of 3.0, 3 years of work experience. Additional exam requirements/recommendations for international students: Required—TOEFL (minimum score 550 paper-based; 79 iBT). Electronic applications accepted.

University of Phoenix–San Antonio Campus, School of Business, San Antonio, TX 78230. Offers accounting (MBA); business administration (MBA); e-business (MBA); global management (MBA); human resources management (MBA, MM); management (MM); marketing (MBA); public administration (MBA, MM). *Accreditation:* ACBSP.

Section 5
Entrepreneurship

This section contains a directory of institutions offering graduate work in entrepreneurship. Additional information about programs listed in the directory but not augmented by an in-depth entry may be obtained by writing directly to the dean of a graduate school or chair of a department at the address given in the directory.

For programs offering related work, see also in this book *Business Administration and Management, International Business,* and *Education (Business Education)*

CONTENTS

Program Directory

Entrepreneurship

Albizu University, Miami Campus, Graduate Programs, Miami, FL 33172-2209. Offers clinical psychology (PhD, Psy D); entrepreneurship (MBA); exceptional student education (MS); human services (PhD); industrial/organizational psychology (MS); marriage and family therapy (MS); mental health counseling (MS); nonprofit management (MBA); organizational management (MBA); school counseling (MS); speech and language pathology (MS); teaching English for speakers of other languages (MS). *Accreditation:* APA. *Program availability:* Part-time, evening/weekend, 100% online, blended/hybrid learning. *Faculty:* 32 full-time (24 women), 27 part-time/adjunct (15 women). *Students:* 479 full-time (410 women), 146 part-time (126 women); includes 539 minority (42 Black or African American, non-Hispanic/Latino; 2 Asian, non-Hispanic/Latino; 490 Hispanic/Latino; 5 Two or more races, non-Hispanic/Latino), 22 international. Average age 33. 314 applicants, 45% accepted, 92 enrolled. In 2018, 101 master's, 64 doctorates awarded. Terminal master's awarded for partial completion of doctoral program. *Degree requirements:* For master's, comprehensive exam (for some programs), integrative project (for MBA); research project (for exceptional student education, teaching English as a second language); for doctorate, comprehensive exam, thesis/dissertation, comprehensive examinations, internship, project/dissertation. *Entrance requirements:* For master's, GRE/EXADEP, bachelor's degree from accredited institution, minimum GPA of 3.0, 3 letters of recommendation, interview, resume, statement of purpose, official transcripts; for doctorate, GRE (for Psy D), 3 letters of recommendation, resume, interview, statement of purpose, official transcripts; bachelor's degree and minimum GPA of 3.25 (for Psy D); master's degree and minimum GPA of 3.0 (for PhD). Additional exam requirements/recommendations for international students: Required—Michigan Test of English Language Proficiency. *Application deadline:* For fall admission, 4/1 priority date for domestic students, 5/1 priority date for international students; for spring admission, 11/1 priority date for domestic students, 9/1 priority date for international students. Applications are processed on a rolling basis. Application fee: $50. Electronic applications accepted. Application fee is waived when completed online. *Expenses:* Contact institution. *Financial support:* In 2018–19, 141 students received support. Federal Work-Study, scholarships/grants, unspecified assistantships, and tuition discounts available. Financial award application deadline: 6/1; financial award applicants required to submit FAFSA. *Faculty research:* Psychotherapy, forensic psychology, neuropsychology, special education, speech-language pathology, criminal justice, human services. *Unit head:* Dr. Jose Pons-Madera, PhD, President, 305-593-1223 Ext. 3120, Fax: 305-477-8983, E-mail: jpons@albizu.edu. *Application contact:* Nancy Alvarez, Director of Enrollment Management, 305-593-1223 Ext. 3136, Fax: 305-593-1854, E-mail: nalvarez@albizu.edu.

American College of Thessaloniki, Department of Business Administration, Pylea, Greece. Offers banking and finance (MBA); entrepreneurship (MBA, Certificate); finance (Certificate); management (MBA, Certificate); marketing (MBA, Certificate). *Program availability:* Part-time, evening/weekend. *Degree requirements:* For master's, thesis. *Entrance requirements:* For master's, bachelor's degree. Additional exam requirements/recommendations for international students: Recommended—TOEFL. Electronic applications accepted.

American University, School of International Service, Washington, DC 20016-8071. Offers comparative and regional studies (Certificate); cross-cultural communication (Certificate); development management (MS); ethics, peace, and global affairs (MA); European studies (Certificate); global environmental policy (MA, Certificate); global information technology (Certificate); global media (MA); international affairs (MA), including comparative and regional studies, global governance, politics, and security, international economic relations, natural resources and sustainable development, U.S. foreign policy and national security; international arts management (Certificate); international communication (MA, Certificate); international development (MA); international economic policy (Certificate); international economic relations (Certificate); international economics (MA); international peace and conflict resolution (MA, Certificate); international politics (Certificate); international relations (MA, PhD); international service (MIS); peacebuilding (Certificate); social enterprise (MA); the Americas (Certificate); United States foreign policy (Certificate); JD/MA. *Program availability:* Part-time, evening/weekend, 100% online, blended/hybrid learning. *Faculty:* 115 full-time (48 women), 50 part-time/adjunct (22 women). *Students:* 496 full-time (320 women), 477 part-time (242 women); includes 410 minority (83 Black or African American, non-Hispanic/Latino; 2 American Indian or Alaska Native, non-Hispanic/Latino; 51 Asian, non-Hispanic/Latino; 242 Hispanic/Latino; 32 Two or more races, non-Hispanic/Latino), 93 international. Average age 30. 1,280 applicants, 82% accepted, 356 enrolled. In 2018, 400 master's, 3 doctorates, 8 other advanced degrees awarded. Terminal master's awarded for partial completion of doctoral program. *Degree requirements:* For master's, one foreign language, comprehensive exam, thesis or alternative; for doctorate, one foreign language, comprehensive exam, thesis/dissertation. *Entrance requirements:* For master's, Please visit the website for details: https://www.american.edu/sis/admissions/, transcripts, resume, 2 letters of recommendation, statement of purpose; for doctorate, GRE, transcripts, resume, 3 letters of recommendation, statement of purpose. Additional exam requirements/recommendations for international students: Required—TOEFL. Application fee: $55. Electronic applications accepted. *Expenses:* Contact institution. *Financial support:* Research assistantships, teaching assistantships, institutionally sponsored loans, scholarships/grants, and unspecified assistantships available. Financial award applicants required to submit FAFSA. *Unit head:* Christine BN Chin, 202-885-1600, E-mail: sisgrad@american.edu. *Application contact:* Jia Jiang, Director, Graduate Enrollment Management, 202-885-1689, E-mail: jiang@american.edu. Website: http://www.american.edu/sis/

Anaheim University, Programs in Business Administration, Anaheim, CA 92806-5150. Offers entrepreneurship (ME, DBA); global sustainable management (MBA); international business (MBA, DBA, Certificate, Diploma); management (DBA); sustainable management (DBA, Certificate, Diploma). *Program availability:* Part-time, evening/weekend, online only, 100% online. In 2018, 3 master's, 4 doctorates awarded. *Application deadline:* Applications are processed on a rolling basis. Electronic applications accepted. *Unit head:* Dr. Robert Robertson, Dean, Graduate School of Business, 714-772-3330, Fax: 714-772-3331, E-mail: admissions@anaheim.edu. *Application contact:* Dr. Robert Robertson, Dean, Graduate School of Business, 714-772-3330, Fax: 714-772-3331, E-mail: admissions@anaheim.edu.

Arizona State University at the Tempe campus, W. P. Carey School of Business, Program in Business Administration, Tempe, AZ 85287-4906. Offers entrepreneurship (MBA); finance (MBA); health sector management (MBA); international business (MBA); leadership (MBA); marketing (MBA); organizational behavior (PhD); strategic management (PhD); supply chain management (MBA, PhD); JD/MBA; MBA/M Acc; MBA/M Arch. *Accreditation:* AACSB. *Program availability:* Part-time, evening/weekend, online learning. Terminal master's awarded for partial completion of doctoral program. *Degree requirements:* For master's, thesis or alternative, internship, interactive Program

of Study (iPOS) submitted before completing 50 percent of required credit hours; for doctorate, comprehensive exam, thesis/dissertation, interactive Program of Study (iPOS) submitted before completing 50 percent of required credit hours. *Entrance requirements:* For master's, GMAT, minimum GPA of 3.0 in last 2 years of work leading to bachelor's degree, 2 letters of recommendation, professional resume, official transcripts, 3 essays; for doctorate, GMAT or GRE, minimum GPA of 3.0 in last 2 years of work leading to bachelor's degree, 3 letters of recommendation, resume, personal statement/essay. Additional exam requirements/recommendations for international students: Required—TOEFL (minimum score 550 paper-based; 80 iBT), IELTS (minimum score 6.5). Electronic applications accepted. *Expenses:* Contact institution.

Ashland University, Dauch College of Business and Economics, Ashland, OH 44805-3702. Offers accounting (MBA); business analytics (MBA); entrepreneurship (MBA); financial management (MBA); global management (MBA); health care management and leadership (MBA); human resource management (MBA); human resources (MBA); management information systems (MBA); project management (MBA); sport management (MBA); supply chain management (MBA). *Accreditation:* ACBSP. *Program availability:* Part-time, evening/weekend, 100% online, blended/hybrid learning. Terminal master's awarded for partial completion of doctoral program. *Degree requirements:* For master's, thesis optional, capstone course. *Entrance requirements:* For master's, 2 years of full-time work experience. Additional exam requirements/recommendations for international students: Required—TOEFL (minimum score 550 paper-based; 78 iBT). Electronic applications accepted. *Expenses:* Contact institution. *Faculty research:* Relationship marketing strategy, executive compensation and company performance, online marketplaces in electronic commerce, diversity training in campus recreation departments, entrepreneurship in developing and emerging economies.

Azusa Pacific University, School of Business and Management, Azusa, CA 91702-7000. Offers accounting (MBA); business administration (MBA); entrepreneurship (MBA); finance (MBA); international business (MBA); marketing (MBA); organizational science (MBA); professional accountancy (M Acc); sport management (MBA). *Program availability:* Part-time, evening/weekend. *Degree requirements:* For master's, thesis (for some programs), final project. *Entrance requirements:* For master's, GMAT, minimum GPA of 3.0. Additional exam requirements/recommendations for international students: Required—TOEFL (minimum score 600 paper-based). *Expenses:* Contact institution. *Faculty research:* Gender issues, financial risk, leadership and ethics, marketing strategy.

Babson College, F. W. Olin Graduate School of Business, Babson Park, MA 02457-0310. Offers accounting (MSA); advanced management (Certificate); business administration (MBA); business analytics (MS); finance (MS); global entrepreneurship (MS); technological entrepreneurship (MS). *Accreditation:* AACSB. *Program availability:* Part-time, evening/weekend, online learning. *Entrance requirements:* For master's, GMAT, 2 years of work experience, resume, letters of recommendation. Additional exam requirements/recommendations for international students: Required—TOEFL (minimum score 100 iBT), IELTS (minimum score 6.5). Electronic applications accepted. *Faculty research:* Entrepreneurship, sustainability, global markets, process of innovation, social media and advertising.

Bakke Graduate University, Programs in Pastoral Ministry and Business, Dallas, TX 75243-7039. Offers business administration (MBA); church and ministry multiplication (D Min); global urban leadership (MA); leadership (D Min); ministry in complex contexts (D Min); social and civic entrepreneurship (MA); theology of work (D Min); theology reflection (D Min); transformational leadership (DTL); urban youth ministry (D Min). *Program availability:* Part-time, online learning. *Degree requirements:* For master's, thesis; for doctorate, thesis/dissertation. *Entrance requirements:* For master's, 2 years of ministry experience, BA in Biblical studies or theology; for doctorate, 3 years of ministry experience, M Div. Additional exam requirements/recommendations for international students: Required—TOEFL. Electronic applications accepted. *Faculty research:* Theological systems, church management, worship.

Baruch College of the City University of New York, Zicklin School of Business, Department of Management, New York, NY 10010-5585. Offers entrepreneurship (MBA); management (PhD); operations management (MBA); organizational behavior/human resources management (MBA); sustainable business (MBA). PhD offered jointly with Graduate School and University Center of the City University of New York. *Program availability:* Part-time, evening/weekend. *Degree requirements:* For doctorate, comprehensive exam, thesis/dissertation. *Entrance requirements:* For master's, GMAT, 2 letters of recommendation, resume, 2 years of work experience; for doctorate, GMAT. Additional exam requirements/recommendations for international students: Required—TOEFL (minimum score 590 paper-based), TWE.

Baruch College of the City University of New York, Zicklin School of Business, International Executive MS Programs, New York, NY 10010-5585. Offers entrepreneurship (MS). *Program availability:* Part-time, evening/weekend. *Entrance requirements:* For master's, GMAT, 2 letters of recommendation, resume, 2 years of work experience. Additional exam requirements/recommendations for international students: Required—TOEFL (minimum score 590 paper-based), TWE (minimum score 5).

Baylor University, Graduate School, Hankamer School of Business, Department of Entrepreneurship, Waco, TX 76798. Offers PhD. *Students:* 6 full-time (2 women), 3 international. *Entrance requirements:* For doctorate, GMAT or GRE. *Unit head:* Kendall Artz, Chairman, E-mail: kendall_artz@baylor.edu. *Application contact:* Laurie Wilson, Director, Graduate Business Programs, 254-710-4163, Fax: 254-710-1066, E-mail: laurie_wilson@baylor.edu. Website: http://www.baylor.edu/business/entrepreneurship/

Bay Path University, Program in Entrepreneurial Thinking and Innovative Practices, Longmeadow, MA 01106-2292. Offers MBA. *Program availability:* Part-time, 100% online. *Students:* 21 full-time (17 women), 51 part-time (43 women); includes 31 minority (17 Black or African American, non-Hispanic/Latino; 2 Asian, non-Hispanic/Latino; 11 Hispanic/Latino; 1 Two or more races, non-Hispanic/Latino). Average age 34. *Entrance requirements:* For master's, completed application; official undergraduate and graduate transcripts (a GPA of 3.0 or higher is preferred); original essay of at least 250 words on the topic: "Why the MBA in Entrepreneurial Thinking & Innovative Practices is important to my personal and professional goals"; current resume; 2 recommendations. *Application deadline:* Applications are processed on a rolling basis. Electronic applications accepted. Application fee is waived when completed online. *Expenses:* Contact institution. *Financial support:* Unspecified assistantships available. Financial award applicants required to submit FAFSA. *Unit head:* Mo Sattar, Program Director, 413-5651228, E-mail: msattar@baypath.edu. *Application contact:* Sheryl Kosakowski, Executive Director of Graduate Admissions, 413-565-1075, Fax: 413-565-1250, E-mail: skosakowski@baypath.edu. Website: https://www.baypath.edu/academics/graduate-programs/entrepreneurial-thinking-innovative-practices-mba/

Benedictine University, Graduate Programs, Program in Business Administration, Lisle, IL 60532. Offers accounting (MBA); entrepreneurship and managing innovation (MBA); financial management (MBA); health administration (MBA); human resource management (MBA); information systems security (MBA); international business (MBA); management consulting (MBA); management information systems (MBA); marketing management (MBA); operations management and logistics (MBA); organizational leadership (MBA). *Program availability:* Part-time, evening/weekend, 100% online, blended/hybrid learning. *Faculty:* 7 full-time (1 woman), 36 part-time/adjunct (10 women). *Students:* 110 full-time (71 women), 500 part-time (302 women); includes 104 minority (34 Black or African American, non-Hispanic/Latino; 1 American Indian or Alaska Native, non-Hispanic/Latino; 41 Asian, non-Hispanic/Latino; 23 Hispanic/Latino; 5 Native Hawaiian or other Pacific Islander, non-Hispanic/Latino), 7 international. Average age 33. 251 applicants, 84% accepted, 202 enrolled. In 2018, 345 master's awarded. *Entrance requirements:* For master's, GMAT or GRE test scores or completed test waiver form, official transcripts; 2 letters of reference from individuals familiar with the applicant's professional or academic work, excluding family or personal friends; a 1-2 page essay addressing educational and career goals; current résumé listing chronological work history; personal interview may be required prior to an admission decision. Additional exam requirements/recommendations for international students: Required—TOEFL (minimum score 550 paper-based; 79 iBT), IELTS (minimum score 6.5). *Application deadline:* Applications are processed on a rolling basis. Application fee: $40. Electronic applications accepted. *Unit head:* Ricky Holman, Assistant Professor, 630-829-1936, E-mail: rholman@ben.edu. *Application contact:* Ricky Holman, Assistant Professor, 630-829-1936, E-mail: rholman@ben.edu.

Brandeis University, Rabb School of Continuing Studies, Division of Graduate Professional Studies, Master of Science in Digital Innovation for Finance Technology Program, Waltham, MA 02454-9110. Offers MS. *Program availability:* Part-time-only. *Entrance requirements:* For master's, undergraduate coursework in general finance or economics and at least some basic experience with a programming language; four-year bachelor's degree from regionally-accredited U.S. institution or equivalent; official transcript(s) from every college or university attended; resume or curriculum vitae; statement of goals; letter of recommendation. Additional exam requirements/recommendations for international students: Required—TWE (minimum score 4.5), TOEFL (minimum scores: 600 paper-based, 100 iBT), IELTS (7), or PTE (68). Electronic applications accepted. *Expenses:* Contact institution.

Brandman University, School of Business and Professional Studies, Irvine, CA 92618. Offers accounting (MBA); business administration (MBA); business intelligence and data analytics (MBA); e-business strategic management (MBA); entrepreneurship (MBA); finance (MBA); health administration (MBA); human resources (MBA, MS); international business (MBA); marketing (MBA); organizational leadership (MA, MBA, MPA); public administration (MPA).

Brigham Young University, Graduate Studies, BYU Marriott School of Business, MBA Program, Provo, UT 84602. Offers entrepreneurship (MBA); finance (MBA); global supply chain management (MBA); marketing (MBA); strategic human resources (MBA); JD/MBA; MBA/MS. *Accreditation:* AACSB. *Entrance requirements:* For master's, GMAT or GRE, commitment to BYU Honor Code, undergraduate degree. Additional exam requirements/recommendations for international students: Required—TOEFL (minimum score 590 paper-based; 100 iBT), IELTS (minimum score 7). Electronic applications accepted. *Expenses:* Contact institution. *Faculty research:* Finance, marketing, supply chain management, entrepreneurship, strategic human resources.

Cairn University, School of Business, Langhorne, PA 19047-2990. Offers accounting (MBA); business administration (MBA); international entrepreneurship (MBA); nonprofit leadership (MBA); organizational leadership (MSOL, Postbaccalaureate Certificate). *Program availability:* Part-time, evening/weekend, 100% online, blended/hybrid learning. *Entrance requirements:* Additional exam requirements/recommendations for international students: Required—TOEFL (minimum score 550 paper-based). Electronic applications accepted. Application fee is waived when completed online. *Expenses:* Contact institution.

California Institute of Advanced Management, The MBA Program, El Monte, CA 91731. Offers executive management and entrepreneurship (MBA).

California Intercontinental University, School of Business, Irvine, CA 92614. Offers banking and finance (MBA); entrepreneurship and business management (DBA); global business leadership (DBA); international management and marketing (MBA); organizational management and human resource management (MBA).

California Lutheran University, Graduate Studies, School of Management, Thousand Oaks, CA 91360-2787. Offers business (IMBA); entrepreneurship (MBA, Certificate); finance (MBA, Certificate); financial planning (MBA, MS, Certificate); human capital management (MBA, Certificate); information technology (MS); information technology management (MBA, Certificate); international business (MBA, Certificate); management (MS); marketing (MBA, Certificate); public policy and administration (MPPA); quantitative economics (MS). *Program availability:* Part-time, evening/weekend, 100% online, blended/hybrid learning. *Degree requirements:* For master's, comprehensive exam (for some programs). *Entrance requirements:* For master's, GMAT, interview, minimum GPA of 3.0. Electronic applications accepted. *Expenses:* Contact institution.

California State University, San Bernardino, Graduate Studies, College of Business and Public Administration, Program in Business Administration, San Bernardino, CA 92407. Offers accounting (MBA); entrepreneurship (MBA); finance (MBA); global business (MBA); information management (MBA); information security (MBA); management (MBA); supply chain management (MBA). *Accreditation:* AACSB. *Program availability:* Part-time, evening/weekend, online learning. *Faculty:* 5 full-time (4 women), 7 part-time/adjunct (3 women). *Students:* 40 full-time (14 women), 163 part-time (72 women); includes 99 minority (7 Black or African American, non-Hispanic/Latino; 15 Asian, non-Hispanic/Latino; 71 Hispanic/Latino; 6 Two or more races, non-Hispanic/Latino), 58 international. Average age 32. 342 applicants, 52% accepted, 91 enrolled. In 2018, 106 master's awarded. *Degree requirements:* For master's, comprehensive exam, thesis. *Entrance requirements:* Additional exam requirements/recommendations for international students: Required—TOEFL. *Application deadline:* For fall admission, 7/16 for domestic students, 7/20 for international students; for winter admission, 10/23 for domestic students, 10/20 for international students; for spring admission, 1/22 for domestic students, 1/20 for international students. Application fee: $55. *Expenses:* Contact institution. *Financial support:* Application deadline: 3/1. *Unit head:* Dr. Lawrence C. Rose, Dean, 909-537-3703, Fax: 909-537-7026, E-mail: lrose@csusb.edu. *Application contact:* Ernest Silvers, MBA Program Director, 909-537-5703, E-mail: esilvers@csusb.edu.
Website: http://mba.csusb.edu/

California University of Pennsylvania, School of Graduate Studies and Research, Eberly College of Science and Technology, Program in Business Administration, California, PA 15419-1394. Offers business analytics (MBA); entrepreneurship (MBA); healthcare management (MBA). *Program availability:* Part-time, evening/weekend. *Degree requirements:* For master's, comprehensive exam. *Entrance requirements:* For master's, minimum GPA of 3.0, official transcripts. Additional exam requirements/recommendations for international students: Required—TOEFL (minimum score 550 paper-based). Electronic applications accepted. *Faculty research:* Economics, applied economics, consumer behavior, technology and business, impact of technology.

Cambridge College, School of Management, Boston, MA 02129. Offers business administration (MBA); business negotiation and conflict resolution (M Mgt); general business (M Mgt); health care (MBA); health care management (M Mgt); small business development (M Mgt); technology management (M Mgt). *Program availability:* Part-time, evening/weekend, 100% online, blended/hybrid learning. *Degree requirements:* For master's, thesis, seminars. *Entrance requirements:* For master's, resume, 2 professional references. Additional exam requirements/recommendations for international students: Required—TOEFL (minimum score 550 paper-based; 79 iBT), Michigan English Language Assessment Battery (minimum score 85); Recommended—IELTS (minimum score 6). *Application deadline:* Applications are processed on a rolling basis. Application fee: $50 ($100 for international students). Electronic applications accepted. *Expenses:* Contact institution. *Financial support:* Career-related internships or fieldwork, Federal Work-Study, and scholarships/grants available. Financial award applicants required to submit FAFSA. *Faculty research:* Negotiation, mediation and conflict resolution; leadership; management of diverse organizations; case studies and simulation methodologies for management education, digital as a second language: social networking for digital immigrants, non-profit and public management. *Unit head:* Joseph Miglio, Interim Dean, E-mail: joseph.miglio@cambridgecollege.edu. *Application contact:* Salvadore Liberto, Interim Assistant Vice President of Enrollment, 800-877-4723, E-mail: admissions@cambridgecollege.edu.
Website: https://www.cambridgecollege.edu/school/school-management

Cameron University, Office of Graduate Studies, Program in Entrepreneurial Studies, Lawton, OK 73505-6377. Offers MS. *Program availability:* Part-time, evening/weekend, online learning. *Degree requirements:* For master's, comprehensive exam. *Entrance requirements:* Additional exam requirements/recommendations for international students: Required—TOEFL (minimum score 550 paper-based). Electronic applications accepted. *Faculty research:* Entrepreneurial competition, new venture creation, legal issues, electronic commerce.

Capella University, School of Business and Technology, Doctoral Programs in Business, Minneapolis, MN 55402. Offers accounting (DBA, PhD); business intelligence (DBA); finance (DBA, PhD); general business management (PhD); human resource management (DBA, PhD); leadership (DBA, PhD); management education (PhD); marketing (DBA, PhD); project management (DBA, PhD); strategy and innovation (DBA, PhD). *Accreditation:* ACBSP.

Capella University, School of Business and Technology, Master's Programs in Business, Minneapolis, MN 55402. Offers accounting (MBA); business analysis (MS); business intelligence (MBA); entrepreneurship (MBA); finance (MBA); general business administration (MBA); general human resource management (MS); general leadership (MS); health care management (MBA); human resource management (MBA); marketing (MBA); project management (MBA, MS). *Accreditation:* ACBSP.

Carnegie Mellon University, Dietrich College of Humanities and Social Sciences, Department of Social and Decision Sciences, Pittsburgh, PA 15213-3891. Offers behavioral decision research (PhD); social and decision science (PhD); strategy, entrepreneurship, and technological change (PhD). Terminal master's awarded for partial completion of doctoral program. *Degree requirements:* For doctorate, comprehensive exam, thesis/dissertation, research paper. *Entrance requirements:* For doctorate, GRE General Test. Additional exam requirements/recommendations for international students: Required—TOEFL. Electronic applications accepted. *Faculty research:* Organization theory, political science, sociology, technology studies.

City Vision University, Program in Technology and Ministry, Kansas City, MO 64109-1845. Offers MS. *Program availability:* Online learning. *Degree requirements:* For master's, capstone project.

Clarion University of Pennsylvania, College of Business Administration and Information Sciences, Master of Business Administration Program, Clarion, PA 16214. Offers accounting (MBA); finance (MBA); health care administration (MBA); innovation and entrepreneurship (MBA); non-profit business (MBA). *Accreditation:* AACSB. *Program availability:* Part-time, evening/weekend, online only, 100% online. *Faculty:* 7 full-time (0 women), 1 part-time/adjunct (0 women). *Students:* 21 full-time (7 women), 67 part-time (34 women); includes 11 minority (5 Black or African American, non-Hispanic/Latino; 5 Hispanic/Latino; 1 Two or more races, non-Hispanic/Latino), 2 international. Average age 31. 90 applicants, 51% accepted, 38 enrolled. In 2018, 39 master's awarded. *Entrance requirements:* For master's, If GPA is below 3.0 submit the GMAT, minimum QPA of 2.75. Additional exam requirements/recommendations for international students: Required—TOEFL (minimum score 550 paper-based; 80 iBT), Or IELTS score of at least 7.0. Bachelor's degree accredited U.S. college or university is acceptable evidence of English language proficiency. *Application deadline:* For fall admission, 8/1 priority date for domestic students, 7/15 priority date for international students; for winter admission, 11/1 priority date for domestic students; for spring admission, 12/1 priority date for domestic students, 11/15 priority date for international students; for summer admission, 4/1 priority date for domestic students. Applications are processed on a rolling basis. Application fee: $40. Electronic applications accepted. *Expenses: Tuition, area resident:* Part-time $516 per credit hour. Tuition, state resident: part-time $516 per credit hour. Tuition, nonresident: part-time $774 per credit hour. *Required fees:* $159 per credit hour. One-time fee: $50 part-time. Tuition and fees vary according to degree level, campus/location and program. *Financial support:* Federal Work-Study, institutionally sponsored loans, and scholarships/grants available. Financial award application deadline: 3/1; financial award applicants required to submit FAFSA. *Unit head:* Juanice Vega, Assistant to the Dean, 814-393-2600, Fax: 814-393-1910, E-mail: mba@clarion.edu. *Application contact:* Susan Staub, Graduate Admissions Counselor, 814-393-2337, Fax: 814-393-2722, E-mail: gradstudies@clarion.edu.
Website: http://www.clarion.edu/admissions/graduate/index.html

Clemson University, Graduate School, College of Business, Department of Management, Clemson, SC 29634. Offers business administration (PhD), including management information systems, strategy, entrepreneurship and organizational behavior, supply chain and operations management; management (MS). *Accreditation:* AACSB. *Faculty:* 26 full-time (9 women). *Students:* 14 full-time (5 women), 4 part-time (2 women); includes 1 minority (Asian, non-Hispanic/Latino), 10 international. Average age 30. 53 applicants, 36% accepted, 8 enrolled. In 2018, 2 master's, 4 doctorates awarded. Terminal master's awarded for partial completion of doctoral program. *Degree requirements:* For master's, comprehensive exam, thesis optional; for doctorate, comprehensive exam, thesis/dissertation. *Entrance requirements:* For master's and doctorate, GMAT or GRE General Test, unofficial transcripts, two letters of reference, curriculum vitae. Additional exam requirements/recommendations for international students: Required—TOEFL (minimum score 80 paper-based; 94 iBT); Recommended—IELTS (minimum score 7), TSE (minimum score 64). *Application deadline:* For fall admission, 4/15 priority date for international students; for spring admission, 10/15 priority date for international students. Applications are processed on a rolling basis. Application fee: $80 ($90 for international students). Electronic applications accepted. *Expenses:* $6823 per semester full-time resident, $14023 per semester full-time non-resident, $833 per credit hour part-time resident, $1731 per credit hour part-

time non-resident, online $1264 per credit hour, $4938 doctoral programs resident, $10405 doctoral programs non-resident, $1144 full-time graduate assistant, other fees may apply per session. *Financial support:* In 2018–19, 10 students received support, including 1 fellowship with full and partial tuition reimbursement available (averaging $1,500 per year), 6 research assistantships with full and partial tuition reimbursements available (averaging $25,000 per year), 17 teaching assistantships with full and partial tuition reimbursements available (averaging $25,000 per year); career-related internships or fieldwork and unspecified assistantships also available. *Faculty research:* Effective use of information technology in business, manufacturing and service operations strategy, lean operations and quality management, healthcare operations, behavioral market design. *Total annual research expenditures:* $131,333. *Unit head:* Dr. Craig Wallace, Department Chair, 864-656-9963, E-mail: CW74@clemson.edu. *Application contact:* Dr. Janis Miller, Graduate Program Coordinator, 864-656-3757, E-mail: janism@clemson.edu.
Website: https://www.clemson.edu/business/departments/management/

Clemson University, Graduate School, College of Business, Master of Business Administration Program, Greenville, SC 29601. Offers business administration (MBA); business analytics (MBA); entrepreneurship and innovation (MBA). *Accreditation:* AACSB. *Program availability:* Part-time, evening/weekend, 100% online. *Faculty:* 2 full-time (1 woman), 10 part-time/adjunct (1 woman). *Students:* 113 full-time (55 women), 406 part-time (135 women); includes 88 minority (42 Black or African American, non-Hispanic/Latino; 2 American Indian or Alaska Native, non-Hispanic/Latino; 12 Asian, non-Hispanic/Latino; 22 Hispanic/Latino; 1 Native Hawaiian or other Pacific Islander, non-Hispanic/Latino; 9 Two or more races, non-Hispanic/Latino), 13 international. Average age 31. 404 applicants, 91% accepted, 261 enrolled. In 2018, 209 master's awarded. *Entrance requirements:* For master's, GMAT, resume, unofficial transcripts, personal statement, letters of recommendation. Additional exam requirements/recommendations for international students: Required—TOEFL (minimum score 80 paper-based; 80 iBT); Recommended—IELTS (minimum score 6.5), TSE (minimum score 54). *Application deadline:* For fall admission, 4/15 for international students; for spring admission, 10/15 for international students. Applications are processed on a rolling basis. Application fee: $80 ($90 for international students). Electronic applications accepted. *Expenses:* $9901 per semester full-time resident, $16051 per semester full-time non-resident, $1031 per credit hour part-time resident, $1283 per credit hour part-time non-resident, Concentration in Entrepreneurship & Innovation: $11694 full time all students. *Unit head:* Dr. Greg Pickett, Director and Associate Dean, 864-656-3975, E-mail: pgregor@clemson.edu. *Application contact:* Jane Layton, Academic Program Director, 864-656-8175, E-mail: elayton@clemson.edu.
Website: https://www.clemson.edu/business/departments/mba/

Cogswell Polytechnical College, Program in Entrepreneurship and Innovation, San Jose, CA 95134. Offers MA.

Columbia University, Graduate School of Business, MBA Program, New York, NY 10027. Offers accounting (MBA); decision, risk, and operations (MBA); entrepreneurship (MBA); finance and economics (MBA); healthcare and pharmaceutical management (MBA); human resource management (MBA); international business (MBA); leadership and ethics (MBA); management (MBA); marketing (MBA); media (MBA); private equity (MBA); real estate (MBA); social enterprise (MBA); value investing (MBA); DDS/MBA; JD/MBA; MBA/MIA; MBA/MPH; MBA/MS; MD/MBA. *Entrance requirements:* For master's, GMAT, 2 letters of recommendation. Additional exam requirements/recommendations for international students: Required—TOEFL. Electronic applications accepted. *Expenses:* Contact institution. *Faculty research:* Human decision making and behavioral research; real estate market and mortgage defaults; financial crisis and corporate governance; international business; security analysis and accounting.

Dallas Baptist University, College of Business, Management Program, Dallas, TX 75211-9299. Offers conflict resolution management (MA); general management (MA, MS); health care management (MA); human resource management (MA); professional sales and management optimization (MA). *Program availability:* Part-time, evening/weekend, online learning. *Application deadline:* Applications are processed on a rolling basis. Application fee: $25. Electronic applications accepted. Application fee is waived when completed online. *Expenses: Tuition:* Full-time $17,262; part-time $959 per credit hour. *Required fees:* $1000; $500 per semester. Tuition and fees vary according to course load and degree level. *Unit head:* Dr. Sandra Reid, Chair, Graduate School of Business, 214-333-6860, E-mail: sandra@dbu.edu. *Application contact:* Dr. Justin Gandy, Program Director, 214-333-6840, E-mail: justing@dbu.edu.
Website: https://www.dbu.edu/graduate/degree-programs/ma-management

Dartmouth College, Thayer School of Engineering, PhD in Innovation Program, Hanover, NH 03755. Offers PhD. *Degree requirements:* For doctorate, internship. *Entrance requirements:* For doctorate, curriculum vitae.

Delaware Valley University, MBA Program, Doylestown, PA 18901-2697. Offers accounting (MBA); entrepreneurship (MBA); finance (MBA); food and agribusiness (MBA); general business (MBA); global executive leadership (MBA); human resource management (MBA); supply chain management (MBA). *Program availability:* Part-time, evening/weekend, online learning. *Entrance requirements:* For master's, minimum undergraduate GPA of 3.0. Electronic applications accepted. *Expenses:* Contact institution.

DePaul University, Kellstadt Graduate School of Business, Chicago, IL 60604. Offers accountancy (MBA, MSA); applied economics (MBA); audit and advisory services (MS); business administration (DBA); business analytics (MS); business strategy and decision-making (MBA); computational finance (MS); economics and policy analysis (MS); enterprise risk management (MS); entrepreneurship (MBA, MS); finance (MBA, MS); general business (MBA); hospitality leadership (MBA); hospitality leadership and operational performance (MS); human resources (MS); international business (MBA); management (MBA, MS); management information systems (MBA); marketing (MBA, MS); marketing analysis (MS); marketing strategy and planning (MBA); real estate (MS); real estate finance and investment (MBA); strategy, execution and valuation (MBA); supply chain management (MS); sustainable management (MS); taxation (MS); JD/MBA. *Accreditation:* AACSB. *Program availability:* Part-time, evening/weekend, online learning. *Entrance requirements:* For master's, GMAT/GRE, 2 letters of recommendation, resume, essay, official transcripts. Additional exam requirements/recommendations for international students: Required—TOEFL (minimum score 550 paper-based; 80 iBT). Electronic applications accepted. *Expenses:* Contact institution.

Dickinson State University, Department of Teacher Education, Dickinson, ND 58601-4896. Offers master of arts in teaching (MAT); master of entrepreneurship (ME); middle school education (MAT); reading (MAT). *Program availability:* Part-time, blended/hybrid learning. *Faculty:* 2 full-time (both women). *Students:* 2 full-time (1 woman), 15 part-time (9 women); includes 1 minority (Hispanic/Latino). Average age 36. 8 applicants, 100% accepted, 8 enrolled. *Degree requirements:* For master's, comprehensive exam (for some programs). *Entrance requirements:* For master's, additional admission requirements for the Master of Entrepreneurship Program: complete the SoBE ME Peregrine Entrance Examination, personal statement; transcripts; additional admission requirements for the Master of Entrepreneurship Program: 2 letters of reference in support of their admission to the program. Reference letters should be from prior academic advisors, faculty, professional colleagues, or supervisors. Additional exam requirements/recommendations for international students: Required—TOEFL (minimum score 71 iBT). *Application deadline:* For fall admission, 8/1 for domestic students, 7/1 for international students; for spring admission, 12/1 for domestic students, 11/15 for international students. Applications are processed on a rolling basis. Application fee: $35. Electronic applications accepted. *Expenses: Tuition, area resident:* Full-time $3735; part-time $311 per credit hour. Tuition, state resident: full-time $3735; part-time $311 per credit hour. Tuition, nonresident: full-time $3735; part-time $311 per credit hour. *Required fees:* $138; $138 per credit hour. *Financial support:* Application deadline: 12/1; applicants required to submit FAFSA. *Unit head:* Dr. Deborah Secord, Chair, Department of Teacher Education, 701-483-2178, E-mail: Deborah.Secord@dickinsonstate.edu. *Application contact:* Pamela Krueger, Graduate Studies Coordinator, 701-483-5631, E-mail: Pamela.j.krueger@dickinsonstate.edu.
Website: https://dickinsonstate.edu/academics/fields-of-study/graduate-studies/

Drexel University, Goodwin College of Professional Studies, School of Technology and Professional Studies, Philadelphia, PA 19104-2875. Offers construction management (MS); creativity and innovation (MS); engineering technology (MS); food science (MS); hospitality management (MS); professional studies: creativity studies (MS); professional studies: e-learning leadership (MS); professional studies: homeland security management (MS); project management (MS); property management (MS); sport management (MS). *Program availability:* Part-time, evening/weekend. *Entrance requirements:* Additional exam requirements/recommendations for international students: Required—TOEFL, IELTS. Electronic applications accepted. Application fee is waived when completed online.

Duke University, The Fuqua School of Business, The Duke MBA-Daytime Program, Durham, NC 27708. Offers academic excellence in finance (Certificate); business administration (MBA); decision sciences (MBA); energy and environment (MBA); energy finance (MBA); entrepreneurship and innovation (MBA); finance (MBA); financial analysis (MBA); health sector management (Certificate); leadership and ethics (MBA); management (MBA); management science and technology management (Certificate); marketing (MBA); operations management (MBA); social entrepreneurship (MBA); strategy (MBA). *Faculty:* 100 full-time (21 women), 55 part-time/adjunct (12 women). *Students:* 875 full-time (335 women); includes 188 minority (44 Black or African American, non-Hispanic/Latino; 4 American Indian or Alaska Native, non-Hispanic/Latino; 90 Asian, non-Hispanic/Latino; 43 Hispanic/Latino; 1 Native Hawaiian or other Pacific Islander, non-Hispanic/Latino; 6 Two or more races, non-Hispanic/Latino), 276 international. Average age 29. In 2018, 429 master's awarded. *Entrance requirements:* For master's, GMAT or GRE, transcripts, essays, resume, recommendation letters, interview. *Application deadline:* For fall admission, 9/19 for domestic and international students; for winter admission, 10/14 for domestic and international students; for spring admission, 1/6 for domestic and international students; for summer admission, 3/11 for domestic and international students. Application fee: $225. Electronic applications accepted. *Expenses:* Contact institution. *Financial support:* Scholarships/grants available. Financial award applicants required to submit FAFSA. *Unit head:* Steve Misuraca, Assistant Dean, Daytime MBA Program. *Application contact:* Shari Hubert, Associate Dean, Office of Admissions, 919-660-7705, Fax: 919-681-8026, E-mail: admissions-info@fuqua.duke.edu.
Website: https://www.fuqua.duke.edu/programs/daytime-mba

Duke University, The Fuqua School of Business, The Duke MBA-Global Executive Program, Durham, NC 27708. Offers business administration (MBA); energy and environment (MBA); entrepreneurship and innovation (MBA); finance (MBA); health sector management (Certificate); marketing (MBA); strategy (MBA). *Faculty:* 100 full-time (21 women), 55 part-time/adjunct (12 women). *Students:* 141 full-time (43 women); includes 43 minority (12 Black or African American, non-Hispanic/Latino; 25 Asian, non-Hispanic/Latino; 4 Hispanic/Latino; 1 Native Hawaiian or other Pacific Islander, non-Hispanic/Latino; 1 Two or more races, non-Hispanic/Latino), 34 international. Average age 35. In 2018, 159 master's awarded. *Entrance requirements:* For master's, Executive Assessment, GMAT, or GRE, or waived, transcripts, essays, resume, recommendation letters, letter of company support, interview. *Application deadline:* For fall admission, 10/16 priority date for domestic and international students; for winter admission, 12/4 priority date for domestic and international students; for spring admission, 3/11 priority date for domestic and international students; for summer admission, 5/27 for domestic and international students. Applications are processed on a rolling basis. Application fee: $225. Electronic applications accepted. *Expenses:* Contact institution. *Financial support:* Scholarships/grants available. Financial award applicants required to submit FAFSA. *Unit head:* Karen Courtney, Associate Dean, Executive Programs. *Application contact:* Shari Hubert, Associate Dean, Office of Admissions, 919-660-7705, Fax: 919-681-8026, E-mail: admissions-info@fuqua.duke.edu.
Website: https://www.fuqua.duke.edu/programs/global-executive-mba

Duke University, The Fuqua School of Business, The Duke MBA-Weekend Executive Program, Durham, NC 27708. Offers business administration (MBA); energy and environment (MBA); entrepreneurship and innovation (MBA); finance (MBA); health sector management (Certificate); marketing (MBA); strategy (MBA). *Faculty:* 100 full-time (21 women), 55 part-time/adjunct (12 women). *Students:* 251 full-time (67 women); includes 79 minority (13 Black or African American, non-Hispanic/Latino; 2 American Indian or Alaska Native, non-Hispanic/Latino; 46 Asian, non-Hispanic/Latino; 12 Hispanic/Latino; 1 Native Hawaiian or other Pacific Islander, non-Hispanic/Latino; 5 Two or more races, non-Hispanic/Latino), 32 international. Average age 35. In 2018, 120 master's awarded. *Entrance requirements:* For master's, Executive Assessment, GMAT, or GRE, or waived, transcripts, essays, resume, recommendation letters, letter of company support, interview. *Application deadline:* For fall admission, 9/18 priority date for domestic and international students; for winter admission, 12/4 priority date for domestic and international students; for spring admission, 1/22 priority date for domestic and international students; for summer admission, 3/11 for domestic and international students. Applications are processed on a rolling basis. Application fee: $225. Electronic applications accepted. *Expenses:* Contact institution. *Financial support:* Scholarships/grants available. Financial award applicants required to submit FAFSA. *Unit head:* Karen Courtney, Associate Dean, Executive Programs. *Application contact:* Shari Hubert, Associate Dean, Office of Admissions, 919-660-7705, Fax: 919-681-8026, E-mail: admissions-info@fuqua.duke.edu.
Website: https://www.fuqua.duke.edu/programs/weekend-executive-mba

Eastern Michigan University, Graduate School, College of Business, Department of Management, Ypsilanti, MI 48197. Offers entrepreneurship (Postbaccalaureate Certificate); human resources management and organizational development (MSHROD). *Program availability:* Part-time, evening/weekend, online learning. *Faculty:* 21 full-time (12 women). *Students:* 5 full-time (4 women), 68 part-time (54 women); includes 29 minority (19 Black or African American, non-Hispanic/Latino; 4 Asian, non-Hispanic/Latino; 4 Hispanic/Latino; 2 Two or more races, non-Hispanic/Latino), 3 international. Average age 32. 47 applicants, 81% accepted, 18 enrolled. In 2018, 62 master's awarded. *Entrance requirements:* For master's, GMAT. Additional exam requirements/recommendations for international students: Required—TOEFL. *Application deadline:* For fall admission, 5/15 priority date for domestic students, 2/15 priority date for international students; for winter admission, 10/15 priority date for

domestic students, 9/1 priority date for international students; for summer admission, 3/15 priority date for domestic students, 3/1 priority date for international students. Applications are processed on a rolling basis. Application fee: $45. *Financial support:* Fellowships, research assistantships with full tuition reimbursements, teaching assistantships with full tuition reimbursements, career-related internships or fieldwork, Federal Work-Study, institutionally sponsored loans, scholarships/grants, tuition waivers (partial), and unspecified assistantships available. Support available to part-time students. Financial award applicants required to submit FAFSA. *Unit head:* Dr. Stephanie Newell, Interim Department Head, 734-487-0141, Fax: 734-487-4100, E-mail: snewell@emich.edu. *Application contact:* Dr. Stephanie Newell, Interim Department Head, 734-487-0141, Fax: 734-487-4100, E-mail: snewell@emich.edu.

Eastern Michigan University, Graduate School, College of Business, Programs in Business Administration, Ypsilanti, MI 48197. Offers business administration (MBA, Graduate Certificate); computer information systems (Graduate Certificate); e-business (MBA, Graduate Certificate); enterprise business intelligence (MBA); entrepreneurship (MBA, Graduate Certificate); finance (MBA, Graduate Certificate); human resources (MBA); human resources management (Graduate Certificate); information systems (MBA); internal auditing (MBA); international business (MBA, Graduate Certificate); marketing management (Graduate Certificate); nonprofit management (MBA); organizational development (Graduate Certificate); supply chain management (MBA, Graduate Certificate). *Accreditation:* AACSB. *Program availability:* Part-time, online learning. *Students:* 69 full-time (38 women), 251 part-time (140 women); includes 100 minority (63 Black or African American, non-Hispanic/Latino; 1 American Indian or Alaska Native, non-Hispanic/Latino; 12 Asian, non-Hispanic/Latino; 14 Hispanic/Latino; 10 Two or more races, non-Hispanic/Latino), 28 international. Average age 32. 199 applicants, 75% accepted, 83 enrolled. In 2018, 75 master's, 50 other advanced degrees awarded. *Entrance requirements:* For master's, GMAT (minimum score 450), minimum cumulative undergraduate GPA of 2.75. Additional exam requirements/recommendations for international students: Required—TOEFL. *Application deadline:* For fall admission, 5/15 priority date for domestic students, 2/15 priority date for international students; for winter admission, 10/15 priority date for domestic students, 9/1 priority date for international students; for summer admission, 3/15 priority date for domestic students, 3/1 priority date for international students. Applications are processed on a rolling basis. Application fee: $45. *Financial support:* Fellowships, research assistantships with full tuition reimbursements, teaching assistantships with full tuition reimbursements, career-related internships or fieldwork, Federal Work-Study, institutionally sponsored loans, scholarships/grants, tuition waivers (partial), and unspecified assistantships available. Support available to part-time students. Financial award applicants required to submit FAFSA. *Unit head:* K. Michelle Henry, Director, Graduate Business Programs, 734-487-4444, Fax: 734-483-1316, E-mail: cob.graduate@emich.edu. *Application contact:* K. Michelle Henry, Director, Graduate Business Programs, 734-487-4444, Fax: 734-483-1316, E-mail: cob.graduate@emich.edu.
Website: http://www.emich.edu/cob/mba/

East Tennessee State University, School of Graduate Studies, College of Business and Technology, Department of Management and Marketing, Johnson City, TN 37614. Offers business administration (MBA, Postbaccalaureate Certificate); digital marketing (MS); entrepreneurial leadership (Postbaccalaureate Certificate); health care management (Postbaccalaureate Certificate). *Program availability:* Part-time, evening/weekend. *Degree requirements:* For master's, comprehensive exam, capstone. *Entrance requirements:* For master's, GMAT, minimum GPA of 2.5 (for MBA), 3.0 (for MS); current resume; three letters of recommendation; for Postbaccalaureate Certificate, minimum GPA of 2.5, undergraduate degree. Additional exam requirements/recommendations for international students: Required—TOEFL (minimum score 550 paper-based; 79 iBT). Electronic applications accepted. *Faculty research:* Sustainability, healthcare effectiveness, consumer behavior, merchandising trends, organizational management issues.

Elms College, Division of Business, Chicopee, MA 01013-2839. Offers accounting (MBA); accounting and finance (MS); financial planning (MBA, Certificate); healthcare leadership (MBA); lean entrepreneurship (MBA); management (MBA). *Program availability:* Part-time, evening/weekend. *Faculty:* 4 full-time (all women), 5 part-time/adjunct (3 women). *Students:* 36 part-time (22 women); includes 9 minority (5 Black or African American, non-Hispanic/Latino; 4 Hispanic/Latino), 1 international. Average age 35. 13 applicants, 85% accepted, 9 enrolled. In 2018, 29 master's awarded. *Entrance requirements:* For master's, minimum GPA of 3.0. *Application deadline:* Applications are processed on a rolling basis. Application fee: $30. Electronic applications accepted. *Expenses: Tuition:* Full-time $14,328; part-time $796 per credit. *Required fees:* $200. Tuition and fees vary according to degree level and program. *Unit head:* Kim Kenney-Rockwal, MBA Program Director, 413-265-2572, E-mail: kenneyrockwalk@elms.edu. *Application contact:* MBA Program Coordinator, 413-265-2592, E-mail: mba@elms.edu.

Embry-Riddle Aeronautical University–Worldwide, Department of Engineering and Technology, Daytona Beach, FL 32114-3900. Offers aerospace engineering (MS); entrepreneurship in technology (MS); systems engineering (M Sys E), including engineering management, technical. *Program availability:* Part-time, evening/weekend, 100% online, blended/hybrid learning. *Entrance requirements:* For master's, GRE (for MS in aerospace engineering). Additional exam requirements/recommendations for international students: Required—TOEFL (minimum score 550 paper-based; 79 iBT), IELTS (minimum score 6). Electronic applications accepted. *Expenses:* Contact institution.

Emory University, Goizueta Business School, Full Time MBA Program, Atlanta, GA 30322-1100. Offers accounting (MBA); alternative investments (MBA); business process consulting (MBA); business technology management (MBA); capital markets (MBA); corporate finance (MBA); customer relationship management (MBA); decision analytics (MBA); entrepreneurship (MBA); finance (MBA); global management (MBA); investment banking (MBA); management consulting (MBA); marketing (MBA); marketing analytics (MBA); marketing consulting (MBA); operations management (MBA); organization and management (MBA); product and brand management (MBA); real estate (MBA); social enterprise (MBA); strategy consulting (MBA). *Accreditation:* AACSB. *Faculty:* 74 full-time (18 women), 18 part-time/adjunct (6 women). *Students:* 349 full-time (105 women); includes 81 minority (26 Black or African American, non-Hispanic/Latino; 1 American Indian or Alaska Native, non-Hispanic/Latino; 35 Asian, non-Hispanic/Latino; 16 Hispanic/Latino; 3 Two or more races, non-Hispanic/Latino), 97 international. Average age 29. 1,380 applicants, 34% accepted, 172 enrolled. In 2018, 180 master's awarded. *Degree requirements:* For master's, 1 leadership course; 2 mid-semester module programs; 2 global components. *Entrance requirements:* For master's, GMAT/GRE, essays; recommendation letters; undergraduate degree; interview. Additional exam requirements/recommendations for international students: Required—TOEFL (minimum score 100 iBT), IELTS (minimum score 7), PTE (minimum score 68). *Application deadline:* For fall admission, 10/6 for domestic and international students; for winter admission, 11/17 for domestic and international students; for spring admission, 1/3 priority date for domestic and international students; for summer admission, 3/9 for domestic and international students. Application fee: $150. Electronic applications accepted. *Expenses:* Contact institution. *Financial support:* In 2018–19, 273 students received support. Career-related internships or fieldwork, institutionally sponsored loans, and scholarships/grants available. Financial award application deadline: 4/1; financial award applicants required to submit FAFSA. *Faculty research:* Corporate finance, information systems, digital marketing, asset pricing, sports management. *Unit head:* Brian Mitchell, Associate Dean, 404-727-4824, Fax: 404-712-9648, E-mail: brian.mitchell@emory.edu. *Application contact:* Melissa Rapp, Associate Dean, 404-727-7583, Fax: 404-727-4612, E-mail: mbaadmissions@emory.edu.
Website: http://www.goizueta.emory.edu

Everglades University, Graduate Programs, Program in Entrepreneurship, Boca Raton, FL 33431. Offers MS. *Program availability:* Part-time, evening/weekend, 100% online. *Degree requirements:* For master's, capstone course. *Entrance requirements:* For master's, GMAT (minimum score of 400) or GRE (minimum score of 290), bachelor's or graduate degree from college accredited by an agency recognized by the U.S. Department of Education; minimum cumulative GPA of 2.0 at the baccalaureate level, 3.0 at the master's level. Additional exam requirements/recommendations for international students: Recommended—TOEFL (minimum score 500 paper-based). Electronic applications accepted. *Expenses:* Contact institution.

Fairleigh Dickinson University, Florham Campus, Silberman College of Business, Departments of Management, Marketing, and Entrepreneurial Studies, Program in Entrepreneurial Studies, Madison, NJ 07940-1099. Offers MBA, Certificate.

Fairleigh Dickinson University, Metropolitan Campus, Silberman College of Business, Departments of Management, Marketing, and Entrepreneurial Studies, Program in Entrepreneurial Studies, Teaneck, NJ 07666-1914. Offers MBA, Certificate.

Felician University, Program in Business, Lodi, NJ 07644-2117. Offers business administration (DBA); innovation and entrepreneurial leadership (MBA). *Program availability:* Part-time-only, evening/weekend, online learning. Terminal master's awarded for partial completion of doctoral program. *Degree requirements:* For master's, comprehensive exam, thesis, presentation; for doctorate, thesis/dissertation, scholarly project. *Entrance requirements:* For master's and doctorate, GMAT, resume, personal statement, graduation from accredited baccalaureate program. Additional exam requirements/recommendations for international students: Required—TOEFL (minimum score 550 paper-based; 79 iBT), IELTS (minimum score 6.5), PTE (minimum score 56). Electronic applications accepted. Application fee is waived when completed online. *Expenses:* Contact institution. *Faculty research:* Social media, assessment, small business management, mission integration.

Florida Atlantic University, College of Business, Department of Management, Boca Raton, FL 33431-0991. Offers business administration (MBA); entrepreneurship (MBA); health administration (MBA); international business (MBA); sport management (MBA). *Faculty:* 8 full-time (3 women). *Students:* 109 full-time (81 women), 82 part-time (58 women); includes 106 minority (52 Black or African American, non-Hispanic/Latino; 8 Asian, non-Hispanic/Latino; 40 Hispanic/Latino; 6 Two or more races, non-Hispanic/Latino), 1 international. Average age 35. 113 applicants, 85% accepted, 72 enrolled. In 2018, 120 master's awarded. *Entrance requirements:* For master's, GMAT or GRE General Test, minimum GPA of 3.0 in last 60 hours of course work. Additional exam requirements/recommendations for international students: Required—TOEFL (minimum score 600 paper-based; 61 iBT), IELTS (minimum score 6). *Application deadline:* For fall admission, 7/25 for domestic students, 2/15 for international students; for spring admission, 12/10 for domestic students, 7/15 for international students. Applications are processed on a rolling basis. Application fee: $30. Electronic applications accepted. *Expenses: Tuition, area resident:* Full-time $7400; part-time $369.82 per credit. Tuition, state resident: full-time $7400; part-time $369.82 per credit. Tuition, nonresident: full-time $20,496; part-time $1024.81 per credit. *Financial support:* Research assistantships with full tuition reimbursements, career-related internships or fieldwork, tuition waivers (partial), and unspecified assistantships available. *Faculty research:* Sports administration, healthcare, policy, finance, real estate, senior living. *Unit head:* Dr. Roland Kidwell, Chair, 561-297-4507, E-mail: kidwellr@fau.edu. *Application contact:* Dr. Roland Kidwell, Chair, 561-297-4507, E-mail: kidwellr@fau.edu.
Website: http://business.fau.edu/departments/management/index.aspx

Fordham University, Gabelli School of Business, New York, NY 10023. Offers accounting (MBA, MS); applied statistics and decision-making (MS); business economics (DPS); capital markets (DPS); communications and media management (MBA); electronic business (MBA); entrepreneurship (MBA); finance (MBA, PhD); global finance (MS); global sustainability (MBA); health administration (MS); healthcare management (MBA); information systems (MBA, MS); investor relations (MS); management (EMBA, MBA, MS, PhD); marketing (MBA); marketing intelligence (MS); media management (MS); nonprofit leadership (MS); quantitative finance (MS); strategy and decision-making (DPS); taxation (MS); JD/MBA; MS/MBA. *Accreditation:* AACSB. *Program availability:* Part-time, evening/weekend. Terminal master's awarded for partial completion of doctoral program. *Degree requirements:* For master's, internships (for some degrees); for doctorate, comprehensive exam (for some programs), thesis/dissertation. *Entrance requirements:* For master's, GMAT/GRE, 2 letters of recommendation, resume, 2 essays, transcripts, interview. Additional exam requirements/recommendations for international students: Required—TOEFL (minimum score 100 iBT), IELTS (minimum score 7). Electronic applications accepted. *Expenses:* Contact institution.

Georgia State University, J. Mack Robinson College of Business, Department of Managerial Sciences, Atlanta, GA 30302-3083. Offers business analysis (MBA, MS); entrepreneurship (MBA); human resources management (MBA, MS); operations management (MBA, MS); organization behavior/human resource management (PhD); organization management (MBA); organizational change (MS); strategic management (PhD). *Accreditation:* AACSB. *Program availability:* Part-time, evening/weekend. *Faculty:* 11 full-time (2 women), 1 part-time/adjunct (0 women). *Students:* 11 full-time (6 women); includes 5 minority (3 Black or African American, non-Hispanic/Latino; 1 Asian, non-Hispanic/Latino; 1 Two or more races, non-Hispanic/Latino), 3 international. Average age 29. 54 applicants, 20% accepted, 8 enrolled. In 2018, 9 master's, 3 doctorates awarded. *Entrance requirements:* For master's, GRE or GMAT, transcripts from all institutions attended, resume, essays; for doctorate, GMAT, three letters of recommendation, personal statement, transcripts from all institutions attended, resume. Additional exam requirements/recommendations for international students: Required—TOEFL (minimum score 610 paper-based; 101 iBT), IELTS (minimum score 7). *Application deadline:* For fall admission, 5/1 priority date for domestic students, 2/1 priority date for international students; for spring admission, 9/15 priority date for domestic students, 4/1 priority date for international students. Applications are processed on a rolling basis. Application fee: $50. Electronic applications accepted. *Expenses: Tuition, area resident:* Full-time $9360; part-time $390 per credit hour. Tuition, state resident: full-time $9360; part-time $390 per credit hour. Tuition, nonresident: full-time $30,024; part-time $1251 per credit hour. *International tuition:* $30,024 full-time. *Required fees:* $2128. *Financial support:* Research assistantships, teaching assistantships, scholarships/grants, tuition waivers, and unspecified assistantships available. Financial award applicants required to submit FAFSA. *Faculty research:* Entrepreneurship and innovation; strategy process; workplace interactions, relationships, and processes; leadership and culture; supply chain management. *Unit head:* Dr. Pamela S. Barr, Chair, 404-413-7525, Fax: 404-413-7571. *Application*

contact: Toby McChesney, Assistant Dean for Graduate Recruiting and Student Services, 404-413-7167, Fax: 404-413-7162, E-mail: rcbgradadmissions@gsu.edu.
Website: http://mgmt.robinson.gsu.edu/

Georgia State University, J. Mack Robinson College of Business, Institute of International Business, Atlanta, GA 30303. Offers international business (GMBA, MBA, MIB); international business and information technology (MBA); international entrepreneurship (MBA); MIB/MIA. *Program availability:* Part-time, evening/weekend. *Faculty:* 5 full-time (3 women). *Students:* 18 full-time (8 women); includes 6 minority (3 Black or African American, non-Hispanic/Latino; 1 Asian, non-Hispanic/Latino; 1 Hispanic/Latino; 1 Two or more races, non-Hispanic/Latino), 8 international. Average age 29. 48 applicants, 73% accepted, 22 enrolled. In 2018, 40 master's awarded. *Entrance requirements:* For master's, GRE or GMAT, transcripts from all institutions attended, resume, essays. Additional exam requirements/recommendations for international students: Required—TOEFL (minimum score 610 paper-based; 101 iBT), IELTS (minimum score 7). *Application deadline:* For fall admission, 5/1 priority date for domestic students, 2/1 priority date for international students; for spring admission, 9/15 priority date for domestic students, 5/1 priority date for international students. Applications are processed on a rolling basis. Application fee: $50. Electronic applications accepted. *Expenses: Tuition, area resident:* Full-time $9360; part-time $390 per credit hour. Tuition, state resident: full-time $9360; part-time $390 per credit hour. Tuition, nonresident: full-time $30,024; part-time $1251 per credit hour. *International tuition:* $30,024 full-time. *Required fees:* $2128. *Financial support:* Research assistantships, teaching assistantships, scholarships/grants, tuition waivers (partial), and unspecified assistantships available. Financial award application deadline: 5/1. *Faculty research:* Business challenges in emerging markets (especially in India and China); interorganizational relationships in an international context, such as strategic alliances and global supply chain relations; globalization and entry mode strategy or new (or emerging) multinationals; emerging market development and business environments; cross-cultural effects on business processes and performance. *Unit head:* Dr. Daniel Bello, Professor/Director of the Institute of International Business, 404-413-7275, Fax: 404-413-7276. *Application contact:* Toby McChesney, Assistant Dean for Graduate Recruiting and Student Services, 404-413-7167, Fax: 404-413-7162, E-mail: rcbgradadmissions@gsu.edu.
Website: http://iib.gsu.edu/

Golden Gate University, Ageno School of Business, San Francisco, CA 94105-2968. Offers accounting (MBA); adaptive leadership (MBA); advanced financial planning (MS); business administration (EMBA, MBA, DBA); business analytics (MBA, MS); entrepreneurship (MBA); finance (MBA, MS, Certificate); financial life planning (Certificate); financial planning (MS, Certificate); global supply chain management (MBA, Certificate); human resource management (MBA, MS, Certificate); information technology management (MBA, MS, Certificate); international business (MBA); marketing (MBA, MS, Certificate); project management (MBA, MS, Certificate); psychology (MA, Certificate); public administration (EMPA, MBA); public administration leadership (Certificate); JD/MBA. *Program availability:* Part-time, evening/weekend. *Degree requirements:* For doctorate, thesis/dissertation, qualifying examination. *Entrance requirements:* For master's, GMAT (for MBA), minimum GPA of 2.5 (MS). Additional exam requirements/recommendations for international students: Required—TOEFL (minimum score 550 paper-based; 79 iBT). Electronic applications accepted. *Expenses:* Contact institution.

Grand Canyon University, Colangelo College of Business, Phoenix, AZ 85017-1097. Offers accounting (MBA, MS); business analytics (MS); disaster preparedness and executive fire service leadership (MS); finance (MBA); general management (MBA); health systems management (MBA); information technology management (MS); leadership (MBA, MS); marketing (MBA); organizational leadership and entrepreneurship (MS); project management (MBA); sports business (MBA); strategic human resource management (MBA). *Accreditation:* ACBSP. *Program availability:* Part-time, evening/weekend, online learning. *Entrance requirements:* For master's, equivalent of two years' full-time professional work experience. Additional exam requirements/recommendations for international students: Required—TOEFL (minimum score 575 paper-based; 90 iBT), IELTS (minimum score 7). Electronic applications accepted.

Harrisburg University of Science and Technology, Program in Information Systems Engineering and Management, Harrisburg, PA 17101. Offers analytics (MS); digital government (MS); digital health (MS); entrepreneurship (MS); information security (MS); software engineering and systems development (MS). *Program availability:* Part-time, evening/weekend. *Degree requirements:* For master's, thesis optional. *Entrance requirements:* For master's, baccalaureate degree. Additional exam requirements/recommendations for international students: Required—TOEFL (minimum score 520 paper-based; 80 iBT); Recommended—IELTS (minimum score 6). Electronic applications accepted. *Faculty research:* Healthcare Informatics, material analysis, enterprise systems, circuit design, enterprise architectures.

Harrisburg University of Science and Technology, Program in Techpreneurship, Philadelphia, PA 19130. Offers MS.

HEC Montreal, School of Business Administration, Graduate Diploma Programs in Administration, Montréal, QC H3T 2A7, Canada. Offers business administration (Graduate Diploma); business analysis - information technology (Graduate Diploma); e-business (Graduate Diploma); entrepreneurship (Graduate Diploma); financial professions (Graduate Diploma); human resources (Graduate Diploma); management (Graduate Diploma); management and sustainable development (Graduate Diploma); management of cultural organizations (Graduate Diploma); marketing communication (Graduate Diploma); organizational development (Graduate Diploma); professional accounting (Graduate Diploma); supply chain management (Graduate Diploma); taxation (Graduate Diploma). All courses are given in French. *Students:* 412 full-time (242 women), 885 part-time (552 women). 834 applicants, 65% accepted, 351 enrolled. In 2018, 611 Graduate Diplomas awarded. *Entrance requirements:* For degree, bachelor's degree. Application fee: $91 Canadian dollars ($191 Canadian dollars for international students). Electronic applications accepted. *Expenses: Tuition, area resident:* Full-time $3052.80 Canadian dollars; part-time $84.80 Canadian dollars per credit. Tuition, state resident: full-time $3816 Canadian dollars; part-time $264.67 Canadian dollars per credit. Tuition, nonresident: full-time $11,910 Canadian dollars. *International tuition:* $20,905.20 Canadian dollars full-time. *Required fees:* $1805.34 Canadian dollars; $43.62 Canadian dollars per credit. $71.78 Canadian dollars per term. Tuition and fees vary according to degree level and program. *Financial support:* Research assistantships, teaching assistantships, and scholarships/grants available. Financial award application deadline: 9/2. *Faculty research:* Art management, business policy, entrepreneurship, new technologies, transportation. *Unit head:* Renaud Lachance, Director, 514-340-6428, E-mail: renaud.lachance@hec.ca. *Application contact:* Anny Caron, Administrative Director, 514-340-6000, Fax: 514-340-6411, E-mail: aide@hec.ca.
Website: http://www.hec.ca/programmes/dess/index.html

HEC Montreal, School of Business Administration, Master of Science Programs in Administration, Montréal, QC H3T 2A7, Canada. Offers accounting, management, control, and audit (M Sc); applied economics (M Sc); applied financial economics (M Sc); business analysis and information technologies (M Sc); business analytics (M Sc); business intelligence (M Sc); electronic commerce (M Sc); entrepreneurship-intrapreneurship-innovation (M Sc); finance (M Sc); financial engineering (M Sc); global supply chain management (M Sc); human resources management (M Sc); international business (M Sc); international logistics (M Sc); management (M Sc); management and social innovations (M Sc); management control (M Sc); marketing (M Sc); operations management (M Sc); organizational development (M Sc); strategy (M Sc); user experience in business context (M Sc). Most courses are given in French. *Accreditation:* AACSB. *Students:* 1,051 full-time (516 women), 293 part-time (149 women). 1,143 applicants, 61% accepted, 438 enrolled. In 2018, 425 master's awarded. *Entrance requirements:* For master's, bachelor's degree in business administration or equivalent. Additional exam requirements/recommendations for international students: Required—TAGE MAGE (minimum recommended score of 300), GMAT (minimum recommended score of 630), or GRE. Application fee: $91 Canadian dollars ($191 Canadian dollars for international students). Electronic applications accepted. *Expenses: Tuition, area resident:* Full-time $3052.80 Canadian dollars; part-time $84.80 Canadian dollars per credit. Tuition, state resident: full-time $3816 Canadian dollars; part-time $264.67 Canadian dollars per credit. Tuition, nonresident: full-time $11,910 Canadian dollars. *International tuition:* $20,905.20 Canadian dollars full-time. *Required fees:* $1805.34 Canadian dollars; $43.62 Canadian dollars per credit. $71.78 Canadian dollars per term. Tuition and fees vary according to degree level and program. *Financial support:* Research assistantships, teaching assistantships, and scholarships/grants available. Financial award application deadline: 9/2. *Unit head:* Dr. Sihem Taboubi, Director, 514-340-6428, E-mail: sihem.taboubi@hec.ca. *Application contact:* Marianne de Moura, Administrative Director, 514-340-6000, Fax: 514-340-6411, E-mail: aide@hec.ca.
Website: http://www.hec.ca/programmes/maitrises/index.html

Hult International Business School, Graduate Programs, Cambridge, MA 02141. Offers business administration (EMBA); business analytics (MBA, MIB); business statistics (MBS); disruptive innovation (MDI); entrepreneurship (MBA, MIB); family business (MBA, MIB); finance (MBA, MF, MIB); international marketing (MIM); marketing (MBA, MIB); project management (MBA, MIB). MDI and MBS offered in San Francisco; MBA also offered in Boston, San Francisco, Dubai, Shanghai, and New York. *Entrance requirements:* For master's, GMAT, 3 years of work experience. Additional exam requirements/recommendations for international students: Required—TOEFL. Electronic applications accepted. *Expenses:* Contact institution.

IGlobal University, Graduate Programs, Vienna, VA 22182. Offers accounting (MBA); data management and analytics (MSIT); entrepreneurship (MBA); finance (MBA); global business management (MBA); health care management (MBA); hospitality and tourism management (MBA); human resources management (MBA); information technology (MBA); information technology systems and management (MSIT); leadership and management (MBA); project management (MBA); public service and administration (MBA); software design and management (MSIT).

Illinois Institute of Technology, Stuart School of Business, Program in Technological Entrepreneurship, Chicago, IL 60616. Offers MTE.

Indiana University–Purdue University Indianapolis, Kelley School of Business, Evening MBA Program, Indianapolis, IN 46202-5151. Offers accounting (MBA); entrepreneurship (MBA); finance (MBA); general administration (MBA); marketing (MBA); supply chain management (MBA); MBA/JD; MBA/MD; MBA/MHA; MBA/MS; MBA/MSA; MBA/MSE. *Program availability:* Part-time-only, evening/weekend, online learning. *Entrance requirements:* For master's, GMAT or GRE, 2 years of professional work experience. Additional exam requirements/recommendations for international students: Required—TOEFL or IELTS. Electronic applications accepted. *Expenses:* Contact institution. *Faculty research:* Entrepreneurship; corporate finance; international business; consumer behavior; supply chain; business law.

International University in Geneva, Business Programs, Geneva, Switzerland. Offers business administration (MBA, DBA); entrepreneurship (MBA); international business (MIB); international trade (MIT); sales and marketing (MBA). *Accreditation:* ACBSP. *Program availability:* Part-time, evening/weekend. *Degree requirements:* For master's, comprehensive exam. *Entrance requirements:* For master's, GMAT. Additional exam requirements/recommendations for international students: Required—TOEFL. Electronic applications accepted.

The International University of Monaco, Graduate Programs, Monte Carlo, Monaco. Offers entrepreneurship (EMBA, MBA); financial engineering (M Sc); hedge fund and private equity (M Sc); international marketing (EMBA, MBA); international wealth management (M Sc); luxury goods and services (EMBA, M Sc, MBA); wealth and asset management (EMBA, MBA). *Program availability:* Part-time. *Degree requirements:* For master's, comprehensive exam (for some programs), applied research project. *Entrance requirements:* Additional exam requirements/recommendations for international students: Required—TOEFL (minimum score 550 paper-based), IELTS. Electronic applications accepted. *Faculty research:* Gaming, leadership, disintermediation.

James Madison University, The Graduate School, College of Business, Program in Business Administration, Harrisonburg, VA 22807. Offers business (MBA), including executive leadership, information security, innovation. *Accreditation:* AACSB. *Program availability:* Part-time, evening/weekend, blended/hybrid learning. *Students:* 37 full-time (10 women), 82 part-time (34 women); includes 28 minority (9 Black or African American, non-Hispanic/Latino; 7 Asian, non-Hispanic/Latino; 10 Hispanic/Latino; 2 Two or more races, non-Hispanic/Latino), 7 international. Average age 30. In 2018, 38 master's awarded. Application fee: $6. Electronic applications accepted. *Expenses:* Tuition, state resident: full-time $10,848. Tuition, nonresident: full-time $27,888. *Required fees:* $1128. *Financial support:* In 2018–19, 2 students received support. Federal Work-Study and 1 assistantship (averaging $7911) available. Financial award application deadline: 3/1; financial award applicants required to submit FAFSA. *Unit head:* Dr. Matthew A. Rutherford, Department Head, 540-568-8777, E-mail: rutherma@jmu.edu. *Application contact:* Lynette D. Michael, Director of Graduate Admissions, 540-568-6131 Ext. 6395, Fax: 540-568-7860, E-mail: michaeld@jmu.edu.
Website: http://www.jmu.edu/cob/graduate/mba/index.shtml

Kansas State University, Graduate School, College of Business, Program in Business Administration, Manhattan, KS 66506. Offers data analytics (MBA); finance (MBA); management (MBA); marketing (MBA); technology entrepreneurship (MBA). *Accreditation:* AACSB. *Program availability:* Part-time, 100% online. *Entrance requirements:* For master's, GMAT (minimum score of 500), minimum undergraduate GPA of 3.0. Additional exam requirements/recommendations for international students: Required—TOEFL (minimum score 550 paper-based; 79 iBT); Recommended—IELTS (minimum score 7). Electronic applications accepted. *Expenses:* Contact institution. *Faculty research:* Organizational citizenship behavior, service marketing, impression management, human resources management, lean manufacturing and supply chain management, financial market behavior and investment management, data analytics, corporate responsibility, technology entrepreneurship.

Lehigh University, P.C. Rossin College of Engineering and Applied Science, Technical Entrepreneurship Program, Bethlehem, PA 18015. Offers M Eng. *Faculty:* 3 full-time (1 woman). *Students:* 21 full-time (11 women), 1 (woman) part-time; includes 9 minority (5 Black or African American, non-Hispanic/Latino; 3 Hispanic/Latino; 1 Two or more races,

non-Hispanic/Latino), 3 international. Average age 24. 26 applicants, 100% accepted, 21 enrolled. In 2018, 23 master's awarded. *Entrance requirements:* For master's, bachelor's degree. Additional exam requirements/recommendations for international students: Required—TOEFL (minimum score 79 iBT), TOEFL required for students who native language is not English. *Application deadline:* For fall admission, 4/15 for domestic and international students. Application fee: $75. Electronic applications accepted. Tuition and fees vary according to program. *Financial support:* Application deadline: 2/15. *Unit head:* Marsha Timmerman, Director, 610-758-4770, E-mail: mwt217@lehigh.edu. *Application contact:* Jodie L. Johnson, Assistant Director, 610-758-4789, Fax: 610-758-6131, E-mail: jlk4@lehigh.edu.
Website: http://www.lehigh.edu/innovate

Lenoir-Rhyne University, Graduate Programs, Charles M. Snipes School of Business, Hickory, NC 28601. Offers accounting (MBA); business analytics and information technology (MBA); entrepreneurship (MBA); global business (MBA); healthcare administration (MBA); innovation and change management (MBA); leadership development (MBA). *Accreditation:* ACBSP. *Program availability:* Part-time, evening/weekend, online learning. *Degree requirements:* For master's, capstone course. *Entrance requirements:* For master's, GMAT, GRE, MAT, minimum undergraduate GPA of 2.7, graduate 3.0. Additional exam requirements/recommendations for international students: Required—TOEFL (minimum score 600 paper-based). Electronic applications accepted. *Expenses:* Contact institution.

Lindenwood University, Graduate Programs, Plaster School of Business and Entrepreneurship, St. Charles, MO 63301-1695. Offers M Acc, MA, MBA, MS. *Accreditation:* ACBSP. *Program availability:* Part-time, evening/weekend, 100% online. *Faculty:* 14 full-time (4 women), 26 part-time/adjunct (9 women). *Students:* 234 full-time (133 women), 221 part-time (139 women); includes 121 minority (95 Black or African American, non-Hispanic/Latino; 1 American Indian or Alaska Native, non-Hispanic/Latino; 3 Asian, non-Hispanic/Latino; 12 Hispanic/Latino; 10 Two or more races, non-Hispanic/Latino), 53 international. Average age 32. 251 applicants, 38% accepted, 95 enrolled. In 2018, 210 master's awarded. *Degree requirements:* For master's, comprehensive exam (for some programs), thesis (for some programs), minimum GPA of 3.0. *Entrance requirements:* For master's, interview, minimum undergraduate cumulative GPA of 3.0, letter of recommendation. Additional exam requirements/recommendations for international students: Required—TOEFL (minimum score 553 paper-based; 81 iBT); Recommended—IELTS (minimum score 6.5). *Application deadline:* For fall admission, 8/9 priority date for domestic students, 6/1 priority date for international students; for winter admission, 12/20 priority date for domestic students, 11/1 priority date for international students; for spring admission, 2/28 priority date for domestic students, 1/3 priority date for international students; for summer admission, 5/15 priority date for domestic students, 3/27 priority date for international students. Applications are processed on a rolling basis. Application fee: $0 ($100 for international students). Electronic applications accepted. *Expenses:* Contact institution. *Financial support:* In 2018–19, 283 students received support. Career-related internships or fieldwork, Federal Work-Study, institutionally sponsored loans, scholarships/grants, tuition waivers (partial), and unspecified assistantships available. Financial award application deadline: 6/30; financial award applicants required to submit FAFSA. *Unit head:* Roger Ellis, Dean, School of Business and Entrepreneurship, 636-949-4839, E-mail: rellis@lindenwood.edu. *Application contact:* Kara Schilli, Assistant Vice President, University Admissions, 636-949-4349, Fax: 636-949-4109, E-mail: adultadmissions@lindenwood.edu.
Website: https://www.lindenwood.edu/academics/academic-schools/robert-w-plaster-school-of-business-entrepreneurship/

Loyola University Chicago, Quinlan School of Business, MBA Programs, Chicago, IL 60611. Offers accounting (MBA); business ethics (MBA); derivative markets (MBA); economics (MBA); entrepreneurship (MBA); finance (MBA); healthcare management (MBA); human resources management (MBA); information systems management (MBA); international business (MBA); management (MBA); marketing (MBA); risk management (MBA); supply chain management (MBA). *Program availability:* Part-time, evening/weekend. *Entrance requirements:* For master's, GMAT or GRE, official transcripts, two letters of recommendation, statement of purpose, resume. Additional exam requirements/recommendations for international students: Required—TOEFL (minimum score 90 iBT) or IELTS (minimum score 6.5). Electronic applications accepted. Application fee is waived when completed online. *Expenses:* Contact institution. *Faculty research:* Social enterprise and responsibility, emerging markets, supply chain management, risk management.

Manhattanville College, School of Education, Program in Education Entrepreneurship, Purchase, NY 10577-2132. Offers education entrepreneurship (M Ed). The 30 credit Master of Education in Entrepreneurship is a joint venture between the School of Professional Studies and the School of Education. Core courses include Education, human development, ethics in education settings, and multicultural perspectives. There are core business courses along with marketing, analytical, and financial tools. Students can take electives in education or business. *Program availability:* Part-time, evening/weekend. *Faculty:* 6 part-time/adjunct (2 women). *Students:* 1 applicant. *Degree requirements:* For master's, comprehensive exam (for some programs), thesis (for some programs), student teaching, research seminars, portfolios, internships, writing assessment. *Entrance requirements:* For master's, for programs leading to certification, candidates must submit scores from GRE or MAT(Miller Analogies Test), minimum undergraduate GPA of 3.0, all transcripts from all colleges and universities attended, 2 letters of recommendation, interview, essay (2-3 page personal statement that describes reasons for choosing education as profession and personal philosophy of education), proof of immunization (for those born after 1957). Additional exam requirements/recommendations for international students: Required—TOEFL (minimum score 600 paper-based; 110 iBT); Recommended—IELTS (minimum score 8). *Application deadline:* Applications are processed on a rolling basis. Application fee: $75. Electronic applications accepted. *Expenses:* 935 per credit. *Financial support:* Teaching assistantships, career-related internships or fieldwork, Federal Work-Study, institutionally sponsored loans, scholarships/grants, and unspecified assistantships available. Financial award application deadline: 3/15; financial award applicants required to submit FAFSA. *Unit head:* Dr. Shelley Wepner, Dean, 914-323-3153, Fax: 914-323-5493, E-mail: Shelley.Wepner@mville.edu. *Application contact:* Alissa Wilson, Director, SOE Graduate Enrollment Management, 914-323-3150, Fax: 914-694-1732, E-mail: edschool@mville.edu.
Website: http://www.mville.edu/programs/educational-studies-education-entrepreneurship

Marlboro College, Graduate and Professional Studies, Program in Business Administration, Marlboro, VT 05344. Offers mission-driven organizations (MBA); project management (MBA); social innovation (MBA). *Program availability:* Part-time, evening/weekend, blended/hybrid learning. *Degree requirements:* For master's, 45 credits including a Master Workshop. *Entrance requirements:* For master's, letter of intent, essay, transcripts, 2 letters of recommendation. Electronic applications accepted. *Expenses:* Contact institution.

Marlboro College, Graduate and Professional Studies, Program in Management, Marlboro, VT 05344. Offers mission-driven organizations (MS); project management (MS); social innovation (MS). *Program availability:* Part-time, evening/weekend, blended/hybrid learning. *Degree requirements:* For master's, capstone project. *Entrance requirements:* For master's, statement of intent, 2 letters of recommendation. Additional exam requirements/recommendations for international students: Recommended—TOEFL (minimum score 577 paper-based; 90 iBT), IELTS (minimum score 7). Electronic applications accepted. *Expenses:* Contact institution.

Marquette University, Graduate School of Management, Program in Business Administration, Milwaukee, WI 53201-1881. Offers business administration (MBA); economics (MBA); entrepreneurship (Certificate); finance (MBA); human resources (MBA); international business (MBA); management information systems (MBA); marketing (MBA); operations and supply chain management (MBA); sports business (MBA); JD/MBA; MBA/MA; MBA/MSN. *Accreditation:* AACSB. *Program availability:* Part-time, evening/weekend. *Degree requirements:* For Certificate, business plan. *Entrance requirements:* For master's, GMAT or GRE, letters of recommendation. Additional exam requirements/recommendations for international students: Required—TOEFL (minimum score 550 paper-based; 88 iBT), IELTS (minimum score 6.5), PTE. Electronic applications accepted. *Faculty research:* Ethics in the professions, services marketing, technology impact on decision-making, mentoring.

McGill University, Faculty of Graduate and Postdoctoral Studies, Desautels Faculty of Management, Montréal, QC H3A 2T5, Canada. Offers administration (PhD); entrepreneurial studies (MBA); finance (MBA); general management (Post Master's Certificate); global manufacturing and supply chain management (MMM); information systems (MBA); international business (MBA); international practicing management (MM); management (MBA); management for development (MBA); marketing (MBA); operations management (MBA); public accountancy (Diploma); strategic management (MBA); MBA/LL B; MD/MBA. MMM offered jointly with Faculty of Engineering; PhD with Concordia University, HEC Montreal, Université de Montréal, Université du Québec à Montréal.

Mercer University, Graduate Studies, Cecil B. Day Campus, Eugene W. Stetson School of Business and Economics (Atlanta), Atlanta, GA 30341. Offers accounting (M Acc); innovation (PMBA), including entrepreneurship; international business (MBA); DPT/MBA; M Div/MBA; MBA/M Acc; Pharm D/MBA. *Accreditation:* AACSB. *Program availability:* Part-time, evening/weekend, 100% online, blended/hybrid learning. *Entrance requirements:* For master's, GMAT or GRE. Additional exam requirements/recommendations for international students: Required—TOEFL (minimum score 550 paper-based, 80 iBT) or IELTS. Electronic applications accepted. *Expenses:* Contact institution. *Faculty research:* Entrepreneurship, market studies, international business strategy, financial analysis.

Mercyhurst University, Graduate Studies, Program in Organizational Leadership, Erie, PA 16546. Offers accounting (MS); higher education administration (MS); human resources (MS); organizational leadership (MS, Certificate); sports leadership (MS); strategy and innovation (MS). *Program availability:* Part-time, evening/weekend. *Degree requirements:* For master's, thesis. *Entrance requirements:* For master's, GRE General Test or MAT, interview, resume, essay, three professional references, transcripts. Additional exam requirements/recommendations for international students: Required—TOEFL (minimum score 80 iBT), IELTS (minimum score 6.5). Electronic applications accepted. *Faculty research:* Leadership training, organizational communication, leadership pedagogy.

Midwest University, Graduate Programs, Wentzville, MO 63385. Offers asset management/investment/real estate (MBA); Christian counseling (D Min); Christian education (D Min); counseling (MA), including marriage and family counseling, school counseling; divinity (M Div); education (MA), including brain and gifted education, Christian education; global business management (MBA); global leadership (MBA); leadership (PhD), including brain and gifted educational leadership, entrepreneurial leadership, international aviation leadership, organizational leadership, political leadership; mission studies (D Min); music (MM, DMA); pastoral theology (D Min); public policy/administration (MBA); teaching English to speakers of other languages (MA). *Program availability:* Part-time, online learning. *Degree requirements:* For master's, thesis (for some programs); for doctorate, thesis/dissertation. *Entrance requirements:* Additional exam requirements/recommendations for international students: Recommended—TOEFL (minimum score 550 paper-based).

Monroe College, King Graduate School, Bronx, NY 10468. Offers accounting (MS); business administration (MBA), including entrepreneurship, finance, general business administration, healthcare management, human resources, information technology, marketing; computer science (MS); criminal justice (MS); hospitality management (MS); public health (MPH), including biostatistics and epidemiology, community health, health administration and leadership. *Program availability:* Online learning.

Nebraska Christian College of Hope International University, Graduate Programs, Papillion, NE 68046. Offers biblical studies (M Div); business as mission/social entrepreneurship (MBA); children, youth, and family (M Div); church planting (M Div); counseling psychology (MS); educational administration (MA); elementary education (M Ed); general management (MBA); gifted and talented education (M Ed); intercultural studies (M Div); international development (MBA); marketing management (MBA); ministry (MA); ministry and leadership (M Div); music education (M Ed); non-profit management (MBA); pastoral care (M Div); secondary education (M Ed); spiritual formation (M Div); worship ministry (M Div).

North Carolina State University, Graduate School, Poole College of Management, Program in Business Administration, Raleigh, NC 27695. Offers biosciences management (MBA); entrepreneurship and technology commercialization (MBA); financial management (MBA); innovation management (MBA); marketing management (MBA); services management (MBA); supply chain management (MBA). *Accreditation:* AACSB. *Program availability:* Part-time. *Degree requirements:* For master's, thesis optional. *Entrance requirements:* For master's, GMAT, interview, 3 letters of recommendation. Additional exam requirements/recommendations for international students: Required—TOEFL (minimum score 600 paper-based; 100 iBT). Electronic applications accepted. *Faculty research:* Manufacturing strategy, information systems, technology commercialization, managing research and development, historical stock returns.

Northeastern University, D'Amore-McKim School of Business, Boston, MA 02115-5096. Offers accounting (MS); business administration (EMBA, MBA); finance (MS); innovation (MS); international business (MS); international management (MS); taxation (MS); technological entrepreneurship (MS); JD/MBA; LL M/MBA; MBA/MSN; MS/MBA. *Accreditation:* AACSB. *Program availability:* Part-time, evening/weekend, online learning. *Entrance requirements:* For master's, GMAT or GRE. Electronic applications accepted. *Expenses:* Contact institution.

Northwestern University, The Graduate School, Kellogg School of Management, Management Programs, Evanston, IL 60208. Offers accounting information and management (MBA, PhD); analytical finance (MBA); business administration (MBA); decision sciences (MBA); entrepreneurship and innovation (MBA); finance (MBA, PhD); health enterprise management (MBA); human resources management (MBA); international business (MBA); management and organizations (MBA, PhD); management and organizations and sociology (PhD); management and strategy (MBA);

management studies (MS); managerial analytics (MBA); managerial economics (MBA); managerial economics and strategy (PhD); marketing (MBA, PhD); marketing management (MBA); media management (MBA); operations management (MBA, PhD); real estate (MBA); social enterprise at Kellogg (MBA); JD/MBA. *Program availability:* Part-time, evening/weekend. Terminal master's awarded for partial completion of doctoral program. *Degree requirements:* For doctorate, thesis/dissertation, 2 years of coursework, qualifying (field) exam and candidacy, summer research papers and presentations to faculty, proposal defense, final exam/defense. *Entrance requirements:* For master's, GMAT, GRE, interview, 2 letters of recommendation, college transcripts, resume, essays, Kellogg honor code; for doctorate, GMAT, GRE, statement of purpose, transcripts, 2 letters of recommendation, resume, interview. Additional exam requirements/recommendations for international students: Required—TOEFL, IELTS. Electronic applications accepted. *Expenses:* Contact institution. *Faculty research:* Business cycles and international finance, health policy, networks, non-market strategy, consumer psychology.

Nova Southeastern University, H. Wayne Huizenga College of Business and Entrepreneurship, Fort Lauderdale, FL 33314-7796. Offers accounting (M Acc); business (MBA); business intelligence/analytics (MBA); complex health systems (MBA); enterprise informatics (MBA); entrepreneurship (MBA); finance (MBA); human resource management (MBA); international business (MBA); management (MBA); marketing (MBA); process improvement (MBA); public administration (MPA); real estate development (MS); sport revenue generation (MBA); supply chain management (MBA). *Accreditation:* NASPAA. *Program availability:* Part-time, evening/weekend, 100% online, blended/hybrid learning. *Entrance requirements:* For master's, GMAT or GRE (depending on undergraduate GPA), official transcripts from all schools attended while in pursuit of bachelor's degree; minimum GPA of 2.5 from regionally-accredited institution. Additional exam requirements/recommendations for international students: Required—TOEFL (minimum score 550 paper-based; 79 iBT), IELTS (minimum score 6), PTE (minimum score 54). Electronic applications accepted. *Expenses:* Contact institution. *Faculty research:* Entrepreneurship and venture capital, ethics and social responsibility, global commerce and cultures, business process management.

Oakland University, Graduate Study and Lifelong Learning, School of Business Administration, Department of Management and Marketing, Rochester, MI 48309-4401. Offers business administration (MBA); entrepreneurship (Certificate); general management (Certificate); human resource management (Certificate); international business (Certificate); management and marketing (EMBA); marketing (Certificate).

Oklahoma State University, Spears School of Business, School of Entrepreneurship, Stillwater, OK 74078. Offers MBA, MS, PhD. *Program availability:* Part-time. *Faculty:* 8 full-time (0 women). *Students:* 9 full-time (5 women), 28 part-time (5 women); includes 8 minority (2 Black or African American, non-Hispanic/Latino; 1 American Indian or Alaska Native, non-Hispanic/Latino; 5 Hispanic/Latino), 5 international. Average age 31. 9 applicants, 78% accepted, 7 enrolled. In 2018, 10 master's, 1 doctorate awarded. *Entrance requirements:* For master's and doctorate, GMAT. Additional exam requirements/recommendations for international students: Required—TOEFL (minimum score 550 paper-based; 89 iBT). *Application deadline:* For fall admission, 3/1 priority date for international students; for spring admission, 8/1 priority date for international students. Applications are processed on a rolling basis. Application fee: $40 ($75 for international students). Electronic applications accepted. *Expenses: Tuition, area resident:* Full-time $4148. Tuition, state resident: full-time $4148. Tuition, nonresident: full-time $10,517. *International tuition:* $10,517 full-time. *Required fees:* $4394; $2929 per credit hour. Tuition and fees vary according to course load and program. *Financial support:* Research assistantships, teaching assistantships, career-related internships or fieldwork, Federal Work-Study, scholarships/grants, health care benefits, tuition waivers (partial), and unspecified assistantships available. Support available to part-time students. Financial award application deadline: 3/1; financial award applicants required to submit FAFSA. *Unit head:* Dr. Bruce Barringer, Department Head, 405-744-9702, E-mail: bruce.barringer@okstate.edu. *Application contact:* Dr. Sheryl Tucker, Dean, 405-744-6368, Fax: 405-744-0355, E-mail: gradi@okstate.edu.
Website: https://business.okstate.edu/entrepreneurship/

Old Dominion University, College of Arts and Letters, Institute for the Humanities, Norfolk, VA 23529. Offers arts and entrepreneurship (Certificate); cultural and human geography (MA); cultural studies (MA); gender and sexuality studies (MA); health, communication and culture (Certificate); media and popular culture studies (MA); philosophy and religious studies (MA); social justice and entrepreneurship (Certificate); visual studies (MA); world cultures (MA). *Program availability:* Part-time, evening/weekend. *Degree requirements:* For master's, thesis optional, project. *Entrance requirements:* For master's, GRE General Test, minimum GPA of 3.25. Electronic applications accepted. *Faculty research:* Media studies, cultural studies, gender studies, American literature, philosophy, art history, cultural geography.

Oral Roberts University, School of Business, Tulsa, OK 74171. Offers accounting (MBA); entrepreneurship (MBA); finance (MBA); international business (MBA); management (MBA); marketing (MBA); not for profit management (MNM). *Accreditation:* ACBSP. *Program availability:* Part-time, online learning. *Degree requirements:* For master's, thesis optional. *Entrance requirements:* For master's, minimum cumulative GPA of 3.0 from regionally-accredited institution. Electronic applications accepted. Application fee is waived when completed online. *Faculty research:* Social media, international business and marketing.

Pace University, Lubin School of Business, Program in Management, New York, NY 10038. Offers entrepreneurial studies (MBA); entrepreneurship (MS); human resource management (MBA, MS); strategic management (MBA, MS). *Program availability:* Part-time, evening/weekend. *Students:* 63 full-time (38 women), 57 part-time (41 women); includes 41 minority (18 Black or African American, non-Hispanic/Latino; 8 Asian, non-Hispanic/Latino; 11 Hispanic/Latino; 1 Native Hawaiian or other Pacific Islander, non-Hispanic/Latino; 3 Two or more races, non-Hispanic/Latino), 34 international. Average age 30. 125 applicants, 66% accepted, 42 enrolled. In 2018, 55 master's awarded. *Entrance requirements:* For master's, GMAT, GRE (GMAT not required for MS in Human Resources Management with 3 years of HR experience in a management position), undergraduate degree, transcripts from all accredited colleges/universities attended, two letters of recommendation, resume, personal statement. Additional exam requirements/recommendations for international students: Required—TOEFL (minimum score 90 iBT), IELTS (minimum score 7) or PTE (minimum score 61). *Application deadline:* For fall admission, 8/1 priority date for domestic students, 6/1 for international students; for spring admission, 12/1 for domestic students, 10/1 for international students. Applications are processed on a rolling basis. Application fee: $70. Electronic applications accepted. *Financial support:* Research assistantships, career-related internships or fieldwork, Federal Work-Study, and unspecified assistantships available. Support available to part-time students. Financial award application deadline: 2/15; financial award applicants required to submit FAFSA. *Unit head:* Dr. Ibraiz Tarique, Chairperson, Management and Management of Science, 212-618-6583, E-mail: itarique@pace.edu. *Application contact:* Susan Ford-Goldschein, Director of Graduate Admissions, 212-346-1531, Fax: 212-346-1585, E-mail: graduateadmission@pace.edu.
Website: http://www.pace.edu/lubin/sections/explore-programs/graduate-programs

Penn State Great Valley, Graduate Studies, Management Division, Malvern, PA 19355-1488. Offers business administration (MBA); cyber security (Certificate); data analytics (MPS, MS, Certificate); distributed energy and grid modernization (Certificate); finance (M Fin); health sector management (Certificate); human resource management (Certificate); information science (MSIS); leadership development (MLD); new ventures and entrepreneurship (Certificate); sustainable management practices (Certificate). *Accreditation:* AACSB.

Penn State University Park, Graduate School, College of Engineering, Program in Engineering Leadership and Innovation Management, University Park, PA 16802. Offers M Eng.

Peru State College, Graduate Programs, Program in Organizational Management, Peru, NE 68421. Offers MS. Program offered online only. *Program availability:* Part-time, online learning. *Degree requirements:* For master's, thesis (for some programs). *Expenses:* Contact institution. *Faculty research:* Emotional intelligence.

Point Loma Nazarene University, Fermanian School of Business, San Diego, CA 92106-2899. Offers general business (MBA); healthcare management (MBA); innovation and entrepreneurship (MBA); organizational leadership (MBA); project management (MBA). *Accreditation:* ACBSP. *Program availability:* Part-time, evening/weekend. *Entrance requirements:* For master's, GMAT, letters of recommendation, essay, interview. Additional exam requirements/recommendations for international students: Required—TOEFL. Electronic applications accepted. *Expenses:* Contact institution.

Pontificia Universidad Catolica Madre y Maestra, Graduate School, Faculty of Social and Administrative Sciences, Santiago, Dominican Republic. Offers business administration (MBA), including business development, finance, international business, management skills (M Mgmt, MBA), marketing, operations, strategic cost management, strategy, tourist destination planning and management; law (LL M), including civil law, corporate business law, criminal law, international relations, real estate law; management (M Mgmt), including higher financial management, insurance program administration, management skills (M Mgmt, MBA); psychology (MA), including clinical child and adolescent psychology, forensic psychology; strategic human resources (EMBA).

Purchase College, State University of New York, School of the Arts, Purchase, NY 10577-1400. Offers entrepreneurship in the arts (MA). *Program availability:* Part-time. *Degree requirements:* For master's, thesis. *Expenses: Tuition, area resident:* Full-time $11,090; part-time $462 per credit hour. Tuition, state resident: full-time $11,310. Tuition, nonresident: full-time $23,100; part-time $944 per credit hour. *Required fees:* $1883; $75.57 per credit hour. One-time fee: $210 full-time.

Purdue University Global, School of Business, Davenport, IA 52807. Offers business administration (MBA); change leadership (MS); entrepreneurship (MBA); finance (MBA); health care management (MBA, MS); human resource (MBA); international business (MBA); management (MS); marketing (MBA); project management (MBA, MS); supply chain management and logistics (MBA, MS). *Accreditation:* ACBSP. *Program availability:* Part-time, evening/weekend, online learning. *Entrance requirements:* Additional exam requirements/recommendations for international students: Required—TOEFL (minimum score 550 paper-based; 80 iBT). Electronic applications accepted.

Queen's University at Kingston, Smith School of Business, Program in Business Administration, Kingston, ON K7L 3N6, Canada. Offers consulting and project management (MBA); finance (MBA); innovation and entrepreneurship (MBA); marketing (MBA). *Degree requirements:* For master's, thesis optional, research project. *Entrance requirements:* For master's, GMAT, minimum B+ average. Additional exam requirements/recommendations for international students: Required—TOEFL. Electronic applications accepted. *Faculty research:* Management fundamentals, strategic thinking, global business, innovation and change, leadership.

Regent University, Graduate School, School of Business and Leadership, Virginia Beach, VA 23464-9800. Offers business administration (MBA), including accounting, economics, entrepreneurship, finance and investing, general management, healthcare management (MA, MBA), human resource management (MA, MBA), innovation management, leadership, marketing, not-for-profit management (MA, MBA); business analytics (MS); business and design management (MA); church leadership (MA); leadership (Certificate); organizational leadership (MA, PhD), including ecclesial leadership (DSL, PhD), entrepreneurial leadership (PhD), healthcare management (MA, MBA), human resource development (PhD), human resource management (MA, MBA), individualized studies (DSL, PhD), interdisciplinary studies (MA), leadership coaching and mentoring (MA), not-for-profit management (MA, MBA), organizational development consulting (MA), servant leadership (MA, DSL); strategic leadership (DSL), including ecclesial leadership (DSL, PhD), global consulting, healthcare leadership, individualized studies (DSL, PhD), leadership coaching, servant leadership (MA, DSL), strategic foresight. *Program availability:* Part-time, evening/weekend, 100% online, blended/hybrid learning. *Degree requirements:* For master's, thesis or alternative, 3-credit hour culminating experience; for doctorate, thesis/dissertation. *Entrance requirements:* For master's, college transcripts, resume, essay; for doctorate, college transcripts, resume, essay, writing sample; for Certificate, writing sample, resume, transcripts. Additional exam requirements/recommendations for international students: Required—TOEFL (minimum score 577 paper-based). Electronic applications accepted. *Expenses:* Contact institution. *Faculty research:* Servant leadership, global business, team effectiveness, technology utilization, leadership development.

Rensselaer Polytechnic Institute, Graduate School, Lally School of Management, Program in Technology Commercialization and Entrepreneurship, Troy, NY 12180-3590. Offers MS, MS/MBA. *Program availability:* Part-time. *Faculty:* 36 full-time (9 women), 5 part-time/adjunct (0 women). *Students:* 9 full-time (5 women), 1 part-time (0 women); includes 7 minority (4 Black or African American, non-Hispanic/Latino; 2 Hispanic/Latino; 1 Two or more races, non-Hispanic/Latino), 1 international. Average age 23. 13 applicants, 77% accepted, 2 enrolled. *Entrance requirements:* For master's, GMAT or GRE, personal statement. Additional exam requirements/recommendations for international students: Required—TOEFL (minimum score 570 paper-based; 88 iBT), IELTS (minimum score 6.5), PTE (minimum score 60). *Application deadline:* For fall admission, 1/1 for domestic and international students. Applications are processed on a rolling basis. Application fee: $75. Electronic applications accepted. *Financial support:* Scholarships/grants available. Financial award application deadline: 1/1. *Unit head:* Dr. Hao Zhao, Graduate Program Director, 518-276-6818, E-mail: zhaoh@rpi.edu. *Application contact:* Jarron Decker, Director of Graduate Admissions, 518-276-6216, Fax: 518-276-4072, E-mail: gradadmissions@rpi.edu.
Website: https://lallyschool.rpi.edu/graduate-programs/ms-tce

Rochester Institute of Technology, Graduate Enrollment Services, Saunders College of Business, Marketing and Management Department, MS Program in Entrepreneurship and Innovative Ventures, Rochester, NY 14623-5603. Offers MS. *Program availability:* Part-time, evening/weekend. *Students:* 11 full-time (5 women), 4 part-time (2 women), 2 international. Average age 29. 15 applicants, 27% accepted, 2 enrolled. In 2018, 3 master's awarded. *Entrance requirements:* For master's, GMAT or GRE, minimum GPA of 3.0 (recommended), resume, essay. Additional exam requirements/recommendations for international students: Required—TOEFL (minimum score 580 paper-based; 92 iBT),

IELTS (minimum score 7), PTE (minimum score 63). *Application deadline:* Applications are processed on a rolling basis. Application fee: $65. Electronic applications accepted. *Financial support:* In 2018–19, 2 students received support. Research assistantships with partial tuition reimbursements available, teaching assistantships with partial tuition reimbursements available, career-related internships or fieldwork, scholarships/grants, and unspecified assistantships available. Support available to part-time students. Financial award applicants required to submit FAFSA. *Faculty research:* Technology management, creativity, and innovation; corporate social responsibility and business ethics; entrepreneurship; leadership; social capital/work relationships; social media and entrepreneurship. *Unit head:* Matt Cornwell, Assistant Director of Student Services and Outreach, 585-475-6916, E-mail: mcornwell@saunders.rit.edu. *Application contact:* Diane Ellison, Senior Associate Vice President, Graduate Enrollment Services, 585-475-2229, Fax: 585-475-7164, E-mail: gradinfo@rit.edu.
Website: https://www.rit.edu/study/entrepreneurship-and-innovative-ventures-ms

Rockhurst University, Helzberg School of Management, Kansas City, MO 64110-2561. Offers accounting (MBA); business intelligence (MBA, Certificate); business intelligence and analytics (MS); data science (MBA, Certificate); entrepreneurship (MBA); finance (MBA); fundraising leadership (MBA, Certificate); healthcare management (MBA, Certificate); human capital (Certificate); international business (Certificate); management (MA, MBA, Certificate); nonprofit administration (Certificate); organizational development (Certificate); science leadership (Certificate). *Accreditation:* AACSB. *Program availability:* Part-time, evening/weekend. *Entrance requirements:* For master's, GMAT or GRE. Additional exam requirements/recommendations for international students: Required—TOEFL (minimum score 550 paper-based; 79 iBT). Electronic applications accepted. *Faculty research:* Offshoring/outsourcing, systems analysis/synthesis, work teams, multilateral trade, path dependencies/creation.

Rollins College, Crummer Graduate School of Business, Winter Park, FL 32789-4499. Offers entrepreneurship (MBA); finance (MBA); international business (MBA); management (MBA). *Accreditation:* AACSB. *Program availability:* Part-time, evening/weekend, online learning. *Degree requirements:* For master's, minimum GPA of 2.85. *Entrance requirements:* For master's, GMAT or GRE, official transcripts, two letters of recommendation, essay, current resume/curriculum vitae, interview. Additional exam requirements/recommendations for international students: Required—TOEFL (minimum score 100 iBT) or IELTS (minimum score 7). Electronic applications accepted. *Expenses:* Contact institution. *Faculty research:* Sustainability, world financial markets, international business, market research, strategic marketing.

Salve Regina University, Program in Business Administration, Newport, RI 02840-4192. Offers cybersecurity issues in business (MBA); entrepreneurial enterprise (MBA); health care administration and management (MBA); nonprofit management (MBA); social ventures (MBA). *Program availability:* Part-time, evening/weekend, online learning. *Entrance requirements:* For master's, GMAT, GRE General Test, or MAT, 6 undergraduate credits each in accounting, economics, quantitative analysis and calculus or statistics. Additional exam requirements/recommendations for international students: Required—TOEFL (minimum score 600 paper-based; 100 iBT) or IELTS. Electronic applications accepted. *Expenses: Tuition:* Full-time $10,530; part-time $585 per credit. *Required fees:* $60 per term. Tuition and fees vary according to course level, course load, degree level and program.

Samford University, Brock School of Business, Birmingham, AL 35229. Offers accountancy (M Acc); entrepreneurship (MBA); finance (MBA); marketing (MBA); JD/M Acc; JD/MBA; MBA/M Acc; MBA/M Div; MBA/MSEM; MBA/Pharm D. Programs offered jointly with Cumberland School of Law, Beeson School of Divinity, Howard College of Arts and Sciences, and McWhorter School of Pharmacy. *Accreditation:* AACSB. *Program availability:* Part-time, 100% online, blended/hybrid learning. *Faculty:* 7 full-time (1 woman), 4 part-time/adjunct (0 women). *Students:* 76 full-time (30 women), 20 part-time (11 women); includes 8 minority (4 Black or African American, non-Hispanic/Latino; 1 Asian, non-Hispanic/Latino; 1 Hispanic/Latino; 2 Two or more races, non-Hispanic/Latino), 7 international. Average age 28. 41 applicants, 88% accepted, 26 enrolled. In 2018, 74 master's awarded. *Degree requirements:* For master's, capstone course. *Entrance requirements:* For master's, GMAT or GRE, resume, transcripts, WES or ECE Evaluation (international applicants only), essay (international applicants only). Additional exam requirements/recommendations for international students: Required—TOEFL (minimum score 90 iBT), IELTS (minimum score 6.5). *Application deadline:* For fall admission, 8/1 for domestic and international students; for spring admission, 1/1 for domestic and international students. Applications are processed on a rolling basis. Application fee: $35. Electronic applications accepted. Application fee is waived when completed online. *Expenses: Tuition:* Full-time $17,255; part-time $837 per credit. *Required fees:* $610; $305 per term. Tuition and fees vary according to course load, degree level, program and student level. *Financial support:* In 2018–19, 46 students received support. Scholarships/grants available. Financial award application deadline: 2/15; financial award applicants required to submit FAFSA. *Unit head:* Dr. Barbara Cartledge, Assistant Dean, 205-726-2935, Fax: 205-726-2540, E-mail: bhcartle@samford.edu. *Application contact:* Elizabeth Gambrell, Associate Director, 205-726-2040, Fax: 205-726-2540, E-mail: eagambre@samford.edu.
Website: http://www.samford.edu/business

San Diego State University, Graduate and Research Affairs, Fowler College of Business, Department of Management, San Diego, CA 92182. Offers entrepreneurship (MS); human resources management (MS); management science (MS). *Program availability:* Part-time, evening/weekend. *Degree requirements:* For master's, thesis or alternative. *Entrance requirements:* For master's, GMAT, resume, letters of reference. Additional exam requirements/recommendations for international students: Required—TOEFL. Electronic applications accepted.

San Francisco State University, Division of Graduate Studies, College of Business, Program in Business Administration, San Francisco, CA 94132-1722. Offers decision sciences/operations research (MBA); ethics and compliance (MBA); finance (MBA); global business and innovation (MBA); healthcare administration (MBA); hospitality and tourism management (MBA); information systems (MBA); leadership (MBA); marketing (MBA); nonprofit and social enterprise leadership (MBA); sustainable business (MBA). *Accreditation:* AACSB. *Program availability:* Part-time, evening/weekend. *Degree requirements:* For master's, thesis, essay test. *Entrance requirements:* For master's, GMAT, minimum GPA of 2.7 in last 60 units. Additional exam requirements/recommendations for international students: Required—TOEFL (minimum score 550 paper-based).

Seton Hall University, Stillman School of Business, Programs in Business Administration, South Orange, NJ 07079-2697. Offers accounting (MBA); entrepreneurial studies (Certificate); finance (MBA); financial decision making (Certificate); information technology management (MBA); international business (MBA); management (MBA); marketing (MBA); sport management (MBA); supply chain management (MBA, Certificate). *Program availability:* Part-time, evening/weekend. *Faculty:* 27 full-time (5 women), 18 part-time/adjunct (2 women). *Students:* 85 full-time (40 women), 363 part-time (147 women); includes 78 minority (22 Black or African American, non-Hispanic/Latino; 4 Asian, non-Hispanic/Latino; 18 Hispanic/Latino; 29 Native Hawaiian or other Pacific Islander, non-Hispanic/Latino; 5 Two or more races, non-Hispanic/Latino), 282 international. Average age 34. 483 applicants, 85% accepted, 302 enrolled. In 2018, 96 master's awarded. *Degree requirements:* For master's, 20 hours of community service (Social Responsibility Project). *Entrance requirements:* For master's, GMAT or CPA, GRE (waived based on work experience or advanced degree from AACSB institution), MS in business discipline, professional degree or designation (MD, JD, PhD, DVM, DDS, CPA, etc.), minimum undergraduate GPA of 3.0. Additional exam requirements/recommendations for international students: Required—TOEFL (minimum score 607 paper-based; 80 iBT), IELTS (minimum score 6), PTE. *Application deadline:* For fall admission, 5/31 priority date for domestic students, 4/30 priority date for international students; for spring admission, 10/31 priority date for domestic students, 9/30 priority date for international students; for summer admission, 3/31 priority date for domestic students. Applications are processed on a rolling basis. Application fee: $75. Electronic applications accepted. Application fee is waived when completed online. *Expenses:* Tuition is $1,305 per credit hour and the overall MBA is a 40 credit hour program. University fees are $115 per semester. The university also has a technology that is $125 per semester. *Financial support:* In 2018–19, 44 students received support, including 25 research assistantships with partial tuition reimbursements available (averaging $3,644 per year); career-related internships or fieldwork, scholarships/grants, and unspecified assistantships also available. Financial award application deadline: 6/30; financial award applicants required to submit FAFSA. *Faculty research:* Sport, hedge funds, executive compensation, social media, legal studies. *Unit head:* Dr. Joyce Strawser, Dean, 973-761-9013, Fax: 973-761-9217, E-mail: joyce.strawser@shu.edu. *Application contact:* Alfred Ayoub, Director of Graduate Admissions, 973-761-9262, Fax: 973-761-9208, E-mail: alfred.ayoub@shu.edu.
Website: http://www.shu.edu/business/mba-programs.cfm

Seton Hill University, MBA Program, Greensburg, PA 15601. Offers entrepreneurship (MBA); forensic accounting and fraud examination (MBA); healthcare administration (MBA); management (MBA). *Program availability:* Part-time, evening/weekend. *Entrance requirements:* For master's, resume, 3 letters of recommendation, personal statement, transcripts. Additional exam requirements/recommendations for international students: Required—TOEFL (minimum score 600 paper-based; 100 iBT), IELTS (minimum score 6.5). *Application deadline:* Applications are processed on a rolling basis. Application fee: $0. Electronic applications accepted. *Financial support:* Federal Work-Study, scholarships/grants, and tuition discounts available. Financial award application deadline: 8/15; financial award applicants required to submit FAFSA. *Unit head:* Dr. Douglas Nelson, Associate Professor, Business/MBA Program Director, E-mail: dnelson@setonhill.edu. *Application contact:* Dr. Douglas Nelson, Associate Professor, Business/MBA Program Director, E-mail: dnelson@setonhill.edu.
Website: http://www.setonhill.edu/academics/graduate_programs/mba

SIT Graduate Institute, Graduate Programs, Master's Program in Global Leadership and Social Innovation, Brattleboro, VT 05302-0676. Offers MA. *Program availability:* Online learning.

South Carolina State University, College of Graduate and Professional Studies, Department of Business Administration, Orangeburg, SC 29117-0001. Offers agribusiness (MBA); entrepreneurship (MBA); general business administration (MBA); healthcare management (MBA). *Program availability:* Part-time, evening/weekend. *Faculty:* 7 full-time (2 women). *Students:* 20 full-time (9 women), 6 part-time (2 women); all minorities (all Black or African American, non-Hispanic/Latino). Average age 28. 12 applicants, 92% accepted, 9 enrolled. In 2018, 14 master's awarded. *Degree requirements:* For master's, comprehensive exam, business plan. *Entrance requirements:* For master's, GMAT, minimum GPA of 2.8. Additional exam requirements/recommendations for international students: Required—TOEFL. *Application deadline:* For fall admission, 6/15 for domestic and international students; for spring admission, 11/1 for domestic and international students. Application fee: $25. Electronic applications accepted. *Expenses: Tuition, area resident:* Full-time $9928; part-time $552 per credit hour. Tuition, state resident: full-time $9928. Tuition, nonresident: full-time $21,038; part-time $1169 per credit hour. *Required fees:* $1532; $85 per credit hour. *Financial support:* Fellowships, research assistantships, career-related internships or fieldwork, Federal Work-Study, scholarships/grants, and unspecified assistantships available. Financial award application deadline: 6/1. *Unit head:* Dr. David Jamison, Interim Chair, 803-536-8443, Fax: 803-536-8078, E-mail: djamison@scsu.edu. *Application contact:* Ellen R. Ricoma, MBA Program Director, 803-533-3777, Fax: 803-516-4651, E-mail: ericoma1@scsu.edu.

Southeastern University, Jannetides College of Business and Entrepreneurial Leadership, Lakeland, FL 33801-6099. Offers executive leadership (MBA); global business administration (MBA); healthcare administration (MBA); missional leadership (MBA); organizational leadership (PhD); sport management (MBA); strategic leadership (DSL). *Accreditation:* ACBSP. *Program availability:* Evening/weekend, online learning. *Entrance requirements:* For master's, GMAT, minimum cumulative GPA of 3.0, writing sample. Electronic applications accepted.

Southeast Missouri State University, School of Graduate Studies, Harrison College of Business and Computing, Cape Girardeau, MO 63701-4799. Offers accounting (MBA); entrepreneurship (MBA); financial management (MBA); sport management (MBA). *Accreditation:* AACSB. *Program availability:* Part-time, evening/weekend, 100% online. *Faculty:* 27 full-time (7 women), 1 (woman) part-time/adjunct. *Students:* 94 full-time (50 women), 88 part-time (39 women); includes 18 minority (9 Black or African American, non-Hispanic/Latino; 4 Asian, non-Hispanic/Latino; 5 Hispanic/Latino), 79 international. Average age 29. 80 applicants, 100% accepted, 80 enrolled. In 2018, 62 master's awarded. *Degree requirements:* For master's, variable foreign language requirement, comprehensive exam (for some programs), thesis or alternative. *Entrance requirements:* For master's, GMAT or GRE, minimum undergraduate GPA of 2.5, minimum grade of C in prerequisite courses. Additional exam requirements/recommendations for international students: Required—TOEFL (minimum score 550 paper-based; 79 iBT), IELTS (minimum score 6), PTE (minimum score 53). *Application deadline:* For fall admission, 8/1 for domestic students, 6/1 for international students; for spring admission, 11/21 for domestic students, 10/1 for international students; for summer admission, 5/15 for domestic students. Applications are processed on a rolling basis. Application fee: $30 ($40 for international students). Electronic applications accepted. *Expenses:* Contact institution. *Financial support:* In 2018–19, 16 students received support. Career-related internships or fieldwork, Federal Work-Study, scholarships/grants, traineeships, tuition waivers (full), and unspecified assistantships available. Financial award application deadline: 6/30; financial award applicants required to submit FAFSA. *Faculty research:* Organizational justice, ethics, leadership, corporate finance, generational differences. *Unit head:* Dr. Alberto Davila, Dean, 573-651-2112, E-mail: adavila@semo.edu. *Application contact:* Dr. Alberto Davila, Dean, 573-651-2112, E-mail: adavila@semo.edu.
Website: http://www.semo.edu/mba

Southern Methodist University, Cox School of Business, MBA Program, Dallas, TX 75275. Offers accounting (MBA, PMBA); business (EMBA); business analytics (PMBA); finance (MBA, PMBA); information technology and operations management (MBA, PMBA), including business analytics (MBA), information and operations (MBA); management (MBA, PMBA); marketing (MBA, PMBA); real estate (MBA, PMBA); strategy and entrepreneurship (MBA, PMBA); JD/MBA; MA/MBA. *Program availability:* Part-time, evening/weekend. *Entrance requirements:* For master's, GMAT. Additional

exam requirements/recommendations for international students: Required—TOEFL. Electronic applications accepted. *Expenses:* Contact institution. *Faculty research:* Corporate finance, financial reporting, modeling consumer decision-making, competition between national brands and store brands, institutional determinants of firms' strategy.

Southern New Hampshire University, School of Business, Manchester, NH 03106-1045. Offers accounting (MBA, Graduate Certificate); accounting finance (MS); accounting/auditing (MS); accounting/forensic accounting (MS); accounting/ management accounting (MS); accounting/taxation (MS); applied economics (MS); athletic administration (MBA, Graduate Certificate); business administration (IMBA, Certificate), including business information systems (Certificate), human resource management (Certificate); business analytics (MBA); business intelligence (MBA); communication (MA), including new media and marketing, public relations; community economic development (MBA); criminal justice (MBA); data analytics (MS); economics (MBA); engineering management (MBA); entrepreneurship (MBA); finance (MBA, MS, Graduate Certificate); finance/corporate finance (MS); finance/investments (MS); forensic accounting (MBA); forensic accounting and fraud examination (Graduate Certificate); healthcare informatics (MBA); healthcare management (MBA); human resource management (MS); human resources (MBA); information technology (MS); information technology management (MBA); international business (PhD); Internet marketing (MBA); leadership (MBA); leadership of nonprofit organizations (Graduate Certificate); management (MS); marketing (MBA, MS, Graduate Certificate); music business (MBA); operations and project management (MS); operations and supply chain management (MBA, Graduate Certificate); organizational leadership (MS); project management (MBA, Graduate Certificate); public administration (MBA, Graduate Certificate); quantitative analysis (MBA); Six Sigma (Graduate Certificate); Six Sigma quality (MBA); social media marketing (MBA, Graduate Certificate); sport management (MBA, MS, Graduate Certificate); sustainability and environmental compliance (MBA); MBA/Certificate. *Accreditation:* ACBSP. *Program availability:* Part-time, evening/ weekend, online learning. Terminal master's awarded for partial completion of doctoral program. *Degree requirements:* For master's, one foreign language, comprehensive exam (for some programs), thesis or alternative; for doctorate, one foreign language, comprehensive exam, thesis/dissertation. *Entrance requirements:* For master's, minimum GPA of 2.5; for doctorate, GMAT. Additional exam requirements/ recommendations for international students: Required—TOEFL (minimum score 500 paper-based). Electronic applications accepted.

South University, Graduate Programs, College of Business, Savannah, GA 31406. Offers corrections (MBA); entrepreneurship and small business (MBA); healthcare administration (MBA); hospitality management (MBA); leadership (MS); public administration (MPA); sustainability (MBA).

Stevens Institute of Technology, Graduate School, School of Business, Program in Business Administration, Hoboken, NJ 07030. Offers business intelligence and analytics (MBA); engineering management (MBA); finance (MBA); information systems (MBA); innovation and entrepreneurship (MBA); marketing (MBA); pharmaceutical management (MBA); project management (MBA, Certificate); technology management (MBA); telecommunications management (MBA). *Accreditation:* AACSB. *Program availability:* Part-time, evening/weekend. *Faculty:* 58 full-time (8 women), 18 part-time/adjunct (3 women). *Students:* 44 full-time (23 women), 202 part-time (90 women); includes 56 minority (12 Black or African American, non-Hispanic/Latino; 2 American Indian or Alaska Native, non-Hispanic/Latino; 40 Asian, non-Hispanic/Latino; 2 Hispanic/Latino), 28 international. Average age 37. In 2018, 45 master's awarded. Terminal master's awarded for partial completion of doctoral program. *Degree requirements:* For master's, thesis optional, minimum B average in major field and overall; for Certificate, minimum B average. *Entrance requirements:* For master's, GRE/GMAT scores: GRE scores are required for all applicants applying to a full-time graduate program in the Schaefer School of Engineering and Science (SES). International applicants must submit TOEFL/ IELTS scores and fulfill the English Language Proficiency Requirements in order to be considered. Additional exam requirements/recommendations for international students: Required—TOEFL (minimum score 74 iBT), IELTS (minimum score 6). *Application deadline:* For fall admission, 4/1 for domestic and international students; for spring admission, 11/1 for domestic and international students; for summer admission, 5/1 for domestic students. Applications are processed on a rolling basis. Application fee: $60. Electronic applications accepted. *Expenses: Tuition:* Full-time $35,960; part-time $1620 per credit. *Required fees:* $1290; $600 per semester. Tuition and fees vary according to course load. *Financial support:* Fellowships, research assistantships, teaching assistantships, career-related internships or fieldwork, Federal Work-Study, scholarships/grants, and unspecified assistantships available. Financial award application deadline: 2/15; financial award applicants required to submit FAFSA. *Unit head:* Dr. Gregory Prastacos, Dean, 201-216-8366, E-mail: gprastac@stevens.edu. *Application contact:* Graduate Admissions, 888-783-8367, Fax: 888-511-1306, E-mail: graduate@stevens.edu.
Website: https://www.stevens.edu/school-business/masters-programs/mbaemba

Stevens Institute of Technology, Graduate School, School of Business, Program in Information Systems, Hoboken, NJ 07030. Offers computer science (MS); e-commerce (MS); enterprise systems (MS); entrepreneurial information technology (MS); information architecture (MS); information management (MS, Certificate); information security (MS); information technology in financial services industry (MS); information technology in the pharmaceutical industry (MS); information technology outsourcing management (MS); project management (MS, Certificate); software engineering (MS); telecommunications (MS). *Program availability:* Part-time, evening/weekend. *Students:* 248 full-time (87 women), 54 part-time (20 women); includes 25 minority (8 Black or African American, non-Hispanic/Latino; 17 Asian, non-Hispanic/Latino), 245 international. Average age 27. In 2018, 202 master's, 16 other advanced degrees awarded. Terminal master's awarded for partial completion of doctoral program. *Degree requirements:* For master's, thesis optional, minimum B average in major field and overall; for Certificate, minimum B average. *Entrance requirements:* For master's, GRE/ GMAT scores: GRE scores are required for all applicants applying to a full-time graduate program in the Schaefer School of Engineering and Science (SES). International applicants must submit TOEFL/IELTS scores and fulfill the English Language Proficiency Requirements in order to be considered. Additional exam requirements/ recommendations for international students: Required—TOEFL (minimum score 74 iBT), IELTS (minimum score 6). *Application deadline:* For fall admission, 4/1 for domestic and international students; for spring admission, 11/1 for domestic and international students; for summer admission, 5/1 for domestic students. Applications are processed on a rolling basis. Application fee: $60. Electronic applications accepted. *Expenses: Tuition:* Full-time $35,960; part-time $1620 per credit. *Required fees:* $1290; $600 per semester. Tuition and fees vary according to course load. *Financial support:* Fellowships, research assistantships, teaching assistantships, career-related internships or fieldwork, Federal Work-Study, scholarships/grants, and unspecified assistantships available. Financial award application deadline: 2/15; financial award applicants required to submit FAFSA. *Unit head:* Dr. Gregory Prastacos, Dean of SB, 201-216-8366, E-mail: gprastac@stevens.edu. *Application contact:* Graduate Admissions, 888-783-8367, Fax: 888-511-1306, E-mail: graduate@stevens.edu.
Website: https://www.stevens.edu/school-business/masters-programs/information-systems

Stony Brook University, State University of New York, Graduate School, College of Business, Program in Business Administration, Stony Brook, NY 11794. Offers accounting (MBA); business administration (MBA); finance (MBA, Certificate); health care management (MBA); human resources (MBA); innovation (MBA); management (MBA); marketing (MBA); operations management (MBA). *Faculty:* 38 full-time (13 women), 8 part-time/adjunct (3 women). *Students:* 153 full-time (74 women), 148 part-time (76 women); includes 76 minority (16 Black or African American, non-Hispanic/Latino; 29 Asian, non-Hispanic/Latino; 27 Hispanic/Latino; 4 Two or more races, non-Hispanic/Latino), 36 international. Average age 28. 128 applicants, 78% accepted, 75 enrolled. In 2018, 76 master's awarded. *Entrance requirements:* For master's, GMAT, 3 letters of recommendation from current or former employers or professors, transcripts, personal statement, resume. Additional exam requirements/recommendations for international students: Required—TOEFL (minimum score 550 paper-based; 80 iBT), IELTS (minimum score 6.5). *Application deadline:* For fall admission, 5/15 for domestic students, 3/15 for international students; for spring admission, 12/1 for domestic students, 10/15 for international students. Application fee: $100. *Expenses:* Contact institution. *Financial support:* Teaching assistantships available. *Total annual research expenditures:* $2,070. *Unit head:* Dr. Manuel London, Dean, 631-632-7159, E-mail: manuel.london@stonybrook.edu. *Application contact:* Dr. Dmytro Holod, Associate Dean for Academic Programs/Graduate Director, 631-632-7183, Fax: 631-632-8181, E-mail: dmytro.holod@stonybrook.edu.
Website: https://www.stonybrook.edu/commcms/business/

Suffolk University, Sawyer Business School, Master of Business Administration Program, Boston, MA 02108-2770. Offers accounting (MBA); entrepreneurship (MBA); executive business administration (EMBA); finance (MBA); global business administration (GMBA); health administration (MBA); international business (MBA); marketing (MBA); nonprofit management (MBA); organizational behavior (MBA); strategic management (MBA); supply chain management (MBA); taxation (MBA); JD/MBA; MBA/MHA; MBA/ MSA; MBA/MSF; MBA/MST. *Accreditation:* AACSB. *Program availability:* Part-time, evening/weekend, 100% online. *Faculty:* 18 full-time (5 women), 5 part-time/adjunct (0 women). *Students:* 79 full-time (46 women), 193 part-time (107 women); includes 69 minority (17 Black or African American, non-Hispanic/Latino; 18 Asian, non-Hispanic/ Latino; 28 Hispanic/Latino; 6 Two or more races, non-Hispanic/Latino), 40 international. Average age 30. 274 applicants, 67% accepted, 83 enrolled. In 2018, 125 master's awarded. *Entrance requirements:* For master's, GMAT, minimum undergraduate GPA of 2.75 (MBA), 5 years of managerial experience (EMBA). Additional exam requirements/ recommendations for international students: Required—TOEFL (minimum score 550 paper-based; 80 iBT). *Application deadline:* For fall admission, 3/15 priority date for domestic students, 10/15 priority date for international students; for spring admission, 10/ 15 priority date for domestic and international students. Applications are processed on a rolling basis. Application fee: $50. Electronic applications accepted. *Expenses:* Contact institution. *Financial support:* In 2018–19, 170 students received support, including 4 fellowships (averaging $2,906 per year); career-related internships or fieldwork, Federal Work-Study, institutionally sponsored loans, and scholarships/grants also available. Support available to part-time students. Financial award application deadline: 4/1; financial award applicants required to submit FAFSA. *Faculty research:* Foreign investments; career strategies and boundaryless careers; corporate ethics codes; interest rates, inflation, and growth options; innovation and product development performance. *Unit head:* Jodi Detjen, Director of MBA Programs, 617-573-8306, E-mail: jdetjen@suffolk.edu. *Application contact:* Mara Marzocchi, Associate Director of Graduate Admissions, 617-573-8302, Fax: 617-305-1733, E-mail: grad.admission@suffolk.edu.
Website: http://www.suffolk.edu/mba

Syracuse University, Martin J. Whitman School of Management, Master of Business Administration Program, Syracuse, NY 13244. Offers accounting (MBA); business analytics (MBA); entrepreneurship (MBA); marketing management (MBA); real estate (MBA); supply chain management (MBA); JD/MBA. *Program availability:* Part-time, 100% online. *Students:* Average age 32. 1,086 applicants, 73% accepted, 516 enrolled. In 2018, 84 master's awarded. *Entrance requirements:* For master's, GMAT or GRE, resume, essay, 5-minute video interview, two letters of recommendation, transcripts (unofficial). Additional exam requirements/recommendations for international students: Required—TOEFL (minimum score 100 iBT), IELTS (minimum score 7), PTE (minimum score 68). *Application deadline:* For fall admission, 11/30 for domestic students, 11/30 priority date for international students; for winter admission, 1/1 for domestic students, 1/ 1 priority date for international students; for spring admission, 2/15 for domestic and international students; for summer admission, 4/19 for domestic students. Application fee: $75. Electronic applications accepted. *Expenses:* Contact institution. *Financial support:* In 2018–19, 22 students received support. Merit scholarships available. Financial award application deadline: 2/15. *Faculty research:* Data analysis, economics of international business, financial markets and institutions, operations management, supply chain management. *Unit head:* Dr. Alexander McKelvie, Associate Dean for Undergraduate and Full-time Master's Education, 315-443-7252, E-mail: mckelvie@syr.edu. *Application contact:* Shri Ramakrishnan, Assistant Director, Graduate Recruitment, 315-443-3497, Fax: 315-443-9517, E-mail: busgrad@syr.edu.
Website: http://whitman.syr.edu/ftmba/

Syracuse University, Martin J. Whitman School of Management, MS in Entrepreneurship Program, Syracuse, NY 13244. Offers MS. *Program availability:* Part-time, 100% online. *Students:* Average age 22. 24 applicants, 38% accepted, 4 enrolled. In 2018, 7 master's awarded. *Entrance requirements:* For master's, GMAT or GRE, resume, essay, one-page business plan, 5-minute video interview, two letters of recommendation, transcripts (unofficial). Additional exam requirements/ recommendations for international students: Required—TOEFL (minimum score 100 iBT), IELTS (minimum score 7), PTE (minimum score 68), GMAT or GRE. *Application deadline:* For fall admission, 11/30 for domestic students, 11/30 priority date for international students; for winter admission, 1/1 for domestic students, 1/1 priority date for international students; for spring admission, 2/15 for domestic and international students; for summer admission, 4/19 for domestic students. Application fee: $75. Electronic applications accepted. *Expenses:* Contact institution. *Financial support:* In 2018–19, 4 students received support. Merit scholarships available. Financial award application deadline: 2/15. *Faculty research:* Entrepreneurship, emerging enterprises, financial markets and institutions, competitive strategy, opportunity recognition and ideation. *Unit head:* Dr. Alexander McKelvie, Chair, Department of Entrepreneurship and Emerging Enterprises, 315-443-7252, E-mail: mckelvie@syr.edu. *Application contact:* Shri Ramakrishnan, Assistant Director, Graduate Recruitment, 315-443-3497, Fax: 315-443-9517, E-mail: sramak01@syr.edu.
Website: http://whitman.syr.edu/programs-and-academics/programs/ms/eee/index.aspx

Temple University, Fox School of Business, Doctoral Programs in Business, Philadelphia, PA 19122-6096. Offers accounting (PhD); entrepreneurship (PhD); finance (PhD); international business (PhD); management information systems (PhD); marketing (PhD); risk management and insurance (PhD); statistics (PhD); strategic management (PhD); tourism and sport (PhD). *Accreditation:* AACSB. *Degree requirements:* For doctorate, thesis/dissertation. *Entrance requirements:* For doctorate, GRE General Test, GMAT, minimum GPA of 3.0, master's degree. Additional exam requirements/recommendations for international students: Required—TOEFL (minimum score 600 paper-based; 100 iBT), IELTS (minimum score 7.5). Electronic applications accepted.

Temple University, Fox School of Business, Specialized Master's Programs, Philadelphia, PA 19122-6096. Offers accountancy (MS); actuarial science (MS); finance (MS); financial engineering (MS); human resource management (MS); innovation management and entrepreneurship (MS); marketing (MS); statistics (MS). MS in innovation management and entrepreneurship delivered jointly with College of Engineering. *Accreditation:* AACSB. *Program availability:* Part-time. *Entrance requirements:* For master's, GRE General Test or GMAT, minimum undergraduate GPA of 3.0. Additional exam requirements/recommendations for international students: Required—TOEFL (minimum score 600 paper-based; 100 iBT), IELTS (minimum score 7.5).

Texas A&M University, Mays Business School, Department of Management, College Station, TX 77843. Offers entrepreneurial leadership (MS); human resource management (MS). *Faculty:* 30. *Students:* 103 full-time (79 women), 1 part-time (0 women); includes 20 minority (2 Black or African American, non-Hispanic/Latino; 5 Asian, non-Hispanic/Latino; 13 Hispanic/Latino), 6 international. Average age 26. 131 applicants, 39% accepted, 40 enrolled. In 2018, 48 master's awarded. Terminal master's awarded for partial completion of doctoral program. *Degree requirements:* For master's, comprehensive exam. *Entrance requirements:* For master's, GMAT or GRE. Additional exam requirements/recommendations for international students: Required—TOEFL (minimum score 550 paper-based; 80 iBT), IELTS (minimum score 6), PTE (minimum score 53). *Application deadline:* For fall admission, 5/26 for domestic and international students. Applications are processed on a rolling basis. Application fee: $50 ($90 for international students). Electronic applications accepted. *Expenses:* Contact institution. *Financial support:* In 2018–19, 86 students received support, including 30 research assistantships with tuition reimbursements available (averaging $10,805 per year), 19 teaching assistantships with tuition reimbursements available (averaging $7,111 per year); career-related internships or fieldwork, institutionally sponsored loans, scholarships/grants, traineeships, health care benefits, tuition waivers (full and partial), and unspecified assistantships also available. Support available to part-time students. Financial award application deadline: 3/15; financial award applicants required to submit FAFSA. *Faculty research:* Strategic and human resource management, business and public policy, organizational behavior, organizational theory. *Unit head:* Dr. Wendy R. Boswell, Head, 979-845-4045, Fax: 979-845-9641, E-mail: wboswell@mays.tamu.edu. *Application contact:* Kristi R. Mora, Senior Academic Advisor II, 979-845-6127, Fax: 979-845-9641, E-mail: kmora@mays.tamu.edu.
Website: http://mays.tamu.edu/mgmt/

Tufts University, School of Engineering, The Gordon Institute, Medford, MA 02155. Offers engineering management (MS); innovation and management (MS). *Program availability:* Part-time. *Entrance requirements:* Additional exam requirements/recommendations for international students: Required—TOEFL (minimum score 550 paper-based; 80 iBT), IELTS (minimum score 6.5). Electronic applications accepted. *Expenses:* Contact institution. *Faculty research:* Engineering management, engineering leadership.

Tulane University, A. B. Freeman School of Business, New Orleans, LA 70118-5669. Offers accounting (M Acct); analytics (MBA); banking and financial services (M Fin); energy (M Fin, MBA); entrepreneurship (MBA); finance (MBA, PhD); financial accounting (PhD); international business (MBA); international management (MBA); strategic management and leadership (MBA); JD/M Acct; JD/MBA; MBA/M Acc; MBA/MA; MBA/MD; MBA/ME; MBA/MPH. *Accreditation:* AACSB. *Program availability:* Part-time, evening/weekend. *Faculty:* 43 full-time (11 women), 45 part-time/adjunct (8 women). *Students:* 432 full-time (218 women), 533 part-time (262 women); includes 99 minority (32 Black or African American, non-Hispanic/Latino; 1 American Indian or Alaska Native, non-Hispanic/Latino; 26 Asian, non-Hispanic/Latino; 35 Hispanic/Latino; 5 Two or more races, non-Hispanic/Latino), 644 international. Average age 28. 1,911 applicants, 77% accepted, 411 enrolled. In 2018, 728 master's, 4 doctorates awarded. Terminal master's awarded for partial completion of doctoral program. *Degree requirements:* For master's, one foreign language, comprehensive exam (for some programs); for doctorate, one foreign language, comprehensive exam, thesis/dissertation. *Entrance requirements:* For master's and doctorate, GMAT or GRE, interview. Additional exam requirements/recommendations for international students: Required—TOEFL or IELTS. *Application deadline:* For fall admission, 11/1 priority date for domestic students, 11/1 for international students; for winter admission, 1/6 for domestic and international students; for spring admission, 3/1 priority date for domestic students, 3/1 for international students; for summer admission, 5/5 for domestic students. Applications are processed on a rolling basis. Application fee: $125. Electronic applications accepted. *Expenses:* Contact institution. *Financial support:* In 2018–19, 153 students received support. Fellowships with tuition reimbursements available, research assistantships, teaching assistantships, career-related internships or fieldwork, Federal Work-Study, tuition waivers (full and partial), and unspecified assistantships available. Support available to part-time students. Financial award application deadline: 4/15; financial award applicants required to submit FAFSA. *Faculty research:* Corporate finance, managerial accounting and financial reporting, strategic management and leadership, consumer behavior and decision making, organizational behavior and human resource management. *Unit head:* Ira Solomon, PhD, Dean, 504-865-5407, Fax: 504-865-5491, E-mail: businessdean@tulane.edu. *Application contact:* Melissa Booth, Assistant Dean for Graduate Admissions, 800-223-5402, E-mail: freeman.admissions@tulane.edu.
Website: http://www.freeman.tulane.edu

United States International University–Africa, School of Business Administration, Nairobi, Kenya. Offers business administration (GEMBA); entrepreneurship (MBA); finance (MBA); human resource management (MBA); information technology management (MBA); integrated studies (MBA); international business administration (MBA); management and organizational development (MS); marketing (MBA); organizational development (EMS); strategic management (MBA). *Program availability:* Part-time, evening/weekend. *Degree requirements:* For master's, thesis. *Entrance requirements:* For master's, GMAT, 2 letters of reference, resume. Additional exam requirements/recommendations for international students: Required—TOEFL (minimum score 550 paper-based). *Faculty research:* Marketing in small business enterprises, total quality management in Kenya.

Université Laval, Faculty of Administrative Sciences, Programs in Business Administration, Québec, QC G1K 7P4, Canada. Offers accounting (MBA); agri-food management (MBA); electronic business (MBA, Diploma); factory management and logistics (MBA); finance (MBA); firm management (MBA); geomatic management (MBA); information technology management (MBA); international management (MBA); management (MBA); management accounting (MBA, Diploma); marketing (MBA); modeling and organizational decision (MBA); occupational health and safety management (MBA); pharmacy management (MBA); social and environmental responsibility (MBA); technological entrepreneurship (Diploma). *Accreditation:* AACSB. *Program availability:* Part-time, evening/weekend, online learning. *Entrance requirements:* For master's and Diploma, knowledge of French and English. Electronic applications accepted.

University at Albany, State University of New York, School of Business, MBA Programs, Albany, NY 12222-0001. Offers business administration (MBA); cyber security (MBA); entrepreneurship (MBA); finance (MBA); human resource information systems (MBA); information systems and business analytics (MBA); marketing (MBA); JD/MBA. JD/MBA offered jointly with Albany Law School. *Program availability:* Part-time, evening/weekend. *Faculty:* 29 full-time (13 women), 9 part-time/adjunct (2 women). *Students:* 103 full-time (36 women), 188 part-time (69 women); includes 76 minority (27 Black or African American, non-Hispanic/Latino; 33 Asian, non-Hispanic/Latino; 16 Hispanic/Latino), 16 international. Average age 25. 181 applicants, 80% accepted, 114 enrolled. In 2018, 103 master's awarded. *Degree requirements:* For master's, thesis (for some programs), field or research project. *Entrance requirements:* For master's, GMAT, minimum undergraduate GPA of 3.0; 3 letters of recommendation; resume; statement of goals. Additional exam requirements/recommendations for international students: Required—TOEFL (minimum score 100 iBT); Recommended—IELTS (minimum score 7). *Application deadline:* For fall admission, 4/1 priority date for domestic students, 2/15 for international students; for spring admission, 12/1 for domestic students; for summer admission, 5/1 for domestic students. Applications are processed on a rolling basis. Application fee: $75. Electronic applications accepted. *Expenses:* 16818. *Financial support:* In 2018–19, 25 students received support, including 7 fellowships with partial tuition reimbursements available (averaging $6,000 per year), 4 research assistantships with partial tuition reimbursements available, 21 teaching assistantships with partial tuition reimbursements available; unspecified assistantships also available. Financial award application deadline: 4/1; financial award applicants required to submit FAFSA. *Faculty research:* Social goods, information assurance, social computing, corporate entrepreneurship, asset pricing. *Total annual research expenditures:* $136,000. *Unit head:* Dr. Nilanjan Sen, Dean, 518-956-8370, Fax: 518-442-3273, E-mail: nsen@albany.edu. *Application contact:* Zina Mega Lawrence, Assistant Dean of Graduate Student Services, 518-956-8320, Fax: 518-442-4042, E-mail: zlawrence@albany.edu.
Website: https://graduatebusiness.albany.edu/

The University of Alabama in Huntsville, School of Graduate Studies, College of Business Administration, Programs in Business and Management, Huntsville, AL 35899. Offers business analytics (MSMS); federal contracting and procurement management (Certificate); human resource management (MSM); management (MBA), including acquisition management, entrepreneurship, federal contract accounting, finance, human resource management, logistics and supply chain management, marketing, project management; supply chain management (Certificate); technology and innovation management (Certificate). *Accreditation:* AACSB. *Program availability:* Part-time. *Faculty:* 8 full-time (3 women). *Students:* 57 full-time (25 women), 152 part-time (76 women); includes 37 minority (20 Black or African American, non-Hispanic/Latino; 2 American Indian or Alaska Native, non-Hispanic/Latino; 6 Asian, non-Hispanic/Latino; 8 Hispanic/Latino; 1 Two or more races, non-Hispanic/Latino), 24 international. Average age 33. 178 applicants, 80% accepted, 84 enrolled. In 2018, 96 master's, 1 other advanced degree awarded. *Degree requirements:* For master's, comprehensive exam, thesis or alternative. *Entrance requirements:* For master's, GMAT (minimum score 500), minimum AACSB index of 1080. Additional exam requirements/recommendations for international students: Required—TOEFL (minimum score 550 paper-based; 80 iBT), IELTS (minimum score 6.5). *Application deadline:* For fall admission, 7/15 priority date for domestic students, 4/1 priority date for international students; for spring admission, 11/30 priority date for domestic students, 9/1 priority date for international students. Applications are processed on a rolling basis. Application fee: $50. Electronic applications accepted. *Expenses: Tuition, area resident:* Full-time $10,632; part-time $412 per credit hour. *Tuition, state resident:* full-time $10,632. *Tuition, nonresident:* full-time $23,604; part-time $412 per credit hour. *Required fees:* $582; $582. Tuition and fees vary according to course load and program. *Financial support:* In 2018–19, 15 students received support, including 15 teaching assistantships with full tuition reimbursements available (averaging $4,871 per year); research assistantships with full tuition reimbursements available, career-related internships or fieldwork, Federal Work-Study, institutionally sponsored loans, scholarships/grants, health care benefits, tuition waivers (full and partial), and unspecified assistantships also available. Support available to part-time students. Financial award application deadline: 4/1; financial award applicants required to submit FAFSA. *Faculty research:* Supply chain management, management of research and development, international marketing and branding, organizational behavior and human resource management, social networks and computational economics. *Unit head:* Dr. Fan Tseng, Chair, 256-824-6804, Fax: 256-824-6328, E-mail: fan.tseng@uah.edu. *Application contact:* Jennifer Pettitt, Director of Advising, 256-824-6681, Fax: 256-824-7571, E-mail: jennifer.pettitt@uah.edu.

University of Arkansas at Little Rock, Graduate School, George W. Donaghey College of Engineering and Information Technology, Graduate Certificate in Technology Innovation Program, Little Rock, AR 72204-1099. Offers Graduate Certificate. *Program availability:* Part-time, evening/weekend. *Degree requirements:* For Graduate Certificate, 1 year of full-time study. *Entrance requirements:* For degree, minimum GPA of 2.75 on undergraduate work or 3.0 in the last 60 hours of undergraduate credit. Additional exam requirements/recommendations for international students: Required—TOEFL (minimum score 525 paper-based). Electronic applications accepted. *Faculty research:* Web computing, robotics, text mining, technology foresight, biotechnology.

University of Baltimore, Graduate School, Merrick School of Business, Department of Marketing and Entrepreneurship, Baltimore, MD 21201-5779. Offers innovation management and technology commercialization (MS). *Program availability:* Part-time, evening/weekend. *Entrance requirements:* For master's, GMAT. Additional exam requirements/recommendations for international students: Required—TOEFL (minimum score 550 paper-based). Electronic applications accepted.

University of Bridgeport, School of Business, Bridgeport, CT 06604. Offers accounting (MBA); finance (MBA); general business (MBA); global financial services (MBA); human resource management (MBA); information systems and knowledge management (MBA); international business (MBA); management (MBA); marketing (MBA); operations management (MBA); small business and entrepreneurship (MBA); specialized business (MBA). *Accreditation:* ACBSP. *Program availability:* Part-time, evening/weekend. *Degree requirements:* For master's, thesis optional. *Entrance requirements:* For master's, GMAT. Additional exam requirements/recommendations for international students: Recommended—TOEFL (minimum score 550 paper-based; 80 iBT), IELTS (minimum score 6.5). Electronic applications accepted. *Expenses:* Contact institution.

University of California, Davis, Graduate School of Management, Full-Time MBA Program, Davis, CA 95616. Offers business analytics and technologies (MBA); entrepreneurship and innovation (MBA); finance and accounting (MBA); general management (MBA); marketing (MBA); organizational behavior (MBA); public health management (MBA); strategy (MBA); technology management (MBA); DVM/MBA; JD/MBA; M Engr/MBA; MBA/MPH; MBA/MS; MD/MBA; MSN/MBA; PhD/MBA. *Faculty:* 31 full-time (10 women). *Students:* 89 full-time (35 women); includes 21 minority (1 Black or African American, non-Hispanic/Latino; 14 Asian, non-Hispanic/Latino; 6 Hispanic/Latino), 43 international. Average age 28. 290 applicants, 39% accepted, 44 enrolled. In 2018, 45 master's awarded. *Degree requirements:* For master's, comprehensive exam, integrated management project. *Entrance requirements:* For master's, GMAT or GRE, letters of recommendation, resume, essays, equivalent of a 4-year U.S. undergraduate degree, transcript. Additional exam requirements/recommendations for international

students: Required—TOEFL (minimum score 600 paper-based; 100 iBT), IELTS (minimum score 7). *Application deadline:* For fall admission, 9/15 priority date for domestic and international students. Applications are processed on a rolling basis. Application fee: $125. Electronic applications accepted. *Expenses:* Contact institution. *Financial support:* In 2018–19, 85 students received support. Fellowships with full and partial tuition reimbursements available, research assistantships with partial tuition reimbursements available, teaching assistantships with partial tuition reimbursements available, institutionally sponsored loans, scholarships/grants, health care benefits, tuition waivers (partial), and unspecified assistantships available. Financial award application deadline: 3/1; financial award applicants required to submit FAFSA. *Faculty research:* Finance, marketing, management, business analytics, accounting. *Unit head:* Amanda Opperman, Assistant Dean of Student Affairs, 530-752-7658, Fax: 530-754-9355, E-mail: admissions@gsm.ucdavis.edu. *Application contact:* Andrea Shaw, Senior Director of Admissions, 530-754-5476, Fax: 530-754-9355, E-mail: admissions@gsm.ucdavis.edu.
Website: http://gsm.ucdavis.edu/daytime-mba-program

University of California, Davis, Graduate School of Management, MBA Programs in Sacramento and San Francisco Bay Area, Davis, CA 95616. Offers business analytics and technologies (MBA); entrepreneurship and innovation (MBA); finance and accounting (MBA); general management (MBA); marketing (MBA); organizational behavior (MBA); public health management (MBA); strategy (MBA); technology management (MBA). *Program availability:* Part-time-only, evening/weekend. *Faculty:* 17 full-time (7 women), 42 part-time/adjunct (11 women). *Students:* 279 part-time (107 women); includes 146 minority (12 Black or African American, non-Hispanic/Latino; 3 American Indian or Alaska Native, non-Hispanic/Latino; 102 Asian, non-Hispanic/Latino; 29 Hispanic/Latino), 24 international. Average age 30. 158 applicants, 83% accepted, 91 enrolled. In 2018, 91 master's awarded. *Degree requirements:* For master's, integrated management project. *Entrance requirements:* For master's, GMAT or GRE, letters of recommendation, resume, equivalent of a 4-year undergraduate degree. Additional exam requirements/recommendations for international students: Required—TOEFL (minimum score 600 paper-based; 100 iBT), IELTS (minimum score 7). *Application deadline:* For fall admission, 9/15 priority date for domestic and international students. Applications are processed on a rolling basis. Application fee: $125. Electronic applications accepted. *Expenses:* Contact institution. *Financial support:* In 2018–19, 89 students received support. Fellowships, teaching assistantships with partial tuition reimbursements available, scholarships/grants, and unspecified assistantships available. Support available to part-time students. Financial award application deadline: 3/1; financial award applicants required to submit FAFSA. *Faculty research:* Accounting, finance, marketing, management, business analytics. *Unit head:* Amanda Opperman, Assistant Dean of Student Affairs, 530-752-7658, Fax: 530-754-9355, E-mail: admissions@gsm.ucdavis.edu. *Application contact:* Andrea Shaw, Senior Director of Admissions, 530-754-5476, Fax: 530-754-9355, E-mail: admissions@gsm.ucdavis.edu.
Website: http://gsm.ucdavis.edu/mba-programs

University of California, Merced, Graduate Division, School of Engineering, Merced, CA 95343. Offers biological engineering and small scale technologies (MS, PhD); electrical engineering and computer science (MS, PhD); environmental systems (MS, PhD); management of innovation, sustainability, and technology (MM); mechanical engineering (MS); mechanical engineering and applied mechanics (PhD). *Faculty:* 60 full-time (16 women). *Students:* 219 full-time (72 women), 1 part-time (0 women); includes 43 minority (2 Black or African American, non-Hispanic/Latino; 17 Asian, non-Hispanic/Latino; 20 Hispanic/Latino; 1 Native Hawaiian or other Pacific Islander, non-Hispanic/Latino; 3 Two or more races, non-Hispanic/Latino), 145 international. Average age 28. 371 applicants, 46% accepted, 75 enrolled. In 2018, 30 master's, 17 doctorates awarded. Terminal master's awarded for partial completion of doctoral program. *Degree requirements:* For master's, variable foreign language requirement, comprehensive exam, thesis or alternative, oral defense; for doctorate, variable foreign language requirement, comprehensive exam, thesis/dissertation, oral defense. *Entrance requirements:* For master's and doctorate, GRE. Additional exam requirements/recommendations for international students: Required—TOEFL (minimum score 550 paper-based; 80 iBT); Recommended—IELTS (minimum score 6.5). *Application deadline:* For fall admission, 1/15 priority date for domestic and international students. Application fee: $105 ($125 for international students). Electronic applications accepted. *Expenses:* In-state tuition $11442 per year; Out-of-state tuition $26544 per year; Student Fees $1765 per year. *Financial support:* In 2018–19, 200 students received support, including 14 fellowships with full tuition reimbursements available (averaging $20,851 per year), 70 research assistantships with full tuition reimbursements available (averaging $18,334 per year), 116 teaching assistantships with full tuition reimbursements available (averaging $19,841 per year); scholarships/grants, traineeships, and health care benefits also available. *Faculty research:* Sustainability systems engineering and resource management: food, energy, water; biomolecular engineering and biotechnology; computational science and data analytics; artificial intelligence, machine learning, internet of things, human computer interface; cyber-physical systems and automation. *Total annual research expenditures:* $3.1 million. *Unit head:* Dr. Mark Matsumoto, Dean, 209-228-4047, Fax: 209-228-4047, E-mail: mmatsumoto@ucmerced.edu. *Application contact:* Tsu Ya, Director of Admissions and Academic Services, 209-228-4521, Fax: 209-228-6906, E-mail: tya@ucmerced.edu.

University of Central Florida, College of Arts and Humanities, School of Visual Arts and Design, Orlando, FL 32816. Offers digital media (MA); emerging media (MFA), including animation and visual effects, digital media, entrepreneurial digital cinema, studio art and the computer. *Program availability:* Part-time. *Students:* 24 full-time (11 women), 5 part-time (3 women); includes 12 minority (3 Black or African American, non-Hispanic/Latino; 1 Asian, non-Hispanic/Latino; 8 Hispanic/Latino), 3 international. Average age 32. 45 applicants, 64% accepted, 13 enrolled. In 2018, 7 master's awarded. *Degree requirements:* For master's, comprehensive exam, thesis or alternative. *Entrance requirements:* For master's, GRE, letter of recommendation. Additional exam requirements/recommendations for international students: Required—TOEFL. *Application deadline:* For fall admission, 7/1 for domestic students. Application fee: $30. Electronic applications accepted. *Financial support:* In 2018–19, 14 students received support, including 7 fellowships with partial tuition reimbursements available (averaging $9,286 per year), 2 research assistantships with partial tuition reimbursements available (averaging $9,122 per year), 12 teaching assistantships with partial tuition reimbursements available (averaging $8,253 per year); scholarships/grants, health care benefits, and unspecified assistantships also available. Financial award application deadline: 3/1; financial award applicants required to submit FAFSA. *Unit head:* Dr. Rudy McDaniel, Director, 407-823-3145, E-mail: rudy@ucf.edu. *Application contact:* Associate Director, Graduate Admissions, 407-823-2766, Fax: 407-823-6442, E-mail: gradadmissions@ucf.edu.
Website: http://svad.cah.ucf.edu/

University of Central Florida, College of Business Administration, Department of Management, Orlando, FL 32816. Offers entrepreneurship (Graduate Certificate); management (MSM); technology ventures (Graduate Certificate). *Accreditation:* AACSB. *Program availability:* Part-time. *Students:* 95 part-time (45 women); includes 43 minority (11 Black or African American, non-Hispanic/Latino; 10 Asian, non-Hispanic/Latino; 17 Hispanic/Latino; 5 Two or more races, non-Hispanic/Latino). Average age 30. 66 applicants, 79% accepted, 41 enrolled. In 2018, 15 master's, 16 other advanced degrees awarded. *Entrance requirements:* For master's, GMAT, minimum GPA of 3.0 in last 60 hours, letters of recommendation, resume, goal statement. Additional exam requirements/recommendations for international students: Required—TOEFL. *Application deadline:* For fall admission, 6/15 for domestic students; for spring admission, 11/15 for domestic students. Application fee: $30. Electronic applications accepted. *Financial support:* Fellowships available. Financial award application deadline: 3/1; financial award applicants required to submit FAFSA. *Unit head:* Dr. Stephen Goodman, Chair, 407-823-2675, Fax: 407-823-3725, E-mail: sgoodman@ucf.edu. *Application contact:* Associate Director, Graduate Admissions, 407-823-2766, Fax: 407-823-6442, E-mail: gradadmissions@ucf.edu.
Website: http://business.ucf.edu/departments-schools/management/

University of Chicago, Booth School of Business, Full-Time MBA Program, Chicago, IL 60637. Offers accounting (MBA); analytic finance (MBA); analytic management (MBA); econometrics and statistics (MBA); economics (MBA); entrepreneurship (MBA); finance (MBA); general management (MBA); health administration and policy (Certificate); international business (MBA); managerial and organizational behavior (MBA); marketing analytics (MBA); marketing management (MBA); operations management (MBA); strategic management (MBA); MBA/AM; MBA/JD; MBA/MA; MBA/MD; MBA/MPP. *Accreditation:* AACSB. *Entrance requirements:* For master's, GMAT or GRE, transcripts, resume, 2 letters of recommendation, essays, interview. Additional exam requirements/recommendations for international students: Required—TOEFL, IELTS, or PTE. Electronic applications accepted. *Expenses:* Contact institution.

University of Colorado Denver, Business School, Program in Information Systems, Denver, CO 80217. Offers accounting and information systems audit and control (MS); business intelligence systems (MS); digital health entrepreneurship (MS); enterprise risk management (MS); enterprise technology management (MS); geographic information systems (MS); health information technology (MS); technology innovation and entrepreneurship (MS); Web and mobile computing (MS). *Program availability:* Part-time, evening/weekend, online learning. *Degree requirements:* For master's, 30 credit hours. *Entrance requirements:* For master's, GMAT, resume, essay, two letters of recommendation, financial statements (for international applicants). Additional exam requirements/recommendations for international students: Required—TOEFL (minimum score 525 paper-based; 71 iBT); Recommended—IELTS (minimum score 6.5). Electronic applications accepted. *Expenses:* Contact institution. *Faculty research:* Human-computer interaction, expert systems, database management, electronic commerce, object-oriented software development.

University of Colorado Denver, Business School, Program in Management and Organization, Denver, CO 80217. Offers business strategy (MS); change and innovation (MS); enterprise technology management (MS); entrepreneurship and innovation (MS); global management (MS); leadership (MS); managing for sustainability (MS); managing human resources (MS); sports and entertainment (MS); strategic management (MS). *Accreditation:* AACSB. *Program availability:* Part-time, evening/weekend, online learning. *Degree requirements:* For master's, 30 semester hours (12 of required courses, 12 of management electives, and 6 of free electives). *Entrance requirements:* For master's, GMAT, resume, two letters of recommendation, essay, financial statements (for international applicants). Additional exam requirements/recommendations for international students: Required—TOEFL (minimum score 525 paper-based; 71 iBT); Recommended—IELTS (minimum score 6.5). Electronic applications accepted. *Expenses:* Contact institution. *Faculty research:* Human resource management, management of catastrophe, turnaround strategies.

University of Delaware, Alfred Lerner College of Business and Economics, Department of Economics, Newark, DE 19716. Offers economic education (PhD); economics (MA, MS, PhD); economics for entrepreneurship and educators (MA); MA/MBA. *Program availability:* Part-time. *Degree requirements:* For master's, comprehensive exam, thesis (for some programs), mathematics review exam, research project; for doctorate, comprehensive exam, thesis/dissertation, field exam. *Entrance requirements:* For master's, GMAT or GRE General Test, minimum GPA of 2.5; for doctorate, GRE General Test, minimum GPA of 3.5 in graduate economics course work. Additional exam requirements/recommendations for international students: Required—TOEFL (minimum score 550 paper-based). Electronic applications accepted. *Faculty research:* Applied quantitative economics, industrial organization, resource economics, monetary economics, labor economics.

University of Florida, Graduate School, Warrington College of Business Administration, Hough Graduate School of Business, Department of Finance, Insurance and Real Estate, Gainesville, FL 32611. Offers entrepreneurship (MS); finance (MS, PhD); financial services (Certificate); insurance (PhD); quantitative finance (PhD); real estate (MS); real estate and urban analysis (PhD); JD/MBA; JD/MS. Terminal master's awarded for partial completion of doctoral program. *Degree requirements:* For master's, comprehensive exam, thesis; for doctorate, comprehensive exam, thesis/dissertation. *Entrance requirements:* For master's, GMAT (minimum score of 465) or GRE General Test, minimum GPA of 3.0 for last 60 hours of undergraduate degree, work experience (preferred); for doctorate, GMAT (minimum score of 465) or GRE General Test, minimum GPA of 3.0. Additional exam requirements/recommendations for international students: Required—TOEFL (minimum score 550 paper-based; 80 iBT), IELTS (minimum score 6). Electronic applications accepted. *Faculty research:* Banking, empirical corporate finance, hedge funds.

University of Hawaii at Manoa, Office of Graduate Education, Shidler College of Business, The Pacific Asian Center for Entrepreneurship and E-Business (PACE), Honolulu, HI 96822. Offers entrepreneurship (Graduate Certificate). *Program availability:* Part-time. *Entrance requirements:* Additional exam requirements/recommendations for international students: Required—TOEFL (minimum score 500 paper-based; 61 iBT).

University of Hawaii at Manoa, Office of Graduate Education, Shidler College of Business, Program in Business Administration, Honolulu, HI 96822. Offers Asian business studies (MBA); Chinese business studies (MBA); decision sciences (MBA); entrepreneurship (MBA); finance (MBA); finance and banking (MBA); human resources management (MBA); information management (MBA); information technology (MBA); international business (MBA); Japanese business studies (MBA); marketing (MBA); organizational behavior (MBA); organizational management (MBA); real estate (MBA); student-designed track (MBA). *Accreditation:* AACSB. *Program availability:* Part-time, evening/weekend. *Degree requirements:* For master's, thesis optional. *Entrance requirements:* For master's, GMAT, minimum GPA of 3.0. Additional exam requirements/recommendations for international students: Required—TOEFL (minimum score 600 paper-based; 100 iBT), IELTS (minimum score 7). *Expenses:* Contact institution.

University of Houston–Victoria, School of Business Administration, Victoria, TX 77901-4450. Offers accounting (MBA); economic development and entrepreneurship (MS); finance (GMBA, MBA); general business (MBA); international business (MBA); management (GMBA, MBA); marketing (MBA). *Accreditation:* AACSB. *Program availability:* Part-time, evening/weekend, online learning. *Entrance requirements:* For master's, GMAT. Additional exam requirements/recommendations for international

students: Required—TOEFL (minimum score 550 paper-based). Electronic applications accepted. *Expenses: Tuition, area resident:* Full-time $6154; part-time $3077 per semester. Tuition, state resident: full-time $6154; part-time $3077 per semester. Tuition, nonresident: full-time $13,624; part-time $6812 per semester. *International tuition:* $13,624 full-time. *Required fees:* $1405; $847 per semester. $423 per semester. Tuition and fees vary according to program. *Faculty research:* Economic development, marketing, finance.

University of Louisiana at Lafayette, BI Moody III College of Business Administration, Lafayette, LA 70504. Offers accounting (MS); business administration (MBA); entrepreneurship (MBA); finance (MBA); global management (MBA); health care administration (MBA); hospitality management (MBA); human resource management (MBA); project management (MBA); sales leadership (MBA). *Accreditation:* AACSB. *Program availability:* Part-time, evening/weekend. *Entrance requirements:* For master's, GRE General Test. Additional exam requirements/recommendations for international students: Required—TOEFL (minimum score 550 paper-based).

University of Louisville, Graduate School, College of Business, MBA Programs, Louisville, KY 40292-0001. Offers entrepreneurship (MBA); global business (MBA); health sector management (MBA). *Accreditation:* AACSB. *Program availability:* Part-time, evening/weekend, 100% online, blended/hybrid learning. *Students:* 227 full-time (82 women), 28 part-time (13 women); includes 58 minority (32 Black or African American, non-Hispanic/Latino; 1 American Indian or Alaska Native, non-Hispanic/Latino; 13 Asian, non-Hispanic/Latino; 9 Hispanic/Latino; 3 Two or more races, non-Hispanic/Latino), 34 international. Average age 32. 236 applicants, 69% accepted, 126 enrolled. In 2018, 102 master's awarded. *Degree requirements:* For master's, international learning experience. *Entrance requirements:* For master's, GMAT, 2 letters of reference, personal interview, resume, personal statement, college transcript(s). Additional exam requirements/recommendations for international students: Required—TOEFL (minimum score 83 iBT). *Application deadline:* For fall admission, 7/1 for domestic students; for spring admission, 12/1 for domestic students. Applications are processed on a rolling basis. Application fee: $65. *Expenses: Tuition, area resident:* Full-time $6500; part-time $723 per credit hour. Tuition, state resident: full-time $6500. Tuition, nonresident: full-time $13,557; part-time $1507 per credit hour. Tuition and fees vary according to course load and program. *Financial support:* In 2018–19, 105 students received support. Fellowships with full tuition reimbursements available, research assistantships with full tuition reimbursements available, health care benefits, and unspecified assistantships available. Financial award application deadline: 3/31; financial award applicants required to submit FAFSA. *Faculty research:* Entrepreneurship, venture capital, retailing/franchising, corporate governance and leadership, supply chain management. *Total annual research expenditures:* $859,000. *Unit head:* Dr. Todd Mooradian, Dean, 502-852-6443, Fax: 502-852-7557, E-mail: todd.mooradian@louisville.edu. *Application contact:* Susan E. Hildebrand, Program Director, 502-852-7257, Fax: 502-852-4901, E-mail: s.hildebrand@louisville.edu. Website: http://business.louisville.edu/mba

University of Louisville, Graduate School, College of Business, PhD Program in Entrepreneurship, Louisville, KY 40292-0001. Offers PhD. *Faculty:* 4 full-time (1 woman). *Students:* 9 full-time (2 women); includes 1 minority (Black or African American, non-Hispanic/Latino), 2 international. Average age 37. 2 applicants. In 2018, 2 doctorates awarded. *Degree requirements:* For doctorate, comprehensive exam, thesis/dissertation, paper of sufficient quality for journal publication. *Entrance requirements:* For doctorate, GMAT, 3 letters of recommendation, curriculum vitae, personal interview. Additional exam requirements/recommendations for international students: Required—TOEFL (minimum score 83 iBT). *Application deadline:* For fall admission, 12/31 priority date for domestic students, 3/31 for international students. Applications are processed on a rolling basis. Application fee: $65. Electronic applications accepted. *Expenses: Tuition, area resident:* Full-time $6500; part-time $723 per credit hour. Tuition, state resident: full-time $6500. Tuition, nonresident: full-time $13,557; part-time $1507 per credit hour. Tuition and fees vary according to course load and program. *Financial support:* In 2018–19, 7 students received support. Fellowships with full tuition reimbursements available, research assistantships with full tuition reimbursements available, teaching assistantships with full tuition reimbursements available, scholarships/grants, health care benefits, and unspecified assistantships available. Financial award application deadline: 3/15; financial award applicants required to submit FAFSA. *Faculty research:* Entrepreneurship, supply chain management, venture capital, retailing/franchising, corporate governance. *Total annual research expenditures:* $133,436. *Unit head:* Dr. Todd Mooradian, Dean, 502-852-6443, Fax: 502-852-7557, E-mail: todd.mooradian@louisville.edu. *Application contact:* Susan E. Hildebrand, Program Director, 502-852-7257, Fax: 502-852-4901, E-mail: s.hildebrand@louisville.edu. Website: http://business.louisville.edu/entrepreneurshipphd

University of Louisville, J. B. Speed School of Engineering, Department of Bioengineering, Louisville, KY 40292-0001. Offers advancing bioengineering technologies through entrepreneurship (PhD); bioengineering (M Eng, PhD). *Accreditation:* ABET. *Students:* 19 full-time (12 women), 21 part-time (8 women); includes 7 minority (1 Black or African American, non-Hispanic/Latino; 3 Asian, non-Hispanic/Latino; 1 Hispanic/Latino; 2 Two or more races, non-Hispanic/Latino). Average age 25. 2 applicants, 100% accepted, 2 enrolled. In 2018, 6 master's awarded. *Degree requirements:* For master's, thesis; for doctorate, comprehensive exam, thesis/dissertation. *Entrance requirements:* For master's, GRE, 2 letters of recommendation; for doctorate, GRE, Three letters of recommendation, written statement describing previous experience related to bioengineering, a written statement as to how the PhD in Bioengineering will allow the applicant to fulfill their career goals. Additional exam requirements/recommendations for international students: Required—TOEFL (minimum score 550 paper-based; 80 iBT), IELTS (minimum score 6.5), GRE. *Application deadline:* For fall admission, 5/1 priority date for domestic and international students; for spring admission, 11/1 priority date for domestic and international students; for summer admission, 3/1 priority date for domestic and international students. Applications are processed on a rolling basis. Application fee: $65. Electronic applications accepted. *Expenses: Tuition, area resident:* Full-time $6500; part-time $723 per credit hour. Tuition, state resident: full-time $6500. Tuition, nonresident: full-time $13,557; part-time $1507 per credit hour. Tuition and fees vary according to course load and program. *Financial support:* In 2018–19, 18 students received support. Fellowships with full tuition reimbursements available, research assistantships with full tuition reimbursements available, teaching assistantships with full tuition reimbursements available, scholarships/grants, and health care benefits available. Financial award application deadline: 2/3. *Faculty research:* Bioimaging, Biomedical Devices, Drug, Gene & Protein Delivery, Bioinstrumentation & Controls Research & Development, Injury Risk Assessment and Prevention. *Total annual research expenditures:* $5.2 million. *Unit head:* Dr. Ayman El-Baz, Chair, 502-852-5092, E-mail: aymen.elbaz@louisville.edu. *Application contact:* Gina Bertocci, Director of Graduate Studies, 502-852-0296, E-mail: gina.bertocci@louisville.edu. Website: https://louisville.edu/speed/bioengineering

The University of Manchester, Alliance Manchester Business School, M15 6PB, United Kingdom. Offers accounting and finance (M Sc); business (M Ent); business

analysis and strategic management (M Sc); business analytics: operational research and risk analysis (M Sc); business psychology (M Sc); corporate communications and reputation management (M Sc); finance (M Sc); finance and business economics (M Sc); human resource management and industrial relations (M Sc); innovation management and entrepreneurship (M Sc); international business and management (M Sc); international human resource management and comparative industrial relations (M Sc); management (M Sc); marketing (M Sc); operations, project and supply chain management (M Sc); organizational psychology (M Sc); quantitative finance (M Sc). *Entrance requirements:* For master's, UK 2:1 honours degree or overseas equivalent. Additional exam requirements/recommendations for international students: Required—TOEFL (minimum score 100 iBT), IELTS (minimum score 7), PTE. Electronic applications accepted. *Faculty research:* Accounting and finance, management sciences and marketing, people management and organization, innovation management and policy, decision sciences.

University of Massachusetts Amherst, Graduate School, Isenberg School of Management, Program in Management, Amherst, MA 01003. Offers accounting (PhD); business administration (MBA); entrepreneurship (MBA); finance (MBA, PhD); healthcare administration (MBA); hospitality and tourism management (PhD); management science (PhD); marketing (MBA, PhD); organization studies (PhD); sport management (PhD); strategic management (PhD); MBA/MS. *Accreditation:* AACSB. *Program availability:* Part-time, evening/weekend, online learning. Terminal master's awarded for partial completion of doctoral program. *Degree requirements:* For doctorate, comprehensive exam, thesis/dissertation. *Entrance requirements:* For master's and doctorate, GMAT or GRE General Test. Additional exam requirements/recommendations for international students: Required—TOEFL (minimum score 550 paper-based; 80 iBT), IELTS (minimum score 6.5). Electronic applications accepted.

University of Massachusetts Lowell, Manning School of Business, Lowell, MA 01854. Offers business administration (MBA, PhD); healthcare innovation and entrepreneurship (MS). *Accreditation:* AACSB. *Program availability:* Part-time, evening/weekend. *Entrance requirements:* For master's, GMAT.

University of Minnesota, Twin Cities Campus, Carlson School of Management, Doctoral Program in Business Administration, Minneapolis, MN 55455-0213. Offers accounting (PhD); finance (PhD); information and decision sciences (PhD); marketing (PhD); strategic management and entrepreneurship (PhD); supply chain and operations (PhD); work and organizations (PhD). *Faculty:* 106 full-time (33 women). *Students:* 88 full-time (34 women); includes 9 minority (2 Black or African American, non-Hispanic/Latino; 6 Asian, non-Hispanic/Latino; 1 Hispanic/Latino), 66 international. Average age 30. 306 applicants, 8% accepted, 15 enrolled. In 2018, 14 doctorates awarded. *Degree requirements:* For doctorate, comprehensive exam, thesis/dissertation, written and oral preliminary exams, proposal defense, final defense. *Entrance requirements:* For doctorate, GMAT or GRE, minimum undergraduate GPA of 3.0, graduate 3.5 (recommended). Additional exam requirements/recommendations for international students: Required—Either or: TOEFL or IELTS; Recommended—TOEFL, IELTS. *Application deadline:* For fall admission, 12/15 for domestic students, 12/15 priority date for international students. Applications are processed on a rolling basis. Application fee: $75 ($95 for international students). Electronic applications accepted. *Financial support:* In 2018–19, 80 students received support, including 80 fellowships with full tuition reimbursements available (averaging $12,500 per year), 72 research assistantships with full tuition reimbursements available (averaging $7,800 per year), 72 teaching assistantships with full tuition reimbursements available (averaging $7,800 per year); health care benefits, unspecified assistantships, and full student service fee waivers also available. Financial award application deadline: 12/15. *Faculty research:* Finance, strategy and entrepreneurship, marketing, information and decision science, operations, accounting, supply chain, human resources and industrial relations, organizational behavior. *Unit head:* Dr. Shawn P. Curley, Director, 612-624-6546, Fax: 612-624-8221, E-mail: curley@umn.edu. *Application contact:* Sandy Herzan, Associate Director, 612-624-0875, Fax: 612-624-8221, E-mail: herza002@umn.edu. Website: http://carlsonschool.umn.edu/degrees/phd

University of New Brunswick Fredericton, School of Graduate Studies, Faculty of Business Administration, Fredericton, NB E3B 5A3, Canada. Offers business administration (MBA); engineering management (MBA); entrepreneurship (MBA); sports and recreation management (MBA); MBA/LL B. *Program availability:* Part-time. *Degree requirements:* For master's, thesis optional. *Entrance requirements:* For master's, GMAT (minimum score 550), minimum GPA of 3.0; 3-5 years of work experience; 3 letters of reference with at least one academic reference. Additional exam requirements/recommendations for international students: Required—TOEFL (minimum score 580 paper-based; 92 iBT) or IELTS (minimum score 7). Electronic applications accepted. *Faculty research:* Entrepreneurship, finance, law, sport and recreation management, engineering management.

University of New Mexico, Anderson School of Management, Department of Finance, International, Technology and Entrepreneurship, Albuquerque, NM 87131-1221. Offers entrepreneurship (MBA); finance (MBA); international management (MBA); international management in Latin America (MBA); management of technology (MBA). *Program availability:* Part-time. *Faculty:* 15 full-time (1 woman), 8 part-time/adjunct (2 women). In 2018, 29 master's awarded. *Entrance requirements:* For master's, GMAT or GRE, minimum GPA of 3.0 on last 60 hours of coursework; bachelor's degree from regionally-accredited college or university in U.S. or its equivalent in another country. Additional exam requirements/recommendations for international students: Required—TOEFL (minimum score 550 paper-based; 79 iBT), IELTS (minimum score 6.5). *Application deadline:* For fall admission, 4/1 priority date for domestic and international students; for spring admission, 10/1 priority date for domestic and international students. Applications are processed on a rolling basis. Application fee: $50. Electronic applications accepted. *Expenses:* For MBA (not EMBA): $531.34 per credit hour resident, $1197.98 per credit hour non-resident. *Financial support:* In 2018–19, 17 students received support, including 9 fellowships (averaging $18,720 per year), 12 research assistantships with partial tuition reimbursements available (averaging $15,291 per year); career-related internships or fieldwork, Federal Work-Study, scholarships/grants, and unspecified assistantships also available. Support available to part-time students. Financial award application deadline: 6/1; financial award applicants required to submit FAFSA. *Faculty research:* Corporate finance, investments, management in Latin America, management of technology, entrepreneurship. *Unit head:* Dr. Raul Gouvea, Chair, 505-277-6471, E-mail: rauldg@unm.edu. *Application contact:* Lisa Beauchene, Student Recruitment Specialist, 505-277-6471, E-mail: andersonadvising@unm.edu. Website: https://www.mgt.unm.edu/fite/default.asp?mm-faculty

University of Notre Dame, Mendoza College of Business, Master of Business Administration Program, Notre Dame, IN 46556. Offers business analytics (MBA); business leadership (MBA); consulting (MBA); corporate finance (MBA); innovation and entrepreneurship (MBA); investments (MBA); marketing (MBA); MBA/MSBA. *Accreditation:* AACSB. *Entrance requirements:* For master's, GMAT or GRE, work experience, essay, four-slide presentation, two recommendations, transcripts from all colleges and/or universities attended, interview. Additional exam requirements/recommendations for international students: Required—PTE (minimum score 68), TOEFL (minimum iBT score of 109), IELTS (7.5), or documentation of at least six

semesters of full-time university education in English. Electronic applications accepted. *Expenses:* Contact institution. *Faculty research:* Market micro-structure; marketing and public policy; corporate finance and accounting; corporate governance and ethical behavior; high performing organizations.

University of Oklahoma, Price College of Business, Norman, OK 73019. Offers accounting (M Acc); business administration (MBA, PMBA, PhD), including business administration (EMBA, MBA, PMBA, PhD); business entrepreneurship (Graduate Certificate); digital technologies (Graduate Certificate), including digital technologies; energy (EMBA), including business administration (EMBA, MBA, PMBA, PhD); foundations of business (Graduate Certificate); management information technology (MS), including management of information technology; the business of energy (Graduate Certificate); JD/MBA; MBA/MA; MBA/MLIS; MBA/MPH; MBA/MS. *Program availability:* Part-time, evening/weekend, 100% online. *Faculty:* 58 full-time (16 women), 6 part-time/adjunct (0 women). *Students:* 108 full-time (31 women), 267 part-time (84 women); includes 92 minority (16 Black or African American, non-Hispanic/Latino; 9 American Indian or Alaska Native, non-Hispanic/Latino; 16 Asian, non-Hispanic/Latino; 33 Hispanic/Latino; 1 Native Hawaiian or other Pacific Islander, non-Hispanic/Latino; 17 Two or more races, non-Hispanic/Latino), 38 international. Average age 33. 265 applicants, 44% accepted, 83 enrolled. In 2018, 132 master's, 5 doctorates, 41 other advanced degrees awarded. *Degree requirements:* For doctorate, comprehensive exam, thesis/dissertation. *Entrance requirements:* For master's, GMAT/GRE; for doctorate, GMAT. Additional exam requirements/recommendations for international students: Required—TOEFL (minimum score 100 iBT) or IELTS (minimum score 7.0). *Application deadline:* Applications are processed on a rolling basis. Application fee: $50 ($100 for international students). Electronic applications accepted. *Expenses:* Contact institution. *Financial support:* Fellowships, research assistantships, teaching assistantships, career-related internships or fieldwork, scholarships/grants, health care benefits, and unspecified assistantships available. Support available to part-time students. Financial award application deadline: 6/1; financial award applicants required to submit FAFSA. *Unit head:* Wayne Thomas, Interim Dean, 405-325-0100, Fax: 405-325-3421, E-mail: wthomas@ou.edu. *Application contact:* Amber Hasbrook, Academic Counselor, 405-325-5815, Fax: 405-325-7753, E-mail: ahasbrook@ou.edu.
Website: http://www.ou.edu/price

University of Pennsylvania, Graduate School of Education, Division of Teaching, Learning, and Leadership, Program in Education Entrepreneurship, Philadelphia, PA 19104. Offers MS Ed. *Program availability:* Evening/weekend. *Degree requirements:* For master's, thesis or alternative, capstone project. *Entrance requirements:* For master's, bachelor's degree; at least 3 years of work experience. Additional exam requirements/recommendations for international students: Required—TOEFL, IELTS. *Application deadline:* For summer admission, 2/1 priority date for domestic and international students. Application fee: $75. Electronic applications accepted. *Financial support:* Scholarships/grants available. *Unit head:* Dr. Jenny Zapf, Director, 215-898-3265, E-mail: jzapf@upenn.edu. *Application contact:* Ayoung Lee, Administrative Coordinator, 215-573-8149, E-mail: ayoungl@upenn.edu.
Website: http://www.gse.upenn.edu/tll/ee

University of Pennsylvania, School of Engineering and Applied Science, Program in Integrated Product Design, Philadelphia, PA 19104. Offers MIPD, MSE. *Program availability:* Part-time. *Students:* 25 full-time (12 women), 3 part-time (0 women); includes 6 minority (1 Black or African American, non-Hispanic/Latino; 2 Asian, non-Hispanic/Latino; 2 Hispanic/Latino; 1 Two or more races, non-Hispanic/Latino), 11 international. Average age 26. 117 applicants, 32% accepted, 18 enrolled. In 2018, 18 master's awarded. *Degree requirements:* For master's, comprehensive exam, thesis optional. *Entrance requirements:* For master's, GRE, bachelor's degree, letters of recommendation, resume, personal statement, portfolio. Additional exam requirements/recommendations for international students: Required—TOEFL (minimum score 100 iBT), IELTS (minimum score 7). *Application deadline:* For fall admission, 2/1 priority date for domestic and international students. Applications are processed on a rolling basis. Application fee: $80. Electronic applications accepted. *Expenses:* Contact institution. *Faculty research:* Technology and manufacturing processes, mechatronics, product design and design thinking. *Application contact:* William Fenton, Assistant Director of Graduate Admissions, 215-898-4542, Fax: 215-573-5577, E-mail: gradstudies@seas.upenn.edu.
Website: http://ipd.me.upenn.edu/

University of Pikeville, Coleman College of Business, Pikeville, KY 41501. Offers business (MBA); entrepreneurship (MBA); healthcare (MBA). *Program availability:* Part-time, evening/weekend. *Degree requirements:* For master's, comprehensive exam (for some programs). *Entrance requirements:* For master's, official transcripts, two professional letters of recommendation, three years of work experience. *Expenses:* Contact institution.

University of Portland, Dr. Robert B. Pamplin, Jr. School of Business, Portland, OR 97203-5798. Offers entrepreneurship (MBA); finance (MBA, MS); health care management (MBA); marketing (MBA); nonprofit management (EMBA); operations and technology management (MBA, MS); sustainability (MBA). *Accreditation:* AACSB. *Program availability:* Part-time, evening/weekend. *Faculty:* 26 full-time (5 women), 8 part-time/adjunct (1 woman). *Students:* 35 full-time (16 women), 114 part-time (47 women); includes 21 minority (3 Black or African American, non-Hispanic/Latino; 2 American Indian or Alaska Native, non-Hispanic/Latino; 8 Asian, non-Hispanic/Latino; 8 Hispanic/Latino), 24 international. Average age 32. In 2018, 55 master's awarded. *Entrance requirements:* For master's, GMAT or GRE, minimum GPA of 3.0, resume, statement of goals, 2 letters of recommendation. Additional exam requirements/recommendations for international students: Required—TOEFL (minimum score 88 iBT), IELTS (minimum score 7). *Application deadline:* For fall admission, 7/19 priority date for domestic and international students; for spring admission, 12/7 priority date for domestic and international students; for summer admission, 4/12 priority date for domestic and international students. Applications are processed on a rolling basis. Application fee: $0. Electronic applications accepted. *Expenses:* Contact institution. *Financial support:* Application deadline: 3/1; applicants required to submit FAFSA. *Unit head:* Melissa McCarthy, Director, 503-943-7224, E-mail: mba-up@up.edu. *Application contact:* Melissa McCarthy, Director, 503-943-7224, E-mail: mba-up@up.edu.

University of Rhode Island, Graduate School, College of Business, Kingston, RI 02881. Offers accounting (MS); business administration (MBA, PhD), including finance (MBA), general business (MBA), management (MBA), marketing, operations and supply chain management (PhD), supply chain management (MBA); finance (MBA, MS, PhD); general business (MBA); health care management (MBA); labor research (MS, Graduate Certificate), including labor relations and human resources; management (MBA); marketing (MBA); strategic innovation (MBA); supply chain management (MBA); textiles, fashion merchandising and design (MS, Certificate), including fashion merchandising (Certificate), master seamstress (Certificate), textiles, fashion merchandising and design (MS); MS/JD; Pharm D/MBA. *Accreditation:* AACSB. *Program availability:* Part-time, evening/weekend. *Faculty:* 61 full-time (30 women), 1 (woman) part-time/adjunct. *Students:* 85 full-time (35 women), 196 part-time (89 women); includes 43 minority (14 Black or African American, non-Hispanic/Latino; 1 American Indian or Alaska Native, non-Hispanic/Latino; 14 Asian, non-Hispanic/Latino;

10 Hispanic/Latino; 1 Native Hawaiian or other Pacific Islander, non-Hispanic/Latino; 3 Two or more races, non-Hispanic/Latino), 23 international. 155 applicants, 85% accepted, 105 enrolled. In 2018, 127 master's, 5 doctorates, 23 other advanced degrees awarded. *Entrance requirements:* Additional exam requirements/recommendations for international students: Required—TOEFL. Application fee: $65. Electronic applications accepted. *Expenses: Tuition, area resident:* Full-time $13,226; part-time $735 per credit. Tuition, state resident: full-time $13,226; part-time $735 per credit. Tuition, nonresident: full-time $25,854; part-time $1436 per credit. *International tuition:* $25,854 full-time. *Required fees:* $1698; $50 per credit. $35 per semester. One-time fee: $165. *Financial support:* In 2018–19, 15 teaching assistantships with tuition reimbursements (averaging $17,739 per year) were awarded; research assistantships also available. Financial award applicants required to submit FAFSA. *Unit head:* Dr. Maling Ebrahimpour, Dean, 401-874-4348, Fax: 401-874-4312, E-mail: mebrahimpour@uri.edu. *Application contact:* Lisa Lancellotta, Coordinator, MBA Programs, 401-874-4241, Fax: 401-874-4312, E-mail: mba@uri.edu.
Website: https://web.uri.edu/business/

University of Rochester, Hajim School of Engineering and Applied Sciences, Master of Science in Technical Entrepreneurship and Management Program, Rochester, NY 14627. Offers biomedical engineering (MS). Program offered in collaboration with the Simon School of Business and administered by the University of Rochester Ain Center for Entrepreneurship. *Program availability:* Part-time. *Students:* 39 full-time (13 women), 6 part-time (2 women); includes 5 minority (3 Black or African American, non-Hispanic/Latino; 1 Asian, non-Hispanic/Latino; 1 Hispanic/Latino), 30 international. Average age 25. 220 applicants, 73% accepted, 23 enrolled. In 2018, 14 master's awarded. *Degree requirements:* For master's, comprehensive exam. *Entrance requirements:* For master's, GRE or GMAT (strongly recommended), 3 letters of recommendation, personal statement, official transcript. Additional exam requirements/recommendations for international students: Required—TOEFL (minimum score 90 paper-based), IELTS (minimum score 6.5). *Application deadline:* For fall admission, 2/1 for domestic and international students. Application fee: $60. Electronic applications accepted. *Expenses: Tuition:* Full-time $52,974; part-time $1654 per credit hour. *Required fees:* $612. One-time fee: $30 part-time. Tuition and fees vary according to campus/location and program. *Financial support:* Career-related internships or fieldwork, scholarships/grants, health care benefits, and tuition waivers (partial) available. Support available to part-time students. Financial award application deadline: 2/1. *Unit head:* Duncan T. Moore, Vice Provost for Entrepreneurship, 585-275-5248, E-mail: duncan.moore@rochester.edu. *Application contact:* Andrea Barrett, Executive Director, 585-276-3407, E-mail: andrea.barrett@rochester.edu.
Website: http://www.rochester.edu/team/

University of Rochester, Simon Business School, Full-Time Master's Program in Business Administration, Rochester, NY 14627. Offers business systems consulting (MBA); competitive and organizational strategy (MBA); computers and information systems (MBA); corporate accounting (MBA); entrepreneurship (MBA); finance (MBA); health sciences management (MBA); marketing (MBA); operations management (MBA); public accounting (MBA); strategy and organizations (MBA). *Accreditation:* AACSB. *Entrance requirements:* For master's, GMAT or GRE. *Expenses: Tuition:* Full-time $52,974; part-time $1654 per credit hour. *Required fees:* $612. One-time fee: $30 part-time. Tuition and fees vary according to campus/location and program. *Faculty research:* Empirical industrial organization, risk management, financial disclosure and regulation, social media, health care management.

University of Rochester, Simon Business School, Part-Time MBA Program, Rochester, NY 14627. Offers business systems consulting (MBA); competitive and organizational strategy (MBA); computers and information systems (MBA); corporate accounting (MBA); entrepreneurship (MBA); finance (MBA); health sciences management (MBA); marketing (MBA), including brand management, marketing strategy, pricing; operations management (MBA); public accounting (MBA). *Program availability:* Part-time-only, evening/weekend. *Entrance requirements:* For master's, GRE or GMAT. Electronic applications accepted. *Expenses:* Contact institution.

University of San Francisco, School of Management, Master in Global Entrepreneurial Management Program, San Francisco, CA 94117. Offers MGEM. Program offered jointly with IQS in Barcelona, Spain and Fu Jen Catholic University in Taipei, Taiwan. *Students:* 10 full-time (4 women); includes 8 minority (1 Black or African American, non-Hispanic/Latino; 2 Asian, non-Hispanic/Latino; 4 Hispanic/Latino; 1 Native Hawaiian or other Pacific Islander, non-Hispanic/Latino). Average age 24. 78 applicants, 97% accepted, 39 enrolled. In 2018, 37 master's awarded. *Entrance requirements:* For master's, resume, transcripts from each college or university attended, two letters of recommendation, personal statement. Additional exam requirements/recommendations for international students: Required—TOEFL (minimum score 550 paper-based, 79 iBT), IELTS (minimum score 6), or PTE (minimum score 53). *Application deadline:* For fall admission, 5/15 for domestic students. Application fee: $55. Electronic applications accepted. *Expenses:* Contact institution. *Financial support:* Application deadline: 3/2; applicants required to submit FAFSA. *Unit head:* Dr. Gleb Nikitenko, Director, 415-422-2221, E-mail: management@usfca.edu. *Application contact:* Office of Graduate Recruiting and Admissions, 415-422-2221, E-mail: management@usfca.edu.
Website: http://www.usfca.edu/mgem

University of San Francisco, School of Management, Master of Business Administration Program, San Francisco, CA 94117. Offers entrepreneurship and innovation (MBA); finance (MBA); marketing (MBA); organization development (MBA); DDS/MBA; JD/MBA; MBA/MAPS. *Accreditation:* AACSB. *Program availability:* Part-time, evening/weekend. *Students:* 136 full-time (67 women), 7 part-time (2 women); includes 57 minority (5 Black or African American, non-Hispanic/Latino; 29 Asian, non-Hispanic/Latino; 14 Hispanic/Latino; 1 Native Hawaiian or other Pacific Islander, non-Hispanic/Latino; 8 Two or more races, non-Hispanic/Latino), 27 international. Average age 29. 226 applicants, 61% accepted, 56 enrolled. In 2018, 76 master's awarded. *Entrance requirements:* For master's, GMAT or GRE, resume (two years of professional work experience required for part-time students, preferred for full-time), transcripts from each college or university attended, two letters of recommendation, personal statement, interview. Additional exam requirements/recommendations for international students: Required—TOEFL (minimum score 600 paper-based, 100 iBT), IELTS (minimum score 7) or PTE (minimum score 68). *Application deadline:* For fall admission, 6/5 for domestic students, 5/15 for international students; for spring admission, 11/30 for domestic students. Application fee: $55. Electronic applications accepted. *Expenses:* Contact institution. *Financial support:* Fellowships and scholarships/grants available. Financial award application deadline: 3/2; financial award applicants required to submit FAFSA. *Faculty research:* International financial markets, technology transfer licensing, international marketing, strategic planning. *Total annual research expenditures:* $50,000. *Unit head:* Dr. Frank Fletcher, Director, 415-422-2221, E-mail: management@usfca.edu. *Application contact:* Office of Graduate Recruiting and Admissions, 415-422-2221, E-mail: management@usfca.edu.
Website: http://www.usfca.edu/mba

University of San Francisco, School of Management, Master of Science in Entrepreneurship and Innovation Program, San Francisco, CA 94117. Offers MS. *Students:* 45 full-time (24 women); includes 6 minority (1 Black or African American,

non-Hispanic/Latino; 5 Asian, non-Hispanic/Latino), 30 international. Average age 24. 165 applicants, 69% accepted, 45 enrolled. *Application deadline:* For fall admission, 11/15 priority date for domestic students. *Expenses:* Contact institution. *Unit head:* Dr. Gleb Nikitenko, Director, 415-422-2151, E-mail: nikitenko@usfca.edu. *Application contact:* Dr. Gleb Nikitenko, Director, 415-422-2151, E-mail: nikitenko@usfca.edu.
Website: https://www.usfca.edu/management/graduate-programs/entrepreneurship-innovation

University of Sioux Falls, Vucurevich School of Business, Sioux Falls, SD 57105-1699. Offers entrepreneurial leadership (MBA); general management (MBA); health care management (MBA); marketing (MBA). *Program availability:* Part-time, evening/weekend. *Degree requirements:* For master's, project. *Entrance requirements:* For master's, minimum GPA of 3.0. Additional exam requirements/recommendations for international students: Required—TOEFL. *Expenses:* Contact institution.

University of Southern California, Graduate School, Marshall School of Business, Program in Entrepreneurship and Innovation, Los Angeles, CA 90089. Offers MS.

University of South Florida, Innovative Education, Tampa, FL 33620-9951. Offers adult, career and higher education (Graduate Certificate), including college teaching, leadership in developing human resources, leadership in higher education; Africana studies (Graduate Certificate), including diasporas and health disparities, genocide and human rights; aging studies (Graduate Certificate), including gerontology; art research (Graduate Certificate), including museum studies; business foundations (Graduate Certificate); chemical and biomedical engineering (Graduate Certificate), including materials science and engineering, water, health and sustainability; child and family studies (Graduate Certificate), including positive behavior support; civil and industrial engineering (Graduate Certificate), including transportation systems analysis; community and family health (Graduate Certificate), including maternal and child health, social marketing and public health, violence and injury: prevention and intervention, women's health; criminology (Graduate Certificate), including criminal justice administration; data science for public administration (Graduate Certificate); digital humanities (Graduate Certificate); educational measurement and research (Graduate Certificate), including evaluation; English (Graduate Certificate), including comparative literary studies, creative writing, professional and technical communication; entrepreneurship (Graduate Certificate); environmental health (Graduate Certificate), including safety management; epidemiology and biostatistics (Graduate Certificate), including applied biostatistics, biostatistics, concepts and tools of epidemiology, epidemiology, epidemiology of infectious diseases; geography, environment and planning (Graduate Certificate), including community development, environmental policy and management, geographical information systems; geology (Graduate Certificate), including hydrogeology; global health (Graduate Certificate), including disaster management, global health and Latin American and Caribbean studies, global health practice, humanitarian assistance, infection control; government and international affairs (Graduate Certificate), including Cuban studies, globalization studies; health policy and management (Graduate Certificate), including health management and leadership, public health policy and programs; hearing specialist: early intervention (Graduate Certificate); industrial and management systems engineering (Graduate Certificate), including systems engineering, technology management; information studies (Graduate Certificate), including school library media specialist; information systems/decision sciences (Graduate Certificate), including analytics and business intelligence; instructional technology (Graduate Certificate), including distance education, Florida digital/virtual educator, instructional design, multimedia design, Web design; internal medicine, bioethics and medical humanities (Graduate Certificate), including biomedical ethics; Latin American and Caribbean studies (Graduate Certificate); leadership for coastal resiliency planning (Graduate Certificate); mass communications (Graduate Certificate), including multimedia journalism; mathematics and statistics (Graduate Certificate), including mathematics; medicine (Graduate Certificate), including aging and neuroscience, bioinformatics, biotechnology, brain fitness and memory management, clinical investigation, hand and upper limb rehabilitation, health informatics, health sciences, integrative weight management, intellectual property, medicine and gender, metabolic and nutritional medicine, metabolic cardiology, pharmacy sciences; national and competitive intelligence (Graduate Certificate); nursing (Graduate Certificate), including simulation based academic fellowship in advanced pain management; psychological and social foundations (Graduate Certificate), including career counseling, college teaching, diversity in education, mental health counseling, school counseling; public affairs (Graduate Certificate), including nonprofit management, public management, research administration; public health (Graduate Certificate), including assessing chemical toxicity and public health risks, health equity, pharmacoepidemiology, public health generalist, toxicology, translational research in adolescent behavioral health; public health practices (Graduate Certificate), including planning for healthy communities; rehabilitation and mental health counseling (Graduate Certificate), including integrative mental health care, marriage and family therapy, rehabilitation technology; secondary education (Graduate Certificate), including ESOL, foreign language education: culture and content, foreign language education: professional; social work (Graduate Certificate), including geriatric social work/clinical gerontology; special education (Graduate Certificate), including autism spectrum disorder, disabilities education: severe/profound; world languages (Graduate Certificate), including teaching English as a second language (TESL) or foreign language. *Expenses:* Tuition, state resident: full-time $6350. Tuition, nonresident: full-time $19,048. *International tuition:* $19,048 full-time. *Required fees:* $2079. *Unit head:* Dr. Cynthia DeLuca, Associate Vice President and Assistant Vice Provost, 813-974-3077, Fax: 813-974-7061, E-mail: deluca@usf.edu. *Application contact:* Owen Hooper, Director, Summer and Alternative Calendar Programs, 813-974-6917, E-mail: hooper@usf.edu.
Website: http://www.usf.edu/innovative-education/

University of South Florida, Muma College of Business, Center for Entrepreneurship, Tampa, FL 33620-9951. Offers entrepreneurship and applied technologies (MS). *Program availability:* Part-time, evening/weekend. *Faculty:* 4 full-time (2 women), 1 part-time/adjunct (0 women). *Students:* 3. In 2018, 55 master's awarded. *Degree requirements:* For master's, comprehensive exam, thesis optional. *Entrance requirements:* For master's, GMAT or GRE (preferred), MCAT or LSAT, 3.0 GPA, 2 letters of recommendation, letter of interest, interview. Demonstrated competence in statistics, accounting, and finance. Additional exam requirements/recommendations for international students: Required—TOEFL, TOEFL (minimum score 550 paper-based; 79 iBT) or IELTS (minimum score 6.5). *Application deadline:* For fall admission, 6/1 for domestic students, 2/1 for international students; for spring admission, 10/15 for domestic students, 7/1 for international students. Applications are processed on a rolling basis. Application fee: $30. Electronic applications accepted. *Expenses:* Tuition, state resident: full-time $6350. Tuition, nonresident: full-time $19,048. *International tuition:* $19,048 full-time. *Required fees:* $2079. *Faculty research:* Underlying success factors which drive the creation, growth and failures of businesses and technologies in the life sciences industry; influences of individual company geographic location, financial parameters, intellectual property, FDA and regulatory compliance, and press coverage on stock performance of over 1,000 publicly-traded life sciences companies. *Total annual research expenditures:* $37,313. *Unit head:* Dr. Michael W. Fountain, Director, Center for Entrepreneurship, 813-974-7825, Fax: 813-974-6175, E-mail: fountain@usf.edu. *Application contact:* Dr. Tapas Das, Assistant Director/Professor, 813-974-5585, Fax: 813-974-5953, E-mail: das@usf.edu.
Website: http://www.ce.usf.edu/

University of South Florida, Patel College of Global Sustainability, Tampa, FL 33620-9951. Offers energy, global, water and sustainable tourism (Graduate Certificate); global sustainability (MA), including building sustainable enterprise, climate change and sustainability, coastal sustainability, entrepreneurship, food sustainability and security, sustainability policy, sustainable energy, sustainable tourism, water. *Faculty:* 1 full-time (0 women). *Students:* 64 full-time (33 women), 92 part-time (57 women); includes 32 minority (8 Black or African American, non-Hispanic/Latino; 3 Asian, non-Hispanic/Latino; 15 Hispanic/Latino; 6 Two or more races, non-Hispanic/Latino), 50 international. Average age 29. 119 applicants, 75% accepted, 60 enrolled. In 2018, 91 master's awarded. *Degree requirements:* For master's, comprehensive exam (for some programs), thesis or alternative, internship. *Entrance requirements:* For master's, GPA of at least 3.25 or greater; alternatively a GPA of at least 3.00 along with a GRE Verbal score of 153 (61 percentile) or higher, Quantitative of 153 (51 percentile) or higher and Analytical Writing of 3.5 or higher, all taken within 5 years of application; at least 2 letters of recommendation from professors or supervisors. Additional exam requirements/recommendations for international students: Required—TOEFL (minimum score 550 paper-based; 79 iBT). *Application deadline:* For fall admission, 6/1 for domestic students, 5/1 for international students; for spring admission, 10/15 for domestic students, 9/15 for international students. Electronic applications accepted. *Expenses:* Tuition, state resident: full-time $6350. Tuition, nonresident: full-time $19,048. *International tuition:* $19,048 full-time. *Required fees:* $2079. *Financial support:* In 2018–19, 35 students received support. *Faculty research:* Global sustainability, integrated resource management, systems thinking, green communities, entrepreneurship, ecotourism. *Total annual research expenditures:* $174,608. *Unit head:* Dr. Govindan Parayil, Dean, 813-974-9694, E-mail: gparayil@usf.edu. *Application contact:* Dr. Govindan Parayil, Dean, 813-974-9694, E-mail: gparayil@usf.edu.
Website: http://psgs.usf.edu/

The University of Tampa, Sykes College of Business, Tampa, FL 33606-1490. Offers accounting (MS); business analytics (MBA); cybersecurity (MBA, MS); entrepreneurship (MBA, MS); finance (MBA, MS); information systems management (MBA); innovation management (MBA); international business (MBA); marketing (MBA, MS); nonprofit management (MBA, Certificate). *Accreditation:* AACSB. *Program availability:* Part-time, evening/weekend. *Faculty:* 61 full-time (13 women), 11 part-time/adjunct (3 women). *Students:* 361 full-time (153 women), 122 part-time (52 women); includes 101 minority (31 Black or African American, non-Hispanic/Latino; 5 Asian, non-Hispanic/Latino; 57 Hispanic/Latino; 1 Native Hawaiian or other Pacific Islander, non-Hispanic/Latino; 7 Two or more races, non-Hispanic/Latino), 144 international. Average age 29. 1,079 applicants, 57% accepted, 263 enrolled. In 2018, 281 master's, 12 other advanced degrees awarded. *Degree requirements:* For master's, capstone. *Entrance requirements:* For master's, GMAT or GRE, official transcripts from all colleges and/or universities previously attended, resume, personal statement, letters of recommendation. Additional exam requirements/recommendations for international students: Required—TOEFL (minimum score 577 paper-based; 90 iBT), IELTS (minimum score 7.5). *Application deadline:* Applications are processed on a rolling basis. Application fee: $40. Electronic applications accepted. *Expenses:* Contact institution. *Financial support:* In 2018–19, 123 students received support. Career-related internships or fieldwork, scholarships/grants, and unspecified assistantships available. Financial award applicants required to submit FAFSA. *Faculty research:* Job market signaling, on-line shopping behaviors and social media, the Tampa Bay economy, digital literacy, entrepreneurship in small businesses. *Unit head:* Dr. Natasha F. Veltri, Associate Dean, 813-253-6289, E-mail: nveltri@ut.edu. *Application contact:* Ashley Russell, Staff Assistant, Admissions for Graduate and Continuing Studies, 813-253-6249, E-mail: arussell@ut.edu.
Website: http://www.ut.edu/business/

The University of Texas at Austin, Graduate School, McCombs School of Business, Program in Technology Commercialization, Austin, TX 78712-1111. Offers MS. Twelve-month program, beginning in May, with classes held every other Friday and Saturday. *Program availability:* Evening/weekend, online learning. *Degree requirements:* For master's, year-long global teaming project. *Entrance requirements:* For master's, GRE General Test or GMAT. Additional exam requirements/recommendations for international students: Required—TOEFL (minimum score 550 paper-based; 79 iBT). Electronic applications accepted. *Expenses:* Contact institution. *Faculty research:* Technology transfer; entrepreneurship; commercialization; research, development and innovation.

The University of Texas at Dallas, Naveen Jindal School of Management, Program in Organizations, Strategy and International Management, Richardson, TX 75080. Offers business administration (MBA); executive business administration (EMBA); global leadership (EMBA); healthcare leadership and management (MS); healthcare management (EMBA); innovation and entrepreneurship (MS); international management studies (MS, PhD); management science (MS, PhD); project management (EMBA); systems engineering and management (MS); MS/MBA. *Program availability:* Part-time, evening/weekend. *Faculty:* 19 full-time (6 women), 33 part-time/adjunct (12 women). *Students:* 587 full-time (237 women), 777 part-time (361 women); includes 456 minority (83 Black or African American, non-Hispanic/Latino; 226 Asian, non-Hispanic/Latino; 110 Hispanic/Latino; 37 Two or more races, non-Hispanic/Latino), 316 international. Average age 34. 1,452 applicants, 43% accepted, 376 enrolled. In 2018, 556 master's, 23 doctorates awarded. *Degree requirements:* For doctorate, thesis/dissertation. *Entrance requirements:* For master's and doctorate, GMAT. Additional exam requirements/recommendations for international students: Required—TOEFL (minimum score 550 paper-based). *Application deadline:* For fall admission, 7/15 for domestic students, 5/1 priority date for international students; for spring admission, 11/15 for domestic students, 9/1 priority date for international students. Applications are processed on a rolling basis. Application fee: $50 ($100 for international students). Electronic applications accepted. *Expenses: Tuition, area resident:* Full-time $13,458. Tuition, state resident: full-time $13,458. Tuition, nonresident: full-time $26,852. *International tuition:* $26,852 full-time. Tuition and fees vary according to course load. *Financial support:* In 2018–19, 102 students received support, including 24 research assistantships with partial tuition reimbursements available (averaging $37,400 per year), 83 teaching assistantships with partial tuition reimbursements available (averaging $25,119 per year); Federal Work-Study, institutionally sponsored loans, scholarships/grants, and unspecified assistantships also available. Support available to part-time students. Financial award application deadline: 4/30; financial award applicants required to submit FAFSA. *Faculty research:* International accounting, international trade and finance, economic development, international economics. *Unit head:* Dr. Seung-Hyun Lee, Area Coordinator, 972-883-6267, Fax: 972-883-5977, E-mail: sxl029100@utdallas.edu. *Application contact:* Dr. Seung-Hyun Lee, Area Coordinator, 972-883-6267, Fax: 972-883-5977, E-mail: sxl029100@utdallas.edu.
Website: http://jindal.utdallas.edu/osim/

University of Washington, Graduate School, Michael G. Foster School of Business, Seattle, WA 98195-3200. Offers auditing and assurance (MP Acc); business

administration (MBA, PhD); entrepreneurship (MS); executive business administration (MBA); global executive business administration (MBA); information systems (MSIS); supply chain management (MSSCM); taxation (MP Acc); technology management (MBA); JD/MBA; MBA/MAIS; MBA/MHA. *Accreditation:* AACSB. *Program availability:* Part-time, evening/weekend, blended/hybrid learning. Terminal master's awarded for partial completion of doctoral program. *Degree requirements:* For doctorate, comprehensive exam, thesis/dissertation. *Entrance requirements:* For master's and doctorate, GMAT, GRE. Additional exam requirements/recommendations for international students: Required—TOEFL (minimum score 600 paper-based; 100 iBT). Electronic applications accepted. *Expenses:* Contact institution. *Faculty research:* Finance, consumer behavior, marketing analytics, technology management, supply chain.

University of Waterloo, Graduate Studies and Postdoctoral Affairs, Faculty of Engineering, Conrad School of Entrepreneurship and Business, Waterloo, ON N2L 3G1, Canada. Offers MBET. *Entrance requirements:* For master's, honors degree. Additional exam requirements/recommendations for international students: Required—TOEFL (minimum score 90 iBT), IELTS (minimum score 7), PTE (minimum score 63). *Application deadline:* Applications are processed on a rolling basis. Application fee: $125. Electronic applications accepted. *Application contact:* Tracie Wilkinson, Administrative Liaison and Support, 519-888-4567 Ext. 37167, Fax: 519-747-7287, E-mail: twilkins@uwaterloo.ca.
Website: https://uwaterloo.ca/conrad-business-entrepreneurship-technology/

The University of Western Ontario, Ivey Business School, London, ON N6A 3K7, Canada. Offers business (EMBA, PhD); corporate strategy and leadership elective (MBA); entrepreneurship elective (MBA); finance elective (MBA); health sector stream (MBA); international management elective (MBA); marketing elective (MBA); JD/MBA. *Degree requirements:* For master's, thesis (for some programs); for doctorate, thesis/dissertation. *Entrance requirements:* For master's, GMAT, 2 years of full-time work experience, interview. Additional exam requirements/recommendations for international students: Required—TOEFL (minimum score 100 iBT) or IELTS (minimium score 6). Electronic applications accepted. *Faculty research:* Strategy, organizational behavior, international business, finance, operations management.

University of West Los Angeles, School of Business, Inglewood, CA 90301. Offers organizational leadership and business innovation (MS).

University of Wisconsin–Milwaukee, Graduate School, Lubar School of Business, Milwaukee, WI 53201. Offers business administration (MBA); executive business administration (EMBA); management science (MS, PhD, Graduate Certificate), including business analytics (Graduate Certificate), enterprise resource planning (Graduate Certificate), information technology management (MS), investment management (Graduate Certificate), nonprofit management (Graduate Certificate), nonprofit management and leadership (MS), state and local taxation (Graduate Certificate); technology entrepreneurship (Graduate Certificate). *Accreditation:* AACSB. *Program availability:* Part-time, evening/weekend. *Students:* 282 full-time (122 women), 280 part-time (115 women); includes 95 minority (19 Black or African American, non-Hispanic/Latino; 2 American Indian or Alaska Native, non-Hispanic/Latino; 35 Asian, non-Hispanic/Latino; 7 Hispanic/Latino; 32 Two or more races, non-Hispanic/Latino), 65 international. Average age 32. 389 applicants, 66% accepted, 191 enrolled. In 2018, 212 master's, 2 doctorates, 18 other advanced degrees awarded. *Degree requirements:* For master's, comprehensive exam (for some programs); for doctorate, comprehensive exam, thesis/dissertation. *Entrance requirements:* For master's and doctorate, GMAT or GRE General Test. Additional exam requirements/recommendations for international students: Required—TOEFL (minimum score 550 paper-based; 79 iBT), IELTS (minimum score 6.5). *Application deadline:* For fall admission, 1/1 priority date for domestic students; for spring admission, 9/1 for domestic students. Application fee: $56 ($96 for international students). Electronic applications accepted. *Expenses:* Contact institution. *Financial support:* Fellowships with full tuition reimbursements, research assistantships with full tuition reimbursements, teaching assistantships with full tuition reimbursements, career-related internships or fieldwork, Federal Work-Study, health care benefits, unspecified assistantships, and project assistantships available. Support available to part-time students. Financial award application deadline: 4/15; financial award applicants required to submit FAFSA. *Faculty research:* Applied management research in finance, management information systems, marketing, operations research, organizational sciences. *Unit head:* V. Kanti Prasad, Dean, 414-229-6256, E-mail: dean-prasad@uwm.edu. *Application contact:* Business Graduate Student Services, 414-229-5403, E-mail: mba-ms@uwm.edu.
Website: https://uwm.edu/business/

Ursuline College, School of Graduate and Professional Studies, Program in Business Administration, Pepper Pike, OH 44124-4398. Offers ethical and entrepreneurial leadership (MBA); financial planning and accounting (MBA); health services management (MBA); management (MBA); management and leadership (MBA); marketing and communications management (MBA). *Program availability:* Part-time, evening/weekend. *Faculty:* 2 full-time (both women), 2 part-time/adjunct (1 woman). *Students:* 17 full-time (all women), 5 part-time (3 women); includes 10 minority (9 Black or African American, non-Hispanic/Latino; 1 Two or more races, non-Hispanic/Latino). Average age 40. 33 applicants, 100% accepted, 6 enrolled. In 2018, 16 master's awarded. *Degree requirements:* For master's, comprehensive exam (for some programs). *Entrance requirements:* For master's, GRE. Additional exam requirements/recommendations for international students: Required—TOEFL (minimum score 500 paper-based) or GRE. *Application deadline:* For fall admission, 8/1 for domestic students. Applications are processed on a rolling basis. Application fee: $25. Electronic applications accepted. *Expenses:* 36 hours at $903/per. *Financial support:* In 2018–19, 2 students received support. Campus work-study available. Financial award application deadline: 8/1; financial award applicants required to submit FAFSA. *Faculty research:* Gift economy; sharing economy; cooperative business models; collaborative leadership; corporate social responsibility and the triple bottom line, defined as the three P's: people, planet and profit. *Unit head:* Dr. Debra Fleming, Professor, 440-440-720-3864, Fax: 440-684-6088, E-mail: dfleming@ursuline.edu. *Application contact:* Melanie Steele, Director of Graduate Admission, 440-646-8146, Fax: 440-684-6138, E-mail: graduateadmissions@ursuline.edu.

Virginia International University, School of Business, Fairfax, VA 22030. Offers accounting (MBA, MS); entrepreneurship (MBA); executive management (Graduate Certificate); global logistics (MBA); health care management (MBA); hospitality and tourism management (MBA); human resources management (MBA); international business management (MBA); international finance (MBA); marketing management (MBA); mass media and public relations (MBA); project management (MBA, MS). *Program availability:* Part-time, online learning. *Entrance requirements:* For master's and Graduate Certificate, bachelor's degree. Additional exam requirements/recommendations for international students: Required—TOEFL (minimum score 550 paper-based; 80 iBT), IELTS (minimum score 6). Electronic applications accepted.

Walden University, Graduate Programs, School of Management, Minneapolis, MN 55401. Offers accounting (MBA, MS, DBA), including accounting for the professional (MS), accounting with CPA emphasis (MS), self-designed (MS); advanced project management (Graduate Certificate); applied project management (Graduate Certificate); auditing (Graduate Certificate); bridge to business administration (Post-Doctoral Certificate); bridge to management (Post-Doctoral Certificate); business management (Graduate Certificate); communication (MBA); corporate finance (MBA); digital marketing (Graduate Certificate); entrepreneurship (DBA); entrepreneurship and small business (MBA); finance (MS, DBA), including finance for the professional (MS), finance with CFA/investment (MS), finance with CPA emphasis (MS); global supply chain management (DBA); healthcare management (MBA, DBA); human resource management (MBA, MS, Graduate Certificate), including functional human resource management (MS), general program (MS), integrating functional and strategic human resource management (MS), organizational strategy (MS); human resources management (DBA); information systems management (DBA); international business (MBA, DBA); leadership (MBA, MS, DBA, Graduate Certificate), including general program (MS), human resource leadership (MS), leader development (MS), self-designed (MS); management (MS, PhD), including communications (MS), finance (PhD), general program (MS), healthcare management (MS), human resource management (MS), human resources management (PhD), information systems management (PhD), international business (MS), leadership (MS), leadership and organizational change (PhD), marketing (MS), project management (MS), strategy and operations (MS); managerial accounting (Graduate Certificate); marketing (MBA, MS, DBA); project management (MBA, MS, DBA); self-designed (MBA, DBA); social impact management (DBA); technology entrepreneurship (DBA). *Accreditation:* ACBSP. *Program availability:* Part-time, evening/weekend, online only, 100% online. *Degree requirements:* For master's, thesis (for some programs), residency (for EMBA); for doctorate, thesis/dissertation (for some programs), residency. *Entrance requirements:* For master's, bachelor's degree or higher; minimum GPA of 2.5; official transcripts; goal statement (for some programs); access to computer and Internet; for doctorate, master's degree or higher; three years of related professional or academic experience (preferred); minimum GPA of 3.0; goal statement and current resume (for select programs); official transcripts; access to computer and Internet; for other advanced degree, relevant work experience; access to computer and Internet. Additional exam requirements/recommendations for international students: Required—TOEFL (minimum score 550 paper-based, 79 iBT), IELTS (minimum score 6.5), Michigan English Language Assessment Battery (minimum score 82), or PTE (minimum score 53). Electronic applications accepted.

Washington University in St. Louis, School of Medicine, Program in Clinical Investigation, St. Louis, MO 63130-4899. Offers clinical investigation (MS), including bioethics, entrepreneurship, genetics/genomics, translational medicine. *Program availability:* Part-time, evening/weekend. *Degree requirements:* For master's, thesis. *Entrance requirements:* For master's, doctoral-level degree or in process of obtaining doctoral-level degree. Electronic applications accepted. *Faculty research:* Anesthesiology, infectious diseases, neurology, obstetrics and gynecology, orthopedic surgery.

Wayne State University, Mike Ilitch School of Business, Detroit, MI 48202. Offers accounting (MS, MSA, Postbaccalaureate Certificate); business (EMS, Graduate Certificate); business administration (MBA, PhD); data science (MS), including business analytics; entrepreneurship and innovation (Postbaccalaureate Certificate); finance (MS); information systems management (Postbaccalaureate Certificate); taxation (MST); JD/MBA. Application deadline for PhD is February 15. *Accreditation:* AACSB. *Program availability:* Part-time, evening/weekend. *Faculty:* 31. *Students:* 286 full-time (152 women), 1,166 part-time (533 women); includes 409 minority (236 Black or African American, non-Hispanic/Latino; 83 Asian, non-Hispanic/Latino; 53 Hispanic/Latino; 37 Two or more races, non-Hispanic/Latino), 74 international. Average age 30. 1,212 applicants, 38% accepted, 294 enrolled. In 2018, 285 master's, 6 doctorates, 7 other advanced degrees awarded. *Degree requirements:* For doctorate, thesis/dissertation. *Entrance requirements:* For master's, GMAT, GRE, LSAT, MCAT, at least three years of relevant work experience that shows increased responsibility, or minimum GPA of 3.0 from AACSB-accredited program or 3.2 from regionally-accredited program, undergraduate degree from accredited institution; undergraduate degree in accounting, business administration, or area of business administration (for MS and MST); for doctorate, GMAT (minimum score of 600), minimum undergraduate GPA of 3.0, 3.5 upper-division or graduate; three letters of recommendation; brief essay; undergraduate degree from accredited institution; personal statement; for other advanced degree, bachelor's degree from accredited institution. Additional exam requirements/recommendations for international students: Required—TOEFL (minimum score 550 paper-based; 79 iBT), Michigan English Language Assessment Battery (minimum score 85); Recommended—IELTS (minimum score 6.5), TWE (minimum score 5.5). *Application deadline:* For fall admission, 7/1 for domestic students, 5/1 priority date for international students; for winter admission, 11/1 for domestic students, 9/1 priority date for international students; for spring admission, 3/1 for domestic students, 1/1 priority date for international students. Applications are processed on a rolling basis. Application fee: $50. Electronic applications accepted. *Expenses:* Contact institution. *Financial support:* In 2018–19, 175 students received support, including 1 fellowship with tuition reimbursement available (averaging $20,000 per year), 5 research assistantships with tuition reimbursements available (averaging $21,393 per year); teaching assistantships with tuition reimbursements available, scholarships/grants, health care benefits, and unspecified assistantships also available. Support available to part-time students. Financial award applicants required to submit FAFSA. *Faculty research:* Executive compensation and stock performance, consumer reactions to pricing strategies, communication across the automotive supply chain, performance of firms in sub-Saharan Africa, implementation issues with ERP software. *Unit head:* Dr. Robert Forsythe, Dean, School of Business Administration, 313-577-4501, E-mail: robert.forsythe@wayne.edu. *Application contact:* Kiantee N. Rupert-Jones, Director, 313-577-4511, Fax: 313-577-9442, E-mail: gradbusiness@wayne.edu.
Website: http://ilitchbusiness.wayne.edu/

Western Carolina University, Graduate School, College of Business, Program in Entrepreneurship, Cullowhee, NC 28723. Offers ME. *Program availability:* Part-time, evening/weekend, online learning. *Entrance requirements:* For master's, GMAT or GRE General Test. Additional exam requirements/recommendations for international students: Required—TOEFL (minimum score 550 paper-based; 79 iBT). *Expenses: Tuition, area resident:* Full-time $4435. Tuition, state resident: full-time $4435. Tuition, nonresident: full-time $14,842. *International tuition:* $14,842 full-time. *Required fees:* $2979. Part-time tuition and fees vary according to course load, degree level and program.

Wichita State University, Graduate School, Institute for Interdisciplinary Creativity, Wichita, KS 67260. Offers innovation design (MID). *Unit head:* Dr. Jeremy Patterson, Graduate Coordinator, 316-978-3010, E-mail: jeremy.patterson@wichita.edu. *Application contact:* Jordan Oleson, Admissions Coordinator, 316-978-3095, Fax: 316-978-3253, E-mail: jordan.oleson@wichita.edu.
Website: http://www.wichita.edu/iic

Wilkes University, College of Graduate and Professional Studies, Jay S. Sidhu School of Business and Leadership, Wilkes-Barre, PA 18766-0002. Offers accounting (MBA); global business (MBA); human resource management (MBA); international business (MBA); leadership (MBA); management (MBA); operations management (MBA);

organizational leadership and development (MBA). *Accreditation:* ACBSP. *Program availability:* Part-time, evening/weekend. *Students:* 16 full-time (9 women), 64 part-time (33 women); includes 11 minority (3 Black or African American, non-Hispanic/Latino; 3 Asian, non-Hispanic/Latino; 3 Hispanic/Latino; 2 Two or more races, non-Hispanic/Latino), 7 international. Average age 30. In 2018, 49 master's awarded. *Entrance requirements:* For master's, GMAT. Additional exam requirements/recommendations for international students: Required—TOEFL (minimum score 550 paper-based; 79 iBT). *Application deadline:* Applications are processed on a rolling basis. Application fee: $45 ($65 for international students). Electronic applications accepted. *Expenses:* Contact institution. *Financial support:* Unspecified assistantships available. Financial award application deadline: 3/1; financial award applicants required to submit FAFSA. *Unit head:* Dr. Abel Adekola, Dean, 570-408-4701, Fax: 570-408-7846, E-mail: abel.adekola@wilkes.edu. *Application contact:* Kristin Donati, Associate Director of Graduate Admissions, 570-408-3338, Fax: 570-408-7846, E-mail: kristin.donati@wilkes.edu.
Website: http://www.wilkes.edu/academics/colleges/sidhu-school-of-business-leadership/index.aspx

William Paterson University of New Jersey, Cotsakos College of Business, Wayne, NJ 07470-8420. Offers applied business analytics (MS); business administration (MBA), including accounting, entrepreneurship, finance, general business administration, human resource management, marketing, music and entertainment management; MBA pathways (Certificate); sales leadership (MS). *Accreditation:* AACSB. *Program availability:* Part-time, evening/weekend. *Faculty:* 21 full-time (6 women), 5 part-time/adjunct (1 woman). *Students:* 78 full-time (40 women), 250 part-time (113 women); includes 161 minority (39 Black or African American, non-Hispanic/Latino; 1 American Indian or Alaska Native, non-Hispanic/Latino; 23 Asian, non-Hispanic/Latino; 82 Hispanic/Latino; 16 Two or more races, non-Hispanic/Latino), 14 international. Average age 31. 222 applicants, 86% accepted, 136 enrolled. In 2018, 95 master's awarded. *Degree requirements:* For master's, Programs Differ see: https://academiccatalog.wpunj.edu/content.php?catoid=1&navoid=68. *Entrance requirements:* For master's, program details: https://www.wpunj.edu/admissions/graduate/admission-deadlines-and-requirements/. Additional exam requirements/recommendations for international students: Required—TOEFL (minimum score 550 paper-based; 79 iBT), IELTS (minimum score 6). *Application deadline:* For fall admission, 6/1 for domestic students, 3/1 for international students; for spring admission, 11/1 for domestic students, 10/1 for international students. Applications are processed on a rolling basis. Application fee: $50. Electronic applications accepted. *Expenses: Tuition, area resident:* Full-time $14,714; part-time $727 per credit. Tuition, state resident: full-time $14,714; part-time $727 per credit. Tuition, nonresident: full-time $22,952; part-time $727 per credit. *International tuition:* $22,952 full-time. *Required fees:* $4 per semester. Tuition and fees vary according to course load, degree level and program. *Financial support:* In 2018–19, 18 students received support. Career-related internships or fieldwork, Federal Work-Study, scholarships/grants, tuition waivers, and unspecified assistantships available. Support available to part-time students. Financial award application deadline: 3/15; financial award applicants required to submit FAFSA. *Faculty research:* Labor markets, job characteristics and ethical behavior, institutional trading of stocks and bonds, education funding, pricing strategies in business-to-business markets. *Unit head:* Dr. Siamack Shojai, Dean, 973-720-2964, Fax: 973-720-2809, E-mail: shojais@wpunj.edu. *Application contact:* Tinu Adeniran, Assistant Director, Graduate Admissions, 973-720-2764, Fax: 973-720-2035, E-mail: adenirant@wpunj.edu.
Website: http://www.wpunj.edu/ccob

Wingate University, Porter B. Byrum School of Business, Wingate, NC 28174. Offers accounting (MAC); corporate innovation (MBA); finance (MBA); general management (MBA); healthcare management (MBA); marketing (MBA); project management (MBA). *Accreditation:* ACBSP. *Program availability:* Part-time, evening/weekend. *Entrance requirements:* For master's, GMAT, work experience, 2 letters of recommendation. Electronic applications accepted. *Expenses:* Contact institution. *Faculty research:* Stochastic processes, business ethics, regional economic development, municipal finance, consumer behavior.

Section 6
Facilities and Entertainment Management

This section contains a directory of institutions offering graduate work in facilities management. Additional information about programs listed in the directory but not augmented by an in-depth entry may be obtained by writing directly to the dean of a graduate school or chair of a department at the address given in the directory.

For programs offering related work, see also in this book *Business Administration and Management.*

CONTENTS

Program Directories

Entertainment Management

Berklee College of Music, Berklee Graduate Programs, Boston, MA 46013, Spain. Offers contemporary performance (MM), including global jazz, production; global entertainment and music business (MA); music production, technology, and innovation (MM); scoring for film, television, and video games (MM). Contemporary performance - production concentration; global entertainment and music business; music production, technology, and innovation; and scoring for film, television, and video games programs offered at Valencia, Spain campus. *Program availability:* Part-time, blended/hybrid learning. *Faculty:* 42 full-time (10 women), 53 part-time/adjunct (13 women). *Students:* 222 full-time (92 women), 7 part-time (all women); includes 44 minority (13 Black or African American, non-Hispanic/Latino; 5 Asian, non-Hispanic/Latino; 19 Hispanic/Latino; 7 Two or more races, non-Hispanic/Latino), 118 international. Average age 26. 736 applicants, 36% accepted, 171 enrolled. In 2018, 170 master's awarded. *Degree requirements:* For master's, thesis, culminating experience project. *Entrance requirements:* For master's, https://www.berklee.edu/admissions/graduate/eligibility-requirements. Additional exam requirements/recommendations for international students: Required—TOEFL (minimum score 600 paper-based; 100 iBT), IELTS (minimum score 7.5), PTE (minimum score 73). *Application deadline:* For fall admission, 1/15 for domestic and international students. Application fee: $150. Electronic applications accepted. *Expenses:* Contact institution. *Financial support:* In 2018–19, fellowships with full and partial tuition reimbursements (averaging $12,453 per year), 21 research assistantships (averaging $4,332 per year) were awarded; career-related internships or fieldwork, scholarships/grants, and tuition waivers (full and partial) also available. Support available to part-time students. Financial award application deadline: 1/15; financial award applicants required to submit CSS PROFILE or FAFSA. *Faculty research:* Neuroscience, integrative medicine, music therapy practice, music cognition, ethnomusicology. *Unit head:* Rob Lagueux, PhD, Associate Vice President for Academic Affairs, 617-747-6908, E-mail: rlagueux@berklee.edu. *Application contact:* Office of Admissions, 617-747-2221, E-mail: admissions@berklee.edu.
Website: https://www.berklee.edu/graduate

California Intercontinental University, Hollywood College of the Entertainment Industry, Irvine, CA 92614. Offers Hollywood and entertainment management (MBA).

California State University, Northridge, Graduate Studies, Tseng College, Northridge, CA 91330. Offers business administration (Graduate Certificate); health administration (MPA); health education (MPH); knowledge management (MKM); music industry administration (MA); nonprofit-sector management (Graduate Certificate); public administration (MPA); public sector management and leadership (MPA); social work (MSW); taxation (MS); tourism, hospitality and recreation management (MS). *Entrance requirements:* For master's, GRE (if cumulative undergraduate GPA less than 3.0).

Carnegie Mellon University, Heinz College, School of Public Policy and Management, Master of Entertainment Industry Management Program, Pittsburgh, PA 15213-3891. Offers MEIM. *Accreditation:* AACSB. *Entrance requirements:* For master's, GRE or GMAT, college-level course in advanced algebra/pre-calculus; college-level courses in economics and statistics (recommended). Additional exam requirements/recommendations for international students: Required—TOEFL or IELTS.

Columbia College Chicago, School of Graduate Studies, Business and Entrepreneurship Department, Chicago, IL 60605-1996. Offers arts, entertainment and media management (MAM). *Entrance requirements:* For master's, self-assessment essay, resume, letters of recommendation, transcripts. Additional exam requirements/recommendations for international students: Required—TOEFL, IELTS. Electronic applications accepted. *Expenses:* Contact institution.

Full Sail University, Entertainment Business Master of Science Program - Campus, Winter Park, FL 32792-7437. Offers MS.

Full Sail University, Entertainment Business Master of Science Program - Online, Winter Park, FL 32792-7437. Offers MS. *Program availability:* Online learning. *Entrance requirements:* Additional exam requirements/recommendations for international students: Required—TOEFL (minimum score 550 paper-based; 79 iBT).

Hofstra University, Frank G. Zarb School of Business, Programs in Management and General Business, Hempstead, NY 11549. Offers business administration (MBA), including health services management, management, sports and entertainment management, strategic business management, strategic healthcare management; general management (Advanced Certificate); human resource management (MS, Advanced Certificate). *Program availability:* Part-time, evening/weekend, blended/hybrid learning. *Students:* 121 full-time (48 women), 112 part-time (52 women); includes 96 minority (18 Black or African American, non-Hispanic/Latino; 1 American Indian or Alaska Native, non-Hispanic/Latino; 34 Asian, non-Hispanic/Latino; 38 Hispanic/Latino; 5 Two or more races, non-Hispanic/Latino), 16 international. Average age 33. 290 applicants, 75% accepted, 89 enrolled. In 2018, 110 master's awarded. *Degree requirements:* For master's, thesis optional, capstone course (for MBA), thesis (for MS), minimum GPA of 3.0. *Entrance requirements:* For master's, GMAT/GRE, 2 letters of recommendation, resume, essay. Additional exam requirements/recommendations for international students: Required—TOEFL (minimum score 550 paper-based; 80 iBT); Recommended—IELTS (minimum score 6). *Application deadline:* Applications are processed on a rolling basis. Application fee: $75. Electronic applications accepted. *Expenses:* $1,375 per credit plus fees. *Financial support:* In 2018–19, 91 students received support, including 84 fellowships with full and partial tuition reimbursements available (averaging $4,279 per year), 1 research assistantship with full and partial tuition reimbursement available (averaging $9,179 per year); career-related internships or fieldwork, Federal Work-Study, institutionally sponsored loans, scholarships/grants, tuition waivers (full and partial), unspecified assistantships, and scholarships and endowed scholarships also available. Support available to part-time students. Financial award applicants required to submit FAFSA. *Faculty research:* Organizational behavior; sustainability; entrepreneurial spawning; family business; global supply chain strategies. *Unit head:* Dr. Kaushik Sengupta, Chairperson, 516-463-7825, Fax: 516-463-4834, E-mail: kaushik.sengupta@hofstra.edu. *Application contact:* Sunil Samuel, Assistant Vice President of Admissions, 516-463-4723, Fax: 516-463-4664, E-mail: graduateadmission@hofstra.edu.
Website: http://www.hofstra.edu/business/

Point Park University, Rowland School of Business, Program in Business Administration, Pittsburgh, PA 15222-1984. Offers business analytics (MBA); global management and administration (MBA); health systems management (MBA); international business (MBA); management (MBA); management information systems (MBA); sports, arts and entertainment management (MBA). *Program availability:* Evening/weekend, 100% online.

Southern New Hampshire University, School of Business, Manchester, NH 03106-1045. Offers accounting (MBA, Graduate Certificate); accounting finance (MS); accounting/auditing (MS); accounting/forensic accounting (MS); accounting/management accounting (MS); accounting/taxation (MS); applied economics (MS); athletic administration (MBA, Graduate Certificate); business administration (IMBA, Certificate), including business information systems (Certificate), human resource management (Certificate); business analytics (MBA); business intelligence (MBA); communication (MA), including new media and marketing, public relations; community economic development (MBA); criminal justice (MBA); data analytics (MS); economics (MBA); engineering management (MBA); entrepreneurship (MBA); finance (MBA, MS, Graduate Certificate); finance/corporate finance (MS); finance/investments (MS); forensic accounting (MBA); forensic accounting and fraud examination (Graduate Certificate); healthcare informatics (MBA); healthcare management (MBA); human resource management (MS); human resources (MBA); information technology (MS); information technology management (MBA); international business (PhD); Internet marketing (MBA); leadership (MBA); leadership of nonprofit organizations (Graduate Certificate); management (MS); marketing (MBA, MS, Graduate Certificate); music business (MBA); operations and project management (MS); operations and supply chain management (MBA, Graduate Certificate); organizational leadership (MS); project management (MBA, Graduate Certificate); public administration (MBA, Graduate Certificate); quantitative analysis (MBA); Six Sigma (Graduate Certificate); Six Sigma quality (MBA); social media marketing (MBA, Graduate Certificate); sport management (MBA, MS, Graduate Certificate); sustainability and environmental compliance (MBA); MBA/Certificate. *Accreditation:* ACBSP. *Program availability:* Part-time, evening/weekend, online learning. Terminal master's awarded for partial completion of doctoral program. *Degree requirements:* For master's, one foreign language, comprehensive exam (for some programs), thesis or alternative; for doctorate, one foreign language, comprehensive exam, thesis/dissertation. *Entrance requirements:* For master's, minimum GPA of 2.5; for doctorate, GMAT. Additional exam requirements/recommendations for international students: Required—TOEFL (minimum score 500 paper-based). Electronic applications accepted.

Syracuse University, College of Visual and Performing Arts, MA Program in Audio Arts, Syracuse, NY 13244. Offers audio arts (MA), including audio recording, music industry, music video, radio horizons. Program taught in conjunction with the S.I. Newhouse School of Public Communications. *Entrance requirements:* For master's, resume, sample of work, personal statement, three letters of recommendation. Additional exam requirements/recommendations for international students: Required—TOEFL (minimum score 100 iBT). *Application deadline:* For summer admission, 2/1 priority date for domestic and international students. Application fee: $75. Electronic applications accepted. *Financial support:* Fellowships, teaching assistantships, and scholarships/grants available. Financial award application deadline: 1/1. *Faculty research:* Audio practice, music industry, audio recording, radio horizons, music video. *Unit head:* Prof. James Abbott, Professor of Practice, Music Industry and Technologies/Program Coordinator, Sound Recording Technology, 315-443-4107, E-mail: jsabbott@syr.edu. *Application contact:* Caitlin Jarvis, Graduate Recruitment Specialist, 315-443-2769, E-mail: admissg@syr.edu.
Website: http://vpa.syr.edu/academics/setnor/graduate/audio-arts/

Universidad Autonoma de Guadalajara, Graduate Programs, Guadalajara, Mexico. Offers administrative law and justice (LL M); advertising and corporate communications (MA); architecture (M Arch); business (MBA); computational science (MCC); education (Ed M, Ed D); English-Spanish translation (MA); entrepreneurship and management (MBA); integrated management of digital animation (MA); international business (MIB); international corporate law (LL M); Internet technologies (MS); manufacturing systems (MMS); occupational health (MS); philosophy (MA, PhD); power electronics (MS); quality systems (MQS); renewable energy (MS); social evaluation of projects (MBA); strategic market research (MBA); tax law (MA); teaching mathematics (MA).

University of Colorado Denver, Business School, Program in Management and Organization, Denver, CO 80217. Offers business strategy (MS); change and innovation (MS); enterprise technology management (MS); entrepreneurship and innovation (MS); global management (MS); leadership (MS); managing for sustainability (MS); managing human resources (MS); sports and entertainment (MS); strategic management (MS). *Accreditation:* AACSB. *Program availability:* Part-time, evening/weekend, online learning. *Degree requirements:* For master's, 30 semester hours (12 of required courses, 12 of management electives, and 6 of free electives). *Entrance requirements:* For master's, GMAT, resume, two letters of recommendation, essay, financial statements (for international applicants). Additional exam requirements/recommendations for international students: Required—TOEFL (minimum score 525 paper-based; 71 iBT); Recommended—IELTS (minimum score 6.5). Electronic applications accepted. *Expenses:* Contact institution. *Faculty research:* Human resource management, management of catastrophe, turnaround strategies.

University of Colorado Denver, Business School, Program in Marketing, Denver, CO 80217. Offers advanced market analytics in a big data world (MS); brand communication in the digital era (MS); global marketing (MS); high-tech and entrepreneurial marketing (MS); marketing and global sustainability (MS); marketing intelligence and strategy in the 21st century (MS); sports and entertainment business (MS). *Program availability:* Part-time, evening/weekend. *Degree requirements:* For master's, 30 semester hours (21 of marketing core courses, 9 of marketing electives). *Entrance requirements:* For master's, GMAT, resume, essay, two letters of recommendation, financial statements (for international applicants). Additional exam requirements/recommendations for international students: Required—TOEFL (minimum score 525 paper-based; 71 iBT); Recommended—IELTS (minimum score 6.5). Electronic applications accepted. *Expenses:* Contact institution. *Faculty research:* Marketing issues in the Chinese environment, impact of individual difference and contextual factors on the risk-taking behaviors of managers making new-business creation decisions, attribution theory perspective of conflict between marketers and engineers, organizational identity and identification, international market entry strategies.

University of Dallas, Satish and Yasmin Gupta College of Business, Irving, TX 75062. Offers accounting (MBA, MS); business administration (DBA); business analytics (MS); business management (MBA); corporate finance (MBA); cybersecurity (MS); finance (MS); financial services (MBA); global business (MBA, MS); health services management (MBA); human resource management (MBA); information and technology management (MS); information assurance (MBA); information technology (MBA); information technology service management (MBA); marketing management (MBA); organization development (MBA); project management (MBA); sports and entertainment management (MBA); strategic leadership (MBA); supply chain management (MBA). *Accreditation:* AACSB. *Program availability:* Part-time, evening/weekend, 100% online. *Students:* 147 full-time (56 women), 584 part-time (232 women); includes 402 minority (204 Black or African American, non-Hispanic/Latino; 95 Asian, non-Hispanic/Latino; 92 Hispanic/Latino; 2 Native Hawaiian or other Pacific Islander, non-Hispanic/Latino; 9 Two

or more races, non-Hispanic/Latino), 113 international. Average age 34. 992 applicants, 30% accepted, 157 enrolled. In 2018, 336 master's, 5 doctorates awarded. *Degree requirements:* For doctorate, thesis/dissertation. *Entrance requirements:* For master's and doctorate, U.S. bachelor's degree with a minimum cumulative GPA of 2.0 from a regionally accredited college or university (or comparable foreign degree); minimum 3.0 GPA in any graduate-level coursework completed; good academic standing with all colleges attended. Additional exam requirements/recommendations for international students: Required—TOEFL (minimum score 80 iBT), IELTS (minimum score 6.5), PTE (minimum score 67). *Application deadline:* Applications are processed on a rolling basis. Application fee: $50. Electronic applications accepted. *Expenses:* $1250 per credit hour. *Financial support:* In 2018–19, 291 students received support. Research assistantships, teaching assistantships, scholarships/grants, and unspecified assistantships available. Support available to part-time students. Financial award application deadline: 2/15; financial award applicants required to submit FAFSA. *Unit head:* Brett J.L. Landry, Dean, 972-721-5356, E-mail: blandry@udallas.edu. *Application contact:* Breonna Collins, Director, Graduate Admissions, 972-7215304, E-mail: bcollins@udallas.edu. Website: http://www.udallas.edu/cob/

University of Massachusetts Amherst, Graduate School, Interdisciplinary Programs, Dual Degree Programs in Management and Engineering, Amherst, MA 01003. Offers MBA/MIE, MBA/MSEWRE, MSCE/MBA, MSME/MBA. *Program availability:* Part-time. *Entrance requirements:* Additional exam requirements/recommendations for international students: Required—TOEFL (minimum score 600 paper-based; 100 iBT), IELTS (minimum score 7). Electronic applications accepted.

University of South Carolina, The Graduate School, College of Hospitality, Retail, and Sport Management, Department of Sport and Entertainment Management, Columbia, SC 29208. Offers live sport and entertainment events (MS); public assembly facilities management (MS). *Program availability:* Part-time. *Degree requirements:* For master's, comprehensive exam, thesis optional. *Entrance requirements:* For master's, GRE General Test or GMAT (preferred), minimum GPA of 3.0. Additional exam requirements/recommendations for international students: Required—TOEFL (minimum score 570 paper-based; 70 iBT). Electronic applications accepted. *Expenses:* Contact institution. *Faculty research:* Public assembly marketing, operations, box office, booking and scheduling, law/economic impacts.

Valparaiso University, Graduate School and Continuing Education, Program in Arts and Entertainment Administration, Valparaiso, IN 46383. Offers MA. *Program availability:* Part-time, evening/weekend. *Degree requirements:* For master's, internship or research project. *Entrance requirements:* Additional exam requirements/

recommendations for international students: Required—TOEFL (minimum score 550 paper-based; 80 iBT), IELTS (minimum score 6). Electronic applications accepted.

William Paterson University of New Jersey, Cotsakos College of Business, Wayne, NJ 07470-8420. Offers applied business analytics (MS); business administration (MBA), including accounting, entrepreneurship, finance, general business administration, human resource management, marketing, music and entertainment management; MBA pathways (Certificate); sales leadership (MS). *Accreditation:* AACSB. *Program availability:* Part-time, evening/weekend. *Faculty:* 21 full-time (6 women), 5 part-time/adjunct (1 woman). *Students:* 78 full-time (40 women), 250 part-time (113 women); includes 161 minority (39 Black or African American, non-Hispanic/Latino; 1 American Indian or Alaska Native, non-Hispanic/Latino; 23 Asian, non-Hispanic/Latino; 82 Hispanic/Latino; 16 Two or more races, non-Hispanic/Latino), 14 international. Average age 31. 222 applicants, 86% accepted, 136 enrolled. In 2018, 95 master's awarded. *Degree requirements:* For master's, Programs Differ see: https://academiccatalog.wpunj.edu/content.php?catoid=1&navoid=68. *Entrance requirements:* For master's, program details: https://www.wpunj.edu/admissions/graduate/admission-deadlines-and-requirements/. Additional exam requirements/recommendations for international students: Required—TOEFL (minimum score 550 paper-based; 79 iBT), IELTS (minimum score 6). *Application deadline:* For fall admission, 6/1 for domestic students, 3/1 for international students; for spring admission, 11/1 for domestic students, 10/1 for international students. Applications are processed on a rolling basis. Application fee: $50. Electronic applications accepted. *Expenses: Tuition, area resident:* Full-time $14,714; part-time $727 per credit. Tuition, state resident: full-time $14,714; part-time $727 per credit. Tuition, nonresident: full-time $22,952; part-time $727 per credit. *International tuition:* $22,952 full-time. *Required fees:* $4 per semester. Tuition and fees vary according to course load, degree level and program. *Financial support:* In 2018–19, 18 students received support. Career-related internships or fieldwork, Federal Work-Study, scholarships/grants, tuition waivers, and unspecified assistantships available. Support available to part-time students. Financial award application deadline: 3/15; financial award applicants required to submit FAFSA. *Faculty research:* Labor markets, job characteristics and ethical behavior, institutional trading of stocks and bonds, education funding, pricing strategies in business-to-business markets. *Unit head:* Dr. Siamack Shojai, Dean, 973-720-2964, Fax: 973-720-2809, E-mail: shojais@wpunj.edu. *Application contact:* Tinu Adeniran, Assistant Director, Graduate Admissions, 973-720-2764, Fax: 973-720-2035, E-mail: adenirant@wpunj.edu. Website: http://www.wpunj.edu/ccob

Facilities Management

Cornell University, Graduate School, Graduate Fields of Human Ecology, Field of Design and Environmental Analysis, Ithaca, NY 14853. Offers applied research in human-environment relations (MS); facilities planning and management (MS); housing and design (MS); human factors and ergonomics (MS); human-environment relations (MS); interior design (MA, MPS). *Degree requirements:* For master's, thesis. *Entrance requirements:* For master's, GRE General Test, portfolio or slides of recent work; bachelor's degree in interior design, architecture or related design discipline; 2 letters of recommendation. Additional exam requirements/recommendations for international students: Required—TOEFL (minimum score 600 paper-based; 105 iBT). Electronic applications accepted. *Faculty research:* Facility planning and management, environmental psychology, housing, interior design, ergonomics and human factors.

Liberty University, School of Business, Lynchburg, VA 24515. Offers accounting (MBA, MS), including audit and financial reporting (MS), business (MS), financial services (MS), forensic accounting (MS), leadership (MS), taxation (MS); cyber security (MS); executive leadership (MA); international business (DBA); leadership (DBA); marketing (MBA, MS, DBA), including digital marketing and advertising (MS), project management (MS), public relations (MS), sports marketing and media (MS); project management (MBA, DBA); public relations (MBA). *Program availability:* Part-time, online learning. *Students:* 2,871 full-time (1,496 women), 4,437 part-time (1,969 women); includes 2,069 minority (1,424 Black or African American, non-Hispanic/Latino; 44 American Indian or Alaska Native, non-Hispanic/Latino; 133 Asian, non-Hispanic/Latino; 282 Hispanic/Latino; 16 Native Hawaiian or other Pacific Islander, non-Hispanic/Latino; 170 Two or more races, non-Hispanic/Latino), 154 international. Average age 36. 8,980 applicants, 45% accepted, 2009 enrolled. In 2018, 1,988 master's, 25 doctorates awarded. *Entrance requirements:* For master's, minimum undergraduate GPA of 3.0, 15 hours of upper-level business courses. Additional exam requirements/recommendations for international students: Required—TOEFL (minimum score 600 paper-based; 100 iBT). *Application deadline:* Applications are processed on a rolling basis. Application fee: $50. Electronic applications accepted. *Expenses:* Contact institution. *Financial support:* In 2018–19, 990 students received support. Teaching assistantships and Federal Work-Study available. Financial award applicants required to submit FAFSA. *Unit head:* Dr. Dave Bratt, Dean, 434-592-7321, E-mail: dabrat@liberty.edu. *Application contact:* Jay Bridge, Director of Graduate Admissions, 800-424-9595, Fax: 800-628-7977, E-mail: gradadmissions@liberty.edu. Website: https://www.liberty.edu/business/

Maastricht School of Management, Graduate Programs, Maastricht, Netherlands. Offers business administration (MBA, DBA, PhD); facility management (Exec MBA); management (M Sc); sustainability (Exec MBA).

Massachusetts Maritime Academy, Program in Facilities Management, Buzzards Bay, MA 02532-1803. Offers MS. *Program availability:* Evening/weekend. *Students:* 36 full-time (2 women). In 2018, 20 master's awarded. *Application deadline:* Applications are processed on a rolling basis. Electronic applications accepted. *Expenses:* Contact institution. *Unit head:* James McDonald, Dean, Graduate and Continuing Education, 508-830-5096, E-mail: dce@maritime.edu. *Application contact:* Anna Woringer, Staff Assistant, 508-830-5019, E-mail: dce@maritime.edu.

Pratt Institute, School of Architecture, Program in Facilities Management, New York, NY 10011. Offers MS. *Program availability:* Part-time. *Students:* 7 full-time (6 women), 2 part-time (0 women); includes 5 minority (2 Black or African American, non-Hispanic/Latino; 1 Asian, non-Hispanic/Latino; 1 Hispanic/Latino; 1 Two or more races, non-Hispanic/Latino), 4 international. Average age 32. 8 applicants, 50% accepted, 1 enrolled. In 2018, 5 master's awarded. *Degree requirements:* For master's, thesis. *Entrance requirements:* For master's, writing sample, bachelor's degree, transcripts, letters of recommendation, portfolio. Additional exam requirements/recommendations for international students: Required—TOEFL (minimum score 550 paper-based; 79 iBT). *Application deadline:* For fall admission, 1/5 for domestic and international students; for

spring admission, 10/1 for domestic and international students. Application fee: $50 ($90 for international students). Electronic applications accepted. *Expenses: Tuition:* Full-time $33,246; part-time $1847 per credit. *Required fees:* $1980. *Financial support:* Career-related internships or fieldwork, Federal Work-Study, institutionally sponsored loans, scholarships/grants, health care benefits, and unspecified assistantships available. Support available to part-time students. Financial award application deadline: 2/1; financial award applicants required to submit FAFSA. *Faculty research:* Benchmarking, organizational studies, resource planning and management, computer-aided facilities management, value analysis. *Unit head:* Regina Ford Cahill, Chairperson, 212-647-7524, E-mail: rcahill8@pratt.edu. *Application contact:* Natalie Capannelli, Director of Graduate Admissions, 718-636-3551, Fax: 718-399-4242, E-mail: ncapanne@pratt.edu. Website: https://www.pratt.edu/academics/architecture/facilities-management/

Purdue University Fort Wayne, College of Engineering, Technology, and Computer Science, Program in Technology, Fort Wayne, IN 46805-1499. Offers facilities/construction management (MS); industrial technology/manufacturing (MS); information technology/advanced computer applications (MS). *Program availability:* Part-time. *Entrance requirements:* For master's, minimum GPA of 3.0. Additional exam requirements/recommendations for international students: Required—TOEFL (minimum score 550 paper-based; 79 iBT), TWE. Electronic applications accepted.

Université Laval, Faculty of Administrative Sciences, Programs in Business Administration, Québec, QC G1K 7P4, Canada. Offers accounting (MBA); agri-food management (MBA); electronic business (MBA, Diploma); factory management and logistics (MBA); finance (MBA); firm management (MBA); geomatic management (MBA); information technology management (MBA); international management (MBA); management (MBA); management accounting (MBA, Diploma); marketing (MBA); modeling and organizational decision (MBA); occupational health and safety management (MBA); pharmacy management (MBA); social and environmental responsibility (MBA); technological entrepreneurship (Diploma). *Accreditation:* AACSB. *Program availability:* Part-time, evening/weekend, online learning. *Entrance requirements:* For master's and Diploma, knowledge of French and English. Electronic applications accepted.

University of California, Berkeley, UC Berkeley Extension, Certificate Programs in Engineering, Construction and Facilities Management, Berkeley, CA 94720. Offers construction management (Certificate); HVAC (Certificate); integrated circuit design and techniques (online) (Certificate). *Program availability:* Online learning.

University of New Haven, Graduate School, College of Business, Program in Sport Management, West Haven, CT 06516. Offers collegiate athletic administration (MS); facility management (MS); sport analytics (MS); sport management (Graduate Certificate). *Program availability:* Part-time, evening/weekend. *Students:* 24 full-time (12 women), 3 part-time (0 women); includes 3 minority (1 Black or African American, non-Hispanic/Latino; 1 American Indian or Alaska Native, non-Hispanic/Latino; 1 Hispanic/Latino), 5 international. Average age 25. 41 applicants, 98% accepted, 23 enrolled. In 2018, 14 master's awarded. *Entrance requirements:* For master's, GMAT. Additional exam requirements/recommendations for international students: Required—TOEFL (minimum score 80 iBT), IELTS, PTE. *Application deadline:* Applications are processed on a rolling basis. Application fee: $50. Electronic applications accepted. Application fee is waived when completed online. *Expenses: Tuition:* Full-time $16,470; part-time $915 per credit hour. *Required fees:* $230; $95 per term. *Financial support:* Research assistantships with partial tuition reimbursements, teaching assistantships with partial tuition reimbursements, Federal Work-Study, scholarships/grants, and unspecified assistantships available. Support available to part-time students. Financial award applicants required to submit FAFSA. *Unit head:* Gil B. Fried, Professor, 203-932-7081, E-mail: gfried@newhaven.edu. *Application contact:* Selina O'Toole, Senior Associate Director of Graduate Admissions, 203-932-7337, E-mail: SOToole@newhaven.edu. Website: https://www.newhaven.edu/business/graduate-programs/sport-management/

Facilities Management

The University of North Carolina at Charlotte, William States Lee College of Engineering, Department of Engineering Technology and Construction Management, Charlotte, NC 28223-0001. Offers applied energy (Graduate Certificate); applied energy and electromechanical systems (MS); construction and facilities management (MS); fire protection and administration (MS). *Program availability:* Part-time. *Students:* 54 full-time (17 women), 17 part-time (3 women); includes 9 minority (3 Black or African American, non-Hispanic/Latino; 2 Asian, non-Hispanic/Latino; 3 Hispanic/Latino; 1 Two or more races, non-Hispanic/Latino), 40 international. Average age 26. 97 applicants, 81% accepted, 22 enrolled. In 2018, 31 master's awarded. *Entrance requirements:* For master's, GRE, minimum undergraduate GPA of 3.0, recommendations, statistics; integral and differential calculus (for students pursuing fire protection concentration or applied energy and electromechanical systems program); for Graduate Certificate, bachelor's degree in engineering, engineering technology, construction management or a closely-related technical or scientific field; undergraduate coursework of at least 3 semesters in engineering analysis or calculus; minimum GPA of 3.0. Additional exam requirements/recommendations for international students: Required—TOEFL (minimum score 523 paper-based; 70 iBT), IELTS (minimum score 6), TOEFL (minimum score 523 paper-based, 70 iBT) or IELTS (6). *Application deadline:* Applications are processed on a rolling basis. Application fee: $75. Electronic applications accepted. *Expenses:* Contact institution. *Financial support:* Research assistantships, career-related internships or fieldwork, institutionally sponsored loans, scholarships/grants, and unspecified assistantships available. Support available to part-time students. Financial award application deadline: 3/1; financial award applicants required to submit FAFSA. *Total annual research expenditures:* $1.7 million. *Unit head:* Dr. Anthony Brizendine, Chair, 704-687-5050, E-mail: albrizen@uncc.edu. *Application contact:* Kathy B. Giddings, Director of Graduate Admissions, 704-687-5503, Fax: 704-687-1668, E-mail: gradadm@uncc.edu.
Website: http://et.uncc.edu/

Wentworth Institute of Technology, Master of Science in Facility Management Program, Boston, MA 02115-5998. Offers MS. *Program availability:* Part-time, evening/weekend, online only, 100% online, blended/hybrid learning. *Degree requirements:* For master's, thesis optional, capstone. *Entrance requirements:* For master's, current resume; two professional recommendation forms from current or former employer; statement of purpose; undergraduate degree in one of the following: architecture, facility management, engineering, construction management, business or interior design; one year of professional experience in technical role and/or technical organization. Additional exam requirements/recommendations for international students: Recommended—TOEFL (minimum score 550 paper-based). Electronic applications accepted. *Expenses:* Contact institution.

Section 7
Hospitality Management

This section contains a directory of institutions offering graduate work in hospitality management. Additional information about programs listed in the directory may be obtained by writing directly to the dean of a graduate school or chair of a department at the address given in the directory.

For programs offering related work, see also in this book *Business Administration and Management* and *Advertising and Public Relations*.

In the other guides in this series:

Graduate Programs in the Biological/Biomedical Sciences & Health-Related Medical Professions

See *Health Services*

Graduate Programs in the Physical Sciences, Mathematics, Agricultural Sciences, the Environment & Natural Resources

See *Agricultural and Food Sciences (Food Science and Technology)*

CONTENTS

Program Directories

Hospitality Management

Alabama Agricultural and Mechanical University, School of Graduate Studies, College of Agricultural, Life and Natural Sciences, Department of Family and Consumer Sciences, Huntsville, AL 35811. Offers apparel, merchandising and design (MS); family and consumer sciences (MS); human development and family studies (MS); nutrition and hospitality management (MS). *Program availability:* Part-time, evening/weekend. *Degree requirements:* For master's, comprehensive exam, thesis optional. *Entrance requirements:* For master's, GRE General Test. Additional exam requirements/recommendations for international students: Required—TOEFL (minimum score 500 paper-based; 61 iBT). Electronic applications accepted. *Faculty research:* Food biotechnology, nutrition, food microbiology, food engineering, food chemistry.

American International College, School of Business, Arts and Sciences, Springfield, MA 01109-3189. Offers accounting and taxation (MS); business administration (MBA); clinical psychology (MA); educational psychology (Ed D); forensic psychology (MS); general psychology (MA, CAGS); management (CAGS); resort and casino management (MBA, CAGS). *Program availability:* Part-time, evening/weekend. *Degree requirements:* For master's, practicum; for doctorate, comprehensive exam, thesis/dissertation, practicum. *Entrance requirements:* For master's, BS or BA, minimum undergraduate GPA of 2.75, 2 letters of recommendation, official transcripts, personal goal statement or essay; for doctorate, 3 letters of recommendation; BS or BA; minimum undergraduate GPA of 3.0 (3.25 recommended); official transcripts; personal goal statement or essay. Additional exam requirements/recommendations for international students: Required—TOEFL (minimum score 550 paper-based; 80 iBT). *Expenses:* Contact institution. *Faculty research:* Substance abuse, forensic psychology, special education.

Boston University, School of Hospitality Administration, Boston, MA 02215. Offers MMH. *Program availability:* Part-time. *Faculty:* 9 full-time, 17 part-time/adjunct. *Students:* 45 full-time (37 women), 8 part-time (6 women); includes 8 minority (3 Asian, non-Hispanic/Latino; 5 Hispanic/Latino), 28 international. Average age 26. In 2018, 29 master's awarded. *Entrance requirements:* Additional exam requirements/recommendations for international students: Required—TOEFL (minimum score 84 iBT), IELTS (minimum score 6.5). *Application deadline:* For fall admission, 2/1 priority date for domestic and international students. Applications are processed on a rolling basis. Application fee: $95. Electronic applications accepted. Application fee is waived when completed online. *Financial support:* In 2018–19, 43 students received support. Scholarships/grants and unspecified assistantships available. Financial award application deadline: 2/1; financial award applicants required to submit FAFSA. *Faculty research:* Revenue Management, Air BnB, Food and Beverage Management, Hospitality Finance. *Unit head:* Dr. Arun Upneja, Dean, 617-353-3261, E-mail: aupneja@bu.edu. *Application contact:* Micah Sieber, Director of Graduate Affairs, 617-353-1011, E-mail: shagrad@bu.edu.
Website: http://www.bu.edu/hospitality/

California State Polytechnic University, Pomona, Program in Hospitality Management, Pomona, CA 91768-2557. Offers hospitality management (MS). *Program availability:* Part-time, evening/weekend. *Students:* 21 full-time (11 women), 20 part-time (12 women); includes 16 minority (4 Black or African American, non-Hispanic/Latino; 9 Asian, non-Hispanic/Latino; 2 Hispanic/Latino; 1 Two or more races, non-Hispanic/Latino), 20 international. Average age 29. 29 applicants, 72% accepted, 15 enrolled. In 2018, 17 master's awarded. *Degree requirements:* For master's, thesis or professional paper. *Entrance requirements:* Additional exam requirements/recommendations for international students: Required—TOEFL (minimum score 550 paper-based). *Application deadline:* Applications are processed on a rolling basis. Application fee: $55. Electronic applications accepted. *Expenses:* Contact institution. *Financial support:* Application deadline: 3/2; applicants required to submit FAFSA. *Unit head:* Dr. Neha Singh, Associate Professor/MSHM Program Director, 909-869-4565, Fax: 909-869-4805, E-mail: nsingh@cpp.edu. *Application contact:* Dr. Neha Singh, Associate Professor/MSHM Program Director, 909-869-4565, Fax: 909-869-4805, E-mail: nsingh@cpp.edu.
Website: http://www.cpp.edu/~ceu/degree-programs/hospitality-management/index.shtml

California State University, Northridge, Graduate Studies, College of Health and Human Development, Department of Recreation and Tourism Management, Northridge, CA 91330. Offers hospitality and tourism (MS); recreational sport management/campus recreation (MS). *Degree requirements:* For master's, thesis (for some programs). *Entrance requirements:* For master's, GRE (if cumulative undergraduate GPA less than 3.0). Additional exam requirements/recommendations for international students: Required—TOEFL.

California State University, Northridge, Graduate Studies, Tseng College, Northridge, CA 91330. Offers business administration (Graduate Certificate); health administration (MPA); health education (MPH); knowledge management (MKM); music industry administration (MA); nonprofit-sector management (Graduate Certificate); public administration (MPA); public sector management and leadership (MPA); social work (MSW); taxation (MS); tourism, hospitality and recreation management (MS). *Entrance requirements:* For master's, GRE (if cumulative undergraduate GPA less than 3.0).

Cornell University, Graduate School, Field of Hotel Administration, Ithaca, NY 14853. Offers hospitality management (MMH); hotel administration (MS, PhD). Terminal master's awarded for partial completion of doctoral program. *Degree requirements:* For master's, thesis (MS); for doctorate, comprehensive exam, thesis/dissertation. *Entrance requirements:* For master's and doctorate, GMAT, 1 academic and 1 employer letter of recommendation, 2 interviews. Additional exam requirements/recommendations for international students: Required—TOEFL (minimum score 600 paper-based). Electronic applications accepted. *Faculty research:* Hospitality finance; property-asset management; real estate; management, strategy, and human resources; organizational communication.

Cornell University, Graduate School, Graduate Fields of Agriculture and Life Sciences, Field of Applied Economics and Management, Ithaca, NY 14853. Offers agricultural finance (MS, PhD); applied econometrics and qualitative analysis (MS, PhD); economics of development (MS, PhD); environmental economics (MS, PhD); environmental management (MPS); farm management and production economics (MS, PhD); marketing and food distribution (MS, PhD); public policy analysis (MS, PhD); resource economics (PhD). *Entrance requirements:* For master's and doctorate, GRE. Additional exam requirements/recommendations for international students: Required—TOEFL.

DePaul University, Kellstadt Graduate School of Business, Chicago, IL 60604. Offers accountancy (MBA, MSA); applied economics (MBA); audit and advisory services (MS); business administration (DBA); business analytics (MS); business strategy and decision-making (MBA); computational finance (MS); economics and policy analysis (MS); enterprise risk management (MS); entrepreneurship (MBA, MS); finance (MBA, MS); general business (MBA); hospitality leadership (MBA); hospitality leadership and

operational performance (MS); human resources (MS); international business (MBA); management (MBA, MS); management information systems (MBA); marketing (MBA, MS); marketing analysis (MS); marketing strategy and planning (MBA); real estate (MS); real estate finance and investment (MBA); strategy, execution and valuation (MBA); supply chain management (MS); sustainable management (MS); taxation (MS); JD/MBA. *Accreditation:* AACSB. *Program availability:* Part-time, evening/weekend, online learning. *Entrance requirements:* For master's, GMAT/GRE, 2 letters of recommendation, resume, essay, official transcripts. Additional exam requirements/recommendations for international students: Required—TOEFL (minimum score 550 paper-based; 80 iBT). Electronic applications accepted. *Expenses:* Contact institution.

Drexel University, Goodwin College of Professional Studies, School of Technology and Professional Studies, Philadelphia, PA 19104-2875. Offers construction management (MS); creativity and innovation (MS); engineering technology (MS); food science (MS); hospitality management (MS); professional studies: creativity studies (MS); professional studies: e-learning leadership (MS); professional studies: homeland security management (MS); project management (MS); property management (MS); sport management (MS). *Program availability:* Part-time, evening/weekend. *Entrance requirements:* Additional exam requirements/recommendations for international students: Required—TOEFL, IELTS. Electronic applications accepted. Application fee is waived when completed online.

East Carolina University, Graduate School, College of Business, School of Hospitality Leadership, Greenville, NC 27858-4353. Offers hospitality management (Postbaccalaureate Certificate); sustainable tourism and hospitality (MS). *Expenses:* Tuition, area resident: Full-time $4749. Tuition, state resident: full-time $4749. Tuition, nonresident: full-time $17,898. *International tuition:* $17,898 full-time. *Required fees:* $2787. Part-time tuition and fees vary according to course load and program. *Unit head:* Dr. Robert M O'Halloran, Director, 252-737-1604, E-mail: ohalloranr@ecu.edu. *Application contact:* Graduate School Admissions, 252-328-6012, Fax: 252-328-6071, E-mail: gradschool@ecu.edu.
Website: http://www.ecu.edu/business/shl/

Eastern Michigan University, Graduate School, College of Engineering and Technology, School of Technology and Professional Services Management, Program in Hotel and Restaurant Management, Ypsilanti, MI 48197. Offers Graduate Certificate. *Program availability:* Part-time, evening/weekend, online learning. *Students:* 1 applicant, 100% accepted. *Entrance requirements:* Additional exam requirements/recommendations for international students: Required—TOEFL. *Application deadline:* Applications are processed on a rolling basis. Application fee: $45. *Financial support:* Fellowships, research assistantships with full tuition reimbursements, teaching assistantships with full tuition reimbursements, career-related internships or fieldwork, Federal Work-Study, institutionally sponsored loans, scholarships/grants, tuition waivers (partial), and unspecified assistantships available. Support available to part-time students. Financial award applicants required to submit FAFSA. *Application contact:* Dr. Tierney Orfgen McCleary, Program Advisor, 734-487-2326, Fax: 734-487-7690, E-mail: cot_hrm@emich.edu.

Ecole Hôtelière de Lausanne, Program in Hospitality Administration, Lausanne, Switzerland. Offers MHA. *Degree requirements:* For master's, project.

ESSEC Business School, Graduate Programs, Paris, France. Offers business administration (PhD); executive business administration (MBA); global business administration (MBA); hospitality management (MBA); international luxury brand management (MBA); management (MSM).

Fairleigh Dickinson University, Florham Campus, Anthony J. Petrocelli College of Continuing Studies, International School of Hospitality and Tourism Management, Madison, NJ 07940-1099. Offers hospitality management studies (MS).

Fairleigh Dickinson University, Metropolitan Campus, Anthony J. Petrocelli College of Continuing Studies, International School of Hospitality and Tourism Management, Teaneck, NJ 07666-1914. Offers hospitality management (MS).

Florida International University, Chaplin School of Hospitality and Tourism Management, North Miami, FL 33181-3000. Offers MS. *Program availability:* Part-time, evening/weekend, online learning. *Faculty:* 25 full-time (6 women), 38 part-time/adjunct (12 women). *Students:* 183 full-time (119 women), 92 part-time (65 women); includes 105 minority (24 Black or African American, non-Hispanic/Latino; 7 Asian, non-Hispanic/Latino; 69 Hispanic/Latino; 5 Two or more races, non-Hispanic/Latino), 134 international. Average age 27. 214 applicants, 78% accepted, 109 enrolled. In 2018, 140 master's awarded. *Degree requirements:* For master's, thesis (for some programs). *Entrance requirements:* For master's, minimum GPA of 3.0, 5 years of management experience (for executive track). Additional exam requirements/recommendations for international students: Required—TOEFL (minimum score 550 paper-based; 80 iBT). *Application deadline:* For fall admission, 6/1 for domestic students, 4/1 for international students; for spring admission, 10/1 for domestic students, 9/1 for international students. Applications are processed on a rolling basis. Application fee: $30. Electronic applications accepted. *Financial support:* Institutionally sponsored loans and scholarships/grants available. Financial award application deadline: 3/1; financial award applicants required to submit FAFSA. *Faculty research:* Environmental sustainability in hospitality/lodging, casino marketing and management, management philosophy, strategic management and competitive advantage, legal liabilities of hotels and resorts for waterfront amenities. *Unit head:* Dr. Michael Cheng, Interim Dean, 305-919-4506, E-mail: michael.cheng@fiu.edu. *Application contact:* Nanett Rojas, Manager, Admissions Operations, 305-348-7464, Fax: 305-348-7441, E-mail: gradadm@fiu.edu.
Website: http://hospitality.fiu.edu/

Georgetown University, Graduate School of Arts and Sciences, School of Continuing Studies, Washington, DC 20057. Offers American studies (MALS); applied intelligence (MPS); Catholic studies (MALS); classical civilizations (MALS); emergency and disaster management (MPS); ethics and the professions (MALS); global strategic communications (MPS); hospitality management (MPS); human resources management (MPS); humanities (MALS); individualized study (MALS); integrated marketing communications (MPS); international affairs (MALS); Islam and Muslim-Christian relations (MALS); journalism (MPS); liberal studies (DLS); literature and society (MALS); medieval and early modern European studies (MALS); public relations and corporate communications (MPS); real estate (MPS); religious studies (MALS); social and public policy (MALS); sports industry management (MPS); systems engineering management (MPS); technology management (MPS); the theory and practice of American democracy (MALS); urban and regional planning (MPS); visual culture (MALS). MPS in systems engineering management offered jointly with Stevens Institute of Technology. *Entrance requirements:* Additional exam requirements/recommendations for international students: Required—TOEFL.

The George Washington University, School of Business, Department of Tourism and Hospitality Management, Washington, DC 20052. Offers destination management (Professional Certificate); event and meeting management (MTA); event management (Professional Certificate); hospitality management (MTA); individualized studies (MTA); sport management (MTA); sustainable tourism destination management (MTA); tourism and hospitality management (MBA). *Program availability:* Part-time, online learning. *Students:* 79 full-time (46 women), 35 part-time (28 women); includes 37 minority (21 Black or African American, non-Hispanic/Latino; 5 Asian, non-Hispanic/Latino; 9 Hispanic/Latino; 2 Two or more races, non-Hispanic/Latino), 40 international. Average age 28. 161 applicants, 76% accepted, 47 enrolled. In 2018, 50 master's awarded. *Degree requirements:* For master's, comprehensive exam, thesis. *Entrance requirements:* For master's, GRE General Test. Additional exam requirements/recommendations for international students: Required—TOEFL. *Application deadline:* For fall admission, 4/1 priority date for domestic students; for spring admission, 10/1 for domestic students. Applications are processed on a rolling basis. Application fee: $75. *Financial support:* In 2018–19, 32 students received support. Fellowships, teaching assistantships, career-related internships or fieldwork, Federal Work-Study, institutionally sponsored loans, and tuition waivers (partial) available. Financial award application deadline: 4/1. *Faculty research:* Tourism policy, tourism impact forecasting, geotourism. *Unit head:* Prof. Lisa Delpy Neirotti, Faculty Director, 202-994-6623, E-mail: delpy@gwu.edu. *Application contact:* Christopher Storer, Executive Director, Graduate Admissions, 202-994-1212, E-mail: gwmba@gwu.edu.
Website: http://business.gwu.edu/tourism/

Glion Institute of Higher Education, Graduate Programs, Glion-sur-Montreux, Switzerland. Offers hospitality organizational training (M Ed); hotel management with leadership (MBA); hotel management with marketing (MBA); international hospitality management (MBA). *Program availability:* Evening/weekend.

Husson University, Master of Business Administration Program, Bangor, ME 04401-2999. Offers athletic administration (MBA); biotechnology and innovation (MBA); general business administration (MBA); healthcare management (MBA); hospitality and tourism management (MBA); organizational management (MBA); risk management (MBA). *Program availability:* Part-time, evening/weekend, 100% online, blended/hybrid learning. *Degree requirements:* For master's, comprehensive exam (for some programs), thesis optional. *Entrance requirements:* For master's, minimum GPA of 3.0, letter of recommendation. Additional exam requirements/recommendations for international students: Required—TOEFL (minimum score 550 paper-based; 80 iBT), IELTS (minimum score 6.5). Electronic applications accepted. *Expenses:* Contact institution.

IGlobal University, Graduate Programs, Vienna, VA 22182. Offers accounting (MBA); data management and analytics (MSIT); entrepreneurship (MBA); finance (MBA); global business management (MBA); health care management (MBA); hospitality and tourism management (MBA); human resources management (MBA); information technology (MBA); information technology systems and management (MSIT); leadership and management (MBA); project management (MBA); public service and administration (MBA); software design and management (MSIT).

Johnson & Wales University, Graduate Studies, MBA Program, Providence, RI 02903-3703. Offers accounting (MBA); business administration (MBA); finance (MBA); global fashion merchandising and management (MBA); hospitality (MBA); human resource management (MBA); information security/assurance (MBA); information technology (MBA); nonprofit management (MBA); operations and supply chain management (MBA); organizational leadership (MBA); organizational psychology (MBA); sport leadership (MBA). Program also offered on Denver campus. *Program availability:* Part-time, online learning. *Entrance requirements:* For master's, minimum GPA of 2.75. Additional exam requirements/recommendations for international students: Required—TOEFL (minimum score 550 paper-based); Recommended—IELTS, TWE. *Faculty research:* International banking, global economy, international trade, cultural differences.

Kansas State University, Graduate School, College of Human Ecology, Department of Hospitality Management, Manhattan, KS 66506. Offers hospitality and dietetics administration (MS). *Program availability:* Part-time. *Degree requirements:* For master's, comprehensive exam (for some programs), thesis or alternative, residency. *Entrance requirements:* For master's, GRE or GMAT. Additional exam requirements/recommendations for international students: Required—TOEFL (minimum score 550 paper-based; 79 iBT). Electronic applications accepted. *Expenses:* Contact institution. *Faculty research:* Food and beverage management; lodging management; event management; sustainability; customer behaviors; human resource management; food safety in food service operations; gerontology and the hospitality industry; education, training, and career development in hospitality administration.

Kansas State University, Graduate School, College of Human Ecology, Doctorate in Human Ecology Program, Manhattan, KS 66506-1407. Offers apparel and textiles (PhD); applied family sciences (PhD); couple and family therapy (PhD); hospitality administration (PhD); kinesiology (PhD); life-span human development (PhD). *Program availability:* Part-time. *Degree requirements:* For doctorate, thesis/dissertation. *Entrance requirements:* Additional exam requirements/recommendations for international students: Required—TOEFL. Electronic applications accepted.

Kent State University, College of Education, Health and Human Services, School of Foundations, Leadership and Administration, Program in Hospitality and Tourism Management, Kent, OH 44242-0001. Offers MS. *Program availability:* Part-time. *Faculty:* 7 full-time (4 women), 5 part-time/adjunct (1 woman). *Students:* 12 full-time (7 women), 16 part-time (10 women); includes 5 minority (1 Black or African American, non-Hispanic/Latino; 3 Asian, non-Hispanic/Latino; 1 Hispanic/Latino), 11 international. 35 applicants, 43% accepted. In 2018, 6 master's awarded. *Degree requirements:* For master's, thesis optional. *Entrance requirements:* For master's, minimum GPA of 3.0, 3 letters of recommendation, resume, goals statement. Additional exam requirements/recommendations for international students: Required—TOEFL (minimum score 550 paper-based; 80 iBT). *Application deadline:* Applications are processed on a rolling basis. Application fee: $45 ($60 for international students). Electronic applications accepted. *Expenses:* Tuition, state resident: full-time $11,766; part-time $536 per credit. Tuition, nonresident: full-time $21,952; part-time $999 per credit. *International tuition:* $21,952 full-time. Tuition and fees vary according to course load. *Financial support:* In 2018–19, 4 students received support, including 8 research assistantships with full tuition reimbursements available (averaging $8,500 per year); teaching assistantships, Federal Work-Study, scholarships/grants, and unspecified assistantships also available. Financial award application deadline: 2/1; financial award applicants required to submit FAFSA. *Faculty research:* Training human service workers, health care services for older adults, early adolescent development, care-giving arrangements with aging families, peace and war. *Unit head:* Aviad Israeli, Coordinator, 330-672-2075, E-mail: aisraeli@kent.edu. *Application contact:* Cheryl Slusarczyk, Academic Program Director, Office of Graduate Student Services, 330-672-2576, Fax: 330-672-9162, E-mail: ogs@kent.edu.

Lasell College, Graduate and Professional Studies in Management, Newton, MA 02466-2709. Offers business administration (MBA); elder care management (MSM); hospitality and event management (MSM); human resources management (MSM, Graduate Certificate); management (MSM, Graduate Certificate); marketing (MS, Graduate Certificate); project management (MSM, Graduate Certificate). *Accreditation:* ACBSP. *Program availability:* Part-time, evening/weekend, 100% online, blended/hybrid learning. *Faculty:* 7 full-time (4 women), 14 part-time/adjunct (9 women). *Students:* 37 full-time (28 women), 76 part-time (48 women); includes 22 minority (12 Black or African American, non-Hispanic/Latino; 1 Asian, non-Hispanic/Latino; 9 Hispanic/Latino), 20 international. Average age 32. 68 applicants, 54% accepted, 20 enrolled. In 2018, 62 master's, 1 other advanced degree awarded. *Degree requirements:* For master's, minimum GPA of 3.0; internship or research paper (for MSM). *Entrance requirements:* For master's, one-page personal statement, 2 letters of recommendation, resume, bachelor's degree transcript; proof of microeconomics and statistics (for MBA); for Graduate Certificate, bachelor's degree transcript, 2 letters of recommendation, 1-page personal statement, resume. Additional exam requirements/recommendations for international students: Required—TOEFL (minimum score 550 paper-based, 79 iBT) or IELTS (minimum score 6). *Application deadline:* For fall admission, 8/31 priority date for domestic students, 6/30 priority date for international students; for spring admission, 12/31 priority date for domestic students, 10/31 priority date for international students. Applications are processed on a rolling basis. Electronic applications accepted. *Expenses: Tuition:* Part-time $600 per credit. *Required fees:* $40 per course. *Financial support:* Federal Work-Study, scholarships/grants, and tuition discounts available. Support available to part-time students. Financial award application deadline: 8/31; financial award applicants required to submit FAFSA. *Unit head:* Eric Turner, Vice President of Graduate and Professional Studies, 617-243-2071, Fax: 617-243-2450, E-mail: gradinfo@lasell.edu. *Application contact:* Adrienne Franciosi, Assistant Vice President of Graduate and Professional Studies, 617-243-2214, Fax: 617-243-2450, E-mail: gradinfo@lasell.edu.
Website: http://www.lasell.edu/academics/graduate-and-professional-studies/programs-of-study/master-of-science-in-management.html

Lasell College, Graduate and Professional Studies in Sport Management, Newton, MA 02466-2709. Offers athletic administration (MS); parks and recreation (MS); sport leadership (MS, Graduate Certificate); sport tourism and hospitality (MS). *Program availability:* Part-time, evening/weekend, online only, 100% online. *Faculty:* 4 full-time (1 woman), 4 part-time/adjunct (2 women). *Students:* 15 full-time (7 women), 32 part-time (11 women); includes 17 minority (12 Black or African American, non-Hispanic/Latino; 4 Hispanic/Latino; 1 Two or more races, non-Hispanic/Latino). Average age 29. 36 applicants, 39% accepted, 11 enrolled. In 2018, 20 master's awarded. *Degree requirements:* For master's, minimum GPA of 3.0; internship or thesis. *Entrance requirements:* For master's, one-page personal statement, 2 letters of recommendation, resume, bachelor's degree transcript; for Graduate Certificate, bachelor's degree transcript, 2 letters of recommendation, 1-page personal statement, resume. Additional exam requirements/recommendations for international students: Required—TOEFL (minimum score 550 paper-based, 79 iBT) or IELTS (minimum score 6). *Application deadline:* For fall admission, 8/31 priority date for domestic students, 6/30 priority date for international students; for spring admission, 12/31 priority date for domestic students, 10/31 priority date for international students. Applications are processed on a rolling basis. Electronic applications accepted. *Expenses: Tuition:* Part-time $600 per credit. *Required fees:* $40 per course. *Financial support:* Federal Work-Study, scholarships/grants, and tuition discounts available. Support available to part-time students. Financial award application deadline: 8/31; financial award applicants required to submit FAFSA. *Faculty research:* How do fans attribute team failure; investigating cross-cultural difference in attribution; sense of ownership as a key predictor of fan loyalty; fans' normative beliefs about sponsorship and sponsors; investigation of new attitudinal variables in sponsorship. *Unit head:* Eric Turner, Vice President of Graduate and Professional Studies, 617-243-2071, Fax: 617-243-2450, E-mail: gradinfo@lasell.edu. *Application contact:* Adrienne Franciosi, Assistant Vice President of Graduate and Professional Studies, 617-243-2214, Fax: 617-243-2450, E-mail: gradinfo@lasell.edu.
Website: http://www.lasell.edu/academics/graduate-and-professional-studies/programs-of-study/master-of-science-in-sport-management.html

Les Roches International School of Hotel Management, Program in Hospitality Management, Bluche, Switzerland. Offers MBA. Available only at Switzerland campus.

Michigan State University, The Graduate School, Eli Broad College of Business, The School of Hospitality Business, East Lansing, MI 48224. Offers foodservice business management (MS); hospitality business management (MS). *Degree requirements:* For master's, comprehensive exam, research project. *Entrance requirements:* For master's, GMAT or GRE, minimum GPA of 3.0 in last 2 years of undergraduate course work, resume, 3 letters of recommendation, 2 official transcripts, at least 1 year of professional work experience. Additional exam requirements/recommendations for international students: Required—TOEFL (minimum score 580 paper-based; 87 iBT). Electronic applications accepted. *Faculty research:* Corporate food service management, entrepreneurial and food service management, hospitality business.

Monroe College, King Graduate School, Bronx, NY 10468. Offers accounting (MS); business administration (MBA), including entrepreneurship, finance, general business administration, healthcare management, human resources, information technology, marketing; computer science (MS); criminal justice (MS); hospitality management (MS); public health (MPH), including biostatistics and epidemiology, community health, health administration and leadership. *Program availability:* Online learning.

Morgan State University, School of Graduate Studies, Earl G. Graves School of Business and Management, Program in Hospitality Management, Baltimore, MD 21251. Offers MS.

New York University, School of Professional Studies, Jonathan M. Tisch Center of Hospitality, Program in Hospitality Industry Studies, New York, NY 10012-1019. Offers hospitality industry studies (MS), including brand strategy, hotel finance, lodging operations, revenue management. *Program availability:* Part-time, evening/weekend. *Degree requirements:* For master's, thesis. *Entrance requirements:* For master's, GRE or GMAT (only upon request), bachelor's degree, resume with relevant professional work, internship or volunteer experience, two letters of recommendation, statement of purpose. Additional exam requirements/recommendations for international students: Required—TOEFL (minimum score 600 paper-based; 100 iBT), IELTS (minimum score 7). Electronic applications accepted. *Expenses:* Contact institution.

New York University, Steinhardt School of Culture, Education, and Human Development, Department of Nutrition, Food Studies, and Public Health, Program in Food Studies, New York, NY 10012. Offers food studies (MA, PhD), including food culture (MA), food systems (MA). *Program availability:* Part-time. *Degree requirements:* For master's, thesis (for some programs); for doctorate, thesis/dissertation. *Entrance requirements:* For doctorate, GRE General Test, interview. Additional exam requirements/recommendations for international students: Required—TOEFL (minimum score 100 iBT). Electronic applications accepted. *Faculty research:* Cultural and social history of food, food systems and agriculture, food and aesthetics, political economy of food.

North Carolina Agricultural and Technical State University, The Graduate College, College of Agriculture and Environmental Sciences, Department of Agribusiness, Applied Economics, and Agriscience Education, Greensboro, NC 27411. Offers

agribusiness and food industry management (MS); agricultural education (MS). *Accreditation:* NCATE. *Program availability:* Part-time, evening/weekend. *Degree requirements:* For master's, comprehensive exam, thesis or alternative, qualifying exam. *Entrance requirements:* For master's, GRE General Test, minimum GPA of 3.0. *Faculty research:* Aid for small farmers, agricultural technology resources, labor force mobility, agrology.

Oklahoma State University, College of Human Sciences, School of Hospitality and Tourism Management, Stillwater, OK 74078. Offers MS, PhD. *Faculty:* 16 full-time (9 women), 7 part-time/adjunct (1 woman). *Students:* 18 full-time (11 women), 19 part-time (10 women); includes 3 minority (all Asian, non-Hispanic/Latino), 30 international. Average age 28. 17 applicants, 65% accepted, 8 enrolled. In 2018, 9 master's awarded. *Entrance requirements:* For master's and doctorate, GRE or GMAT. Additional exam requirements/recommendations for international students: Required—TOEFL (minimum score 550 paper-based; 79 iBT). *Application deadline:* For fall admission, 3/1 priority date for international students; for spring admission, 8/1 priority date for international students. Applications are processed on a rolling basis. Application fee: $40 ($75 for international students). Electronic applications accepted. *Expenses: Tuition, area resident:* Full-time $4148. Tuition, state resident: full-time $4148. Tuition, nonresident: full-time $10,517. *International tuition:* $10,517 full-time. *Required fees:* $4394; $2929 per credit hour. Tuition and fees vary according to course load and program. *Financial support:* Research assistantships, teaching assistantships, career-related internships or fieldwork, Federal Work-Study, scholarships/grants, health care benefits, tuition waivers (partial), and unspecified assistantships available. Support available to part-time students. Financial award application deadline: 3/1; financial award applicants required to submit FAFSA. *Faculty research:* Hotel operations and management, restaurant/food service management, hospitality education, hospitality human resources management, tourism. *Unit head:* Dr. Li Miao, Interim Director, 405-744-6713, Fax: 405-744-6299, E-mail: htm@okstate.edu. *Application contact:* Dr. Li Miao, Graduate Coordinator, 405-744-1277, Fax: 405-744-6299, E-mail: lm@okstate.edu.
Website: https://humansciences.okstate.edu/htm/index.html

Penn State University Park, Graduate School, College of Health and Human Development, School of Hospitality Management, University Park, PA 16802. Offers MS, PhD.

Pontificia Universidad Catolica Madre y Maestra, Graduate School, Faculty of Social and Administrative Sciences, Santiago, Dominican Republic. Offers business administration (MBA), including business development, finance, international business, management skills (M Mgmt, MBA), marketing, operations, strategic cost management, strategy, tourist destination planning and management; law (LL M), including civil law, corporate business law, criminal law, international relations, real estate law; management (M Mgmt), including higher financial management, insurance program administration, management skills (M Mgmt, MBA); psychology (MA), including clinical child and adolescent psychology, forensic psychology; strategic human resources (EMBA).

Purdue University, Graduate School, College of Health and Human Sciences, School of Hospitality and Tourism Management, West Lafayette, IN 47907. Offers MS, PhD. *Program availability:* Online learning. *Faculty:* 14 full-time (6 women). *Students:* 35 full-time (25 women), 64 part-time (46 women); includes 26 minority (11 Black or African American, non-Hispanic/Latino; 8 Asian, non-Hispanic/Latino; 4 Hispanic/Latino; 3 Two or more races, non-Hispanic/Latino), 39 international. Average age 31. 111 applicants, 64% accepted, 35 enrolled. In 2018, 13 master's, 5 doctorates awarded. *Degree requirements:* For master's, thesis; for doctorate, thesis/dissertation. *Entrance requirements:* For master's, GMAT (minimum score of 550) or GRE General Test (minimum combined verbal and quantitative score of 290 new scoring, minimum of 145 each section, or 1000 with 500 each section, old scoring), minimum GPA of 3.0; for doctorate, GMAT (minimum score of 550) or GRE General Test (minimum combined verbal and quantitative score of 290 new scoring, minimum of 145 each section, or 1000 with 500 each section, old scoring), minimum undergraduate GPA of 3.0; master's degree with minimum GPA of 3.0 or equivalent. Additional exam requirements/recommendations for international students: Required—TOEFL (minimum score 77 iBT), TWE. *Application deadline:* For fall admission, 3/5 priority date for domestic and international students; for spring admission, 9/20 for domestic and international students. Applications are processed on a rolling basis. Application fee: $60 ($75 for international students). Electronic applications accepted. *Financial support:* Research assistantships, teaching assistantships, and career-related internships or fieldwork available. Support available to part-time students. Financial award applicants required to submit FAFSA. *Faculty research:* Human resources, marketing, hotel and restaurant operations, food product and equipment development, tourism development. *Unit head:* Dr. Richard F. Ghiselli, Head, 765-494-2636, E-mail: ghiselli@purdue.edu. *Application contact:* Ayrielle K. Espinosa, Graduate Contact, 765-494-9811, E-mail: camposm@purdue.edu.
Website: http://www.purdue.edu/hhs/htm/

Rochester Institute of Technology, Graduate Enrollment Services, College of Applied Science and Technology, School of International Hospitality and Service Innovation, MS Program in Hospitality and Tourism Management, Rochester, NY 14623-5603. Offers MS. *Program availability:* Part-time, evening/weekend. *Students:* 13 full-time (9 women), 2 part-time (both women); includes 4 minority (2 Black or African American, non-Hispanic/Latino; 1 Asian, non-Hispanic/Latino; 1 Two or more races, non-Hispanic/Latino), 7 international. Average age 29. 20 applicants, 65% accepted, 5 enrolled. In 2018, 6 master's awarded. *Degree requirements:* For master's, comprehensive exam (for some programs), thesis or alternative, Thesis, Project, or Comprehensive Exam options. *Entrance requirements:* For master's, minimum GPA of 3.0 (recommended). Additional exam requirements/recommendations for international students: Required—TOEFL (minimum score 570 paper-based; 80 iBT), IELTS (minimum score 6.5), PTE (minimum score 61). *Application deadline:* Applications are processed on a rolling basis. Application fee: $65. Electronic applications accepted. *Financial support:* In 2018–19, 10 students received support. Teaching assistantships with partial tuition reimbursements available, career-related internships or fieldwork, scholarships/grants, and unspecified assistantships available. Support available to part-time students. Financial award applicants required to submit FAFSA. *Faculty research:* Service innovation and technology integration, innovative food product development, hospitality employees' occupational health and wellness, tourist behaviors, destination management. *Unit head:* Matthew Cornwell, Assistant Director of Student Services and Outreach, 585-475-6916, E-mail: mcornwell@saunders.rit.edu. *Application contact:* Diane Ellison, Senior Associate Vice President, Graduate Enrollment Services, 585-475-2229, Fax: 585-475-7164, E-mail: gradinfo@rit.edu.
Website: https://www.rit.edu/study/hospitality-and-tourism-management-ms

Rochester Institute of Technology, Graduate Enrollment Services, College of Applied Science and Technology, School of International Hospitality and Service Innovation, MS Program in Service Leadership and Innovation, Rochester, NY 14623-5603. Offers MS. *Program availability:* Part-time, evening/weekend, 100% online. *Students:* 1 full-time, 38 part-time (24 women); includes 3 minority (1 Black or African American, non-Hispanic/Latino; 1 Asian, non-Hispanic/Latino; 1 Hispanic/Latino), 1 international. Average age 30. 6 applicants, 67% accepted, 2 enrolled. In 2018, 4 master's awarded. *Degree requirements:* For master's, thesis or alternative, Project, Comprehensive Exam, and Thesis options available. *Entrance requirements:* For master's, Have a minimum cumulative GPA of 3.0 (or equivalent), or evidence of relevant professional performance. Additional exam requirements/recommendations for international students: Required—TOEFL (minimum score 570 paper-based; 88 iBT), IELTS (minimum score 6.5), PTE (minimum score 62). *Application deadline:* Applications are processed on a rolling basis. Application fee: $65. Electronic applications accepted. *Financial support:* In 2018–19, 4 students received support. Teaching assistantships with partial tuition reimbursements available, career-related internships or fieldwork, scholarships/grants, and unspecified assistantships available. Support available to part-time students. Financial award applicants required to submit FAFSA. *Faculty research:* Leadership development, customer service/patient satisfaction, program evaluation, knowledge construction, diversity, individual creativity, healthcare applications. *Unit head:* Dr. Linda Underhill, Department Chair, 585-475-7359, E-mail: lmuism@rit.edu. *Application contact:* Diane Ellison, Senior Associate Vice President, Graduate Enrollment Services, 585-475-2229, Fax: 585-475-7164, E-mail: gradinfo@rit.edu.
Website: https://www.rit.edu/study/service-leadership-and-innovation-ms

Roosevelt University, Graduate Division, Walter E. Heller College of Business, Program in Hospitality and Tourism Management, Chicago, IL 60605. Offers MS. *Program availability:* Part-time, evening/weekend. *Degree requirements:* For master's, thesis. Electronic applications accepted. *Expenses:* Contact institution.

San Diego State University, Graduate and Research Affairs, College of Professional Studies and Fine Arts, L. Robert Payne School of Hospitality and Tourism Management, San Diego, CA 92182. Offers hospitality and tourism (MA); meeting and event management (MA).

San Francisco State University, Division of Graduate Studies, College of Business, Program in Business Administration, San Francisco, CA 94132-1722. Offers decision sciences/operations research (MBA); ethics and compliance (MBA); finance (MBA); global business and innovation (MBA); healthcare administration (MBA); hospitality and tourism management (MBA); information systems (MBA); leadership (MBA); marketing (MBA); nonprofit and social enterprise leadership (MBA); sustainable business (MBA). *Accreditation:* AACSB. *Program availability:* Part-time, evening/weekend. *Degree requirements:* For master's, thesis, essay test. *Entrance requirements:* For master's, GMAT, minimum GPA of 2.7 in last 60 units. Additional exam requirements/recommendations for international students: Required—TOEFL (minimum score 550 paper-based).

San Ignacio University, Graduate Programs, Doral, FL 33178. Offers business administration (MBA), including human resources management, international business, marketing management; education (M Ed), including early childhood education, educational leadership, special education; hospitality management (MA), including gastronomy and restaurant management, tourism management.

Schiller International University, MBA Programs, Florida, Program in International Hotel and Tourism Management, Largo, FL 33771. Offers MBA. *Degree requirements:* For master's, thesis optional. *Entrance requirements:* Additional exam requirements/recommendations for international students: Required—TOEFL (minimum score 550 paper-based).

South University, Graduate Programs, College of Business, Savannah, GA 31406. Offers corrections (MBA); entrepreneurship and small business (MBA); healthcare administration (MBA); hospitality management (MBA); leadership (MS); public administration (MPA); sustainability (MBA).

Stratford University, Program in International Hospitality Management, Baltimore, MD 21202. Offers MS. *Program availability:* Part-time, evening/weekend, online learning.

Strayer University, Graduate Studies, Washington, DC 20005-2603. Offers accounting (MS); acquisition (MBA); business administration (MBA); communications technology (MS); educational management (M Ed); finance (MBA); health services administration (MHSA); hospitality and tourism management (MBA); human resource management (MBA); information systems (MS), including computer security management, decision support system management, enterprise resource management, network management, software engineering management, systems development management; management (MBA); management information systems (MS); marketing (MBA); professional accounting (MS), including accounting information systems, controllership, taxation; public administration (MPA); supply chain management (MBA); technology in education (M Ed). Programs also offered at campus locations in Birmingham, AL; Chamblee, GA; Cobb County, GA; Morrow, GA; White Marsh, MD; Charleston, SC; Columbia, SC; Greensboro, NC; Greenville, SC; Lexington, KY; Louisville, KY; Nashville, TN; North Raleigh, NC; Washington, DC. *Accreditation:* ACBSP. *Program availability:* Part-time, evening/weekend, online learning. *Degree requirements:* For master's, thesis. *Entrance requirements:* For master's, GMAT, GRE General Test, bachelor's degree from an accredited college or university, minimum undergraduate GPA of 2.75. Electronic applications accepted.

Syracuse University, David B. Falk College of Sport and Human Dynamics, Program in Food Studies, Syracuse, NY 13244. Offers MS, CAS. *Program availability:* Part-time. *Entrance requirements:* For master's, GRE, three letters of recommendation, resume, personal statement, official transcripts. *Application deadline:* For fall admission, 2/15 priority date for domestic and international students; for spring admission, 11/15 priority date for domestic and international students. Application fee: $75. Electronic applications accepted. *Financial support:* Fellowships, research assistantships, teaching assistantships, career-related internships or fieldwork, and scholarships/grants available. Financial award application deadline: 1/1. *Faculty research:* Food and nutrition systems and economies, linkages between sustainable agriculture and development, human rights and the right to adequate food and nutrition, food sovereignty, urban-rural food linkages in terms of production for trade and household consumption. *Unit head:* Anne C. Bellows, Director, 315-443-4228, E-mail: acbellow@syr.edu. *Application contact:* Felicia Otero, Director of College Admissions, 315-443-5555, Fax: 315-443-2562, E-mail: falk@syr.edu.
Website: https://falk.syr.edu/food-studies/academic-programs/#msfs

Temple University, Fox School of Business, Doctoral Programs in Business, Philadelphia, PA 19122-6096. Offers accounting (PhD); entrepreneurship (PhD); finance (PhD); international business (PhD); management information systems (PhD); marketing (PhD); risk management and insurance (PhD); statistics (PhD); strategic management (PhD); tourism and sport (PhD). *Accreditation:* AACSB. *Degree requirements:* For doctorate, thesis/dissertation. *Entrance requirements:* For doctorate, GRE General Test, GMAT, minimum GPA of 3.0, master's degree. Additional exam requirements/recommendations for international students: Required—TOEFL (minimum score 600 paper-based; 100 iBT), IELTS (minimum score 7.5). Electronic applications accepted.

Temple University, School of Sport, Tourism and Hospitality Management, Philadelphia, PA 19122-6096. Offers sport business (MS); tourism and hospitality management (MTHM); tourism and sport (PhD); travel and tourism (MS). *Program availability:* Part-time, evening/weekend, online learning. *Faculty:* 24 full-time (9 women), 11 part-time/adjunct (4 women). *Students:* 153 full-time (70 women), 56 part-

time (25 women); includes 48 minority (28 Black or African American, non-Hispanic/Latino; 5 Asian, non-Hispanic/Latino; 10 Hispanic/Latino; 5 Two or more races, non-Hispanic/Latino), 33 international. 215 applicants, 76% accepted, 107 enrolled. In 2018, 71 master's awarded. *Entrance requirements:* For master's, GMAT or GRE, 500-word statement of goals, 2 letters of recommendation, resume. Additional exam requirements/recommendations for international students: Required—TOEFL, IELTS, PTE, one of three is required. *Application deadline:* For fall admission, 12/15 priority date for domestic students, 3/1 for international students; for spring admission, 11/1 for domestic students, 8/1 for international students. Applications are processed on a rolling basis. Application fee: $60. Electronic applications accepted. *Expenses:* Contact institution. *Financial support:* Scholarships/grants, health care benefits, and unspecified assistantships available. Financial award application deadline: 3/1; financial award applicants required to submit FAFSA. *Unit head:* Ronald C. Anderson, Dean, 215-204-8701, E-mail: sthm@temple.edu. *Application contact:* Michelle Rosar, Assistant Director of Graduate Enrollment, 215-204-3315, E-mail: michelle.rosar@temple.edu. Website: http://sthm.temple.edu/

Texas Tech University, Graduate School, College of Human Sciences, Department of Hospitality and Retail Management, Lubbock, TX 79409-1240. Offers hospitality administration (PhD); hospitality and retail management (MS). *Program availability:* Part-time, evening/weekend. *Faculty:* 23 full-time (10 women), 1 (woman) part-time/adjunct. *Students:* 28 full-time (17 women), 5 part-time (0 women); includes 4 minority (3 Hispanic/Latino; 1 Two or more races, non-Hispanic/Latino), 9 international. Average age 29. 16 applicants, 63% accepted, 7 enrolled. In 2018, 7 master's, 6 doctorates awarded. Terminal master's awarded for partial completion of doctoral program. *Degree requirements:* For master's, thesis or alternative; for doctorate, thesis/dissertation. *Entrance requirements:* For master's, GRE, professional experience (restaurant, hotel, and institutional management); for doctorate, GRE General Test, professional experience. Additional exam requirements/recommendations for international students: Required—TOEFL (minimum score 550 paper-based; 79 iBT), IELTS (minimum score 6.5). *Application deadline:* For fall admission, 6/1 priority date for domestic students, 1/15 priority date for international students; for spring admission, 9/1 priority date for domestic students, 6/15 priority date for international students. Applications are processed on a rolling basis. Application fee: $65. Electronic applications accepted. *Expenses:* Contact institution. *Financial support:* In 2018–19, 35 students received support, including 33 fellowships (averaging $5,022 per year), 5 research assistantships (averaging $11,519 per year), 25 teaching assistantships (averaging $10,008 per year); Federal Work-Study and scholarships/grants also available. Financial award application deadline: 4/15; financial award applicants required to submit FAFSA. *Faculty research:* Cultural and emotional intelligence, tourism, consumer behavior, wine, sustainability. *Total annual research expenditures:* $55,120. *Unit head:* Dr. Robert Paul Jones, Chairperson/Associate Professor, 806-834-8922, Fax: 806-742-3042, E-mail: robert.p.jones@ttu.edu. *Application contact:* Dr. Jessica Yuan, Graduate Coordinator, Hospitality and Retail Management, 806-834-8446, Fax: 806-742-3042, E-mail: jessica.yuan@ttu.edu.
Website: www.depts.ttu.edu/hs/hrm/

Thomas Edison State University, School of Business and Management, Program in Hospitality Management, Trenton, NJ 08608. Offers MS. *Program availability:* Online learning.

The University of Alabama, Graduate School, College of Human Environmental Sciences, Department of Human Nutrition and Hospitality Management, Tuscaloosa, AL 35487. Offers MSHES. *Program availability:* Part-time, online only, 100% online. *Degree requirements:* For master's, comprehensive exam, thesis optional. *Entrance requirements:* For master's, minimum GPA of 3.0. Additional exam requirements/recommendations for international students: Required—TOEFL, IELTS. Electronic applications accepted. *Faculty research:* Maternal and child nutrition, childhood obesity, community nutrition interventions, geriatric nutrition, family eating patterns, food chemistry, phytochemicals, dietary antioxidants.

The University of Alabama, Graduate School, College of Human Environmental Sciences, Program in Human Environmental Science, Tuscaloosa, AL 35487. Offers interactive technology (MS); quality management (MS); restaurant and meeting management (MS); rural community health (MS); sport management (MS). *Program availability:* Part-time, evening/weekend, online learning. *Degree requirements:* For master's, comprehensive exam. *Entrance requirements:* For master's, GRE (for some specializations), minimum GPA of 3.0. Additional exam requirements/recommendations for international students: Required—TOEFL. Electronic applications accepted. *Faculty research:* Rural health, hospitality management, sport management, interactive technology, consumer quality management, environmental health and safety.

University of Central Florida, Rosen College of Hospitality Management, Orlando, FL 32816. Offers destination marketing and management (Certificate); event management (Certificate); hospitality and tourism management (MS); hospitality management (PhD). *Program availability:* Part-time. *Faculty:* 71 full-time (27 women), 26 part-time/adjunct (10 women). *Students:* 82 full-time (53 women), 168 part-time (113 women); includes 70 minority (30 Black or African American, non-Hispanic/Latino; 1 American Indian or Alaska Native, non-Hispanic/Latino; 8 Asian, non-Hispanic/Latino; 27 Hispanic/Latino; 4 Two or more races, non-Hispanic/Latino), 40 international. Average age 30. 226 applicants, 64% accepted, 92 enrolled. In 2018, 58 master's, 2 doctorates, 44 other advanced degrees awarded. *Degree requirements:* For master's, thesis or alternative; for doctorate, thesis/dissertation, candidacy exam. *Entrance requirements:* For master's and doctorate, GMAT or GRE, letters of recommendation, goal statement, resume. Additional exam requirements/recommendations for international students: Required—TOEFL. *Application deadline:* For fall admission, 7/15 for domestic students; for spring admission, 12/1 for domestic students. Application fee: $30. Electronic applications accepted. *Financial support:* In 2018–19, 36 students received support, including 17 fellowships with partial tuition reimbursements available (averaging $14,760 per year), 1 research assistantship with partial tuition reimbursement available (averaging $9,882 per year), 26 teaching assistantships with partial tuition reimbursements available (averaging $11,242 per year); health care benefits also available. Financial award application deadline: 3/1; financial award applicants required to submit FAFSA. *Unit head:* Dr. Abraham C. Pizam, Dean, 407-903-8010, E-mail: abraham.pizam@ucf.edu. *Application contact:* Associate Director, Graduate Admissions, 407-823-2766, Fax: 407-823-6442, E-mail: gradadmissions@ucf.edu.
Website: http://www.hospitality.ucf.edu/

University of Delaware, Alfred Lerner College of Business and Economics, Program in Hospitality Information Management, Newark, DE 19716. Offers MS. *Entrance requirements:* Additional exam requirements/recommendations for international students: Required—TOEFL (minimum score 550 paper-based). Electronic applications accepted. *Faculty research:* Foodservice, lodging and tourism management.

The University of Findlay, Office of Graduate Admissions, Findlay, OH 45840-3653. Offers applied security and analytics (MSAS); athletic training (MAT); business (MBA), including certified management accountant, certified public accountant, health care management, hospitality management; education (MA Ed, Ed D), including children's literature (MA Ed), curriculum and teaching (MA Ed), education (MA Ed), educational administration (MA Ed), human resource development (MA Ed), mathematics (MA Ed),

reading (MA Ed), science education (MA Ed), superintendent (Ed D), teaching (Ed D), technology (MA Ed); environmental, safety, and health management (MSEM); health informatics (MS); occupational therapy (MOT); pharmacy (Pharm D); physical therapy (DPT); physician assistant (MPA); rhetoric and writing (MA); teaching English to speakers of other languages (TESOL) and applied linguistics (MA). *Program availability:* Part-time, evening/weekend, 100% online, blended/hybrid learning. *Degree requirements:* For master's, comprehensive exam (for some programs), thesis (for some programs), cumulative project, capstone project; for doctorate, thesis/dissertation (for some programs). *Entrance requirements:* For master's, GRE/GMAT, bachelor's degree from accredited institution, minimum undergraduate GPA of 2.5 in last 64 hours of course work; for doctorate, GRE, MAT, minimum cumulative GPA of 3.0. Additional exam requirements/recommendations for international students: Required—TOEFL (minimum score 79 iBT), IELTS (minimum score 7), PTE (minimum score 61). Electronic applications accepted.

University of Guelph, Office of Graduate and Postdoctoral Studies, College of Management and Economics, MBA Program, Guelph, ON N1G 2W1, Canada. Offers food and agribusiness management (MBA); hospitality and tourism management (MBA). *Program availability:* Part-time, evening/weekend, online learning. *Entrance requirements:* For master's, minimum B-average, minimum of 3 years of relevant work experience. Additional exam requirements/recommendations for international students: Required—TOEFL (minimum score 550 paper-based). Electronic applications accepted. *Faculty research:* Marketing, operations management, business policy, financial management, organizational behavior.

University of Houston, Conrad N. Hilton College of Hotel and Restaurant Management, Houston, TX 77204. Offers hospitality management (MS). *Program availability:* Part-time. *Degree requirements:* For master's, practicum or thesis. *Entrance requirements:* For master's, GMAT or GRE General Test. Additional exam requirements/recommendations for international students: Required—TOEFL (minimum score 100 iBT) or IELTS (minimum score 7). Electronic applications accepted. *Faculty research:* Catering, tourism, hospitality marketing, security and risk management, purchasing and financial information usage.

University of Kentucky, Graduate School, College of Agriculture, Food and Environment, Program in Hospitality and Dietetics Administration, Lexington, KY 40506-0032. Offers MS. *Degree requirements:* For master's, comprehensive exam, thesis optional. *Entrance requirements:* For master's, GRE General Test, minimum undergraduate GPA of 2.75. Additional exam requirements/recommendations for international students: Required—TOEFL (minimum score 550 paper-based). Electronic applications accepted.

University of Louisiana at Lafayette, BI Moody III College of Business Administration, Lafayette, LA 70504. Offers accounting (MS); business administration (MBA); entrepreneurship (MBA); finance (MBA); global management (MBA); health care administration (MBA); hospitality management (MBA); human resource management (MBA); project management (MBA); sales leadership (MBA). *Accreditation:* AACSB. *Program availability:* Part-time, evening/weekend. *Entrance requirements:* For master's, GRE General Test. Additional exam requirements/recommendations for international students: Required—TOEFL (minimum score 550 paper-based).

University of Massachusetts Amherst, Graduate School, Isenberg School of Management, Program in Management, Amherst, MA 01003. Offers accounting (PhD); business administration (MBA); entrepreneurship (MBA); finance (MBA, PhD); healthcare administration (MBA); hospitality and tourism management (PhD); management science (PhD); marketing (MBA, PhD); organization studies (PhD); sport management (PhD); strategic management (PhD); MBA/MS. *Accreditation:* AACSB. *Program availability:* Part-time, evening/weekend, online learning. Terminal master's awarded for partial completion of doctoral program. *Degree requirements:* For doctorate, comprehensive exam, thesis/dissertation. *Entrance requirements:* For master's and doctorate, GMAT or GRE General Test. Additional exam requirements/recommendations for international students: Required—TOEFL (minimum score 550 paper-based; 80 iBT), IELTS (minimum score 6.5). Electronic applications accepted.

University of Memphis, Graduate School, Kemmons Wilson School of Hospitality and Resort Management, Memphis, TN 38152. Offers hospitality management specialist (Graduate Certificate); sports commerce (MS). *Program availability:* Part-time. *Faculty:* 9 full-time (3 women), 3 part-time/adjunct (1 woman). *Students:* 33 full-time (13 women), 28 part-time (8 women); includes 26 minority (23 Black or African American, non-Hispanic/Latino; 1 Asian, non-Hispanic/Latino; 2 Two or more races, non-Hispanic/Latino), 2 international. Average age 28. 35 applicants, 80% accepted, 28 enrolled. In 2018, 30 master's awarded. *Degree requirements:* For master's, comprehensive exam, thesis or alternative. *Entrance requirements:* For master's, letters of recommendation, curriculum vitae or resume, statement of goals, minimum undergraduate GPA of 2.5. Additional exam requirements/recommendations for international students: Required—TOEFL (minimum score 550 paper-based; 79 iBT). *Application deadline:* For fall admission, 7/1 for domestic students, 5/1 for international students; for spring admission, 12/1 for domestic students, 9/1 for international students; for summer admission, 5/1 for domestic students, 2/1 for international students. Application fee: $35 ($60 for international students). Electronic applications accepted. *Expenses:* Tuition, area resident: Full-time $10,240; part-time $503 per credit hour. Tuition, state resident: full-time $10,464. Tuition, nonresident: full-time $20,224; part-time $991 per credit hour. *Required fees:* $850; $106 per credit hour. *Financial support:* Research assistantships, teaching assistantships, career-related internships or fieldwork, Federal Work-Study, scholarships/grants, and unspecified assistantships available. Support available to part-time students. Financial award application deadline: 2/1; financial award applicants required to submit FAFSA. *Unit head:* Dr. Radesh Palakurthi, Dean, 901-678-3430, E-mail: rplkrthi@memphis.edu. *Application contact:* Dr. Tim Ryan, Coordinator of Graduate Studies, 901-678-5003, E-mail: tdryan@memphis.edu.
Website: http://www.memphis.edu/wilson

University of Mississippi, Graduate School, School of Applied Sciences, University, MS 38677. Offers communicative disorders (MS); criminal justice (MCJ); exercise science (MS); food and nutrition services (MS); health and kinesiology (PhD); health promotion (MS); nutrition and hospitality management (PhD); park and recreation management (MA); social welfare (PhD); social work (MSW). *Faculty:* 66 full-time (36 women), 27 part-time/adjunct (13 women). *Students:* 192 full-time (148 women), 40 part-time (25 women); includes 50 minority (41 Black or African American, non-Hispanic/Latino; 1 American Indian or Alaska Native, non-Hispanic/Latino; 1 Asian, non-Hispanic/Latino; 5 Hispanic/Latino; 2 Two or more races, non-Hispanic/Latino), 16 international. Average age 26. In 2018, 72 master's, 5 doctorates awarded. *Entrance requirements:* For master's, GRE General Test, minimum GPA of 3.0. Additional exam requirements/recommendations for international students: Required—TOEFL. *Application deadline:* Applications are processed on a rolling basis. Application fee: $50. Electronic applications accepted. *Financial support:* Scholarships/grants available. Financial award application deadline: 3/1; financial award applicants required to submit FAFSA. *Unit head:* Dr. Peter Grandjean, Dean of Applied Sciences, 662-915-7900, Fax: 662-915-7901, E-mail: applsci@olemiss.edu. *Application contact:* Temeka Smith, Graduate Activities Specialist for Admissions, 662-915-7474, Fax: 662-915-7577, E-mail: gschool@olemiss.edu.

Hospitality Management

University of Missouri, Office of Research and Graduate Studies, College of Agriculture, Food and Natural Resources, Department of Food Science, Columbia, MO 65211. Offers MS, PhD. Terminal master's awarded for partial completion of doctoral program. *Entrance requirements:* For master's, GRE General Test (minimum score: Verbal and Quantitative 1000 with neither section below 400, 297 combined under new scoring; Analytical 3.5), minimum GPA of 3.0; BS in food science from accredited university; for doctorate, GRE General Test (minimum score: Verbal and Quantitative 1000 with neither section below 400, Analytical 3.5), minimum GPA of 3.0; BS and MS in food science from accredited university. *Faculty research:* Food chemistry, food analysis, food microbiology, food engineering and process control, functional foods, meat science and processing technology.

University of Nevada, Las Vegas, Graduate College, William F. Harrah College of Hospitality, Las Vegas, NV 89154-6013. Offers hospitality administration (MHA, PhD); hotel administration (MS). *Program availability:* Part-time, evening/weekend, 100% online, blended/hybrid learning. *Faculty:* 16 full-time (6 women), 3 part-time/adjunct (0 women). *Students:* 43 full-time (24 women), 51 part-time (28 women); includes 20 minority (4 Black or African American, non-Hispanic/Latino; 9 Asian, non-Hispanic/Latino; 4 Hispanic/Latino; 3 Two or more races, non-Hispanic/Latino), 32 international. Average age 34. 118 applicants, 40% accepted, 28 enrolled. In 2018, 36 master's, 1 doctorate awarded. *Degree requirements:* For master's, thesis (for some programs), professional paper, oral examination; for doctorate, comprehensive exam, thesis/dissertation, dissertation defense. *Entrance requirements:* For master's, GRE or GMAT, bachelor's degree with minimum GPA 2.75; minimum of one year of full-time work experience; brief essay; 2 letters of recommendation; for doctorate, GRE or GMAT, master's degree with minimum GPA of 3.0; statement of purpose; 3 letters of recommendation. Additional exam requirements/recommendations for international students: Required—TOEFL (minimum score 550 paper-based; 80 iBT), IELTS (minimum score 7). Application fee: $60 ($95 for international students). Electronic applications accepted. *Expenses:* Contact institution. *Financial support:* In 2018–19, 35 students received support, including 4 research assistantships with full tuition reimbursements available (averaging $12,188 per year), 31 teaching assistantships with full tuition reimbursements available (averaging $13,306 per year); institutionally sponsored loans, scholarships/grants, health care benefits, and unspecified assistantships also available. Financial award application deadline: 3/15; financial award applicants required to submit FAFSA. *Faculty research:* Marketing, human resources, financial analysis, tourism, gaming. *Total annual research expenditures:* $12,152. *Unit head:* Dr. Stowe Shoemaker, Dean, 702-895-3308, Fax: 702-895-4109, E-mail: hospitality.dean@unlv.edu. *Application contact:* Dr. Stowe Shoemaker, Dean, 702-895-3308, Fax: 702-895-4109, E-mail: hospitality.dean@unlv.edu.
Website: http://hotel.unlv.edu/

University of New Orleans, Graduate School, College of Business Administration, Lester E. Kabacoff School of Hotel, Restaurant, and Tourism Administration, New Orleans, LA 70148. Offers hospitality and tourism management (MS). *Entrance requirements:* Additional exam requirements/recommendations for international students: Required—TOEFL (minimum score 550 paper-based; 79 iBT). Electronic applications accepted.

University of North Texas, Toulouse Graduate School, Denton, TX 76203-5459. Offers accounting (MS); applied anthropology (MA, MS); applied behavior analysis (Certificate); applied geography (MA); applied technology and performance improvement (M Ed, MS); art education (MA); art history (MA); arts leadership (Certificate); audiology (Au D); behavior analysis (MS); behavioral science (PhD); biochemistry and molecular biology (MS); biology (MA, MS); biomedical engineering (MS); business analysis (MS); chemistry (MS); clinical health psychology (PhD); communication studies (MA, MS); computer engineering (MS); computer science (MS); counseling (M Ed, MS), including clinical mental health counseling (MS), college and university counseling, elementary school counseling, secondary school counseling; creative writing (MA); criminal justice (MS); curriculum and instruction (M Ed); decision sciences (MBA); design (MA, MFA), including fashion design (MFA), innovation studies, interior design (MFA); early childhood studies (MS); economics (MS); educational leadership (M Ed, Ed D); educational psychology (MS, PhD), including family studies (MS), gifted and talented (MS), human development (MS), learning and cognition (MS), research, measurement and evaluation (MS); electrical engineering (MS); emergency management (MPA); engineering technology (MS); English (MA); English as a second language (MA); environmental science (MS); finance (MBA, MS); financial management (MPA); French (MA); health services management (MBA); higher education (M Ed, Ed D); history (MA, MS); hospitality management (MS); human resources management (MPA); information science (MS); information systems (PhD); information technologies (MBA); interdisciplinary studies (MA, MS); international studies (MA); international sustainable tourism (MS); jazz studies (MM); journalism (MA, MJ, Graduate Certificate), including interactive and virtual digital communication (Graduate Certificate), narrative journalism (Graduate Certificate), public relations (Graduate Certificate); kinesiology (MS); linguistics (MA); local government management (MPA); logistics (PhD); logistics and supply chain management (MBA); long-term care, senior housing, and aging services (MA); management (PhD); marketing (MBA); mathematics (MA, MS); mechanical and energy engineering (MS, PhD); music (MA), including ethnomusicology, music theory, musicology, performance; music composition (PhD); music education (MM Ed, PhD); nonprofit management (MPA); operations and supply chain management (MBA); performance (MM, DMA); philosophy (MA); political science (MA); professional and technical communication (MA); radio, television and film (MA, MFA); rehabilitation counseling (Certificate); sociology (MA); Spanish (MA); special education (M Ed); speech-language pathology (MA); strategic management (MBA); studio art (MFA); teaching (M Ed); MBA/MS. *Program availability:* Part-time, evening/weekend, online learning. Terminal master's awarded for partial completion of doctoral program. *Degree requirements:* For master's, variable foreign language requirement, comprehensive exam (for some programs), thesis (for some programs); for doctorate, variable foreign language requirement, comprehensive exam (for some programs), thesis/dissertation; for other advanced degree, variable foreign language requirement, comprehensive exam (for some programs). *Entrance requirements:* For master's and doctorate, GRE, GMAT. Additional exam requirements/recommendations for international students: Required—TOEFL (minimum score 550 paper-based; 79 iBT). Electronic applications accepted.

University of South Carolina, The Graduate School, College of Hospitality, Retail, and Sport Management, School of Hotel, Restaurant and Tourism Management, Columbia, SC 29208. Offers MIHTM. *Entrance requirements:* For master's, GMAT or GRE General Test, minimum GPA of 3.0, 2 letters of recommendation. Electronic applications accepted. *Faculty research:* Corporate strategy and management practices, sustainable tourism, club management, tourism technology, revenue management.

University of South Florida Sarasota-Manatee, College of Hospitality and Technology Leadership, Sarasota, FL 34243. Offers hospitality management (MS). *Program availability:* Part-time. *Faculty:* 4 full-time (1 woman). *Students:* 8 full-time (6 women), 7 part-time (3 women); includes 3 minority (1 Asian, non-Hispanic/Latino; 2 Hispanic/Latino), 4 international. Average age 35. 18 applicants, 33% accepted, 5 enrolled. In 2018, 7 master's awarded. *Degree requirements:* For master's, thesis optional. *Entrance requirements:* For master's, GRE or GMAT (taken within last five years) if overall or upper-division GPA is less than 3.0, current resume, essay, and 3 letters of recommendation. Additional exam requirements/recommendations for international students: Required—TOEFL (minimum score 550 paper-based; 79 iBT), IELTS (minimum score 6.5). *Application deadline:* For fall admission, 6/1 priority date for domestic students, 6/1 for international students; for spring admission, 10/1 priority date for domestic students, 10/1 for international students; for summer admission, 3/1 priority date for domestic students, 3/1 for international students. Applications are processed on a rolling basis. Application fee: $30. Electronic applications accepted. *Expenses: Tuition, area resident:* Full-time $8350; part-time $348 per credit hour. Tuition, state resident: full-time $8350; part-time $348 per credit hour. Tuition, nonresident: full-time $19,048; part-time $794 per credit hour. *Required fees:* $1689; $70 per credit hour. $5 per semester. Tuition and fees vary according to program. *Financial support:* In 2018–19, 3 research assistantships (averaging $13,478 per year) were awarded; teaching assistantships with tuition reimbursements, career-related internships or fieldwork, institutionally sponsored loans, health care benefits, and unspecified assistantships also available. Support available to part-time students. Financial award application deadline: 6/30; financial award applicants required to submit FAFSA. *Faculty research:* Technology's impact on the hospitality industry, hospitality accounting, and cost control, international tourism development, service quality. *Unit head:* Dr. Pat Moreo, Dean, 941-359-4327, E-mail: pmoreo@sar.usf.edu. *Application contact:* Brandon Avery, Director, Admissions, 941-359-4331, E-mail: bavery@sar.usf.edu.
Website: http://www.usfsm.edu/chtl/

The University of Tennessee, Graduate School, College of Education, Health and Human Sciences, Department of Consumer and Industry Services Management, Program in Hotel, Restaurant, and Tourism Management, Knoxville, TN 37996. Offers hospitality management (MS); tourism (MS). *Program availability:* Part-time. *Degree requirements:* For master's, thesis or alternative. *Entrance requirements:* For master's, GRE General Test, minimum GPA of 2.7. Additional exam requirements/recommendations for international students: Required—TOEFL. Electronic applications accepted.

University of the Pacific, College of the Pacific, Program in Food Studies, Stockton, CA 95211-0197. Offers MA.

Virginia International University, School of Business, Fairfax, VA 22030. Offers accounting (MBA, MS); entrepreneurship (MBA); executive management (Graduate Certificate); global logistics (MBA); health care management (MBA); hospitality and tourism management (MBA); human resources management (MBA); international business management (MBA); international finance (MBA); marketing management (MBA); mass media and public relations (MBA); project management (MBA, MS). *Program availability:* Part-time, online learning. *Entrance requirements:* For master's and Graduate Certificate, bachelor's degree. Additional exam requirements/recommendations for international students: Required—TOEFL (minimum score 550 paper-based; 80 iBT), IELTS (minimum score 6). Electronic applications accepted.

Travel and Tourism

Arizona State University at the Tempe campus, College of Public Programs, School of Community Resources and Development, Phoenix, AZ 85004-0685. Offers community resources and development (MS, PhD); nonprofit leadership and management (Graduate Certificate); nonprofit studies (MNpS); sustainable tourism (MAS). *Program availability:* Part-time, evening/weekend. Terminal master's awarded for partial completion of doctoral program. *Degree requirements:* For master's, thesis or alternative, interactive Program of Study (iPOS) submitted before completing 50 percent of required credit hours; for doctorate, comprehensive exam, thesis/dissertation, interactive Program of Study (iPOS) submitted before completing 50 percent of required credit hours. *Entrance requirements:* For master's and doctorate, GRE, minimum GPA of 3.0 or equivalent in last 2 years of work leading to bachelor's degree. Additional exam requirements/recommendations for international students: Required—TOEFL, IELTS, or PTE. Electronic applications accepted. *Expenses:* Contact institution.

Boston University, Metropolitan College, Department of Administrative Sciences, Boston, MA 02215. Offers applied business analytics (MS); economic development and tourism management (MSAS); enterprise risk management (MS); financial management (MS); global marketing management (MS); innovation and technology (MSAS); insurance management (MS); project management (MS); supply chain management (MS). *Accreditation:* AACSB. *Program availability:* Part-time, evening/weekend, 100% online, blended/hybrid learning. *Faculty:* 27 full-time (5 women), 39 part-time/adjunct (5 women). *Students:* 617 full-time (351 women), 574 part-time (290 women); includes 196 minority (47 Black or African American, non-Hispanic/Latino; 2 American Indian or Alaska Native, non-Hispanic/Latino; 75 Asian, non-Hispanic/Latino; 60 Hispanic/Latino; 12 Two or more races, non-Hispanic/Latino), 730 international. Average age 28. 2,259 applicants, 76% accepted, 594 enrolled. In 2018, 441 master's awarded. *Degree requirements:* For master's, thesis optional. *Entrance requirements:* For master's, 1 year of work experience, minimum GPA of 3.0. Additional exam requirements/recommendations for international students: Required—TOEFL (minimum score 84 iBT). *Application deadline:* For fall admission, 8/1 priority date for domestic students, 6/1 priority date for international students; for spring admission, 12/1 priority date for domestic students, 11/15 priority date for international students; for summer admission, 4/1 priority date for domestic students, 3/1 priority date for international students. Applications are processed on a rolling basis. Application fee: $85. Electronic applications accepted. *Expenses:* Contact institution. *Financial support:* In 2018–19, 15 students received support, including 16 research assistantships (averaging $8,400 per year), 30 teaching assistantships (averaging $3,400 per year); career-related internships or fieldwork, Federal Work-Study, and unspecified assistantships also available. Financial award applicants required to submit FAFSA. *Faculty research:* International business, innovative process. *Unit head:* Dr. John Sullivan, Chair, 617-353-3016, E-mail: adminsc@bu.edu. *Application contact:* Enrollment Services, 617-358-8162, E-mail: met@bu.edu.
Website: http://www.bu.edu/met/academic-community/departments/administrative-sciences/

California State University, Chico, Office of Graduate Studies, College of Communication and Education, Recreation, Hospitality and Parks Management Department, Chico, CA 95929-0722. Offers recreation, parks, and tourism (MS). *Program availability:* Part-time. *Faculty:* 1 full-time (0 women), 3 part-time/adjunct (all women). *Students:* 2 full-time (0 women), 10 part-time (6 women); includes 3 minority (1 American Indian or Alaska Native, non-Hispanic/Latino; 1 Asian, non-Hispanic/Latino; 1 Hispanic/Latino). 4 applicants, 100% accepted, 4 enrolled. In 2018, 1 master's awarded. *Degree requirements:* For master's, thesis or project. *Entrance requirements:* For master's, GRE General Test, 3 letters of recommendation, statement of purpose, resume. Additional exam requirements/recommendations for international students: Required—TOEFL (minimum score 550 paper-based; 80 iBT), IELTS (minimum score 6.5), PTE. Application fee: $55. Electronic applications accepted. *Expenses: Tuition, area resident:* Full-time $4622; part-time $3116 per unit. Tuition, state resident: full-time $4622; part-time $3116 per unit. Tuition, nonresident: full-time $10,634. *Required fees:* $2160; $1620 per year. Tuition and fees vary according to class time and program. *Financial support:* Fellowships, research assistantships, teaching assistantships, career-related internships or fieldwork, Federal Work-Study, scholarships/grants, traineeships, health care benefits, unspecified assistantships, and stipends available. Support available to part-time students. Financial award application deadline: 3/2; financial award applicants required to submit FAFSA. *Unit head:* Dr. Emilyn Sheffield, Chair, 530-898-6408, Fax: 530-898-6557, E-mail: recr@csuchico.edu. *Application contact:* Micah Lehner, Graduate Admissions Coordinator, 530-898-5416, Fax: 530-898-3342, E-mail: mlehner@csuchico.edu.
Website: https://www.csuchico.edu/rhpm/degrees-options/masters.shtml

California State University, East Bay, Office of Graduate Studies, College of Education and Allied Studies, Department of Hospitality, Recreation and Tourism, Hayward, CA 94542-3000. Offers recreation and tourism (MS). *Program availability:* Part-time, evening/weekend, online learning. *Degree requirements:* For master's, thesis optional. *Entrance requirements:* For master's, minimum GPA of 2.75; 2 years' related work experience; 3 letters of recommendation; resume; baccalaureate degree. Additional exam requirements/recommendations for international students: Required—TOEFL (minimum score 550 paper-based). Electronic applications accepted. *Faculty research:* Leisure, online vs. face-to-face (F2F) learning, risk management, leadership, tourism consumer behavior.

California State University, Fullerton, Graduate Studies, College of Communications, Department of Communications, Fullerton, CA 92831-3599. Offers communications in tourism and entertainment (MA); mass communications research and theory (MA); professional communications (MA). *Program availability:* Part-time. *Entrance requirements:* For master's, GRE General Test.

California State University, Northridge, Graduate Studies, College of Health and Human Development, Department of Recreation and Tourism Management, Northridge, CA 91330. Offers hospitality and tourism (MS); recreational sport management/campus recreation (MS). *Degree requirements:* For master's, thesis (for some programs). *Entrance requirements:* For master's, GRE (if cumulative undergraduate GPA less than 3.0). Additional exam requirements/recommendations for international students: Required—TOEFL.

Clemson University, Graduate School, College of Behavioral, Social and Health Sciences, Department of Parks, Recreation, and Tourism Management, Clemson, SC 29634-0735. Offers international parks and tourism (Certificate); parks, recreation and tourism management (MS, PhD), including recreational therapy (PhD); public administration (MPA, Certificate); recreational therapy (MS); youth development leadership (MS, Certificate). *Program availability:* Part-time, evening/weekend, 100% online. *Faculty:* 31 full-time (10 women), 3 part-time/adjunct (0 women). *Students:* 84 full-time (58 women), 227 part-time (140 women); includes 62 minority (45 Black or African American, non-Hispanic/Latino; 1 American Indian or Alaska Native, non-Hispanic/Latino; 1 Asian, non-Hispanic/Latino; 9 Hispanic/Latino; 6 Two or more races, non-Hispanic/Latino), 18 international. Average age 31. 275 applicants, 80% accepted, 135 enrolled. In 2018, 72 master's, 9 doctorates, 26 other advanced degrees awarded. *Degree requirements:* For master's, comprehensive exam (for some programs), thesis (for some programs); for doctorate, comprehensive exam, thesis/dissertation; for Certificate, portfolio. *Entrance requirements:* For master's and doctorate, GRE General Test, unofficial transcripts, letter of intent, letters of reference; for Certificate, letter of recommendation, unofficial transcripts, personal statement, resume. Additional exam requirements/recommendations for international students: Required—TOEFL (minimum score 80 paper-based; 80 iBT); Recommended—IELTS (minimum score 6.5), TSE (minimum score 54). *Application deadline:* For fall admission, 4/15 priority date for international students; for spring admission, 10/15 priority date for international students. Applications are processed on a rolling basis. Application fee: $80 ($90 for international students). Electronic applications accepted. *Expenses: Tuition, area resident:* Full-time $11,270; part-time $8688 per credit hour. Tuition, state resident: full-time $11,796. Tuition, nonresident: full-time $23,802; part-time $17,412 per credit hour. *International tuition:* $23,246 full-time. *Required fees:* $1196; $497 per semester. Tuition and fees vary according to course load, degree level, campus/location and program. *Financial support:* In 2018–19, 59 students received support, including 1 research assistantship with full and partial tuition reimbursement available (averaging $4,324 per year), 55 teaching assistantships with full and partial tuition reimbursements available (averaging $10,318 per year); career-related internships or fieldwork and unspecified assistantships also available. *Faculty research:* Land use, recreational therapy, sustainability, tourism, public administration. *Total annual research expenditures:* $532,593. *Unit head:* Dr. Fran McGuire, Interim Chair, 864-656-3036, E-mail: lefty@clemson.edu. *Application contact:* Dr. Jeff Hallo, Graduate Coordinator, 864-656-3237, E-mail: jhallo@clemson.edu.
Website: http://www.clemson.edu/hehd/departments/prtm/

Colorado State University, Warner College of Natural Resources, Department of Human Dimensions of Natural Resources, Fort Collins, CO 80523-1480. Offers human dimensions of natural resources (MS, PhD); tourism management (MTM). *Program availability:* Part-time, evening/weekend, 100% online. Terminal master's awarded for partial completion of doctoral program. *Degree requirements:* For master's, thesis (for some programs); for doctorate, comprehensive exam, thesis/dissertation. *Entrance requirements:* For master's, GRE General Test, minimum GPA of 3.0, 3 letters of recommendation, statement of interest, official transcripts; for doctorate, GRE General Test, minimum GPA of 3.0, 3 letters of recommendation, copy of master's thesis or professional paper, statement of interest, official transcripts. Electronic applications accepted. *Expenses:* Contact institution. *Faculty research:* Biocultural approaches to conservation; conservation governance; dimensions of wildlife management; marine conservation; park recreation and management.

The George Washington University, School of Business, Department of Tourism and Hospitality Management, Washington, DC 20052. Offers destination management (Professional Certificate); event and meeting management (MTA); event management (Professional Certificate); hospitality management (MTA); individualized studies (MTA); sport management (MTA); sustainable tourism destination management (MTA); tourism and hospitality management (MBA). *Program availability:* Part-time, online learning. *Students:* 79 full-time (46 women), 35 part-time (28 women); includes 37 minority (21

Black or African American, non-Hispanic/Latino; 5 Asian, non-Hispanic/Latino; 9 Hispanic/Latino; 2 Two or more races, non-Hispanic/Latino), 40 international. Average age 28. 161 applicants, 76% accepted, 47 enrolled. In 2018, 50 master's awarded. *Degree requirements:* For master's, comprehensive exam, thesis. *Entrance requirements:* For master's, GRE General Test. Additional exam requirements/recommendations for international students: Required—TOEFL. *Application deadline:* For fall admission, 4/1 priority date for domestic students; for spring admission, 10/1 for domestic students. Applications are processed on a rolling basis. Application fee: $75. *Financial support:* In 2018–19, 32 students received support. Fellowships, teaching assistantships, career-related internships or fieldwork, Federal Work-Study, institutionally sponsored loans, and tuition waivers (partial) available. Financial award application deadline: 4/1. *Faculty research:* Tourism policy, tourism impact forecasting, geotourism. *Unit head:* Prof. Lisa Delpy Neirotti, Faculty Director, 202-994-6623, E-mail: delpy@gwu.edu. *Application contact:* Christopher Storer, Executive Director, Graduate Admissions, 202-994-1212, E-mail: gwmba@gwu.edu.
Website: http://business.gwu.edu/tourism/

IGlobal University, Graduate Programs, Vienna, VA 22182. Offers accounting (MBA); data management and analytics (MSIT); entrepreneurship (MBA); finance (MBA); global business management (MBA); health care management (MBA); hospitality and tourism management (MBA); human resources management (MBA); information technology (MBA); information technology systems and management (MSIT); leadership and management (MBA); project management (MBA); public service and administration (MBA); software design and management (MSIT).

Indiana University Bloomington, School of Public Health, Department of Recreation, Park, and Tourism Studies, Bloomington, IN 47405-7000. Offers leisure behavior (PhD); outdoor recreation (MS); park and public lands management (MS); recreation administration (MS); recreational sports administration (MS); recreational therapy (MS); tourism management (MS). Terminal master's awarded for partial completion of doctoral program. *Degree requirements:* For master's, thesis optional; for doctorate, comprehensive exam, thesis/dissertation. *Entrance requirements:* For master's, GRE General Test, minimum GPA of 2.8; for doctorate, GRE General Test, minimum GPA of 3.0 (undergraduate), 3.5 (graduate). Additional exam requirements/recommendations for international students: Required—TOEFL (minimum score 550 paper-based; 80 iBT). Electronic applications accepted. *Faculty research:* Leisure counseling, gerontology, special populations, planning and development.

Johnson & Wales University, Graduate Studies, MS Program in Global Tourism and Sustainable Economic Development, Providence, RI 02903-3703. Offers MS. *Program availability:* Online learning.

Kent State University, College of Education, Health and Human Services, School of Foundations, Leadership and Administration, Program in Hospitality and Tourism Management, Kent, OH 44242-0001. Offers MS. *Program availability:* Part-time. *Faculty:* 7 full-time (4 women), 5 part-time/adjunct (1 woman). *Students:* 12 full-time (7 women), 16 part-time (10 women); includes 5 minority (1 Black or African American, non-Hispanic/Latino; 3 Asian, non-Hispanic/Latino; 1 Hispanic/Latino), 11 international. 35 applicants, 43% accepted. In 2018, 6 master's awarded. *Degree requirements:* For master's, thesis optional. *Entrance requirements:* For master's, minimum GPA of 3.0, 3 letters of recommendation, resume, goals statement. Additional exam requirements/recommendations for international students: Required—TOEFL (minimum score 550 paper-based; 80 iBT). *Application deadline:* Applications are processed on a rolling basis. Application fee: $45 ($60 for international students). Electronic applications accepted. *Expenses:* Tuition, state resident: full-time $11,766; part-time $536 per credit. Tuition, nonresident: full-time $21,952; part-time $999 per credit. *International tuition:* $21,952 full-time. Tuition and fees vary according to course load. *Financial support:* In 2018–19, 4 students received support, including 8 research assistantships with full tuition reimbursements available (averaging $8,500 per year); teaching assistantships, Federal Work-Study, scholarships/grants, and unspecified assistantships also available. Financial award application deadline: 2/1; financial award applicants required to submit FAFSA. *Faculty research:* Training human service workers, health care services for older adults, early adolescent development, care-giving arrangements with aging families, peace and war. *Unit head:* Aviad Israeli, Coordinator, 330-672-2075, E-mail: aisraeli@kent.edu. *Application contact:* Cheryl Slusarczyk, Academic Program Director, Office of Graduate Student Services, 330-672-2576, Fax: 330-672-9162, E-mail: ogs@kent.edu.

Lasell College, Graduate and Professional Studies in Management, Newton, MA 02466-2709. Offers business administration (MBA); elder care management (MSM); hospitality and event management (MSM); human resources management (MSM, Graduate Certificate); management (MSM, Graduate Certificate); marketing (MS, Graduate Certificate); project management (MSM, Graduate Certificate). *Accreditation:* ACBSP. *Program availability:* Part-time, evening/weekend, 100% online, blended/hybrid learning. *Faculty:* 7 full-time (4 women), 14 part-time/adjunct (9 women). *Students:* 37 full-time (28 women), 76 part-time (48 women); includes 22 minority (12 Black or African American, non-Hispanic/Latino; 1 Asian, non-Hispanic/Latino; 9 Hispanic/Latino), 20 international. Average age 32. 68 applicants, 54% accepted, 20 enrolled. In 2018, 62 master's, 1 other advanced degree awarded. *Degree requirements:* For master's, minimum GPA of 3.0; internship or research paper (for MSM). *Entrance requirements:* For master's, one-page personal statement, 2 letters of recommendation, resume, bachelor's degree transcript; proof of microeconomics and statistics (for MBA); for Graduate Certificate, bachelor's degree transcript, 2 letters of recommendation, 1-page personal statement, resume. Additional exam requirements/recommendations for international students: Required—TOEFL (minimum score 550 paper-based, 79 iBT) or IELTS (minimum score 6). *Application deadline:* For fall admission, 8/31 priority date for domestic students, 6/30 priority date for international students; for spring admission, 12/31 priority date for domestic students, 10/31 priority date for international students. Applications are processed on a rolling basis. Electronic applications accepted. *Expenses: Tuition:* Part-time $600 per credit. *Required fees:* $40 per course. *Financial support:* Federal Work-Study, scholarships/grants, and tuition discounts available. Support available to part-time students. Financial award application deadline: 8/31; financial award applicants required to submit FAFSA. *Unit head:* Eric Turner, Vice President of Graduate and Professional Studies, 617-243-2071, Fax: 617-243-2450, E-mail: gradinfo@lasell.edu. *Application contact:* Adrienne Franciosi, Assistant Vice President of Graduate and Professional Studies, 617-243-2214, Fax: 617-243-2450, E-mail: gradinfo@lasell.edu.
Website: http://www.lasell.edu/academics/graduate-and-professional-studies/programs-of-study/master-of-science-in-management.html

Lasell College, Graduate and Professional Studies in Sport Management, Newton, MA 02466-2709. Offers athletic administration (MS); parks and recreation (MS); sport leadership (MS, Graduate Certificate); sport tourism and hospitality (MS). *Program availability:* Part-time, evening/weekend, online only, 100% online. *Faculty:* 4 full-time (1 woman), 4 part-time/adjunct (2 women). *Students:* 15 full-time (7 women), 32 part-time (11 women); includes 17 minority (12 Black or African American, non-Hispanic/Latino; 4 Hispanic/Latino; 1 Two or more races, non-Hispanic/Latino). Average age 29. 36 applicants, 39% accepted, 11 enrolled. In 2018, 20 master's awarded. *Degree requirements:* For master's, minimum GPA of 3.0; internship or thesis. *Entrance*

requirements: For master's, one-page personal statement, 2 letters of recommendation, resume, bachelor's degree transcript; for Graduate Certificate, bachelor's degree transcript, 2 letters of recommendation, 1-page personal statement, resume. Additional exam requirements/recommendations for international students: Required—TOEFL (minimum score 550 paper-based, 79 iBT) or IELTS (minimum score 6). *Application deadline:* For fall admission, 8/31 priority date for domestic students, 6/30 priority date for international students; for spring admission, 12/31 priority date for domestic students, 10/31 priority date for international students. Applications are processed on a rolling basis. Electronic applications accepted. *Expenses: Tuition:* Part-time $600 per credit. *Required fees:* $40 per course. *Financial support:* Federal Work-Study, scholarships/grants, and tuition discounts available. Support available to part-time students. Financial award application deadline: 8/31; financial award applicants required to submit FAFSA. *Faculty research:* How do fans attribute team failure; investigating cross-cultural difference in attribution; sense of ownership as a key predictor of fan loyalty; fans' normative beliefs about sponsorship and sponsors; investigation of new attitudinal variables in sponsorship. *Unit head:* Eric Turner, Vice President of Graduate and Professional Studies, 617-243-2071, Fax: 617-243-2450, E-mail: gradinfo@lasell.edu. *Application contact:* Adrienne Franciosi, Assistant Vice President of Graduate and Professional Studies, 617-243-2214, Fax: 617-243-2450, E-mail: gradinfo@lasell.edu. Website: http://www.lasell.edu/academics/graduate-and-professional-studies/programs-of-study/master-of-science-in-sport-management.html

New Mexico State University, College of Agricultural, Consumer and Environmental Sciences, Department of Family and Consumer Sciences, Las Cruces, NM 88003-8001. Offers clothing, textiles, and merchandising (MS); family and child science (MS); family and consumer science education (MS); family and consumer sciences (MS); food science and technology (MS); hotel, restaurant, and tourism management (MS); human nutrition and dietetic sciences (MS). *Program availability:* Part-time. *Faculty:* 11 full-time (8 women), 1 (woman) part-time/adjunct. *Students:* 35 full-time (27 women), 7 part-time (6 women); includes 28 minority (2 Black or African American, non-Hispanic/Latino; 25 Hispanic/Latino; 1 Two or more races, non-Hispanic/Latino), 1 international. Average age 30. 21 applicants, 76% accepted, 14 enrolled. In 2018, 19 master's awarded. *Degree requirements:* For master's, comprehensive exam (for some programs), thesis (for some programs), oral exam. *Entrance requirements:* For master's, GRE, 3 letters of reference from faculty members or employers, resume, letter of interest. Additional exam requirements/recommendations for international students: Required—TOEFL (minimum score 550 paper-based; 79 iBT), IELTS (minimum score 6.5). *Application deadline:* For fall admission, 2/1 priority date for domestic and international students; for spring admission, 10/1 for domestic and international students. Applications are processed on a rolling basis. Application fee: $40 ($50 for international students). Electronic applications accepted. *Expenses: Tuition, area resident:* Full-time $4216.70; part-time $252.70 per credit hour. Tuition, state resident: full-time $4216.70; part-time $252.70 per credit hour. Tuition, nonresident: full-time $12,769; part-time $881.10 per credit hour. *International tuition:* $12,769.30 full-time. *Required fees:* $878.40; $48.80 per credit hour. Full-time tuition and fees vary according to course load and reciprocity agreements. *Financial support:* In 2018–19, 27 students received support, including 6 research assistantships (averaging $11,417 per year), 8 teaching assistantships (averaging $11,913 per year); career-related internships or fieldwork, Federal Work-Study, scholarships/grants, traineeships, health care benefits, and unspecified assistantships also available. Support available to part-time students. Financial award application deadline: 3/1. *Faculty research:* Food product analysis, childhood obesity, dietary decision-making, military families, equine assisted psychotherapy. *Total annual research expenditures:* $432,486. *Application contact:* Dr. Kourtney Vaillancourt, Graduate Program Contact, 575-646-3383, Fax: 575-646-1889, E-mail: kvaillan@nmsu.edu.
Website: http://aces.nmsu.edu/academics/fcs

New York University, School of Professional Studies, Jonathan M. Tisch Center of Hospitality, Program in Tourism Management, New York, NY 10012-1019. Offers MS. *Program availability:* Part-time, evening/weekend. *Degree requirements:* For master's, thesis. *Entrance requirements:* For master's, GRE or GMAT (only upon request), bachelor's degree, resume with relevant professional work, internship or volunteer experience, two letters of recommendation, statement of purpose. Additional exam requirements/recommendations for international students: Required—TOEFL (minimum score 600 paper-based; 100 iBT), IELTS (minimum score 7). Electronic applications accepted. *Expenses:* Contact institution.

North Carolina State University, Graduate School, College of Natural Resources, Department of Parks, Recreation and Tourism Management, Raleigh, NC 27695. Offers natural resource management (MPRTM, MS); park and recreation management (MPRTM, MS); parks, recreation and tourism management (PhD); recreational sport management (MPRTM, MS); spatial information science (MPRTM, MS); tourism policy and development (MPRTM, MS). *Degree requirements:* For master's, thesis (for some programs); for doctorate, thesis/dissertation. *Entrance requirements:* For master's and doctorate, GRE General Test. Additional exam requirements/recommendations for international students: Required—TOEFL. Electronic applications accepted. *Faculty research:* Tourism policy and development, spatial information systems, natural resource management, recreational sports management, park and recreation management.

Old Dominion University, Darden College of Education, Program in Park, Recreation and Tourism Studies, Norfolk, VA 23529. Offers park, recreation and tourism (MS). *Program availability:* Part-time, evening/weekend, blended/hybrid learning. *Degree requirements:* For master's, comprehensive exam, thesis or alternative, research project. *Entrance requirements:* For master's, GRE, minimum GPA of 2.8 overall, 3.0 in major. Additional exam requirements/recommendations for international students: Required—TOEFL (minimum score 500 paper-based). Electronic applications accepted. *Faculty research:* Outdoor recreation and education, recreation programming, sustainable tourism, sense of community and urban parks.

Penn State University Park, Graduate School, College of Health and Human Development, Department of Recreation, Park and Tourism Management, University Park, PA 16802. Offers MS, PhD.

Pontificia Universidad Catolica Madre y Maestra, Graduate School, Faculty of Social and Administrative Sciences, Santiago, Dominican Republic. Offers business administration (MBA), including business development, finance, international business, management skills (M Mgmt, MBA), marketing, operations, strategic cost management, strategy, tourist destination planning and management; law (LL M), including civil law, corporate business law, criminal law, international relations, real estate law; management (M Mgmt), including higher financial management, insurance program administration, management skills (M Mgmt, MBA); psychology (MA), including clinical child and adolescent psychology, forensic psychology; strategic human resources (EMBA).

Purdue University, Graduate School, College of Health and Human Sciences, School of Hospitality and Tourism Management, West Lafayette, IN 47907. Offers MS, PhD. *Program availability:* Online learning. *Faculty:* 14 full-time (6 women). *Students:* 35 full-time (25 women), 64 part-time (46 women); includes 26 minority (11 Black or African American, non-Hispanic/Latino; 8 Asian, non-Hispanic/Latino; 4 Hispanic/Latino; 3 Two or more races, non-Hispanic/Latino), 39 international. Average age 31. 111 applicants, 64% accepted, 35 enrolled. In 2018, 13 master's, 5 doctorates awarded. *Degree requirements:* For master's, thesis; for doctorate, thesis/dissertation. *Entrance requirements:* For master's, GMAT (minimum score of 550) or GRE General Test (minimum combined verbal and quantitative score of 290 new scoring, minimum of 145 each section, or 1000 with 500 each section, old scoring), minimum GPA of 3.0; for doctorate, GMAT (minimum score of 550) or GRE General Test (minimum combined verbal and quantitative score of 290 new scoring, minimum of 145 each section, or 1000 with 500 each section, old scoring), minimum undergraduate GPA of 3.0; master's degree with minimum GPA of 3.0 or equivalent. Additional exam requirements/recommendations for international students: Required—TOEFL (minimum score 77 iBT), TWE. *Application deadline:* For fall admission, 3/5 priority date for domestic and international students; for spring admission, 9/20 for domestic and international students. Applications are processed on a rolling basis. Application fee: $60 ($75 for international students). Electronic applications accepted. *Financial support:* Research assistantships, teaching assistantships, and career-related internships or fieldwork available. Support available to part-time students. Financial award applicants required to submit FAFSA. *Faculty research:* Human resources, marketing, hotel and restaurant operations, food product and equipment development, tourism development. *Unit head:* Dr. Richard F. Ghiselli, Head, 765-494-2636, E-mail: ghiselli@purdue.edu. *Application contact:* Ayrielle K. Espinosa, Graduate Contact, 765-494-9811, E-mail: camposm@purdue.edu.
Website: http://www.purdue.edu/hhs/htm/

Rochester Institute of Technology, Graduate Enrollment Services, College of Applied Science and Technology, School of International Hospitality and Service Innovation, MS Program in Hospitality and Tourism Management, Rochester, NY 14623-5603. Offers MS. *Program availability:* Part-time, evening/weekend. *Students:* 13 full-time (9 women), 2 part-time (both women); includes 4 minority (2 Black or African American, non-Hispanic/Latino; 1 Asian, non-Hispanic/Latino; 1 Two or more races, non-Hispanic/Latino), 7 international. Average age 29. 20 applicants, 65% accepted, 5 enrolled. In 2018, 6 master's awarded. *Degree requirements:* For master's, comprehensive exam (for some programs), thesis or alternative, Thesis, Project, or Comprehensive Exam options. *Entrance requirements:* For master's, minimum GPA of 3.0 (recommended). Additional exam requirements/recommendations for international students: Required—TOEFL (minimum score 570 paper-based; 80 iBT), IELTS (minimum score 6.5), PTE (minimum score 61). *Application deadline:* Applications are processed on a rolling basis. Application fee: $65. Electronic applications accepted. *Financial support:* In 2018–19, 10 students received support. Teaching assistantships with partial tuition reimbursements available, career-related internships or fieldwork, scholarships/grants, and unspecified assistantships available. Support available to part-time students. Financial award applicants required to submit FAFSA. *Faculty research:* Service innovation and technology integration, innovative food product development, hospitality employees' occupational health and wellness, tourist behaviors, destination management. *Unit head:* Matthew Cornwell, Assistant Director of Student Services and Outreach, 585-475-6916, E-mail: mcornwell@saunders.rit.edu. *Application contact:* Diane Ellison, Senior Associate Vice President, Graduate Enrollment Services, 585-475-2229, Fax: 585-475-7164, E-mail: gradinfo@rit.edu.
Website: https://www.rit.edu/study/hospitality-and-tourism-management-ms

Rochester Institute of Technology, Graduate Enrollment Services, College of Applied Science and Technology, School of International Hospitality and Service Innovation, MS Program in Service Leadership and Innovation, Rochester, NY 14623-5603. Offers MS. *Program availability:* Part-time, evening/weekend, 100% online. *Students:* 1 full-time, 38 part-time (24 women); includes 3 minority (1 Black or African American, non-Hispanic/Latino; 1 Asian, non-Hispanic/Latino; 1 Hispanic/Latino), 1 international. Average age 30. 6 applicants, 67% accepted, 2 enrolled. In 2018, 4 master's awarded. *Degree requirements:* For master's, thesis or alternative, Project, Comprehensive Exam, and Thesis options available. *Entrance requirements:* For master's, Have a minimum cumulative GPA of 3.0 (or equivalent), or evidence of relevant professional performance. Additional exam requirements/recommendations for international students: Required—TOEFL (minimum score 570 paper-based; 88 iBT), IELTS (minimum score 6.5), PTE (minimum score 62). *Application deadline:* Applications are processed on a rolling basis. Application fee: $65. Electronic applications accepted. *Financial support:* In 2018–19, 4 students received support. Teaching assistantships with partial tuition reimbursements available, career-related internships or fieldwork, scholarships/grants, and unspecified assistantships available. Support available to part-time students. Financial award applicants required to submit FAFSA. *Faculty research:* Leadership development, customer service/patient satisfaction, program evaluation, knowledge construction, diversity, individual creativity, healthcare applications. *Unit head:* Dr. Linda Underhill, Department Chair, 585-475-7359, E-mail: lmuism@rit.edu. *Application contact:* Diane Ellison, Senior Associate Vice President, Graduate Enrollment Services, 585-475-2229, Fax: 585-475-7164, E-mail: gradinfo@rit.edu.
Website: https://www.rit.edu/study/service-leadership-and-innovation-ms

Royal Roads University, Graduate Studies, Tourism and Hospitality Management Program, Victoria, BC V9B 5Y2, Canada. Offers tourism management (MA, Graduate Certificate). *Expenses: Tuition, area resident:* Full-time $27,000 Canadian dollars. Tuition, state resident: full-time $27,000 Canadian dollars. Tuition, nonresident: full-time $33,000 Canadian dollars. *Required fees:* $662 Canadian dollars.

San Diego State University, Graduate and Research Affairs, College of Professional Studies and Fine Arts, L. Robert Payne School of Hospitality and Tourism Management, San Diego, CA 92182. Offers hospitality and tourism (MA); meeting and event management (MA).

San Francisco State University, Division of Graduate Studies, College of Business, Program in Business Administration, San Francisco, CA 94132-1722. Offers decision sciences/operations research (MBA); ethics and compliance (MBA); finance (MBA); global business and innovation (MBA); healthcare administration (MBA); hospitality and tourism management (MBA); information systems (MBA); leadership (MBA); marketing (MBA); nonprofit and social enterprise leadership (MBA); sustainable business (MBA). *Accreditation:* AACSB. *Program availability:* Part-time, evening/weekend. *Degree requirements:* For master's, thesis, essay test. *Entrance requirements:* For master's, GMAT, minimum GPA of 2.7 in last 60 units. Additional exam requirements/recommendations for international students: Required—TOEFL (minimum score 550 paper-based).

San Francisco State University, Division of Graduate Studies, College of Health and Social Sciences, Department of Recreation, Parks, and Tourism, San Francisco, CA 94132-1722. Offers MS. *Program availability:* Part-time. *Application deadline:* Applications are processed on a rolling basis. *Financial support:* Career-related internships or fieldwork available. *Unit head:* Dr. Erik Rosegard, Chair, 415-338-7529, Fax: 415-338-0543, E-mail: rosegard@sfsu.edu. *Application contact:* Dr. Jackson Wilson, Graduate Coordinator, 415-338-1487, Fax: 415-338-0543, E-mail: wilsonj@sfsu.edu.
Website: http://recdept.sfsu.edu/graduate

San Ignacio University, Graduate Programs, Doral, FL 33178. Offers business administration (MBA), including human resources management, international business,

marketing management; education (M Ed), including early childhood education, educational leadership, special education; hospitality management (MA), including gastronomy and restaurant management, tourism management.

Savannah College of Art and Design, Program in Themed Entertainment Design, Savannah, GA 31402-3146. Offers MFA. *Program availability:* Part-time. *Faculty:* 1 full-time (0 women). *Students:* 36 full-time (27 women), 5 part-time (2 women); includes 6 minority (1 Asian, non-Hispanic/Latino; 5 Hispanic/Latino), 10 international. Average age 26. 33 applicants, 64% accepted, 14 enrolled. In 2018, 8 master's awarded. *Degree requirements:* For master's, thesis. *Entrance requirements:* For master's, GRE (recommended), portfolio (submitted in digital format), audition or writing submission, resume, statement of purpose, two letters of recommendation. Additional exam requirements/recommendations for international students: Recommended—TOEFL (minimum score 550 paper-based; 85 iBT), IELTS (minimum score 6.5). *Application deadline:* For fall admission, 4/1 for domestic and international students. Applications are processed on a rolling basis. Application fee: $40. Electronic applications accepted. *Expenses:* Tuition: Full-time $37,530; part-time $4170 per course. One-time fee: $500. *Financial support:* Career-related internships or fieldwork, Federal Work-Study, and scholarships/grants available. Financial award application deadline: 4/1; financial award applicants required to submit FAFSA. *Unit head:* Andra Reeve-Raab, Dean, school of entertainment arts. *Application contact:* Jenny Jaquillard, Executive Director of Admission Recruitment, 912-525-5100, E-mail: admission@scad.edu. Website: http://www.scad.edu/academics/programs/themed-entertainment-design

Schiller International University, MBA Programs, Florida, Program in International Hotel and Tourism Management, Largo, FL 33771. Offers MBA. *Degree requirements:* For master's, thesis optional. *Entrance requirements:* Additional exam requirements/recommendations for international students: Required—TOEFL (minimum score 550 paper-based).

Strayer University, Graduate Studies, Washington, DC 20005-2603. Offers accounting (MS); acquisition (MBA); business administration (MBA); communications technology (MS); educational management (M Ed); finance (MBA); health services administration (MHSA); hospitality and tourism management (MBA); human resource management (MBA); information systems (MS), including computer security management, decision support system management, enterprise resource management, network management, software engineering management, systems development management; management (MBA); management information systems (MS); marketing (MBA); professional accounting (MS), including accounting information systems, controllership, taxation; public administration (MPA); supply chain management (MBA); technology in education (M Ed). Programs also offered at campus locations in Birmingham, AL; Chamblee, GA; Cobb County, GA; Morrow, GA; White Marsh, MD; Charleston, SC; Columbia, SC; Greensboro, NC; Greenville, SC; Lexington, KY; Louisville, KY; Nashville, TN; North Raleigh, NC; Washington, DC. *Accreditation:* ACBSP. *Program availability:* Part-time, evening/weekend, online learning. *Degree requirements:* For master's, thesis. *Entrance requirements:* For master's, GMAT, GRE General Test, bachelor's degree from an accredited college or university, minimum undergraduate GPA of 2.75. Electronic applications accepted.

Syracuse University, David B, Falk College of Sport and Human Dynamics, MS Program in Sport Venue and Event Management, Syracuse, NY 13244. Offers MS. *Entrance requirements:* For master's, GRE, undergraduate transcripts, three recommendations, resume, personal statement. Additional exam requirements/recommendations for international students: Required—TOEFL (minimum score 100 iBT). *Application deadline:* For fall admission, 2/15 for domestic students; for spring admission, 11/1 priority date for domestic and international students. Application fee: $75. Electronic applications accepted. *Financial support:* Fellowships, research assistantships, teaching assistantships, and career-related internships or fieldwork available. Financial award application deadline: 1/1; financial award applicants required to submit FAFSA. *Faculty research:* Managing and operating sport and entertainment facilities and events, sociology of sport, psychological and social issues in sport. *Unit head:* Jeff Pauline, Graduate Program Director, 315-443-0364, Fax: 315-443-9811, E-mail: jspaulin@syr.edu. *Application contact:* Felicia Otero, Director of Admissions, 315-443-5555, E-mail: falk@syr.edu. Website: https://falk.syr.edu/sport-management/academic-programs/#mssvem

Temple University, School of Sport, Tourism and Hospitality Management, Philadelphia, PA 19122-6096. Offers sport business (MS); tourism and hospitality management (MTHM); tourism and sport (PhD); travel and tourism (MS). *Program availability:* Part-time, evening/weekend, online learning. *Faculty:* 24 full-time (9 women), 11 part-time/adjunct (4 women). *Students:* 153 full-time (70 women), 56 part-time (25 women); includes 48 minority (28 Black or African American, non-Hispanic/Latino; 5 Asian, non-Hispanic/Latino; 10 Hispanic/Latino; 5 Two or more races, non-Hispanic/Latino), 33 international. 215 applicants, 76% accepted, 107 enrolled. In 2018, 71 master's awarded. *Entrance requirements:* For master's, GMAT or GRE, 500-word statement of goals, 2 letters of recommendation, resume. Additional exam requirements/recommendations for international students: Required—TOEFL, IELTS, PTE, one of three is required. *Application deadline:* For fall admission, 12/15 priority date for domestic students, 3/1 for international students; for spring admission, 11/1 for domestic students, 8/1 for international students. Applications are processed on a rolling basis. Application fee: $60. Electronic applications accepted. *Expenses:* Contact institution. *Financial support:* Scholarships/grants, health care benefits, and unspecified assistantships available. Financial award application deadline: 3/1; financial award applicants required to submit FAFSA. *Unit head:* Ronald C. Anderson, Dean, 215-204-8701, E-mail: sthm@temple.edu. *Application contact:* Michelle Rosar, Assistant Director of Graduate Enrollment, 215-204-3315, E-mail: michelle.rosar@temple.edu. Website: http://sthm.temple.edu/

Tropical Agriculture Research and Higher Education Center, Graduate School, Turrialba, Costa Rica. Offers agribusiness management (MS); agroforestry systems (PhD); development practices (MS); ecological agriculture (MS); environmental socioeconomics (MS); forestry in tropical and subtropical zones (PhD); integrated watershed management (MS); international sustainable tourism (MS); management and conservation of tropical rainforests and biodiversity (MS); tropical agriculture (PhD); tropical agroforestry (MS). *Entrance requirements:* For master's, GRE, 2 years of related professional experience, letters of recommendation; for doctorate, GRE, 4 letters of recommendation, letter of support from employing organization, master's degree in agronomy, biological sciences, forestry, natural resources or related field. Additional exam requirements/recommendations for international students: Required—TOEFL (minimum score 550 paper-based). Electronic applications accepted. *Faculty research:* Biodiversity in fragmented landscapes, ecosystem management, integrated pest management, environmental livestock production, biotechnology carbon balances in diverse land uses.

Université du Québec à Trois-Rivières, Graduate Programs, Program in Leisure, Culture and Tourism Sciences, Trois-Rivières, QC G9A 5H7, Canada. Offers MA, DESS. *Program availability:* Part-time. *Degree requirements:* For master's, thesis optional. *Entrance requirements:* For master's, appropriate bachelor's degree, proficiency in French.

University of Central Florida, Rosen College of Hospitality Management, Orlando, FL 32816. Offers destination marketing and management (Certificate); event management (Certificate); hospitality and tourism management (MS); hospitality management (PhD). *Program availability:* Part-time. *Faculty:* 71 full-time (27 women), 26 part-time/adjunct (10 women). *Students:* 82 full-time (53 women), 168 part-time (113 women); includes 70 minority (30 Black or African American, non-Hispanic/Latino; 1 American Indian or Alaska Native, non-Hispanic/Latino; 8 Asian, non-Hispanic/Latino; 27 Hispanic/Latino; 4 Two or more races, non-Hispanic/Latino), 40 international. Average age 30. 226 applicants, 64% accepted, 92 enrolled. In 2018, 58 master's, 2 doctorates, 44 other advanced degrees awarded. *Degree requirements:* For master's, thesis or alternative; for doctorate, thesis/dissertation, candidacy exam. *Entrance requirements:* For master's and doctorate, GMAT or GRE, letters of recommendation, goal statement, resume. Additional exam requirements/recommendations for international students: Required—TOEFL. *Application deadline:* For fall admission, 7/15 for domestic students; for spring admission, 12/1 for domestic students. Application fee: $30. Electronic applications accepted. *Financial support:* In 2018–19, 36 students received support, including 17 fellowships with partial tuition reimbursements available (averaging $14,760 per year), 1 research assistantship with partial tuition reimbursement available (averaging $9,882 per year), 26 teaching assistantships with partial tuition reimbursements available (averaging $11,242 per year); health care benefits also available. Financial award application deadline: 3/1; financial award applicants required to submit FAFSA. *Unit head:* Dr. Abraham C. Pizam, Dean, 407-903-8010, E-mail: abraham.pizam@ucf.edu. *Application contact:* Associate Director, Graduate Admissions, 407-823-2766, Fax: 407-823-6442, E-mail: gradadmissions@ucf.edu. Website: http://www.hospitality.ucf.edu/

University of Florida, Graduate School, College of Health and Human Performance, Department of Tourism, Recreation and Sport Management, Gainesville, FL 32611. Offers health and human performance (PhD), including historic preservation (MS, PhD), recreation, parks and tourism (MS, PhD), sport management; recreation, parks and tourism (MS), including historic preservation (MS, PhD), natural resource recreation, recreation, parks and tourism (MS, PhD), therapeutic recreation, tourism, tropical conservation and development; sport management (MS), including historic preservation (MS, PhD), tropical conservation and development; JD/MS; MSM/MS. *Degree requirements:* For master's, comprehensive exam (for some programs), thesis (for some programs); for doctorate, comprehensive exam, thesis/dissertation. *Entrance requirements:* For master's and doctorate, GRE General Test, minimum GPA of 3.0. Additional exam requirements/recommendations for international students: Required—TOEFL (minimum score 550 paper-based; 80 iBT), IELTS (minimum score 6). Electronic applications accepted. *Faculty research:* Hospitality, natural resource management, sport management, tourism.

University of Hawaii at Manoa, Office of Graduate Education, School of Travel Industry Management, Honolulu, HI 96822. Offers MS. *Program availability:* Part-time. *Degree requirements:* For master's, thesis optional. *Entrance requirements:* For master's, GRE General Test, minimum GPA of 3.0. Additional exam requirements/recommendations for international students: Required—TOEFL (minimum score 560 paper-based; 83 iBT), IELTS (minimum score 5). Electronic applications accepted. *Faculty research:* Travel information technology, tourism development and policy, transportation management and policy, hospitality management, sustainable tourism development.

University of Idaho, College of Graduate Studies, College of Education, Health and Human Sciences, Department of Movement Sciences, Moscow, ID 83844-2401. Offers athletic training (MSAT, DAT); exercise science and health (MS); physical education teacher education (M Ed, MS); recreation, sport, and tourism management (MS). *Faculty:* 19. *Students:* 89 full-time, 9 part-time. Average age 26. In 2018, 43 master's awarded. *Degree requirements:* For doctorate, thesis/dissertation. *Entrance requirements:* For master's and doctorate, minimum GPA of 3.0. Additional exam requirements/recommendations for international students: Required—TOEFL. *Application deadline:* For fall admission, 8/1 for domestic students; for spring admission, 12/15 for domestic students. Applications are processed on a rolling basis. Application fee: $60. Electronic applications accepted. *Expenses:* Tuition, state resident: full-time $7266.44; part-time $474.50 per credit hour. Tuition, nonresident: full-time $24,902; part-time $1453.50 per credit hour. *Required fees:* $2085.56; $45.50 per credit hour. *Financial support:* Research assistantships and teaching assistantships available. Financial award applicants required to submit FAFSA. *Unit head:* Dr. Philip W. Scruggs, Chair, 208-885-7921, E-mail: movementsciences@uidaho.edu. *Application contact:* Dr. Philip W. Scruggs, Chair, 208-885-7921, E-mail: movementsciences@uidaho.edu. Website: https://www.uidaho.edu/ed/mvsc

University of Massachusetts Amherst, Graduate School, Isenberg School of Management, Program in Management, Amherst, MA 01003. Offers accounting (PhD); business administration (MBA); entrepreneurship (MBA); finance (MBA, PhD); healthcare administration (MBA); hospitality and tourism management (PhD); management science (PhD); marketing (MBA, PhD); organization studies (PhD); sport management (PhD); strategic management (PhD); MBA/MS. *Accreditation:* AACSB. *Program availability:* Part-time, evening/weekend, online learning. Terminal master's awarded for partial completion of doctoral program. *Degree requirements:* For doctorate, comprehensive exam, thesis/dissertation. *Entrance requirements:* For master's and doctorate, GMAT or GRE General Test. Additional exam requirements/recommendations for international students: Required—TOEFL (minimum score 550 paper-based; 80 iBT), IELTS (minimum score 6.5). Electronic applications accepted.

University of Minnesota, Twin Cities Campus, Graduate School, College of Food, Agricultural and Natural Resource Sciences, Program in Natural Resources Science and Management, St. Paul, MN 55108. Offers assessment, monitoring, and geospatial analysis (MS, PhD); economics, policy, management, and society (MS, PhD); forest hydrology and watershed management (MS, PhD); forest products (MS, PhD); forests: biology, ecology, conservation, and management (MS, PhD); natural resources science and management (MS, PhD); paper science and engineering (MS, PhD); recreation resources, tourism, and environmental education (MS, PhD). *Program availability:* Part-time. Terminal master's awarded for partial completion of doctoral program. *Degree requirements:* For master's, comprehensive exam, thesis (for some programs); for doctorate, comprehensive exam, thesis/dissertation. *Entrance requirements:* For master's and doctorate, GRE General Test. Additional exam requirements/recommendations for international students: Required—TOEFL (minimum score 550 paper-based; 79 iBT); Recommended—IELTS (minimum score 6.5). Electronic applications accepted. *Faculty research:* Forest hydrology, biology, ecology, conservation, and management; recreation resources and environmental education; wildlife ecology; economics, policy, and society; geographic information systems (GIS); forest products and paper science.

University of New Orleans, Graduate School, College of Business Administration, Lester E. Kabacoff School of Hotel, Restaurant, and Tourism Administration, New Orleans, LA 70148. Offers hospitality and tourism management (MS). *Entrance requirements:* Additional exam requirements/recommendations for international students: Required—TOEFL (minimum score 550 paper-based; 79 iBT). Electronic applications accepted.

Travel and Tourism

University of North Texas, Toulouse Graduate School, Denton, TX 76203-5459. Offers accounting (MS); applied anthropology (MA, MS); applied behavior analysis (Certificate); applied geography (MA); applied technology and performance improvement (M Ed, MS); art education (MA); art history (MA); arts leadership (Certificate); audiology (Au D); behavior analysis (MS); behavioral science (PhD); biochemistry and molecular biology (MS); biology (MA, MS); biomedical engineering (MS); business analysis (MS); chemistry (MS); clinical health psychology (PhD); communication studies (MA, MS); computer engineering (MS); computer science (MS); counseling (M Ed, MS), including clinical mental health counseling (MS), college and university counseling, elementary school counseling, secondary school counseling; creative writing (MA); criminal justice (MS); curriculum and instruction (M Ed); decision sciences (MBA); design (MA, MFA), including fashion design (MFA), innovation studies, interior design (MFA); early childhood studies (MS); economics (MS); educational leadership (M Ed, Ed D); educational psychology (MS, PhD), including family studies (MS), gifted and talented (MS), human development (MS), learning and cognition (MS), research, measurement and evaluation (MS); electrical engineering (MS); emergency management (MPA); engineering technology (MS); English (MA); English as a second language (MA); environmental science (MS); finance (MBA, MS); financial management (MPA); French (MA); health services management (MBA); higher education (M Ed, Ed D); history (MA, MS); hospitality management (MS); human resources management (MPA); information science (MS); information systems (PhD); information technologies (MBA); interdisciplinary studies (MA, MS); international studies (MA); international sustainable tourism (MS); jazz studies (MM); journalism (MA, MJ, Graduate Certificate), including interactive and virtual digital communication (Graduate Certificate), narrative journalism (Graduate Certificate), public relations (Graduate Certificate); kinesiology (MS); linguistics (MA); local government management (MPA); logistics (PhD); logistics and supply chain management (MBA); long-term care, senior housing, and aging services (MA); management (PhD); marketing (MBA); mathematics (MA, MS); mechanical and energy engineering (MS, PhD); music (MA), including ethnomusicology, music theory, musicology, performance; music composition (PhD); music education (MM Ed, PhD); nonprofit management (MPA); operations and supply chain management (MBA); performance (MM, DMA); philosophy (MA); political science (MA); professional and technical communication (MA); radio, television and film (MA, MFA); rehabilitation counseling (Certificate); sociology (MA); Spanish (MA); special education (M Ed); speech-language pathology (MA); strategic management (MBA); studio art (MFA); teaching (M Ed); MBA/MS. *Program availability:* Part-time, evening/weekend, online learning. Terminal master's awarded for partial completion of doctoral program. *Degree requirements:* For master's, variable foreign language requirement, comprehensive exam (for some programs), thesis (for some programs); for doctorate, variable foreign language requirement, comprehensive exam (for some programs), thesis/dissertation; for other advanced degree, variable foreign language requirement, comprehensive exam (for some programs). *Entrance requirements:* For master's and doctorate, GRE, GMAT. Additional exam requirements/recommendations for international students: Required—TOEFL (minimum score 550 paper-based; 79 iBT). Electronic applications accepted.

University of South Africa, College of Economic and Management Sciences, Pretoria, South Africa. Offers accounting (D Admin, D Com); accounting science (DA); auditing (D Admin, D Com); business administration (M Tech); business economics (D Admin); business leadership (DBL); business management (D Admin, D Com); economic management analysis (M Tech); economics (D Admin, D Com, PhD); human resource development (M Tech); industrial psychology (D Admin, D Com, PhD); logistics (D Com); marketing (M Tech); public administration (D Admin, D Com, DPA, PhD); public management (M Tech); quantitative management (D Admin, D Com); real estate (M Tech); statistics (D Admin, PhD); tourism management (D Admin, D Com); transport economics (D Admin, D Com).

University of South Carolina, The Graduate School, College of Hospitality, Retail, and Sport Management, School of Hotel, Restaurant and Tourism Management, Columbia, SC 29208. Offers MIHTM. *Entrance requirements:* For master's, GMAT or GRE General Test, minimum GPA of 3.0, 2 letters of recommendation. Electronic applications accepted. *Faculty research:* Corporate strategy and management practices, sustainable tourism, club management, tourism technology, revenue management.

University of South Florida, Patel College of Global Sustainability, Tampa, FL 33620-9951. Offers energy, global, water and sustainable tourism (Graduate Certificate); global sustainability (MA), including building sustainable enterprise, climate change and sustainability, coastal sustainability, entrepreneurship, food sustainability and security, sustainability policy, sustainable energy, sustainable tourism, water. *Faculty:* 1 full-time (0 women). *Students:* 64 full-time (33 women), 92 part-time (57 women); includes 32 minority (8 Black or African American, non-Hispanic/Latino; 3 Asian, non-Hispanic/Latino; 15 Hispanic/Latino; 6 Two or more races, non-Hispanic/Latino), 50 international. Average age 29. 119 applicants, 75% accepted, 60 enrolled. In 2018, 91 master's awarded. *Degree requirements:* For master's, comprehensive exam (for some programs), thesis or alternative, internship. *Entrance requirements:* For master's, GPA of at least 3.25 or greater; alternatively a GPA of at least 3.00 along with a GRE Verbal score of 153 (61 percentile) or higher, Quantitative of 153 (51 percentile) or higher and Analytical Writing of 3.5 or higher, all taken within 5 years of application; at least 2 letters of recommendation from professors or supervisors. Additional exam requirements/recommendations for international students: Required—TOEFL (minimum score 550 paper-based; 79 iBT). *Application deadline:* For fall admission, 6/1 for domestic students, 5/1 for international students; for spring admission, 10/15 for domestic students, 9/15 for international students. Electronic applications accepted. *Expenses:* Tuition, state resident: full-time $6350. Tuition, nonresident: full-time $19,048. *International tuition:* $19,048 full-time. *Required fees:* $2079. *Financial support:* In 2018–19, 35 students received support. *Faculty research:* Global sustainability, integrated resource management, systems thinking, green communities, entrepreneurship, ecotourism. *Total annual research expenditures:* $174,608. *Unit head:* Dr. Govindan Parayil, Dean, 813-974-9694, E-mail: gparayil@usf.edu. *Application contact:* Dr. Govindan Parayil, Dean, 813-974-9694, E-mail: gparayil@usf.edu. Website: http://psgs.usf.edu/

The University of Tennessee, Graduate School, College of Education, Health and Human Sciences, Department of Consumer and Industry Services Management, Program in Hotel, Restaurant, and Tourism Management, Knoxville, TN 37996. Offers hospitality management (MS); tourism (MS). *Program availability:* Part-time. *Degree requirements:* For master's, thesis or alternative. *Entrance requirements:* For master's, GRE General Test, minimum GPA of 2.7. Additional exam requirements/recommendations for international students: Required—TOEFL. Electronic applications accepted.

Western Illinois University, School of Graduate Studies, College of Education and Human Services, Department of Recreation, Park, and Tourism Administration, Macomb, IL 61455-1390. Offers MS. *Program availability:* Part-time. *Students:* 24 full-time (16 women), 7 part-time (5 women); includes 6 minority (all Black or African American, non-Hispanic/Latino), 3 international. Average age 26. 28 applicants, 93% accepted, 21 enrolled. In 2018, 17 master's awarded. *Entrance requirements:* Additional exam requirements/recommendations for international students: Required—TOEFL (minimum score 550 paper-based; 80 iBT). *Application deadline:* Applications are processed on a rolling basis. Application fee: $30. Electronic applications accepted. *Financial support:* Unspecified assistantships available. Financial award applicants required to submit FAFSA. *Unit head:* Dr. Michael Lukkarinene, Interim Chairperson, 309-298-1967. *Application contact:* Dr. Mark Mossman, Director of Graduate Studies, 309-298-1806, Fax: 309-298-2345, E-mail: grad-office@wiu.edu. Website: http://www.wiu.edu/rpta

West Virginia University, Davis College of Agriculture, Forestry and Consumer Sciences, Morgantown, WV 26506. Offers agricultural and extension education (MS, PhD); agriculture and resource management (MS); agriculture, natural resources and design (M Agr); agronomy (MS); animal and food science (PhD); animal physiology (MS); applied and environmental microbiology (MS); design and merchandising (MS); entomology (MS); forest resource science (PhD); forestry (MSF); genetics and developmental biology (MS, PhD); horticulture (MS); human and community development (PhD); landscape architecture (MLA); natural resource economics (PhD); nutritional and food science (MS); plant and soil science (PhD); plant pathology (MS); recreation, parks and tourism resources (MS); reproductive physiology (MS, PhD); wildlife and fisheries resources (PhD). *Accreditation:* ASLA. *Program availability:* Part-time. *Students:* 188 full-time (86 women), 47 part-time (30 women); includes 22 minority (5 Black or African American, non-Hispanic/Latino; 5 Asian, non-Hispanic/Latino; 8 Hispanic/Latino; 4 Two or more races, non-Hispanic/Latino), 60 international. In 2018, 56 master's, 14 doctorates awarded. *Degree requirements:* For master's, thesis; for doctorate, thesis/dissertation. *Entrance requirements:* Additional exam requirements/recommendations for international students: Required—TOEFL (minimum score 550 paper-based). *Application deadline:* For fall admission, 6/1 priority date for domestic students, 6/1 for international students; for spring admission, 1/5 for domestic and international students. Applications are processed on a rolling basis. Application fee: $60. Electronic applications accepted. *Financial support:* Fellowships, research assistantships, teaching assistantships, career-related internships or fieldwork, Federal Work-Study, institutionally sponsored loans, tuition waivers (full and partial), and unspecified assistantships available. Financial award application deadline: 2/1; financial award applicants required to submit FAFSA. *Faculty research:* Reproductive physiology, soil and water quality, human nutrition, aquaculture, wildlife management. *Unit head:* Dr. Ken Blemings, Interim Dean, 304-293-2395, Fax: 304-293-3740, E-mail: ken.blemings@mail.wvu.edu. *Application contact:* Dr. J. Todd Petty, Associate Dean, 304-293-2278, Fax: 304-293-3740, E-mail: jtpetty@mail.wvu.edu. Website: https://www.davis.wvu.edu

Section 8
Human Resources

This section contains a directory of institutions offering graduate work in human resources, followed by in-depth entries submitted by institutions that chose to prepare detailed program descriptions. Additional information about programs listed in the directory but not augmented by an in-depth entry may be obtained by writing directly to the dean of a graduate school or chair of a department at the address given in the directory.

For programs offering related work, see also in this book *Business Administration and Management, Advertising and Public Relations, Hospitality Management, Industrial and Manufacturing Management,* and *Organizational Behavior.* In another guide in this series:

CONTENTS

Program Directories

Human Resources Development

Abilene Christian University, College of Graduate and Professional Studies, Program in Organizational Development, Addison, TX 79699. Offers MS. *Program availability:* Part-time, evening/weekend, online only, 100% online. *Students:* 39 full-time (29 women), 12 part-time (10 women); includes 26 minority (16 Black or African American, non-Hispanic/Latino; 2 Asian, non-Hispanic/Latino; 7 Hispanic/Latino; 1 Two or more races, non-Hispanic/Latino). 15 applicants, 93% accepted, 13 enrolled. In 2018, 31 master's awarded. *Degree requirements:* For master's, thesis. *Entrance requirements:* Additional exam requirements/recommendations for international students: Required—TOEFL (minimum score 80 iBT), IELTS (minimum score 6), PTE. *Application deadline:* For fall admission, 10/7 for domestic students; for winter admission, 12/20 for domestic students; for spring admission, 2/24 for domestic students; for summer admission, 4/20 for domestic students. Applications are processed on a rolling basis. Application fee: $50. Electronic applications accepted. *Expenses:* $775 per hour. *Financial support:* In 2018–19, 17 students received support. Scholarships/grants available. Support available to part-time students. Financial award application deadline: 7/1; financial award applicants required to submit FAFSA. *Unit head:* Dr. Kipi Fleming, Program Director, 214-305-9451, E-mail: klw07b@acu.edu. *Application contact:* Graduate Advisor, 855-219-7300, E-mail: onlineadmissions@acu.edu.
Website: http://www.acu.edu/online/academics/organizational-development.html

Amberton University, Graduate School, Program in Human Relations and Business, Garland, TX 75041-5595. Offers MS. *Program availability:* Part-time, evening/weekend. *Entrance requirements:* For master's, minimum GPA of 3.0.

Amberton University, Graduate School, Program in Human Resources Training and Development, Garland, TX 75041-5595. Offers MS.

Antioch University Los Angeles, Program in Leadership, Management and Business, Culver City, CA 90230. Offers human resource development (MA); leadership (MA); organizational development (MA). *Program availability:* Part-time, evening/weekend. *Entrance requirements:* For master's, interview. Additional exam requirements/recommendations for international students: Required—TOEFL. *Faculty research:* Systems thinking and chaos theory, technology and organizational structure, nonprofit management, power and empowerment.

Barry University, School of Education, Program in Human Resource Development and Administration, Miami Shores, FL 33161-6695. Offers MS. *Program availability:* Part-time, evening/weekend. *Degree requirements:* For master's, comprehensive exam, practicum. *Entrance requirements:* For master's, GRE General Test or MAT, minimum GPA of 3.0. Electronic applications accepted.

Barry University, School of Education, Program in Leadership and Education, Miami Shores, FL 33161-6695. Offers educational technology (PhD); exceptional student education (PhD); higher education administration (PhD); human resource development (PhD); leadership (PhD). *Program availability:* Part-time, evening/weekend. *Degree requirements:* For doctorate, thesis/dissertation. *Entrance requirements:* For doctorate, GRE General Test, minimum GPA of 3.25. Electronic applications accepted.

Bowie State University, Graduate Programs, Program in Human Resource Development, Bowie, MD 20715-9465. Offers MA. *Program availability:* Part-time, evening/weekend. *Degree requirements:* For master's, comprehensive exam, thesis optional, research paper. *Entrance requirements:* For master's, minimum GPA of 2.5. Electronic applications accepted.

California State University, Sacramento, College of Business Administration, Sacramento, CA 95819. Offers accountancy (MS); business administration (IMBA, MBA); human resources (MBA); urban land development (MBA). *Accreditation:* AACSB. *Program availability:* Part-time, evening/weekend, 100% online, blended/hybrid learning. *Degree requirements:* For master's, comprehensive exam, project, thesis, or writing proficiency exam. *Entrance requirements:* For master's, GMAT. Additional exam requirements/recommendations for international students: Required—TOEFL (minimum score 550 paper-based; 80 iBT). Electronic applications accepted. *Expenses:* Contact institution.

Claremont Graduate University, Graduate Programs, School of Social Science, Policy and Evaluation, Department of Psychology, Claremont, CA 91711-6160. Offers advanced study in evaluation (Certificate); cognitive psychology (MA, PhD); developmental psychology (MA, PhD); evaluation and applied research methods (MA, PhD); health behavior research and evaluation (MA, PhD); human resource development and evaluation (MA); industrial/organizational psychology (MA, PhD); organizational behavior (MA, PhD); organizational psychology (MA, PhD); social psychology (MA, PhD); MBA/PhD. *Program availability:* Part-time. Terminal master's awarded for partial completion of doctoral program. *Entrance requirements:* For master's and doctorate, GRE General Test. Additional exam requirements/recommendations for international students: Required—TOEFL (minimum score 75 iBT). Electronic applications accepted. *Faculty research:* Social intervention, diversity in organizations, eyewitness memory, aging and cognition, drug policy.

Clemson University, Graduate School, College of Education, Department of Educational and Organizational Leadership Development, Clemson, SC 29634. Offers administration and supervision (M Ed, Ed S); athletic leadership (MS, Certificate); education systems improvement science (Ed D); educational leadership (PhD), including higher education, P-12; human resource development (MHRD), including human resource development; leadership (Certificate); student affairs (M Ed). *Program availability:* Part-time, evening/weekend, 100% online. *Faculty:* 17 full-time (11 women). *Students:* 105 full-time (64 women), 265 part-time (170 women); includes 76 minority (61 Black or African American, non-Hispanic/Latino; 1 American Indian or Alaska Native, non-Hispanic/Latino; 3 Asian, non-Hispanic/Latino; 5 Hispanic/Latino; 6 Two or more races, non-Hispanic/Latino). Average age 32. 204 applicants, 83% accepted, 123 enrolled. In 2018, 93 master's, 17 doctorates, 28 other advanced degrees awarded. *Degree requirements:* For master's, thesis (for some programs); for doctorate, comprehensive exam, thesis/dissertation. *Entrance requirements:* For master's, doctorate, and other advanced degree, GRE General Test, unofficial transcripts, letters of recommendation. Additional exam requirements/recommendations for international students: Required—TOEFL (minimum score 80 paper-based; 80 iBT); Recommended—IELTS (minimum score 6.5), TSE (minimum score 54). *Application deadline:* For fall admission, 4/15 priority date for international students; for spring admission, 10/15 priority date for international students. Applications are processed on a rolling basis. Application fee: $80 ($90 for international students). Electronic applications accepted. *Expenses:* $5198 per semester full-time resident, $10123 per semester full-time non-resident, $556 per credit hour part-time resident, $1109 per credit hour part-time non-resident, online $770 per credit hour, $4938 doctoral programs resident, $10405 doctoral programs non-resident, $1144 full-time graduate assistant, other fees may apply per session. *Financial support:* In 2018–19, 30 students received support,

including 8 fellowships with full and partial tuition reimbursements available (averaging $4,525 per year), 3 research assistantships with full and partial tuition reimbursements available (averaging $7,500 per year); career-related internships or fieldwork and unspecified assistantships also available. *Faculty research:* Leadership, ethics, policy development, performance improvement. *Total annual research expenditures:* $79,638. *Unit head:* Dr. Roy Jones, Interim Department Chair, 864-656-7915, E-mail: royj@clemson.edu. *Application contact:* Alison Search, Student Services Program Coordinator, 864-250-8880, E-mail: alisonp@clemson.edu.
Website: http://www.clemson.edu/education/departments/educational-organizational-leadership-development/index.html

The College of New Rochelle, Graduate School, Division of Human Services, Program in Career Development, New Rochelle, NY 10805-2308. Offers MS, Advanced Certificate. *Program availability:* Part-time. *Degree requirements:* For master's and Advanced Certificate, internship. *Entrance requirements:* For master's, interview, minimum GPA of 3.0, writing sample.

Drexel University, Goodwin College of Professional Studies, School of Education, Philadelphia, PA 19104-2875. Offers applied behavior analysis (MS); creativity and innovation (MS); education improvement and transformation (MS); educational administration (MS); educational leadership and management (Ed D); educational leadership development and learning technologies (PhD); global and international education (MS); higher education (MS); human resources development (MS); learning technologies (MS); mathematics, learning and teaching (MS); special education (MS); teaching, learning and curriculum (MS). *Program availability:* Part-time, evening/weekend, online learning. *Degree requirements:* For doctorate, thesis/dissertation. *Entrance requirements:* For doctorate, GRE or GMAT. Additional exam requirements/recommendations for international students: Required—TOEFL, IELTS. Electronic applications accepted. Application fee is waived when completed online. *Expenses:* Contact institution. *Faculty research:* Leadership development, mathematics education, literacy, autism, educational technology.

Florida International University, College of Arts, Sciences, and Education, Department of Leadership and Professional Studies, Miami, FL 33199. Offers adult education and human resource development (MS, Ed D); counseling (MS), including rehabilitation counseling, school counseling; counselor education (MS), including clinical mental health counseling; educational administration and supervision (Ed D); educational leadership (MS, Certificate, Ed S); higher education (Ed D); higher education administration (MS); international and comparative education (MS); recreation and sport management (MS), including recreation and sport management, recreational therapy; school psychology (Ed S); urban education (MS), including instruction in urban settings, learning technologies, multicultural/bilingual, multicultural/TESOL, urban education. *Program availability:* Part-time, evening/weekend. *Faculty:* 64 full-time (43 women), 104 part-time/adjunct (76 women). *Students:* 258 full-time (196 women), 217 part-time (155 women); includes 387 minority (118 Black or African American, non-Hispanic/Latino; 8 Asian, non-Hispanic/Latino; 249 Hispanic/Latino; 12 Two or more races, non-Hispanic/Latino), 11 international. Average age 31. 345 applicants, 57% accepted, 126 enrolled. In 2018, 172 master's, 11 doctorates awarded. *Entrance requirements:* For master's, minimum GPA of 3.0; for doctorate and other advanced degree, GRE General Test. Additional exam requirements/recommendations for international students: Required—TOEFL (minimum score 550 paper-based; 80 iBT), IELTS (minimum score 6.3). *Application deadline:* For fall admission, 6/1 priority date for domestic students, 4/1 for international students; for winter admission, 10/1 priority date for domestic students, 9/1 for international students; for spring admission, 3/1 priority date for domestic students, 2/1 for international students. Applications are processed on a rolling basis. Application fee: $30. Electronic applications accepted. *Financial support:* Fellowships, research assistantships, teaching assistantships, Federal Work-Study, and tuition waivers (full and partial) available. Support available to part-time students. Financial award applicants required to submit FAFSA. *Unit head:* Dr. Benjamin Baez, Chair, 305-348-3214, Fax: 305-348-1515, E-mail: benjamin.baez@fiu.edu. *Application contact:* Nanett Rojas, Manager, Admissions Operations, 305-348-7464, Fax: 305-348-7441, E-mail: gradadm@fiu.edu.
Website: http://education.fiu.edu

The George Washington University, Graduate School of Education and Human Development, Department of Human and Organizational Learning, Program in Human Resource Development, Washington, DC 20052. Offers MA. *Program availability:* Part-time, evening/weekend. *Students:* 1 (woman) part-time. Average age 50. *Entrance requirements:* For master's, GRE, MAT, or GMAT, two letters of recommendation, statement of purpose, official transcripts, resume. Additional exam requirements/recommendations for international students: Required—TOEFL or IELTS. Electronic applications accepted. *Financial support:* Fellowships available. *Unit head:* Kristin Furio, Program Manager, 202-994-1040, E-mail: kfurio@gwu.edu. *Application contact:* Sarah Lang, Director of Graduate Admissions, 202-994-1447, Fax: 202-994-7207, E-mail: slang@gwu.edu.
Website: http://gsehd.gwu.edu/

The George Washington University, Graduate School of Education and Human Development, Department of Human and Organizational Learning, Program in Leadership Development, Washington, DC 20052. Offers Graduate Certificate. *Students:* 17 part-time (13 women); includes 5 minority (1 Black or African American, non-Hispanic/Latino; 4 Asian, non-Hispanic/Latino), 1 international. Average age 40. 7 applicants, 71% accepted, 5 enrolled. In 2018, 14 Graduate Certificates awarded. *Entrance requirements:* For degree, two letters of recommendation, resume, statement of purpose. Electronic applications accepted. *Unit head:* Michael Feuer, Dean, 202-994-6161, E-mail: mjfeuer@gwu.edu. *Application contact:* Sarah Lang, Director of Graduate Admissions, 202-994-1447, Fax: 202-994-7207, E-mail: slang@gwu.edu.
Website: http://gsehd.gwu.edu/academics/programs/certificates/leadership-development/overview

The George Washington University, Graduate School of Education and Human Development, Department of Human and Organizational Learning, Programs in Human and Organizational Learning, Washington, DC 20052. Offers Ed D, Ed S. *Students:* 31 full-time (22 women), 99 part-time (60 women); includes 56 minority (35 Black or African American, non-Hispanic/Latino; 4 Asian, non-Hispanic/Latino; 10 Hispanic/Latino; 7 Two or more races, non-Hispanic/Latino), 6 international. Average age 46. 46 applicants, 72% accepted, 21 enrolled. In 2018, 36 doctorates, 1 other advanced degree awarded. *Degree requirements:* For doctorate, comprehensive exam, thesis/dissertation; for Ed S, comprehensive exam. *Entrance requirements:* For doctorate, GRE General Test or MAT, interview, minimum GPA of 3.3; for Ed S, GRE General Test or MAT, minimum GPA of 3.3. *Application deadline:* For fall admission, 1/15 priority date for domestic students; for spring admission, 10/1 for domestic students. Applications are processed

on a rolling basis. Application fee: $75. *Financial support:* Fellowships, research assistantships, teaching assistantships, career-related internships or fieldwork, Federal Work-Study, and tuition waivers (partial) available. Financial award application deadline: 1/15; financial award applicants required to submit FAFSA. *Faculty research:* Organizational learning, program evaluation. *Unit head:* David Schwandt, Program Manager, 571-553-3770, E-mail: schwandt@gwu.edu. *Application contact:* Sarah Lang, Director of Graduate Admissions, 202-994-1447, E-mail: slang@gwu.edu.
Website: http://gsehd.gwu.edu/

Grantham University, Mark Skousen School of Business, Lenexa, KS 66219. Offers business administration (MBA); business intelligence (MS); human resources (Certificate); information management (MBA); performance improvement (MS); project management (MBA, Certificate). *Program availability:* Part-time, evening/weekend, online only, 100% online. *Students:* 556 full-time (238 women), 301 part-time (122 women); includes 369 minority (268 Black or African American, non-Hispanic/Latino; 5 American Indian or Alaska Native, non-Hispanic/Latino; 16 Asian, non-Hispanic/Latino; 50 Hispanic/Latino; 4 Native Hawaiian or other Pacific Islander, non-Hispanic/Latino; 26 Two or more races, non-Hispanic/Latino), 1 international. Average age 40. 206 applicants, 90% accepted, 159 enrolled. In 2018, 284 master's, 16 other advanced degrees awarded. *Degree requirements:* For master's, comprehensive exam (for some programs), PMP Prep Exams throughout the term (for MBA in project management); for Certificate, comprehensive exam (for some programs), PMP Prep Exam (for project management). *Entrance requirements:* For master's, baccalaureate or master's degree with minimum cumulative GPA of 2.5 from institution accredited by agency recognized by ED or foreign equivalent; official transcripts showing proof of degree. Additional exam requirements/recommendations for international students: Required—TOEFL (minimum score 530 paper-based; 71 iBT), IELTS (minimum score 6.5), PTE (minimum score 50). *Application deadline:* Applications are processed on a rolling basis. Application fee: $0. Electronic applications accepted. *Expenses: Tuition:* Full-time $4200; part-time $350 per credit hour. *Required fees:* $50; $50 per credit hour. *Financial support:* Scholarships/grants available. Financial award applicants required to submit FAFSA. *Faculty research:* How chronic diseases contribute to the rising costs of healthcare, marketing for entrepreneurs, managers' hiring practices of workers with disability, organizational structures, organizational change, online pedagogy, impact of instructor video tips in the online classroom, decision-making techniques. *Unit head:* Dr. David Marker, Dean of the Mark Skousen School of Business, 913-309-4747, Fax: 844-260-6287, E-mail: dmarker@grantham.edu. *Application contact:* Lauren Cook, Director of Admissions, 800-955-2527 Ext. 803, Fax: 877-304-4467, E-mail: admissions@grantham.edu.
Website: https://www.grantham.edu/school-of-business/

HEC Montreal, School of Business Administration, Graduate Diploma Programs in Administration, Montréal, QC H3T 2A7, Canada. Offers business administration (Graduate Diploma); business analysis - information technology (Graduate Diploma); e-business (Graduate Diploma); entrepreneurship (Graduate Diploma); financial professions (Graduate Diploma); human resources (Graduate Diploma); management (Graduate Diploma); management and sustainable development (Graduate Diploma); management of cultural organizations (Graduate Diploma); marketing communication (Graduate Diploma); organizational development (Graduate Diploma); professional accounting (Graduate Diploma); supply chain management (Graduate Diploma); taxation (Graduate Diploma). All courses are given in French. *Students:* 412 full-time (242 women), 885 part-time (552 women). 834 applicants, 65% accepted, 351 enrolled. In 2018, 611 Graduate Diplomas awarded. *Entrance requirements:* For degree, bachelor's degree. Application fee: $91 Canadian dollars ($191 Canadian dollars for international students). Electronic applications accepted. *Expenses: Tuition, area resident:* Full-time $3052.80 Canadian dollars; part-time $84.80 Canadian dollars per credit. Tuition, state resident: full-time $3816 Canadian dollars; part-time $264.67 Canadian dollars per credit. Tuition, nonresident: full-time $11,910 Canadian dollars. *International tuition:* $20,905.20 Canadian dollars full-time. *Required fees:* $1805.34 Canadian dollars; $43.62 Canadian dollars per credit. $71.78 Canadian dollars per term. Tuition and fees vary according to degree level and program. *Financial support:* Research assistantships, teaching assistantships, and scholarships/grants available. Financial award application deadline: 9/2. *Faculty research:* Art management, business policy, entrepreneurship, new technologies, transportation. *Unit head:* Renaud Lachance, Director, 514-340-6428, E-mail: renaud.lachance@hec.ca. *Application contact:* Anny Caron, Administrative Director, 514-340-6000, Fax: 514-340-6411, E-mail: aide@hec.ca.
Website: http://www.hec.ca/programmes/dess/index.html

Illinois Institute of Technology, Graduate College, Lewis College of Human Sciences, Department of Psychology, Chicago, IL 60616. Offers clinical psychology (PhD); industrial and organizational psychology (PhD); personnel and human resource development (MS); rehabilitation and mental health counseling (MS); rehabilitation counseling education (PhD). *Accreditation:* APA (one or more programs are accredited); CORE. *Program availability:* Part-time, evening/weekend. Terminal master's awarded for partial completion of doctoral program. *Degree requirements:* For master's, thesis (for some programs); for doctorate, comprehensive exam, thesis/dissertation, minimum of 107 credit hours, 1-year full-time internship. *Entrance requirements:* For master's, GRE General Test (minimum score 298 Quantitative and Verbal, 3.0 Analytical Writing), minimum GPA of 3.0; 3 letters of recommendation; bachelor's degree from accredited institution (for personnel and human resource development); for doctorate, GRE General Test (minimum score 298 Quantitative and Verbal, 3.0 Analytical Writing), bachelor's or master's degree from accredited institution, recommendations. Additional exam requirements/recommendations for international students: Required—TOEFL (minimum score 550 paper-based; 80 iBT). Electronic applications accepted. *Faculty research:* Clinical psychology, rehabilitation and mental health counseling, industrial organizational psychology.

Indiana State University, College of Graduate and Professional Studies, College of Technology, Department of Human Resource Development and Performance Technologies, Terre Haute, IN 47809. Offers career and technical education (MS); human resource development (MS).

Indiana Tech, Program in Business Administration, Fort Wayne, IN 46803-1297. Offers accounting (MBA); health care management (MBA); human resources (MBA); management (MBA); marketing (MBA). *Program availability:* Part-time, evening/weekend, online learning. *Entrance requirements:* For master's, GMAT, bachelor's degree from regionally-accredited university; minimum undergraduate GPA of 2.5; 2 years of significant work experience; 3 letters of recommendation. Electronic applications accepted.

Indiana University of Pennsylvania, School of Graduate Studies and Research, College of Education and Communications, Department of Adult and Community Education, Program in Business/Workforce Development, Indiana, PA 15705. Offers M Ed. *Program availability:* Part-time. *Faculty:* 2 full-time (both women). *Students:* 3 full-time (1 woman), 3 part-time (1 woman). Average age 37. 4 applicants, 75% accepted, 3 enrolled. In 2018, 4 master's awarded. *Degree requirements:* For master's, thesis optional. *Entrance requirements:* For master's, GMAT or GRE. Additional exam requirements/recommendations for international students: Required—TOEFL (minimum score 540 paper-based). *Application deadline:* Applications are processed on a rolling basis. Application fee: $50. Electronic applications accepted. *Expenses:* Tuition, state resident: full-time $12,384; part-time $516 per credit hour. Tuition, nonresident: full-time $18,576; part-time $774 per credit hour. *Required fees:* $4454; $186 per credit hour. $65 per semester. Tuition and fees vary according to program and reciprocity agreements. *Financial support:* In 2018–19, 1 research assistantship with tuition reimbursement (averaging $5,000 per year) was awarded; career-related internships or fieldwork and Federal Work-Study also available. Support available to part-time students. Financial award application deadline: 4/15; financial award applicants required to submit FAFSA. *Unit head:* Prof. Jacqueline McGinty, Coordinator, 724-357-2470, E-mail: jacqueline.mcginty@iup.edu. *Application contact:* Prof. Jacqueline McGinty, Coordinator, 724-357-2470, E-mail: jacqueline.mcginty@iup.edu.
Website: http://www.iup.edu/ace/grad/default.aspx

Inter American University of Puerto Rico, Metropolitan Campus, Graduate Programs, Program in Human Resources, San Juan, PR 00919-1293. Offers MBA. *Degree requirements:* For master's, comprehensive exam. *Entrance requirements:* For master's, GRE or EXADEP, interview. Electronic applications accepted.

Inter American University of Puerto Rico, San Germán Campus, Graduate Studies Center, Program in Business Administration, San Germán, PR 00683-5008. Offers accounting (MBA); finance (MBA); general business administration (MBA); human resources (MBA, PhD); industrial relations (MBA); information systems (MBA); international and interregional business (PhD); management (MBA); marketing (MBA). *Program availability:* Part-time, evening/weekend. *Degree requirements:* For master's, comprehensive exam. *Entrance requirements:* For master's, GRE General Test or EXADEP, minimum GPA of 3.0. *Expenses: Tuition:* Full-time $212; part-time $212 per credit. *Required fees:* $366 per semester. One-time fee: $31. Tuition and fees vary according to degree level and program.

Iowa State University of Science and Technology, Department of Educational Leadership and Policy Studies, Ames, IA 50011. Offers counselor education (M Ed, MS); educational administration (M Ed, MS); educational leadership (PhD); higher education (M Ed, MS); organizational learning and human resource development (M Ed, MS); research and evaluation (MS); student affairs (MS). *Degree requirements:* For master's, thesis or alternative; for doctorate, thesis/dissertation. *Entrance requirements:* For master's and doctorate, GRE General Test. Additional exam requirements/recommendations for international students: Required—TOEFL (minimum score 560 paper-based; 83 iBT), IELTS (minimum score 6.5). Electronic applications accepted.

La Salle University, School of Business, Program in Human Capital Development, Philadelphia, PA 19141-1199. Offers MS, Certificate. *Program availability:* Part-time, evening/weekend, online only, 100% online. *Degree requirements:* For master's, capstone project. *Entrance requirements:* For master's and Certificate, professional resume; 2 letters of recommendation; 500-word essay stating interest in program and goals; baccalaureate degree. Additional exam requirements/recommendations for international students: Required—TOEFL. Electronic applications accepted. Application fee is waived when completed online. *Expenses:* Contact institution.

Lawrence Technological University, College of Arts and Sciences, Southfield, MI 48075-1058. Offers bioinformatics (Graduate Certificate); computer science (MS), including data science, big data, and data mining, intelligent systems; educational technology (MA), including robotics; instructional design, communication, and presentation (Graduate Certificate); integrated science (MA); science education (MA); technical and professional communication (MS, Graduate Certificate); writing for the digital age (Graduate Certificate). *Program availability:* Part-time, evening/weekend. *Degree requirements:* For master's, thesis (for some programs). *Entrance requirements:* Additional exam requirements/recommendations for international students: Required—TOEFL (minimum score 550 paper-based; 79 iBT), IELTS (minimum score 6.5). Electronic applications accepted. *Faculty research:* Computer analysis of music, machine learning of literature and lyrics, customer sentiments and response analysis through social media, peta-scale computing in astronomical databases, early detection of diseases with pattern recognition.

Lincoln Memorial University, Carter and Moyers School of Education, Harrogate, TN 37752-1901. Offers administration and supervision (M Ed, Ed S); counseling and guidance (M Ed); curriculum and instruction (M Ed, Ed D, Ed S); English (M Ed); executive leadership (Ed D); higher education administration (Ed D); human resource development (Ed D); leadership and administration (Ed D). *Program availability:* Part-time, evening/weekend, online learning. *Degree requirements:* For master's, comprehensive exam, thesis optional; for Ed S, comprehensive exam. *Entrance requirements:* For master's, PRAXIS, NTE, GRE, MAT, letters of recommendation; for Ed S, graduate transcripts. Additional exam requirements/recommendations for international students: Recommended—TOEFL. *Faculty research:* Brain compatible teaching and learning; poverty in Appalachia; leadership for change; ethics, moral responsibility and social justice; human and organizational learning.

Louisiana State University and Agricultural & Mechanical College, Graduate School, College of Human Sciences and Education, School of Human Resource Education and Workforce Development, Baton Rouge, LA 70803. Offers agriculture and extension education and youth development (MS, PhD); career and technical education (MS, PhD); comprehensive vocational education (MS, PhD); extension and international education (MS, PhD); human resource and leadership development (MS, PhD); industrial education (MS); vocational agriculture education (MS, PhD); vocational business education (MS); vocational home economics education (MS). *Accreditation:* NCATE.

Marquette University, Graduate School of Management, Program in Human Resources, Milwaukee, WI 53201-1881. Offers MSHR. *Program availability:* Part-time, evening/weekend. *Entrance requirements:* For master's, GMAT or GRE General Test, letters of recommendation. Additional exam requirements/recommendations for international students: Required—TOEFL (minimum score 550 paper-based; 88 iBT), IELTS (minimum score 6.5), PTE. Electronic applications accepted. *Faculty research:* Diversity, mentoring, executive compensation.

McDaniel College, Graduate and Professional Studies, Program in Human Resources Development, Westminster, MD 21157-4390. Offers MS. *Program availability:* Part-time, evening/weekend. *Degree requirements:* For master's, portfolio, internship. *Entrance requirements:* For master's, 3 recommendations; essay. Additional exam requirements/recommendations for international students: Required—TOEFL (minimum score 79 iBT), IELTS (minimum score 6). Electronic applications accepted.

Midwestern State University, Billie Doris McAda Graduate School, West College of Education, Program in Counseling, Wichita Falls, TX 76308. Offers counseling (MA); human resource development (MA); school counseling (M Ed); training and development (MA). *Program availability:* Part-time, evening/weekend. *Degree requirements:* For master's, comprehensive exam, thesis (for some programs). *Entrance requirements:* For master's, GRE General Test, MAT, or GMAT, valid teaching certificate (M Ed). Additional exam requirements/recommendations for international students: Required—TOEFL (minimum score 550 paper-based). Electronic applications accepted. *Faculty research:* Social development of students with disabilities, autism, criminal justice counseling, conflict resolution issues, leadership.

Human Resources Development

Mississippi State University, College of Education, Department of Instructional Systems and Workforce Development, Mississippi State, MS 39762. Offers instructional systems and workforce development (MSIT, PhD); technology (MST, Ed S). *Faculty:* 9 full-time (5 women). *Students:* 11 full-time (5 women), 45 part-time (34 women); includes 32 minority (31 Black or African American, non-Hispanic/Latino; 1 Two or more races, non-Hispanic/Latino). Average age 36. 11 applicants, 36% accepted, 3 enrolled. In 2018, 3 master's, 6 doctorates, 2 other advanced degrees awarded. *Degree requirements:* For master's, thesis optional, comprehensive oral or written exam; for doctorate, thesis/dissertation, comprehensive oral and written exam; for Ed S, thesis, comprehensive written exam. *Entrance requirements:* For master's, GRE, minimum GPA of 2.75 on undergraduate work, 3.0 graduate; for doctorate, GRE, minimum GPA of 3.4 on graduate work; for Ed S, GRE, minimum GPA of 3.2, master's degree. Additional exam requirements/recommendations for international students: Required—TOEFL (minimum score 550 paper-based; 79 iBT); Recommended—IELTS (minimum score 6.5). *Application deadline:* For fall admission, 7/1 for domestic students, 5/1 for international students; for spring admission, 11/1 for domestic students, 9/1 for international students. Applications are processed on a rolling basis. Application fee: $60 ($80 for international students). Electronic applications accepted. *Expenses:* Tuition, state resident: full-time $8450; part-time $360.59 per credit hour. Tuition, nonresident: full-time $23,140; part-time $969.09 per credit hour. *Required fees:* $110. One-time fee: $55 full-time. Part-time tuition and fees vary according to course load, degree level, campus/location and reciprocity agreements. *Financial support:* In 2018–19, 1 teaching assistantship with full tuition reimbursement (averaging $10,800 per year) was awarded; Federal Work-Study, institutionally sponsored loans, scholarships/grants, and unspecified assistantships also available. Financial award application deadline: 4/1; financial award applicants required to submit FAFSA. *Faculty research:* Computer technology, nontraditional students, interactive video, instructional technology, educational leadership. *Unit head:* Dr. Trey Martindale, Associate Professor and Head, 662-325-7258, Fax: 662-325-7599, E-mail: tmartindale@colled.msstate.edu. *Application contact:* Angie Campbell, Admissions and Enrollment Assistant, 662-325-9514, E-mail: acampbell@grad.msstate.edu.
Website: http://www.iswd.msstate.edu

National Louis University, College of Management and Business, Chicago, IL 60603. Offers business administration (MBA); human resource management and development (MS); management (MS). *Program availability:* Part-time, evening/weekend. *Entrance requirements:* For master's, college-administered critical thinking and writing skills test, minimum GPA of 3.0, resume, 3 references. Additional exam requirements/recommendations for international students: Required—TOEFL (minimum score 550 paper-based; 79 iBT).

New York University, School of Professional Studies, Division of Programs in Business, Program in Leadership and Human Capital Management, New York, NY 10012-1019. Offers human resource management and development (MS), including global talent management, human resource management, learning, development, and executive coaching, organizational effectiveness. *Program availability:* Part-time, evening/weekend, 100% online, blended/hybrid learning. *Degree requirements:* For master's, thesis. *Entrance requirements:* For master's, GRE or GMAT (only upon request), bachelor's degree, resume with relevant professional work, internship or volunteer experience, two letters of recommendation, statement of purpose. Additional exam requirements/recommendations for international students: Required—TOEFL (minimum score 600 paper-based; 100 iBT), IELTS (minimum score 7). Electronic applications accepted. *Expenses:* Contact institution.

North Carolina State University, Graduate School, College of Education, Department of Educational Leadership, Policy, and Human Development, Program in Human Resource Development, Raleigh, NC 27695. Offers MS. *Degree requirements:* For master's, thesis. *Entrance requirements:* For master's, GRE, 3 letters of recommendation, resume.

Northeastern Illinois University, College of Graduate Studies and Research, Daniel L. Goodwin College of Education, Program in Human Resource Development, Chicago, IL 60625. Offers human resource development (MA). *Program availability:* Part-time, evening/weekend. *Entrance requirements:* For master's, minimum GPA of 2.75, BA in human resource development. Additional exam requirements/recommendations for international students: Required—TOEFL (minimum score 550 paper-based; 79 iBT). Electronic applications accepted. *Faculty research:* Analogics, development of expertise, case-based instruction, action science organizational development, theoretical model building.

Ottawa University, Graduate Studies-Kansas City, Overland Park, KS 66211. Offers business administration (MBA); human resources (MA). *Program availability:* Part-time, evening/weekend, online learning. *Degree requirements:* For master's, thesis or alternative. *Entrance requirements:* For master's, resume, 3 letters of recommendation. Additional exam requirements/recommendations for international students: Required—TOEFL (minimum score 550 paper-based). Electronic applications accepted. *Expenses:* Contact institution.

Penn State Great Valley, Graduate Studies, Management Division, Malvern, PA 19355-1488. Offers business administration (MBA); cyber security (Certificate); data analytics (MPS, MS, Certificate); distributed energy and grid modernization (Certificate); finance (M Fin); health sector management (Certificate); human resource management (Certificate); information science (MSIS); leadership development (MLD); new ventures and entrepreneurship (Certificate); sustainable management practices (Certificate). *Accreditation:* AACSB.

Penn State University Park, Graduate School, College of the Liberal Arts, School of Labor and Employment Relations, University Park, PA 16802. Offers human resources and employment relations (MS); labor and global workers' rights (MPS).

Pittsburg State University, Graduate School, College of Technology, Department of Technology and Workforce Learning, Program in Human Resource Development, Pittsburg, KS 66762. Offers MS. *Program availability:* Part-time, online only, 100% online. *Degree requirements:* For master's, thesis or alternative. *Entrance requirements:* Additional exam requirements/recommendations for international students: Required—TOEFL (minimum score 520 paper-based; 68 iBT), IELTS (minimum score 6), PTE (minimum score 47). Electronic applications accepted. *Expenses:* Contact institution.

Regent University, Graduate School, School of Business and Leadership, Virginia Beach, VA 23464-9800. Offers business administration (MBA), including accounting, economics, entrepreneurship, finance and investing, general management, healthcare management (MA, MBA), human resource management (MA, MBA), innovation management, leadership, marketing, not-for-profit management (MA, MBA); business analytics (MS); business and design management (MA); church leadership (MA); leadership (Certificate); organizational leadership (MA, PhD), including ecclesial leadership (DSL, PhD), entrepreneurial leadership (PhD), healthcare management (MA, MBA), human resource development (PhD), human resource management (MA, MBA), individualized studies (DSL, PhD), interdisciplinary studies (MA), leadership coaching and mentoring (MA), not-for-profit management (MA, MBA), organizational development consulting (MA), servant leadership (MA, DSL); strategic leadership (DSL), including ecclesial leadership (DSL, PhD), global consulting, healthcare leadership, individualized studies (DSL, PhD), leadership coaching, servant leadership (MA, DSL), strategic foresight. *Program availability:* Part-time, evening/weekend, 100% online, blended/hybrid learning. *Degree requirements:* For master's, thesis or alternative, 3-credit hour culminating experience; for doctorate, thesis/dissertation. *Entrance requirements:* For master's, college transcripts, resume, essay; for doctorate, college transcripts, resume, essay, writing sample; for Certificate, writing sample, resume, transcripts. Additional exam requirements/recommendations for international students: Required—TOEFL (minimum score 577 paper-based). Electronic applications accepted. *Expenses:* Contact institution. *Faculty research:* Servant leadership, global business, team effectiveness, technology utilization, leadership development.

Rochester Institute of Technology, Graduate Enrollment Services, College of Applied Science and Technology, School of International Hospitality and Service Innovation, MS Program in Human Resources Development, Rochester, NY 14623-5603. Offers MS. *Program availability:* Part-time, evening/weekend, 100% online. *Students:* 13 full-time (6 women), 14 part-time (10 women); includes 1 minority (Asian, non-Hispanic/Latino), 9 international. Average age 30. 21 applicants, 57% accepted, 3 enrolled. In 2018, 8 master's awarded. *Degree requirements:* For master's, thesis or alternative, Thesis, Project, and Comprehensive Exam options available. *Entrance requirements:* For master's, minimum GPA of 3.0 (recommended). Additional exam requirements/recommendations for international students: Required—TOEFL (minimum score 570 paper-based; 88 iBT), IELTS (minimum score 6.5), PTE (minimum score 62). *Application deadline:* Applications are processed on a rolling basis. Application fee: $65. Electronic applications accepted. *Financial support:* In 2018–19, 5 students received support. Teaching assistantships with partial tuition reimbursements available, career-related internships or fieldwork, scholarships/grants, and unspecified assistantships available. Support available to part-time students. Financial award applicants required to submit FAFSA. *Faculty research:* Diversity recruitment: higher education and corporate America; equity and social justice issues in graduate employability; leadership development. *Unit head:* Dr. Linda Underhill, Director, 585-475-7359, Fax: 585-475-5099, E-mail: lmuism@rit.edu. *Application contact:* Diane Ellison, Senior Associate Vice President, Graduate Enrollment Services, 585-475-2229, Fax: 585-475-7164, E-mail: gradinfo@rit.edu.
Website: https://www.rit.edu/study/human-resource-development-ms

Rockhurst University, Helzberg School of Management, Kansas City, MO 64110-2561. Offers accounting (MBA); business intelligence (MBA, Certificate); business intelligence and analytics (MS); data science (MBA, Certificate); entrepreneurship (MBA); finance (MBA); fundraising leadership (MBA, Certificate); healthcare management (MBA, Certificate); human capital (Certificate); international business (Certificate); management (MA, MBA, Certificate); nonprofit administration (Certificate); organizational development (Certificate); science leadership (Certificate). *Accreditation:* AACSB. *Program availability:* Part-time, evening/weekend. *Entrance requirements:* For master's, GMAT or GRE. Additional exam requirements/recommendations for international students: Required—TOEFL (minimum score 550 paper-based; 79 iBT). Electronic applications accepted. *Faculty research:* Offshoring/outsourcing, systems analysis/synthesis, work teams, multilateral trade, path dependencies/creation.

Rollins College, Hamilton Holt School, Master of Human Resources Program, Winter Park, FL 32789. Offers MHR. *Program availability:* Part-time, evening/weekend. *Degree requirements:* For master's, thesis optional. *Entrance requirements:* For master's, GMAT or GRE, official transcripts, two letters of recommendation, essay, current resume. Additional exam requirements/recommendations for international students: Required—TOEFL (minimum score 550 paper-based; 80 iBT). *Expenses:* Contact institution.

Roosevelt University, Graduate Division, College of Education, Program in Training and Development, Chicago, IL 60605. Offers MA. *Program availability:* Part-time, evening/weekend. Electronic applications accepted. *Expenses:* Contact institution.

South Dakota State University, Graduate School, College of Education and Human Sciences, Department of Counseling and Human Development, Brookings, SD 57007. Offers counseling and human resource development (M Ed, MS); human sciences (MS). *Accreditation:* ACA (one or more programs are accredited); NCATE. *Program availability:* Part-time, evening/weekend. *Degree requirements:* For master's, comprehensive exam, thesis (for some programs), oral exams. *Entrance requirements:* For master's, minimum GPA of 2.75. Additional exam requirements/recommendations for international students: Required—TOEFL (minimum score 525 paper-based; 71 iBT). *Faculty research:* Rural mental health, family issues, character education, student affairs, solution focused therapy.

Texas A&M University, College of Education and Human Development, Department of Educational Administration and Human Resource Development, College Station, TX 77843. Offers educational administration (M Ed, MS, Ed D); educational human resource development (PhD). *Program availability:* Part-time. *Faculty:* 33. *Students:* 177 full-time (143 women), 262 part-time (165 women); includes 182 minority (47 Black or African American, non-Hispanic/Latino; 1 American Indian or Alaska Native, non-Hispanic/Latino; 13 Asian, non-Hispanic/Latino; 118 Hispanic/Latino; 1 Native Hawaiian or other Pacific Islander, non-Hispanic/Latino; 2 Two or more races, non-Hispanic/Latino), 30 international. Average age 36. 261 applicants, 57% accepted, 129 enrolled. In 2018, 85 master's, 29 doctorates awarded. *Degree requirements:* For master's, thesis optional; for doctorate, thesis/dissertation. *Entrance requirements:* For master's, GRE General Test, writing exam, interview, professional experience; for doctorate, GRE General Test, writing exam, interview/presentation, professional experience. Additional exam requirements/recommendations for international students: Required—TOEFL (minimum score 550 paper-based; 80 iBT), IELTS (minimum score 6), PTE (minimum score 53). *Application deadline:* For fall admission, 12/1 for domestic and international students; for spring admission, 8/15 for domestic and international students. Application fee: $50 ($90 for international students). Electronic applications accepted. *Expenses:* Contact institution. *Financial support:* In 2018–19, 77 students received support, including 6 fellowships with tuition reimbursements available (averaging $2,583 per year), 55 research assistantships with tuition reimbursements available (averaging $12,390 per year), 22 teaching assistantships with tuition reimbursements available (averaging $14,003 per year); career-related internships or fieldwork, institutionally sponsored loans, scholarships/grants, traineeships, health care benefits, tuition waivers (full and partial), and unspecified assistantships also available. Support available to part-time students. Financial award application deadline: 3/15; financial award applicants required to submit FAFSA. *Faculty research:* Higher education administration, public school administration, student affairs. *Unit head:* Dr. Fred M. Nafukho, Head, 979-862-3395, Fax: 979-862-4347, E-mail: fnafukho@tamu.edu. *Application contact:* Joyce Nelson, Director of Academic Advising, 979-845-3017, Fax: 979-862-4347, E-mail: eahradvisor@tamu.edu.
Website: http://eahr.tamu.edu

Towson University, College of Liberal Arts, Program in Human Resource Development, Towson, MD 21252-0001. Offers education leadership (MS); general human resource management (MS). *Program availability:* Part-time, evening/weekend. *Degree requirements:* For master's, comprehensive exam. *Entrance requirements:* For master's, bachelor's degree, 2 letters of recommendation, minimum GPA of 3.0, essay, resume. Additional exam requirements/recommendations for international students:

Required—TOEFL. Electronic applications accepted. *Expenses: Tuition, area resident:* Full-time $9196; part-time $418 per unit. Tuition, state resident: full-time $9196; part-time $418 per unit. Tuition, nonresident: full-time $19,030; part-time $865 per unit. *International tuition:* $19,030 full-time. *Required fees:* $3102; $141 per year. $423 per term. Tuition and fees vary according to campus/location and program.

Tusculum University, Program in Talent Development, Greeneville, TN 37743-9997. Offers MA. *Program availability:* Online learning.

Universidad Central del Este, Graduate School, San Pedro de Macoris, Dominican Republic. Offers environmental engineering (ME); financial management (M Ad); higher education (M Ed), including higher education management, higher education pedagogy; human resources (M Ad). *Entrance requirements:* For master's, letters of recommendation.

Universidad Iberoamericana, Graduate School, Santo Domingo D.N., Dominican Republic. Offers business administration (MBA, PMBA); constitutional law (LL M); dentistry (DMD); educational management (MA); integrated marketing communication (MA); psychopedagogical intervention (M Ed); real estate law (LL M); strategic management of human talent (MM).

University of Arkansas, Graduate School, College of Education and Health Professions, Department of Rehabilitation, Human Resources and Communication Disorders, Fayetteville, AR 72701. Offers adult and lifelong learning (M Ed, Ed D); communication disorders (MS); counselor education (MS, PhD); educational statistics and research methods (MS, PhD); higher education (M Ed, Ed D, Ed S); human resource and workforce development education (M Ed, Ed D); rehabilitation (MS, PhD). *Program availability:* Part-time. In 2018, 211 master's, 56 doctorates, 10 other advanced degrees awarded. *Application deadline:* For fall admission, 8/1 for domestic students, 4/1 for international students; for spring admission, 12/1 for domestic students, 10/1 for international students; for summer admission, 4/15 for domestic students, 3/1 for international students. Applications are processed on a rolling basis. Application fee: $60. Electronic applications accepted. *Financial support:* In 2018–19, 55 research assistantships, 3 teaching assistantships were awarded; fellowships with tuition reimbursements, career-related internships or fieldwork, and Federal Work-Study also available. Support available to part-time students. Financial award application deadline: 4/1; financial award applicants required to submit FAFSA. *Unit head:* Dr. Michael Hevel, Department Head, 479-575-4924, Fax: 479-575-3319, E-mail: hevel@uark.edu. *Application contact:* Vicki Dieffenderfer, Graduate Program Coordinator, 479-575-5239, Fax: 575-3319, E-mail: vmdieffe@uark.edu.
Website: http://rhrc.uark.edu/

University of Bridgeport, School of Arts and Sciences, Department of Counseling, Bridgeport, CT 06604. Offers clinical mental health counseling (MS); college student personnel (MS); community counseling (MS); human resource development (MS); human service (MS). *Program availability:* Part-time, evening/weekend. *Degree requirements:* For master's, thesis, project. *Entrance requirements:* Additional exam requirements/recommendations for international students: Recommended—TOEFL (minimum score 550 paper-based; 80 iBT), IELTS (minimum score 6.5). Electronic applications accepted. *Expenses:* Contact institution.

University of Houston, College of Technology, Department of Human Development and Consumer Sciences, Houston, TX 77204. Offers future studies in commerce (MS); human resources development (MS). *Program availability:* Part-time. *Degree requirements:* For master's, project or thesis. *Entrance requirements:* For master's, GMAT, MAT. Additional exam requirements/recommendations for international students: Required—TOEFL (minimum score 550 paper-based; 79 iBT). Electronic applications accepted.

University of Louisville, Graduate School, College of Education and Human Development, Department of Educational Leadership, Evaluation and Organizational Development, Louisville, KY 40292-0001. Offers educational leadership and organizational development (Ed D, PhD), including evaluation (PhD), human resource development (PhD), P-12 administration (PhD), post-secondary administration (PhD), sport administration (MA, PhD); health professions education (Certificate); higher education administration (MA), including sport administration (MA, PhD); human resources and organization development (MS), including health professions education, human resource leadership, workplace learning and performance; P-12 educational administration (Ed S), including principalship, supervisor of instruction. *Accreditation:* NCATE. *Program availability:* Part-time, evening/weekend, 100% online, blended/hybrid learning. *Students:* 200 full-time (82 women), 474 part-time (262 women); includes 218 minority (127 Black or African American, non-Hispanic/Latino; 1 American Indian or Alaska Native, non-Hispanic/Latino; 18 Asian, non-Hispanic/Latino; 46 Hispanic/Latino; 2 Native Hawaiian or other Pacific Islander, non-Hispanic/Latino; 24 Two or more races, non-Hispanic/Latino), 5 international. Average age 36. 257 applicants, 77% accepted, 170 enrolled. In 2018, 111 master's, 10 doctorates, 22 other advanced degrees awarded. Terminal master's awarded for partial completion of doctoral program. *Degree requirements:* For master's, comprehensive exam (for some programs), thesis (for some programs); for doctorate, comprehensive exam (for some programs), thesis/dissertation. *Entrance requirements:* For master's, GRE (for most programs), PRAXIS (for educator preparation programs), professional statement, recommendation letters, resume, transcripts; for doctorate and other advanced degree, GRE, professional statement, recommendation letters, resume, transcripts. Additional exam requirements/recommendations for international students: Required—TOEFL (minimum score 550 paper-based; 79 iBT); Recommended—IELTS (minimum score 6.5). *Application deadline:* For fall admission, 6/1 priority date for domestic students, 5/1 priority date for international students; for spring admission, 10/1 priority date for domestic students, 11/1 priority date for international students; for summer admission, 3/1 for domestic students, 4/1 priority date for international students. Application fee: $65. *Expenses: Tuition, area resident:* Full-time $6500; part-time $723 per credit hour. Tuition, state resident: full-time $6500. Tuition, nonresident: full-time $13,557; part-time $1507 per credit hour. Tuition and fees vary according to course load and program. *Financial support:* In 2018–19, 144 students received support, including fellowships (averaging $21,024 per year), research assistantships with full tuition reimbursements available (averaging $21,024 per year), teaching assistantships with full tuition reimbursements available (averaging $21,024 per year); Federal Work-Study, scholarships/grants, health care benefits, tuition waivers (full), and unspecified assistantships also available. Financial award application deadline: 3/1; financial award applicants required to submit FAFSA. *Faculty research:* Human resources and organizational development; career, technical, health professions, and economic education; health professions education; community and military partnerships; higher education. *Unit head:* Dr. Sharron Kerrick, Chair, 502-852-6475, E-mail: lead@louisville.edu. *Application contact:* Dr. Margaret Pentecost, Assistant Dean for Graduate Student Success, 502-852-6437, Fax: 502-852-1417, E-mail: gedadm@louisville.edu.
Website: http://louisville.edu/education/departments/eleod

University of Louisville, Graduate School, College of Education and Human Development, Departments of Early Childhood and Elementary Education, Middle and Secondary Education, and Special Education, Louisville, KY 40292-0001. Offers art education (MAT); autism and applied behavior analysis (Certificate); curriculum and instruction (PhD); early elementary education (MAT); exercise physiology (MS); health and physical education (MAT); health professions education (Certificate); higher education (MA); human resources and organization development (MS); instructional technology (M Ed); interdisciplinary early childhood education (MAT); middle school education (MAT); music education (MAT); secondary education (MAT); special education (MAT); sport administration (MS); teacher leadership (M Ed). *Program availability:* Part-time, evening/weekend, 100% online, blended/hybrid learning. *Faculty:* 97 full-time (64 women), 131 part-time/adjunct (86 women). *Students:* 109 full-time (72 women), 139 part-time (87 women); includes 43 minority (18 Black or African American, non-Hispanic/Latino; 6 Asian, non-Hispanic/Latino; 10 Hispanic/Latino; 9 Two or more races, non-Hispanic/Latino), 9 international. Average age 29. 108 applicants, 75% accepted, 59 enrolled. In 2018, 64 master's awarded. Terminal master's awarded for partial completion of doctoral program. *Degree requirements:* For master's, comprehensive exam (for some programs), thesis optional; for doctorate, comprehensive exam (for some programs), thesis/dissertation. *Entrance requirements:* For master's, GRE (for most programs), PRAXIS (for educator preparation programs), professional statement, recommendation letters, resume, transcripts; for doctorate and Certificate, GRE, professional statement, recommendation letters, resume, transcripts. Additional exam requirements/recommendations for international students: Required—TOEFL (minimum score 550 paper-based; 79 iBT); Recommended—IELTS (minimum score 6.5). *Application deadline:* For fall admission, 6/1 priority date for domestic students, 5/1 priority date for international students; for spring admission, 10/1 for domestic students, 11/1 priority date for international students; for summer admission, 3/1 priority date for domestic students, 4/1 priority date for international students. Application fee: $65. *Expenses: Tuition, area resident:* Full-time $6500; part-time $723 per credit hour. Tuition, state resident: full-time $6500. Tuition, nonresident: full-time $13,557; part-time $1507 per credit hour. Tuition and fees vary according to course load and program. *Financial support:* In 2018–19, 144 students received support, including fellowships with full tuition reimbursements available (averaging $21,024 per year), research assistantships with full tuition reimbursements available (averaging $21,024 per year), teaching assistantships with full tuition reimbursements available (averaging $21,024 per year); Federal Work-Study, scholarships/grants, health care benefits, tuition waivers (full), and unspecified assistantships also available. Financial award application deadline: 3/1; financial award applicants required to submit FAFSA. *Faculty research:* Children's early reading and writing development, crelevance of basic facts in elementary mathematics instruction, clinical model of teacher education, cultural and linguistic context of diverse learners, and STEM-integrated curriculum design and development. STEM teaching and learning, content literacy for English language learners, social justice in teacher education, adolescent literacy, mathematics teacher development. Classroom and behavior management; moderate/severe disabilities, autism. *Unit head:* Dr. Amy Lingo, Interim Dean, 502-852-3235, Fax: 502-852-1464, E-mail: cehdinfo@louisville.edu. *Application contact:* Dr. Margaret Pentecost, Assistant Dean for Graduate Student Success, 502-852-6437, Fax: 502-852-1417, E-mail: gedadm@louisville.edu.
Website: http://louisville.edu/delphi

University of Minnesota, Twin Cities Campus, Graduate School, College of Education and Human Development, Department of Organizational Leadership, Policy and Development, Program in Human Resource Development, Minneapolis, MN 55455-0213. Offers M Ed, MA, Ed D, PhD, Certificate. *Students:* 78 full-time (51 women), 43 part-time (31 women); includes 24 minority (5 Black or African American, non-Hispanic/Latino; 1 American Indian or Alaska Native, non-Hispanic/Latino; 11 Asian, non-Hispanic/Latino; 3 Hispanic/Latino; 4 Two or more races, non-Hispanic/Latino), 42 international. Average age 34. 87 applicants, 69% accepted, 45 enrolled. In 2018, 31 master's, 4 doctorates, 12 other advanced degrees awarded. Application fee: $75 ($95 for international students). *Unit head:* Dr. Kenneth Bartlett, Chair, 612-624-1006, E-mail: bartlett@umn.edu. *Application contact:* Dr. Jeremy J. Hernandez, Director of Graduate Studies, 612-626-9377, E-mail: olpd@umn.edu.
Website: http://www.cehd.umn.edu/OLPD/grad-programs/HRD/

University of Nebraska at Omaha, Graduate Studies, College of Arts and Sciences, Department of Psychology, Omaha, NE 68182. Offers applied behavior analysis (Certificate); human resources and training (Certificate); industrial/organizational psychology (MS); psychology (MA, PhD); school psychology (MS, Ed S). *Program availability:* Part-time. *Degree requirements:* For master's, comprehensive exam, thesis (for some programs); for doctorate, comprehensive exam, thesis/dissertation. *Entrance requirements:* For master's and doctorate, GRE, minimum GPA of 3.0, official transcripts, 3 letters of recommendation, statement of purpose, writing sample, resume. Additional exam requirements/recommendations for international students: Required—TOEFL, IELTS, PTE. Electronic applications accepted.

University of Nebraska at Omaha, Graduate Studies, College of Business Administration, Program in Business Administration, Omaha, NE 68182. Offers business administration (MBA); business for bioscientists (Certificate); executive business administration (EMBA); human resources and training (Certificate). *Accreditation:* AACSB. *Program availability:* Part-time, evening/weekend. *Degree requirements:* For master's, thesis (for some programs), capstone course. *Entrance requirements:* For master's, GMAT or GRE, minimum GPA of 3.0, official transcripts, resume; for Certificate, minimum GPA of 3.0, official transcripts, resume, letter of recommendation, statement of purpose. Additional exam requirements/recommendations for international students: Required—TOEFL, IELTS, PTE. Electronic applications accepted.

University of Nebraska at Omaha, Graduate Studies, College of Communication, Fine Arts and Media, School of Communication, Omaha, NE 68182. Offers communication (MA); human resources and training (Certificate); technical communication (Certificate). *Program availability:* Part-time, evening/weekend. *Degree requirements:* For master's, comprehensive exam, thesis (for some programs). *Entrance requirements:* For master's, minimum GPA of 3.0, 15 undergraduate communication courses, resume, statement of purpose, 3 letters of recommendation. Additional exam requirements/recommendations for international students: Required—TOEFL, IELTS, PTE. Electronic applications accepted.

University of Regina, Faculty of Graduate Studies and Research, Faculty of Education, Department of Human Resource Development, Regina, SK S4S 0A2, Canada. Offers MHRD. *Program availability:* Part-time. *Students:* 7 full-time (3 women), 6 part-time (5 women). Average age 30. 11 applicants, 45% accepted. In 2018, 5 master's awarded. *Degree requirements:* For master's, thesis (for some programs), course, project. *Entrance requirements:* For master's, 4-year undergraduate degree in related field (e.g. adult education or administration); at least 2 years of teaching or other relevant professional experience preferred; minimum grade point average of 70 percent. Additional exam requirements/recommendations for international students: Required—TOEFL (minimum score 580 paper-based; 80 iBT), IELTS (minimum score 6.5), PTE (minimum score 59), other options are CAEL, MELAB, Cantest and U of R ESL. *Application deadline:* For fall admission, 2/15 for domestic and international students; for winter admission, 10/15 for domestic and international students; for spring admission, 2/15 for domestic and international students. Application fee: $100 Canadian dollars. Electronic applications accepted. *Expenses:* Estimated tuition and fees for one academic year is 6,702.90 for master's. The fee will vary base on your choice program.

For doctoral program one academic year is estimated 14,129.40. International students will pay additional 1,191.75 for international surcharge per semester. *Financial support:* Fellowships, research assistantships, teaching assistantships, career-related internships or fieldwork, Federal Work-Study, scholarships/grants, unspecified assistantships, and travel award and Graduate Scholarship Base funds available. Support available to part-time students. Financial award application deadline: 9/30. *Faculty research:* Foundations of adult development, theory and practice of adult education and human resource development, design and assessment of curriculum and instruction, planning and curriculum development, learning and the workplace. *Unit head:* Dr. Twyla Salm, Associate Dean, Research & Graduate Programs, 306-585-4604, Fax: 306-585-4006, E-mail: Twyla.Salm@uregina.ca. *Application contact:* Linda Jiang, Graduate Program Coordinator, 306-585-4506, Fax: 306-585-5387, E-mail: ed.grad.programs@uregina.ca.
Website: http://www.uregina.ca/education/

The University of Scranton, Panuska College of Professional Studies, Department of Health Administration and Human Resources, Program in Human Resources, Scranton, PA 18510. Offers MS. *Program availability:* Part-time, evening/weekend, 100% online.

University of South Africa, College of Economic and Management Sciences, Pretoria, South Africa. Offers accounting (D Admin, D Com); accounting science (DA); auditing (D Admin, D Com); business administration (M Tech); business economics (D Admin); business leadership (DBL); business management (D Admin, D Com); economic management analysis (M Tech); economics (D Admin, D Com, PhD); human resource development (M Tech); industrial psychology (D Admin, D Com, PhD); logistics (D Com); marketing (M Tech); public administration (D Admin, D Com, DPA, PhD); public management (M Tech); quantitative management (D Admin, D Com); real estate (M Tech); statistics (D Admin, PhD); tourism management (D Admin, D Com); transport economics (D Admin, D Com).

University of South Florida, Innovative Education, Tampa, FL 33620-9951. Offers adult, career and higher education (Graduate Certificate), including college teaching, leadership in developing human resources, leadership in higher education; Africana studies (Graduate Certificate), including diasporas and health disparities, genocide and human rights; aging studies (Graduate Certificate), including gerontology; art research (Graduate Certificate), including museum studies; business foundations (Graduate Certificate); chemical and biomedical engineering (Graduate Certificate), including materials science and engineering, water, health and sustainability; child and family studies (Graduate Certificate), including positive behavior support; civil and industrial engineering (Graduate Certificate), including transportation systems analysis; community and family health (Graduate Certificate), including maternal and child health, social marketing and public health, violence and injury: prevention and intervention, women's health; criminology (Graduate Certificate), including criminal justice administration; data science for public administration (Graduate Certificate); digital humanities (Graduate Certificate); educational measurement and research (Graduate Certificate), including evaluation; English (Graduate Certificate), including comparative literary studies, creative writing, professional and technical communication; entrepreneurship (Graduate Certificate); environmental health (Graduate Certificate), including safety management; epidemiology and biostatistics (Graduate Certificate), including applied biostatistics, biostatistics, concepts and tools of epidemiology, epidemiology, epidemiology of infectious diseases; geography, environment and planning (Graduate Certificate), including community development, environmental policy and management, geographical information systems; geology (Graduate Certificate), including hydrogeology; global health (Graduate Certificate), including disaster management, global health and Latin American and Caribbean studies, global health practice, humanitarian assistance, infection control; government and international affairs (Graduate Certificate), including Cuban studies, globalization studies; health policy and management (Graduate Certificate), including health management and leadership, public health policy and programs; hearing specialist: early intervention (Graduate Certificate); industrial and management systems engineering (Graduate Certificate), including systems engineering, technology management; information studies (Graduate Certificate), including school library media specialist; information systems/decision sciences (Graduate Certificate), including analytics and business intelligence; instructional technology (Graduate Certificate), including distance education, Florida digital/virtual educator, instructional design, multimedia design, Web design; internal medicine, bioethics and medical humanities (Graduate Certificate), including biomedical ethics; Latin American and Caribbean studies (Graduate Certificate); leadership for coastal resiliency planning (Graduate Certificate); mass communications (Graduate Certificate), including multimedia journalism; mathematics and statistics (Graduate Certificate), including mathematics; medicine (Graduate Certificate), including aging and neuroscience, bioinformatics, biotechnology, brain fitness and memory management, clinical investigation, hand and upper limb rehabilitation, health informatics, health sciences, integrative weight management, intellectual property, medicine and gender, metabolic and nutritional medicine, metabolic cardiology, pharmacy sciences; national and competitive intelligence (Graduate Certificate); nursing (Graduate Certificate), including simulation based academic fellowship in advanced pain management; psychological and social foundations (Graduate Certificate), including career counseling, college teaching, diversity in education, mental health counseling, school counseling; public affairs (Graduate Certificate), including nonprofit management, public management, research administration; public health (Graduate Certificate), including assessing chemical toxicity and public health risks, health equity, pharmacoepidemiology, public health generalist, toxicology, translational research in adolescent behavioral health; public health practices (Graduate Certificate), including planning for healthy communities; rehabilitation and mental health counseling (Graduate Certificate), including integrative mental health care, marriage and family therapy, rehabilitation technology; secondary education (Graduate Certificate), including ESOL, foreign language education: culture and content, foreign language education: professional; social work (Graduate Certificate), including geriatric social work/clinical gerontology; special education (Graduate Certificate), including autism spectrum disorder, disabilities education: severe/profound; world languages (Graduate Certificate), including teaching English as a second language (TESL) or foreign language. *Expenses:* Tuition, state resident: full-time $6350. Tuition, nonresident: full-time $19,048. *International tuition:* $19,048 full-time. *Required fees:* $2079. *Unit head:* Dr. Cynthia DeLuca, Associate Vice President and Assistant Vice Provost, 813-974-3077, Fax: 813-974-7061, E-mail: deluca@usf.edu. *Application contact:* Owen Hooper, Director, Summer and Alternative Calendar Programs, 813-974-6917, E-mail: hooper@usf.edu.
Website: http://www.usf.edu/innovative-education/

The University of Tennessee, Graduate School, College of Business Administration, Program in Human Resource Development, Knoxville, TN 37996. Offers teacher licensure (MS); training and development (MS). *Program availability:* Part-time. *Degree requirements:* For master's, thesis. *Entrance requirements:* For master's, GRE General Test, minimum GPA of 2.7. Electronic applications accepted.

The University of Texas at Tyler, Soules College of Business, Department of Human Resource Development, Tyler, TX 75799-0001. Offers MS, PhD. *Program availability:* Part-time, evening/weekend, online learning. *Students:* Average age 35. 34 applicants, 97% accepted, 23 enrolled. In 2018, 31 master's awarded. *Entrance requirements:* For master's, GRE General Test or MAT. Additional exam requirements/recommendations for international students: Required—TOEFL. *Application deadline:* For fall admission, 8/17 priority date for domestic students, 5/30 for international students; for spring admission, 12/21 priority date for domestic students, 10/30 for international students. Application fee: $25 ($50 for international students). Electronic applications accepted. *Financial support:* Career-related internships or fieldwork, institutionally sponsored loans, scholarships/grants, and health care benefits available. Support available to part-time students. Financial award application deadline: 7/1. *Faculty research:* Human resource development. *Unit head:* Dr. Mark Miller, Chair, 903-566-7186, E-mail: mmiller@uttyler.edu. *Application contact:* Dr. Mark Miller, Chair, 903-566-7186, E-mail: mmiller@uttyler.edu.
Website: https://www.uttyler.edu/cbt/hrd/

University of Wisconsin–Stout, Graduate School, College of Management, Program in Training and Human Resource Development, Menomonie, WI 54751. Offers MS. *Program availability:* Part-time, online learning. *Degree requirements:* For master's, thesis. *Entrance requirements:* For master's, minimum GPA of 2.75. Additional exam requirements/recommendations for international students: Required—TOEFL (minimum score 500 paper-based; 61 iBT). Electronic applications accepted. *Faculty research:* Organizational behavior, performance, learning and performance, strategic planning.

Villanova University, Graduate School of Liberal Arts and Sciences, Department of Human Resource Development, Villanova, PA 19085-1699. Offers MS. *Program availability:* Part-time, evening/weekend, 100% online. *Degree requirements:* For master's, comprehensive exam. *Entrance requirements:* For master's, GRE General Test, minimum GPA of 3.0, statement of goals, resume, 3 letters of recommendation. Additional exam requirements/recommendations for international students: Required—TOEFL. Electronic applications accepted.

Virginia Commonwealth University, Graduate School, School of Education, Program in Adult Learning, Richmond, VA 23284-9005. Offers adult literacy (M Ed); human resource development (M Ed); teaching and learning with technology (M Ed). *Accreditation:* NCATE. *Program availability:* Part-time. *Entrance requirements:* For master's, GRE General Test or MAT. Additional exam requirements/recommendations for international students: Required—TOEFL (minimum score 600 paper-based; 100 iBT). Electronic applications accepted. *Faculty research:* Adult development and learning, program planning and evaluation.

Waldorf University, Program in Organizational Leadership, Forest City, IA 50436. Offers criminal justice leadership (MA); emergency management leadership (MA); fire/rescue executive leadership (MA); human resource development (MA); public administration (MA); sport management (MA); teacher leader (MA).

Webster University, George Herbert Walker School of Business and Technology, Department of Business, St. Louis, MO 63119-3194. Offers business and organizational security management (MBA); decision support systems (MBA); environmental management (MBA); finance (MBA, MS); forensic accounting (MS); gerontology (MBA); human resources development (MBA); human resources management (MBA); information technology management (MBA); international business (MA, MBA); international relations (MBA); management and leadership (MBA); marketing (MBA); media communications (MBA); procurement and acquisitions management (MBA); Web services (MBA). *Accreditation:* ACBSP. *Program availability:* Part-time, evening/weekend, online learning. *Degree requirements:* For master's, comprehensive exam (for some programs), thesis (for some programs). *Entrance requirements:* Additional exam requirements/recommendations for international students: Required—TOEFL. *Expenses: Tuition:* Full-time $22,500; part-time $750 per credit hour. Tuition and fees vary according to degree level, campus/location and program.

Webster University, George Herbert Walker School of Business and Technology, Department of Management, St. Louis, MO 63119-3194. Offers business and organizational security management (MA); digital marketing management (Graduate Certificate); government contracting (Graduate Certificate); health administration (MHA); health care management (MA); health services management (MA); human resources development (MA); human resources management (MA); information technology management (MA, MS); management (D Mgt); management and leadership (MA); marketing (MA); nonprofit leadership (MA); nonprofit revenue development (Graduate Certificate); organizational development (Graduate Certificate); procurement and acquisitions management (MA); public administration (MPA); space systems operations management (MS). *Program availability:* Part-time, evening/weekend, online learning. *Degree requirements:* For master's, thesis (for some programs); for doctorate, thesis/dissertation, written exam. *Entrance requirements:* For doctorate, GMAT, 3 years of work experience, MBA. Additional exam requirements/recommendations for international students: Required—TOEFL. *Expenses: Tuition:* Full-time $22,500; part-time $750 per credit hour. Tuition and fees vary according to degree level, campus/location and program.

Western Seminary, Graduate Programs, Program in Ministry and Leadership, Portland, OR 97215-3367. Offers chaplaincy (MA); coaching (MA); Jewish ministry (MA); pastoral care to women (MA); youth ministry (MA). *Degree requirements:* For master's, practicum. *Entrance requirements:* Additional exam requirements/recommendations for international students: Required—TOEFL.

William Woods University, Graduate and Adult Studies, Fulton, MO 65251-1098. Offers administration (M Ed, Ed S); athletic/activities administration (M Ed); curriculum and instruction (M Ed, Ed S); educational leadership (Ed D); equestrian education (M Ed); health management (MBA); human resources (MBA); leadership (MBA); marketing, advertising, and public relations (MBA); teaching and technology (M Ed). *Program availability:* Part-time, evening/weekend. *Degree requirements:* For master's, capstone course (MBA), action research (M Ed); for Ed S, field experience. *Entrance requirements:* Additional exam requirements/recommendations for international students: Required—TOEFL (minimum score 550 paper-based). Electronic applications accepted. *Expenses:* Contact institution.

Xavier University, College of Professional Sciences, School of Education, Department of Educational Leadership and Human Resource Development, Cincinnati, OH 45207. Offers educational administration (M Ed); human resource development (MS). *Program availability:* Part-time, evening/weekend. *Degree requirements:* For master's, internship; for doctorate, comprehensive exam, thesis/dissertation. *Entrance requirements:* For master's, GRE or MAT, resume; 2 letters of recommendation; goal statement; official transcript; for doctorate, GRE, GMAT, LSAT or MAT, official transcript; 1,000-word goal statement; resume; 3 letters of recommendation. Additional exam requirements/recommendations for international students: Required—TOEFL (minimum score 550 paper-based; 79 iBT). Electronic applications accepted. Application fee is waived when completed online. *Expenses:* Contact institution.

Human Resources Management

Adelphi University, Robert B. Willumstad School of Business, Certificate Program in Human Resource Management, Garden City, NY 11530-0701. Offers Certificate. *Program availability:* Part-time, evening/weekend. *Students:* 3 part-time (2 women); all minorities (1 Black or African American, non-Hispanic/Latino; 1 Asian, non-Hispanic/Latino; 1 Hispanic/Latino). Average age 34. 8 applicants, 50% accepted, 3 enrolled. In 2018, 12 Certificates awarded. *Entrance requirements:* For degree, GMAT or master's degree, GRE. Additional exam requirements/recommendations for international students: Required—TOEFL (minimum score 550 paper-based; 80 iBT), IELTS (minimum score 6.5). *Application deadline:* For fall admission, 5/1 for international students; for spring admission, 11/1 for international students. Applications are processed on a rolling basis. Application fee: $50. Electronic applications accepted. *Expenses:* Contact institution. *Financial support:* Career-related internships or fieldwork, Federal Work-Study, tuition waivers, and unspecified assistantships available. Financial award application deadline: 3/1; financial award applicants required to submit FAFSA. *Unit head:* Dr. Rajib Sanyal, Dean, 516-877-4690, E-mail: rsanyal@adelphi.edu. *Application contact:* Dr. Rajib Sanyal, Dean, 516-877-4690, E-mail: rsanyal@adelphi.edu.
Website: http://business.adelphi.edu/academics/certificate-programs/advanced-certificate-in-human-resource-management/

Adelphi University, Robert B. Willumstad School of Business, MBA Program, Garden City, NY 11530-0701. Offers accounting (MBA); finance (MBA); health services administration (MBA); human resource management (MBA); management (MBA); management information systems (MBA); marketing (MBA); sport management (MBA). *Accreditation:* AACSB. *Program availability:* Part-time, evening/weekend. *Students:* 343 full-time (132 women), 101 part-time (56 women); includes 75 minority (22 Black or African American, non-Hispanic/Latino; 2 American Indian or Alaska Native, non-Hispanic/Latino; 20 Asian, non-Hispanic/Latino; 23 Hispanic/Latino; 1 Native Hawaiian or other Pacific Islander, non-Hispanic/Latino; 7 Two or more races, non-Hispanic/Latino), 275 international. Average age 29. 389 applicants, 59% accepted, 187 enrolled. In 2018, 171 master's awarded. *Entrance requirements:* For master's, GMAT, official transcripts, bachelor's degree, 500 word essay, 2 letters of recommendation, resume. Additional exam requirements/recommendations for international students: Required—TOEFL (minimum score 550 paper-based; 80 iBT), IELTS (minimum score 6.5). *Application deadline:* For fall admission, 4/1 for international students; for spring admission, 11/1 for international students. Applications are processed on a rolling basis. Application fee: $50. Electronic applications accepted. *Financial support:* Research assistantships with partial tuition reimbursements, career-related internships or fieldwork, Federal Work-Study, institutionally sponsored loans, scholarships/grants, tuition waivers (partial), and unspecified assistantships available. Financial award application deadline: 3/1; financial award applicants required to submit FAFSA. *Faculty research:* Supply chain management, distribution channels, productivity benchmark analysis, data envelopment analysis, financial portfolio analysis. *Unit head:* Britt'ny Brown, Director of Graduate Programs, 516-877-4605. *Application contact:* Britt'ny Brown, Director of Graduate Programs, 516-877-4605.
Website: https://business.adelphi.edu/

Albany State University, College of Arts and Humanities, Albany, GA 31705-2717. Offers criminal justice (MS); English education (M Ed); public administration (MPA), including community and economic development, criminal justice administration, health administration and policy, human resources management, public management, public policy, water resources management and policy; social work (MSW). *Accreditation:* NASPAA. *Program availability:* Part-time. *Degree requirements:* For master's, comprehensive exam, professional portfolio (for MPA), internship, capstone report. *Entrance requirements:* For master's, GRE, MAT, minimum GPA of 3.0, official transcript, pre-medical record/certificate of immunization, letters of reference. Electronic applications accepted. *Faculty research:* HIV prevention for minority students.

Albertus Magnus College, Master of Business Administration Program, New Haven, CT 06511-1189. Offers accounting (MBA); general management (MBA); health care management (MBA); human resource management (MBA); leadership (MBA); project management (MBA). Program also offered in East Hartford, CT. *Program availability:* Part-time, evening/weekend, 100% online, blended/hybrid learning. *Degree requirements:* For master's, thesis, capstone project, business plan, minimum cumulative GPA of 3.0, completion of all requirements within seven years of matriculation. *Entrance requirements:* For master's, 3 years of management or related experience, minimum GPA of 2.5, 2 letters of recommendation, official transcripts. Additional exam requirements/recommendations for international students: Recommended—TOEFL (minimum score 550 paper-based; 80 iBT). Electronic applications accepted. *Expenses:* Contact institution. *Faculty research:* Finance, project management, accounting, business administration, generalist.

Amberton University, Graduate School, Program in Human Relations and Business, Garland, TX 75041-5595. Offers MS. *Program availability:* Part-time, evening/weekend. *Entrance requirements:* For master's, minimum GPA of 3.0.

American InterContinental University Online, Program in Business Administration, Schaumburg, IL 60173. Offers accounting and finance (MBA); finance (MBA); healthcare management (MBA); human resource management (MBA); international business (MBA); management (MBA); marketing (MBA); operations management (MBA); organizational psychology and development (MBA); project management (MBA). *Accreditation:* ACBSP. *Program availability:* Evening/weekend, online learning. *Entrance requirements:* Additional exam requirements/recommendations for international students: Required—TOEFL (minimum score 550 paper-based). Electronic applications accepted.

American University, School of Professional and Extended Studies, Washington, DC 20016. Offers agile project management (MS); healthcare management (MS, Graduate Certificate); human resource analytics and management (MS, Graduate Certificate); instructional design and learning analytics (MS); measurement and evaluation (MS); project monitoring and evaluation (Graduate Certificate); sports analytics and management (MS, Graduate Certificate). *Program availability:* Part-time, evening/weekend, 100% online, blended/hybrid learning. *Faculty:* 27 full-time (14 women), 33 part-time/adjunct (20 women). *Students:* 2 full-time (both women), 113 part-time (68 women); includes 6 minority (4 Black or African American, non-Hispanic/Latino; 1 Asian, non-Hispanic/Latino; 1 Hispanic/Latino). Average age 31. 156 applicants, 93% accepted, 66 enrolled. In 2018, 1 master's, 6 other advanced degrees awarded. *Entrance requirements:* For master's, Please visit website: https://www.american.edu/spexs/, official transcript(s), resume. Additional exam requirements/recommendations for international students: Required—TOEFL. *Application deadline:* Applications are processed on a rolling basis. Application fee: $55. Electronic applications accepted. *Expenses:* Contact institution. *Financial support:* Applicants required to submit FAFSA.

Unit head: Jill Klein, Dean, 202-895-4900, E-mail: spexs@american.edu. *Application contact:* Emily Emily, Assistant Director for Recruitment and Admission, 202-885-4910, E-mail: aronoff@american.edu.
Website: http://www.american.edu/spexs/

American University of Beirut, Graduate Programs, Suliman S. Olayan School of Business, Master in Human Resource Management Program, Beirut, Lebanon. Offers MHRM. *Program availability:* Part-time. *Faculty:* 5 full-time (3 women), 4 part-time/adjunct (2 women). *Students:* 10 full-time (9 women). Average age 27. 62 applicants, 58% accepted, 10 enrolled. In 2018, 10 master's awarded. *Degree requirements:* For master's, thesis. *Entrance requirements:* Additional exam requirements/recommendations for international students: Required—TOEFL (minimum score 79 iBT), IELTS (minimum score 6). *Application deadline:* For fall admission, 6/30 for domestic and international students. Applications are processed on a rolling basis. Application fee: $50. Electronic applications accepted. *Expenses: Tuition:* Full-time $17,748; part-time $986 per credit. *Required fees:* $762. Tuition and fees vary according to course load and program. *Financial support:* In 2018–19, 2 research assistantships with partial tuition reimbursements (averaging $21,000 per year) were awarded; fellowships, teaching assistantships, tuition waivers, and unspecified assistantships also available. Financial award application deadline: 6/30; financial award applicants required to submit CSS PROFILE. *Unit head:* Maya El Helou, Director of Graduate Programs, 961-1-350000 Ext. 3955, E-mail: helou@aub.edu.lb. *Application contact:* Maya El-Helou, Director of Graduate Programs, 961-1-350000 Ext. 3955, E-mail: helou@aub.edu.lb.
Website: http://www.aub.edu.lb/osb/MHRM/Pages/default.aspx

Anderson University, College of Business, Anderson, SC 29621-4035. Offers business administration (MBA); healthcare leadership (MBA); human resources (MBA); marketing (MBA); organizational leadership (MOL); supply chain management (MBA). *Accreditation:* ACBSP. *Application deadline:* Applications are processed on a rolling basis. Electronic applications accepted. *Expenses: Tuition:* Full-time $400; part-time $400 per credit. *Required fees:* $200; $200 per semester. Tuition and fees vary according to course load. *Financial support:* Scholarships/grants and tuition waivers available. Financial award application deadline: 3/1; financial award applicants required to submit FAFSA. *Unit head:* Steve Nail, Dean, 864-MBA-6000. *Application contact:* Sharon Vargo, Graduate Admission Counselor, 864-231-2000, E-mail: svargo@andersonuniversity.edu.
Website: http://www.andersonuniversity.edu/business

Ashland University, Dauch College of Business and Economics, Ashland, OH 44805-3702. Offers accounting (MBA); business analytics (MBA); entrepreneurship (MBA); financial management (MBA); global management (MBA); health care management and leadership (MBA); human resource management (MBA); human resources (MBA); management information systems (MBA); project management (MBA); sport management (MBA); supply chain management (MBA). *Accreditation:* ACBSP. *Program availability:* Part-time, evening/weekend, 100% online, blended/hybrid learning. Terminal master's awarded for partial completion of doctoral program. *Degree requirements:* For master's, thesis optional, capstone course. *Entrance requirements:* For master's, 2 years of full-time work experience. Additional exam requirements/recommendations for international students: Required—TOEFL (minimum score 550 paper-based; 78 iBT). Electronic applications accepted. *Expenses:* Contact institution. *Faculty research:* Relationship marketing strategy, executive compensation and company performance, online marketplaces in electronic commerce, diversity training in campus recreation departments, entrepreneurship in developing and emerging economies.

Ashworth College, Graduate Programs, Norcross, GA 30092. Offers business administration (MBA); criminal justice (MS); health care administration (MBA, MS); human resource management (MBA, MS); international business (MBA); management (MS); marketing (MBA, MS).

Assumption College, Business Studies Program, Worcester, MA 01609-1296. Offers accounting (MBA); business studies (CAGS); finance/economics (MBA); human resources (MBA); international business (MBA); management (MBA); marketing (MBA); nonprofit leadership (MBA). *Program availability:* Part-time, evening/weekend. *Degree requirements:* For master's, capstone. *Entrance requirements:* For master's, bachelor's degree, three letters of recommendation, official transcripts, personal statement, current resume; for CAGS, MBA or equivalent degree in a closely related field, three letters of recommendation, official transcripts, personal statement, current resume. Additional exam requirements/recommendations for international students: Required—TOEFL (minimum score 540 paper-based; 76 iBT), IELTS (minimum score 6). Electronic applications accepted. *Faculty research:* Workplace diversity, dynamics of team interaction, utilization of leased employees, experiential learning project on due diligence market for prostheses.

Averett University, Master of Business Administration Program, Danville, VA 24541-3692. Offers business administration (MBA); human resources management (MBA); leadership (MBA); marketing (MBA). *Program availability:* Part-time. *Faculty:* 7 full-time (1 woman), 10 part-time/adjunct (2 women). *Students:* 156 full-time (93 women), 2 part-time (1 woman); includes 61 minority (51 Black or African American, non-Hispanic/Latino; 2 American Indian or Alaska Native, non-Hispanic/Latino; 3 Asian, non-Hispanic/Latino; 3 Hispanic/Latino; 2 Two or more races, non-Hispanic/Latino), 2 international. Average age 35. 61 applicants, 70% accepted, 35 enrolled. In 2018, 62 master's awarded. *Degree requirements:* For master's, 41-credit core curriculum, minimum GPA of 3.0 throughout program, no more than 2 grades of C, completion of degree requirements within six years from start of program. *Entrance requirements:* For master's, minimum cumulative GPA of 3.0 over the last 60 semester hours of undergraduate study toward a baccalaureate degree, official transcripts, three years of full-time work experience, three letters of recommendation, current resume. Additional exam requirements/recommendations for international students: Required—TOEFL (minimum score 600 paper-based; 100 iBT). *Application deadline:* Applications are processed on a rolling basis. Electronic applications accepted. *Expenses:* Contact institution. *Financial support:* Application deadline: 3/1; applicants required to submit FAFSA. *Unit head:* Dr. Peggy C. Wright, Chair, Business Department, 434-791-7118, E-mail: pwright@averett.edu. *Application contact:* Christy Davis, Assistant Director of Admissions, 434-791-7133, E-mail: cdavis@averett.edu.
Website: https://gps.averett.edu/online/business/

Avila University, School of Professional Studies, Kansas City, MO 64145-1698. Offers executive leadership (MS); fundraising (MA); instructional design and technology (MA, MS); leadership coaching (MS); project management (MA); strategic human resources (MS). *Program availability:* Part-time-only, evening/weekend, 100% online, blended/hybrid learning. *Faculty:* 14 part-time/adjunct (8 women). *Students:* 69 full-time (49 women), 48 part-time (42 women); includes 45 minority (38 Black or African American,

non-Hispanic/Latino; 5 Hispanic/Latino; 2 Two or more races, non-Hispanic/Latino), 5 international. Average age 39. 63 applicants, 60% accepted, 29 enrolled. In 2018, 34 master's awarded. *Degree requirements:* For master's, thesis optional. *Entrance requirements:* For master's, 2 letters of recommendation, minimum GPA of 3.0 during last 60 hours, resume, statement of intent. Additional exam requirements/recommendations for international students: Required—TOEFL (minimum score 550 paper-based; 79 iBT). *Application deadline:* Applications are processed on a rolling basis. Application fee: $0. Electronic applications accepted. *Expenses:* Contact institution. *Financial support:* In 2018–19, 12 students received support. Unspecified assistantships available. Support available to part-time students. Financial award applicants required to submit FAFSA. *Unit head:* Sarah Sullivan, Coordinator, 816-501-0429, Fax: 816-941-4650, E-mail: advantage@avila.edu. *Application contact:* Jessica Burson, Graduate Admission Advisor, 816-501-2482, Fax: 816-941-4650, E-mail: advantage@avila.edu.
Website: https://www.avila.edu/mrk/advantage-3

Baker College Center for Graduate Studies–Online, Graduate Programs, Flint, MI 48507. Offers accounting (MBA); business administration (DBA); finance (MBA); general business (MBA); health care management (MBA); human resources management (MBA); information management (MBA); leadership studies (MBA); management information systems (MSIS); marketing (MBA); occupational therapy (MOT). *Program availability:* Part-time, evening/weekend, online learning. *Degree requirements:* For master's, portfolio. *Entrance requirements:* For master's, 3 years of work experience, minimum undergraduate GPA of 2.5, writing sample, 3 letters of recommendation; for doctorate, MBA or acceptable related master's degree from accredited association, 5 years work experience, minimum graduate GPA of 3.25, writing sample, 3 professional references. Additional exam requirements/recommendations for international students: Required—TOEFL (minimum score 550 paper-based). Electronic applications accepted.

Baldwin Wallace University, Graduate Programs, School of Business, Program in Human Resources, Berea, OH 44017-2088. Offers MBA. *Program availability:* Part-time, evening/weekend. *Students:* 9 full-time (all women), 21 part-time (14 women); includes 10 minority (7 Black or African American, non-Hispanic/Latino; 2 Asian, non-Hispanic/Latino; 1 Hispanic/Latino). Average age 37. 12 applicants, 33% accepted, 3 enrolled. In 2018, 13 master's awarded. *Degree requirements:* For master's, minimum overall GPA of 3.0. *Entrance requirements:* For master's, GMAT or minimum GPA of 3.0, bachelor's degree in any field, work experience. Additional exam requirements/recommendations for international students: Required—TOEFL (minimum score 550 paper-based; 79 iBT), IELTS can be accepted in place of TOEFL. *Application deadline:* For fall admission, 7/25 priority date for domestic students, 4/30 priority date for international students; for spring admission, 12/15 priority date for domestic students, 9/30 priority date for international students; for summer admission, 4/15 priority date for domestic students. Applications are processed on a rolling basis. Application fee: $0. Electronic applications accepted. *Expenses:* $31,284 to complete program. *Financial support:* Scholarships/grants and tuition discounts available. Financial award applicants required to submit FAFSA. *Unit head:* Dr. Susan Kuznik, Associate Dean, Graduate Business Programs, 440-826-2053, Fax: 440-826-3868, E-mail: skuznik@bw.edu. *Application contact:* Laura Spencer, Graduate Business Admission Specialist, 440-826-2191, Fax: 440-826-3868, E-mail: lspencer@bw.edu.
Website: http://www.bw.edu/graduate/business/mba/

Barry University, School of Education, Graduate Certificate Programs, Miami Shores, FL 33161-6695. Offers advanced teaching and learning with technology (Certificate); distance education (Certificate); higher education technology integration (Certificate); human resources: not for profit and religious organizations (Certificate); K-12 technology integration (Certificate).

Baruch College of the City University of New York, Zicklin School of Business, Department of Management, New York, NY 10010-5585. Offers entrepreneurship (MBA); management (PhD); operations management (MBA); organizational behavior/human resources management (MBA); sustainable business (MBA). PhD offered jointly with Graduate School and University Center of the City University of New York. *Program availability:* Part-time, evening/weekend. *Degree requirements:* For doctorate, comprehensive exam, thesis/dissertation. *Entrance requirements:* For master's, GMAT, 2 letters of recommendation, resume, 2 years of work experience; for doctorate, GMAT. Additional exam requirements/recommendations for international students: Required—TOEFL (minimum score 590 paper-based), TWE.

Belhaven University, School of Business, Jackson, MS 39202-1789. Offers business administration (MBA); health administration (MBA, MHA); human resources (MBA, MSL); leadership (MBA); public administration (MPA); sports administration (MBA, MSA). *Program availability:* Part-time, evening/weekend, 100% online. *Students:* Average age 35. 574 applicants, 75% accepted, 306 enrolled. In 2018, 326 master's awarded. *Degree requirements:* For master's, comprehensive exam (for some programs), thesis or alternative. *Entrance requirements:* For master's, minimum GPA of 2.8 (for MBA and MHA), 2.5 (for MSL, MPA and MSA). *Application deadline:* Applications are processed on a rolling basis. Application fee: $25. Electronic applications accepted. *Expenses:* Contact institution. *Financial support:* Applicants required to submit FAFSA. *Unit head:* Dr. Ralph Mason, Dean, 601-968-8949, Fax: 601-968-8951, E-mail: cmason@belhaven.edu. *Application contact:* Dr. Audrey Kelleher, Vice President of Adult and Graduate Marketing and Development, 407-804-1424, Fax: 407-620-5210, E-mail: akelleher@belhaven.edu.
Website: http://www.belhaven.edu/campuses/index.htm

Bellevue University, Graduate School, College of Business, Bellevue, NE 68005-3098. Offers acquisition and contract management (MS); business administration (MBA); finance (MS); human capital management (PhD); management (MSM).

Benedictine University, Graduate Programs, Program in Business Administration, Lisle, IL 60532. Offers accounting (MBA); entrepreneurship and managing innovation (MBA); financial management (MBA); health administration (MBA); human resource management (MBA); information systems security (MBA); international business (MBA); management consulting (MBA); management information systems (MBA); marketing management (MBA); operations management and logistics (MBA); organizational leadership (MBA). *Program availability:* Part-time, evening/weekend, 100% online, blended/hybrid learning. *Faculty:* 7 full-time (1 woman), 36 part-time/adjunct (10 women). *Students:* 110 full-time (71 women), 500 part-time (302 women); includes 104 minority (34 Black or African American, non-Hispanic/Latino; 1 American Indian or Alaska Native, non-Hispanic/Latino; 41 Asian, non-Hispanic/Latino; 23 Hispanic/Latino; 5 Native Hawaiian or other Pacific Islander, non-Hispanic/Latino), 7 international. Average age 33. 251 applicants, 84% accepted, 202 enrolled. In 2018, 345 master's awarded. *Entrance requirements:* For master's, GMAT or GRE test scores or completed test waiver form, official transcripts; 2 letters of reference from individuals familiar with the applicant's professional or academic work, excluding family or personal friends; a 1-2 page essay addressing educational and career goals; current résumé listing chronological work history; personal interview may be required prior to an admission decision. Additional exam requirements/recommendations for international students: Required—TOEFL (minimum score 550 paper-based; 79 iBT), IELTS (minimum score 6.5). *Application deadline:* Applications are processed on a rolling basis. Application fee: $40. Electronic applications accepted. *Unit head:* Ricky Holman, Assistant Professor, 630-829-1936, E-mail: rholman@ben.edu. *Application contact:* Ricky Holman, Assistant Professor, 630-829-1936, E-mail: rholman@ben.edu.

Brandman University, School of Business and Professional Studies, Irvine, CA 92618. Offers accounting (MBA); business administration (MBA); business intelligence and data analytics (MBA); e-business strategic management (MBA); entrepreneurship (MBA); finance (MBA); health administration (MBA); human resources (MBA, MS); international business (MBA); marketing (MBA); organizational leadership (MA, MBA, MPA); public administration (MPA).

Brigham Young University, Graduate Studies, BYU Marriott School of Business, MBA Program, Provo, UT 84602. Offers entrepreneurship (MBA); finance (MBA); global supply chain management (MBA); marketing (MBA); strategic human resources (MBA); JD/MBA; MBA/MS. *Accreditation:* AACSB. *Entrance requirements:* For master's, GMAT or GRE, commitment to BYU Honor Code, undergraduate degree. Additional exam requirements/recommendations for international students: Required—TOEFL (minimum score 590 paper-based; 100 iBT), IELTS (minimum score 7). Electronic applications accepted. *Expenses:* Contact institution. *Faculty research:* Finance, marketing, supply chain management, entrepreneurship, strategic human resources.

Bryan College, MBA Program, Dayton, TN 37321. Offers business administration (MBA); healthcare administration (MBA); human resources (MBA); marketing (MBA); ministry (MBA); sports management (MBA). *Program availability:* Online only, 100% online. *Entrance requirements:* For master's, resume, 2 letters of recommendation. Additional exam requirements/recommendations for international students: Required—TOEFL. Electronic applications accepted. *Expenses:* Contact institution.

Buffalo State College, State University of New York, The Graduate School, School of Education, Department of Adult Education, Buffalo, NY 14222-1095. Offers adult education (MS, Certificate); human resource development (Certificate). *Program availability:* Part-time, evening/weekend, online learning. *Degree requirements:* For master's, comprehensive exam. *Entrance requirements:* Additional exam requirements/recommendations for international students: Required—TOEFL (minimum score 550 paper-based).

California Coast University, School of Administration and Management, Santa Ana, CA 92701. Offers business marketing (MBA); health care management (MBA); human resource management (MBA); management (MBA, MS). *Program availability:* Online learning. Electronic applications accepted.

California Intercontinental University, School of Business, Irvine, CA 92614. Offers banking and finance (MBA); entrepreneurship and business management (DBA); global business leadership (DBA); international management and marketing (MBA); organizational management and human resource management (MBA).

California State University, East Bay, Office of Graduate Studies, College of Business and Economics, MBA Program, Option in Human Resources and Organizational Behavior, Hayward, CA 94542-3000. Offers MBA. *Program availability:* Part-time, evening/weekend. *Degree requirements:* For master's, comprehensive exam or thesis. *Entrance requirements:* For master's, GMAT, minimum GPA of 2.75. Additional exam requirements/recommendations for international students: Required—TOEFL (minimum score 550 paper-based). Electronic applications accepted.

California State University, Sacramento, College of Business Administration, Sacramento, CA 95819. Offers accountancy (MS); business administration (IMBA, MBA); human resources (MBA); urban land development (MBA). *Accreditation:* AACSB. *Program availability:* Part-time, evening/weekend, 100% online, blended/hybrid learning. *Degree requirements:* For master's, comprehensive exam, project, thesis, or writing proficiency exam. *Entrance requirements:* For master's, GMAT. Additional exam requirements/recommendations for international students: Required—TOEFL (minimum score 550 paper-based; 80 iBT). Electronic applications accepted. *Expenses:* Contact institution.

Capella University, School of Business and Technology, Doctoral Programs in Business, Minneapolis, MN 55402. Offers accounting (DBA, PhD); business intelligence (DBA); finance (DBA, PhD); general business management (PhD); human resource management (DBA, PhD); leadership (DBA, PhD); management education (PhD); marketing (DBA, PhD); project management (DBA, PhD); strategy and innovation (DBA, PhD). *Accreditation:* ACBSP.

Capella University, School of Business and Technology, Master's Programs in Business, Minneapolis, MN 55402. Offers accounting (MBA); business analysis (MS); business intelligence (MBA); entrepreneurship (MBA); finance (MBA); general business administration (MBA); general human resource management (MS); general leadership (MS); health care management (MBA); human resource management (MBA); marketing (MBA); project management (MBA, MS). *Accreditation:* ACBSP.

Caribbean University, Graduate School, Bayamón, PR 00960-0493. Offers administration and supervision (MA Ed); criminal justice (MA); curriculum and instruction (MA Ed, PhD), including elementary education (MA Ed), English education (MA Ed), history education (MA Ed), mathematics education (MA Ed), primary education (MA Ed), science education (MA Ed), Spanish education (MA Ed); educational technology in instructional systems (MA Ed); gerontology (MSN); human resources (MBA); museology, archiving and art history (MA Ed); neonatal pediatrics (MSN); physical education (MA Ed); special education (MA Ed). *Entrance requirements:* For master's, interview, minimum GPA of 2.5.

Carlow University, College of Leadership and Social Change, MBA Program, Pittsburgh, PA 15213-3165. Offers fraud and forensics (MBA); healthcare management (MBA); human resource management (MBA); leadership and management (MBA); project management (MBA). *Program availability:* Part-time, evening/weekend, 100% online, blended/hybrid learning. *Students:* 64 full-time (47 women), 35 part-time (25 women); includes 37 minority (31 Black or African American, non-Hispanic/Latino; 1 Asian, non-Hispanic/Latino; 1 Hispanic/Latino; 4 Two or more races, non-Hispanic/Latino). Average age 33. 34 applicants, 100% accepted, 22 enrolled. In 2018, 38 master's awarded. *Entrance requirements:* For master's, minimum undergraduate GPA of 3.0 (preferred); personal essay; resume; official transcripts; two professional recommendations. Additional exam requirements/recommendations for international students: Required—TOEFL (minimum score 550 paper-based). *Application deadline:* Applications are processed on a rolling basis. Electronic applications accepted. *Expenses: Tuition:* Full-time $13,090; part-time $5100 per semester. *Required fees:* $215; $84. Tuition and fees vary according to course load, degree level and program. *Financial support:* Application deadline: 4/1; applicants required to submit FAFSA. *Unit head:* Dr. Howard Stern, Program Director, MBA Program, 412-578-8828, E-mail: hastern@carlow.edu. *Application contact:* Dr. Howard Stern, Program Director, MBA Program, 412-578-8828, E-mail: hastern@carlow.edu.
Website: http://www.carlow.edu/Business_Administration.aspx

The Catholic University of America, Busch School of Business and Economics, Washington, DC 20064. Offers accounting (MS); business analysis (MSBA); integral economic development management (MA); integral economic development policy (MA); management (MS), including Federal contract management, human resource management, leadership and management, project management, sales management. *Program availability:* Part-time. *Faculty:* 38 full-time (8 women), 21 part-time/adjunct (9

women). *Students:* 57 full-time (11 women), 1 (woman) part-time; includes 24 minority (3 Black or African American, non-Hispanic/Latino; 1 American Indian or Alaska Native, non-Hispanic/Latino; 8 Asian, non-Hispanic/Latino; 7 Hispanic/Latino; 5 Two or more races, non-Hispanic/Latino), 1 international. Average age 33. 96 applicants, 79% accepted, 56 enrolled. In 2018, 58 master's awarded. *Degree requirements:* For master's, comprehensive exam (for some programs). *Entrance requirements:* For master's, GRE General Test, statement of purpose, official copies of academic transcripts, three letters of recommendation. Additional exam requirements/recommendations for international students: Required—TOEFL (minimum score 550 paper-based; 80 iBT). *Application deadline:* For fall admission, 7/15 priority date for domestic students, 7/1 for international students; for spring admission, 11/15 priority date for domestic students, 11/1 for international students. Applications are processed on a rolling basis. Application fee: $55. Electronic applications accepted. *Expenses:* Contact institution. *Financial support:* Fellowships, research assistantships, teaching assistantships, Federal Work-Study, scholarships/grants, tuition waivers (full and partial), and unspecified assistantships available. Financial award application deadline: 2/1; financial award applicants required to submit FAFSA. *Faculty research:* Integrity of the marketing process, economics of energy and the environment, emerging markets, social change, international finance and economic development. *Unit head:* Dr. Andrew Abela, Dean, 202-319-6130, E-mail: DeanAbela@cua.edu. *Application contact:* Dr. Steven Brown, Director of Graduate Admissions, 202-319-5057, Fax: 202-319-6533, E-mail: cua-admissions@cua.edu.
Website: https://business.catholic.edu/

Central Michigan University, Central Michigan University Global Campus, Program in Administration, Mount Pleasant, MI 48859. Offers acquisitions administration (MSA, Certificate); engineering management administration (MSA, Certificate); general administration (MSA, Certificate); health services administration (MSA, Certificate); human resources administration (MSA, Certificate); information resource management (MSA); information resource management administration (Certificate); international administration (MSA, Certificate); leadership (MSA, Certificate); philanthropy and fundraising administration (MSA, Certificate); public administration (MSA, Certificate); recreation and park administration (MSA); research administration (MSA, Certificate). *Program availability:* Part-time, evening/weekend, online learning. *Entrance requirements:* For master's, minimum GPA of 2.7 in major. Electronic applications accepted.

Central Michigan University, Central Michigan University Global Campus, Program in Business Administration, Mount Pleasant, MI 48859. Offers enterprise resource planning (MBA, Certificate); human resource management (MBA); logistics management (MBA, Certificate); marketing (MBA); value-driven organization (MBA). *Program availability:* Part-time, evening/weekend. *Entrance requirements:* For master's, GMAT.

Central Michigan University, College of Graduate Studies, College of Business Administration, MBA Program, Mount Pleasant, MI 48859. Offers accounting (MBA); business economics (MBA); consulting (MBA); finance (MBA); general business (MBA); human resource management (MBA); information systems (MBA); international business (MBA); logistics management (MBA); marketing (MBA); value-driven organization (MBA). *Program availability:* Part-time, evening/weekend, online learning. Electronic applications accepted. *Faculty research:* Accounting, consulting, international business, marketing, information systems.

Central Michigan University, College of Graduate Studies, Interdisciplinary Administration Programs, Mount Pleasant, MI 48859. Offers acquisitions administration (MSA, Graduate Certificate); general administration (MSA, Graduate Certificate); health services administration (MSA, Graduate Certificate); human resource administration (Graduate Certificate); human resources administration (MSA); information resource management (MSA, Graduate Certificate); international administration (MSA, Graduate Certificate); leadership (MSA, Graduate Certificate); public administration (MSA, Graduate Certificate); research administration (Graduate Certificate); sport administration (MSA). *Accreditation:* AACSB. *Program availability:* Part-time, evening/weekend, online learning. *Degree requirements:* For master's, thesis or alternative. *Entrance requirements:* For master's, bachelor's degree with minimum GPA of 2.7. Electronic applications accepted. *Faculty research:* Interdisciplinary studies in acquisitions administration, health services administration, sport administration, recreation and park administration, and international administration.

Charleston Southern University, College of Business, Charleston, SC 29423-8087. Offers accounting (MBA); finance (MBA); general management (MBA); human resource management (MS); leadership (MBA); management information systems (MBA); organizational leadership (MA). *Program availability:* Part-time, evening/weekend. *Degree requirements:* For master's, thesis optional. *Entrance requirements:* For master's, GMAT. Additional exam requirements/recommendations for international students: Required—TOEFL (minimum score 550 paper-based; 79 iBT). Electronic applications accepted.

City University of Seattle, Graduate Division, School of Management, Seattle, WA 98121. Offers accounting (Certificate); change leadership (MBA, Certificate); computer systems (MS); finance (Certificate); financial management (MBA); general management (MBA); general management-Europe (MBA); global marketing (MBA); human resources management (Certificate); individualized study (MBA); information security (MS); information systems (MBA); leadership (MA); marketing (MBA, Certificate); project management (MBA, MS, Certificate); sustainable business (Certificate); technology management (MBA, Certificate). *Program availability:* Part-time, evening/weekend, online learning. *Degree requirements:* For master's, comprehensive exam (for some programs), thesis (for some programs). *Entrance requirements:* For master's, baccalaureate degree or equivalent from an accredited or otherwise recognized institution. Additional exam requirements/recommendations for international students: Required—TOEFL (minimum score 567 paper-based; 87 iBT); Recommended—IELTS. Electronic applications accepted.

Claremont Graduate University, Graduate Programs, School of Social Science, Policy and Evaluation, Human Resource Management Program, Claremont, CA 91711-6160. Offers MS. *Program availability:* Part-time, evening/weekend. *Entrance requirements:* For master's, GMAT or GRE General Test. Additional exam requirements/recommendations for international students: Required—TOEFL (minimum score 75 iBT). Electronic applications accepted.

Clarkson University, David D. Reh School of Business, Master's Program in Business Administration, Potsdam, NY 13699. Offers business administration (MBA); business fundamentals (Advanced Certificate); global supply chain management (Advanced Certificate); human resource management (Advanced Certificate); management and leadership (Advanced Certificate). *Accreditation:* AACSB. *Program availability:* Part-time, evening/weekend, 100% online, blended/hybrid learning. *Faculty:* 36 full-time (7 women), 8 part-time/adjunct (2 women). *Students:* 68 full-time (30 women), 63 part-time (29 women); includes 17 minority (2 Black or African American, non-Hispanic/Latino; 2 American Indian or Alaska Native, non-Hispanic/Latino; 6 Asian, non-Hispanic/Latino; 4 Hispanic/Latino; 3 Two or more races, non-Hispanic/Latino), 11 international. 119 applicants, 74% accepted, 67 enrolled. In 2018, 89 master's, 2 other advanced degrees awarded. *Entrance requirements:* For master's, GRE or GMAT. Additional exam requirements/recommendations for international students: Required—TOEFL (minimum score 550 paper-based, 80 iBT) or IELTS (6.5). *Application deadline:* Applications are processed on a rolling basis. Application fee: $50. Electronic applications accepted. *Expenses: Tuition:* Full-time $24,984; part-time $1388 per credit hour. *Required fees:* $225. Tuition and fees vary according to campus/location and program. *Financial support:* Scholarships/grants available. *Unit head:* Dr. Dennis Yu, Associate Dean of Graduate Programs & Research, 315-268-2300, E-mail: dyu@clarkson.edu. *Application contact:* Dan Capogna, Director of Graduate Admissions & Recruitment, 518-631-9910, E-mail: graduate@clarkson.edu.
Website: https://www.clarkson.edu/academics/graduate

Clayton State University, School of Graduate Studies, College of Business, Program in Business Administration, Morrow, GA 30260-0285. Offers accounting (MBA); human resource leadership (MBA); international business (MBA); sports and entertainment management (MBA); supply chain management (MBA). *Accreditation:* AACSB. *Program availability:* Part-time, evening/weekend. *Degree requirements:* For master's, thesis. *Entrance requirements:* For master's, GMAT, 3 letters of recommendation; statement of purpose; 2 official transcripts. Additional exam requirements/recommendations for international students: Required—TOEFL (minimum score 550 paper-based; 80 iBT). Electronic applications accepted. *Expenses:* Contact institution.

Cleveland State University, College of Graduate Studies, Monte Ahuja College of Business, Department of Management, Cleveland, OH 44115. Offers health care administration (MBA); labor relations and human resources (MLRHR). *Program availability:* Part-time, evening/weekend. *Faculty:* 6 full-time (3 women), 8 part-time/adjunct (1 woman). *Students:* 10 full-time (9 women), 17 part-time (15 women); includes 9 minority (3 Black or African American, non-Hispanic/Latino; 1 American Indian or Alaska Native, non-Hispanic/Latino; 2 Asian, non-Hispanic/Latino; 3 Hispanic/Latino), 2 international. Average age 28. In 2018, 15 master's awarded. *Entrance requirements:* For master's, GMAT or GRE, minimum GPA of 3.0. Additional exam requirements/recommendations for international students: Required—TOEFL (minimum score 550 paper-based; 78 iBT). *Application deadline:* For fall admission, 7/15 for domestic students; for spring admission, 12/15 for domestic students. Applications are processed on a rolling basis. Application fee: $40. Electronic applications accepted. *Expenses:* Tuition, state resident: full-time $7232.55; part-time $6676 per credit hour. Tuition, nonresident: full-time $12,375. *International tuition:* $18,914 full-time. *Required fees:* $80; $80 $40. Tuition and fees vary according to program. *Financial support:* In 2018–19, 3 students received support. Career-related internships or fieldwork, scholarships/grants, and unspecified assistantships available. Financial award application deadline: 5/1; financial award applicants required to submit FAFSA. *Faculty research:* Employee selection, individual differences, leadership, emotions, interviews. *Unit head:* Dr. Kenneth J. Dunegan, Chairperson, 216-687-4747, Fax: 216-687-4708, E-mail: t.degroot@csuohio.edu. *Application contact:* Lisa Marie Sample, Administrative Assistant, 216-687-4726, Fax: 216-687-6888, E-mail: l.m.sample@csuohio.edu.
Website: https://www.csuohio.edu/business/management/management

College of Saint Elizabeth, Department of Business Administration and Management, Morristown, NJ 07960-6989. Offers human resource management (MS); organizational change (MS). *Program availability:* Part-time. *Degree requirements:* For master's, thesis. *Entrance requirements:* Additional exam requirements/recommendations for international students: Required—TOEFL (minimum score 550 paper-based; 79 iBT), IELTS (minimum score 6.5). Electronic applications accepted. Application fee is waived when completed online.

Colorado State University–Global Campus, Graduate Programs, Greenwood Village, CO 80111. Offers criminal justice and law enforcement administration (MS); education leadership (MS); finance (MS); healthcare administration and management (MS); human resource management (MHRM); information technology management (MITM); international management (MS); management (MS); organizational leadership (MS); professional accounting (MPA); project management (MS); teaching and learning (MS). *Accreditation:* ACBSP. *Program availability:* Online learning.

Colorado Technical University Aurora, Programs in Business Administration and Management, Aurora, CO 80014. Offers accounting (MBA); business administration (MBA); business administration and management (EMBA); finance (MBA); human resource management (MBA); marketing (MBA); mediation and dispute resolution (MBA); operations management (MBA); project management (MBA); technology management (MBA). *Program availability:* Part-time, evening/weekend. *Degree requirements:* For master's, thesis or alternative. *Entrance requirements:* For master's, minimum undergraduate GPA of 3.0, resume.

Colorado Technical University Colorado Springs, Graduate Studies, Program in Management, Colorado Springs, CO 80907. Offers accounting (MBA, MSA); business administration (MBA); finance (MBA); human resources management (MBA); logistics/supply chain management (MBA); management (DM); marketing (MBA); mediation and dispute resolution (MBA); operations management (MBA); project management (MBA); technology management (MBA). *Accreditation:* ACBSP. *Program availability:* Part-time, evening/weekend, online learning. *Degree requirements:* For master's, thesis or alternative; for doctorate, thesis/dissertation. *Entrance requirements:* For doctorate, minimum graduate GPA of 3.0, 5 years of related work experience. *Faculty research:* Sexual harassment, performance evaluation, critical thinking.

Columbia College, Master of Business Administration Program, Columbia, MO 65216-0002. Offers accounting (MBA); business administration (MBA); human resources (MBA). *Program availability:* Part-time, evening/weekend, 100% online, blended/hybrid learning. *Faculty:* 1 full-time (0 women), 55 part-time/adjunct (16 women). *Students:* 60 full-time (32 women), 335 part-time (201 women); includes 121 minority (67 Black or African American, non-Hispanic/Latino; 1 American Indian or Alaska Native, non-Hispanic/Latino; 6 Asian, non-Hispanic/Latino; 24 Hispanic/Latino; 1 Native Hawaiian or other Pacific Islander, non-Hispanic/Latino; 22 Two or more races, non-Hispanic/Latino), 31 international. Average age 37. 443 applicants, 92% accepted, 127 enrolled. In 2018, 195 master's awarded. *Entrance requirements:* For master's, 3 letters of recommendation, minimum cumulative undergraduate GPA of 3.0, resume, goal statement. Additional exam requirements/recommendations for international students: Required—TOEFL (minimum score 550 paper-based; 79 iBT). *Application deadline:* For fall admission, 8/9 priority date for domestic and international students; for spring admission, 12/27 priority date for domestic and international students. Applications are processed on a rolling basis. Application fee: $0. Electronic applications accepted. *Expenses:* 17640 - tuition (all fees included). *Financial support:* In 2018–19, 54 students received support. Scholarships/grants, tuition waivers (full and partial), and unspecified assistantships available. Financial award application deadline: 3/1; financial award applicants required to submit FAFSA. *Application contact:* Stephanie Johnson, Associate Vice President for Recruiting & Admissions Division, 573-875-7352, Fax: 573-875-7506, E-mail: sjohnson@ccis.edu.
Website: http://www.ccis.edu/graduate/academics/degrees.asp?MBA

Columbia Southern University, MBA Program, Orange Beach, AL 36561. Offers finance (MBA); health care management (MBA); human resource management (MBA); marketing (MBA); project management (MBA); public administration (MBA). *Program*

availability: Part-time, evening/weekend, online learning. *Entrance requirements:* For master's, bachelor's degree from accredited/approved institution. Additional exam requirements/recommendations for international students: Required—TOEFL. Electronic applications accepted.

Columbia University, Graduate School of Business, MBA Program, New York, NY 10027. Offers accounting (MBA); decision, risk, and operations (MBA); entrepreneurship (MBA); finance and economics (MBA); healthcare and pharmaceutical management (MBA); human resource management (MBA); international business (MBA); leadership and ethics (MBA); management (MBA); marketing (MBA); media (MBA); private equity (MBA); real estate (MBA); social enterprise (MBA); value investing (MBA); DDS/MBA; JD/MBA; MBA/MIA; MBA/MPH; MBA/MS; MD/MBA. *Entrance requirements:* For master's, GMAT, 2 letters of recommendation. Additional exam requirements/ recommendations for international students: Required—TOEFL. Electronic applications accepted. *Expenses:* Contact institution. *Faculty research:* Human decision making and behavioral research; real estate market and mortgage defaults; financial crisis and corporate governance; international business; security analysis and accounting.

Columbus State University, Graduate Studies, Turner College of Business, Columbus, GA 31907-5645. Offers applied computer science (MS), including informational assurance, modeling and simulation, software development; business administration (MBA); cyber security (MS); human resource management (Certificate); information systems security (Certificate); modeling and simulation (Certificate); organizational leadership (MS), including human resource management, leader development, servant leadership; servant leadership (Certificate). *Accreditation:* AACSB. *Program availability:* Part-time, evening/weekend, 100% online, blended/hybrid learning. *Faculty:* 10 full-time (3 women), 1 part-time/adjunct (0 women). *Students:* 79 full-time (24 women), 136 part-time (47 women); includes 73 minority (40 Black or African American, non-Hispanic/ Latino; 1 American Indian or Alaska Native, non-Hispanic/Latino; 8 Asian, non-Hispanic/ Latino; 15 Hispanic/Latino; 9 Two or more races, non-Hispanic/Latino), 27 international. Average age 31. 237 applicants, 51% accepted, 64 enrolled. In 2018, 113 master's, 10 other advanced degrees awarded. *Entrance requirements:* For master's, GMAT, GRE, minimum undergraduate GPA of 2.75, letters of recommendation. Additional exam requirements/recommendations for international students: Required—TOEFL (minimum score 550 paper-based; 79 iBT). *Application deadline:* For fall admission, 6/30 for domestic students, 5/1 for international students; for spring admission, 11/1 for domestic and international students; for summer admission, 3/1 for domestic and international students. Applications are processed on a rolling basis. Application fee: $50. Electronic applications accepted. *Expenses:* Contact institution. *Financial support:* In 2018–19, 18 students received support, including 20 research assistantships (averaging $3,000 per year); Federal Work-Study also available. Financial award application deadline: 5/1; financial award applicants required to submit FAFSA. *Unit head:* Dr. Linda U. Hadley, Dean, 706-507-8153, Fax: 706-568-2184, E-mail: hadley_linda@columbusstate.edu. *Application contact:* Catrina Smith-Edmond, Assistant Director for Graduate and Global Admission, 706-507-8824, Fax: 706-568-5091, E-mail: smithedmond_catrina@ columbusstate.edu.
Website: http://turner.columbusstate.edu/

Concordia University, St. Paul, College of Business and Technology, St. Paul, MN 55104-5494. Offers business administration (MBA), including cyber-security leadership; health care management (MBA); human resource management (MA); information technology (MBA); leadership and management (MA); strategic communication management (MA). *Accreditation:* ACBSP. *Program availability:* Part-time, evening/ weekend, 100% online, blended/hybrid learning. *Faculty:* 12 full-time (5 women), 28 part-time/adjunct (14 women). *Students:* 448 full-time (289 women), 30 part-time (17 women); includes 135 minority (58 Black or African American, non-Hispanic/Latino; 2 American Indian or Alaska Native, non-Hispanic/Latino; 46 Asian, non-Hispanic/Latino; 13 Hispanic/Latino; 16 Two or more races, non-Hispanic/Latino), 40 international. Average age 32. 328 applicants, 96% accepted, 149 enrolled. In 2018, 205 master's awarded. *Degree requirements:* For master's, thesis (for some programs). *Entrance requirements:* For master's, official transcripts from regionally-accredited institution stating the conferral of a bachelor's degree with minimum cumulative GPA of 3.0; personal statement; professional resume. Additional exam requirements/ recommendations for international students: Recommended—TOEFL (minimum score 547 paper-based; 78 iBT), IELTS (minimum score 6). *Application deadline:* For fall admission, 8/1 for domestic and international students; for spring admission, 12/1 for domestic and international students; for summer admission, 5/1 for domestic and international students. Applications are processed on a rolling basis. Application fee: $0. Electronic applications accepted. *Expenses:* $625 a credit for 42 credits (for MBA), $475 a credit for 36 credits (for MA/MS). *Financial support:* In 2018–19, 267 students received support. Federal Work-Study, scholarships/grants, and unspecified assistantships available. Financial award applicants required to submit FAFSA. *Faculty research:* Leadership in transition and polarity, managing the evolution of a software product line, decision making and behavioral economics, strength based coaching and the relationship with student success, three-way XML merging. *Unit head:* Dr. Kevin Hall, Dean, 651-603-6165, Fax: 651-641-8807, E-mail: khall@csp.edu. *Application contact:* Amber Faletti, Director of Enrollment Management, 651-641-8838, Fax: 651-603-6320, E-mail: faletti@csp.edu.

Concordia University Wisconsin, Graduate Programs, Batterman School of Business, MBA Program, Mequon, WI 53097-2402. Offers finance (MBA); health care administration (MBA); human resource management (MBA); international business (MBA); international business-bilingual English/Chinese (MBA); management (MBA); management information systems (MBA); managerial communications (MBA); marketing (MBA); public administration (MBA); risk management (MBA). *Program availability:* Online learning. *Degree requirements:* For master's, comprehensive exam, thesis or alternative. *Entrance requirements:* Additional exam requirements/ recommendations for international students: Required—TOEFL. *Expenses:* Contact institution.

Cornell University, Graduate School, Graduate Fields of Industrial and Labor Relations, Ithaca, NY 14853. Offers collective bargaining, labor law and labor history (MILR, MPS, MS, PhD); economic and social statistics (MILR); human resource studies (MILR, MPS, MS, PhD); industrial and labor relations problems (MILR, MPS, MS, PhD); international and comparative labor (MILR, MPS, MS, PhD); labor economics (MILR, MPS, MS, PhD); organizational behavior (MILR, MPS, MS, PhD). *Degree requirements:* For master's, thesis (MS); for doctorate, comprehensive exam, thesis/dissertation, teaching experience. *Entrance requirements:* For master's and doctorate, GMAT or GRE General Test, 2 academic recommendations. Additional exam requirements/ recommendations for international students: Required—TOEFL (minimum score 550 paper-based; 77 iBT). Electronic applications accepted. *Expenses:* Contact institution.

Dallas Baptist University, College of Business, Management Program, Dallas, TX 75211-9299. Offers conflict resolution management (MA); general management (MA, MS); health care management (MA); human resource management (MA); professional sales and management optimization (MA). *Program availability:* Part-time, evening/ weekend, online learning. *Application deadline:* Applications are processed on a rolling basis. Application fee: $25. Electronic applications accepted. Application fee is waived when completed online. *Expenses: Tuition:* Full-time $17,262; part-time $959 per credit hour. *Required fees:* $1000; $500 per semester. Tuition and fees vary according to course load and degree level. *Unit head:* Dr. Sandra Reid, Chair, Graduate School of Business, 214-333-6860, E-mail: sandra@dbu.edu. *Application contact:* Dr. Justin Gandy, Program Director, 214-333-6840, E-mail: justing@dbu.edu.
Website: https://www.dbu.edu/graduate/degree-programs/ma-management

Davenport University, Sneden Graduate School, Grand Rapids, MI 49512. Offers accounting (MBA); business administration (EMBA); finance (MBA); health care management (MBA); human resources (MBA); information assurance (MS); occupational therapy (MSOT); public health (MPH); strategic management (MBA). *Program availability:* Evening/weekend. *Entrance requirements:* For master's, GMAT, minimum undergraduate GPA of 2.75. Additional exam requirements/recommendations for international students: Required—TOEFL. Electronic applications accepted. *Faculty research:* Leadership, management, marketing, organizational culture.

Delaware Valley University, MBA Program, Doylestown, PA 18901-2697. Offers accounting (MBA); entrepreneurship (MBA); finance (MBA); food and agribusiness (MBA); general business (MBA); global executive leadership (MBA); human resource management (MBA); supply chain management (MBA). *Program availability:* Part-time, evening/weekend, online learning. *Entrance requirements:* For master's, minimum undergraduate GPA of 3.0. Electronic applications accepted. *Expenses:* Contact institution.

DePaul University, Kellstadt Graduate School of Business, Chicago, IL 60604. Offers accountancy (MBA, MSA); applied economics (MBA); audit and advisory services (MS); business administration (DBA); business analytics (MS); business strategy and decision-making (MBA); computational finance (MS); economics and policy analysis (MS); enterprise risk management (MS); entrepreneurship (MBA, MS); finance (MBA, MS); general business (MBA); hospitality leadership (MBA); hospitality leadership and operational performance (MS); human resources (MS); international business (MBA); management (MBA, MS); management information systems (MBA); marketing (MBA, MS); marketing analysis (MS); marketing strategy and planning (MBA); real estate (MS); real estate finance and investment (MBA); strategy, execution and valuation (MBA); supply chain management (MS); sustainable management (MS); taxation (MS); JD/ MBA. *Accreditation:* AACSB. *Program availability:* Part-time, evening/weekend, online learning. *Entrance requirements:* For master's, GMAT/GRE, 2 letters of recommendation, resume, essay, official transcripts. Additional exam requirements/ recommendations for international students: Required—TOEFL (minimum score 550 paper-based; 80 iBT). Electronic applications accepted. *Expenses:* Contact institution.

DeSales University, Division of Business, Center Valley, PA 18034-9568. Offers accounting (MBA); computer information systems (MBA); finance (MBA); health care systems management (MBA); human resources management (MBA); management (MBA); marketing (MBA); project management (MBA); self-design (MBA); supply chain management (MBA); DNP/MBA; MSN/MBA. *Accreditation:* ACBSP. *Program availability:* Part-time, evening/weekend, 100% online, blended/hybrid learning. *Entrance requirements:* For master's, GMAT (waived if undergraduate GPA is 3.0 or better), minimum GPA of 3.0 in undergraduate work, literacy in basic software, background or interest in the field of study, personal statement, 2 years of work experience. Additional exam requirements/recommendations for international students: Required—TOEFL. Electronic applications accepted. *Expenses:* Contact institution. *Faculty research:* Quality improvement, executive development, productivity, cross-cultural managerial differences, leadership.

DeVry University–Folsom Campus, Graduate Programs, Folsom, CA 95630. Offers accounting (M Acc); accounting and financial management (MAFM); business administration (MBA); curriculum leadership (M Ed); educational leadership (M Ed); educational technology (M Ed); higher education leadership (M Ed); human resource management (MHRM); information systems management (MISM); network and communications management (MNCM); project management (MPM); public administration (MPA).

East Central University, School of Graduate Studies, Department of Professional Programs in Human Services, Ada, OK 74820. Offers clinical rehabilitation and clinical mental health counseling (MSHR); criminal justice (MSHR); human resources (MSHR). *Accreditation:* CORE. *Program availability:* Part-time, evening/weekend. *Degree requirements:* For master's, thesis optional. *Entrance requirements:* For master's, GRE General Test, MAT, minimum GPA of 2.5. Electronic applications accepted.

Eastern Michigan University, Graduate School, College of Business, Department of Management, Program in Human Resources Management and Organizational Development, Ypsilanti, MI 48197. Offers MSHROD. *Program availability:* Part-time, evening/weekend, online learning. *Students:* 5 full-time (4 women), 68 part-time (54 women); includes 29 minority (19 Black or African American, non-Hispanic/Latino; 4 Asian, non-Hispanic/Latino; 4 Hispanic/Latino; 2 Two or more races, non-Hispanic/ Latino), 3 international. Average age 32. 47 applicants, 81% accepted, 18 enrolled. In 2018, 62 master's awarded. *Entrance requirements:* For master's, GMAT. Additional exam requirements/recommendations for international students: Required—TOEFL. *Application deadline:* Applications are processed on a rolling basis. Application fee: $45. *Financial support:* Fellowships, research assistantships with full tuition reimbursements, teaching assistantships with full tuition reimbursements, career-related internships or fieldwork, Federal Work-Study, institutionally sponsored loans, scholarships/grants, tuition waivers (partial), and unspecified assistantships available. Support available to part-time students. Financial award applicants required to submit FAFSA. *Unit head:* Dr. Fraya Wagner-Marsh, Department Head, 734-487-3240, Fax: 734-487-4100, E-mail: fwagnerm@emich.edu. *Application contact:* Dr. Fraya Wagner-Marsh, Department Head, 734-487-3240, Fax: 734-487-4100, E-mail: fwagnerm@emich.edu.
Website: http://www.emich.edu/cob/departments_centers/management/mshrod.php

Eastern Michigan University, Graduate School, College of Business, Programs in Business Administration, Ypsilanti, MI 48197. Offers business administration (MBA, Graduate Certificate); computer information systems (Graduate Certificate); e-business (MBA, Graduate Certificate); enterprise business intelligence (MBA); entrepreneurship (MBA, Graduate Certificate); finance (MBA, Graduate Certificate); human resources (MBA); human resources management (Graduate Certificate); information systems (MBA); internal auditing (MBA); international business (MBA, Graduate Certificate); marketing management (Graduate Certificate); nonprofit management (MBA); organizational development (Graduate Certificate); supply chain management (MBA, Graduate Certificate). *Accreditation:* AACSB. *Program availability:* Part-time, online learning. *Students:* 69 full-time (38 women), 251 part-time (140 women); includes 100 minority (63 Black or African American, non-Hispanic/Latino; 1 American Indian or Alaska Native, non-Hispanic/Latino; 12 Asian, non-Hispanic/Latino; 14 Hispanic/Latino; 10 Two or more races, non-Hispanic/Latino), 28 international. Average age 32. 199 applicants, 75% accepted, 83 enrolled. In 2018, 75 master's, 50 other advanced degrees awarded. *Entrance requirements:* For master's, GMAT (minimum score 450), minimum cumulative undergraduate GPA of 2.75. Additional exam requirements/ recommendations for international students: Required—TOEFL. *Application deadline:* For fall admission, 5/15 priority date for domestic students, 2/15 priority date for international students; for winter admission, 10/15 priority date for domestic students, 9/ 1 priority date for international students; for summer admission, 3/15 priority date for

domestic students, 3/1 priority date for international students. Applications are processed on a rolling basis. Application fee: $45. *Financial support:* Fellowships, research assistantships with full tuition reimbursements, teaching assistantships with full tuition reimbursements, career-related internships or fieldwork, Federal Work-Study, institutionally sponsored loans, scholarships/grants, tuition waivers (partial), and unspecified assistantships available. Support available to part-time students. Financial award applicants required to submit FAFSA. *Unit head:* K. Michelle Henry, Director, Graduate Business Programs, 734-487-4444, Fax: 734-483-1316, E-mail: cob.graduate@emich.edu. *Application contact:* K. Michelle Henry, Director, Graduate Business Programs, 734-487-4444, Fax: 734-483-1316, E-mail: cob.graduate@emich.edu.
Website: http://www.emich.edu/cob/mba/

Embry-Riddle Aeronautical University–Daytona, College of Business, Daytona Beach, FL 32114-3900. Offers airline management (MBA); airport management (MBA); aviation finance (MSAF); aviation human resources (MBA); aviation management (MBA-AM); aviation system management (MBA); finance (MBA). *Accreditation:* ACBSP. *Degree requirements:* For master's, thesis (for some programs). *Entrance requirements:* For master's, GRE (for some programs). Additional exam requirements/recommendations for international students: Required—TOEFL (minimum score 550 paper-based, 79 iBT) or IELTS (6). Electronic applications accepted.

Embry-Riddle Aeronautical University–Worldwide, Department of Decision Sciences, Daytona Beach, FL 32114-3900. Offers aviation and aerospace (MSPM); aviation/aerospace management (MSEM); financial management (MSEM, MSPM); general management (MSPM); global management (MSPM); human resources management (MSPM); information systems (MSPM); leadership (MSEM, MSPM); logistics and supply chain management (MSEM, MSLSCM, MSPM); management (MSEM, MSPM); project management (MSEM); systems engineering (MSEM, MSPM); technical management (MSPM). *Program availability:* Part-time, evening/weekend, EagleVision Classroom (between classrooms), EagleVision Home (faculty and students at home), and a blend of Classroom or Home. *Degree requirements:* For master's, comprehensive exam (for some programs), thesis (for some programs). *Entrance requirements:* Additional exam requirements/recommendations for international students: Required—TOEFL (minimum score 550 paper-based; 79 iBT), IELTS (minimum score 6). Electronic applications accepted. *Expenses:* Contact institution.

Emmanuel College, Graduate and Professional Programs, Graduate Programs in Human Resource Management, Boston, MA 02115. Offers MS, Graduate Certificate. *Program availability:* Part-time, evening/weekend, blended/hybrid learning. *Degree requirements:* For master's, 36 credits. *Entrance requirements:* For master's and Graduate Certificate, transcripts from all regionally-accredited institutions attended (showing proof of bachelor's degree completion), 2 letters of recommendation, essay, resume. Additional exam requirements/recommendations for international students: Required—TOEFL. Electronic applications accepted. *Expenses:* Contact institution.

Everglades University, Graduate Programs, Program in Business Administration, Boca Raton, FL 33431. Offers accounting for managers (MBA); aviation management (MBA); human resource management (MBA); project management (MBA). *Program availability:* Part-time, evening/weekend, 100% online. *Entrance requirements:* For master's, GMAT (minimum score of 400) or GRE (minimum score of 290), bachelor's or graduate degree from college accredited by an agency recognized by the U.S. Department of Education; minimum cumulative GPA of 2.0 at the baccalaureate level, 3.0 at the master's level. Additional exam requirements/recommendations for international students: Recommended—TOEFL (minimum score 500 paper-based). Electronic applications accepted. *Expenses:* Contact institution.

Fairleigh Dickinson University, Florham Campus, Silberman College of Business, Center for Human Resource Management Studies, Program in Human Resource Management, Madison, NJ 07940-1099. Offers MBA, MA/MBA.

Fairleigh Dickinson University, Metropolitan Campus, Silberman College of Business, Center for Human Resources Management Studies, Program in Human Resource Management, Teaneck, NJ 07666-1914. Offers MBA, Certificate.

Fitchburg State University, Division of Graduate and Continuing Education, Program in Business Administration, Fitchburg, MA 01420-2697. Offers accounting (MBA); human resources management (MBA); management (MBA). *Program availability:* Part-time, evening/weekend, 100% online. *Entrance requirements:* Additional exam requirements/recommendations for international students: Required—TOEFL (minimum score 550 paper-based; 79 iBT). Electronic applications accepted. *Expenses:* Contact institution.

Florida Institute of Technology, Aberdeen Education Center (Maryland), Program in Management, Melbourne, FL 32901-6975. Offers acquisition and contract management (MS, PMBA); business administration (MS, PMBA); contracts management (PMBA); financial management (MPA); global management (PMBA); health management (MS); human resources management (MS, PMBA); information systems (PMBA); logistics management (MS); management (MS), including information systems, operations research; materials acquisition management (MS); operations research (MS); public administration (MPA); research (PMBA); space systems (MS); space systems management (MS). *Expenses: Tuition:* Full-time $22,338; part-time $1241 per credit hour. Tuition and fees vary according to degree level, campus/location and program. *Financial support:* Application deadline: 3/1. *Application contact:* Online Learning and Off-Campus Programs Admissions, 321-674-8263, E-mail: gradadm-olocp@fit.edu.
Website: https://www.fit.edu/education-centers/degrees-and-programs/management-ms/

Florida International University, Chapman Graduate School of Business, Department of Management and International Business, Miami, FL 33199. Offers human resources management (MSHRM); international business (MIB); management and international business (EMBA, IMBA, MBA, PhD). *Program availability:* Part-time, evening/weekend. *Faculty:* 19 full-time (7 women), 27 part-time/adjunct (10 women). *Students:* 892 full-time (530 women), 555 part-time (285 women); includes 1,094 minority (237 Black or African American, non-Hispanic/Latino; 47 Asian, non-Hispanic/Latino; 779 Hispanic/Latino; 4 Native Hawaiian or other Pacific Islander, non-Hispanic/Latino; 27 Two or more races, non-Hispanic/Latino), 153 international. Average age 32. 1,377 applicants, 50% accepted, 476 enrolled. In 2018, 792 master's, 6 doctorates awarded. *Degree requirements:* For doctorate, comprehensive exam, thesis/dissertation. *Entrance requirements:* For master's, GMAT or GRE (depending on program), minimum GPA of 3.0 in upper-level coursework; for doctorate, GMAT or GRE, letter of intent; 3 letters of recommendation; resume. Additional exam requirements/recommendations for international students: Required—TOEFL (minimum score 550 paper-based; 80 iBT) or IELTS (minimum score 6.5). *Application deadline:* For fall admission, 6/1 for domestic students, 4/1 for international students; for spring admission, 10/1 for domestic students, 9/1 for international students. Applications are processed on a rolling basis. Application fee: $30. Electronic applications accepted. *Expenses:* Contact institution. *Financial support:* Institutionally sponsored loans and scholarships/grants available. Financial award application deadline: 3/1; financial award applicants required to submit FAFSA. *Faculty research:* International business, strategy, entrepreneurship, human resource management. *Unit head:* Dr. Willam Newbury, Chair, 305-348-1103, E-mail: newburry@fiu.edu. *Application contact:* Nanett Rojas, Manager, Admissions Operations, 305-348-7464, Fax: 305-348-7441, E-mail: gradadm@fiu.edu.

Florida State University, The Graduate School, College of Business, Tallahassee, FL 32306-1110. Offers accounting (M Acc), including assurance and advisory services, generalist, taxation; business administration (MBA, PhD), including accounting (PhD), finance (PhD), management information systems (PhD), marketing (PhD), organizational behavior and human resources (PhD), risk management and insurance (PhD), strategy (PhD); finance (MS); management information systems (MS); risk management and insurance (MS); JD/MBA; MSW/MBA. *Accreditation:* AACSB. *Program availability:* Part-time, 100% online. *Students:* Average age 31. 300 applicants, 61% accepted, 133 enrolled. In 2018, 268 master's, 9 doctorates awarded. Terminal master's awarded for partial completion of doctoral program. *Degree requirements:* For doctorate, comprehensive exam, thesis/dissertation. *Entrance requirements:* For master's, GMAT, GRE (for all except MS in finance), work experience (MBA, MS); minimum GPA of 3.0, letters of recommendation; for doctorate, GMAT, GRE (for marketing, organizational behavior, risk management and insurance, management information systems, and human resources only), minimum graduate GPA of 3.5, letters of recommendation. Additional exam requirements/recommendations for international students: Required—TOEFL (minimum score 600 paper-based; 85 iBT); Recommended—IELTS (minimum score 6). *Application deadline:* For fall admission, 6/1 for domestic and international students; for spring admission, 10/1 for domestic and international students; for summer admission, 3/1 for domestic and international students. Applications are processed on a rolling basis. Application fee: $30. Electronic applications accepted. *Expenses:* Contact institution. *Financial support:* In 2018–19, 146 students received support, including 26 fellowships (averaging $1,500 per year), 77 research assistantships with full tuition reimbursements available (averaging $20,000 per year), 43 teaching assistantships with full tuition reimbursements available (averaging $20,000 per year); career-related internships or fieldwork, scholarships/grants, health care benefits, tuition waivers (full and partial), and unspecified assistantships also available. Support available to part-time students. Financial award application deadline: 1/1; financial award applicants required to submit FAFSA. *Faculty research:* Business strategy, marketing, finance, accounting, business analytics. *Total annual research expenditures:* $1.4 million. *Unit head:* Dr. Michael Hartline, Dean, 850-644-4405, Fax: 850-644-0915, E-mail: mhartline@business.fsu.edu. *Application contact:* Jennifer Clark, Director, 850-644-6458, E-mail: gradprograms@business.fsu.edu.
Website: http://business.fsu.edu/

Framingham State University, Graduate Studies, Program in Human Resource Management, Framingham, MA 01701-9101. Offers MHR. *Program availability:* Part-time, evening/weekend.

Franklin Pierce University, Graduate and Professional Studies, Rindge, NH 03461-0060. Offers curriculum and instruction (M Ed); elementary education (MS Ed); emerging network technologies (Graduate Certificate); energy and sustainability studies (MBA, Graduate Certificate); health administration (MBA, Graduate Certificate); human resource management (MBA, Graduate Certificate); information technology (MBA); leadership (MBA); nursing education (MS); nursing leadership (MS); physical therapy (DPT); physician assistant studies (MPAS); special education (M Ed); sports management (MBA). *Accreditation:* APTA. *Program availability:* Part-time, 100% online, blended/hybrid learning. *Degree requirements:* For master's, concentrated original research projects; student teaching; fieldwork and/or internship; leadership project; PRAXIS I and II (for M Ed); for doctorate, concentrated original research projects, clinical fieldwork and/or internship, leadership project. *Entrance requirements:* For master's, minimum GPA of 2.5, 3 letters of recommendation; competencies in accounting, economics, statistics, and computer skills through life experience or undergraduate coursework (for MBA); certification/e-portfolio, minimum C grade in all education courses (for M Ed); license to practice as RN (for MS); for doctorate, GRE, 80 hours of observation/work in PT settings; completion of anatomy, chemistry, physics, and statistics; minimum GPA of 3.0. Additional exam requirements/recommendations for international students: Required—TOEFL (minimum score 550 paper-based; 61 iBT). Electronic applications accepted. *Faculty research:* Evidence-based practice in sports physical therapy, human resource management in economic crisis, leadership in nursing, innovation in sports facility management, differentiated learning and understanding by design.

Gannon University, School of Graduate Studies, College of Engineering and Business, Dahlkemper School of Business, Program in Business Administration, Erie, PA 16541-0001. Offers business administration (MBA); finance (MBA); human resources management (MBA); marketing (MBA). *Accreditation:* ACBSP. *Program availability:* Part-time, evening/weekend, 100% online, blended/hybrid learning. *Entrance requirements:* For master's, GMAT, bachelor's degree in any discipline from any accredited college or university, resume, transcripts, 3 letters of recommendation. Additional exam requirements/recommendations for international students: Required—TOEFL (minimum score 79 iBT). Electronic applications accepted. Application fee is waived when completed online.

George Fox University, College of Business, Newberg, OR 97132-2697. Offers accounting (DBA); finance (MBA); management (DBA); management and leadership (MBA); marketing (DBA); organizational strategy (MBA); strategic human resource management (MBA). MBA offered in Newberg, OR and in Portland, OR. *Accreditation:* ACBSP. *Program availability:* Part-time, evening/weekend, online learning. *Degree requirements:* For master's, capstone project; for doctorate, credit-applied research project. *Entrance requirements:* For master's, resume (5 years of professional experience); 3 professional references; interview; financial e-learning course; official transcripts; for doctorate, GRE or GMAT, resume; personal mission statement; academic research writing sample; official transcript from each college/university attended; three professional references. Additional exam requirements/recommendations for international students: Required—TOEFL (minimum score 577 paper-based; 90 iBT) or IELTS (minimum score 7). Electronic applications accepted. *Expenses:* Contact institution.

George Mason University, Schar School of Policy and Government, Program in Organization Development and Knowledge Management, Arlington, VA 22201. Offers MS. *Faculty:* 2 full-time (1 woman), 4 part-time/adjunct (2 women). *Students:* 2 full-time (both women), 38 part-time (31 women); includes 16 minority (5 Black or African American, non-Hispanic/Latino; 6 Asian, non-Hispanic/Latino; 2 Hispanic/Latino; 3 Two or more races, non-Hispanic/Latino), 4 international. Average age 34. 32 applicants, 97% accepted, 21 enrolled. In 2018, 25 master's awarded. *Degree requirements:* For master's, thesis or alternative, internship. *Entrance requirements:* For master's, GRE (for students seeking merit-based scholarships), bachelor's degree with minimum GPA of 3.0, current resume, 2 letters of recommendation, expanded goals statement, 2 copies of official transcripts. Additional exam requirements/recommendations for international students: Required—TOEFL (minimum score 575 paper-based; 88 iBT), IELTS (minimum score 6.5), PTE (minimum score 59). *Application deadline:* For fall admission, 2/1 priority date for domestic and international students. Applications are processed on a rolling basis. Application fee: $75 ($80 for international students). Electronic applications accepted. *Expenses:* $689 per credit in-state tuition, $1,446.75

per credit out-of-state tuition. *Financial support:* Career-related internships or fieldwork, Federal Work-Study, scholarships/grants, unspecified assistantships, and health care benefits (for full-time research or teaching assistantship recipients) available. Financial award application deadline: 3/1; financial award applicants required to submit FAFSA. *Faculty research:* Organization development; appreciative intelligence; leadership; collaborative learning; knowledge management. *Unit head:* Tojo Joseph Thatchenkery, Director, 703-993-3808, Fax: 703-993-8215, E-mail: thatchen@gmu.edu. *Application contact:* Stephanie Ellis, Graduate Admissions Coordinator, 703-993-4478, E-mail: sellis11@gmu.edu.
Website: http://spgia.gmu.edu/programs/graduate-degrees/organization-development-knowledge-management-odkm/

Georgetown University, Graduate School of Arts and Sciences, School of Continuing Studies, Washington, DC 20057. Offers American studies (MALS); applied intelligence (MPS); Catholic studies (MALS); classical civilizations (MALS); emergency and disaster management (MPS); ethics and the professions (MALS); global strategic communications (MPS); hospitality management (MPS); human resources management (MPS); humanities (MALS); individualized study (MALS); integrated marketing communications (MPS); international affairs (MALS); Islam and Muslim-Christian relations (MALS); journalism (MPS); liberal studies (DLS); literature and society (MALS); medieval and early modern European studies (MALS); public relations and corporate communications (MPS); real estate (MPS); religious studies (MALS); social and public policy (MALS); sports industry management (MPS); systems engineering management (MPS); technology management (MPS); the theory and practice of American democracy (MALS); urban and regional planning (MPS); visual culture (MALS). MPS in systems engineering management offered jointly with Stevens Institute of Technology. *Entrance requirements:* Additional exam requirements/recommendations for international students: Required—TOEFL.

The George Washington University, Columbian College of Arts and Sciences, Department of Organizational Sciences and Communication, Washington, DC 20052. Offers human resources management (MA); non-profit management (Graduate Certificate); organizational management (Graduate Certificate). *Program availability:* Part-time, evening/weekend. *Students:* 41 full-time (24 women), 18 part-time (12 women); includes 13 minority (5 Black or African American, non-Hispanic/Latino; 2 Asian, non-Hispanic/Latino; 6 Hispanic/Latino), 16 international. Average age 27. 126 applicants, 71% accepted, 32 enrolled. In 2018, 42 master's, 15 other advanced degrees awarded. *Entrance requirements:* For master's, GRE General Test, minimum GPA of 3.0; for Graduate Certificate, minimum GPA of 3.0. Additional exam requirements/recommendations for international students: Required—TOEFL (minimum score 500 paper-based; 80 iBT). *Application deadline:* For fall admission, 1/15 priority date for domestic and international students; for spring admission, 10/1 priority date for domestic students, 9/1 priority date for international students. Applications are processed on a rolling basis. Application fee: $75. Electronic applications accepted. *Financial support:* Federal Work-Study and institutionally sponsored loans available. *Unit head:* Dr. Lynn Offermann, Chair, 202-994-8507, E-mail: lro@gwu.edu. *Application contact:* Information Contact, 202-994-1878, Fax: 202-994-1881.
Website: http://www.gwu.edu/~orgsci/

Georgia State University, J. Mack Robinson College of Business, Department of Managerial Sciences, Atlanta, GA 30302-3083. Offers business analysis (MBA, MS); entrepreneurship (MBA); human resources management (MBA, MS); operations management (MBA, MS); organization behavior/human resource management (PhD); organization management (MBA); organizational change (MS); strategic management (PhD). *Accreditation:* AACSB. *Program availability:* Part-time, evening/weekend. *Faculty:* 11 full-time (2 women), 1 part-time/adjunct (0 women). *Students:* 11 full-time (6 women); includes 5 minority (3 Black or African American, non-Hispanic/Latino; 1 Asian, non-Hispanic/Latino; 1 Two or more races, non-Hispanic/Latino), 3 international. Average age 29. 54 applicants, 20% accepted, 8 enrolled. In 2018, 9 master's, 3 doctorates awarded. *Entrance requirements:* For master's, GRE or GMAT, transcripts from all institutions attended, resume, essays; for doctorate, GMAT, three letters of recommendation, personal statement, transcripts from all institutions attended, resume. Additional exam requirements/recommendations for international students: Required—TOEFL (minimum score 610 paper-based; 101 iBT), IELTS (minimum score 7). *Application deadline:* For fall admission, 5/1 priority date for domestic students, 2/1 priority date for international students; for spring admission, 9/15 priority date for domestic students, 4/1 priority date for international students. Applications are processed on a rolling basis. Application fee: $50. Electronic applications accepted. *Expenses: Tuition, area resident:* Full-time $9360; part-time $390 per credit hour. Tuition, state resident: full-time $9360; part-time $390 per credit hour. Tuition, nonresident: full-time $30,024; part-time $1251 per credit hour. *International tuition:* $30,024 full-time. *Required fees:* $2128. *Financial support:* Research assistantships, teaching assistantships, scholarships/grants, tuition waivers, and unspecified assistantships available. Financial award applicants required to submit FAFSA. *Faculty research:* Entrepreneurship and innovation; strategy process; workplace interactions, relationships, and processes; leadership and culture; supply chain management. *Unit head:* Dr. Pamela S. Barr, Chair, 404-413-7525, Fax: 404-413-7571. *Application contact:* Toby McChesney, Assistant Dean for Graduate Recruiting and Student Services, 404-413-7167, Fax: 404-413-7162, E-mail: rcbgradadmissions@gsu.edu.
Website: http://mgmt.robinson.gsu.edu/

Golden Gate University, Ageno School of Business, San Francisco, CA 94105-2968. Offers accounting (MBA); adaptive leadership (MBA); advanced financial planning (MS); business administration (EMBA, MBA, DBA); business analytics (MBA, MS); entrepreneurship (MBA); finance (MBA, MS, Certificate); financial life planning (Certificate); financial planning (MS, Certificate); global supply chain management (MBA, Certificate); human resource management (MBA, MS, Certificate); information technology management (MBA, MS, Certificate); international business (MBA); marketing (MBA, MS, Certificate); project management (MBA, MS, Certificate); psychology (MA, Certificate); public administration (EMPA, MBA); public administration leadership (Certificate); JD/MBA. *Program availability:* Part-time, evening/weekend. *Degree requirements:* For doctorate, thesis/dissertation, qualifying examination. *Entrance requirements:* For master's, GMAT (for MBA), minimum GPA of 2.5 (MS). Additional exam requirements/recommendations for international students: Required—TOEFL (minimum score 550 paper-based; 79 iBT). Electronic applications accepted. *Expenses:* Contact institution.

Goldey-Beacom College, Graduate Program, Wilmington, DE 19808-1999. Offers business administration (MBA); finance (MS); financial management (MBA); health care management (MBA); human resource management (MBA); information technology (MBA); international business management (MBA); major finance (MBA); major taxation (MBA); management (MM); marketing management (MBA); taxation (MBA, MS). *Accreditation:* ACBSP. *Program availability:* Part-time, evening/weekend. *Entrance requirements:* For master's, GMAT, MAT, GRE, minimum GPA of 3.0. Additional exam requirements/recommendations for international students: Required—TOEFL (minimum score 65 iBT); Recommended—IELTS (minimum score 6). Electronic applications accepted.

Grambling State University, School of Graduate Studies and Research, College of Arts and Sciences, Department of Political Science and Public Administration, Grambling, LA 71270. Offers health services administration (MPA); human resource management (MPA); public management (MPA); state and local government (MPA). *Accreditation:* NASPAA. *Program availability:* Part-time. *Degree requirements:* For master's, comprehensive exam (for some programs), thesis optional. *Entrance requirements:* For master's, GRE, minimum GPA of 2.75 on last degree. Additional exam requirements/recommendations for international students: Required—TOEFL (minimum score 500 paper-based; 62 iBT). Electronic applications accepted.

Grand Canyon University, Colangelo College of Business, Phoenix, AZ 85017-1097. Offers accounting (MBA, MS); business analytics (MS); disaster preparedness and executive fire service leadership (MS); finance (MBA); general management (MBA); health systems management (MBA); information technology management (MS); leadership (MBA, MS); marketing (MBA); organizational leadership and entrepreneurship (MS); project management (MBA); sports business (MBA); strategic human resource management (MBA). *Accreditation:* ACBSP. *Program availability:* Part-time, evening/weekend, online learning. *Entrance requirements:* For master's, equivalent of two years' full-time professional work experience. Additional exam requirements/recommendations for international students: Required—TOEFL (minimum score 575 paper-based; 90 iBT), IELTS (minimum score 7). Electronic applications accepted.

Grantham University, Mark Skousen School of Business, Lenexa, KS 66219. Offers business administration (MBA); business intelligence (MS); human resources (Certificate); information management (MBA); performance improvement (MS); project management (MBA, Certificate). *Program availability:* Part-time, evening/weekend, online only, 100% online. *Students:* 556 full-time (238 women), 301 part-time (122 women); includes 369 minority (268 Black or African American, non-Hispanic/Latino; 5 American Indian or Alaska Native, non-Hispanic/Latino; 16 Asian, non-Hispanic/Latino; 50 Hispanic/Latino; 4 Native Hawaiian or other Pacific Islander, non-Hispanic/Latino; 26 Two or more races, non-Hispanic/Latino), 1 international. Average age 40. 206 applicants, 90% accepted, 159 enrolled. In 2018, 284 master's, 16 other advanced degrees awarded. *Degree requirements:* For master's, comprehensive exam (for some programs), PMP Prep Exams throughout the term (for MBA in project management); for Certificate, comprehensive exam (for some programs), PMP Prep Exam (for project management). *Entrance requirements:* For master's, baccalaureate or master's degree with minimum cumulative GPA of 2.5 from institution accredited by agency recognized by ED or foreign equivalent; official transcripts showing proof of degree. Additional exam requirements/recommendations for international students: Required—TOEFL (minimum score 530 paper-based; 71 iBT), IELTS (minimum score 6.5), PTE (minimum score 50). *Application deadline:* Applications are processed on a rolling basis. Application fee: $0. Electronic applications accepted. *Expenses: Tuition:* Full-time $4200; part-time $350 per credit hour. *Required fees:* $50; $50 per credit hour. *Financial support:* Scholarships/grants available. Financial award applicants required to submit FAFSA. *Faculty research:* How chronic diseases contribute to the rising costs of healthcare, marketing for entrepreneurs, managers' hiring practices of workers with disability, organizational structures, organizational change, online pedagogy, impact of instructor video tips in the online classroom, decision-making techniques. *Unit head:* Dr. David Marker, Dean of the Mark Skousen School of Business, 913-309-4747, Fax: 844-260-6287, E-mail: dmarker@grantham.edu. *Application contact:* Lauren Cook, Director of Admissions, 800-955-2527 Ext. 803, Fax: 877-304-4467, E-mail: admissions@grantham.edu.
Website: https://www.grantham.edu/school-of-business/

Hawai`i Pacific University, College of Business, Program in Business Administration, Honolulu, HI 96813. Offers finance (MBA); human resource management (MBA); information systems (MBA); international business (MBA); management (MBA); marketing (MBA); organizational change and development (MBA). *Program availability:* Part-time, evening/weekend, 100% online, blended/hybrid learning. *Entrance requirements:* For master's, GMAT or GRE. Additional exam requirements/recommendations for international students: Recommended—TOEFL (minimum score 550 paper-based; 80 iBT), IELTS (minimum score 6), TWE (minimum score 5). Electronic applications accepted.

HEC Montreal, School of Business Administration, Doctoral Program in Administration, Montréal, QC H3T 2A7, Canada. Offers accounting (PhD); applied economics (PhD); data science (PhD); finance (PhD); financial engineering (PhD); information technology (PhD); international business (PhD); logistics and operations management (PhD); management science (PhD); management, strategy and organizations (PhD); marketing (PhD); organizational behaviour and human resources (PhD). Program offered jointly with Concordia University, McGill University, and Universite du Quebec a Montreal. *Accreditation:* AACSB. *Students:* 130 full-time (55 women). 114 applicants, 46% accepted, 31 enrolled. In 2018, 19 doctorates awarded. *Entrance requirements:* For doctorate, TAGE MAGE, GMAT, or GRE, master's degree in administration or related field. *Application deadline:* For fall admission, 1/15 for domestic and international students. Application fee: 91 (191 for international students). Electronic applications accepted. *Expenses: Tuition, area resident:* Full-time $3052.80 Canadian dollars; part-time $84.80 Canadian dollars per credit. Tuition, state resident: full-time $3816 Canadian dollars; part-time $264.67 Canadian dollars per credit. Tuition, nonresident: full-time $11,910 Canadian dollars. *International tuition:* $20,905.20 Canadian dollars full-time. *Required fees:* $1805.34 Canadian dollars; $43.62 Canadian dollars per credit. $71.78 Canadian dollars per term. Tuition and fees vary according to degree level and program. *Financial support:* Research assistantships, teaching assistantships, and scholarships/grants available. Financial award application deadline: 9/2. *Faculty research:* Art management, business policy, entrepreneurship, new technologies, transportation. *Unit head:* Guy Paré, Director, 514-340-6264, E-mail: guy.pare@hec.ca. *Application contact:* Julie Bilodeau, PhD Program Analyst, 514-340-6000, Fax: 514-340-6411, E-mail: analyste.phd@hec.ca.
Website: http://www.hec.ca/en/programs/phd/index.html

HEC Montreal, School of Business Administration, Graduate Diploma Programs in Administration, Montréal, QC H3T 2A7, Canada. Offers business administration (Graduate Diploma); business analysis - information technology (Graduate Diploma); e-business (Graduate Diploma); entrepreneurship (Graduate Diploma); financial professions (Graduate Diploma); human resources (Graduate Diploma); management (Graduate Diploma); management and sustainable development (Graduate Diploma); management of cultural organizations (Graduate Diploma); marketing communication (Graduate Diploma); organizational development (Graduate Diploma); professional accounting (Graduate Diploma); supply chain management (Graduate Diploma); taxation (Graduate Diploma). All courses are given in French. *Students:* 412 full-time (242 women), 885 part-time (552 women). 834 applicants, 65% accepted, 351 enrolled. In 2018, 611 Graduate Diplomas awarded. *Entrance requirements:* For degree, bachelor's degree. Application fee: $91 Canadian dollars ($191 Canadian dollars for international students). Electronic applications accepted. *Expenses: Tuition, area resident:* Full-time $3052.80 Canadian dollars; part-time $84.80 Canadian dollars per credit. Tuition, state resident: full-time $3816 Canadian dollars; part-time $264.67 Canadian dollars per credit. Tuition, nonresident: full-time $11,910 Canadian dollars. *International tuition:* $20,905.20 Canadian dollars full-time. *Required fees:* $1805.34

Canadian dollars; $43.62 Canadian dollars per credit. $71.78 Canadian dollars per term. Tuition and fees vary according to degree level and program. *Financial support:* Research assistantships, teaching assistantships, and scholarships/grants available. Financial award application deadline: 9/2. *Faculty research:* Art management, business policy, entrepreneurship, new technologies, transportation. *Unit head:* Renaud Lachance, Director, 514-340-6428, E-mail: renaud.lachance@hec.ca. *Application contact:* Anny Caron, Administrative Director, 514-340-6000, Fax: 514-340-6411, E-mail: aide@hec.ca.
Website: http://www.hec.ca/programmes/dess/index.html

HEC Montreal, School of Business Administration, Master of Science Programs in Administration, Program in Human Resources Management, Montréal, QC H3T 2A7, Canada. Offers M Sc. All courses are given in French (Thesis stream, Supervised project stream). *Students:* 49 full-time (35 women), 14 part-time (12 women). 37 applicants, 65% accepted, 19 enrolled. In 2018, 30 master's awarded. *Entrance requirements:* For master's, BBA, undergraduate degree in another field, degree deemed equivalent by program director and minimum GPA of 3.0 on 4.3 scale. Additional exam requirements/recommendations for international students: Required— TAGE MAGE (minimum recommended score of 300), GMAT (minimum recommended score of 630), or GRE. *Application deadline:* For fall admission, 3/15 for domestic and international students; for winter admission, 9/15 for domestic and international students. Application fee: $91 Canadian dollars ($191 Canadian dollars for international students). Electronic applications accepted. *Expenses: Tuition, area resident:* Full-time $3052.80 Canadian dollars; part-time $84.80 Canadian dollars per credit. Tuition, state resident: full-time $3816 Canadian dollars; part-time $264.67 Canadian dollars per credit. Tuition, nonresident: full-time $11,910 Canadian dollars. *International tuition:* $20,905.20 Canadian dollars full-time. *Required fees:* $1805.34 Canadian dollars; $43.62 Canadian dollars per credit. $71.78 Canadian dollars per term. Tuition and fees vary according to degree level and program. *Financial support:* Research assistantships, teaching assistantships, and scholarships/grants available. Financial award application deadline: 9/2. *Unit head:* Dr. Sihem Taboubi, Director, 514-340-6428, E-mail: sihem.taboubi@hec.ca. *Application contact:* Marianne de Moura, Administrative Director, 514-340-6000, Fax: 514-340-6411, E-mail: aide@hec.ca.
Website: http://www.hec.ca/programmes/maitrises/maitrise-gestion-ressources-humaines/index.html

Herzing University Online, Program in Business Administration, Menomonee Falls, WI 53051. Offers accounting (MBA); business administration (MBA); business management (MBA); healthcare management (MBA); human resources (MBA); marketing (MBA); project management (MBA); technology management (MBA). *Program availability:* Online learning.

Hofstra University, Frank G. Zarb School of Business, Programs in Management and General Business, Hempstead, NY 11549. Offers business administration (MBA), including health services management, management, sports and entertainment management, strategic business management, strategic healthcare management; general management (Advanced Certificate); human resource management (MS, Advanced Certificate). *Program availability:* Part-time, evening/weekend, blended/hybrid learning. *Students:* 121 full-time (48 women), 112 part-time (52 women); includes 96 minority (18 Black or African American, non-Hispanic/Latino; 1 American Indian or Alaska Native, non-Hispanic/Latino; 34 Asian, non-Hispanic/Latino; 38 Hispanic/Latino; 5 Two or more races, non-Hispanic/Latino), 16 international. Average age 33. 290 applicants, 75% accepted, 89 enrolled. In 2018, 110 master's awarded. *Degree requirements:* For master's, thesis optional, capstone course (for MBA), thesis (for MS), minimum GPA of 3.0. *Entrance requirements:* For master's, GMAT/GRE, 2 letters of recommendation, resume, essay. Additional exam requirements/recommendations for international students: Required—TOEFL (minimum score 550 paper-based; 80 iBT); Recommended—IELTS (minimum score 6). *Application deadline:* Applications are processed on a rolling basis. Application fee: $75. Electronic applications accepted. *Expenses:* $1,375 per credit plus fees. *Financial support:* In 2018–19, 91 students received support, including 84 fellowships with full and partial tuition reimbursements available (averaging $4,279 per year), 1 research assistantship with full and partial tuition reimbursement available (averaging $9,179 per year); career-related internships or fieldwork, Federal Work-Study, institutionally sponsored loans, scholarships/grants, tuition waivers (full and partial), unspecified assistantships, and scholarships and endowed scholarships also available. Support available to part-time students. Financial award applicants required to submit FAFSA. *Faculty research:* Organizational behavior; sustainability; entrepreneurial spawning; family business; global supply chain strategies. *Unit head:* Dr. Kaushik Sengupta, Chairperson, 516-463-7825, Fax: 516-463-4834, E-mail: kaushik.sengupta@hofstra.edu. *Application contact:* Sunil Samuel, Assistant Vice President of Admissions, 516-463-4723, Fax: 516-463-4664, E-mail: graduateadmission@hofstra.edu.
Website: http://www.hofstra.edu/business/

Holy Family University, Graduate and Professional Programs, School of Business Administration, Philadelphia, PA 19114. Offers accountancy (MS); finance (MBA); health care administration (MBA); human resource management (MBA); information systems management (MBA). *Accreditation:* ACBSP. *Program availability:* Part-time, evening/weekend. *Degree requirements:* For master's, comprehensive exam, thesis optional. *Entrance requirements:* For master's, minimum GPA of 3.0, interview, essay/personal statement, current resume, official transcript of all college or university work. Additional exam requirements/recommendations for international students: Required—TOEFL (minimum score 550 paper-based; 79 iBT), IELTS (minimum score 6), PTE (minimum score 54). Electronic applications accepted.

Houston Baptist University, Archie W. Dunham College of Business, Program in Human Resources Management, Houston, TX 77074-3298. Offers MSHRM. *Program availability:* Part-time, evening/weekend, 100% online. *Entrance requirements:* For master's, minimum GPA of 2.5, essay/personal statement, resume, bachelor's degree conferred transcript. Additional exam requirements/recommendations for international students: Required—TOEFL (minimum score 80 iBT), IELTS (minimum score 6.5). Electronic applications accepted. Application fee is waived when completed online. *Expenses:* Contact institution.

Howard University, School of Business, Graduate Programs in Business, Washington, DC 20059-0002. Offers accounting (MBA); entrepreneurship (MBA); finance (MBA); general management (MBA); human resources management (MBA); information systems (MBA); international business (MBA); marketing (MBA); supply chain management (MBA); JD/MBA. *Accreditation:* AACSB. *Program availability:* Part-time, evening/weekend, online learning. *Entrance requirements:* For master's, GMAT, minimum 1 year post undergraduate work experience, resume, 3 letters of recommendation, advanced college algebra. Additional exam requirements/recommendations for international students: Required—TOEFL. *Faculty research:* Marketing research in multi-ethnic populations, U.S. trade policies and international relations, risk management (finance).

Idaho State University, Graduate School, College of Education, Department of Organizational Learning and Performance, Pocatello, ID 83209. Offers human resource development (MS); instructional design (PhD); instructional technology (M Ed). *Program availability:* Part-time. *Degree requirements:* For master's, comprehensive exam, thesis optional, minimum 36 credits; for doctorate, comprehensive exam, thesis/dissertation (for some programs). *Entrance requirements:* For master's, GRE or MAT, bachelor's degree; for doctorate, GRE or MAT, master's degree. Additional exam requirements/ recommendations for international students: Required—TOEFL (minimum score 550 paper-based; 80 iBT). Electronic applications accepted.

IGlobal University, Graduate Programs, Vienna, VA 22182. Offers accounting (MBA); data management and analytics (MSIT); entrepreneurship (MBA); finance (MBA); global business management (MBA); health care management (MBA); hospitality and tourism management (MBA); human resources management (MBA); information technology (MBA); information technology systems and management (MSIT); leadership and management (MBA); project management (MBA); public service and administration (MBA); software design and management (MSIT).

Indiana Tech, Program in Business Administration, Fort Wayne, IN 46803-1297. Offers accounting (MBA); health care management (MBA); human resources (MBA); management (MBA); marketing (MBA). *Program availability:* Part-time, evening/ weekend, online learning. *Entrance requirements:* For master's, GMAT, bachelor's degree from regionally-accredited university; minimum undergraduate GPA of 2.5; 2 years of significant work experience; 3 letters of recommendation. Electronic applications accepted.

Indiana University South Bend, Judd Leighton School of Business and Economics, South Bend, IN 46615. Offers accounting (MSA); business (Graduate Certificate); business administration (MBA), including finance, human resource management, marketing; MBA/MSA. *Program availability:* Part-time, evening/weekend. *Entrance requirements:* For master's, GMAT. Additional exam requirements/recommendations for international students: Required—TOEFL (minimum score 550 paper-based; 79 iBT). Electronic applications accepted. *Expenses:* Contact institution. *Faculty research:* Financial accounting, consumer research, capital budgeting research, business strategy research.

Indiana Wesleyan University, College of Adult and Professional Studies, Graduate Studies in Business, Marion, IN 46953. Offers accounting (MBA, Graduate Certificate); applied management (MBA); business administration (MBA); health care (MBA, Graduate Certificate); human resources (MBA, Graduate Certificate); management (MS); organizational leadership (MA). *Program availability:* Part-time, evening/weekend, online learning. *Degree requirements:* For master's, applied business or management project. *Entrance requirements:* For master's, minimum GPA of 2.5, 2 years of related work experience. Additional exam requirements/recommendations for international students: Required—TOEFL (minimum score 550 paper-based). Electronic applications accepted.

Instituto Tecnologico de Santo Domingo, Graduate School, Area of Business, Santo Domingo, Dominican Republic. Offers banking and securities markets (M Mgmt); corporate finance (M Mgmt); human resources management (M Mgmt, Certificate); international trade management (M Mgmt); marketing (M Mgmt); organizational development (M Mgmt); quality and productivity management (Certificate); tax management and planning (M Mgmt); upper management (M Mgmt).

Instituto Tecnologico de Santo Domingo, Graduate School, Area of Engineering, Santo Domingo, Dominican Republic. Offers construction administration (MS, Certificate); data telecommunications (M Eng, MS, Certificate); industrial engineering (M Eng, Certificate); industrial management (M Mgmt); information technology (Certificate); maintenance engineering (M Eng); occupational hazard prevention (M Mgmt); production management (Certificate); quantitative methods (Certificate); sanitary and environmental engineering (M Eng); structural engineering (M Eng); systems engineering and electronic data processing (Certificate); transportation (Certificate).

Instituto Tecnológico y de Estudios Superiores de Monterrey, Campus Cuernavaca, Programs in Business Administration, Temixco, Mexico. Offers finance (MA); human resources management (MA); international business (MA); marketing (MA).

Inter American University of Puerto Rico, Aguadilla Campus, Graduate School, Aguadilla, PR 00605. Offers accounting (MBA); counseling psychology specializing in family (MS); criminal justice (MA); educative management and leadership (MA); elementary education (M Ed); finance (MBA); human resources (MBA); industrial management (MBA); management information systems (MBA); marketing (MBA). *Program availability:* Part-time, evening/weekend. *Degree requirements:* For master's, comprehensive exam. *Entrance requirements:* For master's, EXADEP, 2 letters of recommendation, minimum GPA of 2.5. Electronic applications accepted.

Inter American University of Puerto Rico, Arecibo Campus, Program in Business Administration, Arecibo, PR 00614-4050. Offers accounting (MBA); finance (MBA); human resources (MBA).

Inter American University of Puerto Rico, Barranquitas Campus, Business Administration Program, Barranquitas, PR 00794. Offers accounting (MBA); human resources (MBA); managerial information systems (MBA). *Program availability:* Part-time, evening/weekend. *Degree requirements:* For master's, 2 foreign languages, comprehensive exam (for some programs), thesis or alternative, minimum GPA of 3.0. *Entrance requirements:* For master's, BBA or its equivalent from accredited institution, official academic transcript from institution that conferred bachelor's degree, minimum GPA of 2.5, interview (for some programs). Electronic applications accepted. *Expenses:* Contact institution.

Inter American University of Puerto Rico, Bayamón Campus, Graduate School, Bayamón, PR 00957. Offers biology (MS), including environmental sciences and ecology, molecular biotechnology; electrical engineering (ME), including control system, potence system; human resources (MBA); mechanical engineering (ME, MS), including aerospace, energy. *Program availability:* Part-time, evening/weekend. *Degree requirements:* For master's, comprehensive exam, research project. *Entrance requirements:* For master's, EXADEP, GRE General Test, letters of recommendation. *Expenses: Tuition:* Full-time $3816; part-time $1908 per trimester. *Required fees:* $735; $642.

Inter American University of Puerto Rico, Fajardo Campus, Graduate Programs, Fajardo, PR 00738-7003. Offers computer science (MS); educational management and leadership (MA Ed); general business (MBA); human resources (MBA); management information systems (MBA); marketing (MBA); special education (MA Ed). *Program availability:* Online learning.

Inter American University of Puerto Rico, Metropolitan Campus, Graduate Programs, Program in Human Resources, San Juan, PR 00919-1293. Offers MBA. *Degree requirements:* For master's, comprehensive exam. *Entrance requirements:* For master's, GRE or EXADEP, interview. Electronic applications accepted.

Inter American University of Puerto Rico, Ponce Campus, Graduate School, Mercedita, PR 00715-1602. Offers accounting (MBA); biology (M Ed); chemistry (M Ed); criminal justice (MA); elementary education (M Ed); English as a Second Language (M Ed); finance (MBA); history (M Ed); human resources (MBA); marketing (MBA); mathematics (M Ed); Spanish (M Ed). *Entrance requirements:* For master's, minimum GPA of 2.5.

Human Resources Management

Inter American University of Puerto Rico, San Germán Campus, Graduate Studies Center, Program in Business Administration, San Germán, PR 00683-5008. Offers accounting (MBA); finance (MBA); general business administration (MBA); human resources (MBA, PhD); industrial relations (MBA); information systems (MBA); international and interregional business (PhD); management (MBA); marketing (MBA). *Program availability:* Part-time, evening/weekend. *Degree requirements:* For master's, comprehensive exam. *Entrance requirements:* For master's, GRE General Test or EXADEP, minimum GPA of 3.0. *Expenses: Tuition:* Full-time $212; part-time $212 per credit. *Required fees:* $366 per semester. One-time fee: $31. Tuition and fees vary according to degree level and program.

Iona College, School of Arts and Science, Department of Psychology, New Rochelle, NY 10801-1890. Offers general-experimental psychology (MA); human resources (Certificate); industrial-organizational psychology (MA); mental health counseling (MA); organizational behavior (Certificate); psychology (MA); school psychology (MA). *Program availability:* Part-time. *Faculty:* 10 full-time (6 women), 9 part-time/adjunct (6 women). *Students:* 74 full-time (56 women), 29 part-time (25 women); includes 49 minority (13 Black or African American, non-Hispanic/Latino; 3 Asian, non-Hispanic/Latino; 31 Hispanic/Latino; 2 Two or more races, non-Hispanic/Latino), 3 international. Average age 25. 126 applicants, 81% accepted, 37 enrolled. In 2018, 39 master's, 4 other advanced degrees awarded. *Degree requirements:* For master's, thesis (for some programs), literature review (for some programs). *Entrance requirements:* For master's, BA in psychology including 3 credits each in psychology statistics and experimental research methods, or 9 credits in psychology including 3 credits each in psychology statistics, psychology research methods and upper-level coursework. Additional exam requirements/recommendations for international students: Required—TOEFL (minimum score 550 paper-based), IELTS (minimum score 6.5). *Application deadline:* For fall admission, 8/15 for domestic students, 5/1 for international students; for spring admission, 1/15 for domestic students, 9/1 for international students. Applications are processed on a rolling basis. Electronic applications accepted. *Expenses: Tuition:* Full-time $14,064; part-time $7032 per credit. *Required fees:* $245 per semester. One-time fee: $250. Tuition and fees vary according to program. *Financial support:* In 2018–19, 4 students received support, including 4 research assistantships with partial tuition reimbursements available (averaging $10,143 per year); tuition waivers (partial) and unspecified assistantships also available. Support available to part-time students. Financial award application deadline: 4/15; financial award applicants required to submit FAFSA. *Faculty research:* Non-suicidal self-injury, trauma response, performance appraisal and evaluation, diversity infusion, assessment and treatment of sexual offenders. *Unit head:* Patricia Oswald, PhD, Chair, 914-633-2374, E-mail: poswald@iona.edu. *Application contact:* Shantell Smith, Associate Director of Graduate Admissions, Arts & Science, 914-633-2440, Fax: 914-633-2277, E-mail: ssmith@iona.edu.
Website: http://www.iona.edu/Academics/School-of-Arts-Science/Departments/Psychology/Graduate-Programs.aspx

Iona College, School of Business, Department of Management, Business Administration and Health Care Management, New Rochelle, NY 10801-1890. Offers health care analytics (AC); human resource management (PMC); management (MBA, PMC). *Program availability:* Part-time, evening/weekend. *Faculty:* 7 full-time (0 women), 1 (woman) part-time/adjunct. *Students:* 38 full-time (22 women), 78 part-time (47 women); includes 48 minority (17 Black or African American, non-Hispanic/Latino; 6 Asian, non-Hispanic/Latino; 24 Hispanic/Latino; 1 Native Hawaiian or other Pacific Islander, non-Hispanic/Latino), 3 international. Average age 27. 89 applicants, 92% accepted, 36 enrolled. In 2018, 59 master's, 66 other advanced degrees awarded. *Entrance requirements:* For master's, GMAT, 2 letters of recommendation, minimum GPA of 3.0; for other advanced degree, GMAT, minimum GPA of 3.0. Additional exam requirements/recommendations for international students: Required—TOEFL (minimum score 550 paper-based; 80 iBT), IELTS (minimum score 6.5). *Application deadline:* For fall admission, 8/15 priority date for domestic students, 8/1 priority date for international students; for winter admission, 11/15 priority date for domestic students, 11/1 priority date for international students; for spring admission, 2/15 priority date for domestic students, 2/1 priority date for international students; for summer admission, 5/15 priority date for domestic students, 5/1 priority date for international students. Applications are processed on a rolling basis. Application fee: $50. Electronic applications accepted. *Expenses:* Contact institution. *Financial support:* In 2018–19, 55 students received support. Scholarships/grants, tuition waivers (partial), and unspecified assistantships available. Support available to part-time students. Financial award application deadline: 4/15; financial award applicants required to submit FAFSA. *Faculty research:* Information systems, strategic management, corporate values and ethics. *Unit head:* George DeFeis, Chair, 914-633-2631, E-mail: gdefeis@iona.edu. *Application contact:* Kimberly Kelly, Director of Graduate Business Admissions, 914-633-2271, Fax: 914-633-2012, E-mail: kkelly@iona.edu.
Website: http://www.iona.edu/Academics/Hagan-School-of-Business/Departments/Management-Business-Administration-Health-Car/Graduate-Programs.aspx

James Madison University, The Graduate School, College of Education, Program in Adult Education and Human Resource Development, Harrisonburg, VA 22807. Offers higher education (MS Ed); human resource management (MS Ed); individualized (MS Ed); instructional design (MS Ed); leadership and facilitation (MS Ed); program evaluation and measurement (MS Ed). *Accreditation:* NCATE. *Program availability:* Part-time, evening/weekend. *Students:* 10 full-time (7 women), 11 part-time (8 women); includes 8 minority (5 Black or African American, non-Hispanic/Latino; 1 American Indian or Alaska Native, non-Hispanic/Latino; 1 Hispanic/Latino; 1 Two or more races, non-Hispanic/Latino), 1 international. Average age 30. In 2018, 10 master's awarded. Application fee: $60. Electronic applications accepted. *Expenses:* Tuition, state resident: full-time $10,848. Tuition, nonresident: full-time $27,888. *Required fees:* $1128. *Financial support:* In 2018–19, 8 students received support. Teaching assistantships, Federal Work-Study, and assistantships (averaging $7911) available. Financial award application deadline: 3/1; financial award applicants required to submit FAFSA. *Unit head:* Dr. Jane B. Thall, Department Head, 540-568-5531, E-mail: thalljb@jmu.edu. *Application contact:* Lynette D. Michael, Director of Graduate Admissions, 540-568-6131 Ext. 6395, Fax: 540-568-7860, E-mail: michaeld@jmu.edu.

John F. Kennedy University, College of Business and Professional Studies, Program in Business Administration, Pleasant Hill, CA 94523-4817. Offers business administration (MBA); finance (MBA); health care (MBA); human resources (MBA); information technology (MBA); management (MBA); sales management (MBA); strategic management (MBA). *Program availability:* Part-time, evening/weekend, online learning. *Degree requirements:* For master's, thesis or alternative. *Entrance requirements:* For master's, interview. Additional exam requirements/recommendations for international students: Required—TOEFL.

Johnson & Wales University, Graduate Studies, MBA Program, Providence, RI 02903-3703. Offers accounting (MBA); business administration (MBA); finance (MBA); global fashion merchandising and management (MBA); hospitality (MBA); human resource management (MBA); information security/assurance (MBA); information technology (MBA); nonprofit management (MBA); operations and supply chain management (MBA); organizational leadership (MBA); organizational psychology (MBA); sport leadership (MBA). Program also offered on Denver campus. *Program availability:* Part-time, online learning. *Entrance requirements:* For master's, minimum GPA of 2.75. Additional exam requirements/recommendations for international students: Required—TOEFL (minimum score 550 paper-based); Recommended—IELTS, TWE. *Faculty research:* International banking, global economy, international trade, cultural differences.

Johnson & Wales University, Graduate Studies, MS Program in Human Resource Management, Providence, RI 02903-3703. Offers MS. *Program availability:* Online learning.

King University, School of Business, Economics, and Technology, Bristol, TN 37620-2699. Offers accounting (MBA); finance (MBA); healthcare management (MBA); human resources management (MBA); leadership (MBA); management (MBA); marketing (MBA); project management (MBA). *Program availability:* Part-time, evening/weekend, 100% online, blended/hybrid learning. *Faculty:* 11 full-time (9 women), 10 part-time/adjunct (7 women). *Students:* 182 full-time (107 women), 8 part-time (6 women); includes 18 minority (7 Black or African American, non-Hispanic/Latino; 4 Hispanic/Latino; 1 Native Hawaiian or other Pacific Islander, non-Hispanic/Latino; 6 Two or more races, non-Hispanic/Latino), 2 international. Average age 32. 143 applicants, 98% accepted, 68 enrolled. In 2018, 125 master's awarded. *Degree requirements:* For master's, comprehensive exam, thesis optional. *Entrance requirements:* For master's, resume which demonstrates a minimum of 2 years of full-time work experience, minimum cumulative grade point average of 3.0 on a 4.0 scale is required. Students who do not meet this requirement may be conditionally accepted. Additional exam requirements/recommendations for international students: Required—TOEFL (minimum score 84 paper-based; 84 iBT). *Application deadline:* Applications are processed on a rolling basis. Application fee: $0 ($50 for international students). Electronic applications accepted. *Expenses: Tuition:* Full-time $13,365; part-time $495 per semester hour. *Required fees:* $900; $100 per course. One-time fee: $175. Tuition and fees vary according to class time, degree level and program. *Financial support:* Unspecified assistantships available. Financial award applicants required to submit FAFSA. *Faculty research:* International monetary policy. *Unit head:* Dr. Mark Pate, Dean, School of Business, Economics, and Technology, 423-652-4814, E-mail: mjpate@king.edu. *Application contact:* Nancy Beverly, Territory Manager/Enrollment Counselor, 423-341-9495, Fax: 423-652-4727, E-mail: nmbeverly@king.edu.

La Roche University, School of Graduate Studies and Adult Education, Program in Human Resources Management, Pittsburgh, PA 15237-5898. Offers MS, Certificate. *Program availability:* Part-time, evening/weekend. *Faculty:* 2 full-time (both women), 5 part-time/adjunct (1 woman). *Students:* 3 full-time (2 women), 32 part-time (19 women); includes 3 minority (1 Black or African American, non-Hispanic/Latino; 1 Hispanic/Latino; 1 Two or more races, non-Hispanic/Latino), 8 international. Average age 31. 83 applicants, 69% accepted, 8 enrolled. In 2018, 9 master's awarded. *Entrance requirements:* For master's, GMAT, GRE or MAT, minimum GPA of 3.0 during previous 2 years, resume, 2 letters of recommendation, interview. Additional exam requirements/recommendations for international students: Recommended—TOEFL (minimum score 550 paper-based). *Application deadline:* For fall admission, 8/15 priority date for domestic students, 8/15 for international students; for spring admission, 12/15 priority date for domestic students, 12/15 for international students. Applications are processed on a rolling basis. Application fee: $50. Electronic applications accepted. *Expenses: Tuition:* Part-time $735 per credit. *Required fees:* $80; $80 per unit. *Financial support:* Unspecified assistantships available. Financial award application deadline: 3/31; financial award applicants required to submit FAFSA. *Faculty research:* Human resources development. *Unit head:* Dr. Jean Forti, Professor, Human Resources Management Program Chair, 412-536-1193, Fax: 412-536-1179, E-mail: fortij1@laroche.edu. *Application contact:* Erin Pottgen, Assistant Director, Graduate Admissions, 412-847-2509, Fax: 412-536-1283, E-mail: erin.pottgen@laroche.edu.

La Salle University, School of Business, Master of Business Administration Program, Philadelphia, PA 19141-1199. Offers accounting (MBA, Post-MBA Certificate); business systems and analytics (MBA, Post-MBA Certificate); finance (MBA, Post-MBA Certificate); general business administration (MBA, Post-MBA Certificate); human resource management (MBA, Post-MBA Certificate); management (MBA, Post-MBA Certificate); marketing (Post-MBA Certificate); MBA/MSN. Program also offered in Switzerland. *Accreditation:* AACSB. *Program availability:* Part-time, evening/weekend, online learning. *Entrance requirements:* For master's, GMAT or GRE, two letters of reference; resume; for Post-MBA Certificate, MBA with minimum GPA of 3.0. Additional exam requirements/recommendations for international students: Required—TOEFL. Electronic applications accepted. Application fee is waived when completed online. *Expenses:* Contact institution.

Lasell College, Graduate and Professional Studies in Management, Newton, MA 02466-2709. Offers business administration (MBA); elder care management (MSM); hospitality and event management (MSM); human resources management (MSM, Graduate Certificate); management (MSM, Graduate Certificate); marketing (MS, Graduate Certificate); project management (MSM, Graduate Certificate). *Accreditation:* ACBSP. *Program availability:* Part-time, evening/weekend, 100% online, blended/hybrid learning. *Faculty:* 7 full-time (4 women), 14 part-time/adjunct (9 women). *Students:* 37 full-time (28 women), 76 part-time (48 women); includes 22 minority (12 Black or African American, non-Hispanic/Latino; 1 Asian, non-Hispanic/Latino; 9 Hispanic/Latino), 20 international. Average age 32. 68 applicants, 54% accepted, 20 enrolled. In 2018, 62 master's, 1 other advanced degree awarded. *Degree requirements:* For master's, minimum GPA of 3.0; internship or research paper (for MSM). *Entrance requirements:* For master's, one-page personal statement, 2 letters of recommendation, resume, bachelor's degree transcript; proof of microeconomics and statistics (for MBA); for Graduate Certificate, bachelor's degree transcript, 2 letters of recommendation, 1-page personal statement, resume. Additional exam requirements/recommendations for international students: Required—TOEFL (minimum score 550 paper-based, 79 iBT) or IELTS (minimum score 6). *Application deadline:* For fall admission, 8/31 priority date for domestic students, 6/30 priority date for international students; for spring admission, 12/31 priority date for domestic students, 10/31 priority date for international students. Applications are processed on a rolling basis. Electronic applications accepted. *Expenses: Tuition:* Part-time $600 per credit. *Required fees:* $40 per course. *Financial support:* Federal Work-Study, scholarships/grants, and tuition discounts available. Support available to part-time students. Financial award application deadline: 8/31; financial award applicants required to submit FAFSA. *Unit head:* Eric Turner, Vice President of Graduate and Professional Studies, 617-243-2071, Fax: 617-243-2450, E-mail: gradinfo@lasell.edu. *Application contact:* Adrienne Franciosi, Assistant Vice President of Graduate and Professional Studies, 617-243-2214, Fax: 617-243-2450, E-mail: gradinfo@lasell.edu.
Website: http://www.lasell.edu/academics/graduate-and-professional-studies/programs-of-study/master-of-science-in-management.html

La Sierra University, School of Business and Management, Riverside, CA 92505. Offers accounting (MBA); finance (MBA); general management (MBA); human resources management (MBA); leadership, values, and ethics for business and management (Certificate); marketing (MBA). *Degree requirements:* For master's, research project. *Entrance requirements:* For master's, GMAT, minimum GPA of 3.0.

Additional exam requirements/recommendations for international students: Required—TOEFL. *Faculty research:* Financial econometrics, institutional assessment and strategic planning, legal issues in management, behavioral finance, content of financial reports.

Lebanon Valley College, Program in Business Administration, Annville, PA 17003-1400. Offers business administration (MBA); healthcare management (MBA); human resources (MBA); leadership and ethics (MBA); project management (MBA). *Program availability:* Part-time, evening/weekend. *Degree requirements:* For master's, capstone course. *Entrance requirements:* For master's, GMAT, 3 years of work experience, resume, professional statement (application form, resume, personal statement, transcripts). Additional exam requirements/recommendations for international students: Required—TOEFL (minimum score 80 iBT), IELTS (minimum score 6.5) or STEP Eiken (grade 1). Electronic applications accepted. *Expenses:* Contact institution. *Faculty research:* Leadership, motivation, BI, information systems strategies, emerging market development, the role of informational business education, economic growth.

Lewis University, College of Business, Program in Business Administration, Romeoville, IL 60446. Offers accounting (MBA); custom elective option (MBA); e-business (MBA); finance (MBA); healthcare management (MBA); human resources management (MBA); international business (MBA); management information systems (MBA); marketing (MBA); project management (MBA); technology and operations management (MBA). *Program availability:* Part-time, evening/weekend. *Students:* 114 full-time (72 women), 143 part-time (87 women); includes 84 minority (21 Black or African American, non-Hispanic/Latino; 2 American Indian or Alaska Native, non-Hispanic/Latino; 11 Asian, non-Hispanic/Latino; 45 Hispanic/Latino; 5 Two or more races, non-Hispanic/Latino), 17 international. Average age 31. In 2018, 99 master's awarded. *Entrance requirements:* For master's, interview, bachelor's degree, resume, two recommendations. Additional exam requirements/recommendations for international students: Required—TOEFL (minimum score 550 paper-based), IELTS. *Application deadline:* For fall admission, 8/15 priority date for domestic students, 5/1 priority date for international students; for spring admission, 11/15 priority date for international students. Applications are processed on a rolling basis. Application fee: $40. Electronic applications accepted. *Financial support:* Career-related internships or fieldwork, Federal Work-Study, scholarships/grants, and unspecified assistantships available. Financial award application deadline: 5/1; financial award applicants required to submit FAFSA. *Unit head:* Dr. Maureen Culleeney, Academic Program Director, 815-838-0500 Ext. 5631, E-mail: culleema@lewisu.edu. *Application contact:* Michele Ryan, Director of Admission, 815-838-0500 Ext. 5384, E-mail: ryanml@lewisu.edu.

Lincoln University, Graduate Studies, Oakland, CA 94612. Offers finance and investments (DBA); finance management (MS); finance management and investments (MBA); general business (MBA); human resource management (MBA, DBA); international business (MBA, MS); management information systems (MBA). *Program availability:* Part-time. *Degree requirements:* For master's, research project (thesis), internship report, or comprehensive exam; for doctorate, comprehensive exam, thesis/dissertation. *Entrance requirements:* For master's, minimum GPA of 2.7; for doctorate, GMAT (minimum score: 550), GRE (minimum score: 1000), or equivalent test results (waived for master's degree with minimum cumulative GPA of 3.3). Additional exam requirements/recommendations for international students: Required—TOEFL minimum score 525 paper-based; 71 iBT or IELTS minimum score 5.5 (for MBA); TOEFL minimum score 550 paper-based; 79 iBT or IELTS minimum score 6 (for MS and DBA). Electronic applications accepted.

Lincoln University, The School of Adult & Continuing Education, Philadelphia, PA 19104. Offers counseling (MSC); early childhood education (M Ed), including PreK-4; early childhood education and special education (M Ed); educational leadership (M Ed), including principal certification; finance (MBA); human resources management (MBA); human services delivery (MAHS). *Program availability:* Part-time, evening/weekend. *Faculty:* 8 full-time (3 women), 22 part-time/adjunct (12 women). *Students:* 192 full-time (154 women), 62 part-time (40 women); includes 230 minority (218 Black or African American, non-Hispanic/Latino; 9 Hispanic/Latino; 3 Two or more races, non-Hispanic/Latino), 3 international. Average age 33. 278 applicants, 58% accepted, 94 enrolled. In 2018, 105 master's awarded. *Degree requirements:* For master's, comprehensive exam, thesis or alternative, capstone, grant proposal. *Entrance requirements:* For master's, GRE/GMAT (Optional), Official academic transcript(s), letters of recommendation, personal statement, resume, supervisor's evaluation form, Application fee. Additional exam requirements/recommendations for international students: Required—TOEFL (minimum score 500 paper-based; 71 iBT); Recommended—IELTS (minimum score 6.5). *Application deadline:* For fall admission, 8/19 for domestic and international students; for spring admission, 12/30 for domestic and international students. Applications are processed on a rolling basis. Application fee: $50. Electronic applications accepted. *Financial support:* Scholarships/grants available. Financial award application deadline: 4/1; financial award applicants required to submit FAFSA. *Unit head:* Dr. Patricia Joseph, Dean of Faculty, 484-365-7659, E-mail: joseph@lincoln.edu. *Application contact:* Jernice Lea, Director, Student Services and Admissions, 215-590-8231, Fax: 215-387-3859, E-mail: jlea@lincoln.edu.
Website: http://www.lincoln.edu/admissions/graduate-admissions

Lindenwood University, Graduate Programs, School of Accelerated Degree Programs, St. Charles, MO 63301-1695. Offers administration (MSA), including management, marketing, project management; business administration (MBA); communications (MA), including digital and multimedia, media management, promotions, training and development; criminal justice and administration (MS); healthcare administration (MS); human resource management (MS); information technology (Certificate); managing information security (MS); managing information technology (MS); managing virtualization and cloud computing (MS); writing (MFA). *Program availability:* Part-time, evening/weekend, 100% online. *Faculty:* 15 full-time (8 women), 62 part-time/adjunct (22 women). *Students:* 652 full-time (398 women), 66 part-time (45 women); includes 241 minority (182 Black or African American, non-Hispanic/Latino; 1 American Indian or Alaska Native, non-Hispanic/Latino; 8 Asian, non-Hispanic/Latino; 25 Hispanic/Latino; 1 Native Hawaiian or other Pacific Islander, non-Hispanic/Latino; 24 Two or more races, non-Hispanic/Latino), 81 international. Average age 36. 359 applicants, 54% accepted, 170 enrolled. In 2018, 416 master's, 2 other advanced degrees awarded. *Degree requirements:* For master's, thesis (for some programs), minimum cumulative GPA of 3.0; for Certificate, minimum cumulative GPA of 3.0. *Entrance requirements:* For master's, resume, personal statement, official undergraduate transcript, minimum undergraduate cumulative GPA of 3.0. Additional exam requirements/recommendations for international students: Required—TOEFL (minimum score 553 paper-based; 81 iBT); Recommended—IELTS (minimum score 6.5). *Application deadline:* For fall admission, 9/30 priority date for domestic and international students; for winter admission, 1/6 priority date for domestic and international students; for spring admission, 4/6 priority date for domestic and international students; for summer admission, 7/8 priority date for domestic and international students. Applications are processed on a rolling basis. Application fee: $0 ($100 for international students). Electronic applications accepted. *Expenses:* Contact institution. *Financial support:* In 2018–19, 372 students received support. Career-related internships or fieldwork, institutionally sponsored loans, scholarships/grants, tuition waivers (partial), and unspecified assistantships available. Financial award application deadline: 6/30; financial award applicants required to submit FAFSA. *Unit head:* Dr. Gina Ganahl, Dean, Accelerated Degree Programs, 636-949-4501, Fax: 636-949-4505, E-mail: gganahl@lindenwood.edu. *Application contact:* Kara Schilli, Assistant Vice President, University Admissions, 636-949-4349, Fax: 636-949-4109, E-mail: adultadmissions@lindenwood.edu.
Website: https://www.lindenwood.edu/academics/academic-schools/school-of-accelerated-degree-programs/

Lindenwood University–Belleville, Graduate Programs, Belleville, IL 62226. Offers business administration (MBA); communications (MA), including digital and multimedia, media management, promotions, training and development; counseling (MA); criminal justice administration (MS); education (MA); healthcare administration (MS); human resource management (MS); school administration (MA); teaching (MAT).

London Metropolitan University, Graduate Programs, London, United Kingdom. Offers applied psychology (M Sc); architecture (MA); biomedical science (M Sc); blood science (M Sc); cancer pharmacology (M Sc); computer networking and cyber security (M Sc); computing and information systems (M Sc); conference interpreting (MA); counter-terrorism studies (M Sc); creative, digital and professional writing (MA); crime, violence and prevention (M Sc); criminology (M Sc); curating contemporary art (MA); data analytics (M Sc); digital media (MA); early childhood studies (MA); education (MA, Ed D); financial services law, regulation and compliance (LL M); food science (M Sc); forensic psychology (M Sc); health and social care management and policy (M Sc); human nutrition (M Sc); human resource management (MA); human rights and international conflict (MA); information technology (M Sc); intelligence and security studies (M Sc); international oil, gas and energy law (LL M); international relations (MA); interpreting (MA); learning and teaching in higher education (MA); legal practice (LL M); media and entertainment law (LL M); organizational and consumer psychology (M Sc); psychological therapy (M Sc); psychology of mental health (M Sc); public health (M Sc); public policy and management (MPA); security studies (M Sc); social work (M Sc); spatial planning and urban design (MA); sports therapy (M Sc); supporting older children and young people with dyslexia (MA); teaching languages (MA), including Arabic, English; translation (MA); woman and child abuse (MA).

Long Island University–LIU Brooklyn, School of Business, Public Administration and Information Sciences, Brooklyn, NY 11201-8423. Offers accounting (MBA); accounting (MS); business administration (MBA); computer science (MS); gerontology (Advanced Certificate); health administration (MPA); human resources management (MS); not-for-profit management (Advanced Certificate); public administration (MPA); taxation (MS). *Program availability:* Part-time, evening/weekend. *Entrance requirements:* Additional exam requirements/recommendations for international students: Required—TOEFL (minimum score 550 paper-based; 75 iBT). Electronic applications accepted. *Faculty research:* Tax policy; public sector budgeting and gender inequities; technology and innovation; game theory; knowledge management.

Loyola University Chicago, Quinlan School of Business, Master of Science in Human Resources Program, Chicago, IL 60611. Offers MSHR. *Program availability:* Part-time, evening/weekend. *Entrance requirements:* For master's, GMAT or GRE, official transcripts, two letters of recommendation, statement of purpose, resume. Additional exam requirements/recommendations for international students: Required—TOEFL (minimum score 90 iBT) or IELTS (minimum score 6.5). Electronic applications accepted. Application fee is waived when completed online. *Expenses:* Contact institution. *Faculty research:* Encouraging innovation with reward programs, alternative dispute resolution, performance appraisal, global human resources, work of Independent contractors.

Loyola University Chicago, Quinlan School of Business, MBA Programs, Chicago, IL 60611. Offers accounting (MBA); business ethics (MBA); derivative markets (MBA); economics (MBA); entrepreneurship (MBA); finance (MBA); healthcare management (MBA); human resources management (MBA); information systems management (MBA); international business (MBA); management (MBA); marketing (MBA); risk management (MBA); supply chain management (MBA). *Program availability:* Part-time, evening/weekend. *Entrance requirements:* For master's, GMAT or GRE, official transcripts, two letters of recommendation, statement of purpose, resume. Additional exam requirements/recommendations for international students: Required—TOEFL (minimum score 90 iBT) or IELTS (minimum score 6.5). Electronic applications accepted. Application fee is waived when completed online. *Expenses:* Contact institution. *Faculty research:* Social enterprise and responsibility, emerging markets, supply chain management, risk management.

Manhattanville College, School of Professional Studies, Master of Science in International Management Program, Purchase, NY 10577-2132. Offers international management (MS, Advanced Certificate), including business leadership (MS), finance (MS), human resource management (MS), marketing communication management (MS). *Program availability:* Part-time, evening/weekend. *Faculty:* 6 part-time/adjunct (3 women). *Students:* 2 full-time (1 woman), 1 part-time (0 women); includes 1 minority (Hispanic/Latino). Average age 24. 9 applicants, 44% accepted, 2 enrolled. In 2018, 5 master's awarded. *Degree requirements:* For master's, thesis (for some programs), final project. *Entrance requirements:* For master's, scores of GRE and GMAT are optional, personal essay, transcripts, 2 letters of recommendation (academic or professional), resume, health form with proof of immunization (for those born after 1957). Additional exam requirements/recommendations for international students: Required—TOEFL (minimum score 563 paper-based; 85 iBT), TOEFL (minimum score 563 paper-based, 85 iBT), IELTS (7), or iTEP (B2); Recommended—IELTS (minimum score 7). *Application deadline:* Applications are processed on a rolling basis. Application fee: $75. Electronic applications accepted. *Expenses:* 935 per credit. *Financial support:* Federal Work-Study, institutionally sponsored loans, scholarships/grants, and unspecified assistantships available. Financial award application deadline: 3/15; financial award applicants required to submit FAFSA. *Unit head:* Laura Persky, Associate Dean, 914-323-5188, E-mail: Laura.Persky@mville.edu. *Application contact:* Monika Pottgen, Assistant Director, Recruitment and Admissions, 914-323-5150, E-mail: business@mville.edu.
Website: https://www.mville.edu/programs/ms-international-management

Marquette University, Graduate School of Management, Executive MBA Program, Milwaukee, WI 53201-1881. Offers economics (MBA); finance (MBA); human resources (MBA); international business (MBA); management information systems (MBA); marketing (MBA); operations and supply chain management (MBA); sports business (MBA). *Accreditation:* AACSB. *Degree requirements:* For master's, international trip. *Entrance requirements:* For master's, GMAT or GRE, two letters of recommendation, official transcripts from current and previous colleges/universities. Additional exam requirements/recommendations for international students: Required—TOEFL (minimum score 550 paper-based; 88 iBT), IELTS (minimum score 6.5), PTE. Electronic applications accepted. *Expenses:* Contact institution. *Faculty research:* International trade and finance, customer relationship management, consumer satisfaction, customer service.

Marquette University, Graduate School of Management, Program in Business Administration, Milwaukee, WI 53201-1881. Offers business administration (MBA);

economics (MBA); entrepreneurship (Certificate); finance (MBA); human resources (MBA); international business (MBA); management information systems (MBA); marketing (MBA); operations and supply chain management (MBA); sports business (MBA); JD/MBA; MBA/MA; MBA/MSN. *Accreditation:* AACSB. *Program availability:* Part-time, evening/weekend. *Degree requirements:* For Certificate, business plan. *Entrance requirements:* For master's, GMAT or GRE, letters of recommendation. Additional exam requirements/recommendations for international students: Required—TOEFL (minimum score 550 paper-based; 88 iBT), IELTS (minimum score 6.5), PTE. Electronic applications accepted. *Faculty research:* Ethics in the professions, services marketing, technology impact on decision-making, mentoring.

Marquette University, Graduate School of Management, Program in Human Resources, Milwaukee, WI 53201-1881. Offers MSHR. *Program availability:* Part-time, evening/weekend. *Entrance requirements:* For master's, GMAT or GRE General Test, letters of recommendation. Additional exam requirements/recommendations for international students: Required—TOEFL (minimum score 550 paper-based; 88 iBT), IELTS (minimum score 6.5), PTE. Electronic applications accepted. *Faculty research:* Diversity, mentoring, executive compensation.

Marshall University, Academic Affairs Division, College of Business, Program in Human Resource Management, Huntington, WV 25755. Offers MS. *Program availability:* Part-time, evening/weekend. *Entrance requirements:* For master's, GMAT or GRE General Test.

Marygrove College, Graduate Studies, Detroit, MI 48221-2599. Offers autism spectrum disorders (M Ed, Certificate); curriculum instruction and assessment (MAT); educational leadership (MA); educational technology (M Ed); effective teaching in the 21st century-classroom focus (MAT); effective teaching in the 21st century-technology focus (MAT); human resource management (MA, Certificate); mathematics 6-8 (MAT); mathematics K-5 (MAT); reading and literacy K-6 (MAT); reading specialist (M Ed); school administrator (Certificate); social justice (MA); special education (MAT); special education - learning disabilities (M Ed); teaching - pre-elementary education (M Ed); teaching - pre-secondary education (M Ed). *Program availability:* Part-time, evening/weekend, 100% online, blended/hybrid learning. *Entrance requirements:* For master's, all official bachelor's transcripts. Additional exam requirements/recommendations for international students: Required—TOEFL (minimum score 550 paper-based; 80 iBT). Electronic applications accepted.

Marymount University, School of Business and Technology, Program in Human Resource Management, Arlington, VA 22207-4299. Offers human resource management (Certificate); human resource management with business administration (MBA/MA); organization development (Certificate); MBA/MA. *Program availability:* Part-time, evening/weekend. *Faculty:* 4 full-time (3 women), 1 (woman) part-time/adjunct. *Students:* 7 full-time (6 women), 21 part-time (16 women); includes 13 minority (2 Black or African American, non-Hispanic/Latino; 1 American Indian or Alaska Native, non-Hispanic/Latino; 3 Asian, non-Hispanic/Latino; 4 Hispanic/Latino; 2 Native Hawaiian or other Pacific Islander, non-Hispanic/Latino; 1 Two or more races, non-Hispanic/Latino), 3 international. Average age 34. 28 applicants, 96% accepted, 12 enrolled. In 2018, 9 Certificates awarded. *Entrance requirements:* For degree, resume. Additional exam requirements/recommendations for international students: Required—TOEFL (minimum score 600 paper-based; 96 iBT), IELTS (minimum score 6.5), PTE (minimum score 58). *Application deadline:* For fall admission, 7/16 priority date for domestic and international students; for spring admission, 11/16 priority date for domestic and international students; for summer admission, 4/16 priority date for domestic and international students. Applications are processed on a rolling basis. Application fee: $40. Electronic applications accepted. *Expenses:* $1,060 per credit. *Financial support:* Research assistantships, teaching assistantships, career-related internships or fieldwork, scholarships/grants, and unspecified assistantships available. Support available to part-time students. Financial award application deadline: 3/1; financial award applicants required to submit FAFSA. *Unit head:* Dr. Virginia Bianco-Mathis, Chair/Director, 703-284-5957, E-mail: virginia.bianco-mathis@marymount.edu. *Application contact:* Rebecca Esposito, Senior Associate Director, Graduate Admissions, 703-284-5901, Fax: 703-527-3815, E-mail: grad.admissions@marymount.edu.
Website: https://www.marymount.edu/Academics/School-of-Business-and-Technology/Graduate-Programs/Human-Resource-Management-(M-A-)

Maryville University of Saint Louis, The John E. Simon School of Business, St. Louis, MO 63141-7299. Offers accounting (MBA, MS, Certificate); business studies (Certificate); cybersecurity (MBA, MS, Certificate); financial services (MBA, Certificate); health administration (MBA); healthcare administration (Certificate); human resource management (MBA); human resources management (Certificate); information technology (MBA); information technology management (Certificate); management (MBA, Certificate); management and leadership (MA); marketing (MBA, Certificate); project management (MBA, Certificate); sport business management (MBA); supply chain management (Certificate); supply chain management/logistics (MBA). *Accreditation:* ACBSP. *Program availability:* Part-time, 100% online, blended/hybrid learning. *Faculty:* 5 full-time (1 woman), 77 part-time/adjunct (19 women). *Students:* 338 full-time (166 women), 739 part-time (356 women); includes 310 minority (161 Black or African American, non-Hispanic/Latino; 6 American Indian or Alaska Native, non-Hispanic/Latino; 59 Asian, non-Hispanic/Latino; 57 Hispanic/Latino; 27 Two or more races, non-Hispanic/Latino), 30 international. Average age 33. In 2018, 143 master's awarded. *Degree requirements:* For master's, capstone course (for MBA). *Entrance requirements:* Additional exam requirements/recommendations for international students: Required—TOEFL (minimum score 563 paper-based; 85 iBT). *Application deadline:* Applications are processed on a rolling basis. Electronic applications accepted. *Expenses:* Tuition varies by program. *Financial support:* Career-related internships or fieldwork, Federal Work-Study, tuition waivers (partial), and campus employment available. Financial award application deadline: 4/1; financial award applicants required to submit FAFSA. *Unit head:* Tammy Gocial, Interim Dean, 314-529-9401, Fax: 314-529-9975, E-mail: tgocial@maryville.edu. *Application contact:* Chris Gourdine, Assistant Dean Business Administration, 314-529-6861, Fax: 314-529-9975, E-mail: cgourdine@maryville.edu.
Website: http://www.maryville.edu/bu/business-administration-masters/

McKendree University, Graduate Programs, Master of Business Administration Program, Lebanon, IL 62254-1299. Offers business administration (MBA); human resource management (MBA); international business (MBA). *Program availability:* Part-time, evening/weekend, online learning. *Entrance requirements:* For master's, official transcripts from all institutions attended, essay, minimum GPA of 3.0, three references, resume. Additional exam requirements/recommendations for international students: Required—TOEFL. Electronic applications accepted.

McMaster University, School of Graduate Studies, DeGroote School of Business, Program in Human Resources and Management, Hamilton, ON L8S 4M2, Canada. Offers MBA, PhD. *Program availability:* Part-time. *Degree requirements:* For doctorate, comprehensive exam, thesis/dissertation. *Entrance requirements:* For master's, GMAT; for doctorate, GMAT or GRE, master's degree, minimum B+ average. Additional exam requirements/recommendations for international students: Required—TOEFL (minimum score 580 paper-based). *Faculty research:* Leadership, occupational mental health, work attitudes, human resources recruitment, change and stress management strategies.

Mercy College, School of Business, Program in Human Resource Management, Dobbs Ferry, NY 10522-1189. Offers MS. *Program availability:* Part-time, evening/weekend, 100% online, blended/hybrid learning. *Students:* 42 full-time (33 women), 30 part-time (26 women); includes 53 minority (21 Black or African American, non-Hispanic/Latino; 4 Asian, non-Hispanic/Latino; 25 Hispanic/Latino; 3 Two or more races, non-Hispanic/Latino), 3 international. Average age 33. 58 applicants, 78% accepted, 24 enrolled. In 2018, 32 master's awarded. *Degree requirements:* For master's, thesis or alternative, Capstone project or thesis required. *Entrance requirements:* For master's, transcript(s); interview. Additional exam requirements/recommendations for international students: Required—TOEFL (minimum score 80 iBT), IELTS (minimum score 6.5). *Application deadline:* Applications are processed on a rolling basis. Application fee: $40. Electronic applications accepted. *Expenses:* Contact institution. *Financial support:* Career-related internships or fieldwork, Federal Work-Study, scholarships/grants, and unspecified assistantships available. Support available to part-time students. Financial award applicants required to submit FAFSA. *Unit head:* Dr. Lloyd Gibson, Dean, School of Business, 914-674-7159, Fax: 914-674-7493, E-mail: lgibson@mercy.edu. *Application contact:* Allison Gurdineer, Executive Director of Admissions, 877-637-2946, Fax: 914-674-7382, E-mail: admissions@mercy.edu.
Website: https://www.mercy.edu/degrees-programs/ms-human-resource-management

Mercyhurst University, Graduate Studies, Program in Organizational Leadership, Erie, PA 16546. Offers accounting (MS); higher education administration (MS); human resources (MS); organizational leadership (MS, Certificate); sports leadership (MS); strategy and innovation (MS). *Program availability:* Part-time, evening/weekend. *Degree requirements:* For master's, thesis. *Entrance requirements:* For master's, GRE General Test or MAT, interview, resume, essay, three professional references, transcripts. Additional exam requirements/recommendations for international students: Required—TOEFL (minimum score 80 iBT), IELTS (minimum score 6.5). Electronic applications accepted. *Faculty research:* Leadership training, organizational communication, leadership pedagogy.

Michigan State University, The Graduate School, College of Social Science, School of Human Resources and Labor Relations, East Lansing, MI 48824. Offers MLRHR, PhD. *Entrance requirements:* Additional exam requirements/recommendations for international students: Required—TOEFL.

Michigan State University, The Graduate School, Eli Broad College of Business, Program in Business Administration, East Lansing, MI 48224. Offers finance (MBA); human resource management (MBA); integrative management (MBA); marketing (MBA); supply chain management (MBA). MBA in integrative management is through Weekend MBA Program; other 4 concentrations are through Full-Time MBA Program. *Program availability:* Evening/weekend. *Degree requirements:* For master's, enrichment experience. *Entrance requirements:* For master's, GMAT or GRE, 4-year bachelor's degree; resume; work experience (minimum of 5 years for Weekend MBA); 2-3 personal essays; 2 letters of recommendation; personal interview. Additional exam requirements/recommendations for international students: Required—PTE (minimum score 70), TOEFL (minimum score 100 iBT) or IELTS (minimum score 7) for full-time MBA applicants. Electronic applications accepted. *Expenses:* Contact institution.

Middle Tennessee State University, College of Graduate Studies, University College, Murfreesboro, TN 37132. Offers advanced studies in teaching and learning (M Ed); human resources leadership (MPS); nursing administration (MSN); nursing education (MSN); strategic leadership (MPS); training and development (MPS). *Program availability:* Part-time, evening/weekend, online learning. *Entrance requirements:* Additional exam requirements/recommendations for international students: Required—TOEFL (minimum score 525 paper-based; 71 iBT) or IELTS (minimum score 6).

Millennia Atlantic University, Graduate Programs, Doral, FL 33178. Offers accounting (MBA); business administration (MBA); health information management (MS); human resource management (MA). *Program availability:* Online learning.

Misericordia University, College of Business, Master of Business Administration Program, Dallas, PA 18612-1098. Offers accounting (MBA); healthcare management (MBA); human resource management (MBA); management (MBA); sport management (MBA). *Program availability:* Part-time, evening/weekend, online learning. *Entrance requirements:* For master's, GMAT, MAT, GRE (50th percentile or higher), or minimum undergraduate GPA of 3.0, interview. Additional exam requirements/recommendations for international students: Required—TOEFL. Electronic applications accepted. Application fee is waived when completed online. *Expenses:* Contact institution.

Misericordia University, College of Business, Program in Organizational Management, Dallas, PA 18612-1098. Offers healthcare management (MS); human resource management (MS); management (MS). *Program availability:* Part-time, evening/weekend, online learning. *Entrance requirements:* For master's, GRE General Test, MAT (35th percentile or higher), or minimum undergraduate GPA of 3.0. Additional exam requirements/recommendations for international students: Required—TOEFL. Electronic applications accepted. Application fee is waived when completed online. *Expenses:* Contact institution.

Monroe College, King Graduate School, Bronx, NY 10468. Offers accounting (MS); business administration (MBA), including entrepreneurship, finance, general business administration, healthcare management, human resources, information technology, marketing; computer science (MS); criminal justice (MS); hospitality management (MS); public health (MPH), including biostatistics and epidemiology, community health, health administration and leadership. *Program availability:* Online learning.

Montclair State University, The Graduate School, Feliciano School of Business, General MBA Program, Montclair, NJ 07043-1624. Offers accounting (MBA); business analytics (MBA); digital marketing (MBA); finance (MBA); general business administration (MBA); human resources management (MBA); management (MBA); management of information and technology (MBA); marketing (MBA); project management (MBA). *Program availability:* Part-time, evening/weekend. *Degree requirements:* For master's, culminating experience. *Entrance requirements:* For master's, GMAT or GRE General Test, 2 letters of recommendation, resume, essay. Additional exam requirements/recommendations for international students: Required—TOEFL (minimum score 83 iBT), IELTS (minimum score 6.5). Electronic applications accepted. *Faculty research:* Accounting, management, marketing.

Moravian College, Graduate and Continuing Studies, Business and Management Programs, Bethlehem, PA 18018-6650. Offers accounting (MBA); business management (MBA); health administration (MHA); HR leadership (MSHRM); supply chain management (MBA). *Program availability:* Part-time, evening/weekend. *Faculty:* 3 full-time (2 women), 13 part-time/adjunct (4 women). *Students:* 13 full-time (12 women), 70 part-time (38 women); includes 10 minority (1 Black or African American, non-Hispanic/Latino; 9 Hispanic/Latino), 1 international. Average age 30. 92 applicants, 85% accepted, 58 enrolled. In 2018, 34 master's awarded. *Entrance requirements:* For master's, current resume, official transcripts, 2 letters of recommendation. Additional exam requirements/recommendations for international students: Required—TOEFL (minimum score 577 paper-based), IELTS (minimum score 6.5). *Application deadline:* For fall admission, 8/1 priority date for domestic and international students; for spring admission, 1/1 priority date for domestic and international students; for summer admission, 5/1 priority date for domestic and international students. Applications are

processed on a rolling basis. Electronic applications accepted. *Financial support:* Research assistantships available. Financial award applicants required to submit FAFSA. *Faculty research:* Leadership, change management, human resources. *Unit head:* Dr. Katie P. Desiderio, Executive Director, Graduate Business Programs, 610-861-1400, Fax: 610-861-1466, E-mail: graduate@moravian.edu. *Application contact:* Kristy Sullivan, Director of Student Recruitment Operations, 610-861-1400, Fax: 610-861-1466, E-mail: graduate@moravian.edu.
Website: https://www.moravian.edu/graduate/programs/business#/

Mount Mercy University, Program in Business Administration, Cedar Rapids, IA 52402-4797. Offers human resource (MBA); quality management (MBA). *Program availability:* Evening/weekend. *Entrance requirements:* For master's, minimum cumulative GPA of 3.0, 2 letters of recommendation, resume. Additional exam requirements/recommendations for international students: Required—TOEFL (minimum score 570 paper-based; 88 iBT). Electronic applications accepted.

Murray State University, Arthur J. Bauernfeind College of Business, MBA Program, Murray, KY 42071. Offers accounting (MBA); finance (MBA); global communications (MBA); human resource management (MBA); marketing (MBA). *Accreditation:* AACSB. *Program availability:* Part-time, evening/weekend, 100% online, blended/hybrid learning. *Entrance requirements:* For master's, GRE or GMAT, minimum university GPA of 2.75. Additional exam requirements/recommendations for international students: Required—TOEFL (minimum score 527 paper-based; 71 iBT). *Faculty research:* Human resource management, e-commerce, supply-chain management, investment management, accounting.

National American University, Roueche Graduate Center, Austin, TX 78731. Offers accounting (MBA); aviation management (MBA, MM); care coordination (MSN); community college leadership (Ed D); criminal justice (MM); e-marketing (MBA, MM); health care administration (MBA, MM); higher education (MM); human resources management (MBA, MM); information technology management (MBA, MM); international business (MBA); leadership (EMBA); management (MBA); nursing administration (MSN); nursing education (MSN); nursing informatics (MSN); operations and configuration management (MBA, MM); project and process management (MBA, MM). Master's programs offered online through the Harold D. Buckingham Graduate School. *Program availability:* Part-time, evening/weekend, online learning. *Entrance requirements:* For master's, minimum undergraduate GPA of 2.75. Additional exam requirements/recommendations for international students: Required—TOEFL, TWE. Electronic applications accepted. *Faculty research:* Tourism, finance, marketing.

National Louis University, College of Management and Business, Chicago, IL 60603. Offers business administration (MBA); human resource management and development (MS); management (MS). *Program availability:* Part-time, evening/weekend. *Entrance requirements:* For master's, college-administered critical thinking and writing skills test, minimum GPA of 3.0, resume, 3 references. Additional exam requirements/recommendations for international students: Required—TOEFL (minimum score 550 paper-based; 79 iBT).

National University, School of Business and Management, La Jolla, CA 92037-1011. Offers accountancy (M Acc, Certificate); business administration (GMBA, MBA); business analytics (MS); cause leadership (MA); global management (MGM); human resource management (MA); management information systems (MS); marketing (MS); organizational leadership (MS). GMBA offered in Spanish. *Program availability:* Part-time, evening/weekend, 100% online, blended/hybrid learning. *Degree requirements:* For master's, thesis (for some programs). *Entrance requirements:* For master's, interview, minimum GPA of 2.5. Additional exam requirements/recommendations for international students: Required—TOEFL (minimum score 550 paper-based; 79 iBT), IELTS (minimum score 6). Electronic applications accepted. *Expenses: Tuition:* Full-time $10,320; part-time $430 per unit. Tuition and fees vary according to degree level.

National University, School of Professional Studies, La Jolla, CA 92037-1011. Offers criminal justice (MCJ); digital cinema production (MFA); digital journalism (MA); homeland security and emergency management (MS); juvenile justice (MS); professional screenwriting (MFA); public administration (MPA), including human resource management, organizational leadership. *Program availability:* Part-time, evening/weekend, 100% online, blended/hybrid learning. *Degree requirements:* For master's, thesis (for some programs). *Entrance requirements:* For master's, interview, minimum GPA of 2.5. Additional exam requirements/recommendations for international students: Required—TOEFL (minimum score 550 paper-based; 79 iBT), IELTS (minimum score 6). Electronic applications accepted. *Expenses: Tuition:* Full-time $10,320; part-time $430 per unit. Tuition and fees vary according to degree level.

Nazareth College of Rochester, Graduate Studies, Department of Business, Program in Human Resource Management, Rochester, NY 14618. Offers MS. *Program availability:* Part-time, evening/weekend. *Entrance requirements:* For master's, minimum GPA of 3.0. Additional exam requirements/recommendations for international students: Required—TOEFL (minimum score 550 paper-based, 79 iBT) or IELTS (6.5). Electronic applications accepted.

New Mexico Highlands University, Graduate Studies, School of Business, Media and Technology, Las Vegas, NM 87701. Offers business administration (MBA), including human resource management, international business, management; media arts and technology (MA), including media arts and computer science. *Accreditation:* ACBSP. *Degree requirements:* For master's, comprehensive exam, thesis or alternative. *Entrance requirements:* For master's, minimum undergraduate GPA of 3.0. Additional exam requirements/recommendations for international students: Required—TOEFL (minimum score 540 paper-based). *Faculty research:* Real estate valuation, studying expert judgments in complex accounting, decision environments, green marketing, environmentalism, marketing research methodology.

New York Institute of Technology, School of Management, Department of Human Resource Management Studies, Old Westbury, NY 11568-8000. Offers human resource management (Advanced Certificate); human resource management and labor relations (MS). *Program availability:* Part-time. *Faculty:* 5 full-time (1 woman), 4 part-time/adjunct (1 woman). *Students:* 14 full-time (8 women), 25 part-time (24 women); includes 17 minority (6 Black or African American, non-Hispanic/Latino; 4 Asian, non-Hispanic/Latino; 7 Hispanic/Latino), 109 international. Average age 30. 54 applicants, 76% accepted, 17 enrolled. In 2018, 26 master's awarded. *Degree requirements:* For master's, thesis or alternative, seminar and comprehensive exam, or thesis. *Entrance requirements:* For master's, bachelor's degree; minimum undergraduate GPA of 3.0; interview; for Advanced Certificate, bachelor's degree; minimum undergraduate GPA of 3.0. Additional exam requirements/recommendations for international students: Required—TOEFL (minimum score 79 iBT), IELTS (minimum score 6), PTE (minimum score 53). *Application deadline:* Applications are processed on a rolling basis. Application fee: $50. Electronic applications accepted. *Expenses: Tuition:* Full-time $1285; part-time $1285 per credit. *Required fees:* $215; $175 per unit. Tuition and fees vary according to course load, degree level and campus/location. *Financial support:* Career-related internships or fieldwork, Federal Work-Study, scholarships/grants, tuition waivers (full and partial), and unspecified assistantships available. Support available to part-time students. Financial award application deadline: 2/15; financial award applicants required to submit FAFSA. *Faculty research:* Conflict resolution; adapting human resource practices to the needs of a global workforce; effect of leadership styles and human resource practices on employee productivity; human resource management practices as a source of competitive advantage; influence of personality on work-life balance and work-home domain boundaries. *Unit head:* Dr. Maya Kroumova, Chairperson, 212-261-1667, Fax: 516-686-7425, E-mail: mkroumov@nyit.edu. *Application contact:* Alice Dolitsky, Director, Graduate Admissions, 516-686-7520, Fax: 516-686-1116, E-mail: admissions@nyit.edu.
Website: http://www.nyit.edu/degrees/human_resources_management_labor_relations_ms

New York University, School of Professional Studies, Division of Programs in Business, Program in Leadership and Human Capital Management, New York, NY 10012-1019. Offers human resource management and development (MS), including global talent management, human resource management, learning, development, and executive coaching, organizational effectiveness. *Program availability:* Part-time, evening/weekend, 100% online, blended/hybrid learning. *Degree requirements:* For master's, thesis. *Entrance requirements:* For master's, GRE or GMAT (only upon request), bachelor's degree, resume with relevant professional work, internship or volunteer experience, two letters of recommendation, statement of purpose. Additional exam requirements/recommendations for international students: Required—TOEFL (minimum score 600 paper-based; 100 iBT), IELTS (minimum score 7). Electronic applications accepted. *Expenses:* Contact institution.

Niagara University, Graduate Division of Business Administration, Niagara University, NY 14109. Offers accounting (MBA); business administration (MBA); finance (MBA, MS); financial planning (MBA); healthcare administration (MBA, MHA); human resources (MBA); international business (MBA); marketing (MBA); professional accountancy (MBA); strategic management (MBA); supply chain management (MBA). *Accreditation:* AACSB. *Program availability:* Part-time, evening/weekend, 100% online, blended/hybrid learning. *Students:* 224 full-time (116 women), 56 part-time (22 women); includes 36 minority (9 Black or African American, non-Hispanic/Latino; 2 American Indian or Alaska Native, non-Hispanic/Latino; 6 Asian, non-Hispanic/Latino; 12 Hispanic/Latino; 7 Two or more races, non-Hispanic/Latino), 82 international. Average age 26. In 2018, 134 master's awarded. *Entrance requirements:* For master's, GMAT. Additional exam requirements/recommendations for international students: Required—TOEFL (minimum score 550 paper-based; 79 iBT), IELTS (minimum score 6). *Application deadline:* For fall admission, 8/1 for domestic students; for spring admission, 11/1 for domestic students. Applications are processed on a rolling basis. Electronic applications accepted. *Expenses:* Contact institution. *Financial support:* Research assistantships, teaching assistantships, career-related internships or fieldwork, Federal Work-Study, scholarships/grants, and unspecified assistantships available. Support available to part-time students. Financial award application deadline: 4/15; financial award applicants required to submit FAFSA. *Faculty research:* Capital flows, Federal Reserve policy, human resource management, public policy, issues in marketing, auctions, economics of information, risk and capital markets, management strategy, consumer behavior, Internet and social media marketing. *Unit head:* Dr. Paul Richardson, MBA Director/Chair of the Marketing Department, 716-286-8169, Fax: 716-286-8206, E-mail: mba@niagara.edu. *Application contact:* Evan Pierce, Associate Director for Graduate Recruitment, 716-286-8327, Fax: 716-286-8710, E-mail: epierce@niagara.edu.
Website: http://mba.niagara.edu

North Carolina Agricultural and Technical State University, The Graduate College, College of Business and Economics, Greensboro, NC 27411. Offers accounting (MBA); business education (MAT); human resources management (MBA); supply chain systems (MBA).

North Central College, School of Graduate and Professional Studies, Program in Business Administration, Naperville, IL 60566-7063. Offers change management (MBA); finance (MBA); human resource management (MBA); management (MBA). *Program availability:* Part-time, evening/weekend. *Degree requirements:* For master's, thesis optional, project. *Entrance requirements:* For master's, interview. Additional exam requirements/recommendations for international students: Required—TOEFL (minimum score 550 paper-based; 80 iBT), IELTS (minimum score 6.5). Electronic applications accepted. Application fee is waived when completed online. *Expenses:* Contact institution.

North Greenville University, T. Walter Brashier Graduate School, Greer, SC 29651. Offers Christian ministry (MCM, D Min); education (M Ed, MAT); financial planning (MBA); human resources (MBA). *Program availability:* Part-time, evening/weekend, online learning. *Degree requirements:* For master's, comprehensive exam (for some programs), thesis or alternative, capstone course. *Entrance requirements:* For master's, minimum GPA of 2.25 overall, 2.5 in major; for doctorate, MAT. Additional exam requirements/recommendations for international students: Required—TOEFL (minimum score 550 paper-based). Electronic applications accepted. *Faculty research:* Organizational behavior, church growth, homiletics, human resources, business strategy.

Northwestern University, The Graduate School, Kellogg School of Management, Management Programs, Evanston, IL 60208. Offers accounting information and management (MBA, PhD); analytical finance (MBA); business administration (MBA); decision sciences (MBA); entrepreneurship and innovation (MBA); finance (MBA, PhD); health enterprise management (MBA); human resources management (MBA); international business (MBA); management and organizations (MBA, PhD); management and organizations and sociology (PhD); management and strategy (MBA); management studies (MS); managerial analytics (MBA); managerial economics (MBA); managerial economics and strategy (PhD); marketing (MBA, PhD); marketing management (MBA); media management (MBA); operations management (MBA, PhD); real estate (MBA); social enterprise at Kellogg (MBA); JD/MBA. *Program availability:* Part-time, evening/weekend. Terminal master's awarded for partial completion of doctoral program. *Degree requirements:* For doctorate, thesis/dissertation, 2 years of coursework, qualifying (field) exam and candidacy, summer research papers and presentations to faculty, proposal defense, final exam/defense. *Entrance requirements:* For master's, GMAT, GRE, interview, 2 letters of recommendation, college transcripts, resume, essays, Kellogg honor code; for doctorate, GMAT, GRE, statement of purpose, transcripts, 2 letters of recommendation, resume, interview. Additional exam requirements/recommendations for international students: Required—TOEFL, IELTS. Electronic applications accepted. *Expenses:* Contact institution. *Faculty research:* Business cycles and international finance, health policy, networks, non-market strategy, consumer psychology.

Northwest Missouri State University, Graduate School, Melvin and Valorie Booth College of Business and Professional Studies, Maryville, MO 64468-6001. Offers agricultural economics (MBA); business decision and analytics (MBA); general management (MBA); human resource management (MBA); marketing (MBA). *Program availability:* Part-time. *Faculty:* 24 full-time (12 women). *Students:* 56 full-time (31 women), 220 part-time (126 women); includes 47 minority (23 Black or African American, non-Hispanic/Latino; 6 Asian, non-Hispanic/Latino; 10 Hispanic/Latino; 8 Two or more races, non-Hispanic/Latino), 15 international. Average age 32. 154 applicants, 75% accepted, 104 enrolled. In 2018, 53 master's awarded. *Degree requirements:* For master's, comprehensive exam. *Entrance requirements:* For master's, GMAT, GRE,

minimum GPA of 2.5. Additional exam requirements/recommendations for international students: Required—TOEFL (minimum score 550 paper-based). *Application deadline:* For fall admission, 7/1 for domestic and international students; for spring admission, 11/15 for domestic and international students; for summer admission, 4/1 for domestic and international students. Applications are processed on a rolling basis. Application fee: $0 ($50 for international students). Electronic applications accepted. *Expenses:* $13,530 to complete degree (online MBA program); 401.06/credit hour in-state& 653.92/credit hour out-of-state. *Financial support:* Research assistantships with full tuition reimbursements, teaching assistantships with full tuition reimbursements, career-related internships or fieldwork, unspecified assistantships, and administrative assistantships, tutorial assistantships available. Financial award application deadline: 4/1; financial award applicants required to submit FAFSA. *Unit head:* Dr. Steve Ludwig, Director of the Melvin And Valorie Booth School of Business, 660-562-1749, Fax: 660-562-1096, E-mail: sludwig@nwmissouri.edu. *Application contact:* Dr. Steve Ludwig, Director of the Melvin And Valorie Booth School of Business, 660-562-1749, Fax: 660-562-1096, E-mail: sludwig@nwmissouri.edu.
Website: https://www.nwmissouri.edu/business/index.htm

Norwich University, College of Graduate and Continuing Studies, Master of Science in Leadership Program, Northfield, VT 05663. Offers leadership (MS), including human resources leadership, leading change management consulting, organizational leadership, public sector/government/military leadership. *Program availability:* Evening/weekend, online only, mostly all online with a week-long residency requirement. *Degree requirements:* For master's, capstone. *Entrance requirements:* For master's, minimum undergraduate GPA of 2.75. Additional exam requirements/recommendations for international students: Required—TOEFL (minimum score 550 paper-based; 80 iBT), IELTS (minimum score 6.5). Electronic applications accepted. *Expenses:* Contact institution.

Nova Southeastern University, H. Wayne Huizenga College of Business and Entrepreneurship, Fort Lauderdale, FL 33314-7796. Offers accounting (M Acc); business (MBA); business intelligence/analytics (MBA); complex health systems (MBA); enterprise informatics (MBA); entrepreneurship (MBA); finance (MBA); human resource management (MBA); international business (MBA); management (MBA); marketing (MBA); process improvement (MBA); public administration (MPA); real estate development (MS); sport revenue generation (MBA); supply chain management (MBA). *Accreditation:* NASPAA. *Program availability:* Part-time, evening/weekend, 100% online, blended/hybrid learning. *Entrance requirements:* For master's, GMAT or GRE (depending on undergraduate GPA), official transcripts from all schools attended while in pursuit of bachelor's degree; minimum GPA of 2.5 from regionally-accredited institution. Additional exam requirements/recommendations for international students: Required—TOEFL (minimum score 550 paper-based; 79 iBT), IELTS (minimum score 6), PTE (minimum score 54). Electronic applications accepted. *Expenses:* Contact institution. *Faculty research:* Entrepreneurship and venture capital, ethics and social responsibility, global commerce and cultures, business process management.

Oakland University, Graduate Study and Lifelong Learning, School of Business Administration, Department of Management and Marketing, Rochester, MI 48309-4401. Offers business administration (MBA); entrepreneurship (Certificate); general management (Certificate); human resource management (Certificate); international business (Certificate); management and marketing (EMBA); marketing (Certificate).

Ohio Christian University, Graduate Programs, Circleville, OH 43113. Offers accounting (MBA); business administration (MBA); digital marketing (MBA); finance (MBA); healthcare management (MBA); human resources (MBA); management (MM); organizational leadership (MBA); pastoral care and counseling (MAM); practical theology (MAM).

The Ohio State University, Graduate School, Max M. Fisher College of Business, Program in Human Resource Management, Columbus, OH 43210. Offers human resource management (MHRM, PhD); labor and human resources (PhD). *Program availability:* Part-time. *Faculty:* 25. *Students:* 76 full-time (60 women), 27 part-time (20 women). Average age 26. In 2018, 56 master's awarded. *Degree requirements:* For doctorate, thesis/dissertation. *Entrance requirements:* For master's and doctorate, GRE General Test or GMAT. Additional exam requirements/recommendations for international students: Required—Michigan English Language Assessment Battery (minimum score 86); Recommended—TOEFL (minimum score 600 paper-based; 100 iBT), IELTS (minimum score 7). *Application deadline:* For fall admission, 11/15 priority date for domestic and international students. Applications are processed on a rolling basis. Application fee: $60 ($70 for international students). Electronic applications accepted. *Financial support:* Fellowships with tuition reimbursements, research assistantships with tuition reimbursements, and teaching assistantships with tuition reimbursements available. *Unit head:* Dr. Bennett J. Tepper, Chair, 614-688-2129, E-mail: tepper.15@osu.edu. *Application contact:* Graduate and Professional Admissions, 614-292-9444, Fax: 614-292-3895, E-mail: gpadmissions@osu.edu.
Website: http://fisher.osu.edu/departments/management-and-hr/

Oklahoma Christian University, Graduate School of Business, Oklahoma City, OK 73136-1100. Offers accounting (M Acc, MBA); financial services (MBA); general business (MBA); health services management (MBA); human resources (MBA); international business (MBA); leadership and organizational development (MBA); marketing (MBA); nonprofit management (MBA); project management (MBA). *Accreditation:* ACBSP. *Program availability:* Part-time, 100% online. *Entrance requirements:* For master's, bachelor's degree. Additional exam requirements/recommendations for international students: Required—TOEFL (minimum score 550 paper-based). Electronic applications accepted. *Expenses:* Contact institution.

Ottawa University, Graduate Studies-Arizona, Programs in Business, Ottawa, KS 66067-3399. Offers business administration (MBA); finance (MBA); human resources (MA, MBA); leadership (MBA); marketing (MBA). Programs offered in Mesa, Phoenix, Tempe and West Valley, AZ. *Program availability:* Part-time, evening/weekend, online learning. *Degree requirements:* For master's, thesis or alternative. *Entrance requirements:* For master's, minimum undergraduate GPA of 3.0. Additional exam requirements/recommendations for international students: Required—TOEFL (minimum score 550 paper-based). Electronic applications accepted.

Pace University, Lubin School of Business, Program in Management, New York, NY 10038. Offers entrepreneurial studies (MBA); entrepreneurship (MS); human resource management (MBA, MS); strategic management (MBA, MS). *Program availability:* Part-time, evening/weekend. *Students:* 63 full-time (38 women), 57 part-time (41 women); includes 41 minority (18 Black or African American, non-Hispanic/Latino; 8 Asian, non-Hispanic/Latino; 11 Hispanic/Latino; 1 Native Hawaiian or other Pacific Islander, non-Hispanic/Latino; 3 Two or more races, non-Hispanic/Latino), 34 international. Average age 30. 125 applicants, 66% accepted, 42 enrolled. In 2018, 55 master's awarded. *Entrance requirements:* For master's, GMAT, GRE (GMAT not required for MS in Human Resources Management with 3 years of HR experience in a management position), undergraduate degree, transcripts from all accredited colleges/universities attended, two letters of recommendation, resume, personal statement. Additional exam requirements/recommendations for international students: Required—TOEFL (minimum score 90 iBT), IELTS (minimum score 7) or PTE (minimum score 61). *Application deadline:* For fall admission, 8/1 priority date for domestic students, 6/1 for international students; for spring admission, 12/1 for domestic students, 10/1 for international students. Applications are processed on a rolling basis. Application fee: $70. Electronic applications accepted. *Financial support:* Research assistantships, career-related internships or fieldwork, Federal Work-Study, and unspecified assistantships available. Support available to part-time students. Financial award application deadline: 2/15; financial award applicants required to submit FAFSA. *Unit head:* Dr. Ibraiz Tarique, Chairperson, Management and Management of Science, 212-618-6583, E-mail: itarique@pace.edu. *Application contact:* Susan Ford-Goldschein, Director of Graduate Admissions, 212-346-1531, Fax: 212-346-1585, E-mail: graduateadmission@pace.edu.
Website: http://www.pace.edu/lubin/sections/explore-programs/graduate-programs

Penn State Great Valley, Graduate Studies, Management Division, Malvern, PA 19355-1488. Offers business administration (MBA); cyber security (Certificate); data analytics (MPS, MS, Certificate); distributed energy and grid modernization (Certificate); finance (M Fin); health sector management (Certificate); human resource management (Certificate); information science (MSIS); leadership development (MLD); new ventures and entrepreneurship (Certificate); sustainable management practices (Certificate). *Accreditation:* AACSB.

Penn State Harrisburg, Graduate School, School of Public Affairs, Middletown, PA 17057. Offers criminal justice (MA); health administration (MHA); health administration: long term care (Certificate); homeland security (MPS, Certificate); public administration (MPA, PhD); public administration: non-profit administration (Certificate); public budgeting and financial management (Certificate); public sector human resource management (Certificate). *Accreditation:* NASPAA.

Penn State University Park, Graduate School, College of the Liberal Arts, School of Labor and Employment Relations, University Park, PA 16802. Offers human resources and employment relations (MS); labor and global workers' rights (MPS).

Polytechnic University of Puerto Rico, Miami Campus, Graduate School, Miami, FL 33166. Offers accounting (MBA); business administration (MBA); construction management (MEM); environmental management (MEM); finance (MBA); human resources management (MBA); logistics and supply chain management (MBA); management of international enterprises (MBA); manufacturing management (MEM); marketing management (MBA); project management (MBA). *Program availability:* Part-time, evening/weekend, online learning. *Entrance requirements:* For master's, minimum GPA of 3.0. Electronic applications accepted.

Polytechnic University of Puerto Rico, Orlando Campus, Graduate School, Orlando, FL 32825. Offers accounting (MBA); business administration (MBA); construction management (MEM); engineering management (MEM); environmental management (MEM); finance (MBA); human resources management (MBA); management of international enterprises (MBA); management of technology (MBA); manufacturing management (MEM). *Program availability:* Part-time, evening/weekend, online learning. *Entrance requirements:* For master's, minimum GPA of 3.0. Additional exam requirements/recommendations for international students: Recommended—TOEFL. Electronic applications accepted.

Pontifical Catholic University of Puerto Rico, College of Business Administration, Program in Human Resources, Ponce, PR 00717-0777. Offers MBA, Professional Certificate. *Program availability:* Part-time, evening/weekend. *Degree requirements:* For master's, thesis. *Entrance requirements:* For master's, GRE, interview, minimum GPA of 2.75.

Pontificia Universidad Catolica Madre y Maestra, Graduate School, Faculty of Social and Administrative Sciences, Santiago, Dominican Republic. Offers business administration (MBA), including business development, finance, international business, management skills (M Mgmt, MBA), marketing, operations, strategic cost management, strategy, tourist destination planning and management; law (LL M), including civil law, corporate business law, criminal law, international relations, real estate law; management (M Mgmt), including higher financial management, insurance program administration, management skills (M Mgmt, MBA); psychology (MA), including clinical child and adolescent psychology, forensic psychology; strategic human resources (EMBA).

Portland State University, Graduate Studies, College of Urban and Public Affairs, Hatfield School of Government, Department of Public Administration, Portland, OR 97207-0751. Offers collaborative governance (Certificate); energy policy and management (Certificate); global management and leadership (MPA); health administration (MPA); human resource management (MPA); local government (MPA); natural resource policy and administration (MPA); nonprofit and public management (Certificate); nonprofit management (MPA); public administration (EMPA); public affairs and policy (PhD); sustainable food systems (Certificate). *Accreditation:* CAHME; NASPAA (one or more programs are accredited). *Program availability:* Part-time, evening/weekend. *Degree requirements:* For master's, integrative field experience (MPA), practicum (MPH); for doctorate, comprehensive exam, thesis/dissertation. *Entrance requirements:* For master's, GRE (minimum scores: verbal 150, quantitative 149, and analytic writing 4.5), minimum GPA of 3.0, 3 recommendation letters, resume, 500-word statement of intent; for doctorate, GRE, 3 recommendation letters, resume, 500-word personal essay. Additional exam requirements/recommendations for international students: Required—TOEFL (minimum score 550 paper-based; 80 iBT), IELTS (minimum score 7). *Faculty research:* Public budgeting, program evaluation, nonprofit management, natural resources policy and administration.

Purdue University, Graduate School, Krannert School of Management, Doctoral Program in Organizational Behavior and Human Resource Management, West Lafayette, IN 47907-2056. Offers PhD. *Degree requirements:* For doctorate, comprehensive exam, thesis/dissertation, dissertation proposal, dissertation defense. *Entrance requirements:* For doctorate, GMAT or GRE, bachelor's degree, two semesters of calculus, one semester each of linear algebra and statistics. Additional exam requirements/recommendations for international students: Required—TOEFL (minimum score 575 paper-based); Recommended—TWE. Electronic applications accepted. *Faculty research:* Human resource management, organizational behavior.

Purdue University, Graduate School, Krannert School of Management, Master of Science in Human Resource Management Program, West Lafayette, IN 47907. Offers MSHRM. *Entrance requirements:* For master's, GMAT or GRE, essays, recommendation letters, work experience/internship, minimum GPA of 3.0, four-year baccalaureate degree. Additional exam requirements/recommendations for international students: Required—TOEFL (minimum score 600 paper-based, 93 iBT), IELTS (minimum score 7.5), or PTE (minimum score 70). Electronic applications accepted. *Expenses:* Contact institution. *Faculty research:* Performance periods and the dynamics of the performance-risk relationship, reactions to unfair events in computer-mediated groups: a test of uncertainty management theory, influences on job search self-efficacy of spouses of military personnel, cross-cultural social intelligence: an assessment for employees working in cross-national contexts.

Purdue University Global, School of Business, Davenport, IA 52807. Offers business administration (MBA); change leadership (MS); entrepreneurship (MBA); finance (MBA); health care management (MBA, MS); human resource (MBA); international business

(MBA); management (MS); marketing (MBA); project management (MBA, MS); supply chain management and logistics (MBA, MS). *Accreditation:* ACBSP. *Program availability:* Part-time, evening/weekend, online learning. *Entrance requirements:* Additional exam requirements/recommendations for international students: Required—TOEFL (minimum score 550 paper-based; 80 iBT). Electronic applications accepted.

Regent's University London, Webster Graduate School, London, United Kingdom. Offers business (MBA); finance (MS); human resources (MA); information technology management (MA); international business (MA); international non-governmental organizations (MA); international relations (MA); management and leadership (MA); marketing (MA). *Program availability:* Part-time.

Regent University, Graduate School, School of Business and Leadership, Virginia Beach, VA 23464-9800. Offers business administration (MBA), including accounting, economics, entrepreneurship, finance and investing, general management, healthcare management (MA, MBA), human resource management (MA, MBA), innovation management, leadership, marketing, not-for-profit management (MA, MBA); business analytics (MS); business and design management (MA); church leadership (MA); leadership (Certificate); organizational leadership (MA, PhD), including ecclesial leadership (DSL, PhD), entrepreneurial leadership (PhD), healthcare management (MA, MBA), human resource development (PhD), human resource management (MA, MBA), individualized studies (DSL, PhD), interdisciplinary studies (MA), leadership coaching and mentoring (MA), not-for-profit management (MA, MBA), organizational development consulting (MA), servant leadership (MA, DSL); strategic leadership (DSL), including ecclesial leadership (DSL, PhD), global consulting, healthcare leadership, individualized studies (DSL, PhD), leadership coaching, servant leadership (MA, DSL), strategic foresight. *Program availability:* Part-time, evening/weekend, 100% online, blended/hybrid learning. *Degree requirements:* For master's, thesis or alternative, 3-credit hour culminating experience; for doctorate, thesis/dissertation. *Entrance requirements:* For master's, college transcripts, resume, essay; for doctorate, college transcripts, resume, essay, writing sample; for Certificate, writing sample, resume, transcripts. Additional exam requirements/recommendations for international students: Required—TOEFL (minimum score 577 paper-based). Electronic applications accepted. *Expenses:* Contact institution. *Faculty research:* Servant leadership, global business, team effectiveness, technology utilization, leadership development.

Regent University, Graduate School, School of Law, Virginia Beach, VA 23464-9800. Offers American legal studies (LL M); human rights (LL M); law (MA, JD), including advanced paralegal studies (MA), alternative dispute resolution (MA), business (MA), criminal justice (MA), general legal studies (MA), human resources management (MA), human rights and rule of law (MA), national security (MA), non-profit organizational law (MA), regulatory compliance (MA), wealth management and financial planning (MA); JD/MA; JD/MBA. *Accreditation:* ABA. *Program availability:* Part-time, 100% online, blended/hybrid learning. *Entrance requirements:* For master's, college transcripts, resume, personal statement; for doctorate, LSAT, minimum undergraduate GPA of 3.0, official transcripts, 2 letters of recommendation, resume, personal statement. Additional exam requirements/recommendations for international students: Required—TOEFL (minimum score 600 paper-based). Electronic applications accepted. *Expenses:* Contact institution. *Faculty research:* Family law, Constitutional law, law and culture, evidence and practice, intellectual property.

Regis University, College of Business and Economics, Denver, CO 80221-1099. Offers accounting (MS); executive leadership (Certificate); finance (MS); finance and accounting (MBA); health industry leadership (MBA); human resource management and leadership (MSOL); management (MBA); marketing (MBA); nonprofit leadership (Post-Graduate Certificate); nonprofit management (MNM); nonprofit organizational capacity building (Certificate); operations management (MBA); organizational leadership and management (MSOL); project leadership and management (MS, MSOL); strategic business management (Certificate); strategic human resource integration (Certificate); strategic management (MBA). Programs offered at Colorado Springs Campus, Northwest Denver Campus, Southeast Denver Campus, Fort Collins Campus, Broomfield Campus, Henderson (Nevada) Campus, and Summerlin (Nevada) Campus. *Program availability:* Part-time, evening/weekend, 100% online, blended/hybrid learning. *Degree requirements:* For master's, thesis (for some programs), capstone or final research project. *Entrance requirements:* For master's, official transcript reflecting baccalaureate degree awarded from regionally-accredited college or university, interview, 2 years of full-time related work experience, resume, letters of recommendation. Additional exam requirements/recommendations for international students: Required—TOEFL (minimum score 550 paper-based; 82 iBT). Electronic applications accepted. *Expenses:* Contact institution. *Faculty research:* Impact of information technology on small business regulation of accounting, international project financing, mineral development, delivery of healthcare to rural indigenous communities.

Robert Morris University, School of Business, Moon Township, PA 15108-1189. Offers business administration (MBA); human resource management (MS); taxation (MS); MBA/MS. *Accreditation:* AACSB. *Program availability:* Part-time-only, evening/weekend, 100% online. *Faculty:* 18 full-time (7 women), 1 (woman) part-time/adjunct. *Students:* 214 part-time (84 women); includes 12 minority (6 Black or African American, non-Hispanic/Latino; 5 Asian, non-Hispanic/Latino; 1 Two or more races, non-Hispanic/Latino), 7 international. Average age 30. 77 applicants, 97% accepted, 71 enrolled. In 2018, 83 master's awarded. *Degree requirements:* For master's, Completion of 36 or 30 credit hours depending upon program. *Entrance requirements:* For master's, GMAT, GRE, letters of recommendation, work experience. Additional exam requirements/recommendations for international students: Required—TOEFL (minimum score 550 paper-based; 79 iBT). *Application deadline:* For fall admission, 7/1 priority date for domestic and international students; for spring admission, 11/1 priority date for domestic and international students. Applications are processed on a rolling basis. Application fee: $35. Electronic applications accepted. Application fee is waived when completed online. *Expenses: Tuition:* Part-time $925 per credit hour. *Required fees:* $80 per credit hour. Tuition and fees vary according to degree level. *Financial support:* Institutionally sponsored loans available. Support available to part-time students. Financial award application deadline: 5/1; financial award applicants required to submit FAFSA. *Unit head:* Dr. Michelle L. Patrick, Dean, 412-397-5445, Fax: 412-397-2585, E-mail: patrick@rmu.edu. *Application contact:* Dr. Jodi Potter, Director, MBA Program, 412-397-6387, E-mail: potterj@rmu.edu.
Website: http://sbus.rmu.edu

Robert Morris University Illinois, Morris Graduate School of Management, Chicago, IL 60605. Offers accounting (MBA); accounting/finance (MBA); business analytics (MIS); health care administration (MM); higher education administration (MM); human performance (MS); human resource management (MBA); information security (MIS); information systems management (MIS); law enforcement administration (MM); management (MBA); management/finance (MBA); management/human resource management (MBA); sports administration (MM). *Program availability:* Part-time, evening/weekend. *Entrance requirements:* For master's, official transcripts and letters of recommendation (for some programs); written personal statement. Additional exam requirements/recommendations for international students: Required—TOEFL (minimum score 550 paper-based). Electronic applications accepted.

Rollins College, Hamilton Holt School, Master of Human Resources Program, Winter Park, FL 32789. Offers MHR. *Program availability:* Part-time, evening/weekend. *Degree requirements:* For master's, thesis optional. *Entrance requirements:* For master's, GMAT or GRE, official transcripts, two letters of recommendation, essay, current resume. Additional exam requirements/recommendations for international students: Required—TOEFL (minimum score 550 paper-based; 80 iBT). *Expenses:* Contact institution.

Roosevelt University, Graduate Division, Walter E. Heller College of Business, Program in Human Resource Management, Chicago, IL 60605. Offers MSHRM. *Program availability:* Part-time, evening/weekend. Electronic applications accepted.

Rutgers University–Newark, Graduate School, Program in Public Administration, Newark, NJ 07102. Offers health care administration (MPA); human resources administration (MPA); public administration (PhD); public management (MPA); public policy analysis (MPA); urban systems and issues (MPA). *Accreditation:* NASPAA (one or more programs are accredited). *Program availability:* Part-time, evening/weekend. *Degree requirements:* For master's, comprehensive exam, thesis or alternative; for doctorate, thesis/dissertation. *Entrance requirements:* For master's, GRE, minimum undergraduate B average; for doctorate, GRE, MPA, minimum B average. Electronic applications accepted. *Faculty research:* Government finance, municipal and state government, public productivity.

Rutgers University–New Brunswick, School of Management and Labor Relations, Program in Human Resource Management, Piscataway, NJ 08854-8097. Offers MHRM. *Program availability:* Part-time, evening/weekend. *Entrance requirements:* For master's, GMAT or GRE General Test, 3 letters of recommendation. Additional exam requirements/recommendations for international students: Required—TOEFL (minimum score 575 paper-based). Electronic applications accepted. *Expenses:* Contact institution. *Faculty research:* Human resource policy and planning, employee ownership and profit sharing, compensation and appraisal of performance, law and public policy, computers and decision making.

Rutgers University–New Brunswick, School of Management and Labor Relations, Program in Industrial Relations and Human Resources, Piscataway, NJ 08854-8097. Offers PhD. *Program availability:* Part-time. *Degree requirements:* For doctorate, comprehensive exam, thesis/dissertation. *Entrance requirements:* For doctorate, GRE or GMAT, 3 letters of recommendation. Additional exam requirements/recommendations for international students: Required—TOEFL (minimum score 575 paper-based; 91 iBT). Electronic applications accepted. *Faculty research:* Strategic human resources, labor relations, organizational change, worker representation.

Sacred Heart University, Graduate Programs, Jack Welch College of Business, Department of Management, Fairfield, CT 06825. Offers administration (MBA); human resource management (MS, Graduate Certificate); management (Graduate Certificate). *Program availability:* Part-time, evening/weekend. *Degree requirements:* For master's, capstone project. *Entrance requirements:* For master's, GMAT/GRE, bachelor's degree. Additional exam requirements/recommendations for international students: Required—TOEFL (minimum score 570 paper-based, 80 iBT), TWE, or IELTS (6.5). Electronic applications accepted. *Expenses:* Contact institution.

St. Ambrose University, College of Business, Program in Business Administration, Davenport, IA 52803-2898. Offers business administration (DBA); health care (MBA); human resources (MBA). *Accreditation:* ACBSP. *Program availability:* Part-time, evening/weekend. *Degree requirements:* For master's, comprehensive exam (for some programs), thesis or alternative, capstone seminar; for doctorate, comprehensive exam, thesis/dissertation, oral and written exams. *Entrance requirements:* For master's, GMAT; for doctorate, GMAT, master's degree. Additional exam requirements/recommendations for international students: Required—TOEFL. Electronic applications accepted. *Expenses:* Contact institution.

Saint Francis University, School of Business, Loretto, PA 15940-0600. Offers business administration (MBA); human resource management (MHRM). *Program availability:* Part-time, evening/weekend. *Degree requirements:* For master's, comprehensive exam (for some programs), thesis (for some programs). *Entrance requirements:* For master's, GMAT (waived if undergraduate QPA is 3.3 or above), 2 letters of recommendation, minimum GPA of 2.75, two essays. Additional exam requirements/recommendations for international students: Required—TOEFL (minimum score 550 paper-based; 57 iBT). Electronic applications accepted. *Expenses:* Contact institution.

St. Joseph's College, Long Island Campus, Programs in Management, Field in Human Resources Management, Patchogue, NY 11772-2399. Offers MS. *Program availability:* Part-time, evening/weekend, 100% online, blended/hybrid learning. *Faculty:* 13 full-time (5 women), 23 part-time/adjunct (8 women). *Students:* 7 full-time (5 women), 34 part-time (26 women); includes 12 minority (2 Black or African American, non-Hispanic/Latino; 10 Hispanic/Latino). Average age 33. 29 applicants, 62% accepted, 12 enrolled. In 2018, 7 master's awarded. *Entrance requirements:* For master's, Application, $25 application fee, official transcripts, two letters of recommendation, current resume, 250 word written statement. Additional exam requirements/recommendations for international students: Required—TOEFL (minimum score 80 iBT). *Application deadline:* Applications are processed on a rolling basis. Application fee: $25. Electronic applications accepted. *Expenses: Tuition:* Full-time $18,450; part-time $1025 per credit. *Required fees:* $414. *Financial support:* In 2018–19, 7 students received support. *Unit head:* Mary A. Chance, Assistant Professor/Interim Director of Graduate Management Studies, 631-687-1297, E-mail: mchance@sjcny.edu. *Application contact:* Mary A. Chance, Assistant Professor/Interim Director of Graduate Management Studies, 631-687-1297, E-mail: mchance@sjcny.edu.

St. Joseph's College, New York, Programs in Management, Field in Human Resources Management, Brooklyn, NY 11205-3688. Offers MS. *Program availability:* Part-time, evening/weekend, 100% online, blended/hybrid learning. *Faculty:* 5 part-time/adjunct (4 women). *Students:* 1 full-time (0 women), 14 part-time (10 women); includes 10 minority (6 Black or African American, non-Hispanic/Latino; 2 Asian, non-Hispanic/Latino; 1 Hispanic/Latino; 1 Two or more races, non-Hispanic/Latino). Average age 40. 8 applicants, 88% accepted, 2 enrolled. In 2018, 7 master's awarded. *Entrance requirements:* For master's, Application, $25 application fee, two letters of recommendation, current resume, 250 word essay, official transcripts. Additional exam requirements/recommendations for international students: Required—TOEFL (minimum score 80 iBT). *Application deadline:* Applications are processed on a rolling basis. Application fee: $25. Electronic applications accepted. *Expenses: Tuition:* Full-time $18,450; part-time $1025 per credit. *Required fees:* $414. *Financial support:* In 2018–19, 1 student received support. *Unit head:* Sharon Didier, Assistant Chair/Co-Director of Graduate Management Studies/Associate Professor, 718-940-5790, E-mail: sdidier@sjcny.edu. *Application contact:* Sharon Didier, Assistant Chair/Co-Director of Graduate Management Studies/Associate Professor, 718-940-5790, E-mail: sdidier@sjcny.edu.
Website: https://www.sjcny.edu

Saint Joseph's University, Erivan K. Haub School of Business, Strategic Human Resource Management Program, Philadelphia, PA 19131-1395. Offers strategic human resources management (MS). *Program availability:* Part-time, online learning. *Degree requirements:* For master's, minimum GPA of 3.0. *Entrance requirements:* For master's,

MAT, GRE, or GMAT, 2 letters of recommendation, resume, personal statement, official undergraduate and graduate transcripts. Additional exam requirements/ recommendations for international students: Required—PTE, TOEFL, IELTS, or PTE. Electronic applications accepted. *Expenses:* Contact institution.

Saint Leo University, Graduate Studies in Business, Saint Leo, FL 33574-6665. Offers accounting (M Acc); cybersecurity management (MBA); health care management (MBA); human resource management (MBA); marketing (MBA); marketing research and social media analytics (MBA); software engineering (MS). *Accreditation:* ACBSP. *Program availability:* Part-time, evening/weekend, 100% online, blended/hybrid learning. *Faculty:* 51 full-time (16 women), 54 part-time/adjunct (22 women). *Students:* 8 full-time (3 women), 2,209 part-time (1,288 women); includes 1,046 minority (691 Black or African American, non-Hispanic/Latino; 10 American Indian or Alaska Native, non-Hispanic/Latino; 47 Asian, non-Hispanic/Latino; 249 Hispanic/Latino; 5 Native Hawaiian or other Pacific Islander, non-Hispanic/Latino; 44 Two or more races, non-Hispanic/ Latino), 71 international. Average age 37. 760 applicants, 83% accepted, 498 enrolled. In 2018, 763 master's, 14 doctorates awarded. *Degree requirements:* For doctorate, comprehensive exam, thesis/dissertation. *Entrance requirements:* For master's, GMAT with minimum score 500 (for M Acc), official transcripts, current resume, 2 professional recommendations, personal statement, bachelor's degree from regionally-accredited university; undergraduate degree in accounting and minimum undergraduate GPA of 3.0 (for M Acc); minimum undergraduate GPA of 3.0 in final 2 years of undergraduate study and 2 years' work experience (for MBA); for doctorate, GMAT (minimum score of 550) if master's GPA is under 3.25, official transcripts, current resume, 2 professional recommendations, personal statement, master's degree from regionally-accredited university with minimum GPA of 3.25, 3 years' work experience, interview. Additional exam requirements/recommendations for international students: Required—TOEFL (minimum score 550 paper-based; 78 iBT). *Application deadline:* For fall admission, 7/1 priority date for domestic and international students; for spring admission, 11/12 priority date for domestic students, 11/1 for international students. Applications are processed on a rolling basis. Application fee: $80. Electronic applications accepted. *Expenses:* Onground Master of Accounting $555 per credit, Online Master of Accounting $720 per credit, Onground MBA $555 per credit, Onground MBA Intl/Experiential $720 per credit, Online MBA/Cybersecurity military rate $555 per credit, Online MBA civilian rate $720, MS Cybersecurity civilian rate $770, DBA $900 per credit. *Financial support:* In 2018–19, 213 students received support. Scholarships/grants, unspecified assistantships, and tuition remission for Saint Leo employees and their dependents available. Financial award application deadline: 3/1; financial award applicants required to submit FAFSA. *Faculty research:* Servant leadership, work/life balance, emotional intelligence, pricing, marketing. *Unit head:* Dr. Robyn Parker, Dean, School of Business, 352-588-8599, Fax: 352-588-8912, E-mail: mbaslu@saintleo.edu. *Application contact:* Mark Russum, Assistant Vice President, Enrollment, 800-707-8846, Fax: 352-588-7873, E-mail: grad.admissions@saintleo.edu.
Website: https://www.saintleo.edu/college-of-business

Saint Mary's University of Minnesota, Schools of Graduate and Professional Programs, Graduate School of Business and Technology, Human Resource Management Program, Winona, MN 55987-1399. Offers MA. *Unit head:* Holly Tapper, Director, 612-238-4547, E-mail: htapper@smumn.edu. *Application contact:* Laurie Roy, Director of Admission of Schools of Graduate and Professional Programs, 507-457-8606, Fax: 612-728-5121, E-mail: lroy@smumn.edu.
Website: http://www.smumn.edu/graduate-home/areas-of-study/graduate-school-of-business-technology/ma-in-human-resource-management

Saint Peter's University, Graduate Business Programs, MBA Program, Jersey City, NJ 07306-5997. Offers finance (MBA); health care administration (MBA); human resource management (MBA); international business (MBA); management (MBA); management information systems (MBA); marketing (MBA); risk management (MBA); MBA/MS. *Program availability:* Part-time, evening/weekend. *Entrance requirements:* Additional exam requirements/recommendations for international students: Required—TOEFL. Electronic applications accepted. *Faculty research:* Finance, health care management, human resource management, international business, management, management information systems, marketing, risk management.

St. Thomas University, School of Business, Department of Management, Miami Gardens, FL 33054-6459. Offers accounting (MBA); general management (MSM, Certificate); health management (MBA, MSM, Certificate); human resource management (MBA, MSM, Certificate); international business (MBA, MIB, MSM, Certificate); justice administration (MSM, Certificate); management accounting (MSM, Certificate); public management (MSM, Certificate); sports administration (MS). *Program availability:* Part-time, evening/weekend. *Degree requirements:* For master's, comprehensive exam. *Entrance requirements:* For master's, interview, minimum GPA of 3.0 or GMAT. Additional exam requirements/recommendations for international students: Required—TOEFL (minimum score 550 paper-based; 79 iBT). Electronic applications accepted.

Salve Regina University, Program in Management, Newport, RI 02840-4192. Offers business studies (CGS); human resource management (CGS); innovation and strategic management (MS); management (CGS); nonprofit management (CGS); social entrepreneurship (CGS). *Program availability:* Part-time, evening/weekend, online learning. *Entrance requirements:* For master's, GMAT, GRE General Test, or MAT. Additional exam requirements/recommendations for international students: Required—TOEFL (minimum score 600 paper-based; 100 iBT). Electronic applications accepted. *Expenses: Tuition:* Full-time $10,530; part-time $585 per credit. *Required fees:* $60 per term. Tuition and fees vary according to course level, course load, degree level and program.

San Diego State University, Graduate and Research Affairs, Fowler College of Business, Department of Management, San Diego, CA 92182. Offers entrepreneurship (MS); human resources management (MS); management science (MS). *Program availability:* Part-time, evening/weekend. *Degree requirements:* For master's, thesis or alternative. *Entrance requirements:* For master's, GMAT, resume, letters of reference. Additional exam requirements/recommendations for international students: Required—TOEFL. Electronic applications accepted.

San Ignacio University, Graduate Programs, Doral, FL 33178. Offers business administration (MBA), including human resources management, international business, marketing management; education (M Ed), including early childhood education, educational leadership, special education; hospitality management (MA), including gastronomy and restaurant management, tourism management.

Savannah State University, Master of Public Administration Program, Savannah, GA 31404. Offers city management (MPA); human resources (MPA). *Accreditation:* NASPAA. *Program availability:* Part-time. *Degree requirements:* For master's, comprehensive exam, thesis, public service internship, capstone seminar. *Entrance requirements:* For master's, GRE General Test, GMAT, or MAT, minimum cumulative GPA of 2.5, 3 letters of recommendation, essay, official transcripts, resume, essay of 500-1000 words detailing reasons for pursuing degree. Additional exam requirements/recommendations for international students: Required—TOEFL. Electronic applications accepted. *Expenses:* Contact institution. *Faculty research:* Community development, human resources, leadership, conflict resolution, city management, non-profit management.

Seattle Pacific University, Master of Arts in Management Program, Seattle, WA 98119-1997. Offers business intelligence and data analytics (MA); cybersecurity (MA); faith and business (MA); human resources (MA); social and sustainable management (MA). *Students:* 12 part-time (9 women); includes 3 minority (2 Black or African American, non-Hispanic/Latino; 1 Asian, non-Hispanic/Latino), 4 international. Average age 31. 11 applicants, 45% accepted, 2 enrolled. *Entrance requirements:* For master's, GMAT scores above 500 (25 verbal; 30 quantitative; 4.4 analytical writing) are preferred. https://spu.edu/academics/school-of-business-and-economics/graduate-programs/ mba#application, bachelor's degree from accredited college or university, resume, essay, official transcript. *Application deadline:* For fall admission, 8/1 for domestic students, 6/1 for international students; for winter admission, 11/1 for domestic students, 9/1 for international students; for spring admission, 2/1 for domestic students, 12/1 for international students; for summer admission, 5/1 for domestic students. Application fee: $50.
Website: http://spu.edu/academics/school-of-business-and-economics/graduate-programs/ma-management

Southern New Hampshire University, School of Business, Manchester, NH 03106-1045. Offers accounting (MBA, Graduate Certificate); accounting finance (MS); accounting/auditing (MS); accounting/forensic accounting (MS); accounting/ management accounting (MS); accounting/taxation (MS); applied economics (MS); athletic administration (MBA, Graduate Certificate); business administration (IMBA, Certificate), including business information systems (Certificate), human resource management (Certificate); business analytics (MBA); business intelligence (MBA); communication (MA), including new media and marketing, public relations; community economic development (MBA); criminal justice (MBA); data analytics (MS); economics (MBA); engineering management (MBA); entrepreneurship (MBA); finance (MBA, MS, Graduate Certificate); finance/corporate finance (MS); finance/investments (MS); forensic accounting (MBA); forensic accounting and fraud examination (Graduate Certificate); healthcare informatics (MBA); healthcare management (MBA); human resource management (MS); human resources (MBA); information technology (MS); information technology management (MBA); international business (PhD); Internet marketing (MBA); leadership (MBA); leadership of nonprofit organizations (Graduate Certificate); management (MS); marketing (MBA, MS, Graduate Certificate); music business (MBA); operations and project management (MS); operations and supply chain management (MBA, Graduate Certificate); organizational leadership (MS); project management (MBA, Graduate Certificate); public administration (MBA, Graduate Certificate); quantitative analysis (MBA); Six Sigma (Graduate Certificate); Six Sigma quality (MBA); social media marketing (MBA, Graduate Certificate); sport management (MBA, MS, Graduate Certificate); sustainability and environmental compliance (MBA); MBA/Certificate. *Accreditation:* ACBSP. *Program availability:* Part-time, evening/ weekend, online learning. Terminal master's awarded for partial completion of doctoral program. *Degree requirements:* For master's, one foreign language, comprehensive exam (for some programs), thesis or alternative; for doctorate, one foreign language, comprehensive exam, thesis/dissertation. *Entrance requirements:* For master's, minimum GPA of 2.5; for doctorate, GMAT. Additional exam requirements/ recommendations for international students: Required—TOEFL (minimum score 500 paper-based). Electronic applications accepted.

State University of New York Polytechnic Institute, MBA Program in Technology Management, Utica, NY 13502. Offers accounting and finance (MBA); business management (MBA); health informatics (MBA); human resource management (MBA); marketing management (MBA). *Program availability:* Part-time, 100% online. *Students:* 29 full-time (13 women), 85 part-time (41 women); includes 18 minority (4 Black or African American, non-Hispanic/Latino; 8 Asian, non-Hispanic/Latino; 6 Hispanic/ Latino). Average age 32. 54 applicants, 54% accepted, 26 enrolled. In 2018, 29 master's awarded. *Degree requirements:* For master's, comprehensive exam, capstone project. *Entrance requirements:* For master's, GMAT or approved GMAT waiver, resume, letter of reference. Additional exam requirements/recommendations for international students: Required—TOEFL (minimum score 79 iBT), IELTS (minimum score 6.5), PTE (minimum score 53), TOEFL, IELTS, or PTE; GMAT or approved GMAT waiver. *Application deadline:* For fall admission, 7/1 priority date for domestic students, 7/1 for international students; for spring admission, 12/1 for domestic students, 11/1 for international students. Applications are processed on a rolling basis. Application fee: $60. Electronic applications accepted. *Expenses:* Contact institution. *Financial support:* Fellowships, research assistantships, and unspecified assistantships available. Financial award application deadline: 6/1; financial award applicants required to submit FAFSA. *Faculty research:* Entrepreneurial capacity development. *Unit head:* Dr. Rafael Romero, Coordinator, 315-792-7207, E-mail: rafael.romero@sunypoly.edu. *Application contact:* Alicia Foster, Director of Graduate Admissions, 315-792-7347, E-mail: fostera3@ sunypoly.edu.
Website: https://sunypoly.edu/academics/majors-and-programs/technology-management.html

Stevens Institute of Technology, Graduate School, School of Business, Program in Management, Hoboken, NJ 07030. Offers general management (MS); global innovation management (MS); human resource management (MS); information management (MS); project management (MS); technology commercialization (MS); technology management (MS). *Program availability:* Part-time, evening/weekend. *Faculty:* 58 full-time (8 women), 18 part-time/adjunct (3 women). *Students:* 101 full-time (41 women), 66 part-time (34 women); includes 14 minority (4 Black or African American, non-Hispanic/ Latino; 9 Asian, non-Hispanic/Latino; 1 Hispanic/Latino), 115 international. Average age 28. In 2018, 70 master's awarded. Terminal master's awarded for partial completion of doctoral program. *Degree requirements:* For master's, thesis optional, minimum B average in major field and overall. *Entrance requirements:* For master's, GRE/GMAT scores: GRE scores are required for all applicants applying to a full-time graduate program in the Schaefer School of Engineering and Science (SES). International applicants must submit TOEFL/IELTS scores and fulfill the English Language Proficiency Requirements in order to be considered. Additional exam requirements/ recommendations for international students: Required—TOEFL (minimum score 74 iBT), IELTS (minimum score 6). *Application deadline:* For fall admission, 4/1 for domestic and international students; for spring admission, 11/1 for domestic and international students; for summer admission, 5/1 for domestic students. Applications are processed on a rolling basis. Application fee: $60. Electronic applications accepted. *Expenses: Tuition:* Full-time $35,960; part-time $1620 per credit. *Required fees:* $1290; $600 per semester. Tuition and fees vary according to course load. *Financial support:* Fellowships, research assistantships, teaching assistantships, career-related internships or fieldwork, Federal Work-Study, scholarships/grants, and unspecified assistantships available. Financial award application deadline: 2/15; financial award applicants required to submit FAFSA. *Unit head:* Dr. Gregory Prascatos, Dean of SB, 201-216 8366, E-mail: gprastac@stevens.edu. *Application contact:* Graduate Admissions, 888-783-8367, Fax: 888-511-1306, E-mail: graduate@stevens.edu.
Website: https://www.stevens.edu/school-business/masters-programs/management

Stony Brook University, State University of New York, Graduate School, College of Business, Program in Business Administration, Stony Brook, NY 11794. Offers accounting (MBA); business administration (MBA); finance (MBA, Certificate); health care management (MBA); human resources (MBA); innovation (MBA); management (MBA); marketing (MBA); operations management (MBA). *Faculty:* 38 full-time (13 women), 8 part-time/adjunct (3 women). *Students:* 153 full-time (74 women), 148 part-time (76 women); includes 76 minority (16 Black or African American, non-Hispanic/Latino; 29 Asian, non-Hispanic/Latino; 27 Hispanic/Latino; 4 Two or more races, non-Hispanic/Latino), 36 international. Average age 28. 128 applicants, 78% accepted, 75 enrolled. In 2018, 76 master's awarded. *Entrance requirements:* For master's, GMAT, 3 letters of recommendation from current or former employers or professors, transcripts, personal statement, resume. Additional exam requirements/recommendations for international students: Required—TOEFL (minimum score 550 paper-based; 80 iBT), IELTS (minimum score 6.5). *Application deadline:* For fall admission, 5/15 for domestic students, 3/15 for international students; for spring admission, 12/1 for domestic students, 10/15 for international students. Application fee: $100. *Expenses:* Contact institution. *Financial support:* Teaching assistantships available. *Total annual research expenditures:* $2,070. *Unit head:* Dr. Manuel London, Dean, 631-632-7159, E-mail: manuel.london@stonybrook.edu. *Application contact:* Dr. Dmytro Holod, Associate Dean for Academic Programs/Graduate Director, 631-632-7183, Fax: 631-632-8181, E-mail: dmytro.holod@stonybrook.edu.
Website: https://www.stonybrook.edu/commcms/business/

Stony Brook University, State University of New York, School of Professional Development, Stony Brook, NY 11794. Offers coaching (Graduate Certificate); environmental management (MPS); German (MAT); higher education administration (MA, Certificate); human resource management (MS, Graduate Certificate); Italian (MAT); liberal studies (MA); mathematics (MAT); school district business leadership (Advanced Certificate); social studies (MAT); Spanish (MAT). *Program availability:* Part-time, evening/weekend, online learning. *Faculty:* 3 full-time (2 women), 94 part-time/adjunct (40 women). *Students:* 214 full-time (138 women), 1,100 part-time (813 women); includes 313 minority (117 Black or African American, non-Hispanic/Latino; 2 American Indian or Alaska Native, non-Hispanic/Latino; 32 Asian, non-Hispanic/Latino; 140 Hispanic/Latino; 3 Native Hawaiian or other Pacific Islander, non-Hispanic/Latino; 19 Two or more races, non-Hispanic/Latino), 7 international. Average age 33. 483 applicants, 89% accepted, 337 enrolled. In 2018, 315 master's, 178 other advanced degrees awarded. *Entrance requirements:* Additional exam requirements/recommendations for international students: Required—TOEFL (minimum score 85 iBT). *Application deadline:* For fall admission, 1/15 for domestic students, 6/1 for international students; for spring admission, 10/1 for domestic and international students. Applications are processed on a rolling basis. Application fee: $100. *Expenses:* Contact institution. *Financial support:* Fellowships, research assistantships, teaching assistantships, and career-related internships or fieldwork available. Support available to part-time students. *Unit head:* Patricia Malone, Associate Vice President for Professional Education and Assistant Provost for Engaged Learning, 631-632-7512, Fax: 631-632-9046, E-mail: patricia.malone@stonybrook.edu. *Application contact:* Melissa Jordan, Assistant Dean, 631-632-7751, E-mail: melissa.jordan@stonybrook.edu.
Website: http://www.stonybrook.edu/spd/

Strayer University, Graduate Studies, Washington, DC 20005-2603. Offers accounting (MS); acquisition (MBA); business administration (MBA); communications technology (MS); educational management (M Ed); finance (MBA); health services administration (MHSA); hospitality and tourism management (MBA); human resource management (MBA); information systems (MS), including computer security management, decision support system management, enterprise resource management, network management, software engineering management, systems development management; management (MBA); management information systems (MS); marketing (MBA); professional accounting (MS), including accounting information systems, controllership, taxation; public administration (MPA); supply chain management (MBA); technology in education (M Ed). Programs also offered at campus locations in Birmingham, AL; Chamblee, GA; Cobb County, GA; Morrow, GA; White Marsh, MD; Charleston, SC; Columbia, SC; Greensboro, NC; Greenville, SC; Lexington, KY; Louisville, KY; Nashville, TN; North Raleigh, NC; Washington, DC. *Accreditation:* ACBSP. *Program availability:* Part-time, evening/weekend, online learning. *Degree requirements:* For master's, thesis. *Entrance requirements:* For master's, GMAT, GRE General Test, bachelor's degree from an accredited college or university, minimum undergraduate GPA of 2.75. Electronic applications accepted.

Tarleton State University, College of Graduate Studies, College of Business Administration, Department of Management, Stephenville, TX 76402. Offers human resources management (MS). *Program availability:* Part-time, evening/weekend, 100% online, blended/hybrid learning. *Faculty:* 9 full-time (1 woman), 3 part-time/adjunct (1 woman). *Students:* 5 full-time (all women), 115 part-time (92 women). Average age 35. 46 applicants, 85% accepted, 26 enrolled. In 2018, 37 master's awarded. *Degree requirements:* For master's, comprehensive exam, thesis (for some programs). *Entrance requirements:* For master's, GRE, GMAT, minimum GPA of 3.0. Additional exam requirements/recommendations for international students: Required—TOEFL (minimum score 520 paper-based; 69 iBT); Recommended—IELTS (minimum score 6), TSE (minimum score 50). *Application deadline:* For fall admission, 8/15 priority date for domestic students; for spring admission, 1/7 for domestic students. Applications are processed on a rolling basis. Application fee: $50 ($130 for international students). Electronic applications accepted. *Expenses:* Contact institution. *Financial support:* Research assistantships, teaching assistantships, Federal Work-Study, scholarships/grants, and unspecified assistantships available. Financial award application deadline: 5/1; financial award applicants required to submit FAFSA. *Unit head:* Dr. Reggie Hall, Department Chair, 254-968-9654, E-mail: rhall@tarleton.edu. *Application contact:* Information Contact, 254-968-9104, Fax: 254-968-9670, E-mail: gradoffice@tarleton.edu.

Temple University, Fox School of Business, MBA Programs, Philadelphia, PA 19122-6096. Offers accounting (MBA); business management (MBA); financial management (MBA); healthcare and life sciences innovation (MBA); human resource management (MBA); international business (IMBA); IT management (MBA); marketing management (MBA); pharmaceutical management (MBA); strategic management (EMBA, MBA). EMBA offered in Philadelphia, PA and Tokyo, Japan. *Accreditation:* AACSB. *Program availability:* Part-time, evening/weekend, online learning. *Entrance requirements:* For master's, GMAT, minimum undergraduate GPA of 3.0. Additional exam requirements/recommendations for international students: Required—TOEFL (minimum score 600 paper-based; 100 iBT), IELTS (minimum score 7.5).

Temple University, Fox School of Business, Specialized Master's Programs, Philadelphia, PA 19122-6096. Offers accountancy (MS); actuarial science (MS); finance (MS); financial engineering (MS); human resource management (MS); innovation management and entrepreneurship (MS); marketing (MS); statistics (MS). MS in innovation management and entrepreneurship delivered jointly with College of Engineering. *Accreditation:* AACSB. *Program availability:* Part-time. *Entrance requirements:* For master's, GRE General Test or GMAT, minimum undergraduate GPA of 3.0. Additional exam requirements/recommendations for international students: Required—TOEFL (minimum score 600 paper-based; 100 iBT), IELTS (minimum score 7.5).

Tennessee State University, The School of Graduate Studies and Research, College of Public Service, Nashville, TN 37209-1561. Offers human resource management (MPS); public administration (MPA, PhD); social work (MSW); strategic leadership (MPS); training and development (MPS). *Accreditation:* NASPAA (one or more programs are accredited). *Program availability:* Part-time, evening/weekend. *Degree requirements:* For master's, comprehensive exam, thesis optional; for doctorate, comprehensive exam, thesis/dissertation. *Entrance requirements:* For master's, GRE General Test, minimum GPA of 2.5, writing sample; for doctorate, GRE General Test, minimum GPA of 3.25, writing sample. *Faculty research:* Total quality management and process improvement, national health care policy and administration, starting non-profit ventures, public service ethics, state education financing across the U.S. public.

Tennessee Technological University, College of Graduate Studies, College of Business, MBA Program, Cookeville, TN 38505. Offers finance (MBA); human resource management (MBA); international business (MBA); management information systems (MBA). *Program availability:* Part-time, evening/weekend. *Students:* 32 full-time (10 women), 156 part-time (66 women); includes 16 minority (7 Black or African American, non-Hispanic/Latino; 1 Asian, non-Hispanic/Latino; 5 Hispanic/Latino; 3 Two or more races, non-Hispanic/Latino), 5 international. 115 applicants, 68% accepted, 57 enrolled. In 2018, 88 master's awarded. *Entrance requirements:* For master's, GMAT or GRE. *Financial support:* In 2018–19, 2 research assistantships, 3 teaching assistantships were awarded; fellowships and unspecified assistantships also available. Financial award application deadline: 4/1; financial award applicants required to submit FAFSA. *Unit head:* Kate Nicewicz, Director, 931-372-3600, E-mail: knicewicz@tntech.edu. *Application contact:* Shelia K. Kendrick, Coordinator of Graduate Studies, 931-372-3808, Fax: 931-372-3497, E-mail: skendrick@tntech.edu.
Website: https://www.tntech.edu/cob/mba/

Tennessee Technological University, College of Graduate Studies, College of Interdisciplinary Studies, School of Professional Studies, Cookeville, TN 38505. Offers health care administration (MPS); human resources leadership (MPS); public safety (MPS); strategic leadership (MPS); teaching English to speakers of other languages (MPS); training and development (MPS). *Program availability:* Part-time, evening/weekend, online learning. *Students:* 23 full-time (8 women), 80 part-time (48 women); includes 20 minority (13 Black or African American, non-Hispanic/Latino; 3 Hispanic/Latino; 4 Two or more races, non-Hispanic/Latino), 1 international. 49 applicants, 73% accepted, 29 enrolled. In 2018, 33 master's awarded. *Degree requirements:* For master's, comprehensive exam, thesis or alternative. *Entrance requirements:* For master's, GRE. Additional exam requirements/recommendations for international students: Required—TOEFL (minimum score 527 paper-based; 71 iBT), IELTS (minimum score 5.5), PTE (minimum score 48), or TOEIC (Test of English as an International Communication). *Application deadline:* For fall admission, 7/1 for domestic students, 5/1 for international students; for spring admission, 11/1 for domestic students, 10/1 for international students; for summer admission, 5/1 for domestic students, 2/1 for international students. Applications are processed on a rolling basis. Application fee: $35 ($40 for international students). Electronic applications accepted. *Financial support:* Application deadline: 4/1. *Unit head:* Dr. Joseph Roberts, Interim Director, School of Professional Studies, 931-372-6223, E-mail: jmroberts@tntech.edu. *Application contact:* Shelia K. Kendrick, Coordinator of Graduate Studies, 931-372-3808, Fax: 931-372-3497, E-mail: skendrick@tntech.edu.
Website: https://www.tntech.edu/is/sps/

Texas A&M University, Mays Business School, Department of Management, College Station, TX 77843. Offers entrepreneurial leadership (MS); human resource management (MS). *Faculty:* 30. *Students:* 103 full-time (79 women), 1 part-time (0 women); includes 20 minority (2 Black or African American, non-Hispanic/Latino; 5 Asian, non-Hispanic/Latino; 13 Hispanic/Latino), 6 international. Average age 26. 131 applicants, 39% accepted, 40 enrolled. In 2018, 48 master's awarded. Terminal master's awarded for partial completion of doctoral program. *Degree requirements:* For master's, comprehensive exam. *Entrance requirements:* For master's, GMAT or GRE. Additional exam requirements/recommendations for international students: Required—TOEFL (minimum score 550 paper-based; 80 iBT), IELTS (minimum score 6), PTE (minimum score 53). *Application deadline:* For fall admission, 5/26 for domestic and international students. Applications are processed on a rolling basis. Application fee: $50 ($90 for international students). Electronic applications accepted. *Expenses:* Contact institution. *Financial support:* In 2018–19, 86 students received support, including 30 research assistantships with tuition reimbursements available (averaging $10,805 per year), 19 teaching assistantships with tuition reimbursements available (averaging $7,111 per year); career-related internships or fieldwork, institutionally sponsored loans, scholarships/grants, traineeships, health care benefits, tuition waivers (full and partial), and unspecified assistantships also available. Support available to part-time students. Financial award application deadline: 3/15; financial award applicants required to submit FAFSA. *Faculty research:* Strategic and human resource management, business and public policy, organizational behavior, organizational theory. *Unit head:* Dr. Wendy R. Boswell, Head, 979-845-4045, Fax: 979-845-9641, E-mail: wboswell@mays.tamu.edu. *Application contact:* Kristi R. Mora, Senior Academic Advisor II, 979-845-6127, Fax: 979-845-9641, E-mail: kmora@mays.tamu.edu.
Website: http://mays.tamu.edu/mgmt/

Texas A&M University–Central Texas, Graduate Studies and Research, Killeen, TX 76549. Offers accounting (MS); business administration (MBA); clinical mental health counseling (MS); criminal justice (MCJ); curriculum and instruction (M Ed); educational administration (M Ed); educational psychology - experimental psychology (MS); history (MA); human resource management (MS); information systems (MS); liberal studies (MS); management and leadership (MS); marriage and family therapy (MS); mathematics (MS); political science (MA); school counseling (M Ed); school psychology (Ed S).

Texas State University, The Graduate College, Emmett and Miriam McCoy College of Business Administration, Program in Human Resource Management, San Marcos, TX 78666. Offers MS. *Program availability:* Part-time. *Faculty:* 11 full-time (2 women). *Students:* 5 full-time (3 women), 13 part-time (8 women); includes 10 minority (4 Black or African American, non-Hispanic/Latino; 5 Hispanic/Latino; 1 Two or more races, non-Hispanic/Latino), 1 international. Average age 29. 20 applicants, 45% accepted, 9 enrolled. In 2018, 9 master's awarded. *Degree requirements:* For master's, comprehensive exam. *Entrance requirements:* For master's, official GRE (general test only) or GMAT required with competitive scores, baccalaureate degree from regionally-accredited university (business administration or a related field preferred); a competitive GPA in your last 60 hours of undergraduate course work (plus any completed graduate courses); 2 letters of recommendation; resume. Additional exam requirements/recommendations for international students: Required—TOEFL (minimum score 550 paper-based; 78 iBT), IELTS (minimum score 6.5). *Application deadline:* For fall admission, 1/15 priority date for domestic and international students; for spring admission, 10/1 for domestic and international students. Application fee: $55 ($90 for international students). Electronic applications accepted. *Expenses:* Tuition, state

resident: full-time $8102; part-time $4051 per semester. Tuition, nonresident: full-time $18,229; part-time $9115 per semester. *International tuition:* $18,229 full-time. *Required fees:* $2116; $120 per credit hour. Tuition and fees vary according to course load. *Financial support:* In 2018–19, 8 students received support, including 4 teaching assistantships (averaging $13,086 per year); research assistantships, Federal Work-Study, institutionally sponsored loans, scholarships/grants, health care benefits, and unspecified assistantships also available. Support available to part-time students. Financial award application deadline: 1/15; financial award applicants required to submit FAFSA. *Unit head:* Dr. William Chittenden, Associate Dean, 512-245-3591, Fax: 512-245-8365, E-mail: businessgraduate@txstate.edu. *Application contact:* Dr. Andrea Golato, Dean of Graduate School, 512-245-2581, Fax: 512-245-8365, E-mail: gradcollege@txstate.edu.
Website: https://graduate.mccoy.txstate.edu/grad_programs/MSHRM.html

Texas Woman's University, Graduate School, College of Business, Denton, TX 76204. Offers business administration (MBA), including accounting, business analytics, healthcare administration (MBA, MHA), human resources management, management; health systems management (MHSM); healthcare administration (MHA), including healthcare administration (MBA, MHA). *Accreditation:* ACBSP. *Program availability:* Part-time, 100% online, blended/hybrid learning. *Faculty:* 26 full-time (9 women), 14 part-time/adjunct (7 women). *Students:* 483 full-time (429 women), 445 part-time (373 women); includes 643 minority (325 Black or African American, non-Hispanic/Latino; 4 American Indian or Alaska Native, non-Hispanic/Latino; 134 Asian, non-Hispanic/Latino; 152 Hispanic/Latino; 1 Native Hawaiian or other Pacific Islander, non-Hispanic/Latino; 27 Two or more races, non-Hispanic/Latino), 38 international. Average age 33. 401 applicants, 84% accepted, 251 enrolled. In 2018, 471 master's awarded. *Degree requirements:* For master's, thesis or alternative, capstone. *Entrance requirements:* For master's, minimum GPA of 3.0 in last 60 hours of undergraduate coursework and prior graduate coursework, resume. Additional exam requirements/recommendations for international students: Required—TOEFL (minimum score 550 paper-based; 79 iBT); Recommended—IELTS (minimum score 6.5), TSE (minimum score 53). *Application deadline:* Applications are processed on a rolling basis. Application fee: $50 ($75 for international students). Electronic applications accepted. *Expenses: Tuition, area resident:* Full-time $4852; part-time $270 per semester hour. Tuition, state resident: full-time $4852; part-time $270 per semester hour. Tuition, nonresident: full-time $12,322; part-time $685 per semester hour. *International tuition:* $12,322 full-time. *Required fees:* $2714; $113 per semester hour. $296 per semester. Tuition and fees vary according to course level, course load, degree level, campus/location and program. *Financial support:* In 2018–19, 138 students received support, including 12 teaching assistantships (averaging $10,666 per year); career-related internships or fieldwork, Federal Work-Study, institutionally sponsored loans, scholarships/grants, traineeships, health care benefits, and unspecified assistantships also available. Support available to part-time students. Financial award application deadline: 3/1; financial award applicants required to submit FAFSA. *Faculty research:* Marketing and market research, economics, accounting, logistics and supply chain management, health systems. *Unit head:* Dr. James R. Lumpkin, Dean, 940-898-2458, Fax: 940-898-2120, E-mail: mba@twu.edu. *Application contact:* Korie Hawkins, Associate Director of Admissions, Graduate Recruitment, 940-898-3188, Fax: 940-898-3081, E-mail: admissions@twu.edu.
Website: http://www.twu.edu/business/

Thomas College, Graduate School, Programs in Business, Waterville, ME 04901-5097. Offers business (MBA); computer technology education (MS); education (MS); human resource management (MBA). *Program availability:* Part-time, evening/weekend. *Entrance requirements:* For master's, GMAT, GRE, MAT or minimum GPA of 3.3 in first 3 graduate-level courses. Additional exam requirements/recommendations for international students: Recommended—TOEFL.

Thomas Edison State University, School of Business and Management, Program in Human Resources Management, Trenton, NJ 08608. Offers MSHRM. *Program availability:* Part-time, online learning. *Degree requirements:* For master's, final/capstone project. *Entrance requirements:* For master's, bachelor's degree from a regionally-accredited college or university; minimum 2 letters of recommendation; 3-5 years of related working experience; current resume. Additional exam requirements/recommendations for international students: Required—TOEFL (minimum score 550 paper-based; 79 iBT). Electronic applications accepted.

Tiffin University, Program in Business Administration, Tiffin, OH 44883-2161. Offers finance (MBA); general management (MBA); healthcare administration (MBA); human resource management (MBA); international business (MBA); leadership (MBA); marketing (MBA); non-profit management (MBA); sports management (MBA). *Accreditation:* ACBSP. *Program availability:* Part-time, evening/weekend, online learning. *Entrance requirements:* For master's, minimum undergraduate GPA of 2.5, work experience. Additional exam requirements/recommendations for international students: Required—TOEFL (minimum score 550 paper-based; 79 iBT), IELTS. Electronic applications accepted. Application fee is waived when completed online. *Faculty research:* Small business, executive development operations, research and statistical analysis, market research, management information systems.

Towson University, College of Liberal Arts, Program in Human Resource Development, Towson, MD 21252-0001. Offers education leadership (MS); general human resource management (MS). *Program availability:* Part-time, evening/weekend. *Degree requirements:* For master's, comprehensive exam. *Entrance requirements:* For master's, bachelor's degree, 2 letters of recommendation, minimum GPA of 3.0, essay, resume. Additional exam requirements/recommendations for international students: Required—TOEFL. Electronic applications accepted. *Expenses: Tuition, area resident:* Full-time $9196; part-time $418 per unit. Tuition, state resident: full-time $9196; part-time $418 per unit. Tuition, nonresident: full-time $19,030; part-time $865 per unit. *International tuition:* $19,030 full-time. *Required fees:* $3102; $141 per year. $423 per term. Tuition and fees vary according to campus/location and program.

Trident University International, College of Business Administration, Program in Business Administration, Cypress, CA 90630. Offers business administration (PhD); conflict and negotiation management (MBA); criminal justice administration (MBA); entrepreneurship (MBA); finance (MBA); general management (MBA); government accounting (MBA); human resource management (MBA); information security and digital assurance management (MBA); information technology management (MBA); international business (MBA); logistics management (MBA); marketing (MBA); project management (MBA); public management (MBA); quality management (MBA); strategic leadership (MBA). *Program availability:* Part-time, evening/weekend, online learning. *Degree requirements:* For doctorate, comprehensive exam, thesis/dissertation, defense of dissertation. *Entrance requirements:* For master's, minimum GPA of 2.5 (students with GPA 3.0 or greater may transfer up to 30% of graduate level credits); for doctorate, minimum GPA of 3.4, curriculum vitae, course work in research methods or statistics. Additional exam requirements/recommendations for international students: Required—TOEFL. Electronic applications accepted.

Trinity International University, Trinity Law School, Santa Ana, CA 92705. Offers bioethics (MLS); church and ministry management (MLS); general legal studies (MLS); human resources management (MLS); human rights (MLS); law (JD); nonprofit organizations (MLS). *Program availability:* Part-time, evening/weekend. *Entrance requirements:* For doctorate, LSAT. Additional exam requirements/recommendations for international students: Required—TOEFL (minimum score 580 paper-based). *Expenses:* Contact institution.

Trinity Washington University, School of Business and Graduate Studies, Washington, DC 20017-1094. Offers business administration (MBA); communication (MA); international security studies (MA); organizational management (MSA), including federal program management, human resource management, nonprofit management, organizational development, public and community health. *Program availability:* Part-time, evening/weekend. *Degree requirements:* For master's, thesis (for some programs), capstone project (MSA). *Entrance requirements:* For master's, minimum GPA of 2.5. Additional exam requirements/recommendations for international students: Required—TOEFL (minimum score 550 paper-based).

Troy University, Graduate School, College of Business, Program in Human Resources Management, Troy, AL 36082. Offers MS. *Program availability:* Part-time, evening/weekend. *Faculty:* 8 full-time (2 women), 1 part-time/adjunct (0 women). *Students:* 76 full-time (58 women), 298 part-time (227 women); includes 123 minority (114 Black or African American, non-Hispanic/Latino; 1 Asian, non-Hispanic/Latino; 3 Hispanic/Latino; 5 Two or more races, non-Hispanic/Latino). Average age 34. 203 applicants, 92% accepted, 123 enrolled. In 2018, 90 master's awarded. *Degree requirements:* For master's, minimum GPA of 3.0; admission to candidacy. *Entrance requirements:* For master's, GRE (minimum score of 900 on old exam or 294 on new exam) or GMAT (minimum score of 500), bachelor's degree; minimum undergraduate GPA of 2.5 or 3.0 on last 30 semester hours, letter of recommendation. Additional exam requirements/recommendations for international students: Required—TOEFL (minimum score 523 paper-based; 70 iBT), IELTS (minimum score 6). *Application deadline:* Applications are processed on a rolling basis. Application fee: $50. Electronic applications accepted. *Expenses: Tuition, area resident:* Full-time $425; part-time $425 per credit hour. Tuition, state resident: full-time $425; part-time $425 per credit hour. Tuition, nonresident: full-time $850; part-time $850 per credit hour. *International tuition:* $850 full-time. *Required fees:* $50 per semester. Tuition and fees vary according to campus/location and program. *Financial support:* Fellowships, career-related internships or fieldwork, and scholarships/grants available. Support available to part-time students. Financial award applicants required to submit FAFSA. *Unit head:* Dr. Bill Heisler, Director, 757-846-4203, Fax: 334-241-0378, E-mail: wheisler@troy.edu. *Application contact:* Jessica A. Kimbro, Assistant Director of Graduate Programs, 334-670-3189, E-mail: jacord@troy.edu.
Website: https://www.troy.edu/academics/academic-programs/graduate/human-resource-management.html

United States International University–Africa, School of Business Administration, Nairobi, Kenya. Offers business administration (GEMBA); entrepreneurship (MBA); finance (MBA); human resource management (MBA); information technology management (MBA); integrated studies (MBA); international business administration (MBA); management and organizational development (MS); marketing (MBA); organizational development (EMS); strategic management (MBA). *Program availability:* Part-time, evening/weekend. *Degree requirements:* For master's, thesis. *Entrance requirements:* For master's, GMAT, 2 letters of reference, resume. Additional exam requirements/recommendations for international students: Required—TOEFL (minimum score 550 paper-based). *Faculty research:* Marketing in small business enterprises, total quality management in Kenya.

Universidad del Este, Graduate School, Carolina, PR 00984. Offers accounting (MBA); adult education (M Ed); agribusiness (MBA); criminal justice and criminology (MA); curriculum and instruction - early education (M Ed); curriculum and instruction - elementary (M Ed); curriculum and instruction - English (M Ed); curriculum and instruction - Spanish (M Ed); human resources (MBA); information security management (MBA); information technology and Web business development (MBA); management (MBA); public policy (MPA); social work (MA), including clinical social work; special education (M Ed); strategic leadership (MBA).

Universidad del Turabo, Graduate Programs, School of Business and Entrepreneurship, Program in Human Resources, Gurabo, PR 00778-3030. Offers MBA. *Entrance requirements:* For master's, GRE, EXADEP or GMAT, interview, essay, official transcript, recommendation letters. Electronic applications accepted.

Universidad Metropolitana, School of Business Administration, Program in Human Resources Management, San Juan, PR 00928-1150. Offers MBA. *Program availability:* Part-time.

University at Albany, State University of New York, Nelson A. Rockefeller College of Public Affairs and Policy, Department of Public Administration and Policy, Albany, NY 12222-0001. Offers financial management and public economics (MPA); financial market regulation (MPA); health policy (MPA); healthcare management (MPA); homeland security (MPA); human resources management (MPA); information strategy and management (MPA); local government management (MPA); nonprofit management (MPA); nonprofit management and leadership (Certificate); organizational behavior and theory (MPA, PhD); planning and policy analysis (CAS); policy analysis (MPA); politics and administration (PhD); public finance (PhD); public management (PhD); public policy (PhD); public sector management (Certificate); women and public policy (Certificate); JD/MPA. JD/MPA offered jointly with Albany Law School. *Accreditation:* NASPAA (one or more programs are accredited). *Faculty:* 24 full-time (10 women), 19 part-time/adjunct (10 women). *Students:* 117 full-time (62 women), 101 part-time (58 women); includes 56 minority (20 Black or African American, non-Hispanic/Latino; 8 Asian, non-Hispanic/Latino; 20 Hispanic/Latino; 8 Two or more races, non-Hispanic/Latino), 28 international. 236 applicants, 69% accepted, 86 enrolled. In 2018, 57 master's, 1 doctorate, 14 other advanced degrees awarded. *Degree requirements:* For doctorate, one foreign language, thesis/dissertation. *Entrance requirements:* For doctorate, GRE General Test. Additional exam requirements/recommendations for international students: Required—TOEFL (minimum score 550 paper-based). *Application deadline:* For fall admission, 2/1 priority date for domestic students, 5/1 for international students; for spring admission, 12/1 for domestic students. Applications are processed on a rolling basis. Application fee: $75. Electronic applications accepted. *Financial support:* Application deadline: 2/1. *Unit head:* Victor Asal, Chair, 518-591-8729, E-mail: vasal@albany.edu. *Application contact:* Victor Asal, Chair, 518-591-8729, E-mail: vasal@albany.edu.
Website: http://www.albany.edu/rockefeller/pad.shtml

University at Albany, State University of New York, School of Business, MBA Programs, Albany, NY 12222-0001. Offers business administration (MBA); cyber security (MBA); entrepreneurship (MBA); finance (MBA); human resource information systems (MBA); information systems and business analytics (MBA); marketing (MBA); JD/MBA. JD/MBA offered jointly with Albany Law School. *Program availability:* Part-time, evening/weekend. *Faculty:* 29 full-time (13 women), 9 part-time/adjunct (2 women). *Students:* 103 full-time (36 women), 188 part-time (69 women); includes 76 minority (27 Black or African American, non-Hispanic/Latino; 33 Asian, non-Hispanic/Latino; 16 Hispanic/Latino), 16 international. Average age 25. 181 applicants, 80% accepted, 114 enrolled. In 2018, 103 master's awarded. *Degree requirements:* For master's, thesis (for some programs), field or research project. *Entrance requirements:* For master's, GMAT, minimum undergraduate GPA of 3.0; 3 letters of recommendation;

resume; statement of goals. Additional exam requirements/recommendations for international students: Required—TOEFL (minimum score 100 iBT); Recommended—IELTS (minimum score 7). *Application deadline:* For fall admission, 4/1 priority date for domestic students, 2/15 for international students; for spring admission, 12/1 for domestic students; for summer admission, 5/1 for domestic students. Applications are processed on a rolling basis. Application fee: $75. Electronic applications accepted. *Expenses:* 16818. *Financial support:* In 2018–19, 25 students received support, including 7 fellowships with partial tuition reimbursements available (averaging $6,000 per year), 4 research assistantships with partial tuition reimbursements available, 21 teaching assistantships with partial tuition reimbursements available; unspecified assistantships also available. Financial award application deadline: 4/1; financial award applicants required to submit FAFSA. *Faculty research:* Social goods, information assurance, social computing, corporate entrepreneurship, asset pricing. *Total annual research expenditures:* $136,000. *Unit head:* Dr. Nilanjan Sen, Dean, 518-956-8370, Fax: 518-442-3273, E-mail: nsen@albany.edu. *Application contact:* Zina Mega Lawrence, Assistant Dean of Graduate Student Services, 518-956-8320, Fax: 518-442-4042, E-mail: zlawrence@albany.edu.
Website: https://graduatebusiness.albany.edu/

University at Buffalo, the State University of New York, Graduate School, Graduate School of Education, Department of Educational Leadership and Policy, Buffalo, NY 14260. Offers economics and education policy analysis (MA); education studies (Ed M); educational administration (Ed M, Ed D, PhD); educational culture, policy and society (PhD); higher education administration (Ed M, PhD); school building leadership (Certificate); school business and human resource administration (Certificate); school district business leadership (Certificate); school district leadership (Certificate). *Program availability:* Part-time, evening/weekend. *Faculty:* 16 full-time (10 women), 11 part-time/adjunct (4 women). *Students:* 73 full-time (50 women), 128 part-time (82 women); includes 40 minority (21 Black or African American, non-Hispanic/Latino; 7 Asian, non-Hispanic/Latino; 11 Hispanic/Latino; 1 Two or more races, non-Hispanic/Latino), 19 international. Average age 34. 136 applicants, 69% accepted, 53 enrolled. In 2018, 39 master's, 20 doctorates, 25 other advanced degrees awarded. *Degree requirements:* For master's, comprehensive exam (for some programs), thesis optional; for doctorate, comprehensive exam, thesis/dissertation. *Entrance requirements:* For master's, interview, letters of reference; for doctorate, GRE General Test or MAT, writing sample, letters of reference. Additional exam requirements/recommendations for international students: Required—TOEFL (minimum score 600 paper-based; 79 iBT), IELTS (minimum score 6.5), PTE (minimum score 55). *Application deadline:* For fall admission, 2/1 priority date for domestic students, 2/1 for international students; for spring admission, 11/15 priority date for domestic students, 10/1 for international students. Applications are processed on a rolling basis. Application fee: $50. Electronic applications accepted. *Financial support:* In 2018–19, 18 fellowships (averaging $5,673 per year), 34 research assistantships with tuition reimbursements (averaging $12,055 per year) were awarded; career-related internships or fieldwork, Federal Work-Study, institutionally sponsored loans, scholarships/grants, health care benefits, tuition waivers (full and partial), and unspecified assistantships also available. Financial award application deadline: 3/15; financial award applicants required to submit FAFSA. *Faculty research:* College access and choice, school leadership preparation and practice, public policy, curriculum and pedagogy, comparative and international education. *Total annual research expenditures:* $637,951. *Unit head:* Dr. Nathan Daun-Barnett, Department Chair, 716-645-1096, Fax: 716-645-2481, E-mail: nbarnett@buffalo.edu. *Application contact:* Renad Aref, Assistant Director of Admission Recruitment, 716-645-2110, Fax: 716-645-7937, E-mail: gseinfo@buffalo.edu.
Website: http://gse.buffalo.edu/elp

The University of Alabama in Huntsville, School of Graduate Studies, College of Business Administration, Programs in Business and Management, Huntsville, AL 35899. Offers business analytics (MSMS); federal contracting and procurement management (Certificate); human resource management (MSM); management (MBA), including acquisition management, entrepreneurship, federal contract accounting, finance, human resource management, logistics and supply chain management, marketing, project management; supply chain management (Certificate); technology and innovation management (Certificate). *Accreditation:* AACSB. *Program availability:* Part-time. *Faculty:* 8 full-time (3 women). *Students:* 57 full-time (25 women), 152 part-time (76 women); includes 37 minority (20 Black or African American, non-Hispanic/Latino; 2 American Indian or Alaska Native, non-Hispanic/Latino; 6 Asian, non-Hispanic/Latino; 8 Hispanic/Latino; 1 Two or more races, non-Hispanic/Latino), 24 international. Average age 33. 178 applicants, 80% accepted, 84 enrolled. In 2018, 96 master's, 1 other advanced degree awarded. *Degree requirements:* For master's, comprehensive exam, thesis or alternative. *Entrance requirements:* For master's, GMAT (minimum score 500), minimum AACSB index of 1080. Additional exam requirements/recommendations for international students: Required—TOEFL (minimum score 550 paper-based; 80 iBT), IELTS (minimum score 6.5). *Application deadline:* For fall admission, 7/15 priority date for domestic students, 4/1 priority date for international students; for spring admission, 11/30 priority date for domestic students, 9/1 priority date for international students. Applications are processed on a rolling basis. Application fee: $50. Electronic applications accepted. *Expenses: Tuition, area resident:* Full-time $10,632; part-time $412 per credit hour. Tuition, state resident: full-time $10,632. Tuition, nonresident: full-time $23,604; part-time $412 per credit hour. *Required fees:* $582; $582. Tuition and fees vary according to course load and program. *Financial support:* In 2018–19, 15 students received support, including 15 teaching assistantships with full tuition reimbursements available (averaging $4,871 per year); research assistantships with full tuition reimbursements available, career-related internships or fieldwork, Federal Work-Study, institutionally sponsored loans, scholarships/grants, health care benefits, tuition waivers (full and partial), and unspecified assistantships also available. Support available to part-time students. Financial award application deadline: 4/1; financial award applicants required to submit FAFSA. *Faculty research:* Supply chain management, management of research and development, international marketing and branding, organizational behavior and human resource management, social networks and computational economics. *Unit head:* Dr. Fan Tseng, Chair, 256-824-6804, Fax: 256-824-6328, E-mail: fan.tseng@uah.edu. *Application contact:* Jennifer Pettitt, Director of Advising, 256-824-6681, Fax: 256-824-7571, E-mail: jennifer.pettitt@uah.edu.

University of Bridgeport, School of Business, Bridgeport, CT 06604. Offers accounting (MBA); finance (MBA); general business (MBA); global financial services (MBA); human resource management (MBA); information systems and knowledge management (MBA); international business (MBA); management (MBA); marketing (MBA); operations management (MBA); small business and entrepreneurship (MBA); specialized business (MBA). *Accreditation:* ACBSP. *Program availability:* Part-time, evening/weekend. *Degree requirements:* For master's, thesis optional. *Entrance requirements:* For master's, GMAT. Additional exam requirements/recommendations for international students: Recommended—TOEFL (minimum score 550 paper-based; 80 iBT), IELTS (minimum score 6.5). Electronic applications accepted. *Expenses:* Contact institution.

University of California, Berkeley, UC Berkeley Extension, Certificate Programs in Business, Berkeley, CA 94720. Offers accounting (Certificate); business administration (Certificate); finance (Certificate); human resource management (Certificate); management (Certificate); marketing (Certificate); project management (Certificate). *Accreditation:* AACSB. *Program availability:* Online learning.

University of Cincinnati, Carl H. Lindner College of Business, MA Program, Cincinnati, OH 45221. Offers human resources (MA). *Program availability:* Part-time, evening/weekend. *Faculty:* 19 full-time (10 women), 28 part-time/adjunct (4 women). *Students:* 3 full-time (all women), 9 part-time (5 women); includes 4 minority (3 Black or African American, non-Hispanic/Latino; 1 Hispanic/Latino), 2 international. Average age 29. 16 applicants, 75% accepted, 12 enrolled. In 2018, 12 master's awarded. *Degree requirements:* For master's, capstone. *Entrance requirements:* For master's, GRE or GMAT. Additional exam requirements/recommendations for international students: Required—TOEFL (minimum score 577 paper-based; 90 iBT), IELTS (minimum score 6.5). *Application deadline:* For fall admission, 6/30 priority date for domestic students, 3/15 priority date for international students; for spring admission, 12/15 for domestic students, 9/15 for international students; for summer admission, 4/15 for domestic and international students. Applications are processed on a rolling basis. Application fee: $65 ($70 for international students). Electronic applications accepted. *Expenses:* Full-time resident $10,479 per term, full-time nonresident $14,398 per term, part-time $890 per credit hour. *Financial support:* In 2018–19, 4 students received support. Scholarships/grants and tuition waivers (partial) available. Financial award application deadline: 3/15. *Total annual research expenditures:* $39,943. *Unit head:* Dr. Marianne Lewis, Dean, 513-556-7001, Fax: 513-556-4891, E-mail: marianne.lewis@uc.edu. *Application contact:* Dona Clary, Executive Director, Graduate Programs, 513-556-3546, Fax: 513-558-7006, E-mail: dona.clary@uc.edu.
Website: http://business.uc.edu/graduate/masters/ma-human-resources.html

University of Colorado Denver, Business School, Program in Management and Organization, Denver, CO 80217. Offers business strategy (MS); change and innovation (MS); enterprise technology management (MS); entrepreneurship and innovation (MS); global management (MS); leadership (MS); managing for sustainability (MS); managing human resources (MS); sports and entertainment (MS); strategic management (MS). *Accreditation:* AACSB. *Program availability:* Part-time, evening/weekend, online learning. *Degree requirements:* For master's, 30 semester hours (12 of required courses, 12 of management electives, and 6 of free electives). *Entrance requirements:* For master's, GMAT, resume, two letters of recommendation, essay, financial statements (for international applicants). Additional exam requirements/recommendations for international students: Required—TOEFL (minimum score 525 paper-based; 71 iBT); Recommended—IELTS (minimum score 6.5). Electronic applications accepted. *Expenses:* Contact institution. *Faculty research:* Human resource management, management of catastrophe, turnaround strategies.

University of Connecticut, Graduate School, eCampus, Program in Human Resource Management, Storrs, CT 06269. Offers MS.

University of Connecticut, Graduate School, School of Business, Storrs, CT 06269. Offers accounting (MS, PhD); business (PhD); business administration (MBA); business analytics and project management (MS); finance (PhD); financial risk management (MS); health care management and insurance studies (MBA); human resource management (MS); management (PhD); management consulting (MBA); marketing (PhD); marketing intelligence (MBA); operations and information management (PhD). *Accreditation:* AACSB. *Degree requirements:* For master's, comprehensive exam; for doctorate, thesis/dissertation. *Entrance requirements:* For master's and doctorate, GMAT. Additional exam requirements/recommendations for international students: Required—TOEFL (minimum score 550 paper-based). Electronic applications accepted.

University of Dallas, Satish and Yasmin Gupta College of Business, Irving, TX 75062. Offers accounting (MBA, MS); business administration (DBA); business analytics (MS); business management (MBA); corporate finance (MBA); cybersecurity (MS); finance (MS); financial services (MBA); global business (MBA, MS); health services management (MBA); human resource management (MBA); information and technology management (MS); information assurance (MBA); information technology (MBA); information technology service management (MBA); marketing management (MBA); organization development (MBA); project management (MBA); sports and entertainment management (MBA); strategic leadership (MBA); supply chain management (MBA). *Accreditation:* AACSB. *Program availability:* Part-time, evening/weekend, 100% online. *Students:* 147 full-time (56 women), 584 part-time (232 women); includes 402 minority (204 Black or African American, non-Hispanic/Latino; 95 Asian, non-Hispanic/Latino; 92 Hispanic/Latino; 2 Native Hawaiian or other Pacific Islander, non-Hispanic/Latino; 9 Two or more races, non-Hispanic/Latino), 113 international. Average age 34. 992 applicants, 30% accepted, 157 enrolled. In 2018, 336 master's, 5 doctorates awarded. *Degree requirements:* For doctorate, thesis/dissertation. *Entrance requirements:* For master's and doctorate, U.S. bachelor's degree with a minimum cumulative GPA of 2.0 from a regionally accredited college or university (or comparable foreign degree); minimum 3.0 GPA in any graduate-level coursework completed; good academic standing with all colleges attended. Additional exam requirements/recommendations for international students: Required—TOEFL (minimum score 80 iBT), IELTS (minimum score 6.5), PTE (minimum score 67). *Application deadline:* Applications are processed on a rolling basis. Application fee: $50. Electronic applications accepted. *Expenses:* $1250 per credit hour. *Financial support:* In 2018–19, 291 students received support. Research assistantships, teaching assistantships, scholarships/grants, and unspecified assistantships available. Support available to part-time students. Financial award application deadline: 2/15; financial award applicants required to submit FAFSA. *Unit head:* Brett J.L. Landry, Dean, 972-721-5356, E-mail: blandry@udallas.edu. *Application contact:* Breonna Collins, Director, Graduate Admissions, 972-7215304, E-mail: bcollins@udallas.edu.
Website: http://www.udallas.edu/cob/

University of Denver, University College, Denver, CO 80208. Offers arts and culture (MA, Certificate); communication management (MS, Certificate), including translation studies (Certificate), world history and culture (Certificate); environmental policy and management (MS); geographic information systems (MS); global affairs (MA, Certificate), including human capital in organizations (Certificate), philanthropic leadership (Certificate), project management (Certificate), strategic innovation and change (Certificate); healthcare leadership (MS); information communications and technology (MS); leadership and organizations (MS); professional creative writing (MA, Certificate), including emergency planning and response (Certificate), organizational security (Certificate); security management (MS, Certificate); strategic human resources (Certificate). *Program availability:* Part-time, evening/weekend, 100% online, blended/hybrid learning. *Faculty:* 4 full-time (2 women), 108 part-time/adjunct (51 women). *Students:* 51 full-time (26 women), 1,291 part-time (733 women); includes 337 minority (112 Black or African American, non-Hispanic/Latino; 6 American Indian or Alaska Native, non-Hispanic/Latino; 46 Asian, non-Hispanic/Latino; 132 Hispanic/Latino; 3 Native Hawaiian or other Pacific Islander, non-Hispanic/Latino; 38 Two or more races, non-Hispanic/Latino), 75 international. Average age 34. 834 applicants, 87% accepted, 423 enrolled. In 2018, 443 master's, 232 other advanced degrees awarded. *Degree requirements:* For master's, capstone project. *Entrance requirements:* For master's, baccalaureate degree, transcripts, two letters of recommendation, personal statement, resume, writing sample (Master of Arts in Professional Creative Writing). Additional exam requirements/recommendations for international students: Required—TOEFL (minimum score 550 paper-based; 80 iBT). *Application deadline:* For fall admission, 6/19

priority date for domestic students, 6/14 priority date for international students; for winter admission, 10/25 priority date for domestic students, 9/27 priority date for international students; for spring admission, 2/7 priority date for domestic students, 1/10 priority date for international students; for summer admission, 4/24 priority date for domestic students, 3/27 priority date for international students. Applications are processed on a rolling basis. Application fee: $75. Electronic applications accepted. *Expenses:* $8,280 per year half-time. *Financial support:* In 2018–19, 38 students received support. Teaching assistantships available. Financial award applicants required to submit FAFSA. *Unit head:* Dr. Michael McGuire, Dean, 303-871-3518, E-mail: michael.mcguire@du.edu. *Application contact:* Admission Team, 303-871-2291, E-mail: ucoladm@du.edu.
Website: http://universitycollege.du.edu/

University of Florida, Graduate School, Warrington College of Business Administration, Hough Graduate School of Business, Programs in Business Administration, Gainesville, FL 32611. Offers business administration (MA, MS, PhD); competitive strategy (MBA); finance (MBA); global management (MBA); Graham-Buffett security analysis (MBA); human resource management (MBA); information systems and operations management (MBA); international studies (MBA); management (MBA); real estate (MBA); JD/MBA; MBA/MS; MBA/PhD; MBA/Pharm D; MD/MBA. *Accreditation:* AACSB. *Program availability:* Part-time, evening/weekend, online learning. *Degree requirements:* For master's, capstone course. *Entrance requirements:* For master's and doctorate, GMAT (minimum score 465), minimum GPA of 3.0, interview. Additional exam requirements/recommendations for international students: Required—TOEFL (minimum score 550 paper-based; 80 iBT), IELTS (minimum score 6). Electronic applications accepted. *Faculty research:* Accounting, finance, insurance, management, real estate, urban analysis marketing.

University of Hawaii at Manoa, Office of Graduate Education, Shidler College of Business, Program in Business Administration, Honolulu, HI 96822. Offers Asian business studies (MBA); Chinese business studies (MBA); decision sciences (MBA); entrepreneurship (MBA); finance (MBA); finance and banking (MBA); human resources management (MBA); information management (MBA); information technology (MBA); international business (MBA); Japanese business studies (MBA); marketing (MBA); organizational behavior (MBA); organizational management (MBA); real estate (MBA); student-designed track (MBA). *Accreditation:* AACSB. *Program availability:* Part-time, evening/weekend. *Degree requirements:* For master's, thesis optional. *Entrance requirements:* For master's, GMAT, minimum GPA of 3.0. Additional exam requirements/recommendations for international students: Required—TOEFL (minimum score 600 paper-based; 100 iBT), IELTS (minimum score 7). *Expenses:* Contact institution.

University of Hawaii at Manoa, Office of Graduate Education, Shidler College of Business, Program in Human Resources Management, Honolulu, HI 96822. Offers MHRM. *Program availability:* Part-time. *Entrance requirements:* Additional exam requirements/recommendations for international students: Required—TOEFL (minimum score 600 paper-based; 100 iBT), IELTS (minimum score 7). *Expenses:* Contact institution.

University of Houston–Clear Lake, School of Business, Program in Administrative Science, Houston, TX 77058-1002. Offers environmental management (MS); human resource management (MA). *Program availability:* Part-time, evening/weekend. *Degree requirements:* For master's, thesis optional. *Entrance requirements:* For master's, GMAT. Additional exam requirements/recommendations for international students: Required—TOEFL (minimum score 550 paper-based). Electronic applications accepted.

University of Houston–Downtown, Marilyn Davies College of Business, MBA Program, Houston, TX 77002. Offers accounting (MBA); finance (MBA); human resource management (MBA); international business (MBA); investment management (MBA); leadership (MBA); project management and process improvement (MBA); sales management and business development (MBA); supply chain management (MBA). *Accreditation:* AACSB. *Program availability:* Part-time, evening/weekend. *Entrance requirements:* For master's, GMAT, two letters of recommendation from professional references, personal statement, resume. Additional exam requirements/recommendations for international students: Required—TOEFL (minimum score 81 iBT). Electronic applications accepted. *Expenses:* Contact institution.

University of Illinois at Urbana–Champaign, Graduate College, College of Education, Department of Education Policy, Organization, and Leadership, Champaign, IL 61820. Offers educational organization and leadership (Ed M, MS, Ed D, PhD, CAS); educational policy studies (Ed M, MA, PhD); human resource education (Ed M, MS, Ed D, PhD, CAS). *Program availability:* Part-time, online learning.

University of Illinois at Urbana–Champaign, Graduate College, School of Labor and Employment Relations, Champaign, IL 61820. Offers human resources and industrial relations (MHRIR, PhD); MHRIR/JD; MHRIR/MBA. Terminal master's awarded for partial completion of doctoral program.

The University of Kansas, Graduate Studies, School of Business, Program in Business, Lawrence, KS 66045. Offers business and organizational leadership (MS); decision sciences and supply chain management (PhD); finance (PhD); human resources management (PhD); marketing (PhD); organizational behavior (PhD); strategic management (PhD); supply chain management and logistics (MS). *Accreditation:* AACSB. *Program availability:* Part-time. *Students:* 69 full-time (20 women), 150 part-time (62 women); includes 42 minority (14 Black or African American, non-Hispanic/Latino; 2 American Indian or Alaska Native, non-Hispanic/Latino; 6 Asian, non-Hispanic/Latino; 7 Hispanic/Latino; 13 Two or more races, non-Hispanic/Latino), 24 international. Average age 32. 306 applicants, 51% accepted, 132 enrolled. In 2018, 22 master's, 1 doctorate awarded. *Entrance requirements:* For master's, GMAT, official transcript, three letters of recommendation, resume, statement of purpose; for doctorate, GMAT or GRE, official transcript, three letters of recommendation, resume, statement of purpose. Additional exam requirements/recommendations for international students: Required—TOEFL, IELTS. *Application deadline:* For fall admission, 1/10 for domestic and international students. Application fee: $65 ($85 for international students). Electronic applications accepted. *Financial support:* Fellowships, research assistantships, teaching assistantships, scholarships/grants, health care benefits, tuition waivers (full), and unspecified assistantships available. Financial award application deadline: 1/10. *Faculty research:* Strategic human resource management, business ethics, organizational theory/behavior, corporate strategy, international business, supply chain management, Bayesian networks, game theory, decision analysis and time/series analysis, pricing, consumer effects, advertising and emotion. *Unit head:* Charly Edmonds, Director, 785-864-3841, E-mail: cedmonds@ku.edu. *Application contact:* Andrea Noltner, Graduate Admission Contact, 785-864-7556, E-mail: anoltner@ku.edu.
Website: http://www.business.ku.edu/

University of La Verne, College of Business and Public Management, Program in Leadership and Management, La Verne, CA 91750-4443. Offers human resource management (Certificate); leadership and management (MS), including human resource management, nonprofit management, organizational development; nonprofit management (Certificate); organizational leadership (Certificate). *Program availability:* Part-time. *Entrance requirements:* For master's, bachelor's degree, minimum undergraduate GPA of 2.75, 2 letters of recommendation, interview, resume. Additional exam requirements/recommendations for international students: Required—TOEFL (minimum score 550 paper-based).

University of La Verne, Regional and Online Campuses, Graduate Programs, Inland Empire Campus, Ontario, CA 91730. Offers business administration (MBA, MBA-EP), including accounting (MBA), finance (MBA), health services management (MBA-EP), information technology (MBA-EP), international business (MBA), managed care (MBA), management and leadership (MBA-EP), marketing (MBA-EP), supply chain management (MBA); leadership and management (MS), including human resource management, nonprofit management, organizational development. *Program availability:* Part-time, evening/weekend. *Expenses:* Contact institution.

University of Lethbridge, School of Graduate Studies, Lethbridge, AB T1K 3M4, Canada. Offers addictions counseling (M Sc); agricultural biotechnology (M Sc); agricultural studies (M Sc, MA); anthropology (MA); archaeology (M Sc, MA); art (MA, MFA); biochemistry (M Sc); biological sciences (M Sc); biomolecular science (PhD); biosystems and biodiversity (PhD); Canadian studies (MA); chemistry (M Sc); computer science (M Sc); computer science and geographical information science (M Sc); counseling (MC); counseling psychology (M Ed); dramatic arts (MA); earth, space, and physical science (PhD); economics (MA); education (MA, PhD); educational leadership (M Ed); English (MA); environmental science (M Sc); evolution and behavior (PhD); exercise science (M Sc); French (MA); French/German (MA); French/Spanish (MA); general education (M Ed); geography (M Sc, MA); German (MA); health sciences (M Sc); individualized multidisciplinary (M Sc, MA); kinesiology (M Sc, MA); management (M Sc), including accounting, finance, human resource management and labor relations, information systems, international management, marketing, policy and strategy; mathematics (M Sc); music (M Mus, MA); Native American studies (MA); neuroscience (M Sc, PhD); new media (MA, MFA); nursing (M Sc, MN); philosophy (MA); physics (M Sc); political science (MA); psychology (M Sc, MA); religious studies (MA); sociology (MA); theatre and dramatic arts (MFA); theoretical and computational science (PhD); urban and regional studies (MA); women and gender studies (MA). *Program availability:* Part-time, evening/weekend. *Degree requirements:* For master's, thesis (for some programs); for doctorate, comprehensive exam, thesis/dissertation. *Entrance requirements:* For master's, GMAT (for M Sc in management), bachelor's degree in related field, minimum GPA of 3.0 during previous 20 graded semester courses, 2 years' teaching or related experience (M Ed); for doctorate, master's degree, minimum graduate GPA of 3.5. Additional exam requirements/recommendations for international students: Required—TOEFL (minimum score 580 paper-based; 93 iBT). Electronic applications accepted. *Faculty research:* Movement and brain plasticity, gibberellin physiology, photosynthesis, carbon cycling, molecular properties of main-group ring components.

University of Louisiana at Lafayette, BI Moody III College of Business Administration, Lafayette, LA 70504. Offers accounting (MS); business administration (MBA); entrepreneurship (MBA); finance (MBA); global management (MBA); health care administration (MBA); hospitality management (MBA); human resource management (MBA); project management (MBA); sales leadership (MBA). *Accreditation:* AACSB. *Program availability:* Part-time, evening/weekend. *Entrance requirements:* For master's, GRE General Test. Additional exam requirements/recommendations for international students: Required—TOEFL (minimum score 550 paper-based).

University of Louisville, Graduate School, College of Arts and Sciences, Department of Urban and Public Affairs, Louisville, KY 40208. Offers public administration (MPA), including human resources management, non-profit management, public policy and administration; urban and public affairs (PhD), including urban planning and development, urban policy and administration; urban planning (MUP), including administration of planning organizations, housing and community development, land use and environmental planning, spatial analysis. *Program availability:* Part-time, evening/weekend. *Faculty:* 12 full-time (6 women), 7 part-time/adjunct (2 women). *Students:* 39 full-time (18 women), 20 part-time (12 women); includes 14 minority (5 Black or African American, non-Hispanic/Latino; 1 Asian, non-Hispanic/Latino; 2 Hispanic/Latino; 6 Two or more races, non-Hispanic/Latino), 5 international. Average age 32. 38 applicants, 66% accepted, 16 enrolled. In 2018, 9 master's awarded. Terminal master's awarded for partial completion of doctoral program. *Degree requirements:* For master's, internship; for doctorate, comprehensive exam, thesis/dissertation. *Entrance requirements:* For master's, GRE General Test, minimum GPA of 3.0; for doctorate, GRE General Test, master's degree in appropriate field. Additional exam requirements/recommendations for international students: Required—TOEFL (minimum score 550 paper-based; 79 iBT). *Application deadline:* Applications are processed on a rolling basis. Application fee: $65. *Expenses:* Contact institution. *Financial support:* In 2018–19, 27 students received support. Fellowships, research assistantships, tuition waivers (full and partial), and unspecified assistantships available. Financial award application deadline: 2/1. *Faculty research:* Urban theory, sustainability, public administration, urban planning, urban management. *Total annual research expenditures:* $240,308. *Unit head:* Dr. David Simpson, Chair, 502-852-8019, Fax: 502-852-4558, E-mail: dave.simpson@louisville.edu.
Website: http://supa.louisville.edu

University of Louisville, Graduate School, College of Education and Human Development, Department of Educational Leadership, Evaluation and Organizational Development, Louisville, KY 40292-0001. Offers educational leadership and organizational development (Ed D, PhD), including evaluation (PhD), human resource development (PhD), P-12 administration (PhD), post-secondary administration (PhD), sport administration (MA, PhD); health professions education (Certificate); higher education administration (MA), including sport administration (MA, PhD); human resources and organization development (MS), including health professions education, human resource leadership, workplace learning and performance; P-12 educational administration (Ed S), including principalship, supervisor of instruction. *Accreditation:* NCATE. *Program availability:* Part-time, evening/weekend, 100% online, blended/hybrid learning. *Students:* 200 full-time (82 women), 474 part-time (262 women); includes 218 minority (127 Black or African American, non-Hispanic/Latino; 1 American Indian or Alaska Native, non-Hispanic/Latino; 18 Asian, non-Hispanic/Latino; 46 Hispanic/Latino; 2 Native Hawaiian or other Pacific Islander, non-Hispanic/Latino; 24 Two or more races, non-Hispanic/Latino), 5 international. Average age 36. 257 applicants, 77% accepted, 170 enrolled. In 2018, 111 master's, 10 doctorates, 22 other advanced degrees awarded. Terminal master's awarded for partial completion of doctoral program. *Degree requirements:* For master's, comprehensive exam (for some programs), thesis (for some programs); for doctorate, comprehensive exam (for some programs), thesis/dissertation. *Entrance requirements:* For master's, GRE (for most programs), PRAXIS (for educator preparation programs), professional statement, recommendation letters, resume, transcripts; for doctorate and other advanced degree, GRE, professional statement, recommendation letters, resume, transcripts. Additional exam requirements/recommendations for international students: Required—TOEFL (minimum score 550 paper-based; 79 iBT); Recommended—IELTS (minimum score 6.5). *Application deadline:* For fall admission, 6/1 priority date for domestic students, 5/1 priority date for international students; for spring admission, 10/1 priority date for domestic students, 11/1 priority date for international students; for summer admission, 3/1 for domestic

students, 4/1 priority date for international students. Application fee: $65. *Expenses: Tuition, area resident:* Full-time $6500; part-time $723 per credit hour. *Tuition, state resident:* full-time $6500. Tuition, nonresident: full-time $13,557; part-time $1507 per credit hour. Tuition and fees vary according to course load and program. *Financial support:* In 2018–19, 144 students received support, including fellowships (averaging $21,024 per year), research assistantships with full tuition reimbursements available (averaging $21,024 per year), teaching assistantships with full tuition reimbursements available (averaging $21,024 per year); Federal Work-Study, scholarships/grants, health care benefits, tuition waivers (full), and unspecified assistantships also available. Financial award application deadline: 3/1; financial award applicants required to submit FAFSA. *Faculty research:* Human resources and organizational development; career, technical, health professions, and economic education; health professions education; community and military partnerships; higher education. *Unit head:* Dr. Sharron Kerrick, Chair, 502-852-6475, E-mail: lead@louisville.edu. *Application contact:* Dr. Margaret Pentecost, Assistant Dean for Graduate Student Success, 502-852-6437, Fax: 502-852-1417, E-mail: gedadm@louisville.edu.
Website: http://louisville.edu/education/departments/eleod

University of Louisville, Graduate School, College of Education and Human Development, Departments of Early Childhood and Elementary Education, Middle and Secondary Education, and Special Education, Louisville, KY 40292-0001. Offers art education (MAT); autism and applied behavior analysis (Certificate); curriculum and instruction (PhD); early elementary education (MAT); exercise physiology (MS); health and physical education (MAT); health professions education (Certificate); higher education (MA); human resources and organization development (MS); instructional technology (M Ed); interdisciplinary early childhood education (MAT); middle school education (MAT); music education (MAT); secondary education (MAT); special education (MAT); sport administration (MS); teacher leadership (M Ed). *Program availability:* Part-time, evening/weekend, 100% online, blended/hybrid learning. *Faculty:* 97 full-time (64 women), 131 part-time/adjunct (86 women). *Students:* 109 full-time (72 women), 139 part-time (87 women); includes 43 minority (18 Black or African American, non-Hispanic/Latino; 6 Asian, non-Hispanic/Latino; 10 Hispanic/Latino; 9 Two or more races, non-Hispanic/Latino), 9 international. Average age 29. 108 applicants, 75% accepted, 59 enrolled. In 2018, 64 master's awarded. Terminal master's awarded for partial completion of doctoral program. *Degree requirements:* For master's, comprehensive exam (for some programs), thesis optional; for doctorate, comprehensive exam (for some programs), thesis/dissertation. *Entrance requirements:* For master's, GRE (for most programs), PRAXIS (for educator preparation programs), professional statement, recommendation letters, resume, transcripts; for doctorate and Certificate, GRE, professional statement, recommendation letters, resume, transcripts. Additional exam requirements/recommendations for international students: Required— TOEFL (minimum score 550 paper-based; 79 iBT); Recommended—IELTS (minimum score 6.5). *Application deadline:* For fall admission, 6/1 priority date for domestic students, 5/1 priority date for international students; for spring admission, 10/1 for domestic students, 11/1 priority date for international students; for summer admission, 3/1 priority date for domestic students, 4/1 priority date for international students. Application fee: $65. *Expenses: Tuition, area resident:* Full-time $6500; part-time $723 per credit hour. *Tuition, state resident:* full-time $6500. Tuition, nonresident: full-time $13,557; part-time $1507 per credit hour. Tuition and fees vary according to course load and program. *Financial support:* In 2018–19, 144 students received support, including fellowships with full tuition reimbursements available (averaging $21,024 per year), research assistantships with full tuition reimbursements available (averaging $21,024 per year), teaching assistantships with full tuition reimbursements available (averaging $21,024 per year); Federal Work-Study, scholarships/grants, health care benefits, tuition waivers (full), and unspecified assistantships also available. Financial award application deadline: 3/1; financial award applicants required to submit FAFSA. *Faculty research:* Children's early reading and writing development, crelevance of basic facts in elementary mathematics instruction, clinical model of teacher education, cultural and linguistic context of diverse learners, and STEM-integrated curriculum design and development. STEM teaching and learning, content literacy for English language learners, social justice in teacher education, adolescent literacy, mathematics teacher development. Classroom and behavior management; moderate/severe disabilities, autism. *Unit head:* Dr. Amy Lingo, Interim Dean, 502-852-3235, Fax: 502-852-1464, E-mail: cehdinfo@louisville.edu. *Application contact:* Dr. Margaret Pentecost, Assistant Dean for Graduate Student Success, 502-852-6437, Fax: 502-852-1417, E-mail: gedadm@louisville.edu.
Website: http://louisville.edu/delphi

The University of Manchester, Alliance Manchester Business School, M15 6PB, United Kingdom. Offers accounting and finance (M Sc); business (M Ent); business analysis and strategic management (M Sc); business analytics: operational research and risk analysis (M Sc); business psychology (M Sc); corporate communications and reputation management (M Sc); finance (M Sc); finance and business economics (M Sc); human resource management and industrial relations (M Sc); innovation management and entrepreneurship (M Sc); international business and management (M Sc); international human resource management and comparative industrial relations (M Sc); management (M Sc); marketing (M Sc); operations, project and supply chain management (M Sc); organizational psychology (M Sc); quantitative finance (M Sc). *Entrance requirements:* For master's, UK 2:1 honours degree or overseas equivalent. Additional exam requirements/recommendations for international students: Required— TOEFL (minimum score 100 iBT), IELTS (minimum score 7), PTE. Electronic applications accepted. *Faculty research:* Accounting and finance, management sciences and marketing, people management and organization, innovation management and policy, decision sciences.

University of Mary, Gary Tharaldson School of Business, Bismarck, ND 58504-9652. Offers business administration (MBA); energy management (MBA, MS); executive (MBA, MS); health care (MBA, MS); human resource management (MBA); project management (MBA, MPM); virtuous leadership (MBA, MPM, MS). *Program availability:* Part-time, evening/weekend. *Entrance requirements:* For master's, minimum GPA of 2.5. Additional exam requirements/recommendations for international students: Required—TOEFL (minimum score 550 paper-based; 80 iBT). Electronic applications accepted.

University of Memphis, Graduate School, University College, Memphis, TN 38152. Offers human resources leadership (MPS); liberal studies (MALS, Graduate Certificate); strategic leadership (MPS, Graduate Certificate); training and development (MPS). *Program availability:* Part-time, evening/weekend. *Faculty:* 3 full-time (2 women). *Students:* 15 full-time (9 women), 85 part-time (63 women); includes 71 minority (67 Black or African American, non-Hispanic/Latino; 2 Hispanic/Latino; 2 Two or more races, non-Hispanic/Latino), 1 international. Average age 40. 57 applicants, 77% accepted, 44 enrolled. In 2018, 25 master's, 5 other advanced degrees awarded. *Degree requirements:* For master's, comprehensive exam, thesis (for some programs). *Entrance requirements:* For master's, GRE (for MPS), resume, letters of recommendation, personal essay, interview, minimum undergraduate GPA of 2.75 (for MALS); portfolio in lieu of GRE (for MPS applicants with substantial professional work experience); for Graduate Certificate, essay, letter of recommendation. Additional exam requirements/ recommendations for international students: Required—TOEFL (minimum score 550

paper-based; 79 iBT). *Application deadline:* For fall admission, 7/1 for domestic students, 5/1 for international students; for spring admission, 11/1 for domestic students, 9/15 for international students. Applications are processed on a rolling basis. Application fee: $35 ($60 for international students). Electronic applications accepted. *Expenses: Tuition, area resident:* Full-time $10,240; part-time $503 per credit hour. Tuition, state resident: full-time $10,464. Tuition, nonresident: full-time $20,224; part-time $991 per credit hour. *Required fees:* $850; $106 per credit hour. *Financial support:* Research assistantships with full tuition reimbursements, teaching assistantships with tuition reimbursements, Federal Work-Study, scholarships/grants, and unspecified assistantships available. Financial award application deadline: 2/3; financial award applicants required to submit FAFSA. *Faculty research:* Media ethics, history of psychiatry, public relations. *Unit head:* Dr. Richard Irwin, Executive Dean, 901-678-2716, E-mail: rirwin@memphis.edu. *Application contact:* Dr. Colin Chapell, Graduate Advisor, 901-678-3066, E-mail: cbchpell@memphis.edu.
Website: http://www.memphis.edu/univcoll/

University of Minnesota, Twin Cities Campus, Carlson School of Management, Master of Arts Program in Human Resources and Industrial Relations, Minneapolis, MN 55455-0213. Offers MA. *Accreditation:* AACSB. *Program availability:* Part-time, evening/ weekend. *Faculty:* 17 full-time (9 women), 14 part-time/adjunct (7 women). *Students:* 121 full-time (87 women), 33 part-time (28 women); includes 17 minority (5 Black or African American, non-Hispanic/Latino; 1 American Indian or Alaska Native, non-Hispanic/Latino; 9 Asian, non-Hispanic/Latino; 2 Hispanic/Latino), 62 international. Average age 25. 152 applicants, 93% accepted, 71 enrolled. In 2018, 67 master's awarded. *Degree requirements:* For master's, thesis or alternative, 48 course credits. *Entrance requirements:* For master's, GMAT or GRE General Test, undergraduate degree from accredited institution, course in microeconomics. Additional exam requirements/recommendations for international students: Required—TOEFL (minimum score 550 paper-based; 79 iBT), IELTS (minimum score 6.5). *Application deadline:* For fall admission, 2/1 for domestic and international students. Applications are processed on a rolling basis. Application fee: $75 ($95 for international students). Electronic applications accepted. *Expenses:* Contact institution. *Financial support:* In 2018–19, 71 students received support, including 60 fellowships (averaging $7,500 per year), 1 research assistantship with partial tuition reimbursement available (averaging $16,225 per year), 5 teaching assistantships with partial tuition reimbursements available (averaging $9,000 per year); scholarships/grants, health care benefits, tuition waivers (partial), and unspecified assistantships also available. Financial award application deadline: 2/1; financial award applicants required to submit FAFSA. *Faculty research:* Staffing, training, and development; compensation and benefits; organization theory; collective bargaining. *Total annual research expenditures:* $78,590. *Unit head:* Stacy Doepner-Hove, Director, 612-625-8732, Fax: 612-624-8360, E-mail: doepn002@umn.edu. *Application contact:* Amy Danzeisen, Assistant Director for Admissions and Recruiting, 612-624-5704, Fax: 612-624-8360, E-mail: hrirgrad@umn.edu.
Website: https://carlsonschool.umn.edu/degrees/master-arts-human-resources-industrial-relations

University of Missouri–St. Louis, College of Business Administration, St. Louis, MO 63121. Offers accounting (M Acc); business administration (MBA, DBA, PhD, Certificate), including logistics and supply chain management (PhD); business intelligence (Certificate); cybersecurity (Certificate); digital and social media marketing (Certificate); human resources management (Certificate); information systems (MS); logistics and supply chain management (Certificate); marketing management (Certificate). *Program availability:* Part-time, evening/weekend. *Degree requirements:* For doctorate, thesis/dissertation. *Entrance requirements:* For master's, GMAT, 2 letters of recommendation; for doctorate, GMAT or GRE, 3 letters of recommendation. Additional exam requirements/recommendations for international students: Recommended—TOEFL (minimum score 550 paper-based; 79 iBT), IELTS (minimum score 6.5). Electronic applications accepted. *Faculty research:* Statistical decision aids, commercial banking, corporate finance, operations management, information systems.

University of Nebraska at Kearney, College of Business and Technology, Department of Business, Kearney, NE 68849-0001. Offers accounting (MBA); generalist (MBA); human resources (MBA); human services (MBA); marketing (MBA). *Accreditation:* AACSB. *Program availability:* Part-time, evening/weekend. *Degree requirements:* For master's, thesis optional, capstone course. *Entrance requirements:* For master's, GRE or GMAT (if no significant managerial experience), letters of recommendation, essay, resume. Additional exam requirements/recommendations for international students: Recommended—TOEFL (minimum score 550 paper-based; 79 iBT), IELTS (minimum score 6.5). Electronic applications accepted. *Faculty research:* Small business financial management, employment law, expert systems, international trade and marketing, environmental economics.

University of New Haven, Graduate School, College of Arts and Sciences, Program in Industrial and Organizational Psychology, West Haven, CT 06516. Offers conflict management (MA); industrial organizational psychology (MA); industrial-human resources psychology (MA); organizational development and consultation (MA); psychology of conflict management (Graduate Certificate). *Program availability:* Part-time, evening/weekend. *Students:* 63 full-time (37 women), 3 part-time (2 women); includes 15 minority (8 Black or African American, non-Hispanic/Latino; 2 Asian, non-Hispanic/Latino; 5 Hispanic/Latino), 9 international. Average age 27. 80 applicants, 78% accepted, 31 enrolled. In 2018, 41 master's awarded. *Degree requirements:* For master's, thesis or alternative, internship or practicum. *Entrance requirements:* Additional exam requirements/recommendations for international students: Required— TOEFL (minimum score 80 iBT), IELTS, PTE. *Application deadline:* Applications are processed on a rolling basis. Application fee: $50. Electronic applications accepted. Application fee is waived when completed online. *Expenses:* Contact institution. *Financial support:* Research assistantships with partial tuition reimbursements, teaching assistantships with partial tuition reimbursements, career-related internships or fieldwork, Federal Work-Study, scholarships/grants, and unspecified assistantships available. Support available to part-time students. Financial award applicants required to submit FAFSA. *Unit head:* Dr. Eric Marcus, Distinguished Lecturer, 203-932-1242, E-mail: emarcus@newhaven.edu. *Application contact:* Selina O'Toole, Senior Associate Director of Graduate Admissions, 203-932-7337, E-mail: SOToole@newhaven.edu.
Website: https://www.newhaven.edu/arts-sciences/graduate-programs/industrial-organizational-psychology/

University of New Haven, Graduate School, College of Business, Program in Business Administration, West Haven, CT 06516. Offers accounting (MBA); business administration (MBA); business intelligence (MBA); business policy and strategic leadership (MBA); finance (MBA), including chartered financial analyst; global marketing (MBA); human resources management (MBA); sport management (MBA). *Accreditation:* AACSB. *Program availability:* Part-time, evening/weekend. *Students:* 151 full-time (73 women), 70 part-time (30 women); includes 51 minority (23 Black or African American, non-Hispanic/Latino; 13 Asian, non-Hispanic/Latino; 14 Hispanic/Latino; 1 Two or more races, non-Hispanic/Latino), 74 international. Average age 28. 197 applicants, 91% accepted, 82 enrolled. In 2018, 70 master's awarded. *Entrance requirements:* For master's, GMAT. Additional exam requirements/recommendations for international students: Required—TOEFL (minimum score 80 iBT), IELTS, PTE. *Application*

deadline: Applications are processed on a rolling basis. Application fee: $50. Electronic applications accepted. Application fee is waived when completed online. *Expenses: Tuition:* Full-time $16,470; part-time $915 per credit hour. *Required fees:* $230; $95 per term. *Financial support:* Research assistantships with partial tuition reimbursements, teaching assistantships with partial tuition reimbursements, career-related internships or fieldwork, Federal Work-Study, scholarships/grants, and unspecified assistantships available. Support available to part-time students. Financial award applicants required to submit FAFSA. *Unit head:* Darell Singleterry, Director, 203-932-7386, E-mail: dsingleterry@newhaven.edu. *Application contact:* Selina O'Toole, Senior Associate Director of Graduate Admissions, 203-932-7337, E-mail: SOToole@newhaven.edu.
Website: http://www.newhaven.edu/business/graduate-programs/mba/index.php

University of New Mexico, Anderson School of Management, Department of Organizational Studies, Albuquerque, NM 87131. Offers organizational behavior and human resources management (MBA); strategic management and policy (MBA). *Program availability:* Part-time. *Faculty:* 15 full-time (11 women), 16 part-time/adjunct (8 women). In 2018, 21 master's awarded. *Entrance requirements:* For master's, GMAT or GRE, minimum GPA of 3.0 on last 60 hours of coursework; bachelor's degree from regionally-accredited college or university in U.S. or its equivalent in another country. Additional exam requirements/recommendations for international students: Required—TOEFL (minimum score 550 paper-based; 79 iBT), IELTS (minimum score 6.5). *Application deadline:* For fall admission, 4/1 priority date for domestic and international students; for spring admission, 10/1 priority date for domestic and international students. Applications are processed on a rolling basis. Application fee: $50. Electronic applications accepted. *Expenses:* $531.34 per credit resident tuition and fees, $1197.98 per credit non-resident tuition and fees (both are non-EMBA tuition). *Financial support:* In 2018–19, 14 students received support, including 4 fellowships (averaging $18,200 per year), 11 research assistantships with partial tuition reimbursements available (averaging $15,488 per year); career-related internships or fieldwork, Federal Work-Study, scholarships/grants, and unspecified assistantships also available. Support available to part-time students. Financial award application deadline: 6/1; financial award applicants required to submit FAFSA. *Faculty research:* Business ethics and social corporate responsibility, diversity, human resources, organizational strategy, organizational behavior. *Unit head:* Dr. Michelle Arthur, Chair, 505-277-6471, E-mail: arthurm@unm.edu. *Application contact:* Lisa Beauchene-Lawson, Supervisor, Graduate Advisement, 505-277-6471, E-mail: andersongrad@unm.edu.
Website: https://www.mgt.unm.edu/dos/default.asp?mm-faculty

University of Northern Colorado, Graduate School, Monfort College of Business, Greeley, CO 80639. Offers accounting (MA); general business management (MBA); healthcare administration (MBA); human resources management (MBA). *Accreditation:* AACSB.

University of North Florida, Coggin College of Business, MBA Program, Jacksonville, FL 32224. Offers accounting (MBA); construction management (MBA); e-commerce (MBA); economics (MBA); finance (MBA); human resource management (MBA); international business (MBA); logistics (MBA); management applications (MBA). *Accreditation:* AACSB. *Program availability:* Part-time, evening/weekend. *Faculty:* 40 full-time (14 women). *Students:* 368 part-time (158 women); includes 83 minority (30 Black or African American, non-Hispanic/Latino; 20 Asian, non-Hispanic/Latino; 16 Hispanic/Latino; 17 Two or more races, non-Hispanic/Latino), 28 international. Average age 30. 311 applicants, 51% accepted, 99 enrolled. In 2018, 151 master's awarded. *Entrance requirements:* For master's, GMAT or GRE, U.S. bachelor's degree from regionally-accredited university or equivalent foreign degree. Additional exam requirements/recommendations for international students: Required—TOEFL (minimum score 550 paper-based; 79 iBT). *Application deadline:* For fall admission, 8/1 priority date for domestic students, 5/1 for international students; for spring admission, 12/1 priority date for domestic students, 10/1 for international students; for summer admission, 4/29 priority date for domestic students, 2/1 for international students. Application fee: $30. *Expenses: Tuition, area resident:* Part-time $408.10 per credit hour. Tuition, state resident: part-time $408.10 per credit hour. Tuition, nonresident: part-time $932.61 per credit hour. *Required fees:* $111.81 per credit hour. Tuition and fees vary according to course load, campus/location and program. *Financial support:* In 2018–19, 41 students received support, including 1 research assistantship (averaging $2,143 per year); teaching assistantships, Federal Work-Study, and tuition waivers (partial) also available. Support available to part-time students. Financial award application deadline: 4/1; financial award applicants required to submit FAFSA. *Faculty research:* Performance measures, costing, and inventory issues in logistics and supply chain management; inter-organizational systems; international management and marketing practices; e-commerce; organizational learning and socialization processes. *Unit head:* Dr. Parvez Ahmed, Graduate Program Director, 904-620-1678, E-mail: pahmed@unf.edu. *Application contact:* Amy Bishop, MSM Advisor, 904-620-2575, Fax: 904-620-2832, E-mail: coggin.students@unf.edu.
Website: http://www.unf.edu/graduateschool/academics/programs/MBA.aspx

University of North Texas, Toulouse Graduate School, Denton, TX 76203-5459. Offers accounting (MS); applied anthropology (MA, MS); applied behavior analysis (Certificate); applied geography (MA); applied technology and performance improvement (M Ed, MS); art education (MA); art history (MA); arts leadership (Certificate); audiology (Au D); behavior analysis (MS); behavioral science (PhD); biochemistry and molecular biology (MS); biology (MA, MS); biomedical engineering (MS); business analysis (MS); chemistry (MS); clinical health psychology (PhD); communication studies (MA, MS); computer engineering (MS); computer science (MS); counseling (M Ed, MS), including clinical mental health counseling (MS), college and university counseling, elementary school counseling, secondary school counseling; creative writing (MA); criminal justice (MS); curriculum and instruction (M Ed); decision sciences (MBA); design (MA, MFA), including fashion design (MFA), innovation studies, interior design (MFA); early childhood studies (MS); economics (MS); educational leadership (M Ed, Ed D); educational psychology (MS, PhD), including family studies (MS), gifted and talented (MS), human development (MS), learning and cognition (MS), research, measurement and evaluation (MS); electrical engineering (MS); emergency management (MPA); engineering technology (MS); English (MA); English as a second language (MA); environmental science (MS); finance (MBA, MS); financial management (MPA); French (MA); health services management (MBA); higher education (M Ed, Ed D); history (MA, MS); hospitality management (MS); human resources management (MPA); information science (MS); information systems (PhD); information technologies (MBA); interdisciplinary studies (MA, MS); international studies (MA); international sustainable tourism (MS); jazz studies (MM); journalism (MA, MJ, Graduate Certificate), including interactive and virtual digital communication (Graduate Certificate), narrative journalism (Graduate Certificate), public relations (Graduate Certificate); kinesiology (MS); linguistics (MA); local government management (MPA); logistics (PhD); logistics and supply chain management (MBA); long-term care, senior housing, and aging services (MA); management (PhD); marketing (MBA); mathematics (MA, MS); mechanical and energy engineering (MS, PhD); music (MA), including ethnomusicology, music theory, musicology, performance; music composition (PhD); music education (MM Ed, PhD); nonprofit management (MPA); operations and supply chain management (MBA); performance (MM, DMA); philosophy (MA); political science (MA); professional and technical communication (MA); radio, television and film (MA, MFA); rehabilitation counseling (Certificate); sociology (MA); Spanish (MA); special education (M Ed); speech-language pathology (MA); strategic management (MBA); studio art (MFA); teaching (M Ed); MBA/MS. *Program availability:* Part-time, evening/weekend, online learning. Terminal master's awarded for partial completion of doctoral program. *Degree requirements:* For master's, variable foreign language requirement, comprehensive exam (for some programs), thesis (for some programs); for doctorate, variable foreign language requirement, comprehensive exam (for some programs), thesis/dissertation; for other advanced degree, variable foreign language requirement, comprehensive exam (for some programs). *Entrance requirements:* For master's and doctorate, GRE, GMAT. Additional exam requirements/recommendations for international students: Required—TOEFL (minimum score 550 paper-based; 79 iBT). Electronic applications accepted.

University of North Texas at Dallas, Graduate School, Dallas, TX 75241. Offers accounting (MBA); counseling (M Ed, MS); criminal justice (MS); curriculum and instruction (M Ed); educational administration (M Ed); human resources and organizational behavior (MBA); public leadership (MS); strategic management (MBA).

University of Oklahoma, College of Arts and Sciences, Department of Human Relations, Norman, OK 73019-0390. Offers clinical mental health (MHR); helping skills in human relations (Graduate Certificate); human relations (MHR); human resource diversity and development (Graduate Certificate); human resources (MHR); licensed professional counselor (MHR). *Program availability:* Part-time, evening/weekend. *Faculty:* 18 full-time (10 women), 8 part-time/adjunct (4 women). *Students:* 256 full-time (178 women), 317 part-time (205 women); includes 268 minority (121 Black or African American, non-Hispanic/Latino; 23 American Indian or Alaska Native, non-Hispanic/Latino; 20 Asian, non-Hispanic/Latino; 58 Hispanic/Latino; 3 Native Hawaiian or other Pacific Islander, non-Hispanic/Latino; 43 Two or more races, non-Hispanic/Latino), 12 international. Average age 35. 130 applicants, 91% accepted, 84 enrolled. In 2018, 222 master's, 99 other advanced degrees awarded. *Entrance requirements:* For degree, minimum GPA of 3.0. Additional exam requirements/recommendations for international students: Required—TOEFL (minimum score 79 iBT) or IELTS (minimum score 6.5). *Application deadline:* For fall admission, 8/21 for domestic and international students; for spring admission, 1/23 for domestic and international students; for summer admission, 6/5 for domestic and international students. Application fee: $50 ($100 for international students). Electronic applications accepted. *Expenses:* Tuition, state resident: full-time $5683.20; part-time $236.80 per credit hour. Tuition, nonresident: full-time $20,342; part-time $847.60 per credit hour. *International tuition:* $20,342.40 full-time. *Required fees:* $2894.20; $110.05 per credit hour. $126.50 per semester. Tuition and fees vary according to course load and program. *Financial support:* In 2018–19, 101 students received support, including 6 research assistantships with full tuition reimbursements available (averaging $11,124 per year), 4 teaching assistantships with full tuition reimbursements available (averaging $12,468 per year); scholarships/grants also available. Financial award application deadline: 6/1; financial award applicants required to submit FAFSA. *Faculty research:* At-risk youth, strength model, women's health, adolescent addiction and recovery, group psychotherapy. *Unit head:* Dr. Wesley Long, Chair of Department of Human Relations, 405-325-1756, Fax: 405-325-4402, E-mail: wlong@ou.edu. *Application contact:* Lawana Miller, Admissions Coordinator, 405-325-1756, Fax: 405-325-4402, E-mail: lmiller@ou.edu.
Website: http://www.ou.edu/cas/humanrelations

University of Oklahoma, College of Arts and Sciences, Department of Psychology, Norman, OK 73019. Offers organizational dynamics (MA, Graduate Certificate), including human resource management (Graduate Certificate), organizational dynamics (MA), project management (Graduate Certificate); psychology (MS, PhD), including psychology. *Faculty:* 19 full-time (9 women), 1 (woman) part-time/adjunct. *Students:* 63 full-time (41 women), 33 part-time (22 women); includes 22 minority (3 Black or African American, non-Hispanic/Latino; 3 American Indian or Alaska Native, non-Hispanic/Latino; 3 Asian, non-Hispanic/Latino; 8 Hispanic/Latino; 5 Two or more races, non-Hispanic/Latino), 8 international. Average age 30. 95 applicants, 20% accepted, 17 enrolled. In 2018, 23 master's, 8 doctorates, 15 other advanced degrees awarded. Terminal master's awarded for partial completion of doctoral program. *Degree requirements:* For master's, comprehensive exam, thesis; for doctorate, comprehensive exam, thesis/dissertation. *Entrance requirements:* For master's and doctorate, GRE. Additional exam requirements/recommendations for international students: Required—TOEFL (minimum score 79 iBT) or IELTS (minimum score 6.5). *Application deadline:* For fall admission, 1/1 for domestic and international students. Application fee: $50 ($100 for international students). Electronic applications accepted. *Expenses:* Tuition, state resident: full-time $5683.20; part-time $236.80 per credit hour. Tuition, nonresident: full-time $20,342; part-time $847.60 per credit hour. *International tuition:* $20,342.40 full-time. *Required fees:* $2894.20; $110.05 per credit hour. $126.50 per semester. Tuition and fees vary according to course load and program. *Financial support:* Fellowships, research assistantships, and teaching assistantships available. Financial award application deadline: 6/1; financial award applicants required to submit FAFSA. *Faculty research:* Behavioral statistics; leadership for innovation; eyewitness testimony; risk assessment and literacy; theory of mind. *Unit head:* Dr. Eric Day, Chair, 405-325-4511, Fax: 405-325-4737, E-mail: eday@ou.edu. *Application contact:* Dr. Shane Connelly, Professor/Chair, 405-325-4580, Fax: 405-325-4737, E-mail: sconnelly@ou.edu.
Website: http://www.ou.edu/cas/psychology

University of Phoenix–Bay Area Campus, School of Business, San Jose, CA 95134-1805. Offers accountancy (MS); accounting (MBA); business administration (MBA, DBA); energy management (MBA); global management (MBA); health care management (MBA); human resource management (MBA); human resources management (MM); management (MM); marketing (MBA); organizational leadership (DM); project management (MBA); public administration (MPA); technology management (MBA). *Accreditation:* ACBSP. *Program availability:* Evening/weekend, online learning. *Degree requirements:* For master's, thesis (for some programs). *Entrance requirements:* For master's, minimum undergraduate GPA of 3.0, 3 years of work experience. Additional exam requirements/recommendations for international students: Required—TOEFL (minimum score 550 paper-based; 79 iBT). Electronic applications accepted.

University of Phoenix–Central Valley Campus, School of Business, Fresno, CA 93720-1552. Offers accounting (MBA); business administration (MBA); global management (MBA); human resources management (MBA, MM); management (MM); marketing (MBA); public administration (MBA, MM). *Accreditation:* ACBSP.

University of Phoenix–Dallas Campus, School of Business, Dallas, TX 75251. Offers accounting (MBA); business administration (MBA); global management (MBA); human resources management (MBA, MM); management (MM); marketing (MBA); public administration (MBA, MM). *Accreditation:* ACBSP. *Program availability:* Evening/weekend, online learning. *Degree requirements:* For master's, thesis (for some programs). *Entrance requirements:* For master's, 3 years of work experience, minimum undergraduate GPA of 3.0. Additional exam requirements/recommendations for international students: Required—TOEFL (minimum score 550 paper-based; 79 iBT). Electronic applications accepted.

University of Phoenix–Hawaii Campus, School of Business, Honolulu, HI 96813-3800. Offers accounting (MBA); business administration (MBA); global management (MBA); human resources management (MBA, MM); management (MM); marketing (MBA); public administration (MBA, MM). *Accreditation:* ACBSP. *Program availability:* Evening/weekend. *Degree requirements:* For master's, thesis (for some programs). *Entrance requirements:* For master's, minimum undergraduate GPA of 3.0, 3 years of work experience. Additional exam requirements/recommendations for international students: Required—TOEFL (minimum score 550 paper-based; 79 iBT). Electronic applications accepted.

University of Phoenix–Houston Campus, School of Business, Houston, TX 77079-2004. Offers accounting (MBA); business administration (MBA); global management (MBA); human resources management (MBA, MM); management (MM); marketing (MBA); public administration (MBA, MM). *Accreditation:* ACBSP. *Program availability:* Evening/weekend, online learning. *Degree requirements:* For master's, thesis (for some programs). *Entrance requirements:* For master's, 3 years of work experience, minimum undergraduate GPA of 3.0. Additional exam requirements/recommendations for international students: Required—TOEFL (minimum score 550 paper-based; 79 iBT). Electronic applications accepted.

University of Phoenix–Las Vegas Campus, School of Business, Las Vegas, NV 89135. Offers accounting (MBA); business administration (MBA); global management (MBA); human resources management (MBA, MM); management (MM); marketing (MBA); public administration (MM). *Accreditation:* ACBSP. *Program availability:* Evening/weekend, online learning. *Degree requirements:* For master's, thesis (for some programs). *Entrance requirements:* For master's, minimum undergraduate GPA of 3.0, 3 years of work experience. Additional exam requirements/recommendations for international students: Required—TOEFL (minimum score 550 paper-based; 79 iBT). Electronic applications accepted.

University of Phoenix–Online Campus, School of Business, Phoenix, AZ 85034-7209. Offers accountancy (MS); accounting (MBA, Certificate); business administration (MBA); energy management (MBA); global management (MBA); health care management (MBA); human resource management (MBA, Certificate); human resources management (MM); management (MM); marketing (MBA, Certificate); project management (MBA, Certificate); public administration (MBA, MM); technology management (MBA). *Program availability:* Evening/weekend, online learning. *Entrance requirements:* Additional exam requirements/recommendations for international students: Required—TOEFL, TOEIC (Test of English as an International Communication), Berlitz Online English Proficiency Exam, PTE, or IELTS. Electronic applications accepted. *Expenses:* Contact institution.

University of Phoenix–Phoenix Campus, School of Business, Tempe, AZ 85282-2371. Offers accounting (MBA, MS, Certificate); business administration (MBA); energy management (MBA); global management (MBA); health care management (MBA); human resource management (MBA, Certificate); management (MM); marketing (MBA); project management (MBA); technology management (MBA). *Program availability:* Evening/weekend, online learning. *Entrance requirements:* Additional exam requirements/recommendations for international students: Required—TOEFL, TOEIC (Test of English as an International Communication), Berlitz Online English Proficiency Exam, PTE, or IELTS. Electronic applications accepted. *Expenses:* Contact institution.

University of Phoenix–Sacramento Valley Campus, School of Business, Sacramento, CA 95833-4334. Offers accounting (MBA); business administration (MBA); global management (MBA); human resources management (MBA, MM); management (MM); marketing (MBA); public administration (MBA, MM). *Accreditation:* ACBSP. *Program availability:* Evening/weekend. *Degree requirements:* For master's, thesis (for some programs). *Entrance requirements:* For master's, minimum undergraduate GPA of 3.0, 3 years work experience. Additional exam requirements/recommendations for international students: Required—TOEFL (minimum score 550 paper-based; 79 iBT). Electronic applications accepted.

University of Phoenix–San Antonio Campus, School of Business, San Antonio, TX 78230. Offers accounting (MBA); business administration (MBA); e-business (MBA); global management (MBA); human resources management (MBA, MM); management (MM); marketing (MBA); public administration (MBA, MM). *Accreditation:* ACBSP.

University of Phoenix–San Diego Campus, School of Business, San Diego, CA 92123. Offers accounting (MBA); business administration (MBA); global management (MBA); human resources management (MBA, MM); management (MM); marketing (MBA); public administration (MBA). *Accreditation:* ACBSP. *Program availability:* Evening/weekend. *Degree requirements:* For master's, thesis (for some programs). *Entrance requirements:* For master's, 3 years of work experience, minimum undergraduate GPA of 3.0. Additional exam requirements/recommendations for international students: Required—TOEFL (minimum score 550 paper-based; 79 iBT). Electronic applications accepted.

University of Pittsburgh, Katz Graduate School of Business, Doctoral Program in Business Administration, Pittsburgh, PA 15260. Offers accounting (PhD); business analytics and operations (PhD); finance (PhD); information systems and technology management (PhD); marketing (PhD); organizational behavior and human resources (PhD); strategic management (PhD). *Accreditation:* AACSB. *Program availability:* Evening/weekend. *Degree requirements:* For doctorate, comprehensive exam, thesis/dissertation, student teaching. *Entrance requirements:* For doctorate, GMAT or GRE, 3 recommendations, statement of purpose, transcripts of all previous course work and degrees. Additional exam requirements/recommendations for international students: Required—TOEFL (minimum score 100 iBT) or IELTS (minimum score 7.0). Electronic applications accepted. *Faculty research:* Accounting systems/financial reporting, corporate finance, shopper marketing/consumer behavior, management information systems, organizational behavior and entrepreneurship.

University of Pittsburgh, Katz Graduate School of Business, Master of Business Administration Programs, Pittsburgh, PA 15260. Offers finance (MBA); information systems (MBA); marketing (MBA); operations (MBA); organizational behavior and human resources (MBA); strategy, environment and organizations (MBA); MBA/JD; MBA/MID; MBA/MIS; MBA/MSE. *Accreditation:* AACSB. *Program availability:* Part-time, evening/weekend, blended/hybrid learning. *Degree requirements:* For master's, minimum GPA of 3.0. *Entrance requirements:* For master's, GMAT, GRE. Additional exam requirements/recommendations for international students: Required—TOEFL (minimum score 100 iBT) or IELTS (minimum score 7.0). Electronic applications accepted. *Faculty research:* Accounting systems/financial reporting, corporate finance, shopper marketing/consumer behavior, management information systems, organizational behavior and entrepreneurship.

University of Puerto Rico–Mayagüez, Graduate Studies, College of Business Administration, Mayagüez, PR 00681-9000. Offers business administration (MBA); finance (MBA); human resources (MBA); industrial management (MBA). *Program availability:* Part-time, evening/weekend. *Degree requirements:* For master's, one foreign language, comprehensive exam, thesis (for some programs). *Entrance requirements:* For master's, GMAT or EXADEP, bachelor's degree with courses in calculus, microeconomics, accounting and statistics. Additional exam requirements/recommendations for international students: Required—TOEFL (minimum score 500 paper-based), GMAT or EXADEP.

Electronic applications accepted. *Faculty research:* Organizational studies, management, accounting, entrepreneurship, leadership and motivation.

University of Puerto Rico–Río Piedras, College of Business Administration, San Juan, PR 00931-3300. Offers accounting (MBA); finance (MBA, PhD); general business (MBA); human resources management (MBA); international trade and business (MBA, PhD); marketing (MBA); operations management (MBA); quantitative methods (MBA). *Accreditation:* AACSB. *Program availability:* Part-time. *Degree requirements:* For master's, comprehensive exam, thesis or alternative, research project. *Entrance requirements:* For master's, GMAT or PAEG, minimum GPA of 3.0, letter of recommendation; for doctorate, GMAT, PAEG, minimum GPA of 3.0, master degree. *Faculty research:* Management.

University of Regina, Faculty of Graduate Studies and Research, Kenneth Levene Graduate School of Business, Program in Human Resources Management, Regina, SK S4S 0A2, Canada. Offers MHRM, Master's Certificate. *Program availability:* Part-time. *Students:* 29 full-time (27 women), 12 part-time (9 women). Average age 30. 79 applicants, 32% accepted, 8 enrolled. In 2018, 21 master's, 2 other advanced degrees awarded. *Degree requirements:* For master's, project, Research paper. *Entrance requirements:* For master's, two years of relevant work experience. post secondary transcripts, 2 letter of recommendations. Additional exam requirements/recommendations for international students: Required—TOEFL (minimum score 580 paper-based; 80 iBT), IELTS (minimum score 6.5), PTE (minimum score 59), other option is CAEL, MELAB and U of R ESL. *Application deadline:* For fall admission, 3/1 for domestic and international students; for winter admission, 7/1 for domestic and international students; for spring admission, 10/1 for domestic and international students; for summer admission, 10/1 for domestic and international students. Application fee: $100 Canadian dollars. Electronic applications accepted. *Expenses:* One academic year is 13,354. International students will pay additional 1,191.75 for International surcharge per semester. *Financial support:* Fellowships, research assistantships, teaching assistantships, career-related internships or fieldwork, Federal Work-Study, scholarships/grants, unspecified assistantships, and travel award and Graduate Scholarship Base funds available. Support available to part-time students. Financial award application deadline: 9/30. *Faculty research:* Human behavior in organizations, labor relations and collective bargaining, organization theory, staffing organizations, human resources systems analysis. *Unit head:* Dr. Gina Grandy, Dean, 306-585-4435, Fax: 306-585-5361, E-mail: business.dean@uregina.ca. *Application contact:* Dr. Adrian Pitariu, Associate Dean, Research and Graduate Programs, 306-3585-6294, Fax: 306-585-5361, E-mail: business.AD.levene@uregina.ca.
Website: http://www.uregina.ca/business/levene/

University of Rhode Island, Graduate School, College of Business, Schmidt Labor Research Center, Kingston, RI 02881. Offers labor relations and human resources (MS, Graduate Certificate); MS/JD. *Program availability:* Part-time, evening/weekend. *Faculty:* 1 part-time/adjunct (0 women). *Students:* 5 full-time (4 women), 16 part-time (14 women); includes 8 minority (3 Black or African American, non-Hispanic/Latino; 3 Hispanic/Latino; 1 Native Hawaiian or other Pacific Islander, non-Hispanic/Latino; 1 Two or more races, non-Hispanic/Latino). 21 applicants, 95% accepted, 9 enrolled. In 2018, 5 master's, 23 other advanced degrees awarded. *Entrance requirements:* Additional exam requirements/recommendations for international students: Required—TOEFL. *Application deadline:* For fall admission, 7/15 for domestic students, 2/1 for international students; for spring admission, 11/15 for domestic students, 7/15 for international students; for summer admission, 4/15 for domestic students. Application fee: $65. Electronic applications accepted. *Expenses: Tuition, area resident:* Full-time $13,226; part-time $735 per credit. Tuition, state resident: Full-time $13,226; part-time $735 per credit. Tuition, nonresident: full-time $25,854; part-time $1436 per credit. International tuition: $25,854 full-time. Required fees: $1698; $50 per credit. $35 per semester. One-time fee: $165. *Financial support:* In 2018–19, 2 teaching assistantships with tuition reimbursements (averaging $17,724 per year) were awarded. Financial award application deadline: 2/1; financial award applicants required to submit FAFSA. *Unit head:* Dr. Aimee Phelps, Acting Director, 401-874-4693, E-mail: aimee@uri.edu. *Application contact:* Dr. Aimee Phelps, Acting Director, 401-874-4693, E-mail: aimee@uri.edu.
Website: https://web.uri.edu/lrc/

University of St. Francis, College of Business and Health Administration, Joliet, IL 60435-6169. Offers accounting (MBA, Certificate); business analytics (MBA, Certificate); e-learning (Certificate); finance (MBA, Certificate); health administration (MBA, MS); human resource management (MBA, Certificate); logistics (Certificate); management (MBA, MSM); management of training and development (Certificate); supply chain management (MBA); training and development (MBA); training specialist (Certificate). *Program availability:* Part-time, evening/weekend, 100% online, blended/hybrid learning. *Faculty:* 13 full-time (6 women), 20 part-time/adjunct (7 women). *Students:* 139 full-time (94 women), 206 part-time (159 women); includes 86 minority (51 Black or African American, non-Hispanic/Latino; 1 American Indian or Alaska Native, non-Hispanic/Latino; 11 Asian, non-Hispanic/Latino; 21 Hispanic/Latino; 2 Two or more races, non-Hispanic/Latino), 24 international. Average age 37. 261 applicants, 63% accepted, 98 enrolled. In 2018, 129 master's, 3 other advanced degrees awarded. *Degree requirements:* For master's, comprehensive exam (for some programs). *Entrance requirements:* Additional exam requirements/recommendations for international students: Required—TOEFL (minimum score 550 paper-based; 79 iBT), IELTS (minimum score 6). *Application deadline:* Applications are processed on a rolling basis. Electronic applications accepted. Application fee is waived when completed online. *Expenses:* Contact institution. *Financial support:* In 2018–19, 126 students received support. Scholarships/grants and tuition waivers (partial) available. Support available to part-time students. Financial award applicants required to submit FAFSA. *Unit head:* Dr. Orlando Griego, Dean, 815-740-3395, Fax: 815-740-3452, E-mail: ogriego@stfrancis.edu. *Application contact:* Sandee Sloka, Director Adult & Graduate Admissions, 800-735-7500, E-mail: ssloka@stfrancis.edu.
Website: https://www.stfrancis.edu/business-health-administration/

University of Saint Mary, Graduate Programs, Program in Business Administration, Leavenworth, KS 66048-5082. Offers enterprise risk management (MBA); finance (MBA); general management (MBA); health care management (MBA); human resources management (MBA); marketing and advertising management (MBA). *Program availability:* Part-time, evening/weekend, 100% online, blended/hybrid learning. *Faculty:* 1 full-time, 23 part-time/adjunct (7 women). *Students:* 177 full-time (116 women), 50 part-time (29 women); includes 73 minority (30 Black or African American, non-Hispanic/Latino; 3 American Indian or Alaska Native, non-Hispanic/Latino; 12 Asian, non-Hispanic/Latino; 18 Hispanic/Latino; 1 Native Hawaiian or other Pacific Islander, non-Hispanic/Latino; 9 Two or more races, non-Hispanic/Latino), 2 international. Average age 33. *Degree requirements:* For master's, thesis. *Entrance requirements:* For master's, Minimum undergraduate GPA of 2.75, official transcripts. *Application deadline:* Applications are processed on a rolling basis. Application fee: $25. Electronic applications accepted. *Expenses:* Contact institution. *Financial support:* Applicants required to submit FAFSA. *Unit head:* Mark Harvey, Director of Graduate Business Programs, 913-319-3011, E-mail: mark.harvey@stmary.edu. *Application contact:* Mark Harvey, Director of Graduate Business Programs, 913-319-3011, E-mail: mark.harvey@stmary.edu.
Website: https://www.stmary.edu/mba

Human Resources Management

University of South Carolina, The Graduate School, Darla Moore School of Business, Human Resources Program, Columbia, SC 29208. Offers MHR, JD/MHR. *Program availability:* Part-time. *Degree requirements:* For master's, internship. *Entrance requirements:* For master's, GMAT or GRE, minimum GPA of 3.0. Additional exam requirements/recommendations for international students: Required—TOEFL (minimum score 100 iBT); Recommended—IELTS. Electronic applications accepted. *Expenses:* Contact institution. *Faculty research:* Management and compensation, performance appraisal, work values, grievance systems, union formation, group behavior.

University of South Dakota, Graduate School, College of Arts and Sciences, Program in Administrative Studies, Vermillion, SD 57069. Offers addiction studies (MSA); criminal justice studies (MSA); health services administration (MSA); human resources (MSA); interdisciplinary studies (MSA); long term care administration (MSA); organizational leadership (MSA). *Program availability:* Part-time, evening/weekend, 100% online. *Degree requirements:* For master's, thesis or alternative. *Entrance requirements:* For master's, 3 years of work or experience, minimum GPA of 2.7, resume. Additional exam requirements/recommendations for international students: Required—TOEFL (minimum score 550 paper-based; 79 iBT). Electronic applications accepted.

University of Southern Indiana, Graduate Studies, Romain College of Business, Program in Business Administration, Evansville, IN 47712-3590. Offers accounting (MBA); data analytics (MBA); engineering management (MBA); general business administration (MBA); healthcare administration (MBA); human resource management (MBA). *Accreditation:* AACSB. *Program availability:* Part-time, evening/weekend, 100% online, blended/hybrid learning. *Entrance requirements:* For master's, GMAT or GRE, minimum GPA of 2.5, resume, 3 professional references. Additional exam requirements/recommendations for international students: Required—TOEFL (minimum score 550 paper-based; 79 iBT), IELTS (minimum score 6). Electronic applications accepted.

University of South Florida, Muma College of Business, Department of Management, Tampa, FL 33620-9951. Offers management (MS), including human resources, management information systems. *Accreditation:* AACSB. *Program availability:* Part-time, online learning. *Faculty:* 4 full-time (2 women). *Students:* 22 full-time (10 women), 36 part-time (23 women); includes 21 minority (6 Black or African American, non-Hispanic/Latino; 1 Asian, non-Hispanic/Latino; 14 Hispanic/Latino), 14 international. Average age 31. 81 applicants, 63% accepted, 27 enrolled. In 2018, 43 master's awarded. Terminal master's awarded for partial completion of doctoral program. *Degree requirements:* For master's, comprehensive exam, thesis (for some programs). *Entrance requirements:* For master's, GMAT, letters of recommendation, resume, statement of purpose, relevant work experience. Additional exam requirements/recommendations for international students: Required—TOEFL (minimum score 550 paper-based; 79 iBT) or IELTS (minimum score 6.5). *Application deadline:* For fall admission, 6/1 for domestic students, 2/1 for international students; for spring admission, 10/15 for domestic students, 7/1 for international students. Application fee: $30. Electronic applications accepted. *Expenses:* Tuition, state resident: full-time $6350. Tuition, nonresident: full-time $19,048. *International tuition:* $19,048 full-time. *Required fees:* $2079. *Financial support:* In 2018–19, 6 students received support, including 1 research assistantship with tuition reimbursement available (averaging $9,002 per year), 3 teaching assistantships with tuition reimbursements available (averaging $9,002 per year); tuition waivers also available. Financial award applicants required to submit FAFSA. *Faculty research:* Leadership and employment relations, time management, personal motivation, crew resource management in aviation, psychology of gambling, organizational culture, issues of fairness, employment law, marketing strategy/implementation, organizational diversity, ethics, environmentally-friendly business practices, green business, sustainable business plans, institutional theory, social movement theory, diffusion of innovations, stakeholder human resources management, social responsibility. *Total annual research expenditures:* $24,235. *Unit head:* Dr. Sally Fuller, Interim Department Chair/Associate Professor, 813-974-1766, Fax: 813-905-9964, E-mail: sfuller@usf.edu. *Application contact:* Stacee Bender, Academic Services Administrator, 813-974-4516, Fax: 813-974-9964, E-mail: staceebender@usf.edu.
Website: http://www.usf.edu/business/graduate/masters/management/

The University of Texas at Arlington, Graduate School, College of Business, Department of Management, Arlington, TX 76019. Offers human resources (MSHRM). *Program availability:* Part-time, evening/weekend. *Degree requirements:* For master's, thesis optional. *Entrance requirements:* For master's, GMAT/GRE. Additional exam requirements/recommendations for international students: Required—TOEFL (minimum score 550 paper-based; 79 iBT). *Faculty research:* Compensations, training, diversity, strategic human resources.

University of the Sacred Heart, Graduate Programs, Department of Business Administration, Program in Human Resource Management, San Juan, PR 00914-0383. Offers MBA. *Program availability:* Part-time, evening/weekend. *Degree requirements:* For master's, thesis. *Entrance requirements:* For master's, EXADEP, minimum undergraduate GPA of 2.75, interview.

University of Toronto, School of Graduate Studies, Faculty of Arts and Science, Centre for Industrial Relations and Human Resources, Toronto, ON M5S 1A1, Canada. Offers MIRHR, PhD. *Program availability:* Part-time. *Degree requirements:* For doctorate, thesis/dissertation. *Entrance requirements:* For master's, GRE or GMAT (for applicants who completed degree outside of Canada), minimum B+ in final 2 years of bachelor's degree completion, 2 letters of reference, resume; for doctorate, GRE or GMAT, MIR or equivalent, minimum B+ average, 3 letters of reference, resume. Additional exam requirements/recommendations for international students: Required—TOEFL (minimum score 600 paper-based; 100 iBT), IELTS, TWE (minimum score 5), Michigan English Language Assessment Battery, or COPE. Electronic applications accepted. *Expenses:* Contact institution.

University of Wisconsin–Madison, Graduate School, Wisconsin School of Business, Doctoral Program in Management and Human Resources, Madison, WI 53706-1380. Offers PhD. *Degree requirements:* For doctorate, comprehensive exam, thesis/dissertation. *Entrance requirements:* For doctorate, GMAT or GRE. Additional exam requirements/recommendations for international students: Recommended—TOEFL (minimum score 623 paper-based; 106 iBT), IELTS (minimum score 7.5), TSE. Electronic applications accepted. *Expenses:* Contact institution. *Faculty research:* Employee compensation, performance for work groups, small business management, venture financing, arts industry, entrepreneurship, development economics, corporate finance, work motivation, diversity/discrimination, organizational justice.

University of Wisconsin–Madison, Graduate School, Wisconsin School of Business, Wisconsin Full-Time MBA Program, Madison, WI 53706-1380. Offers applied security analysis (MBA); arts administration (MBA); brand and product management (MBA); corporate finance and investment banking (MBA); marketing research (MBA); operations and technology management (MBA); real estate (MBA); risk management and insurance (MBA); strategic human resource management (MBA); supply chain management (MBA). *Faculty:* 137 full-time (36 women), 39 part-time/adjunct (11 women). *Students:* 183 full-time (59 women); includes 31 minority (5 Black or African American, non-Hispanic/Latino; 1 American Indian or Alaska Native, non-Hispanic/Latino; 6 Asian, non-Hispanic/Latino; 13 Hispanic/Latino; 6 Two or more races, non-Hispanic/Latino), 40 international. Average age 28. 465 applicants, 33% accepted, 79 enrolled. In 2018, 104 master's awarded. *Entrance requirements:* For master's, GMAT or GRE, bachelor's or equivalent degree, essay, letter of recommendation, resume. Additional exam requirements/recommendations for international students: Required—TOEFL (minimum score 100 iBT), IELTS (minimum score 7.5), TOEFL is not required for international students whose undergraduate training was in English. *Application deadline:* For fall admission, 11/1 for domestic and international students; for winter admission, 1/10 for domestic and international students; for spring admission, 3/1 for domestic and international students; for summer admission, 4/10 for domestic students, 4/10 priority date for international students. Applications are processed on a rolling basis. Application fee: $75 ($81 for international students). Electronic applications accepted. *Expenses:* Wisconsin Resident tuition and fees - $39,156; Nonresident tuition and fees - $76,635. *Financial support:* In 2018–19, 148 students received support, including 7 fellowships with full tuition reimbursements available (averaging $25,871 per year), 7 research assistantships with full tuition reimbursements available (averaging $14,832 per year), 47 teaching assistantships with full tuition reimbursements available (averaging $14,832 per year); scholarships/grants, health care benefits, tuition waivers (full and partial), and unspecified assistantships also available. Financial award application deadline: 6/1. *Faculty research:* Ecology, environmental studies, and business; decision making; tax policy; diversity and inclusion in governance boards; marketing and social media. *Unit head:* Dr. Enno Siemsen, Associate Dean of the MBA and Masters Programs, 608-890-3130, E-mail: esiemsen@wisc.edu. *Application contact:* Betsy Kacizak, Director of Admissions and Recruiting, Full-time MBA Program, 608-262-4000, E-mail: betsy.kacizak@wisc.edu.
Website: https://wsb.wisc.edu/

University of Wisconsin–Milwaukee, Graduate School, College of Letters and Science, Interdepartmental Program in Human Resources and Labor Relations, Milwaukee, WI 53201-0413. Offers human resources and labor relations (MHRLR); international human resources and labor relations (Graduate Certificate); mediation and negotiation (Graduate Certificate). *Program availability:* Part-time. *Students:* 16 full-time (9 women), 33 part-time (28 women); includes 15 minority (4 Black or African American, non-Hispanic/Latino; 2 Asian, non-Hispanic/Latino; 1 Hispanic/Latino; 8 Two or more races, non-Hispanic/Latino), 1 international. Average age 31. 29 applicants, 76% accepted, 17 enrolled. In 2018, 11 master's, 5 other advanced degrees awarded. *Entrance requirements:* For master's, GMAT or GRE General Test. Additional exam requirements/recommendations for international students: Required—TOEFL (minimum score 80 iBT), IELTS (minimum score 6.5). Application fee: $56 ($96 for international students). Electronic applications accepted. *Financial support:* Career-related internships or fieldwork available. Support available to part-time students. Financial award application deadline: 4/15; financial award applicants required to submit FAFSA. *Unit head:* Susan M. Donohue-Davies, Assistant Director, 414-299-4009, Fax: 414-229-5915, E-mail: suedono@uwm.edu. *Application contact:* Susan M. Donohue-Davies, Assistant Director, 414-299-4009, Fax: 414-229-5915, E-mail: suedono@uwm.edu.
Website: http://uwm.edu/human-resources-labor-relations/

Upper Iowa University, Online Master's Programs, Fayette, IA 52142-1857. Offers accounting (MBA); corporate financial management (MBA); emergency management and homeland security (MPA); general management (MBA); general studies (MPA); government administration (MPA); health and human services (MPA); human resources management (MBA); nonprofit organizational management (MPA); organizational development (MBA); public management (MPA); sport administration (MSA). MBA also available at Madison, WI campus. *Program availability:* Part-time, online learning. *Degree requirements:* For master's, research project. *Entrance requirements:* For master's, GMAT, GRE, or minimum GPA of 2.7 during last 60 hours. Additional exam requirements/recommendations for international students: Required—TOEFL (minimum score 570 paper-based). Electronic applications accepted. *Faculty research:* Total quality management, teams, organization culture and climate, management.

Utah State University, School of Graduate Studies, Jon M. Huntsman School of Business, Program in Human Resources, Logan, UT 84322. Offers MHR. *Program availability:* Part-time, evening/weekend, online learning. *Entrance requirements:* For master's, GMAT or GRE, minimum GPA of 3.0. Additional exam requirements/recommendations for international students: Required—TOEFL. Electronic applications accepted. *Expenses:* Contact institution. *Faculty research:* International human resources, aging workforce.

Virginia Commonwealth University, Graduate School, L. Douglas Wilder School of Government and Public Affairs, Program in Public Administration, Richmond, VA 23284-9005. Offers financial management (MPA); human resource management (MPA); state and local government management (MPA). *Accreditation:* NASPAA. *Program availability:* Part-time. *Entrance requirements:* For master's, GRE, GMAT or LSAT. Additional exam requirements/recommendations for international students: Required—TOEFL (minimum score 600 paper-based; 100 iBT); Recommended—IELTS (minimum score 6.5). Electronic applications accepted. *Faculty research:* Environmental policy, executive leadership, human resource management, local government management, nonprofit management, public financial management, public policy analysis and evaluation.

Virginia International University, School of Business, Fairfax, VA 22030. Offers accounting (MBA, MS); entrepreneurship (MBA); executive management (Graduate Certificate); global logistics (MBA); health care management (MBA); hospitality and tourism management (MBA); human resources management (MBA); international business management (MBA); international finance (MBA); marketing management (MBA); mass media and public relations (MBA); project management (MBA, MS). *Program availability:* Part-time, online learning. *Entrance requirements:* For master's and Graduate Certificate, bachelor's degree. Additional exam requirements/recommendations for international students: Required—TOEFL (minimum score 550 paper-based; 80 iBT), IELTS (minimum score 6). Electronic applications accepted.

Walden University, Graduate Programs, School of Management, Minneapolis, MN 55401. Offers accounting (MBA, MS, DBA), including accounting for the professional (MS), accounting with CPA emphasis (MS), self-designed (MS); advanced project management (Graduate Certificate); applied project management (Graduate Certificate); auditing (Graduate Certificate); bridge to business administration (Post-Doctoral Certificate); bridge to management (Post-Doctoral Certificate); business management (Graduate Certificate); communication (MBA); corporate finance (MBA); digital marketing (Graduate Certificate); entrepreneurship (DBA); entrepreneurship and small business (MBA); finance (MS, DBA), including finance for the professional (MS), finance with CFA/investment (MS), finance with CPA emphasis (MS); global supply chain management (DBA); healthcare management (MBA, DBA); human resource management (MBA, MS, Graduate Certificate), including functional human resource management (MS), general program (MS), integrating functional and strategic human resource management (MS), organizational strategy (MS); human resources management (DBA); information systems management (DBA); international business (MBA, DBA); leadership (MBA, MS, DBA, Graduate Certificate), including general program (MS), human resource leadership (MS), leader development (MS), self-designed (MS); management (MS, PhD), including communications (MS), finance (PhD), general program (MS), healthcare management (MS), human resource management (MS), human resources management (PhD), information systems

management (PhD), international business (MS), leadership (MS), leadership and organizational change (PhD), marketing (MS), project management (MS), strategy and operations (MS); managerial accounting (Graduate Certificate); marketing (MBA, MS, DBA); project management (MBA, MS, DBA); self-designed (MBA, DBA); social impact management (DBA); technology entrepreneurship (DBA). *Accreditation:* ACBSP. *Program availability:* Part-time, evening/weekend, online only, 100% online. *Degree requirements:* For master's, thesis (for some programs), residency (for EMBA); for doctorate, thesis/dissertation (for some programs), residency. *Entrance requirements:* For master's, bachelor's degree or higher; minimum GPA of 2.5; official transcripts; goal statement (for some programs); access to computer and Internet; for doctorate, master's degree or higher; three years of related professional or academic experience (preferred); minimum GPA of 3.0; goal statement and current resume (for select programs); official transcripts; access to computer and Internet; for other advanced degree, relevant work experience; access to computer and Internet. Additional exam requirements/recommendations for international students: Required—TOEFL (minimum score 550 paper-based, 79 iBT), IELTS (minimum score 6.5), Michigan English Language Assessment Battery (minimum score 82), or PTE (minimum score 53). Electronic applications accepted.

Walsh College of Accountancy and Business Administration, Graduate Programs, Program in Management, Troy, MI 48083. Offers human resources management (MS); international business (MS); strategic management (MS). *Program availability:* Part-time, evening/weekend, 100% online, blended/hybrid learning. *Faculty:* 8 full-time (4 women), 7 part-time/adjunct (4 women). *Students:* 1 (woman) full-time, 38 part-time (28 women); includes 15 minority (12 Black or African American, non-Hispanic/Latino; 1 Asian, non-Hispanic/Latino; 2 Hispanic/Latino), 1 international. Average age 37. 19 applicants, 84% accepted, 7 enrolled. In 2018, 17 master's awarded. *Entrance requirements:* For master's, minimum overall cumulative GPA of 2.750 from all colleges previously attended. Additional exam requirements/recommendations for international students: Required—TOEFL (minimum score 550 paper-based, 79-80 internet based), IELTS (6.5), Michigan Test of English Language Proficiency, or MTELP (80). *Application deadline:* Applications are processed on a rolling basis. Application fee: $35. Electronic applications accepted. *Expenses:* $785 per credit hour plus $175 student support fee per semester. International students pay $785 per credit hour plus $175 student support fee and $275 international student fee per semester. *Financial support:* In 2018–19, 3 students received support. Scholarships/grants and Tuition Exchange Program available. Financial award application deadline: 6/30; financial award applicants required to submit FAFSA. *Faculty research:* Strategy practice and process, management learning and decision-making, human capital development, global leadership and citizenship, use of systems and complexity theory and management practice. *Unit head:* Dr. Ann Saurbier, Chair, Management, 248-823-1635, Fax: 248-689-0920, E-mail: asaurbie@walshcollege.edu. *Application contact:* Karen Mahaffy, Executive Director, Admissions and Enrollment Services, 248-823-1610, Fax: 248-823-1611, E-mail: kmahaffy@walshcollege.edu.

Warner University, School of Business, Lake Wales, FL 33859. Offers accounting (MBA); business administration (MBA); human resource management (MBA); international business (MBA); management (MSMC). *Program availability:* Part-time, evening/weekend, online learning. *Degree requirements:* For master's, comprehensive exam, thesis. *Entrance requirements:* For master's, minimum GPA of 3.0, 2 letters of recommendation. Additional exam requirements/recommendations for international students: Required—TOEFL. Electronic applications accepted.

Wayland Baptist University, Graduate Programs, Program in Education, Plainview, TX 79072-6998. Offers education administration (M Ed); education diagnostics (M Ed); education literacy (M Ed); elementary certification (M Ed); English (M Ed); English as a second language (M Ed); higher education administration (M Ed); human resources (M Ed); instructional leadership (M Ed); instructional technology (M Ed); leadership training and development (M Ed); science education (M Ed); secondary certification (M Ed); social studies (M Ed); special education (M Ed); sports administration and management (M Ed). *Program availability:* Part-time, evening/weekend, 100% online. *Degree requirements:* For master's, comprehensive exam, capstone course. *Entrance requirements:* For master's, GRE, GMAT or MAT. Additional exam requirements/recommendations for international students: Required—TOEFL (minimum score 500 paper-based; 61 iBT). Electronic applications accepted.

Wayland Baptist University, Graduate Programs, Programs in Business Administration/Management, Plainview, TX 79072-6998. Offers accounting (MBA); general business (MBA); health care administration (MAM, MBA); human resource management (MAM, MBA); international management (MBA); management (MBA, D Mgt); management information systems (MBA); organization management (MAM); project management (MBA). *Program availability:* Part-time, evening/weekend, online learning. *Degree requirements:* For master's, capstone course. *Entrance requirements:* For master's, GMAT, GRE or MAT. Additional exam requirements/recommendations for international students: Required—TOEFL (minimum score 500 paper-based; 61 iBT). Electronic applications accepted.

Waynesburg University, Graduate and Professional Studies, Canonsburg, PA 15370. Offers business (MBA), including energy management, finance, health systems, human resources, leadership, market development; counseling (MA), including addictions counseling, clinical mental health; counselor education and supervision (PhD); criminal investigation (MA); education (M Ed), including autism, curriculum and instruction, educational leadership, online teaching; nursing (MSN), including administration, education, informatics; nursing practice (DNP); special education (M Ed); technology (M Ed); MSN/MBA. *Accreditation:* AACN. *Program availability:* Part-time, evening/weekend. *Degree requirements:* For doctorate, thesis/dissertation. *Entrance requirements:* Additional exam requirements/recommendations for international students: Required—TOEFL. Electronic applications accepted.

Wayne State University, College of Liberal Arts and Sciences, Department of Political Science, Detroit, MI 48202. Offers political science (MA, PhD); public administration (MPA), including economic development policy and management, health and human services policy and management, human and fiscal resource management, nonprofit policy and management, organizational behavior and management, urban and metropolitan policy and management; JD/MA. *Accreditation:* NASPAA. *Faculty:* 18. *Students:* 61 full-time (26 women), 51 part-time (27 women); includes 31 minority (22 Black or African American, non-Hispanic/Latino; 3 Asian, non-Hispanic/Latino; 1 Hispanic/Latino; 5 Two or more races, non-Hispanic/Latino), 12 international. Average age 32. 103 applicants, 39% accepted, 20 enrolled. In 2018, 32 master's, 5 doctorates awarded. *Degree requirements:* For master's, comprehensive exam (for some programs), thesis (for some programs); for doctorate, thesis/dissertation. *Entrance requirements:* For master's, GRE General Test, substantial undergraduate preparation in the social sciences, minimum upper-division undergraduate GPA of 3.0, two letters of recommendation, personal statement; for doctorate, GRE General Test, 3 letters of recommendation; personal statement; interview. Additional exam requirements/recommendations for international students: Required—TOEFL (minimum score 550 paper-based; 79 iBT), TWE (minimum score 5.5), Michigan English Language Assessment Battery (minimum score 85); Recommended—IELTS (minimum score 6.5). *Application deadline:* For fall admission, 5/15 for domestic students, 5/1 priority date for

international students; for winter admission, 10/15 for domestic students, 9/1 priority date for international students. Applications are processed on a rolling basis. Application fee: $50. Electronic applications accepted. *Expenses:* Contact institution. *Financial support:* In 2018–19, 46 students received support, including 4 fellowships with tuition reimbursements available (averaging $17,000 per year), 1 research assistantship with tuition reimbursement available (averaging $23,119 per year), 12 teaching assistantships with tuition reimbursements available (averaging $19,267 per year); scholarships/grants, health care benefits, and unspecified assistantships also available. Financial award applicants required to submit FAFSA. *Faculty research:* American government and politics, comparative politics, political methodology, political theory, public administration, public law, public policy, world politics/international relations, formal theory/modeling, gender and politics, international law, peace research, political economy, political psychology, politics of developing countries, race, religion, and ethnicity, urban politics. *Unit head:* Dr. Daniel Geller, Professor and Chair, 313-577-6328, E-mail: dgeller@wayne.edu. *Application contact:* Dr. Sharon Lean, Graduate Director, 313-577-2630, E-mail: gradpolisci@wayne.edu. Website: http://clas.wayne.edu/politicalscience/

Webster University, George Herbert Walker School of Business and Technology, Department of Business, St. Louis, MO 63119-3194. Offers business and organizational security management (MBA); decision support systems (MBA); environmental management (MBA); finance (MBA, MS); forensic accounting (MS); gerontology (MBA); human resources development (MBA); human resources management (MBA); information technology management (MBA); international business (MA, MBA); international relations (MBA); management and leadership (MBA); marketing (MBA); media communications (MBA); procurement and acquisitions management (MBA); Web services (MBA). *Accreditation:* ACBSP. *Program availability:* Part-time, evening/weekend, online learning. *Degree requirements:* For master's, comprehensive exam (for some programs), thesis (for some programs). *Entrance requirements:* Additional exam requirements/recommendations for international students: Required—TOEFL. *Expenses: Tuition:* Full-time $22,500; part-time $750 per credit hour. Tuition and fees vary according to degree level, campus/location and program.

Webster University, George Herbert Walker School of Business and Technology, Department of Management, St. Louis, MO 63119-3194. Offers business and organizational security management (MA); digital marketing management (Graduate Certificate); government contracting (Graduate Certificate); health administration (MHA); health care management (MA); health services management (MA); human resources development (MA); human resources management (MA); information technology management (MA, MS); management (D Mgt); management and leadership (MA); marketing (MA); nonprofit leadership (MA); nonprofit revenue development (Graduate Certificate); organizational development (Graduate Certificate); procurement and acquisitions management (MA); public administration (MPA); space systems operations management (MS). *Program availability:* Part-time, evening/weekend, online learning. *Degree requirements:* For master's, thesis (for some programs); for doctorate, thesis/dissertation, written exam. *Entrance requirements:* For doctorate, GMAT, 3 years of work experience, MBA. Additional exam requirements/recommendations for international students: Required—TOEFL. *Expenses: Tuition:* Full-time $22,500; part-time $750 per credit hour. Tuition and fees vary according to degree level, campus/location and program.

West Chester University of Pennsylvania, College of Business and Public Management, Department of Management, West Chester, PA 19383. Offers human resource management (MS, Certificate). *Program availability:* Part-time, evening/weekend, online only, 100% online. *Degree requirements:* For master's, capstone project. *Entrance requirements:* For master's, GMAT or GRE, bachelor's degree or above in any major/field from accredited institution; at least two years of professional experience in human resources (preferred). Additional exam requirements/recommendations for international students: Required—TOEFL or IELTS. Electronic applications accepted. *Faculty research:* Organizational behavior, employment law, labor relations, compensation.

Wilfrid Laurier University, Faculty of Graduate and Postdoctoral Studies, Lazaridis School of Business and Economics, Department of Business, Waterloo, ON N2L 3C5, Canada. Offers accounting (PhD); finance (M Fin); financial economics (PhD); marketing (PhD); operations and supply chain management (PhD); organizational behavior and human resource management (M Sc); organizational behaviour and human resource management (PhD); supply chain management (M Sc); technology management (EMTM). *Accreditation:* AACSB. *Program availability:* Part-time, evening/weekend. *Degree requirements:* For master's, thesis optional; for doctorate, comprehensive exam, thesis/dissertation. *Entrance requirements:* For master's, GMAT, 4-year honors degree with minimum B+ average; for doctorate, GMAT, master's degree, minimum B+ average. Additional exam requirements/recommendations for international students: Required—TOEFL (minimum score 89 iBT). Electronic applications accepted. *Faculty research:* Financial economics, management and organizational behavior, operations and supply chain management.

Wilkes University, College of Graduate and Professional Studies, Jay S. Sidhu School of Business and Leadership, Wilkes-Barre, PA 18766-0002. Offers accounting (MBA); global business (MBA); human resource management (MBA); international business (MBA); leadership (MBA); management (MBA); operations management (MBA); organizational leadership and development (MBA). *Accreditation:* ACBSP. *Program availability:* Part-time, evening/weekend. *Students:* 16 full-time (9 women), 64 part-time (33 women); includes 11 minority (3 Black or African American, non-Hispanic/Latino; 3 Asian, non-Hispanic/Latino; 3 Hispanic/Latino; 2 Two or more races, non-Hispanic/Latino), 7 international. Average age 30. In 2018, 49 master's awarded. *Entrance requirements:* For master's, GMAT. Additional exam requirements/recommendations for international students: Required—TOEFL (minimum score 550 paper-based; 79 iBT). *Application deadline:* Applications are processed on a rolling basis. Application fee: $45 ($65 for international students). Electronic applications accepted. *Expenses:* Contact institution. *Financial support:* Unspecified assistantships available. Financial award application deadline: 3/1; financial award applicants required to submit FAFSA. *Unit head:* Dr. Abel Adekola, Dean, 570-408-4701, Fax: 570-408-7846, E-mail: abel.adekola@wilkes.edu. *Application contact:* Kristin Donati, Associate Director of Graduate Admissions, 570-408-3338, Fax: 570-408-7846, E-mail: kristin.donati@wilkes.edu.
Website: http://www.wilkes.edu/academics/colleges/sidhu-school-of-business-leadership/index.aspx

William Paterson University of New Jersey, Cotsakos College of Business, Wayne, NJ 07470-8420. Offers applied business analytics (MS); business administration (MBA), including accounting, entrepreneurship, finance, general business administration, human resource management, marketing, music and entertainment management; MBA pathways (Certificate); sales leadership (MS). *Accreditation:* AACSB. *Program availability:* Part-time, evening/weekend. *Faculty:* 21 full-time (6 women), 5 part-time/adjunct (1 woman). *Students:* 78 full-time (40 women), 250 part-time (113 women); includes 161 minority (39 Black or African American, non-Hispanic/Latino; 1 American Indian or Alaska Native, non-Hispanic/Latino; 23 Asian, non-Hispanic/Latino; 82 Hispanic/Latino; 16 Two or more races, non-Hispanic/Latino), 14 international. Average

Human Resources Management

age 31. 222 applicants, 86% accepted, 136 enrolled. In 2018, 95 master's awarded. *Degree requirements:* For master's, Programs Differ see: https://academiccatalog.wpunj.edu/content.php?catoid=1&navoid=68. *Entrance requirements:* For master's, program details: https://www.wpunj.edu/admissions/graduate/admission-deadlines-and-requirements/. Additional exam requirements/recommendations for international students: Required—TOEFL (minimum score 550 paper-based; 79 iBT), IELTS (minimum score 6). *Application deadline:* For fall admission, 6/1 for domestic students, 3/1 for international students; for spring admission, 11/1 for domestic students, 10/1 for international students. Applications are processed on a rolling basis. Application fee: $50. Electronic applications accepted. *Expenses: Tuition, area resident:* Full-time $14,714; part-time $727 per credit. Tuition, state resident: full-time $14,714; part-time $727 per credit. Tuition, nonresident: full-time $22,952; part-time $727 per credit. *International tuition:* $22,952 full-time. *Required fees:* $4 per semester. Tuition and fees vary according to course load, degree level and program. *Financial support:* In 2018–19, 18 students received support. Career-related internships or fieldwork, Federal Work-Study, scholarships/grants, tuition waivers, and unspecified assistantships available. Support available to part-time students. Financial award application deadline: 3/15; financial award applicants required to submit FAFSA. *Faculty research:* Labor markets, job characteristics and ethical behavior, institutional trading of stocks and bonds, education funding, pricing strategies in business-to-business markets. *Unit head:* Dr. Siamack Shojai, Dean, 973-720-2964, Fax: 973-720-2809, E-mail: shojais@wpunj.edu. *Application contact:* Tinu Adeniran, Assistant Director, Graduate Admissions, 973-720-2764, Fax: 973-720-2035, E-mail: adenirant@wpunj.edu. *Website:* http://www.wpunj.edu/ccob

Wilmington University, College of Business, New Castle, DE 19720-6491. Offers accounting (MBA, MS); business administration (MBA, DBA); environmental stewardship (MBA); finance (MBA); health care administration (MBA, MSM); homeland security (MBA, MSM); human resource management (MSM); management information systems (MBA, MSN); marketing (MSM); marketing management (MBA); military leadership (MSM); organizational leadership (MBA, MSM); public administration (MSM). *Program availability:* Part-time, evening/weekend. *Entrance requirements:* Additional exam requirements/recommendations for international students: Required—TOEFL (minimum score 500 paper-based). Electronic applications accepted.

York University, Faculty of Graduate Studies, Faculty of Liberal Arts and Professional Studies, Program in Human Resources Management, Toronto, ON M3J 1P3, Canada. Offers MHRM, PhD. *Program availability:* Part-time. *Degree requirements:* For master's, thesis or alternative. *Entrance requirements:* Additional exam requirements/recommendations for international students: Required—TOEFL (minimum score 600 paper-based). Electronic applications accepted.

Section 9
Industrial and Manufacturing Management

This section contains a directory of institutions offering graduate work in industrial and manufacturing management. Additional information about programs listed in the directory but not augmented by an in-depth entry may be obtained by writing directly to the dean of a graduate school or chair of a department at the address given in the directory.

For programs offering related work, see also in this book *Business Administration and Management* and *Human Resources*. In another guide in this series:
Graduate Programs in the Humanities, Arts & Social Sciences

See *Public, Regional, and Industrial Affairs (Industrial* and *Labor Relations)*

CONTENTS

Program Directory

Industrial and Manufacturing Management

American InterContinental University Online, Program in Business Administration, Schaumburg, IL 60173. Offers accounting and finance (MBA); finance (MBA); healthcare management (MBA); human resource management (MBA); international business (MBA); management (MBA); marketing (MBA); operations management (MBA); organizational psychology and development (MBA); project management (MBA). *Accreditation:* ACBSP. *Program availability:* Evening/weekend, online learning. *Entrance requirements:* Additional exam requirements/recommendations for international students: Required—TOEFL (minimum score 550 paper-based). Electronic applications accepted.

Baruch College of the City University of New York, Zicklin School of Business, Department of Management, New York, NY 10010-5585. Offers entrepreneurship (MBA); management (PhD); operations management (MBA); organizational behavior/human resources management (MBA); sustainable business (MBA). PhD offered jointly with Graduate School and University Center of the City University of New York. *Program availability:* Part-time, evening/weekend. *Degree requirements:* For doctorate, comprehensive exam, thesis/dissertation. *Entrance requirements:* For master's, GMAT, 2 letters of recommendation, resume, 2 years of work experience; for doctorate, GMAT. Additional exam requirements/recommendations for international students: Required—TOEFL (minimum score 590 paper-based), TWE.

Bluffton University, Graduate Programs in Business, Bluffton, OH 45817. Offers accounting and financial management (MBA); health care management (MBA); leadership (MAOM, MBA); production and operations management (MBA); sustainability management (MBA). *Program availability:* Evening/weekend, blended/hybrid learning, videoconference. *Faculty:* 4 full-time (2 women), 5 part-time/adjunct (1 woman). *Students:* 38 full-time (22 women), 1 part-time (0 women); includes 11 minority (6 Black or African American, non-Hispanic/Latino; 3 Hispanic/Latino; 2 Two or more races, non-Hispanic/Latino). Average age 33. In 2018, 25 master's awarded. *Degree requirements:* For master's, integrated research project (for some programs). *Entrance requirements:* For master's, current resume, official transcript, bachelor's degree, minimum GPA of 3.0, personal essay. Additional exam requirements/recommendations for international students: Recommended—TOEFL (minimum score 550 paper-based). *Application deadline:* For fall admission, 7/31 priority date for domestic and international students. Applications are processed on a rolling basis. Electronic applications accepted. *Expenses:* Contact institution. *Financial support:* Unspecified assistantships and faculty/staff grants available. Financial award applicants required to submit FAFSA. *Unit head:* Dr. Melissa Green, Director of Graduate Programs in Business, 419-358-3447, E-mail: greenm@bluffton.edu. *Application contact:* Shelby Koenig, Enrollment Counselor for Graduate Program, 419-3583684, E-mail: koenigs@bluffton.edu.
Website: https://www.bluffton.edu/ags/index.aspx

California State University, East Bay, Office of Graduate Studies, College of Business and Economics, MBA Program, Option in Operations and Supply Chain Management, Hayward, CA 94542-3000. Offers MBA. *Degree requirements:* For master's, comprehensive exam or thesis. *Entrance requirements:* For master's, GMAT, minimum GPA of 2.75. Additional exam requirements/recommendations for international students: Required—TOEFL (minimum score 550 paper-based). Electronic applications accepted.

Carnegie Mellon University, Carnegie Institute of Technology and School of Design, Program in Product Development, Pittsburgh, PA 15213-3891. Offers MPD. *Entrance requirements:* For master's, GRE General Test, undergraduate degree in engineering, industrial design, or related fields, 3 letters of reference, 2 years of professional experience. Additional exam requirements/recommendations for international students: Required—TOEFL or TSE.

Carnegie Mellon University, College of Fine Arts, School of Design, Pittsburgh, PA 15213-3891. Offers design (MA, D Des, PhD); design for interaction (M Des); design theory (PhD); new product development (PhD); product development (MPD); typography and information design (PhD).

Carnegie Mellon University, Tepper School of Business, Program in Operations Management, Pittsburgh, PA 15213-3891. Offers PhD. *Degree requirements:* For doctorate, thesis/dissertation.

Case Western Reserve University, Weatherhead School of Management, Department of Operations, Cleveland, OH 44106. Offers operations and supply chain management (MSM); operations research (PhD); MBA/MSM. *Program availability:* Part-time. *Degree requirements:* For doctorate, thesis/dissertation. *Entrance requirements:* For master's, GRE General Test; for doctorate, GMAT, GRE General Test. *Expenses: Tuition:* Full-time $45,168; part-time $1939 per credit hour. *Required fees:* $36; $18 per semester. $18 per semester. *Faculty research:* Mathematical finance, mathematical programming, scheduling, stochastic optimization, environmental/energy models.

Cedarville University, Graduate Programs, Cedarville, OH 45314. Offers business administration (MBA); family nurse practitioner (MSN); global ministry (M Div); global public health nursing (MSN); healthcare administration (MBA); ministry (M Min); nurse educator (MSN); operations management (MBA); pharmacy (Pharm D). *Program availability:* Part-time, evening/weekend, 100% online, blended/hybrid learning. *Faculty:* 55 full-time (19 women), 18 part-time/adjunct (8 women). *Students:* 341 full-time (201 women), 60 part-time (41 women); includes 88 minority (51 Black or African American, non-Hispanic/Latino; 2 American Indian or Alaska Native, non-Hispanic/Latino; 22 Asian, non-Hispanic/Latino; 2 Hispanic/Latino; 11 Two or more races, non-Hispanic/Latino), 3 international. Average age 26. 354 applicants, 38% accepted, 113 enrolled. In 2018, 65 master's, 34 doctorates awarded. *Degree requirements:* For master's, portfolio; for doctorate, comprehensive exam. *Entrance requirements:* For master's, GRE, 2 professional recommendations; for doctorate, PCAT, professional recommendation from a practicing pharmacist or current employer/supervisor, resume, essay, interview. Additional exam requirements/recommendations for international students: Required—TOEFL (minimum score 550 paper-based; 80 iBT). *Application deadline:* For fall admission, 5/1 priority date for domestic and international students; for spring admission, 11/1 priority date for domestic and international students. Applications are processed on a rolling basis. Application fee: $0. Electronic applications accepted. *Expenses: Tuition:* Full-time $12,594; part-time $566 per credit. One-time fee: $100 full-time. Tuition and fees vary according to degree level and program. *Financial support:* Scholarships/grants and unspecified assistantships available. Support available to part-time students. Financial award application deadline: 1/30; financial award applicants required to submit FAFSA. *Faculty research:* Establishing competencies of clinical reasoning for nursing students in Taiwan, social determinants of health in pediatric primary care, meeting needs of palliative care populations, natural product utility in cancer, monoclonal antibodies directed at angiogenesis regulation. *Unit head:* Dr. Janice Supplee, Dean of Graduate Studies, 937-766-7700, E-mail: suppleej@cedarville.edu. *Application contact:* Alexis McKay, Director of Graduate Admissions, 937-766-7878, Fax: 937-766-7700, E-mail: amckay@cedarville.edu.
Website: https://www.cedarville.edu/Admissions/Graduate/Graduate-Programs.aspx

Central Connecticut State University, School of Graduate Studies, School of Engineering, Science and Technology, Department of Manufacturing and Construction Management, New Britain, CT 06050-4010. Offers construction management (MS, Certificate); lean manufacturing and Six Sigma (Certificate); supply chain and logistics (Certificate); technology management (MS). *Program availability:* Part-time, evening/weekend. *Faculty:* 6 full-time (0 women), 2 part-time/adjunct (0 women). *Students:* 14 full-time (7 women), 82 part-time (18 women); includes 28 minority (11 Black or African American, non-Hispanic/Latino; 2 Asian, non-Hispanic/Latino; 12 Hispanic/Latino; 3 Two or more races, non-Hispanic/Latino), 6 international. Average age 32. 70 applicants, 71% accepted, 29 enrolled. In 2018, 51 master's, 5 other advanced degrees awarded. *Degree requirements:* For master's, comprehensive exam, special project; for Certificate, qualifying exam. *Entrance requirements:* For master's, minimum undergraduate GPA of 2.7. Additional exam requirements/recommendations for international students: Required—TOEFL (minimum score 550 paper-based; 79 iBT); Recommended—IELTS (minimum score 6.5). *Application deadline:* For fall admission, 8/1 for domestic students, 5/1 for international students; for spring admission, 12/1 for domestic students, 11/1 for international students; for summer admission, 5/1 for domestic students. Applications are processed on a rolling basis. Application fee: $50. Electronic applications accepted. *Expenses: Tuition, area resident:* Full-time $7027; part-time $388 per credit. Tuition, state resident: full-time $9750; part-time $388 per credit. Tuition, nonresident: full-time $18,102; part-time $388 per credit. *International tuition:* $18,102 full-time. *Required fees:* $266 per semester. *Financial support:* In 2018–19, 7 students received support. Career-related internships or fieldwork, Federal Work-Study, scholarships/grants, and unspecified assistantships available. Support available to part-time students. Financial award application deadline: 3/1; financial award applicants required to submit FAFSA. *Faculty research:* All aspects of middle management, technical supervision in the workplace. *Unit head:* Dr. Ravindra Thamma, Chair, 860-832-1830, E-mail: thammarav@ccsu.edu. *Application contact:* Patricia Gardner, Associate Director of Graduate Studies, 860-832-2350, Fax: 860-832-2362.
Website: http://www.ccsu.edu/mcm/

Central Michigan University, College of Graduate Studies, College of Science and Engineering, School of Engineering and Technology, Mount Pleasant, MI 48859. Offers industrial management and technology (MA). *Program availability:* Part-time. *Degree requirements:* For master's, thesis or alternative. Electronic applications accepted. *Faculty research:* Computer applications, manufacturing process control, mechanical engineering automation, industrial technology.

Colorado Technical University Aurora, Programs in Business Administration and Management, Aurora, CO 80014. Offers accounting (MBA); business administration (MBA); business administration and management (EMBA); finance (MBA); human resource management (MBA); marketing (MBA); mediation and dispute resolution (MBA); operations management (MBA); project management (MBA); technology management (MBA). *Program availability:* Part-time, evening/weekend. *Degree requirements:* For master's, thesis or alternative. *Entrance requirements:* For master's, minimum undergraduate GPA of 3.0, resume.

Colorado Technical University Colorado Springs, Graduate Studies, Program in Management, Colorado Springs, CO 80907. Offers accounting (MBA, MSA); business administration (MBA); finance (MBA); human resources management (MBA); logistics/supply chain management (MBA); management (DM); marketing (MBA); mediation and dispute resolution (MBA); operations management (MBA); project management (MBA); technology management (MBA). *Accreditation:* ACBSP. *Program availability:* Part-time, evening/weekend, online learning. *Degree requirements:* For master's, thesis or alternative; for doctorate, thesis/dissertation. *Entrance requirements:* For doctorate, minimum graduate GPA of 3.0, 5 years of related work experience. *Faculty research:* Sexual harassment, performance evaluation, critical thinking.

Duke University, The Fuqua School of Business, The Duke MBA-Daytime Program, Durham, NC 27708. Offers academic excellence in finance (Certificate); business administration (MBA); decision sciences (MBA); energy and environment (MBA); energy finance (MBA); entrepreneurship and innovation (MBA); finance (MBA); financial analysis (MBA); health sector management (Certificate); leadership and ethics (MBA); management (MBA); management science and technology management (Certificate); marketing (MBA); operations management (MBA); social entrepreneurship (MBA); strategy (MBA). *Faculty:* 100 full-time (21 women), 55 part-time/adjunct (12 women). *Students:* 875 full-time (335 women); includes 188 minority (44 Black or African American, non-Hispanic/Latino; 4 American Indian or Alaska Native, non-Hispanic/Latino; 90 Asian, non-Hispanic/Latino; 43 Hispanic/Latino; 1 Native Hawaiian or other Pacific Islander, non-Hispanic/Latino; 6 Two or more races, non-Hispanic/Latino), 276 international. Average age 29. In 2018, 429 master's awarded. *Entrance requirements:* For master's, GMAT or GRE, transcripts, essays, resume, recommendation letters, interview. *Application deadline:* For fall admission, 9/19 for domestic and international students; for winter admission, 10/14 for domestic and international students; for spring admission, 1/6 for domestic and international students; for summer admission, 3/11 for domestic and international students. Application fee: $225. Electronic applications accepted. *Expenses:* Contact institution. *Financial support:* Scholarships/grants available. Financial award applicants required to submit FAFSA. *Unit head:* Steve Misuraca, Assistant Dean, Daytime MBA Program. *Application contact:* Shari Hubert, Associate Dean, Office of Admissions, 919-660-7705, Fax: 919-681-8026, E-mail: admissions-info@fuqua.duke.edu.
Website: https://www.fuqua.duke.edu/programs/daytime-mba

Duke University, The Fuqua School of Business, PhD Program, Durham, NC 27708. Offers accounting (PhD); decision sciences (PhD); finance (PhD); management and organizations (PhD); marketing (PhD); operations management (PhD); strategy (PhD). *Faculty:* 100 full-time (21 women). *Students:* 84 full-time (29 women); includes 4 minority (2 Asian, non-Hispanic/Latino; 2 Hispanic/Latino), 53 international. Average age 28. In 2018, 14 doctorates awarded. *Degree requirements:* For doctorate, comprehensive exam (for some programs), thesis/dissertation, Comprehensive or Qualifying exams are required for some of the 7 areas in Business Administration. *Entrance requirements:* For doctorate, GMAT or GRE, transcripts, essays, recommendation letters, statement of purpose. Additional exam requirements/recommendations for international students: Required—TOEFL, IELTS. *Application deadline:* For fall admission, 12/31 priority date for domestic and international students. Application fee: $90. Electronic applications accepted. *Expenses:* Contact institution. *Financial support:* In 2018–19, 74 fellowships with full tuition reimbursements (averaging $33,300 per year) were awarded; research assistantships with full tuition reimbursements, teaching assistantships, institutionally sponsored loans, scholarships/grants, health care benefits, and tuition waivers (full) also

available. *Unit head:* William Boulding, Dean, 919-660-7822. *Application contact:* Ravi Bansal, Director of Graduate Studies, 919-660-7753, Fax: 919-660-7971, E-mail: fuqua-phd-info@duke.edu.

East Carolina University, Graduate School, College of Engineering and Technology, Department of Technology Systems, Greenville, NC 27858-4353. Offers computer network professional (Certificate); cyber security professional (Certificate); information assurance (Certificate); Lean Six Sigma Black Belt (Certificate); network technology (MS), including computer networking management, digital communications technology, information security, Web technologies; occupational safety (MS); technology management (MS, PhD), including industrial distribution and logistics (MS); Website developer (Certificate). *Application deadline:* For fall admission, 6/1 priority date for domestic students. *Expenses: Tuition, area resident:* Full-time $4749. Tuition, state resident: full-time $4749. Tuition, nonresident: full-time $17,898. *International tuition:* $17,898 full-time. *Required fees:* $2787. Part-time tuition and fees vary according to course load and program. *Financial support:* Application deadline: 6/1. *Unit head:* Dr. Tijjani Mohammed, Chair, 252-328-9668, E-mail: mohammedt@ecu.edu. *Application contact:* Graduate School Admissions, 252-328-6012, Fax: 252-328-6071, E-mail: gradschool@ecu.edu.
Website: http://www.ecu.edu/cs-cet/techsystems/index.cfm

Emory University, Goizueta Business School, Full Time MBA Program, Atlanta, GA 30322-1100. Offers accounting (MBA); alternative investments (MBA); business process consulting (MBA); business technology management (MBA); capital markets (MBA); corporate finance (MBA); customer relationship management (MBA); decision analytics (MBA); entrepreneurship (MBA); finance (MBA); global management (MBA); investment banking (MBA); management consulting (MBA); marketing (MBA); marketing analytics (MBA); marketing consulting (MBA); operations management (MBA); organization and management (MBA); product and brand management (MBA); real estate (MBA); social enterprise (MBA); strategy consulting (MBA). *Accreditation:* AACSB. *Faculty:* 74 full-time (18 women), 18 part-time/adjunct (6 women). *Students:* 349 full-time (105 women); includes 81 minority (26 Black or African American, non-Hispanic/Latino; 1 American Indian or Alaska Native, non-Hispanic/Latino; 35 Asian, non-Hispanic/Latino; 16 Hispanic/Latino; 3 Two or more races, non-Hispanic/Latino), 97 international. Average age 29. 1,380 applicants, 34% accepted, 172 enrolled. In 2018, 180 master's awarded. *Degree requirements:* For master's, 1 leadership course; 2 mid-semester module programs; 2 global components. *Entrance requirements:* For master's, GMAT/GRE, essays; recommendation letters; undergraduate degree; interview. Additional exam requirements/recommendations for international students: Required—TOEFL (minimum score 100 iBT), IELTS (minimum score 7), PTE (minimum score 68). *Application deadline:* For fall admission, 10/6 for domestic and international students; for winter admission, 11/17 for domestic and international students; for spring admission, 1/3 priority date for domestic and international students; for summer admission, 3/9 for domestic and international students. Application fee: $150. Electronic applications accepted. *Expenses:* Contact institution. *Financial support:* In 2018–19, 273 students received support. Career-related internships or fieldwork, institutionally sponsored loans, and scholarships/grants available. Financial award application deadline: 4/1; financial award applicants required to submit FAFSA. *Faculty research:* Corporate finance, information systems, digital marketing, asset pricing, sports management. *Unit head:* Brian Mitchell, Associate Dean, 404-727-4824, Fax: 404-712-9648, E-mail: brian.mitchell@emory.edu. *Application contact:* Melissa Rapp, Associate Dean, 404-727-7583, Fax: 404-727-4612, E-mail: mbaadmissions@emory.edu.
Website: http://www.goizueta.emory.edu

Everglades University, Graduate Programs, Program in Aviation Science, Boca Raton, FL 33431. Offers aviation operations management (MSA); aviation security (MSA); business administration (MSA). *Program availability:* Part-time, evening/weekend, 100% online. *Entrance requirements:* For master's, GMAT (minimum score of 400) or GRE (minimum score of 290), bachelor's or graduate degree from college accredited by an agency recognized by the U.S. Department of Education; minimum cumulative GPA of 2.0 at the baccalaureate level, 3.0 at the master's level. Additional exam requirements/recommendations for international students: Recommended—TOEFL (minimum score 500 paper-based). Electronic applications accepted. *Expenses:* Contact institution.

Georgetown University, Graduate School of Arts and Sciences, Department of Economics, Washington, DC 20057. Offers econometrics (PhD); economic development (PhD); economic theory (PhD); industrial organization (PhD); international macro and finance (PhD); international trade (PhD); labor economics (PhD); macroeconomics (PhD); public economics and political economy (PhD); MA/PhD; MS/MA. *Degree requirements:* For doctorate, comprehensive exam, thesis/dissertation. *Entrance requirements:* For doctorate, GRE General Test. Additional exam requirements/recommendations for international students: Required—TOEFL. *Faculty research:* International economics, economic development.

Harvard University, Harvard Business School, Doctoral Programs in Management, Boston, MA 02163. Offers accounting and management (DBA); business economics (PhD); health policy management (PhD); management (DBA); marketing (DBA); organizational behavior (PhD); science, technology and management (PhD); strategy (DBA); technology and operations management (DBA). *Degree requirements:* For doctorate, comprehensive exam (for some programs), thesis/dissertation. *Entrance requirements:* For doctorate, GRE General Test or GMAT. Additional exam requirements/recommendations for international students: Required—TOEFL.

HEC Montreal, School of Business Administration, Master of Science Programs in Administration, Program in Operations Management, Montréal, QC H3T 2A7, Canada. Offers M Sc. Program offered in French (Thesis Stream, Supervised project Stream). *Students:* 27 full-time (14 women), 5 part-time (1 woman). 40 applicants, 65% accepted, 18 enrolled. In 2018, 9 master's awarded. *Entrance requirements:* For master's, BBA, undergraduate degree in another field, degree deemed equivalent by program director and minimum GPA of 3.0 on 4.3 scale. Additional exam requirements/recommendations for international students: Required—TAGE MAGE (minimum recommended score of 300), GMAT (minimum recommended score of 630), or GRE. *Application deadline:* For fall admission, 3/15 for domestic and international students; for winter admission, 9/15 for domestic and international students. Application fee: $91 Canadian dollars ($191 Canadian dollars for international students). Electronic applications accepted. *Expenses: Tuition, area resident:* Full-time $3052.80 Canadian dollars; part-time $84.80 Canadian dollars per credit. Tuition, state resident: full-time $3816 Canadian dollars; part-time $264.67 Canadian dollars per credit. Tuition, nonresident: full-time $11,910 Canadian dollars. *International tuition:* $20,905.20 Canadian dollars full-time. *Required fees:* $1805.34 Canadian dollars; $43.62 Canadian dollars per credit. $71.78 Canadian dollars per term. Tuition and fees vary according to degree level and program. *Financial support:* Research assistantships, teaching assistantships, and scholarships/grants available. Financial award application deadline: 9/2. *Unit head:* Dr. Sihem Taboubi, Director, 514-340-6428, E-mail: sihem.taboubi@hec.ca. *Application contact:* Marianne de Moura, Administrative Director, 514-340-6000, Fax: 514-340-6411, E-mail: aide@hec.ca.
Website: http://www.hec.ca/programmes/maitrises/maitrise-gestion-operations/index.html

Illinois Institute of Technology, Graduate College, School of Applied Technology, Department of Industrial Technology and Management, Wheaton, IL 60819. Offers MAS. *Program availability:* Part-time, evening/weekend, online learning. *Entrance requirements:* For master's, GRE (minimum score 900 verbal and quantitative; 2.5 analytical writing), bachelor's degree with minimum cumulative undergraduate GPA of 3.0 (or its equivalent) from accredited institution. Additional exam requirements/recommendations for international students: Required—TOEFL (minimum score 523 paper-based; 70 iBT); Recommended—IELTS (minimum score 5.5). Electronic applications accepted. *Faculty research:* Industrial logistics, industrial facilities, manufacturing technology, entrepreneurship, energy options.

Instituto Tecnologico de Santo Domingo, Graduate School, Area of Engineering, Santo Domingo, Dominican Republic. Offers construction administration (MS, Certificate); data telecommunications (M Eng, MS, Certificate); industrial engineering (M Eng, Certificate); industrial management (M Mgmt); information technology (Certificate); maintenance engineering (M Eng); occupational hazard prevention (M Mgmt); production management (Certificate); quantitative methods (Certificate); sanitary and environmental engineering (M Eng); structural engineering (M Eng); systems engineering and electronic data processing (Certificate); transportation (Certificate).

Instituto Tecnológico y de Estudios Superiores de Monterrey, Campus Estado de México, Professional and Graduate Division, Estado de Mexico, Mexico. Offers administration of information technologies (MITA); architecture (M Arch); business administration (GMBA, MBA); computer sciences (MCS, PhD); education (M Ed); educational institution administration (MAD); educational technology and innovation (PhD); electronic commerce (MEC); environmental systems (MS); finance (MAF); humanistic studies (MHS); information sciences and knowledge management (MISKM); information systems (MS); manufacturing systems (MS); marketing (MEM); quality systems and productivity (MS); science and materials engineering (PhD); telecommunications management (MTM). *Program availability:* Part-time, online learning. *Degree requirements:* For master's, one foreign language, thesis (for some programs); for doctorate, one foreign language, thesis/dissertation. *Entrance requirements:* For master's, E-PAEP 500, interview; for doctorate, E-PAEP 500, research proposal. Additional exam requirements/recommendations for international students: Required—TOEFL (minimum score 550 paper-based). *Faculty research:* Surface treatments by plasmas, mechanical properties, robotics, graphical computing, mechatronics security protocols.

Instituto Tecnológico y de Estudios Superiores de Monterrey, Campus Irapuato, Graduate Programs, Irapuato, Mexico. Offers administration (MBA); administration of information technology (MAIT); administration of telecommunications (MAT); architecture (M Arch); computer science (MCS); education (M Ed); educational administration (MEA); educational innovation and technology (DEIT); educational technology (MET); electronic commerce (MBA); environmental administration and planning (MEAP); environmental systems (MES); finances (MBA); humanistic studies (MHS); international management for Latin American executives (MIMLAE); library and information science (MLIS); manufacturing quality management (MMQM); marketing research (MBA).

Inter American University of Puerto Rico, Metropolitan Campus, Graduate Programs, Program in Industrial Management, San Juan, PR 00919-1293. Offers MBA. *Degree requirements:* For master's, comprehensive exam. *Entrance requirements:* For master's, GRE or EXADEP, interview. Electronic applications accepted.

Inter American University of Puerto Rico, San Germán Campus, Graduate Studies Center, Program in Business Administration, San Germán, PR 00683-5008. Offers accounting (MBA); finance (MBA); general business administration (MBA); human resources (MBA, PhD); industrial relations (MBA); information systems (MBA); international and interregional business (PhD); management (MBA); marketing (MBA). *Program availability:* Part-time, evening/weekend. *Degree requirements:* For master's, comprehensive exam. *Entrance requirements:* For master's, GRE General Test or EXADEP, minimum GPA of 3.0. *Expenses: Tuition:* Full-time $212; part-time $212 per credit. *Required fees:* $366 per semester. One-time fee: $31. Tuition and fees vary according to degree level and program.

Lawrence Technological University, College of Engineering, Southfield, MI 48075-1058. Offers architectural engineering (MS); automotive engineering (MS); biomedical engineering (MS); civil engineering (MA, MS, PhD), including environmental engineering (MS), geotechnical engineering (MS), structural engineering (MS), transportation engineering (MS), water resource engineering (MS); construction engineering management (MA); electrical and computer engineering (MS); engineering management (MEM); engineering technology (MS); fire engineering (MS); industrial engineering (MS), including healthcare systems; manufacturing systems (ME); mechanical engineering (MS, DE, PhD), including automotive engineering (MS), energy engineering (MS), manufacturing (DE), solid mechanics (MS), thermal/fluid systems (MS); mechatronic systems engineering (MS). *Program availability:* Part-time, evening/weekend. Terminal master's awarded for partial completion of doctoral program. *Degree requirements:* For master's, thesis optional; for doctorate, comprehensive exam, thesis/dissertation optional. *Entrance requirements:* Additional exam requirements/recommendations for international students: Required—TOEFL (minimum score 550 paper-based; 79 iBT), IELTS (minimum score 6.5). Electronic applications accepted. *Faculty research:* Innovative infrastructure and building structures and materials; connectivity and mobility; automotive systems modeling, simulation and testing; biomedical devices and materials; building mechanical/electrical systems.

Marquette University, Graduate School of Management, Executive MBA Program, Milwaukee, WI 53201-1881. Offers economics (MBA); finance (MBA); human resources (MBA); international business (MBA); management information systems (MBA); marketing (MBA); operations and supply chain management (MBA); sports business (MBA). *Accreditation:* AACSB. *Degree requirements:* For master's, international trip. *Entrance requirements:* For master's, GMAT or GRE, two letters of recommendation, official transcripts from current and previous colleges/universities. Additional exam requirements/recommendations for international students: Required—TOEFL (minimum score 550 paper-based; 88 iBT), IELTS (minimum score 6.5), PTE. Electronic applications accepted. *Expenses:* Contact institution. *Faculty research:* International trade and finance, customer relationship management, consumer satisfaction, customer service.

Marquette University, Graduate School of Management, Program in Business Administration, Milwaukee, WI 53201-1881. Offers business administration (MBA); economics (MBA); entrepreneurship (Certificate); finance (MBA); human resources (MBA); international business (MBA); management information systems (MBA); marketing (MBA); operations and supply chain management (MBA); sports business (MBA); JD/MBA; MBA/MA; MBA/MSN. *Accreditation:* AACSB. *Program availability:* Part-time, evening/weekend. *Degree requirements:* For Certificate, business plan. *Entrance requirements:* For master's, GMAT or GRE, letters of recommendation. Additional exam requirements/recommendations for international students: Required—TOEFL (minimum score 550 paper-based; 88 iBT), IELTS (minimum score 6.5), PTE. Electronic applications accepted. *Faculty research:* Ethics in the professions, services marketing, technology impact on decision-making, mentoring.

Industrial and Manufacturing Management

McGill University, Faculty of Graduate and Postdoctoral Studies, Desautels Faculty of Management, Montréal, QC H3A 2T5, Canada. Offers administration (PhD); entrepreneurial studies (MBA); finance (MBA); general management (Post Master's Certificate); global manufacturing and supply chain management (MMM); information systems (MBA); international business (MBA); international practicing management (MM); management (MBA); management for development (MBA); marketing (MBA); operations management (MBA); public accountancy (Diploma); strategic management (MBA); MBA/LL B; MD/MBA. MMM offered jointly with Faculty of Engineering; PhD with Concordia University, HEC Montreal, Université de Montréal, Université du Québec à Montréal.

McGill University, Faculty of Graduate and Postdoctoral Studies, Faculty of Engineering, Department of Mechanical Engineering, Montréal, QC H3A 2T5, Canada. Offers aerospace (M Eng); manufacturing management (MMM); mechanical engineering (M Eng, M Sc, PhD).

Milligan College, Area of Business Administration, Milligan College, TN 37682. Offers health sector management (MBA, Graduate Certificate); leadership (MBA, Graduate Certificate); operations management (MBA, Graduate Certificate). *Program availability:* Blended/hybrid learning. *Faculty:* 3 full-time (0 women), 5 part-time/adjunct (1 woman). *Students:* 50 full-time (17 women), 1 part-time (0 women); includes 3 minority (1 Black or African American, non-Hispanic/Latino; 1 Asian, non-Hispanic/Latino; 1 Two or more races, non-Hispanic/Latino), 2 international. Average age 36. 42 applicants, 93% accepted, 35 enrolled. In 2018, 29 master's awarded. *Degree requirements:* For master's, thesis or alternative. *Entrance requirements:* For master's, GMAT if undergraduate GPA less than 3.0, undergraduate degree and supporting transcripts, relevant full-time work experience, essay/personal statement, professional recommendations. Additional exam requirements/recommendations for international students: Required—TOEFL (minimum score 550 paper-based, 79 iBT) or IELTS (6.5). *Application deadline:* For fall admission, 8/1 for domestic students, 6/1 for international students; for spring admission, 1/15 for domestic students, 12/1 for international students. Applications are processed on a rolling basis. Application fee: $30. Electronic applications accepted. *Expenses:* Contact institution. *Financial support:* Scholarships/grants available. Financial award application deadline: 12/1; financial award applicants required to submit FAFSA. *Faculty research:* International microfinance; economic development in Appalachia; job satisfaction; business ethics; internal migration. *Unit head:* Dr. David Campbell, Area Chair of Business, 423-461-8674, Fax: 423-461-8677, E-mail: dacampbell@milligan.edu. *Application contact:* Rebecca Banton, Graduate Admissions Recruiter, Business Area, 423-461-8662, Fax: 423-461-8789, E-mail: rbbanton@milligan.edu.
Website: http://www.milligan.edu/GPS

Milwaukee School of Engineering, MS Program in New Product Management, Milwaukee, WI 53202-3109. Offers MS. *Program availability:* Part-time, evening/weekend. *Degree requirements:* For master's, thesis or alternative, thesis defense or capstone project. *Entrance requirements:* For master's, GRE General Test or GMAT if undergraduate GPA less than 2.8, 2 letters of recommendation; bachelor's degree from accredited university; work experience (strongly recommended). Additional exam requirements/recommendations for international students: Required—TOEFL (minimum score 90 iBT), IELTS (minimum score 7). Electronic applications accepted. *Faculty research:* New product development, product research and design, product development.

Mississippi State University, Bagley College of Engineering, Department of Industrial and Systems Engineering, Mississippi State, MS 39762. Offers human factors and ergonomics (MS); industrial and systems engineering (PhD); industrial systems (MS); management systems (MS); manufacturing systems (MS); operations research (MS). *Program availability:* Part-time, blended/hybrid learning. *Faculty:* 12 full-time (2 women). *Students:* 35 full-time (13 women), 66 part-time (16 women); includes 20 minority (7 Black or African American, non-Hispanic/Latino; 6 Asian, non-Hispanic/Latino; 5 Hispanic/Latino; 1 Native Hawaiian or other Pacific Islander, non-Hispanic/Latino; 1 Two or more races, non-Hispanic/Latino), 21 international. Average age 36. 67 applicants, 40% accepted, 18 enrolled. In 2018, 16 master's, 9 doctorates awarded. *Degree requirements:* For master's, comprehensive exam (for some programs), thesis optional, comprehensive oral or written exam; for doctorate, comprehensive exam, thesis/dissertation, candidacy exam. *Entrance requirements:* For master's, GRE (for graduates from program not accredited by EAC/ABET), minimum GPA of 3.0 on junior and senior years; for doctorate, GRE (for graduates from program not accredited by EAC/ABET), minimum GPA of 3.5 on master's degree and junior and senior years of BS. Additional exam requirements/recommendations for international students: Required—TOEFL (minimum score 550 paper-based; 79 iBT); Recommended—IELTS (minimum score 6.5). *Application deadline:* For fall admission, 7/1 for domestic students, 5/1 for international students; for spring admission, 11/1 for domestic students, 9/1 for international students. Applications are processed on a rolling basis. Application fee: $60 ($80 for international students). Electronic applications accepted. *Expenses:* Tuition, state resident: full-time $8450; part-time $360.59 per credit hour. Tuition, nonresident: full-time $23,140; part-time $969.09 per credit hour. *Required fees:* $110. One-time fee: $55 full-time. Part-time tuition and fees vary according to course load, degree level, campus/location and reciprocity agreements. *Financial support:* In 2018–19, 18 research assistantships with full tuition reimbursements (averaging $16,905 per year), 3 teaching assistantships with full tuition reimbursements (averaging $16,033 per year) were awarded; Federal Work-Study, institutionally sponsored loans, and unspecified assistantships also available. Financial award application deadline: 4/1; financial award applicants required to submit FAFSA. *Faculty research:* Operations research, ergonomics, production systems, management systems, transportation. *Total annual research expenditures:* $2 million. *Unit head:* Dr. Kari Babski-Reeves, Professor/Interim Head and Associate Dean for Research & Graduate Studies, 662-325-8430, Fax: 662-325-7618, E-mail: kari@ise.msstate.edu. *Application contact:* Ryan King, Admissions and Enrollment Assistant, 662-325-8951, E-mail: rjk101@grad.msstate.edu.
Website: http://www.ise.msstate.edu/

Northern Illinois University, Graduate School, College of Engineering and Engineering Technology, Department of Technology, De Kalb, IL 60115-2854. Offers industrial management (MS). *Program availability:* Part-time, evening/weekend. *Faculty:* 14 full-time (1 woman), 1 part-time/adjunct (0 women). *Students:* 1 full-time (0 women), 18 part-time (3 women); includes 5 minority (3 Black or African American, non-Hispanic/Latino; 1 Asian, non-Hispanic/Latino; 1 Two or more races, non-Hispanic/Latino). Average age 36. 1 applicant, 100% accepted, 1 enrolled. In 2018, 10 master's awarded. *Degree requirements:* For master's, thesis optional. *Entrance requirements:* For master's, GRE General Test, minimum GPA of 2.75. Additional exam requirements/recommendations for international students: Required—TOEFL (minimum score 550 paper-based). *Application deadline:* For fall admission, 6/1 for domestic students, 5/1 for international students; for spring admission, 11/1 for domestic students, 10/1 for international students. Applications are processed on a rolling basis. Application fee: $40. Electronic applications accepted. *Financial support:* In 2018–19, 3 research assistantships with full tuition reimbursements, 14 teaching assistantships with full tuition reimbursements were awarded; fellowships with full tuition reimbursements, career-related internships or fieldwork, Federal Work-Study, scholarships/grants, tuition waivers (full), and unspecified assistantships also available. Support available to part-time students. Financial award applicants required to submit FAFSA. *Faculty research:* Digital control, intelligent systems, engineering graphic design, occupational safety, ergonomics. *Unit head:* Dr. Abul Azad, Acting Associate Dean, 815-753-1349, Fax: 815-753-3702, E-mail: aazad@niu.edu. *Application contact:* Graduate School Office, 815-753-0395, E-mail: gradsch@niu.edu.
Website: http://www.niu.edu/tech/

Northwestern University, The Graduate School, Kellogg School of Management, Management Programs, Evanston, IL 60208. Offers accounting information and management (MBA, PhD); analytical finance (MBA); business administration (MBA); decision sciences (MBA); entrepreneurship and innovation (MBA); finance (MBA, PhD); health enterprise management (MBA); human resources management (MBA); international business (MBA); management and organizations (MBA, PhD); management and organizations and sociology (PhD); management and strategy (MBA); management studies (MS); managerial analytics (MBA); managerial economics (MBA); managerial economics and strategy (PhD); marketing (MBA, PhD); marketing management (MBA); media management (MBA); operations management (MBA, PhD); real estate (MBA); social enterprise at Kellogg (MBA); JD/MBA. *Program availability:* Part-time, evening/weekend. Terminal master's awarded for partial completion of doctoral program. *Degree requirements:* For doctorate, thesis/dissertation, 2 years of coursework, qualifying (field) exam and candidacy, summer research papers and presentations to faculty, proposal defense, final exam/defense. *Entrance requirements:* For master's, GMAT, GRE, interview, 2 letters of recommendation, college transcripts, resume, essays, Kellogg honor code; for doctorate, GMAT, GRE, statement of purpose, transcripts, 2 letters of recommendation, resume, interview. Additional exam requirements/recommendations for international students: Required—TOEFL, IELTS. Electronic applications accepted. *Expenses:* Contact institution. *Faculty research:* Business cycles and international finance, health policy, networks, non-market strategy, consumer psychology.

Oakland University, Graduate Study and Lifelong Learning, School of Business Administration, Department of Decision and Information Sciences, Rochester, MI 48309-4401. Offers information technology management (MS); management information systems (Certificate); production and operations management (Certificate).

Penn State Erie, The Behrend College, Graduate School, Erie, PA 16563. Offers accounting (MPAC); applied clinical psychology (MA); business administration (MBA); quality and manufacturing management (MMM). *Accreditation:* AACSB. *Program availability:* Part-time. *Entrance requirements:* Additional exam requirements/recommendations for international students: Required—TOEFL (minimum score 550 paper-based; 80 iBT), IELTS. Electronic applications accepted.

Polytechnic University of Puerto Rico, Graduate School, Hato Rey, PR 00918. Offers business administration (MBA), including computer information systems, general management, management of information systems, management of international enterprises; civil engineering (ME, MS); computer engineering (ME, MS); computer science (MCS, MS); electrical engineering (ME, MS); engineering management (MEM); environmental management (MEM); landscape architecture (M Land Arch); manufacturing competitiveness (MMC, MS); manufacturing engineering (ME, MS); mechanical engineering (M Mech E). *Accreditation:* ASLA. *Program availability:* Part-time, evening/weekend. *Entrance requirements:* For master's, 3 letters of recommendation.

Polytechnic University of Puerto Rico, Miami Campus, Graduate School, Miami, FL 33166. Offers accounting (MBA); business administration (MBA); construction management (MEM); environmental management (MEM); finance (MBA); human resources management (MBA); logistics and supply chain management (MBA); management of international enterprises (MBA); manufacturing management (MEM); marketing management (MBA); project management (MBA). *Program availability:* Part-time, evening/weekend, online learning. *Entrance requirements:* For master's, minimum GPA of 3.0. Electronic applications accepted.

Polytechnic University of Puerto Rico, Orlando Campus, Graduate School, Orlando, FL 32825. Offers accounting (MBA); business administration (MBA); construction management (MEM); engineering management (MEM); environmental management (MEM); finance (MBA); human resources management (MBA); management of international enterprises (MBA); management of technology (MBA); manufacturing management (MEM). *Program availability:* Part-time, evening/weekend, online learning. *Entrance requirements:* For master's, minimum GPA of 3.0. Additional exam requirements/recommendations for international students: Recommended—TOEFL. Electronic applications accepted.

Regis University, College of Business and Economics, Denver, CO 80221-1099. Offers accounting (MS); executive leadership (Certificate); finance (MS); finance and accounting (MBA); health industry leadership (MBA); human resource management and leadership (MSOL); management (MBA); marketing (MBA); nonprofit leadership (Post-Graduate Certificate); nonprofit management (MNM); nonprofit organizational capacity building (Certificate); operations management (MBA); organizational leadership and management (MSOL); project leadership and management (MS, MSOL); strategic business management (Certificate); strategic human resource integration (Certificate); strategic management (MBA). Programs offered at Colorado Springs Campus, Northwest Denver Campus, Southeast Denver Campus, Fort Collins Campus, Broomfield Campus, Henderson (Nevada) Campus, and Summerlin (Nevada) Campus. *Program availability:* Part-time, evening/weekend, 100% online, blended/hybrid learning. *Degree requirements:* For master's, thesis (for some programs), capstone or final research project. *Entrance requirements:* For master's, official transcript reflecting baccalaureate degree awarded from regionally-accredited college or university, interview, 2 years of full-time related work experience, resume, letters of recommendation. Additional exam requirements/recommendations for international students: Required—TOEFL (minimum score 550 paper-based; 82 iBT). Electronic applications accepted. *Expenses:* Contact institution. *Faculty research:* Impact of information technology on small business regulation of accounting, international project financing, mineral development, delivery of healthcare to rural indigenous communities.

Rochester Institute of Technology, Graduate Enrollment Services, Kate Gleason College of Engineering, Design, Development and Manufacturing Department, MS Program in Manufacturing Leadership, Rochester, NY 14623-5603. Offers MS. *Program availability:* Part-time, evening/weekend, 100% online. *Students:* 19 part-time (3 women); includes 1 minority (Hispanic/Latino). Average age 34. 8 applicants, 88% accepted, 6 enrolled. In 2018, 2 master's awarded. *Degree requirements:* For master's, capstone. *Entrance requirements:* For master's, GRE is not required, though it will be considered if it is submitted., minimum GPA of 3.0 (recommended), at least two years of experience in a manufacturing-related organization or business environment, resume, one letter of recommendation. Additional exam requirements/recommendations for international students: Required—TOEFL (minimum score 550 paper-based; 79 iBT), IELTS (minimum score 6.5), PTE (minimum score 58). *Application deadline:* Applications are processed on a rolling basis. Application fee: $65. Electronic applications accepted. *Expenses:* Contact institution. *Financial support:* In 2018–19, 1 student received support. Scholarships/grants available. Support available to part-time

students. Financial award applicants required to submit FAFSA. *Faculty research:* Lean manufacturing, Lean Six Sigma, modeling and simulation, supply chain management, project management. *Unit head:* Christine Fisher, Program Coordinator, 585-475-7971, Fax: 585-475-4080, E-mail: christine.fisher@rit.edu. *Application contact:* Diane Ellison, Senior Associate Vice President, Graduate Enrollment Services, 585-475-2229, Fax: 585-475-7164, E-mail: gradinfo@rit.edu.
Website: https://www.rit.edu/study/manufacturing-leadership-ms

San Francisco State University, Division of Graduate Studies, College of Business, Program in Business Administration, San Francisco, CA 94132-1722. Offers decision sciences/operations research (MBA); ethics and compliance (MBA); finance (MBA); global business and innovation (MBA); healthcare administration (MBA); hospitality and tourism management (MBA); information systems (MBA); leadership (MBA); marketing (MBA); nonprofit and social enterprise leadership (MBA); sustainable business (MBA). *Accreditation:* AACSB. *Program availability:* Part-time, evening/weekend. *Degree requirements:* For master's, thesis, essay test. *Entrance requirements:* For master's, GMAT, minimum GPA of 2.7 in last 60 units. Additional exam requirements/recommendations for international students: Required—TOEFL (minimum score 550 paper-based).

Southern New Hampshire University, School of Business, Manchester, NH 03106-1045. Offers accounting (MBA, Graduate Certificate); accounting finance (MS); accounting/auditing (MS); accounting/forensic accounting (MS); accounting/management accounting (MS); accounting/taxation (MS); applied economics (MS); athletic administration (MBA, Graduate Certificate); business administration (IMBA, Certificate), including business information systems (Certificate), human resource management (Certificate); business analytics (MBA); business intelligence (MBA); communication (MA), including new media and marketing, public relations; community economic development (MBA); criminal justice (MBA); data analytics (MS); economics (MBA); engineering management (MBA); entrepreneurship (MBA); finance (MBA, MS, Graduate Certificate); finance/corporate finance (MS); finance/investments (MS); forensic accounting (MBA); forensic accounting and fraud examination (Graduate Certificate); healthcare informatics (MBA); healthcare management (MBA); human resource management (MS); human resources (MBA); information technology (MS); information technology management (MBA); international business (PhD); Internet marketing (MBA); leadership (MBA); leadership of nonprofit organizations (Graduate Certificate); management (MS); marketing (MBA, MS, Graduate Certificate); music business (MBA); operations and project management (MS); operations and supply chain management (MBA, Graduate Certificate); organizational leadership (MS); project management (MBA, Graduate Certificate); public administration (MBA, Graduate Certificate); quantitative analysis (MBA); Six Sigma (Graduate Certificate); Six Sigma quality (MBA); social media marketing (MBA, Graduate Certificate); sport management (MBA, MS, Graduate Certificate); sustainability and environmental compliance (MBA); MBA/Certificate. *Accreditation:* ACBSP. *Program availability:* Part-time, evening/weekend, online learning. Terminal master's awarded for partial completion of doctoral program. *Degree requirements:* For master's, one foreign language, comprehensive exam (for some programs), thesis or alternative; for doctorate, one foreign language, comprehensive exam, thesis/dissertation. *Entrance requirements:* For master's, minimum GPA of 2.5; for doctorate, GMAT. Additional exam requirements/recommendations for international students: Required—TOEFL (minimum score 500 paper-based). Electronic applications accepted.

Stevens Institute of Technology, Graduate School, Charles V. Schaefer Jr. School of Engineering and Science, Department of Mechanical Engineering, Program in Integrated Product Development, Hoboken, NJ 07030. Offers armament engineering (M Eng); computer and electrical engineering (M Eng); manufacturing technologies (M Eng); systems reliability and design (M Eng). *Program availability:* Part-time, evening/weekend. *Faculty:* 32 full-time (4 women), 10 part-time/adjunct (0 women). *Degree requirements:* For master's, thesis optional, minimum B average in major field and overall. *Entrance requirements:* For master's, GRE/GMAT scores: GRE scores are required for all applicants applying to a full-time graduate program in the Schaefer School of Engineering and Science (SES). International applicants must submit TOEFL/IELTS scores and fulfill the English Language Proficiency Requirements in order to be considered. Additional exam requirements/recommendations for international students: Required—TOEFL (minimum score 74 iBT), IELTS (minimum score 6). *Application deadline:* For fall admission, 4/15 for domestic and international students; for spring admission, 11/1 for domestic and international students; for summer admission, 5/1 for domestic students. Applications are processed on a rolling basis. Application fee: $60. Electronic applications accepted. *Expenses: Tuition:* Full-time $35,960; part-time $1620 per credit. *Required fees:* $1290; $600 per semester. Tuition and fees vary according to course load. *Financial support:* Fellowships, research assistantships, teaching assistantships, career-related internships or fieldwork, Federal Work-Study, scholarships/grants, and unspecified assistantships available. Financial award application deadline: 2/15; financial award applicants required to submit FAFSA. *Unit head:* Dr. Jean Zu, Dean of SES, 201-216.8233, Fax: 201-216.8372, E-mail: Jean.Zu@stevens.edu. *Application contact:* Graduate Admissions, 888-783-8367, Fax: 888-511-1306, E-mail: graduate@stevens.edu.

Texas A&M University–Kingsville, College of Graduate Studies, Frank H. Dotterweich College of Engineering, Department of Industrial Management and Technology, Kingsville, TX 78363. Offers industrial management (MS). *Degree requirements:* For master's, variable foreign language requirement, comprehensive exam, thesis (for some programs). *Entrance requirements:* For master's, GRE, MAT, GMAT. Additional exam requirements/recommendations for international students: Required—TOEFL (minimum score 550 paper-based; 79 iBT). Electronic applications accepted.

Universidad de las Américas Puebla, Division of Graduate Studies, School of Engineering, Program in Industrial Engineering, Puebla, Mexico. Offers industrial engineering (MS); production management (M Adm). *Program availability:* Part-time, evening/weekend. *Degree requirements:* For master's, one foreign language, thesis. *Faculty research:* Textile industry, quality control.

Universidad de las Américas Puebla, Division of Graduate Studies, School of Engineering, Program in Manufacturing Administration, Puebla, Mexico. Offers MS. *Faculty research:* Operations research, construction.

The University of Alabama, Graduate School, Manderson Graduate School of Business, Department of Information Systems, Statistics, and Management Science, Program in Operations Management, Tuscaloosa, AL 35487. Offers MS, PhD. *Accreditation:* AACSB. *Program availability:* Online learning. Terminal master's awarded for partial completion of doctoral program. *Degree requirements:* For master's, comprehensive exam, business calculus; for doctorate, comprehensive exam, thesis/dissertation. *Entrance requirements:* For master's, GMAT or GRE; for doctorate, GRE or GMAT. Additional exam requirements/recommendations for international students: Required—TOEFL (minimum score 94 iBT), IELTS (minimum score 7). Electronic applications accepted. *Faculty research:* Supply chain management, inventory, simulation, logistics.

University of Arkansas, Graduate School, College of Engineering, Department of Industrial Engineering, Operations Management Program, Fayetteville, AR 72701. Offers MS. *Program availability:* Part-time, evening/weekend, online learning. *Students:* 137 applicants, 94% accepted. In 2018, 185 master's awarded. *Application deadline:* For fall admission, 8/1 for domestic students, 4/1 for international students; for spring admission, 12/1 for domestic students, 10/1 for international students; for summer admission, 4/15 for domestic students, 3/1 for international students. Applications are processed on a rolling basis. Application fee: $60. Electronic applications accepted. *Financial support:* In 2018–19, 2 research assistantships were awarded; fellowships, teaching assistantships, and institutionally sponsored loans also available. *Unit head:* Ed Pohl, Department Head, 479-575-6029, E-mail: epohl@uark.edu. *Application contact:* Blake Chapman, Marketing and Recruitment Coordinator, 479-575-5192, E-mail: pchapman@uark.edu.
Website: https://operations-management.uark.edu/

University of Bridgeport, School of Business, Bridgeport, CT 06604. Offers accounting (MBA); finance (MBA); general business (MBA); global financial services (MBA); human resource management (MBA); information systems and knowledge management (MBA); international business (MBA); management (MBA); marketing (MBA); operations management (MBA); small business and entrepreneurship (MBA); specialized business (MBA). *Accreditation:* ACBSP. *Program availability:* Part-time, evening/weekend. *Degree requirements:* For master's, thesis optional. *Entrance requirements:* For master's, GMAT. Additional exam requirements/recommendations for international students: Recommended—TOEFL (minimum score 550 paper-based; 80 iBT), IELTS (minimum score 6.5). Electronic applications accepted. *Expenses:* Contact institution.

University of Central Missouri, The Graduate School, Warrensburg, MO 64093. Offers accountancy (MA); accounting (MBA); applied mathematics (MS); aviation safety (MA); biology (MS); business administration (MBA); career and technical education leadership (MS); college student personnel administration (MS); communication (MA); computer science (MS); counseling (MS); criminal justice (MS); educational leadership (Ed D); educational technology (MS); elementary and early childhood education (MSE); English (MA); environmental studies (MA); finance (MBA); history (MA); human services/educational technology (Ed S); human services/learning resources (Ed S); human services/professional counseling (Ed S); industrial hygiene (MS); industrial management (MS); information systems (MBA); information technology (MS); kinesiology (MS); library science and information services (MS); literacy education (MSE); marketing (MBA); mathematics (MS); music (MA); occupational safety management (MS); psychology (MS); rural family nursing (MS); school administration (MSE); social gerontology (MS); sociology (MA); special education (MSE); speech language pathology (MS); superintendency (Ed S); teaching (MAT); teaching English as a second language (MA); technology (MS); technology management (PhD); theatre (MA). *Accreditation:* ASHA. *Program availability:* Part-time, 100% online, blended/hybrid learning. *Degree requirements:* For master's and Ed S, comprehensive exam (for some programs), thesis (for some programs). *Entrance requirements:* Additional exam requirements/recommendations for international students: Required—TOEFL (minimum score 550 paper-based; 79 iBT). Electronic applications accepted.

University of Chicago, Booth School of Business, Full-Time MBA Program, Chicago, IL 60637. Offers accounting (MBA); analytic finance (MBA); analytic management (MBA); econometrics and statistics (MBA); economics (MBA); entrepreneurship (MBA); finance (MBA); general management (MBA); health administration and policy (Certificate); international business (MBA); managerial and organizational behavior (MBA); marketing analytics (MBA); marketing management (MBA); operations management (MBA); strategic management (MBA); MBA/AM; MBA/JD; MBA/MA; MBA/MD; MBA/MPP. *Accreditation:* AACSB. *Entrance requirements:* For master's, GMAT or GRE, transcripts, resume, 2 letters of recommendation, essays, interview. Additional exam requirements/recommendations for international students: Required—TOEFL, IELTS, or PTE. Electronic applications accepted. *Expenses:* Contact institution.

University of Cincinnati, Carl H. Lindner College of Business, PhD Programs, Cincinnati, OH 45221. Offers accounting (PhD); business analytics (PhD); economics (PhD); finance (PhD); information systems (PhD); management (PhD); marketing (PhD); operations and business analytics (PhD); operations research (PhD). *Faculty:* 101 full-time (37 women). *Students:* 15 full-time (5 women), 10 part-time (4 women); includes 4 minority (1 Black or African American, non-Hispanic/Latino; 3 Asian, non-Hispanic/Latino), 20 international. Average age 31. 125 applicants, 12% accepted, 4 enrolled. In 2018, 7 doctorates awarded. *Degree requirements:* For doctorate, comprehensive exam, thesis/dissertation. *Entrance requirements:* For doctorate, GMAT, GRE, transcripts, essays, resume, letters of recommendation. Additional exam requirements/recommendations for international students: Required—TOEFL (minimum score 600 paper-based; 100 iBT), IELTS (minimum score 7). *Application deadline:* For fall admission, 1/15 for domestic and international students. Application fee: $65 ($70 for international students). Electronic applications accepted. *Expenses:* Contact institution. *Financial support:* In 2018–19, 35 students received support, including 25 research assistantships with full tuition reimbursements available (averaging $23,250 per year); scholarships/grants, health care benefits, tuition waivers (full), and unspecified assistantships also available. Financial award application deadline: 1/15; financial award applicants required to submit FAFSA. *Faculty research:* Bayesian Prediction Theory, organizational fairness, consumer insight and market research, consumer insight and market research, density estimation from correlated data. *Unit head:* Dr. Olivier Parent, Director, 513-556-3941, Fax: 513-556-5499, E-mail: olivier.parent@uc.edu. *Application contact:* Angel Elvin, Assistant Director, 513-556-7190, Fax: 513-558-7006, E-mail: angel.elvin@uc.edu.
Website: http://business.uc.edu/graduate/phd.html

The University of Manchester, School of Mechanical, Aerospace and Civil Engineering, Manchester, United Kingdom. Offers advanced manufacturing technology (M Ent); aerospace engineering (M Phil, M Sc, PhD); civil engineering (M Phil, M Sc, PhD); environmental engineering (M Phil, PhD); management of projects (M Phil, M Sc, PhD); mechanical engineering (M Phil, M Sc, PhD); mechanical engineering design (M Ent); nuclear engineering (M Phil, D Eng, PhD).

University of Michigan–Flint, School of Management, Program in Business Administration, Flint, MI 48502-1950. Offers accounting (MBA); computer information systems (MBA); finance (MBA, Post-Master's Certificate); general business (Graduate Certificate); general business administration (MBA); health care management (MBA); international business (MBA, Post-Master's Certificate); lean manufacturing (MBA); marketing (Post-Master's Certificate); marketing and innovation management (MBA); organizational leadership (MBA). *Program availability:* Part-time, evening/weekend, mixed mode format. *Faculty:* 30 full-time (4 women), 10 part-time/adjunct (2 women). *Students:* 24 full-time (14 women), 151 part-time (60 women); includes 45 minority (22 Black or African American, non-Hispanic/Latino; 3 American Indian or Alaska Native, non-Hispanic/Latino; 7 Asian, non-Hispanic/Latino; 9 Hispanic/Latino; 4 Two or more races, non-Hispanic/Latino), 19 international. Average age 36. 160 applicants, 75% accepted, 62 enrolled. In 2018, 50 master's, 1 other advanced degree awarded. *Entrance requirements:* For master's, bachelor's degree in arts, sciences, engineering, or business administration from regionally-accredited college or university; for other advanced degree, bachelor's degree in arts, sciences, engineering, or business administration from regionally-accredited college or university. college-level math, statistics, or quantitative course (for Graduate Certificate); MBA or equivalent degree

from regionally-accredited college or university (for Post Master's Certificate). Additional exam requirements/recommendations for international students: Required—TOEFL (minimum score 84 iBT), IELTS (minimum score 6.5). *Application deadline:* For fall admission, 8/1 for domestic students, 5/1 for international students; for winter admission, 11/15 for domestic students, 9/1 for international students; for spring admission, 3/15 for domestic students, 1/1 for international students; for summer admission, 5/15 for domestic students. Applications are processed on a rolling basis. Application fee: $55. Electronic applications accepted. *Expenses:* Contact institution. *Financial support:* Federal Work-Study, scholarships/grants, and unspecified assistantships available. Support available to part-time students. Financial award application deadline: 3/1; financial award applicants required to submit FAFSA. *Unit head:* Dr. Scott Johnson, Dean, School of Management, 810-762-3164, Fax: 810-237-6685, E-mail: scotjohn@umflint.edu. *Application contact:* Matt Bohlen, Director of Graduate Admissions, 810-762-3171, E-mail: mbohlen@umflint.edu.
Website: http://www.umflint.edu/graduateprograms/business-administration-mba

University of New Haven, Graduate School, Tagliatela College of Engineering, Program in Engineering and Operations Management, West Haven, CT 06516. Offers engineering and operations management (MS); engineering management (MS); Lean Six Sigma (Graduate Certificate). *Program availability:* Part-time. *Students:* 59 full-time (11 women), 25 part-time (3 women); includes 4 minority (2 Black or African American, non-Hispanic/Latino; 1 American Indian or Alaska Native, non-Hispanic/Latino; 1 Asian, non-Hispanic/Latino), 59 international. Average age 27. 288 applicants, 86% accepted, 26 enrolled. In 2018, 45 master's awarded. *Entrance requirements:* Additional exam requirements/recommendations for international students: Required—TOEFL (minimum score 75 iBT), IELTS, PTE (minimum score 50). *Application deadline:* Applications are processed on a rolling basis. Application fee: $50. Electronic applications accepted. Application fee is waived when completed online. *Expenses: Tuition:* Full-time $16,470; part-time $915 per credit hour. *Required fees:* $230; $95 per term. *Financial support:* Applicants required to submit FAFSA. *Unit head:* Dr. Ali Montazer, Professor, 203-932-7050, E-mail: amontazer@newhaven.edu. *Application contact:* Selina O'Toole, Senior Associate Director of Graduate Admissions, 203-932-7337, E-mail: sotoole@newhaven.edu.
Website: https://www.newhaven.edu/engineering/graduate-programs/operations-management/

The University of North Carolina at Charlotte, College of Computing and Informatics, Program in Computing and Information Systems, Charlotte, NC 28223-0001. Offers computing and information systems (PhD), including bioinformatics, business information systems and operations management, computer science, interdisciplinary, software and information systems. *Students:* 99 full-time (27 women), 18 part-time (5 women); includes 4 minority (1 Black or African American, non-Hispanic/Latino; 1 Asian, non-Hispanic/Latino; 1 Hispanic/Latino; 1 Two or more races, non-Hispanic/Latino), 90 international. Average age 30. 86 applicants, 33% accepted, 15 enrolled. In 2018, 17 doctorates awarded. *Entrance requirements:* For doctorate, GRE or GMAT, baccalaureate degree, minimum GPA of 3.0 on courses related to the chosen field of PhD study, essay, reference letters. Additional exam requirements/recommendations for international students: Required—TOEFL (minimum score 523 paper-based; 70 iBT), IELTS (minimum score 6), TOEFL (minimum score 523 paper-based, 70 iBT) or IELTS (6). *Application deadline:* Applications are processed on a rolling basis. Application fee: $75. Electronic applications accepted. Tuition and fees vary according to course load and program. *Financial support:* Career-related internships or fieldwork, institutionally sponsored loans, scholarships/grants, health care benefits, and unspecified assistantships available. Support available to part-time students. Financial award applicants required to submit FAFSA. *Unit head:* Dr. Fatma Mili, Dean, 704-687-8450. *Application contact:* Kathy B. Giddings, Director of Graduate Admissions, 704-687-5503, Fax: 704-687-1668, E-mail: gradadm@uncc.edu.

The University of North Carolina at Charlotte, William States Lee College of Engineering, Department of Systems Engineering and Engineering Management, Charlotte, NC 28223-0001. Offers energy analytics (Graduate Certificate); engineering management (MSEM); Lean Six Sigma (Graduate Certificate); logistics and supply chains (Graduate Certificate); systems analytics (Graduate Certificate). *Program availability:* Part-time, evening/weekend, 100% online, blended/hybrid learning. *Students:* 27 full-time (8 women), 45 part-time (11 women); includes 15 minority (5 Black or African American, non-Hispanic/Latino; 1 American Indian or Alaska Native, non-Hispanic/Latino; 5 Asian, non-Hispanic/Latino; 2 Hispanic/Latino; 2 Two or more races, non-Hispanic/Latino), 27 international. Average age 29. 112 applicants, 77% accepted, 23 enrolled. In 2018, 38 master's, 3 other advanced degrees awarded. *Entrance requirements:* For master's, GRE or GMAT, bachelor's degree in engineering or a closely-related technical or scientific field, or in business, provided relevant technical course requirements have been met; undergraduate coursework in engineering economics, calculus, or statistics; minimum GPA of 3.0; for Graduate Certificate, bachelor's degree in engineering or closely-related technical or scientific field, or in business, provided relevant technical course requirements have been met; minimum GPA of 3.0; undergraduate coursework in engineering economics, calculus, and statistics; written description of work experience. Additional exam requirements/recommendations for international students: Required—TOEFL (minimum score 523 paper-based; 70 iBT), IELTS (minimum score 6), TOEFL (minimum score 523 paper-based, 70 iBT) or IELTS (6). *Application deadline:* Applications are processed on a rolling basis. Application fee: $75. Electronic applications accepted. *Expenses:* Contact institution. *Financial support:* Career-related internships or fieldwork, institutionally sponsored loans, scholarships/grants, and unspecified assistantships available. Support available to part-time students. Financial award application deadline: 3/1; financial award applicants required to submit FAFSA. *Total annual research expenditures:* $186,132. *Unit head:* Dr. Simon M. Hsiang, Chair, 704-687-1958, E-mail: shsiang1@uncc.edu. *Application contact:* Kathy B. Giddings, Director of Graduate Admissions, 704-687-5503, Fax: 704-687-1668, E-mail: gradadm@uncc.edu.
Website: http://seem.uncc.edu/

University of North Texas, Toulouse Graduate School, Denton, TX 76203-5459. Offers accounting (MS); applied anthropology (MA, MS); applied behavior analysis (Certificate); applied geography (MA); applied technology and performance improvement (M Ed, MS); art education (MA); art history (MA); arts leadership (Certificate); audiology (Au D); behavior analysis (MS); behavioral science (PhD); biochemistry and molecular biology (MS); biology (MA, MS); biomedical engineering (MS); business analysis (MS); chemistry (MS); clinical health psychology (PhD); communication studies (MA, MS); computer engineering (MS); computer science (MS); counseling (M Ed, MS), including clinical mental health counseling (MS), college and university counseling, elementary school counseling, secondary school counseling; creative writing (MA); criminal justice (MS); curriculum and instruction (M Ed); decision sciences (MBA); design (MA, MFA), including fashion design (MFA), innovation studies, interior design (MFA); early childhood studies (MS); economics (MS); educational leadership (M Ed, Ed D); educational psychology (MS, PhD), including family studies (MS), gifted and talented (MS), human development (MS), learning and cognition (MS), research, measurement and evaluation (MS); electrical engineering (MS); emergency management (MPA); engineering technology (MS); English (MA); English as a second language (MA); environmental science (MS); finance (MBA, MS); financial management (MPA); French (MA); health services management (MBA); higher education (M Ed, Ed D); history (MA, MS); hospitality management (MS); human resources management (MPA); information science (MS); information systems (PhD); information technologies (MBA); interdisciplinary studies (MA, MS); international studies (MA); international sustainable tourism (MS); jazz studies (MM); journalism (MA, MJ, Graduate Certificate), including interactive and virtual digital communication (Graduate Certificate), narrative journalism (Graduate Certificate), public relations (Graduate Certificate); kinesiology (MS); linguistics (MA); local government management (MPA); logistics (PhD); logistics and supply chain management (MBA); long-term care, senior housing, and aging services (MA); management (PhD); marketing (MBA); mathematics (MA, MS); mechanical and energy engineering (MS, PhD); music (MA), including ethnomusicology, music theory, musicology, performance; music composition (PhD); music education (MM Ed, PhD); nonprofit management (MPA); operations and supply chain management (MBA); performance (MM, DMA); philosophy (MA); political science (MA); professional and technical communication (MA); radio, television and film (MA, MFA); rehabilitation counseling (Certificate); sociology (MA); Spanish (MA); special education (M Ed); speech-language pathology (MA); strategic management (MBA); studio art (MFA); teaching (M Ed); MBA/MS. *Program availability:* Part-time, evening/weekend, online learning. Terminal master's awarded for partial completion of doctoral program. *Degree requirements:* For master's, variable foreign language requirement, comprehensive exam (for some programs), thesis (for some programs); for doctorate, variable foreign language requirement, comprehensive exam (for some programs), thesis/dissertation; for other advanced degree, variable foreign language requirement, comprehensive exam (for some programs). *Entrance requirements:* For master's and doctorate, GRE, GMAT. Additional exam requirements/recommendations for international students: Required—TOEFL (minimum score 550 paper-based; 79 iBT). Electronic applications accepted.

University of Pittsburgh, Katz Graduate School of Business, Master of Business Administration Programs, Pittsburgh, PA 15260. Offers finance (MBA); information systems (MBA); marketing (MBA); operations (MBA); organizational behavior and human resources (MBA); strategy, environment and organizations (MBA); MBA/JD; MBA/MID; MBA/MIS; MBA/MSE. *Accreditation:* AACSB. *Program availability:* Part-time, evening/weekend, blended/hybrid learning. *Degree requirements:* For master's, minimum GPA of 3.0. *Entrance requirements:* For master's, GMAT, GRE. Additional exam requirements/recommendations for international students: Required—TOEFL (minimum score 100 iBT) or IELTS (minimum score 7.0). Electronic applications accepted. *Faculty research:* Accounting systems/financial reporting, corporate finance, shopper marketing/consumer behavior, management information systems, organizational behavior and entrepreneurship.

University of Portland, Dr. Robert B. Pamplin, Jr. School of Business, Portland, OR 97203-5798. Offers entrepreneurship (MBA); finance (MBA, MS); health care management (MBA); marketing (MBA); nonprofit management (EMBA); operations and technology management (MBA, MS); sustainability (MBA). *Accreditation:* AACSB. *Program availability:* Part-time, evening/weekend. *Faculty:* 26 full-time (5 women), 8 part-time/adjunct (1 woman). *Students:* 35 full-time (16 women), 114 part-time (47 women); includes 21 minority (3 Black or African American, non-Hispanic/Latino; 2 American Indian or Alaska Native, non-Hispanic/Latino; 8 Asian, non-Hispanic/Latino; 8 Hispanic/Latino), 24 international. Average age 32. In 2018, 55 master's awarded. *Entrance requirements:* For master's, GMAT or GRE, minimum GPA of 3.0, resume, statement of goals, 2 letters of recommendation. Additional exam requirements/recommendations for international students: Required—TOEFL (minimum score 88 iBT), IELTS (minimum score 7). *Application deadline:* For fall admission, 7/19 priority date for domestic and international students; for spring admission, 12/7 priority date for domestic and international students; for summer admission, 4/12 priority date for domestic and international students. Applications are processed on a rolling basis. Application fee: $0. Electronic applications accepted. *Expenses:* Contact institution. *Financial support:* Application deadline: 3/1; applicants required to submit FAFSA. *Unit head:* Melissa McCarthy, Director, 503-943-7224, E-mail: mba-up@up.edu. *Application contact:* Melissa McCarthy, Director, 503-943-7224, E-mail: mba-up@up.edu.

University of Puerto Rico–Mayagüez, Graduate Studies, College of Business Administration, Mayagüez, PR 00681-9000. Offers business administration (MBA); finance (MBA); human resources (MBA); industrial management (MBA). *Program availability:* Part-time, evening/weekend. *Degree requirements:* For master's, one foreign language, comprehensive exam, thesis (for some programs). *Entrance requirements:* For master's, GMAT or EXADEP, bachelor's degree with courses in calculus, microeconomics, accounting and statistics. Additional exam requirements/recommendations for international students: Required—TOEFL (minimum score 500 paper-based), GMAT or EXADEP. Electronic applications accepted. *Faculty research:* Organizational studies, management, accounting, entrepreneurship, leadership and motivation.

University of Puerto Rico–Río Piedras, College of Business Administration, San Juan, PR 00931-3300. Offers accounting (MBA); finance (MBA, PhD); general business (MBA); human resources management (MBA); international trade and business (MBA, PhD); marketing (MBA); operations management (MBA); quantitative methods (MBA). *Accreditation:* AACSB. *Program availability:* Part-time. *Degree requirements:* For master's, comprehensive exam, thesis or alternative, research project. *Entrance requirements:* For master's, GMAT or PAEG, minimum GPA of 3.0, letter of recommendation; for doctorate, GMAT, PAEG, minimum GPA of 3.0, master degree. *Faculty research:* Management.

University of Rochester, Simon Business School, Doctoral Program in Business Administration, Rochester, NY 14627. Offers accounting (PhD); computer information systems (PhD); finance (PhD); marketing (PhD); operations management (PhD). *Accreditation:* AACSB. *Degree requirements:* For doctorate, comprehensive exam, thesis/dissertation, qualifying exam. *Entrance requirements:* For doctorate, GMAT or GRE. Additional exam requirements/recommendations for international students: Required—TOEFL. Electronic applications accepted. *Expenses:* Contact institution. *Faculty research:* Empirical industrial organization, risk management, financial disclosure and regulation, social media, health care management.

University of Southern Indiana, Graduate Studies, Pott College of Science, Engineering, and Education, Program in Industrial Management, Evansville, IN 47712-3590. Offers MSIM. *Program availability:* Part-time-only, evening/weekend. *Degree requirements:* For master's, project. *Entrance requirements:* For master's, minimum GPA of 2.5, BS in engineering or engineering technology. Additional exam requirements/recommendations for international students: Required—TOEFL (minimum score 550 paper-based; 79 iBT), IELTS (minimum score 6). Electronic applications accepted.

The University of Tennessee, Graduate School, College of Business Administration, Program in Business Administration, Knoxville, TN 37996. Offers accounting (PhD); finance (MBA, PhD); logistics and transportation (MBA, PhD); management (PhD); marketing (MBA, PhD); operations management (MBA); professional business administration (MBA); statistics (PhD); JD/MBA; MS/MBA; Pharm D/MBA. Pharm D/MBA offered jointly with The University of Tennessee Health Science Center. *Accreditation:* AACSB. *Program availability:* Online learning. *Degree requirements:* For

master's, thesis or alternative; for doctorate, thesis/dissertation. *Entrance requirements:* For master's and doctorate, GMAT, minimum GPA of 2.7. Additional exam requirements/recommendations for international students: Required—TOEFL. Electronic applications accepted.

The University of Texas at Austin, Graduate School, McCombs School of Business, Department of Information, Risk, and Operations Management, Austin, TX 78712-1111. Offers information management (MBA); information systems (PhD); information technology and management (MS); risk analysis and decision making (PhD); risk management (MBA); supply chain and operations management (MBA, PhD). *Degree requirements:* For doctorate, thesis/dissertation. *Entrance requirements:* For doctorate, GMAT or GRE. Electronic applications accepted. *Faculty research:* Stochastic processing and queuing, discrete nonlinear and large-scale optimization simulation, quality assurance logistics, distributed artificial intelligence, organizational modeling.

The University of Texas at Dallas, Naveen Jindal School of Management, Program in Organizations, Strategy and International Management, Richardson, TX 75080. Offers business administration (MBA); executive business administration (EMBA); global leadership (EMBA); healthcare leadership and management (MS); healthcare management (EMBA); innovation and entrepreneurship (MS); international management studies (MS, PhD); management science (MS, PhD); project management (EMBA); systems engineering and management (MS); MS/MBA. *Program availability:* Part-time, evening/weekend. *Faculty:* 19 full-time (6 women), 33 part-time/adjunct (12 women). *Students:* 587 full-time (237 women), 777 part-time (361 women); includes 456 minority (83 Black or African American, non-Hispanic/Latino; 226 Asian, non-Hispanic/Latino; 110 Hispanic/Latino; 37 Two or more races, non-Hispanic/Latino), 316 international. Average age 34. 1,452 applicants, 43% accepted, 376 enrolled. In 2018, 556 master's, 23 doctorates awarded. *Degree requirements:* For doctorate, thesis/dissertation. *Entrance requirements:* For master's and doctorate, GMAT. Additional exam requirements/recommendations for international students: Required—TOEFL (minimum score 550 paper-based). *Application deadline:* For fall admission, 7/15 for domestic students, 5/1 for international students; for spring admission, 11/15 for domestic students, 9/1 priority date for international students. Applications are processed on a rolling basis. Application fee: $50 ($100 for international students). Electronic applications accepted. *Expenses: Tuition, area resident:* Full-time $13,458. Tuition, state resident: full-time $13,458. Tuition, nonresident: full-time $26,852. *International tuition:* $26,852 full-time. Tuition and fees vary according to course load. *Financial support:* In 2018–19, 102 students received support, including 24 research assistantships with partial tuition reimbursements available (averaging $37,400 per year), 83 teaching assistantships with partial tuition reimbursements available (averaging $25,119 per year); Federal Work-Study, institutionally sponsored loans, scholarships/grants, and unspecified assistantships also available. Support available to part-time students. Financial award application deadline: 4/30; financial award applicants required to submit FAFSA. *Faculty research:* International accounting, international trade and finance, economic development, international economics. *Unit head:* Dr. Seung-Hyun Lee, Area Coordinator, 972-883-6267, Fax: 972-883-5977, E-mail: sxl029100@utdallas.edu. *Application contact:* Dr. Seung-Hyun Lee, Area Coordinator, 972-883-6267, Fax: 972-883-5977, E-mail: sxl029100@utdallas.edu. Website: http://jindal.utdallas.edu/osim/

The University of Texas at Tyler, Soules College of Business, School of Technology, Tyler, TX 75799-0001. Offers MS. *Program availability:* Online learning. *Entrance requirements:* For master's, GMAT. Electronic applications accepted. *Unit head:* Dr. Mark Miller, Chair, 903-566-7186. *Application contact:* Dr. Mark Miller, Chair, 903-566-7186.
Website: https://www.uttyler.edu/cbt/technology/

University of Utah, Graduate School, David Eccles School of Business, Business Administration Program, Salt Lake City, UT 84112. Offers accounting (PhD); business administration (EMBA, MBA, PMBA); finance (PhD); information systems (PhD); marketing (PhD); operations management (PhD); organizational behavior (PhD); strategic management (PhD); MBA/JD; MBA/MHA; MBA/MS. *Program availability:* Part-time, evening/weekend, online learning. *Students:* 112 full-time (26 women), 7 part-time (2 women); includes 12 minority (1 Asian, non-Hispanic/Latino; 7 Hispanic/Latino; 4 Two or more races, non-Hispanic/Latino), 13 international. Average age 29. 182 applicants, 51% accepted, 58 enrolled. In 2018, 58 master's awarded. *Entrance requirements:* For master's, GMAT or GRE; for doctorate, GMAT. Additional exam requirements/recommendations for international students: Required—TOEFL (minimum score 100 iBT), IELTS (minimum score 7). *Application deadline:* For fall admission, 5/1 for domestic students, 3/1 for international students. Application fee: $55 ($65 for international students). Electronic applications accepted. *Expenses:* Contact institution. *Financial support:* In 2018–19, 57 students received support. Scholarships/grants available. Financial award application deadline: 5/1; financial award applicants required to submit FAFSA. *Faculty research:* Corporate finance, strategy services, consumer behavior, financial disclosures, operations. *Unit head:* Brad Vierig, Associate Dean, MBA Programs & Executive Education. *Application contact:* Stephanie Geisler, Director,

Full-Time MBA, 801-585-6291, E-mail: ftmba@utah.edu.
Website: http://www.business.utah.edu/

University of Utah, Graduate School, David Eccles School of Business, Master of Science in Information Systems Program, Salt Lake City, UT 84112-8939. Offers information systems (MS, Graduate Certificate), including business intelligence and analytics, IT security, product and process management, software and systems architecture. *Program availability:* Part-time, evening/weekend, 100% online, blended/hybrid learning. *Degree requirements:* For master's, capstone project. *Entrance requirements:* For master's, GMAT/GRE, minimum undergraduate GPA of 3.0, 2 letters of recommendation, personal statement, professional resume. Additional exam requirements/recommendations for international students: Required—TOEFL (minimum score 550 paper-based; 80 iBT), IELTS (minimum score 6.5). Electronic applications accepted. *Expenses:* Contact institution. *Faculty research:* Business intelligence and analytics, software and system architecture, product and process management, IT security, Web and data mining, applications and management of IT in healthcare.

Wayne State University, College of Liberal Arts and Sciences, Department of Economics, Detroit, MI 48202. Offers applied macroeconomics (MA, PhD); health economics (MA, PhD); industrial organization (MA, PhD); international economics (MA, PhD); labor and human resources (MA, PhD); JD/MA. *Faculty:* 10. *Students:* 48 full-time (12 women), 5 part-time (1 woman); includes 7 minority (3 Black or African American, non-Hispanic/Latino; 2 Asian, non-Hispanic/Latino; 2 Hispanic/Latino), 21 international. Average age 30. 76 applicants, 39% accepted, 11 enrolled. In 2018, 3 master's, 2 doctorates awarded. *Degree requirements:* For master's, comprehensive exam; for doctorate, comprehensive exam, thesis/dissertation, oral examination on research, completion of course work in quantitative methods, final lecture. *Entrance requirements:* For master's, minimum upper-division GPA of 3.0; prior coursework in intermediate microeconomic and macroeconomic theory, statistics, and elementary calculus; for doctorate, GRE, minimum upper-division GPA of 3.0, prior coursework in intermediate microeconomic and macroeconomic theory, statistics, two courses in calculus, three letters of recommendation from officials or teaching staff at institution(s) most recently attended, statement of purpose. Additional exam requirements/recommendations for international students: Required—TOEFL (minimum score 550 paper-based; 79 iBT), TWE (minimum score 5.5), Michigan English Language Assessment Battery (minimum score 85); Recommended—IELTS (minimum score 6.5). *Application deadline:* For fall admission, 5/1 for domestic and international students; for winter admission, 10/1 priority date for domestic students, 9/1 priority date for international students; for spring admission, 1/1 priority date for domestic and international students. Applications are processed on a rolling basis. Application fee: $50. Electronic applications accepted. *Financial support:* In 2018–19, 34 students received support, including 2 fellowships with tuition reimbursements available (averaging $20,000 per year), 1 research assistantship with tuition reimbursement available (averaging $23,119 per year), 17 teaching assistantships with tuition reimbursements available (averaging $19,267 per year); scholarships/grants, health care benefits, and unspecified assistantships also available. Support available to part-time students. Financial award applicants required to submit FAFSA. *Faculty research:* Health economics, international economics, macroeconomics, urban and labor economics, econometrics. *Unit head:* Dr. Kevin Cotter, Interim Chair, 313-577-3345, E-mail: kevin.cotter@wayne.edu. *Application contact:* Dr. Li Way Lee, Professor and Director of Graduate Studies, 313-577-3345, E-mail: aa1313@wayne.edu.
Website: http://clas.wayne.edu/economics/

Wilkes University, College of Graduate and Professional Studies, Jay S. Sidhu School of Business and Leadership, Wilkes-Barre, PA 18766-0002. Offers accounting (MBA); global business (MBA); human resource management (MBA); international business (MBA); leadership (MBA); management (MBA); operations management (MBA); organizational leadership and development (MBA). *Accreditation:* ACBSP. *Program availability:* Part-time, evening/weekend. *Students:* 16 full-time (9 women), 64 part-time (33 women); includes 11 minority (3 Black or African American, non-Hispanic/Latino; 3 Asian, non-Hispanic/Latino; 3 Hispanic/Latino; 2 Two or more races, non-Hispanic/Latino), 7 international. Average age 30. In 2018, 49 master's awarded. *Entrance requirements:* For master's, GMAT. Additional exam requirements/recommendations for international students: Required—TOEFL (minimum score 550 paper-based; 79 iBT). *Application deadline:* Applications are processed on a rolling basis. Application fee: $45 ($65 for international students). Electronic applications accepted. *Expenses:* Contact institution. *Financial support:* Unspecified assistantships available. Financial award application deadline: 3/1; financial award applicants required to submit FAFSA. *Unit head:* Dr. Abel Adekola, Dean, 570-408-4701, Fax: 570-408-7846, E-mail: abel.adekola@wilkes.edu. *Application contact:* Kristin Donati, Associate Director of Graduate Admissions, 570-408-3338, Fax: 570-408-7846, E-mail: kristin.donati@wilkes.edu.
Website: http://www.wilkes.edu/academics/colleges/sidhu-school-of-business-leadership/index.aspx

Section 10
Insurance, Actuarial Science, and Risk Management

This section contains a directory of institutions offering graduate work in insurance and actuarial science. Additional information about programs listed in the directory but not augmented by an in-depth entry may be obtained by writing directly to the dean of a graduate school or chair of a department at the address given in the directory.

For programs offering related work, see also in this book *Business Administration and Management*.

CONTENTS

Program Directories

Actuarial Science

Ball State University, Graduate School, College of Sciences and Humanities, Department of Mathematical Sciences, Program in Actuarial Science, Muncie, IN 47306. Offers MA. *Program availability:* Part-time. *Entrance requirements:* For master's, minimum baccalaureate GPA of 2.75 or 3.0 in latter half of baccalaureate. Additional exam requirements/recommendations for international students: Required—TOEFL (minimum score 550 paper-based; 79 iBT), IELTS (minimum score 6.5). Electronic applications accepted.

Boston University, Metropolitan College, Department of Actuarial Science, Boston, MA 02215. Offers MS. *Program availability:* Part-time, evening/weekend. *Faculty:* 4 full-time (1 woman), 5 part-time/adjunct (2 women). *Students:* 57 full-time (27 women), 25 part-time (8 women); includes 11 minority (1 Black or African American, non-Hispanic/Latino; 9 Asian, non-Hispanic/Latino; 1 Hispanic/Latino), 65 international. Average age 24. 135 applicants, 78% accepted, 36 enrolled. In 2018, 42 master's awarded. *Entrance requirements:* For master's, prerequisite coursework in calculus. Additional exam requirements/recommendations for international students: Required—TOEFL (minimum score 84 iBT). *Application deadline:* For fall admission, 8/1 priority date for domestic students, 6/1 priority date for international students; for spring admission, 12/1 priority date for domestic students, 11/15 priority date for international students; for summer admission, 4/1 priority date for domestic students, 3/1 priority date for international students. Applications are processed on a rolling basis. Application fee: $85. Electronic applications accepted. *Expenses:* Contact institution. *Financial support:* In 2018–19, 1 research assistantship with partial tuition reimbursement (averaging $8,400 per year) was awarded; teaching assistantships, career-related internships or fieldwork, scholarships/grants, and unspecified assistantships also available. *Unit head:* Hal Tepfer, Director, 617-353-8758, E-mail: hal@bu.edu. *Application contact:* Amy Johnson, Program Manager, 617-353-8758, E-mail: actuary@bu.edu.
Website: http://www.bu.edu/actuary/

California State University, East Bay, Office of Graduate Studies, College of Science, Department of Statistics and Biostatistics, Statistics Program, Hayward, CA 94542-3000. Offers actuarial science (MS); applied statistics (MS); computational statistics (MS); mathematical statistics (MS). *Program availability:* Part-time, evening/weekend. *Degree requirements:* For master's, comprehensive exam. *Entrance requirements:* For master's, letters of recommendation, minimum GPA of 3.0, math through lower-division calculus. Additional exam requirements/recommendations for international students: Required—TOEFL (minimum score 550 paper-based). Electronic applications accepted.

Central Connecticut State University, School of Graduate Studies, School of Engineering, Science and Technology, Department of Mathematical Sciences, New Britain, CT 06050-4010. Offers data mining (MS, Certificate); mathematics (MA, MS), including actuarial science (MA), computer science (MA), statistics (MA); mathematics education leadership (Sixth Year Certificate); mathematics for secondary education (Certificate). *Program availability:* Part-time, evening/weekend, 100% online. *Faculty:* 13 full-time (4 women). *Students:* 14 full-time (9 women), 70 part-time (39 women); includes 21 minority (8 Black or African American, non-Hispanic/Latino; 9 Asian, non-Hispanic/Latino; 3 Hispanic/Latino; 1 Two or more races, non-Hispanic/Latino), 2 international. Average age 33. 57 applicants, 70% accepted, 20 enrolled. In 2018, 20 master's, 3 other advanced degrees awarded. *Degree requirements:* For master's, comprehensive exam, thesis or alternative, special project; for other advanced degree, qualifying exam. *Entrance requirements:* For master's, minimum undergraduate GPA of 2.7; for other advanced degree, minimum undergraduate GPA of 3.0, essay, letters of recommendation. Additional exam requirements/recommendations for international students: Required—TOEFL (minimum score 550 paper-based; 79 iBT); Recommended—IELTS (minimum score 6.5). *Application deadline:* For fall admission, 6/1 for domestic students, 5/1 for international students; for spring admission, 11/1 for domestic and international students. Applications are processed on a rolling basis. Application fee: $50. Electronic applications accepted. *Expenses: Tuition, area resident:* Full-time $7027; part-time $388 per credit. Tuition, state resident: full-time $9750; part-time $388 per credit. Tuition, nonresident: full-time $18,102; part-time $388 per credit. *International tuition:* $18,102 full-time. *Required fees:* $266 per semester. *Financial support:* In 2018–19, 22 students received support. Career-related internships or fieldwork, Federal Work-Study, scholarships/grants, and unspecified assistantships available. Support available to part-time students. Financial award application deadline: 3/1; financial award applicants required to submit FAFSA. *Faculty research:* Statistics, actuarial mathematics, computer systems and engineering, computer programming techniques, operations research. *Unit head:* Dr. Robin Kalder, Chair, 860-832-2835, E-mail: kalderr@ccsu.edu. *Application contact:* Patricia Gardner, Associate Director of Graduate Studies, 860-832-2350, Fax: 860-832-2362.
Website: http://www.ccsu.edu/mathematics

Columbia University, School of Professional Studies, Program in Actuarial Science, New York, NY 10027. Offers MS. *Program availability:* Part-time. *Degree requirements:* For master's, comprehensive exam. *Entrance requirements:* For master's, minimum GPA of 3.0, knowledge of economics, linear algebra, calculus. Additional exam requirements/recommendations for international students: Required—American Language Program placement test. Electronic applications accepted.

Florida State University, The Graduate School, Department of Anthropology, Department of Mathematics, Tallahassee, FL 32306-4510. Offers applied and computational mathematics (MS, PhD); biomathematics (MS, PhD); financial mathematics (MS, PhD), including actuarial science (MS); pure mathematics (MS, PhD). *Program availability:* Part-time. *Students:* 114 full-time (31 women); includes 8 minority (1 Black or African American, non-Hispanic/Latino; 1 Asian, non-Hispanic/Latino; 2 Hispanic/Latino; 4 Two or more races, non-Hispanic/Latino), 74 international. 225 applicants, 45% accepted, 47 enrolled. In 2018, 13 master's, 11 doctorates awarded. Terminal master's awarded for partial completion of doctoral program. *Degree requirements:* For master's, comprehensive exam (for some programs), thesis optional; for doctorate, comprehensive exam, thesis/dissertation, candidacy exam (including written qualifying examinations which differ by degree concentration). *Entrance requirements:* For master's and doctorate, GRE General Test, minimum upper-division GPA of 3.0, 4-year bachelor's degree. Additional exam requirements/recommendations for international students: Required—TOEFL (minimum score 550 paper-based; 80 iBT), IELTS (minimum score 6.5). *Application deadline:* For fall admission, 12/15 priority date for domestic and international students; for spring admission, 4/30 for domestic and international students. Application fee: $30. Electronic applications accepted. *Expenses: Tuition, area resident:* Part-time $479.32 per credit hour. Tuition and fees vary according to campus/location and program. *Financial support:* In 2018–19, 109 students received support, including 2 fellowships with full tuition reimbursements available (averaging $24,053 per year), 10 research assistantships with full tuition reimbursements available (averaging $20,053 per year), 83 teaching assistantships with full tuition reimbursements available (averaging $20,053 per year); career-related internships or fieldwork, scholarships/grants, health care benefits, tuition waivers (full and partial), and unspecified assistantships also available. Financial award application deadline: 12/15; financial award applicants required to submit FAFSA. *Faculty research:* Low-dimensional and geometric topology, mathematical modeling in neuroscience, computational stochastics and Monte Carlo methods, mathematical physics, applied analysis. *Total annual research expenditures:* $1.3 million. *Unit head:* Dr. Philip L. Bowers, Chairperson, 850-644-2202, Fax: 850-644-4053, E-mail: bowers@math.fsu.edu. *Application contact:* Elizabeth Scott, Graduate Advisor and Admissions Coordinator, 850-644-2278, Fax: 850-644-4053, E-mail: emscott2@fsu.edu.
Website: http://www.math.fsu.edu/

Georgia State University, J. Mack Robinson College of Business, Department of Risk Management and Insurance, Program in Actuarial Science, Atlanta, GA 30302-3083. Offers MAS. *Program availability:* Part-time, evening/weekend. *Entrance requirements:* For master's, GRE or GMAT, transcripts from all institutions attended, resume, essays. Additional exam requirements/recommendations for international students: Required—TOEFL (minimum score 610 paper-based; 101 iBT), IELTS (minimum score 7). *Application deadline:* Applications are processed on a rolling basis. Application fee: $50. Electronic applications accepted. *Expenses: Tuition, area resident:* Full-time $9360; part-time $390 per credit hour. Tuition, state resident: full-time $9360; part-time $390 per credit hour. Tuition, nonresident: full-time $30,024; part-time $1251 per credit hour. *International tuition:* $30,024 full-time. *Required fees:* $2128. *Financial support:* Research assistantships, scholarships/grants, tuition waivers, and unspecified assistantships available. *Faculty research:* Quantification and pricing of risk, risk modeling, financial methods in insurance, economic theory, enterprise risk management. *Unit head:* Dr. Haci Akcin, Director, 404-413-7467, Fax: 404-413-7499. *Application contact:* Toby McChesney, Assistant Dean for Graduate Recruiting and Student Services, 404-413-7167, Fax: 404-413-7162, E-mail: rcbgradadmissions@gsu.edu.
Website: http://rmi.robinson.gsu.edu/academic-programs/mas/

Governors State University, College of Arts and Sciences, Program in Mathematics, University Park, IL 60484. Offers actuarial science (MS). *Program availability:* Part-time. *Faculty:* 39 full-time (14 women), 29 part-time/adjunct (12 women). *Students:* 3 full-time (2 women), 20 part-time (13 women); includes 7 minority (5 Black or African American, non-Hispanic/Latino; 2 Hispanic/Latino). Average age 35. 13 applicants, 77% accepted, 7 enrolled. In 2018, 9 master's awarded. *Application deadline:* For fall admission, 4/1 for domestic students. Applications are processed on a rolling basis. Application fee: $50. Electronic applications accepted. *Financial support:* Application deadline: 5/1; applicants required to submit FAFSA. *Unit head:* Mary Carrington, Interim Chair, Division of Science, Mathematics, and Technology, 708-534-5000 Ext. 4532, E-mail: mcarrington@govst.edu. *Application contact:* Mary Carrington, Interim Chair, Division of Science, Mathematics, and Technology, 708-534-5000 Ext. 4532, E-mail: mcarrington@govst.edu.

Lock Haven University of Pennsylvania, College of Natural, Behavioral and Health Sciences, Lock Haven, PA 17745-2390. Offers actuarial science (PSM); athletic training (MS); health promotion/education (MHS); healthcare management (MHS); physician assistant (MHS). Program also offered at the Clearfield, Coudersport, and Harrisburg campuses. *Accreditation:* ARC-PA. *Entrance requirements:* For master's, minimum undergraduate GPA of 3.0. Additional exam requirements/recommendations for international students: Required—TOEFL. Electronic applications accepted.

Maryville University of Saint Louis, College of Arts and Sciences, St. Louis, MO 63141-7299. Offers actuarial science (MS); data science (MS); strategic communication and leadership (MA). *Program availability:* Part-time. *Faculty:* 7 full-time (5 women), 11 part-time/adjunct (5 women). *Students:* 62 full-time (33 women), 37 part-time (28 women); includes 11 minority (5 Black or African American, non-Hispanic/Latino; 3 Asian, non-Hispanic/Latino; 1 Hispanic/Latino; 2 Two or more races, non-Hispanic/Latino), 52 international. Average age 28. In 2018, 32 master's awarded. *Entrance requirements:* For master's, strong mathematics background, 2 letters of recommendation, and personal statement (MS). Additional exam requirements/recommendations for international students: Required—TOEFL (minimum score 550 paper-based; 80 iBT). *Application deadline:* Applications are processed on a rolling basis. Electronic applications accepted. *Expenses:* Tuition varies by program. *Financial support:* Application deadline: 4/1; applicants required to submit FAFSA. *Unit head:* Jennifer Yukna, Interim Dean, 314-529-6858, Fax: 314-529-9965, E-mail: jyukna@maryville.edu. *Application contact:* Shani Lenore-Jenkins, Associate Vice President of Enrollment, 314-529-9359, E-mail: slenore@maryville.edu.
Website: https://www.maryville.edu/as/

Middle Tennessee State University, College of Graduate Studies, College of Basic and Applied Sciences, Program in Professional Science, Murfreesboro, TN 37132. Offers actuarial sciences (MS); biostatistics (MS); biotechnology (MS); engineering management (MS); health care informatics (MS). *Program availability:* Part-time, evening/weekend, online learning. *Degree requirements:* For master's, comprehensive exam. *Entrance requirements:* For master's, GRE. Additional exam requirements/recommendations for international students: Required—TOEFL (minimum score 525 paper-based; 71 iBT) or IELTS (minimum score 6).

The Ohio State University, Graduate School, College of Arts and Sciences, Division of Natural and Mathematical Sciences, Department of Mathematics, Columbus, OH 43210. Offers actuarial and quantitative risk management (MAQRM); computational sciences (MMS); mathematical biosciences (MMS); mathematics (PhD); mathematics for educators (MMS). *Faculty:* 61. *Students:* 150 full-time (32 women); includes 16 minority (9 Asian, non-Hispanic/Latino; 5 Hispanic/Latino; 2 Two or more races, non-Hispanic/Latino), 84 international. Average age 26. In 2018, 24 master's, 21 doctorates awarded. *Degree requirements:* For master's, thesis optional; for doctorate, one foreign language, thesis/dissertation. *Entrance requirements:* For master's, GRE General Test; for doctorate, GRE General Test (recommended), GRE Subject Test (mathematics). Additional exam requirements/recommendations for international students: Required—TOEFL (minimum score 550 paper-based; 79 iBT), Michigan English Language Assessment Battery (minimum score 82); Recommended—IELTS (minimum score 7). *Application deadline:* For fall admission, 12/15 priority date for domestic and international students. Applications are processed on a rolling basis. Application fee: $60 ($70 for international students). Electronic applications accepted. *Financial support:* Fellowships, research assistantships, teaching assistantships, Federal Work-Study, institutionally sponsored loans, and unspecified assistantships available. Support available to part-time students. *Unit head:* Dr. Jean-Francois Lafont, Chair, 614-292-7173, E-mail: lafont.1@osu.edu. *Application contact:* Erin Anthony, Graduate Studies Coordinator, 614-292-6274, Fax: 614-292-1479, E-mail: grad-info@math.osu.edu.
Website: http://www.math.osu.edu/

Oregon State University, College of Science, Program in Mathematics, Corvallis, OR 97331. Offers differential geometry (MA, MS, PhD); financial and actuarial mathematics (MA, MS, PhD); mathematical biology (MA, MS, PhD); mathematics education (MS, PhD); number theory (MA, MS, PhD); numerical analysis (MA, MS, PhD); probability (MA). Terminal master's awarded for partial completion of doctoral program. *Degree requirements:* For master's, thesis or alternative; for doctorate, thesis/dissertation, qualifying exams. *Entrance requirements:* For master's and doctorate, GRE. Additional exam requirements/recommendations for international students: Required—TOEFL (minimum score 100 iBT). Electronic applications accepted.

Roosevelt University, Graduate Division, College of Arts and Sciences, Department of Math, Actuarial Science, and Economics, Chicago, IL 60605. Offers actuarial science (MS); mathematics (MS), including mathematical sciences. Electronic applications accepted.

St. John's University, The Peter J. Tobin College of Business, School of Risk Management, Insurance and Actuarial Science, Queens, NY 11439. Offers actuarial science (MS); business administration (MBA), including risk management and insurance; enterprise risk management (MBA, MS), including enterprise risk management (MS); risk management and insurance (MS). *Entrance requirements:* For master's, GMAT or GRE, 2 letters of recommendation, essay, resume, unofficial transcripts. Additional exam requirements/recommendations for international students: Required—TOEFL (minimum score 80 iBT), IELTS (minimum score 6.5). Electronic applications accepted. *Expenses:* Contact institution. *Faculty research:* Insurance company operations and financial analysis, enterprise risk management, risk theory and modeling, credibility theory and actuarial price modeling, international insurance.

Simon Fraser University, Office of Graduate Studies and Postdoctoral Fellows, Faculty of Science, Department of Statistics and Actuarial Science, Burnaby, BC V5A 1S6, Canada. Offers actuarial science (M Sc); statistics (M Sc, PhD). *Degree requirements:* For master's, participation in consulting, project; for doctorate, comprehensive exam, thesis/dissertation. *Entrance requirements:* For master's, minimum GPA of 3.0 (on scale of 4.33) or 3.33 based on last 60 credits of undergraduate courses; for doctorate, minimum GPA of 3.5 (on scale of 4.33). Additional exam requirements/recommendations for international students: Recommended—TOEFL (minimum score 580 paper-based; 93 iBT), IELTS (minimum score 7), TWE (minimum score 5). Electronic applications accepted. *Faculty research:* Biostatistics, experimental design, envirometrics, statistical computing, statistical theory.

Temple University, Fox School of Business, Specialized Master's Programs, Philadelphia, PA 19122-6096. Offers accountancy (MS); actuarial science (MS); finance (MS); financial engineering (MS); human resource management (MS); innovation management and entrepreneurship (MS); marketing (MS); statistics (MS). MS in innovation management and entrepreneurship delivered jointly with College of Engineering. *Accreditation:* AACSB. *Program availability:* Part-time. *Entrance requirements:* For master's, GRE General Test or GMAT, minimum undergraduate GPA of 3.0. Additional exam requirements/recommendations for international students: Required—TOEFL (minimum score 600 paper-based; 100 iBT), IELTS (minimum score 7.5).

Université du Québec à Montréal, Graduate Programs, Program in Actuarial Sciences, Montréal, QC H3C 3P8, Canada. Offers Diploma. *Program availability:* Part-time. *Entrance requirements:* For degree, appropriate bachelor's degree or equivalent and proficiency in French.

University of Illinois at Urbana–Champaign, Graduate College, College of Liberal Arts and Sciences, Department of Mathematics, Champaign, IL 61820. Offers applied mathematics (MS); applied mathematics: actuarial science (MS); mathematics (MS, PhD); teaching of mathematics (MS).

The University of Iowa, Graduate College, College of Liberal Arts and Sciences, Department of Statistics and Actuarial Science, Iowa City, IA 52242-1316. Offers actuarial science (MS); statistics (MS, PhD). *Degree requirements:* For master's, thesis optional, exam; for doctorate, comprehensive exam, thesis/dissertation. *Entrance requirements:* For master's and doctorate, GRE General Test, minimum GPA of 3.0. Additional exam requirements/recommendations for international students: Required—TOEFL (minimum score 550 paper-based; 81 iBT). Electronic applications accepted.

The University of Manchester, School of Mathematics, Manchester, United Kingdom. Offers actuarial science (PhD); applied mathematics (M Phil, PhD); applied numerical computing (M Phil, PhD); financial mathematics (M Phil, PhD); mathematical logic (M Phil); probability (M Phil, PhD); pure mathematics (M Phil, PhD); statistics (M Phil, PhD).

University of Nebraska–Lincoln, Graduate College, College of Business Administration, Interdepartmental Area of Actuarial Science, Lincoln, NE 68588. Offers MS. *Entrance requirements:* For master's, GRE. Additional exam requirements/recommendations for international students: Required—TOEFL (minimum score 550 paper-based). Electronic applications accepted. *Faculty research:* Risk theory, pensions, actuarial finance, decision theory, stochastic calculus.

The University of Texas at Austin, Graduate School, College of Natural Sciences, Department of Mathematics, Austin, TX 78712-1111. Offers MA, PhD. *Entrance requirements:* For master's and doctorate, GRE General Test. Electronic applications accepted.

The University of Texas at Dallas, School of Natural Sciences and Mathematics, Department of Mathematical Sciences, Richardson, TX 75080. Offers actuarial science (MS); mathematics (MS, PhD), including applied mathematics, data science (MS), engineering mathematics (MS), mathematics (MS); statistics (MS, PhD). *Program availability:* Part-time, evening/weekend. *Faculty:* 29 full-time (6 women), 3 part-time/adjunct (0 women). *Students:* 155 full-time (58 women), 35 part-time (9 women); includes 34 minority (4 Black or African American, non-Hispanic/Latino; 19 Asian, non-Hispanic/Latino; 7 Hispanic/Latino; 4 Two or more races, non-Hispanic/Latino), 116 international. Average age 32. 264 applicants, 37% accepted, 48 enrolled. In 2018, 48 master's, 11 doctorates awarded. *Degree requirements:* For master's, thesis optional;

for doctorate, thesis/dissertation. *Entrance requirements:* For master's, GRE General Test, minimum GPA of 3.0 in upper-level course work in field; for doctorate, GRE General Test, minimum GPA of 3.5 in upper-level course work in field. Additional exam requirements/recommendations for international students: Required—TOEFL (minimum score 550 paper-based). *Application deadline:* For fall admission, 7/15 for domestic students, 5/1 priority date for international students; for spring admission, 11/15 for domestic students, 9/1 priority date for international students. Applications are processed on a rolling basis. Application fee: $50 ($100 for international students). Electronic applications accepted. *Expenses: Tuition, area resident:* Full-time $13,458. Tuition, state resident: Full-time $13,458. Tuition, nonresident: full-time $26,852. *International tuition:* $26,852 full-time. Tuition and fees vary according to course load. *Financial support:* In 2018–19, 92 students received support, including 10 research assistantships (averaging $24,110 per year), 89 teaching assistantships with partial tuition reimbursements available (averaging $17,110 per year); fellowships, career-related internships or fieldwork, Federal Work-Study, institutionally sponsored loans, scholarships/grants, and unspecified assistantships also available. Support available to part-time students. Financial award application deadline: 4/30; financial award applicants required to submit FAFSA. *Faculty research:* Sequential analysis, applications in semiconductor manufacturing, medical image analysis, computational anatomy, information theory, probability theory. *Unit head:* Dr. Vladimir Dragovic, Department Head, 972-883-2161, Fax: 972-883-6622, E-mail: utdmath@utdallas.edu. *Application contact:* Evangelina Bustamante, Graduate Student Coordinator, 972-883-2163, Fax: 972-883-6622, E-mail: utdmath@utdallas.edu.
Website: http://www.utdallas.edu/math

University of Waterloo, Graduate Studies and Postdoctoral Affairs, Faculty of Mathematics, Department of Statistics and Actuarial Science, Waterloo, ON N2L 3G1, Canada. Offers actuarial science (M Math, MAS, PhD); biostatistics (PhD); statistics (M Math, PhD); statistics-biostatistics (M Math); statistics-computing (M Math); statistics-finance (M Math). *Degree requirements:* For master's, research paper or thesis; for doctorate, comprehensive exam, thesis/dissertation. *Entrance requirements:* For master's, honors degree in field, minimum B+ average; for doctorate, master's degree, minimum B+ average. Additional exam requirements/recommendations for international students: Required—TOEFL, IELTS, PTE. *Application deadline:* Applications are processed on a rolling basis. Application fee: $125 Canadian dollars. Electronic applications accepted. *Financial support:* Fellowships, research assistantships, teaching assistantships, career-related internships or fieldwork, and scholarships/grants available. *Faculty research:* Data analysis, risk theory, inference, stochastic processes, quantitative finance.
Website: https://uwaterloo.ca/statistics-and-actuarial-science/

University of Wisconsin–Madison, Graduate School, Wisconsin School of Business, Doctoral Program in Actuarial Science, Risk Management and Insurance, Madison, WI 53706-1380. Offers PhD. *Degree requirements:* For doctorate, comprehensive exam, thesis/dissertation. *Entrance requirements:* For doctorate, GMAT or GRE General Test. Additional exam requirements/recommendations for international students: Recommended—TOEFL (minimum score 623 paper-based; 106 iBT), IELTS (minimum score 7.5), TSE (minimum score 73). Electronic applications accepted. *Expenses:* Contact institution. *Faculty research:* Actuarial science, regression and business forecasting, panel data, economics of insurance markets, insurance regulation, public economics, behavioral economics, Bayesian methodology related to health insurance, tort reform and government programs, joint and several liability, superfund, predictive modeling, asymmetric information in insurance, psychology and economics, applied microeconomics, insurance markets, risk and decision making.

University of Wisconsin–Milwaukee, Graduate School, College of Letters and Science, Department of Mathematical Sciences, Milwaukee, WI 53201-0413. Offers mathematics (MS, PhD), including actuarial science, algebra (PhD), applied and computational mathematics (PhD), atmospheric science, foundations of advanced studies (MS), industrial mathematics, probability and statistics (PhD), standard mathematics (MS), statistics (MS), topology (PhD). *Students:* 56 full-time (11 women), 10 part-time (2 women); includes 4 minority (2 Black or African American, non-Hispanic/Latino; 1 Asian, non-Hispanic/Latino; 1 Two or more races, non-Hispanic/Latino), 28 international. Average age 30. 136 applicants, 22% accepted, 20 enrolled. In 2018, 16 master's, 8 doctorates awarded. *Degree requirements:* For master's, comprehensive exam, thesis optional; for doctorate, 2 foreign languages, thesis/dissertation. *Entrance requirements:* Additional exam requirements/recommendations for international students: Required—TOEFL (minimum score 550 paper-based; 79 iBT), IELTS (minimum score 6.5). *Application deadline:* For fall admission, 1/1 priority date for domestic students; for spring admission, 9/1 for domestic students. Application fee: $56 ($96 for international students). Electronic applications accepted. *Financial support:* Fellowships, research assistantships, teaching assistantships, career-related internships or fieldwork, health care benefits, and unspecified assistantships available. Support available to part-time students. Financial award application deadline: 4/15; financial award applicants required to submit FAFSA. *Faculty research:* Algebra, applied mathematics, atmospheric science, probability and statistics, topology. *Unit head:* Richard Stockbridge, Department Chair, 414-229-4568, E-mail: stockbri@uwm.edu. *Application contact:* General Information Contact, 414-229-4982, Fax: 414-229-6967, E-mail: gradschool@uwm.edu.
Website: http://www.uwm.edu/dept/math/

Youngstown State University, College of Graduate Studies, College of Science, Technology, Engineering and Mathematics, Department of Mathematics and Statistics, Youngstown, OH 44555-0001. Offers actuarial science (MS); applied mathematics (MS); computer science (MS); mathematics (MS); secondary/community college mathematics (MS); statistics (MS). *Program availability:* Part-time. *Degree requirements:* For master's, comprehensive exam, thesis optional. *Entrance requirements:* For master's, minimum GPA of 2.7 in computer science and mathematics. Additional exam requirements/recommendations for international students: Required—TOEFL. *Faculty research:* Regression analysis, numerical analysis, statistics, Markov chain, topology and fuzzy sets.

Insurance

California State University, Fullerton, Graduate Studies, College of Business and Economics, Program in Business Administration, Fullerton, CA 92831-3599. Offers business administration (MBA); business analytics (MBA); international business (MBA); organizational leadership (MBA); risk management and insurance (MBA). *Accreditation:* AACSB. *Program availability:* Part-time. *Entrance requirements:* For master's, GMAT.

Florida State University, The Graduate School, College of Business, Tallahassee, FL 32306-1110. Offers accounting (M Acc), including assurance and advisory services, generalist, taxation; business administration (MBA, PhD), including accounting (PhD), finance (PhD), management information systems (PhD), marketing (PhD), organizational behavior and human resources (PhD), risk management and insurance (PhD), strategy (PhD); finance (MS); management information systems (MS); risk

management and insurance (MS); JD/MBA; MSW/MBA. *Accreditation:* AACSB. *Program availability:* Part-time, 100% online. *Students:* Average age 31. 300 applicants, 61% accepted, 133 enrolled. In 2018, 268 master's, 9 doctorates awarded. Terminal master's awarded for partial completion of doctoral program. *Degree requirements:* For doctorate, comprehensive exam, thesis/dissertation. *Entrance requirements:* For master's, GMAT, GRE (for all except MS in finance), work experience (MBA, MS); minimum GPA of 3.0, letters of recommendation; for doctorate, GMAT, GRE (for marketing, organizational behavior, risk management and insurance, management information systems, and human resources only), minimum graduate GPA of 3.5, letters of recommendation. Additional exam requirements/recommendations for international students: Required—TOEFL (minimum score 600 paper-based; 85 iBT); Recommended—IELTS (minimum score 6). *Application deadline:* For fall admission, 6/1 for domestic and international students; for spring admission, 10/1 for domestic and international students; for summer admission, 3/1 for domestic and international students. Applications are processed on a rolling basis. Application fee: $30. Electronic applications accepted. *Expenses:* Contact institution. *Financial support:* In 2018–19, 146 students received support, including 26 fellowships (averaging $1,500 per year), 77 research assistantships with full tuition reimbursements available (averaging $20,000 per year), 43 teaching assistantships with full tuition reimbursements available (averaging $20,000 per year); career-related internships or fieldwork, scholarships/grants, health care benefits, tuition waivers (full and partial), and unspecified assistantships also available. Support available to part-time students. Financial award application deadline: 1/1; financial award applicants required to submit FAFSA. *Faculty research:* Business strategy, marketing, finance, accounting, business analytics. *Total annual research expenditures:* $1.4 million. *Unit head:* Dr. Michael Hartline, Dean, 850-644-4405, Fax: 850-644-0915, E-mail: mhartline@business.fsu.edu. *Application contact:* Jennifer Clark, Director, 850-644-6458, E-mail: gradprograms@business.fsu.edu.
Website: http://business.fsu.edu/

Georgia State University, J. Mack Robinson College of Business, Department of Risk Management and Insurance, Program in Risk Management and Insurance, Atlanta, GA 30302-3083. Offers enterprise risk management (MBA, Certificate); financial risk management (MBA); mathematical risk management (MS); risk and insurance (MS); risk management and insurance (MBA, PhD); MAS/MRM. *Program availability:* Part-time, evening/weekend. *Entrance requirements:* For master's, GRE or GMAT, transcripts from all institutions attended, resume, essays. Additional exam requirements/recommendations for international students: Required—TOEFL (minimum score 610 paper-based; 101 iBT), IELTS (minimum score 7). *Application deadline:* Applications are processed on a rolling basis. Application fee: $50. Electronic applications accepted. *Expenses: Tuition, area resident:* Full-time $9360; part-time $390 per credit hour. Tuition, state resident: full-time $9360; part-time $390 per credit hour. Tuition, nonresident: full-time $30,024; part-time $1251 per credit hour. *International tuition:* $30,024 full-time. *Required fees:* $2128. *Financial support:* Research assistantships, scholarships/grants, tuition waivers, and unspecified assistantships available. *Faculty research:* Insurance economics, structure and performance of insurance markets, regulation and policy in insurance markets, asset pricing theory, financial econometrics. *Unit head:* Dr. Haci Akin, Director, 404-413-7467, Fax: 404-413-7467, E-mail: hakcin1@gsu.edu. *Application contact:* Toby McChesney, Graduate Recruiting Contact, 404-413-7167, Fax: 404-413-7162, E-mail: rcbgradadmissions@gsu.edu.
Website: http://rmi.robinson.gsu.edu/academic-programs/ms-rmi/

Olivet College, Master of Business Administration in Insurance Program, Olivet, MI 49076-9701. Offers MBA. *Accreditation:* TEAC. *Program availability:* Part-time, online only, 100% online, blended/hybrid learning. *Degree requirements:* For master's, thesis optional. *Entrance requirements:* For master's, GMAT or CPCU designation, professional resume, official transcript, two letters of recommendation, 2 years of professional experience in field of insurance or risk management after earning undergraduate degree, minimum undergraduate GPA of 3.0. Electronic applications accepted. *Expenses:* Contact institution.

Pontificia Universidad Catolica Madre y Maestra, Graduate School, Faculty of Social and Administrative Sciences, Santiago, Dominican Republic. Offers business administration (MBA), including business development, finance, international business, management skills (M Mgmt, MBA), marketing, operations, strategic cost management, strategy, tourist destination planning and management; law (LL M), including civil law, corporate business law, criminal law, international relations, real estate law; management (M Mgmt), including higher financial management, insurance program administration, management skills (M Mgmt, MBA); psychology (MA), including clinical child and adolescent psychology, forensic psychology; strategic human resources (EMBA).

St. John's University, The Peter J. Tobin College of Business, School of Risk Management, Insurance and Actuarial Science, Queens, NY 11439. Offers actuarial science (MS); business administration (MBA), including risk management and insurance; enterprise risk management (MBA, MS), including enterprise risk management (MS); risk management and insurance (MS). *Entrance requirements:* For master's, GMAT or GRE, 2 letters of recommendation, essay, resume, unofficial transcripts. Additional exam requirements/recommendations for international students: Required—TOEFL (minimum score 80 iBT), IELTS (minimum score 6.5). Electronic applications accepted. *Expenses:* Contact institution. *Faculty research:* Insurance company operations and financial analysis, enterprise risk management, risk theory and modeling, credibility theory and actuarial price modeling, international insurance.

Temple University, Fox School of Business, Doctoral Programs in Business, Philadelphia, PA 19122-6096. Offers accounting (PhD); entrepreneurship (PhD); finance (PhD); international business (PhD); management information systems (PhD); marketing (PhD); risk management and insurance (PhD); statistics (PhD); strategic management (PhD); tourism and sport (PhD). *Accreditation:* AACSB. *Degree requirements:* For doctorate, thesis/dissertation. *Entrance requirements:* For doctorate, GRE General Test, GMAT, minimum GPA of 3.0, master's degree. Additional exam requirements/recommendations for international students: Required—TOEFL (minimum score 600 paper-based; 100 iBT), IELTS (minimum score 7.5). Electronic applications accepted.

University of Colorado Denver, Business School, Program in Finance, Denver, CO 80217. Offers economics (MS); finance (MS); financial analysis and management (MS); financial and commodities risk management (MS); risk management and insurance (MS). *Program availability:* Part-time, evening/weekend. *Degree requirements:* For master's, 30 semester hours (18 of required core courses, 9 of finance electives, and 3 of free elective). *Entrance requirements:* For master's, GMAT, essay, resume, two letters of recommendation; financial statements (for international students). Additional exam requirements/recommendations for international students: Required—TOEFL (minimum score 537 paper-based; 75 iBT); Recommended—IELTS (minimum score 6.5). Electronic applications accepted. *Expenses:* Contact institution. *Faculty research:* Corporate governance, debt maturity policies, regulation and financial markets, option management strategies.

University of Florida, Graduate School, Warrington College of Business Administration, Hough Graduate School of Business, Department of Finance, Insurance and Real Estate, Gainesville, FL 32611. Offers entrepreneurship (MS); finance (MS, PhD); financial services (Certificate); insurance (PhD); quantitative finance (PhD); real estate (MS); real estate and urban analysis (PhD); JD/MBA; JD/MS. Terminal master's awarded for partial completion of doctoral program. *Degree requirements:* For master's, comprehensive exam, thesis; for doctorate, comprehensive exam, thesis/dissertation. *Entrance requirements:* For master's, GMAT (minimum score of 465) or GRE General Test, minimum GPA of 3.0 for last 60 hours of undergraduate degree, work experience (preferred); for doctorate, GMAT (minimum score of 465) or GRE General Test, minimum GPA of 3.0. Additional exam requirements/recommendations for international students: Required—TOEFL (minimum score 550 paper-based; 80 iBT), IELTS (minimum score 6). Electronic applications accepted. *Faculty research:* Banking, empirical corporate finance, hedge funds.

University of Pennsylvania, Wharton School, Insurance and Risk Management Department, Philadelphia, PA 19104. Offers MBA, PhD. *Degree requirements:* For doctorate, thesis/dissertation. *Entrance requirements:* For master's, GMAT; for doctorate, GMAT or GRE. *Faculty research:* Fair rate of return in insurance economics of pension plans, insurance regulation, malpractice insurance, actuarial science, genetic testing and life insurance.

University of Wisconsin–Madison, Graduate School, Wisconsin School of Business, Doctoral Program in Actuarial Science, Risk Management and Insurance, Madison, WI 53706-1380. Offers PhD. *Degree requirements:* For doctorate, comprehensive exam, thesis/dissertation. *Entrance requirements:* For doctorate, GMAT or GRE General Test. Additional exam requirements/recommendations for international students: Recommended—TOEFL (minimum score 623 paper-based; 106 iBT), IELTS (minimum score 7.5), TSE (minimum score 73). Electronic applications accepted. *Expenses:* Contact institution. *Faculty research:* Actuarial science, regression and business forecasting, panel data, economics of insurance markets, insurance regulation, public economics, behavioral economics, Bayesian methodology related to health insurance, tort reform and government programs, joint and several liability, superfund, predictive modeling, asymmetric information in insurance, psychology and economics, applied microeconomics, insurance markets, risk and decision making.

University of Wisconsin–Madison, Graduate School, Wisconsin School of Business, Wisconsin Full-Time MBA Program, Madison, WI 53706-1380. Offers applied security analysis (MBA); arts administration (MBA); brand and product management (MBA); corporate finance and investment banking (MBA); marketing research (MBA); operations and technology management (MBA); real estate (MBA); risk management and insurance (MBA); strategic human resource management (MBA); supply chain management (MBA). *Faculty:* 137 full-time (36 women), 39 part-time/adjunct (11 women). *Students:* 183 full-time (59 women); includes 31 minority (5 Black or African American, non-Hispanic/Latino; 1 American Indian or Alaska Native, non-Hispanic/Latino; 6 Asian, non-Hispanic/Latino; 13 Hispanic/Latino; 6 Two or more races, non-Hispanic/Latino), 40 international. Average age 28. 465 applicants, 33% accepted, 79 enrolled. In 2018, 104 master's awarded. *Entrance requirements:* For master's, GMAT or GRE, bachelor's or equivalent degree, essay, letter of recommendation, resume. Additional exam requirements/recommendations for international students: Required—TOEFL (minimum score 100 iBT), IELTS (minimum score 7.5), TOEFL is not required for international students whose undergraduate training was in English. *Application deadline:* For fall admission, 11/1 for domestic and international students; for winter admission, 1/10 for domestic and international students; for spring admission, 3/1 for domestic and international students; for summer admission, 4/10 for domestic students, 4/10 priority date for international students. Applications are processed on a rolling basis. Application fee: $75 ($81 for international students). Electronic applications accepted. *Expenses:* Wisconsin Resident tuition and fees - $39,156; Nonresident tuition and fees - $76,635. *Financial support:* In 2018–19, 148 students received support, including 7 fellowships with full tuition reimbursements available (averaging $25,871 per year), 7 research assistantships with full tuition reimbursements available (averaging $14,832 per year), 47 teaching assistantships with full tuition reimbursements available (averaging $14,832 per year); scholarships/grants, health care benefits, tuition waivers (full and partial), and unspecified assistantships also available. Financial award application deadline: 6/1. *Faculty research:* Ecology, environmental studies, and business; decision making; tax policy; diversity and inclusion in governance boards; marketing and social media. *Unit head:* Dr. Enno Siemsen, Associate Dean of the MBA and Masters Programs, 608-890-3130, E-mail: esiemsen@wisc.edu. *Application contact:* Betsy Kacizak, Director of Admissions and Recruiting, Full-time MBA Program, 608-262-4000, E-mail: betsy.kacizak@wisc.edu.
Website: https://wsb.wisc.edu/

Western Michigan University Thomas M. Cooley Law School, Graduate Programs, Lansing, MI 48901-3038. Offers administrative law (public law) (JD); business transactions (JD); Canadian law practice (JD); corporate law and finance (LL M); environmental law (public law) (JD); general practice (JD), including solo and small firm; general studies (LL M); homeland and national security law (LL M); insurance law (LL M); intellectual property (JD); intellectual property law (LL M); international law (JD); litigation (JD); taxation (LL M); U.S. legal studies for foreign attorneys (LL M); JD/LL M; JD/MBA; JD/MHA; JD/MPA; JD/MSW. *Accreditation:* ABA. *Program availability:* Part-time, evening/weekend, 100% online, blended/hybrid learning. *Degree requirements:* For master's, thesis (for some programs); for doctorate, minimum of 3 credits of clinical experience. *Entrance requirements:* For master's, JD or LL B; for doctorate, LSAT. Additional exam requirements/recommendations for international students: Required—TOEFL (for U.S. legal studies for foreign attorneys LL M program); Recommended—TOEFL. Electronic applications accepted. *Expenses:* Contact institution. *Faculty research:* Wrongful convictions, civil rights, environmental law, litigation techniques, data mining, intellectual property, practical and skills-based legal education.

Risk Management

Boston University, Metropolitan College, Department of Administrative Sciences, Boston, MA 02215. Offers applied business analytics (MS); economic development and tourism management (MSAS); enterprise risk management (MS); financial management (MS); global marketing management (MS); innovation and technology (MSAS); insurance management (MS); project management (MS); supply chain management (MS). *Accreditation:* AACSB. *Program availability:* Part-time, evening/weekend, 100% online, blended/hybrid learning. *Faculty:* 27 full-time (5 women), 39 part-time/adjunct (5 women). *Students:* 617 full-time (351 women), 574 part-time (290 women); includes 196 minority (47 Black or African American, non-Hispanic/Latino; 2 American Indian or Alaska Native, non-Hispanic/Latino; 75 Asian, non-Hispanic/Latino; 60 Hispanic/Latino; 12 Two or more races, non-Hispanic/Latino), 730 international. Average age 28. 2,259 applicants, 76% accepted, 594 enrolled. In 2018, 441 master's awarded. *Degree requirements:* For master's, thesis optional. *Entrance requirements:* For master's, 1 year of work experience, minimum GPA of 3.0. Additional exam requirements/recommendations for international students: Required—TOEFL (minimum score 84 iBT). *Application deadline:* For fall admission, 8/1 priority date for domestic students, 6/1 priority date for international students; for spring admission, 12/1 priority date for domestic students, 11/15 priority date for international students; for summer admission, 4/1 priority date for domestic students, 3/1 priority date for international students. Applications are processed on a rolling basis. Application fee: $85. Electronic applications accepted. *Expenses:* Contact institution. *Financial support:* In 2018–19, 15 students received support, including 16 research assistantships (averaging $8,400 per year), 30 teaching assistantships (averaging $3,400 per year); career-related internships or fieldwork, Federal Work-Study, and unspecified assistantships also available. Financial award applicants required to submit FAFSA. *Faculty research:* International business, innovative process. *Unit head:* Dr. John Sullivan, Chair, 617-353-3016, E-mail: adminsc@bu.edu. *Application contact:* Enrollment Services, 617-358-8162, E-mail: met@bu.edu.
Website: http://www.bu.edu/met/academic-community/departments/administrative-sciences/

Brandeis University, International Business School (IBS), Master of Science in Finance Program, Waltham, MA 02454-9110. Offers asset management (MSF); corporate finance (MSF); risk management (MSF). *Entrance requirements:* For master's, GMAT or GRE. Additional exam requirements/recommendations for international students: Required—TOEFL (minimum score 600 paper-based; 100 iBT), IELTS (minimum score 7), PTE (minimum score 68). Electronic applications accepted. *Expenses:* Contact institution. *Faculty research:* Asset management, municipal finance, corporate finance, venture capital, international trade.

California State University, Fullerton, Graduate Studies, College of Business and Economics, Program in Business Administration, Fullerton, CA 92831-3599. Offers business administration (MBA); business analytics (MBA); international business (MBA); organizational leadership (MBA); risk management and insurance (MBA). *Accreditation:* AACSB. *Program availability:* Part-time. *Entrance requirements:* For master's, GMAT.

Concordia University Wisconsin, Graduate Programs, Batterman School of Business, MBA Program, Mequon, WI 53097-2402. Offers finance (MBA); health care administration (MBA); human resource management (MBA); international business (MBA); international business-bilingual English/Chinese (MBA); management (MBA); management information systems (MBA); managerial communications (MBA); marketing (MBA); public administration (MBA); risk management (MBA). *Program availability:* Online learning. *Degree requirements:* For master's, comprehensive exam, thesis or alternative. *Entrance requirements:* Additional exam requirements/recommendations for international students: Required—TOEFL. *Expenses:* Contact institution.

DePaul University, Kellstadt Graduate School of Business, Chicago, IL 60604. Offers accountancy (MBA, MSA); applied economics (MBA); audit and advisory services (MS); business administration (DBA); business analytics (MS); business strategy and decision-making (MBA); computational finance (MS); economics and policy analysis (MS); enterprise risk management (MS); entrepreneurship (MBA, MS); finance (MBA, MS); general business (MBA); hospitality leadership (MBA); hospitality leadership and operational performance (MS); human resources (MS); international business (MBA); management (MBA, MS); management information systems (MBA); marketing (MBA, MS); marketing analysis (MS); marketing strategy and planning (MBA); real estate (MS); real estate finance and investment (MBA); strategy, execution and valuation (MBA); supply chain management (MS); sustainable management (MS); taxation (MS); JD/MBA. *Accreditation:* AACSB. *Program availability:* Part-time, evening/weekend, online learning. *Entrance requirements:* For master's, GMAT/GRE, 2 letters of recommendation, resume, essay, official transcripts. Additional exam requirements/recommendations for international students: Required—TOEFL (minimum score 550 paper-based; 80 iBT). Electronic applications accepted. *Expenses:* Contact institution.

Florida State University, The Graduate School, College of Business, Tallahassee, FL 32306-1110. Offers accounting (M Acc), including assurance and advisory services, generalist, taxation; business administration (MBA, PhD), including accounting (PhD), finance (PhD), management information systems (PhD), marketing (PhD), organizational behavior and human resources (PhD), risk management and insurance (PhD), strategy (PhD); finance (MS); management information systems (MS); risk management and insurance (MS); JD/MBA; MSW/MBA. *Accreditation:* AACSB. *Program availability:* Part-time, 100% online. *Students:* Average age 31. 300 applicants, 61% accepted, 133 enrolled. In 2018, 268 master's, 9 doctorates awarded. Terminal master's awarded for partial completion of doctoral program. *Degree requirements:* For doctorate, comprehensive exam, thesis/dissertation. *Entrance requirements:* For master's, GMAT, GRE (for all except MS in finance), work experience (MBA, MS); minimum GPA of 3.0, letters of recommendation; for doctorate, GMAT, GRE (for marketing, organizational behavior, risk management and insurance, management information systems, and human resources only), minimum graduate GPA of 3.5, letters of recommendation. Additional exam requirements/recommendations for international students: Required—TOEFL (minimum score 600 paper-based; 85 iBT); Recommended—IELTS (minimum score 6). *Application deadline:* For fall admission, 6/1 for domestic and international students; for spring admission, 10/1 for domestic and international students; for summer admission, 3/1 for domestic and international students. Applications are processed on a rolling basis. Application fee: $30. Electronic applications accepted. *Expenses:* Contact institution. *Financial support:* In 2018–19, 146 students received support, including 26 fellowships (averaging $1,500 per year), 77 research assistantships with full tuition reimbursements available (averaging $20,000 per year), 43 teaching assistantships with full tuition reimbursements available (averaging $20,000 per year); career-related internships or fieldwork, scholarships/grants, health care benefits, tuition waivers (full and partial), and unspecified assistantships also available. Support available to part-time students. Financial award application deadline: 1/1; financial award applicants required to submit FAFSA. *Faculty research:* Business strategy, marketing, finance, accounting, business analytics. *Total annual research expenditures:* $1.4 million. *Unit head:* Dr. Michael Hartline, Dean, 850-644-4405, Fax: 850-644-0915, E-mail: mhartline@business.fsu.edu. *Application contact:* Jennifer Clark, Director, 850-644-6458, E-mail: gradprograms@business.fsu.edu.
Website: http://business.fsu.edu/

Georgia State University, J. Mack Robinson College of Business, Department of Risk Management and Insurance, Program in Risk Management and Insurance, Atlanta, GA 30302-3083. Offers enterprise risk management (MBA, Certificate); financial risk management (MBA); mathematical risk management (MS); risk and insurance (MS); risk management and insurance (MBA, PhD); MAS/MRM. *Program availability:* Part-time, evening/weekend. *Entrance requirements:* For master's, GRE or GMAT, transcripts from all institutions attended, resume, essays. Additional exam requirements/recommendations for international students: Required—TOEFL (minimum score 610 paper-based; 101 iBT), IELTS (minimum score 7). *Application deadline:* Applications are processed on a rolling basis. Application fee: $50. Electronic applications accepted. *Expenses: Tuition, area resident:* Full-time $9360; part-time $390 per credit hour. Tuition, state resident: full-time $9360; part-time $390 per credit hour. Tuition, nonresident: full-time $30,024; part-time $1251 per credit hour. *International tuition:* $30,024 full-time. *Required fees:* $2128. *Financial support:* Research assistantships, scholarships/grants, tuition waivers, and unspecified assistantships available. *Faculty research:* Insurance economics, structure and performance of insurance markets, regulation and policy in insurance markets, asset pricing theory, financial econometrics. *Unit head:* Dr. Haci Akin, Director, 404-413-7467, Fax: 404-413-7467, E-mail: hakcin1@gsu.edu. *Application contact:* Toby McChesney, Graduate Recruiting Contact, 404-413-7167, Fax: 404-413-7162, E-mail: rcbgradadmissions@gsu.edu.
Website: http://rmi.robinson.gsu.edu/academic-programs/ms-rmi/

Husson University, Master of Business Administration Program, Bangor, ME 04401-2999. Offers athletic administration (MBA); biotechnology and innovation (MBA); general business administration (MBA); healthcare management (MBA); hospitality and tourism management (MBA); organizational management (MBA); risk management (MBA). *Program availability:* Part-time, evening/weekend, 100% online, blended/hybrid learning. *Degree requirements:* For master's, comprehensive exam (for some programs), thesis optional. *Entrance requirements:* For master's, minimum GPA of 3.0, letter of recommendation. Additional exam requirements/recommendations for international students: Required—TOEFL (minimum score 550 paper-based; 80 iBT), IELTS (minimum score 6.5). Electronic applications accepted. *Expenses:* Contact institution.

Iona College, School of Business, Department of Information Systems, New Rochelle, NY 10801-1890. Offers accounting and information systems (MS); business continuity and risk management (AC); information systems (MBA, MS, PMC); project management (MS). *Program availability:* Part-time, evening/weekend. *Faculty:* 5 full-time (0 women). *Students:* 12 full-time (7 women), 9 part-time (4 women); includes 7 minority (3 Black or African American, non-Hispanic/Latino; 2 Asian, non-Hispanic/Latino; 2 Hispanic/Latino), 1 international. Average age 28. 9 applicants, 89% accepted, 2 enrolled. In 2018, 12 master's awarded. *Entrance requirements:* For master's, GMAT, 2 letters of recommendation, minimum GPA of 3.0; for other advanced degree, GMAT, minimum GPA of 3.0. Additional exam requirements/recommendations for international students: Required—TOEFL (minimum score 550 paper-based; 80 iBT), IELTS (minimum score 6.5). *Application deadline:* For fall admission, 8/15 priority date for domestic students, 8/1 priority date for international students; for winter admission, 11/15 priority date for domestic students, 11/1 priority date for international students; for spring admission, 2/15 priority date for domestic students, 2/1 priority date for international students; for summer admission, 5/15 priority date for domestic students, 5/1 priority date for international students. Applications are processed on a rolling basis. Application fee: $50. Electronic applications accepted. *Expenses:* Contact institution. *Financial support:* In 2018–19, 12 students received support. Scholarships/grants, tuition waivers (partial), and unspecified assistantships available. Support available to part-time students. Financial award application deadline: 4/15; financial award applicants required to submit FAFSA. *Faculty research:* Fuzzy sets, risk management, computer security, competence set analysis, investment strategies. *Unit head:* Dr. Shoshana Altschuller, Department Chair, 914-637-7726, E-mail: saltschuller@iona.edu. *Application contact:* Kimberly Kelly, Director of Graduate Business Admissions, 914-633-2271, Fax: 914-633-2012, E-mail: kkelly@iona.edu.
Website: http://www.iona.edu/Academics/Hagan-School-of-Business/Departments/Information-Systems/Graduate-Programs.aspx

Johns Hopkins University, Carey Business School, MS in Business Analytics and Risk Management Program, Baltimore, MD 21218. Offers MS. *Students:* 73 full-time (42 women), 9 part-time (3 women). 156 applicants, 70% accepted, 50 enrolled. In 2018, 13 master's awarded. *Degree requirements:* For master's, 36 credits. *Entrance requirements:* For master's, GMAT or GRE. Additional exam requirements/recommendations for international students: Required—TOEFL, IELTS. *Application deadline:* For fall admission, 4/3 for domestic and international students. Applications are processed on a rolling basis. Application fee: $100. Electronic applications accepted. *Expenses:* Contact institution. *Financial support:* In 2018–19, 20 students received support. Scholarships/grants available. Financial award application deadline: 4/15; financial award applicants required to submit FAFSA. *Faculty research:* Emerging issues in business analytics and risk management. *Unit head:* Dr. Kevin Frick, Vice Dean of Education, 410-234-9272, E-mail: kfrick@jhu.edu. *Application contact:* Office of Admissions, 410-234-9220, Fax: 443-529-1554, E-mail: carey.admissions@jhu.edu.

Loyola University Chicago, Quinlan School of Business, MBA Programs, Chicago, IL 60611. Offers accounting (MBA); business ethics (MBA); derivative markets (MBA); economics (MBA); entrepreneurship (MBA); finance (MBA); healthcare management (MBA); human resources management (MBA); information systems management (MBA); international business (MBA); management (MBA); marketing (MBA); risk management (MBA); supply chain management (MBA). *Program availability:* Part-time, evening/weekend. *Entrance requirements:* For master's, GMAT or GRE, official transcripts, two letters of recommendation, statement of purpose, resume. Additional exam requirements/recommendations for international students: Required—TOEFL (minimum score 90 iBT) or IELTS (minimum score 6.5). Electronic applications accepted. Application fee is waived when completed online. *Expenses:* Contact institution. *Faculty research:* Social enterprise and responsibility, emerging markets, supply chain management, risk management.

Metropolitan College of New York, Program in Business Administration, New York, NY 10006. Offers financial services (MBA); general management (MBA); healthcare systems and risk management (MBA); media management (MBA). *Accreditation:*

ACBSP. *Program availability:* Evening/weekend. *Degree requirements:* For master's, thesis, 10-day study abroad. *Entrance requirements:* For master's, GMAT. Additional exam requirements/recommendations for international students: Required—TOEFL (minimum score 600 paper-based). Electronic applications accepted. *Expenses:* Contact institution.

New York University, School of Professional Studies, Division of Programs in Business, Program in Management and Systems, New York, NY 10012-1019. Offers management and systems (MS), including database technologies, enterprise risk management, strategy and leadership, systems management. *Program availability:* Part-time, evening/weekend, 100% online, blended/hybrid learning. *Degree requirements:* For master's, thesis, capstone project. *Entrance requirements:* For master's, GRE or GMAT (only upon request), bachelor's degree, resume with relevant professional work, internship or volunteer experience, two letters of recommendation, statement of purpose. Additional exam requirements/recommendations for international students: Required—TOEFL (minimum score 600 paper-based; 100 iBT), IELTS (minimum score 7). Electronic applications accepted. *Expenses:* Contact institution.

Ohio Dominican University, Division of Business, Program in Business Administration, Columbus, OH 43219-2099. Offers accounting (MBA); data analytics (MBA); finance (MBA); leadership (MBA); risk management (MBA); sport management (MBA). *Program availability:* Part-time, evening/weekend, 100% online, blended/hybrid learning. *Faculty:* 10 full-time (4 women), 12 part-time/adjunct (1 woman). *Students:* 42 full-time (17 women), 88 part-time (43 women); includes 29 minority (16 Black or African American, non-Hispanic/Latino; 1 American Indian or Alaska Native, non-Hispanic/Latino; 3 Asian, non-Hispanic/Latino; 5 Hispanic/Latino; 4 Two or more races, non-Hispanic/Latino), 14 international. Average age 31. 97 applicants, 44% accepted, 26 enrolled. In 2018, 56 master's awarded. *Entrance requirements:* For master's, minimum overall GPA of 3.0 in undergraduate degree from regionally-accredited institution or 2.75 in last 60 semester hours of bachelor's degree. Additional exam requirements/recommendations for international students: Required—TOEFL (minimum score 550 paper-based), IELTS (minimum score 6.5). *Application deadline:* For fall admission, 8/15 for domestic students, 6/10 for international students; for spring admission, 1/4 for domestic students, 11/2 for international students; for summer admission, 5/30 for domestic students. Applications are processed on a rolling basis. Application fee: $25. Electronic applications accepted. *Expenses: Tuition:* Full-time $10,800; part-time $600 per credit hour. *Required fees:* $450; $225 per semester. Tuition and fees vary according to program. *Financial support:* Applicants required to submit FAFSA. *Unit head:* Dr. Thomas Eveland, Director of Graduate Programs in Business, 614-251-4569, E-mail: evelandt@ohiodominican.edu. *Application contact:* John W. Naughton, Vice President for Enrollment and Student Success, 614-251-4721, Fax: 614-251-6654, E-mail: grad@ohiodominican.edu.
Website: http://www.ohiodominican.edu/academics/graduate/mba

Pace University, Lubin School of Business, Finance Program, New York, NY 10038. Offers financial management (MBA, MS); financial risk management (MS); international finance (MBA); investment management (MBA, MS). *Program availability:* Part-time, evening/weekend. *Students:* 120 full-time (52 women), 79 part-time (30 women); includes 33 minority (10 Black or African American, non-Hispanic/Latino; 14 Asian, non-Hispanic/Latino; 8 Hispanic/Latino; 1 Two or more races, non-Hispanic/Latino), 119 international. Average age 26. 236 applicants, 77% accepted, 64 enrolled. In 2018, 132 master's awarded. *Entrance requirements:* For master's, GMAT, GRE (GMAT not required for MS with passing of Level 1 of Chartered Financial Analyst exam or Level 1 of Financial Risk Manager Exam), Undergrad degree, transcripts from all accredited colleges/universities attended, 2 letters of recommendation, resume, personal statement. If applying to the 1 year fast track MBA in Financial Management, must have a cumulative GPA of 3.30 or above, a grade of B or better for all business core courses from an AACSB-accredited U.S. business school. Additional exam requirements/recommendations for international students: Required—TOEFL (minimum score 90 iBT), IELTS (minimum score 7) or PTE (minimum score 61). *Application deadline:* For fall admission, 8/1 priority date for domestic students, 6/1 for international students; for spring admission, 12/1 for domestic students, 10/1 for international students. Applications are processed on a rolling basis. Application fee: $70. Electronic applications accepted. *Financial support:* Research assistantships, career-related internships or fieldwork, Federal Work-Study, tuition waivers (full and partial), and unspecified assistantships available. Support available to part-time students. Financial award application deadline: 2/15; financial award applicants required to submit FAFSA. *Unit head:* Dr. Aron Gottesman, Chairperson, Finance Department, 212-618-6525, E-mail: agottesman@pace.edu. *Application contact:* Susan Ford-Goldschein, Director of Graduate Admissions, 212-346-1531, Fax: 212-346-1585, E-mail: graduateadmissions@pace.edu.
Website: http://www.pace.edu/lubin/sections/explore-programs/graduate-programs

Queens College of the City University of New York, Division of Social Sciences, Department of Economics, Queens, NY 11367-1597. Offers risk management: accounting (MS); risk management: dynamic financial analysis (MS); risk management: finance (MS). Risk Management is a graduate program offered jointly by the Departments of Economics and Accounting & Information Systems. *Faculty:* 23 full-time (8 women), 42 part-time/adjunct (9 women). *Students:* 3 full-time (2 women), 26 part-time (15 women); includes 24 minority (4 Black or African American, non-Hispanic/Latino; 10 Asian, non-Hispanic/Latino; 7 Hispanic/Latino; 3 Two or more races, non-Hispanic/Latino), 5 international. Average age 30. 24 applicants, 79% accepted, 12 enrolled. In 2018, 20 master's awarded. *Degree requirements:* For master's, thesis, Capstone Class/Thesis Project. *Entrance requirements:* For master's, minimum GPA of 3.0. Additional exam requirements/recommendations for international students: Required—TOEFL (minimum score 100 iBT), IELTS (minimum score 7). *Application deadline:* For fall admission, 6/30 for domestic and international students; for spring admission, 11/30 for domestic and international students. Applications are processed on a rolling basis. Application fee: $75. Electronic applications accepted. *Financial support:* In 2018–19, 1 student received support. Federal Work-Study, institutionally sponsored loans, and scholarships/grants available. Financial award application deadline: 4/1; financial award applicants required to submit FAFSA. *Faculty research:* Business economics, urban economic problems, international economics, economics of nonprofit sector. *Unit head:* Cara Marshall, Program Director, 718-997-5387, E-mail: cara.marshall@qc.cuny.edu. *Application contact:* Elvira Casper, Program Coordinator, 718-997-5507, E-mail: elvira.casper@qc.cuny.edu.

St. John's University, The Peter J. Tobin College of Business, School of Risk Management, Insurance and Actuarial Science, Queens, NY 11439. Offers actuarial science (MS); business administration (MBA), including risk management and insurance; enterprise risk management (MBA, MS), including enterprise risk management (MS); risk management and insurance (MS). *Entrance requirements:* For master's, GMAT or GRE, 2 letters of recommendation, essay, resume, unofficial transcripts. Additional exam requirements/recommendations for international students: Required—TOEFL (minimum score 80 iBT), IELTS (minimum score 6.5). Electronic applications accepted. *Expenses:* Contact institution. *Faculty research:* Insurance company operations and financial analysis, enterprise risk management, risk theory and modeling, credibility theory and actuarial price modeling, international insurance.

Saint Peter's University, Graduate Business Programs, MBA Program, Jersey City, NJ 07306-5997. Offers finance (MBA); health care administration (MBA); human resource management (MBA); international business (MBA); management (MBA); management information systems (MBA); marketing (MBA); risk management (MBA); MBA/MS. *Program availability:* Part-time, evening/weekend. *Entrance requirements:* Additional exam requirements/recommendations for international students: Required—TOEFL. Electronic applications accepted. *Faculty research:* Finance, health care management, human resource management, international business, management, management information systems, marketing, risk management.

Temple University, Fox School of Business, Doctoral Programs in Business, Philadelphia, PA 19122-6096. Offers accounting (PhD); entrepreneurship (PhD); finance (PhD); international business (PhD); management information systems (PhD); marketing (PhD); risk management and insurance (PhD); statistics (PhD); strategic management (PhD); tourism and sport (PhD). *Accreditation:* AACSB. *Degree requirements:* For doctorate, thesis/dissertation. *Entrance requirements:* For doctorate, GRE General Test, GMAT, minimum GPA of 3.0, master's degree. Additional exam requirements/recommendations for international students: Required—TOEFL (minimum score 600 paper-based; 100 iBT), IELTS (minimum score 7.5). Electronic applications accepted.

University of Colorado Denver, Business School, Program in Finance, Denver, CO 80217. Offers economics (MS); finance (MS); financial analysis and management (MS); financial and commodities risk management (MS); risk management and insurance (MS). *Program availability:* Part-time, evening/weekend. *Degree requirements:* For master's, 30 semester hours (18 of required core courses, 9 of finance electives, and 3 of free elective). *Entrance requirements:* For master's, GMAT, essay, resume, two letters of recommendation; financial statements (for international students). Additional exam requirements/recommendations for international students: Required—TOEFL (minimum score 537 paper-based; 75 iBT); Recommended—IELTS (minimum score 6.5). Electronic applications accepted. *Expenses:* Contact institution. *Faculty research:* Corporate governance, debt maturity policies, regulation and financial markets, option management strategies.

University of Connecticut, Graduate School, School of Business, Storrs, CT 06269. Offers accounting (MS, PhD); business (PhD); business administration (MBA); business analytics and project management (MS); finance (PhD); financial risk management (MS); health care management and insurance studies (MBA); human resource management (MS); management (PhD); management consulting (MBA); marketing (PhD); marketing intelligence (MBA); operations and information management (PhD). *Accreditation:* AACSB. *Degree requirements:* For master's, comprehensive exam; for doctorate, thesis/dissertation. *Entrance requirements:* For master's and doctorate, GMAT. Additional exam requirements/recommendations for international students: Required—TOEFL (minimum score 550 paper-based). Electronic applications accepted.

University of Michigan, Rackham Graduate School, College of Literature, Science, and the Arts, Department of Mathematics, Ann Arbor, MI 48109. Offers applied and interdisciplinary mathematics (AM, MS, PhD); mathematics (AM, MS, PhD); quantitative finance and risk management (MS). *Program availability:* Part-time. *Degree requirements:* For doctorate, one foreign language, comprehensive exam, thesis/dissertation, oral defense of dissertation, preliminary exam. *Entrance requirements:* For master's and doctorate, GRE General Test, GRE Subject Test. Additional exam requirements/recommendations for international students: Required—TOEFL (minimum score 560 paper-based; 84 iBT). Electronic applications accepted. *Expenses:* Contact institution. *Faculty research:* Algebra, analysis, topology, applied mathematics, geometry.

University of Pennsylvania, Wharton School, Insurance and Risk Management Department, Philadelphia, PA 19104. Offers MBA, PhD. *Degree requirements:* For doctorate, thesis/dissertation. *Entrance requirements:* For master's, GMAT; for doctorate, GMAT or GRE. *Faculty research:* Fair rate of return in insurance economics of pension plans, insurance regulation, malpractice insurance, actuarial science, genetic testing and life insurance.

University of Saint Mary, Graduate Programs, Program in Business Administration, Leavenworth, KS 66048-5082. Offers enterprise risk management (MBA); finance (MBA); general management (MBA); health care management (MBA); human resources management (MBA); marketing and advertising management (MBA). *Program availability:* Part-time, evening/weekend, 100% online, blended/hybrid learning. *Faculty:* 1 full-time, 23 part-time/adjunct (7 women). *Students:* 177 full-time (116 women), 50 part-time (29 women); includes 73 minority (30 Black or African American, non-Hispanic/Latino; 3 American Indian or Alaska Native, non-Hispanic/Latino; 12 Asian, non-Hispanic/Latino; 18 Hispanic/Latino; 1 Native Hawaiian or other Pacific Islander, non-Hispanic/Latino; 9 Two or more races, non-Hispanic/Latino), 2 international. Average age 33. *Degree requirements:* For master's, thesis. *Entrance requirements:* For master's, Minimum undergraduate GPA of 2.75, official transcripts. *Application deadline:* Applications are processed on a rolling basis. Application fee: $25. Electronic applications accepted. *Expenses:* Contact institution. *Financial support:* Applicants required to submit FAFSA. *Unit head:* Mark Harvey, Director of Graduate Business Programs, 913-319-3011, E-mail: mark.harvey@stmary.edu. *Application contact:* Mark Harvey, Director of Graduate Business Programs, 913-319-3011, E-mail: mark.harvey@stmary.edu.
Website: https://www.stmary.edu/mba

The University of Texas at Austin, Graduate School, McCombs School of Business, Department of Information, Risk, and Operations Management, Austin, TX 78712-1111. Offers information management (MBA); information systems (PhD); information technology and management (MS); risk analysis and decision making (PhD); risk management (MBA); supply chain and operations management (MBA, PhD). *Degree requirements:* For doctorate, thesis/dissertation. *Entrance requirements:* For doctorate, GMAT or GRE. Electronic applications accepted. *Faculty research:* Stochastic processing and queuing, discrete nonlinear and large-scale optimization simulation, quality assurance logistics, distributed artificial intelligence, organizational modeling.

University of Wisconsin–Madison, Graduate School, Wisconsin School of Business, Doctoral Program in Actuarial Science, Risk Management and Insurance, Madison, WI 53706-1380. Offers PhD. *Degree requirements:* For doctorate, comprehensive exam, thesis/dissertation. *Entrance requirements:* For doctorate, GMAT or GRE General Test. Additional exam requirements/recommendations for international students: Recommended—TOEFL (minimum score 623 paper-based; 106 iBT), IELTS (minimum score 7.5), TSE (minimum score 73). Electronic applications accepted. *Expenses:* Contact institution. *Faculty research:* Actuarial science, regression and business forecasting, panel data, economics of insurance markets, insurance regulation, public economics, behavioral economics, Bayesian methodology related to health insurance, tort reform and government programs, joint and several liability, superfund, predictive modeling, asymmetric information in insurance, psychology and economics, applied microeconomics, insurance markets, risk and decision making.

University of Wisconsin–Madison, Graduate School, Wisconsin School of Business, Wisconsin Full-Time MBA Program, Madison, WI 53706-1380. Offers applied security analysis (MBA); arts administration (MBA); brand and product management (MBA);

corporate finance and investment banking (MBA); marketing research (MBA); operations and technology management (MBA); real estate (MBA); risk management and insurance (MBA); strategic human resource management (MBA); supply chain management (MBA). *Faculty:* 137 full-time (36 women), 39 part-time/adjunct (11 women). *Students:* 183 full-time (59 women); includes 31 minority (5 Black or African American, non-Hispanic/Latino; 1 American Indian or Alaska Native, non-Hispanic/Latino; 6 Asian, non-Hispanic/Latino; 13 Hispanic/Latino; 6 Two or more races, non-Hispanic/Latino), 40 international. Average age 28. 465 applicants, 33% accepted, 79 enrolled. In 2018, 104 master's awarded. *Entrance requirements:* For master's, GMAT or GRE, bachelor's or equivalent degree, essay, letter of recommendation, resume. Additional exam requirements/recommendations for international students: Required—TOEFL (minimum score 100 iBT), IELTS (minimum score 7.5), TOEFL is not required for international students whose undergraduate training was in English. *Application deadline:* For fall admission, 11/1 for domestic and international students; for winter admission, 1/10 for domestic and international students; for spring admission, 3/1 for domestic and international students; for summer admission, 4/10 for domestic students, 4/10 priority date for international students. Applications are processed on a rolling basis. Application fee: $75 ($81 for international students). Electronic applications accepted. *Expenses:* Wisconsin Resident tuition and fees - $39,156; Nonresident tuition and fees - $76,635. *Financial support:* In 2018–19, 148 students received support, including 7 fellowships with full tuition reimbursements available (averaging $25,871 per year), 7 research assistantships with full tuition reimbursements available (averaging $14,832 per year), 47 teaching assistantships with full tuition reimbursements available (averaging $14,832 per year); scholarships/grants, health care benefits, tuition waivers (full and partial), and unspecified assistantships also available. Financial award application deadline: 6/1. *Faculty research:* Ecology, environmental studies, and business; decision making; tax policy; diversity and inclusion in governance boards; marketing and social media. *Unit head:* Dr. Enno Siemsen, Associate Dean of the MBA and Masters Programs, 608-890-3130, E-mail: esiemsen@wisc.edu. *Application contact:* Betsy Kacizak, Director of Admissions and Recruiting, Full-time MBA Program, 608-262-4000, E-mail: betsy.kacizak@wisc.edu.
Website: https://wsb.wisc.edu/

Yeshiva University, The Katz School, Program in Enterprise Risk Management, New York, NY 10033-3201. Offers MS. *Program availability:* Part-time, online learning.

Section 11
International Business

This section contains a directory of institutions offering graduate work in international business. Additional information about programs listed in the directory but not augmented by an in-depth entry may be obtained by writing directly to the dean of a graduate school or chair of a department at the address given in the directory.

For programs offering related work, see also in this book *Business Administration and Management, Entrepreneurship, Industrial and Manufacturing Management,* and *Organizational Behavior.* In another guide in this series:

Graduate Programs in the Humanities, Arts & Social Sciences
See *Political Science and International Affairs* and *Public, Regional, and Industrial Affairs*

CONTENTS

Program Directory

International Business

Abilene Christian University, College of Graduate and Professional Studies, Program in Business Administration, Addison, TX 79699. Offers business analytics (MBA); general management (MBA); healthcare administration (MBA); international business (MBA); management: business analytics (MS); management: healthcare administration (MS); management: international business (MS); management: marketing (MS); management: operations and supply chain management (MS); marketing (MBA); nonprofit leadership (MBA). *Program availability:* Part-time, online only, 100% online. *Faculty:* 4 full-time (0 women), 7 part-time/adjunct (3 women). *Students:* 149 full-time (69 women), 53 part-time (25 women); includes 88 minority (42 Black or African American, non-Hispanic/Latino; 2 American Indian or Alaska Native, non-Hispanic/Latino; 4 Asian, non-Hispanic/Latino; 31 Hispanic/Latino; 1 Native Hawaiian or other Pacific Islander, non-Hispanic/Latino; 8 Two or more races, non-Hispanic/Latino), 4 international. 36 applicants, 100% accepted, 32 enrolled. In 2018, 24 master's awarded. *Entrance requirements:* Additional exam requirements/recommendations for international students: Required—TOEFL (minimum score 80 iBT), IELTS (minimum score 6). *Application deadline:* For fall admission, 10/7 for domestic students; for winter admission, 12/20 for domestic students; for spring admission, 2/24 for domestic students; for summer admission, 4/20 for domestic students. Applications are processed on a rolling basis. Application fee: $50. Electronic applications accepted. *Expenses:* $721 per hour. *Financial support:* In 2018–19, 16 students received support. Scholarships/grants available. Financial award application deadline: 7/1; financial award applicants required to submit FAFSA. *Faculty research:* Organizational structure, financial management, cost accounting, unit analysis management. *Unit head:* Dr. Phil Vardiman, Program Director, 325-674-2153, E-mail: pxv02b@acu.edu. *Application contact:* Graduate Advisor, 817-219-7300, E-mail: onlineadmissions@acu.edu. Website: http://www.acu.edu/online/academics/mba-business-administration.html

Amberton University, Graduate School, Department of Business Administration, Garland, TX 75041-5595. Offers agile project management (MS); general business (MBA); international business (MBA); management (MBA); project management (MBA); strategic leadership (MBA). *Program availability:* Part-time, evening/weekend. *Entrance requirements:* For master's, minimum GPA of 3.0.

American Business & Technology University, Programs in Business Administration, Saint Joseph, MO 64506. Offers business administration (MBA); financial management (MBA); global business management (MBA); information systems management (MBA); marketing and social media (MBA); project and operations management (MBA); public accounting (MBA). *Program availability:* Online learning.

American College Dublin, Graduate Programs, Dublin, Ireland. Offers business administration (MBA); creative writing (MFA); international business (MBA); oil and gas management (MBA); performance (MFA).

American InterContinental University Atlanta, Program in Global Technology Management, Atlanta, GA 30328. Offers MBA. *Program availability:* Part-time, evening/weekend, online learning. *Entrance requirements:* For master's, interview. Electronic applications accepted. *Faculty research:* E-commerce, service quality leadership, human resources management.

American InterContinental University Online, Program in Business Administration, Schaumburg, IL 60173. Offers accounting and finance (MBA); finance (MBA); healthcare management (MBA); human resource management (MBA); international business (MBA); management (MBA); marketing (MBA); operations management (MBA); organizational psychology and development (MBA); project management (MBA). *Accreditation:* ACBSP. *Program availability:* Evening/weekend, online learning. *Entrance requirements:* Additional exam requirements/recommendations for international students: Required—TOEFL (minimum score 550 paper-based). Electronic applications accepted.

The American University in Dubai, Graduate Programs, Dubai, United Arab Emirates. Offers construction management (MS); education (M Ed); finance (MBA); generalist (MBA); marketing (MBA). *Program availability:* Part-time, evening/weekend. *Degree requirements:* For master's, thesis optional. *Entrance requirements:* For master's, GMAT (for MBA); GRE (for M Ed and MS), minimum undergraduate GPA of 3.0, official transcripts, two reference forms, curriculum vitae/resume, statement of career objectives, work experience. Additional exam requirements/recommendations for international students: Required—TOEFL (minimum score 550 paper-based; 79 iBT). Electronic applications accepted.

The American University of Paris, Graduate Programs, Paris, France. Offers cross-cultural and sustainable business management (MA); cultural translation (MA); global communications (MA); global communications and civil society (MA); international affairs (MA); international affairs, conflict resolution and civil society development (MA); Middle East and Islamic studies (MA); Middle East and Islamic studies and international affairs (MA); public policy and international affairs (MA); public policy and international law (MA). *Degree requirements:* For master's, thesis (for some programs). *Entrance requirements:* For master's, minimum undergraduate GPA of 3.0. Additional exam requirements/recommendations for international students: Recommended—TOEFL, IELTS. Electronic applications accepted.

Anaheim University, Programs in Business Administration, Anaheim, CA 92806-5150. Offers entrepreneurship (ME, DBA); global sustainable management (MBA); international business (MBA, DBA, Certificate, Diploma); management (DBA); sustainable management (DBA, Certificate, Diploma). *Program availability:* Part-time, evening/weekend, online only, 100% online. In 2018, 3 master's, 4 doctorates awarded. *Application deadline:* Applications are processed on a rolling basis. Electronic applications accepted. *Unit head:* Dr. Robert Robertson, Dean, Graduate School of Business, 714-772-3330, Fax: 714-772-3331, E-mail: admissions@anaheim.edu. *Application contact:* Dr. Robert Robertson, Dean, Graduate School of Business, 714-772-3330, Fax: 714-772-3331, E-mail: admissions@anaheim.edu.

Argosy University, Atlanta, College of Business, Atlanta, GA 30328. Offers accounting (DBA); corporate compliance (MBA); customized professional concentration (MBA, DBA); finance (MBA); healthcare administration (MBA); information systems (DBA); information systems management (MBA); international business (MBA, DBA); management (MBA, MSM, DBA); marketing (MBA, DBA). *Accreditation:* ACBSP.

Argosy University, Chicago, College of Business, Chicago, IL 60601. Offers accounting (DBA); customized professional concentration (MBA, DBA); finance (MBA); fraud examination (MBA); global business sustainability (DBA); healthcare administration (MBA); information systems (DBA); information systems management (MBA); international business (MBA, DBA); management (MBA, MSM, DBA); marketing (MBA, DBA); organizational leadership (Ed D); public administration (MBA); sustainable management (MBA). *Accreditation:* ACBSP. *Program availability:* Online learning.

Argosy University, Hawai`i, College of Business, Honolulu, HI 96813. Offers accounting (DBA); corporate compliance (MBA); customized professional concentration (MBA, DBA); finance (MBA, Certificate); fraud examination (MBA); global business sustainability (DBA); healthcare administration (MBA, Certificate); information systems (DBA); information systems management (MBA, Certificate); international business (MBA, DBA, Certificate); management (MBA, MSM, DBA); marketing (MBA, DBA, Certificate); organizational leadership (Ed D); public administration (MBA); sustainable management (MBA).

Argosy University, Los Angeles, College of Business, Los Angeles, CA 90045. Offers accounting (DBA); corporate compliance (MBA); customized professional concentration (MBA, DBA); finance (MBA); fraud examination (MBA); global business sustainability (DBA); healthcare administration (MBA); information systems (DBA); information systems management (MBA); international business (MBA, DBA); management (MBA, MSM, DBA); marketing (MBA, DBA); organizational leadership (Ed D); public administration (MBA); sustainable management (MBA).

Argosy University, Northern Virginia, College of Business, Arlington, VA 22209. Offers accounting (DBA); customized professional concentration (MBA, DBA); finance (MBA); fraud examination (MBA); global business sustainability (DBA); healthcare administration (MBA); information systems (DBA); information systems management (MBA); international business (MBA, DBA, Certificate); management (MBA, MSM, DBA); marketing (MBA, DBA, Certificate); organizational leadership (Ed D); public administration (MBA); sustainable management (MBA).

Argosy University, Orange County, College of Business, Orange, CA 92868. Offers accounting (DBA, Adv C); corporate compliance (MBA); customized professional concentration (MBA, DBA); finance (MBA, Certificate); fraud examination (MBA); global business sustainability (DBA); healthcare administration (MBA, Certificate); information systems (DBA, Adv C, Certificate); information systems management (MBA); international business (MBA, DBA, Adv C, Certificate); management (MBA, MSM, DBA, Adv C); marketing (MBA, DBA, Adv C, Certificate); organizational leadership (Ed D); public administration (MBA, Certificate); sustainable management (MBA).

Argosy University, Phoenix, College of Business, Phoenix, AZ 85021. Offers accounting (DBA); corporate compliance (MBA); customized professional concentration (MBA, DBA); finance (MBA); fraud examination (MBA); global business sustainability (DBA); healthcare administration (MBA); information systems (DBA); information systems management (MBA); international business (MBA, DBA); management (MBA, DBA); marketing (MBA, DBA); public administration (MBA); sustainable management (MBA).

Argosy University, Seattle, College of Business, Seattle, WA 98121. Offers accounting (DBA); corporate compliance (MBA); customized professional concentration (MBA, DBA); finance (MBA); fraud examination (MBA); global business sustainability (DBA); healthcare administration (MBA); information systems (DBA); information systems management (MBA); international business (MBA, DBA); management (MBA, MSM, DBA); marketing (MBA, DBA); organizational leadership (Ed D); public administration (MBA); sustainable management (MBA).

Argosy University, Tampa, College of Business, Tampa, FL 33607. Offers accounting (DBA); corporate compliance (MBA); customized professional concentration (MBA, DBA); finance (MBA); fraud examination (MBA); global business sustainability (DBA); healthcare administration (MBA); information systems (DBA); information systems management (MBA); international business (MBA, DBA); management (MBA, MSM, DBA); marketing (MBA, DBA); organizational leadership (Ed D); public administration (MBA); sustainable management (MBA).

Argosy University, Twin Cities, College of Business, Eagan, MN 55121. Offers accounting (DBA); customized professional concentration (MBA, DBA); finance (MBA); fraud examination (MBA); global business sustainability (DBA); healthcare administration (MBA); information systems (DBA); information systems management (MBA); international business (MBA, DBA); management (MBA, MSM, DBA); marketing (MBA, DBA); organizational leadership (Ed D); public administration (MBA); sustainable management (MBA).

Arizona State University at the Tempe campus, Thunderbird School of Global Management, Tempe, AZ 85287. Offers global affairs and management (MA); global management (MGM). *Accreditation:* AACSB. *Program availability:* Online learning. *Degree requirements:* For master's, one foreign language. *Entrance requirements:* For master's, GMAT. Additional exam requirements/recommendations for international students: Required—TOEFL.

Arizona State University at the Tempe campus, W. P. Carey School of Business, Program in Business Administration, Tempe, AZ 85287-4906. Offers entrepreneurship (MBA); finance (MBA); health sector management (MBA); international business (MBA); leadership (MBA); marketing (MBA); organizational behavior (PhD); strategic management (PhD); supply chain management (MBA, PhD); JD/MBA; MBA/M Acc; MBA/M Arch. *Accreditation:* AACSB. *Program availability:* Part-time, evening/weekend, online learning. Terminal master's awarded for partial completion of doctoral program. *Degree requirements:* For master's, thesis or alternative, internship, interactive Program of Study (iPOS) submitted before completing 50 percent of required credit hours; for doctorate, comprehensive exam, thesis/dissertation, interactive Program of Study (iPOS) submitted before completing 50 percent of required credit hours. *Entrance requirements:* For master's, GMAT, minimum GPA of 3.0 in last 2 years of work leading to bachelor's degree, 2 letters of recommendation, professional resume, official transcripts, 3 essays; for doctorate, GMAT or GRE, minimum GPA of 3.0 in last 2 years of work leading to bachelor's degree, 3 letters of recommendation, resume, personal statement/essay. Additional exam requirements/recommendations for international students: Required—TOEFL (minimum score 550 paper-based; 80 iBT), IELTS (minimum score 6.5). Electronic applications accepted. *Expenses:* Contact institution.

Ashland University, Dauch College of Business and Economics, Ashland, OH 44805-3702. Offers accounting (MBA); business analytics (MBA); entrepreneurship (MBA); financial management (MBA); global management (MBA); health care management and leadership (MBA); human resource management (MBA); human resources (MBA); management information systems (MBA); project management (MBA); sport management (MBA); supply chain management (MBA). *Accreditation:* ACBSP. *Program availability:* Part-time, evening/weekend, 100% online, blended/hybrid learning. Terminal master's awarded for partial completion of doctoral program. *Degree requirements:* For master's, thesis optional, capstone course. *Entrance requirements:* For master's, 2 years of full-time work experience. Additional exam requirements/recommendations for international students: Required—TOEFL (minimum score 550 paper-based; 78 iBT). Electronic applications accepted. *Expenses:* Contact institution. *Faculty research:* Relationship marketing strategy, executive compensation and company performance, online marketplaces in electronic commerce, diversity training in campus recreation departments, entrepreneurship in developing and emerging economies.

Ashworth College, Graduate Programs, Norcross, GA 30092. Offers business administration (MBA); criminal justice (MS); health care administration (MBA, MS); human resource management (MBA, MS); international business (MBA); management (MS); marketing (MBA, MS).

Assumption College, Business Studies Program, Worcester, MA 01609-1296. Offers accounting (MBA); business studies (CAGS); finance/economics (MBA); human resources (MBA); international business (MBA); management (MBA); marketing (MBA); nonprofit leadership (MBA). *Program availability:* Part-time, evening/weekend. *Degree requirements:* For master's, capstone. *Entrance requirements:* For master's, bachelor's degree, three letters of recommendation, official transcripts, personal statement, current resume; for CAGS, MBA or equivalent degree in a closely related field, three letters of recommendation, official transcripts, personal statement, current resume. Additional exam requirements/recommendations for international students: Required—TOEFL (minimum score 540 paper-based; 76 iBT), IELTS (minimum score 6). Electronic applications accepted. *Faculty research:* Workplace diversity, dynamics of team interaction, utilization of leased employees, experiential learning project on due diligence market for prostheses.

Azusa Pacific University, School of Behavioral and Applied Sciences, Department of Leadership and Organizational Psychology, Program in Leadership, Azusa, CA 91702-7000. Offers executive leadership (MA); leadership development (MA); leadership studies (MA); sport management (MA). *Expenses:* Contact institution.

Azusa Pacific University, School of Business and Management, Azusa, CA 91702-7000. Offers accounting (MBA); business administration (MBA); entrepreneurship (MBA); finance (MBA); international business (MBA); marketing (MBA); organizational science (MBA); professional accountancy (M Acc); sport management (MBA). *Program availability:* Part-time, evening/weekend. *Degree requirements:* For master's, thesis (for some programs), final project. *Entrance requirements:* For master's, GMAT, minimum GPA of 3.0. Additional exam requirements/recommendations for international students: Required—TOEFL (minimum score 600 paper-based). *Expenses:* Contact institution. *Faculty research:* Gender issues, financial risk, leadership and ethics, marketing strategy.

Baldwin Wallace University, Graduate Programs, School of Business, Program in International Management, Berea, OH 44017-2088. Offers MBA. *Program availability:* Part-time-only, evening/weekend. *Students:* 3 full-time (all women), 3 part-time (1 woman); includes 1 minority (Black or African American, non-Hispanic/Latino). Average age 32. 2 applicants. In 2018, 1 master's awarded. *Degree requirements:* For master's, one foreign language, minimum overall GPA of 3.0. *Entrance requirements:* For master's, GMAT or minimum undergraduate GPA of 3.0, interview, work experience, bachelor's degree in any field. Additional exam requirements/recommendations for international students: Required—TOEFL (minimum score 550 paper-based; 79 iBT), IELTS can be accepted in place of TOEFL. *Application deadline:* For fall admission, 7/25 priority date for domestic students, 4/30 priority date for international students; for spring admission, 12/15 priority date for domestic students, 9/30 priority date for international students; for summer admission, 4/15 priority date for domestic students. Applications are processed on a rolling basis. Application fee: $0. Electronic applications accepted. *Expenses:* $31,284 to complete program. *Financial support:* In 2018–19, 1 student received support. Scholarships/grants and tuition discounts available. Financial award applicants required to submit FAFSA. *Faculty research:* International finance, systems approach, international marketing. *Unit head:* Dr. Susan Kuznik, Associate Dean, Graduate Business Programs, 440-826-2053, Fax: 440-826-3868, E-mail: skuznik@bw.edu. *Application contact:* Laura Spencer, Graduate Business Admission Specialist, 440-826-2191, Fax: 440-826-3868, E-mail: lspencer@bw.edu.
Website: http://www.bw.edu/graduate/business/mba/

Barry University, Andreas School of Business, Graduate Certificate Programs, Miami Shores, FL 33161-6695. Offers finance (Certificate); health services administration (Certificate); international business (Certificate); management (Certificate); management information systems (Certificate); marketing (Certificate).

Baruch College of the City University of New York, Zicklin School of Business, Department of Marketing and International Business, New York, NY 10010-5585. Offers international business (MBA); marketing (MBA, MS, PhD). PhD offered jointly with Graduate School and University Center of the City University of New York. *Program availability:* Part-time, evening/weekend. *Degree requirements:* For doctorate, comprehensive exam, thesis/dissertation. *Entrance requirements:* For master's, GMAT, 2 letters of recommendation, resume, 2 years of work experience; for doctorate, GMAT. Additional exam requirements/recommendations for international students: Required—TOEFL (minimum score 590 paper-based), TWE (minimum score 5).

Baruch College of the City University of New York, Zicklin School of Business, International Executive MS Programs, New York, NY 10010-5585. Offers entrepreneurship (MS). *Program availability:* Part-time, evening/weekend. *Entrance requirements:* For master's, GMAT, 2 letters of recommendation, resume, 2 years of work experience. Additional exam requirements/recommendations for international students: Required—TOEFL (minimum score 590 paper-based), TWE (minimum score 5).

Benedictine University, Graduate Programs, Program in Business Administration, Lisle, IL 60532. Offers accounting (MBA); entrepreneurship and managing innovation (MBA); financial management (MBA); health administration (MBA); human resource management (MBA); information systems security (MBA); international business (MBA); management consulting (MBA); management information systems (MBA); marketing management (MBA); operations management and logistics (MBA); organizational leadership (MBA). *Program availability:* Part-time, evening/weekend, 100% online, blended/hybrid learning. *Faculty:* 7 full-time (1 woman), 36 part-time/adjunct (10 women). *Students:* 110 full-time (71 women), 500 part-time (302 women); includes 104 minority (34 Black or African American, non-Hispanic/Latino; 1 American Indian or Alaska Native, non-Hispanic/Latino; 41 Asian, non-Hispanic/Latino; 23 Hispanic/Latino; 5 Native Hawaiian or other Pacific Islander, non-Hispanic/Latino), 7 international. Average age 33. 251 applicants, 84% accepted, 202 enrolled. In 2018, 345 master's awarded. *Entrance requirements:* For master's, GMAT or GRE test scores or completed test waiver form, official transcripts; 2 letters of reference from individuals familiar with the applicant's professional or academic work, excluding family or personal friends; a 1-2 page essay addressing educational and career goals; current résumé listing chronological work history; personal interview may be required prior to an admission decision. Additional exam requirements/recommendations for international students: Required—TOEFL (minimum score 550 paper-based; 79 iBT), IELTS (minimum score 6.5). *Application deadline:* Applications are processed on a rolling basis. Application fee: $40. Electronic applications accepted. *Unit head:* Ricky Holman, Assistant Professor, 630-829-1936, E-mail: rholman@ben.edu. *Application contact:* Ricky Holman, Assistant Professor, 630-829-1936, E-mail: rholman@ben.edu.

Boston University, Metropolitan College, Department of Administrative Sciences, Boston, MA 02215. Offers applied business analytics (MS); economic development and tourism management (MSAS); enterprise risk management (MS); financial management (MS); global marketing management (MS); innovation and technology (MSAS); insurance management (MS); project management (MS); supply chain management (MS). *Accreditation:* AACSB. *Program availability:* Part-time, evening/weekend, 100% online, blended/hybrid learning. *Faculty:* 27 full-time (5 women), 39 part-time/adjunct (5 women). *Students:* 617 full-time (351 women), 574 part-time (290 women); includes 196 minority (47 Black or African American, non-Hispanic/Latino; 2 American Indian or Alaska Native, non-Hispanic/Latino; 75 Asian, non-Hispanic/Latino; 60 Hispanic/Latino; 12 Two or more races, non-Hispanic/Latino), 730 international. Average age 28. 2,259 applicants, 76% accepted, 594 enrolled. In 2018, 441 master's awarded. *Degree requirements:* For master's, thesis optional. *Entrance requirements:* For master's, 1 year of work experience, minimum GPA of 3.0. Additional exam requirements/recommendations for international students: Required—TOEFL (minimum score 84 iBT). *Application deadline:* For fall admission, 8/1 priority date for domestic students, 6/1 priority date for international students; for spring admission, 12/1 priority date for domestic students, 11/15 priority date for international students; for summer admission, 4/1 priority date for domestic students, 3/1 priority date for international students. Applications are processed on a rolling basis. Application fee: $85. Electronic applications accepted. *Expenses:* Contact institution. *Financial support:* In 2018–19, 15 students received support, including 16 research assistantships (averaging $8,400 per year), 30 teaching assistantships (averaging $3,400 per year); career-related internships or fieldwork, Federal Work-Study, and unspecified assistantships also available. Financial award applicants required to submit FAFSA. *Faculty research:* International business, innovative process. *Unit head:* Dr. John Sullivan, Chair, 617-353-3016, E-mail: adminsc@bu.edu. *Application contact:* Enrollment Services, 617-358-8162, E-mail: met@bu.edu.
Website: http://www.bu.edu/met/academic-community/departments/administrative-sciences/

Brandeis University, International Business School (IBS), Waltham, MA 02454-9110. Offers MA, MBA, MSF, PhD. *Degree requirements:* For doctorate, thesis/dissertation. *Entrance requirements:* For master's, GMAT or GRE, minimum two years of full-time work experience (for MBA); for doctorate, GRE, writing sample. Additional exam requirements/recommendations for international students: Required—TOEFL (minimum score 600 paper-based; 100 iBT), IELTS (minimum score 7), PTE (minimum score 68). Electronic applications accepted. *Expenses:* Contact institution. *Faculty research:* Corporate finance, fixed income, monetary policy, business strategy, cross-cultural interaction.

Brandman University, School of Business and Professional Studies, Irvine, CA 92618. Offers accounting (MBA); business administration (MBA); business intelligence and data analytics (MBA); e-business strategic management (MBA); entrepreneurship (MBA); finance (MBA); health administration (MBA); human resources (MBA, MS); international business (MBA); marketing (MBA); organizational leadership (MA, MBA, MPA); public administration (MPA).

Brooklyn College of the City University of New York, School of Business, Brooklyn, NY 11210-2889. Offers accounting (MS); business administration (MS), including economic analysis, general business, global business and finance. *Program availability:* Part-time, evening/weekend. *Degree requirements:* For master's, comprehensive exam, thesis or alternative. *Entrance requirements:* For master's, GMAT, 2 letters of recommendation. Additional exam requirements/recommendations for international students: Required—TOEFL (minimum score 550 paper-based; 79 iBT). Electronic applications accepted. *Faculty research:* Econometrics, environmental economics, microeconomics, macroeconomics, taxation.

California Intercontinental University, School of Business, Irvine, CA 92614. Offers banking and finance (MBA); entrepreneurship and business management (DBA); global business leadership (DBA); international management and marketing (MBA); organizational management and human resource management (MBA).

California Lutheran University, Graduate Studies, School of Management, Thousand Oaks, CA 91360-2787. Offers business (IMBA); entrepreneurship (MBA, Certificate); finance (MBA, Certificate); financial planning (MBA, MS, Certificate); human capital management (MBA, Certificate); information technology (MS); information technology management (MBA, Certificate); international business (MBA, Certificate); management (MS); marketing (MBA, Certificate); public policy and administration (MPPA); quantitative economics (MS). *Program availability:* Part-time, evening/weekend, 100% online, blended/hybrid learning. *Degree requirements:* For master's, comprehensive exam (for some programs). *Entrance requirements:* For master's, GMAT, interview, minimum GPA of 3.0. Electronic applications accepted. *Expenses:* Contact institution.

California State University, Fullerton, Graduate Studies, College of Business and Economics, Program in Business Administration, Fullerton, CA 92831-3599. Offers business administration (MBA); business analytics (MBA); international business (MBA); organizational leadership (MBA); risk management and insurance (MBA). *Accreditation:* AACSB. *Program availability:* Part-time. *Entrance requirements:* For master's, GMAT.

California State University, Los Angeles, Graduate Studies, College of Business and Economics, Department of Marketing, Los Angeles, CA 90032-8530. Offers international business (MBA, MS). *Program availability:* Part-time, evening/weekend. *Degree requirements:* For master's, comprehensive exam (MBA), thesis (MS). *Entrance requirements:* For master's, GMAT, minimum GPA of 2.5 during previous 2 years of course work. Additional exam requirements/recommendations for international students: Required—TOEFL (minimum score 550 paper-based). Electronic applications accepted.

California State University, San Bernardino, Graduate Studies, College of Business and Public Administration, Program in Business Administration, San Bernardino, CA 92407. Offers accounting (MBA); entrepreneurship (MBA); finance (MBA); global business (MBA); information management (MBA); information security (MBA); management (MBA); supply chain management (MBA). *Accreditation:* AACSB. *Program availability:* Part-time, evening/weekend, online learning. *Faculty:* 5 full-time (4 women), 7 part-time/adjunct (3 women). *Students:* 40 full-time (14 women), 163 part-time (72 women); includes 99 minority (7 Black or African American, non-Hispanic/Latino; 15 Asian, non-Hispanic/Latino; 71 Hispanic/Latino; 6 Two or more races, non-Hispanic/Latino), 58 international. Average age 32. 342 applicants, 52% accepted, 91 enrolled. In 2018, 106 master's awarded. *Degree requirements:* For master's, comprehensive exam, thesis. *Entrance requirements:* Additional exam requirements/recommendations for international students: Required—TOEFL. *Application deadline:* For fall admission, 7/16 for domestic students, 7/20 for international students; for winter admission, 10/23 for domestic students, 10/20 for international students; for spring admission, 1/22 for domestic students, 1/20 for international students. Application fee: $55. *Expenses:* Contact institution. *Financial support:* Application deadline: 3/1. *Unit head:* Dr. Lawrence C. Rose, Dean, 909-537-3703, Fax: 909-537-7026, E-mail: lrose@csusb.edu. *Application contact:* Ernest Silvers, MBA Program Director, 909-537-5703, E-mail: esilvers@csusb.edu.
Website: http://mba.csusb.edu/

California University of Management and Sciences, Graduate Programs, Anaheim, CA 92801. Offers business administration (MBA, DBA); computer information systems (MS); economics (MS); international business (MS); sports management (MS).

Canisius College, Graduate Division, Richard J. Wehle School of Business, Department of Management, Buffalo, NY 14208-1098. Offers business administration (MBA); international business (MS). *Accreditation:* AACSB. *Program availability:* Part-

time, evening/weekend. *Faculty:* 8 full-time (3 women), 4 part-time/adjunct (1 woman). *Students:* 85 full-time (38 women), 121 part-time (44 women); includes 19 minority (9 Black or African American, non-Hispanic/Latino; 1 American Indian or Alaska Native, non-Hispanic/Latino; 2 Asian, non-Hispanic/Latino; 2 Hispanic/Latino; 5 Two or more races, non-Hispanic/Latino), 19 international. Average age 28. 125 applicants, 93% accepted, 69 enrolled. In 2018, 116 master's awarded. *Entrance requirements:* For master's, GMAT, GRE, official transcript from colleges attended, current resume. Additional exam requirements/recommendations for international students: Required—TOEFL (minimum score 550 paper-based, 80 iBT), IELTS (minimum score 6.5), or CAEL (minimum score 70). *Application deadline:* For fall admission, 7/1 priority date for domestic students; for spring admission, 11/1 priority date for domestic students. Applications are processed on a rolling basis. Application fee: $0. Electronic applications accepted. *Expenses: Tuition:* Part-time $820 per credit hour. *Required fees:* $25 per semester. One-time fee: $65 part-time. Tuition and fees vary according to program. *Financial support:* In 2018–19, 35 students received support. Career-related internships or fieldwork, Federal Work-Study, scholarships/grants, tuition waivers (partial), and unspecified assistantships available. Support available to part-time students. Financial award application deadline: 4/30; financial award applicants required to submit FAFSA. *Faculty research:* Global leadership effectiveness, global supply chain management, quality management. *Unit head:* Dr. Robyn L. Brouer, Chair/Associate Professor of Management, 716-888-2226, Fax: 716-888-3215, E-mail: brouerr@canisius.edu. *Application contact:* Dr. Robyn L. Brouer, Chair/Associate Professor of Management, 716-888-2226, Fax: 716-888-3215, E-mail: brouerr@canisius.edu.
Website: http://www.canisius.edu/graduate/

Central European University, Department of Legal Studies, Budapest, Hungary. Offers comparative Constitutional law (LL M); human rights (LL M, MA); international business law (LL M); juridical sciences (SJD). Terminal master's awarded for partial completion of doctoral program. *Degree requirements:* For master's, one foreign language, thesis; for doctorate, one foreign language, comprehensive exam, thesis/dissertation. *Entrance requirements:* For master's and doctorate, LSAT. Additional exam requirements/recommendations for international students: Required—TOEFL (minimum score 570 paper-based); Recommended—IELTS (minimum score 6.5). Electronic applications accepted. *Expenses:* Contact institution. *Faculty research:* Institutional, Constitutional and human rights in European Union law; biomedical law and reproductive rights; data protection law; comparative and international business law and the regulation of business environments;.

Central Michigan University, College of Graduate Studies, College of Business Administration, MBA Program, Mount Pleasant, MI 48859. Offers accounting (MBA); business economics (MBA); consulting (MBA); finance (MBA); general business (MBA); human resource management (MBA); information systems (MBA); international business (MBA); logistics management (MBA); marketing (MBA); value-driven organization (MBA). *Program availability:* Part-time, evening/weekend, online learning. Electronic applications accepted. *Faculty research:* Accounting, consulting, international business, marketing, information systems.

Central Michigan University, College of Graduate Studies, Interdisciplinary Administration Programs, Mount Pleasant, MI 48859. Offers acquisitions administration (MSA, Graduate Certificate); general administration (MSA, Graduate Certificate); health services administration (MSA, Graduate Certificate); human resource administration (Graduate Certificate); human resources administration (MSA); information resource management (MSA, Graduate Certificate); international administration (MSA, Graduate Certificate); leadership (MSA, Graduate Certificate); public administration (MSA, Graduate Certificate); research administration (Graduate Certificate); sport administration (MSA). *Accreditation:* AACSB. *Program availability:* Part-time, evening/weekend, online learning. *Degree requirements:* For master's, thesis or alternative. *Entrance requirements:* For master's, bachelor's degree with minimum GPA of 2.7. Electronic applications accepted. *Faculty research:* Interdisciplinary studies in acquisitions administration, health services administration, sport administration, recreation and park administration, and international administration.

Christian Brothers University, School of Business, Memphis, TN 38104-5581. Offers accountancy (M Acc); business (MBA); international business (MIB); project management (Certificate); MBA/MIB. *Program availability:* Part-time, evening/weekend. *Entrance requirements:* For master's, GMAT, GRE. Additional exam requirements/recommendations for international students: Required—TOEFL.

City University of Seattle, Graduate Division, School of Management, Seattle, WA 98121. Offers accounting (Certificate); change leadership (MBA, Certificate); computer systems (MS); finance (Certificate); financial management (MBA); general management (MBA); general management-Europe (MBA); global marketing (MBA); human resources management (Certificate); individualized study (MBA); information security (MS); information systems (MBA); leadership (MA); marketing (MBA, Certificate); project management (MBA, MS, Certificate); sustainable business (Certificate); technology management (MBA, Certificate). *Program availability:* Part-time, evening/weekend, online learning. *Degree requirements:* For master's, comprehensive exam (for some programs), thesis (for some programs). *Entrance requirements:* For master's, baccalaureate degree or equivalent from an accredited or otherwise recognized institution. Additional exam requirements/recommendations for international students: Required—TOEFL (minimum score 567 paper-based; 87 iBT); Recommended—IELTS. Electronic applications accepted.

Clarkson University, David D. Reh School of Business, Master's Program in Business Administration, Potsdam, NY 13699. Offers business administration (MBA); business fundamentals (Advanced Certificate); global supply chain management (Advanced Certificate); human resource management (Advanced Certificate); management and leadership (Advanced Certificate). *Accreditation:* AACSB. *Program availability:* Part-time, evening/weekend, 100% online, blended/hybrid learning. *Faculty:* 36 full-time (7 women), 8 part-time/adjunct (2 women). *Students:* 68 full-time (30 women), 63 part-time (29 women); includes 17 minority (2 Black or African American, non-Hispanic/Latino; 2 American Indian or Alaska Native, non-Hispanic/Latino; 6 Asian, non-Hispanic/Latino; 4 Hispanic/Latino; 3 Two or more races, non-Hispanic/Latino), 11 international. 119 applicants, 74% accepted, 67 enrolled. In 2018, 89 master's, 2 other advanced degrees awarded. *Entrance requirements:* For master's, GRE or GMAT. Additional exam requirements/recommendations for international students: Required—TOEFL (minimum score 550 paper-based, 80 iBT) or IELTS (6.5). *Application deadline:* Applications are processed on a rolling basis. Application fee: $50. Electronic applications accepted. *Expenses: Tuition:* Full-time $24,984; part-time $1388 per credit hour. *Required fees:* $225. Tuition and fees vary according to campus/location and program. *Financial support:* Scholarships/grants available. *Unit head:* Dr. Dennis Yu, Associate Dean of Graduate Programs & Research, 315-268-2300, E-mail: dyu@clarkson.edu. *Application contact:* Dan Capogna, Director of Graduate Admissions & Recruitment, 518-631-9910, E-mail: graduate@clarkson.edu.
Website: https://www.clarkson.edu/academics/graduate

Clayton State University, School of Graduate Studies, College of Business, Program in Business Administration, Morrow, GA 30260-0285. Offers accounting (MBA); human resource leadership (MBA); international business (MBA); sports and entertainment management (MBA); supply chain management (MBA). *Accreditation:* AACSB. *Program availability:* Part-time, evening/weekend. *Degree requirements:* For master's, thesis. *Entrance requirements:* For master's, GMAT, 3 letters of recommendation; statement of purpose; 2 official transcripts. Additional exam requirements/recommendations for international students: Required—TOEFL (minimum score 550 paper-based; 80 iBT). Electronic applications accepted. *Expenses:* Contact institution.

Colorado State University–Global Campus, Graduate Programs, Greenwood Village, CO 80111. Offers criminal justice and law enforcement administration (MS); education leadership (MS); finance (MS); healthcare administration and management (MS); human resource management (MHRM); information technology management (MITM); international management (MS); management (MS); organizational leadership (MS); professional accounting (MPA); project management (MS); teaching and learning (MS). *Accreditation:* ACBSP. *Program availability:* Online learning.

Columbia University, Graduate School of Business, Executive MBA Global Program, New York, NY 10027. Offers EMBA. Program offered jointly with London Business School. *Entrance requirements:* For master's, GMAT, 2 letters of reference, interview, minimum 5 years of work experience, curriculum vitae or resume, employer support. Additional exam requirements/recommendations for international students: Recommended—TOEFL, IELTS. Electronic applications accepted. *Expenses:* Contact institution.

Columbia University, Graduate School of Business, MBA Program, New York, NY 10027. Offers accounting (MBA); decision, risk, and operations (MBA); entrepreneurship (MBA); finance and economics (MBA); healthcare and pharmaceutical management (MBA); human resource management (MBA); international business (MBA); leadership and ethics (MBA); management (MBA); marketing (MBA); media (MBA); private equity (MBA); real estate (MBA); social enterprise (MBA); value investing (MBA); DDS/MBA; JD/MBA; MBA/MIA; MBA/MPH; MBA/MS; MD/MBA. *Entrance requirements:* For master's, GMAT, 2 letters of recommendation. Additional exam requirements/recommendations for international students: Required—TOEFL. Electronic applications accepted. *Expenses:* Contact institution. *Faculty research:* Human decision making and behavioral research; real estate market and mortgage defaults; financial crisis and corporate governance; international business; security analysis and accounting.

Concordia University Wisconsin, Graduate Programs, Batterman School of Business, MBA Program, Mequon, WI 53097-2402. Offers finance (MBA); health care administration (MBA); human resource management (MBA); international business (MBA); international business-bilingual English/Chinese (MBA); management (MBA); management information systems (MBA); managerial communications (MBA); marketing (MBA); public administration (MBA); risk management (MBA). *Program availability:* Online learning. *Degree requirements:* For master's, comprehensive exam, thesis or alternative. *Entrance requirements:* Additional exam requirements/recommendations for international students: Required—TOEFL. *Expenses:* Contact institution.

Copenhagen Business School, Graduate Programs, Copenhagen, Denmark. Offers business administration (Exec MBA, MBA, PhD); business administration and information systems (M Sc); business, language and culture (M Sc); economics and business administration (M Sc); health management (MHM); international business and politics (M Sc); public administration (MPA); shipping and logistics (Exec MBA); technology, market and organization (MBA).

Daemen College, International Business Program, Amherst, NY 14226-3592. Offers global business (MS), including accounting, global business, management information systems, marketing. *Program availability:* Part-time, evening/weekend. *Faculty:* 3 full-time (2 women), 3 part-time/adjunct (1 woman). *Students:* 4 full-time (2 women), 5 part-time (3 women); includes 1 minority (Black or African American, non-Hispanic/Latino), 2 international. Average age 34. 7 applicants, 57% accepted, 2 enrolled. In 2018, 4 master's awarded. *Degree requirements:* For master's, minimum GPA of 3.0. *Entrance requirements:* For master's, GMAT if undergraduate GPA is less than 3.0, baccalaureate degree from an accredited college or university with a major concentration in a business related field, such as accounting, business administration, economics, management, or marketing; official transcripts; undergrad GPA 3.0 higher or needs to take the GMAT; resume; 2 letters of recommendation; personal statement. Additional exam requirements/recommendations for international students: Required—TOEFL (minimum score 77 paper-based), IELTS (minimum score 6.5). *Application deadline:* Applications are processed on a rolling basis. Application fee: $25. Electronic applications accepted. Application fee is waived when completed online. *Expenses: Tuition:* Part-time $977 per credit hour. *Required fees:* $125; $14 per credit hour. *Financial support:* Scholarships/grants and unspecified assistantships available. Support available to part-time students. Financial award applicants required to submit FAFSA. *Unit head:* Dr. Torsten Doering, Director of International Business Program, 716-839-8239, E-mail: tdoering@daemen.edu. *Application contact:* Megan Beardi, Senior Assistant Director of Graduate Admissions, 716-566-7861, Fax: 716-839-8229, E-mail: mbeardi@daemen.edu.
Website: https://www.daemen.edu/academics/areas-study/international-business

Dallas Baptist University, College of Business, Master of Business Administration Program, Dallas, TX 75211-9299. Offers health care management (MBA); international business (MBA); management information systems (MBA). *Accreditation:* ACBSP. *Program availability:* Part-time, evening/weekend, 100% online, blended/hybrid learning. *Application deadline:* Applications are processed on a rolling basis. Application fee: $25. Electronic applications accepted. Application fee is waived when completed online. *Expenses: Tuition:* Full-time $17,262; part-time $959 per credit hour. *Required fees:* $1000; $500 per semester. Tuition and fees vary according to course load and degree level. *Unit head:* Dr. Sandra Reid, Chair of Graduate Business Programs, Program Director, 214-333-5280, E-mail: sandra@dbu.edu. *Application contact:* Dr. Sandra Reid, Chair of Graduate Business Programs, Program Director, 214-333-5280, E-mail: sandra@dbu.edu.
Website: https://www.dbu.edu/graduate/degree-programs/mba

Dallas Baptist University, Gary Cook School of Leadership, Program in International Studies, Dallas, TX 75211-9299. Offers East Asian studies (MA); European studies (MA); general international studies (MA); global business (MA); international immersion (MA); international ministry (MA); international relations (MA). *Program availability:* Part-time, evening/weekend. *Application deadline:* Applications are processed on a rolling basis. Application fee: $25. Electronic applications accepted. Application fee is waived when completed online. *Expenses: Tuition:* Full-time $17,262; part-time $959 per credit hour. *Required fees:* $1000; $500 per semester. Tuition and fees vary according to course load and degree level. *Unit head:* Dr. Jack Goodyear, Dean, 214-333-5595, Fax: 214-333-6809, E-mail: jackg@dbu.edu. *Application contact:* Lee Bratcher, Program Director, 214-333-5808, E-mail: leeb@dbu.edu.
Website: https://www.dbu.edu/graduate/degree-programs/ma-international-studies

Dallas Baptist University, Graduate School of Ministry, Program in Global Leadership, Dallas, TX 75211-9299. Offers church planting (MA); East Asian Studies (MA); English as a second language (MA); general studies (MA); global communication (MA); global studies (MA); international business (MA); leading the nonprofit organization (MA); missions (MA); small group ministry (MA); urban ministry (MA). *Program availability:* Part-time, evening/weekend, online learning. *Application deadline:* Applications are processed on a rolling basis. Application fee: $25. Electronic applications accepted.

Application fee is waived when completed online. *Expenses: Tuition:* Full-time $17,262; part-time $959 per credit hour. *Required fees:* $1000; $500 per semester. Tuition and fees vary according to course load and degree level. *Unit head:* Dr. Robert R. Brooks, Dean, 214-333-5494, Fax: 214-333-5673, E-mail: bobb@dbu.edu. *Application contact:* Dr. Brent Thomason, Program Director, 214-333-5236, E-mail: brentt@dbu.edu.
Website: http://www.dbu.edu/ministry/degree-programs/m-a-in-global-leadership

Delaware Valley University, MBA Program, Doylestown, PA 18901-2697. Offers accounting (MBA); entrepreneurship (MBA); finance (MBA); food and agribusiness (MBA); general business (MBA); global executive leadership (MBA); human resource management (MBA); supply chain management (MBA). *Program availability:* Part-time, evening/weekend, online learning. *Entrance requirements:* For master's, minimum undergraduate GPA of 3.0. Electronic applications accepted. *Expenses:* Contact institution.

DePaul University, Kellstadt Graduate School of Business, Chicago, IL 60604. Offers accountancy (MBA, MSA); applied economics (MBA); audit and advisory services (MS); business administration (DBA); business analytics (MS); business strategy and decision-making (MBA); computational finance (MS); economics and policy analysis (MS); enterprise risk management (MS); entrepreneurship (MBA, MS); finance (MBA, MS); general business (MBA); hospitality leadership (MBA); hospitality leadership and operational performance (MS); human resources (MS); international business (MBA); management (MBA, MS); management information systems (MBA); marketing (MBA, MS); marketing analysis (MS); marketing strategy and planning (MBA); real estate (MS); real estate finance and investment (MBA); strategy, execution and valuation (MBA); supply chain management (MS); sustainable management (MS); taxation (MS); JD/MBA. *Accreditation:* AACSB. *Program availability:* Part-time, evening/weekend, online learning. *Entrance requirements:* For master's, GMAT/GRE, 2 letters of recommendation, resume, essay, official transcripts. Additional exam requirements/recommendations for international students: Required—TOEFL (minimum score 550 paper-based; 80 iBT). Electronic applications accepted. *Expenses:* Contact institution.

Duke University, The Fuqua School of Business, The Duke MBA-Global Executive Program, Durham, NC 27708. Offers business administration (MBA); energy and environment (MBA); entrepreneurship and innovation (MBA); finance (MBA); health sector management (Certificate); marketing (MBA); strategy (MBA). *Faculty:* 100 full-time (21 women), 55 part-time/adjunct (12 women). *Students:* 141 full-time (43 women); includes 43 minority (12 Black or African American, non-Hispanic/Latino; 25 Asian, non-Hispanic/Latino; 4 Hispanic/Latino; 1 Native Hawaiian or other Pacific Islander, non-Hispanic/Latino; 1 Two or more races, non-Hispanic/Latino), 34 international. Average age 35. In 2018, 159 master's awarded. *Entrance requirements:* For master's, Executive Assessment, GMAT, or GRE, or waived, transcripts, essays, resume, recommendation letters, letter of company support, interview. *Application deadline:* For fall admission, 10/16 priority date for domestic and international students; for winter admission, 12/4 priority date for domestic and international students; for spring admission, 3/11 priority date for domestic and international students; for summer admission, 5/27 for domestic and international students. Applications are processed on a rolling basis. Application fee: $225. Electronic applications accepted. *Expenses:* Contact institution. *Financial support:* Scholarships/grants available. Financial award applicants required to submit FAFSA. *Unit head:* Karen Courtney, Associate Dean, Executive Programs. *Application contact:* Shari Hubert, Associate Dean, Office of Admissions, 919-660-7705, Fax: 919-681-8026, E-mail: admissions-info@fuqua.duke.edu.
Website: https://www.fuqua.duke.edu/programs/global-executive-mba

Duke University, The Fuqua School of Business, MMS: Duke Kunshan University Program, Durham, NC 27708. Offers MMS. Duke Kunshan University. *Faculty:* 100 full-time (21 women), 55 part-time/adjunct (12 women). *Students:* 64 full-time (38 women); includes 2 minority (1 American Indian or Alaska Native, non-Hispanic/Latino; 1 Asian, non-Hispanic/Latino), 57 international. Average age 23. In 2018, 56 master's awarded. *Entrance requirements:* For master's, GMAT or GRE, transcripts, essays, resume, recommendation letter, interview. *Application deadline:* For fall admission, 10/28 for domestic and international students; for winter admission, 1/22 for domestic and international students; for spring admission, 3/5 for domestic and international students; for summer admission, 4/13 for domestic and international students. Electronic applications accepted. *Financial support:* Applicants required to submit FAFSA. *Unit head:* Steve Misuraca, Assistant Dean, 919-660-7778. *Application contact:* Shari Hubert, Associate Dean, Office of Admissions, 919-660-7705, E-mail: mms-dku-info@fuqua.duke.edu.
Website: https://www.fuqua.duke.edu/programs/mms-duke-kunshan-university

D'Youville College, Department of Business, Buffalo, NY 14201-1084. Offers business administration (MBA); international business (MS). *Program availability:* Part-time, evening/weekend. *Degree requirements:* For master's, one foreign language, project or thesis. *Entrance requirements:* For master's, minimum GPA of 3.0. Additional exam requirements/recommendations for international students: Required—TOEFL (minimum score 500 paper-based). Electronic applications accepted. *Faculty research:* Assessment, accreditation, supply chain, online learning, adult learning.

Eastern Michigan University, Graduate School, College of Arts and Sciences, Department of World Languages, Program in Language and International Trade, Ypsilanti, MI 48197. Offers MA. *Program availability:* Evening/weekend. *Students:* 1 (woman) part-time; minority (Black or African American, non-Hispanic/Latino). Average age 30. 1 applicant, 100% accepted, 1 enrolled. *Entrance requirements:* Additional exam requirements/recommendations for international students: Required—TOEFL. *Application deadline:* Applications are processed on a rolling basis. Application fee: $45. *Financial support:* Fellowships, research assistantships with full tuition reimbursements, teaching assistantships with full tuition reimbursements, career-related internships or fieldwork, Federal Work-Study, institutionally sponsored loans, scholarships/grants, tuition waivers (partial), and unspecified assistantships available. Support available to part-time students. Financial award applicants required to submit FAFSA. *Application contact:* Dr. Genevieve Peden, Program Advisor, 734-487-1498, Fax: 734-487-3411, E-mail: gpeden@emich.edu.

Eastern Michigan University, Graduate School, College of Business, Department of Marketing, Ypsilanti, MI 48197. Offers e-business (MBA); integrated marketing communications (MS, Postbaccalaureate Certificate); international business (MBA); marketing management (MBA); supply chain management (MBA). *Program availability:* Part-time, evening/weekend, online learning. *Faculty:* 22 full-time (7 women). *Students:* 31 full-time (25 women), 33 part-time (22 women); includes 25 minority (15 Black or African American, non-Hispanic/Latino; 1 Asian, non-Hispanic/Latino; 9 Hispanic/Latino). Average age 30. 32 applicants, 84% accepted, 16 enrolled. In 2018, 23 master's awarded. *Entrance requirements:* For master's, GMAT. Additional exam requirements/recommendations for international students: Required—TOEFL. *Application deadline:* For fall admission, 5/15 priority date for domestic students, 2/15 priority date for international students; for winter admission, 10/15 priority date for domestic students, 9/1 priority date for international students; for summer admission, 3/15 priority date for domestic students, 3/1 priority date for international students. Applications are processed on a rolling basis. Application fee: $45. *Financial support:* Fellowships, research assistantships with full tuition reimbursements, teaching assistantships with full tuition reimbursements, career-related internships or fieldwork, Federal Work-Study, institutionally sponsored loans, scholarships/grants, tuition waivers (partial), and unspecified assistantships available. Support available to part-time students. Financial award applicants required to submit FAFSA. *Unit head:* Dr. Lewis Hershey, Department Head, 734-487-3323, Fax: 734-487-7099, E-mail: lhershe1@emich.edu. *Application contact:* K. Michelle Henry, Director, Graduate Business Programs, 734-487-4444, Fax: 734-483-1316, E-mail: cob.graduate@emich.edu.
Website: http://www.mkt.emich.edu/index.html

Eastern Michigan University, Graduate School, College of Business, Programs in Business Administration, Ypsilanti, MI 48197. Offers business administration (MBA, Graduate Certificate); computer information systems (Graduate Certificate); e-business (MBA, Graduate Certificate); enterprise business intelligence (MBA); entrepreneurship (MBA, Graduate Certificate); finance (MBA, Graduate Certificate); human resources (MBA); human resources management (Graduate Certificate); information systems (MBA); internal auditing (MBA); international business (MBA, Graduate Certificate); marketing management (Graduate Certificate); nonprofit management (MBA); organizational development (Graduate Certificate); supply chain management (MBA, Graduate Certificate). *Accreditation:* AACSB. *Program availability:* Part-time, online learning. *Students:* 69 full-time (38 women), 251 part-time (140 women); includes 100 minority (63 Black or African American, non-Hispanic/Latino; 1 American Indian or Alaska Native, non-Hispanic/Latino; 12 Asian, non-Hispanic/Latino; 14 Hispanic/Latino; 10 Two or more races, non-Hispanic/Latino), 28 international. Average age 32. 199 applicants, 75% accepted, 83 enrolled. In 2018, 75 master's, 50 other advanced degrees awarded. *Entrance requirements:* For master's, GMAT (minimum score 450), minimum cumulative undergraduate GPA of 2.75. Additional exam requirements/recommendations for international students: Required—TOEFL. *Application deadline:* For fall admission, 5/15 priority date for domestic students, 2/15 priority date for international students; for winter admission, 10/15 priority date for domestic students, 9/1 priority date for international students; for summer admission, 3/15 priority date for domestic students, 3/1 priority date for international students. Applications are processed on a rolling basis. Application fee: $45. *Financial support:* Fellowships, research assistantships with full tuition reimbursements, teaching assistantships with full tuition reimbursements, career-related internships or fieldwork, Federal Work-Study, institutionally sponsored loans, scholarships/grants, tuition waivers (partial), and unspecified assistantships available. Support available to part-time students. Financial award applicants required to submit FAFSA. *Unit head:* K. Michelle Henry, Director, Graduate Business Programs, 734-487-4444, Fax: 734-483-1316, E-mail: cob.graduate@emich.edu. *Application contact:* K. Michelle Henry, Director, Graduate Business Programs, 734-487-4444, Fax: 734-483-1316, E-mail: cob.graduate@emich.edu.
Website: http://www.emich.edu/cob/mba/

Embry-Riddle Aeronautical University–Worldwide, Department of Decision Sciences, Daytona Beach, FL 32114-3900. Offers aviation and aerospace (MSPM); aviation/aerospace management (MSEM); financial management (MSEM, MSPM); general management (MSPM); global management (MSPM); human resources management (MSPM); information systems (MSPM); leadership (MSEM, MSPM); logistics and supply chain management (MSEM, MSLSCM, MSPM); management (MSEM, MSPM); project management (MSEM); systems engineering (MSEM, MSPM); technical management (MSPM). *Program availability:* Part-time, evening/weekend, EagleVision Classroom (between classrooms), EagleVision Home (faculty and students at home), and a blend of Classroom or Home. *Degree requirements:* For master's, comprehensive exam (for some programs), thesis (for some programs). *Entrance requirements:* Additional exam requirements/recommendations for international students: Required—TOEFL (minimum score 550 paper-based; 79 iBT), IELTS (minimum score 6). Electronic applications accepted. *Expenses:* Contact institution.

Emory University, Goizueta Business School, Full Time MBA Program, Atlanta, GA 30322-1100. Offers accounting (MBA); alternative investments (MBA); business process consulting (MBA); business technology management (MBA); capital markets (MBA); corporate finance (MBA); customer relationship management (MBA); decision analytics (MBA); entrepreneurship (MBA); finance (MBA); global management (MBA); investment banking (MBA); management consulting (MBA); marketing (MBA); marketing analytics (MBA); marketing consulting (MBA); operations management (MBA); organization and management (MBA); product and brand management (MBA); real estate (MBA); social enterprise (MBA); strategy consulting (MBA). *Accreditation:* AACSB. *Faculty:* 74 full-time (18 women), 18 part-time/adjunct (6 women). *Students:* 349 full-time (105 women); includes 81 minority (26 Black or African American, non-Hispanic/Latino; 1 American Indian or Alaska Native, non-Hispanic/Latino; 35 Asian, non-Hispanic/Latino; 16 Hispanic/Latino; 3 Two or more races, non-Hispanic/Latino), 97 international. Average age 29. 1,380 applicants, 34% accepted, 172 enrolled. In 2018, 180 master's awarded. *Degree requirements:* For master's, 1 leadership course; 2 mid-semester module programs; 2 global components. *Entrance requirements:* For master's, GMAT/GRE, essays; recommendation letters; undergraduate degree; interview. Additional exam requirements/recommendations for international students: Required—TOEFL (minimum score 100 iBT), IELTS (minimum score 7), PTE (minimum score 68). *Application deadline:* For fall admission, 10/6 for domestic and international students; for winter admission, 11/17 for domestic and international students; for spring admission, 1/3 priority date for domestic and international students; for summer admission, 3/9 for domestic and international students. Application fee: $150. Electronic applications accepted. *Expenses:* Contact institution. *Financial support:* In 2018–19, 273 students received support. Career-related internships or fieldwork, institutionally sponsored loans, and scholarships/grants available. Financial award application deadline: 4/1; financial award applicants required to submit FAFSA. *Faculty research:* Corporate finance, information systems, digital marketing, asset pricing, sports management. *Unit head:* Brian Mitchell, Associate Dean, 404-727-4824, Fax: 404-712-9648, E-mail: brian.mitchell@emory.edu. *Application contact:* Melissa Rapp, Associate Dean, 404-727-7583, Fax: 404-727-4612, E-mail: mbaadmissions@emory.edu.
Website: http://www.goizueta.emory.edu

ESSEC Business School, Graduate Programs, Paris, France. Offers business administration (PhD); executive business administration (MBA); global business administration (MBA); hospitality management (MBA); international luxury brand management (MBA); management (MSM).

Fairleigh Dickinson University, Florham Campus, Silberman College of Business, Department of Economics, Finance, and International Business, Program in International Business, Madison, NJ 07940-1099. Offers MBA, Certificate.

Fairleigh Dickinson University, Metropolitan Campus, Silberman College of Business, Department of Economics, Finance and International Business, Program in International Business, Teaneck, NJ 07666-1914. Offers MBA.

Florida Atlantic University, College of Business, Department of Management, Boca Raton, FL 33431-0991. Offers business administration (MBA); entrepreneurship (MBA); health administration (MBA); international business (MBA); sport management (MBA). *Faculty:* 8 full-time (3 women). *Students:* 109 full-time (81 women), 82 part-time (58 women); includes 106 minority (52 Black or African American, non-Hispanic/Latino; 8 Asian, non-Hispanic/Latino; 40 Hispanic/Latino; 6 Two or more races, non-Hispanic/Latino), 1 international. Average age 35. 113 applicants, 85% accepted, 72 enrolled. In

2018, 120 master's awarded. *Entrance requirements:* For master's, GMAT or GRE General Test, minimum GPA of 3.0 in last 60 hours of course work. Additional exam requirements/recommendations for international students: Required—TOEFL (minimum score 600 paper-based; 61 iBT), IELTS (minimum score 6). *Application deadline:* For fall admission, 7/25 for domestic students, 2/15 for international students; for spring admission, 12/10 for domestic students, 7/15 for international students. Applications are processed on a rolling basis. Application fee: $30. Electronic applications accepted. *Expenses: Tuition, area resident:* Full-time $7400; part-time $369.82 per credit. Tuition, state resident: full-time $7400; part-time $369.82 per credit. Tuition, nonresident: full-time $20,496; part-time $1024.81 per credit. *Financial support:* Research assistantships with full tuition reimbursements, career-related internships or fieldwork, tuition waivers (partial), and unspecified assistantships available. *Faculty research:* Sports administration, healthcare, policy, finance, real estate, senior living. *Unit head:* Dr. Roland Kidwell, Chair, 561-297-4507, E-mail: kidwellr@fau.edu. *Application contact:* Dr. Roland Kidwell, Chair, 561-297-4507, E-mail: kidwellr@fau.edu.
Website: http://business.fau.edu/departments/management/index.aspx

Florida Institute of Technology, Aberdeen Education Center (Maryland), Program in Management, Melbourne, FL 32901-6975. Offers acquisition and contract management (MS, PMBA); business administration (MS, PMBA); contracts management (PMBA); financial management (MPA); global management (PMBA); health management (MS); human resources management (MS, PMBA); information systems (PMBA); logistics management (MS); management (MS), including information systems, operations research; materials acquisition management (MS); operations research (MS); public administration (MPA); research (PMBA); space systems (MS); space systems management (MS). *Expenses: Tuition:* Full-time $22,338; part-time $1241 per credit hour. Tuition and fees vary according to degree level, campus/location and program. *Financial support:* Application deadline: 3/1. *Application contact:* Online Learning and Off-Campus Programs Admissions, 321-674-8263, E-mail: gradadm-olocp@fit.edu.
Website: https://www.fit.edu/education-centers/degrees-and-programs/management-ms/

Florida International University, Chapman Graduate School of Business, Department of Management and International Business, Miami, FL 33199. Offers human resources management (MSHRM); international business (MIB); management and international business (EMBA, IMBA, MBA, PhD). *Program availability:* Part-time, evening/weekend. *Faculty:* 19 full-time (7 women), 27 part-time/adjunct (10 women). *Students:* 892 full-time (530 women), 555 part-time (285 women); includes 1,094 minority (237 Black or African American, non-Hispanic/Latino; 47 Asian, non-Hispanic/Latino; 779 Hispanic/Latino; 4 Native Hawaiian or other Pacific Islander, non-Hispanic/Latino; 27 Two or more races, non-Hispanic/Latino), 153 international. Average age 32. 1,377 applicants, 50% accepted, 476 enrolled. In 2018, 792 master's, 6 doctorates awarded. *Degree requirements:* For doctorate, comprehensive exam, thesis/dissertation. *Entrance requirements:* For master's, GMAT or GRE (depending on program), minimum GPA of 3.0 in upper-level coursework; for doctorate, GMAT or GRE, letter of intent; 3 letters of recommendation; resume. Additional exam requirements/recommendations for international students: Required—TOEFL (minimum score 550 paper-based; 80 iBT) or IELTS (minimum score 6.5). *Application deadline:* For fall admission, 6/1 for domestic students, 4/1 for international students; for spring admission, 10/1 for domestic students, 9/1 for international students. Applications are processed on a rolling basis. Application fee: $30. Electronic applications accepted. *Expenses:* Contact institution. *Financial support:* Institutionally sponsored loans and scholarships/grants available. Financial award application deadline: 3/1; financial award applicants required to submit FAFSA. *Faculty research:* International business, strategy, entrepreneurship, human resource management. *Unit head:* Dr. Willam Newburry, Chair, 305-348-1103, E-mail: newburry@fiu.edu. *Application contact:* Nanett Rojas, Manager, Admissions Operations, 305-348-7464, Fax: 305-348-7441, E-mail: gradadm@fiu.edu.

Franklin University Switzerland, The Taylor Institute for Global Enterprise Management, 6924 Sorengo, Switzerland. Offers international management (MS).

George Mason University, College of Education and Human Development, School of Recreation, Health and Tourism, Manassas, VA 20110. Offers athletic training (MS); exercise, fitness, and health promotion (MS), including advanced practitioner, wellness practitioner; international sport management (Certificate); recreation, health and tourism (Certificate); sport management (MS), including sport and recreation studies. *Program availability:* Part-time, evening/weekend. *Faculty:* 33 full-time (15 women), 84 part-time/adjunct (44 women). *Students:* 76 full-time (33 women), 21 part-time (5 women); includes 32 minority (25 Black or African American, non-Hispanic/Latino; 1 American Indian or Alaska Native, non-Hispanic/Latino; 1 Asian, non-Hispanic/Latino; 3 Hispanic/Latino; 1 Native Hawaiian or other Pacific Islander, non-Hispanic/Latino; 1 Two or more races, non-Hispanic/Latino), 17 international. Average age 26. 77 applicants, 88% accepted, 41 enrolled. In 2018, 26 master's, 1 other advanced degree awarded. *Entrance requirements:* For master's, 3 letters of recommendation; official transcripts; expanded goals statement; undergraduate course in statistics and minimum GPA of 3.0 in last 60 credit hours and overall (for MS in sport and recreation studies); baccalaureate degree related to kinesiology, exercise science or athletic training (for MS in exercise, fitness and health promotion). Additional exam requirements/recommendations for international students: Required—TOEFL (minimum score 575 paper-based; 88 iBT), IELTS (minimum score 6.5), PTE (minimum score 59). *Application deadline:* For fall admission, 4/2 priority date for domestic and international students; for spring admission, 11/1 for domestic and international students. Application fee: $75 ($80 for international students). Electronic applications accepted. *Financial support:* In 2018–19, 6 students received support, including 6 research assistantships with tuition reimbursements available (averaging $7,242 per year); career-related internships or fieldwork, Federal Work-Study, scholarships/grants, unspecified assistantships, and health care benefits (for full-time research or teaching assistantship recipients) also available. Support available to part-time students. Financial award application deadline: 3/1; financial award applicants required to submit FAFSA. *Faculty research:* Sport for development and peace, sport analytics, leadership and coaching, diversity and inclusion in sport, sport communication. *Total annual research expenditures:* $826,386. *Unit head:* Martin Ford, Senior Associate Dean, 703-993-2004, E-mail: mford@gmu.edu. *Application contact:* Lindsey Olson, Office Assistant, 703-993-2098, Fax: 703-993-2025, E-mail: lolson7@gmu.edu.
Website: http://rht.gmu.edu/

Georgetown University, Graduate School of Arts and Sciences, Department of Economics, Washington, DC 20057. Offers econometrics (PhD); economic development (PhD); economic theory (PhD); industrial organization (PhD); international macro and finance (PhD); international trade (PhD); labor economics (PhD); macroeconomics (PhD); public economics and political economy (PhD); MA/PhD; MS/MA. *Degree requirements:* For doctorate, comprehensive exam, thesis/dissertation. *Entrance requirements:* For doctorate, GRE General Test. Additional exam requirements/recommendations for international students: Required—TOEFL. *Faculty research:* International economics, economic development.

Georgetown University, Law Center, Washington, DC 20001. Offers environmental law (LL M); global health law (LL M); global health law and international institutions (LL M); individualized study (LL M); international business and economic law (LL M); law (JD, SJD); national security law (LL M); securities and financial regulation (LL M); taxation (LL M); JD/LL M; JD/MA; JD/MBA; JD/MPH; JD/PhD. *Accreditation:* ABA. *Program availability:* Part-time, evening/weekend. *Degree requirements:* For master's, thesis; for doctorate, thesis/dissertation (for some programs). *Entrance requirements:* For master's, JD, LL B, or first law degree earned in country of origin; for doctorate, LSAT (for JD). Additional exam requirements/recommendations for international students: Required—TOEFL. *Expenses:* Contact institution. *Faculty research:* Constitutional law, legal history, jurisprudence.

The George Washington University, Elliott School of International Affairs, Program in International Trade and Investment Policy, Washington, DC 20052. Offers MA. *Program availability:* Part-time. *Students:* 35 full-time (17 women), 9 part-time (6 women); includes 12 minority (5 Black or African American, non-Hispanic/Latino; 2 Asian, non-Hispanic/Latino; 3 Hispanic/Latino; 2 Two or more races, non-Hispanic/Latino), 19 international. Average age 26. 76 applicants, 71% accepted, 23 enrolled. In 2018, 19 master's awarded. *Degree requirements:* For master's, one foreign language, capstone project. *Entrance requirements:* For master's, GRE General Test, 2 years of a modern foreign language, 2 semesters of introductory economics. Additional exam requirements/recommendations for international students: Required—TOEFL (minimum score 100 iBT), IELTS (minimum score 7). *Application deadline:* For fall admission, 1/15 priority date for domestic and international students; for spring admission, 10/1 for domestic students. Application fee: $75. Electronic applications accepted. *Financial support:* In 2018–19, 11 students received support. Fellowships with partial tuition reimbursements available, Federal Work-Study, and scholarships/grants available. Financial award application deadline: 1/15. *Unit head:* Prof. Michael Moore, Director, 202-994-5230, E-mail: itip@gwu.edu. *Application contact:* Nicole A. Campbell, Director of Graduate Admissions, 202-994-7050, Fax: 202-994-9537, E-mail: esiagrad@gwu.edu.
Website: http://elliott.gwu.edu/international-trade-investment-policy

The George Washington University, School of Business, Department of International Business, Washington, DC 20052. Offers PhD. *Program availability:* Part-time, evening/weekend. *Students:* 7 applicants, 86% accepted. *Entrance requirements:* For doctorate, GMAT or GRE. Additional exam requirements/recommendations for international students: Required—TOEFL. *Application deadline:* For fall admission, 4/1 priority date for domestic students; for spring admission, 10/1 for domestic students. Applications are processed on a rolling basis. Application fee: $75. *Financial support:* Fellowships, teaching assistantships, career-related internships or fieldwork, Federal Work-Study, and institutionally sponsored loans available. Financial award application deadline: 4/1. *Faculty research:* International trade, competitiveness, business management. *Unit head:* Robert Weiner, Chair, 202-994-5981, E-mail: rweiner@gwu.edu. *Application contact:* Christopher Storer, Executive Director, Graduate Admissions, 202-994-1212, E-mail: gwmba@gwu.edu.
Website: http://business.gwu.edu/about-us/departments/department-of-international-business/

Georgia Institute of Technology, Graduate Studies, Scheller College of Business, Program in Business Administration, Atlanta, GA 30332-0001. Offers business administration (MBA); global business (MBA); management of technology (MBA). *Accreditation:* AACSB. *Program availability:* Part-time, evening/weekend. *Entrance requirements:* For master's, GMAT, two essays, three letters of recommendation, transcript from each college/university attended. Additional exam requirements/recommendations for international students: Required—TOEFL (minimum score 600 paper-based; 100 iBT). Electronic applications accepted. *Expenses:* Contact institution.

Georgia State University, J. Mack Robinson College of Business, Institute of International Business, Atlanta, GA 30303. Offers international business (GMBA, MBA, MIB); international business and information technology (MBA); international entrepreneurship (MBA); MIB/MIA. *Program availability:* Part-time, evening/weekend. *Faculty:* 5 full-time (3 women). *Students:* 18 full-time (8 women); includes 6 minority (3 Black or African American, non-Hispanic/Latino; 1 Asian, non-Hispanic/Latino; 1 Hispanic/Latino; 1 Two or more races, non-Hispanic/Latino), 8 international. Average age 29. 48 applicants, 73% accepted, 22 enrolled. In 2018, 40 master's awarded. *Entrance requirements:* For master's, GRE or GMAT, transcripts from all institutions attended, resume, essays. Additional exam requirements/recommendations for international students: Required—TOEFL (minimum score 610 paper-based; 101 iBT), IELTS (minimum score 7). *Application deadline:* For fall admission, 5/1 priority date for domestic students, 2/1 priority date for international students; for spring admission, 9/15 priority date for domestic students, 5/1 priority date for international students. Applications are processed on a rolling basis. Application fee: $50. Electronic applications accepted. *Expenses: Tuition, area resident:* Full-time $9360; part-time $390 per credit hour. Tuition, state resident: full-time $9360; part-time $390 per credit hour. Tuition, nonresident: full-time $30,024; part-time $1251 per credit hour. *International tuition:* $30,024 full-time. *Required fees:* $2128. *Financial support:* Research assistantships, teaching assistantships, scholarships/grants, tuition waivers (partial), and unspecified assistantships available. Financial award application deadline: 5/1. *Faculty research:* Business challenges in emerging markets (especially in India and China); interorganizational relationships in an international context, such as strategic alliances and global supply chain relations; globalization and entry mode strategy or new (or emerging) multinationals; emerging market development and business environments; cross-cultural effects on business processes and performance. *Unit head:* Dr. Daniel Bello, Professor/Director of the Institute of International Business, 404-413-7275, Fax: 404-413-7276. *Application contact:* Toby McChesney, Assistant Dean for Graduate Recruiting and Student Services, 404-413-7167, Fax: 404-413-7162, E-mail: rcbgradadmissions@gsu.edu.
Website: http://iib.gsu.edu/

Golden Gate University, Ageno School of Business, San Francisco, CA 94105-2968. Offers accounting (MBA); adaptive leadership (MBA); advanced financial planning (MS); business administration (EMBA, MBA, DBA); business analytics (MBA, MS); entrepreneurship (MBA); finance (MBA, MS, Certificate); financial life planning (Certificate); financial planning (MS, Certificate); global supply chain management (MBA, Certificate); human resource management (MBA, MS, Certificate); information technology management (MBA, MS, Certificate); international business (MBA); marketing (MBA, MS, Certificate); project management (MBA, MS, Certificate); psychology (MA, Certificate); public administration (EMPA, MBA); public administration leadership (Certificate); JD/MBA. *Program availability:* Part-time, evening/weekend. *Degree requirements:* For doctorate, thesis/dissertation, qualifying examination. *Entrance requirements:* For master's, GMAT (for MBA), minimum GPA of 2.5 (MS). Additional exam requirements/recommendations for international students: Required—TOEFL (minimum score 550 paper-based; 79 iBT). Electronic applications accepted. *Expenses:* Contact institution.

Goldey-Beacom College, Graduate Program, Wilmington, DE 19808-1999. Offers business administration (MBA); finance (MS); financial management (MBA); health care management (MBA); human resource management (MBA); information technology (MBA); international business management (MBA); major finance (MBA); major taxation (MBA); management (MM); marketing management (MBA); taxation (MBA, MS). *Accreditation:* ACBSP. *Program availability:* Part-time, evening/weekend. *Entrance*

requirements: For master's, GMAT, MAT, GRE, minimum GPA of 3.0. Additional exam requirements/recommendations for international students: Required—TOEFL (minimum score 65 iBT); Recommended—IELTS (minimum score 6). Electronic applications accepted.

Hallmark University, School of Business, San Antonio, TX 78230. Offers global management (MBA). *Degree requirements:* For master's, thesis (for some programs). *Entrance requirements:* For master's, bachelor's degree; minimum undergraduate GPA of 2.5; completion of one course each in college-level statistics, quanitative methods, and calculus or pre-calculus; official undergraduate transcripts; professional resume; personal statement; two letters of recommendation; two 200-word typed essays. Additional exam requirements/recommendations for international students: Required—TOEFL (minimum score 450 paper-based; 45 iBT). *Expenses:* Contact institution.

Harding University, Paul R. Carter College of Business Administration, Searcy, AR 72149-0001. Offers international business (MBA); leadership and organizational management (MBA). *Accreditation:* ACBSP. *Program availability:* Part-time, evening/weekend, 100% online. *Degree requirements:* For master's, portfolio. *Entrance requirements:* For master's, GMAT (minimum score of 500) or GRE (minimum score of 300), minimum GPA of 3.0, 2 letters of recommendation, resume, 3 essays, all official transcripts. Additional exam requirements/recommendations for international students: Required—TOEFL (minimum score 550 paper-based; 79 iBT).

Hawai`i Pacific University, College of Business, Program in Business Administration, Honolulu, HI 96813. Offers finance (MBA); human resource management (MBA); information systems (MBA); international business (MBA); management (MBA); marketing (MBA); organizational change and development (MBA). *Program availability:* Part-time, evening/weekend, 100% online, blended/hybrid learning. *Entrance requirements:* For master's, GMAT or GRE. Additional exam requirements/recommendations for international students: Recommended—TOEFL (minimum score 550 paper-based; 80 iBT), IELTS (minimum score 6), TWE (minimum score 5). Electronic applications accepted.

HEC Montreal, School of Business Administration, Doctoral Program in Administration, Montréal, QC H3T 2A7, Canada. Offers accounting (PhD); applied economics (PhD); data science (PhD); finance (PhD); financial engineering (PhD); information technology (PhD); international business (PhD); logistics and operations management (PhD); management science (PhD); management, strategy and organizations (PhD); marketing (PhD); organizational behaviour and human resources (PhD). Program offered jointly with Concordia University, McGill University, and Universite du Quebec a Montreal. *Accreditation:* AACSB. *Students:* 130 full-time (55 women). 114 applicants, 46% accepted, 31 enrolled. In 2018, 19 doctorates awarded. *Entrance requirements:* For doctorate, TAGE MAGE, GMAT, or GRE, master's degree in administration or related field. *Application deadline:* For fall admission, 1/15 for domestic and international students. Application fee: 91 (191 for international students). Electronic applications accepted. *Expenses: Tuition, area resident:* Full-time $3052.80 Canadian dollars; part-time $84.80 Canadian dollars per credit. Tuition, state resident: full-time $3816 Canadian dollars; part-time $264.67 Canadian dollars per credit. Tuition, nonresident: full-time $11,910 Canadian dollars. *International tuition:* $20,905.20 Canadian dollars full-time. *Required fees:* $1805.34 Canadian dollars; $43.62 Canadian dollars per credit. $71.78 Canadian dollars per term. Tuition and fees vary according to degree level and program. *Financial support:* Research assistantships, teaching assistantships, and scholarships/grants available. Financial award application deadline: 9/2. *Faculty research:* Art management, business policy, entrepreneurship, new technologies, transportation. *Unit head:* Guy Paré, Director, 514-340-6264, E-mail: guy.pare@hec.ca. *Application contact:* Julie Bilodeau, PhD Program Analyst, 514-340-6000, Fax: 514-340-6411, E-mail: analyste.phd@hec.ca.
Website: http://www.hec.ca/en/programs/phd/index.html

HEC Montreal, School of Business Administration, Master of Science Programs in Administration, Program in International Business, Montréal, QC H3T 2A7, Canada. Offers M Sc. Program offered in French and also in English (Supervised project stream, Thesis Stream). *Students:* 104 full-time (61 women), 6 part-time (4 women). 125 applicants, 66% accepted, 39 enrolled. In 2018, 36 master's awarded. *Entrance requirements:* For master's, BBA, undergraduate degree in another field, degree deemed equivalent by program director and minimum GPA of 3.0 on 4.3 scale. Additional exam requirements/recommendations for international students: Required—TAGE MAGE (minimum recommended score of 300), GMAT (minimum recommended score of 630), or GRE. *Application deadline:* For fall admission, 3/15 for domestic and international students; for winter admission, 9/15 for domestic and international students. Application fee: $91 Canadian dollars ($191 Canadian dollars for international students). Electronic applications accepted. *Expenses: Tuition, area resident:* Full-time $3052.80 Canadian dollars; part-time $84.80 Canadian dollars per credit. Tuition, state resident: full-time $3816 Canadian dollars; part-time $264.67 Canadian dollars per credit. Tuition, nonresident: full-time $11,910 Canadian dollars. *International tuition:* $20,905.20 Canadian dollars full-time. *Required fees:* $1805.34 Canadian dollars; $43.62 Canadian dollars per credit. $71.78 Canadian dollars per term. Tuition and fees vary according to degree level and program. *Financial support:* Research assistantships, teaching assistantships, and scholarships/grants available. Financial award application deadline: 9/2. *Unit head:* Dr. Sihem Taboubi, Director, 514-340-6428, E-mail: sihem.taboubi@hec.ca. *Application contact:* Marianne de Moura, Administrative Director, 514-340-6000, Fax: 514-340-6411, E-mail: aide@hec.ca.
Website: http://www.hec.ca/en/programs/masters/master-international-business/index.html

Hofstra University, Frank G. Zarb School of Business, Programs in Marketing and International Business, Hempstead, NY 11549. Offers business administration (MBA), including international business, marketing; international business (Advanced Certificate); marketing (MS, Advanced Certificate); marketing research (MS). *Program availability:* Part-time, evening/weekend, blended/hybrid learning. *Students:* 65 full-time (35 women), 19 part-time (11 women); includes 11 minority (2 Black or African American, non-Hispanic/Latino; 5 Asian, non-Hispanic/Latino; 4 Hispanic/Latino), 51 international. Average age 26. 168 applicants, 68% accepted, 35 enrolled. In 2018, 54 master's awarded. *Degree requirements:* For master's, thesis (for some programs), capstone course (for MBA), thesis (for MS), minimum GPA of 3.0. *Entrance requirements:* For master's, GMAT/GRE, 2 letters of recommendation, resume, essay. Additional exam requirements/recommendations for international students: Required—TOEFL (minimum score 550 paper-based; 80 iBT); Recommended—IELTS (minimum score 6). *Application deadline:* Applications are processed on a rolling basis. Application fee: $75. Electronic applications accepted. *Expenses:* $1,375 per credit plus fees. *Financial support:* In 2018–19, 34 students received support, including 21 fellowships with full and partial tuition reimbursements available (averaging $5,450 per year), 3 research assistantships with full and partial tuition reimbursements available (averaging $4,477 per year); career-related internships or fieldwork, Federal Work-Study, institutionally sponsored loans, scholarships/grants, tuition waivers (full and partial), unspecified assistantships, and scholarships and endowed scholarships also available. Support available to part-time students. Financial award applicants required to submit FAFSA. *Faculty research:* Cross-cultural consumer behavior; social, digital, global, and strategic issues in marketing; consumer health/well-being; ethnocentrism and animosity. *Unit head:* Dr. Anil Mathur, Chairperson, 516-463-5346, Fax: 516-463-4834, E-mail: anil.mathur@hofstra.edu. *Application contact:* Sunil Samuel, Assistant Vice President of Admissions, 516-463-4723, Fax: 516-463-4664, E-mail: graduateadmission@hofstra.edu.
Website: http://www.hofstra.edu/business/

Hope International University, School of Graduate and Professional Studies, Program in Business Administration, Fullerton, CA 92831-3138. Offers general management (MBA, MSM); international development (MBA, MSM); marketing management (MBA, MSM); non-profit management (MBA, MSM). *Program availability:* Part-time, online learning. *Degree requirements:* For master's, comprehensive exam (for some programs), thesis (for some programs), project. *Entrance requirements:* For master's, minimum GPA of 3.0; 2 references. Additional exam requirements/recommendations for international students: Required—TOEFL (minimum score 550 paper-based; 86 iBT); Recommended—IELTS (minimum score 6.5). Electronic applications accepted. *Expenses:* Contact institution.

Houston Baptist University, Archie W. Dunham College of Business, Program in International Business, Houston, TX 77074-3298. Offers MIB. *Program availability:* Part-time, evening/weekend. *Entrance requirements:* For master's, minimum GPA of 2.5, bachelor's degree conferred transcript, essay/personal statement, resume. Additional exam requirements/recommendations for international students: Required—TOEFL (minimum score 80 iBT), IELTS (minimum score 6.5). Electronic applications accepted. Application fee is waived when completed online. *Expenses:* Contact institution.

Howard University, School of Business, Graduate Programs in Business, Washington, DC 20059-0002. Offers accounting (MBA); entrepreneurship (MBA); finance (MBA); general management (MBA); human resources management (MBA); information systems (MBA); international business (MBA); marketing (MBA); supply chain management (MBA); JD/MBA. *Accreditation:* AACSB. *Program availability:* Part-time, evening/weekend, online learning. *Entrance requirements:* For master's, GMAT, minimum 1 year post undergraduate work experience, resume, 3 letters of recommendation, advanced college algebra. Additional exam requirements/recommendations for international students: Required—TOEFL. *Faculty research:* Marketing research in multi-ethnic populations, U.S. trade policies and international relations, risk management (finance).

Hult International Business School, Graduate Programs, Cambridge, MA 02141. Offers business administration (EMBA); business analytics (MBA, MIB); business statistics (MBS); disruptive innovation (MDI); entrepreneurship (MBA, MIB); family business (MBA, MIB); finance (MBA, MF, MIB); international marketing (MIM); marketing (MBA, MIB); project management (MBA, MIB). MDI and MBS offered in San Francisco; MBA also offered in Boston, San Francisco, Dubai, Shanghai, and New York. *Entrance requirements:* For master's, GMAT, 3 years of work experience. Additional exam requirements/recommendations for international students: Required—TOEFL. Electronic applications accepted. *Expenses:* Contact institution.

IGlobal University, Graduate Programs, Vienna, VA 22182. Offers accounting (MBA); data management and analytics (MSIT); entrepreneurship (MBA); finance (MBA); global business management (MBA); health care management (MBA); hospitality and tourism management (MBA); human resources management (MBA); information technology (MBA); information technology systems and management (MSIT); leadership and management (MBA); project management (MBA); public service and administration (MBA); software design and management (MSIT).

Indiana Tech, Program in Global Leadership, Fort Wayne, IN 46803-1297. Offers PhD. *Program availability:* Part-time, evening/weekend, online only, 100% online. *Entrance requirements:* For doctorate, GMAT, LSAT, GRE, or MAT, official transcripts of all previous undergraduate and graduate work including evidence of completion of a master's degree at regionally-accredited institution; original essay addressing the candidate's interest in the program and intended goals; current resume including educational record, employment history and relevant accomplishments; interview. Electronic applications accepted.

Instituto Tecnologico de Santo Domingo, Graduate School, Area of Business, Santo Domingo, Dominican Republic. Offers banking and securities markets (M Mgmt); corporate finance (M Mgmt); human resources management (M Mgmt, Certificate); international trade management (M Mgmt); marketing (M Mgmt); organizational development (M Mgmt); quality and productivity management (Certificate); tax management and planning (M Mgmt); upper management (M Mgmt).

Instituto Tecnologico de Santo Domingo, Graduate School, Area of Humanities and Social Sciences, Santo Domingo, Dominican Republic. Offers accounting (Certificate); adult education (Certificate); applied linguistics (MA); economics (MA); education (M Ed); educational psychology (MA, Certificate); gender and development (MA, Certificate); humanistic studies (MA); international marketing management (Certificate); international relations in the Caribbean basin (Certificate); intervention systems in family therapy (MA); linguistic and literary communication (Certificate); pedagogical support (MA); social science education (M Ed); sustainable human development (MA); terminal illness and death psychology (Certificate); youth and adult education (M Ed).

Instituto Tecnológico y de Estudios Superiores de Monterrey, Campus Central de Veracruz, Graduate Programs, Córdoba, Mexico. Offers administration (MA); administration of information technologies (MTI); computer sciences (MCC); education (MEE); educational institution administration (MAD); educational technology (MTE); electronic commerce (MCE); finance (MAF); humanistic studies (MEH); international business for Latin America (MNL); marketing (MMT); science (MCP). *Program availability:* Part-time, evening/weekend, online learning. *Degree requirements:* For master's, thesis (for some programs). *Entrance requirements:* For master's, PAEP College Board. Electronic applications accepted.

Instituto Tecnológico y de Estudios Superiores de Monterrey, Campus Chihuahua, Graduate Programs, Chihuahua, Mexico. Offers computer systems engineering (Ingeniero); electrical engineering (Ingeniero); electromechanical engineering (Ingeniero); electronic engineering (Ingeniero); engineering administration (MEA); industrial engineering (MIE, Ingeniero); international trade (MIT); mechanical engineering (Ingeniero).

Instituto Tecnológico y de Estudios Superiores de Monterrey, Campus Ciudad de México, Virtual University Division, Ciudad de Mexico, Mexico. Offers administration of information technologies (MA); computer sciences (MA); education (MA, PhD); educational technology (MA); environmental engineering (MA); environmental systems (MA); humanistic studies (MA); industrial engineering (MA); international business for Latin America (MA); quality systems (MA); quality systems and productivity (MA). *Program availability:* Part-time, evening/weekend, online learning. *Entrance requirements:* For master's and doctorate, Instituto entrance exam. Additional exam requirements/recommendations for international students: Required—TOEFL.

Instituto Tecnológico y de Estudios Superiores de Monterrey, Campus Cuernavaca, Programs in Business Administration, Temixco, Mexico. Offers finance (MA); human resources management (MA); international business (MA); marketing (MA).

International Business

Instituto Tecnológico y de Estudios Superiores de Monterrey, Campus Irapuato, Graduate Programs, Irapuato, Mexico. Offers administration (MBA); administration of information technology (MAIT); administration of telecommunications (MAT); architecture (M Arch); computer science (MCS); education (M Ed); educational administration (MEA); educational innovation and technology (DEIT); educational technology (MET); electronic commerce (MBA); environmental administration and planning (MEAP); environmental systems (MES); finances (MBA); humanistic studies (MHS); international management for Latin American executives (MIMLAE); library and information science (MLIS); manufacturing quality management (MMQM); marketing research (MBA).

Instituto Tecnológico y de Estudios Superiores de Monterrey, Campus Monterrey, Graduate School of Business Administration and Leadership, Program in Business Administration, Monterrey, Mexico. Offers business administration (MA, MBA); finance (M Sc); international business (M Sc); marketing (M Sc). *Program availability:* Part-time. *Degree requirements:* For master's, one foreign language, thesis. *Entrance requirements:* For master's, GMAT. Additional exam requirements/recommendations for international students: Required—TOEFL. *Faculty research:* Technology management, quality management, organizational theory and behavior.

Inter American University of Puerto Rico, Metropolitan Campus, Graduate Programs, Program in International Business, San Juan, PR 00919-1293. Offers international business (MIB); interregional and international business (PhD).

Inter American University of Puerto Rico, San Germán Campus, Graduate Studies Center, Program in Business Administration, San Germán, PR 00683-5008. Offers accounting (MBA); finance (MBA); general business administration (MBA); human resources (MBA, PhD); industrial relations (MBA); information systems (MBA); international and interregional business (PhD); management (MBA); marketing (MBA). *Program availability:* Part-time, evening/weekend. *Degree requirements:* For master's, comprehensive exam. *Entrance requirements:* For master's, GRE General Test or EXADEP, minimum GPA of 3.0. *Expenses: Tuition:* Full-time $212; part-time $212 per credit. *Required fees:* $366 per semester. One-time fee: $31. Tuition and fees vary according to degree level and program.

International University in Geneva, Business Programs, Geneva, Switzerland. Offers business administration (MBA, DBA); entrepreneurship (MBA); international business (MIB); international trade (MIT); sales and marketing (MBA). *Accreditation:* ACBSP. *Program availability:* Part-time, evening/weekend. *Degree requirements:* For master's, comprehensive exam. *Entrance requirements:* For master's, GMAT. Additional exam requirements/recommendations for international students: Required—TOEFL. Electronic applications accepted.

The International University of Monaco, Graduate Programs, Monte Carlo, Monaco. Offers entrepreneurship (EMBA, MBA); financial engineering (M Sc); hedge fund and private equity (M Sc); international marketing (EMBA, MBA); international wealth management (M Sc); luxury goods and services (EMBA, M Sc, MBA); wealth and asset management (EMBA, MBA). *Program availability:* Part-time. *Degree requirements:* For master's, comprehensive exam (for some programs), applied research project. *Entrance requirements:* Additional exam requirements/recommendations for international students: Required—TOEFL (minimum score 550 paper-based), IELTS. Electronic applications accepted. *Faculty research:* Gaming, leadership, disintermediation.

Iona College, School of Business, Department of Finance, Business Economics and Legal Studies, New Rochelle, NY 10801-1890. Offers finance (MS); financial management (MBA, PMC); financial services (MS); international finance (MS). *Program availability:* Part-time, evening/weekend. *Faculty:* 5 full-time (1 woman). *Students:* 38 full-time (10 women), 34 part-time (12 women); includes 24 minority (11 Black or African American, non-Hispanic/Latino; 2 Asian, non-Hispanic/Latino; 11 Hispanic/Latino), 7 international. Average age 26. 52 applicants, 96% accepted, 27 enrolled. In 2018, 52 master's awarded. *Entrance requirements:* For master's, GMAT, 2 letters of recommendation, minimum GPA of 3.0; for PMC, minimum GPA of 3.0. Additional exam requirements/recommendations for international students: Required—TOEFL (minimum score 550 paper-based; 80 iBT), IELTS (minimum score 6.5). *Application deadline:* For fall admission, 8/15 priority date for domestic students, 8/1 priority date for international students; for winter admission, 11/15 priority date for domestic students, 11/1 priority date for international students; for spring admission, 2/15 priority date for domestic students, 2/1 priority date for international students; for summer admission, 5/15 priority date for domestic students, 5/1 priority date for international students. Applications are processed on a rolling basis. Application fee: $50. Electronic applications accepted. *Expenses:* Contact institution. *Financial support:* In 2018–19, 45 students received support. Scholarships/grants, tuition waivers (partial), and unspecified assistantships available. Support available to part-time students. Financial award application deadline: 4/15; financial award applicants required to submit FAFSA. *Faculty research:* Options, insurance financing, asset depreciation ranges, international finance, emerging markets. *Unit head:* Dr. John F. Manley, Department Chair, 914-633-2284, E-mail: jmanley@iona.edu. *Application contact:* Kimberly Kelly, Director of Graduate Business Admissions, 914-633-2271, Fax: 914-633-2012, E-mail: kkelly@iona.edu.
Website: http://www.iona.edu/Academics/Hagan-School-of-Business/Departments/Finance-Business-Economics-Legal-Studies/Graduate-Programs.aspx

Iona College, School of Business, Department of Marketing and International Business, New Rochelle, NY 10801-1890. Offers international business (AC, PMC); marketing (MBA); sports and entertainment management (AC). *Program availability:* Part-time, evening/weekend. *Faculty:* 3 full-time (1 woman), 3 part-time/adjunct (1 woman). *Students:* 14 full-time (10 women), 26 part-time (13 women); includes 17 minority (4 Black or African American, non-Hispanic/Latino; 1 Asian, non-Hispanic/Latino; 12 Hispanic/Latino), 3 international. Average age 25. 15 applicants, 93% accepted, 8 enrolled. In 2018, 13 master's, 78 other advanced degrees awarded. *Entrance requirements:* For master's, GMAT, 2 letters of recommendation, minimum GPA of 3.0; for other advanced degree, GMAT, minimum GPA of 3.0. Additional exam requirements/recommendations for international students: Required—TOEFL (minimum score 550 paper-based; 80 iBT), IELTS (minimum score 6.5). *Application deadline:* For fall admission, 8/15 priority date for domestic students, 8/1 priority date for international students; for winter admission, 11/15 priority date for domestic students, 11/1 priority date for international students; for spring admission, 2/15 priority date for domestic students, 2/1 priority date for international students; for summer admission, 5/15 for domestic students, 5/1 priority date for international students. Applications are processed on a rolling basis. Application fee: $50. Electronic applications accepted. *Expenses:* Contact institution. *Financial support:* In 2018–19, 38 students received support. Scholarships/grants, tuition waivers (partial), and unspecified assistantships available. Support available to part-time students. Financial award application deadline: 4/15; financial award applicants required to submit FAFSA. *Faculty research:* Business ethics, international retailing, mega-marketing, consumer behavior and consumer confidence. *Unit head:* Dr. Susan G. Rozensher, Department Chair, 914-637-2748, E-mail: srozensher@iona.edu. *Application contact:* Kimberly Kelly, Director of Graduate Business Admissions, 914-633-2271, Fax: 914-633-2012, E-mail: kkelly@iona.edu.
Website: http://www.iona.edu/Academics/Hagan-School-of-Business/Departments/Marketing/Graduate-Programs.aspx

John Brown University, Soderquist College of Business, Siloam Springs, AR 72761-2121. Offers international business (MBA); leadership and ethics (MBA, MS). *Accreditation:* ACBSP. *Program availability:* Part-time, evening/weekend, online only, 100% online, blended/hybrid learning. *Entrance requirements:* For master's, MAT, GMAT or GRE if undergraduate GPA is less than 3.0, recommendation forms from three people, 200-word essay describing professional plans and reason for seeking acceptance. Additional exam requirements/recommendations for international students: Required—TOEFL (minimum score 550 paper-based; 79 iBT). Electronic applications accepted. *Faculty research:* Ethical leadership.

Kean University, College of Business and Public Management, Program in Global Management, Union, NJ 07083. Offers executive management (MBA); global management (MBA). *Program availability:* Part-time, evening/weekend. *Faculty:* 2 full-time (0 women). *Students:* 60 full-time (33 women), 30 part-time (19 women); includes 58 minority (16 Black or African American, non-Hispanic/Latino; 6 Asian, non-Hispanic/Latino; 34 Hispanic/Latino; 1 Native Hawaiian or other Pacific Islander, non-Hispanic/Latino; 1 Two or more races, non-Hispanic/Latino), 12 international. Average age 32. 47 applicants, 100% accepted, 29 enrolled. In 2018, 24 master's awarded. *Degree requirements:* For master's, one foreign language, internship or consulting project. *Entrance requirements:* For master's, GMAT (minimum score of 500) or GRE (minimum Quantitative and Verbal scores of 152), minimum GPA of 3.0, 2 letters of recommendation, personal essay, resume; 5 years of experience (for executive management option). Additional exam requirements/recommendations for international students: Required—TOEFL (minimum score 550 paper-based; 79 iBT), IELTS (minimum score 6.5). *Application deadline:* For fall admission, 6/30 for domestic and international students; for spring admission, 12/1 for domestic and international students. Applications are processed on a rolling basis. Application fee: $75. Electronic applications accepted. *Expenses:* Tuition, state resident: full-time $15,025; part-time $733.50 per credit. Tuition, nonresident: full-time $19,890; part-time $884.50 per credit. *Required fees:* $2107.50; $89.50 per credit. Tuition and fees vary according to course level, course load, degree level and program. *Financial support:* Scholarships/grants and unspecified assistantships available. Financial award applicants required to submit FAFSA. *Unit head:* Dr. Veysel Yucetepe, Program Coordinator, 908-737-4762, E-mail: vyucetep@kean.edu. *Application contact:* Pedro Lopes, Admissions Counselor, 908-737-7100, E-mail: gradadmissions@kean.edu.
Website: http://grad.kean.edu/masters-programs/mba-global-management

Keiser University, Doctor of Business Administration Program, Fort Lauderdale, FL 33309. Offers global business (DBA); global management (DBA); marketing (DBA).

Keiser University, Master of Business Administration Program, Fort Lauderdale, FL 33309. Offers accounting (MBA); health services administration (MBA); international business (MBA); management (MBA); marketing (MBA); technology management (MBA). All concentrations except technology management also offered in Mandarin. *Program availability:* Part-time, online learning.

Lake Forest Graduate School of Management, The Immersion MBA Program (iMBA), Lake Forest, IL 60045. Offers global business (MBA). *Program availability:* Online learning.

Lake Forest Graduate School of Management, The Leadership MBA Program, Lake Forest, IL 60045. Offers finance (MBA); global business (MBA); healthcare management (MBA); management (MBA); marketing (MBA); organizational behavior (MBA). *Program availability:* Part-time, evening/weekend. *Entrance requirements:* For master's, 4 years of work experience in field, interview, 2 letters of recommendation. Electronic applications accepted.

La Salle University, School of Business, Philadelphia, PA 19141-1199. Offers business administration (MBA, Post-MBA Certificate), including accounting, business systems and analytics, finance, general business administration, human resource management, management, marketing (Post-MBA Certificate); human capital development (MS, Certificate); international business (Post-MBA Certificate); nonprofit leadership (MS); MBA/MSN. *Accreditation:* AACSB. *Program availability:* Part-time, evening/weekend, 100% online, blended/hybrid learning. *Entrance requirements:* Additional exam requirements/recommendations for international students: Required—TOEFL. Electronic applications accepted. Application fee is waived when completed online. *Expenses:* Contact institution.

Lenoir-Rhyne University, Graduate Programs, Charles M. Snipes School of Business, Hickory, NC 28601. Offers accounting (MBA); business analytics and information technology (MBA); entrepreneurship (MBA); global business (MBA); healthcare administration (MBA); innovation and change management (MBA); leadership development (MBA). *Accreditation:* ACBSP. *Program availability:* Part-time, evening/weekend, online learning. *Degree requirements:* For master's, capstone course. *Entrance requirements:* For master's, GMAT, GRE, MAT, minimum undergraduate GPA of 2.7, graduate 3.0. Additional exam requirements/recommendations for international students: Required—TOEFL (minimum score 600 paper-based). Electronic applications accepted. *Expenses:* Contact institution.

Lewis University, College of Business, Program in Business Administration, Romeoville, IL 60446. Offers accounting (MBA); custom elective option (MBA); e-business (MBA); finance (MBA); healthcare management (MBA); human resources management (MBA); international business (MBA); management information systems (MBA); marketing (MBA); project management (MBA); technology and operations management (MBA). *Program availability:* Part-time, evening/weekend. *Students:* 114 full-time (72 women), 143 part-time (87 women); includes 84 minority (21 Black or African American, non-Hispanic/Latino; 2 American Indian or Alaska Native, non-Hispanic/Latino; 11 Asian, non-Hispanic/Latino; 45 Hispanic/Latino; 5 Two or more races, non-Hispanic/Latino), 17 international. Average age 31. In 2018, 99 master's awarded. *Entrance requirements:* For master's, interview, bachelor's degree, resume, two recommendations. Additional exam requirements/recommendations for international students: Required—TOEFL (minimum score 550 paper-based), IELTS. *Application deadline:* For fall admission, 8/15 priority date for domestic students, 5/1 priority date for international students; for spring admission, 11/15 priority date for international students. Applications are processed on a rolling basis. Application fee: $40. Electronic applications accepted. *Financial support:* Career-related internships or fieldwork, Federal Work-Study, scholarships/grants, and unspecified assistantships available. Financial award application deadline: 5/1; financial award applicants required to submit FAFSA. *Unit head:* Dr. Maureen Culleeney, Academic Program Director, 815-838-0500 Ext. 5631, E-mail: culleema@lewisu.edu. *Application contact:* Michele Ryan, Director of Admission, 815-838-0500 Ext. 5384, E-mail: ryanml@lewisu.edu.

Liberty University, School of Business, Lynchburg, VA 24515. Offers accounting (MBA, MS), including audit and financial reporting (MS), business (MS), financial services (MS), forensic accounting (MS), leadership (MS), taxation (MS); cyber security (MS); executive leadership (MA); international business (DBA); leadership (DBA); marketing (MBA, MS, DBA), including digital marketing and advertising (MS), project management (MS), public relations (MS), sports marketing and media (MS); project management (MBA, DBA); public relations (MBA). *Program availability:* Part-time, online learning. *Students:* 2,871 full-time (1,496 women), 4,437 part-time (1,969 women); includes 2,069 minority (1,424 Black or African American, non-Hispanic/Latino; 44

American Indian or Alaska Native, non-Hispanic/Latino; 133 Asian, non-Hispanic/Latino; 282 Hispanic/Latino; 16 Native Hawaiian or other Pacific Islander, non-Hispanic/Latino; 170 Two or more races, non-Hispanic/Latino), 154 international. Average age 36. 8,980 applicants, 45% accepted, 2009 enrolled. In 2018, 1,988 master's, 25 doctorates awarded. *Entrance requirements:* For master's, minimum undergraduate GPA of 3.0, 15 hours of upper-level business courses. Additional exam requirements/recommendations for international students: Required—TOEFL (minimum score 600 paper-based; 100 iBT). *Application deadline:* Applications are processed on a rolling basis. Application fee: $50. Electronic applications accepted. *Expenses:* Contact institution. *Financial support:* In 2018–19, 990 students received support. Teaching assistantships and Federal Work-Study available. Financial award applicants required to submit FAFSA. *Unit head:* Dr. Dave Bratt, Dean, 434-592-7321, E-mail: dabrat@liberty.edu. *Application contact:* Jay Bridge, Director of Graduate Admissions, 800-424-9595, Fax: 800-628-7977, E-mail: gradadmissions@liberty.edu.
Website: https://www.liberty.edu/business/

Lincoln University, Graduate Studies, Oakland, CA 94612. Offers finance and investments (DBA); finance management (MS); finance management and investments (MBA); general business (MBA); human resource management (MBA, DBA); international business (MBA, MS); management information systems (MBA). *Program availability:* Part-time. *Degree requirements:* For master's, research project (thesis), internship report, or comprehensive exam; for doctorate, comprehensive exam, thesis/dissertation. *Entrance requirements:* For master's, minimum GPA of 2.7; for doctorate, GMAT (minimum score: 550), GRE (minimum score: 1000), or equivalent test results (waived for master's degree with minimum cumulative GPA of 3.3). Additional exam requirements/recommendations for international students: Required—TOEFL minimum score 525 paper-based; 71 iBT or IELTS minimum score 5.5 (for MBA); TOEFL minimum score 550 paper-based; 79 iBT or IELTS minimum score 6 (for MS and DBA). Electronic applications accepted.

Long Island University–LIU Post, College of Management, Brookville, NY 11548-1300. Offers accountancy (MS); finance (MBA); information systems (MS); international business (MBA); management (MBA); management engineering (MS); marketing (MBA); taxation (MS); technical project management (MS); JD/MBA. *Accreditation:* AACSB. *Program availability:* Part-time, evening/weekend, blended/hybrid learning. *Entrance requirements:* For master's, GMAT, GRE, or LSAT. Additional exam requirements/recommendations for international students: Required—TOEFL (minimum score 550 paper-based, 75 iBT) or IELTS. Electronic applications accepted. *Faculty research:* Innovation and property rights, knowledge sourcing, sustainability and firm performance, China and growth markets, corporate social responsibility, workforce compensation and issues.

Loyola University Chicago, Quinlan School of Business, MBA Programs, Chicago, IL 60611. Offers accounting (MBA); business ethics (MBA); derivative markets (MBA); economics (MBA); entrepreneurship (MBA); finance (MBA); healthcare management (MBA); human resources management (MBA); information systems management (MBA); international business (MBA); management (MBA); marketing (MBA); risk management (MBA); supply chain management (MBA). *Program availability:* Part-time, evening/weekend. *Entrance requirements:* For master's, GMAT or GRE, official transcripts, two letters of recommendation, statement of purpose, resume. Additional exam requirements/recommendations for international students: Required—TOEFL (minimum score 90 iBT) or IELTS (minimum score 6.5). Electronic applications accepted. Application fee is waived when completed online. *Expenses:* Contact institution. *Faculty research:* Social enterprise and responsibility, emerging markets, supply chain management, risk management.

Madonna University, School of Business, Livonia, MI 48150-1173. Offers business administration (MBA); international business (MSBA); leadership studies (MSBA); leadership studies in criminal justice (MSBA); quality and operations management (MSBA). *Program availability:* Part-time, evening/weekend, online learning. *Degree requirements:* For master's, thesis (for some programs), foreign language proficiency (international business). *Entrance requirements:* For master's, GMAT, GRE General Test, minimum GPA of 3.0. Electronic applications accepted. *Expenses: Tuition:* Full-time $15,030; part-time $835 per credit hour. Tuition and fees vary according to degree level and program. *Faculty research:* Management, women in management, future studies.

Maine Maritime Academy, Loeb-Sullivan School of International Business and Logistics, Castine, ME 04420. Offers global logistics and maritime management (MS); international logistics management (MS). *Program availability:* Part-time, 100% online. *Degree requirements:* For master's, capstone course. *Entrance requirements:* For master's, GMAT or GRE, letter of recommendation. Additional exam requirements/recommendations for international students: Required—TOEFL, IELTS. Electronic applications accepted. Application fee is waived when completed online. *Faculty research:* Internet of things, trait intelligence, port operations, location theory.

Marconi International University, Graduate Programs, Miami, FL 33132. Offers business administration (DBA); education leadership (Ed D); education leadership, management and emerging technologies (M Ed); international business administration (IMBA).

Marquette University, Graduate School of Management, Executive MBA Program, Milwaukee, WI 53201-1881. Offers economics (MBA); finance (MBA); human resources (MBA); international business (MBA); management information systems (MBA); marketing (MBA); operations and supply chain management (MBA); sports business (MBA). *Accreditation:* AACSB. *Degree requirements:* For master's, international trip. *Entrance requirements:* For master's, GMAT or GRE, two letters of recommendation, official transcripts from current and previous colleges/universities. Additional exam requirements/recommendations for international students: Required—TOEFL (minimum score 550 paper-based; 88 iBT), IELTS (minimum score 6.5), PTE. Electronic applications accepted. *Expenses:* Contact institution. *Faculty research:* International trade and finance, customer relationship management, consumer satisfaction, customer service.

Marquette University, Graduate School of Management, Program in Business Administration, Milwaukee, WI 53201-1881. Offers business administration (MBA); economics (MBA); entrepreneurship (Certificate); finance (MBA); human resources (MBA); international business (MBA); management information systems (MBA); marketing (MBA); operations and supply chain management (MBA); sports business (MBA); JD/MBA; MBA/MA; MBA/MSN. *Accreditation:* AACSB. *Program availability:* Part-time, evening/weekend. *Degree requirements:* For Certificate, business plan. *Entrance requirements:* For master's, GMAT or GRE, letters of recommendation. Additional exam requirements/recommendations for international students: Required—TOEFL (minimum score 550 paper-based; 88 iBT), IELTS (minimum score 6.5), PTE. Electronic applications accepted. *Faculty research:* Ethics in the professions, services marketing, technology impact on decision-making, mentoring.

McGill University, Faculty of Graduate and Postdoctoral Studies, Desautels Faculty of Management, Montréal, QC H3A 2T5, Canada. Offers administration (PhD); entrepreneurial studies (MBA); finance (MBA); general management (Post Master's Certificate); global manufacturing and supply chain management (MMM); information systems (MBA); international business (MBA); international practicing management (MM); management (MBA); management for development (MBA); marketing (MBA); operations management (MBA); public accountancy (Diploma); strategic management (MBA); MBA/LL B; MD/MBA. MMM offered jointly with Faculty of Engineering; PhD with Concordia University, HEC Montreal, Université de Montréal, Université du Québec à Montréal.

McKendree University, Graduate Programs, Master of Business Administration Program, Lebanon, IL 62254-1299. Offers business administration (MBA); human resource management (MBA); international business (MBA). *Program availability:* Part-time, evening/weekend, online learning. *Entrance requirements:* For master's, official transcripts from all institutions attended, essay, minimum GPA of 3.0, three references, resume. Additional exam requirements/recommendations for international students: Required—TOEFL. Electronic applications accepted.

Midwest University, Graduate Programs, Wentzville, MO 63385. Offers asset management/investment/real estate (MBA); Christian counseling (D Min); Christian education (D Min); counseling (MA), including marriage and family counseling, school counseling; divinity (M Div); education (MA), including brain and gifted education, Christian education; global business management (MBA); global leadership (MBA); leadership (PhD), including brain and gifted educational leadership, entrepreneurial leadership, international aviation leadership, organizational leadership, political leadership; mission studies (D Min); music (MM, DMA); pastoral theology (D Min); public policy/administration (MBA); teaching English to speakers of other languages (MA). *Program availability:* Part-time, online learning. *Degree requirements:* For master's, thesis (for some programs); for doctorate, thesis/dissertation. *Entrance requirements:* Additional exam requirements/recommendations for international students: Recommended—TOEFL (minimum score 550 paper-based).

Milwaukee School of Engineering, MS Program in Marketing and Export Management, Milwaukee, WI 53202-3109. Offers MS. *Program availability:* Part-time, evening/weekend. *Degree requirements:* For master's, thesis or alternative, thesis defense or capstone project. *Entrance requirements:* For master's, GRE or GMAT if undergraduate GPA less than 2.8, 2 letters of recommendation; bachelor's degree from accredited university; work experience (strongly recommended). Additional exam requirements/recommendations for international students: Required—TOEFL (minimum score 90 iBT), IELTS (minimum score 7). Electronic applications accepted.

National American University, Roueche Graduate Center, Austin, TX 78731. Offers accounting (MBA); aviation management (MBA, MM); care coordination (MSN); community college leadership (Ed D); criminal justice (MM); e-marketing (MBA, MM); health care administration (MBA, MM); higher education (MM); human resources management (MBA, MM); information technology management (MBA, MM); international business (MBA); leadership (EMBA); management (MBA); nursing administration (MSN); nursing education (MSN); nursing informatics (MSN); operations and configuration management (MBA, MM); project and process management (MBA, MM). Master's programs offered online through the Harold D. Buckingham Graduate School. *Program availability:* Part-time, evening/weekend, online learning. *Entrance requirements:* For master's, minimum undergraduate GPA of 2.75. Additional exam requirements/recommendations for international students: Required—TOEFL, TWE. Electronic applications accepted. *Faculty research:* Tourism, finance, marketing.

National University, School of Business and Management, La Jolla, CA 92037-1011. Offers accountancy (M Acc, Certificate); business administration (GMBA, MBA); business analytics (MS); cause leadership (MA); global management (MGM); human resource management (MA); management information systems (MS); marketing (MS); organizational leadership (MS). GMBA offered in Spanish. *Program availability:* Part-time, evening/weekend, 100% online, blended/hybrid learning. *Degree requirements:* For master's, thesis (for some programs). *Entrance requirements:* For master's, interview, minimum GPA of 2.5. Additional exam requirements/recommendations for international students: Required—TOEFL (minimum score 550 paper-based; 79 iBT), IELTS (minimum score 6). Electronic applications accepted. *Expenses: Tuition:* Full-time $10,320; part-time $430 per unit. Tuition and fees vary according to degree level.

Nebraska Christian College of Hope International University, Graduate Programs, Papillion, NE 68046. Offers biblical studies (M Div); business as mission/social entrepreneurship (MBA); children, youth, and family (M Div); church planting (M Div); counseling psychology (MS); educational administration (MA); elementary education (M Ed); general management (MBA); gifted and talented education (M Ed); intercultural studies (M Div); international development (MBA); marketing management (MBA); ministry (MA); ministry and leadership (M Div); music education (M Ed); non-profit management (MBA); pastoral care (M Div); secondary education (M Ed); spiritual formation (M Div); worship ministry (M Div).

Newman University, MBA Program, Wichita, KS 67213-2097. Offers finance (MBA); international business (MBA); leadership (MBA); management (MBA); management information technology (MBA). *Program availability:* Part-time. *Degree requirements:* For master's, thesis optional. *Entrance requirements:* For master's, minimum GPA of 3.0; 2 letters of recommendation; course work in algebra, statistics, macroeconomics, and financial accounting. Additional exam requirements/recommendations for international students: Required—TOEFL (minimum score 600 paper-based; 100 iBT). Electronic applications accepted. *Expenses:* Contact institution.

New Mexico Highlands University, Graduate Studies, School of Business, Media and Technology, Las Vegas, NM 87701. Offers business administration (MBA), including human resource management, international business, management; media arts and technology (MA), including media arts and computer science. *Accreditation:* ACBSP. *Degree requirements:* For master's, comprehensive exam, thesis or alternative. *Entrance requirements:* For master's, minimum undergraduate GPA of 3.0. Additional exam requirements/recommendations for international students: Required—TOEFL (minimum score 540 paper-based). *Faculty research:* Real estate valuation, studying expert judgments in complex accounting, decision environments, green marketing, environmentalism, marketing research methodology.

New York University, Graduate School of Arts and Science, Department of Politics, New York, NY 10012-1019. Offers political campaign management (MA); politics (MA, PhD); JD/MA; MBA/MA. *Program availability:* Part-time. *Students:* 93 full-time (35 women), 17 part-time (6 women); includes 15 minority (1 Black or African American, non-Hispanic/Latino; 5 Asian, non-Hispanic/Latino; 8 Hispanic/Latino; 1 Two or more races, non-Hispanic/Latino), 64 international. Average age 27. 401 applicants, 60% accepted, 25 enrolled. In 2018, 31 master's, 10 doctorates awarded. Terminal master's awarded for partial completion of doctoral program. *Degree requirements:* For master's, one foreign language, thesis or alternative; for doctorate, 2 foreign languages, comprehensive exam, thesis/dissertation. *Entrance requirements:* For master's and doctorate, GRE General Test. Additional exam requirements/recommendations for international students: Required—TOEFL, IELTS. *Application deadline:* For fall admission, 12/18 priority date for domestic students, 12/18 for international students. Application fee: $110. *Financial support:* Fellowships, teaching assistantships, career-related internships or fieldwork, Federal Work-Study, and institutionally sponsored loans available. Financial award application deadline: 12/18; financial award applicants required to submit FAFSA. *Faculty research:* Comparative politics, democratic theory

and practice, rational choice, political economy, international relations. *Unit head:* Sanford Gordon, Director of Graduate Studies, PhD Program, 212-998-8500, Fax: 212-995-4184, E-mail: politics.phd@nyu.edu. *Application contact:* Nicole Simonelli, Director of Graduate Studies, Master's Program, 212-998-8500, Fax: 212-995-4184, E-mail: politics.masters@nyu.edu.
Website: http://www.nyu.edu/gsas/dept/politics/

Niagara University, Graduate Division of Business Administration, Niagara University, NY 14109. Offers accounting (MBA); business administration (MBA); finance (MBA, MS); financial planning (MBA); healthcare administration (MBA, MHA); human resources (MBA); international business (MBA); marketing (MBA); professional accountancy (MBA); strategic management (MBA); supply chain management (MBA). *Accreditation:* AACSB. *Program availability:* Part-time, evening/weekend, 100% online, blended/hybrid learning. *Students:* 224 full-time (116 women), 56 part-time (22 women); includes 36 minority (9 Black or African American, non-Hispanic/Latino; 2 American Indian or Alaska Native, non-Hispanic/Latino; 6 Asian, non-Hispanic/Latino; 12 Hispanic/Latino; 7 Two or more races, non-Hispanic/Latino), 82 international. Average age 26. In 2018, 134 master's awarded. *Entrance requirements:* For master's, GMAT. Additional exam requirements/recommendations for international students: Required—TOEFL (minimum score 550 paper-based; 79 iBT), IELTS (minimum score 6). *Application deadline:* For fall admission, 8/1 for domestic students; for spring admission, 11/1 for domestic students. Applications are processed on a rolling basis. Electronic applications accepted. *Expenses:* Contact institution. *Financial support:* Research assistantships, teaching assistantships, career-related internships or fieldwork, Federal Work-Study, scholarships/grants, and unspecified assistantships available. Support available to part-time students. Financial award application deadline: 4/15; financial award applicants required to submit FAFSA. *Faculty research:* Capital flows, Federal Reserve policy, human resource management, public policy, issues in marketing, auctions, economics of information, risk and capital markets, management strategy, consumer behavior, Internet and social media marketing. *Unit head:* Dr. Paul Richardson, MBA Director/Chair of the Marketing Department, 716-286-8169, Fax: 716-286-8206, E-mail: mba@niagara.edu. *Application contact:* Evan Pierce, Associate Director for Graduate Recruitment, 716-286-8327, Fax: 716-286-8710, E-mail: epierce@niagara.edu.
Website: http://mba.niagara.edu

Northeastern University, D'Amore-McKim School of Business, Boston, MA 02115-5096. Offers accounting (MS); business administration (EMBA, MBA); finance (MS); innovation (MS); international business (MS); international management (MS); taxation (MS); technological entrepreneurship (MS); JD/MBA; LL M/MBA; MBA/MSN; MS/MBA. *Accreditation:* AACSB. *Program availability:* Part-time, evening/weekend, online learning. *Entrance requirements:* For master's, GMAT or GRE. Electronic applications accepted. *Expenses:* Contact institution.

Northern Arizona University, Office of the Provost, Business and Administration Program (NAU-Yuma), Yuma, AZ 85365. Offers global business administration (MGBA). *Program availability:* Part-time, blended/hybrid learning. *Degree requirements:* For master's, variable foreign language requirement, comprehensive exam (for some programs), thesis (for some programs). *Entrance requirements:* Additional exam requirements/recommendations for international students: Required—TOEFL (minimum score 80 iBT), IELTS (minimum score 6.5). Electronic applications accepted.

Northwestern University, The Graduate School, Kellogg School of Management, Management Programs, Evanston, IL 60208. Offers accounting information and management (MBA, PhD); analytical finance (MBA); business administration (MBA); decision sciences (MBA); entrepreneurship and innovation (MBA); finance (MBA, PhD); health enterprise management (MBA); human resources management (MBA); international business (MBA); management and organizations (MBA, PhD); management and organizations and sociology (PhD); management and strategy (MBA); management studies (MS); managerial analytics (MBA); managerial economics (MBA); managerial economics and strategy (PhD); marketing (MBA, PhD); marketing management (MBA); media management (MBA); operations management (MBA, PhD); real estate (MBA); social enterprise at Kellogg (MBA); JD/MBA. *Program availability:* Part-time, evening/weekend. Terminal master's awarded for partial completion of doctoral program. *Degree requirements:* For doctorate, thesis/dissertation, 2 years of coursework, qualifying (field) exam and candidacy, summer research papers and presentations to faculty, proposal defense, final exam/defense. *Entrance requirements:* For master's, GMAT, GRE, interview, 2 letters of recommendation, college transcripts, resume, essays, Kellogg honor code; for doctorate, GMAT, GRE, statement of purpose, transcripts, 2 letters of recommendation, resume, interview. Additional exam requirements/recommendations for international students: Required—TOEFL, IELTS. Electronic applications accepted. *Expenses:* Contact institution. *Faculty research:* Business cycles and international finance, health policy, networks, non-market strategy, consumer psychology.

Northwest University, College of Business, Kirkland, WA 98033. Offers business administration (MBA); international business (MBA); project management (MBA); social entrepreneurship (MBA). *Accreditation:* ACBSP. *Program availability:* Part-time, evening/weekend. *Degree requirements:* For master's, formalized research. *Entrance requirements:* For master's, GMAT. Additional exam requirements/recommendations for international students: Required—TOEFL (minimum score 550 paper-based; 75 iBT). Electronic applications accepted. *Expenses:* Contact institution.

Norwich University, College of Graduate and Continuing Studies, Master of Arts in Diplomacy Program, Northfield, VT 05663. Offers diplomacy (MA), including cyber diplomacy - policy, cyber diplomacy - technical, international commerce, international conflict management, international terrorism. *Program availability:* Evening/weekend, online only, mostly all online with a week-long residency requirement. *Degree requirements:* For master's, comprehensive exam, thesis optional. *Entrance requirements:* For master's, minimum undergraduate GPA of 2.75. Additional exam requirements/recommendations for international students: Required—TOEFL (minimum score 550 paper-based; 80 iBT), IELTS (minimum score 6.5). Electronic applications accepted. *Expenses:* Contact institution.

Nova Southeastern University, H. Wayne Huizenga College of Business and Entrepreneurship, Fort Lauderdale, FL 33314-7796. Offers accounting (M Acc); business (MBA); business intelligence/analytics (MBA); complex health systems (MBA); enterprise informatics (MBA); entrepreneurship (MBA); finance (MBA); human resource management (MBA); international business (MBA); management (MBA); marketing (MBA); process improvement (MBA); public administration (MPA); real estate development (MS); sport revenue generation (MBA); supply chain management (MBA). *Accreditation:* NASPAA. *Program availability:* Part-time, evening/weekend, 100% online, blended/hybrid learning. *Entrance requirements:* For master's, GMAT or GRE (depending on undergraduate GPA), official transcripts from all schools attended while in pursuit of bachelor's degree; minimum GPA of 2.5 from regionally-accredited institution. Additional exam requirements/recommendations for international students: Required—TOEFL (minimum score 550 paper-based; 79 iBT), IELTS (minimum score 6), PTE (minimum score 54). Electronic applications accepted. *Expenses:* Contact institution. *Faculty research:* Entrepreneurship and venture capital, ethics and social responsibility, global commerce and cultures, business process management.

Oakland University, Graduate Study and Lifelong Learning, School of Business Administration, Department of Management and Marketing, Rochester, MI 48309-4401. Offers business administration (MBA); entrepreneurship (Certificate); general management (Certificate); human resource management (Certificate); international business (Certificate); management and marketing (EMBA); marketing (Certificate).

Oklahoma Christian University, Graduate School of Business, Oklahoma City, OK 73136-1100. Offers accounting (M Acc, MBA); financial services (MBA); general business (MBA); health services management (MBA); human resources (MBA); international business (MBA); leadership and organizational development (MBA); marketing (MBA); nonprofit management (MBA); project management (MBA). *Accreditation:* ACBSP. *Program availability:* Part-time, 100% online. *Entrance requirements:* For master's, bachelor's degree. Additional exam requirements/recommendations for international students: Required—TOEFL (minimum score 550 paper-based). Electronic applications accepted. *Expenses:* Contact institution.

Oklahoma State University, Spears School of Business, School of Marketing and International Business, Stillwater, OK 74078. Offers business administration (PhD), including marketing; marketing (MBA). *Program availability:* Part-time. *Faculty:* 21 full-time (5 women), 5 part-time/adjunct (2 women). *Students:* 71 full-time (22 women), 34 part-time (17 women); includes 8 minority (1 Black or African American, non-Hispanic/Latino; 3 Asian, non-Hispanic/Latino; 4 Hispanic/Latino), 74 international. Average age 27. 234 applicants, 20% accepted, 42 enrolled. In 2018, 39 master's awarded. *Entrance requirements:* For master's and doctorate, GRE or GMAT. Additional exam requirements/recommendations for international students: Required—TOEFL (minimum score 550 paper-based; 79 iBT). *Application deadline:* For fall admission, 3/1 priority date for international students; for spring admission, 8/1 priority date for international students. Applications are processed on a rolling basis. Application fee: $40 ($75 for international students). Electronic applications accepted. *Expenses: Tuition, area resident:* Full-time $4148. Tuition, state resident: full-time $4148. Tuition, nonresident: full-time $10,517. *International tuition:* $10,517 full-time. *Required fees:* $4394; $2929 per credit hour. Tuition and fees vary according to course load and program. *Financial support:* Research assistantships, teaching assistantships, career-related internships or fieldwork, Federal Work-Study, scholarships/grants, health care benefits, tuition waivers (partial), and unspecified assistantships available. Support available to part-time students. Financial award application deadline: 3/1; financial award applicants required to submit FAFSA. *Faculty research:* Decision-making (consumer, managerial, cross-functional), communication effects, services marketing, public policy and marketing, corporate image. *Unit head:* Dr. Tom Brown, Department Head, 405-744-5113, Fax: 405-744-5180, E-mail: tom.brown@okstate.edu. *Application contact:* Dr. Kevin Voss, PhD Coordinator, 405-744-5106, Fax: 405-744-5180, E-mail: kevin.voss@okstate.edu.
Website: https://business.okstate.edu/marketing/

Old Dominion University, Strome College of Business, Program in Maritime Trade and Supply Chain Management, Norfolk, VA 23529. Offers MS. *Program availability:* Part-time, evening/weekend. *Degree requirements:* For master's, capstone course. *Entrance requirements:* For master's, GRE or GMAT, bachelor's degree, official transcripts, two letters of recommendation, current resume, statement of professional goals. Additional exam requirements/recommendations for international students: Required—TOEFL (minimum score 550 paper-based; 79 iBT), IELTS (minimum score 6.5). Electronic applications accepted.

Oral Roberts University, School of Business, Tulsa, OK 74171. Offers accounting (MBA); entrepreneurship (MBA); finance (MBA); international business (MBA); management (MBA); marketing (MBA); not for profit management (MNM). *Accreditation:* ACBSP. *Program availability:* Part-time, online learning. *Degree requirements:* For master's, thesis optional. *Entrance requirements:* For master's, minimum cumulative GPA of 3.0 from regionally-accredited institution. Electronic applications accepted. Application fee is waived when completed online. *Faculty research:* Social media, international business and marketing.

Pace University, Lubin School of Business, Advanced Professional Certificate Program, New York, NY 10038. Offers business economics (APC); e-business (APC); financial management (APC); international business (APC); international economics (APC); investment management (APC); marketing (APC); public accounting (APC). *Program availability:* Part-time, evening/weekend. *Entrance requirements:* For degree, MBA or MS in business discipline, relevant professional experience. Additional exam requirements/recommendations for international students: Required—TOEFL (minimum score 90 iBT), IELTS (minimum score 7) or PTE (minimum score 61). *Application deadline:* For fall admission, 8/1 priority date for domestic students, 6/1 for international students; for spring admission, 12/1 for domestic students, 10/1 for international students. Applications are processed on a rolling basis. Application fee: $70. Electronic applications accepted. *Unit head:* Dr. Ibraiz Tarique, Chairperson, 212-618-6583, E-mail: itarique@pace.edu. *Application contact:* Susan Ford-Goldschein, Director of Graduate Admissions, 212-346-1531, Fax: 212-346-1585, E-mail: graduateadmission@pace.edu.
Website: http://www.pace.edu/lubin/agc

Pace University, Lubin School of Business, Finance Program, New York, NY 10038. Offers financial management (MBA, MS); financial risk management (MS); international finance (MBA); investment management (MBA, MS). *Program availability:* Part-time, evening/weekend. *Students:* 120 full-time (52 women), 79 part-time (30 women); includes 33 minority (10 Black or African American, non-Hispanic/Latino; 14 Asian, non-Hispanic/Latino; 8 Hispanic/Latino; 1 Two or more races, non-Hispanic/Latino), 119 international. Average age 26. 236 applicants, 77% accepted, 64 enrolled. In 2018, 132 master's awarded. *Entrance requirements:* For master's, GMAT, GRE (GMAT not required for MS with passing of Level 1 of Chartered Financial Analyst exam or Level 1 of Financial Risk Manager Exam), Undergrad degree, transcripts from all accredited colleges/universities attended, 2 letters of recommendation, resume, personal statement. If applying to the 1 year fast track MBA in Financial Management, must have a cumulative GPA of 3.30 or above, a grade of B or better for all business core courses from an AACSB-accredited U.S. business school. Additional exam requirements/recommendations for international students: Required—TOEFL (minimum score 90 iBT), IELTS (minimum score 7) or PTE (minimum score 61). *Application deadline:* For fall admission, 8/1 priority date for domestic students, 6/1 for international students; for spring admission, 12/1 for domestic students, 10/1 for international students. Applications are processed on a rolling basis. Application fee: $70. Electronic applications accepted. *Financial support:* Research assistantships, career-related internships or fieldwork, Federal Work-Study, tuition waivers (full and partial), and unspecified assistantships available. Support available to part-time students. Financial award application deadline: 2/15; financial award applicants required to submit FAFSA. *Unit head:* Dr. Aron Gottesman, Chairperson, Finance Department, 212-618-6525, E-mail: agottesman@pace.edu. *Application contact:* Susan Ford-Goldschein, Director of Graduate Admissions, 212-346-1531, Fax: 212-346-1585, E-mail: graduateadmissions@pace.edu.
Website: http://www.pace.edu/lubin/sections/explore-programs/graduate-programs

Pace University, Lubin School of Business, International Business Program, New York, NY 10038. Offers MBA. *Program availability:* Part-time, evening/weekend. *Students:* 6 full-time (all women), 5 part-time (2 women); includes 4 minority (2 Black or African

American, non-Hispanic/Latino; 1 Asian, non-Hispanic/Latino; 1 Hispanic/Latino), 5 international. Average age 29. 24 applicants, 42% accepted, 1 enrolled. In 2018, 3 master's awarded. *Entrance requirements:* For master's, GMAT, GRE, undergraduate degree, transcripts from all accredited colleges/universities attended, two letters of recommendation, resume, personal statement. Additional exam requirements/recommendations for international students: Required—TOEFL (minimum score 90 iBT), IELTS (minimum score 7) or PTE (minimum score 61). *Application deadline:* For fall admission, 8/1 priority date for domestic students, 6/1 for international students; for spring admission, 12/1 for domestic students, 10/1 for international students. Applications are processed on a rolling basis. Application fee: $70. Electronic applications accepted. *Financial support:* Research assistantships, career-related internships or fieldwork, Federal Work-Study, and unspecified assistantships available. Support available to part-time students. Financial award application deadline: 2/15; financial award applicants required to submit FAFSA. *Unit head:* Dr. Ibraiz Tarique, Chairperson, Management and Management Science, 212-618-6583, E-mail: itarique@pace.edu. *Application contact:* Susan Ford-Goldschein, Director of Graduate Admissions, 212-346-1531, Fax: 212-346-1585, E-mail: graduateadmission@pace.edu. Website: http://www.pace.edu/lubin/mba-in-international-business

Pacific States University, College of Business, Los Angeles, CA 90010. Offers accounting (MBA, Certificate); beauty management (MBA); finance (MBA); international business (MBA); management of information technology (MBA); project management (Certificate); real estate management (MBA). *Program availability:* Part-time, evening/weekend, online learning. *Entrance requirements:* For master's, minimum undergraduate GPA of 2.5 during last 90 quarter units of course work, bachelor's degree in business administration or economics. Additional exam requirements/recommendations for international students: Required—TOEFL (minimum score 500 paper-based; 61 iBT), IELTS (minimum score 5.5).

Park University, School of Graduate and Professional Studies, Kansas City, MO 54105. Offers adult education (M Ed); business and government leadership (Graduate Certificate); business, government, and global society (MPA); communication and leadership (MA); creative and life writing (Graduate Certificate); disaster and emergency management (MPA, Graduate Certificate); educational leadership (M Ed); finance (MBA, Graduate Certificate); general business (MBA); global business (Graduate Certificate); healthcare administration (MHA); healthcare services management and leadership (Graduate Certificate); international business (MBA); language and literacy (M Ed), including English for speakers of other languages, special reading teacher/literacy coach; leadership of international healthcare organizations (Graduate Certificate); management information systems (MBA, Graduate Certificate); music performance (ADP, Graduate Certificate), including cello (MM, ADP), piano (MM, ADP), viola (MM, ADP), violin (MM, ADP); nonprofit and community services management (MPA); nonprofit leadership (Graduate Certificate); performance (MM), including cello (MM, ADP), piano (MM, ADP), viola (MM, ADP), violin (MM, ADP); public management (MPA); social work (MSW); teacher leadership (M Ed), including curriculum and assessment, instructional leader. *Program availability:* Part-time, evening/weekend, online learning. *Degree requirements:* For master's, comprehensive exam (for some programs), thesis (for some programs), internship (for some programs); exam (for some programs). *Entrance requirements:* For master's, GRE or GMAT (for some programs), teacher certification (for some M Ed programs), letters of recommendation, essay, resume (for some programs). Additional exam requirements/recommendations for international students: Required—TOEFL (minimum score 550 paper-based; 79 iBT), IELTS (minimum score 6). Electronic applications accepted.

Pittsburg State University, Graduate School, Kelce College of Business, Department of Management and Marketing, Pittsburg, KS 66762. Offers general administration (MBA); international business (MBA). *Accreditation:* AACSB. *Program availability:* Part-time. *Degree requirements:* For master's, thesis or alternative. *Entrance requirements:* For master's, GMAT or GRE. Additional exam requirements/recommendations for international students: Required—TOEFL (minimum score 550 paper-based; 79 iBT), IELTS (minimum score 6.5), PTE (minimum score 53). Electronic applications accepted. *Expenses:* Contact institution. *Faculty research:* Consumer behavior, productions management, forecasting interest rate swaps, strategy management.

Point Park University, Rowland School of Business, Program in Business Administration, Pittsburgh, PA 15222-1984. Offers business analytics (MBA); global management and administration (MBA); health systems management (MBA); international business (MBA); management (MBA); management information systems (MBA); sports, arts and entertainment management (MBA). *Program availability:* Evening/weekend, 100% online.

Polytechnic University of Puerto Rico, Graduate School, Hato Rey, PR 00918. Offers business administration (MBA), including computer information systems, general management, management of information systems, management of international enterprises; civil engineering (ME, MS); computer engineering (ME, MS); computer science (MCS, MS); electrical engineering (ME, MS); engineering management (MEM); environmental management (MEM); landscape architecture (M Land Arch); manufacturing competitiveness (MMC, MS); manufacturing engineering (ME, MS); mechanical engineering (M Mech E). *Accreditation:* ASLA. *Program availability:* Part-time, evening/weekend. *Entrance requirements:* For master's, 3 letters of recommendation.

Polytechnic University of Puerto Rico, Miami Campus, Graduate School, Miami, FL 33166. Offers accounting (MBA); business administration (MBA); construction management (MEM); environmental management (MEM); finance (MBA); human resources management (MBA); logistics and supply chain management (MBA); management of international enterprises (MBA); manufacturing management (MEM); marketing management (MBA); project management (MBA). *Program availability:* Part-time, evening/weekend, online learning. *Entrance requirements:* For master's, minimum GPA of 3.0. Electronic applications accepted.

Polytechnic University of Puerto Rico, Orlando Campus, Graduate School, Orlando, FL 32825. Offers accounting (MBA); business administration (MBA); construction management (MEM); engineering management (MEM); environmental management (MEM); finance (MBA); human resources management (MBA); management of international enterprises (MBA); management of technology (MBA); manufacturing management (MEM). *Program availability:* Part-time, evening/weekend, online learning. *Entrance requirements:* For master's, minimum GPA of 3.0. Additional exam requirements/recommendations for international students: Recommended—TOEFL. Electronic applications accepted.

Pontifical Catholic University of Puerto Rico, College of Business Administration, Program in International Business, Ponce, PR 00717-0777. Offers MBA. *Program availability:* Part-time, evening/weekend. *Entrance requirements:* For master's, GRE, interview, minimum GPA of 2.75.

Pontificia Universidad Catolica Madre y Maestra, Graduate School, Faculty of Social and Administrative Sciences, Santiago, Dominican Republic. Offers business administration (MBA), including business development, finance, international business, management skills (M Mgmt, MBA), marketing, operations, strategic cost management, strategy, tourist destination planning and management; law (LL M), including civil law, corporate business law, criminal law, international relations, real estate law; management (M Mgmt), including higher financial management, insurance program administration, management skills (M Mgmt, MBA); psychology (MA), including clinical child and adolescent psychology, forensic psychology; strategic human resources (EMBA).

Portland State University, Graduate Studies, The School of Business, Program in International Management, Portland, OR 97207-0751. Offers MIM. *Program availability:* Part-time, evening/weekend. *Degree requirements:* For master's, one foreign language, field study trip to China and Japan, international consulting project. *Entrance requirements:* For master's, GMAT, GRE General Test, minimum GPA of 2.75, resume, 2 letters of recommendation, essay. Additional exam requirements/recommendations for international students: Required—TOEFL (minimum score 550 paper-based; 80 iBT). Electronic applications accepted. *Expenses:* Contact institution.

Providence College, School of Business, Providence, RI 02918. Offers accounting (MBA); finance (MBA); international business (MBA); management (MBA); marketing (MBA). *Accreditation:* AACSB. *Program availability:* Part-time, evening/weekend. *Entrance requirements:* For master's, GMAT. Additional exam requirements/recommendations for international students: Required—TOEFL (minimum score 577 paper-based; 90 iBT). *Expenses:* Contact institution.

Purdue University, Graduate School, Krannert School of Management, IMM Global Executive MBA Program, West Lafayette, IN 47906. Offers MBA. *Entrance requirements:* For master's, GMAT or GRE, resume (minimum 5 years' work experience), official transcripts, two recommendations, interview. Additional exam requirements/recommendations for international students: Required—TOEFL, IELTS. Electronic applications accepted. *Expenses:* Contact institution. *Faculty research:* Dimensions of trust, communities of practice and networks, business in Latin America.

Purdue University Global, School of Business, Davenport, IA 52807. Offers business administration (MBA); change leadership (MS); entrepreneurship (MBA); finance (MBA); health care management (MBA, MS); human resource (MBA); international business (MBA); management (MS); marketing (MBA); project management (MBA, MS); supply chain management and logistics (MBA, MS). *Accreditation:* ACBSP. *Program availability:* Part-time, evening/weekend, online learning. *Entrance requirements:* Additional exam requirements/recommendations for international students: Required—TOEFL (minimum score 550 paper-based; 80 iBT). Electronic applications accepted.

Queen's University at Kingston, Smith School of Business, Program in International Business, Kingston, ON K7L 3N6, Canada. Offers MIB.

Regent's University London, Webster Graduate School, London, United Kingdom. Offers business (MBA); finance (MS); human resources (MA); information technology management (MA); international business (MA); international non-governmental organizations (MA); international relations (MA); management and leadership (MA); marketing (MA). *Program availability:* Part-time.

Rochester Institute of Technology, Graduate Enrollment Services, Saunders College of Business, Marketing and Management Department, MS Program in Management, Rochester, NY 14623-5603. Offers MS. *Program availability:* Part-time. *Students:* 9 full-time (7 women), 8 part-time (4 women); includes 1 minority (Two or more races, non-Hispanic/Latino), 8 international. Average age 28. 39 applicants, 67% accepted, 8 enrolled. In 2018, 4 master's awarded. *Entrance requirements:* For master's, GRE or GMAT. GMAT may be waived if applicant has a GPA of 3.25 or higher or can present evidence of at least six years of professional work experience., minimum GPA of 3.0 (recommended), resume, essay. Additional exam requirements/recommendations for international students: Required—TOEFL (minimum score 580 paper-based; 92 iBT), IELTS (minimum score 7), PTE (minimum score 63). *Application deadline:* Applications are processed on a rolling basis. Application fee: $65. Electronic applications accepted. *Financial support:* In 2018–19, 17 students received support. Research assistantships with partial tuition reimbursements available, teaching assistantships with partial tuition reimbursements available, career-related internships or fieldwork, scholarships/grants, and unspecified assistantships available. Support available to part-time students. Financial award applicants required to submit FAFSA. *Faculty research:* Impacts of clinical IT adoption in the U.S. healthcare system; social media and entrepreneurship; cybersecurity. *Unit head:* Matt Cornwell, Assistant Director of Student Services and Outreach, 585-475-6916, E-mail: mcornwell@saunders.rit.edu. *Application contact:* Diane Ellison, Senior Associate Vice President, Graduate Enrollment Services, 585-475-2229, Fax: 585-475-7164, E-mail: gradinfo@rit.edu. Website: https://www.rit.edu/study/management-ms

Rockhurst University, Helzberg School of Management, Kansas City, MO 64110-2561. Offers accounting (MBA); business intelligence (MBA, Certificate); business intelligence and analytics (MS); data science (MBA, Certificate); entrepreneurship (MBA); finance (MBA); fundraising leadership (MBA, Certificate); healthcare management (MBA, Certificate); human capital (Certificate); international business (Certificate); management (MA, MBA, Certificate); nonprofit administration (Certificate); organizational development (Certificate); science leadership (Certificate). *Accreditation:* AACSB. *Program availability:* Part-time, evening/weekend. *Entrance requirements:* For master's, GMAT or GRE. Additional exam requirements/recommendations for international students: Required—TOEFL (minimum score 550 paper-based; 79 iBT). Electronic applications accepted. *Faculty research:* Offshoring/outsourcing, systems analysis/synthesis, work teams, multilateral trade, path dependencies/creation.

Rollins College, Crummer Graduate School of Business, Winter Park, FL 32789-4499. Offers entrepreneurship (MBA); finance (MBA); international business (MBA); management (MBA). *Accreditation:* AACSB. *Program availability:* Part-time, evening/weekend, online learning. *Degree requirements:* For master's, minimum GPA of 2.85. *Entrance requirements:* For master's, GMAT or GRE, official transcripts, two letters of recommendation, essay, current resume/curriculum vitae, interview. Additional exam requirements/recommendations for international students: Required—TOEFL (minimum score 100 iBT) or IELTS (minimum score 7). Electronic applications accepted. *Expenses:* Contact institution. *Faculty research:* Sustainability, world financial markets, international business, market research, strategic marketing.

Rutgers University–Newark, Graduate School, Program in Management, Newark, NJ 07102. Offers accounting (PhD); accounting information systems (PhD); computer information systems (PhD); finance (PhD); information technology (PhD); international business (PhD); management science (PhD); marketing (PhD); organization management (PhD). Program offered jointly with New Jersey Institute of Technology. *Accreditation:* AACSB. *Degree requirements:* For doctorate, thesis/dissertation, cumulative exams. *Entrance requirements:* For doctorate, GMAT or GRE General Test, minimum undergraduate B average. Additional exam requirements/recommendations for international students: Required—TOEFL. Electronic applications accepted. *Faculty research:* Technology management, leadership and teams, consumer behavior, financial and markets, logistics.

Rutgers University–Newark, Rutgers Business School–Newark and New Brunswick, Doctoral Programs in Management, Newark, NJ 07102. Offers accounting (PhD); accounting information systems (PhD); economics (PhD); finance (PhD); individualized study (PhD); information technology (PhD); international business (PhD); management

science (PhD); marketing science (PhD); organizational management (PhD); science, technology and management (PhD); supply chain management (PhD). *Degree requirements:* For doctorate, comprehensive exam, thesis/dissertation. *Entrance requirements:* For doctorate, GRE or GMAT. Additional exam requirements/recommendations for international students: Required—TOEFL (minimum score 550 paper-based; 79 iBT). Electronic applications accepted.

St. John's University, The Peter J. Tobin College of Business, Program in International Business, Queens, NY 11439. Offers business administration (MBA), including international business. *Entrance requirements:* For master's, GMAT or GRE, 2 letters of recommendation, essay, resume, unofficial transcripts. Additional exam requirements/recommendations for international students: Required—TOEFL (minimum score 80 iBT), IELTS (minimum score 6.5). Electronic applications accepted. *Expenses:* Contact institution.

Saint Joseph's University, Erivan K. Haub School of Business, MBA Program, Philadelphia, PA 19131-1395. Offers accounting (MBA); business intelligence analytics (MBA); finance (MBA); financial analysis reporting (Postbaccalaureate Certificate); general business (MBA); health and medical services administration (MBA); international business (MBA); international marketing (MBA); leading (MBA); marketing (MBA); DO/MBA. DO/MBA offered jointly with Philadelphia College of Osteopathic Medicine. *Program availability:* Part-time-only, evening/weekend, 100% online. *Degree requirements:* For master's, minimum GPA of 3.0. *Entrance requirements:* For master's, GMAT or GRE, 2 letters of recommendation, resume, personal statement, official undergraduate and graduate transcripts. Additional exam requirements/recommendations for international students: Required—PTE, TOEFL, IELTS, or PTE. Electronic applications accepted. *Expenses:* Contact institution.

Saint Joseph's University, Erivan K. Haub School of Business, MS Program in Marketing, Philadelphia, PA 19131-1395. Offers customer analytics and insights (MS); international marketing (MS). *Program availability:* Part-time, evening/weekend, 100% online. *Degree requirements:* For master's, minimum GPA of 3.0. *Entrance requirements:* For master's, GMAT or GRE, 2 letters of recommendation, resume, personal statement, official undergraduate and graduate transcripts. Additional exam requirements/recommendations for international students: Required—PTE, TOEFL, IELTS, or PTE. Electronic applications accepted.

Saint Louis University, Graduate Programs, John Cook School of Business, Boeing Institute of International Business, St. Louis, MO 63103. Offers business administration (PhD), including international business and marketing; executive international business (EMIB); international business (MBA). *Program availability:* Part-time, evening/weekend. *Degree requirements:* For master's, thesis, study abroad; for doctorate, comprehensive exam, thesis/dissertation. *Entrance requirements:* For master's, GMAT, work experience. Additional exam requirements/recommendations for international students: Required—TOEFL (minimum score 525 paper-based). *Expenses:* Contact institution. *Faculty research:* Foreign direct investment, technology transfer, emerging markets, Asian business, Latin American business.

Saint Peter's University, Graduate Business Programs, MBA Program, Jersey City, NJ 07306-5997. Offers finance (MBA); health care administration (MBA); human resource management (MBA); international business (MBA); management (MBA); management information systems (MBA); marketing (MBA); risk management (MBA); MBA/MS. *Program availability:* Part-time, evening/weekend. *Entrance requirements:* Additional exam requirements/recommendations for international students: Required—TOEFL. Electronic applications accepted. *Faculty research:* Finance, health care management, human resource management, international business, management, management information systems, marketing, risk management.

St. Thomas University, School of Business, Department of Management, Miami Gardens, FL 33054-6459. Offers accounting (MBA); general management (MSM, Certificate); health management (MBA, MSM, Certificate); human resource management (MBA, MSM, Certificate); international business (MBA, MIB, MSM, Certificate); justice administration (MSM, Certificate); management accounting (MSM, Certificate); public management (MSM, Certificate); sports administration (MS). *Program availability:* Part-time, evening/weekend. *Degree requirements:* For master's, comprehensive exam. *Entrance requirements:* For master's, interview, minimum GPA of 3.0 or GMAT. Additional exam requirements/recommendations for international students: Required—TOEFL (minimum score 550 paper-based; 79 iBT). Electronic applications accepted.

Salem International University, School of Business, Salem, WV 26426-0500. Offers information security (MBA); international business (MBA). *Program availability:* Part-time, online learning. *Entrance requirements:* For master's, minimum undergraduate GPA of 2.5, course work in business, resume. Additional exam requirements/recommendations for international students: Recommended—TOEFL (minimum score 550 paper-based), IELTS (minimum score 6.5). Electronic applications accepted. *Expenses:* Contact institution. *Faculty research:* Organizational behavior strategy, marketing services.

San Francisco State University, Division of Graduate Studies, College of Business, Program in Business Administration, San Francisco, CA 94132-1722. Offers decision sciences/operations research (MBA); ethics and compliance (MBA); finance (MBA); global business and innovation (MBA); healthcare administration (MBA); hospitality and tourism management (MBA); information systems (MBA); leadership (MBA); marketing (MBA); nonprofit and social enterprise leadership (MBA); sustainable business (MBA). *Accreditation:* AACSB. *Program availability:* Part-time, evening/weekend. *Degree requirements:* For master's, thesis, essay test. *Entrance requirements:* For master's, GMAT, minimum GPA of 2.7 in last 60 units. Additional exam requirements/recommendations for international students: Required—TOEFL (minimum score 550 paper-based).

San Ignacio University, Graduate Programs, Doral, FL 33178. Offers business administration (MBA), including human resources management, international business, marketing management; education (M Ed), including early childhood education, educational leadership, special education; hospitality management (MA), including gastronomy and restaurant management, tourism management.

Schiller International University, MBA Program, Madrid, Spain, Madrid, Spain. Offers international business (MBA). *Program availability:* Part-time. *Degree requirements:* For master's, comprehensive exam, thesis optional. *Entrance requirements:* Additional exam requirements/recommendations for international students: Required—TOEFL (minimum score 550 paper-based).

Schiller International University, MBA Program Paris, France, Paris, France. Offers international business (MBA). Bilingual French/English MBA available for native French speakers. *Program availability:* Part-time, evening/weekend, online learning. *Degree requirements:* For master's, comprehensive exam, thesis or alternative. *Entrance requirements:* Additional exam requirements/recommendations for international students: Required—TOEFL (minimum score 550 paper-based).

Schiller International University, MBA Programs, Florida, Program in International Business, Largo, FL 33771. Offers MBA. *Program availability:* Part-time, evening/weekend, online learning. *Degree requirements:* For master's, thesis optional. *Entrance requirements:* Additional exam requirements/recommendations for international students: Required—TOEFL (minimum score 550 paper-based).

Schiller International University, MBA Programs, Heidelberg, Germany, Heidelberg, Germany. Offers international business (MBA, MIM); management of information technology (MBA). *Program availability:* Part-time, evening/weekend. *Degree requirements:* For master's, thesis optional. *Entrance requirements:* Additional exam requirements/recommendations for international students: Required—TOEFL (minimum score 550 paper-based). *Faculty research:* Leadership, international economy, foreign direct investment.

Seton Hall University, Stillman School of Business, Programs in Business Administration, South Orange, NJ 07079-2697. Offers accounting (MBA); entrepreneurial studies (Certificate); finance (MBA); financial decision making (Certificate); information technology management (MBA); international business (MBA); management (MBA); marketing (MBA); sport management (MBA); supply chain management (MBA, Certificate). *Program availability:* Part-time, evening/weekend. *Faculty:* 27 full-time (5 women), 18 part-time/adjunct (2 women). *Students:* 85 full-time (40 women), 363 part-time (147 women); includes 78 minority (22 Black or African American, non-Hispanic/Latino; 4 Asian, non-Hispanic/Latino; 18 Hispanic/Latino; 29 Native Hawaiian or other Pacific Islander, non-Hispanic/Latino; 5 Two or more races, non-Hispanic/Latino), 282 international. Average age 34. 483 applicants, 85% accepted, 302 enrolled. In 2018, 96 master's awarded. *Degree requirements:* For master's, 20 hours of community service (Social Responsibility Project). *Entrance requirements:* For master's, GMAT or CPA, GRE (waived based on work experience or advanced degree from AACSB institution), MS in business discipline, professional degree or designation (MD, JD, PhD, DVM, DDS, CPA, etc.), minimum undergraduate GPA of 3.0. Additional exam requirements/recommendations for international students: Required—TOEFL (minimum score 607 paper-based; 80 iBT), IELTS (minimum score 6), PTE. *Application deadline:* For fall admission, 5/31 priority date for domestic students, 4/30 priority date for international students; for spring admission, 10/31 priority date for domestic students, 9/30 priority date for international students; for summer admission, 3/31 priority date for domestic students. Applications are processed on a rolling basis. Application fee: $75. Electronic applications accepted. Application fee is waived when completed online. *Expenses:* Tuition is $1,305 per credit hour and the overall MBA is a 40 credit hour program. University fees are $115 per semester. The university also has a technology that is $125 per semester. *Financial support:* In 2018–19, 44 students received support, including 25 research assistantships with partial tuition reimbursements available (averaging $3,644 per year); career-related internships or fieldwork, scholarships/grants, and unspecified assistantships also available. Financial award application deadline: 6/30; financial award applicants required to submit FAFSA. *Faculty research:* Sport, hedge funds, executive compensation, social media, legal studies. *Unit head:* Dr. Joyce Strawser, Dean, 973-761-9013, Fax: 973-761-9217, E-mail: joyce.strawser@shu.edu. *Application contact:* Alfred Ayoub, Director of Graduate Admissions, 973-761-9262, Fax: 973-761-9208, E-mail: alfred.ayoub@shu.edu.
Website: http://www.shu.edu/business/mba-programs.cfm

SIT Graduate Institute, Graduate Programs, Master's Programs in Intercultural Service, Leadership, and Management, Brattleboro, VT 05302-0676. Offers intercultural service, leadership, and management (self-designed) (MA); international education (MA); peace and justice leadership (MA); sustainable development (MA). *Program availability:* Online learning. *Degree requirements:* For master's, one foreign language, thesis. *Entrance requirements:* For master's, 3 letters of reference. Additional exam requirements/recommendations for international students: Required—TOEFL, IELTS. *Faculty research:* Intercultural communication, conflict resolution, international education, world issues, international affairs.

Southeastern University, Jannetides College of Business and Entrepreneurial Leadership, Lakeland, FL 33801-6099. Offers executive leadership (MBA); global business administration (MBA); healthcare administration (MBA); missional leadership (MBA); organizational leadership (PhD); sport management (MBA); strategic leadership (DSL). *Accreditation:* ACBSP. *Program availability:* Evening/weekend, online learning. *Entrance requirements:* For master's, GMAT, minimum cumulative GPA of 3.0, writing sample. Electronic applications accepted.

Southern New Hampshire University, School of Business, Manchester, NH 03106-1045. Offers accounting (MBA, Graduate Certificate); accounting finance (MS); accounting/auditing (MS); accounting/forensic accounting (MS); accounting/management accounting (MS); accounting/taxation (MS); applied economics (MS); athletic administration (MBA, Graduate Certificate); business administration (IMBA, Certificate), including business information systems (Certificate), human resource management (Certificate); business analytics (MBA); business intelligence (MBA); communication (MA), including new media and marketing, public relations; community economic development (MBA); criminal justice (MBA); data analytics (MS); economics (MBA); engineering management (MBA); entrepreneurship (MBA); finance (MBA, MS, Graduate Certificate); finance/corporate finance (MS); finance/investments (MS); forensic accounting (MBA); forensic accounting and fraud examination (Graduate Certificate); healthcare informatics (MBA); healthcare management (MBA); human resource management (MS); human resources (MBA); information technology (MS); information technology management (MBA); international business (PhD); Internet marketing (MBA); leadership (MBA); leadership of nonprofit organizations (Graduate Certificate); management (MS); marketing (MBA, MS, Graduate Certificate); music business (MBA); operations and project management (MS); operations and supply chain management (MBA, Graduate Certificate); organizational leadership (MS); project management (MBA, Graduate Certificate); public administration (MBA, Graduate Certificate); quantitative analysis (MBA); Six Sigma (Graduate Certificate); Six Sigma quality (MBA); social media marketing (MBA, Graduate Certificate); sport management (MBA, MS, Graduate Certificate); sustainability and environmental compliance (MBA); MBA/Certificate. *Accreditation:* ACBSP. *Program availability:* Part-time, evening/weekend, online learning. Terminal master's awarded for partial completion of doctoral program. *Degree requirements:* For master's, one foreign language, comprehensive exam (for some programs), thesis or alternative; for doctorate, one foreign language, comprehensive exam, thesis/dissertation. *Entrance requirements:* For master's, minimum GPA of 2.5; for doctorate, GMAT. Additional exam requirements/recommendations for international students: Required—TOEFL (minimum score 500 paper-based). Electronic applications accepted.

Southern Oregon University, Graduate Studies, School of Business, Ashland, OR 97520. Offers accounting (Postbaccalaureate Certificate); business administration (MBA); international management (MIM). *Accreditation:* ACBSP. *Program availability:* Part-time, evening/weekend, online learning. *Degree requirements:* For master's, comprehensive exam. *Entrance requirements:* For master's, GMAT, minimum cumulative GPA of 3.0 in the last 90 quarter credits (60 semester credits) of undergraduate coursework. Additional exam requirements/recommendations for international students: Required—TOEFL (minimum score 540 paper-based; 76 iBT), IELTS (minimum score 6), ELPT (minimum score 964) or ELS (minimum score 112). Electronic applications accepted.

State University of New York Empire State College, School for Graduate Studies, Program in Business Administration, Saratoga Springs, NY 12866-4391. Offers global

leadership (MBA); management (MBA). *Program availability:* Part-time, online learning. *Degree requirements:* For master's, thesis or alternative. *Entrance requirements:* For master's, previous course work in statistics, macroeconomics, microeconomics, and accounting. Additional exam requirements/recommendations for international students: Required—TOEFL (minimum score 600 paper-based). Electronic applications accepted. *Expenses:* Contact institution. *Faculty research:* Corporate strategy, managerial competencies, decision analysis, economics in transition, organizational communication.

Stevens Institute of Technology, Graduate School, School of Business, Program in Management, Hoboken, NJ 07030. Offers general management (MS); global innovation management (MS); human resource management (MS); information management (MS); project management (MS); technology commercialization (MS); technology management (MS). *Program availability:* Part-time, evening/weekend. *Faculty:* 58 full-time (8 women), 18 part-time/adjunct (3 women). *Students:* 101 full-time (41 women), 66 part-time (34 women); includes 14 minority (4 Black or African American, non-Hispanic/Latino; 9 Asian, non-Hispanic/Latino; 1 Hispanic/Latino), 115 international. Average age 28. In 2018, 70 master's awarded. Terminal master's awarded for partial completion of doctoral program. *Degree requirements:* For master's, thesis optional, minimum B average in major field and overall. *Entrance requirements:* For master's, GRE/GMAT scores: GRE scores are required for all applicants applying to a full-time graduate program in the Schaefer School of Engineering and Science (SES). International applicants must submit TOEFL/IELTS scores and fulfill the English Language Proficiency Requirements in order to be considered. Additional exam requirements/recommendations for international students: Required—TOEFL (minimum score 74 iBT), IELTS (minimum score 6). *Application deadline:* For fall admission, 4/1 for domestic and international students; for spring admission, 11/1 for domestic and international students; for summer admission, 5/1 for domestic students. Applications are processed on a rolling basis. Application fee: $60. Electronic applications accepted. *Expenses: Tuition:* Full-time $35,960; part-time $1620 per credit. *Required fees:* $1290; $600 per semester. Tuition and fees vary according to course load. *Financial support:* Fellowships, research assistantships, teaching assistantships, career-related internships or fieldwork, Federal Work-Study, scholarships/grants, and unspecified assistantships available. Financial award application deadline: 2/15; financial award applicants required to submit FAFSA. *Unit head:* Dr. Gregory Prascatos, Dean of SB, 201-216 8366, E-mail: gprastac@stevens.edu. *Application contact:* Graduate Admissions, 888-783-8367, Fax: 888-511-1306, E-mail: graduate@stevens.edu.
Website: https://www.stevens.edu/school-business/masters-programs/management

Suffolk University, Sawyer Business School, Master of Business Administration Program, Boston, MA 02108-2770. Offers accounting (MBA); entrepreneurship (MBA); executive business administration (EMBA); finance (MBA); global business administration (GMBA); health administration (MBA); international business (MBA); marketing (MBA); nonprofit management (MBA); organizational behavior (MBA); strategic management (MBA); supply chain management (MBA); taxation (MBA); JD/MBA; MBA/MHA; MBA/MSA; MBA/MSF; MBA/MST. *Accreditation:* AACSB. *Program availability:* Part-time, evening/weekend, 100% online. *Faculty:* 18 full-time (5 women), 5 part-time/adjunct (0 women). *Students:* 79 full-time (46 women), 193 part-time (107 women); includes 69 minority (17 Black or African American, non-Hispanic/Latino; 18 Asian, non-Hispanic/Latino; 28 Hispanic/Latino; 6 Two or more races, non-Hispanic/Latino), 40 international. Average age 30. 274 applicants, 67% accepted, 83 enrolled. In 2018, 125 master's awarded. *Entrance requirements:* For master's, GMAT, minimum undergraduate GPA of 2.75 (MBA), 5 years of managerial experience (EMBA). Additional exam requirements/recommendations for international students: Required—TOEFL (minimum score 550 paper-based; 80 iBT). *Application deadline:* For fall admission, 3/15 priority date for domestic students, 10/15 priority date for international students; for spring admission, 10/15 priority date for domestic and international students. Applications are processed on a rolling basis. Application fee: $50. Electronic applications accepted. *Expenses:* Contact institution. *Financial support:* In 2018–19, 170 students received support, including 4 fellowships (averaging $2,906 per year); career-related internships or fieldwork, Federal Work-Study, institutionally sponsored loans, and scholarships/grants also available. Support available to part-time students. Financial award application deadline: 4/1; financial award applicants required to submit FAFSA. *Faculty research:* Foreign investments; career strategies and boundaryless careers; corporate ethics codes; interest rates, inflation, and growth options; innovation and product development performance. *Unit head:* Jodi Detjen, Director of MBA Programs, 617-573-8306, E-mail: jdetjen@suffolk.edu. *Application contact:* Mara Marzocchi, Associate Director of Graduate Admissions, 617-573-8302, Fax: 617-305-1733, E-mail: grad.admission@suffolk.edu.
Website: http://www.suffolk.edu/mba

Temple University, Fox School of Business, Doctoral Programs in Business, Philadelphia, PA 19122-6096. Offers accounting (PhD); entrepreneurship (PhD); finance (PhD); international business (PhD); management information systems (PhD); marketing (PhD); risk management and insurance (PhD); statistics (PhD); strategic management (PhD); tourism and sport (PhD). *Accreditation:* AACSB. *Degree requirements:* For doctorate, thesis/dissertation. *Entrance requirements:* For doctorate, GRE General Test, GMAT, minimum GPA of 3.0, master's degree. Additional exam requirements/recommendations for international students: Required—TOEFL (minimum score 600 paper-based; 100 iBT), IELTS (minimum score 7.5). Electronic applications accepted.

Temple University, Fox School of Business, MBA Programs, Philadelphia, PA 19122-6096. Offers accounting (MBA); business management (MBA); financial management (MBA); healthcare and life sciences innovation (MBA); human resource management (MBA); international business (IMBA); IT management (MBA); marketing management (MBA); pharmaceutical management (MBA); strategic management (EMBA, MBA). EMBA offered in Philadelphia, PA and Tokyo, Japan. *Accreditation:* AACSB. *Program availability:* Part-time, evening/weekend, online learning. *Entrance requirements:* For master's, GMAT, minimum undergraduate GPA of 3.0. Additional exam requirements/recommendations for international students: Required—TOEFL (minimum score 600 paper-based; 100 iBT), IELTS (minimum score 7.5).

Tennessee Technological University, College of Graduate Studies, College of Business, MBA Program, Cookeville, TN 38505. Offers finance (MBA); human resource management (MBA); international business (MBA); management information systems (MBA). *Program availability:* Part-time, evening/weekend. *Students:* 32 full-time (10 women), 156 part-time (66 women); includes 16 minority (7 Black or African American, non-Hispanic/Latino; 1 Asian, non-Hispanic/Latino; 5 Hispanic/Latino; 3 Two or more races, non-Hispanic/Latino), 5 international. 115 applicants, 68% accepted, 57 enrolled. In 2018, 88 master's awarded. *Entrance requirements:* For master's, GMAT or GRE. *Financial support:* In 2018–19, 2 research assistantships, 3 teaching assistantships were awarded; fellowships and unspecified assistantships also available. Financial award application deadline: 4/1; financial award applicants required to submit FAFSA. *Unit head:* Kate Nicewicz, Director, 931-372-3600, E-mail: knicewicz@tntech.edu. *Application contact:* Shelia K. Kendrick, Coordinator of Graduate Studies, 931-372-3808, Fax: 931-372-3497, E-mail: skendrick@tntech.edu.
Website: https://www.tntech.edu/cob/mba/

Texas A&M International University, Office of Graduate Studies and Research, A.R. Sanchez, Jr. School of Business, Division of International Business and Technology Studies, Laredo, TX 78041. Offers information systems (MSIS); international business management (MBA, PhD). *Degree requirements:* For master's, thesis (for some programs). *Entrance requirements:* For master's, GMAT or GRE General Test. Additional exam requirements/recommendations for international students: Required—TOEFL (minimum score 550 paper-based; 79 iBT).

Texas A&M University–Corpus Christi, College of Graduate Studies, College of Business, Corpus Christi, TX 78412. Offers accounting (M Acc); business (MBA); finance (MBA); health care administration (MBA); international business (MBA). *Accreditation:* AACSB. *Program availability:* Part-time, evening/weekend, 100% online, blended/hybrid learning. *Degree requirements:* For master's, 30 to 42 hours (for MBA; varies by concentration area, delivery format, and necessity for foundational courses for students with nonbusiness degrees). *Entrance requirements:* For master's, GMAT, GRE. Additional exam requirements/recommendations for international students: Required—TOEFL (minimum score 550 paper-based; 79 iBT), IELTS (minimum score 6.5). Electronic applications accepted.

Thomas Edison State University, School of Business and Management, Program in International Business Finance, Trenton, NJ 08608. Offers MS. *Program availability:* Online learning. *Entrance requirements:* For master's, undergraduate coursework in financial accounting, microeconomics, finance and statistics.

Tiffin University, Program in Business Administration, Tiffin, OH 44883-2161. Offers finance (MBA); general management (MBA); healthcare administration (MBA); human resource management (MBA); international business (MBA); leadership (MBA); marketing (MBA); non-profit management (MBA); sports management (MBA). *Accreditation:* ACBSP. *Program availability:* Part-time, evening/weekend, online learning. *Entrance requirements:* For master's, minimum undergraduate GPA of 2.5, work experience. Additional exam requirements/recommendations for international students: Required—TOEFL (minimum score 550 paper-based; 79 iBT), IELTS. Electronic applications accepted. Application fee is waived when completed online. *Faculty research:* Small business, executive development operations, research and statistical analysis, market research, management information systems.

Trident University International, College of Business Administration, Program in Business Administration, Cypress, CA 90630. Offers business administration (PhD); conflict and negotiation management (MBA); criminal justice administration (MBA); entrepreneurship (MBA); finance (MBA); general management (MBA); government accounting (MBA); human resource management (MBA); information security and digital assurance management (MBA); information technology management (MBA); international business (MBA); logistics management (MBA); marketing (MBA); project management (MBA); public management (MBA); quality management (MBA); strategic leadership (MBA). *Program availability:* Part-time, evening/weekend, online learning. *Degree requirements:* For doctorate, comprehensive exam, thesis/dissertation, defense of dissertation. *Entrance requirements:* For master's, minimum GPA of 2.5 (students with GPA 3.0 or greater may transfer up to 30% of graduate level credits); for doctorate, minimum GPA of 3.4, curriculum vitae, course work in research methods or statistics. Additional exam requirements/recommendations for international students: Required—TOEFL. Electronic applications accepted.

Trinity Western University, School of Graduate Studies, Program in Business Administration, Langley, BC V2Y 1Y1, Canada. Offers international business (MBA); management of the growing enterprise (MBA); non-profit and charitable organization management (MBA). *Program availability:* Part-time, online learning. *Degree requirements:* For master's, thesis or alternative, applied project. *Entrance requirements:* For master's, GMAT (minimum score of 550 recommended). Additional exam requirements/recommendations for international students: Required—TOEFL (minimum score 600 paper-based; 100 iBT), IELTS (minimum score 7). *Application deadline:* For spring admission, 4/30 for domestic and international students. Applications are processed on a rolling basis. Electronic applications accepted. *Financial support:* Scholarships/grants available. *Unit head:* Dr. Mark A. Lee, Director, MBA Program, 604-888-7511 Ext. 3474, Fax: 604-513-2042, E-mail: mark.lee@twu.ca. *Application contact:* Phil Kay, Director of Graduate and International Admissions, 604-513-2121 Ext. 3444, E-mail: phil.kay@twu.edu.
Website: http://www.twu.ca/mba

Tufts University, The Fletcher School of Law and Diplomacy, Medford, MA 02155. Offers economics and public policy (PhD); international affairs (PhD); international business (MIB); international law (LL M); law and diplomacy (MA, MALD); transatlantic affairs (MA); DVM/MA; JD/MALD; MALD/MA; MALD/MBA; MALD/MS; MD/MA. MA in transatlantic affairs offered jointly with The College of Europe; PhD in economics and public policy with Tufts' Graduate School of Arts and Sciences. *Program availability:* Online learning. *Degree requirements:* For master's, one foreign language, thesis; for doctorate, one foreign language, comprehensive exam, thesis/dissertation, dissertation defense. *Entrance requirements:* For master's and doctorate, GMAT or GRE General Test. Additional exam requirements/recommendations for international students: Required—TOEFL (minimum score 600 paper-based; 100 iBT), IELTS (minimum score 7). Electronic applications accepted. *Expenses:* Contact institution. *Faculty research:* Negotiation and conflict resolution, international organizations, international business and economic law, security studies, development economics.

Tulane University, A. B. Freeman School of Business, New Orleans, LA 70118-5669. Offers accounting (M Acct); analytics (MBA); banking and financial services (M Fin); energy (M Fin, MBA); entrepreneurship (MBA); finance (MBA, PhD); financial accounting (PhD); international business (MBA); international management (MBA); strategic management and leadership (MBA); JD/M Acct; JD/MBA; MBA/M Acc; MBA/MA; MBA/MD; MBA/ME; MBA/MPH. *Accreditation:* AACSB. *Program availability:* Part-time, evening/weekend. *Faculty:* 43 full-time (11 women), 45 part-time/adjunct (8 women). *Students:* 432 full-time (218 women), 533 part-time (262 women); includes 99 minority (32 Black or African American, non-Hispanic/Latino; 1 American Indian or Alaska Native, non-Hispanic/Latino; 26 Asian, non-Hispanic/Latino; 35 Hispanic/Latino; 5 Two or more races, non-Hispanic/Latino), 644 international. Average age 28. 1,911 applicants, 77% accepted, 411 enrolled. In 2018, 728 master's, 4 doctorates awarded. Terminal master's awarded for partial completion of doctoral program. *Degree requirements:* For master's, one foreign language, comprehensive exam (for some programs); for doctorate, one foreign language, comprehensive exam, thesis/dissertation. *Entrance requirements:* For master's and doctorate, GMAT or GRE, interview. Additional exam requirements/recommendations for international students: Required—TOEFL or IELTS. *Application deadline:* For fall admission, 11/1 priority date for domestic students, 11/1 for international students; for winter admission, 1/6 for domestic and international students; for spring admission, 3/1 priority date for domestic students, 3/1 for international students; for summer admission, 5/5 for domestic students. Applications are processed on a rolling basis. Application fee: $125. Electronic applications accepted. *Expenses:* Contact institution. *Financial support:* In 2018–19, 153 students received support. Fellowships with tuition reimbursements available, research assistantships, teaching assistantships, career-related internships or fieldwork, Federal Work-Study, tuition waivers (full and partial), and unspecified assistantships available. Support available to part-time students. Financial award application deadline:

4/15; financial award applicants required to submit FAFSA. *Faculty research:* Corporate finance, managerial accounting and financial reporting, strategic management and leadership, consumer behavior and decision making, organizational behavior and human resource management. *Unit head:* Ira Solomon, PhD, Dean, 504-865-5407, Fax: 504-865-5491, E-mail: businessdean@tulane.edu. *Application contact:* Melissa Booth, Assistant Dean for Graduate Admissions, 800-223-5402, E-mail: freeman.admissions@tulane.edu.
Website: http://www.freeman.tulane.edu

United States International University–Africa, School of Business Administration, Nairobi, Kenya. Offers business administration (GEMBA); entrepreneurship (MBA); finance (MBA); human resource management (MBA); information technology management (MBA); integrated studies (MBA); international business administration (MBA); management and organizational development (MS); marketing (MBA); organizational development (EMS); strategic management (MBA). *Program availability:* Part-time, evening/weekend. *Degree requirements:* For master's, thesis. *Entrance requirements:* For master's, GMAT, 2 letters of reference, resume. Additional exam requirements/recommendations for international students: Required—TOEFL (minimum score 550 paper-based). *Faculty research:* Marketing in small business enterprises, total quality management in Kenya.

Universidad Autonoma de Guadalajara, Graduate Programs, Guadalajara, Mexico. Offers administrative law and justice (LL M); advertising and corporate communications (MA); architecture (M Arch); business (MBA); computational science (MCC); education (Ed M, Ed D); English-Spanish translation (MA); entrepreneurship and management (MBA); integrated management of digital animation (MA); international business (MIB); international corporate law (LL M); Internet technologies (MS); manufacturing systems (MMS); occupational health (MS); philosophy (MA, PhD); power electronics (MS); quality systems (MQS); renewable energy (MS); social evaluation of projects (MBA); strategic market research (MBA); tax law (MA); teaching mathematics (MA).

Universidad Metropolitana, School of Business Administration, Program in International Business, San Juan, PR 00928-1150. Offers MBA.

Université de Sherbrooke, Faculty of Administration, Program in International Business, Sherbrooke, QC J1K 2R1, Canada. Offers M Sc. *Degree requirements:* For master's, one foreign language, thesis. *Entrance requirements:* For master's, bachelor's degree in related field, minimum GPA of 3.0 (on 4.3 scale). Electronic applications accepted.

Université du Québec, École nationale d'administration publique, Graduate Programs in Public Administration, Program in International Administration, Quebec, QC G1K 9E5, Canada. Offers MAP, Diploma. *Program availability:* Part-time. *Entrance requirements:* For degree, appropriate bachelor's degree, proficiency in French.

Université Laval, Faculty of Administrative Sciences, Programs in Business Administration, Québec, QC G1K 7P4, Canada. Offers accounting (MBA); agri-food management (MBA); electronic business (MBA, Diploma); factory management and logistics (MBA); finance (MBA); firm management (MBA); geomatic management (MBA); information technology management (MBA); international management (MBA); management (MBA); management accounting (MBA, Diploma); marketing (MBA); modeling and organizational decision (MBA); occupational health and safety management (MBA); pharmacy management (MBA); social and environmental responsibility (MBA); technological entrepreneurship (Diploma). *Accreditation:* AACSB. *Program availability:* Part-time, evening/weekend, online learning. *Entrance requirements:* For master's and Diploma, knowledge of French and English. Electronic applications accepted.

University at Buffalo, the State University of New York, Graduate School, College of Arts and Sciences, Department of Geography, Buffalo, NY 14260. Offers earth systems science (MA, MS); economic geography and business geographics (MS); environmental modeling and analysis (MA); geographic information science (MA, MS); geography (MA, PhD); health geography (MS); international trade (MA); urban and regional analysis (MA). *Program availability:* Part-time. Terminal master's awarded for partial completion of doctoral program. *Degree requirements:* For master's, thesis (for some programs), project or portfolio; for doctorate, thesis/dissertation. *Entrance requirements:* For master's, GRE General Test, minimum GPA of 2.9; for doctorate, GRE General Test, minimum GPA of 3.0. Additional exam requirements/recommendations for international students: Required—TOEFL (minimum score 550 paper-based; 79 iBT). Electronic applications accepted. *Expenses:* Contact institution. *Faculty research:* International business and world trade, geographic information systems and cartography, transportation, urban and regional analysis, physical and environmental geography.

University at Buffalo, the State University of New York, Graduate School, School of Management, Buffalo, NY 14260. Offers accounting (MS); analytics (MBA); business administration (PMBA); consulting (MBA); finance (MBA, MS), including financial risk management (MS), quantitative finance (MS); healthcare (MBA); information assurance (MBA); information systems (MBA); international management (MBA); management (EMBA, PhD); management information systems (MS); marketing (MBA); supply chain and operations (MBA); supply chains and operations management (MS); Au D/MBA; DDS/MBA; JD/MBA; M Arch/MBA; MD/MBA; MPH/MBA; MSW/MBA; Pharm D/MBA. *Accreditation:* AACSB. *Program availability:* Part-time, evening/weekend. *Degree requirements:* For master's, capstone courses or projects; for doctorate, comprehensive exam, thesis/dissertation. *Entrance requirements:* For master's, GMAT (for MS in accounting, finance); GRE or GMAT (for MBA, MS in management information systems, supply chains and operations management), essays, letters of recommendation; for doctorate, GMAT or GRE, essays, writing sample, letters of recommendation. Additional exam requirements/recommendations for international students: Required—TOEFL (minimum score 95 iBT) or IELTS (minimum score 6.5); Recommended—TSE (minimum score 73). Electronic applications accepted. *Expenses:* Contact institution. *Faculty research:* Data analytics, accounting and law, rate finance, consumer behavior, supply chain logistics, leadership and team effectiveness.

University of Alberta, Faculty of Graduate Studies and Research, Program in Business Administration, Edmonton, AB T6G 2E1, Canada. Offers international business (MBA); leisure and sport management (MBA); natural resources and energy (MBA); technology commercialization (MBA); MBA/LL B; MBA/M Ag; MBA/M Eng; MBA/MF; MBA/PhD. *Accreditation:* AACSB. *Program availability:* Part-time, evening/weekend. *Degree requirements:* For master's, thesis or alternative. *Entrance requirements:* For master's, GMAT. Additional exam requirements/recommendations for international students: Required—TOEFL (minimum score 600 paper-based). Electronic applications accepted. *Faculty research:* Natural resources and energy/management and policy/family enterprise/international business/healthcare research management.

University of Baltimore, Graduate School, Merrick School of Business, Department of Management and International Business, Baltimore, MD 21201-5779. Offers global leadership (MS).

University of Bridgeport, School of Business, Bridgeport, CT 06604. Offers accounting (MBA); finance (MBA); general business (MBA); global financial services (MBA); human resource management (MBA); information systems and knowledge management (MBA); international business (MBA); management (MBA); marketing (MBA); operations management (MBA); small business and entrepreneurship (MBA); specialized business (MBA). *Accreditation:* ACBSP. *Program availability:* Part-time, evening/weekend. *Degree requirements:* For master's, thesis optional. *Entrance requirements:* For master's, GMAT. Additional exam requirements/recommendations for international students: Recommended—TOEFL (minimum score 550 paper-based; 80 iBT), IELTS (minimum score 6.5). Electronic applications accepted. *Expenses:* Contact institution.

University of California, Berkeley, UC Berkeley Extension, International Diploma Programs, Berkeley, CA 94720. Offers business administration (Certificate); finance (Certificate); global business management (Certificate); marketing (Certificate); project management (Certificate). *Accreditation:* AACSB.

University of California, San Diego, Graduate Division, School of Global Policy and Strategy, Master of International Affairs Program, La Jolla, CA 92093. Offers international development and nonprofit management (MIA); international economics (MIA); international environmental policy (MIA); international management (MIA); international politics (MIA). Students will choose one of the following country/regional specializations: China, Japan, Korea, Latin America, or Southeast Asia. *Degree requirements:* For master's, one foreign language. *Entrance requirements:* For master's, GMAT or GRE General Test. Additional exam requirements/recommendations for international students: Required—TOEFL (minimum score 90 iBT), IELTS (minimum score 7). Electronic applications accepted.

University of Chicago, Booth School of Business, Executive MBA Program Asia (Hong Kong), 238466, Singapore. Offers MBA. *Program availability:* Part-time. *Entrance requirements:* For master's, GMAT, GRE, or Executive Assessment, letter of company support, letters of recommendation, essays, resume, interview. Electronic applications accepted. *Expenses:* Contact institution.

University of Chicago, Booth School of Business, Executive MBA Program Europe (London), EC2V 5HA, United Kingdom. Offers MBA. *Program availability:* Part-time. *Entrance requirements:* For master's, GMAT, GRE, or Executive Assessment, letter of company support, letters of recommendation, essays, resume, interview. Electronic applications accepted. *Expenses:* Contact institution.

University of Chicago, Booth School of Business, Executive MBA Program North America, Chicago, IL 60611. Offers MBA. *Program availability:* Part-time. *Entrance requirements:* For master's, GMAT, GRE, or Executive Assessment, letter of company support, letters of recommendation, essays, resume, interview. Electronic applications accepted. *Expenses:* Contact institution.

University of Chicago, Booth School of Business, Full-Time MBA Program, Chicago, IL 60637. Offers accounting (MBA); analytic finance (MBA); analytic management (MBA); econometrics and statistics (MBA); economics (MBA); entrepreneurship (MBA); finance (MBA); general management (MBA); health administration and policy (Certificate); international business (MBA); managerial and organizational behavior (MBA); marketing analytics (MBA); marketing management (MBA); operations management (MBA); strategic management (MBA); MBA/AM; MBA/JD; MBA/MA; MBA/MD; MBA/MPP. *Accreditation:* AACSB. *Entrance requirements:* For master's, GMAT or GRE, transcripts, resume, 2 letters of recommendation, essays, interview. Additional exam requirements/recommendations for international students: Required—TOEFL, IELTS, or PTE. Electronic applications accepted. *Expenses:* Contact institution.

University of Colorado Denver, Business School, Program in Global Energy Management, Denver, CO 80217. Offers MS. *Program availability:* Online learning. *Degree requirements:* For master's, 36 semester credit hours. *Entrance requirements:* For master's, GMAT if less than three years of experience in the energy industry (waived for students already holding a graduate degree), minimum of 5 years' experience in energy industry; resume; letters of recommendation; essays. Additional exam requirements/recommendations for international students: Required—TOEFL (minimum score 525 paper-based; 71 iBT); Recommended—IELTS (minimum score 6). Electronic applications accepted. *Expenses:* Contact institution.

University of Colorado Denver, Business School, Program in International Business, Denver, CO 80217. Offers MS. *Program availability:* Part-time, evening/weekend. *Degree requirements:* For master's, 42 credit hours; thesis, internship or international field study. *Entrance requirements:* For master's, GMAT, resume, essay, two letters of recommendation, financial statements (for international applicants). Additional exam requirements/recommendations for international students: Required—TOEFL (minimum score 525 paper-based; 71 iBT); Recommended—IELTS (minimum score 6.5). Electronic applications accepted. *Expenses:* Contact institution. *Faculty research:* Foreign direct investment, international business strategies, cross-cultural management, internationalization of research and development, global leadership development.

University of Colorado Denver, Business School, Program in Management and Organization, Denver, CO 80217. Offers business strategy (MS); change and innovation (MS); enterprise technology management (MS); entrepreneurship and innovation (MS); global management (MS); leadership (MS); managing for sustainability (MS); managing human resources (MS); sports and entertainment (MS); strategic management (MS). *Accreditation:* AACSB. *Program availability:* Part-time, evening/weekend, online learning. *Degree requirements:* For master's, 30 semester hours (12 of required courses, 12 of management electives, and 6 of free electives). *Entrance requirements:* For master's, GMAT, resume, two letters of recommendation, essay, financial statements (for international applicants). Additional exam requirements/recommendations for international students: Required—TOEFL (minimum score 525 paper-based; 71 iBT); Recommended—IELTS (minimum score 6.5). Electronic applications accepted. *Expenses:* Contact institution. *Faculty research:* Human resource management, management of catastrophe, turnaround strategies.

University of Colorado Denver, Business School, Program in Marketing, Denver, CO 80217. Offers advanced market analytics in a big data world (MS); brand communication in the digital era (MS); global marketing (MS); high-tech and entrepreneurial marketing (MS); marketing and global sustainability (MS); marketing intelligence and strategy in the 21st century (MS); sports and entertainment business (MS). *Program availability:* Part-time, evening/weekend. *Degree requirements:* For master's, 30 semester hours (21 of marketing core courses, 9 of marketing electives). *Entrance requirements:* For master's, GMAT, resume, essay, two letters of recommendation, financial statements (for international applicants). Additional exam requirements/recommendations for international students: Required—TOEFL (minimum score 525 paper-based; 71 iBT); Recommended—IELTS (minimum score 6.5). Electronic applications accepted. *Expenses:* Contact institution. *Faculty research:* Marketing issues in the Chinese environment, impact of individual difference and contextual factors on the risk-taking behaviors of managers making new-business creation decisions, attribution theory perspective of conflict between marketers and engineers, organizational identity and identification, international market entry strategies.

University of Dallas, Satish and Yasmin Gupta College of Business, Irving, TX 75062. Offers accounting (MBA, MS); business administration (DBA); business analytics (MS); business management (MBA); corporate finance (MBA); cybersecurity (MS); finance (MS); financial services (MBA); global business (MBA, MS); health services management (MBA); human resource management (MBA); information and technology management (MS); information assurance (MBA); information technology (MBA);

information technology service management (MBA); marketing management (MBA); organization development (MBA); project management (MBA); sports and entertainment management (MBA); strategic leadership (MBA); supply chain management (MBA). *Accreditation:* AACSB. *Program availability:* Part-time, evening/weekend, 100% online. *Students:* 147 full-time (56 women), 584 part-time (232 women); includes 402 minority (204 Black or African American, non-Hispanic/Latino; 95 Asian, non-Hispanic/Latino; 92 Hispanic/Latino; 2 Native Hawaiian or other Pacific Islander, non-Hispanic/Latino; 9 Two or more races, non-Hispanic/Latino), 113 international. Average age 34. 992 applicants, 30% accepted, 157 enrolled. In 2018, 336 master's, 5 doctorates awarded. *Degree requirements:* For doctorate, thesis/dissertation. *Entrance requirements:* For master's and doctorate, U.S. bachelor's degree with a minimum cumulative GPA of 2.0 from a regionally accredited college or university (or comparable foreign degree); minimum 3.0 GPA in any graduate-level coursework completed; good academic standing with all colleges attended. Additional exam requirements/recommendations for international students: Required—TOEFL (minimum score 80 iBT), IELTS (minimum score 6.5), PTE (minimum score 67). *Application deadline:* Applications are processed on a rolling basis. Application fee: $50. Electronic applications accepted. *Expenses:* $1250 per credit hour. *Financial support:* In 2018–19, 291 students received support. Research assistantships, teaching assistantships, scholarships/grants, and unspecified assistantships available. Support available to part-time students. Financial award application deadline: 2/15; financial award applicants required to submit FAFSA. *Unit head:* Brett J.L. Landry, Dean, 972-721-5356, E-mail: blandry@udallas.edu. *Application contact:* Breonna Collins, Director, Graduate Admissions, 972-7215304, E-mail: bcollins@udallas.edu. Website: http://www.udallas.edu/cob/

University of Florida, Graduate School, Warrington College of Business Administration, Hough Graduate School of Business, Department of Management, Gainesville, FL 32611. Offers health care risk management (MS); international business (MA); management (MS, PhD). *Accreditation:* AACSB. *Program availability:* Online learning. *Degree requirements:* For master's, comprehensive exam, thesis. *Entrance requirements:* For master's, GMAT (minimum score of 465) or GRE General Test, minimum GPA of 3.0. Additional exam requirements/recommendations for international students: Required—TOEFL (minimum score 550 paper-based; 80 iBT), IELTS (minimum score 6). Electronic applications accepted. *Faculty research:* Job attitudes, personality and individual differences, organizational entry and exit, knowledge management, competitive dynamics.

University of Florida, Graduate School, Warrington College of Business Administration, Hough Graduate School of Business, Programs in Business Administration, Gainesville, FL 32611. Offers business administration (MA, MS, PhD); competitive strategy (MBA); finance (MBA); global management (MBA); Graham-Buffett security analysis (MBA); human resource management (MBA); information systems and operations management (MBA); international studies (MBA); management (MBA); real estate (MBA); JD/MBA; MBA/MS; MBA/PhD; MBA/Pharm D; MD/MBA. *Accreditation:* AACSB. *Program availability:* Part-time, evening/weekend, online learning. *Degree requirements:* For master's, capstone course. *Entrance requirements:* For master's and doctorate, GMAT (minimum score 465), minimum GPA of 3.0, interview. Additional exam requirements/recommendations for international students: Required—TOEFL (minimum score 550 paper-based; 80 iBT), IELTS (minimum score 6). Electronic applications accepted. *Faculty research:* Accounting, finance, insurance, management, real estate, urban analysis marketing.

University of Florida, Levin College of Law, Gainesville, FL 32611. Offers comparative law (LL M), including tropical conservation and development; environmental and land use law (LL M); international taxation (LL M); law (JD); taxation (LL M, SJD). *Accreditation:* ABA. *Entrance requirements:* For doctorate, LSAT (for JD). Electronic applications accepted. *Faculty research:* Environmental and land use law, taxation, dispute resolution, family law, Constitutional law.

University of Hawaii at Manoa, Office of Graduate Education, Shidler College of Business, Program in Business Administration, Honolulu, HI 96822. Offers Asian business studies (MBA); Chinese business studies (MBA); decision sciences (MBA); entrepreneurship (MBA); finance (MBA); finance and banking (MBA); human resources management (MBA); information management (MBA); information technology (MBA); international business (MBA); Japanese business studies (MBA); marketing (MBA); organizational behavior (MBA); organizational management (MBA); real estate (MBA); student-designed track (MBA). *Accreditation:* AACSB. *Program availability:* Part-time, evening/weekend. *Degree requirements:* For master's, thesis optional. *Entrance requirements:* For master's, GMAT, minimum GPA of 3.0. Additional exam requirements/recommendations for international students: Required—TOEFL (minimum score 600 paper-based; 100 iBT), IELTS (minimum score 7). *Expenses:* Contact institution.

University of Hawaii at Manoa, Office of Graduate Education, Shidler College of Business, Program in International Management, Honolulu, HI 96822. Offers Asian finance (PhD); global information technology management (PhD); international accounting (PhD); international marketing (PhD); international organization and strategy (PhD). *Program availability:* Part-time. *Degree requirements:* For doctorate, comprehensive exam, thesis/dissertation. *Entrance requirements:* For doctorate, GMAT or GRE General Test, minimum GPA of 3.0. Additional exam requirements/recommendations for international students: Required—TOEFL (minimum score 600 paper-based; 100 iBT), IELTS (minimum score 7). *Expenses:* Contact institution.

University of Houston–Downtown, Marilyn Davies College of Business, MBA Program, Houston, TX 77002. Offers accounting (MBA); finance (MBA); human resource management (MBA); international business (MBA); investment management (MBA); leadership (MBA); project management and process improvement (MBA); sales management and business development (MBA); supply chain management (MBA). *Accreditation:* AACSB. *Program availability:* Part-time, evening/weekend. *Entrance requirements:* For master's, GMAT, two letters of recommendation from professional references, personal statement, resume. Additional exam requirements/recommendations for international students: Required—TOEFL (minimum score 81 iBT). Electronic applications accepted. *Expenses:* Contact institution.

University of Houston–Victoria, School of Business Administration, Victoria, TX 77901-4450. Offers accounting (MBA); economic development and entrepreneurship (MS); finance (GMBA, MBA); general business (MBA); international business (MBA); management (GMBA, MBA); marketing (MBA). *Accreditation:* AACSB. *Program availability:* Part-time, evening/weekend, online learning. *Entrance requirements:* For master's, GMAT. Additional exam requirements/recommendations for international students: Required—TOEFL (minimum score 550 paper-based). Electronic applications accepted. *Expenses: Tuition, area resident:* Full-time $6154; part-time $3077 per semester. Tuition, state resident: full-time $6154; part-time $3077 per semester. Tuition, nonresident: full-time $13,624; part-time $6812 per semester. *International tuition:* $13,624 full-time. *Required fees:* $1405; $847 per semester. $423 per semester. Tuition and fees vary according to program. *Faculty research:* Economic development, marketing, finance.

University of Kentucky, Graduate School, Patterson School of Diplomacy and International Commerce, Lexington, KY 40506-0027. Offers MA. *Degree requirements:* For master's, one foreign language, comprehensive exam, statistics. *Entrance requirements:* For master's, GRE General Test, minimum undergraduate GPA of 3.0. Additional exam requirements/recommendations for international students: Required—TOEFL (minimum score 550 paper-based; 79 iBT). Electronic applications accepted. *Faculty research:* International relations, foreign and defense policy, cross-cultural negotiation, international science and technology, diplomacy, international economics and development, geopolitical modeling.

University of La Verne, College of Business and Public Management, Graduate Programs in Business Administration, La Verne, CA 91750-4443. Offers accounting (MBA, MBA-EP); finance (MBA, MBA-EP); health services management (MBA); information technology (MBA, MBA-EP); international business (MBA, MBA-EP); management and leadership (MBA, MBA-EP); marketing (MBA, MBA-EP); supply chain management (MBA, MBA-EP). *Program availability:* Part-time, evening/weekend. *Entrance requirements:* For master's, GMAT, MAT, or GRE, minimum undergraduate GPA of 3.0, 2 letters of recommendation, resume, statement of purpose. Additional exam requirements/recommendations for international students: Required—TOEFL (minimum score 550 paper-based; 85 iBT).

University of La Verne, Regional and Online Campuses, Graduate Programs, Inland Empire Campus, Ontario, CA 91730. Offers business administration (MBA, MBA-EP), including accounting (MBA), finance (MBA), health services management (MBA-EP), information technology (MBA-EP), international business (MBA), managed care (MBA), management and leadership (MBA-EP), marketing (MBA-EP), supply chain management (MBA); leadership and management (MS), including human resource management, nonprofit management, organizational development. *Program availability:* Part-time, evening/weekend. *Expenses:* Contact institution.

University of Lethbridge, School of Graduate Studies, Lethbridge, AB T1K 3M4, Canada. Offers addictions counseling (M Sc); agricultural biotechnology (M Sc); agricultural studies (M Sc, MA); anthropology (MA); archaeology (M Sc, MA); art (MA, MFA); biochemistry (M Sc); biological sciences (M Sc); biomolecular science (PhD); biosystems and biodiversity (PhD); Canadian studies (MA); chemistry (M Sc); computer science (M Sc); computer science and geographical information science (M Sc); counseling (MC); counseling psychology (M Ed); dramatic arts (MA); earth, space, and physical science (PhD); economics (MA); education (MA, PhD); educational leadership (M Ed); English (MA); environmental science (M Sc); evolution and behavior (PhD); exercise science (M Sc); French (MA); French/German (MA); French/Spanish (MA); general education (M Ed); geography (M Sc, MA); German (MA); health sciences (M Sc); individualized multidisciplinary (M Sc, MA); kinesiology (M Sc, MA); management (M Sc), including accounting, finance, human resource management and labor relations, information systems, international management, marketing, policy and strategy; mathematics (M Sc); music (M Mus, MA); Native American studies (MA); neuroscience (M Sc, PhD); new media (MA, MFA); nursing (M Sc, MN); philosophy (MA); physics (M Sc); political science (MA); psychology (M Sc, MA); religious studies (MA); sociology (MA); theatre and dramatic arts (MFA); theoretical and computational science (PhD); urban and regional studies (MA); women and gender studies (MA). *Program availability:* Part-time, evening/weekend. *Degree requirements:* For master's, thesis (for some programs); for doctorate, comprehensive exam, thesis/dissertation. *Entrance requirements:* For master's, GMAT (for M Sc in management), bachelor's degree in related field, minimum GPA of 3.0 during previous 20 graded semester courses, 2 years' teaching or related experience (M Ed); for doctorate, master's degree, minimum graduate GPA of 3.5. Additional exam requirements/recommendations for international students: Required—TOEFL (minimum score 580 paper-based; 93 iBT). Electronic applications accepted. *Faculty research:* Movement and brain plasticity, gibberellin physiology, photosynthesis, carbon cycling, molecular properties of main-group ring components.

University of Louisiana at Lafayette, BI Moody III College of Business Administration, Lafayette, LA 70504. Offers accounting (MS); business administration (MBA); entrepreneurship (MBA); finance (MBA); global management (MBA); health care administration (MBA); hospitality management (MBA); human resource management (MBA); project management (MBA); sales leadership (MBA). *Accreditation:* AACSB. *Program availability:* Part-time, evening/weekend. *Entrance requirements:* For master's, GRE General Test. Additional exam requirements/recommendations for international students: Required—TOEFL (minimum score 550 paper-based).

University of Louisville, Graduate School, College of Business, MBA Programs, Louisville, KY 40292-0001. Offers entrepreneurship (MBA); global business (MBA); health sector management (MBA). *Accreditation:* AACSB. *Program availability:* Part-time, evening/weekend, 100% online, blended/hybrid learning. *Students:* 227 full-time (82 women), 28 part-time (13 women); includes 58 minority (32 Black or African American, non-Hispanic/Latino; 1 American Indian or Alaska Native, non-Hispanic/Latino; 13 Asian, non-Hispanic/Latino; 9 Hispanic/Latino; 3 Two or more races, non-Hispanic/Latino), 34 international. Average age 32. 236 applicants, 69% accepted, 126 enrolled. In 2018, 102 master's awarded. *Degree requirements:* For master's, international learning experience. *Entrance requirements:* For master's, GMAT, 2 letters of reference, personal interview, resume, personal statement, college transcript(s). Additional exam requirements/recommendations for international students: Required—TOEFL (minimum score 83 iBT). *Application deadline:* For fall admission, 7/1 for domestic students; for spring admission, 12/1 for domestic students. Applications are processed on a rolling basis. Application fee: $65. *Expenses: Tuition, area resident:* Full-time $6500; part-time $723 per credit hour. Tuition, state resident: full-time $6500. Tuition, nonresident: full-time $13,557; part-time $1507 per credit hour. Tuition and fees vary according to course load and program. *Financial support:* In 2018–19, 105 students received support. Fellowships with full tuition reimbursements available, research assistantships with full tuition reimbursements available, health care benefits, and unspecified assistantships available. Financial award application deadline: 3/31; financial award applicants required to submit FAFSA. *Faculty research:* Entrepreneurship, venture capital, retailing/franchising, corporate governance and leadership, supply chain management. *Total annual research expenditures:* $859,000. *Unit head:* Dr. Todd Mooradian, Dean, 502-852-6443, Fax: 502-852-7557, E-mail: todd.mooradian@louisville.edu. *Application contact:* Susan E. Hildebrand, Program Director, 502-852-7257, Fax: 502-852-4901, E-mail: s.hildebrand@louisville.edu. Website: http://business.louisville.edu/mba

The University of Manchester, Alliance Manchester Business School, M15 6PB, United Kingdom. Offers accounting and finance (M Sc); business (M Ent); business analysis and strategic management (M Sc); business analytics: operational research and risk analysis (M Sc); business psychology (M Sc); corporate communications and reputation management (M Sc); finance (M Sc); finance and business economics (M Sc); human resource management and industrial relations (M Sc); innovation management and entrepreneurship (M Sc); international business and management (M Sc); international human resource management and comparative industrial relations (M Sc); management (M Sc); marketing (M Sc); operations, project and supply chain management (M Sc); organizational psychology (M Sc); quantitative finance (M Sc). *Entrance requirements:* For master's, UK 2:1 honours degree or overseas equivalent. Additional exam requirements/recommendations for international students: Required—TOEFL (minimum score 100 iBT), IELTS (minimum score 7), PTE. Electronic

applications accepted. *Faculty research:* Accounting and finance, management sciences and marketing, people management and organization, innovation management and policy, decision sciences.

University of Mary Hardin-Baylor, Graduate Studies in Business Administration, Belton, TX 76513. Offers accounting (MBA); information systems management (MBA); international business (MBA); management (MBA). *Program availability:* Part-time, evening/weekend. *Degree requirements:* For master's, comprehensive exam. *Entrance requirements:* For master's, minimum GPA of 3.0, interview. Additional exam requirements/recommendations for international students: Required—TOEFL (minimum score 60 iBT), IELTS (minimum score 4.5). Electronic applications accepted. *Faculty research:* Financial management, financial markets, supply chain management.

University of Massachusetts Boston, College of Management, Program in International Management, Boston, MA 02125-3393. Offers MS. *Faculty:* 17 full-time (7 women), 15 part-time/adjunct (7 women). *Students:* 1 part-time (0 women). Average age 33. 1 applicant, 100% accepted, 1 enrolled. In 2018, 3 master's awarded. *Expenses: Tuition, area resident:* Full-time $17,896. Tuition, state resident: full-time $17,896. Tuition, nonresident: full-time $34,932. *International tuition:* $34,932 full-time. *Required fees:* $355. *Unit head:* Dr. Alessia Contu, Chair, 617-287.6388, E-mail: alessia.contu@umb.edu. *Application contact:* Graduate Admissions Coordinator, 617-287-6400, Fax: 617-287-6236, E-mail: graduate.admissions@umb.edu.

University of Miami, Miami Business School, Coral Gables, FL 33146. Offers accounting (M Acc); business (PhD); business administration (MBA); business analytics (MSBA); economics (PhD); finance (MSF); health administration (MHA); international business (MIBS); real estate (MBA); taxation (MS Tax); JD/MBA; MD/MBA. *Accreditation:* AACSB; CAHME (one or more programs are accredited). *Program availability:* Part-time, evening/weekend, 100% online, blended/hybrid learning. *Faculty:* 155 full-time (47 women), 14 part-time/adjunct (5 women). *Students:* 1,083 full-time (469 women); includes 422 minority (79 Black or African American, non-Hispanic/Latino; 1 American Indian or Alaska Native, non-Hispanic/Latino; 43 Asian, non-Hispanic/Latino; 274 Hispanic/Latino; 3 Native Hawaiian or other Pacific Islander, non-Hispanic/Latino; 22 Two or more races, non-Hispanic/Latino), 282 international. Average age 30. 2,564 applicants, 38% accepted, 450 enrolled. In 2018, 558 master's, 5 doctorates awarded. Terminal master's awarded for partial completion of doctoral program. *Degree requirements:* For master's, comprehensive exam; for doctorate, comprehensive exam, thesis/dissertation. *Entrance requirements:* For master's, GMAT or GRE; for doctorate, GRE General Test. Additional exam requirements/recommendations for international students: Required—TOEFL (minimum score 94 iBT), IELTS (minimum score 7), TOEFL (minimum score 587 paper-based, 94 iBT) or IELTS (7). *Application deadline:* For fall admission, 6/30 priority date for domestic students, 5/30 priority date for international students; for spring admission, 10/31 priority date for domestic students, 9/30 priority date for international students. Applications are processed on a rolling basis. Application fee: $48. Electronic applications accepted. *Expenses:* Contact institution. *Financial support:* In 2018–19, 643 students received support, including 1 fellowship with full tuition reimbursement available (averaging $20,000 per year), 47 research assistantships with full and partial tuition reimbursements available (averaging $28,826 per year), 6 teaching assistantships with full and partial tuition reimbursements available (averaging $2,183 per year); career-related internships or fieldwork, Federal Work-Study, institutionally sponsored loans, scholarships/grants, and unspecified assistantships also available. Support available to part-time students. Financial award application deadline: 3/26; financial award applicants required to submit FAFSA. *Faculty research:* Behavioral finance; computational economics; consumer research; risk perception; consumer behavior; consumer choice research; behavioral decision theory; business analytics; point processes; longitudinal data analyses; international business; global business strategy, joint ventures, and alliances; emerging economies; global economic growth and development, money and financial markets, and computed dynamic models; health policy; innovative payment mechanisms. *Total annual research expenditures:* $703,773. *Unit head:* Dr. John Quelch, Dean, 305-284-6515, Fax: 305-284-6526, E-mail: jquelch@miami.edu. *Application contact:* Loubna Bouamane, Director of Graduate Business Recruiting and Admissions, 305-284-2510, Fax: 305-284-5905, E-mail: loubna@miami.edu.
Website: www.mbs.miami.edu

University of Michigan–Flint, School of Management, Program in Business Administration, Flint, MI 48502-1950. Offers accounting (MBA); computer information systems (MBA); finance (MBA, Post-Master's Certificate); general business (Graduate Certificate); general business administration (MBA); health care management (MBA); international business (MBA, Post-Master's Certificate); lean manufacturing (MBA); marketing (Post-Master's Certificate); marketing and innovation management (MBA); organizational leadership (MBA). *Program availability:* Part-time, evening/weekend, mixed mode format. *Faculty:* 30 full-time (4 women), 10 part-time/adjunct (2 women). *Students:* 24 full-time (14 women), 151 part-time (60 women); includes 45 minority (22 Black or African American, non-Hispanic/Latino; 3 American Indian or Alaska Native, non-Hispanic/Latino; 7 Asian, non-Hispanic/Latino; 9 Hispanic/Latino; 4 Two or more races, non-Hispanic/Latino), 19 international. Average age 36. 160 applicants, 75% accepted, 62 enrolled. In 2018, 50 master's, 1 other advanced degree awarded. *Entrance requirements:* For master's, bachelor's degree in arts, sciences, engineering, or business administration from regionally-accredited college or university; for other advanced degree, bachelor's degree in arts, sciences, engineering, or business administration from regionally-accredited college or university. college-level math, statistics, or quantitative course (for Graduate Certificate); MBA or equivalent degree from regionally-accredited college or university (for Post Master's Certificate). Additional exam requirements/recommendations for international students: Required—TOEFL (minimum score 84 iBT), IELTS (minimum score 6.5). *Application deadline:* For fall admission, 8/1 for domestic students, 5/1 for international students; for winter admission, 11/15 for domestic students, 9/1 for international students; for spring admission, 3/15 for domestic students, 1/1 for international students; for summer admission, 5/15 for domestic students. Applications are processed on a rolling basis. Application fee: $55. Electronic applications accepted. *Expenses:* Contact institution. *Financial support:* Federal Work-Study, scholarships/grants, and unspecified assistantships available. Support available to part-time students. Financial award application deadline: 3/1; financial award applicants required to submit FAFSA. *Unit head:* Dr. Scott Johnson, Dean, School of Management, 810-762-3164, Fax: 810-237-6685, E-mail: scotjohn@umflint.edu. *Application contact:* Matt Bohlen, Director of Graduate Admissions, 810-762-3171, E-mail: mbohlen@umflint.edu.
Website: http://www.umflint.edu/graduateprograms/business-administration-mba

University of New Brunswick Saint John, Faculty of Business, Saint John, NB E2L 4L5, Canada. Offers administration (MBA); electronic commerce (MBA); international business (MBA); natural resource management (MBA). *Program availability:* Part-time. *Entrance requirements:* For master's, GMAT (minimum score of 550) or GRE (minimum 54th percentile), minimum GPA of 3.0. Additional exam requirements/recommendations for international students: Required—TOEFL (minimum score 580 paper-based; 93 iBT), TWE (minimum score 4.5). Electronic applications accepted. *Expenses:* Contact institution. *Faculty research:* International business, project management, innovation and technology management; business use of Weblogs and podcasts to communicate; corporate governance; high-involvement work systems; international competitiveness; supply chain management and logistics.

University of New Haven, Graduate School, College of Business, Program in Business Administration, West Haven, CT 06516. Offers accounting (MBA); business administration (MBA); business intelligence (MBA); business policy and strategic leadership (MBA); finance (MBA), including chartered financial analyst; global marketing (MBA); human resources management (MBA); sport management (MBA). *Accreditation:* AACSB. *Program availability:* Part-time, evening/weekend. *Students:* 151 full-time (73 women), 70 part-time (30 women); includes 51 minority (23 Black or African American, non-Hispanic/Latino; 13 Asian, non-Hispanic/Latino; 14 Hispanic/Latino; 1 Two or more races, non-Hispanic/Latino), 74 international. Average age 28. 197 applicants, 91% accepted, 82 enrolled. In 2018, 70 master's awarded. *Entrance requirements:* For master's, GMAT. Additional exam requirements/recommendations for international students: Required—TOEFL (minimum score 80 iBT), IELTS, PTE. *Application deadline:* Applications are processed on a rolling basis. Application fee: $50. Electronic applications accepted. Application fee is waived when completed online. *Expenses: Tuition:* Full-time $16,470; part-time $915 per credit hour. *Required fees:* $230; $95 per term. *Financial support:* Research assistantships with partial tuition reimbursements, teaching assistantships with partial tuition reimbursements, career-related internships or fieldwork, Federal Work-Study, scholarships/grants, and unspecified assistantships available. Support available to part-time students. Financial award applicants required to submit FAFSA. *Unit head:* Darell Singleterry, Director, 203-932-7386, E-mail: dsingleterry@newhaven.edu. *Application contact:* Selina O'Toole, Senior Associate Director of Graduate Admissions, 203-932-7337, E-mail: SOToole@newhaven.edu.
Website: http://www.newhaven.edu/business/graduate-programs/mba/index.php

University of New Mexico, Anderson School of Management, Department of Finance, International, Technology and Entrepreneurship, Albuquerque, NM 87131-1221. Offers entrepreneurship (MBA); finance (MBA); international management (MBA); international management in Latin America (MBA); management of technology (MBA). *Program availability:* Part-time. *Faculty:* 15 full-time (1 woman), 8 part-time/adjunct (2 women). In 2018, 29 master's awarded. *Entrance requirements:* For master's, GMAT or GRE, minimum GPA of 3.0 on last 60 hours of coursework; bachelor's degree from regionally-accredited college or university in U.S. or its equivalent in another country. Additional exam requirements/recommendations for international students: Required—TOEFL (minimum score 550 paper-based; 79 iBT), IELTS (minimum score 6.5). *Application deadline:* For fall admission, 4/1 priority date for domestic and international students; for spring admission, 10/1 priority date for domestic and international students. Applications are processed on a rolling basis. Application fee: $50. Electronic applications accepted. *Expenses:* For MBA (not EMBA): $531.34 per credit hour resident, $1197.98 per credit hour non-resident. *Financial support:* In 2018–19, 17 students received support, including 9 fellowships (averaging $18,720 per year), 12 research assistantships with partial tuition reimbursements available (averaging $15,291 per year); career-related internships or fieldwork, Federal Work-Study, scholarships/grants, and unspecified assistantships also available. Support available to part-time students. Financial award application deadline: 6/1; financial award applicants required to submit FAFSA. *Faculty research:* Corporate finance, investments, management in Latin America, management of technology, entrepreneurship. *Unit head:* Dr. Raul Gouvea, Chair, 505-277-6471, E-mail: rauldg@unm.edu. *Application contact:* Lisa Beauchene, Student Recruitment Specialist, 505-277-6471, E-mail: andersonadvising@unm.edu.
Website: https://www.mgt.unm.edu/fite/default.asp?mm-faculty

University of North Alabama, College of Business, Florence, AL 35632-0001. Offers business administration (MBA), including accounting, enterprise resource planning systems, executive, finance, health care management, information systems, international business, project management. *Accreditation:* AACSB; ACBSP. *Program availability:* Part-time, 100% online, blended/hybrid learning. *Entrance requirements:* For master's, GMAT, GRE, minimum GPA of 2.75 in last 60 hours, 2.5 overall (on a 3.0 scale); 27 hours of course work in business and economics. Additional exam requirements/recommendations for international students: Required—TOEFL (minimum score 79 iBT), IELTS (minimum score 6), PTE (minimum score 54). Electronic applications accepted.

The University of North Carolina Wilmington, Cameron School of Business, Business Administration Program, Wilmington, NC 28403-3297. Offers business administration (MBA); business administration - international (MBA); business administration - professional (MBA). *Accreditation:* AACSB. *Program availability:* Part-time-only. *Degree requirements:* For master's, thesis (for some programs), written case analysis and oral presentation (for professional), oral competency (for international). *Entrance requirements:* For master's, GMAT (for some programs), 2 years of appropriate work experience (for professional option), baccalaureate degree in the area of business and/or economics or six business prerequisite courses (for international option), resume, 3 letters of recommendation. Additional exam requirements/recommendations for international students: Required—TOEFL (minimum score 550 paper-based; 79 iBT), IELTS (minimum score 6.5). Electronic applications accepted. *Expenses:* Contact institution.

University of North Florida, Coggin College of Business, MBA Program, Jacksonville, FL 32224. Offers accounting (MBA); construction management (MBA); e-commerce (MBA); economics (MBA); finance (MBA); human resource management (MBA); international business (MBA); logistics (MBA); management applications (MBA). *Accreditation:* AACSB. *Program availability:* Part-time, evening/weekend. *Faculty:* 40 full-time (14 women). *Students:* 368 part-time (158 women); includes 83 minority (30 Black or African American, non-Hispanic/Latino; 20 Asian, non-Hispanic/Latino; 16 Hispanic/Latino; 17 Two or more races, non-Hispanic/Latino), 28 international. Average age 30. 311 applicants, 51% accepted, 99 enrolled. In 2018, 151 master's awarded. *Entrance requirements:* For master's, GMAT or GRE, U.S. bachelor's degree from regionally-accredited university or equivalent foreign degree. Additional exam requirements/recommendations for international students: Required—TOEFL (minimum score 550 paper-based; 79 iBT). *Application deadline:* For fall admission, 8/1 priority date for domestic students, 5/1 for international students; for spring admission, 12/1 priority date for domestic students, 10/1 for international students; for summer admission, 4/29 priority date for domestic students, 2/1 for international students. Application fee: $30. *Expenses: Tuition, area resident:* Part-time $408.10 per credit hour. Tuition, state resident: part-time $408.10 per credit hour. Tuition, nonresident: part-time $932.61 per credit hour. *Required fees:* $111.81 per credit hour. Tuition and fees vary according to course load, campus/location and program. *Financial support:* In 2018–19, 41 students received support, including 1 research assistantship (averaging $2,143 per year); teaching assistantships, Federal Work-Study, and tuition waivers (partial) also available. Support available to part-time students. Financial award application deadline: 4/1; financial award applicants required to submit FAFSA. *Faculty research:* Performance measures, costing, and inventory issues in logistics and supply chain management; inter-organizational systems; international management and marketing practices; e-commerce; organizational learning and socialization processes. *Unit head:* Dr. Parvez Ahmed, Graduate Program Director, 904-620-1678, E-mail: pahmed@unf.edu. *Application contact:* Amy Bishop, MSM Advisor, 904-620-2575, Fax: 904-620-2832, E-mail: coggin.students@unf.edu.
Website: http://www.unf.edu/graduateschool/academics/programs/MBA.aspx

University of Pennsylvania, School of Arts and Sciences and Wharton School, Joseph H. Lauder Institute of Management and International Studies, Philadelphia, PA 19104. Offers international studies (MA); management and international studies (MBA); MBA/MA. Applications must be made concurrently and separately to the Wharton MBA program. *Degree requirements:* For master's, one foreign language, thesis. *Entrance requirements:* For master's, GMAT or GRE, advanced proficiency in a non-native language (Arabic, Chinese, French, German, Hindi, Japanese, Portuguese, Russian, or Spanish). Additional exam requirements/recommendations for international students: Required—TOEFL. Electronic applications accepted. *Expenses:* Contact institution. *Faculty research:* Finance, marketing, strategy, operations management, multinational management.

University of Phoenix–Bay Area Campus, School of Business, San Jose, CA 95134-1805. Offers accountancy (MS); accounting (MBA); business administration (MBA, DBA); energy management (MBA); global management (MBA); health care management (MBA); human resource management (MBA); human resources management (MM); management (MM); marketing (MBA); organizational leadership (DM); project management (MBA); public administration (MPA); technology management (MBA). *Accreditation:* ACBSP. *Program availability:* Evening/weekend, online learning. *Degree requirements:* For master's, thesis (for some programs). *Entrance requirements:* For master's, minimum undergraduate GPA of 3.0, 3 years of work experience. Additional exam requirements/recommendations for international students: Required—TOEFL (minimum score 550 paper-based; 79 iBT). Electronic applications accepted.

University of Phoenix–Central Valley Campus, School of Business, Fresno, CA 93720-1552. Offers accounting (MBA); business administration (MBA); global management (MBA); human resources management (MBA, MM); management (MM); marketing (MBA); public administration (MBA, MM). *Accreditation:* ACBSP.

University of Phoenix–Dallas Campus, School of Business, Dallas, TX 75251. Offers accounting (MBA); business administration (MBA); global management (MBA); human resources management (MBA, MM); management (MM); marketing (MBA); public administration (MBA, MM). *Accreditation:* ACBSP. *Program availability:* Evening/weekend, online learning. *Degree requirements:* For master's, thesis (for some programs). *Entrance requirements:* For master's, 3 years of work experience, minimum undergraduate GPA of 3.0. Additional exam requirements/recommendations for international students: Required—TOEFL (minimum score 550 paper-based; 79 iBT). Electronic applications accepted.

University of Phoenix–Hawaii Campus, School of Business, Honolulu, HI 96813-3800. Offers accounting (MBA); business administration (MBA); global management (MBA); human resources management (MBA, MM); management (MM); marketing (MBA); public administration (MBA, MM). *Accreditation:* ACBSP. *Program availability:* Evening/weekend. *Degree requirements:* For master's, thesis (for some programs). *Entrance requirements:* For master's, minimum undergraduate GPA of 3.0, 3 years of work experience. Additional exam requirements/recommendations for international students: Required—TOEFL (minimum score 550 paper-based; 79 iBT). Electronic applications accepted.

University of Phoenix–Houston Campus, School of Business, Houston, TX 77079-2004. Offers accounting (MBA); business administration (MBA); global management (MBA); human resources management (MBA, MM); management (MM); marketing (MBA); public administration (MBA, MM). *Accreditation:* ACBSP. *Program availability:* Evening/weekend, online learning. *Degree requirements:* For master's, thesis (for some programs). *Entrance requirements:* For master's, 3 years of work experience, minimum undergraduate GPA of 3.0. Additional exam requirements/recommendations for international students: Required—TOEFL (minimum score 550 paper-based; 79 iBT). Electronic applications accepted.

University of Phoenix–Las Vegas Campus, School of Business, Las Vegas, NV 89135. Offers accounting (MBA); business administration (MBA); global management (MBA); human resources management (MBA, MM); management (MM); marketing (MBA); public administration (MM). *Accreditation:* ACBSP. *Program availability:* Evening/weekend, online learning. *Degree requirements:* For master's, thesis (for some programs). *Entrance requirements:* For master's, minimum undergraduate GPA of 3.0, 3 years of work experience. Additional exam requirements/recommendations for international students: Required—TOEFL (minimum score 550 paper-based; 79 iBT). Electronic applications accepted.

University of Phoenix–Online Campus, School of Business, Phoenix, AZ 85034-7209. Offers accountancy (MS); accounting (MBA, Certificate); business administration (MBA); energy management (MBA); global management (MBA); health care management (MBA); human resource management (MBA, Certificate); human resources management (MM); management (MM); marketing (MBA, Certificate); project management (MBA, Certificate); public administration (MBA, MM); technology management (MBA). *Program availability:* Evening/weekend, online learning. *Entrance requirements:* Additional exam requirements/recommendations for international students: Required—TOEFL, TOEIC (Test of English as an International Communication), Berlitz Online English Proficiency Exam, PTE, or IELTS. Electronic applications accepted. *Expenses:* Contact institution.

University of Phoenix–Phoenix Campus, School of Business, Tempe, AZ 85282-2371. Offers accounting (MBA, MS, Certificate); business administration (MBA); energy management (MBA); global management (MBA); health care management (MBA); human resource management (MBA, Certificate); management (MM); marketing (MBA); project management (MBA); technology management (MBA). *Program availability:* Evening/weekend, online learning. *Entrance requirements:* Additional exam requirements/recommendations for international students: Required—TOEFL, TOEIC (Test of English as an International Communication), Berlitz Online English Proficiency Exam, PTE, or IELTS. Electronic applications accepted. *Expenses:* Contact institution.

University of Phoenix–Sacramento Valley Campus, School of Business, Sacramento, CA 95833-4334. Offers accounting (MBA); business administration (MBA); global management (MBA); human resources management (MBA, MM); management (MM); marketing (MBA); public administration (MBA, MM). *Accreditation:* ACBSP. *Program availability:* Evening/weekend. *Degree requirements:* For master's, thesis (for some programs). *Entrance requirements:* For master's, minimum undergraduate GPA of 3.0, 3 years work experience. Additional exam requirements/recommendations for international students: Required—TOEFL (minimum score 550 paper-based; 79 iBT). Electronic applications accepted.

University of Phoenix–San Antonio Campus, School of Business, San Antonio, TX 78230. Offers accounting (MBA); business administration (MBA); e-business (MBA); global management (MBA); human resources management (MBA, MM); management (MM); marketing (MBA); public administration (MBA, MM). *Accreditation:* ACBSP.

University of Phoenix–San Diego Campus, School of Business, San Diego, CA 92123. Offers accounting (MBA); business administration (MBA); global management (MBA); human resources management (MBA, MM); management (MM); marketing (MBA); public administration (MBA). *Accreditation:* ACBSP. *Program availability:* Evening/weekend. *Degree requirements:* For master's, thesis (for some programs). *Entrance requirements:* For master's, 3 years of work experience, minimum undergraduate GPA of 3.0. Additional exam requirements/recommendations for international students: Required—TOEFL (minimum score 550 paper-based; 79 iBT). Electronic applications accepted.

University of Pittsburgh, Katz Graduate School of Business, Augsburg Executive Fellows Program, Pittsburgh, PA 15260. Offers Certificate. Students nominated by Augsburg where they earn an MBA. *Entrance requirements:* Additional exam requirements/recommendations for international students: Required—TOEFL (minimum score 100 iBT) or IELTS (minimum score 7.0). Electronic applications accepted. *Expenses:* Contact institution. *Faculty research:* Accounting systems/financial reporting, corporate finance, shopper marketing/consumer behavior, management information systems, organizational behavior and entrepreneurship.

University of Pittsburgh, Katz Graduate School of Business, MBA/Master of International Business Dual Degree Program, Pittsburgh, PA 15260. Offers MBA/MIB. *Program availability:* Part-time, evening/weekend. *Entrance requirements:* Additional exam requirements/recommendations for international students: Required—TOEFL (minimum score 100 iBT) or IELTS (minimum score 7.0). Electronic applications accepted. *Faculty research:* Accounting systems/financial reporting, corporate finance, shopper marketing/consumer behavior, management information systems, organizational behavior and entrepreneurship.

University of Puerto Rico–Río Piedras, College of Business Administration, San Juan, PR 00931-3300. Offers accounting (MBA); finance (MBA, PhD); general business (MBA); human resources management (MBA); international trade and business (MBA, PhD); marketing (MBA); operations management (MBA); quantitative methods (MBA). *Accreditation:* AACSB. *Program availability:* Part-time. *Degree requirements:* For master's, comprehensive exam, thesis or alternative, research project. *Entrance requirements:* For master's, GMAT or PAEG, minimum GPA of 3.0, letter of recommendation; for doctorate, GMAT, PAEG, minimum GPA of 3.0, master degree. *Faculty research:* Management.

University of Regina, Faculty of Graduate Studies and Research, Kenneth Levene Graduate School of Business, Program in Business Administration, Regina, SK S4S 0A2, Canada. Offers business foundations (PGD); engineering management (MBA); executive business administration (EMBA); international business (MBA); leadership (M Admin); organizational leadership (Master's Certificate); project management (Master's Certificate); public safety management (MBA). *Program availability:* Part-time, evening/weekend. *Students:* 30 full-time (14 women), 9 part-time (5 women). Average age 30. In 2018, 23 master's awarded. *Degree requirements:* For master's, project (for some programs). workplacement for Co-op concentration. *Entrance requirements:* For master's, GMAT, 3 years of relevant work experience, four-year undergraduate degree, post secondary transcript, 2 letters of recommendation; for other advanced degree, GMAT (for PGD), four-year undergraduate degree and 2 years of relevant work experience (for Master's Certificate); 3 years' work experience (for PGD). Additional exam requirements/recommendations for international students: Required—TOEFL (minimum score 580 paper-based; 80 iBT), IELTS (minimum score 6.5), PTE (minimum score 59), other options are CAEL, MELAB, CANTEST or U of R ESI; GMAT is mandatory. *Application deadline:* For fall admission, 3/1 for domestic and international students; for winter admission, 7/1 for domestic and international students; for spring admission, 10/1 for domestic and international students; for summer admission, 10/1 for domestic and international students. Applications are processed on a rolling basis. Application fee: $100. Electronic applications accepted. *Expenses:* One academic year is 18,752. International students will pay additional 1,191.75 for International surcharge per semester. *Financial support:* Fellowships, research assistantships, teaching assistantships, career-related internships or fieldwork, Federal Work-Study, scholarships/grants, unspecified assistantships, and travel award and Graduate scholarship Base Funds available. Support available to part-time students. Financial award application deadline: 9/30. *Faculty research:* Business policy and strategy, production and operations management, human behavior in organizations, financial management, social issues in business. *Unit head:* Dr. Gina Grandy, Dean, 306-585-4435, Fax: 306-585-5361, E-mail: business.dean@uregina.ca. *Application contact:* Adrian Pitariu, Associate Dean, Research and Graduate Programs, 306-585-6294, Fax: 306-585-5361, E-mail: business.AD.levene@uregina.ca.
Website: http://www.uregina.ca/business/levene/

University of St. Thomas, Cameron School of Business, Houston, TX 77006-4696. Offers MBA, MCTM, MIB, MSA, MSF. *Program availability:* Part-time, evening/weekend. *Degree requirements:* For master's, capstone (for some programs), additional course requirements for those sitting for state accountancy exam. *Entrance requirements:* For master's, minimum GPA of 2.5, 3 letters of recommendation. Additional exam requirements/recommendations for international students: Required—TOEFL (minimum score 550 paper-based; 79 iBT), IELTS (minimum score 6.5), PTE (minimum score 53). Electronic applications accepted.

University of San Francisco, School of Law, Master of Law Programs, San Francisco, CA 94117. Offers intellectual property and technology law (LL M); international transactions and comparative law (LL M). *Program availability:* Part-time. *Students:* 11 full-time (5 women), 3 part-time (1 woman); includes 3 minority (2 Hispanic/Latino; 1 Two or more races, non-Hispanic/Latino), 10 international. Average age 32. 60 applicants, 92% accepted, 13 enrolled. In 2018, 14 master's awarded. *Entrance requirements:* For master's, law degree from U.S. or foreign school (intellectual property and technology law); law degree from foreign school (international transactions and comparative law). Additional exam requirements/recommendations for international students: Required—TOEFL (minimum score 90 paper-based; 90 iBT). *Application deadline:* For fall admission, 2/15 for domestic students. Applications are processed on a rolling basis. Application fee: $70. Electronic applications accepted. *Financial support:* In 2018–19, 28 students received support. Scholarships/grants available. Financial award applicants required to submit FAFSA. *Unit head:* Olivera Jovanovic, Director, 415-422-6900. *Application contact:* Margaret Mullane, Assistant Director, 415-422-6658, E-mail: masterlaws@usfca.edu.
Website: http://www.usfca.edu/law/llm/

University of San Francisco, School of Management, Master in Global Entrepreneurial Management Program, San Francisco, CA 94117. Offers MGEM. Program offered jointly with IQS in Barcelona, Spain and Fu Jen Catholic University in Taipei, Taiwan. *Students:* 10 full-time (4 women); includes 8 minority (1 Black or African American, non-Hispanic/Latino; 2 Asian, non-Hispanic/Latino; 4 Hispanic/Latino; 1 Native Hawaiian or other Pacific Islander, non-Hispanic/Latino). Average age 24. 78 applicants, 97% accepted, 39 enrolled. In 2018, 37 master's awarded. *Entrance requirements:* For master's, resume, transcripts from each college or university attended, two letters of recommendation, personal statement. Additional exam requirements/recommendations for international students: Required—TOEFL (minimum score 550 paper-based, 79 iBT), IELTS (minimum score 6), or PTE (minimum score 53). *Application deadline:* For fall admission, 5/15 for domestic students. Application fee: $55. Electronic applications accepted. *Expenses:* Contact institution. *Financial support:* Application deadline: 3/2; applicants required to submit FAFSA. *Unit head:* Dr. Gleb Nikitenko, Director, 415-422-2221, E-mail: management@usfca.edu. *Application contact:* Office of Graduate Recruiting and Admissions, 415-422-2221, E-mail: management@usfca.edu.
Website: http://www.usfca.edu/mgem

International Business

The University of Scranton, Kania School of Management, Program in Business Administration, Scranton, PA 18510. Offers accounting (MBA); finance (MBA); general business administration (MBA); health care management (MBA); international business (MBA); management information systems (MBA); marketing (MBA); operations management (MBA). *Accreditation:* AACSB. *Program availability:* Part-time, evening/weekend, 100% online. *Entrance requirements:* For master's, GMAT (for MBA). *Faculty research:* Financial markets, strategic impact of total quality management, internal accounting controls, consumer preference, information systems and the Internet.

University of South Carolina, The Graduate School, Darla Moore School of Business, International Business Administration Program, Columbia, SC 29208. Offers IMBA. *Degree requirements:* For master's, one foreign language, field consulting project/internship. *Entrance requirements:* For master's, GMAT or GRE, minimum two years of work experience. Additional exam requirements/recommendations for international students: Required—TOEFL (minimum score 100 iBT); Recommended—IELTS. Electronic applications accepted. *Expenses:* Contact institution.

The University of Tampa, Sykes College of Business, Tampa, FL 33606-1490. Offers accounting (MS); business analytics (MBA); cybersecurity (MBA, MS); entrepreneurship (MBA, MS); finance (MBA, MS); information systems management (MBA); innovation management (MBA); international business (MBA); marketing (MBA, MS); nonprofit management (MBA, Certificate). *Accreditation:* AACSB. *Program availability:* Part-time, evening/weekend. *Faculty:* 61 full-time (13 women), 11 part-time/adjunct (3 women). *Students:* 361 full-time (153 women), 122 part-time (52 women); includes 101 minority (31 Black or African American, non-Hispanic/Latino; 5 Asian, non-Hispanic/Latino; 57 Hispanic/Latino; 1 Native Hawaiian or other Pacific Islander, non-Hispanic/Latino; 7 Two or more races, non-Hispanic/Latino), 144 international. Average age 29. 1,079 applicants, 57% accepted, 263 enrolled. In 2018, 281 master's, 12 other advanced degrees awarded. *Degree requirements:* For master's, capstone. *Entrance requirements:* For master's, GMAT or GRE, official transcripts from all colleges and/or universities previously attended, resume, personal statement, letters of recommendation. Additional exam requirements/recommendations for international students: Required—TOEFL (minimum score 577 paper-based; 90 iBT), IELTS (minimum score 7.5). *Application deadline:* Applications are processed on a rolling basis. Application fee: $40. Electronic applications accepted. *Expenses:* Contact institution. *Financial support:* In 2018–19, 123 students received support. Career-related internships or fieldwork, scholarships/grants, and unspecified assistantships available. Financial award applicants required to submit FAFSA. *Faculty research:* Job market signaling, on-line shopping behaviors and social media, the Tampa Bay economy, digital literacy, entrepreneurship in small businesses. *Unit head:* Dr. Natasha F. Veltri, Associate Dean, 813-253-6289, E-mail: nveltri@ut.edu. *Application contact:* Ashley Russell, Staff Assistant, Admissions for Graduate and Continuing Studies, 813-253-6249, E-mail: arussell@ut.edu.
Website: http://www.ut.edu/business/

The University of Texas at Dallas, Naveen Jindal School of Management, Program in Organizations, Strategy and International Management, Richardson, TX 75080. Offers business administration (MBA); executive business administration (EMBA); global leadership (EMBA); healthcare leadership and management (MS); healthcare management (EMBA); innovation and entrepreneurship (MS); international management studies (MS, PhD); management science (MS, PhD); project management (EMBA); systems engineering and management (MS); MS/MBA. *Program availability:* Part-time, evening/weekend. *Faculty:* 19 full-time (6 women), 33 part-time/adjunct (12 women). *Students:* 587 full-time (237 women), 777 part-time (361 women); includes 456 minority (83 Black or African American, non-Hispanic/Latino; 226 Asian, non-Hispanic/Latino; 110 Hispanic/Latino; 37 Two or more races, non-Hispanic/Latino), 316 international. Average age 34. 1,452 applicants, 43% accepted, 376 enrolled. In 2018, 556 master's, 23 doctorates awarded. *Degree requirements:* For doctorate, thesis/dissertation. *Entrance requirements:* For master's and doctorate, GMAT. Additional exam requirements/recommendations for international students: Required—TOEFL (minimum score 550 paper-based). *Application deadline:* For fall admission, 7/15 for domestic students, 5/1 priority date for international students; for spring admission, 11/15 for domestic students, 9/1 priority date for international students. Applications are processed on a rolling basis. Application fee: $50 ($100 for international students). Electronic applications accepted. *Expenses: Tuition, area resident:* Full-time $13,458. Tuition, state resident: full-time $13,458. Tuition, nonresident: full-time $26,852. *International tuition:* $26,852 full-time. Tuition and fees vary according to course load. *Financial support:* In 2018–19, 102 students received support, including 24 research assistantships with partial tuition reimbursements available (averaging $37,400 per year), 83 teaching assistantships with partial tuition reimbursements available (averaging $25,119 per year); Federal Work-Study, institutionally sponsored loans, scholarships/grants, and unspecified assistantships also available. Support available to part-time students. Financial award application deadline: 4/30; financial award applicants required to submit FAFSA. *Faculty research:* International accounting, international trade and finance, economic development, international economics. *Unit head:* Dr. Seung-Hyun Lee, Area Coordinator, 972-883-6267, Fax: 972-883-5977, E-mail: sxl029100@utdallas.edu. *Application contact:* Dr. Seung-Hyun Lee, Area Coordinator, 972-883-6267, Fax: 972-883-5977, E-mail: sxl029100@utdallas.edu.
Website: http://jindal.utdallas.edu/osim/

The University of Texas at El Paso, Graduate School, College of Business Administration, Programs in Business Administration, El Paso, TX 79968-0001. Offers business administration (MBA, Certificate); international business (PhD). *Accreditation:* AACSB. *Program availability:* Part-time, evening/weekend, online learning. *Degree requirements:* For master's, comprehensive exam. *Entrance requirements:* For master's and doctorate, GMAT. Additional exam requirements/recommendations for international students: Required—TOEFL. Electronic applications accepted. *Faculty research:* Cross-border modeling, human resources, and outsourcing and manufacturing; global information technology transfer; international investments and risk management.

University of the West, Department of Business Administration, Rosemead, CA 91770. Offers business administration (EMBA); computer information systems (MBA); finance (MBA); international business (MBA); nonprofit organization management (MBA). *Program availability:* Part-time, evening/weekend. *Entrance requirements:* Additional exam requirements/recommendations for international students: Required—TOEFL.

The University of Toledo, College of Graduate Studies, College of Business and Innovation, Department of Marketing and International Business, Toledo, OH 43606-3390. Offers MBA. *Program availability:* Part-time, evening/weekend. *Entrance requirements:* For master's, GMAT, GRE, or LSAT, minimum GPA of 2.7 for all prior academic work, three letters of recommendation, statement of purpose, transcripts from all prior institutions attended. Additional exam requirements/recommendations for international students: Required—TOEFL (minimum score 550 paper-based; 80 iBT). Electronic applications accepted.

University of Virginia, McIntire School of Commerce, M.S. in Global Commerce, Charlottesville, VA 22903. Offers global commerce (MS); global strategic management (MS); international management (Certificate). ESADE Business School at Ramon Lull University (Barcelona, Spain); Lingnan (University) College at Sun Yat-sen University (Guangzhou, China). *Faculty:* 26 full-time (11 women). *Students:* 54 full-time (27 women); includes 2 minority (both Asian, non-Hispanic/Latino), 32 international. Average age 24. 150 applicants, 50% accepted, 54 enrolled. In 2018, 2 master's, 1 other advanced degree awarded. *Entrance requirements:* For master's, GMAT or GRE, Must have a bachelor's degree in business administration, marketing, finance, supply chain, management, or equivalent. Additional exam requirements/recommendations for international students: Required—TOEFL (minimum score 600 paper-based; 100 iBT), IELTS (minimum score 7.5). *Application deadline:* For fall admission, 10/15 for domestic students; for winter admission, 1/15 for domestic students; for spring admission, 3/15 for domestic students; for summer admission, 6/15 for domestic students. Applications are processed on a rolling basis. Application fee: $75. Electronic applications accepted. *Financial support:* Federal Work-Study, scholarships/grants, and unspecified assistantships available. Financial award application deadline: 3/15; financial award applicants required to submit FAFSA. *Faculty research:* Global strategic management, international finance, supply chain, business communication, marketing. *Unit head:* Amanda Cowen, Program Director, 434-243-8753, Fax: 434-924-7074, E-mail: msglobal@virginia.edu. *Application contact:* Emma Candelier, Assistant Dean of Graduate Recruiting, 434-243-4992, Fax: 434-924-4511, E-mail: ecandelier@virginia.edu.
Website: https://www.commerce.virginia.edu/ms-global

University of Washington, Graduate School, Interdisciplinary Program in Global Trade, Transportation and Logistics Studies, Seattle, WA 98195. Offers Certificate.

University of Washington, Graduate School, Michael G. Foster School of Business, Seattle, WA 98195-3200. Offers auditing and assurance (MP Acc); business administration (MBA, PhD); entrepreneurship (MS); executive business administration (MBA); global executive business administration (MBA); information systems (MSIS); supply chain management (MSSCM); taxation (MP Acc); technology management (MBA); JD/MBA; MBA/MAIS; MBA/MHA. *Accreditation:* AACSB. *Program availability:* Part-time, evening/weekend, blended/hybrid learning. Terminal master's awarded for partial completion of doctoral program. *Degree requirements:* For doctorate, comprehensive exam, thesis/dissertation. *Entrance requirements:* For master's and doctorate, GMAT, GRE. Additional exam requirements/recommendations for international students: Required—TOEFL (minimum score 600 paper-based; 100 iBT). Electronic applications accepted. *Expenses:* Contact institution. *Faculty research:* Finance, consumer behavior, marketing analytics, technology management, supply chain.

The University of Western Ontario, Ivey Business School, London, ON N6A 3K7, Canada. Offers business (EMBA, PhD); corporate strategy and leadership elective (MBA); entrepreneurship elective (MBA); finance elective (MBA); health sector stream (MBA); international management elective (MBA); marketing elective (MBA); JD/MBA. *Degree requirements:* For master's, thesis (for some programs); for doctorate, thesis/dissertation. *Entrance requirements:* For master's, GMAT, 2 years of full-time work experience, interview. Additional exam requirements/recommendations for international students: Required—TOEFL (minimum score 100 iBT) or IELTS (minimium score 6). Electronic applications accepted. *Faculty research:* Strategy, organizational behavior, international business, finance, operations management.

University of Wisconsin–Oshkosh, Graduate Studies, College of Business, Program in Global Business Administration, Oshkosh, WI 54901. Offers GMBA. *Degree requirements:* For master's, integrative seminar, study abroad. *Entrance requirements:* For master's, GMAT, GRE, letters of recommendation. Additional exam requirements/recommendations for international students: Required—TOEFL (minimum score 79 iBT).

Vancouver Island University, Master of Business Administration Program, Nanaimo, BC V9R 5S5, Canada. Offers international business (MBA), including finance, marketing. Program offered jointly with University of Hertfordshire. *Accreditation:* ACBSP. *Program availability:* Part-time. *Degree requirements:* For master's, thesis. *Entrance requirements:* Additional exam requirements/recommendations for international students: Required—TOEFL (minimum score 88 iBT), IELTS (minimum score 6.5). Electronic applications accepted. *Expenses:* Contact institution. *Faculty research:* Tourism development, entrepreneurship, organizational development, strategic planning, international business strategy, intercultural team work.

Villanova University, Villanova School of Business, MBA - The Fast Track Program, Villanova, PA 19085. Offers finance (MBA); healthcare (MBA); international business (MBA); strategic management (MBA). *Accreditation:* AACSB. *Program availability:* Part-time, evening/weekend. *Faculty:* 101 full-time (38 women), 36 part-time/adjunct (9 women). *Students:* 111 part-time (47 women); includes 20 minority (3 Black or African American, non-Hispanic/Latino; 7 Asian, non-Hispanic/Latino; 9 Hispanic/Latino; 1 Two or more races, non-Hispanic/Latino), 4 international. Average age 30. 45 applicants, 80% accepted, 26 enrolled. In 2018, 55 master's awarded. *Degree requirements:* For master's, minimum GPA of 3.0. *Entrance requirements:* For master's, GMAT or GRE, Application, official transcripts, 2 letters of recommendation, resume, 2 essays. Additional exam requirements/recommendations for international students: Required—TOEFL (minimum score 550 paper-based; 100 iBT). *Application deadline:* For fall admission, 7/31 for domestic and international students. Applications are processed on a rolling basis. Application fee: $65. Electronic applications accepted. *Expenses:* Contact institution. *Financial support:* Scholarships/grants available. Financial award application deadline: 6/30; financial award applicants required to submit FAFSA. *Faculty research:* Real Estate, Business Analytics, Global Leadership, Marketing and Consumer Insights, Church management. *Unit head:* Dr. Joyce E. A. Russell, Dean of Villanova School of Business, 610-519-6082, Fax: 610-519-6273, E-mail: joyce.russell@villanova.edu. *Application contact:* Daniel Guertin, Assistant Director, Recruitment, 610-519-8031, Fax: 610-519-6273, E-mail: daniel.guertin@villanova.edu.
Website: http://www1.villanova.edu/villanova/business/graduate/mba.html

Villanova University, Villanova School of Business, MBA - The Flex Track Program, Villanova, PA 19085. Offers healthcare (MBA); international business (MBA); marketing (MBA); real estate (MBA); strategic management (MBA); JD/MBA. *Accreditation:* AACSB. *Program availability:* Part-time, evening/weekend, online learning. *Faculty:* 101 full-time (38 women), 36 part-time/adjunct (9 women). *Students:* 13 full-time (5 women), 427 part-time (157 women); includes 74 minority (12 Black or African American, non-Hispanic/Latino; 29 Asian, non-Hispanic/Latino; 23 Hispanic/Latino; 10 Two or more races, non-Hispanic/Latino), 12 international. Average age 32. 156 applicants, 92% accepted, 139 enrolled. In 2018, 124 master's awarded. *Degree requirements:* For master's, minimum GPA of 3.0. *Entrance requirements:* For master's, GMAT or GRE, Application, official transcripts, 2 letters of recommendation, resume, 2 essays. Additional exam requirements/recommendations for international students: Required—TOEFL (minimum score 550 paper-based; 100 iBT). *Application deadline:* For fall admission, 7/31 for domestic and international students; for spring admission, 11/30 for domestic and international students; for summer admission, 4/30 for domestic and international students. Applications are processed on a rolling basis. Application fee: $65. Electronic applications accepted. *Expenses:* Contact institution. *Financial support:* Research assistantships and scholarships/grants available. Financial award application deadline: 6/30; financial award applicants required to submit FAFSA. *Faculty research:* Real Estate, Business Analytics, Global Leadership, Marketing and Consumer Insights, Church management. *Unit head:* Dr. Joyce E. A. Russell, Dean of Villanova School of

Business, 610-519-6082, Fax: 610-519-6273, E-mail: joyce.russell@villanova.edu. *Application contact:* Daniel Guertin, Assistant Director, Recruitment, 610-519-8031, Fax: 610-519-6273, E-mail: daniel.guertin@villanova.edu.
Website: http://www1.villanova.edu/villanova/business/graduate/mba.html

Virginia International University, School of Business, Fairfax, VA 22030. Offers accounting (MBA, MS); entrepreneurship (MBA); executive management (Graduate Certificate); global logistics (MBA); health care management (MBA); hospitality and tourism management (MBA); human resources management (MBA); international business management (MBA); international finance (MBA); marketing management (MBA); mass media and public relations (MBA); project management (MBA, MS). *Program availability:* Part-time, online learning. *Entrance requirements:* For master's and Graduate Certificate, bachelor's degree. Additional exam requirements/recommendations for international students: Required—TOEFL (minimum score 550 paper-based; 80 iBT), IELTS (minimum score 6). Electronic applications accepted.

Viterbo University, Master of Business Administration Program, La Crosse, WI 54601-4797. Offers general business administration (MBA); health care management (MBA); international business (MBA); leadership (MBA); project management (MBA). *Accreditation:* ACBSP. *Program availability:* Part-time, evening/weekend. *Degree requirements:* For master's, 34 semester credits. *Entrance requirements:* For master's, bachelor's degree, transcripts, minimum undergraduate cumulative GPA of 3.0, 2 letters of reference, 3-5 page essay. Additional exam requirements/recommendations for international students: Recommended—TOEFL (minimum score 550 paper-based). Electronic applications accepted. *Expenses:* Contact institution.

Walden University, Graduate Programs, School of Management, Minneapolis, MN 55401. Offers accounting (MBA, MS, DBA), including accounting for the professional (MS), accounting with CPA emphasis (MS), self-designed (MS); advanced project management (Graduate Certificate); applied project management (Graduate Certificate); auditing (Graduate Certificate); bridge to business administration (Post-Doctoral Certificate); bridge to management (Post-Doctoral Certificate); business management (Graduate Certificate); communication (MBA); corporate finance (MBA); digital marketing (Graduate Certificate); entrepreneurship (DBA); entrepreneurship and small business (MBA); finance (MS, DBA), including finance for the professional (MS), finance with CFA/investment (MS), finance with CPA emphasis (MS); global supply chain management (DBA); healthcare management (MBA, DBA); human resource management (MBA, MS, Graduate Certificate), including functional human resource management (MS), general program (MS), integrating functional and strategic human resource management (MS), organizational strategy (MS); human resources management (DBA); information systems management (DBA); international business (MBA, DBA); leadership (MBA, MS, DBA, Graduate Certificate), including general program (MS), human resource leadership (MS), leader development (MS), self-designed (MS); management (MS, PhD), including communications (MS), finance (PhD), general program (MS), healthcare management (MS), human resource management (MS), human resources management (PhD), information systems management (PhD), international business (MS), leadership (MS), leadership and organizational change (PhD), marketing (MS), project management (MS), strategy and operations (MS); managerial accounting (Graduate Certificate); marketing (MBA, MS, DBA); project management (MBA, MS, DBA); self-designed (MBA, DBA); social impact management (DBA); technology entrepreneurship (DBA). *Accreditation:* ACBSP. *Program availability:* Part-time, evening/weekend, online only, 100% online. *Degree requirements:* For master's, thesis (for some programs), residency (for EMBA); for doctorate, thesis/dissertation (for some programs), residency. *Entrance requirements:* For master's, bachelor's degree or higher; minimum GPA of 2.5; official transcripts; goal statement (for some programs); access to computer and Internet; for doctorate, master's degree or higher; three years of related professional or academic experience (preferred); minimum GPA of 3.0; goal statement and current resume (for select programs); official transcripts; access to computer and Internet; for other advanced degree, relevant work experience; access to computer and Internet. Additional exam requirements/recommendations for international students: Required—TOEFL (minimum score 550 paper-based, 79 iBT), IELTS (minimum score 6.5), Michigan English Language Assessment Battery (minimum score 82), or PTE (minimum score 53). Electronic applications accepted.

Walsh College of Accountancy and Business Administration, Graduate Programs, Program in Management, Troy, MI 48083. Offers human resources management (MS); international business (MS); strategic management (MS). *Program availability:* Part-time, evening/weekend, 100% online, blended/hybrid learning. *Faculty:* 8 full-time (4 women), 7 part-time/adjunct (4 women). *Students:* 1 (woman) full-time, 38 part-time (28 women); includes 15 minority (12 Black or African American, non-Hispanic/Latino; 1 Asian, non-Hispanic/Latino; 2 Hispanic/Latino), 1 international. Average age 37. 19 applicants, 84% accepted, 7 enrolled. In 2018, 17 master's awarded. *Entrance requirements:* For master's, minimum overall cumulative GPA of 2.750 from all colleges previously attended. Additional exam requirements/recommendations for international students: Required—TOEFL (minimum score 550 paper-based, 79-80 internet based), IELTS (6.5), Michigan Test of English Language Proficiency, or MTELP (80). *Application deadline:* Applications are processed on a rolling basis. Application fee: $35. Electronic applications accepted. *Expenses:* $785 per credit hour plus $175 student support fee per semester. International students pay $785 per credit hour plus $175 student support fee and $275 international student fee per semester. *Financial support:* In 2018–19, 3 students received support. Scholarships/grants and Tuition Exchange Program available. Financial award application deadline: 6/30; financial award applicants required to submit FAFSA. *Faculty research:* Strategy practice and process, management learning and decision-making, human capital development, global leadership and citizenship, use of systems and complexity theory and management practice. *Unit head:* Dr. Ann Saurbier, Chair, Management, 248-823-1635, Fax: 248-689-0920, E-mail: asaurbie@walshcollege.edu. *Application contact:* Karen Mahaffy, Executive Director, Admissions and Enrollment Services, 248-823-1610, Fax: 248-823-1611, E-mail: kmahaffy@walshcollege.edu.

Warner University, School of Business, Lake Wales, FL 33859. Offers accounting (MBA); business administration (MBA); human resource management (MBA); international business (MBA); management (MSMC). *Program availability:* Part-time, evening/weekend, online learning. *Degree requirements:* For master's, comprehensive exam, thesis. *Entrance requirements:* For master's, minimum GPA of 3.0, 2 letters of recommendation. Additional exam requirements/recommendations for international students: Required—TOEFL. Electronic applications accepted.

Wayland Baptist University, Graduate Programs, Programs in Business Administration/Management, Plainview, TX 79072-6998. Offers accounting (MBA); general business (MBA); health care administration (MAM, MBA); human resource management (MAM, MBA); international management (MBA); management (MBA, D Mgt); management information systems (MBA); organization management (MAM); project management (MBA). *Program availability:* Part-time, evening/weekend, online learning. *Degree requirements:* For master's, capstone course. *Entrance requirements:* For master's, GMAT, GRE or MAT. Additional exam requirements/recommendations for international students: Required—TOEFL (minimum score 500 paper-based; 61 iBT). Electronic applications accepted.

Webber International University, Graduate School of Business, Babson Park, FL 33827. Offers accounting (MBA); business (MBA); criminal justice management (MBA); international business (MBA); sport business management (MBA). *Program availability:* Part-time, evening/weekend, 100% online, blended/hybrid learning. *Faculty:* 11 full-time (5 women), 1 part-time/adjunct (0 women). *Students:* 69 full-time (34 women), 11 part-time (5 women); includes 26 minority (17 Black or African American, non-Hispanic/Latino; 1 Asian, non-Hispanic/Latino; 8 Hispanic/Latino), 10 international. Average age 24. 64 applicants, 61% accepted, 32 enrolled. In 2018, 17 master's awarded. *Degree requirements:* For master's, International Learning Experience required for the master in International Business, other majors have a practicum project. *Entrance requirements:* For master's, three recommendation letters, resume, essay, official transcripts from all colleges and universities attended. Additional exam requirements/recommendations for international students: Recommended—TOEFL (minimum score 500 paper-based; 61 iBT), IELTS (minimum score 6). *Application deadline:* For fall admission, 8/1 for domestic students, 6/1 for international students; for spring admission, 1/1 for domestic students. Applications are processed on a rolling basis. Application fee: $0. Electronic applications accepted. *Financial support:* In 2018–19, 11 students received support. Scholarships/grants and unspecified assistantships available. Financial award application deadline: 8/1; financial award applicants required to submit FAFSA. *Unit head:* Dr. Nikos Orphanoudakis, Dean, 863-638-2910, Fax: 863-638-1591, E-mail: orphanoudakisn@webber.edu. *Application contact:* Lacy Edwards, Admissions Counselor and MBA Coordinator, 863-638-2910, Fax: 863-638-1591, E-mail: admissions@webber.edu.
Website: www.webber.edu

Webster University, George Herbert Walker School of Business and Technology, Department of Business, St. Louis, MO 63119-3194. Offers business and organizational security management (MBA); decision support systems (MBA); environmental management (MBA); finance (MBA, MS); forensic accounting (MS); gerontology (MBA); human resources development (MBA); human resources management (MBA); information technology management (MBA); international business (MA, MBA); international relations (MBA); management and leadership (MBA); marketing (MBA); media communications (MBA); procurement and acquisitions management (MBA); Web services (MBA). *Accreditation:* ACBSP. *Program availability:* Part-time, evening/weekend, online learning. *Degree requirements:* For master's, comprehensive exam (for some programs), thesis (for some programs). *Entrance requirements:* Additional exam requirements/recommendations for international students: Required—TOEFL. *Expenses: Tuition:* Full-time $22,500; part-time $750 per credit hour. Tuition and fees vary according to degree level, campus/location and program.

Wilkes University, College of Graduate and Professional Studies, Jay S. Sidhu School of Business and Leadership, Wilkes-Barre, PA 18766-0002. Offers accounting (MBA); global business (MBA); human resource management (MBA); international business (MBA); leadership (MBA); management (MBA); operations management (MBA); organizational leadership and development (MBA). *Accreditation:* ACBSP. *Program availability:* Part-time, evening/weekend. *Students:* 16 full-time (9 women), 64 part-time (33 women); includes 11 minority (3 Black or African American, non-Hispanic/Latino; 3 Asian, non-Hispanic/Latino; 3 Hispanic/Latino; 2 Two or more races, non-Hispanic/Latino), 7 international. Average age 30. In 2018, 49 master's awarded. *Entrance requirements:* For master's, GMAT. Additional exam requirements/recommendations for international students: Required—TOEFL (minimum score 550 paper-based; 79 iBT). *Application deadline:* Applications are processed on a rolling basis. Application fee: $45 ($65 for international students). Electronic applications accepted. *Expenses:* Contact institution. *Financial support:* Unspecified assistantships available. Financial award application deadline: 3/1; financial award applicants required to submit FAFSA. *Unit head:* Dr. Abel Adekola, Dean, 570-408-4701, Fax: 570-408-7846, E-mail: abel.adekola@wilkes.edu. *Application contact:* Kristin Donati, Associate Director of Graduate Admissions, 570-408-3338, Fax: 570-408-7846, E-mail: kristin.donati@wilkes.edu.
Website: http://www.wilkes.edu/academics/colleges/sidhu-school-of-business-leadership/index.aspx

Xavier University, Williams College of Business, Master of Business Administration Program, Cincinnati, OH 45207. Offers business administration (Exec MBA, MBA); business intelligence (MBA); finance (MBA); health industry (MBA); international business (MBA); marketing (MBA); values-based leadership (MBA); MBA/MHSA; MSN/MBA. *Accreditation:* AACSB. *Program availability:* Part-time, evening/weekend. *Degree requirements:* For master's, capstone course. *Entrance requirements:* For master's, GMAT or GRE, official transcript; resume. Additional exam requirements/recommendations for international students: Required—TOEFL (minimum score 550 paper-based; 79 iBT). Electronic applications accepted. Application fee is waived when completed online. *Expenses:* Contact institution.

York University, Faculty of Graduate Studies, Schulich School of Business, Toronto, ON M3J 1P3, Canada. Offers accounting (M Acc); administration (PhD); business (MBA); business analytics (MBA); finance (MF); international business (IMBA); MBA/JD; MBA/MA; MBA/MFA. *Program availability:* Part-time, evening/weekend. *Degree requirements:* For master's, advanced proficiency in a second language, work term (IMBA); for doctorate, comprehensive exam, thesis/dissertation. *Entrance requirements:* For master's, GMAT or GRE, minimum GPA of 3.0 (3.3 for MF, MBA in business analytics, and IMBA); for doctorate, GMAT or GRE, minimum GPA of 3.3. Additional exam requirements/recommendations for international students: Required—TOEFL (minimum score 600 paper-based; 100 iBT), IELTS (minimum score 7), York English Language Test (minimum score 1); PearsonVUE (minimum score 64). Electronic applications accepted. *Faculty research:* Accounting, finance, marketing, operations management and information systems, organizational studies, strategic management.

Section 12
Management Information Systems

This section contains a directory of institutions offering graduate work in management information systems. Additional information about programs listed in the directory but not augmented by an in-depth entry may be obtained by writing directly to the dean of a graduate school or chair of a department at the address given in the directory.

For programs offering related work, see also in this book *Business Administration and Management*. In another guide in this series:

Graduate Programs in Engineering & Applied Sciences
See *Computer Science and Information Technology* and *Management of Engineering and Technology*

CONTENTS

Program Directory

Management Information Systems

Adelphi University, Robert B. Willumstad School of Business, MBA Program, Garden City, NY 11530-0701. Offers accounting (MBA); finance (MBA); health services administration (MBA); human resource management (MBA); management (MBA); management information systems (MBA); marketing (MBA); sport management (MBA). *Accreditation:* AACSB. *Program availability:* Part-time, evening/weekend. *Students:* 343 full-time (132 women), 101 part-time (56 women); includes 75 minority (22 Black or African American, non-Hispanic/Latino; 2 American Indian or Alaska Native, non-Hispanic/Latino; 20 Asian, non-Hispanic/Latino; 23 Hispanic/Latino; 1 Native Hawaiian or other Pacific Islander, non-Hispanic/Latino; 7 Two or more races, non-Hispanic/Latino), 275 international. Average age 29. 389 applicants, 59% accepted, 187 enrolled. In 2018, 171 master's awarded. *Entrance requirements:* For master's, GMAT, official transcripts, bachelor's degree, 500 word essay, 2 letters of recommendation, resume. Additional exam requirements/recommendations for international students: Required—TOEFL (minimum score 550 paper-based; 80 iBT), IELTS (minimum score 6.5). *Application deadline:* For fall admission, 4/1 for international students; for spring admission, 11/1 for international students. Applications are processed on a rolling basis. Application fee: $50. Electronic applications accepted. *Financial support:* Research assistantships with partial tuition reimbursements, career-related internships or fieldwork, Federal Work-Study, institutionally sponsored loans, scholarships/grants, tuition waivers (partial), and unspecified assistantships available. Financial award application deadline: 3/1; financial award applicants required to submit FAFSA. *Faculty research:* Supply chain management, distribution channels, productivity benchmark analysis, data envelopment analysis, financial portfolio analysis. *Unit head:* Britt'ny Brown, Director of Graduate Programs, 516-877-4605. *Application contact:* Britt'ny Brown, Director of Graduate Programs, 516-877-4605.
Website: https://business.adelphi.edu/

Air Force Institute of Technology, Graduate School of Engineering and Management, Department of Systems and Engineering Management, Dayton, OH 45433-7765. Offers cost analysis (MS); environmental and engineering management (MS); environmental engineering science (MS); information resource/systems management (MS). *Accreditation:* ABET. *Program availability:* Part-time. *Degree requirements:* For master's, thesis. *Entrance requirements:* For master's, GRE, GMAT, minimum GPA of 3.0.

American Business & Technology University, Programs in Business Administration, Saint Joseph, MO 64506. Offers business administration (MBA); financial management (MBA); global business management (MBA); information systems management (MBA); marketing and social media (MBA); project and operations management (MBA); public accounting (MBA). *Program availability:* Online learning.

American InterContinental University Atlanta, Program in Information Technology, Atlanta, GA 30328. Offers MIT. *Program availability:* Part-time, evening/weekend. *Degree requirements:* For master's, technical proficiency demonstration. *Entrance requirements:* For master's, Computer Programmer Aptitude Battery Exam, interview. Electronic applications accepted. *Faculty research:* Operating systems, security issues, networks and routing, computer hardware.

American Sentinel University, Graduate Programs, Aurora, CO 80014. Offers business administration (MBA); business intelligence (MS); computer science (MSCS); health information management (MS); healthcare (MBA); information systems (MSIS); nursing (MSN). *Program availability:* Part-time, evening/weekend, online learning. *Entrance requirements:* Additional exam requirements/recommendations for international students: Required—TOEFL (minimum score 600 paper-based). Electronic applications accepted.

American University, Kogod School of Business, Department of Information Technology and Analytics, Washington, DC 20016-8044. Offers analytics (MS). *Faculty:* 14 full-time (3 women), 17 part-time/adjunct (5 women). *Students:* 97 full-time (52 women), 111 part-time (46 women); includes 74 minority (33 Black or African American, non-Hispanic/Latino; 1 American Indian or Alaska Native, non-Hispanic/Latino; 19 Asian, non-Hispanic/Latino; 14 Hispanic/Latino; 7 Two or more races, non-Hispanic/Latino), 48 international. Average age 30. 254 applicants, 72% accepted, 88 enrolled. In 2018, 57 master's awarded. *Degree requirements:* For master's, comprehensive exam (for some programs). *Entrance requirements:* For master's, GMAT or GRE; Please see website: https://www.american.edu/kogod/. Additional exam requirements/recommendations for international students: Required—TOEFL (minimum score 100 iBT). Application fee: $100. Electronic applications accepted. *Expenses:* Contact institution. *Financial support:* Scholarships/grants available. Financial award applicants required to submit FAFSA. *Unit head:* Edward Wasil, Chair, 202-885-1900, E-mail: kogodgrad@american.edu. *Application contact:* Jason Garner, Director of Admissions, 202-885-1926, E-mail: jgarner@american.edu.

American University, School of International Service, Washington, DC 20016-8071. Offers comparative and regional studies (Certificate); cross-cultural communication (Certificate); development management (MS); ethics, peace, and global affairs (MA); European studies (Certificate); global environmental policy (MA, Certificate); global information technology (Certificate); global media (MA); international affairs (MA), including comparative and regional studies, global governance, politics, and security, international economic relations, natural resources and sustainable development, U.S. foreign policy and national security; international arts management (Certificate); international communication (MA, Certificate); international development (MA); international economic policy (Certificate); international economic relations (Certificate); international economics (MA); international peace and conflict resolution (MA, Certificate); international politics (Certificate); international relations (MA, PhD); international service (MIS); peacebuilding (Certificate); social enterprise (MA); the Americas (Certificate); United States foreign policy (Certificate); JD/MA. *Program availability:* Part-time, evening/weekend, 100% online, blended/hybrid learning. *Faculty:* 115 full-time (48 women), 50 part-time/adjunct (22 women). *Students:* 496 full-time (320 women), 477 part-time (242 women); includes 410 minority (83 Black or African American, non-Hispanic/Latino; 2 American Indian or Alaska Native, non-Hispanic/Latino; 51 Asian, non-Hispanic/Latino; 242 Hispanic/Latino; 32 Two or more races, non-Hispanic/Latino), 93 international. Average age 30. 1,280 applicants, 82% accepted, 356 enrolled. In 2018, 400 master's, 3 doctorates, 8 other advanced degrees awarded. Terminal master's awarded for partial completion of doctoral program. *Degree requirements:* For master's, one foreign language, comprehensive exam, thesis or alternative; for doctorate, one foreign language, comprehensive exam, thesis/dissertation. *Entrance requirements:* For master's, Please visit the website for details: https://www.american.edu/sis/admissions/, transcripts, resume, 2 letters of recommendation, statement of purpose; for doctorate, GRE, transcripts, resume, 3 letters of recommendation, statement of purpose. Additional exam requirements/recommendations for international students: Required—TOEFL. Application fee: $55.

Electronic applications accepted. *Expenses:* Contact institution. *Financial support:* Research assistantships, teaching assistantships, institutionally sponsored loans, scholarships/grants, and unspecified assistantships available. Financial award applicants required to submit FAFSA. *Unit head:* Christine BN Chin, 202-885-1600, E-mail: sisgrad@american.edu. *Application contact:* Jia Jiang, Director, Graduate Enrollment Management, 202-885-1689, E-mail: jiang@american.edu.
Website: http://www.american.edu/sis/

American University of Armenia, Graduate Programs, Yerevan, Armenia. Offers business administration (MBA); computer and information science (MS), including business management, design and manufacturing, energy (ME, MS), industrial engineering and systems management; economics (MS); industrial engineering and systems management (ME), including business, computer aided design/manufacturing, energy (ME, MS), information technology; law (LL M); political science and international affairs (MPSIA); public health (MPH); teaching English as a foreign language (MA). *Program availability:* Part-time, evening/weekend. *Degree requirements:* For master's, thesis (for some programs), capstone/project. *Entrance requirements:* For master's, GRE, GMAT, or LSAT. Additional exam requirements/recommendations for international students: Recommended—TOEFL (minimum score 79 iBT), IELTS (minimum score 6.5). *Faculty research:* Microfinance, finance (rural/development, international, corporate), firm life cycle theory, TESOL, language proficiency testing, public policy, administrative law, economic development, cryptography, artificial intelligence, energy efficiency/renewable energy, computer-aided design/manufacturing, health financing, tuberculosis control, mother/child health, preventive ophthalmology, post-earthquake psychopathological investigations, tobacco control, environmental health risk assessments.

Argosy University, Atlanta, College of Business, Atlanta, GA 30328. Offers accounting (DBA); corporate compliance (MBA); customized professional concentration (MBA, DBA); finance (MBA); healthcare administration (MBA); information systems (DBA); information systems management (MBA); international business (MBA, DBA); management (MBA, MSM, DBA); marketing (MBA, DBA). *Accreditation:* ACBSP.

Argosy University, Chicago, College of Business, Chicago, IL 60601. Offers accounting (DBA); customized professional concentration (MBA, DBA); finance (MBA); fraud examination (MBA); global business sustainability (DBA); healthcare administration (MBA); information systems (DBA); information systems management (MBA); international business (MBA, DBA); management (MBA, MSM, DBA); marketing (MBA, DBA); organizational leadership (Ed D); public administration (MBA); sustainable management (MBA). *Accreditation:* ACBSP. *Program availability:* Online learning.

Argosy University, Hawai'i, College of Business, Honolulu, HI 96813. Offers accounting (DBA); corporate compliance (MBA); customized professional concentration (MBA, DBA); finance (MBA, Certificate); fraud examination (MBA); global business sustainability (DBA); healthcare administration (MBA, Certificate); information systems (DBA); information systems management (MBA, Certificate); international business (MBA, DBA, Certificate); management (MBA, MSM, DBA); marketing (MBA, DBA, Certificate); organizational leadership (Ed D); public administration (MBA); sustainable management (MBA).

Argosy University, Los Angeles, College of Business, Los Angeles, CA 90045. Offers accounting (DBA); corporate compliance (MBA); customized professional concentration (MBA, DBA); finance (MBA); fraud examination (MBA); global business sustainability (DBA); healthcare administration (MBA); information systems (DBA); information systems management (MBA); international business (MBA, DBA); management (MBA, MSM, DBA); marketing (MBA, DBA); organizational leadership (Ed D); public administration (MBA); sustainable management (MBA).

Argosy University, Northern Virginia, College of Business, Arlington, VA 22209. Offers accounting (DBA); customized professional concentration (MBA, DBA); finance (MBA); fraud examination (MBA); global business sustainability (DBA); healthcare administration (MBA); information systems (DBA); information systems management (MBA); international business (MBA, DBA, Certificate); management (MBA, MSM, DBA); marketing (MBA, DBA, Certificate); organizational leadership (Ed D); public administration (MBA); sustainable management (MBA).

Argosy University, Orange County, College of Business, Orange, CA 92868. Offers accounting (DBA, Adv C); corporate compliance (MBA); customized professional concentration (MBA, DBA); finance (MBA, Certificate); fraud examination (MBA); global business sustainability (DBA); healthcare administration (MBA, Certificate); information systems (DBA, Adv C, Certificate); information systems management (MBA); international business (MBA, DBA, Adv C, Certificate); management (MBA, MSM, DBA, Adv C); marketing (MBA, DBA, Adv C, Certificate); organizational leadership (Ed D); public administration (MBA, Certificate); sustainable management (MBA).

Argosy University, Phoenix, College of Business, Phoenix, AZ 85021. Offers accounting (DBA); corporate compliance (MBA); customized professional concentration (MBA, DBA); finance (MBA); fraud examination (MBA); global business sustainability (DBA); healthcare administration (MBA); information systems (DBA); information systems management (MBA); international business (MBA, DBA); management (MBA, DBA); marketing (MBA, DBA); public administration (MBA); sustainable management (MBA).

Argosy University, Seattle, College of Business, Seattle, WA 98121. Offers accounting (DBA); corporate compliance (MBA); customized professional concentration (MBA, DBA); finance (MBA); fraud examination (MBA); global business sustainability (DBA); healthcare administration (MBA); information systems (DBA); information systems management (MBA); international business (MBA, DBA); management (MBA, MSM, DBA); marketing (MBA, DBA); organizational leadership (Ed D); public administration (MBA); sustainable management (MBA).

Argosy University, Tampa, College of Business, Tampa, FL 33607. Offers accounting (DBA); corporate compliance (MBA); customized professional concentration (MBA, DBA); finance (MBA); fraud examination (MBA); global business sustainability (DBA); healthcare administration (MBA); information systems (DBA); information systems management (MBA); international business (MBA, DBA); management (MBA, MSM, DBA); marketing (MBA, DBA); organizational leadership (Ed D); public administration (MBA); sustainable management (MBA).

Argosy University, Twin Cities, College of Business, Eagan, MN 55121. Offers accounting (DBA); customized professional concentration (MBA, DBA); finance (MBA); fraud examination (MBA); global business sustainability (DBA); healthcare administration (MBA); information systems (DBA); information systems management (MBA); international business (MBA, DBA); management (MBA, MSM, DBA); marketing (MBA, DBA); organizational leadership (Ed D); public administration (MBA); sustainable management (MBA).

Arizona State University at the Tempe campus, Ira A. Fulton Schools of Engineering, The Polytechnic School, Programs in Technology Management, Mesa, AZ 85212. Offers aviation management and human factors (MS); environmental technology management (MS); global technology and development (MS); graphic information technology (MS); management of technology (MS). *Program availability:* Part-time, evening/weekend, online learning. *Degree requirements:* For master's, thesis or applied project and oral defense; interactive Program of Study (iPOS) submitted before completing 50 percent of required credit hours. *Entrance requirements:* For master's, GRE, minimum GPA of 3.0 or equivalent in last 2 years of work leading to bachelor's degree. Additional exam requirements/recommendations for international students: Required—TOEFL, IELTS, or PTE. Electronic applications accepted. *Faculty research:* Digital imaging, digital publishing, Internet development/e-commerce, information aviation human factors, pilot selection, databases, multimedia, commercial digital photography, digital workflow, computer graphics modeling and animation, information design, sociotechnology, visual and technical literacy, environmental management, quality management, project management, industrial ethics, hazardous materials, environmental chemistry.

Arizona State University at the Tempe campus, W. P. Carey School of Business, Department of Information Systems, Tempe, AZ 85287-4606. Offers business administration (PhD), including information systems; information management (MS); MBA/MS. *Program availability:* Evening/weekend, online learning. Terminal master's awarded for partial completion of doctoral program. *Degree requirements:* For master's, thesis or alternative, applied project, interactive Program of Study (iPOS) submitted before completing 50 percent of required credit hours; for doctorate, comprehensive exam, thesis/dissertation, interactive Program of Study (iPOS) submitted before completing 50 percent of required credit hours. *Entrance requirements:* For master's, 2 years of full-time related work experience, bachelor's degree in related field from accredited university, resume, essay, 2 letters of recommendation, official transcripts; for doctorate, GMAT, MBA, 2 years of full-time related work experience (recommended), bachelor's degree in related field from accredited university, 3 letters of recommendation, resume, personal statement. Additional exam requirements/recommendations for international students: Required—TOEFL (minimum score 550 paper-based; 80 iBT), IELTS (minimum score 6.5). Electronic applications accepted. *Expenses:* Contact institution. *Faculty research:* Strategy and technology, technology investments and firm valuation, Internet e-commerce, IT enablement for emergency preparedness and response, information supply chain, collaborative computing and security/privacy issues for e-health, enterprise information systems and their application to management control systems.

Arkansas State University, Graduate School, College of Business, Department of Computer and Information Technology, State University, AR 72467. Offers business administration education (SCCT); business technology education (SCCT). *Program availability:* Part-time. *Entrance requirements:* Additional exam requirements/recommendations for international students: Required—TOEFL (minimum score 550 paper-based; 79 iBT), IELTS (minimum score 6), PTE (minimum score 56). Electronic applications accepted. *Expenses:* Contact institution.

Ashland University, Dauch College of Business and Economics, Ashland, OH 44805-3702. Offers accounting (MBA); business analytics (MBA); entrepreneurship (MBA); financial management (MBA); global management (MBA); health care management and leadership (MBA); human resource management (MBA); human resources (MBA); management information systems (MBA); project management (MBA); sport management (MBA); supply chain management (MBA). *Accreditation:* ACBSP. *Program availability:* Part-time, evening/weekend, 100% online, blended/hybrid learning. Terminal master's awarded for partial completion of doctoral program. *Degree requirements:* For master's, thesis optional, capstone course. *Entrance requirements:* For master's, 2 years of full-time work experience. Additional exam requirements/recommendations for international students: Required—TOEFL (minimum score 550 paper-based; 78 iBT). Electronic applications accepted. *Expenses:* Contact institution. *Faculty research:* Relationship marketing strategy, executive compensation and company performance, online marketplaces in electronic commerce, diversity training in campus recreation departments, entrepreneurship in developing and emerging economies.

Aspen University, Programs in Information Management, Denver, CO 80246-1930. Offers information management (MS); information systems (Certificate). *Program availability:* Part-time, evening/weekend, online only, 100% online. *Faculty:* 10 part-time/adjunct (5 women). *Students:* 27 part-time. Average age 37. In 2018, 6 master's awarded. *Degree requirements:* For master's, comprehensive exam. *Entrance requirements:* For master's and Certificate, www.aspen.edu, www.aspen.edu. *Application deadline:* Applications are processed on a rolling basis. Application fee: $0. Electronic applications accepted. *Financial support:* Applicants required to submit FAFSA. *Unit head:* Kevin Thrasher, Provost, E-mail: kevin.thrasher@aspen.edu. *Application contact:* Enrollment Advisor, 800-373-7814.

Auburn University at Montgomery, College of Business, Department of Information Systems, Montgomery, AL 36124-4023. Offers information systems management (MS). *Students:* Average age 30. 31 applicants, 71% accepted, 8 enrolled. In 2018, 11 master's awarded. *Entrance requirements:* For master's, GMAT or GRE General Test. Additional exam requirements/recommendations for international students: Required—TOEFL (minimum score 500 paper-based; 61 iBT), IELTS (minimum score 5.5), PTE (minimum score 44). *Application deadline:* Applications are processed on a rolling basis. Application fee: $25 ($0 for international students). Electronic applications accepted. *Expenses:* Tuition, area resident: Full-time $7146; part-time $4764 per credit hour. Tuition, state resident: full-time $7146; part-time $4764 per credit hour. Tuition, nonresident: full-time $16,056; part-time $10,704 per credit hour. *International tuition:* $16,056 full-time. *Required fees:* $766. One-time fee: $25 full-time. *Financial support:* Application deadline: 3/1; applicants required to submit FAFSA. *Unit head:* Dr. David Ang, Head, 334-244-3455, Fax: 334-244-3792, E-mail: dang@aum.edu. *Application contact:* Dr. Joseph Newman, Associate Dean/Graduate Coordinator, 334-244-3905, Fax: 334-244-3792, E-mail: jnewman3@aum.edu. Website: http://business.aum.edu/academic-programs/undergraduate-programs/information-systems

Baker College Center for Graduate Studies–Online, Graduate Programs, Flint, MI 48507. Offers accounting (MBA); business administration (DBA); finance (MBA); general business (MBA); health care management (MBA); human resources management (MBA); information management (MBA); leadership studies (MBA); management information systems (MSIS); marketing (MBA); occupational therapy (MOT). *Program availability:* Part-time, evening/weekend, online learning. *Degree requirements:* For master's, portfolio. *Entrance requirements:* For master's, 3 years of work experience, minimum undergraduate GPA of 2.5, writing sample, 3 letters of recommendation; for doctorate, MBA or acceptable related master's degree from accredited association, 5 years work experience, minimum graduate GPA of 3.25, writing sample, 3 professional references. Additional exam requirements/recommendations for international students: Required—TOEFL (minimum score 550 paper-based). Electronic applications accepted.

Ball State University, Graduate School, College of Communication, Information, and Media, Center for Information and Communication Sciences, Muncie, IN 47306. Offers information and communication sciences (MS); information and communication technologies (Certificate). *Program availability:* Part-time, 100% online. *Entrance requirements:* For master's, minimum baccalaureate GPA of 2.75 or 3.0 in latter half of baccalaureate, statement of goals. Additional exam requirements/recommendations for international students: Required—TOEFL (minimum score 550 paper-based; 79 iBT), IELTS (minimum score 6.5). Electronic applications accepted.

Ball State University, Graduate School, Miller College of Business, Department of Information Systems and Operations Management, Muncie, IN 47306. Offers business education (MA); information systems security management (Certificate). *Accreditation:* NCATE (one or more programs are accredited). *Program availability:* Part-time, online only, 100% online. *Entrance requirements:* For master's, minimum baccalaureate GPA of 2.75 or 3.0 in latter half of baccalaureate. Additional exam requirements/recommendations for international students: Required—TOEFL (minimum score 550 paper-based; 79 iBT), IELTS (minimum score 6.5). Electronic applications accepted. *Expenses:* Contact institution.

Barry University, Andreas School of Business, Graduate Certificate Programs, Miami Shores, FL 33161-6695. Offers finance (Certificate); health services administration (Certificate); international business (Certificate); management (Certificate); management information systems (Certificate); marketing (Certificate).

Baruch College of the City University of New York, Zicklin School of Business, Department of Statistics and Computer Information Systems, Program in Information Systems, New York, NY 10010-5585. Offers MBA, MS, PhD. *Program availability:* Part-time, evening/weekend. Terminal master's awarded for partial completion of doctoral program. *Degree requirements:* For master's, thesis or alternative; for doctorate, comprehensive exam, thesis/dissertation. *Entrance requirements:* For master's, GMAT, 2 letters of recommendation, resume, 2 years of work experience; for doctorate, GMAT. Additional exam requirements/recommendations for international students: Required—TOEFL (minimum score 590 paper-based), TWE (minimum score 5).

Baylor University, Graduate School, Hankamer School of Business, Department of Information Systems, Waco, TX 76798. Offers information systems (PhD); information systems management (MBA); MBA/MSIS. *Students:* 24 full-time (11 women), 3 part-time (1 woman); includes 4 minority (3 Hispanic/Latino; 1 Two or more races, non-Hispanic/Latino), 14 international. In 2018, 20 master's, 5 doctorates awarded. *Entrance requirements:* For master's, GMAT; for doctorate, GMAT, GRE. Additional exam requirements/recommendations for international students: Required—TOEFL. *Application deadline:* Applications are processed on a rolling basis. Application fee: $25. *Financial support:* Research assistantships, career-related internships or fieldwork, and Federal Work-Study available. *Faculty research:* Computer personnel, group systems, information technology standards and infrastructure, international information systems, technology and the learning environment. *Unit head:* Dr. Timothy Kayworth, Associate Dean, 254-710-4091, Fax: 254-710-1091, E-mail: timothy_kayworth@baylor.edu. *Application contact:* Laurie Wilson, Director, Graduate Business Programs, 254-710-4163, Fax: 254-710-1066, E-mail: laurie_wilson@baylor.edu. Website: http://hsb.baylor.edu/isy/

Bay Path University, Program in Communications and Information Management, Longmeadow, MA 01106-2292. Offers MS. *Program availability:* Part-time, evening/weekend, 100% online. *Students:* 7 full-time (all women), 8 part-time (6 women); includes 4 minority (all Hispanic/Latino), 1 international. Average age 35. *Entrance requirements:* For master's, completed application, official undergraduate and graduate transcripts (a GPA of 3.0 or higher is preferred), original essay of at least 250 words on the topic: "Why the MS in Communications & Information Management is important to my personal and professional goals", current resume, 2 recommendations. *Application deadline:* Applications are processed on a rolling basis. Electronic applications accepted. Application fee is waived when completed online. *Expenses:* Contact institution. *Financial support:* Unspecified assistantships available. Financial award applicants required to submit FAFSA. *Unit head:* Robin Saunders, Program Director, 413-565-1009, E-mail: rsaunders@baypath.edu. *Application contact:* Elise Carrier, Assistant Director of Graduate Admissions, 413-565-1621, Fax: 413-565-1250, E-mail: ecarrier@baypath.edu. Website: https://www.baypath.edu/academics/graduate-programs/communications-information-management-ms/

Bay Path University, Program in Information Management, Longmeadow, MA 01106-2292. Offers MS. *Program availability:* Part-time, 100% online. *Students:* 1 (woman) full-time, 4 part-time (2 women); includes 1 minority (Hispanic/Latino). Average age 36. *Entrance requirements:* For master's, completed application; official undergraduate and graduate transcripts (a GPA of 3.0 or higher is preferred); original essay of at least 250 words on the topic: "Why the MS in Information Management is important to my personal and professional goals"; current resume; 2 recommendations. *Application deadline:* Applications are processed on a rolling basis. Electronic applications accepted. Application fee is waived when completed online. *Expenses:* Contact institution. *Financial support:* Unspecified assistantships available. Financial award applicants required to submit FAFSA. *Unit head:* Robin Saunders, Director, 413-565-1009, E-mail: rsaunders@baypath.edu. *Application contact:* Elise Carrier, Assistant Director of Graduate Admissions, 413-565-1621, Fax: 413-565-1250, E-mail: ecarrier@baypath.edu. Website: https://www.baypath.edu/academics/graduate-programs/information-management-ms/

Bellevue University, Graduate School, College of Information Technology, Bellevue, NE 68005-3098. Offers computer information systems (MS); cybersecurity (MS); management of information systems (MS); project management (MPM).

Benedictine University, Graduate Programs, Program in Business Administration, Lisle, IL 60532. Offers accounting (MBA); entrepreneurship and managing innovation (MBA); financial management (MBA); health administration (MBA); human resource management (MBA); information systems security (MBA); international business (MBA); management consulting (MBA); management information systems (MBA); marketing management (MBA); operations management and logistics (MBA); organizational leadership (MBA). *Program availability:* Part-time, evening/weekend, 100% online, blended/hybrid learning. *Faculty:* 7 full-time (1 woman), 36 part-time/adjunct (10 women). *Students:* 110 full-time (71 women), 500 part-time (302 women); includes 104 minority (34 Black or African American, non-Hispanic/Latino; 1 American Indian or Alaska Native, non-Hispanic/Latino; 41 Asian, non-Hispanic/Latino; 23 Hispanic/Latino; 5 Native Hawaiian or other Pacific Islander, non-Hispanic/Latino), 7 international. Average age 33. 251 applicants, 84% accepted, 202 enrolled. In 2018, 345 master's awarded. *Entrance requirements:* For master's, GMAT or GRE test scores or completed test waiver form, official transcripts; 2 letters of reference from individuals familiar with the applicant's professional or academic work, excluding family or personal friends; a 1-2 page essay addressing educational and career goals; current résumé listing chronological work history; personal interview may be required prior to an admission decision. Additional exam requirements/recommendations for international students: Required—TOEFL (minimum score 550 paper-based; 79 iBT), IELTS (minimum score 6.5). *Application deadline:* Applications are processed on a rolling basis. Application fee: $40. Electronic applications accepted. *Unit head:* Ricky Holman, Assistant Professor, 630-829-1936, E-mail: rholman@ben.edu. *Application contact:* Ricky Holman, Assistant Professor, 630-829-1936, E-mail: rholman@ben.edu.

Management Information Systems

Benedictine University, Graduate Programs, Program in Management Information Systems, Lisle, IL 60532. Offers MS, MBA/MS, MPH/MS. *Program availability:* Part-time, evening/weekend. *Faculty:* 2 full-time (1 woman), 3 part-time/adjunct (0 women). *Students:* 92 part-time (42 women); includes 4 minority (all Asian, non-Hispanic/Latino). Average age 30. 81 applicants, 88% accepted, 70 enrolled. In 2018, 70 master's awarded. *Entrance requirements:* For master's, GMAT or GRE test scores or completed test waiver form, official transcripts; 2 letters of reference from individuals familiar with the applicant's professional or academic work, excluding family or personal friends; a 1-2 page essay addressing educational and career goals; résumé; personal interview may be required prior to an admission decision. Additional exam requirements/recommendations for international students: Required—TOEFL (minimum score 550 paper-based; 79 iBT), IELTS (minimum score 6.5). *Application deadline:* Applications are processed on a rolling basis. Application fee: $40. Electronic applications accepted. *Unit head:* Dr. Barbara Ozog, Program Director, 630-829-6218, E-mail: bozog@ben.edu. *Application contact:* Dr. Barbara Ozog, Program Director, 630-829-6218, E-mail: bozog@ben.edu.

Binghamton University, State University of New York, Graduate School, School of Management, Program in Management, Binghamton, NY 13902-6000. Offers finance (PhD); management information systems (PhD); marketing (PhD); organizational studies (PhD); supply chain management (PhD). *Degree requirements:* For doctorate, thesis/dissertation. *Entrance requirements:* For doctorate, GMAT.

Boston University, Metropolitan College, Department of Computer Science, Boston, MA 02215. Offers computer information systems (MS), including computer networks, data analytics, database management and business intelligence, health informatics, IT project management, security, Web application development; computer networks (Certificate); computer science (MS); data analytics (Certificate); digital forensics (Certificate); health informatics (Certificate); information technology project management (Certificate); software development (MS); software engineering in health care systems (Certificate); telecommunications (MS), including security. *Program availability:* Part-time, evening/weekend, online learning. *Faculty:* 16 full-time (3 women), 52 part-time/adjunct (5 women). *Students:* 201 full-time (57 women), 953 part-time (252 women); includes 285 minority (57 Black or African American, non-Hispanic/Latino; 2 American Indian or Alaska Native, non-Hispanic/Latino; 139 Asian, non-Hispanic/Latino; 67 Hispanic/Latino; 1 Native Hawaiian or other Pacific Islander, non-Hispanic/Latino; 19 Two or more races, non-Hispanic/Latino), 333 international. Average age 31. 1,079 applicants, 72% accepted, 297 enrolled. In 2018, 395 master's awarded. *Entrance requirements:* For master's and Certificate, official transcripts from regionally-accredited bachelor's degree program, 3 letters of recommendation, professional resume, personal statement. Additional exam requirements/recommendations for international students: Required—TOEFL (minimum score 84 iBT), IELTS. *Application deadline:* For fall admission, 8/1 priority date for domestic students, 6/1 priority date for international students; for spring admission, 12/1 priority date for domestic students, 11/15 priority date for international students; for summer admission, 4/1 priority date for domestic students, 3/1 priority date for international students. Applications are processed on a rolling basis. Application fee: $85. Electronic applications accepted. *Expenses:* Contact institution. *Financial support:* In 2018–19, 11 research assistantships (averaging $8,400 per year), 23 teaching assistantships (averaging $3,400 per year) were awarded; unspecified assistantships also available. Support available to part-time students. Financial award applicants required to submit FAFSA. *Faculty research:* Artificial intelligence and machine learning, security and forensics, web technologies, software engineering, programming languages, medical informatics, information systems and IT project management. *Unit head:* Dr. Anatoly Temkin, Chair, 617-353-2566, Fax: 617-353-2367, E-mail: csinfo@bu.edu. *Application contact:* Enrollment Services, 617-353-6004, E-mail: met@bu.edu. Website: http://www.bu.edu/csmet/

Bowie State University, Graduate Programs, Program in Management Information Systems, Bowie, MD 20715-9465. Offers information systems analyst (Certificate); management information systems (MS). *Program availability:* Part-time, evening/weekend. *Degree requirements:* For master's, comprehensive exam, thesis optional, research paper. *Entrance requirements:* For master's, minimum GPA of 2.5. Electronic applications accepted.

Brandeis University, Rabb School of Continuing Studies, Division of Graduate Professional Studies, Master of Science in Technology Management Program, Waltham, MA 02454-9110. Offers MS. *Program availability:* Part-time-only. *Entrance requirements:* For master's, four-year bachelor's degree from regionally-accredited U.S. institution or equivalent; official transcript(s) from every college or university attended; resume or curriculum vitae; statement of goals; letter of recommendation. Additional exam requirements/recommendations for international students: Required—TWE (minimum score 4.5), TOEFL (minimum scores: 600 paper-based, 100 iBT), IELTS (7), or PTE (68). Electronic applications accepted. *Expenses:* Contact institution.

Broadview University–West Jordan, Graduate Programs, West Jordan, UT 84088. Offers business administration (MBA); health care management (MSM); information technology (MSM); managerial leadership (MSM).

California Intercontinental University, School of Information Technology, Irvine, CA 92614. Offers information systems and enterprise resource management (DBA); information systems and knowledge management (MBA); project and quality management (MBA).

California Lutheran University, Graduate Studies, School of Management, Thousand Oaks, CA 91360-2787. Offers business (IMBA); entrepreneurship (MBA, Certificate); finance (MBA, Certificate); financial planning (MBA, MS, Certificate); human capital management (MBA, Certificate); information technology (MS); information technology management (MBA, Certificate); international business (MBA, Certificate); management (MS); marketing (MBA, Certificate); public policy and administration (MPPA); quantitative economics (MS). *Program availability:* Part-time, evening/weekend, 100% online, blended/hybrid learning. *Degree requirements:* For master's, comprehensive exam (for some programs). *Entrance requirements:* For master's, GMAT, interview, minimum GPA of 3.0. Electronic applications accepted. *Expenses:* Contact institution.

California State Polytechnic University, Pomona, Master of Science in Business Administration Program, Pomona, CA 91768-2557. Offers business administration (MS). *Accreditation:* AACSB. *Program availability:* Part-time, evening/weekend. *Students:* 15 full-time (5 women), 9 part-time (3 women); includes 11 minority (1 Black or African American, non-Hispanic/Latino; 6 Asian, non-Hispanic/Latino; 4 Hispanic/Latino), 3 international. Average age 31. 39 applicants, 67% accepted, 18 enrolled. *Entrance requirements:* Additional exam requirements/recommendations for international students: Required—TOEFL (minimum score 550 paper-based). *Application deadline:* Applications are processed on a rolling basis. Application fee: $55. Electronic applications accepted. *Expenses:* Contact institution. *Financial support:* Application deadline: 3/2; applicants required to submit FAFSA. *Unit head:* Dr. Tarique Hossain, Associate Professor/Director of Graduate Programs, 909-869-2362, Fax: 909-869-4559, E-mail: tmhossain@cpp.edu. *Application contact:* Dr. Tarique Hossain, Associate Professor/Director of Graduate Programs, 909-869-2362, Fax: 909-869-4559, E-mail: tmhossain@cpp.edu.
Website: http://www.cpp.edu/~cba/graduate-business-programs/programs/MSBA.shtml

California State University, Fullerton, Graduate Studies, College of Business and Economics, Department of Information Systems and Decision Sciences, Fullerton, CA 92831-3599. Offers decision science (MBA); information systems (MBA, MS); information systems and decision sciences (MS); information systems and e-commerce (MS); information technology (MS). *Program availability:* Part-time. *Entrance requirements:* For master's, GMAT, minimum AACSB index of 950.

California State University, Los Angeles, Graduate Studies, College of Business and Economics, Department of Information Systems, Los Angeles, CA 90032-8530. Offers management (MS). *Program availability:* Part-time, evening/weekend. *Degree requirements:* For master's, comprehensive exam (MBA), thesis (MS). *Entrance requirements:* For master's, GMAT, minimum GPA of 2.5 during previous 2 years of course work. Additional exam requirements/recommendations for international students: Required—TOEFL (minimum score 550 paper-based). Electronic applications accepted.

California State University, Monterey Bay, College of Science, School of Computing and Design, Seaside, CA 93955-8001. Offers MS, MSMIT. MSMIT offered in conjunction with College of Business. *Degree requirements:* For master's, capstone or thesis. *Entrance requirements:* For master's, GRE, 2 letters of recommendation, minimum GPA of 3.0, technology screening assessment. Additional exam requirements/recommendations for international students: Required—TOEFL (minimum score 550 paper-based; 71 iBT). Electronic applications accepted. *Faculty research:* Electronic commerce, e-learning, knowledge management, international business, business and public policy.

California State University, San Bernardino, Graduate Studies, College of Business and Public Administration, Program in Business Administration, San Bernardino, CA 92407. Offers accounting (MBA); entrepreneurship (MBA); finance (MBA); global business (MBA); information management (MBA); information security (MBA); management (MBA); supply chain management (MBA). *Accreditation:* AACSB. *Program availability:* Part-time, evening/weekend, online learning. *Faculty:* 5 full-time (4 women), 7 part-time/adjunct (3 women). *Students:* 40 full-time (14 women), 163 part-time (72 women); includes 99 minority (7 Black or African American, non-Hispanic/Latino; 15 Asian, non-Hispanic/Latino; 71 Hispanic/Latino; 6 Two or more races, non-Hispanic/Latino), 58 international. Average age 32. 342 applicants, 52% accepted, 91 enrolled. In 2018, 106 master's awarded. *Degree requirements:* For master's, comprehensive exam, thesis. *Entrance requirements:* Additional exam requirements/recommendations for international students: Required—TOEFL. *Application deadline:* For fall admission, 7/16 for domestic students, 7/20 for international students; for winter admission, 10/23 for domestic students, 10/20 for international students; for spring admission, 1/22 for domestic students, 1/20 for international students. Application fee: $55. *Expenses:* Contact institution. *Financial support:* Application deadline: 3/1. *Unit head:* Dr. Lawrence C. Rose, Dean, 909-537-3703, Fax: 909-537-7026, E-mail: lrose@csusb.edu. *Application contact:* Ernest Silvers, MBA Program Director, 909-537-5703, E-mail: esilvers@csusb.edu.
Website: http://mba.csusb.edu/

California University of Management and Sciences, Graduate Programs, Anaheim, CA 92801. Offers business administration (MBA, DBA); computer information systems (MS); economics (MS); international business (MS); sports management (MS).

Capella University, School of Business and Technology, Doctoral Programs in Technology, Minneapolis, MN 55402. Offers general information technology (PhD); global operations and supply chain management (DBA); information assurance and security (PhD); information technology education (PhD); information technology management (DBA, PhD).

Capella University, School of Business and Technology, Master's Programs in Technology, Minneapolis, MN 55402. Offers enterprise software architecture (MS); general information systems and technology management (MS); global operations and supply chain management (MBA); information assurance and security (MS); information technology management (MBA); network management (MS).

Capitol Technology University, Graduate Programs, Laurel, MD 20708-9759. Offers business administration (MBA); computer science (MS); electrical engineering (MS); information and telecommunications systems management (MS); information architecture (MS); network security (MS). *Program availability:* Part-time, evening/weekend, online learning. *Entrance requirements:* For master's, minimum GPA of 3.0. Electronic applications accepted.

Carnegie Mellon University, Heinz College Australia, Master of Science in Information Technology Program (Adelaide, South Australia), Adelaide SA 5000, Australia. Offers MSIT. *Entrance requirements:* For master's, GRE or GMAT, college-level course in advanced algebra/pre-calculus; college-level courses in economics and statistics (recommended). Additional exam requirements/recommendations for international students: Required—TOEFL or IELTS.

Carnegie Mellon University, Heinz College, School of Information Systems and Management, Master of Information Systems Management Program, Pittsburgh, PA 15213-3891. Offers MISM. *Entrance requirements:* For master's, GRE or GMAT, college-level course in advanced algebra/pre-calculus; college-level courses in economics and statistics (recommended). Additional exam requirements/recommendations for international students: Required—TOEFL or IELTS.

Carnegie Mellon University, Heinz College, School of Information Systems and Management, Master of Science in Information Security Policy and Management Program, Pittsburgh, PA 15213-3891. Offers MSISPM. *Entrance requirements:* For master's, GRE or GMAT, college-level course in advanced algebra/pre-calculus; college-level courses in economics and statistics (recommended). Additional exam requirements/recommendations for international students: Required—TOEFL or IELTS.

Carnegie Mellon University, Heinz College, School of Information Systems and Management, Program in Information Technology, Pittsburgh, PA 15213-3891. Offers MSIT.

Carnegie Mellon University, Tepper School of Business, Program in Business Technologies, Pittsburgh, PA 15213-3891. Offers PhD. *Degree requirements:* For doctorate, thesis/dissertation. *Entrance requirements:* For doctorate, GRE General Test.

The Catholic University of America, School of Engineering, Program in Engineering Management, Washington, DC 20064. Offers engineering management (MSE, Certificate), including engineering management and organization (MSE), project and systems engineering management (MSE), technology management (MSE); program management (Certificate); systems engineering and management of information technology (Certificate). *Program availability:* Part-time. *Faculty:* 6 part-time/adjunct (1 woman). *Students:* 16 full-time (1 woman), 19 part-time (7 women); includes 3 minority (1 Asian, non-Hispanic/Latino; 2 Two or more races, non-Hispanic/Latino), 17 international. Average age 31. 48 applicants, 85% accepted, 19 enrolled. In 2018, 17 master's awarded. *Degree requirements:* For master's, minimum GPA of 3.0. *Entrance requirements:* For master's and Certificate, statement of purpose, official copies of academic transcripts, two letters of recommendation. Additional exam requirements/recommendations for international students: Required—TOEFL (minimum score 550 paper-based; 80 iBT). *Application deadline:* For fall admission, 7/15 priority date for domestic students, 7/1 for international students; for spring admission, 11/15 priority

date for domestic students, 11/1 for international students. Applications are processed on a rolling basis. Application fee: $55. Electronic applications accepted. *Expenses:* Contact institution. *Financial support:* Fellowships, research assistantships, teaching assistantships, Federal Work-Study, scholarships/grants, tuition waivers (full and partial), and unspecified assistantships available. Financial award application deadline: 2/1; financial award applicants required to submit FAFSA. *Faculty research:* Engineering management and organization, project and systems engineering management, technology management. *Unit head:* Melvin G. Williams, Jr., Director, 202-319-5191, Fax: 202-319-6860, E-mail: williamsme@cua.edu. *Application contact:* Dr. Steven Brown, Director of Graduate Admissions, 202-319-5057, Fax: 202-319-6533, E-mail: cua-admissions@cua.edu.
Website: https://engineering.catholic.edu/management/index.html

Central Michigan University, Central Michigan University Global Campus, Program in Administration, Mount Pleasant, MI 48859. Offers acquisitions administration (MSA, Certificate); engineering management administration (MSA, Certificate); general administration (MSA, Certificate); health services administration (MSA, Certificate); human resources administration (MSA, Certificate); information resource management (MSA); information resource management administration (Certificate); international administration (MSA, Certificate); leadership (MSA, Certificate); philanthropy and fundraising administration (MSA, Certificate); public administration (MSA, Certificate); recreation and park administration (MSA); research administration (MSA, Certificate). *Program availability:* Part-time, evening/weekend, online learning. *Entrance requirements:* For master's, minimum GPA of 2.7 in major. Electronic applications accepted.

Central Michigan University, College of Graduate Studies, College of Business Administration, Department of Business Information Systems, Mount Pleasant, MI 48859. Offers business computing (Graduate Certificate); information systems (MS), including accounting information systems, business informatics, enterprise systems using SAP software, information systems. *Program availability:* Part-time, evening/weekend. *Degree requirements:* For master's, thesis or alternative. Electronic applications accepted. *Faculty research:* Enterprise software, electronic commerce, decision support systems, ethical issues in information systems, information technology management and teaching issues.

Central Michigan University, College of Graduate Studies, College of Business Administration, MBA Program, Mount Pleasant, MI 48859. Offers accounting (MBA); business economics (MBA); consulting (MBA); finance (MBA); general business (MBA); human resource management (MBA); information systems (MBA); international business (MBA); logistics management (MBA); marketing (MBA); value-driven organization (MBA). *Program availability:* Part-time, evening/weekend, online learning. Electronic applications accepted. *Faculty research:* Accounting, consulting, international business, marketing, information systems.

Central Michigan University, College of Graduate Studies, Interdisciplinary Administration Programs, Mount Pleasant, MI 48859. Offers acquisitions administration (MSA, Graduate Certificate); general administration (MSA, Graduate Certificate); health services administration (MSA, Graduate Certificate); human resource administration (Graduate Certificate); human resources administration (MSA); information resource management (MSA, Graduate Certificate); international administration (MSA, Graduate Certificate); leadership (MSA, Graduate Certificate); public administration (MSA, Graduate Certificate); research administration (Graduate Certificate); sport administration (MSA). *Accreditation:* AACSB. *Program availability:* Part-time, evening/weekend, online learning. *Degree requirements:* For master's, thesis or alternative. *Entrance requirements:* For master's, bachelor's degree with minimum GPA of 2.7. Electronic applications accepted. *Faculty research:* Interdisciplinary studies in acquisitions administration, health services administration, sport administration, recreation and park administration, and international administration.

Central Penn College, Graduate Programs, Summerdale, PA 17093-0309. Offers information systems management (MPS); organizational development (MPS). Programs offered in Harrisburg, PA. *Program availability:* Evening/weekend.

Charleston Southern University, College of Business, Charleston, SC 29423-8087. Offers accounting (MBA); finance (MBA); general management (MBA); human resource management (MS); leadership (MBA); management information systems (MBA); organizational leadership (MA). *Program availability:* Part-time, evening/weekend. *Degree requirements:* For master's, thesis optional. *Entrance requirements:* For master's, GMAT. Additional exam requirements/recommendations for international students: Required—TOEFL (minimum score 550 paper-based; 79 iBT). Electronic applications accepted.

City College of the City University of New York, Graduate School, Grove School of Engineering, Department of Computer Science, New York, NY 10031-9198. Offers computer science (MS, PhD); information systems (MIS). PhD program offered jointly with Graduate School and University Center of the City University of New York. *Degree requirements:* For master's, thesis optional; for doctorate, one foreign language, comprehensive exam, thesis/dissertation. *Entrance requirements:* For master's and doctorate, GRE General Test. Additional exam requirements/recommendations for international students: Required—TOEFL (minimum score 500 paper-based; 61 iBT). *Faculty research:* Complexities of algebraic research, human issues in computer science, scientific computing, super compilers, parallel algorithms.

City University of Seattle, Graduate Division, School of Management, Seattle, WA 98121. Offers accounting (Certificate); change leadership (MBA, Certificate); computer systems (MS); finance (Certificate); financial management (MBA); general management (MBA); general management-Europe (MBA); global marketing (MBA); human resources management (Certificate); individualized study (MBA); information security (MS); information systems (MBA); leadership (MA); marketing (MBA, Certificate); project management (MBA, MS, Certificate); sustainable business (Certificate); technology management (MBA, Certificate). *Program availability:* Part-time, evening/weekend, online learning. *Degree requirements:* For master's, comprehensive exam (for some programs), thesis (for some programs). *Entrance requirements:* For master's, baccalaureate degree or equivalent from an accredited or otherwise recognized institution. Additional exam requirements/recommendations for international students: Required—TOEFL (minimum score 567 paper-based; 87 iBT); Recommended—IELTS. Electronic applications accepted.

Claremont Graduate University, Graduate Programs, Center for Information Systems and Technology, Claremont, CA 91711-6160. Offers cybersecurity and networking (MS); data science and analytics (MS); electronic commerce (PhD); geographic information systems (MS); health informatics (MS); information systems (Certificate); IT strategy and innovation (MS); knowledge management (PhD); systems development (PhD); telecommunications and networking (PhD); MBA/MS. *Program availability:* Part-time. *Degree requirements:* For doctorate, comprehensive exam, thesis/dissertation, portfolio. *Entrance requirements:* For master's and doctorate, GMAT, GRE General Test. Additional exam requirements/recommendations for international students: Required—TOEFL (minimum score 75 iBT). Electronic applications accepted. *Faculty research:* Man-machine interaction, organizational aspects of computing, implementation of information systems, information systems practice.

Clark University, Graduate School, Graduate School of Management, Business Administration Program, Worcester, MA 01610-1477. Offers accounting (MBA); finance (MBA); information management and business analytics (MBA); management (MBA); marketing (MBA); social change (MBA); sustainability (MBA). *Accreditation:* AACSB. *Program availability:* Part-time, evening/weekend. *Degree requirements:* For master's, thesis optional. *Entrance requirements:* For master's, GMAT or GRE, 2 references, resume or curriculum vitae, personal statement. Additional exam requirements/recommendations for international students: Required—TOEFL (minimum score 575 paper-based; 90 iBT), IELTS (minimum score 6.5). Electronic applications accepted. *Expenses:* Contact institution. *Faculty research:* Marketing, accounting, human resource management, management information systems, business finance.

Clemson University, Graduate School, College of Business, Department of Management, Clemson, SC 29634. Offers business administration (PhD), including management information systems, strategy, entrepreneurship and organizational behavior, supply chain and operations management; management (MS). *Accreditation:* AACSB. *Faculty:* 26 full-time (9 women). *Students:* 14 full-time (5 women), 4 part-time (2 women); includes 1 minority (Asian, non-Hispanic/Latino), 10 international. Average age 30. 53 applicants, 36% accepted, 8 enrolled. In 2018, 2 master's, 4 doctorates awarded. Terminal master's awarded for partial completion of doctoral program. *Degree requirements:* For master's, comprehensive exam, thesis optional; for doctorate, comprehensive exam, thesis/dissertation. *Entrance requirements:* For master's and doctorate, GMAT or GRE General Test, unofficial transcripts, two letters of reference, curriculum vitae. Additional exam requirements/recommendations for international students: Required—TOEFL (minimum score 80 paper-based; 94 iBT); Recommended—IELTS (minimum score 7), TSE (minimum score 64). *Application deadline:* For fall admission, 4/15 priority date for international students; for spring admission, 10/15 priority date for international students. Applications are processed on a rolling basis. Application fee: $80 ($90 for international students). Electronic applications accepted. *Expenses:* $6823 per semester full-time resident, $14023 per semester full-time non-resident, $833 per credit hour part-time resident, $1731 per credit hour part-time non-resident, online $1264 per credit hour, $4938 doctoral programs resident, $10405 doctoral programs non-resident, $1144 full-time graduate assistant, other fees may apply per session. *Financial support:* In 2018–19, 10 students received support, including 1 fellowship with full and partial tuition reimbursement available (averaging $1,500 per year), 6 research assistantships with full and partial tuition reimbursements available (averaging $25,000 per year), 17 teaching assistantships with full and partial tuition reimbursements available (averaging $25,000 per year); career-related internships or fieldwork and unspecified assistantships also available. *Faculty research:* Effective use of information technology in business, manufacturing and service operations strategy, lean operations and quality management, healthcare operations, behavioral market design. *Total annual research expenditures:* $131,333. *Unit head:* Dr. Craig Wallace, Department Chair, 864-656-9963, E-mail: CW74@clemson.edu. *Application contact:* Dr. Janis Miller, Graduate Program Coordinator, 864-656-3757, E-mail: janism@clemson.edu.
Website: https://www.clemson.edu/business/departments/management/

Cleveland State University, College of Graduate Studies, Monte Ahuja College of Business, Doctor of Business Administration Program, Cleveland, OH 44115. Offers information systems (DBA); marketing (DBA). *Accreditation:* AACSB. *Program availability:* Part-time, evening/weekend. *Faculty:* 50 full-time (11 women). *Students:* 8 full-time (4 women), 20 part-time (11 women); includes 7 minority (3 Black or African American, non-Hispanic/Latino; 3 Asian, non-Hispanic/Latino; 1 Hispanic/Latino), 7 international. Average age 37. In 2018, 2 doctorates awarded. *Degree requirements:* For doctorate, comprehensive exam, thesis/dissertation, oral dissertation defense. *Entrance requirements:* For doctorate, GMAT, MBA or equivalent. Additional exam requirements/recommendations for international students: Required—TOEFL (minimum score 550 paper-based; 78 iBT). *Application deadline:* For fall admission, 2/1 for domestic and international students. Application fee: $40. Electronic applications accepted. *Expenses:* Tuition, state resident: full-time $7232.55; part-time $6676 per credit hour. Tuition, nonresident: full-time $12,375. *International tuition:* $18,914 full-time. *Required fees:* $80; $80 $40. Tuition and fees vary according to program. *Financial support:* In 2018–19, 5 research assistantships with full tuition reimbursements (averaging $12,700 per year), 4 teaching assistantships with full tuition reimbursements (averaging $12,700 per year) were awarded; tuition waivers (full) and unspecified assistantships also available. Financial award applicants required to submit FAFSA. *Faculty research:* Supply chain management, international business, strategic management, risk analysis, consumer behavior. *Unit head:* Dr. Raj Shekhar G. Javalgi, Director, 216-687-3786, Fax: 216-687-9354, E-mail: r.javalgi@csuohio.edu. *Application contact:* Melinda J. Arnold, Administrative Secretary, 216-687-6952, Fax: 216-687-9257, E-mail: m.arnold@csuohio.edu.
Website: http://www.csuohio.edu/business/academics/mbajuris-doctor

Coastal Carolina University, College of Science, Conway, SC 29528-6054. Offers applied computing and information systems (Certificate); coastal marine and wetland studies (MS); information systems technology (MS); marine science (PhD); sports management (MS). *Program availability:* Part-time, evening/weekend, 100% online. *Degree requirements:* For master's, thesis or internship; for doctorate, comprehensive exam, thesis/dissertation. *Entrance requirements:* For master's, GRE, 3 letters of recommendation, resume, official transcripts, written statement of educational and career goals, baccalaureate degree; for doctorate, GRE, official transcripts; baccalaureate or master's degree; minimum GPA of 3.0 for all collegiate coursework; successful completion of at least two semesters of college-level calculus, physics, and chemistry; 3 letters of recommendation; written statement of educational and career goals; resume; for Certificate, 2 letters of reference, official transcripts, minimum GPA of 3.0 in all computing and information systems courses, documentation of graduation from accredited four-year college or university. Additional exam requirements/recommendations for international students: Required—TOEFL (minimum score 550 paper-based; 79 iBT), IELTS (minimum score 6.5). Electronic applications accepted.

College of Charleston, Graduate School, School of Sciences and Mathematics, Program in Computer and Information Sciences, Charleston, SC 29424-0001. Offers MS. Program offered jointly with The Citadel, The Military College of South Carolina. *Program availability:* Part-time, evening/weekend. *Degree requirements:* For master's, thesis optional. *Entrance requirements:* For master's, GRE. Additional exam requirements/recommendations for international students: Required—TOEFL (minimum score 81 iBT). Electronic applications accepted.

The College of St. Scholastica, Graduate Studies, Department of Computer Information Systems, Duluth, MN 55811-4199. Offers MA, Certificate. *Program availability:* Part-time, online learning. *Degree requirements:* For master's, thesis. *Entrance requirements:* Additional exam requirements/recommendations for international students: Required—TOEFL (minimum score 550 paper-based; 79 iBT). Electronic applications accepted. Application fee is waived when completed online. *Expenses:* Contact institution. *Faculty research:* Organization acceptance of software development methodologies.

Colorado State University, College of Business, Department of Computer Information Systems, Fort Collins, CO 80523-1277. Offers MCIS. *Program availability:* Part-time,

evening/weekend, 100% online, blended/hybrid learning. *Entrance requirements:* For master's, GMAT (minimum score of 550) or GRE, minimum GPA of 3.0; bachelor's degree; letters of recommendation; resume; statement of purpose. Additional exam requirements/recommendations for international students: Required—TOEFL (minimum score 86 iBT), IELTS (minimum score 6.5), PTE (minimum score 58). Electronic applications accepted. *Expenses:* Contact institution. *Faculty research:* Learning and effectively using information technology; predictors of programmer performance; he impact of information systems on identity and culture dynamics.

Colorado State University–Global Campus, Graduate Programs, Greenwood Village, CO 80111. Offers criminal justice and law enforcement administration (MS); education leadership (MS); finance (MS); healthcare administration and management (MS); human resource management (MHRM); information technology management (MITM); international management (MS); management (MS); organizational leadership (MS); professional accounting (MPA); project management (MS); teaching and learning (MS). *Accreditation:* ACBSP. *Program availability:* Online learning.

Concordia University Wisconsin, Graduate Programs, Batterman School of Business, MBA Program, Mequon, WI 53097-2402. Offers finance (MBA); health care administration (MBA); human resource management (MBA); international business (MBA); international business-bilingual English/Chinese (MBA); management (MBA); management information systems (MBA); managerial communications (MBA); marketing (MBA); public administration (MBA); risk management (MBA). *Program availability:* Online learning. *Degree requirements:* For master's, comprehensive exam, thesis or alternative. *Entrance requirements:* Additional exam requirements/recommendations for international students: Required—TOEFL. *Expenses:* Contact institution.

Copenhagen Business School, Graduate Programs, Copenhagen, Denmark. Offers business administration (Exec MBA, MBA, PhD); business administration and information systems (M Sc); business, language and culture (M Sc); economics and business administration (M Sc); health management (MHM); international business and politics (M Sc); public administration (MPA); shipping and logistics (Exec MBA); technology, market and organization (MBA).

Daemen College, International Business Program, Amherst, NY 14226-3592. Offers global business (MS), including accounting, global business, management information systems, marketing. *Program availability:* Part-time, evening/weekend. *Faculty:* 3 full-time (2 women), 3 part-time/adjunct (1 woman). *Students:* 4 full-time (2 women), 5 part-time (3 women); includes 1 minority (Black or African American, non-Hispanic/Latino), 2 international. Average age 34. 7 applicants, 57% accepted, 2 enrolled. In 2018, 4 master's awarded. *Degree requirements:* For master's, minimum GPA of 3.0. *Entrance requirements:* For master's, GMAT if undergraduate GPA is less than 3.0, baccalaureate degree from an accredited college or university with a major concentration in a business related field, such as accounting, business administration, economics, management, or marketing; official transcripts; undergrad GPA 3.0 higher or needs to take the GMAT; resume; 2 letters of recommendation; personal statement. Additional exam requirements/recommendations for international students: Required—TOEFL (minimum score 77 paper-based), IELTS (minimum score 6.5). *Application deadline:* Applications are processed on a rolling basis. Application fee: $25. Electronic applications accepted. Application fee is waived when completed online. *Expenses:* Tuition: Part-time $977 per credit hour. *Required fees:* $125; $14 per credit hour. *Financial support:* Scholarships/grants and unspecified assistantships available. Support available to part-time students. Financial award applicants required to submit FAFSA. *Unit head:* Dr. Torsten Doering, Director of International Business Program, 716-839-8239, E-mail: tdoering@daemen.edu. *Application contact:* Megan Beardi, Senior Assistant Director of Graduate Admissions, 716-566-7861, Fax: 716-839-8229, E-mail: mbeardi@daemen.edu. Website: https://www.daemen.edu/academics/areas-study/international-business

Dakota State University,.College of Business and Information Systems, Madison, SD 57042-1799. Offers analytics (MSA); business analytics (Graduate Certificate); general management (MBA); health informatics (MSHI); information systems (MSIS, D Sc IS); information technology (Graduate Certificate). *Accreditation:* ACBSP. *Program availability:* Part-time, evening/weekend, 100% online, blended/hybrid learning. *Faculty:* 27 full-time (10 women). *Students:* 40 full-time (11 women), 165 part-time (60 women); includes 56 minority (21 Black or African American, non-Hispanic/Latino; 4 American Indian or Alaska Native, non-Hispanic/Latino; 19 Asian, non-Hispanic/Latino; 10 Hispanic/Latino; 1 Native Hawaiian or other Pacific Islander, non-Hispanic/Latino; 1 Two or more races, non-Hispanic/Latino), 38 international. Average age 38. 246 applicants, 47% accepted, 63 enrolled. In 2018, 62 master's, 7 doctorates, 9 other advanced degrees awarded. *Degree requirements:* For master's, comprehensive exam, thesis optional, Examination, integrative project; for doctorate, comprehensive exam, thesis/dissertation, portfolio. *Entrance requirements:* For master's, GRE General Test, Demonstration of information systems skills, minimum GPA of 2.7; for doctorate, GRE General Test, Demonstration of information systems skills; for Graduate Certificate, GMAT. Additional exam requirements/recommendations for international students: Required—PTE (minimum score 53), TOEFL (minimum score 550 paper-based, 76 iBT) or IELTS (6.0). *Application deadline:* For fall admission, 6/15 for domestic students, 4/15 for international students; for spring admission, 11/15 for domestic students, 9/15 priority date for international students; for summer admission, 4/15 for domestic and international students. Applications are processed on a rolling basis. Application fee: $35. Electronic applications accepted. *Expenses:* Contact institution. *Financial support:* In 2018–19, 20 students received support. Research assistantships with partial tuition reimbursements available, teaching assistantships with partial tuition reimbursements available, career-related internships or fieldwork, Federal Work-Study, scholarships/grants, and unspecified assistantships available. Support available to part-time students. Financial award applicants required to submit FAFSA. *Faculty research:* Data mining and analytics, biometrics and information assurance, decision support systems, health informatics, STEM education for K-12 teachers/students and underrepresented populations. *Unit head:* Dr. Dorine Bennett, Dean of College of Business and Information Systems, 605-256-5176, E-mail: dorine.bennett@dsu.edu. *Application contact:* Erin Blankespoor, Senior Secretary, Office of Graduate Studies and Research, 605-256-5799, E-mail: erin.blankespoor@dsu.edu. Website: http://dsu.edu/academics/colleges/college-of-business-and-information-systems

Dalhousie University, Faculty of Management, Centre for Advanced Management Education, Halifax, NS B3H 3J5, Canada. Offers financial services (MBA); information management (MIM); management (MPA); natural resources (MBA). *Program availability:* Part-time, online learning. *Entrance requirements:* For master's, GMAT, minimum GPA of 3.0, resume. Additional exam requirements/recommendations for international students: Required—TOEFL, IELTS, CANTEST, CAEL, or Michigan English Language Assessment Battery. Electronic applications accepted.

Dallas Baptist University, College of Business, Master of Business Administration Program, Dallas, TX 75211-9299. Offers health care management (MBA); international business (MBA); management information systems (MBA). *Accreditation:* ACBSP. *Program availability:* Part-time, evening/weekend, 100% online, blended/hybrid learning. *Application deadline:* Applications are processed on a rolling basis. Application fee: $25. Electronic applications accepted. Application fee is waived when completed online.

Expenses: Tuition: Full-time $17,262; part-time $959 per credit hour. *Required fees:* $1000; $500 per semester. Tuition and fees vary according to course load and degree level. *Unit head:* Dr. Sandra Reid, Chair of Graduate Business Programs, Program Director, 214-333-5280, E-mail: sandra@dbu.edu. *Application contact:* Dr. Sandra Reid, Chair of Graduate Business Programs, Program Director, 214-333-5280, E-mail: sandra@dbu.edu. Website: https://www.dbu.edu/graduate/degree-programs/mba

DePaul University, College of Computing and Digital Media, Chicago, IL 60604. Offers animation (MA, MFA); applied technology (MS); business information technology (MS); computational finance (MS); computer and information sciences (PhD); computer science (MS); creative producing (MFA); cybersecurity (MS); data science (MS); digital communication and media arts (MA); documentary (MFA); e-commerce technology (MS); experience design (MA); film and television (MS); film and television directing (MFA); game design (MFA); game programming (MS); health informatics (MS); human centered design (PhD); human-computer interaction (MS); information systems (MS); network engineering and security (MS); product innovation and computing (MS); screenwriting (MFA); software engineering (MS); JD/MS. *Program availability:* Part-time, evening/weekend, online learning. *Degree requirements:* For master's, thesis (for some programs); for doctorate, comprehensive exam, thesis/dissertation. *Entrance requirements:* For master's, GRE or GMAT (for MS in computational finance only), bachelor's degree, resume (MS in predictive analytics only), IT experience (MS in information technology project management only), portfolio review (all MFA programs and MA in animation); for doctorate, GRE, master's degree in computer science. Additional exam requirements/recommendations for international students: Required—TOEFL (minimum score 590 paper-based; 80 iBT), IELTS (minimum score 6.5), PTE (minimum score 53). Electronic applications accepted. *Expenses:* Contact institution. *Faculty research:* Data mining, computer science, human-computer interaction, security, animation and film.

DePaul University, Kellstadt Graduate School of Business, Chicago, IL 60604. Offers accountancy (MBA, MSA); applied economics (MBA); audit and advisory services (MS); business administration (DBA); business analytics (MS); business strategy and decision-making (MBA); computational finance (MS); economics and policy analysis (MS); enterprise risk management (MS); entrepreneurship (MBA, MS); finance (MBA, MS); general business (MBA); hospitality leadership (MBA); hospitality leadership and operational performance (MS); human resources (MS); international business (MBA); management (MBA, MS); management information systems (MBA); marketing (MBA, MS); marketing analysis (MS); marketing strategy and planning (MBA); real estate (MS); real estate finance and investment (MBA); strategy, execution and valuation (MBA); supply chain management (MS); sustainable management (MS); taxation (MS); JD/MBA. *Accreditation:* AACSB. *Program availability:* Part-time, evening/weekend, online learning. *Entrance requirements:* For master's, GMAT/GRE, 2 letters of recommendation, resume, essay, official transcripts. Additional exam requirements/recommendations for international students: Required—TOEFL (minimum score 550 paper-based; 80 iBT). Electronic applications accepted. *Expenses:* Contact institution.

DeSales University, Division of Business, Center Valley, PA 18034-9568. Offers accounting (MBA); computer information systems (MBA); finance (MBA); health care systems management (MBA); human resources management (MBA); management (MBA); marketing (MBA); project management (MBA); self-design (MBA); supply chain management (MBA); DNP/MBA; MSN/MBA. *Accreditation:* ACBSP. *Program availability:* Part-time, evening/weekend, 100% online, blended/hybrid learning. *Entrance requirements:* For master's, GMAT (waived if undergraduate GPA is 3.0 or better), minimum GPA of 3.0 in undergraduate work, literacy in basic software, background or interest in the field of study, personal statement, 2 years of work experience. Additional exam requirements/recommendations for international students: Required—TOEFL. Electronic applications accepted. *Expenses:* Contact institution. *Faculty research:* Quality improvement, executive development, productivity, cross-cultural managerial differences, leadership.

DeSales University, Division of Science and Mathematics, Center Valley, PA 18034-9568. Offers cyber security (Postbaccalaureate Certificate); data analytics (Postbaccalaureate Certificate); information systems (MS), including cyber security, digital forensics, healthcare information management, project management. *Program availability:* Part-time, evening/weekend, 100% online, blended/hybrid learning. *Entrance requirements:* For master's, GRE or GMAT, bachelor's degree in computer-related discipline from accredited college or university, minimum undergraduate GPA of 3.0, personal statement, three letters of recommendation. Additional exam requirements/recommendations for international students: Required—TOEFL. Electronic applications accepted. *Expenses:* Contact institution.

DeVry University–Folsom Campus, Graduate Programs, Folsom, CA 95630. Offers accounting (M Acc); accounting and financial management (MAFM); business administration (MBA); curriculum leadership (M Ed); educational leadership (M Ed); educational technology (M Ed); higher education leadership (M Ed); human resource management (MHRM); information systems management (MISM); network and communications management (MNCM); project management (MPM); public administration (MPA).

Dominican University, School of Information Studies, River Forest, IL 60305-1099. Offers information management (MSIM); knowledge management (Certificate); library and information science (MLIS, MPS, PhD); special studies (CSS); MBA/MLIS; MLIS/MA. MLIS/M Div offered jointly with McCormick Theological Seminary, MLIS/MA with Loyola University Chicago, MLIS/MM with Northwestern University. *Accreditation:* ALA (one or more programs are accredited). *Program availability:* Part-time, evening/weekend, 100% online, blended/hybrid learning. *Degree requirements:* For doctorate, thesis/dissertation. *Entrance requirements:* For master's, minimum GPA of 3.0, GRE General Test, or MAT; for doctorate, MLIS or related MA, minimum GPA of 3.0, GRE General Test, or MAT. Additional exam requirements/recommendations for international students: Required—TOEFL. *Expenses:* Contact institution. *Faculty research:* Productivity and the information environment, bibliometrics, library history, subject access, library materials and services for children.

Drexel University, College of Computing and Informatics, Department of Information Science, Philadelphia, PA 19104-2875. Offers health informatics (MS); information science (PhD, Post-Master's Certificate, Postbaccalaureate Certificate); information systems (MS); library and information science (MS). *Accreditation:* ALA. *Program availability:* Part-time, evening/weekend, 100% online. *Faculty:* 24 full-time (11 women), 18 part-time/adjunct (9 women). *Students:* 153 full-time (92 women), 212 part-time (137 women); includes 85 minority (29 Black or African American, non-Hispanic/Latino; 22 Asian, non-Hispanic/Latino; 19 Hispanic/Latino; 15 Two or more races, non-Hispanic/Latino), 66 international. Average age 33. 570 applicants, 45% accepted, 136 enrolled. In 2018, 144 master's, 8 doctorates, 8 other advanced degrees awarded. *Degree requirements:* For doctorate, thesis/dissertation. *Entrance requirements:* For master's and doctorate, GRE General Test. Additional exam requirements/recommendations for international students: Required—TOEFL (minimum score 90 iBT), IELTS (minimum score 6.5). *Application deadline:* For fall admission, 8/15 for domestic students, 7/15 for international students; for spring admission, 3/1 for domestic students, 2/1 for international students. Applications are processed on a rolling basis. Application fee:

$65. Electronic applications accepted. *Financial support:* Fellowships, research assistantships, teaching assistantships, career-related internships or fieldwork, scholarships/grants, and tuition waivers (partial) available. Support available to part-time students. Financial award application deadline: 3/1; financial award applicants required to submit FAFSA. *Unit head:* Dr. Yi Deng, Dean/Professor, 215-895-2474, Fax: 215-895-2494, E-mail: yd362@drexel.edu. *Application contact:* Matthew Lechtenberg, Director, Recruitment, 215-895-2474, Fax: 215-895-2303, E-mail: cciinfo@drexel.edu. Website: http://cci.drexel.edu/academics/graduate-programs/ms-in-health-informatics

Duquesne University, Palumbo-Donahue School of Business, Pittsburgh, PA 15282-0001. Offers accounting (M Acc); finance (MBA); information systems management (MSISM); management (MBA, MS); marketing (MBA); sports business (MS); supply chain management (MS); sustainability (MBA); JD/MBA; MBA/M Acc; MBA/MA; MBA/MES; MBA/MHMS; MSISM/MBA; Pharm D/MBA. *Accreditation:* AACSB. *Program availability:* Part-time, evening/weekend, 100% online, blended/hybrid learning. *Faculty:* 59 full-time (23 women), 25 part-time/adjunct (6 women). *Students:* 214 full-time (74 women), 42 part-time (20 women); includes 39 minority (12 Black or African American, non-Hispanic/Latino; 13 Asian, non-Hispanic/Latino; 8 Hispanic/Latino; 6 Two or more races, non-Hispanic/Latino), 23 international. Average age 29. 228 applicants, 88% accepted, 118 enrolled. In 2018, 149 master's awarded. *Entrance requirements:* For master's, GMAT or GRE, all official transcripts, two letters of recommendation, current resume, essays. Additional exam requirements/recommendations for international students: Required—TOEFL (minimum score 90 iBT), IELTS (minimum score 7). *Application deadline:* For fall admission, 7/1 priority date for domestic and international students; for spring admission, 12/1 for domestic and international students; for summer admission, 4/1 for domestic and international students. Applications are processed on a rolling basis. Application fee: $0. Electronic applications accepted. *Expenses:* $1,284/credit hour (business), $953/credit hour (management). *Financial support:* In 2018–19, 174 students received support, including 6 fellowships with partial tuition reimbursements available (averaging $24,750 per year); career-related internships or fieldwork, scholarships/grants, and unspecified assistantships also available. Support available to part-time students. Financial award application deadline: 7/1; financial award applicants required to submit FAFSA. *Faculty research:* Investment management, business ethics, technology management, supply chain management, entrepreneurship. *Unit head:* Dr. Karen Donovan, Associate Dean of Graduate Programs and Executive Education, 412-396-5788, Fax: 412-396-1726, E-mail: donovan6@duq.edu. *Application contact:* Chris Rouhier, Director of Graduate Admissions, 412-396-6244, Fax: 412-396-1726, E-mail: rouhierc@duq.edu. Website: http://www.duq.edu/business/grad

East Carolina University, Graduate School, College of Engineering and Technology, Department of Technology Systems, Greenville, NC 27858-4353. Offers computer network professional (Certificate); cyber security professional (Certificate); information assurance (Certificate); Lean Six Sigma Black Belt (Certificate); network technology (MS), including computer networking management, digital communications technology, information security, Web technologies; occupational safety (MS); technology management (MS, PhD), including industrial distribution and logistics (MS); Website developer (Certificate). *Application deadline:* For fall admission, 6/1 priority date for domestic students. *Expenses: Tuition, area resident:* Full-time $4749. Tuition, state resident: full-time $4749. Tuition, nonresident: full-time $17,898. *International tuition:* $17,898 full-time. *Required fees:* $2787. Part-time tuition and fees vary according to course load and program. *Financial support:* Application deadline: 6/1. *Unit head:* Dr. Tijjani Mohammed, Chair, 252-328-9668, E-mail: mohammedt@ecu.edu. *Application contact:* Graduate School Admissions, 252-328-6012, Fax: 252-328-6071, E-mail: gradschool@ecu.edu. Website: http://www.ecu.edu/cs-cet/techsystems/index.cfm

Eastern Michigan University, Graduate School, College of Business, Department of Computer Information Systems, Ypsilanti, MI 48197. Offers MS. *Program availability:* Part-time, evening/weekend. *Faculty:* 6 full-time (0 women). *Students:* 13 full-time (7 women), 12 part-time (7 women); includes 3 minority (1 Asian, non-Hispanic/Latino; 1 Hispanic/Latino; 1 Two or more races, non-Hispanic/Latino), 15 international. Average age 31. 51 applicants, 47% accepted, 4 enrolled. In 2018, 18 master's awarded. *Entrance requirements:* Additional exam requirements/recommendations for international students: Required—TOEFL. *Application deadline:* For fall admission, 5/15 priority date for domestic students, 2/15 priority date for international students; for winter admission, 10/15 priority date for domestic students, 9/1 priority date for international students; for summer admission, 3/15 priority date for domestic students, 3/1 priority date for international students. Applications are processed on a rolling basis. Application fee: $45. *Financial support:* Fellowships, research assistantships with full tuition reimbursements, teaching assistantships with full tuition reimbursements, career-related internships or fieldwork, Federal Work-Study, institutionally sponsored loans, scholarships/grants, tuition waivers (partial), and unspecified assistantships available. Support available to part-time students. Financial award applicants required to submit FAFSA. *Unit head:* Dr. Hung-Lian Tang, Interim Department Head, 734-487-2454, Fax: 734-487-1941, E-mail: hung_lian.tang@emich.edu. *Application contact:* Dr. Hung-Lian Tang, Interim Department Head, 734-487-2454, Fax: 734-487-1941, E-mail: hung_lian.tang@emich.edu. Website: http://www.cis.emich.edu

Eastern Michigan University, Graduate School, College of Business, Programs in Business Administration, Ypsilanti, MI 48197. Offers business administration (MBA, Graduate Certificate); computer information systems (Graduate Certificate); e-business (MBA, Graduate Certificate); enterprise business intelligence (MBA); entrepreneurship (MBA, Graduate Certificate); finance (MBA, Graduate Certificate); human resources (MBA); human resources management (Graduate Certificate); information systems (MBA); internal auditing (MBA); international business (MBA, Graduate Certificate); marketing management (Graduate Certificate); nonprofit management (MBA); organizational development (Graduate Certificate); supply chain management (MBA, Graduate Certificate). *Accreditation:* AACSB. *Program availability:* Part-time, online learning. *Students:* 69 full-time (38 women), 251 part-time (140 women); includes 100 minority (63 Black or African American, non-Hispanic/Latino; 1 American Indian or Alaska Native, non-Hispanic/Latino; 12 Asian, non-Hispanic/Latino; 14 Hispanic/Latino; 10 Two or more races, non-Hispanic/Latino), 28 international. Average age 32. 199 applicants, 75% accepted, 83 enrolled. In 2018, 75 master's, 50 other advanced degrees awarded. *Entrance requirements:* For master's, GMAT (minimum score 450), minimum cumulative undergraduate GPA of 2.75. Additional exam requirements/recommendations for international students: Required—TOEFL. *Application deadline:* For fall admission, 5/15 priority date for domestic students, 2/15 priority date for international students; for winter admission, 10/15 priority date for domestic students, 9/1 priority date for international students; for summer admission, 3/15 priority date for domestic students, 3/1 priority date for international students. Applications are processed on a rolling basis. Application fee: $45. *Financial support:* Fellowships, research assistantships with full tuition reimbursements, teaching assistantships with full tuition reimbursements, career-related internships or fieldwork, Federal Work-Study, institutionally sponsored loans, scholarships/grants, tuition waivers (partial), and unspecified assistantships available. Support available to part-time students. Financial award applicants required to submit FAFSA. *Unit head:* K. Michelle Henry, Director,

Graduate Business Programs, 734-487-4444, Fax: 734-483-1316, E-mail: cob.graduate@emich.edu. *Application contact:* K. Michelle Henry, Director, Graduate Business Programs, 734-487-4444, Fax: 734-483-1316, E-mail: cob.graduate@emich.edu. Website: http://www.emich.edu/cob/mba/

ECPI University, Graduate Programs, Virginia Beach, VA 23462. Offers business administration (MBA); cybersecurity (MS); information systems (MS).

Elmhurst College, Graduate Programs, Program in Computer Information Technology, Elmhurst, IL 60126-3296. Offers MS. *Program availability:* Part-time, evening/weekend, 100% online, blended/hybrid learning. *Faculty:* 2 full-time (0 women). *Students:* 1 full-time (0 women), 25 part-time (6 women); includes 9 minority (3 Black or African American, non-Hispanic/Latino; 2 Asian, non-Hispanic/Latino; 3 Hispanic/Latino; 1 Two or more races, non-Hispanic/Latino), 6 international. Average age 34. 29 applicants, 34% accepted, 9 enrolled. In 2018, 13 master's awarded. *Entrance requirements:* For master's, 3 recommendations, resume, statement of purpose. Additional exam requirements/recommendations for international students: Required—TOEFL (minimum score 550 paper-based; 79 iBT), IELTS (minimum score 6.5). *Application deadline:* Applications are processed on a rolling basis. Application fee: $0. Electronic applications accepted. *Expenses:* $795 per semester hour. *Financial support:* In 2018–19, 11 students received support. Scholarships/grants available. Support available to part-time students. Financial award applicants required to submit FAFSA. *Unit head:* Ali Ghane, Director, 630-617-3366, E-mail: alig@elmhurst.edu. *Application contact:* Timothy J. Panfil, Senior Director of Graduate Admission and Enrollment Management, 630-617-3300 Ext. 3256, Fax: 630-617-6471, E-mail: panfilt@elmhurst.edu. Website: http://www.elmhurst.edu/cis

Embry-Riddle Aeronautical University–Worldwide, Department of Decision Sciences, Daytona Beach, FL 32114-3900. Offers aviation and aerospace (MSPM); aviation/aerospace management (MSEM); financial management (MSEM, MSPM); general management (MSPM); global management (MSPM); human resources management (MSPM); information systems (MSPM); leadership (MSEM, MSPM); logistics and supply chain management (MSEM, MSLSCM, MSPM); management (MSEM, MSPM); project management (MSEM); systems engineering (MSEM, MSPM); technical management (MSPM). *Program availability:* Part-time, evening/weekend, EagleVision Classroom (between classrooms), EagleVision Home (faculty and students at home), and a blend of Classroom or Home. *Degree requirements:* For master's, comprehensive exam (for some programs), thesis (for some programs). *Entrance requirements:* Additional exam requirements/recommendations for international students: Required—TOEFL (minimum score 550 paper-based; 79 iBT), IELTS (minimum score 6). Electronic applications accepted. *Expenses:* Contact institution.

Embry-Riddle Aeronautical University–Worldwide, Department of Technology Management, Daytona Beach, FL 32114-3900. Offers information and security assurance (MS); management information systems (MS). *Program availability:* Part-time, evening/weekend, EagleVision Classroom (between classrooms), EagleVision Home (faculty and students at home), and a blend of Classroom or Home. *Entrance requirements:* Additional exam requirements/recommendations for international students: Required—TOEFL (minimum score 550 paper-based; 79 iBT), IELTS (minimum score 6). Electronic applications accepted. *Expenses:* Tuition: Full-time $7980; part-time $665 per credit hour. Tuition and fees vary according to course load, degree level and program.

Emory University, Goizueta Business School, Doctoral Program in Business, Atlanta, GA 30322. Offers accounting (PhD); finance (PhD); information systems and operations management (PhD); marketing (PhD); organization and management (PhD). *Faculty:* 67 full-time (22 women). *Students:* 45 full-time (21 women); includes 5 minority (2 Black or African American, non-Hispanic/Latino; 3 Hispanic/Latino), 31 international. Average age 29. 143 applicants, 19% accepted, 10 enrolled. In 2018, 7 doctorates awarded. *Degree requirements:* For doctorate, comprehensive exam, thesis/dissertation. *Entrance requirements:* For doctorate, GMAT, interview. Additional exam requirements/recommendations for international students: Required—TOEFL (minimum score 600 paper-based; 100 iBT), IELTS, We will take either TOEFL or IELTS. *Application deadline:* For fall admission, 1/3 priority date for domestic and international students. Applications are processed on a rolling basis. Application fee: $75. Electronic applications accepted. *Expenses:* Our students are required to pay approximately $400 in their fall and spring terms; approximately $200 in summer terms in fees. All tuition is scholarshiped 100%. *Financial support:* In 2018–19, 45 students received support, including 11 fellowships (averaging $1,000 per year); scholarships/grants, health care benefits, and Fellowships are both the Sheth Fellows and Goizueta Fellows whom are named each year based on certain milestones. also available. Financial award application deadline: 1/3. *Faculty research:* Financial and managerial accounting, asset pricing strategy and organizational behavior, information technology marketing analytics and consumer behavior. *Unit head:* Kathryn Kadous, Associate Dean, 404-727-2306, Fax: 404-727-5337, E-mail: kathryn.kadous@emory.edu. *Application contact:* Allison Gilmore, Director of Admissions and Student Services, 404-727-6353, Fax: 404-727-5337, E-mail: allison.gilmore@emory.edu. Website: https://goizueta.emory.edu/degree/phd/index.html

Emory University, Goizueta Business School, Full Time MBA Program, Atlanta, GA 30322-1100. Offers accounting (MBA); alternative investments (MBA); business process consulting (MBA); business technology management (MBA); capital markets (MBA); corporate finance (MBA); customer relationship management (MBA); decision analytics (MBA); entrepreneurship (MBA); finance (MBA); global management (MBA); investment banking (MBA); management consulting (MBA); marketing (MBA); marketing analytics (MBA); marketing consulting (MBA); operations management (MBA); organization and management (MBA); product and brand management (MBA); real estate (MBA); social enterprise (MBA); strategy consulting (MBA). *Accreditation:* AACSB. *Faculty:* 74 full-time (18 women), 18 part-time/adjunct (6 women). *Students:* 349 full-time (105 women); includes 81 minority (26 Black or African American, non-Hispanic/Latino; 1 American Indian or Alaska Native, non-Hispanic/Latino; 35 Asian, non-Hispanic/Latino; 16 Hispanic/Latino; 3 Two or more races, non-Hispanic/Latino), 97 international. Average age 29. 1,380 applicants, 34% accepted, 172 enrolled. In 2018, 180 master's awarded. *Degree requirements:* For master's, 1 leadership course; 2 mid-semester module programs; 2 global components. *Entrance requirements:* For master's, GMAT/GRE, essays; recommendation letters; undergraduate degree; interview. Additional exam requirements/recommendations for international students: Required—TOEFL (minimum score 100 iBT), IELTS (minimum score 7), PTE (minimum score 68). *Application deadline:* For fall admission, 10/6 for domestic and international students; for winter admission, 11/17 for domestic and international students; for spring admission, 1/3 priority date for domestic and international students; for summer admission, 3/9 for domestic and international students. Application fee: $150. Electronic applications accepted. *Expenses:* Contact institution. *Financial support:* In 2018–19, 273 students received support. Career-related internships or fieldwork, institutionally sponsored loans, and scholarships/grants available. Financial award application deadline: 4/1; financial award applicants required to submit FAFSA. *Faculty research:* Corporate finance, information systems, digital marketing, asset pricing, sports management. *Unit head:* Brian Mitchell, Associate Dean, 404-727-4824, Fax: 404-712-9648, E-mail:

brian.mitchell@emory.edu. *Application contact:* Melissa Rapp, Associate Dean, 404-727-7583, Fax: 404-727-4612, E-mail: mbaadmissions@emory.edu.
Website: http://www.goizueta.emory.edu

Endicott College, Van Loan School of Graduate and Professional Studies, Program in Information Technology, Beverly, MA 01915-2096. Offers MSIT. *Program availability:* Part-time, evening/weekend. *Degree requirements:* For master's, thesis. *Entrance requirements:* For master's, GRE or MAT, two letters of recommendation, undergraduate transcript. Additional exam requirements/recommendations for international students: Required—TOEFL. Electronic applications accepted. *Expenses:* Contact institution.

Fairfield University, Dolan School of Business, Fairfield, CT 06824. Offers accounting (MBA, MS, CAS); business analytics (MS); finance (MBA, MS, CAS); information systems and business analytics (MBA); management (MBA, CAS); marketing (MBA, CAS); taxation (CAS). *Accreditation:* AACSB. *Program availability:* Part-time, evening/weekend. *Degree requirements:* For master's, capstone course. *Entrance requirements:* For master's, GMAT (minimum score 500), 2 letters of reference, resume, minimum GPA of 3.0. Additional exam requirements/recommendations for international students: Required—TOEFL (minimum score 550 paper-based; 80 iBT) or IELTS (minimum score 6.5). Electronic applications accepted. *Expenses:* Contact institution. *Faculty research:* International finance, leadership and careers, ethics in accounting, emotions in consumer behavior and organizations, data analytics.

Fairleigh Dickinson University, Metropolitan Campus, Silberman College of Business, Departments of Management, Marketing, and Entrepreneurial Studies, Program in Management, Teaneck, NJ 07666-1914. Offers management (MBA); management information systems (Certificate). *Accreditation:* AACSB.

Fairleigh Dickinson University, Metropolitan Campus, University College: Arts, Sciences, and Professional Studies, School of Computer Sciences and Engineering, Program in Management Information Systems, Teaneck, NJ 07666-1914. Offers MS.

Ferris State University, College of Business, Big Rapids, MI 49307. Offers design and innovation management (MBA); lean systems and leadership (MBA); project management (MBA); supply chain management and lean logistics (MBA). *Accreditation:* ACBSP. *Program availability:* Part-time, evening/weekend, 100% online, blended/hybrid learning. *Faculty:* 20 full-time (7 women). *Students:* 14 full-time (9 women), 96 part-time (51 women); includes 12 minority (4 Black or African American, non-Hispanic/Latino; 1 American Indian or Alaska Native, non-Hispanic/Latino; 3 Asian, non-Hispanic/Latino; 2 Hispanic/Latino; 2 Two or more races, non-Hispanic/Latino), 8 international. Average age 33. 48 applicants, 88% accepted, 32 enrolled. In 2018, 39 master's awarded. *Degree requirements:* For master's, comprehensive exam, thesis. *Entrance requirements:* For master's, GRE or GMAT, minimum GPA of 3.0 overall and in junior-/senior-level classes; statement of purpose; 3 letters of reference; resume; transcripts. Additional exam requirements/recommendations for international students: Required—TOEFL (minimum score 500 paper-based; 70 iBT), IELTS (minimum score 6.5). *Application deadline:* For fall admission, 7/1 priority date for domestic students, 6/15 for international students; for winter admission, 11/1 priority date for domestic students, 10/15 for international students; for spring admission, 3/1 priority date for domestic students, 2/15 for international students. Applications are processed on a rolling basis. Application fee: $0 ($30 for international students). Electronic applications accepted. *Expenses:* $610 per credit hour; $12 per credit hour online fee; 33 credits for MISI $20,526; 39 credits for MBA $24,258. *Financial support:* In 2018–19, 17 students received support. Career-related internships or fieldwork, Federal Work-Study, scholarships/grants, and unspecified assistantships available. Support available to part-time students. Financial award applicants required to submit FAFSA. *Faculty research:* Digital forensics, security issues with internet of things, cybersecurity education. *Total annual research expenditures:* $130,000. *Unit head:* Dr. David Nicol, College of Business Dean, 231-591-2168, Fax: 231-591-3521, E-mail: davidnicol@ferris.edu. *Application contact:* Dr. Greg Gogolin, Professor, 231-591-3159, Fax: 231-591-3521, E-mail: greggogolin@ferris.edu.
Website: http://cbgp.ferris.edu/

Florida Agricultural and Mechanical University, Division of Graduate Studies, Research, and Continuing Education, School of Business and Industry, Tallahassee, FL 32307-3200. Offers accounting (MBA); finance (MBA); management information systems (MBA); marketing (MBA). *Accreditation:* ACBSP. *Degree requirements:* For master's, residency. *Entrance requirements:* For master's, GMAT, minimum GPA of 3.0.

Florida Atlantic University, College of Business, Department of Information Technology and Operations Management, Boca Raton, FL 33431-0991. Offers information technology management (MS). *Faculty:* 13 full-time (4 women). *Students:* 23 full-time (9 women), 31 part-time (9 women); includes 28 minority (9 Black or African American, non-Hispanic/Latino; 2 Asian, non-Hispanic/Latino; 16 Hispanic/Latino; 1 Two or more races, non-Hispanic/Latino), 6 international. Average age 29. 41 applicants, 63% accepted, 23 enrolled. In 2018, 26 master's awarded. *Entrance requirements:* For master's, GMAT, minimum GPA of 3.0. Additional exam requirements/recommendations for international students: Required—TOEFL (minimum score 600 paper-based; 61 iBT), IELTS (minimum score 6). *Application deadline:* For fall admission, 7/1 priority date for domestic students, 2/15 priority date for international students; for spring admission, 4/1 priority date for domestic students, 1/15 priority date for international students. Applications are processed on a rolling basis. Application fee: $30. Electronic applications accepted. *Expenses: Tuition, area resident:* Full-time $7400; part-time $369.82 per credit. Tuition, state resident: full-time $7400; part-time $369.82 per credit. Tuition, nonresident: full-time $20,496; part-time $1024.81 per credit. *Financial support:* Research assistantships, teaching assistantships, career-related internships or fieldwork, Federal Work-Study, institutionally sponsored loans, tuition waivers (partial), and unspecified assistantships available. Support available to part-time students. Financial award application deadline: 3/1; financial award applicants required to submit FAFSA. *Unit head:* Dr. Tamara Dinev, Chair, 561-297-3181, E-mail: tdinev@fau.edu. *Application contact:* Dr. Tamara Dinev, Chair, 561-297-3181, E-mail: tdinev@fau.edu.
Website: http://business.fau.edu/departments/information-technology-operations-management/index.aspx

Florida Gulf Coast University, Lutgert College of Business, Program in Information Systems and Analytics, Fort Myers, FL 33965-6565. Offers MS. *Entrance requirements:* For master's, GMAT or GRE. Additional exam requirements/recommendations for international students: Required—TOEFL (minimum score 550 paper-based). Electronic applications accepted.

Florida Institute of Technology, Aberdeen Education Center (Maryland), Program in Management, Melbourne, FL 32901-6975. Offers acquisition and contract management (MS, PMBA); business administration (MS, PMBA); contracts management (PMBA); financial management (MPA); global management (PMBA); health management (MS); human resources management (MS, PMBA); information systems (PMBA); logistics management (MS); management (MS), including information systems, operations research; materials acquisition management (MS); operations research (MS); public administration (MPA); research (PMBA); space systems (MS); space systems management (MS). *Expenses: Tuition:* Full-time $22,338; part-time $1241 per credit hour. Tuition and fees vary according to degree level, campus/location and program. *Financial support:* Application deadline: 3/1. *Application contact:* Online Learning and Off-Campus Programs Admissions, 321-674-8263, E-mail: gradadm-olocp@fit.edu.
Website: https://www.fit.edu/education-centers/degrees-and-programs/management-ms/

Florida International University, Chapman Graduate School of Business, Department of Decision Sciences and Information Systems, Miami, FL 33199. Offers decision sciences and information systems (PhD); health information management systems (MS); systems management (MS). *Program availability:* Part-time, evening/weekend. *Faculty:* 29 full-time (10 women), 10 part-time/adjunct (2 women). *Students:* 62 full-time (28 women), 60 part-time (33 women); includes 98 minority (27 Black or African American, non-Hispanic/Latino; 1 American Indian or Alaska Native, non-Hispanic/Latino; 4 Asian, non-Hispanic/Latino; 63 Hispanic/Latino; 3 Two or more races, non-Hispanic/Latino), 18 international. Average age 34. 299 applicants, 39% accepted, 71 enrolled. In 2018, 75 master's awarded. *Entrance requirements:* For master's, GMAT or GRE, minimum GPA of 3.0 in upper-level coursework; letter of intent; resume. Additional exam requirements/recommendations for international students: Required—TOEFL (minimum score 550 paper-based; 80 iBT) or IELTS. *Application deadline:* For fall admission, 6/1 for domestic students, 4/1 for international students; for spring admission, 10/1 for domestic students, 9/1 for international students. Applications are processed on a rolling basis. Application fee: $30. Electronic applications accepted. *Expenses:* Contact institution. *Financial support:* Institutionally sponsored loans and scholarships/grants available. Financial award application deadline: 3/1; financial award applicants required to submit FAFSA. *Faculty research:* Artificial intelligence, data warehouses, operations management. *Unit head:* Dr. Richard Klein, Jr., Interim Chair, 305-348-2156, E-mail: rklein@fiu.edu. *Application contact:* Nanett Rojas, Manager, Admissions Operations, 305-348-7464, Fax: 305-348-7441, E-mail: gradadm@fiu.edu.

Florida International University, College of Engineering and Computing, School of Computing and Information Sciences, Miami, FL 33199. Offers computer science (MS, PhD); cybersecurity (MS); data science (MS); information technology (MS); telecommunications and networking (MS). *Program availability:* Part-time, evening/weekend. *Faculty:* 49 full-time (13 women), 31 part-time/adjunct (7 women). *Students:* 182 full-time (53 women), 132 part-time (28 women); includes 168 minority (13 Black or African American, non-Hispanic/Latino; 1 American Indian or Alaska Native, non-Hispanic/Latino; 10 Asian, non-Hispanic/Latino; 137 Hispanic/Latino; 7 Two or more races, non-Hispanic/Latino), 123 international. Average age 30. 393 applicants, 47% accepted, 92 enrolled. In 2018, 81 master's, 9 doctorates awarded. *Degree requirements:* For master's, thesis or alternative; for doctorate, comprehensive exam, thesis/dissertation. *Entrance requirements:* For master's and doctorate, GRE General Test, 3 letters of recommendation, minimum GPA of 3.0. Additional exam requirements/recommendations for international students: Required—TOEFL (minimum score 550 paper-based; 80 iBT). *Application deadline:* For fall admission, 6/1 for domestic students, 4/1 for international students; for spring admission, 10/1 for domestic students, 9/1 for international students. Applications are processed on a rolling basis. Application fee: $30. Electronic applications accepted. *Financial support:* Research assistantships, teaching assistantships, institutionally sponsored loans, scholarships/grants, and unspecified assistantships available. Financial award application deadline: 3/1; financial award applicants required to submit FAFSA. *Faculty research:* Database systems, software engineering, operating systems, networks. *Unit head:* Dr. Sundararaj S. Iyengar, Director, 305-348-3947, Fax: 305-348-3549, E-mail: sundararaj.iyengar@fiu.edu. *Application contact:* Nanett Rojas, Manager, Admissions Operations, 305-348-7464, Fax: 305-348-7441, E-mail: gradadm@fiu.edu.

Florida State University, The Graduate School, College of Business, Tallahassee, FL 32306-1110. Offers accounting (M Acc), including assurance and advisory services, generalist, taxation; business administration (MBA, PhD), including accounting (PhD), finance (PhD), management information systems (PhD), marketing (PhD), organizational behavior and human resources (PhD), risk management and insurance (PhD), strategy (PhD); finance (MS); management information systems (MS); risk management and insurance (MS); JD/MBA; MSW/MBA. *Accreditation:* AACSB. *Program availability:* Part-time, 100% online. *Students:* Average age 31. 300 applicants, 61% accepted, 133 enrolled. In 2018, 268 master's, 9 doctorates awarded. Terminal master's awarded for partial completion of doctoral program. *Degree requirements:* For doctorate, comprehensive exam, thesis/dissertation. *Entrance requirements:* For master's, GMAT, GRE (for all except MS in finance), work experience (MBA, MS); minimum GPA of 3.0, letters of recommendation; for doctorate, GMAT, GRE (for marketing, organizational behavior, risk management and insurance, management information systems, and human resources only), minimum graduate GPA of 3.5, letters of recommendation. Additional exam requirements/recommendations for international students: Required—TOEFL (minimum score 600 paper-based; 85 iBT); Recommended—IELTS (minimum score 6). *Application deadline:* For fall admission, 6/1 for domestic and international students; for spring admission, 10/1 for domestic and international students; for summer admission, 3/1 for domestic and international students. Applications are processed on a rolling basis. Application fee: $30. Electronic applications accepted. *Expenses:* Contact institution. *Financial support:* In 2018–19, 146 students received support, including 26 fellowships (averaging $1,500 per year), 77 research assistantships with full tuition reimbursements available (averaging $20,000 per year), 43 teaching assistantships with full tuition reimbursements available (averaging $20,000 per year); career-related internships or fieldwork, scholarships/grants, health care benefits, tuition waivers (full and partial), and unspecified assistantships also available. Support available to part-time students. Financial award application deadline: 1/1; financial award applicants required to submit FAFSA. *Faculty research:* Business strategy, marketing, finance, accounting, business analytics. *Total annual research expenditures:* $1.4 million. *Unit head:* Dr. Michael Hartline, Dean, 850-644-4405, Fax: 850-644-0915, E-mail: mhartline@business.fsu.edu. *Application contact:* Jennifer Clark, Director, 850-644-6458, E-mail: gradprograms@business.fsu.edu.
Website: http://business.fsu.edu/

Florida State University, The Graduate School, College of Communication and Information, School of Information, Tallahassee, FL 32306-2100. Offers information (MA, MS, PhD, Specialist); information technology (MS). *Accreditation:* ALA (one or more programs are accredited). *Program availability:* Part-time, evening/weekend, 100% online, blended/hybrid learning. *Faculty:* 29 full-time (16 women), 9 part-time/adjunct (5 women). *Students:* 40 full-time (23 women), 331 part-time (217 women); includes 135 minority (45 Black or African American, non-Hispanic/Latino; 15 Asian, non-Hispanic/Latino; 47 Hispanic/Latino; 1 Native Hawaiian or other Pacific Islander, non-Hispanic/Latino; 27 Two or more races, non-Hispanic/Latino), 20 international. Average age 35. 301 applicants, 60% accepted, 130 enrolled. In 2018, 124 master's, 2 other advanced degrees awarded. Terminal master's awarded for partial completion of doctoral program. *Degree requirements:* For master's, thesis optional, minimum GPA of 3.0, 36 hours (MSI); 32 hours (MSIT); for doctorate, comprehensive exam, thesis/dissertation, dissertation defense, manuscript clearance, minimum GPA of 3.0; for Specialist, minimum GPA of 3.0; 30 hours. *Entrance requirements:* For master's, GRE (recommended minimum percentile of 50 on each of the verbal and quantitative portions and writing score of 4.0), minimum GPA of 3.0 on last 2 years of baccalaureate degree, resume, statement of goals, two letters of recommendation, official transcripts from

every college-level institution attended; for doctorate, GRE (recommended minimum percentile of 50 on each of the verbal and quantitative portions and writing score of 4.0), minimum GPA of 3.0 on last degree program, resume, 3 letters of recommendation, personal/goals statement, writing sample, brief digital video, official transcripts from all college-level institutions attended; for Specialist, GRE (recommended minimum percentile of 50 on each of the verbal and quantitative portions and writing score of 4.0), minimum graduate GPA of 3.2, resume, statement of goals, 2 letters of recommendation, writing sample, official transcripts from every college-level institution attended. Additional exam requirements/recommendations for international students: Required—TOEFL (minimum score 94 paper-based; 94 iBT), IELTS (minimum score 6.5). *Application deadline:* For fall admission, 7/1 for domestic and international students; for spring admission, 11/1 for domestic and international students. Applications are processed on a rolling basis. Application fee: $30. Electronic applications accepted. *Expenses:* $479.32 per credit hour in-state; $1,590.04 per credit hour out-of-state. *Financial support:* In 2018–19, 106 students received support, including 8 research assistantships with full tuition reimbursements available (averaging $20,076 per year), 25 teaching assistantships with full tuition reimbursements available (averaging $20,076 per year); career-related internships or fieldwork, health care benefits, tuition waivers (full), and unspecified assistantships also available. Financial award application deadline: 3/1; financial award applicants required to submit FAFSA. *Faculty research:* Information technology, social informatics, health information, human information behavior, youth services. *Total annual research expenditures:* $288,132. *Unit head:* Dr. Kathleen Burnett, Director/Professor, 850-644-5775, Fax: 850-644-9763, E-mail: kburnett@fsu.edu. *Application contact:* Student Services, 850-645-3280, Fax: 850-644-9763, E-mail: ischooladvising@admin.fsu.edu.
Website: http://ischool.cci.fsu.edu

Fordham University, Gabelli School of Business, New York, NY 10023. Offers accounting (MBA, MS); applied statistics and decision-making (MS); business economics (DPS); capital markets (DPS); communications and media management (MBA); electronic business (MBA); entrepreneurship (MBA); finance (MBA, PhD); global finance (MS); global sustainability (MBA); health administration (MS); healthcare management (MBA); information systems (MBA, MS); investor relations (MS); management (EMBA, MBA, MS, PhD); marketing (MBA); marketing intelligence (MS); media management (MS); nonprofit leadership (MS); quantitative finance (MS); strategy and decision-making (DPS); taxation (MS); JD/MBA; MS/MBA. *Accreditation:* AACSB. *Program availability:* Part-time, evening/weekend. Terminal master's awarded for partial completion of doctoral program. *Degree requirements:* For master's, internships (for some degrees); for doctorate, comprehensive exam (for some programs), thesis/dissertation. *Entrance requirements:* For master's, GMAT/GRE, 2 letters of recommendation, resume, 2 essays, transcripts, interview. Additional exam requirements/recommendations for international students: Required—TOEFL (minimum score 100 iBT), IELTS (minimum score 7). Electronic applications accepted. *Expenses:* Contact institution.

Franklin Pierce University, Graduate and Professional Studies, Rindge, NH 03461-0060. Offers curriculum and instruction (M Ed); elementary education (MS Ed); emerging network technologies (Graduate Certificate); energy and sustainability studies (MBA, Graduate Certificate); health administration (MBA, Graduate Certificate); human resource management (MBA, Graduate Certificate); information technology (MBA); leadership (MBA); nursing education (MS); nursing leadership (MS); physical therapy (DPT); physician assistant studies (MPAS); special education (M Ed); sports management (MBA). *Accreditation:* APTA. *Program availability:* Part-time, 100% online, blended/hybrid learning. *Degree requirements:* For master's, concentrated original research projects; student teaching; fieldwork and/or internship; leadership project; PRAXIS I and II (for M Ed); for doctorate, concentrated original research projects, clinical fieldwork and/or internship, leadership project. *Entrance requirements:* For master's, minimum GPA of 2.5, 3 letters of recommendation; competencies in accounting, economics, statistics, and computer skills through life experience or undergraduate coursework (for MBA); certification/e-portfolio, minimum C grade in all education courses (for M Ed); license to practice as RN (for MS); for doctorate, GRE, 80 hours of observation/work in PT settings; completion of anatomy, chemistry, physics, and statistics; minimum GPA of 3.0. Additional exam requirements/recommendations for international students: Required—TOEFL (minimum score 550 paper-based; 61 iBT). Electronic applications accepted. *Faculty research:* Evidence-based practice in sports physical therapy, human resource management in economic crisis, leadership in nursing, innovation in sports facility management, differentiated learning and understanding by design.

Friends University, Graduate School, Wichita, KS 67213. Offers family therapy (MSFT); global business administration (MBA), including accounting, business law, change management, health care leadership, management information systems, supply chain management and logistics; health care leadership (MHCL); management information systems (MMIS); professional business administration (MBA), including accounting, business law, change management, health care leadership, management information systems, supply chain management and logistics. *Program availability:* Part-time, evening/weekend, online learning. *Degree requirements:* For master's, research project. *Entrance requirements:* For master's, bachelor's degree from accredited institution, official transcripts, interview with program director, letter(s) of recommendation. Additional exam requirements/recommendations for international students: Required—TOEFL (minimum score 560 paper-based). Electronic applications accepted.

George Mason University, School of Business, Program in Management of Secure Information Systems, Fairfax, VA 22030. Offers MS. *Faculty:* 7 full-time (1 woman), 3 part-time/adjunct (1 woman). *Students:* 25 full-time (7 women); includes 9 minority (3 Black or African American, non-Hispanic/Latino; 3 Asian, non-Hispanic/Latino; 2 Hispanic/Latino; 1 Two or more races, non-Hispanic/Latino). Average age 38. In 2018, 18 master's awarded. *Degree requirements:* For master's, thesis, capstone project. *Entrance requirements:* For master's, current resume; official copies of transcripts from all colleges or universities attended; two professional letters of recommendation; goal statement; interview. Additional exam requirements/recommendations for international students: Required—TOEFL (minimum score 650 paper-based; 93 iBT), IELTS, PTE. Application fee: $75 ($80 for international students). Electronic applications accepted. *Expenses:* $1,200 per credit. *Financial support:* Career-related internships or fieldwork, Federal Work-Study, and scholarships/grants available. Support available to part-time students. Financial award applicants required to submit FAFSA. *Unit head:* Kumar Mehta, Director, 703-993-9412, Fax: 703-993-1809, E-mail: kmehta1@gmu.edu. *Application contact:* Jacky Buchy, Assistant Dean of Graduate Enrollment, 703-993-1856, Fax: 703-993-1778, E-mail: jbuchy@gmu.edu.
Website: http://business.gmu.edu/cyber-security-degree/

The George Washington University, School of Business, Department of Information Systems and Technology Management, Washington, DC 20052. Offers information and decision systems (PhD); information systems (MSIST); information systems development (MSIST); information systems management (MBA); information systems project management (MSIST); management information systems (MSIST); management of science, technology, and innovation (MBA, PhD). Programs also offered in Ashburn and Arlington, VA. *Program availability:* Part-time, evening/weekend, online learning. *Students:* 98 full-time (49 women), 47 part-time (19 women); includes 33 minority (12 Black or African American, non-Hispanic/Latino; 14 Asian, non-Hispanic/Latino; 2 Hispanic/Latino; 5 Two or more races, non-Hispanic/Latino), 91 international. Average age 29. 328 applicants, 67% accepted, 55 enrolled. In 2018, 98 master's awarded. *Entrance requirements:* For master's, GMAT. Additional exam requirements/recommendations for international students: Required—TOEFL. *Application deadline:* For fall admission, 4/1 priority date for domestic students; for spring admission, 10/1 for domestic students. Applications are processed on a rolling basis. Application fee: $75. *Financial support:* In 2018–19, 35 students received support. Fellowships, teaching assistantships, career-related internships or fieldwork, Federal Work-Study, institutionally sponsored loans, and tuition waivers available. Financial award application deadline: 4/1. *Faculty research:* Expert systems, decision support systems. *Unit head:* Richard Donnelly, Chair, 202-994-7155, E-mail: rgd@gwu.edu. *Application contact:* Christopher Storer, Executive Director, Graduate Admissions, 202-994-1212, E-mail: gwmba@gwu.edu.

Georgia College & State University, Graduate School, The J. Whitney Bunting School of Business, Program in Management Information Systems, Milledgeville, GA 31061. Offers MMIS. *Program availability:* Part-time-only, blended/hybrid learning. *Degree requirements:* For master's, minimum GPA of 3.0, complete program within 7 years of start date. *Entrance requirements:* For master's, GRE or GMAT (not required for students who attended an AACSB accredited business school and maintained an overall undergraduate GPA of 3.2), transcript, certificate of immunization. Electronic applications accepted. *Expenses:* Contact institution.

Georgia Institute of Technology, Graduate Studies, Scheller College of Business, Program in Business Administration, Atlanta, GA 30332-0001. Offers business administration (MBA); global business (MBA); management of technology (MBA). *Accreditation:* AACSB. *Program availability:* Part-time, evening/weekend. *Entrance requirements:* For master's, GMAT, two essays, three letters of recommendation, transcript from each college/university attended. Additional exam requirements/recommendations for international students: Required—TOEFL (minimum score 600 paper-based; 100 iBT). Electronic applications accepted. *Expenses:* Contact institution.

Georgia Southern University, Jack N. Averitt College of Graduate Studies, Allen E. Paulson College of Engineering and Computing, Department of Information Technology, Statesboro, GA 30458. Offers MSAE. *Program availability:* Part-time. *Degree requirements:* For master's, comprehensive exam, thesis (for some programs). *Entrance requirements:* For master's, undergraduate major or equivalent in proposed study area. Additional exam requirements/recommendations for international students: Required—TOEFL (minimum score 550 paper-based; 80 iBT), IELTS (minimum score 6). Electronic applications accepted. *Expenses: Tuition, area resident:* Part-time $3324 per semester. Tuition, state resident: full-time $5814; part-time $3324 per semester. Tuition, nonresident: full-time $23,204; part-time $13,260 per semester. *Required fees:* $2092; $2092. Tuition and fees vary according to course load, degree level, campus/location and program. *Faculty research:* Electrical systems, information technology, electromagnetics, digital control systems, applied engineering.

Georgia Southern University, Jack N. Averitt College of Graduate Studies, Parker College of Business, Enterprise Resources Planning Certificate Program, Statesboro, GA 30458. Offers Graduate Certificate. *Program availability:* Part-time-only, online only, 100% online, blended/hybrid learning. *Faculty:* 11 full-time (2 women). *Students:* 3 part-time (1 woman); includes 1 minority (Black or African American, non-Hispanic/Latino). Average age 45. 5 applicants, 100% accepted, 3 enrolled. In 2018, 4 Graduate Certificates awarded. *Entrance requirements:* For degree, bachelor's degree or equivalent with minimum cumulative GPA of 2.7; official copies of all transcripts; resume with three references; personal statement. Additional exam requirements/recommendations for international students: Required—TOEFL (minimum score 550 paper-based), IELTS (minimum score 6). *Application deadline:* For fall admission, 6/15 for domestic students. Applications are processed on a rolling basis. Application fee: $50. Electronic applications accepted. *Expenses:* Contact institution. *Financial support:* In 2018–19, 1 student received support. Application deadline: 4/20; applicants required to submit FAFSA. *Faculty research:* Enterprise resource planning (ERP) and business intelligence (BI) synergies, cloud-based and on-demand ERP solutions, IT artifact in ERP-centered supply chain information systems, impact of bring your own device (BYOD) policies on deployment of enterprise systems mobile applications, career readiness of SAP University Alliances students for positions in ERP user and consulting firms. *Unit head:* Dr. Camille Rogers, Program Coordinator, 912-478-4747, E-mail: cfrogers@georgiasouthern.edu. *Application contact:* Dr. Camille Rogers, Program Coordinator, 912-478-4747, E-mail: cfrogers@georgiasouthern.edu.
Website: http://cob.georgiasouthern.edu/is/degrees/online-erp-program/

Georgia Southern University, Jack N. Averitt College of Graduate Studies, Parker College of Business, Program in Applied Economics, Statesboro, GA 30460. Offers applied economics (MS); information systems (Graduate Certificate). *Program availability:* Part-time-only, online only, 100% online. *Entrance requirements:* For master's, GRE, minimum GPA of 3.0, current knowledge of calculus and statistics, introductory micro and macro courses. Additional exam requirements/recommendations for international students: Required—TOEFL (minimum score 550 paper-based; 80 iBT), IELTS (minimum score 6). Electronic applications accepted. *Expenses: Tuition, area resident:* Part-time $3324 per semester. Tuition, state resident: full-time $5814; part-time $3324 per semester. Tuition, nonresident: full-time $23,204; part-time $13,260 per semester. *Required fees:* $2092; $2092. Tuition and fees vary according to course load, degree level, campus/location and program. *Faculty research:* Analytical capabilities in economic development, financial economics, regulatory issues, market analysis, economic development.

Georgia Southwestern State University, School of Computing and Mathematics, Americus, GA 31709-4693. Offers computer information systems (Graduate Certificate); computer science (MS). *Program availability:* Part-time, 100% online, blended/hybrid learning. *Degree requirements:* For master's, thesis optional, minimum cumulative GPA of 3.0; maximum of 6 credit hours with C grade; no courses with D grade; degree must be completed within 7 calendar years from date of initial enrollment in graduate course work; for Graduate Certificate, minimum cumulative GPA of 3.0; maximum of 6 credit hours with C grade; no courses with D grade; degree must be completed within 7 calendar years from date of initial enrollment in graduate course work. *Entrance requirements:* For master's and Graduate Certificate, GRE, bachelor's degree from regionally-accredited college; minimum undergraduate GPA of 2.5 as reported on official final transcripts from all institutions attended; letters of recommendation. Additional exam requirements/recommendations for international students: Required—TOEFL (minimum score 523 paper-based; 69 iBT), IELTS (minimum score 6.5). Electronic applications accepted. *Expenses:* Contact institution.

Georgia State University, J. Mack Robinson College of Business, Department of Computer Information Systems, Atlanta, GA 30302-3083. Offers computer information systems (PhD); health informatics (MBA, MS); information systems (MSIS, Certificate); information systems development and project management (MBA); information systems management (MBA); managing information technology (Exec MS); the wireless organization (MBA). *Program availability:* Part-time, evening/weekend. *Faculty:* 13 full-

time (1 woman), 4 part-time/adjunct (all women). *Students:* 126 full-time (60 women), 6 part-time (0 women); includes 32 minority (20 Black or African American, non-Hispanic/Latino; 9 Asian, non-Hispanic/Latino; 2 Hispanic/Latino; 1 Two or more races, non-Hispanic/Latino), 90 international. Average age 30. 409 applicants, 62% accepted, 86 enrolled. In 2018, 156 master's, 5 doctorates awarded. *Entrance requirements:* For master's, GRE or GMAT, transcripts from all institutions attended, resume, essays; for doctorate, GRE or GMAT, three letters of recommendation, personal statement, transcripts from all institutions attended, resume. Additional exam requirements/recommendations for international students: Required—TOEFL (minimum score 610 paper-based; 101 iBT), IELTS (minimum score 7). *Application deadline:* For fall admission, 5/1 priority date for domestic students, 2/1 priority date for international students; for spring admission, 9/15 priority date for domestic students, 4/1 priority date for international students. Applications are processed on a rolling basis. Application fee: $50. Electronic applications accepted. *Expenses: Tuition, area resident:* Full-time $9360; part-time $390 per credit hour. Tuition, state resident: full-time $9360; part-time $390 per credit hour. Tuition, nonresident: full-time $30,024; part-time $1251 per credit hour. *International tuition:* $30,024 full-time. *Required fees:* $2128. *Financial support:* Research assistantships, teaching assistantships, scholarships/grants, tuition waivers, and unspecified assistantships available. Financial award applicants required to submit FAFSA. *Faculty research:* Process and technological innovation, strategic IT management, intelligent systems, information systems security, software project risk. *Unit head:* Dr. Ephraim R. McLean, Professor/Chair, 404-413-7360, Fax: 404-413-7394. *Application contact:* Toby McChesney, Assistant Dean for Graduate Recruiting and Student Services, 404-413-7167, Fax: 404-413-7167, E-mail: rcbgradadmissions@gsu.edu.
Website: http://cis.robinson.gsu.edu/

Georgia State University, J. Mack Robinson College of Business, Institute of International Business, Atlanta, GA 30303. Offers international business (GMBA, MBA, MIB); international business and information technology (MBA); international entrepreneurship (MBA); MIB/MIA. *Program availability:* Part-time, evening/weekend. *Faculty:* 5 full-time (3 women). *Students:* 18 full-time (8 women); includes 6 minority (3 Black or African American, non-Hispanic/Latino; 1 Asian, non-Hispanic/Latino; 1 Hispanic/Latino; 1 Two or more races, non-Hispanic/Latino), 8 international. Average age 29. 48 applicants, 73% accepted, 22 enrolled. In 2018, 40 master's awarded. *Entrance requirements:* For master's, GRE or GMAT, transcripts from all institutions attended, resume, essays. Additional exam requirements/recommendations for international students: Required—TOEFL (minimum score 610 paper-based; 101 iBT), IELTS (minimum score 7). *Application deadline:* For fall admission, 5/1 priority date for domestic students, 2/1 priority date for international students; for spring admission, 9/15 priority date for domestic students, 5/1 priority date for international students. Applications are processed on a rolling basis. Application fee: $50. Electronic applications accepted. *Expenses: Tuition, area resident:* Full-time $9360; part-time $390 per credit hour. Tuition, state resident: full-time $9360; part-time $390 per credit hour. Tuition, nonresident: full-time $30,024; part-time $1251 per credit hour. *International tuition:* $30,024 full-time. *Required fees:* $2128. *Financial support:* Research assistantships, teaching assistantships, scholarships/grants, tuition waivers (partial), and unspecified assistantships available. Financial award application deadline: 5/1. *Faculty research:* Business challenges in emerging markets (especially in India and China); interorganizational relationships in an international context, such as strategic alliances and global supply chain relations; globalization and entry mode strategy or new (or emerging) multinationals; emerging market development and business environments; cross-cultural effects on business processes and performance. *Unit head:* Dr. Daniel Bello, Professor/Director of the Institute of International Business, 404-413-7275, Fax: 404-413-7276. *Application contact:* Toby McChesney, Assistant Dean for Graduate Recruiting and Student Services, 404-413-7167, Fax: 404-413-7162, E-mail: rcbgradadmissions@gsu.edu.
Website: http://iib.gsu.edu/

Golden Gate University, Ageno School of Business, San Francisco, CA 94105-2968. Offers accounting (MBA); adaptive leadership (MBA); advanced financial planning (MS); business administration (EMBA, MBA, DBA); business analytics (MBA, MS); entrepreneurship (MBA); finance (MBA, MS, Certificate); financial life planning (Certificate); financial planning (MS, Certificate); global supply chain management (MBA, Certificate); human resource management (MBA, MS, Certificate); information technology management (MBA, MS, Certificate); international business (MBA); marketing (MBA, MS, Certificate); project management (MBA, MS, Certificate); psychology (MA, Certificate); public administration (EMPA, MBA); public administration leadership (Certificate); JD/MBA. *Program availability:* Part-time, evening/weekend. *Degree requirements:* For doctorate, thesis/dissertation, qualifying examination. *Entrance requirements:* For master's, GMAT (for MBA), minimum GPA of 2.5 (MS). Additional exam requirements/recommendations for international students: Required—TOEFL (minimum score 550 paper-based; 79 iBT). Electronic applications accepted. *Expenses:* Contact institution.

Goldey-Beacom College, Graduate Program, Wilmington, DE 19808-1999. Offers business administration (MBA); finance (MS); financial management (MBA); health care management (MBA); human resource management (MBA); information technology (MBA); international business management (MBA); major finance (MBA); major taxation (MBA); management (MM); marketing management (MBA); taxation (MBA, MS). *Accreditation:* ACBSP. *Program availability:* Part-time, evening/weekend. *Entrance requirements:* For master's, GMAT, MAT, GRE, minimum GPA of 3.0. Additional exam requirements/recommendations for international students: Required—TOEFL (minimum score 65 iBT); Recommended—IELTS (minimum score 6). Electronic applications accepted.

Governors State University, College of Business, Program in Management Information Systems, University Park, IL 60484. Offers MS. *Program availability:* Part-time. *Faculty:* 14 full-time (10 women), 17 part-time/adjunct (10 women). *Students:* 6 full-time (1 woman), 10 part-time (3 women); includes 10 minority (6 Black or African American, non-Hispanic/Latino; 2 Asian, non-Hispanic/Latino; 1 Hispanic/Latino; 1 Two or more races, non-Hispanic/Latino), 1 international. Average age 40. 24 applicants, 38% accepted, 8 enrolled. In 2018, 11 master's awarded. *Application deadline:* For fall admission, 4/1 for domestic students. Applications are processed on a rolling basis. Application fee: $50. Electronic applications accepted. *Expenses:* $406/credit hour; $4,872 in tuition/term; $6,002 in tuition and fees/term; $12,004/year. *Financial support:* Application deadline: 5/1; applicants required to submit FAFSA. *Unit head:* David Green, Chair, Division of Accounting, Finance, Management Information Systems, and Economics, 708-534-5000 Ext. 4967, E-mail: dgreen@govst.edu. *Application contact:* David Green, Chair, Division of Accounting, Finance, Management Information Systems, and Economics, 708-534-5000 Ext. 4967, E-mail: dgreen@govst.edu.

The Graduate Center, City University of New York, Graduate Studies, Program in Business, New York, NY 10016-4039. Offers accounting (PhD); behavioral science (PhD); finance (PhD); management planning systems (PhD). *Degree requirements:* For doctorate, thesis/dissertation. *Entrance requirements:* For doctorate, GMAT, writing sample (15 pages). Additional exam requirements/recommendations for international students: Required—TOEFL. Electronic applications accepted.

Grand Valley State University, Padnos College of Engineering and Computing, School of Computing and Information Systems, Allendale, MI 49401-9403. Offers computer information systems (MS), including databases, distributed systems, management of information systems, object-oriented systems, software engineering. *Program availability:* Part-time, evening/weekend. *Faculty:* 10 full-time (0 women). *Students:* 26 full-time (10 women), 53 part-time (7 women); includes 10 minority (2 Black or African American, non-Hispanic/Latino; 6 Asian, non-Hispanic/Latino; 1 Hispanic/Latino; 1 Two or more races, non-Hispanic/Latino), 21 international. Average age 29. 56 applicants, 70% accepted, 15 enrolled. In 2018, 23 master's awarded. *Entrance requirements:* For master's, GRE (recommended with GPA below 3.0), minimum GPA of 3.0; knowledge of a programming language; coursework or experience in: computer architecture and/or organization, data structures and algorithms, databases, discrete math, networking, operating systems, and software engineering; minimum of 2 letters of recommendation; resume; personal statement. Additional exam requirements/recommendations for international students: Required—Michigan English Language Assessment Battery (minimum score 77), TOEFL (minimum iBT score of 80), or IELTS (6.5); GRE. *Application deadline:* For fall admission, 6/1 for international students; for winter admission, 9/1 for international students. Applications are processed on a rolling basis. Application fee: $30. Electronic applications accepted. *Expenses:* $712 per credit hour, 33 credit hours. *Financial support:* In 2018–19, 13 students received support, including 6 fellowships, 5 research assistantships with full and partial tuition reimbursements available (averaging $8,000 per year). *Faculty research:* Object technology, distributed computing, information systems management database, software engineering. *Unit head:* Dr. Paul Leidig, Director, 616-331-2060, Fax: 616-331-2144, E-mail: leidigp@gvsu.edu. *Application contact:* Dr. D. Robert Adams, Graduate Program Director, 616-331-3885, Fax: 616-331-2144, E-mail: adamsr@gvsu.edu.
Website: http://www.cis.gvsu.edu/

Grantham University, College of Engineering and Computer Science, Lenexa, KS 66219. Offers information management (MS), including project management; information management technology (MS); information technology (MS). *Program availability:* Part-time, evening/weekend, online only, 100% online. *Students:* 168 full-time (40 women), 65 part-time (19 women); includes 102 minority (73 Black or African American, non-Hispanic/Latino; 1 American Indian or Alaska Native, non-Hispanic/Latino; 10 Asian, non-Hispanic/Latino; 10 Hispanic/Latino; 8 Two or more races, non-Hispanic/Latino). Average age 40. 52 applicants, 96% accepted, 44 enrolled. In 2018, 84 master's awarded. *Degree requirements:* For master's, comprehensive exam (for some programs), Project Management: PMP Prep Exam (for information management). *Entrance requirements:* For master's, baccalaureate or master's degree with minimum cumulative GPA of 2.5 from institution accredited by agency recognized by U.S. ED or foreign equivalent; official transcripts showing proof of degree. Additional exam requirements/recommendations for international students: Required—TOEFL (minimum score 530 paper-based; 71 iBT), IELTS (minimum score 6.5), PTE (minimum score 50). *Application deadline:* Applications are processed on a rolling basis. Application fee: $0. Electronic applications accepted. *Expenses:* $350 per credit hour plus $50 per credit hour technology fee and books. Military, first responders and their families receive reduced tuition ($250 per credit hour) and technology fee and books fees are waived. *Financial support:* Scholarships/grants available. Financial award applicants required to submit FAFSA. *Faculty research:* Sensor networks and security, grid technologies, cloud computing. *Unit head:* Dr. Nancy Miller, Dean of the College of Engineering and Computer Science, 913-309-4738, Fax: 855-681-5201, E-mail: nmiller@grantham.edu. *Application contact:* Lauren Cook, Director of Admissions, 800-955-2527 Ext. 803, Fax: 877-304-4467, E-mail: admissions@grantham.edu.
Website: http://www.grantham.edu/engineering-and-computer-science/

Grantham University, Mark Skousen School of Business, Lenexa, KS 66219. Offers business administration (MBA); business intelligence (MS); human resources (Certificate); information management (MBA); performance improvement (MS); project management (MBA, Certificate). *Program availability:* Part-time, evening/weekend, online only, 100% online. *Students:* 556 full-time (238 women), 301 part-time (122 women); includes 369 minority (268 Black or African American, non-Hispanic/Latino; 5 American Indian or Alaska Native, non-Hispanic/Latino; 16 Asian, non-Hispanic/Latino; 50 Hispanic/Latino; 4 Native Hawaiian or other Pacific Islander, non-Hispanic/Latino; 26 Two or more races, non-Hispanic/Latino), 1 international. Average age 40. 206 applicants, 90% accepted, 159 enrolled. In 2018, 284 master's, 16 other advanced degrees awarded. *Degree requirements:* For master's, comprehensive exam (for some programs), PMP Prep Exams throughout the term (for MBA in project management); for Certificate, comprehensive exam (for some programs), PMP Prep Exam (for project management). *Entrance requirements:* For master's, baccalaureate or master's degree with minimum cumulative GPA of 2.5 from institution accredited by agency recognized by ED or foreign equivalent; official transcripts showing proof of degree. Additional exam requirements/recommendations for international students: Required—TOEFL (minimum score 530 paper-based; 71 iBT), IELTS (minimum score 6.5), PTE (minimum score 50). *Application deadline:* Applications are processed on a rolling basis. Application fee: $0. Electronic applications accepted. *Expenses: Tuition:* Full-time $4200; part-time $350 per credit hour. *Required fees:* $50; $50 per credit hour. *Financial support:* Scholarships/grants available. Financial award applicants required to submit FAFSA. *Faculty research:* How chronic diseases contribute to the rising costs of healthcare, marketing for entrepreneurs, managers' hiring practices of workers with disability, organizational structures, organizational change, online pedagogy, impact of instructor video tips in the online classroom, decision-making techniques. *Unit head:* Dr. David Marker, Dean of the Mark Skousen School of Business, 913-309-4747, Fax: 844-260-6287, E-mail: dmarker@grantham.edu. *Application contact:* Lauren Cook, Director of Admissions, 800-955-2527 Ext. 803, Fax: 877-304-4467, E-mail: admissions@grantham.edu.
Website: https://www.grantham.edu/school-of-business/

Harrisburg University of Science and Technology, Program in Information Systems Engineering and Management, Harrisburg, PA 17101. Offers analytics (MS); digital government (MS); digital health (MS); entrepreneurship (MS); information security (MS); software engineering and systems development (MS). *Program availability:* Part-time, evening/weekend. *Degree requirements:* For master's, thesis optional. *Entrance requirements:* For master's, baccalaureate degree. Additional exam requirements/recommendations for international students: Required—TOEFL (minimum score 520 paper-based; 80 iBT); Recommended—IELTS (minimum score 6). Electronic applications accepted. *Faculty research:* Healthcare Informatics, material analysis, enterprise systems, circuit design, enterprise architectures.

Hawai`i Pacific University, College of Business, Program in Business Administration, Honolulu, HI 96813. Offers finance (MBA); human resource management (MBA); information systems (MBA); international business (MBA); management (MBA); marketing (MBA); organizational change and development (MBA). *Program availability:* Part-time, evening/weekend, 100% online, blended/hybrid learning. *Entrance requirements:* For master's, GMAT or GRE. Additional exam requirements/recommendations for international students: Recommended—TOEFL (minimum score 550 paper-based; 80 iBT), IELTS (minimum score 6), TWE (minimum score 5). Electronic applications accepted.

Hawai`i Pacific University, College of Business, Program in Information Systems, Honolulu, HI 96813. Offers MSIS. *Program availability:* Part-time, evening/weekend. *Entrance requirements:* For master's, GMAT or GRE. Additional exam requirements/ recommendations for international students: Recommended—TOEFL (minimum score 550 paper-based; 80 iBT), IELTS (minimum score 6), TWE (minimum score 5). Electronic applications accepted.

HEC Montreal, School of Business Administration, Graduate Diploma Programs in Administration, Montréal, QC H3T 2A7, Canada. Offers business administration (Graduate Diploma); business analysis - information technology (Graduate Diploma); e-business (Graduate Diploma); entrepreneurship (Graduate Diploma); financial professions (Graduate Diploma); human resources (Graduate Diploma); management (Graduate Diploma); management and sustainable development (Graduate Diploma); management of cultural organizations (Graduate Diploma); marketing communication (Graduate Diploma); organizational development (Graduate Diploma); professional accounting (Graduate Diploma); supply chain management (Graduate Diploma); taxation (Graduate Diploma). All courses are given in French. *Students:* 412 full-time (242 women), 885 part-time (552 women). 834 applicants, 65% accepted, 351 enrolled. In 2018, 611 Graduate Diplomas awarded. *Entrance requirements:* For degree, bachelor's degree. Application fee: $91 Canadian dollars ($191 Canadian dollars for international students). Electronic applications accepted. *Expenses: Tuition, area resident:* Full-time $3052.80 Canadian dollars; part-time $84.80 Canadian dollars per credit. Tuition, state resident: full-time $3816 Canadian dollars; part-time $264.67 Canadian dollars per credit. Tuition, nonresident: full-time $11,910 Canadian dollars. *International tuition:* $20,905.20 Canadian dollars full-time. *Required fees:* $1805.34 Canadian dollars; $43.62 Canadian dollars per credit. $71.78 Canadian dollars per term. Tuition and fees vary according to degree level and program. *Financial support:* Research assistantships, teaching assistantships, and scholarships/grants available. Financial award application deadline: 9/2. *Faculty research:* Art management, business policy, entrepreneurship, new technologies, transportation. *Unit head:* Renaud Lachance, Director, 514-340-6428, E-mail: renaud.lachance@hec.ca. *Application contact:* Anny Caron, Administrative Director, 514-340-6000, Fax: 514-340-6411, E-mail: aide@hec.ca.
Website: http://www.hec.ca/programmes/dess/index.html

HEC Montreal, School of Business Administration, Master of Science Programs in Administration, Digital Transformation of Organizations, Montréal, QC H3T 2A7, Canada. Offers M Sc. All courses are given in French (Thesis Stream, Supervised project Stream offered). *Students:* 15 full-time (5 women), 5 part-time (1 woman). 17 applicants, 65% accepted, 8 enrolled. In 2018, 15 master's awarded. *Entrance requirements:* For master's, BBA, undergraduate degree in another field, degree deemed equivalent by program director and minimum GPA of 3.0 on 4.3 scale. Additional exam requirements/recommendations for international students: Required—TAGE MAGE (minimum recommended score of 300), GMAT (minimum recommended score of 630), or GRE. *Application deadline:* For fall admission, 3/15 for domestic and international students. Application fee: $91 Canadian dollars ($191 Canadian dollars for international students). Electronic applications accepted. *Expenses: Tuition, area resident:* Full-time $3052.80 Canadian dollars; part-time $84.80 Canadian dollars per credit. Tuition, state resident: full-time $3816 Canadian dollars; part-time $264.67 Canadian dollars per credit. Tuition, nonresident: full-time $11,910 Canadian dollars. *International tuition:* $20,905.20 Canadian dollars full-time. *Required fees:* $1805.34 Canadian dollars; $43.62 Canadian dollars per credit. $71.78 Canadian dollars per term. Tuition and fees vary according to degree level and program. *Financial support:* Research assistantships, teaching assistantships, and scholarships/grants available. Financial award application deadline: 9/2. *Unit head:* Dr. Sihem Taboubi, Director, 514-340-6428, E-mail: sihem.taboubi@hec.ca. *Application contact:* Marianne de Moura, Administrative Director, 514-340-600, Fax: 514-340-6411, E-mail: aide@hec.ca.
Website: http://www.hec.ca/programmes/maitrises/maitrise-technologies-information/index.html

Hodges University, Graduate Programs, Naples, FL 34119. Offers accounting (M Acc); business administration (MBA); clinical mental health counseling (MS); health services administration (MS); information systems management (MIS); legal studies (MS); management (MSM). *Program availability:* Part-time, evening/weekend, 100% online, blended/hybrid learning. *Degree requirements:* For master's, comprehensive exam (for some programs), thesis (for some programs). *Entrance requirements:* For master's, essay. Additional exam requirements/recommendations for international students: Recommended—TOEFL. Electronic applications accepted.

Hofstra University, Frank G. Zarb School of Business, Programs in Information Systems, Hempstead, NY 11549. Offers business administration (MBA), including business analytics, information systems, quality management; business analytics (MS); information systems (MS, Advanced Certificate). *Program availability:* Part-time, evening/weekend, blended/hybrid learning. *Students:* 85 full-time (35 women), 31 part-time (16 women); includes 17 minority (2 Black or African American, non-Hispanic/Latino; 9 Asian, non-Hispanic/Latino; 6 Hispanic/Latino), 76 international. Average age 27. 152 applicants, 69% accepted, 27 enrolled. In 2018, 52 master's awarded. *Degree requirements:* For master's, thesis (for some programs), capstone course (for MBA), thesis (for MS), minimum GPA of 3.0. *Entrance requirements:* For master's, GMAT/GRE, 2 letters of recommendation, resume, essay; for Advanced Certificate, GMAT/GRE, 2 letters of recommendation, resume. Additional exam requirements/recommendations for international students: Required—TOEFL (minimum score 550 paper-based; 80 iBT); Recommended—IELTS (minimum score 6). *Application deadline:* Applications are processed on a rolling basis. Application fee: $75. Electronic applications accepted. *Expenses:* $1,375 per credit plus fees. *Financial support:* In 2018–19, 32 students received support, including 27 fellowships with full and partial tuition reimbursements available (averaging $5,630 per year); research assistantships with full and partial tuition reimbursements available, career-related internships or fieldwork, Federal Work-Study, institutionally sponsored loans, scholarships/grants, tuition waivers (full and partial), unspecified assistantships, and scholarships and endowed scholarships also available. Support available to part-time students. Financial award applicants required to submit FAFSA. *Faculty research:* Big data and social media, healthcare IT and analytics, machine learning and artificial intelligence, inventory system and quality management, cybersecurity and information privacy. *Unit head:* Dr. Hak Kim, Chairperson, 516-463-5716, Fax: 516-463-4834, E-mail: hak.j.kim@hofstra.edu. *Application contact:* Sunil Samuel, Assistant Vice President of Admissions, 516-463-4723, Fax: 516-463-4664, E-mail: graduateadmission@hofstra.edu.
Website: http://www.hofstra.edu/business/

Holy Family University, Graduate and Professional Programs, School of Business Administration, Philadelphia, PA 19114. Offers accountancy (MS); finance (MBA); health care administration (MBA); human resource management (MBA); information systems management (MBA). *Accreditation:* ACBSP. *Program availability:* Part-time, evening/weekend. *Degree requirements:* For master's, comprehensive exam, thesis optional. *Entrance requirements:* For master's, minimum GPA of 3.0, interview, essay/personal statement, current resume, official transcript of all college or university work. Additional exam requirements/recommendations for international students: Required—TOEFL (minimum score 550 paper-based; 79 iBT), IELTS (minimum score 6), PTE (minimum score 54). Electronic applications accepted.

Hood College, Graduate School, Department of Economics and Business Administration, Frederick, MD 21701-8575. Offers accounting (MBA); information systems (MBA); organizational management (Certificate). *Accreditation:* ACBSP. *Program availability:* Part-time, evening/weekend. *Faculty:* 3 full-time (2 women), 6 part-time/adjunct (1 woman). *Students:* 23 full-time (12 women), 176 part-time (120 women); includes 44 minority (17 Black or African American, non-Hispanic/Latino; 5 Asian, non-Hispanic/Latino; 19 Hispanic/Latino; 3 Two or more races, non-Hispanic/Latino), 13 international. Average age 35. 23 applicants, 96% accepted, 13 enrolled. In 2018, 36 master's, 2 other advanced degrees awarded. *Degree requirements:* For master's, capstone/final research project. *Entrance requirements:* For master's, minimum GPA of 3.0 (or resume and two letters of recommendation), copy of official transcripts; for Certificate, copy of official transcripts, Statement of Intent (250 words). Additional exam requirements/recommendations for international students: Required—TOEFL (minimum score 575 paper-based; 89 iBT), IELTS (minimum score 6.5). *Application deadline:* For fall admission, 8/15 for domestic students, 8/5 for international students; for spring admission, 12/1 for domestic and international students; for summer admission, 5/1 for domestic students, 4/15 for international students. Applications are processed on a rolling basis. Application fee: $50 ($100 for international students). Electronic applications accepted. *Expenses:* Business Programs: Tuition $605 per credit hour, Comprehensive Fee $115 per semester. *Financial support:* Tuition waivers (partial) and unspecified assistantships available. Financial award applicants required to submit FAFSA. *Faculty research:* Corporate strategy and sustainable competitive advantages, business ethics, entrepreneurship, investments management, economic development. *Unit head:* Dr. April M. Boulton, Dean of the Graduate School, 301-696-3600, Fax: 301-696-3597, E-mail: gofurther@hood.edu. *Application contact:* Christian DiGregorio, Director of Graduate Admissions, 301-696-3604, E-mail: gofurther@hood.edu.

Howard University, School of Business, Graduate Programs in Business, Washington, DC 20059-0002. Offers accounting (MBA); entrepreneurship (MBA); finance (MBA); general management (MBA); human resources management (MBA); information systems (MBA); international business (MBA); marketing (MBA); supply chain management (MBA); JD/MBA. *Accreditation:* AACSB. *Program availability:* Part-time, evening/weekend, online learning. *Entrance requirements:* For master's, GMAT, minimum 1 year post undergraduate work experience, resume, 3 letters of recommendation, advanced college algebra. Additional exam requirements/recommendations for international students: Required—TOEFL. *Faculty research:* Marketing research in multi-ethnic populations, U.S. trade policies and international relations, risk management (finance).

Idaho State University, Graduate School, College of Business, Pocatello, ID 83209-8020. Offers business administration (MBA, Postbaccalaureate Certificate); computer information systems (MS, Postbaccalaureate Certificate). *Accreditation:* AACSB. *Program availability:* Part-time. *Degree requirements:* For master's, comprehensive exam, thesis (for some programs), oral exam; for Postbaccalaureate Certificate, comprehensive exam, thesis (for some programs), 6 hours of clerkship. *Entrance requirements:* For master's, GMAT, GRE General Test, minimum GPA of 3.0, resume outlining work experience, 2 letters of reference; for Postbaccalaureate Certificate, GMAT, GRE General Test, minimum upper-level GPA of 3.0, resume of work experience. Additional exam requirements/recommendations for international students: Required—TOEFL (minimum score 550 paper-based; 80 iBT). Electronic applications accepted. *Faculty research:* Information assurance, computer information technology, finance management, marketing.

IGlobal University, Graduate Programs, Vienna, VA 22182. Offers accounting (MBA); data management and analytics (MSIT); entrepreneurship (MBA); finance (MBA); global business management (MBA); health care management (MBA); hospitality and tourism management (MBA); human resources management (MBA); information technology (MBA); information technology systems and management (MSIT); leadership and management (MBA); project management (MBA); public service and administration (MBA); software design and management (MSIT).

Illinois Institute of Technology, Graduate College, College of Science, Department of Computer Science, Chicago, IL 60616. Offers business (MCS); computational intelligence (MCS); computer science (MCS, MS, PhD); cyber-physical systems (MCS); data analytics (MCS); data science (MAS); database systems (MCS); distributed and cloud computing (MCS); education (MCS); finance (MCS); information security and assurance (MCS); networking and communications (MCS); software engineering (MCS); telecommunications and software engineering (MAS); MS/MAS. *Program availability:* Part-time, evening/weekend, online learning. Terminal master's awarded for partial completion of doctoral program. *Degree requirements:* For master's, thesis optional; for doctorate, comprehensive exam, thesis/dissertation. *Entrance requirements:* For master's, GRE General Test with minimum scores of 298 Quantitative and Verbal, 3.0 Analytical Writing (for MS); GRE General Test with minimum scores of 292 Quantitative and Verbal, 2.5 Analytical Writing (for MAS), minimum undergraduate GPA of 3.0; for doctorate, GRE General Test (minimum scores: 304 Quantitative and Verbal, 3.5 Analytical Writing), minimum undergraduate GPA of 3.0. Additional exam requirements/recommendations for international students: Required—TOEFL (minimum score 523 paper-based; 70 iBT). Electronic applications accepted. *Faculty research:* Parallel and distributed processing, high-performance computing, computational linguistics, information retrieval, data mining, grid computing.

Illinois Institute of Technology, Graduate College, Lewis College of Human Sciences, Department of Humanities, Chicago, IL 60616. Offers information architecture (MS); technical communication (PhD); technical communication and information design (MS). *Program availability:* Part-time. *Degree requirements:* For master's, comprehensive exam, thesis or alternative; for doctorate, comprehensive exam, thesis/dissertation. *Entrance requirements:* For master's, GRE General Test (minimum score 144 Quantitative, 153 Verbal, and 4.0 Analytical Writing), minimum undergraduate GPA of 3.0; 2 letters of recommendation from faculty or supervisors; professional statement discussing academic goals; for doctorate, GRE General Test (minimum score 144 Quantitative, 153 Verbal, and 4.0 Analytical Writing), bachelor's or master's degree in a field that, in combination with the 27-credit hour technical core, would provide a solid basis for advanced academic work leading to original research in the field; 3 letters of recommendation from faculty or supervisors; professional statement discussing academic goals. Additional exam requirements/recommendations for international students: Required—TOEFL (minimum score 95 iBT); Recommended—IELTS (minimum score 7). Electronic applications accepted. *Faculty research:* Linguistics, punishment theory, political communication, gender and technology, philosophical and ethical issues in neuroscience.

Illinois Institute of Technology, Graduate College, School of Applied Technology, Department of Information Technology and Management, Wheaton, IL 60189. Offers cyber forensics and security (MAS); information technology and management (MAS). *Program availability:* Part-time, evening/weekend, online learning. *Entrance requirements:* For master's, GRE (minimum score 300 Quantitative and Verbal, 2.5 Analytical Writing), bachelor's degree with minimum cumulative undergraduate GPA of 3.0 (or its equivalent) from accredited institution. Additional exam requirements/

recommendations for international students: Required—TOEFL (minimum score 523 paper-based; 70 iBT); Recommended—IELTS (minimum score 5.5). Electronic applications accepted. *Faculty research:* Database design, voice over IP, process engineering, object-oriented programming, computer networking, online design, system administration.

Illinois State University, Graduate School, College of Applied Science and Technology, School of Information Technology, Normal, IL 61790. Offers MS. *Faculty:* 22 full-time (8 women), 18 part-time/adjunct (5 women). *Students:* 43 full-time (19 women), 14 part-time (2 women); includes 3 minority (2 Black or African American, non-Hispanic/Latino; 1 Asian, non-Hispanic/Latino), 39 international. Average age 28. 51 applicants, 88% accepted, 16 enrolled. In 2018, 22 master's awarded. *Degree requirements:* For master's, thesis or alternative. *Entrance requirements:* For master's, GRE General Test, minimum GPA of 3.0 in last 60 hours; proficiency in COBOL, FORTRAN, Pascal, or P12. *Application deadline:* Applications are processed on a rolling basis. Application fee: $40. *Expenses: Tuition, area resident:* Full-time $7264.62. Tuition, state resident: full-time $9466. Tuition, nonresident: full-time $17,290. *International tuition:* $15,089.40 full-time. *Required fees:* $1481.04. *Financial support:* In 2018–19, 1 research assistantship, 15 teaching assistantships were awarded; tuition waivers (full) and unspecified assistantships also available. Financial award application deadline: 4/1. *Faculty research:* Graduate practicum training in network support. *Unit head:* Dr. Mary Elaine Califf, School Director, 309-438-8338, E-mail: mecalif@illinoisState.edu. *Application contact:* Dr. Yongining Tang, Graduate Coordinator, 309-438-8002, E-mail: ytang@illinoisState.edu.
Website: http://www.acs.ilstu.edu/

Indiana University Bloomington, School of Public and Environmental Affairs, Public Affairs Programs, Bloomington, IN 47405. Offers economic development (MPA); energy (MPA); environmental policy (PhD); environmental policy and natural resource management (MPA); information systems (MPA); international development (MPA); local government management (MPA); nonprofit management (MPA, Certificate); policy analysis (MPA); public budgeting and financial management (Certificate); public finance (PhD); public financial administration (MPA); public management (MPA, PhD, Certificate); public policy analysis (PhD); social entrepreneurship (Certificate); specialized public affairs (MPA); sustainability and sustainable development (MPA); JD/MPA; MPA/MA; MPA/MIS; MPA/MLS; MSES/MPA. *Accreditation:* NASPAA (one or more programs are accredited). *Program availability:* Part-time. *Degree requirements:* For master's, capstone, internship; for doctorate, comprehensive exam, thesis/dissertation. *Entrance requirements:* For master's, GRE General Test or GMAT, official transcripts, 3 letters of recommendation, resume, personal statement; for doctorate, GRE General Test, official transcripts, 3 letters of recommendation, statement of purpose. Additional exam requirements/recommendations for international students: Required—TOEFL (minimum score 600 paper-based; 96 iBT); Recommended—IELTS (minimum score 7). Electronic applications accepted. *Faculty research:* International development, environmental policy and resource management, policy analysis, public finance, public management, urban management, nonprofit management, energy policy, social policy, public finance.

Indiana University Northwest, College of Arts and Sciences, Gary, IN 46408. Offers clinical counseling (MS), including drug and alcohol counseling; community development/urban studies (Graduate Certificate); computer information systems (Graduate Certificate); liberal studies (MLS); race-ethnic studies (Graduate Certificate); women's and gender studies (Graduate Certificate). *Program availability:* Part-time, evening/weekend. *Entrance requirements:* For master's, GRE (recommended for MS), minimum undergraduate GPA of 3.0, bachelor's degree from accredited university (for MS). Electronic applications accepted. *Expenses:* Contact institution.

Instituto Tecnológico y de Estudios Superiores de Monterrey, Campus Central de Veracruz, Graduate Programs, Córdoba, Mexico. Offers administration (MA); administration of information technologies (MTI); computer sciences (MCC); education (MEE); educational institution administration (MAD); educational technology (MTE); electronic commerce (MCE); finance (MAF); humanistic studies (MEH); international business for Latin America (MNL); marketing (MMT); science (MCP). *Program availability:* Part-time, evening/weekend, online learning. *Degree requirements:* For master's, thesis (for some programs). *Entrance requirements:* For master's, PAEP College Board. Electronic applications accepted.

Instituto Tecnológico y de Estudios Superiores de Monterrey, Campus Ciudad de México, Virtual University Division, Ciudad de Mexico, Mexico. Offers administration of information technologies (MA); computer sciences (MA); education (MA, PhD); educational technology (MA); environmental engineering (MA); environmental systems (MA); humanistic studies (MA); industrial engineering (MA); international business for Latin America (MA); quality systems (MA); quality systems and productivity (MA). *Program availability:* Part-time, evening/weekend, online learning. *Entrance requirements:* For master's and doctorate, Instituto entrance exam. Additional exam requirements/recommendations for international students: Required—TOEFL.

Instituto Tecnológico y de Estudios Superiores de Monterrey, Campus Ciudad Juárez, Program in Administration of Information Technology, Ciudad Juárez, Mexico. Offers MAIT.

Instituto Tecnológico y de Estudios Superiores de Monterrey, Campus Ciudad Obregón, Program in Administration of Information Technology, Ciudad Obregón, Mexico. Offers MATI.

Instituto Tecnológico y de Estudios Superiores de Monterrey, Campus Estado de México, Professional and Graduate Division, Estado de Mexico, Mexico. Offers administration of information technologies (MITA); architecture (M Arch); business administration (GMBA, MBA); computer sciences (MCS, PhD); education (M Ed); educational institution administration (MAD); educational technology and innovation (PhD); electronic commerce (MEC); environmental systems (MS); finance (MAF); humanistic studies (MHS); information sciences and knowledge management (MISKM); information systems (MS); manufacturing systems (MS); marketing (MEM); quality systems and productivity (MS); science and materials engineering (PhD); telecommunications management (MTM). *Program availability:* Part-time, online learning. *Degree requirements:* For master's, one foreign language, thesis (for some programs); for doctorate, one foreign language, thesis/dissertation. *Entrance requirements:* For master's, E-PAEP 500, interview; for doctorate, E-PAEP 500, research proposal. Additional exam requirements/recommendations for international students: Required—TOEFL (minimum score 550 paper-based). *Faculty research:* Surface treatments by plasmas, mechanical properties, robotics, graphical computing, mechatronics security protocols.

Instituto Tecnológico y de Estudios Superiores de Monterrey, Campus Irapuato, Graduate Programs, Irapuato, Mexico. Offers administration (MBA); administration of information technology (MAIT); administration of telecommunications (MAT); architecture (M Arch); computer science (MCS); education (M Ed); educational administration (MEA); educational innovation and technology (DEIT); educational technology (MET); electronic commerce (MBA); environmental administration and planning (MEAP); environmental systems (MES); finances (MBA); humanistic studies (MHS); international management for Latin American executives (MIMLAE); library and information science (MLIS); manufacturing quality management (MMQM); marketing research (MBA).

Instituto Tecnológico y de Estudios Superiores de Monterrey, Campus Laguna, Graduate School, Torreón, Mexico. Offers business administration (MBA); industrial engineering (MIE); management information systems (MS). *Program availability:* Part-time. *Entrance requirements:* For master's, GMAT. *Faculty research:* Computer communications from home to the university.

Inter American University of Puerto Rico, Aguadilla Campus, Graduate School, Aguadilla, PR 00605. Offers accounting (MBA); counseling psychology specializing in family (MS); criminal justice (MA); educative management and leadership (MA); elementary education (M Ed); finance (MBA); human resources (MBA); industrial management (MBA); management information systems (MBA); marketing (MBA). *Program availability:* Part-time, evening/weekend. *Degree requirements:* For master's, comprehensive exam. *Entrance requirements:* For master's, EXADEP, 2 letters of recommendation, minimum GPA of 2.5. Electronic applications accepted.

Inter American University of Puerto Rico, Fajardo Campus, Graduate Programs, Fajardo, PR 00738-7003. Offers computer science (MS); educational management and leadership (MA Ed); general business (MBA); human resources (MBA); management information systems (MBA); marketing (MBA); special education (MA Ed). *Program availability:* Online learning.

Inter American University of Puerto Rico, Metropolitan Campus, Graduate Programs, Program in Management Information Systems, San Juan, PR 00919-1293. Offers MBA.

Inter American University of Puerto Rico, San Germán Campus, Graduate Studies Center, Program in Business Administration, San Germán, PR 00683-5008. Offers accounting (MBA); finance (MBA); general business administration (MBA); human resources (MBA, PhD); industrial relations (MBA); information systems (MBA); international and interregional business (PhD); management (MBA); marketing (MBA). *Program availability:* Part-time, evening/weekend. *Degree requirements:* For master's, comprehensive exam. *Entrance requirements:* For master's, GRE General Test or EXADEP, minimum GPA of 3.0. *Expenses: Tuition:* Full-time $212; part-time $212 per credit. *Required fees:* $366 per semester. One-time fee: $31. Tuition and fees vary according to degree level and program.

Iona College, School of Business, Department of Accounting, New Rochelle, NY 10801-1890. Offers accounting and information systems (MS); general accounting (MBA, AC); public accounting (MBA, MS, AC). *Program availability:* Part-time, evening/weekend. *Faculty:* 6 full-time (2 women), 2 part-time/adjunct (both women). *Students:* 25 full-time (10 women), 43 part-time (20 women); includes 23 minority (1 Black or African American, non-Hispanic/Latino; 2 American Indian or Alaska Native, non-Hispanic/Latino; 5 Asian, non-Hispanic/Latino; 14 Hispanic/Latino; 1 Two or more races, non-Hispanic/Latino), 3 international. Average age 29. 32 applicants, 94% accepted, 19 enrolled. In 2018, 55 master's awarded. *Entrance requirements:* For master's and AC, minimum GPA of 3.0. Additional exam requirements/recommendations for international students: Required—TOEFL (minimum score 550 paper-based; 80 iBT), IELTS (minimum score 6.5). *Application deadline:* For fall admission, 8/15 priority date for domestic students, 8/1 priority date for international students; for winter admission, 11/15 priority date for domestic students, 11/1 priority date for international students; for spring admission, 2/15 priority date for domestic students, 2/1 priority date for international students; for summer admission, 5/15 priority date for domestic students, 5/1 priority date for international students. Applications are processed on a rolling basis. Application fee: $0. Electronic applications accepted. *Expenses: Tuition:* Full-time $14,064; part-time $7032 per credit. *Required fees:* $245 per semester. One-time fee: $250. Tuition and fees vary according to program. *Financial support:* In 2018–19, 38 students received support. Scholarships/grants, tuition waivers (partial), and unspecified assistantships available. Support available to part-time students. Financial award application deadline: 4/15; financial award applicants required to submit FAFSA. *Faculty research:* Tax policy, investment returns, international accounting standards. *Unit head:* Katherine Kinkela, LLM, Chair, Accounting Department, 914-633-2267, E-mail: kkinkela@iona.edu. *Application contact:* Kimberly Kelly, Director of Graduate Business Admissions, 914-633-2271, Fax: 914-633-2012, E-mail: kkelly@iona.edu.
Website: https://www.iona.edu/academics/school-of-business/departments/accounting.aspx

Iowa State University of Science and Technology, Program in Business and Technology, Ames, IA 50011. Offers PhD. *Entrance requirements:* Additional exam requirements/recommendations for international students: Required—TOEFL (minimum score 600 paper-based; 100 iBT), IELTS (minimum score 7). Electronic applications accepted.

Iowa State University of Science and Technology, Program in Information Systems, Ames, IA 50011. Offers information systems (MS). *Degree requirements:* For master's, thesis or alternative. *Entrance requirements:* For master's, GMAT. Additional exam requirements/recommendations for international students: Recommended—TOEFL (minimum score 600 paper-based; 100 iBT), IELTS (minimum score 7). Electronic applications accepted. *Expenses:* Contact institution.

James Madison University, The Graduate School, College of Business, Program in Business Administration, Harrisonburg, VA 22807. Offers business (MBA), including executive leadership, information security, innovation. *Accreditation:* AACSB. *Program availability:* Part-time, evening/weekend, blended/hybrid learning. *Students:* 37 full-time (10 women), 82 part-time (34 women); includes 28 minority (9 Black or African American, non-Hispanic/Latino; 7 Asian, non-Hispanic/Latino; 10 Hispanic/Latino; 2 Two or more races, non-Hispanic/Latino), 7 international. Average age 30. In 2018, 38 master's awarded. Application fee: $6. Electronic applications accepted. *Expenses:* Tuition, state resident: full-time $10,848. Tuition, nonresident: full-time $27,888. *Required fees:* $1128. *Financial support:* In 2018–19, 2 students received support. Federal Work-Study and 1 assistantship (averaging $7911) available. Financial award application deadline: 3/1; financial award applicants required to submit FAFSA. *Unit head:* Dr. Matthew A. Rutherford, Department Head, 540-568-8777, E-mail: rutherma@jmu.edu. *Application contact:* Lynette D. Michael, Director of Graduate Admissions, 540-568-6131 Ext. 6395, Fax: 540-568-7860, E-mail: michaeld@jmu.edu.
Website: http://www.jmu.edu/cob/graduate/mba/index.shtml

Johns Hopkins University, Carey Business School, MS in Information Systems Program, Baltimore, MD 21218. Offers MS. *Students:* 72 full-time (39 women), 11 part-time (1 woman). 276 applicants, 59% accepted, 64 enrolled. In 2018, 87 master's awarded. *Degree requirements:* For master's, 36 credits. *Entrance requirements:* For master's, GMAT or GRE. Additional exam requirements/recommendations for international students: Required—TOEFL, IELTS. *Application deadline:* For fall admission, 5/1 for domestic and international students. Applications are processed on a rolling basis. Application fee: $100. Electronic applications accepted. *Expenses:* Contact institution. *Financial support:* In 2018–19, 7 students received support. Scholarships/grants available. Support available to part-time students. Financial award application deadline: 4/15; financial award applicants required to submit FAFSA. *Faculty research:* Digital innovations in healthcare, digital marketplaces, healthcare information systems, information technology and strategy. *Unit head:* Dr. Kevin Frick, Vice Dean of Education,

410-234-9272, E-mail: kfrick@jhu.edu. *Application contact:* Office of Admissions, 410-234-9220, Fax: 443-529-1554, E-mail: carey.admissions@jhu.edu.
Website: http://carey.jhu.edu/academics/master-of-science/ms-in-information-systems/

Johns Hopkins University, Engineering Program for Professionals, Part-time Program in Information Systems Engineering, Baltimore, MD 21218. Offers MS, Graduate Certificate, Post-Master's Certificate. *Program availability:* Part-time, evening/weekend, 100% online, blended/hybrid learning. *Faculty:* 7 part-time/adjunct (3 women). *Students:* 91 part-time (18 women). 43 applicants, 37% accepted, 13 enrolled. In 2018, 37 master's, 1 other advanced degree awarded. *Entrance requirements:* Additional exam requirements/recommendations for international students: Required—TOEFL (minimum score 600 paper-based; 100 iBT). *Application deadline:* Applications are processed on a rolling basis. Application fee: $0. Electronic applications accepted. *Unit head:* Dr. John Piorkowski, Program Chair, 443-778-6372, E-mail: jpiorko2@jhu.edu. *Application contact:* Doug Schiller, Admissions Director, 410-516-2300, Fax: 410-579-8049, E-mail: schiller@jhu.edu.
Website: http://www.ep.jhu.edu/

Johnson & Wales University, Graduate Studies, MBA Program, Providence, RI 02903-3703. Offers accounting (MBA); business administration (MBA); finance (MBA); global fashion merchandising and management (MBA); hospitality (MBA); human resource management (MBA); information security/assurance (MBA); information technology (MBA); nonprofit management (MBA); operations and supply chain management (MBA); organizational leadership (MBA); organizational psychology (MBA); sport leadership (MBA). Program also offered on Denver campus. *Program availability:* Part-time, online learning. *Entrance requirements:* For master's, minimum GPA of 2.75. Additional exam requirements/recommendations for international students: Required—TOEFL (minimum score 550 paper-based); Recommended—IELTS, TWE. *Faculty research:* International banking, global economy, international trade, cultural differences.

Kean University, College of Natural, Applied and Health Sciences, Program in Computer Information Systems, Union, NJ 07083. Offers MS. *Program availability:* Part-time, 100% online. *Faculty:* 12 full-time (6 women). *Students:* 14 full-time (6 women), 5 part-time (1 woman); includes 8 minority (4 Black or African American, non-Hispanic/Latino; 3 Asian, non-Hispanic/Latino; 1 Hispanic/Latino), 10 international. Average age 28. 15 applicants, 80% accepted, 6 enrolled. In 2018, 13 master's awarded. *Entrance requirements:* For master's, baccalaureate degree in computer science or closely-related field from accredited college or university; minimum cumulative GPA of 3.0; official transcripts from all institutions attended; two letters of recommendation; professional resume/curriculum vitae; personal statement. Additional exam requirements/recommendations for international students: Required—TOEFL (minimum score 550 paper-based; 79 iBT), IELTS (minimum score 6.5). *Application deadline:* For fall admission, 6/30 for domestic and international students; for spring admission, 12/1 for domestic and international students. Applications are processed on a rolling basis. Application fee: $75. Electronic applications accepted. *Expenses:* Tuition, state resident: full-time $15,025; part-time $733.50 per credit. Tuition, nonresident: full-time $19,890; part-time $884.50 per credit. *Required fees:* $2107.50; $89.50 per credit. Tuition and fees vary according to course level, course load, degree level and program. *Financial support:* Scholarships/grants and unspecified assistantships available. Financial award applicants required to submit FAFSA. *Unit head:* Dr. Jing-Chiou Liou, Program Coordinator, 908-737-3803, E-mail: jliou@kean.edu. *Application contact:* Pedro Lopes, Admissions Counselor, 908-737-7100, E-mail: gradadmissions@kean.edu.
Website: http://grad.kean.edu/masters-programs/computer-information-systems

Keiser University, MS in Information Technology Leadership Program, Fort Lauderdale, FL 33309. Offers MS.

Kent State University, College of Business Administration, Doctoral Program in Management Systems, Kent, OH 44242. Offers PhD. *Faculty:* 9 full-time (3 women). *Students:* 11 full-time (7 women), 7 international. Average age 34. 26 applicants, 35% accepted, 5 enrolled. In 2018, 2 doctorates awarded. *Degree requirements:* For doctorate, comprehensive exam, thesis/dissertation, oral defense. *Entrance requirements:* For doctorate, GMAT or GRE. Additional exam requirements/recommendations for international students: Required—TOEFL (minimum score 600 paper-based; 100 iBT), IELTS (minimum score 7). *Application deadline:* For fall admission, 1/1 for domestic students, 2/1 for international students. Application fee: $45 ($70 for international students). Electronic applications accepted. *Expenses:* Contact institution. *Financial support:* In 2018–19, 7 students received support, including 7 teaching assistantships with full tuition reimbursements available (averaging $23,000 per year). Financial award application deadline: 2/1; financial award applicants required to submit FAFSA. *Unit head:* Dr. O. Felix Offodile, Chair and Professor, 330-672-2750, Fax: 330-672-2953, E-mail: foffodil@kent.edu. *Application contact:* Felecia A. Urbanek, Assistant Director, 330-672-2282, Fax: 330-672-7303, E-mail: gradbus@kent.edu.
Website: http://www.kent.edu/business/phd

Lake Erie College, School of Business, Painesville, OH 44077-3389. Offers general management (MBA); health care administration (MBA); information technology management (MBA). *Program availability:* Part-time, evening/weekend. *Entrance requirements:* For master's, GMAT or minimum GPA of 3.0, resume, personal statement. Additional exam requirements/recommendations for international students: Required—TOEFL (minimum score 550 paper-based; 79 iBT), IELTS (minimum score 6), STEP Eiken 1st and pre-1st grade level (for Japanese students). Electronic applications accepted. Application fee is waived when completed online. *Expenses:* Contact institution.

Le Moyne College, Madden School of Business, Syracuse, NY 13214. Offers business administration (MBA); information systems (MS). *Accreditation:* AACSB. *Program availability:* Part-time, evening/weekend. *Faculty:* 18 full-time (5 women), 5 part-time/adjunct (1 woman). *Students:* 48 full-time (21 women), 63 part-time (30 women); includes 11 minority (3 Black or African American, non-Hispanic/Latino; 1 American Indian or Alaska Native, non-Hispanic/Latino; 3 Asian, non-Hispanic/Latino; 4 Hispanic/Latino), 4 international. Average age 27. 69 applicants, 94% accepted, 61 enrolled. In 2018, 60 master's awarded. *Degree requirements:* For master's, thesis (for some programs), capstone-level course. *Entrance requirements:* For master's, GMAT or GRE General Test, bachelor's degree with minimum GPA of 3.0, resume, 2 letters of recommendation, personal statement, transcripts, interview; GMAT/GRE. Additional exam requirements/recommendations for international students: Required—TOEFL (minimum score 79 iBT); Recommended—IELTS (minimum score 6.5). *Application deadline:* For fall admission, 7/1 priority date for domestic and international students; for spring admission, 11/1 priority date for domestic and international students; for summer admission, 4/1 priority date for domestic and international students. Applications are processed on a rolling basis. Application fee: $0. Electronic applications accepted. *Expenses:* $835 per credit hour; wellness fee $70 per semester for full-time graduate students taking 9+ credit hours; technology fee $75 per semester for full-time graduate students taking 9+ credit hours, $25 per semester for part-time students. *Financial support:* In 2018–19, 35 students received support. Career-related internships or fieldwork, scholarships/grants, health care benefits, and unspecified assistantships available. Support available to part-time students. Financial award applicants required to submit FAFSA. *Faculty research:* Performance evaluation outcomes assessment, technology outsourcing, international business, systems for Web-based information-seeking, non-profit business practices, business sustainability practices, management/leadership development, operations management optimization applications. *Unit head:* James Joseph, Dean of Madden School of Business, 315-445-4280, Fax: 315-445-4787, E-mail: josepjae@lemoyne.edu. *Application contact:* Teresa M. Renn, Senior Assistant Director for Graduate Admission, 315-445-5444, Fax: 315-445-6092, E-mail: renntm@lemoyne.edu.
Website: http://www.lemoyne.edu/madden

Lenoir-Rhyne University, Graduate Programs, Charles M. Snipes School of Business, Hickory, NC 28601. Offers accounting (MBA); business analytics and information technology (MBA); entrepreneurship (MBA); global business (MBA); healthcare administration (MBA); innovation and change management (MBA); leadership development (MBA). *Accreditation:* ACBSP. *Program availability:* Part-time, evening/weekend, online learning. *Degree requirements:* For master's, capstone course. *Entrance requirements:* For master's, GMAT, GRE, MAT, minimum undergraduate GPA of 2.7, graduate 3.0. Additional exam requirements/recommendations for international students: Required—TOEFL (minimum score 600 paper-based). Electronic applications accepted. *Expenses:* Contact institution.

Lewis University, College of Business, Program in Business Administration, Romeoville, IL 60446. Offers accounting (MBA); custom elective option (MBA); e-business (MBA); finance (MBA); healthcare management (MBA); human resources management (MBA); international business (MBA); management information systems (MBA); marketing (MBA); project management (MBA); technology and operations management (MBA). *Program availability:* Part-time, evening/weekend. *Students:* 114 full-time (72 women), 143 part-time (87 women); includes 84 minority (21 Black or African American, non-Hispanic/Latino; 2 American Indian or Alaska Native, non-Hispanic/Latino; 11 Asian, non-Hispanic/Latino; 45 Hispanic/Latino; 5 Two or more races, non-Hispanic/Latino), 17 international. Average age 31. In 2018, 99 master's awarded. *Entrance requirements:* For master's, interview, bachelor's degree, resume, two recommendations. Additional exam requirements/recommendations for international students: Required—TOEFL (minimum score 550 paper-based), IELTS. *Application deadline:* For fall admission, 8/15 priority date for domestic students, 5/1 priority date for international students; for spring admission, 11/15 priority date for international students. Applications are processed on a rolling basis. Application fee: $40. Electronic applications accepted. *Financial support:* Career-related internships or fieldwork, Federal Work-Study, scholarships/grants, and unspecified assistantships available. Financial award application deadline: 5/1; financial award applicants required to submit FAFSA. *Unit head:* Dr. Maureen Culleeney, Academic Program Director, 815-838-0500 Ext. 5631, E-mail: culleema@lewisu.edu. *Application contact:* Michele Ryan, Director of Admission, 815-838-0500 Ext. 5384, E-mail: ryanml@lewisu.edu.

Lincoln University, Graduate Studies, Oakland, CA 94612. Offers finance and investments (DBA); finance management (MS); finance management and investments (MBA); general business (MBA); human resource management (MBA, DBA); international business (MBA, MS); management information systems (MBA). *Program availability:* Part-time. *Degree requirements:* For master's, research project (thesis), internship report, or comprehensive exam; for doctorate, comprehensive exam, thesis/dissertation. *Entrance requirements:* For master's, minimum GPA of 2.7; for doctorate, GMAT (minimum score: 550), GRE (minimum score: 1000), or equivalent test results (waived for master's degree with minimum cumulative GPA of 3.3). Additional exam requirements/recommendations for international students: Required—TOEFL minimum score 525 paper-based; 71 iBT or IELTS minimum score 5.5 (for MBA); TOEFL minimum score 550 paper-based; 79 iBT or IELTS minimum score 6 (for MS and DBA). Electronic applications accepted.

Lindenwood University, Graduate Programs, School of Accelerated Degree Programs, St. Charles, MO 63301-1695. Offers administration (MSA), including management, marketing, project management; business administration (MBA); communications (MA), including digital and multimedia, media management, promotions, training and development; criminal justice and administration (MS); healthcare administration (MS); human resource management (MS); information technology (Certificate); managing information security (MS); managing information technology (MS); managing virtualization and cloud computing (MS); writing (MFA). *Program availability:* Part-time, evening/weekend, 100% online. *Faculty:* 15 full-time (8 women), 62 part-time/adjunct (22 women). *Students:* 652 full-time (398 women), 66 part-time (45 women); includes 241 minority (182 Black or African American, non-Hispanic/Latino; 1 American Indian or Alaska Native, non-Hispanic/Latino; 8 Asian, non-Hispanic/Latino; 25 Hispanic/Latino; 1 Native Hawaiian or other Pacific Islander, non-Hispanic/Latino; 24 Two or more races, non-Hispanic/Latino), 81 international. Average age 36. 359 applicants, 54% accepted, 170 enrolled. In 2018, 416 master's, 2 other advanced degrees awarded. *Degree requirements:* For master's, thesis (for some programs), minimum cumulative GPA of 3.0; for Certificate, minimum cumulative GPA of 3.0. *Entrance requirements:* For master's, resume, personal statement, official undergraduate transcript, minimum undergraduate cumulative GPA of 3.0. Additional exam requirements/recommendations for international students: Required—TOEFL (minimum score 553 paper-based; 81 iBT); Recommended—IELTS (minimum score 6.5). *Application deadline:* For fall admission, 9/30 priority date for domestic and international students; for winter admission, 1/6 priority date for domestic and international students; for spring admission, 4/6 priority date for domestic and international students; for summer admission, 7/8 priority date for domestic and international students. Applications are processed on a rolling basis. Application fee: $0 ($100 for international students). Electronic applications accepted. *Expenses:* Contact institution. *Financial support:* In 2018–19, 372 students received support. Career-related internships or fieldwork, institutionally sponsored loans, scholarships/grants, tuition waivers (partial), and unspecified assistantships available. Financial award application deadline: 6/30; financial award applicants required to submit FAFSA. *Unit head:* Dr. Gina Ganahl, Dean, Accelerated Degree Programs, 636-949-4501, Fax: 636-949-4505, E-mail: gganahl@lindenwood.edu. *Application contact:* Kara Schilli, Assistant Vice President, University Admissions, 636-949-4349, Fax: 636-949-4109, E-mail: adultadmissions@lindenwood.edu.
Website: https://www.lindenwood.edu/academics/academic-schools/school-of-accelerated-degree-programs/

Lipscomb University, College of Computing and Technology, Nashville, TN 37204-3951. Offers data science (MS, Certificate); information technology (MS, Certificate), including data science (MS), information security (MS), information technology management (MS), software engineering (MS); software engineering (MS, Certificate). *Program availability:* Part-time, evening/weekend. *Degree requirements:* For master's, capstone project. *Entrance requirements:* For master's, GRE, 2 references, transcripts, resume, personal statement. Additional exam requirements/recommendations for international students: Required—TOEFL (minimum score 570 paper-based; 80 iBT). Electronic applications accepted. *Expenses:* Contact institution.

London Metropolitan University, Graduate Programs, London, United Kingdom. Offers applied psychology (M Sc); architecture (MA); biomedical science (M Sc); blood science (M Sc); cancer pharmacology (M Sc); computer networking and cyber security

(M Sc); computing and information systems (M Sc); conference interpreting (MA); counter-terrorism studies (M Sc); creative, digital and professional writing (MA); crime, violence and prevention (M Sc); criminology (M Sc); curating contemporary art (MA); data analytics (M Sc); digital media (MA); early childhood studies (MA); education (MA, Ed D); financial services law, regulation and compliance (LL M); food science (M Sc); forensic psychology (M Sc); health and social care management and policy (M Sc); human nutrition (M Sc); human resource management (MA); human rights and international conflict (MA); information technology (M Sc); intelligence and security studies (M Sc); international oil, gas and energy law (LL M); international relations (MA); interpreting (MA); learning and teaching in higher education (MA); legal practice (LL M); media and entertainment law (LL M); organizational and consumer psychology (M Sc); psychological therapy (M Sc); psychology of mental health (M Sc); public health (M Sc); public policy and management (MPA); security studies (M Sc); social work (M Sc); spatial planning and urban design (MA); sports therapy (M Sc); supporting older children and young people with dyslexia (MA); teaching languages (MA), including Arabic, English; translation (MA); woman and child abuse (MA).

Long Island University–LIU Post, College of Management, Brookville, NY 11548-1300. Offers accountancy (MS); finance (MBA); information systems (MS); international business (MBA); management (MBA); management engineering (MS); marketing (MBA); taxation (MS); technical project management (MS); JD/MBA. *Accreditation:* AACSB. *Program availability:* Part-time, evening/weekend, blended/hybrid learning. *Entrance requirements:* For master's, GMAT, GRE, or LSAT. Additional exam requirements/recommendations for international students: Required—TOEFL (minimum score 550 paper-based, 75 iBT) or IELTS. Electronic applications accepted. *Faculty research:* Innovation and property rights, knowledge sourcing, sustainability and firm performance, China and growth markets, corporate social responsibility, workforce compensation and issues.

Louisiana State University and Agricultural & Mechanical College, Graduate School, E. J. Ourso College of Business, Department of Information Systems and Decision Sciences, Baton Rouge, LA 70803. Offers MS, PhD.

Louisiana Tech University, Graduate School, College of Business, Ruston, LA 71272. Offers accounting (M Acc, DBA); computer information systems (DBA); finance (MBA, DBA); information assurance (MBA); innovation (MBA); management (DBA); marketing (MBA, DBA). *Accreditation:* AACSB. *Program availability:* Part-time, evening/weekend, 100% online, blended/hybrid learning. *Degree requirements:* For doctorate, thesis/dissertation. *Entrance requirements:* For master's and doctorate, GMAT, transcript with bachelor's degree awarded. Additional exam requirements/recommendations for international students: Required—TOEFL (minimum score 550 paper-based; 80 iBT), IELTS (minimum score 6.5). Electronic applications accepted. *Faculty research:* Consumer environmental behavior; identifying and analyzing current issues and future concerns in real estate; information assurance and related areas in business for Northwest Louisiana and the United States (business continuity, disaster recovery, accounting controls, auditing, computer forensics, and security attribution); value creation driven by the consumer and employee interface within exchange environments.

Loyola University Chicago, Quinlan School of Business, Master of Science in Information Systems Management Program, Chicago, IL 60611. Offers information systems (MS, Certificate). *Program availability:* Part-time, evening/weekend. *Entrance requirements:* For master's, GMAT or GRE, a completed application form, official transcripts, two letters of recommendation, a statement of purpose, a resume. Additional exam requirements/recommendations for international students: Required—the minimum total score on the Internet-Based Test (IBT) of the TOEFL exam is 90. The minimum acceptable total score on the IELTS exam is 6.5. Electronic applications accepted. Application fee is waived when completed online. *Expenses:* Contact institution. *Faculty research:* Strategic use of IT, database design data warehousing, e-business, applications of data mining.

Loyola University Chicago, Quinlan School of Business, MBA Programs, Chicago, IL 60611. Offers accounting (MBA); business ethics (MBA); derivative markets (MBA); economics (MBA); entrepreneurship (MBA); finance (MBA); healthcare management (MBA); human resources management (MBA); information systems management (MBA); international business (MBA); management (MBA); marketing (MBA); risk management (MBA); supply chain management (MBA). *Program availability:* Part-time, evening/weekend. *Entrance requirements:* For master's, GMAT or GRE, official transcripts, two letters of recommendation, statement of purpose, resume. Additional exam requirements/recommendations for international students: Required—TOEFL (minimum score 90 iBT) or IELTS (minimum score 6.5). Electronic applications accepted. Application fee is waived when completed online. *Expenses:* Contact institution. *Faculty research:* Social enterprise and responsibility, emerging markets, supply chain management, risk management.

Loyola University Maryland, Graduate Programs, Sellinger School of Business, Professional MBA Program, Baltimore, MD 21210-2699. Offers finance (MBA); information systems (MBA); investments and applied portfolio management (MBA); management (MBA); marketing (MBA). *Accreditation:* AACSB. *Program availability:* Part-time, evening/weekend. *Entrance requirements:* For master's, GMAT, resume, essay, official transcripts, professional letter of recommendation. Additional exam requirements/recommendations for international students: Required—TOEFL (minimum score 550 paper-based, 80 iBT) or IELTS (minimum score 7). Electronic applications accepted. *Expenses:* Contact institution.

Marist College, Graduate Programs, School of Computer Science and Mathematics, Poughkeepsie, NY 12601-1387. Offers business analytics (Adv C); computer science/software development (MS); information systems (MS, Adv C). *Program availability:* Part-time, evening/weekend, online learning. *Entrance requirements:* For master's, resume. Additional exam requirements/recommendations for international students: Required—TOEFL (minimum score 550 paper-based; 80 iBT); Recommended—IELTS (minimum score 6.5). Electronic applications accepted. *Faculty research:* Data quality, artificial intelligence, imaging, analysis of algorithms, distributed systems and applications.

Marquette University, Graduate School of Management, Executive MBA Program, Milwaukee, WI 53201-1881. Offers economics (MBA); finance (MBA); human resources (MBA); international business (MBA); management information systems (MBA); marketing (MBA); operations and supply chain management (MBA); sports business (MBA). *Accreditation:* AACSB. *Degree requirements:* For master's, international trip. *Entrance requirements:* For master's, GMAT or GRE, two letters of recommendation, official transcripts from current and previous colleges/universities. Additional exam requirements/recommendations for international students: Required—TOEFL (minimum score 550 paper-based; 88 iBT), IELTS (minimum score 6.5), PTE. Electronic applications accepted. *Expenses:* Contact institution. *Faculty research:* International trade and finance, customer relationship management, consumer satisfaction, customer service.

Marquette University, Graduate School of Management, Program in Business Administration, Milwaukee, WI 53201-1881. Offers business administration (MBA); economics (MBA); entrepreneurship (Certificate); finance (MBA); human resources (MBA); international business (MBA); management information systems (MBA); marketing (MBA); operations and supply chain management (MBA); sports business (MBA); JD/MBA; MBA/MA; MBA/MSN. *Accreditation:* AACSB. *Program availability:* Part-time, evening/weekend. *Degree requirements:* For Certificate, business plan. *Entrance requirements:* For master's, GMAT or GRE, letters of recommendation. Additional exam requirements/recommendations for international students: Required—TOEFL (minimum score 550 paper-based; 88 iBT), IELTS (minimum score 6.5), PTE. Electronic applications accepted. *Faculty research:* Ethics in the professions, services marketing, technology impact on decision-making, mentoring.

Marymount University, School of Business and Technology, Program in Information Technology, Arlington, VA 22207-4299. Offers health care informatics (Certificate); information technology (MS, Certificate), including cybersecurity (MS), health care informatics (MS), project management and technology leadership (MS), software engineering (MS); information technology project management and technology leadership (Certificate); information technology with business administration (MS/MBA); information technology with health care management (MS/MS); MS/MBA; MS/MS. *Program availability:* Part-time, evening/weekend. *Faculty:* 5 full-time (3 women), 7 part-time/adjunct (0 women). *Students:* 29 full-time (17 women), 36 part-time (19 women); includes 25 minority (15 Black or African American, non-Hispanic/Latino; 5 Asian, non-Hispanic/Latino; 5 Hispanic/Latino), 24 international. Average age 30. 66 applicants, 98% accepted, 22 enrolled. In 2018, 35 master's, 3 other advanced degrees awarded. *Degree requirements:* For master's, thesis or alternative. *Entrance requirements:* For master's, resume, bachelor's degree in computer-related field or degree in another subject with a certificate in a computer-related field or related work experience. Software Engineering Track: bachelor's degree in Computer Science or work in software development. Project Mgmt/Tech Leadership Track: minimum 2 years of IT experience. Additional exam requirements/recommendations for international students: Required—TOEFL (minimum score 600 paper-based; 96 iBT), IELTS (minimum score 6.5), PTE (minimum score 58). *Application deadline:* For fall admission, 7/16 priority date for domestic and international students; for spring admission, 11/16 priority date for domestic and international students; for summer admission, 4/16 priority date for domestic and international students. Applications are processed on a rolling basis. Application fee: $40. Electronic applications accepted. *Expenses:* $1,060 per credit. *Financial support:* In 2018–19, 1 student received support. Research assistantships, teaching assistantships, career-related internships or fieldwork, scholarships/grants, and unspecified assistantships available. Support available to part-time students. Financial award application deadline: 3/1; financial award applicants required to submit FAFSA. *Unit head:* Dr. Diane Murphy, Chair/Director, Information Technology, Management Sciences and Cybersecurity, 703-284-5958, E-mail: diane.murphy@marymount.edu. *Application contact:* Rebecca Esposito, Senior Associate Director, Graduate Admissions, 703-284-5901, Fax: 703-527-3815, E-mail: grad.admissions@marymount.edu.
Website: https://www.marymount.edu/Academics/School-of-Business-and-Technology/Graduate-Programs/Information-Technology-(M-S-)

Marywood University, Academic Affairs, Munley College of Liberal Arts and Sciences, School of Business and Global Innovation, Emphasis in Management Information Systems, Scranton, PA 18509-1598. Offers MBA, MS. *Program availability:* Part-time. Electronic applications accepted.

McGill University, Faculty of Graduate and Postdoctoral Studies, Desautels Faculty of Management, Montréal, QC H3A 2T5, Canada. Offers administration (PhD); entrepreneurial studies (MBA); finance (MBA); general management (Post Master's Certificate); global manufacturing and supply chain management (MMM); information systems (MBA); international business (MBA); international practicing management (MM); management (MBA); management for development (MBA); marketing (MBA); operations management (MBA); public accountancy (Diploma); strategic management (MBA); MBA/LL B; MD/MBA. MMM offered jointly with Faculty of Engineering; PhD with Concordia University, HEC Montreal, Université de Montréal, Université du Québec à Montréal.

McMaster University, School of Graduate Studies, DeGroote School of Business, Program in Information Systems, Hamilton, ON L8S 4M2, Canada. Offers PhD. *Program availability:* Part-time. *Degree requirements:* For doctorate, comprehensive exam, thesis/dissertation. *Entrance requirements:* For doctorate, GMAT or GRE General Test, master's degree, minimum B+ average. Additional exam requirements/recommendations for international students: Required—TOEFL (minimum score 580 paper-based). *Faculty research:* Information systems, operations management, web-based decision support systems, web-based agents, financial engineering.

Metropolitan State University, College of Management, St. Paul, MN 55106-5000. Offers business administration (MBA, DBA); business analytics (Graduate Certificate); database administration (Graduate Certificate); global supply chain management (Graduate Certificate); information assurance security (Graduate Certificate); management information systems (MMIS); MIS generalist (Graduate Certificate); MIS systems analysis and design (Graduate Certificate); project management (Graduate Certificate). *Program availability:* Part-time, evening/weekend. *Degree requirements:* For master's, thesis optional, computer language (MMIS). *Entrance requirements:* For master's, GMAT (for MBA), resume. Additional exam requirements/recommendations for international students: Required—TOEFL (minimum score 550 paper-based). Electronic applications accepted. *Faculty research:* Yugoslav economic system, workers' cooperatives, participative management and job enrichment, global business systems.

Michigan State University, The Graduate School, College of Communication Arts and Sciences, Department of Media and Information, East Lansing, MI 48824. Offers media and information management (MA); serious game design (MA). *Entrance requirements:* Additional exam requirements/recommendations for international students: Required—TOEFL. Electronic applications accepted.

Michigan State University, The Graduate School, Eli Broad College of Business, Department of Accounting and Information Systems, East Lansing, MI 48224. Offers accounting (MS, PhD), including information systems (MS), public and corporate accounting (MS), taxation (MS); business information systems (PhD). *Accreditation:* AACSB. *Degree requirements:* For doctorate, comprehensive exam, thesis/dissertation. *Entrance requirements:* For master's, GMAT (minimum score 550), bachelor's degree in accounting; minimum cumulative GPA of 3.0 at any institution attended and in any junior-/senior-level accounting courses taken; 3 letters of recommendation (at least 1 from faculty); working knowledge of computers including word processing, spreadsheets, networking, and database management system; for doctorate, GMAT (minimum score 600), bachelor's degree; transcripts; 3 letters of recommendation; statement of purpose; resume; on-campus interview; personal qualifications of sound character, perseverance, intellectual curiosity, and interest in scholarly research. Additional exam requirements/recommendations for international students: Required—TOEFL (minimum score 600 paper-based; 100 iBT), IELTS (minimum score 7) accepted for MS only. Electronic applications accepted.

Middle Georgia State University, Office of Graduate Studies, Macon, GA 31206. Offers adult/gerontology acute care nurse practitioner (MSN); information technology (MS), including health informatics, information security and digital forensics, software

development. *Entrance requirements:* For master's, GRE. Additional exam requirements/recommendations for international students: Required—TOEFL (minimum score 523 paper-based; 69 iBT). *Expenses:* Contact institution.

Middle Tennessee State University, College of Graduate Studies, Jennings A. Jones College of Business, Department of Computer Information Systems, Murfreesboro, TN 37132. Offers MS. *Program availability:* Part-time, evening/weekend, online learning. *Entrance requirements:* Additional exam requirements/recommendations for international students: Required—TOEFL (minimum score 525 paper-based; 71 iBT) or IELTS (minimum score 6). Electronic applications accepted. *Faculty research:* Safety and security, project management.

Minot State University, Graduate School, Information Systems Program, Minot, ND 58707-0002. Offers MSIS. *Program availability:* Part-time, online learning. *Entrance requirements:* Additional exam requirements/recommendations for international students: Required—TOEFL (minimum score 79 iBT), IELTS (minimum score 6).

Mississippi State University, Bagley College of Engineering, Department of Industrial and Systems Engineering, Mississippi State, MS 39762. Offers human factors and ergonomics (MS); industrial and systems engineering (PhD); industrial systems (MS); management systems (MS); manufacturing systems (MS); operations research (MS). *Program availability:* Part-time, blended/hybrid learning. *Faculty:* 12 full-time (2 women). *Students:* 35 full-time (13 women), 66 part-time (16 women); includes 20 minority (7 Black or African American, non-Hispanic/Latino; 6 Asian, non-Hispanic/Latino; 5 Hispanic/Latino; 1 Native Hawaiian or other Pacific Islander, non-Hispanic/Latino; 1 Two or more races, non-Hispanic/Latino), 21 international. Average age 36. 67 applicants, 40% accepted, 18 enrolled. In 2018, 16 master's, 9 doctorates awarded. *Degree requirements:* For master's, comprehensive exam (for some programs), thesis optional, comprehensive oral or written exam; for doctorate, comprehensive exam, thesis/dissertation, candidacy exam. *Entrance requirements:* For master's, GRE (for graduates from program not accredited by EAC/ABET), minimum GPA of 3.0 on junior and senior years; for doctorate, GRE (for graduates from program not accredited by EAC/ABET), minimum GPA of 3.5 on master's degree and junior and senior years of BS. Additional exam requirements/recommendations for international students: Required—TOEFL (minimum score 550 paper-based; 79 iBT); Recommended—IELTS (minimum score 6.5). *Application deadline:* For fall admission, 7/1 for domestic students, 5/1 for international students; for spring admission, 11/1 for domestic students, 9/1 for international students. Applications are processed on a rolling basis. Application fee: $60 ($80 for international students). Electronic applications accepted. *Expenses:* Tuition, state resident: full-time $8450; part-time $360.59 per credit hour. Tuition, nonresident: full-time $23,140; part-time $969.09 per credit hour. *Required fees:* $110. One-time fee: $55 full-time. Part-time tuition and fees vary according to course load, degree level, campus/location and reciprocity agreements. *Financial support:* In 2018–19, 18 research assistantships with full tuition reimbursements (averaging $16,905 per year), 3 teaching assistantships with full tuition reimbursements (averaging $16,033 per year) were awarded; Federal Work-Study, institutionally sponsored loans, and unspecified assistantships also available. Financial award application deadline: 4/1; financial award applicants required to submit FAFSA. *Faculty research:* Operations research, ergonomics, production systems, management systems, transportation. *Total annual research expenditures:* $2 million. *Unit head:* Dr. Kari Babski-Reeves, Professor/Interim Head and Associate Dean for Research & Graduate Studies, 662-325-8430, Fax: 662-325-7618, E-mail: kari@ise.msstate.edu. *Application contact:* Ryan King, Admissions and Enrollment Assistant, 662-325-8951, E-mail: rjk101@grad.msstate.edu. Website: http://www.ise.msstate.edu/

Mississippi State University, College of Business, Department of Management and Information Systems, Mississippi State, MS 39762. Offers business administration (MBA); information systems (MSIS, PhD); management (PhD); project management (MBA). *Program availability:* Part-time. *Faculty:* 16 full-time (3 women), 1 part-time/adjunct (0 women). *Students:* 62 full-time (21 women), 189 part-time (50 women); includes 25 minority (13 Black or African American, non-Hispanic/Latino; 3 Asian, non-Hispanic/Latino; 9 Hispanic/Latino), 18 international. Average age 30. 136 applicants, 59% accepted, 46 enrolled. In 2018, 105 master's, 2 doctorates awarded. *Degree requirements:* For master's, comprehensive exam; for doctorate, comprehensive exam, thesis/dissertation. *Entrance requirements:* For master's, GMAT, minimum GPA of 3.0 in last 60 hours of undergraduate course work; for doctorate, GMAT (minimum score of 550), minimum GPA of 3.25 on all graduate work; BS with minimum GPA of 3.0 cumulative and last 60 hours. Additional exam requirements/recommendations for international students: Required—TOEFL (minimum score 575 paper-based; 84 iBT); Recommended—IELTS (minimum score 7). *Application deadline:* For fall admission, 7/1 for domestic students, 5/1 for international students; for spring admission, 11/1 for domestic students, 9/1 for international students. Applications are processed on a rolling basis. Application fee: $60 ($80 for international students). Electronic applications accepted. *Expenses:* Tuition, state resident: full-time $8450; part-time $360.59 per credit hour. Tuition, nonresident: full-time $23,140; part-time $969.09 per credit hour. *Required fees:* $110. One-time fee: $55 full-time. Part-time tuition and fees vary according to course load, degree level, campus/location and reciprocity agreements. *Financial support:* Career-related internships or fieldwork, Federal Work-Study, institutionally sponsored loans, scholarships/grants, and unspecified assistantships available. Financial award applicants required to submit FAFSA. *Faculty research:* Electronic commerce, management of information technology. *Total annual research expenditures:* $1.4 million. *Unit head:* Dr. James J. Chrisman, Professor and Head, 662-325-1991, Fax: 662-325-8651, E-mail: jchrisman@business.msstate.edu. *Application contact:* Robbie Salters, Admissions and Enrollment Assistant, 662-325-7400, E-mail: rsalters@grad.msstate.edu.
Website: http://www.business.msstate.edu/programs/mis/index.php

Montclair State University, The Graduate School, Feliciano School of Business, General MBA Program, Montclair, NJ 07043-1624. Offers accounting (MBA); business analytics (MBA); digital marketing (MBA); finance (MBA); general business administration (MBA); human resources management (MBA); management (MBA); management of information and technology (MBA); marketing (MBA); project management (MBA). *Program availability:* Part-time, evening/weekend. *Degree requirements:* For master's, culminating experience. *Entrance requirements:* For master's, GMAT or GRE General Test, 2 letters of recommendation, resume, essay. Additional exam requirements/recommendations for international students: Required—TOEFL (minimum score 83 iBT), IELTS (minimum score 6.5). Electronic applications accepted. *Faculty research:* Accounting, management, marketing.

Morehead State University, Graduate School, Elmer R. Smith College of Business and Technology, Department of Engineering and Technology Management, Morehead, KY 40351. Offers career and technical education (MS); computer information systems and analytics (MS); engineering and technology (MS). *Entrance requirements:* For master's, GRE, GMAT. Additional exam requirements/recommendations for international students: Required—TOEFL (minimum score 525 paper-based). Electronic applications accepted.

Morgan State University, School of Graduate Studies, Earl G. Graves School of Business and Management, PhD Program in Business Administration, Baltimore, MD 21251. Offers business administration (PhD), including accounting, information systems,

management and marketing. *Accreditation:* AACSB. *Entrance requirements:* For doctorate, GMAT. Additional exam requirements/recommendations for international students: Required—TOEFL (minimum score 550 paper-based).

Murray State University, Arthur J. Bauernfeind College of Business, Department of Computer Science and Information Systems, Murray, KY 42071. Offers MSIS. *Program availability:* Part-time, evening/weekend, 100% online, blended/hybrid learning. *Entrance requirements:* For master's, GRE or GMAT, minimum university GPA of 2.75. Additional exam requirements/recommendations for international students: Required—TOEFL (minimum score 527 paper-based; 71 iBT). Electronic applications accepted.

National American University, Roueche Graduate Center, Austin, TX 78731. Offers accounting (MBA); aviation management (MBA, MM); care coordination (MSN); community college leadership (Ed D); criminal justice (MM); e-marketing (MBA, MM); health care administration (MBA, MM); higher education (MM); human resources management (MBA, MM); information technology management (MBA, MM); international business (MBA); leadership (EMBA); management (MBA); nursing administration (MSN); nursing education (MSN); nursing informatics (MSN); operations and configuration management (MBA, MM); project and process management (MBA, MM). Master's programs offered online through the Harold D. Buckingham Graduate School. *Program availability:* Part-time, evening/weekend, online learning. *Entrance requirements:* For master's, minimum undergraduate GPA of 2.75. Additional exam requirements/recommendations for international students: Required—TOEFL, TWE. Electronic applications accepted. *Faculty research:* Tourism, finance, marketing.

National University, School of Business and Management, La Jolla, CA 92037-1011. Offers accountancy (M Acc, Certificate); business administration (GMBA, MBA); business analytics (MS); cause leadership (MA); global management (MGM); human resource management (MA); management information systems (MS); marketing (MS); organizational leadership (MS). GMBA offered in Spanish. *Program availability:* Part-time, evening/weekend, 100% online, blended/hybrid learning. *Degree requirements:* For master's, thesis (for some programs). *Entrance requirements:* For master's, interview, minimum GPA of 2.5. Additional exam requirements/recommendations for international students: Required—TOEFL (minimum score 550 paper-based; 79 iBT), IELTS (minimum score 6). Electronic applications accepted. *Expenses: Tuition:* Full-time $10,320; part-time $430 per unit. Tuition and fees vary according to degree level.

National University, School of Engineering and Computing, La Jolla, CA 92037-1011. Offers computer science (MS), including advanced computing; cyber security and information assurance (MS); data analytics (MS); electrical engineering (MS); engineering management (MS); information technology management (MS); management information systems (MS); sustainability management (MS). *Program availability:* Part-time, evening/weekend, 100% online, blended/hybrid learning. *Degree requirements:* For master's, thesis (for some programs). *Entrance requirements:* For master's, interview, minimum GPA of 2.5. Additional exam requirements/recommendations for international students: Required—TOEFL (minimum score 550 paper-based; 79 iBT), IELTS (minimum score 6). Electronic applications accepted. *Expenses: Tuition:* Full-time $10,320; part-time $430 per unit. Tuition and fees vary according to degree level. *Faculty research:* Educational technology, scholarships in science.

Naval Postgraduate School, Departments and Academic Groups, Department of Information Sciences, Monterey, CA 93943. Offers electronic warfare systems engineering (MS); information sciences (PhD); information systems and operations (MS); information technology management (MS); information warfare systems engineering (MS); knowledge superiority (Certificate); remote sensing intelligence (MS); system technology (command, control and communications) (MS). Program open only to commissioned officers of the United States and friendly nations and selected United States federal civilian employees. *Program availability:* Part-time. *Degree requirements:* For master's, thesis (for some programs); for doctorate, thesis/dissertation. *Faculty research:* Designing inter-organisational collectivities for dynamic fit: stability, manoeuvrability and application in disaster relief endeavours; system self-awareness and related methods for Improving the use and understanding of data within DoD; evaluating a macrocognition model of team collaboration using real-world data from the Haiti relief effort; cyber distortion in command and control; performance and QoS in service-based systems.

Naval Postgraduate School, Departments and Academic Groups, Graduate School of Business and Public Policy, Monterey, CA 93943. Offers acquisition and contract management (MBA); business administration (EMBA, MBA); contract management (MS); defense business management (MBA); defense systems analysis (MS), including management; defense systems management (international) (MBA); financial management (MBA); information management (MBA); manpower systems analysis (MS); material logistics support management (MBA); program management (MS); resource planning and management for international defense (MBA); supply chain management (MBA); systems acquisition management (MBA); transportation management (MBA). Program only open to commissioned officers of the United States and friendly nations and selected United States federal civilian employees. *Accreditation:* AACSB; NASPAA. *Program availability:* Part-time, online learning. *Degree requirements:* For master's, thesis (for some programs), terminal project/capstone (for some programs). *Faculty research:* U.S. and European public procurement policies for small and medium-sized enterprises, examining external validity criticisms in the choice of students as subjects in accounting experiment studies, assurance of learning in contract management education, contracting for cloud computing: opportunities and risks, NPS, Apple App Store as a business model supporting U.S. Navy requirements.

New England Institute of Technology, Program in Information Technology, East Greenwich, RI 02818. Offers MS. *Program availability:* Part-time, evening/weekend, 100% online, blended/hybrid learning. *Students:* 14 full-time (6 women), 7 part-time (1 woman), 7 international. Average age 31. *Entrance requirements:* For master's, Minimum GPA of 2.5 awarded Bachelor's degree in related field from an accredited institution plus personal statement and a professional resume. Additional exam requirements/recommendations for international students: Required—TOEFL. *Application deadline:* Applications are processed on a rolling basis. Application fee: $25. Electronic applications accepted. *Expenses:* $565.00 x 45 credits to complete this program. Tuition is $25,425.00. Visit https://www.neit.edu/Financial-Aid/Tuition-and-Fees for more information. *Unit head:* Dr. Douglas H. Sherman, Senior Vice President and Provost, 401-739-5000 Ext. 3481, Fax: 401-886-0859, E-mail: dsherman@neit.edu. *Application contact:* Lynn M Fawthrop, Vice President of Enrollment Management and Marketing, 401-739-5000 Ext. 3315, Fax: 401-886-0859, E-mail: lmfawthrop@neit.edu. Website: http://www.neit.edu/Programs/Masters-Degree/Information-Technology

New Jersey Institute of Technology, Ying Wu College of Computing, Newark, NJ 07102. Offers big data management and mining (Certificate); business and information systems (Certificate); computer science (PhD); computing and business (MS); data mining (Certificate); data science (MS); information security (Certificate); information systems (PhD); information technology administration and security (MS); IT administration (Certificate); network security and information assurance (Certificate); software engineering (MS), including information systems; software engineering

analysis/design (Certificate); Web systems development (Certificate). *Program availability:* Part-time, evening/weekend. *Faculty:* 69 full-time (13 women), 38 part-time/adjunct (4 women). *Students:* 699 full-time (229 women), 269 part-time (67 women); includes 260 minority (44 Black or African American, non-Hispanic/Latino; 145 Asian, non-Hispanic/Latino; 59 Hispanic/Latino; 12 Two or more races, non-Hispanic/Latino), 614 international. Average age 26. 2,216 applicants, 55% accepted, 366 enrolled. In 2018, 418 master's, 5 doctorates, 13 other advanced degrees awarded. Terminal master's awarded for partial completion of doctoral program. *Degree requirements:* For master's, thesis optional; for doctorate, thesis/dissertation. *Entrance requirements:* For master's, GRE General Test; for doctorate, GRE General Test, minimum graduate GPA of 3.5. Additional exam requirements/recommendations for international students: Required—TOEFL (minimum score 550 paper-based; 79 iBT), IELTS (minimum score 6.5). *Application deadline:* For fall admission, 6/1 priority date for domestic students, 5/1 priority date for international students; for spring admission, 11/15 priority date for domestic and international students. Applications are processed on a rolling basis. Application fee: $75. Electronic applications accepted. *Expenses:* $22,690 per year (in-state), $32,136 per year (out-of-state). *Financial support:* In 2018–19, 366 students received support, including 10 fellowships with full tuition reimbursements available (averaging $22,000 per year), 47 research assistantships with full tuition reimbursements available (averaging $22,000 per year), 28 teaching assistantships with full tuition reimbursements available (averaging $22,000 per year); career-related internships or fieldwork, Federal Work-Study, scholarships/grants, and unspecified assistantships also available. Financial award application deadline: 1/15. *Faculty research:* Computer systems, communications and networking, artificial intelligence, database engineering, systems analysis, analytics and optimization in crowdsourcing. *Total annual research expenditures:* $4.9 million. *Unit head:* Dr. Craig Gotsman, Dean, 973-596-3366, Fax: 973-596-5777, E-mail: craig.gotsman@njit.edu. *Application contact:* Stephen Eck, Director of Admissions, 973-596-3300, Fax: 973-596-3461, E-mail: admissions@njit.edu.
Website: http://computing.njit.edu/

Newman University, MBA Program, Wichita, KS 67213-2097. Offers finance (MBA); international business (MBA); leadership (MBA); management (MBA); management information technology (MBA). *Program availability:* Part-time. *Degree requirements:* For master's, thesis optional. *Entrance requirements:* For master's, minimum GPA of 3.0; 2 letters of recommendation; course work in algebra, statistics, macroeconomics, and financial accounting. Additional exam requirements/recommendations for international students: Required—TOEFL (minimum score 600 paper-based; 100 iBT). Electronic applications accepted. *Expenses:* Contact institution.

New Mexico State University, College of Business, MBA Program, Las Cruces, NM 88003-8001. Offers agribusiness (MBA); finance (MBA); information systems (MBA). *Accreditation:* AACSB. *Program availability:* Part-time-only, evening/weekend, online with required 2-3 day orientation and 2-3 day concluding session in Las Cruces. *Students:* Average age 33. 166 applicants, 82% accepted, 19 enrolled. In 2018, 79 master's awarded. *Entrance requirements:* For master's, GMAT or GRE (depending upon undergraduate or graduate degree institution and GPA), minimum GPA of 3.5 from AACSB international or ACBSP-accredited institution or graduate degree from regionally-accredited U.S. university (without GMAT or GRE). Additional exam requirements/recommendations for international students: Required—TOEFL (minimum score 550 paper-based; 79 iBT), IELTS (minimum score 6.5). *Application deadline:* For fall admission, 7/15 priority date for domestic students, 4/15 priority date for international students; for spring admission, 4/15 priority date for domestic students, 9/15 priority date for international students; for summer admission, 4/15 for domestic students, 1/15 for international students. Applications are processed on a rolling basis. Application fee: $40 ($50 for international students). Electronic applications accepted. *Expenses: Tuition, area resident:* Full-time $4216.70; part-time $252.70 per credit hour. Tuition, state resident: full-time $4216.70; part-time $252.70 per credit hour. Tuition, nonresident: full-time $12,769; part-time $881.10 per credit hour. *International tuition:* $12,769.30 full-time. *Required fees:* $878.40; $48.80 per credit hour. Full-time tuition and fees vary according to course load and reciprocity agreements. *Financial support:* In 2018–19, 29 students received support. Fellowships, Federal Work-Study, institutionally sponsored loans, scholarships/grants, health care benefits, and unspecified assistantships available. Financial award application deadline: 3/1. *Unit head:* Dr. Kathy Brook, Associate Dean, 575-646-8003, Fax: 575-646-7977, E-mail: kbrook@nmsu.edu. *Application contact:* John Shonk, MBA Advisor, 575-646-8003, Fax: 575-646-7977, E-mail: mbaprog@nmsu.edu.
Website: http://business.nmsu.edu/mba

New York University, Leonard N. Stern School of Business, Department of Information, Operations and Management Sciences, New York, NY 10012-1019. Offers information systems (MBA, PhD); operations management (MBA, PhD); statistics (MBA, PhD). *Faculty research:* Knowledge management, economics of information, computer-supported groups and communities financial information systems, data mining and business intelligence.

New York University, School of Professional Studies, Division of Programs in Business, Program in Management and Systems, New York, NY 10012-1019. Offers management and systems (MS), including database technologies, enterprise risk management, strategy and leadership, systems management. *Program availability:* Part-time, evening/weekend, 100% online, blended/hybrid learning. *Degree requirements:* For master's, thesis, capstone project. *Entrance requirements:* For master's, GRE or GMAT (only upon request), bachelor's degree, resume with relevant professional work, internship or volunteer experience, two letters of recommendation, statement of purpose. Additional exam requirements/recommendations for international students: Required—TOEFL (minimum score 600 paper-based; 100 iBT), IELTS (minimum score 7). Electronic applications accepted. *Expenses:* Contact institution.

Northeastern University, College of Computer and Information Science, Boston, MA 02115-5096. Offers computer science (MS, PhD); data science (MS); game science and design (MS); health informatics (MS); information assurance (MS); network science (PhD); personal health informatics (PhD). *Program availability:* Part-time, evening/weekend. Terminal master's awarded for partial completion of doctoral program. *Degree requirements:* For master's, thesis optional; for doctorate, comprehensive exam, thesis/dissertation. Electronic applications accepted. *Expenses:* Contact institution.

Northeastern University, College of Engineering, Boston, MA 02115-5096. Offers bioengineering (MS, PhD); chemical engineering (MS, PhD); civil engineering (MS, PhD); computer engineering (PhD); computer systems engineering (MS); electrical and computer engineering (MS); electrical and computer engineering leadership (MS); electrical engineering (PhD); energy systems (MS); engineering and public policy (MS); engineering management (MS, Certificate); environmental engineering (MS); industrial engineering (MS, PhD); information assurance (PhD); information systems (MS); interdisciplinary engineering (PhD); mechanical engineering (PhD); operations research (MS); telecommunication systems management (MS). *Program availability:* Part-time, online learning. Electronic applications accepted. *Expenses:* Contact institution.

Northern Illinois University, Graduate School, College of Business, Department of Operations Management and Information Systems, De Kalb, IL 60115-2854. Offers management information systems (MS). *Program availability:* Part-time. *Faculty:* 11 full-time (3 women), 3 part-time/adjunct (0 women). *Students:* 115 full-time (45 women), 42 part-time (13 women); includes 21 minority (7 Black or African American, non-Hispanic/Latino; 5 Asian, non-Hispanic/Latino; 7 Hispanic/Latino; 2 Two or more races, non-Hispanic/Latino), 118 international. Average age 28. 234 applicants, 73% accepted, 45 enrolled. In 2018, 112 master's awarded. *Entrance requirements:* For master's, GMAT, minimum GPA of 2.75. Additional exam requirements/recommendations for international students: Required—TOEFL (minimum score 550 paper-based). *Application deadline:* For fall admission, 6/1 for domestic students, 5/1 for international students; for spring admission, 11/1 for domestic students, 10/1 for international students. Applications are processed on a rolling basis. Application fee: $40. Electronic applications accepted. *Financial support:* In 2018–19, 9 research assistantships with full tuition reimbursements, 21 teaching assistantships with full tuition reimbursements were awarded; fellowships with full tuition reimbursements, career-related internships or fieldwork, Federal Work-Study, scholarships/grants, tuition waivers (full), and unspecified assistantships also available. Support available to part-time students. Financial award applicants required to submit FAFSA. *Faculty research:* Affordability of home ownership, Web portal competition intranet, electronic commerce, corporate-academic alliances. *Unit head:* Dr. Chang Liu, Chair, 815-753-3021, Fax: 815-753-7460. *Application contact:* Steven Kispert, Office of Graduate Studies in Business, 815-753-6372, E-mail: skispert@niu.edu.
Website: http://www.cob.niu.edu/omis/

Northwestern University, School of Professional Studies, Program in Information Systems, Evanston, IL 60208. Offers analytics and business intelligence (MS); database and Internet technologies (MS); information systems (MS); information systems management (MS); information systems security (MS); medical informatics (MS); software project management and development (MS). *Program availability:* Part-time, evening/weekend.

Northwest Missouri State University, Graduate School, School of Computer Science and Information Systems, Maryville, MO 64468-6001. Offers applied computer science (MS); information systems (MS); instructional technology (MS). *Program availability:* Part-time. *Faculty:* 13 full-time (5 women). *Students:* 205 full-time (82 women), 36 part-time (14 women); includes 1 minority (Two or more races, non-Hispanic/Latino), 233 international. Average age 24. 459 applicants, 79% accepted, 116 enrolled. In 2018, 185 master's awarded. *Degree requirements:* For master's, comprehensive exam. *Entrance requirements:* For master's, GRE General Test, minimum GPA of 3.0. Additional exam requirements/recommendations for international students: Required—TOEFL (minimum score 550 paper-based). *Application deadline:* Applications are processed on a rolling basis. Application fee: $0 ($75 for international students). *Expenses: Tuition, area resident:* Full-time $4551; part-time $252.86 per credit hour. Tuition, state resident: full-time $4551; part-time $252.86 per credit hour. Tuition, nonresident: full-time $9103; part-time $505.72 per credit hour. *International tuition:* $9103 full-time. *Required fees:* $2668; $148.20 per credit hour. Tuition and fees vary according to program. *Financial support:* Research assistantships, teaching assistantships with full tuition reimbursements, and unspecified assistantships available. Financial award application deadline: 4/1; financial award applicants required to submit FAFSA. *Unit head:* Dr. Douglas Hawley, Director of School of Computer Science and Information Systems, 660-562-1200, Fax: 660-562-1963, E-mail: hawley@nwmissouri.edu. *Application contact:* Dr. Gregory Haddock, Dean of Graduate School, 660-562-1145, Fax: 660-562-1096, E-mail: gradsch@nwmissouri.edu.
Website: http://www.nwmissouri.edu/csis/

Nova Southeastern University, College of Engineering and Computing, Fort Lauderdale, FL 33314-7796. Offers computer science (MS, PhD); information assurance (PhD); information assurance and cybersecurity (MS); information systems (PhD); information technology (MS); management information systems (MS). *Program availability:* Part-time, evening/weekend, blended/hybrid learning. Terminal master's awarded for partial completion of doctoral program. *Degree requirements:* For master's, thesis optional; for doctorate, thesis/dissertation. *Entrance requirements:* For master's, minimum undergraduate GPA of 2.5; for doctorate, master's degree, minimum graduate GPA of 3.25. Additional exam requirements/recommendations for international students: Required—TOEFL (minimum score 80 iBT), IELTS (minimum score 6), PTE (minimum score 54). Electronic applications accepted. *Expenses:* Contact institution. *Faculty research:* Artificial intelligence, database management, human-computer interaction, business intelligence and data analytics, information assurance and cybersecurity.

Oakland University, Graduate Study and Lifelong Learning, School of Business Administration, Department of Decision and Information Sciences, Rochester, MI 48309-4401. Offers information technology management (MS); management information systems (Certificate); production and operations management (Certificate).

Oakland University, Graduate Study and Lifelong Learning, School of Engineering and Computer Science, Department of Computer Science and Engineering, Rochester, MI 48309-4401. Offers computer science (MS); computer science and informatics (PhD); software engineering and information technology (MS). *Program availability:* Part-time, evening/weekend. *Entrance requirements:* For master's, minimum GPA of 3.0. Electronic applications accepted. *Expenses:* Contact institution.

The Ohio State University, Graduate School, Max M. Fisher College of Business, Department of Accounting and Management Information Systems, Columbus, OH 43210. Offers accounting (M Acc); management information systems (PhD). *Accreditation:* AACSB. *Faculty:* 21. *Students:* 107 (55 women). Average age 24. In 2018, 64 master's, 1 doctorate awarded. Terminal master's awarded for partial completion of doctoral program. *Degree requirements:* For doctorate, thesis/dissertation. *Entrance requirements:* For master's, GMAT (minimum score of 550 recommended, 600 preferred) or GRE; for doctorate, GMAT. Additional exam requirements/recommendations for international students: Required—TOEFL (minimum score 600 paper-based; 100 iBT), Michigan English Language Assessment Battery (minimum score 86); Recommended—IELTS (minimum score 7). *Application deadline:* For fall admission, 11/15 priority date for domestic and international students. Applications are processed on a rolling basis. Application fee: $60 ($70 for international students). Electronic applications accepted. *Financial support:* Fellowships with tuition reimbursements, research assistantships with tuition reimbursements, teaching assistantships with tuition reimbursements, career-related internships or fieldwork, Federal Work-Study, and institutionally sponsored loans available. Support available to part-time students. *Faculty research:* Artificial intelligence, protocol analysis, database design in decision-supporting systems. *Unit head:* Dr. Brian Mittendorf, Chair and Professor, 614-292-1720, E-mail: mittendorf.3@osu.edu. *Application contact:* Graduate and Professional Admissions, 614-292-6031, Fax: 614-292-3656, E-mail: gpadmissions@osu.edu.
Website: https://fisher.osu.edu/academic-departments/amis

Oklahoma State University, Spears School of Business, Department of Management Science and Information Systems, Stillwater, OK 74078. Offers management information systems (MS); management science and information systems (PhD); telecommunications management (MS). *Program availability:* Part-time, online learning. *Faculty:* 15 full-time (1 woman), 6 part-time/adjunct (3 women). *Students:* 57 full-time (18 women), 76 part-time (16 women); includes 15 minority (3 Black or African American, non-Hispanic/Latino; 3 American Indian or Alaska Native, non-Hispanic/

Latino; 3 Asian, non-Hispanic/Latino; 2 Hispanic/Latino; 1 Native Hawaiian or other Pacific Islander, non-Hispanic/Latino; 3 Two or more races, non-Hispanic/Latino), 73 international. Average age 29. 391 applicants, 27% accepted, 65 enrolled. In 2018, 50 master's awarded. *Entrance requirements:* For master's and doctorate, GRE or GMAT. Additional exam requirements/recommendations for international students: Required— TOEFL (minimum score 550 paper-based; 79 iBT). *Application deadline:* For fall admission, 3/1 priority date for international students; for spring admission, 8/1 priority date for international students. Applications are processed on a rolling basis. Application fee: $40 ($75 for international students). Electronic applications accepted. *Expenses: Tuition, area resident:* Full-time $4148. Tuition, state resident: full-time $4148. Tuition, nonresident: full-time $10,517. *International tuition:* $10,517 full-time. *Required fees:* $4394; $2929 per credit hour. Tuition and fees vary according to course load and program. *Financial support:* Research assistantships, teaching assistantships, career-related internships or fieldwork, Federal Work-Study, scholarships/grants, health care benefits, tuition waivers (partial), and unspecified assistantships available. Support available to part-time students. Financial award application deadline: 3/1; financial award applicants required to submit FAFSA. *Unit head:* Dr. Rick Wilson, Department Head, 405-744-3551, Fax: 405-744-5180, E-mail: rick.wilson@okstate.edu. *Application contact:* Dr. Rathin Sarathy, Graduate Coordinator, 405-744-8646, Fax: 405-744-5180, E-mail: rathin.sarathy@okstate.edu.
Website: https://business.okstate.edu/msis/

Old Dominion University, College of Sciences, Program in Computer Science, Norfolk, VA 23529. Offers computer information systems (MS); computer science (MS, PhD). *Program availability:* Part-time, 100% online. Terminal master's awarded for partial completion of doctoral program. *Degree requirements:* For master's, comprehensive exam, thesis optional, 34 credit hours; for doctorate, comprehensive exam, thesis/dissertation, 48 credit hours beyond the MS. *Entrance requirements:* For master's, GRE General Test, minimum GPA of 3.0; for doctorate, GRE General Test, MS in computer science. Additional exam requirements/recommendations for international students: Required—TOEFL (minimum score 550 paper-based; 79 iBT), IELTS (minimum score 6.5). Electronic applications accepted. *Faculty research:* Machine intelligence and data science, Web science and digital libraries, cyber-physical systems, bioinformatics, scientific computing.

Our Lady of the Lake University, School of Business and Leadership, Program in Information Systems and Security, San Antonio, TX 78207-4689. Offers MS. *Program availability:* Part-time, online only, 100% online. *Faculty:* 3 full-time (all women), 1 part-time/adjunct (0 women). *Students:* 28 full-time (11 women), 2 part-time (0 women); includes 16 minority (all Hispanic/Latino). Average age 36. 10 applicants, 100% accepted, 9 enrolled. In 2018, 13 master's awarded. *Entrance requirements:* For master's, GRE or GMAT, official transcripts showing baccalaureate degree from regionally-accredited institution in technical discipline and minimum GPA of 3.0 for cumulative undergraduate work or 3.2 in the major field (technical discipline) of study. Additional exam requirements/recommendations for international students: Required— TOEFL. *Application deadline:* For fall admission, 6/15 for domestic and international students; for spring admission, 11/15 for domestic and international students; for summer admission, 4/15 for domestic and international students. Applications are processed on a rolling basis. Application fee: $40 ($50 for international students). Electronic applications accepted. Application fee is waived when completed online. *Expenses: Tuition:* Full-time $16,326; part-time $907 per credit. *Financial support:* In 2018–19, 9 students received support. Federal Work-Study, scholarships/grants, unspecified assistantships, and tuition discounts available. Support available to part-time students. Financial award application deadline: 5/1; financial award applicants required to submit FAFSA. *Faculty research:* Computer information systems implementation and best practices, computer and network security, cyber security legal issues, information assurance, and information technology education. *Unit head:* Carol Jeffries-Horner, Chair, Computer Information Systems and Security Department, 210-528-6730, E-mail: cjeffries@ollusa.edu. *Application contact:* Office of Graduate Admissions, 210-431-3995, Fax: 210-431-3945, E-mail: gradadm@ollusa.edu.
Website: http://www.ollusa.edu/s/1190/hybrid/default-hybrid-ollu.aspx?sid-1190&gid-1&pgid-7901

Pace University, Lubin School of Business, Information Systems Program, New York, NY 10038. Offers MBA. *Program availability:* Part-time, evening/weekend. *Students:* 10 full-time (5 women), 3 part-time (1 woman); includes 7 minority (2 Black or African American, non-Hispanic/Latino; 2 Asian, non-Hispanic/Latino; 2 Hispanic/Latino; 1 Two or more races, non-Hispanic/Latino), 3 international. Average age 30. 15 applicants, 73% accepted, 5 enrolled. In 2018, 7 master's awarded. *Entrance requirements:* For master's, GMAT, GRE, undergraduate degree, transcripts from all accredited colleges/universities attended, two letters of recommendation, resume, personal statement. Additional exam requirements/recommendations for international students: Required— TOEFL (minimum score 90 iBT), IELTS (minimum score 7) or PTE (minimum score 61). *Application deadline:* For fall admission, 8/1 priority date for domestic students, 6/1 for international students; for spring admission, 12/1 for domestic students, 10/1 for international students. Applications are processed on a rolling basis. Application fee: $70. Electronic applications accepted. *Financial support:* Research assistantships, career-related internships or fieldwork, Federal Work-Study, and unspecified assistantships available. Support available to part-time students. Financial award application deadline: 2/15; financial award applicants required to submit FAFSA. *Unit head:* Dr. Li-Chiou Chen, Chairperson, 914-773-3907, E-mail: lchen@pace.edu. *Application contact:* Susan Ford-Goldschein, Director of Graduate Admissions, 212-346-1531, Fax: 212-346-1585, E-mail: graduateadmission@pace.edu.
Website: http://www.pace.edu/lubin/mba-in-information-systems

Pace University, Seidenberg School of Computer Science and Information Systems, New York, NY 10038. Offers chief information security officer (APC); computer science (MS, PhD); enterprise analytics (MS); information and communication technology strategy and innovation (APC); information systems (MS, APC); information technology (MS); professional studies in computing (DPS); secure software and information engineering (APC); security and information assurance (Certificate); software development and engineering (MS, Certificate); telecommunications systems and networks (MS, Certificate). *Program availability:* Part-time, evening/weekend, online only, 100% online, blended/hybrid learning. *Faculty:* 26 full-time (7 women), 7 part-time/adjunct (2 women). *Students:* 515 full-time (172 women), 288 part-time (90 women); includes 183 minority (67 Black or African American, non-Hispanic/Latino; 3 American Indian or Alaska Native, non-Hispanic/Latino; 50 Asian, non-Hispanic/Latino; 52 Hispanic/Latino; 1 Native Hawaiian or other Pacific Islander, non-Hispanic/Latino; 10 Two or more races, non-Hispanic/Latino), 497 international. Average age 30. 817 applicants, 93% accepted, 235 enrolled. In 2018, 383 master's, 15 doctorates, 1 other advanced degree awarded. *Degree requirements:* For master's, thesis or alternative, capstone course; for doctorate, comprehensive exam (for some programs), thesis/dissertation. *Entrance requirements:* Additional exam requirements/recommendations for international students: Required—TOEFL (minimum score 78 iBT), IELTS (minimum score 6.5) or PTE (minimum score 52). *Application deadline:* For fall admission, 8/1 priority date for domestic students, 6/1 for international students; for spring admission, 12/1 for domestic students, 10/1 for international students. Applications are processed on a rolling basis. Application fee: $70. Electronic applications accepted. *Expenses:*

Contact institution. *Financial support:* In 2018–19, 45 students received support. Research assistantships, career-related internships or fieldwork, scholarships/grants, and unspecified assistantships available. Support available to part-time students. Financial award application deadline: 2/15; financial award applicants required to submit FAFSA. *Faculty research:* Cyber security/digital forensics; mobile app development; big data/enterprise analytics; artificial intelligence; software development. *Total annual research expenditures:* $584,594. *Unit head:* Dr. Jonathan Hill, Dean, Seidenberg School of Computer Science and Information Systems, 212-346-1864, E-mail: jhill@pace.edu. *Application contact:* Susan Ford-Goldschein, Director of Graduate Admissions, 914-422-4283, Fax: 212-346-1585, E-mail: graduateadmission@pace.edu.
Website: http://www.pace.edu/seidenberg

Pacific States University, College of Business, Los Angeles, CA 90010. Offers accounting (MBA, Certificate); beauty management (MBA); finance (MBA); international business (MBA); management of information technology (MBA); project management (Certificate); real estate management (MBA). *Program availability:* Part-time, evening/weekend, online learning. *Entrance requirements:* For master's, minimum undergraduate GPA of 2.5 during last 90 quarter units of course work, bachelor's degree in business administration or economics. Additional exam requirements/recommendations for international students: Required—TOEFL (minimum score 500 paper-based; 61 iBT), IELTS (minimum score 5.5).

Pacific States University, College of Computer Science and Information Systems, Los Angeles, CA 90010. Offers computer science (MS); information systems (MS). *Program availability:* Part-time, evening/weekend. *Entrance requirements:* For master's, bachelor's degree in physics, engineering, computer science, information systems, or applied mathematics; minimum undergraduate GPA of 2.5 during last 90 quarter units of course work. Additional exam requirements/recommendations for international students: Required—TOEFL (minimum score 500 paper-based; 61 iBT), IELTS (minimum score 5.5).

Park University, School of Graduate and Professional Studies, Kansas City, MO 54105. Offers adult education (M Ed); business and government leadership (Graduate Certificate); business, government, and global society (MPA); communication and leadership (MA); creative and life writing (Graduate Certificate); disaster and emergency management (MPA, Graduate Certificate); educational leadership (M Ed); finance (MBA, Graduate Certificate); general business (MBA); global business (Graduate Certificate); healthcare administration (MHA); healthcare services management and leadership (Graduate Certificate); international business (MBA); language and literacy (M Ed), including English for speakers of other languages, special reading teacher/literacy coach; leadership of international healthcare organizations (Graduate Certificate); management information systems (MBA, Graduate Certificate); music performance (ADP, Graduate Certificate), including cello (MM, ADP), piano (MM, ADP), viola (MM, ADP), violin (MM, ADP); nonprofit and community services management (MPA); nonprofit leadership (Graduate Certificate); performance (MM), including cello (MM, ADP), piano (MM, ADP), viola (MM, ADP), violin (MM, ADP); public management (MPA); social work (MSW); teacher leadership (M Ed), including curriculum and assessment, instructional leader. *Program availability:* Part-time, evening/weekend, online learning. *Degree requirements:* For master's, comprehensive exam (for some programs), thesis (for some programs), internship (for some programs); exam (for some programs). *Entrance requirements:* For master's, GRE or GMAT (for some programs), teacher certification (for some M Ed programs), letters of recommendation, essay, resume (for some programs). Additional exam requirements/recommendations for international students: Required—TOEFL (minimum score 550 paper-based; 79 iBT), IELTS (minimum score 6). Electronic applications accepted.

Penn State Harrisburg, Graduate School, School of Business Administration, Middletown, PA 17057. Offers accounting (MPAC, Certificate); business administration (MBA); information systems (MS); operations and supply chain management (Certificate). *Program availability:* Part-time, evening/weekend.

Penn State University Park, Graduate School, College of Information Sciences and Technology, University Park, PA 16802. Offers information sciences (MPS); information sciences and technology (MS, PhD). *Program availability:* Part-time, evening/weekend. *Entrance requirements:* Additional exam requirements/recommendations for international students: Required—TOEFL (minimum score 550 paper-based; 80 iBT), IELTS. Electronic applications accepted. *Expenses:* Contact institution.

Point Park University, Rowland School of Business, Program in Business Administration, Pittsburgh, PA 15222-1984. Offers business analytics (MBA); global management and administration (MBA); health systems management (MBA); international business (MBA); management (MBA); management information systems (MBA); sports, arts and entertainment management (MBA). *Program availability:* Evening/weekend, 100% online.

Polytechnic University of Puerto Rico, Graduate School, Hato Rey, PR 00918. Offers business administration (MBA), including computer information systems, general management, management of information systems, management of international enterprises; civil engineering (ME, MS); computer engineering (ME, MS); computer science (MCS, MS); electrical engineering (ME, MS); engineering management (MEM); environmental management (MEM); landscape architecture (M Land Arch); manufacturing competitiveness (MMC, MS); manufacturing engineering (ME, MS); mechanical engineering (M Mech E). *Accreditation:* ASLA. *Program availability:* Part-time, evening/weekend. *Entrance requirements:* For master's, 3 letters of recommendation.

Pontifical Catholic University of Puerto Rico, College of Business Administration, Program in Management Information Systems, Ponce, PR 00717-0777. Offers MBA, Professional Certificate. *Program availability:* Part-time, evening/weekend. *Degree requirements:* For master's, thesis. *Entrance requirements:* For master's, GRE, interview, minimum GPA of 2.75.

Prairie View A&M University, College of Engineering, Prairie View, TX 77446. Offers computer information systems (MSCIS); computer science (MSCS); electrical engineering (MSEE, PhDEE); general engineering (MS Engr). *Program availability:* Part-time, evening/weekend. *Faculty:* 29 full-time (8 women), 1 part-time/adjunct (0 women). *Students:* 134 full-time (34 women), 67 part-time (24 women); includes 84 minority (67 Black or African American, non-Hispanic/Latino; 12 Asian, non-Hispanic/Latino; 5 Hispanic/Latino), 102 international. Average age 31. 130 applicants, 80% accepted, 52 enrolled. In 2018, 67 master's, 3 doctorates awarded. *Degree requirements:* For master's, thesis optional; for doctorate, comprehensive exam, thesis/dissertation. *Entrance requirements:* For master's, GRE General Test (minimum score of 900), bachelor's degree in engineering from ABET-accredited institution; for doctorate, minimum GPA of 3.0. Additional exam requirements/recommendations for international students: Required—TOEFL (minimum score 550 paper-based; 79 iBT). *Application deadline:* For fall admission, 5/1 priority date for domestic and international students; for spring admission, 10/1 priority date for domestic students, 9/1 priority date for international students; for summer admission, 3/1 priority date for domestic students, 2/1 priority date for international students. Applications are processed on a rolling basis. Application fee: $50. Electronic applications accepted. *Expenses: Tuition, area resident:* Full-time $3172; part-time $317 per credit. Tuition, state resident: full-time $3172; part-

time $317 per credit. Tuition, nonresident: full-time $7965; part-time $796 per credit. *Required fees:* $4847; $485 per credit. *Financial support:* Fellowships, research assistantships, teaching assistantships, career-related internships or fieldwork, institutionally sponsored loans, scholarships/grants, health care benefits, tuition waivers (full), and unspecified assistantships available. Financial award application deadline: 4/1; financial award applicants required to submit FAFSA. *Faculty research:* Electrical and computer engineering: big data analysis, wireless communications, bioinformatics and computational biology, space radiation; computer science: cloud computing, cyber security; chemical engineering: thermochemical processing of biofuel, photochemical modeling; civil and environmental engineering: environmental sustainability, water resources, structure; mechanical engineering: thermal science, nanocomposites, computational fluid dynamics. *Unit head:* Dr. Pamela H Obiomon, Dean, 936-261-9890, Fax: 936-261-9868, E-mail: phobiomon@pvamu.edu. *Application contact:* Pauline Walker, Administrative Assistant II, Research and Graduate Studies, 936-261-3521, Fax: 936-261-3529, E-mail: gradadmissions@pvamu.edu.

Purdue University, Graduate School, Purdue Polytechnic Institute, Department of Computer and Information Technology, West Lafayette, IN 47907. Offers MS. *Faculty:* 26 full-time (8 women), 2 part-time/adjunct (both women). *Students:* 46 full-time (20 women), 56 part-time (20 women); includes 13 minority (2 Black or African American, non-Hispanic/Latino; 5 Asian, non-Hispanic/Latino; 5 Hispanic/Latino; 1 Two or more races, non-Hispanic/Latino), 49 international. Average age 30. 344 applicants, 17% accepted, 34 enrolled. In 2018, 46 master's awarded. *Entrance requirements:* For master's, GRE, minimum GPA of 3.0 or equivalent. *Application deadline:* For fall admission, 4/1 for domestic and international students; for spring admission, 10/1 for domestic students, 9/1 for international students; for summer admission, 4/1 for domestic students, 2/15 for international students. Applications are processed on a rolling basis. Application fee: $60 ($75 for international students). Electronic applications accepted. *Unit head:* Thomas J. Hacker, Head of the Graduate Program, 765-494-4465, E-mail: hacker@purdue.edu. *Application contact:* Stacy Lane, Graduate Contact, 765-494-4545, E-mail: smlane@purdue.edu.
Website: http://www.tech.purdue.edu/cit/

Purdue University Global, School of Information Technology, Davenport, IA 52807. Offers decision support systems (MS); information security and assurance (MS). *Program availability:* Part-time, evening/weekend, online learning. *Entrance requirements:* Additional exam requirements/recommendations for international students: Required—TOEFL (minimum score 550 paper-based; 80 iBT).

Queen's University at Kingston, Smith School of Business, Doctoral Program in Management, Kingston, ON K7L 3N6, Canada. Offers analytics (PhD); business economics (PhD); finance (PhD); management information systems (PhD); marketing (PhD); organizational behavior (PhD); strategy (PhD).

Queen's University at Kingston, Smith School of Business, Master of Science in Management Program, Kingston, ON K7L 3N6, Canada. Offers analytics (M Sc); business economics (M Sc); finance (M Sc); management information systems (M Sc); marketing (M Sc); organizational behavior (M Sc); strategy (M Sc).

Radford University, College of Graduate Studies and Research, Program in Data and Information Management, Radford, VA 24142. Offers MS. *Program availability:* Part-time. *Faculty:* 4 full-time (0 women). *Students:* 4 full-time (1 woman), 3 part-time (0 women); includes 1 minority (Asian, non-Hispanic/Latino), 3 international. Average age 30. 4 applicants, 50% accepted, 1 enrolled. In 2018, 5 master's awarded. *Entrance requirements:* For master's, GRE (minimum scores of 152 on quantitative portion and 148 on verbal portion, or 650 and 420, respectively, under old scoring system), minimum GPA of 3.0 overall from accredited educational institution, three letters of reference from faculty members familiar with academic performance in major coursework or from colleagues or supervisors familiar with work. Additional exam requirements/recommendations for international students: Required—TOEFL (minimum score 567 paper-based). *Application deadline:* Applications are processed on a rolling basis. Application fee: $50. Electronic applications accepted. *Expenses: Tuition, area resident:* Full-time $8915; part-time $371 per credit hour. Tuition, state resident: full-time $8915; part-time $371 per credit hour. Tuition, nonresident: full-time $17,441. *Required fees:* $3288; $138 per credit hour. *Financial support:* In 2018–19, 3 students received support, including 3 teaching assistantships (averaging $10,000 per year); scholarships/grants and unspecified assistantships also available. Support available to part-time students. Financial award application deadline: 3/1; financial award applicants required to submit FAFSA. *Unit head:* Dr. Jeff Pittges, Graduate Coordinator and Director, 540-831-5381, E-mail: jpittges@radford.edu. *Application contact:* Dr. Jeff Pittges, Graduate Coordinator and Director, 540-831-5381, E-mail: jpittges@radford.edu.
Website: http://www.radford.edu/content/csat/home/daim.html

Regent's University London, Webster Graduate School, London, United Kingdom. Offers business (MBA); finance (MS); human resources (MA); information technology management (MA); international business (MA); international non-governmental organizations (MA); international relations (MA); management and leadership (MA); marketing (MA). *Program availability:* Part-time.

Regis University, College of Computer and Information Sciences, Denver, CO 80221-1099. Offers agile technologies (Certificate); cybersecurity (Certificate); data science (M Sc); database administration with Oracle (Certificate); database development (Certificate); database technologies (M Sc); enterprise Java software development (Certificate); enterprise resource planning (Certificate); executive information technology (Certificate); health care informatics (Certificate); health care informatics and information management (M Sc); information assurance (M Sc); information assurance policy management (Certificate); information technology management (M Sc); mobile software development (Certificate); software engineering (M Sc, Certificate); software engineering and database technology (M Sc); storage area networks (Certificate); systems engineering (M Sc, Certificate). *Program availability:* Part-time, evening/weekend, 100% online, blended/hybrid learning. *Degree requirements:* For master's, thesis (for some programs), final research project. *Entrance requirements:* For master's, official transcript reflecting baccalaureate degree awarded from regionally-accredited college or university, 2 years of related experience, resume, interview. Additional exam requirements/recommendations for international students: Required—TOEFL (minimum score 550 paper-based; 82 iBT). Electronic applications accepted. *Expenses:* Contact institution. *Faculty research:* Information policy, knowledge management, software architectures, data science.

Rivier University, School of Graduate Studies, Department of Computer Information Systems, Nashua, NH 03060. Offers MS. *Program availability:* Part-time.

Robert Morris University, School of Informatics, Humanities and Social Sciences, Moon Township, PA 15108-1189. Offers communication and information systems (MS); cyber security (MS); data analytics (MS); information security and assurance (MS); information systems and communications (D Sc); information systems management (MS); information technology project management (MS); Internet information systems (MS); organizational leadership (MS). *Program availability:* Part-time-only, evening/weekend, 100% online. *Faculty:* 22 full-time (7 women), 10 part-time/adjunct (0 women). *Students:* 262 part-time (94 women); includes 57 minority (31 Black or African American, non-Hispanic/Latino; 13 Asian, non-Hispanic/Latino; 8 Hispanic/Latino; 5 Two or more races, non-Hispanic/Latino), 43 international. Average age 35. 150 applicants, 92% accepted, 79 enrolled. In 2018, 133 master's, 11 doctorates awarded. *Degree requirements:* For master's, Completion of 30 credits; for doctorate, thesis/dissertation, Completion of 63 credits. *Entrance requirements:* For doctorate, employer letter of endorsement, interview. Additional exam requirements/recommendations for international students: Required—TOEFL (minimum score 550 paper-based; 79 iBT). *Application deadline:* For fall admission, 7/1 priority date for domestic and international students; for spring admission, 11/1 priority date for domestic and international students. Applications are processed on a rolling basis. Application fee: $35. Electronic applications accepted. Application fee is waived when completed online. *Expenses:* Master's $920/credit plus $80/credit fees; D.Sc. $28,290/year. *Financial support:* Institutionally sponsored loans available. Support available to part-time students. Financial award application deadline: 5/1; financial award applicants required to submit FAFSA. *Unit head:* Jon A. Radermacher, Interim Dean, School of Informatics, Humanities and Social Sciences, 412-397-4088, E-mail: radermacher@rmu.edu. *Application contact:* Jon A. Radermacher, Interim Dean, School of Informatics, Humanities and Social Sciences, 412-397-4088, E-mail: radermacher@rmu.edu.
Website: https://www.rmu.edu/academics/schools/sihss

Robert Morris University Illinois, Morris Graduate School of Management, Chicago, IL 60605. Offers accounting (MBA); accounting/finance (MBA); business analytics (MIS); health care administration (MM); higher education administration (MM); human performance (MS); human resource management (MBA); information security (MIS); information systems management (MIS); law enforcement administration (MM); management (MBA); management/finance (MBA); management/human resource management (MBA); sports administration (MM). *Program availability:* Part-time, evening/weekend. *Entrance requirements:* For master's, official transcripts and letters of recommendation (for some programs); written personal statement. Additional exam requirements/recommendations for international students: Required—TOEFL (minimum score 550 paper-based). Electronic applications accepted.

Rochester Institute of Technology, Graduate Enrollment Services, Golisano College of Computing and Information Sciences, Information Science and Technologies Department, Advanced Certificate Program in Networking, Planning and Design, Rochester, NY 14623-5603. Offers Advanced Certificate. *Program availability:* Part-time, evening/weekend, 100% online. In 2018, 1 Advanced Certificate awarded. *Entrance requirements:* For degree, GRE is recommended for students whose GPA does not meet the minimum requirement., minimum GPA of 3.0 (recommended), Hold a relevant baccalaureate degree. Additional exam requirements/recommendations for international students: Required—TOEFL (minimum score 570 paper-based; 88 iBT), IELTS (minimum score 6.5), PTE (minimum score 61). *Application deadline:* Applications are processed on a rolling basis. Application fee: $65. Electronic applications accepted. *Financial support:* Available to part-time students. Applicants required to submit FAFSA. *Faculty research:* Enterprise network architectures and administration, emerging network technologies, the network design process, and project management. *Unit head:* Qi Yu, Graduate Program Director, 585-475-6929, E-mail: informaticsgrad@rit.edu. *Application contact:* Diane Ellison, Senior Associate Vice President, Graduate Enrollment Services, 585-475-2229, Fax: 585-475-7164, E-mail: gradinfo@rit.edu.
Website: https://www.rit.edu/study/networking-planning-and-design-adv-cert

Rose-Hulman Institute of Technology, Graduate Studies, Department of Electrical and Computer Engineering, Terre Haute, IN 47803-3999. Offers electrical and computer engineering (M Eng); electrical engineering (MS); systems engineering and management (MS). *Program availability:* Part-time. *Faculty:* 19 full-time (2 women), 1 (woman) part-time/adjunct. *Students:* 4 full-time (0 women), 4 part-time (2 women), 7 international. Average age 26. 9 applicants, 44% accepted, 4 enrolled. In 2018, 2 master's awarded. *Degree requirements:* For master's, thesis (for some programs). *Entrance requirements:* For master's, GRE, minimum GPA of 3.0. Additional exam requirements/recommendations for international students: Required—TOEFL (minimum score 580 paper-based; 94 iBT), IELTS (minimum score 7). *Application deadline:* For fall admission, 2/1 priority date for domestic and international students; for winter admission, 10/1 for domestic students, 4/1 for international students; for spring admission, 1/15 for domestic students, 11/1 for international students. Applications are processed on a rolling basis. Application fee: $0. Electronic applications accepted. *Expenses: Tuition:* Full-time $46,641. *Financial support:* In 2018–19, 7 students received support. Fellowships with tuition reimbursements available, research assistantships with tuition reimbursements available, institutionally sponsored loans, scholarships/grants, and tuition waivers (full and partial) available. *Faculty research:* VLSI, power systems, analog electronics, communications, electromagnetics. *Total annual research expenditures:* $55,933. *Unit head:* Dr. Mario Simoni, Department Head, 812-877-8341, Fax: 812-877-8895, E-mail: simoni@rose-hulman.edu. *Application contact:* Dr. Craig Downing, Associate Dean of the Faculty, 812-877-8822, E-mail: downing@rose-hulman.edu.
Website: https://www.rose-hulman.edu/academics/academic-departments/electrical-computer-engineering/index.html

Rutgers University–Newark, Graduate School, Program in Management, Newark, NJ 07102. Offers accounting (PhD); accounting information systems (PhD); computer information systems (PhD); finance (PhD); information technology (PhD); international business (PhD); management science (PhD); marketing (PhD); organization management (PhD). Program offered jointly with New Jersey Institute of Technology. *Accreditation:* AACSB. *Degree requirements:* For doctorate, thesis/dissertation, cumulative exams. *Entrance requirements:* For doctorate, GMAT or GRE General Test, minimum undergraduate B average. Additional exam requirements/recommendations for international students: Required—TOEFL. Electronic applications accepted. *Faculty research:* Technology management, leadership and teams, consumer behavior, financial and markets, logistics.

Rutgers University–Newark, Rutgers Business School–Newark and New Brunswick, Doctoral Programs in Management, Newark, NJ 07102. Offers accounting (PhD); accounting information systems (PhD); economics (PhD); finance (PhD); individualized study (PhD); information technology (PhD); international business (PhD); management science (PhD); marketing science (PhD); organizational management (PhD); science, technology and management (PhD); supply chain management (PhD). *Degree requirements:* For doctorate, comprehensive exam, thesis/dissertation. *Entrance requirements:* For doctorate, GRE or GMAT. Additional exam requirements/recommendations for international students: Required—TOEFL (minimum score 550 paper-based; 79 iBT). Electronic applications accepted.

Rutgers University–Newark, Rutgers Business School–Newark and New Brunswick, Program in Information Technology, Newark, NJ 07102. Offers MIT. *Entrance requirements:* For master's, GMAT. Additional exam requirements/recommendations for international students: Required—TOEFL.

St. John's University, The Peter J. Tobin College of Business, Department of Business Analytics and Information Systems, Queens, NY 11439. Offers MBA. *Entrance requirements:* For master's, GMAT or GRE, 2 letters of recommendation, essay, resume, unofficial transcripts. Additional exam requirements/recommendations for international students: Required—TOEFL (minimum score 80 iBT), IELTS (minimum score 6.5). Electronic applications accepted. *Expenses:* Contact institution.

Saint Peter's University, Graduate Business Programs, MBA Program, Jersey City, NJ 07306-5997. Offers finance (MBA); health care administration (MBA); human resource management (MBA); international business (MBA); management (MBA); management information systems (MBA); marketing (MBA); risk management (MBA); MBA/MS. *Program availability:* Part-time, evening/weekend. *Entrance requirements:* Additional exam requirements/recommendations for international students: Required—TOEFL. Electronic applications accepted. *Faculty research:* Finance, health care management, human resource management, international business, management, management information systems, marketing, risk management.

San Diego State University, Graduate and Research Affairs, Fowler College of Business, Department of Management Information Systems, San Diego, CA 92182. Offers information systems (MS). *Program availability:* Evening/weekend. *Degree requirements:* For master's, thesis or alternative. *Entrance requirements:* For master's, GMAT, resume, letters of reference. Additional exam requirements/recommendations for international students: Required—TOEFL. Electronic applications accepted.

San Francisco State University, Division of Graduate Studies, College of Business, Program in Business Administration, San Francisco, CA 94132-1722. Offers decision sciences/operations research (MBA); ethics and compliance (MBA); finance (MBA); global business and innovation (MBA); healthcare administration (MBA); hospitality and tourism management (MBA); information systems (MBA); leadership (MBA); marketing (MBA); nonprofit and social enterprise leadership (MBA); sustainable business (MBA). *Accreditation:* AACSB. *Program availability:* Part-time, evening/weekend. *Degree requirements:* For master's, thesis, essay test. *Entrance requirements:* For master's, GMAT, minimum GPA of 2.7 in last 60 units. Additional exam requirements/recommendations for international students: Required—TOEFL (minimum score 550 paper-based).

Santa Clara University, Leavey School of Business, Santa Clara, CA 95053. Offers business administration (MBA); business analytics (MS); finance (MS); information systems (MS); supply chain management and analytics (MS); JD/MBA. *Accreditation:* AACSB. *Program availability:* Part-time, online learning. *Faculty:* 101 full-time (32 women), 47 part-time/adjunct (15 women). *Students:* 487 full-time (278 women), 326 part-time (139 women); includes 295 minority (14 Black or African American, non-Hispanic/Latino; 207 Asian, non-Hispanic/Latino; 39 Hispanic/Latino; 35 Two or more races, non-Hispanic/Latino), 294 international. Average age 31. 694 applicants, 65% accepted, 281 enrolled. In 2018, 195 master's awarded. *Entrance requirements:* For master's, Varies based on program. Additional exam requirements/recommendations for international students: Required—TOEFL (minimum score 90 iBT). Application fee: $100 ($150 for international students). Electronic applications accepted. *Financial support:* In 2018–19, 192 students received support. Fellowships, Federal Work-Study, and scholarships/grants available. Support available to part-time students. Financial award applicants required to submit FAFSA. *Unit head:* Caryn Beck-Dudley, Dean, 408-554-4523, E-mail: cbeckdudley@scu.edu. *Application contact:* Caryn Beck-Dudley, Dean, 408-554-4523, E-mail: cbeckdudley@scu.edu.
Website: http://www.scu.edu/business/

Schiller International University, MBA Programs, Florida, Program in Information Technology, Largo, FL 33771. Offers MBA. *Entrance requirements:* Additional exam requirements/recommendations for international students: Required—TOEFL.

Schiller International University, MBA Programs, Heidelberg, Germany, Heidelberg, Germany. Offers international business (MBA, MIM); management of information technology (MBA). *Program availability:* Part-time, evening/weekend. *Degree requirements:* For master's, thesis optional. *Entrance requirements:* Additional exam requirements/recommendations for international students: Required—TOEFL (minimum score 550 paper-based). *Faculty research:* Leadership, international economy, foreign direct investment.

Seattle Pacific University, Master of Science in Information Systems Management Program, Seattle, WA 98119-1997. Offers MS. *Program availability:* Part-time. *Students:* 2 full-time (both women), 20 part-time (11 women); includes 7 minority (4 Black or African American, non-Hispanic/Latino; 2 Asian, non-Hispanic/Latino; 1 Hispanic/Latino), 10 international. Average age 32. 18 applicants, 61% accepted, 9 enrolled. In 2018, 10 master's awarded. *Entrance requirements:* For master's, GMAT (minimum score of 500 preferred; 25 verbal, 30 quantitative, 4.4 analytical writing), GRE (minimum score of 295 preferred; 150 verbal/450 old scoring, 145 quantitative/525 old scoring), BA, resume as evidence of substantive work experience. Additional exam requirements/recommendations for international students: Required—TOEFL. *Application deadline:* For fall admission, 8/1 for domestic students, 6/1 for international students; for winter admission, 11/1 for domestic and international students; for spring admission, 2/1 for domestic students, 12/1 for international students; for summer admission, 5/1 for domestic students. Applications are processed on a rolling basis. Application fee: $50. Electronic applications accepted. *Financial support:* Applicants required to submit FAFSA. *Unit head:* Gary Karns, Associate Dean for Graduate Studies, 206-281-2948, Fax: 206-281-2733. *Application contact:* Gary Karns, Associate Dean for Graduate Studies, 206-281-2948, Fax: 206-281-2733.
Website: https://spu.edu/academics/school-of-business-and-economics/graduate-programs/ms-is

Shippensburg University of Pennsylvania, School of Graduate Studies, John L. Grove College of Business, Shippensburg, PA 17257-2299. Offers advanced studies in business (Certificate); advanced supply chain and logistics management (Certificate); business administration (MBA, DBA), including business administration (MBA), business analytics (MBA), finance (MBA), healthcare management (MBA), management information systems (MBA), supply chain management (MBA); finance (Certificate); health care management (Certificate); management information systems (Certificate). *Accreditation:* AACSB. *Program availability:* Part-time, evening/weekend, 100% online, blended/hybrid learning. *Faculty:* 20 full-time (4 women), 2 part-time/adjunct (0 women). *Students:* 31 full-time (14 women), 174 part-time (67 women); includes 33 minority (17 Black or African American, non-Hispanic/Latino; 6 Asian, non-Hispanic/Latino; 7 Hispanic/Latino; 3 Two or more races, non-Hispanic/Latino), 13 international. Average age 33. 149 applicants, 61% accepted, 60 enrolled. In 2018, 104 master's, 1 other advanced degree awarded. *Degree requirements:* For master's, comprehensive exam (for some programs), thesis optional, practicum capstone course; for doctorate, comprehensive exam, thesis/dissertation, comprehensive exam dissertation. *Entrance requirements:* For master's, GMAT (minimum score 450 if less than 5 years of mid-level experience, including management experience), current resume; relevant work/classroom experience; 500-word statement of purpose; prerequisites of quantitative analysis, computer usage, and oral and written communications; laptop computer; for doctorate, GMAT (minimum score of 600 if less than 5 years of substantive professional or teaching experience), 2 letters of recommendation from professionals in academia or industry; 2-3 page personal and professional statement; interview; resume. Additional exam requirements/recommendations for international students: Required—TOEFL (minimum score 550 paper-based; 68 iBT), IELTS (minimum score 6), TOEFL (minimum score 550 paper-based, 68 iBT) or IELTS (minimum score 6). *Application deadline:* For fall admission, 4/30 for international students; for spring admission, 9/30 for international students. Applications are processed on a rolling basis. Application fee: $45. Electronic applications accepted. *Expenses:* Tuition, state resident: part-time $516 per credit.

Tuition, nonresident: part-time $750 per credit. *Required fees:* $149 per credit. *Financial support:* In 2018–19, 15 students received support. Career-related internships or fieldwork, scholarships/grants, unspecified assistantships, and resident hall director and student payroll positions available. Support available to part-time students. Financial award application deadline: 3/1; financial award applicants required to submit FAFSA. *Unit head:* Dr. John G. Kooti, Dean of the College of Business, 717-477-1435, Fax: 717-477-4003, E-mail: jgkooti@ship.edu. *Application contact:* Maya T. Mapp, Director of Admissions, 717-477-1231, Fax: 717-477-4016, E-mail: mtmapp@ship.edu.
Website: http://www.ship.edu/business

Southeastern Oklahoma State University, School of Arts and Sciences, Durant, OK 74701-0609. Offers biology (MT); computer information systems (MT); occupational safety and health (MT). *Program availability:* Part-time, evening/weekend. *Degree requirements:* For master's, thesis optional. *Entrance requirements:* For master's, minimum GPA of 3.0 in last 60 hours or 2.75 overall. Additional exam requirements/recommendations for international students: Required—TOEFL (minimum score 550 paper-based; 79 iBT). Electronic applications accepted.

Southern Illinois University Edwardsville, Graduate School, School of Business, Department of Computer Management and Information Systems, Edwardsville, IL 62026. Offers MS. *Program availability:* Part-time, evening/weekend. *Degree requirements:* For master's, thesis or alternative, final exam. *Entrance requirements:* For master's, GMAT. Additional exam requirements/recommendations for international students: Required—TOEFL (minimum score 550 paper-based; 79 iBT), IELTS (minimum score 6.5). Electronic applications accepted.

Southern Illinois University Edwardsville, Graduate School, School of Business, Program in Business Administration, Edwardsville, IL 62026. Offers business analytics (MBA); management information systems (MBA); project management (MBA). *Accreditation:* AACSB. *Program availability:* Part-time, evening/weekend. *Degree requirements:* For master's, comprehensive exam. *Entrance requirements:* For master's, GMAT. Additional exam requirements/recommendations for international students: Required—TOEFL (minimum score 550 paper-based; 79 iBT), IELTS (minimum score 6.5). Electronic applications accepted.

Southern Methodist University, Cox School of Business, MBA Program, Dallas, TX 75275. Offers accounting (MBA, PMBA); business (EMBA); business analytics (PMBA); finance (MBA, PMBA); information technology and operations management (MBA, PMBA), including business analytics (MBA), information and operations (MBA); management (MBA, PMBA); marketing (MBA, PMBA); real estate (MBA, PMBA); strategy and entrepreneurship (MBA, PMBA); JD/MBA; MA/MBA. *Program availability:* Part-time, evening/weekend. *Entrance requirements:* For master's, GMAT. Additional exam requirements/recommendations for international students: Required—TOEFL. Electronic applications accepted. *Expenses:* Contact institution. *Faculty research:* Corporate finance, financial reporting, modeling consumer decision-making, competition between national brands and store brands, institutional determinants of firms' strategy.

Southern New Hampshire University, School of Business, Manchester, NH 03106-1045. Offers accounting (MBA, Graduate Certificate); accounting finance (MS); accounting/auditing (MS); accounting/forensic accounting (MS); accounting/management accounting (MS); accounting/taxation (MS); applied economics (MS); athletic administration (MBA, Graduate Certificate); business administration (IMBA, Certificate), including business information systems (Certificate), human resource management (Certificate); business analytics (MBA); business intelligence (MBA); communication (MA), including new media and marketing, public relations; community economic development (MBA); criminal justice (MBA); data analytics (MS); economics (MBA); engineering management (MBA); entrepreneurship (MBA); finance (MBA, MS, Graduate Certificate); finance/corporate finance (MS); finance/investments (MS); forensic accounting (MBA); forensic accounting and fraud examination (Graduate Certificate); healthcare informatics (MBA); healthcare management (MBA); human resource management (MS); human resources (MBA); information technology (MS); information technology management (MBA); international business (PhD); Internet marketing (MBA); leadership (MBA); leadership of nonprofit organizations (Graduate Certificate); management (MS); marketing (MBA, MS, Graduate Certificate); music business (MBA); operations and project management (MS); operations and supply chain management (MBA, Graduate Certificate); organizational leadership (MS); project management (MBA, Graduate Certificate); public administration (MBA, Graduate Certificate); quantitative analysis (MBA); Six Sigma (Graduate Certificate); Six Sigma quality (MBA); social media marketing (MBA, Graduate Certificate); sport management (MBA, MS, Graduate Certificate); sustainability and environmental compliance (MBA); MBA/Certificate. *Accreditation:* ACBSP. *Program availability:* Part-time, evening/weekend, online learning. Terminal master's awarded for partial completion of doctoral program. *Degree requirements:* For master's, one foreign language, comprehensive exam (for some programs), thesis or alternative; for doctorate, one foreign language, comprehensive exam, thesis/dissertation. *Entrance requirements:* For master's, minimum GPA of 2.5; for doctorate, GMAT. Additional exam requirements/recommendations for international students: Required—TOEFL (minimum score 500 paper-based). Electronic applications accepted.

Southern University at New Orleans, School of Graduate Studies, New Orleans, LA 70126-1009. Offers criminal justice (MA); management information systems (MS); museum studies (MA); social work (MSW). *Accreditation:* CSWE. *Program availability:* Part-time, evening/weekend. *Degree requirements:* For master's, thesis. *Entrance requirements:* For master's, GRE/GMAT. Additional exam requirements/recommendations for international students: Required—TOEFL.

South University, Program in Information Systems and Technology, Round Rock, TX 78681. Offers MS.

South University, Program in Information Systems and Technology, Montgomery, AL 36116-1120. Offers MS.

South University, Program in Information Systems and Technology, Tampa, FL 33614. Offers MS.

South University, Program in Information Systems and Technology, Virginia Beach, VA 23452. Offers MS.

South University, Program in Information Systems and Technology, Royal Palm Beach, FL 33411. Offers MS.

Stevens Institute of Technology, Graduate School, School of Business, Program in Business Administration, Hoboken, NJ 07030. Offers business intelligence and analytics (MBA); engineering management (MBA); finance (MBA); information systems (MBA); innovation and entrepreneurship (MBA); marketing (MBA); pharmaceutical management (MBA); project management (MBA, Certificate); technology management (MBA); telecommunications management (MBA). *Accreditation:* AACSB. *Program availability:* Part-time, evening/weekend. *Faculty:* 58 full-time (8 women), 18 part-time/adjunct (3 women). *Students:* 44 full-time (23 women), 202 part-time (90 women); includes 56 minority (12 Black or African American, non-Hispanic/Latino; 2 American Indian or Alaska Native, non-Hispanic/Latino; 40 Asian, non-Hispanic/Latino; 2 Hispanic/Latino), 28 international. Average age 37. In 2018, 45 master's awarded. Terminal master's awarded for partial completion of doctoral program. *Degree requirements:* For master's,

thesis optional, minimum B average in major field and overall; for Certificate, minimum B average. *Entrance requirements:* For master's, GRE/GMAT scores: GRE scores are required for all applicants applying to a full-time graduate program in the Schaefer School of Engineering and Science (SES). International applicants must submit TOEFL/IELTS scores and fulfill the English Language Proficiency Requirements in order to be considered. Additional exam requirements/recommendations for international students: Required—TOEFL (minimum score 74 iBT), IELTS (minimum score 6). *Application deadline:* For fall admission, 4/1 for domestic and international students; for spring admission, 11/1 for domestic and international students; for summer admission, 5/1 for domestic students. Applications are processed on a rolling basis. Application fee: $60. Electronic applications accepted. *Expenses: Tuition:* Full-time $35,960; part-time $1620 per credit. *Required fees:* $1290; $600 per semester. Tuition and fees vary according to course load. *Financial support:* Fellowships, research assistantships, teaching assistantships, career-related internships or fieldwork, Federal Work-Study, scholarships/grants, and unspecified assistantships available. Financial award application deadline: 2/15; financial award applicants required to submit FAFSA. *Unit head:* Dr. Gregory Prastacos, Dean, 201-216-8366, E-mail: gprastac@stevens.edu. *Application contact:* Graduate Admissions, 888-783-8367, Fax: 888-511-1306, E-mail: graduate@stevens.edu.
Website: https://www.stevens.edu/school-business/masters-programs/mbaemba

Stevens Institute of Technology, Graduate School, School of Business, Program in Information Systems, Hoboken, NJ 07030. Offers computer science (MS); e-commerce (MS); enterprise systems (MS); entrepreneurial information technology (MS); information architecture (MS); information management (MS, Certificate); information security (MS); information technology in financial services industry (MS); information technology in the pharmaceutical industry (MS); information technology outsourcing management (MS); project management (MS, Certificate); software engineering (MS); telecommunications (MS). *Program availability:* Part-time, evening/weekend. *Students:* 248 full-time (87 women), 54 part-time (20 women); includes 25 minority (8 Black or African American, non-Hispanic/Latino; 17 Asian, non-Hispanic/Latino), 245 international. Average age 27. In 2018, 202 master's, 16 other advanced degrees awarded. Terminal master's awarded for partial completion of doctoral program. *Degree requirements:* For master's, thesis optional, minimum B average in major field and overall; for Certificate, minimum B average. *Entrance requirements:* For master's, GRE/GMAT scores: GRE scores are required for all applicants applying to a full-time graduate program in the Schaefer School of Engineering and Science (SES). International applicants must submit TOEFL/IELTS scores and fulfill the English Language Proficiency Requirements in order to be considered. Additional exam requirements/recommendations for international students: Required—TOEFL (minimum score 74 iBT), IELTS (minimum score 6). *Application deadline:* For fall admission, 4/1 for domestic and international students; for spring admission, 11/1 for domestic and international students; for summer admission, 5/1 for domestic students. Applications are processed on a rolling basis. Application fee: $60. Electronic applications accepted. *Expenses: Tuition:* Full-time $35,960; part-time $1620 per credit. *Required fees:* $1290; $600 per semester. Tuition and fees vary according to course load. *Financial support:* Fellowships, research assistantships, teaching assistantships, career-related internships or fieldwork, Federal Work-Study, scholarships/grants, and unspecified assistantships available. Financial award application deadline: 2/15; financial award applicants required to submit FAFSA. *Unit head:* Dr. Gregory Prastacos, Dean of SB, 201-216-8366, E-mail: gprastac@stevens.edu. *Application contact:* Graduate Admissions, 888-783-8367, Fax: 888-511-1306, E-mail: graduate@stevens.edu.
Website: https://www.stevens.edu/school-business/masters-programs/information-systems

Stevens Institute of Technology, Graduate School, School of Business, Program in Management, Hoboken, NJ 07030. Offers general management (MS); global innovation management (MS); human resource management (MS); information management (MS); project management (MS); technology commercialization (MS); technology management (MS). *Program availability:* Part-time, evening/weekend. *Faculty:* 58 full-time (8 women), 18 part-time/adjunct (3 women). *Students:* 101 full-time (41 women), 66 part-time (34 women); includes 14 minority (4 Black or African American, non-Hispanic/Latino; 9 Asian, non-Hispanic/Latino; 1 Hispanic/Latino), 115 international. Average age 28. In 2018, 70 master's awarded. Terminal master's awarded for partial completion of doctoral program. *Degree requirements:* For master's, thesis optional, minimum B average in major field and overall. *Entrance requirements:* For master's, GRE/GMAT scores: GRE scores are required for all applicants applying to a full-time graduate program in the Schaefer School of Engineering and Science (SES). International applicants must submit TOEFL/IELTS scores and fulfill the English Language Proficiency Requirements in order to be considered. Additional exam requirements/recommendations for international students: Required—TOEFL (minimum score 74 iBT), IELTS (minimum score 6). *Application deadline:* For fall admission, 4/1 for domestic and international students; for spring admission, 11/1 for domestic and international students; for summer admission, 5/1 for domestic students. Applications are processed on a rolling basis. Application fee: $60. Electronic applications accepted. *Expenses: Tuition:* Full-time $35,960; part-time $1620 per credit. *Required fees:* $1290; $600 per semester. Tuition and fees vary according to course load. *Financial support:* Fellowships, research assistantships, teaching assistantships, career-related internships or fieldwork, Federal Work-Study, scholarships/grants, and unspecified assistantships available. Financial award application deadline: 2/15; financial award applicants required to submit FAFSA. *Unit head:* Dr. Gregory Prascatos, Dean of SB, 201-216 8366, E-mail: gprastac@stevens.edu. *Application contact:* Graduate Admissions, 888-783-8367, Fax: 888-511-1306, E-mail: graduate@stevens.edu.
Website: https://www.stevens.edu/school-business/masters-programs/management

Stevens Institute of Technology, Graduate School, School of Business, Program in Technology Management, Hoboken, NJ 07030. Offers information management (PhD); technology management (PhD); telecommunications management (PhD). *Program availability:* Part-time, evening/weekend, online learning. *Faculty:* 58 full-time (8 women), 18 part-time/adjunct (3 women). *Students:* 6 full-time (0 women), 23 part-time (6 women); includes 10 minority (4 Black or African American, non-Hispanic/Latino; 6 Asian, non-Hispanic/Latino), 4 international. Average age 38. In 2018, 1 doctorate awarded. Terminal master's awarded for partial completion of doctoral program. *Degree requirements:* For doctorate, comprehensive exam (for some programs), thesis/dissertation. *Entrance requirements:* Additional exam requirements/recommendations for international students: Required—TOEFL (minimum score 74 iBT), IELTS (minimum score 6). *Application deadline:* For fall admission, 4/1 for domestic and international students; for spring admission, 11/1 for domestic and international students; for summer admission, 5/1 for domestic students. Applications are processed on a rolling basis. Application fee: $60. Electronic applications accepted. *Expenses: Tuition:* Full-time $35,960; part-time $1620 per credit. *Required fees:* $1290; $600 per semester. Tuition and fees vary according to course load. *Financial support:* Fellowships, research assistantships, teaching assistantships, career-related internships or fieldwork, Federal Work-Study, scholarships/grants, and unspecified assistantships available. Financial award application deadline: 2/15; financial award applicants required to submit FAFSA. *Unit head:* Dr. Gregory Prascatos, Dean of SB, 201-216 8366, Fax: 201-216-5385, E-mail: gprastac@stevens.edu. *Application contact:* Graduate Admissions, 888-783-8367, Fax: 888-511-1306, E-mail: graduate@stevens.edu.
Website: https://www.stevens.edu/school-business/phd-business-administration

Stratford University, School of Graduate Studies, Falls Church, VA 22043. Offers accounting (MS); business administration (MBA, DBA); cyber security (MS); cyber security leadership and policy (MS); digital forensics (MS); healthcare administration (MS); information systems (MS); information technology (DIT); networking and telecommunications (MS); software engineering (MS). *Program availability:* Part-time, evening/weekend, 100% online, blended/hybrid learning. *Degree requirements:* For master's, comprehensive exam, capstone project. *Entrance requirements:* For master's, GRE or GMAT, baccalaureate degree. Additional exam requirements/recommendations for international students: Required—TOEFL (minimum score 79 iBT), IELTS (minimum score 6.5), PTE (minimum score 5). Electronic applications accepted. *Expenses: Tuition:* Full-time $22,275; part-time $11,137 per year. One-time fee: $385.

Strayer University, Graduate Studies, Washington, DC 20005-2603. Offers accounting (MS); acquisition (MBA); business administration (MBA); communications technology (MS); educational management (M Ed); finance (MBA); health services administration (MHSA); hospitality and tourism management (MBA); human resource management (MBA); information systems (MS), including computer security management, decision support system management, enterprise resource management, network management, software engineering management, systems development management; management (MBA); management information systems (MS); marketing (MBA); professional accounting (MS), including accounting information systems, controllership, taxation; public administration (MPA); supply chain management (MBA); technology in education (M Ed). Programs also offered at campus locations in Birmingham, AL; Chamblee, GA; Cobb County, GA; Morrow, GA; White Marsh, MD; Charleston, SC; Columbia, SC; Greensboro, NC; Greenville, SC; Lexington, KY; Louisville, KY; Nashville, TN; North Raleigh, NC; Washington, DC. *Accreditation:* ACBSP. *Program availability:* Part-time, evening/weekend, online learning. *Degree requirements:* For master's, thesis. *Entrance requirements:* For master's, GMAT, GRE General Test, bachelor's degree from an accredited college or university, minimum undergraduate GPA of 2.75. Electronic applications accepted.

Suffolk University, Sawyer Business School, Department of Public Administration, Boston, MA 02108-2770. Offers community health (MPA); information systems, performance management, and big data analytics (MPA); nonprofit management (MPA); state and local government (MPA); JD/MPA; MPA/MS; MPA/MSCJ; MPA/MSMHC; MPA/MSPS. *Accreditation:* NASPAA (one or more programs are accredited). *Program availability:* Part-time, evening/weekend. *Faculty:* 9 full-time (5 women), 4 part-time/adjunct (2 women). *Students:* 21 full-time (14 women), 85 part-time (57 women); includes 37 minority (20 Black or African American, non-Hispanic/Latino; 5 Asian, non-Hispanic/Latino; 9 Hispanic/Latino; 3 Two or more races, non-Hispanic/Latino), 3 international. Average age 35. 106 applicants, 83% accepted, 34 enrolled. In 2018, 42 master's awarded. *Entrance requirements:* Additional exam requirements/recommendations for international students: Required—TOEFL (minimum score 550 paper-based; 80 iBT). *Application deadline:* For fall admission, 3/15 priority date for domestic and international students; for spring admission, 10/15 priority date for domestic and international students. Applications are processed on a rolling basis. Application fee: $50. Electronic applications accepted. *Expenses:* Contact institution. *Financial support:* In 2018–19, 76 students received support, including 2 fellowships (averaging $4,650 per year); career-related internships or fieldwork, Federal Work-Study, institutionally sponsored loans, and scholarships/grants also available. Support available to part-time students. Financial award application deadline: 4/1; financial award applicants required to submit FAFSA. *Faculty research:* Local government, health care, federal policy, mental health, HIV/AIDS. *Unit head:* Brenda Bond, Director/Department Chair, 617-305-1768, E-mail: bbond@suffolk.edu. *Application contact:* Mara Marzocchi, Associate Director of Graduate Admissions, 617-573-8302, Fax: 617-305-1733, E-mail: grad.admission@suffolk.edu.
Website: http://www.suffolk.edu/mpa

Syracuse University, Martin J. Whitman School of Management, PhD Programs, Syracuse, NY 13244. Offers finance (PhD); management information systems (PhD). In 2018, 2 doctorates awarded. *Degree requirements:* For doctorate, comprehensive exam, thesis/dissertation, summer research paper. *Entrance requirements:* For doctorate, GMAT (preferred) or GRE, master's degree (preferred), transcripts, three recommendation letters, personal statement. Additional exam requirements/recommendations for international students: Required—TOEFL (minimum score 600 paper-based; 100 iBT). *Application deadline:* For fall admission, 1/15 for domestic and international students. Application fee: $75. Electronic applications accepted. *Financial support:* Fellowships with full tuition reimbursements, research assistantships with full tuition reimbursements, teaching assistantships with full tuition reimbursements, and scholarships/grants available. *Faculty research:* Marketing models, market microstructure, supply chain, auditing, corporate governance. *Unit head:* Dr. Michel Benaroch, Associate Dean for Research and PhD Programs, 315-443-3492, E-mail: mbenaroc@syr.edu. *Application contact:* Lisa Svegl, Executive Assistant for Development and PhD Programs, 315-443-9141, E-mail: lmsvegl@syr.edu.

Syracuse University, School of Information Studies, CAS Program in Information Security Management, Syracuse, NY 13244. Offers CAS. *Program availability:* Part-time, evening/weekend, online learning. *Students:* Average age 26. *Entrance requirements:* For degree, resume, personal statement, official transcripts. Additional exam requirements/recommendations for international students: Required—TOEFL (minimum score 100 iBT). *Application deadline:* For fall admission, 1/1 priority date for domestic and international students; for spring admission, 10/15 priority date for domestic and international students; for summer admission, 2/1 priority date for domestic and international students. Applications are processed on a rolling basis. Application fee: $75. Electronic applications accepted. *Financial support:* Application deadline: 1/1. *Faculty research:* Information security, digital forensics, Internet security, risk management, security policy. *Unit head:* Carsten Oesterlund, Program Director, 315-443-2911, E-mail: igrad@syr.edu. *Application contact:* Susan Corieri, Director of Enrollment Management, 315-443-2575, E-mail: ischool@syr.edu.
Website: https://ischool.syr.edu/academics/graduate/cas/cas-information-security-management/

Syracuse University, School of Information Studies, MS Program in Enterprise Data Systems, Syracuse, NY 13244. Offers MS. *Program availability:* Part-time, evening/weekend, online learning. *Entrance requirements:* For master's, GRE General Test, official academic credentials, 500-word personal statement, two letters of recommendation, resume or curriculum vitae. Additional exam requirements/recommendations for international students: Required—TOEFL (minimum iBT score 100) or IELTS. *Application deadline:* For fall admission, 6/1 priority date for domestic and international students. Applications are processed on a rolling basis. Application fee: $75. Electronic applications accepted. *Financial support:* Research assistantships, teaching assistantships, career-related internships or fieldwork, institutionally sponsored loans, and scholarships/grants available. Financial award application deadline: 2/1. *Faculty research:* Information environments, telecommunications and enterprise network management, information architecture. *Unit head:* Carsten Oesterlund, Program Director, 315-443-2911, E-mail: igrad@syr.edu. *Application contact:* Susan Corieri, Assistant Dean for Enrollment Management, 315-443-2575, E-mail: igrad@syr.edu.
Website: https://ischool.syr.edu/academics/graduate/masters-degrees/ms-in-enterprise-data-systems/

Syracuse University, School of Information Studies, MS Program in Information Management, Syracuse, NY 13244. Offers MS. *Program availability:* Part-time, evening/weekend, online learning. *Entrance requirements:* For master's, GRE General Test, personal statement, two letters of recommendation, resume. Additional exam requirements/recommendations for international students: Required—TOEFL (minimum score 100 iBT). *Application deadline:* For fall admission, 2/1 priority date for domestic and international students; for spring admission, 10/15 priority date for domestic and international students. Applications are processed on a rolling basis. Application fee: $75. Electronic applications accepted. *Financial support:* Fellowships with full tuition reimbursements, research assistantships with partial tuition reimbursements, teaching assistantships with partial tuition reimbursements, and scholarships/grants available. Financial award application deadline: 1/1; financial award applicants required to submit FAFSA. *Faculty research:* Increasing the effectiveness of managers and executives who work with information resources, designing and managing mission-critical information technologies within organizations, developing corporate and government policies to maximize the benefits resulting from the widespread use of these technologies. *Unit head:* Carsten Oesterlund, Program Director, 315-443-2911, Fax: 315-443-6886, E-mail: igrad@syr.edu. *Application contact:* Susan Corieri, Assistant Dean for Enrollment Management, 315-443-2575, E-mail: igrad@syr.edu.
Website: https://ischool.syr.edu/academics/graduate/masters-degrees/ms-in-information-management/

Tarleton State University, College of Graduate Studies, College of Business Administration, Department of Marketing and Computer Information Systems, Stephenville, TX 76402. Offers information systems (MS). *Program availability:* Part-time, evening/weekend, 100% online, blended/hybrid learning. *Faculty:* 8 full-time (1 woman), 1 part-time/adjunct (0 women). *Students:* 13 full-time (5 women), 46 part-time (15 women). Average age 34. 27 applicants, 100% accepted, 22 enrolled. In 2018, 6 master's awarded. *Degree requirements:* For master's, comprehensive exam, thesis (for some programs). *Entrance requirements:* For master's, GRE, minimum GPA of 3.0. Additional exam requirements/recommendations for international students: Required—TOEFL (minimum score 520 paper-based; 69 iBT); Recommended—IELTS (minimum score 6), TSE (minimum score 50). *Application deadline:* For fall admission, 8/15 priority date for domestic students; for spring admission, 1/7 for domestic students. Applications are processed on a rolling basis. Application fee: $50 ($130 for international students). Electronic applications accepted. *Expenses:* Contact institution. *Financial support:* Research assistantships and teaching assistantships available. Financial award application deadline: 5/1; financial award applicants required to submit FAFSA. *Unit head:* Dr. Leah Schultz, Interim Department Head, 254-968-9169, E-mail: lschult@tarleton.edu. *Application contact:* Information Contact, 254-968-9104, Fax: 254-968-9670, E-mail: gradoffice@tarleton.edu.
Website: http://www.tarleton.edu/cis/

Temple University, College of Education, Department of Teaching and Learning, Philadelphia, PA 19122-6096. Offers career and technical education (Ed M), including business, computing, and information technology, industrial education, marketing education; middle grades education (Ed M), including math and language arts, math and science, science and language arts; secondary education (Ed M), including English, math, social studies; teaching English to speakers of other languages (MS Ed); urban education (Ed M). *Program availability:* Part-time, evening/weekend. *Faculty:* 27 full-time (19 women), 71 part-time/adjunct (51 women). *Students:* 181 full-time (126 women), 128 part-time (78 women); includes 71 minority (25 Black or African American, non-Hispanic/Latino; 1 American Indian or Alaska Native, non-Hispanic/Latino; 20 Asian, non-Hispanic/Latino; 19 Hispanic/Latino; 1 Native Hawaiian or other Pacific Islander, non-Hispanic/Latino; 5 Two or more races, non-Hispanic/Latino), 12 international. 234 applicants, 67% accepted, 103 enrolled. In 2018, 148 master's awarded. *Degree requirements:* For master's, thesis (for some programs). *Entrance requirements:* For master's, statement of goals, 2 letters of recommendation. Additional exam requirements/recommendations for international students: Required—TOEFL (minimum score 79 iBT), IELTS, PTE, one of three is required. Application fee: $60. Electronic applications accepted. *Financial support:* Fellowships, research assistantships, teaching assistantships, career-related internships or fieldwork, Federal Work-Study, scholarships/grants, health care benefits, and unspecified assistantships available. Financial award applicants required to submit FAFSA. *Faculty research:* Career & technical education, early childhood education, middle grades education, secondary education, special education. *Unit head:* Matthew Tincani, Prof. of Applied Behavior Analysis and Dept. Chairperson, 215-204-8073, E-mail: matthew.tincani@temple.edu. *Application contact:* Stacey Sanginette, Academic Coordinator, 215-204-6143, E-mail: stacey.sangtinette@temple.edu.
Website: http://education.temple.edu/tl

Temple University, Fox School of Business, Doctoral Programs in Business, Philadelphia, PA 19122-6096. Offers accounting (PhD); entrepreneurship (PhD); finance (PhD); international business (PhD); management information systems (PhD); marketing (PhD); risk management and insurance (PhD); statistics (PhD); strategic management (PhD); tourism and sport (PhD). *Accreditation:* AACSB. *Degree requirements:* For doctorate, thesis/dissertation. *Entrance requirements:* For doctorate, GRE General Test, GMAT, minimum GPA of 3.0, master's degree. Additional exam requirements/recommendations for international students: Required—TOEFL (minimum score 600 paper-based; 100 iBT), IELTS (minimum score 7.5). Electronic applications accepted.

Tennessee Technological University, College of Graduate Studies, College of Business, MBA Program, Cookeville, TN 38505. Offers finance (MBA); human resource management (MBA); international business (MBA); management information systems (MBA). *Program availability:* Part-time, evening/weekend. *Students:* 32 full-time (10 women), 156 part-time (66 women); includes 16 minority (7 Black or African American, non-Hispanic/Latino; 1 Asian, non-Hispanic/Latino; 5 Hispanic/Latino; 3 Two or more races, non-Hispanic/Latino), 5 international. 115 applicants, 68% accepted, 57 enrolled. In 2018, 88 master's awarded. *Entrance requirements:* For master's, GMAT or GRE. *Financial support:* In 2018–19, 2 research assistantships, 3 teaching assistantships were awarded; fellowships and unspecified assistantships also available. Financial award application deadline: 4/1; financial award applicants required to submit FAFSA. *Unit head:* Kate Nicewicz, Director, 931-372-3600, E-mail: knicewicz@tntech.edu. *Application contact:* Shelia K. Kendrick, Coordinator of Graduate Studies, 931-372-3808, Fax: 931-372-3497, E-mail: skendrick@tntech.edu.
Website: https://www.tntech.edu/cob/mba/

Texas A&M International University, Office of Graduate Studies and Research, A.R. Sanchez, Jr. School of Business, Division of International Business and Technology Studies, Laredo, TX 78041. Offers information systems (MSIS); international business management (MBA, PhD). *Degree requirements:* For master's, thesis (for some programs). *Entrance requirements:* For master's, GMAT or GRE General Test. Additional exam requirements/recommendations for international students: Required—TOEFL (minimum score 550 paper-based; 79 iBT).

Texas A&M University, Mays Business School, Department of Information and Operations Management, College Station, TX 77843. Offers management information systems (MS). *Faculty:* 17. *Students:* 259 full-time (118 women), 3 part-time (1 woman);

includes 20 minority (5 Black or African American, non-Hispanic/Latino; 10 Asian, non-Hispanic/Latino; 5 Hispanic/Latino), 194 international. Average age 26. 441 applicants, 49% accepted, 75 enrolled. In 2018, 156 master's awarded. Terminal master's awarded for partial completion of doctoral program. *Degree requirements:* For master's, comprehensive exam. *Entrance requirements:* For master's, GMAT. Additional exam requirements/recommendations for international students: Required—TOEFL (minimum score 550 paper-based; 80 iBT), IELTS (minimum score 6), PTE (minimum score 53). *Application deadline:* For fall admission, 12/1 priority date for domestic students, 2/15 for international students. Applications are processed on a rolling basis. Application fee: $50 ($90 for international students). Electronic applications accepted. *Expenses:* Contact institution. *Financial support:* In 2018–19, 213 students received support, including 50 research assistantships with tuition reimbursements available (averaging $7,801 per year), 47 teaching assistantships with tuition reimbursements available (averaging $7,505 per year); career-related internships or fieldwork, institutionally sponsored loans, scholarships/grants, traineeships, health care benefits, tuition waivers, and unspecified assistantships also available. Support available to part-time students. Financial award application deadline: 3/15; financial award applicants required to submit FAFSA. *Unit head:* Dr. Rich Metters, Head, 979-845-1148, Fax: 979-845-1148, E-mail: rmetters@mays.tamu.edu. *Application contact:* Andre Araujo, Graduate Advisor, 979-845-0809, Fax: 979-845-1148, E-mail: aaraujo@mays.tamu.edu.
Website: http://mays.tamu.edu/info/

Texas A&M University–Central Texas, Graduate Studies and Research, Killeen, TX 76549. Offers accounting (MS); business administration (MBA); clinical mental health counseling (MS); criminal justice (MCJ); curriculum and instruction (M Ed); educational administration (M Ed); educational psychology - experimental psychology (MS); history (MA); human resource management (MS); information systems (MS); liberal studies (MS); management and leadership (MS); marriage and family therapy (MS); mathematics (MS); political science (MA); school counseling (M Ed); school psychology (Ed S).

Texas Southern University, Jesse H. Jones School of Business, Program in Management Information Systems, Houston, TX 77004-4584. Offers MS. Electronic applications accepted.

Texas State University, The Graduate College, Emmett and Miriam McCoy College of Business Administration, Program in Accounting and Information Technology, San Marcos, TX 78666. Offers MS. *Program availability:* Part-time. *Faculty:* 8 full-time (2 women). *Students:* 9 full-time (4 women), 9 part-time (6 women); includes 11 minority (1 Black or African American, non-Hispanic/Latino; 2 Asian, non-Hispanic/Latino; 7 Hispanic/Latino; 1 Native Hawaiian or other Pacific Islander, non-Hispanic/Latino), 2 international. Average age 36. 8 applicants, 50% accepted, 3 enrolled. In 2018, 5 master's awarded. *Degree requirements:* For master's, comprehensive exam. *Entrance requirements:* For master's, official GMAT or GRE (general test only) required with competitive scores, baccalaureate degree from regionally-accredited university; a competitive GPA in your last 60 hours of undergraduate course work; two letters or forms of recommendation; essay; resume showing work experience, extracurricular and community activities, and honors and achievements. Additional exam requirements/recommendations for international students: Required—TOEFL (minimum score 550 paper-based; 78 iBT), IELTS (minimum score 6.5). *Application deadline:* For fall admission, 1/15 priority date for domestic and international students; for spring admission, 10/1 for domestic and international students. Application fee: $55 ($90 for international students). Electronic applications accepted. *Expenses:* Tuition, state resident: full-time $8102; part-time $4051 per semester. Tuition, nonresident: full-time $18,229; part-time $9115 per semester. International tuition: $18,229 full-time. *Required fees:* $2116; $120 per credit hour. Tuition and fees vary according to course load. *Financial support:* In 2018–19, 10 students received support, including 5 teaching assistantships (averaging $11,981 per year); research assistantships, Federal Work-Study, institutionally sponsored loans, scholarships/grants, health care benefits, and unspecified assistantships also available. Support available to part-time students. Financial award application deadline: 1/15; financial award applicants required to submit FAFSA. *Unit head:* Dr. William Chittenden, Associate Dean, 512-245-3591, Fax: 512-245-8365, E-mail: wc10@txstate.edu. *Application contact:* Dr. Andrea Golato, Dean of Graduate School, 512-245-2581, Fax: 512-245-8365, E-mail: gradcollege@txstate.edu.
Website: https://www.cis.txstate.edu/prospective/msait.html

Texas Tech University, Rawls College of Business Administration, Lubbock, TX 79409-2101. Offers accounting (MSA, PhD), including audit/financial reporting (MSA), taxation (MSA); data science (MS); finance (PhD); general business (MBA); healthcare management (MS); information systems and operations management (PhD); management (PhD); marketing (PhD); STEM (MBA); JD/MBA; JD/MSA; MBA/M Arch; MBA/MD; MBA/MS; MBA/Pharm D. *Accreditation:* AACSB. *Program availability:* Evening/weekend, 100% online, blended/hybrid learning. *Degree requirements:* For master's, thesis (for MS); capstone course; for doctorate, comprehensive exam, thesis/dissertation, qualifying exams. *Entrance requirements:* For master's, GMAT, GRE, MCAT, PCAT, LSAT, or DAT, holistic review of academic credentials, resume, essay, letters of recommendation; for doctorate, GMAT, GRE, holistic review of academic credentials, resume, statement of purpose, letters of recommendation. Additional exam requirements/recommendations for international students: Required—TOEFL (minimum score 550 paper-based; 79 iBT), IELTS (minimum score 6.5), PTE (minimum score 60). Electronic applications accepted. *Expenses:* Contact institution. *Faculty research:* Governmental and nonprofit accounting, securities and options futures, statistical analysis and design, leadership, consumer behavior.

Touro College, Graduate School of Technology, New York, NY 10010. Offers information systems (MS); instructional technology (MS); Web and multimedia design (MA). *Entrance requirements:* Additional exam requirements/recommendations for international students: Required—TOEFL (minimum score 83 iBT), IELTS (minimum score 6.5), PTE (minimum score 58).

Trident University International, College of Business Administration, Program in Business Administration, Cypress, CA 90630. Offers business administration (PhD); conflict and negotiation management (MBA); criminal justice administration (MBA); entrepreneurship (MBA); finance (MBA); general management (MBA); government accounting (MBA); human resource management (MBA); information security and digital assurance management (MBA); information technology management (MBA); international business (MBA); logistics management (MBA); marketing (MBA); project management (MBA); public management (MBA); quality management (MBA); strategic leadership (MBA). *Program availability:* Part-time, evening/weekend, online learning. *Degree requirements:* For doctorate, comprehensive exam, thesis/dissertation, defense of dissertation. *Entrance requirements:* For master's, minimum GPA of 2.5 (students with GPA 3.0 or greater may transfer up to 30% of graduate level credits); for doctorate, minimum GPA of 3.4, curriculum vitae, course work in research methods or statistics. Additional exam requirements/recommendations for international students: Required—TOEFL. Electronic applications accepted.

Trident University International, College of Information Systems, Cypress, CA 90630. Offers business intelligence (Certificate); information technology management (MS). *Program availability:* Part-time, evening/weekend, online learning. *Entrance requirements:* For master's, minimum GPA of 2.5 (students with GPA 3.0 or greater may

transfer up to 30% of graduate level credits); undergraduate degree completed within the past 5 years. Additional exam requirements/recommendations for international students: Required—TOEFL (minimum score 525 paper-based). Electronic applications accepted.

Trine University, Program in Information Studies, Angola, IN 46703-1764. Offers MS.

Troy University, Graduate School, College of Business, Program in Business Administration, Troy, AL 36082. Offers accounting (EMBA, MBA); criminal justice (EMBA); finance (MBA); general management (EMBA, MBA); healthcare management (EMBA); information systems (EMBA, MBA); international economic development (MBA). *Accreditation:* ACBSP. *Program availability:* Part-time, evening/weekend. *Faculty:* 12 full-time (1 woman), 1 part-time/adjunct (0 women). *Students:* 27 full-time (16 women), 93 part-time (44 women); includes 31 minority (27 Black or African American, non-Hispanic/Latino; 1 Asian, non-Hispanic/Latino; 3 Hispanic/Latino), 29 international. Average age 30. 108 applicants, 37% accepted, 22 enrolled. In 2018, 74 master's awarded. *Degree requirements:* For master's, minimum GPA of 3.0, capstone course, research course. *Entrance requirements:* For master's, GMAT (minimum score 500) or GRE (minimum score 900 on old exam or 294 on new exam), bachelor's degree; minimum undergraduate GPA of 2.5 or 3.0 on last 30 semester hours, letter of recommendation. Additional exam requirements/recommendations for international students: Required—TOEFL (minimum score 523 paper-based; 70 iBT), IELTS (minimum score 6). *Application deadline:* Applications are processed on a rolling basis. Application fee: $50. Electronic applications accepted. *Expenses: Tuition, area resident:* Full-time $425; part-time $425 per credit hour. Tuition, state resident: full-time $425; part-time $425 per credit hour. Tuition, nonresident: full-time $850; part-time $850 per credit hour. *International tuition:* $850 full-time. *Required fees:* $50 per semester. Tuition and fees vary according to campus/location and program. *Financial support:* Fellowships, career-related internships or fieldwork, and scholarships/grants available. Support available to part-time students. Financial award applicants required to submit FAFSA. *Unit head:* Dr. Robert Wheatley, Professor, Director of Graduate Business Programs, 334-670-3194, Fax: 334-670-3708, E-mail: rwheat@troy.edu. *Application contact:* Jessica A. Kimbro, Assistant Director of Graduate Programs, 334-670-3189, E-mail: jacord@troy.edu.
Website: https://www.troy.edu/academics/academic-programs/sorrell-college-business-programs.php

Tulane University, School of Professional Advancement, New Orleans, LA 70118-5669. Offers health and wellness management (MPS); homeland security studies (MPS); information technology management (MPS); liberal arts (MLA). *Program availability:* Part-time. *Degree requirements:* For master's, thesis. *Entrance requirements:* For master's, GRE General Test, minimum B average in undergraduate course work. Additional exam requirements/recommendations for international students: Required—TOEFL. *Expenses: Tuition:* Full-time $52,856; part-time $2937 per credit hour. *Required fees:* $2040; $44.50 per credit hour. $580 per term. Tuition and fees vary according to course load, degree level and program.

Tuskegee University, Graduate Programs, Andrew F. Brimmer College of Business and Information Science, Tuskegee, AL 36088. Offers information systems and security management (MS). *Degree requirements:* For master's, thesis. *Entrance requirements:* For master's, GRE or GMAT, baccalaureate degree in computer science, management information systems, accounting, finance, management, information technology, or a closely-related field.

United States International University–Africa, School of Business Administration, Nairobi, Kenya. Offers business administration (GEMBA); entrepreneurship (MBA); finance (MBA); human resource management (MBA); information technology management (MBA); integrated studies (MBA); international business administration (MBA); management and organizational development (MS); marketing (MBA); organizational development (EMS); strategic management (MBA). *Program availability:* Part-time, evening/weekend. *Degree requirements:* For master's, thesis. *Entrance requirements:* For master's, GMAT, 2 letters of reference, resume. Additional exam requirements/recommendations for international students: Required—TOEFL (minimum score 550 paper-based). *Faculty research:* Marketing in small business enterprises, total quality management in Kenya.

Universidad del Este, Graduate School, Carolina, PR 00984. Offers accounting (MBA); adult education (M Ed); agribusiness (MBA); criminal justice and criminology (MA); curriculum and instruction - early education (M Ed); curriculum and instruction - elementary (M Ed); curriculum and instruction - English (M Ed); curriculum and instruction - Spanish (M Ed); human resources (MBA); information security management (MBA); information technology and Web business development (MBA); management (MBA); public policy (MPA); social work (MA), including clinical social work; special education (M Ed); strategic leadership (MBA).

Universidad del Turabo, Graduate Programs, School of Business and Entrepreneurship, Program in Management of Information Systems, Gurabo, PR 00778-3030. Offers DBA. *Entrance requirements:* For doctorate, GRE, EXADEP or GMAT, official transcript, recommendation letters, essay, curriculum vitae, interview. Electronic applications accepted.

Universidad Metropolitana, School of Business Administration, Program in Management Information Systems, San Juan, PR 00928-1150. Offers MBA.

Université de Sherbrooke, Faculty of Administration, Program in Governance, Audit and Security of Information Technology, Longueuil, QC J4K0A8, Canada. Offers M Adm. *Program availability:* Part-time, evening/weekend, online learning. *Degree requirements:* For master's, thesis. *Entrance requirements:* For master's, bachelor's degree, related work experience. Electronic applications accepted.

Université de Sherbrooke, Faculty of Administration, Program in Management Information Systems, Sherbrooke, QC J1K 2R1, Canada. Offers M Sc. *Degree requirements:* For master's, one foreign language, thesis. *Entrance requirements:* For master's, bachelor's degree in related field, minimum GPA of 3.0 (on 4.3 scale). Electronic applications accepted. *Faculty research:* Project management in IT, IT governance, business intelligence, IT performance.

Université de Sherbrooke, Faculty of Sciences, Centre de Formation en Technologies de L'information, Sherbrooke, QC J1K 2R1, Canada. Offers M Sc, Diploma. Electronic applications accepted.

Université du Québec à Montréal, Graduate Programs, Program in Management Information Systems, Montréal, QC H3C 3P8, Canada. Offers M Sc, M Sc A. *Program availability:* Part-time. *Entrance requirements:* For master's, appropriate bachelor's degree or equivalent and proficiency in French.

Université Laval, Faculty of Administrative Sciences, Programs in Business Administration, Québec, QC G1K 7P4, Canada. Offers accounting (MBA); agri-food management (MBA); electronic business (MBA, Diploma); factory management and logistics (MBA); finance (MBA); firm management (MBA); geomatic management (MBA); information technology management (MBA); international management (MBA); management (MBA); management accounting (MBA, Diploma); marketing (MBA); modeling and organizational decision (MBA); occupational health and safety management (MBA); pharmacy management (MBA); social and environmental responsibility (MBA); technological entrepreneurship (Diploma). *Accreditation:* AACSB. *Program availability:* Part-time, evening/weekend, online learning. *Entrance requirements:* For master's and Diploma, knowledge of French and English. Electronic applications accepted.

University at Albany, State University of New York, Nelson A. Rockefeller College of Public Affairs and Policy, Department of Public Administration and Policy, Albany, NY 12222-0001. Offers financial management and public economics (MPA); financial market regulation (MPA); health policy (MPA); healthcare management (MPA); homeland security (MPA); human resources management (MPA); information strategy and management (MPA); local government management (MPA); nonprofit management (MPA); nonprofit management and leadership (Certificate); organizational behavior and theory (MPA, PhD); planning and policy analysis (CAS); policy analysis (MPA); politics and administration (PhD); public finance (PhD); public management (PhD); public policy (PhD); public sector management (Certificate); women and public policy (Certificate); JD/MPA. JD/MPA offered jointly with Albany Law School. *Accreditation:* NASPAA (one or more programs are accredited). *Faculty:* 24 full-time (10 women), 19 part-time/adjunct (10 women). *Students:* 117 full-time (62 women), 101 part-time (58 women); includes 56 minority (20 Black or African American, non-Hispanic/Latino; 8 Asian, non-Hispanic/Latino; 20 Hispanic/Latino; 8 Two or more races, non-Hispanic/Latino), 28 international. 236 applicants, 69% accepted, 86 enrolled. In 2018, 57 master's, 1 doctorate, 14 other advanced degrees awarded. *Degree requirements:* For doctorate, one foreign language, thesis/dissertation. *Entrance requirements:* For doctorate, GRE General Test. Additional exam requirements/recommendations for international students: Required—TOEFL (minimum score 550 paper-based). *Application deadline:* For fall admission, 2/1 priority date for domestic students, 5/1 for international students; for spring admission, 12/1 for domestic students. Applications are processed on a rolling basis. Application fee: $75. Electronic applications accepted. *Financial support:* Application deadline: 2/1. *Unit head:* Victor Asal, Chair, 518-591-8729, E-mail: vasal@albany.edu. *Application contact:* Victor Asal, Chair, 518-591-8729, E-mail: vasal@albany.edu.
Website: http://www.albany.edu/rockefeller/pad.shtml

University at Albany, State University of New York, School of Business, MBA Programs, Albany, NY 12222-0001. Offers business administration (MBA); cyber security (MBA); entrepreneurship (MBA); finance (MBA); human resource information systems (MBA); information systems and business analytics (MBA); marketing (MBA); JD/MBA. JD/MBA offered jointly with Albany Law School. *Program availability:* Part-time, evening/weekend. *Faculty:* 29 full-time (13 women), 9 part-time/adjunct (2 women). *Students:* 103 full-time (36 women), 188 part-time (69 women); includes 76 minority (27 Black or African American, non-Hispanic/Latino; 33 Asian, non-Hispanic/Latino; 16 Hispanic/Latino), 16 international. Average age 25. 181 applicants, 80% accepted, 114 enrolled. In 2018, 103 master's awarded. *Degree requirements:* For master's, thesis (for some programs), field or research project. *Entrance requirements:* For master's, GMAT, minimum undergraduate GPA of 3.0; 3 letters of recommendation; resume; statement of goals. Additional exam requirements/recommendations for international students: Required—TOEFL (minimum score 100 iBT); Recommended—IELTS (minimum score 7). *Application deadline:* For fall admission, 4/1 priority date for domestic students, 2/15 for international students; for spring admission, 12/1 for domestic students; for summer admission, 5/1 for domestic students. Applications are processed on a rolling basis. Application fee: $75. Electronic applications accepted. *Expenses:* 16818. *Financial support:* In 2018–19, 25 students received support, including 7 fellowships with partial tuition reimbursements available (averaging $6,000 per year), 4 research assistantships with partial tuition reimbursements available, 21 teaching assistantships with partial tuition reimbursements available; unspecified assistantships also available. Financial award application deadline: 4/1; financial award applicants required to submit FAFSA. *Faculty research:* Social goods, information assurance, social computing, corporate entrepreneurship, asset pricing. *Total annual research expenditures:* $136,000. *Unit head:* Dr. Nilanjan Sen, Dean, 518-956-8370, Fax: 518-442-3273, E-mail: nsen@albany.edu. *Application contact:* Zina Mega Lawrence, Assistant Dean of Graduate Student Services, 518-956-8320, Fax: 518-442-4042, E-mail: zlawrence@albany.edu.
Website: https://graduatebusiness.albany.edu/

University at Buffalo, the State University of New York, Graduate School, School of Engineering and Applied Sciences, Department of Computer Science and Engineering, Buffalo, NY 14260. Offers computer science and engineering (MS, PhD); information assurance (Certificate). *Program availability:* Part-time. Terminal master's awarded for partial completion of doctoral program. *Degree requirements:* For master's, thesis or alternative; for doctorate, thesis/dissertation, comprehensive qualifying exam. *Entrance requirements:* For master's and doctorate, GRE General Test. Additional exam requirements/recommendations for international students: Required—TOEFL (minimum score 550 paper-based; 79 iBT). Electronic applications accepted. *Faculty research:* Theory and algorithms, databases and information retrieval, data mining and data science, artificial intelligence and machine learning, computer security and information assurance, computing education, cyber-physical systens (Internet of Things), distributed systems and networks, hardware and architecture, high-performance and computing and computational science, medical applications and bioinformatics, mobile systems, programming languages and software systems.

University at Buffalo, the State University of New York, Graduate School, School of Management, Buffalo, NY 14260. Offers accounting (MS); analytics (MBA); business administration (PMBA); consulting (MBA); finance (MBA, MS), including financial risk management (MS), quantitative finance (MS); healthcare (MBA); information assurance (MBA); information systems (MBA); international management (MBA); management (EMBA, PhD); management information systems (MS); marketing (MBA); supply chain and operations (MBA); supply chains and operations management (MS); Au D/MBA; DDS/MBA; JD/MBA; M Arch/MBA; MD/MBA; MPH/MBA; MSW/MBA; Pharm D/MBA. *Accreditation:* AACSB. *Program availability:* Part-time, evening/weekend. *Degree requirements:* For master's, capstone courses or projects; for doctorate, comprehensive exam, thesis/dissertation. *Entrance requirements:* For master's, GMAT (for MS in accounting, finance); GRE or GMAT (for MBA, MS in management information systems, supply chains and operations management), essays, letters of recommendation; for doctorate, GMAT or GRE, essays, writing sample, letters of recommendation. Additional exam requirements/recommendations for international students: Required—TOEFL (minimum score 95 iBT) or IELTS (minimum score 6.5); Recommended—TSE (minimum score 73). Electronic applications accepted. *Expenses:* Contact institution. *Faculty research:* Data analytics, accounting and law, rate finance, consumer behavior, supply chain logistics, leadership and team effectiveness.

The University of Akron, Graduate School, College of Business Administration, Department of Management, Program in Information Systems Management, Akron, OH 44325. Offers MSM. *Entrance requirements:* For master's, GMAT, GRE, MCAT, LSAT, PCAT, or CAT, undergraduate degree in information systems, minimum GPA of 3.0, two letters of recommendation, statement of purpose, resume. Additional exam requirements/recommendations for international students: Required—TOEFL (minimum score 79 iBT), IELTS (minimum score 6.5). Electronic applications accepted.

The University of Alabama at Birmingham, Collat School of Business, Program in Business Administration, Birmingham, AL 35294. Offers business administration (MBA),

including finance, health care management, information technology management, marketing; MD/MBA. *Program availability:* Part-time, evening/weekend, 100% online, blended/hybrid learning. *Entrance requirements:* For master's, GMAT. Additional exam requirements/recommendations for international students: Required—TOEFL (minimum score 80 iBT), IELTS (minimum score 6.5). Electronic applications accepted. *Expenses: Tuition, area resident:* Full-time $8100; part-time $8100 per year. Tuition, state resident: full-time $8100. Tuition, nonresident: full-time $19,188; part-time $19,188 per year. Tuition and fees vary according to program. *Faculty research:* Open innovation, workplace issues, leadership, supply chain management, capital markets.

The University of Alabama at Birmingham, Collat School of Business, Program in Management Information Systems, Birmingham, AL 35294. Offers management information systems (MS), including cybersecurity management, information technology management. *Program availability:* Part-time, evening/weekend, online only, 100% online. *Faculty:* 7 full-time (1 woman), 4 part-time/adjunct (2 women). *Students:* 8 full-time (0 women), 116 part-time (38 women); includes 49 minority (35 Black or African American, non-Hispanic/Latino; 1 American Indian or Alaska Native, non-Hispanic/Latino; 5 Asian, non-Hispanic/Latino; 3 Hispanic/Latino; 5 Two or more races, non-Hispanic/Latino), 1 international. Average age 37. 47 applicants, 94% accepted, 36 enrolled. In 2018, 35 master's awarded. *Entrance requirements:* For master's, GMAT or GRE. Additional exam requirements/recommendations for international students: Required—TOEFL (minimum score 80 iBT), IELTS (minimum score 6.5). *Application deadline:* For fall admission, 8/1 for domestic and international students; for spring admission, 12/1 for domestic and international students; for summer admission, 5/1 for domestic and international students. Applications are processed on a rolling basis. Application fee: $70 ($85 for international students). Electronic applications accepted. *Expenses: Tuition, area resident:* Full-time $8100; part-time $8100 per year. Tuition, state resident: full-time $8100. Tuition, nonresident: full-time $19,188; part-time $19,188 per year. Tuition and fees vary according to program. *Faculty research:* Open innovation, information security, online communities, privacy, business analytics. *Unit head:* Dr. Jack Howard, Department Chair, 205-934-8846, Fax: 205-934-8886, E-mail: jlhoward@uab.edu. *Application contact:* Wendy England, Online Program Coordinator, 205-934-8813, Fax: 205-975-4429.
Website: https://businessdegrees.uab.edu/mis-degree-masters/

The University of Alabama in Huntsville, School of Graduate Studies, College of Business Administration, Program in Accounting, Huntsville, AL 35899. Offers accounting (M Acc), including CPA preparatory with an emphasis in taxation, CPA preparatory with emphasis in assurance and financial reporting, general accounting, information systems audit and control (ISAC). *Accreditation:* AACSB. *Program availability:* Part-time. *Faculty:* 3 full-time (1 woman). *Students:* 14 full-time (6 women), 25 part-time (18 women); includes 5 minority (2 Black or African American, non-Hispanic/Latino; 2 Asian, non-Hispanic/Latino; 1 Hispanic/Latino), 3 international. Average age 29. 40 applicants, 73% accepted, 17 enrolled. In 2018, 12 master's awarded. *Degree requirements:* For master's, comprehensive exam, thesis or alternative. *Entrance requirements:* For master's, GMAT (minimum score 500), minimum AACSB index of 1080. Additional exam requirements/recommendations for international students: Required—TOEFL (minimum score 550 paper-based; 80 iBT), IELTS (minimum score 6.5). *Application deadline:* For fall admission, 7/15 priority date for domestic students, 4/1 priority date for international students; for spring admission, 11/30 priority date for domestic students, 9/1 priority date for international students. Applications are processed on a rolling basis. Application fee: $50. Electronic applications accepted. *Expenses: Tuition, area resident:* Full-time $10,632; part-time $412 per credit hour. Tuition, state resident: full-time $10,632. Tuition, nonresident: full-time $23,604; part-time $412 per credit hour. *Required fees:* $582; $582. Tuition and fees vary according to course load and program. *Financial support:* In 2018–19, 4 students received support, including 3 teaching assistantships with full tuition reimbursements available (averaging $5,100 per year); career-related internships or fieldwork, Federal Work-Study, institutionally sponsored loans, scholarships/grants, health care benefits, and unspecified assistantships also available. Support available to part-time students. Financial award application deadline: 4/1; financial award applicants required to submit FAFSA. *Faculty research:* Accounting information systems, managerial accounting, behavioral accounting, state and local taxation, financial accounting. *Unit head:* Dr. Allen Wilhite, Interim Chair, 256-824-6591, Fax: 256-824-2929, E-mail: allen.wilhite@uah.edu. *Application contact:* Jennifer Pettitt, Director of Graduate Programs, 256-824-6681, Fax: 256-824-7571, E-mail: jennifer.pettitt@uah.edu.

The University of Alabama in Huntsville, School of Graduate Studies, College of Business Administration, Programs in Information Systems, Huntsville, AL 35899. Offers cybersecurity (MS, Certificate); enterprise resource planning (Certificate); information systems (MSIS); supply chain and logistics management (MS); supply chain management (Certificate). *Program availability:* Part-time. *Faculty:* 4 full-time. *Students:* 33 full-time (9 women), 89 part-time (34 women); includes 23 minority (13 Black or African American, non-Hispanic/Latino; 3 Asian, non-Hispanic/Latino; 5 Hispanic/Latino; 2 Two or more races, non-Hispanic/Latino), 3 international. Average age 35. 117 applicants, 69% accepted, 46 enrolled. In 2018, 39 master's, 3 other advanced degrees awarded. *Degree requirements:* For master's, comprehensive exam, thesis or alternative. *Entrance requirements:* For master's, GMAT (minimum score 500), minimum AACSB index of 1080. Additional exam requirements/recommendations for international students: Required—TOEFL (minimum score 550 paper-based; 80 iBT), IELTS (minimum score 6.5). *Application deadline:* For fall admission, 7/15 priority date for domestic students, 4/1 priority date for international students; for spring admission, 11/30 priority date for domestic students, 9/1 priority date for international students. Applications are processed on a rolling basis. Application fee: $50. Electronic applications accepted. *Expenses: Tuition, area resident:* Full-time $10,632; part-time $412 per credit hour. Tuition, state resident: full-time $10,632. Tuition, nonresident: full-time $23,604; part-time $412 per credit hour. *Required fees:* $582; $582. Tuition and fees vary according to course load and program. *Financial support:* Research assistantships with full tuition reimbursements, teaching assistantships with full tuition reimbursements, career-related internships or fieldwork, Federal Work-Study, institutionally sponsored loans, scholarships/grants, health care benefits, and unspecified assistantships available. Support available to part-time students. Financial award application deadline: 4/1; financial award applicants required to submit FAFSA. *Faculty research:* Supply chain information systems, information assurance and security, databases and conceptual schema, workflow management, inter-organizational information sharing. *Unit head:* Dr. Fan Tseng, Chair, 256-824-6804, Fax: 256-824-6328, E-mail: fan.tseng@uah.edu. *Application contact:* Jennifer Pettitt, Director of Advising, 256-824-6681, Fax: 256-824-7571, E-mail: jennifer.pettitt@uah.edu.

The University of Arizona, Eller College of Management, Department of Management Information Systems, Tucson, AZ 85721. Offers MS, Graduate Certificate. *Degree requirements:* For master's, thesis or alternative. *Entrance requirements:* For master's, GMAT or GRE General Test, 2 letters of recommendation, resume. Additional exam requirements/recommendations for international students: Required—TOEFL (minimum score 550 paper-based; 80 iBT). Electronic applications accepted. *Faculty research:* Group decision support systems, domestic and international computing issues, expert systems, data management and structures.

University of Arkansas, Graduate School, Sam M. Walton College of Business Administration, Department of Information Systems, Fayetteville, AR 72701. Offers MIS. *Program availability:* Part-time, evening/weekend. In 2018, 30 master's awarded. *Entrance requirements:* For master's, GMAT. *Application deadline:* For fall admission, 8/1 for domestic students, 4/1 for international students; for spring admission, 12/1 for domestic students, 10/1 for international students; for summer admission, 4/15 for domestic students, 3/1 for international students. Application fee: $60. Electronic applications accepted. *Financial support:* In 2018–19, 18 research assistantships, 7 teaching assistantships were awarded; fellowships with tuition reimbursements also available. Financial award application deadline: 4/1. *Unit head:* Dr. Rajiv Sabherwal, Department Chair, 479-575-2216, Fax: 479-575-4168, E-mail: rsabherwal@walton.uark.edu. *Application contact:* Alice Frizzell, Assistant Director of ISYS Graduate Programs, 479-575-2393, E-mail: afrizzell@walton.uark.edu.
Website: https://information-systems.uark.edu/

University of Arkansas at Little Rock, Graduate School, College of Business, Little Rock, AR 72204-1099. Offers business administration (MBA); business information systems (MS, Graduate Certificate); management (Graduate Certificate). *Accreditation:* AACSB. *Program availability:* Part-time, evening/weekend. *Entrance requirements:* For master's, GMAT, minimum undergraduate GPA of 2.7. Additional exam requirements/recommendations for international students: Required—TOEFL (minimum score 525 paper-based).

University of Baltimore, Graduate School, Merrick School of Business, Department of Accounting, Baltimore, MD 21201-5779. Offers accounting and business advisory services (MS); accounting fundamentals (Graduate Certificate); forensic accounting (Graduate Certificate); taxation (MS). *Program availability:* Part-time, evening/weekend. *Entrance requirements:* For master's, GMAT. Additional exam requirements/recommendations for international students: Required—TOEFL (minimum score 550 paper-based). Electronic applications accepted. *Faculty research:* Health care, accounting and administration, managerial accounting, financial accounting theory, accounting information.

University of Baltimore, Graduate School, Merrick School of Business, Department of Information Systems and Decision Science, Baltimore, MD 21201-5779. Offers accounting and business advisory services (MS).

University of Bridgeport, School of Business, Bridgeport, CT 06604. Offers accounting (MBA); finance (MBA); general business (MBA); global financial services (MBA); human resource management (MBA); information systems and knowledge management (MBA); international business (MBA); management (MBA); marketing (MBA); operations management (MBA); small business and entrepreneurship (MBA); specialized business (MBA). *Accreditation:* ACBSP. *Program availability:* Part-time, evening/weekend. *Degree requirements:* For master's, thesis optional. *Entrance requirements:* For master's, GMAT. Additional exam requirements/recommendations for international students: Recommended—TOEFL (minimum score 550 paper-based; 80 iBT), IELTS (minimum score 6.5). Electronic applications accepted. *Expenses:* Contact institution.

The University of British Columbia, Sauder School of Business, Doctoral Program in Business Administration, Vancouver, BC V6T 1Z2, Canada. Offers accounting (PhD); finance (PhD); management information systems (PhD); management science (PhD); marketing (PhD); organizational behavior (PhD); strategy and business economics (PhD); transportation and logistics (PhD); urban land economics (PhD). *Degree requirements:* For doctorate, comprehensive exam, thesis/dissertation. *Entrance requirements:* For doctorate, GMAT or GRE. Additional exam requirements/recommendations for international students: Required—TOEFL (minimum score 600 paper-based; 100 iBT). Electronic applications accepted. *Expenses:* Contact institution.

University of California, Berkeley, Graduate Division, School of Information, Program in Information Management and Systems, Berkeley, CA 94720. Offers MIMS, PhD. Electronic applications accepted.

University of California, Berkeley, UC Berkeley Extension, Certificate Programs in Computer Technology and Information Management, Berkeley, CA 94720. Offers information systems and management (Postbaccalaureate Certificate); UNIX/LINUX system administration (Certificate). *Program availability:* Online learning.

University of Central Missouri, The Graduate School, Warrensburg, MO 64093. Offers accountancy (MA); accounting (MBA); applied mathematics (MS); aviation safety (MA); biology (MS); business administration (MBA); career and technical education leadership (MS); college student personnel administration (MS); communication (MA); computer science (MS); counseling (MS); criminal justice (MS); educational leadership (Ed D); educational technology (MS); elementary and early childhood education (MSE); English (MA); environmental studies (MA); finance (MBA); history (MA); human services/educational technology (Ed S); human services/learning resources (Ed S); human services/professional counseling (Ed S); industrial hygiene (MS); industrial management (MS); information systems (MBA); information technology (MS); kinesiology (MS); library science and information services (MS); literacy education (MSE); marketing (MBA); mathematics (MS); music (MA); occupational safety management (MS); psychology (MS); rural family nursing (MS); school administration (MSE); social gerontology (MS); sociology (MA); special education (MSE); speech language pathology (MS); superintendency (Ed S); teaching (MAT); teaching English as a second language (MA); technology (MS); technology management (PhD); theatre (MA). *Accreditation:* ASHA. *Program availability:* Part-time, 100% online, blended/hybrid learning. *Degree requirements:* For master's and Ed S, comprehensive exam (for some programs), thesis (for some programs). *Entrance requirements:* Additional exam requirements/recommendations for international students: Required—TOEFL (minimum score 550 paper-based; 79 iBT). Electronic applications accepted.

University of Cincinnati, Carl H. Lindner College of Business, MS Program, Cincinnati, OH 45221. Offers accounting (MS); applied economics (MS); business analytics (MS); finance (MS); information systems (MS); marketing (MS); taxation (MS). *Program availability:* Part-time, evening/weekend. *Faculty:* 98 full-time (27 women), 28 part-time/adjunct (4 women). *Students:* 305 full-time (123 women), 190 part-time (83 women); includes 35 minority (13 Black or African American, non-Hispanic/Latino; 1 American Indian or Alaska Native, non-Hispanic/Latino; 10 Asian, non-Hispanic/Latino; 6 Hispanic/Latino; 5 Two or more races, non-Hispanic/Latino), 309 international. Average age 29. 1,219 applicants, 55% accepted, 495 enrolled. In 2018, 355 master's awarded. *Degree requirements:* For master's, thesis (for some programs), capstone. *Entrance requirements:* For master's, GMAT, GRE, resume, transcripts, essays, letters of recommendation. Additional exam requirements/recommendations for international students: Required—TOEFL (minimum score 577 paper-based; 90 iBT), IELTS (minimum score 6.5). *Application deadline:* For fall admission, 6/30 priority date for domestic students, 3/15 for international students; for spring admission, 12/15 for domestic students, 9/15 for international students; for summer admission, 4/15 for domestic and international students. Applications are processed on a rolling basis. Application fee: $65 ($70 for international students). Electronic applications accepted. *Expenses:* Full-time resident $10,479 per term, full-time nonresident $14,398 per term, part-time $890 per credit hour. *Financial support:* In 2018–19, 251 students received support, including 12 teaching assistantships with full and partial tuition reimbursements available (averaging $3,500 per year); scholarships/grants, tuition waivers (full and

partial), and unspecified assistantships also available. Financial award application deadline: 2/1; financial award applicants required to submit FAFSA. *Faculty research:* Business analytics, financial management, organizational behavior, financial accounting, consumer insights. *Total annual research expenditures:* $39,943. *Unit head:* Dr. Marianne Lewis, Dean, 513-556-7001, Fax: 513-556-4891, E-mail: marianne.lewis@uc.edu. *Application contact:* Dona Clary, Executive Director, Graduate Programs, 513-556-3546, Fax: 513-558-7006, E-mail: dona.clary@uc.edu.
Website: http://business.uc.edu/graduate/masters.html

University of Cincinnati, Carl H. Lindner College of Business, PhD Programs, Cincinnati, OH 45221. Offers accounting (PhD); business analytics (PhD); economics (PhD); finance (PhD); information systems (PhD); management (PhD); marketing (PhD); operations and business analytics (PhD); operations research (PhD). *Faculty:* 101 full-time (37 women). *Students:* 15 full-time (5 women), 10 part-time (4 women); includes 4 minority (1 Black or African American, non-Hispanic/Latino; 3 Asian, non-Hispanic/Latino), 20 international. Average age 31. 125 applicants, 12% accepted, 4 enrolled. In 2018, 7 doctorates awarded. *Degree requirements:* For doctorate, comprehensive exam, thesis/dissertation. *Entrance requirements:* For doctorate, GMAT, GRE, transcripts, essays, resume, letters of recommendation. Additional exam requirements/recommendations for international students: Required—TOEFL (minimum score 600 paper-based; 100 iBT), IELTS (minimum score 7). *Application deadline:* For fall admission, 1/15 for domestic and international students. Application fee: $65 ($70 for international students). Electronic applications accepted. *Expenses:* Contact institution. *Financial support:* In 2018–19, 35 students received support, including 25 research assistantships with full tuition reimbursements available (averaging $23,250 per year); scholarships/grants, health care benefits, tuition waivers (full), and unspecified assistantships also available. Financial award application deadline: 1/15; financial award applicants required to submit FAFSA. *Faculty research:* Bayesian Prediction Theory, organizational fairness, consumer insight and market research, consumer insight and market research, density estimation from correlated data. *Unit head:* Dr. Olivier Parent, Director, 513-556-3941, Fax: 513-556-5499, E-mail: olivier.parent@uc.edu. *Application contact:* Angel Elvin, Assistant Director, 513-556-7190, Fax: 513-558-7006, E-mail: angel.elvin@uc.edu.
Website: http://business.uc.edu/graduate/phd.html

University of Colorado Denver, Business School, Program in Computer Science and Information Systems, Denver, CO 80217. Offers PhD. *Degree requirements:* For doctorate, comprehensive exam, thesis/dissertation. *Entrance requirements:* For doctorate, GMAT or GRE General Test, letters of recommendation, portfolio, essay describing applicant's motivation and initial plan for doctoral study, resume. Additional exam requirements/recommendations for international students: Required—TOEFL (minimum score 525 paper-based; 71 iBT); Recommended—IELTS (minimum score 6.5). Electronic applications accepted. *Expenses:* Contact institution. *Faculty research:* Design science of information systems, information system economics, organizational impacts of information technology, high performance parallel and distributed systems, performance measurement and prediction.

University of Colorado Denver, Business School, Program in Information Systems, Denver, CO 80217. Offers accounting and information systems audit and control (MS); business intelligence systems (MS); digital health entrepreneurship (MS); enterprise risk management (MS); enterprise technology management (MS); geographic information systems (MS); health information technology (MS); technology innovation and entrepreneurship (MS); Web and mobile computing (MS). *Program availability:* Part-time, evening/weekend, online learning. *Degree requirements:* For master's, 30 credit hours. *Entrance requirements:* For master's, GMAT, resume, essay, two letters of recommendation, financial statements (for international applicants). Additional exam requirements/recommendations for international students: Required—TOEFL (minimum score 525 paper-based; 71 iBT); Recommended—IELTS (minimum score 6.5). Electronic applications accepted. *Expenses:* Contact institution. *Faculty research:* Human-computer interaction, expert systems, database management, electronic commerce, object-oriented software development.

University of Connecticut, Graduate School, School of Business, Storrs, CT 06269. Offers accounting (MS, PhD); business (PhD); business administration (MBA); business analytics and project management (MS); finance (PhD); financial risk management (MS); health care management and insurance studies (MBA); human resource management (MS); management (PhD); management consulting (MBA); marketing (PhD); marketing intelligence (MBA); operations and information management (PhD). *Accreditation:* AACSB. *Degree requirements:* For master's, comprehensive exam; for doctorate, thesis/dissertation. *Entrance requirements:* For master's and doctorate, GMAT. Additional exam requirements/recommendations for international students: Required—TOEFL (minimum score 550 paper-based). Electronic applications accepted.

University of Dallas, Satish and Yasmin Gupta College of Business, Irving, TX 75062. Offers accounting (MBA, MS); business administration (DBA); business analytics (MS); business management (MBA); corporate finance (MBA); cybersecurity (MS); finance (MS); financial services (MBA); global business (MBA, MS); health services management (MBA); human resource management (MBA); information and technology management (MS); information assurance (MBA); information technology (MBA); information technology service management (MBA); marketing management (MBA); organization development (MBA); project management (MBA); sports and entertainment management (MBA); strategic leadership (MBA); supply chain management (MBA). *Accreditation:* AACSB. *Program availability:* Part-time, evening/weekend, 100% online. *Students:* 147 full-time (56 women), 584 part-time (232 women); includes 402 minority (204 Black or African American, non-Hispanic/Latino; 95 Asian, non-Hispanic/Latino; 92 Hispanic/Latino; 2 Native Hawaiian or other Pacific Islander, non-Hispanic/Latino; 9 Two or more races, non-Hispanic/Latino), 113 international. Average age 34. 992 applicants, 30% accepted, 157 enrolled. In 2018, 336 master's, 5 doctorates awarded. *Degree requirements:* For doctorate, thesis/dissertation. *Entrance requirements:* For master's and doctorate, U.S. bachelor's degree with a minimum cumulative GPA of 2.0 from a regionally accredited college or university (or comparable foreign degree); minimum 3.0 GPA in any graduate-level coursework completed; good academic standing with all colleges attended. Additional exam requirements/recommendations for international students: Required—TOEFL (minimum score 80 iBT), IELTS (minimum score 6.5), PTE (minimum score 67). *Application deadline:* Applications are processed on a rolling basis. Application fee: $50. Electronic applications accepted. *Expenses:* $1250 per credit hour. *Financial support:* In 2018–19, 291 students received support. Research assistantships, teaching assistantships, scholarships/grants, and unspecified assistantships available. Support available to part-time students. Financial award application deadline: 2/15; financial award applicants required to submit FAFSA. *Unit head:* Brett J.L. Landry, Dean, 972-721-5356, E-mail: blandry@udallas.edu. *Application contact:* Breonna Collins, Director, Graduate Admissions, 972-7215304, E-mail: bcollins@udallas.edu.
Website: http://www.udallas.edu/cob/

University of Delaware, Alfred Lerner College of Business and Economics, Department of Accounting and Management Information Systems and Department of Electrical and Computer Engineering, Program in Information Systems and Technology Management, Newark, DE 19716. Offers MS. *Program availability:* Part-time, evening/weekend. *Entrance requirements:* For master's, GRE or GMAT, 2 letters of recommendation, resume, minimum GPA of 2.75. Additional exam requirements/recommendations for international students: Required—TOEFL (minimum score 600 paper-based). *Faculty research:* Security, developer trust, XML.

University of Delaware, Alfred Lerner College of Business and Economics, Program in Financial Service Analytics, Newark, DE 19716. Offers PhD. Program admits students every other year.

University of Detroit Mercy, College of Liberal Arts and Education, Detroit, MI 48221. Offers addiction counseling (MA); addiction studies (Certificate); clinical mental health counseling (MA); clinical psychology (MA, PhD); computer and information systems (MS); criminal justice (MA); curriculum and instruction (MA); economics (MA); educational administration (MA); financial economics (MA); industrial/organizational psychology (MA); information assurance (MS); intelligence analysis (MA); liberal studies (MALS); religious studies (MA); school counseling (MA, Certificate); school psychology (Spec); security administration (MS); special education: emotionally impaired/behaviorally disordered (MA); special education: learning disabilities (MA). *Program availability:* Part-time, evening/weekend. *Degree requirements:* For doctorate, departmental qualifying exam. *Faculty research:* Psychology of aging, history of technology, Renaissance humanism, U.S. and Japanese economic relations.

University of Florida, Graduate School, Warrington College of Business Administration, Hough Graduate School of Business, Department of Information Systems and Operations Management, Gainesville, FL 32611. Offers information systems and operations management (PhD); supply chain management (Certificate). Terminal master's awarded for partial completion of doctoral program. *Degree requirements:* For doctorate, thesis/dissertation. *Entrance requirements:* For master's, GMAT or GRE General Test, minimum GPA of 3.0; for doctorate, GMAT (minimum score 650) or GRE General Test, minimum GPA of 3.0. Additional exam requirements/recommendations for international students: Required—TOEFL (minimum score 550 paper-based; 80 iBT), IELTS (minimum score 6). *Faculty research:* Expert systems, nonconvex optimization, manufacturing management, production and operation management, telecommunication.

University of Florida, Graduate School, Warrington College of Business Administration, Hough Graduate School of Business, Programs in Business Administration, Gainesville, FL 32611. Offers business administration (MA, MS, PhD); competitive strategy (MBA); finance (MBA); global management (MBA); Graham-Buffett security analysis (MBA); human resource management (MBA); information systems and operations management (MBA); international studies (MBA); management (MBA); real estate (MBA); JD/MBA; MBA/MS; MBA/PhD; MBA/Pharm D; MD/MBA. *Accreditation:* AACSB. *Program availability:* Part-time, evening/weekend, online learning. *Degree requirements:* For master's, capstone course. *Entrance requirements:* For master's and doctorate, GMAT (minimum score 465), minimum GPA of 3.0, interview. Additional exam requirements/recommendations for international students: Required—TOEFL (minimum score 550 paper-based; 80 iBT), IELTS (minimum score 6). Electronic applications accepted. *Faculty research:* Accounting, finance, insurance, management, real estate, urban analysis marketing.

University of Hawaii at Manoa, Office of Graduate Education, College of Social Sciences, School of Communications, Program in Telecommunication and Information Resource Management, Honolulu, HI 96822. Offers Graduate Certificate. *Program availability:* Part-time. *Entrance requirements:* Additional exam requirements/recommendations for international students: Required—TOEFL (minimum score 500 paper-based; 61 iBT), IELTS (minimum score 5).

University of Hawaii at Manoa, Office of Graduate Education, Shidler College of Business, Program in Accounting, Honolulu, HI 96822. Offers accounting (M Acc); accounting law (M Acc); information systems (M Acc); taxation (M Acc). *Program availability:* Part-time. *Entrance requirements:* For master's, GMAT, bachelor's degree in accounting, minimum GPA of 3.0. Additional exam requirements/recommendations for international students: Required—TOEFL (minimum score 550 paper-based; 79 iBT), IELTS (minimum score 5). *Faculty research:* International accounting, current tax topics, insurance industry financial reporting, behavioral accounting, auditing.

University of Hawaii at Manoa, Office of Graduate Education, Shidler College of Business, Program in Business Administration, Honolulu, HI 96822. Offers Asian business studies (MBA); Chinese business studies (MBA); decision sciences (MBA); entrepreneurship (MBA); finance (MBA); finance and banking (MBA); human resources management (MBA); information management (MBA); information technology (MBA); international business (MBA); Japanese business studies (MBA); marketing (MBA); organizational behavior (MBA); organizational management (MBA); real estate (MBA); student-designed track (MBA). *Accreditation:* AACSB. *Program availability:* Part-time, evening/weekend. *Degree requirements:* For master's, thesis optional. *Entrance requirements:* For master's, GMAT, minimum GPA of 3.0. Additional exam requirements/recommendations for international students: Required—TOEFL (minimum score 600 paper-based; 100 iBT), IELTS (minimum score 7). *Expenses:* Contact institution.

University of Hawaii at Manoa, Office of Graduate Education, Shidler College of Business, Program in International Management, Honolulu, HI 96822. Offers Asian finance (PhD); global information technology management (PhD); international accounting (PhD); international marketing (PhD); international organization and strategy (PhD). *Program availability:* Part-time. *Degree requirements:* For doctorate, comprehensive exam, thesis/dissertation. *Entrance requirements:* For doctorate, GMAT or GRE General Test, minimum GPA of 3.0. Additional exam requirements/recommendations for international students: Required—TOEFL (minimum score 600 paper-based; 100 iBT), IELTS (minimum score 7). *Expenses:* Contact institution.

University of Houston–Clear Lake, School of Business, Program in Management Information Systems, Houston, TX 77058-1002. Offers MS. *Program availability:* Part-time. *Entrance requirements:* For master's, GMAT. Additional exam requirements/recommendations for international students: Required—TOEFL (minimum score 550 paper-based).

University of Houston–Victoria, School of Arts and Sciences, Department of Computer Science, Victoria, TX 77901-4450. Offers computer information systems (MS); computer science (MS). *Program availability:* Part-time, evening/weekend, online learning. *Degree requirements:* For master's, comprehensive exam (for some programs), thesis (for some programs). *Entrance requirements:* For master's, GRE. Additional exam requirements/recommendations for international students: Required—TOEFL (minimum score 550 paper-based). *Expenses: Tuition, area resident:* Full-time $6154; part-time $3077 per semester. Tuition, state resident: full-time $6154; part-time $3077 per semester. Tuition, nonresident: full-time $13,624; part-time $6812 per semester. *International tuition:* $13,624 full-time. *Required fees:* $1405; $847 per semester. $423 per semester. Tuition and fees vary according to program.

University of Illinois at Chicago, Liautaud Graduate School of Business, Department of Information and Decision Sciences, Chicago, IL 60607-7128. Offers management information systems (PhD). *Program availability:* Part-time, evening/weekend. *Degree requirements:* For doctorate, thesis/dissertation. *Entrance requirements:* For doctorate, GMAT, minimum GPA of 2.75. Additional exam requirements/recommendations for

international students: Required—TOEFL. Electronic applications accepted. *Expenses:* Contact institution. *Faculty research:* Information management/technology and innovation, data and analytics, health informatics, risk management, business statistics and forecasting.

University of Illinois at Springfield, Graduate Programs, College of Business and Management, Program in Management Information Systems, Springfield, IL 62703-5407. Offers MS. *Program availability:* Part-time, evening/weekend, 100% online, blended/hybrid learning. *Faculty:* 9 full-time (1 woman), 2 part-time/adjunct (1 woman). *Students:* 71 full-time (35 women), 101 part-time (37 women); includes 40 minority (11 Black or African American, non-Hispanic/Latino; 16 Asian, non-Hispanic/Latino; 9 Hispanic/Latino; 4 Two or more races, non-Hispanic/Latino), 80 international. Average age 32. 322 applicants, 39% accepted, 30 enrolled. In 2018, 132 master's awarded. *Degree requirements:* For master's, thesis or alternative, thesis or closure seminar. *Entrance requirements:* For master's, GMAT or GRE General Test, courses in managerial and financial accounting, production/operations management, statistics, linear algebra or mathematics; competency in a structured, high-level programming language; minimum undergraduate GPA of 2.75. Additional exam requirements/recommendations for international students: Required—TOEFL (minimum score 500 paper-based; 61 iBT). *Application deadline:* Applications are processed on a rolling basis. Application fee: $60 ($75 for international students). Electronic applications accepted. *Expenses:* Contact institution. *Financial support:* In 2018–19, research assistantships with full tuition reimbursements (averaging $10,384 per year), teaching assistantships with full tuition reimbursements (averaging $10,303 per year) were awarded; fellowships, career-related internships or fieldwork, Federal Work-Study, scholarships/grants, health care benefits, and unspecified assistantships also available. Support available to part-time students. Financial award application deadline: 11/15; financial award applicants required to submit FAFSA. *Unit head:* Dr. Rassule Hadidi, Program Administrator, 217-206-6067, Fax: 217-206-7541, E-mail: rhadi1@uis.edu. *Application contact:* Dr. Rassule Hadidi, Program Administrator, 217-206-6067, Fax: 217-206-7541, E-mail: rhadi1@uis.edu.
Website: mis@uis.edu

University of Illinois at Urbana–Champaign, Graduate College, School of Information Sciences, Champaign, IL 61820. Offers bioinformatics (MS); digital libraries (CAS); information management (MS); library and information science (MS, PhD, CAS). *Accreditation:* ALA (one or more programs are accredited). *Program availability:* Part-time, online learning. *Entrance requirements:* For degree, master's degree in library and information science or related field with minimum GPA of 3.0.

The University of Kansas, Graduate Studies, School of Engineering, Program in Information Technology, Lawrence, KS 66045. Offers MS. *Program availability:* Part-time, evening/weekend. *Students:* 1 full-time (0 women), 24 part-time (7 women); includes 7 minority (6 Black or African American, non-Hispanic/Latino; 1 Asian, non-Hispanic/Latino), 2 international. Average age 38. 24 applicants, 67% accepted, 9 enrolled. In 2018, 3 master's awarded. *Entrance requirements:* For master's, GRE, official transcript, three recommendations, statement of academic objectives, resume. Additional exam requirements/recommendations for international students: Required—TOEFL (minimum score 600 paper-based; 100 iBT), IELTS (minimum score 6). *Application deadline:* For fall admission, 8/1 for domestic and international students; for spring admission, 1/1 for domestic and international students. Application fee: $65 ($85 for international students). Electronic applications accepted. *Faculty research:* Information security and privacy, game theory, graph theory, software process improvement, resilient and survivable networks, object orientation technology. *Unit head:* Erik Perrins, Chair, 785-864-4486, E-mail: perrins@ku.edu. *Application contact:* Joy Grisafe-Gross, Assistant to Graduate Director, 785-864-4487, Fax: 785-864-3226, E-mail: jgrisafe@ku.edu.

University of La Verne, College of Business and Public Management, Graduate Programs in Business Administration, La Verne, CA 91750-4443. Offers accounting (MBA, MBA-EP); finance (MBA, MBA-EP); health services management (MBA); information technology (MBA, MBA-EP); international business (MBA, MBA-EP); management and leadership (MBA, MBA-EP); marketing (MBA, MBA-EP); supply chain management (MBA, MBA-EP). *Program availability:* Part-time, evening/weekend. *Entrance requirements:* For master's, GMAT, MAT, or GRE, minimum undergraduate GPA of 3.0, 2 letters of recommendation, resume, statement of purpose. Additional exam requirements/recommendations for international students: Required—TOEFL (minimum score 550 paper-based; 85 iBT).

University of La Verne, Regional and Online Campuses, Graduate Programs, Central Coast/Vandenberg Air Force Base Campuses, La Verne, CA 91750-4443. Offers business administration for experienced professionals (MBA), including health services management, information technology; leadership and management (MS). *Program availability:* Part-time. *Expenses:* Contact institution.

University of La Verne, Regional and Online Campuses, Graduate Programs, Inland Empire Campus, Ontario, CA 91730. Offers business administration (MBA, MBA-EP), including accounting (MBA), finance (MBA), health services management (MBA-EP), information technology (MBA-EP), international business (MBA), managed care (MBA), management and leadership (MBA-EP), marketing (MBA-EP), supply chain management (MBA); leadership and management (MS), including human resource management, nonprofit management, organizational development. *Program availability:* Part-time, evening/weekend. *Expenses:* Contact institution.

University of Lethbridge, School of Graduate Studies, Lethbridge, AB T1K 3M4, Canada. Offers addictions counseling (M Sc); agricultural biotechnology (M Sc); agricultural studies (M Sc, MA); anthropology (MA); archaeology (M Sc, MA); art (MA, MFA); biochemistry (M Sc); biological sciences (M Sc); biomolecular science (PhD); biosystems and biodiversity (PhD); Canadian studies (MA); chemistry (M Sc); computer science (M Sc); computer science and geographical information science (M Sc); counseling (MC); counseling psychology (M Ed); dramatic arts (MA); earth, space, and physical science (PhD); economics (MA); education (MA, PhD); educational leadership (M Ed); English (MA); environmental science (M Sc); evolution and behavior (PhD); exercise science (M Sc); French (MA); French/German (MA); French/Spanish (MA); general education (M Ed); geography (M Sc, MA); German (MA); health sciences (M Sc); individualized multidisciplinary (M Sc, MA); kinesiology (M Sc, MA); management (M Sc), including accounting, finance, human resource management and labor relations, information systems, international management, marketing, policy and strategy; mathematics (M Sc); music (M Mus, MA); Native American studies (MA); neuroscience (M Sc, PhD); new media (MA, MFA); nursing (M Sc, MN); philosophy (MA); physics (M Sc); political science (MA); psychology (M Sc, MA); religious studies (MA); sociology (MA); theatre and dramatic arts (MFA); theoretical and computational science (PhD); urban and regional studies (MA); women and gender studies (MA). *Program availability:* Part-time, evening/weekend. *Degree requirements:* For master's, thesis (for some programs); for doctorate, comprehensive exam, thesis/dissertation. *Entrance requirements:* For master's, GMAT (for M Sc in management), bachelor's degree in related field, minimum GPA of 3.0 during previous 20 graded semester courses, 2 years' teaching or related experience (M Ed); for doctorate, master's degree, minimum graduate GPA of 3.5. Additional exam requirements/recommendations for international students: Required—TOEFL (minimum score 580 paper-based; 93 iBT). Electronic applications accepted. *Faculty research:* Movement and brain plasticity, gibberellin physiology, photosynthesis, carbon cycling, molecular properties of main-group ring components.

University of Management and Technology, Program in Information Technology, Arlington, VA 22209-1609. Offers MS, Advanced Certificate. *Expenses: Tuition:* Full-time $7020; part-time $1170 per course.

University of Mary Hardin-Baylor, Graduate Studies in Business Administration, Belton, TX 76513. Offers accounting (MBA); information systems management (MBA); international business (MBA); management (MBA). *Program availability:* Part-time, evening/weekend. *Degree requirements:* For master's, comprehensive exam. *Entrance requirements:* For master's, minimum GPA of 3.0, interview. Additional exam requirements/recommendations for international students: Required—TOEFL (minimum score 60 iBT), IELTS (minimum score 4.5). Electronic applications accepted. *Faculty research:* Financial management, financial markets, supply chain management.

University of Mary Hardin-Baylor, Graduate Studies in Information Systems, Belton, TX 76513. Offers MS. *Program availability:* Part-time, evening/weekend. *Degree requirements:* For master's, comprehensive exam. *Entrance requirements:* For master's, minimum GPA of 3.0, interview. Additional exam requirements/recommendations for international students: Required—TOEFL (minimum score 60 iBT), IELTS (minimum score 4.5). Electronic applications accepted. *Faculty research:* Sports statistical use, faith in the technology arena, ERP implementations.

University of Maryland University College, The Graduate School, Program in Accounting and Information Systems, Adelphi, MD 20783. Offers MS, Certificate. *Accreditation:* AACSB. *Program availability:* Part-time, evening/weekend, online learning. *Degree requirements:* For master's, thesis or alternative, capstone course. Electronic applications accepted.

University of Massachusetts Boston, College of Management, Program in Information Technology, Boston, MA 02125-3393. Offers MS. *Students:* 12 full-time (2 women), 14 part-time (6 women); includes 9 minority (3 Black or African American, non-Hispanic/Latino; 5 Asian, non-Hispanic/Latino; 1 Hispanic/Latino), 10 international. Average age 34. 25 applicants, 64% accepted, 7 enrolled. In 2018, 29 master's awarded. *Application deadline:* For fall admission, 7/1 for domestic students; for spring admission, 11/15 for domestic students. *Expenses: Tuition, area resident:* Full-time $17,896. Tuition, state resident: full-time $17,896. Tuition, nonresident: full-time $34,932. *International tuition:* $34,932 full-time. *Required fees:* $355. *Unit head:* Dr. Noushin Ashrafi, Professor, 617-287.7883, E-mail: Noushin.Ashrafi@umb.edu. *Application contact:* Graduate Admissions Coordinator, 617-287-6400, Fax: 617-287-6236, E-mail: graduate.admissions@umb.edu.

University of Memphis, Graduate School, Fogelman College of Business and Economics, Department of Business Information and Technology, Memphis, TN 38152. Offers MS, PhD, Graduate Certificate. *Students:* 22 full-time (17 women), 51 part-time (20 women); includes 35 minority (25 Black or African American, non-Hispanic/Latino; 7 Asian, non-Hispanic/Latino; 1 Hispanic/Latino; 2 Two or more races, non-Hispanic/Latino), 23 international. Average age 34. 28 applicants, 100% accepted, 20 enrolled. In 2018, 50 other advanced degrees awarded. *Expenses: Tuition, area resident:* Full-time $10,240; part-time $503 per credit hour. Tuition, state resident: full-time $10,464. Tuition, nonresident: full-time $20,224; part-time $991 per credit hour. *Required fees:* $850; $106 per credit hour. *Financial support:* Research assistantships and teaching assistantships available. *Unit head:* Dr. Chen Zhang, Interim Chair, 901-678-5671, E-mail: czhang12@memphis.edu. *Application contact:* Dr. Sandra Richardson, Master's Program Advisor, 901-678-4614, E-mail: srchrdsn@memphis.edu.
Website: http://www.memphis.edu/bitm/

University of Michigan–Dearborn, College of Business, MS Program in Information Systems, Dearborn, MI 48126. Offers MS. *Program availability:* Part-time, evening/weekend. *Faculty:* 41 full-time (17 women), 9 part-time/adjunct (6 women). *Students:* 6 full-time (5 women), 11 part-time (3 women); includes 2 minority (both Asian, non-Hispanic/Latino), 7 international. Average age 31. 33 applicants, 39% accepted, 5 enrolled. In 2018, 18 master's awarded. *Entrance requirements:* For master's, GRE or GMAT, equivalent of four-year U.S. bachelor's degree from regionally-accredited institution, undergraduate course in finite math, pre-calculus, or calculus. Additional exam requirements/recommendations for international students: Required—TOEFL (minimum score 560 paper-based; 84 iBT), IELTS (minimum score 6.5). *Application deadline:* For fall admission, 8/1 for domestic students, 5/1 for international students; for winter admission, 12/1 for domestic students, 9/1 for international students; for spring admission, 4/1 for domestic students, 1/1 for international students. Applications are processed on a rolling basis. Application fee: $60. Electronic applications accepted. *Expenses:* $15,740 per academic year (typical full-time in-state); $24,308 per academic year (typical full-time out-of-state). *Financial support:* In 2018–19, 5 students received support. Scholarships/grants and non-resident tuition scholarships available. Financial award application deadline: 3/1; financial award applicants required to submit FAFSA. *Faculty research:* Business intelligence, behavioral finance, brand management and new media, management education, operations strategy. *Unit head:* Dr. Michael Kamen, Director, Graduate Programs, 313-593-5460, E-mail: mkamen@umich.edu. *Application contact:* Joan Doherty, Academic Advisor/Counselor, 313-593-5460, Fax: 313-271-9838, E-mail: umd-gradbusiness@umich.edu.
Website: http://umdearborn.edu/cob/ms-information-systems/

University of Michigan–Dearborn, College of Education, Health, and Human Services, Master of Science Program in Health Information Technology, Dearborn, MI 48126. Offers MS. *Program availability:* Part-time, evening/weekend. *Faculty:* 2 part-time/adjunct (both women). *Students:* 3 full-time (all women), 16 part-time (11 women); includes 9 minority (5 Black or African American, non-Hispanic/Latino; 2 Asian, non-Hispanic/Latino; 1 Hispanic/Latino; 1 Two or more races, non-Hispanic/Latino), 4 international. Average age 35. 13 applicants, 46% accepted, 4 enrolled. In 2018, 11 master's awarded. *Entrance requirements:* Additional exam requirements/recommendations for international students: Required—TOEFL (minimum score 560 paper-based; 84 iBT), IELTS (minimum score 6.5). *Application deadline:* For fall admission, 3/1 for domestic and international students. Application fee: $60. Electronic applications accepted. *Expenses:* $12,140 per academic year (typical full-time in-state); $20,708 per academic year (typical full-time out-of-state). *Financial support:* In 2018–19, 5 students received support. Career-related internships or fieldwork and scholarships/grants available. Financial award application deadline: 3/1; financial award applicants required to submit FAFSA. *Faculty research:* Race and health, urban education, data analysis, economics. *Unit head:* Dr. Paul Fossum, Director, Master's Programs, 313-593-0982, E-mail: pfossum@umich.edu. *Application contact:* Office of Graduate Studies, 313-583-6321, E-mail: umd-graduatestudies@umich.edu.
Website: http://umdearborn.edu/cehhs/cehhs_m_hit/

University of Michigan–Dearborn, College of Engineering and Computer Science, MS Program in Information Systems and Technology, Dearborn, MI 48128. Offers MS. *Program availability:* Part-time, evening/weekend, 100% online. *Faculty:* 17 full-time (4 women), 9 part-time/adjunct (1 woman). *Students:* 7 full-time (5 women), 31 part-time (6 women); includes 10 minority (4 Black or African American, non-Hispanic/Latino; 3 Asian, non-Hispanic/Latino; 1 Hispanic/Latino; 2 Two or more races, non-Hispanic/

Latino), 12 international. Average age 35. 33 applicants, 52% accepted, 6 enrolled. In 2018, 18 master's awarded. *Entrance requirements:* For master's, bachelor's degree in engineering, a physical science, computer science, applied mathematics, business administration, or liberal arts with minimum cumulative GPA of 3.0. Additional exam requirements/recommendations for international students: Required—TOEFL (minimum score 560 paper-based; 84 iBT), IELTS (minimum score 6.5). *Application deadline:* For fall admission, 8/1 for domestic students, 5/1 for international students; for winter admission, 12/1 for domestic students, 9/1 for international students; for spring admission, 4/1 for domestic students, 1/1 for international students. Applications are processed on a rolling basis. Application fee: $60. Electronic applications accepted. *Expenses:* Tuition, state resident: full-time $15,380; part-time $88 per credit hour. Tuition, nonresident: full-time $23,948; part-time $1377 per credit hour. *Required fees:* $780; $780 $390. Tuition and fees vary according to course level, course load, degree level, program, reciprocity agreements and student level. *Financial support:* In 2018–19, 9 students received support. Scholarships/grants, unspecified assistantships, and non-resident tuition scholarships available. Support available to part-time students. Financial award application deadline: 3/1; financial award applicants required to submit FAFSA. *Faculty research:* Operations Research and Decision Science, Quality and Reliability Engineering, Manufacturing, Human Factors and Ergonomics, Transportation Safety. *Unit head:* Dr. Armen Zakarian, Chair, 313-593-5361, E-mail: zakarian@umich.edu. *Application contact:* Office of Graduate Studies, 313-583-6321, E-mail: umd-graduatestudies@umich.edu.
Website: https://umdearborn.edu/cecs/departments/industrial-and-manufacturing-systems-engineering/graduate-programs/ms-information-systems-and-technology

University of Michigan–Flint, College of Arts and Sciences, Program in Computer Science and Information Systems, Flint, MI 48502-1950. Offers computer science (MS); information systems (MS), including business information systems, health information systems. *Program availability:* Part-time, evening/weekend, 100% online. *Faculty:* 15 full-time (5 women), 7 part-time/adjunct (3 women). *Students:* 33 full-time (14 women), 56 part-time (17 women); includes 17 minority (4 Black or African American, non-Hispanic/Latino; 1 American Indian or Alaska Native, non-Hispanic/Latino; 3 Asian, non-Hispanic/Latino; 6 Hispanic/Latino; 1 Native Hawaiian or other Pacific Islander, non-Hispanic/Latino; 2 Two or more races, non-Hispanic/Latino), 39 international. Average age 30. 310 applicants, 66% accepted, 21 enrolled. In 2018, 29 master's awarded. *Degree requirements:* For master's, thesis optional, Non Thesis option available. *Entrance requirements:* For master's, BS from regionally-accredited institution in computer science, computer information systems, or computer engineering (preferred); minimum overall undergraduate GPA of 3.0. Additional exam requirements/recommendations for international students: Required—TOEFL (minimum score 84 iBT), IELTS (minimum score 6.5). *Application deadline:* For fall admission, 8/1 for domestic students, 5/1 for international students; for winter admission, 10/1 for domestic students, 8/1 for international students; for spring admission, 3/15 for domestic students, 1/1 for international students. Applications are processed on a rolling basis. Application fee: $55. Electronic applications accepted. *Expenses:* Contact institution. *Financial support:* Federal Work-Study, scholarships/grants, and unspecified assistantships available. Financial award application deadline: 3/1; financial award applicants required to submit FAFSA. *Faculty research:* Computer network systems, database management systems, artificial intelligence and controlled systems. *Unit head:* Dr. Mike Farmer, Department Chair, 810-762-3423, Fax: 810-766-6780, E-mail: farmerme@umflint.edu. *Application contact:* Matt Bohlen, Director of Graduate Admissions, 810-762-3171, Fax: 810-766-6789, E-mail: mbohlen@umflint.edu.
Website: http://www.umflint.edu/graduateprograms/computer-science-information-systems-ms

University of Michigan–Flint, School of Management, Program in Business Administration, Flint, MI 48502-1950. Offers accounting (MBA); computer information systems (MBA); finance (MBA, Post-Master's Certificate); general business (Graduate Certificate); general business administration (MBA); health care management (MBA); international business (MBA, Post-Master's Certificate); lean manufacturing (MBA); marketing (Post-Master's Certificate); marketing and innovation management (MBA); organizational leadership (MBA). *Program availability:* Part-time, evening/weekend, mixed mode format. *Faculty:* 30 full-time (4 women), 10 part-time/adjunct (2 women). *Students:* 24 full-time (14 women), 151 part-time (60 women); includes 45 minority (22 Black or African American, non-Hispanic/Latino; 3 American Indian or Alaska Native, non-Hispanic/Latino; 7 Asian, non-Hispanic/Latino; 9 Hispanic/Latino; 4 Two or more races, non-Hispanic/Latino), 19 international. Average age 36. 160 applicants, 75% accepted, 62 enrolled. In 2018, 50 master's, 1 other advanced degree awarded. *Entrance requirements:* For master's, bachelor's degree in arts, sciences, engineering, or business administration from regionally-accredited college or university; for other advanced degree, bachelor's degree in arts, sciences, engineering, or business administration from regionally-accredited college or university. college-level math, statistics, or quantitative course (for Graduate Certificate); MBA or equivalent degree from regionally-accredited college or university (for Post Master's Certificate). Additional exam requirements/recommendations for international students: Required—TOEFL (minimum score 84 iBT), IELTS (minimum score 6.5). *Application deadline:* For fall admission, 8/1 for domestic students, 5/1 for international students; for winter admission, 11/15 for domestic students, 9/1 for international students; for spring admission, 3/15 for domestic students, 1/1 for international students; for summer admission, 5/15 for domestic students. Applications are processed on a rolling basis. Application fee: $55. Electronic applications accepted. *Expenses:* Contact institution. *Financial support:* Federal Work-Study, scholarships/grants, and unspecified assistantships available. Support available to part-time students. Financial award application deadline: 3/1; financial award applicants required to submit FAFSA. *Unit head:* Dr. Scott Johnson, Dean, School of Management, 810-762-3164, Fax: 810-237-6685, E-mail: scotjohn@umflint.edu. *Application contact:* Matt Bohlen, Director of Graduate Admissions, 810-762-3171, E-mail: mbohlen@umflint.edu.
Website: http://www.umflint.edu/graduateprograms/business-administration-mba

University of Minnesota, Twin Cities Campus, Carlson School of Management, Carlson Full-Time MBA Program, Minneapolis, MN 55455. Offers finance (MBA); information technology (MBA); management (MBA); marketing (MBA); medical industry orientation (MBA); supply chain and operations (MBA); JD/MBA; MBA/MPP; MBA/MSBA; MD/MBA; MHA/MBA; Pharm D/MBA. *Accreditation:* AACSB. *Faculty:* 150 full-time (43 women), 21 part-time/adjunct (5 women). *Students:* 169 full-time (57 women); includes 32 minority (6 Black or African American, non-Hispanic/Latino; 4 American Indian or Alaska Native, non-Hispanic/Latino; 14 Asian, non-Hispanic/Latino; 8 Hispanic/Latino), 36 international. Average age 29. 529 applicants, 39% accepted, 92 enrolled. In 2018, 76 master's awarded. *Degree requirements:* For master's, None are required for MBA. *Entrance requirements:* For master's, GMAT or GRE, 2 recommendations, personal statement, resume. Additional exam requirements/recommendations for international students: Required—TOEFL (minimum score 580 paper-based; 84 iBT), IELTS (minimum score 7), PTE. *Application deadline:* For fall admission, 4/1 for domestic students, 2/1 for international students. Application fee: $75. Electronic applications accepted. *Expenses:* FTMBA Tuition; Collegiate fee; Student Services fee; Hospitalization. *Financial support:* In 2018–19, 139 students received support. Teaching assistantships with partial tuition reimbursements available, scholarships/grants, and unspecified assistantships available. Financial award application deadline: 4/1. *Faculty research:* Market regulation and asset pricing, social networks and data analytics, consumer behavior, innovation and entrepreneurship, workplace wellbeing and labor relationships. *Total annual research expenditures:* $577,440. *Unit head:* Philip J. Miller, Assistant Dean, MBA and MS Programs, 612-625-5555, Fax: 612-625-1012, E-mail: mba@umn.edu. *Application contact:* Linh Gilles, Director of Admissions and Recruiting, 612-625-5555, Fax: 612-625-1012, E-mail: ftmba@umn.edu.
Website: http://www.csom.umn.edu/MBA/full-time/

University of Minnesota, Twin Cities Campus, Carlson School of Management, Carlson Part-Time MBA Program, Minneapolis, MN 55455. Offers finance (MBA); information technology (MBA); management (MBA); marketing (MBA); medical industry orientation (MBA); supply chain and operations (MBA). *Program availability:* Part-time-only, evening/weekend, 100% online, blended/hybrid learning. *Faculty:* 150 full-time (43 women), 23 part-time/adjunct (6 women). *Students:* 822 part-time (260 women); includes 122 minority (18 Black or African American, non-Hispanic/Latino; 11 American Indian or Alaska Native, non-Hispanic/Latino; 67 Asian, non-Hispanic/Latino; 24 Hispanic/Latino; 2 Native Hawaiian or other Pacific Islander, non-Hispanic/Latino), 41 international. Average age 29. 204 applicants, 83% accepted, 141 enrolled. In 2018, 257 master's awarded. *Degree requirements:* For master's, None for MBA. *Entrance requirements:* For master's, GMAT or GRE, 2 recommendations, personal statement, current resume. Additional exam requirements/recommendations for international students: Required—TOEFL (minimum score 580 paper-based; 84 iBT), IELTS (minimum score 7), PTE. *Application deadline:* For fall admission, 5/15 priority date for domestic and international students; for spring admission, 10/15 priority date for domestic and international students. Applications are processed on a rolling basis. Application fee: $75. Electronic applications accepted. *Expenses:* PTMBA tuition; Collegiate fee. *Financial support:* Applicants required to submit FAFSA. *Faculty research:* Market regulation and asset pricing, social networks and data analytics, consumer behavior, innovation and entrepreneurship, workplace wellbeing and labor relationships. *Total annual research expenditures:* $577,440. *Unit head:* Philip J. Miller, Assistant Dean, MBA and MS Programs, 612-624-2039, Fax: 612-625-1012, E-mail: mba@umn.edu. *Application contact:* Linh Gilles, Director of Admissions and Recruiting, 612-625-5555, Fax: 612-625-1012, E-mail: ptmba@umn.edu.
Website: http://www.carlsonschool.umn.edu/ptmba

University of Minnesota, Twin Cities Campus, Carlson School of Management, Doctoral Program in Business Administration, Minneapolis, MN 55455-0213. Offers accounting (PhD); finance (PhD); information and decision sciences (PhD); marketing (PhD); strategic management and entrepreneurship (PhD); supply chain and operations (PhD); work and organizations (PhD). *Faculty:* 106 full-time (33 women). *Students:* 88 full-time (34 women); includes 9 minority (2 Black or African American, non-Hispanic/Latino; 6 Asian, non-Hispanic/Latino; 1 Hispanic/Latino), 66 international. Average age 30. 306 applicants, 8% accepted, 15 enrolled. In 2018, 14 doctorates awarded. *Degree requirements:* For doctorate, comprehensive exam, thesis/dissertation, written and oral preliminary exams, proposal defense, final defense. *Entrance requirements:* For doctorate, GMAT or GRE, minimum undergraduate GPA of 3.0, graduate 3.5 (recommended). Additional exam requirements/recommendations for international students: Required—Either or: TOEFL or IELTS; Recommended—TOEFL, IELTS. *Application deadline:* For fall admission, 12/15 for domestic students, 12/15 priority date for international students. Applications are processed on a rolling basis. Application fee: $75 ($95 for international students). Electronic applications accepted. *Financial support:* In 2018–19, 80 students received support, including 80 fellowships with full tuition reimbursements available (averaging $12,500 per year), 72 research assistantships with full tuition reimbursements available (averaging $7,800 per year), 72 teaching assistantships with full tuition reimbursements available (averaging $7,800 per year); health care benefits, unspecified assistantships, and full student service fee waivers also available. Financial award application deadline: 12/15. *Faculty research:* Finance, strategy and entrepreneurship, marketing, information and decision science, operations, accounting, supply chain, human resources and industrial relations, organizational behavior. *Unit head:* Dr. Shawn P. Curley, Director, 612-624-6546, Fax: 612-624-8221, E-mail: curley@umn.edu. *Application contact:* Sandy Herzan, Associate Director, 612-624-0875, Fax: 612-624-8221, E-mail: herza002@umn.edu.
Website: http://carlsonschool.umn.edu/degrees/phd

University of Mississippi, Graduate School, School of Business Administration, University, MS 38677. Offers business administration (MBA, PhD); finance (PhD); management (PhD); management information systems (PhD); marketing (PhD); JD/MBA. *Accreditation:* AACSB. *Faculty:* 60 full-time (18 women), 7 part-time/adjunct (1 woman). *Students:* 62 full-time (18 women), 83 part-time (20 women); includes 13 minority (4 Black or African American, non-Hispanic/Latino; 3 Asian, non-Hispanic/Latino; 4 Hispanic/Latino; 2 Two or more races, non-Hispanic/Latino), 14 international. Average age 30. In 2018, 83 master's, 11 doctorates awarded. *Entrance requirements:* For master's, GMAT, minimum GPA of 3.0; for doctorate, GMAT. Additional exam requirements/recommendations for international students: Required—TOEFL. *Application deadline:* Applications are processed on a rolling basis. Application fee: $50. Electronic applications accepted. *Financial support:* Fellowships, career-related internships or fieldwork, scholarships/grants, tuition waivers (full), and unspecified assistantships available. Financial award application deadline: 3/1; financial award applicants required to submit FAFSA. *Unit head:* Dr. Ken Cyree, Dean, 662-915-5820, Fax: 662-915-5821, E-mail: info@bus.olemiss.edu. *Application contact:* Temeka Smith, Graduate Activities Specialist for Admissions, 662-915-7474, Fax: 662-915-7577, E-mail: gschool@olemiss.edu.
Website: http://www.olemissbusiness.com/

University of Missouri–St. Louis, College of Business Administration, St. Louis, MO 63121. Offers accounting (M Acc); business administration (MBA, DBA, PhD, Certificate), including logistics and supply chain management (PhD); business intelligence (Certificate); cybersecurity (Certificate); digital and social media marketing (Certificate); human resources management (Certificate); information systems (MS); logistics and supply chain management (Certificate); marketing management (Certificate). *Program availability:* Part-time, evening/weekend. *Degree requirements:* For doctorate, thesis/dissertation. *Entrance requirements:* For master's, GMAT, 2 letters of recommendation; for doctorate, GMAT or GRE, 3 letters of recommendation. Additional exam requirements/recommendations for international students: Recommended—TOEFL (minimum score 550 paper-based; 79 iBT), IELTS (minimum score 6.5). Electronic applications accepted. *Faculty research:* Statistical decision aids, commercial banking, corporate finance, operations management, information systems.

University of Nebraska at Kearney, College of Education, Department of Teacher Education, Kearney, NE 68849-0001. Offers curriculum and instruction (MA Ed), including early childhood education, elementary education, English as a second language, instructional effectiveness, reading/special education, secondary education; instructional technology (MS Ed), including information technology, instructional technology, school librarian; reading PK-12 (MA Ed); special education (MA Ed), including advanced practitioner: assistive technology specialist, advanced practitioner: behavioral interventionist, advanced practitioner: inclusive collaboration specialist, gifted, teacher education. *Program availability:* Part-time, evening/weekend, online only,

100% online. *Degree requirements:* For master's, comprehensive exam, thesis optional. *Entrance requirements:* For master's, portfolio or GRE. Additional exam requirements/recommendations for international students: Recommended—TOEFL (minimum score 550 paper-based; 79 iBT), IELTS (minimum score 6.5). Electronic applications accepted. *Expenses:* Contact institution.

University of Nebraska at Omaha, Graduate Studies, College of Information Science and Technology, Department of Information Systems and Quantitative Analysis, Omaha, NE 68182. Offers data analytics (Certificate); information assurance (Certificate); information technology (MIT, PhD); management information systems (MS); project management (Certificate); systems analysis and design (Certificate). *Program availability:* Part-time, evening/weekend. *Degree requirements:* For master's, comprehensive exam, thesis (for some programs); for doctorate, comprehensive exam, thesis/dissertation. *Entrance requirements:* For master's, GRE General Test, minimum GPA of 3.0, 3 letters of recommendation, writing sample, resume, official transcripts; for doctorate, GMAT or GRE General Test, minimum GPA of 3.0, 3 letters of recommendation, writing sample, resume, official transcripts; for Certificate, minimum GPA of 3.0, official transcripts. Additional exam requirements/recommendations for international students: Required—TOEFL, IELTS, PTE. Electronic applications accepted.

University of Nebraska–Lincoln, Graduate College, College of Agricultural Sciences and Natural Resources, Program in Mechanized Systems Management, Lincoln, NE 68588. Offers MS. *Degree requirements:* For master's, thesis optional. *Entrance requirements:* For master's, GRE General Test. Additional exam requirements/recommendations for international students: Required—TOEFL (minimum score 550 paper-based). Electronic applications accepted. *Faculty research:* Irrigation management, agricultural power and machinery systems, sensors and controls, food/industrial materials handling and processing systems.

University of Nevada, Las Vegas, Graduate College, Lee Business School, Department of Management, Entrepreneurship and Technology, Las Vegas, NV 89154-6034. Offers data analytics (Certificate); data analytics and applied economics (MS); hotel administration/management information systems (MS/MS); management (Certificate); management information systems (MS, Certificate); new venture management (Certificate); MS/MS. *Program availability:* Part-time, evening/weekend. *Faculty:* 10 full-time (1 woman), 1 part-time/adjunct (0 women). *Students:* 59 full-time (21 women), 36 part-time (15 women); includes 27 minority (5 Black or African American, non-Hispanic/Latino; 14 Asian, non-Hispanic/Latino; 4 Hispanic/Latino; 4 Two or more races, non-Hispanic/Latino), 32 international. Average age 30. 85 applicants, 84% accepted, 44 enrolled. In 2018, 28 master's, 5 other advanced degrees awarded. *Degree requirements:* For master's, thesis optional. *Entrance requirements:* For master's, GMAT or GRE, bachelor's degree with minimum GPA 3.0; 2 letters of recommendation; for Certificate, GMAT or GRE. Additional exam requirements/recommendations for international students: Required—TOEFL (minimum score 550 paper-based; 80 iBT), IELTS (minimum score 7). *Application deadline:* For fall admission, 8/1 for domestic students, 5/1 for international students; for spring admission, 11/15 for domestic students, 10/1 for international students. Application fee: $60 ($95 for international students). Electronic applications accepted. *Expenses:* Contact institution. *Financial support:* In 2018–19, 25 students received support, including 8 research assistantships with full tuition reimbursements available (averaging $11,286 per year), 7 teaching assistantships with full tuition reimbursements available (averaging $11,429 per year); institutionally sponsored loans, scholarships/grants, health care benefits, and unspecified assistantships also available. Financial award application deadline: 3/15; financial award applicants required to submit FAFSA. *Faculty research:* Decision-making, publish or perish, ethical issues in information systems, IT-enabled decision making, business ethics. *Total annual research expenditures:* $28,971. *Unit head:* Dr. Rajiv Kishore, Chair/ Professor, 702-895-1709, Fax: 702-895-4370, E-mail: met.chair@unlv.edu. *Application contact:* Dr. Greg Moody, Graduate Coordinator, 702-895-1365, Fax: 702-895-4370, E-mail: met.gradcoord@unlv.edu. Website: https://www.unlv.edu/met

University of Nevada, Reno, Graduate School, College of Business, Department of Information Systems, Reno, NV 89557. Offers MS. *Degree requirements:* For master's, thesis optional. *Entrance requirements:* For master's, GRE or GMAT, minimum GPA of 2.75. Additional exam requirements/recommendations for international students: Required—TOEFL (minimum score 500 paper-based; 61 iBT), IELTS (minimum score 6). Electronic applications accepted.

University of New Hampshire, Graduate School Manchester Campus, Manchester, NH 03101. Offers business administration (MBA); cybersecurity policy and risk management (MS); educational administration and supervision (Ed S); educational studies (M Ed); elementary education (M Ed); information technology (MS); public administration (MPA); public health (MPH, Certificate); secondary education (M Ed, MAT); social work (MSW); substance use disorders (Certificate). *Program availability:* Part-time, evening/weekend. *Entrance requirements:* Additional exam requirements/recommendations for international students: Required—TOEFL (minimum score 550 paper-based; 80 iBT). Electronic applications accepted.

University of North Alabama, College of Business, Florence, AL 35632-0001. Offers business administration (MBA), including accounting, enterprise resource planning systems, executive, finance, health care management, information systems, international business, project management. *Accreditation:* AACSB; ACBSP. *Program availability:* Part-time, 100% online, blended/hybrid learning. *Entrance requirements:* For master's, GMAT, GRE, minimum GPA of 2.75 in last 60 hours, 2.5 overall (on a 3.0 scale); 27 hours of course work in business and economics. Additional exam requirements/recommendations for international students: Required—TOEFL (minimum score 79 iBT), IELTS (minimum score 6), PTE (minimum score 54). Electronic applications accepted.

The University of North Carolina at Chapel Hill, Kenan-Flagler Business School, Doctoral Program in Business Administration, Chapel Hill, NC 27599. Offers accounting (PhD); finance (PhD); marketing (PhD); operations management (PhD); organizational behavior (PhD); strategy (PhD). *Accreditation:* AACSB. *Degree requirements:* For doctorate, thesis/dissertation. *Entrance requirements:* For doctorate, GMAT or GRE General Test. Electronic applications accepted. *Expenses:* Contact institution.

The University of North Carolina at Charlotte, College of Computing and Informatics, Department of Software and Information Systems, Charlotte, NC 28223-0001. Offers advanced databases and knowledge discovery (Graduate Certificate); game design and development (Graduate Certificate); information security and privacy (Graduate Certificate); information technology (MS); management of information technology (Graduate Certificate); network security (Graduate Certificate); secure software development (Graduate Certificate). *Program availability:* Part-time, evening/weekend. *Students:* 122 full-time (57 women), 102 part-time (39 women); includes 44 minority (24 Black or African American, non-Hispanic/Latino; 8 Asian, non-Hispanic/Latino; 10 Hispanic/Latino; 2 Two or more races, non-Hispanic/Latino), 126 international. Average age 28. 308 applicants, 82% accepted, 98 enrolled. In 2018, 107 master's, 18 other advanced degrees awarded. *Entrance requirements:* For master's, GRE or GMAT, undergraduate or equivalent course work in data structures, object-oriented programming in C++, C#, or Java with minimum GPA of 3.0; for Graduate Certificate, bachelor's degree from accredited institution in computing, mathematical, engineering or business discipline with minimum overall GPA of 2.8, junior/senior 3.0; substantial knowledge of data structures and object-oriented programming in C++, C# or Java. Additional exam requirements/recommendations for international students: Required—TOEFL (minimum score 523 paper-based; 70 iBT), IELTS (minimum score 6), TOEFL (minimum score 523 paper-based, 70 iBT) or IELTS (6). *Application deadline:* Applications are processed on a rolling basis. Application fee: $75. Electronic applications accepted. *Expenses:* Contact institution. *Financial support:* Fellowships, research assistantships, teaching assistantships, career-related internships or fieldwork, institutionally sponsored loans, scholarships/grants, and unspecified assistantships available. Support available to part-time students. Financial award application deadline: 3/1; financial award applicants required to submit FAFSA. *Total annual research expenditures:* $3.1 million. *Unit head:* Dr. Mary Lou Maher, Chair, 704-687-1940, E-mail: mmaher9@uncc.edu. *Application contact:* Kathy B. Giddings, Director of Graduate Admissions, 704-687-5503, Fax: 704-687-1668, E-mail: gradadm@uncc.edu. Website: http://sis.uncc.edu/

The University of North Carolina at Charlotte, College of Computing and Informatics, Program in Computing and Information Systems, Charlotte, NC 28223-0001. Offers computing and information systems (PhD), including bioinformatics, business information systems and operations management, computer science, interdisciplinary, software and information systems. *Students:* 99 full-time (27 women), 18 part-time (5 women); includes 4 minority (1 Black or African American, non-Hispanic/Latino; 1 Asian, non-Hispanic/Latino; 1 Hispanic/Latino; 1 Two or more races, non-Hispanic/Latino), 90 international. Average age 30. 86 applicants, 33% accepted, 15 enrolled. In 2018, 17 doctorates awarded. *Entrance requirements:* For doctorate, GRE or GMAT, baccalaureate degree, minimum GPA of 3.0 on courses related to the chosen field of PhD study, essay, reference letters. Additional exam requirements/recommendations for international students: Required—TOEFL (minimum score 523 paper-based; 70 iBT), IELTS (minimum score 6), TOEFL (minimum score 523 paper-based, 70 iBT) or IELTS (6). *Application deadline:* Applications are processed on a rolling basis. Application fee: $75. Electronic applications accepted. Tuition and fees vary according to course load and program. *Financial support:* Career-related internships or fieldwork, institutionally sponsored loans, scholarships/grants, health care benefits, and unspecified assistantships available. Support available to part-time students. Financial award applicants required to submit FAFSA. *Unit head:* Dr. Fatma Mili, Dean, 704-687-8450. *Application contact:* Kathy B. Giddings, Director of Graduate Admissions, 704-687-5503, Fax: 704-687-1668, E-mail: gradadm@uncc.edu.

The University of North Carolina at Greensboro, Graduate School, Bryan School of Business and Economics, Department of Information Systems and Supply Chain Management, Greensboro, NC 27412-5001. Offers information systems (PhD); information technology (Certificate); information technology and management (MS); supply chain management (Certificate). *Entrance requirements:* For master's, GMAT, GRE General Test. Additional exam requirements/recommendations for international students: Required—TOEFL. Electronic applications accepted.

The University of North Carolina Wilmington, Interdisciplinary Program in Computer Science and Information Systems, Wilmington, NC 28403-3297. Offers computer science and information systems (MS); data science (MS). *Degree requirements:* For master's, thesis or alternative, research project. *Entrance requirements:* For master's, GMAT or GRE, 3 letters of recommendation, resume, statement of interest; baccalaureate degree in a computational field preferred (for data science). Additional exam requirements/recommendations for international students: Required—TOEFL (minimum score 550 paper-based; 79 iBT), IELTS (minimum score 6.5). Electronic applications accepted. *Expenses:* Contact institution.

University of North Florida, College of Computing, Engineering, and Construction, School of Computing, Jacksonville, FL 32224. Offers computer science (MS); information systems (MS); software engineering (MS). *Program availability:* Part-time. *Faculty:* 13 full-time (1 woman). *Students:* 14 full-time (4 women), 35 part-time (9 women); includes 14 minority (1 Black or African American, non-Hispanic/Latino; 8 Asian, non-Hispanic/Latino; 3 Hispanic/Latino; 2 Two or more races, non-Hispanic/Latino), 8 international. Average age 33. 33 applicants, 45% accepted, 11 enrolled. In 2018, 48 master's awarded. *Degree requirements:* For master's, thesis. *Entrance requirements:* For master's, GRE General Test, minimum GPA of 3.0 in last 60 hours of course work. Additional exam requirements/recommendations for international students: Required—TOEFL (minimum score 500 paper-based; 61 iBT). *Application deadline:* For fall admission, 8/1 priority date for domestic students, 5/1 for international students; for spring admission, 12/1 priority date for domestic students, 10/1 for international students; for summer admission, 3/15 priority date for domestic students, 2/1 for international students. Application fee: $30. Electronic applications accepted. *Expenses: Tuition, area resident:* Part-time $408.10 per credit hour. *Tuition, state resident:* part-time $408.10 per credit hour. *Tuition, nonresident:* part-time $932.61 per credit hour. *Required fees:* $111.81 per credit hour. Tuition and fees vary according to course load, campus/location and program. *Financial support:* In 2018–19, 8 students received support, including 6 research assistantships (averaging $3,134 per year), 1 teaching assistantship (averaging $2,666 per year); Federal Work-Study, scholarships/grants, and unspecified assistantships also available. Financial award application deadline: 4/1; financial award applicants required to submit FAFSA. *Total annual research expenditures:* $86,396. *Unit head:* Dr. Sherif Elfayoumy, Director/Professor, 904-620-2985, E-mail: selfayou@unf.edu. *Application contact:* Dr. Amanda Pascale, Director, The Graduate School, 904-620-1360, Fax: 904-620-1362, E-mail: graduateschool@unf.edu. Website: http://www.unf.edu/ccec/computing/

University of North Texas, Toulouse Graduate School, Denton, TX 76203-5459. Offers accounting (MS); applied anthropology (MA, MS); applied behavior analysis (Certificate); applied geography (MA); applied technology and performance improvement (M Ed, MS); art education (MA); art history (MA); arts leadership (Certificate); audiology (Au D); behavior analysis (MS); behavioral science (PhD); biochemistry and molecular biology (MS); biology (MA, MS); biomedical engineering (MS); business analysis (MS); chemistry (MS); clinical health psychology (PhD); communication studies (MA, MS); computer engineering (MS); computer science (MS); counseling (M Ed, MS), including clinical mental health counseling (MS), college and university counseling, elementary school counseling, secondary school counseling; creative writing (MA); criminal justice (MS); curriculum and instruction (M Ed); decision sciences (MBA); design (MA, MFA), including fashion design (MFA), innovation studies, interior design (MFA); early childhood studies (MS); economics (MS); educational leadership (M Ed, Ed D); educational psychology (MS, PhD), including family studies (MS), gifted and talented (MS), human development (MS), learning and cognition (MS), research, measurement and evaluation (MS); electrical engineering (MS); emergency management (MPA); engineering technology (MS); English (MA); English as a second language (MA); environmental science (MS); finance (MBA, MS); financial management (MPA); French (MA); health services management (MBA); higher education (M Ed, Ed D); history (MA, MS); hospitality management (MS); human resources management (MPA); information science (MS); information systems (PhD); information technologies

(MBA); interdisciplinary studies (MA, MS); international studies (MA); international sustainable tourism (MS); jazz studies (MM); journalism (MA, MJ, Graduate Certificate), including interactive and virtual digital communication (Graduate Certificate), narrative journalism (Graduate Certificate), public relations (Graduate Certificate); kinesiology (MS); linguistics (MA); local government management (MPA); logistics (PhD); logistics and supply chain management (MBA); long-term care, senior housing, and aging services (MA); management (PhD); marketing (MBA); mathematics (MA, MS); mechanical and energy engineering (MS, PhD); music (MA), including ethnomusicology, music theory, musicology, performance; music composition (PhD); music education (MM Ed, PhD); nonprofit management (MPA); operations and supply chain management (MBA); performance (MM, DMA); philosophy (MA); political science (MA); professional and technical communication (MA); radio, television and film (MA, MFA); rehabilitation counseling (Certificate); sociology (MA); Spanish (MA); special education (M Ed); speech-language pathology (MA); strategic management (MBA); studio art (MFA); teaching (M Ed); MBA/MS. *Program availability:* Part-time, evening/weekend, online learning. Terminal master's awarded for partial completion of doctoral program. *Degree requirements:* For master's, variable foreign language requirement, comprehensive exam (for some programs), thesis (for some programs); for doctorate, variable foreign language requirement, comprehensive exam (for some programs), thesis/dissertation; for other advanced degree, variable foreign language requirement, comprehensive exam (for some programs). *Entrance requirements:* For master's and doctorate, GRE, GMAT. Additional exam requirements/recommendations for international students: Required—TOEFL (minimum score 550 paper-based; 79 iBT). Electronic applications accepted.

University of Oklahoma, Price College of Business, Norman, OK 73019. Offers accounting (M Acc); business administration (MBA, PMBA, PhD), including business administration (EMBA, MBA, PMBA, PhD); business entrepreneurship (Graduate Certificate); digital technologies (Graduate Certificate), including digital technologies; energy (EMBA), including business administration (EMBA, MBA, PMBA, PhD); foundations of business (Graduate Certificate); management information technology (MS), including management of information technology; the business of energy (Graduate Certificate); JD/MBA; MBA/MA; MBA/MLIS; MBA/MPH; MBA/MS. *Program availability:* Part-time, evening/weekend, 100% online. *Faculty:* 58 full-time (16 women), 6 part-time/adjunct (0 women). *Students:* 108 full-time (31 women), 267 part-time (84 women); includes 92 minority (16 Black or African American, non-Hispanic/Latino; 9 American Indian or Alaska Native, non-Hispanic/Latino; 16 Asian, non-Hispanic/Latino; 33 Hispanic/Latino; 1 Native Hawaiian or other Pacific Islander, non-Hispanic/Latino; 17 Two or more races, non-Hispanic/Latino), 38 international. Average age 33. 265 applicants, 44% accepted, 83 enrolled. In 2018, 132 master's, 5 doctorates, 41 other advanced degrees awarded. *Degree requirements:* For doctorate, comprehensive exam, thesis/dissertation. *Entrance requirements:* For master's, GMAT/GRE; for doctorate, GMAT. Additional exam requirements/recommendations for international students: Required—TOEFL (minimum score 100 iBT) or IELTS (minimum score 7.0). *Application deadline:* Applications are processed on a rolling basis. Application fee: $50 ($100 for international students). Electronic applications accepted. *Expenses:* Contact institution. *Financial support:* Fellowships, research assistantships, teaching assistantships, career-related internships or fieldwork, scholarships/grants, health care benefits, and unspecified assistantships available. Support available to part-time students. Financial award application deadline: 6/1; financial award applicants required to submit FAFSA. *Unit head:* Wayne Thomas, Interim Dean, 405-325-0100, Fax: 405-325-3421, E-mail: wthomas@ou.edu. *Application contact:* Amber Hasbrook, Academic Counselor, 405-325-5815, Fax: 405-325-7753, E-mail: ahasbrook@ou.edu.
Website: http://www.ou.edu/price

University of Oregon, Graduate School, Interdisciplinary Program in Applied Information Management, Eugene, OR 97403. Offers MS. *Program availability:* Part-time, online learning. *Degree requirements:* For master's, project. *Entrance requirements:* Additional exam requirements/recommendations for international students: Required—TOEFL. Electronic applications accepted. *Expenses:* Contact institution. *Faculty research:* Business management, information design.

University of Pennsylvania, Wharton School, Operations and Information Management Department, Philadelphia, PA 19104. Offers MBA, PhD. Terminal master's awarded for partial completion of doctoral program. *Degree requirements:* For master's, thesis, preliminary exams; for doctorate, thesis/dissertation, preliminary exams. *Entrance requirements:* For master's, GMAT, GRE; for doctorate, GRE. Electronic applications accepted. *Faculty research:* Supply chain management, operations research, economics of information systems, risk analysis, electronic commerce.

University of Phoenix–Bay Area Campus, College of Information Systems and Technology, San Jose, CA 95134-1805. Offers information systems (MIS); organizational leadership/information systems and technology (DM). *Program availability:* Evening/weekend. *Degree requirements:* For master's, thesis (for some programs). *Entrance requirements:* For master's, minimum undergraduate GPA of 3.0, 3 years of work experience. Additional exam requirements/recommendations for international students: Required—TOEFL (minimum score 550 paper-based; 79 iBT). Electronic applications accepted.

University of Phoenix–Central Valley Campus, College of Information Systems and Technology, Fresno, CA 93720-1552. Offers information systems (MIS); technology management (MBA).

University of Phoenix–Dallas Campus, College of Information Systems and Technology, Dallas, TX 75251. Offers e-business (MBA); information systems (MIS); technology management (MBA). *Program availability:* Evening/weekend. *Degree requirements:* For master's, thesis (for some programs). *Entrance requirements:* For master's, minimum undergraduate GPA of 3.0, 3 years of work experience. Additional exam requirements/recommendations for international students: Required—TOEFL (minimum score 550 paper-based; 79 iBT). Electronic applications accepted.

University of Phoenix–Hawaii Campus, College of Information Systems and Technology, Honolulu, HI 96813-3800. Offers information systems (MIS); technology management (MBA). *Program availability:* Evening/weekend. *Degree requirements:* For master's, thesis (for some programs). *Entrance requirements:* For master's, minimum undergraduate GPA of 3.0, 3 years of work experience. Additional exam requirements/recommendations for international students: Required—TOEFL (minimum score 550 paper-based; 79 iBT). Electronic applications accepted.

University of Phoenix–Houston Campus, College of Information Systems and Technology, Houston, TX 77079-2004. Offers e-business (MBA); information systems (MIS); technology management (MBA). *Program availability:* Evening/weekend, online learning. *Degree requirements:* For master's, comprehensive exam (for some programs), thesis. *Entrance requirements:* For master's, minimum undergraduate GPA of 3.0, 3 years of work experience. Additional exam requirements/recommendations for international students: Required—TOEFL (minimum score 550 paper-based; 79 iBT). Electronic applications accepted.

University of Phoenix–Las Vegas Campus, College of Information Systems and Technology, Las Vegas, NV 89135. Offers information systems (MIS); technology management (MBA). *Program availability:* Evening/weekend. *Degree requirements:* For master's, thesis (for some programs). *Entrance requirements:* For master's, minimum undergraduate GPA of 3.0, 3 years of work experience. Additional exam requirements/recommendations for international students: Required—TOEFL (minimum score 550 paper-based; 79 iBT). Electronic applications accepted.

University of Phoenix–Online Campus, College of Information Systems and Technology, Phoenix, AZ 85034-7209. Offers MIS. *Program availability:* Evening/weekend, online learning. *Entrance requirements:* Additional exam requirements/recommendations for international students: Required—TOEFL, TOEIC (Test of English as an International Communication), Berlitz Online English Proficiency Exam, PTE, or IELTS. Electronic applications accepted. *Expenses:* Contact institution.

University of Phoenix–Sacramento Valley Campus, College of Information Systems and Technology, Sacramento, CA 95833-4334. Offers management (MIS); technology management (MBA). *Program availability:* Evening/weekend. *Degree requirements:* For master's, thesis (for some programs). *Entrance requirements:* For master's, minimum undergraduate GPA of 3.0, 3 years work experience. Additional exam requirements/recommendations for international students: Required—TOEFL (minimum score 550 paper-based; 79 iBT). Electronic applications accepted.

University of Phoenix–San Antonio Campus, College of Information Systems and Technology, San Antonio, TX 78230. Offers information systems (MIS); technology management (MBA).

University of Phoenix–San Diego Campus, College of Information Systems and Technology, San Diego, CA 92123. Offers management (MIS); technology management (MBA). *Program availability:* Evening/weekend. *Degree requirements:* For master's, thesis (for some programs). *Entrance requirements:* For master's, minimum undergraduate GPA of 3.0, 3 years work experience. Additional exam requirements/recommendations for international students: Required—TOEFL (minimum score 550 paper-based; 79 iBT). Electronic applications accepted.

University of Pittsburgh, Katz Graduate School of Business, Doctoral Program in Business Administration, Pittsburgh, PA 15260. Offers accounting (PhD); business analytics and operations (PhD); finance (PhD); information systems and technology management (PhD); marketing (PhD); organizational behavior and human resources (PhD); strategic management (PhD). *Accreditation:* AACSB. *Program availability:* Evening/weekend. *Degree requirements:* For doctorate, comprehensive exam, thesis/dissertation, student teaching. *Entrance requirements:* For doctorate, GMAT or GRE, 3 recommendations, statement of purpose, transcripts of all previous course work and degrees. Additional exam requirements/recommendations for international students: Required—TOEFL (minimum score 100 iBT) or IELTS (minimum score 7.0). Electronic applications accepted. *Faculty research:* Accounting systems/financial reporting, corporate finance, shopper marketing/consumer behavior, management information systems, organizational behavior and entrepreneurship.

University of Pittsburgh, Katz Graduate School of Business, Master of Business Administration Programs, Pittsburgh, PA 15260. Offers finance (MBA); information systems (MBA); marketing (MBA); operations (MBA); organizational behavior and human resources (MBA); strategy, environment and organizations (MBA); MBA/JD; MBA/MID; MBA/MIS; MBA/MSE. *Accreditation:* AACSB. *Program availability:* Part-time, evening/weekend, blended/hybrid learning. *Degree requirements:* For master's, minimum GPA of 3.0. *Entrance requirements:* For master's, GMAT, GRE. Additional exam requirements/recommendations for international students: Required—TOEFL (minimum score 100 iBT) or IELTS (minimum score 7.0). Electronic applications accepted. *Faculty research:* Accounting systems/financial reporting, corporate finance, shopper marketing/consumer behavior, management information systems, organizational behavior and entrepreneurship.

University of Pittsburgh, Katz Graduate School of Business, Master of Science in Management Information Systems Program, Pittsburgh, PA 15260. Offers MS. *Degree requirements:* For master's, minimum GPA of 3.0. *Entrance requirements:* For master's, GMAT, GRE. Additional exam requirements/recommendations for international students: Required—TOEFL (minimum score 100 iBT), IELTS (minimum score 7). Electronic applications accepted. *Faculty research:* Accounting systems/financial reporting, corporate finance, shopper marketing/consumer behavior, management information systems, organizational behavior and entrepreneurship.

University of Pittsburgh, Katz Graduate School of Business, MBA/MS in Management of Information Systems Program, Pittsburgh, PA 15260. Offers MBA/MS. *Program availability:* Part-time, evening/weekend. *Entrance requirements:* Additional exam requirements/recommendations for international students: Required—TOEFL (minimum score 100 iBT) or IELTS (minimum score 7.0). Electronic applications accepted. *Faculty research:* Accounting systems/financial reporting, corporate finance, shopper marketing/consumer behavior, management information systems, organizational behavior and entrepreneurship.

University of Redlands, School of Business, Redlands, CA 92373-0999. Offers business (MBA); information technology (MS); management (MA). *Program availability:* Evening/weekend. *Entrance requirements:* For master's, minimum GPA of 3.0, 2 letters of recommendation. *Faculty research:* Human resources management, educational leadership, humanities, teacher education.

University of Rochester, Simon Business School, Doctoral Program in Business Administration, Rochester, NY 14627. Offers accounting (PhD); computer information systems (PhD); finance (PhD); marketing (PhD); operations management (PhD). *Accreditation:* AACSB. *Degree requirements:* For doctorate, comprehensive exam, thesis/dissertation, qualifying exam. *Entrance requirements:* For doctorate, GMAT or GRE. Additional exam requirements/recommendations for international students: Required—TOEFL. Electronic applications accepted. *Expenses:* Contact institution. *Faculty research:* Empirical industrial organization, risk management, financial disclosure and regulation, social media, health care management.

University of Rochester, Simon Business School, Full-Time Master's Program in Business Administration, Rochester, NY 14627. Offers business systems consulting (MBA); competitive and organizational strategy (MBA); computers and information systems (MBA); corporate accounting (MBA); entrepreneurship (MBA); finance (MBA); health sciences management (MBA); marketing (MBA); operations management (MBA); public accounting (MBA); strategy and organizations (MBA). *Accreditation:* AACSB. *Entrance requirements:* For master's, GMAT or GRE. *Expenses: Tuition:* Full-time $52,974; part-time $1654 per credit hour. *Required fees:* $612. One-time fee: $30 part-time. Tuition and fees vary according to campus/location and program. *Faculty research:* Empirical industrial organization, risk management, financial disclosure and regulation, social media, health care management.

University of Rochester, Simon Business School, Part-Time MBA Program, Rochester, NY 14627. Offers business systems consulting (MBA); competitive and organizational strategy (MBA); computers and information systems (MBA); corporate accounting (MBA); entrepreneurship (MBA); finance (MBA); health sciences management (MBA); marketing (MBA), including brand management, marketing strategy, pricing; operations management (MBA); public accounting (MBA). *Program availability:* Part-time-only, evening/weekend. *Entrance requirements:* For master's, GRE or GMAT. Electronic applications accepted. *Expenses:* Contact institution.

University of San Francisco, School of Management, Master of Science in Information Systems Program, San Francisco, CA 94117. Offers MS. *Program availability:* Part-time, evening/weekend. *Students:* 47 full-time (16 women); includes 26 minority (4 Black or African American, non-Hispanic/Latino; 11 Asian, non-Hispanic/Latino; 7 Hispanic/Latino; 1 Native Hawaiian or other Pacific Islander, non-Hispanic/Latino; 3 Two or more races, non-Hispanic/Latino), 7 international. Average age 33. 33 applicants, 76% accepted, 14 enrolled. In 2018, 10 master's awarded. *Degree requirements:* For master's, thesis. *Entrance requirements:* For master's, resume demonstrating minimum of two years of professional work experience, transcripts from each college or university attended, two letters of recommendation, personal statement. Additional exam requirements/recommendations for international students: Required—TOEFL (minimum score 600 paper-based, 100 iBT), IELTS (minimum score 7) or PTE (minimum score 68). *Application deadline:* For fall admission, 6/15 for domestic students, 5/15 for international students. Application fee: $55. Electronic applications accepted. *Expenses:* Contact institution. *Financial support:* Scholarships/grants available. Financial award application deadline: 3/2; financial award applicants required to submit FAFSA. *Unit head:* Thomas Grossman, Director, E-mail: tagrossman@usfca.edu. *Application contact:* Office of Graduate Recruiting and Admissions, 415-422-2221, E-mail: management@usfca.edu.
Website: http://www.usfca.edu/msis

The University of Scranton, Kania School of Management, Program in Business Administration, Scranton, PA 18510. Offers accounting (MBA); finance (MBA); general business administration (MBA); health care management (MBA); international business (MBA); management information systems (MBA); marketing (MBA); operations management (MBA). *Accreditation:* AACSB. *Program availability:* Part-time, evening/weekend, 100% online. *Entrance requirements:* For master's, GMAT (for MBA). *Faculty research:* Financial markets, strategic impact of total quality management, internal accounting controls, consumer preference, information systems and the Internet.

University of South Africa, College of Science, Engineering and Technology, Pretoria, South Africa. Offers chemical engineering (M Tech); information technology (M Tech).

University of South Alabama, School of Computing, Mobile, AL 36688. Offers computer science (MS); information systems (MS). *Program availability:* Part-time, evening/weekend. *Degree requirements:* For master's, comprehensive exam, project, thesis, or coursework only with additional credit hours earned; for doctorate, comprehensive exam, thesis/dissertation, minimum GPA of 3.0. *Entrance requirements:* For master's, GRE General Test, undergraduate degree, official transcripts, three letters of recommendation, statement of purpose; for doctorate, GRE, master's degree in related discipline, minimum graduate GPA of 3.5, statement of purpose, three letters of recommendation, curriculum vitae, official transcripts. Additional exam requirements/recommendations for international students: Required—TOEFL (minimum score 525 paper-based; 71 iBT). Electronic applications accepted. *Faculty research:* Artificial intelligence, big data/data mining, STEM education, visual analytics.

University of South Florida, College of Engineering, Department of Industrial and Management Systems Engineering, Tampa, FL 33620-9951. Offers engineering management (MSEM); industrial engineering (MSIE, PhD); information technology (MSIT); materials science and engineering (MSMSE). *Program availability:* Part-time, online learning. *Faculty:* 30 full-time (3 women), 1 part-time/adjunct (0 women). *Students:* 84 full-time (25 women), 60 part-time (15 women); includes 13 minority (2 Black or African American, non-Hispanic/Latino; 4 Asian, non-Hispanic/Latino; 7 Hispanic/Latino), 100 international. Average age 27. 280 applicants, 54% accepted, 37 enrolled. In 2018, 72 master's, 3 doctorates awarded. Terminal master's awarded for partial completion of doctoral program. *Degree requirements:* For master's, comprehensive exam, thesis (for some programs); for doctorate, comprehensive exam, thesis/dissertation, 2 tools of research as specified by dissertation committee. *Entrance requirements:* For master's, GRE General Test, BS in engineering (or equivalent), letters of recommendation, resume, two years professional experience or internship may be required; statement of purpose; for doctorate, GRE General Test, minimum GPA of 3.0, 3 letters of recommendation, statement of purpose, strong background in scientific and engineering principles. Ph.D. students must complete their total doctoral major as full-time Tampa campus students. Additional exam requirements/recommendations for international students: Required—TOEFL, TOEFL (minimum score 550 paper-based; 79 iBT) or IELTS (minimum score 6.5). *Application deadline:* For fall admission, 2/15 for domestic and international students; for spring admission, 10/15 for domestic students, 9/15 for international students; for summer admission, 2/15 for domestic students, 1/15 for international students. Application fee: $30. Electronic applications accepted. *Expenses:* Tuition, state resident: full-time $6350. Tuition, nonresident: full-time $19,048. *International tuition:* $19,048 full-time. *Required fees:* $2079. *Financial support:* In 2018–19, 26 students received support, including 20 research assistantships with partial tuition reimbursements available (averaging $16,748 per year), 11 teaching assistantships with partial tuition reimbursements available (averaging $15,000 per year); tuition waivers (partial) also available. Financial award applicants required to submit FAFSA. *Faculty research:* Healthcare, healthcare systems, public health policies, energy and environment, manufacturing, logistics, transportation. *Total annual research expenditures:* $368,578. *Unit head:* Dr. Tapas K. Das, Professor and Department Chair, 813-974-5585, Fax: 813-974-5953, E-mail: das@usf.edu. *Application contact:* Dr. Alex Savachkin, Associate Professor and Graduate Director, 813-974-5577, Fax: 813-974-5953, E-mail: alexs@usf.edu.
Website: http://imse.eng.usf.edu

University of South Florida, Innovative Education, Tampa, FL 33620-9951. Offers adult, career and higher education (Graduate Certificate), including college teaching, leadership in developing human resources, leadership in higher education; Africana studies (Graduate Certificate), including diasporas and health disparities, genocide and human rights; aging studies (Graduate Certificate), including gerontology; art research (Graduate Certificate), including museum studies; business foundations (Graduate Certificate); chemical and biomedical engineering (Graduate Certificate), including materials science and engineering, water, health and sustainability; child and family studies (Graduate Certificate), including positive behavior support; civil and industrial engineering (Graduate Certificate), including transportation systems analysis; community and family health (Graduate Certificate), including maternal and child health, social marketing and public health, violence and injury: prevention and intervention, women's health; criminology (Graduate Certificate), including criminal justice administration; data science for public administration (Graduate Certificate); digital humanities (Graduate Certificate); educational measurement and research (Graduate Certificate), including evaluation; English (Graduate Certificate), including comparative literary studies, creative writing, professional and technical communication; entrepreneurship (Graduate Certificate); environmental health (Graduate Certificate), including safety management; epidemiology and biostatistics (Graduate Certificate), including applied biostatistics, biostatistics, concepts and tools of epidemiology, epidemiology, epidemiology of infectious diseases; geography, environment and planning (Graduate Certificate), including community development, environmental policy and management, geographical information systems; geology (Graduate Certificate), including hydrogeology; global health (Graduate Certificate), including disaster management, global health and Latin American and Caribbean studies, global health practice, humanitarian assistance, infection control; government and international affairs (Graduate Certificate), including Cuban studies, globalization studies; health policy and management (Graduate Certificate), including health management and leadership, public health policy and programs; hearing specialist: early intervention (Graduate Certificate); industrial and management systems engineering (Graduate Certificate), including systems engineering, technology management; information studies (Graduate Certificate), including school library media specialist; information systems/decision sciences (Graduate Certificate), including analytics and business intelligence; instructional technology (Graduate Certificate), including distance education, Florida digital/virtual educator, instructional design, multimedia design, Web design; internal medicine, bioethics and medical humanities (Graduate Certificate), including biomedical ethics; Latin American and Caribbean studies (Graduate Certificate); leadership for coastal resiliency planning (Graduate Certificate); mass communications (Graduate Certificate), including multimedia journalism; mathematics and statistics (Graduate Certificate), including mathematics; medicine (Graduate Certificate), including aging and neuroscience, bioinformatics, biotechnology, brain fitness and memory management, clinical investigation, hand and upper limb rehabilitation, health informatics, health sciences, integrative weight management, intellectual property, medicine and gender, metabolic and nutritional medicine, metabolic cardiology, pharmacy sciences; national and competitive intelligence (Graduate Certificate); nursing (Graduate Certificate), including simulation based academic fellowship in advanced pain management; psychological and social foundations (Graduate Certificate), including career counseling, college teaching, diversity in education, mental health counseling, school counseling; public affairs (Graduate Certificate), including nonprofit management, public management, research administration; public health (Graduate Certificate), including assessing chemical toxicity and public health risks, health equity, pharmacoepidemiology, public health generalist, toxicology, translational research in adolescent behavioral health; public health practices (Graduate Certificate), including planning for healthy communities; rehabilitation and mental health counseling (Graduate Certificate), including integrative mental health care, marriage and family therapy, rehabilitation technology; secondary education (Graduate Certificate), including ESOL, foreign language education: culture and content, foreign language education: professional; social work (Graduate Certificate), including geriatric social work/clinical gerontology; special education (Graduate Certificate), including autism spectrum disorder, disabilities education: severe/profound; world languages (Graduate Certificate), including teaching English as a second language (TESL) or foreign language. *Expenses:* Tuition, state resident: full-time $6350. Tuition, nonresident: full-time $19,048. *International tuition:* $19,048 full-time. *Required fees:* $2079. *Unit head:* Dr. Cynthia DeLuca, Associate Vice President and Assistant Vice Provost, 813-974-3077, Fax: 813-974-7061, E-mail: deluca@usf.edu. *Application contact:* Owen Hooper, Director, Summer and Alternative Calendar Programs, 813-974-6917, E-mail: hooper@usf.edu.
Website: http://www.usf.edu/innovative-education/

University of South Florida, Muma College of Business, Department of Information Systems and Decision Sciences, Tampa, FL 33620-9951. Offers business administration (PhD), including information systems; business analytics and information systems (MS), including analytics and business intelligence, information assurance. *Program availability:* Part-time. *Faculty:* 25 full-time (4 women). *Students:* 193 full-time (66 women), 130 part-time (38 women); includes 36 minority (9 Black or African American, non-Hispanic/Latino; 18 Asian, non-Hispanic/Latino; 7 Hispanic/Latino; 2 Two or more races, non-Hispanic/Latino), 245 international. Average age 29. 668 applicants, 65% accepted, 131 enrolled. In 2018, 189 master's awarded. Terminal master's awarded for partial completion of doctoral program. *Degree requirements:* For master's, comprehensive exam, thesis (for some programs), thesis or practicum project; for doctorate, comprehensive exam, thesis/dissertation. *Entrance requirements:* For master's, GMAT, GRE or other standardized scores for graduate programs, letters of recommendation, statement of purpose, relevant work experience; for doctorate, GMAT or GRE, letters of recommendation, personal statement, interview. Additional exam requirements/recommendations for international students: Required—TOEFL, TOEFL (minimum score 550 paper-based; 79 iBT) or IELTS (minimum score 6.5). *Application deadline:* For fall admission, 6/1 for domestic students, 2/1 for international students; for spring admission, 10/15 for domestic students, 9/15 for international students. Applications are processed on a rolling basis. Application fee: $30. Electronic applications accepted. *Expenses:* Tuition, state resident: full-time $6350. Tuition, nonresident: full-time $19,048. *International tuition:* $19,048 full-time. *Required fees:* $2079. *Financial support:* In 2018–19, 43 students received support, including 8 research assistantships with tuition reimbursements available (averaging $11,972 per year), 22 teaching assistantships with tuition reimbursements available (averaging $9,002 per year); scholarships/grants, health care benefits, and unspecified assistantships also available. Financial award applicants required to submit FAFSA. *Faculty research:* Data mining, business intelligence, bioterrorism surveillance, health informatics/informatics, software engineering, agent-based modeling, distributed systems, statistics, electronic markets, e-commerce, business process improvement, operations management, supply chain, LEAN management, global information systems, organizational impacts of IT, enterprise resource planning, business intelligence, Web and mobile technologies, social networks, information security. *Total annual research expenditures:* $423,775. *Unit head:* Dr. Kaushal Chari, Chair and Professor, 813-974-6768, Fax: 813-974-6749, E-mail: kchari@usf.edu. *Application contact:* Barber Warner, 813-974-6776, Fax: 813-974-6749, E-mail: bwarner@usf.edu.
Website: http://business.usf.edu/departments/isds/

University of South Florida, Muma College of Business, Department of Management, Tampa, FL 33620-9951. Offers management (MS), including human resources, management information systems. *Accreditation:* AACSB. *Program availability:* Part-time, online learning. *Faculty:* 4 full-time (2 women). *Students:* 22 full-time (10 women), 36 part-time (23 women); includes 21 minority (6 Black or African American, non-Hispanic/Latino; 1 Asian, non-Hispanic/Latino; 14 Hispanic/Latino), 14 international. Average age 31. 81 applicants, 63% accepted, 27 enrolled. In 2018, 43 master's awarded. Terminal master's awarded for partial completion of doctoral program. *Degree requirements:* For master's, comprehensive exam, thesis (for some programs). *Entrance requirements:* For master's, GMAT, letters of recommendation, resume, statement of purpose, relevant work experience. Additional exam requirements/recommendations for international students: Required—TOEFL (minimum score 550 paper-based; 79 iBT) or IELTS (minimum score 6.5). *Application deadline:* For fall admission, 6/1 for domestic students, 2/1 for international students; for spring admission, 10/15 for domestic students, 7/1 for international students. Application fee: $30. Electronic applications accepted. *Expenses:* Tuition, state resident: full-time $6350. Tuition, nonresident: full-time $19,048. *International tuition:* $19,048 full-time. *Required fees:* $2079. *Financial support:* In 2018–19, 6 students received support, including 1 research assistantship with tuition reimbursement available (averaging $9,002 per year), 3 teaching assistantships with tuition reimbursements available (averaging $9,002 per year); tuition waivers also available. Financial award applicants required to submit FAFSA. *Faculty research:* Leadership and employment relations, time management, personal motivation, crew resource management in aviation, psychology of gambling, organizational culture, issues of fairness, employment law, marketing strategy/

implementation, organizational diversity, ethics, environmentally-friendly business practices, green business, sustainable business plans, institutional theory, social movement theory, diffusion of innovations, stakeholder human resources management, social responsibility. *Total annual research expenditures:* $24,235. *Unit head:* Dr. Sally Fuller, Interim Department Chair/Associate Professor, 813-974-1766, Fax: 813-905-9964, E-mail: sfuller@usf.edu. *Application contact:* Stacee Bender, Academic Services Administrator, 813-974-4516, Fax: 813-974-9964, E-mail: staceebender@usf.edu.
Website: http://www.usf.edu/business/graduate/masters/management/

The University of Tampa, Sykes College of Business, Tampa, FL 33606-1490. Offers accounting (MS); business analytics (MBA); cybersecurity (MBA, MS); entrepreneurship (MBA, MS); finance (MBA, MS); information systems management (MBA); innovation management (MBA); international business (MBA); marketing (MBA, MS); nonprofit management (MBA, Certificate). *Accreditation:* AACSB. *Program availability:* Part-time, evening/weekend. *Faculty:* 61 full-time (13 women), 11 part-time/adjunct (3 women). *Students:* 361 full-time (153 women), 122 part-time (52 women); includes 101 minority (31 Black or African American, non-Hispanic/Latino; 5 Asian, non-Hispanic/Latino; 57 Hispanic/Latino; 1 Native Hawaiian or other Pacific Islander, non-Hispanic/Latino; 7 Two or more races, non-Hispanic/Latino), 144 international. Average age 29. 1,079 applicants, 57% accepted, 263 enrolled. In 2018, 281 master's, 12 other advanced degrees awarded. *Degree requirements:* For master's, capstone. *Entrance requirements:* For master's, GMAT or GRE, official transcripts from all colleges and/or universities previously attended, resume, personal statement, letters of recommendation. Additional exam requirements/recommendations for international students: Required—TOEFL (minimum score 577 paper-based; 90 iBT), IELTS (minimum score 7.5). *Application deadline:* Applications are processed on a rolling basis. Application fee: $40. Electronic applications accepted. *Expenses:* Contact institution. *Financial support:* In 2018–19, 123 students received support. Career-related internships or fieldwork, scholarships/grants, and unspecified assistantships available. Financial award applicants required to submit FAFSA. *Faculty research:* Job market signaling, on-line shopping behaviors and social media, the Tampa Bay economy, digital literacy, entrepreneurship in small businesses. *Unit head:* Dr. Natasha F. Veltri, Associate Dean, 813-253-6289, E-mail: nveltri@ut.edu. *Application contact:* Ashley Russell, Staff Assistant, Admissions for Graduate and Continuing Studies, 813-253-6249, E-mail: arussell@ut.edu.
Website: http://www.ut.edu/business/

The University of Texas at Arlington, Graduate School, College of Business, Department of Information Systems and Operations Management, Arlington, TX 76019. Offers information systems (MS, PhD). *Program availability:* Part-time, evening/weekend. *Degree requirements:* For master's, thesis optional; for doctorate, comprehensive exam, thesis/dissertation. *Entrance requirements:* For master's, GMAT, minimum GPA of 3.0; for doctorate, GMAT/GRE. Additional exam requirements/recommendations for international students: Required—TOEFL (minimum score 550 paper-based; 79 iBT). *Faculty research:* Database modeling, strategic issues in information systems, simulations, production operations management.

The University of Texas at Austin, Graduate School, McCombs School of Business, Department of Information, Risk, and Operations Management, Austin, TX 78712-1111. Offers information management (MBA); information systems (PhD); information technology and management (MS); risk analysis and decision making (PhD); risk management (MBA); supply chain and operations management (MBA, PhD). *Degree requirements:* For doctorate, thesis/dissertation. *Entrance requirements:* For doctorate, GMAT or GRE. Electronic applications accepted. *Faculty research:* Stochastic processing and queuing, discrete nonlinear and large-scale optimization simulation, quality assurance logistics, distributed artificial intelligence, organizational modeling.

The University of Texas at Dallas, Naveen Jindal School of Management, Program in Information Systems, Richardson, TX 75080. Offers business analytics (MS); information technology and management (MS). *Program availability:* Part-time, evening/weekend. *Faculty:* 19 full-time (2 women), 29 part-time/adjunct (5 women). *Students:* 1,313 full-time (523 women), 504 part-time (202 women); includes 177 minority (16 Black or African American, non-Hispanic/Latino; 128 Asian, non-Hispanic/Latino; 28 Hispanic/Latino; 1 Native Hawaiian or other Pacific Islander, non-Hispanic/Latino; 4 Two or more races, non-Hispanic/Latino), 1,523 international. Average age 27. 2,623 applicants, 76% accepted, 760 enrolled. In 2018, 983 master's awarded. *Degree requirements:* For master's, thesis optional. *Entrance requirements:* For master's, GMAT. Additional exam requirements/recommendations for international students: Required—TOEFL (minimum score 550 paper-based). *Application deadline:* For fall admission, 7/15 for domestic students, 5/1 priority date for international students; for spring admission, 11/15 for domestic students, 9/1 priority date for international students. Applications are processed on a rolling basis. Application fee: $50 ($100 for international students). Electronic applications accepted. *Expenses: Tuition, area resident:* Full-time $13,458. Tuition, state resident: full-time $13,458. Tuition, nonresident: full-time $26,852. *International tuition:* $26,852 full-time. Tuition and fees vary according to course load. *Financial support:* In 2018–19, 1 research assistantship with partial tuition reimbursement (averaging $13,400 per year), 26 teaching assistantships with partial tuition reimbursements (averaging $10,050 per year) were awarded; career-related internships or fieldwork, Federal Work-Study, institutionally sponsored loans, scholarships/grants, and unspecified assistantships also available. Support available to part-time students. Financial award application deadline: 4/30; financial award applicants required to submit FAFSA. *Faculty research:* Electronic commerce, decision support systems, data quality. *Unit head:* Dr. Syam Menon, Area Coordinator, 972-883-4779, E-mail: syam@utdallas.edu. *Application contact:* Dr. Syam Menon, Area Coordinator, 972-883-4779, E-mail: syam@utdallas.edu.
Website: https://jindal.utdallas.edu/information-systems-programs/

The University of Texas Rio Grande Valley, College of Engineering and Computer Science, Department of Computer Science, Edinburg, TX 78539. Offers computer science (MS); information technology (MS). *Program availability:* Part-time, evening/weekend, online learning. *Degree requirements:* For master's, comprehensive exam, thesis optional. *Entrance requirements:* For master's, GRE General Test. Additional exam requirements/recommendations for international students: Required—TOEFL (minimum score 550 paper-based, 79 iBT) or IELTS (6.5). Electronic applications accepted. *Expenses: Tuition, area resident:* Full-time $6888. Tuition, state resident: full-time $6888. Tuition, nonresident: full-time $14,484. *International tuition:* $14,484 full-time. *Required fees:* $1468. *Faculty research:* Artificial intelligence, distributed systems, Internet computing, theoretical computer sciences, information visualization.

University of the Sacred Heart, Graduate Programs, Department of Business Administration, Program in Information Systems Management, San Juan, PR 00914-0383. Offers MBA. *Program availability:* Part-time, evening/weekend. *Degree requirements:* For master's, thesis. *Entrance requirements:* For master's, EXADEP, minimum undergraduate GPA of 2.75, interview.

University of the West, Department of Business Administration, Rosemead, CA 91770. Offers business administration (EMBA); computer information systems (MBA); finance (MBA); international business (MBA); nonprofit organization management (MBA). *Program availability:* Part-time, evening/weekend. *Entrance requirements:* Additional exam requirements/recommendations for international students: Required—TOEFL.

University of Utah, Graduate School, David Eccles School of Business, Business Administration Program, Salt Lake City, UT 84112. Offers accounting (PhD); business administration (EMBA, MBA, PMBA); finance (PhD); information systems (PhD); marketing (PhD); operations management (PhD); organizational behavior (PhD); strategic management (PhD); MBA/JD; MBA/MHA; MBA/MS. *Program availability:* Part-time, evening/weekend, online learning. *Students:* 112 full-time (26 women), 7 part-time (2 women); includes 12 minority (1 Asian, non-Hispanic/Latino; 7 Hispanic/Latino; 4 Two or more races, non-Hispanic/Latino), 13 international. Average age 29. 182 applicants, 51% accepted, 58 enrolled. In 2018, 58 master's awarded. *Entrance requirements:* For master's, GMAT or GRE; for doctorate, GMAT. Additional exam requirements/recommendations for international students: Required—TOEFL (minimum score 100 iBT), IELTS (minimum score 7). *Application deadline:* For fall admission, 5/1 for domestic students, 3/1 for international students. Application fee: $55 ($65 for international students). Electronic applications accepted. *Expenses:* Contact institution. *Financial support:* In 2018–19, 57 students received support. Scholarships/grants available. Financial award application deadline: 5/1; financial award applicants required to submit FAFSA. *Faculty research:* Corporate finance, strategy services, consumer behavior, financial disclosures, operations. *Unit head:* Brad Vierig, Associate Dean, MBA Programs & Executive Education. *Application contact:* Stephanie Geisler, Director, Full-Time MBA, 801-585-6291, E-mail: ftmba@utah.edu.
Website: http://www.business.utah.edu/

University of Utah, Graduate School, David Eccles School of Business, Master of Science in Information Systems Program, Salt Lake City, UT 84112-8939. Offers information systems (MS, Graduate Certificate), including business intelligence and analytics, IT security, product and process management, software and systems architecture. *Program availability:* Part-time, evening/weekend, 100% online, blended/hybrid learning. *Degree requirements:* For master's, capstone project. *Entrance requirements:* For master's, GMAT/GRE, minimum undergraduate GPA of 3.0, 2 letters of recommendation, personal statement, professional resume. Additional exam requirements/recommendations for international students: Required—TOEFL (minimum score 550 paper-based; 80 iBT), IELTS (minimum score 6.5). Electronic applications accepted. *Expenses:* Contact institution. *Faculty research:* Business intelligence and analytics, software and system architecture, product and process management, IT security, Web and data mining, applications and management of IT in healthcare.

University of Washington, Graduate School, Michael G. Foster School of Business, Seattle, WA 98195-3200. Offers auditing and assurance (MP Acc); business administration (MBA, PhD); entrepreneurship (MS); executive business administration (MBA); global executive business administration (MBA); information systems (MSIS); supply chain management (MSSCM); taxation (MP Acc); technology management (MBA); JD/MBA; MBA/MAIS; MBA/MHA. *Accreditation:* AACSB. *Program availability:* Part-time, evening/weekend, blended/hybrid learning. Terminal master's awarded for partial completion of doctoral program. *Degree requirements:* For doctorate, comprehensive exam, thesis/dissertation. *Entrance requirements:* For master's and doctorate, GMAT, GRE. Additional exam requirements/recommendations for international students: Required—TOEFL (minimum score 600 paper-based; 100 iBT). Electronic applications accepted. *Expenses:* Contact institution. *Faculty research:* Finance, consumer behavior, marketing analytics, technology management, supply chain.

University of Wisconsin–Madison, Graduate School, Wisconsin School of Business, Doctoral Program in Accounting and Information Systems, Madison, WI 53706-1380. Offers PhD. *Accreditation:* AACSB. *Degree requirements:* For doctorate, comprehensive exam, thesis/dissertation. *Entrance requirements:* For doctorate, GMAT or GRE. Additional exam requirements/recommendations for international students: Recommended—TOEFL (minimum score 623 paper-based; 106 iBT), IELTS (minimum score 7.5). Electronic applications accepted. *Expenses:* Contact institution. *Faculty research:* Auditing, financial reporting, economic theory, strategy, computer models, Internal audit and fraud, health care fiscal management, tax reporting, incentives used in nonprofit hospitals, CFO compensation, state and local taxation, audit quality, FASB pronouncements, financial statement analysis.

University of Wisconsin–Madison, Graduate School, Wisconsin School of Business, Doctoral Program in Operations and Information Management, Madison, WI 53706-1380. Offers information systems (PhD); operations management (PhD). *Degree requirements:* For doctorate, comprehensive exam, thesis/dissertation. *Entrance requirements:* For doctorate, GMAT or GRE General Test. Additional exam requirements/recommendations for international students: Recommended—TOEFL (minimum score 623 paper-based; 106 iBT), IELTS (minimum score 7.5), TSE (minimum score 73). Electronic applications accepted. *Expenses:* Contact institution. *Faculty research:* Supply chain management, reorganization of the factory, creating continuous innovation, transportation economics, organizational economics, health care operations management, econometric analysis, forecasting, project management.

Utah State University, School of Graduate Studies, Jon M. Huntsman School of Business, Department of Management Information Systems, Logan, UT 84322. Offers MMIS. *Program availability:* Part-time. *Degree requirements:* For master's, thesis optional. *Entrance requirements:* For master's, GMAT, minimum GPA of 3.2. Additional exam requirements/recommendations for international students: Required—TOEFL. *Faculty research:* Oral and written communication, methods of teaching, CASE tools, object-oriented programming, decision support systems.

Valparaiso University, Graduate School and Continuing Education, Program in Information Technology, Valparaiso, IN 46383. Offers computing (MS); management (MS); security8441 (MS). *Program availability:* Part-time, evening/weekend. *Entrance requirements:* For master's, minimum GPA of 3.0; minor or equivalent in computer science, information technology, or a related field. Additional exam requirements/recommendations for international students: Required—TOEFL (minimum score 550 paper-based; 80 iBT), IELTS (minimum score 6). Electronic applications accepted.

Virginia Commonwealth University, Graduate School, School of Business, Program in Information Systems, Richmond, VA 23284-9005. Offers MS. *Entrance requirements:* For master's, GMAT. Additional exam requirements/recommendations for international students: Required—TOEFL (minimum score 600 paper-based; 100 iBT); Recommended—IELTS (minimum score 6.5). Electronic applications accepted.

Virginia International University, School of Computer Information Systems, Fairfax, VA 22030. Offers business intelligence (Graduate Certificate); business intelligence and data analytics (MIS); computer science (MS), including computer animation and gaming, cybersecurity, data management networking, intelligent systems, software applications development, software engineering; cybersecurity (MIS); data management (MIS); enterprise project management (MIS); health informatics (MIS); information assurance (MIS); information systems (Graduate Certificate); information systems management (MS, Graduate Certificate); information technology (MS); information technology audit and compliance (Graduate Certificate); knowledge management (MIS); software engineering (MS). *Program availability:* Part-time, online learning. *Entrance requirements:* For master's, bachelor's degree. Additional exam requirements/recommendations for international students: Required—TOEFL (minimum score 550 paper-based; 80 iBT), IELTS. Electronic applications accepted.

Virginia Polytechnic Institute and State University, Graduate School, Intercollege, Blacksburg, VA 24061. Offers genetics, bioinformatics, and computational biology (PhD); information technology (MIT); macromolecular science and engineering (MS, PhD); translational biology, medicine, and health (PhD). *Students:* 189 full-time (92 women), 685 part-time (206 women); includes 260 minority (65 Black or African American, non-Hispanic/Latino; 106 Asian, non-Hispanic/Latino; 54 Hispanic/Latino; 2 Native Hawaiian or other Pacific Islander, non-Hispanic/Latino; 33 Two or more races, non-Hispanic/Latino), 98 international. Average age 33. 531 applicants, 75% accepted, 274 enrolled. In 2018, 138 master's, 20 doctorates awarded. *Degree requirements:* For master's, comprehensive exam (for some programs), thesis (for some programs); for doctorate, comprehensive exam (for some programs), thesis/dissertation (for some programs). *Entrance requirements:* For master's and doctorate, GRE/GMAT. Additional exam requirements/recommendations for international students: Required—TOEFL (minimum score 90 iBT). *Application deadline:* For fall admission, 8/1 for domestic students, 4/1 for international students; for spring admission, 1/1 for domestic students, 9/1 for international students. Applications are processed on a rolling basis. Application fee: $75. Electronic applications accepted. *Expenses:* Tuition, state resident: full-time $15,510; part-time $739.50 per credit hour. Tuition, nonresident: full-time $29,629; part-time $1490.25 per credit hour. *Required fees:* $2804; $550 per semester. Tuition and fees vary according to course load, campus/location and program. *Financial support:* In 2018–19, 3 fellowships with full and partial tuition reimbursements (averaging $18,380 per year), 158 research assistantships with full tuition reimbursements (averaging $22,336 per year), 21 teaching assistantships with full tuition reimbursements (averaging $19,355 per year) were awarded; scholarships/grants also available. Financial award application deadline: 3/1; financial award applicants required to submit FAFSA. *Unit head:* Dr. Karen P. DePauw, Vice President and Dean for Graduate Education, 540-231-7581, Fax: 540-231-1670, E-mail: kpdepauw@vt.edu. *Application contact:* Dr. Karen P. DePauw, Vice President and Dean for Graduate Education, 540-231-7581, Fax: 540-231-1670, E-mail: kpdepauw@vt.edu.

Virginia Polytechnic Institute and State University, Graduate School, Pamplin College of Business, Blacksburg, VA 24061. Offers accounting and information systems (MACIS, PhD); business administration (MS), including business analytics, hospitality and tourism management; business information technology (PhD); executive business research (PhD); finance (PhD); marketing (PhD), including marketing; MS/MBA. *Faculty:* 141 full-time (42 women), 2 part-time/adjunct (1 woman). *Students:* 227 full-time (89 women), 217 part-time (75 women); includes 131 minority (30 Black or African American, non-Hispanic/Latino; 58 Asian, non-Hispanic/Latino; 25 Hispanic/Latino; 18 Two or more races, non-Hispanic/Latino), 81 international. Average age 32. 361 applicants, 55% accepted, 152 enrolled. In 2018, 181 master's, 8 doctorates awarded. *Degree requirements:* For master's, comprehensive exam (for some programs), thesis (for some programs); for doctorate, comprehensive exam (for some programs), thesis/dissertation (for some programs). *Entrance requirements:* For master's and doctorate, GRE/GMAT. Additional exam requirements/recommendations for international students: Required—TOEFL (minimum score 90 iBT). *Application deadline:* For fall admission, 8/1 for domestic students, 4/1 for international students; for spring admission, 1/1 for domestic students, 9/1 for international students. Applications are processed on a rolling basis. Application fee: $75. Electronic applications accepted. *Expenses:* Tuition, state resident: full-time $15,510; part-time $739.50 per credit hour. Tuition, nonresident: full-time $29,629; part-time $1490.25 per credit hour. *Required fees:* $2804; $550 per semester. Tuition and fees vary according to course load, campus/location and program. *Financial support:* In 2018–19, 1 fellowship with full tuition reimbursement (averaging $3,999 per year), 4 research assistantships with full tuition reimbursements (averaging $20,163 per year), 66 teaching assistantships with full tuition reimbursements (averaging $19,822 per year) were awarded; scholarships/grants and unspecified assistantships also available. Financial award application deadline: 3/1; financial award applicants required to submit FAFSA. *Total annual research expenditures:* $3.1 million. *Unit head:* Dr. Robert T. Sumichrast, Dean, 540-231-6601, Fax: 540-231-4487, E-mail: busdean@vt.edu. *Application contact:* Kimberly Ridpath, Executive Assistant, 540-231-9647, Fax: 540-231-4487, E-mail: ridpathk@vt.edu.
Website: http://www.pamplin.vt.edu/

Virginia Polytechnic Institute and State University, VT Online, Blacksburg, VA 24061. Offers advanced transportation systems (Certificate); aerospace engineering (MS); agricultural and life sciences (MSLFS); business information systems (Graduate Certificate); career and technical education (MS); civil engineering (MS); computer engineering (M Eng, MS); decision support systems (Graduate Certificate); eLearning leadership (MA); electrical engineering (M Eng, MS); engineering administration (MEA); environmental engineering (Certificate); environmental politics and policy (Graduate Certificate); environmental sciences and engineering (MS); foundations of political analysis (Graduate Certificate); health product risk management (Graduate Certificate); industrial and systems engineering (MS); information policy and society (Graduate Certificate); information security (Graduate Certificate); information technology (MIT); instructional technology (MA); integrative STEM education (MA Ed); liberal arts (Graduate Certificate); life sciences: health product risk management (MS); natural resources (MNR, Graduate Certificate); networking (Graduate Certificate); nonprofit and nongovernmental organization management (Graduate Certificate); ocean engineering (MS); political science (MA); security studies (Graduate Certificate); software development (Graduate Certificate). *Expenses:* Tuition, state resident: full-time $15,510; part-time $739.50 per credit hour. Tuition, nonresident: full-time $29,629; part-time $1490.25 per credit hour. *Required fees:* $2804; $550 per semester. Tuition and fees vary according to course load, campus/location and program. *Application contact:* Graduate Admissions and Academic Progress, 540-231-8636, E-mail: grads@vt.edu.
Website: http://www.vto.vt.edu/

Walden University, Graduate Programs, School of Information Systems and Technology, Minneapolis, MN 55401. Offers information systems (Graduate Certificate); information systems management (MISM); information technology (MS, DIT), including health informatics (MS), information assurance and cyber security (MS), information systems (MS), software engineering (MS). *Program availability:* Part-time, evening/weekend, online only, 100% online. *Degree requirements:* For doctorate, thesis/dissertation (for some programs), residency. *Entrance requirements:* For master's, bachelor's degree or higher; minimum GPA of 2.5; official transcripts; goal statement (for some programs); access to computer and Internet; for doctorate, master's degree or higher; three years of related professional or academic experience (preferred); minimum GPA of 3.0; goal statement and current resume (for select programs); official transcripts; access to computer and Internet; for Graduate Certificate, relevant work experience; access to computer and Internet. Additional exam requirements/recommendations for international students: Required—TOEFL (minimum score 550 paper-based, 79 iBT), IELTS (minimum score 6.5), Michigan English Language Assessment Battery (minimum score 82), or PTE (minimum score 53). Electronic applications accepted.

Walden University, Graduate Programs, School of Management, Minneapolis, MN 55401. Offers accounting (MBA, MS, DBA), including accounting for the professional (MS), accounting with CPA emphasis (MS), self-designed (MS); advanced project management (Graduate Certificate); applied project management (Graduate Certificate); auditing (Graduate Certificate); bridge to business administration (Post-Doctoral Certificate); bridge to management (Post-Doctoral Certificate); business management (Graduate Certificate); communication (MBA); corporate finance (MBA); digital marketing (Graduate Certificate); entrepreneurship (DBA); entrepreneurship and small business (MBA); finance (MS, DBA), including finance for the professional (MS), finance with CFA/investment (MS), finance with CPA emphasis (MS); global supply chain management (DBA); healthcare management (MBA, DBA); human resource management (MBA, MS, Graduate Certificate), including functional human resource management (MS), general program (MS), integrating functional and strategic human resource management (MS), organizational strategy (MS); human resources management (DBA); information systems management (DBA); international business (MBA, DBA); leadership (MBA, MS, DBA, Graduate Certificate), including general program (MS), human resource leadership (MS), leader development (MS), self-designed (MS); management (MS, PhD), including communications (MS), finance (PhD), general program (MS), healthcare management (MS), human resource management (MS), human resources management (PhD), information systems management (PhD), international business (MS), leadership (MS), leadership and organizational change (PhD), marketing (MS), project management (MS), strategy and operations (MS); managerial accounting (Graduate Certificate); marketing (MBA, MS, DBA); project management (MBA, MS, DBA); self-designed (MBA, DBA); social impact management (DBA); technology entrepreneurship (DBA). *Accreditation:* ACBSP. *Program availability:* Part-time, evening/weekend, online only, 100% online. *Degree requirements:* For master's, thesis (for some programs), residency (for EMBA); for doctorate, thesis/dissertation (for some programs), residency. *Entrance requirements:* For master's, bachelor's degree or higher; minimum GPA of 2.5; official transcripts; goal statement (for some programs); access to computer and Internet; for doctorate, master's degree or higher; three years of related professional or academic experience (preferred); minimum GPA of 3.0; goal statement and current resume (for select programs); official transcripts; access to computer and Internet; for other advanced degree, relevant work experience; access to computer and Internet. Additional exam requirements/recommendations for international students: Required—TOEFL (minimum score 550 paper-based, 79 iBT), IELTS (minimum score 6.5), Michigan English Language Assessment Battery (minimum score 82), or PTE (minimum score 53). Electronic applications accepted.

Wayland Baptist University, Graduate Programs, Programs in Business Administration/Management, Plainview, TX 79072-6998. Offers accounting (MBA); general business (MBA); health care administration (MAM, MBA); human resource management (MAM, MBA); international management (MBA); management (MBA, D Mgt); management information systems (MBA); organization management (MAM); project management (MBA). *Program availability:* Part-time, evening/weekend, online learning. *Degree requirements:* For master's, capstone course. *Entrance requirements:* For master's, GMAT, GRE or MAT. Additional exam requirements/recommendations for international students: Required—TOEFL (minimum score 500 paper-based; 61 iBT). Electronic applications accepted.

Wayne State University, Mike Ilitch School of Business, Detroit, MI 48202. Offers accounting (MS, MSA, Postbaccalaureate Certificate); business (EMS, Graduate Certificate); business administration (MBA, PhD); data science (MS), including business analytics; entrepreneurship and innovation (Postbaccalaureate Certificate); finance (MS); information systems management (Postbaccalaureate Certificate); taxation (MST); JD/MBA. Application deadline for PhD is February 15. *Accreditation:* AACSB. *Program availability:* Part-time, evening/weekend. *Faculty:* 31. *Students:* 286 full-time (152 women), 1,166 part-time (533 women); includes 409 minority (236 Black or African American, non-Hispanic/Latino; 83 Asian, non-Hispanic/Latino; 53 Hispanic/Latino; 37 Two or more races, non-Hispanic/Latino), 74 international. Average age 30. 1,212 applicants, 38% accepted, 294 enrolled. In 2018, 285 master's, 6 doctorates, 7 other advanced degrees awarded. *Degree requirements:* For doctorate, thesis/dissertation. *Entrance requirements:* For master's, GMAT, GRE, LSAT, MCAT, at least three years of relevant work experience that shows increased responsibility, or minimum GPA of 3.0 from AACSB-accredited program or 3.2 from regionally-accredited program, undergraduate degree from accredited institution; undergraduate degree in accounting, business administration, or area of business administration (for MS and MST); for doctorate, GMAT (minimum score of 600), minimum undergraduate GPA of 3.0, 3.5 upper-division or graduate; three letters of recommendation; brief essay; undergraduate degree from accredited institution; personal statement; for other advanced degree, bachelor's degree from accredited institution. Additional exam requirements/recommendations for international students: Required—TOEFL (minimum score 550 paper-based; 79 iBT), Michigan English Language Assessment Battery (minimum score 85); Recommended—IELTS (minimum score 6.5), TWE (minimum score 5.5). *Application deadline:* For fall admission, 7/1 for domestic students, 5/1 priority date for international students; for winter admission, 11/1 for domestic students, 9/1 priority date for international students; for spring admission, 3/1 for domestic students, 1/1 priority date for international students. Applications are processed on a rolling basis. Application fee: $50. Electronic applications accepted. *Expenses:* Contact institution. *Financial support:* In 2018–19, 175 students received support, including 1 fellowship with tuition reimbursement available (averaging $20,000 per year), 5 research assistantships with tuition reimbursements available (averaging $21,393 per year); teaching assistantships with tuition reimbursements available, scholarships/grants, health care benefits, and unspecified assistantships also available. Support available to part-time students. Financial award applicants required to submit FAFSA. *Faculty research:* Executive compensation and stock performance, consumer reactions to pricing strategies, communication across the automotive supply chain, performance of firms in sub-Saharan Africa, implementation issues with ERP software. *Unit head:* Dr. Robert Forsythe, Dean, School of Business Administration, 313-577-4501, E-mail: robert.forsythe@wayne.edu. *Application contact:* Kiantee N. Rupert-Jones, Director, 313-577-4511, Fax: 313-577-9442, E-mail: gradbusiness@wayne.edu.
Website: http://ilitchbusiness.wayne.edu/

Wayne State University, School of Information Sciences, Detroit, MI 48202. Offers archival administration (Graduate Certificate); information management (MS, Graduate Certificate); library and information science (MLIS, Graduate Certificate, Spec); public library services to children and young adults (Graduate Certificate); MLIS/MA. WSU History Department. *Accreditation:* ALA (one or more programs are accredited). *Program availability:* Part-time, evening/weekend, 100% online, blended/hybrid learning. *Faculty:* 12 full-time (9 women), 17 part-time/adjunct (12 women). *Students:* 85 full-time (74 women), 316 part-time (258 women); includes 77 minority (42 Black or African American, non-Hispanic/Latino; 2 American Indian or Alaska Native, non-Hispanic/Latino; 3 Asian, non-Hispanic/Latino; 19 Hispanic/Latino; 1 Native Hawaiian or other Pacific Islander, non-Hispanic/Latino; 10 Two or more races, non-Hispanic/Latino), 1 international. Average age 33. 258 applicants, 60% accepted, 100 enrolled. In 2018, 149 master's, 34 other advanced degrees awarded. *Degree requirements:* For master's and other advanced degree, e-portfolio. *Entrance requirements:* For master's, GRE or MAT (if undergraduate GPA is between 2.5 and 2.99), minimum undergraduate GPA of 3.0 or graduate degree, personal statement, resume or curriculum vitae; for other advanced degree, GRE or MAT (if undergraduate GPA is between 2.5 and 2.99), minimum undergraduate GPA of 3.0 or graduate degree, personal statement, resume or curriculum vitae, MLIS (for specialist certificate). Additional exam requirements/recommendations for international students: Required—TOEFL (minimum score 550

Management Information Systems

paper-based; 79 iBT); Recommended—IELTS (minimum score 6.5), TWE (minimum score 5.5). *Application deadline:* For fall admission, 7/1 for domestic students, 5/1 priority date for international students; for winter admission, 10/1 priority date for domestic students, 9/1 priority date for international students; for spring admission, 2/1 priority date for domestic students, 1/1 priority date for international students. Applications are processed on a rolling basis. Application fee: $50. Electronic applications accepted. *Expenses:* 15,000/year. *Financial support:* In 2018–19, 133 students received support. Fellowships with tuition reimbursements available, scholarships/grants, health care benefits, and unspecified assistantships available. Support available to part-time students. Financial award applicants required to submit FAFSA. *Faculty research:* Library services, information management issues, digital content management, library/community engagement, archives and preservation. *Unit head:* Dr. Jon Cawthorne, Dean, 313-577-4020, E-mail: jon.cawthorne@wayne.edu. *Application contact:* Academic Services Officer II, 313-577-1825, E-mail: asklis@wayne.edu.
Website: http://slis.wayne.edu/

Webster University, George Herbert Walker School of Business and Technology, Department of Business, St. Louis, MO 63119-3194. Offers business and organizational security management (MBA); decision support systems (MBA); environmental management (MBA); finance (MBA, MS); forensic accounting (MS); gerontology (MBA); human resources development (MBA); human resources management (MBA); information technology management (MBA); international business (MA, MBA); international relations (MBA); management and leadership (MBA); marketing (MBA); media communications (MBA); procurement and acquisitions management (MBA); Web services (MBA). *Accreditation:* ACBSP. *Program availability:* Part-time, evening/weekend, online learning. *Degree requirements:* For master's, comprehensive exam (for some programs), thesis (for some programs). *Entrance requirements:* Additional exam requirements/recommendations for international students: Required—TOEFL. *Expenses: Tuition:* Full-time $22,500; part-time $750 per credit hour. Tuition and fees vary according to degree level, campus/location and program.

Webster University, George Herbert Walker School of Business and Technology, Department of Management, St. Louis, MO 63119-3194. Offers business and organizational security management (MA); digital marketing management (Graduate Certificate); government contracting (Graduate Certificate); health administration (MHA); health care management (MA); health services management (MA); human resources development (MA); human resources management (MA); information technology management (MA, MS); management (D Mgt); management and leadership (MA); marketing (MA); nonprofit leadership (MA); nonprofit revenue development (Graduate Certificate); organizational development (Graduate Certificate); procurement and acquisitions management (MA); public administration (MPA); space systems operations management (MS). *Program availability:* Part-time, evening/weekend, online learning. *Degree requirements:* For master's, thesis (for some programs); for doctorate, thesis/dissertation, written exam. *Entrance requirements:* For doctorate, GMAT, 3 years of work experience, MBA. Additional exam requirements/recommendations for international students: Required—TOEFL. *Expenses: Tuition:* Full-time $22,500; part-time $750 per credit hour. Tuition and fees vary according to degree level, campus/location and program.

West Chester University of Pennsylvania, College of the Sciences and Mathematics, Department of Computer Science, West Chester, PA 19383. Offers computer science (MS); computer security (information assurance) (Certificate); information systems (Certificate); Web technology (Certificate). *Program availability:* Part-time, evening/weekend. *Degree requirements:* For master's, thesis optional, 33 credits; for Certificate, 12 credits. *Entrance requirements:* For master's, GRE, two letters of reference; for Certificate, BS. Additional exam requirements/recommendations for international students: Required—TOEFL or IELTS. Electronic applications accepted. *Faculty research:* Security in mobile ad-hoc networks, intrusion detection, security and trust in pervasive computing, cloud computing, wireless sensor networks, cloud computing and data mining.

Western Governors University, College of Business, Salt Lake City, UT 84107. Offers accounting (MS); information technology management (MBA); management and leadership (MS); management and strategy (MBA); strategic leadership (MBA). *Program availability:* Evening/weekend, online learning. *Degree requirements:* For master's, capstone project. *Entrance requirements:* For master's, transcripts. Additional exam requirements/recommendations for international students: Required—TOEFL (minimum score 450 paper-based; 80 iBT). Electronic applications accepted. Application fee is waived when completed online.

Wichita State University, Graduate School, W. Frank Barton School of Business, School of Accountancy, Wichita, KS 67260. Offers accounting information systems (M Acc); taxation (M Acc). *Accreditation:* AACSB. *Program availability:* Part-time, evening/weekend. *Unit head:* Dr. Jeffrey Bryant, Director, 316-978-3215, Fax: 316-978-3660, E-mail: jeffrey.bryant@wichita.edu. *Application contact:* Jordan Oleson, Admissions Coordinator, 316-978-3095, Fax: 316-978-3253, E-mail: jordan.oleson@wichita.edu.
Website: http://www.wichita.edu/acct

Wilmington University, College of Business, New Castle, DE 19720-6491. Offers accounting (MBA, MS); business administration (MBA, DBA); environmental stewardship (MBA); finance (MBA); health care administration (MBA, MSM); homeland security (MBA, MSM); human resource management (MSM); management information systems (MBA, MSN); marketing (MSM); management management (MBA); military leadership (MSM); organizational leadership (MBA, MSM); public administration (MSM). *Program availability:* Part-time, evening/weekend. *Entrance requirements:* Additional exam requirements/recommendations for international students: Required—TOEFL (minimum score 500 paper-based). Electronic applications accepted.

Wilmington University, College of Technology, New Castle, DE 19720-6491. Offers cybersecurity (MS); information assurance (MS); information systems technologies (MS); management and management information systems (MS); technology project management (MS); Web design (MS). *Program availability:* Part-time, evening/weekend. *Entrance requirements:* Additional exam requirements/recommendations for international students: Required—TOEFL (minimum score 500 paper-based). Electronic applications accepted.

Winston-Salem State University, Program in Computer Science and Information Technology, Winston-Salem, NC 27110-0003. Offers MS. *Program availability:* Part-time. *Degree requirements:* For master's, thesis optional. *Entrance requirements:* For master's, GRE, resume. Electronic applications accepted. *Faculty research:* Artificial intelligence, network protocols, software engineering.

Worcester Polytechnic Institute, Graduate Admissions, Foisie Business School, Worcester, MA 01609-2280. Offers business administration (PhD); information technology (MS), including information security management; management (MS, Graduate Certificate); marketing and innovation (MS); operations analytics and management (MS); supply chain management (MS). *Accreditation:* AACSB. *Program availability:* Part-time, evening/weekend, 100% online, blended/hybrid learning. *Students:* 136 full-time (74 women), 214 part-time (85 women); includes 29 minority (4 Black or African American, non-Hispanic/Latino; 11 Asian, non-Hispanic/Latino; 9 Hispanic/Latino; 5 Two or more races, non-Hispanic/Latino), 189 international. Average age 29. 636 applicants, 64% accepted, 104 enrolled. In 2018, 165 master's, 1 doctorate, 10 other advanced degrees awarded. *Degree requirements:* For master's, thesis optional. *Entrance requirements:* For master's and Graduate Certificate, GMAT or GRE General Test, 3 letters of recommendation, statement of purpose, resume. Additional exam requirements/recommendations for international students: Required—TOEFL (minimum score 563 paper-based; 84 iBT), IELTS (minimum score 7). *Application deadline:* For fall admission, 6/1 priority date for domestic and international students; for spring admission, 11/1 priority date for domestic students, 10/1 priority date for international students. Applications are processed on a rolling basis. Application fee: $70. Electronic applications accepted. *Financial support:* Career-related internships or fieldwork, institutionally sponsored loans, scholarships/grants, and unspecified assistantships available. Financial award application deadline: 6/1. *Unit head:* Melissa Terrio, Director of Graduate Recruitment & Admissions, 508-831-4665, Fax: 508-831-5866, E-mail: biz@wpi.edu. *Application contact:* Amy Trakimas, Associate Director of Graduate Recruitment & Admissions, 508-831-4665, Fax: 508-831-5866, E-mail: atrakimas@wpi.edu.
Website: https://www.wpi.edu/academics/business

Wright State University, Graduate School, Raj Soin College of Business, Department of Information Systems and Operations Management, Information Systems Program, Dayton, OH 45435. Offers MIS.

Section 13
Management Strategy and Policy

This section contains a directory of institutions offering graduate work in management strategy and policy. Additional information about programs listed in the directory but not augmented by an in-depth entry may be obtained by writing directly to the dean of a graduate school or chair of a department at the address given in the directory.

For programs offering related work, see also in this book *Business Administration and Management.* In another guide in this series:

Graduate Programs in the Humanities, Arts & Social Sciences
See *Public, Regional, and Industrial Affairs (Industrial and Labor Relations)*

CONTENTS

Program Directories

Management Strategy and Policy

Amberton University, Graduate School, Department of Business Administration, Garland, TX 75041-5595. Offers agile project management (MS); general business (MBA); international business (MBA); management (MBA); project management (MBA); strategic leadership (MBA). *Program availability:* Part-time, evening/weekend. *Entrance requirements:* For master's, minimum GPA of 3.0.

Antioch University Santa Barbara, Program in Business Administration, Santa Barbara, CA 93101-1581. Offers non-profit management (MBA); social business (MBA); strategic leadership (MBA).

Arizona State University at the Tempe campus, W. P. Carey School of Business, Program in Business Administration, Tempe, AZ 85287-4906. Offers entrepreneurship (MBA); finance (MBA); health sector management (MBA); international business (MBA); leadership (MBA); marketing (MBA); organizational behavior (PhD); strategic management (PhD); supply chain management (MBA, PhD); JD/MBA; MBA/M Acc; MBA/M Arch. *Accreditation:* AACSB. *Program availability:* Part-time, evening/weekend, online learning. Terminal master's awarded for partial completion of doctoral program. *Degree requirements:* For master's, thesis or alternative, internship, interactive Program of Study (iPOS) submitted before completing 50 percent of required credit hours; for doctorate, comprehensive exam, thesis/dissertation, interactive Program of Study (iPOS) submitted before completing 50 percent of required credit hours. *Entrance requirements:* For master's, GMAT, minimum GPA of 3.0 in last 2 years of work leading to bachelor's degree, 2 letters of recommendation, professional resume, official transcripts, 3 essays; for doctorate, GMAT or GRE, minimum GPA of 3.0 in last 2 years of work leading to bachelor's degree, 3 letters of recommendation, resume, personal statement/essay. Additional exam requirements/recommendations for international students: Required—TOEFL (minimum score 550 paper-based; 80 iBT), IELTS (minimum score 6.5). Electronic applications accepted. *Expenses:* Contact institution.

Bay Path University, Program in Leadership and Negotiation, Longmeadow, MA 01106-2292. Offers MS. *Program availability:* Part-time, 100% online, blended/hybrid learning. *Students:* 4 full-time (3 women), 26 part-time (25 women); includes 9 minority (7 Black or African American, non-Hispanic/Latino; 1 Asian, non-Hispanic/Latino; 1 Hispanic/Latino). Average age 38. *Entrance requirements:* For master's, completed application; official undergraduate and graduate transcripts (a GPA of 3.0 or higher preferred); original essay of at least 250 words on the topic: "Why the MS in Leadership & Negotiation is important to my personal and professional goals"; current resume; 2 recommendations. *Application deadline:* Applications are processed on a rolling basis. Electronic applications accepted. Application fee is waived when completed online. *Expenses:* Contact institution. *Financial support:* Unspecified assistantships available. Financial award applicants required to submit FAFSA. *Unit head:* Dr. Joshua Weiss, Director, E-mail: joweiss@baypath.edu. *Application contact:* Elise Carrier, Assistant Dean of Graduate Director, 413-565-1621, Fax: 413-565-1250, E-mail: ecarrier@baypath.edu.
Website: https://www.baypath.edu/academics/graduate-programs/leadership-negotiation-ms/

Black Hills State University, Graduate Studies, Program in Strategic Leadership, Spearfish, SD 57799. Offers MS. *Program availability:* Part-time, evening/weekend. *Entrance requirements:* Additional exam requirements/recommendations for international students: Required—TOEFL (minimum score 500 paper-based; 60 iBT).

Boston University, Metropolitan College, Department of Computer Science, Boston, MA 02215. Offers computer information systems (MS), including computer networks, data analytics, database management and business intelligence, health informatics, IT project management, security, Web application development; computer networks (Certificate); computer science (MS); data analytics (Certificate); digital forensics (Certificate); health informatics (Certificate); information technology project management (Certificate); software development (MS); software engineering in health care systems (Certificate); telecommunications (MS), including security. *Program availability:* Part-time, evening/weekend, online learning. *Faculty:* 16 full-time (3 women), 52 part-time/adjunct (5 women). *Students:* 201 full-time (57 women), 953 part-time (252 women); includes 285 minority (57 Black or African American, non-Hispanic/Latino; 2 American Indian or Alaska Native, non-Hispanic/Latino; 139 Asian, non-Hispanic/Latino; 67 Hispanic/Latino; 1 Native Hawaiian or other Pacific Islander, non-Hispanic/Latino; 19 Two or more races, non-Hispanic/Latino), 333 international. Average age 31. 1,079 applicants, 72% accepted, 297 enrolled. In 2018, 395 master's awarded. *Entrance requirements:* For master's and Certificate, official transcripts from regionally-accredited bachelor's degree program, 3 letters of recommendation, professional resume, personal statement. Additional exam requirements/recommendations for international students: Required—TOEFL (minimum score 84 iBT), IELTS. *Application deadline:* For fall admission, 8/1 priority date for domestic students, 6/1 priority date for international students; for spring admission, 12/1 priority date for domestic students, 11/15 priority date for international students; for summer admission, 4/1 priority date for domestic students, 3/1 priority date for international students. Applications are processed on a rolling basis. Application fee: $85. Electronic applications accepted. *Expenses:* Contact institution. *Financial support:* In 2018–19, 11 research assistantships (averaging $8,400 per year), 23 teaching assistantships (averaging $3,400 per year) were awarded; unspecified assistantships also available. Support available to part-time students. Financial award applicants required to submit FAFSA. *Faculty research:* Artificial intelligence and machine learning, security and forensics, web technologies, software engineering, programming languages, medical informatics, information systems and IT project management. *Unit head:* Dr. Anatoly Temkin, Chair, 617-353-2566, Fax: 617-353-2367, E-mail: csinfo@bu.edu. *Application contact:* Enrollment Services, 617-353-6004, E-mail: met@bu.edu.
Website: http://www.bu.edu/csmet/

Brandeis University, Rabb School of Continuing Studies, Division of Graduate Professional Studies, Master of Science in Strategic Analytics Program, Waltham, MA 02454-9110. Offers MS. *Program availability:* Part-time-only. *Entrance requirements:* For master's, four-year bachelor's degree from regionally-accredited U.S. institution or equivalent; official transcript(s) from every college or university attended; resume or curriculum vitae; statement of goals; letter of recommendation. Additional exam requirements/recommendations for international students: Required—TWE (minimum score 4.5), TOEFL (minimum scores: 600 paper-based, 100 iBT), IELTS (7), or PTE (68). Electronic applications accepted. *Expenses:* Contact institution.

California Miramar University, Program in Strategic Leadership, San Diego, CA 92108. Offers MS. *Degree requirements:* For master's, capstone project.

California State University, East Bay, Office of Graduate Studies, College of Business and Economics, MBA Program, Option in Strategy and Innovation, Hayward, CA 94542-3000. Offers MBA. *Program availability:* Part-time, evening/weekend. *Degree requirements:* For master's, comprehensive exam or thesis. *Entrance requirements:* For master's, GMAT, minimum GPA of 2.75. Additional exam requirements/recommendations for international students: Required—TOEFL (minimum score 550 paper-based).

Capella University, School of Business and Technology, Doctoral Programs in Business, Minneapolis, MN 55402. Offers accounting (DBA, PhD); business intelligence (DBA); finance (DBA, PhD); general business management (PhD); human resource management (DBA, PhD); leadership (DBA, PhD); management education (PhD); marketing (DBA, PhD); project management (DBA, PhD); strategy and innovation (DBA, PhD). *Accreditation:* ACBSP.

Capella University, School of Business and Technology, Master's Programs in Business, Minneapolis, MN 55402. Offers accounting (MBA); business analysis (MS); business intelligence (MBA); entrepreneurship (MBA); finance (MBA); general business administration (MBA); general human resource management (MS); general leadership (MS); health care management (MBA); human resource management (MBA); marketing (MBA); project management (MBA, MS). *Accreditation:* ACBSP.

Claremont Graduate University, Graduate Programs, Peter F. Drucker and Masatoshi Ito Graduate School of Management, Program in Executive Management, Claremont, CA 91711-6160. Offers advanced management (MS); executive management (EMBA); leadership (Certificate); management (MA, PhD, Certificate); strategy (Certificate). *Accreditation:* AACSB. *Program availability:* Part-time. *Entrance requirements:* Additional exam requirements/recommendations for international students: Required—TOEFL (minimum score 75 iBT). Electronic applications accepted. *Expenses:* Contact institution. *Faculty research:* Strategy and leadership, brand management, cost management and control, organizational transformation, general management.

Cleary University, Online Program in Business Administration, Howell, MI 48843. Offers analytics, technology, and innovation (MBA, Graduate Certificate); financial planning (Graduate Certificate); global leadership (MBA, Graduate Certificate); health care leadership (MBA, Graduate Certificate). *Program availability:* Part-time, evening/weekend, online learning. *Degree requirements:* For master's, thesis. *Entrance requirements:* For master's, bachelor's degree; minimum GPA of 2.5; professional resume indicating minimum of 2 years of management or related experience; undergraduate degree from accredited college or university with at least 18 quarter hours (or 12 semester hours) of accounting study (for MBA in accounting). Additional exam requirements/recommendations for international students: Required—TOEFL (minimum score 550 paper-based; 79 iBT), Michigan English Language Assessment Battery (minimum score 75). Electronic applications accepted.

College of Staten Island of the City University of New York, Graduate Programs, School of Business, Program in Business Management, Staten Island, NY 10314-6600. Offers large scale data analysis (MS); strategic management (MS). *Program availability:* Part-time, evening/weekend. *Faculty:* 4. *Students:* 39. 52 applicants, 56% accepted, 26 enrolled. In 2018, 21 master's awarded. *Degree requirements:* For master's, 30 credit hours, or ten courses at three credits each. *Entrance requirements:* For master's, GMAT or the GRE. CSI graduates with a 3.2 GPA or higher in their accounting/business major may be exempt from the GMAT/GRE. The TOEFL or IELTS is required for students whose second language is English., baccalaureate degree in business or related field, overall GPA of 3.0 or higher, letter of intent, two letters of recommendation. 2 courses in accounting,1 course in communications, 1 course in computer fundamentals, 2 courses in economics, 2 courses in quantitative methods, 1 course in management, 1 course in marketing. Additional exam requirements/recommendations for international students: Required—TOEFL (minimum score 550 paper-based; 79 iBT), IELTS (minimum score 6.5). *Application deadline:* For fall admission, 6/30 priority date for domestic students, 6/30 for international students; for spring admission, 11/25 priority date for domestic students, 11/25 for international students. Applications are processed on a rolling basis. Application fee: $75. Electronic applications accepted. *Expenses: Tuition, area resident:* Full-time $10,770; part-time $455 per credit. Tuition, state resident: full-time $10,770; part-time $455 per credit. Tuition, nonresident: full-time $19,920; part-time $830 per credit. *International tuition:* $19,920 full-time. *Required fees:* $559.20; $181.10 per semester. Tuition and fees vary according to program. *Faculty research:* Knowledge integration, management innovation, organizational decision-making, Human Resource Management, Behavioral Economics. *Unit head:* Dr. Heidi Bertels, Assistant Professor, 718-982-2924, E-mail: heidi.bertels@csi.cuny.edu. *Application contact:* Sasha Spence, Associate Director for Graduate Admissions, 718-982-2019, Fax: 718-982-2500, E-mail: sasha.spence@csi.cuny.edu.
Website: https://www.csi.cuny.edu/sites/default/files/pdf/admissions/grad/pdf/Business%20Management%20Fact%20Sheet.pdf

Davenport University, Sneden Graduate School, Grand Rapids, MI 49512. Offers accounting (MBA); business administration (EMBA); finance (MBA); health care management (MBA); human resources (MBA); information assurance (MS); occupational therapy (MSOT); public health (MPH); strategic management (MBA). *Program availability:* Evening/weekend. *Entrance requirements:* For master's, GMAT, minimum undergraduate GPA of 2.75. Additional exam requirements/recommendations for international students: Required—TOEFL. Electronic applications accepted. *Faculty research:* Leadership, management, marketing, organizational culture.

Defiance College, Program in Business Administration, Defiance, OH 43512-1610. Offers leadership (MBA). *Program availability:* Part-time, evening/weekend. *Degree requirements:* For master's, thesis. *Entrance requirements:* For master's, minimum GPA of 2.75. Additional exam requirements/recommendations for international students: Recommended—TOEFL. Electronic applications accepted.

DePaul University, Kellstadt Graduate School of Business, Chicago, IL 60604. Offers accountancy (MBA, MSA); applied economics (MBA); audit and advisory services (MS); business administration (DBA); business analytics (MS); business strategy and decision-making (MBA); computational finance (MS); economics and policy analysis (MS); enterprise risk management (MS); entrepreneurship (MBA, MS); finance (MBA, MS); general business (MBA); hospitality leadership (MBA); hospitality leadership and operational performance (MS); human resources (MS); international business (MBA); management (MBA, MS); management information systems (MBA); marketing (MBA, MS); marketing analysis (MS); marketing strategy and planning (MBA); real estate (MS); real estate finance and investment (MBA); strategy, execution and valuation (MBA); supply chain management (MS); sustainable management (MS); taxation (MS); JD/MBA. *Accreditation:* AACSB. *Program availability:* Part-time, evening/weekend, online learning. *Entrance requirements:* For master's, GMAT/GRE, 2 letters of recommendation, resume, essay, official transcripts. Additional exam requirements/recommendations for international students: Required—TOEFL (minimum score 550 paper-based; 80 iBT). Electronic applications accepted. *Expenses:* Contact institution.

Drexel University, LeBow College of Business, Program in Business Administration, Philadelphia, PA 19104-2875. Offers business administration (MBA, PhD, APC), including accounting (MBA, PhD), decision sciences (PhD), economics (MBA, PhD), finance (MBA, PhD), legal studies (MBA), management (MBA), marketing (MBA, PhD), organizational sciences (PhD), quantitative methods (MBA), strategic management (PhD). *Accreditation:* AACSB. *Program availability:* Part-time, evening/weekend, online learning. Terminal master's awarded for partial completion of doctoral program. *Entrance requirements:* For master's, GMAT, minimum GPA of 2.75; for doctorate, GMAT. Additional exam requirements/recommendations for international students: Required—TOEFL. Electronic applications accepted. *Faculty research:* Decision support systems, individual and group behavior, operations research, techniques and strategy.

Duke University, The Fuqua School of Business, The Duke MBA-Daytime Program, Durham, NC 27708. Offers academic excellence in finance (Certificate); business administration (MBA); decision sciences (MBA); energy and environment (MBA); energy finance (MBA); entrepreneurship and innovation (MBA); finance (MBA); financial analysis (MBA); health sector management (Certificate); leadership and ethics (MBA); management (MBA); management science and technology management (Certificate); marketing (MBA); operations management (MBA); social entrepreneurship (MBA); strategy (MBA). *Faculty:* 100 full-time (21 women), 55 part-time/adjunct (12 women). *Students:* 875 full-time (335 women); includes 188 minority (44 Black or African American, non-Hispanic/Latino; 4 American Indian or Alaska Native, non-Hispanic/Latino; 90 Asian, non-Hispanic/Latino; 43 Hispanic/Latino; 1 Native Hawaiian or other Pacific Islander, non-Hispanic/Latino; 6 Two or more races, non-Hispanic/Latino), 276 international. Average age 29. In 2018, 429 master's awarded. *Entrance requirements:* For master's, GMAT or GRE, transcripts, essays, resume, recommendation letters, interview. *Application deadline:* For fall admission, 9/19 for domestic and international students; for winter admission, 10/14 for domestic and international students; for spring admission, 1/6 for domestic and international students; for summer admission, 3/11 for domestic and international students. Application fee: $225. Electronic applications accepted. *Expenses:* Contact institution. *Financial support:* Scholarships/grants available. Financial award applicants required to submit FAFSA. *Unit head:* Steve Misuraca, Assistant Dean, Daytime MBA Program. *Application contact:* Shari Hubert, Associate Dean, Office of Admissions, 919-660-7705, Fax: 919-681-8026, E-mail: admissions-info@fuqua.duke.edu.
Website: https://www.fuqua.duke.edu/programs/daytime-mba

Duke University, The Fuqua School of Business, The Duke MBA-Global Executive Program, Durham, NC 27708. Offers business administration (MBA); energy and environment (MBA); entrepreneurship and innovation (MBA); finance (MBA); health sector management (Certificate); marketing (MBA); strategy (MBA). *Faculty:* 100 full-time (21 women), 55 part-time/adjunct (12 women). *Students:* 141 full-time (43 women); includes 43 minority (12 Black or African American, non-Hispanic/Latino; 25 Asian, non-Hispanic/Latino; 4 Hispanic/Latino; 1 Native Hawaiian or other Pacific Islander, non-Hispanic/Latino; 1 Two or more races, non-Hispanic/Latino), 34 international. Average age 35. In 2018, 159 master's awarded. *Entrance requirements:* For master's, Executive Assessment, GMAT, or GRE, or waived, transcripts, essays, resume, recommendation letters, letter of company support, interview. *Application deadline:* For fall admission, 10/16 priority date for domestic and international students; for winter admission, 12/4 priority date for domestic and international students; for spring admission, 3/11 priority date for domestic and international students; for summer admission, 5/27 for domestic and international students. Applications are processed on a rolling basis. Application fee: $225. Electronic applications accepted. *Expenses:* Contact institution. *Financial support:* Scholarships/grants available. Financial award applicants required to submit FAFSA. *Unit head:* Karen Courtney, Associate Dean, Executive Programs. *Application contact:* Shari Hubert, Associate Dean, Office of Admissions, 919-660-7705, Fax: 919-681-8026, E-mail: admissions-info@fuqua.duke.edu.
Website: https://www.fuqua.duke.edu/programs/global-executive-mba

Duke University, The Fuqua School of Business, The Duke MBA-Weekend Executive Program, Durham, NC 27708. Offers business administration (MBA); energy and environment (MBA); entrepreneurship and innovation (MBA); finance (MBA); health sector management (Certificate); marketing (MBA); strategy (MBA). *Faculty:* 100 full-time (21 women), 55 part-time/adjunct (12 women). *Students:* 251 full-time (67 women); includes 79 minority (13 Black or African American, non-Hispanic/Latino; 2 American Indian or Alaska Native, non-Hispanic/Latino; 46 Asian, non-Hispanic/Latino; 12 Hispanic/Latino; 1 Native Hawaiian or other Pacific Islander, non-Hispanic/Latino; 5 Two or more races, non-Hispanic/Latino), 32 international. Average age 35. In 2018, 120 master's awarded. *Entrance requirements:* For master's, Executive Assessment, GMAT, or GRE, or waived, transcripts, essays, resume, recommendation letters, letter of company support, interview. *Application deadline:* For fall admission, 9/18 priority date for domestic and international students; for winter admission, 12/4 priority date for domestic and international students; for spring admission, 1/22 priority date for domestic and international students; for summer admission, 3/11 for domestic and international students. Applications are processed on a rolling basis. Application fee: $225. Electronic applications accepted. *Expenses:* Contact institution. *Financial support:* Scholarships/grants available. Financial award applicants required to submit FAFSA. *Unit head:* Karen Courtney, Associate Dean, Executive Programs. *Application contact:* Shari Hubert, Associate Dean, Office of Admissions, 919-660-7705, Fax: 919-681-8026, E-mail: admissions-info@fuqua.duke.edu.
Website: https://www.fuqua.duke.edu/programs/weekend-executive-mba

Duke University, The Fuqua School of Business, Master of Quantitative Management Program: Business Analytics, Durham, NC 27708. Offers finance (MQM); forensics (MQM); marketing (MQM); strategy (MQM). *Faculty:* 100 full-time (21 women), 55 part-time/adjunct (12 women). *Students:* 136 full-time (56 women); includes 15 minority (1 Black or African American, non-Hispanic/Latino; 14 Asian, non-Hispanic/Latino), 99 international. Average age 23. In 2018, 136 master's awarded. *Entrance requirements:* For master's, GMAT/GRE, transcripts, essays, resume, recommendation letter, interview. *Application deadline:* For fall admission, 10/21 for domestic and international students; for winter admission, 1/15 for domestic and international students; for spring admission, 2/27 for domestic and international students; for summer admission, 4/6 for domestic and international students. Application fee: $125. Electronic applications accepted. *Expenses:* Contact institution. *Financial support:* Scholarships/grants available. Financial award applicants required to submit FAFSA. *Unit head:* Jeremy Petranka, Associate Dean, 919-660-7778. *Application contact:* Shari Hubert, Associate Dean, Office of Admissions, 919-660-7705, Fax: 919-681-8026, E-mail: mqmbusinessanalytics@fuqua.duke.edu.
Website: https://www.fuqua.duke.edu/programs/mqm-business-analytics

Duke University, The Fuqua School of Business, PhD Program, Durham, NC 27708. Offers accounting (PhD); decision sciences (PhD); finance (PhD); management and organizations (PhD); marketing (PhD); operations management (PhD); strategy (PhD). *Faculty:* 100 full-time (21 women). *Students:* 84 full-time (29 women); includes 4 minority (2 Asian, non-Hispanic/Latino; 2 Hispanic/Latino), 53 international. Average age 28. In 2018, 14 doctorates awarded. *Degree requirements:* For doctorate, comprehensive exam (for some programs), thesis/dissertation, Comprehensive or Qualifying exams are required for some of the 7 areas in Business Administration. *Entrance requirements:* For doctorate, GMAT or GRE, transcripts, essays, recommendation letters, statement of purpose. Additional exam requirements/recommendations for international students: Required—TOEFL, IELTS. *Application deadline:* For fall admission, 12/31 priority date for domestic and international students. Application fee: $90. Electronic applications accepted. *Expenses:* Contact institution. *Financial support:* In 2018–19, 74 fellowships with full tuition reimbursements (averaging $33,300 per year) were awarded; research assistantships with full tuition reimbursements, teaching assistantships, institutionally sponsored loans, scholarships/grants, health care benefits, and tuition waivers (full) also available. *Unit head:* William Boulding, Dean, 919-660-7822. *Application contact:* Ravi Bansal, Director of Graduate Studies, 919-660-7753, Fax: 919-660-7971, E-mail: fuqua-phd-info@duke.edu.

East Tennessee State University, School of Graduate Studies, School of Continuing Studies and Academic Outreach, Johnson City, TN 37614. Offers archival studies (Postbaccalaureate Certificate); liberal studies (MALS); reinforcing education through artistic learning (Postbaccalaureate Certificate); strategic leadership (MPS); training and development (MPS). *Program availability:* Part-time, online learning. *Degree requirements:* For master's, comprehensive exam, thesis (for some programs), professional project. *Entrance requirements:* For master's, GRE General Test, minimum GPA of 2.75, professional portfolio, three letters of recommendation, interview, writing sample; for Postbaccalaureate Certificate, minimum GPA of 2.5, three letters of recommendation, interview. Additional exam requirements/recommendations for international students: Required—TOEFL (minimum score 550 paper-based; 79 iBT). Electronic applications accepted. *Faculty research:* Appalachian studies, women's and gender studies, interdisciplinary theory, regional and Southern cultures.

Fisher College, Master of Business Administration Program, Boston, MA 02116-1500. Offers strategic leadership (MBA). *Program availability:* Part-time, evening/weekend, online only, 100% online. *Degree requirements:* For master's, comprehensive exam. *Entrance requirements:* Additional exam requirements/recommendations for international students: Required—TOEFL (minimum score 80 iBT), IELTS (minimum score 6.5). Electronic applications accepted. *Faculty research:* Humanistic management, the role of human resources in employee engagement.

Florida State University, The Graduate School, College of Business, Tallahassee, FL 32306-1110. Offers accounting (M Acc), including assurance and advisory services, generalist, taxation; business administration (MBA, PhD), including accounting (PhD), finance (PhD), management information systems (PhD), marketing (PhD), organizational behavior and human resources (PhD), risk management and insurance (PhD), strategy (PhD); finance (MS); management information systems (MS); risk management and insurance (MS); JD/MBA; MSW/MBA. *Accreditation:* AACSB. *Program availability:* Part-time, 100% online. *Students:* Average age 31. 300 applicants, 61% accepted, 133 enrolled. In 2018, 268 master's, 9 doctorates awarded. Terminal master's awarded for partial completion of doctoral program. *Degree requirements:* For doctorate, comprehensive exam, thesis/dissertation. *Entrance requirements:* For master's, GMAT, GRE (for all except MS in finance), work experience (MBA, MS); minimum GPA of 3.0, letters of recommendation; for doctorate, GMAT, GRE (for marketing, organizational behavior, risk management and insurance, management information systems, and human resources only), minimum graduate GPA of 3.5, letters of recommendation. Additional exam requirements/recommendations for international students: Required—TOEFL (minimum score 600 paper-based; 85 iBT); Recommended—IELTS (minimum score 6). *Application deadline:* For fall admission, 6/1 for domestic and international students; for spring admission, 10/1 for domestic and international students; for summer admission, 3/1 for domestic and international students. Applications are processed on a rolling basis. Application fee: $30. Electronic applications accepted. *Expenses:* Contact institution. *Financial support:* In 2018–19, 146 students received support, including 26 fellowships (averaging $1,500 per year), 77 research assistantships with full tuition reimbursements available (averaging $20,000 per year), 43 teaching assistantships with full tuition reimbursements available (averaging $20,000 per year); career-related internships or fieldwork, scholarships/grants, health care benefits, tuition waivers (full and partial), and unspecified assistantships also available. Support available to part-time students. Financial award application deadline: 1/1; financial award applicants required to submit FAFSA. *Faculty research:* Business strategy, marketing, finance, accounting, business analytics. *Total annual research expenditures:* $1.4 million. *Unit head:* Dr. Michael Hartline, Dean, 850-644-4405, Fax: 850-644-0915, E-mail: mhartline@business.fsu.edu. *Application contact:* Jennifer Clark, Director, 850-644-6458, E-mail: gradprograms@business.fsu.edu.
Website: http://business.fsu.edu/

Freed-Hardeman University, Program in Business Administration, Henderson, TN 38340-2399. Offers accounting (MBA); corporate responsibility (MBA); leadership (MBA). *Accreditation:* ACBSP. *Program availability:* Part-time, evening/weekend, online learning. *Entrance requirements:* For master's, GMAT. Additional exam requirements/recommendations for international students: Required—TOEFL (minimum score 500 paper-based).

Friends University, Graduate School, Wichita, KS 67213. Offers family therapy (MSFT); global business administration (MBA), including accounting, business law, change management, health care leadership, management information systems, supply chain management and logistics; health care leadership (MHCL); management information systems (MMIS); professional business administration (MBA), including accounting, business law, change management, health care leadership, management information systems, supply chain management and logistics. *Program availability:* Part-time, evening/weekend, online learning. *Degree requirements:* For master's, research project. *Entrance requirements:* For master's, bachelor's degree from accredited institution, official transcripts, interview with program director, letter(s) of recommendation. Additional exam requirements/recommendations for international students: Required—TOEFL (minimum score 560 paper-based). Electronic applications accepted.

The George Washington University, School of Business, Department of Decision Sciences, Washington, DC 20052. Offers business analytics (MS, Certificate); project management (MS). *Program availability:* Online learning. *Students:* 109 full-time (62 women), 132 part-time (71 women); includes 54 minority (25 Black or African American, non-Hispanic/Latino; 1 American Indian or Alaska Native, non-Hispanic/Latino; 16 Asian, non-Hispanic/Latino; 10 Hispanic/Latino; 2 Two or more races, non-Hispanic/Latino), 137 international. Average age 31. 1,081 applicants, 44% accepted, 108 enrolled. In 2018, 89 master's, 60 other advanced degrees awarded. Application fee: $75. *Financial support:* Tuition waivers available. *Unit head:* Prof. Refik Soyer, Chair, 202-994-6445, E-mail: soyer@gwu.edu. *Application contact:* Christopher Storer, Executive Director, Graduate Admissions, 202-994-1212, E-mail: gwmba@gwu.edu.
Website: http://business.gwu.edu/decisionsciences/

The George Washington University, School of Business, Department of Strategic Management and Public Policy, Washington, DC 20052. Offers MBA, PhD. *Accreditation:* NASPAA. *Program availability:* Part-time, evening/weekend. *Students:* 129 full-time (53 women); includes 26 minority (8 Black or African American, non-Hispanic/Latino; 6 Asian, non-Hispanic/Latino; 10 Hispanic/Latino; 2 Two or more races,

non-Hispanic/Latino), 53 international. Average age 29. 292 applicants, 60% accepted, 49 enrolled. In 2018, 89 master's awarded. *Entrance requirements:* For master's, GMAT; for doctorate, GMAT or GRE. Additional exam requirements/recommendations for international students: Required—TOEFL. *Application deadline:* For fall admission, 4/1 priority date for domestic students; for spring admission, 10/1 for domestic students. Applications are processed on a rolling basis. Application fee: $75. *Financial support:* In 2018–19, 1 student received support. Fellowships, teaching assistantships, career-related internships or fieldwork, Federal Work-Study, and institutionally sponsored loans available. Financial award application deadline: 4/1. *Unit head:* Dr. Jennifer Griffin, Chair, 202-994-2536, E-mail: jgriffin@gwu.edu. *Application contact:* Christopher Storer, Executive Director, Graduate Admissions, 202-994-1212, E-mail: gwmba@gwu.edu.
Website: http://business.gwu.edu/smpp/

Georgia State University, J. Mack Robinson College of Business, Department of Managerial Sciences, Atlanta, GA 30302-3083. Offers business analysis (MBA, MS); entrepreneurship (MBA); human resources management (MBA, MS); operations management (MBA, MS); organization behavior/human resource management (PhD); organization management (MBA); organizational change (MS); strategic management (PhD). *Accreditation:* AACSB. *Program availability:* Part-time, evening/weekend. *Faculty:* 11 full-time (2 women), 1 part-time/adjunct (0 women). *Students:* 11 full-time (6 women); includes 5 minority (3 Black or African American, non-Hispanic/Latino; 1 Asian, non-Hispanic/Latino; 1 Two or more races, non-Hispanic/Latino), 3 international. Average age 29. 54 applicants, 20% accepted, 8 enrolled. In 2018, 9 master's, 3 doctorates awarded. *Entrance requirements:* For master's, GRE or GMAT, transcripts from all institutions attended, resume, essays; for doctorate, GMAT, three letters of recommendation, personal statement, transcripts from all institutions attended, resume. Additional exam requirements/recommendations for international students: Required—TOEFL (minimum score 610 paper-based; 101 iBT), IELTS (minimum score 7). *Application deadline:* For fall admission, 5/1 priority date for domestic students, 2/1 priority date for international students; for spring admission, 9/15 priority date for domestic students, 4/1 priority date for international students. Applications are processed on a rolling basis. Application fee: $50. Electronic applications accepted. *Expenses: Tuition, area resident:* Full-time $9360; part-time $390 per credit hour. Tuition, state resident: full-time $9360; part-time $390 per credit hour. Tuition, nonresident: full-time $30,024; part-time $1251 per credit hour. *International tuition:* $30,024 full-time. *Required fees:* $2128. *Financial support:* Research assistantships, teaching assistantships, scholarships/grants, tuition waivers, and unspecified assistantships available. Financial award applicants required to submit FAFSA. *Faculty research:* Entrepreneurship and innovation; strategy process; workplace interactions, relationships, and processes; leadership and culture; supply chain management. *Unit head:* Dr. Pamela S. Barr, Chair, 404-413-7525, Fax: 404-413-7571. *Application contact:* Toby McChesney, Assistant Dean for Graduate Recruiting and Student Services, 404-413-7167, Fax: 404-413-7162, E-mail: rcbgradadmissions@gsu.edu.
Website: http://mgmt.robinson.gsu.edu/

Grantham University, Mark Skousen School of Business, Lenexa, KS 66219. Offers business administration (MBA); business intelligence (MS); human resources (Certificate); information management (MBA); performance improvement (MS); project management (MBA, Certificate). *Program availability:* Part-time, evening/weekend, online only, 100% online. *Students:* 556 full-time (238 women), 301 part-time (122 women); includes 369 minority (268 Black or African American, non-Hispanic/Latino; 5 American Indian or Alaska Native, non-Hispanic/Latino; 16 Asian, non-Hispanic/Latino; 50 Hispanic/Latino; 4 Native Hawaiian or other Pacific Islander, non-Hispanic/Latino; 26 Two or more races, non-Hispanic/Latino), 1 international. Average age 40. 206 applicants, 90% accepted, 159 enrolled. In 2018, 284 master's, 16 other advanced degrees awarded. *Degree requirements:* For master's, comprehensive exam (for some programs), PMP Prep Exams throughout the term (for MBA in project management); for Certificate, comprehensive exam (for some programs), PMP Prep Exam (for project management). *Entrance requirements:* For master's, baccalaureate or master's degree with minimum cumulative GPA of 2.5 from institution accredited by agency recognized by ED or foreign equivalent; official transcripts showing proof of degree. Additional exam requirements/recommendations for international students: Required—TOEFL (minimum score 530 paper-based; 71 iBT), IELTS (minimum score 6.5), PTE (minimum score 50). *Application deadline:* Applications are processed on a rolling basis. Application fee: $0. Electronic applications accepted. *Expenses: Tuition:* Full-time $4200; part-time $350 per credit hour. *Required fees:* $50; $50 per credit hour. *Financial support:* Scholarships/grants available. Financial award applicants required to submit FAFSA. *Faculty research:* How chronic diseases contribute to the rising costs of healthcare, marketing for entrepreneurs, managers' hiring practices of workers with disability, organizational structures, organizational change, online pedagogy, impact of instructor video tips in the online classroom, decision-making techniques. *Unit head:* Dr. David Marker, Dean of the Mark Skousen School of Business, 913-309-4747, Fax: 844-260-6287, E-mail: dmarker@grantham.edu. *Application contact:* Lauren Cook, Director of Admissions, 800-955-2527 Ext. 803, Fax: 877-304-4467, E-mail: admissions@grantham.edu.
Website: https://www.grantham.edu/school-of-business/

Gwynedd Mercy University, School of Graduate and Professional Studies, Gwynedd Valley, PA 19437-0901. Offers health care administration (MBA); management (MSM); strategic management and leadership (MBA). *Program availability:* Part-time, evening/weekend. *Degree requirements:* For master's, thesis. *Entrance requirements:* For master's, minimum GPA of 3.0. *Expenses:* Contact institution.

Harrisburg University of Science and Technology, Program in Information Systems Engineering and Management, Harrisburg, PA 17101. Offers analytics (MS); digital government (MS); digital health (MS); entrepreneurship (MS); information security (MS); software engineering and systems development (MS). *Program availability:* Part-time, evening/weekend. *Degree requirements:* For master's, thesis optional. *Entrance requirements:* For master's, baccalaureate degree. Additional exam requirements/recommendations for international students: Required—TOEFL (minimum score 520 paper-based; 80 iBT); Recommended—IELTS (minimum score 6). Electronic applications accepted. *Faculty research:* Healthcare Informatics, material analysis, enterprise systems, circuit design, enterprise architectures.

Harvard University, Harvard Business School, Doctoral Programs in Management, Boston, MA 02163. Offers accounting and management (DBA); business economics (PhD); health policy management (PhD); management (DBA); marketing (DBA); organizational behavior (PhD); science, technology and management (PhD); strategy (DBA); technology and operations management (DBA). *Degree requirements:* For doctorate, comprehensive exam (for some programs), thesis/dissertation. *Entrance requirements:* For doctorate, GRE General Test or GMAT. Additional exam requirements/recommendations for international students: Required—TOEFL.

HEC Montreal, School of Business Administration, Master of Science Programs in Administration, Program in Business Intelligence, Montréal, QC H3T 2A7, Canada. Offers M Sc. All courses are given in French (Thesis stream, Supervised project stream). *Students:* 89 full-time (31 women), 38 part-time (15 women). 53 applicants, 85% accepted, 37 enrolled. In 2018, 36 master's awarded. *Degree requirements:* For master's, thesis. *Entrance requirements:* For master's, BBA, undergraduate degree in another field, degree deemed equivalent by program director and minimum GPA of 3.0 on 4.3 scale. Additional exam requirements/recommendations for international students: Required—TAGE MAGE (minimum recommended score of 300), GMAT (minimum recommended score of 630), or GRE. *Application deadline:* For fall admission, 3/15 for domestic and international students; for winter admission, 9/15 for domestic and international students. Application fee: $91 Canadian dollars ($191 Canadian dollars for international students). Electronic applications accepted. *Expenses: Tuition, area resident:* Full-time $3052.80 Canadian dollars; part-time $84.80 Canadian dollars per credit. Tuition, state resident: full-time $3816 Canadian dollars; part-time $264.67 Canadian dollars per credit. Tuition, nonresident: full-time $11,910 Canadian dollars. *International tuition:* $20,905.20 Canadian dollars full-time. *Required fees:* $1805.34 Canadian dollars; $43.62 Canadian dollars per credit. $71.78 Canadian dollars per term. Tuition and fees vary according to degree level and program. *Financial support:* Research assistantships, teaching assistantships, and scholarships/grants available. Financial award application deadline: 9/2. *Unit head:* Dr. Sihem Taboubi, Director, 514-340-6428, E-mail: sihem.taboubi@hec.ca. *Application contact:* Marianne de Moura, Administrative Director, 514-340-6000, Fax: 514-340-6411, E-mail: aide@hec.ca.
Website: http://www.hec.ca/programmes/maitrises/maitrise-intelligence-affaires/index.html

HEC Montreal, School of Business Administration, Master of Science Programs in Administration, Program in Strategy, Montréal, QC H3T 2A7, Canada. Offers M Sc. Program offered in French (Thesis Stream, Supervised project Stream). *Students:* 81 full-time (32 women), 14 part-time (8 women). 55 applicants, 60% accepted, 24 enrolled. In 2018, 38 master's awarded. *Entrance requirements:* For master's, BBA, undergraduate degree in another field, degree deemed equivalent by program director and minimum GPA of 3.0 on 4.3 scale. Additional exam requirements/recommendations for international students: Required—TAGE MAGE (minimum recommended score of 300), GMAT (minimum recommended score of 630), or GRE. *Application deadline:* For fall admission, 3/15 for domestic and international students; for winter admission, 9/15 for domestic and international students. Application fee: $91 Canadian dollars ($191 Canadian dollars for international students). Electronic applications accepted. *Expenses: Tuition, area resident:* Full-time $3052.80 Canadian dollars; part-time $84.80 Canadian dollars per credit. Tuition, state resident: full-time $3816 Canadian dollars; part-time $264.67 Canadian dollars per credit. Tuition, nonresident: full-time $11,910 Canadian dollars. *International tuition:* $20,905.20 Canadian dollars full-time. *Required fees:* $1805.34 Canadian dollars; $43.62 Canadian dollars per credit. $71.78 Canadian dollars per term. Tuition and fees vary according to degree level and program. *Financial support:* Research assistantships, teaching assistantships, and scholarships/grants available. Financial award application deadline: 9/2. *Unit head:* Dr. Sihem Taboubi, Director, 514-340-6428, E-mail: sihem.taboubi@hec.ca. *Application contact:* Marianne de Moura, Administrative Director, 514-340-6000, Fax: 514-340-6411, E-mail: aide@hec.ca.
Website: http://www.hec.ca/programmes/maitrises/maitrise-strategie/index.html

Hofstra University, Frank G. Zarb School of Business, Programs in Information Systems, Hempstead, NY 11549. Offers business administration (MBA), including business analytics, information systems, quality management; business analytics (MS); information systems (MS, Advanced Certificate). *Program availability:* Part-time, evening/weekend, blended/hybrid learning. *Students:* 85 full-time (35 women), 31 part-time (16 women); includes 17 minority (2 Black or African American, non-Hispanic/Latino; 9 Asian, non-Hispanic/Latino; 6 Hispanic/Latino), 76 international. Average age 27. 152 applicants, 69% accepted, 27 enrolled. In 2018, 52 master's awarded. *Degree requirements:* For master's, thesis (for some programs), capstone course (for MBA), thesis (for MS), minimum GPA of 3.0. *Entrance requirements:* For master's, GMAT/GRE, 2 letters of recommendation, resume, essay; for Advanced Certificate, GMAT/GRE, 2 letters of recommendation, resume. Additional exam requirements/recommendations for international students: Required—TOEFL (minimum score 550 paper-based; 80 iBT); Recommended—IELTS (minimum score 6). *Application deadline:* Applications are processed on a rolling basis. Application fee: $75. Electronic applications accepted. *Expenses:* $1,375 per credit plus fees. *Financial support:* In 2018–19, 32 students received support, including 27 fellowships with full and partial tuition reimbursements available (averaging $5,630 per year); research assistantships with full and partial tuition reimbursements available, career-related internships or fieldwork, Federal Work-Study, institutionally sponsored loans, scholarships/grants, tuition waivers (full and partial), unspecified assistantships, and scholarships and endowed scholarships also available. Support available to part-time students. Financial award applicants required to submit FAFSA. *Faculty research:* Big data and social media, healthcare IT and analytics, machine learning and artificial intelligence, inventory system and quality management, cybersecurity and information privacy. *Unit head:* Dr. Hak Kim, Chairperson, 516-463-5716, Fax: 516-463-4834, E-mail: hak.j.kim@hofstra.edu. *Application contact:* Sunil Samuel, Assistant Vice President of Admissions, 516-463-4723, Fax: 516-463-4664, E-mail: graduateadmission@hofstra.edu.
Website: http://www.hofstra.edu/business/

Hofstra University, Frank G. Zarb School of Business, Programs in Management and General Business, Hempstead, NY 11549. Offers business administration (MBA), including health services management, management, sports and entertainment management, strategic business management, strategic healthcare management; general management (Advanced Certificate); human resource management (MS, Advanced Certificate). *Program availability:* Part-time, evening/weekend, blended/hybrid learning. *Students:* 121 full-time (48 women), 112 part-time (52 women); includes 96 minority (18 Black or African American, non-Hispanic/Latino; 1 American Indian or Alaska Native, non-Hispanic/Latino; 34 Asian, non-Hispanic/Latino; 38 Hispanic/Latino; 5 Two or more races, non-Hispanic/Latino), 16 international. Average age 33. 290 applicants, 75% accepted, 89 enrolled. In 2018, 110 master's awarded. *Degree requirements:* For master's, thesis optional, capstone course (for MBA), thesis (for MS), minimum GPA of 3.0. *Entrance requirements:* For master's, GMAT/GRE, 2 letters of recommendation, resume, essay. Additional exam requirements/recommendations for international students: Required—TOEFL (minimum score 550 paper-based; 80 iBT); Recommended—IELTS (minimum score 6). *Application deadline:* Applications are processed on a rolling basis. Application fee: $75. Electronic applications accepted. *Expenses:* $1,375 per credit plus fees. *Financial support:* In 2018–19, 91 students received support, including 84 fellowships with full and partial tuition reimbursements available (averaging $4,279 per year), 1 research assistantship with full and partial tuition reimbursement available (averaging $9,179 per year); career-related internships or fieldwork, Federal Work-Study, institutionally sponsored loans, scholarships/grants, tuition waivers (full and partial), unspecified assistantships, and scholarships and endowed scholarships also available. Support available to part-time students. Financial award applicants required to submit FAFSA. *Faculty research:* Organizational behavior; sustainability; entrepreneurial spawning; family business; global supply chain strategies. *Unit head:* Dr. Kaushik Sengupta, Chairperson, 516-463-7825, Fax: 516-463-4834, E-mail: kaushik.sengupta@hofstra.edu. *Application contact:* Sunil Samuel, Assistant Vice President of Admissions, 516-463-4723, Fax: 516-463-4664, E-mail: graduateadmission@hofstra.edu.
Website: http://www.hofstra.edu/business/

James Madison University, The Graduate School, College of Business, Program in Strategic Leadership, Harrisonburg, VA 22807. Offers postsecondary analysis and

leadership (PhD), including nonprofit and community leadership, organizational science and leadership, postsecondary analysis and leadership. *Program availability:* Part-time, evening/weekend, online learning. *Students:* 13 full-time (6 women), 32 part-time (13 women); includes 5 minority (2 Black or African American, non-Hispanic/Latino; 1 Asian, non-Hispanic/Latino; 2 Hispanic/Latino), 4 international. Average age 30. In 2018, 7 doctorates awarded. Application fee: $60. Electronic applications accepted. *Expenses:* Tuition, state resident: full-time $10,848. Tuition, nonresident: full-time $27,888. *Required fees:* $1128. *Financial support:* In 2018–19, 9 students received support. Fellowships, career-related internships or fieldwork, Federal Work-Study, unspecified assistantships, and doctoral assistantships (stipend varies) available. Financial award application deadline: 3/1; financial award applicants required to submit FAFSA. *Unit head:* Dr. Karen A. Ford, Director of Strategic Leadership Studies, 540-568-7020, Fax: 540-568-7117, E-mail: fordka@jmu.edu. *Application contact:* Lynette D. Michael, Director of Graduate Admissions, 540-568-6131 Ext. 6395, Fax: 540-568-7860, E-mail: michaeld@jmu.edu.
Website: http://www.jmu.edu/leadership/

John F. Kennedy University, College of Business and Professional Studies, Program in Business Administration, Pleasant Hill, CA 94523-4817. Offers business administration (MBA); finance (MBA); health care (MBA); human resources (MBA); information technology (MBA); management (MBA); sales management (MBA); strategic management (MBA). *Program availability:* Part-time, evening/weekend, online learning. *Degree requirements:* For master's, thesis or alternative. *Entrance requirements:* For master's, interview. Additional exam requirements/recommendations for international students: Required—TOEFL.

Lawrence Technological University, College of Management, Southfield, MI 48075-1058. Offers business administration (MBA, DBA), including business analytics (MBA, MS), cybersecurity (MBA, MS), finance (MBA), information systems (MBA), information technology (MBA), marketing (MBA), project management (MBA, MS); cybersecurity (Graduate Certificate); health IT management (Graduate Certificate); information assurance management (Graduate Certificate); information systems (MS), including enterprise resource planning, enterprise security management, project management (MBA, MS); information technology (MS, DM), including business analytics (MBA, MS), cybersecurity (MBA, MS), information assurance (MS), project management (MBA, MS); management (PhD); nonprofit management and leadership (Graduate Certificate); operations management (MS), including manufacturing operations, service operations; project management (Graduate Certificate). *Accreditation:* ACBSP. *Program availability:* Part-time, evening/weekend, 100% online. Terminal master's awarded for partial completion of doctoral program. *Degree requirements:* For master's, thesis (for some programs); for doctorate, comprehensive exam, thesis/dissertation. *Entrance requirements:* Additional exam requirements/recommendations for international students: Required—TOEFL (minimum score 550 paper-based; 79 iBT), IELTS (minimum score 6.5). Electronic applications accepted. *Faculty research:* Cybersecurity; risk management; IT governance; security controls and countermeasures; threat modeling cyber resilience; autonomous cars; natural language processing; text mining; machine learning; reflective leadership; emerging leadership theories and practice; motivational studies; teaching effectiveness strategies; teamwork; organization development; strategic planning; strengths-based and positive organizational scholarship; global leadership; globalization; corporate governance.

Lenoir-Rhyne University, Graduate Programs, Charles M. Snipes School of Business, Hickory, NC 28601. Offers accounting (MBA); business analytics and information technology (MBA); entrepreneurship (MBA); global business (MBA); healthcare administration (MBA); innovation and change management (MBA); leadership development (MBA). *Accreditation:* ACBSP. *Program availability:* Part-time, evening/weekend, online learning. *Degree requirements:* For master's, capstone course. *Entrance requirements:* For master's, GMAT, GRE, MAT, minimum undergraduate GPA of 2.7, graduate 3.0. Additional exam requirements/recommendations for international students: Required—TOEFL (minimum score 600 paper-based). Electronic applications accepted. *Expenses:* Contact institution.

LeTourneau University, Graduate Programs, Longview, TX 75607-7001. Offers business administration (MBA); counseling (MA); curriculum and instruction (M Ed); educational administration (M Ed); engineering (ME, MS); engineering management (MEM); health care administration (MS); marriage and family therapy (MA); psychology (MA); strategic leadership (MSL); teacher leadership (M Ed); teaching and learning (M Ed). *Program availability:* Part-time, 100% online, blended/hybrid learning. *Students:* 61 full-time (47 women), 311 part-time (248 women); includes 184 minority (117 Black or African American, non-Hispanic/Latino; 3 American Indian or Alaska Native, non-Hispanic/Latino; 1 Asian, non-Hispanic/Latino; 35 Hispanic/Latino; 28 Two or more races, non-Hispanic/Latino), 2 international. Average age 37. In 2018, 97 master's awarded. *Entrance requirements:* Additional exam requirements/recommendations for international students: Required—TOEFL (minimum score 525 paper-based; 80 iBT), IELTS (minimum score 6), Either a TOEFL or IELTS is required for graduate students. One or the other. *Application deadline:* Applications are processed on a rolling basis. Electronic applications accepted. *Financial support:* Research assistantships, teaching assistantships, unspecified assistantships, and employee tuition waivers and institutionally sponsored loans available. Financial award applicants required to submit FAFSA.
Website: http://www.letu.edu

Lipscomb University, Program in Organizational Leadership, Nashville, TN 37204-3951. Offers aging services leadership (Certificate); global leadership (Certificate); organizational leadership (MPS); performance coaching (Certificate); strategic leadership (Certificate). *Program availability:* Part-time, online only, blended/hybrid learning. *Entrance requirements:* For master's, GRE or GMAT, two references, resume, interview. Additional exam requirements/recommendations for international students: Required—TOEFL (minimum score 550 paper-based). Electronic applications accepted. *Expenses:* Contact institution.

McGill University, Faculty of Graduate and Postdoctoral Studies, Desautels Faculty of Management, Montréal, QC H3A 2T5, Canada. Offers administration (PhD); entrepreneurial studies (MBA); finance (MBA); general management (Post Master's Certificate); global manufacturing and supply chain management (MMM); information systems (MBA); international business (MBA); international practicing management (MM); management (MBA); management for development (MBA); marketing (MBA); operations management (MBA); public accountancy (Diploma); strategic management (MBA); MBA/LL B; MD/MBA. MMM offered jointly with Faculty of Engineering; PhD with Concordia University, HEC Montréal, Université de Montréal, Université du Québec à Montréal.

Mercyhurst University, Graduate Studies, Program in Organizational Leadership, Erie, PA 16546. Offers accounting (MS); higher education administration (MS); human resources (MS); organizational leadership (MS, Certificate); sports leadership (MS); strategy and innovation (MS). *Program availability:* Part-time, evening/weekend. *Degree requirements:* For master's, thesis. *Entrance requirements:* For master's, GRE General Test or MAT, interview, resume, essay, three professional references, transcripts. Additional exam requirements/recommendations for international students: Required—TOEFL (minimum score 80 iBT), IELTS (minimum score 6.5). Electronic applications accepted. *Faculty research:* Leadership training, organizational communication, leadership pedagogy.

Messiah College, Program in Business and Leadership, Mechanicsburg, PA 17055. Offers leadership (MBA, Certificate); management (Certificate); strategic leadership (MA). *Program availability:* Online learning.

Michigan State University, The Graduate School, Eli Broad College of Business, Department of Management, East Lansing, MI 48224. Offers management (PhD); management, strategy, and leadership (MS). *Program availability:* Part-time, online learning. *Degree requirements:* For doctorate, comprehensive exam, thesis/dissertation. *Entrance requirements:* For master's, full-time managerial experience in a supervisory role; for doctorate, GMAT or GRE, letters of recommendation, experience in teaching and conducting research, work experience in business contexts, personal essay. Additional exam requirements/recommendations for international students: Required—TOEFL (minimum score 600 paper-based). Electronic applications accepted.

Middle Tennessee State University, College of Graduate Studies, University College, Murfreesboro, TN 37132. Offers advanced studies in teaching and learning (M Ed); human resources leadership (MPS); nursing administration (MSN); nursing education (MSN); strategic leadership (MPS); training and development (MPS). *Program availability:* Part-time, evening/weekend, online learning. *Entrance requirements:* Additional exam requirements/recommendations for international students: Required—TOEFL (minimum score 525 paper-based; 71 iBT) or IELTS (minimum score 6).

Mount Mercy University, Program in Strategic Leadership, Cedar Rapids, IA 52402-4797. Offers MSL. *Program availability:* Evening/weekend.

Neumann University, Program in Organizational and Strategic Leadership, Aston, PA 19014-1298. Offers MS. *Program availability:* Part-time, evening/weekend, 100% online, blended/hybrid learning. *Degree requirements:* For master's, project. *Entrance requirements:* For master's, official transcripts from all institutions attended, current resume, letter of intent, letter of recommendation. Additional exam requirements/recommendations for international students: Required—TOEFL (minimum score 70 iBT). Electronic applications accepted. *Expenses:* Contact institution.

New England College, Program in Management, Henniker, NH 03242-3293. Offers accounting (MSA); healthcare administration (MS); international relations (MA); marketing management (MS); nonprofit leadership (MS); project management (MS); strategic leadership (MS). *Program availability:* Part-time, evening/weekend. *Degree requirements:* For master's, independent research project. Electronic applications accepted.

The New School, Parsons School of Design, Program in Strategic Design and Management, New York, NY 10011. Offers business of design (Advanced Certificate); strategic design and management (MS). *Program availability:* Part-time, 100% online. *Degree requirements:* For master's, thesis or alternative, integrative studio. *Entrance requirements:* For master's, transcripts, resume, statement of purpose, recommendation letters, essay, interview. Additional exam requirements/recommendations for international students: Required—TOEFL (minimum score 92 iBT), IELTS (minimum score 7), PTE (minimum score 63). Electronic applications accepted. *Expenses:* Contact institution.

New York University, Leonard N. Stern School of Business, Department of Management and Organizations, New York, NY 10012-1019. Offers management organizations (MBA); organization theory (PhD); organizational behavior (PhD); strategy (PhD). *Faculty research:* Strategic management, managerial cognition, interpersonal processes, conflict and negotiation.

Niagara University, Graduate Division of Business Administration, Niagara University, NY 14109. Offers accounting (MBA); business administration (MBA); finance (MBA, MS); financial planning (MBA); healthcare administration (MBA, MHA); human resources (MBA); international business (MBA); marketing (MBA); professional accountancy (MBA); strategic management (MBA); supply chain management (MBA). *Accreditation:* AACSB. *Program availability:* Part-time, evening/weekend, 100% online, blended/hybrid learning. *Students:* 224 full-time (116 women), 56 part-time (22 women); includes 36 minority (9 Black or African American, non-Hispanic/Latino; 2 American Indian or Alaska Native, non-Hispanic/Latino; 6 Asian, non-Hispanic/Latino; 12 Hispanic/Latino; 7 Two or more races, non-Hispanic/Latino), 82 international. Average age 26. In 2018, 134 master's awarded. *Entrance requirements:* For master's, GMAT. Additional exam requirements/recommendations for international students: Required—TOEFL (minimum score 550 paper-based; 79 iBT), IELTS (minimum score 6). *Application deadline:* For fall admission, 8/1 for domestic students; for spring admission, 11/1 for domestic students. Applications are processed on a rolling basis. Electronic applications accepted. *Expenses:* Contact institution. *Financial support:* Research assistantships, teaching assistantships, career-related internships or fieldwork, Federal Work-Study, scholarships/grants, and unspecified assistantships available. Support available to part-time students. Financial award application deadline: 4/15; financial award applicants required to submit FAFSA. *Faculty research:* Capital flows, Federal Reserve policy, human resource management, public policy, issues in marketing, auctions, economics of information, risk and capital markets, management strategy, consumer behavior, Internet and social media marketing. *Unit head:* Dr. Paul Richardson, MBA Director/Chair of the Marketing Department, 716-286-8169, Fax: 716-286-8206, E-mail: mba@niagara.edu. *Application contact:* Evan Pierce, Associate Director for Graduate Recruitment, 716-286-8327, Fax: 716-286-8710, E-mail: epierce@niagara.edu.
Website: http://mba.niagara.edu

North Central College, School of Graduate and Professional Studies, Program in Business Administration, Naperville, IL 60566-7063. Offers change management (MBA); finance (MBA); human resource management (MBA); management (MBA). *Program availability:* Part-time, evening/weekend. *Degree requirements:* For master's, thesis optional, project. *Entrance requirements:* For master's, interview. Additional exam requirements/recommendations for international students: Required—TOEFL (minimum score 550 paper-based; 80 iBT), IELTS (minimum score 6.5). Electronic applications accepted. Application fee is waived when completed online. *Expenses:* Contact institution.

Northwestern University, The Graduate School, Kellogg School of Management, Department of Management and Strategy, Evanston, IL 60208. Offers PhD.

Northwestern University, The Graduate School, Kellogg School of Management, Department of Managerial Economics and Decision Sciences, Evanston, IL 60208. Offers PhD. Admissions and degree offered through The Graduate School. *Degree requirements:* For doctorate, comprehensive exam, thesis/dissertation. *Entrance requirements:* For doctorate, GMAT or GRE General Test. Additional exam requirements/recommendations for international students: Required—TOEFL. Electronic applications accepted. *Faculty research:* Competitive strategy and organization, managerial economics, decision sciences, game theory, operations management.

Northwestern University, The Graduate School, Kellogg School of Management, Management Programs, Evanston, IL 60208. Offers accounting information and management (MBA, PhD); analytical finance (MBA); business administration (MBA); decision sciences (MBA); entrepreneurship and innovation (MBA); finance (MBA, PhD);

health enterprise management (MBA); human resources management (MBA); international business (MBA); management and organizations (MBA, PhD); management and organizations and sociology (PhD); management and strategy (MBA); management studies (MS); managerial analytics (MBA); managerial economics (MBA); managerial economics and strategy (PhD); marketing (MBA, PhD); marketing management (MBA); media management (MBA); operations management (MBA, PhD); real estate (MBA); social enterprise at Kellogg (MBA); JD/MBA. *Program availability:* Part-time, evening/weekend. Terminal master's awarded for partial completion of doctoral program. *Degree requirements:* For doctorate, thesis/dissertation, 2 years of coursework, qualifying (field) exam and candidacy, summer research papers and presentations to faculty, proposal defense, final exam/defense. *Entrance requirements:* For master's, GMAT, GRE, interview, 2 letters of recommendation, college transcripts, resume, essays, Kellogg honor code; for doctorate, GMAT, GRE, statement of purpose, transcripts, 2 letters of recommendation, resume, interview. Additional exam requirements/recommendations for international students: Required—TOEFL, IELTS. Electronic applications accepted. *Expenses:* Contact institution. *Faculty research:* Business cycles and international finance, health policy, networks, non-market strategy, consumer psychology.

Northwestern University, School of Professional Studies, Program in Information Systems, Evanston, IL 60208. Offers analytics and business intelligence (MS); database and Internet technologies (MS); information systems (MS); information systems management (MS); information systems security (MS); medical informatics (MS); software project management and development (MS). *Program availability:* Part-time, evening/weekend.

Norwich University, College of Graduate and Continuing Studies, Master of Science in Leadership Program, Northfield, VT 05663. Offers leadership (MS), including human resources leadership, leading change management consulting, organizational leadership, public sector/government/military leadership. *Program availability:* Evening/weekend, online only, mostly all online with a week-long residency requirement. *Degree requirements:* For master's, capstone. *Entrance requirements:* For master's, minimum undergraduate GPA of 2.75. Additional exam requirements/recommendations for international students: Required—TOEFL (minimum score 550 paper-based; 80 iBT), IELTS (minimum score 6.5). Electronic applications accepted. *Expenses:* Contact institution.

Nova Southeastern University, H. Wayne Huizenga College of Business and Entrepreneurship, Fort Lauderdale, FL 33314-7796. Offers accounting (M Acc); business (MBA); business intelligence/analytics (MBA); complex health systems (MBA); enterprise informatics (MBA); entrepreneurship (MBA); finance (MBA); human resource management (MBA); international business (MBA); management (MBA); marketing (MBA); process improvement (MBA); public administration (MPA); real estate development (MS); sport revenue generation (MBA); supply chain management (MBA). *Accreditation:* NASPAA. *Program availability:* Part-time, evening/weekend, 100% online, blended/hybrid learning. *Entrance requirements:* For master's, GMAT or GRE (depending on undergraduate GPA), official transcripts from all schools attended while in pursuit of bachelor's degree; minimum GPA of 2.5 from regionally-accredited institution. Additional exam requirements/recommendations for international students: Required—TOEFL (minimum score 550 paper-based; 79 iBT), IELTS (minimum score 6), PTE (minimum score 54). Electronic applications accepted. *Expenses:* Contact institution. *Faculty research:* Entrepreneurship and venture capital, ethics and social responsibility, global commerce and cultures, business process management.

Oakland City University, School of Business, Oakland City, IN 47660-1099. Offers business administration (MBA); strategic management (MS). *Program availability:* Part-time, evening/weekend. *Degree requirements:* For master's, thesis or alternative. *Entrance requirements:* For master's, GMAT, GRE, or MAT, appropriate bachelor's degree, computer literacy. Additional exam requirements/recommendations for international students: Required—TOEFL. *Faculty research:* Leadership and management styles, international business, new technologies.

Ohio Dominican University, Division of Business, Columbus, OH 43219-2099. Offers business administration (MBA), including accounting, data analytics, finance, leadership, risk management, sport management; healthcare administration (MS); sport management (MS). *Accreditation:* ACBSP. *Program availability:* Part-time, evening/weekend, 100% online, blended/hybrid learning. *Faculty:* 13 full-time (4 women), 17 part-time/adjunct (3 women). *Students:* 60 full-time (24 women), 100 part-time (48 women); includes 38 minority (24 Black or African American, non-Hispanic/Latino; 1 American Indian or Alaska Native, non-Hispanic/Latino; 4 Asian, non-Hispanic/Latino; 5 Hispanic/Latino; 4 Two or more races, non-Hispanic/Latino), 22 international. Average age 30. 141 applicants, 43% accepted, 38 enrolled. In 2018, 70 master's awarded. *Degree requirements:* For master's, thesis or alternative. *Entrance requirements:* Additional exam requirements/recommendations for international students: Required—TOEFL (minimum score 550 paper-based), IELTS (minimum score 6.5). *Application deadline:* For fall admission, 8/15 for domestic students, 6/10 for international students; for spring admission, 1/4 for domestic students, 11/2 for international students. Applications are processed on a rolling basis. Application fee: $25. Electronic applications accepted. *Expenses: Tuition:* Full-time $10,800; part-time $600 per credit hour. *Required fees:* $450; $225 per semester. Tuition and fees vary according to program. *Financial support:* Applicants required to submit FAFSA. *Unit head:* Dr. Kenneth C. Fah, Chair, 614-251-4566, E-mail: fahk@ohiodominican.edu. *Application contact:* John W. Naughton, Vice President for Enrollment & Student Success, 614-251-4721, Fax: 614-251-6654, E-mail: grad@ohiodominican.edu.
Website: http://www.ohiodominican.edu/academics/graduate/mba

Oklahoma Wesleyan University, Professional Studies Division, Bartlesville, OK 74006-6299. Offers nursing administration (MSN); nursing education (MSN); strategic leadership (MS); theology and apologetics (MA).

Pace University, Lubin School of Business, Program in Management, New York, NY 10038. Offers entrepreneurial studies (MBA); entrepreneurship (MS); human resource management (MBA, MS); strategic management (MBA, MS). *Program availability:* Part-time, evening/weekend. *Students:* 63 full-time (38 women), 57 part-time (41 women); includes 41 minority (18 Black or African American, non-Hispanic/Latino; 8 Asian, non-Hispanic/Latino; 11 Hispanic/Latino; 1 Native Hawaiian or other Pacific Islander, non-Hispanic/Latino; 3 Two or more races, non-Hispanic/Latino), 34 international. Average age 30. 125 applicants, 66% accepted, 42 enrolled. In 2018, 55 master's awarded. *Entrance requirements:* For master's, GMAT, GRE (GMAT not required for MS in Human Resources Management with 3 years of HR experience in a management position), undergraduate degree, transcripts from all accredited colleges/universities attended, two letters of recommendation, resume, personal statement. Additional exam requirements/recommendations for international students: Required—TOEFL (minimum score 90 iBT), IELTS (minimum score 7) or PTE (minimum score 61). *Application deadline:* For fall admission, 8/1 priority date for domestic students, 6/1 for international students; for spring admission, 12/1 for domestic students, 10/1 for international students. Applications are processed on a rolling basis. Application fee: $70. Electronic applications accepted. *Financial support:* Research assistantships, career-related internships or fieldwork, Federal Work-Study, and unspecified assistantships available. Support available to part-time students. Financial award application deadline: 2/15; financial award applicants required to submit FAFSA. *Unit head:* Dr. Ibraiz Tarique, Chairperson, Management and Management of Science, 212-618-6583, E-mail: itarique@pace.edu. *Application contact:* Susan Ford-Goldschein, Director of Graduate Admissions, 212-346-1531, Fax: 212-346-1585, E-mail: graduateadmission@pace.edu.
Website: http://www.pace.edu/lubin/sections/explore-programs/graduate-programs

Pontificia Universidad Catolica Madre y Maestra, Graduate School, Faculty of Social and Administrative Sciences, Santiago, Dominican Republic. Offers business administration (MBA), including business development, finance, international business, management skills (M Mgmt, MBA), marketing, operations, strategic cost management, strategy, tourist destination planning and management; law (LL M), including civil law, corporate business law, criminal law, international relations, real estate law; management (M Mgmt), including higher financial management, insurance program administration, management skills (M Mgmt, MBA); psychology (MA), including clinical child and adolescent psychology, forensic psychology; strategic human resources (EMBA).

Queen's University at Kingston, Smith School of Business, Doctoral Program in Management, Kingston, ON K7L 3N6, Canada. Offers analytics (PhD); business economics (PhD); finance (PhD); management information systems (PhD); marketing (PhD); organizational behavior (PhD); strategy (PhD).

Queen's University at Kingston, Smith School of Business, Master of Science in Management Program, Kingston, ON K7L 3N6, Canada. Offers analytics (M Sc); business economics (M Sc); finance (M Sc); management information systems (M Sc); marketing (M Sc); organizational behavior (M Sc); strategy (M Sc).

Regent University, Graduate School, School of Business and Leadership, Virginia Beach, VA 23464-9800. Offers business administration (MBA), including accounting, economics, entrepreneurship, finance and investing, general management, healthcare management (MA, MBA), human resource management (MA, MBA), innovation management, leadership, marketing, not-for-profit management (MA, MBA); business analytics (MS); business and design management (MA); church leadership (MA); leadership (Certificate); organizational leadership (MA, PhD), including ecclesial leadership (DSL, PhD), entrepreneurial leadership (PhD), healthcare management (MA, MBA), human resource development (PhD), human resource management (MA, MBA), individualized studies (DSL, PhD), interdisciplinary studies (MA), leadership coaching and mentoring (MA), not-for-profit management (MA, MBA), organizational development consulting (MA), servant leadership (MA, DSL); strategic leadership (DSL), including ecclesial leadership (DSL, PhD), global consulting, healthcare leadership, individualized studies (DSL, PhD), leadership coaching, servant leadership (MA, DSL), strategic foresight. *Program availability:* Part-time, evening/weekend, 100% online, blended/hybrid learning. *Degree requirements:* For master's, thesis or alternative, 3-credit hour culminating experience; for doctorate, thesis/dissertation. *Entrance requirements:* For master's, college transcripts, resume, essay; for doctorate, college transcripts, resume, essay, writing sample; for Certificate, writing sample, resume, transcripts. Additional exam requirements/recommendations for international students: Required—TOEFL (minimum score 577 paper-based). Electronic applications accepted. *Expenses:* Contact institution. *Faculty research:* Servant leadership, global business, team effectiveness, technology utilization, leadership development.

Regis University, College of Business and Economics, Denver, CO 80221-1099. Offers accounting (MS); executive leadership (Certificate); finance (MS); finance and accounting (MBA); health industry leadership (MBA); human resource management and leadership (MSOL); management (MBA); marketing (MBA); nonprofit leadership (Post-Graduate Certificate); nonprofit management (MNM); nonprofit organizational capacity building (Certificate); operations management (MBA); organizational leadership and management (MSOL); project leadership and management (MS, MSOL); strategic business management (Certificate); strategic human resource integration (Certificate); strategic management (MBA). Programs offered at Colorado Springs Campus, Northwest Denver Campus, Southeast Denver Campus, Fort Collins Campus, Broomfield Campus, Henderson (Nevada) Campus, and Summerlin (Nevada) Campus. *Program availability:* Part-time, evening/weekend, 100% online, blended/hybrid learning. *Degree requirements:* For master's, thesis (for some programs), capstone or final research project. *Entrance requirements:* For master's, official transcript reflecting baccalaureate degree awarded from regionally-accredited college or university, interview, 2 years of full-time related work experience, resume, letters of recommendation. Additional exam requirements/recommendations for international students: Required—TOEFL (minimum score 550 paper-based; 82 iBT). Electronic applications accepted. *Expenses:* Contact institution. *Faculty research:* Impact of information technology on small business regulation of accounting, international project financing, mineral development, delivery of healthcare to rural indigenous communities.

Roberts Wesleyan College, Graduate Business Programs, Rochester, NY 14624-1997. Offers strategic leadership (MS); strategic marketing (MS). *Program availability:* Evening/weekend. *Degree requirements:* For master's, thesis or alternative. *Entrance requirements:* For master's, GMAT, minimum GPA of 2.75, verifiable work experience. *Expenses:* Contact institution.

Rockhurst University, Helzberg School of Management, Kansas City, MO 64110-2561. Offers accounting (MBA); business intelligence (MBA, Certificate); business intelligence and analytics (MS); data science (MBA, Certificate); entrepreneurship (MBA); finance (MBA); fundraising leadership (MBA, Certificate); healthcare management (MBA, Certificate); human capital (Certificate); international business (Certificate); management (MA, MBA, Certificate); nonprofit administration (Certificate); organizational development (Certificate); science leadership (Certificate). *Accreditation:* AACSB. *Program availability:* Part-time, evening/weekend. *Entrance requirements:* For master's, GMAT or GRE. Additional exam requirements/recommendations for international students: Required—TOEFL (minimum score 550 paper-based; 79 iBT). Electronic applications accepted. *Faculty research:* Offshoring/outsourcing, systems analysis/synthesis, work teams, multilateral trade, path dependencies/creation.

St. John's University, The Peter J. Tobin College of Business, Department of Management, Queens, NY 11439. Offers business administration (MBA), including strategic management. *Entrance requirements:* For master's, GMAT or GRE, 2 letters of recommendation, essay, resume, unofficial transcripts. Additional exam requirements/recommendations for international students: Required—TOEFL (minimum score 80 iBT), IELTS (minimum score 6.5). Electronic applications accepted. *Expenses:* Contact institution.

Saint Mary-of-the-Woods College, Master of Leadership Development Program, Saint Mary of the Woods, IN 47876. Offers not-for-profit leadership (MLD); organizational leadership (MLD). *Program availability:* Part-time. *Degree requirements:* For master's, thesis. Electronic applications accepted. *Expenses:* Contact institution.

Salve Regina University, Program in Management, Newport, RI 02840-4192. Offers business studies (CGS); human resource management (CGS); innovation and strategic management (MS); management (CGS); nonprofit management (CGS); social entrepreneurship (CGS). *Program availability:* Part-time, evening/weekend, online learning. *Entrance requirements:* For master's, GMAT, GRE General Test, or MAT. Additional exam requirements/recommendations for international students: Required—TOEFL (minimum score 600 paper-based; 100 iBT). Electronic applications accepted. *Expenses: Tuition:* Full-time $10,530; part-time $585 per credit. *Required fees:* $60 per term. Tuition and fees vary according to course level, course load, degree level and program.

Southeastern University, Jannetides College of Business and Entrepreneurial Leadership, Lakeland, FL 33801-6099. Offers executive leadership (MBA); global business administration (MBA); healthcare administration (MBA); missional leadership (MBA); organizational leadership (PhD); sport management (MBA); strategic leadership (DSL). *Accreditation:* ACBSP. *Program availability:* Evening/weekend, online learning. *Entrance requirements:* For master's, GMAT, minimum cumulative GPA of 3.0, writing sample. Electronic applications accepted.

Southern Methodist University, Cox School of Business, MBA Program, Dallas, TX 75275. Offers accounting (MBA, PMBA); business (EMBA); business analytics (PMBA); finance (MBA, PMBA); information technology and operations management (MBA, PMBA), including business analytics (MBA); information and operations (MBA); management (MBA, PMBA); marketing (MBA, PMBA); real estate (MBA, PMBA); strategy and entrepreneurship (MBA, PMBA); JD/MBA; MA/MBA. *Program availability:* Part-time, evening/weekend. *Entrance requirements:* For master's, GMAT. Additional exam requirements/recommendations for international students: Required—TOEFL. Electronic applications accepted. *Expenses:* Contact institution. *Faculty research:* Corporate finance, financial reporting, modeling consumer decision-making, competition between national brands and store brands, institutional determinants of firms' strategy.

Stevens Institute of Technology, Graduate School, School of Business, Program in Management, Hoboken, NJ 07030. Offers general management (MS); global innovation management (MS); human resource management (MS); information management (MS); project management (MS); technology commercialization (MS); technology management (MS). *Program availability:* Part-time, evening/weekend. *Faculty:* 58 full-time (8 women), 18 part-time/adjunct (3 women). *Students:* 101 full-time (41 women), 66 part-time (34 women); includes 14 minority (4 Black or African American, non-Hispanic/Latino; 9 Asian, non-Hispanic/Latino; 1 Hispanic/Latino), 115 international. Average age 28. In 2018, 70 master's awarded. Terminal master's awarded for partial completion of doctoral program. *Degree requirements:* For master's, thesis optional, minimum B average in major field and overall. *Entrance requirements:* For master's, GRE/GMAT scores: GRE scores are required for all applicants applying to a full-time graduate program in the Schaefer School of Engineering and Science (SES). International applicants must submit TOEFL/IELTS scores and fulfill the English Language Proficiency Requirements in order to be considered. Additional exam requirements/recommendations for international students: Required—TOEFL (minimum score 74 iBT), IELTS (minimum score 6). *Application deadline:* For fall admission, 4/1 for domestic and international students; for spring admission, 11/1 for domestic and international students; for summer admission, 5/1 for domestic students. Applications are processed on a rolling basis. Application fee: $60. Electronic applications accepted. *Expenses: Tuition:* Full-time $35,960; part-time $1620 per credit. *Required fees:* $1290; $600 per semester. Tuition and fees vary according to course load. *Financial support:* Fellowships, research assistantships, teaching assistantships, career-related internships or fieldwork, Federal Work-Study, scholarships/grants, and unspecified assistantships available. Financial award application deadline: 2/15; financial award applicants required to submit FAFSA. *Unit head:* Dr. Gregory Prascatos, Dean of SB, 201-216 8366, E-mail: gprastac@stevens.edu. *Application contact:* Graduate Admissions, 888-783-8367, Fax: 888-511-1306, E-mail: graduate@stevens.edu. Website: https://www.stevens.edu/school-business/masters-programs/management

Stockton University, Office of Graduate Studies, Program in Data Science and Strategic Analytics, Galloway, NJ 08205-9441. Offers MS. *Program availability:* Part-time, online learning. *Faculty:* 6 full-time (2 women), 3 part-time/adjunct (1 woman). *Students:* 23 full-time (9 women), 8 part-time (3 women); includes 6 minority (1 Black or African American, non-Hispanic/Latino; 4 Asian, non-Hispanic/Latino; 1 Two or more races, non-Hispanic/Latino), 2 international. Average age 30. 41 applicants, 76% accepted, 26 enrolled. *Expenses: Tuition, area resident:* Full-time $11,226; part-time $623.69 per credit hour. Tuition, state resident: full-time $11,226; part-time $623.69 per credit hour. Tuition, nonresident: full-time $17,282; part-time $960.10 per credit hour. *International tuition:* $17,282 full-time. *Required fees:* $3376; $187.56 per credit hour. *Unit head:* Dr. J. Russell Manson, Director, 609-652-4354. *Application contact:* Tara Williams, Assistant Director of Graduate Enrollment, 609-626-3640, Fax: 609-626-6050, E-mail: gradschool@stockton.edu. Website: https://stockton.edu/graduate/data-science_strategic-analytics.html

Suffolk University, Sawyer Business School, Master of Business Administration Program, Boston, MA 02108-2770. Offers accounting (MBA); entrepreneurship (MBA); executive business administration (EMBA); finance (MBA); global business administration (GMBA); health administration (MBA); international business (MBA); marketing (MBA); nonprofit management (MBA); organizational behavior (MBA); strategic management (MBA); supply chain management (MBA); taxation (MBA); JD/MBA; MBA/MHA; MBA/MSA; MBA/MSF; MBA/MST. *Accreditation:* AACSB. *Program availability:* Part-time, evening/weekend, 100% online. *Faculty:* 18 full-time (5 women), 5 part-time/adjunct (0 women). *Students:* 79 full-time (46 women), 193 part-time (107 women); includes 69 minority (17 Black or African American, non-Hispanic/Latino; 18 Asian, non-Hispanic/Latino; 28 Hispanic/Latino; 6 Two or more races, non-Hispanic/Latino), 40 international. Average age 30. 274 applicants, 67% accepted, 83 enrolled. In 2018, 125 master's awarded. *Entrance requirements:* For master's, GMAT, minimum undergraduate GPA of 2.75 (MBA), 5 years of managerial experience (EMBA). Additional exam requirements/recommendations for international students: Required—TOEFL (minimum score 550 paper-based; 80 iBT). *Application deadline:* For fall admission, 3/15 priority date for domestic students, 10/15 priority date for international students; for spring admission, 10/15 priority date for domestic and international students. Applications are processed on a rolling basis. Application fee: $50. Electronic applications accepted. *Expenses:* Contact institution. *Financial support:* In 2018–19, 170 students received support, including 4 fellowships (averaging $2,906 per year); career-related internships or fieldwork, Federal Work-Study, institutionally sponsored loans, and scholarships/grants also available. Support available to part-time students. Financial award application deadline: 4/1; financial award applicants required to submit FAFSA. *Faculty research:* Foreign investments; career strategies and boundaryless careers; corporate ethics codes; interest rates, inflation, and growth options; innovation and product development performance. *Unit head:* Jodi Detjen, Director of MBA Programs, 617-573-8306, E-mail: jdetjen@suffolk.edu. *Application contact:* Mara Marzocchi, Associate Director of Graduate Admissions, 617-573-8302, Fax: 617-305-1733, E-mail: grad.admission@suffolk.edu. Website: http://www.suffolk.edu/mba

Temple University, Fox School of Business, Doctoral Programs in Business, Philadelphia, PA 19122-6096. Offers accounting (PhD); entrepreneurship (PhD); finance (PhD); international business (PhD); management information systems (PhD); marketing (PhD); risk management and insurance (PhD); statistics (PhD); strategic management (PhD); tourism and sport (PhD). *Accreditation:* AACSB. *Degree requirements:* For doctorate, thesis/dissertation. *Entrance requirements:* For doctorate, GRE General Test, GMAT, minimum GPA of 3.0, master's degree. Additional exam requirements/recommendations for international students: Required—TOEFL (minimum score 600 paper-based; 100 iBT), IELTS (minimum score 7.5). Electronic applications accepted.

Tennessee State University, The School of Graduate Studies and Research, College of Public Service, Nashville, TN 37209-1561. Offers human resource management (MPS); public administration (MPA, PhD); social work (MSW); strategic leadership (MPS); training and development (MPS). *Accreditation:* NASPAA (one or more programs are accredited). *Program availability:* Part-time, evening/weekend. *Degree requirements:* For master's, comprehensive exam, thesis optional; for doctorate, comprehensive exam, thesis/dissertation. *Entrance requirements:* For master's, GRE General Test, minimum GPA of 2.5, writing sample; for doctorate, GRE General Test, minimum GPA of 3.25, writing sample. *Faculty research:* Total quality management and process improvement, national health care policy and administration, starting non-profit ventures, public service ethics, state education financing across the U.S. public.

Tennessee Technological University, College of Graduate Studies, College of Interdisciplinary Studies, School of Professional Studies, Cookeville, TN 38505. Offers health care administration (MPS); human resources leadership (MPS); public safety (MPS); strategic leadership (MPS); teaching English to speakers of other languages (MPS); training and development (MPS). *Program availability:* Part-time, evening/weekend, online learning. *Students:* 23 full-time (8 women), 80 part-time (48 women); includes 20 minority (13 Black or African American, non-Hispanic/Latino; 3 Hispanic/Latino; 4 Two or more races, non-Hispanic/Latino), 1 international. 49 applicants, 73% accepted, 29 enrolled. In 2018, 33 master's awarded. *Degree requirements:* For master's, comprehensive exam, thesis or alternative. *Entrance requirements:* For master's, GRE. Additional exam requirements/recommendations for international students: Required—TOEFL (minimum score 527 paper-based; 71 iBT), IELTS (minimum score 5.5), PTE (minimum score 48), or TOEIC (Test of English as an International Communication). *Application deadline:* For fall admission, 7/1 for domestic students, 5/1 for international students; for spring admission, 11/1 for domestic students, 10/1 for international students; for summer admission, 5/1 for domestic students, 2/1 for international students. Applications are processed on a rolling basis. Application fee: $35 ($40 for international students). Electronic applications accepted. *Financial support:* Application deadline: 4/1. *Unit head:* Dr. Joseph Roberts, Interim Director, School of Professional Studies, 931-372-6223, E-mail: jmroberts@tntech.edu. *Application contact:* Shelia K. Kendrick, Coordinator of Graduate Studies, 931-372-3808, Fax: 931-372-3497, E-mail: skendrick@tntech.edu. Website: https://www.tntech.edu/is/sps/

Thomas Jefferson University, Kanbar College of Design, Engineering and Commerce, Innovation MBA Program, Philadelphia, PA 19107. Offers business analytics (MBA); general business (MBA); management (MBA); marketing (MBA); strategy and design thinking (MBA); MBA/MS. *Program availability:* Part-time, evening/weekend, online learning. *Entrance requirements:* For master's, GMAT. Additional exam requirements/recommendations for international students: Required—TOEFL (minimum score 550 paper-based; 79 iBT).

Thomas Jefferson University, School of Continuing and Professional Studies, Philadelphia, PA 19107. Offers strategic leadership (D Mgt).

Tufts University, Graduate School of Arts and Sciences, Graduate Certificate Programs, Program Evaluation Program, Medford, MA 02155. Offers Certificate. *Program availability:* Part-time, evening/weekend. Electronic applications accepted. *Expenses:* Contact institution.

Tulane University, A. B. Freeman School of Business, New Orleans, LA 70118-5669. Offers accounting (M Acct); analytics (MBA); banking and financial services (M Fin); energy (M Fin, MBA); entrepreneurship (MBA); finance (MBA, PhD); financial accounting (PhD); international business (MBA); international management (MBA); strategic management and leadership (MBA); JD/M Acct; JD/MBA; MBA/M Acc; MBA/MA; MBA/MD; MBA/ME; MBA/MPH. *Accreditation:* AACSB. *Program availability:* Part-time, evening/weekend. *Faculty:* 43 full-time (11 women), 45 part-time/adjunct (8 women). *Students:* 432 full-time (218 women), 533 part-time (262 women); includes 99 minority (32 Black or African American, non-Hispanic/Latino; 1 American Indian or Alaska Native, non-Hispanic/Latino; 26 Asian, non-Hispanic/Latino; 35 Hispanic/Latino; 5 Two or more races, non-Hispanic/Latino), 644 international. Average age 28. 1,911 applicants, 77% accepted, 411 enrolled. In 2018, 728 master's, 4 doctorates awarded. Terminal master's awarded for partial completion of doctoral program. *Degree requirements:* For master's, one foreign language, comprehensive exam (for some programs); for doctorate, one foreign language, comprehensive exam, thesis/dissertation. *Entrance requirements:* For master's and doctorate, GMAT or GRE, interview. Additional exam requirements/recommendations for international students: Required—TOEFL or IELTS. *Application deadline:* For fall admission, 11/1 priority date for domestic students, 11/1 for international students; for winter admission, 1/6 for domestic and international students; for spring admission, 3/1 priority date for domestic students, 3/1 for international students; for summer admission, 5/5 for domestic students. Applications are processed on a rolling basis. Application fee: $125. Electronic applications accepted. *Expenses:* Contact institution. *Financial support:* In 2018–19, 153 students received support. Fellowships with tuition reimbursements available, research assistantships, teaching assistantships, career-related internships or fieldwork, Federal Work-Study, tuition waivers (full and partial), and unspecified assistantships available. Support available to part-time students. Financial award application deadline: 4/15; financial award applicants required to submit FAFSA. *Faculty research:* Corporate finance, managerial accounting and financial reporting, strategic management and leadership, consumer behavior and decision making, organizational behavior and human resource management. *Unit head:* Ira Solomon, PhD, Dean, 504-865-5407, Fax: 504-865-5491, E-mail: businessdean@tulane.edu. *Application contact:* Melissa Booth, Assistant Dean for Graduate Admissions, 800-223-5402, E-mail: freeman.admissions@tulane.edu. Website: http://www.freeman.tulane.edu

United States International University–Africa, School of Business Administration, Nairobi, Kenya. Offers business administration (GEMBA); entrepreneurship (MBA); finance (MBA); human resource management (MBA); information technology management (MBA); integrated studies (MBA); international business administration (MBA); management and organizational development (MS); marketing (MBA); organizational development (EMS); strategic management (MBA). *Program availability:* Part-time, evening/weekend. *Degree requirements:* For master's, thesis. *Entrance requirements:* For master's, GMAT, 2 letters of reference, resume. Additional exam requirements/recommendations for international students: Required—TOEFL (minimum score 550 paper-based). *Faculty research:* Marketing in small business enterprises, total quality management in Kenya.

Universidad del Este, Graduate School, Carolina, PR 00984. Offers accounting (MBA); adult education (M Ed); agribusiness (MBA); criminal justice and criminology (MA); curriculum and instruction - early education (M Ed); curriculum and instruction - elementary (M Ed); curriculum and instruction - English (M Ed); curriculum and instruction - Spanish (M Ed); human resources (MBA); information security management (MBA); information technology and Web business development (MBA); management (MBA); public policy (MPA); social work (MA), including clinical social work; special education (M Ed); strategic leadership (MBA).

Management Strategy and Policy

The University of Arizona, Eller College of Management, Department of Management and Organizations, Tucson, AZ 85721. Offers MS, PhD. *Program availability:* Evening/weekend. *Entrance requirements:* Additional exam requirements/recommendations for international students: Required—TOEFL (minimum score 550 paper-based; 79 iBT). Electronic applications accepted. *Faculty research:* Organizational behavior, human resources, decision-making, health economics and finance, immigration.

The University of British Columbia, Sauder School of Business, Doctoral Program in Business Administration, Vancouver, BC V6T 1Z2, Canada. Offers accounting (PhD); finance (PhD); management information systems (PhD); management science (PhD); marketing (PhD); organizational behavior (PhD); strategy and business economics (PhD); transportation and logistics (PhD); urban land economics (PhD). *Degree requirements:* For doctorate, comprehensive exam, thesis/dissertation. *Entrance requirements:* For doctorate, GMAT or GRE. Additional exam requirements/recommendations for international students: Required—TOEFL (minimum score 600 paper-based; 100 iBT). Electronic applications accepted. *Expenses:* Contact institution.

University of Calgary, Faculty of Graduate Studies, Faculty of Arts, Program in Military and Strategic Studies, Calgary, AB T2N 1N4, Canada. Offers MSS, PhD. PhD offered in special cases only. *Program availability:* Part-time. *Degree requirements:* For master's, thesis; for doctorate, comprehensive exam, thesis/dissertation. *Entrance requirements:* For master's, minimum GPA of 3.4. Additional exam requirements/recommendations for international students: Recommended—TOEFL (minimum score 550 paper-based). *Faculty research:* Military history, Israeli studies, strategic studies, int'l relations, Arctic security.

University of California, Davis, Graduate School of Management, Full-Time MBA Program, Davis, CA 95616. Offers business analytics and technologies (MBA); entrepreneurship and innovation (MBA); finance and accounting (MBA); general management (MBA); marketing (MBA); organizational behavior (MBA); public health management (MBA); strategy (MBA); technology management (MBA); DVM/MBA; JD/MBA; M Engr/MBA; MBA/MPH; MBA/MS; MD/MBA; MSN/MBA; PhD/MBA. *Faculty:* 31 full-time (10 women). *Students:* 89 full-time (35 women); includes 21 minority (1 Black or African American, non-Hispanic/Latino; 14 Asian, non-Hispanic/Latino; 6 Hispanic/Latino), 43 international. Average age 28. 290 applicants, 39% accepted, 44 enrolled. In 2018, 45 master's awarded. *Degree requirements:* For master's, comprehensive exam, integrated management project. *Entrance requirements:* For master's, GMAT or GRE, letters of recommendation, resume, essays, equivalent of a 4-year U.S. undergraduate degree, transcript. Additional exam requirements/recommendations for international students: Required—TOEFL (minimum score 600 paper-based; 100 iBT), IELTS (minimum score 7). *Application deadline:* For fall admission, 9/15 priority date for domestic and international students. Applications are processed on a rolling basis. Application fee: $125. Electronic applications accepted. *Expenses:* Contact institution. *Financial support:* In 2018–19, 85 students received support. Fellowships with full and partial tuition reimbursements available, research assistantships with partial tuition reimbursements available, teaching assistantships with partial tuition reimbursements available, institutionally sponsored loans, scholarships/grants, health care benefits, tuition waivers (partial), and unspecified assistantships available. Financial award application deadline: 3/1; financial award applicants required to submit FAFSA. *Faculty research:* Finance, marketing, management, business analytics, accounting. *Unit head:* Amanda Opperman, Assistant Dean of Student Affairs, 530-752-7658, Fax: 530-754-9355, E-mail: admissions@gsm.ucdavis.edu. *Application contact:* Andrea Shaw, Senior Director of Admissions, 530-754-5476, Fax: 530-754-9355, E-mail: admissions@gsm.ucdavis.edu.
Website: http://gsm.ucdavis.edu/daytime-mba-program

University of California, Davis, Graduate School of Management, MBA Programs in Sacramento and San Francisco Bay Area, Davis, CA 95616. Offers business analytics and technologies (MBA); entrepreneurship and innovation (MBA); finance and accounting (MBA); general management (MBA); marketing (MBA); organizational behavior (MBA); public health management (MBA); strategy (MBA); technology management (MBA). *Program availability:* Part-time-only, evening/weekend. *Faculty:* 17 full-time (7 women), 42 part-time/adjunct (11 women). *Students:* 279 part-time (107 women); includes 146 minority (12 Black or African American, non-Hispanic/Latino; 3 American Indian or Alaska Native, non-Hispanic/Latino; 102 Asian, non-Hispanic/Latino; 29 Hispanic/Latino), 24 international. Average age 30. 158 applicants, 83% accepted, 91 enrolled. In 2018, 91 master's awarded. *Degree requirements:* For master's, integrated management project. *Entrance requirements:* For master's, GMAT or GRE, letters of recommendation, resume, equivalent of a 4-year undergraduate degree. Additional exam requirements/recommendations for international students: Required—TOEFL (minimum score 600 paper-based; 100 iBT), IELTS (minimum score 7). *Application deadline:* For fall admission, 9/15 priority date for domestic and international students. Applications are processed on a rolling basis. Application fee: $125. Electronic applications accepted. *Expenses:* Contact institution. *Financial support:* In 2018–19, 89 students received support. Fellowships, teaching assistantships with partial tuition reimbursements available, scholarships/grants, and unspecified assistantships available. Support available to part-time students. Financial award application deadline: 3/1; financial award applicants required to submit FAFSA. *Faculty research:* Accounting, finance, marketing, management, business analytics. *Unit head:* Amanda Opperman, Assistant Dean of Student Affairs, 530-752-7658, Fax: 530-754-9355, E-mail: admissions@gsm.ucdavis.edu. *Application contact:* Andrea Shaw, Senior Director of Admissions, 530-754-5476, Fax: 530-754-9355, E-mail: admissions@gsm.ucdavis.edu.
Website: http://gsm.ucdavis.edu/mba-programs

University of California, Los Angeles, Graduate Division, UCLA Anderson School of Management, Los Angeles, CA 90095-1481. Offers accounting (PhD); behavioral decision making (PhD); business administration (EMBA, MBA); business administration/computer science (MBA/MSCS); business administration/latin american studies (MBA/MLAS); business administration/law (MBA/JD); business administration/library science (MBA/MLIS); business administration/medicine (MBA/MD); business administration/nursing (MBA/MN); business administration/public health (MBA/MPH); business administration/public policy (MBA/MPP); business administration/urban and regional planning (MBA/MURP); business analytics (MSBA); decisions, operations, and technology management (PhD); finance (PhD); financial engineering (MFE); global economics and management (PhD); management and organizations (PhD); marketing (PhD); strategy and policy (PhD); DDS/MBA; MBA/JD; MBA/MD; MBA/MLAS; MBA/MLIS; MBA/MN; MBA/MPH; MBA/MPP; MBA/MSCS; MBA/MURP. UCLA-NUS EMBA: UCLA Anderson and the National University of Singapore. *Accreditation:* AACSB. *Program availability:* Part-time, evening/weekend. *Faculty:* 86 full-time (19 women), 102 part-time/adjunct (16 women). *Students:* 1,040 full-time (378 women), 1,262 part-time (391 women); includes 784 minority (47 Black or African American, non-Hispanic/Latino; 1 American Indian or Alaska Native, non-Hispanic/Latino; 539 Asian, non-Hispanic/Latino; 116 Hispanic/Latino; 5 Native Hawaiian or other Pacific Islander, non-Hispanic/Latino; 76 Two or more races, non-Hispanic/Latino), 609 international. Average age 31. 6,708 applicants, 27% accepted, 949 enrolled. In 2018, 885 master's, 13 doctorates awarded. Terminal master's awarded for partial completion of doctoral program. *Degree requirements:* For master's, comprehensive exam, field consulting project (for MBA, FEMBA, EMBA, UCLA-NUS EMBA, MFE, and MSBA); internship (for MBA only); for doctorate, comprehensive exam, thesis/dissertation, oral and written qualifying exams.

Entrance requirements: For master's, GMAT or GRE (for MBA, MFE, MSBA); Executive Assessment (EA) for candidates with 10+ years of work experience (FEMBA); Executive Assessment (EA) or STEM Master's degree or JD, MBA, CPA (EMBA), 4-year bachelor's degree or equivalent; 2 letters of recommendation; interview (invitation only); 2 essays; average 4-8 years of full-time work experience (for FEMBA); minimum 8 years of work experience with at least 3 years at management level (for EMBA); 10 years of full-time high managerial responsibility work experience (UCLA-NUS EMBA); for doctorate, GMAT or GRE, bachelor's degree from college or university of fully-recognized standing, minimum B average during junior and senior undergraduate years, 3 letters of recommendation, statement of purpose. Additional exam requirements/recommendations for international students: Required—TOEFL (minimum score 560 paper-based; 87 iBT), IELTS (minimum score 7), TOEFL with minimum iBT score of 100 (for MSBA). *Application deadline:* For fall admission, 10/2 for domestic and international students; for winter admission, 1/8 for domestic and international students; for spring admission, 4/16 for domestic and international students. Applications are processed on a rolling basis. Application fee: $200. Electronic applications accepted. *Expenses:* Per Year - MBA: $64,292, FEMBA: $42,420, EMBA: $81,120, UCLA-NUS EMBA (UC Portion only): $57,500, MFE: $75,816, MSBA: $64,1,43, PhD: $32,049. *Financial support:* Fellowships, research assistantships with partial tuition reimbursements, teaching assistantships with partial tuition reimbursements, career-related internships or fieldwork, institutionally sponsored loans, and scholarships/grants available. Support available to part-time students. *Faculty research:* Finance/global economics, entrepreneurship, accounting, human resources/organizational behavior, marketing and behavioral decision making. *Total annual research expenditures:* $2 million. *Unit head:* Dr. Antonio Bernardo, Dean & John E. Anderson Chair in Management, 310-825-7982, Fax: 310-206-2073, E-mail: a.bernardo@anderson.ucla.edu. *Application contact:* Alex Lawrence, Assistant Dean and Director of MBA Admissions, 310-825-6944, Fax: 310-825-8582, E-mail: mba.admissions@anderson.ucla.edu.
Website: http://www.anderson.ucla.edu/

University of Charleston, Master of Science in Strategic Leadership Program, Charleston, WV 25304-1099. Offers MS. *Entrance requirements:* For master's, bachelor's degree from regionally-accredited college or university with minimum GPA of 3.0. Electronic applications accepted.

University of Chicago, Booth School of Business, Full-Time MBA Program, Chicago, IL 60637. Offers accounting (MBA); analytic finance (MBA); analytic management (MBA); econometrics and statistics (MBA); economics (MBA); entrepreneurship (MBA); finance (MBA); general management (MBA); health administration and policy (Certificate); international business (MBA); managerial and organizational behavior (MBA); marketing analytics (MBA); marketing management (MBA); operations management (MBA); strategic management (MBA); MBA/AM; MBA/JD; MBA/MA; MBA/MD; MBA/MPP. *Accreditation:* AACSB. *Entrance requirements:* For master's, GMAT or GRE, transcripts, resume, 2 letters of recommendation, essays, interview. Additional exam requirements/recommendations for international students: Required—TOEFL, IELTS, or PTE. Electronic applications accepted. *Expenses:* Contact institution.

University of Colorado Denver, Business School, Program in Management and Organization, Denver, CO 80217. Offers business strategy (MS); change and innovation (MS); enterprise technology management (MS); entrepreneurship and innovation (MS); global management (MS); leadership (MS); managing for sustainability (MS); managing human resources (MS); sports and entertainment (MS); strategic management (MS). *Accreditation:* AACSB. *Program availability:* Part-time, evening/weekend, online learning. *Degree requirements:* For master's, 30 semester hours (12 of required courses, 12 of management electives, and 6 of free electives). *Entrance requirements:* For master's, GMAT, resume, two letters of recommendation, essay, financial statements (for international applicants). Additional exam requirements/recommendations for international students: Required—TOEFL (minimum score 525 paper-based; 71 iBT); Recommended—IELTS (minimum score 6.5). Electronic applications accepted. *Expenses:* Contact institution. *Faculty research:* Human resource management, management of catastrophe, turnaround strategies.

University of Dallas, Satish and Yasmin Gupta College of Business, Irving, TX 75062. Offers accounting (MBA, MS); business administration (DBA); business analytics (MS); business management (MBA); corporate finance (MBA); cybersecurity (MS); finance (MS); financial services (MBA); global business (MBA, MS); health services management (MBA); human resource management (MBA); information and technology management (MS); information assurance (MBA); information technology (MBA); information technology service management (MBA); marketing management (MBA); organization development (MBA); project management (MBA); sports and entertainment management (MBA); strategic leadership (MBA); supply chain management (MBA). *Accreditation:* AACSB. *Program availability:* Part-time, evening/weekend, 100% online. *Students:* 147 full-time (56 women), 584 part-time (232 women); includes 402 minority (204 Black or African American, non-Hispanic/Latino; 95 Asian, non-Hispanic/Latino; 92 Hispanic/Latino; 2 Native Hawaiian or other Pacific Islander, non-Hispanic/Latino; 9 Two or more races, non-Hispanic/Latino), 113 international. Average age 34. 992 applicants, 30% accepted, 157 enrolled. In 2018, 336 master's, 5 doctorates awarded. *Degree requirements:* For doctorate, thesis/dissertation. *Entrance requirements:* For master's and doctorate, U.S. bachelor's degree with a minimum cumulative GPA of 2.0 from a regionally accredited college or university (or comparable foreign degree); minimum 3.0 GPA in any graduate-level coursework completed; good academic standing with all colleges attended. Additional exam requirements/recommendations for international students: Required—TOEFL (minimum score 80 iBT), IELTS (minimum score 6.5), PTE (minimum score 67). *Application deadline:* Applications are processed on a rolling basis. Application fee: $50. Electronic applications accepted. *Expenses:* $1250 per credit hour. *Financial support:* In 2018–19, 291 students received support. Research assistantships, teaching assistantships, scholarships/grants, and unspecified assistantships available. Support available to part-time students. Financial award application deadline: 2/15; financial award applicants required to submit FAFSA. *Unit head:* Brett J.L. Landry, Dean, 972-721-5356, E-mail: blandry@udallas.edu. *Application contact:* Breonna Collins, Director, Graduate Admissions, 972-7215304, E-mail: bcollins@udallas.edu.
Website: http://www.udallas.edu/cob/

University of Detroit Mercy, College of Business Administration, Detroit, MI 48221. Offers business administration (MBA); business fundamentals (Certificate); business turnaround management (Certificate); ethical leadership and change management (Certificate); finance (Certificate); forensic accounting (Certificate); JD/MBA; MBA/MHSA. *Program availability:* Part-time, evening/weekend, 100% online, blended/hybrid learning. *Entrance requirements:* For master's, GMAT, resume, letter of recommendation, transcripts; for Certificate, resume, letter of recommendation, transcripts. Electronic applications accepted. Application fee is waived when completed online. *Expenses:* Contact institution. *Faculty research:* Ethics, international finance, trade policy, leadership, information technology.

University of Illinois at Urbana–Champaign, Graduate College, College of Education, Department of Education Policy, Organization, and Leadership, Champaign, IL 61820. Offers educational organization and leadership (Ed M, MS, Ed D, PhD, CAS); educational policy studies (Ed M, MA, PhD); human resource education (Ed M, MS, Ed D, PhD, CAS). *Program availability:* Part-time, online learning.

The University of Kansas, Graduate Studies, School of Business, Program in Business, Lawrence, KS 66045. Offers business and organizational leadership (MS); decision sciences and supply chain management (PhD); finance (PhD); human resources management (PhD); marketing (PhD); organizational behavior (PhD); strategic management (PhD); supply chain management and logistics (MS). *Accreditation:* AACSB. *Program availability:* Part-time. *Students:* 69 full-time (20 women), 150 part-time (62 women); includes 42 minority (14 Black or African American, non-Hispanic/Latino; 2 American Indian or Alaska Native, non-Hispanic/Latino; 6 Asian, non-Hispanic/Latino; 7 Hispanic/Latino; 13 Two or more races, non-Hispanic/Latino), 24 international. Average age 32. 306 applicants, 51% accepted, 132 enrolled. In 2018, 22 master's, 1 doctorate awarded. *Entrance requirements:* For master's, GMAT, official transcript, three letters of recommendation, resume, statement of purpose; for doctorate, GMAT or GRE, official transcript, three letters of recommendation, resume, statement of purpose. Additional exam requirements/recommendations for international students: Required—TOEFL, IELTS. *Application deadline:* For fall admission, 1/10 for domestic and international students. Application fee: $65 ($85 for international students). Electronic applications accepted. *Financial support:* Fellowships, research assistantships, teaching assistantships, scholarships/grants, health care benefits, tuition waivers (full), and unspecified assistantships available. Financial award application deadline: 1/10. *Faculty research:* Strategic human resource management, business ethics, organizational theory/behavior, corporate strategy, international business, supply chain management, Bayesian networks, game theory, decision analysis and time/series analysis, pricing, consumer effects, advertising and emotion. *Unit head:* Charly Edmonds, Director, 785-864-3841, E-mail: cedmonds@ku.edu. *Application contact:* Andrea Noltner, Graduate Admission Contact, 785-864-7556, E-mail: anoltner@ku.edu.
Website: http://www.business.ku.edu/

University of Lethbridge, School of Graduate Studies, Lethbridge, AB T1K 3M4, Canada. Offers addictions counseling (M Sc); agricultural biotechnology (M Sc); agricultural studies (M Sc, MA); anthropology (MA); archaeology (M Sc, MA); art (MA, MFA); biochemistry (M Sc); biological sciences (M Sc); biomolecular science (PhD); biosystems and biodiversity (PhD); Canadian studies (MA); chemistry (M Sc); computer science (M Sc); computer science and geographical information science (M Sc); counseling (MC); counseling psychology (M Ed); dramatic arts (MA); earth, space, and physical science (PhD); economics (MA); education (MA, PhD); educational leadership (M Ed); English (MA); environmental science (M Sc); evolution and behavior (PhD); exercise science (M Sc); French (MA); French/German (MA); French/Spanish (MA); general education (M Ed); geography (M Sc, MA); German (MA); health sciences (M Sc); individualized multidisciplinary (M Sc, MA); kinesiology (M Sc, MA); management (M Sc), including accounting, finance, human resource management and labor relations, information systems, international management, marketing, policy and strategy; mathematics (M Sc); music (M Mus, MA); Native American studies (MA); neuroscience (M Sc, PhD); new media (MA, MFA); nursing (M Sc, MN); philosophy (MA); physics (M Sc); political science (MA); psychology (M Sc, MA); religious studies (MA); sociology (MA); theatre and dramatic arts (MFA); theoretical and computational science (PhD); urban and regional studies (MA); women and gender studies (MA). *Program availability:* Part-time, evening/weekend. *Degree requirements:* For master's, thesis (for some programs); for doctorate, comprehensive exam, thesis/dissertation. *Entrance requirements:* For master's, GMAT (for M Sc in management), bachelor's degree in related field, minimum GPA of 3.0 during previous 20 graded semester courses, 2 years' teaching or related experience (M Ed); for doctorate, master's degree, minimum graduate GPA of 3.5. Additional exam requirements/recommendations for international students: Required—TOEFL (minimum score 580 paper-based; 93 iBT). Electronic applications accepted. *Faculty research:* Movement and brain plasticity, gibberellin physiology, photosynthesis, carbon cycling, molecular properties of main-group ring components.

The University of Manchester, Alliance Manchester Business School, M15 6PB, United Kingdom. Offers accounting and finance (M Sc); business (M Ent); business analysis and strategic management (M Sc); business analytics: operational research and risk analysis (M Sc); business psychology (M Sc); corporate communications and reputation management (M Sc); finance (M Sc); finance and business economics (M Sc); human resource management and industrial relations (M Sc); innovation management and entrepreneurship (M Sc); international business and management (M Sc); international human resource management and comparative industrial relations (M Sc); management (M Sc); marketing (M Sc); operations, project and supply chain management (M Sc); organizational psychology (M Sc); quantitative finance (M Sc). *Entrance requirements:* For master's, UK 2:1 honours degree or overseas equivalent. Additional exam requirements/recommendations for international students: Required—TOEFL (minimum score 100 iBT), IELTS (minimum score 7), PTE. Electronic applications accepted. *Faculty research:* Accounting and finance, management sciences and marketing, people management and organization, innovation management and policy, decision sciences.

University of Massachusetts Amherst, Graduate School, Isenberg School of Management, Program in Management, Amherst, MA 01003. Offers accounting (PhD); business administration (MBA); entrepreneurship (MBA); finance (MBA, PhD); healthcare administration (MBA); hospitality and tourism management (PhD); management science (PhD); marketing (MBA, PhD); organization studies (PhD); sport management (PhD); strategic management (PhD); MBA/MS. *Accreditation:* AACSB. *Program availability:* Part-time, evening/weekend, online learning. Terminal master's awarded for partial completion of doctoral program. *Degree requirements:* For doctorate, comprehensive exam, thesis/dissertation. *Entrance requirements:* For master's and doctorate, GMAT or GRE General Test. Additional exam requirements/recommendations for international students: Required—TOEFL (minimum score 550 paper-based; 80 iBT), IELTS (minimum score 6.5). Electronic applications accepted.

University of Memphis, Graduate School, University College, Memphis, TN 38152. Offers human resources leadership (MPS); liberal studies (MALS, Graduate Certificate); strategic leadership (MPS, Graduate Certificate); training and development (MPS). *Program availability:* Part-time, evening/weekend. *Faculty:* 3 full-time (2 women). *Students:* 15 full-time (9 women), 85 part-time (63 women); includes 71 minority (67 Black or African American, non-Hispanic/Latino; 2 Hispanic/Latino; 2 Two or more races, non-Hispanic/Latino), 1 international. Average age 40. 57 applicants, 77% accepted, 44 enrolled. In 2018, 25 master's, 5 other advanced degrees awarded. *Degree requirements:* For master's, comprehensive exam, thesis (for some programs). *Entrance requirements:* For master's, GRE (for MPS), resume, letters of recommendation, personal essay, interview, minimum undergraduate GPA of 2.75 (for MALS); portfolio in lieu of GRE (for MPS applicants with substantial professional work experience); for Graduate Certificate, essay, letter of recommendation. Additional exam requirements/recommendations for international students: Required—TOEFL (minimum score 550 paper-based; 79 iBT). *Application deadline:* For fall admission, 7/1 for domestic students, 5/1 for international students; for spring admission, 11/1 for domestic students, 9/15 for international students. Applications are processed on a rolling basis. Application fee: $35 ($60 for international students). Electronic applications accepted. *Expenses: Tuition, area resident:* Full-time $10,240; part-time $503 per credit hour. Tuition, state resident: full-time $10,464. Tuition, nonresident: full-time $20,224; part-time $991 per credit hour. *Required fees:* $850; $106 per credit hour. *Financial support:* Research assistantships with full tuition reimbursements, teaching assistantships with tuition reimbursements, Federal Work-Study, scholarships/grants, and unspecified assistantships available. Financial award application deadline: 2/3; financial award applicants required to submit FAFSA. *Faculty research:* Media ethics, history of psychiatry, public relations. *Unit head:* Dr. Richard Irwin, Executive Dean, 901-678-2716, E-mail: rirwin@memphis.edu. *Application contact:* Dr. Colin Chapell, Graduate Advisor, 901-678-3066, E-mail: cbchpell@memphis.edu.
Website: http://www.memphis.edu/univcoll/

University of Minnesota, Twin Cities Campus, Carlson School of Management, Doctoral Program in Business Administration, Minneapolis, MN 55455-0213. Offers accounting (PhD); finance (PhD); information and decision sciences (PhD); marketing (PhD); strategic management and entrepreneurship (PhD); supply chain and operations (PhD); work and organizations (PhD). *Faculty:* 106 full-time (33 women). *Students:* 88 full-time (34 women); includes 9 minority (2 Black or African American, non-Hispanic/Latino; 6 Asian, non-Hispanic/Latino; 1 Hispanic/Latino), 66 international. Average age 30. 306 applicants, 8% accepted, 15 enrolled. In 2018, 14 doctorates awarded. *Degree requirements:* For doctorate, comprehensive exam, thesis/dissertation, written and oral preliminary exams, proposal defense, final defense. *Entrance requirements:* For doctorate, GMAT or GRE, minimum undergraduate GPA of 3.0, graduate 3.5 (recommended). Additional exam requirements/recommendations for international students: Required—Either or: TOEFL or IELTS; Recommended—TOEFL, IELTS. *Application deadline:* For fall admission, 12/15 for domestic students, 12/15 priority date for international students. Applications are processed on a rolling basis. Application fee: $75 ($95 for international students). Electronic applications accepted. *Financial support:* In 2018–19, 80 students received support, including 80 fellowships with full tuition reimbursements available (averaging $12,500 per year), 72 research assistantships with full tuition reimbursements available (averaging $7,800 per year), 72 teaching assistantships with full tuition reimbursements available (averaging $7,800 per year); health care benefits, unspecified assistantships, and full student service fee waivers also available. Financial award application deadline: 12/15. *Faculty research:* Finance, strategy and entrepreneurship, marketing, information and decision science, operations, accounting, supply chain, human resources and industrial relations, organizational behavior. *Unit head:* Dr. Shawn P. Curley, Director, 612-624-6546, Fax: 612-624-8221, E-mail: curley@umn.edu. *Application contact:* Sandy Herzan, Associate Director, 612-624-0875, Fax: 612-624-8221, E-mail: herza002@umn.edu.
Website: http://carlsonschool.umn.edu/degrees/phd

University of New Haven, Graduate School, College of Business, Program in Business Administration, West Haven, CT 06516. Offers accounting (MBA); business administration (MBA); business intelligence (MBA); business policy and strategic leadership (MBA); finance (MBA), including chartered financial analyst; global marketing (MBA); human resources management (MBA); sport management (MBA). *Accreditation:* AACSB. *Program availability:* Part-time, evening/weekend. *Students:* 151 full-time (73 women), 70 part-time (30 women); includes 51 minority (23 Black or African American, non-Hispanic/Latino; 13 Asian, non-Hispanic/Latino; 14 Hispanic/Latino; 1 Two or more races, non-Hispanic/Latino), 74 international. Average age 28. 197 applicants, 91% accepted, 82 enrolled. In 2018, 70 master's awarded. *Entrance requirements:* For master's, GMAT. Additional exam requirements/recommendations for international students: Required—TOEFL (minimum score 80 iBT), IELTS, PTE. *Application deadline:* Applications are processed on a rolling basis. Application fee: $50. Electronic applications accepted. Application fee is waived when completed online. *Expenses: Tuition:* Full-time $16,470; part-time $915 per credit hour. *Required fees:* $230; $95 per term. *Financial support:* Research assistantships with partial tuition reimbursements, teaching assistantships with partial tuition reimbursements, career-related internships or fieldwork, Federal Work-Study, scholarships/grants, and unspecified assistantships available. Support available to part-time students. Financial award applicants required to submit FAFSA. *Unit head:* Darell Singleterry, Director, 203-932-7386, E-mail: dsingleterry@newhaven.edu. *Application contact:* Selina O'Toole, Senior Associate Director of Graduate Admissions, 203-932-7337, E-mail: SOToole@newhaven.edu.
Website: http://www.newhaven.edu/business/graduate-programs/mba/index.php

University of New Mexico, Anderson School of Management, Department of Marketing, Information Systems, Information Assurance, and Operations Management, Albuquerque, NM 87131. Offers information assurance (MBA); information systems and assurance (MS); management information systems (MBA); marketing management (MBA); operations management (MBA). *Program availability:* Part-time. *Faculty:* 17 full-time (6 women), 12 part-time/adjunct (5 women). In 2018, 59 master's awarded. *Entrance requirements:* For master's, GMAT or GRE, minimum GPA of 3.0 on last 60 hours of coursework; bachelor's degree from regionally-accredited college or university in U.S. or its equivalent in another country. Additional exam requirements/recommendations for international students: Required—TOEFL (minimum score 550 paper-based; 79 iBT), IELTS (minimum score 6.5). *Application deadline:* For fall admission, 4/1 priority date for domestic and international students; for spring admission, 10/1 priority date for domestic and international students. Applications are processed on a rolling basis. Application fee: $50. Electronic applications accepted. *Expenses:* $531.34 per credit hour resident, $1197.98 per credit hour non-resident. *Financial support:* In 2018–19, 23 students received support, including 13 fellowships (averaging $16,320 per year), 12 research assistantships with partial tuition reimbursements available (averaging $15,180 per year); career-related internships or fieldwork, Federal Work-Study, scholarships/grants, and unspecified assistantships also available. Support available to part-time students. Financial award application deadline: 6/1; financial award applicants required to submit FAFSA. *Faculty research:* Marketing, operations management, information systems, information assurance. *Unit head:* Dr. Mary Margaret Rogers, Chair, 505-277-6471, E-mail: mmrogers@unm.edu. *Application contact:* Lisa Beauchene-Lawson, Supervisor, Graduate Advisement, 505-277-6471, E-mail: andersongrad@unm.edu.
Website: https://www.mgt.unm.edu/mids/default.asp?mm-faculty

University of New Mexico, Anderson School of Management, Department of Organizational Studies, Albuquerque, NM 87131. Offers organizational behavior and human resources management (MBA); strategic management and policy (MBA). *Program availability:* Part-time. *Faculty:* 15 full-time (11 women), 16 part-time/adjunct (8 women). In 2018, 21 master's awarded. *Entrance requirements:* For master's, GMAT or GRE, minimum GPA of 3.0 on last 60 hours of coursework; bachelor's degree from regionally-accredited college or university in U.S. or its equivalent in another country. Additional exam requirements/recommendations for international students: Required—TOEFL (minimum score 550 paper-based; 79 iBT), IELTS (minimum score 6.5). *Application deadline:* For fall admission, 4/1 priority date for domestic and international students; for spring admission, 10/1 priority date for domestic and international students. Applications are processed on a rolling basis. Application fee: $50. Electronic applications accepted. *Expenses:* $531.34 per credit resident tuition and fees, $1197.98 per credit non-resident tuition and fees (both are non-EMBA tuition). *Financial support:* In 2018–19, 14 students received support, including 4 fellowships (averaging $18,200 per year), 11 research assistantships with partial tuition reimbursements available (averaging $15,488 per year); career-related internships or fieldwork, Federal Work-Study, scholarships/grants, and unspecified assistantships also available. Support available to part-time students. Financial award application deadline: 6/1; financial

award applicants required to submit FAFSA. *Faculty research:* Business ethics and social corporate responsibility, diversity, human resources, organizational strategy, organizational behavior. *Unit head:* Dr. Michelle Arthur, Chair, 505-277-6471, E-mail: arthurm@unm.edu. *Application contact:* Lisa Beauchene-Lawson, Supervisor, Graduate Advisement, 505-277-6471, E-mail: andersongrad@unm.edu.
Website: https://www.mgt.unm.edu/dos/default.asp?mm-faculty

The University of North Carolina at Chapel Hill, Kenan-Flagler Business School, Doctoral Program in Business Administration, Chapel Hill, NC 27599. Offers accounting (PhD); finance (PhD); marketing (PhD); operations management (PhD); organizational behavior (PhD); strategy (PhD). *Accreditation:* AACSB. *Degree requirements:* For doctorate, thesis/dissertation. *Entrance requirements:* For doctorate, GMAT or GRE General Test. Electronic applications accepted. *Expenses:* Contact institution.

University of North Texas, Toulouse Graduate School, Denton, TX 76203-5459. Offers accounting (MS); applied anthropology (MA, MS); applied behavior analysis (Certificate); applied geography (MA); applied technology and performance improvement (M Ed, MS); art education (MA); art history (MA); arts leadership (Certificate); audiology (Au D); behavior analysis (MS); behavioral science (PhD); biochemistry and molecular biology (MS); biology (MA, MS); biomedical engineering (MS); business analysis (MS); chemistry (MS); clinical health psychology (PhD); communication studies (MA, MS); computer engineering (MS); computer science (MS); counseling (M Ed, MS), including clinical mental health counseling (MS), college and university counseling, elementary school counseling, secondary school counseling; creative writing (MA); criminal justice (MS); curriculum and instruction (M Ed); decision sciences (MBA); design (MA, MFA), including fashion design (MFA), innovation studies, interior design (MFA); early childhood studies (MS); economics (MS); educational leadership (M Ed, Ed D); educational psychology (MS, PhD), including family studies (MS), gifted and talented (MS), human development (MS), learning and cognition (MS), research, measurement and evaluation (MS); electrical engineering (MS); emergency management (MPA); engineering technology (MS); English (MA); English as a second language (MA); environmental science (MS); finance (MBA, MS); financial management (MPA); French (MA); health services management (MBA); higher education (M Ed, Ed D); history (MA, MS); hospitality management (MS); human resources management (MPA); information science (MS); information systems (PhD); information technologies (MBA); interdisciplinary studies (MA, MS); international studies (MA); international sustainable tourism (MS); jazz studies (MM); journalism (MA, MJ, Graduate Certificate), including interactive and virtual digital communication (Graduate Certificate), narrative journalism (Graduate Certificate), public relations (Graduate Certificate); kinesiology (MS); linguistics (MA); local government management (MPA); logistics (PhD); logistics and supply chain management (MBA); long-term care, senior housing, and aging services (MA); management (PhD); marketing (MBA); mathematics (MA, MS); mechanical and energy engineering (MS, PhD); music (MA), including ethnomusicology, music theory, musicology, performance; music composition (PhD); music education (MM Ed, PhD); nonprofit management (MPA); operations and supply chain management (MBA); performance (MM, DMA); philosophy (MA); political science (MA); professional and technical communication (MA); radio, television and film (MA, MFA); rehabilitation counseling (Certificate); sociology (MA); Spanish (MA); special education (M Ed); speech-language pathology (MA); strategic management (MBA); studio art (MFA); teaching (M Ed); MBA/MS. *Program availability:* Part-time, evening/weekend, online learning. Terminal master's awarded for partial completion of doctoral program. *Degree requirements:* For master's, variable foreign language requirement, comprehensive exam (for some programs), thesis (for some programs); for doctorate, variable foreign language requirement, comprehensive exam (for some programs), thesis/dissertation; for other advanced degree, variable foreign language requirement, comprehensive exam (for some programs). *Entrance requirements:* For master's and doctorate, GRE, GMAT. Additional exam requirements/recommendations for international students: Required—TOEFL (minimum score 550 paper-based; 79 iBT). Electronic applications accepted.

University of North Texas at Dallas, Graduate School, Dallas, TX 75241. Offers accounting (MBA); counseling (M Ed, MS); criminal justice (MS); curriculum and instruction (M Ed); educational administration (M Ed); human resources and organizational behavior (MBA); public leadership (MS); strategic management (MBA).

University of Pittsburgh, Katz Graduate School of Business, Doctoral Program in Business Administration, Pittsburgh, PA 15260. Offers accounting (PhD); business analytics and operations (PhD); finance (PhD); information systems and technology management (PhD); marketing (PhD); organizational behavior and human resources (PhD); strategic management (PhD). *Accreditation:* AACSB. *Program availability:* Evening/weekend. *Degree requirements:* For doctorate, comprehensive exam, thesis/dissertation, student teaching. *Entrance requirements:* For doctorate, GMAT or GRE, 3 recommendations, statement of purpose, transcripts of all previous course work and degrees. Additional exam requirements/recommendations for international students: Required—TOEFL (minimum score 100 iBT) or IELTS (minimum score 7.0). Electronic applications accepted. *Faculty research:* Accounting systems/financial reporting, corporate finance, shopper marketing/consumer behavior, management information systems, organizational behavior and entrepreneurship.

University of Pittsburgh, Katz Graduate School of Business, Master of Business Administration Programs, Pittsburgh, PA 15260. Offers finance (MBA); information systems (MBA); marketing (MBA); operations (MBA); organizational behavior and human resources (MBA); strategy, environment and organizations (MBA); MBA/JD; MBA/MID; MBA/MIS; MBA/MSE. *Accreditation:* AACSB. *Program availability:* Part-time, evening/weekend, blended/hybrid learning. *Degree requirements:* For master's, minimum GPA of 3.0. *Entrance requirements:* For master's, GMAT, GRE. Additional exam requirements/recommendations for international students: Required—TOEFL (minimum score 100 iBT) or IELTS (minimum score 7.0). Electronic applications accepted. *Faculty research:* Accounting systems/financial reporting, corporate finance, shopper marketing/consumer behavior, management information systems, organizational behavior and entrepreneurship.

University of Rhode Island, Graduate School, College of Business, Kingston, RI 02881. Offers accounting (MS); business administration (MBA, PhD), including finance (MBA), general business (MBA), management (MBA), marketing, operations and supply chain management (PhD), supply chain management (MBA); finance (MBA, MS, PhD); general business (MBA); health care management (MBA); labor research (MS, Graduate Certificate), including labor relations and human resources; management (MBA); marketing (MBA); strategic innovation (MBA); supply chain management (MBA); textiles, fashion merchandising and design (MS, Certificate), including fashion merchandising (Certificate), master seamstress (Certificate), textiles, fashion merchandising and design (MS); MS/JD; Pharm D/MBA. *Accreditation:* AACSB. *Program availability:* Part-time, evening/weekend. *Faculty:* 61 full-time (30 women), 1 (woman) part-time/adjunct. *Students:* 85 full-time (35 women), 196 part-time (89 women); includes 43 minority (14 Black or African American, non-Hispanic/Latino; 1 American Indian or Alaska Native, non-Hispanic/Latino; 14 Asian, non-Hispanic/Latino; 10 Hispanic/Latino; 1 Native Hawaiian or other Pacific Islander, non-Hispanic/Latino; 3 Two or more races, non-Hispanic/Latino), 23 international. 155 applicants, 85% accepted, 105 enrolled. In 2018, 127 master's, 5 doctorates, 23 other advanced degrees awarded. *Entrance requirements:* Additional exam requirements/recommendations for international students: Required—TOEFL. Application fee: $65. Electronic applications accepted. *Expenses: Tuition, area resident:* Full-time $13,226; part-time $735 per credit. Tuition, state resident: full-time $13,226; part-time $735 per credit. Tuition, nonresident: full-time $25,854; part-time $1436 per credit. *International tuition:* $25,854 full-time. *Required fees:* $1698; $50 per credit. $35 per semester. One-time fee: $165. *Financial support:* In 2018–19, 15 teaching assistantships with tuition reimbursements (averaging $17,739 per year) were awarded; research assistantships also available. Financial award applicants required to submit FAFSA. *Unit head:* Dr. Maling Ebrahimpour, Dean, 401-874-4348, Fax: 401-874-4312, E-mail: mebrahimpour@uri.edu. *Application contact:* Lisa Lancellotta, Coordinator, MBA Programs, 401-874-4241, Fax: 401-874-4312, E-mail: mba@uri.edu.
Website: https://web.uri.edu/business/

University of Rochester, Simon Business School, Full-Time Master's Program in Business Administration, Rochester, NY 14627. Offers business systems consulting (MBA); competitive and organizational strategy (MBA); computers and information systems (MBA); corporate accounting (MBA); entrepreneurship (MBA); finance (MBA); health sciences management (MBA); marketing (MBA); operations management (MBA); public accounting (MBA); strategy and organizations (MBA). *Accreditation:* AACSB. *Entrance requirements:* For master's, GMAT or GRE. *Expenses: Tuition:* Full-time $52,974; part-time $1654 per credit hour. *Required fees:* $612. One-time fee: $30 part-time. Tuition and fees vary according to campus/location and program. *Faculty research:* Empirical industrial organization, risk management, financial disclosure and regulation, social media, health care management.

University of Rochester, Simon Business School, Part-Time MBA Program, Rochester, NY 14627. Offers business systems consulting (MBA); competitive and organizational strategy (MBA); computers and information systems (MBA); corporate accounting (MBA); entrepreneurship (MBA); finance (MBA); health sciences management (MBA); marketing (MBA), including brand management, marketing strategy, pricing; operations management (MBA); public accounting (MBA). *Program availability:* Part-time-only, evening/weekend. *Entrance requirements:* For master's, GRE or GMAT. Electronic applications accepted. *Expenses:* Contact institution.

University of South Florida, Innovative Education, Tampa, FL 33620-9951. Offers adult, career and higher education (Graduate Certificate), including college teaching, leadership in developing human resources, leadership in higher education; Africana studies (Graduate Certificate), including diasporas and health disparities, genocide and human rights; aging studies (Graduate Certificate), including gerontology; art research (Graduate Certificate), including museum studies; business foundations (Graduate Certificate); chemical and biomedical engineering (Graduate Certificate), including materials science and engineering, water, health and sustainability; child and family studies (Graduate Certificate), including positive behavior support; civil and industrial engineering (Graduate Certificate), including transportation systems analysis; community and family health (Graduate Certificate), including maternal and child health, social marketing and public health, violence and injury: prevention and intervention, women's health; criminology (Graduate Certificate), including criminal justice administration; data science for public administration (Graduate Certificate); digital humanities (Graduate Certificate); educational measurement and research (Graduate Certificate), including evaluation; English (Graduate Certificate), including comparative literary studies, creative writing, professional and technical communication; entrepreneurship (Graduate Certificate); environmental health (Graduate Certificate), including safety management; epidemiology and biostatistics (Graduate Certificate), including applied biostatistics, biostatistics, concepts and tools of epidemiology, epidemiology, epidemiology of infectious diseases; geography, environment and planning (Graduate Certificate), including community development, environmental policy and management, geographical information systems; geology (Graduate Certificate), including hydrogeology; global health (Graduate Certificate), including disaster management, global health and Latin American and Caribbean studies, global health practice, humanitarian assistance, infection control; government and international affairs (Graduate Certificate), including Cuban studies, globalization studies; health policy and management (Graduate Certificate), including health management and leadership, public health policy and programs; hearing specialist: early intervention (Graduate Certificate); industrial and management systems engineering (Graduate Certificate), including systems engineering, technology management; information studies (Graduate Certificate), including school library media specialist; information systems/decision sciences (Graduate Certificate), including analytics and business intelligence; instructional technology (Graduate Certificate), including distance education, Florida digital/virtual educator, instructional design, multimedia design, Web design; internal medicine, bioethics and medical humanities (Graduate Certificate), including biomedical ethics; Latin American and Caribbean studies (Graduate Certificate); leadership for coastal resiliency planning (Graduate Certificate); mass communications (Graduate Certificate), including multimedia journalism; mathematics and statistics (Graduate Certificate), including mathematics; medicine (Graduate Certificate), including aging and neuroscience, bioinformatics, biotechnology, brain fitness and memory management, clinical investigation, hand and upper limb rehabilitation, health informatics, health sciences, integrative weight management, intellectual property, medicine and gender, metabolic and nutritional medicine, metabolic cardiology, pharmacy sciences; national and competitive intelligence (Graduate Certificate); nursing (Graduate Certificate), including simulation based academic fellowship in advanced pain management; psychological and social foundations (Graduate Certificate), including career counseling, college teaching, diversity in education, mental health counseling, school counseling; public affairs (Graduate Certificate), including nonprofit management, public management, research administration; public health (Graduate Certificate), including assessing chemical toxicity and public health risks, health equity, pharmacoepidemiology, public health generalist, toxicology, translational research in adolescent behavioral health; public health practices (Graduate Certificate), including planning for healthy communities; rehabilitation and mental health counseling (Graduate Certificate), including integrative mental health care, marriage and family therapy, rehabilitation technology; secondary education (Graduate Certificate), including ESOL, foreign language education: culture and content, foreign language education: professional; social work (Graduate Certificate), including geriatric social work/clinical gerontology; special education (Graduate Certificate), including autism spectrum disorder, disabilities education: severe/profound; world languages (Graduate Certificate), including teaching English as a second language (TESL) or foreign language. *Expenses:* Tuition, state resident: full-time $6350. Tuition, nonresident: full-time $19,048. *International tuition:* $19,048 full-time. *Required fees:* $2079. *Unit head:* Dr. Cynthia DeLuca, Associate Vice President and Assistant Vice Provost, 813-974-3077, Fax: 813-974-7061, E-mail: deluca@usf.edu. *Application contact:* Owen Hooper, Director, Summer and Alternative Calendar Programs, 813-974-6917, E-mail: hooper@usf.edu.
Website: http://www.usf.edu/innovative-education/

University of South Florida, Muma College of Business, Department of Information Systems and Decision Sciences, Tampa, FL 33620-9951. Offers business administration (PhD), including information systems; business analytics and information systems (MS), including analytics and business intelligence, information assurance.

Program availability: Part-time. *Faculty:* 25 full-time (4 women). *Students:* 193 full-time (66 women), 130 part-time (38 women); includes 36 minority (9 Black or African American, non-Hispanic/Latino; 18 Asian, non-Hispanic/Latino; 7 Hispanic/Latino; 2 Two or more races, non-Hispanic/Latino), 245 international. Average age 29. 668 applicants, 65% accepted, 131 enrolled. In 2018, 189 master's awarded. Terminal master's awarded for partial completion of doctoral program. *Degree requirements:* For master's, comprehensive exam, thesis (for some programs), thesis or practicum project; for doctorate, comprehensive exam, thesis/dissertation. *Entrance requirements:* For master's, GMAT, GRE or other standardized scores for graduate programs, letters of recommendation, statement of purpose, relevant work experience; for doctorate, GMAT or GRE, letters of recommendation, personal statement, interview. Additional exam requirements/recommendations for international students: Required—TOEFL, TOEFL (minimum score 550 paper-based; 79 iBT) or IELTS (minimum score 6.5). *Application deadline:* For fall admission, 6/1 for domestic students, 2/1 for international students; for spring admission, 10/15 for domestic students, 9/15 for international students. Applications are processed on a rolling basis. Application fee: $30. Electronic applications accepted. *Expenses:* Tuition, state resident: full-time $6350. Tuition, nonresident: full-time $19,048. International tuition: $19,048 full-time. *Required fees:* $2079. *Financial support:* In 2018–19, 43 students received support, including 8 research assistantships with tuition reimbursements available (averaging $11,972 per year), 22 teaching assistantships with tuition reimbursements available (averaging $9,002 per year); scholarships/grants, health care benefits, and unspecified assistantships also available. Financial award applicants required to submit FAFSA. *Faculty research:* Data mining, business intelligence, bioterrorism surveillance, health informatics/informatics, software engineering, agent-based modeling, distributed systems, statistics, electronic markets, e-commerce, business process improvement, operations management, supply chain, LEAN management, global information systems, organizational impacts of IT, enterprise resource planning, business intelligence, Web and mobile technologies, social networks, information security. *Total annual research expenditures:* $423,775. *Unit head:* Dr. Kaushal Chari, Chair and Professor, 813-974-6768, Fax: 813-974-6749, E-mail: kchari@usf.edu. *Application contact:* Barber Warner, 813-974-6776, Fax: 813-974-6749, E-mail: bwarner@usf.edu.
Website: http://business.usf.edu/departments/isds/

The University of Texas at Dallas, Naveen Jindal School of Management, Program in Information Systems, Richardson, TX 75080. Offers business analytics (MS); information technology and management (MS). *Program availability:* Part-time, evening/weekend. *Faculty:* 19 full-time (2 women), 29 part-time/adjunct (5 women). *Students:* 1,313 full-time (523 women), 504 part-time (202 women); includes 177 minority (16 Black or African American, non-Hispanic/Latino; 128 Asian, non-Hispanic/Latino; 28 Hispanic/Latino; 1 Native Hawaiian or other Pacific Islander, non-Hispanic/Latino; 4 Two or more races, non-Hispanic/Latino), 1,523 international. Average age 27. 2,623 applicants, 76% accepted, 760 enrolled. In 2018, 983 master's awarded. *Degree requirements:* For master's, thesis optional. *Entrance requirements:* For master's, GMAT. Additional exam requirements/recommendations for international students: Required—TOEFL (minimum score 550 paper-based). *Application deadline:* For fall admission, 7/15 for domestic students, 5/1 priority date for international students; for spring admission, 11/15 for domestic students, 9/1 priority date for international students. Applications are processed on a rolling basis. Application fee: $50 ($100 for international students). Electronic applications accepted. *Expenses: Tuition, area resident:* Full-time $13,458. Tuition, state resident: full-time $13,458. Tuition, nonresident: full-time $26,852. *International tuition:* $26,852 full-time. Tuition and fees vary according to course load. *Financial support:* In 2018–19, 1 research assistantship with partial tuition reimbursement (averaging $13,400 per year), 26 teaching assistantships with partial tuition reimbursements (averaging $10,050 per year) were awarded; career-related internships or fieldwork, Federal Work-Study, institutionally sponsored loans, scholarships/grants, and unspecified assistantships also available. Support available to part-time students. Financial award application deadline: 4/30; financial award applicants required to submit FAFSA. *Faculty research:* Electronic commerce, decision support systems, data quality. *Unit head:* Dr. Syam Menon, Area Coordinator, 972-883-4779, E-mail: syam@utdallas.edu. *Application contact:* Dr. Syam Menon, Area Coordinator, 972-883-4779, E-mail: syam@utdallas.edu.
Website: https://jindal.utdallas.edu/information-systems-programs/

University of Utah, Graduate School, David Eccles School of Business, Business Administration Program, Salt Lake City, UT 84112. Offers accounting (PhD); business administration (EMBA, MBA, PMBA); finance (PhD); information systems (PhD); marketing (PhD); operations management (PhD); organizational behavior (PhD); strategic management (PhD); MBA/JD; MBA/MHA; MBA/MS. *Program availability:* Part-time, evening/weekend, online learning. *Students:* 112 full-time (26 women), 7 part-time (2 women); includes 12 minority (1 Asian, non-Hispanic/Latino; 7 Hispanic/Latino; 4 Two or more races, non-Hispanic/Latino), 13 international. Average age 29. 182 applicants, 51% accepted, 58 enrolled. In 2018, 58 master's awarded. *Entrance requirements:* For master's, GMAT or GRE; for doctorate, GMAT. Additional exam requirements/recommendations for international students: Required—TOEFL (minimum score 100 iBT), IELTS (minimum score 7). *Application deadline:* For fall admission, 5/1 for domestic students, 3/1 for international students. Application fee: $55 ($65 for international students). Electronic applications accepted. *Expenses:* Contact institution. *Financial support:* In 2018–19, 57 students received support. Scholarships/grants available. Financial award application deadline: 5/1; financial award applicants required to submit FAFSA. *Faculty research:* Corporate finance, strategy services, consumer behavior, financial disclosures, operations. *Unit head:* Brad Vierig, Associate Dean, MBA Programs & Executive Education. *Application contact:* Stephanie Geisler, Director, Full-Time MBA, 801-585-6291, E-mail: ftmba@utah.edu.
Website: http://www.business.utah.edu/

University of Utah, Graduate School, David Eccles School of Business, Master of Science in Information Systems Program, Salt Lake City, UT 84112-8939. Offers information systems (MS, Graduate Certificate), including business intelligence and analytics, IT security, product and process management, software and systems architecture. *Program availability:* Part-time, evening/weekend, 100% online, blended/hybrid learning. *Degree requirements:* For master's, capstone project. *Entrance requirements:* For master's, GMAT/GRE, minimum undergraduate GPA of 3.0, 2 letters of recommendation, personal statement, professional resume. Additional exam requirements/recommendations for international students: Required—TOEFL (minimum score 550 paper-based; 80 iBT), IELTS (minimum score 6.5). Electronic applications accepted. *Expenses:* Contact institution. *Faculty research:* Business intelligence and analytics, software and system architecture, product and process management, IT security, Web and data mining, applications and management of IT in healthcare.

University of Virginia, McIntire School of Commerce, M.S. in Global Commerce, Charlottesville, VA 22903. Offers global commerce (MS); global strategic management (MS); international management (Certificate). ESADE Business School at Ramon Lull University (Barcelona, Spain); Lingnan (University) College at Sun Yat-sen University (Guangzhou, China). *Faculty:* 26 full-time (11 women). *Students:* 54 full-time (27 women); includes 2 minority (both Asian, non-Hispanic/Latino), 32 international. Average age 24. 150 applicants, 50% accepted, 54 enrolled. In 2018, 2 master's, 1 other advanced degree awarded. *Entrance requirements:* For master's, GMAT or GRE, Must

have a bachelor's degree in business administration, marketing, finance, supply chain, management, or equivalent. Additional exam requirements/recommendations for international students: Required—TOEFL (minimum score 600 paper-based; 100 iBT), IELTS (minimum score 7.5). *Application deadline:* For fall admission, 10/15 for domestic students; for winter admission, 1/15 for domestic students; for spring admission, 3/15 for domestic students; for summer admission, 6/15 for domestic students. Applications are processed on a rolling basis. Application fee: $75. Electronic applications accepted. *Financial support:* Federal Work-Study, scholarships/grants, and unspecified assistantships available. Financial award application deadline: 3/15; financial award applicants required to submit FAFSA. *Faculty research:* Global strategic management, international finance, supply chain, business communication, marketing. *Unit head:* Amanda Cowen, Program Director, 434-243-8753, Fax: 434-924-7074, E-mail: msglobal@virginia.edu. *Application contact:* Emma Candelier, Assistant Dean of Graduate Recruiting, 434-243-4992, Fax: 434-924-4511, E-mail: ecandelier@virginia.edu.
Website: https://www.commerce.virginia.edu/ms-global

The University of Western Ontario, Ivey Business School, London, ON N6A 3K7, Canada. Offers business (EMBA, PhD); corporate strategy and leadership elective (MBA); entrepreneurship elective (MBA); finance elective (MBA); health sector stream (MBA); international management elective (MBA); marketing elective (MBA); JD/MBA. *Degree requirements:* For master's, thesis (for some programs); for doctorate, thesis/dissertation. *Entrance requirements:* For master's, GMAT, 2 years of full-time work experience, interview. Additional exam requirements/recommendations for international students: Required—TOEFL (minimum score 100 iBT) or IELTS (minimum score 6). Electronic applications accepted. *Faculty research:* Strategy, organizational behavior, international business, finance, operations management.

University of Wisconsin–Madison, Graduate School, College of Engineering, Department of Industrial and Systems Engineering, Madison, WI 53706. Offers industrial engineering (MS, PhD), including human factors and health systems engineering (MS), systems engineering and analytics (MS). *Program availability:* Part-time. *Faculty:* 20 full-time (6 women). *Students:* 87 full-time (33 women), 12 part-time (8 women); includes 4 minority (1 Black or African American, non-Hispanic/Latino; 3 Asian, non-Hispanic/Latino), 63 international. Average age 26. 372 applicants, 21% accepted, 18 enrolled. In 2018, 35 master's, 9 doctorates awarded. Terminal master's awarded for partial completion of doctoral program. *Degree requirements:* For master's, thesis optional, 30 credits; minimum GPA of 3.0; for doctorate, comprehensive exam, thesis/dissertation, minimum of 51 credits; minimum GPA of 3.0. *Entrance requirements:* For master's and doctorate, GRE General Test, minimum GPA of 3.0, BS in engineering or equivalent, course work in computer programming and statistics. Additional exam requirements/recommendations for international students: Required—TOEFL (minimum score 580 paper-based; 92 iBT), IELTS (minimum score 7). *Application deadline:* For fall admission, 12/15 for domestic and international students; for spring admission, 10/1 for domestic and international students; for summer admission, 12/15 for domestic and international students. Application fee: $75 ($81 for international students). Electronic applications accepted. *Financial support:* In 2018–19, 66 students received support, including 2 fellowships with full tuition reimbursements available (averaging $27,816 per year), 39 research assistantships with full tuition reimbursements available (averaging $24,456 per year), 21 teaching assistantships with full tuition reimbursements available (averaging $19,788 per year); career-related internships or fieldwork, Federal Work-Study, institutionally sponsored loans, scholarships/grants, traineeships, health care benefits, and unspecified assistantships also available. Financial award application deadline: 12/1; financial award applicants required to submit FAFSA. *Faculty research:* Operations research; human factors and ergonomics; health systems engineering; manufacturing and production systems. *Total annual research expenditures:* $13.9 million. *Unit head:* Dr. Jeff Lindroth, Chair, 608-262-2686, E-mail: ie@engr.wisc.edu. *Application contact:* Pam Peterson, Student Services Coordinator, 608-263-4025, Fax: 608-890-2204, E-mail: prpeterson@wisc.edu.
Website: http://www.engr.wisc.edu/department/industrial-systems-engineering/

University of Wisconsin–Milwaukee, Graduate School, Lubar School of Business, Milwaukee, WI 53201. Offers business administration (MBA); executive business administration (EMBA); management science (MS, PhD, Graduate Certificate), including business analytics (Graduate Certificate), enterprise resource planning (Graduate Certificate), information technology management (MS), investment management (Graduate Certificate), nonprofit management (Graduate Certificate), nonprofit management and leadership (MS), state and local taxation (Graduate Certificate), technology entrepreneurship (Graduate Certificate). *Accreditation:* AACSB. *Program availability:* Part-time, evening/weekend. *Students:* 282 full-time (122 women), 280 part-time (115 women); includes 95 minority (19 Black or African American, non-Hispanic/Latino; 2 American Indian or Alaska Native, non-Hispanic/Latino; 35 Asian, non-Hispanic/Latino; 7 Hispanic/Latino; 32 Two or more races, non-Hispanic/Latino), 65 international. Average age 32. 389 applicants, 66% accepted, 191 enrolled. In 2018, 212 master's, 2 doctorates, 18 other advanced degrees awarded. *Degree requirements:* For master's, comprehensive exam (for some programs); for doctorate, comprehensive exam, thesis/dissertation. *Entrance requirements:* For master's and doctorate, GMAT or GRE General Test. Additional exam requirements/recommendations for international students: Required—TOEFL (minimum score 550 paper-based; 79 iBT), IELTS (minimum score 6.5). *Application deadline:* For fall admission, 1/1 priority date for domestic students; for spring admission, 9/1 for domestic students. Application fee: $56 ($96 for international students). Electronic applications accepted. *Expenses:* Contact institution. *Financial support:* Fellowships with full tuition reimbursements, research assistantships with full tuition reimbursements, teaching assistantships with full tuition reimbursements, career-related internships or fieldwork, Federal Work-Study, health care benefits, unspecified assistantships, and project assistantships available. Support available to part-time students. Financial award application deadline: 4/15; financial award applicants required to submit FAFSA. *Faculty research:* Applied management research in finance, management information systems, marketing, operations research, organizational sciences. *Unit head:* V. Kanti Prasad, Dean, 414-229-6256, E-mail: dean-prasad@uwm.edu. *Application contact:* Business Graduate Student Services, 414-229-5403, E-mail: mba-ms@uwm.edu.
Website: https://uwm.edu/business/

Valparaiso University, Graduate School and Continuing Education, College of Business, Valparaiso, IN 46383. Offers business administration (MBA); business decision-making (Certificate); business intelligence (Certificate); engineering management (Certificate); finance (Certificate); general business (Certificate); leading the global enterprise (Certificate); management (Certificate); JD/MBA; MSN/MBA. *Accreditation:* AACSB. *Program availability:* Part-time, evening/weekend, online learning. *Students:* 7 full-time (5 women), 43 part-time (16 women); includes 5 minority (4 Black or African American, non-Hispanic/Latino; 1 Two or more races, non-Hispanic/Latino). Average age 31. *Entrance requirements:* For master's, GMAT, GRE, minimum GPA of 3.0. Additional exam requirements/recommendations for international students: Required—TOEFL (minimum score 550 paper-based; 80 iBT), IELTS (minimum score 6). *Application deadline:* Applications are processed on a rolling basis. Application fee: $30 ($50 for international students). Electronic applications accepted. *Expenses:* Contact institution. *Financial support:* Available to part-time students. Applicants

required to submit FAFSA. *Unit head:* Jim Brodzinski, Dean, 219-464-5035, E-mail: jim.brodzinski@valpo.edu. *Application contact:* Cindy Scanlan, Director of Graduate Programs in Management, 219-465-7952, Fax: 219-464-5789, E-mail: cindy.scanlan@valpo.edu.
Website: http://www.valpo.edu/college-of-business/

Vanderbilt University, Vanderbilt University Owen Graduate School of Management, Vanderbilt MBA Program, Nashville, TN 37203. Offers accounting (MBA); finance (MBA); general management (MBA); health care (MBA); human and organizational performance (MBA); marketing (MBA); operations (MBA); strategy (MBA); MBA/JD; MBA/M Div; MBA/MD; MBA/MSN; MBA/MTS; MBA/PhD. *Accreditation:* AACSB. *Degree requirements:* For master's, 62 credit hours of coursework; completion of ethics course; minimum GPA of 3.0. *Entrance requirements:* For master's, GMAT (preferred) or GRE, 2 years of work experience (recommended). Additional exam requirements/recommendations for international students: Required—TOEFL (minimum score 100 iBT). Electronic applications accepted. *Expenses:* Contact institution. *Faculty research:* Accounting and finance, business strategy and economics, marketing, operations management, organization studies.

Villanova University, Villanova School of Business, MBA - The Fast Track Program, Villanova, PA 19085. Offers finance (MBA); healthcare (MBA); international business (MBA); strategic management (MBA). *Accreditation:* AACSB. *Program availability:* Part-time, evening/weekend. *Faculty:* 101 full-time (38 women), 36 part-time/adjunct (9 women). *Students:* 111 part-time (47 women); includes 20 minority (3 Black or African American, non-Hispanic/Latino; 7 Asian, non-Hispanic/Latino; 9 Hispanic/Latino; 1 Two or more races, non-Hispanic/Latino), 4 international. Average age 30. 45 applicants, 80% accepted, 26 enrolled. In 2018, 55 master's awarded. *Degree requirements:* For master's, minimum GPA of 3.0. *Entrance requirements:* For master's, GMAT or GRE, Application, official transcripts, 2 letters of recommendation, resume, 2 essays. Additional exam requirements/recommendations for international students: Required—TOEFL (minimum score 550 paper-based; 100 iBT). *Application deadline:* For fall admission, 7/31 for domestic and international students. Applications are processed on a rolling basis. Application fee: $65. Electronic applications accepted. *Expenses:* Contact institution. *Financial support:* Scholarships/grants available. Financial award application deadline: 6/30; financial award applicants required to submit FAFSA. *Faculty research:* Real Estate, Business Analytics, Global Leadership, Marketing and Consumer Insights, Church management. *Unit head:* Dr. Joyce E. A. Russell, Dean of Villanova School of Business, 610-519-6082, Fax: 610-519-6273, E-mail: joyce.russell@villanova.edu. *Application contact:* Daniel Guertin, Assistant Director, Recruitment, 610-519-8031, Fax: 610-519-6273, E-mail: daniel.guertin@villanova.edu.
Website: http://www1.villanova.edu/villanova/business/graduate/mba.html

Villanova University, Villanova School of Business, MBA - The Flex Track Program, Villanova, PA 19085. Offers healthcare (MBA); international business (MBA); marketing (MBA); real estate (MBA); strategic management (MBA); JD/MBA. *Accreditation:* AACSB. *Program availability:* Part-time, evening/weekend, online learning. *Faculty:* 101 full-time (38 women), 36 part-time/adjunct (9 women). *Students:* 13 full-time (5 women), 427 part-time (157 women); includes 74 minority (12 Black or African American, non-Hispanic/Latino; 29 Asian, non-Hispanic/Latino; 23 Hispanic/Latino; 10 Two or more races, non-Hispanic/Latino), 12 international. Average age 32. 156 applicants, 92% accepted, 139 enrolled. In 2018, 124 master's awarded. *Degree requirements:* For master's, minimum GPA of 3.0. *Entrance requirements:* For master's, GMAT or GRE, Application, official transcripts, 2 letters of recommendation, resume, 2 essays. Additional exam requirements/recommendations for international students: Required—TOEFL (minimum score 550 paper-based; 100 iBT). *Application deadline:* For fall admission, 7/31 for domestic and international students; for spring admission, 11/30 for domestic and international students; for summer admission, 4/30 for domestic and international students. Applications are processed on a rolling basis. Application fee: $65. Electronic applications accepted. *Expenses:* Contact institution. *Financial support:* Research assistantships and scholarships/grants available. Financial award application deadline: 6/30; financial award applicants required to submit FAFSA. *Faculty research:* Real Estate, Business Analytics, Global Leadership, Marketing and Consumer Insights, Church management. *Unit head:* Dr. Joyce E. A. Russell, Dean of Villanova School of Business, 610-519-6082, Fax: 610-519-6273, E-mail: joyce.russell@villanova.edu. *Application contact:* Daniel Guertin, Assistant Director, Recruitment, 610-519-8031, Fax: 610-519-6273, E-mail: daniel.guertin@villanova.edu.
Website: http://www1.villanova.edu/villanova/business/graduate/mba.html

Walsh College of Accountancy and Business Administration, Graduate Programs, Program in Management, Troy, MI 48083. Offers human resources management (MS); international business (MS); strategic management (MS). *Program availability:* Part-time, evening/weekend, 100% online, blended/hybrid learning. *Faculty:* 8 full-time (4 women), 7 part-time/adjunct (4 women). *Students:* 1 (woman) full-time, 38 part-time (28 women); includes 15 minority (12 Black or African American, non-Hispanic/Latino; 1 Asian, non-Hispanic/Latino; 2 Hispanic/Latino), 1 international. Average age 37. 19 applicants, 84% accepted, 7 enrolled. In 2018, 17 master's awarded. *Entrance requirements:* For master's, minimum overall cumulative GPA of 2.750 from all colleges previously attended. Additional exam requirements/recommendations for international students: Required—TOEFL (minimum score 550 paper-based, 79-80 internet based), IELTS (6.5), Michigan Test of English Language Proficiency, or MTELP (80). *Application deadline:* Applications are processed on a rolling basis. Application fee: $35. Electronic applications accepted. *Expenses:* $785 per credit hour plus $175 student support fee per semester. International students pay $785 per credit hour plus $175 student support fee and $275 international student fee per semester. *Financial support:* In 2018–19, 3 students received support. Scholarships/grants and Tuition Exchange Program available. Financial award application deadline: 6/30; financial award applicants required to submit FAFSA. *Faculty research:* Strategy practice and process, management learning and decision-making, human capital development, global leadership and citizenship, use of systems and complexity theory and management practice. *Unit head:* Dr. Ann Saurbier, Chair, Management, 248-823-1635, Fax: 248-689-0920, E-mail: asaurbie@walshcollege.edu. *Application contact:* Karen Mahaffy, Executive Director, Admissions and Enrollment Services, 248-823-1610, Fax: 248-823-1611, E-mail: kmahaffy@walshcollege.edu.

Wayne State University, College of Engineering, Department of Computer Science, Detroit, MI 48202. Offers computer science (MS, PhD), including bioinformatics and computational biology (PhD); data science and business analytics (MS). Application deadline for PhD is February 17. *Faculty:* 23. *Students:* 107 full-time (41 women), 39 part-time (11 women); includes 11 minority (2 Black or African American, non-Hispanic/Latino; 6 Asian, non-Hispanic/Latino; 2 Hispanic/Latino; 1 Two or more races, non-Hispanic/Latino), 99 international. Average age 30. 237 applicants, 28% accepted, 35 enrolled. In 2018, 27 master's, 7 doctorates awarded. *Degree requirements:* For master's, thesis (for some programs), practicum (for MS in data science and business analytics); for doctorate, thesis/dissertation. *Entrance requirements:* For master's, GRE (GMAT accepted for MS in data science and business analytics), minimum GPA of 3.0, three letters of recommendation, adequate preparation in computer science and mathematics courses, personal statement, resume (for MS in data science and business analytics); for doctorate, GRE, bachelor's or master's degree in computer science or related field; minimum GPA of 3.3 in most recent degree; three letters of recommendation; personal statement; adequate preparation in computer science and mathematics courses. Additional exam requirements/recommendations for international students: Required—TOEFL (minimum score 550 paper-based; 79 iBT), TWE (minimum score 5.5); Recommended—IELTS (minimum score 6.5). *Application deadline:* For fall admission, 6/1 priority date for domestic students, 5/1 priority date for international students; for winter admission, 10/1 priority date for domestic students, 9/1 priority date for international students; for spring admission, 2/1 priority date for domestic students, 1/2 priority date for international students. Applications are processed on a rolling basis. Application fee: $50. Electronic applications accepted. *Expenses:* Contact institution. *Financial support:* In 2018–19, 91 students received support, including 5 fellowships with tuition reimbursements available (averaging $20,000 per year), 18 research assistantships with tuition reimbursements available (averaging $20,383 per year), 27 teaching assistantships with tuition reimbursements available (averaging $20,166 per year); scholarships/grants, health care benefits, and unspecified assistantships also available. Financial award application deadline: 2/17; financial award applicants required to submit FAFSA. *Faculty research:* Software engineering, databases, bioinformatics, artificial intelligence, networking, distributed and parallel computing, security, graphics, visualizations. *Total annual research expenditures:* $1.1 million. *Unit head:* Dr. Loren Schwiebert, Chair, 313-577-5474, E-mail: loren@wayne.edu. *Application contact:* Areej Salaymeh, Graduate Advisor, 313-577-2477, E-mail: csgradadvisor@cs.wayne.edu.
Website: http://engineering.wayne.edu/cs/

Wayne State University, College of Engineering, Department of Industrial and Systems Engineering, Detroit, MI 48202. Offers data science and business analytics (MS); engineering management (MS); industrial engineering (MS, PhD); manufacturing engineering (MS); systems engineering (Certificate). *Program availability:* Online learning. *Faculty:* 11. *Students:* 178 full-time (40 women), 109 part-time (30 women); includes 42 minority (20 Black or African American, non-Hispanic/Latino; 16 Asian, non-Hispanic/Latino; 6 Hispanic/Latino), 167 international. Average age 29. 539 applicants, 40% accepted, 68 enrolled. In 2018, 172 master's, 9 doctorates awarded. *Entrance requirements:* For master's, GRE or GMAT (for applicants to MS in data science and business analytics), BS from ABET-accredited institution; for doctorate, GRE, graduate degree in engineering or related discipline with minimum graduate GPA of 3.5, statement of purpose, resume/curriculum vitae, three letters of recommendation; for Certificate, GRE (for applicants from non-ABET institutions), BS in engineering or other technical field from ABET-accredited institution with minimum GPA of 3.0 in upper-division course work, at least one year of full-time work experience as practicing engineer or technical leader. Additional exam requirements/recommendations for international students: Required—TOEFL (minimum score 550 paper-based; 79 iBT), TWE (minimum score 5.5), Michigan English Language Assessment Battery (minimum score 85); GRE; Recommended—IELTS (minimum score 6.5). *Application deadline:* Applications are processed on a rolling basis. Application fee: $50. Electronic applications accepted. *Expenses:* Contact institution. *Financial support:* In 2018–19, 135 students received support, including 2 fellowships with tuition reimbursements available (averaging $20,000 per year), 5 research assistantships with tuition reimbursements available (averaging $23,260 per year), 8 teaching assistantships with tuition reimbursements available (averaging $20,166 per year); scholarships/grants, tuition waivers (full), and unspecified assistantships also available. Financial award applicants required to submit FAFSA. *Faculty research:* Manufacturing systems, infrastructure, and management. *Total annual research expenditures:* $320,400. *Unit head:* Dr. Leslie Monplaisir, Associate Professor/Chair, 313-577-3821, Fax: 313-577-8833, E-mail: leslie.monplaisir@wayne.edu. *Application contact:* Eric Scimeca, Graduate Program Coordinator, 313-577-0412, E-mail: eric.scimeca@wayne.edu.
Website: http://engineering.wayne.edu/ise/

Wayne State University, Mike Ilitch School of Business, Detroit, MI 48202. Offers accounting (MS, MSA, Postbaccalaureate Certificate); business (EMS, Graduate Certificate); business administration (MBA, PhD); data science (MS), including business analytics; entrepreneurship and innovation (Postbaccalaureate Certificate); finance (MS); information systems management (Postbaccalaureate Certificate); taxation (MST); JD/MBA. Application deadline for PhD is February 15. *Accreditation:* AACSB. *Program availability:* Part-time, evening/weekend. *Faculty:* 31. *Students:* 286 full-time (152 women), 1,166 part-time (533 women); includes 409 minority (236 Black or African American, non-Hispanic/Latino; 83 Asian, non-Hispanic/Latino; 53 Hispanic/Latino; 37 Two or more races, non-Hispanic/Latino), 74 international. Average age 30. 1,212 applicants, 38% accepted, 294 enrolled. In 2018, 285 master's, 6 doctorates, 7 other advanced degrees awarded. *Degree requirements:* For doctorate, thesis/dissertation. *Entrance requirements:* For master's, GMAT, GRE, LSAT, MCAT, at least three years of relevant work experience that shows increased responsibility, or minimum GPA of 3.0 from AACSB-accredited program or 3.2 from regionally-accredited program, undergraduate degree from accredited institution; undergraduate degree in accounting, business administration, or area of business administration (for MS and MST); for doctorate, GMAT (minimum score of 600), minimum undergraduate GPA of 3.0, 3.5 upper-division or graduate; three letters of recommendation; brief essay; undergraduate degree from accredited institution; personal statement; for other advanced degree, bachelor's degree from accredited institution. Additional exam requirements/recommendations for international students: Required—TOEFL (minimum score 550 paper-based; 79 iBT), Michigan English Language Assessment Battery (minimum score 85); Recommended—IELTS (minimum score 6.5), TWE (minimum score 5.5). *Application deadline:* For fall admission, 7/1 for domestic students, 5/1 priority date for international students; for winter admission, 11/1 for domestic students, 9/1 priority date for international students; for spring admission, 3/1 for domestic students, 1/1 priority date for international students. Applications are processed on a rolling basis. Application fee: $50. Electronic applications accepted. *Expenses:* Contact institution. *Financial support:* In 2018–19, 175 students received support, including 1 fellowship with tuition reimbursement available (averaging $20,000 per year), 5 research assistantships with tuition reimbursements available (averaging $21,393 per year); teaching assistantships with tuition reimbursements available, scholarships/grants, health care benefits, and unspecified assistantships also available. Support available to part-time students. Financial award applicants required to submit FAFSA. *Faculty research:* Executive compensation and stock performance, consumer reactions to pricing strategies, communication across the automotive supply chain, performance of firms in sub-Saharan Africa, implementation issues with ERP software. *Unit head:* Dr. Robert Forsythe, Dean, School of Business Administration, 313-577-4501, E-mail: robert.forsythe@wayne.edu. *Application contact:* Kiantee N. Rupert-Jones, Director, 313-577-4511, Fax: 313-577-9442, E-mail: gradbusiness@wayne.edu.
Website: http://ilitchbusiness.wayne.edu/

Western Governors University, College of Business, Salt Lake City, UT 84107. Offers accounting (MS); information technology management (MBA); management and leadership (MS); management and strategy (MBA); strategic leadership (MBA). *Program availability:* Evening/weekend, online learning. *Degree requirements:* For master's, capstone project. *Entrance requirements:* For master's, transcripts. Additional exam requirements/recommendations for international students: Required—TOEFL (minimum score 450 paper-based; 80 iBT). Electronic applications accepted. Application fee is waived when completed online.

Xavier University, Williams College of Business, Master of Business Administration Program, Cincinnati, OH 45207. Offers business administration (Exec MBA, MBA); business intelligence (MBA); finance (MBA); health industry (MBA); international business (MBA); marketing (MBA); values-based leadership (MBA); MBA/MHSA; MSN/MBA. *Accreditation:* AACSB. *Program availability:* Part-time, evening/weekend. *Degree requirements:* For master's, capstone course. *Entrance requirements:* For master's, GMAT or GRE, official transcript; resume. Additional exam requirements/recommendations for international students: Required—TOEFL (minimum score 550 paper-based; 79 iBT). Electronic applications accepted. Application fee is waived when completed online. *Expenses:* Contact institution.

Sustainability Management

Adler University, Graduate Programs, Master of Public Administration Program, Chicago, IL 60602. Offers criminal justice (MPA); sustainable communities (MPA). *Program availability:* Part-time, evening/weekend.

American University, Kogod School of Business, Sustainability, Washington, DC 20016. Offers MS. *Students:* 17 full-time (13 women), 17 part-time (11 women); includes 6 minority (1 Black or African American, non-Hispanic/Latino; 2 Asian, non-Hispanic/Latino; 2 Hispanic/Latino; 1 Native Hawaiian or other Pacific Islander, non-Hispanic/Latino), 5 international. Average age 27. 35 applicants, 14% accepted, 16 enrolled. In 2018, 9 master's awarded. *Entrance requirements:* For master's, GMAT/GRE; Please see website: https://www.american.edu/kogod/, resume, personal statement, 2 letters of recommendation, transcripts. Additional exam requirements/recommendations for international students: Required—TOEFL (minimum score 100 iBT). Application fee: $100. *Expenses:* Contact institution. *Financial support:* Applicants required to submit FAFSA. *Application contact:* Jason Garner, Director of Admissions, 202-885-1926, E-mail: jgarner@american.edu.
Website: http://www.kogod.american.edu

Anaheim University, Programs in Business Administration, Anaheim, CA 92806-5150. Offers entrepreneurship (ME, DBA); global sustainable management (MBA); international business (MBA, DBA, Certificate, Diploma); management (DBA); sustainable management (DBA, Certificate, Diploma). *Program availability:* Part-time, evening/weekend, online only, 100% online. In 2018, 3 master's, 4 doctorates awarded. *Application deadline:* Applications are processed on a rolling basis. Electronic applications accepted. *Unit head:* Dr. Robert Robertson, Dean, Graduate School of Business, 714-772-3330, Fax: 714-772-3331, E-mail: admissions@anaheim.edu. *Application contact:* Dr. Robert Robertson, Dean, Graduate School of Business, 714-772-3330, Fax: 714-772-3331, E-mail: admissions@anaheim.edu.

Antioch University New England, Graduate School, Department of Management, Program in Sustainability (Green MBA), Keene, NH 03431-3552. Offers MBA. *Program availability:* Part-time. *Entrance requirements:* For master's, GRE, resume, 3 letters of recommendation. Additional exam requirements/recommendations for international students: Required—TOEFL (minimum score 600 paper-based).

Aquinas College, School of Management, Grand Rapids, MI 49506. Offers marketing management (MM); organizational leadership (MM); sustainable business (MM). *Program availability:* Part-time, evening/weekend. *Faculty:* 4 full-time (1 woman), 5 part-time/adjunct (0 women). *Students:* 12 full-time (4 women), 32 part-time (19 women); includes 3 minority (1 Black or African American, non-Hispanic/Latino; 1 Asian, non-Hispanic/Latino; 1 Hispanic/Latino), 2 international. Average age 31. In 2018, 19 master's awarded. *Entrance requirements:* For master's, GMAT, minimum undergraduate GPA of 2.75, 2 years of work experience. Additional exam requirements/recommendations for international students: Required—TOEFL (minimum score 550 paper-based). *Application deadline:* Applications are processed on a rolling basis. Application fee: $0. *Expenses: Tuition:* Part-time $593 per credit hour. *Required fees:* $120; $120. *Financial support:* Scholarships/grants available. Support available to part-time students. Financial award application deadline: 3/15; financial award applicants required to submit FAFSA. *Unit head:* Dr. Linda Hagan, Interim Dean of Business Division, 616-632-2193, Fax: 616-732-4489, E-mail: lmh010@aquinas.edu. *Application contact:* Lynn Atkins-Rykert, Program Coordinator, 616-632-2925, Fax: 616-732-4489, E-mail: atkinlyn@aquinas.edu.

Argosy University, Chicago, College of Business, Chicago, IL 60601. Offers accounting (DBA); customized professional concentration (MBA, DBA); finance (MBA); fraud examination (MBA); global business sustainability (DBA); healthcare administration (MBA); information systems (DBA); information systems management (MBA); international business (MBA, DBA); management (MBA, MSM, DBA); marketing (MBA, DBA); organizational leadership (Ed D); public administration (MBA); sustainable management (MBA). *Accreditation:* ACBSP. *Program availability:* Online learning.

Argosy University, Hawai`i, College of Business, Honolulu, HI 96813. Offers accounting (DBA); corporate compliance (MBA); customized professional concentration (MBA, DBA); finance (MBA, Certificate); fraud examination (MBA); global business sustainability (DBA); healthcare administration (MBA, Certificate); information systems (DBA); information systems management (MBA, Certificate); international business (MBA, DBA, Certificate); management (MBA, MSM, DBA); marketing (MBA, DBA, Certificate); organizational leadership (Ed D); public administration (MBA); sustainable management (MBA).

Argosy University, Los Angeles, College of Business, Los Angeles, CA 90045. Offers accounting (DBA); corporate compliance (MBA); customized professional concentration (MBA, DBA); finance (MBA); fraud examination (MBA); global business sustainability (DBA); healthcare administration (MBA); information systems (DBA); information systems management (MBA); international business (MBA, DBA); management (MBA, MSM, DBA); marketing (MBA, DBA); organizational leadership (Ed D); public administration (MBA); sustainable management (MBA).

Argosy University, Northern Virginia, College of Business, Arlington, VA 22209. Offers accounting (DBA); customized professional concentration (MBA, DBA); finance (MBA); fraud examination (MBA); global business sustainability (DBA); healthcare administration (MBA); information systems (DBA); information systems management (MBA); international business (MBA, DBA, Certificate); management (MBA, MSM, DBA); marketing (MBA, DBA, Certificate); organizational leadership (Ed D); public administration (MBA); sustainable management (MBA).

Argosy University, Orange County, College of Business, Orange, CA 92868. Offers accounting (DBA, Adv C); corporate compliance (MBA); customized professional concentration (MBA, DBA); finance (MBA, Certificate); fraud examination (MBA); global business sustainability (DBA); healthcare administration (MBA, Certificate); information systems (DBA, Adv C, Certificate); information systems management (MBA); international business (MBA, DBA, Adv C, Certificate); management (MBA, MSM, DBA, Adv C); marketing (MBA, DBA, Adv C, Certificate); organizational leadership (Ed D); public administration (MBA, Certificate); sustainable management (MBA).

Argosy University, Phoenix, College of Business, Phoenix, AZ 85021. Offers accounting (DBA); corporate compliance (MBA); customized professional concentration (MBA, DBA); finance (MBA); fraud examination (MBA); global business sustainability (DBA); healthcare administration (MBA); information systems (DBA); information systems management (MBA); international business (MBA, DBA); management (MBA, DBA); marketing (MBA, DBA); public administration (MBA); sustainable management (MBA).

Argosy University, Seattle, College of Business, Seattle, WA 98121. Offers accounting (DBA); corporate compliance (MBA); customized professional concentration (MBA, DBA); finance (MBA); fraud examination (MBA); global business sustainability (DBA); healthcare administration (MBA); information systems (DBA); information systems management (MBA); international business (MBA, DBA); management (MBA, MSM, DBA); marketing (MBA, DBA); organizational leadership (Ed D); public administration (MBA); sustainable management (MBA).

Argosy University, Tampa, College of Business, Tampa, FL 33607. Offers accounting (DBA); corporate compliance (MBA); customized professional concentration (MBA, DBA); finance (MBA); fraud examination (MBA); global business sustainability (DBA); healthcare administration (MBA); information systems (DBA); information systems management (MBA); international business (MBA, DBA); management (MBA, MSM, DBA); marketing (MBA, DBA); organizational leadership (Ed D); public administration (MBA); sustainable management (MBA).

Argosy University, Twin Cities, College of Business, Eagan, MN 55121. Offers accounting (DBA); customized professional concentration (MBA, DBA); finance (MBA); fraud examination (MBA); global business sustainability (DBA); healthcare administration (MBA); information systems (DBA); information systems management (MBA); international business (MBA, DBA); management (MBA, MSM, DBA); marketing (MBA, DBA); organizational leadership (Ed D); public administration (MBA); sustainable management (MBA).

Bard College, Bard Center for Environmental Policy, Annandale-on-Hudson, NY 12504. Offers climate science and policy (MS, Professional Certificate), including agriculture (MS), ecosystems (MS); environmental policy (MS, Professional Certificate); sustainability (MBA); MS/JD; MS/MAT. *Program availability:* Part-time. *Degree requirements:* For master's, thesis, 4-month, full-time internship. *Entrance requirements:* For master's, GRE, coursework in statistics, chemistry and one other semester of college science; personal statement; curriculum vitae; 3 letters of recommendation; sample of written work. Additional exam requirements/recommendations for international students: Required—TOEFL (minimum score 600 paper-based; 100 iBT). Electronic applications accepted. *Expenses:* Contact institution. *Faculty research:* Climate and agriculture, alternative energy, environmental economics, environmental toxicology, EPA law, sustainable development, international relations, literature and composition, human rights, agronomy, advocacy, leadership.

Baruch College of the City University of New York, Zicklin School of Business, Department of Management, New York, NY 10010-5585. Offers entrepreneurship (MBA); management (PhD); operations management (MBA); organizational behavior/human resources management (MBA); sustainable business (MBA). PhD offered jointly with Graduate School and University Center of the City University of New York. *Program availability:* Part-time, evening/weekend. *Degree requirements:* For doctorate, comprehensive exam, thesis/dissertation. *Entrance requirements:* For master's, GMAT, 2 letters of recommendation, resume, 2 years of work experience; for doctorate, GMAT. Additional exam requirements/recommendations for international students: Required—TOEFL (minimum score 590 paper-based), TWE.

Bluffton University, Graduate Programs in Business, Bluffton, OH 45817. Offers accounting and financial management (MBA); health care management (MBA); leadership (MAOM, MBA); production and operations management (MBA); sustainability management (MBA). *Program availability:* Evening/weekend, blended/hybrid learning, videoconference. *Faculty:* 4 full-time (2 women), 5 part-time/adjunct (1 woman). *Students:* 38 full-time (22 women), 1 part-time (0 women); includes 11 minority (6 Black or African American, non-Hispanic/Latino; 3 Hispanic/Latino; 2 Two or more races, non-Hispanic/Latino). Average age 33. In 2018, 25 master's awarded. *Degree requirements:* For master's, integrated research project (for some programs). *Entrance requirements:* For master's, current resume, official transcript, bachelor's degree, minimum GPA of 3.0, personal essay. Additional exam requirements/recommendations for international students: Recommended—TOEFL (minimum score 550 paper-based). *Application deadline:* For fall admission, 7/31 priority date for domestic and international students. Applications are processed on a rolling basis. Electronic applications accepted. *Expenses:* Contact institution. *Financial support:* Unspecified assistantships and faculty/staff grants available. Financial award applicants required to submit FAFSA. *Unit head:* Dr. Melissa Green, Director of Graduate Programs in Business, 419-358-3447, E-mail: greenm@bluffton.edu. *Application contact:* Shelby Koenig, Enrollment Counselor for Graduate Program, 419-3583684, E-mail: koenigs@bluffton.edu.
Website: https://www.bluffton.edu/ags/index.aspx

Case Western Reserve University, Weatherhead School of Management, Department of Design and Innovation, Cleveland, OH 44106. Offers designing sustainable systems (PhD). *Program availability:* Part-time, evening/weekend. *Degree requirements:* For doctorate, thesis/dissertation. *Entrance requirements:* For doctorate, GMAT. *Expenses: Tuition:* Full-time $45,168; part-time $1939 per credit hour. *Required fees:* $36; $18 per semester. $18 per semester. *Faculty research:* Decision support, business forecasting systems, design and use of information systems, artificial intelligence, executive information systems.

Chatham University, Program in Business Administration, Pittsburgh, PA 15232-2826. Offers business administration (MBA); healthcare management (MBA); sustainability (MBA); women's leadership (MBA). *Program availability:* Part-time, evening/weekend. *Entrance requirements:* For master's, minimum GPA of 3.0, letters of recommendation. Additional exam requirements/recommendations for international students: Required—TOEFL (minimum score 600 paper-based; 100 iBT), IELTS (minimum score 7), TWE. Electronic applications accepted. Application fee is waived when completed online. *Expenses:* Contact institution.

Sustainability Management

City University of Seattle, Graduate Division, School of Management, Seattle, WA 98121. Offers accounting (Certificate); change leadership (MBA, Certificate); computer systems (MS); finance (Certificate); financial management (MBA); general management (MBA); general management-Europe (MBA); global marketing (MBA); human resources management (Certificate); individualized study (MBA); information security (MS); information systems (MBA); leadership (MA); marketing (MBA, Certificate); project management (MBA, MS, Certificate); sustainable business (Certificate); technology management (MBA, Certificate). *Program availability:* Part-time, evening/weekend, online learning. *Degree requirements:* For master's, comprehensive exam (for some programs), thesis (for some programs). *Entrance requirements:* For master's, baccalaureate degree or equivalent from an accredited or otherwise recognized institution. Additional exam requirements/recommendations for international students: Required—TOEFL (minimum score 567 paper-based; 87 iBT); Recommended—IELTS. Electronic applications accepted.

Clark University, Graduate School, Graduate School of Management, Business Administration Program, Worcester, MA 01610-1477. Offers accounting (MBA); finance (MBA); information management and business analytics (MBA); management (MBA); marketing (MBA); social change (MBA); sustainability (MBA). *Accreditation:* AACSB. *Program availability:* Part-time, evening/weekend. *Degree requirements:* For master's, thesis optional. *Entrance requirements:* For master's, GMAT or GRE, 2 references, resume or curriculum vitae, personal statement. Additional exam requirements/recommendations for international students: Required—TOEFL (minimum score 575 paper-based; 90 iBT), IELTS (minimum score 6.5). Electronic applications accepted. *Expenses:* Contact institution. *Faculty research:* Marketing, accounting, human resource management, management information systems, business finance.

Colorado State University, Warner College of Natural Resources, Department of Ecosystem Science and Sustainability, Fort Collins, CO 80523-1476. Offers greenhouse gas management and accounting (MGMA); watershed science (MS). *Degree requirements:* For master's, thesis (for some programs). *Entrance requirements:* For master's, GRE (70th percentile or higher), minimum GPA of 3.0; resume; transcript; letters of recommendation; statement of purpose; undergraduate degree in a related field. Additional exam requirements/recommendations for international students: Required—TOEFL (minimum score 550 paper-based; 80 iBT), IELTS (minimum score 6.5). Electronic applications accepted. *Expenses:* Contact institution. *Faculty research:* Animal-habitat relationships; pastoral ecology and simulation; solving applied problems in ecosystem science and sustainable ecosystem management; intersections and boundaries of human activities, physical processes, and ecosystems; theoretical and applied ecology.

Columbia University, School of Professional Studies, Program in Sustainability Management, New York, NY 10027. Offers MS. Program offered in collaboration with Columbia University's Earth Institute. *Program availability:* Part-time. Electronic applications accepted.

DePaul University, Kellstadt Graduate School of Business, Chicago, IL 60604. Offers accountancy (MBA, MSA); applied economics (MBA); audit and advisory services (MS); business administration (DBA); business analytics (MS); business strategy and decision-making (MBA); computational finance (MS); economics and policy analysis (MS); enterprise risk management (MS); entrepreneurship (MBA, MS); finance (MBA, MS); general business (MBA); hospitality leadership (MBA); hospitality leadership and operational performance (MS); human resources (MS); international business (MBA); management (MBA, MS); management information systems (MBA); marketing (MBA, MS); marketing analysis (MS); marketing strategy and planning (MBA); real estate (MS); real estate finance and investment (MBA); strategy, execution and valuation (MBA); supply chain management (MS); sustainable management (MS); taxation (MS); JD/MBA. *Accreditation:* AACSB. *Program availability:* Part-time, evening/weekend, online learning. *Entrance requirements:* For master's, GMAT/GRE, 2 letters of recommendation, resume, essay, official transcripts. Additional exam requirements/recommendations for international students: Required—TOEFL (minimum score 550 paper-based; 80 iBT). Electronic applications accepted. *Expenses:* Contact institution.

Duquesne University, Palumbo-Donahue School of Business, Pittsburgh, PA 15282-0001. Offers accounting (M Acc); finance (MBA); information systems management (MSISM); management (MBA, MS); marketing (MBA); sports business (MS); supply chain management (MS); sustainability (MBA); JD/MBA; MBA/M Acc; MBA/MA; MBA/MES; MBA/MHMS; MSISM/MBA; Pharm D/MBA. *Accreditation:* AACSB. *Program availability:* Part-time, evening/weekend, 100% online, blended/hybrid learning. *Faculty:* 59 full-time (23 women), 25 part-time/adjunct (6 women). *Students:* 214 full-time (74 women), 42 part-time (20 women); includes 39 minority (12 Black or African American, non-Hispanic/Latino; 13 Asian, non-Hispanic/Latino; 8 Hispanic/Latino; 6 Two or more races, non-Hispanic/Latino), 23 international. Average age 29. 228 applicants, 88% accepted, 118 enrolled. In 2018, 149 master's awarded. *Entrance requirements:* For master's, GMAT or GRE, all official transcripts, two letters of recommendation, current resume, essays. Additional exam requirements/recommendations for international students: Required—TOEFL (minimum score 90 iBT), IELTS (minimum score 7). *Application deadline:* For fall admission, 7/1 priority date for domestic and international students; for spring admission, 12/1 for domestic and international students; for summer admission, 4/1 for domestic and international students. Applications are processed on a rolling basis. Application fee: $0. Electronic applications accepted. *Expenses:* $1,284/credit hour (business), $953/credit hour (management). *Financial support:* In 2018–19, 174 students received support, including 6 fellowships with partial tuition reimbursements available (averaging $24,750 per year); career-related internships or fieldwork, scholarships/grants, and unspecified assistantships also available. Support available to part-time students. Financial award application deadline: 7/1; financial award applicants required to submit FAFSA. *Faculty research:* Investment management, business ethics, technology management, supply chain management, entrepreneurship. *Unit head:* Dr. Karen Donovan, Associate Dean of Graduate Programs and Executive Education, 412-396-5788, Fax: 412-396-1726, E-mail: donovan6@duq.edu. *Application contact:* Chris Rouhier, Director of Graduate Admissions, 412-396-6244, Fax: 412-396-1726, E-mail: rouhierc@duq.edu.
Website: http://www.duq.edu/business/grad

Edgewood College, Program in Business, Madison, WI 53711-1997. Offers accountancy (MS); sustainability leadership (MBA). *Accreditation:* ACBSP. *Program availability:* Part-time, evening/weekend. *Students:* 74 full-time (34 women), 47 part-time (28 women); includes 19 minority (5 Black or African American, non-Hispanic/Latino; 2 American Indian or Alaska Native, non-Hispanic/Latino; 1 Asian, non-Hispanic/Latino; 8 Hispanic/Latino; 1 Native Hawaiian or other Pacific Islander, non-Hispanic/Latino; 2 Two or more races, non-Hispanic/Latino), 5 international. Average age 28. In 2018, 43 master's awarded. *Entrance requirements:* For master's, GMAT (minimum score 430), minimum GPA of 2.75, 2 letters of recommendation. Additional exam requirements/recommendations for international students: Required—TOEFL. *Application deadline:* For fall admission, 8/15 for domestic students, 5/1 for international students; for spring admission, 1/8 for domestic students, 11/1 for international students. Applications are processed on a rolling basis. Application fee: $30. Electronic applications accepted. *Expenses: Tuition:* Part-time $963 per credit. *Financial support:* Career-related internships or fieldwork and scholarships/grants available. *Unit head:* Dean, 608-663-2224, Fax: 608-663-3291. *Application contact:* Joann Eastman, Admissions Counselor, 608-663-3250, Fax: 608-663-2214, E-mail: gps@edgewood.edu.
Website: https://www.edgewood.edu/academics/schools/school-of-business

Edgewood College, Program in Social Innovation and Sustainability Leadership, Madison, WI 53711-1997. Offers MA. *Program availability:* Part-time, evening/weekend. *Faculty:* 1 full-time (0 women), 2 part-time/adjunct (1 woman). *Students:* 10 full-time (6 women), 7 part-time (4 women); includes 1 minority (Black or African American, non-Hispanic/Latino). Average age 36. 15 applicants, 100% accepted, 12 enrolled. In 2018, 4 master's awarded. *Entrance requirements:* Additional exam requirements/recommendations for international students: Required—TOEFL. *Application deadline:* For fall admission, 7/1 for domestic students. Application fee: $30. *Expenses:* Contact institution. *Financial support:* In 2018–19, 14 students received support. Scholarships/grants available. Support available to part-time students. Financial award application deadline: 5/1; financial award applicants required to submit FAFSA. *Faculty research:* Community development, collaborative decision-making, leadership, community well-being, organizational change. *Unit head:* Dr. Stephan Gilchrist, Director, 608-663-6991, E-mail: sgilchrist@edgewood.edu. *Application contact:* Joann Eastman, Assistant Director of Graduate Admissions, 608-663-3250, E-mail: jeastman@edgewood.edu.
Website: https://www.edgewood.edu/academics/programs/details/social-innovation-and-sustainability-leadership/graduate

Fairleigh Dickinson University, Florham Campus, Silberman College of Business, Certificate Program in Managing Sustainability, Madison, NJ 07940-1099. Offers Certificate.

Franklin Pierce University, Graduate and Professional Studies, Rindge, NH 03461-0060. Offers curriculum and instruction (M Ed); elementary education (MS Ed); emerging network technologies (Graduate Certificate); energy and sustainability studies (MBA, Graduate Certificate); health administration (MBA, Graduate Certificate); human resource management (MBA, Graduate Certificate); information technology (MBA); leadership (MBA); nursing education (MS); nursing leadership (MS); physical therapy (DPT); physician assistant studies (MPAS); special education (M Ed); sports management (MBA). *Accreditation:* APTA. *Program availability:* Part-time, 100% online, blended/hybrid learning. *Degree requirements:* For master's, concentrated original research projects; student teaching; fieldwork and/or internship; leadership project; PRAXIS I and II (for M Ed); for doctorate, concentrated original research projects, clinical fieldwork and/or internship, leadership project. *Entrance requirements:* For master's, minimum GPA of 2.5, 3 letters of recommendation; competencies in accounting, economics, statistics, and computer skills through life experience or undergraduate coursework (for MBA); certification/e-portfolio, minimum C grade in all education courses (for M Ed); license to practice as RN (for MS); for doctorate, GRE, 80 hours of observation/work in PT settings; completion of anatomy, chemistry, physics, and statistics; minimum GPA of 3.0. Additional exam requirements/recommendations for international students: Required—TOEFL (minimum score 550 paper-based; 61 iBT). Electronic applications accepted. *Faculty research:* Evidence-based practice in sports physical therapy, human resource management in economic crisis, leadership in nursing, innovation in sports facility management, differentiated learning and understanding by design.

Goddard College, Graduate Division, Master of Arts in Social Innovation and Sustainability Program, Plainfield, VT 05667-9432. Offers MA. *Program availability:* Part-time, online learning. *Degree requirements:* For master's, thesis. *Entrance requirements:* For master's, 3 letters of recommendation, relevant prior training or experience, interview. Electronic applications accepted.

Illinois Institute of Technology, Stuart School of Business, Program in Business Administration, Chicago, IL 60661. Offers sustainability (MBA); JD/MBA; M Des/MBA; MBA/MS. *Accreditation:* AACSB. *Program availability:* Part-time, evening/weekend. *Entrance requirements:* For master's, GRE (minimum score 298) or GMAT (500). Additional exam requirements/recommendations for international students: Required—TOEFL (minimum score 600 paper-based; 85 iBT); Recommended—IELTS (minimum score 7). Electronic applications accepted. *Expenses:* Contact institution. *Faculty research:* Global management and marketing strategy, technological innovation, management science, financial management, knowledge management.

Indiana University Bloomington, School of Public and Environmental Affairs, Public Affairs Programs, Bloomington, IN 47405. Offers economic development (MPA); energy (MPA); environmental policy (PhD); environmental policy and natural resource management (MPA); information systems (MPA); international development (MPA); local government management (MPA); nonprofit management (MPA, Certificate); policy analysis (MPA); public budgeting and financial management (Certificate); public finance (PhD); public financial administration (MPA); public management (MPA, PhD, Certificate); public policy analysis (PhD); social entrepreneurship (Certificate); specialized public affairs (MPA); sustainability and sustainable development (MPA); JD/MPA; MPA/MA; MPA/MIS; MPA/MLS; MSES/MPA. *Accreditation:* NASPAA (one or more programs are accredited). *Program availability:* Part-time. *Degree requirements:* For master's, capstone, internship; for doctorate, comprehensive exam, thesis/dissertation. *Entrance requirements:* For master's, GRE General Test or GMAT, official transcripts, 3 letters of recommendation, resume, personal statement; for doctorate, GRE General Test, official transcripts, 3 letters of recommendation, statement of purpose. Additional exam requirements/recommendations for international students: Required—TOEFL (minimum score 600 paper-based; 96 iBT); Recommended—IELTS (minimum score 7). Electronic applications accepted. *Faculty research:* International development, environmental policy and resource management, policy analysis, public finance, public management, urban management, nonprofit management, energy policy, social policy, public finance.

James Madison University, The Graduate School, College of Integrated Science and Engineering, Program in Environmental Management and Sustainability, Harrisonburg, VA 22807. Offers MS. *Students:* 3 part-time (1 woman), 1 international. Average age 30. In 2018, 15 master's awarded. Electronic applications accepted. *Expenses:* Tuition, state resident: full-time $10,848. Tuition, nonresident: full-time $27,888. *Required fees:* $1128. *Financial support:* Fellowships, Federal Work-Study, and unspecified assistantships available. Financial award application deadline: 3/1; financial award applicants required to submit FAFSA. *Unit head:* Dr. Eric H. Maslen, Department Head, 540-568-2740, E-mail: masleneh@jmu.edu. *Application contact:* Lynette D. Michael, Director of Graduate Admissions, 540-568-6131 Ext. 6395, Fax: 540-568-7860, E-mail: michaeld@jmu.edu.
Website: http://www.jmu.edu/mems-malta/index.shtml

Maastricht School of Management, Graduate Programs, Maastricht, Netherlands. Offers business administration (MBA, DBA, PhD); facility management (Exec MBA); management (M Sc); sustainability (Exec MBA).

Maharishi University of Management, Graduate Studies, Program in Business Administration, Fairfield, IA 52557. Offers accounting (MBA); management (PhD); sustainability (MBA). *Program availability:* Evening/weekend, online learning. *Degree requirements:* For doctorate, thesis/dissertation. *Entrance requirements:* For master's, GMAT, minimum GPA of 3.0; for doctorate, minimum GPA of 3.0. Additional exam requirements/recommendations for international students: Required—TOEFL.

Expenses: Tuition: Full-time $29,000; part-time $4800 per credit hour. *Required fees:* $530. *Faculty research:* Leadership, effects of the group dynamics of consciousness on the economy, innovation, employee development, cooperative strategy.

Michigan Technological University, Graduate School, Interdisciplinary Programs, Houghton, MI 49931. Offers automotive systems and controls (Graduate Certificate); biochemistry and molecular biology (PhD); computational science and engineering (PhD); data science (Graduate Certificate); sustainability (Graduate Certificate). *Program availability:* Part-time. *Faculty:* 120 full-time (25 women), 8 part-time/adjunct. *Students:* 67 full-time (28 women), 24 part-time; includes 5 minority (2 Black or African American, non-Hispanic/Latino; 1 American Indian or Alaska Native, non-Hispanic/Latino; 2 Two or more races, non-Hispanic/Latino), 59 international. Average age 29. 479 applicants, 24% accepted, 17 enrolled. In 2018, 19 master's, 8 doctorates, 10 other advanced degrees awarded. Terminal master's awarded for partial completion of doctoral program. *Degree requirements:* For master's, comprehensive exam (for some programs), thesis (for some programs); for doctorate, comprehensive exam, thesis/dissertation. *Entrance requirements:* For master's, doctorate, and Graduate Certificate, GRE, statement of purpose, personal statement, official transcripts, 2-3 letters of recommendation. Additional exam requirements/recommendations for international students: Required—TOEFL or IELTS. *Application deadline:* Applications are processed on a rolling basis. Electronic applications accepted. *Expenses: Tuition, area resident:* Full-time $18,126; part-time $1007 per credit. Tuition, state resident: full-time $18,126; part-time $1007 per credit. Tuition, nonresident: full-time $18,126; part-time $1007 per credit. International tuition: $18,126 full-time. *Required fees:* $248; $124 per semester. Tuition and fees vary according to course load and program. *Financial support:* In 2018–19, 64 students received support, including 14 fellowships with tuition reimbursements available (averaging $16,590 per year), 14 research assistantships with tuition reimbursements available (averaging $16,590 per year), 12 teaching assistantships with tuition reimbursements available (averaging $16,590 per year); career-related internships or fieldwork, Federal Work-Study, scholarships/grants, health care benefits, unspecified assistantships, and cooperative program also available. Financial award applicants required to submit FAFSA. *Faculty research:* Big data, atmospheric sciences, bioinformatics and systems biology, molecular dynamics, environmental studies. *Unit head:* Dr. Pushpalatha Murthy, Dean of the Graduate School/Associate Provost for Graduate Education, 906-487-3007, Fax: 906-487-2284, E-mail: ppmurthy@mtu.edu. *Application contact:* Carol T. Wingerson, Administrative Aide, 906-487-2328, Fax: 906-487-2284, E-mail: gradadms@mtu.edu.

Naropa University, Graduate Programs, Program in Resilient Leadership, Boulder, CO 80302-6697. Offers MA. *Degree requirements:* For master's, applied leadership project. *Entrance requirements:* For master's, interview; letter of interest; resume/curriculum vitae with pertinent academic, employment and volunteer activity; 2 letters of recommendation; transcripts. Additional exam requirements/recommendations for international students: Required—TOEFL (minimum score 550 paper-based; 80 iBT). Electronic applications accepted. *Expenses:* Contact institution.

National University, School of Engineering and Computing, La Jolla, CA 92037-1011. Offers computer science (MS), including advanced computing; cyber security and information assurance (MS); data analytics (MS); electrical engineering (MS); engineering management (MS); information technology management (MS); management information systems (MS); sustainability management (MS). *Program availability:* Part-time, evening/weekend, 100% online, blended/hybrid learning. *Degree requirements:* For master's, thesis (for some programs). *Entrance requirements:* For master's, interview, minimum GPA of 2.5. Additional exam requirements/recommendations for international students: Required—TOEFL (minimum score 550 paper-based; 79 iBT), IELTS (minimum score 6). Electronic applications accepted. *Expenses: Tuition:* Full-time $10,320; part-time $430 per unit. Tuition and fees vary according to degree level. *Faculty research:* Educational technology, scholarships in science.

The New School, Schools of Public Engagement, Program in Environmental Policy and Sustainability Management, New York, NY 10011. Offers environmental policy and sustainability management (MS). *Program availability:* Part-time, evening/weekend. *Degree requirements:* For master's, thesis. *Entrance requirements:* For master's, two letters of recommendation, statement of purpose, resume, transcripts. Additional exam requirements/recommendations for international students: Required—TOEFL (minimum score 92 iBT), IELTS (minimum score 7), PTE (minimum score 68). Electronic applications accepted. *Expenses:* Contact institution.

Oklahoma State University, Graduate College, Stillwater, OK 74078. Offers aerospace security (Graduate Certificate); bioenergy and sustainable technology (Graduate Certificate); business data mining (Graduate Certificate); business sustainability (Graduate Certificate); environmental science (MS); international studies (MS); non-profit management (Graduate Certificate); teaching English to speakers of other languages (Graduate Certificate); telecommunications management (MS). Programs are interdisciplinary. *Degree requirements:* For master's, thesis (for some programs); for doctorate, comprehensive exam, thesis/dissertation. *Entrance requirements:* For master's and doctorate, GRE or GMAT. Additional exam requirements/recommendations for international students: Required—TOEFL (minimum score 550 paper-based; 79 iBT). Electronic applications accepted. *Expenses: Tuition, area resident:* Full-time $4148. Tuition, state resident: full-time $4148. Tuition, nonresident: full-time $10,517. International tuition: $10,517 full-time. *Required fees:* $4394; $2929 per credit hour. Tuition and fees vary according to course load and program.

Oregon State University, College of Forestry, Program in Forest Ecosystems and Society, Corvallis, OR 97331. Offers forest biology (MF); forest, wildlife and landscape ecology (MS, PhD); genetics and physiology (MS, PhD); integrated social and ecological systems (MS, PhD); science of conservation, restoration and sustainable management (MS, PhD); silviculture (MF); social science, policy, and natural resources (MS, PhD); soil-plant-atmosphere continuum (MS, PhD); sustainable recreation and tourism (MS). *Program availability:* Part-time. *Entrance requirements:* For master's and doctorate, GRE. Additional exam requirements/recommendations for international students: Required—TOEFL (minimum score 80 iBT), IELTS (minimum score 6.5). *Faculty research:* Ecosystem structure and function, nutrient cycling, biotechnology, vegetation management, integrated forest protection.

Oregon State University, College of Forestry, Program in Sustainable Forest Management, Corvallis, OR 97331. Offers engineering for sustainable forestry (MF, MS, PhD). *Program availability:* Part-time. *Entrance requirements:* For master's and doctorate, GRE. Additional exam requirements/recommendations for international students: Required—TOEFL (minimum score 80 iBT), IELTS (minimum score 6.5).

Penn State Great Valley, Graduate Studies, Management Division, Malvern, PA 19355-1488. Offers business administration (MBA); cyber security (Certificate); data analytics (MPS, MS, Certificate); distributed energy and grid modernization (Certificate); finance (M Fin); health sector management (Certificate); human resource management (Certificate); information science (MSIS); leadership development (MLD); new ventures and entrepreneurship (Certificate); sustainable management practices (Certificate). *Accreditation:* AACSB.

Presidio Graduate School, Graduate Programs - San Francisco, San Francisco, CA 94129. Offers sustainable energy management (Certificate); sustainable management (MBA, MPA, Certificate); MBA/JD; MBA/MPA. MBA/JD offered in conjunction with the University of California, Hastings College of the Law.

Presidio Graduate School, MBA Programs - Seattle, San Francisco, CA 94129. Offers cooperative management (Certificate); sustainable business (MBA); sustainable systems (MBA). *Program availability:* Part-time, evening/weekend, blended/hybrid learning. *Entrance requirements:* For master's and Certificate, Quantitative Assessment Summary, GRE, or GMAT, resume, two letters of recommendation, essay, transcripts. Additional exam requirements/recommendations for international students: Required—TOEFL (minimum score 90 iBT), IELTS (minimum score 6.5). Electronic applications accepted.

Rochester Institute of Technology, Graduate Enrollment Services, Golisano Institute for Sustainability, Rochester, NY 14623-5603. Offers M Arch, MS, PhD. *Program availability:* Part-time. *Students:* 62 full-time (33 women), 21 part-time (10 women); includes 5 minority (1 Asian, non-Hispanic/Latino; 3 Hispanic/Latino; 1 Two or more races, non-Hispanic/Latino), 51 international. Average age 29. 164 applicants, 55% accepted, 22 enrolled. In 2018, 9 master's, 1 doctorate awarded. *Entrance requirements:* For master's and doctorate, GRE, minimum GPA of 3.0 (recommended). *Application deadline:* For fall admission, 2/15 priority date for domestic and international students; for spring admission, 12/15 priority date for domestic and international students. Applications are processed on a rolling basis. Application fee: $65. Electronic applications accepted. *Expenses:* Contact institution. *Financial support:* In 2018–19, 73 students received support. Research assistantships with tuition reimbursements available, teaching assistantships with tuition reimbursements available, career-related internships or fieldwork, scholarships/grants, unspecified assistantships, and health care benefits (for PhD program only) available. Support available to part-time students. Financial award applicants required to submit FAFSA. *Faculty research:* Environmentally responsive architecture and passive/natural building design and systems; renewable energy; advanced manufacturing technology; built environments; eco-friendly electronics and e-waste; energy generation, storage, and systems; pollution prevention; transportation and interconnected smart city systems. *Unit head:* Dr. Nabil Nasr, Associate Provost and Director, 585-475-5101, E-mail: info@sustainability.rit.edu. *Application contact:* Diane Ellison, Senior Associate Vice President, Graduate Enrollment Services, 585-475-2229, Fax: 585-475-7164, E-mail: gradinfo@rit.edu. Website: http://www.rit.edu/gis/

Royal Roads University, Graduate Studies, Environment and Sustainability Program, Victoria, BC V9B 5Y2, Canada. Offers environment and management (M Sc, MA); environment and sustainability (MAIS); environmental education and communication (MA, G Dip, Graduate Certificate); MA/MS. *Program availability:* Blended/hybrid learning. *Degree requirements:* For master's, thesis. *Entrance requirements:* For master's, 5-7 years of related work experience. Electronic applications accepted. *Expenses: Tuition, area resident:* Full-time $27,000 Canadian dollars. Tuition, state resident: full-time $27,000 Canadian dollars. Tuition, nonresident: full-time $33,000 Canadian dollars. *Required fees:* $662 Canadian dollars. *Faculty research:* Sustainable development, atmospheric processes, sustainable communities, chemical fate and transport of persistent organic pollutants, educational technology.

San Francisco State University, Division of Graduate Studies, College of Business, Program in Business Administration, San Francisco, CA 94132-1722. Offers decision sciences/operations research (MBA); ethics and compliance (MBA); finance (MBA); global business and innovation (MBA); healthcare administration (MBA); hospitality and tourism management (MBA); information systems (MBA); leadership (MBA); marketing (MBA); nonprofit and social enterprise leadership (MBA); sustainable business (MBA). *Accreditation:* AACSB. *Program availability:* Part-time, evening/weekend. *Degree requirements:* For master's, thesis, essay test. *Entrance requirements:* For master's, GMAT, minimum GPA of 2.7 in last 60 units. Additional exam requirements/recommendations for international students: Required—TOEFL (minimum score 550 paper-based).

Seattle Pacific University, Master of Arts in Management Program, Seattle, WA 98119-1997. Offers business intelligence and data analytics (MA); cybersecurity (MA); faith and business (MA); human resources (MA); social and sustainable management (MA). *Students:* 12 part-time (9 women); includes 3 minority (2 Black or African American, non-Hispanic/Latino; 1 Asian, non-Hispanic/Latino), 4 international. Average age 31. 11 applicants, 45% accepted, 2 enrolled. *Entrance requirements:* For master's, GMAT scores above 500 (25 verbal; 30 quantitative; 4.4 analytical writing) are preferred. https://spu.edu/academics/school-of-business-and-economics/graduate-programs/mba#application, bachelor's degree from accredited college or university, resume, essay, official transcript. *Application deadline:* For fall admission, 8/1 for domestic students, 6/1 for international students; for winter admission, 11/1 for domestic students, 9/1 for international students; for spring admission, 2/1 for domestic students, 12/1 for international students; for summer admission, 5/1 for domestic students. Application fee: $50. Website: http://spu.edu/academics/school-of-business-and-economics/graduate-programs/ma-management

Seattle Pacific University, Master of Business Administration Program, Seattle, WA 98119-1997. Offers business administration (MBA); social and sustainable enterprise (MBA). *Accreditation:* AACSB. *Program availability:* Part-time. *Students:* 2 full-time (1 woman), 40 part-time (25 women); includes 13 minority (4 Black or African American, non-Hispanic/Latino; 5 Asian, non-Hispanic/Latino; 2 Hispanic/Latino; 2 Two or more races, non-Hispanic/Latino), 9 international. Average age 32. 36 applicants, 53% accepted, 7 enrolled. In 2018, 14 master's awarded. *Entrance requirements:* For master's, GMAT (minimum preferred scores of 500; 25 verbal; 30 quantitative; 4.4 analytical writing), BA, resume as evidence of substantive work experience. Additional exam requirements/recommendations for international students: Required—TOEFL (minimum score 90 iBT), IELTS (minimum score 7). *Application deadline:* For fall admission, 8/1 for domestic and international students; for winter admission, 11/1 for domestic and international students; for spring admission, 2/1 for domestic and international students. Applications are processed on a rolling basis. Application fee: $50. Electronic applications accepted. *Financial support:* Scholarships/grants available. Financial award applicants required to submit FAFSA. *Unit head:* Gary Karns, Associate Dean for Graduate Studies, 206-281-2948, Fax: 206-281-2733. *Application contact:* Gary Karns, Associate Dean for Graduate Studies, 206-281-2948, Fax: 206-281-2733. Website: http://spu.edu/academics/school-of-business-and-economics/graduate-programs/mba

SIT Graduate Institute, Graduate Programs, Master's Program in Climate Change and Global Sustainability, Brattleboro, VT 05302-0676. Offers MA.

Southeastern Louisiana University, College of Arts, Humanities and Social Sciences, Department of Sociology and Criminal Justice, Hammond, LA 70402. Offers criminal justice (MS); globalization and sustainability (MS). *Program availability:* Part-time, evening/weekend. *Faculty:* 11 full-time (4 women). *Students:* 17 full-time (8 women), 10 part-time (5 women); includes 9 minority (4 Black or African American, non-Hispanic/Latino; 3 Hispanic/Latino; 2 Two or more races, non-Hispanic/Latino), 1 international.

Sustainability Management

Average age 27. 22 applicants, 64% accepted, 11 enrolled. In 2018, 2 master's awarded. *Degree requirements:* For master's, thesis, internship report instead of thesis for those on internship track. *Entrance requirements:* For master's, GRE, letter of application, short autobiographical essay, resume, 2 letters of recommendation. Additional exam requirements/recommendations for international students: Required—TOEFL (minimum score 500 paper-based; 61 iBT). *Application deadline:* For fall admission, 7/15 priority date for domestic students, 6/1 priority date for international students; for spring admission, 12/1 priority date for domestic students, 10/1 priority date for international students. Applications are processed on a rolling basis. Application fee: $20 ($30 for international students). Electronic applications accepted. *Expenses: Tuition, area resident:* Full-time $6684. Tuition, state resident: full-time $6684. Tuition, nonresident: full-time $19,162. *Required fees:* $2097. *Financial support:* In 2018–19, 13 students received support, including 5 research assistantships with tuition reimbursements available (averaging $8,329 per year); career-related internships or fieldwork, Federal Work-Study, institutionally sponsored loans, scholarships/grants, and unspecified assistantships also available. Support available to part-time students. Financial award application deadline: 5/1; financial award applicants required to submit FAFSA. *Faculty research:* Criminology and criminal justice; environmental/green sociology; globalization; disaster management; race, gender, class, and sexuality. *Unit head:* Dr. Kenneth Bolton, Department Head, 985-549-2110, Fax: 985-549-5961, E-mail: kbolton@southeastern.edu. *Application contact:* Office of Admissions, 985-549-5637, Fax: 985-549-5632, E-mail: admissions@southeastern.edu.
Website: http://www.southeastern.edu/acad_research/depts/soc_cj/grad_degree/index.html

Southern New Hampshire University, School of Business, Manchester, NH 03106-1045. Offers accounting (MBA, Graduate Certificate); accounting finance (MS); accounting/auditing (MS); accounting/forensic accounting (MS); accounting/management accounting (MS); accounting/taxation (MS); applied economics (MS); athletic administration (MBA, Graduate Certificate); business administration (IMBA, Certificate), including business information systems (Certificate), human resource management (Certificate); business analytics (MBA); business intelligence (MBA); communication (MA), including new media and marketing, public relations; community economic development (MBA); criminal justice (MBA); data analytics (MS); economics (MBA); engineering management (MBA); entrepreneurship (MBA); finance (MBA, MS, Graduate Certificate); finance/corporate finance (MS); finance/investments (MS); forensic accounting (MBA); forensic accounting and fraud examination (Graduate Certificate); healthcare informatics (MBA); healthcare management (MBA); human resource management (MS); human resources (MBA); information technology (MS); information technology management (MBA); international business (PhD); Internet marketing (MBA); leadership (MBA); leadership of nonprofit organizations (Graduate Certificate); management (MS); marketing (MBA, MS, Graduate Certificate); music business (MBA); operations and project management (MS); operations and supply chain management (MBA, Graduate Certificate); organizational leadership (MS); project management (MBA, Graduate Certificate); public administration (MBA, Graduate Certificate); quantitative analysis (MBA); Six Sigma (Graduate Certificate); Six Sigma quality (MBA); social media marketing (MBA, Graduate Certificate); sport management (MBA, MS, Graduate Certificate); sustainability and environmental compliance (MBA); MBA/Certificate. *Accreditation:* ACBSP. *Program availability:* Part-time, evening/weekend, online learning. Terminal master's awarded for partial completion of doctoral program. *Degree requirements:* For master's, one foreign language, comprehensive exam (for some programs), thesis or alternative; for doctorate, one foreign language, comprehensive exam, thesis/dissertation. *Entrance requirements:* For master's, minimum GPA of 2.5; for doctorate, GMAT. Additional exam requirements/recommendations for international students: Required—TOEFL (minimum score 500 paper-based). Electronic applications accepted.

South University, Graduate Programs, College of Business, Savannah, GA 31406. Offers corrections (MBA); entrepreneurship and small business (MBA); healthcare administration (MBA); hospitality management (MBA); leadership (MS); public administration (MPA); sustainability (MBA).

State University of New York College of Environmental Science and Forestry, Department of Paper and Bioprocess Engineering, Syracuse, NY 13210-2779. Offers biomaterials engineering (MS, PhD); bioprocess engineering (MPS, MS, PhD); bioprocessing (Advanced Certificate); paper science and engineering (MPS, MS, PhD); sustainable engineering management (MPS). *Program availability:* Part-time. *Faculty:* 13 full-time (2 women), 1 part-time/adjunct (0 women). *Students:* 20 full-time (11 women), 1 part-time (0 women); includes 29 minority (28 American Indian or Alaska Native, non-Hispanic/Latino; 1 Hispanic/Latino), 14 international. Average age 28. 18 applicants, 100% accepted, 11 enrolled. In 2018, 2 master's awarded. Terminal master's awarded for partial completion of doctoral program. *Degree requirements:* For master's, thesis; for doctorate, comprehensive exam, thesis/dissertation; for Advanced Certificate, 15 credit hours. *Entrance requirements:* For master's and doctorate, GRE General Test, minimum GPA of 3.0; for Advanced Certificate, BS, calculus plus science major. Additional exam requirements/recommendations for international students: Required—TOEFL (minimum score 550 paper-based; 80 iBT), IELTS (minimum score 6). *Application deadline:* For fall admission, 2/1 priority date for domestic and international students; for spring admission, 11/1 priority date for domestic and international students. Applications are processed on a rolling basis. Application fee: $60. Electronic applications accepted. *Expenses: Tuition, area resident:* Full-time $11,090; part-time $462 per credit hour. Tuition, state resident: full-time $11,090; part-time $462 per credit hour. Tuition, nonresident: full-time $22,650; part-time $944 per credit hour. *International tuition:* $22,650 full-time. *Required fees:* $1733; $178.58 per credit hour. *Financial support:* In 2018–19, 17 students received support. Unspecified assistantships available. Financial award application deadline: 6/30; financial award applicants required to submit FAFSA. *Faculty research:* Sustainable products and processes, biorefinery, pulping and papermaking, nanocellulose, bioconversions, process control and modeling. *Total annual research expenditures:* $237,793. *Unit head:* Dr. Bandaru Ramarao, Interim Chair, 315-470-6502, Fax: 315-470-6945, E-mail: bvramara@esf.edu. *Application contact:* Scott Shannon, Associate Provost and Dean, Instruction and Graduate Studies, 315-470-6599, Fax: 315-470-6978, E-mail: esfgrad@esf.edu.
Website: http://www.esf.edu/pbe/

Syracuse University, College of Engineering and Computer Science, CAS Program in Sustainable Enterprise, Syracuse, NY 13244. Offers CAS. *Unit head:* Dr. Todd Moss, Faculty Director, Sustainable Enterprise Partnership, 315-443-9215, E-mail: tmoss@syr.edu. *Application contact:* Kathleen Joyce, Assistant Dean, 315-443-2219, E-mail: topgrads@syr.edu.
Website: http://eng-cs.syr.edu/our-departments/mechanical-and-aerospace-engineering/graduate/academic-programs/?programID-1549&degree-graduate_certificate

Tufts University, The Gerald J. and Dorothy R. Friedman School of Nutrition Science and Policy, Boston, MA 02111. Offers agriculture, food and environment (MS, PhD); biochemical and molecular nutrition (MS, PhD); dietetic internship (MS); food and nutrition policy (MS, PhD); humanitarian assistance (MAHA); nutrition (MS, PhD); nutrition data science (MS, PhD); nutrition interventions, communication, and behavior change (MS, PhD); sustainable water management (MS). *Program availability:* Part-time. *Degree requirements:* For doctorate, comprehensive exam, thesis/dissertation. *Entrance requirements:* For master's and doctorate, GRE General Test. Additional exam requirements/recommendations for international students: Required—TOEFL. Electronic applications accepted. *Expenses:* Contact institution. *Faculty research:* Nutritional biochemistry and metabolism, cell and molecular biochemistry, epidemiology, policy/planning, applied nutrition.

The University of British Columbia, Faculty of Forestry, Program in Sustainable Forest Management, Vancouver, BC V6T 1Z1, Canada. Offers MSFM.

The University of British Columbia, Faculty of Science, Institute for Resources, Environment and Sustainability, Vancouver, BC V6T 1Z4, Canada. Offers M Sc, MA, PhD. *Degree requirements:* For master's, thesis; for doctorate, comprehensive exam, thesis/dissertation. *Entrance requirements:* Additional exam requirements/recommendations for international students: Required—TOEFL. Electronic applications accepted. *Expenses:* Contact institution. *Faculty research:* Land management, water resources, energy, environmental assessment, risk evaluation.

University of California, Berkeley, UC Berkeley Extension, Certificate Programs in Sustainability Studies, Berkeley, CA 94720. Offers leadership in sustainability and environmental management (Professional Certificate); solar energy and green building (Professional Certificate); sustainable design (Professional Certificate).

University of California, Merced, Graduate Division, School of Engineering, Merced, CA 95343. Offers biological engineering and small scale technologies (MS, PhD); electrical engineering and computer science (MS, PhD); environmental systems (MS, PhD); management of innovation, sustainability, and technology (MM); mechanical engineering (MS); mechanical engineering and applied mechanics (PhD). *Faculty:* 60 full-time (16 women). *Students:* 219 full-time (72 women), 1 part-time (0 women); includes 43 minority (2 Black or African American, non-Hispanic/Latino; 17 Asian, non-Hispanic/Latino; 20 Hispanic/Latino; 1 Native Hawaiian or other Pacific Islander, non-Hispanic/Latino; 3 Two or more races, non-Hispanic/Latino), 145 international. Average age 28. 371 applicants, 46% accepted, 75 enrolled. In 2018, 30 master's, 17 doctorates awarded. Terminal master's awarded for partial completion of doctoral program. *Degree requirements:* For master's, variable foreign language requirement, comprehensive exam, thesis or alternative, oral defense; for doctorate, variable foreign language requirement, comprehensive exam, thesis/dissertation, oral defense. *Entrance requirements:* For master's and doctorate, GRE. Additional exam requirements/recommendations for international students: Required—TOEFL (minimum score 550 paper-based; 80 iBT); Recommended—IELTS (minimum score 6.5). *Application deadline:* For fall admission, 1/15 priority date for domestic and international students. Application fee: $105 ($125 for international students). Electronic applications accepted. *Expenses:* In-state tuition $11442 per year; Out-of-state tuition $26544 per year; Student Fees $1765 per year. *Financial support:* In 2018–19, 200 students received support, including 14 fellowships with full tuition reimbursements available (averaging $20,851 per year), 70 research assistantships with full tuition reimbursements available (averaging $18,334 per year), 116 teaching assistantships with full tuition reimbursements available (averaging $19,841 per year); scholarships/grants, traineeships, and health care benefits also available. *Faculty research:* Sustainability systems engineering and resource management: food, energy, water; biomolecular engineering and biotechnology; computational science and data analytics; artificial intelligence, machine learning, internet of things, human computer interface; cyber-physical systems and automation. *Total annual research expenditures:* $3.1 million. *Unit head:* Dr. Mark Matsumoto, Dean, 209-228-4047, Fax: 209-228-4047, E-mail: mmatsumoto@ucmerced.edu. *Application contact:* Tsu Ya, Director of Admissions and Academic Services, 209-228-4521, Fax: 209-228-6906, E-mail: tya@ucmerced.edu.

University of Colorado Denver, Business School, Program in Management and Organization, Denver, CO 80217. Offers business strategy (MS); change and innovation (MS); enterprise technology management (MS); entrepreneurship and innovation (MS); global management (MS); leadership (MS); managing for sustainability (MS); managing human resources (MS); sports and entertainment (MS); strategic management (MS). *Accreditation:* AACSB. *Program availability:* Part-time, evening/weekend, online learning. *Degree requirements:* For master's, 30 semester hours (12 of required courses, 12 of management electives, and 6 of free electives). *Entrance requirements:* For master's, GMAT, resume, two letters of recommendation, essay, financial statements (for international applicants). Additional exam requirements/recommendations for international students: Required—TOEFL (minimum score 525 paper-based; 71 iBT); Recommended—IELTS (minimum score 6.5). Electronic applications accepted. *Expenses:* Contact institution. *Faculty research:* Human resource management, management of catastrophe, turnaround strategies.

University of Louisville, School of Interdisciplinary and Graduate Studies, Louisville, KY 40292. Offers interdisciplinary studies (MA, MS, PhD), including bioethics and medical humanities (MA), bioinformatics (PhD), sustainability (MA, MS), translational bioengineering (PhD), translational neuroscience (PhD). *Program availability:* Part-time. *Students:* 27 full-time (13 women), 11 part-time (5 women); includes 4 minority (1 Black or African American, non-Hispanic/Latino; 2 Hispanic/Latino; 1 Two or more races, non-Hispanic/Latino), 11 international. Average age 32. 19 applicants, 68% accepted, 8 enrolled. In 2018, 2 master's awarded. *Degree requirements:* For master's, variable foreign language requirement, comprehensive exam (for some programs), thesis (for some programs); for doctorate, variable foreign language requirement, comprehensive exam, thesis/dissertation. *Entrance requirements:* For master's and doctorate, GRE General Test, 3 letters of recommendation, transcripts from previous post-secondary educational institutions. Additional exam requirements/recommendations for international students: Required—TOEFL (minimum score 550 paper-based; 79 iBT), IELTS (minimum score 6.5). *Application deadline:* For fall admission, 12/1 priority date for domestic and international students; for winter admission, 11/1 for domestic students, 6/1 for international students; for spring admission, 11/1 for domestic students, 6/1 for international students; for summer admission, 4/1 for domestic students, 1/1 for international students. Applications are processed on a rolling basis. Application fee: $65. Electronic applications accepted. *Expenses: Tuition, area resident:* Full-time $6500; part-time $723 per credit hour. Tuition, state resident: full-time $6500. Tuition, nonresident: full-time $13,557; part-time $1507 per credit hour. Tuition and fees vary according to course load and program. *Financial support:* In 2018–19, 30 students received support, including 120 fellowships with full tuition reimbursements available (averaging $20,000 per year). Financial award application deadline: 1/15. *Unit head:* Dr. Paul DeMarco, Acting Dean and Acting Vice Provost for Graduate Affairs, 502-852-5110, E-mail: paul.demarco@louisville.edu. *Application contact:* Dr. Barbara Clark, Acting Associate Dean, 502-852-6498, E-mail: gradadm@louisville.edu.
Website: http://www.graduate.louisville.edu

University of New Hampshire, Graduate School, College of Liberal Arts, Department of Political Science, Durham, NH 03824. Offers political science (MA, Postbaccalaureate Certificate), including political science (MA), sustainability politics and policy (Postbaccalaureate Certificate). *Program availability:* Part-time. *Entrance requirements:* For master's, GRE General Test. Additional exam requirements/recommendations for international students: Required—TOEFL (minimum score 550 paper-based; 80 iBT). Electronic applications accepted.

University of Portland, Dr. Robert B. Pamplin, Jr. School of Business, Portland, OR 97203-5798. Offers entrepreneurship (MBA); finance (MBA, MS); health care management (MBA); marketing (MBA); nonprofit management (EMBA); operations and technology management (MBA, MS); sustainability (MBA). *Accreditation:* AACSB. *Program availability:* Part-time, evening/weekend. *Faculty:* 26 full-time (5 women), 8 part-time/adjunct (1 woman). *Students:* 35 full-time (16 women), 114 part-time (47 women); includes 21 minority (3 Black or African American, non-Hispanic/Latino; 2 American Indian or Alaska Native, non-Hispanic/Latino; 8 Asian, non-Hispanic/Latino; 8 Hispanic/Latino), 24 international. Average age 32. In 2018, 55 master's awarded. *Entrance requirements:* For master's, GMAT or GRE, minimum GPA of 3.0, resume, statement of goals, 2 letters of recommendation. Additional exam requirements/recommendations for international students: Required—TOEFL (minimum score 88 iBT), IELTS (minimum score 7). *Application deadline:* For fall admission, 7/19 priority date for domestic and international students; for spring admission, 12/7 priority date for domestic and international students; for summer admission, 4/12 priority date for domestic and international students. Applications are processed on a rolling basis. Application fee: $0. Electronic applications accepted. *Expenses:* Contact institution. *Financial support:* Application deadline: 3/1; applicants required to submit FAFSA. *Unit head:* Melissa McCarthy, Director, 503-943-7224, E-mail: mba-up@up.edu. *Application contact:* Melissa McCarthy, Director, 503-943-7224, E-mail: mba-up@up.edu.

University of Saint Francis, Graduate School, Keith Busse School of Business and Entrepreneurial Leadership, Fort Wayne, IN 46808-3994. Offers business administration (MBA), including sustainability; environmental health (MEH); healthcare administration (MHA); organizational leadership (MOL). *Accreditation:* ACBSP. *Program availability:* Part-time, evening/weekend, online only, 100% online. *Faculty:* 4 full-time (3 women), 11 part-time/adjunct (1 woman). *Students:* 62 full-time (33 women), 94 part-time (53 women); includes 40 minority (23 Black or African American, non-Hispanic/Latino; 1 American Indian or Alaska Native, non-Hispanic/Latino; 10 Hispanic/Latino; 1 Native Hawaiian or other Pacific Islander, non-Hispanic/Latino; 5 Two or more races, non-Hispanic/Latino). Average age 33. 72 applicants, 96% accepted, 51 enrolled. In 2018, 112 master's awarded. *Application deadline:* For fall admission, 7/1 for international students; for spring admission, 11/1 for international students; for summer admission, 3/1 for international students. Applications are processed on a rolling basis. Application fee: $0. Electronic applications accepted. *Expenses: Tuition:* Full-time $935 per credit hour. *Required fees:* $330 per semester. Tuition and fees vary according to degree level, campus/location and program. *Unit head:* Dr. Robert W. Lee, Dean, 260-399-7700 Ext. 8304, Fax: 260-399-8174, E-mail: rlee@sf.edu. *Application contact:* Kyle Richardson, Associate Director of Enrollment Services for Adult Learning, 260-399-7700 Ext. 6310, Fax: 260-399-8152, E-mail: krichardson@sf.edu. Website: https://admissions.sf.edu/graduate/

University of Saskatchewan, College of Graduate and Postdoctoral Studies, School of Environment and Sustainability, Saskatoon, SK S7N 5A2, Canada. Offers MES, PhD.

University of Southern Maine, College of Management and Human Service, School of Business, Portland, ME 04104-9300. Offers accounting (MBA); business administration (MBA); finance (MBA); health management and policy (MBA); sustainability (MBA); JD/MBA; MBA/MSA; MBA/MSN; MS/MBA. *Accreditation:* AACSB. *Program availability:* Part-time, evening/weekend. *Entrance requirements:* For master's, GMAT or GRE, minimum AACSB index of 1100. Additional exam requirements/recommendations for international students: Required—TOEFL (minimum score 550 paper-based; 79 iBT). Electronic applications accepted. *Faculty research:* Economic development, management information systems, real options, system dynamics, simulation.

University of South Florida, Patel College of Global Sustainability, Tampa, FL 33620-9951. Offers energy, global, water and sustainable tourism (Graduate Certificate); global sustainability (MA), including building sustainable enterprise, climate change and sustainability, coastal sustainability, entrepreneurship, food sustainability and security, sustainability policy, sustainable energy, sustainable tourism, water. *Faculty:* 1 full-time (0 women). *Students:* 64 full-time (33 women), 92 part-time (57 women); includes 32 minority (8 Black or African American, non-Hispanic/Latino; 3 Asian, non-Hispanic/Latino; 15 Hispanic/Latino; 6 Two or more races, non-Hispanic/Latino), 50 international. Average age 29. 119 applicants, 75% accepted, 60 enrolled. In 2018, 91 master's awarded. *Degree requirements:* For master's, comprehensive exam (for some programs), thesis or alternative, internship. *Entrance requirements:* For master's, GPA of at least 3.25 or greater; alternatively a GPA of at least 3.00 along with a GRE Verbal score of 153 (61 percentile) or higher, Quantitative of 153 (51 percentile) or higher and Analytical Writing of 3.5 or higher, all taken within 5 years of application; at least 2 letters of recommendation from professors or supervisors. Additional exam requirements/recommendations for international students: Required—TOEFL (minimum score 550 paper-based; 79 iBT). *Application deadline:* For fall admission, 6/1 for domestic students, 5/1 for international students; for spring admission, 10/15 for domestic students, 9/15 for international students. Electronic applications accepted. *Expenses:* Tuition, state resident: full-time $6350. Tuition, nonresident: full-time $19,048. *International tuition:* $19,048 full-time. *Required fees:* $2079. *Financial support:* In 2018–19, 35 students received support. *Faculty research:* Global sustainability, integrated resource management, systems thinking, green communities, entrepreneurship, ecotourism. *Total annual research expenditures:* $174,608. *Unit head:* Dr. Govindan Parayil, Dean, 813-974-9694, E-mail: gparayil@usf.edu. *Application contact:* Dr. Govindan Parayil, Dean, 813-974-9694, E-mail: gparayil@usf.edu. Website: http://psgs.usf.edu/

University of Vermont, Graduate College, Grossman School of Business, Program in Sustainable Innovation, Burlington, VT 05405. Offers MBA, MBA/JD. MBA/JD offered in collaboration with Vermont Law School. *Entrance requirements:* For master's, GMAT or GRE, resume. Additional exam requirements/recommendations for international students: Required—TOEFL (minimum iBT score of 90) or IELTS (6.5). Electronic applications accepted. *Expenses:* Contact institution.

University of Wisconsin–Green Bay, Graduate Studies, Program in Sustainable Management, Green Bay, WI 54311-7001. Offers MS. Program held jointly with four other University of Wisconsin System campuses: Oshkosh, Parkside, Stout, and Superior. *Program availability:* Part-time, evening/weekend, online only, 100% online. *Degree requirements:* For master's, capstone project. *Entrance requirements:* For master's, bachelor's degree from nationally-accredited university with minimum cumulative GPA of 3.0. Additional exam requirements/recommendations for international students: Required—TOEFL. Electronic applications accepted.

University of Wisconsin–Parkside, College of Natural and Health Sciences, Program in Sustainable Management, Kenosha, WI 53141-2000. Offers MS. *Program availability:* Online learning.

University of Wisconsin–Stout, Graduate School, College of Management, Program in Sustainable Management, Menomonie, WI 54751. Offers MS. Program offered in collaboration with University of Wisconsin-Parkside, University of Wisconsin-River Falls and University of Wisconsin-Superior. *Program availability:* Online learning.

University of Wisconsin–Superior, Graduate Division, Department of Business and Economics, Superior, WI 54880-4500. Offers sustainable management (MS). Electronic applications accepted.

Section 14
Marketing

This section contains a directory of institutions offering graduate work in marketing, followed by an in-depth entry submitted by an institution that chose to prepare a detailed program description. Additional information about programs listed in the directory but not augmented by an in-depth entry may be obtained by writing directly to the dean of a graduate school or chair of a department at the address given in the directory.

For programs offering related work, see also in this book *Advertising and Public Relations, Business Administration and Management,* and *Hospitality Management.* In another guide in this series:

Graduate Programs in the Humanities, Arts & Social Sciences
See *Communication and Media* and *Public, Regional, and Industrial Affairs*

CONTENTS

Program Directories

Marketing

Abilene Christian University, College of Graduate and Professional Studies, Program in Business Administration, Addison, TX 79699. Offers business analytics (MBA); general management (MBA); healthcare administration (MBA); international business (MBA); management: business analytics (MS); management: healthcare administration (MS); management: international business (MS); management: marketing (MS); management: operations and supply chain management (MS); marketing (MBA); nonprofit leadership (MBA). *Program availability:* Part-time, online only, 100% online. *Faculty:* 4 full-time (0 women), 7 part-time/adjunct (3 women). *Students:* 149 full-time (69 women), 53 part-time (25 women); includes 88 minority (42 Black or African American, non-Hispanic/Latino; 2 American Indian or Alaska Native, non-Hispanic/Latino; 4 Asian, non-Hispanic/Latino; 31 Hispanic/Latino; 1 Native Hawaiian or other Pacific Islander, non-Hispanic/Latino; 8 Two or more races, non-Hispanic/Latino), 4 international. 36 applicants, 100% accepted, 32 enrolled. In 2018, 24 master's awarded. *Entrance requirements:* Additional exam requirements/recommendations for international students: Required—TOEFL (minimum score 80 iBT), IELTS (minimum score 6). *Application deadline:* For fall admission, 10/7 for domestic students; for winter admission, 12/20 for domestic students; for spring admission, 2/24 for domestic students; for summer admission, 4/20 for domestic students. Applications are processed on a rolling basis. Application fee: $50. Electronic applications accepted. *Expenses:* $721 per hour. *Financial support:* In 2018–19, 16 students received support. Scholarships/grants available. Financial award application deadline: 7/1; financial award applicants required to submit FAFSA. *Faculty research:* Organizational structure, financial management, cost accounting, unit analysis management. *Unit head:* Dr. Phil Vardiman, Program Director, 325-674-2153, E-mail: pxv02b@acu.edu. *Application contact:* Graduate Advisor, 817-219-7300, E-mail: onlineadmissions@acu.edu. Website: http://www.acu.edu/online/academics/mba-business-administration.html

Adelphi University, Robert B. Willumstad School of Business, MBA Program, Garden City, NY 11530-0701. Offers accounting (MBA); finance (MBA); health services administration (MBA); human resource management (MBA); management (MBA); management information systems (MBA); marketing (MBA); sport management (MBA). *Accreditation:* AACSB. *Program availability:* Part-time, evening/weekend. *Students:* 343 full-time (132 women), 101 part-time (56 women); includes 75 minority (22 Black or African American, non-Hispanic/Latino; 2 American Indian or Alaska Native, non-Hispanic/Latino; 20 Asian, non-Hispanic/Latino; 23 Hispanic/Latino; 1 Native Hawaiian or other Pacific Islander, non-Hispanic/Latino; 7 Two or more races, non-Hispanic/Latino), 275 international. Average age 29. 389 applicants, 59% accepted, 187 enrolled. In 2018, 171 master's awarded. *Entrance requirements:* For master's, GMAT, official transcripts, bachelor's degree, 500 word essay, 2 letters of recommendation, resume. Additional exam requirements/recommendations for international students: Required—TOEFL (minimum score 550 paper-based; 80 iBT), IELTS (minimum score 6.5). *Application deadline:* For fall admission, 4/1 for international students; for spring admission, 11/1 for international students. Applications are processed on a rolling basis. Application fee: $50. Electronic applications accepted. *Financial support:* Research assistantships with partial tuition reimbursements, career-related internships or fieldwork, Federal Work-Study, institutionally sponsored loans, scholarships/grants, tuition waivers (partial), and unspecified assistantships available. Financial award application deadline: 3/1; financial award applicants required to submit FAFSA. *Faculty research:* Supply chain management, distribution channels, productivity benchmark analysis, data envelopment analysis, financial portfolio analysis. *Unit head:* Britt'ny Brown, Director of Graduate Programs, 516-877-4605. *Application contact:* Britt'ny Brown, Director of Graduate Programs, 516-877-4605. Website: https://business.adelphi.edu/

American Business & Technology University, Programs in Business Administration, Saint Joseph, MO 64506. Offers business administration (MBA); financial management (MBA); global business management (MBA); information systems management (MBA); marketing and social media (MBA); project and operations management (MBA); public accounting (MBA). *Program availability:* Online learning.

American College of Thessaloniki, Department of Business Administration, Pylea, Greece. Offers banking and finance (MBA); entrepreneurship (MBA, Certificate); finance (Certificate); management (MBA, Certificate); marketing (MBA, Certificate). *Program availability:* Part-time, evening/weekend. *Degree requirements:* For master's, thesis. *Entrance requirements:* For master's, bachelor's degree. Additional exam requirements/recommendations for international students: Recommended—TOEFL. Electronic applications accepted.

American InterContinental University Online, Program in Business Administration, Schaumburg, IL 60173. Offers accounting and finance (MBA); finance (MBA); healthcare management (MBA); human resource management (MBA); international business (MBA); management (MBA); marketing (MBA); operations management (MBA); organizational psychology and development (MBA); project management (MBA). *Accreditation:* ACBSP. *Program availability:* Evening/weekend, online learning. *Entrance requirements:* Additional exam requirements/recommendations for international students: Required—TOEFL (minimum score 550 paper-based). Electronic applications accepted.

American University, Kogod School of Business, Department of Marketing, Washington, DC 20016-8001. Offers MS. *Program availability:* Part-time, evening/weekend. *Faculty:* 12 full-time (4 women), 3 part-time/adjunct (2 women). *Students:* 23 full-time (15 women), 3 part-time (1 woman); includes 8 minority (3 Black or African American, non-Hispanic/Latino; 4 Hispanic/Latino; 1 Two or more races, non-Hispanic/Latino), 10 international. Average age 23. 91 applicants, 57% accepted, 23 enrolled. In 2018, 19 master's awarded. *Entrance requirements:* For master's, GMAT/GRE; Please see website: https://www.american.edu/kogod/, resume, personal statement, 2 letters of recommendation, transcripts, interview. Additional exam requirements/recommendations for international students: Required—TOEFL (minimum score 550 paper-based; 100 iBT). Application fee: $100. *Expenses:* Contact institution. *Financial support:* Applicants required to submit FAFSA. *Faculty research:* Internet marketing, database marketing, consumer behavior, advertising research, public policy in marketing. *Unit head:* Dr. Sonya Grier, Department Chair, 202-885-1900, E-mail: kogodgrad@american.edu. *Application contact:* Jason Garner, Director, Graduate Admissions, 202-885-1922, E-mail: jgarner@american.edu. Website: https://www.american.edu/kogod/graduate/marketing/

The American University in Dubai, Graduate Programs, Dubai, United Arab Emirates. Offers construction management (MS); education (M Ed); finance (MBA); generalist (MBA); marketing (MBA). *Program availability:* Part-time, evening/weekend. *Degree requirements:* For master's, thesis optional. *Entrance requirements:* For master's, GMAT (for MBA); GRE (for M Ed and MS), minimum undergraduate GPA of 3.0, official transcripts, two reference forms, curriculum vitae/resume, statement of career

objectives, work experience. Additional exam requirements/recommendations for international students: Required—TOEFL (minimum score 550 paper-based; 79 iBT). Electronic applications accepted.

Anderson University, College of Business, Anderson, SC 29621-4035. Offers business administration (MBA); healthcare leadership (MBA); human resources (MBA); marketing (MBA); organizational leadership (MOL); supply chain management (MBA). *Accreditation:* ACBSP. *Application deadline:* Applications are processed on a rolling basis. Electronic applications accepted. *Expenses: Tuition:* Full-time $400; part-time $400 per credit. *Required fees:* $200; $200 per semester. Tuition and fees vary according to course load. *Financial support:* Scholarships/grants and tuition waivers available. Financial award application deadline: 3/1; financial award applicants required to submit FAFSA. *Unit head:* Steve Nail, Dean, 864-MBA-6000. *Application contact:* Sharon Vargo, Graduate Admission Counselor, 864-231-2000, E-mail: svargo@andersonuniversity.edu. Website: http://www.andersonuniversity.edu/business

Aquinas College, School of Management, Grand Rapids, MI 49506. Offers marketing management (MM); organizational leadership (MM); sustainable business (MM). *Program availability:* Part-time, evening/weekend. *Faculty:* 4 full-time (1 woman), 5 part-time/adjunct (0 women). *Students:* 12 full-time (4 women), 32 part-time (19 women); includes 3 minority (1 Black or African American, non-Hispanic/Latino; 1 Asian, non-Hispanic/Latino; 1 Hispanic/Latino), 2 international. Average age 31. In 2018, 19 master's awarded. *Entrance requirements:* For master's, GMAT, minimum undergraduate GPA of 2.75, 2 years of work experience. Additional exam requirements/recommendations for international students: Required—TOEFL (minimum score 550 paper-based). *Application deadline:* Applications are processed on a rolling basis. Application fee: $0. *Expenses: Tuition:* Part-time $593 per credit hour. *Required fees:* $120; $120. *Financial support:* Scholarships/grants available. Support available to part-time students. Financial award application deadline: 3/15; financial award applicants required to submit FAFSA. *Unit head:* Dr. Linda Hagan, Interim Dean of Business Division, 616-632-2193, Fax: 616-732-4489, E-mail: lmh010@aquinas.edu. *Application contact:* Lynn Atkins-Rykert, Program Coordinator, 616-632-2925, Fax: 616-732-4489, E-mail: atkinlyn@aquinas.edu.

Argosy University, Atlanta, College of Business, Atlanta, GA 30328. Offers accounting (DBA); corporate compliance (MBA); customized professional concentration (MBA, DBA); finance (MBA); healthcare administration (MBA); information systems (DBA); information systems management (MBA); international business (MBA, DBA); management (MBA, MSM, DBA); marketing (MBA, DBA). *Accreditation:* ACBSP.

Argosy University, Chicago, College of Business, Chicago, IL 60601. Offers accounting (DBA); customized professional concentration (MBA, DBA); finance (MBA); fraud examination (MBA); global business sustainability (DBA); healthcare administration (MBA); information systems (DBA); information systems management (MBA); international business (MBA, DBA); management (MBA, MSM, DBA); marketing (MBA, DBA); organizational leadership (Ed D); public administration (MBA); sustainable management (MBA). *Accreditation:* ACBSP. *Program availability:* Online learning.

Argosy University, Hawai`i, College of Business, Honolulu, HI 96813. Offers accounting (DBA); corporate compliance (MBA); customized professional concentration (MBA, DBA); finance (MBA, Certificate); fraud examination (MBA); global business sustainability (DBA); healthcare administration (MBA, Certificate); information systems (DBA); information systems management (MBA, Certificate); international business (MBA, DBA, Certificate); management (MBA, MSM, DBA); marketing (MBA, DBA, Certificate); organizational leadership (Ed D); public administration (MBA); sustainable management (MBA).

Argosy University, Los Angeles, College of Business, Los Angeles, CA 90045. Offers accounting (DBA); corporate compliance (MBA); customized professional concentration (MBA, DBA); finance (MBA); fraud examination (MBA); global business sustainability (DBA); healthcare administration (MBA); information systems (DBA); information systems management (MBA); international business (MBA, DBA); management (MBA, MSM, DBA); marketing (MBA, DBA); organizational leadership (Ed D); public administration (MBA); sustainable management (MBA).

Argosy University, Northern Virginia, College of Business, Arlington, VA 22209. Offers accounting (DBA); customized professional concentration (MBA, DBA); finance (MBA); fraud examination (MBA); global business sustainability (DBA); healthcare administration (MBA); information systems (DBA); information systems management (MBA); international business (MBA, DBA, Certificate); management (MBA, MSM, DBA); marketing (MBA, DBA, Certificate); organizational leadership (Ed D); public administration (MBA); sustainable management (MBA).

Argosy University, Orange County, College of Business, Orange, CA 92868. Offers accounting (DBA, Adv C); corporate compliance (MBA); customized professional concentration (MBA, DBA); finance (MBA, Certificate); fraud examination (MBA); global business sustainability (DBA); healthcare administration (MBA, Certificate); information systems (DBA, Adv C, Certificate); information systems management (MBA); international business (MBA, DBA, Adv C, Certificate); management (MBA, MSM, DBA, Adv C); marketing (MBA, DBA, Adv C, Certificate); organizational leadership (Ed D); public administration (MBA, Certificate); sustainable management (MBA).

Argosy University, Phoenix, College of Business, Phoenix, AZ 85021. Offers accounting (DBA); corporate compliance (MBA); customized professional concentration (MBA, DBA); finance (MBA); fraud examination (MBA); global business sustainability (DBA); healthcare administration (MBA); information systems (DBA); information systems management (MBA); international business (MBA, DBA); management (MBA, DBA); marketing (MBA, DBA); public administration (MBA); sustainable management (MBA).

Argosy University, Seattle, College of Business, Seattle, WA 98121. Offers accounting (DBA); corporate compliance (MBA); customized professional concentration (MBA, DBA); finance (MBA); fraud examination (MBA); global business sustainability (DBA); healthcare administration (MBA); information systems (DBA); information systems management (MBA); international business (MBA, DBA); management (MBA, MSM, DBA); marketing (MBA, DBA); organizational leadership (Ed D); public administration (MBA); sustainable management (MBA).

Argosy University, Tampa, College of Business, Tampa, FL 33607. Offers accounting (DBA); corporate compliance (MBA); customized professional concentration (MBA, DBA); finance (MBA); fraud examination (MBA); global business sustainability (DBA); healthcare administration (MBA); information systems (DBA); information systems management (MBA); international business (MBA, DBA); management (MBA, MSM, DBA); marketing (MBA, DBA); organizational leadership (Ed D); public administration (MBA); sustainable management (MBA).

Argosy University, Twin Cities, College of Business, Eagan, MN 55121. Offers accounting (DBA); customized professional concentration (MBA, DBA); finance (MBA); fraud examination (MBA); global business sustainability (DBA); healthcare administration (MBA); information systems (DBA); information systems management (MBA); international business (MBA, DBA); management (MBA, MSM, DBA); marketing (MBA, DBA); organizational leadership (Ed D); public administration (MBA); sustainable management (MBA).

Arizona State University at the Tempe campus, W. P. Carey School of Business, Department of Marketing, Tempe, AZ 85287-4106. Offers business administration (PhD), including marketing; real estate development (MRED). *Program availability:* Part-time, evening/weekend, online learning. *Degree requirements:* For master's, thesis or alternative, capstone project, interactive Program of Study (iPOS) submitted before completing 50 percent of required credit hours; for doctorate, comprehensive exam, thesis/dissertation, interactive Program of Study (iPOS) submitted before completing 50 percent of required credit hours. *Entrance requirements:* For master's, GMAT, GRE, or LSAT, minimum GPA of 3.0 in last 2 years of work leading to bachelor's degree, 3 personal references, resume, official transcripts, personal statement; for doctorate, GMAT, minimum GPA of 3.0 in last 2 years of work leading to bachelor's degree, 3 letters of recommendation, personal statement/essay. Additional exam requirements/recommendations for international students: Required—TOEFL (minimum score 550 paper-based; 80 iBT), IELTS (minimum score 6.5). Electronic applications accepted. *Expenses:* Contact institution. *Faculty research:* Service marketing and management, strategic marketing, customer portfolio management, characteristics and skills of high-performing managers, market orientation, market segmentation, consumer behavior, marketing strategy, new product development, management of innovation, social influences on consumption, e-commerce, market research methodology.

Arizona State University at the Tempe campus, W. P. Carey School of Business, Program in Business Administration, Tempe, AZ 85287-4906. Offers entrepreneurship (MBA); finance (MBA); health sector management (MBA); international business (MBA); leadership (MBA); marketing (MBA); organizational behavior (PhD); strategic management (PhD); supply chain management (MBA, PhD); JD/MBA; MBA/M Acc; MBA/M Arch. *Accreditation:* AACSB. *Program availability:* Part-time, evening/weekend, online learning. Terminal master's awarded for partial completion of doctoral program. *Degree requirements:* For master's, thesis or alternative, internship, interactive Program of Study (iPOS) submitted before completing 50 percent of required credit hours; for doctorate, comprehensive exam, thesis/dissertation, interactive Program of Study (iPOS) submitted before completing 50 percent of required credit hours. *Entrance requirements:* For master's, GMAT, minimum GPA of 3.0 in last 2 years of work leading to bachelor's degree, 2 letters of recommendation, professional resume, official transcripts, 3 essays; for doctorate, GMAT or GRE, minimum GPA of 3.0 in last 2 years of work leading to bachelor's degree, 3 letters of recommendation, resume, personal statement/essay. Additional exam requirements/recommendations for international students: Required—TOEFL (minimum score 550 paper-based; 80 iBT), IELTS (minimum score 6.5). Electronic applications accepted. *Expenses:* Contact institution.

Ashworth College, Graduate Programs, Norcross, GA 30092. Offers business administration (MBA); criminal justice (MS); health care administration (MBA, MS); human resource management (MBA, MS); international business (MBA); management (MS); marketing (MBA, MS).

Assumption College, Business Studies Program, Worcester, MA 01609-1296. Offers accounting (MBA); business studies (CAGS); finance/economics (MBA); human resources (MBA); international business (MBA); management (MBA); marketing (MBA); nonprofit leadership (MBA). *Program availability:* Part-time, evening/weekend. *Degree requirements:* For master's, capstone. *Entrance requirements:* For master's, bachelor's degree, three letters of recommendation, official transcripts, personal statement, current resume; for CAGS, MBA or equivalent degree in a closely related field, three letters of recommendation, official transcripts, personal statement, current resume. Additional exam requirements/recommendations for international students: Required—TOEFL (minimum score 540 paper-based; 76 iBT), IELTS (minimum score 6). Electronic applications accepted. *Faculty research:* Workplace diversity, dynamics of team interaction, utilization of leased employees, experiential learning project on due diligence market for prostheses.

Averett University, Master of Business Administration Program, Danville, VA 24541-3692. Offers business administration (MBA); human resources management (MBA); leadership (MBA); marketing (MBA). *Program availability:* Part-time. *Faculty:* 7 full-time (1 woman), 10 part-time/adjunct (2 women). *Students:* 156 full-time (93 women), 2 part-time (1 woman); includes 61 minority (51 Black or African American, non-Hispanic/Latino; 2 American Indian or Alaska Native, non-Hispanic/Latino; 3 Asian, non-Hispanic/Latino; 3 Hispanic/Latino; 2 Two or more races, non-Hispanic/Latino), 2 international. Average age 35. 61 applicants, 70% accepted, 35 enrolled. In 2018, 62 master's awarded. *Degree requirements:* For master's, 41-credit core curriculum, minimum GPA of 3.0 throughout program, no more than 2 grades of C, completion of degree requirements within six years from start of program. *Entrance requirements:* For master's, minimum cumulative GPA of 3.0 over the last 60 semester hours of undergraduate study toward a baccalaureate degree, official transcripts, three years of full-time work experience, three letters of recommendation, current resume. Additional exam requirements/recommendations for international students: Required—TOEFL (minimum score 600 paper-based; 100 iBT). *Application deadline:* Applications are processed on a rolling basis. Electronic applications accepted. *Expenses:* Contact institution. *Financial support:* Application deadline: 3/1; applicants required to submit FAFSA. *Unit head:* Dr. Peggy C. Wright, Chair, Business Department, 434-791-7118, E-mail: pwright@averett.edu. *Application contact:* Christy Davis, Assistant Director of Admissions, 434-791-7133, E-mail: cdavis@averett.edu.
Website: https://gps.averett.edu/online/business/

Azusa Pacific University, School of Business and Management, Azusa, CA 91702-7000. Offers accounting (MBA); business administration (MBA); entrepreneurship (MBA); finance (MBA); international business (MBA); marketing (MBA); organizational science (MBA); professional accountancy (M Acc); sport management (MBA). *Program availability:* Part-time, evening/weekend. *Degree requirements:* For master's, thesis (for some programs), final project. *Entrance requirements:* For master's, GMAT, minimum GPA of 3.0. Additional exam requirements/recommendations for international students: Required—TOEFL (minimum score 600 paper-based). *Expenses:* Contact institution. *Faculty research:* Gender issues, financial risk, leadership and ethics, marketing strategy.

Baker College Center for Graduate Studies–Online, Graduate Programs, Flint, MI 48507. Offers accounting (MBA); business administration (DBA); finance (MBA); general business (MBA); health care management (MBA); human resources management (MBA); information management (MBA); leadership studies (MBA); management information systems (MSIS); marketing (MBA); occupational therapy (MOT). *Program availability:* Part-time, evening/weekend, online learning. *Degree requirements:* For master's, portfolio. *Entrance requirements:* For master's, 3 years of work experience, minimum undergraduate GPA of 2.5, writing sample, 3 letters of recommendation; for doctorate, MBA or acceptable related master's degree from accredited association, 5 years work experience, minimum graduate GPA of 3.25, writing sample, 3 professional references. Additional exam requirements/recommendations for international students: Required—TOEFL (minimum score 550 paper-based). Electronic applications accepted.

Barry University, Andreas School of Business, Graduate Certificate Programs, Miami Shores, FL 33161-6695. Offers finance (Certificate); health services administration (Certificate); international business (Certificate); management (Certificate); management information systems (Certificate); marketing (Certificate).

Baruch College of the City University of New York, Zicklin School of Business, Department of Marketing and International Business, New York, NY 10010-5585. Offers international business (MBA); marketing (MBA, MS, PhD). PhD offered jointly with Graduate School and University Center of the City University of New York. *Program availability:* Part-time, evening/weekend. *Degree requirements:* For doctorate, comprehensive exam, thesis/dissertation. *Entrance requirements:* For master's, GMAT, 2 letters of recommendation, resume, 2 years of work experience; for doctorate, GMAT. Additional exam requirements/recommendations for international students: Required—TOEFL (minimum score 590 paper-based), TWE (minimum score 5).

Bayamón Central University, Graduate Programs, Program in Business Administration, Bayamón, PR 00960-1725. Offers accounting (MBA); finance (MBA); general business (MBA); management (MBA); marketing (MBA). *Program availability:* Part-time, evening/weekend. *Degree requirements:* For master's, comprehensive exam (for some programs). *Entrance requirements:* For master's, EXADEP, bachelor's degree in business or related field.

Benedictine University, Graduate Programs, Program in Business Administration, Lisle, IL 60532. Offers accounting (MBA); entrepreneurship and managing innovation (MBA); financial management (MBA); health administration (MBA); human resource management (MBA); information systems security (MBA); international business (MBA); management consulting (MBA); management information systems (MBA); marketing management (MBA); operations management and logistics (MBA); organizational leadership (MBA). *Program availability:* Part-time, evening/weekend, 100% online, blended/hybrid learning. *Faculty:* 7 full-time (1 woman), 36 part-time/adjunct (10 women). *Students:* 110 full-time (71 women), 500 part-time (302 women); includes 104 minority (34 Black or African American, non-Hispanic/Latino; 1 American Indian or Alaska Native, non-Hispanic/Latino; 41 Asian, non-Hispanic/Latino; 23 Hispanic/Latino; 5 Native Hawaiian or other Pacific Islander, non-Hispanic/Latino), 7 international. Average age 33. 251 applicants, 84% accepted, 202 enrolled. In 2018, 345 master's awarded. *Entrance requirements:* For master's, GMAT or GRE test scores or completed test waiver form, official transcripts; 2 letters of reference from individuals familiar with the applicant's professional or academic work, excluding family or personal friends; a 1-2 page essay addressing educational and career goals; current résumé listing chronological work history; personal interview may be required prior to an admission decision. Additional exam requirements/recommendations for international students: Required—TOEFL (minimum score 550 paper-based; 79 iBT), IELTS (minimum score 6.5). *Application deadline:* Applications are processed on a rolling basis. Application fee: $40. Electronic applications accepted. *Unit head:* Ricky Holman, Assistant Professor, 630-829-1936, E-mail: rholman@ben.edu. *Application contact:* Ricky Holman, Assistant Professor, 630-829-1936, E-mail: rholman@ben.edu.

Bentley University, McCallum Graduate School of Business, Masters in Marketing Analytics, Waltham, MA 02452-4705. Offers MSMA. *Program availability:* Part-time, evening/weekend. *Faculty:* 118 full-time (38 women), 25 part-time/adjunct (4 women). *Students:* 55 full-time (38 women), 25 part-time (17 women); includes 6 minority (2 Black or African American, non-Hispanic/Latino; 3 Asian, non-Hispanic/Latino; 1 Hispanic/Latino), 51 international. Average age 25. 145 applicants, 73% accepted, 27 enrolled. In 2018, 47 master's awarded. *Entrance requirements:* For master's, GMAT or GRE General Test (may be waived for qualified applicants), Transcripts; Resume; Two essays; Two letters of recommendation; Interview (may be requested by Bentley). Additional exam requirements/recommendations for international students: Required—TOEFL (minimum score 100) or IELTS (minimum score 7). *Application deadline:* For fall admission, 7/31 for domestic students, 6/30 for international students; for spring admission, 1/1 for domestic students, 11/1 for international students. Applications are processed on a rolling basis. Application fee: $150. Electronic applications accepted. *Financial support:* In 2018–19, 44 students received support. Scholarships/grants available. Financial award application deadline: 6/1; financial award applicants required to submit FAFSA. *Faculty research:* Marketing information processing; blogging and social media; customer lifetime value and customer relationship management; measuring and improving productivity; online consumer behavior. *Unit head:* Dr. Paul D. Berger, Visiting Professor MSMA Director, 781-891-2746, E-mail: pberger@bentley.edu. *Application contact:* Office of Graduate Admissions, 781-891-2108, E-mail: applygrad@bentley.edu.
Website: https://www.bentley.edu/academics/graduate-programs/masters-marketing-analytics

Binghamton University, State University of New York, Graduate School, School of Management, Program in Management, Binghamton, NY 13902-6000. Offers finance (PhD); management information systems (PhD); marketing (PhD); organizational studies (PhD); supply chain management (PhD). *Degree requirements:* For doctorate, thesis/dissertation. *Entrance requirements:* For doctorate, GMAT.

Brandeis University, International Business School (IBS), Master of Business Administration Program, Waltham, MA 02454-9110. Offers data analytics (MBA); finance (MBA); marketing (MBA); real estate (MBA). *Entrance requirements:* For master's, GMAT or GRE, minimum two years of full-time work experience. Additional exam requirements/recommendations for international students: Required—TOEFL (minimum score 600 paper-based; 100 iBT), IELTS (minimum score 7), PTE (minimum score 68). Electronic applications accepted. *Expenses:* Contact institution. *Faculty research:* Strategic alliances, IPO and venture capital financing, real estate, risk management, data analytics.

Brandman University, School of Business and Professional Studies, Irvine, CA 92618. Offers accounting (MBA); business administration (MBA); business intelligence and data analytics (MBA); e-business strategic management (MBA); entrepreneurship (MBA); finance (MBA); health administration (MBA); human resources (MBA, MS); international business (MBA); marketing (MBA); organizational leadership (MA, MBA, MPA); public administration (MPA).

Brigham Young University, Graduate Studies, BYU Marriott School of Business, MBA Program, Provo, UT 84602. Offers entrepreneurship (MBA); finance (MBA); global supply chain management (MBA); marketing (MBA); strategic human resources (MBA); JD/MBA; MBA/MS. *Accreditation:* AACSB. *Entrance requirements:* For master's, GMAT or GRE, commitment to BYU Honor Code, undergraduate degree. Additional exam requirements/recommendations for international students: Required—TOEFL (minimum score 590 paper-based; 100 iBT), IELTS (minimum score 7). Electronic applications accepted. *Expenses:* Contact institution. *Faculty research:* Finance, marketing, supply chain management, entrepreneurship, strategic human resources.

Bryan College, MBA Program, Dayton, TN 37321. Offers business administration (MBA); healthcare administration (MBA); human resources (MBA); marketing (MBA); ministry (MBA); sports management (MBA). *Program availability:* Online only, 100% online. *Entrance requirements:* For master's, resume, 2 letters of recommendation. Additional exam requirements/recommendations for international students: Required—TOEFL. Electronic applications accepted. *Expenses:* Contact institution.

Marketing

California Coast University, School of Administration and Management, Santa Ana, CA 92701. Offers business marketing (MBA); health care management (MBA); human resource management (MBA); management (MBA, MS). *Program availability:* Online learning. Electronic applications accepted.

California Intercontinental University, School of Business, Irvine, CA 92614. Offers banking and finance (MBA); entrepreneurship and business management (DBA); global business leadership (DBA); international management and marketing (MBA); organizational management and human resource management (MBA).

California Lutheran University, Graduate Studies, School of Management, Thousand Oaks, CA 91360-2787. Offers business (IMBA); entrepreneurship (MBA, Certificate); finance (MBA, Certificate); financial planning (MBA, MS, Certificate); human capital management (MBA, Certificate); information technology (MS); information technology management (MBA, Certificate); international business (MBA, Certificate); management (MS); marketing (MBA, Certificate); public policy and administration (MPPA); quantitative economics (MS). *Program availability:* Part-time, evening/weekend, 100% online, blended/hybrid learning. *Degree requirements:* For master's, comprehensive exam (for some programs). *Entrance requirements:* For master's, GMAT, interview, minimum GPA of 3.0. Electronic applications accepted. *Expenses:* Contact institution.

California State University, East Bay, Office of Graduate Studies, College of Business and Economics, MBA Program, Option in Marketing Management, Hayward, CA 94542-3000. Offers MBA. *Program availability:* Part-time, evening/weekend. *Degree requirements:* For master's, comprehensive exam or thesis. *Entrance requirements:* For master's, GMAT, minimum GPA of 2.75. Additional exam requirements/recommendations for international students: Required—TOEFL (minimum score 550 paper-based). Electronic applications accepted.

California State University, Los Angeles, Graduate Studies, College of Business and Economics, Department of Marketing, Los Angeles, CA 90032-8530. Offers international business (MBA, MS). *Program availability:* Part-time, evening/weekend. *Degree requirements:* For master's, comprehensive exam (MBA), thesis (MS). *Entrance requirements:* For master's, GMAT, minimum GPA of 2.5 during previous 2 years of course work. Additional exam requirements/recommendations for international students: Required—TOEFL (minimum score 550 paper-based). Electronic applications accepted.

California State University, San Bernardino, Graduate Studies, College of Arts and Letters, Program in Communication Studies, San Bernardino, CA 92407. Offers communication studies (MA); integrated marketing communication (MA). *Faculty:* 4 full-time (2 women). *Students:* 10 full-time (6 women), 22 part-time (16 women); includes 14 minority (3 Black or African American, non-Hispanic/Latino; 2 Asian, non-Hispanic/Latino; 8 Hispanic/Latino; 1 Two or more races, non-Hispanic/Latino), 2 international. Average age 31. 33 applicants, 58% accepted, 9 enrolled. In 2018, 15 master's awarded. *Degree requirements:* For master's, comprehensive exam. *Entrance requirements:* Additional exam requirements/recommendations for international students: Required—TOEFL. *Application deadline:* For fall admission, 5/15 for domestic students. Application fee: $55. *Unit head:* Ahlam Muhtaseb, Graduate Coordinator, 909-537-5897, Fax: 909-537-7585, E-mail: amuhtase@csusb.edu. *Application contact:* Dr. Dorota Huizinga, Dean of Graduate Studies, 909-537-3064, Fax: 909-537-7034, E-mail: dorota.huizinga@csusb.edu.

Capella University, School of Business and Technology, Doctoral Programs in Business, Minneapolis, MN 55402. Offers accounting (DBA, PhD); business intelligence (DBA); finance (DBA, PhD); general business management (PhD); human resource management (DBA, PhD); leadership (DBA, PhD); management education (PhD); marketing (DBA, PhD); project management (DBA, PhD); strategy and innovation (DBA, PhD). *Accreditation:* ACBSP.

Capella University, School of Business and Technology, Master's Programs in Business, Minneapolis, MN 55402. Offers accounting (MBA); business analysis (MS); business intelligence (MBA); entrepreneurship (MBA); finance (MBA); general business administration (MBA); general human resource management (MS); general leadership (MS); health care management (MBA); human resource management (MBA); marketing (MBA); project management (MBA, MS). *Accreditation:* ACBSP.

Cardinal Stritch University, College of Business and Management, Milwaukee, WI 53217-3985. Offers cyber security (MBA); healthcare management (MBA); justice administration (MBA); marketing (MBA). *Accreditation:* ACBSP. *Program availability:* Part-time, evening/weekend, 100% online, blended/hybrid learning. *Degree requirements:* For master's, thesis. *Entrance requirements:* For master's, 3 years of management or related experience, minimum GPA of 2.5. Additional exam requirements/recommendations for international students: Required—TOEFL (minimum score 79 iBT), IELTS (minimum score 6.5). Electronic applications accepted. *Expenses:* Contact institution.

Carnegie Mellon University, Tepper School of Business, Program in Marketing, Pittsburgh, PA 15213-3891. Offers PhD. *Degree requirements:* For doctorate, thesis/dissertation.

Central Michigan University, Central Michigan University Global Campus, Program in Business Administration, Mount Pleasant, MI 48859. Offers enterprise resource planning (MBA, Certificate); human resource management (MBA); logistics management (MBA, Certificate); marketing (MBA); value-driven organization (MBA). *Program availability:* Part-time, evening/weekend. *Entrance requirements:* For master's, GMAT.

Central Michigan University, College of Graduate Studies, College of Business Administration, MBA Program, Mount Pleasant, MI 48859. Offers accounting (MBA); business economics (MBA); consulting (MBA); finance (MBA); general business (MBA); human resource management (MBA); information systems (MBA); international business (MBA); logistics management (MBA); marketing (MBA); value-driven organization (MBA). *Program availability:* Part-time, evening/weekend, online learning. Electronic applications accepted. *Faculty research:* Accounting, consulting, international business, marketing, information systems.

City College of the City University of New York, Graduate School, Division of Humanities and the Arts, Department of Media and Communication Arts, Program in Branding and Integrated Communications, New York, NY 10031. Offers MPS. *Entrance requirements:* Additional exam requirements/recommendations for international students: Required—TOEFL (minimum score 90 iBT).

City University of Seattle, Graduate Division, School of Management, Seattle, WA 98121. Offers accounting (Certificate); change leadership (MBA, Certificate); computer systems (MS); finance (Certificate); financial management (MBA); general management (MBA); general management-Europe (MBA); global marketing (MBA); human resources management (Certificate); individualized study (MBA); information security (MS); information systems (MBA); leadership (MA); marketing (MBA, Certificate); project management (MBA, MS, Certificate); sustainable business (Certificate); technology management (MBA, Certificate). *Program availability:* Part-time, evening/weekend, online learning. *Degree requirements:* For master's, comprehensive exam (for some programs), thesis (for some programs). *Entrance requirements:* For master's, baccalaureate degree or equivalent from an accredited or otherwise recognized institution. Additional exam requirements/recommendations for international students: Required—TOEFL (minimum score 567 paper-based; 87 iBT); Recommended—IELTS. Electronic applications accepted.

Clark University, Graduate School, Graduate School of Management, Business Administration Program, Worcester, MA 01610-1477. Offers accounting (MBA); finance (MBA); information management and business analytics (MBA); management (MBA); marketing (MBA); social change (MBA); sustainability (MBA). *Accreditation:* AACSB. *Program availability:* Part-time, evening/weekend. *Degree requirements:* For master's, thesis optional. *Entrance requirements:* For master's, GMAT or GRE, 2 references, resume or curriculum vitae, personal statement. Additional exam requirements/recommendations for international students: Required—TOEFL (minimum score 575 paper-based; 90 iBT), IELTS (minimum score 6.5). Electronic applications accepted. *Expenses:* Contact institution. *Faculty research:* Marketing, accounting, human resource management, management information systems, business finance.

Clemson University, Graduate School, College of Business, Department of Marketing, Clemson, SC 29634. Offers MS. *Program availability:* Part-time, evening/weekend. *Faculty:* 17 full-time (7 women), 1 part-time/adjunct (0 women). *Students:* 14 full-time (7 women), 4 part-time (all women); includes 2 minority (1 Asian, non-Hispanic/Latino; 1 Hispanic/Latino), 9 international. Average age 25. 91 applicants, 80% accepted, 15 enrolled. In 2018, 6 master's awarded. *Degree requirements:* For master's, research project. *Entrance requirements:* For master's, GRE General Test or GMAT, unofficial transcripts, letters of recommendation. Additional exam requirements/recommendations for international students: Required—TOEFL (minimum score 80 paper-based; 90 iBT); Recommended—IELTS (minimum score 6), TSE (minimum score 54). *Application deadline:* For fall admission, 4/15 for international students; for spring admission, 10/15 for international students. Applications are processed on a rolling basis. Application fee: $80 ($90 for international students). Electronic applications accepted. *Expenses:* $6823 per semester full-time resident, $14023 per semester full-time non-resident, $833 per credit hour part-time resident, $1731 per credit hour part-time non-resident, online $1264 per credit hour, $4938 doctoral programs resident, $10405 doctoral programs non-resident, $1144 full-time graduate assistant, other fees may apply per session. *Financial support:* In 2018–19, 16 students received support. Career-related internships or fieldwork and unspecified assistantships available. *Faculty research:* Consumer behavior, sales, relationship marketing, research methodology, services. *Unit head:* Dr. Jesse Moore, Department Chair, 864-656-1086, E-mail: jessem@clemson.edu. *Application contact:* Dr. Michael Dorsch, Graduate Program Coordinator, 864-656-5288, E-mail: mdorsch@clemson.edu.
Website: https://www.clemson.edu/business/departments/marketing/

Cleveland State University, College of Graduate Studies, Monte Ahuja College of Business, Doctor of Business Administration Program, Cleveland, OH 44115. Offers information systems (DBA); marketing (DBA). *Accreditation:* AACSB. *Program availability:* Part-time, evening/weekend. *Faculty:* 50 full-time (11 women). *Students:* 8 full-time (4 women), 20 part-time (11 women); includes 7 minority (3 Black or African American, non-Hispanic/Latino; 3 Asian, non-Hispanic/Latino; 1 Hispanic/Latino), 7 international. Average age 37. In 2018, 2 doctorates awarded. *Degree requirements:* For doctorate, comprehensive exam, thesis/dissertation, oral dissertation defense. *Entrance requirements:* For doctorate, GMAT, MBA or equivalent. Additional exam requirements/recommendations for international students: Required—TOEFL (minimum score 550 paper-based; 78 iBT). *Application deadline:* For fall admission, 2/1 for domestic and international students. Application fee: $40. Electronic applications accepted. *Expenses:* Tuition, state resident: full-time $7232.55; part-time $6676 per credit hour. Tuition, nonresident: full-time $12,375. *International tuition:* $18,914 full-time. *Required fees:* $80; $80 $40. Tuition and fees vary according to program. *Financial support:* In 2018–19, 5 research assistantships with full tuition reimbursements (averaging $12,700 per year), 4 teaching assistantships with full tuition reimbursements (averaging $12,700 per year) were awarded; tuition waivers (full) and unspecified assistantships also available. Financial award applicants required to submit FAFSA. *Faculty research:* Supply chain management, international business, strategic management, risk analysis, consumer behavior. *Unit head:* Dr. Raj Shekhar G. Javalgi, Director, 216-687-3786, Fax: 216-687-9354, E-mail: r.javalgi@csuohio.edu. *Application contact:* Melinda J. Arnold, Administrative Secretary, 216-687-6952, Fax: 216-687-9257, E-mail: m.arnold@csuohio.edu.
Website: http://www.csuohio.edu/business/academics/mbajuris-doctor

Colorado Technical University Aurora, Programs in Business Administration and Management, Aurora, CO 80014. Offers accounting (MBA); business administration (MBA); business administration and management (EMBA); finance (MBA); human resource management (MBA); marketing (MBA); mediation and dispute resolution (MBA); operations management (MBA); project management (MBA); technology management (MBA). *Program availability:* Part-time, evening/weekend. *Degree requirements:* For master's, thesis or alternative. *Entrance requirements:* For master's, minimum undergraduate GPA of 3.0, resume.

Colorado Technical University Colorado Springs, Graduate Studies, Program in Management, Colorado Springs, CO 80907. Offers accounting (MBA, MSA); business administration (MBA); finance (MBA); human resources management (MBA); logistics/supply chain management (MBA); management (DM); marketing (MBA); mediation and dispute resolution (MBA); operations management (MBA); project management (MBA); technology management (MBA). *Accreditation:* ACBSP. *Program availability:* Part-time, evening/weekend, online learning. *Degree requirements:* For master's, thesis or alternative; for doctorate, thesis/dissertation. *Entrance requirements:* For doctorate, minimum graduate GPA of 3.0, 5 years of related work experience. *Faculty research:* Sexual harassment, performance evaluation, critical thinking.

Columbia Southern University, MBA Program, Orange Beach, AL 36561. Offers finance (MBA); health care management (MBA); human resource management (MBA); marketing (MBA); project management (MBA); public administration (MBA). *Program availability:* Part-time, evening/weekend, online learning. *Entrance requirements:* For master's, bachelor's degree from accredited/approved institution. Additional exam requirements/recommendations for international students: Required—TOEFL. Electronic applications accepted.

Columbia University, Graduate School of Business, Doctoral Program in Business, New York, NY 10027. Offers business (PhD), including accounting, decision, risk, and operations, finance and economics, management, marketing. *Accreditation:* AACSB. *Degree requirements:* For doctorate, comprehensive exam, thesis/dissertation, major field exam, research paper, thesis proposal. *Entrance requirements:* For doctorate, GMAT or GRE (finance), 2 letters of reference, resume. Additional exam requirements/recommendations for international students: Required—TOEFL. Electronic applications accepted. *Expenses:* Contact institution. *Faculty research:* Human decision making and behavioral research; real estate market and mortgage defaults; financial crisis and corporate governance; international business; security analysis and accounting.

Columbia University, Graduate School of Business, MBA Program, New York, NY 10027. Offers accounting (MBA); decision, risk, and operations (MBA); entrepreneurship (MBA); finance and economics (MBA); healthcare and pharmaceutical management (MBA); human resource management (MBA); international business (MBA); leadership and ethics (MBA); management (MBA); marketing (MBA); media (MBA); private equity

(MBA); real estate (MBA); social enterprise (MBA); value investing (MBA); DDS/MBA; JD/MBA; MBA/MIA; MBA/MPH; MBA/MS; MD/MBA. *Entrance requirements:* For master's, GMAT, 2 letters of recommendation. Additional exam requirements/recommendations for international students: Required—TOEFL. Electronic applications accepted. *Expenses:* Contact institution. *Faculty research:* Human decision making and behavioral research; real estate market and mortgage defaults; financial crisis and corporate governance; international business; security analysis and accounting.

Concordia University, School of Graduate Studies, John Molson School of Business, Montreal, QC H3H 0A1, Canada. Offers administration (M Sc), including finance, management, marketing; business administration (MBA, PhD, Certificate, Diploma); executive business administration (EMBA); supply chain management (MSCM). PhD program offered jointly with HEC Montreal, McGill University, and Université du Québec à Montréal. *Program availability:* Part-time, evening/weekend. *Degree requirements:* For master's, one foreign language, thesis (for some programs), research project; for doctorate, one foreign language, thesis/dissertation; for other advanced degree, one foreign language. *Entrance requirements:* For master's, GMAT, minimum 2 years of work experience (for MBA); letters of recommendation, bachelor's degree from recognized university with minimum GPA of 3.0, curriculum vitae; for doctorate, GMAT (minimum score of 600), official transcripts, curriculum vitae, 3 letters of reference, statement of purpose; for other advanced degree, minimum GPA of 2.7, 2 letters of reference, statement of purpose, resume. Additional exam requirements/recommendations for international students: Required—TOEFL (minimum score 90 iBT), IELTS (minimum score 7). Electronic applications accepted. *Expenses:* Contact institution. *Faculty research:* General business, capital markets, international business.

Concordia University Wisconsin, Graduate Programs, Batterman School of Business, MBA Program, Mequon, WI 53097-2402. Offers finance (MBA); health care administration (MBA); human resource management (MBA); international business (MBA); international business-bilingual English/Chinese (MBA); management (MBA); management information systems (MBA); managerial communications (MBA); marketing (MBA); public administration (MBA); risk management (MBA). *Program availability:* Online learning. *Degree requirements:* For master's, comprehensive exam, thesis or alternative. *Entrance requirements:* Additional exam requirements/recommendations for international students: Required—TOEFL. *Expenses:* Contact institution.

Cornell University, Graduate School, Graduate Field of Management, Ithaca, NY 14853. Offers accounting (PhD); finance (PhD); marketing (PhD); organizational behavior (PhD); production and operations management (PhD). *Accreditation:* AACSB. *Degree requirements:* For doctorate, comprehensive exam, thesis/dissertation. *Entrance requirements:* For doctorate, GMAT or GRE General Test. Additional exam requirements/recommendations for international students: Required—TOEFL (minimum score 600 paper-based; 77 iBT). Electronic applications accepted. *Expenses:* Contact institution. *Faculty research:* Operations and manufacturing.

Daemen College, International Business Program, Amherst, NY 14226-3592. Offers global business (MS), including accounting, global business, management information systems, marketing. *Program availability:* Part-time, evening/weekend. *Faculty:* 3 full-time (2 women), 3 part-time/adjunct (1 woman). *Students:* 4 full-time (2 women), 5 part-time (3 women); includes 1 minority (Black or African American, non-Hispanic/Latino), 2 international. Average age 34. 7 applicants, 57% accepted, 2 enrolled. In 2018, 4 master's awarded. *Degree requirements:* For master's, minimum GPA of 3.0. *Entrance requirements:* For master's, GMAT if undergraduate GPA is less than 3.0, baccalaureate degree from an accredited college or university with a major concentration in a business related field, such as accounting, business administration, economics, management, or marketing; official transcripts; undergrad GPA 3.0 higher or needs to take the GMAT; resume; 2 letters of recommendation; personal statement. Additional exam requirements/recommendations for international students: Required—TOEFL (minimum score 77 paper-based), IELTS (minimum score 6.5). *Application deadline:* Applications are processed on a rolling basis. Application fee: $25. Electronic applications accepted. Application fee is waived when completed online. *Expenses:* Tuition: Part-time $977 per credit hour. *Required fees:* $125; $14 per credit hour. *Financial support:* Scholarships/grants and unspecified assistantships available. Support available to part-time students. Financial award applicants required to submit FAFSA. *Unit head:* Dr. Torsten Doering, Director of International Business Program, 716-839-8239, E-mail: tdoering@daemen.edu. *Application contact:* Megan Beardi, Senior Assistant Director of Graduate Admissions, 716-566-7861, Fax: 716-839-8229, E-mail: mbeardi@daemen.edu. Website: https://www.daemen.edu/academics/areas-study/international-business

DePaul University, Kellstadt Graduate School of Business, Chicago, IL 60604. Offers accountancy (MBA, MSA); applied economics (MBA); audit and advisory services (MS); business administration (DBA); business analytics (MS); business strategy and decision-making (MBA); computational finance (MS); economics and policy analysis (MS); enterprise risk management (MS); entrepreneurship (MBA, MS); finance (MBA, MS); general business (MBA); hospitality leadership (MBA); hospitality leadership and operational performance (MS); human resources (MS); international business (MBA); management (MBA, MS); management information systems (MBA); marketing (MBA, MS); marketing analysis (MS); marketing strategy and planning (MBA); real estate (MS); real estate finance and investment (MBA); strategy, execution and valuation (MBA); supply chain management (MS); sustainable management (MS); taxation (MS); JD/MBA. *Accreditation:* AACSB. *Program availability:* Part-time, evening/weekend, online learning. *Entrance requirements:* For master's, GMAT/GRE, 2 letters of recommendation, resume, essay, official transcripts. Additional exam requirements/recommendations for international students: Required—TOEFL (minimum score 550 paper-based; 80 iBT). Electronic applications accepted. *Expenses:* Contact institution.

DEREE - The American College of Greece, Graduate Programs, Athens, Greece. Offers applied psychology (MS); communication (MA); leadership (MS); marketing (MS).

DeSales University, Division of Business, Center Valley, PA 18034-9568. Offers accounting (MBA); computer information systems (MBA); finance (MBA); health care systems management (MBA); human resources management (MBA); management (MBA); marketing (MBA); project management (MBA); self-design (MBA); supply chain management (MBA); DNP/MBA; MSN/MBA. *Accreditation:* ACBSP. *Program availability:* Part-time, evening/weekend, 100% online, blended/hybrid learning. *Entrance requirements:* For master's, GMAT (waived if undergraduate GPA is 3.0 or better), minimum GPA of 3.0 in undergraduate work, literacy in basic software, background or interest in the field of study, personal statement, 2 years of work experience. Additional exam requirements/recommendations for international students: Required—TOEFL. Electronic applications accepted. *Expenses:* Contact institution. *Faculty research:* Quality improvement, executive development, productivity, cross-cultural managerial differences, leadership.

Drexel University, LeBow College of Business, Program in Business Administration, Philadelphia, PA 19104-2875. Offers business administration (MBA, PhD, APC), including accounting (MBA, PhD), decision sciences (PhD), economics (MBA, PhD), finance (MBA, PhD), legal studies (MBA), management (MBA), marketing (MBA, PhD), organizational sciences (PhD), quantitative methods (MBA), strategic management (PhD). *Accreditation:* AACSB. *Program availability:* Part-time, evening/weekend, online

learning. Terminal master's awarded for partial completion of doctoral program. *Entrance requirements:* For master's, GMAT, minimum GPA of 2.75; for doctorate, GMAT. Additional exam requirements/recommendations for international students: Required—TOEFL. Electronic applications accepted. *Faculty research:* Decision support systems, individual and group behavior, operations research, techniques and strategy.

Duke University, The Fuqua School of Business, The Duke MBA-Daytime Program, Durham, NC 27708. Offers academic excellence in finance (Certificate); business administration (MBA); decision sciences (MBA); energy and environment (MBA); energy finance (MBA); entrepreneurship and innovation (MBA); finance (MBA); financial analysis (MBA); health sector management (Certificate); leadership and ethics (MBA); management (MBA); management science and technology management (Certificate); marketing (MBA); operations management (MBA); social entrepreneurship (MBA); strategy (MBA). *Faculty:* 100 full-time (21 women), 55 part-time/adjunct (12 women). *Students:* 875 full-time (335 women); includes 188 minority (44 Black or African American, non-Hispanic/Latino; 4 American Indian or Alaska Native, non-Hispanic/Latino; 90 Asian, non-Hispanic/Latino; 43 Hispanic/Latino; 1 Native Hawaiian or other Pacific Islander, non-Hispanic/Latino; 6 Two or more races, non-Hispanic/Latino), 276 international. Average age 29. In 2018, 429 master's awarded. *Entrance requirements:* For master's, GMAT or GRE, transcripts, essays, resume, recommendation letters, interview. *Application deadline:* For fall admission, 9/19 for domestic and international students; for winter admission, 10/14 for domestic and international students; for spring admission, 1/6 for domestic and international students; for summer admission, 3/11 for domestic and international students. Application fee: $225. Electronic applications accepted. *Expenses:* Contact institution. *Financial support:* Scholarships/grants available. Financial award applicants required to submit FAFSA. *Unit head:* Steve Misuraca, Assistant Dean, Daytime MBA Program. *Application contact:* Shari Hubert, Associate Dean, Office of Admissions, 919-660-7705, Fax: 919-681-8026, E-mail: admissions-info@fuqua.duke.edu. Website: https://www.fuqua.duke.edu/programs/daytime-mba

Duke University, The Fuqua School of Business, The Duke MBA-Global Executive Program, Durham, NC 27708. Offers business administration (MBA); energy and environment (MBA); entrepreneurship and innovation (MBA); finance (MBA); health sector management (Certificate); marketing (MBA); strategy (MBA). *Faculty:* 100 full-time (21 women), 55 part-time/adjunct (12 women). *Students:* 141 full-time (43 women); includes 43 minority (12 Black or African American, non-Hispanic/Latino; 25 Asian, non-Hispanic/Latino; 4 Hispanic/Latino; 1 Native Hawaiian or other Pacific Islander, non-Hispanic/Latino; 1 Two or more races, non-Hispanic/Latino), 34 international. Average age 35. In 2018, 159 master's awarded. *Entrance requirements:* For master's, Executive Assessment, GMAT, or GRE, or waived, transcripts, essays, resume, recommendation letters, letter of company support, interview. *Application deadline:* For fall admission, 10/16 priority date for domestic and international students; for winter admission, 12/4 priority date for domestic and international students; for spring admission, 3/11 priority date for domestic and international students; for summer admission, 5/27 for domestic and international students. Applications are processed on a rolling basis. Application fee: $225. Electronic applications accepted. *Expenses:* Contact institution. *Financial support:* Scholarships/grants available. Financial award applicants required to submit FAFSA. *Unit head:* Karen Courtney, Associate Dean, Executive Programs. *Application contact:* Shari Hubert, Associate Dean, Office of Admissions, 919-660-7705, Fax: 919-681-8026, E-mail: admissions-info@fuqua.duke.edu. Website: https://www.fuqua.duke.edu/programs/global-executive-mba

Duke University, The Fuqua School of Business, The Duke MBA-Weekend Executive Program, Durham, NC 27708. Offers business administration (MBA); energy and environment (MBA); entrepreneurship and innovation (MBA); finance (MBA); health sector management (Certificate); marketing (MBA); strategy (MBA). *Faculty:* 100 full-time (21 women), 55 part-time/adjunct (12 women). *Students:* 251 full-time (67 women); includes 79 minority (13 Black or African American, non-Hispanic/Latino; 2 American Indian or Alaska Native, non-Hispanic/Latino; 46 Asian, non-Hispanic/Latino; 12 Hispanic/Latino; 1 Native Hawaiian or other Pacific Islander, non-Hispanic/Latino; 5 Two or more races, non-Hispanic/Latino), 32 international. Average age 35. In 2018, 120 master's awarded. *Entrance requirements:* For master's, Executive Assessment, GMAT, or GRE, or waived, transcripts, essays, resume, recommendation letters, letter of company support, interview. *Application deadline:* For fall admission, 9/18 priority date for domestic and international students; for winter admission, 12/4 priority date for domestic and international students; for spring admission, 1/22 priority date for domestic and international students; for summer admission, 3/11 for domestic and international students. Applications are processed on a rolling basis. Application fee: $225. Electronic applications accepted. *Expenses:* Contact institution. *Financial support:* Scholarships/grants available. Financial award applicants required to submit FAFSA. *Unit head:* Karen Courtney, Associate Dean, Executive Programs. *Application contact:* Shari Hubert, Associate Dean, Office of Admissions, 919-660-7705, Fax: 919-681-8026, E-mail: admissions-info@fuqua.duke.edu. Website: https://www.fuqua.duke.edu/programs/weekend-executive-mba

Duke University, The Fuqua School of Business, Master of Quantitative Management Program: Business Analytics, Durham, NC 27708. Offers finance (MQM); forensics (MQM); marketing (MQM); strategy (MQM). *Faculty:* 100 full-time (21 women), 55 part-time/adjunct (12 women). *Students:* 136 full-time (56 women); includes 15 minority (1 Black or African American, non-Hispanic/Latino; 14 Asian, non-Hispanic/Latino), 99 international. Average age 23. In 2018, 136 master's awarded. *Entrance requirements:* For master's, GMAT/GRE, transcripts, essays, resume, recommendation letter, interview. *Application deadline:* For fall admission, 10/21 for domestic and international students; for winter admission, 1/15 for domestic and international students; for spring admission, 2/27 for domestic and international students; for summer admission, 4/6 for domestic and international students. Application fee: $125. Electronic applications accepted. *Expenses:* Contact institution. *Financial support:* Scholarships/grants available. Financial award applicants required to submit FAFSA. *Unit head:* Jeremy Petranka, Associate Dean, 919-660-7778. *Application contact:* Shari Hubert, Associate Dean, Office of Admissions, 919-660-7705, Fax: 919-681-8026, E-mail: mqmbusinessanalytics@fuqua.duke.edu. Website: https://www.fuqua.duke.edu/programs/mqm-business-analytics

Duke University, The Fuqua School of Business, PhD Program, Durham, NC 27708. Offers accounting (PhD); decision sciences (PhD); finance (PhD); management and organizations (PhD); marketing (PhD); operations management (PhD); strategy (PhD). *Faculty:* 100 full-time (21 women). *Students:* 84 full-time (29 women); includes 4 minority (2 Asian, non-Hispanic/Latino; 2 Hispanic/Latino), 53 international. Average age 28. In 2018, 14 doctorates awarded. *Degree requirements:* For doctorate, comprehensive exam (for some programs), thesis/dissertation, Comprehensive or Qualifying exams are required for some of the 7 areas in Business Administration. *Entrance requirements:* For doctorate, GMAT or GRE, transcripts, essays, recommendation letters, statement of purpose. Additional exam requirements/recommendations for international students: Required—TOEFL, IELTS. *Application deadline:* For fall admission, 12/31 priority date for domestic and international students. Application fee: $90. Electronic applications accepted. *Expenses:* Contact institution. *Financial support:* In 2018–19, 74 fellowships

with full tuition reimbursements (averaging $33,300 per year) were awarded; research assistantships with full tuition reimbursements, teaching assistantships, institutionally sponsored loans, scholarships/grants, health care benefits, and tuition waivers (full) also available. *Unit head:* William Boulding, Dean, 919-660-7822. *Application contact:* Ravi Bansal, Director of Graduate Studies, 919-660-7753, Fax: 919-660-7971, E-mail: fuqua-phd-info@duke.edu.

Duquesne University, Palumbo-Donahue School of Business, Pittsburgh, PA 15282-0001. Offers accounting (M Acc); finance (MBA); information systems management (MSISM); management (MBA, MS); marketing (MBA); sports business (MS); supply chain management (MS); sustainability (MBA); JD/MBA; MBA/M Acc; MBA/MA; MBA/MES; MBA/MHMS; MSISM/MBA; Pharm D/MBA. *Accreditation:* AACSB. *Program availability:* Part-time, evening/weekend, 100% online, blended/hybrid learning. *Faculty:* 59 full-time (23 women), 25 part-time/adjunct (6 women). *Students:* 214 full-time (74 women), 42 part-time (20 women); includes 39 minority (12 Black or African American, non-Hispanic/Latino; 13 Asian, non-Hispanic/Latino; 8 Hispanic/Latino; 6 Two or more races, non-Hispanic/Latino), 23 international. Average age 29. 228 applicants, 88% accepted, 118 enrolled. In 2018, 149 master's awarded. *Entrance requirements:* For master's, GMAT or GRE, all official transcripts, two letters of recommendation, current resume, essays. Additional exam requirements/recommendations for international students: Required—TOEFL (minimum score 90 iBT), IELTS (minimum score 7). *Application deadline:* For fall admission, 7/1 priority date for domestic and international students; for spring admission, 12/1 for domestic and international students; for summer admission, 4/1 for domestic and international students. Applications are processed on a rolling basis. Application fee: $0. Electronic applications accepted. *Expenses:* $1,284/credit hour (business), $953/credit hour (management). *Financial support:* In 2018–19, 174 students received support, including 6 fellowships with partial tuition reimbursements available (averaging $24,750 per year); career-related internships or fieldwork, scholarships/grants, and unspecified assistantships also available. Support available to part-time students. Financial award application deadline: 7/1; financial award applicants required to submit FAFSA. *Faculty research:* Investment management, business ethics, technology management, supply chain management, entrepreneurship. *Unit head:* Dr. Karen Donovan, Associate Dean of Graduate Programs and Executive Education, 412-396-5788, Fax: 412-396-1726, E-mail: donovan6@duq.edu. *Application contact:* Chris Rouhier, Director of Graduate Admissions, 412-396-6244, Fax: 412-396-1726, E-mail: rouhierc@duq.edu.
Website: http://www.duq.edu/business/grad

Eastern Michigan University, Graduate School, Academic and Student Affairs Division, Ypsilanti, MI 48197. Offers individualized studies (MA, MS); integrated marketing communications (MS). *Faculty:* 1 full-time (0 women). *Students:* 1 part-time (0 women). Average age 33. 40 applicants, 90% accepted, 13 enrolled. In 2018, 1 master's awarded. *Entrance requirements:* Additional exam requirements/recommendations for international students: Required—TOEFL. Application fee: $45. *Unit head:* Dr. Wade Tornquist, Interim Dean, 734-487-0042, Fax: 734-487-0050, E-mail: wade.tornquist@emich.edu. *Application contact:* Graduate Admissions, 734-487-2400, Fax: 734-487-6559, E-mail: graduate.admissions@emich.edu.

Eastern Michigan University, Graduate School, College of Business, Department of Marketing, Program in Integrated Marketing Communications, Ypsilanti, MI 48197. Offers MS, Postbaccalaureate Certificate. *Students:* 31 full-time (25 women), 33 part-time (22 women); includes 25 minority (15 Black or African American, non-Hispanic/Latino; 1 Asian, non-Hispanic/Latino; 9 Hispanic/Latino). Average age 30. 32 applicants, 84% accepted, 16 enrolled. In 2018, 23 master's awarded. Application fee: $45. *Application contact:* K. Michelle Henry, Director, Graduate Business Programs, 734-487-4444, Fax: 734-478-1316, E-mail: cob.graduate@emich.edu.

Eastern Michigan University, Graduate School, College of Business, Programs in Business Administration, Ypsilanti, MI 48197. Offers business administration (MBA, Graduate Certificate); computer information systems (Graduate Certificate); e-business (MBA, Graduate Certificate); enterprise business intelligence (MBA); entrepreneurship (MBA, Graduate Certificate); finance (MBA, Graduate Certificate); human resources (MBA); human resources management (Graduate Certificate); information systems (MBA); internal auditing (MBA); international business (MBA, Graduate Certificate); marketing management (Graduate Certificate); nonprofit management (MBA); organizational development (Graduate Certificate); supply chain management (MBA, Graduate Certificate). *Accreditation:* AACSB. *Program availability:* Part-time, online learning. *Students:* 69 full-time (38 women), 251 part-time (140 women); includes 100 minority (63 Black or African American, non-Hispanic/Latino; 1 American Indian or Alaska Native, non-Hispanic/Latino; 12 Asian, non-Hispanic/Latino; 14 Hispanic/Latino; 10 Two or more races, non-Hispanic/Latino), 28 international. Average age 32. 199 applicants, 75% accepted, 83 enrolled. In 2018, 75 master's, 50 other advanced degrees awarded. *Entrance requirements:* For master's, GMAT (minimum score 450), minimum cumulative undergraduate GPA of 2.75. Additional exam requirements/recommendations for international students: Required—TOEFL. *Application deadline:* For fall admission, 5/15 priority date for domestic students, 2/15 priority date for international students; for winter admission, 10/15 priority date for domestic students, 9/1 priority date for international students; for summer admission, 3/15 priority date for domestic students, 3/1 priority date for international students. Applications are processed on a rolling basis. Application fee: $45. *Financial support:* Fellowships, research assistantships with full tuition reimbursements, teaching assistantships with full tuition reimbursements, career-related internships or fieldwork, Federal Work-Study, institutionally sponsored loans, scholarships/grants, tuition waivers (partial), and unspecified assistantships available. Support available to part-time students. Financial award applicants required to submit FAFSA. *Unit head:* K. Michelle Henry, Director, Graduate Business Programs, 734-487-4444, Fax: 734-483-1316, E-mail: cob.graduate@emich.edu. *Application contact:* K. Michelle Henry, Director, Graduate Business Programs, 734-487-4444, Fax: 734-483-1316, E-mail: cob.graduate@emich.edu.
Website: http://www.emich.edu/cob/mba/

East Tennessee State University, School of Graduate Studies, College of Business and Technology, Department of Management and Marketing, Johnson City, TN 37614. Offers business administration (MBA, Postbaccalaureate Certificate); digital marketing (MS); entrepreneurial leadership (Postbaccalaureate Certificate); health care management (Postbaccalaureate Certificate). *Program availability:* Part-time, evening/weekend. *Degree requirements:* For master's, comprehensive exam, capstone. *Entrance requirements:* For master's, GMAT, minimum GPA of 2.5 (for MBA), 3.0 (for MS); current resume; three letters of recommendation; for Postbaccalaureate Certificate, minimum GPA of 2.5, undergraduate degree. Additional exam requirements/recommendations for international students: Required—TOEFL (minimum score 550 paper-based; 79 iBT). Electronic applications accepted. *Faculty research:* Sustainability, healthcare effectiveness, consumer behavior, merchandising trends, organizational management issues.

Emory University, Goizueta Business School, Doctoral Program in Business, Atlanta, GA 30322. Offers accounting (PhD); finance (PhD); information systems and operations management (PhD); marketing (PhD); organization and management (PhD). *Faculty:* 67 full-time (22 women). *Students:* 45 full-time (21 women); includes 5 minority (2 Black or African American, non-Hispanic/Latino; 3 Hispanic/Latino), 31 international. Average age 29. 143 applicants, 19% accepted, 10 enrolled. In 2018, 7 doctorates awarded. *Degree requirements:* For doctorate, comprehensive exam, thesis/dissertation. *Entrance requirements:* For doctorate, GMAT, interview. Additional exam requirements/recommendations for international students: Required—TOEFL (minimum score 600 paper-based; 100 iBT), IELTS, We will take either TOEFL or IELTS. *Application deadline:* For fall admission, 1/3 priority date for domestic and international students. Applications are processed on a rolling basis. Application fee: $75. Electronic applications accepted. *Expenses:* Our students are required to pay approximately $400 in their fall and spring terms; approximately $200 in summer terms in fees. All tuition is scholarshiped 100%. *Financial support:* In 2018–19, 45 students received support, including 11 fellowships (averaging $1,000 per year); scholarships/grants, health care benefits, and Fellowships are both the Sheth Fellows and Goizueta Fellows whom are named each year based on certain milestones. also available. Financial award application deadline: 1/3. *Faculty research:* Financial and managerial accounting, asset pricing strategy and organizational behavior, information technology marketing analytics and consumer behavior. *Unit head:* Kathryn Kadous, Associate Dean, 404-727-2306, Fax: 404-727-5337, E-mail: kathryn.kadous@emory.edu. *Application contact:* Allison Gilmore, Director of Admissions and Student Services, 404-727-6353, Fax: 404-727-5337, E-mail: allison.gilmore@emory.edu.
Website: https://goizueta.emory.edu/degree/phd/index.html

Emory University, Goizueta Business School, Full Time MBA Program, Atlanta, GA 30322-1100. Offers accounting (MBA); alternative investments (MBA); business process consulting (MBA); business technology management (MBA); capital markets (MBA); corporate finance (MBA); customer relationship management (MBA); decision analytics (MBA); entrepreneurship (MBA); finance (MBA); global management (MBA); investment banking (MBA); management consulting (MBA); marketing (MBA); marketing analytics (MBA); marketing consulting (MBA); operations management (MBA); organization and management (MBA); product and brand management (MBA); real estate (MBA); social enterprise (MBA); strategy consulting (MBA). *Accreditation:* AACSB. *Faculty:* 74 full-time (18 women), 18 part-time/adjunct (6 women). *Students:* 349 full-time (105 women); includes 81 minority (26 Black or African American, non-Hispanic/Latino; 1 American Indian or Alaska Native, non-Hispanic/Latino; 35 Asian, non-Hispanic/Latino; 16 Hispanic/Latino; 3 Two or more races, non-Hispanic/Latino), 97 international. Average age 29. 1,380 applicants, 34% accepted, 172 enrolled. In 2018, 180 master's awarded. *Degree requirements:* For master's, 1 leadership course; 2 mid-semester module programs; 2 global components. *Entrance requirements:* For master's, GMAT/GRE, essays; recommendation letters; undergraduate degree; interview. Additional exam requirements/recommendations for international students: Required—TOEFL (minimum score 100 iBT), IELTS (minimum score 7), PTE (minimum score 68). *Application deadline:* For fall admission, 10/6 for domestic and international students; for winter admission, 11/17 for domestic and international students; for spring admission, 1/3 priority date for domestic and international students; for summer admission, 3/9 for domestic and international students. Application fee: $150. Electronic applications accepted. *Expenses:* Contact institution. *Financial support:* In 2018–19, 273 students received support. Career-related internships or fieldwork, institutionally sponsored loans, and scholarships/grants available. Financial award application deadline: 4/1; financial award applicants required to submit FAFSA. *Faculty research:* Corporate finance, information systems, digital marketing, asset pricing, sports management. *Unit head:* Brian Mitchell, Associate Dean, 404-727-4824, Fax: 404-712-9648, E-mail: brian.mitchell@emory.edu. *Application contact:* Melissa Rapp, Associate Dean, 404-727-7583, Fax: 404-727-4612, E-mail: mbaadmissions@emory.edu.
Website: http://www.goizueta.emory.edu

Fairfield University, Dolan School of Business, Fairfield, CT 06824. Offers accounting (MBA, MS, CAS); business analytics (MS); finance (MBA, MS, CAS); information systems and business analytics (MBA); management (MBA, CAS); marketing (MBA, CAS); taxation (CAS). *Accreditation:* AACSB. *Program availability:* Part-time, evening/weekend. *Degree requirements:* For master's, capstone course. *Entrance requirements:* For master's, GMAT (minimum score 500), 2 letters of reference, resume, minimum GPA of 3.0. Additional exam requirements/recommendations for international students: Required—TOEFL (minimum score 550 paper-based; 80 iBT) or IELTS (minimum score 6.5). Electronic applications accepted. *Expenses:* Contact institution. *Faculty research:* International finance, leadership and careers, ethics in accounting, emotions in consumer behavior and organizations, data analytics.

Fairleigh Dickinson University, Florham Campus, Silberman College of Business, Departments of Management, Marketing, and Entrepreneurial Studies, Program in Marketing, Madison, NJ 07940-1099. Offers MBA, Certificate. *Entrance requirements:* For master's, GMAT.

Fairleigh Dickinson University, Metropolitan Campus, Silberman College of Business, Departments of Management, Marketing, and Entrepreneurial Studies, Program in Marketing, Teaneck, NJ 07666-1914. Offers MBA, Certificate.

Fashion Institute of Technology, School of Graduate Studies, Program in Cosmetics and Fragrance Marketing and Management, New York, NY 10001-5992. Offers MPS. *Degree requirements:* For master's, capstone seminar. *Entrance requirements:* Additional exam requirements/recommendations for international students: Required—TOEFL (minimum score 550 paper-based). Electronic applications accepted.

Florida Agricultural and Mechanical University, Division of Graduate Studies, Research, and Continuing Education, School of Business and Industry, Tallahassee, FL 32307-3200. Offers accounting (MBA); finance (MBA); management information systems (MBA); marketing (MBA). *Accreditation:* ACBSP. *Degree requirements:* For master's, residency. *Entrance requirements:* For master's, GMAT, minimum GPA of 3.0.

Florida International University, Chapman Graduate School of Business, Department of Marketing and Logistics, Miami, FL 33199. Offers marketing (MS). *Program availability:* Evening/weekend. *Faculty:* 24 full-time (12 women), 15 part-time/adjunct (7 women). *Students:* 128 full-time, 1 part-time; includes 162 minority (20 Black or African American, non-Hispanic/Latino; 1 American Indian or Alaska Native, non-Hispanic/Latino; 2 Asian, non-Hispanic/Latino; 137 Hispanic/Latino; 2 Two or more races, non-Hispanic/Latino), 21 international. Average age 31. 318 applicants, 60% accepted, 167 enrolled. In 2018, 123 master's awarded. *Entrance requirements:* For master's, GMAT/GRE or 3 years of work experience, minimum AACSB index of 1000, minimum GPA of 3.0. Application fee: $30. *Unit head:* Anthony Miyazaki, Chair, 305-348-2571, Fax: 305-348-3792, E-mail: anthony.miyazaki@fiu.edu. *Application contact:* Nanett Rojas, Manager, Admissions Operations, 305-348-7464, Fax: 305-348-7441, E-mail: gradadm@fiu.edu.

Florida National University, Program in Business Administration, Hialeah, FL 33012. Offers accounting (MBA); finance (MBA); general management (MBA); health services administration (MBA); marketing (MBA); public management and leadership (MBA). *Program availability:* Part-time, blended/hybrid learning. *Faculty:* 3 full-time (1 woman), 4 part-time/adjunct (2 women). *Students:* 15 full-time (5 women), 15 part-time (6 women); all minorities (7 Black or African American, non-Hispanic/Latino; 21 Hispanic/Latino; 2 Two or more races, non-Hispanic/Latino), 1 international. Average age 35. 8 applicants, 88% accepted, 7 enrolled. In 2018, 27 master's awarded. *Degree requirements:* For

master's, capstone. *Entrance requirements:* For master's, writing assessment, bachelor's degree from accredited institution; official undergraduate transcripts; minimum undergraduate GPA of 2.5, GMAT (minimum score of 400), or GRE (minimum score of 900); two letters of recommendation; resume. Additional exam requirements/recommendations for international students: Required—TOEFL (minimum score 500 paper-based; 62 iBT), IELTS (minimum score 5.5). *Application deadline:* Applications are processed on a rolling basis. Electronic applications accepted. *Expenses:* Contact institution. *Financial support:* Federal Work-Study, institutionally sponsored loans, scholarships/grants, and tuition waivers (full and partial) available. Financial award applicants required to submit FAFSA. *Unit head:* Dr. Ernesto Gonzalez, Business and Economics Department Head, 305-821-3333 Ext. 1070, Fax: 305-362-0595, E-mail: egonzalez@fnu.edu. *Application contact:* Dr. Ernesto Gonzalez, Business and Economics Department Head, 305-821-3333 Ext. 1070, Fax: 305-362-0595, E-mail: egonzalez@fnu.edu.
Website: https://www.fnu.edu/prospective-students/our-programs/select-a-program/master-of-business-administration/business-administration-mba-masters/

Florida State University, The Graduate School, College of Business, Tallahassee, FL 32306-1110. Offers accounting (M Acc), including assurance and advisory services, generalist, taxation; business administration (MBA, PhD), including accounting (PhD), finance (PhD), management information systems (PhD), marketing (PhD), organizational behavior and human resources (PhD), risk management and insurance (PhD), strategy (PhD); finance (MS); management information systems (MS); risk management and insurance (MS); JD/MBA; MSW/MBA. *Accreditation:* AACSB. *Program availability:* Part-time, 100% online. *Students:* Average age 31. 300 applicants, 61% accepted, 133 enrolled. In 2018, 268 master's, 9 doctorates awarded. Terminal master's awarded for partial completion of doctoral program. *Degree requirements:* For doctorate, comprehensive exam, thesis/dissertation. *Entrance requirements:* For master's, GMAT, GRE (for all except MS in finance), work experience (MBA, MS); minimum GPA of 3.0, letters of recommendation; for doctorate, GMAT, GRE (for marketing, organizational behavior, risk management and insurance, management information systems, and human resources only), minimum graduate GPA of 3.5, letters of recommendation. Additional exam requirements/recommendations for international students: Required—TOEFL (minimum score 600 paper-based; 85 iBT); Recommended—IELTS (minimum score 6). *Application deadline:* For fall admission, 6/1 for domestic and international students; for spring admission, 10/1 for domestic and international students; for summer admission, 3/1 for domestic and international students. Applications are processed on a rolling basis. Application fee: $30. Electronic applications accepted. *Expenses:* Contact institution. *Financial support:* In 2018–19, 146 students received support, including 26 fellowships (averaging $1,500 per year), 77 research assistantships with full tuition reimbursements available (averaging $20,000 per year), 43 teaching assistantships with full tuition reimbursements available (averaging $20,000 per year); career-related internships or fieldwork, scholarships/grants, health care benefits, tuition waivers (full and partial), and unspecified assistantships also available. Support available to part-time students. Financial award application deadline: 1/1; financial award applicants required to submit FAFSA. *Faculty research:* Business strategy, marketing, finance, accounting, business analytics. *Total annual research expenditures:* $1.4 million. *Unit head:* Dr. Michael Hartline, Dean, 850-644-4405, Fax: 850-644-0915, E-mail: mhartline@business.fsu.edu. *Application contact:* Jennifer Clark, Director, 850-644-6458, E-mail: gradprograms@business.fsu.edu.
Website: http://business.fsu.edu/

Florida State University, The Graduate School, College of Communication and Information, School of Communication, Tallahassee, FL 32306. Offers communication theory and research (PhD); integrated marketing communication (MA, MS); media and communication studies (MA, MS); public interest media and communication (MA, MS). *Program availability:* Part-time. *Faculty:* 23 full-time (13 women), 1 part-time/adjunct (0 women). *Students:* 19 full-time (16 women), 121 part-time (84 women); includes 73 minority (22 Black or African American, non-Hispanic/Latino; 15 Asian, non-Hispanic/Latino; 27 Hispanic/Latino; 9 Two or more races, non-Hispanic/Latino). Average age 24. 196 applicants, 54% accepted, 48 enrolled. In 2018, 65 master's, 5 doctorates awarded. *Degree requirements:* For master's, thesis (for some programs); for doctorate, comprehensive exam, thesis/dissertation. *Entrance requirements:* For master's, GRE General Test, minimum GPA of 3.0; for doctorate, GRE General Test, minimum GPA of 3.3 in graduate course work. Additional exam requirements/recommendations for international students: Required—TOEFL (minimum score 600 paper-based; 100 iBT), IELTS (minimum score 7). *Application deadline:* For fall admission, 7/1 priority date for domestic students, 5/1 priority date for international students; for spring admission, 11/1 priority date for domestic and international students; for summer admission, 3/1 priority date for domestic and international students. Applications are processed on a rolling basis. Application fee: $30. Electronic applications accepted. *Expenses:* Contact institution. *Financial support:* In 2018–19, 109 students received support, including 20 research assistantships with full tuition reimbursements available (averaging $12,726 per year), 139 teaching assistantships with full tuition reimbursements available (averaging $10,602 per year); scholarships/grants, tuition waivers (full and partial), and unspecified assistantships also available. Financial award application deadline: 11/1; financial award applicants required to submit FAFSA. *Faculty research:* Communication in the public interest; strategic communication; media and technology; multicultural, intercultural, and international communication. *Total annual research expenditures:* $41,657. *Unit head:* Dr. Jennifer Proffitt, Director, 850-644-5034, Fax: 850-644-8642, E-mail: jennifer.proffitt@cci.fsu.edu. *Application contact:* Natashia Hinson-Turner, Graduate Coordinator, 850-644-5034, Fax: 850-644-8642, E-mail: comgradadvising@cci.fsu.edu.
Website: http://www.cci.fsu.edu

Fordham University, Gabelli School of Business, New York, NY 10023. Offers accounting (MBA, MS); applied statistics and decision-making (MS); business economics (DPS); capital markets (DPS); communications and media management (MBA); electronic business (MBA); entrepreneurship (MBA); finance (MBA, PhD); global finance (MS); global sustainability (MBA); health administration (MS); healthcare management (MBA); information systems (MBA, MS); investor relations (MS); management (EMBA, MBA, MS, PhD); marketing (MBA); marketing intelligence (MS); media management (MS); nonprofit leadership (MS); quantitative finance (MS); strategy and decision-making (DPS); taxation (MS); JD/MBA; MS/MBA. *Accreditation:* AACSB. *Program availability:* Part-time, evening/weekend. Terminal master's awarded for partial completion of doctoral program. *Degree requirements:* For master's, internships (for some degrees); for doctorate, comprehensive exam (for some programs), thesis/dissertation. *Entrance requirements:* For master's, GMAT/GRE, 2 letters of recommendation, resume, 2 essays, transcripts, interview. Additional exam requirements/recommendations for international students: Required—TOEFL (minimum score 100 iBT), IELTS (minimum score 7). Electronic applications accepted. *Expenses:* Contact institution.

Franklin University, Marketing and Communication Program, Columbus, OH 43215-5399. Offers MS. *Program availability:* Part-time, evening/weekend. *Entrance requirements:* For master's, minimum undergraduate GPA of 2.75. Additional exam requirements/recommendations for international students: Required—TOEFL (minimum score 550 paper-based). Electronic applications accepted.

Full Sail University, Internet Marketing Master of Science Program - Online, Winter Park, FL 32792-7437. Offers MS. *Program availability:* Online learning.

Gannon University, School of Graduate Studies, College of Engineering and Business, Dahlkemper School of Business, Program in Business Administration, Erie, PA 16541-0001. Offers business administration (MBA); finance (MBA); human resources management (MBA); marketing (MBA). *Accreditation:* ACBSP. *Program availability:* Part-time, evening/weekend, 100% online, blended/hybrid learning. *Entrance requirements:* For master's, GMAT, bachelor's degree in any discipline from any accredited college or university, resume, transcripts, 3 letters of recommendation. Additional exam requirements/recommendations for international students: Required—TOEFL (minimum score 79 iBT). Electronic applications accepted. Application fee is waived when completed online.

Geneva College, Program in Business Administration, Beaver Falls, PA 15010-3599. Offers business administration (MBA); finance (MBA); marketing (MBA); operations (MBA). *Accreditation:* ACBSP. *Program availability:* Part-time, evening/weekend. *Degree requirements:* For master's, 36 credit hours of course work (30 of which are required of all students). *Entrance requirements:* For master's, GMAT (if college GPA less than 2.5), undergraduate transcript, 2 letters of recommendation, resume, goals statement. Additional exam requirements/recommendations for international students: Required—TOEFL. Electronic applications accepted. *Expenses:* Contact institution.

George Fox University, College of Business, Newberg, OR 97132-2697. Offers accounting (DBA); finance (MBA); management (DBA); management and leadership (MBA); marketing (DBA); organizational strategy (MBA); strategic human resource management (MBA). MBA offered in Newberg, OR and in Portland, OR. *Accreditation:* ACBSP. *Program availability:* Part-time, evening/weekend, online learning. *Degree requirements:* For master's, capstone project; for doctorate, credit-applied research project. *Entrance requirements:* For master's, resume (5 years of professional experience); 3 professional references; interview; financial e-learning course; official transcripts; for doctorate, GRE or GMAT, resume; personal mission statement; academic research writing sample; official transcript from each college/university attended; three professional references. Additional exam requirements/recommendations for international students: Required—TOEFL (minimum score 577 paper-based; 90 iBT) or IELTS (minimum score 7). Electronic applications accepted. *Expenses:* Contact institution.

The George Washington University, School of Business, Department of Marketing, Washington, DC 20052. Offers MBA, PhD. *Program availability:* Part-time, evening/weekend. *Students:* 4 part-time (all women); includes 3 minority (2 Hispanic/Latino; 1 Two or more races, non-Hispanic/Latino). Average age 26. 15 applicants, 80% accepted, 1 enrolled. *Entrance requirements:* For master's, GMAT; for doctorate, GMAT or GRE. Additional exam requirements/recommendations for international students: Required—TOEFL. *Application deadline:* For fall admission, 4/1 priority date for domestic students; for spring admission, 10/1 for domestic students. Applications are processed on a rolling basis. Application fee: $60. *Financial support:* Fellowships, teaching assistantships, career-related internships or fieldwork, Federal Work-Study, and institutionally sponsored loans available. Financial award application deadline: 4/1. *Faculty research:* Strategic marketing, marketing and public policy, marketing management. *Unit head:* Pradeep Rau, Chairman, 202-994-4989, E-mail: prau@gwu.edu. *Application contact:* Christopher Storer, Executive Director, Graduate Admissions, 202-994-1212, E-mail: gwmba@gwu.edu.
Website: http://business.gwu.edu/marketing/

Georgia State University, J. Mack Robinson College of Business, Department of Marketing, Atlanta, GA 30302-3083. Offers MBA, MS, PhD. *Program availability:* Part-time, evening/weekend. *Faculty:* 9 full-time (2 women), 1 (woman) part-time/adjunct. *Students:* 55 full-time (36 women), 1 (woman) part-time; includes 23 minority (13 Black or African American, non-Hispanic/Latino; 2 Asian, non-Hispanic/Latino; 6 Hispanic/Latino; 2 Two or more races, non-Hispanic/Latino), 20 international. Average age 30. 33 applicants, 12% accepted, 3 enrolled. In 2018, 29 master's, 5 doctorates awarded. *Entrance requirements:* For master's, GRE or GMAT, transcripts from all institutions attended, resume, essays; for doctorate, GRE or GMAT, three letters of recommendation, personal statement, transcripts from all institutions attended, resume. Additional exam requirements/recommendations for international students: Required—TOEFL (minimum score 610 paper-based; 101 iBT), IELTS (minimum score 7). *Application deadline:* For fall admission, 5/1 priority date for domestic students, 2/1 priority date for international students; for spring admission, 9/15 priority date for domestic students, 4/1 priority date for international students. Applications are processed on a rolling basis. Application fee: $50. Electronic applications accepted. *Expenses: Tuition, area resident:* Full-time $9360; part-time $390 per credit hour. *Tuition, state resident:* full-time $9360; part-time $390 per credit hour. *Tuition, nonresident:* full-time $30,024; part-time $1251 per credit hour. *International tuition:* $30,024 full-time. *Required fees:* $2128. *Financial support:* Research assistantships, teaching assistantships, scholarships/grants, tuition waivers (partial), and unspecified assistantships available. Financial award applicants required to submit FAFSA. *Faculty research:* Marketing strategy, market in science, brand and customer management, digital and social media marketing, global marketing. *Unit head:* Dr. Naveen Donthu, Professor/Chair of the Department of Marketing, 404-413-7650, Fax: 404-413-7699. *Application contact:* Toby McChesney, Assistant Dean for Graduate Recruiting and Student Services, 404-413-7167, Fax: 404-413-7162, E-mail: rcbgradadmissions@gsu.edu.
Website: http://robinson.gsu.edu/marketing/

Golden Gate University, Ageno School of Business, San Francisco, CA 94105-2968. Offers accounting (MBA); adaptive leadership (MBA); advanced financial planning (MS); business administration (EMBA, MBA, DBA); business analytics (MBA, MS); entrepreneurship (MBA); finance (MBA, MS, Certificate); financial life planning (Certificate); financial planning (MS, Certificate); global supply chain management (MBA, Certificate); human resource management (MBA, MS, Certificate); information technology management (MBA, MS, Certificate); international business (MBA); marketing (MBA, MS, Certificate); project management (MBA, MS, Certificate); psychology (MA, Certificate); public administration (EMPA, MBA); public administration leadership (Certificate); JD/MBA. *Program availability:* Part-time, evening/weekend. *Degree requirements:* For doctorate, thesis/dissertation, qualifying examination. *Entrance requirements:* For master's, GMAT (for MBA), minimum GPA of 2.5 (MS). Additional exam requirements/recommendations for international students: Required—TOEFL (minimum score 550 paper-based; 79 iBT). Electronic applications accepted. *Expenses:* Contact institution.

Goldey-Beacom College, Graduate Program, Wilmington, DE 19808-1999. Offers business administration (MBA); finance (MS); financial management (MBA); health care management (MBA); human resource management (MBA); information technology (MBA); international business management (MBA); major finance (MBA); major taxation (MBA); management (MM); marketing management (MBA); taxation (MBA, MS). *Accreditation:* ACBSP. *Program availability:* Part-time, evening/weekend. *Entrance*

requirements: For master's, GMAT, MAT, GRE, minimum GPA of 3.0. Additional exam requirements/recommendations for international students: Required—TOEFL (minimum score 65 iBT); Recommended—IELTS (minimum score 6). Electronic applications accepted.

Grand Canyon University, Colangelo College of Business, Phoenix, AZ 85017-1097. Offers accounting (MBA, MS); business analytics (MS); disaster preparedness and executive fire service leadership (MS); finance (MBA); general management (MBA); health systems management (MBA); information technology management (MS); leadership (MBA, MS); marketing (MBA); organizational leadership and entrepreneurship (MS); project management (MBA); sports business (MBA); strategic human resource management (MBA). *Accreditation:* ACBSP. *Program availability:* Part-time, evening/weekend, online learning. *Entrance requirements:* For master's, equivalent of two years' full-time professional work experience. Additional exam requirements/recommendations for international students: Required—TOEFL (minimum score 575 paper-based; 90 iBT), IELTS (minimum score 7). Electronic applications accepted.

Grand Canyon University, College of Doctoral Studies, Phoenix, AZ 85017-1097. Offers data analytics (DBA); general psychology (PhD), including cognition and instruction, industrial and organizational psychology, integrating technology, learning, and psychology, performance psychology; management (DBA); marketing (DBA); organizational leadership (Ed D), including behavioral health, Christian ministry, health care administration, organizational development. *Degree requirements:* For doctorate, comprehensive exam, thesis/dissertation. *Entrance requirements:* For doctorate, minimum GPA of 3.4 on earned advanced degree from regionally-accredited institution; transcripts; goals statement.

Harvard University, Harvard Business School, Doctoral Programs in Management, Boston, MA 02163. Offers accounting and management (DBA); business economics (PhD); health policy management (PhD); management (DBA); marketing (DBA); organizational behavior (PhD); science, technology and management (PhD); strategy (DBA); technology and operations management (DBA). *Degree requirements:* For doctorate, comprehensive exam (for some programs), thesis/dissertation. *Entrance requirements:* For doctorate, GRE General Test or GMAT. Additional exam requirements/recommendations for international students: Required—TOEFL.

Hawai'i Pacific University, College of Business, Program in Business Administration, Honolulu, HI 96813. Offers finance (MBA); human resource management (MBA); information systems (MBA); international business (MBA); management (MBA); marketing (MBA); organizational change and development (MBA). *Program availability:* Part-time, evening/weekend, 100% online, blended/hybrid learning. *Entrance requirements:* For master's, GMAT or GRE. Additional exam requirements/recommendations for international students: Recommended—TOEFL (minimum score 550 paper-based; 80 iBT), IELTS (minimum score 6), TWE (minimum score 5). Electronic applications accepted.

HEC Montreal, School of Business Administration, Doctoral Program in Administration, Montréal, QC H3T 2A7, Canada. Offers accounting (PhD); applied economics (PhD); data science (PhD); finance (PhD); financial engineering (PhD); information technology (PhD); international business (PhD); logistics and operations management (PhD); management science (PhD); management, strategy and organizations (PhD); marketing (PhD); organizational behaviour and human resources (PhD). Program offered jointly with Concordia University, McGill University, and Universite du Quebec a Montreal. *Accreditation:* AACSB. *Students:* 130 full-time (55 women). 114 applicants, 46% accepted, 31 enrolled. In 2018, 19 doctorates awarded. *Entrance requirements:* For doctorate, TAGE MAGE, GMAT, or GRE, master's degree in administration or related field. *Application deadline:* For fall admission, 1/15 for domestic and international students. Application fee: 91 (191 for international students). Electronic applications accepted. *Expenses:* Tuition, area resident: Full-time $3052.80 Canadian dollars; part-time $84.80 Canadian dollars per credit. Tuition, state resident: full-time $3816 Canadian dollars; part-time $264.67 Canadian dollars per credit. Tuition, nonresident: full-time $11,910 Canadian dollars. *International tuition:* $20,905.20 Canadian dollars full-time. *Required fees:* $1805.34 Canadian dollars; $43.62 Canadian dollars per credit. $71.78 Canadian dollars per term. Tuition and fees vary according to degree level and program. *Financial support:* Research assistantships, teaching assistantships, and scholarships/grants available. Financial award application deadline: 9/2. *Faculty research:* Art management, business policy, entrepreneurship, new technologies, transportation. *Unit head:* Guy Paré, Director, 514-340-6264, E-mail: guy.pare@hec.ca. *Application contact:* Julie Bilodeau, PhD Program Analyst, 514-340-6000, Fax: 514-340-6411, E-mail: analyste.phd@hec.ca.
Website: http://www.hec.ca/en/programs/phd/index.html

HEC Montreal, School of Business Administration, Master of Science Programs in Administration, Program in Marketing, Montréal, QC H3T 2A7, Canada. Offers M Sc. Program offered in French (Thesis stream, Supervised project Stream). *Students:* 77 full-time (57 women), 19 part-time (13 women). 78 applicants, 51% accepted, 28 enrolled. In 2018, 42 master's awarded. *Entrance requirements:* For master's, BBA, undergraduate degree in another field, degree deemed equivalent by program director and minimum GPA of 3.0 on 4.3 scale. Additional exam requirements/recommendations for international students: Required—TAGE MAGE (minimum recommended score of 300), GMAT (minimum recommended score of 630), or GRE. *Application deadline:* For fall admission, 3/15 for domestic and international students; for winter admission, 9/15 for domestic and international students. Application fee: $91 Canadian dollars ($191 Canadian dollars for international students). Electronic applications accepted. *Expenses: Tuition, area resident:* Full-time $3052.80 Canadian dollars; part-time $84.80 Canadian dollars per credit. Tuition, state resident: full-time $3816 Canadian dollars; part-time $264.67 Canadian dollars per credit. Tuition, nonresident: full-time $11,910 Canadian dollars. *International tuition:* $20,905.20 Canadian dollars full-time. *Required fees:* $1805.34 Canadian dollars; $43.62 Canadian dollars per credit. $71.78 Canadian dollars per term. Tuition and fees vary according to degree level and program. *Financial support:* Research assistantships, teaching assistantships, and scholarships/grants available. Financial award application deadline: 9/2. *Unit head:* Dr. Sihem Taboubi, Director, 514-340-6428, E-mail: sihem.taboubi@hec.ca. *Application contact:* Marianne de Moura, Administrative Director, 514-340-6000, Fax: 514-340-6411, E-mail: aide@hec.ca.
Website: http://www.hec.ca/programmes/maitrises/maitrise-marketing/index.html

Herzing University Online, Program in Business Administration, Menomonee Falls, WI 53051. Offers accounting (MBA); business administration (MBA); business management (MBA); healthcare management (MBA); human resources (MBA); marketing (MBA); project management (MBA); technology management (MBA). *Program availability:* Online learning.

Hofstra University, Frank G. Zarb School of Business, Programs in Marketing and International Business, Hempstead, NY 11549. Offers business administration (MBA), including international business, marketing; international business (Advanced Certificate); marketing (MS, Advanced Certificate); marketing research (MS). *Program availability:* Part-time, evening/weekend, blended/hybrid learning. *Students:* 65 full-time (35 women), 19 part-time (11 women); includes 11 minority (2 Black or African American, non-Hispanic/Latino; 5 Asian, non-Hispanic/Latino; 4 Hispanic/Latino), 51 international. Average age 26. 168 applicants, 68% accepted, 35 enrolled. In 2018, 54 master's awarded. *Degree requirements:* For master's, thesis (for some programs), capstone course (for MBA), thesis (for MS), minimum GPA of 3.0. *Entrance requirements:* For master's, GMAT/GRE, 2 letters of recommendation, resume, essay. Additional exam requirements/recommendations for international students: Required—TOEFL (minimum score 550 paper-based; 80 iBT); Recommended—IELTS (minimum score 6). *Application deadline:* Applications are processed on a rolling basis. Application fee: $75. Electronic applications accepted. *Expenses:* $1,375 per credit plus fees. *Financial support:* In 2018–19, 34 students received support, including 21 fellowships with full and partial tuition reimbursements available (averaging $5,450 per year), 3 research assistantships with full and partial tuition reimbursements available (averaging $4,477 per year); career-related internships or fieldwork, Federal Work-Study, institutionally sponsored loans, scholarships/grants, tuition waivers (full and partial), unspecified assistantships, and scholarships and endowed scholarships also available. Support available to part-time students. Financial award applicants required to submit FAFSA. *Faculty research:* Cross-cultural consumer behavior; social, digital, global, and strategic issues in marketing; consumer health/well-being; ethnocentrism and animosity. *Unit head:* Dr. Anil Mathur, Chairperson, 516-463-5346, Fax: 516-463-4834, E-mail: anil.mathur@hofstra.edu. *Application contact:* Sunil Samuel, Assistant Vice President of Admissions, 516-463-4723, Fax: 516-463-4664, E-mail: graduateadmission@hofstra.edu.
Website: http://www.hofstra.edu/business/

Holy Names University, Graduate Division, Department of Business, Oakland, CA 94619-1699. Offers finance (MBA); management and leadership (MBA); marketing (MBA). *Program availability:* Part-time, evening/weekend. *Students:* 26 full-time (15 women), 16 part-time (14 women); includes 28 minority (13 Black or African American, non-Hispanic/Latino; 6 Asian, non-Hispanic/Latino; 9 Hispanic/Latino), 4 international. Average age 31. 38 applicants, 61% accepted, 17 enrolled. In 2018, 11 master's awarded. *Entrance requirements:* For master's, minimum undergraduate GPA of 2.6 overall, 3.0 in major; two recommendations (letter or form) from previous professors or current or previous work supervisors; 1-3 page personal statement; resume. Additional exam requirements/recommendations for international students: Required—TOEFL (minimum score 550 paper-based; 79 iBT). *Application deadline:* For fall admission, 8/1 priority date for domestic students, 7/15 for international students; for spring admission, 12/1 priority date for domestic students, 12/1 for international students; for summer admission, 5/1 priority date for domestic students, 5/1 for international students. Applications are processed on a rolling basis. Application fee: $65. Electronic applications accepted. Application fee is waived when completed online. *Expenses:* Contact institution. *Financial support:* Career-related internships or fieldwork, Federal Work-Study, scholarships/grants, and unspecified assistantships available. Support available to part-time students. Financial award application deadline: 3/2; financial award applicants required to submit FAFSA. *Faculty research:* Business ethics, sustainable economics, accounting models, cross-cultural management, diversity in organizations. *Unit head:* Morris Hamm, MBA Program Director, E-mail: hamm@hnu.edu. *Application contact:* 800-430-1321, Fax: 510-436-1325, E-mail: graduateadmissions@hnu.edu.
Website: http://www.hnu.edu

Hope International University, School of Graduate and Professional Studies, Program in Business Administration, Fullerton, CA 92831-3138. Offers general management (MBA, MSM); international development (MBA, MSM); marketing management (MBA, MSM); non-profit management (MBA, MSM). *Program availability:* Part-time, online learning. *Degree requirements:* For master's, comprehensive exam (for some programs), thesis (for some programs), project. *Entrance requirements:* For master's, minimum GPA of 3.0; 2 references. Additional exam requirements/recommendations for international students: Required—TOEFL (minimum score 550 paper-based; 86 iBT); Recommended—IELTS (minimum score 6.5). Electronic applications accepted. *Expenses:* Contact institution.

Howard University, School of Business, Graduate Programs in Business, Washington, DC 20059-0002. Offers accounting (MBA); entrepreneurship (MBA); finance (MBA); general management (MBA); human resources management (MBA); information systems (MBA); international business (MBA); marketing (MBA); supply chain management (MBA); JD/MBA. *Accreditation:* AACSB. *Program availability:* Part-time, evening/weekend, online learning. *Entrance requirements:* For master's, GMAT, minimum 1 year post undergraduate work experience, resume, 3 letters of recommendation, advanced college algebra. Additional exam requirements/recommendations for international students: Required—TOEFL. *Faculty research:* Marketing research in multi-ethnic populations, U.S. trade policies and international relations, risk management (finance).

Hult International Business School, Graduate Programs, Cambridge, MA 02141. Offers business administration (EMBA); business analytics (MBA, MIB); business statistics (MBS); disruptive innovation (MDI); entrepreneurship (MBA, MIB); family business (MBA, MIB); finance (MBA, MF, MIB); international marketing (MIM); marketing (MBA, MIB); project management (MBA, MIB). MDI and MBS offered in San Francisco; MBA also offered in Boston, San Francisco, Dubai, Shanghai, and New York. *Entrance requirements:* For master's, GMAT, 3 years of work experience. Additional exam requirements/recommendations for international students: Required—TOEFL. Electronic applications accepted. *Expenses:* Contact institution.

Illinois Institute of Technology, Stuart School of Business, Program in Marketing Analytics and Communication, Chicago, IL 60661. Offers MS, MBA/MS. *Program availability:* Part-time, evening/weekend. *Entrance requirements:* For master's, GRE (minimum score 1000) or GMAT (500). Additional exam requirements/recommendations for international students: Required—TOEFL (minimum score 600 paper-based; 85 iBT); Recommended—IELTS (minimum score 7). Electronic applications accepted. *Expenses:* Contact institution.

Indiana Tech, Program in Business Administration, Fort Wayne, IN 46803-1297. Offers accounting (MBA); health care management (MBA); human resources (MBA); management (MBA); marketing (MBA). *Program availability:* Part-time, evening/weekend, online learning. *Entrance requirements:* For master's, GMAT, bachelor's degree from regionally-accredited university; minimum undergraduate GPA of 2.5; 2 years of significant work experience; 3 letters of recommendation. Electronic applications accepted.

Indiana University–Purdue University Indianapolis, Kelley School of Business, Evening MBA Program, Indianapolis, IN 46202-5151. Offers accounting (MBA); entrepreneurship (MBA); finance (MBA); general administration (MBA); marketing (MBA); supply chain management (MBA); MBA/JD; MBA/MD; MBA/MHA; MBA/MS; MBA/MSA; MBA/MSE. *Program availability:* Part-time-only, evening/weekend, online learning. *Entrance requirements:* For master's, GMAT or GRE, 2 years of professional work experience. Additional exam requirements/recommendations for international students: Required—TOEFL or IELTS. Electronic applications accepted. *Expenses:* Contact institution. *Faculty research:* Entrepreneurship; corporate finance; international business; consumer behavior; supply chain; business law.

Indiana University South Bend, Judd Leighton School of Business and Economics, South Bend, IN 46615. Offers accounting (MSA); business (Graduate Certificate); business administration (MBA), including finance, human resource management, marketing; MBA/MSA. *Program availability:* Part-time, evening/weekend. *Entrance requirements:* For master's, GMAT. Additional exam requirements/recommendations for international students: Required—TOEFL (minimum score 550 paper-based; 79 iBT). Electronic applications accepted. *Expenses:* Contact institution. *Faculty research:* Financial accounting, consumer research, capital budgeting research, business strategy research.

Instituto Tecnologico de Santo Domingo, Graduate School, Area of Business, Santo Domingo, Dominican Republic. Offers banking and securities markets (M Mgmt); corporate finance (M Mgmt); human resources management (M Mgmt, Certificate); international trade management (M Mgmt); marketing (M Mgmt); organizational development (M Mgmt); quality and productivity management (Certificate); tax management and planning (M Mgmt); upper management (M Mgmt).

Instituto Tecnologico de Santo Domingo, Graduate School, Area of Humanities and Social Sciences, Santo Domingo, Dominican Republic. Offers accounting (Certificate); adult education (Certificate); applied linguistics (MA); economics (MA); education (M Ed); educational psychology (MA, Certificate); gender and development (MA, Certificate); humanistic studies (MA); international marketing management (Certificate); international relations in the Caribbean basin (Certificate); intervention systems in family therapy (MA); linguistic and literary communication (Certificate); pedagogical support (MA); social science education (M Ed); sustainable human development (MA); terminal illness and death psychology (Certificate); youth and adult education (M Ed).

Instituto Tecnológico y de Estudios Superiores de Monterrey, Campus Central de Veracruz, Graduate Programs, Córdoba, Mexico. Offers administration (MA); administration of information technologies (MTI); computer sciences (MCC); education (MEE); educational institution administration (MAD); educational technology (MTE); electronic commerce (MCE); finance (MAF); humanistic studies (MEH); international business for Latin America (MNL); marketing (MMT); science (MCP). *Program availability:* Part-time, evening/weekend, online learning. *Degree requirements:* For master's, thesis (for some programs). *Entrance requirements:* For master's, PAEP College Board. Electronic applications accepted.

Instituto Tecnológico y de Estudios Superiores de Monterrey, Campus Ciudad Obregón, Program in Marketing Technology, Ciudad Obregón, Mexico. Offers MMT.

Instituto Tecnológico y de Estudios Superiores de Monterrey, Campus Cuernavaca, Programs in Business Administration, Temixco, Mexico. Offers finance (MA); human resources management (MA); international business (MA); marketing (MA).

Instituto Tecnológico y de Estudios Superiores de Monterrey, Campus Estado de México, Professional and Graduate Division, Estado de Mexico, Mexico. Offers administration of information technologies (MITA); architecture (M Arch); business administration (GMBA, MBA); computer sciences (MCS, PhD); education (M Ed); educational institution administration (MAD); educational technology and innovation (PhD); electronic commerce (MEC); environmental systems (MS); finance (MAF); humanistic studies (MHS); information sciences and knowledge management (MISKM); information systems (MS); manufacturing systems (MS); marketing (MEM); quality systems and productivity (MS); science and materials engineering (PhD); telecommunications management (MTM). *Program availability:* Part-time, online learning. *Degree requirements:* For master's, one foreign language, thesis (for some programs); for doctorate, one foreign language, thesis/dissertation. *Entrance requirements:* For master's, E-PAEP 500, interview; for doctorate, E-PAEP 500, research proposal. Additional exam requirements/recommendations for international students: Required—TOEFL (minimum score 550 paper-based). *Faculty research:* Surface treatments by plasmas, mechanical properties, robotics, graphical computing, mechatronics security protocols.

Instituto Tecnológico y de Estudios Superiores de Monterrey, Campus Monterrey, Graduate School of Business Administration and Leadership, Program in Business Administration, Monterrey, Mexico. Offers business administration (MA, MBA); finance (M Sc); international business (M Sc); marketing (M Sc). *Program availability:* Part-time. *Degree requirements:* For master's, one foreign language, thesis. *Entrance requirements:* For master's, GMAT. Additional exam requirements/recommendations for international students: Required—TOEFL. *Faculty research:* Technology management, quality management, organizational theory and behavior.

Inter American University of Puerto Rico, Aguadilla Campus, Graduate School, Aguadilla, PR 00605. Offers accounting (MBA); counseling psychology specializing in family (MS); criminal justice (MA); educative management and leadership (MA); elementary education (M Ed); finance (MBA); human resources (MBA); industrial management (MBA); management information systems (MBA); marketing (MBA). *Program availability:* Part-time, evening/weekend. *Degree requirements:* For master's, comprehensive exam. *Entrance requirements:* For master's, EXADEP, 2 letters of recommendation, minimum GPA of 2.5. Electronic applications accepted.

Inter American University of Puerto Rico, Fajardo Campus, Graduate Programs, Fajardo, PR 00738-7003. Offers computer science (MS); educational management and leadership (MA Ed); general business (MBA); human resources (MBA); management information systems (MBA); marketing (MBA); special education (MA Ed). *Program availability:* Online learning.

Inter American University of Puerto Rico, Guayama Campus, Department of Business Administration, Guayama, PR 00785. Offers marketing (MBA).

Inter American University of Puerto Rico, Metropolitan Campus, Graduate Programs, Program in Marketing, San Juan, PR 00919-1293. Offers MBA. *Degree requirements:* For master's, comprehensive exam. *Entrance requirements:* For master's, GRE or EXADEP, interview. Electronic applications accepted.

Inter American University of Puerto Rico, Ponce Campus, Graduate School, Mercedita, PR 00715-1602. Offers accounting (MBA); biology (M Ed); chemistry (M Ed); criminal justice (MA); elementary education (M Ed); English as a Second Language (M Ed); finance (MBA); history (M Ed); human resources (MBA); marketing (MBA); mathematics (M Ed); Spanish (M Ed). *Entrance requirements:* For master's, minimum GPA of 2.5.

Inter American University of Puerto Rico, San Germán Campus, Graduate Studies Center, Program in Business Administration, San Germán, PR 00683-5008. Offers accounting (MBA); finance (MBA); general business administration (MBA); human resources (MBA, PhD); industrial relations (MBA); information systems (MBA); international and interregional business (PhD); management (MBA); marketing (MBA). *Program availability:* Part-time, evening/weekend. *Degree requirements:* For master's, comprehensive exam. *Entrance requirements:* For master's, GRE General Test or EXADEP, minimum GPA of 3.0. *Expenses: Tuition:* Full-time $212; part-time $212 per credit. *Required fees:* $366 per semester. One-time fee: $31. Tuition and fees vary according to degree level and program.

International University in Geneva, Business Programs, Geneva, Switzerland. Offers business administration (MBA, DBA); entrepreneurship (MBA); international business (MIB); international trade (MIT); sales and marketing (MBA). *Accreditation:* ACBSP. *Program availability:* Part-time, evening/weekend. *Degree requirements:* For master's, comprehensive exam. *Entrance requirements:* For master's, GMAT. Additional exam requirements/recommendations for international students: Required—TOEFL. Electronic applications accepted.

The International University of Monaco, Graduate Programs, Monte Carlo, Monaco. Offers entrepreneurship (EMBA, MBA); financial engineering (M Sc); hedge fund and private equity (M Sc); international marketing (EMBA, MBA); international wealth management (M Sc); luxury goods and services (EMBA, M Sc, MBA); wealth and asset management (EMBA, MBA). *Program availability:* Part-time. *Degree requirements:* For master's, comprehensive exam (for some programs), applied research project. *Entrance requirements:* Additional exam requirements/recommendations for international students: Required—TOEFL (minimum score 550 paper-based), IELTS. Electronic applications accepted. *Faculty research:* Gaming, leadership, disintermediation.

Iona College, School of Business, Department of Marketing and International Business, New Rochelle, NY 10801-1890. Offers international business (AC, PMC); marketing (MBA); sports and entertainment management (AC). *Program availability:* Part-time, evening/weekend. *Faculty:* 3 full-time (1 woman), 3 part-time/adjunct (1 woman). *Students:* 14 full-time (10 women), 26 part-time (13 women); includes 17 minority (4 Black or African American, non-Hispanic/Latino; 1 Asian, non-Hispanic/Latino; 12 Hispanic/Latino), 3 international. Average age 25. 15 applicants, 93% accepted, 8 enrolled. In 2018, 13 master's, 78 other advanced degrees awarded. *Entrance requirements:* For master's, GMAT, 2 letters of recommendation, minimum GPA of 3.0; for other advanced degree, GMAT, minimum GPA of 3.0. Additional exam requirements/recommendations for international students: Required—TOEFL (minimum score 550 paper-based; 80 iBT), IELTS (minimum score 6.5). *Application deadline:* For fall admission, 8/15 priority date for domestic students, 8/1 priority date for international students; for winter admission, 11/15 priority date for domestic students, 11/1 priority date for international students; for spring admission, 2/15 priority date for domestic students, 2/1 priority date for international students; for summer admission, 5/15 for domestic students, 5/1 priority date for international students. Applications are processed on a rolling basis. Application fee: $50. Electronic applications accepted. *Expenses:* Contact institution. *Financial support:* In 2018–19, 38 students received support. Scholarships/grants, tuition waivers (partial), and unspecified assistantships available. Support available to part-time students. Financial award application deadline: 4/15; financial award applicants required to submit FAFSA. *Faculty research:* Business ethics, international retailing, mega-marketing, consumer behavior and consumer confidence. *Unit head:* Dr. Susan G. Rozensher, Department Chair, 914-637-2748, E-mail: srozensher@iona.edu. *Application contact:* Kimberly Kelly, Director of Graduate Business Admissions, 914-633-2271, Fax: 914-633-2012, E-mail: kkelly@iona.edu. Website: http://www.iona.edu/Academics/Hagan-School-of-Business/Departments/Marketing/Graduate-Programs.aspx

Jacksonville University, Davis College of Business, Accelerated Day-time MBA Program, Jacksonville, FL 32211. Offers accounting and finance (MBA); business administration (MBA); consumer goods and services marketing (MBA); management (MBA); management accounting (MBA). *Entrance requirements:* For master's, GMAT or GRE, bachelor's degree from regionally-accredited institution, original transcripts of academic work, statement of intent, resume, 3 letters of recommendation; 3 years of work experience (recommended); interview with program advisor. Additional exam requirements/recommendations for international students: Required—TOEFL (minimum score 550 paper-based; 79 iBT), IELTS (minimum score 6), PTE (minimum score 53). Electronic applications accepted. *Expenses:* Contact institution. *Faculty research:* Behavioral finance, game theory, regional economic integration, information sabotage, public choice and public finance.

Jacksonville University, Davis College of Business, Executive Master of Business Administration Program, Jacksonville, FL 32211. Offers consumer goods and services marketing (MBA); leadership development (MBA). *Accreditation:* AACSB. *Program availability:* Evening/weekend. *Entrance requirements:* For master's, resume, 5-7 years of professional experience, 3 letters of recommendation, corporate letter of support, statement of purpose, interview. Additional exam requirements/recommendations for international students: Required—TOEFL (minimum score 550 paper-based; 79 iBT), IELTS (minimum score 6), PTE (minimum score 53). Electronic applications accepted. *Expenses:* Contact institution. *Faculty research:* Data analytics, emerging markets and economic development, high-performing teams, government deficit, learning from corporate failure.

Jacksonville University, Davis College of Business, FLEX Master of Business Administration Program, Jacksonville, FL 32211. Offers accounting and finance (MBA); business management (MBA); consumer goods and services marketing (MBA); management (MBA); management accounting (MBA); JD/MBA; MBA/MPP; MSN/MBA. MBA/JD offered jointly with Florida School of Law; MSN/MBA offered jointly with JU's Keigwin School of Nursing; MBA/MPP offered jointly with JU's Public Policy Institute. *Accreditation:* AACSB. *Program availability:* Part-time, evening/weekend, blended/hybrid learning. *Entrance requirements:* For master's, GMAT or GRE, bachelor's degree from regionally-accredited institution, 3 years of full-time work experience (recommended), resume, statement of intent, 3 letters of recommendation, interview with program advisor. Additional exam requirements/recommendations for international students: Required—TOEFL (minimum score 550 paper-based; 79 iBT), IELTS (minimum score 6), PTE (minimum score 53). Electronic applications accepted. *Expenses:* Contact institution. *Faculty research:* Downsizing with integrity; impact of YouTube videos; game theory; analysis of effective tax rates; creativity innovation and change.

Johns Hopkins University, Carey Business School, MS in Marketing Program, Baltimore, MD 21218. Offers MS. *Program availability:* Part-time, evening/weekend. *Students:* 159 full-time (125 women), 14 part-time (10 women). 636 applicants, 71% accepted, 176 enrolled. In 2018, 153 master's awarded. *Entrance requirements:* For master's, GMAT or GRE. Additional exam requirements/recommendations for international students: Required—TOEFL, IELTS. *Application deadline:* For fall admission, 4/3 for domestic and international students. Applications are processed on a rolling basis. Application fee: $100. Electronic applications accepted. *Expenses:* Contact institution. *Financial support:* In 2018–19, 61 students received support. Scholarships/grants available. Support available to part-time students. Financial award application deadline: 4/15; financial award applicants required to submit FAFSA. *Faculty research:* Decision making, marketing management, marketing strategy. *Unit head:* Dr. Kevin Frick, Vice Dean of Education, 410-234-9272, E-mail: kfrick@jhu.edu. *Application contact:* Office of Admissions, 410-234-9220, Fax: 443-529-1554, E-mail: carey.admissions@jhu.edu.
Website: http://carey.jhu.edu/academics/master-of-science/ms-in-marketing/

Kansas State University, Graduate School, College of Business, Program in Business Administration, Manhattan, KS 66506. Offers data analytics (MBA); finance (MBA); management (MBA); marketing (MBA); technology entrepreneurship (MBA). *Accreditation:* AACSB. *Program availability:* Part-time, 100% online. *Entrance*

requirements: For master's, GMAT (minimum score of 500), minimum undergraduate GPA of 3.0. Additional exam requirements/recommendations for international students: Required—TOEFL (minimum score 550 paper-based; 79 iBT); Recommended—IELTS (minimum score 7). Electronic applications accepted. *Expenses:* Contact institution. *Faculty research:* Organizational citizenship behavior, service marketing, impression management, human resources management, lean manufacturing and supply chain management, financial market behavior and investment management, data analytics, corporate responsibility, technology entrepreneurship.

Keiser University, Doctor of Business Administration Program, Fort Lauderdale, FL 33309. Offers global business (DBA); global management (DBA); marketing (DBA).

Keiser University, Master of Business Administration Program, Fort Lauderdale, FL 33309. Offers accounting (MBA); health services administration (MBA); international business (MBA); management (MBA); marketing (MBA); technology management (MBA). All concentrations except technology management also offered in Mandarin. *Program availability:* Part-time, online learning.

Kent State University, College of Business Administration, Doctoral Program in Marketing, Kent, OH 44242. Offers PhD. *Faculty:* 4 full-time (1 woman). *Students:* 8 full-time (4 women), 7 international. Average age 31. 14 applicants, 43% accepted, 3 enrolled. *Degree requirements:* For doctorate, comprehensive exam, thesis/dissertation, oral defense. *Entrance requirements:* For doctorate, GMAT or GRE. Additional exam requirements/recommendations for international students: Required—TOEFL (minimum score 600 paper-based; 100 iBT), IELTS (minimum score 7). *Application deadline:* For fall admission, 1/1 for domestic students, 2/1 for international students. Application fee: $45 ($70 for international students). Electronic applications accepted. *Expenses:* Contact institution. *Financial support:* In 2018–19, 8 students received support, including 8 teaching assistantships with full tuition reimbursements available (averaging $23,000 per year). Financial award application deadline: 2/1; financial award applicants required to submit FAFSA. *Faculty research:* Advertising effects, satisfaction, international marketing, high-tech marketing, personality and consumer behavior. *Unit head:* Dr. Robert Jewell, Chair and Professor, 330-672-2170, Fax: 330-672-5006, E-mail: rjewell1@kent.edu. *Application contact:* Felecia A. Urbanek, Assistant Director, 330-672-2282, Fax: 330-672-7303, E-mail: gradbus@kent.edu.
Website: http://www.kent.edu/business/phd

King University, School of Business, Economics, and Technology, Bristol, TN 37620-2699. Offers accounting (MBA); finance (MBA); healthcare management (MBA); human resources management (MBA); leadership (MBA); management (MBA); marketing (MBA); project management (MBA). *Program availability:* Part-time, evening/weekend, 100% online, blended/hybrid learning. *Faculty:* 11 full-time (9 women), 10 part-time/adjunct (7 women). *Students:* 182 full-time (107 women), 8 part-time (6 women); includes 18 minority (7 Black or African American, non-Hispanic/Latino; 4 Hispanic/Latino; 1 Native Hawaiian or other Pacific Islander, non-Hispanic/Latino; 6 Two or more races, non-Hispanic/Latino), 2 international. Average age 32. 143 applicants, 98% accepted, 68 enrolled. In 2018, 125 master's awarded. *Degree requirements:* For master's, comprehensive exam, thesis optional. *Entrance requirements:* For master's, resume which demonstrates a minimum of 2 years of full-time work experience, minimum cumulative grade point average of 3.0 on a 4.0 scale is required. Students who do not meet this requirement may be conditionally accepted. Additional exam requirements/recommendations for international students: Required—TOEFL (minimum score 84 paper-based; 84 iBT). *Application deadline:* Applications are processed on a rolling basis. Application fee: $0 ($50 for international students). Electronic applications accepted. *Expenses: Tuition:* Full-time $13,365; part-time $495 per semester hour. *Required fees:* $900; $100 per course. One-time fee: $175. Tuition and fees vary according to class time, degree level and program. *Financial support:* Unspecified assistantships available. Financial award applicants required to submit FAFSA. *Faculty research:* International monetary policy. *Unit head:* Dr. Mark Pate, Dean, School of Business, Economics and Technology, 423-652-4814, E-mail: mjpate@king.edu. *Application contact:* Nancy Beverly, Territory Manager/Enrollment Counselor, 423-341-9495, Fax: 423-652-4727, E-mail: nmbeverly@king.edu.

Lake Forest Graduate School of Management, The Leadership MBA Program, Lake Forest, IL 60045. Offers finance (MBA); global business (MBA); healthcare management (MBA); management (MBA); marketing (MBA); organizational behavior (MBA). *Program availability:* Part-time, evening/weekend. *Entrance requirements:* For master's, 4 years of work experience in field, interview, 2 letters of recommendation. Electronic applications accepted.

La Salle University, School of Business, Master of Business Administration Program, Philadelphia, PA 19141-1199. Offers accounting (MBA, Post-MBA Certificate); business systems and analytics (MBA, Post-MBA Certificate); finance (MBA, Post-MBA Certificate); general business administration (MBA, Post-MBA Certificate); human resource management (MBA, Post-MBA Certificate); management (MBA, Post-MBA Certificate); marketing (Post-MBA Certificate); MBA/MSN. Program also offered in Switzerland. *Accreditation:* AACSB. *Program availability:* Part-time, evening/weekend, online learning. *Entrance requirements:* For master's, GMAT or GRE, two letters of reference; resume; for Post-MBA Certificate, MBA with minimum GPA of 3.0. Additional exam requirements/recommendations for international students: Required—TOEFL. Electronic applications accepted. Application fee is waived when completed online. *Expenses:* Contact institution.

Lasell College, Graduate and Professional Studies in Communication, Newton, MA 02466-2709. Offers health communication (MSC, Graduate Certificate); integrated marketing communication (MSC, Graduate Certificate); public relations (MSC, Graduate Certificate). *Program availability:* Part-time, evening/weekend, 100% online, blended/hybrid learning. *Faculty:* 5 full-time (4 women), 8 part-time/adjunct (4 women). *Students:* 27 full-time (18 women), 28 part-time (23 women); includes 12 minority (5 Black or African American, non-Hispanic/Latino; 6 Hispanic/Latino; 1 Two or more races, non-Hispanic/Latino), 17 international. Average age 30. 55 applicants, 44% accepted, 21 enrolled. In 2018, 34 master's, 2 other advanced degrees awarded. *Degree requirements:* For master's, comprehensive exam, thesis or alternative, minimum GPA of 3.0; special project or internship. *Entrance requirements:* For master's, one-page personal statement, 2 letters of recommendation, resume, bachelor's degree transcript; for Graduate Certificate, bachelor's degree transcript, 2 letters of recommendation, 1-page personal statement, resume. Additional exam requirements/recommendations for international students: Required—TOEFL (minimum score 550 paper-based, 79 iBT) or IELTS (minimum score 6). *Application deadline:* For fall admission, 8/31 priority date for domestic students, 6/30 priority date for international students; for spring admission, 12/31 priority date for domestic students, 10/31 priority date for international students. Applications are processed on a rolling basis. Electronic applications accepted. *Expenses: Tuition:* Part-time $600 per credit. *Required fees:* $40 per course. *Financial support:* Federal Work-Study, scholarships/grants, and tuition discounts available. Support available to part-time students. Financial award application deadline: 8/31; financial award applicants required to submit FAFSA. *Faculty research:* Terrorists' use of the Internet; refugees' use of cell phones as means of communication in Jordan and Germany; political communication; analysis of the media coverage of the conflict and peace process in northern Ireland; interpersonal communication; strategies to address bullying in online communities, in schools and in the workplace. *Unit head:* Eric Turner, Vice President of Graduate and Professional Studies, 617-243-2071, Fax: 617-243-2450, E-mail: gradinfo@lasell.edu. *Application contact:* Adrienne Franciosi, Assistant Vice President of Graduate and Professional Studies, 617-243-2214, Fax: 617-243-2450, E-mail: gradinfo@lasell.edu.
Website: http://www.lasell.edu/academics/graduate-and-professional-studies/programs-of-study/master-of-science-in-communication.html

Lasell College, Graduate and Professional Studies in Management, Newton, MA 02466-2709. Offers business administration (MBA); elder care management (MSM); hospitality and event management (MSM); human resources management (MSM, Graduate Certificate); management (MSM, Graduate Certificate); marketing (MS, Graduate Certificate); project management (MSM, Graduate Certificate). *Accreditation:* ACBSP. *Program availability:* Part-time, evening/weekend, 100% online, blended/hybrid learning. *Faculty:* 7 full-time (4 women), 14 part-time/adjunct (9 women). *Students:* 37 full-time (28 women), 76 part-time (48 women); includes 22 minority (12 Black or African American, non-Hispanic/Latino; 1 Asian, non-Hispanic/Latino; 9 Hispanic/Latino), 20 international. Average age 32. 68 applicants, 54% accepted, 20 enrolled. In 2018, 62 master's, 1 other advanced degree awarded. *Degree requirements:* For master's, minimum GPA of 3.0; internship or research paper (for MSM). *Entrance requirements:* For master's, one-page personal statement, 2 letters of recommendation, resume, bachelor's degree transcript; proof of microeconomics and statistics (for MBA); for Graduate Certificate, bachelor's degree transcript, 2 letters of recommendation, 1-page personal statement, resume. Additional exam requirements/recommendations for international students: Required—TOEFL (minimum score 550 paper-based, 79 iBT) or IELTS (minimum score 6). *Application deadline:* For fall admission, 8/31 priority date for domestic students, 6/30 priority date for international students; for spring admission, 12/31 priority date for domestic students, 10/31 priority date for international students. Applications are processed on a rolling basis. Electronic applications accepted. *Expenses: Tuition:* Part-time $600 per credit. *Required fees:* $40 per course. *Financial support:* Federal Work-Study, scholarships/grants, and tuition discounts available. Support available to part-time students. Financial award application deadline: 8/31; financial award applicants required to submit FAFSA. *Unit head:* Eric Turner, Vice President of Graduate and Professional Studies, 617-243-2071, Fax: 617-243-2450, E-mail: gradinfo@lasell.edu. *Application contact:* Adrienne Franciosi, Assistant Vice President of Graduate and Professional Studies, 617-243-2214, Fax: 617-243-2450, E-mail: gradinfo@lasell.edu.
Website: http://www.lasell.edu/academics/graduate-and-professional-studies/programs-of-study/master-of-science-in-management.html

La Sierra University, School of Business and Management, Riverside, CA 92505. Offers accounting (MBA); finance (MBA); general management (MBA); human resources management (MBA); leadership, values, and ethics for business and management (Certificate); marketing (MBA). *Degree requirements:* For master's, research project. *Entrance requirements:* For master's, GMAT, minimum GPA of 3.0. Additional exam requirements/recommendations for international students: Required—TOEFL. *Faculty research:* Financial econometrics, institutional assessment and strategic planning, legal issues in management, behavioral finance, content of financial reports.

Lawrence Technological University, College of Management, Southfield, MI 48075-1058. Offers business administration (MBA, DBA), including business analytics (MBA, MS), cybersecurity (MBA, MS), finance (MBA), information systems (MBA), information technology (MBA), marketing (MBA), project management (MBA, MS); cybersecurity (Graduate Certificate); health IT management (Graduate Certificate); information assurance management (Graduate Certificate); information systems (MS), including enterprise resource planning, enterprise security management, project management (MBA, MS); information technology (MS, DM), including business analytics (MBA, MS), cybersecurity (MBA, MS), information assurance (MS), project management (MBA, MS); management (PhD); nonprofit management and leadership (Graduate Certificate); operations management (MS), including manufacturing operations, service operations; project management (Graduate Certificate). *Accreditation:* ACBSP. *Program availability:* Part-time, evening/weekend, 100% online. Terminal master's awarded for partial completion of doctoral program. *Degree requirements:* For master's, thesis (for some programs); for doctorate, comprehensive exam, thesis/dissertation. *Entrance requirements:* Additional exam requirements/recommendations for international students: Required—TOEFL (minimum score 550 paper-based; 79 iBT), IELTS (minimum score 6.5). Electronic applications accepted. *Faculty research:* Cybersecurity; risk management; IT governance; security controls and countermeasures; threat modeling cyber resilience; autonomous cars; natural language processing; text mining; machine learning; reflective leadership; emerging leadership theories and practice; motivational studies; teaching effectiveness strategies; teamwork; organization development; strategic planning; strengths-based and positive organizational scholarship; global leadership; globalization; corporate governance.

Lewis University, College of Business, Program in Business Administration, Romeoville, IL 60446. Offers accounting (MBA); custom elective option (MBA); e-business (MBA); finance (MBA); healthcare management (MBA); human resources management (MBA); international business (MBA); management information systems (MBA); marketing (MBA); project management (MBA); technology and operations management (MBA). *Program availability:* Part-time, evening/weekend. *Students:* 114 full-time (72 women), 143 part-time (87 women); includes 84 minority (21 Black or African American, non-Hispanic/Latino; 2 American Indian or Alaska Native, non-Hispanic/Latino; 11 Asian, non-Hispanic/Latino; 45 Hispanic/Latino; 5 Two or more races, non-Hispanic/Latino), 17 international. Average age 31. In 2018, 99 master's awarded. *Entrance requirements:* For master's, interview, bachelor's degree, resume, two recommendations. Additional exam requirements/recommendations for international students: Required—TOEFL (minimum score 550 paper-based), IELTS. *Application deadline:* For fall admission, 8/15 priority date for domestic students, 5/1 priority date for international students; for spring admission, 11/15 priority date for international students. Applications are processed on a rolling basis. Application fee: $40. Electronic applications accepted. *Financial support:* Career-related internships or fieldwork, Federal Work-Study, scholarships/grants, and unspecified assistantships available. Financial award application deadline: 5/1; financial award applicants required to submit FAFSA. *Unit head:* Dr. Maureen Culleeney, Academic Program Director, 815-838-0500 Ext. 5631, E-mail: culleema@lewisu.edu. *Application contact:* Michele Ryan, Director of Admission, 815-838-0500 Ext. 5384, E-mail: ryanml@lewisu.edu.

Liberty University, School of Business, Lynchburg, VA 24515. Offers accounting (MBA, MS), including audit and financial reporting (MS), business (MS), financial services (MS), forensic accounting (MS), leadership (MS), taxation (MS); cyber security (MS); executive leadership (MA); international business (DBA); leadership (DBA); marketing (MBA, MS, DBA), including digital marketing and advertising (MS), project management (MS), public relations (MS), sports marketing and media (MS); project management (MBA, DBA); public relations (MBA). *Program availability:* Part-time, online learning. *Students:* 2,871 full-time (1,496 women), 4,437 part-time (1,969 women); includes 2,069 minority (1,424 Black or African American, non-Hispanic/Latino; 44 American Indian or Alaska Native, non-Hispanic/Latino; 133 Asian, non-Hispanic/Latino; 282 Hispanic/Latino; 16 Native Hawaiian or other Pacific Islander, non-Hispanic/Latino;

170 Two or more races, non-Hispanic/Latino), 154 international. Average age 36. 8,980 applicants, 45% accepted, 2009 enrolled. In 2018, 1,988 master's, 25 doctorates awarded. *Entrance requirements:* For master's, minimum undergraduate GPA of 3.0, 15 hours of upper-level business courses. Additional exam requirements/recommendations for international students: Required—TOEFL (minimum score 600 paper-based; 100 iBT). *Application deadline:* Applications are processed on a rolling basis. Application fee: $50. Electronic applications accepted. *Expenses:* Contact institution. *Financial support:* In 2018–19, 990 students received support. Teaching assistantships and Federal Work-Study available. Financial award applicants required to submit FAFSA. *Unit head:* Dr. Dave Bratt, Dean, 434-592-7321, E-mail: dabrat@liberty.edu. *Application contact:* Jay Bridge, Director of Graduate Admissions, 800-424-9595, Fax: 800-628-7977, E-mail: gradadmissions@liberty.edu.
Website: https://www.liberty.edu/business/

LIM College, MPS Program, New York, NY 10022-5268. Offers business of fashion (MPS); fashion marketing (MPS); fashion merchandising and retail management (MPS); global fashion supply chain management (MPS). *Accreditation:* ACBSP. *Program availability:* Part-time, 100% online. *Faculty:* 2 full-time, 21 part-time/adjunct. *Students:* 125 full-time (109 women), 45 part-time (44 women); includes 64 minority (31 Black or African American, non-Hispanic/Latino; 15 Asian, non-Hispanic/Latino; 18 Hispanic/Latino), 67 international. Average age 25. 292 applicants, 67% accepted, 125 enrolled. In 2018, 146 master's awarded. *Entrance requirements:* Additional exam requirements/recommendations for international students: Required—TOEFL (minimum score 550 paper-based), IELTS (minimum score 6.5), PTE (minimum score 55). *Application deadline:* Applications are processed on a rolling basis. Application fee: $40. Electronic applications accepted. *Expenses: Tuition:* Full-time $28,500; part-time $950 per credit hour. *Required fees:* $500; $100 per semester. *Faculty research:* Marketing, Strategy, Brand Management, Entrepreneurship, Social Media. *Unit head:* John Keane, Chair of Graduate Studies, E-mail: graduatestudies@limcollege.edu. *Application contact:* George Toledo, Assistant Director of Graduate Admissions, 212-310-0634, E-mail: graduateadmissions@limcollege.edu.
Website: http://www.limcollege.edu/academics/graduate

Lindenwood University, Graduate Programs, School of Accelerated Degree Programs, St. Charles, MO 63301-1695. Offers administration (MSA), including management, marketing, project management; business administration (MBA); communications (MA), including digital and multimedia, media management, promotions, training and development; criminal justice and administration (MS); healthcare administration (MS); human resource management (MS); information technology (Certificate); managing information security (MS); managing information technology (MS); managing virtualization and cloud computing (MS); writing (MFA). *Program availability:* Part-time, evening/weekend, 100% online. *Faculty:* 15 full-time (8 women), 62 part-time/adjunct (22 women). *Students:* 652 full-time (398 women), 66 part-time (45 women); includes 241 minority (182 Black or African American, non-Hispanic/Latino; 1 American Indian or Alaska Native, non-Hispanic/Latino; 8 Asian, non-Hispanic/Latino; 25 Hispanic/Latino; 1 Native Hawaiian or other Pacific Islander, non-Hispanic/Latino; 24 Two or more races, non-Hispanic/Latino), 81 international. Average age 36. 359 applicants, 54% accepted, 170 enrolled. In 2018, 416 master's, 2 other advanced degrees awarded. *Degree requirements:* For master's, thesis (for some programs), minimum cumulative GPA of 3.0; for Certificate, minimum cumulative GPA of 3.0. *Entrance requirements:* For master's, resume, personal statement, official undergraduate transcript, minimum undergraduate cumulative GPA of 3.0. Additional exam requirements/recommendations for international students: Required—TOEFL (minimum score 553 paper-based; 81 iBT); Recommended—IELTS (minimum score 6.5). *Application deadline:* For fall admission, 9/30 priority date for domestic and international students; for winter admission, 1/6 priority date for domestic and international students; for spring admission, 4/6 priority date for domestic and international students; for summer admission, 7/8 priority date for domestic and international students. Applications are processed on a rolling basis. Application fee: $0 ($100 for international students). Electronic applications accepted. *Expenses:* Contact institution. *Financial support:* In 2018–19, 372 students received support. Career-related internships or fieldwork, institutionally sponsored loans, scholarships/grants, tuition waivers (partial), and unspecified assistantships available. Financial award application deadline: 6/30; financial award applicants required to submit FAFSA. *Unit head:* Dr. Gina Ganahl, Dean, Accelerated Degree Programs, 636-949-4501, Fax: 636-949-4505, E-mail: gganahl@lindenwood.edu. *Application contact:* Kara Schilli, Assistant Vice President, University Admissions, 636-949-4349, Fax: 636-949-4109, E-mail: adultadmissions@lindenwood.edu.
Website: https://www.lindenwood.edu/academics/academic-schools/school-of-accelerated-degree-programs/

Long Island University–LIU Post, College of Management, Brookville, NY 11548-1300. Offers accountancy (MS); finance (MBA); information systems (MS); international business (MBA); management (MBA); management engineering (MS); marketing (MBA); taxation (MS); technical project management (MS); JD/MBA. *Accreditation:* AACSB. *Program availability:* Part-time, evening/weekend, blended/hybrid learning. *Entrance requirements:* For master's, GMAT, GRE, or LSAT. Additional exam requirements/recommendations for international students: Required—TOEFL (minimum score 550 paper-based, 75 iBT) or IELTS. Electronic applications accepted. *Faculty research:* Innovation and property rights, knowledge sourcing, sustainability and firm performance, China and growth markets, corporate social responsibility, workforce compensation and issues.

Louisiana Tech University, Graduate School, College of Business, Ruston, LA 71272. Offers accounting (M Acc, DBA); computer information systems (DBA); finance (MBA, DBA); information assurance (MBA); innovation (MBA); management (DBA); marketing (MBA, DBA). *Accreditation:* AACSB. *Program availability:* Part-time, evening/weekend, 100% online, blended/hybrid learning. *Degree requirements:* For doctorate, thesis/dissertation. *Entrance requirements:* For master's and doctorate, GMAT, transcript with bachelor's degree awarded. Additional exam requirements/recommendations for international students: Required—TOEFL (minimum score 550 paper-based; 80 iBT), IELTS (minimum score 6.5). Electronic applications accepted. *Faculty research:* Consumer environmental behavior; identifying and analyzing current issues and future concerns in real estate; information assurance and related areas in business for Northwest Louisiana and the United States (business continuity, disaster recovery, accounting controls, auditing, computer forensics, and security attribution); value creation driven by the consumer and employee interface within exchange environments.

Loyola University Chicago, Quinlan School of Business, Master of Science in Integrated Marketing Communications Program, Chicago, IL 60611. Offers MS. *Program availability:* Part-time, evening/weekend. *Entrance requirements:* For master's, GMAT or GRE, official transcripts, two letters of recommendation, statement of purpose, resume. Additional exam requirements/recommendations for international students: Required—TOEFL (minimum score 90 iBT) or IELTS (minimum score 6.5). Electronic applications accepted. Application fee is waived when completed online. *Expenses:* Contact institution. *Faculty research:* Brand strategy, consumer behavior, digital/interactive marketing, international marketing.

Loyola University Chicago, Quinlan School of Business, MBA Programs, Chicago, IL 60611. Offers accounting (MBA); business ethics (MBA); derivative markets (MBA); economics (MBA); entrepreneurship (MBA); finance (MBA); healthcare management (MBA); human resources management (MBA); information systems management (MBA); international business (MBA); management (MBA); marketing (MBA); risk management (MBA); supply chain management (MBA). *Program availability:* Part-time, evening/weekend. *Entrance requirements:* For master's, GMAT or GRE, official transcripts, two letters of recommendation, statement of purpose, resume. Additional exam requirements/recommendations for international students: Required—TOEFL (minimum score 90 iBT) or IELTS (minimum score 6.5). Electronic applications accepted. Application fee is waived when completed online. *Expenses:* Contact institution. *Faculty research:* Social enterprise and responsibility, emerging markets, supply chain management, risk management.

Loyola University Maryland, Graduate Programs, Sellinger School of Business, Professional MBA Program, Baltimore, MD 21210-2699. Offers finance (MBA); information systems (MBA); investments and applied portfolio management (MBA); management (MBA); marketing (MBA). *Accreditation:* AACSB. *Program availability:* Part-time, evening/weekend. *Entrance requirements:* For master's, GMAT, resume, essay, official transcripts, professional letter of recommendation. Additional exam requirements/recommendations for international students: Required—TOEFL (minimum score 550 paper-based, 80 iBT) or IELTS (minimum score 7). Electronic applications accepted. *Expenses:* Contact institution.

Marist College, Graduate Programs, School of Communication and the Arts, Program in Integrated Marketing Communication, Poughkeepsie, NY 12601-1387. Offers MA. *Entrance requirements:* For master's, GRE or GMAT, official undergraduate/graduate transcripts from all institutions attended; current resume; completed recommendation forms for three references; personal statement.

Marquette University, Graduate School of Management, Executive MBA Program, Milwaukee, WI 53201-1881. Offers economics (MBA); finance (MBA); human resources (MBA); international business (MBA); management information systems (MBA); marketing (MBA); operations and supply chain management (MBA); sports business (MBA). *Accreditation:* AACSB. *Degree requirements:* For master's, international trip. *Entrance requirements:* For master's, GMAT or GRE, two letters of recommendation, official transcripts from current and previous colleges/universities. Additional exam requirements/recommendations for international students: Required—TOEFL (minimum score 550 paper-based; 88 iBT), IELTS (minimum score 6.5), PTE. Electronic applications accepted. *Expenses:* Contact institution. *Faculty research:* International trade and finance, customer relationship management, consumer satisfaction, customer service.

Marquette University, Graduate School of Management, Program in Business Administration, Milwaukee, WI 53201-1881. Offers business administration (MBA); economics (MBA); entrepreneurship (Certificate); finance (MBA); human resources (MBA); international business (MBA); management information systems (MBA); marketing (MBA); operations and supply chain management (MBA); sports business (MBA); JD/MBA; MBA/MA; MBA/MSN. *Accreditation:* AACSB. *Program availability:* Part-time, evening/weekend. *Degree requirements:* For Certificate, business plan. *Entrance requirements:* For master's, GMAT or GRE, letters of recommendation. Additional exam requirements/recommendations for international students: Required—TOEFL (minimum score 550 paper-based; 88 iBT), IELTS (minimum score 6.5), PTE. Electronic applications accepted. *Faculty research:* Ethics in the professions, services marketing, technology impact on decision-making, mentoring.

Maryville University of Saint Louis, The John E. Simon School of Business, St. Louis, MO 63141-7299. Offers accounting (MBA, MS, Certificate); business studies (Certificate); cybersecurity (MBA, MS, Certificate); financial services (MBA, Certificate); health administration (MBA); healthcare administration (Certificate); human resource management (MBA); human resources management (Certificate); information technology (MBA); information technology management (Certificate); management (MBA, Certificate); management and leadership (MA); marketing (MBA, Certificate); project management (MBA, Certificate); sport business management (MBA); supply chain management (Certificate); supply chain management/logistics (MBA). *Accreditation:* ACBSP. *Program availability:* Part-time, 100% online, blended/hybrid learning. *Faculty:* 5 full-time (1 woman), 77 part-time/adjunct (19 women). *Students:* 338 full-time (166 women), 739 part-time (356 women); includes 310 minority (161 Black or African American, non-Hispanic/Latino; 6 American Indian or Alaska Native, non-Hispanic/Latino; 59 Asian, non-Hispanic/Latino; 57 Hispanic/Latino; 27 Two or more races, non-Hispanic/Latino), 30 international. Average age 33. In 2018, 143 master's awarded. *Degree requirements:* For master's, capstone course (for MBA). *Entrance requirements:* Additional exam requirements/recommendations for international students: Required—TOEFL (minimum score 563 paper-based; 85 iBT). *Application deadline:* Applications are processed on a rolling basis. Electronic applications accepted. *Expenses:* Tuition varies by program. *Financial support:* Career-related internships or fieldwork, Federal Work-Study, tuition waivers (partial), and campus employment available. Financial award application deadline: 4/1; financial award applicants required to submit FAFSA. *Unit head:* Tammy Gocial, Interim Dean, 314-529-9401, Fax: 314-529-9975, E-mail: tgocial@maryville.edu. *Application contact:* Chris Gourdine, Assistant Dean Business Administration, 314-529-6861, Fax: 314-529-9975, E-mail: cgourdine@maryville.edu.
Website: http://www.maryville.edu/bu/business-administration-masters/

McGill University, Faculty of Graduate and Postdoctoral Studies, Desautels Faculty of Management, Montréal, QC H3A 2T5, Canada. Offers administration (PhD); entrepreneurial studies (MBA); finance (MBA); general management (Post Master's Certificate); global manufacturing and supply chain management (MMM); information systems (MBA); international business (MBA); international practicing management (MM); management (MBA); management for development (MBA); marketing (MBA); operations management (MBA); public accountancy (Diploma); strategic management (MBA); MBA/LL B; MD/MBA. MMM offered jointly with Faculty of Engineering; PhD with Concordia University, HEC Montreal, Université de Montréal, Université du Québec à Montréal.

Melbourne Business School, Graduate Programs, Carlton, Australia. Offers business administration (Exec MBA, MBA); management (PhD); management science (PhD); marketing (PhD); social impact (Graduate Certificate); JD/MBA.

Michigan State University, The Graduate School, Eli Broad College of Business, Department of Marketing, East Lansing, MI 48224. Offers marketing (PhD); marketing research (MS). *Degree requirements:* For doctorate, comprehensive exam, thesis/dissertation. *Entrance requirements:* For master's, GMAT, bachelor's degree with minimum GPA of 3.0 in last 2 years of undergraduate work; transcripts; 3 letters of recommendation; statement of purpose; resume; working knowledge of computers; basic understanding of accounting, finance, marketing, and the management of people; laptop capable of running Windows software; for doctorate, GMAT (taken within past 5 years), bachelor's degree; letters of recommendation; statement of purpose; previous work experience; personal qualifications of sound character, perseverance, intellectual curiosity, and an interest in scholarly research. Additional exam requirements/recommendations for international students: Required—TOEFL (minimum score 100 iBT), PTE (minimum score 70), IELTS (minimum score 7) accepted for MS only.

Marketing

Michigan State University, The Graduate School, Eli Broad College of Business, Program in Business Administration, East Lansing, MI 48224. Offers finance (MBA); human resource management (MBA); integrative management (MBA); marketing (MBA); supply chain management (MBA). MBA in integrative management is through Weekend MBA Program; other 4 concentrations are through Full-Time MBA Program. *Program availability:* Evening/weekend. *Degree requirements:* For master's, enrichment experience. *Entrance requirements:* For master's, GMAT or GRE, 4-year bachelor's degree; resume; work experience (minimum of 5 years for Weekend MBA); 2-3 personal essays; 2 letters of recommendation; personal interview. Additional exam requirements/recommendations for international students: Required—PTE (minimum score 70), TOEFL (minimum score 100 iBT) or IELTS (minimum score 7) for full-time MBA applicants. Electronic applications accepted. *Expenses:* Contact institution.

Milwaukee School of Engineering, MS Program in Marketing and Export Management, Milwaukee, WI 53202-3109. Offers MS. *Program availability:* Part-time, evening/weekend. *Degree requirements:* For master's, thesis or alternative, thesis defense or capstone project. *Entrance requirements:* For master's, GRE or GMAT if undergraduate GPA less than 2.8, 2 letters of recommendation; bachelor's degree from accredited university; work experience (strongly recommended). Additional exam requirements/recommendations for international students: Required—TOEFL (minimum score 90 iBT), IELTS (minimum score 7). Electronic applications accepted.

Mississippi State University, College of Business, Department of Marketing, Quantitative Analysis and Business Law, Mississippi State, MS 39762. Offers business administration (PhD), including marketing. *Program availability:* Part-time, evening/weekend. *Faculty:* 13 full-time (4 women). *Students:* 6 full-time (3 women), 2 part-time (1 woman); includes 2 minority (1 Black or African American, non-Hispanic/Latino; 1 Asian, non-Hispanic/Latino), 2 international. Average age 30. 14 applicants, 21% accepted, 3 enrolled. In 2018, 4 doctorates awarded. *Degree requirements:* For doctorate, comprehensive exam, thesis/dissertation. *Entrance requirements:* For doctorate, GMAT (taken within last five years with minimum score of 550), minimum GPA of 3.25 on all prior graduate work. Additional exam requirements/recommendations for international students: Required—TOEFL (minimum score 575 paper-based; 84 iBT); Recommended—IELTS (minimum score 6.5). *Application deadline:* For fall admission, 7/1 for domestic students, 5/1 for international students; for spring admission, 11/1 for domestic students, 9/1 for international students. Applications are processed on a rolling basis. Application fee: $60 ($80 for international students). Electronic applications accepted. *Expenses:* Tuition, state resident: full-time $8450; part-time $360.59 per credit hour. Tuition, nonresident: full-time $23,140; part-time $969.09 per credit hour. *Required fees:* $110. One-time fee: $55 full-time. Part-time tuition and fees vary according to course load, degree level, campus/location and reciprocity agreements. *Financial support:* Federal Work-Study, institutionally sponsored loans, and scholarships/grants available. Financial award application deadline: 4/1; financial award applicants required to submit FAFSA. *Unit head:* Dr. Melissa Moore, Professor and Head, 662-325-8556, Fax: 662-325-7012, E-mail: mmoore@business.msstate.edu. *Application contact:* Robbie Salters, Admissions and Enrollment Assistant, 662-325-7400, E-mail: rsalters@grad.msstate.edu.
Website: http://www.business.msstate.edu/programs/marketing/index.php

Molloy College, Graduate Business Program, Rockville Centre, NY 11571-5002. Offers accounting (MBA); finance (MBA, Post-Master's Certificate, Postbaccalaureate Certificate); healthcare (MBA, Post-Master's Certificate, Postbaccalaureate Certificate); management (MBA); marketing (MBA, Post-Master's Certificate, Postbaccalaureate Certificate); personal financial planning (MBA). *Program availability:* Part-time, evening/weekend. *Faculty:* 9 full-time (2 women), 20 part-time/adjunct (8 women). *Students:* 75 full-time (45 women), 164 part-time (88 women); includes 100 minority (45 Black or African American, non-Hispanic/Latino; 21 Asian, non-Hispanic/Latino; 30 Hispanic/Latino; 1 Native Hawaiian or other Pacific Islander, non-Hispanic/Latino; 3 Two or more races, non-Hispanic/Latino), 3 international. Average age 40. 97 applicants, 78% accepted, 65 enrolled. In 2018, 91 master's, 1 other advanced degree awarded. *Entrance requirements:* Additional exam requirements/recommendations for international students: Required—TOEFL (minimum score 550 paper-based; 79 iBT). *Application deadline:* Applications are processed on a rolling basis. Application fee: $60. Electronic applications accepted. *Expenses: Tuition:* Full-time $20,790; part-time $1155 per credit. *Required fees:* $1060; $900. Tuition and fees vary according to course load and degree level. *Financial support:* Application deadline: 3/1; applicants required to submit FAFSA. *Faculty research:* Graduate education - pedagogy and the capstone experience; Freedom of Speech in the workplace; employer liability for sexual harassment in the workplace; educational economics and industrial organization; corporate governance and distressed debt analysis; social network analysis; market segmentation. *Unit head:* Dr. Maureen Mackenzie, Dean, Division of Business/Director of Graduate Programs, 516-323-3080, E-mail: mmackenzie@molloy.edu. *Application contact:* Faye Hood, Assistant Director for Admissions, 516-323-4009, E-mail: fhood@molloy.edu.
Website: http://www.molloy.edu/academics/graduate-programs/graduate-business

Monmouth University, Graduate Studies, Leon Hess Business School, West Long Branch, NJ 07764-1898. Offers accounting (MBA, Certificate); business administration (MBA); finance (MBA); management (MBA); marketing (MBA); real estate (MBA). *Accreditation:* AACSB. *Program availability:* Part-time, evening/weekend. *Faculty:* 22 full-time (5 women), 8 part-time/adjunct (1 woman). *Students:* 91 full-time (47 women), 87 part-time (35 women); includes 17 minority (2 Black or African American, non-Hispanic/Latino; 6 Asian, non-Hispanic/Latino; 7 Hispanic/Latino; 2 Two or more races, non-Hispanic/Latino), 12 international. Average age 29. In 2018, 79 master's, 1 other advanced degree awarded. *Degree requirements:* For master's, capstone course. *Entrance requirements:* For master's, GMAT or GRE, current resume; essay (500 words or less). Additional exam requirements/recommendations for international students: Required—TOEFL (minimum score 550 paper-based; 79 iBT), IELTS (minimum score 6), Michigan English Language Assessment Battery (minimum score 77) or Certificate of Advanced English (minimum score 160). *Application deadline:* For fall admission, 7/15 priority date for domestic students, 6/1 for international students; for spring admission, 12/1 priority date for domestic students, 11/1 for international students; for summer admission, 5/1 for domestic students. Applications are processed on a rolling basis. Application fee: $50. Electronic applications accepted. *Expenses: Tuition:* Part-time $1233 per credit. *Required fees:* $178 per term. *Financial support:* In 2018–19, 131 students received support. Institutionally sponsored loans, scholarships/grants, and unspecified assistantships available. Support available to part-time students. Financial award applicants required to submit FAFSA. *Faculty research:* Information technology and marketing, behavioral research in accounting, human resources, management of technology. *Unit head:* Dr. Susan Gupta, MBA Program Director, 732-571-3639, Fax: 732-263-5517, E-mail: sgupta@monmouth.edu. *Application contact:* Laurie Kuhn, Associate Director of Graduate Admission, 732-571-3452, Fax: 732-263-5123, E-mail: gradadm@monmouth.edu.
Website: https://www.monmouth.edu/business-school/leon-hess-business-school.aspx

Monroe College, King Graduate School, Bronx, NY 10468. Offers accounting (MS); business administration (MBA), including entrepreneurship, finance, general business administration, healthcare management, human resources, information technology, marketing; computer science (MS); criminal justice (MS); hospitality management (MS); public health (MPH), including biostatistics and epidemiology, community health, health administration and leadership. *Program availability:* Online learning.

Montclair State University, The Graduate School, Feliciano School of Business, General MBA Program, Montclair, NJ 07043-1624. Offers accounting (MBA); business analytics (MBA); digital marketing (MBA); finance (MBA); general business administration (MBA); human resources management (MBA); management (MBA); management of information and technology (MBA); marketing (MBA); project management (MBA). *Program availability:* Part-time, evening/weekend. *Degree requirements:* For master's, culminating experience. *Entrance requirements:* For master's, GMAT or GRE General Test, 2 letters of recommendation, resume, essay. Additional exam requirements/recommendations for international students: Required—TOEFL (minimum score 83 iBT), IELTS (minimum score 6.5). Electronic applications accepted. *Faculty research:* Accounting, management, marketing.

Morgan State University, School of Graduate Studies, Earl G. Graves School of Business and Management, PhD Program in Business Administration, Baltimore, MD 21251. Offers business administration (PhD), including accounting, information systems, management and marketing. *Accreditation:* AACSB. *Entrance requirements:* For doctorate, GMAT. Additional exam requirements/recommendations for international students: Required—TOEFL (minimum score 550 paper-based).

Murray State University, Arthur J. Bauernfeind College of Business, MBA Program, Murray, KY 42071. Offers accounting (MBA); finance (MBA); global communications (MBA); human resource management (MBA); marketing (MBA). *Accreditation:* AACSB. *Program availability:* Part-time, evening/weekend, 100% online, blended/hybrid learning. *Entrance requirements:* For master's, GRE or GMAT, minimum university GPA of 2.75. Additional exam requirements/recommendations for international students: Required—TOEFL (minimum score 527 paper-based; 71 iBT). *Faculty research:* Human resource management, e-commerce, supply-chain management, investment management, accounting.

National American University, Roueche Graduate Center, Austin, TX 78731. Offers accounting (MBA); aviation management (MBA, MM); care coordination (MSN); community college leadership (Ed D); criminal justice (MM); e-marketing (MBA, MM); health care administration (MBA, MM); higher education (MM); human resources management (MBA, MM); information technology management (MBA, MM); international business (MBA); leadership (EMBA); management (MBA); nursing administration (MSN); nursing education (MSN); nursing informatics (MSN); operations and configuration management (MBA, MM); project and process management (MBA, MM). Master's programs offered online through the Harold D. Buckingham Graduate School. *Program availability:* Part-time, evening/weekend, online learning. *Entrance requirements:* For master's, minimum undergraduate GPA of 2.75. Additional exam requirements/recommendations for international students: Required—TOEFL, TWE. Electronic applications accepted. *Faculty research:* Tourism, finance, marketing.

National University, School of Business and Management, La Jolla, CA 92037-1011. Offers accountancy (M Acc, Certificate); business administration (GMBA, MBA); business analytics (MS); cause leadership (MA); global management (MGM); human resource management (MA); management information systems (MS); marketing (MS); organizational leadership (MS). GMBA offered in Spanish. *Program availability:* Part-time, evening/weekend, 100% online, blended/hybrid learning. *Degree requirements:* For master's, thesis (for some programs). *Entrance requirements:* For master's, interview, minimum GPA of 2.5. Additional exam requirements/recommendations for international students: Required—TOEFL (minimum score 550 paper-based; 79 iBT), IELTS (minimum score 6). Electronic applications accepted. *Expenses: Tuition:* Full-time $10,320; part-time $430 per unit. Tuition and fees vary according to degree level.

National University College, Graduate Programs, Bayamón, PR 00960. Offers digital marketing (MBA); general business (MBA); special education (M Ed).

Nebraska Christian College of Hope International University, Graduate Programs, Papillion, NE 68046. Offers biblical studies (M Div); business as mission/social entrepreneurship (MBA); children, youth, and family (M Div); church planting (M Div); counseling psychology (MS); educational administration (MA); elementary education (M Ed); general management (MBA); gifted and talented education (M Ed); intercultural studies (M Div); international development (MBA); marketing management (MBA); ministry (MA); ministry and leadership (M Div); music education (M Ed); non-profit management (MBA); pastoral care (M Div); secondary education (M Ed); spiritual formation (M Div); worship ministry (M Div).

New England College, Program in Management, Henniker, NH 03242-3293. Offers accounting (MSA); healthcare administration (MS); international relations (MA); marketing management (MS); nonprofit leadership (MS); project management (MS); strategic leadership (MS). *Program availability:* Part-time, evening/weekend. *Degree requirements:* For master's, independent research project. Electronic applications accepted.

New Jersey City University, School of Business, Program in Marketing, Jersey City, NJ 07305-1597. Offers MBA.

New York Institute of Technology, School of Management, Department of Business Administration, Old Westbury, NY 11568-8000. Offers executive management (MBA), including finance, marketing, operations and supply chain management. *Accreditation:* AACSB. *Program availability:* Part-time. *Faculty:* 25 full-time (4 women), 20 part-time/adjunct (6 women). *Students:* 296 full-time (126 women), 91 part-time (45 women); includes 42 minority (6 Black or African American, non-Hispanic/Latino; 1 American Indian or Alaska Native, non-Hispanic/Latino; 17 Asian, non-Hispanic/Latino; 12 Hispanic/Latino; 1 Native Hawaiian or other Pacific Islander, non-Hispanic/Latino; 5 Two or more races, non-Hispanic/Latino), 298 international. Average age 30. 550 applicants, 67% accepted, 111 enrolled. In 2018, 291 master's awarded. *Entrance requirements:* For master's, bachelor's degree; minimum undergraduate GPA of 3.0. Additional exam requirements/recommendations for international students: Required—TOEFL (minimum score 79 iBT), IELTS (minimum score 6), PTE (minimum score 53). *Application deadline:* Applications are processed on a rolling basis. Application fee: $50. Electronic applications accepted. *Expenses: Tuition:* Full-time $1285; part-time $1285 per credit. *Required fees:* $215; $175 per unit. Tuition and fees vary according to course load, degree level and campus/location. *Financial support:* Career-related internships or fieldwork, Federal Work-Study, scholarships/grants, tuition waivers (full and partial), and unspecified assistantships available. Support available to part-time students. Financial award application deadline: 2/15; financial award applicants required to submit FAFSA. *Faculty research:* Accounting, economics, finance, management, marketing. *Unit head:* Dr. Jess Boronico, Dean, 516-686-7838, E-mail: som@nyit.edu. *Application contact:* Alice Dolitsky, Director, Graduate Admissions, 516-686-7520, Fax: 516-686-1116, E-mail: admissions@nyit.edu.
Website: http://www.nyit.edu/degrees/management_mba

New York University, Leonard N. Stern School of Business, Department of Marketing, New York, NY 10012-1019. Offers entertainment, media and technology (MBA); general marketing (MBA); marketing (PhD); product management (MBA).

New York University, School of Professional Studies, Division of Programs in Business, Program in Integrated Marketing, New York, NY 10012-1019. Offers integrated marketing (MS), including brand management, digital marketing, marketing analytics. *Program availability:* Part-time, evening/weekend. *Degree requirements:* For master's, thesis, capstone project. *Entrance requirements:* For master's, GRE or GMAT (only upon request), bachelor's degree, resume with relevant professional work, internship or volunteer experience, two letters of recommendation, statement of purpose. Additional exam requirements/recommendations for international students: Required—TOEFL (minimum score 600 paper-based; 100 iBT), IELTS (minimum score 7). Electronic applications accepted. *Expenses:* Contact institution.

New York University, School of Professional Studies, Division of Programs in Business, Programs in Marketing and Public Relations, New York, NY 10012-1019. Offers public relations and corporate communication (MS), including corporate and organizational communication, public relations management. *Program availability:* Part-time, evening/weekend. *Degree requirements:* For master's, thesis. *Entrance requirements:* For master's, GRE or GMAT (only upon request), bachelor's degree, resume with relevant professional work, internship or volunteer experience, two letters of recommendation, statement of purpose. Additional exam requirements/recommendations for international students: Required—TOEFL (minimum score 600 paper-based; 100 iBT), IELTS (minimum score 7). Electronic applications accepted. *Expenses:* Contact institution.

New York University, School of Professional Studies, Preston Robert Tisch Institute for Global Sport, New York, NY 10012-1019. Offers sports business (MS), including global sports media, professional and collegiate sports operations, sports law, sports marketing and sales. *Program availability:* Part-time, evening/weekend. *Degree requirements:* For master's, thesis. *Entrance requirements:* For master's, GRE or GMAT (only upon request), bachelor's degree, resume with relevant professional work, internship or volunteer experience, two letters of recommendation, statement of purpose. Additional exam requirements/recommendations for international students: Required—TOEFL (minimum score 600 paper-based; 100 iBT), IELTS (minimum score 7). Electronic applications accepted. *Expenses:* Contact institution.

Niagara University, Graduate Division of Business Administration, Niagara University, NY 14109. Offers accounting (MBA); business administration (MBA); finance (MBA, MS); financial planning (MBA); healthcare administration (MBA, MHA); human resources (MBA); international business (MBA); marketing (MBA); professional accountancy (MBA); strategic management (MBA); supply chain management (MBA). *Accreditation:* AACSB. *Program availability:* Part-time, evening/weekend, 100% online, blended/hybrid learning. *Students:* 224 full-time (116 women), 56 part-time (22 women); includes 36 minority (9 Black or African American, non-Hispanic/Latino; 2 American Indian or Alaska Native, non-Hispanic/Latino; 6 Asian, non-Hispanic/Latino; 12 Hispanic/Latino; 7 Two or more races, non-Hispanic/Latino), 82 international. Average age 26. In 2018, 134 master's awarded. *Entrance requirements:* For master's, GMAT. Additional exam requirements/recommendations for international students: Required—TOEFL (minimum score 550 paper-based; 79 iBT), IELTS (minimum score 6). *Application deadline:* For fall admission, 8/1 for domestic students; for spring admission, 11/1 for domestic students. Applications are processed on a rolling basis. Electronic applications accepted. *Expenses:* Contact institution. *Financial support:* Research assistantships, teaching assistantships, career-related internships or fieldwork, Federal Work-Study, scholarships/grants, and unspecified assistantships available. Support available to part-time students. Financial award application deadline: 4/15; financial award applicants required to submit FAFSA. *Faculty research:* Capital flows, Federal Reserve policy, human resource management, public policy, issues in marketing, auctions, economics of information, risk and capital markets, management strategy, consumer behavior, Internet and social media marketing. *Unit head:* Dr. Paul Richardson, MBA Director/Chair of the Marketing Department, 716-286-8169, Fax: 716-286-8206, E-mail: mba@niagara.edu. *Application contact:* Evan Pierce, Associate Director for Graduate Recruitment, 716-286-8327, Fax: 716-286-8710, E-mail: epierce@niagara.edu. Website: http://mba.niagara.edu

Northwestern University, The Graduate School, Kellogg School of Management, Department of Marketing, Evanston, IL 60208. Offers PhD. Admissions and degree offered through The Graduate School. *Degree requirements:* For doctorate, comprehensive exam, thesis/dissertation. *Entrance requirements:* For doctorate, GMAT or GRE General Test. Additional exam requirements/recommendations for international students: Required—TOEFL. Electronic applications accepted. *Faculty research:* Choice models, database and high-tech marketing, consumer information processing, ethnographic analysis of consumption, psychometric analysis of consumer behavior.

Northwestern University, The Graduate School, Kellogg School of Management, Management Programs, Evanston, IL 60208. Offers accounting information and management (MBA, PhD); analytical finance (MBA); business administration (MBA); decision sciences (MBA); entrepreneurship and innovation (MBA); finance (MBA, PhD); health enterprise management (MBA); human resources management (MBA); international business (MBA); management and organizations (MBA, PhD); management and organizations and sociology (PhD); management and strategy (MBA); management studies (MS); managerial analytics (MBA); managerial economics (MBA); managerial economics and strategy (PhD); marketing (MBA, PhD); marketing management (MBA); media management (MBA); operations management (MBA, PhD); real estate (MBA); social enterprise at Kellogg (MBA); JD/MBA. *Program availability:* Part-time, evening/weekend. Terminal master's awarded for partial completion of doctoral program. *Degree requirements:* For doctorate, thesis/dissertation, 2 years of coursework, qualifying (field) exam and candidacy, summer research papers and presentations to faculty, proposal defense, final exam/defense. *Entrance requirements:* For master's, GMAT, GRE, interview, 2 letters of recommendation, college transcripts, resume, essays, Kellogg honor code; for doctorate, GMAT, GRE, statement of purpose, transcripts, 2 letters of recommendation, resume, interview. Additional exam requirements/recommendations for international students: Required—TOEFL, IELTS. Electronic applications accepted. *Expenses:* Contact institution. *Faculty research:* Business cycles and international finance, health policy, networks, non-market strategy, consumer psychology.

Northwestern University, Medill School of Journalism, Media, and Integrated Marketing Communications, Integrated Marketing Communications Program, Evanston, IL 60208. Offers brand strategy (MSIMC); content marketing (MSIMC); direct and interactive marketing (MSIMC); marketing analytics (MSIMC); strategic communications (MSIMC). *Program availability:* Part-time. *Entrance requirements:* For master's, GRE General Test or GMAT, full-time work experience (preferred). Additional exam requirements/recommendations for international students: Required—TOEFL. Electronic applications accepted. *Faculty research:* Data mining, business to business marketing, values in advertising, political advertising.

Northwest Missouri State University, Graduate School, Melvin and Valorie Booth College of Business and Professional Studies, Maryville, MO 64468-6001. Offers agricultural economics (MBA); business decision and analytics (MBA); general management (MBA); human resource management (MBA); marketing (MBA). *Program availability:* Part-time. *Faculty:* 24 full-time (12 women). *Students:* 56 full-time (31 women), 220 part-time (126 women); includes 47 minority (23 Black or African American, non-Hispanic/Latino; 6 Asian, non-Hispanic/Latino; 10 Hispanic/Latino; 8 Two or more races, non-Hispanic/Latino), 15 international. Average age 32. 154 applicants, 75% accepted, 104 enrolled. In 2018, 53 master's awarded. *Degree requirements:* For master's, comprehensive exam. *Entrance requirements:* For master's, GMAT, GRE, minimum GPA of 2.5. Additional exam requirements/recommendations for international students: Required—TOEFL (minimum score 550 paper-based). *Application deadline:* For fall admission, 7/1 for domestic and international students; for spring admission, 11/15 for domestic and international students; for summer admission, 4/1 for domestic and international students. Applications are processed on a rolling basis. Application fee: $0 ($50 for international students). Electronic applications accepted. *Expenses:* $13,530 to complete degree (online MBA program); 401.06/credit hour in-state & 653.92/credit hour out-of-state. *Financial support:* Research assistantships with full tuition reimbursements, teaching assistantships with full tuition reimbursements, career-related internships or fieldwork, unspecified assistantships, and administrative assistantships, tutorial assistantships available. Financial award application deadline: 4/1; financial award applicants required to submit FAFSA. *Unit head:* Dr. Steve Ludwig, Director of the Melvin And Valorie Booth School of Business, 660-562-1749, Fax: 660-562-1096, E-mail: sludwig@nwmissouri.edu. *Application contact:* Dr. Steve Ludwig, Director of the Melvin And Valorie Booth School of Business, 660-562-1749, Fax: 660-562-1096, E-mail: sludwig@nwmissouri.edu. Website: https://www.nwmissouri.edu/business/index.htm

Nova Southeastern University, H. Wayne Huizenga College of Business and Entrepreneurship, Fort Lauderdale, FL 33314-7796. Offers accounting (M Acc); business (MBA); business intelligence/analytics (MBA); complex health systems (MBA); enterprise informatics (MBA); entrepreneurship (MBA); finance (MBA); human resource management (MBA); international business (MBA); management (MBA); marketing (MBA); process improvement (MBA); public administration (MPA); real estate development (MS); sport revenue generation (MBA); supply chain management (MBA). *Accreditation:* NASPAA. *Program availability:* Part-time, evening/weekend, 100% online, blended/hybrid learning. *Entrance requirements:* For master's, GMAT or GRE (depending on undergraduate GPA), official transcripts from all schools attended while in pursuit of bachelor's degree; minimum GPA of 2.5 from regionally-accredited institution. Additional exam requirements/recommendations for international students: Required—TOEFL (minimum score 550 paper-based; 79 iBT), IELTS (minimum score 6), PTE (minimum score 54). Electronic applications accepted. *Expenses:* Contact institution. *Faculty research:* Entrepreneurship and venture capital, ethics and social responsibility, global commerce and cultures, business process management.

Oakland University, Graduate Study and Lifelong Learning, School of Business Administration, Department of Management and Marketing, Rochester, MI 48309-4401. Offers business administration (MBA); entrepreneurship (Certificate); general management (Certificate); human resource management (Certificate); international business (Certificate); management and marketing (EMBA); marketing (Certificate).

Ohio Christian University, Graduate Programs, Circleville, OH 43113. Offers accounting (MBA); business administration (MBA); digital marketing (MBA); finance (MBA); healthcare management (MBA); human resources (MBA); management (MM); organizational leadership (MBA); pastoral care and counseling (MAM); practical theology (MAM).

Oklahoma Christian University, Graduate School of Business, Oklahoma City, OK 73136-1100. Offers accounting (M Acc, MBA); financial services (MBA); general business (MBA); health services management (MBA); human resources (MBA); international business (MBA); leadership and organizational development (MBA); marketing (MBA); nonprofit management (MBA); project management (MBA). *Accreditation:* ACBSP. *Program availability:* Part-time, 100% online. *Entrance requirements:* For master's, bachelor's degree. Additional exam requirements/recommendations for international students: Required—TOEFL (minimum score 550 paper-based). Electronic applications accepted. *Expenses:* Contact institution.

Oklahoma State University, Spears School of Business, School of Marketing and International Business, Stillwater, OK 74078. Offers business administration (PhD), including marketing; marketing (MBA). *Program availability:* Part-time. *Faculty:* 21 full-time (5 women), 5 part-time/adjunct (2 women). *Students:* 71 full-time (22 women), 34 part-time (17 women); includes 8 minority (1 Black or African American, non-Hispanic/Latino; 3 Asian, non-Hispanic/Latino; 4 Hispanic/Latino), 74 international. Average age 27. 234 applicants, 20% accepted, 42 enrolled. In 2018, 39 master's awarded. *Entrance requirements:* For master's and doctorate, GRE or GMAT. Additional exam requirements/recommendations for international students: Required—TOEFL (minimum score 550 paper-based; 79 iBT). *Application deadline:* For fall admission, 3/1 priority date for international students; for spring admission, 8/1 priority date for international students. Applications are processed on a rolling basis. Application fee: $40 ($75 for international students). Electronic applications accepted. *Expenses: Tuition, area resident:* Full-time $4148. Tuition, state resident: full-time $4148. Tuition, nonresident: full-time $10,517. *International tuition:* $10,517 full-time. *Required fees:* $4394; $2929 per credit hour. Tuition and fees vary according to course load and program. *Financial support:* Research assistantships, teaching assistantships, career-related internships or fieldwork, Federal Work-Study, scholarships/grants, health care benefits, tuition waivers (partial), and unspecified assistantships available. Support available to part-time students. Financial award application deadline: 3/1; financial award applicants required to submit FAFSA. *Faculty research:* Decision-making (consumer, managerial, cross-functional), communication effects, services marketing, public policy and marketing, corporate image. *Unit head:* Dr. Tom Brown, Department Head, 405-744-5113, Fax: 405-744-5180, E-mail: tom.brown@okstate.edu. *Application contact:* Dr. Kevin Voss, PhD Coordinator, 405-744-5106, Fax: 405-744-5180, E-mail: kevin.voss@okstate.edu. Website: https://business.okstate.edu/marketing/

Old Dominion University, College of Health Sciences, School of Dental Hygiene, Norfolk, VA 23529. Offers dental hygiene (MS), including community/public health, education, generalist, global health, marketing, modeling and simulation, research. *Program availability:* Part-time, evening/weekend, blended/hybrid learning. *Degree requirements:* For master's, comprehensive exam, thesis optional, writing proficiency exam, responsible conduct of research training. *Entrance requirements:* For master's, Dental Hygiene National Board Examination or copy of license to practice dental hygiene, BS or certificate in dental hygiene or related area, minimum GPA of 2.8 (3.0 in major), 4 letters of recommendation. Additional exam requirements/recommendations for international students: Required—TOEFL (minimum score 550 paper-based, 79 iBT) or IELTS (minimum score 6.5). Electronic applications accepted. *Expenses:* Contact institution. *Faculty research:* Clinical dental hygiene, dental hygiene client health behaviors, dental hygiene education interventions, oral product testing, cold plasma.

Old Dominion University, Strome College of Business, Doctoral Program in Business Administration, Norfolk, VA 23529. Offers business administration (PhD), including finance, IT and supply chain management, marketing, strategic management. *Accreditation:* AACSB. *Degree requirements:* For doctorate, comprehensive exam, thesis/dissertation. *Entrance requirements:* For doctorate, GMAT or GRE. Additional exam requirements/recommendations for international students: Required—TOEFL (minimum score 550 paper-based; 79 iBT). Electronic applications accepted. *Faculty research:* International business, buyer behavior, financial markets, strategy, operations research.

Marketing

Oral Roberts University, School of Business, Tulsa, OK 74171. Offers accounting (MBA); entrepreneurship (MBA); finance (MBA); international business (MBA); management (MBA); marketing (MBA); not for profit management (MNM). *Accreditation:* ACBSP. *Program availability:* Part-time, online learning. *Degree requirements:* For master's, thesis optional. *Entrance requirements:* For master's, minimum cumulative GPA of 3.0 from regionally-accredited institution. Electronic applications accepted. Application fee is waived when completed online. *Faculty research:* Social media, international business and marketing.

Ottawa University, Graduate Studies-Arizona, Programs in Business, Ottawa, KS 66067-3399. Offers business administration (MBA); finance (MBA); human resources (MA, MBA); leadership (MBA); marketing (MBA). Programs offered in Mesa, Phoenix, Tempe and West Valley, AZ. *Program availability:* Part-time, evening/weekend, online learning. *Degree requirements:* For master's, thesis or alternative. *Entrance requirements:* For master's, minimum undergraduate GPA of 3.0. Additional exam requirements/recommendations for international students: Required—TOEFL (minimum score 550 paper-based). Electronic applications accepted.

Pace University, Lubin School of Business, Advanced Professional Certificate Program, New York, NY 10038. Offers business economics (APC); e-business (APC); financial management (APC); international business (APC); international economics (APC); investment management (APC); marketing (APC); public accounting (APC). *Program availability:* Part-time, evening/weekend. *Entrance requirements:* For degree, MBA or MS in business discipline, relevant professional experience. Additional exam requirements/recommendations for international students: Required—TOEFL (minimum score 90 iBT), IELTS (minimum score 7) or PTE (minimum score 61). *Application deadline:* For fall admission, 8/1 priority date for domestic students, 6/1 for international students; for spring admission, 12/1 for domestic students, 10/1 for international students. Applications are processed on a rolling basis. Application fee: $70. Electronic applications accepted. *Unit head:* Dr. Ibraiz Tarique, Chairperson, 212-618-6583, E-mail: itarique@pace.edu. *Application contact:* Susan Ford-Goldschein, Director of Graduate Admissions, 212-346-1531, Fax: 212-346-1585, E-mail: graduateadmission@pace.edu.
Website: http://www.pace.edu/lubin/agc

Pace University, Lubin School of Business, Doctor of Professional Studies Program, New York, NY 10038. Offers finance (DPS); management (DPS); marketing (DPS). *Program availability:* Part-time, blended/hybrid learning. *Students:* 9 full-time (3 women), 63 part-time (31 women); includes 20 minority (11 Black or African American, non-Hispanic/Latino; 4 Asian, non-Hispanic/Latino; 4 Hispanic/Latino; 1 Two or more races, non-Hispanic/Latino), 4 international. Average age 50. 29 applicants, 79% accepted, 12 enrolled. In 2018, 8 doctorates awarded. *Degree requirements:* For doctorate, thesis/dissertation, oral and written exam. *Entrance requirements:* For doctorate, MBA or similar master's degree, 10 years of experience in business, transcripts from all accredited colleges/universities attended, 4 letters of recommendation, interview. Additional exam requirements/recommendations for international students: Required—TOEFL (minimum score 90 iBT), IELTS (minimum score 7) or PTE (minimum score 61). *Application deadline:* For fall admission, 6/1 priority date for domestic students, 6/1 for international students. Applications are processed on a rolling basis. Application fee: $70. Electronic applications accepted. *Unit head:* Dr. Noushi Rahman, Director, Doctoral Program in Business, 212-618-6661, E-mail: nrahman@pace.edu. *Application contact:* Margaret Hanson, Program Coordinator for Doctoral Programs, 212-618-6660, E-mail: dps.bus@pace.edu.
Website: http://www.pace.edu/lubin/dps/

Pace University, Lubin School of Business, Marketing Program, New York, NY 10038. Offers customer intelligence & analytics (MS); marketing management (MBA); social media and mobile marketing (MS). *Program availability:* Part-time, evening/weekend. *Students:* 72 full-time (52 women), 32 part-time (25 women); includes 13 minority (2 Black or African American, non-Hispanic/Latino; 5 Asian, non-Hispanic/Latino; 5 Hispanic/Latino; 1 Two or more races, non-Hispanic/Latino), 60 international. Average age 26. 176 applicants, 70% accepted, 50 enrolled. In 2018, 25 master's awarded. *Entrance requirements:* For master's, GMAT, GRE, undergraduate degree, transcripts from all accredited colleges/universities attended, 2 letters of recommendation, resume, personal statement. For 1 year fast track MBA in Marketing Management, must have a cumulative GPA of 3.30 or above, a grade of B or better for all business core courses from an AACSB-accredited U.S. business school. Additional exam requirements/recommendations for international students: Required—TOEFL (minimum score 90 iBT), IELTS (minimum score 7) or PTE (minimum score 61). *Application deadline:* For fall admission, 8/1 priority date for domestic students, 6/1 for international students; for spring admission, 12/1 for domestic students, 10/1 for international students. Applications are processed on a rolling basis. Application fee: $70. Electronic applications accepted. *Financial support:* Research assistantships, career-related internships or fieldwork, Federal Work-Study, and unspecified assistantships available. Support available to part-time students. Financial award application deadline: 2/15; financial award applicants required to submit FAFSA. *Unit head:* Dr. Pradeep Gopalakrishna, Chairperson, Marketing Department, 212-618-6456, E-mail: pgopalakrishna@pace.edu. *Application contact:* Susan Ford-Goldschein, Director of Graduate Admissions, 212-346-1531, Fax: 212-346-1585, E-mail: graduateadmission@pace.edu.
Website: http://www.pace.edu/lubin/sections/explore-programs/graduate-programs

Polytechnic University of Puerto Rico, Miami Campus, Graduate School, Miami, FL 33166. Offers accounting (MBA); business administration (MBA); construction management (MEM); environmental management (MEM); finance (MBA); human resources management (MBA); logistics and supply chain management (MBA); management of international enterprises (MBA); manufacturing management (MEM); marketing management (MBA); project management (MBA). *Program availability:* Part-time, evening/weekend, online learning. *Entrance requirements:* For master's, minimum GPA of 3.0. Electronic applications accepted.

Pontifical Catholic University of Puerto Rico, College of Business Administration, Program in Marketing, Ponce, PR 00717-0777. Offers MBA. *Program availability:* Part-time, evening/weekend. *Degree requirements:* For master's, thesis. *Entrance requirements:* For master's, GRE, interview, minimum GPA of 2.75.

Pontificia Universidad Catolica Madre y Maestra, Graduate School, Faculty of Social and Administrative Sciences, Santiago, Dominican Republic. Offers business administration (MBA), including business development, finance, international business, management skills (M Mgmt, MBA), marketing, operations, strategic cost management, strategy, tourist destination planning and management; law (LL M), including civil law, corporate business law, criminal law, international relations, real estate law; management (M Mgmt), including higher financial management, insurance program administration, management skills (M Mgmt, MBA); psychology (MA), including clinical child and adolescent psychology, forensic psychology; strategic human resources (EMBA).

Post University, Program in Business Administration, Waterbury, CT 06723-2540. Offers accounting (MSA); business administration (MBA); corporate finance (MBA); corporate innovation (MBA); healthcare systems leadership (MBA); leadership (MBA); marketing (MBA); project management (MBA, MS). *Accreditation:* ACBSP. *Program availability:* Online learning. *Entrance requirements:* For master's, resume. *Expenses:* Tuition: Full-time $8300; part-time $570 per credit. *Required fees:* $140 per term. Tuition and fees vary according to course level, campus/location and program.

Providence College, School of Business, Providence, RI 02918. Offers accounting (MBA); finance (MBA); international business (MBA); management (MBA); marketing (MBA). *Accreditation:* AACSB. *Program availability:* Part-time, evening/weekend. *Entrance requirements:* For master's, GMAT. Additional exam requirements/recommendations for international students: Required—TOEFL (minimum score 577 paper-based; 90 iBT). *Expenses:* Contact institution.

Purdue University Global, School of Business, Davenport, IA 52807. Offers business administration (MBA); change leadership (MS); entrepreneurship (MBA); finance (MBA); health care management (MBA, MS); human resource (MBA); international business (MBA); management (MS); marketing (MBA); project management (MBA, MS); supply chain management and logistics (MBA, MS). *Accreditation:* ACBSP. *Program availability:* Part-time, evening/weekend, online learning. *Entrance requirements:* Additional exam requirements/recommendations for international students: Required—TOEFL (minimum score 550 paper-based; 80 iBT). Electronic applications accepted.

Queen's University at Kingston, Smith School of Business, Doctoral Program in Management, Kingston, ON K7L 3N6, Canada. Offers analytics (PhD); business economics (PhD); finance (PhD); management information systems (PhD); marketing (PhD); organizational behavior (PhD); strategy (PhD).

Queen's University at Kingston, Smith School of Business, Master of Science in Management Program, Kingston, ON K7L 3N6, Canada. Offers analytics (M Sc); business economics (M Sc); finance (M Sc); management information systems (M Sc); marketing (M Sc); organizational behavior (M Sc); strategy (M Sc).

Queen's University at Kingston, Smith School of Business, Program in Business Administration, Kingston, ON K7L 3N6, Canada. Offers consulting and project management (MBA); finance (MBA); innovation and entrepreneurship (MBA); marketing (MBA). *Degree requirements:* For master's, thesis optional, research project. *Entrance requirements:* For master's, GMAT, minimum B+ average. Additional exam requirements/recommendations for international students: Required—TOEFL. Electronic applications accepted. *Faculty research:* Management fundamentals, strategic thinking, global business, innovation and change, leadership.

Regent's University London, Webster Graduate School, London, United Kingdom. Offers business (MBA); finance (MS); human resources (MA); information technology management (MA); international business (MA); international non-governmental organizations (MA); international relations (MA); management and leadership (MA); marketing (MA). *Program availability:* Part-time.

Regent University, Graduate School, School of Business and Leadership, Virginia Beach, VA 23464-9800. Offers business administration (MBA), including accounting, economics, entrepreneurship, finance and investing, general management, healthcare management (MA, MBA), human resource management (MA, MBA), innovation management, leadership, marketing, not-for-profit management (MA, MBA); business analytics (MS); business and design management (MA); church leadership (MA); leadership (Certificate); organizational leadership (MA, PhD), including ecclesial leadership (DSL, PhD), entrepreneurial leadership (PhD), healthcare management (MA, MBA), human resource development (PhD), human resource management (MA, MBA), individualized studies (DSL, PhD), interdisciplinary studies (MA), leadership coaching and mentoring (MA), not-for-profit management (MA, MBA), organizational development consulting (MA), servant leadership (MA, DSL); strategic leadership (DSL), including ecclesial leadership (DSL, PhD), global consulting, healthcare leadership, individualized studies (DSL, PhD), leadership coaching, servant leadership (MA, DSL), strategic foresight. *Program availability:* Part-time, evening/weekend, 100% online, blended/hybrid learning. *Degree requirements:* For master's, thesis or alternative, 3-credit hour culminating experience; for doctorate, thesis/dissertation. *Entrance requirements:* For master's, college transcripts, resume, essay; for doctorate, college transcripts, resume, essay, writing sample; for Certificate, writing sample, resume, transcripts. Additional exam requirements/recommendations for international students: Required—TOEFL (minimum score 577 paper-based). Electronic applications accepted. *Expenses:* Contact institution. *Faculty research:* Servant leadership, global business, team effectiveness, technology utilization, leadership development.

Regis University, College of Business and Economics, Denver, CO 80221-1099. Offers accounting (MS); executive leadership (Certificate); finance (MS); finance and accounting (MBA); health industry leadership (MBA); human resource management and leadership (MSOL); management (MBA); marketing (MBA); nonprofit leadership (Post-Graduate Certificate); nonprofit management (MNM); nonprofit organizational capacity building (Certificate); operations management (MBA); organizational leadership and management (MSOL); project leadership and management (MS, MSOL); strategic business management (Certificate); strategic human resource integration (Certificate); strategic management (MBA). Programs offered at Colorado Springs Campus, Northwest Denver Campus, Southeast Denver Campus, Fort Collins Campus, Broomfield Campus, Henderson (Nevada) Campus, and Summerlin (Nevada) Campus. *Program availability:* Part-time, evening/weekend, 100% online, blended/hybrid learning. *Degree requirements:* For master's, thesis (for some programs), capstone or final research project. *Entrance requirements:* For master's, official transcript reflecting baccalaureate degree awarded from regionally-accredited college or university, interview, 2 years of full-time related work experience, resume, letters of recommendation. Additional exam requirements/recommendations for international students: Required—TOEFL (minimum score 550 paper-based; 82 iBT). Electronic applications accepted. *Expenses:* Contact institution. *Faculty research:* Impact of information technology on small business regulation of accounting, international project financing, mineral development, delivery of healthcare to rural indigenous communities.

Roberts Wesleyan College, Graduate Business Programs, Rochester, NY 14624-1997. Offers strategic leadership (MS); strategic marketing (MS). *Program availability:* Evening/weekend. *Degree requirements:* For master's, thesis or alternative. *Entrance requirements:* For master's, GMAT, minimum GPA of 2.75, verifiable work experience. *Expenses:* Contact institution.

Roosevelt University, Graduate Division, College of Arts and Sciences, Department of Communication, Chicago, IL 60605. Offers integrated marketing communications (MSIMC). *Program availability:* Part-time, evening/weekend. Electronic applications accepted.

Rowan University, Graduate School, College of Communication and Creative Arts, Integrated Marketing Communication and New Media Certificate of Graduate Study Program, Glassboro, NJ 08028-1701. Offers CGS. Electronic applications accepted.

Rutgers University–Newark, Graduate School, Program in Management, Newark, NJ 07102. Offers accounting (PhD); accounting information systems (PhD); computer information systems (PhD); finance (PhD); information technology (PhD); international business (PhD); management science (PhD); marketing (PhD); organization management (PhD). Program offered jointly with New Jersey Institute of Technology. *Accreditation:* AACSB. *Degree requirements:* For doctorate, thesis/dissertation,

cumulative exams. *Entrance requirements:* For doctorate, GMAT or GRE General Test, minimum undergraduate B average. Additional exam requirements/recommendations for international students: Required—TOEFL. Electronic applications accepted. *Faculty research:* Technology management, leadership and teams, consumer behavior, financial and markets, logistics.

Rutgers University–Newark, Rutgers Business School–Newark and New Brunswick, Doctoral Programs in Management, Newark, NJ 07102. Offers accounting (PhD); accounting information systems (PhD); economics (PhD); finance (PhD); individualized study (PhD); information technology (PhD); international business (PhD); management science (PhD); marketing science (PhD); organizational management (PhD); science, technology and management (PhD); supply chain management (PhD). *Degree requirements:* For doctorate, comprehensive exam, thesis/dissertation. *Entrance requirements:* For doctorate, GRE or GMAT. Additional exam requirements/recommendations for international students: Required—TOEFL (minimum score 550 paper-based; 79 iBT). Electronic applications accepted.

Sacred Heart University, Graduate Programs, Jack Welch College of Business, Department of Marketing, Fairfield, CT 06825. Offers digital marketing (MS); marketing (MBA, Graduate Certificate). *Program availability:* Part-time, evening/weekend. *Degree requirements:* For master's, capstone project. *Entrance requirements:* For master's, GMAT, bachelor's degree from accredited institution with minimum GPA of 3.0. Additional exam requirements/recommendations for international students: Required—TOEFL (minimum score 570 paper-based, 80 iBT), TWE, or IELTS (6.5); Recommended—TSE. Electronic applications accepted. *Expenses:* Contact institution.

St. Bonaventure University, School of Graduate School, Jandoli School of Communication, Program in Integrated Marketing Communications, St. Bonaventure, NY 14778-2284. Offers MA. *Program availability:* Part-time, evening/weekend, online only, 100% online. *Faculty:* 4 full-time (3 women), 4 part-time/adjunct (2 women). *Students:* 15 full-time (8 women), 37 part-time (26 women); includes 10 minority (4 Black or African American, non-Hispanic/Latino; 6 Hispanic/Latino). Average age 27. 20 applicants, 100% accepted, 14 enrolled. In 2018, 27 master's awarded. *Degree requirements:* For master's, campaign project. *Entrance requirements:* For master's, official transcripts, personal statement describing desire to pursue the IMC program. Additional exam requirements/recommendations for international students: Required—TOEFL (minimum score 550 paper-based; 79 iBT). *Application deadline:* For fall admission, 3/15 for domestic students, 2/1 for international students; for spring admission, 10/15 for domestic students, 7/1 for international students. Applications are processed on a rolling basis. Application fee: $0. Electronic applications accepted. *Expenses:* Contact institution. *Financial support:* In 2018–19, 8 students received support. Scholarships/grants, health care benefits, and unspecified assistantships available. Support available to part-time students. Financial award application deadline: 4/15; financial award applicants required to submit FAFSA. *Faculty research:* Advancing women in leadership, professional wellness. *Unit head:* Heather Harris, Director, 716-375-2075, Fax: 716-375-2588, E-mail: hharris@sbu.edu. *Application contact:* Matthew Retchless, Director of Graduate Admissions, 716-375-2021, Fax: 716-375-4015, E-mail: gradsch@sbu.edu.
Website: http://www.sbu.edu/academics/schools/journalism-and-mass-communications/graduate-degrees/ma-integrated-marketing-communications

St. Catherine University, Graduate Programs, Program in Business Administration, St. Paul, MN 55105. Offers healthcare (MBA); integrated marketing communications (MBA); management (MBA). *Program availability:* Part-time, evening/weekend. *Entrance requirements:* For master's, GMAT (if undergraduate GPA is less than 3.0), 2+ years' work or volunteer experience in professional setting(s). Additional exam requirements/recommendations for international students: Required—TOEFL. *Expenses:* Contact institution.

St. John's University, The Peter J. Tobin College of Business, Department of Marketing, Queens, NY 11439. Offers business administration (MBA), including marketing management. *Entrance requirements:* For master's, GMAT or GRE, 2 letters of recommendation, essay, resume, unofficial transcripts. Additional exam requirements/recommendations for international students: Required—TOEFL (minimum score 80 iBT), IELTS (minimum score 6.5). Electronic applications accepted. *Expenses:* Contact institution.

Saint Joseph's University, Erivan K. Haub School of Business, Graduate Food Marketing Program, Philadelphia, PA 19131-1395. Offers MBA, MS. *Program availability:* Part-time, evening/weekend, online learning. *Degree requirements:* For master's, minimum GPA of 3.0. *Entrance requirements:* For master's, 4 years of industry experience, interview or GMAT/GRE, letter of recommendation, resume, official transcripts, personal statement. Additional exam requirements/recommendations for international students: Required—TOEFL, IELTS or PTE. Electronic applications accepted. *Expenses:* Contact institution.

Saint Joseph's University, Erivan K. Haub School of Business, MBA Program, Philadelphia, PA 19131-1395. Offers accounting (MBA); business intelligence analytics (MBA); finance (MBA); financial analysis reporting (Postbaccalaureate Certificate); general business (MBA); health and medical services administration (MBA); international business (MBA); international marketing (MBA); leading (MBA); marketing (MBA); DO/MBA. DO/MBA offered jointly with Philadelphia College of Osteopathic Medicine. *Program availability:* Part-time-only, evening/weekend, 100% online. *Degree requirements:* For master's, minimum GPA of 3.0. *Entrance requirements:* For master's, GMAT or GRE, 2 letters of recommendation, resume, personal statement, official undergraduate and graduate transcripts. Additional exam requirements/recommendations for international students: Required—PTE, TOEFL, IELTS, or PTE. Electronic applications accepted. *Expenses:* Contact institution.

Saint Joseph's University, Erivan K. Haub School of Business, MS Program in Marketing, Philadelphia, PA 19131-1395. Offers customer analytics and insights (MS); international marketing (MS). *Program availability:* Part-time, evening/weekend, 100% online. *Degree requirements:* For master's, minimum GPA of 3.0. *Entrance requirements:* For master's, GMAT or GRE, 2 letters of recommendation, resume, personal statement, official undergraduate and graduate transcripts. Additional exam requirements/recommendations for international students: Required—PTE, TOEFL, IELTS, or PTE. Electronic applications accepted.

Saint Joseph's University, Erivan K. Haub School of Business, Pharmaceutical and Healthcare Marketing MBA Program, Philadelphia, PA 19131-1395. Offers MBA, Post Master's Certificate. *Program availability:* Part-time, evening/weekend, 100% online. *Degree requirements:* For master's, minimum GPA of 3.0. *Entrance requirements:* For master's, 4 years of industry experience, letter of recommendation, resume, interview, official transcripts; for Post Master's Certificate, MBA, 4 years of industry experience, resume. Additional exam requirements/recommendations for international students: Required—PTE, TOEFL, IELTS, or PTE. Electronic applications accepted. *Expenses:* Contact institution.

Saint Leo University, Graduate Studies in Business, Saint Leo, FL 33574-6665. Offers accounting (M Acc); cybersecurity management (MBA); health care management (MBA); human resource management (MBA); marketing (MBA); marketing research and social media analytics (MBA); software engineering (MS). *Accreditation:* ACBSP. *Program availability:* Part-time, evening/weekend, 100% online, blended/hybrid learning. *Faculty:* 51 full-time (16 women), 54 part-time/adjunct (22 women). *Students:* 8 full-time (3 women), 2,209 part-time (1,288 women); includes 1,046 minority (691 Black or African American, non-Hispanic/Latino; 10 American Indian or Alaska Native, non-Hispanic/Latino; 47 Asian, non-Hispanic/Latino; 249 Hispanic/Latino; 5 Native Hawaiian or other Pacific Islander, non-Hispanic/Latino; 44 Two or more races, non-Hispanic/Latino), 71 international. Average age 37. 760 applicants, 83% accepted, 498 enrolled. In 2018, 763 master's, 14 doctorates awarded. *Degree requirements:* For doctorate, comprehensive exam, thesis/dissertation. *Entrance requirements:* For master's, GMAT with minimum score 500 (for M Acc), official transcripts, current resume, 2 professional recommendations, personal statement, bachelor's degree from regionally-accredited university; undergraduate degree in accounting and minimum undergraduate GPA of 3.0 (for M Acc); minimum undergraduate GPA of 3.0 in final 2 years of undergraduate study and 2 years' work experience (for MBA); for doctorate, GMAT (minimum score of 550) if master's GPA is under 3.25, official transcripts, current resume, 2 professional recommendations, personal statement, master's degree from regionally-accredited university with minimum GPA of 3.25, 3 years' work experience, interview. Additional exam requirements/recommendations for international students: Required—TOEFL (minimum score 550 paper-based; 78 iBT). *Application deadline:* For fall admission, 7/1 priority date for domestic and international students; for spring admission, 11/12 priority date for domestic students, 11/1 for international students. Applications are processed on a rolling basis. Application fee: $80. Electronic applications accepted. *Expenses:* Onground Master of Accounting $555 per credit, Online Master of Accounting $720 per credit, Onground MBA $555 per credit, Onground MBA Intl/Experiential $720 per credit, Online MBA/Cybersecurity military rate $555 per credit, Online MBA civilian rate $720, MS Cybersecurity civilian rate $770, DBA $900 per credit. *Financial support:* In 2018–19, 213 students received support. Scholarships/grants, unspecified assistantships, and tuition remission for Saint Leo employees and their dependents available. Financial award application deadline: 3/1; financial award applicants required to submit FAFSA. *Faculty research:* Servant leadership, work/life balance, emotional intelligence, pricing, marketing. *Unit head:* Dr. Robyn Parker, Dean, School of Business, 352-588-8599, Fax: 352-588-8912, E-mail: mbaslu@saintleo.edu. *Application contact:* Mark Russum, Assistant Vice President, Enrollment, 800-707-8846, Fax: 352-588-7873, E-mail: grad.admissions@saintleo.edu.
Website: https://www.saintleo.edu/college-of-business

Saint Peter's University, Graduate Business Programs, MBA Program, Jersey City, NJ 07306-5997. Offers finance (MBA); health care administration (MBA); human resource management (MBA); international business (MBA); management (MBA); management information systems (MBA); marketing (MBA); risk management (MBA); MBA/MS. *Program availability:* Part-time, evening/weekend. *Entrance requirements:* Additional exam requirements/recommendations for international students: Required—TOEFL. Electronic applications accepted. *Faculty research:* Finance, health care management, human resource management, international business, management, management information systems, marketing, risk management.

St. Thomas Aquinas College, Division of Business Administration, Sparkill, NY 10976. Offers business administration (MBA); finance (MBA); management (MBA); marketing (MBA). *Program availability:* Part-time, evening/weekend. *Entrance requirements:* For master's, GMAT. Additional exam requirements/recommendations for international students: Required—TOEFL. Electronic applications accepted.

Saint Xavier University, Graduate Studies, Graham School of Management, Chicago, IL 60655-3105. Offers employee health benefits (Certificate); finance (MBA); financial fraud examination and management (MBA, Certificate); financial planning (MBA, Certificate); generalist/individualized (MBA); health administration (MBA); managed care (Certificate); management (MBA); marketing (MBA); project management (MBA, Certificate); MBA/MS. *Accreditation:* AACSB. *Program availability:* Part-time, evening/weekend. *Entrance requirements:* For master's, GMAT, minimum GPA of 3.0, 2 years of work experience. Electronic applications accepted. *Expenses:* Contact institution.

Samford University, Brock School of Business, Birmingham, AL 35229. Offers accountancy (M Acc); entrepreneurship (MBA); finance (MBA); marketing (MBA); JD/M Acc; JD/MBA; MBA/M Acc; MBA/M Div; MBA/MSEM; MBA/Pharm D. Programs offered jointly with Cumberland School of Law, Beeson School of Divinity, Howard College of Arts and Sciences, and McWhorter School of Pharmacy. *Accreditation:* AACSB. *Program availability:* Part-time, 100% online, blended/hybrid learning. *Faculty:* 7 full-time (1 woman), 4 part-time/adjunct (0 women). *Students:* 76 full-time (30 women), 20 part-time (11 women); includes 8 minority (4 Black or African American, non-Hispanic/Latino; 1 Asian, non-Hispanic/Latino; 1 Hispanic/Latino; 2 Two or more races, non-Hispanic/Latino), 7 international. Average age 28. 41 applicants, 88% accepted, 26 enrolled. In 2018, 74 master's awarded. *Degree requirements:* For master's, capstone course. *Entrance requirements:* For master's, GMAT or GRE, resume, transcripts, WES or ECE Evaluation (international applicants only), essay (international applicants only). Additional exam requirements/recommendations for international students: Required—TOEFL (minimum score 90 iBT), IELTS (minimum score 6.5). *Application deadline:* For fall admission, 8/1 for domestic and international students; for spring admission, 1/1 for domestic and international students. Applications are processed on a rolling basis. Application fee: $35. Electronic applications accepted. Application fee is waived when completed online. *Expenses: Tuition:* Full-time $17,255; part-time $837 per credit. *Required fees:* $610; $305 per term. Tuition and fees vary according to course load, degree level, program and student level. *Financial support:* In 2018–19, 46 students received support. Scholarships/grants available. Financial award application deadline: 2/15; financial award applicants required to submit FAFSA. *Unit head:* Dr. Barbara Cartledge, Assistant Dean, 205-726-2935, Fax: 205-726-2540, E-mail: bhcartle@samford.edu. *Application contact:* Elizabeth Gambrell, Associate Director, 205-726-2040, Fax: 205-726-2540, E-mail: eagambre@samford.edu.
Website: http://www.samford.edu/business

San Diego State University, Graduate and Research Affairs, Fowler College of Business, Department of Marketing, San Diego, CA 92182. Offers MS. *Program availability:* Part-time, evening/weekend. *Degree requirements:* For master's, thesis or alternative. *Entrance requirements:* For master's, GMAT, resume, letters of reference. Additional exam requirements/recommendations for international students: Required—TOEFL. Electronic applications accepted.

San Francisco State University, Division of Graduate Studies, College of Business, Program in Business Administration, San Francisco, CA 94132-1722. Offers decision sciences/operations research (MBA); ethics and compliance (MBA); finance (MBA); global business and innovation (MBA); healthcare administration (MBA); hospitality and tourism management (MBA); information systems (MBA); leadership (MBA); marketing (MBA); nonprofit and social enterprise leadership (MBA); sustainable business (MBA). *Accreditation:* AACSB. *Program availability:* Part-time, evening/weekend. *Degree requirements:* For master's, thesis, essay test. *Entrance requirements:* For master's, GMAT, minimum GPA of 2.7 in last 60 units. Additional exam requirements/recommendations for international students: Required—TOEFL (minimum score 550 paper-based).

San Ignacio University, Graduate Programs, Doral, FL 33178. Offers business administration (MBA), including human resources management, international business,

marketing management; education (M Ed), including early childhood education, educational leadership, special education; hospitality management (MA), including gastronomy and restaurant management, tourism management.

Seton Hall University, Stillman School of Business, Programs in Business Administration, South Orange, NJ 07079-2697. Offers accounting (MBA); entrepreneurial studies (Certificate); finance (MBA); financial decision making (Certificate); information technology management (MBA); international business (MBA); management (MBA); marketing (MBA); sport management (MBA); supply chain management (MBA, Certificate). *Program availability:* Part-time, evening/weekend. *Faculty:* 27 full-time (5 women), 18 part-time/adjunct (2 women). *Students:* 85 full-time (40 women), 363 part-time (147 women); includes 78 minority (22 Black or African American, non-Hispanic/Latino; 4 Asian, non-Hispanic/Latino; 18 Hispanic/Latino; 29 Native Hawaiian or other Pacific Islander, non-Hispanic/Latino; 5 Two or more races, non-Hispanic/Latino), 282 international. Average age 34. 483 applicants, 85% accepted, 302 enrolled. In 2018, 96 master's awarded. *Degree requirements:* For master's, 20 hours of community service (Social Responsibility Project). *Entrance requirements:* For master's, GMAT or CPA, GRE (waived based on work experience or advanced degree from AACSB institution), MS in business discipline, professional degree or designation (MD, JD, PhD, DVM, DDS, CPA, etc.), minimum undergraduate GPA of 3.0. Additional exam requirements/recommendations for international students: Required—TOEFL (minimum score 607 paper-based; 80 iBT), IELTS (minimum score 6), PTE. *Application deadline:* For fall admission, 5/31 priority date for domestic students, 4/30 priority date for international students; for spring admission, 10/31 priority date for domestic students, 9/30 priority date for international students; for summer admission, 3/31 priority date for domestic students. Applications are processed on a rolling basis. Application fee: $75. Electronic applications accepted. Application fee is waived when completed online. *Expenses:* Tuition is $1,305 per credit hour and the overall MBA is a 40 credit hour program. University fees are $115 per semester. The university also has a technology that is $125 per semester. *Financial support:* In 2018–19, 44 students received support, including 25 research assistantships with partial tuition reimbursements available (averaging $3,644 per year); career-related internships or fieldwork, scholarships/grants, and unspecified assistantships also available. Financial award application deadline: 6/30; financial award applicants required to submit FAFSA. *Faculty research:* Sport, hedge funds, executive compensation, social media, legal studies. *Unit head:* Dr. Joyce Strawser, Dean, 973-761-9013, Fax: 973-761-9217, E-mail: joyce.strawser@shu.edu. *Application contact:* Alfred Ayoub, Director of Graduate Admissions, 973-761-9262, Fax: 973-761-9208, E-mail: alfred.ayoub@shu.edu.
Website: http://www.shu.edu/business/mba-programs.cfm

Slippery Rock University of Pennsylvania, Graduate Studies (Recruitment), College of Business, School of Business, Slippery Rock, PA 16057-1383. Offers accounting/finance (MBA); general (MBA); marketing/management (MBA). *Program availability:* Part-time, evening/weekend. *Faculty:* 12 full-time (7 women), 1 part-time/adjunct (0 women). *Students:* 21 full-time (8 women), 22 part-time (15 women); includes 3 minority (1 Black or African American, non-Hispanic/Latino; 1 Asian, non-Hispanic/Latino; 1 Hispanic/Latino). Average age 29. 53 applicants, 62% accepted, 23 enrolled. In 2018, 23 master's awarded. *Degree requirements:* For master's, comprehensive exam (for some programs), thesis (for some programs). *Entrance requirements:* For master's, minimum cumulative GPA of 3.0, official transcripts, three references. Additional exam requirements/recommendations for international students: Required—TOEFL (minimum score 550 paper-based; 80 iBT). *Application deadline:* For fall admission, 3/1 priority date for domestic students, 5/1 priority date for international students; for spring admission, 10/1 priority date for domestic students, 9/1 priority date for international students. Applications are processed on a rolling basis. Application fee: $25 ($30 for international students). Electronic applications accepted. *Expenses:* Contact institution. *Financial support:* In 2018–19, 9 students received support. Career-related internships or fieldwork, Federal Work-Study, institutionally sponsored loans, scholarships/grants, tuition waivers (partial), and unspecified assistantships available. Support available to part-time students. Financial award application deadline: 5/1; financial award applicants required to submit FAFSA. *Unit head:* Dr. Larry McCarthy, Graduate Coordinator, 724-738-2552, Fax: 724-738-2959, E-mail: larry.mccarthy@sru.edu. *Application contact:* Brandi Weber-Mortimer, Director of Graduate Admissions, 724-738-2051, Fax: 724-738-2146, E-mail: graduate.admissions@sru.edu.
Website: http://www.sru.edu/academics/graduate-programs/mba-master-of-business-administration

Southeastern Louisiana University, College of Arts, Humanities and Social Sciences, Department of Communication and Media Studies, Hammond, LA 70402. Offers health communications (MA); journalism (MA); marketing (MA); public relations (MA); sociology (MA). *Program availability:* Part-time, evening/weekend. *Faculty:* 8 full-time (6 women). *Students:* 3 full-time (2 women), 15 part-time (11 women); includes 9 minority (6 Black or African American, non-Hispanic/Latino; 2 Hispanic/Latino; 1 Two or more races, non-Hispanic/Latino). Average age 30. 12 applicants, 75% accepted, 4 enrolled. In 2018, 6 master's awarded. *Degree requirements:* For master's, comprehensive exam. *Entrance requirements:* For master's, GRE (minimum score 148 on Verbal section, 3.5 Written). Additional exam requirements/recommendations for international students: Required—TOEFL (minimum score 525 paper-based; 75 iBT). *Application deadline:* For fall admission, 7/15 priority date for domestic students, 6/1 priority date for international students; for spring admission, 12/1 priority date for domestic students, 10/1 priority date for international students. Applications are processed on a rolling basis. Application fee: $20 ($30 for international students). Electronic applications accepted. *Expenses: Tuition, area resident:* Full-time $6684. Tuition, state resident: full-time $6684. Tuition, nonresident: full-time $19,162. *Required fees:* $2097. *Financial support:* In 2018–19, 13 students received support, including 4 research assistantships with tuition reimbursements available (averaging $8,963 per year); career-related internships or fieldwork, Federal Work-Study, institutionally sponsored loans, scholarships/grants, traineeships, health care benefits, tuition waivers (full), and unspecified assistantships also available. Financial award application deadline: 5/1; financial award applicants required to submit FAFSA. *Faculty research:* Communicate with the millennial generation to enhance organizational effectiveness, conflict resolution and mediation among nations, journalism history, media law, media writing, media convergence, external compliances accreditation and strategic planning. *Unit head:* Dr. James O'Connor, Department Head, 985-549-5310, Fax: 985-549-3088, E-mail: james.oconnor@selu.edu. *Application contact:* Office of Admissions, 985-549-5637, Fax: 985-549-5632, E-mail: admissions@southeastern.edu.
Website: http://www.southeastern.edu/acad_research/depts/comm/index.html

Southern Adventist University, School of Business, Collegedale, TN 37315-0370. Offers accounting (MBA); computer information systems (MBA); finance (MBA); healthcare administration (MBA); management (MBA). *Program availability:* Part-time, evening/weekend, 100% online. *Faculty:* 7 full-time (2 women). *Students:* 23 applicants, 48% accepted, 8 enrolled. In 2018, 8 master's awarded. *Entrance requirements:* For master's, GMAT, minimum cumulative undergraduate GPA of 3.0. Additional exam requirements/recommendations for international students: Required—TOEFL (minimum score 100 iBT). *Application deadline:* For fall admission, 7/1 for domestic students, 5/1 for international students; for winter admission, 11/1 for domestic students, 9/1 for international students; for summer admission, 4/1 for domestic students, 2/1 for international students. Applications are processed on a rolling basis. Application fee: $40. Electronic applications accepted. *Financial support:* Scholarships/grants and unspecified assistantships available. Financial award application deadline: 9/1; financial award applicants required to submit FAFSA. *Unit head:* Dr. Stephanie Sheehan, Dean, 423-236-2659, Fax: 423-236-1527, E-mail: ssheehan@southern.edu. *Application contact:* Teshia Price, Graduate Studies Coordinator, 423-236-2751, Fax: 423-236-1527, E-mail: tprice@southern.edu.
Website: https://www.southern.edu/academics/business.html

Southern Methodist University, Cox School of Business, MBA Program, Dallas, TX 75275. Offers accounting (MBA, PMBA); business (EMBA); business analytics (PMBA); finance (MBA, PMBA); information technology and operations management (MBA, PMBA), including business analytics (MBA), information and operations (MBA); management (MBA, PMBA); marketing (MBA, PMBA); real estate (MBA, PMBA); strategy and entrepreneurship (MBA, PMBA); JD/MBA; MA/MBA. *Program availability:* Part-time, evening/weekend. *Entrance requirements:* For master's, GMAT. Additional exam requirements/recommendations for international students: Required—TOEFL. Electronic applications accepted. *Expenses:* Contact institution. *Faculty research:* Corporate finance, financial reporting, modeling consumer decision-making, competition between national brands and store brands, institutional determinants of firms' strategy.

Southern New Hampshire University, School of Business, Manchester, NH 03106-1045. Offers accounting (MBA, Graduate Certificate); accounting finance (MS); accounting/auditing (MS); accounting/forensic accounting (MS); accounting/management accounting (MS); accounting/taxation (MS); applied economics (MS); athletic administration (MBA, Graduate Certificate); business administration (IMBA, Certificate), including business information systems (Certificate), human resource management (Certificate); business analytics (MBA); business intelligence (MBA); communication (MA), including new media and marketing, public relations; community economic development (MBA); criminal justice (MBA); data analytics (MS); economics (MBA); engineering management (MBA); entrepreneurship (MBA); finance (MBA, MS, Graduate Certificate); finance/corporate finance (MS); finance/investments (MS); forensic accounting (MBA); forensic accounting and fraud examination (Graduate Certificate); healthcare informatics (MBA); healthcare management (MBA); human resource management (MS); human resources (MBA); information technology (MS); information technology management (MBA); international business (PhD); Internet marketing (MBA); leadership (MBA); leadership of nonprofit organizations (Graduate Certificate); management (MS); marketing (MBA, MS, Graduate Certificate); music business (MBA); operations and project management (MS); operations and supply chain management (MBA, Graduate Certificate); organizational leadership (MS); project management (MBA, Graduate Certificate); public administration (MBA, Graduate Certificate); quantitative analysis (MBA); Six Sigma (Graduate Certificate); Six Sigma quality (MBA); social media marketing (MBA, Graduate Certificate); sport management (MBA, MS, Graduate Certificate); sustainability and environmental compliance (MBA); MBA/Certificate. *Accreditation:* ACBSP. *Program availability:* Part-time, evening/weekend, online learning. Terminal master's awarded for partial completion of doctoral program. *Degree requirements:* For master's, one foreign language, comprehensive exam (for some programs), thesis or alternative; for doctorate, one foreign language, comprehensive exam, thesis/dissertation. *Entrance requirements:* For master's, minimum GPA of 2.5; for doctorate, GMAT. Additional exam requirements/recommendations for international students: Required—TOEFL (minimum score 500 paper-based). Electronic applications accepted.

Southwest Minnesota State University, Department of Business and Public Affairs, Marshall, MN 56258. Offers leadership (MBA); management (MBA); marketing (MBA). *Program availability:* Part-time, evening/weekend, online learning. *Degree requirements:* For master's, thesis. *Entrance requirements:* For master's, GMAT (minimum score: 450). Additional exam requirements/recommendations for international students: Recommended—TOEFL (minimum score 550 paper-based; 79 iBT), IELTS. Electronic applications accepted.

State University of New York Polytechnic Institute, MBA Program in Technology Management, Utica, NY 13502. Offers accounting and finance (MBA); business management (MBA); health informatics (MBA); human resource management (MBA); marketing management (MBA). *Program availability:* Part-time, 100% online. *Students:* 29 full-time (13 women), 85 part-time (41 women); includes 18 minority (4 Black or African American, non-Hispanic/Latino; 8 Asian, non-Hispanic/Latino; 6 Hispanic/Latino). Average age 32. 54 applicants, 54% accepted, 26 enrolled. In 2018, 29 master's awarded. *Degree requirements:* For master's, comprehensive exam, capstone project. *Entrance requirements:* For master's, GMAT or approved GMAT waiver, resume, letter of reference. Additional exam requirements/recommendations for international students: Required—TOEFL (minimum score 79 iBT), IELTS (minimum score 6.5), PTE (minimum score 53), TOEFL, IELTS, or PTE; GMAT or approved GMAT waiver. *Application deadline:* For fall admission, 7/1 priority date for domestic students, 7/1 for international students; for spring admission, 12/1 for domestic students, 11/1 for international students. Applications are processed on a rolling basis. Application fee: $60. Electronic applications accepted. *Expenses:* Contact institution. *Financial support:* Fellowships, research assistantships, and unspecified assistantships available. Financial award application deadline: 6/1; financial award applicants required to submit FAFSA. *Faculty research:* Entrepreneurial capacity development. *Unit head:* Dr. Rafael Romero, Coordinator, 315-792-7207, E-mail: rafael.romero@sunypoly.edu. *Application contact:* Alicia Foster, Director of Graduate Admissions, 315-792-7347, E-mail: fostera3@sunypoly.edu.
Website: https://sunypoly.edu/academics/majors-and-programs/technology-management.html

Stephen F. Austin State University, Graduate School, Nelson Rusche College of Business, Program in Business Administration, Nacogdoches, TX 75962. Offers business (MBA); management and marketing (MBA). *Accreditation:* AACSB. *Program availability:* Part-time, evening/weekend. *Degree requirements:* For master's, comprehensive exam. *Entrance requirements:* For master's, GMAT, minimum AACSB index of 1000. Additional exam requirements/recommendations for international students: Required—TOEFL (minimum score 550 paper-based). *Faculty research:* Strategic implications, information search, multinational firms, philosophical guidance.

Stevens Institute of Technology, Graduate School, School of Business, Program in Business Administration, Hoboken, NJ 07030. Offers business intelligence and analytics (MBA); engineering management (MBA); finance (MBA); information systems (MBA); innovation and entrepreneurship (MBA); marketing (MBA); pharmaceutical management (MBA); project management (MBA, Certificate); technology management (MBA); telecommunications management (MBA). *Accreditation:* AACSB. *Program availability:* Part-time, evening/weekend. *Faculty:* 58 full-time (8 women), 18 part-time/adjunct (3 women). *Students:* 44 full-time (23 women), 202 part-time (90 women); includes 56 minority (12 Black or African American, non-Hispanic/Latino; 2 American Indian or Alaska Native, non-Hispanic/Latino; 40 Asian, non-Hispanic/Latino; 2 Hispanic/Latino), 28 international. Average age 37. In 2018, 45 master's awarded. Terminal master's awarded for partial completion of doctoral program. *Degree requirements:* For master's, thesis optional, minimum B average in major field and overall; for Certificate, minimum B average. *Entrance requirements:* For master's, GRE/GMAT scores: GRE scores are

required for all applicants applying to a full-time graduate program in the Schaefer School of Engineering and Science (SES). International applicants must submit TOEFL/IELTS scores and fulfill the English Language Proficiency Requirements in order to be considered. Additional exam requirements/recommendations for international students: Required—TOEFL (minimum score 74 iBT), IELTS (minimum score 6). *Application deadline:* For fall admission, 4/1 for domestic and international students; for spring admission, 11/1 for domestic and international students; for summer admission, 5/1 for domestic students. Applications are processed on a rolling basis. Application fee: $60. Electronic applications accepted. *Expenses: Tuition:* Full-time $35,960; part-time $1620 per credit. *Required fees:* $1290; $600 per semester. Tuition and fees vary according to course load. *Financial support:* Fellowships, research assistantships, teaching assistantships, career-related internships or fieldwork, Federal Work-Study, scholarships/grants, and unspecified assistantships available. Financial award application deadline: 2/15; financial award applicants required to submit FAFSA. *Unit head:* Dr. Gregory Prastacos, Dean, 201-216-8366, E-mail: gprastac@stevens.edu. *Application contact:* Graduate Admissions, 888-783-8367, Fax: 888-511-1306, E-mail: graduate@stevens.edu.
Website: https://www.stevens.edu/school-business/masters-programs/mbaemba

Stony Brook University, State University of New York, Graduate School, College of Business, Program in Business Administration, Stony Brook, NY 11794. Offers accounting (MBA); business administration (MBA); finance (MBA, Certificate); health care management (MBA); human resources (MBA); innovation (MBA); management (MBA); marketing (MBA); operations management (MBA). *Faculty:* 38 full-time (13 women), 8 part-time/adjunct (3 women). *Students:* 153 full-time (74 women), 148 part-time (76 women); includes 76 minority (16 Black or African American, non-Hispanic/Latino; 29 Asian, non-Hispanic/Latino; 27 Hispanic/Latino; 4 Two or more races, non-Hispanic/Latino), 36 international. Average age 28. 128 applicants, 78% accepted, 75 enrolled. In 2018, 76 master's awarded. *Entrance requirements:* For master's, GMAT, 3 letters of recommendation from current or former employers or professors, transcripts, personal statement, resume. Additional exam requirements/recommendations for international students: Required—TOEFL (minimum score 550 paper-based; 80 iBT), IELTS (minimum score 6.5). *Application deadline:* For fall admission, 5/15 for domestic students, 3/15 for international students; for spring admission, 12/1 for domestic students, 10/15 for international students. Application fee: $100. *Expenses:* Contact institution. *Financial support:* Teaching assistantships available. *Total annual research expenditures:* $2,070. *Unit head:* Dr. Manuel London, Dean, 631-632-7159, E-mail: manuel.london@stonybrook.edu. *Application contact:* Dr. Dmytro Holod, Associate Dean for Academic Programs/Graduate Director, 631-632-7183, Fax: 631-632-8181, E-mail: dmytro.holod@stonybrook.edu.
Website: https://www.stonybrook.edu/commcms/business/

Strayer University, Graduate Studies, Washington, DC 20005-2603. Offers accounting (MS); acquisition (MBA); business administration (MBA); communications technology (MS); educational management (M Ed); finance (MBA); health services administration (MHSA); hospitality and tourism management (MBA); human resource management (MBA); information systems (MS), including computer security management, decision support system management, enterprise resource management, network management, software engineering management, systems development management; management (MBA); management information systems (MS); marketing (MBA); professional accounting (MS), including accounting information systems, controllership, taxation; public administration (MPA); supply chain management (MBA); technology in education (M Ed). Programs also offered at campus locations in Birmingham, AL; Chamblee, GA; Cobb County, GA; Morrow, GA; White Marsh, MD; Charleston, SC; Columbia, SC; Greensboro, NC; Greenville, SC; Lexington, KY; Louisville, KY; Nashville, TN; North Raleigh, NC; Washington, DC. *Accreditation:* ACBSP. *Program availability:* Part-time, evening/weekend, online learning. *Degree requirements:* For master's, thesis. *Entrance requirements:* For master's, GMAT, GRE General Test, bachelor's degree from an accredited college or university, minimum undergraduate GPA of 2.75. Electronic applications accepted.

Suffolk University, College of Arts and Sciences, Advertising and Public Relations Department, Boston, MA 02108-2770. Offers communication studies (MAC); integrated marketing communication (MAC); public relations and advertising (MAC). *Program availability:* Part-time, evening/weekend. *Faculty:* 9 full-time (8 women). *Students:* 19 full-time (16 women), 9 part-time (6 women); includes 5 minority (1 Black or African American, non-Hispanic/Latino; 1 Asian, non-Hispanic/Latino; 2 Hispanic/Latino; 1 Two or more races, non-Hispanic/Latino), 9 international. Average age 26. 54 applicants, 69% accepted, 10 enrolled. In 2018, 20 master's awarded. *Degree requirements:* For master's, thesis optional. *Entrance requirements:* For master's, GRE General Test, MAT, or GMAT, 2 letters of recommendation, resume. Additional exam requirements/recommendations for international students: Required—TOEFL (minimum score 550 paper-based; 80 iBT). *Application deadline:* For fall admission, 3/15 priority date for domestic and international students; for spring admission, 10/15 priority date for domestic and international students. Applications are processed on a rolling basis. Application fee: $50. Electronic applications accepted. *Expenses:* Contact institution. *Financial support:* In 2018–19, 31 students received support. Fellowships, career-related internships or fieldwork, Federal Work-Study, institutionally sponsored loans, and scholarships/grants available. Support available to part-time students. Financial award application deadline: 4/1; financial award applicants required to submit FAFSA. *Faculty research:* Branding law and management, health care communication, gender roles and violence in video games, new media, political communication. *Unit head:* Robert Rosenthal, Chair, 617-573-8502, E-mail: rrosenthal@suffolk.edu. *Application contact:* Mara Marzocchi, Associate Director of Graduate Admissions, 617-573-8302, Fax: 617-305-1733, E-mail: grad.admission@suffolk.edu.
Website: http://www.suffolk.edu/college/graduate/69298.php

Suffolk University, Sawyer Business School, Master of Business Administration Program, Boston, MA 02108-2770. Offers accounting (MBA); entrepreneurship (MBA); executive business administration (EMBA); finance (MBA); global business administration (GMBA); health administration (MBA); international business (MBA); marketing (MBA); nonprofit management (MBA); organizational behavior (MBA); strategic management (MBA); supply chain management (MBA); taxation (MBA); JD/MBA; MBA/MHA; MBA/MSA; MBA/MSF; MBA/MST. *Accreditation:* AACSB. *Program availability:* Part-time, evening/weekend, 100% online. *Faculty:* 18 full-time (5 women), 5 part-time/adjunct (0 women). *Students:* 79 full-time (46 women), 193 part-time (107 women); includes 69 minority (17 Black or African American, non-Hispanic/Latino; 18 Asian, non-Hispanic/Latino; 28 Hispanic/Latino; 6 Two or more races, non-Hispanic/Latino), 40 international. Average age 30. 274 applicants, 67% accepted, 83 enrolled. In 2018, 125 master's awarded. *Entrance requirements:* For master's, GMAT, minimum undergraduate GPA of 2.75 (MBA), 5 years of managerial experience (EMBA). Additional exam requirements/recommendations for international students: Required—TOEFL (minimum score 550 paper-based; 80 iBT). *Application deadline:* For fall admission, 3/15 priority date for domestic students, 10/15 priority date for international students; for spring admission, 10/15 priority date for domestic and international students. Applications are processed on a rolling basis. Application fee: $50. Electronic applications accepted. *Expenses:* Contact institution. *Financial support:* In 2018–19, 170 students received support, including 4 fellowships (averaging $2,906 per year); career-related internships or fieldwork, Federal Work-Study, institutionally sponsored loans, and scholarships/grants also available. Support available to part-time students. Financial award application deadline: 4/1; financial award applicants required to submit FAFSA. *Faculty research:* Foreign investments; career strategies and boundaryless careers; corporate ethics codes; interest rates, inflation, and growth options; innovation and product development performance. *Unit head:* Jodi Detjen, Director of MBA Programs, 617-573-8306, E-mail: jdetjen@suffolk.edu. *Application contact:* Mara Marzocchi, Associate Director of Graduate Admissions, 617-573-8302, Fax: 617-305-1733, E-mail: grad.admission@suffolk.edu.
Website: http://www.suffolk.edu/mba

Suffolk University, Sawyer Business School, Program in Marketing, Boston, MA 02108-2770. Offers global marketing (MS); market research and customer insights (MS); product management (MS). *Students:* 13 full-time (9 women), 9 part-time (4 women); includes 5 minority (1 Black or African American, non-Hispanic/Latino; 2 Asian, non-Hispanic/Latino; 2 Hispanic/Latino), 10 international. Average age 23. 99 applicants, 61% accepted, 22 enrolled. In 2018, 9 master's awarded. *Entrance requirements:* Additional exam requirements/recommendations for international students: Required—TOEFL (minimum score 550 paper-based; 80 iBT). *Application deadline:* For fall admission, 3/15 priority date for domestic and international students; for spring admission, 10/15 priority date for domestic and international students. Applications are processed on a rolling basis. Application fee: $50. Electronic applications accepted. *Expenses:* Contact institution. *Financial support:* In 2018–19, 13 students received support, including 11 fellowships (averaging $3,029 per year). Financial award application deadline: 4/1; financial award applicants required to submit FAFSA. *Unit head:* Elizabeth Wilson, DR, Director of Programs, Master of Science in Marketing, 617-994-4248, E-mail: ewilson@suffolk.edu. *Application contact:* Mara Marzocchi, Associate Director of Graduate Admissions, 617-573-8302, Fax: 617-305-1733, E-mail: grad.admission@suffolk.edu.

Syracuse University, Martin J. Whitman School of Management, Master of Business Administration Program, Syracuse, NY 13244. Offers accounting (MBA); business analytics (MBA); entrepreneurship (MBA); marketing management (MBA); real estate (MBA); supply chain management (MBA); JD/MBA. *Program availability:* Part-time, 100% online. *Students:* Average age 32. 1,086 applicants, 73% accepted, 516 enrolled. In 2018, 84 master's awarded. *Entrance requirements:* For master's, GMAT or GRE, resume, essay, 5-minute video interview, two letters of recommendation, transcripts (unofficial). Additional exam requirements/recommendations for international students: Required—TOEFL (minimum score 100 iBT), IELTS (minimum score 7), PTE (minimum score 68). *Application deadline:* For fall admission, 11/30 for domestic students, 11/30 priority date for international students; for winter admission, 1/1 for domestic students, 1/1 priority date for international students; for spring admission, 2/15 for domestic and international students; for summer admission, 4/19 for domestic students. Application fee: $75. Electronic applications accepted. *Expenses:* Contact institution. *Financial support:* In 2018–19, 22 students received support. Merit scholarships available. Financial award application deadline: 2/15. *Faculty research:* Data analysis, economics of international business, financial markets and institutions, operations management, supply chain management. *Unit head:* Dr. Alexander McKelvie, Associate Dean for Undergraduate and Full-time Master's Education, 315-443-7252, E-mail: mckelvie@syr.edu. *Application contact:* Shri Ramakrishnan, Assistant Director, Graduate Recruitment, 315-443-3497, Fax: 315-443-9517, E-mail: busgrad@syr.edu.
Website: http://whitman.syr.edu/ftmba/

Tarleton State University, College of Graduate Studies, College of Business Administration, Department of Marketing and Computer Information Systems, Stephenville, TX 76402. Offers information systems (MS). *Program availability:* Part-time, evening/weekend, 100% online, blended/hybrid learning. *Faculty:* 8 full-time (1 woman), 1 part-time/adjunct (0 women). *Students:* 13 full-time (5 women), 46 part-time (15 women). Average age 34. 27 applicants, 100% accepted, 22 enrolled. In 2018, 6 master's awarded. *Degree requirements:* For master's, comprehensive exam, thesis (for some programs). *Entrance requirements:* For master's, GRE, minimum GPA of 3.0. Additional exam requirements/recommendations for international students: Required—TOEFL (minimum score 520 paper-based; 69 iBT); Recommended—IELTS (minimum score 6), TSE (minimum score 50). *Application deadline:* For fall admission, 8/15 priority date for domestic students; for spring admission, 1/7 for domestic students. Applications are processed on a rolling basis. Application fee: $50 ($130 for international students). Electronic applications accepted. *Expenses:* Contact institution. *Financial support:* Research assistantships and teaching assistantships available. Financial award application deadline: 5/1; financial award applicants required to submit FAFSA. *Unit head:* Dr. Leah Schultz, Interim Department Head, 254-968-9169, E-mail: lschult@tarleton.edu. *Application contact:* Information Contact, 254-968-9104, Fax: 254-968-9670, E-mail: gradoffice@tarleton.edu.
Website: http://www.tarleton.edu/cis/

Temple University, Fox School of Business, Doctoral Programs in Business, Philadelphia, PA 19122-6096. Offers accounting (PhD); entrepreneurship (PhD); finance (PhD); international business (PhD); management information systems (PhD); marketing (PhD); risk management and insurance (PhD); statistics (PhD); strategic management (PhD); tourism and sport (PhD). *Accreditation:* AACSB. *Degree requirements:* For doctorate, thesis/dissertation. *Entrance requirements:* For doctorate, GRE General Test, GMAT, minimum GPA of 3.0, master's degree. Additional exam requirements/recommendations for international students: Required—TOEFL (minimum score 600 paper-based; 100 iBT), IELTS (minimum score 7.5). Electronic applications accepted.

Temple University, Fox School of Business, MBA Programs, Philadelphia, PA 19122-6096. Offers accounting (MBA); business management (MBA); financial management (MBA); healthcare and life sciences innovation (MBA); human resource management (MBA); international business (IMBA); IT management (MBA); marketing management (MBA); pharmaceutical management (MBA); strategic management (EMBA, MBA). EMBA offered in Philadelphia, PA and Tokyo, Japan. *Accreditation:* AACSB. *Program availability:* Part-time, evening/weekend, online learning. *Entrance requirements:* For master's, GMAT, minimum undergraduate GPA of 3.0. Additional exam requirements/recommendations for international students: Required—TOEFL (minimum score 600 paper-based; 100 iBT), IELTS (minimum score 7.5).

Temple University, Fox School of Business, Specialized Master's Programs, Philadelphia, PA 19122-6096. Offers accountancy (MS); actuarial science (MS); finance (MS); financial engineering (MS); human resource management (MS); innovation management and entrepreneurship (MS); marketing (MS); statistics (MS). MS in innovation management and entrepreneurship delivered jointly with College of Engineering. *Accreditation:* AACSB. *Program availability:* Part-time. *Entrance requirements:* For master's, GRE General Test or GMAT, minimum undergraduate GPA of 3.0. Additional exam requirements/recommendations for international students: Required—TOEFL (minimum score 600 paper-based; 100 iBT), IELTS (minimum score 7.5).

Texas A&M University, Mays Business School, Department of Marketing, College Station, TX 77843. Offers MS. *Faculty:* 13. *Students:* 63 full-time (43 women), 1 (woman) part-time; includes 6 minority (1 Asian, non-Hispanic/Latino; 4 Hispanic/Latino;

1 Two or more races, non-Hispanic/Latino), 18 international. Average age 25. 131 applicants, 22% accepted, 19 enrolled. In 2018, 43 master's awarded. Terminal master's awarded for partial completion of doctoral program. *Degree requirements:* For master's, comprehensive exam. *Entrance requirements:* For master's, GMAT or GRE. Additional exam requirements/recommendations for international students: Required—TOEFL (minimum score 550 paper-based; 80 iBT), IELTS (minimum score 6), PTE (minimum score 53). *Application deadline:* Applications are processed on a rolling basis. Application fee: $50 ($90 for international students). Electronic applications accepted. *Expenses:* Contact institution. *Financial support:* In 2018–19, 61 students received support, including 13 research assistantships with tuition reimbursements available (averaging $17,466 per year), 30 teaching assistantships with tuition reimbursements available (averaging $5,938 per year); career-related internships or fieldwork, institutionally sponsored loans, scholarships/grants, traineeships, health care benefits, tuition waivers (full and partial), and unspecified assistantships also available. Support available to part-time students. Financial award application deadline: 3/15; financial award applicants required to submit FAFSA. *Faculty research:* Consumer behavior, innovation and product management, international marketing, marketing management and strategy, services marketing. *Unit head:* Dr. Mark B. Houston, Head, 979-845-7257, E-mail: mhouston@mays.tamu.edu. *Application contact:* Stephen W. McDaniel, Master's Advisor, 979-845-5801, E-mail: smcdaniel@mays.tamu.edu.
Website: http://mays.tamu.edu/mktg/

Texas A&M University–Commerce, College of Business, Commerce, TX 75429. Offers accounting (MSA); business administration (MBA); business analytics (MS); finance (MSF); management (MS); marketing (MS). *Accreditation:* AACSB. *Program availability:* Part-time, evening/weekend, 100% online, blended/hybrid learning. *Faculty:* 48 full-time (15 women), 2 part-time/adjunct (1 woman). *Students:* 391 full-time (209 women), 948 part-time (511 women); includes 583 minority (249 Black or African American, non-Hispanic/Latino; 4 American Indian or Alaska Native, non-Hispanic/Latino; 89 Asian, non-Hispanic/Latino; 205 Hispanic/Latino; 1 Native Hawaiian or other Pacific Islander, non-Hispanic/Latino; 35 Two or more races, non-Hispanic/Latino), 156 international. Average age 33. 930 applicants, 58% accepted, 355 enrolled. In 2018, 628 master's awarded. *Degree requirements:* For master's, comprehensive exam. *Entrance requirements:* For master's, GRE General Test, GMAT, letter of recommendation. Additional exam requirements/recommendations for international students: Required—TOEFL (minimum score 550 paper-based; 79 iBT), IELTS (minimum score 6), PTE (minimum score 53). *Application deadline:* For fall admission, 6/1 priority date for international students; for spring admission, 10/15 priority date for international students; for summer admission, 3/15 priority date for international students. Applications are processed on a rolling basis. Application fee: $50 ($75 for international students). Electronic applications accepted. *Expenses: Tuition, area resident:* Full-time $3630. Tuition, state resident: full-time $3630. Tuition, nonresident: full-time $11,100. *International tuition:* $11,100 full-time. *Required fees:* $2794. Tuition and fees vary according to course load, degree level and program. *Financial support:* In 2018–19, 61 students received support, including 57 research assistantships with partial tuition reimbursements available (averaging $3,286 per year); Federal Work-Study, institutionally sponsored loans, scholarships/grants, health care benefits, and unspecified assistantships also available. Financial award application deadline: 5/1; financial award applicants required to submit FAFSA. *Faculty research:* Strategic management and organizational behavior phenomena; marketing and big data decisions of product choice behavior and channel behavior of consumers; international accounting in governmental sectors; finance research on banking, investments, financial institutions and risk management; applied economics with emphasis on industries that are important to the region including health and energy. *Unit head:* Dr. Shanan Gwaltney Gibson, Dean of College of Business, 903-886-5191, Fax: 903-886-5650, E-mail: shanan.gibson@tamuc.edu. *Application contact:* Shanna Hoskison, Director, Graduate Advising, 903-886-5190, E-mail: shanna.hoskison@tamuc.edu.
Website: https://new.tamuc.edu/business/

Texas Tech University, Rawls College of Business Administration, Lubbock, TX 79409-2101. Offers accounting (MSA, PhD), including audit/financial reporting (MSA), taxation (MSA); data science (MS); finance (PhD); general business (MBA); healthcare management (MS); information systems and operations management (PhD); management (PhD); marketing (PhD); STEM (MBA); JD/MBA; JD/MSA; MBA/M Arch; MBA/MD; MBA/MS; MBA/Pharm D. *Accreditation:* AACSB. *Program availability:* Evening/weekend, 100% online, blended/hybrid learning. *Degree requirements:* For master's, thesis (for MS); capstone course; for doctorate, comprehensive exam, thesis/dissertation, qualifying exams. *Entrance requirements:* For master's, GMAT, GRE, MCAT, PCAT, LSAT, or DAT, holistic review of academic credentials, resume, essay, letters of recommendation; for doctorate, GMAT, GRE, holistic review of academic credentials, resume, statement of purpose, letters of recommendation. Additional exam requirements/recommendations for international students: Required—TOEFL (minimum score 550 paper-based; 79 iBT), IELTS (minimum score 6.5), PTE (minimum score 60). Electronic applications accepted. *Expenses:* Contact institution. *Faculty research:* Governmental and nonprofit accounting, securities and options futures, statistical analysis and design, leadership, consumer behavior.

Thomas Jefferson University, Kanbar College of Design, Engineering and Commerce, Innovation MBA Program, Philadelphia, PA 19107. Offers business analytics (MBA); general business (MBA); management (MBA); marketing (MBA); strategy and design thinking (MBA); MBA/MS. *Program availability:* Part-time, evening/weekend, online learning. *Entrance requirements:* For master's, GMAT. Additional exam requirements/recommendations for international students: Required—TOEFL (minimum score 550 paper-based; 79 iBT).

Tiffin University, Program in Business Administration, Tiffin, OH 44883-2161. Offers finance (MBA); general management (MBA); healthcare administration (MBA); human resource management (MBA); international business (MBA); leadership (MBA); marketing (MBA); non-profit management (MBA); sports management (MBA). *Accreditation:* ACBSP. *Program availability:* Part-time, evening/weekend, online learning. *Entrance requirements:* For master's, minimum undergraduate GPA of 2.5, work experience. Additional exam requirements/recommendations for international students: Required—TOEFL (minimum score 550 paper-based; 79 iBT), IELTS. Electronic applications accepted. Application fee is waived when completed online. *Faculty research:* Small business, executive development operations, research and statistical analysis, market research, management information systems.

Trident University International, College of Business Administration, Program in Business Administration, Cypress, CA 90630. Offers business administration (PhD); conflict and negotiation management (MBA); criminal justice administration (MBA); entrepreneurship (MBA); finance (MBA); general management (MBA); government accounting (MBA); human resource management (MBA); information security and digital assurance management (MBA); information technology management (MBA); international business (MBA); logistics management (MBA); marketing (MBA); project management (MBA); public management (MBA); quality management (MBA); strategic leadership (MBA). *Program availability:* Part-time, evening/weekend, online learning. *Degree requirements:* For doctorate, comprehensive exam, thesis/dissertation, defense of dissertation. *Entrance requirements:* For master's, minimum GPA of 2.5 (students with GPA 3.0 or greater may transfer up to 30% of graduate level credits); for doctorate, minimum GPA of 3.4, curriculum vitae, course work in research methods or statistics. Additional exam requirements/recommendations for international students: Required—TOEFL. Electronic applications accepted.

United States International University–Africa, School of Business Administration, Nairobi, Kenya. Offers business administration (GEMBA); entrepreneurship (MBA); finance (MBA); human resource management (MBA); information technology management (MBA); integrated studies (MBA); international business administration (MBA); management and organizational development (MS); marketing (MBA); organizational development (EMS); strategic management (MBA). *Program availability:* Part-time, evening/weekend. *Degree requirements:* For master's, thesis. *Entrance requirements:* For master's, GMAT, 2 letters of reference, resume. Additional exam requirements/recommendations for international students: Required—TOEFL (minimum score 550 paper-based). *Faculty research:* Marketing in small business enterprises, total quality management in Kenya.

Universidad del Turabo, Graduate Programs, School of Business and Entrepreneurship, Program in Marketing, Gurabo, PR 00778-3030. Offers MBA. *Program availability:* Part-time, evening/weekend. *Entrance requirements:* For master's, GRE, EXADEP or GMAT, interview, essay, official transcript, recommendation letters. Electronic applications accepted.

Universidad Iberoamericana, Graduate School, Santo Domingo D.N., Dominican Republic. Offers business administration (MBA, PMBA); constitutional law (LL M); dentistry (DMD); educational management (MA); integrated marketing communication (MA); psychopedagogical intervention (M Ed); real estate law (LL M); strategic management of human talent (MM).

Universidad Metropolitana, School of Business Administration, Program in Marketing, San Juan, PR 00928-1150. Offers MBA. *Program availability:* Part-time. *Degree requirements:* For master's, thesis or alternative. *Entrance requirements:* For master's, GMAT, PAEG, interview. Electronic applications accepted.

Université de Sherbrooke, Faculty of Administration, Program in Marketing, Sherbrooke, QC J1K 2R1, Canada. Offers M Sc. *Degree requirements:* For master's, one foreign language, thesis. *Entrance requirements:* For master's, bachelor's degree in related field, minimum GPA of 3.0 (on 4.3 scale). Electronic applications accepted. *Faculty research:* Consumer behavior, sales force, branding, prices management.

Université Laval, Faculty of Administrative Sciences, Programs in Business Administration, Québec, QC G1K 7P4, Canada. Offers accounting (MBA); agri-food management (MBA); electronic business (MBA, Diploma); factory management and logistics (MBA); finance (MBA); firm management (MBA); geomatic management (MBA); information technology management (MBA); international management (MBA); management (MBA); management accounting (MBA, Diploma); marketing (MBA); modeling and organizational decision (MBA); occupational health and safety management (MBA); pharmacy management (MBA); social and environmental responsibility (MBA); technological entrepreneurship (Diploma). *Accreditation:* AACSB. *Program availability:* Part-time, evening/weekend, online learning. *Entrance requirements:* For master's and Diploma, knowledge of French and English. Electronic applications accepted.

University at Albany, State University of New York, School of Business, MBA Programs, Albany, NY 12222-0001. Offers business administration (MBA); cyber security (MBA); entrepreneurship (MBA); finance (MBA); human resource information systems (MBA); information systems and business analytics (MBA); marketing (MBA); JD/MBA. JD/MBA offered jointly with Albany Law School. *Program availability:* Part-time, evening/weekend. *Faculty:* 29 full-time (13 women), 9 part-time/adjunct (2 women). *Students:* 103 full-time (36 women), 188 part-time (69 women); includes 76 minority (27 Black or African American, non-Hispanic/Latino; 33 Asian, non-Hispanic/Latino; 16 Hispanic/Latino), 16 international. Average age 25. 181 applicants, 80% accepted, 114 enrolled. In 2018, 103 master's awarded. *Degree requirements:* For master's, thesis (for some programs), field or research project. *Entrance requirements:* For master's, GMAT, minimum undergraduate GPA of 3.0; 3 letters of recommendation; resume; statement of goals. Additional exam requirements/recommendations for international students: Required—TOEFL (minimum score 100 iBT); Recommended—IELTS (minimum score 7). *Application deadline:* For fall admission, 4/1 priority date for domestic students, 2/15 for international students; for spring admission, 12/1 for domestic students; for summer admission, 5/1 for domestic students. Applications are processed on a rolling basis. Application fee: $75. Electronic applications accepted. *Expenses:* 16818. *Financial support:* In 2018–19, 25 students received support, including 7 fellowships with partial tuition reimbursements available (averaging $6,000 per year), 4 research assistantships with partial tuition reimbursements available, 21 teaching assistantships with partial tuition reimbursements available; unspecified assistantships also available. Financial award application deadline: 4/1; financial award applicants required to submit FAFSA. *Faculty research:* Social goods, information assurance, social computing, corporate entrepreneurship, asset pricing. *Total annual research expenditures:* $136,000. *Unit head:* Dr. Nilanjan Sen, Dean, 518-956-8370, Fax: 518-442-3273, E-mail: nsen@albany.edu. *Application contact:* Zina Mega Lawrence, Assistant Dean of Graduate Student Services, 518-956-8320, Fax: 518-442-4042, E-mail: zlawrence@albany.edu.
Website: https://graduatebusiness.albany.edu/

University at Buffalo, the State University of New York, Graduate School, School of Management, Buffalo, NY 14260. Offers accounting (MS); analytics (MBA); business administration (PMBA); consulting (MBA); finance (MBA, MS), including financial risk management (MS), quantitative finance (MS); healthcare (MBA); information assurance (MBA); information systems (MBA); international management (MBA); management (EMBA, PhD); management information systems (MS); marketing (MBA); supply chain and operations (MBA); supply chains and operations management (MS); Au D/MBA; DDS/MBA; JD/MBA; M Arch/MBA; MD/MBA; MPH/MBA; MSW/MBA; Pharm D/MBA. *Accreditation:* AACSB. *Program availability:* Part-time, evening/weekend. *Degree requirements:* For master's, capstone courses or projects; for doctorate, comprehensive exam, thesis/dissertation. *Entrance requirements:* For master's, GMAT (for MS in accounting, finance); GRE or GMAT (for MBA, MS in management information systems, supply chains and operations management), essays, letters of recommendation; for doctorate, GMAT or GRE, essays, writing sample, letters of recommendation. Additional exam requirements/recommendations for international students: Required—TOEFL (minimum score 95 iBT) or IELTS (minimum score 6.5); Recommended—TSE (minimum score 73). Electronic applications accepted. *Expenses:* Contact institution. *Faculty research:* Data analytics, accounting and law, rate finance, consumer behavior, supply chain logistics, leadership and team effectiveness.

The University of Akron, Graduate School, College of Business Administration, Department of Marketing, Akron, OH 44325. Offers MBA. *Program availability:* Part-time, evening/weekend. *Entrance requirements:* For master's, GMAT, GRE, MCAT, LSAT, PCAT, or CAT, minimum GPA of 3.0 (preferred), two letters of recommendation, resume, statement of purpose. Additional exam requirements/recommendations for international students: Required—TOEFL (minimum score 79 iBT), IELTS (minimum score 6.5). Electronic applications accepted. *Faculty research:* Multi-channel marketing, direct interactive marketing, strategic retailing, marketing strategy and telemarketing.

The University of Alabama, Graduate School, Manderson Graduate School of Business, Department of Marketing, Tuscaloosa, AL 35487. Offers MS, PhD. *Accreditation:* AACSB. Terminal master's awarded for partial completion of doctoral program. *Degree requirements:* For master's, internship; for doctorate, comprehensive exam, thesis/dissertation. *Entrance requirements:* For master's, GRE or GMAT; for doctorate, GRE or GMAT, minimum GPA of 3.0. Electronic applications accepted. *Faculty research:* Relationship marketing, consumer behavior, services marketing, professional selling, supply chain management.

The University of Alabama at Birmingham, Collat School of Business, Program in Business Administration, Birmingham, AL 35294. Offers business administration (MBA), including finance, health care management, information technology management, marketing; MD/MBA. *Program availability:* Part-time, evening/weekend, 100% online, blended/hybrid learning. *Entrance requirements:* For master's, GMAT. Additional exam requirements/recommendations for international students: Required—TOEFL (minimum score 80 iBT), IELTS (minimum score 6.5). Electronic applications accepted. *Expenses: Tuition, area resident:* Full-time $8100; part-time $8100 per year. Tuition, state resident: full-time $8100. Tuition, nonresident: full-time $19,188; part-time $19,188 per year. Tuition and fees vary according to program. *Faculty research:* Open innovation, workplace issues, leadership, supply chain management, capital markets.

The University of Alabama in Huntsville, School of Graduate Studies, College of Business Administration, Programs in Business and Management, Huntsville, AL 35899. Offers business analytics (MSMS); federal contracting and procurement management (Certificate); human resource management (MSM); management (MBA), including acquisition management, entrepreneurship, federal contract accounting, finance, human resource management, logistics and supply chain management, marketing, project management; supply chain management (Certificate); technology and innovation management (Certificate). *Accreditation:* AACSB. *Program availability:* Part-time. *Faculty:* 8 full-time (3 women). *Students:* 57 full-time (25 women), 152 part-time (76 women); includes 37 minority (20 Black or African American, non-Hispanic/Latino; 2 American Indian or Alaska Native, non-Hispanic/Latino; 6 Asian, non-Hispanic/Latino; 8 Hispanic/Latino; 1 Two or more races, non-Hispanic/Latino), 24 international. Average age 33. 178 applicants, 80% accepted, 84 enrolled. In 2018, 96 master's, 1 other advanced degree awarded. *Degree requirements:* For master's, comprehensive exam, thesis or alternative. *Entrance requirements:* For master's, GMAT (minimum score 500), minimum AACSB index of 1080. Additional exam requirements/recommendations for international students: Required—TOEFL (minimum score 550 paper-based; 80 iBT), IELTS (minimum score 6.5). *Application deadline:* For fall admission, 7/15 priority date for domestic students, 4/1 priority date for international students; for spring admission, 11/30 priority date for domestic students, 9/1 priority date for international students. Applications are processed on a rolling basis. Application fee: $50. Electronic applications accepted. *Expenses: Tuition, area resident:* Full-time $10,632; part-time $412 per credit hour. Tuition, state resident: full-time $10,632. Tuition, nonresident: full-time $23,604; part-time $412 per credit hour. *Required fees:* $582; $582. Tuition and fees vary according to course load and program. *Financial support:* In 2018–19, 15 students received support, including 15 teaching assistantships with full tuition reimbursements available (averaging $4,871 per year); research assistantships with full tuition reimbursements available, career-related internships or fieldwork, Federal Work-Study, institutionally sponsored loans, scholarships/grants, health care benefits, tuition waivers (full and partial), and unspecified assistantships also available. Support available to part-time students. Financial award application deadline: 4/1; financial award applicants required to submit FAFSA. *Faculty research:* Supply chain management, management of research and development, international marketing and branding, organizational behavior and human resource management, social networks and computational economics. *Unit head:* Dr. Fan Tseng, Chair, 256-824-6804, Fax: 256-824-6328, E-mail: fan.tseng@uah.edu. *Application contact:* Jennifer Pettitt, Director of Advising, 256-824-6681, Fax: 256-824-7571, E-mail: jennifer.pettitt@uah.edu.

University of Alberta, Faculty of Graduate Studies and Research, Doctoral Program in Business, Edmonton, AB T6G 2E1, Canada. Offers accounting (PhD); finance (PhD); human resources/industrial relations (PhD); management science (PhD); marketing (PhD); organizational analysis (PhD); MBA/PhD. *Accreditation:* AACSB. *Program availability:* Part-time. *Degree requirements:* For doctorate, comprehensive exam, thesis/dissertation. *Entrance requirements:* For doctorate, GMAT. Additional exam requirements/recommendations for international students: Required—TOEFL (minimum score 550 paper-based). Electronic applications accepted. *Faculty research:* Accounting, capital markets and corporate finance, organizational change and human resource management, marketing, strategic management.

The University of Arizona, Eller College of Management, Department of Marketing, Tucson, AZ 85721. Offers MBA, MS, PhD. *Degree requirements:* For doctorate, comprehensive exam, thesis/dissertation. *Entrance requirements:* For doctorate, GMAT (minimum score 600). Additional exam requirements/recommendations for international students: Required—TOEFL (minimum score 600 paper-based). Electronic applications accepted. *Faculty research:* Consumer behavior, customer relationship management, research methods, brand strategy, public policy.

University of Baltimore, Graduate School, Merrick School of Business, Department of Marketing and Entrepreneurship, Baltimore, MD 21201-5779. Offers innovation management and technology commercialization (MS). *Program availability:* Part-time, evening/weekend. *Entrance requirements:* For master's, GMAT. Additional exam requirements/recommendations for international students: Required—TOEFL (minimum score 550 paper-based). Electronic applications accepted.

University of Bridgeport, School of Business, Bridgeport, CT 06604. Offers accounting (MBA); finance (MBA); general business (MBA); global financial services (MBA); human resource management (MBA); information systems and knowledge management (MBA); international business (MBA); management (MBA); marketing (MBA); operations management (MBA); small business and entrepreneurship (MBA); specialized business (MBA). *Accreditation:* ACBSP. *Program availability:* Part-time, evening/weekend. *Degree requirements:* For master's, thesis optional. *Entrance requirements:* For master's, GMAT. Additional exam requirements/recommendations for international students: Recommended—TOEFL (minimum score 550 paper-based; 80 iBT), IELTS (minimum score 6.5). Electronic applications accepted. *Expenses:* Contact institution.

The University of British Columbia, Sauder School of Business, Doctoral Program in Business Administration, Vancouver, BC V6T 1Z2, Canada. Offers accounting (PhD); finance (PhD); management information systems (PhD); management science (PhD); marketing (PhD); organizational behavior (PhD); strategy and business economics (PhD); transportation and logistics (PhD); urban land economics (PhD). *Degree requirements:* For doctorate, comprehensive exam, thesis/dissertation. *Entrance requirements:* For doctorate, GMAT or GRE. Additional exam requirements/recommendations for international students: Required—TOEFL (minimum score 600 paper-based; 100 iBT). Electronic applications accepted. *Expenses:* Contact institution.

University of California, Berkeley, Graduate Division, Haas School of Business, PhD in Business Administration Program, Berkeley, CA 94720. Offers accounting (PhD); business and public policy (PhD); finance (PhD); management of organizations (PhD); marketing (PhD); real estate (PhD). *Accreditation:* AACSB. *Degree requirements:* For doctorate, comprehensive exam, thesis/dissertation, written preliminary exams, oral qualifying exam. *Entrance requirements:* For doctorate, GMAT or GRE, minimum GPA of 3.0 in undergraduate and graduate coursework. Additional exam requirements/recommendations for international students: Required—TOEFL (minimum score 570 paper-based; 70 iBT), IELTS (minimum score 7). Electronic applications accepted. *Expenses:* Contact institution. *Faculty research:* Accounting, business and public policy, entrepreneurship, finance, management of organizations, marketing, operations and information technology management, real estate.

University of California, Berkeley, UC Berkeley Extension, Certificate Programs in Business, Berkeley, CA 94720. Offers accounting (Certificate); business administration (Certificate); finance (Certificate); human resource management (Certificate); management (Certificate); marketing (Certificate); project management (Certificate). *Accreditation:* AACSB. *Program availability:* Online learning.

University of California, Berkeley, UC Berkeley Extension, International Diploma Programs, Berkeley, CA 94720. Offers business administration (Certificate); finance (Certificate); global business management (Certificate); marketing (Certificate); project management (Certificate). *Accreditation:* AACSB.

University of California, Davis, Graduate School of Management, Full-Time MBA Program, Davis, CA 95616. Offers business analytics and technologies (MBA); entrepreneurship and innovation (MBA); finance and accounting (MBA); general management (MBA); marketing (MBA); organizational behavior (MBA); public health management (MBA); strategy (MBA); technology management (MBA); DVM/MBA; JD/MBA; M Engr/MBA; MBA/MPH; MBA/MS; MD/MBA; MSN/MBA; PhD/MBA. *Faculty:* 31 full-time (10 women). *Students:* 89 full-time (35 women); includes 21 minority (1 Black or African American, non-Hispanic/Latino; 14 Asian, non-Hispanic/Latino; 6 Hispanic/Latino), 43 international. Average age 28. 290 applicants, 39% accepted, 44 enrolled. In 2018, 45 master's awarded. *Degree requirements:* For master's, comprehensive exam, integrated management project. *Entrance requirements:* For master's, GMAT or GRE, letters of recommendation, resume, essays, equivalent of a 4-year U.S. undergraduate degree, transcript. Additional exam requirements/recommendations for international students: Required—TOEFL (minimum score 600 paper-based; 100 iBT), IELTS (minimum score 7). *Application deadline:* For fall admission, 9/15 priority date for domestic and international students. Applications are processed on a rolling basis. Application fee: $125. Electronic applications accepted. *Expenses:* Contact institution. *Financial support:* In 2018–19, 85 students received support. Fellowships with full and partial tuition reimbursements available, research assistantships with partial tuition reimbursements available, teaching assistantships with partial tuition reimbursements available, institutionally sponsored loans, scholarships/grants, health care benefits, tuition waivers (partial), and unspecified assistantships available. Financial award application deadline: 3/1; financial award applicants required to submit FAFSA. *Faculty research:* Finance, marketing, management, business analytics, accounting. *Unit head:* Amanda Opperman, Assistant Dean of Student Affairs, 530-752-7658, Fax: 530-754-9355, E-mail: admissions@gsm.ucdavis.edu. *Application contact:* Andrea Shaw, Senior Director of Admissions, 530-754-5476, Fax: 530-754-9355, E-mail: admissions@gsm.ucdavis.edu.
Website: http://gsm.ucdavis.edu/daytime-mba-program

University of California, Davis, Graduate School of Management, MBA Programs in Sacramento and San Francisco Bay Area, Davis, CA 95616. Offers business analytics and technologies (MBA); entrepreneurship and innovation (MBA); finance and accounting (MBA); general management (MBA); marketing (MBA); organizational behavior (MBA); public health management (MBA); strategy (MBA); technology management (MBA). *Program availability:* Part-time-only, evening/weekend. *Faculty:* 17 full-time (7 women), 42 part-time/adjunct (11 women). *Students:* 279 part-time (107 women); includes 146 minority (12 Black or African American, non-Hispanic/Latino; 3 American Indian or Alaska Native, non-Hispanic/Latino; 102 Asian, non-Hispanic/Latino; 29 Hispanic/Latino), 24 international. Average age 30. 158 applicants, 83% accepted, 91 enrolled. In 2018, 91 master's awarded. *Degree requirements:* For master's, integrated management project. *Entrance requirements:* For master's, GMAT or GRE, letters of recommendation, resume, equivalent of a 4-year undergraduate degree. Additional exam requirements/recommendations for international students: Required—TOEFL (minimum score 600 paper-based; 100 iBT), IELTS (minimum score 7). *Application deadline:* For fall admission, 9/15 priority date for domestic and international students. Applications are processed on a rolling basis. Application fee: $125. Electronic applications accepted. *Expenses:* Contact institution. *Financial support:* In 2018–19, 89 students received support. Fellowships, teaching assistantships with partial tuition reimbursements available, scholarships/grants, and unspecified assistantships available. Support available to part-time students. Financial award application deadline: 3/1; financial award applicants required to submit FAFSA. *Faculty research:* Accounting, finance, marketing, management, business analytics. *Unit head:* Amanda Opperman, Assistant Dean of Student Affairs, 530-752-7658, Fax: 530-754-9355, E-mail: admissions@gsm.ucdavis.edu. *Application contact:* Andrea Shaw, Senior Director of Admissions, 530-754-5476, Fax: 530-754-9355, E-mail: admissions@gsm.ucdavis.edu.
Website: http://gsm.ucdavis.edu/mba-programs

University of California, Los Angeles, Graduate Division, UCLA Anderson School of Management, Los Angeles, CA 90095-1481. Offers accounting (PhD); behavioral decision making (PhD); business administration (EMBA, MBA); business administration/computer science (MBA/MSCS); business administration/latin american studies (MBA/MLAS); business administration/law (MBA/JD); business administration/library science (MBA/MLIS); business administration/medicine (MBA/MD); business administration/nursing (MBA/MN); business administration/public health (MBA/MPH); business administration/public policy (MBA/MPP); business administration/urban and regional planning (MBA/MURP); business analytics (MSBA); decisions, operations, and technology management (PhD); finance (PhD); financial engineering (MFE); global economics and management (PhD); management and organizations (PhD); marketing (PhD); strategy and policy (PhD); DDS/MBA; MBA/JD; MBA/MD; MBA/MLAS; MBA/MLIS; MBA/MN; MBA/MPH; MBA/MPP; MBA/MSCS; MBA/MURP. UCLA-NUS EMBA: UCLA Anderson and the National University of Singapore. *Accreditation:* AACSB. *Program availability:* Part-time, evening/weekend. *Faculty:* 86 full-time (19 women), 102 part-time/adjunct (16 women). *Students:* 1,040 full-time (378 women), 1,262 part-time (391 women); includes 784 minority (47 Black or African American, non-Hispanic/Latino; 1 American Indian or Alaska Native, non-Hispanic/Latino; 539 Asian, non-Hispanic/Latino; 116 Hispanic/Latino; 5 Native Hawaiian or other Pacific Islander, non-Hispanic/Latino; 76 Two or more races, non-Hispanic/Latino), 609 international. Average age 31. 6,708 applicants, 27% accepted, 949 enrolled. In 2018, 885 master's, 13 doctorates awarded. Terminal master's awarded for partial completion of doctoral program. *Degree requirements:* For master's, comprehensive exam, field consulting project (for MBA, FEMBA, EMBA, UCLA-NUS EMBA, MFE, and MSBA); internship (for MBA only); for doctorate, comprehensive exam, thesis/dissertation, oral and written qualifying exams. *Entrance requirements:* For master's, GMAT or GRE (for MBA, MFE, MSBA); Executive Assessment (EA) for candidates with 10+ years of work experience (FEMBA); Executive Assessment (EA) or STEM Master's degree or JD, MBA, CPA (EMBA), 4-year bachelor's degree or equivalent; 2 letters of recommendation; interview (invitation only); 2 essays; average 4-8 years of full-time work experience (for FEMBA); minimum 8 years

of work experience with at least 3 years at management level (for EMBA); 10 years of full-time high managerial responsibility work experience (UCLA-NUS EMBA); for doctorate, GMAT or GRE, bachelor's degree from college or university of fully-recognized standing, minimum B average during junior and senior undergraduate years, 3 letters of recommendation, statement of purpose. Additional exam requirements/recommendations for international students: Required—TOEFL (minimum score 560 paper-based; 87 iBT), IELTS (minimum score 7), TOEFL with minimum iBT score of 100 (for MSBA). *Application deadline:* For fall admission, 10/2 for domestic and international students; for winter admission, 1/8 for domestic and international students; for spring admission, 4/16 for domestic and international students. Applications are processed on a rolling basis. Application fee: $200. Electronic applications accepted. *Expenses:* Per Year - MBA: $64,292, FEMBA: $42,420, EMBA: $81,120, UCLA-NUS EMBA (UC Portion only): $57,500, MFE: $75,816, MSBA: $64,1,43, PhD: $32,049. *Financial support:* Fellowships, research assistantships with partial tuition reimbursements, teaching assistantships with partial tuition reimbursements, career-related internships or fieldwork, institutionally sponsored loans, and scholarships/grants available. Support available to part-time students. *Faculty research:* Finance/global economics, entrepreneurship, accounting, human resources/organizational behavior, marketing and behavioral decision making. *Total annual research expenditures:* $2 million. *Unit head:* Dr. Antonio Bernardo, Dean & John E. Anderson Chair in Management, 310-825-7982, Fax: 310-206-2073, E-mail: a.bernardo@anderson.ucla.edu. *Application contact:* Alex Lawrence, Assistant Dean and Director of MBA Admissions, 310-825-6944, Fax: 310-825-8582, E-mail: mba.admissions@anderson.ucla.edu.
Website: http://www.anderson.ucla.edu/

University of Central Missouri, The Graduate School, Warrensburg, MO 64093. Offers accountancy (MA); accounting (MBA); applied mathematics (MS); aviation safety (MA); biology (MS); business administration (MBA); career and technical education leadership (MS); college student personnel administration (MS); communication (MA); computer science (MS); counseling (MS); criminal justice (MS); educational leadership (Ed D); educational technology (MS); elementary and early childhood education (MSE); English (MA); environmental studies (MA); finance (MBA); history (MA); human services/educational technology (Ed S); human services/learning resources (Ed S); human services/professional counseling (Ed S); industrial hygiene (MS); industrial management (MS); information systems (MBA); information technology (MS); kinesiology (MS); library science and information services (MS); literacy education (MSE); marketing (MBA); mathematics (MS); music (MA); occupational safety management (MS); psychology (MS); rural family nursing (MS); school administration (MSE); social gerontology (MS); sociology (MA); special education (MSE); speech language pathology (MS); superintendency (Ed S); teaching (MAT); teaching English as a second language (MA); technology (MS); technology management (PhD); theatre (MA). *Accreditation:* ASHA. *Program availability:* Part-time, 100% online, blended/hybrid learning. *Degree requirements:* For master's and Ed S, comprehensive exam (for some programs), thesis (for some programs). *Entrance requirements:* Additional exam requirements/recommendations for international students: Required—TOEFL (minimum score 550 paper-based; 79 iBT). Electronic applications accepted.

University of Chicago, Booth School of Business, Full-Time MBA Program, Chicago, IL 60637. Offers accounting (MBA); analytic finance (MBA); analytic management (MBA); econometrics and statistics (MBA); economics (MBA); entrepreneurship (MBA); finance (MBA); general management (MBA); health administration and policy (Certificate); international business (MBA); managerial and organizational behavior (MBA); marketing analytics (MBA); marketing management (MBA); operations management (MBA); strategic management (MBA); MBA/AM; MBA/JD; MBA/MA; MBA/MD; MBA/MPP. *Accreditation:* AACSB. *Entrance requirements:* For master's, GMAT or GRE, transcripts, resume, 2 letters of recommendation, essays, interview. Additional exam requirements/recommendations for international students: Required—TOEFL, IELTS, or PTE. Electronic applications accepted. *Expenses:* Contact institution.

University of Cincinnati, Carl H. Lindner College of Business, MS Program, Cincinnati, OH 45221. Offers accounting (MS); applied economics (MS); business analytics (MS); finance (MS); information systems (MS); marketing (MS); taxation (MS). *Program availability:* Part-time, evening/weekend. *Faculty:* 98 full-time (27 women), 28 part-time/adjunct (4 women). *Students:* 305 full-time (123 women), 190 part-time (83 women); includes 35 minority (13 Black or African American, non-Hispanic/Latino; 1 American Indian or Alaska Native, non-Hispanic/Latino; 10 Asian, non-Hispanic/Latino; 6 Hispanic/Latino; 5 Two or more races, non-Hispanic/Latino), 309 international. Average age 29. 1,219 applicants, 55% accepted, 495 enrolled. In 2018, 355 master's awarded. *Degree requirements:* For master's, thesis (for some programs), capstone. *Entrance requirements:* For master's, GMAT, GRE, resume, transcripts, essays, letters of recommendation. Additional exam requirements/recommendations for international students: Required—TOEFL (minimum score 577 paper-based; 90 iBT), IELTS (minimum score 6.5). *Application deadline:* For fall admission, 6/30 priority date for domestic students, 3/15 for international students; for spring admission, 12/15 for domestic students, 9/15 for international students; for summer admission, 4/15 for domestic and international students. Applications are processed on a rolling basis. Application fee: $65 ($70 for international students). Electronic applications accepted. *Expenses:* Full-time resident $10,479 per term, full-time nonresident $14,398 per term, part-time $890 per credit hour. *Financial support:* In 2018–19, 251 students received support, including 12 teaching assistantships with full and partial tuition reimbursements available (averaging $3,500 per year); scholarships/grants, tuition waivers (full and partial), and unspecified assistantships also available. Financial award application deadline: 2/1; financial award applicants required to submit FAFSA. *Faculty research:* Business analytics, financial management, organizational behavior, financial accounting, consumer insights. *Total annual research expenditures:* $39,943. *Unit head:* Dr. Marianne Lewis, Dean, 513-556-7001, Fax: 513-556-4891, E-mail: marianne.lewis@uc.edu. *Application contact:* Dona Clary, Executive Director, Graduate Programs, 513-556-3546, Fax: 513-558-7006, E-mail: dona.clary@uc.edu.
Website: http://business.uc.edu/graduate/masters.html

University of Cincinnati, Carl H. Lindner College of Business, PhD Programs, Cincinnati, OH 45221. Offers accounting (PhD); business analytics (PhD); economics (PhD); finance (PhD); information systems (PhD); management (PhD); marketing (PhD); operations and business analytics (PhD); operations research (PhD). *Faculty:* 101 full-time (37 women). *Students:* 15 full-time (5 women), 10 part-time (4 women); includes 4 minority (1 Black or African American, non-Hispanic/Latino; 3 Asian, non-Hispanic/Latino), 20 international. Average age 31. 125 applicants, 12% accepted, 4 enrolled. In 2018, 7 doctorates awarded. *Degree requirements:* For doctorate, comprehensive exam, thesis/dissertation. *Entrance requirements:* For doctorate, GMAT, GRE, transcripts, essays, resume, letters of recommendation. Additional exam requirements/recommendations for international students: Required—TOEFL (minimum score 600 paper-based; 100 iBT), IELTS (minimum score 7). *Application deadline:* For fall admission, 1/15 for domestic and international students. Application fee: $65 ($70 for international students). Electronic applications accepted. *Expenses:* Contact institution. *Financial support:* In 2018–19, 35 students received support, including 25 research assistantships with full tuition reimbursements available (averaging $23,250 per year); scholarships/grants, health care benefits, tuition waivers (full), and unspecified assistantships also available. Financial award application deadline: 1/15; financial award applicants required to submit FAFSA. *Faculty research:* Bayesian Prediction Theory, organizational fairness, consumer insight and market research, consumer insight and market research, density estimation from correlated data. *Unit head:* Dr. Olivier Parent, Director, 513-556-3941, Fax: 513-556-5499, E-mail: olivier.parent@uc.edu. *Application contact:* Angel Elvin, Assistant Director, 513-556-7190, Fax: 513-558-7006, E-mail: angel.elvin@uc.edu.
Website: http://business.uc.edu/graduate/phd.html

University of Colorado Denver, Business School, Program in Marketing, Denver, CO 80217. Offers advanced market analytics in a big data world (MS); brand communication in the digital era (MS); global marketing (MS); high-tech and entrepreneurial marketing (MS); marketing and global sustainability (MS); marketing intelligence and strategy in the 21st century (MS); sports and entertainment business (MS). *Program availability:* Part-time, evening/weekend. *Degree requirements:* For master's, 30 semester hours (21 of marketing core courses, 9 of marketing electives). *Entrance requirements:* For master's, GMAT, resume, essay, two letters of recommendation, financial statements (for international applicants). Additional exam requirements/recommendations for international students: Required—TOEFL (minimum score 525 paper-based; 71 iBT); Recommended—IELTS (minimum score 6.5). Electronic applications accepted. *Expenses:* Contact institution. *Faculty research:* Marketing issues in the Chinese environment, impact of individual difference and contextual factors on the risk-taking behaviors of managers making new-business creation decisions, attribution theory perspective of conflict between marketers and engineers, organizational identity and identification, international market entry strategies.

University of Connecticut, Graduate School, School of Business, Storrs, CT 06269. Offers accounting (MS, PhD); business (PhD); business administration (MBA); business analytics and project management (MS); finance (PhD); financial risk management (MS); health care management and insurance studies (MBA); human resource management (MS); management (PhD); management consulting (MBA); marketing (PhD); marketing intelligence (MBA); operations and information management (PhD). *Accreditation:* AACSB. *Degree requirements:* For master's, comprehensive exam; for doctorate, thesis/dissertation. *Entrance requirements:* For master's and doctorate, GMAT. Additional exam requirements/recommendations for international students: Required—TOEFL (minimum score 550 paper-based). Electronic applications accepted.

University of Dallas, Satish and Yasmin Gupta College of Business, Irving, TX 75062. Offers accounting (MBA, MS); business administration (DBA); business analytics (MS); business management (MBA); corporate finance (MBA); cybersecurity (MS); finance (MS); financial services (MBA); global business (MBA, MS); health services management (MBA); human resource management (MBA); information and technology management (MS); information assurance (MBA); information technology (MBA); information technology service management (MBA); marketing management (MBA); organization development (MBA); project management (MBA); sports and entertainment management (MBA); strategic leadership (MBA); supply chain management (MBA). *Accreditation:* AACSB. *Program availability:* Part-time, evening/weekend, 100% online. *Students:* 147 full-time (56 women), 584 part-time (232 women); includes 402 minority (204 Black or African American, non-Hispanic/Latino; 95 Asian, non-Hispanic/Latino; 92 Hispanic/Latino; 2 Native Hawaiian or other Pacific Islander, non-Hispanic/Latino; 9 Two or more races, non-Hispanic/Latino), 113 international. Average age 34. 992 applicants, 30% accepted, 157 enrolled. In 2018, 336 master's, 5 doctorates awarded. *Degree requirements:* For doctorate, thesis/dissertation. *Entrance requirements:* For master's and doctorate, U.S. bachelor's degree with a minimum cumulative GPA of 2.0 from a regionally accredited college or university (or comparable foreign degree); minimum 3.0 GPA in any graduate-level coursework completed; good academic standing with all colleges attended. Additional exam requirements/recommendations for international students: Required—TOEFL (minimum score 80 iBT), IELTS (minimum score 6.5), PTE (minimum score 67). *Application deadline:* Applications are processed on a rolling basis. Application fee: $50. Electronic applications accepted. *Expenses:* $1250 per credit hour. *Financial support:* In 2018–19, 291 students received support. Research assistantships, teaching assistantships, scholarships/grants, and unspecified assistantships available. Support available to part-time students. Financial award application deadline: 2/15; financial award applicants required to submit FAFSA. *Unit head:* Brett J.L. Landry, Dean, 972-721-5356, E-mail: blandry@udallas.edu. *Application contact:* Breonna Collins, Director, Graduate Admissions, 972-7215304, E-mail: bcollins@udallas.edu.
Website: http://www.udallas.edu/cob/

University of Dayton, School of Business Administration, Dayton, OH 45469. Offers accounting (MBA); cyber security (MBA); finance (MBA); marketing (MBA); JD/MBA. *Accreditation:* AACSB. *Program availability:* Part-time, evening/weekend, blended/hybrid learning. *Entrance requirements:* For master's, GMAT (minimum score of 500 total, 19 verbal); GRE (minimum score of 149 verbal, 146 quantitative), minimum GPA of 3.0, current resume. Additional exam requirements/recommendations for international students: Required—TOEFL (minimum score 550 paper-based; 80 iBT); Recommended—IELTS (minimum score 6.5). Electronic applications accepted. *Expenses:* Contact institution. *Faculty research:* Management information systems, economics, finance, marketing, entrepreneurship, accounting, cyber security, analytics.

University of Denver, Daniels College of Business, Department of Marketing, Denver, CO 80208. Offers MBA, MS. *Program availability:* Part-time, evening/weekend. *Faculty:* 15 full-time (7 women), 4 part-time/adjunct (2 women). *Students:* 27 full-time (16 women), 23 part-time (19 women); includes 12 minority (2 Black or African American, non-Hispanic/Latino; 1 Asian, non-Hispanic/Latino; 4 Hispanic/Latino; 5 Two or more races, non-Hispanic/Latino), 12 international. Average age 26. 142 applicants, 46% accepted, 27 enrolled. In 2018, 32 master's awarded. *Entrance requirements:* For master's, GRE General Test or GMAT, bachelor's degree, transcripts, essays, resume, interview. Additional exam requirements/recommendations for international students: Required—TOEFL (minimum score 575 paper-based; 94 iBT). *Application deadline:* For fall admission, 10/15 priority date for domestic and international students. Applications are processed on a rolling basis. Application fee: $100. Electronic applications accepted. *Expenses:* $49,695 per year full-time; $1,372 per credit. *Financial support:* In 2018–19, 42 students received support. Teaching assistantships with tuition reimbursements available, career-related internships or fieldwork, Federal Work-Study, institutionally sponsored loans, scholarships/grants, and unspecified assistantships available. Support available to part-time students. Financial award application deadline: 2/15; financial award applicants required to submit FAFSA. *Faculty research:* Behavorial judgement and decision making, value cocreation, experiential consumption and consumer decision making, the effect of electronic word of mouth on sales, effectivness of pedigoical approaches to business education. *Unit head:* Dr. Don Bacon, Professor and Director, 303-871-3317, E-mail: dbacon@du.edu. *Application contact:* Gabby Barcenas, Assistant to the Chair, 303-871-3317, E-mail: gabriela.barcenas@du.edu.
Website: https://daniels.du.edu/marketing

University of Florida, Graduate School, Warrington College of Business Administration, Hough Graduate School of Business, Department of Marketing, Gainesville, FL 32611. Offers MA, MS, PhD. Terminal master's awarded for partial completion of doctoral program. *Degree requirements:* For master's, comprehensive exam, thesis optional; for doctorate, comprehensive exam, thesis/dissertation. *Entrance requirements:* For master's and doctorate, GMAT (minimum score of 465) or GRE

General Test, minimum GPA of 3.0. Additional exam requirements/recommendations for international students: Required—TOEFL (minimum score 550 paper-based; 80 iBT), IELTS (minimum score 6). Electronic applications accepted. *Faculty research:* Consumer behavior, decision-making, behavioral decision theory, marketing models, marketing strategy.

University of Hawaii at Manoa, Office of Graduate Education, Shidler College of Business, Program in Business Administration, Honolulu, HI 96822. Offers Asian business studies (MBA); Chinese business studies (MBA); decision sciences (MBA); entrepreneurship (MBA); finance (MBA); finance and banking (MBA); human resources management (MBA); information management (MBA); information technology (MBA); international business (MBA); Japanese business studies (MBA); marketing (MBA); organizational behavior (MBA); organizational management (MBA); real estate (MBA); student-designed track (MBA). *Accreditation:* AACSB. *Program availability:* Part-time, evening/weekend. *Degree requirements:* For master's, thesis optional. *Entrance requirements:* For master's, GMAT, minimum GPA of 3.0. Additional exam requirements/recommendations for international students: Required—TOEFL (minimum score 600 paper-based; 100 iBT), IELTS (minimum score 7). *Expenses:* Contact institution.

University of Hawaii at Manoa, Office of Graduate Education, Shidler College of Business, Program in International Management, Honolulu, HI 96822. Offers Asian finance (PhD); global information technology management (PhD); international accounting (PhD); international marketing (PhD); international organization and strategy (PhD). *Program availability:* Part-time. *Degree requirements:* For doctorate, comprehensive exam, thesis/dissertation. *Entrance requirements:* For doctorate, GMAT or GRE General Test, minimum GPA of 3.0. Additional exam requirements/recommendations for international students: Required—TOEFL (minimum score 600 paper-based; 100 iBT), IELTS (minimum score 7). *Expenses:* Contact institution.

University of Houston, Bauer College of Business, Marketing Program, Houston, TX 77204. Offers PhD. *Program availability:* Part-time, evening/weekend. *Degree requirements:* For doctorate, comprehensive exam, thesis/dissertation. *Entrance requirements:* For doctorate, GMAT or GRE. *Faculty research:* Accountancy and taxation, finance, international business, management.

University of Houston–Victoria, School of Business Administration, Victoria, TX 77901-4450. Offers accounting (MBA); economic development and entrepreneurship (MS); finance (GMBA, MBA); general business (MBA); international business (MBA); management (GMBA, MBA); marketing (MBA). *Accreditation:* AACSB. *Program availability:* Part-time, evening/weekend, online learning. *Entrance requirements:* For master's, GMAT. Additional exam requirements/recommendations for international students: Required—TOEFL (minimum score 550 paper-based). Electronic applications accepted. *Expenses: Tuition, area resident:* Full-time $6154; part-time $3077 per semester. Tuition, state resident: full-time $6154; part-time $3077 per semester. Tuition, nonresident: full-time $13,624; part-time $6812 per semester. *International tuition:* $13,624 full-time. *Required fees:* $1405; $847 per semester. $423 per semester. Tuition and fees vary according to program. *Faculty research:* Economic development, marketing, finance.

The University of Iowa, Tippie College of Business, Department of Marketing, Iowa City, IA 52242-1316. Offers PhD. *Degree requirements:* For doctorate, comprehensive exam, thesis/dissertation. *Entrance requirements:* Additional exam requirements/recommendations for international students: Required—TOEFL (minimum iBT score 100) or IELTS (minimum score 7.0). Electronic applications accepted. *Faculty research:* Judgments and decision-making under certainty; consumer behavior: cognitive neuroscience, attitudes and evaluation; hierarchical Bayesian estimation; marketing-finance interface; advertising effects.

The University of Iowa, Tippie College of Business, Professional MBA Program, Iowa City, IA 52242-1316. Offers business administration (MBA); business analytics (MBA); finance (MBA); leadership (MBA); marketing (MBA). *Program availability:* Part-time-only, evening/weekend. *Degree requirements:* For master's, successful completion of nine required courses and six electives totaling 45 credits, minimum GPA of 2.75. *Entrance requirements:* For master's, GMAT or GRE. Additional exam requirements/recommendations for international students: Required—TOEFL (minimum score 600 paper-based; 100 iBT), IELTS (minimum score 7). Electronic applications accepted. *Expenses:* Contact institution. *Faculty research:* Capital markets; analytics techniques and applications; organizational and market systems analysis; applied econometrics; talent effectiveness.

The University of Kansas, Graduate Studies, School of Business, Program in Business, Lawrence, KS 66045. Offers business and organizational leadership (MS); decision sciences and supply chain management (PhD); finance (PhD); human resources management (PhD); marketing (PhD); organizational behavior (PhD); strategic management (PhD); supply chain management and logistics (MS). *Accreditation:* AACSB. *Program availability:* Part-time. *Students:* 69 full-time (20 women), 150 part-time (62 women); includes 42 minority (14 Black or African American, non-Hispanic/Latino; 2 American Indian or Alaska Native, non-Hispanic/Latino; 6 Asian, non-Hispanic/Latino; 7 Hispanic/Latino; 13 Two or more races, non-Hispanic/Latino), 24 international. Average age 32. 306 applicants, 51% accepted, 132 enrolled. In 2018, 22 master's, 1 doctorate awarded. *Entrance requirements:* For master's, GMAT, official transcript, three letters of recommendation, resume, statement of purpose; for doctorate, GMAT or GRE, official transcript, three letters of recommendation, resume, statement of purpose. Additional exam requirements/recommendations for international students: Required—TOEFL, IELTS. *Application deadline:* For fall admission, 1/10 for domestic and international students. Application fee: $65 ($85 for international students). Electronic applications accepted. *Financial support:* Fellowships, research assistantships, teaching assistantships, scholarships/grants, health care benefits, tuition waivers (full), and unspecified assistantships available. Financial award application deadline: 1/10. *Faculty research:* Strategic human resource management, business ethics, organizational theory/behavior, corporate strategy, international business, supply chain management, Bayesian networks, game theory, decision analysis and time/series analysis, pricing, consumer effects, advertising and emotion. *Unit head:* Charly Edmonds, Director, 785-864-3841, E-mail: cedmonds@ku.edu. *Application contact:* Andrea Noltner, Graduate Admission Contact, 785-864-7556, E-mail: anoltner@ku.edu.
Website: http://www.business.ku.edu/

University of La Verne, College of Business and Public Management, Graduate Programs in Business Administration, La Verne, CA 91750-4443. Offers accounting (MBA, MBA-EP); finance (MBA, MBA-EP); health services management (MBA); information technology (MBA, MBA-EP); international business (MBA, MBA-EP); management and leadership (MBA, MBA-EP); marketing (MBA, MBA-EP); supply chain management (MBA, MBA-EP). *Program availability:* Part-time, evening/weekend. *Entrance requirements:* For master's, GMAT, MAT, or GRE, minimum undergraduate GPA of 3.0, 2 letters of recommendation, resume, statement of purpose. Additional exam requirements/recommendations for international students: Required—TOEFL (minimum score 550 paper-based; 85 iBT).

University of La Verne, Regional and Online Campuses, Graduate Programs, Inland Empire Campus, Ontario, CA 91730. Offers business administration (MBA, MBA-EP), including accounting (MBA), finance (MBA), health services management (MBA-EP), information technology (MBA-EP), international business (MBA), managed care (MBA), management and leadership (MBA-EP), marketing (MBA-EP), supply chain management (MBA); leadership and management (MS), including human resource management, nonprofit management, organizational development. *Program availability:* Part-time, evening/weekend. *Expenses:* Contact institution.

University of Lethbridge, School of Graduate Studies, Lethbridge, AB T1K 3M4, Canada. Offers addictions counseling (M Sc); agricultural biotechnology (M Sc); agricultural studies (M Sc, MA); anthropology (MA); archaeology (M Sc, MA); art (MA, MFA); biochemistry (M Sc); biological sciences (M Sc); biomolecular science (PhD); biosystems and biodiversity (PhD); Canadian studies (MA); chemistry (M Sc); computer science (M Sc); computer science and geographical information science (M Sc); counseling (MC); counseling psychology (M Ed); dramatic arts (MA); earth, space, and physical science (PhD); economics (MA); education (MA, PhD); educational leadership (M Ed); English (MA); environmental science (M Sc); evolution and behavior (PhD); exercise science (M Sc); French (MA); French/German (MA); French/Spanish (MA); general education (M Ed); geography (M Sc, MA); German (MA); health sciences (M Sc); individualized multidisciplinary (M Sc, MA); kinesiology (M Sc, MA); management (M Sc), including accounting, finance, human resource management and labor relations, information systems, international management, marketing, policy and strategy; mathematics (M Sc); music (M Mus, MA); Native American studies (MA); neuroscience (M Sc, PhD); new media (MA, MFA); nursing (M Sc, MN); philosophy (MA); physics (M Sc); political science (MA); psychology (M Sc, MA); religious studies (MA); sociology (MA); theatre and dramatic arts (MFA); theoretical and computational science (PhD); urban and regional studies (MA); women and gender studies (MA). *Program availability:* Part-time, evening/weekend. *Degree requirements:* For master's, thesis (for some programs); for doctorate, comprehensive exam, thesis/dissertation. *Entrance requirements:* For master's, GMAT (for M Sc in management), bachelor's degree in related field, minimum GPA of 3.0 during previous 20 graded semester courses, 2 years' teaching or related experience (M Ed); for doctorate, master's degree, minimum graduate GPA of 3.5. Additional exam requirements/recommendations for international students: Required—TOEFL (minimum score 580 paper-based; 93 iBT). Electronic applications accepted. *Faculty research:* Movement and brain plasticity, gibberellin physiology, photosynthesis, carbon cycling, molecular properties of main-group ring components.

The University of Manchester, Alliance Manchester Business School, M15 6PB, United Kingdom. Offers accounting and finance (M Sc); business (M Ent); business analysis and strategic management (M Sc); business analytics: operational research and risk analysis (M Sc); business psychology (M Sc); corporate communications and reputation management (M Sc); finance (M Sc); finance and business economics (M Sc); human resource management and industrial relations (M Sc); innovation management and entrepreneurship (M Sc); international business and management (M Sc); international human resource management and comparative industrial relations (M Sc); management (M Sc); marketing (M Sc); operations, project and supply chain management (M Sc); organizational psychology (M Sc); quantitative finance (M Sc). *Entrance requirements:* For master's, UK 2:1 honours degree or overseas equivalent. Additional exam requirements/recommendations for international students: Required—TOEFL (minimum score 100 iBT), IELTS (minimum score 7), PTE. Electronic applications accepted. *Faculty research:* Accounting and finance, management sciences and marketing, people management and organization, innovation management and policy, decision sciences.

University of Massachusetts Amherst, Graduate School, Isenberg School of Management, Program in Management, Amherst, MA 01003. Offers accounting (PhD); business administration (MBA); entrepreneurship (MBA); finance (MBA, PhD); healthcare administration (MBA); hospitality and tourism management (PhD); management science (PhD); marketing (MBA, PhD); organization studies (PhD); sport management (PhD); strategic management (PhD); MBA/MS. *Accreditation:* AACSB. *Program availability:* Part-time, evening/weekend, online learning. Terminal master's awarded for partial completion of doctoral program. *Degree requirements:* For doctorate, comprehensive exam, thesis/dissertation. *Entrance requirements:* For master's and doctorate, GMAT or GRE General Test. Additional exam requirements/recommendations for international students: Required—TOEFL (minimum score 550 paper-based; 80 iBT), IELTS (minimum score 6.5). Electronic applications accepted.

University of Memphis, Graduate School, Fogelman College of Business and Economics, Program in Business Administration, Memphis, TN 38152. Offers accounting (MBA, PhD); business administration (IMBA); economics (PhD); executive business administration (MBA); finance (PhD); management (PhD); marketing (MS); marketing and supply chain management (PhD); real estate development (MS); JD/MBA. *Accreditation:* AACSB. *Students:* 189 full-time (96 women), 364 part-time (151 women); includes 178 minority (89 Black or African American, non-Hispanic/Latino; 1 American Indian or Alaska Native, non-Hispanic/Latino; 68 Asian, non-Hispanic/Latino; 12 Hispanic/Latino; 8 Two or more races, non-Hispanic/Latino), 102 international. Average age 32. 298 applicants, 72% accepted, 139 enrolled. In 2018, 200 master's, 3 doctorates awarded. *Degree requirements:* For master's, comprehensive exam; for doctorate, comprehensive exam, thesis/dissertation. *Entrance requirements:* For master's, GMAT, resume; for doctorate, GMAT, interview, minimum GPA of 3.4, resume, letter of recommendation. Additional exam requirements/recommendations for international students: Required—TOEFL (minimum score 550 paper-based). *Application deadline:* For fall admission, 8/1 for domestic students; for spring admission, 12/1 for domestic students. Application fee: $35 ($60 for international students). *Expenses: Tuition, area resident:* Full-time $10,240; part-time $503 per credit hour. Tuition, state resident: full-time $10,464. Tuition, nonresident: full-time $20,224; part-time $991 per credit hour. *Required fees:* $850; $106 per credit hour. *Financial support:* Research assistantships with full tuition reimbursements, teaching assistantships with full tuition reimbursements, career-related internships or fieldwork, Federal Work-Study, scholarships/grants, and unspecified assistantships available. Financial award application deadline: 2/15; financial award applicants required to submit FAFSA. *Faculty research:* Competitive business strategy, finance microstructures, supply chain management innovations, health care economics, litigation risks and corporate audits. *Unit head:* Dr. Balaji Krishnan, Director, MBA Programs, 901-678-2786, E-mail: krishnan@memphis.edu. *Application contact:* Dr. Balaji Krishnan, Director, MBA Programs, 901-678-2786, E-mail: krishnan@memphis.edu.
Website: https://www.memphis.edu/mba/index.php

University of Michigan–Flint, School of Management, Program in Business Administration, Flint, MI 48502-1950. Offers accounting (MBA); computer information systems (MBA); finance (MBA, Post-Master's Certificate); general business (Graduate Certificate); general business administration (MBA); health care management (MBA); international business (MBA, Post-Master's Certificate); lean manufacturing (MBA); marketing (Post-Master's Certificate); marketing and innovation management (MBA); organizational leadership (MBA). *Program availability:* Part-time, evening/weekend, mixed mode format. *Faculty:* 30 full-time (4 women), 10 part-time/adjunct (2 women). *Students:* 24 full-time (14 women), 151 part-time (60 women); includes 45 minority (22 Black or African American, non-Hispanic/Latino; 3 American Indian or Alaska Native,

non-Hispanic/Latino; 7 Asian, non-Hispanic/Latino; 9 Hispanic/Latino; 4 Two or more races, non-Hispanic/Latino), 19 international. Average age 36. 160 applicants, 75% accepted, 62 enrolled. In 2018, 50 master's, 1 other advanced degree awarded. *Entrance requirements:* For master's, bachelor's degree in arts, sciences, engineering, or business administration from regionally-accredited college or university; for other advanced degree, bachelor's degree in arts, sciences, engineering, or business administration from regionally-accredited college or university. college-level math, statistics, or quantitative course (for Graduate Certificate); MBA or equivalent degree from regionally-accredited college or university (for Post Master's Certificate). Additional exam requirements/recommendations for international students: Required—TOEFL (minimum score 84 iBT), IELTS (minimum score 6.5). *Application deadline:* For fall admission, 8/1 for domestic students, 5/1 for international students; for winter admission, 11/15 for domestic students, 9/1 for international students; for spring admission, 3/15 for domestic students, 1/1 for international students; for summer admission, 5/15 for domestic students. Applications are processed on a rolling basis. Application fee: $55. Electronic applications accepted. *Expenses:* Contact institution. *Financial support:* Federal Work-Study, scholarships/grants, and unspecified assistantships available. Support available to part-time students. Financial award application deadline: 3/1; financial award applicants required to submit FAFSA. *Unit head:* Dr. Scott Johnson, Dean, School of Management, 810-762-3164, Fax: 810-237-6685, E-mail: scotjohn@umflint.edu. *Application contact:* Matt Bohlen, Director of Graduate Admissions, 810-762-3171, E-mail: mbohlen@umflint.edu.
Website: http://www.umflint.edu/graduateprograms/business-administration-mba

University of Minnesota, Twin Cities Campus, Carlson School of Management, Carlson Full-Time MBA Program, Minneapolis, MN 55455. Offers finance (MBA); information technology (MBA); management (MBA); marketing (MBA); medical industry orientation (MBA); supply chain and operations (MBA); JD/MBA; MBA/MPP; MBA/MSBA; MD/MBA; MHA/MBA; Pharm D/MBA. *Accreditation:* AACSB. *Faculty:* 150 full-time (43 women), 21 part-time/adjunct (5 women). *Students:* 169 full-time (57 women); includes 32 minority (6 Black or African American, non-Hispanic/Latino; 4 American Indian or Alaska Native, non-Hispanic/Latino; 14 Asian, non-Hispanic/Latino; 8 Hispanic/Latino), 36 international. Average age 29. 529 applicants, 39% accepted, 92 enrolled. In 2018, 76 master's awarded. *Degree requirements:* For master's, None are required for MBA. *Entrance requirements:* For master's, GMAT or GRE, 2 recommendations, personal statement, resume. Additional exam requirements/recommendations for international students: Required—TOEFL (minimum score 580 paper-based; 84 iBT), IELTS (minimum score 7), PTE. *Application deadline:* For fall admission, 4/1 for domestic students, 2/1 for international students. Application fee: $75. Electronic applications accepted. *Expenses:* FTMBA Tuition; Collegiate fee; Student Services fee; Hospitalization. *Financial support:* In 2018–19, 139 students received support. Teaching assistantships with partial tuition reimbursements available, scholarships/grants, and unspecified assistantships available. Financial award application deadline: 4/1. *Faculty research:* Market regulation and asset pricing, social networks and data analytics, consumer behavior, innovation and entrepreneurship, workplace wellbeing and labor relationships. *Total annual research expenditures:* $577,440. *Unit head:* Philip J. Miller, Assistant Dean, MBA and MS Programs, 612-625-5555, Fax: 612-625-1012, E-mail: mba@umn.edu. *Application contact:* Linh Gilles, Director of Admissions and Recruiting, 612-625-5555, Fax: 612-625-1012, E-mail: ftmba@umn.edu.
Website: http://www.csom.umn.edu/MBA/full-time/

University of Minnesota, Twin Cities Campus, Carlson School of Management, Carlson Part-Time MBA Program, Minneapolis, MN 55455. Offers finance (MBA); information technology (MBA); management (MBA); marketing (MBA); medical industry orientation (MBA); supply chain and operations (MBA). *Program availability:* Part-time-only, evening/weekend, 100% online, blended/hybrid learning. *Faculty:* 150 full-time (43 women), 23 part-time/adjunct (6 women). *Students:* 822 part-time (260 women); includes 122 minority (18 Black or African American, non-Hispanic/Latino; 11 American Indian or Alaska Native, non-Hispanic/Latino; 67 Asian, non-Hispanic/Latino; 24 Hispanic/Latino; 2 Native Hawaiian or other Pacific Islander, non-Hispanic/Latino), 41 international. Average age 29. 204 applicants, 83% accepted, 141 enrolled. In 2018, 257 master's awarded. *Degree requirements:* For master's, None for MBA. *Entrance requirements:* For master's, GMAT or GRE, 2 recommendations, personal statement, current resume. Additional exam requirements/recommendations for international students: Required—TOEFL (minimum score 580 paper-based; 84 iBT), IELTS (minimum score 7), PTE. *Application deadline:* For fall admission, 5/15 priority date for domestic and international students; for spring admission, 10/15 priority date for domestic and international students. Applications are processed on a rolling basis. Application fee: $75. Electronic applications accepted. *Expenses:* PTMBA tuition; Collegiate fee. *Financial support:* Applicants required to submit FAFSA. *Faculty research:* Market regulation and asset pricing, social networks and data analytics, consumer behavior, innovation and entrepreneurship, workplace wellbeing and labor relationships. *Total annual research expenditures:* $577,440. *Unit head:* Philip J. Miller, Assistant Dean, MBA and MS Programs, 612-624-2039, Fax: 612-625-1012, E-mail: mba@umn.edu. *Application contact:* Linh Gilles, Director of Admissions and Recruiting, 612-625-5555, Fax: 612-625-1012, E-mail: ptmba@umn.edu.
Website: http://www.carlsonschool.umn.edu/ptmba

University of Minnesota, Twin Cities Campus, Carlson School of Management, Doctoral Program in Business Administration, Minneapolis, MN 55455-0213. Offers accounting (PhD); finance (PhD); information and decision sciences (PhD); marketing (PhD); strategic management and entrepreneurship (PhD); supply chain and operations (PhD); work and organizations (PhD). *Faculty:* 106 full-time (33 women). *Students:* 88 full-time (34 women); includes 9 minority (2 Black or African American, non-Hispanic/Latino; 6 Asian, non-Hispanic/Latino; 1 Hispanic/Latino), 66 international. Average age 30. 306 applicants, 8% accepted, 15 enrolled. In 2018, 14 doctorates awarded. *Degree requirements:* For doctorate, comprehensive exam, thesis/dissertation, written and oral preliminary exams, proposal defense, final defense. *Entrance requirements:* For doctorate, GMAT or GRE, minimum undergraduate GPA of 3.0, graduate 3.5 (recommended). Additional exam requirements/recommendations for international students: Required—Either or: TOEFL or IELTS; Recommended—TOEFL, IELTS. *Application deadline:* For fall admission, 12/15 for domestic students, 12/15 priority date for international students. Applications are processed on a rolling basis. Application fee: $75 ($95 for international students). Electronic applications accepted. *Financial support:* In 2018–19, 80 students received support, including 80 fellowships with full tuition reimbursements available (averaging $12,500 per year), 72 research assistantships with full tuition reimbursements available (averaging $7,800 per year), 72 teaching assistantships with full tuition reimbursements available (averaging $7,800 per year); health care benefits, unspecified assistantships, and full student service fee waivers also available. Financial award application deadline: 12/15. *Faculty research:* Finance, strategy and entrepreneurship, marketing, information and decision science, operations, accounting, supply chain, human resources and industrial relations, organizational behavior. *Unit head:* Dr. Shawn P. Curley, Director, 612-624-6546, Fax: 612-624-8221, E-mail: curley@umn.edu. *Application contact:* Sandy Herzan, Associate Director, 612-624-0875, Fax: 612-624-8221, E-mail: herza002@umn.edu.
Website: http://carlsonschool.umn.edu/degrees/phd

University of Mississippi, Graduate School, School of Business Administration, University, MS 38677. Offers business administration (MBA, PhD); finance (PhD); management (PhD); management information systems (PhD); marketing (PhD); JD/MBA. *Accreditation:* AACSB. *Faculty:* 60 full-time (18 women), 7 part-time/adjunct (1 woman). *Students:* 62 full-time (18 women), 83 part-time (20 women); includes 13 minority (4 Black or African American, non-Hispanic/Latino; 3 Asian, non-Hispanic/Latino; 4 Hispanic/Latino; 2 Two or more races, non-Hispanic/Latino), 14 international. Average age 30. In 2018, 83 master's, 11 doctorates awarded. *Entrance requirements:* For master's, GMAT, minimum GPA of 3.0; for doctorate, GMAT. Additional exam requirements/recommendations for international students: Required—TOEFL. *Application deadline:* Applications are processed on a rolling basis. Application fee: $50. Electronic applications accepted. *Financial support:* Fellowships, career-related internships or fieldwork, scholarships/grants, tuition waivers (full), and unspecified assistantships available. Financial award application deadline: 3/1; financial award applicants required to submit FAFSA. *Unit head:* Dr. Ken Cyree, Dean, 662-915-5820, Fax: 662-915-5821, E-mail: info@bus.olemiss.edu. *Application contact:* Temeka Smith, Graduate Activities Specialist for Admissions, 662-915-7474, Fax: 662-915-7577, E-mail: gschool@olemiss.edu.
Website: http://www.olemissbusiness.com/

University of Missouri–St. Louis, College of Business Administration, St. Louis, MO 63121. Offers accounting (M Acc); business administration (MBA, DBA, PhD, Certificate), including logistics and supply chain management (PhD); business intelligence (Certificate); cybersecurity (Certificate); digital and social media marketing (Certificate); human resources management (Certificate); information systems (MS); logistics and supply chain management (Certificate); marketing management (Certificate). *Program availability:* Part-time, evening/weekend. *Degree requirements:* For doctorate, thesis/dissertation. *Entrance requirements:* For master's, GMAT, 2 letters of recommendation; for doctorate, GMAT or GRE, 3 letters of recommendation. Additional exam requirements/recommendations for international students: Recommended—TOEFL (minimum score 550 paper-based; 79 iBT), IELTS (minimum score 6.5). Electronic applications accepted. *Faculty research:* Statistical decision aids, commercial banking, corporate finance, operations management, information systems.

University of Nebraska at Kearney, College of Business and Technology, Department of Business, Kearney, NE 68849-0001. Offers accounting (MBA); generalist (MBA); human resources (MBA); human services (MBA); marketing (MBA). *Accreditation:* AACSB. *Program availability:* Part-time, evening/weekend. *Degree requirements:* For master's, thesis optional, capstone course. *Entrance requirements:* For master's, GRE or GMAT (if no significant managerial experience), letters of recommendation, essay, resume. Additional exam requirements/recommendations for international students: Recommended—TOEFL (minimum score 550 paper-based; 79 iBT), IELTS (minimum score 6.5). Electronic applications accepted. *Faculty research:* Small business financial management, employment law, expert systems, international trade and marketing, environmental economics.

University of Nebraska–Lincoln, Graduate College, College of Arts and Sciences, Department of Communication Studies, Lincoln, NE 68588. Offers instructional communication (MA, PhD); interpersonal communication (MA, PhD); marketing, communication studies, and advertising (MA, PhD); organizational communication (MA, PhD); rhetoric and culture (MA, PhD). *Degree requirements:* For master's, thesis optional; for doctorate, comprehensive exam, thesis/dissertation. *Entrance requirements:* For master's and doctorate, GRE General Test, writing sample. Additional exam requirements/recommendations for international students: Required—TOEFL (minimum score 600 paper-based). Electronic applications accepted. *Faculty research:* Message strategies, gender communication, political communication, organizational communication, instructional communication.

University of Nebraska–Lincoln, Graduate College, College of Business Administration, Interdepartmental Area of Business, Department of Marketing, Lincoln, NE 68588. Offers business (MA, PhD). *Degree requirements:* For doctorate, comprehensive exam, thesis/dissertation. *Entrance requirements:* For master's and doctorate, GMAT. Additional exam requirements/recommendations for international students: Required—TOEFL. Electronic applications accepted. *Faculty research:* Channel information, marketing research methodology, sales management, cross-cultural marketing, impact of new technology.

University of Nebraska–Lincoln, Graduate College, College of Journalism and Mass Communications, Lincoln, NE 68588. Offers marketing, communication and advertising (MA); professional journalism (MA). *Program availability:* Online learning. *Degree requirements:* For master's, thesis. *Entrance requirements:* For master's, samples of work. Additional exam requirements/recommendations for international students: Required—TOEFL (minimum score 600 paper-based). Electronic applications accepted. *Faculty research:* Interactive media and the Internet, community newspapers, children's radio, advertising involvement, telecommunications policy.

University of New Brunswick Fredericton, School of Graduate Studies, Faculty of Forestry and Environmental Management, Fredericton, NB E3B 5A3, Canada. Offers ecological foundations of forest management (PhD); environmental management (MEM); forest engineering (M Sc FE, MFE); forest products marketing (MBA); forest resources (M Sc F, MF, PhD). *Program availability:* Part-time. *Degree requirements:* For master's, thesis; for doctorate, thesis/dissertation. *Entrance requirements:* For master's and doctorate, minimum GPA of 3.0. Additional exam requirements/recommendations for international students: Required—TOEFL (minimum score 550 paper-based; 80 iBT), IELTS (minimum score 7), TWE (minimum score 4). Electronic applications accepted. *Faculty research:* Forest machines, soils, and ecosystems; integrated forest management; forest meteorology; wood engineering; stream ecosystems dynamics; forest and natural resources policy; forest operations planning; wood technology and mechanics; forest road construction and engineering; forest, wildlife, insect, bird, and fire ecology; remote sensing; insect impacts; silviculture; LiDAR analytics; integrated pest management; forest tree genetics; genetic resource conservation and sustainable management.

University of New Haven, Graduate School, College of Business, Program in Business Administration, West Haven, CT 06516. Offers accounting (MBA); business administration (MBA); business intelligence (MBA); business policy and strategic leadership (MBA); finance (MBA), including chartered financial analyst; global marketing (MBA); human resources management (MBA); sport management (MBA). *Accreditation:* AACSB. *Program availability:* Part-time, evening/weekend. *Students:* 151 full-time (73 women), 70 part-time (30 women); includes 51 minority (23 Black or African American, non-Hispanic/Latino; 13 Asian, non-Hispanic/Latino; 14 Hispanic/Latino; 1 Two or more races, non-Hispanic/Latino), 74 international. Average age 28. 197 applicants, 91% accepted, 82 enrolled. In 2018, 70 master's awarded. *Entrance requirements:* For master's, GMAT. Additional exam requirements/recommendations for international students: Required—TOEFL (minimum score 80 iBT), IELTS, PTE. *Application deadline:* Applications are processed on a rolling basis. Application fee: $50. Electronic applications accepted. Application fee is waived when completed online. *Expenses:* *Tuition:* Full-time $16,470; part-time $915 per credit hour. *Required fees:* $230; $95 per term. *Financial support:* Research assistantships with partial tuition reimbursements, teaching assistantships with partial tuition reimbursements, career-related internships or

fieldwork, Federal Work-Study, scholarships/grants, and unspecified assistantships available. Support available to part-time students. Financial award applicants required to submit FAFSA. *Unit head:* Darell Singleterry, Director, 203-932-7386, E-mail: dsingleterry@newhaven.edu. *Application contact:* Selina O'Toole, Senior Associate Director of Graduate Admissions, 203-932-7337, E-mail: SOToole@newhaven.edu. Website: http://www.newhaven.edu/business/graduate-programs/mba/index.php

The University of North Carolina at Chapel Hill, Kenan-Flagler Business School, Doctoral Program in Business Administration, Chapel Hill, NC 27599. Offers accounting (PhD); finance (PhD); marketing (PhD); operations management (PhD); organizational behavior (PhD); strategy (PhD). *Accreditation:* AACSB. *Degree requirements:* For doctorate, thesis/dissertation. *Entrance requirements:* For doctorate, GMAT or GRE General Test. Electronic applications accepted. *Expenses:* Contact institution.

The University of North Carolina at Greensboro, Graduate School, Bryan School of Business and Economics, Department of Consumer, Apparel, and Retail Studies, Greensboro, NC 27412-5001. Offers MS, PhD. *Degree requirements:* For master's, one foreign language; for doctorate, one foreign language, thesis/dissertation. *Entrance requirements:* For master's and doctorate, GRE General Test. Additional exam requirements/recommendations for international students: Required—TOEFL. Electronic applications accepted. *Faculty research:* Impact of phosphate removal, protective clothing for pesticide workers, fabric hand: subjective and objective measurements.

University of North Texas, Toulouse Graduate School, Denton, TX 76203-5459. Offers accounting (MS); applied anthropology (MA, MS); applied behavior analysis (Certificate); applied geography (MA); applied technology and performance improvement (M Ed, MS); art education (MA); art history (MA); arts leadership (Certificate); audiology (Au D); behavior analysis (MS); behavioral science (PhD); biochemistry and molecular biology (MS); biology (MA, MS); biomedical engineering (MS); business analysis (MS); chemistry (MS); clinical health psychology (PhD); communication studies (MA, MS); computer engineering (MS); computer science (MS); counseling (M Ed, MS), including clinical mental health counseling (MS), college and university counseling, elementary school counseling, secondary school counseling; creative writing (MA); criminal justice (MS); curriculum and instruction (M Ed); decision sciences (MBA); design (MA, MFA), including fashion design (MFA), innovation studies, interior design (MFA); early childhood studies (MS); economics (MS); educational leadership (M Ed, Ed D); educational psychology (MS, PhD), including family studies (MS), gifted and talented (MS), human development (MS), learning and cognition (MS), research, measurement and evaluation (MS); electrical engineering (MS); emergency management (MPA); engineering technology (MS); English (MA); English as a second language (MA); environmental science (MS); finance (MBA, MS); financial management (MPA); French (MA); health services management (MBA); higher education (M Ed, Ed D); history (MA, MS); hospitality management (MS); human resources management (MPA); information science (MS); information systems (PhD); information technologies (MBA); interdisciplinary studies (MA, MS); international studies (MA); international sustainable tourism (MS); jazz studies (MM); journalism (MA, MJ, Graduate Certificate), including interactive and virtual digital communication (Graduate Certificate), narrative journalism (Graduate Certificate), public relations (Graduate Certificate); kinesiology (MS); linguistics (MA); local government management (MPA); logistics (PhD); logistics and supply chain management (MBA); long-term care, senior housing, and aging services (MA); management (PhD); marketing (MBA); mathematics (MA, MS); mechanical and energy engineering (MS, PhD); music (MA), including ethnomusicology, music theory, musicology, performance; music composition (PhD); music education (MM Ed, PhD); nonprofit management (MPA); operations and supply chain management (MBA); performance (MM, DMA); philosophy (MA); political science (MA); professional and technical communication (MA); radio, television and film (MA, MFA); rehabilitation counseling (Certificate); sociology (MA); Spanish (MA); special education (M Ed); speech-language pathology (MA); strategic management (MBA); studio art (MFA); teaching (M Ed); MBA/MS. *Program availability:* Part-time, evening/weekend, online learning. Terminal master's awarded for partial completion of doctoral program. *Degree requirements:* For master's, variable foreign language requirement, comprehensive exam (for some programs), thesis (for some programs); for doctorate, variable foreign language requirement, comprehensive exam (for some programs), thesis/dissertation; for other advanced degree, variable foreign language requirement, comprehensive exam (for some programs). *Entrance requirements:* For master's and doctorate, GRE, GMAT. Additional exam requirements/recommendations for international students: Required—TOEFL (minimum score 550 paper-based; 79 iBT). Electronic applications accepted.

University of Notre Dame, Mendoza College of Business, Master of Business Administration Program, Notre Dame, IN 46556. Offers business analytics (MBA); business leadership (MBA); consulting (MBA); corporate finance (MBA); innovation and entrepreneurship (MBA); investments (MBA); marketing (MBA); MBA/MSBA. *Accreditation:* AACSB. *Entrance requirements:* For master's, GMAT or GRE, work experience, essay, four-slide presentation, two recommendations, transcripts from all colleges and/or universities attended, interview. Additional exam requirements/recommendations for international students: Required—PTE (minimum score 68), TOEFL (minimum iBT score of 109), IELTS (7.5), or documentation of at least six semesters of full-time university education in English. Electronic applications accepted. *Expenses:* Contact institution. *Faculty research:* Market micro-structure; marketing and public policy; corporate finance and accounting; corporate governance and ethical behavior; high performing organizations.

University of Oregon, Graduate School, Charles H. Lundquist College of Business, Department of Marketing, Eugene, OR 97403. Offers PhD. *Program availability:* Part-time. *Degree requirements:* For doctorate, thesis/dissertation, 2 comprehensive exams. *Entrance requirements:* For doctorate, GMAT. Additional exam requirements/recommendations for international students: Required—TOEFL. *Faculty research:* Consumer behavior, marketing research, international marketing, marketing management, price quality.

University of Pennsylvania, Wharton School, Marketing Department, Philadelphia, PA 19104. Offers MBA, PhD. Terminal master's awarded for partial completion of doctoral program. *Degree requirements:* For master's, thesis optional; for doctorate, thesis/dissertation. *Entrance requirements:* For doctorate, GMAT or GRE. *Faculty research:* Scanner data, consumer preferences, decision-making theory, modeling for marketing and e-business.

University of Phoenix–Bay Area Campus, School of Business, San Jose, CA 95134-1805. Offers accountancy (MS); accounting (MBA); business administration (MBA, DBA); energy management (MBA); global management (MBA); health care management (MBA); human resource management (MBA); human resources management (MM); management (MM); marketing (MBA); organizational leadership (DM); project management (MBA); public administration (MPA); technology management (MBA). *Accreditation:* ACBSP. *Program availability:* Evening/weekend, online learning. *Degree requirements:* For master's, thesis (for some programs). *Entrance requirements:* For master's, minimum undergraduate GPA of 3.0, 3 years of work experience. Additional exam requirements/recommendations for international students: Required—TOEFL (minimum score 550 paper-based; 79 iBT). Electronic applications accepted.

University of Phoenix–Central Valley Campus, School of Business, Fresno, CA 93720-1552. Offers accounting (MBA); business administration (MBA); global management (MBA); human resources management (MBA, MM); management (MM); marketing (MBA); public administration (MBA, MM). *Accreditation:* ACBSP.

University of Phoenix–Dallas Campus, School of Business, Dallas, TX 75251. Offers accounting (MBA); business administration (MBA); global management (MBA); human resources management (MBA, MM); management (MM); marketing (MBA); public administration (MBA, MM). *Accreditation:* ACBSP. *Program availability:* Evening/weekend, online learning. *Degree requirements:* For master's, thesis (for some programs). *Entrance requirements:* For master's, 3 years of work experience, minimum undergraduate GPA of 3.0. Additional exam requirements/recommendations for international students: Required—TOEFL (minimum score 550 paper-based; 79 iBT). Electronic applications accepted.

University of Phoenix–Hawaii Campus, School of Business, Honolulu, HI 96813-3800. Offers accounting (MBA); business administration (MBA); global management (MBA); human resources management (MBA, MM); management (MM); marketing (MBA); public administration (MBA, MM). *Accreditation:* ACBSP. *Program availability:* Evening/weekend. *Degree requirements:* For master's, thesis (for some programs). *Entrance requirements:* For master's, minimum undergraduate GPA of 3.0, 3 years of work experience. Additional exam requirements/recommendations for international students: Required—TOEFL (minimum score 550 paper-based; 79 iBT). Electronic applications accepted.

University of Phoenix–Houston Campus, School of Business, Houston, TX 77079-2004. Offers accounting (MBA); business administration (MBA); global management (MBA); human resources management (MBA, MM); management (MM); marketing (MBA); public administration (MBA, MM). *Accreditation:* ACBSP. *Program availability:* Evening/weekend, online learning. *Degree requirements:* For master's, thesis (for some programs). *Entrance requirements:* For master's, 3 years of work experience, minimum undergraduate GPA of 3.0. Additional exam requirements/recommendations for international students: Required—TOEFL (minimum score 550 paper-based; 79 iBT). Electronic applications accepted.

University of Phoenix–Las Vegas Campus, School of Business, Las Vegas, NV 89135. Offers accounting (MBA); business administration (MBA); global management (MBA); human resources management (MBA, MM); management (MM); marketing (MBA); public administration (MM). *Accreditation:* ACBSP. *Program availability:* Evening/weekend, online learning. *Degree requirements:* For master's, thesis (for some programs). *Entrance requirements:* For master's, minimum undergraduate GPA of 3.0, 3 years of work experience. Additional exam requirements/recommendations for international students: Required—TOEFL (minimum score 550 paper-based; 79 iBT). Electronic applications accepted.

University of Phoenix–Online Campus, School of Business, Phoenix, AZ 85034-7209. Offers accountancy (MS); accounting (MBA, Certificate); business administration (MBA); energy management (MBA); global management (MBA); health care management (MBA); human resource management (MBA, Certificate); human resources management (MM); management (MM); marketing (MBA, Certificate); project management (MBA, Certificate); public administration (MBA, MM); technology management (MBA). *Program availability:* Evening/weekend, online learning. *Entrance requirements:* Additional exam requirements/recommendations for international students: Required—TOEFL, TOEIC (Test of English as an International Communication), Berlitz Online English Proficiency Exam, PTE, or IELTS. Electronic applications accepted. *Expenses:* Contact institution.

University of Phoenix–Phoenix Campus, School of Business, Tempe, AZ 85282-2371. Offers accounting (MBA, MS, Certificate); business administration (MBA); energy management (MBA); global management (MBA); health care management (MBA); human resource management (MBA, Certificate); management (MM); marketing (MBA); project management (MBA); technology management (MBA). *Program availability:* Evening/weekend, online learning. *Entrance requirements:* Additional exam requirements/recommendations for international students: Required—TOEFL, TOEIC (Test of English as an International Communication), Berlitz Online English Proficiency Exam, PTE, or IELTS. Electronic applications accepted. *Expenses:* Contact institution.

University of Phoenix–Sacramento Valley Campus, School of Business, Sacramento, CA 95833-4334. Offers accounting (MBA); business administration (MBA); global management (MBA); human resources management (MBA, MM); management (MM); marketing (MBA); public administration (MBA, MM). *Accreditation:* ACBSP. *Program availability:* Evening/weekend. *Degree requirements:* For master's, thesis (for some programs). *Entrance requirements:* For master's, minimum undergraduate GPA of 3.0, 3 years work experience. Additional exam requirements/recommendations for international students: Required—TOEFL (minimum score 550 paper-based; 79 iBT). Electronic applications accepted.

University of Phoenix–San Antonio Campus, School of Business, San Antonio, TX 78230. Offers accounting (MBA); business administration (MBA); e-business (MBA); global management (MBA); human resources management (MBA, MM); management (MM); marketing (MBA); public administration (MBA, MM). *Accreditation:* ACBSP.

University of Phoenix–San Diego Campus, School of Business, San Diego, CA 92123. Offers accounting (MBA); business administration (MBA); global management (MBA); human resources management (MBA, MM); management (MM); marketing (MBA); public administration (MBA). *Accreditation:* ACBSP. *Program availability:* Evening/weekend. *Degree requirements:* For master's, thesis (for some programs). *Entrance requirements:* For master's, 3 years of work experience, minimum undergraduate GPA of 3.0. Additional exam requirements/recommendations for international students: Required—TOEFL (minimum score 550 paper-based; 79 iBT). Electronic applications accepted.

University of Pittsburgh, Katz Graduate School of Business, Doctoral Program in Business Administration, Pittsburgh, PA 15260. Offers accounting (PhD); business analytics and operations (PhD); finance (PhD); information systems and technology management (PhD); marketing (PhD); organizational behavior and human resources (PhD); strategic management (PhD). *Accreditation:* AACSB. *Program availability:* Evening/weekend. *Degree requirements:* For doctorate, comprehensive exam, thesis/dissertation, student teaching. *Entrance requirements:* For doctorate, GMAT or GRE, 3 recommendations, statement of purpose, transcripts of all previous course work and degrees. Additional exam requirements/recommendations for international students: Required—TOEFL (minimum score 100 iBT) or IELTS (minimum score 7.0). Electronic applications accepted. *Faculty research:* Accounting systems/financial reporting, corporate finance, shopper marketing/consumer behavior, management information systems, organizational behavior and entrepreneurship.

University of Pittsburgh, Katz Graduate School of Business, Master of Business Administration Programs, Pittsburgh, PA 15260. Offers finance (MBA); information systems (MBA); marketing (MBA); operations (MBA); organizational behavior and human resources (MBA); strategy, environment and organizations (MBA); MBA/JD;

Marketing

MBA/MID; MBA/MIS; MBA/MSE. *Accreditation:* AACSB. *Program availability:* Part-time, evening/weekend, blended/hybrid learning. *Degree requirements:* For master's, minimum GPA of 3.0. *Entrance requirements:* For master's, GMAT, GRE. Additional exam requirements/recommendations for international students: Required—TOEFL (minimum score 100 iBT) or IELTS (minimum score 7.0). Electronic applications accepted. *Faculty research:* Accounting systems/financial reporting, corporate finance, shopper marketing/consumer behavior, management information systems, organizational behavior and entrepreneurship.

University of Pittsburgh, Katz Graduate School of Business, Master of Science in Marketing Science Program, Pittsburgh, PA 15260. Offers MS. *Program availability:* Part-time, evening/weekend. *Degree requirements:* For master's, minimum GPA of 3.0. *Entrance requirements:* For master's, GMAT, GRE. Additional exam requirements/recommendations for international students: Required—TOEFL (minimum score 100 iBT), IELTS (minimum score 7). Electronic applications accepted. *Expenses:* Contact institution. *Faculty research:* Accounting systems/financial reporting, corporate finance, shopper marketing/consumer behavior, management information systems, organizational behavior and entrepreneurship.

University of Portland, Dr. Robert B. Pamplin, Jr. School of Business, Portland, OR 97203-5798. Offers entrepreneurship (MBA); finance (MBA, MS); health care management (MBA); marketing (MBA); nonprofit management (EMBA); operations and technology management (MBA, MS); sustainability (MBA). *Accreditation:* AACSB. *Program availability:* Part-time, evening/weekend. *Faculty:* 26 full-time (5 women), 8 part-time/adjunct (1 woman). *Students:* 35 full-time (16 women), 114 part-time (47 women); includes 21 minority (3 Black or African American, non-Hispanic/Latino; 2 American Indian or Alaska Native, non-Hispanic/Latino; 8 Asian, non-Hispanic/Latino; 8 Hispanic/Latino), 24 international. Average age 32. In 2018, 55 master's awarded. *Entrance requirements:* For master's, GMAT or GRE, minimum GPA of 3.0, resume, statement of goals, 2 letters of recommendation. Additional exam requirements/recommendations for international students: Required—TOEFL (minimum score 88 iBT), IELTS (minimum score 7). *Application deadline:* For fall admission, 7/19 priority date for domestic and international students; for spring admission, 12/7 priority date for domestic and international students; for summer admission, 4/12 priority date for domestic and international students. Applications are processed on a rolling basis. Application fee: $0. Electronic applications accepted. *Expenses:* Contact institution. *Financial support:* Application deadline: 3/1; applicants required to submit FAFSA. *Unit head:* Melissa McCarthy, Director, 503-943-7224, E-mail: mba-up@up.edu. *Application contact:* Melissa McCarthy, Director, 503-943-7224, E-mail: mba-up@up.edu.

University of Puerto Rico–Río Piedras, College of Business Administration, San Juan, PR 00931-3300. Offers accounting (MBA); finance (MBA, PhD); general business (MBA); human resources management (MBA); international trade and business (MBA, PhD); marketing (MBA); operations management (MBA); quantitative methods (MBA). *Accreditation:* AACSB. *Program availability:* Part-time. *Degree requirements:* For master's, comprehensive exam, thesis or alternative, research project. *Entrance requirements:* For master's, GMAT or PAEG, minimum GPA of 3.0, letter of recommendation; for doctorate, GMAT, PAEG, minimum GPA of 3.0, master degree. *Faculty research:* Management.

University of Rhode Island, Graduate School, College of Business, Program in Business Administration, Kingston, RI 02881. Offers finance (MBA); general business (MBA); management (MBA); marketing (MBA, PhD); operations and supply chain management (PhD); supply chain management (MBA); Pharm D/MBA. *Faculty:* 33 full-time (17 women). *Students:* 54 full-time (21 women), 161 part-time (64 women); includes 30 minority (11 Black or African American, non-Hispanic/Latino; 11 Asian, non-Hispanic/Latino; 6 Hispanic/Latino; 1 Native Hawaiian or other Pacific Islander, non-Hispanic/Latino; 1 Two or more races, non-Hispanic/Latino), 17 international. 92 applicants, 87% accepted, 74 enrolled. In 2018, 90 master's, 5 doctorates awarded. *Entrance requirements:* Additional exam requirements/recommendations for international students: Required—TOEFL. *Application deadline:* For fall admission, 6/30 for domestic students; for spring admission, 10/31 for domestic students; for summer admission, 3/31 for domestic students. Electronic applications accepted. *Expenses: Tuition, area resident:* Full-time $13,226; part-time $735 per credit. *Tuition, state resident:* full-time $13,226; part-time $735 per credit. *Tuition, nonresident:* full-time $25,854; part-time $1436 per credit. *International tuition:* $25,854 full-time. *Required fees:* $1698; $50 per credit. $35 per semester. One-time fee: $165. *Financial support:* In 2018–19, 15 teaching assistantships (averaging $17,739 per year) were awarded. Financial award application deadline: 2/1. *Unit head:* Lisa Lancellotta, Coordinator, MBA Programs, 401-874-4241, E-mail: mba@uri.edu. *Application contact:* Lisa Lancellotta, Coordinator, MBA Programs, 401-874-4241, E-mail: mba@uri.edu.

University of Rochester, Simon Business School, Doctoral Program in Business Administration, Rochester, NY 14627. Offers accounting (PhD); computer information systems (PhD); finance (PhD); marketing (PhD); operations management (PhD). *Accreditation:* AACSB. *Degree requirements:* For doctorate, comprehensive exam, thesis/dissertation, qualifying exam. *Entrance requirements:* For doctorate, GMAT or GRE. Additional exam requirements/recommendations for international students: Required—TOEFL. Electronic applications accepted. *Expenses:* Contact institution. *Faculty research:* Empirical industrial organization, risk management, financial disclosure and regulation, social media, health care management.

University of Rochester, Simon Business School, Full-Time Master's Program in Business Administration, Rochester, NY 14627. Offers business systems consulting (MBA); competitive and organizational strategy (MBA); computers and information systems (MBA); corporate accounting (MBA); entrepreneurship (MBA); finance (MBA); health sciences management (MBA); marketing (MBA); operations management (MBA); public accounting (MBA); strategy and organizations (MBA). *Accreditation:* AACSB. *Entrance requirements:* For master's, GMAT or GRE. *Expenses: Tuition:* Full-time $52,974; part-time $1654 per credit hour. *Required fees:* $612. One-time fee: $30 part-time. Tuition and fees vary according to campus/location and program. *Faculty research:* Empirical industrial organization, risk management, financial disclosure and regulation, social media, health care management.

University of Rochester, Simon Business School, Part-Time MBA Program, Rochester, NY 14627. Offers business systems consulting (MBA); competitive and organizational strategy (MBA); computers and information systems (MBA); corporate accounting (MBA); entrepreneurship (MBA); finance (MBA); health sciences management (MBA); marketing (MBA), including brand management, marketing strategy, pricing; operations management (MBA); public accounting (MBA). *Program availability:* Part-time-only, evening/weekend. *Entrance requirements:* For master's, GRE or GMAT. Electronic applications accepted. *Expenses:* Contact institution.

University of Saint Mary, Graduate Programs, Program in Business Administration, Leavenworth, KS 66048-5082. Offers enterprise risk management (MBA); finance (MBA); general management (MBA); health care management (MBA); human resources management (MBA); marketing and advertising management (MBA). *Program availability:* Part-time, evening/weekend, 100% online, blended/hybrid learning. *Faculty:* 1 full-time, 23 part-time/adjunct (7 women). *Students:* 177 full-time (116 women), 50 part-time (29 women); includes 73 minority (30 Black or African American, non-Hispanic/

Latino; 3 American Indian or Alaska Native, non-Hispanic/Latino; 12 Asian, non-Hispanic/Latino; 18 Hispanic/Latino; 1 Native Hawaiian or other Pacific Islander, non-Hispanic/Latino; 9 Two or more races, non-Hispanic/Latino), 2 international. Average age 33. *Degree requirements:* For master's, thesis. *Entrance requirements:* For master's, Minimum undergraduate GPA of 2.75, official transcripts. *Application deadline:* Applications are processed on a rolling basis. Application fee: $25. Electronic applications accepted. *Expenses:* Contact institution. *Financial support:* Applicants required to submit FAFSA. *Unit head:* Mark Harvey, Director of Graduate Business Programs, 913-319-3011, E-mail: mark.harvey@stmary.edu. *Application contact:* Mark Harvey, Director of Graduate Business Programs, 913-319-3011, E-mail: mark.harvey@stmary.edu.
Website: https://www.stmary.edu/mba

University of San Francisco, School of Management, Master of Business Administration Program, San Francisco, CA 94117. Offers entrepreneurship and innovation (MBA); finance (MBA); marketing (MBA); organization development (MBA); DDS/MBA; JD/MBA; MBA/MAPS. *Accreditation:* AACSB. *Program availability:* Part-time, evening/weekend. *Students:* 136 full-time (67 women), 7 part-time (2 women); includes 57 minority (5 Black or African American, non-Hispanic/Latino; 29 Asian, non-Hispanic/Latino; 14 Hispanic/Latino; 1 Native Hawaiian or other Pacific Islander, non-Hispanic/Latino; 8 Two or more races, non-Hispanic/Latino), 27 international. Average age 29. 226 applicants, 61% accepted, 56 enrolled. In 2018, 76 master's awarded. *Entrance requirements:* For master's, GMAT or GRE, resume (two years of professional work experience required for part-time students, preferred for full-time), transcripts from each college or university attended, two letters of recommendation, personal statement, interview. Additional exam requirements/recommendations for international students: Required—TOEFL (minimum score 600 paper-based, 100 iBT), IELTS (minimum score 7) or PTE (minimum score 68). *Application deadline:* For fall admission, 6/5 for domestic students, 5/15 for international students; for spring admission, 11/30 for domestic students. Application fee: $55. Electronic applications accepted. *Expenses:* Contact institution. *Financial support:* Fellowships and scholarships/grants available. Financial award application deadline: 3/2; financial award applicants required to submit FAFSA. *Faculty research:* International financial markets, technology transfer licensing, international marketing, strategic planning. *Total annual research expenditures:* $50,000. *Unit head:* Dr. Frank Fletcher, Director, 415-422-2221, E-mail: management@usfca.edu. *Application contact:* Office of Graduate Recruiting and Admissions, 415-422-2221, E-mail: management@usfca.edu.
Website: http://www.usfca.edu/mba

University of Saskatchewan, College of Graduate and Postdoctoral Studies, Edwards School of Business, Department of Management and Marketing, Saskatoon, SK S7N 5A2, Canada. Offers marketing (M Sc). *Program availability:* Part-time. *Degree requirements:* For master's, thesis. *Entrance requirements:* For master's, GMAT. Additional exam requirements/recommendations for international students: Required—TOEFL.

The University of Scranton, Kania School of Management, Program in Business Administration, Scranton, PA 18510. Offers accounting (MBA); finance (MBA); general business administration (MBA); health care management (MBA); international business (MBA); management information systems (MBA); marketing (MBA); operations management (MBA). *Accreditation:* AACSB. *Program availability:* Part-time, evening/weekend, 100% online. *Entrance requirements:* For master's, GMAT (for MBA). *Faculty research:* Financial markets, strategic impact of total quality management, internal accounting controls, consumer preference, information systems and the Internet.

University of Sioux Falls, Vucurevich School of Business, Sioux Falls, SD 57105-1699. Offers entrepreneurial leadership (MBA); general management (MBA); health care management (MBA); marketing (MBA). *Program availability:* Part-time, evening/weekend. *Degree requirements:* For master's, project. *Entrance requirements:* For master's, minimum GPA of 3.0. Additional exam requirements/recommendations for international students: Required—TOEFL. *Expenses:* Contact institution.

University of South Africa, College of Economic and Management Sciences, Pretoria, South Africa. Offers accounting (D Admin, D Com); accounting science (DA); auditing (D Admin, D Com); business administration (M Tech); business economics (D Admin); business leadership (DBL); business management (D Admin, D Com); economic management analysis (M Tech); economics (D Admin, D Com, PhD); human resource development (M Tech); industrial psychology (D Admin, D Com, PhD); logistics (D Com); marketing (M Tech); public administration (D Admin, D Com, DPA, PhD); public management (M Tech); quantitative management (D Admin, D Com); real estate (M Tech); statistics (D Admin, PhD); tourism management (D Admin, D Com); transport economics (D Admin, D Com).

University of South Alabama, Mitchell College of Business, Program in Business Administration, Mobile, AL 36688. Offers business administration (MBA); management (DBA); marketing (DBA). *Accreditation:* AACSB. *Program availability:* Part-time, evening/weekend. *Degree requirements:* For master's, comprehensive exam; for doctorate, comprehensive exam, thesis/dissertation. *Entrance requirements:* For master's, GMAT (minimum score of 450, 3.0 in Analytical Writing section), minimum undergraduate GPA of 3.0; for doctorate, MBA/specialized master's degree, 5 years of professional experience, 3 letters of reference, curriculum vitae, interview. Additional exam requirements/recommendations for international students: Required—TOEFL (minimum score 525 paper-based; 71 iBT). Electronic applications accepted. *Expenses:* Contact institution.

University of South Dakota, Graduate School, Beacom School of Business, Department of Business Administration, Vermillion, SD 57069. Offers business administration (MBA); business analytics (MBA, Graduate Certificate); health services administration (MBA); long term care management (Graduate Certificate); marketing (MBA, Graduate Certificate); operations and supply chain management (MBA, Graduate Certificate); JD/MBA. *Accreditation:* AACSB. *Program availability:* Part-time, blended/hybrid learning. *Degree requirements:* For master's, thesis or alternative. *Entrance requirements:* For master's, GMAT, minimum GPA of 2.7, resume. Additional exam requirements/recommendations for international students: Required—TOEFL (minimum score 550 paper-based; 79 iBT), IELTS (minimum score 6). Electronic applications accepted. *Expenses:* Contact institution.

University of South Florida, Muma College of Business, Department of Marketing, Tampa, FL 33620-9951. Offers business administration (PhD), including marketing; marketing (MSM); sport and entertainment management (MS). *Program availability:* Part-time, evening/weekend. *Faculty:* 16 full-time (4 women). *Students:* 44 full-time (24 women), 29 part-time (18 women); includes 12 minority (3 Black or African American, non-Hispanic/Latino; 8 Hispanic/Latino; 1 Two or more races, non-Hispanic/Latino), 39 international. Average age 26. 99 applicants, 63% accepted, 33 enrolled. In 2018, 35 master's awarded. Terminal master's awarded for partial completion of doctoral program. *Degree requirements:* For master's, comprehensive exam, thesis (for some programs); for doctorate, comprehensive exam, thesis/dissertation. *Entrance requirements:* For master's, GMAT (preferred) or GRE; MCAT or LSAT may be substituted, minimum GPA of 3.0; letters of recommendation; letter of interest; statement of purpose. Entrepreneurship: Demonstrated competence in Statistics, Accounting, and

Finance. Marketing: resume; relevant professional work experience. Sport Mgmt: interview; admission to MBA with Conc in Sport Business; for doctorate, GMAT or GRE, personal statement, recommendations, interview. Additional exam requirements/recommendations for international students: Required—TOEFL, TOEFL (minimum score 550 paper-based; 79 iBT) or IELTS (minimum score 6.5). *Application deadline:* For fall admission, 1/2 for domestic and international students; for spring admission, 10/15 for domestic students, 7/1 for international students. Applications are processed on a rolling basis. Application fee: $30. Electronic applications accepted. *Expenses:* Tuition, state resident: full-time $6350. Tuition, nonresident: full-time $19,048. *International tuition:* $19,048 full-time. *Required fees:* $2079. *Financial support:* In 2018–19, 12 students received support, including 5 research assistantships (averaging $14,943 per year), 6 teaching assistantships (averaging $11,972 per year); health care benefits and unspecified assistantships also available. *Faculty research:* Branding; consumer behavior; marketing communications' effectiveness; customer satisfaction; customer delight; consumer reactions to new technology, products and services; consumer emotions; brand strategies; communications; advertising effectiveness; green alliances; strategic marketing; international business; international marketing; consumer research; customer service branding; focus group research; market surveys; market research; promotion; services marketing; strategic planning. *Total annual research expenditures:* $24,235. *Unit head:* Dr. Doug Hughes, Chair, Professor, 813-974-6215, Fax: 813-974-6175, E-mail: dehughes1@usf.edu. *Application contact:* Stacee Bender, Academic Services Administrator, 813-974-4516, Fax: 813-974-6175, E-mail: staceebender@usf.edu.
Website: http://business.usf.edu/departments/marketing/

The University of Tampa, Sykes College of Business, Tampa, FL 33606-1490. Offers accounting (MS); business analytics (MBA); cybersecurity (MBA, MS); entrepreneurship (MBA, MS); finance (MBA, MS); information systems management (MBA); innovation management (MBA); international business (MBA); marketing (MBA, MS); nonprofit management (MBA, Certificate). *Accreditation:* AACSB. *Program availability:* Part-time, evening/weekend. *Faculty:* 61 full-time (13 women), 11 part-time/adjunct (3 women). *Students:* 361 full-time (153 women), 122 part-time (52 women); includes 101 minority (31 Black or African American, non-Hispanic/Latino; 5 Asian, non-Hispanic/Latino; 57 Hispanic/Latino; 1 Native Hawaiian or other Pacific Islander, non-Hispanic/Latino; 7 Two or more races, non-Hispanic/Latino), 144 international. Average age 29. 1,079 applicants, 57% accepted, 263 enrolled. In 2018, 281 master's, 12 other advanced degrees awarded. *Degree requirements:* For master's, capstone. *Entrance requirements:* For master's, GMAT or GRE, official transcripts from all colleges and/or universities previously attended, resume, personal statement, letters of recommendation. Additional exam requirements/recommendations for international students: Required—TOEFL (minimum score 577 paper-based; 90 iBT), IELTS (minimum score 7.5). *Application deadline:* Applications are processed on a rolling basis. Application fee: $40. Electronic applications accepted. *Expenses:* Contact institution. *Financial support:* In 2018–19, 123 students received support. Career-related internships or fieldwork, scholarships/grants, and unspecified assistantships available. Financial award applicants required to submit FAFSA. *Faculty research:* Job market signaling, on-line shopping behaviors and social media, the Tampa Bay economy, digital literacy, entrepreneurship in small businesses. *Unit head:* Dr. Natasha F. Veltri, Associate Dean, 813-253-6289, E-mail: nveltri@ut.edu. *Application contact:* Ashley Russell, Staff Assistant, Admissions for Graduate and Continuing Studies, 813-253-6249, E-mail: arussell@ut.edu.
Website: http://www.ut.edu/business/

The University of Tennessee, Graduate School, College of Business Administration, Program in Business Administration, Knoxville, TN 37996. Offers accounting (PhD); finance (MBA, PhD); logistics and transportation (MBA, PhD); management (PhD); marketing (MBA, PhD); operations management (MBA); professional business administration (MBA); statistics (PhD); JD/MBA; MS/MBA; Pharm D/MBA. Pharm D/MBA offered jointly with The University of Tennessee Health Science Center. *Accreditation:* AACSB. *Program availability:* Online learning. *Degree requirements:* For master's, thesis or alternative; for doctorate, thesis/dissertation. *Entrance requirements:* For master's and doctorate, GMAT, minimum GPA of 2.7. Additional exam requirements/recommendations for international students: Required—TOEFL. Electronic applications accepted.

The University of Texas at Arlington, Graduate School, College of Business, Department of Marketing, Arlington, TX 76019. Offers marketing (MBA); marketing research (MS). *Program availability:* Part-time, evening/weekend. *Degree requirements:* For master's, thesis optional. *Entrance requirements:* For master's, GMAT, GRE. Additional exam requirements/recommendations for international students: Required—TOEFL (minimum score 550 paper-based; 79 iBT). Electronic applications accepted. *Faculty research:* Marketing strategy, marketing research, international marketing.

The University of Texas at Austin, Graduate School, McCombs School of Business, Department of Marketing, Austin, TX 78712-1111. Offers MBA, MS, PhD. *Degree requirements:* For doctorate, comprehensive exam, thesis/dissertation. *Entrance requirements:* For doctorate, GMAT or GRE. Electronic applications accepted. *Faculty research:* Internet marketing, strategic marketing, buy behavior.

The University of Texas at Dallas, Naveen Jindal School of Management, Program in Marketing, Richardson, TX 75080. Offers marketing (MS). *Program availability:* Part-time, evening/weekend. *Faculty:* 11 full-time (2 women), 8 part-time/adjunct (1 woman). *Students:* 102 full-time (68 women), 45 part-time (34 women); includes 45 minority (3 Black or African American, non-Hispanic/Latino; 1 American Indian or Alaska Native, non-Hispanic/Latino; 20 Asian, non-Hispanic/Latino; 17 Hispanic/Latino; 4 Two or more races, non-Hispanic/Latino), 61 international. Average age 27. 205 applicants, 75% accepted, 66 enrolled. In 2018, 57 master's awarded. *Degree requirements:* For master's, thesis optional. *Entrance requirements:* For master's, GMAT, minimum GPA of 3.0 in upper-level coursework in field. Additional exam requirements/recommendations for international students: Required—TOEFL (minimum score 550 paper-based). *Application deadline:* For fall admission, 7/15 for domestic students, 5/1 priority date for international students; for spring admission, 11/15 for domestic students, 9/1 priority date for international students. Applications are processed on a rolling basis. Application fee: $50 ($100 for international students). Electronic applications accepted. *Expenses: Tuition, area resident:* Full-time $13,458. *Tuition, state resident:* full-time $13,458. *Tuition, nonresident:* full-time $26,852. *International tuition:* $26,852 full-time. Tuition and fees vary according to course load. *Financial support:* In 2018–19, 2 teaching assistantships with partial tuition reimbursements (averaging $10,050 per year) were awarded; fellowships, research assistantships with partial tuition reimbursements, career-related internships or fieldwork, Federal Work-Study, institutionally sponsored loans, scholarships/grants, and unspecified assistantships also available. Support available to part-time students. Financial award application deadline: 4/30; financial award applicants required to submit FAFSA. *Faculty research:* Inventory control and risk management. *Unit head:* Dr. Nanda Kumar, Area Coordinator, 972-883-6426, E-mail: nkumar@utdallas.edu. *Application contact:* Dr. Nanda Kumar, Area Coordinator, 972-883-6426, E-mail: nkumar@utdallas.edu.
Website: http://jindal.utdallas.edu/marketing/

The University of Texas at San Antonio, College of Business, Department of Marketing, San Antonio, TX 78249-0617. Offers marketing (PhD); marketing management (MBA); tourism destination development (MBA). *Program availability:* Part-time, evening/weekend. *Degree requirements:* For master's, comprehensive exam (for some programs), thesis (for some programs). *Entrance requirements:* For master's, GMAT, minimum GPA of 3.0. Additional exam requirements/recommendations for international students: Required—TOEFL (minimum score 550 paper-based; 79 iBT). Electronic applications accepted. *Faculty research:* Consumer behavior, cross-cultural research, psycholinguistics, pricing, mass media and materialism.

The University of Texas at Tyler, Soules College of Business, Department of Management and Marketing, Tyler, TX 75799-0001. Offers cyber security (MBA); engineering management (MBA); general management (MBA); healthcare management (MBA); internal assurance and consulting (MBA); marketing (MBA); oil, gas and energy (MBA); organizational development (MBA); quality management (MBA). *Accreditation:* AACSB. *Program availability:* Part-time, online learning. *Students:* Average age 29. 73 applicants, 96% accepted, 35 enrolled. In 2018, 37 master's awarded. *Entrance requirements:* Additional exam requirements/recommendations for international students: Required—TOEFL (minimum score 550 paper-based). *Application deadline:* For fall admission, 8/17 priority date for domestic students, 7/1 priority date for international students; for spring admission, 12/21 priority date for domestic students, 11/1 priority date for international students. Application fee: $25 ($50 for international students). *Faculty research:* General business, inventory control, institutional markets, service marketing, product distribution, accounting fraud, financial reporting and recognition. *Unit head:* Dr. Krist Swimberghe, Chair, 903-565-5803, E-mail: kswimberghe@uttyler.edu. *Application contact:* Dr. Krist Swimberghe, Chair, 903-565-5803, E-mail: kswimberghe@uttyler.edu.
Website: https://www.uttyler.edu/cbt/manamark/

The University of Texas Rio Grande Valley, Robert C. Vackar College of Business and Entrepreneurship, Program in Business Administration, Edinburg, TX 78539. Offers business administration (MBA); finance (PhD); management (PhD); marketing (PhD). *Program availability:* Part-time, evening/weekend, online learning. *Degree requirements:* For master's, thesis optional. *Entrance requirements:* For master's, GMAT, minimum GPA of 3.0. Additional exam requirements/recommendations for international students: Required—TOEFL (minimum score 500 paper-based). Electronic applications accepted. *Expenses: Tuition, area resident:* Full-time $6888. *Tuition, state resident:* full-time $6888. *Tuition, nonresident:* full-time $14,484. *International tuition:* $14,484 full-time. *Required fees:* $1468. *Faculty research:* Human resources, border region, entrepreneurship, marketing.

University of the Cumberlands, Graduate Programs in Education, Williamsburg, KY 40769-1372. Offers all grades (P-12) (M Ed); business and marketing (MA Ed, MAT); counselor education and supervision (Ed D); director of pupil personnel (Certificate); director of special education (Certificate); educational administration and supervision (Ed S); educational leadership (Ed D); elementary education (MA Ed, MAT); instructional leadership - principalship (MA Ed); instructional leadership - school principal (Certificate); middle school education (MA Ed, MAT); reading and writing (MA Ed); school counseling (MA Ed); school superintendent (Certificate); secondary education (MA Ed, MAT); special education (MAT); supervisor of instruction (Certificate); teacher leader (MA Ed). *Program availability:* Part-time, evening/weekend, online learning. *Degree requirements:* For master's, comprehensive exam. Electronic applications accepted.

University of the Sacred Heart, Graduate Programs, Department of Business Administration, Program in International Marketing, San Juan, PR 00914-0383. Offers MBA. *Program availability:* Part-time, evening/weekend. *Degree requirements:* For master's, thesis. *Entrance requirements:* For master's, EXADEP, minimum undergraduate GPA of 2.75, interview.

The University of Toledo, College of Graduate Studies, College of Business and Innovation, Department of Marketing and International Business, Toledo, OH 43606-3390. Offers MBA. *Program availability:* Part-time, evening/weekend. *Entrance requirements:* For master's, GMAT, GRE, or LSAT, minimum GPA of 2.7 for all prior academic work, three letters of recommendation, statement of purpose, transcripts from all prior institutions attended. Additional exam requirements/recommendations for international students: Required—TOEFL (minimum score 550 paper-based; 80 iBT). Electronic applications accepted.

University of Utah, Graduate School, David Eccles School of Business, Business Administration Program, Salt Lake City, UT 84112. Offers accounting (PhD); business administration (EMBA, MBA, PMBA); finance (PhD); information systems (PhD); marketing (PhD); operations management (PhD); organizational behavior (PhD); strategic management (PhD); MBA/JD; MBA/MHA; MBA/MS. *Program availability:* Part-time, evening/weekend, online learning. *Students:* 112 full-time (26 women), 7 part-time (2 women); includes 12 minority (1 Asian, non-Hispanic/Latino; 7 Hispanic/Latino; 4 Two or more races, non-Hispanic/Latino), 13 international. Average age 29. 182 applicants, 51% accepted, 58 enrolled. In 2018, 58 master's awarded. *Entrance requirements:* For master's, GMAT or GRE; for doctorate, GMAT. Additional exam requirements/recommendations for international students: Required—TOEFL (minimum score 100 iBT), IELTS (minimum score 7). *Application deadline:* For fall admission, 5/1 for domestic students, 3/1 for international students. Application fee: $55 ($65 for international students). Electronic applications accepted. *Expenses:* Contact institution. *Financial support:* In 2018–19, 57 students received support. Scholarships/grants available. Financial award application deadline: 5/1; financial award applicants required to submit FAFSA. *Faculty research:* Corporate finance, strategy services, consumer behavior, financial disclosures, operations. *Unit head:* Brad Vierig, Associate Dean, MBA Programs & Executive Education. *Application contact:* Stephanie Geisler, Director, Full-Time MBA, 801-585-6291, E-mail: ftmba@utah.edu.
Website: http://www.business.utah.edu/

University of Virginia, McIntire School of Commerce, M.S. in Commerce, Charlottesville, VA 22903. Offers business analytics (MSC); finance (MSC); marketing and management (MSC). *Faculty:* 24 full-time (5 women). *Students:* 123 full-time (50 women). Average age 22. 448 applicants, 40% accepted, 123 enrolled. In 2018, 120 master's awarded. *Entrance requirements:* For master's, GMAT or GRE, 2 letters of recommendation; prerequisite course work in financial accounting, microeconomics, and introduction to statistics. Additional exam requirements/recommendations for international students: Required—TOEFL (minimum score 600 paper-based; 100 iBT), IELTS (minimum score 7.5). *Application deadline:* For fall admission, 11/1 priority date for domestic students, 1/1 priority date for international students; for winter admission, 2/1 for domestic students; for spring admission, 3/15 for domestic students; for summer admission, 6/1 for domestic students. Applications are processed on a rolling basis. Application fee: $75. Electronic applications accepted. *Expenses:* Contact institution. *Financial support:* In 2018–19, 30 students received support. Scholarships/grants available. Financial award application deadline: 2/1; financial award applicants required to submit FAFSA. *Faculty research:* Management, marketing, finance, analytics, and communication. *Unit head:* Ira C. Harris, Program Director, 434-924-8816, Fax: 434-924-7074, E-mail: ich3x@comm.virginia.edu. *Application contact:* Emma Candelier, Assistant Dean of Graduate Recruiting, 434-243-4992, Fax: 434-924-4511, E-mail: ecandelier@virginia.edu.
Website: https://www.commerce.virginia.edu/ms-commerce

Marketing

The University of Western Ontario, Ivey Business School, London, ON N6A 3K7, Canada. Offers business (EMBA, PhD); corporate strategy and leadership elective (MBA); entrepreneurship elective (MBA); finance elective (MBA); health sector stream (MBA); international management elective (MBA); marketing elective (MBA); JD/MBA. *Degree requirements:* For master's, thesis (for some programs); for doctorate, thesis/dissertation. *Entrance requirements:* For master's, GMAT, 2 years of full-time work experience, interview. Additional exam requirements/recommendations for international students: Required—TOEFL (minimum score 100 iBT) or IELTS (minimium score 6). Electronic applications accepted. *Faculty research:* Strategy, organizational behavior, international business, finance, operations management.

University of Wisconsin–Madison, Graduate School, Wisconsin School of Business, Doctoral Program in Marketing, Madison, WI 53706-1380. Offers PhD. *Degree requirements:* For doctorate, comprehensive exam, thesis/dissertation. *Entrance requirements:* For doctorate, GMAT or GRE. Additional exam requirements/recommendations for international students: Recommended—TOEFL (minimum score 623 paper-based; 106 iBT), IELTS (minimum score 7.5), TSE (minimum score 73). Electronic applications accepted. *Expenses:* Contact institution. *Faculty research:* Marketing strategy, consumer behavior, channels of distribution, advertising, price promotions, behavioral and experimental economics, creativity and design, extensions of research involving the sense of touch, ethics.

University of Wisconsin–Whitewater, School of Graduate Studies, College of Business and Economics, Program in Business and Marketing Education, Whitewater, WI 53190-1790. Offers MS. *Accreditation:* NCATE. *Program availability:* Part-time, evening/weekend, online learning. *Degree requirements:* For master's, thesis or alternative. *Entrance requirements:* For master's, interview, teaching license. Additional exam requirements/recommendations for international students: Required—TOEFL (minimum score 550 paper-based; 80 iBT), IELTS (minimum score 6). Electronic applications accepted.

Ursuline College, School of Graduate and Professional Studies, Program in Business Administration, Pepper Pike, OH 44124-4398. Offers ethical and entrepreneurial leadership (MBA); financial planning and accounting (MBA); health services management (MBA); management (MBA); management and leadership (MBA); marketing and communications management (MBA). *Program availability:* Part-time, evening/weekend. *Faculty:* 2 full-time (both women), 2 part-time/adjunct (1 woman). *Students:* 17 full-time (all women), 5 part-time (3 women); includes 10 minority (9 Black or African American, non-Hispanic/Latino; 1 Two or more races, non-Hispanic/Latino). Average age 40. 33 applicants, 100% accepted, 6 enrolled. In 2018, 16 master's awarded. *Degree requirements:* For master's, comprehensive exam (for some programs). *Entrance requirements:* For master's, GRE. Additional exam requirements/recommendations for international students: Required—TOEFL (minimum score 500 paper-based) or GRE. *Application deadline:* For fall admission, 8/1 for domestic students. Applications are processed on a rolling basis. Application fee: $25. Electronic applications accepted. *Expenses:* 36 hours at $903/per. *Financial support:* In 2018–19, 2 students received support. Campus work-study available. Financial award application deadline: 8/1; financial award applicants required to submit FAFSA. *Faculty research:* Gift economy; sharing economy; cooperative business models; collaborative leadership; corporate social responsibility and the triple bottom line, defined as the three P's: people, planet and profit. *Unit head:* Dr. Debra Fleming, Professor, 440-440-720-3864, Fax: 440-684-6088, E-mail: dfleming@ursuline.edu. *Application contact:* Melanie Steele, Director of Graduate Admission, 440-646-8146, Fax: 440-684-6138, E-mail: graduateadmissions@ursuline.edu.

Vancouver Island University, Master of Business Administration Program, Nanaimo, BC V9R 5S5, Canada. Offers international business (MBA), including finance, marketing. Program offered jointly with University of Hertfordshire. *Accreditation:* ACBSP. *Program availability:* Part-time. *Degree requirements:* For master's, thesis. *Entrance requirements:* Additional exam requirements/recommendations for international students: Required—TOEFL (minimum score 88 iBT), IELTS (minimum score 6.5). Electronic applications accepted. *Expenses:* Contact institution. *Faculty research:* Tourism development, entrepreneurship, organizational development, strategic planning, international business strategy, intercultural team work.

Vanderbilt University, Vanderbilt University Owen Graduate School of Management, Master of Marketing Program, Nashville, TN 37240-1001. Offers M Mark. *Entrance requirements:* For master's, GMAT, resume, two essays, two letters of recommendation, interview. Additional exam requirements/recommendations for international students: Required—TOEFL or IELTS. Electronic applications accepted. *Expenses: Tuition:* Full-time $47,208; part-time $2026 per credit hour. *Required fees:* $478.

Vanderbilt University, Vanderbilt University Owen Graduate School of Management, Vanderbilt MBA Program, Nashville, TN 37203. Offers accounting (MBA); finance (MBA); general management (MBA); health care (MBA); human and organizational performance (MBA); marketing (MBA); operations (MBA); strategy (MBA); MBA/JD; MBA/M Div; MBA/MD; MBA/MSN; MBA/MTS; MBA/PhD. *Accreditation:* AACSB. *Degree requirements:* For master's, 62 credit hours of coursework; completion of ethics course; minimum GPA of 3.0. *Entrance requirements:* For master's, GMAT (preferred) or GRE, 2 years of work experience (recommended). Additional exam requirements/recommendations for international students: Required—TOEFL (minimum score 100 iBT). Electronic applications accepted. *Expenses:* Contact institution. *Faculty research:* Accounting and finance, business strategy and economics, marketing, operations management, organization studies.

Villanova University, Villanova School of Business, MBA - The Flex Track Program, Villanova, PA 19085. Offers healthcare (MBA); international business (MBA); marketing (MBA); real estate (MBA); strategic management (MBA); JD/MBA. *Accreditation:* AACSB. *Program availability:* Part-time, evening/weekend, online learning. *Faculty:* 101 full-time (38 women), 36 part-time/adjunct (9 women). *Students:* 13 full-time (5 women), 427 part-time (157 women); includes 74 minority (12 Black or African American, non-Hispanic/Latino; 29 Asian, non-Hispanic/Latino; 23 Hispanic/Latino; 10 Two or more races, non-Hispanic/Latino), 12 international. Average age 32. 156 applicants, 92% accepted, 139 enrolled. In 2018, 124 master's awarded. *Degree requirements:* For master's, minimum GPA of 3.0. *Entrance requirements:* For master's, GMAT or GRE, Application, official transcripts, 2 letters of recommendation, resume, 2 essays. Additional exam requirements/recommendations for international students: Required—TOEFL (minimum score 550 paper-based; 100 iBT). *Application deadline:* For fall admission, 7/31 for domestic and international students; for spring admission, 11/30 for domestic and international students; for summer admission, 4/30 for domestic and international students. Applications are processed on a rolling basis. Application fee: $65. Electronic applications accepted. *Expenses:* Contact institution. *Financial support:* Research assistantships and scholarships/grants available. Financial award application deadline: 6/30; financial award applicants required to submit FAFSA. *Faculty research:* Real Estate, Business Analytics, Global Leadership, Marketing and Consumer Insights, Church management. *Unit head:* Dr. Joyce E. A. Russell, Dean of Villanova School of Business, 610-519-6082, Fax: 610-519-6273, E-mail: joyce.russell@villanova.edu. *Application contact:* Daniel Guertin, Assistant Director, Recruitment, 610-519-8031, Fax: 610-519-6273, E-mail: daniel.guertin@villanova.edu.
Website: http://www1.villanova.edu/villanova/business/graduate/mba.html

Virginia International University, School of Business, Fairfax, VA 22030. Offers accounting (MBA, MS); entrepreneurship (MBA); executive management (Graduate Certificate); global logistics (MBA); health care management (MBA); hospitality and tourism management (MBA); human resources management (MBA); international business management (MBA); international finance (MBA); marketing management (MBA); mass media and public relations (MBA); project management (MBA, MS). *Program availability:* Part-time, online learning. *Entrance requirements:* For master's and Graduate Certificate, bachelor's degree. Additional exam requirements/recommendations for international students: Required—TOEFL (minimum score 550 paper-based; 80 iBT), IELTS (minimum score 6). Electronic applications accepted.

Virginia Polytechnic Institute and State University, Graduate School, Pamplin College of Business, Blacksburg, VA 24061. Offers accounting and information systems (MACIS, PhD); business administration (MS), including business analytics, hospitality and tourism management; business information technology (PhD); executive business research (PhD); finance (PhD); marketing (PhD), including marketing; MS/MBA. *Faculty:* 141 full-time (42 women), 2 part-time/adjunct (1 woman). *Students:* 227 full-time (89 women), 217 part-time (75 women); includes 131 minority (30 Black or African American, non-Hispanic/Latino; 58 Asian, non-Hispanic/Latino; 25 Hispanic/Latino; 18 Two or more races, non-Hispanic/Latino), 81 international. Average age 32. 361 applicants, 55% accepted, 152 enrolled. In 2018, 181 master's, 8 doctorates awarded. *Degree requirements:* For master's, comprehensive exam (for some programs), thesis (for some programs); for doctorate, comprehensive exam (for some programs), thesis/dissertation (for some programs). *Entrance requirements:* For master's and doctorate, GRE/GMAT. Additional exam requirements/recommendations for international students: Required—TOEFL (minimum score 90 iBT). *Application deadline:* For fall admission, 8/1 for domestic students, 4/1 for international students; for spring admission, 1/1 for domestic students, 9/1 for international students. Applications are processed on a rolling basis. Application fee: $75. Electronic applications accepted. *Expenses:* Tuition, state resident: full-time $15,510; part-time $739.50 per credit hour. Tuition, nonresident: full-time $29,629; part-time $1490.25 per credit hour. *Required fees:* $2804; $550 per semester. Tuition and fees vary according to course load, campus/location and program. *Financial support:* In 2018–19, 1 fellowship with full tuition reimbursement (averaging $3,999 per year), 4 research assistantships with full tuition reimbursements (averaging $20,163 per year), 66 teaching assistantships with full tuition reimbursements (averaging $19,822 per year) were awarded; scholarships/grants and unspecified assistantships also available. Financial award application deadline: 3/1; financial award applicants required to submit FAFSA. *Total annual research expenditures:* $3.1 million. *Unit head:* Dr. Robert T. Sumichrast, Dean, 540-231-6601, Fax: 540-231-4487, E-mail: busdean@vt.edu. *Application contact:* Kimberly Ridpath, Executive Assistant, 540-231-9647, Fax: 540-231-4487, E-mail: ridpathk@vt.edu.
Website: http://www.pamplin.vt.edu/

Wagner College, Division of Graduate Studies, Nicolais School of Business, Staten Island, NY 10301-4495. Offers accounting (MS); business administration (MBA); finance (MBA); management (Exec MBA); marketing (MBA); media management (MS). *Accreditation:* ACBSP. *Program availability:* Part-time, evening/weekend. *Degree requirements:* For master's, thesis optional. *Entrance requirements:* For master's, minimum GPA of 2.75, proficiency in computers and math. Additional exam requirements/recommendations for international students: Required—TOEFL (minimum score 550 paper-based; 79 iBT), IELTS (minimum score 6.5).

Walden University, Graduate Programs, School of Management, Minneapolis, MN 55401. Offers accounting (MBA, MS, DBA), including accounting for the professional (MS), accounting with CPA emphasis (MS), self-designed (MS); advanced project management (Graduate Certificate); applied project management (Graduate Certificate); auditing (Graduate Certificate); bridge to business administration (Post-Doctoral Certificate); bridge to management (Post-Doctoral Certificate); business management (Graduate Certificate); communication (MBA); corporate finance (MBA); digital marketing (Graduate Certificate); entrepreneurship (DBA); entrepreneurship and small business (MBA); finance (MS, DBA), including finance for the professional (MS), finance with CFA/investment (MS), finance with CPA emphasis (MS); global supply chain management (DBA); healthcare management (MBA, DBA); human resource management (MBA, MS, Graduate Certificate), including functional human resource management (MS), general program (MS), integrating functional and strategic human resource management (MS), organizational strategy (MS); human resources management (DBA); information systems management (DBA); international business (MBA, DBA); leadership (MBA, MS, DBA, Graduate Certificate), including general program (MS), human resource leadership (MS), leader development (MS), self-designed (MS); management (MS, PhD), including communications (MS), finance (PhD), general program (MS), healthcare management (MS), human resource management (MS), human resources management (PhD), information systems management (PhD), international business (MS), leadership (MS), leadership and organizational change (PhD), marketing (MS), project management (MS), strategy and operations (MS); managerial accounting (Graduate Certificate); marketing (MBA, MS, DBA); project management (MBA, MS, DBA); self-designed (MBA, DBA); social impact management (DBA); technology entrepreneurship (DBA). *Accreditation:* ACBSP. *Program availability:* Part-time, evening/weekend, online only, 100% online. *Degree requirements:* For master's, thesis (for some programs), residency (for EMBA); for doctorate, thesis/dissertation (for some programs), residency. *Entrance requirements:* For master's, bachelor's degree or higher; minimum GPA of 2.5; official transcripts; goal statement (for some programs); access to computer and Internet; for doctorate, master's degree or higher; three years of related professional or academic experience (preferred); minimum GPA of 3.0; goal statement and current resume (for select programs); official transcripts; access to computer and Internet; for other advanced degree, relevant work experience; access to computer and Internet. Additional exam requirements/recommendations for international students: Required—TOEFL (minimum score 550 paper-based, 79 iBT), IELTS (minimum score 6.5), Michigan English Language Assessment Battery (minimum score 82), or PTE (minimum score 53). Electronic applications accepted.

Walsh University, Graduate Programs, MBA Program, North Canton, OH 44720-3396. Offers healthcare management (MBA); management (MBA); marketing (MBA). *Program availability:* Part-time, evening/weekend, online only, 100% online. *Degree requirements:* For master's, capstone course in strategic management. *Entrance requirements:* For master's, GMAT (minimum score of 490), minimum GPA of 3.0. Additional exam requirements/recommendations for international students: Required—TOEFL (minimum score 500 paper-based; 61 iBT). Electronic applications accepted. Application fee is waived when completed online. *Expenses:* Contact institution. *Faculty research:* Medical tourism, familial influence in financial fitness, pedagogy in finance courses, sociocultural aspects of women entrepreneurs, patient satisfaction.

Webster University, George Herbert Walker School of Business and Technology, Department of Business, St. Louis, MO 63119-3194. Offers business and organizational security management (MBA); decision support systems (MBA); environmental management (MBA); finance (MBA, MS); forensic accounting (MS); gerontology (MBA); human resources development (MBA); human resources management (MBA); information technology management (MBA); international business (MA, MBA);

international relations (MBA); management and leadership (MBA); marketing (MBA); media communications (MBA); procurement and acquisitions management (MBA); Web services (MBA). *Accreditation:* ACBSP. *Program availability:* Part-time, evening/weekend, online learning. *Degree requirements:* For master's, comprehensive exam (for some programs), thesis (for some programs). *Entrance requirements:* Additional exam requirements/recommendations for international students: Required—TOEFL. *Expenses: Tuition:* Full-time $22,500; part-time $750 per credit hour. Tuition and fees vary according to degree level, campus/location and program.

Webster University, George Herbert Walker School of Business and Technology, Department of Management, St. Louis, MO 63119-3194. Offers business and organizational security management (MA); digital marketing management (Graduate Certificate); government contracting (Graduate Certificate); health administration (MHA); health care management (MA); health services management (MA); human resources development (MA); human resources management (MA); information technology management (MA, MS); management (D Mgt); management and leadership (MA); marketing (MA); nonprofit leadership (MA); nonprofit revenue development (Graduate Certificate); organizational development (Graduate Certificate); procurement and acquisitions management (MA); public administration (MPA); space systems operations management (MS). *Program availability:* Part-time, evening/weekend, online learning. *Degree requirements:* For master's, thesis (for some programs); for doctorate, thesis/dissertation, written exam. *Entrance requirements:* For doctorate, GMAT, 3 years of work experience, MBA. Additional exam requirements/recommendations for international students: Required—TOEFL. *Expenses: Tuition:* Full-time $22,500; part-time $750 per credit hour. Tuition and fees vary according to degree level, campus/location and program.

West Virginia University, College of Business and Economics, Morgantown, WV 26506. Offers accountancy (M Acc); accounting (PhD); business administration (MBA); business cyber security management (MS); business data analytics (MS); economics (MA, PhD); finance (MS, PhD); forensic and fraud examination (MS); industrial relations (MS); management (PhD); marketing (PhD). *Program availability:* Part-time, online learning. *Students:* 341 full-time (139 women), 44 part-time (13 women); includes 39 minority (10 Black or African American, non-Hispanic/Latino; 12 Asian, non-Hispanic/Latino; 7 Hispanic/Latino; 10 Two or more races, non-Hispanic/Latino), 40 international. In 2018, 208 master's, 20 doctorates awarded. Terminal master's awarded for partial completion of doctoral program. *Degree requirements:* For master's, thesis optional; for doctorate, comprehensive exam, thesis/dissertation. *Entrance requirements:* For doctorate, GRE General Test, minimum GPA of 3.0. Additional exam requirements/recommendations for international students: Required—TOEFL (minimum score 550 paper-based; 92 iBT). *Application deadline:* For fall admission, 10/15 priority date for domestic and international students; for spring admission, 3/1 priority date for domestic and international students. Applications are processed on a rolling basis. Application fee: $60. Electronic applications accepted. *Expenses:* Contact institution. *Financial support:* Fellowships, research assistantships, teaching assistantships, career-related internships or fieldwork, Federal Work-Study, institutionally sponsored loans, scholarships/grants, health care benefits, tuition waivers (full and partial), unspecified assistantships, and administrative assistantships available. Financial award application deadline: 2/1; financial award applicants required to submit FAFSA. *Faculty research:* Regional labor market studies, economic development, market research, economic forecasting, energy analysis. *Unit head:* Dr. Javier Reyes, Dean, 304-293-7800, Fax: 304-293-4056, E-mail: javier.reyes@mail.wvu.edu. *Application contact:* Dr. Virginia F Kleist, Associate Dean for Graduate Programs, 304-293-7939, Fax: 304-293-7188, E-mail: Virginia.Kleist@mail.wvu.edu.
Website: http://www.be.wvu.edu

West Virginia University, Reed College of Media, Morgantown, WV 26506. Offers data marketing communications (MS); integrated marketing communications (MS, Graduate Certificate); journalism (MSJ); media solutions and innovation (MSJ). *Program availability:* Part-time, online learning. *Students:* 128 full-time (97 women), 192 part-time (147 women); includes 58 minority (34 Black or African American, non-Hispanic/Latino; 1 Asian, non-Hispanic/Latino; 18 Hispanic/Latino; 5 Two or more races, non-Hispanic/Latino), 2 international. In 2018, 165 master's awarded. *Degree requirements:* For master's, thesis or alternative. *Entrance requirements:* For master's, GRE General Test, minimum GPA of 3.0, writing samples. Additional exam requirements/recommendations for international students: Required—TOEFL (minimum score 550 paper-based). *Application deadline:* For fall admission, 3/1 priority date for domestic students, 3/1 for international students. Application fee: $60. Electronic applications accepted. *Financial support:* Research assistantships, teaching assistantships, career-related internships or fieldwork, Federal Work-Study, institutionally sponsored loans, health care benefits, tuition waivers (full and partial), and administrative assistantships available. Financial award application deadline: 2/1; financial award applicants required to submit FAFSA. *Faculty research:* History, law, and women in media; press management; public opinion; advertising effectiveness; international advertising. *Unit head:* Dr. Diana Knott Martinelli, Dean, 304-293-6561 Ext. 5409, Fax: 304-293-3072, E-mail: Diana.Martinelli@mail.wvu.edu. *Application contact:* Dr. Steve Urbanski, Director of Graduate Studies/Associate Professor, 304-293-6797, Fax: 304-293-3072, E-mail: steve.urbanski@mail.wvu.edu.
Website: http://reedcollegeofmedia.wvu.edu/

Wilfrid Laurier University, Faculty of Graduate and Postdoctoral Studies, Lazaridis School of Business and Economics, Department of Business, Waterloo, ON N2L 3C5, Canada. Offers accounting (PhD); finance (M Fin); financial economics (PhD); marketing (PhD); operations and supply chain management (PhD); organizational behavior and human resource management (M Sc); organizational behaviour and human resource management (PhD); supply chain management (M Sc); technology management (EMTM). *Accreditation:* AACSB. *Program availability:* Part-time, evening/weekend. *Degree requirements:* For master's, thesis optional; for doctorate, comprehensive exam, thesis/dissertation. *Entrance requirements:* For master's, GMAT, 4-year honors degree with minimum B+ average; for doctorate, GMAT, master's degree, minimum B+ average. Additional exam requirements/recommendations for international students: Required—TOEFL (minimum score 89 iBT). Electronic applications accepted. *Faculty research:* Financial economics, management and organizational behavior, operations and supply chain management.

William Paterson University of New Jersey, Cotsakos College of Business, Wayne, NJ 07470-8420. Offers applied business analytics (MS); business administration (MBA), including accounting, entrepreneurship, finance, general business administration, human resource management, marketing, music and entertainment management; MBA pathways (Certificate); sales leadership (MS). *Accreditation:* AACSB. *Program availability:* Part-time, evening/weekend. *Faculty:* 21 full-time (6 women), 5 part-time/adjunct (1 woman). *Students:* 78 full-time (40 women), 250 part-time (113 women); includes 161 minority (39 Black or African American, non-Hispanic/Latino; 1 American Indian or Alaska Native, non-Hispanic/Latino; 23 Asian, non-Hispanic/Latino; 82 Hispanic/Latino; 16 Two or more races, non-Hispanic/Latino), 14 international. Average age 31. 222 applicants, 86% accepted, 136 enrolled. In 2018, 95 master's awarded. *Degree requirements:* For master's, Programs Differ see: https://academiccatalog.wpunj.edu/content.php?catoid=1&navoid=68. *Entrance requirements:* For master's, program details: https://www.wpunj.edu/admissions/graduate/admission-deadlines-and-requirements/. Additional exam requirements/recommendations for international students: Required—TOEFL (minimum score 550 paper-based; 79 iBT), IELTS (minimum score 6). *Application deadline:* For fall admission, 6/1 for domestic students, 3/1 for international students; for spring admission, 11/1 for domestic students, 10/1 for international students. Applications are processed on a rolling basis. Application fee: $50. Electronic applications accepted. *Expenses: Tuition, area resident:* Full-time $14,714; part-time $727 per credit. Tuition, state resident: full-time $14,714; part-time $727 per credit. Tuition, nonresident: full-time $22,952; part-time $727 per credit. *International tuition:* $22,952 full-time. *Required fees:* $4 per semester. Tuition and fees vary according to course load, degree level and program. *Financial support:* In 2018–19, 18 students received support. Career-related internships or fieldwork, Federal Work-Study, scholarships/grants, tuition waivers, and unspecified assistantships available. Support available to part-time students. Financial award application deadline: 3/15; financial award applicants required to submit FAFSA. *Faculty research:* Labor markets, job characteristics and ethical behavior, institutional trading of stocks and bonds, education funding, pricing strategies in business-to-business markets. *Unit head:* Dr. Siamack Shojai, Dean, 973-720-2964, Fax: 973-720-2809, E-mail: shojais@wpunj.edu. *Application contact:* Tinu Adeniran, Assistant Director, Graduate Admissions, 973-720-2764, Fax: 973-720-2035, E-mail: adenirant@wpunj.edu.
Website: http://www.wpunj.edu/ccob

William Woods University, Graduate and Adult Studies, Fulton, MO 65251-1098. Offers administration (M Ed, Ed S); athletic/activities administration (M Ed); curriculum and instruction (M Ed, Ed S); educational leadership (Ed D); equestrian education (M Ed); health management (MBA); human resources (MBA); leadership (MBA); marketing, advertising, and public relations (MBA); teaching and technology (M Ed). *Program availability:* Part-time, evening/weekend. *Degree requirements:* For master's, capstone course (MBA), action research (M Ed); for Ed S, field experience. *Entrance requirements:* Additional exam requirements/recommendations for international students: Required—TOEFL (minimum score 550 paper-based). Electronic applications accepted. *Expenses:* Contact institution.

Wilmington University, College of Business, New Castle, DE 19720-6491. Offers accounting (MBA, MS); business administration (MBA, DBA); environmental stewardship (MBA); finance (MBA); health care administration (MBA, MSM); homeland security (MBA, MSM); human resource management (MSM); management information systems (MBA, MSN); marketing (MSM); marketing management (MBA); military leadership (MSM); organizational leadership (MBA, MSM); public administration (MSM). *Program availability:* Part-time, evening/weekend. *Entrance requirements:* Additional exam requirements/recommendations for international students: Required—TOEFL (minimum score 500 paper-based). Electronic applications accepted.

Wingate University, Porter B. Byrum School of Business, Wingate, NC 28174. Offers accounting (MAC); corporate innovation (MBA); finance (MBA); general management (MBA); healthcare management (MBA); marketing (MBA); project management (MBA). *Accreditation:* ACBSP. *Program availability:* Part-time, evening/weekend. *Entrance requirements:* For master's, GMAT, work experience, 2 letters of recommendation. Electronic applications accepted. *Expenses:* Contact institution. *Faculty research:* Stochastic processes, business ethics, regional economic development, municipal finance, consumer behavior.

Worcester Polytechnic Institute, Graduate Admissions, Foisie Business School, Worcester, MA 01609-2280. Offers business administration (PhD); information technology (MS), including information security management; management (MS, Graduate Certificate); marketing and innovation (MS); operations analytics and management (MS); supply chain management (MS). *Accreditation:* AACSB. *Program availability:* Part-time, evening/weekend, 100% online, blended/hybrid learning. *Students:* 136 full-time (74 women), 214 part-time (85 women); includes 29 minority (4 Black or African American, non-Hispanic/Latino; 11 Asian, non-Hispanic/Latino; 9 Hispanic/Latino; 5 Two or more races, non-Hispanic/Latino), 189 international. Average age 29. 636 applicants, 64% accepted, 104 enrolled. In 2018, 165 master's, 1 doctorate, 10 other advanced degrees awarded. *Degree requirements:* For master's, thesis optional. *Entrance requirements:* For master's and Graduate Certificate, GMAT or GRE General Test, 3 letters of recommendation, statement of purpose, resume. Additional exam requirements/recommendations for international students: Required—TOEFL (minimum score 563 paper-based; 84 iBT), IELTS (minimum score 7). *Application deadline:* For fall admission, 6/1 priority date for domestic and international students; for spring admission, 11/1 priority date for domestic students, 10/1 priority date for international students. Applications are processed on a rolling basis. Application fee: $70. Electronic applications accepted. *Financial support:* Career-related internships or fieldwork, institutionally sponsored loans, scholarships/grants, and unspecified assistantships available. Financial award application deadline: 6/1. *Unit head:* Melissa Terrio, Director of Graduate Recruitment & Admissions, 508-831-4665, Fax: 508-831-5866, E-mail: biz@wpi.edu. *Application contact:* Amy Trakimas, Associate Director of Graduate Recruitment & Admissions, 508-831-4665, Fax: 508-831-5866, E-mail: atrakimas@wpi.edu.
Website: https://www.wpi.edu/academics/business

Worcester State University, Graduate School, Program in Management, Worcester, MA 01602-2597. Offers accounting (MS); leadership (MS); marketing (MS). *Program availability:* Part-time, evening/weekend. *Faculty:* 6 full-time (3 women), 1 part-time/adjunct (0 women). *Students:* 15 full-time (6 women), 43 part-time (24 women); includes 14 minority (4 Black or African American, non-Hispanic/Latino; 5 Asian, non-Hispanic/Latino; 5 Hispanic/Latino), 7 international. Average age 38. 32 applicants, 100% accepted, 24 enrolled. In 2018, 24 master's awarded. *Degree requirements:* For master's, comprehensive exam (for some programs), thesis (for some programs), For a detail list in Degree Completion requirements please see the graduate catalog at catalog.worcester.edu. *Entrance requirements:* For master's, GMAT, For a detail list of entrance requirements please see the graduate catalog at catalog.worcester.edu. Additional exam requirements/recommendations for international students: Required—TOEFL (minimum score 550 paper-based; 79 iBT), IELTS (minimum score 6). *Application deadline:* For fall admission, 3/1 for domestic and international students; for spring admission, 11/1 for domestic and international students; for summer admission, 3/1 for domestic and international students. Applications are processed on a rolling basis. Application fee: $50. Electronic applications accepted. *Expenses: Tuition, area resident:* Full-time $3042; part-time $169 per credit hour. Tuition, state resident: full-time $3042; part-time $169 per credit hour. Tuition, nonresident: full-time $3042; part-time $169 per credit hour. *International tuition:* $3042 full-time. *Required fees:* $2754; $153 per credit hour. *Financial support:* Career-related internships or fieldwork, scholarships/grants, and unspecified assistantships available. Financial award application deadline: 3/1; financial award applicants required to submit FAFSA. *Unit head:* Dr. Elizabeth Wark, Program Coordinator, 508-929-8743, Fax: 508-929-8048, E-mail: ewark@worcester.edu. *Application contact:* Sara Grady, Associate Dean, Graduate Studies and Professional Development, 508-929-8130, Fax: 508-929-8100, E-mail: sara.grady@worcester.edu.

Xavier University, Williams College of Business, Master of Business Administration Program, Cincinnati, OH 45207. Offers business administration (Exec MBA, MBA);

business intelligence (MBA); finance (MBA); health industry (MBA); international business (MBA); marketing (MBA); values-based leadership (MBA); MBA/MHSA; MSN/MBA. *Accreditation:* AACSB. *Program availability:* Part-time, evening/weekend. *Degree requirements:* For master's, capstone course. *Entrance requirements:* For master's, GMAT or GRE, official transcript; resume. Additional exam requirements/recommendations for international students: Required—TOEFL (minimum score 550 paper-based; 79 iBT). Electronic applications accepted. Application fee is waived when completed online. *Expenses:* Contact institution.

Yale University, Yale School of Management, Doctoral Program in Management, New Haven, CT 06520. Offers accounting (PhD); financial economics (PhD); marketing (PhD); organizations and management (PhD). *Accreditation:* AACSB. *Degree requirements:* For doctorate, comprehensive exam, thesis/dissertation. *Entrance requirements:* For doctorate, GMAT or GRE General Test. Additional exam requirements/recommendations for international students: Required—TOEFL or IELTS. Electronic applications accepted. *Expenses:* Contact institution. *Faculty research:* Pricing of options and futures, term structure of interest rates, use of accounting numbers in debt contracts, product differentiation, e-commerce and marketing, behavioral finance.

Yeshiva University, The Katz School, Program in Marketing, New York, NY 10033-3201. Offers MS. *Program availability:* Part-time, online learning.

Yeshiva University, Sy Syms School of Business, New York, NY 10016. Offers accounting (MS); business (EMBA); marketing (MS); taxation (MS). *Program availability:* Part-time. *Entrance requirements:* For master's, minimum GPA of 3.5 or GMAT.

York College of Pennsylvania, Graham School of Business, York, PA 17403-3651. Offers accounting (M Acc); business (MBA); continuous improvement (MBA); financial management (MBA); health care management (MBA); management (MBA); marketing (MBA); self-designed (MBA). *Accreditation:* ACBSP. *Program availability:* Part-time, evening/weekend. *Faculty:* 11 full-time (5 women), 3 part-time/adjunct (1 woman). *Students:* 13 full-time (4 women), 73 part-time (32 women); includes 11 minority (5 Black or African American, non-Hispanic/Latino; 2 Asian, non-Hispanic/Latino; 2 Hispanic/Latino; 2 Two or more races, non-Hispanic/Latino), 1 international. Average age 35. 57 applicants, 65% accepted, 25 enrolled. In 2018, 8 master's awarded. *Degree requirements:* For master's, directed study. *Entrance requirements:* For master's, GMAT. Additional exam requirements/recommendations for international students: Required—TOEFL (minimum score 530 paper-based; 72 iBT), IELTS (minimum score 6). *Application deadline:* For fall admission, 7/15 priority date for domestic students, 5/1 for international students; for spring admission, 11/15 priority date for domestic students, 9/1 for international students; for summer admission, 4/15 priority date for domestic students. Applications are processed on a rolling basis. Application fee: $0. Electronic applications accepted. *Expenses:* Contact institution. *Financial support:* In 2018–19, 3 students received support. Scholarships/grants available. Financial award applicants required to submit FAFSA. *Unit head:* Nicole Cornell Sadowski, MBA Director, 717-815-1491, Fax: 717-600-3999, E-mail: ncornell@ycp.edu. *Application contact:* MBA Office, 717-815-1491, Fax: 717-600-3999, E-mail: mba@ycp.edu.
Website: http://www.ycp.edu/mba

Marketing Research

Hofstra University, Frank G. Zarb School of Business, Programs in Marketing and International Business, Hempstead, NY 11549. Offers business administration (MBA), including international business, marketing; international business (Advanced Certificate); marketing (MS, Advanced Certificate); marketing research (MS). *Program availability:* Part-time, evening/weekend, blended/hybrid learning. *Students:* 65 full-time (35 women), 19 part-time (11 women); includes 11 minority (2 Black or African American, non-Hispanic/Latino; 5 Asian, non-Hispanic/Latino; 4 Hispanic/Latino), 51 international. Average age 26. 168 applicants, 68% accepted, 35 enrolled. In 2018, 54 master's awarded. *Degree requirements:* For master's, thesis (for some programs), capstone course (for MBA), thesis (for MS), minimum GPA of 3.0. *Entrance requirements:* For master's, GMAT/GRE, 2 letters of recommendation, resume, essay. Additional exam requirements/recommendations for international students: Required—TOEFL (minimum score 550 paper-based; 80 iBT); Recommended—IELTS (minimum score 6). *Application deadline:* Applications are processed on a rolling basis. Application fee: $75. Electronic applications accepted. *Expenses:* $1,375 per credit plus fees. *Financial support:* In 2018–19, 34 students received support, including 21 fellowships with full and partial tuition reimbursements available (averaging $5,450 per year), 3 research assistantships with full and partial tuition reimbursements available (averaging $4,477 per year); career-related internships or fieldwork, Federal Work-Study, institutionally sponsored loans, scholarships/grants, tuition waivers (full and partial), unspecified assistantships, and scholarships and endowed scholarships also available. Support available to part-time students. Financial award applicants required to submit FAFSA. *Faculty research:* Cross-cultural consumer behavior; social, digital, global, and strategic issues in marketing; consumer health/well-being; ethnocentrism and animosity. *Unit head:* Dr. Anil Mathur, Chairperson, 516-463-5346, Fax: 516-463-4834, E-mail: anil.mathur@hofstra.edu. *Application contact:* Sunil Samuel, Assistant Vice President of Admissions, 516-463-4723, Fax: 516-463-4664, E-mail: graduateadmission@hofstra.edu.
Website: http://www.hofstra.edu/business/

Instituto Tecnológico y de Estudios Superiores de Monterrey, Campus Irapuato, Graduate Programs, Irapuato, Mexico. Offers administration (MBA); administration of information technology (MAIT); administration of telecommunications (MAT); architecture (M Arch); computer science (MCS); education (M Ed); educational administration (MEA); educational innovation and technology (DEIT); educational technology (MET); electronic commerce (MBA); environmental administration and planning (MEAP); environmental systems (MES); finances (MBA); humanistic studies (MHS); international management for Latin American executives (MIMLAE); library and information science (MLIS); manufacturing quality management (MMQM); marketing research (MBA).

Marquette University, Graduate School of Management, Department of Economics, Milwaukee, WI 53201-1881. Offers business economics (MSAE); financial economics (MSAE); international economics (MSAE); marketing research (MSAE); real estate economics (MSAE). *Program availability:* Part-time, evening/weekend. *Degree requirements:* For master's, comprehensive exam, professional project. *Entrance requirements:* For master's, GMAT or GRE General Test. Additional exam requirements/recommendations for international students: Required—TOEFL, IELTS, PTE. Electronic applications accepted. *Faculty research:* Monetary and fiscal policy in open economy, housing and regional migration, political economy of taxation and state/local government.

Michigan State University, The Graduate School, Eli Broad College of Business, Department of Marketing, East Lansing, MI 48224. Offers marketing (PhD); marketing research (MS). *Degree requirements:* For doctorate, comprehensive exam, thesis/dissertation. *Entrance requirements:* For master's, GMAT, bachelor's degree with minimum GPA of 3.0 in last 2 years of undergraduate work; transcripts; 3 letters of recommendation; statement of purpose; resume; working knowledge of computers; basic understanding of accounting, finance, marketing, and the management of people; laptop capable of running Windows software; for doctorate, GMAT (taken within past 5 years), bachelor's degree; letters of recommendation; statement of purpose; previous work experience; personal qualifications of sound character, perseverance, intellectual curiosity, and an interest in scholarly research. Additional exam requirements/recommendations for international students: Required—TOEFL (minimum score 100 iBT), PTE (minimum score 70), IELTS (minimum score 7) accepted for MS only.

Pacific Lutheran University, School of Business, Master of Science in Market Research Program, Tacoma, WA 98447. Offers MS. *Entrance requirements:* For master's, GRE or GMAT, two references, official transcripts, resume, statement of professional goals and quantitative skills. Additional exam requirements/recommendations for international students: Required—TOEFL (minimum score 88 iBT) or IELTS (minimum score 6.5).

Saint Leo University, Graduate Studies in Business, Saint Leo, FL 33574-6665. Offers accounting (M Acc); cybersecurity management (MBA); health care management (MBA); human resource management (MBA); marketing (MBA); marketing research and social media analytics (MBA); software engineering (MS). *Accreditation:* ACBSP. *Program availability:* Part-time, evening/weekend, 100% online, blended/hybrid learning. *Faculty:* 51 full-time (16 women), 54 part-time/adjunct (22 women). *Students:* 8 full-time (3 women), 2,209 part-time (1,288 women); includes 1,046 minority (691 Black or African American, non-Hispanic/Latino; 10 American Indian or Alaska Native, non-Hispanic/Latino; 47 Asian, non-Hispanic/Latino; 249 Hispanic/Latino; 5 Native Hawaiian or other Pacific Islander, non-Hispanic/Latino; 44 Two or more races, non-Hispanic/Latino), 71 international. Average age 37. 760 applicants, 83% accepted, 498 enrolled. In 2018, 763 master's, 14 doctorates awarded. *Degree requirements:* For doctorate, comprehensive exam, thesis/dissertation. *Entrance requirements:* For master's, GMAT with minimum score 500 (for M Acc), official transcripts, current resume, 2 professional recommendations, personal statement, bachelor's degree from regionally-accredited university; undergraduate degree in accounting and minimum undergraduate GPA of 3.0 (for M Acc); minimum undergraduate GPA of 3.0 in final 2 years of undergraduate study and 2 years' work experience (for MBA); for doctorate, GMAT (minimum score of 550) if master's GPA is under 3.25, official transcripts, current resume, 2 professional recommendations, personal statement, master's degree from regionally-accredited university with minimum GPA of 3.25, 3 years' work experience, interview. Additional exam requirements/recommendations for international students: Required—TOEFL (minimum score 550 paper-based; 78 iBT). *Application deadline:* For fall admission, 7/1 priority date for domestic and international students; for spring admission, 11/12 priority date for domestic students, 11/1 for international students. Applications are processed on a rolling basis. Application fee: $80. Electronic applications accepted. *Expenses:* Onground Master of Accounting $555 per credit, Online Master of Accounting $720 per credit, Onground MBA $555 per credit, Onground MBA Intl/Experiential $720 per credit, Online MBA/Cybersecurity military rate $555 per credit, Online MBA civilian rate $720, MS Cybersecurity civilian rate $770, DBA $900 per credit. *Financial support:* In 2018–19, 213 students received support. Scholarships/grants, unspecified assistantships, and tuition remission for Saint Leo employees and their dependents available. Financial award application deadline: 3/1; financial award applicants required to submit FAFSA. *Faculty research:* Servant leadership, work/life balance, emotional intelligence, pricing, marketing. *Unit head:* Dr. Robyn Parker, Dean, School of Business, 352-588-8599, Fax: 352-588-8912, E-mail: mbaslu@saintleo.edu. *Application contact:* Mark Russum, Assistant Vice President, Enrollment, 800-707-8846, Fax: 352-588-7873, E-mail: grad.admissions@saintleo.edu.
Website: https://www.saintleo.edu/college-of-business

Southern Illinois University Edwardsville, Graduate School, School of Business, Department of Management and Marketing, Edwardsville, IL 62026. Offers marketing research (MMR). *Program availability:* Part-time, evening/weekend. *Degree requirements:* For master's, comprehensive exam, final exam. *Entrance requirements:* For master's, GMAT. Additional exam requirements/recommendations for international students: Required—TOEFL (minimum score 550 paper-based; 79 iBT), IELTS (minimum score 6.5). Electronic applications accepted.

Towson University, College of Business and Economics, Program in Marketing Intelligence, Towson, MD 21252-0001. Offers MS, Postbaccalaureate Certificate. *Expenses: Tuition, area resident:* Full-time $9196; part-time $418 per unit. Tuition, state resident: full-time $9196; part-time $418 per unit. Tuition, nonresident: full-time $19,030; part-time $865 per unit. *International tuition:* $19,030 full-time. *Required fees:* $3102; $141 per year. $423 per term. Tuition and fees vary according to campus/location and program.

Universidad Autonoma de Guadalajara, Graduate Programs, Guadalajara, Mexico. Offers administrative law and justice (LL M); advertising and corporate communications (MA); architecture (M Arch); business (MBA); computational science (MCC); education (Ed M, Ed D); English-Spanish translation (MA); entrepreneurship and management (MBA); integrated management of digital animation (MA); international business (MIB); international corporate law (LL M); Internet technologies (MS); manufacturing systems (MMS); occupational health (MS); philosophy (MA, PhD); power electronics (MS); quality systems (MQS); renewable energy (MS); social evaluation of projects (MBA); strategic market research (MBA); tax law (MA); teaching mathematics (MA).

Universidad de las Americas, A.C., Program in Business Administration, Mexico City, Mexico. Offers finance (MBA); marketing research (MBA); production and quality (MBA).

University of Missouri–St. Louis, College of Business Administration, St. Louis, MO 63121. Offers accounting (M Acc); business administration (MBA, DBA, PhD, Certificate), including logistics and supply chain management (PhD); business intelligence (Certificate); cybersecurity (Certificate); digital and social media marketing (Certificate); human resources management (Certificate); information systems (MS);

logistics and supply chain management (Certificate); marketing management (Certificate). *Program availability:* Part-time, evening/weekend. *Degree requirements:* For doctorate, thesis/dissertation. *Entrance requirements:* For master's, GMAT, 2 letters of recommendation; for doctorate, GMAT or GRE, 3 letters of recommendation. Additional exam requirements/recommendations for international students: Recommended—TOEFL (minimum score 550 paper-based; 79 iBT), IELTS (minimum score 6.5). Electronic applications accepted. *Faculty research:* Statistical decision aids, commercial banking, corporate finance, operations management, information systems.

University of Rochester, Simon Business School, Master of Science Program in Marketing Analytics, Rochester, NY 14627. Offers MS. *Entrance requirements:* For master's, GMAT or GRE. *Expenses: Tuition:* Full-time $52,974; part-time $1654 per credit hour. *Required fees:* $612. One-time fee: $30 part-time. Tuition and fees vary according to campus/location and program.

The University of Texas at Arlington, Graduate School, College of Business, Department of Marketing, Arlington, TX 76019. Offers marketing (MBA); marketing research (MS). *Program availability:* Part-time, evening/weekend. *Degree requirements:* For master's, thesis optional. *Entrance requirements:* For master's, GMAT, GRE. Additional exam requirements/recommendations for international students: Required— TOEFL (minimum score 550 paper-based; 79 iBT). Electronic applications accepted. *Faculty research:* Marketing strategy, marketing research, international marketing.

University of Wisconsin–Madison, Graduate School, Wisconsin School of Business, Wisconsin Full-Time MBA Program, Madison, WI 53706-1380. Offers applied security analysis (MBA); arts administration (MBA); brand and product management (MBA); corporate finance and investment banking (MBA); marketing research (MBA); operations and technology management (MBA); real estate (MBA); risk management and insurance (MBA); strategic human resource management (MBA); supply chain management (MBA). *Faculty:* 137 full-time (36 women), 39 part-time/adjunct (11 women). *Students:* 183 full-time (59 women); includes 31 minority (5 Black or African American, non-Hispanic/Latino; 1 American Indian or Alaska Native, non-Hispanic/Latino; 6 Asian, non-Hispanic/Latino; 13 Hispanic/Latino; 6 Two or more races, non-Hispanic/Latino), 40 international. Average age 28. 465 applicants, 33% accepted, 79 enrolled. In 2018, 104 master's awarded. *Entrance requirements:* For master's, GMAT or GRE, bachelor's or equivalent degree, essay, letter of recommendation, resume. Additional exam requirements/recommendations for international students: Required— TOEFL (minimum score 100 iBT), IELTS (minimum score 7.5), TOEFL is not required for international students whose undergraduate training was in English. *Application deadline:* For fall admission, 11/1 for domestic and international students; for winter admission, 1/10 for domestic and international students; for spring admission, 3/1 for domestic and international students; for summer admission, 4/10 for domestic students, 4/10 priority date for international students. Applications are processed on a rolling basis. Application fee: $75 ($81 for international students). Electronic applications accepted. *Expenses:* Wisconsin Resident tuition and fees - $39,156; Nonresident tuition and fees - $76,635. *Financial support:* In 2018–19, 148 students received support, including 7 fellowships with full tuition reimbursements available (averaging $25,871 per year), 7 research assistantships with full tuition reimbursements available (averaging $14,832 per year), 47 teaching assistantships with full tuition reimbursements available (averaging $14,832 per year); scholarships/grants, health care benefits, tuition waivers (full and partial), and unspecified assistantships also available. Financial award application deadline: 6/1. *Faculty research:* Ecology, environmental studies, and business; decision making; tax policy; diversity and inclusion in governance boards; marketing and social media. *Unit head:* Dr. Enno Siemsen, Associate Dean of the MBA and Masters Programs, 608-890-3130, E-mail: esiemsen@wisc.edu. *Application contact:* Betsy Kacizak, Director of Admissions and Recruiting, Full-time MBA Program, 608-262-4000, E-mail: betsy.kacizak@wisc.edu.
Website: https://wsb.wisc.edu/

Section 15
Nonprofit Management

This section contains a directory of institutions offering graduate work in nonprofit management. Additional information about programs listed in the directory may be obtained by writing directly to the dean of a graduate school or chair of a department at the address given in the directory.

For programs offering related work, see also in this book *Accounting and Finance* and *Business Administration and Management*. In another guide in this series:

Graduate Programs in the Humanities, Arts & Social Sciences
See *Public, Regional, and Industrial Affairs*

CONTENTS

Program Directory

Nonprofit Management

Abilene Christian University, College of Graduate and Professional Studies, Program in Business Administration, Addison, TX 79699. Offers business analytics (MBA); general management (MBA); healthcare administration (MBA); international business (MBA); management: business analytics (MS); management: healthcare administration (MS); management: international business (MS); management: marketing (MS); management: operations and supply chain management (MS); marketing (MBA); nonprofit leadership (MBA). *Program availability:* Part-time, online only, 100% online. *Faculty:* 4 full-time (0 women), 7 part-time/adjunct (3 women). *Students:* 149 full-time (69 women), 53 part-time (25 women); includes 88 minority (42 Black or African American, non-Hispanic/Latino; 2 American Indian or Alaska Native, non-Hispanic/Latino; 4 Asian, non-Hispanic/Latino; 31 Hispanic/Latino; 1 Native Hawaiian or other Pacific Islander, non-Hispanic/Latino; 8 Two or more races, non-Hispanic/Latino), 4 international. 36 applicants, 100% accepted, 32 enrolled. In 2018, 24 master's awarded. *Entrance requirements:* Additional exam requirements/recommendations for international students: Required—TOEFL (minimum score 80 iBT), IELTS (minimum score 6). *Application deadline:* For fall admission, 10/7 for domestic students; for winter admission, 12/20 for domestic students; for spring admission, 2/24 for domestic students; for summer admission, 4/20 for domestic students. Applications are processed on a rolling basis. Application fee: $50. Electronic applications accepted. *Expenses:* $721 per hour. *Financial support:* In 2018–19, 16 students received support. Scholarships/grants available. Financial award application deadline: 7/1; financial award applicants required to submit FAFSA. *Faculty research:* Organizational structure, financial management, cost accounting, unit analysis management. *Unit head:* Dr. Phil Vardiman, Program Director, 325-674-2153, E-mail: pxv02b@acu.edu. *Application contact:* Graduate Advisor, 817-219-7300, E-mail: onlineadmissions@acu.edu. Website: http://www.acu.edu/online/academics/mba-business-administration.html

Albizu University, Miami Campus, Graduate Programs, Miami, FL 33172-2209. Offers clinical psychology (PhD, Psy D); entrepreneurship (MBA); exceptional student education (MS); human services (PhD); industrial/organizational psychology (MS); marriage and family therapy (MS); mental health counseling (MS); nonprofit management (MBA); organizational management (MBA); school counseling (MS); speech and language pathology (MS); teaching English for speakers of other languages (MS). *Accreditation:* APA. *Program availability:* Part-time, evening/weekend, 100% online, blended/hybrid learning. *Faculty:* 32 full-time (24 women), 27 part-time/adjunct (15 women). *Students:* 479 full-time (410 women), 146 part-time (126 women); includes 539 minority (42 Black or African American, non-Hispanic/Latino; 2 Asian, non-Hispanic/Latino; 490 Hispanic/Latino; 5 Two or more races, non-Hispanic/Latino), 22 international. Average age 33. 314 applicants, 45% accepted, 92 enrolled. In 2018, 101 master's, 64 doctorates awarded. Terminal master's awarded for partial completion of doctoral program. *Degree requirements:* For master's, comprehensive exam (for some programs), integrative project (for MBA); research project (for exceptional student education, teaching English as a second language); for doctorate, comprehensive exam, thesis/dissertation, comprehensive examinations, internship, project/dissertation. *Entrance requirements:* For master's, GRE/EXADEP, bachelor's degree from accredited institution, minimum GPA of 3.0, 3 letters of recommendation, interview, resume, statement of purpose, official transcripts; for doctorate, GRE (for Psy D), 3 letters of recommendation, resume, interview, statement of purpose, official transcripts; bachelor's degree and minimum GPA of 3.25 (for Psy D); master's degree and minimum GPA of 3.0 (for PhD). Additional exam requirements/recommendations for international students: Required—Michigan Test of English Language Proficiency. *Application deadline:* For fall admission, 4/1 priority date for domestic students, 5/1 priority date for international students; for spring admission, 11/1 priority date for domestic students, 9/1 priority date for international students. Applications are processed on a rolling basis. Application fee: $50. Electronic applications accepted. Application fee is waived when completed online. *Expenses:* Contact institution. *Financial support:* In 2018–19, 141 students received support. Federal Work-Study, scholarships/grants, unspecified assistantships, and tuition discounts available. Financial award application deadline: 6/1; financial award applicants required to submit FAFSA. *Faculty research:* Psychotherapy, forensic psychology, neuropsychology, special education, speech-language pathology, criminal justice, human services. *Unit head:* Dr. Jose Pons-Madera, PhD, President, 305-593-1223 Ext. 3120, Fax: 305-477-8983, E-mail: jpons@albizu.edu. *Application contact:* Nancy Alvarez, Director of Enrollment Management, 305-593-1223 Ext. 3136, Fax: 305-593-1854, E-mail: nalvarez@albizu.edu.

American Jewish University, Graduate School of Nonprofit Management, Program in Business Administration, Bel Air, CA 90077-1599. Offers general nonprofit administration (MBA); Jewish nonprofit administration (MBA). *Program availability:* Part-time, evening/weekend. *Degree requirements:* For master's, thesis, internship. *Entrance requirements:* For master's, GMAT or GRE General Test, interview, minimum undergraduate GPA of 3.0. Additional exam requirements/recommendations for international students: Required—TOEFL (minimum score 550 paper-based).

American University, School of Public Affairs, Department of Public Administration and Policy, Washington, DC 20016-8070. Offers organization development (MSOD, Certificate), including leadership for organizational change (Certificate), organization development (MSOD); public administration (MPA, PhD, Certificate), including nonprofit management (Certificate), public financial management (Certificate), public management (Certificate); public administration and policy (MPAP), including public administration policy; public policy (MPP, Certificate), including public policy (MPP), public policy analysis (Certificate); LL M/MPA; MPA/JD; MPP/JD; MPP/LL M. *Program availability:* Part-time, evening/weekend, 100% online, blended/hybrid learning. *Faculty:* 33 full-time (11 women), 18 part-time/adjunct (7 women). *Students:* 235 full-time (153 women), 275 part-time (189 women); includes 123 minority (61 Black or African American, non-Hispanic/Latino; 4 American Indian or Alaska Native, non-Hispanic/Latino; 23 Asian, non-Hispanic/Latino; 18 Hispanic/Latino; 1 Native Hawaiian or other Pacific Islander, non-Hispanic/Latino; 16 Two or more races, non-Hispanic/Latino), 34 international. Average age 29. 710 applicants, 75% accepted, 182 enrolled. In 2018, 202 master's, 5 doctorates, 5 other advanced degrees awarded. *Degree requirements:* For master's, comprehensive exam; for doctorate, comprehensive exam, thesis/dissertation. *Entrance requirements:* For master's, GRE; Please see website: https:// www.american.edu/spa/jlc/, statement of purpose, 2 recommendations, resume, transcript; for doctorate, GRE; Please see website: https://www.american.edu/spa/jlc/, 3 recommendations, statement of purpose, resume, writing sample, transcript; for Certificate, bachelor's degree. Additional exam requirements/recommendations for international students: Required—TOEFL. Application fee: $55. *Expenses:* Contact institution. *Financial support:* Research assistantships, teaching assistantships, institutionally sponsored loans, scholarships/grants, and unspecified assistantships available. Financial award applicants required to submit FAFSA. *Unit head:* Dr. Dave Marcotte, Department Chair, 202-885-2940, E-mail: spagrad@american.edu.

Application contact: Jennifer Forney, Assistant Dean, Graduate Enrollment, 202-885-2940, E-mail: spagrad@american.edu.
Website: http://www.american.edu/spa/dpap/

Antioch University Santa Barbara, Program in Business Administration, Santa Barbara, CA 93101-1581. Offers non-profit management (MBA); social business (MBA); strategic leadership (MBA).

Arizona State University at the Tempe campus, College of Public Programs, School of Community Resources and Development, Phoenix, AZ 85004-0685. Offers community resources and development (MS, PhD); nonprofit leadership and management (Graduate Certificate); nonprofit studies (MNpS); sustainable tourism (MAS). *Program availability:* Part-time, evening/weekend. Terminal master's awarded for partial completion of doctoral program. *Degree requirements:* For master's, thesis or alternative, interactive Program of Study (iPOS) submitted before completing 50 percent of required credit hours; for doctorate, comprehensive exam, thesis/dissertation, interactive Program of Study (iPOS) submitted before completing 50 percent of required credit hours. *Entrance requirements:* For master's and doctorate, GRE, minimum GPA of 3.0 or equivalent in last 2 years of work leading to bachelor's degree. Additional exam requirements/recommendations for international students: Required—TOEFL, IELTS, or PTE. Electronic applications accepted. *Expenses:* Contact institution.

Arizona State University at the Tempe campus, College of Public Programs, School of Public Affairs, Phoenix, AZ 85004-0687. Offers emergency management and homeland security (MA); program evaluation (MS); public administration (MPA, PhD), including nonprofit administration (MPA), urban management (MPA); public policy (MPP); MPA/MSW. *Accreditation:* NASPAA (one or more programs are accredited). *Program availability:* Part-time, evening/weekend. Terminal master's awarded for partial completion of doctoral program. *Degree requirements:* For master's, thesis or alternative, policy analysis or capstone project; interactive Program of Study (iPOS) submitted before completing 50 percent of required credit hours; for doctorate, comprehensive exam, thesis/dissertation, interactive Program of Study (iPOS) submitted before completing 50 percent of required credit hours. *Entrance requirements:* For master's, GRE, minimum GPA of 3.0 or equivalent in last 2 years of work leading to bachelor's degree; for doctorate, GRE, minimum GPA of 3.0 or equivalent in last 2 years of work leading to bachelor's degree, 3 letters of recommendation, resume, statement of goals, samples of research reports. Additional exam requirements/recommendations for international students: Required—TOEFL (minimum score 600 paper-based; 100 iBT), IELTS (minimum score 6.5). Electronic applications accepted. *Expenses:* Contact institution.

Assumption College, Business Studies Program, Worcester, MA 01609-1296. Offers accounting (MBA); business studies (CAGS); finance/economics (MBA); human resources (MBA); international business (MBA); management (MBA); marketing (MBA); nonprofit leadership (MBA). *Program availability:* Part-time, evening/weekend. *Degree requirements:* For master's, capstone. *Entrance requirements:* For master's, bachelor's degree, three letters of recommendation, official transcripts, personal statement, current resume; for CAGS, MBA or equivalent degree in a closely related field, three letters of recommendation, official transcripts, personal statement, current resume. Additional exam requirements/recommendations for international students: Required—TOEFL (minimum score 540 paper-based; 76 iBT), IELTS (minimum score 6). Electronic applications accepted. *Faculty research:* Workplace diversity, dynamics of team interaction, utilization of leased employees, experiential learning project on due diligence market for prostheses.

Avila University, School of Professional Studies, Kansas City, MO 64145-1698. Offers executive leadership (MS); fundraising (MA); instructional design and technology (MA, MS); leadership coaching (MS); project management (MA); strategic human resources (MS). *Program availability:* Part-time-only, evening/weekend, 100% online, blended/hybrid learning. *Faculty:* 14 part-time/adjunct (8 women). *Students:* 69 full-time (49 women), 48 part-time (42 women); includes 45 minority (38 Black or African American, non-Hispanic/Latino; 5 Hispanic/Latino; 2 Two or more races, non-Hispanic/Latino), 5 international. Average age 39. 63 applicants, 60% accepted, 29 enrolled. In 2018, 34 master's awarded. *Degree requirements:* For master's, thesis optional. *Entrance requirements:* For master's, 2 letters of recommendation, minimum GPA of 3.0 during last 60 hours, resume, statement of intent. Additional exam requirements/recommendations for international students: Required—TOEFL (minimum score 550 paper-based; 79 iBT). *Application deadline:* Applications are processed on a rolling basis. Application fee: $0. Electronic applications accepted. *Expenses:* Contact institution. *Financial support:* In 2018–19, 12 students received support. Unspecified assistantships available. Support available to part-time students. Financial award applicants required to submit FAFSA. *Unit head:* Sarah Sullivan, Coordinator, 816-501-0429, Fax: 816-941-4650, E-mail: advantage@avila.edu. *Application contact:* Jessica Burson, Graduate Admission Advisor, 816-501-2482, Fax: 816-941-4650, E-mail: advantage@avila.edu.
Website: https://www.avila.edu/mrk/advantage-3

Baruch College of the City University of New York, Austin W. Marxe School of Public and International Affairs, Program in Public Administration, New York, NY 10010-5585. Offers general public administration (MPA); health care policy (MPA); nonprofit administration (MPA); policy analysis and evaluation (MPA); public management (MPA); urban development and sustainability (MPA); MS/MPA. *Accreditation:* NASPAA. *Program availability:* Part-time, evening/weekend. *Degree requirements:* For master's, thesis, capstone. *Entrance requirements:* For master's, GRE General Test. Additional exam requirements/recommendations for international students: Required—TOEFL. Electronic applications accepted. *Expenses:* Contact institution. *Faculty research:* Urbanization, population and poverty in the developing world, housing and community development, labor unions and housing, government-nongovernment relations, immigration policy, social network analysis, cross-sectoral governance, comparative healthcare systems, program evaluation, social welfare policy, health outcomes, educational policy and leadership, transnationalism, infant health, welfare reform, racial/ethnic disparities in health, urban politics, homelessness, race and ethnic relations.

Bay Path University, Program in Nonprofit Management and Philanthropy, Longmeadow, MA 01106-2292. Offers MS. *Program availability:* Part-time, 100% online. *Students:* 4 full-time (all women), 31 part-time (28 women); includes 16 minority (9 Black or African American, non-Hispanic/Latino; 1 Asian, non-Hispanic/Latino; 4 Hispanic/Latino; 2 Two or more races, non-Hispanic/Latino). Average age 36. *Entrance requirements:* For master's, completed application; official undergraduate and graduate transcripts (a GPA of 3.0 or higher is preferred); original essay of at least 250 words on the topic: "Why the MS in Nonprofit Management & Philanthropy is important to my personal and professional goals"; current resume; 2 recommendations. *Application deadline:* Applications are processed on a rolling basis. Electronic

applications accepted. Application fee is waived when completed online. *Expenses:* Contact institution. *Financial support:* Unspecified assistantships available. Financial award applicants required to submit FAFSA. *Unit head:* Silvia de Haas-Phillips, Program Director, E-mail: sdphillips@baypath.edu. *Application contact:* Jennifer Palma, Director of Graduate Admissions, 413-565-1181, Fax: 413-565-1250, E-mail: jpamla@baypath.edu.
Website: https://www.baypath.edu/academics/graduate-programs/nonprofit-management-philanthropy-ms/

Bay Path University, Program in Strategic Fundraising and Philanthropy, Longmeadow, MA 01106-2292. Offers higher education fundraising (MS); nonprofit fundraising (MS). *Program availability:* Part-time, 100% online. *Students:* 10 part-time (9 women); includes 1 minority (Black or African American, non-Hispanic/Latino). Average age 41. In 2018, 4 master's awarded. *Entrance requirements:* For master's, completed application; official undergraduate and graduate transcripts (a GPA of 3.0 higher is preferred); original essay of at least 250 words on the topic: "Why the MS in Strategic Fundraising & Philanthropy is important to my personal and professional goals?"; current resume; 2 recommendations. *Application deadline:* Applications are processed on a rolling basis. Electronic applications accepted. Application fee is waived when completed online. *Expenses:* Contact institution. *Financial support:* Unspecified assistantships available. Financial award applicants required to submit FAFSA. *Unit head:* Silvia de Haas-Phillips, Program Director, E-mail: sdphillips@baypath.edu. *Application contact:* Jennifer Palma, Director of Graduate Admissions, 413-565-1181, Fax: 413-565-1250, E-mail: jpalma@baypath.edu.
Website: https://www.baypath.edu/academics/graduate-programs/strategic-fundraising-philanthropy-ms/

Bradley University, The Graduate School, College of Education and Health Sciences, Department of Leadership in Education, Nonprofits and Counseling, Peoria, IL 61625-0002. Offers counseling (MA), including clinical mental health counseling, professional school counseling; leadership in educational administration (MA); nonprofit leadership (MA). *Accreditation:* ACA; NCATE. *Program availability:* Part-time, evening/weekend, blended/hybrid learning. *Faculty:* 11 full-time (6 women), 10 part-time/adjunct (6 women). *Students:* 83 full-time (68 women), 166 part-time (137 women); includes 50 minority (26 Black or African American, non-Hispanic/Latino; 2 American Indian or Alaska Native, non-Hispanic/Latino; 4 Asian, non-Hispanic/Latino; 14 Hispanic/Latino; 4 Two or more races, non-Hispanic/Latino), 3 international. Average age 33. 181 applicants, 97% accepted, 54 enrolled. In 2018, 58 master's awarded. *Degree requirements:* For master's, comprehensive exam, thesis optional. *Entrance requirements:* For master's, GRE General Test or MAT, interview, 3 letters of recommendation. Additional exam requirements/recommendations for international students: Required—TOEFL (minimum score 550 paper-based; 79 iBT), IELTS (minimum score 6.5). *Application deadline:* For fall admission, 5/15 priority date for domestic and international students; for spring admission, 10/15 priority date for domestic and international students. Applications are processed on a rolling basis. Application fee: $40 ($50 for international students). Electronic applications accepted. *Expenses:* Tuition: Part-time $890 per credit. *Required fees:* $50 per unit. *Financial support:* In 2018–19, 67 students received support, including 1 fellowship with full tuition reimbursement available (averaging $16,020 per year), 12 research assistantships with full tuition reimbursements available (averaging $14,388 per year); career-related internships or fieldwork, scholarships/grants, tuition waivers (partial), and unspecified assistantships also available. Support available to part-time students. Financial award application deadline: 4/1. *Unit head:* Dean Cantu, Associate Dean and Director, Professor, 309-677-3190, E-mail: dcantu@bradley.edu. *Application contact:* Rachel Webb, Director of On-Campus Graduate Admissions & International Student and Scholar Services, 309-677-2375, E-mail: rkwebb@bradley.edu.
Website: http://www.bradley.edu/academic/departments/lenc/

Brandeis University, The Heller School for Social Policy and Management, Program in Nonprofit Management, Waltham, MA 02454-9110. Offers child, youth, and family management (MBA); health care management (MBA); social impact management (MBA); social policy and management (MBA); sustainable development (MBA); MBA/MA; MBA/MD. MBA/MD program offered in conjunction with Tufts University School of Medicine. *Accreditation:* AACSB. *Program availability:* Part-time. *Degree requirements:* For master's, team consulting project. *Entrance requirements:* For master's, GMAT (preferred) or GRE, 2 letters of recommendation, problem statement analysis, 3-5 years of professional experience. Additional exam requirements/recommendations for international students: Required—TOEFL (minimum score 600 paper-based; 100 iBT). Electronic applications accepted. *Expenses:* Contact institution. *Faculty research:* Health care; children and families; elder and disabled services; social impact management; organizations in the non-profit, for-profit, or public sector.

Brigham Young University, Graduate Studies, BYU Marriott School of Business, Master of Public Administration Program, Provo, UT 84602. Offers healthcare (MPA); local government (MPA); nonprofit management (MPA); state and federal government (MPA); JD/MPA. *Accreditation:* NASPAA. *Entrance requirements:* For master's, GMAT or GRE, commitment to BYU Honor Code. Additional exam requirements/recommendations for international students: Required—TOEFL (minimum score 580 paper-based; 85 iBT). Electronic applications accepted. *Expenses:* Contact institution. *Faculty research:* Taxes, budgeting, nonprofit, ethics, decision modeling, work balance, organizational behavior.

Cairn University, School of Business, Langhorne, PA 19047-2990. Offers accounting (MBA); business administration (MBA); international entrepreneurship (MBA); nonprofit leadership (MBA); organizational leadership (MSOL, Postbaccalaureate Certificate). *Program availability:* Part-time, evening/weekend, 100% online, blended/hybrid learning. *Entrance requirements:* Additional exam requirements/recommendations for international students: Required—TOEFL (minimum score 550 paper-based). Electronic applications accepted. Application fee is waived when completed online. *Expenses:* Contact institution.

California State University, Northridge, Graduate Studies, Tseng College, Program in Nonprofit-Sector Management, Northridge, CA 91330. Offers Graduate Certificate. Offered in collaboration with College of Social and Behavioral Sciences. *Entrance requirements:* For degree, bachelor's degree from accredited college or university with minimum GPA of 2.5 in last 60 semester units or 90 quarter units; at least one year of work experience in the public or non-profit sector.

Capella University, School of Public Service Leadership, Doctoral Programs in Healthcare, Minneapolis, MN 55402. Offers criminal justice (PhD); emergency management (PhD); epidemiology (Dr PH); general health administration (DHA); general public administration (DPA); health advocacy and leadership (Dr PH); health care administration (PhD); health care leadership (DHA); health policy advocacy (DHA); multidisciplinary human services (PhD); nonprofit management and leadership (PhD); public safety leadership (PhD); social and community services (PhD).

Case Western Reserve University, Jack, Joseph and Morton Mandel School of Applied Social Sciences, Cleveland, OH 44087. Offers nonprofit management (MNO); social welfare (PhD); social work (MSSA); JD/MSSA; MSSA/MA; MSSA/MBA; MSSA/MNO. *Accreditation:* CSWE (one or more programs are accredited). *Program availability:* Part-time, evening/weekend, 100% online. *Degree requirements:* For master's, fieldwork; for doctorate, thesis/dissertation. *Entrance requirements:* For master's, minimum undergraduate GPA of 2.7 or GRE/MAT; for doctorate, GRE General Test. Additional exam requirements/recommendations for international students: Required—TOEFL (minimum score 557 paper-based, 90 iBT) or IELTS (minimum score 7). Electronic applications accepted. *Expenses:* Contact institution. *Faculty research:* Urban poverty, community social development, substance abuse, health, child welfare, aging, mental health, behavioral health, policy, mixed income communities, trauma, school social work, adoption.

Case Western Reserve University, Weatherhead School of Management, Mandel Center for Nonprofit Organizations, Cleveland, OH 44106-7167. Offers MNO, CNM, JD/MNO, MNO/MSSA, MSSA/MNO. *Entrance requirements:* For master's, GMAT or GRE. Additional exam requirements/recommendations for international students: Required—TOEFL. *Expenses:* Contact institution. *Faculty research:* Leadership management of non-profit organizations, strategic alliances, economic analysis of non-profit organizations.

Central Michigan University, Central Michigan University Global Campus, Program in Administration, Mount Pleasant, MI 48859. Offers acquisitions administration (MSA, Certificate); engineering management administration (MSA, Certificate); general administration (MSA, Certificate); health services administration (MSA, Certificate); human resources administration (MSA, Certificate); information resource management (MSA); information resource management administration (Certificate); international administration (MSA, Certificate); leadership (MSA, Certificate); philanthropy and fundraising administration (MSA, Certificate); public administration (MSA, Certificate); recreation and park administration (MSA); research administration (MSA, Certificate). *Program availability:* Part-time, evening/weekend, online learning. *Entrance requirements:* For master's, minimum GPA of 2.7 in major. Electronic applications accepted.

Chaminade University of Honolulu, Graduate, Program in Business Administration, Honolulu, HI 96816-1578. Offers accounting (MBA); business (MBA); island business (MBA); not-for-profit (MBA). *Program availability:* Part-time, evening/weekend, 100% online, blended/hybrid learning. *Faculty:* 8 full-time (4 women), 6 part-time/adjunct (2 women). *Students:* 63 full-time (30 women), 45 part-time (29 women); includes 81 minority (8 Black or African American, non-Hispanic/Latino; 4 American Indian or Alaska Native, non-Hispanic/Latino; 34 Asian, non-Hispanic/Latino; 3 Hispanic/Latino; 32 Native Hawaiian or other Pacific Islander, non-Hispanic/Latino), 3 international. Average age 32. 25 applicants, 68% accepted, 15 enrolled. In 2018, 47 master's awarded. *Entrance requirements:* For master's, minimum GPA of 3.0, official transcripts, two years or more of work experience. Additional exam requirements/recommendations for international students: Required—TOEFL (minimum score 550 paper-based; 79 iBT). *Application deadline:* Applications are processed on a rolling basis. Application fee: $40. Electronic applications accepted. *Expenses:* $980 per credit; $93 fee per online course. *Financial support:* Applicants required to submit FAFSA. *Unit head:* Dr. Scott J. Schroeder, Director, 808-739-4612, Fax: 808-735-4734, E-mail: mba@chaminade.edu. *Application contact:* Dr. Scott J. Schroeder, Director, 808-739-4612, Fax: 808-735-4734, E-mail: mba@chaminade.edu.
Website: https://chaminade.edu/academic-program/mba/

Cleveland State University, College of Graduate Studies, Maxine Goodman Levin College of Urban Affairs, Program in Environmental Studies, Cleveland, OH 44115. Offers environmental nonprofit management (MAES); environmental planning (MAES); policy and administration (MAES); sustainable economic development (MAES); urban economic development (Certificate); JD/MAES. *Program availability:* Part-time, evening/weekend. *Faculty:* 16 full-time (8 women), 13 part-time/adjunct (5 women). *Students:* 8 full-time (4 women), 6 part-time (2 women); includes 3 minority (2 Black or African American, non-Hispanic/Latino; 1 Asian, non-Hispanic/Latino). Average age 29. 10 applicants, 100% accepted, 5 enrolled. In 2018, 5 master's awarded. *Degree requirements:* For master's, thesis or alternative, exit project. *Entrance requirements:* For master's, GRE General Test (minimum score: verbal and quantitative combined 40th percentile, analytical writing 4.0), minimum GPA of 3.0. Additional exam requirements/recommendations for international students: Required—TOEFL (minimum score 550 paper-based; 78 iBT), IELTS (6.0), or International Test of English Proficiency (iTEP). *Application deadline:* For fall admission, 7/1 priority date for domestic students, 5/15 for international students; for spring admission, 11/15 for domestic students, 11/1 for international students; for summer admission, 4/1 for domestic students, 3/15 for international students. Applications are processed on a rolling basis. Application fee: $40. Electronic applications accepted. *Expenses:* Contact institution. *Financial support:* In 2018–19, 4 students received support. Research assistantships, teaching assistantships with partial tuition reimbursements available, scholarships/grants, tuition waivers (full and partial), and unspecified assistantships available. Support available to part-time students. Financial award application deadline: 3/1; financial award applicants required to submit FAFSA. *Faculty research:* Environmental policy and administration, environmental planning, geographic information systems (GIS), urban sustainability planning and management, energy policy, land re-use. *Unit head:* Dr. Sanda Kaufman, Professor/Program Director, 216-687-2367, Fax: 216-687-9239, E-mail: s.kaufman@csuohio.edu. *Application contact:* David Arrighi, Graduate Academic Advisor, 216-523-7522, Fax: 216-687-5398, E-mail: d.arrighi@csuohio.edu.
Website: http://urban.csuohio.edu/academics/graduate/maes/

Cleveland State University, College of Graduate Studies, Maxine Goodman Levin College of Urban Affairs, Program in Nonprofit Administration and Leadership, Cleveland, OH 44115. Offers local and urban management (Certificate); nonprofit administration and leadership (MNAL); nonprofit management (Certificate). *Program availability:* Part-time, evening/weekend. *Faculty:* 16 full-time (8 women), 13 part-time/adjunct (5 women). *Students:* 8 full-time (7 women), 16 part-time (12 women); includes 9 minority (8 Black or African American, non-Hispanic/Latino; 1 Hispanic/Latino). Average age 34. 23 applicants, 52% accepted, 3 enrolled. In 2018, 8 master's awarded. *Degree requirements:* For master's, thesis or alternative, capstone course. *Entrance requirements:* For master's, GRE (minimum score: verbal and quantitative combined 40th percentile, analytical writing 4.0), minimum GPA of 3.0. Additional exam requirements/recommendations for international students: Required—TOEFL (minimum score 550 paper-based; 78 iBT), IELTS (6.0), or International Test of English Proficiency (iTEP). *Application deadline:* For fall admission, 7/15 priority date for domestic students, 5/15 for international students; for spring admission, 11/15 for domestic students, 11/1 for international students; for summer admission, 4/1 for domestic students, 3/15 for international students. Applications are processed on a rolling basis. Application fee: $40. Electronic applications accepted. *Expenses:* Contact institution. *Financial support:* In 2018–19, 3 students received support, including 2 research assistantships with full tuition reimbursements available (averaging $7,200 per year), 2 teaching assistantships with partial tuition reimbursements available (averaging $2,400 per year); career-related internships or fieldwork, scholarships/grants, and unspecified assistantships also available. Support available to part-time students. Financial award application deadline: 3/1; financial award applicants required to submit FAFSA. *Faculty research:* Human resource management, volunteerism, performance measurement in nonprofits, government-nonprofit partnerships. *Unit head:* Dr. Mittie Davis Jones, Associate

Nonprofit Management

Professor and Department Chairperson, 216-687-3861, Fax: 216-687-9342, E-mail: m.d.jones97@csuohio.edu. *Application contact:* David Arrighi, Graduate Academic Advisor, 216-523-7522, Fax: 216-687-5398, E-mail: urbanprograms@csuohio.edu.
Website: http://urban.csuohio.edu/academics/graduate/mnal/

Cleveland State University, College of Graduate Studies, Maxine Goodman Levin College of Urban Affairs, Program in Public Administration, Cleveland, OH 44115. Offers economic development (MPA); non-profit management (MPA); public management (MPA); JD/MPA. *Accreditation:* NASPAA. *Program availability:* Part-time, evening/weekend. *Faculty:* 16 full-time (8 women), 13 part-time/adjunct (5 women). *Students:* 17 full-time (10 women), 49 part-time (29 women); includes 16 minority (11 Black or African American, non-Hispanic/Latino; 1 Asian, non-Hispanic/Latino; 2 Hispanic/Latino; 2 Two or more races, non-Hispanic/Latino), 1 international. Average age 32. 79 applicants, 77% accepted, 12 enrolled. In 2018, 24 master's awarded. *Degree requirements:* For master's, thesis or alternative, exit project. *Entrance requirements:* For master's, GRE General Test (minimum scores in 40th percentile verbal and quantitative, 4.0 writing), minimum GPA of 3.0. Additional exam requirements/recommendations for international students: Required—TOEFL (minimum score 550 paper-based; 78 iBT), IELTS (6.0), or International Test of English Proficiency (iTEP). *Application deadline:* For fall admission, 7/1 priority date for domestic students, 5/15 for international students; for spring admission, 11/15 for domestic students, 11/1 for international students; for summer admission, 4/1 for domestic students, 3/15 for international students. Applications are processed on a rolling basis. Application fee: $40. Electronic applications accepted. *Expenses:* Contact institution. *Financial support:* In 2018–19, 16 students received support, including 5 research assistantships with full tuition reimbursements available (averaging $7,200 per year), 1 teaching assistantship with partial tuition reimbursement available (averaging $2,400 per year); scholarships/grants, tuition waivers (full and partial), and unspecified assistantships also available. Support available to part-time students. Financial award application deadline: 3/1; financial award applicants required to submit FAFSA. *Faculty research:* City management, nonprofit management, health care administration, public management, economic development. *Unit head:* Dr. Nicholas Zingale, Director, 216-802-3389, Fax: 216-687-9342, E-mail: n.zingale@csuohio.edu. *Application contact:* David Arrighi, Graduate Academic Advisor, 216-523-7522, Fax: 216-687-5398, E-mail: d.arrighi@csuohio.edu.
Website: http://urban.csuohio.edu/academics/graduate/mpa/

The College at Brockport, State University of New York, School of Business and Management, Department of Public Administration, Brockport, NY 14420-2997. Offers arts administration (AGC); nonprofit management (AGC); public administration (MPA), including health care management, nonprofit management, poverty studies, public management, public safety. *Accreditation:* NASPAA. *Program availability:* Part-time, evening/weekend. *Faculty:* 6 full-time (4 women), 7 part-time/adjunct (2 women). *Students:* 45 full-time (33 women), 113 part-time (71 women); includes 19 minority (14 Black or African American, non-Hispanic/Latino; 1 Asian, non-Hispanic/Latino; 4 Hispanic/Latino). 69 applicants, 93% accepted, 43 enrolled. In 2018, 104 master's, 6 other advanced degrees awarded. *Degree requirements:* For master's, thesis or alternative. *Entrance requirements:* For master's, GRE or minimum GPA of 3.0, letters of recommendation, statement of objectives, current resume. Additional exam requirements/recommendations for international students: Required—TOEFL (minimum score 550 paper-based; 79 iBT), IELTS (minimum score 6.5). *Application deadline:* For fall admission, 8/15 priority date for domestic and international students; for spring admission, 1/15 priority date for domestic and international students; for summer admission, 4/15 priority date for domestic and international students. Application fee: $50. Electronic applications accepted. *Expenses:* Tuition, state resident: part-time $471 per credit. Tuition, nonresident: part-time $963 per credit. *Financial support:* In 2018–19, 1 fellowship with full tuition reimbursement (averaging $7,500 per year), 1 teaching assistantship with full tuition reimbursement (averaging $6,000 per year) were awarded; Federal Work-Study, scholarships/grants, and unspecified assistantships also available. Support available to part-time students. Financial award application deadline: 3/15; financial award applicants required to submit FAFSA. *Faculty research:* E-government, performance management, nonprofits and policy implementation, Medicaid and disabilities. *Unit head:* Dr. Wendy Wright, Graduate Director, 585-395-5570, Fax: 585-395-2172, E-mail: wwright@brockport.edu. *Application contact:* Danielle A. Welch, Graduate Admissions Counselor, 585-395-2525, Fax: 585-395-2515.
Website: https://www.brockport.edu/academics/public_administration/graduate/masters.html

Columbia University, School of Professional Studies, Program in Fundraising Management, New York, NY 10027. Offers MS. *Program availability:* Part-time, evening/weekend. *Degree requirements:* For master's, internship. *Entrance requirements:* For master's, BA with minimum GPA of 3.0. Additional exam requirements/recommendations for international students: Required—American Language Program placement test; Recommended—TOEFL. Electronic applications accepted. *Faculty research:* Fundraising for annual campaigns, capital campaigns, nonprofit financial management, research for fundraising and planned giving.

Corban University, Graduate School, The Corban MBA, Salem, OR 97301-9392. Offers management (MBA); non-profit management (MBA). *Program availability:* Online learning.

Daemen College, Leadership and Innovation Programs, Amherst, NY 14226-3592. Offers business (MS); health professions (MS); not-for-profit organizations (MS). *Program availability:* Part-time-only, evening/weekend. *Faculty:* 1 (woman) full-time, 8 part-time/adjunct (4 women). *Students:* 21 part-time (15 women); includes 3 minority (2 Black or African American, non-Hispanic/Latino; 1 Hispanic/Latino). Average age 38. 10 applicants, 70% accepted, 6 enrolled. In 2018, 8 master's awarded. *Degree requirements:* For master's, thesis, A minimum cumulative grade point average (GPA) of 3.00; A student is allowed a maximum of two repeats before being dismissed. *Entrance requirements:* For master's, bachelor's degree, official transcripts, personal statement, resume, 2 letters of recommendation, interview with program director. Additional exam requirements/recommendations for international students: Required—TOEFL (minimum score 77 paper-based), IELTS (minimum score 6.5). *Application deadline:* Applications are processed on a rolling basis. Application fee: $25. Electronic applications accepted. Application fee is waived when completed online. *Expenses: Tuition:* Part-time $977 per credit hour. *Required fees:* $125; $14 per credit hour. *Financial support:* Scholarships/grants and unspecified assistantships available. Support available to part-time students. Financial award applicants required to submit FAFSA. *Unit head:* Christina Coyle-Lenz, Director, 716-839-8342, E-mail: ccoyle@daemen.edu. *Application contact:* Megan Beardi, Senior Assistant Director of Graduate Admissions, 716-566-7861, Fax: 716-839-8229, E-mail: mbeardi@daemen.edu.
Website: https://www.daemen.edu/academics/areas-study/leadership-and-innovation

Dallas Baptist University, Graduate School of Ministry, Program in Christian Ministry, Dallas, TX 75211-9299. Offers chaplaincy (MA); counseling ministry (MA); family ministry (MA); general ministry (MA); leading the nonprofit organization (MA); ministry leadership (MA); professional life coaching (MA); urban ministry (MA). *Program availability:* Part-time, evening/weekend, online learning. *Application deadline:* Applications are processed on a rolling basis. Application fee: $25. Electronic applications accepted. Application fee is waived when completed online. *Expenses: Tuition:* Full-time $17,262; part-time $959 per credit hour. *Required fees:* $1000; $500 per semester. Tuition and fees vary according to course load and degree level. *Unit head:* Dr. Robert R. Brooks, Dean, 214-333-5494, Fax: 214-333-5673, E-mail: bobb@dbu.edu. *Application contact:* Dr. Jon Choi, Program Director, 214-333-5375, Fax: 214-333-5689, E-mail: jon@dbu.edu.
Website: http://www.dbu.edu/ministry/degree-programs/m-a-in-christian-ministry

Dallas Baptist University, Graduate School of Ministry, Program in Global Leadership, Dallas, TX 75211-9299. Offers church planting (MA); East Asian Studies (MA); English as a second language (MA); general studies (MA); global communication (MA); global studies (MA); international business (MA); leading the nonprofit organization (MA); missions (MA); small group ministry (MA); urban ministry (MA). *Program availability:* Part-time, evening/weekend, online learning. *Application deadline:* Applications are processed on a rolling basis. Application fee: $25. Electronic applications accepted. Application fee is waived when completed online. *Expenses: Tuition:* Full-time $17,262; part-time $959 per credit hour. *Required fees:* $1000; $500 per semester. Tuition and fees vary according to course load and degree level. *Unit head:* Dr. Robert R. Brooks, Dean, 214-333-5494, Fax: 214-333-5673, E-mail: bobb@dbu.edu. *Application contact:* Dr. Brent Thomason, Program Director, 214-333-5236, E-mail: brentt@dbu.edu.
Website: http://www.dbu.edu/ministry/degree-programs/m-a-in-global-leadership

DePaul University, College of Liberal Arts and Social Sciences, Chicago, IL 60614. Offers Arabic (MA); Chinese (MA); critical ethnic studies (MA); English (MA); French (MA); German (MA); history (MA); interdisciplinary studies (MA, MS); international public service (MS); international studies (MA); Italian (MA); Japanese (MA); liberal studies (MA); nonprofit management (MNM); public administration (MPA); public health (MPH); public policy (MPP); public service management (MS); refugee and forced migration studies (MS); social work (MSW); sociology (MA); Spanish (MA); sustainable urban development (MA); women's and gender studies (MA); writing and publishing (MA); writing, rhetoric and discourse (MA); MA/PhD. *Accreditation:* CEPH. *Program availability:* Part-time, evening/weekend, online learning. Terminal master's awarded for partial completion of doctoral program. *Degree requirements:* For master's, variable foreign language requirement, comprehensive exam (for some programs), thesis (for some programs). Electronic applications accepted.

Drury University, Master of Nonprofit and Civic Leadership Program, Springfield, MO 65802. Offers MNCL. *Program availability:* Part-time, evening/weekend. *Faculty:* 3 full-time (1 woman), 2 part-time/adjunct (0 women). *Students:* 19 full-time (16 women). Average age 27. 9 applicants, 100% accepted, 8 enrolled. In 2018, 9 master's awarded. *Entrance requirements:* For master's, bachelor's degree, minimum GPA of 3.0. Additional exam requirements/recommendations for international students: Recommended—TOEFL (minimum score 80 iBT), IELTS (minimum score 6.5). *Application deadline:* For fall admission, 8/4 for domestic and international students; for spring admission, 1/6 for domestic and international students; for summer admission, 5/24 for domestic and international students. Applications are processed on a rolling basis. Application fee: $25. Electronic applications accepted. *Expenses:* Tuition is $462/credit hour. Fees are $7/credit hour. Degree program is 30 hours. *Financial support:* Career-related internships or fieldwork, institutionally sponsored loans, scholarships/grants, and unspecified assistantships available. Financial award application deadline: 6/30; financial award applicants required to submit FAFSA. *Faculty research:* Nonprofit leadership, organizational change, leadership accountability. *Unit head:* Dr. Charles Taylor, Director, 417-873-7391, E-mail: ctaylor@drury.edu. *Application contact:* Dr. Charles Taylor, Director, 417-873-7391, E-mail: ctaylor@drury.edu.
Website: http://www.drury.edu/master-of-nonprofit-and-civic-leadership

Eastern Mennonite University, Program in Business Administration, Harrisonburg, VA 22802-2462. Offers general management (MBA); health services administration (MBA); non-profit leadership (MBA). *Program availability:* Part-time, evening/weekend. *Degree requirements:* For master's, final capstone course. *Entrance requirements:* For master's, GMAT, minimum GPA of 2.5, 2 years of work experience, 2 letters of reference. Additional exam requirements/recommendations for international students: Required—TOEFL (minimum score 500 paper-based). Electronic applications accepted. *Expenses:* Contact institution. *Faculty research:* Information security, Anabaptist/Mennonite experiences and perspectives, limits of multi-cultural education, international development performance criteria.

Eastern Michigan University, Graduate School, College of Arts and Sciences, Department of Political Science, Programs in Public Administration, Ypsilanti, MI 48197. Offers general public management (Graduate Certificate); local government management (Graduate Certificate); management of public healthcare services (Graduate Certificate); nonprofit management (Graduate Certificate); public administration (MPA); public budget management (Graduate Certificate); public land planning and development management (Graduate Certificate); public personnel management (Graduate Certificate); public policy analysis (Graduate Certificate). *Accreditation:* NASPAA. *Students:* 20 full-time (9 women), 32 part-time (15 women); includes 21 minority (14 Black or African American, non-Hispanic/Latino; 1 Asian, non-Hispanic/Latino; 2 Hispanic/Latino; 4 Two or more races, non-Hispanic/Latino), 1 international. Average age 34. 37 applicants, 86% accepted, 13 enrolled. In 2018, 16 master's, 2 other advanced degrees awarded. Application fee: $45. *Application contact:* Dr. Rose Jindal, MPA Coordinator, 734-487-3113, Fax: 734-487-3340, E-mail: rsoliven@emich.edu.
Website: http://www.emich.edu/polisci/

Eastern Michigan University, Graduate School, College of Business, Programs in Business Administration, Ypsilanti, MI 48197. Offers business administration (MBA, Graduate Certificate); computer information systems (Graduate Certificate); e-business (MBA, Graduate Certificate); enterprise business intelligence (MBA); entrepreneurship (MBA, Graduate Certificate); finance (MBA, Graduate Certificate); human resources (MBA); human resources management (Graduate Certificate); information systems (MBA); internal auditing (MBA); international business (MBA, Graduate Certificate); marketing management (Graduate Certificate); nonprofit management (MBA); organizational development (Graduate Certificate); supply chain management (MBA, Graduate Certificate). *Accreditation:* AACSB. *Program availability:* Part-time, online learning. *Students:* 69 full-time (38 women), 251 part-time (140 women); includes 100 minority (63 Black or African American, non-Hispanic/Latino; 1 American Indian or Alaska Native, non-Hispanic/Latino; 12 Asian, non-Hispanic/Latino; 14 Hispanic/Latino; 10 Two or more races, non-Hispanic/Latino), 28 international. Average age 32. 199 applicants, 75% accepted, 83 enrolled. In 2018, 75 master's, 50 other advanced degrees awarded. *Entrance requirements:* For master's, GMAT (minimum score 450), minimum cumulative undergraduate GPA of 2.75. Additional exam requirements/recommendations for international students: Required—TOEFL. *Application deadline:* For fall admission, 5/15 priority date for domestic students, 2/15 priority date for international students; for winter admission, 10/15 priority date for domestic students, 9/1 priority date for international students; for summer admission, 3/15 priority date for domestic students, 3/1 priority date for international students. Applications are processed on a rolling basis. Application fee: $45. *Financial support:* Fellowships, research assistantships with full tuition reimbursements, teaching assistantships with full tuition reimbursements, career-related internships or fieldwork, Federal Work-Study, institutionally sponsored loans, scholarships/grants, tuition waivers (partial), and

unspecified assistantships available. Support available to part-time students. Financial award applicants required to submit FAFSA. *Unit head:* K. Michelle Henry, Director, Graduate Business Programs, 734-487-4444, Fax: 734-483-1316, E-mail: cob.graduate@emich.edu. *Application contact:* K. Michelle Henry, Director, Graduate Business Programs, 734-487-4444, Fax: 734-483-1316, E-mail: cob.graduate@emich.edu.
Website: http://www.emich.edu/cob/mba/

Eastern Michigan University, Graduate School, College of Health and Human Services, Interdisciplinary Program in Non-Profit Management, Ypsilanti, MI 48197. Offers Graduate Certificate. *Unit head:* Dr. Marcia Bombyk, Program Coordinator, 734-487-0393, Fax: 734-487-8536, E-mail: mbombyk@emich.edu. *Application contact:* Dr. Marcia Bombyk, Program Coordinator, 734-487-0393, Fax: 734-487-8536, E-mail: mbombyk@emich.edu.

Eastern University, Program in Organizational Leadership, St. Davids, PA 19087-3696. Offers leadership studies (CAGS); organizational leadership (PhD), including business management, educational administration, public and nonprofit administration. Electronic applications accepted. *Expenses:* Contact institution.

East Tennessee State University, School of Graduate Studies, College of Arts and Sciences, Department of Political Science, International Affairs and Public Administration, Johnson City, TN 37614. Offers economic development (Postbaccalaureate Certificate); economic development and planning (MPA); local government management (MPA); nonprofit and public financial management (MPA); urban planning (Postbaccalaureate Certificate). *Program availability:* Part-time. *Degree requirements:* For master's, internship, capstone. *Entrance requirements:* For master's, GRE General Test, three letters of recommendation. Additional exam requirements/recommendations for international students: Required—TOEFL (minimum score 550 paper-based; 79 iBT). Electronic applications accepted. *Faculty research:* Labor issues, presidency, public law in American politics, East Asian politics, European politics, Middle Eastern politics, development in comparative politics, international political economy, international relations, world politics in international affairs.

Fairleigh Dickinson University, Metropolitan Campus, Anthony J. Petrocelli College of Continuing Studies, Public Administration Institute, Teaneck, NJ 07666-1914. Offers public administration (MPA, Certificate); public non-profit management (Certificate).

Florida Atlantic University, College for Design and Social Inquiry, School of Public Administration, Boca Raton, FL 33431-0991. Offers MPA, PhD. *Accreditation:* NASPAA (one or more programs are accredited). *Program availability:* Part-time, evening/weekend. *Faculty:* 11 full-time (4 women), 1 part-time/adjunct (0 women). *Students:* 20 full-time (13 women), 65 part-time (37 women); includes 36 minority (19 Black or African American, non-Hispanic/Latino; 4 Asian, non-Hispanic/Latino; 11 Hispanic/Latino; 2 Two or more races, non-Hispanic/Latino), 8 international. Average age 35. 46 applicants, 43% accepted, 16 enrolled. In 2018, 42 master's, 2 doctorates awarded. *Degree requirements:* For master's, thesis optional; for doctorate, comprehensive exam, thesis/ dissertation. *Entrance requirements:* For master's, GRE General Test, minimum GPA of 3.0; for doctorate, GRE General Test, faculty reference, scholarly writing samples, letters of recommendation. Additional exam requirements/recommendations for international students: Required—TOEFL (minimum score 500 paper-based; 61 iBT), IELTS (minimum score 6). *Application deadline:* For fall admission, 5/1 priority date for domestic students, 2/15 for international students; for spring admission, 11/1 for domestic students, 7/15 for international students. Applications are processed on a rolling basis. Application fee: $30. *Expenses: Tuition, area resident:* Full-time $7400; part-time $369.82 per credit. Tuition, state resident: full-time $7400; part-time $369.82 per credit. Tuition, nonresident: full-time $20,496; part-time $1024.81 per credit. *Financial support:* Fellowships with full tuition reimbursements, research assistantships with partial tuition reimbursements, teaching assistantships with partial tuition reimbursements, career-related internships or fieldwork, Federal Work-Study, institutionally sponsored loans, and tuition waivers (partial) available. Support available to part-time students. Financial award application deadline: 4/1. *Faculty research:* Public finance and budgeting, public management, evaluation, criminal justice, postmodern public administration. *Unit head:* Leslie Leip, Program Coordinator, 561-297-4153, E-mail: lleip@fau.edu. *Application contact:* Leslie Leip, Program Coordinator, 561-297-4153, E-mail: lleip@fau.edu.
Website: http://www.fau.edu/spa/

Fordham University, Gabelli School of Business, New York, NY 10023. Offers accounting (MBA, MS); applied statistics and decision-making (MS); business economics (DPS); capital markets (DPS); communications and media management (MBA); electronic business (MBA); entrepreneurship (MBA); finance (MBA, PhD); global finance (MS); global sustainability (MBA); health administration (MS); healthcare management (MBA); information systems (MBA, MS); investor relations (MS); management (EMBA, MBA, MS, PhD); marketing (MBA); marketing intelligence (MS); media management (MS); nonprofit leadership (MS); quantitative finance (MS); strategy and decision-making (DPS); taxation (MS); JD/MBA; MS/MBA. *Accreditation:* AACSB. *Program availability:* Part-time, evening/weekend. Terminal master's awarded for partial completion of doctoral program. *Degree requirements:* For master's, internships (for some degrees); for doctorate, comprehensive exam (for some programs), thesis/ dissertation. *Entrance requirements:* For master's, GMAT/GRE, 2 letters of recommendation, resume, 2 essays, transcripts, interview. Additional exam requirements/recommendations for international students: Required—TOEFL (minimum score 100 iBT), IELTS (minimum score 7). Electronic applications accepted. *Expenses:* Contact institution.

Fordham University, Graduate School of Social Service, New York, NY 10023. Offers nonprofit leadership (MS); social work (MSW, PhD); JD/MSW; MSW/MPH. MS program jointly sponsored with Graduate School of Business and conducted through the Fordham Center for Nonprofit Leaders; MSW/MPH offered with Ichan School of Public Health at Mount Sinai. *Accreditation:* CSWE (one or more programs are accredited). *Program availability:* Part-time, evening/weekend, 100% online, blended/hybrid learning. *Degree requirements:* For master's, 1200 hours of field placement; for doctorate, comprehensive exam, thesis/dissertation. *Entrance requirements:* For master's, BA in liberal arts; for doctorate, GRE, master's degree in social work or related field. Additional exam requirements/recommendations for international students: Required—TOEFL (minimum score 600 paper-based; 100 iBT), IELTS. Electronic applications accepted. *Expenses:* Contact institution. *Faculty research:* Aging, children and family, healthcare, domestic violence, substance abuse.

Geneva College, Program in Leadership Studies, Beaver Falls, PA 15010-3599. Offers business management (MS); ministry leadership (MS); non-profit leadership (MS); organizational management (MS); project management (MS). *Program availability:* Online only, 100% online. *Degree requirements:* For master's, thesis or alternative, capstone leadership studies project. *Entrance requirements:* For master's, undergraduate degree from regionally-accredited college or university, one to three years of experience in the workplace, minimum GPA of 3.0 (preferred), resume, essay, two recommendations. Additional exam requirements/recommendations for international students: Required—TOEFL. Electronic applications accepted. *Expenses:* Contact institution. *Faculty research:* Servant leadership, leadership essentials.

The George Washington University, Columbian College of Arts and Sciences, Department of Organizational Sciences and Communication, Washington, DC 20052. Offers human resources management (MA); non-profit management (Graduate Certificate); organizational management (Graduate Certificate). *Program availability:* Part-time, evening/weekend. *Students:* 41 full-time (24 women), 18 part-time (12 women); includes 13 minority (5 Black or African American, non-Hispanic/Latino; 2 Asian, non-Hispanic/Latino; 6 Hispanic/Latino), 16 international. Average age 27. 126 applicants, 71% accepted, 32 enrolled. In 2018, 42 master's, 15 other advanced degrees awarded. *Entrance requirements:* For master's, GRE General Test, minimum GPA of 3.0; for Graduate Certificate, minimum GPA of 3.0. Additional exam requirements/recommendations for international students: Required—TOEFL (minimum score 500 paper-based; 80 iBT). *Application deadline:* For fall admission, 1/15 priority date for domestic and international students; for spring admission, 10/1 priority date for domestic students, 9/1 priority date for international students. Applications are processed on a rolling basis. Application fee: $75. Electronic applications accepted. *Financial support:* Federal Work-Study and institutionally sponsored loans available. *Unit head:* Dr. Lynn Offermann, Chair, 202-994-8507, E-mail: lro@gwu.edu. *Application contact:* Information Contact, 202-994-1878, Fax: 202-994-1881.
Website: http://www.gwu.edu/~orgsci/

Georgian Court University, School of Business and Digital Media, Lakewood, NJ 08701-2697. Offers business (MBA); business essentials (Certificate); nonprofit management (Certificate). *Program availability:* Part-time, evening/weekend. *Faculty:* 5 full-time (1 woman), 6 part-time/adjunct (3 women). *Students:* 27 full-time (13 women), 26 part-time (17 women); includes 15 minority (5 Black or African American, non-Hispanic/Latino; 4 Asian, non-Hispanic/Latino; 5 Hispanic/Latino; 1 Two or more races, non-Hispanic/Latino), 3 international. Average age 30. 59 applicants, 59% accepted, 19 enrolled. In 2018, 23 master's, 3 other advanced degrees awarded. *Entrance requirements:* For master's, GMAT or CPA exam, 3 letters of recommendation. Additional exam requirements/recommendations for international students: Required—TOEFL (minimum score 550 paper-based; 79 iBT). *Application deadline:* For fall admission, 8/15 for domestic students, 5/1 for international students; for spring admission, 1/15 for domestic students, 10/1 for international students. Applications are processed on a rolling basis. Application fee: $40. Electronic applications accepted. *Expenses:* Tuition: Full-time $856; part-time $856 per credit hour. *Required fees:* $968; $496 per unit. $248 per semester. Tuition and fees vary according to campus/location and program. *Financial support:* Scholarships/grants, health care benefits, and unspecified assistantships available. Financial award application deadline: 4/15; financial award applicants required to submit FAFSA. *Unit head:* Dr. Jennifer Edmonds, Dean School of Business and Digital Media, 732-987-2662, Fax: 732-987-2024, E-mail: jedmonds@georgian.edu. *Application contact:* Patrick Givens, Director of Graduate and Professional Studies Admissions, 732-987-2736, Fax: 732-987-2000, E-mail: gps@georgian.edu.
Website: https://georgian.edu/academics/school-of-business-digital-media/

Georgia Southern University, Jack N. Averitt College of Graduate Studies, College of Behavioral and Social Sciences, Department of Public and Nonprofit Studies, Statesboro, GA 30460. Offers public administration (MPA, Graduate Certificate). *Program availability:* Part-time, evening/weekend. *Faculty:* 6 full-time (4 women). *Students:* 30 full-time (20 women), 15 part-time (8 women); includes 16 minority (14 Black or African American, non-Hispanic/Latino; 2 Two or more races, non-Hispanic/ Latino), 10 international. Average age 27. 32 applicants, 94% accepted, 15 enrolled. In 2018, 24 master's awarded. *Degree requirements:* For master's, comprehensive exam. *Entrance requirements:* For master's, GRE General Test and/or GMAT, letters of reference, resume. Additional exam requirements/recommendations for international students: Required—TOEFL (minimum score 550 paper-based; 80 iBT), IELTS (minimum score 6). *Application deadline:* For fall admission, 3/1 priority date for domestic and international students; for spring admission, 10/1 priority date for domestic students, 10/1 for international students. Applications are processed on a rolling basis. Application fee: $50. Electronic applications accepted. *Expenses: Tuition, area resident:* Part-time $3324 per semester. Tuition, state resident: full-time $5814; part-time $3324 per semester. Tuition, nonresident: full-time $23,204; part-time $13,260 per semester. *Required fees:* $2092; $2092. Tuition and fees vary according to course load, degree level, campus/location and program. *Financial support:* In 2018–19, 20 students received support, including 3 fellowships with full tuition reimbursements available (averaging $8,000 per year); Federal Work-Study, scholarships/grants, tuition waivers (full), and unspecified assistantships also available. Support available to part-time students. Financial award application deadline: 4/15; financial award applicants required to submit FAFSA. *Faculty research:* Public administration, public policy, nonprofit management, organizational behavior and leadership, human resource management. *Unit head:* Dr. Trenton Davis, Professor and Chair, 912-478-5430, Fax: 912-478-5348, E-mail: tjdavis@georgiasouthern.edu. *Application contact:* Dr. Trenton Davis, Professor and Chair, 912-467-5430, Fax: 912-478-5348, E-mail: publicadmin@georgiasouthern.edu.
Website: http://cbss.georgiasouthern.edu/publicadmin

Georgia State University, Andrew Young School of Policy Studies, Department of Public Management and Policy, Atlanta, GA 30303. Offers criminal justice (MPA); disaster management (Certificate); disaster policy (MPA); environmental policy (PhD); health policy (PhD); management and finance (MPA); nonprofit management (MPA, Certificate); nonprofit policy (MPA); planning and economic development (MPP, Certificate); policy analysis and evaluation (MPA), including planning and economic development; public and nonprofit management (PhD); public finance and budgeting (PhD), including science and technology policy, urban and regional economic development; public finance policy (MPA), including social policy; public health (MPA). *Accreditation:* NASPAA (one or more programs are accredited). *Program availability:* Part-time. *Faculty:* 13 full-time (6 women), 2 part-time/adjunct (0 women). *Students:* 126 full-time (77 women), 96 part-time (65 women); includes 104 minority (80 Black or African American, non-Hispanic/Latino; 4 Asian, non-Hispanic/Latino; 10 Hispanic/Latino; 10 Two or more races, non-Hispanic/ Latino), 32 international. Average age 32. 304 applicants, 59% accepted, 99 enrolled. In 2018, 57 master's, 7 doctorates, 8 other advanced degrees awarded. Terminal master's awarded for partial completion of doctoral program. *Degree requirements:* For master's, thesis optional; for doctorate, comprehensive exam, thesis/dissertation. *Entrance requirements:* For master's and doctorate, GRE. Additional exam requirements/ recommendations for international students: Required—TOEFL (minimum score 603 paper-based; 100 iBT) or IELTS (minimum score 7). *Application deadline:* For fall admission, 1/15 for domestic and international students. Application fee: $50. Electronic applications accepted. *Expenses: Tuition, area resident:* Full-time $9360; part-time $390 per credit hour. Tuition, state resident: full-time $9360; part-time $390 per credit hour. Tuition, nonresident: full-time $30,024; part-time $1251 per credit hour. *International tuition:* $30,024 full-time. *Required fees:* $2128. *Financial support:* In 2018–19, fellowships (averaging $8,194 per year), research assistantships (averaging $8,068 per year), teaching assistantships (averaging $3,600 per year) were awarded; institutionally sponsored loans, scholarships/grants, health care benefits, and unspecified assistantships also available. Financial award application deadline: 2/1. *Faculty research:* Public budgeting and finance, public management, nonprofit management, performance measurement and management, urban development. *Unit head:* Dr. Greg Lewis, Chair

and Professor, 404-413-0014, Fax: 404-413-0104, E-mail: glewis@gsu.edu. *Application contact:* Dr. Greg Lewis, Chair and Professor, 404-413-0014, Fax: 404-413-0104, E-mail: glewis@gsu.edu.
Website: https://aysps.gsu.edu/public-management-policy/

Grand Valley State University, College of Community and Public Service, School of Public, Nonprofit and Health Administration, Program in Philanthropy and Nonprofit Leadership, Allendale, MI 49401-9403. Offers MPNL. *Program availability:* Part-time, evening/weekend. *Students:* 2 full-time (both women), 13 part-time (all women); includes 2 minority (1 Black or African American, non-Hispanic/Latino; 1 Two or more races, non-Hispanic/Latino). Average age 43. 9 applicants, 67% accepted, 3 enrolled. In 2018, 6 master's awarded. *Degree requirements:* For master's, capstone. *Entrance requirements:* For master's, 3 years of full-time work experience, 3 letters of reference, 250-750 word essay on career and educational objectives, resume. Additional exam requirements/recommendations for international students: Required—TOEFL (minimum iBT score of 80), IELTS (6.5), or Michigan English Language Assessment Battery (77). *Application deadline:* For fall admission, 6/1 for domestic students; for winter admission, 11/1 for domestic students; for spring admission, 4/1 for domestic students. Applications are processed on a rolling basis. Electronic applications accepted. *Expenses:* $651 per credit hour, 36 credit hours. *Financial support:* In 2018–19, 4 students received support, including 3 fellowships, 1 research assistantship with full and partial tuition reimbursement available (averaging $4,000 per year). *Unit head:* Dr. Richard Jelier, Director, 616-331-6575, Fax: 616-331-7120, E-mail: jelierr@gvsu.edu. *Application contact:* Dr. Michelle Wooddell, Graduate Program Director/Recruiting Contact, 616-331-6495, Fax: 616-331-7120, E-mail: wooddelm@gvsu.edu.

Gratz College, Graduate Programs, Program in Nonprofit Management, Melrose Park, PA 19027. Offers MS.

Hamline University, School of Business, St. Paul, MN 55104-1284. Offers business administration (MBA); nonprofit management (MNM); public administration (MPA, DPA); MBA/MNM; MBA/MPA; MPA/MNM. *Program availability:* Part-time, evening/weekend, blended/hybrid learning. *Degree requirements:* For master's, thesis (for some programs); for doctorate, comprehensive exam, thesis/dissertation. *Entrance requirements:* For master's and doctorate, personal statement, official transcripts, resume or curriculum vitae, letters of recommendation, writing sample. Additional exam requirements/recommendations for international students: Required—TOEFL (minimum score 550 paper-based; 80 iBT), IELTS (minimum score 6.5). Electronic applications accepted. *Expenses:* Contact institution. *Faculty research:* Experiential learning, organizational process/politics, gender differences, social equity, pyramid schemes.

Hebrew Union College–Jewish Institute of Religion, School of Jewish Nonprofit Management, Los Angeles, CA 90007. Offers MA.

Hope International University, School of Graduate and Professional Studies, Program in Business Administration, Fullerton, CA 92831-3138. Offers general management (MBA, MSM); international development (MBA, MSM); marketing management (MBA, MSM); non-profit management (MBA, MSM). *Program availability:* Part-time, online learning. *Degree requirements:* For master's, comprehensive exam (for some programs), thesis (for some programs), project. *Entrance requirements:* For master's, minimum GPA of 3.0; 2 references. Additional exam requirements/recommendations for international students: Required—TOEFL (minimum score 550 paper-based; 86 iBT); Recommended—IELTS (minimum score 6.5). Electronic applications accepted. *Expenses:* Contact institution.

Indiana University Bloomington, School of Public and Environmental Affairs, Public Affairs Programs, Bloomington, IN 47405. Offers economic development (MPA); energy (MPA); environmental policy (PhD); environmental policy and natural resource management (MPA); information systems (MPA); international development (MPA); local government management (MPA); nonprofit management (MPA, Certificate); policy analysis (MPA); public budgeting and financial management (Certificate); public finance (PhD); public financial administration (MPA); public management (MPA, PhD, Certificate); public policy analysis (PhD); social entrepreneurship (Certificate); specialized public affairs (MPA); sustainability and sustainable development (MPA); JD/MPA; MPA/MA; MPA/MIS; MPA/MLS; MSES/MPA. *Accreditation:* NASPAA (one or more programs are accredited). *Program availability:* Part-time. *Degree requirements:* For master's, capstone, internship; for doctorate, comprehensive exam, thesis/dissertation. *Entrance requirements:* For master's, GRE General Test or GMAT, official transcripts, 3 letters of recommendation, resume, personal statement; for doctorate, GRE General Test, official transcripts, 3 letters of recommendation, statement of purpose. Additional exam requirements/recommendations for international students: Required—TOEFL (minimum score 600 paper-based; 96 iBT); Recommended—IELTS (minimum score 7). Electronic applications accepted. *Faculty research:* International development, environmental policy and resource management, policy analysis, public finance, public management, urban management, nonprofit management, energy policy, social policy, public finance.

Indiana University Bloomington, University Graduate School, College of Arts and Sciences, Robert A. and Sandra S. Borns Jewish Studies Program, Bloomington, IN 47405. Offers Jewish studies (MA), including nonprofit management; Jewish studies and history (MA). *Degree requirements:* For master's, one foreign language, thesis. *Entrance requirements:* Additional exam requirements/recommendations for international students: Required—TOEFL. Electronic applications accepted. *Faculty research:* Jewish studies, religious studies, history, Holocaust study.

Indiana University Northwest, School of Public and Environmental Affairs, Gary, IN 46408. Offers criminal justice (MPA); environmental affairs (Graduate Certificate); health services (MPA); nonprofit management (Certificate); public management (MPA, Graduate Certificate). *Accreditation:* NASPAA (one or more programs are accredited). *Program availability:* Part-time. *Entrance requirements:* For master's, GRE General Test (minimum combined verbal and quantitative score of 280), GMAT, or LSAT, letters of recommendation. Electronic applications accepted. *Faculty research:* Employment in income security policies, evidence in criminal justice, equal employment law, social welfare policy and welfare reform, public finance in developing countries.

Indiana University of Pennsylvania, School of Graduate Studies and Research, College of Humanities and Social Sciences, Department of Sociology, Program in Administration and Leadership Studies, Indiana, PA 15705. Offers PhD. *Program availability:* Part-time, evening/weekend. *Faculty:* 9 full-time (6 women). *Students:* 7 full-time (6 women), 93 part-time (52 women); includes 23 minority (14 Black or African American, non-Hispanic/Latino; 4 Hispanic/Latino; 1 Native Hawaiian or other Pacific Islander, non-Hispanic/Latino; 4 Two or more races, non-Hispanic/Latino), 1 international. Average age 39. 58 applicants, 84% accepted, 31 enrolled. In 2018, 22 doctorates awarded. *Degree requirements:* For doctorate, comprehensive exam, thesis/dissertation. *Entrance requirements:* For doctorate, GRE, resume, writing sample, 3 letters of recommendation. Additional exam requirements/recommendations for international students: Required—TOEFL (minimum score 540 paper-based). *Application deadline:* For fall admission, 2/15 priority date for domestic students. Applications are processed on a rolling basis. Application fee: $50. Electronic applications accepted. *Expenses:* Contact institution. *Financial support:* In 2018–19, 9 fellowships with full tuition reimbursements (averaging $1,002 per year), 8 research assistantships with tuition reimbursements (averaging $4,500 per year), 1 teaching assistantship with partial tuition reimbursement (averaging $24,425 per year) were awarded; career-related internships or fieldwork, Federal Work-Study, scholarships/grants, and unspecified assistantships also available. Support available to part-time students. Financial award application deadline: 4/15; financial award applicants required to submit FAFSA. *Unit head:* Dr. John A. Anderson, Graduate Coordinator, 724-357-2956, E-mail: jaa@iup.edu. *Application contact:* Dr. John A. Anderson, Graduate Coordinator, 724-357-2956, E-mail: jaa@iup.edu.
Website: http://www.iup.edu/grad/ALS/default.aspx

Indiana University–Purdue University Indianapolis, School of Public and Environmental Affairs, Indianapolis, IN 46202. Offers criminal justice and public safety (MS); homeland security and emergency management (Graduate Certificate); library management (Graduate Certificate); nonprofit management (Graduate Certificate); public affairs (MPA); public management (Graduate Certificate); social entrepreneurship: nonprofit and public benefit organizations (Graduate Certificate); JD/MPA; MLS/NMC; MLS/PMC; MPA/MA. *Accreditation:* CAHME (one or more programs are accredited); NASPAA. *Program availability:* Part-time, evening/weekend, online learning. *Entrance requirements:* For master's, GRE General Test, GMAT or LSAT, minimum GPA of 3.0 (preferred). Additional exam requirements/recommendations for international students: Required—TOEFL (minimum score 93 iBT), IELTS (minimum score 6.5). Electronic applications accepted. *Faculty research:* Nonprofit and public management, public policy, urban policy, sustainability policy, disaster preparedness and recovery, vehicular safety, homicide, offender rehabilitation and re-entry.

Indiana University South Bend, College of Liberal Arts and Sciences, South Bend, IN 46615. Offers advanced computer programming (Graduate Certificate); applied informatics (Graduate Certificate); applied mathematics and computer science (MS); behavior modification (Graduate Certificate); computer applications (Graduate Certificate); computer programming (Graduate Certificate); correctional management and supervision (Graduate Certificate); English (MA); health systems management (Graduate Certificate); international studies (Graduate Certificate); liberal studies (MLS); nonprofit management (Graduate Certificate); paralegal studies (Graduate Certificate); professional writing (Graduate Certificate); public affairs (MPA); public management (Graduate Certificate); social and cultural diversity (Graduate Certificate); strategic sustainability leadership (Graduate Certificate); technology for administration (Graduate Certificate). *Program availability:* Part-time, evening/weekend. *Degree requirements:* For master's, variable foreign language requirement, thesis (for some programs). *Entrance requirements:* For master's, minimum GPA of 3.0. Additional exam requirements/recommendations for international students: Required—TOEFL (minimum score 550 paper-based; 80 iBT). *Expenses:* Contact institution. *Faculty research:* Artificial intelligence, bioinformatics, English language and literature, creative writing, computer networks.

James Madison University, The Graduate School, College of Arts and Letters, Program in Public Administration, Harrisonburg, VA 22807. Offers individualized (MPA); public management (MPA), including international stabilization and recovery, management in international non-governmental organizations, nonprofit management, public management. Public and nonprofit management program offered in Roanoke. *Accreditation:* NASPAA. *Program availability:* Part-time. *Students:* 21 full-time (10 women), 13 part-time (5 women); includes 7 minority (4 Black or African American, non-Hispanic/Latino; 1 Hispanic/Latino; 2 Two or more races, non-Hispanic/Latino). Average age 30. In 2018, 22 master's awarded. Application fee: $60. Electronic applications accepted. *Expenses:* Tuition, state resident: full-time $10,848. Tuition, nonresident: full-time $27,888. *Required fees:* $1128. *Financial support:* In 2018–19, 20 students received support. Fellowships, Federal Work-Study, and assistantships (averaging $7911) available. Financial award application deadline: 3/1; financial award applicants required to submit FAFSA. *Unit head:* Dr. Charles Blake, Department Head, 540-568-6149, E-mail: blakech@jmu.edu. *Application contact:* Lynette D. Michael, Director of Graduate Admissions, 540-568-6131, Fax: 540-568-7860, E-mail: michaeld@jmu.edu.
Website: http://www.jmu.edu/mpa

James Madison University, The Graduate School, College of Business, Program in Strategic Leadership, Harrisonburg, VA 22807. Offers postsecondary analysis and leadership (PhD), including nonprofit and community leadership, organizational science and leadership, postsecondary analysis and leadership. *Program availability:* Part-time, evening/weekend, online learning. *Students:* 13 full-time (6 women), 32 part-time (13 women); includes 5 minority (2 Black or African American, non-Hispanic/Latino; 1 Asian, non-Hispanic/Latino; 2 Hispanic/Latino), 4 international. Average age 30. In 2018, 7 doctorates awarded. Application fee: $60. Electronic applications accepted. *Expenses:* Tuition, state resident: full-time $10,848. Tuition, nonresident: full-time $27,888. *Required fees:* $1128. *Financial support:* In 2018–19, 9 students received support. Fellowships, career-related internships or fieldwork, Federal Work-Study, unspecified assistantships, and doctoral assistantships (stipend varies) available. Financial award application deadline: 3/1; financial award applicants required to submit FAFSA. *Unit head:* Dr. Karen A. Ford, Director of Strategic Leadership Studies, 540-568-7020, Fax: 540-568-7117, E-mail: fordka@jmu.edu. *Application contact:* Lynette D. Michael, Director of Graduate Admissions, 540-568-6131 Ext. 6395, Fax: 540-568-7860, E-mail: michaeld@jmu.edu.
Website: http://www.jmu.edu/leadership/

John Carroll University, Graduate Studies, Program in Nonprofit Administration, University Heights, OH 44118. Offers MA. *Program availability:* Part-time, evening/weekend. *Entrance requirements:* Additional exam requirements/recommendations for international students: Required—TOEFL. *Application deadline:* Applications are processed on a rolling basis. Electronic applications accepted. *Expenses: Tuition:* Full-time $13,140; part-time $730 per credit hour. Tuition and fees vary according to program. *Financial support:* Scholarships/grants and unspecified assistantships available. Financial award applicants required to submit FAFSA. *Unit head:* Dani Robbins, Director, 216-397-4637, E-mail: drobbins@jcu.edu. *Application contact:* Colleen K. Sommerfeld, Assistant Dean for Graduate Admission & Retention, 216-397-4902, Fax: 216-397-1835, E-mail: csommerfeld@jcu.edu.
Website: http://sites.jcu.edu/nonprofit/

Johns Hopkins University, Advanced Academic Programs, Program in Government, Washington, DC 21218. Offers global security studies (MA); government (MA); national securities study (Certificate); nonprofit management (Certificate); public management (MA); research administration (MS); MA/MBA. *Program availability:* Part-time, evening/weekend, online learning. *Students:* 19 full-time (6 women), 154 part-time (52 women). 51 applicants, 88% accepted, 34 enrolled. In 2018, 58 master's awarded. *Entrance requirements:* For master's, minimum GPA of 3.0. Additional exam requirements/recommendations for international students: Required—TOEFL (minimum score 100 iBT). *Application deadline:* For fall admission, 5/31 priority date for domestic students, 4/30 priority date for international students; for spring admission, 10/31 priority date for domestic and international students. Applications are processed on a rolling basis. Application fee: $75. Electronic applications accepted. *Financial support:* Applicants required to submit FAFSA. *Unit head:* Dr. Kathy Wagner, Program Director, 202-452-1953, E-mail: kwagner@jhu.edu. *Application contact:* Melissa Edwards, Admissions Manager, 202-452-1941, Fax: 202-452-1970, E-mail: aapadmissions@jhu.edu.
Website: http://advanced.jhu.edu/academics/graduate-degree-programs/government/

Johnson & Wales University, Graduate Studies, MBA Program, Providence, RI 02903-3703. Offers accounting (MBA); business administration (MBA); finance (MBA); global fashion merchandising and management (MBA); hospitality (MBA); human resource management (MBA); information security/assurance (MBA); information technology (MBA); nonprofit management (MBA); operations and supply chain management (MBA); organizational leadership (MBA); organizational psychology (MBA); sport leadership (MBA). Program also offered on Denver campus. *Program availability:* Part-time, online learning. *Entrance requirements:* For master's, minimum GPA of 2.75. Additional exam requirements/recommendations for international students: Required—TOEFL (minimum score 550 paper-based); Recommended—IELTS, TWE. *Faculty research:* International banking, global economy, international trade, cultural differences.

Johnson & Wales University, Graduate Studies, MS Program in Nonprofit Management, Providence, RI 02903-3703. Offers MS. *Program availability:* Online only, 100% online.

Johnson University, Graduate and Professional Programs, Knoxville, TN 37998-1001. Offers biblical interpretation (Graduate Certificate); business administration (MBA); Christian ministries (Graduate Certificate); clinical mental health counseling (MA); educational technology (MA); intercultural studies (MA); leadership (MBA); leadership studies (PhD); New Testament (MA); nonprofit management (MBA); school counseling (MA); spiritual formation and leadership (Graduate Certificate); strategic ministry (MA); teacher education (MA). *Program availability:* Part-time, evening/weekend, 100% online, blended/hybrid learning. *Degree requirements:* For master's, variable foreign language requirement, comprehensive exam, thesis (for some programs), internships; for doctorate, variable foreign language requirement, comprehensive exam, thesis/dissertation, internships. *Entrance requirements:* For master's, PRAXIS (for MA in teacher education); MAT (for counseling); GRE or GMAT (for MBA), interview, 3 references, transcripts, essay, minimum GPA of 2.5 or 3.0 (depending on program); for doctorate, GRE or MAT (taken not less than 5 years prior), interview, 3 references, transcripts, essay, minimum GPA of 3.0; for Graduate Certificate, interview, 3 references, transcripts, essay, minimum GPA of 3.0. Additional exam requirements/recommendations for international students: Required—TOEFL (minimum score 527 paper-based; 71 iBT). Electronic applications accepted. *Expenses:* Contact institution.

Kean University, College of Business and Public Management, Program in Public Administration, Union, NJ 07083. Offers health services administration (MPA); non-profit management (MPA); public administration (MPA). *Accreditation:* NASPAA. *Program availability:* Part-time. *Faculty:* 16 full-time (5 women). *Students:* 46 full-time (34 women), 48 part-time (31 women); includes 75 minority (40 Black or African American, non-Hispanic/Latino; 10 Asian, non-Hispanic/Latino; 24 Hispanic/Latino; 1 Two or more races, non-Hispanic/Latino), 3 international. Average age 30. 43 applicants, 88% accepted, 22 enrolled. In 2018, 41 master's awarded. *Degree requirements:* For master's, thesis, internship, research seminar. *Entrance requirements:* For master's, minimum cumulative GPA of 3.0, official transcripts from all institutions attended, two letters of recommendation, personal statement, writing sample, professional resume/curriculum vitae. Additional exam requirements/recommendations for international students: Required—TOEFL (minimum score 550 paper-based; 79 iBT), IELTS (minimum score 6.5). *Application deadline:* For fall admission, 6/30 for domestic and international students; for spring admission, 12/1 for domestic and international students. Applications are processed on a rolling basis. Application fee: $75. Electronic applications accepted. *Expenses:* Tuition, state resident: full-time $15,025; part-time $733.50 per credit. Tuition, nonresident: full-time $19,890; part-time $884.50 per credit. *Required fees:* $2107.50; $89.50 per credit. Tuition and fees vary according to course level, course load, degree level and program. *Financial support:* Scholarships/grants and unspecified assistantships available. Financial award applicants required to submit FAFSA. *Unit head:* Dr. Deborah Mohammed-Spigner, Program Coordinator, 908-737-4037, E-mail: demohamm@kean.edu. *Application contact:* Pedro Lopes, Admissions Counselor, 908-737-7100, E-mail: gradadmissions@kean.edu. Website: http://grad.kean.edu/masters-programs/public-administration

La Salle University, School of Business, Program in Nonprofit Leadership, Philadelphia, PA 19141-1199. Offers MS. *Program availability:* Part-time, evening/weekend, online only, 100% online. *Degree requirements:* For master's, completion of all required courses within seven-year period; minimum cumulative GPA of 3.0. *Entrance requirements:* For master's, professional resume; personal statement explaining the applicant's interest in and goals for pursuit of this degree; 2 letters of recommendation. Additional exam requirements/recommendations for international students: Required—TOEFL. Electronic applications accepted. Application fee is waived when completed online. *Expenses:* Contact institution.

Lawrence Technological University, College of Management, Southfield, MI 48075-1058. Offers business administration (MBA, DBA), including business analytics (MBA, MS), cybersecurity (MBA, MS), finance (MBA), information systems (MBA), information technology (MBA), marketing (MBA), project management (MBA, MS); cybersecurity (Graduate Certificate); health IT management (Graduate Certificate); information assurance management (Graduate Certificate); information systems (MS), including enterprise resource planning, enterprise security management, project management (MBA, MS); information technology (MS, DM), including business analytics (MBA, MS), cybersecurity (MBA, MS), information assurance (MS), project management (MBA, MS); management (PhD); nonprofit management and leadership (Graduate Certificate); operations management (MS), including manufacturing operations, service operations; project management (Graduate Certificate). *Accreditation:* ACBSP. *Program availability:* Part-time, evening/weekend, 100% online. Terminal master's awarded for partial completion of doctoral program. *Degree requirements:* For master's, thesis (for some programs); for doctorate, comprehensive exam, thesis/dissertation. *Entrance requirements:* Additional exam requirements/recommendations for international students: Required—TOEFL (minimum score 550 paper-based; 79 iBT), IELTS (minimum score 6.5). Electronic applications accepted. *Faculty research:* Cybersecurity; risk management; IT governance; security controls and countermeasures; threat modeling cyber resilience; autonomous cars; natural language processing; text mining; machine learning; reflective leadership; emerging leadership theories and practice; motivational studies; teaching effectiveness strategies; teamwork; organization development; strategic planning; strengths-based and positive organizational scholarship; global leadership; globalization; corporate governance.

Liberty University, Helms School of Government, Lynchburg, VA 24515. Offers criminal justice (MS), including forensic psychology, homeland security, public administration (MA, MS); international relations (MS); political science (MS); public administration (MPA), including business and government, healthcare, law and public policy, public and non-profit management; public policy (MA), including campaigns and elections, international affairs, Middle East affairs, public administration (MA, MS). *Program availability:* Part-time, online learning. *Students:* 615 full-time (329 women), 975 part-time (408 women); includes 476 minority (330 Black or African American, non-Hispanic/Latino; 6 American Indian or Alaska Native, non-Hispanic/Latino; 15 Asian, non-Hispanic/Latino; 69 Hispanic/Latino; 1 Native Hawaiian or other Pacific Islander, non-Hispanic/Latino; 55 Two or more races, non-Hispanic/Latino), 26 international. Average age 35. 2,345 applicants, 46% accepted, 563 enrolled. In 2018, 291 master's

awarded. *Entrance requirements:* For master's, minimum undergraduate GPA of 3.0. Additional exam requirements/recommendations for international students: Required—TOEFL (minimum score 600 paper-based; 100 iBT). *Application deadline:* Applications are processed on a rolling basis. Application fee: $50. Electronic applications accepted. *Expenses: Tuition:* Full-time $10,851; part-time $562 per credit hour. *Financial support:* In 2018–19, 808 students received support. Teaching assistantships and Federal Work-Study available. *Unit head:* Ron Miller, Dean, 434-592-4986, E-mail: govtdean@liberty.edu. *Application contact:* Jay Bridge, Director of Admissions, 800-424-9595, Fax: 800-628-7977, E-mail: gradadmissions@liberty.edu.
Website: https://www.liberty.edu/government/

Lipscomb University, Nelson and Sue Andrews Institute for Civic Leadership, Nashville, TN 37204-3951. Offers civic leadership (MA, Graduate Certificate); cross sector collaboration (MA); non-profit leadership (MA). *Program availability:* Part-time, evening/weekend. *Degree requirements:* For master's, project, externship. *Entrance requirements:* For master's, GRE, GMAT or MAT, transcripts, 2 references, essay, resume. Additional exam requirements/recommendations for international students: Required—TOEFL (minimum score 570 paper-based; 80 iBT). Electronic applications accepted. *Expenses:* Contact institution.

Long Island University–LIU Brooklyn, School of Business, Public Administration and Information Sciences, Brooklyn, NY 11201-8423. Offers accounting (MBA); accounting (MS); business administration (MBA); computer science (MS); gerontology (Advanced Certificate); health administration (MPA); human resources management (MS); not-for-profit management (Advanced Certificate); public administration (MPA); taxation (MS). *Program availability:* Part-time, evening/weekend. *Entrance requirements:* Additional exam requirements/recommendations for international students: Required—TOEFL (minimum score 550 paper-based; 75 iBT). Electronic applications accepted. *Faculty research:* Tax policy; public sector budgeting and gender inequities; technology and innovation; game theory; knowledge management.

Long Island University–LIU Post, School of Health Professions and Nursing, Brookville, NY 11548-1300. Offers biomedical science (MS); cardiovascular perfusion (MS); clinical lab sciences (MS); clinical laboratory management (MS); dietetic internship (Advanced Certificate); family nurse practitioner (MS, Advanced Certificate); forensic social work (Advanced Certificate); gerontology (Advanced Certificate); health administration (MPA); non-profit management (Advanced Certificate); nursing education (MS); nutrition (MS); public administration (MPA); social work (MSW). *Program availability:* Part-time, blended/hybrid learning. *Degree requirements:* For master's, comprehensive exam (for some programs), thesis (for some programs). *Entrance requirements:* Additional exam requirements/recommendations for international students: Required—TOEFL (minimum score 85 iBT) or IELTS (7.5). Electronic applications accepted. *Faculty research:* Antibiotic resistance, evidence-based practice, family care, interprofessional learning, simulation learning.

Louisiana State University in Shreveport, College of Arts and Sciences, Program in Nonprofit Administration, Shreveport, LA 71115-2399. Offers MS. *Program availability:* Part-time, evening/weekend, online learning. *Degree requirements:* For master's, final project. *Entrance requirements:* For master's, GRE, minimum GPA of 3.0 in last 2 undergraduate years, interview, recommendations. Additional exam requirements/recommendations for international students: Required—TOEFL (minimum score 550 paper-based; 61 iBT). Electronic applications accepted.

Marymount University, School of Business and Technology, Program in Leadership and Management, Arlington, VA 22207-4299. Offers association and nonprofit management (Certificate); leadership and management (MS); management studies (Certificate). *Program availability:* Part-time, evening/weekend. *Faculty:* 1 (woman) full-time. *Students:* 14 part-time (10 women); includes 4 minority (1 Black or African American, non-Hispanic/Latino; 3 Hispanic/Latino). Average age 41. 8 applicants, 88% accepted, 5 enrolled. In 2018, 5 master's, 1 other advanced degree awarded. *Degree requirements:* For master's, thesis or alternative. *Entrance requirements:* For master's, resume, interview, at least 3 years of managerial experience, essay on a topic provided by School of Business and Technology; for Certificate, resume, at least 3 years of managerial experience. Additional exam requirements/recommendations for international students: Required—TOEFL (minimum score 600 paper-based; 96 iBT), IELTS (minimum score 6.5), PTE (minimum score 58). *Application deadline:* For fall admission, 7/16 priority date for domestic and international students; for spring admission, 11/16 priority date for domestic and international students; for summer admission, 4/16 priority date for domestic and international students. Applications are processed on a rolling basis. Application fee: $40. Electronic applications accepted. *Expenses:* $1,060 per credit. *Financial support:* Research assistantships, teaching assistantships, career-related internships or fieldwork, scholarships/grants, and unspecified assistantships available. Support available to part-time students. Financial award application deadline: 3/1; financial award applicants required to submit FAFSA. *Unit head:* Dr. Lorri Cooper, Program Director, Leadership and Management, 703-284-5950, E-mail: lorri.cooper@marymount.edu. *Application contact:* Rebecca Esposito, Senior Associate Director, Graduate Admissions, 703-284-5901, Fax: 703-527-3815, E-mail: grad.admissions@marymount.edu.
Website: https://www.marymount.edu/Academics/School-of-Business-and-Technology/Graduate-Programs/Leadership-Management-(M-S-)

Mercer University, Graduate Studies, Cecil B. Day Campus, Penfield College, Atlanta, GA 30341. Offers certified rehabilitation counseling (MS); clinical mental health (MS); counselor education and supervision (PhD); criminal justice and public safety leadership (MS); health informatics (MS); human services (MS), including child and adolescent services, gerontology services; organizational leadership (MS), including leadership for the health care professional, leadership for the nonprofit organization, organizational development and change; school counseling (MS). *Program availability:* Part-time, evening/weekend, 100% online, blended/hybrid learning. *Degree requirements:* For master's, comprehensive exam (for some programs), thesis (for some programs); for doctorate, thesis/dissertation. *Entrance requirements:* For master's, GRE or MAT, Georgia Professional Standards Commission (GPSC) Certification at the SC-5 level; for doctorate, GRE or MAT. Additional exam requirements/recommendations for international students: Recommended—TOEFL (minimum score 550 paper-based; 80 iBT), IELTS (minimum score 6.5). Electronic applications accepted. Application fee is waived when completed online. *Expenses:* Contact institution. *Faculty research:* Marriage and families issues, leadership and ethics, cyber-bullying, trauma, narrative counseling and theory.

Metropolitan State University, College of Community Studies and Public Affairs, St. Paul, MN 55106-5000. Offers alcohol and drug counseling (MS); co-occurring disorders recovery counseling (MS); public administration (MPA); public and nonprofit administration (MPNA).

Minnesota State University Mankato, College of Graduate Studies and Research, College of Social and Behavioral Sciences, Urban and Regional Studies Institute, Mankato, MN 56001. Offers local government management (Certificate); non-profit leadership (Certificate); urban and regional studies (MA); urban planning (MA, Certificate). *Degree requirements:* For master's, one foreign language, comprehensive exam, thesis or alternative. *Entrance requirements:* For master's, minimum GPA of 3.0

during previous 2 years, 2 letters of recommendation. Additional exam requirements/recommendations for international students: Required—TOEFL. Electronic applications accepted.

Mount Aloysius College, Program in Business Administration, Cresson, PA 16630. Offers accounting (MBA); health and human services administration (MBA); non-profit management (MBA); project management (MBA). *Program availability:* Part-time, evening/weekend. *Entrance requirements:* Additional exam requirements/recommendations for international students: Required—IELTS (minimum score 5.5); Recommended—TOEFL. *Application deadline:* For fall admission, 8/1 for domestic students; for spring admission, 12/1 for domestic students. Applications are processed on a rolling basis. Application fee: $30. Electronic applications accepted. Application fee is waived when completed online. *Financial support:* Unspecified assistantships available. Financial award applicants required to submit FAFSA. *Application contact:* Matthew P. Bodenschatz, Director of Graduate and Continuing Education Admissions, 814-886-6556, Fax: 814-886-6441, E-mail: mbodenschatz@mtaloy.edu.

Murray State University, College of Education and Human Services, Department of Community Leadership and Human Services, Murray, KY 42071. Offers nonprofit leadership studies (MS, Certificate). *Program availability:* Part-time, evening/weekend, 100% online, blended/hybrid learning. *Entrance requirements:* For master's, GRE or GMAT, minimum university GPA of 2.75. Additional exam requirements/recommendations for international students: Required—TOEFL (minimum score 527 paper-based; 71 iBT). Electronic applications accepted. *Faculty research:* Service learning, engaged citizenship, volunteer development, youth programming, philanthropy.

Nebraska Christian College of Hope International University, Graduate Programs, Papillion, NE 68046. Offers biblical studies (M Div); business as mission/social entrepreneurship (MBA); children, youth, and family (M Div); church planting (M Div); counseling psychology (MS); educational administration (MA); elementary education (M Ed); general management (MBA); gifted and talented education (M Ed); intercultural studies (M Div); international development (MBA); marketing management (MBA); ministry (MA); ministry and leadership (M Div); music education (M Ed); non-profit management (MBA); pastoral care (M Div); secondary education (M Ed); spiritual formation (M Div); worship ministry (M Div).

New England College, Program in Management, Henniker, NH 03242-3293. Offers accounting (MSA); healthcare administration (MS); international relations (MA); marketing management (MS); nonprofit leadership (MS); project management (MS); strategic leadership (MS). *Program availability:* Part-time, evening/weekend. *Degree requirements:* For master's, independent research project. Electronic applications accepted.

The New School, Schools of Public Engagement, Program in Nonprofit Management, New York, NY 10011. Offers MS. *Program availability:* Part-time, evening/weekend. *Degree requirements:* For master's, capstone project: Paper of Publishable Quality (PPQ), Professional Decision Report (PDR), or thesis. *Entrance requirements:* For master's, two letters of recommendation, statement of purpose, resume, transcripts. Additional exam requirements/recommendations for international students: Required—TOEFL (minimum score 92 iBT), IELTS (minimum score 7), PTE (minimum score 68). Electronic applications accepted. *Expenses:* Contact institution.

New York University, Wagner Graduate School of Public Service, Program in Public Administration, New York, NY 10012. Offers public administration (PhD); public and nonprofit management and policy (MPA, Advanced Certificate), including financial management and public finance (MPA), international policy and management (MPA), management for public and nonprofit organizations, public policy analysis, social impact, innovation, and investment (MPA); JD/MPA; MBA/MPA; MPA/MA. *Accreditation:* NASPAA (one or more programs are accredited). *Program availability:* Part-time. *Degree requirements:* For master's, thesis or alternative, capstone end event; for doctorate, one foreign language, comprehensive exam, thesis/dissertation, preliminary qualifying examination. *Entrance requirements:* Additional exam requirements/recommendations for international students: Required—TOEFL (minimum score 100 iBT), IELTS (minimum score 7.5), TWE. Electronic applications accepted. *Expenses:* Contact institution.

North Carolina State University, Graduate School, College of Humanities and Social Sciences, School of Public and International Affairs, Raleigh, NC 27695. Offers international studies (MIS); nonprofit management (Certificate); public administration (MPA, PhD). *Accreditation:* NASPAA (one or more programs are accredited). *Program availability:* Part-time, evening/weekend. *Entrance requirements:* For master's, GRE General Test, minimum GPA of 3.0 during previous 2 years. Electronic applications accepted. *Faculty research:* Public sector leadership and ethics, financial management, management systems evaluation, computer applications, service delivery.

Northeastern University, College of Professional Studies, Boston, MA 02115-5096. Offers applied nutrition (MS); college athletics administration (MSL); commerce and economic development (MS); corporate and organizational communication (MS); criminal justice (MS); digital media (MPS); elearning and instructional design (M Ed); elementary education (MAT); geographic information technology (MPS); global studies and international relations (MS); higher education administration (M Ed); homeland security (MA); human services (MS); informatics (MPS); leadership (MS); learning analytics (M Ed); learning and instruction (M Ed); nonprofit management (MS); professional sports administration (MSL); project management (MS); regulatory affairs for drugs, biologics, and medical devices (MS); respiratory care leadership (MS); special education (M Ed); technical communication (MS). *Program availability:* Part-time, evening/weekend, 100% online, blended/hybrid learning. Electronic applications accepted. *Expenses:* Contact institution.

Northern Kentucky University, Office of Graduate Programs, College of Arts and Sciences, Program in Public Administration, Highland Heights, KY 41099. Offers non-profit management (Certificate); public administration (MPA). *Accreditation:* NASPAA. *Program availability:* Part-time. *Degree requirements:* For master's, 39 semester hours, including completion of the capstone course. *Entrance requirements:* For master's, GRE, minimum GPA of 2.5, letters of references, portfolios; for Certificate, minimum GPA of 2.0. Additional exam requirements/recommendations for international students: Required—TOEFL (minimum score 79 iBT); Recommended—IELTS (minimum score 6.5). Electronic applications accepted. *Faculty research:* Nonprofit management, human resource management, urban planning, service-learning, homeland security.

North Park University, School of Business and Nonprofit Management, Chicago, IL 60625-4895. Offers MBA, MHEA, MHRM, MM, MNA. *Program availability:* Part-time, evening/weekend, online learning. *Entrance requirements:* For master's, GMAT, GRE. Additional exam requirements/recommendations for international students: Required—TOEFL. *Expenses:* Contact institution.

Norwich University, College of Graduate and Continuing Studies, Master of Public Administration Program, Northfield, VT 05663. Offers criminal justice and public safety (MPA); fiscal management (MPA); international development and influence (MPA); municipal governance (MPA); nonprofit management (MPA); policy analysis and analytics (MPA); public administration leadership and crisis management (MPA); public works and sustainability (MPA). *Program availability:* Evening/weekend, online only, mostly all online with a week-long residency requirement. *Degree requirements:* For master's, capstone. *Entrance requirements:* For master's, minimum undergraduate GPA of 2.75. Additional exam requirements/recommendations for international students: Required—TOEFL (minimum score 550 paper-based; 80 iBT), IELTS (minimum score 6.5). Electronic applications accepted. *Expenses:* Contact institution.

Notre Dame of Maryland University, Graduate Studies, Program in Nonprofit Management, Baltimore, MD 21210-2476. Offers MA. *Program availability:* Part-time, evening/weekend. *Degree requirements:* For master's, thesis optional. *Entrance requirements:* For master's, minimum GPA of 3.0. Additional exam requirements/recommendations for international students: Required—TOEFL (minimum score 500 paper-based; 61 iBT). Electronic applications accepted.

Oakland University, Graduate Study and Lifelong Learning, College of Arts and Sciences, Department of Political Science, Rochester, MI 48309-4401. Offers local government management (Graduate Certificate); non-profit and organizational management (PMC); public administration (MPA). *Accreditation:* NASPAA. *Program availability:* Part-time, evening/weekend. *Entrance requirements:* For master's, minimum GPA of 3.0. Additional exam requirements/recommendations for international students: Required—TOEFL (minimum score 550 paper-based). Electronic applications accepted.

Oklahoma Christian University, Graduate School of Business, Oklahoma City, OK 73136-1100. Offers accounting (M Acc, MBA); financial services (MBA); general business (MBA); health services management (MBA); human resources (MBA); international business (MBA); leadership and organizational development (MBA); marketing (MBA); nonprofit management (MBA); project management (MBA). *Accreditation:* ACBSP. *Program availability:* Part-time, 100% online. *Entrance requirements:* For master's, bachelor's degree. Additional exam requirements/recommendations for international students: Required—TOEFL (minimum score 550 paper-based). Electronic applications accepted. *Expenses:* Contact institution.

Oklahoma State University, Graduate College, Stillwater, OK 74078. Offers aerospace security (Graduate Certificate); bioenergy and sustainable technology (Graduate Certificate); business data mining (Graduate Certificate); business sustainability (Graduate Certificate); environmental science (MS); international studies (MS); non-profit management (Graduate Certificate); teaching English to speakers of other languages (Graduate Certificate); telecommunications management (MS). Programs are interdisciplinary. *Degree requirements:* For master's, thesis (for some programs); for doctorate, comprehensive exam, thesis/dissertation. *Entrance requirements:* For master's and doctorate, GRE or GMAT. Additional exam requirements/recommendations for international students: Required—TOEFL (minimum score 550 paper-based; 79 iBT). Electronic applications accepted. *Expenses: Tuition, area resident:* Full-time $4148. Tuition, state resident: full-time $4148. Tuition, nonresident: full-time $10,517. *International tuition:* $10,517 full-time. *Required fees:* $4394; $2929 per credit hour. Tuition and fees vary according to course load and program.

Oral Roberts University, School of Business, Tulsa, OK 74171. Offers accounting (MBA); entrepreneurship (MBA); finance (MBA); international business (MBA); management (MBA); marketing (MBA); not for profit management (MNM). *Accreditation:* ACBSP. *Program availability:* Part-time, online learning. *Degree requirements:* For master's, thesis optional. *Entrance requirements:* For master's, minimum cumulative GPA of 3.0 from regionally-accredited institution. Electronic applications accepted. Application fee is waived when completed online. *Faculty research:* Social media, international business and marketing.

Our Lady of the Lake University, School of Business and Leadership, Program in Nonprofit Management, San Antonio, TX 78207-4689. Offers MS. *Program availability:* Part-time, evening/weekend, online only, 100% online. *Faculty:* 4 full-time (2 women), 6 part-time/adjunct (1 woman). *Students:* 30 full-time (22 women), 4 part-time (all women); includes 19 minority (6 Black or African American, non-Hispanic/Latino; 13 Hispanic/Latino). Average age 36. 29 applicants, 90% accepted, 20 enrolled. In 2018, 7 master's awarded. *Entrance requirements:* For master's, official transcripts showing minimum cumulative GPA of 2.5, 2 letters of recommendation, resume. Additional exam requirements/recommendations for international students: Required—TOEFL. *Application deadline:* For fall admission, 6/15 for domestic and international students. Application fee: $40 ($50 for international students). Electronic applications accepted. *Expenses:* Contact institution. *Financial support:* In 2018–19, 2 students received support. Federal Work-Study, scholarships/grants, unspecified assistantships, and tuition discounts available. Support available to part-time students. Financial award application deadline: 5/1; financial award applicants required to submit FAFSA. *Unit head:* Dr. Ronald Crowe, Chair of Business Programs, 210-434-6711 Ext. 2713, E-mail: rcrowe@ollusa.edu. *Application contact:* Office of Graduate Admissions, 210-431-3995, Fax: 210-431-3945, E-mail: gradadm@ollusa.edu.
Website: http://www.ollusa.edu/s/1190/hybrid/default-hybrid-ollu.aspx?sid-1190&gid-1&pgid-7921

Pace University, Dyson College of Arts and Sciences, Department of Public Administration, New York, NY 10038. Offers government management (MPA); health care administration (MPA); not-for-profit management (MPA); JD/MPA. *Program availability:* Part-time, evening/weekend. *Faculty:* 6 full-time (4 women), 4 part-time/adjunct (0 women). *Students:* 38 full-time (21 women), 59 part-time (39 women); includes 57 minority (36 Black or African American, non-Hispanic/Latino; 9 Asian, non-Hispanic/Latino; 10 Hispanic/Latino; 2 Two or more races, non-Hispanic/Latino), 9 international. Average age 32. 57 applicants, 96% accepted, 27 enrolled. In 2018, 47 master's awarded. *Degree requirements:* For master's, comprehensive exam, thesis (for some programs), capstone project. *Entrance requirements:* For master's, 2 letters of recommendation, resume, personal statement, official transcripts, essay. Additional exam requirements/recommendations for international students: Required—TOEFL (minimum score 88 iBT), IELTS (minimum score 7) or PTE (minimum score 60). *Application deadline:* For fall admission, 8/1 priority date for domestic students, 6/1 for international students; for spring admission, 12/1 priority date for domestic students, 10/1 for international students. Applications are processed on a rolling basis. Application fee: $70. Electronic applications accepted. *Financial support:* Research assistantships, career-related internships or fieldwork, Federal Work-Study, and tuition waivers (partial) available. Support available to part-time students. Financial award application deadline: 2/15; financial award applicants required to submit FAFSA. *Unit head:* Dr. Bette Kirschstein, Acting Chair, 914-773-3586, E-mail: bkirschstein@pace.edu. *Application contact:* Susan Ford-Goldschein, Director of Admissions, 914-422-4283, Fax: 212-346-1585, E-mail: graduateadmission@pace.edu.
Website: http://www.pace.edu/dyson/academic-departments-and-programs/public-admin

Park University, School of Graduate and Professional Studies, Kansas City, MO 54105. Offers adult education (M Ed); business and government leadership (Graduate Certificate); business, government, and global society (MPA); communication and leadership (MA); creative and life writing (Graduate Certificate); disaster and emergency management (MPA, Graduate Certificate); educational leadership (M Ed); finance (MBA, Graduate Certificate); general business (MBA); global business (Graduate Certificate); healthcare administration (MHA); healthcare services management and

leadership (Graduate Certificate); international business (MBA); language and literacy (M Ed), including English for speakers of other languages, special reading teacher/literacy coach; leadership of international healthcare organizations (Graduate Certificate); management information systems (MBA, Graduate Certificate); music performance (ADP, Graduate Certificate), including cello (MM, ADP), piano (MM, ADP), viola (MM, ADP), violin (MM, ADP); nonprofit and community services management (MPA); nonprofit leadership (Graduate Certificate); performance (MM), including cello (MM, ADP), piano (MM, ADP), viola (MM, ADP), violin (MM, ADP); public management (MPA); social work (MSW); teacher leadership (M Ed), including curriculum and assessment, instructional leader. *Program availability:* Part-time, evening/weekend, online learning. *Degree requirements:* For master's, comprehensive exam (for some programs), thesis (for some programs), internship (for some programs); exam (for some programs). *Entrance requirements:* For master's, GRE or GMAT (for some programs), teacher certification (for some M Ed programs), letters of recommendation, essay, resume (for some programs). Additional exam requirements/recommendations for international students: Required—TOEFL (minimum score 550 paper-based; 79 iBT), IELTS (minimum score 6). Electronic applications accepted.

Penn State Harrisburg, Graduate School, School of Public Affairs, Middletown, PA 17057. Offers criminal justice (MA); health administration (MHA); health administration: long term care (Certificate); homeland security (MPS, Certificate); public administration (MPA, PhD); public administration: non-profit administration (Certificate); public budgeting and financial management (Certificate); public sector human resource management (Certificate). *Accreditation:* NASPAA.

Portland State University, Graduate Studies, College of Urban and Public Affairs, Hatfield School of Government, Department of Public Administration, Portland, OR 97207-0751. Offers collaborative governance (Certificate); energy policy and management (Certificate); global management and leadership (MPA); health administration (MPA); human resource management (MPA); local government (MPA); natural resource policy and administration (MPA); nonprofit and public management (Certificate); nonprofit management (MPA); public administration (EMPA); public affairs and policy (PhD); sustainable food systems (Certificate). *Accreditation:* CAHME; NASPAA (one or more programs are accredited). *Program availability:* Part-time, evening/weekend. *Degree requirements:* For master's, integrative field experience (MPA), practicum (MPH); for doctorate, comprehensive exam, thesis/dissertation. *Entrance requirements:* For master's, GRE (minimum scores: verbal 150, quantitative 149, and analytic writing 4.5), minimum GPA of 3.0, 3 recommendation letters, resume, 500-word statement of intent; for doctorate, GRE, 3 recommendation letters, resume, 500-word personal essay. Additional exam requirements/recommendations for international students: Required—TOEFL (minimum score 550 paper-based; 80 iBT), IELTS (minimum score 7). *Faculty research:* Public budgeting, program evaluation, nonprofit management, natural resources policy and administration.

Post University, Program in Counseling and Human Services, Waterbury, CT 06723-2540. Offers counseling and human services (MS); counseling and human services/alcohol and drug counseling (MS); counseling and human services/clinical mental health counseling (MS); counseling and human services/forensic mental health counseling (MS); counseling and human services/non-profit management (MS). *Program availability:* Part-time, evening/weekend, online learning. *Entrance requirements:* For master's, resume. *Expenses: Tuition:* Full-time $8300; part-time $570 per credit. *Required fees:* $140 per term. Tuition and fees vary according to course level, campus/location and program.

Regent University, Graduate School, Robertson School of Government, Virginia Beach, VA 23464-9800. Offers government (MA), including American government, healthcare policy and ethics (MA, MPA), international relations, law and public policy, national security studies, political communication, political theory, religion and politics; national security studies (MA), including cybersecurity, homeland security, international security, Middle East politics; public administration (MPA), including emergency management and homeland security, federal government, general public administration, healthcare policy and ethics (MA, MPA), law, nonprofit administration and faith-based organizations, public leadership and management, servant leadership. *Program availability:* Part-time, evening/weekend, 100% online, blended/hybrid learning. *Degree requirements:* For master's, thesis optional, internship. *Entrance requirements:* For master's, GRE General Test or LSAT, personal essay, writing sample, resume, college transcripts. Additional exam requirements/recommendations for international students: Required—TOEFL (minimum score 577 paper-based). Electronic applications accepted. *Expenses:* Contact institution. *Faculty research:* International relations and politics, public administration, leadership and ethics, Biblical law, Constitutional law and Supreme Court.

Regent University, Graduate School, School of Business and Leadership, Virginia Beach, VA 23464-9800. Offers business administration (MBA), including accounting, economics, entrepreneurship, finance and investing, general management, healthcare management (MA, MBA), human resource management (MA, MBA), innovation management, leadership, marketing, not-for-profit management (MA, MBA); business analytics (MS); business and design management (MA); church leadership (MA); leadership (Certificate); organizational leadership (MA, PhD), including ecclesial leadership (DSL, PhD), entrepreneurial leadership (PhD), healthcare management (MA, MBA), human resource development (PhD), human resource management (MA, MBA), individualized studies (DSL, PhD), interdisciplinary studies (MA), leadership coaching and mentoring (MA), not-for-profit management (MA, MBA), organizational development consulting (MA), servant leadership (MA, DSL); strategic leadership (DSL), including ecclesial leadership (DSL, PhD), global consulting, healthcare leadership, individualized studies (DSL, PhD), leadership coaching, servant leadership (MA, DSL), strategic foresight. *Program availability:* Part-time, evening/weekend, 100% online, blended/hybrid learning. *Degree requirements:* For master's, thesis or alternative, 3-credit hour culminating experience; for doctorate, thesis/dissertation. *Entrance requirements:* For master's, college transcripts, resume, essay; for doctorate, college transcripts, resume, essay, writing sample; for Certificate, writing sample, resume, transcripts. Additional exam requirements/recommendations for international students: Required—TOEFL (minimum score 577 paper-based). Electronic applications accepted. *Expenses:* Contact institution. *Faculty research:* Servant leadership, global business, team effectiveness, technology utilization, leadership development.

Regent University, Graduate School, School of Law, Virginia Beach, VA 23464-9800. Offers American legal studies (LL M); human rights (LL M); law (MA, JD), including advanced paralegal studies (MA), alternative dispute resolution (MA), business (MA), criminal justice (MA), general legal studies (MA), human resources management (MA), human rights and rule of law (MA), national security (MA), non-profit organizational law (MA), regulatory compliance (MA), wealth management and financial planning (MA); JD/MA; JD/MBA. *Accreditation:* ABA. *Program availability:* Part-time, 100% online, blended/hybrid learning. *Entrance requirements:* For master's, college transcripts, resume, personal statement; for doctorate, LSAT, minimum undergraduate GPA of 3.0, official transcripts, 2 letters of recommendation, resume, personal statement. Additional exam requirements/recommendations for international students: Required—TOEFL (minimum score 600 paper-based). Electronic applications accepted. *Expenses:* Contact institution. *Faculty research:* Family law, Constitutional law, law and culture, evidence and practice, intellectual property.

Regis University, College of Business and Economics, Denver, CO 80221-1099. Offers accounting (MS); executive leadership (Certificate); finance (MS); finance and accounting (MBA); health industry leadership (MBA); human resource management and leadership (MSOL); management (MBA); marketing (MBA); nonprofit leadership (Post-Graduate Certificate); nonprofit management (MNM); nonprofit organizational capacity building (Certificate); operations management (MBA); organizational leadership and management (MSOL); project leadership and management (MS, MSOL); strategic business management (Certificate); strategic human resource integration (Certificate); strategic management (MBA). Programs offered at Colorado Springs Campus, Northwest Denver Campus, Southeast Denver Campus, Fort Collins Campus, Broomfield Campus, Henderson (Nevada) Campus, and Summerlin (Nevada) Campus. *Program availability:* Part-time, evening/weekend, 100% online, blended/hybrid learning. *Degree requirements:* For master's, thesis (for some programs), capstone or final research project. *Entrance requirements:* For master's, official transcript reflecting baccalaureate degree awarded from regionally-accredited college or university, interview, 2 years of full-time related work experience, resume, letters of recommendation. Additional exam requirements/recommendations for international students: Required—TOEFL (minimum score 550 paper-based; 82 iBT). Electronic applications accepted. *Expenses:* Contact institution. *Faculty research:* Impact of information technology on small business regulation of accounting, international project financing, mineral development, delivery of healthcare to rural indigenous communities.

Rockhurst University, Helzberg School of Management, Kansas City, MO 64110-2561. Offers accounting (MBA); business intelligence (MBA, Certificate); business intelligence and analytics (MS); data science (MBA, Certificate); entrepreneurship (MBA); finance (MBA); fundraising leadership (MBA, Certificate); healthcare management (MBA, Certificate); human capital (Certificate); international business (Certificate); management (MA, MBA, Certificate); nonprofit administration (Certificate); organizational development (Certificate); science leadership (Certificate). *Accreditation:* AACSB. *Program availability:* Part-time, evening/weekend. *Entrance requirements:* For master's, GMAT or GRE. Additional exam requirements/recommendations for international students: Required—TOEFL (minimum score 550 paper-based; 79 iBT). Electronic applications accepted. *Faculty research:* Offshoring/outsourcing, systems analysis/synthesis, work teams, multilateral trade, path dependencies/creation.

Saint Mary-of-the-Woods College, Master of Leadership Development Program, Saint Mary of the Woods, IN 47876. Offers not-for-profit leadership (MLD); organizational leadership (MLD). *Program availability:* Part-time. *Degree requirements:* For master's, thesis. Electronic applications accepted. *Expenses:* Contact institution.

Salve Regina University, Program in Business Administration, Newport, RI 02840-4192. Offers cybersecurity issues in business (MBA); entrepreneurial enterprise (MBA); health care administration and management (MBA); nonprofit management (MBA); social ventures (MBA). *Program availability:* Part-time, evening/weekend, online learning. *Entrance requirements:* For master's, GMAT, GRE General Test, or MAT, 6 undergraduate credits each in accounting, economics, quantitative analysis and calculus or statistics. Additional exam requirements/recommendations for international students: Required—TOEFL (minimum score 600 paper-based; 100 iBT) or IELTS. Electronic applications accepted. *Expenses: Tuition:* Full-time $10,530; part-time $585 per credit. *Required fees:* $60 per term. Tuition and fees vary according to course level, course load, degree level and program.

Salve Regina University, Program in Management, Newport, RI 02840-4192. Offers business studies (CGS); human resource management (CGS); innovation and strategic management (MS); management (CGS); nonprofit management (CGS); social entrepreneurship (CGS). *Program availability:* Part-time, evening/weekend, online learning. *Entrance requirements:* For master's, GMAT, GRE General Test, or MAT. Additional exam requirements/recommendations for international students: Required—TOEFL (minimum score 600 paper-based; 100 iBT). Electronic applications accepted. *Expenses: Tuition:* Full-time $10,530; part-time $585 per credit. *Required fees:* $60 per term. Tuition and fees vary according to course level, course load, degree level and program.

San Francisco State University, Division of Graduate Studies, College of Business, Program in Business Administration, San Francisco, CA 94132-1722. Offers decision sciences/operations research (MBA); ethics and compliance (MBA); finance (MBA); global business and innovation (MBA); healthcare administration (MBA); hospitality and tourism management (MBA); information systems (MBA); leadership (MBA); marketing (MBA); nonprofit and social enterprise leadership (MBA); sustainable business (MBA). *Accreditation:* AACSB. *Program availability:* Part-time, evening/weekend. *Degree requirements:* For master's, thesis, essay test. *Entrance requirements:* For master's, GMAT, minimum GPA of 2.7 in last 60 units. Additional exam requirements/recommendations for international students: Required—TOEFL (minimum score 550 paper-based).

San Francisco State University, Division of Graduate Studies, College of Health and Social Sciences, Public Administration Program, San Francisco, CA 94132-1722. Offers criminal justice administration (MPA); environmental administration and policy (MPA); gerontology (MPA); nonprofit administration (MPA); public management (MPA); public policy (MPA); urban administration (MPA). *Accreditation:* NASPAA.

Seton Hall University, College of Arts and Sciences, Department of Political Science and Public Affairs, South Orange, NJ 07079-2697. Offers nonprofit organization management (Graduate Certificate); public administration (MPA), including data visualization and analytics, health policy and management, nonprofit organization management, public service: leadership, governance, and policy. *Accreditation:* CAHME; NASPAA. *Program availability:* Part-time, evening/weekend. *Degree requirements:* For master's, thesis or alternative, internship or practicum. *Entrance requirements:* Additional exam requirements/recommendations for international students: Required—TOEFL. Electronic applications accepted.

Southern New Hampshire University, School of Business, Manchester, NH 03106-1045. Offers accounting (MBA, Graduate Certificate); accounting finance (MS); accounting/auditing (MS); accounting/forensic accounting (MS); accounting/management accounting (MS); accounting/taxation (MS); applied economics (MS); athletic administration (MBA, Graduate Certificate); business administration (IMBA, Certificate), including business information systems (Certificate), human resource management (Certificate); business analytics (MBA); business intelligence (MBA); communication (MA), including new media and marketing, public relations; community economic development (MBA); criminal justice (MBA); data analytics (MS); economics (MBA); engineering management (MBA); entrepreneurship (MBA); finance (MBA, MS, Graduate Certificate); finance/corporate finance (MS); finance/investments (MS); forensic accounting (MBA); forensic accounting and fraud examination (Graduate Certificate); healthcare informatics (MBA); healthcare management (MBA); human resource management (MS); human resources (MBA); information technology (MS); information technology management (MBA); international business (PhD); Internet marketing (MBA); leadership (MBA); leadership of nonprofit organizations (Graduate Certificate); management (MS); marketing (MBA, MS, Graduate Certificate); music

business (MBA); operations and project management (MS); operations and supply chain management (MBA, Graduate Certificate); organizational leadership (MS); project management (MBA, Graduate Certificate); public administration (MBA, Graduate Certificate); quantitative analysis (MBA); Six Sigma (Graduate Certificate); Six Sigma quality (MBA); social media marketing (MBA, Graduate Certificate); sport management (MBA, MS, Graduate Certificate); sustainability and environmental compliance (MBA); MBA/Certificate. *Accreditation:* ACBSP. *Program availability:* Part-time, evening/weekend, online learning. Terminal master's awarded for partial completion of doctoral program. *Degree requirements:* For master's, one foreign language, comprehensive exam (for some programs), thesis or alternative; for doctorate, one foreign language, comprehensive exam, thesis/dissertation. *Entrance requirements:* For master's, minimum GPA of 2.5; for doctorate, GMAT. Additional exam requirements/recommendations for international students: Required—TOEFL (minimum score 500 paper-based). Electronic applications accepted.

Suffolk University, Sawyer Business School, Department of Public Administration, Boston, MA 02108-2770. Offers community health (MPA); information systems, performance management, and big data analytics (MPA); nonprofit management (MPA); state and local government (MPA); JD/MPA; MPA/MS; MPA/MSCJ; MPA/MSMHC; MPA/MSPS. *Accreditation:* NASPAA (one or more programs are accredited). *Program availability:* Part-time, evening/weekend. *Faculty:* 9 full-time (5 women), 4 part-time/adjunct (2 women). *Students:* 21 full-time (14 women), 85 part-time (57 women); includes 37 minority (20 Black or African American, non-Hispanic/Latino; 5 Asian, non-Hispanic/Latino; 9 Hispanic/Latino; 3 Two or more races, non-Hispanic/Latino), 3 international. Average age 35. 106 applicants, 83% accepted, 34 enrolled. In 2018, 42 master's awarded. *Entrance requirements:* Additional exam requirements/recommendations for international students: Required—TOEFL (minimum score 550 paper-based; 80 iBT). *Application deadline:* For fall admission, 3/15 priority date for domestic and international students; for spring admission, 10/15 priority date for domestic and international students. Applications are processed on a rolling basis. Application fee: $50. Electronic applications accepted. *Expenses:* Contact institution. *Financial support:* In 2018–19, 76 students received support, including 2 fellowships (averaging $4,650 per year); career-related internships or fieldwork, Federal Work-Study, institutionally sponsored loans, and scholarships/grants also available. Support available to part-time students. Financial award application deadline: 4/1; financial award applicants required to submit FAFSA. *Faculty research:* Local government, health care, federal policy, mental health, HIV/AIDS. *Unit head:* Brenda Bond, Director/Department Chair, 617-305-1768, E-mail: bbond@suffolk.edu. *Application contact:* Mara Marzocchi, Associate Director of Graduate Admissions, 617-573-8302, Fax: 617-305-1733, E-mail: grad.admission@suffolk.edu.
Website: http://www.suffolk.edu/mpa

Suffolk University, Sawyer Business School, Master of Business Administration Program, Boston, MA 02108-2770. Offers accounting (MBA); entrepreneurship (MBA); executive business administration (EMBA); finance (MBA); global business administration (GMBA); health administration (MBA); international business (MBA); marketing (MBA); nonprofit management (MBA); organizational behavior (MBA); strategic management (MBA); supply chain management (MBA); taxation (MBA); JD/MBA; MBA/MHA; MBA/MSA; MBA/MSF; MBA/MST. *Accreditation:* AACSB. *Program availability:* Part-time, evening/weekend, 100% online. *Faculty:* 18 full-time (5 women), 5 part-time/adjunct (0 women). *Students:* 79 full-time (46 women), 193 part-time (107 women); includes 69 minority (17 Black or African American, non-Hispanic/Latino; 18 Asian, non-Hispanic/Latino; 28 Hispanic/Latino; 6 Two or more races, non-Hispanic/Latino), 40 international. Average age 30. 274 applicants, 67% accepted, 83 enrolled. In 2018, 125 master's awarded. *Entrance requirements:* For master's, GMAT, minimum undergraduate GPA of 2.75 (MBA), 5 years of managerial experience (EMBA). Additional exam requirements/recommendations for international students: Required—TOEFL (minimum score 550 paper-based; 80 iBT). *Application deadline:* For fall admission, 3/15 priority date for domestic students, 10/15 priority date for international students; for spring admission, 10/15 priority date for domestic and international students. Applications are processed on a rolling basis. Application fee: $50. Electronic applications accepted. *Expenses:* Contact institution. *Financial support:* In 2018–19, 170 students received support, including 4 fellowships (averaging $2,906 per year); career-related internships or fieldwork, Federal Work-Study, institutionally sponsored loans, and scholarships/grants also available. Support available to part-time students. Financial award application deadline: 4/1; financial award applicants required to submit FAFSA. *Faculty research:* Foreign investments; career strategies and boundaryless careers; corporate ethics codes; interest rates, inflation, and growth options; innovation and product development performance. *Unit head:* Jodi Detjen, Director of MBA Programs, 617-573-8306, E-mail: jdetjen@suffolk.edu. *Application contact:* Mara Marzocchi, Associate Director of Graduate Admissions, 617-573-8302, Fax: 617-305-1733, E-mail: grad.admission@suffolk.edu.
Website: http://www.suffolk.edu/mba

Thomas Edison State University, John S. Watson School of Public Service and Continuing Studies, Trenton, NJ 08608. Offers community and economic development (MSM); environmental policy/environmental justice (MSM); homeland security (MSHS, MSM); information and technology for public service (MSM); nonprofit management (MSM); public and municipal finance (MSM); public health (MSM); public service administration and leadership (MSM); public service leadership (MPSL). *Program availability:* Part-time, online learning. *Entrance requirements:* Additional exam requirements/recommendations for international students: Required—TOEFL (minimum score 550 paper-based; 79 iBT). Electronic applications accepted.

Tiffin University, Program in Business Administration, Tiffin, OH 44883-2161. Offers finance (MBA); general management (MBA); healthcare administration (MBA); human resource management (MBA); international business (MBA); leadership (MBA); marketing (MBA); non-profit management (MBA); sports management (MBA). *Accreditation:* ACBSP. *Program availability:* Part-time, evening/weekend, online learning. *Entrance requirements:* For master's, minimum undergraduate GPA of 2.5, work experience. Additional exam requirements/recommendations for international students: Required—TOEFL (minimum score 550 paper-based; 79 iBT), IELTS. Electronic applications accepted. Application fee is waived when completed online. *Faculty research:* Small business, executive development operations, research and statistical analysis, market research, management information systems.

Trinity Washington University, School of Business and Graduate Studies, Washington, DC 20017-1094. Offers business administration (MBA); communication (MA); international security studies (MA); organizational management (MSA), including federal program management, human resource management, nonprofit management, organizational development, public and community health. *Program availability:* Part-time, evening/weekend. *Degree requirements:* For master's, thesis (for some programs), capstone project (MSA). *Entrance requirements:* For master's, minimum GPA of 2.5. Additional exam requirements/recommendations for international students: Required—TOEFL (minimum score 550 paper-based).

Trinity Western University, School of Graduate Studies, Program in Business Administration, Langley, BC V2Y 1Y1, Canada. Offers international business (MBA); management of the growing enterprise (MBA); non-profit and charitable organization management (MBA). *Program availability:* Part-time, online learning. *Degree requirements:* For master's, thesis or alternative, applied project. *Entrance requirements:* For master's, GMAT (minimum score of 550 recommended). Additional exam requirements/recommendations for international students: Required—TOEFL (minimum score 600 paper-based; 100 iBT), IELTS (minimum score 7). *Application deadline:* For spring admission, 4/30 for domestic and international students. Applications are processed on a rolling basis. Electronic applications accepted. *Financial support:* Scholarships/grants available. *Unit head:* Dr. Mark A. Lee, Director, MBA Program, 604-888-7511 Ext. 3474, Fax: 604-513-2042, E-mail: mark.lee@twu.ca. *Application contact:* Phil Kay, Director of Graduate and International Admissions, 604-513-2121 Ext. 3444, E-mail: phil.kay@twu.edu.
Website: http://www.twu.ca/mba

Trinity Western University, School of Graduate Studies, Program in Leadership, Langley, BC V2Y 1Y1, Canada. Offers business (MA, Certificate); Christian ministry (MA); education (MA, Certificate); healthcare (MA, Certificate); non-profit (MA, Certificate). *Program availability:* Online learning. *Degree requirements:* For master's, major project. *Entrance requirements:* For master's, minimum GPA of 2.7. Additional exam requirements/recommendations for international students: Required—TOEFL (minimum score 620 paper-based; 105 iBT). Electronic applications accepted. *Expenses:* Contact institution. *Faculty research:* Servant leadership.

Tufts University, Graduate School of Arts and Sciences, Graduate Certificate Programs, Management of Community Organizations Program, Medford, MA 02155. Offers Certificate. *Program availability:* Part-time, evening/weekend. Electronic applications accepted. *Expenses:* Contact institution.

University at Albany, State University of New York, Nelson A. Rockefeller College of Public Affairs and Policy, Department of Public Administration and Policy, Albany, NY 12222-0001. Offers financial management and public economics (MPA); financial market regulation (MPA); health policy (MPA); healthcare management (MPA); homeland security (MPA); human resources management (MPA); information strategy and management (MPA); local government management (MPA); nonprofit management (MPA); nonprofit management and leadership (Certificate); organizational behavior and theory (MPA, PhD); planning and policy analysis (CAS); policy analysis (MPA); politics and administration (PhD); public finance (PhD); public management (PhD); public policy (PhD); public sector management (Certificate); women and public policy (Certificate); JD/MPA. JD/MPA offered jointly with Albany Law School. *Accreditation:* NASPAA (one or more programs are accredited). *Faculty:* 24 full-time (10 women), 19 part-time/adjunct (10 women). *Students:* 117 full-time (62 women), 101 part-time (58 women); includes 56 minority (20 Black or African American, non-Hispanic/Latino; 8 Asian, non-Hispanic/Latino; 20 Hispanic/Latino; 8 Two or more races, non-Hispanic/Latino), 28 international. 236 applicants, 69% accepted, 86 enrolled. In 2018, 57 master's, 1 doctorate, 14 other advanced degrees awarded. *Degree requirements:* For doctorate, one foreign language, thesis/dissertation. *Entrance requirements:* For doctorate, GRE General Test. Additional exam requirements/recommendations for international students: Required—TOEFL (minimum score 550 paper-based). *Application deadline:* For fall admission, 2/1 priority date for domestic students, 5/1 for international students; for spring admission, 12/1 for domestic students. Applications are processed on a rolling basis. Application fee: $75. Electronic applications accepted. *Financial support:* Application deadline: 2/1. *Unit head:* Victor Asal, Chair, 518-591-8729, E-mail: vasal@albany.edu. *Application contact:* Victor Asal, Chair, 518-591-8729, E-mail: vasal@albany.edu.
Website: http://www.albany.edu/rockefeller/pad.shtml

University of Arkansas at Little Rock, Graduate School, College of Social Sciences and Communication, Program in Nonprofit Management, Little Rock, AR 72204-1099. Offers Graduate Certificate. *Entrance requirements:* For degree, baccalaureate degree, essay, two letters of reference.

University of California, San Diego, Graduate Division, School of Global Policy and Strategy, Master of International Affairs Program, La Jolla, CA 92093. Offers international development and nonprofit management (MIA); international economics (MIA); international environmental policy (MIA); international management (MIA); international politics (MIA). Students will choose one of the following country/regional specializations: China, Japan, Korea, Latin America, or Southeast Asia. *Degree requirements:* For master's, one foreign language. *Entrance requirements:* For master's, GMAT or GRE General Test. Additional exam requirements/recommendations for international students: Required—TOEFL (minimum score 90 iBT), IELTS (minimum score 7). Electronic applications accepted.

University of Central Florida, College of Community Innovation and Education, School of Public Administration, Orlando, FL 32816. Offers emergency management and homeland security (Certificate); fundraising (Certificate); nonprofit management (MNM, Certificate); public administration (MPA); research administration (MRA); urban and regional planning (MS). *Accreditation:* NASPAA. *Program availability:* Part-time, evening/weekend. *Degree requirements:* For master's, comprehensive exam, thesis or alternative, research report. *Entrance requirements:* For master's, letters of recommendation, goal statement, resume. Additional exam requirements/recommendations for international students: Required—TOEFL. Electronic applications accepted.

University of Central Oklahoma, The Jackson College of Graduate Studies, College of Liberal Arts, Department of Political Science, Edmond, OK 73034-5209. Offers political science (MA), including international affairs; public administration (MPA), including public and nonprofit management, urban management. *Program availability:* Part-time. *Degree requirements:* For master's, comprehensive exam (for some programs), thesis (for some programs). *Entrance requirements:* For master's, 18 undergraduate hours in political science. Additional exam requirements/recommendations for international students: Required—TOEFL (minimum score 550 paper-based; 79 iBT), IELTS (minimum score 6.5). Electronic applications accepted.

University of Colorado Denver, School of Public Affairs, Program in Public Affairs and Administration, Denver, CO 80127. Offers public administration (MPA), including domestic violence, emergency management and homeland security, environmental policy, management and law, homeland security and defense, local government, nonprofit management, public administration; public affairs (PhD). *Accreditation:* NASPAA. *Program availability:* Part-time, evening/weekend, online learning. *Expenses:* Tuition, state resident: full-time $6786; part-time $337 per credit hour. Tuition, nonresident: full-time $22,590; part-time $1255 per credit hour. *Required fees:* $1231; $137 per credit hour. Tuition and fees vary according to program and reciprocity agreements.

University of Connecticut, Graduate School, College of Liberal Arts and Sciences, Department of Public Policy, Storrs, CT 06269. Offers public administration (MPA, Graduate Certificate), including nonprofit management (Graduate Certificate), public financial management (Graduate Certificate); survey research (MA, Graduate Certificate), including quantitative research methods (Graduate Certificate), survey research (MA); JD/MPA; MPA/MSW. *Degree requirements:* For master's, comprehensive exam. *Entrance requirements:* For master's, GRE General Test. Additional exam requirements/recommendations for international students: Required—TOEFL (minimum score 550 paper-based). Electronic applications accepted.

University of Florida, Graduate School, College of Agricultural and Life Sciences, Department of Family, Youth, and Community Sciences, Gainesville, FL 32611. Offers community studies (MS); family and youth development (MS); family, youth and community sciences (MS); nonprofit organization development (MS). *Program availability:* Part-time, online learning. *Degree requirements:* For master's, comprehensive exam (for some programs), thesis (for some programs). *Entrance requirements:* For master's, GRE General Test, minimum GPA of 3.0. Additional exam requirements/recommendations for international students: Required—TOEFL (minimum score 550 paper-based; 80 iBT), IELTS (minimum score 6). Electronic applications accepted. *Faculty research:* Adolescent risk behaviors, family risk and resilience, family financial management, community-based organizations/interventions, nutrition and wellness.

University of Georgia, School of Social Work, Athens, GA 30602. Offers MA, MSW, PhD, Certificate, MSW/JD. *Accreditation:* CSWE (one or more programs are accredited). *Program availability:* Part-time, evening/weekend. *Degree requirements:* For master's, thesis or alternative; for doctorate, one foreign language, thesis/dissertation. *Entrance requirements:* For master's and doctorate, GRE General Test. Electronic applications accepted. *Faculty research:* Juvenile justice, substance abuse, civil rights and social justice, gerontology, social policy.

University of Houston–Downtown, College of Humanities and Social Sciences, Department of Social Sciences, Houston, TX 77002. Offers non-profit management (MA). *Program availability:* Part-time, evening/weekend, online only, 100% online. *Degree requirements:* For master's, thesis or capstone project, internship which will include capstone assignments. *Entrance requirements:* For master's, GRE, essay, resume, 3 letters of recommendation, transcripts. Additional exam requirements/recommendations for international students: Required—TOEFL (minimum score 550 paper-based; 50 iBT). Electronic applications accepted. *Expenses:* Contact institution.

University of La Verne, College of Business and Public Management, Master's Program in Public Administration, La Verne, CA 91750-4443. Offers gerontology (MPA); nonprofit (MPA); public health (MPA); urban management and affairs (MPA). *Accreditation:* NASPAA. *Program availability:* Part-time. *Entrance requirements:* For master's, minimum undergraduate GPA of 3.0, statement of purpose, 2 letters of recommendation, resume. Additional exam requirements/recommendations for international students: Required—TOEFL (minimum score 550 paper-based). *Expenses:* Contact institution.

University of La Verne, College of Business and Public Management, Program in Leadership and Management, La Verne, CA 91750-4443. Offers human resource management (Certificate); leadership and management (MS), including human resource management, nonprofit management, organizational development; nonprofit management (Certificate); organizational leadership (Certificate). *Program availability:* Part-time. *Entrance requirements:* For master's, bachelor's degree, minimum undergraduate GPA of 2.75, 2 letters of recommendation, interview, resume. Additional exam requirements/recommendations for international students: Required—TOEFL (minimum score 550 paper-based).

University of La Verne, Regional and Online Campuses, Graduate Programs, Inland Empire Campus, Ontario, CA 91730. Offers business administration (MBA, MBA-EP), including accounting (MBA), finance (MBA), health services management (MBA-EP), information technology (MBA-EP), international business (MBA), managed care (MBA), management and leadership (MBA-EP), marketing (MBA-EP), supply chain management (MBA); leadership and management (MS), including human resource management, nonprofit management, organizational development. *Program availability:* Part-time, evening/weekend. *Expenses:* Contact institution.

University of Louisville, Graduate School, College of Arts and Sciences, Department of Urban and Public Affairs, Louisville, KY 40208. Offers public administration (MPA), including human resources management, non-profit management, public policy and administration; urban and public affairs (PhD), including urban planning and development, urban policy and administration; urban planning (MUP), including administration of planning organizations, housing and community development, land use and environmental planning, spatial analysis. *Program availability:* Part-time, evening/weekend. *Faculty:* 12 full-time (6 women), 7 part-time/adjunct (2 women). *Students:* 39 full-time (18 women), 20 part-time (12 women); includes 14 minority (5 Black or African American, non-Hispanic/Latino; 1 Asian, non-Hispanic/Latino; 2 Hispanic/Latino; 6 Two or more races, non-Hispanic/Latino), 5 international. Average age 32. 38 applicants, 66% accepted, 16 enrolled. In 2018, 9 master's awarded. Terminal master's awarded for partial completion of doctoral program. *Degree requirements:* For master's, internship; for doctorate, comprehensive exam, thesis/dissertation. *Entrance requirements:* For master's, GRE General Test, minimum GPA of 3.0; for doctorate, GRE General Test, master's degree in appropriate field. Additional exam requirements/recommendations for international students: Required—TOEFL (minimum score 550 paper-based; 79 iBT). *Application deadline:* Applications are processed on a rolling basis. Application fee: $65. *Expenses:* Contact institution. *Financial support:* In 2018–19, 27 students received support. Fellowships, research assistantships, tuition waivers (full and partial), and unspecified assistantships available. Financial award application deadline: 2/1. *Faculty research:* Urban theory, sustainability, public administration, urban planning, urban management. *Total annual research expenditures:* $240,308. *Unit head:* Dr. David Simpson, Chair, 502-852-8019, Fax: 502-852-4558, E-mail: dave.simpson@louisville.edu.
Website: http://supa.louisville.edu

University of Lynchburg, Graduate Studies, MA Program in Nonprofit Leadership Studies, Lynchburg, VA 24501-3199. Offers non-profit leadership (MA). *Program availability:* Part-time, evening/weekend, 100% online, blended/hybrid learning. *Degree requirements:* For master's, capstone project. *Entrance requirements:* For master's, GRE. Additional exam requirements/recommendations for international students: Required—TOEFL (minimum score 550 paper-based; 80 iBT), IELTS (minimum score 6). Electronic applications accepted. Application fee is waived when completed online. *Expenses:* Contact institution.

University of Maryland, Baltimore County, The Graduate School, College of Arts, Humanities and Social Sciences, Department of Sociology, Anthropology, and Health Administration and Policy, Baltimore, MD 21250. Offers applied sociology (MA); nonprofit sector (Postbaccalaureate Certificate). *Program availability:* Part-time, evening/weekend. *Degree requirements:* For master's, thesis or alternative. *Entrance requirements:* For master's, minimum GPA of 3.0. Additional exam requirements/recommendations for international students: Required—TOEFL. Electronic applications accepted. *Faculty research:* Health, illness, and medicine; aging and the life course; diversity, gender, and culture; applied research methods.

University of Memphis, Graduate School, College of Arts and Sciences, Division of Public and Nonprofit Administration, Memphis, TN 38152. Offers local government management (Graduate Certificate); philanthropy and nonprofit leadership (Graduate Certificate). *Accreditation:* NASPAA. *Program availability:* Part-time, evening/weekend, blended/hybrid learning. *Students:* 24 full-time (12 women), 39 part-time (25 women); includes 30 minority (25 Black or African American, non-Hispanic/Latino; 1 Asian, non-Hispanic/Latino; 1 Hispanic/Latino; 3 Two or more races, non-Hispanic/Latino), 2 international. Average age 35. 33 applicants, 94% accepted, 28 enrolled. In 2018, 9 master's, 11 other advanced degrees awarded. *Degree requirements:* For master's, comprehensive exam, thesis or alternative, internship. *Entrance requirements:* For master's, GRE General Test, GMAT, MAT, or LSAT, minimum GPA of 3.0, resume, two references, statement of interest. Additional exam requirements/recommendations for international students: Required—TOEFL. *Application deadline:* For fall admission, 7/1 for domestic students, 5/1 for international students; for spring admission, 12/1 for domestic students, 9/15 for international students; for summer admission, 5/1 for domestic students, 2/1 for international students. Applications are processed on a rolling basis. Application fee: $35 ($60 for international students). Electronic applications accepted. *Expenses: Tuition, area resident:* Full-time $10,240; part-time $503 per credit hour. Tuition, state resident: full-time $10,464. Tuition, nonresident: full-time $20,224; part-time $991 per credit hour. *Required fees:* $850; $106 per credit hour. *Financial support:* Fellowships, research assistantships with full tuition reimbursements, career-related internships or fieldwork, Federal Work-Study, scholarships/grants, health care benefits, and unspecified assistantships available. Support available to part-time students. Financial award application deadline: 2/1; financial award applicants required to submit FAFSA. *Faculty research:* Nonprofit organization governance, local government management, community collaboration, urban problems, accountability. *Unit head:* Dr. Sharon Wrobel, Chair, 901-678-4720, Fax: 901-678-2981, E-mail: swrobel@memphis.edu. *Application contact:* Dr. Sharon Wrobel, Chair, 901-678-4720, Fax: 901-678-2981, E-mail: swrobel@memphis.edu.
Website: http://www.memphis.edu/padm

University of Michigan–Flint, Graduate Programs, Program in Public Administration, Flint, MI 48502-1950. Offers administration of non-profit agencies (MPA); criminal justice administration (MPA); educational administration (MPA); general public administration (MPA); healthcare administration (MPA). *Program availability:* Part-time. *Faculty:* 2 part-time/adjunct (1 woman). *Students:* 10 full-time (8 women), 98 part-time (63 women); includes 39 minority (30 Black or African American, non-Hispanic/Latino; 3 American Indian or Alaska Native, non-Hispanic/Latino; 1 Asian, non-Hispanic/Latino; 2 Hispanic/Latino; 3 Two or more races, non-Hispanic/Latino), 3 international. Average age 36. 75 applicants, 69% accepted, 34 enrolled. In 2018, 40 master's awarded. *Degree requirements:* For master's, thesis or alternative, internship. *Entrance requirements:* For master's, bachelor's degree from regionally-accredited institution, minimum overall undergraduate GPA of 3.0 on 4.0 scale. Additional exam requirements/recommendations for international students: Required—TOEFL (minimum score 84 iBT), IELTS (minimum score 6.5). *Application deadline:* For fall admission, 8/1 for domestic students, 5/1 for international students; for winter admission, 11/15 for domestic students, 9/1 for international students; for spring admission, 3/15 for domestic students, 1/1 for international students; for summer admission, 5/15 for domestic students. Applications are processed on a rolling basis. Application fee: $55. Electronic applications accepted. *Expenses:* Contact institution. *Financial support:* Career-related internships or fieldwork, Federal Work-Study, and scholarships/grants available. Support available to part-time students. Financial award application deadline: 3/1; financial award applicants required to submit FAFSA. *Unit head:* Dr. Kim Sacks McManaway, Director, 810-766-6628, E-mail: kimsaks@umflint.edu. *Application contact:* Matt Bohlen, Director of Graduate Admissions, 810-762-3171, Fax: 810-766-6789, E-mail: mbohlen@umflint.edu.
Website: http://www.umflint.edu/graduateprograms/public-administration-mpa

University of Missouri, Office of Research and Graduate Studies, Harry S Truman School of Public Affairs, Columbia, MO 65211. Offers grantsmanship (Graduate Certificate); nonprofit management (Graduate Certificate); organizational change (Graduate Certificate); public affairs (MPA, PhD); public management (Graduate Certificate); science and public policy (Graduate Certificate). *Accreditation:* NASPAA. *Entrance requirements:* For master's, GRE General Test, minimum GPA of 3.0. Additional exam requirements/recommendations for international students: Required—TOEFL, IELTS. Electronic applications accepted.

University of Missouri–St. Louis, Graduate School, Program in Public Policy Administration, St. Louis, MO 63121. Offers local government management (MPPA, Certificate); nonprofit management and leadership (MPPA, Certificate); policy and program evaluation (MPPA, Certificate). *Accreditation:* NASPAA. *Program availability:* Part-time, evening/weekend. *Degree requirements:* For master's, exit project. *Entrance requirements:* For master's, 3 letters of recommendation, personal statement. Additional exam requirements/recommendations for international students: Recommended—TOEFL (minimum score 550 paper-based), IELTS (minimum score 6.5). Electronic applications accepted. *Faculty research:* Urban policy, public finance, evaluation.

University of Nevada, Las Vegas, Graduate College, Greenspun College of Urban Affairs, School of Public Policy and Leadership, Las Vegas, NV 89154-4030. Offers crisis and emergency management (MS); emergency crisis management cybersecurity (Certificate); environmental science (MS, PhD); non-profit management (Certificate); public administration (MPA); public affairs (PhD); public management (Certificate); urban leadership (MA). *Program availability:* Part-time. *Faculty:* 14 full-time (6 women), 11 part-time/adjunct (4 women). *Students:* 61 full-time (33 women), 113 part-time (74 women); includes 95 minority (29 Black or African American, non-Hispanic/Latino; 1 American Indian or Alaska Native, non-Hispanic/Latino; 9 Asian, non-Hispanic/Latino; 41 Hispanic/Latino; 3 Native Hawaiian or other Pacific Islander, non-Hispanic/Latino; 12 Two or more races, non-Hispanic/Latino), 2 international. Average age 37. 96 applicants, 68% accepted, 55 enrolled. In 2018, 59 master's, 6 doctorates, 19 other advanced degrees awarded. *Degree requirements:* For master's, comprehensive exam (for some programs), thesis (for some programs), oral exam; for doctorate, comprehensive exam, thesis/dissertation; for Certificate, portfolio. *Entrance requirements:* For master's, GRE General Test or GMAT, bachelor's degree with minimum GPA 2.75; statement of purpose; 3 letters of recommendation; for doctorate, GRE General Test, master's degree with minimum GPA of 3.5; 3 letters of recommendation; statement of purpose; writing sample; personal interview; for Certificate, bachelor's degree; 2 letters of recommendation; writing sample. Additional exam requirements/recommendations for international students: Required—TOEFL (minimum score 550 paper-based; 80 iBT), IELTS (minimum score 7). *Application deadline:* For fall admission, 6/1 for domestic and international students; for spring admission, 11/1 for domestic and international students; for summer admission, 3/1 for domestic students. Application fee: $60 ($95 for international students). Electronic applications accepted. *Expenses:* Contact institution. *Financial support:* In 2018–19, 23 students received support, including 8 research assistantships with full tuition reimbursements available (averaging $16,719 per year), 15 teaching assistantships with full tuition reimbursements available (averaging $13,500 per year); institutionally sponsored loans, scholarships/grants, health care benefits, and unspecified assistantships also available. Financial award application deadline: 3/15; financial award applicants required to submit FAFSA. *Total annual research expenditures:* $109,177. *Unit head:* Dr. Christopher Stream, Director, 702-895-5120, Fax: 702-895-4436, E-mail: sppl.chair@unlv.edu. *Application contact:* Dr. Jayce Farmer, Graduate Coordinator, 702-895-4828, E-mail: sppl.gradcoord@unlv.edu.
Website: https://www.unlv.edu/publicpolicy

Nonprofit Management

University of New Haven, Graduate School, Henry C. Lee College of Criminal Justice and Forensic Sciences, Program in Public Administration, West Haven, CT 06516. Offers fire and emergency medical services (MPA); municipal management (MPA); nonprofit organization management (MPA); public administration (MPA, Graduate Certificate); public finance (MPA); public safety (MPA). *Program availability:* Part-time, evening/weekend. *Students:* 20 full-time (10 women), 34 part-time (10 women); includes 14 minority (9 Black or African American, non-Hispanic/Latino; 1 Asian, non-Hispanic/Latino; 4 Hispanic/Latino), 5 international. Average age 33. 53 applicants, 85% accepted, 21 enrolled. In 2018, 21 master's, 1 other advanced degree awarded. *Entrance requirements:* Additional exam requirements/recommendations for international students: Required—TOEFL (minimum score 80 iBT), IELTS, PTE. *Application deadline:* Applications are processed on a rolling basis. Application fee: $50. Electronic applications accepted. Application fee is waived when completed online. *Expenses: Tuition:* Full-time $16,470; part-time $915 per credit hour. *Required fees:* $230; $95 per term. *Financial support:* Research assistantships with partial tuition reimbursements, teaching assistantships with partial tuition reimbursements, career-related internships or fieldwork, Federal Work-Study, scholarships/grants, and unspecified assistantships available. Support available to part-time students. Financial award application deadline: 5/1; financial award applicants required to submit FAFSA. *Unit head:* Dr. Christy Smith, Assistant Professor, 203-479-4193, E-mail: cdsmith@newhaven.edu. *Application contact:* Selina O'Toole, Senior Associate Director of Graduate Admissions, 203-932-7337, E-mail: SOToole@newhaven.edu.
Website: http://www.newhaven.edu/lee-college/graduate-programs/public-administration/

The University of North Carolina at Charlotte, College of Liberal Arts and Sciences, Department of Political Science and Public Administration, Charlotte, NC 28223-0001. Offers emergency management (Graduate Certificate); non-profit management (Graduate Certificate); public administration (MPA), including arts administration, emergency management, non-profit management, public budgeting and finance, urban management and policy; public budgeting and finance (Graduate Certificate); urban management and policy (Graduate Certificate). *Accreditation:* NASPAA. *Program availability:* Part-time, evening/weekend. *Students:* 25 full-time (16 women), 55 part-time (39 women); includes 27 minority (18 Black or African American, non-Hispanic/Latino; 1 American Indian or Alaska Native, non-Hispanic/Latino; 7 Hispanic/Latino; 1 Two or more races, non-Hispanic/Latino), 1 international. Average age 29. 45 applicants, 78% accepted, 25 enrolled. In 2018, 26 master's, 13 other advanced degrees awarded. *Entrance requirements:* For master's, GRE General Test, bachelor's degree, or its equivalent, from accredited college or university; minimum undergraduate GPA of 3.0; 3 letters of recommendation; statement of purpose; for Graduate Certificate, statement of purpose (1-2 pages in length) explaining applicant's career goals, how the Graduate Certificate fits into achieving those goals, and any relevant work experience; official transcripts; letters of recommendation. Additional exam requirements/recommendations for international students: Required—TOEFL (minimum score 523 paper-based; 70 iBT), IELTS (minimum score 6), TOEFL (minimum score 523 paper-based, 70 iBT) or IELTS (6). *Application deadline:* Applications are processed on a rolling basis. Application fee: $75. Electronic applications accepted. Tuition and fees vary according to course load and program. *Financial support:* Research assistantships, teaching assistantships, career-related internships or fieldwork, Federal Work-Study, institutionally sponsored loans, scholarships/grants, and unspecified assistantships available. Support available to part-time students. Financial award application deadline: 3/1; financial award applicants required to submit FAFSA. *Total annual research expenditures:* $660,034. *Unit head:* Dr. Greg Weeks, Chair, 704-687-7574, E-mail: gbweeks@uncc.edu. *Application contact:* Kathy B. Giddings, Director of Graduate Admissions, 704-687-5503, Fax: 704-687-1668, E-mail: gradadm@uncc.edu.
Website: http://politicalscience.uncc.edu/

The University of North Carolina at Greensboro, Graduate School, College of Arts and Sciences, Department of Political Science, Greensboro, NC 27412-5001. Offers nonprofit management (Certificate); public affairs (MPA); urban and economic development (Certificate). *Accreditation:* NASPAA. *Degree requirements:* For master's, comprehensive exam. *Entrance requirements:* For master's, GRE General Test. Additional exam requirements/recommendations for international students: Required—TOEFL. Electronic applications accepted. *Faculty research:* U.S. Constitution, Canadian parliament, public management, ethical challenge of public service.

University of Northern Iowa, Graduate College, MA Program in Philanthropy and Nonprofit Development, Cedar Falls, IA 50614. Offers MA. *Entrance requirements:* For master's, minimum GPA of 3.0; 3 letters of recommendation; experience in the philanthropy and/or nonprofit areas. Additional exam requirements/recommendations for international students: Required—TOEFL (minimum score 500 paper-based; 61 iBT). Electronic applications accepted.

University of North Florida, College of Arts and Sciences, Department of Political Science and Public Administration, Jacksonville, FL 32224. Offers nonprofit management (Graduate Certificate); public administration (MPA). *Accreditation:* NASPAA. *Program availability:* Part-time. *Faculty:* 11 full-time (5 women). *Students:* 22 full-time (13 women), 45 part-time (26 women); includes 18 minority (8 Black or African American, non-Hispanic/Latino; 2 Asian, non-Hispanic/Latino; 5 Hispanic/Latino; 3 Two or more races, non-Hispanic/Latino), 3 international. Average age 33. 49 applicants, 57% accepted, 17 enrolled. In 2018, 19 master's awarded. *Degree requirements:* For master's, thesis or alternative, internship. *Entrance requirements:* For master's, GRE General Test, minimum GPA of 3.0 in last 60 hours, 2 letters of recommendation, interview. Additional exam requirements/recommendations for international students: Required—TOEFL (minimum score 500 paper-based; 61 iBT). *Application deadline:* For fall admission, 8/1 priority date for domestic students, 5/1 for international students; for spring admission, 12/1 priority date for domestic students, 10/1 for international students; for summer admission, 3/15 priority date for domestic students, 2/1 for international students. Application fee: $30. Electronic applications accepted. *Expenses: Tuition, area resident:* Part-time $408.10 per credit hour. Tuition, state resident: part-time $408.10 per credit hour. Tuition, nonresident: part-time $932.61 per credit hour. *Required fees:* $111.81 per credit hour. Tuition and fees vary according to course load, campus/location and program. *Financial support:* In 2018–19, 10 students received support. Career-related internships or fieldwork, Federal Work-Study, scholarships/grants, tuition waivers (partial), and unspecified assistantships available. Financial award application deadline: 4/1; financial award applicants required to submit FAFSA. *Faculty research:* America's usage of the Internet, use of information communication technologies by educators and children. *Total annual research expenditures:* $392. *Unit head:* Dr. Matthew T. Corrigan, Chair, 904-620-2997, Fax: 904-620-2979, E-mail: mcorriga@unf.edu. *Application contact:* Dr. Amanda Pascale, Director, The Graduate School, 904-620-1360, Fax: 907-620-1362, E-mail: graduateschool@unf.edu.
Website: http://www.unf.edu/coas/pspa/

University of North Texas, Toulouse Graduate School, Denton, TX 76203-5459. Offers accounting (MS); applied anthropology (MA, MS); applied behavior analysis (Certificate); applied geography (MA); applied technology and performance improvement (M Ed, MS); art education (MA); art history (MA); arts leadership (Certificate); audiology (Au D); behavior analysis (MS); behavioral science (PhD); biochemistry and molecular biology (MS); biology (MA, MS); biomedical engineering (MS); business analysis (MS); chemistry (MS); clinical health psychology (PhD); communication studies (MA, MS); computer engineering (MS); computer science (MS); counseling (M Ed, MS), including clinical mental health counseling (MS), college and university counseling, elementary school counseling, secondary school counseling; creative writing (MA); criminal justice (MS); curriculum and instruction (M Ed); decision sciences (MBA); design (MA, MFA), including fashion design (MFA), innovation studies, interior design (MFA); early childhood studies (MS); economics (MS); educational leadership (M Ed, Ed D); educational psychology (MS, PhD), including family studies (MS), gifted and talented (MS), human development (MS), learning and cognition (MS), research, measurement and evaluation (MS); electrical engineering (MS); emergency management (MPA); engineering technology (MS); English (MA); English as a second language (MA); environmental science (MS); finance (MBA, MS); financial management (MPA); French (MA); health services management (MBA); higher education (M Ed, Ed D); history (MA, MS); hospitality management (MS); human resources management (MPA); information science (MS); information systems (PhD); information technologies (MBA); interdisciplinary studies (MA, MS); international studies (MA); international sustainable tourism (MS); jazz studies (MM); journalism (MA, MJ, Graduate Certificate), including interactive and virtual digital communication (Graduate Certificate), narrative journalism (Graduate Certificate), public relations (Graduate Certificate); kinesiology (MS); linguistics (MA); local government management (MPA); logistics (PhD); logistics and supply chain management (MBA); long-term care, senior housing, and aging services (MA); management (PhD); marketing (MBA); mathematics (MA, MS); mechanical and energy engineering (MS, PhD); music (MA), including ethnomusicology, music theory, musicology, performance; music composition (PhD); music education (MM Ed, PhD); nonprofit management (MPA); operations and supply chain management (MBA); performance (MM, DMA); philosophy (MA); political science (MA); professional and technical communication (MA); radio, television and film (MA, MFA); rehabilitation counseling (Certificate); sociology (MA); Spanish (MA); special education (M Ed); speech-language pathology (MA); strategic management (MBA); studio art (MFA); teaching (M Ed); MBA/MS. *Program availability:* Part-time, evening/weekend, online learning. Terminal master's awarded for partial completion of doctoral program. *Degree requirements:* For master's, variable foreign language requirement, comprehensive exam (for some programs), thesis (for some programs); for doctorate, variable foreign language requirement, comprehensive exam (for some programs), thesis/dissertation; for other advanced degree, variable foreign language requirement, comprehensive exam (for some programs). *Entrance requirements:* For master's and doctorate, GRE, GMAT. Additional exam requirements/recommendations for international students: Required—TOEFL (minimum score 550 paper-based; 79 iBT). Electronic applications accepted.

University of Notre Dame, Mendoza College of Business, Master in Nonprofit Administration Program, Notre Dame, IN 46556. Offers MNA. *Accreditation:* AACSB. *Program availability:* Part-time-only, blended/hybrid learning. *Degree requirements:* For master's, thesis. *Entrance requirements:* For master's, GRE General Test or GMAT (waiver available to qualifying applicants), minimum of two years' nonprofit work experience. Additional exam requirements/recommendations for international students: Required—TOEFL (minimum score 600 paper-based; 100 iBT), IELTS (minimum score 7). Electronic applications accepted. *Expenses:* Contact institution.

University of Oklahoma, College of Arts and Sciences, Department of Political Science, Norman, OK 73019-0390. Offers political science (MA, PhD); public administration (MPA), including general, nonprofit management, public management, public policy. *Faculty:* 31 full-time (12 women). *Students:* 52 full-time (27 women), 53 part-time (34 women); includes 35 minority (8 Black or African American, non-Hispanic/Latino; 3 American Indian or Alaska Native, non-Hispanic/Latino; 3 Asian, non-Hispanic/Latino; 13 Hispanic/Latino; 1 Native Hawaiian or other Pacific Islander, non-Hispanic/Latino; 7 Two or more races, non-Hispanic/Latino), 6 international. Average age 31. 65 applicants, 49% accepted, 22 enrolled. In 2018, 48 master's, 6 doctorates awarded. Terminal master's awarded for partial completion of doctoral program. *Degree requirements:* For master's, comprehensive exam, thesis optional, 36 hours; for doctorate, comprehensive exam, thesis/dissertation, 90 hours. *Entrance requirements:* For master's, GRE, purpose statement, writing sample, and three letters of recommendation (for MA); for doctorate, GRE, purpose statement, writing sample, three letters of recommendation. Additional exam requirements/recommendations for international students: Required—TOEFL (minimum score 100 iBT) or IELTS (minimum score 7.0). *Application deadline:* For fall admission, 2/1 priority date for domestic and international students. Application fee: $50 ($100 for international students). Electronic applications accepted. *Expenses:* Tuition, state resident: full-time $5683.20; part-time $236.80 per credit hour. Tuition, nonresident: full-time $20,342; part-time $847.60 per credit hour. *International tuition:* $20,342.40 full-time. *Required fees:* $2894.20; $110.05 per credit hour. $126.50 per semester. Tuition and fees vary according to course load and program. *Financial support:* Fellowships, research assistantships, teaching assistantships, scholarships/grants, health care benefits, unspecified assistantships, and travel and conference attendance funding available. Financial award application deadline: 6/1; financial award applicants required to submit FAFSA. *Faculty research:* American and comparative politics; public administration and policy; international relations; political theory and research methods. *Unit head:* Prof. Scott Robinson, Chair, 405-325-2061, Fax: 405-325-0718, E-mail: pscgradprog@ou.edu. *Application contact:* Jeff Alexander, Graduate Programs Coordinator, 405-325-1845, Fax: 405-325-0718, E-mail: pscgradprog@ou.edu.
Website: http://www.ou.edu/cas/psc/

University of Oklahoma, College of Professional and Continuing Studies, Norman, OK 73019. Offers administrative leadership (MA, Graduate Certificate), including government and military leadership (MA), organizational leadership (MA), volunteer and non-profit leadership (MA); corrections management (Graduate Certificate); criminal justice (MS); integrated studies (MA), including human and health services administration, integrated studies; museum studies (MA); prevention science (MPS); restorative justice administration (Graduate Certificate). *Program availability:* Part-time, 100% online, blended/hybrid learning. *Degree requirements:* For master's, comprehensive exam, thesis optional, 33 credit hours; project/internship (for museum studies program only); for Graduate Certificate, 12 graduate credit hours (for Graduate Certificate). *Entrance requirements:* For master's and Graduate Certificate, minimum GPA of 3.0 in last 60 undergraduate hours; statement of goals; resume. Additional exam requirements/recommendations for international students: Required—TOEFL (minimum score 79 iBT) or IELTS (minimum score 6.5). Electronic applications accepted. *Expenses:* Tuition, state resident: full-time $5683.20; part-time $236.80 per credit hour. Tuition, nonresident: full-time $20,342; part-time $847.60 per credit hour. *International tuition:* $20,342.40 full-time. *Required fees:* $2894.20; $110.05 per credit hour. $126.50 per semester. Tuition and fees vary according to course load and program. *Faculty research:* Change management and leadership; policing and corrections management; neuro-psychology of addiction; disproportionate minority contact; ethnic identity and nationalism.

University of Oregon, Graduate School, College of Design, School of Planning, Public Policy and Management, Program in Nonprofit Management, Eugene, OR 97403. Offers MNM, Graduate Certificate. *Degree requirements:* For master's, internship, project.

University of Pennsylvania, School of Arts and Sciences, Fels Institute of Government, Philadelphia, PA 19104. Offers economic development and growth (Certificate); government administration (MGA); nonprofit administration (Certificate); organization dynamics (MS); politics (Certificate); public administration (MPA); public finance (Certificate). *Program availability:* Part-time, evening/weekend. *Students:* 30 full-time (15 women), 60 part-time (33 women); includes 25 minority (4 Black or African American, non-Hispanic/Latino; 10 Asian, non-Hispanic/Latino; 8 Hispanic/Latino; 3 Two or more races, non-Hispanic/Latino), 4 international. Average age 32. 757 applicants, 41% accepted, 240 enrolled. In 2018, 48 master's, 10 other advanced degrees awarded. *Financial support:* Application deadline: 1/1.
Website: http://www.fels.upenn.edu/

University of Pittsburgh, Graduate School of Public and International Affairs, Master of Public Administration Program, Pittsburgh, PA 15260. Offers energy and environment (MPA); governance and international public management (MPA); policy research and analysis (MPA); public and nonprofit management (MPA); urban affairs and planning (MPA); JD/MPA; MPH/MPA; MSIS/MPA; MSW/MPA. *Accreditation:* NASPAA. *Program availability:* Part-time, evening/weekend. *Degree requirements:* For master's, thesis optional, capstone seminar. *Entrance requirements:* For master's, GRE General Test or GMAT, 2 letters of recommendation, resume, undergraduate transcripts, personal statement. Additional exam requirements/recommendations for international students: Required—TOEFL (minimum score 80 iBT); Recommended—IELTS (minimum score 7). Electronic applications accepted. *Expenses:* Contact institution. *Faculty research:* Urban affairs and planning, governance and international public management, public and nonprofit management, policy research and analysis, energy and environment.

University of Portland, Dr. Robert B. Pamplin, Jr. School of Business, Portland, OR 97203-5798. Offers entrepreneurship (MBA); finance (MBA, MS); health care management (MBA); marketing (MBA); nonprofit management (EMBA); operations and technology management (MBA, MS); sustainability (MBA). *Accreditation:* AACSB. *Program availability:* Part-time, evening/weekend. *Faculty:* 26 full-time (5 women), 8 part-time/adjunct (1 woman). *Students:* 35 full-time (16 women), 114 part-time (47 women); includes 21 minority (3 Black or African American, non-Hispanic/Latino; 2 American Indian or Alaska Native, non-Hispanic/Latino; 8 Asian, non-Hispanic/Latino; 8 Hispanic/Latino), 24 international. Average age 32. In 2018, 55 master's awarded. *Entrance requirements:* For master's, GMAT or GRE, minimum GPA of 3.0, resume, statement of goals, 2 letters of recommendation. Additional exam requirements/recommendations for international students: Required—TOEFL (minimum score 88 iBT), IELTS (minimum score 7). *Application deadline:* For fall admission, 7/19 priority date for domestic and international students; for spring admission, 12/7 priority date for domestic and international students; for summer admission, 4/12 priority date for domestic and international students. Applications are processed on a rolling basis. Application fee: $0. Electronic applications accepted. *Expenses:* Contact institution. *Financial support:* Application deadline: 3/1; applicants required to submit FAFSA. *Unit head:* Melissa McCarthy, Director, 503-943-7224, E-mail: mba-up@up.edu. *Application contact:* Melissa McCarthy, Director, 503-943-7224, E-mail: mba-up@up.edu.

University of San Diego, School of Leadership and Education Sciences, Department of Leadership Studies, San Diego, CA 92110-2492. Offers higher education leadership (MA); leadership studies (MA, PhD, Certificate); nonprofit leadership and management (MA). *Program availability:* Part-time, evening/weekend. *Faculty:* 8 full-time (3 women), 24 part-time/adjunct (11 women). *Students:* 46 full-time (28 women), 225 part-time (147 women); includes 124 minority (19 Black or African American, non-Hispanic/Latino; 25 Asian, non-Hispanic/Latino; 66 Hispanic/Latino; 14 Two or more races, non-Hispanic/Latino), 17 international. Average age 34. 299 applicants, 67% accepted, 105 enrolled. In 2018, 93 master's, 17 doctorates awarded. *Degree requirements:* For master's, thesis (for some programs), international experience; for doctorate, comprehensive exam, thesis/dissertation, international experience. *Entrance requirements:* For master's, GRE (recommended with GPA less than 3.25); for doctorate, GRE (less than 5 years old) strongly encouraged, master's degree, minimum GPA of 3.5 (graduate coursework), resume. Additional exam requirements/recommendations for international students: Required—TOEFL (minimum score 580 paper-based; 83 iBT), TWE. Application fee: $45. Electronic applications accepted. *Financial support:* In 2018–19, 190 students received support. Career-related internships or fieldwork, Federal Work-Study, institutionally sponsored loans, unspecified assistantships, and stipends available. Support available to part-time students. Financial award application deadline: 4/1; financial award applicants required to submit FAFSA. *Faculty research:* Higher education administration policy and relations, organizational leadership, nonprofits and philanthropy, student affairs leadership. *Unit head:* Dr. Lea Hubbard, Graduate Program Director, 619-260-7818, E-mail: lhubbard@sandiego.edu. *Application contact:* Erika Garwood, Associate Director of Graduate Admissions, 619-260-4524, Fax: 619-260-4158, E-mail: grads@sandiego.edu.
Website: https://www.sandiego.edu/soles/leadership-studies/

University of San Francisco, School of Management, Master of Nonprofit Administration Program, San Francisco, CA 94117. Offers MNA. *Program availability:* Part-time, evening/weekend. *Students:* 32 full-time (27 women), 3 part-time (all women); includes 17 minority (1 Black or African American, non-Hispanic/Latino; 3 Asian, non-Hispanic/Latino; 11 Hispanic/Latino; 2 Two or more races, non-Hispanic/Latino), 1 international. Average age 31. 48 applicants, 77% accepted, 20 enrolled. In 2018, 31 master's awarded. *Degree requirements:* For master's, thesis optional. *Entrance requirements:* For master's, resume demonstrating minimum of two years of professional work experience, transcripts from each college or university attended, two letters of recommendation, personal statement. Additional exam requirements/recommendations for international students: Required—TOEFL (minimum score 600 paper-based, 100 iBT), IELTS (minimum score 7) or PTE (minimum score 68). *Application deadline:* For fall admission, 6/5 for domestic students, 5/15 for international students. Application fee: $55. Electronic applications accepted. *Expenses:* Contact institution. *Financial support:* Scholarships/grants available. Financial award application deadline: 3/2; financial award applicants required to submit FAFSA. *Faculty research:* Philanthropy in ethnic communities. *Unit head:* Dr. Marco Tavanti, Director, 415-422-2221, E-mail: management@usfca.edu. *Application contact:* Office of Graduate Recruiting and Admissions, 415-422-2221, E-mail: management@usfca.edu.
Website: http://www.usfca.edu/mna

University of Southern California, Graduate School, Sol Price School of Public Policy, Master of Public Administration Program, Los Angeles, CA 90089. Offers nonprofit management and policy (Graduate Certificate); political management (Graduate Certificate); public administration (MPA); public management (Graduate Certificate); MPA/JD; MPA/M PI; MPA/MA; MPA/MAJCS; MPA/MS; MPA/MSW. *Accreditation:* NASPAA (one or more programs are accredited). *Program availability:* Part-time, evening/weekend, online learning. Terminal master's awarded for partial completion of doctoral program. *Degree requirements:* For master's, capstone, internship. *Entrance requirements:* For master's, GRE, GMAT. Additional exam requirements/recommendations for international students: Required—TOEFL (minimum score 600 paper-based; 100 iBT). Electronic applications accepted. *Faculty research:* Collaborative governance and decision-making, nonprofit management, environmental management, institutional analysis, local government, civic engagement.

University of Southern Indiana, Graduate Studies, College of Liberal Arts, Program in Public Administration, Evansville, IN 47712-3590. Offers nonprofit administration (MPA); public sector administration (MPA). *Program availability:* Part-time, evening/weekend. *Entrance requirements:* For master's, resume, 2 letters of reference, personal statement, minimum GPA of 3.0. Additional exam requirements/recommendations for international students: Required—TOEFL (minimum score 550 paper-based; 79 iBT), IELTS (minimum score 6). Electronic applications accepted.

University of South Florida, Innovative Education, Tampa, FL 33620-9951. Offers adult, career and higher education (Graduate Certificate), including college teaching, leadership in developing human resources, leadership in higher education; Africana studies (Graduate Certificate), including diasporas and health disparities, genocide and human rights; aging studies (Graduate Certificate), including gerontology; art research (Graduate Certificate), including museum studies; business foundations (Graduate Certificate); chemical and biomedical engineering (Graduate Certificate), including materials science and engineering, water, health and sustainability; child and family studies (Graduate Certificate), including positive behavior support; civil and industrial engineering (Graduate Certificate), including transportation systems analysis; community and family health (Graduate Certificate), including maternal and child health, social marketing and public health, violence and injury: prevention and intervention, women's health; criminology (Graduate Certificate), including criminal justice administration; data science for public administration (Graduate Certificate); digital humanities (Graduate Certificate); educational measurement and research (Graduate Certificate), including evaluation; English (Graduate Certificate), including comparative literary studies, creative writing, professional and technical communication; entrepreneurship (Graduate Certificate); environmental health (Graduate Certificate), including safety management; epidemiology and biostatistics (Graduate Certificate), including applied biostatistics, biostatistics, concepts and tools of epidemiology, epidemiology, epidemiology of infectious diseases; geography, environment and planning (Graduate Certificate), including community development, environmental policy and management, geographical information systems; geology (Graduate Certificate), including hydrogeology; global health (Graduate Certificate), including disaster management, global health and Latin American and Caribbean studies, global health practice, humanitarian assistance, infection control; government and international affairs (Graduate Certificate), including Cuban studies, globalization studies; health policy and management (Graduate Certificate), including health management and leadership, public health policy and programs; hearing specialist: early intervention (Graduate Certificate); industrial and management systems engineering (Graduate Certificate), including systems engineering, technology management; information studies (Graduate Certificate), including school library media specialist; information systems/decision sciences (Graduate Certificate), including analytics and business intelligence; instructional technology (Graduate Certificate), including distance education, Florida digital/virtual educator, instructional design, multimedia design, Web design; internal medicine, bioethics and medical humanities (Graduate Certificate), including biomedical ethics; Latin American and Caribbean studies (Graduate Certificate); leadership for coastal resiliency planning (Graduate Certificate); mass communications (Graduate Certificate), including multimedia journalism; mathematics and statistics (Graduate Certificate), including mathematics; medicine (Graduate Certificate), including aging and neuroscience, bioinformatics, biotechnology, brain fitness and memory management, clinical investigation, hand and upper limb rehabilitation, health informatics, health sciences, integrative weight management, intellectual property, medicine and gender, metabolic and nutritional medicine, metabolic cardiology, pharmacy sciences; national and competitive intelligence (Graduate Certificate); nursing (Graduate Certificate), including simulation based academic fellowship in advanced pain management; psychological and social foundations (Graduate Certificate), including career counseling, college teaching, diversity in education, mental health counseling, school counseling; public affairs (Graduate Certificate), including nonprofit management, public management, research administration; public health (Graduate Certificate), including assessing chemical toxicity and public health risks, health equity, pharmacoepidemiology, public health generalist, toxicology, translational research in adolescent behavioral health; public health practices (Graduate Certificate), including planning for healthy communities; rehabilitation and mental health counseling (Graduate Certificate), including integrative mental health care, marriage and family therapy, rehabilitation technology; secondary education (Graduate Certificate), including ESOL, foreign language education: culture and content, foreign language education: professional; social work (Graduate Certificate), including geriatric social work/clinical gerontology; special education (Graduate Certificate), including autism spectrum disorder, disabilities education: severe/profound; world languages (Graduate Certificate), including teaching English as a second language (TESL) or foreign language. *Expenses:* Tuition, state resident: full-time $6350. Tuition, nonresident: full-time $19,048. *International tuition:* $19,048 full-time. *Required fees:* $2079. *Unit head:* Dr. Cynthia DeLuca, Associate Vice President and Assistant Vice Provost, 813-974-3077, Fax: 813-974-7061, E-mail: deluca@usf.edu. *Application contact:* Owen Hooper, Director, Summer and Alternative Calendar Programs, 813-974-6917, E-mail: hooper@usf.edu.
Website: http://www.usf.edu/innovative-education/

The University of Tampa, Sykes College of Business, Tampa, FL 33606-1490. Offers accounting (MS); business analytics (MBA); cybersecurity (MBA, MS); entrepreneurship (MBA, MS); finance (MBA, MS); information systems management (MBA); innovation management (MBA); international business (MBA); marketing (MBA, MS); nonprofit management (MBA, Certificate). *Accreditation:* AACSB. *Program availability:* Part-time, evening/weekend. *Faculty:* 61 full-time (13 women), 11 part-time/adjunct (3 women). *Students:* 361 full-time (153 women), 122 part-time (52 women); includes 101 minority (31 Black or African American, non-Hispanic/Latino; 5 Asian, non-Hispanic/Latino; 57 Hispanic/Latino; 1 Native Hawaiian or other Pacific Islander, non-Hispanic/Latino; 7 Two or more races, non-Hispanic/Latino), 144 international. Average age 29. 1,079 applicants, 57% accepted, 263 enrolled. In 2018, 281 master's, 12 other advanced degrees awarded. *Degree requirements:* For master's, capstone. *Entrance requirements:* For master's, GMAT or GRE, official transcripts from all colleges and/or universities previously attended, resume, personal statement, letters of recommendation. Additional exam requirements/recommendations for international students: Required—TOEFL (minimum score 577 paper-based; 90 iBT), IELTS (minimum score 7.5). *Application deadline:* Applications are processed on a rolling basis. Application fee: $40. Electronic applications accepted. *Expenses:* Contact institution. *Financial support:* In 2018–19, 123 students received support. Career-related internships or fieldwork, scholarships/grants, and unspecified assistantships available. Financial award applicants required to submit FAFSA. *Faculty research:* Job market signaling, on-line shopping behaviors and social media, the Tampa Bay economy, digital literacy, entrepreneurship in small businesses. *Unit head:* Dr. Natasha F. Veltri, Associate Dean, 813-253-6289, E-mail: nveltri@ut.edu. *Application contact:* Ashley Russell, Staff Assistant, Admissions for Graduate and Continuing Studies, 813-253-6249, E-mail: arussell@ut.edu.
Website: http://www.ut.edu/business/

The University of Tennessee at Chattanooga, Department of Political Science and Public Service, Chattanooga, TN 37403. Offers local government management (MPA);

non-profit management (MPA); public administration (MPA); public administration and non-profit management (Postbaccalaureate Certificate). *Program availability:* Part-time, evening/weekend. *Degree requirements:* For master's, comprehensive exam, thesis or alternative, internship. *Entrance requirements:* For master's, GRE General Test; for Postbaccalaureate Certificate, bachelor's degree with related experience or master's degree. Additional exam requirements/recommendations for international students: Required—TOEFL (minimum score 550 paper-based; 79 iBT), IELTS (minimum score 6). Electronic applications accepted. *Expenses:* Contact institution. *Faculty research:* Organizational cultures and renewal, management theory, public policy, policy analysis, nonprofit organization.

The University of Texas at Dallas, School of Economic, Political and Policy Sciences, Program in Public and Nonprofit Management, Richardson, TX 75080. Offers applied sociology (MS); public affairs (MPA, PhD). *Accreditation:* NASPAA. *Program availability:* Part-time, evening/weekend. *Faculty:* 12 full-time (5 women), 3 part-time/adjunct (1 woman). *Students:* 30 full-time (18 women), 63 part-time (39 women); includes 45 minority (19 Black or African American, non-Hispanic/Latino; 1 American Indian or Alaska Native, non-Hispanic/Latino; 6 Asian, non-Hispanic/Latino; 15 Hispanic/Latino; 4 Two or more races, non-Hispanic/Latino), 10 international. Average age 38. 47 applicants, 66% accepted, 15 enrolled. In 2018, 29 master's, 4 doctorates awarded. *Degree requirements:* For master's, internship; for doctorate, thesis/dissertation. *Entrance requirements:* For master's and doctorate, GRE (minimum combined score of 1000 on verbal and quantitative), minimum GPA of 3.0 in upper-level course work in field. Additional exam requirements/recommendations for international students: Required—TOEFL (minimum score 550 paper-based). *Application deadline:* For fall admission, 7/15 for domestic students, 5/1 priority date for international students; for spring admission, 11/15 for domestic students, 9/1 priority date for international students. Applications are processed on a rolling basis. Application fee: $50 ($100 for international students). Electronic applications accepted. *Expenses: Tuition, area resident:* Full-time $13,458. Tuition, state resident: full-time $13,458. Tuition, nonresident: full-time $26,852. *International tuition:* $26,852 full-time. Tuition and fees vary according to course load. *Financial support:* In 2018–19, 8 students received support, including 1 research assistantship with partial tuition reimbursement available (averaging $18,000 per year), 8 teaching assistantships with partial tuition reimbursements available (averaging $13,500 per year); career-related internships or fieldwork, Federal Work-Study, institutionally sponsored loans, and scholarships/grants also available. Support available to part-time students. Financial award application deadline: 4/30; financial award applicants required to submit FAFSA. *Faculty research:* Corporate citizenship and urban problem solving, policy analysis, presidential decision-making, hazardous material safety, emergency management. *Unit head:* Dr. Meghna Sabharwal, Program Head, 972-883-6473, Fax: 972-883-2735, E-mail: ph.pnm@utdallas.edu. *Application contact:* Rita Medford, Graduate Program Administrator, 972-883-4932, Fax: 972-883-2735, E-mail: medford@utdallas.edu.
Website: https://epps.utdallas.edu/about/programs/public-and-nonprofit-management/

University of the Sacred Heart, Graduate Programs, Program in Nonprofit Organization Administration, San Juan, PR 00914-0383. Offers MBA.

University of the West, Department of Business Administration, Rosemead, CA 91770. Offers business administration (EMBA); computer information systems (MBA); finance (MBA); international business (MBA); nonprofit organization management (MBA). *Program availability:* Part-time, evening/weekend. *Entrance requirements:* Additional exam requirements/recommendations for international students: Required—TOEFL.

The University of Toledo, College of Graduate Studies, College of Languages, Literature and Social Sciences, Department of Political Science and Public Administration, Toledo, OH 43606-3390. Offers health care policy and administration (Certificate); management of non-profit organizations (Certificate); municipal administration (Certificate); political science (MA); public administration (MPA); JD/MPA. *Program availability:* Part-time. *Degree requirements:* For master's, comprehensive exam (for some programs), thesis. *Entrance requirements:* For master's, GRE General Test, minimum cumulative point-hour ratio of 2.7 (3.0 for MPA) for all previous academic work, three letters of recommendation, statement of purpose, transcripts from all prior institutions attended; for Certificate, minimum cumulative point-hour ratio of 2.7 for all previous academic work, three letters of recommendation, statement of purpose, transcripts from all prior institutions attended. Additional exam requirements/recommendations for international students: Required—TOEFL (minimum score 550 paper-based; 80 iBT). Electronic applications accepted. *Faculty research:* Economic development, health care, Third World, criminal justice, Eastern Europe.

University of West Georgia, College of Social Sciences, Carrollton, GA 30118. Offers criminology (MA); data analysis and evaluation methods (Postbaccalaureate Certificate); European Union studies (Postbaccalaureate Certificate); integrative health systems (Postbaccalaureate Certificate); nonprofit management and community development (Postbaccalaureate Certificate); psychology (MA, PhD), including consciousness and society (PhD); public administration (MPA); public management (Postbaccalaureate Certificate); sociology (MA). *Program availability:* Part-time, evening/weekend, 100% online, blended/hybrid learning. *Faculty:* 48 full-time (22 women). *Students:* 105 full-time (68 women), 69 part-time (41 women); includes 66 minority (55 Black or African American, non-Hispanic/Latino; 1 Asian, non-Hispanic/Latino; 6 Hispanic/Latino; 4 Two or more races, non-Hispanic/Latino), 7 international. Average age 32. 97 applicants, 75% accepted, 57 enrolled. In 2018, 50 master's, 7 doctorates, 10 other advanced degrees awarded. *Entrance requirements:* Additional exam requirements/recommendations for international students: Required—TOEFL (minimum score 523 paper-based; 69 iBT); Recommended—IELTS (minimum score 6.5). *Application deadline:* For fall admission, 7/15 for domestic students, 6/1 for international students; for spring admission, 11/30 for domestic students, 10/15 for international students; for summer admission, 5/15 for domestic students, 3/30 for international students. Applications are processed on a rolling basis. Application fee: $40. Electronic applications accepted. Tuition and fees vary according to course load, degree level, campus/location and program. *Financial support:* Fellowships, research assistantships, teaching assistantships, career-related internships or fieldwork, Federal Work-Study, institutionally sponsored loans, scholarships/grants, and unspecified assistantships available. Support available to part-time students. Financial award application deadline: 4/1; financial award applicants required to submit FAFSA. *Unit head:* Dr. Amber Smallwood, Interim Dean of Social Sciences, 678-839-5170, Fax: 678-839-5171, E-mail: amksmall@westga.edu. *Application contact:* Dr. Toby Ziglar, Assistant Dean of the Graduate School, 678-839-1394, Fax: 678-839-1395, E-mail: graduate@westga.edu.
Website: https://www.westga.edu/coss

University of Wisconsin–Milwaukee, Graduate School, College of Letters and Science, Department of Public and Nonprofit Administration, Milwaukee, WI 53201-0413. Offers public administration (MPA), including general public administration, municipal management, non-profit management. *Program availability:* Part-time. *Students:* 19 full-time (8 women), 9 part-time (4 women); includes 6 minority (1 Black or African American, non-Hispanic/Latino; 3 Asian, non-Hispanic/Latino; 1 Hispanic/Latino; 1 Two or more races, non-Hispanic/Latino), 1 international. Average age 29. 22 applicants, 45% accepted, 8 enrolled. In 2018, 13 master's awarded. *Entrance requirements:* For master's, GRE General Test, minimum GPA of 3.0. Additional exam requirements/recommendations for international students: Required—TOEFL (minimum score 550 paper-based; 79 iBT), IELTS (minimum score 6.5). *Application deadline:* For fall admission, 1/1 priority date for domestic students; for spring admission, 9/1 for domestic students. Application fee: $56 ($96 for international students). Electronic applications accepted. *Financial support:* Fellowships, research assistantships, teaching assistantships, career-related internships or fieldwork, health care benefits, and unspecified assistantships available. Support available to part-time students. Financial award application deadline: 4/15; financial award applicants required to submit FAFSA. *Unit head:* Douglas Ihrke, Department Chair, 414-229-4732, E-mail: dihrke@uwm.edu. *Application contact:* General Information Contact, 414-229-4982, Fax: 414-229-6967, E-mail: gradschool@uwm.edu.
Website: https://uwm.edu/public-nonprofit-administration/

University of Wisconsin–Milwaukee, Graduate School, Helen Bader School of Social Welfare, Department of Social Work, Milwaukee, WI 53201-0413. Offers applied gerontology (Graduate Certificate); nonprofit management (Graduate Certificate); social welfare (PhD); social work (MSW, PhD). *Program availability:* Part-time. *Students:* 224 full-time (196 women), 92 part-time (82 women); includes 101 minority (47 Black or African American, non-Hispanic/Latino; 5 American Indian or Alaska Native, non-Hispanic/Latino; 12 Asian, non-Hispanic/Latino; 2 Hispanic/Latino; 35 Two or more races, non-Hispanic/Latino), 3 international. Average age 31. 387 applicants, 59% accepted, 180 enrolled. In 2018, 86 master's, 1 other advanced degree awarded. *Entrance requirements:* For doctorate, GRE, bachelor's degree. Additional exam requirements/recommendations for international students: Required—TOEFL (minimum score 550 paper-based; 79 iBT), IELTS (minimum score 6.5). *Application deadline:* For fall admission, 1/1 priority date for domestic students; for spring admission, 9/1 for domestic students. Application fee: $56 ($96 for international students). Electronic applications accepted. *Financial support:* Fellowships, research assistantships, teaching assistantships, career-related internships or fieldwork, health care benefits, unspecified assistantships, and project assistantships available. Support available to part-time students. Financial award application deadline: 4/15; financial award applicants required to submit FAFSA. *Application contact:* Deb Padgett, Associate Professor, Social Work, 414-229-6452, E-mail: dpadgett@uwm.edu.
Website: http://uwm.edu/socialwelfare/academics/

University of Wisconsin–Milwaukee, Graduate School, Lubar School of Business, Other Business Programs, Milwaukee, WI 53201-0413. Offers business analytics (Graduate Certificate); enterprise resource planning (Graduate Certificate); information technology management (MS); investment management (Graduate Certificate); nonprofit management (Graduate Certificate); nonprofit management and leadership (MS); state and local taxation (Graduate Certificate). *Students:* 132 full-time (63 women), 120 part-time (58 women); includes 45 minority (11 Black or African American, non-Hispanic/Latino; 15 Asian, non-Hispanic/Latino; 4 Hispanic/Latino; 15 Two or more races, non-Hispanic/Latino), 52 international. Average age 31. 196 applicants, 63% accepted, 80 enrolled. In 2018, 108 master's, 18 other advanced degrees awarded. *Entrance requirements:* Additional exam requirements/recommendations for international students: Required—TOEFL (minimum score 550 paper-based; 79 iBT), IELTS (minimum score 6.5). Application fee: $56 ($96 for international students). Electronic applications accepted. *Financial support:* Fellowships, research assistantships, teaching assistantships, health care benefits, unspecified assistantships, and project assistantships available. Financial award applicants required to submit FAFSA. *Application contact:* General Information Contact, 414-229-4982, Fax: 414-229-6967, E-mail: gradschool@uwm.edu.

Upper Iowa University, Online Master's Programs, Fayette, IA 52142-1857. Offers accounting (MBA); corporate financial management (MBA); emergency management and homeland security (MPA); general management (MBA); general studies (MPA); government administration (MPA); health and human services (MPA); human resources management (MBA); nonprofit organizational management (MPA); organizational development (MBA); public management (MPA); sport administration (MSA). MBA also available at Madison, WI campus. *Program availability:* Part-time, online learning. *Degree requirements:* For master's, research project. *Entrance requirements:* For master's, GMAT, GRE, or minimum GPA of 2.7 during last 60 hours. Additional exam requirements/recommendations for international students: Required—TOEFL (minimum score 570 paper-based). Electronic applications accepted. *Faculty research:* Total quality management, teams, organization culture and climate, management.

Villanova University, Graduate School of Liberal Arts and Sciences, Department of Public Administration, Villanova, PA 19085-1699. Offers city management (Certificate); nonprofit management (Certificate); public administration (MPA, Certificate). *Accreditation:* NASPAA. *Program availability:* Part-time, evening/weekend, 100% online. *Degree requirements:* For master's, comprehensive exam. *Entrance requirements:* For master's, GRE General Test, minimum GPA of 3.0, statement of goals, 3 letters of recommendation. Additional exam requirements/recommendations for international students: Required—TOEFL. Electronic applications accepted.

Virginia Commonwealth University, Graduate School, College of Humanities and Sciences, Program in Nonprofit Management, Richmond, VA 23284-9005. Offers Graduate Certificate. *Program availability:* Part-time. *Entrance requirements:* Additional exam requirements/recommendations for international students: Required—TOEFL (minimum score 600 paper-based; 100 iBT); Recommended—IELTS (minimum score 6.5). Electronic applications accepted.

Virginia Polytechnic Institute and State University, VT Online, Blacksburg, VA 24061. Offers advanced transportation systems (Certificate); aerospace engineering (MS); agricultural and life sciences (MSLFS); business information systems (Graduate Certificate); career and technical education (MS); civil engineering (MS); computer engineering (M Eng, MS); decision support systems (Graduate Certificate); eLearning leadership (MA); electrical engineering (M Eng, MS); engineering administration (MEA); environmental engineering (Certificate); environmental politics and policy (Graduate Certificate); environmental sciences and engineering (MS); foundations of political analysis (Graduate Certificate); health product risk management (Graduate Certificate); industrial and systems engineering (MS); information policy and society (Graduate Certificate); information security (Graduate Certificate); information technology (MIT); instructional technology (MA); integrative STEM education (MA Ed); liberal arts (Graduate Certificate); life sciences: health product risk management (MS); natural resources (MNR, Graduate Certificate); networking (Graduate Certificate); nonprofit and nongovernmental organization management (Graduate Certificate); ocean engineering (MS); political science (MA); security studies (Graduate Certificate); software development (Graduate Certificate). *Expenses:* Tuition, state resident: full-time $15,510; part-time $739.50 per credit hour. Tuition, nonresident: full-time $29,629; part-time $1490.25 per credit hour. *Required fees:* $2804; $550 per semester. Tuition and fees vary according to course load, campus/location and program. *Application contact:* Graduate Admissions and Academic Progress, 540-231-8636, E-mail: grads@vt.edu.
Website: http://www.vto.vt.edu/

Walden University, Graduate Programs, School of Public Policy and Administration, Minneapolis, MN 55401. Offers criminal justice (MPA, MPP, MS, Graduate Certificate), including emergency management (MS, PhD), general program (MS), global leadership

(MS, PhD), homeland security and policy coordination (MS, PhD), law and public policy (MS, PhD), policy analysis (MS, PhD), public management and leadership (MS, PhD), self-designed (MS), terrorism, mediation, and peace (MS, PhD); criminal justice and executive management (MS), including global leadership (MS, PhD); criminal justice leadership and executive management (MS), including emergency management (MS, PhD), general program, homeland security and policy coordination (MS, PhD), law and public policy (MS, PhD), policy analysis (MS, PhD), public management and leadership (MS, PhD), self-designed, terrorism, mediation, and peace (MS, PhD); emergency management (MPA, MPP, MS), including criminal justice (MS, PhD), general program (MS), homeland security (MS), public management and leadership (MS, PhD), terrorism and emergency management (MS); general program (MPA, MPP); global leadership (MPA, MPP); government management (Graduate Certificate); health policy (MPA, MPP); homeland security (Graduate Certificate); homeland security and policy coordination (MPA, MPP); international nongovernmental organizations (MPA, MPP); law and public policy (MPA, MPP); local government management for sustainable communities (MPA, MPP); nonprofit management (Graduate Certificate); nonprofit management and leadership (MPA, MPP, MS), including global leadership (MS, PhD); international nongovernmental organization (MS), local government for sustainable communities (MS), self-designed (MS); online teaching in higher education (Post-Master's Certificate); policy analysis (MPA); public management and leadership (MPA, MPP, Graduate Certificate); public policy (Graduate Certificate); public policy and administration (PhD), including criminal justice (MS, PhD), emergency management (MS, PhD), global leadership (MS, PhD), health policy, homeland security and policy coordination (MS, PhD), international nongovernmental organizations, law and public policy (MS, PhD), local government management for sustainable communities, nonprofit management and leadership, policy analysis (MS, PhD), public management and leadership (MS, PhD), terrorism, mediation, and peace (MS, PhD); strategic planning and public policy (Graduate Certificate); terrorism, mediation, and peace (MPA, MPP). *Program availability:* Part-time, evening/weekend, online only, 100% online. *Degree requirements:* For doctorate, thesis/dissertation, residency. *Entrance requirements:* For master's, bachelor's degree or higher; minimum GPA of 2.5; official transcripts; goal statement (for some programs); access to computer and Internet; for doctorate, master's degree or higher; three years of related professional or academic experience (preferred); minimum GPA of 3.0; goal statement and current resume (for select programs); official transcripts; access to computer and Internet; for other advanced degree, relevant work experience; access to computer and Internet. Additional exam requirements/recommendations for international students: Required—TOEFL (minimum score 550 paper-based, 79 iBT), IELTS (minimum score 6.5), Michigan English Language Assessment Battery (minimum score 82), or PTE (minimum score 53). Electronic applications accepted.

Walden University, Graduate Programs, School of Social Work and Human Services, Minneapolis, MN 55401. Offers addictions and social work (DSW); advanced clinical practice (MSW); clinical expertise (DSW); criminal justice (DSW); disaster, crisis, and intervention (DSW); family studies and interventions (DSW); human and social services (PhD), including advanced research, community and social services, community intervention and leadership, conflict management, criminal justice, disaster crisis and intervention, family studies and intervention, gerontology, global social services, higher education, human services and nonprofit administration, mental health facilitation; medical social work (DSW); military social work (MSW); policy practice (DSW); social work (PhD), including addictions and social work, clinical expertise, criminal justice, disaster, crisis and intervention, family studies and interventions, medical social work, policy practice, social work administration; social work administration (DSW); social work in healthcare (MSW); social work with children and families (MSW). *Accreditation:* CSWE. *Program availability:* Part-time, evening/weekend, online only, 100% online. *Degree requirements:* For master's, residency (for some programs); for doctorate, thesis/dissertation, residency. *Entrance requirements:* For master's, bachelor's degree or higher; minimum GPA of 2.5; official transcripts; goal statement (for some programs); access to computer and Internet; for doctorate, master's degree or higher; three years of related professional or academic experience (preferred); minimum GPA of 3.0; goal statement and current resume (for select programs); official transcripts; access to computer and Internet. Additional exam requirements/recommendations for international students: Required—TOEFL (minimum score 550 paper-based, 79 iBT), IELTS (minimum score 6.5), Michigan English Language Assessment Battery (minimum score 82), or PTE (minimum score 53). Electronic applications accepted.

Warner Pacific University, Graduate Programs, Portland, OR 97215-4099. Offers human services (MA); not-for-profit leadership (MS); organizational leadership (MS); teaching (MAT). *Program availability:* Part-time, evening/weekend. *Degree requirements:* For master's, thesis or alternative, presentation of defense. *Entrance requirements:* For master's, interview, minimum GPA of 2.5, letters of recommendation. *Faculty research:* New Testament studies, nineteenth-century Wesleyan theology, preaching and church growth, Christian ethics.

Wayne State University, College of Liberal Arts and Sciences, Department of Political Science, Detroit, MI 48202. Offers political science (MA, PhD); public administration (MPA), including economic development policy and management, health and human services policy and management, human and fiscal resource management, nonprofit policy and management, organizational behavior and management, urban and metropolitan policy and management; JD/MA. *Accreditation:* NASPAA. *Faculty:* 18. *Students:* 61 full-time (26 women), 51 part-time (27 women); includes 31 minority (22 Black or African American, non-Hispanic/Latino; 3 Asian, non-Hispanic/Latino; 1 Hispanic/Latino; 5 Two or more races, non-Hispanic/Latino), 12 international. Average age 32. 103 applicants, 39% accepted, 20 enrolled. In 2018, 32 master's, 5 doctorates awarded. *Degree requirements:* For master's, comprehensive exam (for some programs), thesis (for some programs); for doctorate, thesis/dissertation. *Entrance requirements:* For master's, GRE General Test, substantial undergraduate preparation in the social sciences, minimum upper-division undergraduate GPA of 3.0, two letters of recommendation, personal statement; for doctorate, GRE General Test, 3 letters of recommendation; personal statement; interview. Additional exam requirements/recommendations for international students: Required—TOEFL (minimum score 550

paper-based; 79 iBT), TWE (minimum score 5.5), Michigan English Language Assessment Battery (minimum score 85); Recommended—IELTS (minimum score 6.5). *Application deadline:* For fall admission, 5/15 for domestic students, 5/1 priority date for international students; for winter admission, 10/15 for domestic students, 9/1 priority date for international students. Applications are processed on a rolling basis. Application fee: $50. Electronic applications accepted. *Expenses:* Contact institution. *Financial support:* In 2018–19, 46 students received support, including 4 fellowships with tuition reimbursements available (averaging $17,000 per year), 1 research assistantship with tuition reimbursement available (averaging $23,119 per year), 12 teaching assistantships with tuition reimbursements available (averaging $19,267 per year); scholarships/grants, health care benefits, and unspecified assistantships also available. Financial award applicants required to submit FAFSA. *Faculty research:* American government and politics, comparative politics, political methodology, political theory, public administration, public law, public policy, world politics/international relations, formal theory/modeling, gender and politics, international law, peace research, political economy, political psychology, politics of developing countries, race, religion, and ethnicity, urban politics. *Unit head:* Dr. Daniel Geller, Professor and Chair, 313-577-6328, E-mail: dgeller@wayne.edu. *Application contact:* Dr. Sharon Lean, Graduate Director, 313-577-2630, E-mail: gradpolisci@wayne.edu.
Website: http://clas.wayne.edu/politicalscience/

Webster University, George Herbert Walker School of Business and Technology, Department of Management, St. Louis, MO 63119-3194. Offers business and organizational security management (MA); digital marketing management (Graduate Certificate); government contracting (Graduate Certificate); health administration (MHA); health care management (MA); health services management (MA); human resources development (MA); human resources management (MA); information technology management (MA, MS); management (D Mgt); management and leadership (MA); marketing (MA); nonprofit leadership (MA); nonprofit revenue development (Graduate Certificate); organizational development (Graduate Certificate); procurement and acquisitions management (MA); public administration (MPA); space systems operations management (MS). *Program availability:* Part-time, evening/weekend, online learning. *Degree requirements:* For master's, thesis (for some programs); for doctorate, thesis/dissertation, written exam. *Entrance requirements:* For doctorate, GMAT, 3 years of work experience, MBA. Additional exam requirements/recommendations for international students: Required—TOEFL. *Expenses: Tuition:* Full-time $22,500; part-time $750 per credit hour. Tuition and fees vary according to degree level, campus/location and program.

West Chester University of Pennsylvania, College of Business and Public Management, Department of Public Policy and Administration, West Chester, PA 19383. Offers administration (Certificate); non-profit administration (Certificate); nonprofit administration (MPA); public administration (MPA); public policy and administration (MPA, DPA). *Accreditation:* NASPAA. *Program availability:* Part-time, evening/weekend, 100% online. Terminal master's awarded for partial completion of doctoral program. *Degree requirements:* For master's, capstone project. *Entrance requirements:* For master's, statement of professional goals, resume, two letters of reference, academic transcripts. Additional exam requirements/recommendations for international students: Required—TOEFL or IELTS. Electronic applications accepted. *Faculty research:* Public policy, economic development, research methodology, public administration, nonprofit administration.

Western Michigan University, Graduate College, College of Arts and Sciences, School of Public Affairs and Administration, Kalamazoo, MI 49008. Offers health care administration (MPA, Graduate Certificate); nonprofit leadership and administration (Graduate Certificate); public administration (PhD). *Accreditation:* NASPAA (one or more programs are accredited). *Degree requirements:* For doctorate, thesis/dissertation.

Westfield State University, College of Graduate and Continuing Education, Department of Political Science, Westfield, MA 01086. Offers criminal justice administration (MPA); non-profit management (MPA); public management (MPA). *Program availability:* Part-time, evening/weekend. *Degree requirements:* For master's, comprehensive exam, thesis (for some programs). *Entrance requirements:* For master's, GRE General Test or MAT, minimum undergraduate GPA of 2.8. Additional exam requirements/recommendations for international students: Recommended—TOEFL (minimum score 550 paper-based; 79 iBT).

Worcester State University, Graduate School, Program in Non-Profit Management, Worcester, MA 01602-2597. Offers MS. *Program availability:* Part-time, evening/weekend. *Faculty:* 2 full-time (1 woman). *Students:* 1 full-time (0 women), 9 part-time (6 women). Average age 40. 9 applicants, 100% accepted, 6 enrolled. In 2018, 1 master's awarded. *Degree requirements:* For master's, comprehensive exam (for some programs), thesis, For a detail list in Degree Completion requirements please see the graduate catalog at catalog.worcester.edu. *Entrance requirements:* For master's, GRE General Test or MAT, For a detail list of entrance requirements please see the graduate catalog at catalog.worcester.edu. Additional exam requirements/recommendations for international students: Required—TOEFL (minimum score 550 paper-based; 79 iBT), IELTS (minimum score 6). *Application deadline:* For fall admission, 3/1 for domestic and international students; for spring admission, 11/1 for domestic and international students; for summer admission, 3/1 for domestic and international students. Applications are processed on a rolling basis. Application fee: $50. Electronic applications accepted. *Expenses: Tuition, area resident:* Full-time $3042; part-time $169 per credit hour. Tuition, state resident: full-time $3042; part-time $169 per credit hour. Tuition, nonresident: full-time $3042; part-time $169 per credit hour. *International tuition:* $3042 full-time. *Required fees:* $2754; $153 per credit hour. *Financial support:* Career-related internships or fieldwork, scholarships/grants, and unspecified assistantships available. Financial award application deadline: 3/1; financial award applicants required to submit FAFSA. *Unit head:* Dr. Shiko Gathuo, Program Coordinator, 508-929-8892, Fax: 508-929-8144, E-mail: agathuo@worcester.edu. *Application contact:* Sara Grady, Associate Dean, Graduate Studies and Professional Development, 508-929-8130, Fax: 508-929-8100, E-mail: sara.grady@worcester.edu.

Section 16
Organizational Studies

This section contains a directory of institutions offering graduate work in organizational studies. Additional information about programs listed in the directory but not augmented by an in-depth entry may be obtained by writing directly to the dean of a graduate school or chair of a department at the address given in the directory.

For programs offering related work, see also in this book *Business Administration and Management, Human Resources,* and *Industrial and Manufacturing Management.* In another guide in this series:

Graduate Programs in the Humanities, Arts & Social Sciences
See *Communication and Media* and *Public, Regional, and Industrial Affairs*

CONTENTS

Program Directories

Organizational Behavior

Argosy University, Chicago, Illinois School of Professional Psychology, Doctoral Program in Clinical Psychology, Chicago, IL 60601. Offers child and adolescent psychology (Psy D); client-centered and experiential psychotherapies (Psy D); diversity and multicultural psychology (Psy D); family psychology (Psy D); forensic psychology (Psy D); health psychology (Psy D); neuropsychology (Psy D); organizational consulting (Psy D); psychoanalytic psychology (Psy D); psychology and spirituality (Psy D). *Accreditation:* APA.

Arizona State University at the Tempe campus, W. P. Carey School of Business, Program in Business Administration, Tempe, AZ 85287-4906. Offers entrepreneurship (MBA); finance (MBA); health sector management (MBA); international business (MBA); leadership (MBA); marketing (MBA); organizational behavior (PhD); strategic management (PhD); supply chain management (MBA, PhD); JD/MBA; MBA/M Acc; MBA/M Arch. *Accreditation:* AACSB. *Program availability:* Part-time, evening/weekend, online learning. Terminal master's awarded for partial completion of doctoral program. *Degree requirements:* For master's, thesis or alternative, internship, interactive Program of Study (iPOS) submitted before completing 50 percent of required credit hours; for doctorate, comprehensive exam, thesis/dissertation, interactive Program of Study (iPOS) submitted before completing 50 percent of required credit hours. *Entrance requirements:* For master's, GMAT, minimum GPA of 3.0 in last 2 years of work leading to bachelor's degree, 2 letters of recommendation, professional resume, official transcripts, 3 essays; for doctorate, GMAT or GRE, minimum GPA of 3.0 in last 2 years of work leading to bachelor's degree, 3 letters of recommendation, resume, personal statement/essay. Additional exam requirements/recommendations for international students: Required—TOEFL (minimum score 550 paper-based; 80 iBT), IELTS (minimum score 6.5). Electronic applications accepted. *Expenses:* Contact institution.

A.T. Still University, College of Graduate Health Studies, Kirksville, MO 63501. Offers dental public health (MPH); exercise and sport psychology (Certificate); fundamentals of education (Certificate); geriatric exercise science (Certificate); global health (Certificate); health administration (MHA, DHA); health professions (Ed D); health sciences (DH Sc); kinesiology (MS); leadership and organizational behavior (Certificate); public health (MPH); sports conditioning (Certificate). *Accreditation:* CEPH. *Program availability:* Part-time, evening/weekend, online only, 100% online, blended/hybrid learning. *Faculty:* 50 full-time (38 women), 95 part-time/adjunct (57 women). *Students:* 600 full-time (388 women), 512 part-time (306 women); includes 448 minority (185 Black or African American, non-Hispanic/Latino; 14 American Indian or Alaska Native, non-Hispanic/Latino; 108 Asian, non-Hispanic/Latino; 111 Hispanic/Latino; 1 Native Hawaiian or other Pacific Islander, non-Hispanic/Latino; 29 Two or more races, non-Hispanic/Latino), 31 international. Average age 35. 386 applicants, 82% accepted, 279 enrolled. In 2018, 141 master's, 111 doctorates, 112 other advanced degrees awarded. *Degree requirements:* For master's, thesis, integrated terminal project, practicum; for doctorate, thesis/dissertation. *Entrance requirements:* For master's, minimum GPA of 2.5, bachelor's degree or equivalent, essay, resume, English proficiency; for doctorate, minimum GPA of 2.5, master's or terminal degree, essay, past experience in relevant field, resume, English proficiency. Additional exam requirements/recommendations for international students: Required—TOEFL (minimum score 550 paper-based; 80 iBT). *Application deadline:* For fall admission, 6/25 for domestic and international students; for winter admission, 9/10 for domestic and international students; for spring admission, 12/10 for domestic and international students; for summer admission, 3/4 for domestic and international students. Applications are processed on a rolling basis. Application fee: $70. Electronic applications accepted. *Financial support:* In 2018–19, 8 students received support. Scholarships/grants available. Financial award applicants required to submit FAFSA. *Faculty research:* Public health: influence of availability of comprehensive wellness, resources online, student wellness, oral health care needs assessment of community, oral health knowledge and behaviors of Medicaid-eligible pregnant women and mothers of young children in relations to early childhood caries and tooth decay, alcohol use and alcohol related problems among college students. *Unit head:* Dr. Donald Altman, Dean, 480-219-6008, Fax: 660-626-2826, E-mail: daltman@atsu.edu. *Application contact:* Amie Waldemer, Associate Director, Online Admissions, 480-219-6146, E-mail: awaldemer@atsu.edu.
Website: http://www.atsu.edu/college-of-graduate-health-studies

Baruch College of the City University of New York, Zicklin School of Business, Department of Management, New York, NY 10010-5585. Offers entrepreneurship (MBA); management (PhD); operations management (MBA); organizational behavior/human resources management (MBA); sustainable business (MBA). PhD offered jointly with Graduate School and University Center of the City University of New York. *Program availability:* Part-time, evening/weekend. *Degree requirements:* For doctorate, comprehensive exam, thesis/dissertation. *Entrance requirements:* For master's, GMAT, 2 letters of recommendation, resume, 2 years of work experience; for doctorate, GMAT. Additional exam requirements/recommendations for international students: Required—TOEFL (minimum score 590 paper-based), TWE.

Benedictine University, Graduate Programs, Program in Management and Organizational Behavior, Lisle, IL 60532. Offers MS, PhD, MBA/MS, MPH/MS. *Program availability:* Part-time, evening/weekend, 100% online. *Faculty:* 3 full-time (2 women), 15 part-time/adjunct (6 women). *Students:* 19 full-time (14 women), 73 part-time (53 women); includes 20 minority (11 Black or African American, non-Hispanic/Latino; 1 Asian, non-Hispanic/Latino; 7 Hispanic/Latino; 1 Native Hawaiian or other Pacific Islander, non-Hispanic/Latino), 3 international. Average age 35. 32 applicants, 81% accepted, 24 enrolled. In 2018, 35 master's awarded. *Entrance requirements:* For master's, GMAT or GRE test scores or completed test waiver form, official transcripts; 2 letters of reference from individuals familiar with the applicant's professional or academic work, excluding family or personal friends; a 1-2 page essay addressing educational and career goals; résumé; personal interview may be required prior to an admission decision. Additional exam requirements/recommendations for international students: Required—TOEFL (minimum score 550 paper-based; 79 iBT), IELTS (minimum score 6.5). *Application deadline:* Applications are processed on a rolling basis. Application fee: $40. Electronic applications accepted. *Unit head:* Dr. Peter F. Sorensen, Director, 630-829-6222, E-mail: psorensen@ben.edu. *Application contact:* Dr. Peter F. Sorensen, Director, 630-829-6222, E-mail: psorensen@ben.edu.

Boston College, Carroll School of Management, Department of Management and Organization, Chestnut Hill, MA 02467-3800. Offers PhD. *Degree requirements:* For doctorate, comprehensive exam, thesis/dissertation, teaching experience. *Entrance requirements:* For doctorate, GMAT or GRE, letters of recommendation, resume, transcripts. Additional exam requirements/recommendations for international students: Required—TOEFL (minimum score 100 iBT), IELTS (minimum score 7.5), or PTE (minimum score 68). Electronic applications accepted. *Faculty research:* Organizational transformation, mergers and acquisitions, managerial effectiveness, organizational change, organizational structure.

Brooklyn College of the City University of New York, School of Natural and Behavioral Sciences, Department of Psychology, Brooklyn, NY 11210-2889. Offers experimental psychology (MA); industrial and organizational psychology (MA), including human relations, organizational behavior; mental health counseling (MA); psychology (PhD). *Program availability:* Part-time. *Degree requirements:* For master's, comprehensive exam, thesis (for some programs). *Entrance requirements:* For master's, minimum GPA of 3.0, 2 letters of recommendation, essay; for doctorate, GRE. Additional exam requirements/recommendations for international students: Required—TOEFL (minimum score 520 paper-based; 69 iBT). Electronic applications accepted.

California State University, East Bay, Office of Graduate Studies, College of Business and Economics, MBA Program, Option in Human Resources and Organizational Behavior, Hayward, CA 94542-3000. Offers MBA. *Program availability:* Part-time, evening/weekend. *Degree requirements:* For master's, comprehensive exam or thesis. *Entrance requirements:* For master's, GMAT, minimum GPA of 2.75. Additional exam requirements/recommendations for international students: Required—TOEFL (minimum score 550 paper-based). Electronic applications accepted.

Carnegie Mellon University, Dietrich College of Humanities and Social Sciences, Department of Social and Decision Sciences, Pittsburgh, PA 15213-3891. Offers behavioral decision research (PhD); social and decision science (PhD); strategy, entrepreneurship, and technological change (PhD). Terminal master's awarded for partial completion of doctoral program. *Degree requirements:* For doctorate, comprehensive exam, thesis/dissertation, research paper. *Entrance requirements:* For doctorate, GRE General Test. Additional exam requirements/recommendations for international students: Required—TOEFL. Electronic applications accepted. *Faculty research:* Organization theory, political science, sociology, technology studies.

Carnegie Mellon University, Tepper School of Business, Organizational Behavior and Theory Program, Pittsburgh, PA 15213-3891. Offers PhD. *Degree requirements:* For doctorate, thesis/dissertation. *Entrance requirements:* For doctorate, GMAT or GRE General Test. Additional exam requirements/recommendations for international students: Required—TOEFL. *Faculty research:* Negotiation, organizational learning, interorganizational relations and strategy, group process and performance, communication process and electronic media, group goal setting, uncertainty in organizations, creation and effect of institutions and psychological contracts.

Case Western Reserve University, Weatherhead School of Management, Department of Organizational Behavior, Cleveland, OH 44106. Offers organizational behavior (PhD); positive organization development and change (MS). *Program availability:* Part-time, evening/weekend. *Degree requirements:* For doctorate, thesis/dissertation. *Entrance requirements:* For master's and doctorate, GMAT. *Expenses: Tuition:* Full-time $45,168; part-time $1939 per credit hour. *Required fees:* $36; $18 per semester. $18 per semester. *Faculty research:* Social innovation in global management, competency-based learning, life-long learning, organizational theory, organizational change.

Clemson University, Graduate School, College of Business, Department of Management, Clemson, SC 29634. Offers business administration (PhD), including management information systems, strategy, entrepreneurship and organizational behavior, supply chain and operations management; management (MS). *Accreditation:* AACSB. *Faculty:* 26 full-time (9 women). *Students:* 14 full-time (5 women), 4 part-time (2 women); includes 1 minority (Asian, non-Hispanic/Latino), 10 international. Average age 30. 53 applicants, 36% accepted, 8 enrolled. In 2018, 2 master's, 4 doctorates awarded. Terminal master's awarded for partial completion of doctoral program. *Degree requirements:* For master's, comprehensive exam, thesis optional; for doctorate, comprehensive exam, thesis/dissertation. *Entrance requirements:* For master's and doctorate, GMAT or GRE General Test, unofficial transcripts, two letters of reference, curriculum vitae. Additional exam requirements/recommendations for international students: Required—TOEFL (minimum score 80 paper-based; 94 iBT); Recommended—IELTS (minimum score 7), TSE (minimum score 64). *Application deadline:* For fall admission, 4/15 priority date for international students; for spring admission, 10/15 priority date for international students. Applications are processed on a rolling basis. Application fee: $80 ($90 for international students). Electronic applications accepted. *Expenses:* $6823 per semester full-time resident, $14023 per semester full-time non-resident, $833 per credit hour part-time resident, $1731 per credit hour part-time non-resident, online $1264 per credit hour, $4938 doctoral programs resident, $10405 doctoral programs non-resident, $1144 full-time graduate assistant, other fees may apply per session. *Financial support:* In 2018–19, 10 students received support, including 1 fellowship with full and partial tuition reimbursement available (averaging $1,500 per year), 6 research assistantships with full and partial tuition reimbursements available (averaging $25,000 per year), 17 teaching assistantships with full and partial tuition reimbursements available (averaging $25,000 per year); career-related internships or fieldwork and unspecified assistantships also available. *Faculty research:* Effective use of information technology in business, manufacturing and service operations strategy, lean operations and quality management, healthcare operations, behavioral market design. *Total annual research expenditures:* $131,333. *Unit head:* Dr. Craig Wallace, Department Chair, 864-656-9963, E-mail: CW74@clemson.edu. *Application contact:* Dr. Janis Miller, Graduate Program Coordinator, 864-656-3757, E-mail: janism@clemson.edu.
Website: https://www.clemson.edu/business/departments/management/

Cornell University, Graduate School, Graduate Field of Management, Ithaca, NY 14853. Offers accounting (PhD); finance (PhD); marketing (PhD); organizational behavior (PhD); production and operations management (PhD). *Accreditation:* AACSB. *Degree requirements:* For doctorate, comprehensive exam, thesis/dissertation. *Entrance requirements:* For doctorate, GMAT or GRE General Test. Additional exam requirements/recommendations for international students: Required—TOEFL (minimum score 600 paper-based; 77 iBT). Electronic applications accepted. *Expenses:* Contact institution. *Faculty research:* Operations and manufacturing.

Cornell University, Graduate School, Graduate Fields of Industrial and Labor Relations, Ithaca, NY 14853. Offers collective bargaining, labor law and labor history (MILR, MPS, MS, PhD); economic and social statistics (MILR); human resource studies (MILR, MPS, MS, PhD); industrial and labor relations problems (MILR, MPS, MS, PhD); international and comparative labor (MILR, MPS, MS, PhD); labor economics (MILR, MPS, MS, PhD); organizational behavior (MILR, MPS, MS, PhD). *Degree requirements:* For master's, thesis (MS); for doctorate, comprehensive exam, thesis/dissertation, teaching experience. *Entrance requirements:* For master's and doctorate, GMAT or GRE General Test, 2 academic recommendations. Additional exam requirements/recommendations for international students: Required—TOEFL (minimum score 550 paper-based; 77 iBT). Electronic applications accepted. *Expenses:* Contact institution.

Drexel University, LeBow College of Business, Program in Business Administration, Philadelphia, PA 19104-2875. Offers business administration (MBA, PhD, APC),

including accounting (MBA, PhD), decision sciences (PhD), economics (MBA, PhD), finance (MBA, PhD), legal studies (MBA), management (MBA), marketing (MBA, PhD), organizational sciences (PhD), quantitative methods (MBA), strategic management (PhD). *Accreditation:* AACSB. *Program availability:* Part-time, evening/weekend, online learning. Terminal master's awarded for partial completion of doctoral program. *Entrance requirements:* For master's, GMAT, minimum GPA of 2.75; for doctorate, GMAT. Additional exam requirements/recommendations for international students: Required—TOEFL. Electronic applications accepted. *Faculty research:* Decision support systems, individual and group behavior, operations research, techniques and strategy.

Fairleigh Dickinson University, Florham Campus, Maxwell Becton College of Arts and Sciences, Department of Psychology, Program in Organizational Behavior, Madison, NJ 07940-1099. Offers organizational behavior (MA); organizational leadership (Certificate).

Florida State University, The Graduate School, College of Business, Tallahassee, FL 32306-1110. Offers accounting (M Acc), including assurance and advisory services, generalist, taxation; business administration (MBA, PhD), including accounting (PhD), finance (PhD), management information systems (PhD), marketing (PhD), organizational behavior and human resources (PhD), risk management and insurance (PhD), strategy (PhD); finance (MS); management information systems (MS); risk management and insurance (MS); JD/MBA; MSW/MBA. *Accreditation:* AACSB. *Program availability:* Part-time, 100% online. *Students:* Average age 31. 300 applicants, 61% accepted, 133 enrolled. In 2018, 268 master's, 9 doctorates awarded. Terminal master's awarded for partial completion of doctoral program. *Degree requirements:* For doctorate, comprehensive exam, thesis/dissertation. *Entrance requirements:* For master's, GMAT, GRE (for all except MS in finance), work experience (MBA, MS), minimum GPA of 3.0, letters of recommendation; for doctorate, GMAT, GRE (for marketing, organizational behavior, risk management and insurance, management information systems, and human resources only), minimum graduate GPA of 3.5, letters of recommendation. Additional exam requirements/recommendations for international students: Required—TOEFL (minimum score 600 paper-based; 85 iBT); Recommended—IELTS (minimum score 6). *Application deadline:* For fall admission, 6/1 for domestic and international students; for spring admission, 10/1 for domestic and international students; for summer admission, 3/1 for domestic and international students. Applications are processed on a rolling basis. Application fee: $30. Electronic applications accepted. *Expenses:* Contact institution. *Financial support:* In 2018–19, 146 students received support, including 26 fellowships (averaging $1,500 per year), 77 research assistantships with full tuition reimbursements available (averaging $20,000 per year), 43 teaching assistantships with full tuition reimbursements available (averaging $20,000 per year); career-related internships or fieldwork, scholarships/grants, health care benefits, tuition waivers (full and partial), and unspecified assistantships also available. Support available to part-time students. Financial award application deadline: 1/1; financial award applicants required to submit FAFSA. *Faculty research:* Business strategy, marketing, finance, accounting, business analytics. *Total annual research expenditures:* $1.4 million. *Unit head:* Dr. Michael Hartline, Dean, 850-644-4405, Fax: 850-644-0915, E-mail: mhartline@business.fsu.edu. *Application contact:* Jennifer Clark, Director, 850-644-6458, E-mail: gradprograms@business.fsu.edu.
Website: http://business.fsu.edu/

The Graduate Center, City University of New York, Graduate Studies, Program in Business, New York, NY 10016-4039. Offers accounting (PhD); behavioral science (PhD); finance (PhD); management planning systems (PhD). *Degree requirements:* For doctorate, thesis/dissertation. *Entrance requirements:* For doctorate, GMAT, writing sample (15 pages). Additional exam requirements/recommendations for international students: Required—TOEFL. Electronic applications accepted.

Hampton University, School of Liberal Arts and Education, Program in Sport Administration, Hampton, VA 23668. Offers intercollegiate athletics (MS); international sports (MS); organizational behavior and sport business leadership (MS). *Program availability:* Part-time, evening/weekend. *Students:* 32 full-time (12 women), 3 part-time (1 woman); all minorities (all Black or African American, non-Hispanic/Latino). Average age 25. 20 applicants, 90% accepted, 12 enrolled. In 2018, 17 master's awarded. *Degree requirements:* For master's, thesis (for some programs). *Entrance requirements:* For master's, GRE. Additional exam requirements/recommendations for international students: Required—TOEFL (minimum score 525 paper-based) or IELTS (6.5). *Application deadline:* For fall admission, 6/1 priority date for domestic students, 4/1 priority date for international students; for spring admission, 11/1 priority date for domestic students, 9/1 priority date for international students; for summer admission, 4/1 priority date for domestic students, 2/1 priority date for international students. Applications are processed on a rolling basis. Application fee: $35. Electronic applications accepted. *Expenses:* Contact institution. *Financial support:* Fellowships, research assistantships, teaching assistantships, and career-related internships or fieldwork available. Financial award application deadline: 6/30; financial award applicants required to submit FAFSA. *Faculty research:* International sport, intercollegiate sport, sport leadership, professional sport, event management. *Unit head:* Dr. Aaron Livingston, Program Coordinator, 757-637-2278, E-mail: aaron.livingston@hamptonu.edu. *Application contact:* Dr. Aaron Livingston, Program Coordinator, 757-637-2278, E-mail: aaron.livingston@hamptonu.edu.

Harvard University, Graduate School of Arts and Sciences and Harvard Business School, Committee on Organizational Behavior, Cambridge, MA 02138. Offers PhD. *Entrance requirements:* For doctorate, GRE General Test or GMAT, major in psychology or sociology, course work in statistics or mathematics. Additional exam requirements/recommendations for international students: Required—TOEFL.

Harvard University, Harvard Business School, Doctoral Programs in Management, Boston, MA 02163. Offers accounting and management (DBA); business economics (PhD); health policy management (PhD); management (DBA); marketing (DBA); organizational behavior (PhD); science, technology and management (PhD); strategy (DBA); technology and operations management (DBA). *Degree requirements:* For doctorate, comprehensive exam (for some programs), thesis/dissertation. *Entrance requirements:* For doctorate, GRE General Test or GMAT. Additional exam requirements/recommendations for international students: Required—TOEFL.

International Institute for Restorative Practices, Graduate Programs, Bethlehem, PA 18018. Offers MS, Certificate. *Program availability:* Online learning. *Faculty:* 5 full-time (4 women), 5 part-time/adjunct (2 women). *Students:* 1 (woman) full-time, 66 part-time (49 women). *Expenses:* Contact institution. *Financial support:* Institutionally sponsored loans and scholarships/grants available. *Application contact:* Jamie Kaintz, Registrar, 610-807-9221, E-mail: registrar@iirp.edu.

John Jay College of Criminal Justice of the City University of New York, Graduate Studies, Programs in Criminal Justice, New York, NY 10019. Offers criminal justice (MA, PhD); criminology and deviance (PhD); forensic psychology (PhD); forensic science (PhD); international crime and justice (MA); law and philosophy (PhD); organizational behavior (PhD); public policy (PhD). *Program availability:* Part-time, evening/weekend. Terminal master's awarded for partial completion of doctoral program. *Degree*

requirements: For master's, thesis or alternative; for doctorate, one foreign language, thesis/dissertation. *Entrance requirements:* For master's, GRE General Test, minimum B average; for doctorate, GRE General Test. Additional exam requirements/recommendations for international students: Required—TOEFL (minimum score 500 paper-based).

Lake Forest Graduate School of Management, The Leadership MBA Program, Lake Forest, IL 60045. Offers finance (MBA); global business (MBA); healthcare management (MBA); management (MBA); marketing (MBA); organizational behavior (MBA). *Program availability:* Part-time, evening/weekend. *Entrance requirements:* For master's, 4 years of work experience in field, interview, 2 letters of recommendation. Electronic applications accepted.

New York University, Leonard N. Stern School of Business, Department of Management and Organizations, New York, NY 10012-1019. Offers management organizations (MBA); organization theory (PhD); organizational behavior (PhD); strategy (PhD). *Faculty research:* Strategic management, managerial cognition, interpersonal processes, conflict and negotiation.

Northwestern University, The Graduate School, School of Education and Social Policy, Program in Learning and Organizational Change, Evanston, IL 60208. Offers MS. *Program availability:* Part-time, evening/weekend, online learning. *Degree requirements:* For master's, thesis, practicum. *Entrance requirements:* For master's, GRE or GMAT (recommended), letters of recommendation. Additional exam requirements/recommendations for international students: Required—TOEFL (minimum score 600 paper-based; 100 iBT); Recommended—IELTS (minimum score 7). Electronic applications accepted. *Faculty research:* Strategic change, learning and performance, workplace learning, leadership development, cognitive design, knowledge management.

Phillips Graduate University, Doctoral Program in Organizational Management and Consulting, Chatsworth, CA 91311. Offers Psy D. *Program availability:* Evening/weekend. *Degree requirements:* For doctorate, thesis/dissertation. *Entrance requirements:* For doctorate, minimum GPA of 3.0, interview. Electronic applications accepted.

Purdue University, Graduate School, Krannert School of Management, Doctoral Program in Organizational Behavior and Human Resource Management, West Lafayette, IN 47907-2056. Offers PhD. *Degree requirements:* For doctorate, comprehensive exam, thesis/dissertation, dissertation proposal, dissertation defense. *Entrance requirements:* For doctorate, GMAT or GRE, bachelor's degree, two semesters of calculus, one semester each of linear algebra and statistics. Additional exam requirements/recommendations for international students: Required—TOEFL (minimum score 575 paper-based); Recommended—TWE. Electronic applications accepted. *Faculty research:* Human resource management, organizational behavior.

Queen's University at Kingston, Smith School of Business, Doctoral Program in Management, Kingston, ON K7L 3N6, Canada. Offers analytics (PhD); business economics (PhD); finance (PhD); management information systems (PhD); marketing (PhD); organizational behavior (PhD); strategy (PhD).

Queen's University at Kingston, Smith School of Business, Master of Science in Management Program, Kingston, ON K7L 3N6, Canada. Offers analytics (M Sc); business economics (M Sc); finance (M Sc); management information systems (M Sc); marketing (M Sc); organizational behavior (M Sc); strategy (M Sc).

Saybrook University, School of Organizational Leadership and Transformation, San Francisco, CA 94612. Offers MA. Program offered jointly with Bastyr University. *Degree requirements:* For master's, thesis (for some programs), oral exams. *Entrance requirements:* For master's, bachelor's degree from an accredited college or university. *Faculty research:* Cross-functional work teams, communication, management authority, employee influence, systems theory.

Saybrook University, School of Psychology and Interdisciplinary Inquiry, San Francisco, CA 94612. Offers human science (MA, PhD), including consciousness and spirituality, humanistic and transpersonal psychology, integrative health studies, organizational systems, social transformation; organizational systems (MA, PhD), including consciousness and spirituality, humanistic and transpersonal psychology, integrative health studies, leadership of sustainable systems (MA), organizational systems, social transformation; psychology (MA, PhD), including consciousness and spirituality, creativity studies (MA), humanistic and transpersonal psychology, integrative health studies, Jungian studies, marriage and family therapy (MA), organizational systems, social transformation. *Program availability:* Online learning. Terminal master's awarded for partial completion of doctoral program. *Degree requirements:* For master's, thesis or alternative; for doctorate, thesis/dissertation. *Entrance requirements:* Additional exam requirements/recommendations for international students: Required—TOEFL (minimum score 580 paper-based; 93 iBT). Electronic applications accepted. *Faculty research:* Humanistic theory, health studies, organizational systems, consciousness and spirituality, social transformation.

Suffolk University, Sawyer Business School, Master of Business Administration Program, Boston, MA 02108-2770. Offers accounting (MBA); entrepreneurship (MBA); executive business administration (EMBA); finance (MBA); global business administration (GMBA); health administration (MBA); international business (MBA); marketing (MBA); nonprofit management (MBA); organizational behavior (MBA); strategic management (MBA); supply chain management (MBA); taxation (MBA); JD/MBA; MBA/MHA; MBA/MSA; MBA/MSF; MBA/MST. *Accreditation:* AACSB. *Program availability:* Part-time, evening/weekend, 100% online. *Faculty:* 18 full-time (5 women), 5 part-time/adjunct (0 women). *Students:* 79 full-time (46 women), 193 part-time (107 women); includes 69 minority (17 Black or African American, non-Hispanic/Latino; 18 Asian, non-Hispanic/Latino; 28 Hispanic/Latino; 6 Two or more races, non-Hispanic/Latino), 40 international. Average age 30. 274 applicants, 67% accepted, 83 enrolled. In 2018, 125 master's awarded. *Entrance requirements:* For master's, GMAT, minimum undergraduate GPA of 2.75 (MBA), 5 years of managerial experience (EMBA). Additional exam requirements/recommendations for international students: Required—TOEFL (minimum score 550 paper-based; 80 iBT). *Application deadline:* For fall admission, 3/15 priority date for domestic students, 10/15 priority date for international students; for spring admission, 10/15 priority date for domestic and international students. Applications are processed on a rolling basis. Application fee: $50. Electronic applications accepted. *Expenses:* Contact institution. *Financial support:* In 2018–19, 170 students received support, including 4 fellowships (averaging $2,906 per year); career-related internships or fieldwork, Federal Work-Study, institutionally sponsored loans, and scholarships/grants also available. Support available to part-time students. Financial award application deadline: 4/1; financial award applicants required to submit FAFSA. *Faculty research:* Foreign investments; career strategies and boundaryless careers; corporate ethics codes; interest rates, inflation, and growth options; innovation and product development performance. *Unit head:* Jodi Detjen, Director of MBA Programs, 617-573-8306, E-mail: jdetjen@suffolk.edu. *Application contact:* Mara Marzocchi, Associate Director of Graduate Admissions, 617-573-8302, Fax: 617-305-1733, E-mail: grad.admission@suffolk.edu.
Website: http://www.suffolk.edu/mba

Organizational Behavior

Universidad de las Americas, A.C., Program in International Organizations and Institutions, Mexico City, Mexico. Offers MA.

Université de Sherbrooke, Faculty of Administration, Program in Organizational Change and Intervention, Sherbrooke, QC J1K 2R1, Canada. Offers M Sc. *Degree requirements:* For master's, one foreign language, thesis. *Entrance requirements:* For master's, bachelor's degree in related field, minimum GPA of 3.0 (on 4.3 scale). Electronic applications accepted. *Faculty research:* Organizational change, organizational communication, process approaches and qualitative research, organizational behavior.

University at Albany, State University of New York, Nelson A. Rockefeller College of Public Affairs and Policy, Department of Public Administration and Policy, Albany, NY 12222-0001. Offers financial management and public economics (MPA); financial market regulation (MPA); health policy (MPA); healthcare management (MPA); homeland security (MPA); human resources management (MPA); information strategy and management (MPA); local government management (MPA); nonprofit management (MPA); nonprofit management and leadership (Certificate); organizational behavior and theory (MPA, PhD); planning and policy analysis (CAS); policy analysis (MPA); politics and administration (PhD); public finance (PhD); public management (PhD); public policy (PhD); public sector management (Certificate); women and public policy (Certificate); JD/MPA. JD/MPA offered jointly with Albany Law School. *Accreditation:* NASPAA (one or more programs are accredited). *Faculty:* 24 full-time (10 women), 19 part-time/adjunct (10 women). *Students:* 117 full-time (62 women), 101 part-time (58 women); includes 56 minority (20 Black or African American, non-Hispanic/Latino; 8 Asian, non-Hispanic/Latino; 20 Hispanic/Latino; 8 Two or more races, non-Hispanic/Latino), 28 international. 236 applicants, 69% accepted, 86 enrolled. In 2018, 57 master's, 1 doctorate, 14 other advanced degrees awarded. *Degree requirements:* For doctorate, one foreign language, thesis/dissertation. *Entrance requirements:* For doctorate, GRE General Test. Additional exam requirements/recommendations for international students: Required—TOEFL (minimum score 550 paper-based). *Application deadline:* For fall admission, 2/1 priority date for domestic students, 5/1 for international students; for spring admission, 12/1 for domestic students. Applications are processed on a rolling basis. Application fee: $75. Electronic applications accepted. *Financial support:* Application deadline: 2/1. *Unit head:* Victor Asal, Chair, 518-591-8729, E-mail: vasal@albany.edu. *Application contact:* Victor Asal, Chair, 518-591-8729, E-mail: vasal@albany.edu.
Website: http://www.albany.edu/rockefeller/pad.shtml

The University of British Columbia, Sauder School of Business, Doctoral Program in Business Administration, Vancouver, BC V6T 1Z2, Canada. Offers accounting (PhD); finance (PhD); management information systems (PhD); management science (PhD); marketing (PhD); organizational behavior (PhD); strategy and business economics (PhD); transportation and logistics (PhD); urban land economics (PhD). *Degree requirements:* For doctorate, comprehensive exam, thesis/dissertation. *Entrance requirements:* For doctorate, GMAT or GRE. Additional exam requirements/recommendations for international students: Required—TOEFL (minimum score 600 paper-based; 100 iBT). Electronic applications accepted. *Expenses:* Contact institution.

University of California, Berkeley, Graduate Division, Haas School of Business, PhD in Business Administration Program, Berkeley, CA 94720. Offers accounting (PhD); business and public policy (PhD); finance (PhD); management of organizations (PhD); marketing (PhD); real estate (PhD). *Accreditation:* AACSB. *Degree requirements:* For doctorate, comprehensive exam, thesis/dissertation, written preliminary exams, oral qualifying exam. *Entrance requirements:* For doctorate, GMAT or GRE, minimum GPA of 3.0 in undergraduate and graduate coursework. Additional exam requirements/recommendations for international students: Required—TOEFL (minimum score 570 paper-based; 70 iBT), IELTS (minimum score 7). Electronic applications accepted. *Expenses:* Contact institution. *Faculty research:* Accounting, business and public policy, entrepreneurship, finance, management of organizations, marketing, operations and information technology management, real estate.

University of California, Davis, Graduate School of Management, Full-Time MBA Program, Davis, CA 95616. Offers business analytics and technologies (MBA); entrepreneurship and innovation (MBA); finance and accounting (MBA); general management (MBA); marketing (MBA); organizational behavior (MBA); public health management (MBA); strategy (MBA); technology management (MBA); DVM/MBA; JD/MBA; M Engr/MBA; MBA/MPH; MBA/MS; MD/MBA; MSN/MBA; PhD/MBA. *Faculty:* 31 full-time (10 women). *Students:* 89 full-time (35 women); includes 21 minority (1 Black or African American, non-Hispanic/Latino; 14 Asian, non-Hispanic/Latino; 6 Hispanic/Latino), 43 international. Average age 28. 290 applicants, 39% accepted, 44 enrolled. In 2018, 45 master's awarded. *Degree requirements:* For master's, comprehensive exam, integrated management project. *Entrance requirements:* For master's, GMAT or GRE, letters of recommendation, resume, essays, equivalent of a 4-year U.S. undergraduate degree, transcript. Additional exam requirements/recommendations for international students: Required—TOEFL (minimum score 600 paper-based; 100 iBT), IELTS (minimum score 7). *Application deadline:* For fall admission, 9/15 priority date for domestic and international students. Applications are processed on a rolling basis. Application fee: $125. Electronic applications accepted. *Expenses:* Contact institution. *Financial support:* In 2018–19, 85 students received support. Fellowships with full and partial tuition reimbursements available, research assistantships with partial tuition reimbursements available, teaching assistantships with partial tuition reimbursements available, institutionally sponsored loans, scholarships/grants, health care benefits, tuition waivers (partial), and unspecified assistantships available. Financial award application deadline: 3/1; financial award applicants required to submit FAFSA. *Faculty research:* Finance, marketing, management, business analytics, accounting. *Unit head:* Amanda Opperman, Assistant Dean of Student Affairs, 530-752-7658, Fax: 530-754-9355, E-mail: admissions@gsm.ucdavis.edu. *Application contact:* Andrea Shaw, Senior Director of Admissions, 530-754-5476, Fax: 530-754-9355, E-mail: admissions@gsm.ucdavis.edu.
Website: http://gsm.ucdavis.edu/daytime-mba-program

University of California, Davis, Graduate School of Management, MBA Programs in Sacramento and San Francisco Bay Area, Davis, CA 95616. Offers business analytics and technologies (MBA); entrepreneurship and innovation (MBA); finance and accounting (MBA); general management (MBA); marketing (MBA); organizational behavior (MBA); public health management (MBA); strategy (MBA); technology management (MBA). *Program availability:* Part-time-only, evening/weekend. *Faculty:* 17 full-time (7 women), 42 part-time/adjunct (11 women). *Students:* 279 part-time (107 women); includes 146 minority (12 Black or African American, non-Hispanic/Latino; 3 American Indian or Alaska Native, non-Hispanic/Latino; 102 Asian, non-Hispanic/Latino; 29 Hispanic/Latino), 24 international. Average age 30. 158 applicants, 83% accepted, 91 enrolled. In 2018, 91 master's awarded. *Degree requirements:* For master's, integrated management project. *Entrance requirements:* For master's, GMAT or GRE, letters of recommendation, resume, equivalent of a 4-year U.S. undergraduate degree. Additional exam requirements/recommendations for international students: Required—TOEFL (minimum score 600 paper-based; 100 iBT), IELTS (minimum score 7). *Application deadline:* For fall admission, 9/15 priority date for domestic and international students. Applications are processed on a rolling basis. Application fee: $125. Electronic applications accepted. *Expenses:* Contact institution. *Financial support:* In 2018–19, 89 students received support. Fellowships, teaching assistantships with partial tuition reimbursements available, scholarships/grants, and unspecified assistantships available. Support available to part-time students. Financial award application deadline: 3/1; financial award applicants required to submit FAFSA. *Faculty research:* Accounting, finance, marketing, management, business analytics. *Unit head:* Amanda Opperman, Assistant Dean of Student Affairs, 530-752-7658, Fax: 530-754-9355, E-mail: admissions@gsm.ucdavis.edu. *Application contact:* Andrea Shaw, Senior Director of Admissions, 530-754-5476, Fax: 530-754-9355, E-mail: admissions@gsm.ucdavis.edu.
Website: http://gsm.ucdavis.edu/mba-programs

University of Chicago, Booth School of Business, Full-Time MBA Program, Chicago, IL 60637. Offers accounting (MBA); analytic finance (MBA); analytic management (MBA); econometrics and statistics (MBA); economics (MBA); entrepreneurship (MBA); finance (MBA); general management (MBA); health administration and policy (Certificate); international business (MBA); managerial and organizational behavior (MBA); marketing analytics (MBA); marketing management (MBA); operations management (MBA); strategic management (MBA); MBA/AM; MBA/JD; MBA/MA; MBA/MD; MBA/MPP. *Accreditation:* AACSB. *Entrance requirements:* For master's, GMAT or GRE, transcripts, resume, 2 letters of recommendation, essays, interview. Additional exam requirements/recommendations for international students: Required—TOEFL, IELTS, or PTE. Electronic applications accepted. *Expenses:* Contact institution.

University of Hartford, College of Arts and Sciences, Department of Psychology, Program in Organizational Behavior, West Hartford, CT 06117-1599. Offers MS. *Program availability:* Part-time, evening/weekend. *Entrance requirements:* Additional exam requirements/recommendations for international students: Required—TOEFL (minimum score 550 paper-based). Electronic applications accepted.

University of Hawaii at Manoa, Office of Graduate Education, Shidler College of Business, Program in Business Administration, Honolulu, HI 96822. Offers Asian business studies (MBA); Chinese business studies (MBA); decision sciences (MBA); entrepreneurship (MBA); finance (MBA); finance and banking (MBA); human resources management (MBA); information management (MBA); information technology (MBA); international business (MBA); Japanese business studies (MBA); marketing (MBA); organizational behavior (MBA); organizational management (MBA); real estate (MBA); student-designed track (MBA). *Accreditation:* AACSB. *Program availability:* Part-time, evening/weekend. *Degree requirements:* For master's, thesis optional. *Entrance requirements:* For master's, GMAT, minimum GPA of 3.0. Additional exam requirements/recommendations for international students: Required—TOEFL (minimum score 600 paper-based; 100 iBT), IELTS (minimum score 7). *Expenses:* Contact institution.

The University of Kansas, Graduate Studies, School of Business, Program in Business, Lawrence, KS 66045. Offers business and organizational leadership (MS); decision sciences and supply chain management (PhD); finance (PhD); human resources management (PhD); marketing (PhD); organizational behavior (PhD); strategic management (PhD); supply chain management and logistics (MS). *Accreditation:* AACSB. *Program availability:* Part-time. *Students:* 69 full-time (20 women), 150 part-time (62 women); includes 42 minority (14 Black or African American, non-Hispanic/Latino; 2 American Indian or Alaska Native, non-Hispanic/Latino; 6 Asian, non-Hispanic/Latino; 7 Hispanic/Latino; 13 Two or more races, non-Hispanic/Latino), 24 international. Average age 32. 306 applicants, 51% accepted, 132 enrolled. In 2018, 22 master's, 1 doctorate awarded. *Entrance requirements:* For master's, GMAT, official transcript, three letters of recommendation, resume, statement of purpose; for doctorate, GMAT or GRE, official transcript, three letters of recommendation, resume, statement of purpose. Additional exam requirements/recommendations for international students: Required—TOEFL, IELTS. *Application deadline:* For fall admission, 1/10 for domestic and international students. Application fee: $65 ($85 for international students). Electronic applications accepted. *Financial support:* Fellowships, research assistantships, teaching assistantships, scholarships/grants, health care benefits, tuition waivers (full), and unspecified assistantships available. Financial award application deadline: 1/10. *Faculty research:* Strategic human resource management, business ethics, organizational theory/behavior, corporate strategy, international business, supply chain management, Bayesian networks, game theory, decision analysis and time/series analysis, pricing, consumer effects, advertising and emotion. *Unit head:* Charly Edmonds, Director, 785-864-3841, E-mail: cedmonds@ku.edu. *Application contact:* Andrea Noltner, Graduate Admission Contact, 785-864-7556, E-mail: anoltner@ku.edu.
Website: http://www.business.ku.edu/

University of New Mexico, Anderson School of Management, Department of Organizational Studies, Albuquerque, NM 87131. Offers organizational behavior and human resources management (MBA); strategic management and policy (MBA). *Program availability:* Part-time. *Faculty:* 15 full-time (11 women), 16 part-time/adjunct (8 women). In 2018, 21 master's awarded. *Entrance requirements:* For master's, GMAT or GRE, minimum GPA of 3.0 on last 60 hours of coursework; bachelor's degree from regionally-accredited college or university in U.S. or its equivalent in another country. Additional exam requirements/recommendations for international students: Required—TOEFL (minimum score 550 paper-based; 79 iBT), IELTS (minimum score 6.5). *Application deadline:* For fall admission, 4/1 priority date for domestic and international students; for spring admission, 10/1 priority date for domestic and international students. Applications are processed on a rolling basis. Application fee: $50. Electronic applications accepted. *Expenses:* $531.34 per credit resident tuition and fees, $1197.98 per credit non-resident tuition and fees (both are non-EMBA tuition). *Financial support:* In 2018–19, 14 students received support, including 4 fellowships (averaging $18,200 per year), 11 research assistantships with partial tuition reimbursements available (averaging $15,488 per year); career-related internships or fieldwork, Federal Work-Study, scholarships/grants, and unspecified assistantships also available. Support available to part-time students. Financial award application deadline: 6/1; financial award applicants required to submit FAFSA. *Faculty research:* Business ethics and social corporate responsibility, diversity, human resources, organizational strategy, organizational behavior. *Unit head:* Dr. Michelle Arthur, Chair, 505-277-6471, E-mail: arthurm@unm.edu. *Application contact:* Lisa Beauchene-Lawson, Supervisor, Graduate Advisement, 505-277-6471, E-mail: andersongrad@unm.edu.
Website: https://www.mgt.unm.edu/dos/default.asp?mm-faculty

The University of North Carolina at Chapel Hill, Kenan-Flagler Business School, Doctoral Program in Business Administration, Chapel Hill, NC 27599. Offers accounting (PhD); finance (PhD); marketing (PhD); operations management (PhD); organizational behavior (PhD); strategy (PhD). *Accreditation:* AACSB. *Degree requirements:* For doctorate, thesis/dissertation. *Entrance requirements:* For doctorate, GMAT or GRE General Test. Electronic applications accepted. *Expenses:* Contact institution.

University of North Texas at Dallas, Graduate School, Dallas, TX 75241. Offers accounting (MBA); counseling (M Ed, MS); criminal justice (MS); curriculum and instruction (M Ed); educational administration (M Ed); human resources and organizational behavior (MBA); public leadership (MS); strategic management (MBA).

University of Oklahoma, College of Arts and Sciences, Department of Psychology, Norman, OK 73019. Offers organizational dynamics (MA, Graduate Certificate), including human resource management (Graduate Certificate), organizational dynamics (MA), project management (Graduate Certificate); psychology (MS, PhD), including psychology.

Faculty: 19 full-time (9 women), 1 (woman) part-time/adjunct. *Students:* 63 full-time (41 women), 33 part-time (22 women); includes 22 minority (3 Black or African American, non-Hispanic/Latino; 3 American Indian or Alaska Native, non-Hispanic/Latino; 3 Asian, non-Hispanic/Latino; 8 Hispanic/Latino; 5 Two or more races, non-Hispanic/Latino), 8 international. Average age 30. 95 applicants, 20% accepted, 17 enrolled. In 2018, 23 master's, 8 doctorates, 15 other advanced degrees awarded. Terminal master's awarded for partial completion of doctoral program. *Degree requirements:* For master's, comprehensive exam, thesis; for doctorate, comprehensive exam, thesis/dissertation. *Entrance requirements:* For master's and doctorate, GRE. Additional exam requirements/recommendations for international students: Required—TOEFL (minimum score 79 iBT) or IELTS (minimum score 6.5). *Application deadline:* For fall admission, 1/1 for domestic and international students. Application fee: $50 ($100 for international students). Electronic applications accepted. *Expenses:* Tuition, state resident: full-time $5683.20; part-time $236.80 per credit hour. Tuition, nonresident: full-time $20,342; part-time $847.60 per credit hour. *International tuition:* $20,342.40 full-time. *Required fees:* $2894.20; $110.05 per credit hour. $126.50 per semester. Tuition and fees vary according to course load and program. *Financial support:* Fellowships, research assistantships, and teaching assistantships available. Financial award application deadline: 6/1; financial award applicants required to submit FAFSA. *Faculty research:* Behavioral statistics; leadership for innovation; eyewitness testimony; risk assessment and literacy; theory of mind. *Unit head:* Dr. Eric Day, Chair, 405-325-4511, Fax: 405-325-4737, E-mail: eday@ou.edu. *Application contact:* Dr. Shane Connelly, Professor/Chair, 405-325-4580, Fax: 405-325-4737, E-mail: sconnelly@ou.edu.
Website: http://www.ou.edu/cas/psychology

University of Pittsburgh, Katz Graduate School of Business, Doctoral Program in Business Administration, Pittsburgh, PA 15260. Offers accounting (PhD); business analytics and operations (PhD); finance (PhD); information systems and technology management (PhD); marketing (PhD); organizational behavior and human resources (PhD); strategic management (PhD). *Accreditation:* AACSB. *Program availability:* Evening/weekend. *Degree requirements:* For doctorate, comprehensive exam, thesis/dissertation, student teaching. *Entrance requirements:* For doctorate, GMAT or GRE, 3 recommendations, statement of purpose, transcripts of all previous course work and degrees. Additional exam requirements/recommendations for international students: Required—TOEFL (minimum score 100 iBT) or IELTS (minimum score 7.0). Electronic applications accepted. *Faculty research:* Accounting systems/financial reporting, corporate finance, shopper marketing/consumer behavior, management information systems, organizational behavior and entrepreneurship.

University of Pittsburgh, Katz Graduate School of Business, Master of Business Administration Programs, Pittsburgh, PA 15260. Offers finance (MBA); information systems (MBA); marketing (MBA); operations (MBA); organizational behavior and human resources (MBA); strategy, environment and organizations (MBA); MBA/JD; MBA/MID; MBA/MIS; MBA/MSE. *Accreditation:* AACSB. *Program availability:* Part-time, evening/weekend, blended/hybrid learning. *Degree requirements:* For master's, minimum GPA of 3.0. *Entrance requirements:* For master's, GMAT, GRE. Additional exam requirements/recommendations for international students: Required—TOEFL (minimum score 100 iBT) or IELTS (minimum score 7.0). Electronic applications accepted. *Faculty research:* Accounting systems/financial reporting, corporate finance, shopper marketing/consumer behavior, management information systems, organizational behavior and entrepreneurship.

The University of Texas at Austin, Graduate School, College of Liberal Arts, Program in Human Dimensions of Organizations, Austin, TX 78712-1111. Offers MA. *Program availability:* Evening/weekend, online learning. *Degree requirements:* For master's, capstone project.

University of Utah, Graduate School, David Eccles School of Business, Business Administration Program, Salt Lake City, UT 84112. Offers accounting (PhD); business administration (EMBA, MBA, PMBA); finance (PhD); information systems (PhD); marketing (PhD); operations management (PhD); organizational behavior (PhD); strategic management (PhD); MBA/JD; MBA/MHA; MBA/MS. *Program availability:* Part-time, evening/weekend, online learning. *Students:* 112 full-time (26 women), 7 part-time (2 women); includes 12 minority (1 Asian, non-Hispanic/Latino; 7 Hispanic/Latino; 4 Two or more races, non-Hispanic/Latino), 13 international. Average age 29. 182 applicants, 51% accepted, 58 enrolled. In 2018, 58 master's awarded. *Entrance requirements:* For master's, GMAT or GRE; for doctorate, GMAT. Additional exam requirements/recommendations for international students: Required—TOEFL (minimum score 100 iBT), IELTS (minimum score 7). *Application deadline:* For fall admission, 5/1 for domestic students, 3/1 for international students. Application fee: $55 ($65 for international students). Electronic applications accepted. *Expenses:* Contact institution. *Financial support:* In 2018–19, 57 students received support. Scholarships/grants available. Financial award application deadline: 5/1; financial award applicants required to submit FAFSA. *Faculty research:* Corporate finance, strategy services, consumer behavior, financial disclosures, operations. *Unit head:* Brad Vierig, Associate Dean, MBA Programs & Executive Education. *Application contact:* Stephanie Geisler, Director, Full-Time MBA, 801-585-6291, E-mail: ftmba@utah.edu.
Website: http://www.business.utah.edu/

Wayne State University, College of Liberal Arts and Sciences, Department of Political Science, Detroit, MI 48202. Offers political science (MA, PhD); public administration (MPA), including economic development policy and management, health and human services policy and management, human and fiscal resource management, nonprofit policy and management, organizational behavior and management, urban and metropolitan policy and management; JD/MA. *Accreditation:* NASPAA. *Faculty:* 18. *Students:* 61 full-time (26 women), 51 part-time (27 women); includes 31 minority (22 Black or African American, non-Hispanic/Latino; 3 Asian, non-Hispanic/Latino; 1 Hispanic/Latino; 5 Two or more races, non-Hispanic/Latino), 12 international. Average age 32. 103 applicants, 39% accepted, 20 enrolled. In 2018, 32 master's, 5 doctorates awarded. *Degree requirements:* For master's, comprehensive exam (for some programs), thesis (for some programs); for doctorate, thesis/dissertation. *Entrance requirements:* For master's, GRE General Test, substantial undergraduate preparation in the social sciences, minimum upper-division undergraduate GPA of 3.0, two letters of recommendation, personal statement; for doctorate, GRE General Test, 3 letters of recommendation; personal statement; interview. Additional exam requirements/recommendations for international students: Required—TOEFL (minimum score 550 paper-based; 79 iBT), TWE (minimum score 5.5), Michigan English Language Assessment Battery (minimum score 85); Recommended—IELTS (minimum score 6.5). *Application deadline:* For fall admission, 5/15 for domestic students, 5/1 priority date for international students; for winter admission, 10/15 for domestic students, 9/1 priority date for international students. Applications are processed on a rolling basis. Application fee: $50. Electronic applications accepted. *Expenses:* Contact institution. *Financial support:* In 2018–19, 46 students received support, including 4 fellowships with tuition reimbursements available (averaging $17,000 per year), 1 research assistantship with tuition reimbursement available (averaging $23,119 per year), 12 teaching assistantships with tuition reimbursements available (averaging $19,267 per year); scholarships/grants, health care benefits, and unspecified assistantships also available. Financial award applicants required to submit FAFSA. *Faculty research:* American government and politics, comparative politics, political methodology, political theory, public administration, public law, public policy, world politics/international relations, formal theory/modeling, gender and politics, international law, peace research, political economy, political psychology, politics of developing countries, race, religion, and ethnicity, urban politics. *Unit head:* Dr. Daniel Geller, Professor and Chair, 313-577-6328, E-mail: dgeller@wayne.edu. *Application contact:* Dr. Sharon Lean, Graduate Director, 313-577-2630, E-mail: gradpolisci@wayne.edu.
Website: http://clas.wayne.edu/politicalscience/

Wilfrid Laurier University, Faculty of Graduate and Postdoctoral Studies, Lazaridis School of Business and Economics, Department of Business, Waterloo, ON N2L 3C5, Canada. Offers accounting (PhD); finance (M Fin); financial economics (PhD); marketing (PhD); operations and supply chain management (PhD); organizational behavior and human resource management (M Sc); organizational behaviour and human resource management (PhD); supply chain management (M Sc); technology management (EMTM). *Accreditation:* AACSB. *Program availability:* Part-time, evening/weekend. *Degree requirements:* For master's, thesis optional; for doctorate, comprehensive exam, thesis/dissertation. *Entrance requirements:* For master's, GMAT, 4-year honors degree with minimum B+ average; for doctorate, GMAT, master's degree, minimum B+ average. Additional exam requirements/recommendations for international students: Required—TOEFL (minimum score 89 iBT). Electronic applications accepted. *Faculty research:* Financial economics, management and organizational behavior, operations and supply chain management.

Organizational Management

Albertus Magnus College, Master of Science in Management and Organizational Leadership Program, New Haven, CT 06511-1189. Offers MS. *Program availability:* Part-time, evening/weekend, blended/hybrid learning. *Degree requirements:* For master's, thesis optional, project. *Entrance requirements:* For master's, bachelor's degree from regionally-accredited college or university, minimum GPA of 2.8, three years of professional and/or related experience, official transcripts, essay. Additional exam requirements/recommendations for international students: Recommended—TOEFL (minimum score 550 paper-based; 80 iBT). Electronic applications accepted. *Expenses:* Contact institution. *Faculty research:* Quantitative analysis of decision-making, conflict resolution, scientific method, information literacy, leadership management, principles of organizational management, quality management, business ethics, organizational behavior, human resources, international and global business, critical thinking skills in conducting research including developing hypothesis, evaluating research methods, conducting research, analyzing data, interpreting and presenting findings creative thinking skills.

Albizu University, Miami Campus, Graduate Programs, Miami, FL 33172-2209. Offers clinical psychology (PhD, Psy D); entrepreneurship (MBA); exceptional student education (MS); human services (PhD); industrial/organizational psychology (MS); marriage and family therapy (MS); mental health counseling (MS); nonprofit management (MBA); organizational management (MBA); school counseling (MS); speech and language pathology (MS); teaching English for speakers of other languages (MS). *Accreditation:* APA. *Program availability:* Part-time, evening/weekend, 100% online, blended/hybrid learning. *Faculty:* 32 full-time (24 women), 27 part-time/adjunct (15 women). *Students:* 479 full-time (410 women), 146 part-time (126 women); includes 539 minority (42 Black or African American, non-Hispanic/Latino; 2 Asian, non-Hispanic/Latino; 490 Hispanic/Latino; 5 Two or more races, non-Hispanic/Latino), 22 international. Average age 33. 314 applicants, 45% accepted, 92 enrolled. In 2018, 101 master's, 64 doctorates awarded. Terminal master's awarded for partial completion of doctoral program. *Degree requirements:* For master's, comprehensive exam (for some programs), integrative project (for MBA); research project (for exceptional student education, teaching English as a second language); for doctorate, comprehensive exam, thesis/dissertation, comprehensive examinations, internship, project/dissertation. *Entrance requirements:* For master's, GRE/EXADEP, bachelor's degree from accredited institution, minimum GPA of 3.0, 3 letters of recommendation, interview, resume, statement of purpose, official transcripts; for doctorate, GRE (for Psy D), 3 letters of recommendation, resume, interview, statement of purpose, official transcripts; bachelor's degree and minimum GPA of 3.25 (for Psy D); master's degree and minimum GPA of 3.0 (for PhD). Additional exam requirements/recommendations for international students: Required—Michigan Test of English Language Proficiency. *Application deadline:* For fall admission, 4/1 priority date for domestic students, 5/1 priority date for international students; for spring admission, 11/1 priority date for domestic students, 9/1 priority date for international students. Applications are processed on a rolling basis. Application fee: $50. Electronic applications accepted. Application fee is waived when completed online. *Expenses:* Contact institution. *Financial support:* In 2018–19, 141 students received support. Federal Work-Study, scholarships/grants, unspecified assistantships, and tuition discounts available. Financial award application deadline: 6/1; financial award applicants required to submit FAFSA. *Faculty research:* Psychotherapy, forensic psychology, neuropsychology, special education, speech-language pathology, criminal justice, human services. *Unit head:* Dr. Jose Pons-Madera, PhD, President, 305-593-1223 Ext. 3120, Fax: 305-477-8983, E-mail: jpons@albizu.edu. *Application contact:* Nancy Alvarez, Director of Enrollment Management, 305-593-1223 Ext. 3136, Fax: 305-593-1854, E-mail: nalvarez@albizu.edu.

Alvernia University, School of Graduate Studies, Program in Leadership, Reading, PA 19607-1799. Offers PhD. *Degree requirements:* For doctorate, comprehensive exam, thesis/dissertation (for some programs). *Entrance requirements:* For doctorate, GRE, GMAT, or MAT, minimum GPA of 3.3, 3 letters of recommendation, resume, interview.

The American College of Financial Services, Graduate Programs, Bryn Mawr, PA 19010-2105. Offers financial services (MSFS); leadership (MSM). *Program availability:* Part-time, evening/weekend, online learning. Electronic applications accepted. *Faculty research:* Retirement counseling, social security, aging, family composition, inflation.

Organizational Management

American University, School of Public Affairs, Department of Public Administration and Policy, Washington, DC 20016-8070. Offers organization development (MSOD, Certificate), including leadership for organizational change (Certificate), organization development (MSOD); public administration (MPA, PhD, Certificate), including nonprofit management (Certificate), public financial management (Certificate), public management (Certificate); public administration and policy (MPAP), including public administration policy; public policy (MPP, Certificate), including public policy (MPP), public policy analysis (Certificate); LL M/MPA; MPA/JD; MPP/JD; MPP/LL M. *Program availability:* Part-time, evening/weekend, 100% online, blended/hybrid learning. *Faculty:* 33 full-time (11 women), 18 part-time/adjunct (7 women). *Students:* 235 full-time (153 women), 275 part-time (189 women); includes 123 minority (61 Black or African American, non-Hispanic/Latino; 4 American Indian or Alaska Native, non-Hispanic/Latino; 23 Asian, non-Hispanic/Latino; 18 Hispanic/Latino; 1 Native Hawaiian or other Pacific Islander, non-Hispanic/Latino; 16 Two or more races, non-Hispanic/Latino), 34 international. Average age 29. 710 applicants, 75% accepted, 182 enrolled. In 2018, 202 master's, 5 doctorates, 5 other advanced degrees awarded. *Degree requirements:* For master's, comprehensive exam; for doctorate, comprehensive exam, thesis/dissertation. *Entrance requirements:* For master's, GRE; Please see website: https://www.american.edu/spa/jlc/, statement of purpose, 2 recommendations, resume, transcript; for doctorate, GRE; Please see website: https://www.american.edu/spa/jlc/, 3 recommendations, statement of purpose, resume, writing sample, transcript; for Certificate, bachelor's degree. Additional exam requirements/recommendations for international students: Required—TOEFL. Application fee: $55. *Expenses:* Contact institution. *Financial support:* Research assistantships, teaching assistantships, institutionally sponsored loans, scholarships/grants, and unspecified assistantships available. Financial award applicants required to submit FAFSA. *Unit head:* Dr. Dave Marcotte, Department Chair, 202-885-2940, E-mail: spagrad@american.edu. *Application contact:* Jennifer Forney, Assistant Dean, Graduate Enrollment, 202-885-2940, E-mail: spagrad@american.edu.
Website: http://www.american.edu/spa/dpap/

Anderson University, College of Business, Anderson, SC 29621-4035. Offers business administration (MBA); healthcare leadership (MBA); human resources (MBA); marketing (MBA); organizational leadership (MOL); supply chain management (MBA). *Accreditation:* ACBSP. *Application deadline:* Applications are processed on a rolling basis. Electronic applications accepted. *Expenses: Tuition:* Full-time $400; part-time $400 per credit. *Required fees:* $200; $200 per semester. Tuition and fees vary according to course load. *Financial support:* Scholarships/grants and tuition waivers available. Financial award application deadline: 3/1; financial award applicants required to submit FAFSA. *Unit head:* Steve Nail, Dean, 864-MBA-6000. *Application contact:* Sharon Vargo, Graduate Admission Counselor, 864-231-2000, E-mail: svargo@andersonuniversity.edu.
Website: http://www.andersonuniversity.edu/business

Antioch University Los Angeles, Program in Leadership, Management and Business, Culver City, CA 90230. Offers human resource development (MA); leadership (MA); organizational development (MA). *Program availability:* Part-time, evening/weekend. *Entrance requirements:* For master's, interview. Additional exam requirements/recommendations for international students: Required—TOEFL. *Faculty research:* Systems thinking and chaos theory, technology and organizational structure, nonprofit management, power and empowerment.

Apollos University, School of Business and Management, Great Falls, MT 59401. Offers business administration (MBA, DBA); organizational management (MS).

Aquinas College, School of Management, Grand Rapids, MI 49506. Offers marketing management (MM); organizational leadership (MM); sustainable business (MM). *Program availability:* Part-time, evening/weekend. *Faculty:* 4 full-time (1 woman), 5 part-time/adjunct (0 women). *Students:* 12 full-time (4 women), 32 part-time (19 women); includes 3 minority (1 Black or African American, non-Hispanic/Latino; 1 Asian, non-Hispanic/Latino; 1 Hispanic/Latino), 2 international. Average age 31. In 2018, 19 master's awarded. *Entrance requirements:* For master's, GMAT, minimum undergraduate GPA of 2.75, 2 years of work experience. Additional exam requirements/recommendations for international students: Required—TOEFL (minimum score 550 paper-based). *Application deadline:* Applications are processed on a rolling basis. Application fee: $0. *Expenses: Tuition:* Part-time $593 per credit hour. *Required fees:* $120; $120. *Financial support:* Scholarships/grants available. Support available to part-time students. Financial award application deadline: 3/15; financial award applicants required to submit FAFSA. *Unit head:* Dr. Linda Hagan, Interim Dean of Business Division, 616-632-2193, Fax: 616-732-4489, E-mail: lmh010@aquinas.edu. *Application contact:* Lynn Atkins-Rykert, Program Coordinator, 616-632-2925, Fax: 616-732-4489, E-mail: atkinlyn@aquinas.edu.

Argosy University, Chicago, College of Business, Program in Organizational Leadership, Chicago, IL 60601. Offers Ed D.

Argosy University, Hawai`i, College of Business, Program in Organizational Leadership, Honolulu, HI 96813. Offers Ed D.

Argosy University, Los Angeles, College of Business, Los Angeles, CA 90045. Offers accounting (DBA); corporate compliance (MBA); customized professional concentration (MBA, DBA); finance (MBA); fraud examination (MBA); global business sustainability (DBA); healthcare administration (MBA); information systems (DBA); information systems management (MBA); international business (MBA, DBA); management (MBA, MSM, DBA); marketing (MBA, DBA); organizational leadership (Ed D); public administration (MBA); sustainable management (MBA).

Argosy University, Northern Virginia, College of Business, Arlington, VA 22209. Offers accounting (DBA); customized professional concentration (MBA, DBA); finance (MBA); fraud examination (MBA); global business sustainability (DBA); healthcare administration (MBA); information systems (DBA); information systems management (MBA); international business (MBA, DBA, Certificate); management (MBA, MSM, DBA); marketing (MBA, DBA, Certificate); organizational leadership (Ed D); public administration (MBA); sustainable management (MBA).

Argosy University, Orange County, College of Business, Program in Organizational Leadership, Orange, CA 92868. Offers Ed D.

Argosy University, Seattle, College of Business, Seattle, WA 98121. Offers accounting (DBA); corporate compliance (MBA); customized professional concentration (MBA, DBA); finance (MBA); fraud examination (MBA); global business sustainability (DBA); healthcare administration (MBA); information systems (DBA); information systems management (MBA); international business (MBA, DBA); management (MBA, MSM, DBA); marketing (MBA, DBA); organizational leadership (Ed D); public administration (MBA); sustainable management (MBA).

Argosy University, Tampa, College of Business, Tampa, FL 33607. Offers accounting (DBA); corporate compliance (MBA); customized professional concentration (MBA, DBA); finance (MBA); fraud examination (MBA); global business sustainability (DBA); healthcare administration (MBA); information systems (DBA); information systems management (MBA); international business (MBA, DBA); management (MBA, MSM,

DBA); marketing (MBA, DBA); organizational leadership (Ed D); public administration (MBA); sustainable management (MBA).

Argosy University, Twin Cities, College of Business, Eagan, MN 55121. Offers accounting (DBA); customized professional concentration (MBA, DBA); finance (MBA); fraud examination (MBA); global business sustainability (DBA); healthcare administration (MBA); information systems (DBA); information systems management (MBA); international business (MBA, DBA); management (MBA, MSM, DBA); marketing (MBA, DBA); organizational leadership (Ed D); public administration (MBA); sustainable management (MBA).

Athabasca University, Centre for Interdisciplinary Studies, Athabasca, AB T9S 3A3, Canada. Offers adult education (MA); community studies (MA); cultural studies (MA); educational studies (MA); global change (MA); heritage resource management (Postbaccalaureate Certificate); legislative drafting (Postbaccalaureate Certificate); work, organization, and leadership (MA). *Program availability:* Part-time, evening/weekend, online learning. *Degree requirements:* For master's, project. *Entrance requirements:* Additional exam requirements/recommendations for international students: Required—TOEFL (minimum score 560 paper-based). Electronic applications accepted. *Faculty research:* Women's history, literature and culture studies, sustainable development, labor and education.

Atlantic University, Program in Mindful Leadership, Virginia Beach, VA 23451-2061. Offers global leadership (MA). *Program availability:* Online learning. *Degree requirements:* For master's, capstone project. *Entrance requirements:* For master's, bachelor's degree, official transcripts, minimum undergraduate GPA of 3.0, essay, current resume, interview. *Expenses:* Contact institution.

Augsburg University, Program in Leadership, Minneapolis, MN 55454-1351. Offers MA. *Program availability:* Part-time, evening/weekend. *Degree requirements:* For master's, thesis or alternative. *Entrance requirements:* For master's, MAT, minimum GPA of 3.0. Additional exam requirements/recommendations for international students: Required—TOEFL (minimum score 600 paper-based). *Faculty research:* Soviet leaders, artificial intelligence, homelessness.

Austin Peay State University, College of Graduate Studies, College of Behavioral and Health Sciences, Department of Leadership and Organizational Administration, Clarksville, TN 37044. Offers strategic leadership (MPS). *Program availability:* Part-time, online learning. *Faculty:* 5 full-time (3 women). *Students:* 11 full-time (7 women), 61 part-time (37 women); includes 31 minority (22 Black or African American, non-Hispanic/Latino; 1 American Indian or Alaska Native, non-Hispanic/Latino; 5 Hispanic/Latino; 3 Two or more races, non-Hispanic/Latino). Average age 39. 25 applicants, 92% accepted, 22 enrolled. In 2018, 12 master's awarded. *Degree requirements:* For master's, project. *Entrance requirements:* For master's, GRE General Test, minimum GPA of 2.75. Additional exam requirements/recommendations for international students: Required—TOEFL (minimum score 500 paper-based). *Application deadline:* For fall admission, 8/21 priority date for domestic students. Applications are processed on a rolling basis. Application fee: $45 ($55 for international students). Electronic applications accepted. *Expenses: Tuition,* area resident: Part-time $450 per credit hour. Tuition, state resident: full-time $5987; part-time $450 per credit hour. Tuition, nonresident: full-time $8757; part-time $806 per credit hour. *Required fees:* $1583; $79.15 per credit hour. *Financial support:* Career-related internships or fieldwork, Federal Work-Study, institutionally sponsored loans, scholarships/grants, and unspecified assistantships available. Support available to part-time students. Financial award application deadline: 7/1; financial award applicants required to submit FAFSA. *Unit head:* Dr. William Rayburn, Department Chair, 931-221-6377, E-mail: rayburnw@apsu.edu. *Application contact:* Megan Mitchell, Coordinator of Graduate Admissions, 931-221-6189, Fax: 931-221-7641, E-mail: mitchellm@apsu.edu.
Website: http://www.apsu.edu/leadership

Avila University, School of Professional Studies, Kansas City, MO 64145-1698. Offers executive leadership (MS); fundraising (MA); instructional design and technology (MA, MS); leadership coaching (MS); project management (MA); strategic human resources (MS). *Program availability:* Part-time-only, evening/weekend, 100% online, blended/hybrid learning. *Faculty:* 14 part-time/adjunct (8 women). *Students:* 69 full-time (49 women), 48 part-time (42 women); includes 45 minority (38 Black or African American, non-Hispanic/Latino; 5 Hispanic/Latino; 2 Two or more races, non-Hispanic/Latino), 5 international. Average age 39. 63 applicants, 60% accepted, 29 enrolled. In 2018, 34 master's awarded. *Degree requirements:* For master's, thesis optional. *Entrance requirements:* For master's, 2 letters of recommendation, minimum GPA of 3.0 during last 60 hours, resume, statement of intent. Additional exam requirements/recommendations for international students: Required—TOEFL (minimum score 550 paper-based; 79 iBT). *Application deadline:* Applications are processed on a rolling basis. Application fee: $0. Electronic applications accepted. *Expenses:* Contact institution. *Financial support:* In 2018–19, 12 students received support. Unspecified assistantships available. Support available to part-time students. Financial award applicants required to submit FAFSA. *Unit head:* Sarah Sullivan, Coordinator, 816-501-0429, Fax: 816-941-4650, E-mail: advantage@avila.edu. *Application contact:* Jessica Burson, Graduate Admission Advisor, 816-501-2482, Fax: 816-941-4650, E-mail: advantage@avila.edu.
Website: https://www.avila.edu/mrk/advantage-3

Azusa Pacific University, University College, Azusa, CA 91702-7000. Offers leadership and organizational studies (MA); public health (MPH). *Program availability:* Online learning.

Baker University, School of Professional and Graduate Studies, Programs in Business, Baldwin City, KS 66006-0065. Offers MAOL, MBA, MSM, MSSM. Programs also offered in Overland Park, KS; Topeka, KS; and Wichita, KS. *Program availability:* Part-time, evening/weekend, online learning. *Entrance requirements:* For master's, 2 years of full-time work experience. Additional exam requirements/recommendations for international students: Required—TOEFL (minimum score 600 paper-based; 100 iBT).

Bellevue University, Graduate School, College of Professional Studies, Bellevue, NE 68005-3098. Offers instructional design and development (MS); justice administration and criminal management (MS); leadership (MA); organizational performance (MS); public administration (MPA); security management (MS).

Benedictine University, Graduate Programs, Program in Business Administration, Lisle, IL 60532. Offers accounting (MBA); entrepreneurship and managing innovation (MBA); financial management (MBA); health administration (MBA); human resource management (MBA); information systems security (MBA); international business (MBA); management consulting (MBA); management information systems (MBA); marketing management (MBA); operations management and logistics (MBA); organizational leadership (MBA). *Program availability:* Part-time, evening/weekend, 100% online, blended/hybrid learning. *Faculty:* 7 full-time (1 woman), 36 part-time/adjunct (10 women). *Students:* 110 full-time (71 women), 500 part-time (302 women); includes 104 minority (34 Black or African American, non-Hispanic/Latino; 1 American Indian or Alaska Native, non-Hispanic/Latino; 41 Asian, non-Hispanic/Latino; 23 Hispanic/Latino; 5 Native Hawaiian or other Pacific Islander, non-Hispanic/Latino), 7 international. Average age 33. 251 applicants, 84% accepted, 202 enrolled. In 2018, 345 master's awarded. *Entrance requirements:* For master's, GMAT or GRE test scores or completed

test waiver form, official transcripts; 2 letters of reference from individuals familiar with the applicant's professional or academic work, excluding family or personal friends; a 1-2 page essay addressing educational and career goals; current résumé listing chronological work history; personal interview may be required prior to an admission decision. Additional exam requirements/recommendations for international students: Required—TOEFL (minimum score 550 paper-based; 79 iBT), IELTS (minimum score 6.5). *Application deadline:* Applications are processed on a rolling basis. Application fee: $40. Electronic applications accepted. *Unit head:* Ricky Holman, Assistant Professor, 630-829-1936, E-mail: rholman@ben.edu. *Application contact:* Ricky Holman, Assistant Professor, 630-829-1936, E-mail: rholman@ben.edu.

Benedictine University, Graduate Programs, Program in Organization Development, Lisle, IL 60532. Offers PhD. *Program availability:* Evening/weekend. *Faculty:* 3 full-time (1 woman). *Students:* 34 full-time (20 women); includes 5 minority (4 Black or African American, non-Hispanic/Latino; 1 Asian, non-Hispanic/Latino), 3 international. Average age 45. In 2018, 7 doctorates awarded. *Degree requirements:* For doctorate, thesis/dissertation. *Entrance requirements:* Additional exam requirements/recommendations for international students: Required—TOEFL (minimum score 550 paper-based; 79 iBT), IELTS (minimum score 6.5). Application fee: $75. Electronic applications accepted. *Expenses:* $1,094 per credit hour. *Unit head:* Dr. Peter F. Sorensen, Director, 630-829-6222, E-mail: psorensen@ben.edu. *Application contact:* Dr. Peter F. Sorensen, Director, 630-829-6222, E-mail: psorensen@ben.edu.

Benedictine University, Graduate Programs, Program in Values-Driven Leadership, Lisle, IL 60532. Offers DBA, PhD. *Program availability:* Part-time, evening/weekend. *Faculty:* 2 full-time (0 women). *Students:* 1 (woman) full-time, 23 part-time (10 women); includes 3 minority (2 Black or African American, non-Hispanic/Latino; 1 Hispanic/Latino), 1 international. Average age 49. In 2018, 1 doctorate awarded. *Degree requirements:* For doctorate, thesis/dissertation. *Entrance requirements:* Additional exam requirements/recommendations for international students: Required—TOEFL (minimum score 550 paper-based; 79 iBT), IELTS (minimum score 6.5). *Application deadline:* Applications are processed on a rolling basis. Application fee: $75. Electronic applications accepted. *Expenses:* $1,250 per credit hour. *Unit head:* Dr. James Ludema, Director, 630-829-6229, E-mail: jludema@ben.edu. *Application contact:* Dr. James Ludema, Director, 630-829-6229, E-mail: jludema@ben.edu.

Bethel University, Graduate School, St. Paul, MN 55112-6999. Offers business administration (MBA); classroom management (Certificate); counseling (MA); K-12 education (MA); leadership (Ed D); leadership foundations (Certificate); nurse educator (MS, Certificate); nurse-midwifery (MS); physician assistant (MS); special education (MA); strategic leadership (MA); teaching (MA); teaching and learning (Certificate). *Program availability:* Part-time, evening/weekend, 100% online, blended/hybrid learning. *Faculty:* 23 full-time (17 women), 73 part-time/adjunct (45 women). *Students:* 586 full-time (426 women), 372 part-time (244 women); includes 141 minority (49 Black or African American, non-Hispanic/Latino; 6 American Indian or Alaska Native, non-Hispanic/Latino; 19 Asian, non-Hispanic/Latino; 40 Hispanic/Latino; 2 Native Hawaiian or other Pacific Islander, non-Hispanic/Latino; 25 Two or more races, non-Hispanic/Latino), 25 international. Average age 35. 642 applicants, 39% accepted, 194 enrolled. In 2018, 312 master's, 28 doctorates, 134 other advanced degrees awarded. *Degree requirements:* For master's, comprehensive exam (for some programs), thesis (for some programs); for doctorate, comprehensive exam, thesis/dissertation. *Entrance requirements:* Additional exam requirements/recommendations for international students: Required—TOEFL (minimum score 550 paper-based; 80 iBT), TOEFL (minimum score 550 paper-based, 80 iBT) or IELTS. *Application deadline:* Applications are processed on a rolling basis. Application fee: $0. Electronic applications accepted. *Expenses:* Contact institution. *Financial support:* Teaching assistantships, career-related internships or fieldwork, and scholarships/grants available. Support available to part-time students. Financial award applicants required to submit FAFSA. *Unit head:* Dr. Randy Bergen, Associate Provost, 651-635-8000, Fax: 651-635-8004, E-mail: r-bergen@bethel.edu. *Application contact:* Director of Admissions, 651-635-8000, Fax: 651-635-8004, E-mail: gs@bethel.edu.
Website: https://www.bethel.edu/graduate/

Binghamton University, State University of New York, Graduate School, School of Management, Program in Management, Binghamton, NY 13902-6000. Offers finance (PhD); management information systems (PhD); marketing (PhD); organizational studies (PhD); supply chain management (PhD). *Degree requirements:* For doctorate, thesis/dissertation. *Entrance requirements:* For doctorate, GMAT.

Boise State University, College of Engineering, Department of Organizational Performance and Workplace Learning, Boise, ID 83725-0399. Offers organizational performance and workplace learning (MS); workplace e-learning and performance support (Graduate Certificate); workplace instructional design (Graduate Certificate); workplace performance improvement (Graduate Certificate). *Program availability:* Part-time, 100% online. *Degree requirements:* For master's, thesis optional. *Entrance requirements:* Additional exam requirements/recommendations for international students: Required—TOEFL (minimum score 550 paper-based; 80 iBT), IELTS (minimum score 6). Electronic applications accepted.

Boston College, Carroll School of Management, Department of Management and Organization, Chestnut Hill, MA 02467-3800. Offers PhD. *Degree requirements:* For doctorate, comprehensive exam, thesis/dissertation, teaching experience. *Entrance requirements:* For doctorate, GMAT or GRE, letters of recommendation, resume, transcripts. Additional exam requirements/recommendations for international students: Required—TOEFL (minimum score 100 iBT), IELTS (minimum score 7.5), or PTE (minimum score 68). Electronic applications accepted. *Faculty research:* Organizational transformation, mergers and acquisitions, managerial effectiveness, organizational change, organizational structure.

Boston University, Metropolitan College, Program in Leadership, Boston, MA 02215. Offers MS. Program offered at military locations in Massachusetts and North Carolina. *Faculty:* 2 full-time (0 women), 7 part-time/adjunct (2 women). *Students:* 20 part-time (3 women); includes 3 minority (2 Black or African American, non-Hispanic/Latino; 1 Hispanic/Latino). Average age 36. In 2018, 21 master's awarded. *Application deadline:* Applications are processed on a rolling basis. *Expenses:* Contact institution. *Unit head:* Dr. Lou Chitkushev, Associate Dean, 617-353-3010, Fax: 617-353-6066. *Application contact:* Larry Watson, Director of Military Programs, Virginia and North Carolina, 910-451-5574, E-mail: lwatson@bu.edu.
Website: http://www.bu.edu/met/subject/leadership/

Bowling Green State University, Graduate College, College of Business, Program in Organization Development, Bowling Green, OH 43403. Offers MOD. *Program availability:* Part-time, evening/weekend. *Degree requirements:* For master's, thesis or alternative, internship. *Entrance requirements:* For master's, GMAT or GRE General Test. Additional exam requirements/recommendations for international students: Required—TOEFL. Electronic applications accepted. *Faculty research:* Charismatic leadership, self-managing work teams, knowledge workers, stress, effects of change processes.

Brandman University, School of Business and Professional Studies, Irvine, CA 92618. Offers accounting (MBA); business administration (MBA); business intelligence and data

analytics (MBA); e-business strategic management (MBA); entrepreneurship (MBA); finance (MBA); health administration (MBA); human resources (MBA, MS); international business (MBA); marketing (MBA); organizational leadership (MA, MBA, MPA); public administration (MPA).

Brenau University, Sydney O. Smith Graduate School, College of Business and Mass Communication, Gainesville, GA 30501. Offers accounting (MBA); business administration (MBA); healthcare management (MBA); organizational leadership (MS); project management (MBA). *Accreditation:* ACBSP. *Program availability:* Part-time, evening/weekend, online learning. *Degree requirements:* For master's, comprehensive exam (for some programs). *Entrance requirements:* For master's, resume, minimum undergraduate GPA of 2.5. Additional exam requirements/recommendations for international students: Required—TOEFL (minimum score 500 paper-based; 61 iBT); Recommended—IELTS (minimum score 5). Electronic applications accepted. *Expenses:* Contact institution.

Briercrest Seminary, Graduate Programs, Program in Leadership and Management, Caronport, SK S0H 0S0, Canada. Offers organizational leadership (MA). *Program availability:* Part-time. *Degree requirements:* For master's, comprehensive exam, thesis optional. *Entrance requirements:* Additional exam requirements/recommendations for international students: Required—TOEFL (minimum score 550 paper-based).

Buffalo State College, State University of New York, The Graduate School, School of the Professions, International Center for Studies in Creativity, Buffalo, NY 14222-1095. Offers creative studies (MS). *Program availability:* Part-time, evening/weekend. *Degree requirements:* For master's, thesis, project. *Entrance requirements:* For master's, minimum GPA of 2.5; previous course work in philosophy, psychology, and sociology. Additional exam requirements/recommendations for international students: Required—TOEFL (minimum score 550 paper-based). *Faculty research:* Cognitive styles, small group problem-solving.

Cabrini University, Academic Affairs, Radnor, PA 19087. Offers accounting (M Acc); autism spectrum disorder (M Ed); biological sciences (MS), including civic leadership; criminology and criminal justice (MA); curriculum, instruction, and assessment (M Ed); educational leadership (M Ed, Ed D), including curriculum and instructional leadership (Ed D), preK-12 leadership (Ed D); English as a second language (M Ed); organizational leadership (DBA, PhD); preK to 4 (M Ed); reading specialist (M Ed); secondary education (M Ed), including biology, chemistry, English, English/communication, mathematics, social studies; special education grades 7-12 (M Ed); special education preK-8 (M Ed); teaching and learning (M Ed). *Program availability:* Part-time, evening/weekend. *Degree requirements:* For master's, comprehensive exam (for some programs), thesis (for some programs); for doctorate, comprehensive exam (for some programs), thesis/dissertation. *Entrance requirements:* For master's, professional resume, personal statement, two recommendations, official transcripts; for doctorate, official transcripts, minimum master's GPA of 3.0, two recommendations, interview with admissions committee. Additional exam requirements/recommendations for international students: Required—TOEFL (minimum score 80 iBT). Electronic applications accepted. Application fee is waived when completed online. *Expenses:* Contact institution.

Cairn University, School of Business, Langhorne, PA 19047-2990. Offers accounting (MBA); business administration (MBA); international entrepreneurship (MBA); nonprofit leadership (MBA); organizational leadership (MSOL, Postbaccalaureate Certificate). *Program availability:* Part-time, evening/weekend, 100% online, blended/hybrid learning. *Entrance requirements:* Additional exam requirements/recommendations for international students: Required—TOEFL (minimum score 550 paper-based). Electronic applications accepted. Application fee is waived when completed online. *Expenses:* Contact institution.

California Baptist University, Program in Leadership and Organizational Studies, Riverside, CA 92504-3206. Offers MA. *Program availability:* Part-time. *Faculty:* 3 full-time (0 women), 2 part-time/adjunct (0 women). *Students:* 1 full-time (0 women), 16 part-time (10 women); includes 12 minority (3 Black or African American, non-Hispanic/Latino; 1 Asian, non-Hispanic/Latino; 7 Hispanic/Latino; 1 Two or more races, non-Hispanic/Latino), 1 international. Average age 37. 5 applicants, 100% accepted, 5 enrolled. In 2018, 12 master's awarded. *Entrance requirements:* For master's, minimum undergraduate GPA of 2.75; three recommendations; resume; 500-word essay. Additional exam requirements/recommendations for international students: Required—TOEFL (minimum score 80 iBT). *Application deadline:* For fall admission, 8/1 priority date for domestic students, 7/1 for international students; for spring admission, 11/1 priority date for domestic students, 11/1 for international students. Applications are processed on a rolling basis. Application fee: $45. Electronic applications accepted. *Expenses:* $607 per unit. *Financial support:* In 2018–19, 10 students received support. Federal Work-Study and scholarships/grants available. Financial award applicants required to submit CSS PROFILE or FAFSA. *Faculty research:* Leadership, educational history, assessment. *Unit head:* Dr. Robin Duncan, Dean, School of Education, 951-552-8948, E-mail: rduncan@calbaptist.edu. *Application contact:* Dr. John Shoup, Director, Leadership Institute, 951-343-4205, E-mail: jshoup@calbaptist.edu.
Website: http://www.calbaptist.edu/academics/schools-colleges/school-education/programs/graduate/master-arts-leadership-and-organizational-studies

California Baptist University, Program in Organizational Leadership, Riverside, CA 92504-3206. Offers MA. *Program availability:* Part-time, evening/weekend, 100% online, blended/hybrid learning. *Faculty:* 3 full-time (1 woman), 3 part-time/adjunct (2 women). *Students:* 52 full-time (33 women), 31 part-time (21 women); includes 45 minority (8 Black or African American, non-Hispanic/Latino; 4 Asian, non-Hispanic/Latino; 28 Hispanic/Latino; 1 Native Hawaiian or other Pacific Islander, non-Hispanic/Latino; 4 Two or more races, non-Hispanic/Latino). Average age 38. 62 applicants, 73% accepted, 38 enrolled. In 2018, 54 master's awarded. *Degree requirements:* For master's, capstone project. *Entrance requirements:* For master's, minimum cumulative GPA of 2.25, current resume, two letters of recommendation, comprehensive 500-word essay. Additional exam requirements/recommendations for international students: Required—TOEFL (minimum score 80 iBT). *Application deadline:* For fall admission, 8/1 priority date for domestic students, 7/1 for international students; for spring admission, 12/1 priority date for domestic students, 11/1 for international students. Applications are processed on a rolling basis. Application fee: $45. Electronic applications accepted. *Expenses:* $607 per unit. *Financial support:* In 2018–19, 37 students received support. Federal Work-Study and scholarships/grants available. Financial award applicants required to submit CSS PROFILE or FAFSA. *Faculty research:* Organizational development, public administration, public service motivation, networked governance, finance. *Unit head:* Pamela Daly, Vice President, Online and Professional Studies, 951-343-3901, E-mail: pdaly@calbaptist.edu. *Application contact:* Dr. Jeannette Guignard, Program, MA in Organizational Leadership, 951-343-2458, E-mail: jguignard@calbaptist.edu.
Website: http://www.cbuonline.edu/programs/program/master-of-arts-in-organizational-leadership

California Coast University, School of Education, Santa Ana, CA 92701. Offers administration (M Ed); curriculum and instruction (M Ed); educational administration (Ed D); educational psychology (Ed D); organizational leadership (Ed D). *Program availability:* Online learning.

Organizational Management

California College of the Arts, Graduate Programs, MBA in Design Strategy Program, San Francisco, CA 94107. Offers MBA. *Accreditation:* NASAD. *Faculty:* 1 (woman) full-time, 14 part-time/adjunct (4 women). *Students:* 79 full-time (54 women); includes 24 minority (3 Black or African American, non-Hispanic/Latino; 10 Asian, non-Hispanic/Latino; 10 Hispanic/Latino; 1 Native Hawaiian or other Pacific Islander, non-Hispanic/Latino), 18 international. Average age 31. In 2018, 39 master's awarded. *Degree requirements:* For master's, thesis. *Entrance requirements:* Additional exam requirements/recommendations for international students: Required—TOEFL, IELTS, or PTE. *Application deadline:* For fall admission, 1/31 priority date for domestic and international students. Applications are processed on a rolling basis. Application fee: $70. Electronic applications accepted. *Expenses:* $51,210 per year for full-time students. *Financial support:* Federal Work-Study and scholarships/grants available. Financial award application deadline: 7/31; financial award applicants required to submit FAFSA. *Unit head:* Andy Dong, Program Chair, 800-447-1ART, E-mail: andy@cca.edu. *Application contact:* David Murray, Director of Graduate Admissions, 415-703-9533, Fax: 415-703-9539, E-mail: dmurray@cca.edu.

California Intercontinental University, School of Business, Irvine, CA 92614. Offers banking and finance (MBA); entrepreneurship and business management (DBA); global business leadership (DBA); international management and marketing (MBA); organizational management and human resource management (MBA).

California State University, Fullerton, Graduate Studies, College of Business and Economics, Program in Business Administration, Fullerton, CA 92831-3599. Offers business administration (MBA); business analytics (MBA); international business (MBA); organizational leadership (MBA); risk management and insurance (MBA). *Accreditation:* AACSB. *Program availability:* Part-time. *Entrance requirements:* For master's, GMAT.

Calvary University, Graduate School and Seminary, Kansas City, MO 64147. Offers Bible and theology (MS); Biblical counseling (MA); education (MS), including administration and leadership, Christian education, curriculum and instruction, elementary education; organizational development (MS); pastoral studies (M Div); worship arts (MS). *Program availability:* Part-time, evening/weekend. *Degree requirements:* For master's, variable foreign language requirement, comprehensive exam, thesis or alternative. *Entrance requirements:* For master's, minimum GPA of 2.5, BA or BS, doctrine agreement. Additional exam requirements/recommendations for international students: Required—TOEFL (minimum score 550 paper-based). Electronic applications accepted. *Expenses:* Contact institution.

Capella University, School of Business and Technology, Doctoral Programs in Business, Minneapolis, MN 55402. Offers accounting (DBA, PhD); business intelligence (DBA); finance (DBA, PhD); general business management (PhD); human resource management (DBA, PhD); leadership (DBA, PhD); management education (PhD); marketing (DBA, PhD); project management (DBA, PhD); strategy and innovation (DBA, PhD). *Accreditation:* ACBSP.

Capella University, School of Business and Technology, Master's Programs in Business, Minneapolis, MN 55402. Offers accounting (MBA); business analysis (MS); business intelligence (MBA); entrepreneurship (MBA); finance (MBA); general business administration (MBA); general human resource management (MS); general leadership (MS); health care management (MBA); human resource management (MBA); marketing (MBA); project management (MBA, MS). *Accreditation:* ACBSP.

Carlow University, College of Leadership and Social Change, Pittsburgh, PA 15213-3165. Offers MA, MBA, MS, MSW, Psy D, Certificate, MA/MS. *Program availability:* Part-time, evening/weekend, 100% online, blended/hybrid learning. *Students:* 269 full-time (217 women), 74 part-time (55 women); includes 98 minority (78 Black or African American, non-Hispanic/Latino; 3 Asian, non-Hispanic/Latino; 7 Hispanic/Latino; 10 Two or more races, non-Hispanic/Latino), 1 international. Average age 29. 169 applicants, 97% accepted, 110 enrolled. In 2018, 109 master's, 5 doctorates, 13 other advanced degrees awarded. *Degree requirements:* For doctorate, thesis/dissertation, internship. *Entrance requirements:* For master's, personal essay; resume or curriculum vitae; three recommendations; official transcripts; interview; minimum undergraduate GPA of 3.0; for doctorate, GRE, resume or curriculum vitae; personal essay; reflective essay; official transcripts from all previous undergraduate and graduate institutions; three letters of recommendation; master's degree in closely-related field. Additional exam requirements/recommendations for international students: Required—TOEFL (minimum score 550 paper-based). *Application deadline:* For fall admission, 6/15 priority date for domestic and international students; for spring admission, 11/15 priority date for domestic and international students. Applications are processed on a rolling basis. Application fee: $0. Electronic applications accepted. *Expenses:* Contact institution. *Financial support:* Application deadline: 4/1; applicants required to submit FAFSA. *Unit head:* Dr. Stephanie A. Wilsey, Dean, 412-578-6346, Fax: 412-578-8722, E-mail: sawilsey@carlow.edu. *Application contact:* Dr. Stephanie A. Wilsey, Dean, 412-578-6346, Fax: 412-578-8722, E-mail: sawilsey@carlow.edu.
Website: http://www.carlow.edu/College_of_Leadership_and_Social_Change.aspx

Carson-Newman University, Program in Social Entrepreneurship, Jefferson City, TN 37760. Offers MAASJ. *Program availability:* Part-time, evening/weekend, 100% online, blended/hybrid learning. *Faculty:* 1 part-time/adjunct (0 women). *Students:* 6 part-time (4 women); includes 1 minority (Two or more races, non-Hispanic/Latino), 1 international. Average age 27. 5 applicants, 100% accepted, 5 enrolled. In 2018, 3 master's awarded. *Degree requirements:* For master's, completion of degree within five years of admissions into program. *Entrance requirements:* For master's, GRE (minimum score of 290), minimum GPA of 3.0. Additional exam requirements/recommendations for international students: Recommended—TOEFL (minimum score 79 iBT), IELTS (minimum score 6.5), TSE (minimum score 53). *Application deadline:* For fall admission, 7/15 for domestic students. Applications are processed on a rolling basis. Application fee: $50. *Expenses: Tuition:* Full-time $9036; part-time $502 per credit hour. *Required fees:* $900; $25 per credit hour. $300 per semester. One-time fee: $150. *Financial support:* Federal Work-Study and tuition waivers (full and partial) available. Financial award applicants required to submit FAFSA. *Unit head:* Dr. Laura Wadlington, Department Chair, 865-471-3270. *Application contact:* Nilma Stewart, Graduate Admissions and Services Adviser, 865-471-3223, Fax: 865-471-3875, E-mail: adults@cn.edu.
Website: http://www.cn.edu/graduate-adult-studies/programs/applied-social-justice

Central Penn College, Graduate Programs, Summerdale, PA 17093-0309. Offers information systems management (MPS); organizational development (MPS). Programs offered in Harrisburg, PA. *Program availability:* Evening/weekend.

Charleston Southern University, College of Business, Charleston, SC 29423-8087. Offers accounting (MBA); finance (MBA); general management (MBA); human resource management (MS); leadership (MBA); management information systems (MBA); organizational leadership (MA). *Program availability:* Part-time, evening/weekend. *Degree requirements:* For master's, thesis optional. *Entrance requirements:* For master's, GMAT. Additional exam requirements/recommendations for international students: Required—TOEFL (minimum score 550 paper-based; 79 iBT). Electronic applications accepted.

Charter Oak State College, Program in Organizational Effectiveness and Leadership, New Britain, CT 06053-2142. Offers MS. *Program availability:* Part-time, evening/weekend, online only, 100% online. *Application deadline:* Applications are processed on a rolling basis. Application fee: $50. Electronic applications accepted. *Expenses:* Tuition, state resident: full-time $12,144; part-time $506 per credit. Tuition, nonresident: full-time $12,696; part-time $529 per credit. *Required fees:* $403 per semester. Tuition and fees vary according to course load. *Financial support:* Scholarships/grants available. Financial award applicants required to submit FAFSA. *Unit head:* Dr. Thomas Barron, Director of Organizational Effectiveness and Leadership Program, 860-515-3838, E-mail: tbarron@charteroak.edu. *Application contact:* Dr. Thomas Barron, Director of Organizational Effectiveness and Leadership Program, 860-515-3838, E-mail: tbarron@charteroak.edu.
Website: http://www.charteroak.edu/masters/

The Chicago School of Professional Psychology, Program in Business Psychology, Chicago, IL 60610. Offers business psychology (PhD); industrial and organizational business psychology (Psy D); industrial and organizational psychology (MA); organizational leadership (MA, PhD). *Degree requirements:* For doctorate, thesis/dissertation optional. *Entrance requirements:* For doctorate, GRE. Additional exam requirements/recommendations for international students: Required—TOEFL.

City University of Seattle, Graduate Division, School of Management, Seattle, WA 98121. Offers accounting (Certificate); change leadership (MBA, Certificate); computer systems (MS); finance (Certificate); financial management (MBA); general management (MBA); general management-Europe (MBA); global marketing (MBA); human resources management (Certificate); individualized study (MBA); information security (MS); information systems (MBA); leadership (MA); marketing (MBA, Certificate); project management (MBA, MS, Certificate); sustainable business (Certificate); technology management (MBA, Certificate). *Program availability:* Part-time, evening/weekend, online learning. *Degree requirements:* For master's, comprehensive exam (for some programs), thesis (for some programs). *Entrance requirements:* For master's, baccalaureate degree or equivalent from an accredited or otherwise recognized institution. Additional exam requirements/recommendations for international students: Required—TOEFL (minimum score 567 paper-based; 87 iBT); Recommended—IELTS. Electronic applications accepted.

Clarks Summit University, Baptist Bible Seminary, South Abington Township, PA 18411. Offers Biblical apologetics (MA); Biblical studies (MA); church education (M Min); church planting (M Div, M Min); communication (D Min); counseling and spiritual development (D Min); global ministry (M Min, D Min); ministry (PhD); missions (M Min); organizational leadership (M Min); outreach pastor (M Min); pastoral counseling (M Min); pastoral leadership (M Div, M Min); pastoral ministry (D Min); theological studies (D Min); theology (Th M); youth pastor (M Min). M Min in missions available only for Association of Baptists for World Evangelism missionary personnel. *Program availability:* Part-time, evening/weekend, online learning. Terminal master's awarded for partial completion of doctoral program. *Degree requirements:* For master's, 2 foreign languages, thesis, oral exam (for M Div); for doctorate, 2 foreign languages, comprehensive exam (for some programs), thesis/dissertation, oral exam. *Entrance requirements:* For doctorate, Greek and Hebrew entrance exams (for PhD). Electronic applications accepted.

Clarks Summit University, Online Master's Programs, South Abington Township, PA 18411. Offers Bible (MA); counseling (MA, MS); curriculum and instruction (M Ed); educational administration (M Ed); literature (MA); organizational leadership (MA). *Program availability:* Part-time, evening/weekend, online learning. *Entrance requirements:* Additional exam requirements/recommendations for international students: Required—TOEFL (minimum score 500 paper-based).

College of Saint Elizabeth, Department of Business Administration and Management, Morristown, NJ 07960-6989. Offers human resource management (MS); organizational change (MS). *Program availability:* Part-time. *Degree requirements:* For master's, thesis. *Entrance requirements:* Additional exam requirements/recommendations for international students: Required—TOEFL (minimum score 550 paper-based; 79 iBT), IELTS (minimum score 6.5). Electronic applications accepted. Application fee is waived when completed online.

College of Saint Mary, Program in Organizational Leadership, Omaha, NE 68106. Offers MOL. *Program availability:* Part-time, evening/weekend. *Entrance requirements:* For master's, resume. Electronic applications accepted.

The College of Saint Rose, Graduate Studies, Huether School of Business, Program in Organizational Leadership and Change Management, Albany, NY 12203-1419. Offers Advanced Certificate. *Program availability:* Part-time, evening/weekend. *Students:* 1 full-time. Average age 22. 2 applicants, 50% accepted, 1 enrolled. In 2018, 6 Advanced Certificates awarded. *Entrance requirements:* Additional exam requirements/recommendations for international students: Required—TOEFL (minimum score 550 paper-based; 80 iBT), IELTS (minimum score 6), PTE (minimum score 56). *Application deadline:* For fall admission, 4/1 priority date for domestic and international students; for spring admission, 10/15 priority date for domestic and international students; for summer admission, 3/15 priority date for domestic and international students. Applications are processed on a rolling basis. Application fee: $40. Electronic applications accepted. *Expenses: Tuition:* Full-time $14,382; part-time $799 per credit hour. *Required fees:* $924; $408 per credit. $286. *Financial support:* Career-related internships or fieldwork and scholarships/grants available. Support available to part-time students. Financial award application deadline: 4/15. *Unit head:* Rajarshi Aroskar, Dean, 518-454-5272, E-mail: aroskarr@strose.edu. *Application contact:* Daniel Gallagher, Assistant Vice President for Graduate Recruitment and Enrollment, 518-485-3390, Fax: 518-458-5479, E-mail: grad@strose.edu.
Website: https://www.strose.edu/academics/graduate-programs/graduate-studies/organizational-leadership-and-change-management-certificate/

Colorado State University–Global Campus, Graduate Programs, Greenwood Village, CO 80111. Offers criminal justice and law enforcement administration (MS); education leadership (MS); finance (MS); healthcare administration and management (MS); human resource management (MHRM); information technology management (MITM); international management (MS); management (MS); organizational leadership (MS); professional accounting (MPA); project management (MS); teaching and learning (MS). *Accreditation:* ACBSP. *Program availability:* Online learning.

Columbia College, Graduate Programs, Program in Organizational Leadership, Columbia, SC 29203-5998. Offers organizational change and leadership (MA). *Program availability:* Part-time, evening/weekend, online learning. *Degree requirements:* For master's, thesis, practicum. *Entrance requirements:* For master's, GRE General Test, MAT, 2 letters of recommendation, minimum GPA of 3.2. Additional exam requirements/recommendations for international students: Required—TOEFL. Electronic applications accepted. *Expenses:* Contact institution. *Faculty research:* Envisioning and the resolution of conflict, environmental conflict resolution, crisis negotiation.

Columbia Southern University, Program in Organizational Leadership, Orange Beach, AL 36561. Offers MS.

Columbus State University, Graduate Studies, Turner College of Business, Columbus, GA 31907-5645. Offers applied computer science (MS), including informational assurance, modeling and simulation, software development; business administration

(MBA); cyber security (MS); human resource management (Certificate); information systems security (Certificate); modeling and simulation (Certificate); organizational leadership (MS), including human resource management, leader development, servant leadership; servant leadership (Certificate). *Accreditation:* AACSB. *Program availability:* Part-time, evening/weekend, 100% online, blended/hybrid learning. *Faculty:* 10 full-time (3 women), 1 part-time/adjunct (0 women). *Students:* 79 full-time (24 women), 136 part-time (47 women); includes 73 minority (40 Black or African American, non-Hispanic/Latino; 1 American Indian or Alaska Native, non-Hispanic/Latino; 8 Asian, non-Hispanic/Latino; 15 Hispanic/Latino; 9 Two or more races, non-Hispanic/Latino), 27 international. Average age 31. 237 applicants, 51% accepted, 64 enrolled. In 2018, 113 master's, 10 other advanced degrees awarded. *Entrance requirements:* For master's, GMAT, GRE, minimum undergraduate GPA of 2.75, letters of recommendation. Additional exam requirements/recommendations for international students: Required—TOEFL (minimum score 550 paper-based; 79 iBT). *Application deadline:* For fall admission, 6/30 for domestic students, 5/1 for international students; for spring admission, 11/1 for domestic and international students; for summer admission, 3/1 for domestic and international students. Applications are processed on a rolling basis. Application fee: $50. Electronic applications accepted. *Expenses:* Contact institution. *Financial support:* In 2018–19, 18 students received support, including 20 research assistantships (averaging $3,000 per year); Federal Work-Study also available. Financial award application deadline: 5/1; financial award applicants required to submit FAFSA. *Unit head:* Dr. Linda U. Hadley, Dean, 706-507-8153, Fax: 706-568-2184, E-mail: hadley_linda@columbusstate.edu. *Application contact:* Catrina Smith-Edmond, Assistant Director for Graduate and Global Admission, 706-507-8824, Fax: 706-568-5091, E-mail: smithedmond_catrina@columbusstate.edu.
Website: http://turner.columbusstate.edu/

Concordia College–New York, Program in Business Leadership, Bronxville, NY 10708-1998. Offers MS. *Degree requirements:* For master's, capstone seminar.

Concordia University, School of Graduate Studies, Faculty of Arts and Science, Department of Applied Human Sciences, Montréal, QC H3G 1M8, Canada. Offers human systems intervention (MA); youth work (Graduate Diploma). *Degree requirements:* For master's, 2-week residential laboratory. *Entrance requirements:* For master's, 1 week residential laboratory, 2 full years of work experience. *Faculty research:* Health promotion, adult learning and transitions, applications of group development and small group leadership, adolescent development, generational issues in immigrant families.

Concordia University Ann Arbor, Graduate Programs, Ann Arbor, MI 48105-2797. Offers curriculum and instruction (MS); educational leadership (MS); organizational leadership and administration (MS). *Program availability:* Part-time, evening/weekend. *Degree requirements:* For master's, thesis. *Entrance requirements:* Additional exam requirements/recommendations for international students: Required—TOEFL (minimum score 80 iBT); Recommended—IELTS (minimum score 6.5). Electronic applications accepted.

Concordia University, St. Paul, College of Business and Technology, St. Paul, MN 55104-5494. Offers business administration (MBA), including cyber-security leadership; health care management (MBA); human resource management (MA); information technology (MBA); leadership and management (MA); strategic communication management (MA). *Accreditation:* ACBSP. *Program availability:* Part-time, evening/weekend, 100% online, blended/hybrid learning. *Faculty:* 12 full-time (5 women), 28 part-time/adjunct (14 women). *Students:* 448 full-time (289 women), 30 part-time (17 women); includes 135 minority (58 Black or African American, non-Hispanic/Latino; 2 American Indian or Alaska Native, non-Hispanic/Latino; 46 Asian, non-Hispanic/Latino; 13 Hispanic/Latino; 16 Two or more races, non-Hispanic/Latino), 40 international. Average age 32. 328 applicants, 96% accepted, 149 enrolled. In 2018, 205 master's awarded. *Degree requirements:* For master's, thesis (for some programs). *Entrance requirements:* For master's, official transcripts from regionally-accredited institution stating the conferral of a bachelor's degree with minimum cumulative GPA of 3.0; personal statement; professional resume. Additional exam requirements/recommendations for international students: Recommended—TOEFL (minimum score 547 paper-based; 78 iBT), IELTS (minimum score 6). *Application deadline:* For fall admission, 8/1 for domestic and international students; for spring admission, 12/1 for domestic and international students; for summer admission, 5/1 for domestic and international students. Applications are processed on a rolling basis. Application fee: $0. Electronic applications accepted. *Expenses:* $625 a credit for 42 credits (for MBA), $475 a credit for 36 credits (for MA/MS). *Financial support:* In 2018–19, 267 students received support. Federal Work-Study, scholarships/grants, and unspecified assistantships available. Financial award applicants required to submit FAFSA. *Faculty research:* Leadership in transition and polarity, managing the evolution of a software product line, decision making and behavioral economics, strength based coaching and the relationship with student success, three-way XML merging. *Unit head:* Dr. Kevin Hall, Dean, 651-603-6165, Fax: 651-641-8807, E-mail: khall@csp.edu. *Application contact:* Amber Faletti, Director of Enrollment Management, 651-641-8838, Fax: 651-603-6320, E-mail: faletti@csp.edu.

Concordia University Wisconsin, Graduate Programs, Batterman School of Business, Program in Organizational Leadership Administration, Mequon, WI 53097-2402. Offers MS. *Degree requirements:* For master's, comprehensive exam, thesis or alternative. *Entrance requirements:* Additional exam requirements/recommendations for international students: Required—TOEFL.

Crandall University, Graduate Programs, Moncton, NB E1C 9L7, Canada. Offers literacy education (M Ed); organizational management (MOM); resource education (M Ed).

Creighton University, Graduate School, Department of Interdisciplinary Studies, MS Program in Organizational Leadership, Omaha, NE 68178-0001. Offers MS. *Program availability:* Part-time, online only, 100% online. *Faculty:* 2 full-time (1 woman). *Students:* 8 full-time (3 women), 48 part-time (29 women); includes 9 minority (2 Black or African American, non-Hispanic/Latino; 2 American Indian or Alaska Native, non-Hispanic/Latino; 3 Asian, non-Hispanic/Latino; 2 Hispanic/Latino). Average age 33. 21 applicants, 100% accepted, 11 enrolled. In 2018, 9 master's awarded. *Degree requirements:* For master's, project-based capstone. *Entrance requirements:* For master's, two years of work experience, minimum undergraduate GPA of 3.0, two letters of recommendation, personal statement. Additional exam requirements/recommendations for international students: Required—TOEFL (minimum score 90 iBT), IELTS (minimum score 6.6). *Application deadline:* For fall admission, 7/1 for domestic and international students; for spring admission, 11/1 for domestic and international students; for summer admission, 3/1 for domestic and international students. Applications are processed on a rolling basis. Application fee: $50. Electronic applications accepted. *Expenses:* Tuition - 870/credit hour. *Financial support:* Scholarships/grants available. *Unit head:* Dr. Gretchen Oltman, Director, 402-280-3418, Fax: 402-280-2423, E-mail: gretchenoltman@creighton.edu. *Application contact:* Lindsay Johnson, Director of Graduate and Adult Recruitment, 402-280-2703, Fax: 402-280-2423, E-mail: gradschool@creighton.edu.

Dallas Baptist University, Gary Cook School of Leadership, Program in Educational Leadership, Dallas, TX 75211-9299. Offers higher education leadership (Ed D), including educational ministry leadership, general leadership, higher education leadership. *Program availability:* Part-time. *Degree requirements:* For doctorate, thesis/dissertation. *Application deadline:* Applications are processed on a rolling basis. Application fee: $25. Electronic applications accepted. Application fee is waived when completed online. *Expenses: Tuition:* Full-time $17,262; part-time $959 per credit hour. *Required fees:* $1000; $500 per semester. Tuition and fees vary according to course load and degree level. *Unit head:* Dr. Jack Goodyear, Dean, 214-333-5595, E-mail: jackg@dbu.edu. *Application contact:* Dr. Ozzie Ingram, Program Director, 214-333-6875, E-mail: ozzie@dbu.edu.
Website: http://www4.dbu.edu/leadership/education-leadership-ed-d

Dallas Baptist University, Gary Cook School of Leadership, Program in Leadership, Dallas, TX 75211-9299. Offers MA. *Program availability:* Part-time, evening/weekend. *Application deadline:* Applications are processed on a rolling basis. Application fee: $25. Electronic applications accepted. Application fee is waived when completed online. *Expenses: Tuition:* Full-time $17,262; part-time $959 per credit hour. *Required fees:* $1000; $500 per semester. Tuition and fees vary according to course load and degree level. *Unit head:* Dr. Jack Goodyear, Dean, 214-333-5595, Fax: 214-333-6809, E-mail: jackg@dbu.edu. *Application contact:* Dr. Dale Meinecke, Program Director, 214-333-7169, E-mail: dalem@dbu.edu.
Website: https://www.dbu.edu/graduate/degree-programs/ma-leadership

Duke University, The Fuqua School of Business, The Duke MBA-Daytime Program, Durham, NC 27708. Offers academic excellence in finance (Certificate); business administration (MBA); decision sciences (MBA); energy and environment (MBA); energy finance (MBA); entrepreneurship and innovation (MBA); finance (MBA); financial analysis (MBA); health sector management (Certificate); leadership and ethics (MBA); management (MBA); management science and technology management (Certificate); marketing (MBA); operations management (MBA); social entrepreneurship (MBA); strategy (MBA). *Faculty:* 100 full-time (21 women), 55 part-time/adjunct (12 women). *Students:* 875 full-time (335 women); includes 188 minority (44 Black or African American, non-Hispanic/Latino; 4 American Indian or Alaska Native, non-Hispanic/Latino; 90 Asian, non-Hispanic/Latino; 43 Hispanic/Latino; 1 Native Hawaiian or other Pacific Islander, non-Hispanic/Latino; 6 Two or more races, non-Hispanic/Latino), 276 international. Average age 29. In 2018, 429 master's awarded. *Entrance requirements:* For master's, GMAT or GRE, transcripts, essays, resume, recommendation letters, interview. *Application deadline:* For fall admission, 9/19 for domestic and international students; for winter admission, 10/14 for domestic and international students; for spring admission, 1/6 for domestic and international students; for summer admission, 3/11 for domestic and international students. Application fee: $225. Electronic applications accepted. *Expenses:* Contact institution. *Financial support:* Scholarships/grants available. Financial award applicants required to submit FAFSA. *Unit head:* Steve Misuraca, Assistant Dean, Daytime MBA Program. *Application contact:* Shari Hubert, Associate Dean, Office of Admissions, 919-660-7705, Fax: 919-681-8026, E-mail: admissions-info@fuqua.duke.edu.
Website: https://www.fuqua.duke.edu/programs/daytime-mba

Duke University, The Fuqua School of Business, PhD Program, Durham, NC 27708. Offers accounting (PhD); decision sciences (PhD); finance (PhD); management and organizations (PhD); marketing (PhD); operations management (PhD); strategy (PhD). *Faculty:* 100 full-time (21 women). *Students:* 84 full-time (29 women); includes 4 minority (2 Asian, non-Hispanic/Latino; 2 Hispanic/Latino), 53 international. Average age 28. In 2018, 14 doctorates awarded. *Degree requirements:* For doctorate, comprehensive exam (for some programs), thesis/dissertation, Comprehensive or Qualifying exams are required for some of the 7 areas in Business Administration. *Entrance requirements:* For doctorate, GMAT or GRE, transcripts, essays, recommendation letters, statement of purpose. Additional exam requirements/recommendations for international students: Required—TOEFL, IELTS. *Application deadline:* For fall admission, 12/31 priority date for domestic and international students. Application fee: $90. Electronic applications accepted. *Expenses:* Contact institution. *Financial support:* In 2018–19, 74 fellowships with full tuition reimbursements (averaging $33,300 per year) were awarded; research assistantships with full tuition reimbursements, teaching assistantships, institutionally sponsored loans, scholarships/grants, health care benefits, and tuition waivers (full) also available. *Unit head:* William Boulding, Dean, 919-660-7822. *Application contact:* Ravi Bansal, Director of Graduate Studies, 919-660-7753, Fax: 919-660-7971, E-mail: fuqua-phd-info@duke.edu.

Duquesne University, Graduate School of Liberal Arts, Master of Science in Leadership Program, Pittsburgh, PA 15282-0001. Offers MS. *Program availability:* Part-time, evening/weekend, online only, 100% online. *Students:* 16 full-time (8 women), 21 part-time (11 women); includes 6 minority (all Black or African American, non-Hispanic/Latino), 1 international. Average age 35. 17 applicants, 100% accepted, 11 enrolled. In 2018, 49 master's awarded. *Entrance requirements:* Additional exam requirements/recommendations for international students: Required—TOEFL. *Application deadline:* For fall admission, 8/1 for domestic students; for spring admission, 11/15 priority date for domestic students; for summer admission, 4/15 for domestic students. Applications are processed on a rolling basis. Application fee: $0. Electronic applications accepted. *Expenses: Tuition:* Full-time $23,112; part-time $1284 per credit. Tuition and fees vary according to program. *Financial support:* Available to part-time students. Application deadline: 5/1. *Unit head:* Dr. John Kern, Associate Dean, 412-396-6389, E-mail: kernj@duq.edu. *Application contact:* Linda Rendulic, Assistant to the Dean, 412-396-6400, Fax: 412-396-5265, E-mail: rendulic@duq.edu.
Website: http://duq.edu/academics/schools/liberal-arts/academic-programs/leadership

Eastern Connecticut State University, School of Education and Professional Studies/Graduate Division, Program in Organizational Management, Willimantic, CT 06226-2295. Offers MS. *Program availability:* Part-time, evening/weekend. *Degree requirements:* For master's, comprehensive exam or thesis. *Entrance requirements:* For master's, minimum GPA of 2.7, bachelor's degree from accredited institution. Additional exam requirements/recommendations for international students: Required—TOEFL (minimum score 550 paper-based; 79 iBT); Recommended—IELTS (minimum score 6). Electronic applications accepted.

Eastern Mennonite University, Program in Organizational Leadership, Harrisonburg, VA 22802-2462. Offers MA.

Eastern Michigan University, Graduate School, College of Business, Department of Management, Program in Human Resources Management and Organizational Development, Ypsilanti, MI 48197. Offers MSHROD. *Program availability:* Part-time, evening/weekend, online learning. *Students:* 5 full-time (4 women), 68 part-time (54 women); includes 29 minority (19 Black or African American, non-Hispanic/Latino; 4 Asian, non-Hispanic/Latino; 4 Hispanic/Latino; 2 Two or more races, non-Hispanic/Latino), 3 international. Average age 32. 47 applicants, 81% accepted, 18 enrolled. In 2018, 62 master's awarded. *Entrance requirements:* For master's, GMAT. Additional exam requirements/recommendations for international students: Required—TOEFL. *Application deadline:* Applications are processed on a rolling basis. Application fee: $45. *Financial support:* Fellowships, research assistantships with full tuition reimbursements, teaching assistantships with full tuition reimbursements, career-related internships or fieldwork, Federal Work-Study, institutionally sponsored loans, scholarships/grants, tuition waivers (partial), and unspecified assistantships available. Support available to

part-time students. Financial award applicants required to submit FAFSA. *Unit head:* Dr. Fraya Wagner-Marsh, Department Head, 734-487-3240, Fax: 734-487-4100, E-mail: fwagnerm@emich.edu. *Application contact:* Dr. Fraya Wagner-Marsh, Department Head, 734-487-3240, Fax: 734-487-4100, E-mail: fwagnerm@emich.edu.
Website: http://www.emich.edu/cob/departments_centers/management/mshrod.php

Eastern Michigan University, Graduate School, College of Business, Programs in Business Administration, Ypsilanti, MI 48197. Offers business administration (MBA, Graduate Certificate); computer information systems (Graduate Certificate); e-business (MBA, Graduate Certificate); enterprise business intelligence (MBA); entrepreneurship (MBA, Graduate Certificate); finance (MBA, Graduate Certificate); human resources (MBA); human resources management (Graduate Certificate); information systems (MBA); internal auditing (MBA); international business (MBA, Graduate Certificate); marketing management (Graduate Certificate); nonprofit management (MBA); organizational development (Graduate Certificate); supply chain management (MBA, Graduate Certificate). *Accreditation:* AACSB. *Program availability:* Part-time, online learning. *Students:* 69 full-time (38 women), 251 part-time (140 women); includes 100 minority (63 Black or African American, non-Hispanic/Latino; 1 American Indian or Alaska Native, non-Hispanic/Latino; 12 Asian, non-Hispanic/Latino; 14 Hispanic/Latino; 10 Two or more races, non-Hispanic/Latino), 28 international. Average age 32. 199 applicants, 75% accepted, 83 enrolled. In 2018, 75 master's, 50 other advanced degrees awarded. *Entrance requirements:* For master's, GMAT (minimum score 450), minimum cumulative undergraduate GPA of 2.75. Additional exam requirements/ recommendations for international students: Required—TOEFL. *Application deadline:* For fall admission, 5/15 priority date for domestic students, 2/15 priority date for international students; for winter admission, 10/15 priority date for domestic students, 9/1 priority date for international students; for summer admission, 3/15 priority date for domestic students, 3/1 priority date for international students. Applications are processed on a rolling basis. Application fee: $45. *Financial support:* Fellowships, research assistantships with full tuition reimbursements, teaching assistantships with full tuition reimbursements, career-related internships or fieldwork, Federal Work-Study, institutionally sponsored loans, scholarships/grants, tuition waivers (partial), and unspecified assistantships available. Support available to part-time students. Financial award applicants required to submit FAFSA. *Unit head:* K. Michelle Henry, Director, Graduate Business Programs, 734-487-4444, Fax: 734-483-1316, E-mail: cob.graduate@emich.edu. *Application contact:* K. Michelle Henry, Director, Graduate Business Programs, 734-487-4444, Fax: 734-483-1316, E-mail: cob.graduate@emich.edu.
Website: http://www.emich.edu/cob/mba/

Eastern University, Graduate Programs in Business and Leadership, St. Davids, PA 19087-3696. Offers health administration (MBA); health services management (MS); management (MBA); organizational leadership (MA); social impact (MBA). *Program availability:* Part-time, evening/weekend, online learning. Electronic applications accepted. Application fee is waived when completed online. *Expenses:* Contact institution.

Eastern University, Program in Organizational Leadership, St. Davids, PA 19087-3696. Offers leadership studies (CAGS); organizational leadership (PhD), including business management, educational administration, public and nonprofit administration. Electronic applications accepted. *Expenses:* Contact institution.

Emory & Henry College, Graduate Programs, Emory, VA 24327. Offers American history (MA Ed); education professional studies (M Ed); occupational therapy (MOT); organizational leadership (MCOL); physical therapy (DPT); physician assistant studies (MPAS); reading specialist (MA Ed). *Program availability:* Part-time. *Degree requirements:* For master's, thesis optional; for doctorate, thesis/dissertation optional. *Entrance requirements:* For master's, GRE or PRAXIS I, official transcripts from all colleges previously attended, three professional recommendations, essay. Additional exam requirements/recommendations for international students: Recommended—TOEFL, IELTS (minimum score 6). Electronic applications accepted. *Expenses:* Contact institution.

Emory University, Goizueta Business School, Doctoral Program in Business, Atlanta, GA 30322. Offers accounting (PhD); finance (PhD); information systems and operations management (PhD); marketing (PhD); organization and management (PhD). *Faculty:* 67 full-time (22 women). *Students:* 45 full-time (21 women); includes 5 minority (2 Black or African American, non-Hispanic/Latino; 3 Hispanic/Latino), 31 international. Average age 29. 143 applicants, 19% accepted, 10 enrolled. In 2018, 7 doctorates awarded. *Degree requirements:* For doctorate, comprehensive exam, thesis/dissertation. *Entrance requirements:* For doctorate, GMAT, interview. Additional exam requirements/ recommendations for international students: Required—TOEFL (minimum score 600 paper-based; 100 iBT), IELTS, We will take either TOEFL or IELTS. *Application deadline:* For fall admission, 1/3 priority date for domestic and international students. Applications are processed on a rolling basis. Application fee: $75. Electronic applications accepted. *Expenses:* Our students are required to pay approximately $400 in their fall and spring terms; approximately $200 in summer terms in fees. All tuition is scholarshiped 100%. *Financial support:* In 2018–19, 45 students received support, including 11 fellowships (averaging $1,000 per year); scholarships/grants, health care benefits, and Fellowships are both the Sheth Fellows and Goizueta Fellows whom are named each year based on certain milestones. also available. Financial award application deadline: 1/3. *Faculty research:* Financial and managerial accounting, asset pricing strategy and organizational behavior, information technology marketing analytics and consumer behavior. *Unit head:* Kathryn Kadous, Associate Dean, 404-727-2306, Fax: 404-727-5337, E-mail: kathryn.kadous@emory.edu. *Application contact:* Allison Gilmore, Director of Admissions and Student Services, 404-727-6353, Fax: 404-727-5337, E-mail: allison.gilmore@emory.edu.
Website: https://goizueta.emory.edu/degree/phd/index.html

Emory University, Goizueta Business School, Full Time MBA Program, Atlanta, GA 30322-1100. Offers accounting (MBA); alternative investments (MBA); business process consulting (MBA); business technology management (MBA); capital markets (MBA); corporate finance (MBA); customer relationship management (MBA); decision analytics (MBA); entrepreneurship (MBA); finance (MBA); global management (MBA); investment banking (MBA); management consulting (MBA); marketing (MBA); marketing analytics (MBA); marketing consulting (MBA); operations management (MBA); organization and management (MBA); product and brand management (MBA); real estate (MBA); social enterprise (MBA); strategy consulting (MBA). *Accreditation:* AACSB. *Faculty:* 74 full-time (18 women), 18 part-time/adjunct (6 women). *Students:* 349 full-time (105 women); includes 81 minority (26 Black or African American, non-Hispanic/Latino; 1 American Indian or Alaska Native, non-Hispanic/Latino; 35 Asian, non-Hispanic/Latino; 16 Hispanic/Latino; 3 Two or more races, non-Hispanic/Latino), 97 international. Average age 29. 1,380 applicants, 34% accepted, 172 enrolled. In 2018, 180 master's awarded. *Degree requirements:* For master's, 1 leadership course; 2 mid-semester module programs; 2 global components. *Entrance requirements:* For master's, GMAT/GRE, essays; recommendation letters; undergraduate degree; interview. Additional exam requirements/recommendations for international students: Required—TOEFL (minimum score 100 iBT), IELTS (minimum score 7), PTE (minimum score 68). *Application deadline:* For fall admission, 10/6 for domestic and international students; for winter admission, 11/17 for domestic and international students; for spring admission, 1/3 priority date for domestic and international students; for summer admission, 3/9 for domestic and international students. Application fee: $150. Electronic applications accepted. *Expenses:* Contact institution. *Financial support:* In 2018–19, 273 students received support. Career-related internships or fieldwork, institutionally sponsored loans, and scholarships/grants available. Financial award application deadline: 4/1; financial award applicants required to submit FAFSA. *Faculty research:* Corporate finance, information systems, digital marketing, asset pricing, sports management. *Unit head:* Brian Mitchell, Associate Dean, 404-727-4824, Fax: 404-712-9648, E-mail: brian.mitchell@emory.edu. *Application contact:* Melissa Rapp, Associate Dean, 404-727-7583, Fax: 404-727-4612, E-mail: mbaadmissions@emory.edu.
Website: http://www.goizueta.emory.edu

Endicott College, Van Loan School of Graduate and Professional Studies, Program in Business Administration, Beverly, MA 01915-2096. Offers business administration (MBA); organizational leadership (MBA). *Program availability:* Part-time, evening/weekend, 100% online, blended/hybrid learning. *Degree requirements:* For master's, thesis, project. *Entrance requirements:* For master's, two recommendations, undergraduate transcript, essay. Additional exam requirements/recommendations for international students: Required—TOEFL. Electronic applications accepted. *Expenses:* Contact institution. *Faculty research:* Adult learning and development, supply chain management, marketing, ethics.

Endicott College, Van Loan School of Graduate and Professional Studies, Program in Organizational Management, Beverly, MA 01915-2096. Offers M Ed. *Program availability:* Part-time, evening/weekend, 100% online. *Degree requirements:* For master's, thesis. *Entrance requirements:* For master's, GRE or MAT, two letters of recommendation, personal interview, 250-500 word essay, official transcripts of undergraduate and graduate course work. Additional exam requirements/ recommendations for international students: Required—TOEFL. Electronic applications accepted. *Expenses:* Contact institution.

Evangel University, Organizational Leadership Program, Springfield, MO 65802. Offers MOL. *Program availability:* Part-time, evening/weekend, 100% online, blended/ hybrid learning. *Entrance requirements:* Additional exam requirements/ recommendations for international students: Required—TOEFL (minimum score 550 paper-based). Electronic applications accepted.

Fairleigh Dickinson University, Florham Campus, Maxwell Becton College of Arts and Sciences, Department of Psychology, Program in Organizational Behavior, Madison, NJ 07940-1099. Offers organizational behavior (MA); organizational leadership (Certificate).

Fielding Graduate University, Graduate Programs, School of Leadership Studies, Programs in Evidence Based Coaching, Santa Barbara, CA 93105-3814. Offers comprehensive evidence based coaching (Graduate Certificate); evidence based coaching for organizational leadership (Graduate Certificate). *Program availability:* Part-time, evening/weekend, blended/hybrid learning. *Faculty:* 1 full-time (0 women), 15 part-time/adjunct (8 women). *Students:* 47 part-time (36 women); includes 15 minority (8 Black or African American, non-Hispanic/Latino; 2 Asian, non-Hispanic/Latino; 5 Hispanic/Latino). Average age 48. 17 applicants, 100% accepted, 13 enrolled. In 2018, 23 Graduate Certificates awarded. *Entrance requirements:* For degree, bachelor's degree from regionally-accredited U.S. institution or equivalent, resume, official transcript. *Application deadline:* For fall admission, 7/16 for domestic and international students; for spring admission, 11/21 for domestic and international students; for summer admission, 3/25 for domestic and international students. Application fee: $75. Electronic applications accepted. *Expenses:* Https://www.fielding.edu/how-to-apply/ tuition-financial-aid/tuition-fees/. *Financial support:* Fellowships, research assistantships, teaching assistantships, and tuition waivers available. Financial award applicants required to submit FAFSA. *Faculty research:* Evidence based, coaching, leadership. *Unit head:* Terry Hilderbrand, PhD, Program Faculty Lead, E-mail: thildebrandt@fielding.edu. *Application contact:* Enrollment Coordinator, 800-340-1099 Ext. 4098, Fax: 805-687-9793, E-mail: hodadmission@fielding.edu.
Website: http://www.fielding.edu/our-programs/school-of-leadership-studies/ comprehensive-evidence-based-coaching-certificate/

Gannon University, School of Graduate Studies, College of Humanities, Education, and Social Sciences, School of Humanities, Program in Organizational Learning and Leadership, Erie, PA 16541-0001. Offers PhD. *Program availability:* Part-time, evening/ weekend. *Degree requirements:* For doctorate, thesis/dissertation. *Entrance requirements:* For doctorate, GRE, master's or other post-baccalaureate professional graduate-level degree from regionally-accredited institution of higher education with minimum GPA of 3.5; 2 years of post-baccalaureate work experience; 3 letters of recommendation; transcripts; resume; statement of purpose. Additional exam requirements/recommendations for international students: Required—TOEFL (minimum score 79 iBT). Electronic applications accepted. Application fee is waived when completed online.

Gardner-Webb University, Graduate School, School of Education, Boiling Springs, NC 28017. Offers curriculum and instruction (Ed D); educational leadership (Ed D); executive leadership studies (MA, Ed S); organizational leadership (Ed D); school administration (MA). *Accreditation:* NCATE. *Program availability:* Part-time, evening/ weekend. *Degree requirements:* For master's, comprehensive exam. *Entrance requirements:* For master's, GRE General Test or NTE, PRAXIS, minimum GPA of 2.5. Electronic applications accepted. *Expenses:* Contact institution.

Geneva College, Program in Leadership Studies, Beaver Falls, PA 15010-3599. Offers business management (MS); ministry leadership (MS); non-profit leadership (MS); organizational management (MS); project management (MS). *Program availability:* Online only, 100% online. *Degree requirements:* For master's, thesis or alternative, capstone leadership studies project. *Entrance requirements:* For master's, undergraduate degree from regionally-accredited college or university, one to three years of experience in the workplace, minimum GPA of 3.0 (preferred), resume, essay, two recommendations. Additional exam requirements/recommendations for international students: Required—TOEFL. Electronic applications accepted. *Expenses:* Contact institution. *Faculty research:* Servant leadership, leadership essentials.

George Fox University, College of Business, Newberg, OR 97132-2697. Offers accounting (DBA); finance (MBA); management (DBA); management and leadership (MBA); marketing (DBA); organizational strategy (MBA); strategic human resource management (MBA). MBA offered in Newberg, OR and in Portland, OR. *Accreditation:* ACBSP. *Program availability:* Part-time, evening/weekend, online learning. *Degree requirements:* For master's, capstone project; for doctorate, credit-applied research project. *Entrance requirements:* For master's, resume (5 years of professional experience); 3 professional references; interview; financial e-learning course; official transcripts; for doctorate, GRE or GMAT, resume; personal mission statement; academic research writing sample; official transcript from each college/university attended; three professional references. Additional exam requirements/ recommendations for international students: Required—TOEFL (minimum score 577 paper-based; 90 iBT) or IELTS (minimum score 7). Electronic applications accepted. *Expenses:* Contact institution.

George Mason University, Schar School of Policy and Government, Program in Organization Development and Knowledge Management, Arlington, VA 22201. Offers MS. *Faculty:* 2 full-time (1 woman), 4 part-time/adjunct (2 women). *Students:* 2 full-time (both women), 38 part-time (31 women); includes 16 minority (5 Black or African American, non-Hispanic/Latino; 6 Asian, non-Hispanic/Latino; 2 Hispanic/Latino; 3 Two or more races, non-Hispanic/Latino), 4 international. Average age 34. 32 applicants, 97% accepted, 21 enrolled. In 2018, 25 master's awarded. *Degree requirements:* For master's, thesis or alternative, internship. *Entrance requirements:* For master's, GRE (for students seeking merit-based scholarships), bachelor's degree with minimum GPA of 3.0, current resume, 2 letters of recommendation, expanded goals statement, 2 copies of official transcripts. Additional exam requirements/recommendations for international students: Required—TOEFL (minimum score 575 paper-based; 88 iBT), IELTS (minimum score 6.5), PTE (minimum score 59). *Application deadline:* For fall admission, 2/1 priority date for domestic and international students. Applications are processed on a rolling basis. Application fee: $75 ($80 for international students). Electronic applications accepted. *Expenses:* $689 per credit in-state tuition, $1,446.75 per credit out-of-state tuition. *Financial support:* Career-related internships or fieldwork, Federal Work-Study, scholarships/grants, unspecified assistantships, and health care benefits (for full-time research or teaching assistantship recipients) available. Financial award application deadline: 3/1; financial award applicants required to submit FAFSA. *Faculty research:* Organization development; appreciative intelligence; leadership; collaborative learning; knowledge management. *Unit head:* Tojo Joseph Thatchenkery, Director, 703-993-3808, Fax: 703-993-8215, E-mail: thatchen@gmu.edu. *Application contact:* Stephanie Ellis, Graduate Admissions Coordinator, 703-993-4478, E-mail: sellis11@gmu.edu.
Website: http://spgia.gmu.edu/programs/graduate-degrees/organization-development-knowledge-management-odkm/

The George Washington University, Columbian College of Arts and Sciences, Department of Organizational Sciences and Communication, Washington, DC 20052. Offers human resources management (MA); non-profit management (Graduate Certificate); organizational management (Graduate Certificate). *Program availability:* Part-time, evening/weekend. *Students:* 41 full-time (24 women), 18 part-time (12 women); includes 13 minority (5 Black or African American, non-Hispanic/Latino; 2 Asian, non-Hispanic/Latino; 6 Hispanic/Latino), 16 international. Average age 27. 126 applicants, 71% accepted, 32 enrolled. In 2018, 42 master's, 15 other advanced degrees awarded. *Entrance requirements:* For master's, GRE General Test, minimum GPA of 3.0; for Graduate Certificate, minimum GPA of 3.0. Additional exam requirements/recommendations for international students: Required—TOEFL (minimum score 500 paper-based; 80 iBT). *Application deadline:* For fall admission, 1/15 priority date for domestic and international students; for spring admission, 10/1 priority date for domestic students, 9/1 priority date for international students. Applications are processed on a rolling basis. Application fee: $75. Electronic applications accepted. *Financial support:* Federal Work-Study and institutionally sponsored loans available. *Unit head:* Dr. Lynn Offermann, Chair, 202-994-8507, E-mail: lro@gwu.edu. *Application contact:* Information Contact, 202-994-1878, Fax: 202-994-1881.
Website: http://www.gwu.edu/~orgsci/

The George Washington University, Graduate School of Education and Human Development, Department of Human and Organizational Learning, Program in Organizational Learning and Change, Washington, DC 20052. Offers Graduate Certificate. *Entrance requirements:* For degree, two letters of recommendation, resume, statement of purpose. *Unit head:* Michael Feuer, Dean, 202-994-6161, E-mail: mjfeuer@gwu.edu. *Application contact:* Sarah Lang, Director of Graduate Admissions, 202-994-1447, Fax: 202-994-7207, E-mail: slang@gwu.edu.
Website: http://gsehd.gwu.edu/programs/organizational-learning-change

Georgia State University, J. Mack Robinson College of Business, Department of Managerial Sciences, Atlanta, GA 30302-3083. Offers business analysis (MBA, MS); entrepreneurship (MBA); human resources management (MBA, MS); operations management (MBA, MS); organization behavior/human resource management (PhD); organization management (MBA); organizational change (MS); strategic management (PhD). *Accreditation:* AACSB. *Program availability:* Part-time, evening/weekend. *Faculty:* 11 full-time (2 women), 1 part-time/adjunct (0 women). *Students:* 11 full-time (6 women); includes 5 minority (3 Black or African American, non-Hispanic/Latino; 1 Asian, non-Hispanic/Latino; 1 Two or more races, non-Hispanic/Latino), 3 international. Average age 29. 54 applicants, 20% accepted, 8 enrolled. In 2018, 9 master's, 3 doctorates awarded. *Entrance requirements:* For master's, GRE or GMAT, transcripts from all institutions attended, resume, essays; for doctorate, GMAT, three letters of recommendation, personal statement, transcripts from all institutions attended, resume. Additional exam requirements/recommendations for international students: Required—TOEFL (minimum score 610 paper-based; 101 iBT), IELTS (minimum score 7). *Application deadline:* For fall admission, 5/1 priority date for domestic students, 2/1 priority date for international students; for spring admission, 9/15 priority date for domestic students, 4/1 priority date for international students. Applications are processed on a rolling basis. Application fee: $50. Electronic applications accepted. *Expenses: Tuition, area resident:* Full-time $9360; part-time $390 per credit hour. Tuition, state resident: full-time $9360; part-time $390 per credit hour. Tuition, nonresident: full-time $30,024; part-time $1251 per credit hour. *International tuition:* $30,024 full-time. *Required fees:* $2128. *Financial support:* Research assistantships, teaching assistantships, scholarships/grants, tuition waivers, and unspecified assistantships available. Financial award applicants required to submit FAFSA. *Faculty research:* Entrepreneurship and innovation; strategy process; workplace interactions, relationships, and processes; leadership and culture; supply chain management. *Unit head:* Dr. Pamela S. Barr, Chair, 404-413-7525, Fax: 404-413-7571. *Application contact:* Toby McChesney, Assistant Dean for Graduate Recruiting and Student Services, 404-413-7167, Fax: 404-413-7162, E-mail: rcbgradadmissions@gsu.edu.
Website: http://mgmt.robinson.gsu.edu/

Gonzaga University, School of Leadership Studies, Spokane, WA 99258. Offers communication and leadership (MA); leadership studies (PhD); organizational leadership (MA). *Program availability:* Part-time, evening/weekend, 100% online, blended/hybrid learning, immersion weekends. *Degree requirements:* For master's, leadership seminar; for doctorate, thesis/dissertation. *Entrance requirements:* For master's, MAT or GRE, official transcripts, minimum GPA of 3.0 or MAT/GRE, letter of recommendation, statement of purpose, resume; for doctorate, MAT, GRE, 500-word narrative, short sample of writing, current resume/curriculum vitae, two official transcripts from each college attended, three letters of recommendation, master's degree with minimum GPA of 3.5, interview with department chair and faculty. Additional exam requirements/recommendations for international students: Required—TOEFL (minimum score 88 iBT) or IELTS (minimum score 6.5). Electronic applications accepted. *Expenses:* Contact institution.

Graceland University, School of Nursing, Independence, MO 64050-3434. Offers adult and gerontology acute care (MSN, PMC); family nurse practitioner (MSN, PMC); nurse educator (MSN, PMC); organizational leadership (DNP). *Accreditation:* AACN. *Program availability:* Part-time, online only, 100% online. *Students:* 368 full-time (321 women), 312 part-time (279 women); includes 110 minority (38 Black or African American, non-Hispanic/Latino; 6 American Indian or Alaska Native, non-Hispanic/Latino; 18 Asian, non-Hispanic/Latino; 29 Hispanic/Latino; 19 Two or more races, non-Hispanic/Latino), 2 international. Average age 36. 236 applicants, 68% accepted, 121 enrolled. In 2018, 152 master's, 5 doctorates awarded. *Degree requirements:* For master's, comprehensive exam (for some programs), thesis optional, scholarly project; for doctorate, capstone project. *Entrance requirements:* For master's, BSN from nationally-accredited program, RN license, minimum GPA of 3.0, satisfactory criminal background check, three professional reference letters, professional goals statement of 150 words or less; for doctorate, MSN from nationally-accredited program, RN license, minimum GPA of 3.0, criminal background check. Additional exam requirements/recommendations for international students: Required—TOEFL (minimum score 550 paper-based; 80 iBT). *Application deadline:* For fall admission, 7/1 priority date for domestic students; for winter admission, 11/1 priority date for domestic students; for spring admission, 11/1 priority date for domestic students; for summer admission, 3/1 priority date for domestic students. Applications are processed on a rolling basis. Application fee: $50. Electronic applications accepted. *Expenses:* Tuition, lab fees, university tech fee, program support fee, course fees. *Financial support:* Institutionally sponsored loans available. Support available to part-time students. Financial award application deadline: 6/1; financial award applicants required to submit FAFSA. *Faculty research:* International nursing, family care-giving, health promotion, mental health nursing. *Unit head:* Dr. Sharon Little-Stoetzel, Dean of School of Nursing & Professor of Nursing, 816-423-4670, E-mail: stoetzel@graceland.edu. *Application contact:* Barbie Bell, Admissions Representative, 816-423-4717, Fax: 816-833-2990, E-mail: distancelearning@graceland.edu.
Website: http://www.graceland.edu/nursing

Grand Canyon University, Colangelo College of Business, Phoenix, AZ 85017-1097. Offers accounting (MBA, MS); business analytics (MS); disaster preparedness and executive fire service leadership (MS); finance (MBA); general management (MBA); health systems management (MBA); information technology management (MS); leadership (MBA, MS); marketing (MBA); organizational leadership and entrepreneurship (MS); project management (MBA); sports business (MBA); strategic human resource management (MBA). *Accreditation:* ACBSP. *Program availability:* Part-time, evening/weekend, online learning. *Entrance requirements:* For master's, equivalent of two years' full-time professional work experience. Additional exam requirements/recommendations for international students: Required—TOEFL (minimum score 575 paper-based; 90 iBT), IELTS (minimum score 7). Electronic applications accepted.

Grand Canyon University, College of Doctoral Studies, Phoenix, AZ 85017-1097. Offers data analytics (DBA); general psychology (PhD), including cognition and instruction, industrial and organizational psychology, integrating technology, learning, and psychology, performance psychology; management (DBA); marketing (DBA); organizational leadership (Ed D), including behavioral health, Christian ministry, health care administration, organizational development. *Degree requirements:* For doctorate, comprehensive exam, thesis/dissertation. *Entrance requirements:* For doctorate, minimum GPA of 3.4 on earned advanced degree from regionally-accredited institution; transcripts; goals statement.

Grand View University, Graduate Studies, Des Moines, IA 50316-1599. Offers athletic training (MS); clinical nurse leader (MSN, Post Master's Certificate); nursing education (MSN, Post Master's Certificate); organizational leadership (MS); sport management (MS); teacher leadership (M Ed); urban education (M Ed). *Program availability:* Part-time, evening/weekend. *Degree requirements:* For master's, completion of all required coursework in common core and selected track with minimum cumulative GPA of 3.0 and no more than two grades of C. *Entrance requirements:* For master's, GRE, GMAT, or essay, minimum undergraduate GPA of 3.0, professional resume, 3 letters of recommendation, interview. Additional exam requirements/recommendations for international students: Required—TOEFL (minimum score 550 paper-based). Electronic applications accepted.

Granite State College, MS in Leadership Program, Concord, NH 03301. Offers MS. *Program availability:* Part-time, evening/weekend, 100% online, blended/hybrid learning. *Degree requirements:* For master's, capstone. *Entrance requirements:* For master's, bachelor's degree with minimum GPA of 3.0 on last 60 credit hours, 500-1000 word statement of purpose, two letters of professional or academic reference, resume, official transcripts. Additional exam requirements/recommendations for international students: Required—TOEFL (minimum score 80 iBT), IELTS (minimum score 6.5). Electronic applications accepted.

Harding University, Paul R. Carter College of Business Administration, Searcy, AR 72149-0001. Offers international business (MBA); leadership and organizational management (MBA). *Accreditation:* ACBSP. *Program availability:* Part-time, evening/weekend, 100% online. *Degree requirements:* For master's, portfolio. *Entrance requirements:* For master's, GMAT (minimum score of 500) or GRE (minimum score of 300), minimum GPA of 3.0, 2 letters of recommendation, resume, 3 essays, all official transcripts. Additional exam requirements/recommendations for international students: Required—TOEFL (minimum score 550 paper-based; 79 iBT).

Hawai`i Pacific University, College of Business, Program in Business Administration, Honolulu, HI 96813. Offers finance (MBA); human resource management (MBA); information systems (MBA); international business (MBA); management (MBA); marketing (MBA); organizational change and development (MBA). *Program availability:* Part-time, evening/weekend, 100% online, blended/hybrid learning. *Entrance requirements:* For master's, GMAT or GRE. Additional exam requirements/recommendations for international students: Recommended—TOEFL (minimum score 550 paper-based; 80 iBT), IELTS (minimum score 6), TWE (minimum score 5). Electronic applications accepted.

Hawai`i Pacific University, College of Business, Program in Organizational Change, Honolulu, HI 96813. Offers MA. *Program availability:* Part-time, evening/weekend, 100% online, blended/hybrid learning. *Entrance requirements:* Additional exam requirements/recommendations for international students: Recommended—TOEFL (minimum score 550 paper-based; 80 iBT), IELTS (minimum score 6), TWE (minimum score 5). Electronic applications accepted.

HEC Montreal, School of Business Administration, Master in Management in Cultural Enterprises Program, Montréal, QC H3T 2A7, Canada. Offers MM. All courses are given in French. *Students:* 20 full-time (13 women), 31 part-time (26 women). 43 applicants, 74% accepted, 21 enrolled. In 2018, 19 master's awarded. *Entrance requirements:* For master's, bachelor's degree in cultural field, work experience in cultural or artistic organization. *Application deadline:* For fall admission, 4/15 for domestic and international students; for winter admission, 9/15 for domestic and international students. Application fee: $91 Canadian dollars ($191 Canadian dollars for international students). Electronic applications accepted. *Expenses: Tuition, area resident:* Full-time $3052.80 Canadian dollars; part-time $84.80 Canadian dollars per credit. Tuition, state resident: full-time $3816 Canadian dollars; part-time $264.67 Canadian dollars per credit. Tuition, nonresident: full-time $11,910 Canadian dollars. *International tuition:* $20,905.20 Canadian dollars full-time. *Required fees:* $1805.34 Canadian dollars; $43.62 Canadian dollars per credit. $71.78 Canadian dollars per term. Tuition and fees vary according to degree level and program. *Financial support:* Research

assistantships, teaching assistantships, and scholarships/grants available. Financial award application deadline: 9/2. *Unit head:* Renaud Lachance, Director, 514-340-6428, E-mail: renaud.lachance@hec.ca. *Application contact:* Anny Caron, Administrative Director, 514-340-6000, Fax: 514-340-6411, E-mail: aide@hec.ca.
Website: http://www.hec.ca/programmes/maitrises/maitrise-management-entreprises-culturelles/index.html

HEC Montreal, School of Business Administration, Master of Science Programs in Administration, Program in Organizational Development, Montréal, QC H3T 2A7, Canada. Offers M Sc. Program offered in French (Thesis Stream, Supervised project Stream). *Students:* 72 full-time (53 women), 22 part-time (18 women). 74 applicants, 86% accepted, 39 enrolled. In 2018, 25 master's awarded. *Entrance requirements:* For master's, BBA, undergraduate degree in another field, degree deemed equivalent by program director and minimum GPA of 3.0 on 4.3 scale. Additional exam requirements/recommendations for international students: Required—TAGE MAGE (minimum recommended score of 300), GMAT (minimum recommended score of 630), or GRE. *Application deadline:* For fall admission, 3/15 for domestic and international students; for winter admission, 9/15 for domestic and international students. Application fee: $91 Canadian dollars ($191 Canadian dollars for international students). Electronic applications accepted. *Expenses: Tuition, area resident:* Full-time $3052.80 Canadian dollars; part-time $84.80 Canadian dollars per credit. Tuition, state resident: full-time $3816 Canadian dollars; part-time $264.67 Canadian dollars per credit. Tuition, nonresident: full-time $11,910 Canadian dollars. *International tuition:* $20,905.20 Canadian dollars full-time. *Required fees:* $1805.34 Canadian dollars; $43.62 Canadian dollars per credit. $71.78 Canadian dollars per term. Tuition and fees vary according to degree level and program. *Financial support:* Research assistantships, teaching assistantships, and scholarships/grants available. Financial award application deadline: 9/2. *Unit head:* Dr. Sihem Taboubi, Director, 514-340-6428, E-mail: sihem.taboubi@hec.ca. *Application contact:* Marianne de Moura, Administrative Director, 514-340-6000, Fax: 514-340-6411, E-mail: aide@hec.ca.
Website: http://www.hec.ca/programmes/maitrises/maitrise-developpement-organisationnel/index.html

HEC Montreal, School of Business Administration, Master of Science Programs in Administration, Social Innovation Management, Montréal, QC H3T 2A7, Canada. Offers M Sc. Program offered in French (Thesis stream, Supervised project Stream). *Students:* 31 full-time (22 women), 8 part-time (5 women). 16 applicants, 88% accepted, 9 enrolled. In 2018, 27 master's awarded. *Degree requirements:* For master's, thesis. *Entrance requirements:* For master's, BBA, undergraduate degree in another field, degree deemed equivalent by program director and minimum GPA of 3.0 on 4.3 scale. Additional exam requirements/recommendations for international students: Required—TAGE MAGE (minimum recommended score of 300), GMAT (minimum recommended score of 630), or GRE. *Application deadline:* For fall admission, 3/15 for domestic and international students; for winter admission, 9/15 for domestic and international students. Application fee: $91 Canadian dollars ($191 Canadian dollars for international students). Electronic applications accepted. *Expenses: Tuition, area resident:* Full-time $3052.80 Canadian dollars; part-time $84.80 Canadian dollars per credit. Tuition, state resident: full-time $3816 Canadian dollars; part-time $264.67 Canadian dollars per credit. Tuition, nonresident: full-time $11,910 Canadian dollars. *International tuition:* $20,905.20 Canadian dollars full-time. *Required fees:* $1805.34 Canadian dollars; $43.62 Canadian dollars per credit. $71.78 Canadian dollars per term. Tuition and fees vary according to degree level and program. *Financial support:* Research assistantships, teaching assistantships, and scholarships/grants available. Financial award application deadline: 9/2. *Unit head:* Dr. Sihem Taboubi, Director, 514-340-6428, E-mail: sihem.taboubi@hec.ca. *Application contact:* Marianne de Moura, Administrative Director, 514-340-6000, Fax: 514-340-6411, E-mail: aide@hec.ca.
Website: http://www.hec.ca/programmes/maitrises/maitrise-gestions-en-contexte-innovations-sociales/index.html

Hood College, Graduate School, Department of Economics and Business Administration, Frederick, MD 21701-8575. Offers accounting (MBA); information systems (MBA); organizational management (Certificate). *Accreditation:* ACBSP. *Program availability:* Part-time, evening/weekend. *Faculty:* 3 full-time (2 women), 6 part-time/adjunct (1 woman). *Students:* 23 full-time (12 women), 176 part-time (120 women); includes 44 minority (17 Black or African American, non-Hispanic/Latino; 5 Asian, non-Hispanic/Latino; 19 Hispanic/Latino; 3 Two or more races, non-Hispanic/Latino), 13 international. Average age 35. 23 applicants, 96% accepted, 13 enrolled. In 2018, 36 master's, 2 other advanced degrees awarded. *Degree requirements:* For master's, capstone/final research project. *Entrance requirements:* For master's, minimum GPA of 3.0 (or resume and two letters of recommendation), copy of official transcripts; for Certificate, copy of official transcripts, Statement of Intent (250 words). Additional exam requirements/recommendations for international students: Required—TOEFL (minimum score 575 paper-based; 89 iBT), IELTS (minimum score 6.5). *Application deadline:* For fall admission, 8/15 for domestic students, 8/5 for international students; for spring admission, 12/1 for domestic and international students; for summer admission, 5/1 for domestic students, 4/15 for international students. Applications are processed on a rolling basis. Application fee: $50 ($100 for international students). Electronic applications accepted. *Expenses:* Business Programs: Tuition $605 per credit hour, Comprehensive Fee $115 per semester. *Financial support:* Tuition waivers (partial) and unspecified assistantships available. Financial award applicants required to submit FAFSA. *Faculty research:* Corporate strategy and sustainable competitive advantages, business ethics, entrepreneurship, investments management, economic development. *Unit head:* Dr. April M. Boulton, Dean of the Graduate School, 301-696-3600, Fax: 301-696-3597, E-mail: gofurther@hood.edu. *Application contact:* Christian DiGregorio, Director of Graduate Admissions, 301-696-3604, E-mail: gofurther@hood.edu.

Hood College, Graduate School, Program in Organizational Leadership, Frederick, MD 21701-8575. Offers DBA, DOL. *Program availability:* Part-time-only, evening/weekend. *Faculty:* 2 full-time (1 woman), 5 part-time/adjunct (2 women). *Students:* 53 part-time (31 women); includes 20 minority (15 Black or African American, non-Hispanic/Latino; 2 Asian, non-Hispanic/Latino; 1 Hispanic/Latino; 2 Two or more races, non-Hispanic/Latino). Average age 45. 22 applicants, 100% accepted, 20 enrolled. *Degree requirements:* For doctorate, comprehensive exam, research-based capstone project (R). *Entrance requirements:* For doctorate, master's degree; minimum GPA of 3.25; resume; two letters of recommendation; two essays; standardized test scores (SLLA, GRE, GMAT, or MAT) or evidence of master's-level culminating research experience. *Application deadline:* For fall admission, 4/15 priority date for domestic and international students. Application fee: $50 ($100 for international students). Electronic applications accepted. *Expenses:* Doctorate in Organizational Leadership (DOL): Tuition $940 per credit, Comprehensive Fee $550 per semester; Doctorate in Business Administration (DBA): Tuition $1070 per credit, Comprehensive Fee $550 per semester. *Financial support:* Applicants required to submit FAFSA. *Unit head:* Dr. Kathleen C. Bands, Director, 301-696-3818, E-mail: bands@hood.edu. *Application contact:* Christian DiGregorio, Director of Graduate Admissions, 301-696-3604, E-mail: gofurther@hood.edu.
Website: https://www.hood.edu/graduate

Huntington University, Graduate School, Huntington, IN 46750-1299. Offers adolescent and young adult education (M Ed); business administration (MBA); counseling (MA), including licensed mental health counselor; early adolescent education (M Ed); elementary education (M Ed); global youth ministry (MA); occupational therapy (OTD); organizational leadership (MA); pastoral leadership (MA); TESOL education (M Ed). *Accreditation:* AOTA. *Program availability:* Part-time, online learning. *Degree requirements:* For master's, comprehensive exam (for some programs), thesis (for some programs). *Entrance requirements:* For master's, GRE (for counseling and education students only); for doctorate, GRE (for occupational therapy students). Additional exam requirements/recommendations for international students: Required—TOEFL (minimum score 85 iBT), IELTS (minimum score 6.5). Electronic applications accepted. *Expenses:* Contact institution. *Faculty research:* Leadership, educational technology trends, evangelism, youth ministry, mental health.

Husson University, Master of Business Administration Program, Bangor, ME 04401-2999. Offers athletic administration (MBA); biotechnology and innovation (MBA); general business administration (MBA); healthcare management (MBA); hospitality and tourism management (MBA); organizational management (MBA); risk management (MBA). *Program availability:* Part-time, evening/weekend, 100% online, blended/hybrid learning. *Degree requirements:* For master's, comprehensive exam (for some programs), thesis optional. *Entrance requirements:* For master's, minimum GPA of 3.0, letter of recommendation. Additional exam requirements/recommendations for international students: Required—TOEFL (minimum score 550 paper-based; 80 iBT), IELTS (minimum score 6.5). Electronic applications accepted. *Expenses:* Contact institution.

Immaculata University, College of Graduate Studies, Program in Organization Leadership, Immaculata, PA 19345. Offers MA. *Program availability:* Part-time, evening/weekend. *Degree requirements:* For master's, comprehensive exam, thesis optional. *Entrance requirements:* For master's, GMAT, GRE General Test, MAT. Additional exam requirements/recommendations for international students: Required—TOEFL, IELTS. Electronic applications accepted.

Indiana Tech, Program in Organizational Leadership, Fort Wayne, IN 46803-1297. Offers MS. *Program availability:* Part-time, evening/weekend, online only, 100% online. *Entrance requirements:* For master's, minimum GPA of 2.5, bachelor's degree from regionally-accredited university, minimum three years of work experience, three letters of recommendation, essay, current resume. Electronic applications accepted.

Indiana University Bloomington, School of Public and Environmental Affairs, Public Affairs Programs, Bloomington, IN 47405. Offers economic development (MPA); energy (MPA); environmental policy (PhD); environmental policy and natural resource management (MPA); information systems (MPA); international development (MPA); local government management (MPA); nonprofit management (MPA, Certificate); policy analysis (MPA); public budgeting and financial management (Certificate); public finance (PhD); public financial administration (MPA); public management (MPA, PhD, Certificate); public policy analysis (PhD); social entrepreneurship (Certificate); specialized public affairs (MPA); sustainability and sustainable development (MPA); JD/MPA; MPA/MA; MPA/MIS; MPA/MLS; MSES/MPA. *Accreditation:* NASPAA (one or more programs are accredited). *Program availability:* Part-time. *Degree requirements:* For master's, capstone, internship; for doctorate, comprehensive exam, thesis/dissertation. *Entrance requirements:* For master's, GRE General Test or GMAT, official transcripts, 3 letters of recommendation, resume, personal statement; for doctorate, GRE General Test, official transcripts, 3 letters of recommendation, statement of purpose. Additional exam requirements/recommendations for international students: Required—TOEFL (minimum score 600 paper-based; 96 iBT); Recommended—IELTS (minimum score 7). Electronic applications accepted. *Faculty research:* International development, environmental policy and resource management, policy analysis, public finance, public management, urban management, nonprofit management, energy policy, social policy, public finance.

Indiana University–Purdue University Indianapolis, School of Engineering and Technology, MS in Technology Program, Indianapolis, IN 46202. Offers applied data management and analytics (MS); facilities management (MS); information security and assurance (MS); motorsports (MS); organizational leadership (MS); technical communication (MS). *Program availability:* Online learning.

Indiana University–Purdue University Indianapolis, School of Public and Environmental Affairs, Indianapolis, IN 46202. Offers criminal justice and public safety (MS); homeland security and emergency management (Graduate Certificate); library management (Graduate Certificate); nonprofit management (Graduate Certificate); public affairs (MPA); public management (Graduate Certificate); social entrepreneurship: nonprofit and public benefit organizations (Graduate Certificate); JD/MPA; MLS/NMC; MLS/PMC; MPA/MA. *Accreditation:* CAHME (one or more programs are accredited); NASPAA. *Program availability:* Part-time, evening/weekend, online learning. *Entrance requirements:* For master's, GRE General Test, GMAT or LSAT, minimum GPA of 3.0 (preferred). Additional exam requirements/recommendations for international students: Required—TOEFL (minimum score 93 iBT), IELTS (minimum score 6.5). Electronic applications accepted. *Faculty research:* Nonprofit and public management, public policy, urban policy, sustainability policy, disaster preparedness and recovery, vehicular safety, homicide, offender rehabilitation and re-entry.

Indiana Wesleyan University, College of Adult and Professional Studies, Graduate Studies in Business, Marion, IN 46953. Offers accounting (MBA, Graduate Certificate); applied management (MBA); business administration (MBA); health care (MBA, Graduate Certificate); human resources (MBA, Graduate Certificate); management (MS); organizational leadership (MA). *Program availability:* Part-time, evening/weekend, online learning. *Degree requirements:* For master's, applied business or management project. *Entrance requirements:* For master's, minimum GPA of 2.5, 2 years of related work experience. Additional exam requirements/recommendations for international students: Required—TOEFL (minimum score 550 paper-based). Electronic applications accepted.

Indiana Wesleyan University, College of Adult and Professional Studies, Program in Organizational Leadership, Marion, IN 46953. Offers Ed D. *Program availability:* Part-time, online learning. *Degree requirements:* For doctorate, comprehensive exam, thesis/dissertation, applied field project. *Entrance requirements:* For doctorate, GRE, GMAT. Additional exam requirements/recommendations for international students: Required—TOEFL. *Faculty research:* Organizational leadership as a new structural model for research and teaching, wisdom and its application for leaders, stewardship and its application for leaders, followership and its application for leaders, the importance of a world view in establishing authenticity for leaders.

Instituto Tecnologico de Santo Domingo, Graduate School, Area of Business, Santo Domingo, Dominican Republic. Offers banking and securities markets (M Mgmt); corporate finance (M Mgmt); human resources management (M Mgmt, Certificate); international trade management (M Mgmt); marketing (M Mgmt); organizational development (M Mgmt); quality and productivity management (Certificate); tax management and planning (M Mgmt); upper management (M Mgmt).

Jacksonville University, Davis College of Business, Master of Science in Organizational Leadership Program, Jacksonville, FL 32211. Offers MS. *Program availability:* Part-time-only, evening/weekend, 100% online, blended/hybrid learning.

Entrance requirements: For master's, GMAT or GRE, bachelor's degree from regionally-accredited institution, 3 years of full-time work experience (recommended), resume, statement of intent, 3 letters of recommendation, interview with program advisor. Additional exam requirements/recommendations for international students: Required—TOEFL (minimum score 550 paper-based; 79 iBT), IELTS (minimum score 6), PTE (minimum score 53). Electronic applications accepted. *Expenses:* Contact institution. *Faculty research:* Ethics; science of a start-up culture; organizational culture; sustainability.

James Madison University, The Graduate School, College of Business, Program in Strategic Leadership, Harrisonburg, VA 22807. Offers postsecondary analysis and leadership (PhD), including nonprofit and community leadership, organizational science and leadership, postsecondary analysis and leadership. *Program availability:* Part-time, evening/weekend, online learning. *Students:* 13 full-time (6 women), 32 part-time (13 women); includes 5 minority (2 Black or African American, non-Hispanic/Latino; 1 Asian, non-Hispanic/Latino; 2 Hispanic/Latino), 4 international. Average age 30. In 2018, 7 doctorates awarded. Application fee: $60. Electronic applications accepted. *Expenses:* Tuition, state resident: full-time $10,848. Tuition, nonresident: full-time $27,888. *Required fees:* $1128. *Financial support:* In 2018–19, 9 students received support. Fellowships, career-related internships or fieldwork, Federal Work-Study, unspecified assistantships, and doctoral assistantships (stipend varies) available. Financial award application deadline: 3/1; financial award applicants required to submit FAFSA. *Unit head:* Dr. Karen A. Ford, Director of Strategic Leadership Studies, 540-568-7020, Fax: 540-568-7117, E-mail: fordka@jmu.edu. *Application contact:* Lynette D. Michael, Director of Graduate Admissions, 540-568-6131 Ext. 6395, Fax: 540-568-7860, E-mail: michaeld@jmu.edu.
Website: http://www.jmu.edu/leadership/

Johnson & Wales University, Graduate Studies, MBA Program, Providence, RI 02903-3703. Offers accounting (MBA); business administration (MBA); finance (MBA); global fashion merchandising and management (MBA); hospitality (MBA); human resource management (MBA); information security/assurance (MBA); information technology (MBA); nonprofit management (MBA); operations and supply chain management (MBA); organizational leadership (MBA); organizational psychology (MBA); sport leadership (MBA). Program also offered on Denver campus. *Program availability:* Part-time, online learning. *Entrance requirements:* For master's, minimum GPA of 2.75. Additional exam requirements/recommendations for international students: Required—TOEFL (minimum score 550 paper-based); Recommended—IELTS, TWE. *Faculty research:* International banking, global economy, international trade, cultural differences.

Judson University, Master of Arts in Organizational Leadership, Elgin, IL 60123-1498. Offers MA. *Program availability:* Part-time, evening/weekend, 100% online, blended/hybrid learning. *Faculty:* 7 full-time (4 women), 31 part-time/adjunct (9 women). *Students:* 16 full-time (11 women), 4 part-time (3 women); includes 6 minority (4 Black or African American, non-Hispanic/Latino; 2 Hispanic/Latino). Average age 36. 15 applicants, 73% accepted, 9 enrolled. In 2018, 16 master's awarded. *Degree requirements:* For master's, thesis optional. *Entrance requirements:* For master's, Bachelor's degree with minimum GPA of 2.5; official transcripts; two years of work experience; two letters of reference; professional resume. Additional exam requirements/recommendations for international students: Required—TOEFL (minimum score 550 paper-based). *Application deadline:* Applications are processed on a rolling basis. Application fee: $35. Electronic applications accepted. *Expenses: Required fees:* $250. One-time fee: $125 full-time. Tuition and fees vary according to program. *Financial support:* Institutionally sponsored loans and unspecified assistantships available. Financial award applicants required to submit FAFSA. *Faculty research:* Human resource management, Public affairs, International marketing, Intergenerational leadership. *Unit head:* Karen Love, Chair, 847-628-1524, E-mail: klove@judsonu.edu. *Application contact:* Kim Surin, Enrollment Manager, 847-628-5033, E-mail: kim.surin@info.judsonu.edu.
Website: http://www.judsonu.edu/maol/

Juniata College, Department of Accounting, Business, and Economics, Huntingdon, PA 16652-2119. Offers accounting (M Acc); business administration (MBA); organizational leadership (MOL). *Entrance requirements:* For master's, GMAT.

Keiser University, MS in Organizational Leadership Program, Fort Lauderdale, FL 33309. Offers MSOL.

LaGrange College, Graduate Programs, Program in Organizational Leadership, LaGrange, GA 30240-2999. Offers MA. Program is held on Albany campus. *Program availability:* Evening/weekend. *Entrance requirements:* For master's, GRE or MAT, minimum GPA of 2.5, 3 letters of reference. Additional exam requirements/recommendations for international students: Required—TOEFL (minimum score 500 paper-based; 61 iBT). Electronic applications accepted.

Lenoir-Rhyne University, Graduate Programs, School of Education, Program in Leadership, Hickory, NC 28601. Offers community and nonprofit leadership (MA); general management (MA); higher education leadership (MA); second language community services (MA). *Program availability:* Online learning. *Entrance requirements:* Additional exam requirements/recommendations for international students: Required—TOEFL (minimum score 600 paper-based). Electronic applications accepted. *Expenses:* Contact institution.

Lewis University, College of Arts and Sciences, Program in Organizational Leadership, Romeoville, IL 60446. Offers higher education/student services (MA); organizational and leadership coaching (MA); training and development (MA). *Program availability:* Part-time, evening/weekend, 100% online, blended/hybrid learning. *Students:* 13 full-time (9 women), 150 part-time (115 women); includes 45 minority (28 Black or African American, non-Hispanic/Latino; 3 Asian, non-Hispanic/Latino; 10 Hispanic/Latino; 4 Two or more races, non-Hispanic/Latino), 2 international. Average age 38. *Entrance requirements:* For master's, bachelor's degree, personal statement, minimum GPA of 3.0, letters of recommendation. Additional exam requirements/recommendations for international students: Required—TOEFL (minimum score 550 paper-based; 79 iBT), IELTS (minimum score 6). *Application deadline:* For fall admission, 5/1 priority date for international students; for spring admission, 11/15 priority date for international students. Applications are processed on a rolling basis. Application fee: $40. Electronic applications accepted. *Financial support:* Federal Work-Study, tuition waivers, and unspecified assistantships available. Financial award application deadline: 5/1; financial award applicants required to submit FAFSA. *Unit head:* Dr. Lesley Page, Chair, Organizational Leadership. *Application contact:* Kathy Lisak, Graduate Admission Counselor, 815-836-5610, E-mail: grad@lewisu.edu.

Lincoln Christian University, Graduate Programs, Lincoln, IL 62656-2167. Offers Bible and theology (MA); Biblical studies (MA); church history/historical theology (MA); counseling (MA); formative worship (MA); intercultural studies (MA); ministry (MA); organizational leadership (MA); philosophy and apologetics (MA); spiritual formation (MA); theology (MA). MA in spiritual formation offered in Normal, IL. *Program availability:* Online learning. *Entrance requirements:* For master's, minimum cumulative GPA of 2.5 in undergraduate degree studies. Additional exam requirements/recommendations for international students: Required—TOEFL (minimum score 550 paper-based);

Recommended—IELTS (minimum score 6). Application fee is waived when completed online. *Expenses: Tuition:* Full-time $7920; part-time $5280 per credit hour. *Required fees:* $150; $150 per credit hour. Tuition and fees vary according to program.

Lipscomb University, Nelson and Sue Andrews Institute for Civic Leadership, Nashville, TN 37204-3951. Offers civic leadership (MA, Graduate Certificate); cross sector collaboration (MA); non-profit leadership (MA). *Program availability:* Part-time, evening/weekend. *Degree requirements:* For master's, project, externship. *Entrance requirements:* For master's, GRE, GMAT or MAT, transcripts, 2 references, essay, resume. Additional exam requirements/recommendations for international students: Required—TOEFL (minimum score 570 paper-based; 80 iBT). Electronic applications accepted. *Expenses:* Contact institution.

Lipscomb University, Program in Organizational Leadership, Nashville, TN 37204-3951. Offers aging services leadership (Certificate); global leadership (Certificate); organizational leadership (MPS); performance coaching (Certificate); strategic leadership (Certificate). *Program availability:* Part-time, online only, blended/hybrid learning. *Entrance requirements:* For master's, GRE or GMAT, two references, resume, interview. Additional exam requirements/recommendations for international students: Required—TOEFL (minimum score 550 paper-based). Electronic applications accepted. *Expenses:* Contact institution.

Lourdes University, Graduate School, Sylvania, OH 43560-2898. Offers business (MBA); leadership (M Ed); nurse anesthesia (MSN); nurse educator (MSN); nurse leader (MSN); organizational leadership (MOL); reading (M Ed); teaching and curriculum (M Ed); theology (MA). *Accreditation:* AANA/CANAEP. *Program availability:* Evening/weekend. *Entrance requirements:* Additional exam requirements/recommendations for international students: Required—TOEFL.

Loyola University New Orleans, Joseph A. Butt, S.J., College of Business, Program in Business Administration, New Orleans, LA 70118-6195. Offers organizational performance excellence (MBA); JD/MBA; MBA/MPS. *Accreditation:* AACSB. *Program availability:* Part-time, evening/weekend, online learning. *Faculty:* 14 full-time (6 women), 6 part-time/adjunct (1 woman). *Students:* 48 full-time (25 women), 48 part-time (33 women); includes 34 minority (20 Black or African American, non-Hispanic/Latino; 1 Asian, non-Hispanic/Latino; 11 Hispanic/Latino; 2 Two or more races, non-Hispanic/Latino), 6 international. Average age 34. 79 applicants, 92% accepted, 43 enrolled. In 2018, 22 master's awarded. *Degree requirements:* For master's, capstone project. *Entrance requirements:* For master's, GMAT or GRE, minimum GPA of 3.0, transcript, resume, 2 letters of recommendation, work experience in field, personal statement. Additional exam requirements/recommendations for international students: Required—TOEFL (minimum score 580 paper-based; 92 iBT). *Application deadline:* For fall admission, 6/15 priority date for domestic students, 5/15 priority date for international students; for spring admission, 11/15 priority date for domestic students, 10/15 priority date for international students. Applications are processed on a rolling basis. Application fee: $50. Electronic applications accepted. *Expenses:* $1,005 per credit hour tuition, $733 per semester full-time fees, $376.50 per semester part-time fees. *Financial support:* Research assistantships, scholarships/grants, tuition waivers (partial), and unspecified assistantships available. Financial award application deadline: 5/1; financial award applicants required to submit FAFSA. *Faculty research:* Ethics, international business, entrepreneurship, quality management, risk management. *Unit head:* Dr. J. Patrick O'Brien, Interim Dean, 504-864-7979, Fax: 504-864-7970, E-mail: mba@loyno.edu. *Application contact:* Ashley Francis, Director of Graduate Programs, 504-864-7979, Fax: 504-864-7970, E-mail: mba@loyno.edu.
Website: http://www.business.loyno.edu/mba/programs

Malone University, Graduate Program in Organizational Leadership, Canton, OH 44709. Offers MAOL. *Program availability:* Part-time, evening/weekend. *Entrance requirements:* For master's, minimum GPA of 3.0. Additional exam requirements/recommendations for international students: Required—TOEFL (minimum score 550 paper-based; 79 iBT). *Expenses:* Contact institution. *Faculty research:* Graduates' perceptions of the impact of a Christian higher education.

Manhattan College, Graduate Programs, School of Continuing and Professional Studies, Riverdale, NY 10471. Offers organizational leadership (MS). *Program availability:* Part-time, evening/weekend, 100% online, blended/hybrid learning. *Faculty:* 14 part-time/adjunct (10 women). *Students:* 64 full-time (34 women), 22 part-time (13 women); includes 41 minority (17 Black or African American, non-Hispanic/Latino; 4 Asian, non-Hispanic/Latino; 18 Hispanic/Latino; 2 Two or more races, non-Hispanic/Latino). Average age 33. 36 applicants, 94% accepted, 30 enrolled. In 2018, 28 master's awarded. *Degree requirements:* For master's, capstone project. *Entrance requirements:* For master's, bachelor's degree, minimum cumulative GPA of 2.75, at least three years of work experience; personal statement. Additional exam requirements/recommendations for international students: Required—TOEFL (minimum score 80 paper-based), IELTS (minimum score 6.5). *Application deadline:* For fall admission, 8/1 for domestic students; for spring admission, 11/15 for domestic students. Applications are processed on a rolling basis. Application fee: $75. Electronic applications accepted. *Expenses:* 900 per credit for hybrid coursework; 900 per credit for online coursework (plus fees regardless of program format). *Financial support:* Fellowships, research assistantships, teaching assistantships, and tuition waivers available. Financial award application deadline: 2/15; financial award applicants required to submit FAFSA. *Faculty research:* Quality assurance and program review; students with disabilities; nontraditional students; first-generation students. *Unit head:* Cheryl Harrison, Dean, 718-862-7862, E-mail: cheryl.harrison@manhattan.edu. *Application contact:* William Bisset, Vice President for Enrollment Management, 718-862-7199, Fax: 718-862-8019, E-mail: william.bisset@manhattan.edu.
Website: https://manhattan.edu/academics/schools-and-departments/scps/

Mansfield University of Pennsylvania, Graduate Studies, Program in Organizational Leadership, Mansfield, PA 16933. Offers MA. *Program availability:* Online learning.

Maranatha Baptist University, Program in Organizational Leadership, Watertown, WI 53094. Offers MOL. *Degree requirements:* For master's, capstone project.

Marian University, School of Business and Public Safety, Fond du Lac, WI 54935-4699. Offers organizational leadership (MS). *Program availability:* Part-time, evening/weekend. *Degree requirements:* For master's, comprehensive group project. *Entrance requirements:* For master's, 3 years of managerial experience, minimum GPA of 2.75, letters of professional reference. Additional exam requirements/recommendations for international students: Required—TOEFL (minimum score 525 paper-based; 70 iBT). Electronic applications accepted. *Expenses:* Contact institution. *Faculty research:* Organizational values, statistical decision-making, learning organization, quality planning, customer research.

Marlboro College, Graduate and Professional Studies, Program in Business Administration, Marlboro, VT 05344. Offers mission-driven organizations (MBA); project management (MBA); social innovation (MBA). *Program availability:* Part-time, evening/weekend, blended/hybrid learning. *Degree requirements:* For master's, 45 credits including a Master Workshop. *Entrance requirements:* For master's, letter of intent, essay, transcripts, 2 letters of recommendation. Electronic applications accepted. *Expenses:* Contact institution.

Organizational Management

Marlboro College, Graduate and Professional Studies, Program in Management, Marlboro, VT 05344. Offers mission-driven organizations (MS); project management (MS); social innovation (MS). *Program availability:* Part-time, evening/weekend, blended/hybrid learning. *Degree requirements:* For master's, capstone project. *Entrance requirements:* For master's, statement of intent, 2 letters of recommendation. Additional exam requirements/recommendations for international students: Recommended—TOEFL (minimum score 577 paper-based; 90 iBT), IELTS (minimum score 7). Electronic applications accepted. *Expenses:* Contact institution.

Medaille College, Program in Business Administration - Amherst, Amherst, NY 14221. Offers business administration (MBA); organizational leadership (MA). *Program availability:* Evening/weekend. *Degree requirements:* For master's, thesis or alternative. *Entrance requirements:* For master's, GMAT, minimum undergraduate GPA of 2.7, 3 years of work experience. Additional exam requirements/recommendations for international students: Required—TOEFL (minimum score 550 paper-based). Electronic applications accepted. *Expenses:* Contact institution.

Medaille College, Program in Business Administration - Rochester, Rochester, NY 14623. Offers business administration (MBA); organizational leadership (MA). *Program availability:* Evening/weekend. *Degree requirements:* For master's, thesis or alternative. *Entrance requirements:* For master's, GMAT, 3 years of work experience, minimum undergraduate GPA of 2.7. Additional exam requirements/recommendations for international students: Required—TOEFL (minimum score 550 paper-based). *Expenses:* Contact institution.

Mercer University, Graduate Studies, Cecil B. Day Campus, Penfield College, Atlanta, GA 30341. Offers certified rehabilitation counseling (MS); clinical mental health (MS); counselor education and supervision (PhD); criminal justice and public safety leadership (MS); health informatics (MS); human services (MS), including child and adolescent services, gerontology services; organizational leadership (MS), including leadership for the health care professional, leadership for the nonprofit organization, organizational development and change; school counseling (MS). *Program availability:* Part-time, evening/weekend, 100% online, blended/hybrid learning. *Degree requirements:* For master's, comprehensive exam (for some programs), thesis (for some programs); for doctorate, thesis/dissertation. *Entrance requirements:* For master's, GRE or MAT, Georgia Professional Standards Commission (GPSC) Certification at the SC-5 level; for doctorate, GRE or MAT. Additional exam requirements/recommendations for international students: Recommended—TOEFL (minimum score 550 paper-based; 80 iBT), IELTS (minimum score 6.5). Electronic applications accepted. Application fee is waived when completed online. *Expenses:* Contact institution. *Faculty research:* Marriage and families issues, leadership and ethics, cyber-bullying, trauma, narrative counseling and theory.

Mercy College, School of Business, Program in Organizational Leadership, Dobbs Ferry, NY 10522-1189. Offers MS. *Program availability:* Part-time, evening/weekend, 100% online, blended/hybrid learning. *Students:* 38 full-time (25 women), 16 part-time (13 women); includes 38 minority (20 Black or African American, non-Hispanic/Latino; 3 Asian, non-Hispanic/Latino; 15 Hispanic/Latino), 3 international. Average age 36. 45 applicants, 76% accepted, 20 enrolled. In 2018, 20 master's awarded. *Degree requirements:* For master's, thesis or alternative, Capstone project required. *Entrance requirements:* For master's, transcript(s); work statement or resume. Additional exam requirements/recommendations for international students: Required—TOEFL (minimum score 80 iBT), IELTS (minimum score 6.5). *Application deadline:* Applications are processed on a rolling basis. Application fee: $40. Electronic applications accepted. *Expenses:* Contact institution. *Financial support:* Career-related internships or fieldwork, Federal Work-Study, scholarships/grants, and unspecified assistantships available. Support available to part-time students. Financial award applicants required to submit FAFSA. *Unit head:* Dr. Lloyd Gibson, Dean, School of Business, 914-674-7159, Fax: 914-674-7493, E-mail: lgibson@mercy.edu. *Application contact:* Allison Gurdineer, Executive Director of Admissions, 877-637-2946, E-mail: admissions@mercy.edu. Website: https://www.mercy.edu/degrees-programs/ms-organizational-leadership

Mercyhurst University, Graduate Studies, Program in Organizational Leadership, Erie, PA 16546. Offers accounting (MS); higher education administration (MS); human resources (MS); organizational leadership (MS, Certificate); sports leadership (MS); strategy and innovation (MS). *Program availability:* Part-time, evening/weekend. *Degree requirements:* For master's, thesis. *Entrance requirements:* For master's, GRE General Test or MAT, interview, resume, essay, three professional references, transcripts. Additional exam requirements/recommendations for international students: Required—TOEFL (minimum score 80 iBT), IELTS (minimum score 6.5). Electronic applications accepted. *Faculty research:* Leadership training, organizational communication, leadership pedagogy.

Messiah College, Program in Business and Leadership, Mechanicsburg, PA 17055. Offers leadership (MBA, Certificate); management (Certificate); strategic leadership (MA). *Program availability:* Online learning.

Mid-America Christian University, Program in Leadership, Oklahoma City, OK 73170-4504. Offers MA. *Entrance requirements:* For master's, bachelor's degree from a regionally accredited college or university, minimum overall cumulative GPA of 2.75 of bachelor course work. Additional exam requirements/recommendations for international students: Required—TOEFL (minimum score 550 paper-based).

Midway University, Graduate Programs, Midway, KY 40347-1120. Offers education (MAT); leadership (MBA). *Degree requirements:* For master's, capstone course. *Entrance requirements:* For master's, GMAT (for MBA); GRE or PRAXIS I (for MAT), bachelor's degree; interview; minimum GPA of 3.0 (for MBA), 2.75 (for MAT); 3 years of professional work experience (for MBA). Additional exam requirements/recommendations for international students: Required—TOEFL (minimum score 550 paper-based; 80 iBT).

Midwest University, Graduate Programs, Wentzville, MO 63385. Offers asset management/investment/real estate (MBA); Christian counseling (D Min); Christian education (D Min); counseling (MA), including marriage and family counseling, school counseling; divinity (M Div); education (MA), including brain and gifted education, Christian education; global business management (MBA); global leadership (MBA); leadership (PhD), including brain and gifted educational leadership, entrepreneurial leadership, international aviation leadership, organizational leadership, political leadership; mission studies (D Min); music (MM, DMA); pastoral theology (D Min); public policy/administration (MBA); teaching English to speakers of other languages (MA). *Program availability:* Part-time, online learning. *Degree requirements:* For master's, thesis (for some programs); for doctorate, thesis/dissertation. *Entrance requirements:* Additional exam requirements/recommendations for international students: Recommended—TOEFL (minimum score 550 paper-based).

Misericordia University, College of Business, Program in Organizational Management, Dallas, PA 18612-1098. Offers healthcare management (MS); human resource management (MS); management (MS). *Program availability:* Part-time, evening/weekend, online learning. *Entrance requirements:* For master's, GRE General Test, MAT (35th percentile or higher), or minimum undergraduate GPA of 3.0. Additional exam requirements/recommendations for international students: Required—TOEFL.

Electronic applications accepted. Application fee is waived when completed online. *Expenses:* Contact institution.

Mount St. Joseph University, Master of Science in Organizational Leadership Program, Cincinnati, OH 45233-1670. Offers MS. *Program availability:* Part-time, evening/weekend. *Degree requirements:* For master's, 36 credit hours. *Entrance requirements:* For master's, minimum GPA of 3.0, interview, 3 years of work experience, 2 letters of reference, resume, letter of intent, essay, official transcript. Additional exam requirements/recommendations for international students: Required—TOEFL (minimum score 560 paper-based; 83 iBT). Electronic applications accepted. *Expenses:* Contact institution. *Faculty research:* Gender and cultural effects on management education, group identity formation, leadership skill development, methods for improving instructional effectiveness, technology-based productivity improvement.

National University, School of Business and Management, La Jolla, CA 92037-1011. Offers accountancy (M Acc, Certificate); business administration (GMBA, MBA); business analytics (MS); cause leadership (MA); global management (MGM); human resource management (MA); management information systems (MS); marketing (MS); organizational leadership (MS). GMBA offered in Spanish. *Program availability:* Part-time, evening/weekend, 100% online, blended/hybrid learning. *Degree requirements:* For master's, thesis (for some programs). *Entrance requirements:* For master's, interview, minimum GPA of 2.5. Additional exam requirements/recommendations for international students: Required—TOEFL (minimum score 550 paper-based; 79 iBT), IELTS (minimum score 6). Electronic applications accepted. *Expenses: Tuition:* Full-time $10,320; part-time $430 per unit. Tuition and fees vary according to degree level.

National University, School of Professional Studies, La Jolla, CA 92037-1011. Offers criminal justice (MCJ); digital cinema production (MFA); digital journalism (MA); homeland security and emergency management (MS); juvenile justice (MS); professional screenwriting (MFA); public administration (MPA), including human resource management, organizational leadership. *Program availability:* Part-time, evening/weekend, 100% online, blended/hybrid learning. *Degree requirements:* For master's, thesis (for some programs). *Entrance requirements:* For master's, interview, minimum GPA of 2.5. Additional exam requirements/recommendations for international students: Required—TOEFL (minimum score 550 paper-based; 79 iBT), IELTS (minimum score 6). Electronic applications accepted. *Expenses: Tuition:* Full-time $10,320; part-time $430 per unit. Tuition and fees vary according to degree level.

Neumann University, Program in Organizational and Strategic Leadership, Aston, PA 19014-1298. Offers MS. *Program availability:* Part-time, evening/weekend, 100% online, blended/hybrid learning. *Degree requirements:* For master's, project. *Entrance requirements:* For master's, official transcripts from all institutions attended, current resume, letter of intent, letter of recommendation. Additional exam requirements/recommendations for international students: Required—TOEFL (minimum score 70 iBT). Electronic applications accepted. *Expenses:* Contact institution.

New Jersey City University, School of Business, Program in Organizational Management and Leadership, Jersey City, NJ 07305-1597. Offers MBA.

Newman University, Master of Science in Education Program, Wichita, KS 67213-2097. Offers building leadership (MS Ed); curriculum and instruction (MS Ed), including English as a second language, reading specialist; organizational leadership (MS Ed). *Accreditation:* NCATE. *Program availability:* Part-time, evening/weekend, online learning. *Degree requirements:* For master's, thesis optional. *Entrance requirements:* For master's, 3 years' full-time teaching experience, minimum GPA of 3.0, writing sample, 2 letters of recommendation, evidence of teaching certification. Additional exam requirements/recommendations for international students: Required—TOEFL (minimum score 600 paper-based; 100 iBT). Electronic applications accepted. *Expenses:* Contact institution. *Faculty research:* Online course design and deliver, staff engagement, classroom action.

Newman University, MBA Program, Wichita, KS 67213-2097. Offers finance (MBA); international business (MBA); leadership (MBA); management (MBA); management information technology (MBA). *Program availability:* Part-time. *Degree requirements:* For master's, thesis optional. *Entrance requirements:* For master's, minimum GPA of 3.0; 2 letters of recommendation; course work in algebra, statistics, macroeconomics, and financial accounting. Additional exam requirements/recommendations for international students: Required—TOEFL (minimum score 600 paper-based; 100 iBT). Electronic applications accepted. *Expenses:* Contact institution.

The New School, Schools of Public Engagement, Program in Organizational Change Management, New York, NY 10011. Offers leadership and change (Graduate Certificate); organizational change management (MS); organizational development (Graduate Certificate). *Program availability:* Part-time, evening/weekend. *Degree requirements:* For master's, thesis or alternative, capstone project: Paper of Publishable Quality (PPQ). *Entrance requirements:* For master's, minimum of three years' full-time organizational work experience, two letters of recommendation, statement of purpose, resume, transcripts. Additional exam requirements/recommendations for international students: Required—TOEFL (minimum score 92 iBT), IELTS (minimum score 7), PTE (minimum score 68). Electronic applications accepted. *Expenses:* Contact institution.

New York University, Leonard N. Stern School of Business, Department of Management and Organizations, New York, NY 10012-1019. Offers management organizations (MBA); organization theory (PhD); organizational behavior (PhD); strategy (PhD). *Faculty research:* Strategic management, managerial cognition, interpersonal processes, conflict and negotiation.

New York University, School of Professional Studies, Division of Programs in Business, Program in Leadership and Human Capital Management, New York, NY 10012-1019. Offers human resource management and development (MS), including global talent management, human resource management, learning, development, and executive coaching, organizational effectiveness. *Program availability:* Part-time, evening/weekend, 100% online, blended/hybrid learning. *Degree requirements:* For master's, thesis. *Entrance requirements:* For master's, GRE or GMAT (only upon request), bachelor's degree, resume with relevant professional work, internship or volunteer experience, two letters of recommendation, statement of purpose. Additional exam requirements/recommendations for international students: Required—TOEFL (minimum score 600 paper-based; 100 iBT), IELTS (minimum score 7). Electronic applications accepted. *Expenses:* Contact institution.

Nichols College, Graduate and Professional Studies, Dudley, MA 01571-5000. Offers business administration (MBA); counterterrorism (MS); organizational leadership (MSOL). *Program availability:* Part-time, evening/weekend, online learning. *Degree requirements:* For master's, project (for MOL). *Entrance requirements:* For master's, 2 letters of recommendation, current resume, official transcripts, 800-word personal statement. Additional exam requirements/recommendations for international students: Required—TOEFL (minimum score 500 paper-based). Electronic applications accepted.

Northern Kentucky University, Office of Graduate Programs, College of Business, Program in Executive Leadership and Organizational Change, Highland Heights, KY 41099. Offers MS. *Program availability:* Part-time, evening/weekend. *Entrance requirements:* For master's, resume, current career essay, future career objectives essay, personal statement, 3 letters of recommendation with cover forms, transcripts.

Additional exam requirements/recommendations for international students: Required—TOEFL (minimum score 79 iBT); Recommended—IELTS (minimum score 6.5). Electronic applications accepted. *Expenses:* Contact institution. *Faculty research:* Leadership assessment and development, teams and conflict management, organizational strategy development and systems thinking, organizational consultation.

Northwestern University, The Graduate School, Kellogg School of Management, Department of Management and Organizations, Evanston, IL 60208. Offers PhD. Admissions and degree offered through The Graduate School. *Degree requirements:* For doctorate, comprehensive exam, thesis/dissertation. *Entrance requirements:* For doctorate, GMAT or GRE General Test. Additional exam requirements/recommendations for international students: Required—TOEFL. Electronic applications accepted. *Faculty research:* Bargaining and negotiation, organizational design, decision-making, organizational change, strategic alliances.

Northwestern University, The Graduate School, Kellogg School of Management, Management Programs, Evanston, IL 60208. Offers accounting information and management (MBA, PhD); analytical finance (MBA); business administration (MBA); decision sciences (MBA); entrepreneurship and innovation.(MBA); finance (MBA, PhD); health enterprise management (MBA); human resources management (MBA); international business (MBA); management and organizations (MBA, PhD); management and organizations and sociology (PhD); management and strategy (MBA); management studies (MS); managerial analytics (MBA); managerial economics (MBA); managerial economics and strategy (PhD); marketing (MBA, PhD); marketing management (MBA); media management (MBA); operations management (MBA, PhD); real estate (MBA); social enterprise at Kellogg (MBA); JD/MBA. *Program availability:* Part-time, evening/weekend. Terminal master's awarded for partial completion of doctoral program. *Degree requirements:* For doctorate, thesis/dissertation, 2 years of coursework, qualifying (field) exam and candidacy, summer research papers and presentations to faculty, proposal defense, final exam/defense. *Entrance requirements:* For master's, GMAT, GRE, interview, 2 letters of recommendation, college transcripts, resume, essays, Kellogg honor code; for doctorate, GMAT, GRE, statement of purpose, transcripts, 2 letters of recommendation, resume, interview. Additional exam requirements/recommendations for international students: Required—TOEFL, IELTS. Electronic applications accepted. *Expenses:* Contact institution. *Faculty research:* Business cycles and international finance, health policy, networks, non-market strategy, consumer psychology.

Northwestern University, The Graduate School, School of Education and Social Policy, Program in Learning and Organizational Change, Evanston, IL 60208. Offers MS. *Program availability:* Part-time, evening/weekend, online learning. *Degree requirements:* For master's, thesis, practicum. *Entrance requirements:* For master's, GRE or GMAT (recommended), letters of recommendation. Additional exam requirements/recommendations for international students: Required—TOEFL (minimum score 600 paper-based; 100 iBT); Recommended—IELTS (minimum score 7). Electronic applications accepted. *Faculty research:* Strategic change, learning and performance, workplace learning, leadership development, cognitive design, knowledge management.

Northwest University, College of Business, Kirkland, WA 98033. Offers business administration (MBA); international business (MBA); project management (MBA); social entrepreneurship (MBA). *Accreditation:* ACBSP. *Program availability:* Part-time, evening/weekend. *Degree requirements:* For master's, formalized research. *Entrance requirements:* For master's, GMAT. Additional exam requirements/recommendations for international students: Required—TOEFL (minimum score 550 paper-based; 75 iBT). Electronic applications accepted. *Expenses:* Contact institution.

Norwich University, College of Graduate and Continuing Studies, Master of Business Administration Program, Northfield, VT 05663. Offers construction management (MBA); energy management (MBA); finance (MBA); logistics (MBA); organizational leadership (MBA); project management (MBA); supply chain management (MBA). *Accreditation:* ACBSP. *Program availability:* Evening/weekend, online only, mostly all online with a week-long residency requirement. *Degree requirements:* For master's, comprehensive exam. *Entrance requirements:* For master's, minimum undergraduate GPA of 2.75. Additional exam requirements/recommendations for international students: Required—TOEFL (minimum score 550 paper-based; 80 iBT), IELTS (minimum score 6.5). Electronic applications accepted. *Expenses:* Contact institution.

Norwich University, College of Graduate and Continuing Studies, Master of Science in Executive Leadership Program, Northfield, VT 05663. Offers MS. *Program availability:* Evening/weekend, online only, mostly all online with a week-long residency requirement. *Degree requirements:* For master's, capstone. *Entrance requirements:* For master's, minimum of eight years of formal leadership experience, minimum GPA of 2.75. Additional exam requirements/recommendations for international students: Required—TOEFL (minimum score 550 paper-based; 80 iBT), IELTS (minimum score 6.5). Electronic applications accepted. *Expenses:* Contact institution.

Norwich University, College of Graduate and Continuing Studies, Master of Science in Leadership Program, Northfield, VT 05663. Offers leadership (MS), including human resources leadership, leading change management consulting, organizational leadership, public sector/government/military leadership. *Program availability:* Evening/weekend, online only, mostly all online with a week-long residency requirement. *Degree requirements:* For master's, capstone. *Entrance requirements:* For master's, minimum undergraduate GPA of 2.75. Additional exam requirements/recommendations for international students: Required—TOEFL (minimum score 550 paper-based; 80 iBT), IELTS (minimum score 6.5). Electronic applications accepted. *Expenses:* Contact institution.

Nyack College, School of Business and Leadership, Nyack, NY 10960. Offers business administration (MBA); organizational leadership (MS). *Program availability:* Part-time, evening/weekend, 100% online, blended/hybrid learning. *Students:* 31 full-time (18 women), 10 part-time (6 women); includes 32 minority (20 Black or African American, non-Hispanic/Latino; 1 Asian, non-Hispanic/Latino; 10 Hispanic/Latino; 1 Two or more races, non-Hispanic/Latino), 4 international. Average age 37. In 2018, 26 master's awarded. *Degree requirements:* For master's, thesis (for some programs), capstone project (for MBA). *Entrance requirements:* For master's, transcripts, personal goals statement, recommendations, resume, interview. Additional exam requirements/recommendations for international students: Required—TOEFL (minimum score 550 paper-based; 80 iBT), IELTS (minimum score 6.5). *Application deadline:* Applications are processed on a rolling basis. Application fee: $50. Electronic applications accepted. *Expenses:* MS in Org Ldrshp - $725/credit; MBA - $800/credit. *Financial support:* Scholarships/grants available. Financial award applicants required to submit FAFSA. *Unit head:* Dr. Anita Underwood, Dean, 845-675-4511. *Application contact:* Dr. Anita Underwood, Dean, 845-675-4511.
Website: http://www.nyack.edu/sbl

Nyack College, School of Social Work, Nyack, NY 10960. Offers clinical social work practice (MSW); leadership in organizations and communities (MSW). *Accreditation:* CSWE. *Program availability:* Part-time, evening/weekend. *Students:* 50 full-time (42 women), 38 part-time (30 women); includes 78 minority (48 Black or African American, non-Hispanic/Latino; 5 Asian, non-Hispanic/Latino; 25 Hispanic/Latino; 2 international.

Average age 35. In 2018, 26 master's awarded. *Degree requirements:* For master's, field work. *Entrance requirements:* For master's, official transcripts, academic and professional references, personal statement, essay or case reflection. Additional exam requirements/recommendations for international students: Required—TOEFL (minimum score 550 paper-based; 80 iBT). *Application deadline:* Applications are processed on a rolling basis. Application fee: $45. Electronic applications accepted. *Expenses:* $800/credit. *Financial support:* Scholarships/grants available. Financial award applicants required to submit FAFSA. *Unit head:* Dr. Janet Furness, Director of MSW Program, 646-378-6169. *Application contact:* Dr. Janet Furness, Director of MSW Program, 646-378-6169.
Website: https://www.nyack.edu/msw

Oakland City University, School of Education, Oakland City, IN 47660-1099. Offers building level administration (MS Ed); curriculum and instruction (MS Ed, Ed D); education (MS Ed); elementary education (MAT); organizational management (Ed D); secondary education (MAT); superintendency (Ed D). *Accreditation:* NCATE. Terminal master's awarded for partial completion of doctoral program. *Degree requirements:* For master's, thesis; for doctorate, comprehensive exam, thesis/dissertation. *Entrance requirements:* For master's, MAT, minimum GPA of 3.0, interview, resume, letters of recommendation; for doctorate, MAT, GRE, minimum GPA of 3.2, interview, resume, letters of recommendation. *Expenses:* Contact institution. *Faculty research:* Assessment, cultural diversity, teacher education, education leadership.

Oakland University, Graduate Study and Lifelong Learning, School of Education and Human Services, Department of Organizational Leadership, Rochester, MI 48309-4401. Offers educational leadership (M Ed, PhD); higher education (Certificate); school administration (Ed S). *Entrance requirements:* Additional exam requirements/recommendations for international students: Required—TOEFL (minimum score 550 paper-based).

Ohio Christian University, Graduate Programs, Circleville, OH 43113. Offers accounting (MBA); business administration (MBA); digital marketing (MBA); finance (MBA); healthcare management (MBA); human resources (MBA); management (MM); organizational leadership (MBA); pastoral care and counseling (MAM); practical theology (MAM).

Oklahoma Christian University, Graduate School of Business, Oklahoma City, OK 73136-1100. Offers accounting (M Acc, MBA); financial services (MBA); general business (MBA); health services management (MBA); human resources (MBA); international business (MBA); leadership and organizational development (MBA); marketing (MBA); nonprofit management (MBA); project management (MBA). *Accreditation:* ACBSP. *Program availability:* Part-time, 100% online. *Entrance requirements:* For master's, bachelor's degree. Additional exam requirements/recommendations for international students: Required—TOEFL (minimum score 550 paper-based). Electronic applications accepted. *Expenses:* Contact institution.

Olivet Nazarene University, Program in Organizational Leadership, Bourbonnais, IL 60914. Offers MOL.

Omega Graduate School, Graduate Programs, Dayton, TN 37321-6736. Offers family life education (M Litt); integration of religion and society (D Phil); organizational leadership (M Litt). *Entrance requirements:* For master's, official transcripts, three letters of recommendation, bachelor's degree or its equivalent, minimum undergraduate GPA of 3.0, minimum of 3 years of professional experience; for doctorate, official transcripts, three letters of recommendation, master's degree with minimum GPA of 3.0, minimum of 5 years of professional experience. *Expenses:* Contact institution.

Our Lady of the Lake University, School of Business and Leadership, Program in Leadership Studies, San Antonio, TX 78207-4689. Offers PhD. *Program availability:* Part-time, evening/weekend. *Faculty:* 11 full-time (8 women), 12 part-time/adjunct (4 women). *Students:* 267 full-time (160 women), 7 part-time (3 women); includes 214 minority (29 Black or African American, non-Hispanic/Latino; 4 Asian, non-Hispanic/Latino; 179 Hispanic/Latino; 2 Two or more races, non-Hispanic/Latino), 1 international. Average age 44. 42 applicants, 86% accepted, 27 enrolled. In 2018, 23 doctorates awarded. *Degree requirements:* For doctorate, comprehensive exam, thesis/dissertation. *Entrance requirements:* For doctorate, GRE or MAT, master's degree with minimum of 36 credit hours in appropriate field from regionally-accredited college or university; minimum GPA of 3.3 in all previous master's degree work (preferred); resume; personal statement. Additional exam requirements/recommendations for international students: Required—TOEFL. *Application deadline:* For fall admission, 5/15 for domestic and international students. Application fee: $40 ($50 for international students). Electronic applications accepted. Application fee is waived when completed online. *Expenses:* Contact institution. *Financial support:* In 2018–19, 14 students received support. Federal Work-Study, scholarships/grants, unspecified assistantships, and tuition discounts available. Support available to part-time students. Financial award application deadline: 5/1; financial award applicants required to submit FAFSA. *Unit head:* Dr. Esther Chavez Gergen, Chair of Leadership Department, 210-434-6711 Ext. 2287, E-mail: esgergen@lake.ollusa.edu. *Application contact:* Office of Graduate Admissions, 210-434-3995, Fax: 210-431-3945, E-mail: gradadm@ollusa.edu.
Website: http://www.ollusa.edu/s/1190/hybrid/default-hybrid-ollu.aspx?sid-1190&amp;gid-1&amp;pgid-7956

Our Lady of the Lake University, School of Business and Leadership, Program in Organizational Leadership, San Antonio, TX 78207-4689. Offers MS. *Program availability:* Part-time, evening/weekend. *Faculty:* 11 full-time (8 women), 12 part-time/adjunct (4 women). *Students:* 52 full-time (32 women), 3 part-time (2 women); includes 49 minority (2 Black or African American, non-Hispanic/Latino; 1 Asian, non-Hispanic/Latino; 45 Hispanic/Latino; 1 Native Hawaiian or other Pacific Islander, non-Hispanic/Latino). Average age 35. 29 applicants, 90% accepted, 22 enrolled. In 2018, 30 master's awarded. *Entrance requirements:* For master's, official transcripts showing minimum cumulative GPA of 2.5, 2 letters of recommendation, resume, personal statement. Additional exam requirements/recommendations for international students: Required—TOEFL. *Application deadline:* For fall admission, 6/15 for domestic and international students; for spring admission, 11/15 for domestic and international students. Application fee: $40 ($50 for international students). Electronic applications accepted. *Expenses: Tuition:* Full-time $16,326; part-time $907 per credit. *Financial support:* In 2018–19, 21 students received support. Federal Work-Study, scholarships/grants, unspecified assistantships, and tuition discounts available. Support available to part-time students. Financial award application deadline: 5/1; financial award applicants required to submit FAFSA. *Unit head:* Dr. Esther Chavez Gergen, Leadership Studies Program Chair, 210-434-6711, E-mail: esgergen@ollusa.edu. *Application contact:* Graduate Admission, 210-431-3995, Fax: 210-431-3945, E-mail: gradadm@ollusa.edu.
Website: http://www.ollusa.edu/s/1190/hybrid/default-hybrid-ollu.aspx?sid-1190&amp;gid-1&amp;pgid-7906

Palm Beach Atlantic University, MacArthur School of Leadership, West Palm Beach, FL 33416-4708. Offers MS. *Program availability:* Part-time, evening/weekend, 100% online, blended/hybrid learning. *Faculty:* 8 full-time (3 women), 1 part-time/adjunct (0 women). *Students:* 1 full-time (0 women), 81 part-time (58 women); includes 37 minority (21 Black or African American, non-Hispanic/Latino; 11 Hispanic/Latino; 5 Two or more races, non-Hispanic/Latino), 5 international. Average age 39. In 2018, 17 master's

awarded. *Degree requirements:* For master's, capstone course. *Entrance requirements:* For master's, minimum GPA of 3.0; essay. Additional exam requirements/recommendations for international students: Required—TOEFL (minimum score 550 paper-based; 79 iBT). *Application deadline:* Applications are processed on a rolling basis. Application fee: $50. Electronic applications accepted. *Expenses: Tuition:* Part-time $767 per credit. Tuition and fees vary according to program. *Financial support:* In 2018–19, 44 students received support. Scholarships/grants and employee education grants available. Financial award application deadline: 5/1; financial award applicants required to submit FAFSA. *Faculty research:* Ethics, business strategies, organizational leadership. *Unit head:* Dr. Craig Domeck, Dean, 561-803-2318, E-mail: craig_domeck@pba.edu. *Application contact:* Graduate Admissions, 888-468-6722, E-mail: grad@pba.edu.
Website: http://learn-well.pba.edu/academics/leadership/index.html

Peirce College, Program in Organizational Leadership and Management, Philadelphia, PA 19102-4699. Offers MS. *Degree requirements:* For master's, capstone project. *Entrance requirements:* For master's, official transcripts, current resume, statement of intent, two letters of recommendation.

Penn State University Park, Graduate School, Smeal College of Business, University Park, PA 16802. Offers accounting (M Acc); business administration (MBA, MS, PhD); management and organizational leadership (MPS). *Accreditation:* AACSB. *Program availability:* Part-time, evening/weekend. *Entrance requirements:* Additional exam requirements/recommendations for international students: Required—TOEFL (minimum score 550 paper-based; 80 iBT), IELTS. Electronic applications accepted. *Expenses:* Contact institution.

Peru State College, Graduate Programs, Program in Organizational Management, Peru, NE 68421. Offers MS. Program offered online only. *Program availability:* Part-time, online learning. *Degree requirements:* For master's, thesis (for some programs). *Expenses:* Contact institution. *Faculty research:* Emotional intelligence.

Pfeiffer University, Program in Leadership and Organizational Change, Misenheimer, NC 28109-0960. Offers MS, MBA/MS. *Entrance requirements:* For master's, GRE or GMAT.

Point Loma Nazarene University, College of Extended Learning, Program in Organizational Leadership, San Diego, CA 92106-2899. Offers MA. *Program availability:* Online learning. *Expenses:* Contact institution.

Point Loma Nazarene University, Fermanian School of Business, San Diego, CA 92106-2899. Offers general business (MBA); healthcare management (MBA); innovation and entrepreneurship (MBA); organizational leadership (MBA); project management (MBA). *Accreditation:* ACBSP. *Program availability:* Part-time, evening/weekend. *Entrance requirements:* For master's, GMAT, letters of recommendation, essay, interview. Additional exam requirements/recommendations for international students: Required—TOEFL. Electronic applications accepted. *Expenses:* Contact institution.

Point Park University, Rowland School of Business, Program in Management, Pittsburgh, PA 15222-1984. Offers health care administration and management (MS); leadership (MA). *Program availability:* 100% online.

Purdue University Fort Wayne, College of Engineering, Technology, and Computer Science, Department of Organizational Leadership, Fort Wayne, IN 46805-1499. Offers human resources (MS); leadership (MS); organizational leadership and supervision (Certificate). *Program availability:* Part-time. *Entrance requirements:* For master's, GRE or GMAT (if undergraduate GPA is below 3.0), current resume, 2 recent letters of recommendation, essay. Additional exam requirements/recommendations for international students: Required—TOEFL (minimum score 550 paper-based; 79 iBT); Recommended—TWE. Electronic applications accepted. *Faculty research:* Replication problem and psychology, virtual leadership.

Purdue University Global, School of Business, Davenport, IA 52807. Offers business administration (MBA); change leadership (MS); entrepreneurship (MBA); finance (MBA); health care management (MBA, MS); human resource (MBA); international business (MBA); management (MS); marketing (MBA); project management (MBA, MS); supply chain management and logistics (MBA, MS). *Accreditation:* ACBSP. *Program availability:* Part-time, evening/weekend, online learning. *Entrance requirements:* Additional exam requirements/recommendations for international students: Required—TOEFL (minimum score 550 paper-based; 80 iBT). Electronic applications accepted.

Queens University of Charlotte, McColl School of Business, Charlotte, NC 28274-0002. Offers business administration (EMBA, MBA, PMBA); organization development (MSOD). *Accreditation:* AACSB. *Program availability:* Part-time, evening/weekend, online learning. *Degree requirements:* For master's, capstone course. *Entrance requirements:* For master's, GMAT, minimum GPA of 2.5. Additional exam requirements/recommendations for international students: Required—TOEFL. Electronic applications accepted. *Expenses:* Contact institution.

Quinnipiac University, School of Business, Program in Organizational Leadership, Hamden, CT 06518-1940. Offers MS. *Program availability:* Part-time, evening/weekend, online only, 100% online. *Entrance requirements:* For master's, four years of work experience. Additional exam requirements/recommendations for international students: Required—TOEFL (minimum score 575 paper-based; 90 iBT), IELTS (minimum score 6.5). Electronic applications accepted. *Expenses:* Contact institution. *Faculty research:* Virtual teams, women and leadership, virtual human resources applications and practices, emotional intelligence and its application in the workplace.

Regent University, Graduate School, School of Business and Leadership, Virginia Beach, VA 23464-9800. Offers business administration (MBA), including accounting, economics, entrepreneurship, finance and investing, general management, healthcare management (MA, MBA), human resource management (MA, MBA), innovation management, leadership, marketing, not-for-profit management (MA, MBA); business analytics (MS); business and design management (MA); church leadership (MA); leadership (Certificate); organizational leadership (MA, PhD), including ecclesial leadership (DSL, PhD), entrepreneurial leadership (PhD), healthcare management (MA, MBA), human resource development (PhD), human resource management (MA, MBA), individualized studies (DSL, PhD), interdisciplinary studies (MA), leadership coaching and mentoring (MA), not-for-profit management (MA, MBA), organizational development consulting (MA), servant leadership (MA, DSL); strategic leadership (DSL), including ecclesial leadership (DSL, PhD), global consulting, healthcare leadership, individualized studies (DSL, PhD), leadership coaching, servant leadership (MA, DSL), strategic foresight. *Program availability:* Part-time, evening/weekend, 100% online, blended/hybrid learning. *Degree requirements:* For master's, thesis or alternative, 3-credit hour culminating experience; for doctorate, thesis/dissertation. *Entrance requirements:* For master's, college transcripts, resume, essay; for doctorate, college transcripts, resume, essay, writing sample; for Certificate, writing sample, resume, transcripts. Additional exam requirements/recommendations for international students: Required—TOEFL (minimum score 577 paper-based). Electronic applications accepted. *Expenses:* Contact institution. *Faculty research:* Servant leadership, global business, team effectiveness, technology utilization, leadership development.

Regis University, College of Business and Economics, Denver, CO 80221-1099. Offers accounting (MS); executive leadership (Certificate); finance (MS); finance and accounting (MBA); health industry leadership (MBA); human resource management and leadership (MSOL); management (MBA); marketing (MBA); nonprofit leadership (Post-Graduate Certificate); nonprofit management (MNM); nonprofit organizational capacity building (Certificate); operations management (MBA); organizational leadership and management (MSOL); project leadership and management (MS, MSOL); strategic business management (Certificate); strategic human resource integration (Certificate); strategic management (MBA). Programs offered at Colorado Springs Campus, Northwest Denver Campus, Southeast Denver Campus, Fort Collins Campus, Broomfield Campus, Henderson (Nevada) Campus, and Summerlin (Nevada) Campus. *Program availability:* Part-time, evening/weekend, 100% online, blended/hybrid learning. *Degree requirements:* For master's, thesis (for some programs), capstone or final research project. *Entrance requirements:* For master's, official transcript reflecting baccalaureate degree awarded from regionally-accredited college or university, interview, 2 years of full-time related work experience, resume, letters of recommendation. Additional exam requirements/recommendations for international students: Required—TOEFL (minimum score 550 paper-based; 82 iBT). Electronic applications accepted. *Expenses:* Contact institution. *Faculty research:* Impact of information technology on small business regulation of accounting, international project financing, mineral development, delivery of healthcare to rural indigenous communities.

Rider University, College of Education and Human Services, Program in Organizational Leadership, Lawrenceville, NJ 08648-3001. Offers developing people and organizations (MA); life and career coaching (MA). *Program availability:* Part-time, evening/weekend, 100% online, blended/hybrid learning. *Students:* 10 full-time (7 women), 28 part-time (23 women); includes 21 minority (18 Black or African American, non-Hispanic/Latino; 3 Hispanic/Latino). Average age 31. 37 applicants, 81% accepted, 16 enrolled. In 2018, 9 master's awarded. *Entrance requirements:* For master's, resume, interview, statement of aims and objectives, official prior college transcripts. Additional exam requirements/recommendations for international students: Required—TOEFL (minimum score 540 paper-based; 79 iBT). *Application deadline:* For fall admission, 8/1 for domestic students; for spring admission, 12/1 for domestic students; for summer admission, 5/1 for domestic students. Applications are processed on a rolling basis. Application fee: $50. Electronic applications accepted. *Expenses: Tuition:* Full-time $850; part-time $850 per credit hour. *Required fees:* $50; $50 per course. Tuition and fees vary according to program. *Financial support:* Applicants required to submit FAFSA. *Unit head:* Tricia Nolfi, Program Director, 609-895-5636, E-mail: tnolfi@rider.edu. *Application contact:* Jamie L. Mitchell, Director of Graduate Admissions, 609-896-5036, Fax: 609-895-5680, E-mail: jmitchell@rider.edu.

Robert Morris University, School of Informatics, Humanities and Social Sciences, Moon Township, PA 15108-1189. Offers communication and information systems (MS); cyber security (MS); data analytics (MS); information security and assurance (MS); information systems and communications (D Sc); information systems management (MS); information technology project management (MS); Internet information systems (MS); organizational leadership (MS). *Program availability:* Part-time-only, evening/weekend, 100% online. *Faculty:* 22 full-time (7 women), 10 part-time/adjunct (0 women). *Students:* 262 part-time (94 women); includes 57 minority (31 Black or African American, non-Hispanic/Latino; 13 Asian, non-Hispanic/Latino; 8 Hispanic/Latino; 5 Two or more races, non-Hispanic/Latino), 43 international. Average age 35. 150 applicants, 92% accepted, 79 enrolled. In 2018, 133 master's, 11 doctorates awarded. *Degree requirements:* For master's, Completion of 30 credits; for doctorate, thesis/dissertation, Completion of 63 credits. *Entrance requirements:* For doctorate, employer letter of endorsement, interview. Additional exam requirements/recommendations for international students: Required—TOEFL (minimum score 550 paper-based; 79 iBT). *Application deadline:* For fall admission, 7/1 priority date for domestic and international students; for spring admission, 11/1 priority date for domestic and international students. Applications are processed on a rolling basis. Application fee: $35. Electronic applications accepted. Application fee is waived when completed online. *Expenses:* Master's $920/credit plus $80/credit fees; D.Sc. $28,290/year. *Financial support:* Institutionally sponsored loans available. Support available to part-time students. Financial award application deadline: 5/1; financial award applicants required to submit FAFSA. *Unit head:* Jon A. Radermacher, Interim Dean, School of Informatics, Humanities and Social Sciences, 412-397-4088, E-mail: radermacher@rmu.edu. *Application contact:* Jon A. Radermacher, Interim Dean, School of Informatics, Humanities and Social Sciences, 412-397-4088, E-mail: radermacher@rmu.edu.
Website: https://www.rmu.edu/academics/schools/sihss

Rochester Institute of Technology, Graduate Enrollment Services, College of Applied Science and Technology, School of International Hospitality and Service Innovation, Advanced Certificate Program in Organizational Learning, Rochester, NY 14623-5603. Offers Advanced Certificate. *Program availability:* Part-time, evening/weekend, online only, 100% online. *Entrance requirements:* For degree, minimum GPA of 3.0 (recommended). Additional exam requirements/recommendations for international students: Required—TOEFL (minimum score 570 paper-based; 88 iBT), IELTS (minimum score 6.5), PTE (minimum score 62). *Application deadline:* Applications are processed on a rolling basis. Application fee: $65. Electronic applications accepted. *Expenses:* Contact institution. *Financial support:* Scholarships/grants available. Support available to part-time students. Financial award applicants required to submit FAFSA. *Unit head:* Matthew A Cornwell, Assistant Director of Student Services and Outreach, 585-475-6916, E-mail: mcornwell@saunders.rit.edu. *Application contact:* Diane Ellison, Senior Associate Vice President, Graduate Enrollment Services, 585-475-2229, Fax: 585-475-7164, E-mail: gradinfo@rit.edu.
Website: https://www.rit.edu/study/organizational-learning-adv-cert

Roosevelt University, Graduate Division, Walter E. Heller College of Business, Program in Organization Development, Chicago, IL 60605. Offers MA. *Program availability:* Part-time, evening/weekend. Electronic applications accepted.

Rutgers University–Newark, Rutgers Business School–Newark and New Brunswick, Doctoral Programs in Management, Newark, NJ 07102. Offers accounting (PhD); accounting information systems (PhD); economics (PhD); finance (PhD); individualized study (PhD); information technology (PhD); international business (PhD); management science (PhD); marketing science (PhD); organizational management (PhD); science, technology and management (PhD); supply chain management (PhD). *Degree requirements:* For doctorate, comprehensive exam, thesis/dissertation. *Entrance requirements:* For doctorate, GRE or GMAT. Additional exam requirements/recommendations for international students: Required—TOEFL (minimum score 550 paper-based; 79 iBT). Electronic applications accepted.

Sage Graduate School, School of Management, Program in Organization Management, Troy, NY 12180-4115. Offers MS. *Program availability:* Part-time, evening/weekend, 100% online, blended/hybrid learning. *Faculty:* 5 full-time (3 women), 4 part-time/adjunct (1 woman). *Students:* 1 (woman) full-time, 26 part-time (22 women); includes 5 minority (3 Black or African American, non-Hispanic/Latino; 2 Hispanic/Latino). Average age 34. 22 applicants, 64% accepted, 8 enrolled. In 2018, 10 master's awarded. *Degree requirements:* For master's, capstone seminar. *Entrance requirements:* For master's, minimum GPA of 2.75. Additional exam requirements/

recommendations for international students: Required—TOEFL (minimum score 550 paper-based). *Application deadline:* Applications are processed on a rolling basis. Application fee: $30. Electronic applications accepted. *Financial support:* Fellowships, research assistantships, and unspecified assistantships available. Financial award application deadline: 3/1; financial award applicants required to submit FAFSA. *Unit head:* Dr. Kimberly Fredericks, Dean, School of Management, 518-292-1782, Fax: 518-292-1964, E-mail: fredek1@sage.edu. *Application contact:* Michael Jones, SR Associate Director of Graduate Enrollment Management, 518-292-8615, Fax: 518-292-1912, E-mail: jonesm4@sage.edu.
Website: http://www.sage.edu/academics/management/programs/organization_management/

St. Ambrose University, College of Business, Program in Organizational Leadership, Davenport, IA 52801. Offers MOL. *Program availability:* Part-time, evening/weekend. *Degree requirements:* For master's, comprehensive exam (for some programs), thesis or alternative, integration projects. *Entrance requirements:* Additional exam requirements/recommendations for international students: Required—TOEFL. Electronic applications accepted. *Expenses:* Contact institution.

St. Catherine University, Graduate Programs, Program in Organizational Leadership, St. Paul, MN 55105. Offers MA. *Program availability:* Part-time, evening/weekend. *Degree requirements:* For master's, thesis. *Entrance requirements:* For master's, GMAT, GRE General Test or MAT, 2 years of work experience, minimum GPA of 3.0. Additional exam requirements/recommendations for international students: Required—TOEFL (minimum score 600 paper-based; 100 iBT). *Expenses:* Contact institution. *Faculty research:* Ethics.

St. Edward's University, Bill Munday School of Business, Program in Leadership and Change, Austin, TX 78704. Offers MS. *Program availability:* Part-time-only, evening/weekend. *Entrance requirements:* Additional exam requirements/recommendations for international students: Required—TOEFL, IELTS. Electronic applications accepted.

St. Joseph's College, Long Island Campus, Programs in Management, Field in Organizational Management, Patchogue, NY 11772-2399. Offers MS. *Program availability:* Part-time, evening/weekend, 100% online, blended/hybrid learning. *Faculty:* 13 full-time (5 women), 23 part-time/adjunct (8 women). *Students:* 1 full-time (0 women), 14 part-time (7 women); includes 4 minority (2 Black or African American, non-Hispanic/Latino; 2 Hispanic/Latino). Average age 32. 10 applicants, 40% accepted, 4 enrolled. In 2018, 6 master's awarded. *Entrance requirements:* For master's, Application, $25 application fee, official transcripts, two letters of recommendation, current resume, 250 word written statement. Additional exam requirements/recommendations for international students: Required—TOEFL (minimum score 80 iBT). *Application deadline:* Applications are processed on a rolling basis. Application fee: $25. Electronic applications accepted. *Expenses: Tuition:* Full-time $18,450; part-time $1025 per credit. *Required fees:* $414. *Financial support:* In 2018–19, 3 students received support. *Unit head:* Mary A. Chance, Assistant Professor/Interim Director of Graduate Management Studies, 631-687-1297, E-mail: mchance@sjcny.edu. *Application contact:* Mary A. Chance, Assistant Professor/Interim Director of Graduate Management Studies, 631-687-1297, E-mail: mchance@sjcny.edu.

St. Joseph's College, New York, Programs in Management, Field in Organizational Management, Brooklyn, NY 11205-3688. Offers MS. *Program availability:* Part-time, evening/weekend, 100% online, blended/hybrid learning. *Faculty:* 5 part-time/adjunct (4 women). *Students:* 5 full-time (4 women), 4 part-time (all women); all minorities (5 Black or African American, non-Hispanic/Latino; 1 Asian, non-Hispanic/Latino; 3 Hispanic/Latino). Average age 40. 8 applicants, 75% accepted, 3 enrolled. In 2018, 5 master's awarded. *Entrance requirements:* For master's, Application, $25 application fee, two letters of recommendation, current resume, 250 word essay, official transcripts. Additional exam requirements/recommendations for international students: Required—TOEFL (minimum score 80 iBT). *Application deadline:* Applications are processed on a rolling basis. Application fee: $25. Electronic applications accepted. *Expenses: Tuition:* Full-time $18,450; part-time $1025 per credit. *Required fees:* $414. *Financial support:* In 2018–19, 2 students received support. *Unit head:* Sharon Didier, Assistant Chair/Co-Director of Graduate Management Studies/Associate Professor, 718-940-5790, E-mail: sdidier@sjcny.edu. *Application contact:* Sharon Didier, Assistant Chair/Co-Director of Graduate Management Studies/Associate Professor, 718-940-5790, E-mail: sdidier@sjcny.edu.

Saint Mary-of-the-Woods College, Master of Leadership Development Program, Saint Mary of the Woods, IN 47876. Offers not-for-profit leadership (MLD); organizational leadership (MLD). *Program availability:* Part-time. *Degree requirements:* For master's, thesis. Electronic applications accepted. *Expenses:* Contact institution.

Saint Mary's College of California, Kalmanovitz School of Education, Leadership Programs, Moraga, CA 94556. Offers coaching and facilitation (MA); organizational leadership and change (MA); peacebuilding and conflict transformation (MA); social justice (MA). *Accreditation:* AACSB. *Program availability:* Part-time, evening/weekend, online learning. *Degree requirements:* For master's, research project. *Entrance requirements:* For master's, letters of recommendation, interview. Electronic applications accepted. *Expenses:* Contact institution. *Faculty research:* Leadership, organizational change, values, adult learning, transformative learning.

Saint Mary's University of Minnesota, Schools of Graduate and Professional Programs, Graduate School of Business and Technology, Organizational Leadership Program, Winona, MN 55987-1399. Offers MA. *Program availability:* Online learning. *Unit head:* George Diaz, Director, 612-238-4510, E-mail: gdiaz@smumn.edu. *Application contact:* Laurie Roy, Director of Admission of Schools of Graduate and Professional Programs, 507-457-8606, Fax: 612-728-5121, E-mail: lroy@smumn.edu. Website: http://www.smumn.edu/graduate-home/areas-of-study/graduate-school-of-business-technology/ma-in-organizational-leadership

Salve Regina University, Program in Management, Newport, RI 02840-4192. Offers business studies (CGS); human resource management (CGS); innovation and strategic management (MS); management (CGS); nonprofit management (CGS); social entrepreneurship (CGS). *Program availability:* Part-time, evening/weekend, online learning. *Entrance requirements:* For master's, GMAT, GRE General Test, or MAT. Additional exam requirements/recommendations for international students: Required—TOEFL (minimum score 600 paper-based; 100 iBT). Electronic applications accepted. *Expenses: Tuition:* Full-time $10,530; part-time $585 per credit. *Required fees:* $60 per term. Tuition and fees vary according to course level, course load, degree level and program.

San Diego Christian College, Graduate Programs, Santee, CA 92071. Offers education (MAT); organization (MSL).

Saybrook University, LIOS MA Residential Programs, Kirkland, WA 98033. Offers leadership and organization development (MA); psychology counseling (MA). *Degree requirements:* For master's, thesis (for some programs), oral exams. *Entrance requirements:* For master's, bachelor's degree from an accredited university or college. Additional exam requirements/recommendations for international students: Recommended—TOEFL, IELTS, TWE.

Saybrook University, School of Organizational Leadership and Transformation, San Francisco, CA 94612. Offers MA. Program offered jointly with Bastyr University. *Degree requirements:* For master's, thesis (for some programs), oral exams. *Entrance requirements:* For master's, bachelor's degree from an accredited college or university. *Faculty research:* Cross-functional work teams, communication, management authority, employee influence, systems theory.

Saybrook University, School of Psychology and Interdisciplinary Inquiry, San Francisco, CA 94612. Offers human science (MA, PhD), including consciousness and spirituality, humanistic and transpersonal psychology, integrative health studies, organizational systems, social transformation; organizational systems (MA, PhD), including consciousness and spirituality, humanistic and transpersonal psychology, integrative health studies, leadership of sustainable systems (MA), organizational systems, social transformation; psychology (MA, PhD), including consciousness and spirituality, creativity studies (MA), humanistic and transpersonal psychology, integrative health studies, Jungian studies, marriage and family therapy (MA), organizational systems, social transformation. *Program availability:* Online learning. Terminal master's awarded for partial completion of doctoral program. *Degree requirements:* For master's, thesis or alternative; for doctorate, thesis/dissertation. *Entrance requirements:* Additional exam requirements/recommendations for international students: Required—TOEFL (minimum score 580 paper-based; 93 iBT). Electronic applications accepted. *Faculty research:* Humanistic theory, health studies, organizational systems, consciousness and spirituality, social transformation.

Seattle University, Albers School of Business and Economics, Center for Leadership Formation, Seattle, WA 98122-1090. Offers leadership (EMBA, Certificate). *Program availability:* Evening/weekend. *Faculty:* 2 part-time/adjunct (both women). *Students:* 52 full-time (31 women), 1 (woman) part-time; includes 6 minority (3 Black or African American, non-Hispanic/Latino; 1 Asian, non-Hispanic/Latino; 1 Hispanic/Latino; 1 Two or more races, non-Hispanic/Latino). Average age 42. 40 applicants, 98% accepted, 31 enrolled. In 2018, 25 master's, 16 other advanced degrees awarded. *Entrance requirements:* For master's, GMAT or three online courses, 7 years of continuous professional experience, undergraduate degree with minimum GPA of 3.0, resume, statement of intent/interest, three letters of recommendation; for Certificate, 7 years of continuous professional experience, undergraduate degree with minimum GPA of 3.0, resume, statement of intent/interest, three letters of recommendation. Additional exam requirements/recommendations for international students: Required—TOEFL (minimum score 580 paper-based; 92 iBT), IELTS (minimum score 7), PTE (minimum score 62). *Application deadline:* Applications are processed on a rolling basis. Application fee: $55. Electronic applications accepted. *Expenses:* Contact institution. *Financial support:* In 2018–19, 17 students received support. Scholarships/grants available. Financial award applicants required to submit FAFSA. *Unit head:* Dr. Marilyn Gist, Associate Dean of Executive Education, 206-296-5413, E-mail: gistm@seattleu.edu. *Application contact:* Sommer Harrison, Manager, Graduate Programs Outreach, 206-296-2529, E-mail: emba@seattleu.edu.
Website: https://www.seattleu.edu/albers/executive/

Shippensburg University of Pennsylvania, School of Graduate Studies, College of Arts and Sciences, Department of Sociology and Anthropology, Shippensburg, PA 17257-2299. Offers organizational development and leadership (MS). *Program availability:* Part-time, evening/weekend. *Faculty:* 3 full-time (2 women). *Students:* 9 full-time (7 women), 24 part-time (15 women); includes 13 minority (7 Black or African American, non-Hispanic/Latino; 1 Asian, non-Hispanic/Latino; 4 Hispanic/Latino; 1 Two or more races, non-Hispanic/Latino), 1 international. Average age 30. 28 applicants, 86% accepted, 15 enrolled. In 2018, 18 master's awarded. *Degree requirements:* For master's, thesis, capstone experience including internship. *Entrance requirements:* For master's, interview (if GPA less than 2.75), current resume, personal goals statement, track selection form. Additional exam requirements/recommendations for international students: Required—TOEFL (minimum score 550 paper-based; 68 iBT), IELTS (minimum score 6), TOEFL (minimum score 550 paper-based, 68 iBT) or IELTS (minimum score 6). *Application deadline:* For fall admission, 4/30 for international students; for spring admission, 9/30 for international students. Applications are processed on a rolling basis. Application fee: $45. Electronic applications accepted. *Expenses:* Tuition, state resident: part-time $516 per credit. Tuition, nonresident: part-time $750 per credit. *Required fees:* $149 per credit. *Financial support:* In 2018–19, 13 students received support. Career-related internships or fieldwork, scholarships/grants, unspecified assistantships, and resident hall director and student payroll positions available. Support available to part-time students. Financial award application deadline: 3/1; financial award applicants required to submit FAFSA. *Unit head:* Dr. Barbara J. Denison, Departmental Chair and Program Coordinator, 717-477-1735, Fax: 717-477-4011, E-mail: bjdeni@ship.edu. *Application contact:* Maya T. Mapp, Director of Admissions, 717-477-1231, Fax: 717-477-4016, E-mail: mtmapp@ship.edu. Website: http://www.ship.edu/odl/

Siena Heights University, Graduate College, Adrian, MI 49221-1796. Offers clinical mental health counseling (MA); educational leadership (Specialist); leadership (MA), including health care leadership, organizational leadership; teacher education (MA), including early childhood education, early childhood education: Montessori, education leadership: principal, elementary education: reading K-12, leadership: higher education, secondary education: reading K-12, special education: cognitive impairment, special education: learning disabilities. *Program availability:* Part-time, evening/weekend. *Faculty:* 10 full-time (6 women), 16 part-time/adjunct (6 women). *Students:* 34 full-time (20 women), 183 part-time (126 women); includes 64 minority (38 Black or African American, non-Hispanic/Latino; 2 American Indian or Alaska Native, non-Hispanic/Latino; 4 Asian, non-Hispanic/Latino; 14 Hispanic/Latino; 6 Two or more races, non-Hispanic/Latino). Average age 36. 97 applicants, 41% accepted, 30 enrolled. In 2018, 72 master's awarded. *Degree requirements:* For master's, thesis, Presentation. *Entrance requirements:* For master's, Minimum GPA of 3.0, current resume, essay, all post-secondary transcripts, 3 letters of reference, conviction disclosure form; copy of teaching certificate (for some education programs); for Specialist, Master's degree, minimum GPA of 3.0, current resume, essay, all post-secondary transcripts, 3 letters of reference, conviction disclosure form; copy of teaching certificate (for some education programs). Additional exam requirements/recommendations for international students: Recommended—TOEFL, IELTS, TWE, TSE. *Application deadline:* Applications are processed on a rolling basis. Application fee: $50. Electronic applications accepted. *Expenses: Tuition:* Full-time $11,340; part-time $7560 per year. *Required fees:* $454; $454 per unit. $227 per semester. One-time fee: $100. Tuition and fees vary according to program. *Financial support:* In 2018–19, 55 students received support. Scholarships/grants, tuition waivers (full and partial), unspecified assistantships, and State of Michigan Scholarships/Grants available. Support available to part-time students. Financial award application deadline: 9/1; financial award applicants required to submit FAFSA. *Unit head:* Dr. Cheryl Betz, Dean, College for Professional Studies and Graduate College, 517-264-7234, Fax: 517-264-7714, E-mail: cbetz@sienaheights.edu. *Application contact:* Elizabeth Brooks, Assistant Director, 517-264-7165, Fax: 517-264-7714, E-mail: ebrooks@sienaheights.edu.
Website: http://www.sienaheights.edu

Organizational Management

Simpson University, School of Graduate Studies, Redding, CA 96003-8606. Offers counseling psychology (MA); organizational leadership (MA). *Program availability:* Evening/weekend, 100% online, blended/hybrid learning. *Degree requirements:* For master's, thesis optional, portfolio capstone, integrative essay. *Entrance requirements:* For master's, three letters of recommendation, personal statement, resume, transcripts, personal interview, bachelor's degree in psychology or related field with minimum GPA of 3.0 in final 60 credits (for counseling psychology); two references (for organizational leadership). Additional exam requirements/recommendations for international students: Required—TOEFL (minimum score 550 paper-based; 79 iBT). Electronic applications accepted. *Expenses:* Contact institution. *Faculty research:* Development of executive functioning in young children, cognitive neuropsychology, historical issues in the neurosciences, neurotheology.

SIT Graduate Institute, Graduate Programs, Master's Programs in Intercultural Service, Leadership, and Management, Master's Program in Intercultural Service, Leadership, and Management (Self-Designed), Brattleboro, VT 05302-0676. Offers MA.

Southeastern University, College of Education, Lakeland, FL 33801-6099. Offers curriculum and instruction (Ed D); educational leadership (M Ed); elementary education (M Ed); exceptional student education (M Ed); exceptional student education/ educational therapy (M Ed); kinesiology (M Ed); organizational leadership (Ed D); reading education (M Ed); teaching English to speakers of other languages (M Ed). Electronic applications accepted.

Southeastern University, Jannetides College of Business and Entrepreneurial Leadership, Lakeland, FL 33801-6099. Offers executive leadership (MBA); global business administration (MBA); healthcare administration (MBA); missional leadership (MBA); organizational leadership (PhD); sport management (MBA); strategic leadership (DSL). *Accreditation:* ACBSP. *Program availability:* Evening/weekend, online learning. *Entrance requirements:* For master's, GMAT, minimum cumulative GPA of 3.0, writing sample. Electronic applications accepted.

Southern Arkansas University–Magnolia, School of Graduate Studies, Magnolia, AR 71753. Offers agriculture (MS); business administration (MBA), including agribusiness, social entrepreneurship, supply chain management; clinical and mental health counseling (MS); computer and information sciences (MS), including cyber security and privacy, data science, information technology; gifted and talented (M Ed), including curriculum and instruction, educational administration and supervision, gifted and talented P-8/7-12, instructional specialist P-4; higher, adult and lifelong education (M Ed); kinesiology (M Ed), including coaching; library media and information specialist (M Ed); public administration (MPA); school counseling K-12 (M Ed); student affairs and college counseling (M Ed); teaching (MAT). *Accreditation:* NCATE. *Program availability:* Part-time, 100% online, blended/hybrid learning. *Faculty:* 36 full-time (21 women), 32 part-time/adjunct (15 women). *Students:* 164 full-time (77 women), 762 part-time (510 women); includes 192 minority (163 Black or African American, non-Hispanic/Latino; 7 American Indian or Alaska Native, non-Hispanic/Latino; 13 Asian, non-Hispanic/Latino; 1 Hispanic/Latino; 8 Two or more races, non-Hispanic/Latino), 213 international. Average age 28. 363 applicants, 100% accepted, 237 enrolled. In 2018, 716 master's awarded. *Degree requirements:* For master's, comprehensive exam (for some programs), thesis optional. *Entrance requirements:* For master's, GRE, MAT or GMAT, minimum GPA of 2.5. Additional exam requirements/recommendations for international students: Required—TOEFL (minimum score 550 paper-based), IELTS (minimum score 6). *Application deadline:* For fall admission, 8/1 for domestic and international students; for spring admission, 12/1 for domestic students, 11/15 for international students; for summer admission, 4/1 for domestic students, 5/10 for international students. Applications are processed on a rolling basis. Application fee: $25 ($90 for international students). Electronic applications accepted. *Expenses: Tuition, area resident:* Full-time $5130; part-time $3420 per year. *Tuition, state resident:* full-time $5130; part-time $3420 per year. *Tuition, nonresident:* full-time $7866; part-time $5244 per year. *International tuition:* $7866 full-time. *Required fees:* $1052; $710 per unit. Tuition and fees vary according to course load. *Financial support:* Career-related internships or fieldwork, Federal Work-Study, scholarships/grants, tuition waivers (full), and unspecified assistantships available. Financial award applicants required to submit FAFSA. *Faculty research:* Alternative certification for teachers, supervision of instruction, instructional leadership, counseling. *Unit head:* Dr. Kim Bloss, Dean, School of Graduate Studies, 870-235-4150, Fax: 870-235-5227, E-mail: kkbloss@saumag.edu. *Application contact:* Talia Jett, Admissions Coordinator, 870-2355450, Fax: 870-235-5227, E-mail: taliajett@saumag.edu.
Website: http://www.saumag.edu/graduate

Southern New Hampshire University, School of Business, Manchester, NH 03106-1045. Offers accounting (MBA, Graduate Certificate); accounting finance (MS); accounting/auditing (MS); accounting/forensic accounting (MS); accounting/ management accounting (MS); accounting/taxation (MS); applied economics (MS); athletic administration (MBA, Graduate Certificate); business administration (IMBA, Certificate), including business information systems (Certificate), human resource management (Certificate); business analytics (MBA); business intelligence (MBA); communication (MA), including new media and marketing, public relations; community economic development (MBA); criminal justice (MBA); data analytics (MS); economics (MBA); engineering management (MBA); entrepreneurship (MBA); finance (MBA, MS, Graduate Certificate); finance/corporate finance (MS); finance/investments (MS); forensic accounting (MBA); forensic accounting and fraud examination (Graduate Certificate); healthcare informatics (MBA); healthcare management (MBA); human resource management (MS); human resources (MBA); information technology (MS); information technology management (MBA); international business (PhD); Internet marketing (MBA); leadership (MBA); leadership of nonprofit organizations (Graduate Certificate); management (MS); marketing (MBA, MS, Graduate Certificate); music business (MBA); operations and project management (MS); operations and supply chain management (MBA, Graduate Certificate); organizational leadership (MS); project management (MBA, Graduate Certificate); public administration (MBA, Graduate Certificate); quantitative analysis (MBA); Six Sigma (Graduate Certificate); Six Sigma quality (MBA); social media marketing (MBA, Graduate Certificate); sport management (MBA, MS, Graduate Certificate); sustainability and environmental compliance (MBA); MBA/Certificate. *Accreditation:* ACBSP. *Program availability:* Part-time, evening/ weekend, online learning. Terminal master's awarded for partial completion of doctoral program. *Degree requirements:* For master's, one foreign language, comprehensive exam (for some programs), thesis or alternative; for doctorate, one foreign language, comprehensive exam, thesis/dissertation. *Entrance requirements:* For master's, minimum GPA of 2.5; for doctorate, GMAT. Additional exam requirements/ recommendations for international students: Required—TOEFL (minimum score 500 paper-based). Electronic applications accepted.

South University, Graduate Programs, College of Business, Program in Leadership, Savannah, GA 31406. Offers MS.

South University, Program in Leadership, Virginia Beach, VA 23452. Offers MS.

South University, Program in Leadership, Columbia, SC 29203. Offers MS.

Southwest University, MBA Program, Kenner, LA 70062. Offers business administration (MBA); management (MBA); organizational management (MBA).

Southwest University, Program in Organizational Management, Kenner, LA 70062. Offers MA.

Springfield College, Graduate Programs, Program in Human Services, Springfield, MA 01109-3797. Offers mental health counseling (MS); organizational management and leadership (MS). *Program availability:* Part-time, evening/weekend, blended/hybrid learning. *Degree requirements:* For master's, comprehensive exam, thesis (for some programs), Community Action Research Project. *Entrance requirements:* Additional exam requirements/recommendations for international students: Required—TOEFL (minimum score 550 paper-based). Electronic applications accepted. *Expenses:* Contact institution.

Stockton University, Office of Graduate Studies, Program in Organizational Leadership, Galloway, NJ 08205-9441. Offers Ed D. *Program availability:* Evening/ weekend. *Faculty:* 3 full-time (1 woman). *Students:* 95 part-time (59 women); includes 35 minority (27 Black or African American, non-Hispanic/Latino; 1 American Indian or Alaska Native, non-Hispanic/Latino; 1 Asian, non-Hispanic/Latino; 4 Hispanic/Latino; 2 Two or more races, non-Hispanic/Latino). Average age 44. 36 applicants, 75% accepted, 26 enrolled. *Degree requirements:* For doctorate, thesis/dissertation. *Entrance requirements:* For doctorate, minimum overall GPA of 3.0, three letters of recommendation, essay, resume, official transcripts, personal interview. *Application deadline:* For fall admission, 6/1 for domestic students; for spring admission, 11/16 for domestic students. Application fee: $50. *Expenses:* Contact institution. *Unit head:* Dr. Joseph Marchetti, Director, 609-652-4642. *Application contact:* Tara Williams, Assistant Director of Enrollment Management, 609-626-3640, Fax: 609-626-6050, E-mail: gradschool@stockton.edu.

Syracuse University, Maxwell School of Citizenship and Public Affairs, CAS Program in Leadership of International and Non-Governmental Organizations, Syracuse, NY 13244. Offers CAS. *Program availability:* Part-time. In 2018, 35 CASs awarded. *Entrance requirements:* For degree, resume, three letters of recommendation, personal statement, official transcripts. Additional exam requirements/recommendations for international students: Required—TOEFL (minimum score 100 iBT). *Application deadline:* For fall admission, 2/1 priority date for domestic and international students; for spring admission, 8/15 priority date for domestic and international students. Applications are processed on a rolling basis. Application fee: $75. Electronic applications accepted. *Financial support:* Application deadline: 1/1. *Faculty research:* Managing nongovernment organizations in transitional and development countries, public budgeting, fundamentals of public policy, humanitarian action. *Unit head:* Steven Lux, Director, Executive Education, 315-443-3759, E-mail: sjlux@maxwell.syr.edu. *Application contact:* Margaret Lane, Assistant Director, Executive Education Programs, 315-443-8708, E-mail: melane02@maxwell.syr.edu.
Website: http://www.maxwell.syr.edu/

Thomas Edison State University, School of Business and Management, Program in Management, Trenton, NJ 08608. Offers accounting (MSM); organizational leadership (MSM); project management (MSM). *Program availability:* Part-time, 100% online. *Degree requirements:* For master's, final capstone project. *Entrance requirements:* For master's, bachelor's degree from a regionally-accredited college or university; minimum 2 letters of recommendation; 3-5 years of related working experience; current resume. Additional exam requirements/recommendations for international students: Required—TOEFL (minimum score 550 paper-based; 79 iBT). Electronic applications accepted.

Trevecca Nazarene University, Graduate Business Programs, Nashville, TN 37210-2877. Offers business administration (MBA); health care leadership and innovation (MS); management (MSM). *Program availability:* Evening/weekend, online learning. *Entrance requirements:* For master's, minimum GPA of 2.75, resume, official transcript from regionally accredited institution, minimum math grade of C, minimum English composition grade of C. Additional exam requirements/recommendations for international students: Required—TOEFL (minimum score 550 paper-based; 80 iBT). Electronic applications accepted. *Expenses:* Contact institution.

Trevecca Nazarene University, Graduate Leadership Programs, Nashville, TN 37210-2877. Offers leadership and professional practice (Ed D); organizational leadership (MOL). *Program availability:* Online learning. *Degree requirements:* For master's, capstone course; for doctorate, thesis/dissertation, proposal study, symposium presentation. *Entrance requirements:* For master's, minimum GPA of 2.5, official transcript from regionally accredited institution; for doctorate, minimum GPA of 3.4, official transcript from regionally accredited institution, resume, writing sample, references. Additional exam requirements/recommendations for international students: Required—TOEFL (minimum score 550 paper-based; 80 iBT). Electronic applications accepted. *Expenses:* Contact institution.

Trine University, Lou Holtz Program in Leadership, Angola, IN 46703-1764. Offers MS.

Trinity Washington University, School of Business and Graduate Studies, Washington, DC 20017-1094. Offers business administration (MBA); communication (MA); international security studies (MA); organizational management (MSA), including federal program management, human resource management, nonprofit management, organizational development, public and community health. *Program availability:* Part-time, evening/weekend. *Degree requirements:* For master's, thesis (for some programs), capstone project (MSA). *Entrance requirements:* For master's, minimum GPA of 2.5. Additional exam requirements/recommendations for international students: Required— TOEFL (minimum score 550 paper-based).

Trinity Western University, School of Graduate Studies, Program in Leadership, Langley, BC V2Y 1Y1, Canada. Offers business (MA, Certificate); Christian ministry (MA); education (MA, Certificate); healthcare (MA, Certificate); non-profit (MA, Certificate). *Program availability:* Online learning. *Degree requirements:* For master's, major project. *Entrance requirements:* For master's, minimum GPA of 2.7. Additional exam requirements/recommendations for international students: Required—TOEFL (minimum score 620 paper-based; 105 iBT). Electronic applications accepted. *Expenses:* Contact institution. *Faculty research:* Servant leadership.

Tufts University, Graduate School of Arts and Sciences, Program in Diversity and Inclusion Leadership, Medford, MA 02155. Offers MA. *Program availability:* Part-time. *Degree requirements:* For master's, thesis or capstone project. *Entrance requirements:* Additional exam requirements/recommendations for international students: Required— TOEFL, IELTS. Electronic applications accepted. *Expenses:* Contact institution.

Union Institute & University, Master of Science Program in Organizational Leadership, Cincinnati, OH 45206-1925. Offers MS. *Program availability:* Part-time, online only, 100% online. *Degree requirements:* For master's, capstone project. *Entrance requirements:* For master's, recommendations, transcripts, essay. Additional exam requirements/recommendations for international students: Required—TOEFL. Electronic applications accepted. *Expenses:* Contact institution. *Faculty research:* Leadership.

United States International University–Africa, School of Business Administration, Nairobi, Kenya. Offers business administration (GEMBA); entrepreneurship (MBA); finance (MBA); human resource management (MBA); information technology management (MBA); integrated studies (MBA); international business administration (MBA); management and organizational development (MS); marketing (MBA);

organizational development (EMS); strategic management (MBA). *Program availability:* Part-time, evening/weekend. *Degree requirements:* For master's, thesis. *Entrance requirements:* For master's, GMAT, 2 letters of reference, resume. Additional exam requirements/recommendations for international students: Required—TOEFL (minimum score 550 paper-based). *Faculty research:* Marketing in small business enterprises, total quality management in Kenya.

Université Laval, Faculty of Administrative Sciences, Programs in Business Administration, Québec, QC G1K 7P4, Canada. Offers accounting (MBA); agri-food management (MBA); electronic business (MBA, Diploma); factory management and logistics (MBA); finance (MBA); firm management (MBA); geomatic management (MBA); information technology management (MBA); international management (MBA); management (MBA); management accounting (MBA, Diploma); marketing (MBA); modeling and organizational decision (MBA); occupational health and safety management (MBA); pharmacy management (MBA); social and environmental responsibility (MBA); technological entrepreneurship (Diploma). *Accreditation:* AACSB. *Program availability:* Part-time, evening/weekend, online learning. *Entrance requirements:* For master's and Diploma, knowledge of French and English. Electronic applications accepted.

University of Alberta, Faculty of Graduate Studies and Research, Doctoral Program in Business, Edmonton, AB T6G 2E1, Canada. Offers accounting (PhD); finance (PhD); human resources/industrial relations (PhD); management science (PhD); marketing (PhD); organizational analysis (PhD); MBA/PhD. *Accreditation:* AACSB. *Program availability:* Part-time. *Degree requirements:* For doctorate, comprehensive exam, thesis/dissertation. *Entrance requirements:* For doctorate, GMAT. Additional exam requirements/recommendations for international students: Required—TOEFL (minimum score 550 paper-based). Electronic applications accepted. *Faculty research:* Accounting, capital markets and corporate finance, organizational change and human resource management, marketing, strategic management.

The University of Arizona, Eller College of Management, Department of Management and Organizations, Tucson, AZ 85721. Offers MS, PhD. *Program availability:* Evening/weekend. *Entrance requirements:* Additional exam requirements/recommendations for international students: Required—TOEFL (minimum score 550 paper-based; 79 iBT). Electronic applications accepted. *Faculty research:* Organizational behavior, human resources, decision-making, health economics and finance, immigration.

University of Central Arkansas, Graduate School, Interdisciplinary PhD Program in Leadership Studies, Conway, AR 72035-0001. Offers PhD. *Program availability:* Part-time. *Degree requirements:* For doctorate, thesis/dissertation. *Entrance requirements:* For doctorate, GRE. Additional exam requirements/recommendations for international students: Required—TOEFL. Electronic applications accepted.

University of Charleston, Doctor of Executive Leadership Program, Charleston, WV 25304-1099. Offers DEL. *Entrance requirements:* Additional exam requirements/recommendations for international students: Required—TOEFL. Electronic applications accepted.

University of Cincinnati, Graduate School, McMicken College of Arts and Sciences, Center for Organizational Leadership, Cincinnati, OH 45221. Offers MALER. *Program availability:* Part-time, evening/weekend. *Entrance requirements:* For master's, GRE or GMAT. Additional exam requirements/recommendations for international students: Required—TOEFL (minimum score 520 paper-based; 68 iBT). Electronic applications accepted. *Faculty research:* Leadership and diversity.

University of Colorado Boulder, Graduate School, Master of Science Program in Organizational Leadership, Boulder, CO 80309. Electronic applications accepted.

University of Dallas, Satish and Yasmin Gupta College of Business, Irving, TX 75062. Offers accounting (MBA, MS); business administration (DBA); business analytics (MS); business management (MBA); corporate finance (MBA); cybersecurity (MS); finance (MS); financial services (MBA); global business (MBA, MS); health services management (MBA); human resource management (MBA); information and technology management (MS); information assurance (MBA); information technology (MBA); information technology service management (MBA); marketing management (MBA); organization development (MBA); project management (MBA); sports and entertainment management (MBA); strategic leadership (MBA); supply chain management (MBA). *Accreditation:* AACSB. *Program availability:* Part-time, evening/weekend, 100% online. *Students:* 147 full-time (56 women), 584 part-time (232 women); includes 402 minority (204 Black or African American, non-Hispanic/Latino; 95 Asian, non-Hispanic/Latino; 92 Hispanic/Latino; 2 Native Hawaiian or other Pacific Islander, non-Hispanic/Latino; 9 Two or more races, non-Hispanic/Latino), 113 international. Average age 34. 992 applicants, 30% accepted, 157 enrolled. In 2018, 336 master's, 5 doctorates awarded. *Degree requirements:* For doctorate, thesis/dissertation. *Entrance requirements:* For master's and doctorate, U.S. bachelor's degree with a minimum cumulative GPA of 2.0 from a regionally accredited college or university (or comparable foreign degree); minimum 3.0 GPA in any graduate-level coursework completed; good academic standing with all colleges attended. Additional exam requirements/recommendations for international students: Required—TOEFL (minimum score 80 iBT), IELTS (minimum score 6.5), PTE (minimum score 67). *Application deadline:* Applications are processed on a rolling basis. Application fee: $50. Electronic applications accepted. *Expenses:* $1250 per credit hour. *Financial support:* In 2018–19, 291 students received support. Research assistantships, teaching assistantships, scholarships/grants, and unspecified assistantships available. Support available to part-time students. Financial award application deadline: 2/15; financial award applicants required to submit FAFSA. *Unit head:* Brett J.L. Landry, Dean, 972-721-5356, E-mail: blandry@udallas.edu. *Application contact:* Breonna Collins, Director, Graduate Admissions, 972-7215304, E-mail: bcollins@udallas.edu.
Website: http://www.udallas.edu/cob/

University of Denver, University College, Denver, CO 80208. Offers arts and culture (MA, Certificate); communication management (MS, Certificate), including translation studies (Certificate), world history and culture (Certificate); environmental policy and management (MS); geographic information systems (MS); global affairs (MA, Certificate), including human capital in organizations (Certificate), philanthropic leadership (Certificate), project management (Certificate), strategic innovation and change (Certificate); healthcare leadership (MS); information communications and technology (MS); leadership and organizations (MS); professional creative writing (MA, Certificate), including emergency planning and response (Certificate), organizational security (Certificate); security management (MS, Certificate); strategic human resources (Certificate). *Program availability:* Part-time, evening/weekend, 100% online, blended/hybrid learning. *Faculty:* 4 full-time (2 women), 108 part-time/adjunct (51 women). *Students:* 51 full-time (26 women), 1,291 part-time (733 women); includes 337 minority (112 Black or African American, non-Hispanic/Latino; 6 American Indian or Alaska Native, non-Hispanic/Latino; 46 Asian, non-Hispanic/Latino; 132 Hispanic/Latino; 3 Native Hawaiian or other Pacific Islander, non-Hispanic/Latino; 38 Two or more races, non-Hispanic/Latino), 75 international. Average age 34. 834 applicants, 87% accepted, 423 enrolled. In 2018, 443 master's, 232 other advanced degrees awarded. *Degree requirements:* For master's, capstone project. *Entrance requirements:* For master's, baccalaureate degree, transcripts, two letters of recommendation, personal statement, resume, writing sample (Master of Arts in Professional Creative Writing). Additional exam requirements/recommendations for international students: Required—TOEFL (minimum score 550 paper-based; 80 iBT). *Application deadline:* For fall admission, 6/19 priority date for domestic students, 6/14 priority date for international students; for winter admission, 10/25 priority date for domestic students, 9/27 priority date for international students; for spring admission, 2/7 priority date for domestic students, 1/10 priority date for international students; for summer admission, 4/24 priority date for domestic students, 3/27 priority date for international students. Applications are processed on a rolling basis. Application fee: $75. Electronic applications accepted. *Expenses:* $8,280 per year half-time. *Financial support:* In 2018–19, 38 students received support. Teaching assistantships available. Financial award applicants required to submit FAFSA. *Unit head:* Dr. Michael McGuire, Dean, 303-871-3518, E-mail: michael.mcguire@du.edu. *Application contact:* Admission Team, 303-871-2291, E-mail: ucoladm@du.edu.
Website: http://universitycollege.du.edu/

University of Guelph, Office of Graduate and Postdoctoral Studies, College of Management and Economics, MA (Leadership) Program, Guelph, ON N1G 2W1, Canada. Offers MA. *Program availability:* Part-time, evening/weekend, online learning. *Entrance requirements:* For master's, minimum B-average, minimum 5 years of relevant work experience. Additional exam requirements/recommendations for international students: Required—TOEFL (minimum score 550 paper-based). Electronic applications accepted. *Faculty research:* Theories of leadership, organizational change, ethics in leadership, decision making, politics of organizations.

University of Hawaii at Manoa, Office of Graduate Education, Shidler College of Business, Program in Business Administration, Honolulu, HI 96822. Offers Asian business studies (MBA); Chinese business studies (MBA); decision sciences (MBA); entrepreneurship (MBA); finance (MBA); finance and banking (MBA); human resources management (MBA); information management (MBA); information technology (MBA); international business (MBA); Japanese business studies (MBA); marketing (MBA); organizational behavior (MBA); organizational management (MBA); real estate (MBA); student-designed track (MBA). *Accreditation:* AACSB. *Program availability:* Part-time, evening/weekend. *Degree requirements:* For master's, thesis optional. *Entrance requirements:* For master's, GMAT, minimum GPA of 3.0. Additional exam requirements/recommendations for international students: Required—TOEFL (minimum score 600 paper-based; 100 iBT), IELTS (minimum score 7). *Expenses:* Contact institution.

University of Hawaii at Manoa, Office of Graduate Education, Shidler College of Business, Program in International Management, Honolulu, HI 96822. Offers Asian finance (PhD); global information technology management (PhD); international accounting (PhD); international marketing (PhD); international organization and strategy (PhD). *Program availability:* Part-time. *Degree requirements:* For doctorate, comprehensive exam, thesis/dissertation. *Entrance requirements:* For doctorate, GMAT or GRE General Test, minimum GPA of 3.0. Additional exam requirements/recommendations for international students: Required—TOEFL (minimum score 600 paper-based; 100 iBT), IELTS (minimum score 7). *Expenses:* Contact institution.

The University of Kansas, Graduate Studies, School of Business, Program in Business, Lawrence, KS 66045. Offers business and organizational leadership (MS); decision sciences and supply chain management (PhD); finance (PhD); human resources management (PhD); marketing (PhD); organizational behavior (PhD); strategic management (PhD); supply chain management and logistics (MS). *Accreditation:* AACSB. *Program availability:* Part-time. *Students:* 69 full-time (20 women), 150 part-time (62 women); includes 42 minority (14 Black or African American, non-Hispanic/Latino; 2 American Indian or Alaska Native, non-Hispanic/Latino; 6 Asian, non-Hispanic/Latino; 7 Hispanic/Latino; 13 Two or more races, non-Hispanic/Latino), 24 international. Average age 32. 306 applicants, 51% accepted, 132 enrolled. In 2018, 22 master's, 1 doctorate awarded. *Entrance requirements:* For master's, GMAT, official transcript, three letters of recommendation, resume, statement of purpose; for doctorate, GMAT or GRE, official transcript, three letters of recommendation, resume, statement of purpose. Additional exam requirements/recommendations for international students: Required—TOEFL, IELTS. *Application deadline:* For fall admission, 1/10 for domestic and international students. Application fee: $65 ($85 for international students). Electronic applications accepted. *Financial support:* Fellowships, research assistantships, teaching assistantships, scholarships/grants, health care benefits, tuition waivers (full), and unspecified assistantships available. Financial award application deadline: 1/10. *Faculty research:* Strategic human resource management, business ethics, organizational theory/behavior, corporate strategy, international business, supply chain management, Bayesian networks, game theory, decision analysis and time/series analysis, pricing, consumer effects, advertising and emotion. *Unit head:* Charly Edmonds, Director, 785-864-3841, E-mail: cedmonds@ku.edu. *Application contact:* Andrea Noltner, Graduate Admission Contact, 785-864-7556, E-mail: anoltner@ku.edu.
Website: http://www.business.ku.edu/

The University of Kansas, University of Kansas Medical Center, School of Nursing, Kansas City, KS 66045. Offers adult/gerontological clinical nurse specialist (PMC); adult/gerontological nurse practitioner (PMC); health care informatics (PMC); health professions educator (PMC); nurse midwife (PMC); nursing (MS, DNP, PhD); organizational leadership (PMC); psychiatric/mental health nurse practitioner (PMC); public health nursing (PMC). *Accreditation:* AACN; ACNM/ACME. *Program availability:* Part-time, 100% online, blended/hybrid learning. *Faculty:* 56. *Students:* 55 full-time (49 women), 273 part-time (246 women); includes 62 minority (16 Black or African American, non-Hispanic/Latino; 2 American Indian or Alaska Native, non-Hispanic/Latino; 21 Asian, non-Hispanic/Latino; 9 Hispanic/Latino; 14 Two or more races, non-Hispanic/Latino), 1 international. Average age 36. 76 applicants, 93% accepted, 60 enrolled. In 2018, 19 master's, 28 doctorates, 7 other advanced degrees awarded. Terminal master's awarded for partial completion of doctoral program. *Degree requirements:* For master's, comprehensive exam, thesis (for some programs), general oral exam; for doctorate, thesis/dissertation or alternative, comprehensive oral exam (for DNP); comprehensive written and oral exam, or three publications (for PhD). *Entrance requirements:* For master's, bachelor's degree in nursing, minimum GPA of 3.0, 1 year of clinical experience, RN license in KS and MO; for doctorate, GRE General Test (for PhD only), bachelor's degree in nursing, minimum GPA of 3.5, RN license in KS and MO. Additional exam requirements/recommendations for international students: Required—TOEFL. *Application deadline:* For fall admission, 4/1 for domestic and international students; for spring admission, 9/1 for domestic and international students. Application fee: $75. Electronic applications accepted. *Financial support:* In 2018–19, 5 research assistantships with tuition reimbursements (averaging $20,000 per year), 30 teaching assistantships with tuition reimbursements (averaging $20,000 per year) were awarded; scholarships/grants and traineeships also available. Financial award application deadline: 3/1; financial award applicants required to submit FAFSA. *Faculty research:* Breastfeeding practices of teen mothers, national database of nursing quality indicators, caregiving of families of patients using technology in the home, simulation in nursing education, diaphragm fatigue. *Total annual research expenditures:* $3 million. *Unit head:* Dr. Sally Maliski, Dean, 913-588-1601, Fax: 913-588-1660, E-mail: smaliski@kumc.edu. *Application contact:* Dr. Pamela K. Barnes, Associate Dean, Student Affairs, 913-588-1619, Fax: 913-588-1615, E-mail: pbarnes2@kumc.edu.
Website: http://nursing.kumc.edu

Organizational Management

University of La Verne, College of Business and Public Management, Program in Leadership and Management, La Verne, CA 91750-4443. Offers human resource management (Certificate); leadership and management (MS), including human resource management, nonprofit management, organizational development; nonprofit management (Certificate); organizational leadership (Certificate). *Program availability:* Part-time. *Entrance requirements:* For master's, bachelor's degree, minimum undergraduate GPA of 2.75, 2 letters of recommendation, interview, resume. Additional exam requirements/recommendations for international students: Required—TOEFL (minimum score 550 paper-based).

University of La Verne, LaFetra College of Education, Doctoral Program in Organizational Leadership, La Verne, CA 91750-4443. Offers Ed D. *Program availability:* Part-time. *Entrance requirements:* For doctorate, GRE or MAT, minimum graduate GPA of 3.0, resume or curriculum vitae, 2 endorsement forms. Additional exam requirements/recommendations for international students: Required—TOEFL (minimum score 550 paper-based). *Expenses:* Contact institution.

University of La Verne, Regional and Online Campuses, Graduate Programs, Inland Empire Campus, Ontario, CA 91730. Offers business administration (MBA, MBA-EP), including accounting (MBA), finance (MBA), health services management (MBA-EP), information technology (MBA-EP), international business (MBA), managed care (MBA), management and leadership (MBA-EP), marketing (MBA-EP), supply chain management (MBA); leadership and management (MS), including human resource management, nonprofit management, organizational development. *Program availability:* Part-time, evening/weekend. *Expenses:* Contact institution.

University of La Verne, Regional and Online Campuses, Graduate Programs, Kern County Campus, Bakersfield, CA 93301. Offers business administration for experienced professionals (MBA-EP); education (special emphasis) (M Ed); educational counseling (MS); educational leadership (M Ed); health administration (MHA); leadership and management (MS); mild/moderate education specialist (Credential); multiple subject (elementary) (Credential); organizational leadership (Ed D); preliminary administrative services (Credential); single subject (secondary) (Credential); special education studies (MS). *Program availability:* Part-time, evening/weekend. *Expenses:* Contact institution.

University of Maryland Eastern Shore, Graduate Programs, Program in Organizational Leadership, Princess Anne, MD 21853. Offers PhD. *Program availability:* Evening/weekend. *Degree requirements:* For doctorate, comprehensive exam, thesis/dissertation, internship. *Entrance requirements:* For doctorate, interview, writing sample, successful record of employment or career in organization/profession. Additional exam requirements/recommendations for international students: Required—TOEFL (minimum score 80 iBT). Electronic applications accepted.

University of Massachusetts Amherst, Graduate School, Isenberg School of Management, Program in Management, Amherst, MA 01003. Offers accounting (PhD); business administration (MBA); entrepreneurship (MBA); finance (MBA, PhD); healthcare administration (MBA); hospitality and tourism management (PhD); management science (PhD); marketing (MBA, PhD); organization studies (PhD); sport management (PhD); strategic management (PhD); MBA/MS. *Accreditation:* AACSB. *Program availability:* Part-time, evening/weekend, online learning. Terminal master's awarded for partial completion of doctoral program. *Degree requirements:* For doctorate, comprehensive exam, thesis/dissertation. *Entrance requirements:* For master's and doctorate, GMAT or GRE General Test. Additional exam requirements/recommendations for international students: Required—TOEFL (minimum score 550 paper-based; 80 iBT), IELTS (minimum score 6.5). Electronic applications accepted.

University of Michigan–Flint, School of Management, Program in Business Administration, Flint, MI 48502-1950. Offers accounting (MBA); computer information systems (MBA); finance (MBA, Post-Master's Certificate); general business (Graduate Certificate); general business administration (MBA); health care management (MBA); international business (MBA, Post-Master's Certificate); lean manufacturing (MBA); marketing (Post-Master's Certificate); marketing and innovation management (MBA); organizational leadership (MBA). *Program availability:* Part-time, evening/weekend, mixed mode format. *Faculty:* 30 full-time (4 women), 10 part-time/adjunct (2 women). *Students:* 24 full-time (14 women), 151 part-time (60 women); includes 45 minority (22 Black or African American, non-Hispanic/Latino; 3 American Indian or Alaska Native, non-Hispanic/Latino; 7 Asian, non-Hispanic/Latino; 9 Hispanic/Latino; 4 Two or more races, non-Hispanic/Latino), 19 international. Average age 36. 160 applicants, 75% accepted, 62 enrolled. In 2018, 50 master's, 1 other advanced degree awarded. *Entrance requirements:* For master's, bachelor's degree in arts, sciences, engineering, or business administration from regionally-accredited college or university; for other advanced degree, bachelor's degree in arts, sciences, engineering, or business administration from regionally-accredited college or university. college-level math, statistics, or quantitative course (for Graduate Certificate); MBA or equivalent degree from regionally-accredited college or university (for Post Master's Certificate). Additional exam requirements/recommendations for international students: Required—TOEFL (minimum score 84 iBT), IELTS (minimum score 6.5). *Application deadline:* For fall admission, 8/1 for domestic students, 5/1 for international students; for winter admission, 11/15 for domestic students, 9/1 for international students; for spring admission, 3/15 for domestic students, 1/1 for international students; for summer admission, 5/15 for domestic students. Applications are processed on a rolling basis. Application fee: $55. Electronic applications accepted. *Expenses:* Contact institution. *Financial support:* Federal Work-Study, scholarships/grants, and unspecified assistantships available. Support available to part-time students. Financial award application deadline: 3/1; financial award applicants required to submit FAFSA. *Unit head:* Dr. Scott Johnson, Dean, School of Management, 810-762-3164, Fax: 810-237-6685, E-mail: scotjohn@umflint.edu. *Application contact:* Matt Bohlen, Director of Graduate Admissions, 810-762-3171, E-mail: mbohlen@umflint.edu.
Website: http://www.umflint.edu/graduateprograms/business-administration-mba

University of Michigan–Flint, School of Management, Program in Leadership and Organizational Dynamics, Flint, MI 48502-1950. Offers leadership and organizational dynamics (MS); organizational leadership (Post-Master's Certificate). *Program availability:* Part-time, evening/weekend, mixed mode format. *Faculty:* 30 full-time (4 women), 10 part-time/adjunct (2 women). *Students:* 14 part-time (6 women); includes 1 minority (Black or African American, non-Hispanic/Latino), 2 international. Average age 37. 8 applicants, 100% accepted, 4 enrolled. *Entrance requirements:* For master's, bachelor's degree in arts, sciences, engineering, or business administration from regionally-accredited college or university with minimum GPA of 3.0; minimum of two years of supervisory experience described through resume; for Post-Master's Certificate, MBA or equivalent degree from regionally-accredited college or university (for Post-Master's Certificate). Additional exam requirements/recommendations for international students: Required—TOEFL (minimum score 84 iBT), IELTS (minimum score 6.5). *Application deadline:* For fall admission, 8/1 for domestic students, 5/1 for international students; for winter admission, 11/15 for domestic students, 9/1 for international students; for spring admission, 3/15 for domestic students, 1/1 for international students; for summer admission, 5/15 for domestic students. Applications are processed on a rolling basis. Application fee: $55. Electronic applications accepted. *Expenses:* Contact institution. *Financial support:* Federal Work-Study, scholarships/grants, and unspecified assistantships available. Support available to part-time students. Financial award application deadline: 3/1; financial award applicants required to submit FAFSA. *Unit head:* Dr. Scott Johnson, Dean, School of Management, 810-762-6579, Fax: 810-237-6685, E-mail: scotjohn@umflint.edu. *Application contact:* Matt Bohlen, Director of Graduate Admissions, 810-762-3171, Fax: 810-766-6789, E-mail: mbohlen@umflint.edu.
Website: https://www.umflint.edu/graduateprograms/leadership-organizational-dynamics-ms

University of Missouri, Office of Research and Graduate Studies, Harry S Truman School of Public Affairs, Columbia, MO 65211. Offers grantsmanship (Graduate Certificate); nonprofit management (Graduate Certificate); organizational change (Graduate Certificate); public affairs (MPA, PhD); public management (Graduate Certificate); science and public policy (Graduate Certificate). *Accreditation:* NASPAA. *Entrance requirements:* For master's, GRE General Test, minimum GPA of 3.0. Additional exam requirements/recommendations for international students: Required—TOEFL, IELTS. Electronic applications accepted.

University of Nebraska at Omaha, Graduate Studies, College of Arts and Sciences, Program in Critical and Creative Thinking, Omaha, NE 68182. Offers MA. *Program availability:* Part-time, online learning. *Entrance requirements:* For master's, undergraduate degree with minimum GPA of 3.0. Additional exam requirements/recommendations for international students: Required—TOEFL, IELTS, or PTE. Electronic applications accepted.

University of New Haven, Graduate School, College of Arts and Sciences, Program in Industrial and Organizational Psychology, West Haven, CT 06516. Offers conflict management (MA); industrial organizational psychology (MA); industrial-human resources psychology (MA); organizational development and consultation (MA); psychology of conflict management (Graduate Certificate). *Program availability:* Part-time, evening/weekend. *Students:* 63 full-time (37 women), 3 part-time (2 women); includes 15 minority (8 Black or African American, non-Hispanic/Latino; 2 Asian, non-Hispanic/Latino; 5 Hispanic/Latino), 9 international. Average age 27. 80 applicants, 78% accepted, 31 enrolled. In 2018, 41 master's awarded. *Degree requirements:* For master's, thesis or alternative, internship or practicum. *Entrance requirements:* Additional exam requirements/recommendations for international students: Required—TOEFL (minimum score 80 iBT), IELTS, PTE. *Application deadline:* Applications are processed on a rolling basis. Application fee: $50. Electronic applications accepted. Application fee is waived when completed online. *Expenses:* Contact institution. *Financial support:* Research assistantships with partial tuition reimbursements, teaching assistantships with partial tuition reimbursements, career-related internships or fieldwork, Federal Work-Study, scholarships/grants, and unspecified assistantships available. Support available to part-time students. Financial award applicants required to submit FAFSA. *Unit head:* Dr. Eric Marcus, Distinguished Lecturer, 203-932-1242, E-mail: emarcus@newhaven.edu. *Application contact:* Selina O'Toole, Senior Associate Director of Graduate Admissions, 203-932-7337, E-mail: SOToole@newhaven.edu.
Website: https://www.newhaven.edu/arts-sciences/graduate-programs/industrial-organizational-psychology/

University of Northwestern–St. Paul, Master of Organizational Leadership Program, St. Paul, MN 55113-1598. Offers MOL. *Program availability:* Part-time, evening/weekend, online learning. Electronic applications accepted.

University of Oklahoma, College of Professional and Continuing Studies, Norman, OK 73019. Offers administrative leadership (MA, Graduate Certificate), including government and military leadership (MA), organizational leadership (MA), volunteer and non-profit leadership (MA); corrections management (Graduate Certificate); criminal justice (MS); integrated studies (MA), including human and health services administration, integrated studies; museum studies (MA); prevention science (MPS); restorative justice administration (Graduate Certificate). *Program availability:* Part-time, 100% online, blended/hybrid learning. *Degree requirements:* For master's, comprehensive exam, thesis optional, 33 credit hours; project/internship (for museum studies program only); for Graduate Certificate, 12 graduate credit hours (for Graduate Certificate). *Entrance requirements:* For master's and Graduate Certificate, minimum GPA of 3.0 in last 60 undergraduate hours; statement of goals; resume. Additional exam requirements/recommendations for international students: Required—TOEFL (minimum score 79 iBT) or IELTS (minimum score 6.5). Electronic applications accepted. *Expenses:* Tuition, state resident: full-time $5683.20; part-time $236.80 per credit hour. Tuition, nonresident: full-time $20,342; part-time $847.60 per credit hour. *International tuition:* $20,342.40 full-time. *Required fees:* $2894.20; $110.05 per credit hour. $126.50 per semester. Tuition and fees vary according to course load and program. *Faculty research:* Change management and leadership; policing and corrections management; neuro-psychology of addiction; disproportionate minority contact; ethnic identity and nationalism.

University of Pennsylvania, School of Arts and Sciences, College of Liberal and Professional Studies, Philadelphia, PA 19104. Offers applied geosciences (MSAG); applied positive psychology (MAP); chemical sciences (MCS); environmental studies (MES); individualized study (MLA); liberal arts (M Phil); medical physics (MMP); organization dynamics (M Phil). *Students:* 219 full-time (144 women), 295 part-time (178 women); includes 101 minority (31 Black or African American, non-Hispanic/Latino; 1 American Indian or Alaska Native, non-Hispanic/Latino; 35 Asian, non-Hispanic/Latino; 16 Hispanic/Latino; 1 Native Hawaiian or other Pacific Islander, non-Hispanic/Latino; 17 Two or more races, non-Hispanic/Latino), 103 international. Average age 34. 633 applicants, 52% accepted, 249 enrolled. In 2018, 180 master's awarded. *Unit head:* Nora Lewis, Vice Dean, Professional and Liberal Education, 215-898-7326, E-mail: nlewis@sas.upenn.edu. *Application contact:* Nora Lewis, Vice Dean, Professional and Liberal Education, 215-898-7326, E-mail: nlewis@sas.upenn.edu.
Website: http://www.sas.upenn.edu/lps/graduate

University of Pennsylvania, School of Arts and Sciences, Fels Institute of Government, Philadelphia, PA 19104. Offers economic development and growth (Certificate); government administration (MGA); nonprofit administration (Certificate); organization dynamics (MS); politics (Certificate); public administration (MPA); public finance (Certificate). *Program availability:* Part-time, evening/weekend. *Students:* 30 full-time (15 women); 60 part-time (33 women); includes 25 minority (4 Black or African American, non-Hispanic/Latino; 10 Asian, non-Hispanic/Latino; 8 Hispanic/Latino; 3 Two or more races, non-Hispanic/Latino), 4 international. Average age 32. 757 applicants, 41% accepted, 240 enrolled. In 2018, 48 master's, 10 other advanced degrees awarded. *Financial support:* Application deadline: 1/1.
Website: http://www.fels.upenn.edu/

University of Phoenix–Bay Area Campus, College of Information Systems and Technology, San Jose, CA 95134-1805. Offers information systems (MIS); organizational leadership/information systems and technology (DM). *Program availability:* Evening/weekend. *Degree requirements:* For master's, thesis (for some programs). *Entrance requirements:* For master's, minimum undergraduate GPA of 3.0, 3 years of work experience. Additional exam requirements/recommendations for international students: Required—TOEFL (minimum score 550 paper-based; 79 iBT). Electronic applications accepted.

University of Phoenix–Bay Area Campus, School of Business, San Jose, CA 95134-1805. Offers accountancy (MS); accounting (MBA); business administration (MBA, DBA); energy management (MBA); global management (MBA); health care management (MBA); human resource management (MBA); human resources management (MM); management (MM); marketing (MBA); organizational leadership (DM); project management (MBA); public administration (MPA); technology management (MBA). *Accreditation:* ACBSP. *Program availability:* Evening/weekend, online learning. *Degree requirements:* For master's, thesis (for some programs). *Entrance requirements:* For master's, minimum undergraduate GPA of 3.0, 3 years of work experience. Additional exam requirements/recommendations for international students: Required—TOEFL (minimum score 550 paper-based; 79 iBT). Electronic applications accepted.

University of Phoenix–Online Campus, School of Advanced Studies, Phoenix, AZ 85034-7209. Offers business administration (DBA); education (Ed S); educational leadership (Ed D), including curriculum and instruction, education technology, educational leadership; health administration (DHA); higher education administration (PhD); industrial/organizational psychology (PhD); nursing (PhD); organizational leadership (DM), including information systems and technology, organizational leadership. *Program availability:* Evening/weekend, online learning. *Degree requirements:* For doctorate, thesis/dissertation. *Entrance requirements:* Additional exam requirements/recommendations for international students: Required—TOEFL, TOEIC (Test of English as an International Communication), Berlitz Online English Proficiency Exam, PTE, or IELTS. Electronic applications accepted. *Expenses:* Contact institution.

University of Portland, School of Education, Portland, OR 97203-5798. Offers education (MA, MAT); educational leadership (M Ed); English for speakers of other languages (M Ed); initial administrator licensure (M Ed); neuroeducation (M Ed, Ed D); organizational leadership and development (Ed D); reading (M Ed); school leadership and development (Ed D); special education (M Ed). *Accreditation:* NCATE. *Program availability:* Part-time, evening/weekend. *Students:* 32 full-time (30 women), 239 part-time (187 women); includes 33 minority (7 Black or African American, non-Hispanic/Latino; 3 American Indian or Alaska Native, non-Hispanic/Latino; 13 Asian, non-Hispanic/Latino; 1 Native Hawaiian or other Pacific Islander, non-Hispanic/Latino; 9 Two or more races, non-Hispanic/Latino). Average age 34. 92 applicants, 60% accepted, 42 enrolled. In 2018, 57 master's, 16 doctorates awarded. *Degree requirements:* For doctorate, thesis/dissertation. *Entrance requirements:* For master's, minimum GPA of 3.0, teaching certificate, letters of recommendation, resume, statement of goals, official transcripts; for doctorate, 2 letters of recommendation, resume, essays, official transcripts. Additional exam requirements/recommendations for international students: Required—TOEFL (minimum score 550 paper-based; 80 iBT), IELTS (minimum score 7). *Application deadline:* For fall admission, 7/15 priority date for domestic and international students; for spring admission, 12/15 priority date for domestic and international students; for summer admission, 4/15 for domestic and international students. Applications are processed on a rolling basis. Electronic applications accepted. *Expenses:* MAT degree - $995/credit hour; EDD and Educational Specialist - $813/credit hour; all other degrees and certificates - $663/credit hour. *Financial support:* Fellowships, Federal Work-Study, and scholarships/grants available. Support available to part-time students. Financial award application deadline: 3/1; financial award applicants required to submit FAFSA. *Faculty research:* Multicultural education, supervision/leadership. *Unit head:* Dr. Bruce Weitzel, Associate Dean, 503-943-7135, E-mail: soed@up.edu. *Application contact:* Caitlin Biddulph, Graduate Programs and Admissions Specialist, 503-943-7107, E-mail: biddulph@up.edu.
Website: http://education.up.edu/default.aspx?cid-4318&pid-5590

University of Regina, Faculty of Graduate Studies and Research, Kenneth Levene Graduate School of Business, Program in Business Administration, Regina, SK S4S 0A2, Canada. Offers business foundations (PGD); engineering management (MBA); executive business administration (EMBA); international business (MBA); leadership (M Admin); organizational leadership (Master's Certificate); project management (Master's Certificate); public safety management (MBA). *Program availability:* Part-time, evening/weekend. *Students:* 30 full-time (14 women), 9 part-time (5 women). Average age 30. In 2018, 23 master's awarded. *Degree requirements:* For master's, project (for some programs). workplacement for Co-op concentration. *Entrance requirements:* For master's, GMAT, 3 years of relevant work experience, four-year undergraduate degree, post secondary transcript, 2 letters of recommendation; for other advanced degree, GMAT (for PGD), four-year undergraduate degree and 2 years of relevant work experience (for Master's Certificate); 3 years' work experience (for PGD). Additional exam requirements/recommendations for international students: Required—TOEFL (minimum score 580 paper-based; 80 iBT), IELTS (minimum score 6.5), PTE (minimum score 59), other options are CAEL, MELAB, CANTEST or U of R ESl; GMAT is mandatory. *Application deadline:* For fall admission, 3/1 for domestic and international students; for winter admission, 7/1 for domestic and international students; for spring admission, 10/1 for domestic and international students; for summer admission, 10/1 for domestic and international students. Applications are processed on a rolling basis. Application fee: $100. Electronic applications accepted. *Expenses:* One academic year is 18,752. International students will pay additional 1,191.75 for International surcharge per semester. *Financial support:* Fellowships, research assistantships, teaching assistantships, career-related internships or fieldwork, Federal Work-Study, scholarships/grants, unspecified assistantships, and travel award and Graduate Scholarship Base Funds available. Support available to part-time students. Financial award application deadline: 9/30. *Faculty research:* Business policy and strategy, production and operations management, human behavior in organizations, financial management, social issues in business. *Unit head:* Dr. Gina Grandy, Dean, 306-585-4435, Fax: 306-585-5361, E-mail: business.dean@uregina.ca. *Application contact:* Adrian Pitariu, Associate Dean, Research and Graduate Programs, 306-585-6294, Fax: 306-585-5361, E-mail: business.AD.levene@uregina.ca.
Website: http://www.uregina.ca/business/levene/

University of Saint Francis, Graduate School, Keith Busse School of Business and Entrepreneurial Leadership, Fort Wayne, IN 46808-3994. Offers business administration (MBA), including sustainability; environmental health (MEH); healthcare administration (MHA); organizational leadership (MOL). *Accreditation:* ACBSP. *Program availability:* Part-time, evening/weekend, online only, 100% online. *Faculty:* 4 full-time (3 women), 11 part-time/adjunct (1 woman). *Students:* 62 full-time (33 women), 94 part-time (53 women); includes 40 minority (23 Black or African American, non-Hispanic/Latino; 1 American Indian or Alaska Native, non-Hispanic/Latino; 10 Hispanic/Latino; 1 Native Hawaiian or other Pacific Islander, non-Hispanic/Latino; 5 Two or more races, non-Hispanic/Latino). Average age 33. 72 applicants, 96% accepted, 51 enrolled. In 2018, 112 master's awarded. *Application deadline:* For fall admission, 7/1 for international students; for spring admission, 11/1 for international students; for summer admission, 3/1 for international students. Applications are processed on a rolling basis. Application fee: $0. Electronic applications accepted. *Expenses:* Tuition: Full-time $22,440; part-time $935 per credit hour. *Required fees:* $330 per semester. Tuition and fees vary according to degree level, campus/location and program. *Unit head:* Dr. Robert W. Lee, Dean, 260-399-7700 Ext. 8304, Fax: 260-399-8174, E-mail: rlee@sf.edu. *Application contact:* Kyle Richardson, Associate Director of Enrollment Services for Adult Learning,

260-399-7700 Ext. 6310, Fax: 260-399-8152, E-mail: krichardson@sf.edu.
Website: https://admissions.sf.edu/graduate/

University of St. Thomas, College of Education, Leadership and Counseling, Department of Organization Learning and Development, St. Paul, MN 55105-1096. Offers organization development and change (Ed D). *Program availability:* Part-time, evening/weekend. *Degree requirements:* For doctorate, comprehensive exam, thesis/dissertation. *Entrance requirements:* For doctorate, minimum GPA of 3.5, interview, 5-7 years of organization development or leadership experience. Additional exam requirements/recommendations for international students: Required—TOEFL (minimum score 550 paper-based). Electronic applications accepted. *Expenses:* Contact institution. *Faculty research:* Workplace conflict, physician leaders, virtual teams, technology use in schools/workplace, developing masterful practitioners.

University of San Francisco, School of Management, Master of Business Administration Program, San Francisco, CA 94117. Offers entrepreneurship and innovation (MBA); finance (MBA); marketing (MBA); organization development (MBA); DDS/MBA; JD/MBA; MBA/MAPS. *Accreditation:* AACSB. *Program availability:* Part-time, evening/weekend. *Students:* 136 full-time (67 women), 7 part-time (2 women); includes 57 minority (5 Black or African American, non-Hispanic/Latino; 29 Asian, non-Hispanic/Latino; 14 Hispanic/Latino; 1 Native Hawaiian or other Pacific Islander, non-Hispanic/Latino; 8 Two or more races, non-Hispanic/Latino), 27 international. Average age 29. 226 applicants, 61% accepted, 56 enrolled. In 2018, 76 master's awarded. *Entrance requirements:* For master's, GMAT or GRE, resume (two years of professional work experience required for part-time students, preferred for full-time), transcripts from each college or university attended, two letters of recommendation, personal statement, interview. Additional exam requirements/recommendations for international students: Required—TOEFL (minimum score 600 paper-based, 100 iBT), IELTS (minimum score 7) or PTE (minimum score 68). *Application deadline:* For fall admission, 6/5 for domestic students, 5/15 for international students; for spring admission, 11/30 for domestic students. Application fee: $55. Electronic applications accepted. *Expenses:* Contact institution. *Financial support:* Fellowships and scholarships/grants available. Financial award application deadline: 3/2; financial award applicants required to submit FAFSA. *Faculty research:* International financial markets, technology transfer licensing, international marketing, strategic planning. *Total annual research expenditures:* $50,000. *Unit head:* Dr. Frank Fletcher, Director, 415-422-2221, E-mail: management@usfca.edu. *Application contact:* Office of Graduate Recruiting and Admissions, 415-422-2221, E-mail: management@usfca.edu.
Website: http://www.usfca.edu/mba

University of San Francisco, School of Management, Master of Science in Organization Development Program, San Francisco, CA 94117. Offers MSOD. *Program availability:* Part-time, evening/weekend. *Students:* 83 full-time (63 women), 2 part-time (both women); includes 50 minority (4 Black or African American, non-Hispanic/Latino; 20 Asian, non-Hispanic/Latino; 18 Hispanic/Latino; 2 Native Hawaiian or other Pacific Islander, non-Hispanic/Latino; 6 Two or more races, non-Hispanic/Latino). Average age 34. 66 applicants, 83% accepted, 41 enrolled. In 2018, 43 master's awarded. *Degree requirements:* For master's, thesis. *Entrance requirements:* For master's, resume demonstrating minimum of two years of professional work experience, transcripts from each college or university attended, two letters of recommendation, personal statement. Additional exam requirements/recommendations for international students: Required—TOEFL (minimum score 600 paper-based, 100 iBT), IELTS (minimum score 7) or PTE. *Application deadline:* For fall admission, 6/15 for domestic students, 5/15 for international students. Application fee: $55. Electronic applications accepted. *Expenses:* Contact institution. *Financial support:* In 2018–19, 16 students received support. Scholarships/grants available. Financial award application deadline: 3/2; financial award applicants required to submit FAFSA. *Unit head:* Dr. Rebekah Dibble, Director, 415-422-2221, E-mail: management@usfca.edu. *Application contact:* Office of Graduate Recruiting and Admissions, 415-422-2221, E-mail: management@usfca.edu.
Website: http://www.usfca.edu/msod

University of South Dakota, Graduate School, College of Arts and Sciences, Program in Administrative Studies, Vermillion, SD 57069. Offers addiction studies (MSA); criminal justice studies (MSA); health services administration (MSA); human resources (MSA); interdisciplinary studies (MSA); long term care administration (MSA); organizational leadership (MSA). *Program availability:* Part-time, evening/weekend, 100% online. *Degree requirements:* For master's, thesis or alternative. *Entrance requirements:* For master's, 3 years of work or experience, minimum GPA of 2.7, resume. Additional exam requirements/recommendations for international students: Required—TOEFL (minimum score 550 paper-based; 79 iBT). Electronic applications accepted.

University of Southern California, Graduate School, Sol Price School of Public Policy, Executive Master of Leadership Program, Los Angeles, CA 90089. Offers EML. *Program availability:* Part-time, evening/weekend. *Entrance requirements:* Additional exam requirements/recommendations for international students: Required—TOEFL (minimum score 600 paper-based; 100 iBT). Electronic applications accepted. *Expenses:* Contact institution. *Faculty research:* Strategic planning, organizational transformation, strategic management, leadership.

The University of Texas at San Antonio, College of Business, Department of Management, San Antonio, TX 78249-0617. Offers management and organization studies (PhD). Terminal master's awarded for partial completion of doctoral program. *Degree requirements:* For doctorate, comprehensive exam, thesis/dissertation. *Entrance requirements:* For doctorate, GMAT, GRE. Additional exam requirements/recommendations for international students: Required—TOEFL (minimum score 550 paper-based; 79 iBT), IELTS (minimum score 6.5). Electronic applications accepted.

The University of Texas at Tyler, Soules College of Business, Department of Management and Marketing, Tyler, TX 75799-0001. Offers cyber security (MBA); engineering management (MBA); general management (MBA); healthcare management (MBA); internal assurance and consulting (MBA); marketing (MBA); oil, gas and energy (MBA); organizational development (MBA); quality management (MBA). *Accreditation:* AACSB. *Program availability:* Part-time, online learning. *Students:* Average age 29. 73 applicants, 96% accepted, 35 enrolled. In 2018, 37 master's awarded. *Entrance requirements:* Additional exam requirements/recommendations for international students: Required—TOEFL (minimum score 550 paper-based). *Application deadline:* For fall admission, 8/17 priority date for domestic students, 7/1 priority date for international students; for spring admission, 12/21 priority date for domestic students, 11/1 priority date for international students. Application fee: $25 ($50 for international students). *Faculty research:* General business, inventory control, institutional markets, service marketing, product distribution, accounting fraud, financial reporting and recognition. *Unit head:* Dr. Krist Swimberghe, Chair, 903-565-5803, E-mail: kswimberghe@uttyler.edu. *Application contact:* Dr. Krist Swimberghe, Chair, 903-565-5803, E-mail: kswimberghe@uttyler.edu.
Website: https://www.uttyler.edu/cbt/manamark/

University of the Incarnate Word, School of Professional Studies, San Antonio, TX 78209-6397. Offers communication arts (MAA), including applied administration, communication arts, healthcare administration, industrial and organizational psychology, organizational development; organizational development and leadership (MS);

professional studies (DBA). *Program availability:* Part-time, evening/weekend, 100% online, blended/hybrid learning. *Faculty:* 9 full-time (3 women), 26 part-time/adjunct (10 women). *Students:* 475 full-time (229 women), 358 part-time (151 women); includes 536 minority (122 Black or African American, non-Hispanic/Latino; 5 American Indian or Alaska Native, non-Hispanic/Latino; 19 Asian, non-Hispanic/Latino; 366 Hispanic/Latino; 3 Native Hawaiian or other Pacific Islander, non-Hispanic/Latino; 21 Two or more races, non-Hispanic/Latino). 593 applicants, 91% accepted, 287 enrolled. In 2018, 488 master's, 11 doctorates awarded. *Degree requirements:* For master's, comprehensive exam (for some programs), thesis or alternative. *Entrance requirements:* For master's, GMAT, GRE, official transcripts from all other colleges attended. Additional exam requirements/recommendations for international students: Required—TOEFL (minimum score 560 paper-based; 83 iBT). *Application deadline:* Applications are processed on a rolling basis. Electronic applications accepted. *Expenses: Tuition:* Full-time $22,560; part-time $940 per credit hour. *Required fees:* $2484; $94 per credit hour. Tuition and fees vary according to degree level, program and student level. *Financial support:* Scholarships/grants and unspecified assistantships available. Financial award applicants required to submit FAFSA. *Unit head:* Vincent Porter, Dean, 210-8292770, E-mail: porterv@uiwtx.edu. *Application contact:* Julie Weber, Director of Marketing and Recruitment, 210-318-1876, Fax: 210-829-2756, E-mail: eapadmission@uiwtx.edu. Website: https://sps.uiw.edu/

University of West Los Angeles, School of Business, Inglewood, CA 90301. Offers organizational leadership and business innovation (MS).

University of Wisconsin–Platteville, School of Graduate Studies, Distance Learning Center, Online Master of Science in Organizational Change Leadership Program, Platteville, WI 53818-3099. Offers MS. *Program availability:* Part-time. *Degree requirements:* For master's, capstone, research paper, or thesis research. *Entrance requirements:* Additional exam requirements/recommendations for international students: Required—TOEFL (minimum score 550 paper-based; 79 iBT), IELTS (minimum score 6.5). Electronic applications accepted.

Upper Iowa University, Online Master's Programs, Fayette, IA 52142-1857. Offers accounting (MBA); corporate financial management (MBA); emergency management and homeland security (MPA); general management (MBA); general studies (MPA); government administration (MPA); health and human services (MPA); human resources management (MBA); nonprofit organizational management (MPA); organizational development (MBA); public management (MPA); sport administration (MSA). MBA also available at Madison, WI campus. *Program availability:* Part-time, online learning. *Degree requirements:* For master's, research project. *Entrance requirements:* For master's, GMAT, GRE, or minimum GPA of 2.7 during last 60 hours. Additional exam requirements/recommendations for international students: Required—TOEFL (minimum score 570 paper-based). Electronic applications accepted. *Faculty research:* Total quality management, teams, organization culture and climate, management.

Vanderbilt University, Vanderbilt University Owen Graduate School of Management, Vanderbilt MBA Program, Nashville, TN 37203. Offers accounting (MBA); finance (MBA); general management (MBA); health care (MBA); human and organizational performance (MBA); marketing (MBA); operations (MBA); strategy (MBA); MBA/JD; MBA/M Div; MBA/MD; MBA/MSN; MBA/MTS; MBA/PhD. *Accreditation:* AACSB. *Degree requirements:* For master's, 62 credit hours of coursework; completion of ethics course; minimum GPA of 3.0. *Entrance requirements:* For master's, GMAT (preferred) or GRE, 2 years of work experience (recommended). Additional exam requirements/recommendations for international students: Required—TOEFL (minimum score 100 iBT). Electronic applications accepted. *Expenses:* Contact institution. *Faculty research:* Accounting and finance, business strategy and economics, marketing, operations management, organization studies.

Viterbo University, Master of Arts in Servant Leadership Program, La Crosse, WI 54601-4797. Offers ethical leadership in organizations (Certificate); servant leadership (MA). *Program availability:* Part-time, evening/weekend. *Degree requirements:* For master's, 30 credits (15 credits of Servant Leadership core courses and any combination of 15 elective credits). *Entrance requirements:* For master's, letter of reference, statement of goals, baccalaureate degree, transcript, interview. Additional exam requirements/recommendations for international students: Required—TOEFL (minimum score 525 paper-based). Electronic applications accepted. *Expenses:* Contact institution. *Faculty research:* Organizational culture, community building, ethical decision-making, leadership theory and practice.

Walden University, Graduate Programs, School of Management, Minneapolis, MN 55401. Offers accounting (MBA, MS, DBA), including accounting for the professional (MS), accounting with CPA emphasis (MS), self-designed (MS); advanced project management (Graduate Certificate); applied project management (Graduate Certificate); auditing (Graduate Certificate); bridge to business administration (Post-Doctoral Certificate); bridge to management (Post-Doctoral Certificate); business management (Graduate Certificate); communication (MBA); corporate finance (MBA); digital marketing (Graduate Certificate); entrepreneurship (DBA); entrepreneurship and small business (MBA); finance (MS, DBA), including finance for the professional (MS), finance with CFA/investment (MS), finance with CPA emphasis (MS); global supply chain management (DBA); healthcare management (MBA, DBA); human resource management (MBA, MS, Graduate Certificate), including functional human resource management (MS), general program (MS), integrating functional and strategic human resource management (MS), organizational strategy (MS); human resources management (DBA); information systems management (DBA); international business (MBA, DBA); leadership (MBA, MS, DBA, Graduate Certificate), including general program (MS), human resource leadership (MS), leader development (MS), self-designed (MS); management (MS, PhD), including communications (MS), finance (PhD), general program (MS), healthcare management (MS), human resource management (MS), human resources management (PhD), information systems management (PhD), international business (MS), leadership (MS), leadership and organizational change (PhD), marketing (MS), project management (MS), strategy and operations (MS); managerial accounting (Graduate Certificate); marketing (MBA, MS, DBA); project management (MBA, MS, DBA); self-designed (MBA, DBA); social impact management (DBA); technology entrepreneurship (DBA). *Accreditation:* ACBSP. *Program availability:* Part-time, evening/weekend, online only, 100% online. *Degree requirements:* For master's, thesis (for some programs), residency (for EMBA); for doctorate, thesis/dissertation (for some programs), residency. *Entrance requirements:* For master's, bachelor's degree or higher; minimum GPA of 2.5; official transcripts; goal statement (for some programs); access to computer and Internet; for doctorate, master's degree or higher; three years of related professional or academic experience (preferred); minimum GPA of 3.0; goal statement and current resume (for select programs); official transcripts; access to computer and Internet; for other advanced degree, relevant work experience; access to computer and Internet. Additional exam requirements/recommendations for international students: Required—TOEFL (minimum score 550 paper-based, 79 iBT), IELTS (minimum score 6.5), Michigan English Language Assessment Battery (minimum score 82), or PTE (minimum score 53). Electronic applications accepted.

Walden University, Graduate Programs, School of Public Policy and Administration, Minneapolis, MN 55401. Offers criminal justice (MPA, MPP, MS, Graduate Certificate), including emergency management (MS, PhD), general program (MS), global leadership (MS, PhD), homeland security and policy coordination (MS, PhD), law and public policy (MS, PhD), policy analysis (MS, PhD), public management and leadership (MS, PhD), self-designed (MS), terrorism, mediation, and peace (MS, PhD); criminal justice and executive management (MS), including global leadership (MS, PhD); criminal justice leadership and executive management (MS), including emergency management (MS, PhD), general program, homeland security and policy coordination (MS, PhD), law and public policy (MS, PhD), policy analysis (MS, PhD), public management and leadership (MS, PhD), self-designed, terrorism, mediation, and peace (MS, PhD); emergency management (MPA, MPP, MS), including criminal justice (MS, PhD), general program (MS), homeland security (MS), public management and leadership (MS, PhD), terrorism and emergency management (MS); general program (MPA, MPP); global leadership (MPA, MPP); government management (Graduate Certificate); health policy (MPA, MPP); homeland security (Graduate Certificate); homeland security and policy coordination (MPA, MPP); international nongovernmental organizations (MPA, MPP); law and public policy (MPA, MPP); local government management for sustainable communities (MPA, MPP); nonprofit management (Graduate Certificate); nonprofit management and leadership (MPA, MPP, MS), including global leadership (MS, PhD), international nongovernmental organization (MS), local government for sustainable communities (MS), self-designed (MS); online teaching in higher education (Post-Master's Certificate); policy analysis (MPA); public management and leadership (MPA, MPP, Graduate Certificate); public policy (Graduate Certificate); public policy and administration (PhD), including criminal justice (MS, PhD), emergency management (MS, PhD), global leadership (MS, PhD), health policy, homeland security and policy coordination (MS, PhD), international nongovernmental organizations, law and public policy (MS, PhD), local government management for sustainable communities, nonprofit management and leadership, policy analysis (MS, PhD), public management and leadership (MS, PhD), terrorism, mediation, and peace (MS, PhD); strategic planning and public policy (Graduate Certificate); terrorism, mediation, and peace (MPA, MPP). *Program availability:* Part-time, evening/weekend, online only, 100% online. *Degree requirements:* For doctorate, thesis/dissertation, residency. *Entrance requirements:* For master's, bachelor's degree or higher; minimum GPA of 2.5; official transcripts; goal statement (for some programs); access to computer and Internet; for doctorate, master's degree or higher; three years of related professional or academic experience (preferred); minimum GPA of 3.0; goal statement and current resume (for select programs); official transcripts; access to computer and Internet; for other advanced degree, relevant work experience; access to computer and Internet. Additional exam requirements/recommendations for international students: Required—TOEFL (minimum score 550 paper-based, 79 iBT), IELTS (minimum score 6.5), Michigan English Language Assessment Battery (minimum score 82), or PTE (minimum score 53). Electronic applications accepted.

Waldorf University, Program in Organizational Leadership, Forest City, IA 50436. Offers criminal justice leadership (MA); emergency management leadership (MA); fire/rescue executive leadership (MA); human resource development (MA); public administration (MA); sport management (MA); teacher leader (MA).

Warner Pacific University, Graduate Programs, Portland, OR 97215-4099. Offers human services (MA); not-for-profit leadership (MS); organizational leadership (MS); teaching (MAT). *Program availability:* Part-time, evening/weekend. *Degree requirements:* For master's, thesis or alternative, presentation of defense. *Entrance requirements:* For master's, interview, minimum GPA of 2.5, letters of recommendation. *Faculty research:* New Testament studies, nineteenth-century Wesleyan theology, preaching and church growth, Christian ethics.

Washington University in St. Louis, Olin Business School, Master of Science in Leadership Program, Washington, DC 63130-4899. Offers MS. Program offered in partnership with the Brookings Institution. *Program availability:* Part-time. *Faculty:* 85 full-time (16 women), 46 part-time/adjunct (13 women). *Students:* 53 part-time (23 women); includes 19 minority (12 Black or African American, non-Hispanic/Latino; 3 Asian, non-Hispanic/Latino; 4 Hispanic/Latino). Average age 48. 28 applicants, 54% accepted, 14 enrolled. In 2018, 5 master's awarded. *Degree requirements:* For master's, 30 credit hours, eighteen of those in leadership courses (including five core courses and two residential courses at Washington University in St. Louis). *Entrance requirements:* For master's, bachelor's degree, completed application form, detailed resume, personal statement, phone interview. *Application deadline:* Applications are processed on a rolling basis. Application fee: $0. Electronic applications accepted. *Unit head:* Dr. Kelly Bean, Senior Associate Dean and Professor of Practice in Leadership, 314-935-5000, E-mail: beank@wustl.edu. *Application contact:* Morgan Kaminski, Specialty Program Manager, 202-797-4396, E-mail: MKaminski@brookings.edu.
Website: http://www.olin.wustl.edu/EN-US/academic-programs/Pages/MS-Leadership.aspx

Wayland Baptist University, Graduate Programs, Programs in Business Administration/Management, Plainview, TX 79072-6998. Offers accounting (MBA); general business (MBA); health care administration (MAM, MBA); human resource management (MAM, MBA); international management (MBA); management (MBA, D Mgt); management information systems (MBA); organization management (MAM); project management (MBA). *Program availability:* Part-time, evening/weekend, online learning. *Degree requirements:* For master's, capstone course. *Entrance requirements:* For master's, GMAT, GRE or MAT. Additional exam requirements/recommendations for international students: Required—TOEFL (minimum score 500 paper-based; 61 iBT). Electronic applications accepted.

Waynesburg University, Graduate and Professional Studies, Canonsburg, PA 15370. Offers business (MBA), including energy management, finance, health systems, human resources, leadership, market development; counseling (MA), including addictions counseling, clinical mental health; counselor education and supervision (PhD); criminal investigation (MA); education (M Ed), including autism, curriculum and instruction, educational leadership, online teaching; nursing (MSN), including administration, education, informatics; nursing practice (DNP); special education (M Ed); technology (M Ed); MSN/MBA. *Accreditation:* AACN. *Program availability:* Part-time, evening/weekend. *Degree requirements:* For doctorate, thesis/dissertation. *Entrance requirements:* Additional exam requirements/recommendations for international students: Required—TOEFL. Electronic applications accepted.

Wayne State College, Department of Health, Human Performance and Sport, Wayne, NE 68787. Offers exercise science (MSE); organizational management (MS), including sport management. *Program availability:* Part-time, evening/weekend. *Degree requirements:* For master's, comprehensive exam, thesis optional. *Entrance requirements:* For master's, GRE General Test, minimum GPA of 3.0. Additional exam requirements/recommendations for international students: Required—TOEFL (minimum score 550 paper-based). Electronic applications accepted.

Wayne State University, College of Liberal Arts and Sciences, Department of Political Science, Detroit, MI 48202. Offers political science (MA, PhD); public administration (MPA), including economic development policy and management, health and human services policy and management, human and fiscal resource management, nonprofit policy and management, organizational behavior and management, urban and metropolitan policy and management; JD/MA. *Accreditation:* NASPAA. *Faculty:* 18.

Students: 61 full-time (26 women), 51 part-time (27 women); includes 31 minority (22 Black or African American, non-Hispanic/Latino; 3 Asian, non-Hispanic/Latino; 1 Hispanic/Latino; 5 Two or more races, non-Hispanic/Latino), 12 international. Average age 32. 103 applicants, 39% accepted, 20 enrolled. In 2018, 32 master's, 5 doctorates awarded. *Degree requirements:* For master's, comprehensive exam (for some programs), thesis (for some programs); for doctorate, thesis/dissertation. *Entrance requirements:* For master's, GRE General Test, substantial undergraduate preparation in the social sciences, minimum upper-division undergraduate GPA of 3.0, two letters of recommendation, personal statement; for doctorate, GRE General Test, 3 letters of recommendation; personal statement; interview. Additional exam requirements/recommendations for international students: Required—TOEFL (minimum score 550 paper-based; 79 iBT), TWE (minimum score 5.5), Michigan English Language Assessment Battery (minimum score 85); Recommended—IELTS (minimum score 6.5). *Application deadline:* For fall admission, 5/15 for domestic students, 5/1 priority date for international students; for winter admission, 10/15 for domestic students, 9/1 priority date for international students. Applications are processed on a rolling basis. Application fee: $50. Electronic applications accepted. *Expenses:* Contact institution. *Financial support:* In 2018–19, 46 students received support, including 4 fellowships with tuition reimbursements available (averaging $17,000 per year), 1 research assistantship with tuition reimbursement available (averaging $23,119 per year), 12 teaching assistantships with tuition reimbursements available (averaging $19,267 per year); scholarships/grants, health care benefits, and unspecified assistantships also available. Financial award applicants required to submit FAFSA. *Faculty research:* American government and politics, comparative politics, political methodology, political theory, public administration, public law, public policy, world politics/international relations, formal theory/modeling, gender and politics, international law, peace research, political economy, political psychology, politics of developing countries, race, religion, and ethnicity, urban politics. *Unit head:* Dr. Daniel Geller, Professor and Chair, 313-577-6328, E-mail: dgeller@wayne.edu. *Application contact:* Dr. Sharon Lean, Graduate Director, 313-577-2630, E-mail: gradpolisci@wayne.edu.
Website: http://clas.wayne.edu/politicalscience/

Western New England University, College of Business, Program in Organizational Leadership, Springfield, MA 01119. Offers MS, Pharm D/MS. *Program availability:* Part-time, evening/weekend. *Faculty:* 6 full-time (4 women). *Students:* 13 part-time (7 women). Average age 38. 8 applicants, 100% accepted, 7 enrolled. In 2018, 9 master's awarded. *Entrance requirements:* For master's, GMAT or GRE, transcript, two letters of recommendation, two essays, resume. Additional exam requirements/recommendations for international students: Required—TOEFL (minimum score 79 iBT). *Application deadline:* Applications are processed on a rolling basis. Application fee: $30. Electronic applications accepted. *Expenses:* Contact institution. *Financial support:* Application deadline: 4/15; applicants required to submit FAFSA. *Unit head:* Dr. Sharianne Walker, Dean, 413-782-1389, E-mail: swalker@wne.edu. *Application contact:* Matthew Fox, Executive Director of Graduate Admissions, 413-782-1410, Fax: 413-782-1777, E-mail: study@wne.edu.
Website: http://www1.wne.edu/academics/graduate/organizational-leadership.cfm

West Liberty University, School of Professional Studies, Triadelphia, WV 26059. Offers organizational leadership (MPS). *Entrance requirements:* For master's, bachelor's degree from accredited institution, minimum GPA of 2.5. Additional exam requirements/recommendations for international students: Required—TOEFL.

Wheeling Jesuit University, Department of Social Sciences, Wheeling, WV 26003-6295. Offers MSOL. *Program availability:* Part-time, evening/weekend. *Degree requirements:* For master's, thesis. *Entrance requirements:* For master's, MAT, minimum GPA of 2.75, minimum of three years full-time professional work experience. Additional exam requirements/recommendations for international students: Required—TOEFL (minimum score 600 paper-based; 100 iBT). Electronic applications accepted. Application fee is waived when completed online. *Faculty research:* History, theory and philosophy of leadership; gender roles and leadership; spirituality and leadership.

Wilfrid Laurier University, Faculty of Graduate and Postdoctoral Studies, Lyle S. Hallman Faculty of Social Work, Waterloo, ON N2L 3C5, Canada. Offers Aboriginal studies (MSW); community, policy, planning and organizations (MSW); critical social policy and organizational studies (PhD); individuals, families and groups (MSW); social work practice (individuals, families, groups and communities) (PhD); social work practice: individuals, families, groups and communities (PhD). *Program availability:* Part-time. *Degree requirements:* For master's, thesis optional; for doctorate, thesis/dissertation. *Entrance requirements:* For master's, course work in social science, research methodology, and statistics; honors BA with a minimum B average; for doctorate, master's degree in social work, minimum A- average. Additional exam requirements/recommendations for international students: Required—TOEFL (minimum score 89 iBT). Electronic applications accepted. *Expenses:* Contact institution.

Wilkes University, College of Graduate and Professional Studies, Jay S. Sidhu School of Business and Leadership, Wilkes-Barre, PA 18766-0002. Offers accounting (MBA); global business (MBA); human resource management (MBA); international business (MBA); leadership (MBA); management (MBA); operations management (MBA); organizational leadership and development (MBA). *Accreditation:* ACBSP. *Program availability:* Part-time, evening/weekend. *Students:* 16 full-time (9 women), 64 part-time (33 women); includes 11 minority (3 Black or African American, non-Hispanic/Latino; 3 Asian, non-Hispanic/Latino; 3 Hispanic/Latino; 2 Two or more races, non-Hispanic/Latino), 7 international. Average age 30. In 2018, 49 master's awarded. *Entrance requirements:* For master's, GMAT. Additional exam requirements/recommendations for international students: Required—TOEFL (minimum score 550 paper-based; 79 iBT). *Application deadline:* Applications are processed on a rolling basis. Application fee: $45 ($65 for international students). Electronic applications accepted. *Expenses:* Contact institution. *Financial support:* Unspecified assistantships available. Financial award application deadline: 3/1; financial award applicants required to submit FAFSA. *Unit head:* Dr. Abel Adekola, Dean, 570-408-4701, Fax: 570-408-7846, E-mail: abel.adekola@wilkes.edu. *Application contact:* Kristin Donati, Associate Director of Graduate Admissions, 570-408-3338, Fax: 570-408-7846, E-mail: kristin.donati@wilkes.edu.
Website: http://www.wilkes.edu/academics/colleges/sidhu-school-of-business-leadership/index.aspx

William Penn University, College for Working Adults, Oskaloosa, IA 52577-1799. Offers business leadership (MBL). *Program availability:* Online learning.

Williamson College, Program in Organizational Leadership, Franklin, TN 37067. Offers MA. *Program availability:* Evening/weekend. *Degree requirements:* For master's, capstone project. *Entrance requirements:* For master's, essay, official transcripts, minimum overall GPA of 2.5.

Wilmington University, College of Business, New Castle, DE 19720-6491. Offers accounting (MBA, MS); business administration (MBA, DBA); environmental stewardship (MBA); finance (MBA); health care administration (MBA, MSM); homeland security (MBA, MSM); human resource management (MSM); management information systems (MBA, MSN); marketing (MSM); marketing management (MBA); military leadership (MSM); organizational leadership (MBA, MSM); public administration (MSM). *Program availability:* Part-time, evening/weekend. *Entrance requirements:* Additional exam requirements/recommendations for international students: Required—TOEFL (minimum score 500 paper-based). Electronic applications accepted.

Winona State University, College of Education, Department of Leadership Education, Winona, MN 55987. Offers education leadership (MS, Ed S), including k-12 principal (Ed S), superintendent (Ed S); organizational leadership (MS); professional leadership (MS); sport management (MS). MS in sport management offered in cooperation with Department of Physical Education and Sport Science. *Accreditation:* NCATE. *Program availability:* Part-time, evening/weekend. *Degree requirements:* For master's, comprehensive exam, thesis optional; for Ed S, thesis optional.

Winona State University, College of Nursing and Health Sciences, Winona, MN 55987. Offers adult-gerontology acute care nurse practitioner (MS, DNP, Post Master's Certificate); adult-gerontology clinical nurse specialist (MS, DNP, Post Master's Certificate); adult-gerontology primary care nurse practitioner (MS, DNP, Post Master's Certificate); family nurse practitioner (MS, DNP, Post Master's Certificate); nurse educator (MS); nursing and organizational leadership (MS, DNP, Post Master's Certificate); practice and leadership innovations (DNP, Post Master's Certificate). *Accreditation:* AACN. *Program availability:* Part-time, online learning. *Degree requirements:* For master's, thesis; for doctorate, capstone. *Entrance requirements:* For master's, GRE (if GPA less than 3.0). Additional exam requirements/recommendations for international students: Required—TOEFL (minimum score 550 paper-based).

Woodbury University, School of Business, Program in Organizational Leadership, Burbank, CA 91504-1052. Offers MA. *Program availability:* Evening/weekend. *Entrance requirements:* For master's, GRE General Test (if GPA less than 2.5), 3 recommendations, essay, resume, academic transcripts. Additional exam requirements/recommendations for international students: Required—TOEFL (minimum score 550 paper-based; 83 iBT), IELTS (minimum score 6.5).

Worcester Polytechnic Institute, Graduate Admissions, Foisie Business School, Worcester, MA 01609-2280. Offers business administration (PhD); information technology (MS), including information security management; management (MS, Graduate Certificate); marketing and innovation (MS); operations analytics and management (MS); supply chain management (MS). *Accreditation:* AACSB. *Program availability:* Part-time, evening/weekend, 100% online, blended/hybrid learning. *Students:* 136 full-time (74 women), 214 part-time (85 women); includes 29 minority (4 Black or African American, non-Hispanic/Latino; 11 Asian, non-Hispanic/Latino; 9 Hispanic/Latino; 5 Two or more races, non-Hispanic/Latino), 189 international. Average age 29. 636 applicants, 64% accepted, 104 enrolled. In 2018, 165 master's, 1 doctorate, 10 other advanced degrees awarded. *Degree requirements:* For master's, thesis optional. *Entrance requirements:* For master's and Graduate Certificate, GMAT or GRE General Test, 3 letters of recommendation, statement of purpose, resume. Additional exam requirements/recommendations for international students: Required—TOEFL (minimum score 563 paper-based; 84 iBT), IELTS (minimum score 7). *Application deadline:* For fall admission, 6/1 priority date for domestic and international students; for spring admission, 11/1 priority date for domestic students, 10/1 priority date for international students. Applications are processed on a rolling basis. Application fee: $70. Electronic applications accepted. *Financial support:* Career-related internships or fieldwork, institutionally sponsored loans, scholarships/grants, and unspecified assistantships available. Financial award application deadline: 6/1. *Unit head:* Melissa Terrio, Director of Graduate Recruitment & Admissions, 508-831-4665, Fax: 508-831-5866, E-mail: biz@wpi.edu. *Application contact:* Amy Trakimas, Associate Director of Graduate Recruitment & Admissions, 508-831-4665, Fax: 508-831-5866, E-mail: atrakimas@wpi.edu.
Website: https://www.wpi.edu/academics/business

Worcester State University, Graduate School, Program in Management, Worcester, MA 01602-2597. Offers accounting (MS); leadership (MS); marketing (MS). *Program availability:* Part-time, evening/weekend. *Faculty:* 6 full-time (3 women), 1 part-time/adjunct (0 women). *Students:* 15 full-time (6 women), 43 part-time (24 women); includes 14 minority (4 Black or African American, non-Hispanic/Latino; 5 Asian, non-Hispanic/Latino; 5 Hispanic/Latino), 7 international. Average age 38. 32 applicants, 100% accepted, 24 enrolled. In 2018, 24 master's awarded. *Degree requirements:* For master's, comprehensive exam (for some programs), thesis (for some programs), For a detail list in Degree Completion requirements please see the graduate catalog at catalog.worcester.edu. *Entrance requirements:* For master's, GMAT, For a detail list of entrance requirements please see the graduate catalog at catalog.worcester.edu. Additional exam requirements/recommendations for international students: Required—TOEFL (minimum score 550 paper-based; 79 iBT), IELTS (minimum score 6). *Application deadline:* For fall admission, 3/1 for domestic and international students; for spring admission, 11/1 for domestic and international students; for summer admission, 3/1 for domestic and international students. Applications are processed on a rolling basis. Application fee: $50. Electronic applications accepted. *Expenses: Tuition, area resident:* Full-time $3042; part-time $169 per credit hour. Tuition, state resident: full-time $3042; part-time $169 per credit hour. Tuition, nonresident: full-time $3042; part-time $169 per credit hour. *International tuition:* $3042 full-time. *Required fees:* $2754; $153 per credit hour. *Financial support:* Career-related internships or fieldwork, scholarships/grants, and unspecified assistantships available. Financial award application deadline: 3/1; financial award applicants required to submit FAFSA. *Unit head:* Dr. Elizabeth Wark, Program Coordinator, 508-929-8743, Fax: 508-929-8048, E-mail: ewark@worcester.edu. *Application contact:* Sara Grady, Associate Dean, Graduate Studies and Professional Development, 508-929-8130, Fax: 508-929-8100, E-mail: sara.grady@worcester.edu.

Yale University, Yale School of Management, Doctoral Program in Management, New Haven, CT 06520. Offers accounting (PhD); financial economics (PhD); marketing (PhD); organizations and management (PhD). *Accreditation:* AACSB. *Degree requirements:* For doctorate, comprehensive exam, thesis/dissertation. *Entrance requirements:* For doctorate, GMAT or GRE General Test. Additional exam requirements/recommendations for international students: Required—TOEFL or IELTS. Electronic applications accepted. *Expenses:* Contact institution. *Faculty research:* Pricing of options and futures, term structure of interest rates, use of accounting numbers in debt contracts, product differentiation, e-commerce and marketing, behavioral finance.

Section 17
Project Management

This section contains a directory of institutions offering graduate work in project management. Additional information about programs listed in the directory but not augmented by an in-depth entry may be obtained by writing directly to the dean of a graduate school or chair of a department at the address given in the directory.

For programs offering related work, see also in this book *Business Administration and Management.*

CONTENTS

Project Management

Albertus Magnus College, Master of Business Administration Program, New Haven, CT 06511-1189. Offers accounting (MBA); general management (MBA); health care management (MBA); human resource management (MBA); leadership (MBA); project management (MBA). Program also offered in East Hartford, CT. *Program availability:* Part-time, evening/weekend, 100% online, blended/hybrid learning. *Degree requirements:* For master's, thesis, capstone project, business plan, minimum cumulative GPA of 3.0, completion of all requirements within seven years of matriculation. *Entrance requirements:* For master's, 3 years of management or related experience, minimum GPA of 2.5, 2 letters of recommendation, official transcripts. Additional exam requirements/recommendations for international students: Recommended—TOEFL (minimum score 550 paper-based; 80 iBT). Electronic applications accepted. *Expenses:* Contact institution. *Faculty research:* Finance, project management, accounting, business administration, generalist.

Amberton University, Graduate School, Department of Business Administration, Garland, TX 75041-5595. Offers agile project management (MS); general business (MBA); international business (MBA); management (MBA); project management (MBA); strategic leadership (MBA). *Program availability:* Part-time, evening/weekend. *Entrance requirements:* For master's, minimum GPA of 3.0.

American Business & Technology University, Programs in Business Administration, Saint Joseph, MO 64506. Offers business administration (MBA); financial management (MBA); global business management (MBA); information systems management (MBA); marketing and social media (MBA); project and operations management (MBA); public accounting (MBA). *Program availability:* Online learning.

American InterContinental University Online, Program in Business Administration, Schaumburg, IL 60173. Offers accounting and finance (MBA); finance (MBA); healthcare management (MBA); human resource management (MBA); international business (MBA); management (MBA); marketing (MBA); operations management (MBA); organizational psychology and development (MBA); project management (MBA). *Accreditation:* ACBSP. *Program availability:* Evening/weekend, online learning. *Entrance requirements:* Additional exam requirements/recommendations for international students: Required—TOEFL (minimum score 550 paper-based). Electronic applications accepted.

American InterContinental University Online, Program in Information Technology, Schaumburg, IL 60173. Offers Internet security (MIT); IT project management (MIT). *Program availability:* Evening/weekend, online learning. *Entrance requirements:* Additional exam requirements/recommendations for international students: Required—TOEFL (minimum score 550 paper-based). Electronic applications accepted.

American University, School of Professional and Extended Studies, Washington, DC 20016. Offers agile project management (MS); healthcare management (MS, Graduate Certificate); human resource analytics and management (MS, Graduate Certificate); instructional design and learning analytics (MS); measurement and evaluation (MS); project monitoring and evaluation (Graduate Certificate); sports analytics and management (MS, Graduate Certificate). *Program availability:* Part-time, evening/weekend, 100% online, blended/hybrid learning. *Faculty:* 27 full-time (14 women), 33 part-time/adjunct (20 women). *Students:* 2 full-time (both women), 113 part-time (68 women); includes 6 minority (4 Black or African American, non-Hispanic/Latino; 1 Asian, non-Hispanic/Latino; 1 Hispanic/Latino). Average age 31. 156 applicants, 93% accepted, 66 enrolled. In 2018, 1 master's, 6 other advanced degrees awarded. *Entrance requirements:* For master's, Please visit website: https://www.american.edu/spexs/, official transcript(s), resume. Additional exam requirements/recommendations for international students: Required—TOEFL. *Application deadline:* Applications are processed on a rolling basis. Application fee: $55. Electronic applications accepted. *Expenses:* Contact institution. *Financial support:* Applicants required to submit FAFSA. *Unit head:* Jill Klein, Dean, 202-895-4900, E-mail: spexs@american.edu. *Application contact:* Emily Emily, Assistant Director for Recruitment and Admission, 202-885-4910, E-mail: aronoff@american.edu.
Website: http://www.american.edu/spexs

Ashland University, Dauch College of Business and Economics, Ashland, OH 44805-3702. Offers accounting (MBA); business analytics (MBA); entrepreneurship (MBA); financial management (MBA); global management (MBA); health care management and leadership (MBA); human resource management (MBA); human resources (MBA); management information systems (MBA); project management (MBA); sport management (MBA); supply chain management (MBA). *Accreditation:* ACBSP. *Program availability:* Part-time, evening/weekend, 100% online, blended/hybrid learning. Terminal master's awarded for partial completion of doctoral program. *Degree requirements:* For master's, thesis optional, capstone course. *Entrance requirements:* For master's, 2 years of full-time work experience. Additional exam requirements/recommendations for international students: Required—TOEFL (minimum score 550 paper-based; 78 iBT). Electronic applications accepted. *Expenses:* Contact institution. *Faculty research:* Relationship marketing strategy, executive compensation and company performance, online marketplaces in electronic commerce, diversity training in campus recreation departments, entrepreneurship in developing and emerging economies.

Aspen University, Program in Business Administration, Denver, CO 80246-1930. Offers business administration (MBA); finance (MBA); information management (MBA); project management (MBA, Certificate). *Program availability:* Part-time, evening/weekend, online only, 100% online. *Faculty:* 16 full-time (15 women), 240 part-time/adjunct (120 women). *Students:* 556 part-time. Average age 37. *Degree requirements:* For master's, comprehensive exam. *Entrance requirements:* For master's and Certificate, www.aspen.edu, www.aspen.edu. *Application deadline:* Applications are processed on a rolling basis. Application fee: $0. Electronic applications accepted. *Financial support:* Applicants required to submit FAFSA. *Unit head:* Dr. Kevin Thrasher, Provost, 602-5706708, E-mail: kevin.thrasher@aspen.edu. *Application contact:* Enrollment Advisor, 800-373-7814.
Website: http://www.aspen.edu

Athabasca University, Faculty of Business, Edmonton, AB T5L 4W1, Canada. Offers business administration (MBA); information technology management (MBA), including policing concentration; innovative management (DBA); management (GDM); project management (MBA, GDM). *Program availability:* Part-time, evening/weekend, online learning. *Degree requirements:* For master's, thesis or alternative, applied project. *Entrance requirements:* For master's, 3-8 years of managerial experience, 3 years with undergraduate degree, 5 years' managerial experience with professional designation, 8-10 years' management experience (on exception). Electronic applications accepted. *Expenses:* Contact institution. *Faculty research:* Human resources, project management, operations research, information technology management, corporate stewardship, energy management.

Avila University, School of Professional Studies, Kansas City, MO 64145-1698. Offers executive leadership (MS); fundraising (MA); instructional design and technology (MA, MS); leadership coaching (MS); project management (MA); strategic human resources (MS). *Program availability:* Part-time-only, evening/weekend, 100% online, blended/hybrid learning. *Faculty:* 14 part-time/adjunct (8 women). *Students:* 69 full-time (49 women), 48 part-time (42 women); includes 45 minority (38 Black or African American, non-Hispanic/Latino; 5 Hispanic/Latino; 2 Two or more races, non-Hispanic/Latino), 5 international. Average age 39. 63 applicants, 60% accepted, 29 enrolled. In 2018, 34 master's awarded. *Degree requirements:* For master's, thesis optional. *Entrance requirements:* For master's, 2 letters of recommendation, minimum GPA of 3.0 during last 60 hours, resume, statement of intent. Additional exam requirements/recommendations for international students: Required—TOEFL (minimum score 550 paper-based; 79 iBT). *Application deadline:* Applications are processed on a rolling basis. Application fee: $0. Electronic applications accepted. *Expenses:* Contact institution. *Financial support:* In 2018–19, 12 students received support. Unspecified assistantships available. Support available to part-time students. Financial award applicants required to submit FAFSA. *Unit head:* Sarah Sullivan, Coordinator, 816-501-0429, Fax: 816-941-4650, E-mail: advantage@avila.edu. *Application contact:* Jessica Burson, Graduate Admission Advisor, 816-501-2482, Fax: 816-941-4650, E-mail: advantage@avila.edu.
Website: https://www.avila.edu/mrk/advantage-3

Bellevue University, Graduate School, College of Information Technology, Bellevue, NE 68005-3098. Offers computer information systems (MS); cybersecurity (MS); management of information systems (MS); project management (MPM).

Boston University, Metropolitan College, Department of Administrative Sciences, Boston, MA 02215. Offers applied business analytics (MS); economic development and tourism management (MSAS); enterprise risk management (MS); financial management (MS); global marketing management (MS); innovation and technology (MSAS); insurance management (MS); project management (MS); supply chain management (MS). *Accreditation:* AACSB. *Program availability:* Part-time, evening/weekend, 100% online, blended/hybrid learning. *Faculty:* 27 full-time (5 women), 39 part-time/adjunct (5 women). *Students:* 617 full-time (351 women), 574 part-time (290 women); includes 196 minority (47 Black or African American, non-Hispanic/Latino; 2 American Indian or Alaska Native, non-Hispanic/Latino; 75 Asian, non-Hispanic/Latino; 60 Hispanic/Latino; 12 Two or more races, non-Hispanic/Latino), 730 international. Average age 28. 2,259 applicants, 76% accepted, 594 enrolled. In 2018, 441 master's awarded. *Degree requirements:* For master's, thesis optional. *Entrance requirements:* For master's, 1 year of work experience, minimum GPA of 3.0. Additional exam requirements/recommendations for international students: Required—TOEFL (minimum score 84 iBT). *Application deadline:* For fall admission, 8/1 priority date for domestic students, 6/1 priority date for international students; for spring admission, 12/1 priority date for domestic students, 11/15 priority date for international students; for summer admission, 4/1 priority date for domestic students, 3/1 priority date for international students. Applications are processed on a rolling basis. Application fee: $85. Electronic applications accepted. *Expenses:* Contact institution. *Financial support:* In 2018–19, 15 students received support, including 16 research assistantships (averaging $8,400 per year), 30 teaching assistantships (averaging $3,400 per year); career-related internships or fieldwork, Federal Work-Study, and unspecified assistantships also available. Financial award applicants required to submit FAFSA. *Faculty research:* International business, innovative process. *Unit head:* Dr. John Sullivan, Chair, 617-353-3016, E-mail: adminsc@bu.edu. *Application contact:* Enrollment Services, 617-358-8162, E-mail: met@bu.edu.
Website: http://www.bu.edu/met/academic-community/departments/administrative-sciences/

Boston University, Metropolitan College, Department of Computer Science, Boston, MA 02215. Offers computer information systems (MS), including computer networks, data analytics, database management and business intelligence, health informatics, IT project management, security, Web application development; computer networks (Certificate); computer science (MS); data analytics (Certificate); digital forensics (Certificate); health informatics (Certificate); information technology project management (Certificate); software development (MS); software engineering in health care systems (Certificate); telecommunications (MS), including security. *Program availability:* Part-time, evening/weekend, online learning. *Faculty:* 16 full-time (3 women), 52 part-time/adjunct (5 women). *Students:* 201 full-time (57 women), 953 part-time (252 women); includes 285 minority (57 Black or African American, non-Hispanic/Latino; 2 American Indian or Alaska Native, non-Hispanic/Latino; 139 Asian, non-Hispanic/Latino; 67 Hispanic/Latino; 1 Native Hawaiian or other Pacific Islander, non-Hispanic/Latino; 19 Two or more races, non-Hispanic/Latino), 333 international. Average age 31. 1,079 applicants, 72% accepted, 297 enrolled. In 2018, 395 master's awarded. *Entrance requirements:* For master's and Certificate, official transcripts from regionally-accredited bachelor's degree program, 3 letters of recommendation, professional resume, personal statement. Additional exam requirements/recommendations for international students: Required—TOEFL (minimum score 84 iBT), IELTS. *Application deadline:* For fall admission, 8/1 priority date for domestic students, 6/1 priority date for international students; for spring admission, 12/1 priority date for domestic students, 11/15 priority date for international students; for summer admission, 4/1 priority date for domestic students, 3/1 priority date for international students. Applications are processed on a rolling basis. Application fee: $85. Electronic applications accepted. *Expenses:* Contact institution. *Financial support:* In 2018–19, 11 research assistantships (averaging $8,400 per year), 23 teaching assistantships (averaging $3,400 per year) were awarded; unspecified assistantships also available. Support available to part-time students. Financial award applicants required to submit FAFSA. *Faculty research:* Artificial intelligence and machine learning, security and forensics, web technologies, software engineering, programming languages, medical informatics, information systems and IT project management. *Unit head:* Dr. Anatoly Temkin, Chair, 617-353-2566, Fax: 617-353-2367, E-mail: csinfo@bu.edu. *Application contact:* Enrollment Services, 617-353-6004, E-mail: met@bu.edu.
Website: http://www.bu.edu/csmet/

Brandeis University, Rabb School of Continuing Studies, Division of Graduate Professional Studies, Master of Science Program in Project and Program Management, Waltham, MA 02454-9110. Offers MS. *Program availability:* Part-time-only. *Entrance requirements:* For master's, four-year bachelor's degree from regionally-accredited U.S. institution or equivalent; official transcript(s) from every college or university attended; resume or curriculum vitae; statement of goals; letter of recommendation. Additional exam requirements/recommendations for international students: Required—TWE (minimum score 4.5), TOEFL (minimum scores: 600 paper-based, 100 iBT), IELTS (7), or PTE (68). Electronic applications accepted. *Expenses:* Contact institution.

Brenau University, Sydney O. Smith Graduate School, College of Business and Mass Communication, Gainesville, GA 30501. Offers accounting (MBA); business administration (MBA); healthcare management (MBA); organizational leadership (MS); project management (MBA). *Accreditation:* ACBSP. *Program availability:* Part-time, evening/weekend, online learning. *Degree requirements:* For master's, comprehensive exam (for some programs). *Entrance requirements:* For master's, resume, minimum undergraduate GPA of 2.5. Additional exam requirements/recommendations for international students: Required—TOEFL (minimum score 500 paper-based; 61 iBT); Recommended—IELTS (minimum score 5). Electronic applications accepted. *Expenses:* Contact institution.

California Intercontinental University, School of Information Technology, Irvine, CA 92614. Offers information systems and enterprise resource management (DBA); information systems and knowledge management (MBA); project and quality management (MBA).

Capella University, School of Business and Technology, Doctoral Programs in Business, Minneapolis, MN 55402. Offers accounting (DBA, PhD); business intelligence (DBA); finance (DBA, PhD); general business management (PhD); human resource management (DBA, PhD); leadership (DBA, PhD); management education (PhD); marketing (DBA, PhD); project management (DBA, PhD); strategy and innovation (DBA, PhD). *Accreditation:* ACBSP.

Capella University, School of Business and Technology, Master's Programs in Business, Minneapolis, MN 55402. Offers accounting (MBA); business analysis (MS); business intelligence (MBA); entrepreneurship (MBA); finance (MBA); general business administration (MBA); general human resource management (MS); general leadership (MS); health care management (MBA); human resource management (MBA); marketing (MBA); project management (MBA, MS). *Accreditation:* ACBSP.

Carlow University, College of Leadership and Social Change, MBA Program, Pittsburgh, PA 15213-3165. Offers fraud and forensics (MBA); healthcare management (MBA); human resource management (MBA); leadership and management (MBA); project management (MBA). *Program availability:* Part-time, evening/weekend, 100% online, blended/hybrid learning. *Students:* 64 full-time (47 women), 35 part-time (25 women); includes 37 minority (31 Black or African American, non-Hispanic/Latino; 1 Asian, non-Hispanic/Latino; 1 Hispanic/Latino; 4 Two or more races, non-Hispanic/Latino). Average age 33. 34 applicants, 100% accepted, 22 enrolled. In 2018, 38 master's awarded. *Entrance requirements:* For master's, minimum undergraduate GPA of 3.0 (preferred); personal essay; resume; official transcripts; two professional recommendations. Additional exam requirements/recommendations for international students: Required—TOEFL (minimum score 550 paper-based). *Application deadline:* Applications are processed on a rolling basis. Electronic applications accepted. *Expenses: Tuition:* Full-time $13,090; part-time $5100 per semester. *Required fees:* $215; $84. Tuition and fees vary according to course load, degree level and program. *Financial support:* Application deadline: 4/1; applicants required to submit FAFSA. *Unit head:* Dr. Howard Stern, Program Director, MBA Program, 412-578-8828, E-mail: hastern@carlow.edu. *Application contact:* Dr. Howard Stern, Program Director, MBA Program, 412-578-8828, E-mail: hastern@carlow.edu.
Website: http://www.carlow.edu/Business_Administration.aspx

The Catholic University of America, Busch School of Business and Economics, Washington, DC 20064. Offers accounting (MS); business analysis (MSBA); integral economic development management (MA); integral economic development policy (MA); management (MS), including Federal contract management, human resource management, leadership and management, project management, sales management. *Program availability:* Part-time. *Faculty:* 38 full-time (8 women), 21 part-time/adjunct (9 women). *Students:* 57 full-time (11 women), 1 (woman) part-time; includes 24 minority (3 Black or African American, non-Hispanic/Latino; 1 American Indian or Alaska Native, non-Hispanic/Latino; 8 Asian, non-Hispanic/Latino; 7 Hispanic/Latino; 5 Two or more races, non-Hispanic/Latino), 1 international. Average age 33. 96 applicants, 79% accepted, 56 enrolled. In 2018, 58 master's awarded. *Degree requirements:* For master's, comprehensive exam (for some programs). *Entrance requirements:* For master's, GRE General Test, statement of purpose, official copies of academic transcripts, three letters of recommendation. Additional exam requirements/recommendations for international students: Required—TOEFL (minimum score 550 paper-based; 80 iBT). *Application deadline:* For fall admission, 7/15 priority date for domestic students, 7/1 for international students; for spring admission, 11/15 priority date for domestic students, 11/1 for international students. Applications are processed on a rolling basis. Application fee: $55. Electronic applications accepted. *Expenses:* Contact institution. *Financial support:* Fellowships, research assistantships, teaching assistantships, Federal Work-Study, scholarships/grants, tuition waivers (full and partial), and unspecified assistantships available. Financial award application deadline: 2/1; financial award applicants required to submit FAFSA. *Faculty research:* Integrity of the marketing process, economics of energy and the environment, emerging markets, social change, international finance and economic development. *Unit head:* Dr. Andrew Abela, Dean, 202-319-6130, E-mail: DeanAbela@cua.edu. *Application contact:* Dr. Steven Brown, Director of Graduate Admissions, 202-319-5057, Fax: 202-319-6533, E-mail: cua-admissions@cua.edu.
Website: https://business.catholic.edu/

The Catholic University of America, School of Engineering, Program in Engineering Management, Washington, DC 20064. Offers engineering management (MSE, Certificate), including engineering management and organization (MSE), project and systems engineering management (MSE), technology management (MSE); program management (Certificate); systems engineering and management of information technology (Certificate). *Program availability:* Part-time. *Faculty:* 6 part-time/adjunct (1 woman). *Students:* 16 full-time (1 woman), 19 part-time (7 women); includes 3 minority (1 Asian, non-Hispanic/Latino; 2 Two or more races, non-Hispanic/Latino), 17 international. Average age 31. 48 applicants, 85% accepted, 19 enrolled. In 2018, 17 master's awarded. *Degree requirements:* For master's, minimum GPA of 3.0. *Entrance requirements:* For master's and Certificate, statement of purpose, official copies of academic transcripts, two letters of recommendation. Additional exam requirements/recommendations for international students: Required—TOEFL (minimum score 550 paper-based; 80 iBT). *Application deadline:* For fall admission, 7/15 priority date for domestic students, 7/1 for international students; for spring admission, 11/15 priority date for domestic students, 11/1 for international students. Applications are processed on a rolling basis. Application fee: $55. Electronic applications accepted. *Expenses:* Contact institution. *Financial support:* Fellowships, research assistantships, teaching assistantships, Federal Work-Study, scholarships/grants, tuition waivers (full and partial), and unspecified assistantships available. Financial award application deadline: 2/1; financial award applicants required to submit FAFSA. *Faculty research:* Engineering management and organization, project and systems engineering management, technology management. *Unit head:* Melvin G. Williams, Jr., Director, 202-319-5191, Fax: 202-319-6860, E-mail: williamsme@cua.edu. *Application contact:* Dr. Steven Brown, Director of Graduate Admissions, 202-319-5057, Fax: 202-319-6533, E-mail: cua-admissions@cua.edu.
Website: https://engineering.catholic.edu/management/index.html

Christian Brothers University, School of Business, Memphis, TN 38104-5581. Offers accountancy (M Acc); business (MBA); international business (MIB); project management (Certificate); MBA/MIB. *Program availability:* Part-time, evening/weekend. *Entrance requirements:* For master's, GMAT, GRE. Additional exam requirements/recommendations for international students: Required—TOEFL.

The Citadel, The Military College of South Carolina, Citadel Graduate College, School of Engineering, Department of Engineering Leadership and Program Management, Charleston, SC 29409. Offers project management (MS); systems engineering management (Graduate Certificate); technical program management (Graduate Certificate); technical project management (Graduate Certificate). *Program availability:* Part-time, evening/weekend. *Entrance requirements:* For master's, GRE or GMAT, minimum of one year of professional experience or permission from department head; two letters of reference; resume detailing previous work; for Graduate Certificate, one-page letter of intent; resume detailing previous work. Additional exam requirements/recommendations for international students: Required—TOEFL (minimum score 550 paper-based; 79 iBT). Electronic applications accepted. *Expenses:* Tuition, state resident: part-time $595 per credit hour. Tuition, nonresident: part-time $1020 per credit hour. *Required fees:* $90 per term.

City University of Seattle, Graduate Division, School of Management, Seattle, WA 98121. Offers accounting (Certificate); change leadership (MBA, Certificate); computer systems (MS); finance (Certificate); financial management (MBA); general management (MBA); general management-Europe (MBA); global marketing (MBA); human resources management (Certificate); individualized study (MBA); information security (MS); information systems (MBA); leadership (MA); marketing (MBA, Certificate); project management (MBA, MS, Certificate); sustainable business (Certificate); technology management (MBA, Certificate). *Program availability:* Part-time, evening/weekend, online learning. *Degree requirements:* For master's, comprehensive exam (for some programs), thesis (for some programs). *Entrance requirements:* For master's, baccalaureate degree or equivalent from an accredited or otherwise recognized institution. Additional exam requirements/recommendations for international students: Required—TOEFL (minimum score 567 paper-based; 87 iBT); Recommended—IELTS. Electronic applications accepted.

Colorado Christian University, Program in Business Administration, Lakewood, CO 80226. Offers corporate training (MBA); information security (MA); leadership (MBA); project management (MBA). *Program availability:* Part-time, evening/weekend, online learning. *Degree requirements:* For master's, thesis optional. *Entrance requirements:* For master's, GMAT, 2 letters of recommendation, resume. Additional exam requirements/recommendations for international students: Required—TOEFL. Electronic applications accepted. *Expenses:* Contact institution.

Colorado State University–Global Campus, Graduate Programs, Greenwood Village, CO 80111. Offers criminal justice and law enforcement administration (MS); education leadership (MS); finance (MS); healthcare administration and management (MS); human resource management (MHRM); information technology management (MITM); international management (MS); management (MS); organizational leadership (MS); professional accounting (MPA); project management (MS); teaching and learning (MS). *Accreditation:* ACBSP. *Program availability:* Online learning.

Colorado Technical University Aurora, Programs in Business Administration and Management, Aurora, CO 80014. Offers accounting (MBA); business administration (MBA); business administration and management (EMBA); finance (MBA); human resource management (MBA); marketing (MBA); mediation and dispute resolution (MBA); operations management (MBA); project management (MBA); technology management (MBA). *Program availability:* Part-time, evening/weekend. *Degree requirements:* For master's, thesis or alternative. *Entrance requirements:* For master's, minimum undergraduate GPA of 3.0, resume.

Colorado Technical University Colorado Springs, Graduate Studies, Program in Management, Colorado Springs, CO 80907. Offers accounting (MBA, MSA); business administration (MBA); finance (MBA); human resources management (MBA); logistics/supply chain management (MBA); management (DM); marketing (MBA); mediation and dispute resolution (MBA); operations management (MBA); project management (MBA); technology management (MBA). *Accreditation:* ACBSP. *Program availability:* Part-time, evening/weekend, online learning. *Degree requirements:* For master's, thesis or alternative; for doctorate, thesis/dissertation. *Entrance requirements:* For doctorate, minimum graduate GPA of 3.0, 5 years of related work experience. *Faculty research:* Sexual harassment, performance evaluation, critical thinking.

DeSales University, Division of Business, Center Valley, PA 18034-9568. Offers accounting (MBA); computer information systems (MBA); finance (MBA); health care systems management (MBA); human resources management (MBA); management (MBA); marketing (MBA); project management (MBA); self-design (MBA); supply chain management (MBA); DNP/MBA; MSN/MBA. *Accreditation:* ACBSP. *Program availability:* Part-time, evening/weekend, 100% online, blended/hybrid learning. *Entrance requirements:* For master's, GMAT (waived if undergraduate GPA is 3.0 or better), minimum GPA of 3.0 in undergraduate work, literacy in basic software, background or interest in the field of study, personal statement, 2 years of work experience. Additional exam requirements/recommendations for international students: Required—TOEFL. Electronic applications accepted. *Expenses:* Contact institution. *Faculty research:* Quality improvement, executive development, productivity, cross-cultural managerial differences, leadership.

DeSales University, Division of Science and Mathematics, Center Valley, PA 18034-9568. Offers cyber security (Postbaccalaureate Certificate); data analytics (Postbaccalaureate Certificate); information systems (MS), including cyber security, digital forensics, healthcare information management, project management. *Program availability:* Part-time, evening/weekend, 100% online, blended/hybrid learning. *Entrance requirements:* For master's, GRE or GMAT, bachelor's degree in computer-related discipline from accredited college or university, minimum undergraduate GPA of 3.0, personal statement, three letters of recommendation. Additional exam requirements/recommendations for international students: Required—TOEFL. Electronic applications accepted. *Expenses:* Contact institution.

DeVry University–Folsom Campus, Graduate Programs, Folsom, CA 95630. Offers accounting (M Acc); accounting and financial management (MAFM); business administration (MBA); curriculum leadership (M Ed); educational leadership (M Ed); educational technology (M Ed); higher education leadership (M Ed); human resource management (MHRM); information systems management (MISM); network and communications management (MNCM); project management (MPM); public administration (MPA).

Drexel University, Goodwin College of Professional Studies, School of Technology and Professional Studies, Philadelphia, PA 19104-2875. Offers construction management (MS); creativity and innovation (MS); engineering technology (MS); food science (MS); hospitality management (MS); professional studies: creativity studies (MS); professional studies: e-learning leadership (MS); professional studies: homeland security management (MS); project management (MS); property management (MS); sport management (MS). *Program availability:* Part-time, evening/weekend. *Entrance requirements:* Additional exam requirements/recommendations for international students: Required—TOEFL, IELTS. Electronic applications accepted. Application fee is waived when completed online.

Project Management

Elmhurst College, Graduate Programs, Program in Project Management, Elmhurst, IL 60126-3296. Offers MPM. *Program availability:* Part-time, evening/weekend, 100% online. *Faculty:* 1 full-time (0 women), 4 part-time/adjunct (1 woman). *Students:* 13 part-time (4 women); includes 7 minority (2 Black or African American, non-Hispanic/Latino; 2 Asian, non-Hispanic/Latino; 3 Hispanic/Latino). Average age 32. 40 applicants, 33% accepted, 12 enrolled. *Entrance requirements:* For master's, 3 recommendations, resume, statement of purpose. Additional exam requirements/recommendations for international students: Required—TOEFL (minimum score 550 paper-based; 79 iBT), IELTS (minimum score 6.5). *Application deadline:* Applications are processed on a rolling basis. Application fee: $0. Electronic applications accepted. *Expenses:* $870 per semester hour. *Financial support:* In 2018–19, 11 students received support. Scholarships/grants available. Support available to part-time students. Financial award applicants required to submit FAFSA. *Unit head:* Dr. Bruce Fischer, Director, 630-617-3408, E-mail: brucef@elmhurst.edu. *Application contact:* Timothy J. Panfil, Senior Director of Graduate Admission and Enrollment Management, 630-617-3300 Ext. 3256, Fax: 630-617-6471, E-mail: panfilt@elmhurst.edu.
Website: http://www.elmhurst.edu/master_project_management

Embry-Riddle Aeronautical University–Worldwide, Department of Decision Sciences, Daytona Beach, FL 32114-3900. Offers aviation and aerospace (MSPM); aviation/aerospace management (MSEM); financial management (MSEM, MSPM); general management (MSPM); global management (MSPM); human resources management (MSPM); information systems (MSPM); leadership (MSEM, MSPM); logistics and supply chain management (MSEM, MSLSCM, MSPM); management (MSEM, MSPM); project management (MSEM); systems engineering (MSEM, MSPM); technical management (MSPM). *Program availability:* Part-time, evening/weekend, EagleVision Classroom (between classrooms), EagleVision Home (faculty and students at home), and a blend of Classroom or Home. *Degree requirements:* For master's, comprehensive exam (for some programs), thesis (for some programs). *Entrance requirements:* Additional exam requirements/recommendations for international students: Required—TOEFL (minimum score 550 paper-based; 79 iBT), IELTS (minimum score 6). Electronic applications accepted. *Expenses:* Contact institution.

Everglades University, Graduate Programs, Program in Business Administration, Boca Raton, FL 33431. Offers accounting for managers (MBA); aviation management (MBA); human resource management (MBA); project management (MBA). *Program availability:* Part-time, evening/weekend, 100% online. *Entrance requirements:* For master's, GMAT (minimum score of 400) or GRE (minimum score of 290), bachelor's or graduate degree from college accredited by an agency recognized by the U.S. Department of Education; minimum cumulative GPA of 2.0 at the baccalaureate level, 3.0 at the master's level. Additional exam requirements/recommendations for international students: Recommended—TOEFL (minimum score 500 paper-based). Electronic applications accepted. *Expenses:* Contact institution.

Ferris State University, College of Business, Big Rapids, MI 49307. Offers design and innovation management (MBA); lean systems and leadership (MBA); project management (MBA); supply chain management and lean logistics (MBA). *Accreditation:* ACBSP. *Program availability:* Part-time, evening/weekend, 100% online, blended/hybrid learning. *Faculty:* 20 full-time (7 women). *Students:* 14 full-time (9 women), 96 part-time (51 women); includes 12 minority (4 Black or African American, non-Hispanic/Latino; 1 American Indian or Alaska Native, non-Hispanic/Latino; 3 Asian, non-Hispanic/Latino; 2 Hispanic/Latino; 2 Two or more races, non-Hispanic/Latino), 8 international. Average age 33. 48 applicants, 88% accepted, 32 enrolled. In 2018, 39 master's awarded. *Degree requirements:* For master's, comprehensive exam, thesis. *Entrance requirements:* For master's, GRE or GMAT, minimum GPA of 3.0 overall and in junior-/senior-level classes; statement of purpose; 3 letters of reference; resume; transcripts. Additional exam requirements/recommendations for international students: Required—TOEFL (minimum score 500 paper-based; 70 iBT), IELTS (minimum score 6.5). *Application deadline:* For fall admission, 7/1 priority date for domestic students, 6/15 for international students; for winter admission, 11/1 priority date for domestic students, 10/15 for international students; for spring admission, 3/1 priority date for domestic students, 2/15 for international students. Applications are processed on a rolling basis. Application fee: $0 ($30 for international students). Electronic applications accepted. *Expenses:* $610 per credit hour; $12 per credit hour online fee; 33 credits for MISI $20,526; 39 credits for MBA $24,258. *Financial support:* In 2018–19, 17 students received support. Career-related internships or fieldwork, Federal Work-Study, scholarships/grants, and unspecified assistantships available. Support available to part-time students. Financial award applicants required to submit FAFSA. *Faculty research:* Digital forensics, security issues with internet of things, cybersecurity education. *Total annual research expenditures:* $130,000. *Unit head:* Dr. David Nicol, College of Business Dean, 231-591-2168, Fax: 231-591-3521, E-mail: davidnicol@ferris.edu. *Application contact:* Dr. Greg Gogolin, Professor, 231-591-3159, Fax: 231-591-3521, E-mail: greggogolin@ferris.edu.
Website: http://cbgp.ferris.edu/

Geneva College, Program in Leadership Studies, Beaver Falls, PA 15010-3599. Offers business management (MS); ministry leadership (MS); non-profit leadership (MS); organizational management (MS); project management (MS). *Program availability:* Online only, 100% online. *Degree requirements:* For master's, thesis or alternative, capstone leadership studies project. *Entrance requirements:* For master's, undergraduate degree from regionally-accredited college or university, one to three years of experience in the workplace, minimum GPA of 3.0 (preferred), resume, essay, two recommendations. Additional exam requirements/recommendations for international students: Required—TOEFL. Electronic applications accepted. *Expenses:* Contact institution. *Faculty research:* Servant leadership, leadership essentials.

George Mason University, Volgenau School of Engineering, Sid and Reva Dewberry Department of Civil, Environmental, and Infrastructure Engineering, Fairfax, VA 22030. Offers construction project management (MS); transportation engineering (PhD). *Faculty:* 16 full-time (4 women), 15 part-time/adjunct (4 women). *Students:* 59 full-time (20 women), 69 part-time (19 women); includes 34 minority (9 Black or African American, non-Hispanic/Latino; 14 Asian, non-Hispanic/Latino; 11 Hispanic/Latino), 46 international. Average age 28. 117 applicants, 75% accepted, 31 enrolled. In 2018, 39 master's, 8 doctorates awarded. *Degree requirements:* For master's, thesis (for some programs), 30 credits, departmental seminars; for doctorate, thesis/dissertation, qualifying exams. *Entrance requirements:* For master's, GRE, photocopy of passport; 2 official college transcripts; resume; official bank statement; proof of financial support; expanded goals statement; self-evaluation form; BS in engineering or other related science; 3 letters of recommendation; for doctorate, GRE (for those who received degree outside of the U.S.), photocopy of passport; 2 official college transcripts; resume; official bank statement; proof of financial support; expanded goals statement; self-evaluation form; baccalaureate degree in engineering or related science; master's degree (preferred); 3 letters of recommendation. Additional exam requirements/recommendations for international students: Required—TOEFL (minimum score 575 paper-based; 88 iBT), IELTS (minimum score 6.5), PTE (minimum score 59). *Application deadline:* For fall admission, 12/15 priority date for domestic and international students; for spring admission, 8/15 priority date for domestic and international students. Application fee: $75 ($80 for international students). Electronic applications accepted. *Expenses:* $589 per credit in-state, $1,346.75 per credit out-of-state. *Financial support:* In 2018–19, 37 students received support, including 25 research assistantships with tuition reimbursements available (averaging $19,626 per year), 13 teaching assistantships with tuition reimbursements available (averaging $17,449 per year); career-related internships or fieldwork, Federal Work-Study, scholarships/grants, unspecified assistantships, and health care benefits (for full-time research or teaching assistantship recipients) also available. Support available to part-time students. Financial award application deadline: 3/1; financial award applicants required to submit FAFSA. *Faculty research:* Evolutionary design, infrastructure security, intelligent transportation systems, national transportation networks, water quality modeling. *Total annual research expenditures:* $1.6 million. *Unit head:* LIza Wilson Durant, Acting Chair, 703-993-1687, Fax: 703-993-9790, E-mail: ldurant2@gmu.edu. *Application contact:* Laura Kosoglu, Director, Graduate Program, 703-993-1675, Fax: 703-993-9790, E-mail: ceiegrad@gmu.edu.
Website: http://civil.gmu.edu/

The George Washington University, School of Business, Department of Decision Sciences, Washington, DC 20052. Offers business analytics (MS, Certificate); project management (MS). *Program availability:* Online learning. *Students:* 109 full-time (62 women), 132 part-time (71 women); includes 54 minority (25 Black or African American, non-Hispanic/Latino; 1 American Indian or Alaska Native, non-Hispanic/Latino; 16 Asian, non-Hispanic/Latino; 10 Hispanic/Latino; 2 Two or more races, non-Hispanic/Latino), 137 international. Average age 31. 1,081 applicants, 44% accepted, 108 enrolled. In 2018, 89 master's, 60 other advanced degrees awarded. Application fee: $75. *Financial support:* Tuition waivers available. *Unit head:* Prof. Refik Soyer, Chair, 202-994-6445, E-mail: soyer@gwu.edu. *Application contact:* Christopher Storer, Executive Director, Graduate Admissions, 202-994-1212, E-mail: gwmba@gwu.edu.
Website: http://business.gwu.edu/decisionsciences/

The George Washington University, School of Business, Department of Information Systems and Technology Management, Washington, DC 20052. Offers information and decision systems (PhD); information systems (MSIST); information systems development (MSIST); information systems management (MBA); information systems project management (MSIST); management information systems (MSIST); management of science, technology, and innovation (MBA, PhD). Programs also offered in Ashburn and Arlington, VA. *Program availability:* Part-time, evening/weekend, online learning. *Students:* 98 full-time (49 women), 47 part-time (19 women); includes 33 minority (12 Black or African American, non-Hispanic/Latino; 14 Asian, non-Hispanic/Latino; 2 Hispanic/Latino; 5 Two or more races, non-Hispanic/Latino), 91 international. Average age 29. 328 applicants, 67% accepted, 55 enrolled. In 2018, 98 master's awarded. *Entrance requirements:* For master's, GMAT. Additional exam requirements/recommendations for international students: Required—TOEFL. *Application deadline:* For fall admission, 4/1 priority date for domestic students; for spring admission, 10/1 for domestic students. Applications are processed on a rolling basis. Application fee: $75. *Financial support:* In 2018–19, 35 students received support. Fellowships, teaching assistantships, career-related internships or fieldwork, Federal Work-Study, institutionally sponsored loans, and tuition waivers available. Financial award application deadline: 4/1. *Faculty research:* Expert systems, decision support systems. *Unit head:* Richard Donnelly, Chair, 202-994-7155, E-mail: rgd@gwu.edu. *Application contact:* Christopher Storer, Executive Director, Graduate Admissions, 202-994-1212, E-mail: gwmba@gwu.edu.

Golden Gate University, Ageno School of Business, San Francisco, CA 94105-2968. Offers accounting (MBA); adaptive leadership (MBA); advanced financial planning (MS); business administration (EMBA, MBA, DBA); business analytics (MBA, MS); entrepreneurship (MBA); finance (MBA, MS, Certificate); financial life planning (Certificate); financial planning (MS, Certificate); global supply chain management (MBA, Certificate); human resource management (MBA, MS, Certificate); information technology management (MBA, MS, Certificate); international business (MBA); marketing (MBA, MS, Certificate); project management (MBA, MS, Certificate); psychology (MA, Certificate); public administration (EMPA, MBA); public administration leadership (Certificate); JD/MBA. *Program availability:* Part-time, evening/weekend. *Degree requirements:* For doctorate, thesis/dissertation, qualifying examination. *Entrance requirements:* For master's, GMAT (for MBA), minimum GPA of 2.5 (MS). Additional exam requirements/recommendations for international students: Required—TOEFL (minimum score 550 paper-based; 79 iBT). Electronic applications accepted. *Expenses:* Contact institution.

Grand Canyon University, Colangelo College of Business, Phoenix, AZ 85017-1097. Offers accounting (MBA, MS); business analytics (MS); disaster preparedness and executive fire service leadership (MS); finance (MBA); general management (MBA); health systems management (MBA); information technology management (MS); leadership (MBA, MS); marketing (MBA); organizational leadership and entrepreneurship (MS); project management (MBA); sports business (MBA); strategic human resource management (MBA). *Accreditation:* ACBSP. *Program availability:* Part-time, evening/weekend, online learning. *Entrance requirements:* For master's, equivalent of two years' full-time professional work experience. Additional exam requirements/recommendations for international students: Required—TOEFL (minimum score 575 paper-based; 90 iBT), IELTS (minimum score 7). Electronic applications accepted.

Granite State College, MS in Project Management Program, Concord, NH 03301. Offers MS. *Program availability:* Part-time, 100% online, blended/hybrid learning. *Degree requirements:* For master's, capstone. *Entrance requirements:* For master's, bachelor's degree with minimum GPA of 3.0 on last 60 credit hours, 500-1000 word statement of purpose, two letters of professional or academic reference, resume, official transcripts. Additional exam requirements/recommendations for international students: Required—TOEFL (minimum score 80 iBT), IELTS (minimum score 6.5). Electronic applications accepted.

Grantham University, College of Engineering and Computer Science, Lenexa, KS 66219. Offers information management (MS), including project management; information management technology (MS); information technology (MS). *Program availability:* Part-time, evening/weekend, online only, 100% online. *Students:* 168 full-time (40 women), 65 part-time (19 women); includes 102 minority (73 Black or African American, non-Hispanic/Latino; 1 American Indian or Alaska Native, non-Hispanic/Latino; 10 Asian, non-Hispanic/Latino; 10 Hispanic/Latino; 8 Two or more races, non-Hispanic/Latino). Average age 40. 52 applicants, 96% accepted, 44 enrolled. In 2018, 84 master's awarded. *Degree requirements:* For master's, comprehensive exam (for some programs), Project Management: PMP Prep Exam (for information management). *Entrance requirements:* For master's, baccalaureate or master's degree with minimum cumulative GPA of 2.5 from institution accredited by agency recognized by U.S. ED or foreign equivalent; official transcripts showing proof of degree. Additional exam requirements/recommendations for international students: Required—TOEFL (minimum score 530 paper-based; 71 iBT), IELTS (minimum score 6.5), PTE (minimum score 50). *Application deadline:* Applications are processed on a rolling basis. Application fee: $0. Electronic applications accepted. *Expenses:* $350 per credit hour plus $50 per credit hour technology fee and books. Military, first responders and their families receive reduced tuition ($250 per credit hour) and technology fee and books fees are waived.

Financial support: Scholarships/grants available. Financial award applicants required to submit FAFSA. *Faculty research:* Sensor networks and security, grid technologies, cloud computing. *Unit head:* Dr. Nancy Miller, Dean of the College of Engineering and Computer Science, 913-309-4738, Fax: 855-681-5201, E-mail: nmiller@grantham.edu. *Application contact:* Lauren Cook, Director of Admissions, 800-955-2527 Ext. 803, Fax: 877-304-4467, E-mail: admissions@grantham.edu. Website: http://www.grantham.edu/engineering-and-computer-science/

Grantham University, Mark Skousen School of Business, Lenexa, KS 66219. Offers business administration (MBA); business intelligence (MS); human resources (Certificate); information management (MBA); performance improvement (MS); project management (MBA, Certificate). *Program availability:* Part-time, evening/weekend, online only, 100% online. *Students:* 556 full-time (238 women), 301 part-time (122 women); includes 369 minority (268 Black or African American, non-Hispanic/Latino; 5 American Indian or Alaska Native, non-Hispanic/Latino; 16 Asian, non-Hispanic/Latino; 50 Hispanic/Latino; 4 Native Hawaiian or other Pacific Islander, non-Hispanic/Latino; 26 Two or more races, non-Hispanic/Latino), 1 international. Average age 40. 206 applicants, 90% accepted, 159 enrolled. In 2018, 284 master's, 16 other advanced degrees awarded. *Degree requirements:* For master's, comprehensive exam (for some programs), PMP Prep Exams throughout the term (for MBA in project management); for Certificate, comprehensive exam (for some programs), PMP Prep Exam (for project management). *Entrance requirements:* For master's, baccalaureate or master's degree with minimum cumulative GPA of 2.5 from institution accredited by agency recognized by ED or foreign equivalent; official transcripts showing proof of degree. Additional exam requirements/recommendations for international students: Required—TOEFL (minimum score 530 paper-based; 71 iBT), IELTS (minimum score 6.5), PTE (minimum score 50). *Application deadline:* Applications are processed on a rolling basis. Application fee: $0. Electronic applications accepted. *Expenses: Tuition:* Full-time $4200; part-time $350 per credit hour. *Required fees:* $50; $50 per credit hour. *Financial support:* Scholarships/grants available. Financial award applicants required to submit FAFSA. *Faculty research:* How chronic diseases contribute to the rising costs of healthcare, marketing for entrepreneurs, managers' hiring practices of workers with disability, organizational structures, organizational change, online pedagogy, impact of instructor video tips in the online classroom, decision-making techniques. *Unit head:* Dr. David Marker, Dean of the Mark Skousen School of Business, 913-309-4747, Fax: 844-260-6287, E-mail: dmarker@grantham.edu. *Application contact:* Lauren Cook, Director of Admissions, 800-955-2527 Ext. 803, Fax: 877-304-4467, E-mail: admissions@grantham.edu. Website: https://www.grantham.edu/school-of-business/

Harrisburg University of Science and Technology, Program in Project Management, Harrisburg, PA 17101. Offers information technology (MS). *Program availability:* Part-time, evening/weekend. *Degree requirements:* For master's, thesis optional. *Entrance requirements:* For master's, baccalaureate degree. Additional exam requirements/recommendations for international students: Required—TOEFL (minimum score 520 paper-based; 80 iBT); Recommended—IELTS (minimum score 6). Electronic applications accepted. *Faculty research:* Strategic planning, organizational development.

Herzing University Online, Program in Business Administration, Menomonee Falls, WI 53051. Offers accounting (MBA); business administration (MBA); business management (MBA); healthcare management (MBA); human resources (MBA); marketing (MBA); project management (MBA); technology management (MBA). *Program availability:* Online learning.

Hult International Business School, Graduate Programs, Cambridge, MA 02141. Offers business administration (EMBA); business analytics (MBA, MIB); business statistics (MBS); disruptive innovation (MDI); entrepreneurship (MBA, MIB); family business (MBA, MIB); finance (MBA, MF, MIB); international marketing (MIM); marketing (MBA, MIB); project management (MBA, MIB). MDI and MBS offered in San Francisco; MBA also offered in Boston, San Francisco, Dubai, Shanghai, and New York. *Entrance requirements:* For master's, GMAT, 3 years of work experience. Additional exam requirements/recommendations for international students: Required—TOEFL. Electronic applications accepted. *Expenses:* Contact institution.

IGlobal University, Graduate Programs, Vienna, VA 22182. Offers accounting (MBA); data management and analytics (MSIT); entrepreneurship (MBA); finance (MBA); global business management (MBA); health care management (MBA); hospitality and tourism management (MBA); human resources management (MBA); information technology (MBA); information technology systems and management (MSIT); leadership and management (MBA); project management (MBA); public service and administration (MBA); software design and management (MSIT).

Iona College, School of Business, Department of Information Systems, New Rochelle, NY 10801-1890. Offers accounting and information systems (MS); business continuity and risk management (AC); information systems (MBA, MS, PMC); project management (MS). *Program availability:* Part-time, evening/weekend. *Faculty:* 5 full-time (0 women). *Students:* 12 full-time (7 women), 9 part-time (4 women); includes 7 minority (3 Black or African American, non-Hispanic/Latino; 2 Asian, non-Hispanic/Latino; 2 Hispanic/Latino), 1 international. Average age 28. 9 applicants, 89% accepted, 2 enrolled. In 2018, 12 master's awarded. *Entrance requirements:* For master's, GMAT, 2 letters of recommendation, minimum GPA of 3.0; for other advanced degree, GMAT, minimum GPA of 3.0. Additional exam requirements/recommendations for international students: Required—TOEFL (minimum score 550 paper-based; 80 iBT), IELTS (minimum score 6.5). *Application deadline:* For fall admission, 8/15 priority date for domestic students, 8/1 priority date for international students; for winter admission, 11/15 priority date for domestic students, 11/1 priority date for international students; for spring admission, 2/15 priority date for domestic students, 2/1 priority date for international students; for summer admission, 5/15 priority date for domestic students, 5/1 priority date for international students. Applications are processed on a rolling basis. Application fee: $50. Electronic applications accepted. *Expenses:* Contact institution. *Financial support:* In 2018–19, 12 students received support. Scholarships/grants, tuition waivers (partial), and unspecified assistantships available. Support available to part-time students. Financial award application deadline: 4/15; financial award applicants required to submit FAFSA. *Faculty research:* Fuzzy sets, risk management, computer security, competence set analysis, investment strategies. *Unit head:* Dr. Shoshana Altschuller, Department Chair, 914-637-7726, E-mail: saltschuller@iona.edu. *Application contact:* Kimberly Kelly, Director of Graduate Business Admissions, 914-633-2271, Fax: 914-633-2012, E-mail: kkelly@iona.edu. Website: http://www.iona.edu/Academics/Hagan-School-of-Business/Departments/Information-Systems/Graduate-Programs.aspx

King University, School of Business, Economics, and Technology, Bristol, TN 37620-2699. Offers accounting (MBA); finance (MBA); healthcare management (MBA); human resources management (MBA); leadership (MBA); management (MBA); marketing (MBA); project management (MBA). *Program availability:* Part-time, evening/weekend, 100% online, blended/hybrid learning. *Faculty:* 11 full-time (9 women), 10 part-time/adjunct (7 women). *Students:* 182 full-time (107 women), 8 part-time (6 women); includes 18 minority (7 Black or African American, non-Hispanic/Latino; 4 Hispanic/Latino; 1 Native Hawaiian or other Pacific Islander, non-Hispanic/Latino; 6 Two or more races, non-Hispanic/Latino), 2 international. Average age 32. 143 applicants, 98%

accepted, 68 enrolled. In 2018, 125 master's awarded. *Degree requirements:* For master's, comprehensive exam, thesis optional. *Entrance requirements:* For master's, resume which demonstrates a minimum of 2 years of full-time work experience, minimum cumulative grade point average of 3.0 on a 4.0 scale is required. Students who do not meet this requirement may be conditionally accepted. Additional exam requirements/recommendations for international students: Required—TOEFL (minimum score 84 paper-based; 84 iBT). *Application deadline:* Applications are processed on a rolling basis. Application fee: $0 ($50 for international students). Electronic applications accepted. *Expenses: Tuition:* Full-time $13,365; part-time $495 per semester hour. *Required fees:* $900; $100 per course. One-time fee: $175. Tuition and fees vary according to class time, degree level and program. *Financial support:* Unspecified assistantships available. Financial award applicants required to submit FAFSA. *Faculty research:* International monetary policy. *Unit head:* Dr. Mark Pate, Dean, School of Business, Economics and Technology, 423-652-4814, E-mail: mjpate@king.edu. *Application contact:* Nancy Beverly, Territory Manager/Enrollment Counselor, 423-341-9495, Fax: 423-652-4727, E-mail: nmbeverly@king.edu.

Lakeland University, Graduate Studies Division, Program in Business Administration, Plymouth, WI 53073. Offers accounting (MBA); finance (MBA); healthcare management (MBA); project management (MBA). *Entrance requirements:* For master's, GMAT. *Expenses:* Contact institution.

Lasell College, Graduate and Professional Studies in Management, Newton, MA 02466-2709. Offers business administration (MBA); elder care management (MSM); hospitality and event management (MSM); human resources management (MSM, Graduate Certificate); management (MSM, Graduate Certificate); marketing (MS, Graduate Certificate); project management (MSM, Graduate Certificate). *Accreditation:* ACBSP. *Program availability:* Part-time, evening/weekend, 100% online, blended/hybrid learning. *Faculty:* 7 full-time (4 women), 14 part-time/adjunct (9 women). *Students:* 37 full-time (28 women), 76 part-time (48 women); includes 22 minority (12 Black or African American, non-Hispanic/Latino; 1 Asian, non-Hispanic/Latino; 9 Hispanic/Latino), 20 international. Average age 32. 68 applicants, 54% accepted, 20 enrolled. In 2018, 62 master's, 1 other advanced degree awarded. *Degree requirements:* For master's, minimum GPA of 3.0; internship or research paper (for MSM). *Entrance requirements:* For master's, one-page personal statement, 2 letters of recommendation, resume, bachelor's degree transcript; proof of microeconomics and statistics (for MBA); for Graduate Certificate, bachelor's degree transcript, 2 letters of recommendation, 1-page personal statement, resume. Additional exam requirements/recommendations for international students: Required—TOEFL (minimum score 550 paper-based, 79 iBT) or IELTS (minimum score 6). *Application deadline:* For fall admission, 8/31 priority date for domestic students, 6/30 priority date for international students; for spring admission, 12/31 priority date for domestic students, 10/31 priority date for international students. Applications are processed on a rolling basis. Electronic applications accepted. *Expenses: Tuition:* Part-time $600 per credit. *Required fees:* $40 per course. *Financial support:* Federal Work-Study, scholarships/grants, and tuition discounts available. Support available to part-time students. Financial award application deadline: 8/31; financial award applicants required to submit FAFSA. *Unit head:* Eric Turner, Vice President of Graduate and Professional Studies, 617-243-2071, Fax: 617-243-2450, E-mail: gradinfo@lasell.edu. *Application contact:* Adrienne Franciosi, Assistant Vice President of Graduate and Professional Studies, 617-243-2214, Fax: 617-243-2450, E-mail: gradinfo@lasell.edu. Website: http://www.lasell.edu/academics/graduate-and-professional-studies/programs-of-study/master-of-science-in-management.html

Lawrence Technological University, College of Management, Southfield, MI 48075-1058. Offers business administration (MBA, DBA), including business analytics (MBA, MS), cybersecurity (MBA, MS), finance (MBA), information systems (MBA), information technology (MBA), marketing (MBA), project management (MBA, MS); cybersecurity (Graduate Certificate); health IT management (Graduate Certificate); information assurance management (Graduate Certificate); information systems (MS), including enterprise resource planning, enterprise security management, project management (MBA, MS); information technology (MS, DM), including business analytics (MBA, MS), cybersecurity (MBA, MS), information assurance (MS), project management (MBA, MS); management (PhD); nonprofit management and leadership (Graduate Certificate); operations management (MS), including manufacturing operations, service operations; project management (Graduate Certificate). *Accreditation:* ACBSP. *Program availability:* Part-time, evening/weekend, 100% online. Terminal master's awarded for partial completion of doctoral program. *Degree requirements:* For master's, thesis (for some programs); for doctorate, comprehensive exam, thesis/dissertation. *Entrance requirements:* Additional exam requirements/recommendations for international students: Required—TOEFL (minimum score 550 paper-based; 79 iBT), IELTS (minimum score 6.5). Electronic applications accepted. *Faculty research:* Cybersecurity; risk management; IT governance; security controls and countermeasures; threat modeling cyber resilience; autonomous cars; natural language processing; text mining; machine learning; reflective leadership; emerging leadership theories and practice; motivational studies; teaching effectiveness strategies; teamwork; organization development; strategic planning; strengths-based and positive organizational scholarship; global leadership; globalization; corporate governance.

Lebanon Valley College, Program in Business Administration, Annville, PA 17003-1400. Offers business administration (MBA); healthcare management (MBA); human resources (MBA); leadership and ethics (MBA); project management (MBA). *Program availability:* Part-time, evening/weekend. *Degree requirements:* For master's, capstone course. *Entrance requirements:* For master's, GMAT, 3 years of work experience, resume, professional statement (application form, resume, personal statement, transcripts). Additional exam requirements/recommendations for international students: Required—TOEFL (minimum score 80 iBT), IELTS (minimum score 6.5) or STEP Eiken (grade 1). Electronic applications accepted. *Expenses:* Contact institution. *Faculty research:* Leadership, motivation, BI, information systems strategies, emerging market development, the role of informational business education, economic growth.

Lehigh University, College of Business, Department of Management, Bethlehem, PA 18015. Offers business administration (MBA); project management (MBA); MBA/E; MBA/M Ed. *Accreditation:* AACSB. *Program availability:* Part-time, evening/weekend, synchronous with live classroom. *Faculty:* 11 full-time (3 women), 1 part-time/adjunct (0 women). *Students:* 44 full-time (16 women), 171 part-time (45 women); includes 32 minority (4 Black or African American, non-Hispanic/Latino; 16 Asian, non-Hispanic/Latino; 8 Hispanic/Latino; 1 Native Hawaiian or other Pacific Islander, non-Hispanic/Latino; 3 Two or more races, non-Hispanic/Latino), 23 international. Average age 33. 132 applicants, 77% accepted, 68 enrolled. In 2018, 84 master's awarded. *Entrance requirements:* For master's, GMAT or GRE. Additional exam requirements/recommendations for international students: Required—TOEFL (minimum score 600 paper-based; 94 iBT), IELTS (minimum score 7). *Application deadline:* For fall admission, 7/15 for domestic students, 5/1 for international students; for spring admission, 12/1 for domestic students. Application fee: $75. Tuition and fees vary according to program. *Financial support:* In 2018–19, 33 students received support, including 10 fellowships (averaging $5,250 per year); research assistantships, scholarships/grants, health care benefits, tuition waivers, and unspecified assistantships

also available. Support available to part-time students. Financial award application deadline: 1/15. *Faculty research:* Information systems, organizational behavior, supply chain management, strategic management, entrepreneurship. *Total annual research expenditures:* $26,528. *Unit head:* Dr. Corinne Post, Department Chair, 610-758-5882, Fax: 610-758-6941, E-mail: cgp208@lehigh.edu. *Application contact:* Mary Theresa Taglang, Director of Recruitment and Admissions, 610-758-4386, Fax: 610-758-5283, E-mail: mtt4@lehigh.edu.
Website: https://cbe.lehigh.edu/academics/undergraduate/management

Lewis University, College of Business, Program in Business Administration, Romeoville, IL 60446. Offers accounting (MBA); custom elective option (MBA); e-business (MBA); finance (MBA); healthcare management (MBA); human resources management (MBA); international business (MBA); management information systems (MBA); marketing (MBA); project management (MBA); technology and operations management (MBA). *Program availability:* Part-time, evening/weekend. *Students:* 114 full-time (72 women), 143 part-time (87 women); includes 84 minority (21 Black or African American, non-Hispanic/Latino; 2 American Indian or Alaska Native, non-Hispanic/Latino; 11 Asian, non-Hispanic/Latino; 45 Hispanic/Latino; 5 Two or more races, non-Hispanic/Latino), 17 international. Average age 31. In 2018, 99 master's awarded. *Entrance requirements:* For master's, interview, bachelor's degree, resume, two recommendations. Additional exam requirements/recommendations for international students: Required—TOEFL (minimum score 550 paper-based), IELTS. *Application deadline:* For fall admission, 8/15 priority date for domestic students, 5/1 priority date for international students; for spring admission, 11/15 priority date for international students. Applications are processed on a rolling basis. Application fee: $40. Electronic applications accepted. *Financial support:* Career-related internships or fieldwork, Federal Work-Study, scholarships/grants, and unspecified assistantships available. Financial award application deadline: 5/1; financial award applicants required to submit FAFSA. *Unit head:* Dr. Maureen Culleeney, Academic Program Director, 815-838-0500 Ext. 5631, E-mail: culleema@lewisu.edu. *Application contact:* Michele Ryan, Director of Admission, 815-838-0500 Ext. 5384, E-mail: ryanml@lewisu.edu.

Lewis University, College of Business, Program in Project Management, Romeoville, IL 60446. Offers MS. *Program availability:* Part-time, evening/weekend, 100% online, blended/hybrid learning. *Students:* 6 full-time (2 women), 22 part-time (12 women); includes 8 minority (3 Black or African American, non-Hispanic/Latino; 1 Asian, non-Hispanic/Latino; 4 Hispanic/Latino), 2 international. Average age 37. *Entrance requirements:* For master's, bachelor's degree, interview, resume, statement of purpose, 2 letters of recommendation, minimum GPA of 2.75. Additional exam requirements/recommendations for international students: Required—TOEFL (minimum score 550 paper-based; 80 iBT). *Application deadline:* For fall admission, 5/1 priority date for international students; for spring admission, 11/15 priority date for international students. Applications are processed on a rolling basis. Application fee: $40. Electronic applications accepted. *Financial support:* Career-related internships or fieldwork, Federal Work-Study, and unspecified assistantships available. Support available to part-time students. Financial award application deadline: 5/1; financial award applicants required to submit FAFSA. *Unit head:* Ryan Butt, Program Director. *Application contact:* Office of Graduate Admission, 815-836-5610, E-mail: grad@lewisu.edu.

Liberty University, School of Business, Lynchburg, VA 24515. Offers accounting (MBA, MS), including audit and financial reporting (MS), business (MS), financial services (MS), forensic accounting (MS), leadership (MS), taxation (MS); cyber security (MS); executive leadership (MA); international business (DBA); leadership (DBA); marketing (MBA, MS, DBA), including digital marketing and advertising (MS), project management (MS), public relations (MS), sports marketing and media (MS); project management (MBA, DBA); public relations (MBA). *Program availability:* Part-time, online learning. *Students:* 2,871 full-time (1,496 women), 4,437 part-time (1,969 women); includes 2,069 minority (1,424 Black or African American, non-Hispanic/Latino; 44 American Indian or Alaska Native, non-Hispanic/Latino; 133 Asian, non-Hispanic/Latino; 282 Hispanic/Latino; 16 Native Hawaiian or other Pacific Islander, non-Hispanic/Latino; 170 Two or more races, non-Hispanic/Latino), 154 international. Average age 36. 8,980 applicants, 45% accepted, 2009 enrolled. In 2018, 1,988 master's, 25 doctorates awarded. *Entrance requirements:* For master's, minimum undergraduate GPA of 3.0, 15 hours of upper-level business courses. Additional exam requirements/recommendations for international students: Required—TOEFL (minimum score 600 paper-based; 100 iBT). *Application deadline:* Applications are processed on a rolling basis. Application fee: $50. Electronic applications accepted. *Expenses:* Contact institution. *Financial support:* In 2018–19, 990 students received support. Teaching assistantships and Federal Work-Study available. Financial award applicants required to submit FAFSA. *Unit head:* Dr. Dave Bratt, Dean, 434-592-7321, E-mail: dabrat@liberty.edu. *Application contact:* Jay Bridge, Director of Graduate Admissions, 800-424-9595, Fax: 800-628-7977, E-mail: gradadmissions@liberty.edu.
Website: https://www.liberty.edu/business/

Lindenwood University, Graduate Programs, School of Accelerated Degree Programs, St. Charles, MO 63301-1695. Offers administration (MSA), including management, marketing, project management; business administration (MBA); communications (MA), including digital and multimedia, media management, promotions, training and development; criminal justice and administration (MS); healthcare administration (MS); human resource management (MS); information technology (Certificate); managing information security (MS); managing information technology (MS); managing virtualization and cloud computing (MS); writing (MFA). *Program availability:* Part-time, evening/weekend, 100% online. *Faculty:* 15 full-time (8 women), 62 part-time/adjunct (22 women). *Students:* 652 full-time (398 women), 66 part-time (45 women); includes 241 minority (182 Black or African American, non-Hispanic/Latino; 1 American Indian or Alaska Native, non-Hispanic/Latino; 8 Asian, non-Hispanic/Latino; 25 Hispanic/Latino; 1 Native Hawaiian or other Pacific Islander, non-Hispanic/Latino; 24 Two or more races, non-Hispanic/Latino), 81 international. Average age 36. 359 applicants, 54% accepted, 170 enrolled. In 2018, 416 master's, 2 other advanced degrees awarded. *Degree requirements:* For master's, thesis (for some programs), minimum cumulative GPA of 3.0; for Certificate, minimum cumulative GPA of 3.0. *Entrance requirements:* For master's, resume, personal statement, official undergraduate transcript, minimum undergraduate cumulative GPA of 3.0. Additional exam requirements/recommendations for international students: Required—TOEFL (minimum score 553 paper-based; 81 iBT); Recommended—IELTS (minimum score 6.5). *Application deadline:* For fall admission, 9/30 priority date for domestic and international students; for winter admission, 1/6 priority date for domestic and international students; for spring admission, 4/6 priority date for domestic and international students; for summer admission, 7/8 priority date for domestic and international students. Applications are processed on a rolling basis. Application fee: $0 ($100 for international students). Electronic applications accepted. *Expenses:* Contact institution. *Financial support:* In 2018–19, 372 students received support. Career-related internships or fieldwork, institutionally sponsored loans, scholarships/grants, tuition waivers (partial), and unspecified assistantships available. Financial award application deadline: 6/30; financial award applicants required to submit FAFSA. *Unit head:* Dr. Gina Ganahl, Dean, Accelerated Degree Programs, 636-949-4501, Fax: 636-949-4505, E-mail: gganahl@lindenwood.edu. *Application contact:* Kara Schilli, Assistant Vice President, University Admissions, 636-949-4349, Fax: 636-949-4109, E-mail: adultadmissions@lindenwood.edu.
Website: https://www.lindenwood.edu/academics/academic-schools/school-of-accelerated-degree-programs/

Marlboro College, Graduate and Professional Studies, Program in Business Administration, Marlboro, VT 05344. Offers mission-driven organizations (MBA); project management (MBA); social innovation (MBA). *Program availability:* Part-time, evening/weekend, blended/hybrid learning. *Degree requirements:* For master's, 45 credits including a Master Workshop. *Entrance requirements:* For master's, letter of intent, essay, transcripts, 2 letters of recommendation. Electronic applications accepted. *Expenses:* Contact institution.

Marlboro College, Graduate and Professional Studies, Program in Management, Marlboro, VT 05344. Offers mission-driven organizations (MS); project management (MS); social innovation (MS). *Program availability:* Part-time, evening/weekend, blended/hybrid learning. *Degree requirements:* For master's, capstone project. *Entrance requirements:* For master's, statement of intent, 2 letters of recommendation. Additional exam requirements/recommendations for international students: Recommended—TOEFL (minimum score 577 paper-based; 90 iBT), IELTS (minimum score 7). Electronic applications accepted. *Expenses:* Contact institution.

Marymount University, School of Business and Technology, Program in Information Technology, Arlington, VA 22207-4299. Offers health care informatics (Certificate); information technology (MS, Certificate), including cybersecurity (MS), health care informatics (MS), project management and technology leadership (MS), software engineering (MS); information technology project management and technology leadership (Certificate); information technology with business administration (MS/MBA); information technology with health care management (MS/MS); MS/MBA; MS/MS. *Program availability:* Part-time, evening/weekend. *Faculty:* 5 full-time (3 women), 7 part-time/adjunct (0 women). *Students:* 29 full-time (17 women), 36 part-time (19 women); includes 25 minority (15 Black or African American, non-Hispanic/Latino; 5 Asian, non-Hispanic/Latino; 5 Hispanic/Latino), 24 international. Average age 30. 66 applicants, 98% accepted, 22 enrolled. In 2018, 35 master's, 3 other advanced degrees awarded. *Degree requirements:* For master's, thesis or alternative. *Entrance requirements:* For master's, resume, bachelor's degree in computer-related field or degree in another subject with a certificate in a computer-related field or related work experience. Software Engineering Track: bachelor's degree in Computer Science or work in software development. Project Mgmt/Tech Leadership Track: minimum 2 years of IT experience. Additional exam requirements/recommendations for international students: Required—TOEFL (minimum score 600 paper-based; 96 iBT), IELTS (minimum score 6.5), PTE (minimum score 58). *Application deadline:* For fall admission, 7/16 priority date for domestic and international students; for spring admission, 11/16 priority date for domestic and international students; for summer admission, 4/16 priority date for domestic and international students. Applications are processed on a rolling basis. Application fee: $40. Electronic applications accepted. *Expenses:* $1,060 per credit. *Financial support:* In 2018–19, 1 student received support. Research assistantships, teaching assistantships, career-related internships or fieldwork, scholarships/grants, and unspecified assistantships available. Support available to part-time students. Financial award application deadline: 3/1; financial award applicants required to submit FAFSA. *Unit head:* Dr. Diane Murphy, Chair/Director, Information Technology, Management Sciences and Cybersecurity, 703-284-5958, E-mail: diane.murphy@marymount.edu. *Application contact:* Rebecca Esposito, Senior Associate Director, Graduate Admissions, 703-284-5901, Fax: 703-527-3815, E-mail: grad.admissions@marymount.edu.
Website: https://www.marymount.edu/Academics/School-of-Business-and-Technology/Graduate-Programs/Information-Technology-(M-S-)

Maryville University of Saint Louis, The John E. Simon School of Business, St. Louis, MO 63141-7299. Offers accounting (MBA, MS, Certificate); business studies (Certificate); cybersecurity (MBA, MS, Certificate); financial services (MBA, Certificate); health administration (MBA); healthcare administration (Certificate); human resource management (MBA); human resources management (Certificate); information technology (MBA); information technology management (Certificate); management (MBA, Certificate); management and leadership (MA); marketing (MBA, Certificate); project management (MBA, Certificate); sport business management (MBA); supply chain management (Certificate); supply chain management/logistics (MBA). *Accreditation:* ACBSP. *Program availability:* Part-time, 100% online, blended/hybrid learning. *Faculty:* 5 full-time (1 woman), 77 part-time/adjunct (19 women). *Students:* 338 full-time (166 women), 739 part-time (356 women); includes 310 minority (161 Black or African American, non-Hispanic/Latino; 6 American Indian or Alaska Native, non-Hispanic/Latino; 59 Asian, non-Hispanic/Latino; 57 Hispanic/Latino; 27 Two or more races, non-Hispanic/Latino), 30 international. Average age 33. In 2018, 143 master's awarded. *Degree requirements:* For master's, capstone course (for MBA). *Entrance requirements:* Additional exam requirements/recommendations for international students: Required—TOEFL (minimum score 563 paper-based; 85 iBT). *Application deadline:* Applications are processed on a rolling basis. Electronic applications accepted. *Expenses:* Tuition varies by program. *Financial support:* Career-related internships or fieldwork, Federal Work-Study, tuition waivers (partial), and campus employment available. Financial award application deadline: 4/1; financial award applicants required to submit FAFSA. *Unit head:* Tammy Gocial, Interim Dean, 314-529-9401, Fax: 314-529-9975, E-mail: tgocial@maryville.edu. *Application contact:* Chris Gourdine, Assistant Dean Business Administration, 314-529-6861, Fax: 314-529-9975, E-mail: cgourdine@maryville.edu.
Website: http://www.maryville.edu/bu/business-administration-masters/

Metropolitan State University, College of Management, St. Paul, MN 55106-5000. Offers business administration (MBA, DBA); business analytics (Graduate Certificate); database administration (Graduate Certificate); global supply chain management (Graduate Certificate); information assurance security (Graduate Certificate); management information systems (MMIS); MIS generalist (Graduate Certificate); MIS systems analysis and design (Graduate Certificate); project management (Graduate Certificate). *Program availability:* Part-time, evening/weekend. *Degree requirements:* For master's, thesis optional, computer language (MMIS). *Entrance requirements:* For master's, GMAT (for MBA), resume. Additional exam requirements/recommendations for international students: Required—TOEFL (minimum score 550 paper-based). Electronic applications accepted. *Faculty research:* Yugoslav economic system, workers' cooperatives, participative management and job enrichment, global business systems.

Mississippi State University, College of Business, Department of Management and Information Systems, Mississippi State, MS 39762. Offers business administration (MBA); information systems (MSIS, PhD); management (PhD); project management (MBA). *Program availability:* Part-time. *Faculty:* 16 full-time (3 women), 1 part-time/adjunct (0 women). *Students:* 62 full-time (21 women), 189 part-time (50 women); includes 25 minority (13 Black or African American, non-Hispanic/Latino; 3 Asian, non-Hispanic/Latino; 9 Hispanic/Latino), 18 international. Average age 30. 136 applicants, 59% accepted, 46 enrolled. In 2018, 105 master's, 2 doctorates awarded. *Degree requirements:* For master's, comprehensive exam; for doctorate, comprehensive exam, thesis/dissertation. *Entrance requirements:* For master's, GMAT, minimum GPA of 3.0 in

last 60 hours of undergraduate course work; for doctorate, GMAT (minimum score of 550), minimum GPA of 3.25 on all graduate work; BS with minimum GPA of 3.0 cumulative and last 60 hours. Additional exam requirements/recommendations for international students: Required—TOEFL (minimum score 575 paper-based; 84 iBT); Recommended—IELTS (minimum score 7). *Application deadline:* For fall admission, 7/1 for domestic students, 5/1 for international students; for spring admission, 11/1 for domestic students, 9/1 for international students. Applications are processed on a rolling basis. Application fee: $60 ($80 for international students). Electronic applications accepted. *Expenses:* Tuition, state resident: full-time $8450; part-time $360.59 per credit hour. Tuition, nonresident: full-time $23,140; part-time $969.09 per credit hour. *Required fees:* $110. One-time fee: $55 full-time. Part-time tuition and fees vary according to course load, degree level, campus/location and reciprocity agreements. *Financial support:* Career-related internships or fieldwork, Federal Work-Study, institutionally sponsored loans, scholarships/grants, and unspecified assistantships available. Financial award applicants required to submit FAFSA. *Faculty research:* Electronic commerce, management of information technology. *Total annual research expenditures:* $1.4 million. *Unit head:* Dr. James J. Chrisman, Professor and Head, 662-325-1991, Fax: 662-325-8651, E-mail: jchrisman@business.msstate.edu. *Application contact:* Robbie Salters, Admissions and Enrollment Assistant, 662-325-7400, E-mail: rsalters@grad.msstate.edu.
Website: http://www.business.msstate.edu/programs/mis/index.php

Missouri State University, Graduate College, College of Business, Department of Technology and Construction Management, Springfield, MO 65897. Offers project management (MS). *Program availability:* Part-time. *Faculty:* 4 full-time (0 women), 2 part-time/adjunct (1 woman). *Students:* 24 full-time (13 women), 46 part-time (20 women); includes 12 minority (5 Black or African American, non-Hispanic/Latino; 1 American Indian or Alaska Native, non-Hispanic/Latino; 6 Hispanic/Latino), 13 international. Average age 26. 44 applicants, 68% accepted. In 2018, 25 master's awarded. *Degree requirements:* For master's, thesis or alternative. *Entrance requirements:* For master's, GRE or GMAT, minimum GPA of 2.75. Additional exam requirements/recommendations for international students: Required—TOEFL (minimum score 550 paper-based; 79 iBT), IELTS (minimum score 6). *Application deadline:* For fall admission, 7/20 priority date for domestic students, 5/1 for international students; for spring admission, 12/20 priority date for domestic students, 9/1 for international students; for summer admission, 5/20 priority date for domestic students. Applications are processed on a rolling basis. Application fee: $55 ($60 for international students). Electronic applications accepted. Tuition and fees vary according to class time, course level, course load, degree level, campus/location, program and student level. *Financial support:* Federal Work-Study, institutionally sponsored loans, scholarships/grants, and unspecified assistantships available. Financial award application deadline: 1/31; financial award applicants required to submit FAFSA. *Unit head:* Dr. Richard N. Callahan, Department Head, 417-836-5121, Fax: 417-836-8556, E-mail: indmgt@missouristate.edu. *Application contact:* Lakan Drinker, Director, Graduate Enrollment Management, 417-836-5330, Fax: 417-836-6200, E-mail: lakandrinker@missouristate.edu.
Website: http://tcm.missouristate.edu/

Montana Tech of The University of Montana, Project Engineering and Management Program, Butte, MT 59701-8997. Offers MPEM. *Program availability:* Part-time, evening/weekend, online learning. *Degree requirements:* For master's, comprehensive exam, final project presentation. *Entrance requirements:* For master's, minimum GPA of 3.0. Additional exam requirements/recommendations for international students: Required—TOEFL (minimum score 550 paper-based; 80 iBT), IELTS (minimum score 7). Electronic applications accepted.

Montclair State University, The Graduate School, Feliciano School of Business, General MBA Program, Montclair, NJ 07043-1624. Offers accounting (MBA); business analytics (MBA); digital marketing (MBA); finance (MBA); general business administration (MBA); human resources management (MBA); management (MBA); management of information and technology (MBA); marketing (MBA); project management (MBA). *Program availability:* Part-time, evening/weekend. *Degree requirements:* For master's, culminating experience. *Entrance requirements:* For master's, GMAT or GRE General Test, 2 letters of recommendation, resume, essay. Additional exam requirements/recommendations for international students: Required—TOEFL (minimum score 83 iBT), IELTS (minimum score 6.5). Electronic applications accepted. *Faculty research:* Accounting, management, marketing.

Morgan State University, School of Graduate Studies, Earl G. Graves School of Business and Management, Program in Project Management, Baltimore, MD 21251. Offers MS.

Mount Aloysius College, Program in Business Administration, Cresson, PA 16630. Offers accounting (MBA); health and human services administration (MBA); non-profit management (MBA); project management (MBA). *Program availability:* Part-time, evening/weekend. *Entrance requirements:* Additional exam requirements/recommendations for international students: Required—IELTS (minimum score 5.5); Recommended—TOEFL. *Application deadline:* For fall admission, 8/1 for domestic students; for spring admission, 12/1 for domestic students. Applications are processed on a rolling basis. Application fee: $30. Electronic applications accepted. Application fee is waived when completed online. *Financial support:* Unspecified assistantships available. Financial award applicants required to submit FAFSA. *Application contact:* Matthew P. Bodenschatz, Director of Graduate and Continuing Education Admissions, 814-886-6556, Fax: 814-886-6441, E-mail: mbodenschatz@mtaloy.edu.

National American University, Roueche Graduate Center, Austin, TX 78731. Offers accounting (MBA); aviation management (MBA, MM); care coordination (MSN); community college leadership (Ed D); criminal justice (MM); e-marketing (MBA, MM); health care administration (MBA, MM); higher education (MM); human resources management (MBA, MM); information technology management (MBA, MM); international business (MBA); leadership (EMBA); management (MBA); nursing administration (MSN); nursing education (MSN); nursing informatics (MSN); operations and configuration management (MBA, MM); project and process management (MBA, MM). Master's programs offered online through the Harold D. Buckingham Graduate School. *Program availability:* Part-time, evening/weekend, online learning. *Entrance requirements:* For master's, minimum undergraduate GPA of 2.75. Additional exam requirements/recommendations for international students: Required—TOEFL, TWE. Electronic applications accepted. *Faculty research:* Tourism, finance, marketing.

New England College, Program in Management, Henniker, NH 03242-3293. Offers accounting (MSA); healthcare administration (MS); international relations (MA); marketing management (MS); nonprofit leadership (MS); project management (MS); strategic leadership (MS). *Program availability:* Part-time, evening/weekend. *Degree requirements:* For master's, independent research project. Electronic applications accepted.

New York University, School of Professional Studies, Division of Programs in Business, Program in Project Management, New York, NY 10012-1019. Offers MS. *Program availability:* Part-time, evening/weekend. *Degree requirements:* For master's, thesis. *Entrance requirements:* For master's, GRE or GMAT (only upon request),

bachelor's degree, resume with relevant professional work, internship or volunteer experience, two letters of recommendation, statement of purpose. Additional exam requirements/recommendations for international students: Required—TOEFL (minimum score 600 paper-based; 100 iBT), IELTS (minimum score 7). Electronic applications accepted. *Expenses:* Contact institution.

Northeastern University, College of Professional Studies, Boston, MA 02115-5096. Offers applied nutrition (MS); college athletics administration (MSL); commerce and economic development (MS); corporate and organizational communication (MS); criminal justice (MS); digital media (MPS); elearning and instructional design (M Ed); elementary education (MAT); geographic information technology (MPS); global studies and international relations (MS); higher education administration (M Ed); homeland security (MA); human services (MS); informatics (MPS); leadership (MS); learning analytics (M Ed); learning and instruction (M Ed); nonprofit management (MS); professional sports administration (MSL); project management (MS); regulatory affairs for drugs, biologics, and medical devices (MS); respiratory care leadership (MS); special education (M Ed); technical communication (MS). *Program availability:* Part-time, evening/weekend, 100% online, blended/hybrid learning. Electronic applications accepted. *Expenses:* Contact institution.

Northwestern University, McCormick School of Engineering and Applied Science, Department of Civil and Environmental Engineering, Master of Project Management Program, Evanston, IL 60208. Offers MS. *Program availability:* Part-time, evening/weekend. *Degree requirements:* For master's, capstone report. *Entrance requirements:* Additional exam requirements/recommendations for international students: Required—TOEFL (minimum score 560 paper-based; 83 iBT), IELTS. Electronic applications accepted. *Faculty research:* Construction management, real estate development, sustainability, and transportation management.

Northwestern University, School of Professional Studies, Program in Information Systems, Evanston, IL 60208. Offers analytics and business intelligence (MS); database and Internet technologies (MS); information systems (MS); information systems management (MS); information systems security (MS); medical informatics (MS); software project management and development (MS). *Program availability:* Part-time, evening/weekend.

Northwest University, College of Business, Kirkland, WA 98033. Offers business administration (MBA); international business (MBA); project management (MBA); social entrepreneurship (MBA). *Accreditation:* ACBSP. *Program availability:* Part-time, evening/weekend. *Degree requirements:* For master's, formalized research. *Entrance requirements:* For master's, GMAT. Additional exam requirements/recommendations for international students: Required—TOEFL (minimum score 550 paper-based; 75 iBT). Electronic applications accepted. *Expenses:* Contact institution.

Norwich University, College of Graduate and Continuing Studies, Master of Business Administration Program, Northfield, VT 05663. Offers construction management (MBA); energy management (MBA); finance (MBA); logistics (MBA); organizational leadership (MBA); project management (MBA); supply chain management (MBA). *Accreditation:* ACBSP. *Program availability:* Evening/weekend, online only, mostly all online with a week-long residency requirement. *Degree requirements:* For master's, comprehensive exam. *Entrance requirements:* For master's, minimum undergraduate GPA of 2.75. Additional exam requirements/recommendations for international students: Required—TOEFL (minimum score 550 paper-based; 80 iBT), IELTS (minimum score 6.5). Electronic applications accepted. *Expenses:* Contact institution.

Norwich University, College of Graduate and Continuing Studies, Master of Science in Information Security and Assurance Program, Northfield, VT 05663. Offers information security and assurance (MS), including computer forensic investigation/incident response team management, critical infrastructure protection and cyber crime, cyber law and international perspectives on cyberspace, project management, vulnerability management. *Program availability:* Evening/weekend, online only, mostly all online with a week-long residency requirement. *Entrance requirements:* For master's, minimum undergraduate GPA of 2.75. Additional exam requirements/recommendations for international students: Required—TOEFL (minimum score 550 paper-based; 80 iBT), IELTS (minimum score 6.5). Electronic applications accepted. *Expenses:* Contact institution.

Oklahoma Christian University, Graduate School of Business, Oklahoma City, OK 73136-1100. Offers accounting (M Acc, MBA); financial services (MBA); general business (MBA); health services management (MBA); human resources (MBA); international business (MBA); leadership and organizational development (MBA); marketing (MBA); nonprofit management (MBA); project management (MBA). *Accreditation:* ACBSP. *Program availability:* Part-time, 100% online. *Entrance requirements:* For master's, bachelor's degree. Additional exam requirements/recommendations for international students: Required—TOEFL (minimum score 550 paper-based). Electronic applications accepted. *Expenses:* Contact institution.

Pacific States University, College of Business, Los Angeles, CA 90010. Offers accounting (MBA, Certificate); beauty management (MBA); finance (MBA); international business (MBA); management of information technology (MBA); project management (Certificate); real estate management (MBA). *Program availability:* Part-time, evening/weekend, online learning. *Entrance requirements:* For master's, minimum undergraduate GPA of 2.5 during last 90 quarter units of course work, bachelor's degree in business administration or economics. Additional exam requirements/recommendations for international students: Required—TOEFL (minimum score 500 paper-based; 61 iBT), IELTS (minimum score 5.5).

Point Loma Nazarene University, Fermanian School of Business, San Diego, CA 92106-2899. Offers general business (MBA); healthcare management (MBA); innovation and entrepreneurship (MBA); organizational leadership (MBA); project management (MBA). *Accreditation:* ACBSP. *Program availability:* Part-time, evening/weekend. *Entrance requirements:* For master's, GMAT, letters of recommendation, essay, interview. Additional exam requirements/recommendations for international students: Required—TOEFL. Electronic applications accepted. *Expenses:* Contact institution.

Polytechnic University of Puerto Rico, Miami Campus, Graduate School, Miami, FL 33166. Offers accounting (MBA); business administration (MBA); construction management (MEM); environmental management (MEM); finance (MBA); human resources management (MBA); logistics and supply chain management (MBA); management of international enterprises (MBA); manufacturing management (MEM); marketing management (MBA); project management (MBA). *Program availability:* Part-time, evening/weekend, online learning. *Entrance requirements:* For master's, minimum GPA of 3.0. Electronic applications accepted.

Post University, Program in Business Administration, Waterbury, CT 06723-2540. Offers accounting (MSA); business administration (MBA); corporate finance (MBA); corporate innovation (MBA); healthcare systems leadership (MBA); leadership (MBA); marketing (MBA); project management (MBA, MS). *Accreditation:* ACBSP. *Program availability:* Online learning. *Entrance requirements:* For master's, resume. *Expenses:* Tuition: Full-time $8300; part-time $570 per credit. *Required fees:* $140 per term. Tuition and fees vary according to course level, campus/location and program.

Project Management

Purdue University Global, School of Business, Davenport, IA 52807. Offers business administration (MBA); change leadership (MS); entrepreneurship (MBA); finance (MBA); health care management (MBA, MS); human resource (MBA); international business (MBA); management (MS); marketing (MBA); project management (MBA, MS); supply chain management and logistics (MBA, MS). *Accreditation:* ACBSP. *Program availability:* Part-time, evening/weekend, online learning. *Entrance requirements:* Additional exam requirements/recommendations for international students: Required—TOEFL (minimum score 550 paper-based; 80 iBT). Electronic applications accepted.

Queen's University at Kingston, Smith School of Business, Program in Business Administration, Kingston, ON K7L 3N6, Canada. Offers consulting and project management (MBA); finance (MBA); innovation and entrepreneurship (MBA); marketing (MBA). *Degree requirements:* For master's, thesis optional, research project. *Entrance requirements:* For master's, GMAT, minimum B+ average. Additional exam requirements/recommendations for international students: Required—TOEFL. Electronic applications accepted. *Faculty research:* Management fundamentals, strategic thinking, global business, innovation and change, leadership.

Regis University, College of Business and Economics, Denver, CO 80221-1099. Offers accounting (MS); executive leadership (Certificate); finance (MS); finance and accounting (MBA); health industry leadership (MBA); human resource management and leadership (MSOL); management (MBA); marketing (MBA); nonprofit leadership (Post-Graduate Certificate); nonprofit management (MNM); nonprofit organizational capacity building (Certificate); operations management (MBA); organizational leadership and management (MSOL); project leadership and management (MS, MSOL); strategic business management (Certificate); strategic human resource integration (Certificate); strategic management (MBA). Programs offered at Colorado Springs Campus, Northwest Denver Campus, Southeast Denver Campus, Fort Collins Campus, Broomfield Campus, Henderson (Nevada) Campus, and Summerlin (Nevada) Campus. *Program availability:* Part-time, evening/weekend, 100% online, blended/hybrid learning. *Degree requirements:* For master's, thesis (for some programs), capstone or final research project. *Entrance requirements:* For master's, official transcript reflecting baccalaureate degree awarded from regionally-accredited college or university, interview, 2 years of full-time related work experience, resume, letters of recommendation. Additional exam requirements/recommendations for international students: Required—TOEFL (minimum score 550 paper-based; 82 iBT). Electronic applications accepted. *Expenses:* Contact institution. *Faculty research:* Impact of information technology on small business regulation of accounting, international project financing, mineral development, delivery of healthcare to rural indigenous communities.

Robert Morris University, School of Informatics, Humanities and Social Sciences, Moon Township, PA 15108-1189. Offers communication and information systems (MS); cyber security (MS); data analytics (MS); information security and assurance (MS); information systems and communications (D Sc); information systems management (MS); information technology project management (MS); Internet information systems (MS); organizational leadership (MS). *Program availability:* Part-time-only, evening/weekend, 100% online. *Faculty:* 22 full-time (7 women), 10 part-time/adjunct (0 women). *Students:* 262 part-time (94 women); includes 57 minority (31 Black or African American, non-Hispanic/Latino; 13 Asian, non-Hispanic/Latino; 8 Hispanic/Latino; 5 Two or more races, non-Hispanic/Latino), 43 international. Average age 35. 150 applicants, 92% accepted, 79 enrolled. In 2018, 133 master's, 11 doctorates awarded. *Degree requirements:* For master's, Completion of 30 credits; for doctorate, thesis/dissertation, Completion of 63 credits. *Entrance requirements:* For doctorate, employer letter of endorsement, interview. Additional exam requirements/recommendations for international students: Required—TOEFL (minimum score 550 paper-based; 79 iBT). *Application deadline:* For fall admission, 7/1 priority date for domestic and international students; for spring admission, 11/1 priority date for domestic and international students. Applications are processed on a rolling basis. Application fee: $35. Electronic applications accepted. Application fee is waived when completed online. *Expenses:* Master's $920/credit plus $80/credit fees; D.Sc. $28,290/year. *Financial support:* Institutionally sponsored loans available. Support available to part-time students. Financial award application deadline: 5/1; financial award applicants required to submit FAFSA. *Unit head:* Jon A. Radermacher, Interim Dean, School of Informatics, Humanities and Social Sciences, 412-397-4088, E-mail: radermacher@rmu.edu. *Application contact:* Jon A. Radermacher, Interim Dean, School of Informatics, Humanities and Social Sciences, 412-397-4088, E-mail: radermacher@rmu.edu.
Website: https://www.rmu.edu/academics/schools/sihss

Rochester Institute of Technology, Graduate Enrollment Services, School of Individualized Study, Graduate Programs Department, Advanced Certificate Program in Project Management, Rochester, NY 14623-5603. Offers Advanced Certificate. *Program availability:* Part-time, evening/weekend, 100% online, blended/hybrid learning. *Students:* 8 part-time (6 women); includes 2 minority (1 Hispanic/Latino; 1 Two or more races, non-Hispanic/Latino), 1 international. Average age 36. 11 applicants, 82% accepted, 3 enrolled. In 2018, 23 Advanced Certificates awarded. *Entrance requirements:* For degree, minimum GPA of 3.0 (recommended), personal statement, resume, two letters of recommendation. Additional exam requirements/recommendations for international students: Required—TOEFL (minimum score 550 paper-based; 79 iBT), IELTS (minimum score 6.5), PTE (minimum score 58). *Application deadline:* Applications are processed on a rolling basis. Application fee: $65. Electronic applications accepted. *Expenses:* Contact institution. *Financial support:* In 2018–19, 2 students received support. Available to part-time students. Applicants required to submit FAFSA. *Faculty research:* Risk management; cross-cultural teams; automation of management process; non-traditional management tools; human performance and emotional intelligence. *Unit head:* Peter Boyd, Graduate Program Director, 585-475-6320, E-mail: plbcms@rit.edu. *Application contact:* Diane Ellison, Senior Associate Vice President, Graduate Enrollment Services, 585-475-2229, Fax: 585-475-7164, E-mail: gradinfo@rit.edu.
Website: https://www.rit.edu/study/project-management-adv-cert

Saint Mary's University of Minnesota, Schools of Graduate and Professional Programs, Graduate School of Business and Technology, Project Management Program, Winona, MN 55987-1399. Offers MS, Certificate. *Program availability:* Part-time, evening/weekend, online learning. *Unit head:* William Johnson, Director, 612-728-5178, E-mail: wcjohn06@smumn.edu. *Application contact:* Laurie Roy, Director of Admission of the Schools of Graduate and Professional Programs, 507-457-8606, Fax: 612-728-5121, E-mail: lroy@smumn.edu.
Website: http://www.smumn.edu/graduate-home/areas-of-study/graduate-school-of-business-technology/ms-in-project-management

Saint Xavier University, Graduate Studies, Graham School of Management, Chicago, IL 60655-3105. Offers employee health benefits (Certificate); finance (MBA); financial fraud examination and management (MBA, Certificate); financial planning (MBA, Certificate); generalist/individualized (MBA); health administration (MBA); managed care (Certificate); management (MBA); marketing (MBA); project management (MBA, Certificate); MBA/MS. *Accreditation:* AACSB. *Program availability:* Part-time, evening/weekend. *Entrance requirements:* For master's, GMAT, minimum GPA of 3.0, 2 years of work experience. Electronic applications accepted. *Expenses:* Contact institution.

Sam Houston State University, College of Business Administration, Department of Management and Marketing, Huntsville, TX 77341. Offers project management (MS). *Program availability:* Part-time, online learning. *Entrance requirements:* For master's, GMAT, official transcripts, current resume, essay. Additional exam requirements/recommendations for international students: Required—TOEFL (minimum score 79 iBT), IELTS (minimum score 6.5). Electronic applications accepted.

Southern Illinois University Edwardsville, Graduate School, School of Business, Program in Business Administration, Edwardsville, IL 62026. Offers business analytics (MBA); management information systems (MBA); project management (MBA). *Accreditation:* AACSB. *Program availability:* Part-time, evening/weekend. *Degree requirements:* For master's, comprehensive exam. *Entrance requirements:* For master's, GMAT. Additional exam requirements/recommendations for international students: Required—TOEFL (minimum score 550 paper-based; 79 iBT), IELTS (minimum score 6.5). Electronic applications accepted.

Southern New Hampshire University, School of Business, Manchester, NH 03106-1045. Offers accounting (MBA, Graduate Certificate); accounting finance (MS); accounting/auditing (MS); accounting/forensic accounting (MS); accounting/management accounting (MS); accounting/taxation (MS); applied economics (MS); athletic administration (MBA, Graduate Certificate); business administration (IMBA, Certificate), including business information systems (Certificate), human resource management (Certificate); business analytics (MBA); business intelligence (MBA); communication (MA), including new media and marketing, public relations; community economic development (MBA); criminal justice (MBA); data analytics (MS); economics (MBA); engineering management (MBA); entrepreneurship (MBA); finance (MBA, MS, Graduate Certificate); finance/corporate finance (MS); finance/investments (MS); forensic accounting (MBA); forensic accounting and fraud examination (Graduate Certificate); healthcare informatics (MBA); healthcare management (MBA); human resource management (MS); human resources (MBA); information technology (MS); information technology management (MBA); international business (PhD); Internet marketing (MBA); leadership (MBA); leadership of nonprofit organizations (Graduate Certificate); management (MS); marketing (MBA, MS, Graduate Certificate); music business (MBA); operations and project management (MS); operations and supply chain management (MBA, Graduate Certificate); organizational leadership (MS); project management (MBA, Graduate Certificate); public administration (MBA, Graduate Certificate); quantitative analysis (MBA); Six Sigma (Graduate Certificate); Six Sigma quality (MBA); social media marketing (MBA, Graduate Certificate); sport management (MBA, MS, Graduate Certificate); sustainability and environmental compliance (MBA); MBA/Certificate. *Accreditation:* ACBSP. *Program availability:* Part-time, evening/weekend, online learning. Terminal master's awarded for partial completion of doctoral program. *Degree requirements:* For master's, one foreign language, comprehensive exam (for some programs), thesis or alternative; for doctorate, one foreign language, comprehensive exam, thesis/dissertation. *Entrance requirements:* For master's, minimum GPA of 2.5; for doctorate, GMAT. Additional exam requirements/recommendations for international students: Required—TOEFL (minimum score 500 paper-based). Electronic applications accepted.

Stevens Institute of Technology, Graduate School, School of Business, Program in Business Administration, Hoboken, NJ 07030. Offers business intelligence and analytics (MBA); engineering management (MBA); finance (MBA); information systems (MBA); innovation and entrepreneurship (MBA); marketing (MBA); pharmaceutical management (MBA); project management (MBA, Certificate); technology management (MBA); telecommunications management (MBA). *Accreditation:* AACSB. *Program availability:* Part-time, evening/weekend. *Faculty:* 58 full-time (8 women), 18 part-time/adjunct (3 women). *Students:* 44 full-time (23 women), 202 part-time (90 women); includes 56 minority (12 Black or African American, non-Hispanic/Latino; 2 American Indian or Alaska Native, non-Hispanic/Latino; 40 Asian, non-Hispanic/Latino; 2 Hispanic/Latino), 28 international. Average age 37. In 2018, 45 master's awarded. Terminal master's awarded for partial completion of doctoral program. *Degree requirements:* For master's, thesis optional, minimum B average in major field and overall; for Certificate, minimum B average. *Entrance requirements:* For master's, GRE/GMAT scores: GRE scores are required for all applicants applying to a full-time graduate program in the Schaefer School of Engineering and Science (SES). International applicants must submit TOEFL/IELTS scores and fulfill the English Language Proficiency Requirements in order to be considered. Additional exam requirements/recommendations for international students: Required—TOEFL (minimum score 74 iBT), IELTS (minimum score 6). *Application deadline:* For fall admission, 4/1 for domestic and international students; for spring admission, 11/1 for domestic and international students; for summer admission, 5/1 for domestic students. Applications are processed on a rolling basis. Application fee: $60. Electronic applications accepted. *Expenses: Tuition:* Full-time $35,960; part-time $1620 per credit. *Required fees:* $1290; $600 per semester. Tuition and fees vary according to course load. *Financial support:* Fellowships, research assistantships, teaching assistantships, career-related internships or fieldwork, Federal Work-Study, scholarships/grants, and unspecified assistantships available. Financial award application deadline: 2/15; financial award applicants required to submit FAFSA. *Unit head:* Dr. Gregory Prastacos, Dean, 201-216-8366, E-mail: gprastac@stevens.edu. *Application contact:* Graduate Admissions, 888-783-8367, Fax: 888-511-1306, E-mail: graduate@stevens.edu.
Website: https://www.stevens.edu/school-business/masters-programs/mbaemba

Stevens Institute of Technology, Graduate School, School of Business, Program in Information Systems, Hoboken, NJ 07030. Offers computer science (MS); e-commerce (MS); enterprise systems (MS); entrepreneurial information technology (MS); information architecture (MS); information management (MS, Certificate); information security (MS); information technology in financial services industry (MS); information technology in the pharmaceutical industry (MS); information technology outsourcing management (MS); project management (MS, Certificate); software engineering (MS); telecommunications (MS). *Program availability:* Part-time, evening/weekend. *Students:* 248 full-time (87 women), 54 part-time (20 women); includes 25 minority (8 Black or African American, non-Hispanic/Latino; 17 Asian, non-Hispanic/Latino), 245 international. Average age 27. In 2018, 202 master's, 16 other advanced degrees awarded. Terminal master's awarded for partial completion of doctoral program. *Degree requirements:* For master's, thesis optional, minimum B average in major field and overall; for Certificate, minimum B average. *Entrance requirements:* For master's, GRE/GMAT scores: GRE scores are required for all applicants applying to a full-time graduate program in the Schaefer School of Engineering and Science (SES). International applicants must submit TOEFL/IELTS scores and fulfill the English Language Proficiency Requirements in order to be considered. Additional exam requirements/recommendations for international students: Required—TOEFL (minimum score 74 iBT), IELTS (minimum score 6). *Application deadline:* For fall admission, 4/1 for domestic and international students; for spring admission, 11/1 for domestic and international students; for summer admission, 5/1 for domestic students. Applications are processed on a rolling basis. Application fee: $60. Electronic applications accepted. *Expenses: Tuition:* Full-time $35,960; part-time $1620 per credit. *Required fees:* $1290; $600 per semester. Tuition and fees vary according to course load. *Financial support:* Fellowships, research assistantships, teaching assistantships, career-related internships or fieldwork, Federal Work-Study, scholarships/grants, and unspecified assistantships available. Financial award application deadline: 2/15; financial award

applicants required to submit FAFSA. *Unit head:* Dr. Gregory Prastacos, Dean of SB, 201-216-8366, E-mail: gprastac@stevens.edu. *Application contact:* Graduate Admissions, 888-783-8367, Fax: 888-511-1306, E-mail: graduate@stevens.edu. Website: https://www.stevens.edu/school-business/masters-programs/information-systems

Stevens Institute of Technology, Graduate School, School of Business, Program in Management, Hoboken, NJ 07030. Offers general management (MS); global innovation management (MS); human resource management (MS); information management (MS); project management (MS); technology commercialization (MS); technology management (MS). *Program availability:* Part-time, evening/weekend. *Faculty:* 58 full-time (8 women), 18 part-time/adjunct (3 women). *Students:* 101 full-time (41 women), 66 part-time (34 women); includes 14 minority (4 Black or African American, non-Hispanic/Latino; 9 Asian, non-Hispanic/Latino; 1 Hispanic/Latino), 115 international. Average age 28. In 2018, 70 master's awarded. Terminal master's awarded for partial completion of doctoral program. *Degree requirements:* For master's, thesis optional, minimum B average in major field and overall. *Entrance requirements:* For master's, GRE/GMAT scores: GRE scores are required for all applicants applying to a full-time graduate program in the Schaefer School of Engineering and Science (SES). International applicants must submit TOEFL/IELTS scores and fulfill the English Language Proficiency Requirements in order to be considered. Additional exam requirements/recommendations for international students: Required—TOEFL (minimum score 74 iBT), IELTS (minimum score 6). *Application deadline:* For fall admission, 4/1 for domestic and international students; for spring admission, 11/1 for domestic and international students; for summer admission, 5/1 for domestic students. Applications are processed on a rolling basis. Application fee: $60. Electronic applications accepted. *Expenses: Tuition:* Full-time $35,960; part-time $1620 per credit. *Required fees:* $1290; $600 per semester. Tuition and fees vary according to course load. *Financial support:* Fellowships, research assistantships, teaching assistantships, career-related internships or fieldwork, Federal Work-Study, scholarships/grants, and unspecified assistantships available. Financial award application deadline: 2/15; financial award applicants required to submit FAFSA. *Unit head:* Dr. Gregory Prascatos, Dean of SB, 201-216 8366, E-mail: gprastac@stevens.edu. *Application contact:* Graduate Admissions, 888-783-8367, Fax: 888-511-1306, E-mail: graduate@stevens.edu. Website: https://www.stevens.edu/school-business/masters-programs/management

Stevenson University, Program in Healthcare Management, Owings Mills, MD 21153. Offers project management (MS); quality management and patient safety (MS). *Program availability:* Part-time, online only, 100% online. *Faculty:* 1 (woman) full-time, 7 part-time/adjunct (6 women). *Students:* 4 full-time (1 woman), 36 part-time (30 women); includes 17 minority (11 Black or African American, non-Hispanic/Latino; 2 Asian, non-Hispanic/Latino; 1 Hispanic/Latino; 3 Two or more races, non-Hispanic/Latino). Average age 32. 32 applicants, 41% accepted, 9 enrolled. In 2018, 18 master's awarded. *Degree requirements:* For master's, capstone course. *Entrance requirements:* For master's, official college transcripts from all previous academic work, minimum cumulative GPA of 3.0 in past academic work, minimum grade of B in statistics or an upper-level math and English composition, two professional letters of recommendation with at least one from a current or past supervisor, 250-word personal statement. *Application deadline:* Applications are processed on a rolling basis. Electronic applications accepted. *Expenses:* Contact institution. *Financial support:* Unspecified assistantships available. Financial award applicants required to submit FAFSA. *Unit head:* Sharon Buchbinder, PhD, Coordinator, 443-394-9290, Fax: 443-394-0538, E-mail: sbuchbinder@stevenson.edu. *Application contact:* Amanda Millar, Director, Admissions, 443-352-4243, Fax: 443-394-0538, E-mail: amillar@stevenson.edu. Website: http://www.stevenson.edu

Thomas Edison State University, School of Business and Management, Program in Management, Trenton, NJ 08608. Offers accounting (MSM); organizational leadership (MSM); project management (MSM). *Program availability:* Part-time, 100% online. *Degree requirements:* For master's, final capstone project. *Entrance requirements:* For master's, bachelor's degree from a regionally-accredited college or university; minimum 2 letters of recommendation; 3-5 years of related working experience; current resume. Additional exam requirements/recommendations for international students: Required—TOEFL (minimum score 550 paper-based; 79 iBT). Electronic applications accepted.

Trident University International, College of Business Administration, Program in Business Administration, Cypress, CA 90630. Offers business administration (PhD); conflict and negotiation management (MBA); criminal justice administration (MBA); entrepreneurship (MBA); finance (MBA); general management (MBA); government accounting (MBA); human resource management (MBA); information security and digital assurance management (MBA); information technology management (MBA); international business (MBA); logistics management (MBA); marketing (MBA); project management (MBA); public management (MBA); quality management (MBA); strategic leadership (MBA). *Program availability:* Part-time, evening/weekend, online learning. *Degree requirements:* For doctorate, comprehensive exam, thesis/dissertation, defense of dissertation. *Entrance requirements:* For master's, minimum GPA of 2.5 (students with GPA 3.0 or greater may transfer up to 30% of graduate level credits); for doctorate, minimum GPA of 3.4, curriculum vitae, course work in research methods or statistics. Additional exam requirements/recommendations for international students: Required—TOEFL. Electronic applications accepted.

Universidad del Turabo, Graduate Programs, School of Business and Entrepreneurship, Program in Project Management, Gurabo, PR 00778-3030. Offers MBA. *Entrance requirements:* For master's, GRE, EXADEP or GMAT, interview, essay, official transcript, recommendation letters. Electronic applications accepted.

Universidad Nacional Pedro Henriquez Urena, Graduate School, Santo Domingo, Dominican Republic. Offers agricultural diversity (MS), including horticultural/fruit production, tropical animal production; conservation of monuments and cultural assets (M Arch); ecology and environment (MS); environmental engineering (MEE); international relations (MA); natural resource management (MS); political science (MA); project optimization (MPM); project feasibility (MPM); project management (MPM); sanitation engineering (ME); science for teachers (MS); tropical Caribbean architecture (M Arch).

Université du Québec à Chicoutimi, Graduate Programs, Program in Project Management, Chicoutimi, QC G7H 2B1, Canada. Offers M Sc. *Program availability:* Part-time. *Entrance requirements:* For master's, appropriate bachelor's degree, proficiency in French.

Université du Québec à Montréal, Graduate Programs, Program in Project Management, Montréal, QC H3C 3P8, Canada. Offers MGP, Diploma. *Program availability:* Part-time. *Entrance requirements:* For master's and Diploma, appropriate bachelor's degree or equivalent, proficiency in French.

Université du Québec à Rimouski, Graduate Programs, Program in Project Management, Rimouski, QC G5L 3A1, Canada. Offers M Sc, Diploma. Programs offered jointly with Université du Québec à Chicoutimi, Université du Québec à Trois-Rivières, Université du Québec en Outaouais, Université du Québec en Abitibi-Témiscamingue, and Université du Québec à Montréal. *Program availability:* Part-time. *Entrance requirements:* For master's, proficiency in French, appropriate bachelor's degree.

Université du Québec en Abitibi-Témiscamingue, Graduate Programs, Program in Project Management, Rouyn-Noranda, QC J9X 5E4, Canada. Offers M Sc, DESS. M Sc offered jointly with Université du Québec à Chicoutimi, Université du Québec à Rimouski, Université du Québec à Trois-Rivières, Université du Québec en Outaouais, and Université du Québec à Montréal. *Program availability:* Part-time. *Entrance requirements:* For master's, appropriate bachelor's degree, proficiency in French.

Université du Québec en Outaouais, Graduate Programs, Program in Project Management, Gatineau, QC J8X 3X7, Canada. Offers M Sc, MA, DESS, Diploma. Programs offered jointly with Universite du Quebec a Chicoutimi, Universite du Quebec a Rimouski, Universite du Quebec a Trois-Rivieres, Universite du Quebec en Abitibi-T'miscamingue, and Universite du Quebec a Montreal. *Program availability:* Part-time, evening/weekend. *Degree requirements:* For master's, thesis (for some programs). *Entrance requirements:* For master's, appropriate bachelor's degree, proficiency in French.

The University of Alabama in Huntsville, School of Graduate Studies, College of Business Administration, Programs in Business and Management, Huntsville, AL 35899. Offers business analytics (MSMS); federal contracting and procurement management (Certificate); human resource management (MSM); management (MBA), including acquisition management, entrepreneurship, federal contract accounting, finance, human resource management, logistics and supply chain management, marketing, project management; supply chain management (Certificate); technology and innovation management (Certificate). *Accreditation:* AACSB. *Program availability:* Part-time. *Faculty:* 8 full-time (3 women). *Students:* 57 full-time (25 women), 152 part-time (76 women); includes 37 minority (20 Black or African American, non-Hispanic/Latino; 2 American Indian or Alaska Native, non-Hispanic/Latino; 6 Asian, non-Hispanic/Latino; 8 Hispanic/Latino; 1 Two or more races, non-Hispanic/Latino), 24 international. Average age 33. 178 applicants, 80% accepted, 84 enrolled. In 2018, 96 master's, 1 other advanced degree awarded. *Degree requirements:* For master's, comprehensive exam, thesis or alternative. *Entrance requirements:* For master's, GMAT (minimum score 500), minimum AACSB index of 1080. Additional exam requirements/recommendations for international students: Required—TOEFL (minimum score 550 paper-based; 80 iBT), IELTS (minimum score 6.5). *Application deadline:* For fall admission, 7/15 priority date for domestic students, 4/1 priority date for international students; for spring admission, 11/30 priority date for domestic students, 9/1 priority date for international students. Applications are processed on a rolling basis. Application fee: $50. Electronic applications accepted. *Expenses: Tuition, area resident:* Full-time $10,632; part-time $412 per credit hour. Tuition, state resident: full-time $10,632. Tuition, nonresident: full-time $23,604; part-time $412 per credit hour. *Required fees:* $582; $582. Tuition and fees vary according to course load and program. *Financial support:* In 2018–19, 15 students received support, including 15 teaching assistantships with full tuition reimbursements available (averaging $4,871 per year); research assistantships with full tuition reimbursements available, career-related internships or fieldwork, Federal Work-Study, institutionally sponsored loans, scholarships/grants, health care benefits, tuition waivers (full and partial), and unspecified assistantships also available. Support available to part-time students. Financial award application deadline: 4/1; financial award applicants required to submit FAFSA. *Faculty research:* Supply chain management, management of research and development, international marketing and branding, organizational behavior and human resource management, social networks and computational economics. *Unit head:* Dr. Fan Tseng, Chair, 256-824-6804, Fax: 256-824-6328, E-mail: fan.tseng@uah.edu. *Application contact:* Jennifer Pettitt, Director of Advising, 256-824-6681, Fax: 256-824-7571, E-mail: jennifer.pettitt@uah.edu.

University of Calgary, Faculty of Graduate Studies, Schulich School of Engineering, Program in Civil Engineering, Calgary, AB T2N 1N4, Canada. Offers avalanche mechanics (M Sc, PhD); civil engineering (M Eng, M Sc, PhD); energy and environment engineering (M Eng, M Sc, PhD); environmental engineering (M Eng, M Sc, PhD); geotechnical engineering (M Eng, M Sc, PhD); materials science (M Eng, M Sc, PhD); project management (M Eng, M Sc, PhD); structures and solid mechanics (M Eng, M Sc, PhD); transportation engineering (M Eng, M Sc, PhD); water resources (M Eng, M Sc, PhD). *Program availability:* Part-time. *Degree requirements:* For master's, thesis; for doctorate, thesis/dissertation, written and oral candidacy exam. *Entrance requirements:* For master's, minimum GPA of 3.0; for doctorate, minimum GPA of 3.5. Additional exam requirements/recommendations for international students: Required—TOEFL (minimum score 580 paper-based; 93 iBT), IELTS (minimum score 7). Electronic applications accepted. *Faculty research:* Geotechnical engineering, energy and environment, transportation, project management, structures and solid mechanics.

University of California, Berkeley, UC Berkeley Extension, Certificate Programs in Business, Berkeley, CA 94720. Offers accounting (Certificate); business administration (Certificate); finance (Certificate); human resource management (Certificate); management (Certificate); marketing (Certificate); project management (Certificate). *Accreditation:* AACSB. *Program availability:* Online learning.

University of California, Berkeley, UC Berkeley Extension, International Diploma Programs, Berkeley, CA 94720. Offers business administration (Certificate); finance (Certificate); global business management (Certificate); marketing (Certificate); project management (Certificate). *Accreditation:* AACSB.

University of Connecticut, Graduate School, School of Business, Storrs, CT 06269. Offers accounting (MS, PhD); business (PhD); business administration (MBA); business analytics and project management (MS); finance (PhD); financial risk management (MS); health care management and insurance studies (MBA); human resource management (MS); management (PhD); management consulting (MBA); marketing (PhD); marketing intelligence (MBA); operations and information management (PhD). *Accreditation:* AACSB. *Degree requirements:* For master's, comprehensive exam; for doctorate, thesis/dissertation. *Entrance requirements:* For master's and doctorate, GMAT. Additional exam requirements/recommendations for international students: Required—TOEFL (minimum score 550 paper-based). Electronic applications accepted.

University of Dallas, Satish and Yasmin Gupta College of Business, Irving, TX 75062. Offers accounting (MBA, MS); business administration (DBA); business analytics (MS); business management (MBA); corporate finance (MBA); cybersecurity (MS); finance (MS); financial services (MBA); global business (MBA, MS); health services management (MBA); human resource management (MBA); information and technology management (MS); information assurance (MBA); information technology (MBA); information technology service management (MBA); marketing management (MBA); organization development (MBA); project management (MBA); sports and entertainment management (MBA); strategic leadership (MBA); supply chain management (MBA). *Accreditation:* AACSB. *Program availability:* Part-time, evening/weekend, 100% online. *Students:* 147 full-time (56 women), 584 part-time (232 women); includes 402 minority (204 Black or African American, non-Hispanic/Latino; 95 Asian, non-Hispanic/Latino; 92 Hispanic/Latino; 2 Native Hawaiian or other Pacific Islander, non-Hispanic/Latino; 9 Two or more races, non-Hispanic/Latino), 113 international. Average age 34. 992 applicants, 30% accepted, 157 enrolled. In 2018, 336 master's, 5 doctorates awarded. *Degree requirements:* For doctorate, thesis/dissertation. *Entrance requirements:* For master's and doctorate, U.S. bachelor's degree with a minimum cumulative GPA of 2.0 from a regionally accredited college or university (or comparable foreign degree); minimum 3.0 GPA in any graduate-level coursework completed; good academic standing with all

colleges attended. Additional exam requirements/recommendations for international students: Required—TOEFL (minimum score 80 iBT), IELTS (minimum score 6.5), PTE (minimum score 67). *Application deadline:* Applications are processed on a rolling basis. Application fee: $50. Electronic applications accepted. *Expenses:* $1250 per credit hour. *Financial support:* In 2018–19, 291 students received support. Research assistantships, teaching assistantships, scholarships/grants, and unspecified assistantships available. Support available to part-time students. Financial award application deadline: 2/15; financial award applicants required to submit FAFSA. *Unit head:* Brett J.L. Landry, Dean, 972-721-5356, E-mail: blandry@udallas.edu. *Application contact:* Breonna Collins, Director, Graduate Admissions, 972-7215304, E-mail: bcollins@udallas.edu.
Website: http://www.udallas.edu/cob/

University of Denver, University College, Denver, CO 80208. Offers arts and culture (MA, Certificate); communication management (MS, Certificate), including translation studies (Certificate), world history and culture (Certificate); environmental policy and management (MS); geographic information systems (MS); global affairs (MA, Certificate), including human capital in organizations (Certificate), philanthropic leadership (Certificate), project management (Certificate), strategic innovation and change (Certificate); healthcare leadership (MS); information communications and technology (MS); leadership and organizations (MS); professional creative writing (MA, Certificate), including emergency planning and response (Certificate), organizational security (Certificate); security management (MS, Certificate); strategic human resources (Certificate). *Program availability:* Part-time, evening/weekend, 100% online, blended/hybrid learning. *Faculty:* 4 full-time (2 women), 108 part-time/adjunct (51 women). *Students:* 51 full-time (26 women), 1,291 part-time (733 women); includes 337 minority (112 Black or African American, non-Hispanic/Latino; 6 American Indian or Alaska Native, non-Hispanic/Latino; 46 Asian, non-Hispanic/Latino; 132 Hispanic/Latino; 3 Native Hawaiian or other Pacific Islander, non-Hispanic/Latino; 38 Two or more races, non-Hispanic/Latino), 75 international. Average age 34. 834 applicants, 87% accepted, 423 enrolled. In 2018, 443 master's, 232 other advanced degrees awarded. *Degree requirements:* For master's, capstone project. *Entrance requirements:* For master's, baccalaureate degree, transcripts, two letters of recommendation, personal statement, resume, writing sample (Master of Arts in Professional Creative Writing). Additional exam requirements/recommendations for international students: Required—TOEFL (minimum score 550 paper-based; 80 iBT). *Application deadline:* For fall admission, 6/19 priority date for domestic students, 6/14 priority date for international students; for winter admission, 10/25 priority date for domestic students, 9/27 priority date for international students; for spring admission, 2/7 priority date for domestic students, 1/10 priority date for international students; for summer admission, 4/24 priority date for domestic students, 3/27 priority date for international students. Applications are processed on a rolling basis. Application fee: $75. Electronic applications accepted. *Expenses:* $8,280 per year half-time. *Financial support:* In 2018–19, 38 students received support. Teaching assistantships available. Financial award applicants required to submit FAFSA. *Unit head:* Dr. Michael McGuire, Dean, 303-871-3518, E-mail: michael.mcguire@du.edu. *Application contact:* Admission Team, 303-871-2291, E-mail: ucoladm@du.edu.
Website: http://universitycollege.du.edu/

University of Fairfax, Graduate Programs, Vienna, VA 22182. Offers business administration (DBA); computer science (MCS); cybersecurity (MBA, MS); general business administration (MBA); information technology (MBA); project management (MBA).

University of Houston, College of Technology, Department of Information and Logistics Technology, Houston, TX 77204. Offers information security (MS); supply chain and logistics technology (MS); technology project management (MS). *Program availability:* Part-time. *Degree requirements:* For master's, project or thesis (most programs). *Entrance requirements:* For master's, GMAT. Additional exam requirements/recommendations for international students: Required—TOEFL (minimum score 550 paper-based; 79 iBT). Electronic applications accepted.

University of Houston–Downtown, Marilyn Davies College of Business, MBA Program, Houston, TX 77002. Offers accounting (MBA); finance (MBA); human resource management (MBA); international business (MBA); investment management (MBA); leadership (MBA); project management and process improvement (MBA); sales management and business development (MBA); supply chain management (MBA). *Accreditation:* AACSB. *Program availability:* Part-time, evening/weekend. *Entrance requirements:* For master's, GMAT, two letters of recommendation from professional references, personal statement, resume. Additional exam requirements/recommendations for international students: Required—TOEFL (minimum score 81 iBT). Electronic applications accepted. *Expenses:* Contact institution.

The University of Kansas, Graduate Studies, School of Engineering, Program in Project Management, Overland Park, KS 66045. Offers ME, MS. *Program availability:* Part-time. *Students:* 14 full-time (2 women), 45 part-time (19 women); includes 19 minority (5 Black or African American, non-Hispanic/Latino; 5 Asian, non-Hispanic/Latino; 4 Hispanic/Latino; 5 Two or more races, non-Hispanic/Latino), 3 international. Average age 36. 43 applicants, 91% accepted, 30 enrolled. In 2018, 16 master's awarded. *Entrance requirements:* For master's, undergraduate degree in engineering or closely-related science, minimum undergraduate GPA of 3.0, two years' full-time work experience in engineering or technology-based company (for ME), current resume, official transcript, 3 letters of recommendation. Additional exam requirements/recommendations for international students: Required—TOEFL, IELTS. Application fee: $65 ($85 for international students). Electronic applications accepted. *Unit head:* Herbert R. Tuttle, Assistant Dean, 913-897-8561, E-mail: htuttle@ku.edu. *Application contact:* Jennifer Keleher-Price, Graduate Admissions Contact, 913-897-8635, E-mail: jkeleher-price@ku.edu.
Website: https://edwardscampus.ku.edu/overview-masters-project-management

University of Louisiana at Lafayette, BI Moody III College of Business Administration, Lafayette, LA 70504. Offers accounting (MS); business administration (MBA); entrepreneurship (MBA); finance (MBA); global management (MBA); health care administration (MBA); hospitality management (MBA); human resource management (MBA); project management (MBA); sales leadership (MBA). *Accreditation:* AACSB. *Program availability:* Part-time, evening/weekend. *Entrance requirements:* For master's, GRE General Test. Additional exam requirements/recommendations for international students: Required—TOEFL (minimum score 550 paper-based).

University of Management and Technology, Program in Business Administration, Arlington, VA 22209-1609. Offers general management (MBA, DBA); project management (MBA). *Program availability:* Part-time, 100% online. *Degree requirements:* For master's, comprehensive exam; for doctorate, thesis/dissertation. *Entrance requirements:* For master's, 3 recommendations, resume. Additional exam requirements/recommendations for international students: Required—TOEFL (minimum score 530 paper-based; 71 iBT). Electronic applications accepted. *Expenses: Tuition:* Full-time $7020; part-time $1170 per course.

University of Management and Technology, Program in Computer Science, Arlington, VA 22209-1609. Offers computer science (MS); information technology (AC); project management (AC); software engineering (MS). *Program availability:* Part-time, evening/weekend, online learning. *Entrance requirements:* For master's, 3 recommendations, resume. Additional exam requirements/recommendations for international students: Required—TOEFL (minimum score 530 paper-based; 71 iBT). Electronic applications accepted. *Expenses: Tuition:* Full-time $7020; part-time $1170 per course.

University of Management and Technology, Program in Management, Arlington, VA 22209-1609. Offers acquisition management (MS, AC); criminal justice administration (MS); general management (MS); project management (MS, AC). *Program availability:* Part-time, evening/weekend, online learning. *Entrance requirements:* For master's, 3 recommendations, resume. Additional exam requirements/recommendations for international students: Required—TOEFL (minimum score 530 paper-based; 71 iBT). Electronic applications accepted. *Expenses: Tuition:* Full-time $7020; part-time $1170 per course.

The University of Manchester, Alliance Manchester Business School, M15 6PB, United Kingdom. Offers accounting and finance (M Sc); business (M Ent); business analysis and strategic management (M Sc); business analytics: operational research and risk analysis (M Sc); business psychology (M Sc); corporate communications and reputation management (M Sc); finance (M Sc); finance and business economics (M Sc); human resource management and industrial relations (M Sc); innovation management and entrepreneurship (M Sc); international business and management (M Sc); international human resource management and comparative industrial relations (M Sc); management (M Sc); marketing (M Sc); operations, project and supply chain management (M Sc); organizational psychology (M Sc); quantitative finance (M Sc). *Entrance requirements:* For master's, UK 2:1 honours degree or overseas equivalent. Additional exam requirements/recommendations for international students: Required—TOEFL (minimum score 100 iBT), IELTS (minimum score 7), PTE. Electronic applications accepted. *Faculty research:* Accounting and finance, management sciences and marketing, people management and organization, innovation management and policy, decision sciences.

University of Mary, Gary Tharaldson School of Business, Bismarck, ND 58504-9652. Offers business administration (MBA); energy management (MBA, MS); executive (MBA, MS); health care (MBA, MS); human resource management (MBA); project management (MBA, MPM); virtuous leadership (MBA, MPM, MS). *Program availability:* Part-time, evening/weekend. *Entrance requirements:* For master's, minimum GPA of 2.5. Additional exam requirements/recommendations for international students: Required—TOEFL (minimum score 550 paper-based; 80 iBT). Electronic applications accepted.

University of Michigan–Dearborn, College of Engineering and Computer Science, MS Program in Program and Project Management, Dearborn, MI 48128. Offers MS. *Program availability:* Part-time, evening/weekend, 100% online. *Faculty:* 17 full-time (4 women), 9 part-time/adjunct (1 woman). *Students:* 6 full-time (3 women), 39 part-time (14 women); includes 14 minority (5 Black or African American, non-Hispanic/Latino; 6 Asian, non-Hispanic/Latino; 3 Hispanic/Latino), 9 international. Average age 35. 31 applicants, 61% accepted, 10 enrolled. In 2018, 17 master's awarded. *Entrance requirements:* For master's, regionally-accredited (or international equivalent) undergraduate degree in engineering, business, economics, math, computer science or other physical sciences; at least two years of practical work experience. Additional exam requirements/recommendations for international students: Required—TOEFL (minimum score 560 paper-based; 84 iBT), IELTS (minimum score 6.5). *Application deadline:* For fall admission, 8/1 for domestic students, 5/1 for international students; for winter admission, 12/1 for domestic students, 9/1 for international students; for spring admission, 4/1 for domestic students, 1/1 for international students. Applications are processed on a rolling basis. Application fee: $60. Electronic applications accepted. *Expenses:* Tuition, state resident: full-time $15,380; part-time $88 per credit hour. Tuition, nonresident: full-time $23,948; part-time $1377 per credit hour. *Required fees:* $780; $780 $390. Tuition and fees vary according to course level, course load, degree level, program, reciprocity agreements and student level. *Financial support:* In 2018–19, 9 students received support. Scholarships/grants, unspecified assistantships, and non-resident tuition scholarships available. Support available to part-time students. Financial award application deadline: 3/1; financial award applicants required to submit FAFSA. *Faculty research:* Risk analysis, decision sciences, project scheduling, project optimization, agile project management. *Unit head:* Dr. Armen Zakarian, Chair, 313-593-5361, E-mail: zakarian@umich.edu. *Application contact:* Office of Graduate Studies, 313-583-6321, E-mail: umd-graduatestudies@umich.edu.
Website: https://umdearborn.edu/cecs/departments/industrial-and-manufacturing-systems-engineering/graduate-programs/ms-program-and-project-management

University of Nebraska at Omaha, Graduate Studies, College of Information Science and Technology, Department of Information Systems and Quantitative Analysis, Omaha, NE 68182. Offers data analytics (Certificate); information assurance (Certificate); information technology (MIT, PhD); management information systems (MS); project management (Certificate); systems analysis and design (Certificate). *Program availability:* Part-time, evening/weekend. *Degree requirements:* For master's, comprehensive exam, thesis (for some programs); for doctorate, comprehensive exam, thesis/dissertation. *Entrance requirements:* For master's, GRE General Test, minimum GPA of 3.0, 3 letters of recommendation, writing sample, resume, official transcripts; for doctorate, GMAT or GRE General Test, minimum GPA of 3.0, 3 letters of recommendation, writing sample, resume, official transcripts; for Certificate, minimum GPA of 3.0, official transcripts. Additional exam requirements/recommendations for international students: Required—TOEFL, IELTS, PTE. Electronic applications accepted.

University of North Alabama, College of Business, Florence, AL 35632-0001. Offers business administration (MBA), including accounting, enterprise resource planning systems, executive, finance, health care management, information systems, international business, project management. *Accreditation:* AACSB; ACBSP. *Program availability:* Part-time, 100% online, blended/hybrid learning. *Entrance requirements:* For master's, GMAT, GRE, minimum GPA of 2.75 in last 60 hours, 2.5 overall (on a 3.0 scale); 27 hours of course work in business and economics. Additional exam requirements/recommendations for international students: Required—TOEFL (minimum score 79 iBT), IELTS (minimum score 6), PTE (minimum score 54). Electronic applications accepted.

University of Oklahoma, College of Arts and Sciences, Department of Psychology, Norman, OK 73019. Offers organizational dynamics (MA, Graduate Certificate), including human resource management (Graduate Certificate), organizational dynamics (MA), project management (Graduate Certificate); psychology (MS, PhD), including psychology. *Faculty:* 19 full-time (9 women), 1 (woman) part-time/adjunct. *Students:* 63 full-time (41 women), 33 part-time (22 women); includes 22 minority (3 Black or African American, non-Hispanic/Latino; 3 American Indian or Alaska Native, non-Hispanic/Latino; 3 Asian, non-Hispanic/Latino; 8 Hispanic/Latino; 5 Two or more races, non-Hispanic/Latino), 8 international. Average age 30. 95 applicants, 20% accepted, 17 enrolled. In 2018, 23 master's, 8 doctorates, 15 other advanced degrees awarded. Terminal master's awarded for partial completion of doctoral program. *Degree requirements:* For master's, comprehensive exam, thesis; for doctorate, comprehensive exam, thesis/dissertation. *Entrance requirements:* For master's and doctorate, GRE.

Additional exam requirements/recommendations for international students: Required—TOEFL (minimum score 79 iBT) or IELTS (minimum score 6.5). *Application deadline:* For fall admission, 1/1 for domestic and international students. Application fee: $50 ($100 for international students). Electronic applications accepted. *Expenses:* Tuition, state resident: full-time $5683.20; part-time $236.80 per credit hour. Tuition, nonresident: full-time $20,342; part-time $847.60 per credit hour. *International tuition:* $20,342.40 full-time. *Required fees:* $2894.20; $110.05 per credit hour. $126.50 per semester. Tuition and fees vary according to course load and program. *Financial support:* Fellowships, research assistantships, and teaching assistantships available. Financial award application deadline: 6/1; financial award applicants required to submit FAFSA. *Faculty research:* Behavioral statistics; leadership for innovation; eyewitness testimony; risk assessment and literacy; theory of mind. *Unit head:* Dr. Eric Day, Chair, 405-325-4511, Fax: 405-325-4737, E-mail: eday@ou.edu. *Application contact:* Dr. Shane Connelly, Professor/Chair, 405-325-4580, Fax: 405-325-4737, E-mail: sconnelly@ou.edu.
Website: http://www.ou.edu/cas/psychology

University of Ottawa, Faculty of Graduate and Postdoctoral Studies, Faculty of Engineering, Engineering Management Program, Ottawa, ON K1N 6N5, Canada. Offers engineering management (M Eng); information technology (Certificate); project management (Certificate). *Degree requirements:* For master's, thesis or alternative. *Entrance requirements:* For master's and Certificate, honors degree or equivalent, minimum B average. Electronic applications accepted.

University of Phoenix–Bay Area Campus, School of Business, San Jose, CA 95134-1805. Offers accountancy (MS); accounting (MBA); business administration (MBA, DBA); energy management (MBA); global management (MBA); health care management (MBA); human resource management (MBA); human resources management (MM); management (MM); marketing (MBA); organizational leadership (DM); project management (MBA); public administration (MPA); technology management (MBA). *Accreditation:* ACBSP. *Program availability:* Evening/weekend, online learning. *Degree requirements:* For master's, thesis (for some programs). *Entrance requirements:* For master's, minimum undergraduate GPA of 3.0, 3 years of work experience. Additional exam requirements/recommendations for international students: Required—TOEFL (minimum score 550 paper-based; 79 iBT). Electronic applications accepted.

University of Phoenix–Online Campus, School of Business, Phoenix, AZ 85034-7209. Offers accountancy (MS); accounting (MBA, Certificate); business administration (MBA); energy management (MBA); global management (MBA); health care management (MBA); human resource management (MBA, Certificate); human resources management (MM); management (MM); marketing (MBA, Certificate); project management (MBA, Certificate); public administration (MBA, MM); technology management (MBA). *Program availability:* Evening/weekend, online learning. *Entrance requirements:* Additional exam requirements/recommendations for international students: Required—TOEFL, TOEIC (Test of English as an International Communication), Berlitz Online English Proficiency Exam, PTE, or IELTS. Electronic applications accepted. *Expenses:* Contact institution.

University of Phoenix–Phoenix Campus, School of Business, Tempe, AZ 85282-2371. Offers accounting (MBA, MS, Certificate); business administration (MBA); energy management (MBA); global management (MBA); health care management (MBA); human resource management (MBA, Certificate); management (MM); marketing (MBA); project management (MBA); technology management (MBA). *Program availability:* Evening/weekend, online learning. *Entrance requirements:* Additional exam requirements/recommendations for international students: Required—TOEFL, TOEIC (Test of English as an International Communication), Berlitz Online English Proficiency Exam, PTE, or IELTS. Electronic applications accepted. *Expenses:* Contact institution.

University of Regina, Faculty of Graduate Studies and Research, Kenneth Levene Graduate School of Business, Program in Business Administration, Regina, SK S4S 0A2, Canada. Offers business foundations (PGD); engineering management (MBA); executive business administration (EMBA); international business (MBA); leadership (M Admin); organizational leadership (Master's Certificate); project management (Master's Certificate); public safety management (MBA). *Program availability:* Part-time, evening/weekend. *Students:* 30 full-time (14 women), 9 part-time (5 women). Average age 30. In 2018, 23 master's awarded. *Degree requirements:* For master's, project (for some programs). workplacement for Co-op concentration. *Entrance requirements:* For master's, GMAT, 3 years of relevant work experience, four-year undergraduate degree, post secondary transcript, 2 letters of recommendation; for other advanced degree, GMAT (for PGD), four-year undergraduate degree and 2 years of relevant work experience (for Master's Certificate); 3 years' work experience (for PGD). Additional exam requirements/recommendations for international students: Required—TOEFL (minimum score 580 paper-based; 80 iBT), IELTS (minimum score 6.5), PTE (minimum score 59), other options are CAEL, MELAB, CANTEST or U of R ESl; GMAT is mandatory. *Application deadline:* For fall admission, 3/1 for domestic and international students; for winter admission, 7/1 for domestic and international students; for spring admission, 10/1 for domestic and international students; for summer admission, 10/1 for domestic and international students. Applications are processed on a rolling basis. Application fee: $100. Electronic applications accepted. *Expenses:* One academic year is 18,752. International students will pay additional 1,191.75 for International surcharge per semester. *Financial support:* Fellowships, research assistantships, teaching assistantships, career-related internships or fieldwork, Federal Work-Study, scholarships/grants, unspecified assistantships, and travel award and Graduate scholarship Base Funds available. Support available to part-time students. Financial award application deadline: 9/30. *Faculty research:* Business policy and strategy, production and operations management, human behavior in organizations, financial management, social issues in business. *Unit head:* Dr. Gina Grandy, Dean, 306-585-4435, Fax: 306-585-5361, E-mail: business.dean@uregina.ca. *Application contact:* Adrian Pitariu, Associate Dean, Research and Graduate Programs, 306-585-6294, Fax: 306-585-5361, E-mail: business.AD.levene@uregina.ca.
Website: http://www.uregina.ca/business/levene/

The University of Tennessee at Chattanooga, Engineering Management and Technology Program, Chattanooga, TN 37403. Offers construction management (Graduate Certificate); engineering management (MS); fundamentals of engineering management (Graduate Certificate); leadership and ethics (Graduate Certificate); logistics and supply chain management (Graduate Certificate); power systems management (Graduate Certificate); project and technology management (Graduate Certificate); quality management (Graduate Certificate). *Program availability:* 100% online, blended/hybrid learning. *Degree requirements:* For master's, thesis. *Entrance requirements:* For master's, GRE General Test, letters of recommendation; minimum undergraduate GPA of 2.7 overall or 3.0 in final two years; for Graduate Certificate, baccalaureate degree and professional experience or have already been admitted to engineering/engineering management graduate program. Additional exam requirements/recommendations for international students: Required—TOEFL (minimum score 550 paper-based; 79 iBT), IELTS (minimum score 6). Electronic applications accepted. *Expenses:* Contact institution. *Faculty research:* Plant layout design, lean manufacturing, Six Sigma, value management, product development.

The University of Texas at Dallas, Naveen Jindal School of Management, Program in Organizations, Strategy and International Management, Richardson, TX 75080. Offers business administration (MBA); executive business administration (EMBA); global leadership (EMBA); healthcare leadership and management (MS); healthcare management (EMBA); innovation and entrepreneurship (MS); international management studies (MS, PhD); management science (MS, PhD); project management (EMBA); systems engineering and management (MS); MS/MBA. *Program availability:* Part-time, evening/weekend. *Faculty:* 19 full-time (6 women), 33 part-time/adjunct (12 women). *Students:* 587 full-time (237 women), 777 part-time (361 women); includes 456 minority (83 Black or African American, non-Hispanic/Latino; 226 Asian, non-Hispanic/Latino; 110 Hispanic/Latino; 37 Two or more races, non-Hispanic/Latino), 316 international. Average age 34. 1,452 applicants, 43% accepted, 376 enrolled. In 2018, 556 master's, 23 doctorates awarded. *Degree requirements:* For doctorate, thesis/dissertation. *Entrance requirements:* For master's and doctorate, GMAT. Additional exam requirements/recommendations for international students: Required—TOEFL (minimum score 550 paper-based). *Application deadline:* For fall admission, 7/15 for domestic students, 5/1 priority date for international students; for spring admission, 11/15 for domestic students, 9/1 priority date for international students. Applications are processed on a rolling basis. Application fee: $50 ($100 for international students). Electronic applications accepted. *Expenses: Tuition, area resident:* Full-time $13,458. Tuition, state resident: full-time $13,458. Tuition, nonresident: full-time $26,852. *International tuition:* $26,852 full-time. Tuition and fees vary according to course load. *Financial support:* In 2018–19, 102 students received support, including 24 research assistantships with partial tuition reimbursements available (averaging $37,400 per year), 83 teaching assistantships with partial tuition reimbursements available (averaging $25,119 per year); Federal Work-Study, institutionally sponsored loans, scholarships/grants, and unspecified assistantships also available. Support available to part-time students. Financial award application deadline: 4/30; financial award applicants required to submit FAFSA. *Faculty research:* International accounting, international trade and finance, economic development, international economics. *Unit head:* Dr. Seung-Hyun Lee, Area Coordinator, 972-883-6267, Fax: 972-883-5977, E-mail: sxl029100@utdallas.edu. *Application contact:* Dr. Seung-Hyun Lee, Area Coordinator, 972-883-6267, Fax: 972-883-5977, E-mail: sxl029100@utdallas.edu.
Website: http://jindal.utdallas.edu/osim/

University of Wisconsin–Platteville, School of Graduate Studies, Distance Learning Center, Online Master of Science in Project Management Program, Platteville, WI 53818-3099. Offers MS. *Program availability:* Part-time. *Degree requirements:* For master's, thesis or alternative. *Entrance requirements:* Additional exam requirements/recommendations for international students: Required—TOEFL (minimum score 550 paper-based; 79 iBT), IELTS (minimum score 6.5). Electronic applications accepted.

University of Wisconsin–Stout, Graduate School, College of Management, Program in Operations and Supply Management, Menomonie, WI 54751. Offers operations management (MS); project management (MS); quality management (MS); supply chain management (MS).

Virginia International University, School of Business, Fairfax, VA 22030. Offers accounting (MBA, MS); entrepreneurship (MBA); executive management (Graduate Certificate); global logistics (MBA); health care management (MBA); hospitality and tourism management (MBA); human resources management (MBA); international business management (MBA); international finance (MBA); marketing management (MBA); mass media and public relations (MBA); project management (MBA, MS). *Program availability:* Part-time, online learning. *Entrance requirements:* For master's and Graduate Certificate, bachelor's degree. Additional exam requirements/recommendations for international students: Required—TOEFL (minimum score 550 paper-based; 80 iBT), IELTS (minimum score 6). Electronic applications accepted.

Virginia International University, School of Computer Information Systems, Fairfax, VA 22030. Offers business intelligence (Graduate Certificate); business intelligence and data analytics (MIS); computer science (MS), including computer animation and gaming, cybersecurity, data management networking, intelligent systems, software applications development, software engineering; cybersecurity (MIS); data management (MIS); enterprise project management (MIS); health informatics (MIS); information assurance (MIS); information systems (Graduate Certificate); information systems management (MS, Graduate Certificate); information technology (MS); information technology audit and compliance (Graduate Certificate); knowledge management (MIS); software engineering (MS). *Program availability:* Part-time, online learning. *Entrance requirements:* For master's, bachelor's degree. Additional exam requirements/recommendations for international students: Required—TOEFL (minimum score 550 paper-based; 80 iBT), IELTS. Electronic applications accepted.

Viterbo University, Master of Business Administration Program, La Crosse, WI 54601-4797. Offers general business administration (MBA); health care management (MBA); international business (MBA); leadership (MBA); project management (MBA). *Accreditation:* ACBSP. *Program availability:* Part-time, evening/weekend. *Degree requirements:* For master's, 34 semester credits. *Entrance requirements:* For master's, bachelor's degree, transcripts, minimum undergraduate cumulative GPA of 3.0, 2 letters of reference, 3-5 page essay. Additional exam requirements/recommendations for international students: Recommended—TOEFL (minimum score 550 paper-based). Electronic applications accepted. *Expenses:* Contact institution.

Walden University, Graduate Programs, School of Management, Minneapolis, MN 55401. Offers accounting (MBA, MS, DBA), including accounting for the professional (MS), accounting with CPA emphasis (MS), self-designed (MS); advanced project management (Graduate Certificate); applied project management (Graduate Certificate); auditing (Graduate Certificate); bridge to business administration (Post-Doctoral Certificate); bridge to management (Post-Doctoral Certificate); business management (Graduate Certificate); communication (MBA); corporate finance (MBA); digital marketing (Graduate Certificate); entrepreneurship (DBA); entrepreneurship and small business (MBA); finance (MS, DBA), including finance for the professional (MS), finance with CFA/investment (MS), finance with CPA emphasis (MS); global supply chain management (DBA); healthcare management (MBA, DBA); human resource management (MBA, MS, Graduate Certificate), including functional human resource management (MS), general program (MS), integrating functional and strategic human resource management (MS), organizational strategy (MS); human resources management (DBA); information systems management (DBA); international business (MBA, DBA); leadership (MBA, MS, DBA, Graduate Certificate), including general program (MS), human resource leadership (MS), leader development (MS), self-designed (MS); management (MS, PhD), including communications (MS), finance (PhD), general program (MS), healthcare management (MS), human resource management (MS), human resources management (PhD), information systems management (PhD), international business (MS), leadership (MS), leadership and organizational change (PhD), marketing (MS), project management (MS), strategy and operations (MS); managerial accounting (Graduate Certificate); marketing (MBA, MS, DBA); project management (MBA, MS, DBA); self-designed (MBA, DBA); social impact management (DBA); technology entrepreneurship (DBA). *Accreditation:* ACBSP. *Program availability:* Part-time, evening/weekend, online only, 100% online. *Degree requirements:* For master's, thesis (for some programs), residency (for EMBA); for

Project Management

doctorate, thesis/dissertation (for some programs), residency. *Entrance requirements:* For master's, bachelor's degree or higher; minimum GPA of 2.5; official transcripts; goal statement (for some programs); access to computer and Internet; for doctorate, master's degree or higher; three years of related professional or academic experience (preferred); minimum GPA of 3.0; goal statement and current resume (for select programs); official transcripts; access to computer and Internet; for other advanced degree, relevant work experience; access to computer and Internet. Additional exam requirements/recommendations for international students: Required—TOEFL (minimum score 550 paper-based, 79 iBT), IELTS (minimum score 6.5), Michigan English Language Assessment Battery (minimum score 82), or PTE (minimum score 53). Electronic applications accepted.

Walsh College of Accountancy and Business Administration, Graduate Programs, Program in Information Technology, Troy, MI 48083. Offers chief information officer (MSIT); cybersecurity (MSIT); data science (MSIT); global project and program management (MSIT). *Program availability:* Part-time, evening/weekend. *Faculty:* 2 full-time (1 woman), 10 part-time/adjunct (2 women). *Students:* 3 full-time (1 woman), 66 part-time (25 women); includes 22 minority (14 Black or African American, non-Hispanic/Latino; 4 Asian, non-Hispanic/Latino; 1 Hispanic/Latino; 3 Two or more races, non-Hispanic/Latino), 13 international. Average age 36. 23 applicants, 83% accepted, 13 enrolled. In 2018, 22 master's awarded. *Entrance requirements:* For master's, minimum overall cumulative GPA of 2.75 from all colleges previously attended. Additional exam requirements/recommendations for international students: Required—TOEFL (minimum score 550 paper-based, 79-80 internet based), IELTS (6.5), Michigan Test of English Language Proficiency, or MTELP (80). *Application deadline:* Applications are processed on a rolling basis. Application fee: $35. Electronic applications accepted. *Expenses:* $785 per credit hour plus $175 student support fee per semester. International students pay $785 per credit hour plus $175 student support fee and $275 international student fee per semester. *Financial support:* In 2018–19, 3 students received support. Scholarships/grants and Tuition Exchange Program available. Financial award application deadline: 6/30; financial award applicants required to submit FAFSA. *Faculty research:* Business intelligence, data and decision-making, cyber security, project management, mobile technologies. *Unit head:* Dr. David Schippers, Chair, Information Technology and Decision Sciences, 248-823-1635, Fax: 248-689-0920, E-mail: dschippe@walshcollege.edu. *Application contact:* Karen Mahaffy, Executive Director, Admissions and Enrollment Services, 248-823-1600, Fax: 248-823-1611, E-mail: kmahaffy@walshcollege.edu.

Wayland Baptist University, Graduate Programs, Programs in Business Administration/Management, Plainview, TX 79072-6998. Offers accounting (MBA); general business (MBA); health care administration (MAM, MBA); human resource management (MAM, MBA); international management (MBA); management (MBA, D Mgt); management information systems (MBA); organization management (MAM); project management (MBA). *Program availability:* Part-time, evening/weekend, online learning. *Degree requirements:* For master's, capstone course. *Entrance requirements:* For master's, GMAT, GRE or MAT. Additional exam requirements/recommendations for international students: Required—TOEFL (minimum score 500 paper-based; 61 iBT). Electronic applications accepted.

Western Carolina University, Graduate School, College of Business, Program in Project Management, Cullowhee, NC 28723. Offers MPM, Graduate Certificate. *Program availability:* Part-time, evening/weekend, online learning. *Entrance requirements:* For master's, GMAT or GRE, work experience in project management, appropriate undergraduate degree with minimum GPA of 3.0, employer recommendation, resume. Additional exam requirements/recommendations for international students: Required—TOEFL (minimum score 550 paper-based; 79 iBT). *Expenses: Tuition, area resident:* Full-time $4435. Tuition, state resident: full-time $4435. Tuition, nonresident: full-time $14,842. *International tuition:* $14,842 full-time. *Required fees:* $2979. Part-time tuition and fees vary according to course load, degree level and program.

Wilmington University, College of Technology, New Castle, DE 19720-6491. Offers cybersecurity (MS); information assurance (MS); information systems technologies (MS); management and management information systems (MS); technology project management (MS); Web design (MS). *Program availability:* Part-time, evening/weekend. *Entrance requirements:* Additional exam requirements/recommendations for international students: Required—TOEFL (minimum score 500 paper-based). Electronic applications accepted.

Wingate University, Porter B. Byrum School of Business, Wingate, NC 28174. Offers accounting (MAC); corporate innovation (MBA); finance (MBA); general management (MBA); healthcare management (MBA); marketing (MBA); project management (MBA). *Accreditation:* ACBSP. *Program availability:* Part-time, evening/weekend. *Entrance requirements:* For master's, GMAT, work experience, 2 letters of recommendation. Electronic applications accepted. *Expenses:* Contact institution. *Faculty research:* Stochastic processes, business ethics, regional economic development, municipal finance, consumer behavior.

Section 18
Quality Management

This section contains a directory of institutions offering graduate work in quality management. Additional information about programs listed in the directory may be obtained by writing directly to the dean of a graduate school or chair of a department at the address given in the directory.

For programs offering related work, see also in this book *Business Administration and Management.*

CONTENTS

Program Directory

Quality Management

California Intercontinental University, School of Information Technology, Irvine, CA 92614. Offers information systems and enterprise resource management (DBA); information systems and knowledge management (MBA); project and quality management (MBA).

California State University, Dominguez Hills, College of Extended and International Education, Program in Quality Assurance, Carson, CA 90747-0001. Offers MS. *Program availability:* Part-time, evening/weekend, 100% online. *Degree requirements:* For master's, thesis. *Entrance requirements:* For master's, minimum GPA of 2.75. Additional exam requirements/recommendations for international students: Required—TOEFL. Electronic applications accepted. *Expenses:* Contact institution. *Faculty research:* Six Sigma, lean thinking, risk management, quality management.

Calumet College of Saint Joseph, Program in Quality Assurance, Whiting, IN 46394-2195. Offers MS.

Eastern Michigan University, Graduate School, College of Engineering and Technology, School of Engineering, Programs in Quality Management, Ypsilanti, MI 48197. Offers MS, Graduate Certificate. *Program availability:* Part-time, evening/weekend, online learning. *Students:* 2 full-time (1 woman), 36 part-time (12 women); includes 11 minority (7 Black or African American, non-Hispanic/Latino; 2 Asian, non-Hispanic/Latino; 2 Hispanic/Latino). Average age 45. 13 applicants, 69% accepted, 1 enrolled. In 2018, 12 master's, 1 other advanced degree awarded. *Entrance requirements:* Additional exam requirements/recommendations for international students: Required—TOEFL. *Application deadline:* Applications are processed on a rolling basis. Application fee: $45. *Financial support:* Fellowships, research assistantships with full tuition reimbursements, teaching assistantships with full tuition reimbursements, career-related internships or fieldwork, Federal Work-Study, institutionally sponsored loans, scholarships/grants, tuition waivers (partial), and unspecified assistantships available. Support available to part-time students. Financial award applicants required to submit FAFSA. *Application contact:* Dr. Herman Tang, Program Coordinator, 734-487-2040, Fax: 734-487-8755, E-mail: htang2@emich.edu.

Hofstra University, Frank G. Zarb School of Business, Programs in Information Systems, Hempstead, NY 11549. Offers business administration (MBA), including business analytics, information systems, quality management; business analytics (MS); information systems (MS, Advanced Certificate). *Program availability:* Part-time, evening/weekend, blended/hybrid learning. *Students:* 85 full-time (35 women), 31 part-time (16 women); includes 17 minority (2 Black or African American, non-Hispanic/Latino; 9 Asian, non-Hispanic/Latino; 6 Hispanic/Latino), 76 international. Average age 27. 152 applicants, 69% accepted, 27 enrolled. In 2018, 52 master's awarded. *Degree requirements:* For master's, thesis (for some programs), capstone course (for MBA), thesis (for MS), minimum GPA of 3.0. *Entrance requirements:* For master's, GMAT/GRE, 2 letters of recommendation, resume, essay; for Advanced Certificate, GMAT/GRE, 2 letters of recommendation, resume. Additional exam requirements/recommendations for international students: Required—TOEFL (minimum score 550 paper-based; 80 iBT); Recommended—IELTS (minimum score 6). *Application deadline:* Applications are processed on a rolling basis. Application fee: $75. Electronic applications accepted. *Expenses:* $1,375 per credit plus fees. *Financial support:* In 2018–19, 32 students received support, including 27 fellowships with full and partial tuition reimbursements available (averaging $5,630 per year); research assistantships with full and partial tuition reimbursements available, career-related internships or fieldwork, Federal Work-Study, institutionally sponsored loans, scholarships/grants, tuition waivers (full and partial), unspecified assistantships, and scholarships and endowed scholarships also available. Support available to part-time students. Financial award applicants required to submit FAFSA. *Faculty research:* Big data and social media, healthcare IT and analytics, machine learning and artificial intelligence, inventory system and quality management, cybersecurity and information privacy. *Unit head:* Dr. Hak Kim, Chairperson, 516-463-5716, Fax: 516-463-4834, E-mail: hak.j.kim@hofstra.edu. *Application contact:* Sunil Samuel, Assistant Vice President of Admissions, 516-463-4723, Fax: 516-463-4664, E-mail: graduateadmission@hofstra.edu.
Website: http://www.hofstra.edu/business/

Instituto Tecnologico de Santo Domingo, Graduate School, Area of Business, Santo Domingo, Dominican Republic. Offers banking and securities markets (M Mgmt); corporate finance (M Mgmt); human resources management (M Mgmt, Certificate); international trade management (M Mgmt); marketing (M Mgmt); organizational development (M Mgmt); quality and productivity management (Certificate); tax management and planning (M Mgmt); upper management (M Mgmt).

Instituto Tecnológico y de Estudios Superiores de Monterrey, Campus Ciudad de México, Virtual University Division, Ciudad de Mexico, Mexico. Offers administration of information technologies (MA); computer sciences (MA); education (MA, PhD); educational technology (MA); environmental engineering (MA); environmental systems (MA); humanistic studies (MA); industrial engineering (MA); international business for Latin America (MA); quality systems (MA); quality systems and productivity (MA). *Program availability:* Part-time, evening/weekend, online learning. *Entrance requirements:* For master's and doctorate, Instituto entrance exam. Additional exam requirements/recommendations for international students: Required—TOEFL.

Instituto Tecnológico y de Estudios Superiores de Monterrey, Campus Ciudad Juárez, Program in Quality Management, Ciudad Juárez, Mexico. Offers MQM.

Instituto Tecnológico y de Estudios Superiores de Monterrey, Campus Estado de México, Professional and Graduate Division, Estado de Mexico, Mexico. Offers administration of information technologies (MITA); architecture (M Arch); business administration (GMBA, MBA); computer sciences (MCS, PhD); education (M Ed); educational institution administration (MAD); educational technology and innovation (PhD); electronic commerce (MEC); environmental systems (MS); finance (MAF); humanistic studies (MHS); information sciences and knowledge management (MISKM); information systems (MS); manufacturing systems (MS); marketing (MEM); quality systems and productivity (MS); science and materials engineering (PhD); telecommunications management (MTM). *Program availability:* Part-time, online learning. *Degree requirements:* For master's, one foreign language, thesis (for some programs); for doctorate, one foreign language, thesis/dissertation. *Entrance requirements:* For master's, E-PAEP 500, interview; for doctorate, E-PAEP 500, research proposal. Additional exam requirements/recommendations for international students: Required—TOEFL (minimum score 550 paper-based). *Faculty research:* Surface treatments by plasmas, mechanical properties, robotics, graphical computing, mechatronics security protocols.

Instituto Tecnológico y de Estudios Superiores de Monterrey, Campus Irapuato, Graduate Programs, Irapuato, Mexico. Offers administration (MBA); administration of information technology (MAIT); administration of telecommunications (MAT); architecture (M Arch); computer science (MCS); education (M Ed); educational administration (MEA); educational innovation and technology (DEIT); educational technology (MET); electronic commerce (MBA); environmental administration and planning (MEAP); environmental systems (MES); finances (MBA); humanistic studies (MHS); international management for Latin American executives (MIMLAE); library and information science (MLIS); manufacturing quality management (MMQM); marketing research (MBA).

Madonna University, School of Business, Livonia, MI 48150-1173. Offers business administration (MBA); international business (MSBA); leadership studies (MSBA); leadership studies in criminal justice (MSBA); quality and operations management (MSBA). *Program availability:* Part-time, evening/weekend, online learning. *Degree requirements:* For master's, thesis (for some programs), foreign language proficiency (international business). *Entrance requirements:* For master's, GMAT, GRE General Test, minimum GPA of 3.0. Electronic applications accepted. *Expenses: Tuition:* Full-time $15,030; part-time $835 per credit hour. Tuition and fees vary according to degree level and program. *Faculty research:* Management, women in management, future studies.

Mount Mercy University, Program in Business Administration, Cedar Rapids, IA 52402-4797. Offers human resource (MBA); quality management (MBA). *Program availability:* Evening/weekend. *Entrance requirements:* For master's, minimum cumulative GPA of 3.0, 2 letters of recommendation, resume. Additional exam requirements/recommendations for international students: Required—TOEFL (minimum score 570 paper-based; 88 iBT). Electronic applications accepted.

New England College of Business and Finance, Program in Quality Systems Management, Boston, MA 02111-2645. Offers MS.

Northwestern University, School of Professional Studies, Program in Regulatory Compliance, Evanston, IL 60208. Offers clinical research (MS); healthcare compliance (MS); quality systems (MS). Offered in partnership with Northwestern Univesity's Clinical and Translational Sciences Institute. *Program availability:* Part-time, evening/weekend.

Penn State Erie, The Behrend College, Graduate School, Erie, PA 16563. Offers accounting (MPAC); applied clinical psychology (MA); business administration (MBA); quality and manufacturing management (MMM). *Accreditation:* AACSB. *Program availability:* Part-time. *Entrance requirements:* Additional exam requirements/recommendations for international students: Required—TOEFL (minimum score 550 paper-based; 80 iBT), IELTS. Electronic applications accepted.

Rutgers University–New Brunswick, Graduate School-New Brunswick, Program in Statistics, Piscataway, NJ 08854-8097. Offers applied statistics (MS); biostatistics (MS); data mining (MS); quality and productivity management (MS); statistics (MS, PhD). *Program availability:* Part-time. Terminal master's awarded for partial completion of doctoral program. *Degree requirements:* For master's, comprehensive exam, essay, exam, non-thesis essay paper; for doctorate, one foreign language, thesis/dissertation, qualifying oral and written exams. *Entrance requirements:* For master's, GRE General Test; for doctorate, GRE General Test, GRE Subject Test (recommended). Additional exam requirements/recommendations for international students: Required—TOEFL (minimum score 550 paper-based). Electronic applications accepted. *Faculty research:* Probability, decision theory, linear models, multivariate statistics, statistical computing.

San Jose State University, Program in Aviation and Technology, San Jose, CA 95192-0001. Offers quality assurance (MS). *Entrance requirements:* For master's, GRE. Electronic applications accepted.

Southern New Hampshire University, School of Business, Manchester, NH 03106-1045. Offers accounting (MBA, Graduate Certificate); accounting finance (MS); accounting/auditing (MS); accounting/forensic accounting (MS); accounting/management accounting (MS); accounting/taxation (MS); applied economics (MS); athletic administration (MBA, Graduate Certificate); business administration (IMBA, Certificate), including business information systems (Certificate), human resource management (Certificate); business analytics (MBA); business intelligence (MBA); communication (MA), including new media and marketing, public relations; community economic development (MBA); criminal justice (MBA); data analytics (MS); economics (MBA); engineering management (MBA); entrepreneurship (MBA); finance (MBA, MS, Graduate Certificate); finance/corporate finance (MS); finance/investments (MS); forensic accounting (MBA); forensic accounting and fraud examination (Graduate Certificate); healthcare informatics (MBA); healthcare management (MBA); human resource management (MS); human resources (MBA); information technology (MS); information technology management (MBA); international business (PhD); Internet marketing (MBA); leadership (MBA); leadership of nonprofit organizations (Graduate Certificate); management (MS); marketing (MBA, MS, Graduate Certificate); music business (MBA); operations and project management (MS); operations and supply chain management (MBA, Graduate Certificate); organizational leadership (MS); project management (MBA, Graduate Certificate); public administration (MBA, Graduate Certificate); quantitative analysis (MBA); Six Sigma (Graduate Certificate); Six Sigma quality (MBA); social media marketing (MBA, Graduate Certificate); sport management (MBA, MS, Graduate Certificate); sustainability and environmental compliance (MBA); MBA/Certificate. *Accreditation:* ACBSP. *Program availability:* Part-time, evening/weekend, online learning. Terminal master's awarded for partial completion of doctoral program. *Degree requirements:* For master's, one foreign language, comprehensive exam (for some programs), thesis or alternative; for doctorate, one foreign language, comprehensive exam, thesis/dissertation. *Entrance requirements:* For master's, minimum GPA of 2.5; for doctorate, GMAT. Additional exam requirements/recommendations for international students: Required—TOEFL (minimum score 500 paper-based). Electronic applications accepted.

Stevens Institute of Technology, Graduate School, Charles V. Schaefer Jr. School of Engineering and Science, Department of Civil, Environmental, and Ocean Engineering, Program in Construction Management, Hoboken, NJ 07030. Offers construction management (MS, Certificate), including construction accounting/estimating (Certificate), construction engineering (Certificate), construction law/disputes (Certificate), construction/quality management (Certificate). *Program availability:* Part-time, evening/weekend. *Faculty:* 6 part-time/adjunct (1 woman). *Students:* 109 full-time (19 women), 21 part-time (7 women); includes 12 minority (4 Black or African American, non-Hispanic/Latino; 8 Asian, non-Hispanic/Latino), 100 international. Average age 25. In 2018, 49 master's, 3 other advanced degrees awarded. Terminal master's awarded for partial completion of doctoral program. *Degree requirements:* For master's, thesis optional, minimum B average in major field and overall; for Certificate, minimum B average. *Entrance requirements:* For master's, GRE/GMAT scores: GRE scores are required for all applicants applying to a full-time graduate program in the Schaefer School of Engineering and Science (SES). International applicants must submit TOEFL/

IELTS scores and fulfill the English Language Proficiency Requirements in order to be considered. Additional exam requirements/recommendations for international students: Required—TOEFL (minimum score 74 iBT), IELTS (minimum score 6). *Application deadline:* For fall admission, 4/15 for domestic and international students; for spring admission, 11/1 for domestic and international students; for summer admission, 5/1 for domestic students. Applications are processed on a rolling basis. Application fee: $60. Electronic applications accepted. *Expenses: Tuition:* Full-time $35,960; part-time $1620 per credit. *Required fees:* $1290; $600 per semester. Tuition and fees vary according to course load. *Financial support:* Fellowships, research assistantships, teaching assistantships, career-related internships or fieldwork, Federal Work-Study, scholarships/grants, and unspecified assistantships available. Financial award application deadline: 2/15; financial award applicants required to submit FAFSA. *Unit head:* Dr. Jean Zu, Dean of SES, 201-216.8233, Fax: 201-216.8372, E-mail: Jean.Zu@stevens.edu. *Application contact:* Graduate Admission, 888-783-8367, Fax: 888-511-1306, E-mail: graduate@stevens.edu.

Stevenson University, Program in Healthcare Management, Owings Mills, MD 21153. Offers project management (MS); quality management and patient safety (MS). *Program availability:* Part-time, online only, 100% online. *Faculty:* 1 (woman) full-time, 7 part-time/adjunct (6 women). *Students:* 4 full-time (1 woman), 36 part-time (30 women); includes 17 minority (11 Black or African American, non-Hispanic/Latino; 2 Asian, non-Hispanic/Latino; 1 Hispanic/Latino; 3 Two or more races, non-Hispanic/Latino). Average age 32. 32 applicants, 41% accepted, 9 enrolled. In 2018, 18 master's awarded. *Degree requirements:* For master's, capstone course. *Entrance requirements:* For master's, official college transcripts from all previous academic work, minimum cumulative GPA of 3.0 in past academic work, minimum grade of B in statistics or an upper-level math and English composition, two professional letters of recommendation with at least one from a current or past supervisor, 250-word personal statement. *Application deadline:* Applications are processed on a rolling basis. Electronic applications accepted. *Expenses:* Contact institution. *Financial support:* Unspecified assistantships available. Financial award applicants required to submit FAFSA. *Unit head:* Sharon Buchbinder, PhD, Coordinator, 443-394-9290, Fax: 443-394-0538, E-mail: sbuchbinder@stevenson.edu. *Application contact:* Amanda Millar, Director, Admissions, 443-352-4243, Fax: 443-394-0538, E-mail: amillar@stevenson.edu.
Website: http://www.stevenson.edu

Trident University International, College of Business Administration, Program in Business Administration, Cypress, CA 90630. Offers business administration (PhD); conflict and negotiation management (MBA); criminal justice administration (MBA); entrepreneurship (MBA); finance (MBA); general management (MBA); government accounting (MBA); human resource management (MBA); information security and digital assurance management (MBA); information technology management (MBA); international business (MBA); logistics management (MBA); marketing (MBA); project management (MBA); public management (MBA); quality management (MBA); strategic leadership (MBA). *Program availability:* Part-time, evening/weekend, online learning. *Degree requirements:* For doctorate, comprehensive exam, thesis/dissertation, defense of dissertation. *Entrance requirements:* For master's, minimum GPA of 2.5 (students with GPA 3.0 or greater may transfer up to 30% of graduate level credits); for doctorate, minimum GPA of 3.4, curriculum vitae, course work in research methods or statistics. Additional exam requirements/recommendations for international students: Required—TOEFL. Electronic applications accepted.

Trident University International, College of Health Sciences, Program in Health Sciences, Cypress, CA 90630. Offers clinical research administration (MS, Certificate); emergency and disaster management (MS, Certificate); environmental health science (Certificate); health care administration (PhD); health care management (MS), including health informatics; health education (MS, Certificate); health informatics (Certificate); health sciences (PhD); international health (MS); international health: educator or researcher option (PhD); international health: practitioner option (PhD); law and expert witness studies (MS, Certificate); public health (MS); quality assurance (Certificate). *Program availability:* Part-time, evening/weekend, online learning. *Degree requirements:* For doctorate, comprehensive exam, thesis/dissertation, defense of dissertation. *Entrance requirements:* For master's, minimum GPA of 2.5 (students with GPA 3.0 or greater may transfer up to 30% of graduate level credits); for doctorate, minimum GPA of 3.4, curriculum vitae, course work in research methods or statistics. Additional exam requirements/recommendations for international students: Required—TOEFL. Electronic applications accepted.

Universidad de las Americas, A.C., Program in Business Administration, Mexico City, Mexico. Offers finance (MBA); marketing research (MBA); production and quality (MBA).

Universidad del Turabo, Graduate Programs, School of Business and Entrepreneurship, Program in Quality Management, Gurabo, PR 00778-3030. Offers MBA. *Entrance requirements:* For master's, GRE, EXADEP or GMAT, interview, essay, official transcript, recommendation letters. Electronic applications accepted.

The University of Alabama, Graduate School, College of Human Environmental Sciences, Program in Human Environmental Science, Tuscaloosa, AL 35487. Offers interactive technology (MS); quality management (MS); restaurant and meeting management (MS); rural community health (MS); sport management (MS). *Program availability:* Part-time, evening/weekend, online learning. *Degree requirements:* For master's, comprehensive exam. *Entrance requirements:* For master's, GRE (for some specializations), minimum GPA of 3.0. Additional exam requirements/recommendations for international students: Required—TOEFL. Electronic applications accepted. *Faculty research:* Rural health, hospitality management, sport management, interactive technology, consumer quality management, environmental health and safety.

University of Massachusetts Boston, College of Advancing and Professional Studies, Program in Critical and Creative Thinking, Boston, MA 02125-3393. Offers MA, Certificate. *Program availability:* Part-time, evening/weekend. *Faculty:* 1 part-time/adjunct (0 women). *Students:* 2 full-time (both women), 31 part-time (24 women); includes 6 minority (3 Black or African American, non-Hispanic/Latino; 1 Asian, non-Hispanic/Latino; 1 Hispanic/Latino; 1 Two or more races, non-Hispanic/Latino), 5 international. Average age 35. 10 applicants, 90% accepted, 5 enrolled. In 2018, 12 master's, 12 other advanced degrees awarded. *Entrance requirements:* For master's, GRE General Test or MAT, minimum GPA of 3.0; for Certificate, minimum GPA of 2.75. *Application deadline:* For fall admission, 6/1 for domestic students; for spring admission, 11/1 for domestic students. Application fee: $60 ($100 for international students). Electronic applications accepted. *Expenses: Tuition, area resident:* Full-time $17,896. Tuition, state resident: full-time $17,896. Tuition, nonresident: full-time $34,932. *International tuition:* $34,932 full-time. *Required fees:* $355. *Financial support:* Research assistantships, teaching assistantships, career-related internships or fieldwork, Federal Work-Study, and unspecified assistantships available. Support available to part-time students. Financial award application deadline: 3/1; financial award applicants required to submit FAFSA. *Unit head:* Dr. Peter Taylor, Director, 617-287-7636, E-mail: peter.taylor@umb.edu. *Application contact:* Graduate Admissions Coordinator, 617-287-6400, Fax: 617-287-6236, E-mail: graduate.admissions@umb.edu.

The University of Tennessee at Chattanooga, Engineering Management and Technology Program, Chattanooga, TN 37403. Offers construction management (Graduate Certificate); engineering management (MS); fundamentals of engineering management (Graduate Certificate); leadership and ethics (Graduate Certificate); logistics and supply chain management (Graduate Certificate); power systems management (Graduate Certificate); project and technology management (Graduate Certificate); quality management (Graduate Certificate). *Program availability:* 100% online, blended/hybrid learning. *Degree requirements:* For master's, thesis. *Entrance requirements:* For master's, GRE General Test, letters of recommendation; minimum undergraduate GPA of 2.7 overall or 3.0 in final two years; for Graduate Certificate, baccalaureate degree and professional experience or have already been admitted to engineering/engineering management graduate program. Additional exam requirements/recommendations for international students: Required—TOEFL (minimum score 550 paper-based; 79 iBT), IELTS (minimum score 6). Electronic applications accepted. *Expenses:* Contact institution. *Faculty research:* Plant layout design, lean manufacturing, Six Sigma, value management, product development.

The University of Texas at Tyler, Soules College of Business, Department of Management and Marketing, Tyler, TX 75799-0001. Offers cyber security (MBA); engineering management (MBA); general management (MBA); healthcare management (MBA); internal assurance and consulting (MBA); marketing (MBA); oil, gas and energy (MBA); organizational development (MBA); quality management (MBA). *Accreditation:* AACSB. *Program availability:* Part-time, online learning. *Students:* Average age 29. 73 applicants, 96% accepted, 35 enrolled. In 2018, 37 master's awarded. *Entrance requirements:* Additional exam requirements/recommendations for international students: Required—TOEFL (minimum score 550 paper-based). *Application deadline:* For fall admission, 8/17 priority date for domestic students, 7/1 priority date for international students; for spring admission, 12/21 priority date for domestic students, 11/1 priority date for international students. Application fee: $25 ($50 for international students). *Faculty research:* General business, inventory control, institutional markets, service marketing, product distribution, accounting fraud, financial reporting and recognition. *Unit head:* Dr. Krist Swimberghe, Chair, 903-565-5803, E-mail: kswimberghe@uttyler.edu. *Application contact:* Dr. Krist Swimberghe, Chair, 903-565-5803, E-mail: kswimberghe@uttyler.edu.
Website: https://www.uttyler.edu/cbt/manamark/

University of Wisconsin–Stout, Graduate School, College of Management, Program in Operations and Supply Management, Menomonie, WI 54751. Offers operations management (MS); project management (MS); quality management (MS); supply chain management (MS).

Section 19
Quantitative Analysis and Business Analytics

This section contains a directory of institutions offering graduate work in quantitative analysis. Additional information about programs listed in the directory may be obtained by writing directly to the dean of a graduate school or chair of a department at the address given in the directory.

For programs offering related work, see also in this book *Business Administration and Management.*

CONTENTS

Program Directories

Business Analytics

Abilene Christian University, College of Graduate and Professional Studies, Program in Business Administration, Addison, TX 79699. Offers business analytics (MBA); general management (MBA); healthcare administration (MBA); international business (MBA); management: business analytics (MS); management: healthcare administration (MS); management: international business (MS); management: marketing (MS); management: operations and supply chain management (MS); marketing (MBA); nonprofit leadership (MBA). *Program availability:* Part-time, online only, 100% online. *Faculty:* 4 full-time (0 women), 7 part-time/adjunct (3 women). *Students:* 149 full-time (69 women), 53 part-time (25 women); includes 88 minority (42 Black or African American, non-Hispanic/Latino; 2 American Indian or Alaska Native, non-Hispanic/Latino; 4 Asian, non-Hispanic/Latino; 31 Hispanic/Latino; 1 Native Hawaiian or other Pacific Islander, non-Hispanic/Latino; 8 Two or more races, non-Hispanic/Latino), 4 international. 36 applicants, 100% accepted, 32 enrolled. In 2018, 24 master's awarded. *Entrance requirements:* Additional exam requirements/recommendations for international students: Required—TOEFL (minimum score 80 iBT), IELTS (minimum score 6). *Application deadline:* For fall admission, 10/7 for domestic students; for winter admission, 12/20 for domestic students; for spring admission, 2/24 for domestic students; for summer admission, 4/20 for domestic students. Applications are processed on a rolling basis. Application fee: $50. Electronic applications accepted. *Expenses:* $721 per hour. *Financial support:* In 2018–19, 16 students received support. Scholarships/grants available. Financial award application deadline: 7/1; financial award applicants required to submit FAFSA. *Faculty research:* Organizational structure, financial management, cost accounting, unit analysis management. *Unit head:* Dr. Phil Vardiman, Program Director, 325-674-2153, E-mail: pxv02b@acu.edu. *Application contact:* Graduate Advisor, 817-219-7300, E-mail: onlineadmissions@acu.edu.
Website: http://www.acu.edu/online/academics/mba-business-administration.html

American Public University System, AMU/APU Graduate Programs, Charles Town, WV 25414. Offers accounting (MS); applied business analytics (MS); business administration (MBA); criminal justice (MA); cybersecurity studies (MS); educational leadership (M Ed); environmental policy and management (MS); global security (DGS); health information management (MS); history (MA), including American military history, American Revolution, civil war, war since 1945, World War II; information technology (MS); international relations and conflict resolution (MA), including American politics and government, comparative government and development, general, international relations, public policy; national security studies (MA); nursing (MSN); political science (MA); public policy (MPP); reverse logistics management (MA), including comparative and security issues, conflict resolution, international and transnational security issues, peacekeeping; space studies (MS); sports management (MS); strategic intelligence (DSI); teaching (M Ed), including secondary social studies; transportation and logistics management (MA). *Program availability:* Part-time, evening/weekend, online only, 100% online. *Students:* 406 full-time (180 women), 7,826 part-time (3,329 women); includes 2,781 minority (1,438 Black or African American, non-Hispanic/Latino; 44 American Indian or Alaska Native, non-Hispanic/Latino; 193 Asian, non-Hispanic/Latino; 747 Hispanic/Latino; 53 Native Hawaiian or other Pacific Islander, non-Hispanic/Latino; 306 Two or more races, non-Hispanic/Latino), 121 international. Average age 38. In 2018, 2,717 master's awarded. *Degree requirements:* For master's, comprehensive exam or practicum; for doctorate, practicum. *Entrance requirements:* For master's, official transcript showing earned bachelor's degree from institution accredited by recognized accrediting body. Additional exam requirements/recommendations for international students: Required—TOEFL (minimum score 550 paper-based), IELTS (minimum score 6.5). *Application deadline:* Applications are processed on a rolling basis. Application fee: $0. Electronic applications accepted. *Financial support:* Scholarships/grants available. Financial award applicants required to submit FAFSA. *Unit head:* Dr. Wallace Boston, President, 877-468-6268, Fax: 304-728-2348, E-mail: president@apus.edu. *Application contact:* Yoci Deal, Associate Vice President, Graduate and International Admissions, 877-468-6268, Fax: 304-724-3764, E-mail: info@apus.edu.
Website: http://www.apus.edu

Ashland University, Dauch College of Business and Economics, Ashland, OH 44805-3702. Offers accounting (MBA); business analytics (MBA); entrepreneurship (MBA); financial management (MBA); global management (MBA); health care management and leadership (MBA); human resource management (MBA); human resources (MBA); management information systems (MBA); project management (MBA); sport management (MBA); supply chain management (MBA). *Accreditation:* ACBSP. *Program availability:* Part-time, evening/weekend, 100% online, blended/hybrid learning. Terminal master's awarded for partial completion of doctoral program. *Degree requirements:* For master's, thesis optional, capstone course. *Entrance requirements:* For master's, 2 years of full-time work experience. Additional exam requirements/recommendations for international students: Required—TOEFL (minimum score 550 paper-based; 78 iBT). Electronic applications accepted. *Expenses:* Contact institution. *Faculty research:* Relationship marketing strategy, executive compensation and company performance, online marketplaces in electronic commerce, diversity training in campus recreation departments, entrepreneurship in developing and emerging economies.

Babson College, F. W. Olin Graduate School of Business, Babson Park, MA 02457-0310. Offers accounting (MSA); advanced management (Certificate); business administration (MBA); business analytics (MS); finance (MS); global entrepreneurship (MS); technological entrepreneurship (MS). *Accreditation:* AACSB. *Program availability:* Part-time, evening/weekend, online learning. *Entrance requirements:* For master's, GMAT, 2 years of work experience, resume, letters of recommendation. Additional exam requirements/recommendations for international students: Required—TOEFL (minimum score 100 iBT), IELTS (minimum score 6.5). Electronic applications accepted. *Faculty research:* Entrepreneurship, sustainability, global markets, process of innovation, social media and advertising.

Baldwin Wallace University, Graduate Programs, School of Business, Program in Business Analytics, Berea, OH 44017-2088. Offers MBA. *Program availability:* Part-time-only, evening/weekend, blended/hybrid learning. *Students:* 12 full-time (6 women), 22 part-time (10 women); includes 5 minority (3 Black or African American, non-Hispanic/Latino; 1 Hispanic/Latino; 1 Two or more races, non-Hispanic/Latino), 1 international. Average age 33. 6 applicants, 100% accepted, 4 enrolled. In 2018, 10 master's awarded. *Entrance requirements:* For master's, GMAT or minimum GPA of 3.0, bachelor's degree in any field, work experience. Additional exam requirements/recommendations for international students: Required—TOEFL (minimum score 550 paper-based; 79 iBT), IELTS can be accepted in place of TOEFL. *Application deadline:* For fall admission, 7/25 for domestic students; for spring admission, 12/15 for domestic students; for summer admission, 4/15 for domestic students. Applications are processed on a rolling basis. Application fee: $0. Electronic applications accepted. *Expenses:* $31,284 to complete program. *Financial support:* In 2018–19, 1 student received support. Scholarships/grants and tuition discounts available. Financial award applicants required to submit FAFSA. *Unit head:* Dr. Susan Kuznik, Associate Dean, Graduate Business Programs, 440-826-2053, Fax: 440-826-3868, E-mail: skuznik@bw.edu. *Application contact:* Laura Spencer, Graduate Business Admission Specialist, 440-826-2191, Fax: 440-826-3868, E-mail: lspencer@bw.edu.
Website: business.bw.edu

Bentley University, McCallum Graduate School of Business, Graduate Business Certificate Program, Waltham, MA 02452-4705. Offers accounting (GBC); business analytics (GBC); business ethics (GBC); financial planning (GBC); fraud and forensic accounting (GBC); marketing analytics (GBC); taxation (GBC). *Accreditation:* AACSB. *Program availability:* Part-time, evening/weekend. *Faculty:* 118 full-time (38 women), 25 part-time/adjunct (4 women). *Students:* 10 part-time (6 women); includes 3 minority (all Asian, non-Hispanic/Latino), 1 international. Average age 39. 10 applicants, 90% accepted, 4 enrolled. In 2018, 73 GBCs awarded. *Entrance requirements:* For degree, GMAT or GRE General Test (may be waived for qualified applicants), Transcripts; Resume; 2 essays; Two letters of recommendation; Interview (may be requested by Bentley). Additional exam requirements/recommendations for international students: Required—TOEFL (minimum score 100) or IELTS (minimum score 7). *Application deadline:* For fall admission, 7/31 for domestic students, 6/30 for international students; for spring admission, 1/1 for domestic students, 11/1 for international students. Applications are processed on a rolling basis. Application fee: $150. Electronic applications accepted. *Expenses:* Contact institution. *Financial support:* In 2018–19, 1 student received support. Scholarships/grants available. Financial award application deadline: 6/1; financial award applicants required to submit FAFSA. *Application contact:* Office of Graduate Admissions, 781-891-2108, E-mail: applygrad@bentley.edu.
Website: https://catalog.bentley.edu/graduate/programs/certificates

Bentley University, McCallum Graduate School of Business, Master's Program in Business Analytics, Waltham, MA 02452-4705. Offers MS. *Program availability:* Part-time, evening/weekend. *Faculty:* 118 full-time (38 women), 25 part-time/adjunct (4 women). *Students:* 153 full-time (95 women), 38 part-time (17 women); includes 10 minority (all Asian, non-Hispanic/Latino), 143 international. Average age 26. 397 applicants, 70% accepted, 77 enrolled. In 2018, 49 master's awarded. *Entrance requirements:* For master's, GMAT or GRE General Test (may be waived for qualified applicants), Transcripts; Resume; Two essays; Two letters of recommendation; Interview (may be requested by Bentley). Additional exam requirements/recommendations for international students: Required—TOEFL (minimum score 100) or IELTS (minimum score 7). *Application deadline:* For fall admission, 7/31 for domestic students, 6/30 for international students; for spring admission, 1/1 for domestic students, 11/1 for international students. Applications are processed on a rolling basis. Application fee: $150. Electronic applications accepted. *Financial support:* In 2018–19, 98 students received support. Scholarships/grants and unspecified assistantships available. Financial award application deadline: 6/1; financial award applicants required to submit FAFSA. *Unit head:* Mihaela Predescu, Associate Professor and MSBA Program Director, 781-891-2876, E-mail: mpredescu@bentley.edu. *Application contact:* Office of Graduate Admissions, 781-891-2108, E-mail: applygrad@bentley.edu.
Website: https://www.bentley.edu/academics/graduate-programs/masters-business-analytics

Boston University, Metropolitan College, Department of Administrative Sciences, Boston, MA 02215. Offers applied business analytics (MS); economic development and tourism management (MSAS); enterprise risk management (MS); financial management (MS); global marketing management (MS); innovation and technology (MSAS); insurance management (MS); project management (MS); supply chain management (MS). *Accreditation:* AACSB. *Program availability:* Part-time, evening/weekend, 100% online, blended/hybrid learning. *Faculty:* 27 full-time (5 women), 39 part-time/adjunct (5 women). *Students:* 617 full-time (351 women), 574 part-time (290 women); includes 196 minority (47 Black or African American, non-Hispanic/Latino; 2 American Indian or Alaska Native, non-Hispanic/Latino; 75 Asian, non-Hispanic/Latino; 60 Hispanic/Latino; 12 Two or more races, non-Hispanic/Latino), 730 international. Average age 28. 2,259 applicants, 76% accepted, 594 enrolled. In 2018, 441 master's awarded. *Degree requirements:* For master's, thesis optional. *Entrance requirements:* For master's, 1 year of work experience, minimum GPA of 3.0. Additional exam requirements/recommendations for international students: Required—TOEFL (minimum score 84 iBT). *Application deadline:* For fall admission, 8/1 priority date for domestic students, 6/1 priority date for international students; for spring admission, 12/1 priority date for domestic students, 11/15 priority date for international students; for summer admission, 4/1 priority date for domestic students, 3/1 priority date for international students. Applications are processed on a rolling basis. Application fee: $85. Electronic applications accepted. *Expenses:* Contact institution. *Financial support:* In 2018–19, 15 students received support, including 16 research assistantships (averaging $8,400 per year), 30 teaching assistantships (averaging $3,400 per year); career-related internships or fieldwork, Federal Work-Study, and unspecified assistantships also available. Financial award applicants required to submit FAFSA. *Faculty research:* International business, innovative process. *Unit head:* Dr. John Sullivan, Chair, 617-353-3016, E-mail: adminsc@bu.edu. *Application contact:* Enrollment Services, 617-358-8162, E-mail: met@bu.edu.
Website: http://www.bu.edu/met/academic-community/departments/administrative-sciences/

Boston University, Questrom School of Business, Boston, MA 02215. Offers business (EMBA, MBA); business analytics (MS); management (PhD); management studies (MSMS); mathematical finance (MS, PhD); JD/MBA; MBA/MA; MBA/MPH; MBA/MS; MD/MBA. *Accreditation:* AACSB. *Program availability:* Part-time, evening/weekend. *Faculty:* 85 full-time (23 women), 28 part-time/adjunct (10 women). *Students:* 724 full-time (322 women), 636 part-time (286 women); includes 225 minority (43 Black or African American, non-Hispanic/Latino; 1 American Indian or Alaska Native, non-Hispanic/Latino; 104 Asian, non-Hispanic/Latino; 57 Hispanic/Latino; 20 Two or more races, non-Hispanic/Latino), 451 international. Average age 28. 1,069 applicants, 40% accepted, 164 enrolled. In 2018, 585 master's, 11 doctorates awarded. *Degree requirements:* For doctorate, comprehensive exam, thesis/dissertation. *Entrance requirements:* For master's, GMAT or GRE (for MBA and MS in mathematical finance programs), essay, resume, 2 letters of recommendation, official transcripts; for doctorate, GMAT or GRE, personal statement, resume, 3 letters of recommendation, official transcripts. Additional exam requirements/recommendations for international students: Required—TOEFL (minimum score 600 paper-based, 90 iBT), IELTS (6.5), or PTE. *Application deadline:* For fall admission, 3/18 for domestic and international students; for spring admission, 11/7 for domestic and international students. Application fee: $125. Electronic applications accepted. *Expenses:* Contact institution. *Financial support:* Career-related internships or fieldwork, Federal Work-Study, institutionally sponsored loans, scholarships/grants, and tuition waivers (partial) available. Support

available to part-time students. Financial award applicants required to submit FAFSA. *Faculty research:* Digital innovation, sustainable energy, corporate social responsibility, finance, marketing. *Unit head:* Kenneth W. Freeman, Professor/Dean, 617-353-9720, Fax: 617-353-5581, E-mail: kfreeman@bu.edu. *Application contact:* Meredith C. Siegel, Assistant Dean, Graduate Admissions Office, 617-353-2670, Fax: 617-353-7368, E-mail: mba@bu.edu.
Website: http://www.bu.edu/questrom/

California Polytechnic State University, San Luis Obispo, Orfalea College of Business, Program in Business Analytics, San Luis Obispo, CA 93407. Offers MS. *Students:* 32 full-time (11 women); includes 9 minority (1 Asian, non-Hispanic/Latino; 7 Hispanic/Latino; 1 Two or more races, non-Hispanic/Latino), 9 international. Average age 24. In 2018, 29 master's awarded. *Degree requirements:* For master's, thesis. *Entrance requirements:* For master's, GMAT. Additional exam requirements/recommendations for international students: Required—TOEFL (minimum score 80 iBT). *Application deadline:* For fall admission, 5/1 for domestic students, 4/1 for international students. Applications are processed on a rolling basis. Application fee: $55. Electronic applications accepted. *Expenses: Tuition, area resident:* Full-time $7176; part-time $4164 per year. Tuition, state resident: full-time $10,965. Tuition, nonresident: full-time $10,965. *Required fees:* $6336; $3711. *Financial support:* Fellowships, career-related internships or fieldwork, Federal Work-Study, institutionally sponsored loans, scholarships/grants, and unspecified assistantships available. Support available to part-time students. Financial award application deadline: 3/2; financial award applicants required to submit FAFSA. *Faculty research:* Management of high-tech firms, Pacific Rim, capital market structures, economics of environmental policy, marketing of services. *Unit head:* Dr. Scott Dawson, Dean, 805-756-2705, E-mail: scdawson@calpoly.edu. *Application contact:* Dr. Scott Dawson, Dean, 805-756-2705, E-mail: scdawson@calpoly.edu.
Website: http://www.cob.calpoly.edu/gradbusiness/degree-programs/ms-business-analytics/

California State University, East Bay, Office of Graduate Studies, College of Business and Economics, Program in Business Analytics, Hayward, CA 94542-3000. Offers MS. *Degree requirements:* For master's, comprehensive exam or thesis. *Entrance requirements:* For master's, baccalaureate degree, minimum undergraduate GPA of 2.5. Additional exam requirements/recommendations for international students: Required—TOEFL (minimum score 550 paper-based; 79 iBT), IELTS (minimum score 6.5).

California State University, Fullerton, Graduate Studies, College of Business and Economics, Program in Business Administration, Fullerton, CA 92831-3599. Offers business administration (MBA); business analytics (MBA); international business (MBA); organizational leadership (MBA); risk management and insurance (MBA). *Accreditation:* AACSB. *Program availability:* Part-time. *Entrance requirements:* For master's, GMAT.

California University of Pennsylvania, School of Graduate Studies and Research, Eberly College of Science and Technology, Program in Business Administration, California, PA 15419-1394. Offers business analytics (MBA); entrepreneurship (MBA); healthcare management (MBA). *Program availability:* Part-time, evening/weekend. *Degree requirements:* For master's, comprehensive exam. *Entrance requirements:* For master's, minimum GPA of 3.0, official transcripts. Additional exam requirements/recommendations for international students: Required—TOEFL (minimum score 550 paper-based). Electronic applications accepted. *Faculty research:* Economics, applied economics, consumer behavior, technology and business, impact of technology.

Case Western Reserve University, Weatherhead School of Management, Program in Business Analytics, Cleveland, OH 44106. Offers MSM. *Expenses: Tuition:* Full-time $45,168; part-time $1939 per credit hour. *Required fees:* $36; $18 per semester. $18 per semester.

Central European University, Department of Economics, 1051, Hungary. Offers business administration (PhD); business analytics (M Sc); economic policy in global markets (MA); economics (MA, PhD); finance (MS); global economic relations (MA); technology management and innovation (MS). *Program availability:* Part-time. *Degree requirements:* For master's, one foreign language, thesis; for doctorate, one foreign language, comprehensive exam, thesis/dissertation. *Entrance requirements:* For master's and doctorate, interview. Additional exam requirements/recommendations for international students: Required—TOEFL (minimum score 570 paper-based); Recommended—IELTS (minimum score 6.5). Electronic applications accepted. *Faculty research:* Economic theory (microeconomics and macroeconomics) and econometrics, as well as study of many applied fields, including labor economics, health economics and economics of education, industrial organization, monetary economics, international economics, law and economics, comparative institutional economics, corporate governance, and economics of transition.

Clark University, Graduate School, Graduate School of Management, Business Administration Program, Worcester, MA 01610-1477. Offers accounting (MBA); finance (MBA); information management and business analytics (MBA); management (MBA); marketing (MBA); social change (MBA); sustainability (MBA). *Accreditation:* AACSB. *Program availability:* Part-time, evening/weekend. *Degree requirements:* For master's, thesis optional. *Entrance requirements:* For master's, GMAT or GRE, 2 references, resume or curriculum vitae, personal statement. Additional exam requirements/recommendations for international students: Required—TOEFL (minimum score 575 paper-based; 90 iBT), IELTS (minimum score 6.5). Electronic applications accepted. *Expenses:* Contact institution. *Faculty research:* Marketing, accounting, human resource management, management information systems, business finance.

Clark University, Graduate School, Graduate School of Management, Program in Business Analytics, Worcester, MA 01610-1477. Offers MSBA. *Entrance requirements:* For master's, GMAT or GRE, 2 references, resume or curriculum vitae, personal statement. Additional exam requirements/recommendations for international students: Required—TOEFL (minimum score 575 paper-based; 90 iBT), IELTS (minimum score 6.5). Electronic applications accepted. *Expenses:* Contact institution.

Cleary University, Online Program in Business Administration, Howell, MI 48843. Offers analytics, technology, and innovation (MBA, Graduate Certificate); financial planning (Graduate Certificate); global leadership (MBA, Graduate Certificate); health care leadership (MBA, Graduate Certificate). *Program availability:* Part-time, evening/weekend, online learning. *Degree requirements:* For master's, thesis. *Entrance requirements:* For master's, bachelor's degree; minimum GPA of 2.5; professional resume indicating minimum of 2 years of management or related experience; undergraduate degree from accredited college or university with at least 18 quarter hours (or 12 semester hours) of accounting study (for MBA in accounting). Additional exam requirements/recommendations for international students: Required—TOEFL (minimum score 550 paper-based; 79 iBT), Michigan English Language Assessment Battery (minimum score 75). Electronic applications accepted.

Clemson University, Graduate School, College of Business, Master of Business Administration Program, Greenville, SC 29601. Offers business administration (MBA); business analytics (MBA); entrepreneurship and innovation (MBA). *Accreditation:* AACSB. *Program availability:* Part-time, evening/weekend, 100% online. *Faculty:* 2 full-time (1 woman), 10 part-time/adjunct (1 woman). *Students:* 113 full-time (55 women), 406 part-time (135 women); includes 88 minority (42 Black or African American, non-Hispanic/Latino; 2 American Indian or Alaska Native, non-Hispanic/Latino; 12 Asian, non-Hispanic/Latino; 22 Hispanic/Latino; 1 Native Hawaiian or other Pacific Islander, non-Hispanic/Latino; 9 Two or more races, non-Hispanic/Latino), 13 international. Average age 31. 404 applicants, 91% accepted, 261 enrolled. In 2018, 209 master's awarded. *Entrance requirements:* For master's, GMAT, resume, unofficial transcripts, personal statement, letters of recommendation. Additional exam requirements/recommendations for international students: Required—TOEFL (minimum score 80 paper-based; 80 iBT); Recommended—IELTS (minimum score 6.5), TSE (minimum score 54). *Application deadline:* For fall admission, 4/15 for international students; for spring admission, 10/15 for international students. Applications are processed on a rolling basis. Application fee: $80 ($90 for international students). Electronic applications accepted. *Expenses:* $9901 per semester full-time resident, $16051 per semester full-time non-resident, $1031 per credit hour part-time resident, $1283 per credit hour part-time non-resident, Concentration in Entrepreneurship & Innovation: $11694 full time all students. *Unit head:* Dr. Greg Pickett, Director and Associate Dean, 864-656-3975, E-mail: pgregor@clemson.edu. *Application contact:* Jane Layton, Academic Program Director, 864-656-8175, E-mail: elayton@clemson.edu.
Website: https://www.clemson.edu/business/departments/mba/

The College of Saint Rose, Graduate Studies, Huether School of Business, Program in Business Analytics, Albany, NY 12203-1419. Offers MS. *Program availability:* Part-time, evening/weekend. *Students:* 13 full-time (5 women), 7 part-time (5 women); includes 2 minority (1 Black or African American, non-Hispanic/Latino; 1 Asian, non-Hispanic/Latino), 7 international. Average age 29. 31 applicants, 84% accepted, 12 enrolled. *Entrance requirements:* Additional exam requirements/recommendations for international students: Required—TOEFL (minimum score 550 paper-based; 80 iBT), IELTS (minimum score 6), PTE (minimum score 56). *Application deadline:* For fall admission, 4/1 priority date for domestic students, 4/1 for international students; for spring admission, 10/15 priority date for domestic students, 10/15 for international students; for summer admission, 3/15 priority date for domestic and international students. Application fee: $40. *Expenses: Tuition:* Full-time $14,382; part-time $799 per credit hour. *Required fees:* $924; $408 per credit. $286. *Financial support:* Career-related internships or fieldwork, scholarships/grants, health care benefits, tuition waivers (partial), and unspecified assistantships available. Support available to part-time students. Financial award application deadline: 4/15. *Unit head:* Eyyub Kibis, Assistant Professor, 518-485-3024, E-mail: kibise@strose.edu. *Application contact:* Daniel Gallagher, Assistant Vice President for Graduate Recruitment and Enrollment, 518-485-3390, Fax: 518-458-5479, E-mail: grad@strose.edu.
Website: https://www.strose.edu/business-analytics-ms/

The College of William and Mary, Raymond A. Mason School of Business, Master of Science in Business Analytics Program, Williamsburg, VA 23187-8795. Offers MS. *Faculty:* 7 full-time (1 woman). *Students:* 78 full-time (32 women); includes 12 minority (4 Black or African American, non-Hispanic/Latino; 4 Asian, non-Hispanic/Latino; 4 Hispanic/Latino), 31 international. Average age 24. 476 applicants, 44% accepted, 80 enrolled. In 2018, 83 master's awarded. *Entrance requirements:* For master's, GRE or GMAT (recommended). Additional exam requirements/recommendations for international students: Required—TOEFL (minimum iBT score of 100), IELTS (7), or 4 years of studies in the U.S. *Application deadline:* For fall admission, 12/1 priority date for domestic and international students; for winter admission, 2/1 for domestic and international students; for spring admission, 4/1 for domestic and international students; for summer admission, 6/1 for domestic and international students. Application fee: $100. Electronic applications accepted. *Expenses:* Contact institution. *Financial support:* Fellowships, research assistantships, teaching assistantships, scholarships/grants, and tuition waivers available. Financial award application deadline: 8/1. *Faculty research:* Artificial intelligence, natural language processing, bot and anomaly detection, Healthcare Info Systems/Informatics, machine learning. *Unit head:* Dr. James R. Bradley, Director, 757-221-2802, E-mail: james.bradley@mason.wm.edu. *Application contact:* Brian Nigg, Program Director, 757-221-1763, Fax: 757-221-2884, E-mail: brian.nigg@mason.wm.edu.
Website: http://mason.wm.edu/programs/msba/index.php

Columbia University, Fu Foundation School of Engineering and Applied Science, Program in Business Analytics, New York, NY 10027. Offers MS.

Creighton University, Graduate School, Heider College of Business, Omaha, NE 68178-0001. Offers accounting (MAC); business administration (MBA, DBA); business intelligence and analytics (MS); finance (M Fin); investment management and financial analysis (MIMFA); JD/MBA; MBA/MIMFA; MD/MBA; Pharm D/MBA. *Accreditation:* AACSB. *Program availability:* Part-time, evening/weekend, 100% online, blended/hybrid learning. *Degree requirements:* For master's, thesis optional; for doctorate, thesis/dissertation optional. *Entrance requirements:* For master's, GMAT, resume, 2 letters of recommendation. Additional exam requirements/recommendations for international students: Required—TOEFL (minimum score 90 iBT). Electronic applications accepted. *Expenses:* Contact institution. *Faculty research:* Small business issues, economics, business analytics.

Dakota State University, College of Business and Information Systems, Madison, SD 57042-1799. Offers analytics (MSA); business analytics (Graduate Certificate); general management (MBA); health informatics (MSHI); information systems (MSIS, D Sc IS); information technology (Graduate Certificate). *Accreditation:* ACBSP. *Program availability:* Part-time, evening/weekend, 100% online, blended/hybrid learning. *Faculty:* 27 full-time (10 women). *Students:* 40 full-time (11 women), 165 part-time (60 women); includes 56 minority (21 Black or African American, non-Hispanic/Latino; 4 American Indian or Alaska Native, non-Hispanic/Latino; 19 Asian, non-Hispanic/Latino; 10 Hispanic/Latino; 1 Native Hawaiian or other Pacific Islander, non-Hispanic/Latino; 1 Two or more races, non-Hispanic/Latino), 38 international. Average age 38. 246 applicants, 47% accepted, 63 enrolled. In 2018, 62 master's, 7 doctorates, 9 other advanced degrees awarded. *Degree requirements:* For master's, comprehensive exam, thesis optional, Examination, integrative project; for doctorate, comprehensive exam, thesis/dissertation, portfolio. *Entrance requirements:* For master's, GRE General Test, Demonstration of information systems skills, minimum GPA of 2.7; for doctorate, GRE General Test, Demonstration of information systems skills; for Graduate Certificate, GMAT. Additional exam requirements/recommendations for international students: Required—PTE (minimum score 53), TOEFL (minimum score 550 paper-based, 76 iBT) or IELTS (6.0). *Application deadline:* For fall admission, 6/15 for domestic students, 4/15 for international students; for spring admission, 11/15 for domestic students, 9/15 priority date for international students; for summer admission, 4/15 for domestic and international students. Applications are processed on a rolling basis. Application fee: $35. Electronic applications accepted. *Expenses:* Contact institution. *Financial support:* In 2018–19, 20 students received support. Research assistantships with partial tuition reimbursements available, teaching assistantships with partial tuition reimbursements available, career-related internships or fieldwork, Federal Work-Study, scholarships/grants, and unspecified assistantships available. Support available to part-time students. Financial award applicants required to submit FAFSA. *Faculty research:* Data mining and analytics, biometrics and information assurance, decision support systems, health informatics, STEM education for K-12 teachers/students and underrepresented populations. *Unit head:* Dr. Dorine Bennett, Dean of College of Business and

Business Analytics

Information Systems, 605-256-5176, E-mail: dorine.bennett@dsu.edu. *Application contact:* Erin Blankespoor, Senior Secretary, Office of Graduate Studies and Research, 605-256-5799, E-mail: erin.blankespoor@dsu.edu.
Website: http://dsu.edu/academics/colleges/college-of-business-and-information-systems

DePaul University, Kellstadt Graduate School of Business, Chicago, IL 60604. Offers accountancy (MBA, MSA); applied economics (MBA); audit and advisory services (MS); business administration (DBA); business analytics (MS); business strategy and decision-making (MBA); computational finance (MS); economics and policy analysis (MS); enterprise risk management (MS); entrepreneurship (MBA, MS); finance (MBA, MS); general business (MBA); hospitality leadership (MBA); hospitality leadership and operational performance (MS); human resources (MS); international business (MBA); management (MBA, MS); management information systems (MBA); marketing (MBA, MS); marketing analysis (MS); marketing strategy and planning (MBA); real estate (MS); real estate finance and investment (MBA); strategy, execution and valuation (MBA); supply chain management (MS); sustainable management (MS); taxation (MS); JD/MBA. *Accreditation:* AACSB. *Program availability:* Part-time, evening/weekend, online learning. *Entrance requirements:* For master's, GMAT/GRE, 2 letters of recommendation, resume, essay, official transcripts. Additional exam requirements/recommendations for international students: Required—TOEFL (minimum score 550 paper-based; 80 iBT). Electronic applications accepted. *Expenses:* Contact institution.

Duke University, The Fuqua School of Business, Master of Quantitative Management Program: Business Analytics, Durham, NC 27708. Offers finance (MQM); forensics (MQM); marketing (MQM); strategy (MQM). *Faculty:* 100 full-time (21 women), 55 part-time/adjunct (12 women). *Students:* 136 full-time (56 women); includes 15 minority (1 Black or African American, non-Hispanic/Latino; 14 Asian, non-Hispanic/Latino), 99 international. Average age 23. In 2018, 136 master's awarded. *Entrance requirements:* For master's, GMAT/GRE, transcripts, essays, resume, recommendation letter, interview. *Application deadline:* For fall admission, 10/21 for domestic and international students; for winter admission, 1/15 for domestic and international students; for spring admission, 2/27 for domestic and international students; for summer admission, 4/6 for domestic and international students. Application fee: $125. Electronic applications accepted. *Expenses:* Contact institution. *Financial support:* Scholarships/grants available. Financial award applicants required to submit FAFSA. *Unit head:* Jeremy Petranka, Associate Dean, 919-660-7778. *Application contact:* Shari Hubert, Associate Dean, Office of Admissions, 919-660-7705, Fax: 919-681-8026, E-mail: mqmbusinessanalytics@fuqua.duke.edu.
Website: https://www.fuqua.duke.edu/programs/mqm-business-analytics

Fairfield University, Dolan School of Business, Fairfield, CT 06824. Offers accounting (MBA, MS, CAS); business analytics (MS); finance (MBA, MS, CAS); information systems and business analytics (MBA); management (MBA, CAS); marketing (MBA, CAS); taxation (CAS). *Accreditation:* AACSB. *Program availability:* Part-time, evening/weekend. *Degree requirements:* For master's, capstone course. *Entrance requirements:* For master's, GMAT (minimum score 500), 2 letters of reference, resume, minimum GPA of 3.0. Additional exam requirements/recommendations for international students: Required—TOEFL (minimum score 550 paper-based; 80 iBT) or IELTS (minimum score 6.5). Electronic applications accepted. *Expenses:* Contact institution. *Faculty research:* International finance, leadership and careers, ethics in accounting, emotions in consumer behavior and organizations, data analytics.

The George Washington University, School of Business, Department of Decision Sciences, Washington, DC 20052. Offers business analytics (MS, Certificate); project management (MS). *Program availability:* Online learning. *Students:* 109 full-time (62 women), 132 part-time (71 women); includes 54 minority (25 Black or African American, non-Hispanic/Latino; 1 American Indian or Alaska Native, non-Hispanic/Latino; 16 Asian, non-Hispanic/Latino; 10 Hispanic/Latino; 2 Two or more races, non-Hispanic/Latino), 137 international. Average age 31. 1,081 applicants, 44% accepted, 108 enrolled. In 2018, 89 master's, 60 other advanced degrees awarded. Application fee: $75. *Financial support:* Tuition waivers available. *Unit head:* Prof. Refik Soyer, Chair, 202-994-6445, E-mail: soyer@gwu.edu. *Application contact:* Christopher Storer, Executive Director, Graduate Admissions, 202-994-1212, E-mail: gwmba@gwu.edu.
Website: http://business.gwu.edu/decisionsciences/

Golden Gate University, Ageno School of Business, San Francisco, CA 94105-2968. Offers accounting (MBA); adaptive leadership (MBA); advanced financial planning (MS); business administration (EMBA, MBA, DBA); business analytics (MBA, MS); entrepreneurship (MBA); finance (MBA, MS, Certificate); financial life planning (Certificate); financial planning (MS, Certificate); global supply chain management (MBA, Certificate); human resource management (MBA, MS, Certificate); information technology management (MBA, MS, Certificate); international business (MBA); marketing (MBA, MS, Certificate); project management (MBA, MS, Certificate); psychology (MA, Certificate); public administration (EMPA, MBA); public administration leadership (Certificate); JD/MBA. *Program availability:* Part-time, evening/weekend. *Degree requirements:* For doctorate, thesis/dissertation, qualifying examination. *Entrance requirements:* For master's, GMAT (for MBA), minimum GPA of 2.5 (MS). Additional exam requirements/recommendations for international students: Required—TOEFL (minimum score 550 paper-based; 79 iBT). Electronic applications accepted. *Expenses:* Contact institution.

Grand Canyon University, Colangelo College of Business, Phoenix, AZ 85017-1097. Offers accounting (MBA, MS); business analytics (MS); disaster preparedness and executive fire service leadership (MS); finance (MBA); general management (MBA); health systems management (MBA); information technology management (MS); leadership (MBA, MS); marketing (MBA); organizational leadership and entrepreneurship (MS); project management (MBA); sports business (MBA); strategic human resource management (MBA). *Accreditation:* ACBSP. *Program availability:* Part-time, evening/weekend, online learning. *Entrance requirements:* For master's, equivalent of two years' full-time professional work experience. Additional exam requirements/recommendations for international students: Required—TOEFL (minimum score 575 paper-based; 90 iBT), IELTS (minimum score 7). Electronic applications accepted.

HEC Montreal, School of Business Administration, Master of Science Programs in Administration, Data Science and Business Analytics, Montréal, QC H3T 2A7, Canada. Offers M Sc. Program offered in French and also in English (Thesis stream, Supervised project Stream offered). *Students:* 50 full-time (24 women), 18 part-time (5 women). 90 applicants, 52% accepted, 31 enrolled. In 2018, 16 master's awarded. *Entrance requirements:* For master's, BBA, undergraduate degree in another field, degree deemed equivalent by program director and minimum GPA of 3.0 on 4.3 scale. Additional exam requirements/recommendations for international students: Required—TAGE MAGE (minimum recommended score of 300), GMAT (minimum recommended score of 630), or GRE. *Application deadline:* For fall admission, 3/15 for domestic and international students. Application fee: $91 Canadian dollars ($191 Canadian dollars for international students). Electronic applications accepted. *Expenses: Tuition, area resident:* Full-time $3052.80 Canadian dollars; part-time $84.80 Canadian dollars per credit. Tuition, state resident: full-time $3816 Canadian dollars; part-time $264.67 Canadian dollars per credit. Tuition, nonresident: full-time $11,910 Canadian dollars. *International tuition:* $20,905.20 Canadian dollars full-time. *Required fees:* $1805.34 Canadian dollars; $43.62 Canadian dollars per credit. $71.78 Canadian dollars per term. Tuition and fees vary according to degree level and program. *Financial support:* Research assistantships, teaching assistantships, and scholarships/grants available. Financial award application deadline: 9/2. *Unit head:* Dr. Sihem Taboubi, Director, 514-340-6428, E-mail: sihem.taboubi@hec.ca. *Application contact:* Marianne de Moura, Administrative Director, 514-340-6000, Fax: 514-340-6411, E-mail: aide@hec.ca.
Website: http://www.hec.ca/en/programs/masters/master-business-analytics/index.html

Hult International Business School, Graduate Programs, Cambridge, MA 02141. Offers business administration (EMBA); business analytics (MBA, MIB); business statistics (MBS); disruptive innovation (MDI); entrepreneurship (MBA, MIB); family business (MBA, MIB); finance (MBA, MF, MIB); international marketing (MIM); marketing (MBA, MIB); project management (MBA, MIB). MDI and MBS offered in San Francisco; MBA also offered in Boston, San Francisco, Dubai, Shanghai, and New York. *Entrance requirements:* For master's, GMAT, 3 years of work experience. Additional exam requirements/recommendations for international students: Required—TOEFL. Electronic applications accepted. *Expenses:* Contact institution.

Iowa State University of Science and Technology, Program in Business Analytics, Ames, IA 50011. Offers MS. *Program availability:* Online learning.

Johns Hopkins University, Carey Business School, MS in Business Analytics and Risk Management Program, Baltimore, MD 21218. Offers MS. *Students:* 73 full-time (42 women), 9 part-time (3 women). 156 applicants, 70% accepted, 50 enrolled. In 2018, 13 master's awarded. *Degree requirements:* For master's, 36 credits. *Entrance requirements:* For master's, GMAT or GRE. Additional exam requirements/recommendations for international students: Required—TOEFL, IELTS. *Application deadline:* For fall admission, 4/3 for domestic and international students. Applications are processed on a rolling basis. Application fee: $100. Electronic applications accepted. *Expenses:* Contact institution. *Financial support:* In 2018–19, 20 students received support. Scholarships/grants available. Financial award application deadline: 4/15; financial award applicants required to submit FAFSA. *Faculty research:* Emerging issues in business analytics and risk management. *Unit head:* Dr. Kevin Frick, Vice Dean of Education, 410-234-9272, E-mail: kfrick@jhu.edu. *Application contact:* Office of Admissions, 410-234-9220, Fax: 443-529-1554, E-mail: carey.admissions@jhu.edu.

Kent State University, College of Business Administration, Master of Science Program in Business Analytics, Kent, OH 44242-0001. Offers MS. *Program availability:* Part-time, evening/weekend. *Faculty:* 3 full-time (0 women). *Students:* 21 full-time (11 women), 3 part-time (1 woman); includes 1 minority (Black or African American, non-Hispanic/Latino), 18 international. Average age 28. 62 applicants, 94% accepted, 21 enrolled. In 2018, 9 master's awarded. *Degree requirements:* For master's, 30 credit hours, minimum GPA of 3.0. *Entrance requirements:* For master's, GMAT or GRE, official transcripts, resume, statement of goals and objectives, 3 letters of recommendation. Additional exam requirements/recommendations for international students: Required—TOEFL (minimum score 550 paper-based; 80 iBT), IELTS (minimum score 6.5). *Application deadline:* For fall admission, 3/15 for domestic and international students. Applications are processed on a rolling basis. Application fee: $45 ($70 for international students). Electronic applications accepted. *Expenses:* Contact institution. *Financial support:* Scholarships/grants available. Financial award application deadline: 3/15; financial award applicants required to submit FAFSA. *Faculty research:* Optimization of algorithms to support big data capabilities, Decision Modeling Utilizing Artificial Intelligence, Innovative Systems Development Methodologies. *Unit head:* Dr. O. Felix Offodile, Chair/Professor, 330-672-2750, E-mail: foffodil@kent.edu. *Application contact:* Louise M. Ditchey, Administrative Director, 330-672-2282, Fax: 330-672-7303, E-mail: gradbus@kent.edu.
Website: http://www.kent.edu/business/msba

La Salle University, School of Business, Master of Business Administration Program, Philadelphia, PA 19141-1199. Offers accounting (MBA, Post-MBA Certificate); business systems and analytics (MBA, Post-MBA Certificate); finance (MBA, Post-MBA Certificate); general business administration (MBA, Post-MBA Certificate); human resource management (MBA, Post-MBA Certificate); management (MBA, Post-MBA Certificate); marketing (Post-MBA Certificate); MBA/MSN. Program also offered in Switzerland. *Accreditation:* AACSB. *Program availability:* Part-time, evening/weekend, online learning. *Entrance requirements:* For master's, GMAT or GRE, two letters of reference; resume; for Post-MBA Certificate, MBA with minimum GPA of 3.0. Additional exam requirements/recommendations for international students: Required—TOEFL. Electronic applications accepted. Application fee is waived when completed online. *Expenses:* Contact institution.

Lenoir-Rhyne University, Graduate Programs, Charles M. Snipes School of Business, Hickory, NC 28601. Offers accounting (MBA); business analytics and information technology (MBA); entrepreneurship (MBA); global business (MBA); healthcare administration (MBA); innovation and change management (MBA); leadership development (MBA). *Accreditation:* ACBSP. *Program availability:* Part-time, evening/weekend, online learning. *Degree requirements:* For master's, capstone course. *Entrance requirements:* For master's, GMAT, GRE, MAT, minimum undergraduate GPA of 2.7, graduate 3.0. Additional exam requirements/recommendations for international students: Required—TOEFL (minimum score 600 paper-based). Electronic applications accepted. *Expenses:* Contact institution.

Lewis University, College of Business, Program in Business Analytics, Romeoville, IL 60446. Offers financial analytics (MS); healthcare analytics (MS); marketing analytics (MS); operations analytics (MS). *Program availability:* Part-time, evening/weekend, 100% online, blended/hybrid learning. *Students:* 13 full-time (8 women), 37 part-time (24 women); includes 12 minority (4 Black or African American, non-Hispanic/Latino; 8 Hispanic/Latino), 7 international. Average age 34. *Entrance requirements:* For master's, bachelor's degree, transcripts from each college/university attended, letters of recommendation, resume. Additional exam requirements/recommendations for international students: Required—TOEFL, IELTS. *Application deadline:* Applications are processed on a rolling basis. Electronic applications accepted. *Financial support:* Career-related internships or fieldwork, Federal Work-Study, and unspecified assistantships available. Financial award applicants required to submit FAFSA. *Unit head:* Dr. Ryan Butt, Dean. *Application contact:* Office of Graduate Admission, 815-836-5610, E-mail: grad@lewisu.edu.
Website: http://www.lewisu.edu/academics/business-analytics/

Loyola University Chicago, Quinlan School of Business, Master of Science in Business Data Analytics Program, Chicago, IL 60611. Offers MS, Certificate. *Program availability:* Evening/weekend. *Entrance requirements:* For master's, GMAT or GRE, official transcripts, two letters of recommendation, statement of purpose, resume. Additional exam requirements/recommendations for international students: Required—TOEFL (minimum score 90 iBT), IELTS (minimum score 6.5). Electronic applications accepted. *Expenses:* Contact institution.

Marist College, Graduate Programs, School of Computer Science and Mathematics, Poughkeepsie, NY 12601-1387. Offers business analytics (Adv C); computer science/software development (MS); information systems (MS, Adv C). *Program availability:* Part-time, evening/weekend, online learning. *Entrance requirements:* For master's,

resume. Additional exam requirements/recommendations for international students: Required—TOEFL (minimum score 550 paper-based; 80 iBT); Recommended—IELTS (minimum score 6.5). Electronic applications accepted. *Faculty research:* Data quality, artificial intelligence, imaging, analysis of algorithms, distributed systems and applications.

Merrimack College, Girard School of Business, North Andover, MA 01845-5800. Offers accounting (MS); business analytics (MS); management (MS). *Program availability:* Part-time, evening/weekend, 100% online. *Faculty:* 5 full-time (1 woman), 3 part-time/adjunct (1 woman). *Students:* 81 full-time (33 women), 32 part-time (17 women); includes 11 minority (6 Black or African American, non-Hispanic/Latino; 3 Asian, non-Hispanic/Latino; 2 Two or more races, non-Hispanic/Latino), 11 international. Average age 30. 200 applicants, 75% accepted, 79 enrolled. In 2018, 78 master's awarded. *Degree requirements:* For master's, comprehensive exam (for some programs), thesis optional, capstone. *Entrance requirements:* For master's, official college transcripts, resume, personal statement, 2 recommendations. Additional exam requirements/recommendations for international students: Required—TOEFL (minimum score 84 iBT), IELTS (minimum score 6.5), PTE (minimum score 56). *Application deadline:* For fall admission, 8/24 for domestic students, 7/30 for international students; for spring admission, 1/10 for domestic and international students; for summer admission, 5/10 for domestic students, 4/10 for international students. Applications are processed on a rolling basis. Application fee: $0. Electronic applications accepted. Application fee is waived when completed online. *Expenses:* $885 per credit. *Financial support:* Career-related internships or fieldwork, scholarships/grants, health care benefits, and unspecified assistantships available. Support available to part-time students. Financial award application deadline: 5/1; financial award applicants required to submit FAFSA. *Unit head:* Dr. Catherine Usoff, Dean, 978-837-5044, E-mail: usoffc@merrimack.edu. *Application contact:* Jennifer Greenwood, Graduate Admission Counselor, 978-837-3563, E-mail: graduate@merrimack.edu.
Website: http://www.merrimack.edu/academics/graduate/

Metropolitan State University, College of Management, St. Paul, MN 55106-5000. Offers business administration (MBA, DBA); business analytics (Graduate Certificate); database administration (Graduate Certificate); global supply chain management (Graduate Certificate); information assurance security (Graduate Certificate); management information systems (MMIS); MIS generalist (Graduate Certificate); MIS systems analysis and design (Graduate Certificate); project management (Graduate Certificate). *Program availability:* Part-time, evening/weekend. *Degree requirements:* For master's, thesis optional, computer language (MMIS). *Entrance requirements:* For master's, GMAT (for MBA), resume. Additional exam requirements/recommendations for international students: Required—TOEFL (minimum score 550 paper-based). Electronic applications accepted. *Faculty research:* Yugoslav economic system, workers' cooperatives, participative management and job enrichment, global business systems.

Michigan State University, The Graduate School, Eli Broad College of Business, Program in Business Analytics, East Lansing, MI 48224. Offers MS. Program offered in collaboration with MSU's College of Engineering and College of Natural Science. *Entrance requirements:* For master's, GMAT or GRE, bachelor's degree; minimum cumulative GPA of 3.0 in undergraduate course work and in college-level courses in introductory calculus and statistics; working knowledge of personal computers; knowledge of programming languages; experience in using statistical software program packages; recent laptop computer with MS Office. Additional exam requirements/recommendations for international students: Required—PTE (minimum score 70), TOEFL or IELTS. Electronic applications accepted. *Faculty research:* Artificial intelligence, evolution, and game theory, computational modeling using high performance computing.

Montclair State University, The Graduate School, Feliciano School of Business, General MBA Program, Montclair, NJ 07043-1624. Offers accounting (MBA); business analytics (MBA); digital marketing (MBA); finance (MBA); general business administration (MBA); human resources management (MBA); management (MBA); management of information and technology (MBA); marketing (MBA); project management (MBA). *Program availability:* Part-time, evening/weekend. *Degree requirements:* For master's, culminating experience. *Entrance requirements:* For master's, GMAT or GRE General Test, 2 letters of recommendation, resume, essay. Additional exam requirements/recommendations for international students: Required—TOEFL (minimum score 83 iBT), IELTS (minimum score 6.5). Electronic applications accepted. *Faculty research:* Accounting, management, marketing.

National University, School of Business and Management, La Jolla, CA 92037-1011. Offers accountancy (M Acc, Certificate); business administration (GMBA, MBA); business analytics (MS); cause leadership (MA); global management (MGM); human resource management (MA); management information systems (MS); marketing (MS); organizational leadership (MS). GMBA offered in Spanish. *Program availability:* Part-time, evening/weekend, 100% online, blended/hybrid learning. *Degree requirements:* For master's, thesis (for some programs). *Entrance requirements:* For master's, interview, minimum GPA of 2.5. Additional exam requirements/recommendations for international students: Required—TOEFL (minimum score 550 paper-based; 79 iBT), IELTS (minimum score 6). Electronic applications accepted. *Expenses: Tuition:* Full-time $10,320; part-time $430 per unit. Tuition and fees vary according to degree level.

Northwestern University, The Graduate School, Kellogg School of Management, Management Programs, Evanston, IL 60208. Offers accounting information and management (MBA, PhD); analytical finance (MBA); business administration (MBA); decision sciences (MBA); entrepreneurship and innovation (MBA); finance (MBA, PhD); health enterprise management (MBA); human resources management (MBA); international business (MBA); management and organizations (MBA, PhD); management and organizations and sociology (PhD); management and strategy (MBA); management studies (MS); managerial analytics (MBA); managerial economics (MBA); managerial economics and strategy (PhD); marketing (MBA, PhD); marketing management (MBA); media management (MBA); operations management (MBA, PhD); real estate (MBA); social enterprise at Kellogg (MBA); JD/MBA. *Program availability:* Part-time, evening/weekend. Terminal master's awarded for partial completion of doctoral program. *Degree requirements:* For doctorate, thesis/dissertation, 2 years of coursework, qualifying (field) exam and candidacy, summer research papers and presentations to faculty, proposal defense, final exam/defense. *Entrance requirements:* For master's, GMAT, GRE, interview, 2 letters of recommendation, college transcripts, resume, essays, Kellogg honor code; for doctorate, GMAT, GRE, statement of purpose, transcripts, 2 letters of recommendation, resume, interview. Additional exam requirements/recommendations for international students: Required—TOEFL, IELTS. Electronic applications accepted. *Expenses:* Contact institution. *Faculty research:* Business cycles and international finance, health policy, networks, non-market strategy, consumer psychology.

Northwest Missouri State University, Graduate School, Melvin and Valorie Booth College of Business and Professional Studies, Maryville, MO 64468-6001. Offers agricultural economics (MBA); business decision and analytics (MBA); general management (MBA); human resource management (MBA); marketing (MBA). *Program availability:* Part-time. *Faculty:* 24 full-time (12 women). *Students:* 56 full-time (31 women), 220 part-time (126 women); includes 47 minority (23 Black or African American, non-Hispanic/Latino; 6 Asian, non-Hispanic/Latino; 10 Hispanic/Latino; 8 Two or more races, non-Hispanic/Latino), 15 international. Average age 32. 154 applicants, 75% accepted, 104 enrolled. In 2018, 53 master's awarded. *Degree requirements:* For master's, comprehensive exam. *Entrance requirements:* For master's, GMAT, GRE, minimum GPA of 2.5. Additional exam requirements/recommendations for international students: Required—TOEFL (minimum score 550 paper-based). *Application deadline:* For fall admission, 7/1 for domestic and international students; for spring admission, 11/15 for domestic and international students; for summer admission, 4/1 for domestic and international students. Applications are processed on a rolling basis. Application fee: $0 ($50 for international students). Electronic applications accepted. *Expenses:* $13,530 to complete degree (online MBA program); 401.06/credit hour in-state& 653.92/credit hour out-of-state. *Financial support:* Research assistantships with full tuition reimbursements, teaching assistantships with full tuition reimbursements, career-related internships or fieldwork, unspecified assistantships, and administrative assistantships, tutorial assistantships available. Financial award application deadline: 4/1; financial award applicants required to submit FAFSA. *Unit head:* Dr. Steve Ludwig, Director of the Melvin And Valorie Booth School of Business, 660-562-1749, Fax: 660-562-1096, E-mail: sludwig@nwmissouri.edu. *Application contact:* Dr. Steve Ludwig, Director of the Melvin And Valorie Booth School of Business, 660-562-1749, Fax: 660-562-1096, E-mail: sludwig@nwmissouri.edu.
Website: https://www.nwmissouri.edu/business/index.htm

Nova Southeastern University, H. Wayne Huizenga College of Business and Entrepreneurship, Fort Lauderdale, FL 33314-7796. Offers accounting (M Acc); business (MBA); business intelligence/analytics (MBA); complex health systems (MBA); enterprise informatics (MBA); entrepreneurship (MBA); finance (MBA); human resource management (MBA); international business (MBA); management (MBA); marketing (MBA); process improvement (MBA); public administration (MPA); real estate development (MS); sport revenue generation (MBA); supply chain management (MBA). *Accreditation:* NASPAA. *Program availability:* Part-time, evening/weekend, 100% online, blended/hybrid learning. *Entrance requirements:* For master's, GMAT or GRE (depending on undergraduate GPA), official transcripts from all schools attended while in pursuit of bachelor's degree; minimum GPA of 2.5 from regionally-accredited institution. Additional exam requirements/recommendations for international students: Required—TOEFL (minimum score 550 paper-based; 79 iBT), IELTS (minimum score 6), PTE (minimum score 54). Electronic applications accepted. *Expenses:* Contact institution. *Faculty research:* Entrepreneurship and venture capital, ethics and social responsibility, global commerce and cultures, business process management.

Point Park University, Rowland School of Business, Program in Business Administration, Pittsburgh, PA 15222-1984. Offers business analytics (MBA); global management and administration (MBA); health systems management (MBA); international business (MBA); management (MBA); management information systems (MBA); sports, arts and entertainment management (MBA). *Program availability:* Evening/weekend, 100% online.

Queen's University at Kingston, Smith School of Business, Doctoral Program in Management, Kingston, ON K7L 3N6, Canada. Offers analytics (PhD); business economics (PhD); finance (PhD); management information systems (PhD); marketing (PhD); organizational behavior (PhD); strategy (PhD).

Queen's University at Kingston, Smith School of Business, Master of Science in Management Program, Kingston, ON K7L 3N6, Canada. Offers analytics (M Sc); business economics (M Sc); finance (M Sc); management information systems (M Sc); marketing (M Sc); organizational behavior (M Sc); strategy (M Sc).

Regent University, Graduate School, School of Business and Leadership, Virginia Beach, VA 23464-9800. Offers business administration (MBA), including accounting, economics, entrepreneurship, finance and investing, general management, healthcare management (MA, MBA), human resource management (MA, MBA), innovation management, leadership, marketing, not-for-profit management (MA, MBA); business analytics (MS); business and design management (MA); church leadership (MA); leadership (Certificate); organizational leadership (MA, PhD), including ecclesial leadership (DSL, PhD), entrepreneurial leadership (PhD), healthcare management (MA, MBA), human resource development (PhD), human resource management (MA, MBA), individualized studies (DSL, PhD), interdisciplinary studies (MA), leadership coaching and mentoring (MA), not-for-profit management (MA, MBA), organizational development consulting (MA), servant leadership (MA, DSL); strategic leadership (DSL), including ecclesial leadership (DSL, PhD), global consulting, healthcare leadership, individualized studies (DSL, PhD), leadership coaching, servant leadership (MA, DSL), strategic foresight. *Program availability:* Part-time, evening/weekend, 100% online, blended/hybrid learning. *Degree requirements:* For master's, thesis or alternative, 3-credit hour culminating experience; for doctorate, thesis/dissertation. *Entrance requirements:* For master's, college transcripts, resume, essay; for doctorate, college transcripts, resume, essay, writing sample; for Certificate, writing sample, resume, transcripts. Additional exam requirements/recommendations for international students: Required—TOEFL (minimum score 577 paper-based). Electronic applications accepted. *Expenses:* Contact institution. *Faculty research:* Servant leadership, global business, team effectiveness, technology utilization, leadership development.

Rensselaer Polytechnic Institute, Graduate School, Lally School of Management, Program in Business Analytics, Troy, NY 12180-3590. Offers MS. *Program availability:* Part-time. *Faculty:* 36 full-time (9 women), 5 part-time/adjunct (0 women). *Students:* 51 full-time (28 women), 5 part-time (3 women); includes 5 minority (3 Asian, non-Hispanic/Latino; 2 Two or more races, non-Hispanic/Latino), 44 international. Average age 24. 583 applicants, 23% accepted, 45 enrolled. In 2018, 35 master's awarded. *Entrance requirements:* For master's, GMAT or GRE, personal statement. Additional exam requirements/recommendations for international students: Required—TOEFL, IELTS, PTE, TOEFL (minimum score 570 paper-based; 88 iBT), IELTS (minimum score 6.5), or PTE (minimum score 60). *Application deadline:* For fall admission, 1/1 for domestic and international students. Applications are processed on a rolling basis. Application fee: $75. Electronic applications accepted. *Financial support:* Scholarships/grants available. Financial award application deadline: 1/1. *Total annual research expenditures:* $60,850. *Unit head:* Pindaro Demertzoglou, Graduate Program Director, 518-276-2753, E-mail: demerp@rpi.edu. *Application contact:* Jarron Decker, Director of Graduate Admissions, 518-276-6216, Fax: 518-276-4072, E-mail: gradadmissions@rpi.edu.
Website: https://lallyschool.rpi.edu/ms-business-analytics

Robert Morris University Illinois, Morris Graduate School of Management, Chicago, IL 60605. Offers accounting (MBA); accounting/finance (MBA); business analytics (MIS); health care administration (MM); higher education administration (MM); human performance (MS); human resource management (MBA); information security (MIS); information systems management (MIS); law enforcement administration (MM); management (MBA); management/finance (MBA); management/human resource management (MBA); sports administration (MM). *Program availability:* Part-time, evening/weekend. *Entrance requirements:* For master's, official transcripts and letters of recommendation (for some programs); written personal statement. Additional exam requirements/recommendations for international students: Required—TOEFL (minimum score 550 paper-based). Electronic applications accepted.

Business Analytics

Rockhurst University, Helzberg School of Management, Kansas City, MO 64110-2561. Offers accounting (MBA); business intelligence (MBA, Certificate); business intelligence and analytics (MS); data science (MBA, Certificate); entrepreneurship (MBA); finance (MBA); fundraising leadership (MBA, Certificate); healthcare management (MBA, Certificate); human capital (Certificate); international business (Certificate); management (MA, MBA, Certificate); nonprofit administration (Certificate); organizational development (Certificate); science leadership (Certificate). *Accreditation:* AACSB. *Program availability:* Part-time, evening/weekend. *Entrance requirements:* For master's, GMAT or GRE. Additional exam requirements/recommendations for international students: Required—TOEFL (minimum score 550 paper-based; 79 iBT). Electronic applications accepted. *Faculty research:* Offshoring/outsourcing, systems analysis/synthesis, work teams, multilateral trade, path dependencies/creation.

St. John's University, The Peter J. Tobin College of Business, Department of Business Analytics and Information Systems, Queens, NY 11439. Offers MBA. *Entrance requirements:* For master's, GMAT or GRE, 2 letters of recommendation, essay, resume, unofficial transcripts. Additional exam requirements/recommendations for international students: Required—TOEFL (minimum score 80 iBT), IELTS (minimum score 6.5). Electronic applications accepted. *Expenses:* Contact institution.

Saint Joseph's University, Erivan K. Haub School of Business, MS Program in Business Intelligence and Analytics, Philadelphia, PA 19131-1395. Offers MS. *Program availability:* Part-time, evening/weekend, 100% online. *Degree requirements:* For master's, minimum GPA of 3.0. *Entrance requirements:* For master's, GMAT or GRE, 2 letters of recommendation, resume, personal statement, official undergraduate and graduate transcripts. Additional exam requirements/recommendations for international students: Required—PTE, TOEFL, IELTS, or PTE. Electronic applications accepted.

Saint Mary's College of California, School of Economics and Business Administration, MS in Business Analytics Program, Moraga, CA 94575. Offers MS.

Santa Clara University, Leavey School of Business, Santa Clara, CA 95053. Offers business administration (MBA); business analytics (MS); finance (MS); information systems (MS); supply chain management and analytics (MS); JD/MBA. *Accreditation:* AACSB. *Program availability:* Part-time, online learning. *Faculty:* 101 full-time (32 women), 47 part-time/adjunct (15 women). *Students:* 487 full-time (278 women), 326 part-time (139 women); includes 295 minority (14 Black or African American, non-Hispanic/Latino; 207 Asian, non-Hispanic/Latino; 39 Hispanic/Latino; 35 Two or more races, non-Hispanic/Latino; 294 international. Average age 31. 694 applicants, 65% accepted, 281 enrolled. In 2018, 195 master's awarded. *Entrance requirements:* For master's, Varies based on program. Additional exam requirements/recommendations for international students: Required—TOEFL (minimum score 90 iBT). *Application fee:* $100 ($150 for international students). Electronic applications accepted. *Financial support:* In 2018–19, 192 students received support. Fellowships, Federal Work-Study, and scholarships/grants available. Support available to part-time students. Financial award applicants required to submit FAFSA. *Unit head:* Caryn Beck-Dudley, Dean, 408-554-4523, E-mail: cbeckdudley@scu.edu. *Application contact:* Caryn Beck-Dudley, Dean, 408-554-4523, E-mail: cbeckdudley@scu.edu.
Website: http://www.scu.edu/business/

Seattle University, Albers School of Business and Economics, Master of Science in Business Analytics Program, Seattle, WA 98122-1090. Offers MSBA, Certificate. *Program availability:* Part-time. *Faculty:* 134 full-time (48 women), 34 part-time/adjunct (16 women). *Students:* 45 full-time (27 women), 50 part-time (29 women); includes 19 minority (2 Black or African American, non-Hispanic/Latino; 12 Asian, non-Hispanic/Latino; 4 Hispanic/Latino; 1 Two or more races, non-Hispanic/Latino), 52 international. Average age 28. 163 applicants, 48% accepted, 40 enrolled. In 2018, 22 master's, 20 Certificates awarded. *Entrance requirements:* For master's, GMAT. Additional exam requirements/recommendations for international students: Required—TOEFL or IELTS. *Application deadline:* For fall admission, 7/20 for domestic students, 9/1 for international students; for winter admission, 12/1 for international students; for spring admission, 1/1 for international students; for summer admission, 4/20 for domestic students, 4/1 for international students. Applications are processed on a rolling basis. *Application fee:* $55. Electronic applications accepted. *Expenses:* Contact institution. *Financial support:* In 2018–19, 29 students received support. *Application deadline:* 6/1. *Unit head:* Dr. Carlos De Mello e Souza, Program Director, 206-296-5700, Fax: 206-296-5795, E-mail: albersgrad@seattleu.edu. *Application contact:* Jeff Millard, Assistant Dean of Graduate Programs, 206-296-5700, E-mail: albersgrad@seattleu.edu.
Website: http://www.seattleu.edu/albers/msba/

Shippensburg University of Pennsylvania, School of Graduate Studies, John L. Grove College of Business, Shippensburg, PA 17257-2299. Offers advanced studies in business (Certificate); advanced supply chain and logistics management (Certificate); business administration (MBA, DBA), including business administration (MBA), business analytics (MBA), finance (MBA), healthcare management (MBA), management information systems (MBA), supply chain management (MBA); finance (Certificate); health care management (Certificate); management information systems (Certificate). *Accreditation:* AACSB. *Program availability:* Part-time, evening/weekend, 100% online, blended/hybrid learning. *Faculty:* 20 full-time (4 women), 2 part-time/adjunct (0 women). *Students:* 31 full-time (14 women), 174 part-time (67 women); includes 33 minority (17 Black or African American, non-Hispanic/Latino; 6 Asian, non-Hispanic/Latino; 7 Hispanic/Latino; 3 Two or more races, non-Hispanic/Latino), 13 international. Average age 33. 149 applicants, 61% accepted, 60 enrolled. In 2018, 104 master's, 1 other advanced degree awarded. *Degree requirements:* For master's, comprehensive exam (for some programs), thesis optional, practicum capstone course; for doctorate, comprehensive exam, thesis/dissertation, comprehensive exam dissertation. *Entrance requirements:* For master's, GMAT (minimum score 450 if less than 5 years of mid-level experience, including management experience), current resume; relevant work/classroom experience; 500-word statement of purpose; prerequisites of quantitative analysis, computer usage, and oral and written communications; laptop computer; for doctorate, GMAT (minimum score of 600 if less than 5 years of substantive professional or teaching experience), 2 letters of recommendation from professionals in academia or industry; 2-3 page personal and professional statement; interview; resume. Additional exam requirements/recommendations for international students: Required—TOEFL (minimum score 550 paper-based; 68 iBT), IELTS (minimum score 6), TOEFL (minimum score 550 paper-based, 68 iBT) or IELTS (minimum score 6). *Application deadline:* For fall admission, 4/30 for international students; for spring admission, 9/30 for international students. Applications are processed on a rolling basis. *Application fee:* $45. Electronic applications accepted. *Expenses:* Tuition, state resident: part-time $516 per credit. Tuition, nonresident: part-time $750 per credit. *Required fees:* $149 per credit. *Financial support:* In 2018–19, 15 students received support. Career-related internships or fieldwork, scholarships/grants, unspecified assistantships, and resident hall director and student payroll positions available. Support available to part-time students. Financial award application deadline: 3/1; financial award applicants required to submit FAFSA. *Unit head:* Dr. John G. Kooti, Dean of the College of Business, 717-477-1435, Fax: 717-477-4003, E-mail: jgkooti@ship.edu. *Application contact:* Maya T. Mapp, Director of Admissions, 717-477-1231, Fax: 717-477-4016, E-mail: mtmapp@ship.edu.
Website: http://www.ship.edu/business

Southern Illinois University Edwardsville, Graduate School, School of Business, Program in Business Administration, Edwardsville, IL 62026. Offers business analytics (MBA); management information systems (MBA); project management (MBA). *Accreditation:* AACSB. *Program availability:* Part-time, evening/weekend. *Degree requirements:* For master's, comprehensive exam. *Entrance requirements:* For master's, GMAT. Additional exam requirements/recommendations for international students: Required—TOEFL (minimum score 550 paper-based; 79 iBT), IELTS (minimum score 6.5). Electronic applications accepted.

Southern Methodist University, Cox School of Business, MBA Program, Dallas, TX 75275. Offers accounting (MBA, PMBA); business (EMBA); business analytics (PMBA); finance (MBA, PMBA); information technology and operations management (MBA, PMBA), including business analytics (MBA), information and operations (MBA); management (MBA, PMBA); marketing (MBA, PMBA); real estate (MBA, PMBA); strategy and entrepreneurship (MBA, PMBA); JD/MBA; MA/MBA. *Program availability:* Part-time, evening/weekend. *Entrance requirements:* For master's, GMAT. Additional exam requirements/recommendations for international students: Required—TOEFL. Electronic applications accepted. *Expenses:* Contact institution. *Faculty research:* Corporate finance, financial reporting, modeling consumer decision-making, competition between national brands and store brands, institutional determinants of firms' strategy.

Southern Methodist University, Cox School of Business, Program in Business Analytics, Dallas, TX 75275. Offers MS.

Southern New Hampshire University, School of Business, Manchester, NH 03106-1045. Offers accounting (MBA, Graduate Certificate); accounting finance (MS); accounting/auditing (MS); accounting/forensic accounting (MS); accounting/management accounting (MS); accounting/taxation (MS); applied economics (MS); athletic administration (MBA, Graduate Certificate); business administration (IMBA, Certificate), including business information systems (Certificate), human resource management (Certificate); business analytics (MBA); business intelligence (MBA); communication (MA), including new media and marketing, public relations; community economic development (MBA); criminal justice (MBA); data analytics (MS); economics (MBA); engineering management (MBA); entrepreneurship (MBA); finance (MBA, MS, Graduate Certificate); finance/corporate finance (MS); finance/investments (MS); forensic accounting (MBA); forensic accounting and fraud examination (Graduate Certificate); healthcare informatics (MBA); healthcare management (MBA); human resource management (MS); human resources (MBA); information technology (MS); information technology management (MBA); international business (PhD); Internet marketing (MBA); leadership (MBA); leadership of nonprofit organizations (Graduate Certificate); management (MS); marketing (MBA, MS, Graduate Certificate); music business (MBA); operations and project management (MS); operations and supply chain management (MBA, Graduate Certificate); organizational leadership (MS); project management (MBA, Graduate Certificate); public administration (MBA, Graduate Certificate); quantitative analysis (MBA); Six Sigma (Graduate Certificate); Six Sigma quality (MBA); social media marketing (MBA, Graduate Certificate); sport management (MBA, MS, Graduate Certificate); sustainability and environmental compliance (MBA); MBA/Certificate. *Accreditation:* ACBSP. *Program availability:* Part-time, evening/weekend, online learning. Terminal master's awarded for partial completion of doctoral program. *Degree requirements:* For master's, one foreign language, comprehensive exam (for some programs), thesis or alternative; for doctorate, one foreign language, comprehensive exam, thesis/dissertation. *Entrance requirements:* For master's, minimum GPA of 2.5; for doctorate, GMAT. Additional exam requirements/recommendations for international students: Required—TOEFL (minimum score 500 paper-based). Electronic applications accepted.

Stevens Institute of Technology, Graduate School, School of Business, Program in Business Administration, Hoboken, NJ 07030. Offers business intelligence and analytics (MBA); engineering management (MBA); finance (MBA); information systems (MBA); innovation and entrepreneurship (MBA); marketing (MBA); pharmaceutical management (MBA); project management (MBA, Certificate); technology management (MBA); telecommunications management (MBA). *Accreditation:* AACSB. *Program availability:* Part-time, evening/weekend. *Faculty:* 58 full-time (8 women), 18 part-time/adjunct (3 women). *Students:* 44 full-time (23 women), 202 part-time (90 women); includes 56 minority (12 Black or African American, non-Hispanic/Latino; 2 American Indian or Alaska Native, non-Hispanic/Latino; 40 Asian, non-Hispanic/Latino; 2 Hispanic/Latino), 28 international. Average age 37. In 2018, 45 master's awarded. Terminal master's awarded for partial completion of doctoral program. *Degree requirements:* For master's, thesis optional, minimum B average in major field and overall; for Certificate, minimum B average. *Entrance requirements:* For master's, GRE/GMAT scores: GRE scores are required for all applicants applying to a full-time graduate program in the Schaefer School of Engineering and Science (SES). International applicants must submit TOEFL/IELTS scores and fulfill the English Language Proficiency Requirements in order to be considered. Additional exam requirements/recommendations for international students: Required—TOEFL (minimum score 74 iBT), IELTS (minimum score 6). *Application deadline:* For fall admission, 4/1 for domestic and international students; for spring admission, 11/1 for domestic and international students; for summer admission, 5/1 for domestic students. Applications are processed on a rolling basis. *Application fee:* $60. Electronic applications accepted. *Expenses:* Tuition: Full-time $35,960; part-time $1620 per credit. *Required fees:* $1290; $600 per semester. Tuition and fees vary according to course load. *Financial support:* Fellowships, research assistantships, teaching assistantships, career-related internships or fieldwork, Federal Work-Study, scholarships/grants, and unspecified assistantships available. Financial award application deadline: 2/15; financial award applicants required to submit FAFSA. *Unit head:* Dr. Gregory Prastacos, Dean, 201-216-8366, E-mail: gprastac@stevens.edu. *Application contact:* Graduate Admissions, 888-783-8367, Fax: 888-511-1306, E-mail: graduate@stevens.edu.
Website: https://www.stevens.edu/school-business/masters-programs/mbaemba

Stevens Institute of Technology, Graduate School, School of Business, Program in Business Intelligence and Analytics, Hoboken, NJ 07030. Offers MS, Certificate. *Program availability:* Part-time, evening/weekend. *Faculty:* 58 full-time (8 women), 18 part-time/adjunct (3 women). *Students:* 158 full-time (67 women), 63 part-time (25 women); includes 28 minority (2 Black or African American, non-Hispanic/Latino; 26 Asian, non-Hispanic/Latino), 152 international. Average age 29. In 2018, 121 master's, 67 other advanced degrees awarded. *Degree requirements:* For master's, thesis optional, minimum B average in major field and overall; for Certificate, minimum B average. *Entrance requirements:* For master's, GRE/GMAT scores: GRE scores are required for all applicants applying to a full-time graduate program in the Schaefer School of Engineering and Science (SES). International applicants must submit TOEFL/IELTS scores and fulfill the English Language Proficiency Requirements in order to be considered. Additional exam requirements/recommendations for international students: Required—TOEFL (minimum score 74 iBT), IELTS (minimum score 6). *Application deadline:* For fall admission, 4/1 for domestic and international students; for spring admission, 11/1 for domestic and international students; for summer admission, 5/1 for domestic students. Applications are processed on a rolling basis. *Application fee:* $60. Electronic applications accepted. *Expenses:* Tuition: Full-time $35,960; part-time $1620 per credit. *Required fees:* $1290; $600 per semester. Tuition and fees vary according to

course load. *Financial support:* Fellowships, research assistantships, teaching assistantships, career-related internships or fieldwork, Federal Work-Study, scholarships/grants, and unspecified assistantships available. Financial award application deadline: 2/15; financial award applicants required to submit FAFSA. *Unit head:* Dr. Gregory Prastacos, Dean of SB, 201-216 8366, E-mail: gprastac@stevens.edu. *Application contact:* Graduate Admissions, 888-783-8367, Fax: 888-511-1306, E-mail: graduate@stevens.edu.
Website: https://www.stevens.edu/school-business/masters-programs/business-intelligence-analytics

Suffolk University, Sawyer Business School, Program in Business Analytics, Boston, MA 02108-2770. Offers MS, MSBA, MSBA/MBA, MSBA/MSA. *Program availability:* Part-time, evening/weekend. *Students:* 18 full-time (11 women), 23 part-time (11 women); includes 6 minority (2 Black or African American, non-Hispanic/Latino; 2 Asian, non-Hispanic/Latino; 2 Hispanic/Latino), 29 international. Average age 27. 154 applicants, 71% accepted, 38 enrolled. *Entrance requirements:* For master's, GMAT. Additional exam requirements/recommendations for international students: Required—TOEFL (minimum score 550 paper-based; 80 iBT). *Application deadline:* For fall admission, 3/15 priority date for domestic and international students; for spring admission, 10/15 priority date for domestic and international students. Applications are processed on a rolling basis. Application fee: $50. Electronic applications accepted. *Expenses:* Contact institution. *Financial support:* In 2018–19, 21 students received support, including 1 fellowship (averaging $3,600 per year); career-related internships or fieldwork, Federal Work-Study, institutionally sponsored loans, and scholarships/grants also available. Support available to part-time students. Financial award application deadline: 4/1; financial award applicants required to submit FAFSA. *Unit head:* Ken Hung, DR, Director, Master of Science in Business Analytics, 617-573-8395, E-mail: khung@suffolk.edu. *Application contact:* Mara Marzocchi, Associate Director of Graduate Admissions, 617-573-8302, Fax: 617-305-1733, E-mail: grad.admission@suffolk.edu.

Syracuse University, Martin J. Whitman School of Management, Master of Business Administration Program, Syracuse, NY 13244. Offers accounting (MBA); business analytics (MBA); entrepreneurship (MBA); marketing management (MBA); real estate (MBA); supply chain management (MBA); JD/MBA. *Program availability:* Part-time, 100% online. *Students:* Average age 32. 1,086 applicants, 73% accepted, 516 enrolled. In 2018, 84 master's awarded. *Entrance requirements:* For master's, GMAT or GRE, resume, essay, 5-minute video interview, two letters of recommendation, transcripts (unofficial). Additional exam requirements/recommendations for international students: Required—TOEFL (minimum score 100 iBT), IELTS (minimum score 7), PTE (minimum score 68). *Application deadline:* For fall admission, 11/30 for domestic students, 11/30 priority date for international students; for winter admission, 1/1 for domestic students, 1/1 priority date for international students; for spring admission, 2/15 for domestic and international students; for summer admission, 4/19 for domestic students. Application fee: $75. Electronic applications accepted. *Expenses:* Contact institution. *Financial support:* In 2018–19, 22 students received support. Merit scholarships available. Financial award application deadline: 2/15. *Faculty research:* Data analysis, economics of international business, financial markets and institutions, operations management, supply chain management. *Unit head:* Dr. Alexander McKelvie, Associate Dean for Undergraduate and Full-time Master's Education, 315-443-7252, E-mail: mckelvie@syr.edu. *Application contact:* Shri Ramakrishnan, Assistant Director, Graduate Recruitment, 315-443-3497, Fax: 315-443-9517, E-mail: busgrad@syr.edu.
Website: http://whitman.syr.edu/ftmba/

Syracuse University, Martin J. Whitman School of Management, MS in Business Analytics Program, Syracuse, NY 13244. Offers MS. *Program availability:* Part-time, evening/weekend, 100% online. *Students:* Average age 38. 45 applicants, 82% accepted, 27 enrolled. *Entrance requirements:* For master's, GMAT or GRE, resume, essay, 5-minute video interview, two letters of recommendation, transcripts (unofficial). Additional exam requirements/recommendations for international students: Required—TOEFL (minimum score 100 iBT), IELTS (minimum score 7), PTE (minimum score 68). *Application deadline:* For fall admission, 11/30 for domestic and international students; for winter admission, 1/1 for domestic and international students; for spring admission, 2/15 for domestic and international students; for summer admission, 4/19 for domestic students. Application fee: $75. Electronic applications accepted. *Expenses:* Contact institution. *Financial support:* Merit-based scholarships available. Financial award application deadline: 2/15. *Faculty research:* Data analysis and decision making, business analytics, accounting analytics, financial services analytics, marketing analytics. *Unit head:* Dr. Alexander McKelvie, Associate Dean for Undergraduate and Full-time Master's Education, 315-443-7252, Fax: 315-443-9517, E-mail: mckelvie@syr.edu. *Application contact:* Shri Ramakrishnan, Assistant Director, Graduate Recruitment, 315-443-3497, Fax: 315-443-9517, E-mail: sramak01@syr.edu.

Texas A&M University–Commerce, College of Business, Commerce, TX 75429. Offers accounting (MSA); business administration (MBA); business analytics (MS); finance (MSF); management (MS); marketing (MS). *Accreditation:* AACSB. *Program availability:* Part-time, evening/weekend, 100% online, blended/hybrid learning. *Faculty:* 48 full-time (15 women), 2 part-time/adjunct (1 woman). *Students:* 391 full-time (209 women), 948 part-time (511 women); includes 583 minority (249 Black or African American, non-Hispanic/Latino; 4 American Indian or Alaska Native, non-Hispanic/Latino; 89 Asian, non-Hispanic/Latino; 205 Hispanic/Latino; 1 Native Hawaiian or other Pacific Islander, non-Hispanic/Latino; 35 Two or more races, non-Hispanic/Latino), 156 international. Average age 33. 930 applicants, 58% accepted, 355 enrolled. In 2018, 628 master's awarded. *Degree requirements:* For master's, comprehensive exam. *Entrance requirements:* For master's, GRE General Test, GMAT, letter of recommendation. Additional exam requirements/recommendations for international students: Required—TOEFL (minimum score 550 paper-based; 79 iBT), IELTS (minimum score 6), PTE (minimum score 53). *Application deadline:* For fall admission, 6/1 priority date for international students; for spring admission, 10/15 priority date for international students; for summer admission, 3/15 priority date for international students. Applications are processed on a rolling basis. Application fee: $50 ($75 for international students). Electronic applications accepted. *Expenses:* Tuition, area resident: Full-time $3630. Tuition, state resident: full-time $3630. Tuition, nonresident: full-time $11,100. *International tuition:* $11,100 full-time. *Required fees:* $2794. Tuition and fees vary according to course load, degree level and program. *Financial support:* In 2018–19, 61 students received support, including 57 research assistantships with partial tuition reimbursements available (averaging $3,286 per year); Federal Work-Study, institutionally sponsored loans, scholarships/grants, health care benefits, and unspecified assistantships also available. Financial award application deadline: 5/1; financial award applicants required to submit FAFSA. *Faculty research:* Strategic management and organizational behavior phenomena; marketing and big data decisions of product choice behavior and channel behavior of consumers; international accounting in governmental sectors; finance research on banking, investments, financial institutions and risk management; applied economics with emphasis on industries that are important to the region including health and energy. *Unit head:* Dr. Shanan Gwaltney Gibson, Dean of College of Business, 903-886-5191, Fax: 903-886-5650, E-mail: shanan.gibson@tamuc.edu. *Application contact:* Shanna Hoskison, Director, Graduate

Advising, 903-886-5190, E-mail: shanna.hoskison@tamuc.edu.
Website: https://new.tamuc.edu/business/

Texas Woman's University, Graduate School, College of Business, Program in Healthcare Administration, Houston, TX 76204. Offers healthcare administration (MHA), including business analytics. Program offered at Texas Medical Center in Houston. *Accreditation:* CAHME. *Program availability:* Part-time, evening/weekend, 100% online, blended/hybrid learning. *Faculty:* 4 full-time (1 woman), 7 part-time/adjunct (4 women). *Students:* 82 full-time (73 women), 68 part-time (57 women); includes 115 minority (52 Black or African American, non-Hispanic/Latino; 1 American Indian or Alaska Native, non-Hispanic/Latino; 38 Asian, non-Hispanic/Latino; 20 Hispanic/Latino; 4 Two or more races, non-Hispanic/Latino), 4 international. Average age 30. 45 applicants, 87% accepted, 30 enrolled. In 2018, 50 master's awarded. *Degree requirements:* For master's, thesis or alternative, portfolio. *Entrance requirements:* For master's, GMAT or GRE (optional depending on GPA), interview, resume, 1 letters of reference, interest essay, minimum GPA of 3.0 in last 60 hours of undergraduate degree and in all graduate course work. Additional exam requirements/recommendations for international students: Required—TOEFL (minimum score 79 iBT); Recommended—IELTS (minimum score 6.5), TSE (minimum score 53). *Application deadline:* Applications are processed on a rolling basis. Application fee: $50 ($75 for international students). Electronic applications accepted. *Expenses:* Tuition, area resident: Full-time $4852; part-time $270 per semester hour. Tuition, state resident: full-time $4852; part-time $270 per semester hour. Tuition, nonresident: full-time $12,322; part-time $685 per semester hour. *International tuition:* $12,322 full-time. *Required fees:* $2714; $113 per semester hour. $296 per semester. Tuition and fees vary according to course level, course load, degree level, campus/location and program. *Financial support:* In 2018–19, 33 students received support, including 4 teaching assistantships; career-related internships or fieldwork, Federal Work-Study, institutionally sponsored loans, scholarships/grants, traineeships, health care benefits, and unspecified assistantships also available. Support available to part-time students. Financial award application deadline: 3/1; financial award applicants required to submit FAFSA. *Faculty research:* Patient safety and health policy, competition and market structure on health care quality, performance measurement and promotion. *Unit head:* Dr. Gerald Goodman, Director, 940-898-2458, Fax: 940-898-2120, E-mail: hcahouston@twu.edu. *Application contact:* Korie Hawkins, Associate Director of Admissions, Graduate Recruitment, 940-898-3188, Fax: 940-898-3081, E-mail: admissions@twu.edu.
Website: https://www.twu.edu/business/graduate-programs-college-of-business/master-of-healthcare-administration/

Thomas Jefferson University, Kanbar College of Design, Engineering and Commerce, Innovation MBA Program, Philadelphia, PA 19107. Offers business analytics (MBA); general business (MBA); management (MBA); marketing (MBA); strategy and design thinking (MBA); MBA/MS. *Program availability:* Part-time, evening/weekend, online learning. *Entrance requirements:* For master's, GMAT. Additional exam requirements/recommendations for international students: Required—TOEFL (minimum score 550 paper-based; 79 iBT).

Tulane University, A. B. Freeman School of Business, New Orleans, LA 70118-5669. Offers accounting (M Acct); analytics (MBA); banking and financial services (M Fin); energy (M Fin, MBA); entrepreneurship (MBA); finance (MBA, PhD); financial accounting (PhD); international business (MBA); international management (MBA); strategic management and leadership (MBA); JD/M Acct; JD/MBA; MBA/M Acc; MBA/MA; MBA/MD; MBA/ME; MBA/MPH. *Accreditation:* AACSB. *Program availability:* Part-time, evening/weekend. *Faculty:* 43 full-time (11 women), 45 part-time/adjunct (8 women). *Students:* 432 full-time (218 women), 533 part-time (262 women); includes 99 minority (32 Black or African American, non-Hispanic/Latino; 1 American Indian or Alaska Native, non-Hispanic/Latino; 26 Asian, non-Hispanic/Latino; 35 Hispanic/Latino; 5 Two or more races, non-Hispanic/Latino), 644 international. Average age 28. 1,911 applicants, 77% accepted, 411 enrolled. In 2018, 728 master's, 4 doctorates awarded. Terminal master's awarded for partial completion of doctoral program. *Degree requirements:* For master's, one foreign language, comprehensive exam (for some programs); for doctorate, one foreign language, comprehensive exam, thesis/dissertation. *Entrance requirements:* For master's and doctorate, GMAT or GRE, interview. Additional exam requirements/recommendations for international students: Required—TOEFL or IELTS. *Application deadline:* For fall admission, 11/1 priority date for domestic students, 11/1 for international students; for winter admission, 1/6 for domestic and international students; for spring admission, 3/1 priority date for domestic students, 3/1 for international students; for summer admission, 5/5 for domestic students. Applications are processed on a rolling basis. Application fee: $125. Electronic applications accepted. *Expenses:* Contact institution. *Financial support:* In 2018–19, 153 students received support. Fellowships with tuition reimbursements available, research assistantships, teaching assistantships, career-related internships or fieldwork, Federal Work-Study, tuition waivers (full and partial), and unspecified assistantships available. Support available to part-time students. Financial award application deadline: 4/15; financial award applicants required to submit FAFSA. *Faculty research:* Corporate finance, managerial accounting and financial reporting, strategic management and leadership, consumer behavior and decision making, organizational behavior and human resource management. *Unit head:* Ira Solomon, PhD, Dean, 504-865-5407, Fax: 504-865-5491, E-mail: businessdean@tulane.edu. *Application contact:* Melissa Booth, Assistant Dean for Graduate Admissions, 800-223-5402, E-mail: freeman.admissions@tulane.edu.
Website: http://www.freeman.tulane.edu

University at Albany, State University of New York, School of Business, MBA Programs, Albany, NY 12222-0001. Offers business administration (MBA); cyber security (MBA); entrepreneurship (MBA); finance (MBA); human resource information systems (MBA); information systems and business analytics (MBA); marketing (MBA); JD/MBA. JD/MBA offered jointly with Albany Law School. *Program availability:* Part-time, evening/weekend. *Faculty:* 29 full-time (13 women), 9 part-time/adjunct (2 women). *Students:* 103 full-time (36 women), 188 part-time (69 women); includes 76 minority (27 Black or African American, non-Hispanic/Latino; 33 Asian, non-Hispanic/Latino; 16 Hispanic/Latino), 16 international. Average age 25. 181 applicants, 80% accepted, 114 enrolled. In 2018, 103 master's awarded. *Degree requirements:* For master's, thesis (for some programs), field or research project. *Entrance requirements:* For master's, GMAT, minimum undergraduate GPA of 3.0; 3 letters of recommendation; resume; statement of goals. Additional exam requirements/recommendations for international students: Required—TOEFL (minimum score 100 iBT); Recommended—IELTS (minimum score 7). *Application deadline:* For fall admission, 4/1 priority date for domestic students, 2/15 for international students; for spring admission, 12/1 for domestic students; for summer admission, 5/1 for domestic students. Applications are processed on a rolling basis. Application fee: $75. Electronic applications accepted. *Expenses:* 16818. *Financial support:* In 2018–19, 25 students received support, including 7 fellowships with partial tuition reimbursements available (averaging $6,000 per year), 4 research assistantships with partial tuition reimbursements available, 21 teaching assistantships with partial tuition reimbursements available; unspecified assistantships also available. Financial award application deadline: 4/1; financial award applicants required to submit FAFSA. *Faculty research:* Social goods, information assurance, social computing, corporate entrepreneurship, asset pricing. *Total annual*

research expenditures: $136,000. *Unit head:* Dr. Nilanjan Sen, Dean, 518-956-8370, Fax: 518-442-3273, E-mail: nsen@albany.edu. *Application contact:* Zina Mega Lawrence, Assistant Dean of Graduate Student Services, 518-956-8320, Fax: 518-442-4042, E-mail: zlawrence@albany.edu.
Website: https://graduatebusiness.albany.edu/

University at Buffalo, the State University of New York, Graduate School, School of Management, Buffalo, NY 14260. Offers accounting (MS); analytics (MBA); business administration (PMBA); consulting (MBA); finance (MBA, MS), including financial risk management (MS), quantitative finance (MS); healthcare (MBA); information assurance (MBA); information systems (MBA); international management (MBA); management (EMBA, PhD); management information systems (MS); marketing (MBA); supply chain and operations (MBA); supply chains and operations management (MS); Au D/MBA; DDS/MBA; JD/MBA; M Arch/MBA; MD/MBA; MPH/MBA; MSW/MBA; Pharm D/MBA. *Accreditation:* AACSB. *Program availability:* Part-time, evening/weekend. *Degree requirements:* For master's, capstone courses or projects; for doctorate, comprehensive exam, thesis/dissertation. *Entrance requirements:* For master's, GMAT (for MS in accounting, finance); GRE or GMAT (for MBA, MS in management information systems, supply chains and operations management), essays, letters of recommendation; for doctorate, GMAT or GRE, essays, writing sample, letters of recommendation. Additional exam requirements/recommendations for international students: Required—TOEFL (minimum score 95 iBT) or IELTS (minimum score 6.5); Recommended—TSE (minimum score 73). Electronic applications accepted. *Expenses:* Contact institution. *Faculty research:* Data analytics, accounting and law, rate finance, consumer behavior, supply chain logistics, leadership and team effectiveness.

The University of Alabama in Huntsville, School of Graduate Studies, College of Business Administration, Programs in Business and Management, Huntsville, AL 35899. Offers business analytics (MSMS); federal contracting and procurement management (Certificate); human resource management (MSM); management (MBA), including acquisition management, entrepreneurship, federal contract accounting, finance, human resource management, logistics and supply chain management, marketing, project management; supply chain management (Certificate); technology and innovation management (Certificate). *Accreditation:* AACSB. *Program availability:* Part-time. *Faculty:* 8 full-time (3 women). *Students:* 57 full-time (25 women), 152 part-time (76 women); includes 37 minority (20 Black or African American, non-Hispanic/Latino; 2 American Indian or Alaska Native, non-Hispanic/Latino; 6 Asian, non-Hispanic/Latino; 8 Hispanic/Latino; 1 Two or more races, non-Hispanic/Latino), 24 international. Average age 33. 178 applicants, 80% accepted, 84 enrolled. In 2018, 96 master's, 1 other advanced degree awarded. *Degree requirements:* For master's, comprehensive exam, thesis or alternative. *Entrance requirements:* For master's, GMAT (minimum score 500), minimum AACSB index of 1080. Additional exam requirements/recommendations for international students: Required—TOEFL (minimum score 550 paper-based; 80 iBT), IELTS (minimum score 6.5). *Application deadline:* For fall admission, 7/15 priority date for domestic students, 4/1 priority date for international students; for spring admission, 11/30 priority date for domestic students, 9/1 priority date for international students. Applications are processed on a rolling basis. Application fee: $50. Electronic applications accepted. *Expenses: Tuition, area resident:* Full-time $10,632; part-time $412 per credit hour. Tuition, state resident: full-time $10,632. Tuition, nonresident: full-time $23,604; part-time $412 per credit hour. *Required fees:* $582; $582. Tuition and fees vary according to course load and program. *Financial support:* In 2018–19, 15 students received support, including 15 teaching assistantships with full tuition reimbursements available (averaging $4,871 per year); research assistantships with full tuition reimbursements available, career-related internships or fieldwork, Federal Work-Study, institutionally sponsored loans, scholarships/grants, health care benefits, tuition waivers (full and partial), and unspecified assistantships also available. Support available to part-time students. Financial award application deadline: 4/1; financial award applicants required to submit FAFSA. *Faculty research:* Supply chain management, management of research and development, international marketing and branding, organizational behavior and human resource management, social networks and computational economics. *Unit head:* Dr. Fan Tseng, Chair, 256-824-6804, Fax: 256-824-6328, E-mail: fan.tseng@uah.edu. *Application contact:* Jennifer Pettitt, Director of Advising, 256-824-6681, Fax: 256-824-7571, E-mail: jennifer.pettitt@uah.edu.

The University of British Columbia, Sauder School of Business, Master of Business Analytics Program, Vancouver, BC V6T 1Z2, Canada. Offers MSBA. *Degree requirements:* For master's, industry project. *Entrance requirements:* For master's, GMAT or GRE, strong quantitative or analytical background, bachelor's degree or recognized equivalent from accredited university-level institution, minimum B+ average in undergraduate upper-level course work. Additional exam requirements/recommendations for international students: Required—TOEFL, IELTS or Michigan English Language Assessment Battery. Electronic applications accepted. *Expenses:* Contact institution. *Faculty research:* Operations and logistics.

University of California, Davis, Graduate School of Management, Full-Time MBA Program, Davis, CA 95616. Offers business analytics and technologies (MBA); entrepreneurship and innovation (MBA); finance and accounting (MBA); general management (MBA); marketing (MBA); organizational behavior (MBA); public health management (MBA); strategy (MBA); technology management (MBA); DVM/MBA; JD/MBA; M Engr/MBA; MBA/MPH; MBA/MS; MD/MBA; MSN/MBA; PhD/MBA. *Faculty:* 31 full-time (10 women). *Students:* 89 full-time (35 women); includes 21 minority (1 Black or African American, non-Hispanic/Latino; 14 Asian, non-Hispanic/Latino; 6 Hispanic/Latino), 43 international. Average age 28. 290 applicants, 39% accepted, 44 enrolled. In 2018, 45 master's awarded. *Degree requirements:* For master's, comprehensive exam, integrated management project. *Entrance requirements:* For master's, GMAT or GRE, letters of recommendation, resume, essays, equivalent of a 4-year U.S. undergraduate degree, transcript. Additional exam requirements/recommendations for international students: Required—TOEFL (minimum score 600 paper-based; 100 iBT), IELTS (minimum score 7). *Application deadline:* For fall admission, 9/15 priority date for domestic and international students. Applications are processed on a rolling basis. Application fee: $125. Electronic applications accepted. *Expenses:* Contact institution. *Financial support:* In 2018–19, 85 students received support. Fellowships with full and partial tuition reimbursements available, research assistantships with partial tuition reimbursements available, teaching assistantships with partial tuition reimbursements available, institutionally sponsored loans, scholarships/grants, health care benefits, tuition waivers (partial), and unspecified assistantships available. Financial award application deadline: 3/1; financial award applicants required to submit FAFSA. *Faculty research:* Finance, marketing, management, business analytics, accounting. *Unit head:* Amanda Opperman, Assistant Dean of Student Affairs, 530-752-7658, Fax: 530-754-9355, E-mail: admissions@gsm.ucdavis.edu. *Application contact:* Andrea Shaw, Senior Director of Admissions, 530-754-5476, Fax: 530-754-9355, E-mail: admissions@gsm.ucdavis.edu.
Website: http://gsm.ucdavis.edu/daytime-mba-program

University of California, Davis, Graduate School of Management, Master of Science in Business Analytics Program, San Francisco, CA 94102. Offers MSBA. *Faculty:* 4 full-time (1 woman), 7 part-time/adjunct (0 women). *Students:* 43 full-time (28 women); includes 5 minority (all Asian, non-Hispanic/Latino), 38 international. Average age 24. 845 applicants, 12% accepted, 43 enrolled. In 2018, 38 master's awarded. *Degree requirements:* For master's, comprehensive exam, Practicum. *Entrance requirements:* For master's, GMAT or GRE, resume; equivalent of undergraduate 4-year U.S. degree; essays; coursework in statistics, computer science, and math; letters of recommendation. Additional exam requirements/recommendations for international students: Required—TOEFL (minimum score 600 paper-based; 100 iBT), IELTS (minimum score 7). *Application deadline:* For fall admission, 9/15 priority date for domestic and international students. Application fee: $125. Electronic applications accepted. *Financial support:* In 2018–19, 32 students received support. Fellowships, research assistantships, teaching assistantships with partial tuition reimbursements available, and tuition waivers (partial) available. Financial award application deadline: 3/1; financial award applicants required to submit FAFSA. *Faculty research:* Business analytics, market research, competitive strategy, optimization, network effects. *Unit head:* Amanda Opperman, Assistant Dean of Student Affairs, 530-752-7658, Fax: 530-754-9355, E-mail: admissions@gsm.ucdavis.edu. *Application contact:* Andrea Shaw, Senior Director of Admissions, 530-754-5476, Fax: 530-754-9355, E-mail: admissions@gsm.ucdavis.edu.
Website: https://gsm.ucdavis.edu/msba-masters-science-business-analytics

University of California, Davis, Graduate School of Management, MBA Programs in Sacramento and San Francisco Bay Area, Davis, CA 95616. Offers business analytics and technologies (MBA); entrepreneurship and innovation (MBA); finance and accounting (MBA); general management (MBA); marketing (MBA); organizational behavior (MBA); public health management (MBA); strategy (MBA); technology management (MBA). *Program availability:* Part-time-only, evening/weekend. *Faculty:* 17 full-time (7 women), 42 part-time/adjunct (11 women). *Students:* 279 part-time (107 women); includes 146 minority (12 Black or African American, non-Hispanic/Latino; 3 American Indian or Alaska Native, non-Hispanic/Latino; 102 Asian, non-Hispanic/Latino; 29 Hispanic/Latino), 24 international. Average age 30. 158 applicants, 83% accepted, 91 enrolled. In 2018, 91 master's awarded. *Degree requirements:* For master's, integrated management project. *Entrance requirements:* For master's, GMAT or GRE, letters of recommendation, resume, equivalent of a 4-year undergraduate degree. Additional exam requirements/recommendations for international students: Required—TOEFL (minimum score 600 paper-based; 100 iBT), IELTS (minimum score 7). *Application deadline:* For fall admission, 9/15 priority date for domestic and international students. Applications are processed on a rolling basis. Application fee: $125. Electronic applications accepted. *Expenses:* Contact institution. *Financial support:* In 2018–19, 89 students received support. Fellowships, teaching assistantships with partial tuition reimbursements available, scholarships/grants, and unspecified assistantships available. Support available to part-time students. Financial award application deadline: 3/1; financial award applicants required to submit FAFSA. *Faculty research:* Accounting, finance, marketing, management, business analytics. *Unit head:* Amanda Opperman, Assistant Dean of Student Affairs, 530-752-7658, Fax: 530-754-9355, E-mail: admissions@gsm.ucdavis.edu. *Application contact:* Andrea Shaw, Senior Director of Admissions, 530-754-5476, Fax: 530-754-9355, E-mail: admissions@gsm.ucdavis.edu.
Website: http://gsm.ucdavis.edu/mba-programs

University of California, Irvine, The Paul Merage School of Business, Program in Business Analytics, Irvine, CA 92697. Offers MS. *Students:* 73 full-time (43 women); includes 22 minority (3 Black or African American, non-Hispanic/Latino; 15 Asian, non-Hispanic/Latino; 4 Hispanic/Latino), 47 international. Average age 25. 962 applicants, 17% accepted, 73 enrolled. In 2018, 74 master's awarded. *Application deadline:* For fall admission, 5/15 priority date for domestic students, 4/8 priority date for international students. Application fee: $105 ($125 for international students). *Unit head:* Eric Spangenberg, Dean, 949-824-8470, E-mail: ers@uci.edu. *Application contact:* Burt Slusher, Director, Recruitment and Admissions, 949-824-1609, E-mail: burt.slusher@uci.edu.
Website: http://sites.uci.edu/msbusinessanalytics/

University of California, Los Angeles, Graduate Division, UCLA Anderson School of Management, Los Angeles, CA 90095-1481. Offers accounting (PhD); behavioral decision making (PhD); business administration (EMBA, MBA); business administration/computer science (MBA/MSCS); business administration/latin american studies (MBA/MLAS); business administration/law (MBA/JD); business administration/library science (MBA/MLIS); business administration/medicine (MBA/MD); business administration/nursing (MBA/MN); business administration/public health (MBA/MPH); business administration/public policy (MBA/MPP); business administration/urban and regional planning (MBA/MURP); business analytics (MSBA); decisions, operations, and technology management (PhD); finance (PhD); financial engineering (MFE); global economics and management (PhD); management and organizations (PhD); marketing (PhD); strategy and policy (PhD); DDS/MBA; MBA/JD; MBA/MD; MBA/MLAS; MBA/MLIS; MBA/MN; MBA/MPH; MBA/MPP; MBA/MSCS; MBA/MURP. UCLA-NUS EMBA: UCLA Anderson and the National University of Singapore. *Accreditation:* AACSB. *Program availability:* Part-time, evening/weekend. *Faculty:* 86 full-time (19 women), 102 part-time/adjunct (16 women). *Students:* 1,040 full-time (378 women), 1,262 part-time (391 women); includes 784 minority (47 Black or African American, non-Hispanic/Latino; 1 American Indian or Alaska Native, non-Hispanic/Latino; 539 Asian, non-Hispanic/Latino; 116 Hispanic/Latino; 5 Native Hawaiian or other Pacific Islander, non-Hispanic/Latino; 76 Two or more races, non-Hispanic/Latino), 609 international. Average age 31. 6,708 applicants, 27% accepted, 949 enrolled. In 2018, 885 master's, 13 doctorates awarded. Terminal master's awarded for partial completion of doctoral program. *Degree requirements:* For master's, comprehensive exam, field consulting project (for MBA, FEMBA, EMBA, UCLA-NUS EMBA, MFE, and MSBA); internship (for MBA only); for doctorate, comprehensive exam, thesis/dissertation, oral and written qualifying exams. *Entrance requirements:* For master's, GMAT or GRE (for MBA, MFE, MSBA); Executive Assessment (EA) for candidates with 10+ years of work experience (FEMBA); Executive Assessment (EA) or STEM Master's degree or JD, MBA, CPA (EMBA), 4-year bachelor's degree or equivalent; 2 letters of recommendation; interview (invitation only); 2 essays; average 4-8 years of full-time work experience (for FEMBA); minimum 8 years of work experience with at least 3 years at management level (for EMBA); 10 years of full-time high managerial responsibility work experience (UCLA-NUS EMBA); for doctorate, GMAT or GRE, bachelor's degree from college or university of fully-recognized standing, minimum B average during junior and senior undergraduate years, 3 letters of recommendation, statement of purpose. Additional exam requirements/recommendations for international students: Required—TOEFL (minimum score 560 paper-based; 87 iBT), IELTS (minimum score 7), TOEFL with minimum iBT score of 100 (for MSBA). *Application deadline:* For fall admission, 10/2 for domestic and international students; for winter admission, 1/8 for domestic and international students; for spring admission, 4/16 for domestic and international students. Applications are processed on a rolling basis. Application fee: $200. Electronic applications accepted. *Expenses:* Per Year - MBA: $64,292, FEMBA: $42,420, EMBA: $81,120, UCLA-NUS EMBA (UC Portion only): $57,500, MFE: $75,816, MSBA: $64,1,43, PhD: $32,049. *Financial support:* Fellowships, research assistantships with partial tuition reimbursements, teaching assistantships with partial tuition reimbursements, career-related internships or fieldwork, institutionally sponsored loans, and scholarships/grants available. Support available to part-time students. *Faculty research:* Finance/global economics, entrepreneurship, accounting, human resources/organizational behavior, marketing and

behavioral decision making. *Total annual research expenditures:* $2 million. *Unit head:* Dr. Antonio Bernardo, Dean & John E. Anderson Chair in Management, 310-825-7982, Fax: 310-206-2073, E-mail: a.bernardo@anderson.ucla.edu. *Application contact:* Alex Lawrence, Assistant Dean and Director of MBA Admissions, 310-825-6944, Fax: 310-825-8582, E-mail: mba.admissions@anderson.ucla.edu.
Website: http://www.anderson.ucla.edu/

University of California, San Diego, Graduate Division, Rady School of Management, La Jolla, CA 92093. Offers business administration (MBA); business analytics (MS); finance (MF); management (PhD). *Accreditation:* AACSB. *Program availability:* Part-time, evening/weekend. *Faculty:* 28 full-time (5 women), 5 part-time/adjunct (1 woman). *Students:* 452 full-time (206 women), 158 part-time (91 women). 2,403 applicants, 34% accepted, 336 enrolled. In 2018, 297 master's, 3 doctorates awarded. *Degree requirements:* For master's, capstone project; for doctorate, comprehensive exam, thesis/dissertation. *Entrance requirements:* For master's, GMAT (for MBA); GMAT or GRE General Test (for MF and MPAC); for doctorate, GMAT or GRE General Test. Additional exam requirements/recommendations for international students: Required—TOEFL (minimum score 550 paper-based; 80 iBT), IELTS (minimum score 7). *Application deadline:* Applications are processed on a rolling basis. Application fee: $200. Electronic applications accepted. *Expenses:* Contact institution. *Financial support:* Fellowships, teaching assistantships, and scholarships/grants available. Financial award applicants required to submit FAFSA. *Faculty research:* Innovation technology, operations management, finance, behavioral economics, organizational strategy, marketing, business analytics. *Unit head:* Robert Sullivan, Dean, 858-822-0830, E-mail: rssullivan@ucsd.edu. *Application contact:* Jay Bryant, Director of Graduate Recruitment and Admissions, 858-534-0864, E-mail: radygradadmissions@ucsd.edu.
Website: http://rady.ucsd.edu/

University of Central Oklahoma, The Jackson College of Graduate Studies, College of Business, Edmond, OK 73034-5209. Offers business administration (MBA); business analytics (MS). *Program availability:* Part-time. *Degree requirements:* For master's, comprehensive exam (for some programs), thesis optional. *Entrance requirements:* For master's, GMAT, GRE. Additional exam requirements/recommendations for international students: Required—TOEFL (minimum score 550 paper-based; 79 iBT), IELTS (minimum score 6.5). Electronic applications accepted. *Expenses:* Contact institution.

University of Cincinnati, Carl H. Lindner College of Business, MS Program, Cincinnati, OH 45221. Offers accounting (MS); applied economics (MS); business analytics (MS); finance (MS); information systems (MS); marketing (MS); taxation (MS). *Program availability:* Part-time, evening/weekend. *Faculty:* 98 full-time (27 women), 28 part-time/adjunct (4 women). *Students:* 305 full-time (123 women), 190 part-time (83 women); includes 35 minority (13 Black or African American, non-Hispanic/Latino; 1 American Indian or Alaska Native, non-Hispanic/Latino; 10 Asian, non-Hispanic/Latino; 6 Hispanic/Latino; 5 Two or more races, non-Hispanic/Latino), 309 international. Average age 29. 1,219 applicants, 55% accepted, 495 enrolled. In 2018, 355 master's awarded. *Degree requirements:* For master's, thesis (for some programs), capstone. *Entrance requirements:* For master's, GMAT, GRE, resume, transcripts, essays, letters of recommendation. Additional exam requirements/recommendations for international students: Required—TOEFL (minimum score 577 paper-based; 90 iBT), IELTS (minimum score 6.5). *Application deadline:* For fall admission, 6/30 priority date for domestic students, 3/15 for international students; for spring admission, 12/15 for domestic students, 9/15 for international students; for summer admission, 4/15 for domestic and international students. Applications are processed on a rolling basis. Application fee: $65 ($70 for international students). Electronic applications accepted. *Expenses:* Full-time resident $10,479 per term, full-time nonresident $14,398 per term, part-time $890 per credit hour. *Financial support:* In 2018–19, 251 students received support, including 12 teaching assistantships with full and partial tuition reimbursements available (averaging $3,500 per year); scholarships/grants, tuition waivers (full and partial), and unspecified assistantships also available. Financial award application deadline: 2/1; financial award applicants required to submit FAFSA. *Faculty research:* Business analytics, financial management, organizational behavior, financial accounting, consumer insights. *Total annual research expenditures:* $39,943. *Unit head:* Dr. Marianne Lewis, Dean, 513-556-7001, Fax: 513-556-4891, E-mail: marianne.lewis@uc.edu. *Application contact:* Dona Clary, Executive Director, Graduate Programs, 513-556-3546, Fax: 513-558-7006, E-mail: dona.clary@uc.edu.
Website: http://business.uc.edu/graduate/masters.html

University of Cincinnati, Carl H. Lindner College of Business, PhD Programs, Cincinnati, OH 45221. Offers accounting (PhD); business analytics (PhD); economics (PhD); finance (PhD); information systems (PhD); management (PhD); marketing (PhD); operations and business analytics (PhD); operations research (PhD). *Faculty:* 101 full-time (37 women). *Students:* 15 full-time (5 women), 10 part-time (4 women); includes 4 minority (1 Black or African American, non-Hispanic/Latino; 3 Asian, non-Hispanic/Latino), 20 international. Average age 31. 125 applicants, 12% accepted, 4 enrolled. In 2018, 7 doctorates awarded. *Degree requirements:* For doctorate, comprehensive exam, thesis/dissertation. *Entrance requirements:* For doctorate, GMAT, GRE, transcripts, essays, resume, letters of recommendation. Additional exam requirements/recommendations for international students: Required—TOEFL (minimum score 600 paper-based; 100 iBT), IELTS (minimum score 7). *Application deadline:* For fall admission, 1/15 for domestic and international students. Application fee: $65 ($70 for international students). Electronic applications accepted. *Expenses:* Contact institution. *Financial support:* In 2018–19, 35 students received support, including 25 research assistantships with full tuition reimbursements available (averaging $23,250 per year); scholarships/grants, health care benefits, tuition waivers (full), and unspecified assistantships also available. Financial award application deadline: 1/15; financial award applicants required to submit FAFSA. *Faculty research:* Bayesian Prediction Theory, organizational fairness, consumer insight and market research, consumer insight and market research, density estimation from correlated data. *Unit head:* Dr. Olivier Parent, Director, 513-556-3941, Fax: 513-556-5499, E-mail: olivier.parent@uc.edu. *Application contact:* Angel Elvin, Assistant Director, 513-556-7190, Fax: 513-558-7006, E-mail: angel.elvin@uc.edu.
Website: http://business.uc.edu/graduate/phd.html

University of Connecticut, Graduate School, School of Business, Storrs, CT 06269. Offers accounting (MS, PhD); business (PhD); business administration (MBA); business analytics and project management (MS); finance (PhD); financial risk management (MS); health care management and insurance studies (MBA); human resource management (MS); management (PhD); management consulting (MBA); marketing (PhD); marketing intelligence (MBA); operations and information management (PhD). *Accreditation:* AACSB. *Degree requirements:* For master's, comprehensive exam; for doctorate, thesis/dissertation. *Entrance requirements:* For master's and doctorate, GMAT. Additional exam requirements/recommendations for international students: Required—TOEFL (minimum score 550 paper-based). Electronic applications accepted.

University of Dallas, Satish and Yasmin Gupta College of Business, Irving, TX 75062. Offers accounting (MBA, MS); business administration (DBA); business analytics (MS); business management (MBA); corporate finance (MBA); cybersecurity (MS); finance (MS); financial services (MBA); global business (MBA, MS); health services management (MBA); human resource management (MBA); information and technology management (MS); information assurance (MBA); information technology (MBA); information technology service management (MBA); marketing management (MBA); organization development (MBA); project management (MBA); sports and entertainment management (MBA); strategic leadership (MBA); supply chain management (MBA). *Accreditation:* AACSB. *Program availability:* Part-time, evening/weekend, 100% online. *Students:* 147 full-time (56 women), 584 part-time (232 women); includes 402 minority (204 Black or African American, non-Hispanic/Latino; 95 Asian, non-Hispanic/Latino; 92 Hispanic/Latino; 2 Native Hawaiian or other Pacific Islander, non-Hispanic/Latino; 9 Two or more races, non-Hispanic/Latino), 113 international. Average age 34. 992 applicants, 30% accepted, 157 enrolled. In 2018, 336 master's, 5 doctorates awarded. *Degree requirements:* For doctorate, thesis/dissertation. *Entrance requirements:* For master's and doctorate, U.S. bachelor's degree with a minimum cumulative GPA of 2.0 from a regionally accredited college or university (or comparable foreign degree); minimum 3.0 GPA in any graduate-level coursework completed; good academic standing with all colleges attended. Additional exam requirements/recommendations for international students: Required—TOEFL (minimum score 80 iBT), IELTS (minimum score 6.5), PTE (minimum score 67). *Application deadline:* Applications are processed on a rolling basis. Application fee: $50. Electronic applications accepted. *Expenses:* $1250 per credit hour. *Financial support:* In 2018–19, 291 students received support. Research assistantships, teaching assistantships, scholarships/grants, and unspecified assistantships available. Support available to part-time students. Financial award application deadline: 2/15; financial award applicants required to submit FAFSA. *Unit head:* Brett J.L. Landry, Dean, 972-721-5356, E-mail: blandry@udallas.edu. *Application contact:* Breonna Collins, Director, Graduate Admissions, 972-7215304, E-mail: bcollins@udallas.edu.
Website: http://www.udallas.edu/cob/

University of Denver, Daniels College of Business, Department of Business Information and Analytics, Denver, CO 80208. Offers MBA, MS. *Faculty:* 17 full-time (8 women), 3 part-time/adjunct (0 women). *Students:* 28 full-time (12 women), 26 part-time (12 women); includes 6 minority (1 Asian, non-Hispanic/Latino; 3 Hispanic/Latino; 1 Native Hawaiian or other Pacific Islander, non-Hispanic/Latino; 1 Two or more races, non-Hispanic/Latino), 18 international. Average age 29. 169 applicants, 50% accepted, 25 enrolled. In 2018, 47 master's awarded. *Entrance requirements:* For master's, GRE General Test or GMAT, bachelor's degree, transcripts, essays, resume, interview by invitation only. Additional exam requirements/recommendations for international students: Required—TOEFL (minimum score 575 paper-based; 94 iBT). *Application deadline:* For fall admission, 10/15 priority date for domestic and international students; for spring admission, 9/15 priority date for domestic and international students. Applications are processed on a rolling basis. Application fee: $100. Electronic applications accepted. *Expenses:* $49,695 per year full-time; $1,372 per credit. *Financial support:* In 2018–19, 39 students received support. Teaching assistantships with tuition reimbursements available, career-related internships or fieldwork, Federal Work-Study, institutionally sponsored loans, scholarships/grants, and unspecified assistantships available. Support available to part-time students. Financial award application deadline: 2/15; financial award applicants required to submit FAFSA. *Faculty research:* Information technology strategy, project management, healthcare information systems, distributed knowledge work, complex adaptive systems. *Unit head:* Dr. Andrew Urbaczewski, Associate Professor and Chair, 303-871-4802, E-mail: andrew.urbaczewski@du.edu. *Application contact:* Alicia Lucero, Assistant to the Chair, 303-871-3695, E-mail: alicia.lucero@du.edu.
Website: https://daniels.du.edu/business-information-analytics

University of Georgia, Terry College of Business, Program in Business Analytics, Athens, GA 30602. Offers MSBA.

The University of Iowa, Tippie College of Business, MS Program in Business Analytics, Iowa City, IA 52242-1316. Offers MS. Program offered at the Cedar Rapids, Des Moines and Quad City locations. *Program availability:* Part-time-only, evening/weekend. *Degree requirements:* For master's, 30 hours. *Entrance requirements:* Additional exam requirements/recommendations for international students: Required—TOEFL (minimum score 100 iBT). Electronic applications accepted.

The University of Iowa, Tippie College of Business, Professional MBA Program, Iowa City, IA 52242-1316. Offers business administration (MBA); business analytics (MBA); finance (MBA); leadership (MBA); marketing (MBA). *Program availability:* Part-time-only, evening/weekend. *Degree requirements:* For master's, successful completion of nine required courses and six electives totaling 45 credits, minimum GPA of 2.75. *Entrance requirements:* For master's, GMAT or GRE. Additional exam requirements/recommendations for international students: Required—TOEFL (minimum score 600 paper-based; 100 iBT), IELTS (minimum score 7). Electronic applications accepted. *Expenses:* Contact institution. *Faculty research:* Capital markets; analytics techniques and applications; organizational and market systems analysis; applied econometrics; talent effectiveness.

The University of Manchester, Alliance Manchester Business School, M15 6PB, United Kingdom. Offers accounting and finance (M Sc); business (M Ent); business analysis and strategic management (M Sc); business analytics: operational research and risk analysis (M Sc); business psychology (M Sc); corporate communications and reputation management (M Sc); finance (M Sc); finance and business economics (M Sc); human resource management and industrial relations (M Sc); innovation management and entrepreneurship (M Sc); international business and management (M Sc); international human resource management and comparative industrial relations (M Sc); management (M Sc); marketing (M Sc); operations, project and supply chain management (M Sc); organizational psychology (M Sc); quantitative finance (M Sc). *Entrance requirements:* For master's, UK 2:1 honours degree or overseas equivalent. Additional exam requirements/recommendations for international students: Required—TOEFL (minimum score 100 iBT), IELTS (minimum score 7), PTE. Electronic applications accepted. *Faculty research:* Accounting and finance, management sciences and marketing, people management and organization, innovation management and policy, decision sciences.

University of Massachusetts Boston, College of Management, Program in Business Analytics, Boston, MA 02125-3393. Offers MS. *Students:* 19 full-time (13 women), 15 part-time (8 women); includes 6 minority (3 Asian, non-Hispanic/Latino; 3 Hispanic/Latino), 15 international. Average age 31. 41 applicants, 90% accepted, 21 enrolled. In 2018, 4 master's awarded. *Application deadline:* For fall admission, 7/1 for domestic students; for spring admission, 11/15 for domestic students. *Expenses: Tuition, area resident:* Full-time $17,896. Tuition, state resident: full-time $17,896. Tuition, nonresident: full-time $34,932. *International tuition:* $34,932 full-time. *Required fees:* $355. *Unit head:* Dr. Roger Blake, Associate Chair, 617-287.7692, E-mail: roger.blake@umb.edu. *Application contact:* Graduate Admissions Coordinator, 617-287-6400, Fax: 617-287-6236, E-mail: graduate.admissions@umb.edu.
Website: https://www.umb.edu/academics/cm/masters_programs/degrees/master_of_science_in_business_analytics_msba

University of Miami, Miami Business School, Coral Gables, FL 33146. Offers accounting (M Acc); business (PhD); business administration (MBA); business analytics (MSBA); economics (PhD); finance (MSF); health administration (MHA); international business (MIBS); real estate (MBA); taxation (MS Tax); JD/MBA; MD/MBA.

Accreditation: AACSB; CAHME (one or more programs are accredited). *Program availability:* Part-time, evening/weekend, 100% online, blended/hybrid learning. *Faculty:* 155 full-time (47 women), 14 part-time/adjunct (5 women). *Students:* 1,083 full-time (469 women); includes 422 minority (79 Black or African American, non-Hispanic/Latino; 1 American Indian or Alaska Native, non-Hispanic/Latino; 43 Asian, non-Hispanic/Latino; 274 Hispanic/Latino; 3 Native Hawaiian or other Pacific Islander, non-Hispanic/Latino; 22 Two or more races, non-Hispanic/Latino), 282 international. Average age 30. 2,564 applicants, 38% accepted, 450 enrolled. In 2018, 558 master's, 5 doctorates awarded. Terminal master's awarded for partial completion of doctoral program. *Degree requirements:* For master's, comprehensive exam; for doctorate, comprehensive exam, thesis/dissertation. *Entrance requirements:* For master's, GMAT or GRE; for doctorate, GRE General Test. Additional exam requirements/recommendations for international students: Required—TOEFL (minimum score 94 iBT), IELTS (minimum score 7), TOEFL (minimum score 587 paper-based, 94 iBT) or IELTS (7). *Application deadline:* For fall admission, 6/30 priority date for domestic students, 5/30 priority date for international students; for spring admission, 10/31 priority date for domestic students, 9/30 priority date for international students. Applications are processed on a rolling basis. Application fee: $48. Electronic applications accepted. *Expenses:* Contact institution. *Financial support:* In 2018–19, 643 students received support, including 1 fellowship with full tuition reimbursement available (averaging $20,000 per year), 47 research assistantships with full and partial tuition reimbursements available (averaging $28,826 per year), 6 teaching assistantships with full and partial tuition reimbursements available (averaging $2,183 per year); career-related internships or fieldwork, Federal Work-Study, institutionally sponsored loans, scholarships/grants, and unspecified assistantships also available. Support available to part-time students. Financial award application deadline: 3/26; financial award applicants required to submit FAFSA. *Faculty research:* Behavioral finance; computational economics; consumer research; risk perception; consumer behavior; consumer choice research; behavioral decision theory; business analytics; point processes; longitudinal data analyses; international business; global business strategy, joint ventures, and alliances; emerging economies; global economic growth and development, money and financial markets, and computed dynamic models; health policy; innovative payment mechanisms. *Total annual research expenditures:* $703,773. *Unit head:* Dr. John Quelch, Dean, 305-284-6515, Fax: 305-284-6526, E-mail: jquelch@miami.edu. *Application contact:* Loubna Bouamane, Director of Graduate Business Recruiting and Admissions, 305-284-2510, Fax: 305-284-5905, E-mail: loubna@miami.edu.
Website: www.mbs.miami.edu

University of Michigan–Dearborn, College of Business, MS Program in Business Analytics, Dearborn, MI 48126. Offers MS. *Program availability:* Part-time, evening/weekend. *Faculty:* 41 full-time (17 women), 9 part-time/adjunct (6 women). *Students:* 32 full-time (15 women), 69 part-time (28 women); includes 14 minority (2 Black or African American, non-Hispanic/Latino; 7 Asian, non-Hispanic/Latino; 1 Hispanic/Latino; 4 Two or more races, non-Hispanic/Latino), 55 international. Average age 29. 135 applicants, 48% accepted, 28 enrolled. In 2018, 52 master's awarded. *Entrance requirements:* For master's, GMAT or GRE, equivalent of four-year U.S. bachelor's degree from regionally-accredited institution, undergraduate course in finite math, pre-calculus, or calculus. Additional exam requirements/recommendations for international students: Required—TOEFL (minimum score 560 paper-based; 84 iBT), IELTS (minimum score 6.5). *Application deadline:* For fall admission, 8/1 for domestic students, 5/1 for international students; for winter admission, 12/1 for domestic students, 9/1 for international students; for spring admission, 4/1 for domestic students, 1/1 for international students. Applications are processed on a rolling basis. Application fee: $60. Electronic applications accepted. *Expenses:* $15,740 per academic year (typical full-time in-state); $24,308 per academic year (typical full-time out-of-state). *Financial support:* In 2018–19, 59 students received support. Scholarships/grants and non-resident tuition scholarships available. Financial award application deadline: 3/1; financial award applicants required to submit FAFSA. *Faculty research:* Business intelligence, behavioral finance, brand management and new media, management education, operations strategy. *Unit head:* Dr. Michael Kamen, Director, Graduate Programs, 313-593-5460, E-mail: mkamen@umich.edu. *Application contact:* Joan Doherty, Academic Advisor/Counselor, 313-593-5460, Fax: 313-271-9838, E-mail: umd-gradbusiness@umich.edu.
Website: http://umdearborn.edu/cob/ms-business-analytics/

The University of North Carolina at Charlotte, Belk College of Business, Department of Management, Charlotte, NC 28223-0001. Offers business administration (MBA, DBA, PhD); business analytics (Graduate Certificate); management (MS). *Program availability:* Part-time, evening/weekend. *Students:* 135 full-time (67 women), 266 part-time (86 women); includes 115 minority (45 Black or African American, non-Hispanic/Latino; 1 American Indian or Alaska Native, non-Hispanic/Latino; 35 Asian, non-Hispanic/Latino; 22 Hispanic/Latino; 12 Two or more races, non-Hispanic/Latino), 103 international. Average age 29. 314 applicants, 70% accepted, 147 enrolled. In 2018, 98 master's, 3 doctorates, 5 other advanced degrees awarded. *Degree requirements:* For doctorate, comprehensive exam (for some programs), thesis/dissertation. *Entrance requirements:* For master's, GMAT or GRE, bachelor's degree from regionally-accredited college or university; at least three evaluations from persons familiar with applicant's personal and professional qualifications; essay describing applicant's experience and objectives; resume; for doctorate, GMAT (minimum score of 650) or GRE (minimum 700 on quantitative section, 500 on verbal), baccalaureate or master's degree in business, economics, or related field such as mathematical finance, mathematics, or physics with minimum undergraduate GPA of 3.5 (3.25 graduate); three letters of recommendation; statement of purpose; for Graduate Certificate, transcripts, minimum undergraduate GPA of 2.75, essay describing experience and objectives. Additional exam requirements/recommendations for international students: Required—TOEFL (minimum score 523 paper-based; 70 iBT), IELTS (minimum score 6), TOEFL (minimum score 523 paper-based, 70 iBT) or IELTS (6.0). *Application deadline:* Applications are processed on a rolling basis. Application fee: $75. Electronic applications accepted. *Expenses:* Contact institution. *Financial support:* Research assistantships, teaching assistantships, career-related internships or fieldwork, institutionally sponsored loans, scholarships/grants, and unspecified assistantships available. Support available to part-time students. Financial award application deadline: 3/1; financial award applicants required to submit FAFSA. *Total annual research expenditures:* $167,166. *Unit head:* Dr. David J. Woehr, Department Chair, 704-687-7684, Fax: 704-687-1380, E-mail: dwoehr@uncc.edu. *Application contact:* Kathy B. Giddings, Director of Graduate Admissions, 704-687-5503, Fax: 704-687-1668, E-mail: gradadm@uncc.edu.
Website: https://belkcollege.uncc.edu/departments/management

The University of North Carolina at Charlotte, The Graduate School, Program in Data Science and Business Analytics, Charlotte, NC 28223-0001. Offers MS, PSM, Graduate Certificate. *Program availability:* Part-time, evening/weekend. *Students:* 62 full-time (31 women), 101 part-time (33 women); includes 50 minority (19 Black or African American, non-Hispanic/Latino; 20 Asian, non-Hispanic/Latino; 8 Hispanic/Latino; 3 Two or more races, non-Hispanic/Latino), 52 international. Average age 31. 456 applicants, 32% accepted, 84 enrolled. In 2018, 57 master's, 13 other advanced degrees awarded. *Entrance requirements:* For master's, GRE, GMAT, undergraduate degree in any scientific, engineering or business discipline or a closely-related field; minimum undergraduate GPA of 3.0; three letters of recommendation; statement of purpose outlining goals for pursuing graduate education; current working knowledge of at least one higher-level (procedural) language; for Graduate Certificate, undergraduate degree in any scientific, engineering or business discipline or a closely-related field; minimum undergraduate GPA of 3.0; statement of purpose outlining goals for pursuing graduate education; current working knowledge of at least one higher-level (procedural) language; familiarity with computer applications. Additional exam requirements/recommendations for international students: Required—TOEFL (minimum score 523 paper-based; 70 iBT), IELTS (minimum score 6), TOEFL (minimum score 523 paper-based, 70 iBT) or IELTS (6). *Application deadline:* Applications are processed on a rolling basis. Application fee: $75. Electronic applications accepted. *Expenses:* Contact institution. *Financial support:* Career-related internships or fieldwork, institutionally sponsored loans, scholarships/grants, and unspecified assistantships available. Support available to part-time students. Financial award application deadline: 3/1; financial award applicants required to submit FAFSA. *Unit head:* Carly Mahedy, Director of Student Services, Data Science Initiative, 704-687-0068, E-mail: datascience@uncc.edu. *Application contact:* Kathy B. Giddings, Director of Graduate Admissions, 704-687-5503, Fax: 704-687-1668, E-mail: gradadm@uncc.edu.
Website: http://www.analytics.uncc.edu/

University of Notre Dame, Mendoza College of Business, Master of Business Administration Program, Notre Dame, IN 46556. Offers business analytics (MBA); business leadership (MBA); consulting (MBA); corporate finance (MBA); innovation and entrepreneurship (MBA); investments (MBA); marketing (MBA); MBA/MSBA. *Accreditation:* AACSB. *Entrance requirements:* For master's, GMAT or GRE, work experience, essay, four-slide presentation, two recommendations, transcripts from all colleges and/or universities attended, interview. Additional exam requirements/recommendations for international students: Required—PTE (minimum score 68), TOEFL (minimum iBT score of 109), IELTS (7.5), or documentation of at least six semesters of full-time university education in English. Electronic applications accepted. *Expenses:* Contact institution. *Faculty research:* Market micro-structure; marketing and public policy; corporate finance and accounting; corporate governance and ethical behavior; high performing organizations.

University of Notre Dame, Mendoza College of Business, Master of Science in Business Analytics Program, Notre Dame, IN 46556. Offers MSBA. *Entrance requirements:* For master's, minimum of two years of work experience, evidence of quantitative capabilities to complete a rigorous analytical curriculum. Additional exam requirements/recommendations for international students: Required—TOEFL, IELTS. Electronic applications accepted. *Expenses:* Contact institution. *Faculty research:* Methods and approaches for improving decision making, applied work on decision-making models and processes for accounting; financial management; resource allocation; risk management; the development, improvement and evaluation of statistical methods and measurement issues; supply chain management and integration; design of lean service processes; and adoption of lean manufacturing systems.

University of Oklahoma, Price College of Business, Division of Management Information Systems, Norman, OK 73019. Offers digital technologies (Graduate Certificate); management of information technology (MS), including business analytics. *Program availability:* Part-time, evening/weekend. *Faculty:* 9 full-time (6 women), 3 part-time/adjunct (0 women). *Students:* 23 full-time (8 women), 15 part-time (8 women); includes 8 minority (1 Black or African American, non-Hispanic/Latino; 2 Asian, non-Hispanic/Latino; 2 Hispanic/Latino; 3 Two or more races, non-Hispanic/Latino), 10 international. Average age 27. 28 applicants, 25% accepted, 5 enrolled. In 2018, 17 master's, 4 other advanced degrees awarded. *Degree requirements:* For master's, thesis optional. *Entrance requirements:* For master's and Graduate Certificate, GMAT or GRE, resume, statement of goals, 3 letters of recommendation. Additional exam requirements/recommendations for international students: Required—TOEFL (minimum score 100 iBT) or IELTS (minimum score 7). *Application deadline:* For fall admission, 6/15 for domestic students, 3/1 for international students; for spring admission, 10/1 for domestic students, 8/1 for international students. Applications are processed on a rolling basis. Application fee: $50 ($100 for international students). Electronic applications accepted. *Expenses:* Tuition, state resident: full-time $5683.20; part-time $236.80 per credit hour. Tuition, nonresident: full-time $20,342; part-time $847.60 per credit hour. *International tuition:* $20,342.40 full-time. *Required fees:* $2894.20; $110.05 per credit hour. $126.50 per semester. Tuition and fees vary according to course load and program. *Financial support:* Research assistantships, teaching assistantships, career-related internships or fieldwork, scholarships/grants, and unspecified assistantships available. Support available to part-time students. Financial award application deadline: 6/1; financial award applicants required to submit FAFSA. *Faculty research:* Human-computer interaction and cognition; deception detection in IT-mediated contexts; social media use; computer-mediated collaboration and communication; meaning in discourse about IT and discourse through IT. *Unit head:* Radhika Santhanam, Chair/Division Director, 405-325-0791, E-mail: radhika@ou.edu. *Application contact:* Jennifer Aragon, Academic Advisor, 405-325-2074, Fax: 405-325-7118, E-mail: jhardman@ou.edu.
Website: http://www.ou.edu/content/price/mis/mis_ms_in_mis.html

University of Pittsburgh, Katz Graduate School of Business, Doctoral Program in Business Administration, Pittsburgh, PA 15260. Offers accounting (PhD); business analytics and operations (PhD); finance (PhD); information systems and technology management (PhD); marketing (PhD); organizational behavior and human resources (PhD); strategic management (PhD). *Accreditation:* AACSB. *Program availability:* Evening/weekend. *Degree requirements:* For doctorate, comprehensive exam, thesis/dissertation, student teaching. *Entrance requirements:* For doctorate, GMAT or GRE, 3 recommendations, statement of purpose, transcripts of all previous course work and degrees. Additional exam requirements/recommendations for international students: Required—TOEFL (minimum score 100 iBT) or IELTS (minimum score 7.0). Electronic applications accepted. *Faculty research:* Accounting systems/financial reporting, corporate finance, shopper marketing/consumer behavior, management information systems, organizational behavior and entrepreneurship.

University of St. Francis, College of Business and Health Administration, Joliet, IL 60435-6169. Offers accounting (MBA, Certificate); business analytics (MBA, Certificate); e-learning (Certificate); finance (MBA, Certificate); health administration (MBA, MS); human resource management (MBA, Certificate); logistics (Certificate); management (MBA, MSM); management of training and development (Certificate); supply chain management (MBA); training and development (MBA); training specialist (Certificate). *Program availability:* Part-time, evening/weekend, 100% online, blended/hybrid learning. *Faculty:* 13 full-time (6 women), 20 part-time/adjunct (7 women). *Students:* 139 full-time (94 women), 206 part-time (159 women); includes 86 minority (51 Black or African American, non-Hispanic/Latino; 1 American Indian or Alaska Native, non-Hispanic/Latino; 11 Asian, non-Hispanic/Latino; 21 Hispanic/Latino; 2 Two or more races, non-Hispanic/Latino), 24 international. Average age 37. 261 applicants, 63% accepted, 98 enrolled. In 2018, 129 master's, 3 other advanced degrees awarded. *Degree requirements:* For master's, comprehensive exam (for some programs). *Entrance requirements:* Additional exam requirements/recommendations for international students: Required—TOEFL (minimum score 550 paper-based; 79 iBT), IELTS

(minimum score 6). *Application deadline:* Applications are processed on a rolling basis. Electronic applications accepted. Application fee is waived when completed online. *Expenses:* Contact institution. *Financial support:* In 2018–19, 126 students received support. Scholarships/grants and tuition waivers (partial) available. Support available to part-time students. Financial award applicants required to submit FAFSA. *Unit head:* Dr. Orlando Griego, Dean, 815-740-3395, Fax: 815-740-3452, E-mail: ogriego@stfrancis.edu. *Application contact:* Sandee Sloka, Director Adult & Graduate Admissions, 800-735-7500, E-mail: ssloka@stfrancis.edu.
Website: https://www.stfrancis.edu/business-health-administration/

University of St. Thomas, Opus College of Business, Master of Science in Business Analytics Program, St. Paul, MN 55105-1096. Offers MS. Tuition and fees vary according to course load, degree level and program. *Unit head:* Corey Eakins, Senior Program Director, 651-962-4228, E-mail: cmeakins@stthomas.edu. *Application contact:* Tiffany Cork, Director of Recruiting and Admissions, 651-962-8801, Fax: 651-962-4129, E-mail: ustmba@stthomas.edu.
Website: https://business.stthomas.edu/degrees-programs/specialized-masters/ms-business-analytics/index.html

University of South Dakota, Graduate School, Beacom School of Business, Department of Business Administration, Vermillion, SD 57069. Offers business administration (MBA); business analytics (MBA, Graduate Certificate); health services administration (MBA); long term care management (Graduate Certificate); marketing (MBA, Graduate Certificate); operations and supply chain management (MBA, Graduate Certificate); JD/MBA. *Accreditation:* AACSB. *Program availability:* Part-time, blended/hybrid learning. *Degree requirements:* For master's, thesis or alternative. *Entrance requirements:* For master's, GMAT, minimum GPA of 2.7, resume. Additional exam requirements/recommendations for international students: Required—TOEFL (minimum score 550 paper-based; 79 iBT), IELTS (minimum score 6). Electronic applications accepted. *Expenses:* Contact institution.

The University of Tampa, Sykes College of Business, Tampa, FL 33606-1490. Offers accounting (MS); business analytics (MBA); cybersecurity (MBA, MS); entrepreneurship (MBA, MS); finance (MBA, MS); information systems management (MBA); innovation management (MBA); international business (MBA); marketing (MBA, MS); nonprofit management (MBA, Certificate). *Accreditation:* AACSB. *Program availability:* Part-time, evening/weekend. *Faculty:* 61 full-time (13 women), 11 part-time/adjunct (3 women). *Students:* 361 full-time (153 women), 122 part-time (52 women); includes 101 minority (31 Black or African American, non-Hispanic/Latino; 5 Asian, non-Hispanic/Latino; 57 Hispanic/Latino; 1 Native Hawaiian or other Pacific Islander, non-Hispanic/Latino; 7 Two or more races, non-Hispanic/Latino), 144 international. Average age 29. 1,079 applicants, 57% accepted, 263 enrolled. In 2018, 281 master's, 12 other advanced degrees awarded. *Degree requirements:* For master's, capstone. *Entrance requirements:* For master's, GMAT or GRE, official transcripts from all colleges and/or universities previously attended, resume, personal statement, letters of recommendation. Additional exam requirements/recommendations for international students: Required—TOEFL (minimum score 577 paper-based; 90 iBT), IELTS (minimum score 7.5). *Application deadline:* Applications are processed on a rolling basis. Application fee: $40. Electronic applications accepted. *Expenses:* Contact institution. *Financial support:* In 2018–19, 123 students received support. Career-related internships or fieldwork, scholarships/grants, and unspecified assistantships available. Financial award applicants required to submit FAFSA. *Faculty research:* Job market signaling, on-line shopping behaviors and social media, the Tampa Bay economy, digital literacy, entrepreneurship in small businesses. *Unit head:* Dr. Natasha F. Veltri, Associate Dean, 813-253-6289, E-mail: nveltri@ut.edu. *Application contact:* Ashley Russell, Staff Assistant, Admissions for Graduate and Continuing Studies, 813-253-6249, E-mail: arussell@ut.edu.
Website: http://www.ut.edu/business/

The University of Tulsa, Graduate School, Collins College of Business, Program in Business Analytics, Tulsa, OK 74104-3189. Offers MS. *Program availability:* Part-time. *Students:* 12 full-time (4 women), 14 part-time (4 women); includes 3 minority (1 American Indian or Alaska Native, non-Hispanic/Latino; 2 Asian, non-Hispanic/Latino), 14 international. Average age 26. 34 applicants, 76% accepted, 15 enrolled. *Entrance requirements:* Additional exam requirements/recommendations for international students: Required—TOEFL (minimum score 90 iBT), IELTS. *Application deadline:* Applications are processed on a rolling basis. Application fee: $55. Electronic applications accepted. *Expenses: Tuition:* Full-time $22,230; part-time $1235 per credit hour. *Required fees:* $2100; $6 per credit hour. One-time fee: $400 full-time. Tuition and fees vary according to course level, course load and program. *Financial support:* In 2018–19, 3 students received support, including 3 teaching assistantships with full tuition reimbursements available (averaging $6,321 per year); career-related internships or fieldwork, Federal Work-Study, scholarships/grants, health care benefits, and unspecified assistantships also available. Support available to part-time students. Financial award applicants required to submit FAFSA. *Unit head:* Dr. Ralph Jackson, Associate Dean, 918-631-2213, E-mail: ralph-jackson@utulsa.edu. *Application contact:* Information Contact, 918-631-2242, E-mail: graduate-business@utulsa.edu.
Website: https://business.utulsa.edu/academics/master-science-business-analytics/

University of Wisconsin–Milwaukee, Graduate School, Lubar School of Business, Other Business Programs, Milwaukee, WI 53201-0413. Offers business analytics (Graduate Certificate); enterprise resource planning (Graduate Certificate); information technology management (MS); investment management (Graduate Certificate); nonprofit management (Graduate Certificate); nonprofit management and leadership (MS); state and local taxation (Graduate Certificate). *Students:* 132 full-time (63 women), 120 part-time (58 women); includes 45 minority (11 Black or African American, non-Hispanic/Latino; 15 Asian, non-Hispanic/Latino; 4 Hispanic/Latino; 15 Two or more races, non-Hispanic/Latino), 52 international. Average age 31. 196 applicants, 63% accepted, 80 enrolled. In 2018, 108 master's, 18 other advanced degrees awarded. *Entrance requirements:* Additional exam requirements/recommendations for international students: Required—TOEFL (minimum score 550 paper-based; 79 iBT), IELTS (minimum score 6.5). Application fee: $56 ($96 for international students). Electronic applications accepted. *Financial support:* Fellowships, research assistantships, teaching assistantships, health care benefits, unspecified assistantships, and project assistantships available. Financial award applicants required to submit FAFSA. *Application contact:* General Information Contact, 414-229-4982, Fax: 414-229-6967, E-mail: gradschool@uwm.edu.

Villanova University, Villanova School of Business, Master of Science in Analytics Program, Villanova, PA 19085-1699. Offers MSA. *Program availability:* Part-time-only, evening/weekend, online only, 100% online. *Faculty:* 101 full-time (38 women), 36 part-time/adjunct (9 women). *Students:* 167 part-time (53 women); includes 31 minority (5 Black or African American, non-Hispanic/Latino; 1 American Indian or Alaska Native, non-Hispanic/Latino; 15 Asian, non-Hispanic/Latino; 6 Hispanic/Latino; 4 Two or more races, non-Hispanic/Latino), 4 international. Average age 33. 179 applicants, 75% accepted, 103 enrolled. In 2018, 69 master's awarded. *Degree requirements:* For master's, minimum GPA of 3.0. *Entrance requirements:* For master's, Application, official transcripts, 3 letters of recommendation, resume, 2 essays. Additional exam requirements/recommendations for international students: Required—TOEFL (minimum score 550 paper-based; 100 iBT). *Application deadline:* For fall admission, 7/31 for domestic and international students; for spring admission, 11/30 for domestic and international students. Applications are processed on a rolling basis. Application fee: $65. Electronic applications accepted. *Expenses:* Contact institution. *Financial support:* Scholarships/grants available. Financial award application deadline: 6/30; financial award applicants required to submit FAFSA. *Faculty research:* Real Estate, Business Analytics, Global Leadership, Marketing and Consumer Insights, Church management. *Unit head:* Dr. Joyce Russell, Dean of Villanova School of Business, 610-519-5424, Fax: 610-519-6273, E-mail: joyce.russell@villanova.edu. *Application contact:* Claire Bruno, Director of Recruitment and Enrollment Management, 610-519-6745, Fax: 610-519-6745, E-mail: claire.bruno@villanova.edu.
Website: http://www1.villanova.edu/villanova/business/graduate/specializedprograms/msa.html

Virginia Polytechnic Institute and State University, Graduate School, Pamplin College of Business, Blacksburg, VA 24061. Offers accounting and information systems (MACIS, PhD); business administration (MS), including business analytics, hospitality and tourism management; business information technology (PhD); executive business research (PhD); finance (MS, PhD); marketing (PhD), including marketing; MS/MBA. *Faculty:* 141 full-time (42 women), 2 part-time/adjunct (1 woman). *Students:* 227 full-time (89 women), 217 part-time (75 women); includes 131 minority (30 Black or African American, non-Hispanic/Latino; 58 Asian, non-Hispanic/Latino; 25 Hispanic/Latino; 18 Two or more races, non-Hispanic/Latino), 81 international. Average age 32. 361 applicants, 55% accepted, 152 enrolled. In 2018, 181 master's, 8 doctorates awarded. *Degree requirements:* For master's, comprehensive exam (for some programs), thesis (for some programs); for doctorate, comprehensive exam (for some programs), thesis/dissertation (for some programs). *Entrance requirements:* For master's and doctorate, GRE/GMAT. Additional exam requirements/recommendations for international students: Required—TOEFL (minimum score 90 iBT). *Application deadline:* For fall admission, 8/1 for domestic students, 4/1 for international students; for spring admission, 1/1 for domestic students, 9/1 for international students. Applications are processed on a rolling basis. Application fee: $75. Electronic applications accepted. *Expenses:* Tuition, state resident: full-time $15,510; part-time $739.50 per credit hour. Tuition, nonresident: full-time $29,629; part-time $1490.25 per credit hour. *Required fees:* $2804; $550 per semester. Tuition and fees vary according to course load, campus/location and program. *Financial support:* In 2018–19, 1 fellowship with full tuition reimbursement (averaging $3,999 per year), 4 research assistantships with full tuition reimbursements (averaging $20,163 per year), 66 teaching assistantships with full tuition reimbursements (averaging $19,822 per year) were awarded; scholarships/grants and unspecified assistantships also available. Financial award application deadline: 3/1; financial award applicants required to submit FAFSA. *Total annual research expenditures:* $3.1 million. *Unit head:* Dr. Robert T. Sumichrast, Dean, 540-231-6601, Fax: 540-231-4487, E-mail: busdean@vt.edu. *Application contact:* Kimberly Ridpath, Executive Assistant, 540-231-9647, Fax: 540-231-4487, E-mail: ridpathk@vt.edu.
Website: http://www.pamplin.vt.edu/

Wake Forest University, School of Business, MS in Business Analytics Program, Winston-Salem, NC 27106. Offers MSBA. *Degree requirements:* For master's, 37 credit hours. *Entrance requirements:* For master's, GMAT, bachelor's degree in business, engineering, mathematics, economics, computer science or liberal arts; coursework in calculus and statistics. Additional exam requirements/recommendations for international students: Required—TOEFL (minimum score 600 paper-based). Electronic applications accepted. *Expenses:* Contact institution.

Walsh College of Accountancy and Business Administration, Graduate Programs, Program in Accountancy, Troy, MI 48083. Offers data analytics (MAC); finance (MAC); taxation (MAC). *Program availability:* Part-time, evening/weekend. *Faculty:* 6 full-time (2 women), 14 part-time/adjunct (7 women). *Students:* 14 full-time (3 women), 209 part-time (127 women); includes 51 minority (19 Black or African American, non-Hispanic/Latino; 21 Asian, non-Hispanic/Latino; 10 Hispanic/Latino; 1 Two or more races, non-Hispanic/Latino), 14 international. Average age 33. 67 applicants, 91% accepted, 39 enrolled. In 2018, 84 master's awarded. *Degree requirements:* For master's, thesis optional. *Entrance requirements:* For master's, minimum overall cumulative GPA of 2.75 from all colleges previously attended. Additional exam requirements/recommendations for international students: Required—TOEFL (minimum score 550 paper-based, 79-80 internet based), IELTS (6.5), Michigan Test of English Language Proficiency or MTELP (80). *Application deadline:* Applications are processed on a rolling basis. Application fee: $35. Electronic applications accepted. *Expenses: Tuition:* Full-time $21,195; part-time $14,130 per credit hour. *Required fees:* $525; $525 per semester. $175 per semester. *Financial support:* In 2018–19, 22 students received support. Scholarships/grants available. Financial award application deadline: 6/30; financial award applicants required to submit FAFSA. *Unit head:* John Black, Chair, Accounting, 248-823-1635, Fax: 248-689-0920, E-mail: jblack@walshcollege.edu. *Application contact:* Karen Mahaffy, Executive Director, Admissions and Enrollment Services, 248-823-1600, Fax: 248-823-1611, E-mail: kmahafyy@walshcollege.edu.
Website: https:www.walshcollege.edu/masters-ms-degree-accounting

West Chester University of Pennsylvania, College of Business and Public Management, School of Business, West Chester, PA 19383. Offers business analytics (Certificate); business education (MBA). *Accreditation:* AACSB. *Program availability:* Part-time, evening/weekend, online only, 100% online. *Degree requirements:* For master's, minimum GPA of 3.0. *Entrance requirements:* For master's, GMAT or GRE, statement of professional goals, resume, three letters of recommendation, transcripts. Additional exam requirements/recommendations for international students: Required—TOEFL or IELTS. Electronic applications accepted.

West Virginia University, College of Business and Economics, Morgantown, WV 26506. Offers accountancy (M Acc); accounting (PhD); business administration (MBA); business cyber security management (MS); business data analytics (MS); economics (MA, PhD); finance (MS, PhD); forensic and fraud examination (MS); industrial relations (MS); management (PhD); marketing (PhD). *Program availability:* Part-time, online learning. *Students:* 341 full-time (139 women), 44 part-time (13 women); includes 39 minority (10 Black or African American, non-Hispanic/Latino; 12 Asian, non-Hispanic/Latino; 7 Hispanic/Latino; 10 Two or more races, non-Hispanic/Latino), 40 international. In 2018, 208 master's, 20 doctorates awarded. Terminal master's awarded for partial completion of doctoral program. *Degree requirements:* For master's, thesis optional; for doctorate, comprehensive exam, thesis/dissertation. *Entrance requirements:* For doctorate, GRE General Test, minimum GPA of 3.0. Additional exam requirements/recommendations for international students: Required—TOEFL (minimum score 550 paper-based; 92 iBT). *Application deadline:* For fall admission, 10/15 priority date for domestic and international students; for spring admission, 3/1 priority date for domestic and international students. Applications are processed on a rolling basis. Application fee: $60. Electronic applications accepted. *Expenses:* Contact institution. *Financial support:* Fellowships, research assistantships, teaching assistantships, career-related internships or fieldwork, Federal Work-Study, institutionally sponsored loans, scholarships/grants, health care benefits, tuition waivers (full and partial), unspecified assistantships, and administrative assistantships available. Financial award application deadline: 2/1; financial award applicants required to submit FAFSA. *Faculty research:*

Regional labor market studies, economic development, market research, economic forecasting, energy analysis. *Unit head:* Dr. Javier Reyes, Dean, 304-293-7800, Fax: 304-293-4056, E-mail: javier.reyes@mail.wvu.edu. *Application contact:* Dr. Virginia F Kleist, Associate Dean for Graduate Programs, 304-293-7939, Fax: 304-293-7188, E-mail: Virginia.Kleist@mail.wvu.edu.
Website: http://www.be.wvu.edu

William Paterson University of New Jersey, Cotsakos College of Business, Wayne, NJ 07470-8420. Offers applied business analytics (MS); business administration (MBA), including accounting, entrepreneurship, finance, general business administration, human resource management, marketing, music and entertainment management; MBA pathways (Certificate); sales leadership (MS). *Accreditation:* AACSB. *Program availability:* Part-time, evening/weekend. *Faculty:* 21 full-time (6 women), 5 part-time/adjunct (1 woman). *Students:* 78 full-time (40 women), 250 part-time (113 women); includes 161 minority (39 Black or African American, non-Hispanic/Latino; 1 American Indian or Alaska Native, non-Hispanic/Latino; 23 Asian, non-Hispanic/Latino; 82 Hispanic/Latino; 16 Two or more races, non-Hispanic/Latino), 14 international. Average age 31. 222 applicants, 86% accepted, 136 enrolled. In 2018, 95 master's awarded. *Degree requirements:* For master's, Programs Differ see: https://academiccatalog.wpunj.edu/content.php?catoid=1&navoid=68. *Entrance requirements:* For master's, program details: https://www.wpunj.edu/admissions/graduate/admission-deadlines-and-requirements/. Additional exam requirements/recommendations for international students: Required—TOEFL (minimum score 550 paper-based; 79 iBT), IELTS (minimum score 6). *Application deadline:* For fall admission, 6/1 for domestic students, 3/1 for international students; for spring admission, 11/1 for domestic students, 10/1 for international students. Applications are processed on a rolling basis. Application fee: $50. Electronic applications accepted. *Expenses: Tuition, area resident:* Full-time $14,714; part-time $727 per credit. Tuition, state resident: full-time $14,714; part-time $727 per credit. Tuition, nonresident: full-time $22,952; part-time $727 per credit. *International tuition:* $22,952 full-time. *Required fees:* $4 per semester. Tuition and fees vary according to course load, degree level and program. *Financial support:* In 2018–19, 18 students received support. Career-related internships or fieldwork, Federal Work-Study, scholarships/grants, tuition waivers, and unspecified assistantships available. Support available to part-time students. Financial award application deadline: 3/15; financial award applicants required to submit FAFSA. *Faculty research:* Labor markets, job characteristics and ethical behavior, institutional trading of stocks and bonds, education funding, pricing strategies in business-to-business markets. *Unit head:* Dr. Siamack Shojai, Dean, 973-720-2964, Fax: 973-720-2809, E-mail: shojais@wpunj.edu. *Application contact:* Tinu Adeniran, Assistant Director, Graduate Admissions, 973-720-2764, Fax: 973-720-2035, E-mail: adenirant@wpunj.edu.
Website: http://www.wpunj.edu/ccob

York University, Faculty of Graduate Studies, Schulich School of Business, Toronto, ON M3J 1P3, Canada. Offers accounting (M Acc); administration (PhD); business (MBA); business analytics (MBA); finance (MF); international business (IMBA); MBA/JD; MBA/MA; MBA/MFA. *Program availability:* Part-time, evening/weekend. *Degree requirements:* For master's, advanced proficiency in a second language, work term (IMBA); for doctorate, comprehensive exam, thesis/dissertation. *Entrance requirements:* For master's, GMAT or GRE, minimum GPA of 3.0 (3.3 for MF, MBA in business analytics, and IMBA); for doctorate, GMAT or GRE, minimum GPA of 3.3. Additional exam requirements/recommendations for international students: Required—TOEFL (minimum score 600 paper-based; 100 iBT), IELTS (minimum score 7), York English Language Test (minimum score 1); PearsonVUE (minimum score 64). Electronic applications accepted. *Faculty research:* Accounting, finance, marketing, operations management and information systems, organizational studies, strategic management.

Quantitative Analysis

Baruch College of the City University of New York, Zicklin School of Business, Department of Operations Research and Quantitative Methods, New York, NY 10010-5585. Offers quantitative methods and modeling (MBA, MS). *Program availability:* Part-time.

Baruch College of the City University of New York, Zicklin School of Business, Department of Statistics and Computer Information Systems, Program in Decision Sciences, New York, NY 10010-5585. Offers MBA. *Program availability:* Part-time, evening/weekend. *Entrance requirements:* For master's, GMAT, 2 letters of recommendation, resume, 2 years of work experience. Additional exam requirements/recommendations for international students: Required—TOEFL (minimum score 590 paper-based), TWE (minimum score 5).

Columbia University, Graduate School of Arts and Sciences, New York, NY 10027. Offers African-American studies (MA); American studies (MA); anthropology (MA, PhD); art history and archaeology (MA, PhD); astronomy (PhD); biological sciences (PhD); biotechnology (MA); chemical physics (PhD); chemistry (PhD); classical studies (MA, PhD); classics (MA, PhD); climate and society (MA); conservation biology (MA); earth and environmental sciences (PhD); East Asia: regional studies (MA); East Asian languages and cultures (MA, PhD); ecology, evolution and environmental biology (MA), including conservation biology; ecology, evolution, and environmental biology (PhD), including ecology and evolutionary biology, evolutionary primatology; economics (MA, PhD); English and comparative literature (MA, PhD); French and Romance philology (MA, PhD); Germanic languages (MA, PhD); global French studies (MA); global thought (MA); Hispanic cultural studies (MA); history (PhD); history and literature (MA); human rights studies (MA); Islamic studies (MA); Italian (MA, PhD); Japanese pedagogy (MA); Jewish studies (MA); Latin America and the Caribbean: regional studies (MA); Latin American and Iberian cultures (PhD); mathematics (MA, PhD), including finance (MA); medieval and Renaissance studies (MA); Middle Eastern, South Asian, and African studies (MA, PhD); modern art: critical and curatorial studies (MA); modern European studies (MA); museum anthropology (MA); music (DMA, PhD); oral history (MA); philosophical foundations of physics (MA); philosophy (MA, PhD); physics (PhD); political science (MA, PhD); psychology (PhD); quantitative methods in the social sciences (MA); religion (MA, PhD); Russia, Eurasia and East Europe: regional studies (MA); Russian translation (MA); Slavic cultures (MA); Slavic languages (MA, PhD); sociology (MA, PhD); South Asian studies (MA); statistics (MA, PhD); theatre (PhD). Dual-degree programs require admission to both Graduate School of Arts and Sciences and another Columbia school. *Program availability:* Part-time. Terminal master's awarded for partial completion of doctoral program. *Degree requirements:* For master's, variable foreign language requirement, comprehensive exam (for some programs), thesis (for some programs); for doctorate, variable foreign language requirement, comprehensive exam (for some programs), thesis/dissertation. *Entrance requirements:* For master's and doctorate, GRE General Test, GRE Subject Test (for some programs). Additional exam requirements/recommendations for international students: Required—TOEFL, IELTS. Electronic applications accepted.

Drexel University, LeBow College of Business, Program in Business Administration, Philadelphia, PA 19104-2875. Offers business administration (MBA, PhD, APC), including accounting (MBA, PhD), decision sciences (PhD), economics (MBA, PhD), finance (MBA, PhD), legal studies (MBA), management (MBA), marketing (MBA, PhD), organizational sciences (PhD), quantitative methods (MBA), strategic management (PhD). *Accreditation:* AACSB. *Program availability:* Part-time, evening/weekend, online learning. Terminal master's awarded for partial completion of doctoral program. *Entrance requirements:* For master's, GMAT, minimum GPA of 2.75; for doctorate, GMAT. Additional exam requirements/recommendations for international students: Required—TOEFL. Electronic applications accepted. *Faculty research:* Decision support systems, individual and group behavior, operations research, techniques and strategy.

Duke University, The Fuqua School of Business, The Duke MBA-Daytime Program, Durham, NC 27708. Offers academic excellence in finance (Certificate); business administration (MBA); decision sciences (MBA); energy and environment (MBA); energy finance (MBA); entrepreneurship and innovation (MBA); finance (MBA); financial analysis (MBA); health sector management (Certificate); leadership and ethics (MBA); management (MBA); management science and technology management (Certificate); marketing (MBA); operations management (MBA); social entrepreneurship (MBA); strategy (MBA). *Faculty:* 100 full-time (21 women), 55 part-time/adjunct (12 women). *Students:* 875 full-time (335 women); includes 188 minority (44 Black or African American, non-Hispanic/Latino; 4 American Indian or Alaska Native, non-Hispanic/Latino; 90 Asian, non-Hispanic/Latino; 43 Hispanic/Latino; 1 Native Hawaiian or other Pacific Islander, non-Hispanic/Latino; 6 Two or more races, non-Hispanic/Latino), 276 international. Average age 29. In 2018, 429 master's awarded. *Entrance requirements:* For master's, GMAT or GRE, transcripts, essays, resume, recommendation letters, interview. *Application deadline:* For fall admission, 9/19 for domestic and international students; for winter admission, 10/14 for domestic and international students; for spring admission, 1/6 for domestic and international students; for summer admission, 3/11 for domestic and international students. Application fee: $225. Electronic applications accepted. *Expenses:* Contact institution. *Financial support:* Scholarships/grants available. Financial award applicants required to submit FAFSA. *Unit head:* Steve Misuraca, Assistant Dean, Daytime MBA Program. *Application contact:* Shari Hubert, Associate Dean, Office of Admissions, 919-660-7705, Fax: 919-681-8026, E-mail: admissions-info@fuqua.duke.edu.
Website: https://www.fuqua.duke.edu/programs/daytime-mba

Duke University, The Fuqua School of Business, Master of Quantitative Management Program: Business Analytics, Durham, NC 27708. Offers finance (MQM); forensics (MQM); marketing (MQM); strategy (MQM). *Faculty:* 100 full-time (21 women), 55 part-time/adjunct (12 women). *Students:* 136 full-time (56 women); includes 15 minority (1 Black or African American, non-Hispanic/Latino; 14 Asian, non-Hispanic/Latino), 99 international. Average age 23. In 2018, 136 master's awarded. *Entrance requirements:* For master's, GMAT/GRE, transcripts, essays, resume, recommendation letter, interview. *Application deadline:* For fall admission, 10/21 for domestic and international students; for winter admission, 1/15 for domestic and international students; for spring admission, 2/27 for domestic and international students; for summer admission, 4/6 for domestic and international students. Application fee: $125. Electronic applications accepted. *Expenses:* Contact institution. *Financial support:* Scholarships/grants available. Financial award applicants required to submit FAFSA. *Unit head:* Jeremy Petranka, Associate Dean, 919-660-7778. *Application contact:* Shari Hubert, Associate Dean, Office of Admissions, 919-660-7705, Fax: 919-681-8026, E-mail: mqmbusinessanalytics@fuqua.duke.edu.
Website: https://www.fuqua.duke.edu/programs/mqm-business-analytics

Duke University, The Fuqua School of Business, PhD Program, Durham, NC 27708. Offers accounting (PhD); decision sciences (PhD); finance (PhD); management and organizations (PhD); marketing (PhD); operations management (PhD); strategy (PhD). *Faculty:* 100 full-time (21 women). *Students:* 84 full-time (29 women); includes 4 minority (2 Asian, non-Hispanic/Latino; 2 Hispanic/Latino), 53 international. Average age 28. In 2018, 14 doctorates awarded. *Degree requirements:* For doctorate, comprehensive exam (for some programs), thesis/dissertation, Comprehensive or Qualifying exams are required for some of the 7 areas in Business Administration. *Entrance requirements:* For doctorate, GMAT or GRE, transcripts, essays, recommendation letters, statement of purpose. Additional exam requirements/recommendations for international students: Required—TOEFL, IELTS. *Application deadline:* For fall admission, 12/31 priority date for domestic and international students. Application fee: $90. Electronic applications accepted. *Expenses:* Contact institution. *Financial support:* In 2018–19, 74 fellowships with full tuition reimbursements (averaging $33,300 per year) were awarded; research assistantships with full tuition reimbursements, teaching assistantships, institutionally sponsored loans, scholarships/grants, health care benefits, and tuition waivers (full) also available. *Unit head:* William Boulding, Dean, 919-660-7822. *Application contact:* Ravi Bansal, Director of Graduate Studies, 919-660-7753, Fax: 919-660-7971, E-mail: fuqua-phd-info@duke.edu.

Fordham University, Gabelli School of Business, New York, NY 10023. Offers accounting (MBA, MS); applied statistics and decision-making (MS); business economics (DPS); capital markets (DPS); communications and media management (MBA); electronic business (MBA); entrepreneurship (MBA); finance (MBA, PhD); global finance (MS); global sustainability (MBA); health administration (MS); healthcare management (MBA); information systems (MBA, MS); investor relations (MS); management (EMBA, MBA, MS, PhD); marketing (MBA); marketing intelligence (MS); media management (MS); nonprofit leadership (MS); quantitative finance (MS); strategy and decision-making (DPS); taxation (MS); JD/MBA; MS/MBA. *Accreditation:* AACSB. *Program availability:* Part-time, evening/weekend. Terminal master's awarded for partial completion of doctoral program. *Degree requirements:* For master's, internships (for some degrees); for doctorate, comprehensive exam (for some programs), thesis/dissertation. *Entrance requirements:* For master's, GMAT/GRE, 2 letters of recommendation, resume, 2 essays, transcripts, interview. Additional exam requirements/recommendations for international students: Required—TOEFL (minimum score 100 iBT), IELTS (minimum score 7). Electronic applications accepted. *Expenses:* Contact institution.

The Graduate Center, City University of New York, Graduate Studies, Program in Quantitative Methods in the Social Sciences, New York, NY 10016-4039. Offers MS.

Harvard University, Graduate School of Arts and Sciences, Harvard John A. Paulson School of Engineering and Applied Sciences, Cambridge, MA 02138. Offers applied mathematics (PhD); applied physics (PhD); computational science and engineering (ME, SM); computer science (PhD); data science (SM); design engineering (MDE); engineering science (ME), including electrical engineering (ME, SM, PhD); engineering sciences (SM, PhD), including bioengineering (PhD), electrical engineering (ME, SM, PhD), environmental science and engineering (PhD), materials science and mechanical engineering (PhD). MDE offered in collaboration with Graduate School of Design. *Program availability:* Part-time. Terminal master's awarded for partial completion of doctoral program. *Degree requirements:* For master's, thesis (for ME); for doctorate, comprehensive exam, thesis/dissertation. *Entrance requirements:* For master's and doctorate, GRE General Test, GRE Subject Test (recommended), 3 letters of recommendation. Additional exam requirements/recommendations for international students: Required—TOEFL (minimum score 80 iBT). Electronic applications accepted. *Expenses:* Contact institution. *Faculty research:* Applied mathematics, applied physics, computer science and electrical engineering, environmental engineering, mechanical and biomedical engineering.

Hofstra University, Frank G. Zarb School of Business, Programs in Finance, Hempstead, NY 11549. Offers business administration (MBA), including finance; corporate finance (Advanced Certificate); finance (MS), including financial and risk management, investment analysis; investment management (Advanced Certificate); quantitative finance (MS). *Program availability:* Part-time, evening/weekend, blended/hybrid learning. *Students:* 122 full-time (36 women), 40 part-time (8 women); includes 24 minority (5 Black or African American, non-Hispanic/Latino; 1 American Indian or Alaska Native, non-Hispanic/Latino; 8 Asian, non-Hispanic/Latino; 8 Hispanic/Latino; 2 Two or more races, non-Hispanic/Latino), 90 international. Average age 25. 326 applicants, 78% accepted, 58 enrolled. In 2018, 103 master's awarded. *Degree requirements:* For master's, thesis (for some programs), capstone course (for MBA), thesis (for MS), minimum GPA of 3.0. *Entrance requirements:* For master's, GMAT/GRE, 2 letters of recommendation, resume, essay. Additional exam requirements/recommendations for international students: Required—TOEFL (minimum score 550 paper-based; 80 iBT); Recommended—IELTS (minimum score 6). *Application deadline:* Applications are processed on a rolling basis. Application fee: $75. Electronic applications accepted. *Expenses:* $1,375 per credit plus fees. *Financial support:* In 2018–19, 46 students received support, including 42 fellowships with full and partial tuition reimbursements available (averaging $5,064 per year); research assistantships with full and partial tuition reimbursements available, career-related internships or fieldwork, Federal Work-Study, institutionally sponsored loans, scholarships/grants, tuition waivers (full and partial), unspecified assistantships, and scholarships and endowed scholarships also available. Support available to part-time students. Financial award applicants required to submit FAFSA. *Faculty research:* Sustainable investing; blockchain applications in finance; machine learning in finance; text and data mining in finance; corporate inversions. *Unit head:* Dr. K.G. Viswanathan, Chairperson, 516-463-5699, Fax: 516-463-4834, E-mail: k.g.viswanathan@hofstra.edu. *Application contact:* Sunil Samuel, Assistant Vice President of Admissions, 516-463-4723, Fax: 516-463-4664, E-mail: graduateadmission@hofstra.edu.
Website: http://www.hofstra.edu/business/

Instituto Tecnologico de Santo Domingo, Graduate School, Area of Engineering, Santo Domingo, Dominican Republic. Offers construction administration (MS, Certificate); data telecommunications (M Eng, MS, Certificate); industrial engineering (M Eng, Certificate); industrial management (M Mgmt); information technology (Certificate); maintenance engineering (M Eng); occupational hazard prevention (M Mgmt); production management (Certificate); quantitative methods (Certificate); sanitary and environmental engineering (M Eng); structural engineering (M Eng); systems engineering and electronic data processing (Certificate); transportation (Certificate).

Lehigh University, College of Business, Department of Finance, Bethlehem, PA 18015. Offers analytical finance (MS). *Faculty:* 4 full-time (0 women), 1 (woman) part-time/adjunct. *Students:* 40 full-time (23 women), 1 part-time (0 women), 37 international. Average age 23. 192 applicants, 49% accepted, 22 enrolled. In 2018, 38 master's awarded. *Degree requirements:* For master's, capstone project. *Entrance requirements:* For master's, GMAT or GRE, bachelor's degree from a mathematically rigorous program, minimum GPA of 3.0. Additional exam requirements/recommendations for international students: Required—TOEFL (minimum score 600 paper-based; 94 iBT), IELTS (minimum score 7). *Application deadline:* For fall admission, 7/15 for domestic students, 4/15 for international students. Application fee: $75. Tuition and fees vary according to program. *Financial support:* Fellowships, research assistantships, teaching assistantships, and health care benefits available. *Unit head:* Nandu Nayar, Department Chair, 610-758-4161, E-mail: nan2@lehigh.edu. *Application contact:* Mary Theresa Taglang, Director of Recruitment and Admissions, 610-758-4386, Fax: 610-758-5283, E-mail: mtt4@lehigh.edu.
Website: https://cbe.lehigh.edu/academics/graduate/master-analytical-finance

Rutgers University–Newark, School of Public Health, Newark, NJ 07107-1709. Offers clinical epidemiology (Certificate); dental public health (MPH); general public health (Certificate); public policy and oral health services administration (Certificate); quantitative methods (MPH); urban health (MPH); DMD/MPH; MD/MPH; MS/MPH. *Program availability:* Part-time, evening/weekend. *Degree requirements:* For master's, thesis, internship. *Entrance requirements:* For master's, GRE General Test. Additional exam requirements/recommendations for international students: Required—TOEFL. Electronic applications accepted.

San Francisco State University, Division of Graduate Studies, College of Business, Program in Business Administration, San Francisco, CA 94132-1722. Offers decision sciences/operations research (MBA); ethics and compliance (MBA); finance (MBA); global business and innovation (MBA); healthcare administration (MBA); hospitality and tourism management (MBA); information systems (MBA); leadership (MBA); marketing (MBA); nonprofit and social enterprise leadership (MBA); sustainable business (MBA). *Accreditation:* AACSB. *Program availability:* Part-time, evening/weekend. *Degree requirements:* For master's, thesis, essay test. *Entrance requirements:* For master's, GMAT, minimum GPA of 2.7 in last 60 units. Additional exam requirements/recommendations for international students: Required—TOEFL (minimum score 550 paper-based).

Southern New Hampshire University, School of Business, Manchester, NH 03106-1045. Offers accounting (MBA, Graduate Certificate); accounting finance (MS); accounting/auditing (MS); accounting/forensic accounting (MS); accounting/management accounting (MS); accounting/taxation (MS); applied economics (MS); athletic administration (MBA, Graduate Certificate); business administration (IMBA, Certificate), including business information systems (Certificate), human resource management (Certificate); business analytics (MBA); business intelligence (MBA); communication (MA), including new media and marketing, public relations; community economic development (MBA); criminal justice (MBA); data analytics (MS); economics (MBA); engineering management (MBA); entrepreneurship (MBA); finance (MBA, MS,

Graduate Certificate); finance/corporate finance (MS); finance/investments (MS); forensic accounting (MBA); forensic accounting and fraud examination (Graduate Certificate); healthcare informatics (MBA); healthcare management (MBA); human resource management (MS); human resources (MBA); information technology (MS); information technology management (MBA); international business (PhD); Internet marketing (MBA); leadership (MBA); leadership of nonprofit organizations (Graduate Certificate); management (MS); marketing (MBA, MS, Graduate Certificate); music business (MBA); operations and project management (MS); operations and supply chain management (MBA, Graduate Certificate); organizational leadership (MS); project management (MBA, Graduate Certificate); public administration (MBA, Graduate Certificate); quantitative analysis (MBA); Six Sigma (Graduate Certificate); Six Sigma quality (MBA); social media marketing (MBA, Graduate Certificate); sport management (MBA, MS, Graduate Certificate); sustainability and environmental compliance (MBA); MBA/Certificate. *Accreditation:* ACBSP. *Program availability:* Part-time, evening/weekend, online learning. Terminal master's awarded for partial completion of doctoral program. *Degree requirements:* For master's, one foreign language, comprehensive exam (for some programs), thesis or alternative; for doctorate, one foreign language, comprehensive exam, thesis/dissertation. *Entrance requirements:* For master's, minimum GPA of 2.5; for doctorate, GMAT. Additional exam requirements/recommendations for international students: Required—TOEFL (minimum score 500 paper-based). Electronic applications accepted.

Stockton University, Office of Graduate Studies, Program in Data Science and Strategic Analytics, Galloway, NJ 08205-9441. Offers MS. *Program availability:* Part-time, online learning. *Faculty:* 6 full-time (2 women), 3 part-time/adjunct (1 woman). *Students:* 23 full-time (9 women), 8 part-time (3 women); includes 6 minority (1 Black or African American, non-Hispanic/Latino; 4 Asian, non-Hispanic/Latino; 1 Two or more races, non-Hispanic/Latino), 2 international. Average age 30. 41 applicants, 76% accepted, 26 enrolled. *Expenses: Tuition, area resident:* Full-time $11,226; part-time $623.69 per credit hour. Tuition, state resident: full-time $11,226; part-time $623.69 per credit hour. Tuition, nonresident: full-time $17,282; part-time $960.10 per credit hour. International tuition: $17,282 full-time. Required fees: $3376; $187.56 per credit hour. *Unit head:* Dr. J. Russell Manson, Director, 609-652-4354. *Application contact:* Tara Williams, Assistant Director of Graduate Enrollment, 609-626-3640, Fax: 609-626-6050, E-mail: gradschool@stockton.edu.
Website: https://stockton.edu/graduate/data-science_strategic-analytics.html

University at Buffalo, the State University of New York, Graduate School, School of Management, Buffalo, NY 14260. Offers accounting (MS); analytics (MBA); business administration (PMBA); consulting (MBA); finance (MBA, MS), including financial risk management (MS), quantitative finance (MS); healthcare (MBA); information assurance (MBA); information systems (MBA); international management (MBA); management (EMBA, PhD); management information systems (MS); marketing (MBA); supply chain and operations (MBA); supply chains and operations management (MS); Au D/MBA; DDS/MBA; JD/MBA; M Arch/MBA; MD/MBA; MPH/MBA; MSW/MBA; Pharm D/MBA. *Accreditation:* AACSB. *Program availability:* Part-time, evening/weekend. *Degree requirements:* For master's, capstone courses or projects; for doctorate, comprehensive exam, thesis/dissertation. *Entrance requirements:* For master's, GMAT (for MS in accounting, finance); GRE or GMAT (for MBA, MS in management information systems, supply chains and operations management), essays, letters of recommendation; for doctorate, GMAT or GRE, essays, writing sample, letters of recommendation. Additional exam requirements/recommendations for international students: Required—TOEFL (minimum score 95 iBT) or IELTS (minimum score 6.5); Recommended—TSE (minimum score 73). Electronic applications accepted. *Expenses:* Contact institution. *Faculty research:* Data analytics, accounting and law, rate finance, consumer behavior, supply chain logistics, leadership and team effectiveness.

The University of Alabama at Birmingham, School of Public Health, Program in Health Care Organization and Policy, Birmingham, AL 35294. Offers applied epidemiology and pharmacoepidemiology (MSPH); biostatistics (MPH); clinical and translational science (MSPH); environmental health (MPH); environmental health and toxicology (MSPH); epidemiology (MPH); general theory and practice (MPH); health behavior (MPH); health care organization (MPH, Dr PH); health policy (MPH); industrial hygiene (MPH, MSPH); maternal and child health policy (Dr PH); maternal and child health policy and leadership (MPH); occupational health and safety (MPH); outcomes research (MSPH, Dr PH); public health (PhD); public health preparedness management (MPH). *Accreditation:* CEPH. *Program availability:* Part-time, 100% online, blended/hybrid learning. *Faculty:* 14 full-time (6 women). *Students:* 53 full-time (37 women), 61 part-time (45 women); includes 37 minority (12 Black or African American, non-Hispanic/Latino; 20 Asian, non-Hispanic/Latino; 1 Hispanic/Latino; 4 Two or more races, non-Hispanic/Latino), 17 international. Average age 31. 136 applicants, 59% accepted, 44 enrolled. In 2018, 36 master's, 4 doctorates awarded. *Degree requirements:* For master's, comprehensive exam (for some programs), thesis (for some programs); for doctorate, comprehensive exam, thesis/dissertation. *Entrance requirements:* For doctorate, GRE. Additional exam requirements/recommendations for international students: Required—TOEFL (minimum score 80 iBT), IELTS (minimum score 6.5). *Application deadline:* For fall admission, 4/1 priority date for domestic students, 4/1 for international students; for spring admission, 11/1 for domestic students; for summer admission, 4/1 for domestic students. Application fee: $50 ($60 for international students). Electronic applications accepted. *Expenses: Tuition, area resident:* Full-time $8100; part-time $8100 per year. Tuition, state resident: full-time $8100. Tuition, nonresident: full-time $19,188; part-time $19,188 per year. Tuition and fees vary according to program. *Financial support:* Fellowships, research assistantships, teaching assistantships, scholarships/grants, traineeships, and unspecified assistantships available. Financial award application deadline: 3/1; financial award applicants required to submit FAFSA. *Unit head:* Dr. Martha Wingate, Program Director, 205-934-6783, Fax: 205-975-5484, E-mail: mslay@uab.edu. *Application contact:* Dustin Shaw, Coordinator, Student Admissions and Record, 205-934-3939, E-mail: bcampbel@uab.edu.
Website: http://www.soph.uab.edu

The University of British Columbia, Faculty of Arts, Department of Psychology, Vancouver, BC V6T 1Z4, Canada. Offers behavioral neuroscience (MA, PhD); clinical psychology (MA, PhD); cognitive science (MA, PhD); developmental psychology (MA, PhD); health psychology (MA, PhD); quantitative methods (MA, PhD); social/personality psychology (MA, PhD). *Accreditation:* APA (one or more programs are accredited). Terminal master's awarded for partial completion of doctoral program. *Degree requirements:* For master's, thesis; for doctorate, comprehensive exam, thesis/dissertation. *Entrance requirements:* For master's and doctorate, GRE General Test. Additional exam requirements/recommendations for international students: Required—TOEFL. Electronic applications accepted. *Expenses:* Contact institution. *Faculty research:* Clinical, developmental, social/personality, cognition, behavioral neuroscience.

University of California, Santa Barbara, Graduate Division, College of Letters and Sciences, Division of Mathematics, Life, and Physical Sciences, Department of Geography, Santa Barbara, CA 93106-4060. Offers cognitive science (PhD); geography (MA, PhD); global studies (PhD); quantitative methods in the social sciences (PhD); technology and society (PhD); transportation (PhD); MA/PhD. Terminal master's

awarded for partial completion of doctoral program. *Degree requirements:* For master's, comprehensive exam (for some programs), thesis or alternative; for doctorate, comprehensive exam, thesis/dissertation, 1 quarter of teaching assistantship. *Entrance requirements:* For master's and doctorate, GRE (minimum combined verbal and quantitative scores above 1100 in old scoring system or 301 in new scoring system). Additional exam requirements/recommendations for international students: Required—TOEFL (minimum score 550 paper-based; 80 iBT), IELTS (minimum score 7). Electronic applications accepted. *Faculty research:* Earth system science; human environment relations; modeling, measurement, and computation.

University of California, Santa Barbara, Graduate Division, College of Letters and Sciences, Division of Mathematics, Life, and Physical Sciences, Department of Statistics and Applied Probability, Santa Barbara, CA 93106-3110. Offers bioengineering (PhD); financial mathematics and statistics (PhD); quantitative methods in the social sciences (PhD); statistics (MA), including applied statistics, mathematical statistics; statistics and applied probability (PhD); MA/PhD. Terminal master's awarded for partial completion of doctoral program. *Degree requirements:* For master's, comprehensive exam, thesis optional; for doctorate, comprehensive exam, thesis/dissertation. *Entrance requirements:* For master's and doctorate, GRE General Test. Additional exam requirements/recommendations for international students: Required—TOEFL (minimum score 550 paper-based; 80 iBT), IELTS (minimum score 7). Electronic applications accepted. *Faculty research:* Bayesian inference, financial mathematics, stochastic processes, environmental statistics, biostatistical modeling.

University of California, Santa Barbara, Graduate Division, College of Letters and Sciences, Division of Social Sciences, Department of Communication, Santa Barbara, CA 93106-4020. Offers cognitive science (PhD); communication (PhD); feminist studies (PhD); language, interaction and social organization (PhD); quantitative methods in the social sciences (PhD); society and technology (PhD); MA/PhD. Terminal master's awarded for partial completion of doctoral program. *Degree requirements:* For doctorate, comprehensive exam, thesis/dissertation. *Entrance requirements:* For doctorate, GRE. Additional exam requirements/recommendations for international students: Required—TOEFL (minimum score 80 iBT), IELTS (minimum score 7). Electronic applications accepted. *Faculty research:* Interpersonal, intergroup, intercultural, organizational, health, media.

University of California, Santa Barbara, Graduate Division, College of Letters and Sciences, Division of Social Sciences, Department of Sociology, Santa Barbara, CA 93106-9430. Offers interdisciplinary emphasis: Black studies (PhD); interdisciplinary emphasis: environment and society (PhD); interdisciplinary emphasis: feminist studies (PhD); interdisciplinary emphasis: global studies (PhD); interdisciplinary emphasis: language, interaction and social organization (PhD); interdisciplinary emphasis: quantitative methods in the social sciences (PhD); interdisciplinary emphasis: technology and society (PhD); sociology (PhD); MA/PhD. Terminal master's awarded for partial completion of doctoral program. *Degree requirements:* For doctorate, comprehensive exam, thesis/dissertation. *Entrance requirements:* For doctorate, GRE General Test. Additional exam requirements/recommendations for international students: Required—TOEFL (minimum score 550 paper-based; 80 iBT), IELTS (minimum score 7). Electronic applications accepted. *Faculty research:* Gender and sexualities, race/ethnicity, social movements, conversation analysis, global sociology.

University of Connecticut, Graduate School, College of Liberal Arts and Sciences, Department of Public Policy, Field of Survey Research, Storrs, CT 06269. Offers quantitative research methods (Graduate Certificate); survey research (MA). *Degree requirements:* For master's, comprehensive exam. *Entrance requirements:* For master's, GRE General Test. Additional exam requirements/recommendations for international students: Required—TOEFL (minimum score 550 paper-based). Electronic applications accepted.

University of Florida, Graduate School, College of Liberal Arts and Sciences, Department of Mathematics, Gainesville, FL 32611. Offers mathematics (MAT, MS, MST, PhD), including imaging science and technology (PhD), mathematics (PhD), quantitative finance (PhD). *Program availability:* Part-time. Terminal master's awarded for partial completion of doctoral program. *Degree requirements:* For master's, comprehensive exam, thesis optional, first-year exam; for doctorate, one foreign language, comprehensive exam, thesis/dissertation. *Entrance requirements:* For master's and doctorate, GRE General Test, GRE Subject Test (math), minimum GPA of 3.0. Additional exam requirements/recommendations for international students: Required—TOEFL (minimum score 550 paper-based; 80 iBT), IELTS (minimum score 6). Electronic applications accepted. *Faculty research:* Applied mathematics, including imaging, optimization and biomathematics; analysis and probability; combinatorics and number theory; topology and foundations; group theory.

University of Florida, Graduate School, College of Liberal Arts and Sciences, Department of Statistics, Gainesville, FL 32611. Offers quantitative finance (PhD); statistics (M Stat, MS Stat, PhD). *Program availability:* Part-time. Terminal master's awarded for partial completion of doctoral program. *Degree requirements:* For master's, variable foreign language requirement, comprehensive exam, final oral exam; thesis (for MS Stat); for doctorate, comprehensive exam, thesis/dissertation. *Entrance requirements:* For master's and doctorate, GRE General Test, minimum GPA of 3.0. Additional exam requirements/recommendations for international students: Required—TOEFL (minimum score 550 paper-based; 80 iBT), IELTS (minimum score 6). Electronic applications accepted. *Faculty research:* Bayesian statistics, biostatistics, Markov Chain Monte Carlo (MCMC), nonparametric statistics, statistical genetics/genomics.

University of Florida, Graduate School, Warrington College of Business Administration, Hough Graduate School of Business, Department of Finance, Insurance and Real Estate, Gainesville, FL 32611. Offers entrepreneurship (MS); finance (MS, PhD); financial services (Certificate); insurance (PhD); quantitative finance (PhD); real estate (MS); real estate and urban analysis (PhD); JD/MBA; JD/MS. Terminal master's awarded for partial completion of doctoral program. *Degree requirements:* For master's, comprehensive exam, thesis; for doctorate, comprehensive exam, thesis/dissertation. *Entrance requirements:* For master's, GMAT (minimum score of 465) or GRE General Test, minimum GPA of 3.0 for last 60 hours of undergraduate degree, work experience (preferred); for doctorate, GMAT (minimum score of 465) or GRE General Test, minimum GPA of 3.0. Additional exam requirements/recommendations for international students: Required—TOEFL (minimum score 550 paper-based; 80 iBT), IELTS (minimum score 6). Electronic applications accepted. *Faculty research:* Banking, empirical corporate finance, hedge funds.

The University of Iowa, Graduate College, College of Public Health, Department of Biostatistics, Iowa City, IA 52242-1316. Offers biostatistics (MS, PhD, Certificate); quantitative methods (MPH). *Degree requirements:* For master's, thesis optional, exam; for doctorate, comprehensive exam, thesis/dissertation. *Entrance requirements:* For master's and doctorate, GRE General Test, minimum GPA of 3.0. Additional exam requirements/recommendations for international students: Required—TOEFL (minimum score 600 paper-based; 100 iBT). Electronic applications accepted.

University of Maryland, College Park, Academic Affairs, College of Education, Department of Human Development and Quantitative Methodology, College Park, MD 20742. Offers MA, Ed D, PhD. *Entrance requirements:* Additional exam requirements/recommendations for international students: Required—TOEFL.

University of Michigan, Rackham Graduate School, College of Literature, Science, and the Arts, Department of Mathematics, Ann Arbor, MI 48109. Offers applied and interdisciplinary mathematics (AM, MS, PhD); mathematics (AM, MS, PhD); quantitative finance and risk management (MS). *Program availability:* Part-time. *Degree requirements:* For doctorate, one foreign language, comprehensive exam, thesis/dissertation, oral defense of dissertation, preliminary exam. *Entrance requirements:* For master's and doctorate, GRE General Test, GRE Subject Test. Additional exam requirements/recommendations for international students: Required—TOEFL (minimum score 560 paper-based; 84 iBT). Electronic applications accepted. *Expenses:* Contact institution. *Faculty research:* Algebra, analysis, topology, applied mathematics, geometry.

University of Minnesota, Twin Cities Campus, College of Science and Engineering, School of Mathematics, Minneapolis, MN 55455-0213. Offers mathematics (MS, PhD); quantitative finance (Certificate). *Program availability:* Part-time. Terminal master's awarded for partial completion of doctoral program. *Degree requirements:* For master's, thesis (for some programs); for doctorate, 2 foreign languages, thesis/dissertation. *Entrance requirements:* For master's, GRE Subject Test (recommended); for doctorate, GRE Subject Test. Additional exam requirements/recommendations for international students: Required—TOEFL. Electronic applications accepted. *Faculty research:* Partial and ordinary differential equations, algebra and number theory, geometry, combinatorics, numerical analysis, probability, financial mathematics.

University of New Hampshire, Graduate School, Interdisciplinary Programs, Program in Analytics, Durham, NH 03824. Offers MS, Postbaccalaureate Certificate, MS/MPP. *Entrance requirements:* For master's, minimum GPA of 3.0, statistics course, interview. Additional exam requirements/recommendations for international students: Required—TOEFL (minimum score 550 paper-based; 80 iBT). Electronic applications accepted.

University of New Mexico, Graduate Studies, College of Arts and Sciences, Program in Psychology, Albuquerque, NM 87131-2039. Offers behavioral neuroscience (PhD); clinical psychology (PhD); cognitive neuroimaging (PhD); developmental psychology (PhD); evolution (PhD); health psychology (PhD); quantitative methodology (PhD). *Accreditation:* APA. *Students:* Average age 30. 227 applicants, 11% accepted, 16 enrolled. In 2018, 10 doctorates awarded. *Degree requirements:* For doctorate, comprehensive exam, thesis/dissertation. *Entrance requirements:* For doctorate, GRE General Test, GRE Subject Test (psychology), minimum GPA of 3.0. Additional exam requirements/recommendations for international students: Required—TOEFL (minimum score 550 paper-based; 79 iBT), IELTS (minimum score 6.5). *Application deadline:* For fall admission, 12/15 priority date for domestic and international students. Applications are processed on a rolling basis. Application fee: $50. Electronic applications accepted. *Financial support:* Fellowships, research assistantships, teaching assistantships, career-related internships or fieldwork, Federal Work-Study, institutionally sponsored loans, scholarships/grants, health care benefits, tuition waivers (partial), and unspecified assistantships available. Financial award application deadline: 3/1; financial award applicants required to submit FAFSA. *Faculty research:* Addiction, cognition, brain and behavior, developmental, evolutionary, functioning neuroimaging, health psychology, learning and memory, neuroscience. *Total annual research expenditures:* $727,970. *Unit head:* Dr. Jane Ellen Smith, Department Chair, 505-277-4121, Fax: 505-277-1394. *Application contact:* Rikk Murphy, Graduate Program Coordinator, 505-277-5009, Fax: 505-277-1394, E-mail: advising@unm.edu.
Website: http://psych.unm.edu

University of North Texas, Toulouse Graduate School, Denton, TX 76203-5459. Offers accounting (MS); applied anthropology (MA, MS); applied behavior analysis (Certificate); applied geography (MA); applied technology and performance improvement (M Ed, MS); art education (MA); art history (MA); arts leadership (Certificate); audiology (Au D); behavior analysis (MS); behavioral science (PhD); biochemistry and molecular biology (MS); biology (MA, MS); biomedical engineering (MS); business analysis (MS); chemistry (MS); clinical health psychology (PhD); communication studies (MA, MS); computer engineering (MS); computer science (MS); counseling (M Ed, MS), including clinical mental health counseling (MS), college and university counseling, elementary school counseling, secondary school counseling; creative writing (MA); criminal justice (MS); curriculum and instruction (M Ed); decision sciences (MBA); design (MA, MFA), including fashion design (MFA), innovation studies, interior design (MFA); early childhood studies (MS); economics (MS); educational leadership (M Ed, Ed D); educational psychology (MS, PhD), including family studies (MS), gifted and talented (MS), human development (MS), learning and cognition (MS), research, measurement and evaluation (MS); electrical engineering (MS); emergency management (MPA); engineering technology (MS); English (MA); English as a second language (MA); environmental science (MS); finance (MBA, MS); financial management (MPA); French (MA); health services management (MBA); higher education (M Ed, Ed D); history (MA, MS); hospitality management (MS); human resources management (MPA); information science (MS); information systems (PhD); information technologies (MBA); interdisciplinary studies (MA, MS); international studies (MA); international sustainable tourism (MS); jazz studies (MM); journalism (MA, MJ, Graduate Certificate), including interactive and virtual digital communication (Graduate Certificate), narrative journalism (Graduate Certificate), public relations (Graduate Certificate); kinesiology (MS); linguistics (MA); local government management (MPA); logistics (PhD); logistics and supply chain management (MBA); long-term care, senior housing, and aging services (MA); management (PhD); marketing (MBA); mathematics (MA, MS); mechanical and energy engineering (MS, PhD); music (MA), including ethnomusicology, music theory, musicology, performance; music composition (PhD); music education (MM Ed, PhD); nonprofit management (MPA); operations and supply chain management (MBA); performance (MM, DMA); philosophy (MA); political science (MA); professional and technical communication (MA); radio, television and film (MA, MFA); rehabilitation counseling (Certificate); sociology (MA); Spanish (MA); special education (M Ed); speech-language pathology (MA); strategic management (MBA); studio art (MFA); teaching (M Ed); MBA/MS. *Program availability:* Part-time, evening/weekend, online learning. Terminal master's awarded for partial completion of doctoral program. *Degree requirements:* For master's, variable foreign language requirement, comprehensive exam (for some programs), thesis (for some programs); for doctorate, variable foreign language requirement, comprehensive exam (for some programs), thesis/dissertation; for other advanced degree, variable foreign language requirement, comprehensive exam (for some programs). *Entrance requirements:* For master's and doctorate, GRE, GMAT. Additional exam requirements/recommendations for international students: Required—TOEFL (minimum score 550 paper-based; 79 iBT). Electronic applications accepted.

University of Oregon, Graduate School, Charles H. Lundquist College of Business, Department of Decision Sciences, Eugene, OR 97403. Offers MA, MS. *Entrance requirements:* For master's, GMAT. *Faculty research:* Time-series analysis, production scheduling, nonparametric methods, decision theory.

University of Puerto Rico–Río Piedras, College of Business Administration, San Juan, PR 00931-3300. Offers accounting (MBA); finance (MBA, PhD); general business (MBA); human resources management (MBA); international trade and business (MBA,

PhD); marketing (MBA); operations management (MBA); quantitative methods (MBA). *Accreditation:* AACSB. *Program availability:* Part-time. *Degree requirements:* For master's, comprehensive exam, thesis or alternative, research project. *Entrance requirements:* For master's, GMAT or PAEG, minimum GPA of 3.0, letter of recommendation; for doctorate, GMAT, PAEG, minimum GPA of 3.0, master degree. *Faculty research:* Management.

University of South Africa, College of Economic and Management Sciences, Pretoria, South Africa. Offers accounting (D Admin, D Com); accounting science (DA); auditing (D Admin, D Com); business administration (M Tech); business economics (D Admin); business leadership (DBL); business management (D Admin, D Com); economic management analysis (M Tech); economics (D Admin, D Com, PhD); human resource development (M Tech); industrial psychology (D Admin, D Com, PhD); logistics (D Com); marketing (M Tech); public administration (D Admin, D Com, DPA, PhD); public management (M Tech); quantitative management (D Admin, D Com); real estate (M Tech); statistics (D Admin, PhD); tourism management (D Admin, D Com); transport economics (D Admin, D Com).

University of Southern California, Graduate School, Dana and David Dornsife College of Letters, Arts and Sciences, Department of Psychology, Los Angeles, CA 90089. Offers brain and cognitive science (PhD); clinical science (PhD); developmental psychology (PhD); human behavior (MHB); quantitative methods (PhD); social psychology (PhD). *Accreditation:* APA. *Degree requirements:* For doctorate, comprehensive exam, thesis/dissertation, one-year internship (for clinical science students). *Entrance requirements:* For doctorate, GRE. Additional exam requirements/recommendations for international students: Recommended—TOEFL (minimum score 600 paper-based; 100 iBT). Electronic applications accepted. *Faculty research:* Affective neuroscience; children and families; vision, culture and ethnicity; intergroup relations; aggression and violence; language and reading development; substance abuse.

The University of Texas at Arlington, Graduate School, College of Business, Department of Finance and Real Estate, Arlington, TX 76019. Offers finance (PhD); quantitative finance (MS); real estate (MS). *Program availability:* Part-time, evening/weekend. *Degree requirements:* For master's, thesis optional; for doctorate, comprehensive exam, thesis/dissertation. *Entrance requirements:* For master's, GMAT/GRE, minimum GPA of 3.0; for doctorate, GMAT/GRE. Additional exam requirements/recommendations for international students: Required—TOEFL (minimum score 550 paper-based; 79 iBT).

The University of Texas at Austin, Graduate School, College of Education, Department of Educational Psychology, Austin, TX 78712-1111. Offers academic educational psychology (M Ed, MA); counseling psychology (PhD); counselor education (M Ed); human development, culture and learning sciences (PhD); program evaluation (MA); quantitative methods (M Ed, MA, PhD); school psychology (MA, PhD). *Accreditation:* APA (one or more programs are accredited). *Degree requirements:* For master's, thesis optional; for doctorate, thesis/dissertation. *Entrance requirements:* For master's and doctorate, GRE General Test, 3 letters of recommendation. Additional exam requirements/recommendations for international students: Required—TOEFL.

The University of Texas Health Science Center at Houston, MD Anderson UTHealth Graduate School, Houston, TX 77225-0036. Offers biochemistry and cell biology (PhD); biomedical sciences (MS); cancer biology (PhD); genetic counseling (MS); genetics and epigenetics (PhD); immunology (PhD); medical physics (MS, PhD); microbiology and infectious diseases (PhD); neuroscience (PhD); quantitative sciences (PhD); therapeutics and pharmacology (PhD); MD/PhD. Terminal master's awarded for partial completion of doctoral program. *Degree requirements:* For master's, thesis; for doctorate, thesis/dissertation. *Entrance requirements:* For master's and doctorate, GRE General Test. Additional exam requirements/recommendations for international students: Required—TOEFL. Electronic applications accepted. *Faculty research:* Biomedical sciences.

Vanderbilt University, Peabody College, Department of Psychology and Human Development, Nashville, TN 37240-1001. Offers child studies (M Ed); clinical psychological assessment (M Ed); quantitative methods (M Ed). *Accreditation:* APA. *Program availability:* Part-time. *Faculty:* 35 full-time (21 women), 4 part-time/adjunct (3 women). *Students:* 40 full-time (34 women), 4 part-time (3 women); includes 3 minority (2 Hispanic/Latino; 1 Two or more races, non-Hispanic/Latino), 6 international. Average age 24. 135 applicants, 36% accepted, 26 enrolled. In 2018, 28 master's awarded. *Degree requirements:* For master's, comprehensive exam (for some programs), thesis optional. *Entrance requirements:* For master's, GRE General Test. Additional exam requirements/recommendations for international students: Required—TOEFL (minimum score 550 paper-based; 80 iBT). *Application deadline:* For fall admission, 12/31 for domestic and international students; for spring admission, 11/1 for domestic and international students. Applications are processed on a rolling basis. Application fee: $0. Electronic applications accepted. *Expenses: Tuition:* Full-time $47,208; part-time $2026 per credit hour. *Required fees:* $478. *Financial support:* Fellowships with partial tuition reimbursements, research assistantships with partial tuition reimbursements, teaching assistantships with partial tuition reimbursements, Federal Work-Study, institutionally sponsored loans, scholarships/grants, tuition waivers (partial), and unspecified assistantships available. Financial award application deadline: 1/15; financial award applicants required to submit FAFSA. *Faculty research:* Cognition and language; coping with depression; environmental influences on development; Math and reading development; quantitative methods. *Unit head:* Dr. Bethany Rittle-Johnson, Chair, 615-322-8141, Fax: 615-343-9494, E-mail: Bethany.rittle-johnson@vanderbilt.edu. *Application contact:* Ally Armstead, Educational Coordinator, 615-343-4963, Fax: 615-343-9494, E-mail: ally.armstead@vanderbilt.edu.
Website: http://peabody.vanderbilt.edu/departments/psych/index.php

Virginia Polytechnic Institute and State University, VT Online, Blacksburg, VA 24061. Offers advanced transportation systems (Certificate); aerospace engineering (MS); agricultural and life sciences (MSLFS); business information systems (Graduate Certificate); career and technical education (MS); civil engineering (MS); computer engineering (M Eng, MS); decision support systems (Graduate Certificate); eLearning leadership (MA); electrical engineering (M Eng, MS); engineering administration (MEA); environmental engineering (Certificate); environmental politics and policy (Graduate Certificate); environmental sciences and engineering (MS); foundations of political analysis (Graduate Certificate); health product risk management (Graduate Certificate); industrial and systems engineering (MS); information policy and society (Graduate Certificate); information security (Graduate Certificate); information technology (MIT); instructional technology (MA); integrative STEM education (MA Ed); liberal arts (Graduate Certificate); life sciences: health product risk management (MS); natural resources (MNR, Graduate Certificate); networking (Graduate Certificate); nonprofit and nongovernmental organization management (Graduate Certificate); ocean engineering (MS); political science (MA); security studies (Graduate Certificate); software development (Graduate Certificate). *Expenses:* Tuition, state resident: full-time $15,510; part-time $739.50 per credit hour. Tuition, nonresident: full-time $29,629; part-time $1490.25 per credit hour. *Required fees:* $2804; $550 per semester. Tuition and fees vary according to course load, campus/location and program. *Application contact:* Graduate Admissions and Academic Progress, 540-231-8636, E-mail: grads@vt.edu.
Website: http://www.vto.vt.edu/

Section 20
Real Estate

This section contains a directory of institutions offering graduate work in real estate. Additional information about programs listed in the directory but not augmented by an in-depth entry may be obtained by writing directly to the dean of a graduate school or chair of a department at the address given in the directory.

For programs offering related work, see also in this book *Business Administration and Management*.

CONTENTS

Real Estate

American University, Kogod School of Business, Department of Finance, Washington, DC 20016-8044. Offers finance (MS, Certificate); real estate (MS, Certificate). *Program availability:* Part-time, evening/weekend. *Faculty:* 13 full-time (4 women), 5 part-time/adjunct (2 women). *Students:* 61 full-time (33 women), 26 part-time (10 women); includes 12 minority (5 Black or African American, non-Hispanic/Latino; 4 Asian, non-Hispanic/Latino; 3 Hispanic/Latino), 56 international. Average age 26. 176 applicants, 69% accepted, 40 enrolled. In 2018, 3,349 master's, 4 other advanced degrees awarded. *Degree requirements:* For master's, comprehensive exam (for some programs). *Entrance requirements:* For master's, GMAT/GRE; Please see website: https://www.american.edu/kogod/, resume, personal statement, interview, 2 letters of recommendation, transcripts. Additional exam requirements/recommendations for international students: Required—TOEFL (minimum score 100 iBT). *Application deadline:* Applications are processed on a rolling basis. Application fee: $100. *Expenses:* Contact institution. *Financial support:* Applicants required to submit FAFSA. *Unit head:* Dr. Jeffrey Harris, Department Chair, Finance and Real Estate, 202-885-1900, E-mail: kogodgrad@american.edu. *Application contact:* Jason Garner, Director of Admissions, 202-885-1926, E-mail: jgarner@american.edu.
Website: http://www.american.edu/kogod/

Arizona State University at the Tempe campus, W. P. Carey School of Business, Department of Marketing, Tempe, AZ 85287-4106. Offers business administration (PhD), including marketing; real estate development (MRED). *Program availability:* Part-time, evening/weekend, online learning. *Degree requirements:* For master's, thesis or alternative, capstone project, interactive Program of Study (iPOS) submitted before completing 50 percent of required credit hours; for doctorate, comprehensive exam, thesis/dissertation, interactive Program of Study (iPOS) submitted before completing 50 percent of required credit hours. *Entrance requirements:* For master's, GMAT, GRE, or LSAT, minimum GPA of 3.0 in last 2 years of work leading to bachelor's degree, 3 personal references, resume, official transcripts, personal statement; for doctorate, GMAT, minimum GPA of 3.0 in last 2 years of work leading to bachelor's degree, 3 letters of recommendation, personal statement/essay. Additional exam requirements/recommendations for international students: Required—TOEFL (minimum score 550 paper-based; 80 iBT), IELTS (minimum score 6.5). Electronic applications accepted. *Expenses:* Contact institution. *Faculty research:* Service marketing and management, strategic marketing, customer portfolio management, characteristics and skills of high-performing managers, market orientation, market segmentation, consumer behavior, marketing strategy, new product development, management of innovation, social influences on consumption, e-commerce, market research methodology.

Auburn University, Graduate School, Interdepartmental Programs, Program in Real Estate Development, Auburn University, AL 36849. Offers MRED. *Expenses:* Tuition, state resident: full-time $11,282; part-time $535 per credit hour. Tuition, nonresident: full-time $30,542; part-time $1605 per credit hour. *Required fees:* $826 per semester. Tuition and fees vary according to degree level and program.

Baruch College of the City University of New York, Zicklin School of Business, Department of Real Estate, New York, NY 10010-5585. Offers MBA, MS.

Brandeis University, International Business School (IBS), Master of Business Administration Program, Waltham, MA 02454-9110. Offers data analytics (MBA); finance (MBA); marketing (MBA); real estate (MBA). *Entrance requirements:* For master's, GMAT or GRE, minimum two years of full-time work experience. Additional exam requirements/recommendations for international students: Required—TOEFL (minimum score 600 paper-based; 100 iBT), IELTS (minimum score 7), PTE (minimum score 68). Electronic applications accepted. *Expenses:* Contact institution. *Faculty research:* Strategic alliances, IPO and venture capital financing, real estate, risk management, data analytics.

California State University, Sacramento, College of Business Administration, Sacramento, CA 95819. Offers accountancy (MS); business administration (IMBA, MBA); human resources (MBA); urban land development (MBA). *Accreditation:* AACSB. *Program availability:* Part-time, evening/weekend, 100% online, blended/hybrid learning. *Degree requirements:* For master's, comprehensive exam, project, thesis, or writing proficiency exam. *Entrance requirements:* For master's, GMAT. Additional exam requirements/recommendations for international students: Required—TOEFL (minimum score 550 paper-based; 80 iBT). Electronic applications accepted. *Expenses:* Contact institution.

Clemson University, Graduate School, College of Architecture, Arts, and Humanities, Department of City Planning and Real Estate Development and College of Business, Master of Real Estate Development Program, Greenville, SC 29601. Offers MRED. *Faculty:* 4 full-time (0 women), 11 part-time/adjunct (3 women). *Students:* 46 full-time (9 women), 1 part-time (0 women); includes 10 minority (5 Black or African American, non-Hispanic/Latino; 1 Asian, non-Hispanic/Latino; 4 Hispanic/Latino), 4 international. Average age 26. 36 applicants, 94% accepted, 22 enrolled. In 2018, 19 master's awarded. *Degree requirements:* For master's, practicum. *Entrance requirements:* For master's, GRE General Test or GMAT, 3 letters of recommendation, resume, personal statement, unofficial transcripts, portfolio for 12-month program. Additional exam requirements/recommendations for international students: Required—TOEFL (minimum score 80 paper-based; 80 iBT); Recommended—IELTS (minimum score 6.5), TSE (minimum score 54). *Application deadline:* For fall admission, 4/15 for international students; for spring admission, 10/15 for international students. Applications are processed on a rolling basis. Application fee: $80 ($90 for international students). Electronic applications accepted. *Expenses:* $18384 per semester full-time, $1268 per credit hour part-time, other fees may apply per session. *Financial support:* In 2018–19, 8 students received support, including 8 fellowships (averaging $1,594 per year); career-related internships or fieldwork also available. *Faculty research:* Real estate education, real estate investment/finance, sustainability, public-private partnership. *Unit head:* Dr. John Gaber, Department Chair, 864-656-1208, E-mail: jgaber@clemson.edu. *Application contact:* Ryan Dietz, Program Director, 864-872-1220, E-mail: rbdietz@clemson.edu.
Website: http://www.clemson.edu/caah/departments/real-estate-development/

Cleveland State University, College of Graduate Studies, Maxine Goodman Levin College of Urban Affairs, Program in Urban Planning and Development, Cleveland, OH 44115. Offers economic development (MUPD); environmental sustainability (MUPD); historic preservation (MUPD); housing and neighborhood development (MUPD); real estate development and finance (MUPD); urban economic development (Certificate); urban geographic information systems (MUPD); JD/MUPDD. *Accreditation:* ACSP. *Program availability:* Part-time, evening/weekend. *Faculty:* 16 full-time (8 women), 13 part-time/adjunct (5 women). *Students:* 27 full-time (11 women), 21 part-time (11 women); includes 7 minority (5 Black or African American, non-Hispanic/Latino; 1 Hispanic/Latino; 1 Two or more races, non-Hispanic/Latino), 2 international. Average age 28. 48 applicants, 56% accepted, 14 enrolled. In 2018, 7 master's awarded. *Degree requirements:* For master's, thesis or alternative, exit project. *Entrance requirements:* For master's, GRE General Test (minimum score: 50th percentile combined verbal and quantitative, 4.0 analytical writing), minimum GPA of 3.0. Additional exam requirements/recommendations for international students: Required—TOEFL (minimum score 550 paper-based; 78 iBT), IELTS (6.0), or International Test of English Proficiency (iTEP). *Application deadline:* For fall admission, 7/1 priority date for domestic students, 5/15 for international students; for spring admission, 11/15 for domestic students, 11/1 for international students; for summer admission, 4/1 for domestic students, 3/15 for international students. Applications are processed on a rolling basis. Application fee: $40. Electronic applications accepted. *Expenses:* Contact institution. *Financial support:* In 2018–19, 10 students received support, including 5 research assistantships with full tuition reimbursements available (averaging $7,200 per year), 3 teaching assistantships with partial tuition reimbursements available (averaging $2,400 per year); scholarships/grants, tuition waivers (full and partial), and unspecified assistantships also available. Support available to part-time students. Financial award application deadline: 3/1; financial award applicants required to submit FAFSA. *Faculty research:* Housing and neighborhood development, urban housing policy, environmental sustainability, economic development, GIS and planning decision support. *Unit head:* Dr. Stephanie Ryberg-Webster, Assistant Professor/Program Director, 216-802-3386, Fax: 216-687-2013, E-mail: s.ryberg@csuohio.edu. *Application contact:* David Arrighi, Graduate Academic Advisor, 216-523-7522, Fax: 216-687-5398, E-mail: d.arrighi@csuohio.edu.
Website: http://www.csuohio.edu/urban/mupd/mupd

Columbia University, Graduate School of Architecture, Planning, and Preservation, Program in Real Estate Development, New York, NY 10027. Offers MS. *Degree requirements:* For master's, thesis. *Entrance requirements:* For master's, GRE General Test.

Columbia University, Graduate School of Business, MBA Program, New York, NY 10027. Offers accounting (MBA); decision, risk, and operations (MBA); entrepreneurship (MBA); finance and economics (MBA); healthcare and pharmaceutical management (MBA); human resource management (MBA); international business (MBA); leadership and ethics (MBA); management (MBA); marketing (MBA); media (MBA); private equity (MBA); real estate (MBA); social enterprise (MBA); value investing (MBA); DDS/MBA; JD/MBA; MBA/MIA; MBA/MPH; MBA/MS; MD/MBA. *Entrance requirements:* For master's, GMAT, 2 letters of recommendation. Additional exam requirements/recommendations for international students: Required—TOEFL. Electronic applications accepted. *Expenses:* Contact institution. *Faculty research:* Human decision making and behavioral research; real estate market and mortgage defaults; financial crisis and corporate governance; international business; security analysis and accounting.

Cornell University, Graduate School, Graduate Fields of Architecture, Art and Planning, Field of Real Estate, Ithaca, NY 14853. Offers MPS. *Degree requirements:* For master's, project paper. *Entrance requirements:* For master's, GMAT, 2 letters of recommendation, resume. Additional exam requirements/recommendations for international students: Required—TOEFL (minimum score 600 paper-based; 77 iBT). Electronic applications accepted. *Faculty research:* Smart growth, economic development, urban redevelopment, development financing, securitization of real estate.

DePaul University, Kellstadt Graduate School of Business, Chicago, IL 60604. Offers accountancy (MBA, MSA); applied economics (MBA); audit and advisory services (MS); business administration (DBA); business analytics (MS); business strategy and decision-making (MBA); computational finance (MS); economics and policy analysis (MS); enterprise risk management (MS); entrepreneurship (MBA, MS); finance (MBA, MS); general business (MBA); hospitality leadership (MBA); hospitality leadership and operational performance (MS); human resources (MS); international business (MBA); management (MBA, MS); management information systems (MBA); marketing (MBA, MS); marketing analysis (MS); marketing strategy and planning (MBA); real estate (MS); real estate finance and investment (MBA); strategy, execution and valuation (MBA); supply chain management (MS); sustainable management (MS); taxation (MS); JD/MBA. *Accreditation:* AACSB. *Program availability:* Part-time, evening/weekend, online learning. *Entrance requirements:* For master's, GMAT/GRE, 2 letters of recommendation, resume, essay, official transcripts. Additional exam requirements/recommendations for international students: Required—TOEFL (minimum score 550 paper-based; 80 iBT). Electronic applications accepted. *Expenses:* Contact institution.

Drexel University, Goodwin College of Professional Studies, School of Technology and Professional Studies, Philadelphia, PA 19104-2875. Offers construction management (MS); creativity and innovation (MS); engineering technology (MS); food science (MS); hospitality management (MS); professional studies: creativity studies (MS); professional studies: e-learning leadership (MS); professional studies: homeland security management (MS); project management (MS); property management (MS); sport management (MS). *Program availability:* Part-time, evening/weekend. *Entrance requirements:* Additional exam requirements/recommendations for international students: Required—TOEFL, IELTS. Electronic applications accepted. Application fee is waived when completed online.

Emory University, Goizueta Business School, Full Time MBA Program, Atlanta, GA 30322-1100. Offers accounting (MBA); alternative investments (MBA); business process consulting (MBA); business technology management (MBA); capital markets (MBA); corporate finance (MBA); customer relationship management (MBA); decision analytics (MBA); entrepreneurship (MBA); finance (MBA); global management (MBA); investment banking (MBA); management consulting (MBA); marketing (MBA); marketing analytics (MBA); marketing consulting (MBA); operations management (MBA); organization and management (MBA); product and brand management (MBA); real estate (MBA); social enterprise (MBA); strategy consulting (MBA). *Accreditation:* AACSB. *Faculty:* 74 full-time (18 women), 18 part-time/adjunct (6 women). *Students:* 349 full-time (105 women); includes 81 minority (26 Black or African American, non-Hispanic/Latino; 1 American Indian or Alaska Native, non-Hispanic/Latino; 35 Asian, non-Hispanic/Latino; 16 Hispanic/Latino; 3 Two or more races, non-Hispanic/Latino), 97 international. Average age 29. 1,380 applicants, 34% accepted, 172 enrolled. In 2018, 180 master's awarded. *Degree requirements:* For master's, 1 leadership course; 2 mid-semester module programs; 2 global components. *Entrance requirements:* For master's, GMAT/GRE, essays; recommendation letters; undergraduate degree; interview. Additional exam requirements/recommendations for international students: Required—TOEFL (minimum score 100 iBT), IELTS (minimum score 7), PTE (minimum score 68). *Application deadline:* For fall admission, 10/6 for domestic and international students; for winter admission, 11/17 for domestic and international students; for spring admission, 1/3 priority date for domestic and international students; for summer admission, 3/9 for domestic and international students. Application fee: $150. Electronic applications accepted. *Expenses:* Contact institution. *Financial support:* In 2018–19, 273 students

received support. Career-related internships or fieldwork, institutionally sponsored loans, and scholarships/grants available. Financial award application deadline: 4/1; financial award applicants required to submit FAFSA. *Faculty research:* Corporate finance, information systems, digital marketing, asset pricing, sports management. *Unit head:* Brian Mitchell, Associate Dean, 404-727-4824, Fax: 404-712-9648, E-mail: brian.mitchell@emory.edu. *Application contact:* Melissa Rapp, Associate Dean, 404-727-7583, Fax: 404-727-4612, E-mail: mbaadmissions@emory.edu.
Website: http://www.goizueta.emory.edu

Florida International University, Chapman Graduate School of Business, Hollo School of Real Estate, Miami, FL 33199. Offers international real estate (MS). *Program availability:* Part-time, evening/weekend. *Faculty:* 5 full-time (1 woman), 3 part-time/adjunct (2 women). *Students:* 75 full-time (31 women), 9 part-time (6 women); includes 51 minority (18 Black or African American, non-Hispanic/Latino; 3 Asian, non-Hispanic/Latino; 29 Hispanic/Latino; 1 Two or more races, non-Hispanic/Latino), 11 international. Average age 36. 157 applicants, 64% accepted, 58 enrolled. In 2018, 75 master's awarded. *Entrance requirements:* For master's, GMAT or GRE, letter of intent; resume. Additional exam requirements/recommendations for international students: Required—TOEFL (minimum score 550 paper-based; 80 iBT) or IELTS (minimum score 6.5). *Application deadline:* For fall admission, 4/1 for domestic and international students. Application fee: $30. Electronic applications accepted. *Expenses:* Contact institution. *Financial support:* Institutionally sponsored loans and scholarships/grants available. Financial award application deadline: 3/1; financial award applicants required to submit FAFSA. *Faculty research:* International real estate, real estate investments, commercial real estate. *Unit head:* Eli Beracha, Director, 305-779-7898, E-mail: eli.beracha@fiu.edu. *Application contact:* Nanett Rojas, Manager, Admissions Operations, 305-348-7464, Fax: 305-348-7441, E-mail: gradadm@fiu.edu.

Georgetown University, Graduate School of Arts and Sciences, School of Continuing Studies, Washington, DC 20057. Offers American studies (MALS); applied intelligence (MPS); Catholic studies (MALS); classical civilizations (MALS); emergency and disaster management (MPS); ethics and the professions (MALS); global strategic communications (MPS); hospitality management (MPS); human resources management (MPS); humanities (MALS); individualized study (MALS); integrated marketing communications (MPS); international affairs (MALS); Islam and Muslim-Christian relations (MALS); journalism (MPS); liberal studies (DLS); literature and society (MALS); medieval and early modern European studies (MALS); public relations and corporate communications (MPS); real estate (MPS); religious studies (MALS); social and public policy (MALS); sports industry management (MPS); systems engineering management (MPS); technology management (MPS); the theory and practice of American democracy (MALS); urban and regional planning (MPS); visual culture (MALS). MPS in systems engineering management offered jointly with Stevens Institute of Technology. *Entrance requirements:* Additional exam requirements/recommendations for international students: Required—TOEFL.

The George Washington University, School of Business, Program in Walkable Urban Real Estate Development, Washington, DC 20052. Offers Professional Certificate. *Students:* 4 part-time (1 woman); includes 1 minority (Asian, non-Hispanic/Latino). Average age 40. 6 applicants, 100% accepted, 4 enrolled. In 2018, 1 Professional Certificate awarded. *Unit head:* Robert Valero, Executive Director, 202-994-0920, Fax: 202-994-5966, E-mail: rjvalero@gwu.edu. *Application contact:* Christopher Storer, Executive Director, Graduate Admissions, 202-994-1212, E-mail: gwmba@gwu.edu.

Georgia State University, J. Mack Robinson College of Business, Department of Real Estate, Atlanta, GA 30302-3083. Offers hotel real estate (MBA); real estate (MBA, MS, PhD, Certificate). *Program availability:* Part-time, evening/weekend. *Faculty:* 1 full-time (0 women), 2 part-time/adjunct (0 women). *Students:* 25 full-time (11 women), 2 part-time (0 women); includes 15 minority (8 Black or African American, non-Hispanic/Latino; 2 Asian, non-Hispanic/Latino; 3 Hispanic/Latino; 2 Two or more races, non-Hispanic/Latino), 3 international. Average age 34. 61 applicants, 69% accepted, 24 enrolled. In 2018, 9 master's awarded. *Entrance requirements:* For master's, GRE or GMAT, transcripts from all institutions attended, resume, essays; for doctorate, GRE or GMAT, three letters of recommendation, personal statement, transcripts from all institutions attended, resume. Additional exam requirements/recommendations for international students: Required—TOEFL (minimum score 610 paper-based; 101 iBT), IELTS (minimum score 7). *Application deadline:* For fall admission, 5/1 priority date for domestic students, 2/1 priority date for international students; for spring admission, 9/15 priority date for domestic students, 4/1 priority date for international students. Applications are processed on a rolling basis. Application fee: $50. Electronic applications accepted. *Expenses: Tuition, area resident:* Full-time $9360; part-time $390 per credit hour. Tuition, state resident: full-time $9360; part-time $390 per credit hour. Tuition, nonresident: full-time $30,024; part-time $1251 per credit hour. *International tuition:* $30,024 full-time. *Required fees:* $2128. *Financial support:* Research assistantships, teaching assistantships, scholarships/grants, and unspecified assistantships available. *Faculty research:* International real estate investments, corporate real estate, capital formation, consumer behavior applied to real estate, real estate development. *Application contact:* Toby McChesney, Assistant Dean for Graduate Recruiting and Student Services, 404-413-7167, Fax: 404-413-7162, E-mail: rcbgradadmissions@gsu.edu.
Website: http://realestate.robinson.gsu.edu/

Instituto Centroamericano de Administración de Empresas, Graduate Programs, La Garita, Costa Rica. Offers agribusiness management (MIAM); business administration (EMBA); finance (MBA); real estate management (MGREM); sustainable development (MBA); technology (MBA). *Degree requirements:* For master's, comprehensive exam, essay. *Entrance requirements:* For master's, GMAT or GRE General Test, fluency in Spanish, interview, letters of recommendation, minimum 1 year of work experience. Additional exam requirements/recommendations for international students: Recommended—TOEFL. Electronic applications accepted. *Faculty research:* Competitiveness, production.

Johns Hopkins University, Carey Business School, MS in Real Estate and Infrastructure Program, Baltimore, MD 21218. Offers MS. *Students:* 18 full-time (10 women), 42 part-time (9 women). 76 applicants, 91% accepted, 29 enrolled. In 2018, 45 master's awarded. *Degree requirements:* For master's, 36 credits. *Entrance requirements:* For master's, GMAT or GRE. Additional exam requirements/recommendations for international students: Required—TOEFL, IELTS. *Application deadline:* For fall admission, 5/1 for domestic and international students. Applications are processed on a rolling basis. Application fee: $100. Electronic applications accepted. *Expenses:* Contact institution. *Financial support:* In 2018–19, 60 students received support. Scholarships/grants available. Support available to part-time students. Financial award application deadline: 4/15; financial award applicants required to submit FAFSA. *Faculty research:* Real estate markets and investment, retail businesses and product differentiation, spatial competition in cities, structural modeling and estimation. *Unit head:* Dr. Kevin Frick, Vice Dean of Education, 410-234-9272, E-mail: kfrick@jhu.edu. *Application contact:* Office of Admissions, 410-234-9220, Fax: 443-529-1554, E-mail: carey.admissions@jhu.edu.
Website: http://carey.jhu.edu/academics/master-of-science/ms-in-real-estate-infrastructure/

Longwood University, College of Graduate and Professional Studies, College of Business and Economics, Farmville, VA 23909. Offers general business (MBA); real estate (MBA); retail management (MBA). *Accreditation:* AACSB. *Program availability:* Part-time, online only, 100% online. *Degree requirements:* For master's, internship. *Entrance requirements:* For master's, GMAT or GRE, personal essay, 3 recommendations, official transcripts from all colleges and universities attended. Additional exam requirements/recommendations for international students: Required—TOEFL (minimum score 570 paper-based), IELTS (minimum score 6.5). Electronic applications accepted. *Expenses:* Contact institution.

Marquette University, Graduate School of Management, Department of Economics, Milwaukee, WI 53201-1881. Offers business economics (MSAE); financial economics (MSAE); international economics (MSAE); marketing research (MSAE); real estate economics (MSAE). *Program availability:* Part-time, evening/weekend. *Degree requirements:* For master's, comprehensive exam, professional project. *Entrance requirements:* For master's, GMAT or GRE General Test. Additional exam requirements/recommendations for international students: Required—TOEFL, IELTS, PTE. Electronic applications accepted. *Faculty research:* Monetary and fiscal policy in open economy, housing and regional migration, political economy of taxation and state/local government.

Massachusetts Institute of Technology, School of Architecture and Planning, Center for Real Estate, Cambridge, MA 02139. Offers real estate development (MSRED). *Degree requirements:* For master's, thesis. *Entrance requirements:* For master's, GMAT or GRE General Test. Additional exam requirements/recommendations for international students: Required—TOEFL, IELTS. Electronic applications accepted. *Expenses: Tuition:* Full-time $51,520; part-time $800 per credit hour. *Required fees:* $312. *Faculty research:* Methods, urban economics, entrepreneurship, strategic planning, housing, leadership development, international housing economics and finance, mortgage securitization, innovation, big data, the local tax implications of inefficient land use, post-war neighborhood decline, the supply of workplace flexibility, LinkedIn economic graph.

Midwest University, Graduate Programs, Wentzville, MO 63385. Offers asset management/investment/real estate (MBA); Christian counseling (D Min); Christian education (D Min); counseling (MA), including marriage and family counseling, school counseling; divinity (M Div); education (MA), including brain and gifted education, Christian education; global business management (MBA); global leadership (MBA); leadership (PhD), including brain and gifted educational leadership, entrepreneurial leadership, international aviation leadership, organizational leadership, political leadership; mission studies (D Min); music (MM, DMA); pastoral theology (D Min); public policy/administration (MBA); teaching English to speakers of other languages (MA). *Program availability:* Part-time, online learning. *Degree requirements:* For master's, thesis (for some programs); for doctorate, thesis/dissertation. *Entrance requirements:* Additional exam requirements/recommendations for international students: Recommended—TOEFL (minimum score 550 paper-based).

Monmouth University, Graduate Studies, Leon Hess Business School, West Long Branch, NJ 07764-1898. Offers accounting (MBA, Certificate); business administration (MBA); finance (MBA); management (MBA); marketing (MBA); real estate (MBA). *Accreditation:* AACSB. *Program availability:* Part-time, evening/weekend. *Faculty:* 22 full-time (5 women), 8 part-time/adjunct (1 woman). *Students:* 91 full-time (47 women), 87 part-time (35 women); includes 17 minority (2 Black or African American, non-Hispanic/Latino; 6 Asian, non-Hispanic/Latino; 7 Hispanic/Latino; 2 Two or more races, non-Hispanic/Latino), 12 international. Average age 29. In 2018, 79 master's, 1 other advanced degree awarded. *Degree requirements:* For master's, capstone course. *Entrance requirements:* For master's, GMAT or GRE, current resume; essay (500 words or less). Additional exam requirements/recommendations for international students: Required—TOEFL (minimum score 550 paper-based; 79 iBT), IELTS (minimum score 6), Michigan English Language Assessment Battery (minimum score 77) or Certificate of Advanced English (minimum score 160). *Application deadline:* For fall admission, 7/15 priority date for domestic students, 6/1 for international students; for spring admission, 12/1 priority date for domestic students, 11/1 for international students; for summer admission, 5/1 for domestic students. Applications are processed on a rolling basis. Application fee: $50. Electronic applications accepted. *Expenses: Tuition:* Part-time $1233 per credit. *Required fees:* $178 per term. *Financial support:* In 2018–19, 131 students received support. Institutionally sponsored loans, scholarships/grants, and unspecified assistantships available. Support available to part-time students. Financial award applicants required to submit FAFSA. *Faculty research:* Information technology and marketing, behavioral research in accounting, human resources, management of technology. *Unit head:* Dr. Susan Gupta, MBA Program Director, 732-571-3639, Fax: 732-263-5517, E-mail: sgupta@monmouth.edu. *Application contact:* Laurie Kuhn, Associate Director of Graduate Admission, 732-571-3452, Fax: 732-263-5123, E-mail: gradadm@monmouth.edu.
Website: https://www.monmouth.edu/business-school/leon-hess-business-school.aspx

New York University, School of Professional Studies, Schack Institute of Real Estate, Program in Real Estate, New York, NY 10012-1019. Offers real estate (MS), including finance and investment, real estate asset management. *Program availability:* Part-time, evening/weekend. *Degree requirements:* For master's, thesis, capstone project. *Entrance requirements:* For master's, GRE or GMAT (only upon request), bachelor's degree, resume with relevant professional work, internship or volunteer experience, two letters of recommendation, statement of purpose. Additional exam requirements/recommendations for international students: Required—TOEFL (minimum score 600 paper-based; 100 iBT), IELTS (minimum score 7). Electronic applications accepted. *Expenses:* Contact institution.

New York University, School of Professional Studies, Schack Institute of Real Estate, Program in Real Estate Development, New York, NY 10012-1019. Offers real estate development (MS), including global real estate, sustainable development, the business of development. *Program availability:* Part-time, evening/weekend. *Degree requirements:* For master's, thesis, capstone project. *Entrance requirements:* For master's, GRE or GMAT (only upon request), bachelor's degree, resume with relevant professional work, internship or volunteer experience, two letters of recommendation, statement of purpose. Additional exam requirements/recommendations for international students: Required—TOEFL (minimum score 600 paper-based; 100 iBT), IELTS (minimum score 7). Electronic applications accepted. *Expenses:* Contact institution.

Northwestern University, The Graduate School, Kellogg School of Management, Management Programs, Evanston, IL 60208. Offers accounting information and management (MBA, PhD); analytical finance (MBA); business administration (MBA); decision sciences (MBA); entrepreneurship and innovation (MBA); finance (MBA, PhD); health enterprise management (MBA); human resources management (MBA); international business (MBA); management and organizations (MBA, PhD); management and organizations and sociology (PhD); management and strategy (MBA); management studies (MS); managerial analytics (MBA); managerial economics (MBA); managerial economics and strategy (PhD); marketing (MBA, PhD); marketing management (MBA); media management (MBA); operations management (MBA, PhD); real estate (MBA); social enterprise at Kellogg (MBA); JD/MBA. *Program availability:* Part-time, evening/weekend. Terminal master's awarded for partial completion of doctoral program. *Degree requirements:* For doctorate, thesis/dissertation, 2 years of

coursework, qualifying (field) exam and candidacy, summer research papers and presentations to faculty, proposal defense, final exam/defense. *Entrance requirements:* For master's, GMAT, GRE, interview, 2 letters of recommendation, college transcripts, resume, essays, Kellogg honor code; for doctorate, GMAT, GRE, statement of purpose, transcripts, 2 letters of recommendation, resume, interview. Additional exam requirements/recommendations for international students: Required—TOEFL, IELTS. Electronic applications accepted. *Expenses:* Contact institution. *Faculty research:* Business cycles and international finance, health policy, networks, non-market strategy, consumer psychology.

Pacific States University, College of Business, Los Angeles, CA 90010. Offers accounting (MBA, Certificate); beauty management (MBA); finance (MBA); international business (MBA); management of information technology (MBA); project management (Certificate); real estate management (MBA). *Program availability:* Part-time, evening/weekend, online learning. *Entrance requirements:* For master's, minimum undergraduate GPA of 2.5 during last 90 quarter units of course work, bachelor's degree in business administration or economics. Additional exam requirements/recommendations for international students: Required—TOEFL (minimum score 500 paper-based; 61 iBT), IELTS (minimum score 5.5).

Pontificia Universidad Catolica Madre y Maestra, Graduate School, Faculty of Social and Administrative Sciences, Santiago, Dominican Republic. Offers business administration (MBA), including business development, finance, international business, management skills (M Mgmt, MBA), marketing, operations, strategic cost management, strategy, tourist destination planning and management; law (LL M), including civil law, corporate business law, criminal law, international relations, real estate law; management (M Mgmt), including higher financial management, insurance program administration, management skills (M Mgmt, MBA); psychology (MA), including clinical child and adolescent psychology, forensic psychology; strategic human resources (EMBA).

Portland State University, Graduate Studies, College of Urban and Public Affairs, Nohad A. Toulan School of Urban Studies and Planning, Portland, OR 97207-0751. Offers applied social demography (Certificate); energy policy and management (Certificate); real estate development (Certificate); sustainable food systems (Certificate); transportation (Certificate); urban design (Certificate); urban studies (PhD); urban studies and planning (MRED, MURP, MUS); urban studies: regional science (PhD). *Program availability:* Part-time, evening/weekend. *Degree requirements:* For doctorate, comprehensive exam, thesis/dissertation, residency. *Entrance requirements:* For doctorate, GRE General Test, minimum GPA of 2.75, statement of purpose, 3 letters of recommendation, resume/curriculum vitae. Additional exam requirements/recommendations for international students: Required—TOEFL (minimum score 550 paper-based; 80 iBT). Electronic applications accepted.

Portland State University, Graduate Studies, The School of Business, Master of Real Estate Development Program, Portland, OR 97207-0751. Offers MRED. *Degree requirements:* For master's, real estate development workshop. *Entrance requirements:* For master's, GMAT or GRE, resume, statement of purpose, 2 professional references, transcripts. Additional exam requirements/recommendations for international students: Required—TOEFL (minimum score 550 paper-based; 80 iBT). Electronic applications accepted. *Expenses:* Contact institution.

Pratt Institute, School of Architecture, Program in Real Estate Practice, Brooklyn, NY 11205-3899. Offers MS. *Program availability:* Part-time, evening/weekend. *Students:* 15 full-time (10 women), 1 (woman) part-time; includes 4 minority (2 Black or African American, non-Hispanic/Latino; 1 Hispanic/Latino; 1 Two or more races, non-Hispanic/Latino), 10 international. Average age 29. 27 applicants, 96% accepted, 5 enrolled. In 2018, 7 master's awarded. *Degree requirements:* For master's, thesis optional. *Entrance requirements:* For master's, bachelor's degree in architecture, business, construction management, engineering, or interior design; 500-word statement of purpose. Additional exam requirements/recommendations for international students: Required—TOEFL (minimum score 550 paper-based; 79 iBT), IELTS (minimum score 6.5), PTE. *Application deadline:* For fall admission, 1/5 for domestic students. Application fee: $50 ($90 for international students). Electronic applications accepted. *Expenses: Tuition:* Full-time $33,246; part-time $1847 per credit. *Required fees:* $1980. *Financial support:* Career-related internships or fieldwork, Federal Work-Study, institutionally sponsored loans, scholarships/grants, health care benefits, and unspecified assistantships available. Support available to part-time students. Financial award application deadline: 2/1; financial award applicants required to submit FAFSA. *Unit head:* Howard Albert, Coordinator, 212-647-7524, E-mail: halber11@pratt.edu. *Application contact:* Natalie Capannelli, Director of Graduate Admissions, 718-636-3551, Fax: 718-399-4242, E-mail: ncapanne@pratt.edu.
Website: http://www.pratt.edu/academics/architecture/real-estate-practice/

Roosevelt University, Graduate Division, Walter E. Heller College of Business, School of Real Estate, Chicago, IL 60605. Offers real estate (MS). *Program availability:* Part-time, evening/weekend. Electronic applications accepted.

Rutgers University–Newark, Rutgers Business School–Newark and New Brunswick, Program in Real Estate and Logistics, Newark, NJ 07102. Offers MRE.

Southern Methodist University, Cox School of Business, MBA Program, Dallas, TX 75275. Offers accounting (MBA, PMBA); business (EMBA); business analytics (PMBA); finance (MBA, PMBA); information technology and operations management (MBA, PMBA), including business analytics (MBA), information and operations (MBA); management (MBA, PMBA); marketing (MBA, PMBA); real estate (MBA, PMBA); strategy and entrepreneurship (MBA, PMBA); JD/MBA; MA/MBA. *Program availability:* Part-time, evening/weekend. *Entrance requirements:* For master's, GMAT. Additional exam requirements/recommendations for international students: Required—TOEFL. Electronic applications accepted. *Expenses:* Contact institution. *Faculty research:* Corporate finance, financial reporting, modeling consumer decision-making, competition between national brands and store brands, institutional determinants of firms' strategy.

Syracuse University, Martin J. Whitman School of Management, Master of Business Administration Program, Syracuse, NY 13244. Offers accounting (MBA); business analytics (MBA); entrepreneurship (MBA); marketing management (MBA); real estate (MBA); supply chain management (MBA); JD/MBA. *Program availability:* Part-time, 100% online. *Students:* Average age 32. 1,086 applicants, 73% accepted, 516 enrolled. In 2018, 84 master's awarded. *Entrance requirements:* For master's, GMAT or GRE, resume, essay, 5-minute video interview, two letters of recommendation, transcripts (unofficial). Additional exam requirements/recommendations for international students: Required—TOEFL (minimum score 100 iBT), IELTS (minimum score 7), PTE (minimum score 68). *Application deadline:* For fall admission, 11/30 for domestic students, 11/30 priority date for international students; for winter admission, 1/1 for domestic students, 1/1 priority date for international students; for spring admission, 2/15 for domestic and international students; for summer admission, 4/19 for domestic students. Application fee: $75. Electronic applications accepted. *Expenses:* Contact institution. *Financial support:* In 2018–19, 22 students received support. Merit scholarships available. Financial award application deadline: 2/15. *Faculty research:* Data analysis, economics of international business, financial markets and institutions, operations management, supply chain management. *Unit head:* Dr. Alexander McKelvie, Associate Dean for Undergraduate and Full-time Master's Education, 315-443-7252, E-mail: mckelvie@syr.edu. *Application contact:* Shri Ramakrishnan, Assistant Director, Graduate Recruitment, 315-443-3497, Fax: 315-443-9517, E-mail: busgrad@syr.edu.
Website: http://whitman.syr.edu/ftmba/

Thomas Jefferson University, College of Architecture and the Built Environment, Program in Real Estate Development, Philadelphia, PA 19107. Offers MS.

Universidad Iberoamericana, Graduate School, Santo Domingo D.N., Dominican Republic. Offers business administration (MBA, PMBA); constitutional law (LL M); dentistry (DMD); educational management (MA); integrated marketing communication (MA); psychopedagogical intervention (M Ed); real estate law (LL M); strategic management of human talent (MM).

University at Buffalo, the State University of New York, Graduate School, School of Architecture and Planning, Department of Urban and Regional Planning, Buffalo, NY 14214. Offers economic development (MUP); environment/land use (MUP); health and food systems (MUP); historic preservation (MUP, Certificate); neighborhood/community development (MUP); real estate development (MSRED); urban and regional planning (PhD); urban design (MUP); JD/MUP; M Arch/MUP. *Accreditation:* ACSP. *Program availability:* Part-time. *Faculty:* 13 full-time (5 women), 14 part-time/adjunct (6 women). *Students:* 75 full-time (33 women), 27 part-time (14 women); includes 21 minority (10 Black or African American, non-Hispanic/Latino; 1 Asian, non-Hispanic/Latino; 4 Hispanic/Latino; 6 Two or more races, non-Hispanic/Latino), 19 international. Average age 27. 189 applicants, 21% accepted, 30 enrolled. In 2018, 39 master's, 2 doctorates, 4 other advanced degrees awarded. *Degree requirements:* For master's, thesis or alternative, project; for doctorate, comprehensive exam, thesis/dissertation. *Entrance requirements:* For master's, resume, two letters of recommendation, personal statement, transcripts; for doctorate, GRE, transcripts, three letters of recommendation, resume, research statement, writing sample. Additional exam requirements/recommendations for international students: Required—TOEFL (minimum score 79 iBT), IELTS (minimum score 6.5). *Application deadline:* For fall admission, 3/1 priority date for domestic and international students; for spring admission, 10/31 priority date for domestic students, 10/1 priority date for international students. Applications are processed on a rolling basis. Application fee: $75. Electronic applications accepted. *Financial support:* In 2018–19, 44 students received support, including 3 fellowships with full tuition reimbursements available (averaging $15,600 per year), 2 research assistantships with partial tuition reimbursements available (averaging $10,920 per year), 16 teaching assistantships with partial tuition reimbursements available (averaging $6,563 per year); career-related internships or fieldwork, Federal Work-Study, institutionally sponsored loans, scholarships/grants, health care benefits, tuition waivers (full and partial), and unspecified assistantships also available. Financial award application deadline: 3/1; financial award applicants required to submit FAFSA. *Faculty research:* Economic and international development, environmental and land use planning, GIS and spatial analysis, urban design and physical planning, neighborhood planning and community development, historic preservation. *Total annual research expenditures:* $616,211. *Unit head:* Dr. Daniel B. Hess, Professor and Chair, 716-829-5326, Fax: 716-829-3256, E-mail: dbhess@buffalo.edu. *Application contact:* Norma Everett, Assistant to the Chair, 716-829-3283, Fax: 716-829-3256, E-mail: norma.everett@buffalo.edu.
Website: http://www.ap.buffalo.edu/planning/

University of California, Berkeley, Graduate Division, Haas School of Business, PhD in Business Administration Program, Berkeley, CA 94720. Offers accounting (PhD); business and public policy (PhD); finance (PhD); management of organizations (PhD); marketing (PhD); real estate (PhD). *Accreditation:* AACSB. *Degree requirements:* For doctorate, comprehensive exam, thesis/dissertation, written preliminary exams, oral qualifying exam. *Entrance requirements:* For doctorate, GMAT or GRE, minimum GPA of 3.0 in undergraduate and graduate coursework. Additional exam requirements/recommendations for international students: Required—TOEFL (minimum score 570 paper-based; 70 iBT), IELTS (minimum score 7). Electronic applications accepted. *Expenses:* Contact institution. *Faculty research:* Accounting, business and public policy, entrepreneurship, finance, management of organizations, marketing, operations and information technology management, real estate.

University of Central Florida, College of Business Administration, Dr. P. Phillips School of Real Estate, Orlando, FL 32816. Offers MSRE. *Program availability:* Part-time. *Students:* 9 part-time (2 women); includes 4 minority (1 Black or African American, non-Hispanic/Latino; 1 Asian, non-Hispanic/Latino; 1 Hispanic/Latino; 1 Two or more races, non-Hispanic/Latino). Average age 29. In 2018, 1 master's awarded. *Entrance requirements:* For master's, letters of recommendation, resume. Additional exam requirements/recommendations for international students: Required—TOEFL. *Application deadline:* For fall admission, 7/1 for domestic students. Application fee: $30. Electronic applications accepted. *Financial support:* Application deadline: 3/1; applicants required to submit FAFSA. *Unit head:* Dr. Ajai Singh, Chair and Director, 407-823-5756, Fax: 407-823-6676, E-mail: ajai.singh@ucf.edu. *Application contact:* Associate Director, Graduate Admissions, 407-823-2766, Fax: 407-823-6442, E-mail: gradadmissions@ucf.edu.
Website: http://business.ucf.edu/degree/professional-ms-real-estate/

University of Denver, Daniels College of Business, Franklin L. Burns School of Real Estate and Construction Management, Denver, CO 80208. Offers real estate and the built environment (MBA, MS). *Program availability:* Part-time, evening/weekend. *Faculty:* 7 full-time (1 woman), 5 part-time/adjunct (0 women). *Students:* 26 full-time (6 women), 50 part-time (16 women); includes 12 minority (1 Black or African American, non-Hispanic/Latino; 7 Hispanic/Latino; 4 Two or more races, non-Hispanic/Latino). Average age 33. 60 applicants, 78% accepted, 25 enrolled. In 2018, 47 master's awarded. *Entrance requirements:* For master's, GRE General Test or GMAT, bachelor's degree, transcripts, essays, resume, interview. Additional exam requirements/recommendations for international students: Required—TOEFL (minimum score 575 paper-based; 94 iBT), TWE. *Application deadline:* For fall admission, 10/15 priority date for domestic and international students; for spring admission, 9/15 priority date for domestic and international students. Applications are processed on a rolling basis. Application fee: $100. Electronic applications accepted. *Expenses:* $49,695 per year full-time; $1,372 per credit. *Financial support:* In 2018–19, 56 students received support. Teaching assistantships with tuition reimbursements available, Federal Work-Study, institutionally sponsored loans, scholarships/grants, and unspecified assistantships available. Support available to part-time students. Financial award application deadline: 2/15; financial award applicants required to submit FAFSA. *Unit head:* Dr. Barbara Jackson, Associate Professor and Director, 303-871-3470, E-mail: barbara.jackson@du.edu. *Application contact:* Ceci Smith, Assistant to the Director, 303-871-2145, E-mail: ceci.smith@du.edu.
Website: https://daniels.du.edu/burns-school/

University of Florida, Graduate School, Warrington College of Business Administration, Hough Graduate School of Business, Department of Finance, Insurance and Real Estate, Gainesville, FL 32611. Offers entrepreneurship (MS); finance (MS, PhD); financial services (Certificate); insurance (PhD); quantitative finance (PhD); real estate (MS); real estate and urban analysis (PhD); JD/MBA; JD/MS. Terminal master's awarded for partial completion of doctoral program. *Degree requirements:* For master's,

comprehensive exam, thesis; for doctorate, comprehensive exam, thesis/dissertation. *Entrance requirements:* For master's, GMAT (minimum score of 465) or GRE General Test, minimum GPA of 3.0 for last 60 hours of undergraduate degree, work experience (preferred); for doctorate, GMAT (minimum score of 465) or GRE General Test, minimum GPA of 3.0. Additional exam requirements/recommendations for international students: Required—TOEFL (minimum score 550 paper-based; 80 iBT), IELTS (minimum score 6). Electronic applications accepted. *Faculty research:* Banking, empirical corporate finance, hedge funds.

University of Florida, Graduate School, Warrington College of Business Administration, Hough Graduate School of Business, Programs in Business Administration, Gainesville, FL 32611. Offers business administration (MA, MS, PhD); competitive strategy (MBA); finance (MBA); global management (MBA); Graham-Buffett security analysis (MBA); human resource management (MBA); information systems and operations management (MBA); international studies (MBA); management (MBA); real estate (MBA); JD/MBA; MBA/MS; MBA/PhD; MBA/Pharm D; MD/MBA. *Accreditation:* AACSB. *Program availability:* Part-time, evening/weekend, online learning. *Degree requirements:* For master's, capstone course. *Entrance requirements:* For master's and doctorate, GMAT (minimum score 465), minimum GPA of 3.0, interview. Additional exam requirements/recommendations for international students: Required—TOEFL (minimum score 550 paper-based; 80 iBT), IELTS (minimum score 6). Electronic applications accepted. *Faculty research:* Accounting, finance, insurance, management, real estate, urban analysis marketing.

University of Hawaii at Manoa, Office of Graduate Education, Shidler College of Business, Program in Business Administration, Honolulu, HI 96822. Offers Asian business studies (MBA); Chinese business studies (MBA); decision sciences (MBA); entrepreneurship (MBA); finance (MBA); finance and banking (MBA); human resources management (MBA); information management (MBA); information technology (MBA); international business (MBA); Japanese business studies (MBA); marketing (MBA); organizational behavior (MBA); organizational management (MBA); real estate (MBA); student-designed track (MBA). *Accreditation:* AACSB. *Program availability:* Part-time, evening/weekend. *Degree requirements:* For master's, thesis optional. *Entrance requirements:* For master's, GMAT, minimum GPA of 3.0. Additional exam requirements/recommendations for international students: Required—TOEFL (minimum score 600 paper-based; 100 iBT), IELTS (minimum score 7). *Expenses:* Contact institution.

University of Illinois at Chicago, Liautaud Graduate School of Business, Program in Real Estate, Chicago, IL 60607-7128. Offers MA.

University of Maryland, College Park, Academic Affairs, School of Architecture, Planning and Preservation, Program in Real Estate Development, College Park, MD 20742. Offers MRED.

University of Memphis, Graduate School, Fogelman College of Business and Economics, Program in Business Administration, Memphis, TN 38152. Offers accounting (MBA, PhD); business administration (IMBA); economics (PhD); executive business administration (MBA); finance (PhD); management (PhD); marketing (MS); marketing and supply chain management (PhD); real estate development (MS); JD/MBA. *Accreditation:* AACSB. *Students:* 189 full-time (96 women), 364 part-time (151 women); includes 178 minority (89 Black or African American, non-Hispanic/Latino; 1 American Indian or Alaska Native, non-Hispanic/Latino; 68 Asian, non-Hispanic/Latino; 12 Hispanic/Latino; 8 Two or more races, non-Hispanic/Latino), 102 international. Average age 32. 298 applicants, 72% accepted, 139 enrolled. In 2018, 200 master's, 3 doctorates awarded. *Degree requirements:* For master's, comprehensive exam; for doctorate, comprehensive exam, thesis/dissertation. *Entrance requirements:* For master's, GMAT, resume; for doctorate, GMAT, interview, minimum GPA of 3.4, resume, letter of recommendation. Additional exam requirements/recommendations for international students: Required—TOEFL (minimum score 550 paper-based). *Application deadline:* For fall admission, 8/1 for domestic students; for spring admission, 12/1 for domestic students. Application fee: $35 ($60 for international students). *Expenses: Tuition, area resident:* Full-time $10,240; part-time $503 per credit hour. Tuition, state resident: full-time $10,464. Tuition, nonresident: full-time $20,224; part-time $991 per credit hour. *Required fees:* $850; $106 per credit hour. *Financial support:* Research assistantships with full tuition reimbursements, teaching assistantships with full tuition reimbursements, career-related internships or fieldwork, Federal Work-Study, scholarships/grants, and unspecified assistantships available. Financial award application deadline: 2/15; financial award applicants required to submit FAFSA. *Faculty research:* Competitive business strategy, finance microstructures, supply chain management innovations, health care economics, litigation risks and corporate audits. *Unit head:* Dr. Balaji Krishnan, Director, MBA Programs, 901-678-2786, E-mail: krishnan@memphis.edu. *Application contact:* Dr. Balaji Krishnan, Director, MBA Programs, 901-678-2786, E-mail: krishnan@memphis.edu.
Website: https://www.memphis.edu/mba/index.php

University of Miami, Miami Business School, Coral Gables, FL 33146. Offers accounting (M Acc); business (PhD); business administration (MBA); business analytics (MSBA); economics (PhD); finance (MSF); health administration (MHA); international business (MIBS); real estate (MBA); taxation (MS Tax); JD/MBA; MD/MBA. *Accreditation:* AACSB; CAHME (one or more programs are accredited). *Program availability:* Part-time, evening/weekend, 100% online, blended/hybrid learning. *Faculty:* 155 full-time (47 women), 14 part-time/adjunct (5 women). *Students:* 1,083 full-time (469 women); includes 422 minority (79 Black or African American, non-Hispanic/Latino; 1 American Indian or Alaska Native, non-Hispanic/Latino; 43 Asian, non-Hispanic/Latino; 274 Hispanic/Latino; 3 Native Hawaiian or other Pacific Islander, non-Hispanic/Latino; 22 Two or more races, non-Hispanic/Latino), 282 international. Average age 30. 2,564 applicants, 38% accepted, 450 enrolled. In 2018, 558 master's, 5 doctorates awarded. Terminal master's awarded for partial completion of doctoral program. *Degree requirements:* For master's, comprehensive exam; for doctorate, comprehensive exam, thesis/dissertation. *Entrance requirements:* For master's, GMAT or GRE; for doctorate, GRE General Test. Additional exam requirements/recommendations for international students: Required—TOEFL (minimum score 94 iBT), IELTS (minimum score 7), TOEFL (minimum score 587 paper-based, 94 iBT) or IELTS (7). *Application deadline:* For fall admission, 6/30 priority date for domestic students, 5/30 priority date for international students; for spring admission, 10/31 priority date for domestic students, 9/30 priority date for international students. Applications are processed on a rolling basis. Application fee: $48. Electronic applications accepted. *Expenses:* Contact institution. *Financial support:* In 2018–19, 643 students received support, including 1 fellowship with full tuition reimbursement available (averaging $20,000 per year), 47 research assistantships with full and partial tuition reimbursements available (averaging $28,826 per year), 6 teaching assistantships with full and partial tuition reimbursements available (averaging $2,183 per year); career-related internships or fieldwork, Federal Work-Study, institutionally sponsored loans, scholarships/grants, and unspecified assistantships also available. Support available to part-time students. Financial award application deadline: 3/26; financial award applicants required to submit FAFSA. *Faculty research:* Behavioral finance; computational economics; consumer research; risk perception; consumer behavior; consumer choice research; behavioral decision theory; business analytics; point processes; longitudinal data analyses; international business; global business strategy, joint ventures, and alliances; emerging economies; global economic growth and development, money and financial markets, and computed dynamic models; health policy; innovative payment mechanisms. *Total annual research expenditures:* $703,773. *Unit head:* Dr. John Quelch, Dean, 305-284-6515, Fax: 305-284-6526, E-mail: jquelch@miami.edu. *Application contact:* Loubna Bouamane, Director of Graduate Business Recruiting and Admissions, 305-284-2510, Fax: 305-284-5905, E-mail: loubna@miami.edu.
Website: www.mbs.miami.edu

The University of North Carolina at Charlotte, Belk College of Business, Interdisciplinary Business Programs, Charlotte, NC 28223-0001. Offers mathematical finance (MS); real estate (MS, Graduate Certificate). *Program availability:* Part-time, evening/weekend. *Students:* 59 full-time (17 women), 49 part-time (11 women); includes 18 minority (7 Black or African American, non-Hispanic/Latino; 5 Asian, non-Hispanic/Latino; 3 Hispanic/Latino; 3 Two or more races, non-Hispanic/Latino), 48 international. Average age 33. 130 applicants, 81% accepted, 47 enrolled. In 2018, 69 master's awarded. *Entrance requirements:* For master's, GRE or GMAT, baccalaureate degree in related field with minimum GPA of 3.0 overall and in junior and senior years; transcript of all previous academic work; resume; recommendations; for Graduate Certificate, basic proficiency in using spreadsheet computer software, to be demonstrated by past project or certificate from completion of training course in Excel; previous coursework in financial management. Additional exam requirements/recommendations for international students: Required—TOEFL (minimum score 523 paper-based; 70 iBT), IELTS (minimum score 6), TOEFL (minimum score 523 paper-based, 70 iBT) or IELTS (6). *Application deadline:* Applications are processed on a rolling basis. Application fee: $75. Electronic applications accepted. *Expenses:* Contact institution. *Financial support:* Research assistantships, teaching assistantships, career-related internships or fieldwork, scholarships/grants, and unspecified assistantships available. Support available to part-time students. Financial award application deadline: 3/1; financial award applicants required to submit FAFSA. *Unit head:* Dr. Steven Ott, Dean, 704-687-7577, Fax: 704-687-1393, E-mail: cob-dean@uncc.edu. *Application contact:* Kathy B. Giddings, Director of Graduate Admissions, 704-687-5503, Fax: 704-687-1668, E-mail: gradadm@uncc.edu.
Website: http://belkcollege.uncc.edu/

University of Pennsylvania, Wharton School, Real Estate Department, Philadelphia, PA 19104. Offers MBA, PhD. Terminal master's awarded for partial completion of doctoral program. *Degree requirements:* For doctorate, thesis/dissertation. *Entrance requirements:* For master's, GMAT; for doctorate, GRE General Test. *Faculty research:* Public economics and taxation economics and finance of real estate markets, economics of housing markets, real estate development.

University of San Diego, School of Business, Program in Real Estate, San Diego, CA 92110-2492. Offers MS, MBA/MSRE. *Program availability:* Part-time, evening/weekend. *Students:* 20 full-time (5 women), 11 part-time (2 women); includes 6 minority (2 Asian, non-Hispanic/Latino; 4 Hispanic/Latino), 5 international. Average age 31. In 2018, 13 master's awarded. *Degree requirements:* For master's, capstone course. *Entrance requirements:* For master's, GMAT (minimum score of 550), minimum GPA of 3.0. Additional exam requirements/recommendations for international students: Required—TOEFL (minimum score 580 paper-based; 92 iBT), TWE. *Application deadline:* For fall admission, 11/1 priority date for domestic students. Applications are processed on a rolling basis. Application fee: $80. Electronic applications accepted. *Financial support:* In 2018–19, 19 students received support. Research assistantships, career-related internships or fieldwork, Federal Work-Study, institutionally sponsored loans, and scholarships/grants available. Support available to part-time students. Financial award application deadline: 4/1; financial award applicants required to submit FAFSA. *Faculty research:* Commercial real estate investment, commercial real estate capital markets, sustainable real estate, housing affordability, workplace trends. *Unit head:* Dr. Charles Tu, Academic Director, Real Estate Program, 619-260-5942, E-mail: realestate@sandiego.edu. *Application contact:* Erika Garwood, Associate Director of Graduate Admissions, 619-260-4524, Fax: 619-260-4158, E-mail: grads@sandiego.edu.
Website: http://www.sandiego.edu/business/graduate/ms-real-estate/

University of South Africa, College of Economic and Management Sciences, Pretoria, South Africa. Offers accounting (D Admin, D Com); accounting science (DA); auditing (D Admin, D Com); business administration (M Tech); business economics (D Admin); business leadership (DBL); business management (D Admin, D Com); economic management analysis (M Tech); economics (D Admin, D Com, PhD); human resource development (M Tech); industrial psychology (D Admin, D Com, PhD); logistics (D Com); marketing (M Tech); public administration (D Admin, D Com, DPA, PhD); public management (M Tech); quantitative management (D Admin, D Com); real estate (M Tech); statistics (D Admin, PhD); tourism management (D Admin, D Com); transport economics (D Admin, D Com).

University of Southern California, Graduate School, Sol Price School of Public Policy, Master of Real Estate Development Program, Los Angeles, CA 90089. Offers MRED, JD/MRED, M Pl/MRED, MBA/MRED. *Program availability:* Part-time. *Degree requirements:* For master's, comprehensive exam. *Entrance requirements:* For master's, GRE, GMAT. Additional exam requirements/recommendations for international students: Required—TOEFL (minimum score 600 paper-based; 100 iBT). Electronic applications accepted. *Expenses:* Contact institution. *Faculty research:* Urban development, urban economics, real estate finance, housing markets.

University of South Florida, Muma College of Business, Department of Finance, Tampa, FL 33620-9951. Offers business administration (PhD), including finance; finance (MS); real estate (MSRE). *Program availability:* Part-time, evening/weekend. *Faculty:* 13 full-time (3 women), 1 part-time/adjunct (0 women). *Students:* 83 full-time (33 women), 22 part-time (7 women); includes 7 minority (1 Black or African American, non-Hispanic/Latino; 2 Asian, non-Hispanic/Latino; 4 Hispanic/Latino), 8,594 international. Average age 25. 119 applicants, 55% accepted, 37 enrolled. In 2018, 71 master's awarded. Terminal master's awarded for partial completion of doctoral program. *Degree requirements:* For master's, comprehensive exam, thesis or alternative; for doctorate, comprehensive exam, thesis/dissertation. *Entrance requirements:* For master's, GMAT score of 550 or higher (or equivalent GRE score). Applicants with lower GMAT (GRE) scores may be admitted if the application as a whole convinces the committee that the applicant warrants an admission to the major., minimum undergraduate GPA of 3.0; for doctorate, GMAT or GRE, minimum undergraduate GPA of 3.0 in upper-division coursework, personal statement, recommendations, interview. Additional exam requirements/recommendations for international students: Required—TOEFL, TOEFL (minimum score 550 paper-based; 79 iBT) or IELTS (minimum score 6.5). *Application deadline:* For fall admission, 6/1 for domestic students, 1/2 for international students; for spring admission, 10/15 for domestic students, 7/1 for international students; for summer admission, 2/15 for domestic students, 1/1 for international students. Application fee: $30. Electronic applications accepted. *Expenses:* Tuition, state resident: full-time $6350. Tuition, nonresident: full-time $19,048. *International tuition:* $19,048 full-time. *Required fees:* $2079. *Financial support:* In 2018–19, 12 students received support, including 8 research assistantships (averaging $14,357 per year), 9 teaching assistantships with tuition reimbursements available (averaging $11,972 per year); scholarships/grants,

Real Estate

health care benefits, and unspecified assistantships also available. Financial award application deadline: 6/30. *Faculty research:* International corporate finance, corporate finance, market efficiency, mergers and acquisitions, agency theory, corporate governance, investments, mutual fund industry, mergers and acquisitions, corporate creditworthiness, credit risk issues, empirical asset pricing, financial intermediation, corporate finance theory, public offerings, business strategy. *Total annual research expenditures:* $30,000. *Unit head:* Dr. Scott Besley, Chairperson and Associate Professor, 813-974-6341, Fax: 813-974-3084, E-mail: sbesley@usf.edu. *Application contact:* Yuting DiGiovanni, 813-974-6358, Fax: 813-974-3084, E-mail: yuting2@usf.edu.
Website: http://business.usf.edu/departments/finance/

The University of Texas at Arlington, Graduate School, College of Business, Department of Finance and Real Estate, Arlington, TX 76019. Offers finance (PhD); quantitative finance (MS); real estate (MS). *Program availability:* Part-time, evening/weekend. *Degree requirements:* For master's, thesis optional; for doctorate, comprehensive exam, thesis/dissertation. *Entrance requirements:* For master's, GMAT/GRE, minimum GPA of 3.0; for doctorate, GMAT/GRE. Additional exam requirements/recommendations for international students: Required—TOEFL (minimum score 550 paper-based; 79 iBT).

The University of Texas at Dallas, Naveen Jindal School of Management, Program in Finance and Managerial Economics, Richardson, TX 75080. Offers finance (MS), including energy risk management, enterprise risk management, real estate, risk management insurance. *Program availability:* Part-time, evening/weekend. *Faculty:* 27 full-time (2 women), 19 part-time/adjunct (6 women). *Students:* 244 full-time (87 women), 93 part-time (30 women); includes 57 minority (5 Black or African American, non-Hispanic/Latino; 29 Asian, non-Hispanic/Latino; 15 Hispanic/Latino; 8 Two or more races, non-Hispanic/Latino), 211 international. Average age 27. 452 applicants, 53% accepted, 122 enrolled. In 2018, 181 master's awarded. *Entrance requirements:* For master's, GMAT or GRE. Additional exam requirements/recommendations for international students: Required—TOEFL (minimum score 550 paper-based). *Application deadline:* For fall admission, 7/15 for domestic students, 5/1 priority date for international students; for spring admission, 11/15 for domestic students, 9/1 priority date for international students. Applications are processed on a rolling basis. Application fee: $50 ($100 for international students). Electronic applications accepted. *Expenses: Tuition, area resident:* Full-time $13,458. *Tuition, state resident:* full-time $13,458. Tuition, nonresident: full-time $26,852. *International tuition:* $26,852 full-time. Tuition and fees vary according to course load. *Financial support:* In 2018–19, 10 teaching assistantships with partial tuition reimbursements (averaging $10,050 per year) were awarded; research assistantships with partial tuition reimbursements, career-related internships or fieldwork, Federal Work-Study, institutionally sponsored loans, scholarships/grants, and unspecified assistantships also available. Support available to part-time students. Financial award application deadline: 4/30; financial award applicants required to submit FAFSA. *Faculty research:* Econometrics, industrial organization, auction theory, file-sharing copyrights and bundling, international financial management, entrepreneurial finance. *Unit head:* Dr. Harold Zhang, Area Coordinator, 972-883-4777, E-mail: harold.zhang@utdallas.edu. *Application contact:* Dr. Harold Zhang, Area Coordinator, 972-883-4777, E-mail: harold.zhang@utdallas.edu.
Website: http://jindal.utdallas.edu/finance

University of Utah, Graduate School, David Eccles School of Business, Master in Real Estate Development Program, Salt Lake City, UT 84112. Offers MRED, MRED/JD, MRED/M Arch, MRED/MCMP. MRED/M Arch, MRED/MCMP offered jointly with College of Architecture and Planning; MRED/JD with S.J. Quinney College of Law. *Program availability:* Part-time. *Degree requirements:* For master's, professional project. *Entrance requirements:* For master's, GMAT or GRE, minimum undergraduate GPA of 3.0. Additional exam requirements/recommendations for international students: Required—TOEFL (minimum score 90 iBT), IELTS (minimum score 6.5). Electronic applications accepted. *Expenses:* Contact institution.

University of Wisconsin–Madison, Graduate School, Wisconsin School of Business, Doctoral Program in Real Estate and Urban Land Economics, Madison, WI 53706-1380. Offers PhD. *Degree requirements:* For doctorate, comprehensive exam, thesis/dissertation. *Entrance requirements:* For doctorate, GMAT or GRE. Additional exam requirements/recommendations for international students: Recommended—TOEFL (minimum score 623 paper-based; 106 iBT), IELTS (minimum score 7.5), TSE (minimum score 73). Electronic applications accepted. *Expenses:* Contact institution. *Faculty research:* Real estate finance, real estate equity investments, zoning restructurings, home ownership, international real estate and public policy, real estate economics.

University of Wisconsin–Madison, Graduate School, Wisconsin School of Business, Wisconsin Full-Time MBA Program, Madison, WI 53706-1380. Offers applied security analysis (MBA); arts administration (MBA); brand and product management (MBA); corporate finance and investment banking (MBA); marketing research (MBA); operations and technology management (MBA); real estate (MBA); risk management and insurance (MBA); strategic human resource management (MBA); supply chain management (MBA). *Faculty:* 137 full-time (36 women), 39 part-time/adjunct (11 women). *Students:* 183 full-time (59 women); includes 31 minority (5 Black or African American, non-Hispanic/Latino; 1 American Indian or Alaska Native, non-Hispanic/Latino; 6 Asian, non-Hispanic/Latino; 13 Hispanic/Latino; 6 Two or more races, non-Hispanic/Latino), 40 international. Average age 28. 465 applicants, 33% accepted, 79 enrolled. In 2018, 104 master's awarded. *Entrance requirements:* For master's, GMAT or GRE, bachelor's or equivalent degree, essay, letter of recommendation, resume. Additional exam requirements/recommendations for international students: Required—TOEFL (minimum score 100 iBT), IELTS (minimum score 7.5). TOEFL is not required for international students whose undergraduate training was in English. *Application deadline:* For fall admission, 11/1 for domestic and international students; for winter admission, 1/10 for domestic and international students; for spring admission, 3/1 for domestic and international students; for summer admission, 4/10 for domestic students, 4/10 priority date for international students. Applications are processed on a rolling basis. Application fee: $75 ($81 for international students). Electronic applications accepted. *Expenses:* Wisconsin Resident tuition and fees - $39,156; Nonresident tuition and fees - $76,635. *Financial support:* In 2018–19, 148 students received support, including 7 fellowships with full tuition reimbursements available (averaging $25,871 per year), 7 research assistantships with full tuition reimbursements available (averaging $14,832 per year), 47 teaching assistantships with full tuition reimbursements available (averaging $14,832 per year); scholarships/grants, health care benefits, tuition waivers (full and partial), and unspecified assistantships also available. Financial award application deadline: 6/1. *Faculty research:* Ecology, environmental studies, and business; decision making; tax policy; diversity and inclusion in governance boards; marketing and social media. *Unit head:* Dr. Enno Siemsen, Associate Dean of the MBA and Masters Programs, 608-890-3130, E-mail: esiemsen@wisc.edu. *Application contact:* Betsy Kacizak, Director of Admissions and Recruiting, Full-time MBA Program, 608-262-4000, E-mail: betsy.kacizak@wisc.edu.
Website: https://wsb.wisc.edu/

Villanova University, Villanova School of Business, MBA - The Flex Track Program, Villanova, PA 19085. Offers healthcare (MBA); international business (MBA); marketing (MBA); real estate (MBA); strategic management (MBA); JD/MBA. *Accreditation:* AACSB. *Program availability:* Part-time, evening/weekend, online learning. *Faculty:* 101 full-time (38 women), 36 part-time/adjunct (9 women). *Students:* 13 full-time (5 women), 427 part-time (157 women); includes 74 minority (12 Black or African American, non-Hispanic/Latino; 29 Asian, non-Hispanic/Latino; 23 Hispanic/Latino; 10 Two or more races, non-Hispanic/Latino), 12 international. Average age 32. 156 applicants, 92% accepted, 139 enrolled. In 2018, 124 master's awarded. *Degree requirements:* For master's, minimum GPA of 3.0. *Entrance requirements:* For master's, GMAT or GRE, Application, official transcripts, 2 letters of recommendation, resume, 2 essays. Additional exam requirements/recommendations for international students: Required—TOEFL (minimum score 550 paper-based; 100 iBT). *Application deadline:* For fall admission, 7/31 for domestic and international students; for spring admission, 11/30 for domestic and international students; for summer admission, 4/30 for domestic and international students. Applications are processed on a rolling basis. Application fee: $65. Electronic applications accepted. *Expenses:* Contact institution. *Financial support:* Research assistantships and scholarships/grants available. Financial award application deadline: 6/30; financial award applicants required to submit FAFSA. *Faculty research:* Real Estate, Business Analytics, Global Leadership, Marketing and Consumer Insights, Church management. *Unit head:* Dr. Joyce E. A. Russell, Dean of Villanova School of Business, 610-519-6082, Fax: 610-519-6273, E-mail: joyce.russell@villanova.edu. *Application contact:* Daniel Guertin, Assistant Director, Recruitment, 610-519-8031, Fax: 610-519-6273, E-mail: daniel.guertin@villanova.edu.
Website: http://www1.villanova.edu/villanova/business/graduate/mba.html

Virginia Commonwealth University, Graduate School, School of Business, Program in Real Estate and Urban Land Development, Richmond, VA 23284-9005. Offers Postbaccalaureate Certificate. *Entrance requirements:* Additional exam requirements/recommendations for international students: Required—TOEFL (minimum score 600 paper-based; 100 iBT); Recommended—IELTS (minimum score 6.5). Electronic applications accepted.

Section 21
Transportation Management, Logistics, and Supply Chain Management

This section contains a directory of institutions offering graduate work in real estate, followed by an in-depth entry submitted by an institution that chose to prepare a detailed program description. Additional information about programs listed in the directory but not augmented by an in-depth entry may be obtained by writing directly to the dean of a graduate school or chair of a department at the address given in the directory.

For programs offering related work, see also in this book *Business Administration and Management.*

CONTENTS

Program Directories

Aviation Management

Arizona State University at the Tempe campus, Ira A. Fulton Schools of Engineering, The Polytechnic School, Programs in Technology Management, Mesa, AZ 85212. Offers aviation management and human factors (MS); environmental technology management (MS); global technology and development (MS); graphic information technology (MS); management of technology (MS). *Program availability:* Part-time, evening/weekend, online learning. *Degree requirements:* For master's, thesis or applied project and oral defense; interactive Program of Study (iPOS) submitted before completing 50 percent of required credit hours. *Entrance requirements:* For master's, GRE, minimum GPA of 3.0 or equivalent in last 2 years of work leading to bachelor's degree. Additional exam requirements/recommendations for international students: Required—TOEFL, IELTS, or PTE. Electronic applications accepted. *Faculty research:* Digital imaging, digital publishing, Internet development/e-commerce, information aviation human factors, pilot selection, databases, multimedia, commercial digital photography, digital workflow, computer graphics modeling and animation, information design, sociotechnology, visual and technical literacy, environmental management, quality management, project management, industrial ethics, hazardous materials, environmental chemistry.

Delta State University, Graduate Programs, College of Business, Department of Commercial Aviation, Cleveland, MS 38733-0001. Offers MCA. *Program availability:* Part-time, evening/weekend, online learning. *Degree requirements:* For master's, thesis or alternative. *Entrance requirements:* For master's, GMAT. *Expenses: Tuition, area resident:* Full-time $7076; part-time $393 per credit hour. Tuition, state resident: full-time $7076; part-time $393 per credit hour. Tuition, nonresident: full-time $7076; part-time $393 per credit hour. *International tuition:* $7076 full-time. *Required fees:* $170; $18.90 per credit hour. $9.45 per semester. Part-time tuition and fees vary according to program.

Embry-Riddle Aeronautical University–Worldwide, Department of Business Administration, Daytona Beach, FL 32114-3900. Offers aviation (MBAA); MS/MBA. *Program availability:* Part-time, evening/weekend, online only, EagleVision Classroom (between classrooms), EagleVision Home (faculty and students at home), and a blend of Classroom or Home. *Degree requirements:* For master's, comprehensive exam. *Entrance requirements:* Additional exam requirements/recommendations for international students: Required—TOEFL (minimum score 550 paper-based; 79 iBT), IELTS (minimum score 6). Electronic applications accepted. *Expenses:* Contact institution.

Middle Tennessee State University, College of Graduate Studies, College of Basic and Applied Sciences, Department of Aerospace, Program in Aviation Administration, Murfreesboro, TN 37132. Offers MS. *Program availability:* Part-time, evening/weekend, online learning. *Degree requirements:* For master's, comprehensive exam, thesis optional. *Entrance requirements:* For master's, GRE or MAT. Additional exam requirements/recommendations for international students: Required—TOEFL (minimum score 525 paper-based; 71 iBT) or IELTS (minimum score 6).

Midwest University, Graduate Programs, Wentzville, MO 63385. Offers asset management/investment/real estate (MBA); Christian counseling (D Min); Christian education (D Min); counseling (MA), including marriage and family counseling, school counseling; divinity (M Div); education (MA), including brain and gifted education, Christian education; global business management (MBA); global leadership (MBA); leadership (PhD), including brain and gifted educational leadership, entrepreneurial leadership, international aviation leadership, organizational leadership, political leadership; mission studies (D Min); music (MM, DMA); pastoral theology (D Min); public

policy/administration (MBA); teaching English to speakers of other languages (MA). *Program availability:* Part-time, online learning. *Degree requirements:* For master's, thesis (for some programs); for doctorate, thesis/dissertation. *Entrance requirements:* Additional exam requirements/recommendations for international students: Recommended—TOEFL (minimum score 550 paper-based).

National American University, Roueche Graduate Center, Austin, TX 78731. Offers accounting (MBA); aviation management (MBA, MM); care coordination (MSN); community college leadership (Ed D); criminal justice (MM); e-marketing (MBA, MM); health care administration (MBA, MM); higher education (MM); human resources management (MBA, MM); information technology management (MBA, MM); international business (MBA); leadership (EMBA); management (MBA); nursing administration (MSN); nursing education (MSN); nursing informatics (MSN); operations and configuration management (MBA, MM); project and process management (MBA, MM). Master's programs offered online through the Harold D. Buckingham Graduate School. *Program availability:* Part-time, evening/weekend, online learning. *Entrance requirements:* For master's, minimum undergraduate GPA of 2.75. Additional exam requirements/recommendations for international students: Required—TOEFL, TWE. Electronic applications accepted. *Faculty research:* Tourism, finance, marketing.

Purdue University, Graduate School, Purdue Polytechnic Institute, Department of Aviation Technology, West Lafayette, IN 47907. Offers aviation and aerospace management (MS). *Faculty:* 22 full-time (2 women), 3 part-time/adjunct (all women). *Students:* 37 full-time (13 women), 59 part-time (17 women); includes 16 minority (4 Black or African American, non-Hispanic/Latino; 6 Asian, non-Hispanic/Latino; 3 Hispanic/Latino; 1 Native Hawaiian or other Pacific Islander, non-Hispanic/Latino; 2 Two or more races, non-Hispanic/Latino), 23 international. Average age 29. 61 applicants, 77% accepted, 20 enrolled. In 2018, 47 master's awarded. *Entrance requirements:* For master's, GRE/GMAT, written and spoken communication skills; general knowledge of aviation industry operations and components; entry-level analytical tools and processes; group activity and interpersonal skills. Additional exam requirements/recommendations for international students: Required—TOEFL (minimum score 550 paper-based; 77 iBT); Recommended—TWE. *Application deadline:* For fall admission, 4/1 for domestic and international students; for spring admission, 10/1 for domestic students, 9/1 for international students; for summer admission, 4/1 for domestic students, 2/15 for international students. Applications are processed on a rolling basis. Application fee: $60 ($75 for international students). Electronic applications accepted. *Unit head:* Dr. Manoj S. Patankar, Head of the Graduate Program, 765-496-3136, E-mail: mspatankar@purdue.edu. *Application contact:* Emily Birge, Graduate Contact, 765-494-2884, E-mail: ebirge@purdue.edu.
Website: https://tech.purdue.edu/departments/aviation-technology

Southeastern Oklahoma State University, Department of Aviation Science, Durant, OK 74701-0609. Offers aerospace administration and logistics (MS). *Program availability:* Part-time, evening/weekend. *Entrance requirements:* For master's, minimum GPA of 3.0 in last 60 hours or 2.75 overall. Additional exam requirements/recommendations for international students: Required—TOEFL (minimum score 550 paper-based; 79 iBT). Electronic applications accepted.

Vaughn College of Aeronautics and Technology, Graduate Programs, Flushing, NY 11369. Offers airport management (MS). *Degree requirements:* For master's, project or thesis.

Logistics

Air Force Institute of Technology, Graduate School of Engineering and Management, Department of Operational Sciences, Dayton, OH 45433-7765. Offers logistics management (MS); operations research (MS, PhD); space operations (MS). *Program availability:* Part-time. *Degree requirements:* For master's, thesis; for doctorate, thesis/dissertation. *Entrance requirements:* For doctorate, GRE General Test, minimum GPA of 3.0, U.S. citizenship. *Faculty research:* Optimization, simulation, combat modeling and analysis, reliability and maintainability, resource scheduling.

Albany State University, College of Business, Albany, GA 31705-2717. Offers accounting (MBA); general business administration (MBA); healthcare (MBA); public administration (MBA); supply chain and logistics (MBA). *Accreditation:* ACBSP. *Program availability:* Part-time, evening/weekend. *Degree requirements:* For master's, comprehensive exam, internship, 3 hours of physical education. *Entrance requirements:* For master's, GMAT (minimum score of 450)/GRE (minimum score of 800) for those without earned master's degree or higher, minimum undergraduate GPA of 2.5, 2 letters of reference, official transcript, pre-entrance medical record and certificate of immunization. Electronic applications accepted. *Faculty research:* Diversity issues, ancestry, understanding finance through use of technology.

American Public University System, AMU/APU Graduate Programs, Charles Town, WV 25414. Offers accounting (MS); applied business analytics (MS); business administration (MBA); criminal justice (MA); cybersecurity studies (MS); educational leadership (M Ed); environmental policy and management (MS); global security (DGS); health information management (MS); history (MA), including American military history, American Revolution, civil war, war since 1945, World War II; information technology (MS); international relations and conflict resolution (MA), including American politics and government, comparative government and development, general, international relations, public policy; national security studies (MA); nursing (MSN); political science (MA); public policy (MPP); reverse logistics management (MA), including comparative and security issues, conflict resolution, international and transnational security issues, peacekeeping; space studies (MS); sports management (MS); strategic intelligence (DSI); teaching (M Ed), including secondary social studies; transportation and logistics management (MA). *Program availability:* Part-time, evening/weekend, online only, 100% online. *Students:* 406 full-time (180 women), 7,826 part-time (3,329 women); includes 2,781 minority (1,438 Black or African American, non-Hispanic/Latino; 44 American Indian or Alaska Native, non-Hispanic/Latino; 193 Asian, non-Hispanic/Latino; 747 Hispanic/Latino; 53 Native Hawaiian or other Pacific Islander, non-Hispanic/Latino; 306 Two or more races, non-Hispanic/Latino), 121 international. Average age 38. In 2018, 2,717 master's awarded. *Degree requirements:* For master's, comprehensive exam or practicum; for doctorate, practicum. *Entrance requirements:* For master's, official

transcript showing earned bachelor's degree from institution accredited by recognized accrediting body. Additional exam requirements/recommendations for international students: Required—TOEFL (minimum score 550 paper-based), IELTS (minimum score 6.5). *Application deadline:* Applications are processed on a rolling basis. Application fee: $0. Electronic applications accepted. *Financial support:* Scholarships/grants available. Financial award applicants required to submit FAFSA. *Unit head:* Dr. Wallace Boston, President, 877-468-6268, Fax: 304-728-2348, E-mail: president@apus.edu. *Application contact:* Yoci Deal, Associate Vice President, Graduate and International Admissions, 877-468-6268, Fax: 304-724-3764, E-mail: info@apus.edu.
Website: http://www.apus.edu

Athens State University, Graduate Programs, Athens, AL 35611. Offers career and technical education (M Ed); global logistics and supply chain management (MS); religious studies (MA).

Benedictine University, Graduate Programs, Program in Business Administration, Lisle, IL 60532. Offers accounting (MBA); entrepreneurship and managing innovation (MBA); financial management (MBA); health administration (MBA); human resource management (MBA); information systems security (MBA); international business (MBA); management consulting (MBA); management information systems (MBA); marketing management (MBA); operations management and logistics (MBA); organizational leadership (MBA). *Program availability:* Part-time, evening/weekend, 100% online, blended/hybrid learning. *Faculty:* 7 full-time (1 woman), 36 part-time/adjunct (10 women). *Students:* 110 full-time (71 women), 500 part-time (302 women); includes 104 minority (34 Black or African American, non-Hispanic/Latino; 1 American Indian or Alaska Native, non-Hispanic/Latino; 41 Asian, non-Hispanic/Latino; 23 Hispanic/Latino; 5 Native Hawaiian or other Pacific Islander, non-Hispanic/Latino), 7 international. Average age 33. 251 applicants, 84% accepted, 202 enrolled. In 2018, 345 master's awarded. *Entrance requirements:* For master's, GMAT or GRE test scores or completed test waiver form, official transcripts; 2 letters of reference from individuals familiar with the applicant's professional or academic work, excluding family or personal friends; a 1-2 page essay addressing educational and career goals; current résumé listing chronological work history; personal interview may be required prior to an admission decision. Additional exam requirements/recommendations for international students: Required—TOEFL (minimum score 550 paper-based; 79 iBT), IELTS (minimum score 6.5). *Application deadline:* Applications are processed on a rolling basis. Application fee: $40. Electronic applications accepted. *Unit head:* Ricky Holman, Assistant Professor, 630-829-1936, E-mail: rholman@ben.edu. *Application contact:* Ricky Holman, Assistant Professor, 630-829-1936, E-mail: rholman@ben.edu.

Case Western Reserve University, School of Graduate Studies, Case School of Engineering, Department of Computer and Data Sciences, Cleveland, OH 44106. Offers computer engineering (MS, PhD); computing and information sciences (MS, PhD); electrical engineering (MS, PhD); systems and control engineering (MS, PhD). *Program availability:* Part-time, evening/weekend, online only, 100% online. *Faculty:* 31 full-time (2 women). *Students:* 228 full-time (49 women), 17 part-time (3 women); includes 18 minority (13 Asian, non-Hispanic/Latino; 3 Hispanic/Latino; 2 Two or more races, non-Hispanic/Latino), 180 international. In 2018, 29 master's, 16 doctorates awarded. Terminal master's awarded for partial completion of doctoral program. *Degree requirements:* For master's, thesis; for doctorate, thesis/dissertation, qualifying exam, teaching experience. *Entrance requirements:* For master's and doctorate, GRE General Test. Additional exam requirements/recommendations for international students: Required—TOEFL. *Application deadline:* For fall admission, 2/1 for domestic students; for spring admission, 11/1 for domestic students. Applications are processed on a rolling basis. Application fee: $50. *Expenses: Tuition:* Full-time $45,168; part-time $1939 per credit hour. *Required fees:* $36; $18 per semester. $18 per semester. *Financial support:* In 2018–19, 1 fellowship with tuition reimbursement, 72 research assistantships with tuition reimbursements, 10 teaching assistantships were awarded; career-related internships or fieldwork, Federal Work-Study, and institutionally sponsored loans also available. Support available to part-time students. Financial award application deadline: 3/1; financial award applicants required to submit FAFSA. *Faculty research:* Micro-/nano-systems; robotics and haptics; applied artificial intelligence; automation; computer-aided design and testing of digital systems. *Total annual research expenditures:* $5.1 million. *Unit head:* Jing Li, Interim Department Chair, 216-368-0356, E-mail: jxl175@case.edu. *Application contact:* Angela Beca, Student Affairs Specialist, 216-368-2800, Fax: 216-368-2801, E-mail: angela.beca@case.edu.
Website: www.engineering.case.edu/eecs

Central Connecticut State University, School of Graduate Studies, School of Engineering, Science and Technology, Department of Manufacturing and Construction Management, New Britain, CT 06050-4010. Offers construction management (MS, Certificate); lean manufacturing and Six Sigma (Certificate); supply chain and logistics (Certificate); technology management (MS). *Program availability:* Part-time, evening/weekend. *Faculty:* 6 full-time (0 women), 2 part-time/adjunct (0 women). *Students:* 14 full-time (7 women), 82 part-time (18 women); includes 28 minority (11 Black or African American, non-Hispanic/Latino; 2 Asian, non-Hispanic/Latino; 12 Hispanic/Latino; 3 Two or more races, non-Hispanic/Latino), 6 international. Average age 32. 70 applicants, 71% accepted, 29 enrolled. In 2018, 51 master's, 5 other advanced degrees awarded. *Degree requirements:* For master's, comprehensive exam, special project; for Certificate, qualifying exam. *Entrance requirements:* For master's, minimum undergraduate GPA of 2.7. Additional exam requirements/recommendations for international students: Required—TOEFL (minimum score 550 paper-based; 79 iBT); Recommended—IELTS (minimum score 6.5). *Application deadline:* For fall admission, 8/1 for domestic students, 5/1 for international students; for spring admission, 12/1 for domestic students, 11/1 for international students; for summer admission, 5/1 for domestic students. Applications are processed on a rolling basis. Application fee: $50. Electronic applications accepted. *Expenses: Tuition, area resident:* Full-time $7027; part-time $388 per credit. Tuition, state resident: full-time $9750; part-time $388 per credit. Tuition, nonresident: full-time $18,102; part-time $388 per credit. *International tuition:* $18,102 full-time. *Required fees:* $266 per semester. *Financial support:* In 2018–19, 7 students received support. Career-related internships or fieldwork, Federal Work-Study, scholarships/grants, and unspecified assistantships available. Support available to part-time students. Financial award application deadline: 3/1; financial award applicants required to submit FAFSA. *Faculty research:* All aspects of middle management, technical supervision in the workplace. *Unit head:* Dr. Ravindra Thamma, Chair, 860-832-1830, E-mail: thammarav@ccsu.edu. *Application contact:* Patricia Gardner, Associate Director of Graduate Studies, 860-832-2350, Fax: 860-832-2362.
Website: http://www.ccsu.edu/mcm/

Central Michigan University, Central Michigan University Global Campus, Program in Business Administration, Mount Pleasant, MI 48859. Offers enterprise resource planning (MBA, Certificate); human resource management (MBA); logistics management (MBA, Certificate); marketing (MBA); value-driven organization (MBA). *Program availability:* Part-time, evening/weekend. *Entrance requirements:* For master's, GMAT.

Central Michigan University, College of Graduate Studies, College of Business Administration, MBA Program, Mount Pleasant, MI 48859. Offers accounting (MBA); business economics (MBA); consulting (MBA); finance (MBA); general business (MBA); human resource management (MBA); information systems (MBA); international business (MBA); logistics management (MBA); marketing (MBA); value-driven organization (MBA). *Program availability:* Part-time, evening/weekend, online learning. Electronic applications accepted. *Faculty research:* Accounting, consulting, international business, marketing, information systems.

Colorado Technical University Colorado Springs, Graduate Studies, Program in Management, Colorado Springs, CO 80907. Offers accounting (MBA, MSA); business administration (MBA); finance (MBA); human resources management (MBA); logistics/supply chain management (MBA); management (DM); marketing (MBA); mediation and dispute resolution (MBA); operations management (MBA); project management (MBA); technology management (MBA). *Accreditation:* ACBSP. *Program availability:* Part-time, evening/weekend, online learning. *Degree requirements:* For master's, thesis or alternative; for doctorate, thesis/dissertation. *Entrance requirements:* For doctorate, minimum graduate GPA of 3.0, 5 years of related work experience. *Faculty research:* Sexual harassment, performance evaluation, critical thinking.

Copenhagen Business School, Graduate Programs, Copenhagen, Denmark. Offers business administration (Exec MBA, MBA, PhD); business administration and information systems (M Sc); business, language and culture (M Sc); economics and business administration (M Sc); health management (MHM); international business and politics (M Sc); public administration (MPA); shipping and logistics (Exec MBA); technology, market and organization (MBA).

East Carolina University, Graduate School, College of Engineering and Technology, Department of Technology Systems, Greenville, NC 27858-4353. Offers computer network professional (Certificate); cyber security professional (Certificate); information assurance (Certificate); Lean Six Sigma Black Belt (Certificate); network technology (MS), including computer networking management, digital communications technology, information security, Web technologies; occupational safety (MS); technology management (MS, PhD), including industrial distribution and logistics (MS); Website developer (Certificate). *Application deadline:* For fall admission, 6/1 priority date for domestic students. *Expenses: Tuition, area resident:* Full-time $4749. Tuition, state resident: full-time $4749. Tuition, nonresident: full-time $17,898. *International tuition:* $17,898 full-time. *Required fees:* $2787. Part-time tuition and fees vary according to course load and program. *Financial support:* Application deadline: 6/1. *Unit head:* Dr. Tijani Mohammed, Chair, 252-328-9668, E-mail: mohammedt@ecu.edu. *Application contact:* Graduate School Admissions, 252-328-6012, Fax: 252-328-6071, E-mail: gradschool@ecu.edu.
Website: http://www.ecu.edu/cs-cet/techsystems/index.cfm

Embry-Riddle Aeronautical University–Worldwide, Department of Decision Sciences, Daytona Beach, FL 32114-3900. Offers aviation and aerospace (MSPM); aviation/aerospace management (MSEM); financial management (MSEM, MSPM); general management (MSPM); global management (MSPM); human resources management (MSPM); information systems (MSPM); leadership (MSEM, MSPM); logistics and supply chain management (MSEM, MSLSCM, MSPM); management (MSEM, MSPM); project management (MSEM); systems engineering (MSEM, MSPM); technical management (MSPM). *Program availability:* Part-time, evening/weekend, EagleVision Classroom (between classrooms), EagleVision Home (faculty and students at home), and a blend of Classroom or Home. *Degree requirements:* For master's, comprehensive exam (for some programs), thesis (for some programs). *Entrance requirements:* Additional exam requirements/recommendations for international students: Required—TOEFL (minimum score 550 paper-based; 79 iBT), IELTS (minimum score 6). Electronic applications accepted. *Expenses:* Contact institution.

Florida Institute of Technology, Aberdeen Education Center (Maryland), Program in Management, Melbourne, FL 32901-6975. Offers acquisition and contract management (MS, PMBA); business administration (MS, PMBA); contracts management (PMBA); financial management (MPA); global management (PMBA); health management (MS); human resources management (MS, PMBA); information systems (PMBA); logistics management (MS); management (MS), including information systems, operations research; materials acquisition management (MS); operations research (MS); public administration (MPA); research (PMBA); space systems (MS); space systems management (MS). *Expenses: Tuition:* Full-time $22,338; part-time $1241 per credit hour. Tuition and fees vary according to degree level, campus/location and program. *Financial support:* Application deadline: 3/1. *Application contact:* Online Learning and Off-Campus Programs Admissions, 321-674-8263, E-mail: gradadm-olocp@fit.edu.
Website: https://www.fit.edu/education-centers/degrees-and-programs/management-ms/

Friends University, Graduate School, Wichita, KS 67213. Offers family therapy (MSFT); global business administration (MBA), including accounting, business law, change management, health care leadership, management information systems, supply chain management and logistics; health care leadership (MHCL); management information systems (MMIS); professional business administration (MBA), including accounting, business law, change management, health care leadership, management information systems, supply chain management and logistics. *Program availability:* Part-time, evening/weekend, online learning. *Degree requirements:* For master's, research project. *Entrance requirements:* For master's, bachelor's degree from accredited institution, official transcripts, interview with program director, letter(s) of recommendation. Additional exam requirements/recommendations for international students: Required—TOEFL (minimum score 560 paper-based). Electronic applications accepted.

George Mason University, Schar School of Policy and Government, Program in Transportation Policy, Operations and Logistics, Arlington, VA 22201. Offers MA. *Faculty:* 6 full-time (3 women), 2 part-time/adjunct (0 women). *Students:* 3 full-time (1 woman), 12 part-time (6 women); includes 6 minority (3 Black or African American, non-Hispanic/Latino; 2 Hispanic/Latino; 1 Two or more races, non-Hispanic/Latino), 2 international. Average age 36. 10 applicants, 80% accepted, 1 enrolled. In 2018, 14 master's awarded. *Entrance requirements:* For master's, GRE (for students seeking merit-based scholarships), bachelor's degree with minimum GPA of 3.0, current resume, 2 letters of recommendation, expanded goals statement, 2 copies of official transcripts. Additional exam requirements/recommendations for international students: Required—TOEFL (minimum score 575 paper-based; 88 iBT), IELTS (minimum score 6.5), PTE (minimum score 59). *Application deadline:* For fall admission, 2/1 priority date for domestic and international students; for spring admission, 11/1 priority date for domestic and international students. Application fee: $75 ($80 for international students). Electronic applications accepted. *Expenses:* $689 per credit in-state tuition, $1,446.75 per credit out-of-state tuition. *Financial support:* Career-related internships or fieldwork, Federal Work-Study, and scholarships/grants available. Support available to part-time students. Financial award application deadline: 3/1; financial award applicants required to submit FAFSA. *Unit head:* Laurie Schintler, Director, 703-993-2256, Fax: 703-993-4557, E-mail: lschintl@gmu.edu. *Application contact:* Stephanie Ellis, Graduate Admissions Coordinator, 703-993-4478, E-mail: sellis11@gmu.edu.
Website: http://spgia.gmu.edu/programs/graduate-degrees/transportation-policy-operations-logistics-tpol/

Georgia College & State University, Graduate School, The J. Whitney Bunting School of Business, Logistics Education Center, Milledgeville, GA 31061. Offers MLSCM. *Program availability:* Part-time, evening/weekend. *Degree requirements:* For master's, minimum overall GPA of 3.0 on all business courses taken at Georgia College, complete program within 7 years. *Entrance requirements:* For master's, GRE or GMAT (not required for students who earned business degree at AACSB-accredited business school and maintained minimum overall undergraduate GPA of 3.15), baccalaureate degree, transcript, certification of immunization, resume. Electronic applications accepted. *Expenses:* Contact institution.

Georgia Institute of Technology, Graduate Studies, College of Engineering, H. Milton Stewart School of Industrial and Systems Engineering, Program in International Logistics, Atlanta, GA 30332-0001. Offers MS. *Program availability:* Part-time. *Entrance requirements:* For master's, GRE General Test. Additional exam requirements/recommendations for international students: Required—TOEFL (minimum score 550 paper-based; 79 iBT). Electronic applications accepted. *Expenses:* Contact institution.

Georgia Southern University, Jack N. Averitt College of Graduate Studies, Parker College of Business, Program in Logistics and Supply Chain Management, Statesboro, GA 30458. Offers PhD. *Degree requirements:* For doctorate, comprehensive exam, thesis/dissertation. *Entrance requirements:* For doctorate, GMAT or GRE, minimum of three letters of reference; statement of purpose; resume. Additional exam requirements/recommendations for international students: Required—TOEFL (minimum score 550 paper-based; 80 iBT), IELTS (minimum score 6). Electronic applications accepted. *Expenses: Tuition, area resident:* Part-time $3324 per semester. Tuition, state resident: full-time $5814; part-time $3324 per semester. Tuition, nonresident: full-time $23,204; part-time $13,260 per semester. *Required fees:* $2092; $2092. Tuition and fees vary according to course load, degree level, campus/location and program. *Faculty research:* Buyer-supplier relationships, retail supply chain management, strategic sourcing/outsourcing, supply chain metrics, service scheduling, demand and supply planning, supply chain strategy, operations and supply management, decision sciences.

HEC Montreal, School of Business Administration, Master of Science Programs in Administration, Program in International Logistics, Montréal, QC H3T 2A7, Canada. Offers M Sc. Program offered in French (Thesis stream, Supervised project stream). *Students:* 26 full-time (16 women), 1 part-time (0 women). 25 applicants, 44% accepted, 7 enrolled. In 2018, 14 master's awarded. *Entrance requirements:* For master's, BBA, undergraduate degree in another field, degree deemed equivalent by program director and minimum GPA of 3.0 on 4.3 scale. Additional exam requirements/recommendations for international students: Required—TAGE MAGE (minimum recommended score of 300), GMAT (minimum recommended score of 630), or GRE. *Application deadline:* For fall admission, 3/15 for domestic and international students; for winter admission, 9/15

for domestic and international students. Application fee: $91 Canadian dollars ($191 Canadian dollars for international students). Electronic applications accepted. *Expenses: Tuition, area resident:* Full-time $3052.80 Canadian dollars; part-time $84.80 Canadian dollars per credit. Tuition, state resident: full-time $3816 Canadian dollars; part-time $264.67 Canadian dollars per credit. Tuition, nonresident: full-time $11,910 Canadian dollars. *International tuition:* $20,905.20 Canadian dollars full-time. *Required fees:* $1805.34 Canadian dollars; $43.62 Canadian dollars per credit. $71.78 Canadian dollars per term. Tuition and fees vary according to degree level and program. *Financial support:* Research assistantships, teaching assistantships, and scholarships/grants available. Financial award application deadline: 9/2. *Unit head:* Dr. Sihem Taboubi, Director, 514-340-6428, E-mail: sihem.taboubi@hec.ca. *Application contact:* Marianne de Moura, Administrative Director, 514-340-6000, Fax: 514-340-6411, E-mail: aide@hec.ca.
Website: http://www.hec.ca/programmes/maitrises/maitrise-logistique-internationale/index.html

Maryville University of Saint Louis, The John E. Simon School of Business, St. Louis, MO 63141-7299. Offers accounting (MBA, MS, Certificate); business studies (Certificate); cybersecurity (MBA, MS, Certificate); financial services (MBA, Certificate); health administration (MBA); healthcare administration (Certificate); human resource management (MBA); human resources management (Certificate); information technology (MBA); information technology management (Certificate); management (MBA, Certificate); management and leadership (MA); marketing (MBA, Certificate); project management (MBA, Certificate); sport business management (MBA); supply chain management (Certificate); supply chain management/logistics (MBA). *Accreditation:* ACBSP. *Program availability:* Part-time, 100% online, blended/hybrid learning. *Faculty:* 5 full-time (1 woman), 77 part-time/adjunct (19 women). *Students:* 338 full-time (166 women), 739 part-time (356 women); includes 310 minority (161 Black or African American, non-Hispanic/Latino; 6 American Indian or Alaska Native, non-Hispanic/Latino; 59 Asian, non-Hispanic/Latino; 57 Hispanic/Latino; 27 Two or more races, non-Hispanic/Latino), 30 international. Average age 33. In 2018, 143 master's awarded. *Degree requirements:* For master's, capstone course (for MBA). *Entrance requirements:* Additional exam requirements/recommendations for international students: Required—TOEFL (minimum score 563 paper-based; 85 iBT). *Application deadline:* Applications are processed on a rolling basis. Electronic applications accepted. *Expenses:* Tuition varies by program. *Financial support:* Career-related internships or fieldwork, Federal Work-Study, tuition waivers (partial), and campus employment available. Financial award application deadline: 4/1; financial award applicants required to submit FAFSA. *Unit head:* Tammy Gocial, Interim Dean, 314-529-9401, Fax: 314-529-9975, E-mail: tgocial@maryville.edu. *Application contact:* Chris Gourdine, Assistant Dean Business Administration, 314-529-6861, Fax: 314-529-9975, E-mail: cgourdine@maryville.edu.
Website: http://www.maryville.edu/bu/business-administration-masters/

Massachusetts Institute of Technology, School of Engineering, Supply Chain Management Program, Cambridge, MA 02139-4307. Offers logistics (M Eng). *Degree requirements:* For master's, thesis. *Entrance requirements:* Additional exam requirements/recommendations for international students: Required—TOEFL, IELTS. Electronic applications accepted. *Expenses: Tuition:* Full-time $51,520; part-time $800 per credit hour. *Required fees:* $312. *Faculty research:* Logistics hubs and clusters; supply chain network risk management; urban logistics; carbon efficient supply chains; scenario planning; supply chain strategy alignment; supply chain innovation in emerging markets; supply chain resilience and security.

Michigan State University, The Graduate School, Eli Broad College of Business, Department of Supply Chain Management, East Lansing, MI 48224. Offers logistics (PhD); operations and sourcing management (PhD); supply chain management (MS), including logistics management, operations management, rail management, supply management. *Program availability:* Part-time. *Degree requirements:* For master's, field study/research project; for doctorate, comprehensive exam, thesis/dissertation. *Entrance requirements:* For master's, GMAT (taken within past 5 years), bachelor's degree, minimum GPA of 3.0 in junior/senior years, transcripts, at least 2 years of professional supply chain work experience, 3 letters of recommendation, essays, resume; for doctorate, GMAT or GRE, bachelor's or master's degree, transcripts, strong work experience, 3 letters of recommendation, statement of personal goals, interview. Additional exam requirements/recommendations for international students: Required—TOEFL (minimum score 600 paper-based). Electronic applications accepted. *Expenses:* Contact institution.

Naval Postgraduate School, Departments and Academic Groups, Graduate School of Business and Public Policy, Monterey, CA 93943. Offers acquisition and contract management (MBA); business administration (EMBA, MBA); contract management (MS); defense business management (MBA); defense systems analysis (MS), including management; defense systems management (international) (MBA); financial management (MBA); information management (MBA); manpower systems analysis (MS); material logistics support management (MBA); program management (MS); resource planning and management for international defense (MBA); supply chain management (MBA); systems acquisition management (MBA); transportation management (MBA). Program only open to commissioned officers of the United States and friendly nations and selected United States federal civilian employees. *Accreditation:* AACSB; NASPAA. *Program availability:* Part-time, online learning. *Degree requirements:* For master's, thesis (for some programs), terminal project/capstone (for some programs). *Faculty research:* U.S. and European public procurement policies for small and medium-sized enterprises, examining external validity criticisms in the choice of students as subjects in accounting experiment studies, assurance of learning in contract management education, contracting for cloud computing: opportunities and risks, NPS, Apple App Store as a business model supporting U.S. Navy requirements.

North Dakota State University, College of Graduate and Interdisciplinary Studies, Interdisciplinary Program in Transportation and Logistics, Fargo, ND 58102. Offers managerial logistics (MML); transportation and logistics (PhD); transportation and urban systems (MS). *Entrance requirements:* Additional exam requirements/recommendations for international students: Required—TOEFL.

Norwich University, College of Graduate and Continuing Studies, Master of Business Administration Program, Northfield, VT 05663. Offers construction management (MBA); energy management (MBA); finance (MBA); logistics (MBA); organizational leadership (MBA); project management (MBA); supply chain management (MBA). *Accreditation:* ACBSP. *Program availability:* Evening/weekend, online only, mostly all online with a week-long residency requirement. *Degree requirements:* For master's, comprehensive exam. *Entrance requirements:* For master's, minimum undergraduate GPA of 2.75. Additional exam requirements/recommendations for international students: Required—TOEFL (minimum score 550 paper-based; 80 iBT), IELTS (minimum score 6.5). Electronic applications accepted. *Expenses:* Contact institution.

The Ohio State University, Graduate School, Max M. Fisher College of Business, Program in Business Logistics Engineering, Columbus, OH 43210. Offers MBLE. *Students:* 47 (26 women). Average age 24. In 2018, 20 master's awarded. *Entrance requirements:* For master's, GRE or GMAT. Additional exam requirements/recommendations for international students: Required—TOEFL (minimum score 550 paper-based; 79 iBT), Michigan English Language Assessment Battery (minimum score 82); Recommended—IELTS (minimum score 7). *Application deadline:* For fall admission, 12/13 priority date for domestic students, 11/30 priority date for international students. Applications are processed on a rolling basis. Application fee: $60 ($70 for international students). Electronic applications accepted. *Financial support:* Scholarships/grants available. *Unit head:* Steve DeNunzio, Program Director, 614-769-3155, E-mail: dununzio.4@osu.edu. *Application contact:* Graduate and Professional Admissions, 614-292-9444, Fax: 614-292-3895, E-mail: gpadmissions@osu.edu.
Website: http://fisher.osu.edu/mble

Polytechnic University of Puerto Rico, Miami Campus, Graduate School, Miami, FL 33166. Offers accounting (MBA); business administration (MBA); construction management (MEM); environmental management (MEM); finance (MBA); human resources management (MBA); logistics and supply chain management (MBA); management of international enterprises (MBA); manufacturing management (MEM); marketing management (MBA); project management (MBA). *Program availability:* Part-time, evening/weekend, online learning. *Entrance requirements:* For master's, minimum GPA of 3.0. Electronic applications accepted.

Pontifical Catholic University of Puerto Rico, College of Business Administration, Program in Maritime Logistics and Transportation, Ponce, PR 00717-0777. Offers Professional Certificate.

Pontificia Universidad Catolica Madre y Maestra, Graduate School, Faculty of Engineering Sciences, Santiago, Dominican Republic. Offers earthquake engineering (ME); logistics management (ME).

Purdue University Global, School of Business, Davenport, IA 52807. Offers business administration (MBA); change leadership (MS); entrepreneurship (MBA); finance (MBA); health care management (MBA, MS); human resource (MBA); international business (MBA); management (MS); marketing (MBA); project management (MBA, MS); supply chain management and logistics (MBA, MS). *Accreditation:* ACBSP. *Program availability:* Part-time, evening/weekend, online learning. *Entrance requirements:* Additional exam requirements/recommendations for international students: Required—TOEFL (minimum score 550 paper-based; 80 iBT). Electronic applications accepted.

Rutgers University–Newark, Rutgers Business School–Newark and New Brunswick, Program in Real Estate and Logistics, Newark, NJ 07102. Offers MRE.

Shippensburg University of Pennsylvania, School of Graduate Studies, John L. Grove College of Business, Shippensburg, PA 17257-2299. Offers advanced studies in business (Certificate); advanced supply chain and logistics management (Certificate); business administration (MBA, DBA), including business administration (MBA), business analytics (MBA), finance (MBA), healthcare management (MBA), management information systems (MBA), supply chain management (MBA); finance (Certificate); health care management (Certificate); management information systems (Certificate). *Accreditation:* AACSB. *Program availability:* Part-time, evening/weekend, 100% online, blended/hybrid learning. *Faculty:* 20 full-time (4 women), 2 part-time/adjunct (0 women). *Students:* 31 full-time (14 women), 174 part-time (67 women); includes 33 minority (17 Black or African American, non-Hispanic/Latino; 6 Asian, non-Hispanic/Latino; 7 Hispanic/Latino; 3 Two or more races, non-Hispanic/Latino), 13 international. Average age 33. 149 applicants, 61% accepted, 60 enrolled. In 2018, 104 master's, 1 other advanced degree awarded. *Degree requirements:* For master's, comprehensive exam (for some programs), thesis optional, practicum capstone course; for doctorate, comprehensive exam, thesis/dissertation, comprehensive exam dissertation. *Entrance requirements:* For master's, GMAT (minimum score 450 if less than 5 years of mid-level experience, including management experience), current resume; relevant work/classroom experience; 500-word statement of purpose; prerequisites of quantitative analysis, computer usage, and oral and written communications; laptop computer; for doctorate, GMAT (minimum score of 600 if less than 5 years of substantive professional or teaching experience), 2 letters of recommendation from professionals in academia or industry; 2-3 page personal and professional statement; interview; resume. Additional exam requirements/recommendations for international students: Required—TOEFL (minimum score 550 paper-based; 68 iBT), IELTS (minimum score 6), TOEFL (minimum score 550 paper-based, 68 iBT) or IELTS (minimum score 6). *Application deadline:* For fall admission, 4/30 for international students; for spring admission, 9/30 for international students. Applications are processed on a rolling basis. Application fee: $45. Electronic applications accepted. *Expenses:* Tuition, state resident: part-time $516 per credit. Tuition, nonresident: part-time $750 per credit. *Required fees:* $149 per credit. *Financial support:* In 2018–19, 15 students received support. Career-related internships or fieldwork, scholarships/grants, unspecified assistantships, and resident hall director and student payroll positions available. Support available to part-time students. Financial award application deadline: 3/1; financial award applicants required to submit FAFSA. *Unit head:* Dr. John G. Kooti, Dean of the College of Business, 717-477-1435, Fax: 717-477-4003, E-mail: jgkooti@ship.edu. *Application contact:* Maya T. Mapp, Director of Admissions, 717-477-1231, Fax: 717-477-4016, E-mail: mtmapp@ship.edu.
Website: http://www.ship.edu/business

Trident University International, College of Business Administration, Program in Business Administration, Cypress, CA 90630. Offers business administration (PhD); conflict and negotiation management (MBA); criminal justice administration (MBA); entrepreneurship (MBA); finance (MBA); general management (MBA); government accounting (MBA); human resource management (MBA); information security and digital assurance management (MBA); information technology management (MBA); international business (MBA); logistics management (MBA); marketing (MBA); project management (MBA); public management (MBA); quality management (MBA); strategic leadership (MBA). *Program availability:* Part-time, evening/weekend, online learning. *Degree requirements:* For doctorate, comprehensive exam, thesis/dissertation, defense of dissertation. *Entrance requirements:* For master's, minimum GPA of 2.5 (students with GPA 3.0 or greater may transfer up to 30% of graduate level credits); for doctorate, minimum GPA of 3.4, curriculum vitae, course work in research methods or statistics. Additional exam requirements/recommendations for international students: Required—TOEFL. Electronic applications accepted.

Universidad del Turabo, Graduate Programs, School of Business and Entrepreneurship, Program in Logistics and Materials Management, Gurabo, PR 00778-3030. Offers MBA. *Program availability:* Part-time, evening/weekend. *Entrance requirements:* For master's, GRE, EXADEP or GMAT, interview, essay, official transcript, recommendation letters. Electronic applications accepted.

University at Buffalo, the State University of New York, Graduate School, School of Engineering and Applied Sciences, Program in Sustainable Transportation and Logistics, Buffalo, NY 14260. Offers MS.

University at Buffalo, the State University of New York, Graduate School, School of Management, Buffalo, NY 14260. Offers accounting (MS); analytics (MBA); business administration (PMBA); consulting (MBA); finance (MBA, MS), including financial risk management (MS), quantitative finance (MS); healthcare (MBA); information assurance (MBA); information systems (MBA); international management (MBA); management (EMBA, PhD); management information systems (MS); marketing (MBA); supply chain and operations (MBA); supply chains and operations management (MS); Au D/MBA;

DDS/MBA; JD/MBA; M Arch/MBA; MD/MBA; MPH/MBA; MSW/MBA; Pharm D/MBA. *Accreditation:* AACSB. *Program availability:* Part-time, evening/weekend. *Degree requirements:* For master's, capstone courses or projects; for doctorate, comprehensive exam, thesis/dissertation. *Entrance requirements:* For master's, GMAT (for MS in accounting, finance); GRE or GMAT (for MBA, MS in management information systems, supply chains and operations management), essays, letters of recommendation; for doctorate, GMAT or GRE, essays, writing sample, letters of recommendation. Additional exam requirements/recommendations for international students: Required—TOEFL (minimum score 95 iBT) or IELTS (minimum score 6.5); Recommended—TSE (minimum score 73). Electronic applications accepted. *Expenses:* Contact institution. *Faculty research:* Data analytics, accounting and law, rate finance, consumer behavior, supply chain logistics, leadership and team effectiveness.

The University of Alabama in Huntsville, School of Graduate Studies, College of Business Administration, Programs in Business and Management, Huntsville, AL 35899. Offers business analytics (MSMS); federal contracting and procurement management (Certificate); human resource management (MSM); management (MBA), including acquisition management, entrepreneurship, federal contract accounting, finance, human resource management, logistics and supply chain management, marketing, project management; supply chain management (Certificate); technology and innovation management (Certificate). *Accreditation:* AACSB. *Program availability:* Part-time. *Faculty:* 8 full-time (3 women). *Students:* 57 full-time (25 women), 152 part-time (76 women); includes 37 minority (20 Black or African American, non-Hispanic/Latino; 2 American Indian or Alaska Native, non-Hispanic/Latino; 6 Asian, non-Hispanic/Latino; 8 Hispanic/Latino; 1 Two or more races, non-Hispanic/Latino), 24 international. Average age 33. 178 applicants, 80% accepted, 84 enrolled. In 2018, 96 master's, 1 other advanced degree awarded. *Degree requirements:* For master's, comprehensive exam, thesis or alternative. *Entrance requirements:* For master's, GMAT (minimum score 500), minimum AACSB index of 1080. Additional exam requirements/recommendations for international students: Required—TOEFL (minimum score 550 paper-based; 80 iBT), IELTS (minimum score 6.5). *Application deadline:* For fall admission, 7/15 priority date for domestic students, 4/1 priority date for international students; for spring admission, 11/30 priority date for domestic students, 9/1 priority date for international students. Applications are processed on a rolling basis. Application fee: $50. Electronic applications accepted. *Expenses: Tuition, area resident:* Full-time $10,632; part-time $412 per credit hour. Tuition, state resident: full-time $10,632. Tuition, nonresident: full-time $23,604; part-time $412 per credit hour. *Required fees:* $582; $582. Tuition and fees vary according to course load and program. *Financial support:* In 2018–19, 15 students received support, including 15 teaching assistantships with full tuition reimbursements available (averaging $4,871 per year); research assistantships with full tuition reimbursements available, career-related internships or fieldwork, Federal Work-Study, institutionally sponsored loans, scholarships/grants, health care benefits, tuition waivers (full and partial), and unspecified assistantships also available. Support available to part-time students. Financial award application deadline: 4/1; financial award applicants required to submit FAFSA. *Faculty research:* Supply chain management, management of research and development, international marketing and branding, organizational behavior and human resource management, social networks and computational economics. *Unit head:* Dr. Fan Tseng, Chair, 256-824-6804, Fax: 256-824-6328, E-mail: fan.tseng@uah.edu. *Application contact:* Jennifer Pettitt, Director of Advising, 256-824-6681, Fax: 256-824-7571, E-mail: jennifer.pettitt@uah.edu.

University of Alaska Anchorage, College of Business and Public Policy, Program in Logistics, Anchorage, AK 99508. Offers global supply chain management (MS). *Program availability:* Part-time, evening/weekend, online learning. *Degree requirements:* For master's, thesis or alternative, research project. *Entrance requirements:* Additional exam requirements/recommendations for international students: Required—TOEFL (minimum score 550 paper-based).

University of Dallas, Satish and Yasmin Gupta College of Business, Irving, TX 75062. Offers accounting (MBA, MS); business administration (DBA); business analytics (MS); business management (MBA); corporate finance (MBA); cybersecurity (MS); finance (MS); financial services (MBA); global business (MBA, MS); health services management (MBA); human resource management (MBA); information and technology management (MS); information assurance (MBA); information technology (MBA); information technology service management (MBA); marketing management (MBA); organization development (MBA); project management (MBA); sports and entertainment management (MBA); strategic leadership (MBA); supply chain management (MBA). *Accreditation:* AACSB. *Program availability:* Part-time, evening/weekend, 100% online. *Students:* 147 full-time (56 women), 584 part-time (232 women); includes 402 minority (204 Black or African American, non-Hispanic/Latino; 95 Asian, non-Hispanic/Latino; 92 Hispanic/Latino; 2 Native Hawaiian or other Pacific Islander, non-Hispanic/Latino; 9 Two or more races, non-Hispanic/Latino), 113 international. Average age 34. 992 applicants, 30% accepted, 157 enrolled. In 2018, 336 master's, 5 doctorates awarded. *Degree requirements:* For doctorate, thesis/dissertation. *Entrance requirements:* For master's and doctorate, U.S. bachelor's degree with a minimum cumulative GPA of 2.0 from a regionally accredited college or university (or comparable foreign degree); minimum 3.0 GPA in any graduate-level coursework completed; good academic standing with all colleges attended. Additional exam requirements/recommendations for international students: Required—TOEFL (minimum score 80 iBT), IELTS (minimum score 6.5), PTE (minimum score 67). *Application deadline:* Applications are processed on a rolling basis. Application fee: $50. Electronic applications accepted. *Expenses:* $1250 per credit hour. *Financial support:* In 2018–19, 291 students received support. Research assistantships, teaching assistantships, scholarships/grants, and unspecified assistantships available. Support available to part-time students. Financial award application deadline: 2/15; financial award applicants required to submit FAFSA. *Unit head:* Brett J.L. Landry, Dean, 972-721-5356, E-mail: blandry@udallas.edu. *Application contact:* Breonna Collins, Director, Graduate Admissions, 972-7215304, E-mail: bcollins@udallas.edu. Website: http://www.udallas.edu/cob/

University of Houston, College of Technology, Department of Information and Logistics Technology, Houston, TX 77204. Offers information security (MS); supply chain and logistics technology (MS); technology project management (MS). *Program availability:* Part-time. *Degree requirements:* For master's, project or thesis (most programs). *Entrance requirements:* For master's, GMAT. Additional exam requirements/recommendations for international students: Required—TOEFL (minimum score 550 paper-based; 79 iBT). Electronic applications accepted.

The University of Kansas, Graduate Studies, School of Business, Program in Business, Lawrence, KS 66045. Offers business and organizational leadership (MS); decision sciences and supply chain management (PhD); finance (PhD); human resources management (PhD); marketing (PhD); organizational behavior (PhD); strategic management (PhD); supply chain management and logistics (MS). *Accreditation:* AACSB. *Program availability:* Part-time. *Students:* 69 full-time (20 women), 150 part-time (62 women); includes 42 minority (14 Black or African American, non-Hispanic/Latino; 2 American Indian or Alaska Native, non-Hispanic/Latino; 6 Asian, non-Hispanic/Latino; 7 Hispanic/Latino; 13 Two or more races, non-Hispanic/Latino), 24 international. Average age 32. 306 applicants, 51% accepted, 132 enrolled. In 2018, 22 master's, 1 doctorate awarded. *Entrance requirements:* For master's, GMAT, official transcript, three letters of recommendation, resume, statement of purpose; for doctorate, GMAT or GRE, official transcript, three letters of recommendation, resume, statement of purpose. Additional exam requirements/recommendations for international students: Required—TOEFL, IELTS. *Application deadline:* For fall admission, 1/10 for domestic and international students. Application fee: $65 ($85 for international students). Electronic applications accepted. *Financial support:* Fellowships, research assistantships, teaching assistantships, scholarships/grants, health care benefits, tuition waivers (full), and unspecified assistantships available. Financial award application deadline: 1/10. *Faculty research:* Strategic human resource management, business ethics, organizational theory/behavior, corporate strategy, international business, supply chain management, Bayesian networks, game theory, decision analysis and time/series analysis, pricing, consumer effects, advertising and emotion. *Unit head:* Charly Edmonds, Director, 785-864-3841, E-mail: cedmonds@ku.edu. *Application contact:* Andrea Noltner, Graduate Admission Contact, 785-864-7556, E-mail: anoltner@ku.edu. Website: http://www.business.ku.edu/

University of Louisville, J. B. Speed School of Engineering, Department of Industrial Engineering, Louisville, KY 40292-0001. Offers engineering management (M Eng); industrial engineering (M Eng, MS, PhD); logistics and distribution (Certificate). *Accreditation:* ABET (one or more programs are accredited). *Program availability:* 100% online. *Faculty:* 9 full-time (4 women), 8 part-time/adjunct (2 women). *Students:* 64 full-time (22 women), 147 part-time (35 women); includes 32 minority (13 Black or African American, non-Hispanic/Latino; 9 Asian, non-Hispanic/Latino; 6 Hispanic/Latino; 4 Two or more races, non-Hispanic/Latino), 78 international. Average age 31. 98 applicants, 66% accepted, 53 enrolled. In 2018, 30 master's, 3 doctorates awarded. Terminal master's awarded for partial completion of doctoral program. *Degree requirements:* For master's and Certificate, thesis optional; for doctorate, comprehensive exam, thesis/dissertation. *Entrance requirements:* For master's and doctorate, GRE General Test, two letters of recommendation, official transcripts. Additional exam requirements/recommendations for international students: Required—TOEFL (minimum score 550 paper-based; 80 iBT), IELTS (minimum score 6.5). *Application deadline:* For fall admission, 5/1 priority date for domestic and international students; for spring admission, 11/1 priority date for domestic and international students; for summer admission, 3/1 priority date for domestic and international students. Applications are processed on a rolling basis. Application fee: $65. Electronic applications accepted. *Expenses: Tuition, area resident:* Full-time $6500; part-time $723 per credit hour. Tuition, state resident: full-time $6500. Tuition, nonresident: full-time $13,557; part-time $1507 per credit hour. Tuition and fees vary according to course load and program. *Financial support:* In 2018–19, 38 students received support. Fellowships, research assistantships, teaching assistantships, scholarships/grants, health care benefits, and tuition waivers (full) available. Financial award application deadline: 1/1; financial award applicants required to submit FAFSA. *Faculty research:* Quality and Reliability Assurance, Process Monitoring and Diagnostics, Production Systems Design, Supply Chain Risk Management, Decision Support Systems. *Total annual research expenditures:* $620,986. *Unit head:* Dr. Suraj M. Alexander, Chair, 502-852-6342, Fax: 502-852-5633, E-mail: suraj.alexander@louisville.edu. *Application contact:* Lihui Bai, Director of Graduate Studies, 502-852-1416, E-mail: lihui.bai@louisville.edu. Website: http://www.louisville.edu/speed/industrial/

University of Missouri–St. Louis, College of Business Administration, St. Louis, MO 63121. Offers accounting (M Acc); business administration (MBA, DBA, PhD, Certificate), including logistics and supply chain management (PhD); business intelligence (Certificate); cybersecurity (Certificate); digital and social media marketing (Certificate); human resources management (Certificate); information systems (MS); logistics and supply chain management (Certificate); marketing management (Certificate). *Program availability:* Part-time, evening/weekend. *Degree requirements:* For doctorate, thesis/dissertation. *Entrance requirements:* For master's, GMAT, 2 letters of recommendation; for doctorate, GMAT or GRE, 3 letters of recommendation. Additional exam requirements/recommendations for international students: Recommended—TOEFL (minimum score 550 paper-based; 79 iBT), IELTS (minimum score 6.5). Electronic applications accepted. *Faculty research:* Statistical decision aids, commercial banking, corporate finance, operations management, information systems.

The University of North Carolina at Charlotte, William States Lee College of Engineering, Department of Systems Engineering and Engineering Management, Charlotte, NC 28223-0001. Offers energy analytics (Graduate Certificate); engineering management (MSEM); Lean Six Sigma (Graduate Certificate); logistics and supply chains (Graduate Certificate); systems analytics (Graduate Certificate). *Program availability:* Part-time, evening/weekend, 100% online, blended/hybrid learning. *Students:* 27 full-time (8 women), 45 part-time (11 women); includes 15 minority (5 Black or African American, non-Hispanic/Latino; 1 American Indian or Alaska Native, non-Hispanic/Latino; 5 Asian, non-Hispanic/Latino; 2 Hispanic/Latino; 2 Two or more races, non-Hispanic/Latino), 27 international. Average age 29. 112 applicants, 77% accepted, 23 enrolled. In 2018, 38 master's, 3 other advanced degrees awarded. *Entrance requirements:* For master's, GRE or GMAT, bachelor's degree in engineering or a closely-related technical or scientific field, or in business, provided relevant technical course requirements have been met; undergraduate coursework in engineering economics, calculus, or statistics; minimum GPA of 3.0; for Graduate Certificate, bachelor's degree in engineering or closely-related technical or scientific field, or in business, provided relevant technical course requirements have been met; minimum GPA of 3.0; undergraduate coursework in engineering economics, calculus, and statistics; written description of work experience. Additional exam requirements/recommendations for international students: Required—TOEFL (minimum score 523 paper-based; 70 iBT), IELTS (minimum score 6), TOEFL (minimum score 523 paper-based, 70 iBT) or IELTS (6). *Application deadline:* Applications are processed on a rolling basis. Application fee: $75. Electronic applications accepted. *Expenses:* Contact institution. *Financial support:* Career-related internships or fieldwork, institutionally sponsored loans, scholarships/grants, and unspecified assistantships available. Support available to part-time students. Financial award application deadline: 3/1; financial award applicants required to submit FAFSA. *Total annual research expenditures:* $186,132. *Unit head:* Dr. Simon M. Hsiang, Chair, 704-687-1958, E-mail: shsiang1@uncc.edu. *Application contact:* Kathy B. Giddings, Director of Graduate Admissions, 704-687-5503, Fax: 704-687-1668, E-mail: gradadm@uncc.edu. Website: http://seem.uncc.edu/

University of North Florida, Coggin College of Business, MBA Program, Jacksonville, FL 32224. Offers accounting (MBA); construction management (MBA); e-commerce (MBA); economics (MBA); finance (MBA); human resource management (MBA); international business (MBA); logistics (MBA); management applications (MBA). *Accreditation:* AACSB. *Program availability:* Part-time, evening/weekend. *Faculty:* 40 full-time (14 women). *Students:* 368 part-time (158 women); includes 83 minority (30 Black or African American, non-Hispanic/Latino; 20 Asian, non-Hispanic/Latino; 16 Hispanic/Latino; 17 Two or more races, non-Hispanic/Latino), 28 international. Average age 30. 311 applicants, 51% accepted, 99 enrolled. In 2018, 151 master's awarded. *Entrance requirements:* For master's, GMAT or GRE, U.S. bachelor's degree from regionally-accredited university or equivalent foreign degree. Additional exam requirements/recommendations for international students: Required—TOEFL (minimum score 550 paper-based; 79 iBT). *Application deadline:* For fall admission, 8/1 priority

date for domestic students, 5/1 for international students; for spring admission, 12/1 priority date for domestic students, 10/1 for international students; for summer admission, 4/29 priority date for domestic students, 2/1 for international students. Application fee: $30. *Expenses: Tuition, area resident:* Part-time $408.10 per credit hour. Tuition, state resident: part-time $408.10 per credit hour. Tuition, nonresident: part-time $932.61 per credit hour. *Required fees:* $111.81 per credit hour. Tuition and fees vary according to course load, campus/location and program. *Financial support:* In 2018–19, 41 students received support, including 1 research assistantship (averaging $2,143 per year); teaching assistantships, Federal Work-Study, and tuition waivers (partial) also available. Support available to part-time students. Financial award application deadline: 4/1; financial award applicants required to submit FAFSA. *Faculty research:* Performance measures, costing, and inventory issues in logistics and supply chain management; inter-organizational systems; international management and marketing practices; e-commerce; organizational learning and socialization processes. *Unit head:* Dr. Parvez Ahmed, Graduate Program Director, 904-620-1678, E-mail: pahmed@unf.edu. *Application contact:* Amy Bishop, MSM Advisor, 904-620-2575, Fax: 904-620-2832, E-mail: coggin.students@unf.edu.
Website: http://www.unf.edu/graduateschool/academics/programs/MBA.aspx

University of North Texas, Toulouse Graduate School, Denton, TX 76203-5459. Offers accounting (MS); applied anthropology (MA, MS); applied behavior analysis (Certificate); applied geography (MA); applied technology and performance improvement (M Ed, MS); art education (MA); art history (MA); arts leadership (Certificate); audiology (Au D); behavior analysis (MS); behavioral science (PhD); biochemistry and molecular biology (MS); biology (MA, MS); biomedical engineering (MS); business analysis (MS); chemistry (MS); clinical health psychology (PhD); communication studies (MA, MS); computer engineering (MS); computer science (MS); counseling (M Ed, MS), including clinical mental health counseling (MS), college and university counseling, elementary school counseling, secondary school counseling; creative writing (MA); criminal justice (MS); curriculum and instruction (M Ed); decision sciences (MBA); design (MA, MFA), including fashion design (MFA), innovation studies, interior design (MFA); early childhood studies (MS); economics (MS); educational leadership (M Ed, Ed D); educational psychology (MS, PhD), including family studies (MS), gifted and talented (MS), human development (MS), learning and cognition (MS), research, measurement and evaluation (MS); electrical engineering (MS); emergency management (MPA); engineering technology (MS); English (MA); English as a second language (MA); environmental science (MS); finance (MBA, MS); financial management (MPA); French (MA); health services management (MBA); higher education (M Ed, Ed D); history (MA, MS); hospitality management (MS); human resources management (MPA); information science (MS); information systems (PhD); information technologies (MBA); interdisciplinary studies (MA, MS); international studies (MA); international sustainable tourism (MS); jazz studies (MM); journalism (MA, MJ, Graduate Certificate), including interactive and virtual digital communication (Graduate Certificate), narrative journalism (Graduate Certificate), public relations (Graduate Certificate); kinesiology (MS); linguistics (MA); local government management (MPA); logistics (PhD); logistics and supply chain management (MBA); long-term care, senior housing, and aging services (MA); management (PhD); marketing (MBA); mathematics (MA, MS); mechanical and energy engineering (MS, PhD); music (MA), including ethnomusicology, music theory, musicology, performance; music composition (PhD); music education (MM Ed, PhD); nonprofit management (MPA); operations and supply chain management (MBA); performance (MM, DMA); philosophy (MA); political science (MA); professional and technical communication (MA); radio, television and film (MA, MFA); rehabilitation counseling (Certificate); sociology (MA); Spanish (MA); special education (M Ed); speech-language pathology (MA); strategic management (MBA); studio art (MFA); teaching (M Ed); MBA/MS. *Program availability:* Part-time, evening/weekend, online learning. Terminal master's awarded for partial completion of doctoral program. *Degree requirements:* For master's, variable foreign language requirement, comprehensive exam (for some programs), thesis (for some programs); for doctorate, variable foreign language requirement, comprehensive exam (for some programs), thesis/dissertation; for other advanced degree, variable foreign language requirement, comprehensive exam (for some programs). *Entrance requirements:* For master's and doctorate, GRE, GMAT. Additional exam requirements/recommendations for international students: Required—TOEFL (minimum score 550 paper-based; 79 iBT). Electronic applications accepted.

University of St. Francis, College of Business and Health Administration, Joliet, IL 60435-6169. Offers accounting (MBA, Certificate); business analytics (MBA, Certificate); e-learning (Certificate); finance (MBA, Certificate); health administration (MBA, MS); human resource management (MBA, Certificate); logistics (Certificate); management (MBA, MSM); management of training and development (Certificate); supply chain management (MBA); training and development (MBA); training specialist (Certificate). *Program availability:* Part-time, evening/weekend, 100% online, blended/hybrid learning. *Faculty:* 13 full-time (6 women), 20 part-time/adjunct (7 women). *Students:* 139 full-time (94 women), 206 part-time (159 women); includes 86 minority (51 Black or African American, non-Hispanic/Latino; 1 American Indian or Alaska Native, non-Hispanic/Latino; 11 Asian, non-Hispanic/Latino; 21 Hispanic/Latino; 2 Two or more races, non-Hispanic/Latino), 24 international. Average age 37. 261 applicants, 63% accepted, 98 enrolled. In 2018, 129 master's, 3 other advanced degrees awarded. *Degree requirements:* For master's, comprehensive exam (for some programs). *Entrance requirements:* Additional exam requirements/recommendations for international students: Required—TOEFL (minimum score 550 paper-based; 79 iBT), IELTS (minimum score 6). *Application deadline:* Applications are processed on a rolling basis. Electronic applications accepted. Application fee is waived when completed online. *Expenses:* Contact institution. *Financial support:* In 2018–19, 126 students received support. Scholarships/grants and tuition waivers (partial) available. Support available to part-time students. Financial award applicants required to submit FAFSA. *Unit head:* Dr. Orlando Griego, Dean, 815-740-3395, Fax: 815-740-3452, E-mail: ogriego@stfrancis.edu. *Application contact:* Sandee Sloka, Director Adult & Graduate Admissions, 800-735-7500, E-mail: ssloka@stfrancis.edu.
Website: https://www.stfrancis.edu/business-health-administration/

University of South Africa, College of Economic and Management Sciences, Pretoria, South Africa. Offers accounting (D Admin, D Com); accounting science (DA); auditing (D Admin, D Com); business administration (M Tech); business economics (D Admin); business leadership (DBL); business management (D Admin, D Com); economic management analysis (M Tech); economics (D Admin, D Com, PhD); human resource development (M Tech); industrial psychology (D Admin, D Com, PhD); logistics (D Com); marketing (M Tech); public administration (D Admin, D Com, DPA, PhD); public management (M Tech); quantitative management (D Admin, D Com); real estate (M Tech); statistics (D Admin, PhD); tourism management (D Admin, D Com); transport economics (D Admin, D Com).

University of Southern Mississippi, College of Arts and Sciences, School of Construction and Design, Hattiesburg, MS 39406-0001. Offers logistics, trade and transportation (MS). *Program availability:* Part-time, online learning. *Degree requirements:* For master's, comprehensive exam, thesis optional. *Entrance requirements:* For master's, GMAT or GRE General Test, minimum GPA of 2.75 in last 60 hours. Additional exam requirements/recommendations for international students: Required—TOEFL, IELTS. *Faculty research:* Robotics; CAD/CAM; simulation; computer-integrated manufacturing processes; construction scheduling, estimating, and computer systems.

The University of Tennessee, Graduate School, College of Business Administration, Program in Business Administration, Knoxville, TN 37996. Offers accounting (PhD); finance (MBA, PhD); logistics and transportation (MBA, PhD); management (PhD); marketing (MBA, PhD); operations management (MBA); professional business administration (MBA); statistics (PhD); JD/MBA; MS/MBA; Pharm D/MBA. Pharm D/MBA offered jointly with The University of Tennessee Health Science Center. *Accreditation:* AACSB. *Program availability:* Online learning. *Degree requirements:* For master's, thesis or alternative; for doctorate, thesis/dissertation. *Entrance requirements:* For master's and doctorate, GMAT, minimum GPA of 2.7. Additional exam requirements/recommendations for international students: Required—TOEFL. Electronic applications accepted.

The University of Tennessee at Chattanooga, Engineering Management and Technology Program, Chattanooga, TN 37403. Offers construction management (Graduate Certificate); engineering management (MS); fundamentals of engineering management (Graduate Certificate); leadership and ethics (Graduate Certificate); logistics and supply chain management (Graduate Certificate); power systems management (Graduate Certificate); project and technology management (Graduate Certificate); quality management (Graduate Certificate). *Program availability:* 100% online, blended/hybrid learning. *Degree requirements:* For master's, thesis. *Entrance requirements:* For master's, GRE General Test, letters of recommendation; minimum undergraduate GPA of 2.7 overall or 3.0 in final two years; for Graduate Certificate, baccalaureate degree and professional experience or have already been admitted to engineering/engineering management graduate program. Additional exam requirements/recommendations for international students: Required—TOEFL (minimum score 550 paper-based; 79 iBT), IELTS (minimum score 6). Electronic applications accepted. *Expenses:* Contact institution. *Faculty research:* Plant layout design, lean manufacturing, Six Sigma, value management, product development.

The University of Texas at Arlington, Graduate School, College of Engineering, Department of Industrial, Manufacturing, and Systems Engineering, Program in Logistics, Arlington, TX 76019. Offers MS. *Degree requirements:* For master's, comprehensive exam, thesis optional. *Entrance requirements:* For master's, GRE, GMAT, minimum GPA of 3.0. Additional exam requirements/recommendations for international students: Required—TOEFL (minimum score 550 paper-based).

University of Washington, Graduate School, Interdisciplinary Program in Global Trade, Transportation and Logistics Studies, Seattle, WA 98195. Offers Certificate.

Virginia International University, School of Business, Fairfax, VA 22030. Offers accounting (MBA, MS); entrepreneurship (MBA); executive management (Graduate Certificate); global logistics (MBA); health care management (MBA); hospitality and tourism management (MBA); human resources management (MBA); international business management (MBA); international finance (MBA); marketing management (MBA); mass media and public relations (MBA); project management (MBA, MS). *Program availability:* Part-time, online learning. *Entrance requirements:* For master's and Graduate Certificate, bachelor's degree. Additional exam requirements/recommendations for international students: Required—TOEFL (minimum score 550 paper-based; 80 iBT), IELTS (minimum score 6). Electronic applications accepted.

Wright State University, Graduate School, Raj Soin College of Business, Department of Information Systems and Operations Management, Logistics and Supply Chain Management Program, Dayton, OH 45435. Offers MS.

Supply Chain Management

Abilene Christian University, College of Graduate and Professional Studies, Program in Business Administration, Addison, TX 79699. Offers business analytics (MBA); general management (MBA); healthcare administration (MBA); international business (MBA); management: business analytics (MS); management: healthcare administration (MS); management: international business (MS); management: marketing (MS); management: operations and supply chain management (MS); marketing (MBA); nonprofit leadership (MBA). *Program availability:* Part-time, online only, 100% online. *Faculty:* 4 full-time (0 women), 7 part-time/adjunct (3 women). *Students:* 149 full-time (69 women), 53 part-time (25 women); includes 88 minority (42 Black or African American, non-Hispanic/Latino; 2 American Indian or Alaska Native, non-Hispanic/Latino; 4 Asian, non-Hispanic/Latino; 31 Hispanic/Latino; 1 Native Hawaiian or other Pacific Islander, non-Hispanic/Latino; 8 Two or more races, non-Hispanic/Latino), 4 international. 36 applicants, 100% accepted, 32 enrolled. In 2018, 24 master's awarded. *Entrance requirements:* Additional exam requirements/recommendations for international students: Required—TOEFL (minimum score 80 iBT), IELTS (minimum score 6). *Application deadline:* For fall admission, 10/7 for domestic students; for winter admission, 12/20 for domestic students; for spring admission, 2/24 for domestic students; for summer admission, 4/20 for domestic students. Applications are processed on a rolling basis. Application fee: $50. Electronic applications accepted. *Expenses:* $721 per hour. *Financial support:* In 2018–19, 16 students received support. Scholarships/grants available. Financial award application deadline: 7/1; financial award applicants required to submit FAFSA. *Faculty research:* Organizational structure, financial management, cost accounting, unit analysis management. *Unit head:* Dr. Phil Vardiman, Program Director, 325-674-2153, E-mail: pxv02b@acu.edu. *Application contact:* Graduate Advisor, 817-219-7300, E-mail: onlineadmissions@acu.edu.
Website: http://www.acu.edu/online/academics/mba-business-administration.html

Adelphi University, Robert B. Willumstad School of Business, Program in Supply Chain Management, Garden City, NY 11530-0701. Offers MS. *Program availability:* Part-time, online learning. *Students:* 8 full-time (2 women), 4 part-time (2 women); includes 2 minority (1 Asian, non-Hispanic/Latino; 1 Hispanic/Latino), 8 international.

Average age 31. 37 applicants, 43% accepted, 5 enrolled. In 2018, 2 master's awarded. *Entrance requirements:* For master's, GMAT, official transcripts, bachelor's degree, 500-word essay, letter of recommendation, resume. Additional exam requirements/recommendations for international students: Required—TOEFL (minimum score 550 paper-based; 80 iBT), IELTS (minimum score 6.5). *Application deadline:* For fall admission, 3/1 for domestic and international students; for spring admission, 11/1 for international students. Application fee: $50. *Expenses:* Contact institution. *Unit head:* Anthony Libertella, Dean, 516-877-4661, E-mail: libertel@adelphi.edu. *Application contact:* Anthony Libertella, Dean, 516-877-4661, E-mail: libertel@adelphi.edu. Website: http://business.adelphi.edu/academics/graduate-degree-programs/ms-supply-chain-management/

Albany State University, College of Business, Albany, GA 31705-2717. Offers accounting (MBA); general business administration (MBA); healthcare (MBA); public administration (MBA); supply chain and logistics (MBA). *Accreditation:* ACBSP. *Program availability:* Part-time, evening/weekend. *Degree requirements:* For master's, comprehensive exam, internship, 3 hours of physical education. *Entrance requirements:* For master's, GMAT (minimum score of 450)/GRE (minimum score of 800) for those without earned master's degree or higher, minimum undergraduate GPA of 2.5, 2 letters of reference, official transcript, pre-entrance medical record and certificate of immunization. Electronic applications accepted. *Faculty research:* Diversity issues, ancestry, understanding finance through use of technology.

American Graduate University, Program in Business Administration, Covina, CA 91724. Offers acquisition and contracting (MBA); supply chain management (MBA). *Program availability:* Part-time, online learning. *Degree requirements:* For master's, thesis. *Entrance requirements:* For master's, undergraduate degree from institution accredited by accrediting agency recognized by the U.S. Department of Education. Additional exam requirements/recommendations for international students: Required—TOEFL. Electronic applications accepted.

American Graduate University, Program in Supply Chain Management, Covina, CA 91724. Offers MSCM, Certificate. *Program availability:* Part-time, online learning. *Degree requirements:* For master's, comprehensive exam or project. *Entrance requirements:* For master's, undergraduate degree from institution accredited by accrediting agency recognized by the U.S. Department of Education. Additional exam requirements/recommendations for international students: Required—TOEFL.

Anderson University, College of Business, Anderson, SC 29621-4035. Offers business administration (MBA); healthcare leadership (MBA); human resources (MBA); marketing (MBA); organizational leadership (MOL); supply chain management (MBA). *Accreditation:* ACBSP. *Application deadline:* Applications are processed on a rolling basis. Electronic applications accepted. *Expenses:* Tuition: Full-time $400; part-time $400 per credit. *Required fees:* $200; $200 per semester. Tuition and fees vary according to course load. *Financial support:* Scholarships/grants and tuition waivers available. Financial award application deadline: 3/1; financial award applicants required to submit FAFSA. *Unit head:* Steve Nail, Dean, 864-MBA-6000. *Application contact:* Sharon Vargo, Graduate Admission Counselor, 864-231-2000, E-mail: svargo@andersonuniversity.edu. Website: http://www.andersonuniversity.edu/business

Arizona State University at the Tempe campus, W. P. Carey School of Business, Program in Business Administration, Tempe, AZ 85287-4906. Offers entrepreneurship (MBA); finance (MBA); health sector management (MBA); international business (MBA); leadership (MBA); marketing (MBA); organizational behavior (PhD); strategic management (PhD); supply chain management (MBA, PhD); JD/MBA; MBA/M Acc; MBA/M Arch. *Accreditation:* AACSB. *Program availability:* Part-time, evening/weekend, online learning. Terminal master's awarded for partial completion of doctoral program. *Degree requirements:* For master's, thesis or alternative, internship, interactive Program of Study (iPOS) submitted before completing 50 percent of required credit hours; for doctorate, comprehensive exam, thesis/dissertation, interactive Program of Study (iPOS) submitted before completing 50 percent of required credit hours. *Entrance requirements:* For master's, GMAT, minimum GPA of 3.0 in last 2 years of work leading to bachelor's degree, 2 letters of recommendation, professional resume, official transcripts, 3 essays; for doctorate, GMAT or GRE, minimum GPA of 3.0 in last 2 years of work leading to bachelor's degree, 3 letters of recommendation, resume, personal statement/essay. Additional exam requirements/recommendations for international students: Required—TOEFL (minimum score 550 paper-based; 80 iBT), IELTS (minimum score 6.5). Electronic applications accepted. *Expenses:* Contact institution.

Ashland University, Dauch College of Business and Economics, Ashland, OH 44805-3702. Offers accounting (MBA); business analytics (MBA); entrepreneurship (MBA); financial management (MBA); global management (MBA); health care management and leadership (MBA); human resource management (MBA); human resources (MBA); management information systems (MBA); project management (MBA); sport management (MBA); supply chain management (MBA). *Accreditation:* ACBSP. *Program availability:* Part-time, evening/weekend, 100% online, blended/hybrid learning. Terminal master's awarded for partial completion of doctoral program. *Degree requirements:* For master's, thesis optional, capstone course. *Entrance requirements:* For master's, 2 years of full-time work experience. Additional exam requirements/recommendations for international students: Required—TOEFL (minimum score 550 paper-based; 78 iBT). Electronic applications accepted. *Expenses:* Contact institution. *Faculty research:* Relationship marketing strategy, executive compensation and company performance, online marketplaces in electronic commerce, diversity training in campus recreation departments, entrepreneurship in developing and emerging economies.

Athens State University, Graduate Programs, Athens, AL 35611. Offers career and technical education (M Ed); global logistics and supply chain management (MS); religious studies (MA).

Binghamton University, State University of New York, Graduate School, School of Management, Program in Management, Binghamton, NY 13902-6000. Offers finance (PhD); management information systems (PhD); marketing (PhD); organizational studies (PhD); supply chain management (PhD). *Degree requirements:* For doctorate, thesis/dissertation. *Entrance requirements:* For doctorate, GMAT.

Boston University, Metropolitan College, Department of Administrative Sciences, Boston, MA 02215. Offers applied business analytics (MS); economic development and tourism management (MSAS); enterprise risk management (MS); financial management (MS); global marketing management (MS); innovation and technology (MSAS); insurance management (MS); project management (MS); supply chain management (MS). *Accreditation:* AACSB. *Program availability:* Part-time, evening/weekend, 100% online, blended/hybrid learning. *Faculty:* 27 full-time (5 women), 39 part-time/adjunct (5 women). *Students:* 617 full-time (351 women), 574 part-time (290 women); includes 196 minority (47 Black or African American, non-Hispanic/Latino; 2 American Indian or Alaska Native, non-Hispanic/Latino; 75 Asian, non-Hispanic/Latino; 60 Hispanic/Latino; 12 Two or more races, non-Hispanic/Latino), 730 international. Average age 28. 2,259 applicants, 76% accepted, 594 enrolled. In 2018, 441 master's awarded. *Degree requirements:* For master's, thesis optional. *Entrance requirements:* For master's, 1 year of work experience, minimum GPA of 3.0. Additional exam requirements/recommendations for international students: Required—TOEFL (minimum score 84

iBT). *Application deadline:* For fall admission, 8/1 priority date for domestic students, 6/1 priority date for international students; for spring admission, 12/1 priority date for domestic students, 11/15 priority date for international students; for summer admission, 4/1 priority date for domestic students, 3/1 priority date for international students. Applications are processed on a rolling basis. Application fee: $85. Electronic applications accepted. *Expenses:* Contact institution. *Financial support:* In 2018–19, 15 students received support, including 16 research assistantships (averaging $8,400 per year), 30 teaching assistantships (averaging $3,400 per year); career-related internships or fieldwork, Federal Work-Study, and unspecified assistantships also available. Financial award applicants required to submit FAFSA. *Faculty research:* International business, innovative process. *Unit head:* Dr. John Sullivan, Chair, 617-353-3016, E-mail: adminsc@bu.edu. *Application contact:* Enrollment Services, 617-358-8162, E-mail: met@bu.edu. Website: http://www.bu.edu/met/academic-community/departments/administrative-sciences/

Brigham Young University, Graduate Studies, BYU Marriott School of Business, MBA Program, Provo, UT 84602. Offers entrepreneurship (MBA); finance (MBA); global supply chain management (MBA); marketing (MBA); strategic human resources (MBA); JD/MBA; MBA/MS. *Accreditation:* AACSB. *Entrance requirements:* For master's, GMAT or GRE, commitment to BYU Honor Code, undergraduate degree. Additional exam requirements/recommendations for international students: Required—TOEFL (minimum score 590 paper-based; 100 iBT), IELTS (minimum score 7). Electronic applications accepted. *Expenses:* Contact institution. *Faculty research:* Finance, marketing, supply chain management, entrepreneurship, strategic human resources.

California Polytechnic State University, San Luis Obispo, Orfalea College of Business, Program in Packaging Value Chain, San Luis Obispo, CA 93407. Offers MS. *Program availability:* Online learning. *Degree requirements:* For master's, thesis. *Entrance requirements:* Additional exam requirements/recommendations for international students: Required—TOEFL (minimum score 80 iBT). *Application deadline:* For fall admission, 4/1 for domestic and international students. Applications are processed on a rolling basis. Electronic applications accepted. *Expenses: Tuition, area resident:* Full-time $7176; part-time $4164 per year. Tuition, state resident: full-time $10,965. Tuition, nonresident: full-time $10,965. *Required fees:* $6336; $3711. *Unit head:* Dr. Sanjiv Jaggia, Associate Dean, 805-756-2705, E-mail: sjaggia@calpoly.edu. *Application contact:* Dr. Sanjiv Jaggia, Associate Dean, 805-756-2705, E-mail: sjaggia@calpoly.edu. Website: https://gradbusiness.calpoly.edu/ms-packaging-value-chain/

California State University, East Bay, Office of Graduate Studies, College of Business and Economics, MBA Program, Option in Operations and Supply Chain Management, Hayward, CA 94542-3000. Offers MBA. *Degree requirements:* For master's, comprehensive exam or thesis. *Entrance requirements:* For master's, GMAT, minimum GPA of 2.75. Additional exam requirements/recommendations for international students: Required—TOEFL (minimum score 550 paper-based). Electronic applications accepted.

California State University, San Bernardino, Graduate Studies, College of Business and Public Administration, Program in Business Administration, San Bernardino, CA 92407. Offers accounting (MBA); entrepreneurship (MBA); finance (MBA); global business (MBA); information management (MBA); information security (MBA); management (MBA); supply chain management (MBA). *Accreditation:* AACSB. *Program availability:* Part-time, evening/weekend, online learning. *Faculty:* 5 full-time (4 women), 7 part-time/adjunct (3 women). *Students:* 40 full-time (14 women), 163 part-time (72 women); includes 99 minority (7 Black or African American, non-Hispanic/Latino; 15 Asian, non-Hispanic/Latino; 71 Hispanic/Latino; 6 Two or more races, non-Hispanic/Latino), 58 international. Average age 32. 342 applicants, 52% accepted, 91 enrolled. In 2018, 106 master's awarded. *Degree requirements:* For master's, comprehensive exam, thesis. *Entrance requirements:* Additional exam requirements/recommendations for international students: Required—TOEFL. *Application deadline:* For fall admission, 7/16 for domestic students, 7/20 for international students; for winter admission, 10/23 for domestic students, 10/20 for international students; for spring admission, 1/22 for domestic students, 1/20 for international students. Application fee: $55. *Expenses:* Contact institution. *Financial support:* Application deadline: 3/1. *Unit head:* Dr. Lawrence C. Rose, Dean, 909-537-3703, Fax: 909-537-7026, E-mail: lrose@csusb.edu. *Application contact:* Ernest Silvers, MBA Program Director, 909-537-5703, E-mail: esilvers@csusb.edu. Website: http://mba.csusb.edu/

Capella University, School of Business and Technology, Doctoral Programs in Technology, Minneapolis, MN 55402. Offers general information technology (PhD); global operations and supply chain management (DBA); information assurance and security (PhD); information technology education (PhD); information technology management (DBA, PhD).

Capella University, School of Business and Technology, Master's Programs in Technology, Minneapolis, MN 55402. Offers enterprise software architecture (MS); general information systems and technology management (MS); global operations and supply chain management (MBA); information assurance and security (MS); information technology management (MBA); network management (MS).

Case Western Reserve University, Weatherhead School of Management, Department of Operations, Cleveland, OH 44106. Offers operations and supply chain management (MSM); operations research (PhD); MBA/MSM. *Program availability:* Part-time. *Degree requirements:* For doctorate, thesis/dissertation. *Entrance requirements:* For master's, GRE General Test; for doctorate, GMAT, GRE General Test. *Expenses: Tuition:* Full-time $45,168; part-time $1939 per credit hour. *Required fees:* $36; $18 per semester. $18 per semester. *Faculty research:* Mathematical finance, mathematical programming, scheduling, stochastic optimization, environmental/energy models.

Central Connecticut State University, School of Graduate Studies, School of Engineering, Science and Technology, Department of Manufacturing and Construction Management, New Britain, CT 06050-4010. Offers construction management (MS, Certificate); lean manufacturing and Six Sigma (Certificate); supply chain and logistics (Certificate); technology management (MS). *Program availability:* Part-time, evening/weekend. *Faculty:* 6 full-time (0 women), 2 part-time/adjunct (0 women). *Students:* 14 full-time (7 women), 82 part-time (18 women); includes 28 minority (11 Black or African American, non-Hispanic/Latino; 2 Asian, non-Hispanic/Latino; 12 Hispanic/Latino; 3 Two or more races, non-Hispanic/Latino), 6 international. Average age 32. 70 applicants, 71% accepted, 29 enrolled. In 2018, 51 master's, 5 other advanced degrees awarded. *Degree requirements:* For master's, comprehensive exam, special project; for Certificate, qualifying exam. *Entrance requirements:* For master's, minimum undergraduate GPA of 2.7. Additional exam requirements/recommendations for international students: Required—TOEFL (minimum score 550 paper-based; 79 iBT); Recommended—IELTS (minimum score 6.5). *Application deadline:* For fall admission, 8/1 for domestic students, 5/1 for international students; for spring admission, 12/1 for domestic students, 11/1 for international students; for summer admission, 5/1 for domestic students. Applications are processed on a rolling basis. Application fee: $50. Electronic applications accepted. *Expenses: Tuition, area resident:* Full-time $7027; part-time $388 per credit. Tuition, state resident: full-time $9750; part-time $388 per

credit. Tuition, nonresident: full-time $18,102; part-time $388 per credit. *International tuition:* $18,102 full-time. *Required fees:* $266 per semester. *Financial support:* In 2018–19, 7 students received support. Career-related internships or fieldwork, Federal Work-Study, scholarships/grants, and unspecified assistantships available. Support available to part-time students. Financial award application deadline: 3/1; financial award applicants required to submit FAFSA. *Faculty research:* All aspects of middle management, technical supervision in the workplace. *Unit head:* Dr. Ravindra Thamma, Chair, 860-832-1830, E-mail: thammarav@ccsu.edu. *Application contact:* Patricia Gardner, Associate Director of Graduate Studies, 860-832-2350, Fax: 860-832-2362. Website: http://www.ccsu.edu/mcm/

Clarkson University, David D. Reh School of Business, Master's Program in Business Administration, Potsdam, NY 13699. Offers business administration (MBA); business fundamentals (Advanced Certificate); global supply chain management (Advanced Certificate); human resource management (Advanced Certificate); management and leadership (Advanced Certificate). *Accreditation:* AACSB. *Program availability:* Part-time, evening/weekend, 100% online, blended/hybrid learning. *Faculty:* 36 full-time (7 women), 8 part-time/adjunct (2 women). *Students:* 68 full-time (30 women), 63 part-time (29 women); includes 17 minority (2 Black or African American, non-Hispanic/Latino; 2 American Indian or Alaska Native, non-Hispanic/Latino; 6 Asian, non-Hispanic/Latino; 4 Hispanic/Latino; 3 Two or more races, non-Hispanic/Latino), 11 international. 119 applicants, 74% accepted, 67 enrolled. In 2018, 89 master's, 2 other advanced degrees awarded. *Entrance requirements:* For master's, GRE or GMAT. Additional exam requirements/recommendations for international students: Required—TOEFL (minimum score 550 paper-based, 80 iBT) or IELTS (6.5). *Application deadline:* Applications are processed on a rolling basis. Application fee: $50. Electronic applications accepted. *Expenses: Tuition:* Full-time $24,984; part-time $1388 per credit hour. *Required fees:* $225. Tuition and fees vary according to campus/location and program. *Financial support:* Scholarships/grants available. *Unit head:* Dr. Dennis Yu, Associate Dean of Graduate Programs & Research, 315-268-2300, E-mail: dyu@clarkson.edu. *Application contact:* Dan Capogna, Director of Graduate Admissions & Recruitment, 518-631-9910, E-mail: graduate@clarkson.edu.
Website: https://www.clarkson.edu/academics/graduate

Clayton State University, School of Graduate Studies, College of Business, Program in Business Administration, Morrow, GA 30260-0285. Offers accounting (MBA); human resource leadership (MBA); international business (MBA); sports and entertainment management (MBA); supply chain management (MBA). *Accreditation:* AACSB. *Program availability:* Part-time, evening/weekend. *Degree requirements:* For master's, thesis. *Entrance requirements:* For master's, GMAT, 3 letters of recommendation; statement of purpose; 2 official transcripts. Additional exam requirements/recommendations for international students: Required—TOEFL (minimum score 550 paper-based; 80 iBT). Electronic applications accepted. *Expenses:* Contact institution.

Clemson University, Graduate School, College of Business, Department of Management, Clemson, SC 29634. Offers business administration (PhD), including management information systems, strategy, entrepreneurship and organizational behavior, supply chain and operations management; management (MS). *Accreditation:* AACSB. *Faculty:* 26 full-time (9 women). *Students:* 14 full-time (5 women), 4 part-time (2 women); includes 1 minority (Asian, non-Hispanic/Latino), 10 international. Average age 30. 53 applicants, 36% accepted, 8 enrolled. In 2018, 2 master's, 4 doctorates awarded. Terminal master's awarded for partial completion of doctoral program. *Degree requirements:* For master's, comprehensive exam, thesis optional; for doctorate, comprehensive exam, thesis/dissertation. *Entrance requirements:* For master's and doctorate, GMAT or GRE General Test, unofficial transcripts, two letters of reference, curriculum vitae. Additional exam requirements/recommendations for international students: Required—TOEFL (minimum score 80 paper-based; 94 iBT); Recommended—IELTS (minimum score 7), TSE (minimum score 64). *Application deadline:* For fall admission, 4/15 priority date for international students; for spring admission, 10/15 priority date for international students. Applications are processed on a rolling basis. Application fee: $80 ($90 for international students). Electronic applications accepted. *Expenses:* $6823 per semester full-time resident, $14023 per semester full-time non-resident, $833 per credit hour part-time resident, $1731 per credit hour part-time non-resident, online $1264 per credit hour, $4938 doctoral programs resident, $10405 doctoral programs non-resident, $1144 full-time graduate assistant, other fees may apply per session. *Financial support:* In 2018–19, 10 students received support, including 1 fellowship with full and partial tuition reimbursement available (averaging $1,500 per year), 6 research assistantships with full and partial tuition reimbursements available (averaging $25,000 per year), 17 teaching assistantships with full and partial tuition reimbursements available (averaging $25,000 per year); career-related internships or fieldwork and unspecified assistantships also available. *Faculty research:* Effective use of information technology in business, manufacturing and service operations strategy, lean operations and quality management, healthcare operations, behavioral market design. *Total annual research expenditures:* $131,333. *Unit head:* Dr. Craig Wallace, Department Chair, 864-656-9963, E-mail: CW74@clemson.edu. *Application contact:* Dr. Janis Miller, Graduate Program Coordinator, 864-656-3757, E-mail: janism@clemson.edu.
Website: https://www.clemson.edu/business/departments/management/

Concordia University, School of Graduate Studies, John Molson School of Business, Montreal, QC H3H 0A1, Canada. Offers administration (M Sc), including finance, management, marketing; business administration (MBA, PhD, Certificate, Diploma); executive business administration (EMBA); supply chain management (MSCM). PhD program offered jointly with HEC Montreal, McGill University, and Université du Québec à Montréal. *Program availability:* Part-time, evening/weekend. *Degree requirements:* For master's, one foreign language, thesis (for some programs), research project; for doctorate, one foreign language, thesis/dissertation; for other advanced degree, one foreign language. *Entrance requirements:* For master's, GMAT, minimum 2 years of work experience (for MBA); letters of recommendation, bachelor's degree from recognized university with minimum GPA of 3.0, curriculum vitae; for doctorate, GMAT (minimum score of 600), official transcripts, curriculum vitae, 3 letters of reference, statement of purpose; for other advanced degree, minimum GPA of 2.7, 2 letters of reference, statement of purpose, resume. Additional exam requirements/recommendations for international students: Required—TOEFL (minimum score 90 iBT), IELTS (minimum score 7). Electronic applications accepted. *Expenses:* Contact institution. *Faculty research:* General business, capital markets, international business.

Delaware Valley University, MBA Program, Doylestown, PA 18901-2697. Offers accounting (MBA); entrepreneurship (MBA); finance (MBA); food and agribusiness (MBA); general business (MBA); global executive leadership (MBA); human resource management (MBA); supply chain management (MBA). *Program availability:* Part-time, evening/weekend, online learning. *Entrance requirements:* For master's, minimum undergraduate GPA of 3.0. Electronic applications accepted. *Expenses:* Contact institution.

DePaul University, Kellstadt Graduate School of Business, Chicago, IL 60604. Offers accountancy (MBA, MSA); applied economics (MBA); audit and advisory services (MS); business administration (DBA); business analytics (MS); business strategy and decision-making (MBA); computational finance (MS); economics and policy analysis (MS); enterprise risk management (MS); entrepreneurship (MBA, MS); finance (MBA, MS); general business (MBA); hospitality leadership (MBA); hospitality leadership and operational performance (MS); human resources (MS); international business (MBA); management (MBA, MS); management information systems (MBA); marketing (MBA, MS); marketing analysis (MS); marketing strategy and planning (MBA); real estate (MS); real estate finance and investment (MBA); strategy, execution and valuation (MBA); supply chain management (MS); sustainable management (MS); taxation (MS); JD/MBA. *Accreditation:* AACSB. *Program availability:* Part-time, evening/weekend, online learning. *Entrance requirements:* For master's, GMAT/GRE, 2 letters of recommendation, resume, essay, official transcripts. Additional exam requirements/recommendations for international students: Required—TOEFL (minimum score 550 paper-based; 80 iBT). Electronic applications accepted. *Expenses:* Contact institution.

DeSales University, Division of Business, Center Valley, PA 18034-9568. Offers accounting (MBA); computer information systems (MBA); finance (MBA); health care systems management (MBA); human resources management (MBA); management (MBA); marketing (MBA); project management (MBA); self-design (MBA); supply chain management (MBA); DNP/MBA; MSN/MBA. *Accreditation:* ACBSP. *Program availability:* Part-time, evening/weekend, 100% online, blended/hybrid learning. *Entrance requirements:* For master's, GMAT (waived if undergraduate GPA is 3.0 or better), minimum GPA of 3.0 in undergraduate work, literacy in basic software, background or interest in the field of study, personal statement, 2 years of work experience. Additional exam requirements/recommendations for international students: Required—TOEFL. Electronic applications accepted. *Expenses:* Contact institution. *Faculty research:* Quality improvement, executive development, productivity, cross-cultural managerial differences, leadership.

Duquesne University, Palumbo-Donahue School of Business, Pittsburgh, PA 15282-0001. Offers accounting (M Acc); finance (MBA); information systems management (MSISM); management (MBA, MS); marketing (MBA); sports business (MS); supply chain management (MS); sustainability (MBA); JD/MBA; MBA/M Acc; MBA/MA; MBA/MES; MBA/MHMS; MSISM/MBA; Pharm D/MBA. *Accreditation:* AACSB. *Program availability:* Part-time, evening/weekend, 100% online, blended/hybrid learning. *Faculty:* 59 full-time (23 women), 25 part-time/adjunct (6 women). *Students:* 214 full-time (74 women), 42 part-time (20 women); includes 39 minority (12 Black or African American, non-Hispanic/Latino; 13 Asian, non-Hispanic/Latino; 8 Hispanic/Latino; 6 Two or more races, non-Hispanic/Latino), 23 international. Average age 29. 228 applicants, 88% accepted, 118 enrolled. In 2018, 149 master's awarded. *Entrance requirements:* For master's, GMAT or GRE, all official transcripts, two letters of recommendation, current resume, essays. Additional exam requirements/recommendations for international students: Required—TOEFL (minimum score 90 iBT), IELTS (minimum score 7). *Application deadline:* For fall admission, 7/1 priority date for domestic and international students; for spring admission, 12/1 for domestic and international students; for summer admission, 4/1 for domestic and international students. Applications are processed on a rolling basis. Application fee: $0. Electronic applications accepted. *Expenses:* $1,284/credit hour (business), $953/credit hour (management). *Financial support:* In 2018–19, 174 students received support, including 6 fellowships with partial tuition reimbursements available (averaging $24,750 per year); career-related internships or fieldwork, scholarships/grants, and unspecified assistantships also available. Support available to part-time students. Financial award application deadline: 7/1; financial award applicants required to submit FAFSA. *Faculty research:* Investment management, business ethics, technology management, supply chain management, entrepreneurship. *Unit head:* Dr. Karen Donovan, Associate Dean of Graduate Programs and Executive Education, 412-396-5788, Fax: 412-396-1726, E-mail: donovan6@duq.edu. *Application contact:* Chris Rouhier, Director of Graduate Admissions, 412-396-6244, Fax: 412-396-1726, E-mail: rouhierc@duq.edu.
Website: http://www.duq.edu/business/grad

Eastern Michigan University, Graduate School, College of Business, Department of Marketing, Ypsilanti, MI 48197. Offers e-business (MBA); integrated marketing communications (MS, Postbaccalaureate Certificate); international business (MBA); marketing management (MBA); supply chain management (MBA). *Program availability:* Part-time, evening/weekend, online learning. *Faculty:* 22 full-time (7 women). *Students:* 31 full-time (25 women), 33 part-time (22 women); includes 25 minority (15 Black or African American, non-Hispanic/Latino; 1 Asian, non-Hispanic/Latino; 9 Hispanic/Latino). Average age 30. 32 applicants, 84% accepted, 16 enrolled. In 2018, 23 master's awarded. *Entrance requirements:* For master's, GMAT. Additional exam requirements/recommendations for international students: Required—TOEFL. *Application deadline:* For fall admission, 5/15 priority date for domestic students, 2/15 priority date for international students; for winter admission, 10/15 priority date for domestic students, 9/1 priority date for international students; for summer admission, 3/15 priority date for domestic students, 3/1 priority date for international students. Applications are processed on a rolling basis. Application fee: $45. *Financial support:* Fellowships, research assistantships with full tuition reimbursements, teaching assistantships with full tuition reimbursements, career-related internships or fieldwork, Federal Work-Study, institutionally sponsored loans, scholarships/grants, tuition waivers (partial), and unspecified assistantships available. Support available to part-time students. Financial award applicants required to submit FAFSA. *Unit head:* Dr. Lewis Hershey, Department Head, 734-487-3323, Fax: 734-487-7099, E-mail: lhershe1@emich.edu. *Application contact:* K. Michelle Henry, Director, Graduate Business Programs, 734-487-4444, Fax: 734-483-1316, E-mail: cob.graduate@emich.edu.
Website: http://www.mkt.emich.edu/index.html

Eastern Michigan University, Graduate School, College of Business, Programs in Business Administration, Ypsilanti, MI 48197. Offers business administration (MBA, Graduate Certificate); computer information systems (Graduate Certificate); e-business (MBA, Graduate Certificate); enterprise business intelligence (MBA); entrepreneurship (MBA, Graduate Certificate); finance (MBA, Graduate Certificate); human resources (MBA); human resources management (Graduate Certificate); information systems (MBA); internal auditing (MBA); international business (MBA, Graduate Certificate); marketing management (Graduate Certificate); nonprofit management (MBA); organizational development (Graduate Certificate); supply chain management (MBA, Graduate Certificate). *Accreditation:* AACSB. *Program availability:* Part-time, online learning. *Students:* 69 full-time (38 women), 251 part-time (140 women); includes 100 minority (63 Black or African American, non-Hispanic/Latino; 1 American Indian or Alaska Native, non-Hispanic/Latino; 12 Asian, non-Hispanic/Latino; 14 Hispanic/Latino; 10 Two or more races, non-Hispanic/Latino), 28 international. Average age 32. 199 applicants, 75% accepted, 83 enrolled. In 2018, 75 master's, 50 other advanced degrees awarded. *Entrance requirements:* For master's, GMAT (minimum score 450), minimum cumulative undergraduate GPA of 2.75. Additional exam requirements/recommendations for international students: Required—TOEFL. *Application deadline:* For fall admission, 5/15 priority date for domestic students, 2/15 priority date for international students; for winter admission, 10/15 priority date for domestic students, 9/1 priority date for international students; for summer admission, 3/15 priority date for domestic students, 3/1 priority date for international students. Applications are processed on a rolling basis. Application fee: $45. *Financial support:* Fellowships, research assistantships with full tuition reimbursements, teaching assistantships with full tuition reimbursements, career-related internships or fieldwork, Federal Work-Study,

institutionally sponsored loans, scholarships/grants, tuition waivers (partial), and unspecified assistantships available. Support available to part-time students. Financial award applicants required to submit FAFSA. *Unit head:* K. Michelle Henry, Director, Graduate Business Programs, 734-487-4444, Fax: 734-483-1316, E-mail: cob.graduate@emich.edu. *Application contact:* K. Michelle Henry, Director, Graduate Business Programs, 734-487-4444, Fax: 734-483-1316, E-mail: cob.graduate@emich.edu.
Website: http://www.emich.edu/cob/mba/

Elmhurst College, Graduate Programs, Program in Supply Chain Management, Elmhurst, IL 60126-3296. Offers MS. *Program availability:* Part-time, evening/weekend. *Faculty:* 2 full-time (0 women), 4 part-time/adjunct (0 women). *Students:* 22 part-time (10 women); includes 5 minority (2 Black or African American, non-Hispanic/Latino; 2 Hispanic/Latino; 1 Two or more races, non-Hispanic/Latino), 1 international. Average age 32. 35 applicants, 29% accepted, 10 enrolled. In 2018, 18 master's awarded. *Entrance requirements:* For master's, 3 recommendations, resume, statement of purpose. Additional exam requirements/recommendations for international students: Required—TOEFL (minimum score 550 paper-based; 79 iBT), IELTS (minimum score 6.5). *Application deadline:* Applications are processed on a rolling basis. Application fee: $0. Electronic applications accepted. *Expenses:* $870 per semester hour. *Financial support:* In 2018–19, 9 students received support. Scholarships/grants available. Support available to part-time students. Financial award applicants required to submit FAFSA. *Unit head:* Dr. Roby Thomas, Director, 630-617-3116, E-mail: rthomas@elmhurst.edu. *Application contact:* Timothy J. Panfil, Senior Director of Graduate Admission and Enrollment Management, 630-617-3300 Ext. 3256, Fax: 630-617-6471, E-mail: panfilt@elmhurst.edu.
Website: http://www.elmhurst.edu/scm

Embry-Riddle Aeronautical University–Worldwide, Department of Decision Sciences, Daytona Beach, FL 32114-3900. Offers aviation and aerospace (MSPM); aviation/aerospace management (MSEM); financial management (MSEM, MSPM); general management (MSPM); global management (MSPM); human resources management (MSPM); information systems (MSPM); leadership (MSEM, MSPM); logistics and supply chain management (MSEM, MSLSCM, MSPM); management (MSEM, MSPM); project management (MSEM); systems engineering (MSEM, MSPM); technical management (MSPM). *Program availability:* Part-time, evening/weekend, EagleVision Classroom (between classrooms), EagleVision Home (faculty and students at home), and a blend of Classroom or Home. *Degree requirements:* For master's, comprehensive exam (for some programs), thesis (for some programs). *Entrance requirements:* Additional exam requirements/recommendations for international students: Required—TOEFL (minimum score 550 paper-based; 79 iBT), IELTS (minimum score 6). Electronic applications accepted. *Expenses:* Contact institution.

Fairleigh Dickinson University, Florham Campus, Silberman College of Business, Program in Supply Chain Management, Madison, NJ 07940-1099. Offers MS. *Entrance requirements:* For master's, GMAT.

Ferris State University, College of Business, Big Rapids, MI 49307. Offers design and innovation management (MBA); lean systems and leadership (MBA); project management (MBA); supply chain management and lean logistics (MBA). *Accreditation:* ACBSP. *Program availability:* Part-time, evening/weekend, 100% online, blended/hybrid learning. *Faculty:* 20 full-time (7 women). *Students:* 14 full-time (9 women), 96 part-time (51 women); includes 12 minority (4 Black or African American, non-Hispanic/Latino; 1 American Indian or Alaska Native, non-Hispanic/Latino; 3 Asian, non-Hispanic/Latino; 2 Hispanic/Latino; 2 Two or more races, non-Hispanic/Latino), 8 international. Average age 33. 48 applicants, 88% accepted, 32 enrolled. In 2018, 39 master's awarded. *Degree requirements:* For master's, comprehensive exam, thesis. *Entrance requirements:* For master's, GRE or GMAT, minimum GPA of 3.0 overall and in junior-/senior-level classes; statement of purpose; 3 letters of reference; resume; transcripts. Additional exam requirements/recommendations for international students: Required—TOEFL (minimum score 500 paper-based; 70 iBT), IELTS (minimum score 6.5). *Application deadline:* For fall admission, 7/1 priority date for domestic students, 6/15 for international students; for winter admission, 11/1 priority date for domestic students, 10/15 for international students; for spring admission, 3/1 priority date for domestic students, 2/15 for international students. Applications are processed on a rolling basis. Application fee: $0 ($30 for international students). Electronic applications accepted. *Expenses:* $610 per credit hour; $12 per credit hour online fee; 33 credits for MISI $20,526; 39 credits for MBA $24,258. *Financial support:* In 2018–19, 17 students received support. Career-related internships or fieldwork, Federal Work-Study, scholarships/grants, and unspecified assistantships available. Support available to part-time students. Financial award applicants required to submit FAFSA. *Faculty research:* Digital forensics, security issues with internet of things, cybersecurity education. *Total annual research expenditures:* $130,000. *Unit head:* Dr. David Nicol, College of Business Dean, 231-591-2168, Fax: 231-591-3521, E-mail: davidnicol@ferris.edu. *Application contact:* Dr. Greg Gogolin, Professor, 231-591-3159, Fax: 231-591-3521, E-mail: greggogolin@ferris.edu.
Website: http://cbgp.ferris.edu/

Fontbonne University, Graduate Programs, St. Louis, MO 63105-3098. Offers accounting (MBA, MS); art (MA); art (K-12) (MAT); business (MBA); computer science (MS); deaf education (MA); early intervention in deaf education (MA); education (MA), including autism spectrum disorders, curriculum and instruction, diverse learners, early childhood education, reading, special education; elementary education (MAT); family and consumer sciences (MA), including multidisciplinary health communication studies; fine arts (MFA); instructional design and technology (MS); management and leadership (MM); middle school education (MAT); secondary education (MAT); special education (MAT); speech-language pathology (MS); supply chain management (MS); theatre (MA). *Accreditation:* ASHA. *Program availability:* Part-time, evening/weekend, online learning. *Degree requirements:* For master's, comprehensive exam (for some programs), thesis (for some programs). *Entrance requirements:* Additional exam requirements/recommendations for international students: Required—TOEFL (minimum score 500 paper-based; 65 iBT). Electronic applications accepted.

Friends University, Graduate School, Wichita, KS 67213. Offers family therapy (MSFT); global business administration (MBA), including accounting, business law, change management, health care leadership, management information systems, supply chain management and logistics; health care leadership (MHCL); management information systems (MMIS); professional business administration (MBA), including accounting, business law, change management, health care leadership, management information systems, supply chain management and logistics. *Program availability:* Part-time, evening/weekend, online learning. *Degree requirements:* For master's, research project. *Entrance requirements:* For master's, bachelor's degree from accredited institution, official transcripts, interview with program director, letter(s) of recommendation. Additional exam requirements/recommendations for international students: Required—TOEFL (minimum score 560 paper-based). Electronic applications accepted.

Georgia Southern University, Jack N. Averitt College of Graduate Studies, Parker College of Business, Program in Logistics and Supply Chain Management, Statesboro, GA 30458. Offers PhD. *Degree requirements:* For doctorate, comprehensive exam,

thesis/dissertation. *Entrance requirements:* For doctorate, GMAT or GRE, minimum of three letters of reference; statement of purpose; resume. Additional exam requirements/recommendations for international students: Required—TOEFL (minimum score 550 paper-based; 80 iBT), IELTS (minimum score 6). Electronic applications accepted. *Expenses: Tuition, area resident:* Part-time $3324 per semester. Tuition, state resident: full-time $5814; part-time $3324 per semester. Tuition, nonresident: full-time $23,204; part-time $13,260 per semester. *Required fees:* $2092; $2092. Tuition and fees vary according to course load, degree level, campus/location and program. *Faculty research:* Buyer-supplier relationships, retail supply chain management, strategic sourcing/outsourcing, supply chain metrics, service scheduling, demand and supply planning, supply chain strategy, operations and supply management, decision sciences.

Golden Gate University, Ageno School of Business, San Francisco, CA 94105-2968. Offers accounting (MBA); adaptive leadership (MBA); advanced financial planning (MS); business administration (EMBA, MBA, DBA); business analytics (MBA, MS); entrepreneurship (MBA); finance (MBA, MS, Certificate); financial life planning (Certificate); financial planning (MS, Certificate); global supply chain management (MBA, Certificate); human resource management (MBA, MS, Certificate); information technology management (MBA, MS, Certificate); international business (MBA); marketing (MBA, MS, Certificate); project management (MBA, MS, Certificate); psychology (MA, Certificate); public administration (EMPA, MBA); public administration leadership (Certificate); JD/MBA. *Program availability:* Part-time, evening/weekend. *Degree requirements:* For doctorate, thesis/dissertation, qualifying examination. *Entrance requirements:* For master's, GMAT (for MBA), minimum GPA of 2.5 (MS). Additional exam requirements/recommendations for international students: Required—TOEFL (minimum score 550 paper-based; 79 iBT). Electronic applications accepted. *Expenses:* Contact institution.

HEC Montreal, School of Business Administration, Graduate Diploma Programs in Administration, Program in Supply Chain Management, Montréal, QC H3T 2A7, Canada. Offers Graduate Diploma. All courses are given in French. *Students:* 16 full-time (7 women), 48 part-time (19 women). 42 applicants, 60% accepted, 17 enrolled. In 2018, 13 Graduate Diplomas awarded. *Entrance requirements:* For degree, bachelor's degree, working experience, letters of recommendation. *Application deadline:* For fall admission, 4/15 for domestic and international students; for winter admission, 9/15 for domestic and international students. Application fee: $91 Canadian dollars ($191 Canadian dollars for international students). Electronic applications accepted. *Expenses: Tuition, area resident:* Full-time $3052.80 Canadian dollars; part-time $84.80 Canadian dollars per credit. Tuition, state resident: full-time $3816 Canadian dollars; part-time $264.67 Canadian dollars per credit. Tuition, nonresident: full-time $11,910 Canadian dollars. *International tuition:* $20,905.20 Canadian dollars full-time. *Required fees:* $1805.34 Canadian dollars; $43.62 Canadian dollars per credit. $71.78 Canadian dollars per term. Tuition and fees vary according to degree level and program. *Financial support:* Research assistantships, teaching assistantships, and scholarships/grants available. Financial award application deadline: 9/2. *Unit head:* Renaud Lachance, Director, 514-340-6428, E-mail: renaud.lachance@hec.ca. *Application contact:* Anny Caron, Administrative Director, 514-340-6000, Fax: 514-340-6411, E-mail: aide@hec.ca.
Website: http://www.hec.ca/programmes/dess/dess-gestion-chaine-logistique/index.html

HEC Montreal, School of Business Administration, Master of Science Programs in Administration, Program in Global Supply Chain Management, Montréal, QC H3T 2A7, Canada. Offers M Sc. Program offered in English (Supervised project Stream, Thesis Stream). *Students:* 75 full-time (29 women), 11 part-time (9 women). 73 applicants, 62% accepted, 29 enrolled. In 2018, 28 master's awarded. *Entrance requirements:* For master's, BBA, undergraduate degree in another field, degree deemed equivalent by program director and minimum GPA of 3.0 on 4.3 scale. Additional exam requirements/recommendations for international students: Required—TAGE MAGE (minimum recommended score of 300), GMAT (minimum recommended score of 630), or GRE. *Application deadline:* For fall admission, 3/15 for domestic and international students; for winter admission, 9/15 for domestic and international students. Application fee: $91 Canadian dollars ($191 Canadian dollars for international students). Electronic applications accepted. *Expenses: Tuition, area resident:* Full-time $3052.80 Canadian dollars; part-time $84.80 Canadian dollars per credit. Tuition, state resident: full-time $3816 Canadian dollars; part-time $264.67 Canadian dollars per credit. Tuition, nonresident: full-time $11,910 Canadian dollars. *International tuition:* $20,905.20 Canadian dollars full-time. *Required fees:* $1805.34 Canadian dollars; $43.62 Canadian dollars per credit. $71.78 Canadian dollars per term. Tuition and fees vary according to degree level and program. *Financial support:* Research assistantships, teaching assistantships, and scholarships/grants available. Financial award application deadline: 9/2. *Unit head:* Dr. Sihem Taboubi, Director, 514-340-6428, E-mail: sihem.taboubi@hec.ca. *Application contact:* Marianne de Moura, Administrative Director, 514-340-6000, Fax: 514-340-6411, E-mail: aide@hec.ca.
Website: http://www.hec.ca/en/programs/masters/master-global-supply-chain-management/index.html

Howard University, School of Business, Graduate Programs in Business, Washington, DC 20059-0002. Offers accounting (MBA); entrepreneurship (MBA); finance (MBA); general management (MBA); human resources management (MBA); information systems (MBA); international business (MBA); marketing (MBA); supply chain management (MBA); JD/MBA. *Accreditation:* AACSB. *Program availability:* Part-time, evening/weekend, online learning. *Entrance requirements:* For master's, GMAT, minimum 1 year post undergraduate work experience, resume, 3 letters of recommendation, advanced college algebra. Additional exam requirements/recommendations for international students: Required—TOEFL. *Faculty research:* Marketing research in multi-ethnic populations, U.S. trade policies and international relations, risk management (finance).

Indiana University–Purdue University Indianapolis, Kelley School of Business, Evening MBA Program, Indianapolis, IN 46202-5151. Offers accounting (MBA); entrepreneurship (MBA); finance (MBA); general administration (MBA); marketing (MBA); supply chain management (MBA); MBA/JD; MBA/MD; MBA/MHA; MBA/MS; MBA/MSA; MBA/MSE. *Program availability:* Part-time-only, evening/weekend, online learning. *Entrance requirements:* For master's, GMAT or GRE, 2 years of professional work experience. Additional exam requirements/recommendations for international students: Required—TOEFL or IELTS. Electronic applications accepted. *Expenses:* Contact institution. *Faculty research:* Entrepreneurship; corporate finance; international business; consumer behavior; supply chain; business law.

Johnson & Wales University, Graduate Studies, MBA Program, Providence, RI 02903-3703. Offers accounting (MBA); business administration (MBA); finance (MBA); global fashion merchandising and management (MBA); hospitality (MBA); human resource management (MBA); information security/assurance (MBA); information technology (MBA); nonprofit management (MBA); operations and supply chain management (MBA); organizational leadership (MBA); organizational psychology (MBA); sport leadership (MBA). Program also offered on Denver campus. *Program availability:* Part-time, online learning. *Entrance requirements:* For master's, minimum GPA of 2.75. Additional exam requirements/recommendations for international students:

Required—TOEFL (minimum score 550 paper-based); Recommended—IELTS, TWE. *Faculty research:* International banking, global economy, international trade, cultural differences.

Loyola University Chicago, Quinlan School of Business, Master of Science in Supply Chain Management Program, Chicago, IL 60611. Offers data warehousing (Certificate); supply chain management (MSSCM, Certificate). *Program availability:* Part-time, evening/weekend. *Entrance requirements:* For master's, GMAT or GRE, official transcripts, two letters of recommendation, statement of purpose, resume. Additional exam requirements/recommendations for international students: Required—TOEFL (minimum score 90 iBT), IELTS (minimum score 6.5). Electronic applications accepted. Application fee is waived when completed online. *Expenses:* Contact institution. *Faculty research:* Consistent vehicle routing policies, logistics, operations management.

Loyola University Chicago, Quinlan School of Business, MBA Programs, Chicago, IL 60611. Offers accounting (MBA); business ethics (MBA); derivative markets (MBA); economics (MBA); entrepreneurship (MBA); finance (MBA); healthcare management (MBA); human resources management (MBA); information systems management (MBA); international business (MBA); management (MBA); marketing (MBA); risk management (MBA); supply chain management (MBA). *Program availability:* Part-time, evening/weekend. *Entrance requirements:* For master's, GMAT or GRE, official transcripts, two letters of recommendation, statement of purpose, resume. Additional exam requirements/recommendations for international students: Required—TOEFL (minimum score 90 iBT) or IELTS (minimum score 6.5). Electronic applications accepted. Application fee is waived when completed online. *Expenses:* Contact institution. *Faculty research:* Social enterprise and responsibility, emerging markets, supply chain management, risk management.

Maine Maritime Academy, Loeb-Sullivan School of International Business and Logistics, Castine, ME 04420. Offers global logistics and maritime management (MS); international logistics management (MS). *Program availability:* Part-time, 100% online. *Degree requirements:* For master's, capstone course. *Entrance requirements:* For master's, GMAT or GRE, letter of recommendation. Additional exam requirements/recommendations for international students: Required—TOEFL, IELTS. Electronic applications accepted. Application fee is waived when completed online. *Faculty research:* Internet of things, trait intelligence, port operations, location theory.

Marquette University, Graduate School of Management, Executive MBA Program, Milwaukee, WI 53201-1881. Offers economics (MBA); finance (MBA); human resources (MBA); international business (MBA); management information systems (MBA); marketing (MBA); operations and supply chain management (MBA); sports business (MBA). *Accreditation:* AACSB. *Degree requirements:* For master's, international trip. *Entrance requirements:* For master's, GMAT or GRE, two letters of recommendation, official transcripts from current and previous colleges/universities. Additional exam requirements/recommendations for international students: Required—TOEFL (minimum score 550 paper-based; 88 iBT), IELTS (minimum score 6.5), PTE. Electronic applications accepted. *Expenses:* Contact institution. *Faculty research:* International trade and finance, customer relationship management, consumer satisfaction, customer service.

Marquette University, Graduate School of Management, Program in Business Administration, Milwaukee, WI 53201-1881. Offers business administration (MBA); economics (MBA); entrepreneurship (Certificate); finance (MBA); human resources (MBA); international business (MBA); management information systems (MBA); marketing (MBA); operations and supply chain management (MBA); sports business (MBA); JD/MBA; MBA/MA; MBA/MSN. *Accreditation:* AACSB. *Program availability:* Part-time, evening/weekend. *Degree requirements:* For Certificate, business plan. *Entrance requirements:* For master's, GMAT or GRE, letters of recommendation. Additional exam requirements/recommendations for international students: Required—TOEFL (minimum score 550 paper-based; 88 iBT), IELTS (minimum score 6.5), PTE. Electronic applications accepted. *Faculty research:* Ethics in the professions, services marketing, technology impact on decision-making, mentoring.

Maryville University of Saint Louis, The John E. Simon School of Business, St. Louis, MO 63141-7299. Offers accounting (MBA, MS, Certificate); business studies (Certificate); cybersecurity (MBA, MS, Certificate); financial services (MBA, Certificate); health administration (MBA); healthcare administration (Certificate); human resource management (MBA); human resources management (Certificate); information technology (MBA); information technology management (Certificate); management (MBA, Certificate); management and leadership (MA); marketing (MBA, Certificate); project management (MBA, Certificate); sport business management (MBA); supply chain management (Certificate); supply chain management/logistics (MBA). *Accreditation:* ACBSP. *Program availability:* Part-time, 100% online, blended/hybrid learning. *Faculty:* 5 full-time (1 woman), 77 part-time/adjunct (19 women). *Students:* 338 full-time (166 women), 739 part-time (356 women); includes 310 minority (161 Black or African American, non-Hispanic/Latino; 6 American Indian or Alaska Native, non-Hispanic/Latino; 59 Asian, non-Hispanic/Latino; 57 Hispanic/Latino; 27 Two or more races, non-Hispanic/Latino), 30 international. Average age 33. In 2018, 143 master's awarded. *Degree requirements:* For master's, capstone course (for MBA). *Entrance requirements:* Additional exam requirements/recommendations for international students: Required—TOEFL (minimum score 563 paper-based; 85 iBT). *Application deadline:* Applications are processed on a rolling basis. Electronic applications accepted. *Expenses:* Tuition varies by program. *Financial support:* Career-related internships or fieldwork, Federal Work-Study, tuition waivers (partial), and campus employment available. Financial award application deadline: 4/1; financial award applicants required to submit FAFSA. *Unit head:* Tammy Gocial, Interim Dean, 314-529-9401, Fax: 314-529-9975, E-mail: tgocial@maryville.edu. *Application contact:* Chris Gourdine, Assistant Dean Business Administration, 314-529-6861, Fax: 314-529-9975, E-mail: cgourdine@maryville.edu.
Website: http://www.maryville.edu/bu/business-administration-masters/

McGill University, Faculty of Graduate and Postdoctoral Studies, Desautels Faculty of Management, Montréal, QC H3A 2T5, Canada. Offers administration (PhD); entrepreneurial studies (MBA); finance (MBA); general management (Post Master's Certificate); global manufacturing and supply chain management (MMM); information systems (MBA); international business (MBA); international practicing management (MM); management (MBA); management for development (MBA); marketing (MBA); operations management (MBA); public accountancy (Diploma); strategic management (MBA); MBA/LL B; MD/MBA. MMM offered jointly with Faculty of Engineering; PhD with Concordia University, HEC Montreal, Université de Montréal, Université du Québec à Montréal.

Metropolitan State University, College of Management, St. Paul, MN 55106-5000. Offers business administration (MBA, DBA); business analytics (Graduate Certificate); database administration (Graduate Certificate); global supply chain management (Graduate Certificate); information assurance security (Graduate Certificate); management information systems (MMIS); MIS generalist (Graduate Certificate); MIS systems analysis and design (Graduate Certificate); project management (Graduate Certificate). *Program availability:* Part-time, evening/weekend. *Degree requirements:* For master's, thesis optional, computer language (MMIS). *Entrance requirements:* For master's, GMAT (for MBA), resume. Additional exam requirements/recommendations for international students: Required—TOEFL (minimum score 550 paper-based). Electronic applications accepted. *Faculty research:* Yugoslav economic system, workers' cooperatives, participative management and job enrichment, global business systems.

Michigan State University, The Graduate School, Eli Broad College of Business, Department of Supply Chain Management, East Lansing, MI 48224. Offers logistics (PhD); operations and sourcing management (PhD); supply chain management (MS), including logistics management, operations management, rail management, supply management. *Program availability:* Part-time. *Degree requirements:* For master's, field study/research project; for doctorate, comprehensive exam, thesis/dissertation. *Entrance requirements:* For master's, GMAT (taken within past 5 years), bachelor's degree, minimum GPA of 3.0 in junior/senior years, transcripts, at least 2 years of professional supply chain work experience, 3 letters of recommendation, essays, resume; for doctorate, GMAT or GRE, bachelor's or master's degree, transcripts, strong work experience, 3 letters of recommendation, statement of personal goals, interview. Additional exam requirements/recommendations for international students: Required—TOEFL (minimum score 600 paper-based). Electronic applications accepted. *Expenses:* Contact institution.

Michigan State University, The Graduate School, Eli Broad College of Business, Program in Business Administration, East Lansing, MI 48224. Offers finance (MBA); human resource management (MBA); integrative management (MBA); marketing (MBA); supply chain management (MBA). MBA in integrative management is through Weekend MBA Program; other 4 concentrations are through Full-Time MBA Program. *Program availability:* Evening/weekend. *Degree requirements:* For master's, enrichment experience. *Entrance requirements:* For master's, GMAT or GRE, 4-year bachelor's degree; resume; work experience (minimum of 5 years for Weekend MBA); 2-3 personal essays; 2 letters of recommendation; personal interview. Additional exam requirements/recommendations for international students: Required—PTE (minimum score 70), TOEFL (minimum score 100 iBT) or IELTS (minimum score 7) for full-time MBA applicants. Electronic applications accepted. *Expenses:* Contact institution.

Moravian College, Graduate and Continuing Studies, Business and Management Programs, Bethlehem, PA 18018-6650. Offers accounting (MBA); business management (MBA); health administration (MHA); HR leadership (MSHRM); supply chain management (MBA). *Program availability:* Part-time, evening/weekend. *Faculty:* 3 full-time (2 women), 13 part-time/adjunct (4 women). *Students:* 13 full-time (12 women), 70 part-time (38 women); includes 10 minority (1 Black or African American, non-Hispanic/Latino; 9 Hispanic/Latino), 1 international. Average age 30. 92 applicants, 85% accepted, 58 enrolled. In 2018, 34 master's awarded. *Entrance requirements:* For master's, current resume, official transcripts, 2 letters of recommendation. Additional exam requirements/recommendations for international students: Required—TOEFL (minimum score 577 paper-based), IELTS (minimum score 6.5). *Application deadline:* For fall admission, 8/1 priority date for domestic and international students; for spring admission, 1/1 priority date for domestic and international students; for summer admission, 5/1 priority date for domestic and international students. Applications are processed on a rolling basis. Electronic applications accepted. *Financial support:* Research assistantships available. Financial award applicants required to submit FAFSA. *Faculty research:* Leadership, change management, human resources. *Unit head:* Dr. Katie P. Desiderio, Executive Director, Graduate Business Programs, 610-861-1400, Fax: 610-861-1466, E-mail: graduate@moravian.edu. *Application contact:* Kristy Sullivan, Director of Student Recruitment Operations, 610-861-1400, Fax: 610-861-1466, E-mail: graduate@moravian.edu.
Website: https://www.moravian.edu/graduate/programs/business#/

Naval Postgraduate School, Departments and Academic Groups, Graduate School of Business and Public Policy, Monterey, CA 93943. Offers acquisition and contract management (MBA); business administration (EMBA, MBA); contract management (MS); defense business management (MBA); defense systems analysis (MS), including management; defense systems management (international) (MBA); financial management (MBA); information management (MBA); manpower systems analysis (MS); material logistics support management (MBA); program management (MS); resource planning and management for international defense (MBA); supply chain management (MBA); systems acquisition management (MBA); transportation management (MBA). Program only open to commissioned officers of the United States and friendly nations and selected United States federal civilian employees. *Accreditation:* AACSB; NASPAA. *Program availability:* Part-time, online learning. *Degree requirements:* For master's, thesis (for some programs), terminal project/capstone (for some programs). *Faculty research:* U.S. and European public procurement policies for small and medium-sized enterprises, examining external validity criticisms in the choice of students as subjects in accounting experiment studies, assurance of learning in contract management education, contracting for cloud computing: opportunities and risks, NPS, Apple App Store as a business model supporting U.S. Navy requirements.

New York Institute of Technology, School of Management, Department of Business Administration, Old Westbury, NY 11568-8000. Offers executive management (MBA), including finance, marketing, operations and supply chain management. *Accreditation:* AACSB. *Program availability:* Part-time. *Faculty:* 25 full-time (4 women), 20 part-time/adjunct (6 women). *Students:* 296 full-time (126 women), 91 part-time (45 women); includes 42 minority (6 Black or African American, non-Hispanic/Latino; 1 American Indian or Alaska Native, non-Hispanic/Latino; 17 Asian, non-Hispanic/Latino; 12 Hispanic/Latino; 1 Native Hawaiian or other Pacific Islander, non-Hispanic/Latino; 5 Two or more races, non-Hispanic/Latino), 298 international. Average age 30. 550 applicants, 67% accepted, 111 enrolled. In 2018, 291 master's awarded. *Entrance requirements:* For master's, bachelor's degree; minimum undergraduate GPA of 3.0. Additional exam requirements/recommendations for international students: Required—TOEFL (minimum score 79 iBT), IELTS (minimum score 6), PTE (minimum score 53). *Application deadline:* Applications are processed on a rolling basis. Application fee: $50. Electronic applications accepted. *Expenses: Tuition:* Full-time $1285; part-time $1285 per credit. *Required fees:* $215; $175 per unit. Tuition and fees vary according to course load, degree level and campus/location. *Financial support:* Career-related internships or fieldwork, Federal Work-Study, scholarships/grants, tuition waivers (full and partial), and unspecified assistantships available. Support available to part-time students. Financial award application deadline: 2/15; financial award applicants required to submit FAFSA. *Faculty research:* Accounting, economics, finance, management, marketing. *Unit head:* Dr. Jess Boronico, Dean, 516-686-7838, E-mail: som@nyit.edu. *Application contact:* Alice Dolitsky, Director, Graduate Admissions, 516-686-7520, Fax: 516-686-1116, E-mail: admissions@nyit.edu.
Website: http://www.nyit.edu/degrees/management_mba

Niagara University, Graduate Division of Business Administration, Niagara University, NY 14109. Offers accounting (MBA); business administration (MBA); finance (MBA, MS); financial planning (MBA); healthcare administration (MBA, MHA); human resources (MBA); international business (MBA); marketing (MBA); professional accountancy (MBA); strategic management (MBA); supply chain management (MBA). *Accreditation:* AACSB. *Program availability:* Part-time, evening/weekend, 100% online,

blended/hybrid learning. *Students:* 224 full-time (116 women), 56 part-time (22 women); includes 36 minority (9 Black or African American, non-Hispanic/Latino; 2 American Indian or Alaska Native, non-Hispanic/Latino; 6 Asian, non-Hispanic/Latino; 12 Hispanic/Latino; 7 Two or more races, non-Hispanic/Latino), 82 international. Average age 26. In 2018, 134 master's awarded. *Entrance requirements:* For master's, GMAT. Additional exam requirements/recommendations for international students: Required—TOEFL (minimum score 550 paper-based; 79 iBT), IELTS (minimum score 6). *Application deadline:* For fall admission, 8/1 for domestic students; for spring admission, 11/1 for domestic students. Applications are processed on a rolling basis. Electronic applications accepted. *Expenses:* Contact institution. *Financial support:* Research assistantships, teaching assistantships, career-related internships or fieldwork, Federal Work-Study, scholarships/grants, and unspecified assistantships available. Support available to part-time students. Financial award application deadline: 4/15; financial award applicants required to submit FAFSA. *Faculty research:* Capital flows, Federal Reserve policy, human resource management, public policy, issues in marketing, auctions, economics of information, risk and capital markets, management strategy, consumer behavior, Internet and social media marketing. *Unit head:* Dr. Paul Richardson, MBA Director/Chair of the Marketing Department, 716-286-8169, Fax: 716-286-8206, E-mail: mba@niagara.edu. *Application contact:* Evan Pierce, Associate Director for Graduate Recruitment, 716-286-8327, Fax: 716-286-8710, E-mail: epierce@niagara.edu. Website: http://mba.niagara.edu

North Carolina Agricultural and Technical State University, The Graduate College, College of Business and Economics, Greensboro, NC 27411. Offers accounting (MBA); business education (MAT); human resources management (MBA); supply chain systems (MBA).

North Carolina State University, Graduate School, Poole College of Management, Program in Business Administration, Raleigh, NC 27695. Offers biosciences management (MBA); entrepreneurship and technology commercialization (MBA); financial management (MBA); innovation management (MBA); marketing management (MBA); services management (MBA); supply chain management (MBA). *Accreditation:* AACSB. *Program availability:* Part-time. *Degree requirements:* For master's, thesis optional. *Entrance requirements:* For master's, GMAT, interview, 3 letters of recommendation. Additional exam requirements/recommendations for international students: Required—TOEFL (minimum score 600 paper-based; 100 iBT). Electronic applications accepted. *Faculty research:* Manufacturing strategy, information systems, technology commercialization, managing research and development, historical stock returns.

Norwich University, College of Graduate and Continuing Studies, Master of Business Administration Program, Northfield, VT 05663. Offers construction management (MBA); energy management (MBA); finance (MBA); logistics (MBA); organizational leadership (MBA); project management (MBA); supply chain management (MBA). *Accreditation:* ACBSP. *Program availability:* Evening/weekend, online only, mostly all online with a week-long residency requirement. *Degree requirements:* For master's, comprehensive exam. *Entrance requirements:* For master's, minimum undergraduate GPA of 2.75. Additional exam requirements/recommendations for international students: Required—TOEFL (minimum score 550 paper-based; 80 iBT), IELTS (minimum score 6.5). Electronic applications accepted. *Expenses:* Contact institution.

Nova Southeastern University, H. Wayne Huizenga College of Business and Entrepreneurship, Fort Lauderdale, FL 33314-7796. Offers accounting (M Acc); business (MBA); business intelligence/analytics (MBA); complex health systems (MBA); enterprise informatics (MBA); entrepreneurship (MBA); finance (MBA); human resource management (MBA); international business (MBA); management (MBA); marketing (MBA); process improvement (MBA); public administration (MPA); real estate development (MS); sport revenue generation (MBA); supply chain management (MBA). *Accreditation:* NASPAA. *Program availability:* Part-time, evening/weekend, 100% online, blended/hybrid learning. *Entrance requirements:* For master's, GMAT or GRE (depending on undergraduate GPA), official transcripts from all schools attended while in pursuit of bachelor's degree; minimum GPA of 2.5 from regionally-accredited institution. Additional exam requirements/recommendations for international students: Required—TOEFL (minimum score 550 paper-based; 79 iBT), IELTS (minimum score 6), PTE (minimum score 54). Electronic applications accepted. *Expenses:* Contact institution. *Faculty research:* Entrepreneurship and venture capital, ethics and social responsibility, global commerce and cultures, business process management.

Old Dominion University, Strome College of Business, Program in Maritime Trade and Supply Chain Management, Norfolk, VA 23529. Offers MS. *Program availability:* Part-time, evening/weekend. *Degree requirements:* For master's, capstone course. *Entrance requirements:* For master's, GRE or GMAT, bachelor's degree, official transcripts, two letters of recommendation, current resume, statement of professional goals. Additional exam requirements/recommendations for international students: Required—TOEFL (minimum score 550 paper-based; 79 iBT), IELTS (minimum score 6.5). Electronic applications accepted.

Penn State Harrisburg, Graduate School, School of Business Administration, Middletown, PA 17057. Offers accounting (MPAC, Certificate); business administration (MBA); information systems (MS); operations and supply chain management (Certificate). *Program availability:* Part-time, evening/weekend.

Polytechnic University of Puerto Rico, Miami Campus, Graduate School, Miami, FL 33166. Offers accounting (MBA); business administration (MBA); construction management (MEM); environmental management (MEM); finance (MBA); human resources management (MBA); logistics and supply chain management (MBA); management of international enterprises (MBA); manufacturing management (MEM); marketing management (MBA); project management (MBA). *Program availability:* Part-time, evening/weekend, online learning. *Entrance requirements:* For master's, minimum GPA of 3.0. Electronic applications accepted.

Portland State University, Graduate Studies, The School of Business, MS in Global Supply Chain Management Program, Portland, OR 97207-0751. Offers MS. *Program availability:* Part-time, online learning. *Entrance requirements:* For master's, minimum undergraduate GPA of 3.0; two professional references; unofficial transcript from each college or university attended; statement of purpose; resume. Additional exam requirements/recommendations for international students: Required—TOEFL (minimum score 550 paper-based; 80 iBT). Electronic applications accepted. *Expenses:* Contact institution.

Purdue University Global, School of Business, Davenport, IA 52807. Offers business administration (MBA); change leadership (MS); entrepreneurship (MBA); finance (MBA); health care management (MBA, MS); human resource (MBA); international business (MBA); management (MS); marketing (MBA); project management (MBA, MS); supply chain management and logistics (MBA, MS). *Accreditation:* ACBSP. *Program availability:* Part-time, evening/weekend, online learning. *Entrance requirements:* Additional exam requirements/recommendations for international students: Required—TOEFL (minimum score 550 paper-based; 80 iBT). Electronic applications accepted.

Quinnipiac University, School of Business, Program in Business Administration, Hamden, CT 06518-1940. Offers finance (MBA); health care management (MBA); supply chain management (MBA); JD/MBA. *Accreditation:* AACSB. *Program availability:*

Part-time, evening/weekend, 100% online, blended/hybrid learning. *Entrance requirements:* For master's, GMAT or GRE, minimum GPA of 3.0. Additional exam requirements/recommendations for international students: Required—TOEFL (minimum score 575 paper-based; 90 iBT), IELTS (minimum score 6.5). Electronic applications accepted. *Expenses:* Contact institution. *Faculty research:* Financial markets and investments, international business, supply chain management, health care management, corporate governance.

Rensselaer Polytechnic Institute, Graduate School, Lally School of Management, Program in Supply Chain Management, Troy, NY 12180-3590. Offers MS, MS/MBA. *Program availability:* Part-time. *Faculty:* 36 full-time (9 women), 5 part-time/adjunct (0 women). *Students:* 12 full-time (8 women), 4 part-time (2 women); includes 2 minority (both Hispanic/Latino), 9 international. Average age 23. 79 applicants, 61% accepted, 8 enrolled. In 2018, 14 master's awarded. *Entrance requirements:* For master's, GMAT or GRE, personal statement. Additional exam requirements/recommendations for international students: Required—TOEFL (minimum score 570 paper-based; 88 iBT), IELTS (minimum score 6.8), PTE (minimum score 60). *Application deadline:* For fall admission, 1/1 for domestic and international students. Applications are processed on a rolling basis. Application fee: $75. Electronic applications accepted. *Financial support:* Scholarships/grants available. Financial award application deadline: 1/1. *Unit head:* Dr. T. Ravichandran, Graduate Program Director, 518-276-6842, E-mail: ravit@rpi.edu. *Application contact:* Jarron Decker, Director of Graduate Admissions, 518-276-6216, Fax: 518-276-4072, E-mail: gradadmissions@rpi.edu. Website: https://lallyschool.rpi.edu/graduate-programs/ms-supplychainmanagement

Rutgers University–Newark, Rutgers Business School–Newark and New Brunswick, Doctoral Programs in Management, Newark, NJ 07102. Offers accounting (PhD); accounting information systems (PhD); economics (PhD); finance (PhD); individualized study (PhD); information technology (PhD); international business (PhD); management science (PhD); marketing science (PhD); organizational management (PhD); science, technology and management (PhD); supply chain management (PhD). *Degree requirements:* For doctorate, comprehensive exam, thesis/dissertation. *Entrance requirements:* For doctorate, GRE or GMAT. Additional exam requirements/recommendations for international students: Required—TOEFL (minimum score 550 paper-based; 79 iBT). Electronic applications accepted

St. Norbert College, Master of Business Administration Program, De Pere, WI 54115-2099. Offers business (MBA); health care (MBA); supply chain and manufacturing (MBA). *Program availability:* Part-time-only, evening/weekend. *Faculty:* 11 full-time (3 women), 10 part-time/adjunct (3 women). *Students:* 66 part-time (38 women); includes 6 minority (1 American Indian or Alaska Native, non-Hispanic/Latino; 2 Asian, non-Hispanic/Latino; 2 Hispanic/Latino; 1 Two or more races, non-Hispanic/Latino). Average age 33. 15 applicants, 100% accepted, 14 enrolled. In 2018, 31 master's awarded. *Entrance requirements:* For master's, official transcripts, letters of recommendation, professional resume, essay. *Application deadline:* For fall admission, 8/4 for domestic students; for winter admission, 12/15 for domestic students; for spring admission, 3/2 for domestic students; for summer admission, 4/20 for domestic students. Applications are processed on a rolling basis. Application fee: $50. Electronic applications accepted. *Expenses:* Tuition per credit $725; estimated total cost to complete 39 credits $28,275; technology fee per course $37.50; estimated cost of textbooks for entire program $1,500; application for graduation fee $100; audit-only course, per credit $375. *Financial support:* Federal Work-Study available. Financial award application deadline: 1/1; financial award applicants required to submit FAFSA. *Faculty research:* Urban segregation, religious identity, crisis decision-making, normative ethics, psychological effects of change on individuals and organizations. *Unit head:* Lisa Gray, Coordinator of MBA Program, 920-403-3449, E-mail: lisa.gray@snc.edu. *Application contact:* Brenda Busch, Associate Director of Graduate Recruitment, 920-403-3942, Fax: 920-403-4072, E-mail: brenda.busch@snc.edu. Website: https://schneiderschool.snc.edu/mba/

Santa Clara University, Leavey School of Business, Santa Clara, CA 95053. Offers business administration (MBA); business analytics (MS); finance (MS); information systems (MS); supply chain management and analytics (MS); JD/MBA. *Accreditation:* AACSB. *Program availability:* Part-time, online learning. *Faculty:* 101 full-time (32 women), 47 part-time/adjunct (15 women). *Students:* 487 full-time (278 women), 326 part-time (139 women); includes 295 minority (14 Black or African American, non-Hispanic/Latino; 207 Asian, non-Hispanic/Latino; 39 Hispanic/Latino; 35 Two or more races, non-Hispanic/Latino), 294 international. Average age 31. 694 applicants, 65% accepted, 281 enrolled. In 2018, 195 master's awarded. *Entrance requirements:* For master's, Varies based on program. Additional exam requirements/recommendations for international students: Required—TOEFL (minimum score 90 iBT). Application fee: $100 ($150 for international students). Electronic applications accepted. *Financial support:* In 2018–19, 192 students received support. Fellowships, Federal Work-Study, and scholarships/grants available. Support available to part-time students. Financial award applicants required to submit FAFSA. *Unit head:* Caryn Beck-Dudley, Dean, 408-554-4523, E-mail: cbeckdudley@scu.edu. *Application contact:* Caryn Beck-Dudley, Dean, 408-554-4523, E-mail: cbeckdudley@scu.edu. Website: http://www.scu.edu/business/

Seton Hall University, Stillman School of Business, Programs in Business Administration, South Orange, NJ 07079-2697. Offers accounting (MBA); entrepreneurial studies (Certificate); finance (MBA); financial decision making (Certificate); information technology management (MBA); international business (MBA); management (MBA); marketing (MBA); sport management (MBA); supply chain management (MBA, Certificate). *Program availability:* Part-time, evening/weekend. *Faculty:* 27 full-time (5 women), 18 part-time/adjunct (2 women). *Students:* 85 full-time (40 women), 363 part-time (147 women); includes 78 minority (22 Black or African American, non-Hispanic/Latino; 4 Asian, non-Hispanic/Latino; 18 Hispanic/Latino; 29 Native Hawaiian or other Pacific Islander, non-Hispanic/Latino; 5 Two or more races, non-Hispanic/Latino), 282 international. Average age 34. 483 applicants, 85% accepted, 302 enrolled. In 2018, 96 master's awarded. *Degree requirements:* For master's, 20 hours of community service (Social Responsibility Project). *Entrance requirements:* For master's, GMAT or CPA, GRE (waived based on work experience or advanced degree from AACSB institution), MS in business discipline, professional degree or designation (MD, JD, PhD, DVM, DDS, CPA, etc.), minimum undergraduate GPA of 3.0. Additional exam requirements/recommendations for international students: Required—TOEFL (minimum score 607 paper-based; 80 iBT), IELTS (minimum score 6), PTE. *Application deadline:* For fall admission, 5/31 priority date for domestic students, 4/30 priority date for international students; for spring admission, 10/31 priority date for domestic students, 9/30 priority date for international students; for summer admission, 3/31 priority date for domestic students. Applications are processed on a rolling basis. Application fee: $75. Electronic applications accepted. Application fee is waived when completed online. *Expenses:* Tuition is $1,305 per credit hour and the overall MBA is a 40 credit hour program. University fees are $115 per semester. The university also has a technology that is $125 per semester. *Financial support:* In 2018–19, 44 students received support, including 25 research assistantships with partial tuition reimbursements available (averaging $3,644 per year); career-related internships or fieldwork, scholarships/grants, and unspecified assistantships also available. Financial award application

deadline: 6/30; financial award applicants required to submit FAFSA. *Faculty research:* Sport, hedge funds, executive compensation, social media, legal studies. *Unit head:* Dr. Joyce Strawser, Dean, 973-761-9013, Fax: 973-761-9217, E-mail: joyce.strawser@shu.edu. *Application contact:* Alfred Ayoub, Director of Graduate Admissions, 973-761-9262, Fax: 973-761-9208, E-mail: alfred.ayoub@shu.edu.
Website: http://www.shu.edu/business/mba-programs.cfm

Shippensburg University of Pennsylvania, School of Graduate Studies, John L. Grove College of Business, Shippensburg, PA 17257-2299. Offers advanced studies in business (Certificate); advanced supply chain and logistics management (Certificate); business administration (MBA, DBA), including business administration (MBA), business analytics (MBA), finance (MBA), healthcare management (MBA), management information systems (MBA), supply chain management (MBA); finance (Certificate); health care management (Certificate); management information systems (Certificate). *Accreditation:* AACSB. *Program availability:* Part-time, evening/weekend, 100% online, blended/hybrid learning. *Faculty:* 20 full-time (4 women), 2 part-time/adjunct (0 women). *Students:* 31 full-time (14 women), 174 part-time (67 women); includes 33 minority (17 Black or African American, non-Hispanic/Latino; 6 Asian, non-Hispanic/Latino; 7 Hispanic/Latino; 3 Two or more races, non-Hispanic/Latino), 13 international. Average age 33. 149 applicants, 61% accepted, 60 enrolled. In 2018, 104 master's, 1 other advanced degree awarded. *Degree requirements:* For master's, comprehensive exam (for some programs), thesis optional, practicum capstone course; for doctorate, comprehensive exam, thesis/dissertation, comprehensive exam dissertation. *Entrance requirements:* For master's, GMAT (minimum score 450 if less than 5 years of mid-level experience, including management experience), current resume; relevant work/classroom experience; 500-word statement of purpose; prerequisites of quantitative analysis, computer usage, and oral and written communications; laptop computer; for doctorate, GMAT (minimum score of 600 if less than 5 years of substantive professional or teaching experience), 2 letters of recommendation from professionals in academia or industry; 2-3 page personal and professional statement; interview; resume. Additional exam requirements/recommendations for international students: Required—TOEFL (minimum score 550 paper-based; 68 iBT), IELTS (minimum score 6), TOEFL (minimum score 550 paper-based, 68 iBT) or IELTS (minimum score 6). *Application deadline:* For fall admission, 4/30 for international students; for spring admission, 9/30 for international students. Applications are processed on a rolling basis. Application fee: $45. Electronic applications accepted. *Expenses:* Tuition, state resident: part-time $516 per credit. Tuition, nonresident: part-time $750 per credit. *Required fees:* $149 per credit. *Financial support:* In 2018–19, 15 students received support. Career-related internships or fieldwork, scholarships/grants, unspecified assistantships, and resident hall director and student payroll positions available. Support available to part-time students. Financial award application deadline: 3/1; financial award applicants required to submit FAFSA. *Unit head:* Dr. John G. Kooti, Dean of the College of Business, 717-477-1435, Fax: 717-477-4003, E-mail: jgkooti@ship.edu. *Application contact:* Maya T. Mapp, Director of Admissions, 717-477-1231, Fax: 717-477-4016, E-mail: mtmapp@ship.edu.
Website: http://www.ship.edu/business

Southern Arkansas University–Magnolia, School of Graduate Studies, Magnolia, AR 71753. Offers agriculture (MS); business administration (MBA), including agribusiness, social entrepreneurship, supply chain management; clinical and mental health counseling (MS); computer and information sciences (MS), including cyber security and privacy, data science, information technology; gifted and talented (M Ed), including curriculum and instruction, educational administration and supervision, gifted and talented P-8/7-12, instructional specialist P-4; higher, adult and lifelong education (M Ed); kinesiology (M Ed), including coaching; library media and information specialist (M Ed); public administration (MPA); school counseling K-12 (M Ed); student affairs and college counseling (M Ed); teaching (MAT). *Accreditation:* NCATE. *Program availability:* Part-time, 100% online, blended/hybrid learning. *Faculty:* 36 full-time (21 women), 32 part-time/adjunct (15 women). *Students:* 164 full-time (77 women), 762 part-time (510 women); includes 192 minority (163 Black or African American, non-Hispanic/Latino; 7 American Indian or Alaska Native, non-Hispanic/Latino; 13 Asian, non-Hispanic/Latino; 1 Hispanic/Latino; 8 Two or more races, non-Hispanic/Latino), 213 international. Average age 28. 363 applicants, 100% accepted, 237 enrolled. In 2018, 716 master's awarded. *Degree requirements:* For master's, comprehensive exam (for some programs), thesis optional. *Entrance requirements:* For master's, GRE, MAT or GMAT, minimum GPA of 2.5. Additional exam requirements/recommendations for international students: Required—TOEFL (minimum score 550 paper-based), IELTS (minimum score 6). *Application deadline:* For fall admission, 8/1 for domestic and international students; for spring admission, 12/1 for domestic students, 11/15 for international students; for summer admission, 4/1 for domestic students, 5/10 for international students. Applications are processed on a rolling basis. Application fee: $25 ($90 for international students). Electronic applications accepted. *Expenses: Tuition, area resident:* Full-time $5130; part-time $3420 per year. Tuition, state resident: full-time $5130; part-time $3420 per year. Tuition, nonresident: full-time $7866; part-time $5244 per year. *International tuition:* $7866 full-time. *Required fees:* $1052; $710 per unit. Tuition and fees vary according to course load. *Financial support:* Career-related internships or fieldwork, Federal Work-Study, scholarships/grants, tuition waivers (full), and unspecified assistantships available. Financial award applicants required to submit FAFSA. *Faculty research:* Alternative certification for teachers, supervision of instruction, instructional leadership, counseling. *Unit head:* Dr. Kim Bloss, Dean, School of Graduate Studies, 870-235-4150, Fax: 870-235-5227, E-mail: kkbloss@saumag.edu. *Application contact:* Talia Jett, Admissions Coordinator, 870-2355450, Fax: 870-235-5227, E-mail: taliajett@saumag.edu.
Website: http://www.saumag.edu/graduate

Southern New Hampshire University, School of Business, Manchester, NH 03106-1045. Offers accounting (MBA, Graduate Certificate); accounting finance (MS); accounting/auditing (MS); accounting/forensic accounting (MS); accounting/management accounting (MS); accounting/taxation (MS); applied economics (MS); athletic administration (MBA, Graduate Certificate); business administration (IMBA, Certificate), including business information systems (Certificate), human resource management (Certificate); business analytics (MBA); business intelligence (MBA); communication (MA), including new media and marketing, public relations; community economic development (MBA); criminal justice (MBA); data analytics (MS); economics (MBA); engineering management (MBA); entrepreneurship (MBA); finance (MBA, MS, Graduate Certificate); finance/corporate finance (MS); finance/investments (MS); forensic accounting (MBA); forensic accounting and fraud examination (Graduate Certificate); healthcare informatics (MBA); healthcare management (MBA); human resource management (MS); human resources (MBA); information technology (MS); information technology management (MBA); international business (PhD); Internet marketing (MBA); leadership (MBA); leadership of nonprofit organizations (Graduate Certificate); management (MS); marketing (MBA, MS, Graduate Certificate); music business (MBA); operations and project management (MS); operations and supply chain management (MBA, Graduate Certificate); organizational leadership (MS); project management (MBA, Graduate Certificate); public administration (MBA, Graduate Certificate); quantitative analysis (MBA); Six Sigma (Graduate Certificate); Six Sigma quality (MBA); social media marketing (MBA, Graduate Certificate); sport management (MBA, MS, Graduate Certificate); sustainability and environmental compliance (MBA); MBA/Certificate. *Accreditation:* ACBSP. *Program availability:* Part-time, evening/weekend, online learning. Terminal master's awarded for partial completion of doctoral program. *Degree requirements:* For master's, one foreign language, comprehensive exam (for some programs), thesis or alternative; for doctorate, one foreign language, comprehensive exam, thesis/dissertation. *Entrance requirements:* For master's, minimum GPA of 2.5; for doctorate, GMAT. Additional exam requirements/recommendations for international students: Required—TOEFL (minimum score 500 paper-based). Electronic applications accepted.

Strayer University, Graduate Studies, Washington, DC 20005-2603. Offers accounting (MS); acquisition (MBA); business administration (MBA); communications technology (MS); educational management (M Ed); finance (MBA); health services administration (MHSA); hospitality and tourism management (MBA); human resource management (MBA); information systems (MS), including computer security management, decision support system management, enterprise resource management, network management, software engineering management, systems development management; management (MBA); management information systems (MS); marketing (MBA); professional accounting (MS), including accounting information systems, controllership, taxation; public administration (MPA); supply chain management (MBA); technology in education (M Ed). Programs also offered at campus locations in Birmingham, AL; Chamblee, GA; Cobb County, GA; Morrow, GA; White Marsh, MD; Charleston, SC; Columbia, SC; Greensboro, NC; Greenville, SC; Lexington, KY; Louisville, KY; Nashville, TN; North Raleigh, NC; Washington, DC. *Accreditation:* ACBSP. *Program availability:* Part-time, evening/weekend, online learning. *Degree requirements:* For master's, thesis. *Entrance requirements:* For master's, GMAT, GRE General Test, bachelor's degree from an accredited college or university, minimum undergraduate GPA of 2.75. Electronic applications accepted.

Suffolk University, Sawyer Business School, Master of Business Administration Program, Boston, MA 02108-2770. Offers accounting (MBA); entrepreneurship (MBA); executive business administration (EMBA); finance (MBA); global business administration (GMBA); health administration (MBA); international business (MBA); marketing (MBA); nonprofit management (MBA); organizational behavior (MBA); strategic management (MBA); supply chain management (MBA); taxation (MBA); JD/MBA; MBA/MHA; MBA/MSA; MBA/MSF; MBA/MST. *Accreditation:* AACSB. *Program availability:* Part-time, evening/weekend, 100% online. *Faculty:* 18 full-time (5 women), 5 part-time/adjunct (0 women). *Students:* 79 full-time (46 women), 193 part-time (107 women); includes 69 minority (17 Black or African American, non-Hispanic/Latino; 18 Asian, non-Hispanic/Latino; 28 Hispanic/Latino; 6 Two or more races, non-Hispanic/Latino), 40 international. Average age 30. 274 applicants, 67% accepted, 83 enrolled. In 2018, 125 master's awarded. *Entrance requirements:* For master's, GMAT, minimum undergraduate GPA of 2.75 (MBA), 5 years of managerial experience (EMBA). Additional exam requirements/recommendations for international students: Required—TOEFL (minimum score 550 paper-based; 80 iBT). *Application deadline:* For fall admission, 3/15 priority date for domestic students, 10/15 priority date for international students; for spring admission, 10/15 priority date for domestic and international students. Applications are processed on a rolling basis. Application fee: $50. Electronic applications accepted. *Expenses:* Contact institution. *Financial support:* In 2018–19, 170 students received support, including 4 fellowships (averaging $2,906 per year); career-related internships or fieldwork, Federal Work-Study, institutionally sponsored loans, and scholarships/grants also available. Support available to part-time students. Financial award application deadline: 4/1; financial award applicants required to submit FAFSA. *Faculty research:* Foreign investments; career strategies and boundaryless careers; corporate ethics codes; interest rates, inflation, and growth options; innovation and product development performance. *Unit head:* Jodi Detjen, Director of MBA Programs, 617-573-8306, E-mail: jdetjen@suffolk.edu. *Application contact:* Mara Marzocchi, Associate Director of Graduate Admissions, 617-573-8302, Fax: 617-305-1733, E-mail: grad.admission@suffolk.edu.
Website: http://www.suffolk.edu/mba

Syracuse University, Martin J. Whitman School of Management, Master of Business Administration Program, Syracuse, NY 13244. Offers accounting (MBA); business analytics (MBA); entrepreneurship (MBA); marketing management (MBA); real estate (MBA); supply chain management (MBA); JD/MBA. *Program availability:* Part-time, 100% online. *Students:* Average age 32. 1,086 applicants, 73% accepted, 516 enrolled. In 2018, 84 master's awarded. *Entrance requirements:* For master's, GMAT or GRE, resume, essay, 5-minute video interview, two letters of recommendation, transcripts (unofficial). Additional exam requirements/recommendations for international students: Required—TOEFL (minimum score 100 iBT), IELTS (minimum score 7), PTE (minimum score 68). *Application deadline:* For fall admission, 11/30 for domestic students, 11/30 priority date for international students; for winter admission, 1/1 for domestic students, 1/1 priority date for international students; for spring admission, 2/15 for domestic and international students; for summer admission, 4/19 for domestic students. Application fee: $75. Electronic applications accepted. *Expenses:* Contact institution. *Financial support:* In 2018–19, 22 students received support. Merit scholarships available. Financial award application deadline: 2/15. *Faculty research:* Data analysis, economics of international business, financial markets and institutions, operations management, supply chain management. *Unit head:* Dr. Alexander McKelvie, Associate Dean for Undergraduate and Full-time Master's Education, 315-443-7252, E-mail: mckelvie@syr.edu. *Application contact:* Shri Ramakrishnan, Assistant Director, Graduate Recruitment, 315-443-3497, Fax: 315-443-9517, E-mail: busgrad@syr.edu.
Website: http://whitman.syr.edu/ftmba/

Syracuse University, Martin J. Whitman School of Management, MS Program in Supply Chain Management, Syracuse, NY 13244. Offers MS. *Students:* Average age 22. 72 applicants, 36% accepted, 3 enrolled. In 2018, 5 master's awarded. *Entrance requirements:* For master's, GMAT or GRE, resume, essay, 5-minute video interview, two letters of recommendation, transcripts (unofficial). Additional exam requirements/recommendations for international students: Required—TOEFL (minimum score 100 iBT), IELTS (minimum score 7), PTE (minimum score 68), GMAT or GRE. *Application deadline:* For fall admission, 11/30 for domestic students, 11/30 priority date for international students; for winter admission, 1/1 for domestic students, 1/1 priority date for international students; for spring admission, 2/15 for domestic and international students; for summer admission, 4/19 for domestic students. Application fee: $75. Electronic applications accepted. *Expenses:* Contact institution. *Financial support:* In 2018–19, 3 students received support. Merit scholarships available. Financial award application deadline: 2/15. *Faculty research:* Supply chain management, logistics management, management information systems, risk sharing, buyer-seller alliances. *Unit head:* Fred Easton, Director, Operations Management/Professor of Supply Chain Management, 315-443-3463, E-mail: ffeaston@syr.edu. *Application contact:* Shri Ramakrishnan, Assistant Director, Graduate Recruitment, 315-443-3497, Fax: 315-443-9517, E-mail: sramak01@syr.edu.
Website: http://whitman.syr.edu/Academics/Marketing/SupplyChain/

Towson University, College of Business and Economics, Program in e-Business and Technology Management, Towson, MD 21252-0001. Offers project, program and portfolio management (Postbaccalaureate Certificate); supply chain management (MS). *Entrance requirements:* For master's and Postbaccalaureate Certificate, GRE or GMAT,

bachelor's degree in relevant field and/or three years of post-bachelor's experience working in supply chain related areas; minimum cumulative GPA of 3.0; resume; 2 reference letters. Additional exam requirements/recommendations for international students: Required—TOEFL (minimum score 550 paper-based). Electronic applications accepted. *Expenses: Tuition, area resident:* Full-time $9196; part-time $418 per unit. Tuition, state resident: full-time $9196; part-time $418 per unit. Tuition, nonresident: full-time $19,030; part-time $865 per unit. *International tuition:* $19,030 full-time. *Required fees:* $3102; $141 per year. $423 per term. Tuition and fees vary according to campus/location and program.

University at Buffalo, the State University of New York, Graduate School, School of Management, Buffalo, NY 14260. Offers accounting (MS); analytics (MBA); business administration (PMBA); consulting (MBA); finance (MBA, MS), including financial risk management (MS); quantitative finance (MS); healthcare (MBA); information assurance (MBA); information systems (MBA); international management (MBA); management (EMBA, PhD); management information systems (MS); marketing (MBA); supply chain and operations (MBA); supply chains and operations management (MS); Au D/MBA; DDS/MBA; JD/MBA; M Arch/MBA; MD/MBA; MPH/MBA; MSW/MBA; Pharm D/MBA. *Accreditation:* AACSB. *Program availability:* Part-time, evening/weekend. *Degree requirements:* For master's, capstone courses or projects; for doctorate, comprehensive exam, thesis/dissertation. *Entrance requirements:* For master's, GMAT (for MS in accounting, finance); GRE or GMAT (for MBA, MS in management information systems, supply chains and operations management), essays, letters of recommendation; for doctorate, GMAT or GRE, essays, writing sample, letters of recommendation. Additional exam requirements/recommendations for international students: Required—TOEFL (minimum score 95 iBT) or IELTS (minimum score 6.5); Recommended—TSE (minimum score 73). Electronic applications accepted. *Expenses:* Contact institution. *Faculty research:* Data analytics, accounting and law, rate finance, consumer behavior, supply chain logistics, leadership and team effectiveness.

The University of Akron, Graduate School, College of Business Administration, Department of Management, Program in Supply Chain Management, Akron, OH 44325. Offers MBA. *Program availability:* Part-time. *Entrance requirements:* For master's, GMAT, GRE, MCAT, LSAT, PCAT, or CAT, minimum GPA of 3.0 (preferred), two letters of recommendation, resume, statement of purpose. Additional exam requirements/recommendations for international students: Required—TOEFL (minimum score 79 iBT), IELTS (minimum score 6.5). Electronic applications accepted.

The University of Alabama in Huntsville, School of Graduate Studies, College of Business Administration, Programs in Business and Management, Huntsville, AL 35899. Offers business analytics (MSMS); federal contracting and procurement management (Certificate); human resource management (MSM); management (MBA), including acquisition management, entrepreneurship, federal contract accounting, finance, human resource management, logistics and supply chain management, marketing, project management; supply chain management (Certificate); technology and innovation management (Certificate). *Accreditation:* AACSB. *Program availability:* Part-time. *Faculty:* 8 full-time (3 women). *Students:* 57 full-time (25 women), 152 part-time (76 women); includes 37 minority (20 Black or African American, non-Hispanic/Latino; 2 American Indian or Alaska Native, non-Hispanic/Latino; 6 Asian, non-Hispanic/Latino; 8 Hispanic/Latino; 1 Two or more races, non-Hispanic/Latino), 24 international. Average age 33. 178 applicants, 80% accepted, 84 enrolled. In 2018, 96 master's, 1 other advanced degree awarded. *Degree requirements:* For master's, comprehensive exam, thesis or alternative. *Entrance requirements:* For master's, GMAT (minimum score 500), minimum AACSB index of 1080. Additional exam requirements/recommendations for international students: Required—TOEFL (minimum score 550 paper-based; 80 iBT), IELTS (minimum score 6.5). *Application deadline:* For fall admission, 7/15 priority date for domestic students, 4/1 priority date for international students; for spring admission, 11/30 priority date for domestic students, 9/1 priority date for international students. Applications are processed on a rolling basis. Application fee: $50. Electronic applications accepted. *Expenses: Tuition, area resident:* Full-time $10,632; part-time $412 per credit hour. Tuition, state resident: full-time $10,632. Tuition, nonresident: full-time $23,604; part-time $412 per credit hour. *Required fees:* $582; $582. Tuition and fees vary according to course load and program. *Financial support:* In 2018–19, 15 students received support, including 15 teaching assistantships with full tuition reimbursements available (averaging $4,871 per year); research assistantships with full tuition reimbursements available, career-related internships or fieldwork, Federal Work-Study, institutionally sponsored loans, scholarships/grants, health care benefits, tuition waivers (full and partial), and unspecified assistantships also available. Support available to part-time students. Financial award application deadline: 4/1; financial award applicants required to submit FAFSA. *Faculty research:* Supply chain management, management of research and development, international marketing and branding, organizational behavior and human resource management, social networks and computational economics. *Unit head:* Dr. Fan Tseng, Chair, 256-824-6804, Fax: 256-824-6328, E-mail: fan.tseng@uah.edu. *Application contact:* Jennifer Pettitt, Director of Advising, 256-824-6681, Fax: 256-824-7571, E-mail: jennifer.pettitt@uah.edu.

The University of Alabama in Huntsville, School of Graduate Studies, College of Business Administration, Programs in Information Systems, Huntsville, AL 35899. Offers cybersecurity (MS, Certificate); enterprise resource planning (Certificate); information systems (MSIS); supply chain and logistics management (MS); supply chain management (Certificate). *Program availability:* Part-time. *Faculty:* 4 full-time. *Students:* 33 full-time (9 women), 89 part-time (34 women); includes 23 minority (13 Black or African American, non-Hispanic/Latino; 3 Asian, non-Hispanic/Latino; 5 Hispanic/Latino; 2 Two or more races, non-Hispanic/Latino), 3 international. Average age 35. 117 applicants, 69% accepted, 46 enrolled. In 2018, 39 master's, 3 other advanced degrees awarded. *Degree requirements:* For master's, comprehensive exam, thesis or alternative. *Entrance requirements:* For master's, GMAT (minimum score 500), minimum AACSB index of 1080. Additional exam requirements/recommendations for international students: Required—TOEFL (minimum score 550 paper-based; 80 iBT), IELTS (minimum score 6.5). *Application deadline:* For fall admission, 7/15 priority date for domestic students, 4/1 priority date for international students; for spring admission, 11/30 priority date for domestic students, 9/1 priority date for international students. Applications are processed on a rolling basis. Application fee: $50. Electronic applications accepted. *Expenses: Tuition, area resident:* Full-time $10,632; part-time $412 per credit hour. Tuition, state resident: full-time $10,632. Tuition, nonresident: full-time $23,604; part-time $412 per credit hour. *Required fees:* $582; $582. Tuition and fees vary according to course load and program. *Financial support:* Research assistantships with full tuition reimbursements, teaching assistantships with full tuition reimbursements, career-related internships or fieldwork, Federal Work-Study, institutionally sponsored loans, scholarships/grants, health care benefits, and unspecified assistantships available. Support available to part-time students. Financial award application deadline: 4/1; financial award applicants required to submit FAFSA. *Faculty research:* Supply chain information systems, information assurance and security, databases and conceptual schema, workflow management, inter-organizational information sharing. *Unit head:* Dr. Fan Tseng, Chair, 256-824-6804, Fax: 256-824-6328, E-mail: fan.tseng@uah.edu. *Application contact:* Jennifer Pettitt, Director of Advising, 256-824-6681, Fax: 256-824-7571, E-mail: jennifer.pettitt@uah.edu.

University of Dallas, Satish and Yasmin Gupta College of Business, Irving, TX 75062. Offers accounting (MBA, MS); business administration (DBA); business analytics (MS); business management (MBA); corporate finance (MBA); cybersecurity (MS); finance (MS); financial services (MBA); global business (MBA, MS); health services management (MBA); human resource management (MBA); information and technology management (MS); information assurance (MBA); information technology (MBA); information technology service management (MBA); marketing management (MBA); organization development (MBA); project management (MBA); sports and entertainment management (MBA); strategic leadership (MBA); supply chain management (MBA). *Accreditation:* AACSB. *Program availability:* Part-time, evening/weekend, 100% online. *Students:* 147 full-time (56 women), 584 part-time (232 women); includes 402 minority (204 Black or African American, non-Hispanic/Latino; 95 Asian, non-Hispanic/Latino; 92 Hispanic/Latino; 2 Native Hawaiian or other Pacific Islander, non-Hispanic/Latino; 9 Two or more races, non-Hispanic/Latino), 113 international. Average age 34. 992 applicants, 30% accepted, 157 enrolled. In 2018, 336 master's, 5 doctorates awarded. *Degree requirements:* For doctorate, thesis/dissertation. *Entrance requirements:* For master's and doctorate, U.S. bachelor's degree with a minimum cumulative GPA of 2.0 from a regionally accredited college or university (or comparable foreign degree); minimum 3.0 GPA in any graduate-level coursework completed; good academic standing with all colleges attended. Additional exam requirements/recommendations for international students: Required—TOEFL (minimum score 80 iBT), IELTS (minimum score 6.5), PTE (minimum score 67). *Application deadline:* Applications are processed on a rolling basis. Application fee: $50. Electronic applications accepted. *Expenses:* $1250 per credit hour. *Financial support:* In 2018–19, 291 students received support. Research assistantships, teaching assistantships, scholarships/grants, and unspecified assistantships available. Support available to part-time students. Financial award application deadline: 2/15; financial award applicants required to submit FAFSA. *Unit head:* Brett J.L. Landry, Dean, 972-721-5356, E-mail: blandry@udallas.edu. *Application contact:* Breonna Collins, Director, Graduate Admissions, 972-7215304, E-mail: bcollins@udallas.edu. Website: http://www.udallas.edu/cob/

University of Florida, Graduate School, Warrington College of Business Administration, Hough Graduate School of Business, Department of Information Systems and Operations Management, Gainesville, FL 32611. Offers information systems and operations management (PhD); supply chain management (Certificate). Terminal master's awarded for partial completion of doctoral program. *Degree requirements:* For doctorate, thesis/dissertation. *Entrance requirements:* For master's, GMAT or GRE General Test, minimum GPA of 3.0; for doctorate, GMAT (minimum score 650) or GRE General Test, minimum GPA of 3.0. Additional exam requirements/recommendations for international students: Required—TOEFL (minimum score 550 paper-based; 80 iBT), IELTS (minimum score 6). *Faculty research:* Expert systems, nonconvex optimization, manufacturing management, production and operation management, telecommunication.

University of Houston, College of Technology, Department of Information and Logistics Technology, Houston, TX 77204. Offers information security (MS); supply chain and logistics technology (MS); technology project management (MS). *Program availability:* Part-time. *Degree requirements:* For master's, project or thesis (most programs). *Entrance requirements:* For master's, GMAT. Additional exam requirements/recommendations for international students: Required—TOEFL (minimum score 550 paper-based; 79 iBT). Electronic applications accepted.

University of Houston–Downtown, Marilyn Davies College of Business, MBA Program, Houston, TX 77002. Offers accounting (MBA); finance (MBA); human resource management (MBA); international business (MBA); investment management (MBA); leadership (MBA); project management and process improvement (MBA); sales management and business development (MBA); supply chain management (MBA). *Accreditation:* AACSB. *Program availability:* Part-time, evening/weekend. *Entrance requirements:* For master's, GMAT, two letters of recommendation from professional references, personal statement, resume. Additional exam requirements/recommendations for international students: Required—TOEFL (minimum score 81 iBT). Electronic applications accepted. *Expenses:* Contact institution.

The University of Kansas, Graduate Studies, School of Business, Program in Business, Lawrence, KS 66045. Offers business and organizational leadership (MS); decision sciences and supply chain management (PhD); finance (PhD); human resources management (PhD); marketing (PhD); organizational behavior (PhD); strategic management (PhD); supply chain management and logistics (MS). *Accreditation:* AACSB. *Program availability:* Part-time. *Students:* 69 full-time (20 women), 150 part-time (62 women); includes 42 minority (14 Black or African American, non-Hispanic/Latino; 2 American Indian or Alaska Native, non-Hispanic/Latino; 6 Asian, non-Hispanic/Latino; 7 Hispanic/Latino; 13 Two or more races, non-Hispanic/Latino), 24 international. Average age 32. 306 applicants, 51% accepted, 132 enrolled. In 2018, 22 master's, 1 doctorate awarded. *Entrance requirements:* For master's, GMAT, official transcript, three letters of recommendation, resume, statement of purpose; for doctorate, GMAT or GRE, official transcript, three letters of recommendation, resume, statement of purpose. Additional exam requirements/recommendations for international students: Required—TOEFL, IELTS. *Application deadline:* For fall admission, 1/10 for domestic and international students. Application fee: $65 ($85 for international students). Electronic applications accepted. *Financial support:* Fellowships, research assistantships, teaching assistantships, scholarships/grants, health care benefits, tuition waivers (full), and unspecified assistantships available. Financial award application deadline: 1/10. *Faculty research:* Strategic human resource management, business ethics, organizational theory/behavior, corporate strategy, international business, supply chain management, Bayesian networks, game theory, decision analysis and time/series analysis, pricing, consumer effects, advertising and emotion. *Unit head:* Charly Edmonds, Director, 785-864-3841, E-mail: cedmonds@ku.edu. *Application contact:* Andrea Noltner, Graduate Admission Contact, 785-864-7556, E-mail: anoltner@ku.edu. Website: http://www.business.ku.edu/

University of La Verne, College of Business and Public Management, Graduate Programs in Business Administration, La Verne, CA 91750-4443. Offers accounting (MBA, MBA-EP); finance (MBA, MBA-EP); health services management (MBA); information technology (MBA, MBA-EP); international business (MBA, MBA-EP); management and leadership (MBA, MBA-EP); marketing (MBA, MBA-EP); supply chain management (MBA, MBA-EP). *Program availability:* Part-time, evening/weekend. *Entrance requirements:* For master's, GMAT, MAT, or GRE, minimum undergraduate GPA of 3.0, 2 letters of recommendation, resume, statement of purpose. Additional exam requirements/recommendations for international students: Required—TOEFL (minimum score 550 paper-based; 85 iBT).

University of La Verne, Regional and Online Campuses, Graduate Programs, Inland Empire Campus, Ontario, CA 91730. Offers business administration (MBA, MBA-EP), including accounting (MBA), finance (MBA), health services management (MBA-EP), information technology (MBA-EP), international business (MBA), managed care (MBA), management and leadership (MBA-EP), marketing (MBA-EP), supply chain management (MBA); leadership and management (MS), including human resource management, nonprofit management, organizational development. *Program availability:* Part-time, evening/weekend. *Expenses:* Contact institution.

Supply Chain Management

University of Louisville, J. B. Speed School of Engineering, Department of Industrial Engineering, Louisville, KY 40292-0001. Offers engineering management (M Eng); industrial engineering (M Eng, MS, PhD); logistics and distribution (Certificate). *Accreditation:* ABET (one or more programs are accredited). *Program availability:* 100% online. *Faculty:* 9 full-time (4 women), 8 part-time/adjunct (2 women). *Students:* 64 full-time (22 women), 147 part-time (35 women); includes 32 minority (13 Black or African American, non-Hispanic/Latino; 9 Asian, non-Hispanic/Latino; 6 Hispanic/Latino; 4 Two or more races, non-Hispanic/Latino), 78 international. Average age 31. 98 applicants, 66% accepted, 53 enrolled. In 2018, 30 master's, 3 doctorates awarded. Terminal master's awarded for partial completion of doctoral program. *Degree requirements:* For master's and Certificate, thesis optional; for doctorate, comprehensive exam, thesis/dissertation. *Entrance requirements:* For master's and doctorate, GRE General Test, two letters of recommendation, official transcripts. Additional exam requirements/recommendations for international students: Required—TOEFL (minimum score 550 paper-based; 80 iBT), IELTS (minimum score 6.5). *Application deadline:* For fall admission, 5/1 priority date for domestic and international students; for spring admission, 11/1 priority date for domestic and international students; for summer admission, 3/1 priority date for domestic and international students. Applications are processed on a rolling basis. Application fee: $65. Electronic applications accepted. *Expenses:* Tuition, area resident: Full-time $6500; part-time $723 per credit hour. Tuition, state resident: full-time $6500. Tuition, nonresident: full-time $13,557; part-time $1507 per credit hour. Tuition and fees vary according to course load and program. *Financial support:* In 2018–19, 38 students received support. Fellowships, research assistantships, teaching assistantships, scholarships/grants, health care benefits, and tuition waivers (full) available. Financial award application deadline: 1/1; financial award applicants required to submit FAFSA. *Faculty research:* Quality and Reliability Assurance, Process Monitoring and Diagnostics, Production Systems Design, Supply Chain Risk Management, Decision Support Systems. *Total annual research expenditures:* $620,986. *Unit head:* Dr. Suraj M. Alexander, Chair, 502-852-6342, Fax: 502-852-5633, E-mail: suraj.alexander@louisville.edu. *Application contact:* Lihui Bai, Director of Graduate Studies, 502-852-1416, E-mail: lihui.bai@louisville.edu. Website: http://www.louisville.edu/speed/industrial/

The University of Manchester, Alliance Manchester Business School, M15 6PB, United Kingdom. Offers accounting and finance (M Sc); business (M Ent); business analysis and strategic management (M Sc); business analytics: operational research and risk analysis (M Sc); business psychology (M Sc); corporate communications and reputation management (M Sc); finance (M Sc); finance and business economics (M Sc); human resource management and industrial relations (M Sc); innovation management and entrepreneurship (M Sc); international business and management (M Sc); international human resource management and comparative industrial relations (M Sc); management (M Sc); marketing (M Sc); operations, project and supply chain management (M Sc); organizational psychology (M Sc); quantitative finance (M Sc). *Entrance requirements:* For master's, UK 2:1 honours degree or overseas equivalent. Additional exam requirements/recommendations for international students: Required—TOEFL (minimum score 100 iBT), IELTS (minimum score 7), PTE. Electronic applications accepted. *Faculty research:* Accounting and finance, management sciences and marketing, people management and organization, innovation management and policy, decision sciences.

University of Memphis, Graduate School, Fogelman College of Business and Economics, Program in Business Administration, Memphis, TN 38152. Offers accounting (MBA, PhD); business administration (IMBA); economics (PhD); executive business administration (MBA); finance (PhD); management (PhD); marketing (MS); marketing and supply chain management (PhD); real estate development (MS); JD/MBA. *Accreditation:* AACSB. *Students:* 189 full-time (96 women), 364 part-time (151 women); includes 178 minority (89 Black or African American, non-Hispanic/Latino; 1 American Indian or Alaska Native, non-Hispanic/Latino; 68 Asian, non-Hispanic/Latino; 12 Hispanic/Latino; 8 Two or more races, non-Hispanic/Latino), 102 international. Average age 32. 298 applicants, 72% accepted, 139 enrolled. In 2018, 200 master's, 3 doctorates awarded. *Degree requirements:* For master's, comprehensive exam; for doctorate, comprehensive exam, thesis/dissertation. *Entrance requirements:* For master's, GMAT, resume; for doctorate, GMAT, interview, minimum GPA of 3.4, resume, letter of recommendation. Additional exam requirements/recommendations for international students: Required—TOEFL (minimum score 550 paper-based). *Application deadline:* For fall admission, 8/1 for domestic students; for spring admission, 12/1 for domestic students. Application fee: $35 ($60 for international students). *Expenses:* Tuition, area resident: Full-time $10,240; part-time $503 per credit hour. Tuition, state resident: full-time $10,464. Tuition, nonresident: full-time $20,224; part-time $991 per credit hour. *Required fees:* $850; $106 per credit hour. *Financial support:* Research assistantships with full tuition reimbursements, teaching assistantships with full tuition reimbursements, career-related internships or fieldwork, Federal Work-Study, scholarships/grants, and unspecified assistantships available. Financial award application deadline: 2/15; financial award applicants required to submit FAFSA. *Faculty research:* Competitive business strategy, finance microstructures, supply chain management innovations, health care economics, litigation risks and corporate audits. *Unit head:* Dr. Balaji Krishnan, Director, MBA Programs, 901-678-2786, E-mail: krishnan@memphis.edu. *Application contact:* Dr. Balaji Krishnan, Director, MBA Programs, 901-678-2786, E-mail: krishnan@memphis.edu. Website: https://www.memphis.edu/mba/index.php

University of Michigan, Ross School of Business, Ann Arbor, MI 48109-1234. Offers accounting (M Acc); business (MBA); business administration (PhD); supply chain management (MSCM); JD/MBA; MBA/M Arch; MBA/M Eng; MBA/MA; MBA/MEM; MBA/MHSA; MBA/MM; MBA/MPP; MBA/MS; MBA/MSE; MBA/MSI; MBA/MSW; MBA/MUP; MD/MBA; MHSA/MBA. *Accreditation:* AACSB. *Program availability:* Part-time, evening/weekend. *Degree requirements:* For doctorate, comprehensive exam, thesis/dissertation, oral defense of dissertation, preliminary exam. *Entrance requirements:* For master's, GMAT or GRE, completion of equivalent of four-year U.S. bachelor's degree, two letters of recommendation, essays, resume; for doctorate, GMAT or GRE. Additional exam requirements/recommendations for international students: Required—TOEFL (minimum score 600 paper-based; 100 iBT). Electronic applications accepted. *Faculty research:* Finance and accounting, marketing, technology and operations management, corporate strategy, management and organizations.

University of Michigan–Dearborn, College of Business, MS Program in Supply Chain Management, Dearborn, MI 48126. Offers MS. *Program availability:* Part-time, evening/weekend. *Faculty:* 41 full-time (17 women), 9 part-time/adjunct (6 women). *Students:* 4 full-time (3 women), 9 part-time (3 women); includes 1 minority (Black or African American, non-Hispanic/Latino), 7 international. Average age 26. 27 applicants, 22% accepted, 3 enrolled. In 2018, 9 master's awarded. *Entrance requirements:* For master's, GRE or GMAT, equivalent of four-year U.S. bachelor's degree from regionally-accredited institution, undergraduate course in finite math, pre-calculus, or calculus. Additional exam requirements/recommendations for international students: Required—TOEFL (minimum score 560 paper-based; 84 iBT), IELTS (minimum score 6.5). *Application deadline:* For fall admission, 8/1 for domestic students, 5/1 for international students; for winter admission, 12/1 for domestic students, 9/1 for international students; for spring admission, 4/1 for domestic students, 1/1 for international students. Applications are processed on a rolling

basis. Application fee: $60. Electronic applications accepted. *Expenses:* $15,740 per academic year (typical full-time in-state); $24,308 per academic year (typical full-time out-of-state). *Financial support:* In 2018–19, 8 students received support. Scholarships/grants and non-resident tuition scholarships available. Financial award application deadline: 3/1; financial award applicants required to submit FAFSA. *Faculty research:* Business intelligence, behavioral finance, brand management and new media, management education, operations strategy. *Unit head:* Dr. Michael Kamen, Director, Graduate Programs, 313-593-5460, E-mail: mkamen@umich.edu. *Application contact:* Joan Doherty, Academic Advisor/Counselor, 313-593-5460, Fax: 313-271-9838, E-mail: umd-gradbusiness@umich.edu. Website: http://umdearborn.edu/cob/ms-supply-chain/

University of Minnesota, Twin Cities Campus, Carlson School of Management, Carlson Full-Time MBA Program, Minneapolis, MN 55455. Offers finance (MBA); information technology (MBA); management (MBA); marketing (MBA); medical industry orientation (MBA); supply chain and operations (MBA); JD/MBA; MBA/MPP; MBA/MSBA; MD/MBA; MHA/MBA; Pharm D/MBA. *Accreditation:* AACSB. *Faculty:* 150 full-time (43 women), 21 part-time/adjunct (5 women). *Students:* 169 full-time (57 women); includes 32 minority (6 Black or African American, non-Hispanic/Latino; 4 American Indian or Alaska Native, non-Hispanic/Latino; 14 Asian, non-Hispanic/Latino; 8 Hispanic/Latino), 36 international. Average age 29. 529 applicants, 39% accepted, 92 enrolled. In 2018, 76 master's awarded. *Degree requirements:* For master's, None are required for MBA. *Entrance requirements:* For master's, GMAT or GRE, 2 recommendations, personal statement, resume. Additional exam requirements/recommendations for international students: Required—TOEFL (minimum score 580 paper-based; 84 iBT), IELTS (minimum score 7), PTE. *Application deadline:* For fall admission, 4/1 for domestic students, 2/1 for international students. Application fee: $75. Electronic applications accepted. *Expenses:* FTMBA Tuition; Collegiate fee; Student Services fee; Hospitalization. *Financial support:* In 2018–19, 139 students received support. Teaching assistantships with partial tuition reimbursements available, scholarships/grants, and unspecified assistantships available. Financial award application deadline: 4/1. *Faculty research:* Market regulation and asset pricing, social networks and data analytics, consumer behavior, innovation and entrepreneurship, workplace wellbeing and labor relationships. *Total annual research expenditures:* $577,440. *Unit head:* Philip J. Miller, Assistant Dean, MBA and MS Programs, 612-625-5555, Fax: 612-625-1012, E-mail: mba@umn.edu. *Application contact:* Linh Gilles, Director of Admissions and Recruiting, 612-625-5555, Fax: 612-625-1012, E-mail: ftmba@umn.edu. Website: http://www.csom.umn.edu/MBA/full-time/

University of Minnesota, Twin Cities Campus, Carlson School of Management, Carlson Part-Time MBA Program, Minneapolis, MN 55455. Offers finance (MBA); information technology (MBA); management (MBA); marketing (MBA); medical industry orientation (MBA); supply chain and operations (MBA). *Program availability:* Part-time-only, evening/weekend, 100% online, blended/hybrid learning. *Faculty:* 150 full-time (43 women), 23 part-time/adjunct (6 women). *Students:* 822 part-time (260 women); includes 122 minority (18 Black or African American, non-Hispanic/Latino; 11 American Indian or Alaska Native, non-Hispanic/Latino; 67 Asian, non-Hispanic/Latino; 24 Hispanic/Latino; 2 Native Hawaiian or other Pacific Islander, non-Hispanic/Latino), 41 international. Average age 29. 204 applicants, 83% accepted, 141 enrolled. In 2018, 257 master's awarded. *Degree requirements:* For master's, None for MBA. *Entrance requirements:* For master's, GMAT or GRE, 2 recommendations, personal statement, current resume. Additional exam requirements/recommendations for international students: Required—TOEFL (minimum score 580 paper-based; 84 iBT), IELTS (minimum score 7), PTE. *Application deadline:* For fall admission, 5/15 priority date for domestic and international students; for spring admission, 10/15 priority date for domestic and international students. Applications are processed on a rolling basis. Application fee: $75. Electronic applications accepted. *Expenses:* PTMBA tuition; Collegiate fee. *Financial support:* Applicants required to submit FAFSA. *Faculty research:* Market regulation and asset pricing, social networks and data analytics, consumer behavior, innovation and entrepreneurship, workplace wellbeing and labor relationships. *Total annual research expenditures:* $577,440. *Unit head:* Philip J. Miller, Assistant Dean, MBA and MS Programs, 612-624-2039, Fax: 612-625-1012, E-mail: mba@umn.edu. *Application contact:* Linh Gilles, Director of Admissions and Recruiting, 612-625-5555, Fax: 612-625-1012, E-mail: ptmba@umn.edu. Website: http://www.carlsonschool.umn.edu/ptmba

University of Minnesota, Twin Cities Campus, Carlson School of Management, Doctoral Program in Business Administration, Minneapolis, MN 55455-0213. Offers accounting (PhD); finance (PhD); information and decision sciences (PhD); marketing (PhD); strategic management and entrepreneurship (PhD); supply chain and operations (PhD); work and organizations (PhD). *Faculty:* 106 full-time (33 women). *Students:* 88 full-time (34 women); includes 9 minority (2 Black or African American, non-Hispanic/Latino; 6 Asian, non-Hispanic/Latino; 1 Hispanic/Latino), 66 international. Average age 30. 306 applicants, 8% accepted, 15 enrolled. In 2018, 14 doctorates awarded. *Degree requirements:* For doctorate, comprehensive exam, thesis/dissertation, written and oral preliminary exams, proposal defense, final defense. *Entrance requirements:* For doctorate, GMAT or GRE, minimum undergraduate GPA of 3.0, graduate 3.5 (recommended). Additional exam requirements/recommendations for international students: Required—Either or: TOEFL or IELTS; Recommended—TOEFL, IELTS. *Application deadline:* For fall admission, 12/15 for domestic students, 12/15 priority date for international students. Applications are processed on a rolling basis. Application fee: $75 ($95 for international students). Electronic applications accepted. *Financial support:* In 2018–19, 80 students received support, including 80 fellowships with full tuition reimbursements available (averaging $12,500 per year), 72 research assistantships with full tuition reimbursements available (averaging $7,800 per year), 72 teaching assistantships with full tuition reimbursements available (averaging $7,800 per year); health care benefits, unspecified assistantships, and full student service fee waivers also available. Financial award application deadline: 12/15. *Faculty research:* Finance, strategy and entrepreneurship, marketing, information and decision science, operations, accounting, supply chain, human resources and industrial relations, organizational behavior. *Unit head:* Dr. Shawn P. Curley, Director, 612-624-6546, Fax: 612-624-8221, E-mail: curley@umn.edu. *Application contact:* Sandy Herzan, Associate Director, 612-624-0875, Fax: 612-624-8221, E-mail: herza002@umn.edu. Website: http://carlsonschool.umn.edu/degrees/phd

University of Missouri–St. Louis, College of Business Administration, St. Louis, MO 63121. Offers accounting (M Acc); business administration (MBA, DBA, PhD, Certificate), including logistics and supply chain management (PhD); business intelligence (Certificate); cybersecurity (Certificate); digital and social media marketing (Certificate); human resources management (Certificate); information systems (MS); logistics and supply chain management (Certificate); marketing management (Certificate). *Program availability:* Part-time, evening/weekend. *Degree requirements:* For doctorate, thesis/dissertation. *Entrance requirements:* For master's, GMAT, 2 letters of recommendation; for doctorate, GMAT or GRE, 3 letters of recommendation. Additional exam requirements/recommendations for international students: Recommended—TOEFL (minimum score 550 paper-based; 79 iBT), IELTS (minimum score 6.5). Electronic applications accepted. *Faculty research:* Statistical decision aids, commercial banking, corporate finance, operations management, information systems.

The University of North Carolina at Charlotte, William States Lee College of Engineering, Department of Systems Engineering and Engineering Management, Charlotte, NC 28223-0001. Offers energy analytics (Graduate Certificate); engineering management (MSEM); Lean Six Sigma (Graduate Certificate); logistics and supply chains (Graduate Certificate); systems analytics (Graduate Certificate). *Program availability:* Part-time, evening/weekend, 100% online, blended/hybrid learning. *Students:* 27 full-time (8 women), 45 part-time (11 women); includes 15 minority (5 Black or African American, non-Hispanic/Latino; 1 American Indian or Alaska Native, non-Hispanic/Latino; 5 Asian, non-Hispanic/Latino; 2 Hispanic/Latino; 2 Two or more races, non-Hispanic/Latino), 27 international. Average age 29. 112 applicants, 77% accepted, 23 enrolled. In 2018, 38 master's, 3 other advanced degrees awarded. *Entrance requirements:* For master's, GRE or GMAT, bachelor's degree in engineering or a closely-related technical or scientific field, or in business, provided relevant technical course requirements have been met; undergraduate coursework in engineering economics, calculus, or statistics; minimum GPA of 3.0; for Graduate Certificate, bachelor's degree in engineering or closely-related technical or scientific field, or in business, provided relevant technical course requirements have been met; minimum GPA of 3.0; undergraduate coursework in engineering economics, calculus, and statistics; written description of work experience. Additional exam requirements/recommendations for international students: Required—TOEFL (minimum score 523 paper-based; 70 iBT), IELTS (minimum score 6), TOEFL (minimum score 523 paper-based, 70 iBT) or IELTS (6). *Application deadline:* Applications are processed on a rolling basis. Application fee: $75. Electronic applications accepted. *Expenses:* Contact institution. *Financial support:* Career-related internships or fieldwork, institutionally sponsored loans, scholarships/grants, and unspecified assistantships available. Support available to part-time students. Financial award application deadline: 3/1; financial award applicants required to submit FAFSA. *Total annual research expenditures:* $186,132. *Unit head:* Dr. Simon M. Hsiang, Chair, 704-687-1958, E-mail: shsiang1@uncc.edu. *Application contact:* Kathy B. Giddings, Director of Graduate Admissions, 704-687-5503, Fax: 704-687-1668, E-mail: gradadm@uncc.edu.
Website: http://seem.uncc.edu/

The University of North Carolina at Greensboro, Graduate School, Bryan School of Business and Economics, Department of Information Systems and Supply Chain Management, Greensboro, NC 27412-5001. Offers information systems (PhD); information technology (Certificate); information technology and management (MS); supply chain management (Certificate). *Entrance requirements:* For master's, GMAT, GRE General Test. Additional exam requirements/recommendations for international students: Required—TOEFL. Electronic applications accepted.

University of North Texas, Toulouse Graduate School, Denton, TX 76203-5459. Offers accounting (MS); applied anthropology (MA, MS); applied behavior analysis (Certificate); applied geography (MA); applied technology and performance improvement (M Ed, MS); art education (MA); art history (MA); arts leadership (Certificate); audiology (Au D); behavior analysis (MS); behavioral science (PhD); biochemistry and molecular biology (MS); biology (MA, MS); biomedical engineering (MS); business analysis (MS); chemistry (MS); clinical health psychology (PhD); communication studies (MA, MS); computer engineering (MS); computer science (MS); counseling (M Ed, MS), including clinical mental health counseling (MS), college and university counseling, elementary school counseling, secondary school counseling; creative writing (MA); criminal justice (MS); curriculum and instruction (M Ed); decision sciences (MBA); design (MA, MFA), including fashion design (MFA), innovation studies, interior design (MFA); early childhood studies (MS); economics (MS); educational leadership (M Ed, Ed D); educational psychology (MS, PhD), including family studies (MS), gifted and talented (MS), human development (MS), learning and cognition (MS), research, measurement and evaluation (MS); electrical engineering (MS); emergency management (MPA); engineering technology (MS); English (MA); English as a second language (MA); environmental science (MS); finance (MBA, MS); financial management (MPA); French (MA); health services management (MBA); higher education (M Ed, Ed D); history (MA, MS); hospitality management (MS); human resources management (MPA); information science (MS); information systems (PhD); information technologies (MBA); interdisciplinary studies (MA, MS); international studies (MA); international sustainable tourism (MS); jazz studies (MM); journalism (MA, MJ, Graduate Certificate), including interactive and virtual digital communication (Graduate Certificate), narrative journalism (Graduate Certificate), public relations (Graduate Certificate); kinesiology (MS); linguistics (MA); local government management (MPA); logistics (PhD); logistics and supply chain management (MBA); long-term care, senior housing, and aging services (MA); management (PhD); marketing (MBA); mathematics (MA, MS); mechanical and energy engineering (MS, PhD); music (MA), including ethnomusicology, music theory, musicology, performance; music composition (PhD); music education (MM Ed, PhD); nonprofit management (MPA); operations and supply chain management (MBA); performance (MM, DMA); philosophy (MA); political science (MA); professional and technical communication (MA); radio, television and film (MA, MFA); rehabilitation counseling (Certificate); sociology (MA); Spanish (MA); special education (M Ed); speech-language pathology (MA); strategic management (MBA); studio art (MFA); teaching (M Ed); MBA/MS. *Program availability:* Part-time, evening/weekend, online learning. Terminal master's awarded for partial completion of doctoral program. *Degree requirements:* For master's, variable foreign language requirement, comprehensive exam (for some programs), thesis (for some programs); for doctorate, variable foreign language requirement, comprehensive exam (for some programs), thesis/dissertation; for other advanced degree, variable foreign language requirement, comprehensive exam (for some programs). *Entrance requirements:* For master's and doctorate, GRE, GMAT. Additional exam requirements/recommendations for international students: Required—TOEFL (minimum score 550 paper-based; 79 iBT). Electronic applications accepted.

University of Pittsburgh, Katz Graduate School of Business, Master of Science in Supply Chain Management Program, Pittsburgh, PA 15260. Offers MS. *Degree requirements:* For master's, minimum GPA of 3.0. *Entrance requirements:* For master's, GMAT, GRE. Additional exam requirements/recommendations for international students: Required—TOEFL (minimum score 100 iBT), IELTS (minimum score 7). Electronic applications accepted. *Expenses:* Contact institution. *Faculty research:* Accounting systems/financial reporting, corporate finance, shopper marketing/consumer behavior, management information systems, organizational behavior and entrepreneurship.

University of Rhode Island, Graduate School, College of Business, Program in Business Administration, Kingston, RI 02881. Offers finance (MBA); general business (MBA); management (MBA); marketing (MBA, PhD); operations and supply chain management (PhD); supply chain management (MBA); Pharm D/MBA. *Faculty:* 33 full-time (17 women). *Students:* 54 full-time (21 women), 161 part-time (64 women); includes 30 minority (11 Black or African American, non-Hispanic/Latino; 11 Asian, non-Hispanic/Latino; 6 Hispanic/Latino; 1 Native Hawaiian or other Pacific Islander, non-Hispanic/Latino; 1 Two or more races, non-Hispanic/Latino), 17 international. 92 applicants, 87% accepted, 74 enrolled. In 2018, 90 master's, 5 doctorates awarded. *Entrance requirements:* Additional exam requirements/recommendations for international students: Required—TOEFL. *Application deadline:* For fall admission, 6/30 for domestic students; for spring admission, 10/31 for domestic students; for summer admission, 3/31 for domestic students. Electronic applications accepted. *Expenses: Tuition, area resident:* Full-time $13,226; part-time $735 per credit. Tuition, state resident: full-time $13,226; part-time $735 per credit. Tuition, nonresident: full-time $25,854; part-time $1436 per credit. *International tuition:* $25,854 full-time. *Required fees:* $1698; $50 per credit. $35 per semester. One-time fee: $165. *Financial support:* In 2018–19, 15 teaching assistantships (averaging $17,739 per year) were awarded. Financial award application deadline: 2/1. *Unit head:* Lisa Lancellotta, Coordinator, MBA Programs, 401-874-4241, E-mail: mba@uri.edu. *Application contact:* Lisa Lancellotta, Coordinator, MBA Programs, 401-874-4241, E-mail: mba@uri.edu.

University of St. Francis, College of Business and Health Administration, Joliet, IL 60435-6169. Offers accounting (MBA, Certificate); business analytics (MBA, Certificate); e-learning (Certificate); finance (MBA, Certificate); health administration (MBA, MS); human resource management (MBA, Certificate); logistics (Certificate); management (MBA, MSM); management of training and development (Certificate); supply chain management (MBA); training and development (MBA); training specialist (Certificate). *Program availability:* Part-time, evening/weekend, 100% online, blended/hybrid learning. *Faculty:* 13 full-time (6 women), 20 part-time/adjunct (7 women). *Students:* 139 full-time (94 women), 206 part-time (159 women); includes 86 minority (51 Black or African American, non-Hispanic/Latino; 1 American Indian or Alaska Native, non-Hispanic/Latino; 11 Asian, non-Hispanic/Latino; 21 Hispanic/Latino; 2 Two or more races, non-Hispanic/Latino), 24 international. Average age 37. 261 applicants, 63% accepted, 98 enrolled. In 2018, 129 master's, 3 other advanced degrees awarded. *Degree requirements:* For master's, comprehensive exam (for some programs). *Entrance requirements:* Additional exam requirements/recommendations for international students: Required—TOEFL (minimum score 550 paper-based; 79 iBT), IELTS (minimum score 6). *Application deadline:* Applications are processed on a rolling basis. Electronic applications accepted. Application fee is waived when completed online. *Expenses:* Contact institution. *Financial support:* In 2018–19, 126 students received support. Scholarships/grants and tuition waivers (partial) available. Support available to part-time students. Financial award applicants required to submit FAFSA. *Unit head:* Dr. Orlando Griego, Dean, 815-740-3395, Fax: 815-740-3452, E-mail: ogriego@stfrancis.edu. *Application contact:* Sandee Sloka, Director Adult & Graduate Admissions, 800-735-7500, E-mail: ssloka@stfrancis.edu.
Website: https://www.stfrancis.edu/business-health-administration/

University of South Dakota, Graduate School, Beacom School of Business, Department of Business Administration, Vermillion, SD 57069. Offers business administration (MBA); business analytics (MBA, Graduate Certificate); health services administration (MBA); long term care management (Graduate Certificate); marketing (MBA, Graduate Certificate); operations and supply chain management (MBA, Graduate Certificate); JD/MBA. *Accreditation:* AACSB. *Program availability:* Part-time, blended/hybrid learning. *Degree requirements:* For master's, thesis or alternative. *Entrance requirements:* For master's, GMAT, minimum GPA of 2.7, resume. Additional exam requirements/recommendations for international students: Required—TOEFL (minimum score 550 paper-based; 79 iBT), IELTS (minimum score 6). Electronic applications accepted. *Expenses:* Contact institution.

University of Southern California, Graduate School, Viterbi School of Engineering, Daniel J. Epstein Department of Industrial and Systems Engineering, Los Angeles, CA 90089. Offers digital supply chain management (MS); engineering management (MS); engineering technology communication (Graduate Certificate); health systems operations (Graduate Certificate); industrial and systems engineering (MS, PhD, Engr); manufacturing engineering (MS); operations research engineering (MS); optimization and supply chain management (Graduate Certificate); product development engineering (MS); safety systems and security (MS); systems architecting and engineering (MS, Graduate Certificate); systems safety and security (Graduate Certificate); transportation systems (Graduate Certificate); MS/MBA. *Program availability:* Part-time, evening/weekend, online learning. Terminal master's awarded for partial completion of doctoral program. *Degree requirements:* For master's, thesis optional; for doctorate, thesis/dissertation. *Entrance requirements:* For master's and doctorate, GRE General Test. Additional exam requirements/recommendations for international students: Recommended—TOEFL. Electronic applications accepted. *Faculty research:* Health systems, music cognition and retrieval, transportation and logistics, manufacturing and automation, engineering systems design, risk and economic analysis.

The University of Tennessee at Chattanooga, Engineering Management and Technology Program, Chattanooga, TN 37403. Offers construction management (Graduate Certificate); engineering management (MS); fundamentals of engineering management (Graduate Certificate); leadership and ethics (Graduate Certificate); logistics and supply chain management (Graduate Certificate); power systems management (Graduate Certificate); project and technology management (Graduate Certificate); quality management (Graduate Certificate). *Program availability:* 100% online, blended/hybrid learning. *Degree requirements:* For master's, thesis. *Entrance requirements:* For master's, GRE General Test, letters of recommendation; minimum undergraduate GPA of 2.7 overall or 3.0 in final two years; for Graduate Certificate, baccalaureate degree and professional experience or have already been admitted to engineering/engineering management graduate program. Additional exam requirements/recommendations for international students: Required—TOEFL (minimum score 550 paper-based; 79 iBT), IELTS (minimum score 6). Electronic applications accepted. *Expenses:* Contact institution. *Faculty research:* Plant layout design, lean manufacturing, Six Sigma, value management, product development.

The University of Texas at Austin, Graduate School, McCombs School of Business, Department of Information, Risk, and Operations Management, Austin, TX 78712-1111. Offers information management (MBA); information systems (PhD); information technology and management (MS); risk analysis and decision making (PhD); risk management (MBA); supply chain and operations management (MBA, PhD). *Degree requirements:* For doctorate, thesis/dissertation. *Entrance requirements:* For doctorate, GMAT or GRE. Electronic applications accepted. *Faculty research:* Stochastic processing and queuing, discrete nonlinear and large-scale optimization simulation, quality assurance logistics, distributed artificial intelligence, organizational modeling.

The University of Texas at Dallas, Naveen Jindal School of Management, Program in Operations Management, Richardson, TX 75080. Offers supply chain management (MS). *Faculty:* 15 full-time (3 women), 21 part-time/adjunct (8 women). *Students:* 244 full-time (92 women), 104 part-time (47 women); includes 38 minority (5 Black or African American, non-Hispanic/Latino; 21 Asian, non-Hispanic/Latino; 9 Hispanic/Latino; 3 Two or more races, non-Hispanic/Latino), 267 international. Average age 29. 306 applicants, 73% accepted, 127 enrolled. In 2018, 190 master's awarded. *Entrance requirements:* For master's, GMAT. Additional exam requirements/recommendations for international students: Required—TOEFL (minimum score 550 paper-based). *Application deadline:* For fall admission, 7/15 for domestic students, 5/1 priority date for international students; for spring admission, 11/15 for domestic students, 9/1 priority date for international students. Applications are processed on a rolling basis. Application fee: $50 ($100 for international students). Electronic applications accepted. *Expenses: Tuition, area resident:* Full-time $13,458. Tuition, state resident: full-time $13,458. Tuition, nonresident: full-time $26,852. *International tuition:* $26,852 full-time. Tuition and fees vary according to course load. *Financial support:* In 2018–19, 19 teaching

assistantships with partial tuition reimbursements (averaging $10,050 per year) were awarded; research assistantships, career-related internships or fieldwork, Federal Work-Study, institutionally sponsored loans, scholarships/grants, and unspecified assistantships also available. Support available to part-time students. Financial award application deadline: 4/30; financial award applicants required to submit FAFSA. *Faculty research:* Technology marketing, measuring information work productivity. *Unit head:* Dr. Milind Dawande, Professor, 972-883-2793, E-mail: milind@utdallas.edu. *Application contact:* Dr. Milind Dawande, Professor, 972-883-2793, E-mail: milind@utdallas.edu.
Website: http://jindal.utdallas.edu/isom/operations-scm-programs/

University of Washington, Graduate School, Michael G. Foster School of Business, Seattle, WA 98195-3200. Offers auditing and assurance (MP Acc); business administration (MBA, PhD); entrepreneurship (MS); executive business administration (MBA); global executive business administration (MBA); information systems (MSIS); supply chain management (MSSCM); taxation (MP Acc); technology management (MBA); JD/MBA; MBA/MAIS; MBA/MHA. *Accreditation:* AACSB. *Program availability:* Part-time, evening/weekend, blended/hybrid learning. Terminal master's awarded for partial completion of doctoral program. *Degree requirements:* For doctorate, comprehensive exam, thesis/dissertation. *Entrance requirements:* For master's and doctorate, GMAT, GRE. Additional exam requirements/recommendations for international students: Required—TOEFL (minimum score 600 paper-based; 100 iBT). Electronic applications accepted. *Expenses:* Contact institution. *Faculty research:* Finance, consumer behavior, marketing analytics, technology management, supply chain.

University of Wisconsin–Madison, Graduate School, Wisconsin School of Business, Wisconsin Full-Time MBA Program, Madison, WI 53706-1380. Offers applied security analysis (MBA); arts administration (MBA); brand and product management (MBA); corporate finance and investment banking (MBA); marketing research (MBA); operations and technology management (MBA); real estate (MBA); risk management and insurance (MBA); strategic human resource management (MBA); supply chain management (MBA). *Faculty:* 137 full-time (36 women), 39 part-time/adjunct (11 women). *Students:* 183 full-time (59 women); includes 31 minority (5 Black or African American, non-Hispanic/Latino; 1 American Indian or Alaska Native, non-Hispanic/Latino; 6 Asian, non-Hispanic/Latino; 13 Hispanic/Latino; 6 Two or more races, non-Hispanic/Latino), 40 international. Average age 28. 465 applicants, 33% accepted, 79 enrolled. In 2018, 104 master's awarded. *Entrance requirements:* For master's, GMAT or GRE, bachelor's or equivalent degree, essay, letter of recommendation, resume. Additional exam requirements/recommendations for international students: Required—TOEFL (minimum score 100 iBT), IELTS (minimum score 7.5), TOEFL is not required for international students whose undergraduate training was in English. *Application deadline:* For fall admission, 11/1 for domestic and international students; for winter admission, 1/10 for domestic and international students; for spring admission, 3/1 for domestic and international students; for summer admission, 4/10 for domestic students, 4/10 priority date for international students. Applications are processed on a rolling basis. Application fee: $75 ($81 for international students). Electronic applications accepted. *Expenses:* Wisconsin Resident tuition and fees - $39,156; Nonresident tuition and fees - $76,635. *Financial support:* In 2018–19, 148 students received support, including 7 fellowships with full tuition reimbursements available (averaging $25,871 per year), 7 research assistantships with full tuition reimbursements available (averaging $14,832 per year), 47 teaching assistantships with full tuition reimbursements available (averaging $14,832 per year); scholarships/grants, health care benefits, tuition waivers (full and partial), and unspecified assistantships also available. Financial award application deadline: 6/1. *Faculty research:* Ecology, environmental studies, and business; decision making; tax policy; diversity and inclusion in governance boards; marketing and social media. *Unit head:* Dr. Enno Siemsen, Associate Dean of the MBA and Masters Programs, 608-890-3130, E-mail: esiemsen@wisc.edu. *Application contact:* Betsy Kacizak, Director of Admissions and Recruiting, Full-time MBA Program, 608-262-4000, E-mail: betsy.kacizak@wisc.edu.
Website: https://wsb.wisc.edu/

University of Wisconsin–Platteville, School of Graduate Studies, Distance Learning Center, Online Master of Science in Integrated Supply Chain Management Program, Platteville, WI 53818-3099. Offers MS. *Program availability:* Part-time, online learning. *Entrance requirements:* Additional exam requirements/recommendations for international students: Required—TOEFL (minimum score 550 paper-based; 79 iBT), IELTS (minimum score 6.5). Electronic applications accepted.

University of Wisconsin–Stout, Graduate School, College of Management, Program in Operations and Supply Management, Menomonie, WI 54751. Offers operations management (MS); project management (MS); quality management (MS); supply chain management (MS).

Walden University, Graduate Programs, School of Management, Minneapolis, MN 55401. Offers accounting (MBA, MS, DBA), including accounting for the professional (MS), accounting with CPA emphasis (MS), self-designed (MS); advanced project management (Graduate Certificate); applied project management (Graduate Certificate); auditing (Graduate Certificate); bridge to business administration (Post-Doctoral Certificate); bridge to management (Post-Doctoral Certificate); business management (Graduate Certificate); communication (MBA); corporate finance (MBA); digital marketing (Graduate Certificate); entrepreneurship (DBA); entrepreneurship and small business (MBA); finance (MS, DBA), including finance for the professional (MS), finance with CFA/investment (MS), finance with CPA emphasis (MS); global supply chain management (DBA); healthcare management (MBA, DBA); human resource management (MBA, MS, Graduate Certificate), including functional human resource management (MS), general program (MS), integrating functional and strategic human resource management (MS), organizational strategy (MS); human resources management (DBA); information systems management (DBA); international business (MBA, DBA); leadership (MBA, MS, DBA, Graduate Certificate), including general program (MS), human resource leadership (MS), leader development (MS), self-designed (MS); management (MS, PhD), including communications (MS), finance (PhD), general program (MS), healthcare management (MS), human resource management (MS), human resources management (PhD), information systems management (PhD), international business (MS), leadership (MS), leadership and organizational change (PhD), marketing (MS), project management (MS), strategy and operations (MS); managerial accounting (Graduate Certificate); marketing (MBA, MS, DBA); project management (MBA, MS, DBA); self-designed (MBA, DBA); social impact management (DBA); technology entrepreneurship (DBA). *Accreditation:* ACBSP. *Program availability:* Part-time, evening/weekend, online only, 100% online. *Degree requirements:* For master's, thesis (for some programs), residency (for EMBA); for doctorate, thesis/dissertation (for some programs), residency. *Entrance requirements:* For master's, bachelor's degree or higher; minimum GPA of 2.5; official transcripts; goal statement (for some programs); access to computer and Internet; for doctorate, master's degree or higher; three years of related professional or academic experience (preferred); minimum GPA of 3.0; goal statement and current resume (for select programs); official transcripts; access to computer and Internet; for other advanced degree, relevant work experience; access to computer and Internet. Additional exam requirements/recommendations for international students: Required—TOEFL (minimum score 550 paper-based, 79 iBT), IELTS (minimum score 6.5), Michigan English Language Assessment Battery (minimum score 82), or PTE (minimum score 53). Electronic applications accepted.

Washington University in St. Louis, Olin Business School, Program in Supply Chain Management, St. Louis, MO 63130-4899. Offers MS. *Program availability:* Part-time. *Faculty:* 85 full-time (16 women), 46 part-time/adjunct (13 women). *Students:* 60 full-time (33 women), 2 part-time (0 women); includes 2 minority (both Asian, non-Hispanic/Latino), 59 international. Average age 24. 140 applicants, 24% accepted, 20 enrolled. In 2018, 24 master's awarded. *Degree requirements:* For master's, 36 credit hours. *Entrance requirements:* For master's, GMAT or GRE, U.S. bachelor's degree or equivalent, one letter of recommendation. Additional exam requirements/recommendations for international students: Required—TOEFL, IELTS. *Application deadline:* For fall admission, 10/10 for domestic and international students; for winter admission, 1/15 for domestic students, 1/15 priority date for international students; for spring admission, 3/18 for domestic and international students. Applications are processed on a rolling basis. Application fee: $100. Electronic applications accepted. *Financial support:* Institutionally sponsored loans and scholarships/grants available. Financial award applicants required to submit FAFSA. *Unit head:* Steve Malter, Senior Associate Dean, Undergrad and Graduate Programs, 314-935-6315, Fax: 314-935-9095, E-mail: malter@wustl.edu. *Application contact:* Ruthie Pyles, Asst Dean & Dir of Grad Admissions & Fin Aid, 314-935-7301, E-mail: OlinGradAdmissions@wustl.edu.
Website: http://www.olin.wustl.edu/academicprograms/MSSCM/Pages/default.aspx

Western Illinois University, School of Graduate Studies, College of Business and Technology, Program in Business Administration, Macomb, IL 61455-1390. Offers business administration (MBA, Certificate); supply chain management (Certificate). *Accreditation:* AACSB. *Program availability:* Part-time. *Students:* 32 full-time (15 women), 73 part-time (21 women); includes 14 minority (3 Black or African American, non-Hispanic/Latino; 1 American Indian or Alaska Native, non-Hispanic/Latino; 5 Asian, non-Hispanic/Latino; 3 Hispanic/Latino; 2 Two or more races, non-Hispanic/Latino), 6 international. Average age 33. 76 applicants, 72% accepted, 30 enrolled. In 2018, 38 master's, 3 other advanced degrees awarded. *Entrance requirements:* For master's, GMAT. Additional exam requirements/recommendations for international students: Required—TOEFL (minimum score 550 paper-based; 80 iBT). *Application deadline:* Applications are processed on a rolling basis. Application fee: $30. Electronic applications accepted. *Financial support:* Research assistantships with full tuition reimbursements and unspecified assistantships available. Financial award applicants required to submit FAFSA. *Unit head:* Dr. Tara Feld, Associate Dean, 309-298-2442. *Application contact:* Dr. Mark Mossman, Associate Provost and Director of Graduate Studies, 309-298-1806, Fax: 309-298-2345, E-mail: grad-office@wiu.edu.
Website: http://wiu.edu/cbt

Wichita State University, Graduate School, W. Frank Barton School of Business, Program in Global Supply Chain Management, Wichita, KS 67260. Offers MS. *Unit head:* Dr. Mehmet Barut, Graduate Coordinator, 316-978-6930, E-mail: mehmet.barut@wichita.edu. *Application contact:* Jordan Oleson, Admissions Coordinator, 316-978-3095, Fax: 316-978-3253, E-mail: jordan.oleson@wichita.edu.

Wilfrid Laurier University, Faculty of Graduate and Postdoctoral Studies, Lazaridis School of Business and Economics, Department of Business, Waterloo, ON N2L 3C5, Canada. Offers accounting (PhD); finance (M Fin); financial economics (PhD); marketing (PhD); operations and supply chain management (PhD); organizational behavior and human resource management (M Sc); organizational behaviour and human resource management (PhD); supply chain management (M Sc); technology management (EMTM). *Accreditation:* AACSB. *Program availability:* Part-time, evening/weekend. *Degree requirements:* For master's, thesis optional; for doctorate, comprehensive exam, thesis/dissertation. *Entrance requirements:* For master's, GMAT, 4-year honors degree with minimum B+ average; for doctorate, GMAT, master's degree, minimum B+ average. Additional exam requirements/recommendations for international students: Required—TOEFL (minimum score 89 iBT). Electronic applications accepted. *Faculty research:* Financial economics, management and organizational behavior, operations and supply chain management.

Worcester Polytechnic Institute, Graduate Admissions, Foisie Business School, Worcester, MA 01609-2280. Offers business administration (PhD); information technology (MS), including information security management; management (MS, Graduate Certificate); marketing and innovation (MS); operations analytics and management (MS); supply chain management (MS). *Accreditation:* AACSB. *Program availability:* Part-time, evening/weekend, 100% online, blended/hybrid learning. *Students:* 136 full-time (74 women), 214 part-time (85 women); includes 29 minority (4 Black or African American, non-Hispanic/Latino; 11 Asian, non-Hispanic/Latino; 9 Hispanic/Latino; 5 Two or more races, non-Hispanic/Latino), 189 international. Average age 29. 636 applicants, 64% accepted, 104 enrolled. In 2018, 165 master's, 1 doctorate, 10 other advanced degrees awarded. *Degree requirements:* For master's, thesis optional. *Entrance requirements:* For master's and Graduate Certificate, GMAT or GRE General Test, 3 letters of recommendation, statement of purpose, resume. Additional exam requirements/recommendations for international students: Required—TOEFL (minimum score 563 paper-based; 84 iBT), IELTS (minimum score 7). *Application deadline:* For fall admission, 6/1 priority date for domestic and international students; for spring admission, 11/1 priority date for domestic students, 10/1 priority date for international students. Applications are processed on a rolling basis. Application fee: $70. Electronic applications accepted. *Financial support:* Career-related internships or fieldwork, institutionally sponsored loans, scholarships/grants, and unspecified assistantships available. Financial award application deadline: 6/1. *Unit head:* Melissa Terrio, Director of Graduate Recruitment & Admissions, 508-831-4665, Fax: 508-831-5866, E-mail: biz@wpi.edu. *Application contact:* Amy Trakimas, Associate Director of Graduate Recruitment & Admissions, 508-831-4665, Fax: 508-831-5866, E-mail: atrakimas@wpi.edu.
Website: https://www.wpi.edu/academics/business

Wright State University, Graduate School, Raj Soin College of Business, Department of Information Systems and Operations Management, Logistics and Supply Chain Management Program, Dayton, OH 45435. Offers MS.

Youngstown State University, College of Graduate Studies, Williamson College of Business Administration, Department of Management, Youngstown, OH 44555-0001. Offers enterprise resource planning (Certificate). *Program availability:* Part-time, evening/weekend. *Entrance requirements:* Additional exam requirements/recommendations for international students: Required—TOEFL. *Faculty research:* Organizational behavior, information systems, ethical and social issues, operations management, research design, strategy/policy communication.

Transportation Management

American Public University System, AMU/APU Graduate Programs, Charles Town, WV 25414. Offers accounting (MS); applied business analytics (MS); business administration (MBA); criminal justice (MA); cybersecurity studies (MS); educational leadership (M Ed); environmental policy and management (MS); global security (DGS); health information management (MS); history (MA), including American military history, American Revolution, civil war, war since 1945, World War II; information technology (MS); international relations and conflict resolution (MA), including American politics and government, comparative government and development, general, international relations, public policy; national security studies (MA); nursing (MSN); political science (MA); public policy (MPP); reverse logistics management (MA), including comparative and security issues, conflict resolution, international and transnational security issues, peacekeeping; space studies (MS); sports management (MS); strategic intelligence (DSI); teaching (M Ed), including secondary social studies; transportation and logistics management (MA). *Program availability:* Part-time, evening/weekend, online only, 100% online. *Students:* 406 full-time (180 women), 7,826 part-time (3,329 women); includes 2,781 minority (1,438 Black or African American, non-Hispanic/Latino; 44 American Indian or Alaska Native, non-Hispanic/Latino; 193 Asian, non-Hispanic/Latino; 747 Hispanic/Latino; 53 Native Hawaiian or other Pacific Islander, non-Hispanic/Latino; 306 Two or more races, non-Hispanic/Latino), 121 international. Average age 38. In 2018, 2,717 master's awarded. *Degree requirements:* For master's, comprehensive exam or practicum; for doctorate, practicum. *Entrance requirements:* For master's, official transcript showing earned bachelor's degree from institution accredited by recognized accrediting body. Additional exam requirements/recommendations for international students: Required—TOEFL (minimum score 550 paper-based), IELTS (minimum score 6.5). *Application deadline:* Applications are processed on a rolling basis. Application fee: $0. Electronic applications accepted. *Financial support:* Scholarships/grants available. Financial award applicants required to submit FAFSA. *Unit head:* Dr. Wallace Boston, President, 877-468-6268, Fax: 304-728-2348, E-mail: president@apus.edu. *Application contact:* Yoci Deal, Associate Vice President, Graduate and International Admissions, 877-468-6268, Fax: 304-724-3764, E-mail: info@apus.edu.
Website: http://www.apus.edu

California State University Maritime Academy, Graduate Studies, Vallejo, CA 94590. Offers transportation and engineering management (MS), including engineering management, humanitarian disaster management, transportation. *Program availability:* Evening/weekend, online only, 100% online. *Faculty:* 13 part-time/adjunct (2 women). *Students:* 34 full-time (6 women); includes 10 minority (2 Black or African American, non-Hispanic/Latino; 4 Asian, non-Hispanic/Latino; 4 Hispanic/Latino), 2 international. Average age 38. 21 applicants, 86% accepted, 16 enrolled. In 2018, 19 master's awarded. *Degree requirements:* For master's, comprehensive exam (for some programs), thesis, Minimum GPA of 3.0 in 10 required courses including capstone course and project, demonstrated proficiency in graduate-level writing. *Entrance requirements:* For master's, GMAT/GRE (for applicants with fewer than five years of post-baccalaureate professional experience), Equivalent of four-year U.S. bachelor's degree with minimum GPA of 2.5 during last two years (60 semester units or 90 quarter units) of coursework in degree program. Additional exam requirements/ recommendations for international students: Required—TOEFL (minimum score 550 paper-based). *Application deadline:* Applications are processed on a rolling basis. Application fee: $55. Electronic applications accepted. *Financial support:* Applicants required to submit FAFSA. *Unit head:* Dr. Graham Benton, Associate Vice President, Academic Affairs, 707-654-1147, E-mail: gbenton@csum.edu. *Application contact:* Kathy Arnold, Program Coordinator, 707-654-1271, Fax: 707-654-1158, E-mail: karnold@csum.edu.
Website: http://www.csum.edu/web/industry/graduate-studies

George Mason University, Schar School of Policy and Government, Program in Transportation Policy, Operations and Logistics, Arlington, VA 22201. Offers MA. *Faculty:* 6 full-time (3 women), 2 part-time/adjunct (0 women). *Students:* 3 full-time (1 woman), 12 part-time (6 women); includes 6 minority (3 Black or African American, non-Hispanic/Latino; 2 Hispanic/Latino; 1 Two or more races, non-Hispanic/Latino), 2 international. Average age 36. 10 applicants, 80% accepted, 1 enrolled. In 2018, 14 master's awarded. *Entrance requirements:* For master's, GRE (for students seeking merit-based scholarships), bachelor's degree with minimum GPA of 3.0, current resume, 2 letters of recommendation, expanded goals statement, 2 copies of official transcripts. Additional exam requirements/recommendations for international students: Required—TOEFL (minimum score 575 paper-based; 88 iBT), IELTS (minimum score 6.5), PTE (minimum score 59). *Application deadline:* For fall admission, 2/1 priority date for domestic and international students; for spring admission, 11/1 priority date for domestic and international students. Application fee: $75 ($80 for international students). Electronic applications accepted. *Expenses:* $689 per credit in-state tuition, $1,446.75 per credit out-of-state tuition. *Financial support:* Career-related internships or fieldwork, Federal Work-Study, and scholarships/grants available. Support available to part-time students. Financial award application deadline: 3/1; financial award applicants required to submit FAFSA. *Unit head:* Laurie Schintler, Director, 703-993-2256, Fax: 703-993-4557, E-mail: lschintl@gmu.edu. *Application contact:* Stephanie Ellis, Graduate Admissions Coordinator, 703-993-4478, E-mail: sellis11@gmu.edu.
Website: http://spgia.gmu.edu/programs/graduate-degrees/transportation-policy-operations-logistics-tpol/

Instituto Tecnologico de Santo Domingo, Graduate School, Area of Engineering, Santo Domingo, Dominican Republic. Offers construction administration (MS, Certificate); data telecommunications (M Eng, MS, Certificate); industrial engineering (M Eng, Certificate); industrial management (M Mgmt); information technology (Certificate); maintenance engineering (M Eng); occupational hazard prevention (M Mgmt); production management (Certificate); quantitative methods (Certificate); sanitary and environmental engineering (M Eng); structural engineering (M Eng); systems engineering and electronic data processing (Certificate); transportation (Certificate).

Iowa State University of Science and Technology, Department of Community and Regional Planning, Ames, IA 50011. Offers community and regional planning (MCRP); transportation (MS); M Arch/MCRP; MBA/MCRP; MCRP/MLA; MCRP/MPA. *Accreditation:* ACSP (one or more programs are accredited). *Degree requirements:* For master's, thesis or alternative. *Entrance requirements:* For master's, GRE General Test. Additional exam requirements/recommendations for international students: Required—TOEFL (minimum score 550 paper-based; 79 iBT), IELTS (minimum score 6.5). Electronic applications accepted. *Faculty research:* Economic development, housing, land use, geographic information systems planning in developing nations, regional and community revitalization, transportation planning in developing countries.

Iowa State University of Science and Technology, Program in Transportation, Ames, IA 50011. Offers MS. *Entrance requirements:* For master's, GMAT or GRE General

Test. Additional exam requirements/recommendations for international students: Required—TOEFL (minimum score 550 paper-based; 82 iBT), IELTS (minimum score 6.5). Electronic applications accepted.

Maine Maritime Academy, Loeb-Sullivan School of International Business and Logistics, Castine, ME 04420. Offers global logistics and maritime management (MS); international logistics management (MS). *Program availability:* Part-time, 100% online. *Degree requirements:* For master's, capstone course. *Entrance requirements:* For master's, GMAT or GRE, letter of recommendation. Additional exam requirements/ recommendations for international students: Required—TOEFL, IELTS. Electronic applications accepted. Application fee is waived when completed online. *Faculty research:* Internet of things, trait intelligence, port operations, location theory.

McGill University, Faculty of Graduate and Postdoctoral Studies, Faculty of Engineering, School of Urban Planning, Montréal, QC H3A 2T5, Canada. Offers environmental planning (MUP); housing (MUP); transportation (MUP); urban design (MUP); urban planning, policy and design (PhD).

Naval Postgraduate School, Departments and Academic Groups, Graduate School of Business and Public Policy, Monterey, CA 93943. Offers acquisition and contract management (MBA); business administration (EMBA, MBA); contract management (MS); defense business management (MBA); defense systems analysis (MS), including management; defense systems management (international) (MBA); financial management (MBA); information management (MBA); manpower systems analysis (MS); material logistics support management (MBA); program management (MS); resource planning and management for international defense (MBA); supply chain management (MBA); systems acquisition management (MBA); transportation management (MBA). Program only open to commissioned officers of the United States and friendly nations and selected United States federal civilian employees. *Accreditation:* AACSB; NASPAA. *Program availability:* Part-time, online learning. *Degree requirements:* For master's, thesis (for some programs), terminal project/ capstone (for some programs). *Faculty research:* U.S. and European public procurement policies for small and medium-sized enterprises, examining external validity criticisms in the choice of students as subjects in accounting experiment studies, assurance of learning in contract management education, contracting for cloud computing: opportunities and risks, NPS, Apple App Store as a business model supporting U.S. Navy requirements.

New Jersey Institute of Technology, Newark College of Engineering, Newark, NJ 07102. Offers biomedical engineering (MS, PhD); biopharmaceutical engineering (MS); chemical engineering (MS, PhD); civil engineering (MS, PhD); computer engineering (MS); critical infrastructure systems (MS); electrical engineering (MS, PhD); engineering management (MS); engineering science (MS); environmental engineering (MS, PhD); healthcare systems management (MS); industrial engineering (MS, PhD); internet engineering (MS); manufacturing systems engineering (MS); materials science & engineering (PhD); materials science and engineering (MS); mechanical engineering (MS, PhD); occupational safety and health engineering (MS). *Program availability:* Part-time, evening/weekend. *Faculty:* 147 full-time (26 women), 133 part-time/adjunct (16 women). *Students:* 690 full-time (163 women), 594 part-time (130 women); includes 427 minority (79 Black or African American, non-Hispanic/Latino; 181 Asian, non-Hispanic/Latino; 140 Hispanic/Latino; 27 Two or more races, non-Hispanic/Latino), 553 international. Average age 27. 2,334 applicants, 57% accepted, 452 enrolled. In 2018, 418 master's, 31 doctorates awarded. Terminal master's awarded for partial completion of doctoral program. *Degree requirements:* For master's, thesis (for some programs); for doctorate, thesis/dissertation. *Entrance requirements:* For master's, GRE General Test, minimum GPA 2.8, personal statement, 1 letter of recommendation, transcripts; for doctorate, GRE General Test, minimum GPA of 3.5, personal statement, 3 letters of recommendation, transcripts. Additional exam requirements/recommendations for international students: Required—TOEFL (minimum score 550 paper-based; 79 iBT), IELTS (minimum score 6.5). *Application deadline:* For fall admission, 6/1 priority date for domestic students, 5/1 priority date for international students; for spring admission, 11/ 15 priority date for domestic and international students. Applications are processed on a rolling basis. Application fee: $75. Electronic applications accepted. *Expenses:* $22,690 per year (in-state), $32,136 per year (out-of-state). *Financial support:* In 2018–19, 396 students received support, including 52 fellowships with full tuition reimbursements available (averaging $22,000 per year), 113 research assistantships with full tuition reimbursements available (averaging $22,000 per year), 101 teaching assistantships with full tuition reimbursements available (averaging $22,000 per year); career-related internships or fieldwork, Federal Work-Study, scholarships/grants, and unspecified assistantships also available. Financial award application deadline: 1/15. *Faculty research:* Nonlinear signal processing, intelligent medical image analysis, calibration issues in coherent localization, computer-aided design, neural network for tool wear measurement. *Total annual research expenditures:* $41.7 million. *Unit head:* Dr. Moshe Kam, Dean, 973-596-5534, Fax: 973-596-2316, E-mail: moshe.kam@njit.edu. *Application contact:* Stephen Eck, Director of Admissions, 973-596-3300, Fax: 973-596-3461, E-mail: admissions@njit.edu.
Website: http://engineering.njit.edu/

North Dakota State University, College of Graduate and Interdisciplinary Studies, Interdisciplinary Program in Transportation and Logistics, Fargo, ND 58102. Offers managerial logistics (MML); transportation and logistics (PhD); transportation and urban systems (MS). *Entrance requirements:* Additional exam requirements/ recommendations for international students: Required—TOEFL.

Pontifical Catholic University of Puerto Rico, College of Business Administration, Program in Maritime Logistics and Transportation, Ponce, PR 00717-0777. Offers Professional Certificate.

State University of New York Maritime College, Program in International Transportation Management, Throggs Neck, NY 10465-4198. Offers MS. *Program availability:* Part-time, evening/weekend. *Degree requirements:* For master's, thesis. *Entrance requirements:* For master's, minimum GPA of 2.5. Additional exam requirements/recommendations for international students: Required—TOEFL. *Faculty research:* Ports, intermodal, shipping, logistics, port tax.

Texas A&M University, Galveston Campus, Department of Maritime Administration, College Station, TX 77843. Offers maritime administration and logistics (MMAL). *Program availability:* Part-time, evening/weekend. *Faculty:* 6. *Students:* 51 full-time (16 women), 16 part-time (2 women); includes 13 minority (1 Black or African American, non-Hispanic/Latino; 6 Asian, non-Hispanic/Latino; 3 Hispanic/Latino; 3 Two or more races, non-Hispanic/Latino), 1 international. Average age 28. 17 applicants, 100% accepted, 15 enrolled. In 2018, 35 master's awarded. *Degree requirements:* For master's, comprehensive exam (for some programs), thesis (for some programs). *Entrance requirements:* For master's, GMAT, coursework in statistics, microeconomics,

Transportation Management

organizational behavior, financial and managerial accounting, management information systems. Additional exam requirements/recommendations for international students: Required—TOEFL (minimum score 550 paper-based; 80 iBT), IELTS (minimum score 6). *Application deadline:* For fall admission, 5/1 for domestic and international students; for spring admission, 10/15 for domestic students, 10/1 for international students. Application fee: $50 ($90 for international students). Electronic applications accepted. *Expenses:* Contact institution. *Financial support:* In 2018–19, 33 students received support, including 8 research assistantships (averaging $11,403 per year), 12 teaching assistantships (averaging $14,155 per year); scholarships/grants and unspecified assistantships also available. Financial award application deadline: 3/15; financial award applicants required to submit FAFSA. *Faculty research:* International trade, inland waterways management, brokerage and chartering, organizational behavior, transportation economics, port and terminal management. *Unit head:* Dr. Joan P. Mileski, Professor/Chair of Maritime Administration, 409-740-4978, E-mail: mileskij@tamug.edu. *Application contact:* Nicole Kinslow, Director of Graduate Studies, 409-740-4937, Fax: 409-740-4754, E-mail: kinslown@tamug.edu.
Website: http://www.tamug.edu/mara/

Texas Southern University, School of Science and Technology, Program in Transportation, Planning and Management, Houston, TX 77004-4584. Offers MS. *Program availability:* Part-time, evening/weekend. *Degree requirements:* For master's, comprehensive exam, thesis optional. *Entrance requirements:* For master's, GRE General Test, minimum GPA of 2.5. Additional exam requirements/recommendations for international students: Required—TOEFL. Electronic applications accepted. *Faculty research:* Highway traffic operations, transportation and policy planning, air quality in transportation, transportation modeling.

University at Buffalo, the State University of New York, Graduate School, School of Engineering and Applied Sciences, Program in Sustainable Transportation and Logistics, Buffalo, NY 14260. Offers MS.

The University of British Columbia, Sauder School of Business, Doctoral Program in Business Administration, Vancouver, BC V6T 1Z2, Canada. Offers accounting (PhD); finance (PhD); management information systems (PhD); management science (PhD); marketing (PhD); organizational behavior (PhD); strategy and business economics (PhD); transportation and logistics (PhD); urban land economics (PhD). *Degree requirements:* For doctorate, comprehensive exam, thesis/dissertation. *Entrance requirements:* For doctorate, GMAT or GRE. Additional exam requirements/recommendations for international students: Required—TOEFL (minimum score 600 paper-based; 100 iBT). Electronic applications accepted. *Expenses:* Contact institution.

University of California, Davis, College of Engineering, Graduate Group in Transportation Technology and Policy, Davis, CA 95616. Offers MS, PhD. Terminal master's awarded for partial completion of doctoral program. *Degree requirements:* For master's, comprehensive exam (for some programs), thesis (for some programs); for doctorate, thesis/dissertation. *Entrance requirements:* For master's, GRE General Test, minimum GPA of 3.0; for doctorate, GRE General Test, minimum GPA of 3.5. Additional exam requirements/recommendations for international students: Required—TOEFL (minimum score 550 paper-based). Electronic applications accepted.

University of California, Santa Barbara, Graduate Division, College of Letters and Sciences, Division of Mathematics, Life, and Physical Sciences, Department of Geography, Santa Barbara, CA 93106-4060. Offers cognitive science (PhD); geography (MA, PhD); global studies (PhD); quantitative methods in the social sciences (PhD); technology and society (PhD); transportation (PhD); MA/PhD. Terminal master's awarded for partial completion of doctoral program. *Degree requirements:* For master's, comprehensive exam (for some programs), thesis or alternative; for doctorate, comprehensive exam, thesis/dissertation, 1 quarter of teaching assistantship. *Entrance requirements:* For master's and doctorate, GRE (minimum combined verbal and quantitative scores above 1100 in old scoring system or 301 in new scoring system). Additional exam requirements/recommendations for international students: Required—TOEFL (minimum score 550 paper-based; 80 iBT), IELTS (minimum score 7). Electronic applications accepted. *Faculty research:* Earth system science; human environment relations; modeling, measurement, and computation.

University of Hawaii at Manoa, Office of Graduate Education, College of Social Sciences, Department of Urban and Regional Planning, Honolulu, HI 96822. Offers community planning (MURP); disaster management and humanitarian assistance (Graduate Certificate); environmental planning and sustainability (MURP); international development planning (MURP); land use, transportation and infrastructure planning (MURP); planning studies (Graduate Certificate); urban and regional planning (PhD, Graduate Certificate). *Accreditation:* ACSP. *Program availability:* Part-time. *Entrance requirements:* For master's, GRE General Test, minimum GPA of 3.0; for doctorate, GRE General Test. Additional exam requirements/recommendations for international students: Required—TOEFL (minimum score 500 paper-based; 61 iBT), IELTS (minimum score 5).

University of New Orleans, Graduate School, College of Liberal Arts, Education and Human Development, Department of Planning and Urban Studies, Program in Transportation, New Orleans, LA 70148. Offers MS. *Program availability:* Online learning.

University of Southern Mississippi, College of Arts and Sciences, School of Construction and Design, Hattiesburg, MS 39406-0001. Offers logistics, trade and transportation (MS). *Program availability:* Part-time, online learning. *Degree requirements:* For master's, comprehensive exam, thesis optional. *Entrance requirements:* For master's, GMAT or GRE General Test, minimum GPA of 2.75 in last 60 hours. Additional exam requirements/recommendations for international students: Required—TOEFL, IELTS. *Faculty research:* Robotics; CAD/CAM; simulation; computer-integrated manufacturing processes; construction scheduling, estimating, and computer systems.

The University of Tennessee, Graduate School, College of Business Administration, Program in Business Administration, Knoxville, TN 37996. Offers accounting (PhD); finance (MBA, PhD); logistics and transportation (MBA, PhD); management (PhD); marketing (MBA, PhD); operations management (MBA); professional business administration (MBA); statistics (PhD); JD/MBA; MS/MBA; Pharm D/MBA. Pharm D/MBA offered jointly with The University of Tennessee Health Science Center. *Accreditation:* AACSB. *Program availability:* Online learning. *Degree requirements:* For master's, thesis or alternative; for doctorate, thesis/dissertation. *Entrance requirements:* For master's and doctorate, GMAT, minimum GPA of 2.7. Additional exam requirements/recommendations for international students: Required—TOEFL. Electronic applications accepted.

University of Washington, Graduate School, Interdisciplinary Program in Global Trade, Transportation and Logistics Studies, Seattle, WA 98195. Offers Certificate.

ACADEMIC AND PROFESSIONAL PROGRAMS IN EDUCATION

Section 22
Education

This section contains a directory of institutions offering graduate work in education, followed by in-depth entries submitted by institutions that chose to prepare detailed program descriptions. Additional information about programs listed in the directory but not augmented by an in-depth entry may be obtained by writing directly to the dean of a graduate school or chair of a department at the address given in the directory.

For programs offering related work, see also in this book *Administration, Instruction, and Theory; Instructional Levels; Leisure Studies and Recreation; Physical Education and Kinesiology; Special Focus;* and *Subject Areas.* In other guides in this series:

Graduate Programs in the Humanities, Arts & Social Sciences
See *Psychology and Counseling (School Psychology)*

Graduate Programs in the Biological/Biomedical Sciences and Health-Related Medical Professions
See *Health-Related Professions*

CONTENTS

Education—General

Abilene Christian University, Graduate Programs, College of Education and Human Services, Abilene, TX 79699. Offers M Ed, MS, MSSW, Certificate. *Accreditation:* TEAC. *Faculty:* 5 full-time (4 women), 36 part-time/adjunct (27 women). *Students:* 198 full-time (192 women), 46 part-time (37 women); includes 61 minority (12 Black or African American, non-Hispanic/Latino; 1 American Indian or Alaska Native, non-Hispanic/Latino; 5 Asian, non-Hispanic/Latino; 33 Hispanic/Latino; 1 Native Hawaiian or other Pacific Islander, non-Hispanic/Latino; 9 Two or more races, non-Hispanic/Latino), 3 international. 639 applicants, 45% accepted, 146 enrolled. In 2018, 92 master's, 12 other advanced degrees awarded. *Degree requirements:* For master's, comprehensive exam (for some programs), thesis (for some programs), practicum. *Entrance requirements:* For master's, GRE. Additional exam requirements/recommendations for international students: Required—TOEFL (minimum score 80 iBT), IELTS (minimum score 6), PTE. *Application deadline:* For fall admission, 8/15 priority date for domestic students; for winter admission, 10/1 priority date for domestic students; for spring admission, 12/15 priority date for domestic students; for summer admission, 4/15 for domestic students. Applications are processed on a rolling basis. Application fee: $65. Electronic applications accepted. *Expenses:* Contact institution. *Financial support:* In 2018–19, 118 students received support. Career-related internships or fieldwork, Federal Work-Study, institutionally sponsored loans, and scholarships/grants available. Support available to part-time students. Financial award application deadline: 4/1; financial award applicants required to submit FAFSA. *Unit head:* Dr. Jennifer Shewmaker, Dean, 325-674-2700, Fax: 325-674-3707, E-mail: cehs@acu.edu. *Application contact:* Graduate Admission, 325-674-6911, E-mail: gradinfo@acu.edu. Website: http://www.acu.edu/graduate/academics/education-and-human-services.html

Acacia University, American Graduate School of Education, Tempe, AZ 85284. Offers educational administration (M Ed); elementary education (MA); English as a second language (M Ed); secondary education (MA); special education (M Ed).

Acadia University, Faculty of Professional Studies, Inter-University Doctoral Program in Educational Studies, Wolfville, NS B4P 2R6, Canada. Offers PhD. Program offered jointly with Mount Saint Vincent University and St. Francis Xavier University. *Degree requirements:* For doctorate, thesis/dissertation, comprehensive research/scholarly portfolio.

Acadia University, Faculty of Professional Studies, School of Education, Wolfville, NS B4P 2R6, Canada. Offers counseling (M Ed); curriculum studies (M Ed), including curriculum studies, interprofessional health practice, music education; inclusive education (M Ed); leadership (M Ed). *Entrance requirements:* For master's, B Ed or the equivalent, 2 years of teaching or related experience. Additional exam requirements/recommendations for international students: Required—TOEFL (minimum score 580 paper-based; 93 iBT), IELTS (minimum score 6.5).

Adams State University, Office of Graduate Studies, Department of Teacher Education, Alamosa, CO 81101. Offers teacher education (MA), including adaptive leadership, curriculum and instruction, curriculum and instruction-STEM, educational leadership. *Program availability:* Part-time, online learning. *Degree requirements:* For master's, qualifying exam. *Entrance requirements:* For master's, GRE General Test or MAT, minimum undergraduate GPA of 3.0.

Adelphi University, College of Education & Health Sciences, Garden City, NY 11530-0701. Offers MA, MS, DA, Certificate. *Accreditation:* NCATE. *Program availability:* Part-time, evening/weekend. *Faculty:* 69 full-time (45 women), 88 part-time/adjunct (61 women). *Students:* 460 full-time (369 women), 259 part-time (160 women); includes 197 minority (57 Black or African American, non-Hispanic/Latino; 1 American Indian or Alaska Native, non-Hispanic/Latino; 26 Asian, non-Hispanic/Latino; 106 Hispanic/Latino; 1 Native Hawaiian or other Pacific Islander, non-Hispanic/Latino; 6 Two or more races, non-Hispanic/Latino), 34 international. Average age 27. 1,256 applicants, 59% accepted, 288 enrolled. In 2018, 299 master's, 8 doctorates, 83 other advanced degrees awarded. *Degree requirements:* For doctorate, comprehensive exam, thesis/dissertation, Master's in Speech Language Pathology. *Entrance requirements:* For master's, resume, letters of recommendation, official transcripts, bachelor's degree, 500 word essay; for doctorate, 3 letters of recommendation, transcripts, CV. Additional exam requirements/recommendations for international students: Required—TOEFL (minimum score 550 paper-based; 80 iBT), IELTS (minimum score 6.5). *Application deadline:* For fall admission, 3/1 for international students; for spring admission, 11/1 for international students. Applications are processed on a rolling basis. Application fee: $50. Electronic applications accepted. *Expenses:* Contact institution. *Financial support:* Fellowships, research assistantships, teaching assistantships, career-related internships or fieldwork, Federal Work-Study, scholarships/grants, traineeships, tuition waivers (full and partial), unspecified assistantships, and tuition remission for employees available. Support available to part-time students. Financial award application deadline: 1/1; financial award applicants required to submit FAFSA. *Faculty research:* Multicultural and gender issues, psychometric assessment, quantitative research methods. *Unit head:* Dr. Xiao-Lei Wang, Dean, 516-877-4065, E-mail: xlwang@adelphi.edu. *Application contact:* Kristen Capezza, Vice President for Enrollment Management, 516-877-3021, Fax: 516-877-3039, E-mail: graduateadmissions@adelphi.edu. Website: http://education.adelphi.edu/

Alabama Agricultural and Mechanical University, School of Graduate Studies, College of Education, Humanities, and Behavioral Sciences, Huntsville, AL 35811. Offers M Ed, MS, MS Ed, PhD, Ed S. *Accreditation:* NCATE. *Program availability:* Part-time, evening/weekend. *Degree requirements:* For master's, comprehensive exam. *Entrance requirements:* For master's, GRE General Test. Additional exam requirements/recommendations for international students: Required—TOEFL (minimum score 500 paper-based; 61 iBT). Electronic applications accepted. *Faculty research:* Speech defects, aging, blindness, multicultural education, learning styles.

Alabama State University, College of Education, Montgomery, AL 36101-0271. Offers M Ed, MS, Ed D, PhD, Ed S. *Accreditation:* NCATE. *Program availability:* Part-time. *Faculty:* 7 full-time (4 women), 7 part-time/adjunct (4 women). *Students:* 62 full-time (42 women), 189 part-time (140 women); includes 235 minority (234 Black or African American, non-Hispanic/Latino; 1 Hispanic/Latino), 5 international. Average age 41. 71 applicants, 79% accepted, 21 enrolled. In 2018, 76 master's, 4 doctorates, 17 other advanced degrees awarded. *Degree requirements:* For master's, comprehensive exam; for doctorate, thesis/dissertation; for Ed S, comprehensive exam, thesis. *Entrance requirements:* For master's, GRE General Test, MAT, writing competency test; for Ed S, writing competency test, GRE, MAT. Additional exam requirements/recommendations for international students: Required—TOEFL (minimum score 500 paper-based). *Application deadline:* For fall admission, 4/15 for domestic and international students; for spring admission, 11/15 for domestic and international students; for summer admission, 3/15 for domestic and international students. Applications are processed on a rolling basis. Application fee: $25. Electronic applications accepted. *Expenses:* Contact

institution. *Financial support:* Fellowships, teaching assistantships, career-related internships or fieldwork, scholarships/grants, tuition waivers (partial), and unspecified assistantships available. Financial award application deadline: 6/30; financial award applicants required to submit FAFSA. *Faculty research:* Whole language instruction, African-American children's literature. *Unit head:* Dr. Alethea Hampton, Dean, 334-229-4250, E-mail: ahampton@alasu.edu. *Application contact:* Dr. Ed Brown, Dean of Graduate Studies, 334-229-4274, Fax: 334-229-4928, E-mail: ebrown@alasu.edu. Website: http://www.alasu.edu/Education/

Alaska Pacific University, Graduate Programs, Education Department, Program in Teaching, Anchorage, AK 99508-4672. Offers teaching (K-8) (MAT). *Degree requirements:* For master's, research project. *Entrance requirements:* For master's, GRE or MAT, PRAXIS, minimum GPA of 3.0.

Albany State University, College of Education, Albany, GA 31705-2717. Offers early childhood education (M Ed); educational leadership (Ed S); health and physical education (M Ed); middle grades education (M Ed); school counseling (M Ed); special education (M Ed). *Accreditation:* NCATE. *Program availability:* Part-time, evening/weekend, online learning. *Degree requirements:* For master's, comprehensive exam, internship, GACE Content Exam. *Entrance requirements:* For master's, GRE or MAT. Electronic applications accepted. *Faculty research:* GACE preparation, STEM (science, technology, engineering, and mathematics), technology education, special education, professional teacher development, health implications liberation philosophy, NET-Q, learning community, disabled or at-risk students.

Albertus Magnus College, Master of Science in Education Program, New Haven, CT 06511-1189. Offers MS Ed. *Program availability:* Part-time, evening/weekend, blended/hybrid learning. *Degree requirements:* For master's, thesis, capstone. *Entrance requirements:* For master's, bachelor's degree, official transcripts of all undergraduate work, three letters of recommendation, resume, essay, valid Connecticut initial teacher certificate (preferred). Additional exam requirements/recommendations for international students: Recommended—TOEFL (minimum score 550 paper-based; 80 iBT). *Expenses:* Contact institution. *Faculty research:* Assessment, learning theory, educational leadership, differentiated instruction, multiculturalism.

Albright College, Graduate Division, Reading, PA 19612-5234. Offers early childhood education (MS); elementary education (MS); English as a second language (MA); general education (MA); special education (MS). *Program availability:* Part-time, evening/weekend. *Degree requirements:* For master's, thesis. *Entrance requirements:* For master's, GRE General Test or MAT, minimum undergraduate GPA of 3.0, 2 letters of recommendation, interview. Additional exam requirements/recommendations for international students: Recommended—TOEFL (minimum score 525 paper-based). Electronic applications accepted.

Alcorn State University, School of Graduate Studies, School of Education and Psychology, Lorman, MS 39096-7500. Offers agricultural education (MS Ed); elementary education (MAT, MS Ed, Ed S); guidance and counseling (MS Ed); industrial education (MS Ed); secondary education (MAT, MS Ed), including health and physical education (MS Ed), NCAA compliance and academic progress reporting (MS Ed); special education (MS Ed). *Accreditation:* NCATE. *Degree requirements:* For master's, thesis optional.

Alfred University, Graduate School, Division of Education, Alfred, NY 14802-1205. Offers college student development (MS Ed); literacy (MS Ed). *Accreditation:* TEAC. *Program availability:* Part-time. *Entrance requirements:* For master's, Liberal Arts and Sciences Test (LAST), Assessment of Teaching Skills (written) (ATS-W), Content Specialty Test (CST). Additional exam requirements/recommendations for international students: Required—TOEFL (minimum score 590 paper-based; 90 iBT), IELTS (minimum score 6.5). Electronic applications accepted.

Alliant International University–Los Angeles, Shirley M. Hufstedler School of Education, TeachersCHOICE Preparation Programs, Alhambra, CA 91803. Offers MA, Credential. *Program availability:* Part-time. *Entrance requirements:* For master's, CBEST, CSET, interview; offer of employment as a teacher of record in a California school; minimum GPA of 2.5; 2 letters of recommendation. Additional exam requirements/recommendations for international students: Required—TOEFL (minimum score 550 paper-based). *Faculty research:* Multicultural and bilingual education pedagogy, teacher training pedagogy, curriculum development, instructional strategies.

Alliant International University–Sacramento, Shirley M. Hufstedler School of Education, TeachersCHOICE Preparation Programs, Sacramento, CA 95833. Offers MA, Credential. *Entrance requirements:* For master's, CBEST, CSET, interview; offer of employment as a teacher of record in a California school; minimum GPA of 3.0; 2 letters of recommendation. Electronic applications accepted. *Faculty research:* Innovative teacher education, educational leadership, cross-cultural education.

Alliant International University–San Diego, Shirley M. Hufstedler School of Education, Teacher Education Programs, San Diego, CA 92131. Offers preliminary single subject (Credential); professional clear multiple subject (Credential); professional clear single subject (Credential); teacher education (MA). *Program availability:* Part-time, evening/weekend. *Entrance requirements:* For degree, California Basic Educational Skills Test, minimum GPA of 2.5. Additional exam requirements/recommendations for international students: Required—TOEFL (minimum score 550 paper-based; 80 iBT), TWE (minimum score 5). Electronic applications accepted. *Faculty research:* Curriculum and instructional planning.

Alliant International University–San Francisco, Shirley M. Hufstedler School of Education, Teacher Education Programs, San Francisco, CA 94133. Offers auditory oral education (Certificate); CLAD (Certificate); education specialist: mild/moderate disabilities (Credential); preliminary multiple subject (Credential); preliminary single subject (Credential); professional clear multiple subject (Credential); professional clear single subject (Credential); special education (MA); teaching (MA); TESOL (Certificate). *Program availability:* Part-time, evening/weekend. *Degree requirements:* For master's, thesis. *Entrance requirements:* For degree, California Basic Educational Skills Test, minimum GPA of 2.5. Additional exam requirements/recommendations for international students: Required—TOEFL (minimum score 550 paper-based), TWE (minimum score 5). Electronic applications accepted. *Faculty research:* Curriculum development, first year teachers, cross-cultural issues in teaching, biliteracy.

Alvernia University, School of Graduate Studies, Program in Education, Reading, PA 19607-1799. Offers urban education (M Ed). *Program availability:* Part-time, evening/weekend. *Degree requirements:* For master's, thesis optional. *Entrance requirements:* For master's, GRE or MAT (alumni excluded). Electronic applications accepted.

Alverno College, School of Professional Studies - Education Division, Milwaukee, WI 53234-3922. Offers adaptive education (MA); administrative leadership (MA); adult

education and organizational development (MA); adult educational and instructional design (MA); adult educational and instructional technology (MA); global connections in the humanities (MA); instructional leadership (MA); instructional technology for K-12 settings (MA); professional development (MA); reading education (MA); reading education with adaptive education (MA); science education (MA); special education (MA); teaching in alternative schools (MA). *Accreditation:* NCATE. *Program availability:* Part-time, evening/weekend. *Degree requirements:* For master's, presentation/defense of proposal, conference presentation of inquiry projects. *Entrance requirements:* For master's, bachelor's degree in related field, communication samples from work setting, 3 letters of recommendation. Additional exam requirements/recommendations for international students: Required—TOEFL. Electronic applications accepted. *Expenses:* Contact institution. *Faculty research:* Student self-assessment, self-reflection, integration of curriculum, identifying needs of students in strategic situations and designing appropriate classroom strategies.

American College of Education, Graduate Programs, Indianapolis, IN 46204. Offers curriculum and instruction (M Ed), including bilingual, ESL; educational leadership (M Ed); educational technology (M Ed).

American InterContinental University Online, Program in Education, Schaumburg, IL 60173. Offers curriculum and instruction (M Ed); educational assessment and evaluation (M Ed); instructional technology (M Ed); leadership of educational organizations (M Ed). *Accreditation:* TEAC. *Program availability:* Evening/weekend, online learning. *Entrance requirements:* Additional exam requirements/recommendations for international students: Required—TOEFL (minimum score 550 paper-based). Electronic applications accepted.

American International College, School of Education, Low Residency Programs, Springfield, MA 01109-3189. Offers counseling psychology (MA); educational leadership and supervision (Ed D); professional counseling and supervision (Ed D); teaching and learning (Ed D). *Program availability:* Evening/weekend. *Degree requirements:* For doctorate, thesis/dissertation. *Entrance requirements:* For master's, minimum undergraduate GPA of 3.0, 2 letters of recommendation, personal goal statement, official transcript of all academic work (graduate and undergraduate); for doctorate, minimum master's GPA of 3.0, 3 letters of recommendation, personal goal statement/essay (6-8 pages), official transcript of all academic work (graduate and undergraduate). Additional exam requirements/recommendations for international students: Required—TOEFL. *Expenses:* Contact institution. *Faculty research:* Educational leadership, curriculum, program evaluation, educational policy.

American Jewish University, Graduate School of Education, Program in Education, Bel Air, CA 90077-1599. Offers MA Ed. *Degree requirements:* For master's, one foreign language. *Entrance requirements:* For master's, GRE General Test, interview, minimum GPA of 3.0. Additional exam requirements/recommendations for international students: Required—TOEFL. *Faculty research:* Philosophy of education, curriculum development, teacher training.

American Jewish University, Graduate School of Education, Program in Education for Working Professionals, Bel Air, CA 90077-1599. Offers MA Ed. *Degree requirements:* For master's, comprehensive exam, internships. *Entrance requirements:* For master's, GRE General Test, interview. Additional exam requirements/recommendations for international students: Required—TOEFL.

American University, School of Education, Washington, DC 20016-8030. Offers education (Certificate); education policy and leadership (M Ed); international training and education (MA); special education (MA); teacher education (MAT); M Ed/MPA; M Ed/MPP; MAT/MA. *Accreditation:* NCATE. *Program availability:* Part-time, evening/weekend, 100% online. *Faculty:* 17 full-time (13 women), 33 part-time/adjunct (23 women). *Students:* 53 full-time (46 women), 246 part-time (191 women); includes 139 minority (97 Black or African American, non-Hispanic/Latino; 13 Asian, non-Hispanic/Latino; 23 Hispanic/Latino; 6 Two or more races, non-Hispanic/Latino), 5 international. Average age 29. 361 applicants, 88% accepted, 161 enrolled. In 2018, 73 master's, 2 other advanced degrees awarded. *Degree requirements:* For master's, comprehensive exam, thesis or alternative. *Entrance requirements:* For master's, Please visit website: https://www.american.edu/soe/, bachelor's degree, statement of purpose, transcripts, 2 letters of recommendation. Additional exam requirements/recommendations for international students: Required—TOEFL (minimum score 100 iBT). Application fee: $55. Electronic applications accepted. *Expenses: Tuition:* Full-time $30,744; part-time $1642 per credit hour. *Required fees:* $702; $200 per semester. Tuition and fees vary according to course load, degree level and program. *Financial support:* Research assistantships, teaching assistantships, institutionally sponsored loans, scholarships/grants, and unspecified assistantships available. Financial award application deadline: 2/1; financial award applicants required to submit FAFSA. *Unit head:* Dr. Cheryl Holcomb-McCoy, Dean, 202-885-3720, E-mail: educate@american.edu. *Application contact:* Ashleigh Huseth, Senior Coordinator, Admissions & Onboarding, E-mail: ahuseth@american.edu.
Website: https://www.american.edu/cas/education/

The American University in Cairo, Graduate School of Education, Cairo, Egypt. Offers educational leadership (MA); international and comparative education (MA). *Program availability:* Part-time, evening/weekend. *Degree requirements:* For master's, thesis. *Entrance requirements:* Additional exam requirements/recommendations for international students: Required—TOEFL (minimum score 450 paper-based; 45 iBT), IELTS (minimum score 5). Electronic applications accepted. *Faculty research:* Educational reform.

The American University in Dubai, Graduate Programs, Dubai, United Arab Emirates. Offers construction management (MS); education (M Ed); finance (MBA); generalist (MBA); marketing (MBA). *Program availability:* Part-time, evening/weekend. *Degree requirements:* For master's, thesis optional. *Entrance requirements:* For master's, GMAT (for MBA); GRE (for M Ed and MS), minimum undergraduate GPA of 3.0, official transcripts, two reference forms, curriculum vitae/resume, statement of career objectives, work experience. Additional exam requirements/recommendations for international students: Required—TOEFL (minimum score 550 paper-based; 79 iBT). Electronic applications accepted.

American University of Beirut, Graduate Programs, Faculty of Arts and Sciences, Beirut 1107 2020, Lebanon. Offers anthropology (MA); Arab and Middle Eastern history (PhD); Arabic language and literature (MA, PhD); archaeology (MA); art history and curating (MA); biology (MS); cell and molecular biology (PhD); chemistry (MS); clinical psychology (MA); computational sciences (MS); computer science (MS); economics (MA); education (MA), including administration and policy studies, elementary education, mathematics education, psychology school guidance, psychology test and measurements, science education, teaching English as a foreign language; English language (MA); English literature (MA); environmental policy planning (MS); financial economics (MAFE); general psychology (MA); geology (MS); history (MA); Islamic studies (MA); mathematics (MS); media studies (MA); Middle East studies (MA); philosophy (MA); physics (MS); political studies (MA); public administration (MA); public policy and international affairs (MA); sociology (MA); theoretical physics (PhD). *Program availability:* Part-time. *Faculty:* 187 full-time (64 women), 27 part-time/adjunct (15 women). *Students:* 292 full-time (215 women), 216 part-time (148 women). Average age 27. 422 applicants, 64% accepted, 124 enrolled. In 2018, 90 master's, 3 doctorates awarded. *Degree requirements:* For master's, comprehensive exam, thesis (for some programs), project; for doctorate, comprehensive exam, thesis/dissertation (for some programs). *Entrance requirements:* For master's, GRE General Test (for archaeology, clinical psychology, general psychology, economics, financial economics and biology); for doctorate, GRE General Test for all PhD programs, GRE Subject Test for theoretical physics. Additional exam requirements/recommendations for international students: Required—TOEFL (minimum score 583 paper-based; 97 iBT), IELTS (minimum score 7). *Application deadline:* For fall admission, 3/18 for domestic students; for spring admission, 11/5 for domestic students. Application fee: $50. Electronic applications accepted. *Expenses:* MA/MS: Humanities and social sciences=$912/credit. Sciences=$943/credit. Financial economics=$986/credit. Thesis: Humanities/social sciences=$6565 and sciences=$6865. *Financial support:* In 2018–19, 227 fellowships with full tuition reimbursements, 17 research assistantships with full tuition reimbursements, 83 teaching assistantships with full tuition reimbursements were awarded; scholarships/grants, tuition waivers (full and partial), and unspecified assistantships also available. Financial award application deadline: 3/18. *Faculty research:* Sciences: Physics: High energy, Particle, Polymer and Soft Matter, Thermal, Plasma; String Theory, Mathematical physics, Astrophysics (stellar evolution, planet and galaxy formation and evolution, astrophysical dynamics), Solid State physics/thin films, Spintronics, Magnetic properties of materials, Mineralogy, Petrology, and Geochemistry of Hard Rocks, Geophysics and Petrophysics, Hydrogeology, Micropaleontology, Sedimentology, and Stratigraphy, Structural Geology and Geotectonics, Renewable en. *Total annual research expenditures:* $4.3 million. *Unit head:* Dr. Nadia Maria El Cheikh, Dean, Faculty of Arts and Sciences, 961-1-350000 Ext. 3800, Fax: 961-1-744461, E-mail: nmcheikh@aub.edu.lb. *Application contact:* Adriana Michelle Zanaty, Curriculum and Graduate Studies Officer, 961-1-350000 Ext. 3833, Fax: 961-1-744461, E-mail: az48@aub.edu.lb.
Website: https://www.aub.edu.lb/fas/Pages/default.aspx

American University of Puerto Rico, Program in Education, Bayamon, PR 00960-2037. Offers art education (M Ed); elementary education 4-6 (M Ed); elementary education K-3 (M Ed); general science education (M Ed); physical education (M Ed); special education (M Ed). *Program availability:* Part-time, evening/weekend. *Entrance requirements:* For master's, EXADEP, GRE, or MAT, 2 letters of recommendation, minimum GPA of 2.5.

Anderson University, College of Education, Anderson, SC 29621-4035. Offers administration and supervision (M Ed); education (M Ed); elementary education (MAT). *Accreditation:* NCATE. *Program availability:* 100% online. *Expenses: Tuition:* Full-time $400; part-time $400 per credit. *Required fees:* $200; $200 per semester. Tuition and fees vary according to course load. *Financial support:* Scholarships/grants and tuition waivers available. Financial award application deadline: 3/1; financial award applicants required to submit FAFSA. *Unit head:* Dr. Mark Butler, Dean, 864-231-2042. *Application contact:* Dr. Mark Butler, Dean, 864-231-2042.
Website: https://www.andersonuniversity.edu/education

Anderson University, School of Education, Anderson, IN 46012-3495. Offers M Ed. *Accreditation:* NCATE.

Andrews University, School of Graduate Studies, School of Education, Berrien Springs, MI 49104. Offers MA, MAT, MS, Ed D, PhD, Ed S. *Accreditation:* NCATE. *Program availability:* Part-time. Terminal master's awarded for partial completion of doctoral program. *Degree requirements:* For doctorate, thesis/dissertation. *Entrance requirements:* For master's, GRE Subject Test. Additional exam requirements/recommendations for international students: Required—TOEFL (minimum score 550 paper-based). *Faculty research:* Church planting, bilingual education, leadership development, exercise education.

Anna Maria College, Graduate Division, Program in Education, Paxton, MA 01612. Offers early childhood education (M Ed); education (CAGS); elementary education (M Ed); English language arts (M Ed); visual arts (M Ed). *Program availability:* Part-time, evening/weekend. *Entrance requirements:* For master's, bachelor's degree in liberal arts or sciences, minimum GPA of 3.0. Additional exam requirements/recommendations for international students: Required—TOEFL (minimum score 500 paper-based). Electronic applications accepted.

Antioch University Los Angeles, Program in Education, Culver City, CA 90230. Offers MA. *Program availability:* Evening/weekend. *Entrance requirements:* Additional exam requirements/recommendations for international students: Required—TOEFL.

Antioch University New England, Graduate School, Department of Education, Keene, NH 03431-3552. Offers integrated learning (M Ed), including elementary and early childhood education, elementary education (M Ed, Certificate); teaching (M Ed, PMC), including foundations of education (M Ed), principal certification (PMC); Waldorf teacher training (M Ed, Certificate), including elementary education, foundations of education (M Ed). *Degree requirements:* For master's, thesis (for some programs), internship. *Entrance requirements:* Additional exam requirements/recommendations for international students: Required—TOEFL (minimum score 550 paper-based). Electronic applications accepted. *Expenses:* Contact institution. *Faculty research:* Classroom and school restructuring, problem-based learning, Waldorf collaborative leadership, ecological literacy.

Antioch University Santa Barbara, Program in Education/Teacher Credentialing, Santa Barbara, CA 93101-1581. Offers M Ed, MA. *Program availability:* Part-time. *Entrance requirements:* Additional exam requirements/recommendations for international students: Required—TOEFL (minimum score 550 paper-based). Electronic applications accepted.

Antioch University Seattle, Program in Education, Seattle, WA 98121. Offers adult education (MA); drama therapy (MA); individualized studies (MA); leadership in edible education (MA); teaching (MAT); urban environmental education (MA). *Program availability:* Part-time, evening/weekend. *Degree requirements:* For master's, comprehensive exam (for some programs), thesis. *Entrance requirements:* For master's, WEST-B, WEST-E, current resume, transcripts of undergraduate degree and coursework (or for highest degree completed), two letters of recommendation, proof of fingerprinting and background check, moral character with fitness statement of understanding, documentation of 40 hours' experience in school classroom(s). *Expenses:* Contact institution. *Faculty research:* Visual thinking and science education, K-8 equity and engaged pedagogy in science education, K-12 inquiry-based mathematics education, education in prisons and other institutions of confinement.

Aquinas College, School of Education, Nashville, TN 37205-2005. Offers elementary education (MAT); secondary education (MAT); teaching and learning (M Ed).

Aquinas College, School of Education, Grand Rapids, MI 49506. Offers M Ed, MAT. *Accreditation:* TEAC. *Program availability:* Part-time, evening/weekend. *Faculty:* 4 full-time (all women), 20 part-time/adjunct (16 women). *Students:* 4 full-time (all women), 108 part-time (91 women); includes 10 minority (1 Black or African American, non-Hispanic/Latino; 1 Asian, non-Hispanic/Latino; 8 Hispanic/Latino). Average age 36. In 2018, 8 master's awarded. *Degree requirements:* For master's, teaching project; action research. *Entrance requirements:* For master's, Michigan Basic Skills Test, minimum

undergraduate GPA of 3.0, teaching certificate. Additional exam requirements/recommendations for international students: Required—TOEFL (minimum score 550 paper-based). *Application deadline:* Applications are processed on a rolling basis. Application fee: $0. *Expenses: Tuition:* Part-time $593 per credit hour. *Required fees:* $120; $120. *Financial support:* Scholarships/grants available. Support available to part-time students. Financial award application deadline: 3/15. *Faculty research:* Early Childhood Education, English as a Learned Language, Learning Disabilities. *Unit head:* Dr. Susan English, Dean, 616-632-2800, Fax: 616-732-4465, E-mail: englisus@aquinas.edu. *Application contact:* Michele Mazurek, Certification Officer, Data Records Specialist, 616-632-2427, E-mail: michele.mazurek@aquinas.edu.
Website: http://www.aquinas.edu/education/

Arcadia University, School of Education, Glenside, PA 19038-3295. Offers art education (M Ed); computer education (CAS); curriculum (CAS); curriculum studies (M Ed); early childhood education (M Ed), including individualized, master teacher, research in child development; educational leadership (M Ed, Ed D, CAS); elementary education (M Ed); English education (MA Ed); environmental education (MA Ed); instructional technology (M Ed); language arts (M Ed); library science (M Ed); mathematics education (M Ed, MA Ed); music education (MA Ed); psychology (MA Ed); reading (M Ed, CAS); science education (M Ed, CAS); secondary education (M Ed, CAS); special education (M Ed, Ed D, CAS); theater arts (MA Ed); written communication (MA Ed). *Accreditation:* NASAD. *Program availability:* Part-time, evening/weekend, online learning. *Faculty:* 14 full-time (10 women). *Students:* 35 full-time (24 women), 299 part-time (243 women); includes 72 minority (49 Black or African American, non-Hispanic/Latino; 1 American Indian or Alaska Native, non-Hispanic/Latino; 12 Asian, non-Hispanic/Latino; 8 Hispanic/Latino; 2 Two or more races, non-Hispanic/Latino), 5 international. In 2018, 152 master's, 8 doctorates awarded. *Entrance requirements:* Additional exam requirements/recommendations for international students: Required—Official results from the TOEFL or IELTS are required. *Application deadline:* Applications are processed on a rolling basis. Application fee: $25. Electronic applications accepted. *Expenses:* Contact institution. *Financial support:* Career-related internships or fieldwork, tuition waivers (partial), and unspecified assistantships available. *Unit head:* Kimberly Dean, Chair, 215-572-8629. *Application contact:* 215-572-2925, Fax: 215-572-2126, E-mail: grad@arcadia.edu.

Argosy University, Atlanta, College of Education, Atlanta, GA 30328. Offers educational leadership (MAEd, Ed D, Ed S), including higher education administration (Ed D), K-12 education (Ed D); teaching and learning (MAEd, Ed D, Ed S), including education technology (Ed D), higher education (Ed D), K-12 education (Ed D).

Argosy University, Chicago, College of Education, Chicago, IL 60601. Offers adult education and training (MA Ed); community college executive leadership (Ed D); educational leadership (MA Ed, Ed D, Ed S), including district leadership (Ed D), higher education administration (Ed D), K-12 education (Ed D); instructional leadership (Ed D, Ed S), including higher education (Ed D), K-12 education (Ed D). *Program availability:* Online learning.

Argosy University, Hawai`i, College of Education, Honolulu, HI 96813. Offers adult education and training (MAEd); educational leadership (Ed D), including higher education administration, K-12 education; instructional leadership (Ed D), including higher education, K-12 education; school psychology (MA).

Argosy University, Los Angeles, College of Education, Los Angeles, CA 90045. Offers community college executive leadership (Ed D); educational leadership (MA Ed, Ed D), including higher education administration (Ed D), K-12 education (Ed D); instructional leadership (MA Ed, Ed D), including higher education (Ed D), K-12 education (Ed D), multiple subject teacher preparation (MA Ed), single subject teacher preparation (MA Ed).

Argosy University, Northern Virginia, College of Education, Arlington, VA 22209. Offers community college executive leadership (Ed D); educational leadership (MA Ed, Ed D, Ed S), including higher education administration (Ed D), K-12 education (Ed D); instructional leadership (MA Ed, Ed D, Ed S), including higher education (Ed D), K-12 education (Ed D).

Argosy University, Orange County, College of Education, Orange, CA 92868. Offers community college executive leadership (Ed D); educational leadership (MA Ed, Ed D), including higher education administration (Ed D), K-12 education (Ed D); instructional leadership (MA Ed, Ed D), including education technology (Ed D), higher education (Ed D), K-12 education (Ed D), multiple subject teacher preparation (MA Ed), single subject teacher preparation (MA Ed).

Argosy University, Phoenix, College of Education, Phoenix, AZ 85021. Offers adult education and training (MA Ed); advanced educational administration (Ed D, Ed S); community college executive leadership (Ed D); educational administration (MA Ed); educational leadership (MA Ed, Ed D, Ed S), including education technology (Ed D), higher education administration (Ed D), K-12 education (Ed D); higher and postsecondary education (MA Ed); initial educational administration (Ed D, Ed S); school psychology (MA); teaching and learning (MA Ed, Ed D, Ed S), including education technology (Ed D), higher education (Ed D), K-12 education (Ed D).

Argosy University, Seattle, College of Education, Seattle, WA 98121. Offers adult education and training (MA Ed); community college executive leadership (Ed D); educational leadership (MA Ed, Ed D), including higher education administration (Ed D), K-12 education (Ed D); higher and postsecondary education (MA Ed); instructional leadership (MA Ed, Ed D), including education technology (Ed D), higher education (Ed D), K-12 education (Ed D).

Argosy University, Tampa, College of Education, Tampa, FL 33607. Offers community college executive leadership (Ed D); educational leadership (MA Ed, Ed D, Ed S), including higher education administration (Ed D), K-12 education (Ed D); school counseling (MA); teaching and learning (MA Ed, Ed D, Ed S), including higher education (Ed D), K-12 education (Ed D).

Argosy University, Twin Cities, College of Education, Eagan, MN 55121. Offers advanced educational administration (Ed D, Ed S); educational leadership (MA Ed, Ed D, Ed S), including higher education administration (Ed D), K-12 education (Ed D); higher and postsecondary education (MA Ed); initial educational administration (Ed D, Ed S); instructional leadership (MA Ed, Ed D, Ed S), including education technology (Ed D), higher education (Ed D), K-12 education (Ed D).

Arizona State University at the Tempe campus, Mary Lou Fulton Teachers College, Phoenix, AZ 85069. Offers M Ed, MA, MC, MPE, Ed D, PhD, Graduate Certificate. *Program availability:* Part-time, evening/weekend, online learning. *Degree requirements:* For master's, comprehensive exam (for some programs), thesis (for some programs), interactive Program of Study (iPOS) submitted before completing 50 percent of required credit hours; for doctorate, comprehensive exam, thesis/dissertation, interactive Program of Study (iPOS) submitted before completing 50 percent of required credit hours. *Entrance requirements:* For master's and doctorate, GRE General Test or GMAT, minimum GPA of 3.0 or equivalent in last 2 years of work leading to bachelor's degree. Additional exam requirements/recommendations for international students: Required—TOEFL, IELTS, or PTE. Electronic applications accepted. *Expenses:* Contact institution.

Arkansas State University, Graduate School, College of Education and Behavioral Science, State University, AR 72467. Offers MAT, MRC, MS, MSE, Ed D, Ed S, Graduate Certificate, SCCT. *Accreditation:* NCATE. *Program availability:* Part-time, online learning. *Degree requirements:* For master's and other advanced degree, comprehensive exam, thesis or alternative; for doctorate, comprehensive exam, thesis/dissertation. *Entrance requirements:* For master's, GRE General Test or MAT, appropriate bachelor's degree, interview, letters of reference, official transcripts, immunization records; for doctorate, GRE General Test or MAT, interview, master's degree, letters of reference, official transcript, personal statement, immunization records, writing sample; for other advanced degree, GRE General Test, MAT, interview, master's degree, letters of reference, official transcript, 3 years of teaching experience, teaching license, immunization records. Additional exam requirements/recommendations for international students: Required—TOEFL (minimum score 550 paper-based; 79 iBT), IELTS (minimum score 6), PTE (minimum score 56). Electronic applications accepted.

Arkansas Tech University, College of Education, Russellville, AR 72801. Offers college student personnel (MS); educational leadership (M Ed, Ed S); instructional technology (M Ed); school counseling and leadership (M Ed); school leadership (Ed D); special education K-12 (M Ed); strength and conditioning studies (MS); teaching (MAT); teaching, learning, and leadership (M Ed). *Accreditation:* NCATE. *Program availability:* Part-time, evening/weekend, 100% online, blended/hybrid learning. *Students:* 90 full-time (52 women), 450 part-time (359 women); includes 100 minority (63 Black or African American, non-Hispanic/Latino; 6 American Indian or Alaska Native, non-Hispanic/Latino; 1 Asian, non-Hispanic/Latino; 15 Hispanic/Latino; 15 Two or more races, non-Hispanic/Latino), 4 international. Average age 34. In 2018, 130 master's, 14 doctorates, 1 other advanced degree awarded. *Degree requirements:* For master's, comprehensive exam, thesis optional, action research project; for doctorate, thesis/dissertation. *Entrance requirements:* Additional exam requirements/recommendations for international students: Required—TOEFL (minimum score 550 paper-based; 79 iBT), IELTS (minimum score 6.5), PTE (minimum score 58). *Application deadline:* For fall admission, 3/1 priority date for domestic students, 5/1 priority date for international students; for spring admission, 10/1 priority date for domestic and international students. Applications are processed on a rolling basis. Application fee: $40 ($90 for international students). Electronic applications accepted. *Expenses: Tuition, area resident:* Full-time $6816; part-time $284 per credit hour. Tuition, state resident: full-time $6816; part-time $284 per credit hour. Tuition, nonresident: full-time $13,632; part-time $568 per credit hour. *International tuition:* $13,632 full-time. *Required fees:* $457.50 per semester. Tuition and fees vary according to course load and degree level. *Financial support:* In 2018–19, research assistantships with full and partial tuition reimbursements (averaging $4,800 per year), teaching assistantships with full and partial tuition reimbursements (averaging $4,800 per year) were awarded; career-related internships or fieldwork, Federal Work-Study, scholarships/grants, health care benefits, and unspecified assistantships also available. Support available to part-time students. Financial award application deadline: 4/15; financial award applicants required to submit FAFSA. *Unit head:* Dr. Linda Bean, Dean, 479-964-3217, E-mail: lbean@atu.edu. *Application contact:* Dr. Jeff Robertson, Interim Dean of Graduate College, 479-968-0398, Fax: 479-964-0542, E-mail: gradcollege@atu.edu.
Website: http://www.atu.edu/education/

Arlington Baptist University, Program in Education, Arlington, TX 76012-3425. Offers curriculum and instruction (M Ed); educational leadership (M Ed). *Degree requirements:* For master's, professional portfolio; internship (for educational leadership). *Entrance requirements:* For master's, bachelor's degree from accredited college or university with minimum GPA of 3.0, minimum of 12 hours in Bible; minimum of three years' classroom teaching experience in an accredited K-12 public or private school (for educational leadership only).

Ashland University, Dwight Schar College of Education, Ashland, OH 44805-3702. Offers M Ed, Ed D. *Accreditation:* NCATE. *Program availability:* Part-time. *Degree requirements:* For master's, thesis optional, capstone project; for doctorate, comprehensive exam, thesis/dissertation. *Entrance requirements:* For master's, minimum GPA of 2.75; for doctorate, master's degree, minimum GPA of 3.3, writing sample, letters of recommendation. Additional exam requirements/recommendations for international students: Recommended—TOEFL, IELTS, TSE. Electronic applications accepted. *Expenses: Tuition:* Full-time $6660; part-time $3330 per credit hour. *Required fees:* $360; $180 per credit hour. Tuition and fees vary according to program. *Faculty research:* Teacher performance, administrative performance, collaborative learning groups, talent development, environmental education.

Athabasca University, Centre for Distance Education, Athabasca, AB T9S 3A3, Canada. Offers distance education (MDE, Ed D); distance education technology (Advanced Diploma). *Program availability:* Part-time, online learning. *Degree requirements:* For master's, thesis optional. *Entrance requirements:* For master's, 3- or 4-year baccalaureate degree. Electronic applications accepted. *Expenses:* Contact institution. *Faculty research:* Role development, interaction, educational technology, and communities of practice in distance education; instructional design.

Athabasca University, Centre for Interdisciplinary Studies, Athabasca, AB T9S 3A3, Canada. Offers adult education (MA); community studies (MA); cultural studies (MA); educational studies (MA); global change (MA); heritage resource management (Postbaccalaureate Certificate); legislative drafting (Postbaccalaureate Certificate); work, organization, and leadership (MA). *Program availability:* Part-time, evening/weekend, online learning. *Degree requirements:* For master's, project. *Entrance requirements:* Additional exam requirements/recommendations for international students: Required—TOEFL (minimum score 560 paper-based). Electronic applications accepted. *Faculty research:* Women's history, literature and culture studies, sustainable development, labor and education.

Auburn University, Graduate School, College of Education, Auburn University, AL 36849. Offers M Ed, MS, Ed D, PhD, Ed S, Graduate Certificate. *Accreditation:* NCATE. *Program availability:* Part-time. *Degree requirements:* For master's, thesis (for some programs); for doctorate, thesis/dissertation. *Entrance requirements:* For master's, doctorate, and other advanced degree, GRE General Test. Electronic applications accepted. *Expenses:* Tuition, state resident: full-time $11,282; part-time $535 per credit hour. Tuition, nonresident: full-time $30,542; part-time $1605 per credit hour. *Required fees:* $826 per semester. Tuition and fees vary according to degree level and program. *Faculty research:* Dropout phenomena, high school students and substance use and abuse.

Auburn University at Montgomery, College of Education, Montgomery, AL 36124-4023. Offers M Ed, Ed S. *Accreditation:* NCATE. *Program availability:* Part-time, evening/weekend. *Faculty:* 26 full-time (15 women), 11 part-time/adjunct (all women). *Students:* 82 full-time (66 women), 156 part-time (127 women); includes 91 minority (87 Black or African American, non-Hispanic/Latino; 4 Hispanic/Latino), 2 international. Average age 33. 198 applicants, 71% accepted, 73 enrolled. In 2018, 102 master's awarded. *Degree requirements:* For master's and Ed S, comprehensive exam. *Entrance requirements:* For master's, GRE General Test or MAT, BS in teaching, certification; for Ed S, GRE General Test or MAT, certification. Additional exam requirements/recommendations for international students: Recommended—TOEFL (minimum score

500 paper-based; 61 iBT), IELTS (minimum score 5.5), TSE (minimum score 44). *Application deadline:* For fall admission, 7/1 for international students; for spring admission, 11/1 for international students; for summer admission, 4/15 for international students. Applications are processed on a rolling basis. Application fee: $25. Electronic applications accepted. *Expenses:* Tuition, area resident: Full-time $7146; part-time $4764 per credit hour. Tuition, state resident: full-time $7146; part-time $4764 per credit hour. Tuition, nonresident: full-time $16,056; part-time $10,704 per credit hour. *International tuition:* $16,056 full-time. *Required fees:* $766. One-time fee: $25 full-time. *Financial support:* Teaching assistantships, career-related internships or fieldwork, and scholarships/grants available. Support available to part-time students. Financial award application deadline: 3/1; financial award applicants required to submit FAFSA. *Unit head:* Dr. Sheila Austin, Dean, 334-244-3425, Fax: 334-244-3102, E-mail: saustin1@aum.edu. *Application contact:* Dr. Rhonda Morton, Associate Dean/Graduate Coordinator, 334-224-3287, Fax: 334-244-3978, E-mail: rmorton@aum.edu.
Website: http://www.education.aum.edu/

Augsburg University, Program in Education, Minneapolis, MN 55454-1351. Offers MAE. *Accreditation:* NCATE. *Program availability:* Part-time, evening/weekend. *Degree requirements:* For master's, comprehensive exam, final project. *Entrance requirements:* For master's, minimum GPA of 3.0. Additional exam requirements/recommendations for international students: Required—TOEFL (minimum score 600 paper-based). Electronic applications accepted.

Augustana University, MA in Education Program, Sioux Falls, SD 57197. Offers instructional strategies (MA); reading (MA); special populations (MA); STEM (MA); technology (MA). *Accreditation:* NCATE. *Program availability:* Part-time-only, evening/weekend, online only, 100% online. *Degree requirements:* For master's, thesis. *Entrance requirements:* For master's, appropriate bachelor's degree, minimum GPA of 3.0, teaching certificate. Additional exam requirements/recommendations for international students: Required—TOEFL (minimum score 550 paper-based). Electronic applications accepted. *Expenses:* Contact institution. *Faculty research:* Multicultural education, education of students with autism, well-being in school settings, factors that predict academic hopefulness.

Augusta University, College of Education, Augusta, GA 30912. Offers M Ed, MAT, Ed D, Ed S. *Accreditation:* NCATE. *Program availability:* Part-time, evening/weekend. *Entrance requirements:* For master's, GRE, MAT, minimum GPA of 2.5.

Aurora University, School of Education and Human Performance, Aurora, IL 60506-4892. Offers applied behavioral analysis (MS); bilingual-ESL education (MA); educational leadership with principal endorsement (MA); educational technology (MA); leadership in adult learning higher education (Ed D); leadership in curriculum and instruction (Ed D); leadership in educational administration (Ed D); reading instruction (MA); special education (MA). *Accreditation:* NCATE. *Program availability:* Part-time, evening/weekend, 100% online. *Faculty:* 14 full-time (6 women), 32 part-time/adjunct (17 women). *Students:* 28 full-time (25 women), 537 part-time (359 women); includes 101 minority (25 Black or African American, non-Hispanic/Latino; 8 Asian, non-Hispanic/Latino; 58 Hispanic/Latino; 2 Native Hawaiian or other Pacific Islander, non-Hispanic/Latino; 8 Two or more races, non-Hispanic/Latino), 2 international. Average age 38. 191 applicants, 98% accepted, 133 enrolled. In 2018, 213 master's, 16 doctorates awarded. *Degree requirements:* For master's, student teaching, research seminar, and practicum; for doctorate, comprehensive exam, thesis/dissertation. *Entrance requirements:* For master's, 2 years of teaching experience, valid teaching certificate, resume; for doctorate, appropriate master's degree, two references, curriculum vitae, personal statement, professional project, reflective essay. Additional exam requirements/recommendations for international students: Required—TOEFL (minimum score 550 paper-based; 79 iBT). *Application deadline:* For fall admission, 6/1 for international students; for spring admission, 10/1 for international students. Applications are processed on a rolling basis. Application fee: $0. Electronic applications accepted. *Expenses:* The reported tuition amount is for the program with the greatest enrollment, MA in Educational Leadership with Principal Endorsement. Other programs may require more semester hours, and thus have a greater total cost. The Education doctoral programs are roughly double the amount of the master's programs. *Financial support:* In 2018–19, 31 students received support. Federal Work-Study, scholarships/grants, and unspecified assistantships available. Financial award applicants required to submit FAFSA. *Unit head:* Dr. Jen Buckley, Dean, School of Education and Human Performance, 630-844-1542, Fax: 630-844-6155, E-mail: jbuckley@aurora.edu. *Application contact:* Center for Graduate Studies, 630-947-8955, E-mail: AUadmission@aurora.edu.
Website: http://aurora.edu/education

Austin College, Austin Teacher Program, Sherman, TX 75090-4400. Offers MAT. *Program availability:* Part-time. *Faculty:* 3 full-time (all women), 4 part-time/adjunct (3 women). *Students:* 19 full-time (11 women); includes 7 minority (1 Asian, non-Hispanic/Latino; 5 Hispanic/Latino; 1 Two or more races, non-Hispanic/Latino). Average age 23. In 2018, 13 master's awarded. *Degree requirements:* For master's, one foreign language, thesis or alternative. *Entrance requirements:* For master's, Texas Academic Skills Program Test. Additional exam requirements/recommendations for international students: Required—TOEFL (minimum score 80 paper-based), IELTS (minimum score 6.5). *Application deadline:* For fall admission, 5/1 priority date for domestic students; for spring admission, 1/15 priority date for domestic students. Applications are processed on a rolling basis. Application fee: $35. Electronic applications accepted. Application fee is waived when completed online. *Financial support:* Career-related internships or fieldwork, Federal Work-Study, scholarships/grants, and unspecified assistantships available. Support available to part-time students. Financial award application deadline: 4/1; financial award applicants required to submit FAFSA. *Unit head:* Julia Shahid, Department Chair, 903-813-2457, E-mail: jshahid@austincollege.edu. *Application contact:* Administrative Assistant, 903-813-2327.
Website: http://www.austincollege.edu/academics/atp/

Austin Peay State University, College of Graduate Studies, College of Education, Clarksville, TN 37044. Offers MA Ed, Ed S. *Accreditation:* NCATE. *Program availability:* Part-time, evening/weekend, online learning. *Faculty:* 17 full-time (12 women), 9 part-time/adjunct (5 women). *Students:* 86 full-time (66 women), 181 part-time (141 women); includes 48 minority (29 Black or African American, non-Hispanic/Latino; 3 Asian, non-Hispanic/Latino; 7 Hispanic/Latino; 9 Two or more races, non-Hispanic/Latino), 1 international. Average age 33. 128 applicants, 89% accepted, 98 enrolled. In 2018, 72 master's, 13 Ed Ss awarded. *Degree requirements:* For master's, comprehensive exam, thesis optional. *Entrance requirements:* For master's, GRE General Test, MAT, 3 letters of recommendation, minimum undergraduate GPA of 2.75; for Ed S, GRE General Test, master's degree, minimum graduate GPA of 3.0, 3 letters of recommendation. Additional exam requirements/recommendations for international students: Required—TOEFL (minimum score 500 paper-based). *Application deadline:* For fall admission, 8/21 priority date for domestic students. Applications are processed on a rolling basis. Application fee: $45 ($55 for international students). Electronic applications accepted. *Expenses:* Tuition, area resident: Part-time $450 per credit hour. Tuition, state resident: full-time $5987; part-time $450 per credit hour. Tuition, nonresident: full-time $8757; part-time $806 per credit hour. *Required fees:* $1583; $79.15 per credit hour. *Financial support:* Research assistantships with full tuition reimbursements, career-related internships or fieldwork, Federal Work-Study, institutionally sponsored loans, scholarships/grants, and unspecified assistantships available. Support available to part-time students. Financial award application deadline: 7/1; financial award applicants required to submit FAFSA. *Unit head:* Dr. Prentice Chandler, Dean, 931-221-7511, Fax: 931-221-1292, E-mail: chandlerp@apsu.edu. *Application contact:* Megan Mitchell, Coordinator of Graduate Admissions, 931-221-6189, Fax: 931-221-7641, E-mail: mitchellm@apsu.edu.
Website: http://www.apsu.edu/education/index.php

Averett University, Master in Education Program, Danville, VA 24541-3692. Offers administration and supervision (M Ed); curriculum and instruction (M Ed); special education with endorsement (M Ed); special education with licensure (M Ed). *Program availability:* Part-time, online only, 100% online. *Faculty:* 2 full-time (both women), 14 part-time/adjunct (11 women). *Students:* 141 full-time (108 women), 4 part-time (2 women); includes 31 minority (30 Black or African American, non-Hispanic/Latino; 1 Hispanic/Latino). Average age 37. 106 applicants, 58% accepted, 52 enrolled. In 2018, 52 master's awarded. *Degree requirements:* For master's, 30-credit core curriculum, minimum GPA of 3.0 throughout program, completion of degree requirements within six years from start of program. *Entrance requirements:* For master's, PRAXIS I, GRE, or MAT; writing proficiency test, minimum cumulative GPA of 3.0 over the last 60 hours of undergraduate study toward a baccalaureate degree, three letters of recommendation, Virginia teaching license (or eligibility). Additional exam requirements/recommendations for international students: Required—TOEFL (minimum score 600 paper-based; 100 iBT). *Application deadline:* Applications are processed on a rolling basis. Electronic applications accepted. *Expenses:* Contact institution. *Financial support:* Application deadline: 3/1; applicants required to submit FAFSA. *Unit head:* Dr. Nancy Riddell, Chair of the Education Department; Director of Teacher Education, 434-791-5741, Fax: 434-791-5020, E-mail: nriddell@averett.edu. *Application contact:* Christy Davis, Assistant Director of Admissions, 434-791-7133, E-mail: cdavis@averett.edu.
Website: http://gps.averett.edu/online/education/

Avila University, School of Education, Kansas City, MO 64145-1698. Offers advanced classroom management (MA); elementary education (Teaching Certificate); English language learners (Advanced Certificate); middle school (Teaching Certificate); physical education K-12 (Teaching Certificate); secondary education (Teaching Certificate). *Program availability:* Part-time, evening/weekend, online learning. *Faculty:* 6 full-time (5 women), 9 part-time/adjunct (8 women). *Students:* 83 full-time (71 women), 84 part-time (69 women); includes 13 minority (6 Black or African American, non-Hispanic/Latino; 2 Asian, non-Hispanic/Latino; 4 Hispanic/Latino; 1 Two or more races, non-Hispanic/Latino), 2 international. Average age 40. 92 applicants, 62% accepted, 40 enrolled. In 2018, 21 master's awarded. *Entrance requirements:* For master's, minimum GPA of 3.0, writing sample, recommendation, interview; for other advanced degree, foreign language. Additional exam requirements/recommendations for international students: Required—TOEFL (minimum score 580 paper-based; 92 iBT). *Application deadline:* Applications are processed on a rolling basis. Electronic applications accepted. *Expenses:* Contact institution. *Financial support:* In 2018–19, 12 students received support. Unspecified assistantships available. Financial award applicants required to submit FAFSA. *Unit head:* Dr. Stacy Keith, Director of Graduate Education, 816-501-2446, Fax: 816-501-2915, E-mail: stacy.keith@avila.edu. *Application contact:* Cory Roup, Graduate Education Enrollment and Academic Advisor, 816-501-2464, E-mail: cory.roup@avila.edu.
Website: https://www.avila.edu/academics/graduate-studies/grad-education

Azusa Pacific University, School of Education, Azusa, CA 91702-7000. Offers M Ed, MA, MA Ed, Ed D. *Program availability:* Part-time, evening/weekend. *Degree requirements:* For doctorate, oral defense of dissertation, qualifying exam. *Entrance requirements:* For master's, minimum GPA of 3.0; for doctorate, GRE General Test or MAT, 5 years of experience, writing sample. Additional exam requirements/recommendations for international students: Required—TOEFL.

Baker University, School of Education, Baldwin City, KS 66006-0065. Offers MA Ed, MSSE, MSSL, Ed D. Master's-level programs also offered in Wichita, KS. *Accreditation:* NCATE; TEAC. *Program availability:* Part-time, evening/weekend, 100% online. *Degree requirements:* For master's, portfolio of learning; for doctorate, thesis/dissertation, portfolio of learning. *Entrance requirements:* For master's, one year of full-time work experience, teaching certificate; for doctorate, interview. Additional exam requirements/recommendations for international students: Required—TOEFL (minimum score 600 paper-based; 100 iBT). Electronic applications accepted. *Expenses:* Contact institution.

Baldwin Wallace University, Graduate Programs, School of Education, Berea, OH 44017-2088. Offers leadership in higher education (MA Ed); leadership in technology for teaching and learning (MA Ed); literacy (MA Ed); mild/moderate educational needs (MA Ed); school leadership (MA Ed). *Accreditation:* NCATE. *Program availability:* Part-time, evening/weekend, 100% online, blended/hybrid learning. *Faculty:* 10 full-time (6 women), 8 part-time/adjunct (2 women). *Students:* 81 full-time (60 women), 80 part-time (66 women); includes 22 minority (14 Black or African American, non-Hispanic/Latino; 1 Asian, non-Hispanic/Latino; 1 Hispanic/Latino; 6 Two or more races, non-Hispanic/Latino). Average age 32. 108 applicants, 52% accepted, 45 enrolled. In 2018, 62 master's awarded. *Degree requirements:* For master's, capstone, practica or portfolio. *Entrance requirements:* For master's, bachelor's degree in field, MAT or minimum GPA of 3.0, teaching license (for all but technology program). Additional exam requirements/recommendations for international students: Required—TOEFL (minimum score 550 paper-based; 79 iBT). *Application deadline:* For fall admission, 8/15 priority date for domestic students; for spring admission, 12/15 priority date for domestic students. Applications are processed on a rolling basis. Application fee: $25. Electronic applications accepted. Application fee is waived when completed online. *Expenses:* Contact institution. *Financial support:* Career-related internships or fieldwork available. Financial award applicants required to submit FAFSA. *Faculty research:* Literacy, technology and literacy, diversity in education, assessment, special education, research methodology, leadership, and organization. *Unit head:* Michael J Smith, Interim Dean of EDU/HSC/HPE, 440-826-3137, Fax: 440-826-3779, E-mail: mjsmith@bw.edu. *Application contact:* Amiyra Alveranga, Admission Counselor, 440-826-8005, Fax: 440-826-3830, E-mail: aalveran@bw.edu.
Website: http://www.bw.edu/academics/master-of-arts-in-education

Ball State University, Graduate School, Teachers College, Muncie, IN 47306. Offers MA, MAE, MS, Ed D, PhD, Certificate, Ed S. *Accreditation:* NCATE. *Program availability:* Part-time, evening/weekend, 100% online, blended/hybrid learning. Terminal master's awarded for partial completion of doctoral program. *Degree requirements:* For doctorate, comprehensive exam, thesis/dissertation; for other advanced degree, comprehensive exam, thesis. *Entrance requirements:* For master's, minimum baccalaureate GPA of 2.75 or 3.0 in latter half of baccalaureate; for doctorate, GRE General Test, minimum graduate GPA of 3.2; for other advanced degree, GRE General Test. Additional exam requirements/recommendations for international students: Required—TOEFL (minimum score 550 paper-based; 79 iBT), IELTS (minimum score 6.5). Electronic applications accepted.

Bank Street College of Education, Graduate School, New York, NY 10025. Offers Ed M, MS, MS Ed. *Degree requirements:* For master's, thesis. *Entrance requirements:* For master's, interview, essays. Additional exam requirements/recommendations for international students: Required—TOEFL (minimum score 600 paper-based; 100 iBT),

IELTS (minimum score 7). Electronic applications accepted. *Faculty research:* Understanding developmental variations in inclusive classrooms, urban teacher education and technology, learner-centered education, improving teacher preparation.

Bard College, Master of Arts in Teaching Program, Annandale-on-Hudson, NY 12504. Offers secondary education (MAT), including biology, history, literature, mathematics, Spanish; MS/MAT. *Program availability:* Part-time. *Degree requirements:* For master's, year-long teaching residencies in area middle and high schools. *Entrance requirements:* For master's, GRE General Test, resume, 3 letters of recommendation, personal statement, official transcripts. Additional exam requirements/recommendations for international students: Required—TOEFL. Electronic applications accepted. Application fee is waived when completed online.

Barry University, School of Education, Miami Shores, FL 33161-6695. Offers MS, Ed D, PhD, Certificate, Ed S. *Program availability:* Part-time, evening/weekend, online learning. *Degree requirements:* For master's, comprehensive exam; for doctorate, thesis/dissertation. *Entrance requirements:* For master's, GRE General Test or MAT, minimum GPA of 3.0; for doctorate, GRE General Test, minimum GPA of 3.25; for other advanced degree, GRE General Test, minimum GPA of 3.0. Additional exam requirements/recommendations for international students: Required—TOEFL (minimum score 550 paper-based). Electronic applications accepted.

Bayamón Central University, Graduate Programs, Program in Education, Bayamón, PR 00960-1725. Offers administration and supervision (MA Ed); commercial education (MA Ed); elementary education (K–3) (MA Ed); family counseling (Graduate Certificate); guidance and counseling (MA Ed); pre-elementary teacher (MA Ed); rehabilitation counseling (MA Ed); special education (MA Ed), including attention deficit disorder, education of the autistic, learning disabilities. *Program availability:* Part-time, evening/weekend. *Degree requirements:* For master's, comprehensive exam. *Entrance requirements:* For master's, EXADEP, bachelor's degree in education or related field.

Baylor University, Graduate School, School of Education, Waco, TX 76798. Offers MA, MS Ed, Ed D, PhD, Ed S. *Accreditation:* NCATE. *Program availability:* Part-time. *Faculty:* 42 full-time (26 women), 10 part-time/adjunct (6 women). *Students:* 163 full-time (113 women), 96 part-time (74 women); includes 81 minority (30 Black or African American, non-Hispanic/Latino; 1 American Indian or Alaska Native, non-Hispanic/Latino; 7 Asian, non-Hispanic/Latino; 30 Hispanic/Latino; 13 Two or more races, non-Hispanic/Latino), 9 international. 248 applicants, 35% accepted, 28 enrolled. In 2018, 52 master's, 4 doctorates, 9 other advanced degrees awarded. *Degree requirements:* For master's, variable foreign language requirement, comprehensive exam, thesis optional; for doctorate, variable foreign language requirement, comprehensive exam, thesis/dissertation. *Entrance requirements:* For master's and Ed S, GRE; for doctorate, GRE, 3 letters of recommendation, personal statement. Additional exam requirements/recommendations for international students: Required—TOEFL (minimum score 550 paper-based; 80 iBT), IELTS (minimum score 6.5). *Application deadline:* For fall admission, 2/1 priority date for domestic and international students. Applications are processed on a rolling basis. Application fee: $50. Electronic applications accepted. *Financial support:* In 2018–19, 181 students received support, including 38 research assistantships (averaging $12,050 per year), 68 teaching assistantships (averaging $12,050 per year); career-related internships or fieldwork, Federal Work-Study, institutionally sponsored loans, scholarships/grants, health care benefits, tuition waivers (partial), unspecified assistantships, and stipends also available. Support available to part-time students. Financial award application deadline: 2/1; financial award applicants required to submit FAFSA. *Faculty research:* Quantitative methods, gifted and talented, applied behavior analysis, sport management, marketing, civics/science education. *Total annual research expenditures:* $324,254. *Unit head:* Dr. Terrill F. Saxon, Interim Dean/Associate Dean of Graduate Programs, 254-710-3111, Fax: 254-710-3987, E-mail: terrill_saxon@baylor.edu. *Application contact:* Dr. Terrill F. Saxon, Interim Dean/Associate Dean of Graduate Programs, 254-710-3111, Fax: 254-710-3987, E-mail: terrill_saxon@baylor.edu.
Website: http://www.baylor.edu/soe/

Belhaven University, School of Education, Jackson, MS 39202-1789. Offers education (M Ed, MAT); educational leadership (Ed D, Ed S); reading literacy (M Ed). *Program availability:* Part-time, evening/weekend, 100% online, blended/hybrid learning. *Faculty:* 8 full-time (6 women), 24 part-time/adjunct (20 women). *Students:* 11 full-time (7 women), 452 part-time (360 women); includes 262 minority (244 Black or African American, non-Hispanic/Latino; 1 American Indian or Alaska Native, non-Hispanic/Latino; 3 Asian, non-Hispanic/Latino; 3 Hispanic/Latino; 11 Two or more races, non-Hispanic/Latino), 1 international. Average age 36. 299 applicants, 49% accepted, 103 enrolled. In 2018, 65 master's, 5 other advanced degrees awarded. *Degree requirements:* For master's, comprehensive exam, portfolio; for doctorate, thesis/dissertation. *Entrance requirements:* For master's, PRAXIS I and II, minimum GPA of 2.8; for doctorate, MAT or GRE, master's degree in education or related field with minimum GPA of 3.0; essay; three professional letters of recommendation; minimum three years' experience in a PK-12 education context. *Application deadline:* Applications are processed on a rolling basis. Application fee: $25. Electronic applications accepted. *Expenses:* $525 per credit hour, $75 technology fee per course. *Financial support:* Applicants required to submit FAFSA. *Unit head:* Dr. David Hand, Dean, 601-965-7020, E-mail: dhand@belhaven.edu. *Application contact:* Sean Kirnan, Assistant Vice President for Adult and Graduate Enrollment and Student Services, 601-968-8727, Fax: 601-968-5953, E-mail: gradadmission@belhaven.edu.

Bellarmine University, Annsley Frazier Thornton School of Education, Louisville, KY 40205. Offers education and district leadership (Ed D); education and social change (PhD); elementary education (MA Ed, MAT); leadership in higher education (PhD); middle school education (MA Ed, MAT); principalship (Ed S); reading and writing (MA Ed); secondary education (MAT); teacher leadership (MA Ed). *Accreditation:* NCATE. *Program availability:* Part-time, evening/weekend. *Faculty:* 14 full-time (7 women), 17 part-time/adjunct (11 women). *Students:* 27 full-time (19 women), 205 part-time (156 women); includes 74 minority (53 Black or African American, non-Hispanic/Latino; 6 Asian, non-Hispanic/Latino; 7 Hispanic/Latino; 8 Two or more races, non-Hispanic/Latino). Average age 34. 155 applicants, 71% accepted, 95 enrolled. In 2018, 69 master's, 10 doctorates, 30 other advanced degrees awarded. *Degree requirements:* For master's, comprehensive exam (for some programs), thesis (for some programs); for doctorate, comprehensive exam (for some programs), thesis/dissertation; for Ed S, comprehensive exam (for some programs). *Entrance requirements:* For master's, GRE, baccalaureate degree from accredited institution; minimum cumulative GPA of 2.75; recommendations from employers, supervisors, or professors attesting to applicant's potential as graduate student; statement of intent to pursue graduate degree; for doctorate, GRE, minimum GPA of 3.5 in all graduate coursework; baccalaureate and master's degrees in education or fields directly relevant to education; three letters of recommendation; two essays (no more than 1,000 words each); resume or curriculum vitae; interview; for Ed S, master's degree in education; valid teaching certificate; three years of experience in teaching; three recommendations; minimum GPA of 3.0 in all graduate work; interview; essays; personal goal statement. Additional exam requirements/recommendations for international students: Required—TOEFL (minimum score 80 iBT), IELTS (minimum score 6), TOEFL (minimum score 550 paper-based, 68 iBT), IELTS (minimum score 6), or Michigan English Language Assessment Battery.

Application deadline: For fall admission, 8/1 priority date for domestic and international students; for spring admission, 12/1 priority date for domestic and international students; for summer admission, 4/10 priority date for domestic and international students. Applications are processed on a rolling basis. Application fee: $40. Electronic applications accepted. *Expenses:* Doctor of Education: $855 per credit hour; Educational Specialist: $410 per credit hour; Master of Arts in Education: $410 per credit hour; Master of Arts in Teaching: $665 per credit hour; Master of Arts in Teaching, undergraduate content courses: $410 per credit hour; Master of Education in Higher Education Leadership and Social Justice: $665 per credit hour; Ph.D., Social Change: $855 per credit hour; Ph.D., Leadership in Higher Education: $855 per credit hour; Rank I Programs: $410 per credit hour. *Financial support:* Scholarships/grants available. Financial award applicants required to submit FAFSA. *Faculty research:* Literacy, service-learning, dispositions, educational technology, special education. *Unit head:* Dr. Elizabeth Dinkins, Dean, 502-272-7958, Fax: 502-272-8189, E-mail: edinkins@bellarmine.edu. *Application contact:* Sarah Schuble, Assistant Director of Graduate Student Enrollment, 502-272-8271, Fax: 502-272-8002, E-mail: sschuble@bellarmine.edu.
Website: http://www.bellarmine.edu/education/graduate

Bemidji State University, School of Graduate Studies, Bemidji, MN 56601. Offers biology (MS); education (MS); English (MA, MS); environmental studies (MS); mathematics (MS); mathematics (elementary and middle level education) (MS); special education (M Sp Ed). *Program availability:* Part-time, online learning. *Degree requirements:* For master's, comprehensive exam, thesis (for some programs). *Entrance requirements:* For master's, GRE; GMAT, letters of recommendation, letters of interest. Additional exam requirements/recommendations for international students: Required—TOEFL (minimum score 550 paper-based; 80 iBT). Electronic applications accepted. *Expenses:* Contact institution. *Faculty research:* Human performance, sport, and health: physical education teacher education, continuum models, spiritual health, intellectual health, resiliency, health priorities; psychology: health psychology, college student drinking behavior, micro-aggressions, infant cognition, false memories, leadership assessment; biology: structure and dynamics of forest communities, aquatic and riverine ecology, interaction between animal populations and aquatic environments, cellular motility.

Benedictine College, Master of Arts in Education Program, Atchison, KS 66002-1499. Offers MA. *Program availability:* Part-time, evening/weekend. *Entrance requirements:* For master's, minimum GPA of 3.0 in last two years (60 hours) of college course work from accredited institutions, official transcripts, bachelor's degree, teacher certification/licensure, resume, essay. Additional exam requirements/recommendations for international students: Recommended—TOEFL, IELTS. Electronic applications accepted. Application fee is waived when completed online. *Expenses:* Contact institution.

Berry College, Graduate Programs, Graduate Programs in Education, Mount Berry, GA 30149. Offers curriculum and instruction (M Ed, Ed S); educational leadership (Ed S); middle-grades education and reading (M Ed, MAT), including middle grades education (MAT), middle-grades education (M Ed), reading (M Ed); secondary education (MAT). *Accreditation:* NCATE. *Program availability:* Part-time. *Students:* Average age 41. In 2018, 12 master's, 46 other advanced degrees awarded. *Degree requirements:* For master's and Ed S, thesis, portfolio, oral exams. *Entrance requirements:* For master's, GRE General Test or MAT, minimum GPA of 2.5; for Ed S, M Ed from NCATE-accredited school, minimum GPA of 3.25. Additional exam requirements/recommendations for international students: Required—TOEFL (minimum score 550 paper-based). *Application deadline:* For fall admission, 7/20 for domestic students, 5/1 for international students; for spring admission, 12/1 for domestic students, 10/1 for international students. Applications are processed on a rolling basis. Application fee: $25 ($30 for international students). *Expenses:* Contact institution. *Financial support:* In 2018–19, 3 students received support. Research assistantships with full tuition reimbursements available, scholarships/grants, tuition waivers (partial), and unspecified assistantships available. Support available to part-time students. Financial award application deadline: 3/1; financial award applicants required to submit FAFSA. *Faculty research:* Focus on faculty research, school readiness, literacy, K-12 hiring, education policy, arts education. *Total annual research expenditures:* $11,064. *Unit head:* Dr. Jacqueline McDowell, Dean, Charter School of Education and Human Sciences, 706-236-1717, Fax: 706-238-5827, E-mail: jmcdowell@berry.edu. *Application contact:* Brett Kennedy, Assistant Vice President of Enrollment Management, 706-236-2215, Fax: 706-290-2178, E-mail: admissions@berry.edu.
Website: http://www.berry.edu/academics/education/graduate/

Bethany College, Master of Arts in Teaching Program, Bethany, WV 26032. Offers MAT. *Program availability:* Part-time. *Degree requirements:* For master's, thesis. *Entrance requirements:* For master's, baccalaureate degree from accredited U.S. college/university or international equivalent; minimum undergraduate GPA of 2.75. Additional exam requirements/recommendations for international students: Required—TOEFL (minimum score 500 paper-based; 90 iBT); Recommended—IELTS (minimum score 7). Electronic applications accepted.

Bethel University, Adult and Graduate Programs, Program in Education, Mishawaka, IN 46545-5591. Offers M Ed, MAT. *Accreditation:* NCATE; TEAC. *Program availability:* Part-time. *Entrance requirements:* Additional exam requirements/recommendations for international students: Required—TOEFL (minimum score 540 paper-based). Electronic applications accepted.

Bethel University, Graduate School, St. Paul, MN 55112-6999. Offers business administration (MBA); classroom management (Certificate); counseling (MA); K-12 education (MA); leadership (Ed D); leadership foundations (Certificate); nurse educator (MS, Certificate); nurse-midwifery (MS); physician assistant (MS); special education (MA); strategic leadership (MA); teaching (MA); teaching and learning (Certificate). *Program availability:* Part-time, evening/weekend, 100% online, blended/hybrid learning. *Faculty:* 23 full-time (17 women), 73 part-time/adjunct (45 women). *Students:* 586 full-time (426 women), 372 part-time (244 women); includes 141 minority (49 Black or African American, non-Hispanic/Latino; 6 American Indian or Alaska Native, non-Hispanic/Latino; 19 Asian, non-Hispanic/Latino; 40 Hispanic/Latino; 2 Native Hawaiian or other Pacific Islander, non-Hispanic/Latino; 25 Two or more races, non-Hispanic/Latino), 25 international. Average age 35. 642 applicants, 39% accepted, 194 enrolled. In 2018, 312 master's, 28 doctorates, 134 other advanced degrees awarded. *Degree requirements:* For master's, comprehensive exam (for some programs), thesis (for some programs); for doctorate, comprehensive exam, thesis/dissertation. *Entrance requirements:* Additional exam requirements/recommendations for international students: Required—TOEFL (minimum score 550 paper-based; 80 iBT), TOEFL (minimum score 550 paper-based, 80 iBT) or IELTS. *Application deadline:* Applications are processed on a rolling basis. Application fee: $0. Electronic applications accepted. *Expenses:* Contact institution. *Financial support:* Teaching assistantships, career-related internships or fieldwork, and scholarships/grants available. Support available to part-time students. Financial award applicants required to submit FAFSA. *Unit head:* Dr. Randy Bergen, Associate Provost, 651-635-8000, Fax: 651-635-8004, E-mail: r-bergen@bethel.edu. *Application contact:* Director of Admissions, 651-635-8000, Fax: 651-635-8004, E-mail: gs@bethel.edu.
Website: https://www.bethel.edu/graduate/

Binghamton University, State University of New York, Graduate School, College of Community and Public Affairs, Department of Teaching, Learning and Educational Leadership, Binghamton, NY 13902-6000. Offers adolescence education (MAT, MS Ed), including biology education, chemistry education, earth science education, English education, French education, mathematical sciences education, physics, social studies, Spanish education; childhood and early childhood education (MS Ed); educational leadership (Certificate); educational studies (MS); educational theory and practice (Ed D); literacy education (MS Ed); special education (MS Ed); TESOL education (MA, MS Ed). *Accreditation:* TEAC. *Program availability:* Part-time, evening/weekend. *Degree requirements:* For doctorate, thesis/dissertation. *Entrance requirements:* For master's, GRE General Test, teaching certification; for doctorate, GRE General Test, writing sample. Additional exam requirements/recommendations for international students: Required—TOEFL (minimum score 550 paper-based; 80 iBT). Electronic applications accepted.

Biola University, School of Education, La Mirada, CA 90639-0001. Offers curriculum and instruction (Certificate); early childhood (MA Ed, MAT); multiple subject (MAT); single subject (MAT); special education (MA Ed, MAT, Certificate). *Program availability:* Part-time, evening/weekend, online learning. *Entrance requirements:* For master's, CBEST, CSET, GRE (waived if cumulative GPA is 3.5 or above or if CBEST and all CSET subtests are passed). Additional exam requirements/recommendations for international students: Required—TOEFL (minimum score 100 iBT). Electronic applications accepted. *Faculty research:* Early childhood education, elementary education, special education, curriculum development, teacher preparation.

Bishop's University, School of Education, Sherbrooke, QC J1M 1Z7, Canada. Offers advanced studies in education (Diploma); education (M Ed, MA); teaching English as a second language (Certificate). *Program availability:* Part-time, online learning. *Degree requirements:* For master's, thesis (for some programs). *Entrance requirements:* For master's, teaching license, 2 years of teaching experience. *Faculty research:* Integration of special needs students, multigrade classes/small schools, leadership in organizational development, second language acquisition.

Bloomsburg University of Pennsylvania, School of Graduate Studies, College of Education, Bloomsburg, PA 17815-1301. Offers M Ed, MS, Certificate. *Accreditation:* NCATE. *Program availability:* Part-time. *Degree requirements:* For master's, thesis optional. *Entrance requirements:* For master's, minimum QPA of 3.0. Additional exam requirements/recommendations for international students: Required—TOEFL, IELTS. Electronic applications accepted.

Bluefield College, School of Education, Bluefield, VA 24605-1799. Offers MA Ed. *Accreditation:* TEAC. *Program availability:* Part-time, online only, 100% online. *Degree requirements:* For master's, action research project. *Entrance requirements:* For master's, GRE, MAT or PRAXIS, bachelor's degree from regionally-accredited institution of higher education, minimum GPA of 2.75 in all college work, two letters of recommendation, Pre-Self-Assessment of Professional Temperament and Performance. Additional exam requirements/recommendations for international students: Required—TOEFL. Electronic applications accepted. *Expenses:* Contact institution.

Bluffton University, Programs in Education, Bluffton, OH 45817. Offers intervention specialist (MA Ed); leadership (MA Ed); reading (MA Ed). *Accreditation:* NCATE. *Program availability:* Part-time, 100% online, blended/hybrid learning, videoconference. *Faculty:* 2 full-time (both women), 2 part-time/adjunct (1 woman). *Students:* 14 full-time (7 women), 7 part-time (all women). Average age 31. In 2018, 8 master's awarded. *Degree requirements:* For master's, action research project, public presentation. *Entrance requirements:* For master's, PRAXIS I, bachelor's degree, minimum GPA of 3.0. Additional exam requirements/recommendations for international students: Required—TOEFL. *Application deadline:* For fall admission, 8/15 priority date for domestic students, 6/15 priority date for international students; for spring admission, 12/15 priority date for domestic students, 9/15 priority date for international students. Applications are processed on a rolling basis. Electronic applications accepted. *Expenses:* Contact institution. *Financial support:* Unspecified assistantships available. Financial award application deadline: 9/15; financial award applicants required to submit FAFSA. *Unit head:* Dr. Amy K. Mullins, Director of Graduate Programs in Education, 419-358-3457, E-mail: mullinsa@bluffton.edu. *Application contact:* Shelby Koenig, Enrollment Counselor for Graduate Program, 419-358-3022, E-mail: koenigs@bluffton.edu.
Website: https://www.bluffton.edu/ags/index.aspx

Boise State University, College of Education, Boise, ID 83725-0399. Offers M Ed, MA, MET, MPE, MS, MS Ed, Ed D, Ed S, Graduate Certificate. *Accreditation:* NCATE. *Program availability:* Part-time, 100% online, blended/hybrid learning. Terminal master's awarded for partial completion of doctoral program. *Degree requirements:* For master's, thesis (for some programs); for doctorate, thesis/dissertation. *Entrance requirements:* For master's, minimum GPA of 3.0; for doctorate, GRE General Test, minimum GPA of 3.0. Additional exam requirements/recommendations for international students: Required—TOEFL (minimum score 550 paper-based; 80 iBT), IELTS (minimum score 6). Electronic applications accepted.

Boston College, Lynch School of Education and Human Development, Chestnut Hill, MA 02467-3800. Offers M Ed, MA, MAT, MS, MST, Ed D, PhD, CAES, JD/M Ed, JD/MA, MA/MA, MBA/MA. *Accreditation:* TEAC. *Program availability:* Part-time, 100% online. *Faculty:* 67 full-time (43 women). *Students:* 523 full-time (382 women), 290 part-time (223 women); includes 187 minority (57 Black or African American, non-Hispanic/Latino; 1 American Indian or Alaska Native, non-Hispanic/Latino; 30 Asian, non-Hispanic/Latino; 73 Hispanic/Latino; 26 Two or more races, non-Hispanic/Latino), 129 international. Average age 29. 1,416 applicants, 342 enrolled. In 2018, 267 master's, 29 doctorates, 2 other advanced degrees awarded. Terminal master's awarded for partial completion of doctoral program. *Degree requirements:* For master's, comprehensive exam; for doctorate, comprehensive exam, thesis/dissertation. *Entrance requirements:* For master's, GRE, letters of recommendation, transcripts, personal statement, resume; for doctorate, GRE, letters of recommendation, transcripts, writing sample, personal statement, resume. Additional exam requirements/recommendations for international students: Required—TOEFL (minimum score 600 paper-based; 100 iBT); Recommended—IELTS (minimum score 7). *Application deadline:* For fall admission, 1/9 priority date for domestic and international students; for spring admission, 11/1 for domestic and international students. Applications are processed on a rolling basis. Application fee: $75. Electronic applications accepted. *Financial support:* Fellowships with tuition reimbursements, research assistantships with tuition reimbursements, teaching assistantships with tuition reimbursements, career-related internships or fieldwork, Federal Work-Study, institutionally sponsored loans, scholarships/grants, traineeships, health care benefits, tuition waivers (full and partial), and unspecified assistantships available. Support available to part-time students. Financial award applicants required to submit FAFSA. *Faculty research:* Formative education, teaching and learning, educational change and leadership, assessment and evaluation, counseling and development. *Total annual research expenditures:* $17.1 million. *Unit head:* Dr. Stanton Wortham, Dean, 617-552-4200, Fax: 617-552-0812. *Application contact:* Jessica Rivers, Assistant Dean for Graduate Admissions and Financial Aid, 617-552-4214, Fax: 617-552-0398, E-mail: riversja@bc.edu.
Website: http://www.bc.edu/schools/lsoe

Boston University, Wheelock College of Education and Human Development, Boston, MA 02215. Offers Ed M, MAT, Ed D, PhD, CAGS. *Program availability:* Part-time, evening/weekend. *Faculty:* 85 full-time (59 women), 87 part-time/adjunct (67 women). *Students:* 234 full-time (183 women), 444 part-time (331 women); includes 168 minority (38 Black or African American, non-Hispanic/Latino; 46 Asian, non-Hispanic/Latino; 63 Hispanic/Latino; 1 Native Hawaiian or other Pacific Islander, non-Hispanic/Latino; 20 Two or more races, non-Hispanic/Latino), 53 international. Average age 27. 1,303 applicants, 65% accepted, 346 enrolled. In 2018, 286 master's, 26 doctorates, 6 other advanced degrees awarded. Terminal master's awarded for partial completion of doctoral program. *Degree requirements:* For master's, thesis (for some programs); for doctorate, comprehensive exam, thesis/dissertation; for CAGS, comprehensive exam. *Entrance requirements:* For master's, GRE or MAT (for Ed M in counseling); for doctorate, GRE General Test; for CAGS, GRE General Test or MAT. Additional exam requirements/recommendations for international students: Required—TOEFL (minimum score 84 iBT), IELTS. *Application deadline:* For fall admission, 1/15 priority date for domestic and international students; for spring admission, 9/15 priority date for domestic and international students. Applications are processed on a rolling basis. Application fee: $95. Electronic applications accepted. *Financial support:* In 2018–19, 450 students received support, including 36 fellowships with full tuition reimbursements available (averaging $22,660 per year), 25 research assistantships (averaging $10,000 per year), 32 teaching assistantships with partial tuition reimbursements available (averaging $8,000 per year); career-related internships or fieldwork, Federal Work-Study, and scholarships/grants also available. Support available to part-time students. Financial award applicants required to submit FAFSA. *Faculty research:* Civic engagement and education, human development, language and literacy studies, special education, STEM education. *Total annual research expenditures:* $7 million. *Unit head:* Dr. David J. Chard, Interim Dean, 617-353-3213. *Application contact:* Julia Cocca, Director of Graduate Enrollment, 617-353-4237, E-mail: whegrad@bu.edu.
Website: http://www.bu.edu/wheelock

Bowie State University, Graduate Programs, Program in Teaching, Bowie, MD 20715-9465. Offers MAT. *Accreditation:* NCATE. *Program availability:* Part-time, evening/weekend. *Entrance requirements:* For master's, PRAXIS I. Electronic applications accepted.

Bradley University, The Graduate School, College of Education and Health Sciences, Peoria, IL 61625-0002. Offers MA, MS, MSN, DNP, DPT, Certificate. *Accreditation:* NCATE. *Program availability:* Part-time, evening/weekend, 100% online, blended/hybrid learning. *Faculty:* 54 full-time (40 women), 42 part-time/adjunct (34 women). *Students:* 271 full-time (207 women), 814 part-time (706 women); includes 307 minority (156 Black or African American, non-Hispanic/Latino; 8 American Indian or Alaska Native, non-Hispanic/Latino; 52 Asian, non-Hispanic/Latino; 65 Hispanic/Latino; 1 Native Hawaiian or other Pacific Islander, non-Hispanic/Latino; 25 Two or more races, non-Hispanic/Latino), 22 international. Average age 35. 767 applicants, 95% accepted, 234 enrolled. In 2018, 124 master's, 43 doctorates awarded. *Degree requirements:* For master's, comprehensive exam, thesis optional. *Entrance requirements:* For master's, Minimum GPA of 2.5, Essays, Recommendation letters, Transcripts; for doctorate, GRE, Essays, Recommendation letters, Transcripts. Additional exam requirements/recommendations for international students: Required—TOEFL (minimum score 550 paper-based; 79 iBT), IELTS (minimum score 6.5). *Application deadline:* For fall admission, 5/15 priority date for domestic students, 5/15 for international students; for spring admission, 10/15 priority date for domestic students, 10/15 for international students. Applications are processed on a rolling basis. Application fee: $40 ($50 for international students). Electronic applications accepted. *Expenses: Tuition:* Part-time $890 per credit. *Required fees:* $50 per unit. *Financial support:* In 2018–19, 78 students received support, including 1 fellowship with full tuition reimbursement available (averaging $16,020 per year), 23 research assistantships with full and partial tuition reimbursements available (averaging $12,382 per year); career-related internships or fieldwork, institutionally sponsored loans, scholarships/grants, tuition waivers (partial), and unspecified assistantships also available. Support available to part-time students. Financial award application deadline: 4/1. *Faculty research:* Health care, professional nurse traineeship, gifted education. *Unit head:* Dr. Molly Cluskey, Interim Dean, 309-677-3181, E-mail: mcluskey@bradley.edu. *Application contact:* Rachel Webb, Director of On-Campus Graduate Admissions & International Student and Scholar Services, 309-677-2375, E-mail: rkwebb@bradley.edu.
Website: http://www.bradley.edu/academic/colleges/ehs/

Brandman University, School of Education, Irvine, CA 92618. Offers curriculum and instruction (MAE); educational administration (MAE); educational leadership (MAE); educational leadership and administration (MA); elementary education (MAT); instructional technology: teaching the 21st century learner (MAE); leadership in early childhood education (MAE); organizational leadership (Ed D); school counseling (MA); secondary education (MAT); special education (MA); teaching and learning (MAE).

Brandon University, Faculty of Education, Brandon, MB R7A 6A9, Canada. Offers curriculum and instruction (M Ed, Diploma); educational administration (M Ed, Diploma); guidance and counseling (M Ed, Diploma); special education (M Ed, Diploma). *Degree requirements:* For master's, thesis. *Entrance requirements:* For master's, minimum GPA of 3.0, teaching certificate or equivalent. Additional exam requirements/recommendations for international students: Required—TOEFL. *Faculty research:* Comparative education, environmental studies, parent/school council.

Brenau University, Sydney O. Smith Graduate School, College of Education, Gainesville, GA 30501. Offers early childhood (Ed S); early childhood education (M Ed, MAT); middle grades (Ed S); middle grades education (M Ed, MAT); secondary education (MAT); special education (M Ed, MAT). *Accreditation:* NCATE. *Program availability:* Part-time, evening/weekend, online learning. *Degree requirements:* For master's, thesis optional, comprehensive exam or applied research project, effective portfolio; for Ed S, thesis, applied research project. *Entrance requirements:* For master's, GRE, MAT, interview, minimum GPA of 3.0, 3 references, writing samples; for Ed S, GRE, MAT, master's degree, minimum GPA of 3.0, writing sample, letters of reference. Additional exam requirements/recommendations for international students: Required—TOEFL (minimum score 500 paper-based; 61 iBT); Recommended—IELTS (minimum score 5). Electronic applications accepted. *Expenses:* Contact institution.

Bridgewater State University, College of Graduate Studies, College of Education and Allied Studies, Bridgewater, MA 02325. Offers M Ed, MAT, MS, CAGS. *Accreditation:* NCATE. *Program availability:* Part-time, evening/weekend. *Degree requirements:* For CAGS, comprehensive exam. *Entrance requirements:* For master's, GRE General Test or Massachusetts Test for Educator Licensure; for CAGS, master's degree. Additional exam requirements/recommendations for international students: Required—TOEFL.

Brigham Young University, Graduate Studies, David O. McKay School of Education, Provo, UT 84602. Offers counseling psychology (PhD); doctorate of education (Ed D); school leadership (M Ed); school psychology (Ed S); special education (MS); teacher education (MA). *Accreditation:* TEAC. *Faculty:* 74 full-time (23 women), 10 part-time/adjunct (3 women). *Students:* 159 full-time (106 women), 157 part-time (91 women);

includes 31 minority (3 Black or African American, non-Hispanic/Latino; 4 American Indian or Alaska Native, non-Hispanic/Latino; 8 Asian, non-Hispanic/Latino; 12 Hispanic/Latino; 4 Native Hawaiian or other Pacific Islander, non-Hispanic/Latino), 10 international. Average age 34. 264 applicants, 48% accepted, 109 enrolled. In 2018, 57 master's, 15 doctorates, 9 other advanced degrees awarded. Application fee: $50. Electronic applications accepted. *Financial support:* In 2018–19, 245 students received support. Research assistantships, teaching assistantships, career-related internships or fieldwork, institutionally sponsored loans, scholarships/grants, health care benefits, tuition waivers, and unspecified assistantships available. Support available to part-time students. Financial award applicants required to submit FAFSA. *Unit head:* Dr. Mary Anne Prater, Dean, 801-422-1592, Fax: 801-422-0200, E-mail: prater@byu.edu. *Application contact:* Brandan Beerli, Director, Education Student Services, 801-422-9199, Fax: 801-422-0195.
Website: https://education.byu.edu

Brock University, Faculty of Graduate Studies, Faculty of Education, St. Catharines, ON L2S 3A1, Canada. Offers M Ed, PhD. *Program availability:* Part-time, evening/weekend. *Degree requirements:* For master's, thesis optional; for doctorate, thesis/dissertation. *Entrance requirements:* For master's, 1 year of teaching experience, honors degree; for doctorate, master's degree. Additional exam requirements/recommendations for international students: Required—TOEFL (minimum score 550 paper-based; 80 iBT), IELTS (minimum score 6.5), TWE (minimum score 4). Electronic applications accepted. *Expenses:* Contact institution. *Faculty research:* International and comparative education, early childhood education, educational leadership, adult education.

Brooklyn College of the City University of New York, School of Education, Brooklyn, NY 11210-2889. Offers MA, MAT, MS Ed, AC. *Accreditation:* NCATE. *Program availability:* Part-time, evening/weekend. *Entrance requirements:* For master's, GRE, GMAT, MAT (depending on program). Additional exam requirements/recommendations for international students: Required—TOEFL or IELTS. Electronic applications accepted.

Brown University, Graduate School, Department of Education, Providence, RI 02912. Offers teaching (MAT), including elementary education, English, history/social studies, science, secondary education; urban education policy (AM). *Degree requirements:* For master's, student teaching, portfolio. *Entrance requirements:* For master's, GRE General Test, letters of recommendation, interview. Additional exam requirements/recommendations for international students: Recommended—TOEFL.

Bucknell University, Graduate Studies, College of Arts and Sciences, Department of Education, Lewisburg, PA 17837. Offers college student personnel (MS Ed). *Program availability:* Part-time. *Degree requirements:* For master's, comprehensive exam (for some programs), thesis or alternative. *Entrance requirements:* For master's, GRE General Test, minimum GPA of 3.0. Additional exam requirements/recommendations for international students: Required—TOEFL (minimum score 600 paper-based).

Buena Vista University, School of Education, Storm Lake, IA 50588. Offers curriculum and instruction (M Ed), including effective teaching, TESL; school guidance and counseling (MS Ed). Program offered in summer only. *Program availability:* Part-time, evening/weekend, online learning. *Degree requirements:* For master's, thesis, fieldwork/practicum, capstone portfolio. *Entrance requirements:* For master's, Analytical Writing Assessment (in-house), minimum undergraduate GPA of 2.75. Electronic applications accepted. *Faculty research:* Reading, curriculum, educational psychology, special education.

Buffalo State College, State University of New York, The Graduate School, School of Education, Buffalo, NY 14222-1095. Offers MS, MS Ed, CAS, Certificate, Graduate Certificate. *Program availability:* Part-time, evening/weekend, online learning. *Degree requirements:* For master's, comprehensive exam (for some programs), thesis (for some programs), project; for other advanced degree, internship. *Entrance requirements:* For master's, New York teaching certificate; for other advanced degree, master's degree, New York teaching certificate, 3 years of teaching experience. Additional exam requirements/recommendations for international students: Required—TOEFL (minimum score 550 paper-based).

Butler University, College of Education, Indianapolis, IN 46208-3485. Offers educational administration (MS). *Accreditation:* ACA; NCATE. *Program availability:* Part-time. *Faculty:* 12 full-time (8 women), 12 part-time/adjunct (all women). *Students:* 11 full-time (8 women), 169 part-time (140 women); includes 27 minority (11 Black or African American, non-Hispanic/Latino; 3 Asian, non-Hispanic/Latino; 7 Hispanic/Latino; 6 Two or more races, non-Hispanic/Latino). Average age 34. 74 applicants, 85% accepted, 63 enrolled. In 2018, 51 master's, 32 other advanced degrees awarded. *Degree requirements:* For master's, thesis. *Entrance requirements:* For master's, GRE (minimum score 291) or MAT (minimum score 396) unless undergraduate GPA is a 3.0 or higher, two letters of recommendation, transcripts, interview, professional resume. Additional exam requirements/recommendations for international students: Required—TOEFL (minimum score 550 paper-based; 79 iBT), IELTS (minimum score 6). *Application deadline:* For fall admission, 2/1 for domestic and international students; for spring admission, 11/1 for domestic and international students; for summer admission, 4/1 for domestic and international students. Applications are processed on a rolling basis. Application fee: $0. Electronic applications accepted. Application fee is waived when completed online. *Expenses:* Contact institution. *Financial support:* In 2018–19, 64 students received support. Scholarships/grants, tuition waivers (full and partial), and unspecified assistantships available. Financial award application deadline: 7/15; financial award applicants required to submit FAFSA. *Faculty research:* Educational neuroscience, transformational adult learning, culture and leadership, educational leadership. *Unit head:* Dr. Ena Shelley, Dean, 317-940-9752, Fax: 317-940-6481. *Application contact:* Diane Dubord, Graduate Student Services Specialist, 317-940-8100, Fax: 317-940-8250, E-mail: ddubord@butler.edu.
Website: https://www.butler.edu/coe/graduate-programs

Cairn University, School of Education, Langhorne, PA 19047-2990. Offers applied behavior analysis (MS Sp Ed, Certificate); educational leadership and administration (MS El); instruction (MS Sp Ed); teacher education (MS Ed). *Program availability:* Part-time, evening/weekend, 100% online, blended/hybrid learning. *Entrance requirements:* Additional exam requirements/recommendations for international students: Required—TOEFL (minimum score 550 paper-based). Electronic applications accepted. Application fee is waived when completed online. *Expenses:* Contact institution.

Caldwell University, School of Education, Caldwell, NJ 07006-6195. Offers elementary, secondary or preschool endorsement, special ed, ESL (Postbaccalaureate Certificate). *Program availability:* Part-time, evening/weekend. *Faculty:* 9 full-time (6 women), 18 part-time/adjunct (10 women). *Students:* 35 full-time (29 women), 170 part-time (125 women); includes 45 minority (22 Black or African American, non-Hispanic/Latino; 1 American Indian or Alaska Native, non-Hispanic/Latino; 5 Asian, non-Hispanic/Latino; 14 Hispanic/Latino; 3 Two or more races, non-Hispanic/Latino). Average age 36. 75 applicants, 93% accepted, 42 enrolled. In 2018, 40 master's, 8 doctorates awarded. *Degree requirements:* For master's, comprehensive exam (for some programs), thesis (for some programs); for doctorate, thesis/dissertation. *Entrance requirements:* For master's, PRAXIS, 3 years of work experience (for some programs), prior teaching certification (for some programs); one to two professional references; writing sample (for some programs); personal statement (for some programs); interview (for some programs); bachelor's or graduate degree (for some programs); minimum 3.0 GPA (for some programs); for doctorate, GRE or MAT, 3 years of work experience, prior teaching certification; two letters of recommendation; copy of completed research paper/thesis (or other sample of some type of research writing); resume; interview; master's degree in education or related field; minimum 3.6 GPA in graduate courses; for other advanced degree, PRAXIS (for some programs), bachelor's degree (for some programs); master's degree (for some programs); minimum 3.0 GPA (for some programs); 2 professional references (for some programs); 2 letters of recommendation (for some programs); personal statement; interview; work experience (for some programs); prior certification (for some programs). Additional exam requirements/recommendations for international students: Required—The TOEFL or IELTS is required of international students who were not educated at the Bachelors level in English. Recommended—TOEFL (minimum score 580 paper-based; 92 iBT), IELTS (minimum score 7.5). *Application deadline:* For fall admission, 7/15 for domestic students. Applications are processed on a rolling basis. Application fee: $50. Electronic applications accepted. *Expenses:* $63,450 for full EdD tuition; $77,550 for full PhD tuition; $24,300 for full MA online tuition; $35,820 for full MA tuition. *Financial support:* Unspecified assistantships available. Financial award applicants required to submit FAFSA. *Faculty research:* Curriculum and instruction, secondary education, special education, education and technology, literacy instruction, higher education administration, education leadership. *Unit head:* Dr. Joan Moriarity, Associate Dean, 973-618-3626, E-mail: jmoriarity@caldwell.edu. *Application contact:* Tom Disch, Senior Admissions Counselor, 973-618-3544, E-mail: graduate@caldwell.edu.

California Baptist University, Program in Education, Riverside, CA 92504-3206. Offers educational leadership (MS); educational leadership for faith-based institutions (MS); educational leadership for public institutions (MS); educational technology (MS); instructional computer applications (MS); international education (MS); leadership and adult learning (MS); leadership and organizational studies (MS); online teaching and learning (MS); reading (MS); science education (MA); special education in mild/moderate disabilities (MS); special education in moderate/severe disabilities (MS); teacher leadership (MS); teaching (MS); teaching and learning (MS). *Program availability:* Part-time, evening/weekend, 100% online, blended/hybrid learning. *Faculty:* 26 full-time (13 women), 28 part-time/adjunct (21 women). *Students:* 201 full-time (164 women), 265 part-time (209 women); includes 226 minority (23 Black or African American, non-Hispanic/Latino; 4 American Indian or Alaska Native, non-Hispanic/Latino; 7 Asian, non-Hispanic/Latino; 169 Hispanic/Latino; 6 Native Hawaiian or other Pacific Islander, non-Hispanic/Latino; 17 Two or more races, non-Hispanic/Latino), 2 international. Average age 39. 145 applicants, 97% accepted, 141 enrolled. In 2018, 253 master's awarded. *Degree requirements:* For master's, comprehensive exam, project, or thesis. *Entrance requirements:* For master's, minimum undergraduate GPA of 2.75; 500-word essay; three letters of recommendation; two prerequisite courses completed with minimum C grade. Additional exam requirements/recommendations for international students: Required—TOEFL (minimum score 80 iBT). *Application deadline:* For fall admission, 8/1 priority date for domestic students, 7/1 for international students; for spring admission, 12/1 priority date for domestic students, 11/1 for international students. Applications are processed on a rolling basis. Application fee: $45. Electronic applications accepted. *Expenses:* $634 per unit. *Financial support:* In 2018–19, 312 students received support. Federal Work-Study and scholarships/grants available. Financial award applicants required to submit CSS PROFILE or FAFSA. *Faculty research:* Leadership development, complexity theory, faith and learning, special education, social and philosophical contexts of education. *Unit head:* Dr. Robin Duncan, Dean, School of Education, 951-552-8948, E-mail: rduncan@calbaptist.edu. *Application contact:* Dr. Shari Farris, Program Director, Online MS in Education, 951-343-2455, E-mail: sfarris@calbaptist.edu.
Website: http://www.calbaptist.edu/mastersined/

California Coast University, School of Education, Santa Ana, CA 92701. Offers administration (M Ed); curriculum and instruction (M Ed); educational administration (Ed D); educational psychology (Ed D); organizational leadership (Ed D). *Program availability:* Online learning.

California Lutheran University, Graduate Studies, Graduate School of Education, Thousand Oaks, CA 91360-2787. Offers counseling and guidance (MS), including college student personnel, counseling and guidance; educational leadership (MA, Ed D), including educational leadership (K-12) (Ed D), higher education leadership (Ed D); special education (MS); teacher leadership (M Ed); teaching (M Ed). *Accreditation:* NCATE. *Program availability:* Part-time, evening/weekend. *Degree requirements:* For master's, comprehensive exam or thesis; for doctorate, thesis/dissertation. *Entrance requirements:* For master's, GRE General Test, interview, minimum GPA of 3.0. Electronic applications accepted.

California Polytechnic State University, San Luis Obispo, College of Science and Mathematics, School of Education, San Luis Obispo, CA 93407. Offers MA. *Accreditation:* NCATE. *Program availability:* Part-time, evening/weekend. *Faculty:* 8 full-time (5 women), 8 part-time/adjunct (5 women). *Students:* 68 full-time (49 women), 22 part-time (20 women); includes 11 minority (1 Black or African American, non-Hispanic/Latino; 1 Asian, non-Hispanic/Latino; 9 Hispanic/Latino). Average age 30. 143 applicants, 59% accepted, 72 enrolled. In 2018, 95 master's awarded. *Degree requirements:* For master's, comprehensive exam. *Entrance requirements:* Additional exam requirements/recommendations for international students: Required—TOEFL (minimum score 80 iBT). *Application deadline:* For fall admission, 4/1 for domestic and international students. Applications are processed on a rolling basis. Application fee: $55. Electronic applications accepted. *Expenses: Tuition, area resident:* Full-time $7176; part-time $4164 per year. Tuition, state resident: full-time $10,965. Tuition, nonresident: full-time $10,965. *Required fees:* $6336; $3711. *Financial support:* Fellowships, research assistantships, career-related internships or fieldwork, Federal Work-Study, and institutionally sponsored loans available. Support available to part-time students. Financial award application deadline: 3/2; financial award applicants required to submit FAFSA. *Faculty research:* Rural school counseling, partner school effectiveness, college student affairs, special education, educational leadership and administration. *Unit head:* Dr. Kevin Taylor, Director, 805-756-1503, E-mail: jktaylor@calpoly.edu. *Application contact:* Dr. Kevin Taylor, Director, 805-756-1503, E-mail: jktaylor@calpoly.edu.
Website: http://soe.calpoly.edu/

California State University, Bakersfield, Division of Graduate Studies, School of Social Sciences and Education, Bakersfield, CA 93311. Offers MA, MS, MSW, Ed D. *Accreditation:* NCATE. *Degree requirements:* For master's, thesis or alternative, culminating projects.

California State University, Dominguez Hills, College of Education, Carson, CA 90747-0001. Offers MA, MS. *Accreditation:* NCATE. *Program availability:* Part-time, evening/weekend. *Degree requirements:* For master's, comprehensive exam, thesis or alternative. *Entrance requirements:* For master's, minimum GPA of 2.75. Additional exam requirements/recommendations for international students: Required—TOEFL. *Faculty research:* Science education, literacy, language acquisition, math, social adjustment.

California State University, East Bay, Office of Graduate Studies, College of Education and Allied Studies, Department of Teacher Education, Hayward, CA 94542-3000. Offers education (MS), including curriculum, early childhood education, educational technology and leadership, reading instruction. *Program availability:* Online learning. *Degree requirements:* For master's, project or thesis. *Entrance requirements:* For master's, minimum GPA of 3.0 in field, 2.5 overall; teaching experience; baccalaureate degree; 3 letters of recommendation. Additional exam requirements/recommendations for international students: Required—TOEFL (minimum score 550 paper-based), IELTS. Electronic applications accepted. *Faculty research:* Online, pedagogy, writing, learning, teaching.

California State University, Fresno, Division of Research and Graduate Studies, Kremen School of Education and Human Development, Fresno, CA 93740-8027. Offers MA, MS, Ed D. *Accreditation:* NCATE. *Program availability:* Part-time, evening/weekend. *Degree requirements:* For master's, thesis or alternative; for doctorate, thesis/dissertation. *Entrance requirements:* For master's, GRE General Test, MAT; for doctorate, GRE or MAT, minimum GPA of 3.2, master's degree. Additional exam requirements/recommendations for international students: Required—TOEFL. Electronic applications accepted. *Faculty research:* Adult community education, parenting, gifted and talented curriculum and instruction, peer mediation and conflict resolution.

California State University, Long Beach, Graduate Studies, College of Education, Long Beach, CA 90840. Offers MA, MS, Ed D. *Accreditation:* NCATE. *Program availability:* Part-time, evening/weekend. *Students:* 1,287 full-time (897 women), 694 part-time (518 women); includes 1,236 minority (99 Black or African American, non-Hispanic/Latino; 3 American Indian or Alaska Native, non-Hispanic/Latino; 223 Asian, non-Hispanic/Latino; 825 Hispanic/Latino; 6 Native Hawaiian or other Pacific Islander, non-Hispanic/Latino; 80 Two or more races, non-Hispanic/Latino), 51 international. Average age 30. *Degree requirements:* For master's, comprehensive exam (for some programs). *Entrance requirements:* For master's, GRE General Test, minimum GPA of 2.75. *Application deadline:* Applications are processed on a rolling basis. Application fee: $55. Electronic applications accepted. *Expenses: Required fees:* $2628 per term. Tuition and fees vary according to class time, course level, course load, degree level, campus/location and program. *Financial support:* Federal Work-Study, institutionally sponsored loans, and scholarships/grants available. Financial award application deadline: 3/2; financial award applicants required to submit FAFSA. *Faculty research:* K-16 educational reform and partnership, gender issues related to teaching and learning, urban education (poverty, diversity, language), assessment and standards-based education. *Unit head:* Shireen Pavri, Dean, 562-985-4513, Fax: 562-985-4951. *Application contact:* Megan Duggan, Program Support Specialist, 562-985-5238, Fax: 562-985-7786, E-mail: megan.duggan@csulb.edu.
Website: https://www.csulb.edu/college-of-education

California State University, Los Angeles, Graduate Studies, Charter College of Education, Los Angeles, CA 90032-8530. Offers MA, MS, Ed D, PhD, Graduate Certificate. *Accreditation:* NCATE. *Program availability:* Part-time, evening/weekend. *Degree requirements:* For doctorate, thesis/dissertation. *Entrance requirements:* For master's, minimum GPA of 2.75 in last 90 units of course work, teaching certificate; for doctorate, GRE General Test, master's degree; minimum undergraduate GPA of 3.0, graduate 3.5. Additional exam requirements/recommendations for international students: Required—TOEFL (minimum score 500 paper-based). Electronic applications accepted.

California State University, Monterey Bay, College of Education, Seaside, CA 93955-8001. Offers MAE. *Accreditation:* NCATE. *Program availability:* Part-time, evening/weekend. *Degree requirements:* For master's, one foreign language, thesis, 2 years of teaching experience. *Entrance requirements:* For master's, recommendations. Additional exam requirements/recommendations for international students: Required—TOEFL (minimum score 550 paper-based; 71 iBT). Electronic applications accepted. *Faculty research:* Multicultural education, linguistic diversity, behavior analysis.

California State University, Northridge, Graduate Studies, Michael D. Eisner College of Education, Northridge, CA 91330. Offers MA, MA Ed, MS, Ed D. *Accreditation:* NCATE. *Program availability:* Part-time, evening/weekend. *Entrance requirements:* Additional exam requirements/recommendations for international students: Required—TOEFL. *Faculty research:* Federal teacher center support, bilingual teacher training.

California State University, Sacramento, College of Education, Sacramento, CA 95819. Offers MA, MS, Ed D, Ed S. *Program availability:* Part-time, evening/weekend, blended/hybrid learning. *Degree requirements:* For master's, comprehensive exam, project, thesis, or writing proficiency exam; for doctorate, thesis/dissertation; for Ed S, project/thesis. *Entrance requirements:* For master's and doctorate, GRE. Additional exam requirements/recommendations for international students: Required—TOEFL (minimum score 550 paper-based; 80 iBT); Recommended—IELTS, TSE. Electronic applications accepted.

California State University, San Bernardino, Graduate Studies, College of Education, Program in Education, San Bernardino, CA 92407. Offers MA. *Faculty:* 8 full-time (5 women), 4 part-time/adjunct (3 women). *Students:* 114 full-time (86 women), 174 part-time (134 women); includes 155 minority (16 Black or African American, non-Hispanic/Latino; 1 American Indian or Alaska Native, non-Hispanic/Latino; 11 Asian, non-Hispanic/Latino; 118 Hispanic/Latino; 9 Two or more races, non-Hispanic/Latino), 40 international. Average age 35. 161 applicants, 71% accepted, 90 enrolled. In 2018, 143 master's awarded. *Degree requirements:* For master's, comprehensive exam (for some programs), thesis (for some programs). *Entrance requirements:* Additional exam requirements/recommendations for international students: Required—TOEFL. *Application deadline:* For fall admission, 7/16 for domestic students. Application fee: $55. *Unit head:* Dr. Chinaka DomNwachukwu, Dean, 909-537-5645, E-mail: Chinaka.domnwachukwu@csusb.edu. *Application contact:* Dr. Dorota Huizinga, Dean of Graduate Studies, 909-537-3064, E-mail: dorota.huizinga@csusb.edu.

California State University, San Marcos, College of Education, Health and Human Services, School of Education, San Marcos, CA 92096-0001. Offers education (MA); educational administration (MA); educational leadership (Ed D); literacy education (MA); special education (MA). *Accreditation:* NCATE (one or more programs are accredited). *Program availability:* Part-time, evening/weekend. *Entrance requirements:* For master's, minimum GPA of 3.0, teaching credentials, 1 year of teaching experience. *Application deadline:* For fall admission, 2/1 priority date for domestic students. Applications are processed on a rolling basis. Application fee: $55. *Financial support:* Applicants required to submit FAFSA. *Faculty research:* Multicultural literature, art as knowledge, poetry and second language acquisition, restructuring K–12 education and improving the training of K–8 science teachers. *Unit head:* Pat Stall, Director, 760-750-4386, E-mail: pstall@csusm.edu. *Application contact:* Dr. Wesley Schultz, Dean of Office of Graduate Studies and Research, 760-750-8045, Fax: 760-750-8045, E-mail: apply@csusm.edu.
Website: http://www.csusm.edu/education/

California State University, Stanislaus, College of Education, Kinesiology and Social Work, Turlock, CA 95382. Offers MA, MSW, Ed D. *Accreditation:* NCATE. *Program availability:* Part-time, evening/weekend. *Degree requirements:* For master's, thesis. *Entrance requirements:* For master's, MAT, minimum GPA of 3.0. Additional exam requirements/recommendations for international students: Required—TOEFL (minimum score 550 paper-based).

California University of Pennsylvania, School of Graduate Studies and Research, College of Education and Human Services, California, PA 15419-1394. Offers M Ed, MAT, MS, MSW, Ed D. *Accreditation:* NCATE. *Program availability:* Part-time, evening/weekend, online learning. *Degree requirements:* For master's, comprehensive exam, thesis optional. *Entrance requirements:* For master's, PRAXIS, MAT, minimum GPA of 3.0. Additional exam requirements/recommendations for international students: Required—TOEFL (minimum score 550 paper-based; 80 iBT). Electronic applications accepted. *Faculty research:* Autism counseling, injury and education, early childhood education, National Board certification.

Calvary University, Graduate School and Seminary, Kansas City, MO 64147. Offers Bible and theology (MS); Biblical counseling (MA); education (MS), including administration and leadership, Christian education, curriculum and instruction, elementary education; organizational development (MS); pastoral studies (M Div); worship arts (MS). *Program availability:* Part-time, evening/weekend. *Degree requirements:* For master's, variable foreign language requirement, comprehensive exam, thesis or alternative. *Entrance requirements:* For master's, minimum GPA of 2.5, BA or BS, doctrine agreement. Additional exam requirements/recommendations for international students: Required—TOEFL (minimum score 550 paper-based). Electronic applications accepted. *Expenses:* Contact institution.

Calvin College, Graduate Programs in Education, Grand Rapids, MI 49546-4388. Offers curriculum and instruction (M Ed). *Accreditation:* TEAC. *Program availability:* Part-time. *Degree requirements:* For master's, thesis or seminar. *Entrance requirements:* For master's, teaching certificate. Additional exam requirements/recommendations for international students: Required—TOEFL (minimum score 550 paper-based; 80 iBT). Electronic applications accepted. *Expenses:* Contact institution. *Faculty research:* Literacy, racialized gender and gendered identity, teacher learning, learning disabilities identification, leadership.

Cambridge College, School of Education, Boston, MA 02129. Offers autism specialist (M Ed); autism/behavior analyst (M Ed); behavior analyst (Post-Master's Certificate); curriculum and instruction (CAGS); early childhood teacher (M Ed); educational leadership (M Ed, Ed D); elementary teacher (M Ed); English as a second language (M Ed, Certificate); general science (M Ed); health education (Post-Master's Certificate); interdisciplinary studies (M Ed); library teacher (M Ed); mathematics education (M Ed); mathematics specialist (Certificate); school administration (M Ed, CAGS); school nurse education (M Ed); teacher of students with moderate disabilities (M Ed); teaching skills and methodologies (M Ed). *Program availability:* Part-time, evening/weekend, online learning. *Degree requirements:* For master's, thesis, internship/practicum (licensure program only); for doctorate, thesis/dissertation; for other advanced degree, thesis. *Entrance requirements:* For master's, interview, resume, documentation of licensure, 2 professional references; for doctorate, official transcripts, interview, resume, written personal statement/essay, portfolio of scholarly and professional work, 2 professional references, health insurance, immunizations form; for other advanced degree, official transcripts, interview, resume, written personal statement/essay, 2 professional references, health insurance, immunizations form. Additional exam requirements/recommendations for international students: Required—TOEFL (minimum score 550 paper-based; 79 iBT), Michigan English Language Assessment Battery (minimum score 85); Recommended—IELTS (minimum score 6). *Application deadline:* Applications are processed on a rolling basis. Application fee: $30. Electronic applications accepted. *Expenses:* Contact institution. *Financial support:* Career-related internships or fieldwork, Federal Work-Study, and scholarships/grants available. Financial award applicants required to submit FAFSA. *Faculty research:* Adult education, accelerated learning, mathematics education, brain compatible learning, special education and law. *Unit head:* Dr. Mary Garrity, Interim Dean, 617-873-0168, E-mail: mary.garrity@cambridgecollege.edu. *Application contact:* Salvadore Liberto, Interim Assistant Vice President of Enrollment, 800-877-4723, E-mail: admissions@cambridgecollege.edu.
Website: https://www.cambridgecollege.edu/school/school-education

Cameron University, Office of Graduate Studies, Program in Education, Lawton, OK 73505-6377. Offers M Ed. *Accreditation:* NCATE. *Program availability:* Part-time, evening/weekend. *Degree requirements:* For master's, portfolio. *Entrance requirements:* Additional exam requirements/recommendations for international students: Required—TOEFL (minimum score 550 paper-based). Electronic applications accepted. *Faculty research:* Motivation, computer learning, special education mathematics, inquiry-based learning.

Cameron University, Office of Graduate Studies, Program in Teaching, Lawton, OK 73505-6377. Offers MAT. *Accreditation:* NCATE. *Degree requirements:* For master's, portfolio. *Entrance requirements:* Additional exam requirements/recommendations for international students: Required—TOEFL (minimum score 550 paper-based). Electronic applications accepted. *Faculty research:* Teacher retention/attrition, teacher education.

Campbellsville University, School of Education, Campbellsville, KY 42718-2799. Offers education (MA); school counseling (MA); school improvement (MA); special education (MASE); special education-teacher leader (MA); teacher leader (MA); teaching (MAT), including middle grades biology, middle grades chemistry, middle grades English. *Accreditation:* NCATE. *Program availability:* Part-time, evening/weekend, 100% online, blended/hybrid learning. *Faculty:* 16 full-time (10 women), 13 part-time/adjunct (7 women). *Students:* 154 full-time (122 women), 44 part-time (36 women); includes 18 minority (16 Black or African American, non-Hispanic/Latino; 1 Hispanic/Latino; 1 Two or more races, non-Hispanic/Latino), 1 international. Average age 34. 280 applicants, 30% accepted, 72 enrolled. In 2018, 66 master's awarded. *Degree requirements:* For master's, comprehensive exam (for some programs), thesis, research paper. *Entrance requirements:* For master's, GRE or PRAXIS, minimum undergraduate GPA of 2.75, teaching certificate, professional growth plan, letters of recommendation, interview. Additional exam requirements/recommendations for international students: Recommended—TOEFL (minimum score 550 paper-based; 79 iBT), IELTS (minimum score 6). *Application deadline:* Applications are processed on a rolling basis. Application fee: $25. Electronic applications accepted. Application fee is waived when completed online. *Expenses:* $299/credit hour. *Financial support:* Unspecified assistantships available. Financial award applicants required to submit FAFSA. *Faculty research:* Professional development, curriculum development, school governance, assessment, special education. *Unit head:* Dr. Lisa Allen, Dean of School of Education, 270-789-5344, Fax: 270-789-5206, E-mail: lsallen@campbellsville.edu. *Application contact:* Monica Bamwine, Director of Graduate Admissions, 270-789-5221, Fax: 270-789-5071, E-mail: mkbamwine@campbellsville.edu.

Campbell University, Graduate and Professional Programs, School of Education, Buies Creek, NC 27506. Offers elementary education (M Ed); interdisciplinary studies (M Ed); middle grades education (M Ed); physical education (M Ed); school administration (MSA); school counseling (M Ed); secondary education (M Ed). *Accreditation:* NCATE. *Program availability:* Part-time, evening/weekend. *Degree requirements:* For master's, comprehensive exam. *Entrance requirements:* For master's, GRE General Test, minimum GPA of 2.7. *Faculty research:* Spiritual values and wellness issues in counseling, stress and professional burnout among counselors, thinking strategies, leadership, adaptive technology.

Education—General

Canisius College, Graduate Division, School of Education and Human Services, Buffalo, NY 14208-1098. Offers MS, MS Ed, MSA, Certificate. *Program availability:* Part-time, evening/weekend, 100% online, blended/hybrid learning. *Faculty:* 26 full-time (15 women), 58 part-time/adjunct (39 women). *Students:* 319 full-time (213 women), 323 part-time (212 women); includes 117 minority (68 Black or African American, non-Hispanic/Latino; 1 American Indian or Alaska Native, non-Hispanic/Latino; 7 Asian, non-Hispanic/Latino; 27 Hispanic/Latino; 14 Two or more races, non-Hispanic/Latino), 12 international. Average age 28. 411 applicants, 87% accepted, 236 enrolled. In 2018, 363 master's awarded. *Degree requirements:* For master's, thesis (for some programs). *Entrance requirements:* For master's, GRE (if cumulative GPA less than 2.7), transcripts, BA from accredited institution. Additional exam requirements/recommendations for international students: Required—TOEFL (minimum score 550 paper-based, 79 iBT), IELTS (minimum score 6.5), or CAEL (minimum score 70). *Application deadline:* Applications are processed on a rolling basis. Application fee: $0. Electronic applications accepted. *Expenses: Tuition:* Part-time $820 per credit hour. *Required fees:* $25 per semester. One-time fee: $65 part-time. Tuition and fees vary according to program. *Financial support:* In 2018–19, 590 students received support. Career-related internships or fieldwork, Federal Work-Study, scholarships/grants, tuition waivers (partial), and unspecified assistantships available. Support available to part-time students. Financial award application deadline: 4/30; financial award applicants required to submit FAFSA. *Faculty research:* Asperger's disease, autism, culturally congruent pedagogy in physical education, family as faculty, impact of trauma on adults, information processing and perceptual styles of athletes, integrating digital technologies in the classroom, long term psych-social impact on police officers, private higher education, qualities of effective coaches, reading strategies, student perceptions of online courses, teaching effectiveness, teaching methods, tutorial experiences in modern math. *Unit head:* Dr. Nancy V. Wallace, Dean, 716-888-3205, Fax: 716-888-3164, E-mail: wallacen@canisius.edu. *Application contact:* Lauren M Kicak, Associate Director of Graduate Admissions, 716-888-2109, Fax: 716-888-3290, E-mail: kicakl@canisius.edu.
Website: http://www.canisius.edu/graduate/

Capella University, School of Education, Doctoral Programs in Education, Minneapolis, MN 55402. Offers curriculum and instruction (PhD); educational leadership and management (Ed D); instructional design for online learning (PhD); K-12 studies in education (PhD); leadership for higher education (PhD); leadership in educational administration (PhD); postsecondary and adult education (PhD); professional studies in education (PhD); reading and literacy (Ed D); special education leadership (PhD); training and performance improvement (PhD).

Capella University, School of Education, Master's Programs in Education, Minneapolis, MN 55402. Offers adult education (MS); curriculum and instruction (MS); early childhood education (MS); enrollment management (MS); higher education leadership and management (MS); instructional design for online learning (MS); integrative studies (MS); K-12 studies in education (MS); leadership in educational administration (MS); reading and literacy (MS); special education teaching (MS).

Cardinal Stritch University, College of Education and Leadership, Milwaukee, WI 53217-3985. Offers MA, MS, Ed D, PhD. *Accreditation:* NCATE. *Program availability:* Part-time, evening/weekend, 100% online. *Degree requirements:* For master's, comprehensive exam, thesis (for some programs); for doctorate, thesis/dissertation, practica/field experience. *Entrance requirements:* For doctorate, minimum GPA of 3.5 in master's coursework, portfolio, interview, 3 letters of recommendation. Additional exam requirements/recommendations for international students: Required—TOEFL (minimum score 79 iBT), IELTS (minimum score 6.5). Electronic applications accepted. *Expenses:* Contact institution.

Caribbean University, Graduate School, Bayamón, PR 00960-0493. Offers administration and supervision (MA Ed); criminal justice (MA); curriculum and instruction (MA Ed, PhD), including elementary education (MA Ed), English education (MA Ed), history education (MA Ed), mathematics education (MA Ed), primary education (MA Ed), science education (MA Ed), Spanish education (MA Ed); educational technology in instructional systems (MA Ed); gerontology (MSN); human resources (MBA); museology, archiving and art history (MA Ed); neonatal pediatrics (MSN); physical education (MA Ed); special education (MA Ed). *Entrance requirements:* For master's, interview, minimum GPA of 2.5.

Carlow University, College of Learning and Innovation, Pittsburgh, PA 15213-3165. Offers M Ed, MA, MFA, Certificate, Graduate Certificate. *Program availability:* Part-time, evening/weekend, 100% online, blended/hybrid learning, low-residency. *Students:* 52 full-time (39 women), 37 part-time (34 women); includes 15 minority (12 Black or African American, non-Hispanic/Latino; 1 Asian, non-Hispanic/Latino; 2 Two or more races, non-Hispanic/Latino), 1 international. Average age 32. 42 applicants, 93% accepted, 26 enrolled. In 2018, 34 master's, 6 other advanced degrees awarded. *Entrance requirements:* For master's, personal essay (two for MFA); resume or curriculum vitae; two recommendations; official transcripts; interview; minimum undergraduate GPA of 3.0. Additional exam requirements/recommendations for international students: Required—TOEFL (minimum score 550 paper-based). *Application deadline:* Applications are processed on a rolling basis. Application fee: $0. Electronic applications accepted. *Expenses:* Contact institution. *Financial support:* Application deadline: 4/1; applicants required to submit FAFSA. *Unit head:* Dr. Matthew Gordley, Dean, 412-578-6262, E-mail: megordley@carlow.edu. *Application contact:* Dr. Matthew Gordley, Dean, 412-578-6262, E-mail: megordley@carlow.edu.
Website: http://www.carlow.edu/College_of_Learning_and_Innovation.aspx

Carroll University, Graduate Programs in Education, Waukesha, WI 53186-5593. Offers adult and continuing education (M Ed); educational leadership (MS); PK-12 (M Ed). *Program availability:* Part-time, evening/weekend. *Degree requirements:* For master's, thesis. *Entrance requirements:* For master's, minimum undergraduate GPA of 2.5 in related field. Additional exam requirements/recommendations for international students: Required—TOEFL. Electronic applications accepted. *Faculty research:* Qualitative research methods, whole language approaches to teaching, the writing process, multicultural education, gifted/talented learners.

Carson-Newman University, Graduate Program in Education, Jefferson City, TN 37760. Offers curriculum and instruction (M Ed); educational leadership (M Ed); elementary education (MAT); school counseling (MS); secondary education (MAT); teaching English as a second language (MATESL). *Accreditation:* NCATE. *Program availability:* Part-time, evening/weekend, 100% online, blended/hybrid learning. *Faculty:* 20 full-time (11 women), 16 part-time/adjunct (13 women). *Students:* 14 full-time (8 women), 401 part-time (294 women); includes 45 minority (34 Black or African American, non-Hispanic/Latino; 1 American Indian or Alaska Native, non-Hispanic/Latino; 4 Hispanic/Latino; 1 Native Hawaiian or other Pacific Islander, non-Hispanic/Latino; 5 Two or more races, non-Hispanic/Latino). Average age 36. 223 applicants, 100% accepted, 199 enrolled. In 2018, 211 master's awarded. *Degree requirements:* For master's, thesis or alternative. *Entrance requirements:* For master's, PRAXIS II or GRE with minimum score of 290 on the verbal and quantitative components (for MAT), minimum GPA of 3.0 in major, 2.5 overall. Additional exam requirements/recommendations for international students: Recommended—TOEFL (minimum score 79 iBT), IELTS (minimum score 6.5), TSE (minimum score 53). *Application deadline:* For fall admission, 7/15 priority date for domestic students. Applications are processed on a rolling basis. Application fee: $50. *Expenses: Tuition:* Full-time $9036; part-time $502 per credit hour. *Required fees:* $900; $25 per credit hour. $300 per semester. One-time fee: $150. *Financial support:* Federal Work-Study and unspecified assistantships available. Financial award applicants required to submit FAFSA. *Unit head:* Dr. Kim Hawkins, Chair, 865-471-3314, E-mail: khawkins@cn.edu. *Application contact:* Nilma Stewart, Graduate Admissions and Services Adviser, 865-471-3230, Fax: 865-471-3875, E-mail: adults@cn.edu.
Website: http://www.cn.edu/adult-graduate-studies

Carthage College, Division of Teacher Education, Kenosha, WI 53140. Offers classroom guidance and counseling (M Ed); creative arts (M Ed); gifted and talented children (M Ed); language arts (M Ed); modern language (M Ed); natural sciences (M Ed); reading (M Ed, Certificate); social sciences (M Ed); teacher leadership (M Ed). *Program availability:* Part-time, evening/weekend. *Degree requirements:* For master's, thesis optional. *Entrance requirements:* For master's, MAT, minimum B average, letters of reference.

Castleton University, Division of Graduate Studies, Department of Education, Castleton, VT 05735. Offers curriculum and instruction (MA Ed); educational leadership (MA Ed, CAGS); language arts and reading (MA Ed, CAGS); special education (MA Ed, CAGS). *Program availability:* Part-time, evening/weekend. *Degree requirements:* For master's, thesis or alternative; for CAGS, publishable paper. *Entrance requirements:* For master's, GRE General Test, MAT, interview, minimum undergraduate GPA of 3.0; for CAGS, educational research, master's degree, minimum undergraduate GPA of 3.0. *Faculty research:* Assessment, narrative.

The Catholic University of America, School of Arts and Sciences, Department of Education, Washington, DC 20064. Offers Catholic school leadership (MA); education (Certificate); secondary education (MA); special education (MA), including early childhood, non-categorical. *Accreditation:* NCATE. *Program availability:* Part-time. *Faculty:* 7 full-time (6 women), 7 part-time/adjunct (5 women). *Students:* 12 full-time (11 women), 15 part-time (6 women); includes 3 minority (2 Hispanic/Latino; 1 Two or more races, non-Hispanic/Latino), 2 international. Average age 37. 12 applicants, 75% accepted, 8 enrolled. In 2018, 14 master's awarded. *Degree requirements:* For master's, comprehensive exam, thesis or alternative; for Certificate, action research project. *Entrance requirements:* For master's, GRE General Test or MAT, statement of purpose, official copies of academic transcripts, three letters of recommendation, interview; for Certificate, PRAXIS I, statement of purpose, official copies of academic transcripts, three letters of recommendation, interview. Additional exam requirements/recommendations for international students: Required—TOEFL (minimum score 550 paper-based; 80 iBT). *Application deadline:* For fall admission, 7/15 priority date for domestic students, 7/1 for international students; for spring admission, 11/15 priority date for domestic students, 11/1 for international students. Applications are processed on a rolling basis. Application fee: $55. Electronic applications accepted. *Expenses:* Contact institution. *Financial support:* Fellowships, research assistantships, teaching assistantships, Federal Work-Study, scholarships/grants, tuition waivers (full and partial), and unspecified assistantships available. Financial award application deadline: 2/1; financial award applicants required to submit FAFSA. *Faculty research:* Special education, early childhood education, educational psychology, Catholic school administration, leadership and policy studies, counseling, curriculum and instruction. *Unit head:* Dr. Agnes Cave, Chair, 202-319-5805, Fax: 202-319-5815, E-mail: cave@cua.edu. *Application contact:* Dr. Steven Brown, Director of Graduate Admissions, 202-319-5057, Fax: 202-319-6533, E-mail: cua-admissions@cua.edu.
Website: http://education.cua.edu/

Cedar Crest College, Department of Education, Allentown, PA 18104-6196. Offers M Ed. *Program availability:* Part-time, evening/weekend, 100% online, blended/hybrid learning. *Faculty:* 4 full-time (all women), 13 part-time/adjunct (8 women). *Students:* 11 full-time (all women), 60 part-time (49 women); includes 11 minority (1 Black or African American, non-Hispanic/Latino; 2 Asian, non-Hispanic/Latino; 7 Hispanic/Latino; 1 Two or more races, non-Hispanic/Latino). Average age 34. 14 applicants, 79% accepted, 8 enrolled. In 2018, 21 master's awarded. *Entrance requirements:* Additional exam requirements/recommendations for international students: Required—TOEFL. *Application deadline:* For fall admission, 8/7 priority date for domestic and international students; for winter admission, 11/7 priority date for domestic and international students; for spring admission, 1/8 priority date for domestic and international students. Applications are processed on a rolling basis. Electronic applications accepted. *Expenses:* 516 per credit. *Financial support:* In 2018–19, 60 students received support. Available to part-time students. Applicants required to submit FAFSA. *Faculty research:* Science education, reading, history of Pennsylvania, math education. *Unit head:* Dr. Jill Purdy, Department Chair, 610-606-4666 Ext. 3419, E-mail: jepurdy@cedarcrest.edu. *Application contact:* Nancy Wunderly, Director of School of Adult and Graduate Education, 610-606-4666, E-mail: sage@cedarcrest.edu.

Centenary College of Louisiana, Graduate Programs, Department of Education, Shreveport, LA 71104. Offers elementary education (MAT); secondary education (MAT). *Program availability:* Part-time, evening/weekend. *Degree requirements:* For master's, comprehensive exam. *Entrance requirements:* For master's, PRAXIS I and II (for MAT), undergraduate degree, minimum GPA of 2.5. *Expenses:* Contact institution. *Faculty research:* Teachers as advocates for teachers, portfolio assessment, disabled readers.

Centenary University, Program in Education, Hackettstown, NJ 07840-2100. Offers education practice (M Ed); educational leadership (MA, Ed D); instructional leadership (MA); reading (M Ed); special education (MA). *Accreditation:* TEAC. *Program availability:* Part-time, evening/weekend, online learning. *Degree requirements:* For master's, thesis. *Entrance requirements:* For master's, interview, minimum undergraduate GPA of 2.8.

Central Connecticut State University, School of Graduate Studies, School of Education and Professional Studies, New Britain, CT 06050-4010. Offers MAT, MS, MSN, Ed D, AC, Certificate, Sixth Year Certificate. *Accreditation:* NCATE. *Program availability:* Part-time, evening/weekend. *Faculty:* 44 full-time (26 women), 64 part-time/adjunct (42 women). *Students:* 260 full-time (200 women), 831 part-time (641 women); includes 255 minority (90 Black or African American, non-Hispanic/Latino; 2 American Indian or Alaska Native, non-Hispanic/Latino; 14 Asian, non-Hispanic/Latino; 127 Hispanic/Latino; 1 Native Hawaiian or other Pacific Islander, non-Hispanic/Latino; 21 Two or more races, non-Hispanic/Latino), 2 international. Average age 33. 429 applicants, 69% accepted, 207 enrolled. In 2018, 229 master's, 6 doctorates, 99 other advanced degrees awarded. *Degree requirements:* For master's, comprehensive exam, thesis or alternative; for doctorate, thesis/dissertation; for other advanced degree, qualifying exam. *Entrance requirements:* For master's, minimum undergraduate GPA of 2.7; for doctorate, GRE. Additional exam requirements/recommendations for international students: Required—TOEFL (minimum score 550 paper-based; 79 iBT); Recommended—IELTS (minimum score 6.5). *Application deadline:* For fall admission, 6/1 for domestic students, 5/1 for international students; for spring admission, 11/1 for domestic and international students. Applications are processed on a rolling basis. Application fee: $50. Electronic applications accepted. *Expenses: Tuition, area resident:* Full-time $7027; part-time $388 per credit. Tuition, state resident: full-time $9750; part-time $388 per credit. Tuition, nonresident: full-time $18,102; part-time $388 per credit.

International tuition: $18,102 full-time. *Required fees:* $266 per semester. *Financial support:* In 2018–19, 129 students received support. Career-related internships or fieldwork, Federal Work-Study, scholarships/grants, and unspecified assistantships available. Support available to part-time students. Financial award application deadline: 3/1; financial award applicants required to submit FAFSA. *Unit head:* Dr. Kimberly Kostelis, Dean, 860-832-2101, E-mail: kimberly.kostelis@ccsu.edu. *Application contact:* Patricia Gardner, Associate Director of Graduate Studies, 860-832-2350, Fax: 860-832-2362.
Website: http://www.ccsu.edu/seps/

Central Methodist University, College of Graduate and Extended Studies, Fayette, MO 65248-1198. Offers clinical counseling (MS); clinical nurse leader (MSN); education (M Ed); music education (MME); nurse educator (MSN). *Program availability:* Part-time, evening/weekend, online learning. *Degree requirements:* For master's, thesis. *Entrance requirements:* For master's, GRE General Test, minimum GPA of 2.75. Electronic applications accepted.

Central Michigan University, Central Michigan University Global Campus, Program in Education, Mount Pleasant, MI 48859. Offers college teaching (Graduate Certificate); community college (MA); curriculum and instruction (MA); educational technology (MA, DET); reading and literacy K-12 (MA); school principalship (MA), including charter school leadership; training and development (MA). *Accreditation:* TEAC. *Program availability:* Part-time, evening/weekend. *Entrance requirements:* For master's, minimum GPA of 2.7 in major. Additional exam requirements/recommendations for international students: Required—TOEFL. Electronic applications accepted.

Central Michigan University, College of Graduate Studies, College of Education and Human Services, Mount Pleasant, MI 48859. Offers MA, MS, Ed D, Ed S, Graduate Certificate. *Accreditation:* TEAC. *Program availability:* Part-time, evening/weekend. *Degree requirements:* For master's and other advanced degree, thesis or alternative; for doctorate, thesis/dissertation. Electronic applications accepted.

Central Washington University, School of Graduate Studies and Research, College of Education and Professional Studies, Ellensburg, WA 98926. Offers M Ed, MS. *Program availability:* Part-time. *Entrance requirements:* For master's, minimum GPA of 3.0. Additional exam requirements/recommendations for international students: Required—TOEFL (minimum score 550 paper-based; 79 iBT). Electronic applications accepted.

Chadron State College, School of Professional and Graduate Studies, Department of Education, Chadron, NE 69337. Offers business (MA Ed); community counseling (MA Ed); educational administration (MS Ed, Sp Ed); elementary education (MS Ed); history (MA Ed); language and literature (MA Ed); secondary administration (MS Ed); secondary education (MS Ed). *Accreditation:* NCATE. *Program availability:* Part-time, evening/weekend, online learning. *Degree requirements:* For master's, thesis optional. *Entrance requirements:* For master's, GRE General Test, GRE Writing Test, minimum GPA of 2.75 or 12 graduate hours at CSC with minimum GPA of 3.25. Additional exam requirements/recommendations for international students: Required—TOEFL. Electronic applications accepted. *Faculty research:* Rural education, technology, mental health.

Chaminade University of Honolulu, Graduate, Program in Education, Honolulu, HI 96816-1578. Offers child development (M Ed); early childhood education (Montessori) (MAT); early childhood education (PK-3) (MAT); educational leadership (M Ed); elementary education (MAT); instructional leadership (M Ed); Montessori (M Ed); secondary education (MAT); special education (MAT); teacher leader (M Ed). *Program availability:* Part-time, evening/weekend, 100% online, blended/hybrid learning. *Faculty:* 8 full-time (3 women), 11 part-time/adjunct (8 women). *Students:* 80 full-time (57 women), 100 part-time (77 women); includes 113 minority (6 Black or African American, non-Hispanic/Latino; 4 American Indian or Alaska Native, non-Hispanic/Latino; 45 Asian, non-Hispanic/Latino; 6 Hispanic/Latino; 50 Native Hawaiian or other Pacific Islander, non-Hispanic/Latino; 2 Two or more races, non-Hispanic/Latino), 2 international. Average age 35. 53 applicants, 92% accepted, 40 enrolled. In 2018, 92 master's awarded. *Degree requirements:* For master's, thesis or alternative. *Entrance requirements:* For master's, PRAXIS (for MAT), official transcripts, writing sample (for MAT). Additional exam requirements/recommendations for international students: Required—TOEFL (minimum score 550 paper-based; 79 iBT). *Application deadline:* Applications are processed on a rolling basis. Application fee: $40. Electronic applications accepted. *Expenses:* $780 per credit; $93 fee per online course. *Financial support:* Applicants required to submit FAFSA. *Unit head:* Dr. Dale Fryxell, Dean, 808-739-4652, Fax: 808-739-4607, E-mail: edu-office@chaminade.edu. *Application contact:* 808-739-7478, E-mail: gradserv@chaminade.edu.
Website: https://chaminade.edu/academics/education-behavioral-sciences/

Chapman University, Donna Ford Attallah College of Educational Studies, Orange, CA 92866. Offers counseling (MA), including school counseling (MA, Credential); curriculum and instruction (MA), including elementary education, secondary education; education (PhD), including cultural and curricular studies, disability studies, leadership studies, school psychology (PhD, Credential); educational psychology (MA); leadership development (MA); multiple subjects (Credential), including Spanish/English bilingual; pupil personnel services (Credential), including school counseling (MA, Credential), school psychology (PhD, Credential); school psychology (Ed S); single subject (Credential); special education (MA, Credential), including mild/moderate (Credential), moderate/severe (Credential); teaching (MA), including elementary education, secondary education, secondary music education. *Accreditation:* TEAC. *Program availability:* Part-time, evening/weekend. Electronic applications accepted. *Expenses:* Contact institution.

Charleston Southern University, College of Education, Charleston, SC 29423-8087. Offers elementary administration and supervision (M Ed); elementary education (M Ed); secondary administration and supervision (M Ed). *Accreditation:* NCATE. *Program availability:* Part-time, evening/weekend. *Degree requirements:* For master's, thesis optional. *Entrance requirements:* For master's, GRE or MAT. Additional exam requirements/recommendations for international students: Required—TOEFL (minimum score 550 paper-based; 79 iBT). Electronic applications accepted. *Expenses:* Contact institution.

Chatham University, Program in Education, Pittsburgh, PA 15232-2826. Offers early childhood education (MAT); elementary education (MAT); environmental education (K-12) (MAT); secondary art (MAT); secondary biology education (MAT); secondary chemistry education (MAT); secondary English education (MAT); secondary math education (MAT); secondary physics education (MAT); secondary social studies education (MAT); special education (MAT). *Degree requirements:* For master's, thesis, teaching experience. *Entrance requirements:* For master's, minimum GPA of 3.0, sample of written work, recommendation letters. Additional exam requirements/recommendations for international students: Required—TOEFL (minimum score 600 paper-based; 100 iBT), IELTS (minimum score 7), TWE. Electronic applications accepted. Application fee is waived when completed online. *Faculty research:* Gifted education, environmental education, technology in education, writing as learning, class size and achievement.

Chestnut Hill College, School of Graduate Studies, Department of Education, Philadelphia, PA 19118-2693. Offers early education (M Ed), including early education; educational leadership (M Ed); elementary/middle education (M Ed); reading (M Ed), including reading specialist; secondary education (M Ed); special education (M Ed), including special education. *Program availability:* Part-time, evening/weekend. *Degree requirements:* For master's, thesis optional. *Entrance requirements:* For master's, PRAXIS I or proof of teaching certification, letters of recommendation, writing sample, 6 graduate credits with minimum B grade if undergraduate GPA less than 3.0. Additional exam requirements/recommendations for international students: Required—TOEFL (minimum score 500 paper-based), IELTS (minimum score 6.0), or TWE (minimum score 22). Electronic applications accepted. *Expenses:* Contact institution. *Faculty research:* Culturally responsive pedagogy, gender issues, autism, inclusive education, mentoring and induction programs.

Cheyney University of Pennsylvania, Graduate Programs, Cheyney, PA 19319. Offers M Ed, MPA, Certificate. *Program availability:* Part-time, evening/weekend. *Degree requirements:* For master's and Certificate, thesis or alternative. *Entrance requirements:* For master's and Certificate, GRE General Test, MAT, minimum GPA of 2.75. Electronic applications accepted. *Faculty research:* Teacher motivation, critical thinking.

Chicago State University, School of Graduate and Professional Studies, College of Education, Chicago, IL 60628. Offers M Ed, MA, MAT, MS Ed, Ed D. *Accreditation:* NCATE. *Program availability:* Part-time. *Entrance requirements:* For master's, minimum GPA of 2.75.

Chowan University, School of Graduate Studies, Murfreesboro, NC 27855. Offers education (M Ed). *Entrance requirements:* For master's, official transcripts, three letters of recommendation, personal statement, current teacher license. Additional exam requirements/recommendations for international students: Required—TOEFL. Electronic applications accepted.

Christian Brothers University, School of Arts, Memphis, TN 38104-5581. Offers Catholic studies (MACS); educational leadership (MSEL); teacher-leadership (M Ed); teaching (MAT). *Program availability:* Part-time, evening/weekend. *Entrance requirements:* For master's, GRE, GMAT, PRAXIS II. *Expenses:* Contact institution.

Christopher Newport University, Graduate Studies, Department of Teacher Preparation, Newport News, VA 23606-3072. Offers MAT. *Degree requirements:* For master's, comprehensive exam, thesis or alternative. *Entrance requirements:* For master's, PRAXIS II/Virginia Communication and Literacy Assessment (VCLA)/PRAXIS (core mathematics), minimum GPA of 3.0. Additional exam requirements/recommendations for international students: Required—TOEFL (minimum score 580 paper-based; 92 iBT), IELTS (minimum score 7). Electronic applications accepted. *Faculty research:* Early literacy development, instructional innovations, professional teaching standards, multicultural issues, aesthetic education.

The Citadel, The Military College of South Carolina, Citadel Graduate College, Zucker Family School of Education, Charleston, SC 29409. Offers elementary/secondary school administration and supervision (M Ed); elementary/secondary school counseling (M Ed); interdisciplinary STEM education (M Ed); literacy education (M Ed, Graduate Certificate); middle grades (MAT), including English, mathematics, science, social studies; physical education (grades K-12) (MAT); school superintendency (Ed S); secondary education (MAT), including biology, English, mathematics, social studies; student affairs (Graduate Certificate); student affairs and college counseling (M Ed). *Accreditation:* NCATE. *Program availability:* Part-time, evening/weekend, 100% online, blended/hybrid learning. *Degree requirements:* For master's, comprehensive exam (for some programs). *Entrance requirements:* For master's, GRE (minimum combined verbal and quantitative score of 290) or MAT (minimum score 396). Additional exam requirements/recommendations for international students: Required—TOEFL (minimum score 550 paper-based; 79 iBT). Electronic applications accepted. *Expenses:* Tuition, state resident: part-time $595 per credit hour. Tuition, nonresident: part-time $1020 per credit hour. *Required fees:* $90 per term.

City College of the City University of New York, Graduate School, School of Education, New York, NY 10031-9198. Offers MA, MS, MS Ed, AC. *Accreditation:* NCATE. *Program availability:* Part-time, evening/weekend. *Entrance requirements:* For master's, Liberal Arts and Sciences Test (LAST), Content Specialty Test (CST). Additional exam requirements/recommendations for international students: Required—TOEFL.

City University of Seattle, Graduate Division, Albright School of Education, Seattle, WA 98121. Offers administrator certification (Certificate); curriculum and instruction (M Ed); elementary education (MIT); guidance and counseling (M Ed); leadership (M Ed); reading and literacy (M Ed); school counseling (M Ed); special education (MIT); superintendent certification (Certificate). *Program availability:* Part-time, evening/weekend, online learning. *Degree requirements:* For master's, comprehensive exam (for some programs), thesis (for some programs). *Entrance requirements:* For master's, baccalaureate degree or equivalent from an accredited or otherwise recognized institution. Additional exam requirements/recommendations for international students: Required—TOEFL (minimum score 567 paper-based; 87 iBT); Recommended—IELTS. Electronic applications accepted. *Expenses:* Contact institution.

Claremont Graduate University, Graduate Programs, School of Educational Studies, Claremont, CA 91711-6160. Offers Africana education (Certificate); education and policy (MA, PhD); higher education/student affairs (MA, PhD); human development (MA, PhD); public school administration (MA, PhD); quantitative evaluation (MA, PhD); special education (MA, PhD); teacher education (MA); teaching and learning (MA, PhD); urban leadership (PhD); MBA/PhD. PhD program offered jointly with San Diego State University. *Program availability:* Part-time. Terminal master's awarded for partial completion of doctoral program. *Entrance requirements:* For master's and doctorate, GRE General Test. Additional exam requirements/recommendations for international students: Required—TOEFL (minimum score 75 iBT). Electronic applications accepted. *Faculty research:* Education administration, K-12 and higher education, multicultural education, education policy, diversity in higher education, faculty issues.

Clarion University of Pennsylvania, College of Arts, Education and Sciences, Master of Education Program, Clarion, PA 16214. Offers curriculum and instruction (M Ed); early childhood (M Ed); math education (M Ed); reading (M Ed); science education (M Ed); special education (M Ed); technology (M Ed). *Accreditation:* NCATE. *Program availability:* Part-time, evening/weekend, 100% online, blended/hybrid learning. *Faculty:* 6 full-time (3 women). *Students:* 5 full-time (all women), 85 part-time (73 women); includes 3 minority (2 Black or African American, non-Hispanic/Latino; 1 Two or more races, non-Hispanic/Latino). Average age 30. 57 applicants, 61% accepted, 26 enrolled. In 2018, 51 master's awarded. *Degree requirements:* For master's, comprehensive exam (for some programs), thesis or alternative. *Entrance requirements:* For master's, minimum QPA of 3.0. Additional exam requirements/recommendations for international students: Required—TOEFL (minimum score 550 paper-based; 80 iBT), Or IELTS. Satisfactory completion of a bachelor's degree from an accredited US college or university is also acceptable evidence of English language. *Application deadline:* For fall admission, 8/1 priority date for domestic students, 7/15 priority date for international students; for winter admission, 11/1 priority date for domestic students; for spring admission, 12/1 priority date for domestic students, 11/15 priority date for international students; for summer admission, 4/1 priority date for domestic students. Applications are

processed on a rolling basis. Application fee: $40. Electronic applications accepted. *Expenses: Tuition, area resident:* Part-time $516 per credit hour. Tuition, state resident: part-time $516 per credit hour. Tuition, nonresident: part-time $774 per credit hour. *Required fees:* $159 per credit hour. One-time fee: $50 part-time. Tuition and fees vary according to degree level, campus/location and program. *Financial support:* Federal Work-Study, institutionally sponsored loans, and scholarships/grants available. Financial award application deadline: 3/1; financial award applicants required to submit FAFSA. *Unit head:* Dr. John McCullough, Chair, Department of Education, 814-393-2404, Fax: 814-393-2446, E-mail: gradstudies@clarion.edu. *Application contact:* Susan Staub, Graduate Admissions Counselor, 814-393-2337, Fax: 814-393-2722, E-mail: gradstudies@clarion.edu.

Clark Atlanta University, School of Education, Atlanta, GA 30314. Offers MA, MAT, Ed D, Ed S. *Accreditation:* NCATE. *Program availability:* Part-time, evening/weekend. *Degree requirements:* For master's, comprehensive exam; for doctorate, comprehensive exam, thesis/dissertation. *Entrance requirements:* For master's, GRE General Test, minimum undergraduate GPA of 2.6; for doctorate, GRE General Test, minimum graduate GPA of 3.0. Additional exam requirements/recommendations for international students: Required—TOEFL (minimum score 500 paper-based; 61 iBT). Electronic applications accepted.

Clarke University, Program in Education, Dubuque, IA 52001-3198. Offers instructional leadership (MAE). *Program availability:* Part-time, 100% online, blended/hybrid learning. *Degree requirements:* For master's, thesis optional. *Entrance requirements:* For master's, official transcripts documenting completion of undergraduate degree from accredited college or university, copy of teaching certificates and licenses, two recommendation forms, statement of goals and career plans, minimum GPA of 2.75. Additional exam requirements/recommendations for international students: Required—TOEFL (minimum score 550 paper-based; 80 iBT), IELTS (minimum score 6.5). Electronic applications accepted. *Expenses:* Contact institution.

Clarkson University, Program in Education, Schenectady, NY 13699. Offers MAT. *Accreditation:* TEAC. *Faculty:* 5 full-time (all women), 7 part-time/adjunct (2 women). *Students:* 31 full-time (21 women), 22 part-time (19 women); includes 11 minority (2 Black or African American, non-Hispanic/Latino; 4 Asian, non-Hispanic/Latino; 4 Hispanic/Latino; 1 Two or more races, non-Hispanic/Latino), 10 international. 48 applicants, 88% accepted, 38 enrolled. In 2018, 23 master's awarded. *Degree requirements:* For master's, thesis (for some programs), thesis or project. *Entrance requirements:* For master's, GRE, minimum undergraduate GPA of 3.0. Additional exam requirements/recommendations for international students: Required—TOEFL (minimum score 550 paper-based, 80 iBT) or IELTS (6.5). *Application deadline:* Applications are processed on a rolling basis. Application fee: $50. Electronic applications accepted. *Expenses:* Contact institution. *Financial support:* Scholarships/grants available. *Unit head:* Dr. Catherine Snyder, Chair of Education, 518-631-9870, E-mail: csnyder@clarkson.edu. *Application contact:* Dan Capogna, Director of Graduate Admissions & Recruitment, 518-631-9910, E-mail: graduate@clarkson.edu.
Website: https://www.clarkson.edu/academics/graduate

Clark University, Graduate School, Adam Institute for Urban Teaching and School Practice, Worcester, MA 01610-1477. Offers MAT, PhD. *Degree requirements:* For master's, thesis or alternative, oral exam. *Entrance requirements:* For master's, GRE General Test, minimum GPA of 3.0, professional experience, 2 references, statement of purpose, resume. Additional exam requirements/recommendations for international students: Required—TOEFL (minimum score 575 paper-based; 90 iBT), IELTS (minimum score 6.5). Electronic applications accepted. *Expenses:* Contact institution. *Faculty research:* Developmental learning, instructional theory, educational program management, special education, urban education.

Clayton State University, School of Graduate Studies, College of Arts and Sciences, Program in Education, Morrow, GA 30260-0285. Offers biology (MAT); English (MAT); history (MAT); mathematics (MAT). *Accreditation:* NCATE. *Entrance requirements:* For master's, GRE, GACE, 2 official copies of transcripts, 3 recommendation letters, statement of purpose. Additional exam requirements/recommendations for international students: Required—TOEFL (minimum score 550 paper-based). Electronic applications accepted. *Expenses: Tuition, area resident:* Full-time $3528; part-time $2352 per year. Tuition, state resident: full-time $3528; part-time $2352 per year. Tuition, nonresident: full-time $13,176; part-time $8784 per year. *International tuition:* $13,176 full-time. *Required fees:* $1474; $1474 per unit. Tuition and fees vary according to campus/location and program.

Clemson University, Graduate School, College of Education, Clemson, SC 29634. Offers M Ed, MAT, MHRD, MS, Ed D, PhD, Certificate, Ed S. *Program availability:* Part-time, evening/weekend, 100% online. *Faculty:* 78 full-time (56 women). *Students:* 489 full-time (378 women), 509 part-time (394 women); includes 232 minority (143 Black or African American, non-Hispanic/Latino; 2 American Indian or Alaska Native, non-Hispanic/Latino; 8 Asian, non-Hispanic/Latino; 43 Hispanic/Latino; 36 Two or more races, non-Hispanic/Latino), 11 international. Average age 32. 1,357 applicants, 81% accepted, 870 enrolled. In 2018, 182 master's, 25 doctorates, 62 other advanced degrees awarded. *Degree requirements:* For master's, comprehensive exam (for some programs), thesis (for some programs); for doctorate, comprehensive exam, thesis/dissertation. *Entrance requirements:* For master's, doctorate, and other advanced degree, GRE General Test, unofficial transcripts, letters of recommendation. Additional exam requirements/recommendations for international students: Required—TOEFL (minimum score 80 paper-based; 80 iBT), IELTS (minimum score 6.5), PTE (minimum score 54). *Application deadline:* For fall admission, 4/15 for international students; for spring admission, 10/15 for international students. Applications are processed on a rolling basis. Application fee: $80 ($90 for international students). Electronic applications accepted. *Expenses:* $5198 per semester full-time resident, $10123 per semester full-time non-resident, $556 per credit hour part-time resident, $1109 per credit hour part-time non-resident, online $770 per credit hour, $4938 doctoral programs resident, $10405 doctoral programs non-resident, $1144 full-time graduate assistant, other fees may apply per session. *Financial support:* In 2018–19, 144 students received support, including 10 fellowships with full and partial tuition reimbursements available (averaging $4,620 per year), 6 research assistantships with full and partial tuition reimbursements available (averaging $12,500 per year), 31 teaching assistantships with full and partial tuition reimbursements available (averaging $17,241 per year); career-related internships or fieldwork and unspecified assistantships also available. *Faculty research:* Early literacy and motivation, STEAM education, legal/policy issues in education, leadership, special education interventions/assessment/policy. *Total annual research expenditures:* $2.7 million. *Unit head:* Dr. George J. Petersen, Founding Dean, 864-656-4444, E-mail: soedean@clemson.edu. *Application contact:* Dr. Jeff Marshall, Interim Associate Dean, Academic Affairs & Research, 864-656-2059, E-mail: marsha9@clemson.edu.
Website: http://www.clemson.edu/education/

Cleveland State University, College of Graduate Studies, College of Education and Human Services, Cleveland, OH 44115. Offers M Ed, MPH, PhD, Certificate, Ed S. *Accreditation:* NCATE. *Program availability:* Part-time, evening/weekend, 100% online, blended/hybrid learning. *Faculty:* 86 full-time (60 women), 106 part-time/adjunct (81 women). *Students:* 261 full-time (205 women), 773 part-time (593 women); includes 323 minority (233 Black or African American, non-Hispanic/Latino; 3 American Indian or Alaska Native, non-Hispanic/Latino; 11 Asian, non-Hispanic/Latino; 41 Hispanic/Latino; 1 Native Hawaiian or other Pacific Islander, non-Hispanic/Latino; 34 Two or more races, non-Hispanic/Latino), 33 international. Average age 34. 487 applicants, 58% accepted, 178 enrolled. In 2018, 266 master's, 12 doctorates, 1 other advanced degree awarded. *Degree requirements:* For master's, comprehensive exam (for some programs), thesis optional; for doctorate, one foreign language, comprehensive exam, thesis/dissertation; for other advanced degree, comprehensive exam (for some programs), thesis optional, internship. *Entrance requirements:* For master's, GRE General Test or MAT, minimum undergraduate GPA of 2.75, 3.0 if undergraduate degree is 6 or more years old; for doctorate, GRE General Test, master's degree, minimum graduate GPA of 3.25; for other advanced degree, GRE General Test or MAT, master's degree, minimum graduate GPA of 3.0. Additional exam requirements/recommendations for international students: Required—TOEFL (minimum score 550 paper-based; 78 iBT). *Application deadline:* For fall admission, 7/1 priority date for domestic students, 5/15 for international students; for spring admission, 11/15 priority date for domestic students, 11/1 for international students; for summer admission, 4/1 for domestic students, 3/15 for international students. Applications are processed on a rolling basis. Application fee: $30. Electronic applications accepted. *Expenses:* Tuition, state resident: full-time $7232.55; part-time $6676 per credit hour. Tuition, nonresident: full-time $12,375. *International tuition:* $18,914 full-time. *Required fees:* $80; $80 $40. Tuition and fees vary according to program. *Financial support:* In 2018–19, 64 students received support, including 38 research assistantships with full tuition reimbursements available (averaging $6,960 per year), 2 teaching assistantships with full tuition reimbursements available (averaging $7,800 per year); career-related internships or fieldwork, Federal Work-Study, scholarships/grants, tuition waivers (partial), and unspecified assistantships also available. Support available to part-time students. Financial award application deadline: 8/1; financial award applicants required to submit FAFSA. *Faculty research:* Adult learning and development, counseling theory and practice, equity issues in education (race, ethnicity, gender, socioeconomics), health care and health education, population nursing, urban educational leadership, curriculum and instruction. *Total annual research expenditures:* $7.5 million. *Unit head:* Dr. Sajit Zachariah, Dean, 216-523-7143, Fax: 216-687-5415, E-mail: sajit.zachariah@csuohio.edu. *Application contact:* Patricia Sokolowski, Office Coordinator/Assistant to the Dean, 216-523-7143, Fax: 216-687-5415, E-mail: p.sokolowski@csuohio.edu.
Website: http://www.csuohio.edu/cehs/

Coastal Carolina University, Spadoni College of Education, Conway, SC 29528-6054. Offers education (MAT); educational leadership (M Ed, Ed S); English for speakers of other languages (Certificate); instructional technology (M Ed, Ed S); language, literacy and culture (M Ed); learning and teaching (M Ed); online teaching and training (Certificate); special education (M Ed). *Accreditation:* NCATE. *Program availability:* Part-time, evening/weekend, 100% online, blended/hybrid learning. *Degree requirements:* For master's and other advanced degree, comprehensive exam. *Entrance requirements:* For master's, GRE, GMAT, 2 letters of recommendation, evidence of teacher certification, official transcripts; for other advanced degree, official transcripts, 3 letters of reference, master's degree in related field with minimum overall cumulative GPA of 3.0. Additional exam requirements/recommendations for international students: Required—TOEFL (minimum score 550 paper-based; 79 iBT), IELTS (minimum score 6.5). Electronic applications accepted.

The College at Brockport, State University of New York, School of Education, Health, and Human Services, Department of Education and Human Development, Brockport, NY 14420-2997. Offers adolescence education (MS Ed), including adolescence biology education, adolescence chemistry education, adolescence English, adolescence mathematics, adolescence physics, adolescence physics education, adolescence social studies education; bilingual education (MS Ed, AGC); childhood curriculum specialist (MS Ed); inclusive generalist education (MS Ed, AGC, Advanced Certificate), including biology (MS Ed, AGC), chemistry (MS Ed), English (MS Ed, Advanced Certificate), mathematics (MS Ed, Advanced Certificate), science (MS Ed, Advanced Certificate), social studies (MS Ed, Advanced Certificate); literacy education B-12 (MS Ed). *Accreditation:* NCATE. *Faculty:* 12 full-time (7 women), 10 part-time/adjunct (6 women). *Students:* 60 full-time (39 women), 227 part-time (157 women); includes 9 minority (1 Asian, non-Hispanic/Latino; 8 Hispanic/Latino). 135 applicants, 71% accepted, 59 enrolled. In 2018, 107 master's, 13 AGCs awarded. *Degree requirements:* For master's, thesis or alternative. *Entrance requirements:* For master's, minimum GPA of 3.0, letters of recommendation, interview (for some programs); statement of objectives, current resume. Additional exam requirements/recommendations for international students: Required—TOEFL (minimum score 550 paper-based; 79 iBT), IELTS (minimum score 6.5). *Application deadline:* For fall admission, 3/15 priority date for domestic and international students; for spring admission, 10/15 priority date for domestic and international students; for summer admission, 3/15 priority date for domestic and international students. Application fee: $80. Electronic applications accepted. *Expenses:* Tuition, state resident: part-time $471 per credit. Tuition, nonresident: part-time $963 per credit. *Financial support:* In 2018–19, 1 fellowship with full tuition reimbursement (averaging $7,500 per year), 1 teaching assistantship with full tuition reimbursement (averaging $6,000 per year) were awarded; Federal Work-Study, scholarships/grants, and unspecified assistantships also available. Support available to part-time students. Financial award application deadline: 3/15; financial award applicants required to submit FAFSA. *Faculty research:* Educational assessment, literacy education, inclusive education, teacher preparation, qualitative methodology. *Unit head:* Dr. Janka Szilagyi, Chairperson, 585-395-5945, Fax: 585-395-2172, E-mail: jszilagy@brockport.edu. *Application contact:* Buffie Edick, Graduate Program Director, 585-395-2326, Fax: 585-395-2172, E-mail: bedick@brockport.edu.
Website: https://www.brockport.edu/academics/education_human_development/department.html

College of Charleston, Graduate School, School of Education, Health, and Human Performance, Charleston, SC 29424-0001. Offers M Ed, MAT, Certificate. *Accreditation:* NCATE. *Program availability:* Part-time, evening/weekend. *Degree requirements:* For master's, thesis or alternative, written qualifying exam, student teaching experience (MAT). *Entrance requirements:* For master's, teaching certificate (M Ed). Additional exam requirements/recommendations for international students: Required—TOEFL (minimum score 81 iBT). Electronic applications accepted. *Faculty research:* Computer-assisted instruction, higher education, faculty development, teaching study skills to college students.

The College of Idaho, Department of Education, Caldwell, ID 83605. Offers curriculum and instruction (M Ed); teaching (MAT). *Degree requirements:* For master's, thesis. *Entrance requirements:* For master's, GRE, portfolio, minimum undergraduate GPA of 3.0, interview. *Faculty research:* Discourse analysis, at-risk youth, children's literature, research design, program evaluation.

College of Mount Saint Vincent, School of Professional and Graduate Studies, Department of Teacher Education, Riverdale, NY 10471-1093. Offers instructional technology and global perspectives (Certificate); middle level education (Certificate); multicultural studies (Certificate); teaching English to speakers of other languages (MS Ed); urban and multicultural education (MS Ed). *Accreditation:* TEAC. *Program*

availability: Part-time. *Degree requirements:* For master's, comprehensive exam. *Entrance requirements:* For master's, interview, New York teaching certificate. Additional exam requirements/recommendations for international students: Required—TOEFL.

The College of New Jersey, Office of Graduate and Advancing Education, School of Education, Ewing, NJ 08628. Offers M Ed, MA, MAT, Certificate, Ed S. *Accreditation:* NCATE. *Program availability:* Part-time, evening/weekend. *Students:* 149 full-time (136 women), 208 part-time (167 women); includes 69 minority (17 Black or African American, non-Hispanic/Latino; 3 American Indian or Alaska Native, non-Hispanic/Latino; 14 Asian, non-Hispanic/Latino; 31 Hispanic/Latino; 4 Native Hawaiian or other Pacific Islander, non-Hispanic/Latino), 2 international. 297 applicants, 84% accepted, 202 enrolled. In 2018, 282 master's, 47 other advanced degrees awarded. *Degree requirements:* For master's, comprehensive exam. *Entrance requirements:* For master's, GRE, minimum GPA of 3.0 in field or 2.75 overall; for other advanced degree, previous master's degree or higher. Additional exam requirements/recommendations for international students: Required—TOEFL. *Application deadline:* For fall admission, 2/1 priority date for domestic students; for spring admission, 10/1 priority date for domestic students. Application fee: $75. Electronic applications accepted. *Financial support:* Tuition waivers (partial) and unspecified assistantships available. Financial award application deadline: 5/1; financial award applicants required to submit FAFSA. *Unit head:* Dr. Jeff Passe, Dean, 609-771-3177, Fax: 609-637-5117, E-mail: passej@tcnj.edu. *Application contact:* Susan L. Hydro, Director of Graduate and Intersession Programs, 609-771-2300, Fax: 609-637-5105, E-mail: graduate@tcnj.edu.
Website: https://education.tcnj.edu/

The College of New Rochelle, Graduate School, Division of Education, New Rochelle, NY 10805-2308. Offers art education (MS); childhood education/early childhood education (MS Ed), including childhood education, early childhood education; educational leadership (MS, Advanced Certificate, Advanced Diploma), including school building leader (MS, Advanced Certificate), school district leader (MS, Advanced Diploma); gifted education (Certificate); literacy education (MS Ed); multilingual/multicultural education (MS Ed, Certificate), including bilingual education (Certificate), multilingual/multicultural education (Certificate), teaching English to speakers of other languages; special education (MS Ed). *Program availability:* Part-time, evening/weekend. *Degree requirements:* For master's, comprehensive exam (for some programs), thesis (for some programs). *Entrance requirements:* For master's, interview; minimum GPA of 3.0 in field, 2.7 overall. Electronic applications accepted.

College of Saint Elizabeth, Program in Education, Morristown, NJ 07960-6989. Offers assistive technology (Certificate); education (MA); ESL (Certificate); Holocaust/genocide education (Certificate); middle school science (Certificate); online teaching in the 21st century (Certificate); teaching (Certificate), including K-12, K-6, teacher of students with disabilities. *Program availability:* Part-time. *Degree requirements:* For master's and Certificate, thesis. *Entrance requirements:* For master's, certification. Additional exam requirements/recommendations for international students: Required—TOEFL (minimum score 550 paper-based; 79 iBT), IELTS (minimum score 6.5). Electronic applications accepted. Application fee is waived when completed online.

College of St. Joseph, Graduate Programs, Division of Education, Rutland, VT 05701-3899. Offers elementary education (M Ed); general education (M Ed); reading (M Ed); secondary education (M Ed), including English, social studies; special education (M Ed). *Program availability:* Part-time, evening/weekend. *Degree requirements:* For master's, comprehensive exam. *Entrance requirements:* For master's, PRAXIS I, essay; two letters of reference from academic or professional sources; official transcripts of all graduate and undergraduate study. Additional exam requirements/recommendations for international students: Required—TOEFL (minimum score 550 paper-based). Electronic applications accepted. *Faculty research:* Co-teaching, Response to Intervention (RTI).

College of Saint Mary, Program in Teaching, Omaha, NE 68106. Offers MAT. *Program availability:* Evening/weekend. *Entrance requirements:* For master's, Pre-Professional Skills Tests (PPST), minimum cumulative GPA of 2.5, background check.

The College of Saint Rose, Graduate Studies, Thelma P. Lally School of Education, Albany, NY 12203-1419. Offers MS, MS Ed, Advanced Certificate, Certificate. *Accreditation:* NCATE. *Program availability:* Part-time, evening/weekend, 100% online. *Faculty:* 32 full-time (21 women), 72 part-time/adjunct (39 women). *Students:* 315 full-time (277 women), 975 part-time (773 women); includes 407 minority (164 Black or African American, non-Hispanic/Latino; 1 American Indian or Alaska Native, non-Hispanic/Latino; 31 Asian, non-Hispanic/Latino; 118 Hispanic/Latino; 93 Two or more races, non-Hispanic/Latino), 6 international. Average age 33. 834 applicants, 66% accepted, 390 enrolled. In 2018, 285 master's, 754 other advanced degrees awarded. *Degree requirements:* For master's, comprehensive exam (for some programs), thesis (for some programs), capstone project. *Entrance requirements:* For master's, GRE or MAT, application, statement of purpose, college transcript(s), resume, 2 letters of recommendation, interview required for some programs; for other advanced degree, application, statement of purpose, college transcript(s), resume, 2 letters of recommendation. Additional exam requirements/recommendations for international students: Required—TOEFL (minimum score 550 paper-based; 80 iBT), IELTS (minimum score 6), PTE (minimum score 56). *Application deadline:* For fall admission, 4/1 priority date for domestic and international students; for spring admission, 10/15 priority date for domestic and international students; for summer admission, 3/15 priority date for domestic and international students. Applications are processed on a rolling basis. Application fee: $40. Electronic applications accepted. *Expenses: Tuition:* Full-time $14,382; part-time $799 per credit hour. *Required fees:* $924; $408 per credit. $286. *Financial support:* Career-related internships or fieldwork, scholarships/grants, tuition waivers (partial), and unspecified assistantships available. Support available to part-time students. Financial award application deadline: 4/15. *Unit head:* Dr. Theresa Ward, Interim Dean, 518-454-5125. *Application contact:* Daniel Gallagher, Assistant Vice President for Graduate Recruitment and Enrollment, 518-454-5136, Fax: 518-458-5479, E-mail: grad@strose.edu.
Website: https://www.strose.edu/academics/schools/school-of-education/

The College of St. Scholastica, Graduate Studies, Department of Education, Duluth, MN 55811-4199. Offers M Ed, MS, Certificate. *Accreditation:* TEAC. *Program availability:* Part-time, evening/weekend, online learning. *Entrance requirements:* Additional exam requirements/recommendations for international students: Required—TOEFL (minimum score 550 paper-based; 79 iBT). Electronic applications accepted.

College of Staten Island of the City University of New York, Graduate Programs, School of Education, Staten Island, NY 10314-6600. Offers MS Ed, Advanced Certificate, Post-Master's Certificate. *Accreditation:* NCATE. *Expenses: Tuition, area resident:* Full-time $10,770; part-time $455 per credit. Tuition, state resident: full-time $10,770; part-time $455 per credit. Tuition, nonresident: full-time $19,920; part-time $830 per credit. *International tuition:* $19,920 full-time. *Required fees:* $559.20; $181.10 per semester. Tuition and fees vary according to program. *Unit head:* Dr. Kenneth Gold, Dean of School of Education, 718-982-3737, Fax: 718-982-3743, E-mail: kenneth.gold@csi.cuny.edu. *Application contact:* Sasha Spence, Associate Director for Graduate Admissions, 718-982-2019, Fax: 718-982-2500, E-mail: sasha.spence@csi.cuny.edu.
Website: https://www.csi.cuny.edu/academics-and-research/divisions-schools/school-education

The College of William and Mary, School of Education, Williamsburg, VA 23187-8795. Offers M Ed, MA Ed, Ed D, PhD, Ed S. *Accreditation:* NCATE. *Program availability:* Part-time, evening/weekend, Coursework is online with required residencies. *Faculty:* 47 full-time (25 women), 81 part-time/adjunct (41 women). *Students:* 209 full-time (157 women), 269 part-time (193 women); includes 114 minority (50 Black or African American, non-Hispanic/Latino; 1 American Indian or Alaska Native, non-Hispanic/Latino; 9 Asian, non-Hispanic/Latino; 40 Hispanic/Latino; 14 Two or more races, non-Hispanic/Latino), 16 international. Average age 35. 520 applicants, 64% accepted, 220 enrolled. In 2018, 165 master's, 40 doctorates, 10 other advanced degrees awarded. *Degree requirements:* For master's, project; for doctorate, comprehensive exam, thesis/dissertation; for Ed S, internship. *Entrance requirements:* For master's, GRE, MAT, PRAXIS Core Academic Skills for Educators, minimum GPA of 2.5; for doctorate, GRE or MAT, minimum GPA of 3.5; for Ed S, GRE, minimum GPA of 3.0. Additional exam requirements/recommendations for international students: Required—TOEFL (minimum score 100 iBT), IELTS (minimum score 7). *Application deadline:* For fall admission, 1/15 for domestic and international students; for spring admission, 10/1 for domestic and international students. Application fee: $50. Electronic applications accepted. *Expenses:* 26350 per year full-time in-state tuition and fees; 33354 per year full-time out-of-state tuition and fees; 560 per credit hour part-time in-state tuition plus 115 required student fee; 960 per credit hour part-time out-of-state tuition plus 115 required student fee. *Financial support:* In 2018–19, 132 students received support, including 1 fellowship with full tuition reimbursement available (averaging $20,000 per year), 92 research assistantships with full tuition reimbursements available (averaging $17,382 per year); scholarships/grants and unspecified assistantships also available. Financial award application deadline: 1/15; financial award applicants required to submit FAFSA. *Faculty research:* Gifted education, curriculum and instruction, technology and education, leadership, classroom assessment. *Total annual research expenditures:* $6.7 million. *Unit head:* Dr. Spencer G. Niles, Dean, 757-221-2317, E-mail: sgniles@wm.edu. *Application contact:* Dorothy Smith Osborne, Assistant Dean for Academic Programs and Student Services, 757-221-2317, E-mail: dsosbo@wm.edu.
Website: http://education.wm.edu

See Display on the next page and Close-Up on page 599.

Colorado Christian University, Program in Curriculum and Instruction, Lakewood, CO 80226. Offers corporate education (MACI); early childhood educator (MACI); elementary educator (MACI); instructional technology (MACI); master educator (MACI); online course developer (MACI); online teaching and learning (MACI); special education generalist (MACI). *Program availability:* Part-time, evening/weekend. *Degree requirements:* For master's, thesis optional, practicum. *Entrance requirements:* For master's, interviews, letters of recommendation. Additional exam requirements/recommendations for international students: Required—TOEFL. Electronic applications accepted. *Expenses:* Contact institution.

The Colorado College, Education Department, Colorado Springs, CO 80903-3294. Offers elementary education (MAT), including elementary school teaching; secondary education (MAT), including art teaching (K-12), English teaching, foreign language teaching, mathematics teaching, music teaching, science teaching, social studies teaching; teaching (MAT), including arts and humanities, integrated natural sciences, liberal arts, Southwest studies. *Degree requirements:* For master's, thesis, internship. Electronic applications accepted. *Faculty research:* Geology, environmental resources, urban education, educational psychology, arts integration in the classroom, literacy/early childhood.

Colorado Mesa University, Center for Teacher Education, Grand Junction, CO 81501-3122. Offers educational leadership (MAEd); English for speakers of other languages (MAEd); exceptional learner/special education (MAEd); teacher education (Graduate Certificate); teacher leader (MAEd). *Accreditation:* NCATE. *Program availability:* Part-time. *Degree requirements:* For master's, comprehensive exam (for some programs), capstone presentation. *Entrance requirements:* For master's, 3 professional letters of recommendation, Colorado teaching license, minimum baccalaureate GPA of 3.0; for Graduate Certificate, minimum baccalaureate GPA of 3.0. Additional exam requirements/recommendations for international students: Required—TOEFL (minimum score 550 paper-based). Electronic applications accepted. *Expenses:* Contact institution. *Faculty research:* K-8 STEM instruction, special education inclusion, elementary math literacy, secondary literacy, elementary/early childhood education literacy.

Colorado State University, College of Health and Human Sciences, School of Education, Fort Collins, CO 80523-1588. Offers adult education and training (M Ed); counseling and career development (MA); education and human resources (M Ed); education, equity, and transformation (PhD); higher education leadership (PhD); organizational learning, performance, and change (M Ed, PhD); student affairs in higher education (MS). *Accreditation:* ACA; TEAC. *Program availability:* Part-time, online only, 100% online, blended/hybrid learning. *Degree requirements:* For master's, thesis optional, professional portfolio or capstone project; for doctorate, comprehensive exam, thesis/dissertation. *Entrance requirements:* For master's, bachelor's degree; minimum GPA of 3.0 in last degree earned; for doctorate, GRE; GRE or GMAT (for organizational learning, performance and change only), master's degree; minimum GPA of 3.0 in last degree earned. Additional exam requirements/recommendations for international students: Required—TOEFL (minimum score 550 paper-based; 80 iBT), IELTS (minimum score 6.5), PTE (minimum score 58). Electronic applications accepted. *Expenses:* Contact institution. *Faculty research:* Diversity, equity, and inclusion; STEM education; higher education; occupational learning, performance, and change; teacher education.

Colorado State University–Global Campus, Graduate Programs, Greenwood Village, CO 80111. Offers criminal justice and law enforcement administration (MS); education leadership (MS); finance (MS); healthcare administration and management (MS); human resource management (MHRM); information technology management (MITM); international management (MS); management (MS); organizational leadership (MS); professional accounting (MPA); project management (MS); teaching and learning (MS). *Accreditation:* ACBSP. *Program availability:* Online learning.

Colorado State University–Pueblo, College of Education, Engineering and Professional Studies, Education Program, Pueblo, CO 81001-4901. Offers art education (M Ed); foreign language education (M Ed); health and physical education (M Ed); instructional technology (M Ed); linguistically diverse education (M Ed); music education (M Ed); special education (M Ed). *Accreditation:* TEAC. *Program availability:* Part-time. *Degree requirements:* For master's, portfolio. *Entrance requirements:* For master's, 3 recommendations, teaching license. Additional exam requirements/recommendations for international students: Required—TOEFL (minimum score 500 paper-based). Electronic applications accepted. *Faculty research:* Portfolio assessment, math education, science education.

Columbia College, Graduate Programs, Education Division, Columbia, SC 29203-5998. Offers divergent learning (M Ed); higher education administration (M Ed). *Accreditation:* NCATE. *Program availability:* Part-time, evening/weekend, online learning. *Degree*

requirements: For master's, thesis. *Entrance requirements:* For master's, GRE General Test, MAT, 2 recommendations, current South Carolina teaching certificate, minimum GPA of 3.2. Electronic applications accepted. *Expenses:* Contact institution.

Columbia College, Master of Arts in Teaching Program, Columbia, MO 65216-0002. Offers MAT. *Program availability:* Part-time, evening/weekend, 100% online, blended/hybrid learning. *Faculty:* 5 full-time (3 women), 18 part-time/adjunct (12 women). *Students:* 5 full-time (4 women), 96 part-time (76 women); includes 21 minority (12 Black or African American, non-Hispanic/Latino; 1 Asian, non-Hispanic/Latino; 2 Hispanic/Latino; 6 Two or more races, non-Hispanic/Latino), 3 international. Average age 35. 107 applicants, 82% accepted, 45 enrolled. In 2018, 45 master's awarded. *Entrance requirements:* For master's, 3 letters of recommendation, minimum cumulative undergraduate GPA of 3.0, resume, goal statement. Additional exam requirements/recommendations for international students: Required—TOEFL (minimum score 550 paper-based; 79 iBT). *Application deadline:* For fall admission, 8/9 priority date for domestic and international students; for spring admission, 12/27 priority date for domestic and international students. Applications are processed on a rolling basis. Application fee: $0. Electronic applications accepted. *Expenses: Tuition:* Full-time $13,230; part-time $490 per credit hour. Tuition and fees vary according to reciprocity agreements. *Financial support:* In 2018–19, 34 students received support. Scholarships/grants, tuition waivers (full and partial), and unspecified assistantships available. Financial award application deadline: 3/15; financial award applicants required to submit FAFSA. *Unit head:* Dr. Lisa Ford-Brown, Dean of School of Humanities, Arts and Social Sciences, 573-875-7570, E-mail: labrown@ccis.edu. *Application contact:* Stephanie Johnson, Associate Vice President of Recruitment & Admissions Division, 573-875-7352, Fax: 573-875-7506, E-mail: sjohnson@ccis.edu.
Website: http://www.ccis.edu/graduate/academics/degrees.asp?MAT

Columbia International University, Columbia Graduate School, Columbia, SC 29203. Offers Bible teaching (MABT); counseling (MACN); early childhood and elementary education (MAT); educational administration (M Ed); educational leadership (PhD); instruction and learning (M Ed); teaching English as a foreign language (Certificate); teaching English as a foreign language and intercultural studies (MATF). *Program availability:* Part-time, evening/weekend, online learning. *Degree requirements:* For master's, internships, professional project. *Entrance requirements:* For master's, MAT; GRE (for some programs), minimum GPA of 2.7. Additional exam requirements/recommendations for international students: Required—TOEFL. Electronic applications accepted.

Columbus State University, Graduate Studies, College of Education and Health Professions, Columbus, GA 31907-5645. Offers M Ed, MAT, MS, MSN, Ed D, Ed S. *Accreditation:* ACA (one or more programs are accredited); NCATE. *Program availability:* Part-time, evening/weekend, 100% online, blended/hybrid learning. *Faculty:* 46 full-time (27 women), 42 part-time/adjunct (28 women). *Students:* 193 full-time (141 women), 366 part-time (281 women); includes 263 minority (228 Black or African American, non-Hispanic/Latino; 6 Asian, non-Hispanic/Latino; 17 Hispanic/Latino; 12 Two or more races, non-Hispanic/Latino), 1 international. Average age 36. 338 applicants, 53% accepted, 128 enrolled. In 2018, 168 master's, 25 doctorates, 140 other advanced degrees awarded. *Degree requirements:* For master's, thesis, exit exam; for doctorate, thesis/dissertation; for Ed S, thesis or alternative. *Entrance requirements:* For master's, GRE General Test, minimum undergraduate GPA of 2.75; for doctorate, GRE General Test, minimum graduate GPA of 3.5, four years of professional service; for Ed S, GRE General Test, minimum undergraduate GPA of 2.75, graduate 3.0. Additional exam requirements/recommendations for international students: Required—TOEFL (minimum score 550 paper-based; 79 iBT). *Application deadline:* For fall admission, 6/30 for domestic students, 5/1 for international students; for spring admission, 11/1 for domestic and international students; for summer admission, 3/1 for domestic and international students. Applications are processed on a rolling basis. Application fee: $50. Electronic applications accepted. *Expenses: Tuition, area resident:* Full-time $4924; part-time $618 per credit hour. Tuition, state resident: full-time $4924; part-time $618 per credit hour. Tuition, nonresident: full-time $19,218; part-time $2403 per credit hour. *International tuition:* $19,218 full-time. *Required fees:* $1870; $802. Tuition and fees vary according to course load, degree level and program. *Financial support:* In 2018–19, 63 students received support, including 20 research assistantships with partial tuition reimbursements available (averaging $3,000 per year); career-related internships or fieldwork, Federal Work-Study, institutionally sponsored loans, scholarships/grants, tuition waivers (partial), and unspecified assistantships also available. Support available to part-time students. Financial award application deadline: 5/1; financial award applicants required to submit FAFSA. *Unit head:* Dr. Deirdre Greer, Dean, 706-507-8505, Fax: 706-569-3134, E-mail: greer_deirdre@columbusstate.edu. *Application contact:* Catrina Smith-Edmond, Assistant Director for Graduate and Global Admission, 706-507-8824, Fax: 706-568-5091, E-mail: smithedmond_catrina@columbusstate.edu.
Website: http://coehp.columbusstate.edu/

Concordia College, Program in Education, Moorhead, MN 56562. Offers world language instruction (M Ed). *Degree requirements:* For master's, thesis/seminar. *Entrance requirements:* For master's, 2 professional references, 1 personal reference.

Concordia University, College of Education, Portland, OR 97211-6099. Offers administrative leadership (Ed D); career and technical education (M Ed); curriculum and instruction (M Ed), including adolescent literacy, early childhood education, educational technology leadership, English for speakers of other languages, environmental education, health and physical education, mathematics, methods and curriculum, reading interventionist, science, social studies, STEAM education, teacher leadership, the inclusive classroom, trauma and resilience in educational settings; educational administration (M Ed); educational leadership (M Ed); elementary education (MAT); higher education (Ed D); instructional leadership (Ed D); professional leadership, inquiry, and transformation (Ed D); secondary education (MAT); transformational leadership (Ed D). *Program availability:* Part-time, online learning. *Degree requirements:* For master's, comprehensive exam, work samples/portfolio. *Entrance requirements:* For master's, California Basic Educational Skills Test or PRAXIS I, minimum undergraduate GPA of 2.8, graduate 3.0; 2 letters of recommendation. Additional exam requirements/recommendations for international students: Required—TOEFL (minimum score 525 paper-based). Electronic applications accepted. *Faculty research:* Learner-centered classroom, brain-based learning, future of online learning.

Concordia University, School of Graduate Studies, Faculty of Arts and Science, Department of Education, Montréal, QC H3G 1M8, Canada. Offers adult education (Certificate, Diploma); applied linguistics (MA, Certificate), including applied linguistics (MA), teaching English as a second language (Certificate); child studies (MA); educational studies (MA); educational technology (MA); instructional technology (Diploma). *Degree requirements:* For master's, one foreign language, thesis optional.

Concordia University Chicago, College of Graduate Studies, Program in Teaching, River Forest, IL 60305-1499. Offers elementary education (MAT); secondary education (MAT). *Degree requirements:* For master's, thesis or alternative. *Entrance requirements:* For master's, minimum GPA of 2.9. Additional exam requirements/recommendations for international students: Required—TOEFL (minimum score 550 paper-based). Electronic applications accepted.

Concordia University Irvine, School of Education, Irvine, CA 92612-3299. Offers curriculum and instruction (MA); education and preliminary teaching credential (M Ed); educational administration and preliminary administrative services credential (MA); educational technology (MA); school counseling with pupil personnel services credential (MA). *Program availability:* Part-time, evening/weekend, online learning. *Degree requirements:* For master's, action research project. *Entrance requirements:* For master's, California Basic Educational Skills Test, California Subject Examinations for Teachers (M Ed and MA in educational administration and preliminary administrative services credential), official college transcript(s), signed statement of intent, two references, copy of credential. Additional exam requirements/recommendations for international students: Required—TOEFL. Electronic applications accepted. *Expenses:* Contact institution.

Concordia University, Nebraska, Graduate Programs in Education, Seward, NE 68434. Offers M Ed, MPE, MS. *Accreditation:* NCATE. *Program availability:* Part-time, evening/weekend. *Degree requirements:* For master's, comprehensive exam, thesis or alternative. *Entrance requirements:* For master's, GRE, MAT, or NTE, minimum GPA of 3.0, BS in education or equivalent. Additional exam requirements/recommendations for international students: Required—TOEFL. Electronic applications accepted.

Concordia University, St. Paul, College of Education, St. Paul, MN 55104-5494. Offers classroom instruction (MA Ed), including K-12 reading; differentiated instruction (MA Ed); early childhood education (MA Ed); education (Ed D); educational leadership (MA Ed); educational technology (MA Ed, Certificate); K-12 principal licensure (Ed S); special education (MA Ed), including autism spectrum disorder, emotional and behavioral disorders, learning disabilities; superintendent (Ed S); teaching (MAT). *Accreditation:* NCATE. *Program availability:* Part-time, evening/weekend, 100% online, blended/hybrid learning. *Faculty:* 13 full-time (9 women), 82 part-time/adjunct (51 women). *Students:* 979 full-time (748 women), 40 part-time (28 women); includes 124 minority (49 Black or African American, non-Hispanic/Latino; 6 American Indian or Alaska Native, non-Hispanic/Latino; 34 Asian, non-Hispanic/Latino; 22 Hispanic/Latino; 1 Native Hawaiian or other Pacific Islander, non-Hispanic/Latino; 12 Two or more races, non-Hispanic/Latino), 11 international. Average age 34. 423 applicants, 99% accepted, 335 enrolled. In 2018, 358 master's, 3 doctorates, 119 other advanced degrees awarded. *Degree requirements:* For master's, thesis (for some programs); for doctorate, thesis/dissertation, capstone projects; for other advanced degree, e-folio review of competencies. *Entrance requirements:* For master's, official transcripts from regionally-accredited institution stating the conferral of a bachelor's degree with minimum cumulative GPA of 3.0; personal statement; professional resume; practitioner in field through work or volunteerism; resume; for doctorate, minimum master's or specialist degree GPA of 3.25; transcript; writing sample; three letters of recommendation; current resume; on-campus interview; for other advanced degree, minimum master's or specialist degree GPA of 3.25; transcript; statement covering employment history and long-term academic and professional goals; two letters of recommendation; interview with program director. Additional exam requirements/recommendations for international students: Recommended—TOEFL (minimum score 547 paper-based; 78 iBT), IELTS (minimum score 6). *Application deadline:* For fall admission, 8/1 for domestic and international students; for spring admission, 12/1 for domestic and international students; for summer admission, 5/1 for domestic and international students. Applications are processed on a rolling basis. Application fee: $0. Electronic applications accepted. *Expenses:* $395 per credit for 30 credits (for MA programs), $440 per credit for 42 credits (for MAT), $415 per credit for 30 credits (for EdS), $615 per credit for 64 credits (for EdD). *Financial support:* In 2018–19, 163 students received support. Federal Work-Study, scholarships/grants, and unspecified assistantships available. Financial award applicants required to submit FAFSA. *Faculty research:* School design for innovative learning practices, equine-assisted instruction, best practices for leadership in early childhood education, mental health needs in K-12 focusing on children of incarcerated parents, competency-based education. *Unit head:* Lonn Maly, Dean, 651-641-8203, E-mail: maly@csp.edu. *Application contact:* Amber Faletti, Director of Enrollment Management, 651-641-8838, Fax: 651-603-6320, E-mail: faletti@csp.edu.

Concordia University Texas, College of Education, Austin, TX 78726. Offers M Ed. *Program availability:* Part-time, evening/weekend. *Degree requirements:* For master's, thesis (for some programs), portfolio presentation.

Concordia University Wisconsin, Graduate Programs, School of Education, Mequon, WI 53097-2402. Offers art education (MS Ed); early childhood (MS Ed); educational administration (MS Ed); environmental education (MS Ed); family studies (MS Ed); literacy (MS Ed); school counseling (MS Ed); special education (MS Ed). *Program availability:* Part-time, evening/weekend, online learning. *Degree requirements:* For master's, comprehensive exam, thesis or alternative. *Entrance requirements:* For master's, minimum GPA of 3.0, teaching license. Additional exam requirements/recommendations for international students: Required—TOEFL. *Faculty research:* Motivation, developmental learning, learning styles.

Concord University, Graduate Studies, Athens, WV 24712-1000. Offers educational leadership and supervision (M Ed); health promotion (MA); reading specialist (M Ed); social work (MSW); special education (M Ed); teaching (MAT). *Program availability:* Part-time, evening/weekend, 100% online. *Degree requirements:* For master's, thesis (for some programs). *Entrance requirements:* For master's, GRE or MAT, baccalaureate degree with minimum GPA of 2.5 from regionally-accredited institution; teaching license; 2 letters of recommendation; completed disposition assessment form. Electronic applications accepted.

Coppin State University, School of Graduate Studies, School of Education, Department of Teaching and Learning, Program in Teaching, Baltimore, MD 21216-3698. Offers MAT. *Program availability:* Part-time, evening/weekend, online learning. *Degree requirements:* For master's, thesis, exit portfolio. *Entrance requirements:* For master's, GRE, resume, references.

Corban University, Graduate School, Education Program, Salem, OR 97301-9392. Offers MS Ed.

Cornell University, Graduate School, Graduate Fields of Agriculture and Life Sciences, Field of Education, Ithaca, NY 14853. Offers adult and extension education (MPS, MS, PhD); learning, teaching, and social policy (MPS, MS, PhD); mathematics 7-12 (MS). Terminal master's awarded for partial completion of doctoral program. *Degree requirements:* For master's, thesis (MS); for doctorate, comprehensive exam, thesis/dissertation. *Entrance requirements:* For master's and doctorate, GRE General Test, sample of written work (recommended), 2 letters of recommendation. Additional exam requirements/recommendations for international students: Required—TOEFL (minimum score 550 paper-based; 77 iBT). Electronic applications accepted. *Faculty research:* Moral development and professional ethics, public issues education and community development, socio/political issues in public education, teacher education and curriculum in agricultural science and mathematics, extension research.

Cornerstone University, Graduate Programs, Grand Rapids, MI 49525-5897. Offers business administration (MBA); education (MA Ed); management (MSM); teaching English to speakers of other languages (MA, Graduate Certificate). Programs also offered at Holland, Kalamazoo, and Troy, MI campuses. *Program availability:* Part-time,

online learning. *Degree requirements:* For master's, comprehensive exam (for some programs), thesis (for some programs). *Entrance requirements:* For master's, minimum GPA of 2.5, 2 letters of reference. Additional exam requirements/recommendations for international students: Required—TOEFL (minimum score 575 paper-based). Electronic applications accepted.

Covenant College, Program in Education, Lookout Mountain, GA 30750. Offers M Ed, MAT. *Program availability:* Part-time. *Degree requirements:* For master's, comprehensive exam, special project. *Entrance requirements:* For master's, GRE General Test, 2 professional recommendations, minimum GPA of 3.0, writing sample.

Crandall University, Graduate Programs, Moncton, NB E1C 9L7, Canada. Offers literacy education (M Ed); organizational management (MOM); resource education (M Ed).

Creighton University, Graduate School, College of Arts and Sciences, Department of Education, Omaha, NE 68178-0001. Offers educational leadership (MS), including elementary school administration, secondary school administration, teacher leadership; school counseling and preventive mental health (MS), including elementary school guidance, secondary school guidance; teaching (M Ed), including elementary teaching, secondary teaching. *Accreditation:* NCATE. *Program availability:* Part-time, 100% online, blended/hybrid learning. *Faculty:* 14 full-time (7 women). *Students:* 38 full-time (35 women), 188 part-time (138 women); includes 15 minority (3 Black or African American, non-Hispanic/Latino; 2 American Indian or Alaska Native, non-Hispanic/Latino; 4 Asian, non-Hispanic/Latino; 3 Hispanic/Latino; 2 Native Hawaiian or other Pacific Islander, non-Hispanic/Latino; 1 Two or more races, non-Hispanic/Latino), 4 international. Average age 33. 2 applicants, 100% accepted, 1 enrolled. In 2018, 92 master's awarded. *Degree requirements:* For master's, comprehensive exam (for some programs), portfolio. *Entrance requirements:* For master's, GRE General Test, PPST, 3 letters of recommendation, writing samples, resume. Additional exam requirements/recommendations for international students: Required—TOEFL (minimum score 90 iBT). *Application deadline:* For fall admission, 7/1 priority date for domestic students, 3/1 priority date for international students; for winter admission, 12/1 for domestic students, 7/1 for international students; for spring admission, 4/1 for domestic students, 10/1 for international students; for summer admission, 3/1 for domestic and international students. Application fee: $50. Electronic applications accepted. *Financial support:* Scholarships/grants and tuition waivers (partial) available. Support available to part-time students. Financial award applicants required to submit FAFSA. *Unit head:* Dr. Timothy J. Cook, Chair, 402-280-2561, E-mail: timothycook@creighton.edu. *Application contact:* Lindsay Johnson, Director of Graduate and Adult Recruitment, 402-280-2703, Fax: 402-280-2423, E-mail: gradschool@creighton.edu.

Cumberland University, Program in Education, Lebanon, TN 37087. Offers MAE. *Accreditation:* NCATE. *Program availability:* Part-time, evening/weekend, online learning. *Degree requirements:* For master's, comprehensive exam. *Entrance requirements:* For master's, GRE General Test, MAT, or NTE, 3 letters of recommendation. Additional exam requirements/recommendations for international students: Required—TOEFL (minimum score 500 paper-based).

Curry College, Graduate Studies, Program in Education, Milton, MA 02186-9984. Offers elementary education (M Ed); foundations (non-license) (M Ed); reading (M Ed, Certificate); special education (M Ed). *Program availability:* Part-time, evening/weekend. *Degree requirements:* For master's, project or thesis. *Entrance requirements:* For master's, interview, recommendations, resume, written statement. Additional exam requirements/recommendations for international students: Required—TOEFL (minimum score 550 paper-based; 80 iBT). *Expenses:* Contact institution. *Faculty research:* Classroom trauma, therapeutic writing, inclusionary practices.

Daemen College, Education Programs, Amherst, NY 14226-3592. Offers adolescence education (MS); childhood education (MS); childhood special education (MS); childhood special-alternative certification (MS); early childhood special-alternative certification (MS). *Accreditation:* TEAC. *Program availability:* Part-time. *Faculty:* 16 full-time (12 women), 19 part-time/adjunct (14 women). *Students:* 233 full-time (210 women), 21 part-time (18 women); includes 4 minority (1 Black or African American, non-Hispanic/Latino; 3 Hispanic/Latino), 1 international. Average age 22. 76 applicants, 93% accepted, 68 enrolled. In 2018, 204 master's awarded. *Degree requirements:* For master's, comprehensive exam, A minimum grade of B earned in all courses, thereby resulting in a minimum cumulative grade point average of 3.00. *Entrance requirements:* For master's, Submit scores from taking the Graduate Record Exam (GRE) by no later than December 16 for fall applicants, no later than May 1 for spring applicants, bachelor's degree, GPA of 3.0 or above, resume, letter of intent, 2 letters of recommendation, interview with department chair. Additional exam requirements/recommendations for international students: Required—TOEFL (minimum score 77 paper-based), IELTS (minimum score 6.5). *Application deadline:* Applications are processed on a rolling basis. Application fee: $25. Electronic applications accepted. Application fee is waived when completed online. *Expenses: Tuition:* Part-time $977 per credit hour. *Required fees:* $125; $14 per credit hour. *Financial support:* Scholarships/grants and unspecified assistantships available. Support available to part-time students. Financial award applicants required to submit FAFSA. *Unit head:* Dr. Elizabeth Heilman, Department Chair, 716-839-8553, E-mail: eheilman@daemen.edu. *Application contact:* Megan Beardi, Senior Assistant Director of Graduate Admissions, 716-566-7861, Fax: 716-839-8229, E-mail: mbeardi@daemen.edu.
Website: https://www.daemen.edu/academics/areas-study/education

Dakota State University, College of Education, Madison, SD 57042-1799. Offers educational technology (MSET). *Accreditation:* NCATE. *Program availability:* Part-time-only, evening/weekend, online only, 100% online. *Faculty:* 4 full-time (0 women). *Students:* 20 part-time (15 women); includes 1 minority (American Indian or Alaska Native, non-Hispanic/Latino). Average age 34. 12 applicants, 100% accepted, 10 enrolled. In 2018, 8 master's awarded. *Degree requirements:* For master's, thesis optional, portfolio. *Entrance requirements:* For master's, GRE General Test, demonstration of technology skills, minimum GPA of 2.7. *Application deadline:* For fall admission, 6/15 for domestic students; for spring admission, 11/15 for domestic students; for summer admission, 4/15 for domestic students. Applications are processed on a rolling basis. Application fee: $35. Electronic applications accepted. *Expenses: Tuition, area resident:* Full-time $7666. Tuition, state resident: full-time $7666. Tuition, nonresident: full-time $14,311. *International tuition:* $14,311 full-time. *Required fees:* $953. *Financial support:* In 2018–19, 3 students received support. Career-related internships or fieldwork, Federal Work-Study, scholarships/grants, unspecified assistantships, and administrative assistantships available. Support available to part-time students. Financial award applicants required to submit FAFSA. *Faculty research:* Educational technology evaluation, computer-supported collaborative learning, cognitive theory and visual representation of the effects of ubiquitous wireless computing on student learning and productivity, accessible learning, pedagogies for exceptional children. *Unit head:* Dr. Crystal Pauli, Dean of College of Education, 605-256-5799. *Application contact:* Dr. Kevin Smith, MSET Program Coordinator, 605-256-5175, Fax: 605-256-7300, E-mail: kevin.smith@dsu.edu.
Website: http://dsu.edu/graduate-students/mset

Education—General

Dakota Wesleyan University, Program in Education, Mitchell, SD 57301. Offers curriculum and instruction (MA Ed); educational policy and administration (MA Ed); preK-12 principal certification (MA Ed); secondary certification (MA Ed). *Program availability:* Part-time, evening/weekend, online only, 100% online. *Faculty:* 5 part-time/adjunct (2 women). *Students:* 20 full-time (6 women), 4 part-time (1 woman); includes 8 minority (4 Black or African American, non-Hispanic/Latino; 3 Hispanic/Latino; 1 Two or more races, non-Hispanic/Latino). Average age 26. 12 applicants, 83% accepted, 8 enrolled. In 2018, 13 master's awarded. *Degree requirements:* For master's, comprehensive exam, thesis optional, electronic portfolio. *Entrance requirements:* For master's, minimum GPA of 2.7, elementary statistics course, statement of purpose, official transcripts, resume, three letters of recommendation. Additional exam requirements/recommendations for international students: Required—TOEFL (minimum score 500 paper-based), IELTS (minimum score 6.5). *Application deadline:* For fall admission, 8/1 priority date for domestic and international students; for winter admission, 12/1 priority date for domestic students; for spring admission, 4/1 priority date for domestic students, 12/1 priority date for international students. Applications are processed on a rolling basis. Application fee: $0. Electronic applications accepted. Application fee is waived when completed online. *Expenses:* Contact institution. *Financial support:* Applicants required to submit FAFSA. *Faculty research:* Technology in the classroom, current educational trends, higher education. *Unit head:* Dr. Melissa Weber, Director of Graduate Studies, 605-995-2630, Fax: 605-995-2609, E-mail: melissa.weber@dwu.edu. *Application contact:* Stacy Mock, Coordinator of Adult and Online Admissions, 605-995-2650, Fax: 605-995-2699, E-mail: admissions@dwu.edu. Website: www.dwu.edu

Dallas Baptist University, Dorothy M. Bush College of Education, Teaching Program, Dallas, TX 75211-9299. Offers distance learning (MAT); early childhood through grade 6 certification (MAT); early childhood-12 (MAT); elementary (MAT); English as a second language (MAT); Montessori (MAT); multisensory (MAT); secondary (MAT). *Program availability:* Part-time, evening/weekend, 100% online, blended/hybrid learning. *Application deadline:* Applications are processed on a rolling basis. Application fee: $25. Electronic applications accepted. Application fee is waived when completed online. *Expenses:* Tuition: Full-time $17,262; part-time $959 per credit hour. Required fees: $1000; $500 per semester. Tuition and fees vary according to course load and degree level. *Unit head:* Dr. Neil Dugger, Dean, 214-333-5202, E-mail: neil@dbu.edu. *Application contact:* Dr. DeAnna Jenkins, Program Director, 214-333-5402, E-mail: deannaj@dbu.edu.
Website: https://www.dbu.edu/graduate/degree-programs/ma-teaching

Defiance College, Program in Education, Defiance, OH 43512-1610. Offers education (MAE); sport coaching (MAE). *Program availability:* Part-time-only. *Degree requirements:* For master's, thesis. *Entrance requirements:* For master's, teaching license. Electronic applications accepted.

Delaware State University, Graduate Programs, College of Education, Health and Public Policy, Dover, DE 19901-2277. Offers MA, MS, MSW, Ed D. *Accreditation:* NCATE. *Program availability:* Part-time, evening/weekend. *Degree requirements:* For master's, comprehensive exam, thesis optional. *Entrance requirements:* For master's, GRE General Test, minimum GPA of 3.0 in major, 2.75 overall. Additional exam requirements/recommendations for international students: Required—TOEFL (minimum score 500 paper-based). Electronic applications accepted.

Delta State University, Graduate Programs, College of Education, Cleveland, MS 38733-0001. Offers M Ed, MAT, MS, Ed D, Ed S. *Accreditation:* NCATE. *Program availability:* Part-time, evening/weekend. *Degree requirements:* For master's, thesis optional; for doctorate, thesis/dissertation. *Entrance requirements:* For doctorate, GRE General Test; for Ed S, master's degree, teaching certificate. *Expenses:* Tuition, area resident: Full-time $7076; part-time $393 per credit hour. Tuition, state resident: full-time $7076; part-time $393 per credit hour. Tuition, nonresident: full-time $7076; part-time $393 per credit hour. International tuition: $7076 full-time. Required fees: $170; $18.90 per credit hour. $9.45 per semester. Part-time tuition and fees vary according to program.

DePaul University, College of Education, Chicago, IL 60614. Offers bilingual-bicultural education (M Ed, MA); counseling (M Ed, MA), including clinical mental health counseling, college student development, school counseling; curriculum studies (M Ed, MA, Ed D); early childhood education (M Ed, MA, Ed D); educational leadership (M Ed, MA, Ed D), including Catholic leadership (M Ed, MA), general (M Ed, MA), higher education (M Ed, MA), physical education (M Ed, MA), principal preparation (M Ed); teacher preparation (M Ed); elementary education (M Ed, MA); middle grades education (M Ed); middle school mathematics education (MS); reading specialist (M Ed, MA); secondary education (M Ed, MA); social and cultural foundations in education (M Ed, MA); special education (M Ed); sport, fitness and recreation leadership (MS); value-creating education for global citizenship (M Ed); world languages education (M Ed, MA). *Program availability:* Part-time, evening/weekend, online learning. *Degree requirements:* For doctorate, thesis/dissertation. Electronic applications accepted.

DePaul University, School for New Learning, Chicago, IL 60604. Offers applied professional studies (MA); applied technology (MS); educating adults (MA). *Program availability:* Part-time, evening/weekend. *Degree requirements:* For master's, thesis or alternative. *Entrance requirements:* For master's, resume, interview, official transcript. Electronic applications accepted.

DeSales University, Division of Liberal Arts and Social Sciences, Center Valley, PA 18034-9568. Offers criminal justice (MCJ); digital forensics (MCJ, Postbaccalaureate Certificate); education (M Ed), including instructional technology, secondary education, special education, teaching English to speakers of other languages; investigative forensics (MCJ, Postbaccalaureate Certificate). *Program availability:* Part-time, 100% online, blended/hybrid learning. *Entrance requirements:* For master's, bachelor's degree from accredited institution, minimum undergraduate GPA of 3.0, personal statement showing potential of graduate work, three letters of recommendation, professional goal statement. Additional exam requirements/recommendations for international students: Required—TOEFL. Electronic applications accepted.

Dickinson State University, Department of Teacher Education, Dickinson, ND 58601-4896. Offers master of arts in teaching (MAT); master of entrepreneurship (ME); middle school education (MAT); reading (MAT). *Program availability:* Part-time, blended/hybrid learning. *Faculty:* 2 full-time (both women). *Students:* 2 full-time (1 woman), 15 part-time (9 women); includes 1 minority (Hispanic/Latino). Average age 36. 8 applicants, 100% accepted, 8 enrolled. *Degree requirements:* For master's, comprehensive exam (for some programs). *Entrance requirements:* For master's, additional admission requirements for the Master of Entrepreneurship Program: complete the SoBE ME Peregrine Entrance Examination, personal statement; transcripts; additional admission requirements for the Master of Entrepreneurship Program: 2 letters of reference in support of their admission to the program. Reference letters should be from prior academic advisors, faculty, professional colleagues, or supervisors. Additional exam requirements/recommendations for international students: Required—TOEFL (minimum score 71 iBT). *Application deadline:* For fall admission, 8/1 for domestic students, 7/1 for international students; for spring admission, 12/1 for domestic students, 11/15 for international students. Applications are processed on a rolling basis. Application fee:

$35. Electronic applications accepted. *Expenses: Tuition, area resident:* Full-time $3735; part-time $311 per credit hour. Tuition, state resident: full-time $3735; part-time $311 per credit hour. Tuition, nonresident: full-time $3735; part-time $311 per credit hour. *Required fees:* $138; $138 per credit hour. *Financial support:* Application deadline: 12/1; applicants required to submit FAFSA. *Unit head:* Dr. Deborah Secord, Chair, Department of Teacher Education, 701-483-2178, E-mail: Deborah.Secord@dickinsonstate.edu. *Application contact:* Pamela Krueger, Graduate Studies Coordinator, 701-483-5631, E-mail: Pamela.j.krueger@dickinsonstate.edu.
Website: https://dickinsonstate.edu/academics/fields-of-study/graduate-studies/

Doane University, Program in Education, Crete, NE 68333-2430. Offers curriculum and instruction (M Ed); education (Ed D); education specialist (Ed S); educational leadership (M Ed); school counseling (M Ed). *Accreditation:* NCATE. *Program availability:* Part-time, evening/weekend. *Faculty:* 10 full-time (7 women), 66 part-time/adjunct (50 women). *Students:* 287 full-time (235 women), 474 part-time (363 women); includes 57 minority (20 Black or African American, non-Hispanic/Latino; 1 American Indian or Alaska Native, non-Hispanic/Latino; 5 Asian, non-Hispanic/Latino; 22 Hispanic/Latino; 1 Native Hawaiian or other Pacific Islander, non-Hispanic/Latino; 8 Two or more races, non-Hispanic/Latino), 6 international. Average age 34. In 2018, 247 master's, 9 doctorates, 33 other advanced degrees awarded. *Degree requirements:* For master's, thesis; for doctorate, thesis/dissertation. *Entrance requirements:* For master's, minimum GPA of 2.5. Additional exam requirements/recommendations for international students: Required—TOEFL. *Application deadline:* Applications are processed on a rolling basis. Electronic applications accepted. *Expenses:* Contact institution. *Financial support:* Applicants required to submit FAFSA. *Unit head:* Dr. Lyn C. Forester, Dean, 402-826-8604, Fax: 402-826-8278. *Application contact:* Leah Schaber, Assistant Dean, 402-464-1223, Fax: 402-466-4228, E-mail: leah.schaber@doane.edu.
Website: http://www.doane.edu/masters-degrees

Dominican College, Division of Teacher Education, Orangeburg, NY 10962-1210. Offers education/teaching of individuals with multiple disabilities (MS Ed). *Program availability:* Part-time, evening/weekend, online learning. *Faculty:* 5 part-time/adjunct (all women). *Students:* 4 full-time (all women), 52 part-time (40 women); includes 11 minority (1 Black or African American, non-Hispanic/Latino; 2 Asian, non-Hispanic/Latino; 8 Hispanic/Latino). Average age 33. In 2018, 24 master's awarded. *Degree requirements:* For master's, comprehensive exam (for some programs), thesis. *Entrance requirements:* For master's, 3 letters of recommendation (atleast 1 from a former professor), current resume, Official transcripts (not student copies) of all undergraduate and graduate records, results from GRE/MAT/SAT or ACT scores, interview, State issued teaching certificate & State Certification Exam Scores are Required for TVI program. Additional exam requirements/recommendations for international students: Required—TOEFL (minimum score 90 iBT). *Application deadline:* For fall admission, 8/1 for domestic students, 6/1 for international students. Applications are processed on a rolling basis. Application fee: $50. Electronic applications accepted. *Expenses: Tuition:* Part-time $965 per credit. *Required fees:* $200 per semester. One-time fee: $200. Tuition and fees vary according to course load, degree level and program. *Financial support:* Application deadline: 2/1; applicants required to submit FAFSA. *Unit head:* Dr. Mike Kelly, Director, 845-848-4090, Fax: 845-359-7802, E-mail: mike.kelly@dc.edu. *Application contact:* Heather Karsenty, Assistant Director of Graduate Admissions, 845-848-7908 Ext. 15, Fax: 845-365-3150, E-mail: admissions@dc.edu.

Dominican University, School of Education, River Forest, IL 60305-1099. Offers child life studies (MS); early childhood education (MS); education (MAT); elementary education (MA Ed); English as a second language (MA Ed); reading (MA Ed); secondary education (MAT); special education (MS). *Accreditation:* NCATE. *Program availability:* Part-time, evening/weekend, 100% online, blended/hybrid learning. *Entrance requirements:* For master's, Illinois Test of Basic Skills. Additional exam requirements/recommendations for international students: Required—TOEFL (minimum score 550 paper-based; 79 iBT). *Expenses:* Contact institution. *Faculty research:* Governance of private education institutions, reading and language arts, inclusion, organizational planning, leadership and vision.

Dominican University of California, School of Liberal Arts and Education, San Rafael, CA 94901-2298. Offers MA. *Program availability:* Part-time, evening/weekend. *Degree requirements:* For master's, comprehensive exam (for some programs), thesis (for some programs). *Entrance requirements:* For master's, minimum GPA of 3.0. Additional exam requirements/recommendations for international students: Required—TOEFL (minimum score 550 paper-based; 80 iBT), IELTS (minimum score 6.5). Electronic applications accepted.

Dordt College, Program in Education, Sioux Center, IA 51250-1697. Offers M Ed. *Program availability:* Part-time, online learning. *Degree requirements:* For master's, comprehensive exam, thesis. *Entrance requirements:* For master's, GRE or MAT. Additional exam requirements/recommendations for international students: Required—TOEFL. Electronic applications accepted.

Drake University, School of Education, Des Moines, IA 50311-4516. Offers applied behavior analysis (MS); counseling (MS); education (PhD); education administration (Ed D); educational leadership (MSE, Ed D); effective teaching (MSE); leadership development (MS); literacy (Ed S); literacy education (MSE); rehabilitation administration (MS); rehabilitation placement (MS); special education (MSE); STEM education (MSE); teacher education (5-12) (MAT); teacher education (K-8) (MST); teacher effectiveness and professional development (MSE). *Program availability:* Part-time, evening/weekend, 100% online, blended/hybrid learning. *Students:* 90 full-time (74 women), 690 part-time (532 women); includes 69 minority (30 Black or African American, non-Hispanic/Latino; 1 American Indian or Alaska Native, non-Hispanic/Latino; 9 Asian, non-Hispanic/Latino; 16 Hispanic/Latino; 13 Two or more races, non-Hispanic/Latino). Average age 34. In 2018, 253 master's, 30 doctorates awarded. *Degree requirements:* For master's and Ed S, comprehensive exam, internships (for some programs); for doctorate, comprehensive exam, thesis/dissertation, internships (for some programs). *Entrance requirements:* For master's, GRE General Test, MAT, or Drake Writing Assessment, resume, 2 letters of recommendation; for doctorate, GRE General Test or MAT, master's degree, 3 letters of recommendation; for Ed S, GRE General Test or MAT. Additional exam requirements/recommendations for international students: Required—TOEFL (minimum score 550 paper-based). *Application deadline:* For fall admission, 7/1 priority date for domestic students, 6/1 priority date for international students; for spring admission, 11/1 priority date for domestic students, 10/1 priority date for international students. Applications are processed on a rolling basis. Application fee: $25. Electronic applications accepted. *Expenses:* Contact institution. *Financial support:* Research assistantships, career-related internships or fieldwork, and unspecified assistantships available. Support available to part-time students. *Faculty research:* Counseling and rehabilitation, behavioral supports, inquiry-based science methods, teacher quality enhancement. *Unit head:* Dr. Janet McMahill, Dean, 515-271-3829, E-mail: janet.mcmahill@drake.edu. *Application contact:* Dr. Janet McMahill, Dean, 515-271-3829, E-mail: janet.mcmahill@drake.edu.
Website: http://www.drake.edu/soe/

Drew University, Caspersen School of Graduate Studies, Madison, NJ 07940-1493. Offers conflict resolution and leadership (Certificate), including community leadership, moderation, peace building; education (M Ed); finance (MA); history and culture (MA,

PhD), including American history, book history, British history, European history, intellectual history, Irish history, print culture, public history; K-12 education (MAT), including art, biology, chemistry, elementary education, English, French, Italian, math, secondary education, special education, teacher of students with disabilities; liberal studies (M Litt, D Litt), including history, Irish/Irish-American studies, literature (M Litt, MMH, D Litt, DMH, CMH), religion, spirituality, teaching in the two-year college, writing; medical humanities (MMH, DMH, CMH), including arts, health, healthcare, literature (M Litt, MMH, D Litt, DMH, CMH), scientific research; poetry (MFA). *Program availability:* Part-time, evening/weekend. *Faculty:* 3 full-time (2 women), 27 part-time/adjunct (13 women). *Students:* 66 full-time (38 women), 179 part-time (117 women); includes 37 minority (15 Black or African American, non-Hispanic/Latino; 2 Asian, non-Hispanic/Latino; 15 Hispanic/Latino; 5 Two or more races, non-Hispanic/Latino), 14 international. Average age 42. 157 applicants, 82% accepted, 57 enrolled. In 2018, 34 master's, 24 doctorates, 17 other advanced degrees awarded. Terminal master's awarded for partial completion of doctoral program. *Degree requirements:* For master's and other advanced degree, thesis (for some programs); for doctorate, one foreign language, comprehensive exam (for some programs), thesis/dissertation. *Entrance requirements:* For master's, PRAXIS Core and Subject Area tests (for MAT), GRE/GMAT (for MFin MS in Data Analytics), resume, transcripts, writing sample, personal statement, letters of recommendation; for doctorate, GRE (PhD in history and culture), resume, transcripts, writing sample, personal statement, letters of recommendation; for other advanced degree, resume, transcripts, personal statement. Additional exam requirements/recommendations for international students: Required—TOEFL (minimum score 587 paper-based; 80 iBT), IELTS (minimum score 6), TWE (minimum score 4). *Application deadline:* For fall admission, 8/1 for domestic students, 6/1 for international students; for spring admission, 12/1 for domestic students, 10/1 for international students. Applications are processed on a rolling basis. Application fee: $35. Electronic applications accepted. *Financial support:* Fellowships, research assistantships, teaching assistantships, career-related internships or fieldwork, Federal Work-Study, scholarships/grants, and unspecified assistantships available. Support available to part-time students. Financial award applicants required to submit FAFSA. *Unit head:* Dr. Debra Liebowitz, Provost and Dean of the College of Liberal Arts & Caspersen School of Graduate Studies, 973-4083139, E-mail: dliebowi@drew.edu. *Application contact:* Amo-Augustus Kubeyinje, Associate Vice President for Graduate Enrollment, 973-408-3111, E-mail: akubeyinje@drew.edu.
Website: http://www.drew.edu/caspersen

Drexel University, Goodwin College of Professional Studies, School of Education, Philadelphia, PA 19104-2875. Offers applied behavior analysis (MS); creativity and innovation (MS); education improvement and transformation (MS); educational administration (MS); educational leadership and management (Ed D); educational leadership development and learning technologies (PhD); global and international education (MS); higher education (MS); human resources development (MS); learning technologies (MS); mathematics, learning and teaching (MS); special education (MS); teaching, learning and curriculum (MS). *Program availability:* Part-time, evening/weekend, online learning. *Degree requirements:* For doctorate, thesis/dissertation. *Entrance requirements:* For doctorate, GRE or GMAT. Additional exam requirements/recommendations for international students: Required—TOEFL, IELTS. Electronic applications accepted. Application fee is waived when completed online. *Expenses:* Contact institution. *Faculty research:* Leadership development, mathematics education, literacy, autism, educational technology.

Drury University, Master in Education Program, Springfield, MO 65802. Offers curriculum and instruction (M Ed), including elementary education, middle school education, secondary education; instructional leadership (M Ed); instructional technology (M Ed); integrated learning (M Ed); special education (M Ed); special reading (M Ed). *Accreditation:* NCATE. *Program availability:* Part-time, evening/weekend, 100% online, blended/hybrid learning. *Faculty:* 10 full-time (6 women), 8 part-time/adjunct (6 women). *Students:* 167 full-time (133 women). Average age 32. 92 applicants, 92% accepted, 69 enrolled. In 2018, 44 master's awarded. *Entrance requirements:* For master's, bachelor's degree with minimum GPA of 2.75. Additional exam requirements/recommendations for international students: Recommended—TOEFL (minimum score 80 iBT), IELTS (minimum score 6.5). *Application deadline:* For fall admission, 8/4 priority date for domestic and international students; for spring admission, 1/5 priority date for domestic and international students; for summer admission, 5/26 priority date for domestic and international students. Applications are processed on a rolling basis. Application fee: $25. Electronic applications accepted. *Expenses:* Tuition is $366 per credit hour. Fees are $7 per credit hour. Most M.Ed. degrees are 33 credit hours. *Financial support:* In 2018–19, 5 students received support. Career-related internships or fieldwork, scholarships/grants, and unspecified assistantships available. Financial award application deadline: 6/30; financial award applicants required to submit FAFSA. *Faculty research:* Instructional technology, autism, diversity, and social justice. *Unit head:* Dr. Asikaa Cosgrove, Director, Master in Education Program, 417-873-7806, E-mail: acosgrov@drury.edu. *Application contact:* Dr. Asikaa Cosgrove, Director, Master in Education Program, 417-873-7806, E-mail: acosgrov@drury.edu.
Website: http://www.drury.edu/education-masters

Duke University, Graduate School, Program in Teaching, Durham, NC 27708. Offers MAT. *Accreditation:* NCATE. *Entrance requirements:* For master's, GRE General Test. Additional exam requirements/recommendations for international students: Required—TOEFL (minimum score 577 paper-based; 90 iBT) or IELTS (minimum score 7). Electronic applications accepted.

Duquesne University, School of Education, Pittsburgh, PA 15282-0001. Offers MS Ed, Ed D, PhD, Psy D, Post-Master's Certificate. *Accreditation:* NCATE. *Program availability:* Part-time, evening/weekend, 100% online, blended/hybrid learning. *Faculty:* 52 full-time (31 women), 83 part-time/adjunct (63 women). *Students:* 490 full-time (368 women), 44 part-time (32 women); includes 93 minority (48 Black or African American, non-Hispanic/Latino; 1 American Indian or Alaska Native, non-Hispanic/Latino; 12 Asian, non-Hispanic/Latino; 16 Hispanic/Latino; 16 Two or more races, non-Hispanic/Latino), 63 international. Average age 30. 437 applicants, 85% accepted, 178 enrolled. In 2018, 142 master's, 52 doctorates, 7 other advanced degrees awarded. *Degree requirements:* For master's, comprehensive exam (for some programs); for doctorate, comprehensive exam (for some programs), thesis/dissertation (for some programs); for Post-Master's Certificate, comprehensive exam (for some programs), thesis (for some programs). *Entrance requirements:* For master's, letters of recommendation, essay, personal statement, interview, bachelor's degree; for doctorate, GRE, letters of recommendation, essay, personal statement, interview, master's degree; for Post-Master's Certificate, GRE, letters of recommendation, essay, personal statement, interview, bachelor's/master's degree. Additional exam requirements/recommendations for international students: Required—TOEFL (minimum score 550 paper-based), IELTS (minimum score 7). *Application deadline:* For fall admission, 3/1 for domestic students; for spring admission, 9/1 for domestic students. Applications are processed on a rolling basis. Application fee: $0. Electronic applications accepted. *Expenses: Tuition:* Full-time $23,112; part-time $1284 per credit. Tuition and fees vary according to program. *Financial support:* In 2018–19, 53 research assistantships with full and partial tuition reimbursements (averaging $3,603 per year) were awarded; teaching assistantships, career-related internships or fieldwork, Federal Work-Study, institutionally sponsored loans, and tuition waivers also available. Support available to part-time students. Financial award applicants required to submit FAFSA. *Total annual research expenditures:* $249,745. *Unit head:* Dr. Cindy Walker, Dean, 412-396-6102, Fax: 412-396-5585. *Application contact:* Kelly McGinley, Graduate Admissions Assistant, 412-396-1559, Fax: 412-296-5585, E-mail: mcginleyk@duq.edu.
Website: http://www.duq.edu/academics/schools/education

D'Youville College, Department of Education, Buffalo, NY 14201-1084. Offers educational leadership (Ed D); elementary education (MS Ed); secondary education (MS Ed); special education (MS Ed). *Program availability:* Part-time, evening/weekend. *Degree requirements:* For master's, one foreign language, comprehensive exam, project or thesis. *Entrance requirements:* For master's, GRE (if GPA less than 2.75), minimum GPA of 3.0. Additional exam requirements/recommendations for international students: Required—TOEFL (minimum score 500 paper-based). Electronic applications accepted. *Faculty research:* Developmental disabilities, multiculturalism, early childhood education.

Earlham College, Graduate Programs, Richmond, IN 47374-4095. Offers M Ed, MAT. *Entrance requirements:* For master's, GRE, PRAXIS I, PRAXIS II.

East Carolina University, Graduate School, College of Education, Greenville, NC 27858-4353. Offers MA, MA Ed, MAT, MLS, MS, MSA, Ed D, Certificate, Ed S. *Accreditation:* NCATE. *Program availability:* Part-time, evening/weekend, online learning. *Application deadline:* For fall admission, 8/15 for domestic students, 2/1 for international students; for spring admission, 12/20 for domestic students, 10/1 for international students. *Expenses: Tuition, area resident:* Full-time $4749. Tuition, state resident: full-time $4749. Tuition, nonresident: full-time $17,898. *International tuition:* $17,898 full-time. *Required fees:* $2787. Part-time tuition and fees vary according to course load and program. *Financial support:* Application deadline: 6/1. *Unit head:* Dr. B Grant Hayes, Dean, 252-328-4260, Fax: 252-328-4219, E-mail: hayesb15@ecu.edu. *Application contact:* Graduate School Admissions, 252-328-6012, Fax: 252-328-6071, E-mail: gradschool@ecu.edu.
Website: http://www.ecu.edu/coe

East Central University, School of Graduate Studies, Department of Education, Ada, OK 74820. Offers M Ed. *Accreditation:* NCATE. *Program availability:* Part-time, evening/weekend. *Entrance requirements:* For master's, minimum GPA of 2.5. Electronic applications accepted.

Eastern Connecticut State University, School of Education and Professional Studies/Graduate Division, Willimantic, CT 06226-2295. Offers MS. *Accreditation:* NCATE. *Program availability:* Part-time, evening/weekend. *Degree requirements:* For master's, comprehensive exam, thesis optional. *Entrance requirements:* For master's, PRAXIS I, SAT, ACT, or GRE; PRAXIS II, minimum GPA of 2.7, 3.0 (for education). Additional exam requirements/recommendations for international students: Required—TOEFL (minimum score 550 paper-based; 79 iBT); Recommended—IELTS (minimum score 6). Electronic applications accepted.

Eastern Illinois University, Graduate School, College of Education, Charleston, IL 61920. Offers MS, MS Ed, Ed S. *Accreditation:* NCATE. *Program availability:* Part-time, evening/weekend. *Degree requirements:* For master's and Ed S, comprehensive exam (for some programs), thesis (for some programs). *Entrance requirements:* For master's and Ed S, GMAT or GRE. Additional exam requirements/recommendations for international students: Required—TOEFL (minimum score 500 paper-based; 61 iBT), IELTS (minimum score 6). *Application deadline:* For fall admission, 5/15 for domestic and international students; for spring admission, 10/15 for domestic and international students. Applications are processed on a rolling basis. Application fee: $30. Electronic applications accepted. *Expenses:* Tuition, state resident: part-time $299 per credit hour. Tuition, nonresident: part-time $718 per credit hour. *Required fees:* $214.50 per credit hour. *Financial support:* Research assistantships with full tuition reimbursements, teaching assistantships with full tuition reimbursements, career-related internships or fieldwork, Federal Work-Study, scholarships/grants, and unspecified assistantships available. Support available to part-time students. Financial award application deadline: 3/1; financial award applicants required to submit FAFSA. *Unit head:* Douglas J. Bower, Ph.D., Dean, 217-581-2200, Fax: 217-581-2518, E-mail: djbower@eiu.edu. *Application contact:* Douglas J. Bower, Ph.D., Dean, 217-581-2200, Fax: 217-581-2518, E-mail: djbower@eiu.edu.
Website: http://www.eiu.edu/ceps/programs.php

Eastern Kentucky University, The Graduate School, College of Education, Richmond, KY 40475-3102. Offers MA, MA Ed, MAT. *Accreditation:* NCATE. *Program availability:* Part-time, online learning. *Entrance requirements:* For master's, GRE General Test, minimum GPA of 2.5. *Faculty research:* Dispositions to teach, technology in education, distance learning.

Eastern Mennonite University, Program in Teacher Education, Harrisonburg, VA 22802-2462. Offers curriculum and instruction (MA Ed); diverse needs (MA Ed); literacy (MA Ed); restorative justice in education (MA Ed). *Accreditation:* NCATE. *Program availability:* Part-time. *Degree requirements:* For master's, portfolio, research projects. *Entrance requirements:* For master's, 1 year of teaching experience, interview, minimum undergraduate GPA of 2.75. Additional exam requirements/recommendations for international students: Required—TOEFL (minimum score 550 paper-based). Electronic applications accepted. *Expenses:* Contact institution. *Faculty research:* Effective literacy instruction for middle school English language learners, beginning teacher's emotional experiences, constructivist learning environments, restorative discipline.

Eastern Michigan University, Graduate School, College of Education, Ypsilanti, MI 48197. Offers M Ed, MA, Ed D, PhD, Graduate Certificate, Post Master's Certificate, SPA. *Accreditation:* NCATE. *Program availability:* Part-time, evening/weekend, online learning. *Faculty:* 66 full-time (46 women). *Students:* 195 full-time (159 women), 658 part-time (499 women); includes 207 minority (123 Black or African American, non-Hispanic/Latino; 12 Asian, non-Hispanic/Latino; 40 Hispanic/Latino; 32 Two or more races, non-Hispanic/Latino), 19 international. Average age 33. 618 applicants, 56% accepted, 215 enrolled. In 2018, 253 master's, 19 doctorates, 49 other advanced degrees awarded. *Entrance requirements:* For master's, GRE; for doctorate, GRE General Test. Additional exam requirements/recommendations for international students: Required—TOEFL. *Application deadline:* Applications are processed on a rolling basis. Application fee: $45. *Financial support:* Fellowships, research assistantships with full tuition reimbursements, teaching assistantships with full tuition reimbursements, career-related internships or fieldwork, Federal Work-Study, institutionally sponsored loans, scholarships/grants, tuition waivers (partial), and unspecified assistantships available. Support available to part-time students. Financial award applicants required to submit FAFSA. *Unit head:* Dr. Michael Sayler, Dean, 734-487-1414, Fax: 734-484-6471, E-mail: msayler@emich.edu. *Application contact:* Dr. Michael Sayler, Dean, 734-487-1414, Fax: 734-484-6471, E-mail: msayler@emich.edu.
Website: http://www.emich.edu/coe/

Eastern Nazarene College, Adult and Graduate Studies, Division of Teacher Education, Quincy, MA 02170. Offers administration (M Ed); early childhood education (M Ed, Certificate); elementary education (M Ed, Certificate); English as a second language (Certificate); instructional enrichment and development (Certificate); middle school education (M Ed, Certificate); moderate special needs education (Certificate);

principal (Certificate); program development and supervision (Certificate); secondary education (M Ed, Certificate); special education administrator (Certificate); special needs (M Ed); supervisor (Certificate); teacher of reading (M Ed, Certificate). M Ed also available through weekend program for administration, special needs, and teacher of reading only. *Program availability:* Part-time, evening/weekend. *Entrance requirements:* Additional exam requirements/recommendations for international students: Required—TOEFL (minimum score 550 paper-based).

Eastern New Mexico University, Graduate School, College of Education and Technology, Department of Educational Studies, Portales, NM 88130. Offers counseling (MA); education (M Ed), including educational administration, secondary education; school counseling (M Ed); special education (M Ed, M Sp Ed), including early childhood special education (M Sp Ed), general special education (M Sp Ed), gifted education pedagogy (M Ed), special education pedagogy (M Ed). *Accreditation:* NCATE. *Program availability:* Part-time, evening/weekend, online learning. *Degree requirements:* For master's, comprehensive exam, thesis optional. *Entrance requirements:* For master's, writing assessment, minimum GPA of 3.0, letter of recommendation, photocopy of teaching license; Level II teaching license (for M Ed in educational administration). Additional exam requirements/recommendations for international students: Required—TOEFL (minimum score 550 paper-based; 79 iBT), IELTS (minimum score 6). Electronic applications accepted. *Expenses: Tuition,* area resident: Full-time $6776. Tuition, state resident: full-time $6776; part-time $282 per credit hour. Tuition, nonresident: full-time $8986; part-time $374 per credit hour. *Required fees:* $60 per semester. One-time fee: $25.

Eastern Oregon University, Master of Arts in Teaching Program, La Grande, OR 97850-2899. Offers elementary education (MAT); secondary education (MAT). *Faculty:* 10 full-time (6 women), 5 part-time/adjunct (2 women). *Students:* 48 full-time (26 women), 3 part-time (all women); includes 4 minority (1 Asian, non-Hispanic/Latino; 2 Hispanic/Latino; 1 Two or more races, non-Hispanic/Latino). Average age 32. In 2018, 47 master's awarded. *Degree requirements:* For master's, thesis. *Entrance requirements:* For master's, NTE. Secondary candidates will be required to pass the state approved subject-specific test(s), prior to entry into the program (ORELA/NES or Praxis II, depending upon which is required of your subject). Elementary-Multiple Subjects candidates will be required to pass the state approved Elementary Education, subtest II (ORELA/NES). Additional exam requirements/recommendations for international students: Required—TOEFL (minimum score 550 paper-based; 79 iBT), IELTS (minimum score 6), Can also be satisfied by successful completion of the American Classroom Readiness course. *Application deadline:* For fall admission, 3/1 for domestic students. Applications are processed on a rolling basis. Electronic applications accepted. *Expenses:* $466.50/credit hour. *Financial support:* In 2018–19, 23 students received support. Federal Work-Study, scholarships/grants, and tuition waivers (full and partial) available. Support available to part-time students. *Unit head:* Dr. Matt Seimears, Dean of College of Business and Education, 541-962-3399, Fax: 541-962-3701, E-mail: mseimears@eou.edu. *Application contact:* Janet Frye, Administrative Support, MAT/MS Graduate Admission, 541-962-3772, Fax: 541-962-3701, E-mail: jfrye@eou.edu. Website: https://www.eou.edu/cobe/ed/mat/

Eastern Oregon University, Master of Science Program, La Grande, OR 97850-2899. Offers education (MS). *Program availability:* Part-time, online only, 100% online. *Faculty:* 9 full-time (5 women), 3 part-time/adjunct (1 woman). *Students:* 4 full-time (2 women), 52 part-time (43 women); includes 7 minority (1 American Indian or Alaska Native, non-Hispanic/Latino; 1 Asian, non-Hispanic/Latino; 4 Hispanic/Latino; 1 Native Hawaiian or other Pacific Islander, non-Hispanic/Latino). Average age 37. In 2018, 15 master's awarded. *Degree requirements:* For master's, thesis. *Entrance requirements:* For master's, minimum GPA of 3.0 on last 60 quarter hours completed of undergraduate upper-division coursework or 15 quarter hours of approved graduate-level coursework; two letters of professional reference attesting to applicant's ability to be successful; essay. Additional exam requirements/recommendations for international students: Required—TOEFL (minimum score 500 paper-based; 61 iBT), IELTS (minimum score 5), Can be satisfied with completion of level 112 in an English language school; or successful completion of the American Classroom Readiness course. *Application deadline:* Applications are processed on a rolling basis. Electronic applications accepted. *Expenses:* $466.50 per credit hour. *Financial support:* In 2018–19, 12 students received support. Federal Work-Study, scholarships/grants, and tuition waivers (full and partial) available. Support available to part-time students. *Unit head:* Dr. Matt Seimears, Dean of College of Business and Education, 541-962-3399, Fax: 541-962-3701, E-mail: mseimears@eou.edu. *Application contact:* Janet Frye, Administrative Support, MAT/MS Graduate Admission, 541-962-3772, Fax: 541-962-3701, E-mail: jfrye@eou.edu. Website: https://www.eou.edu/cobe/ed/ms/

Eastern Washington University, Graduate Studies, College of Arts, Letters and Education, Department of Education, Cheney, WA 99004-2431. Offers adult education (M Ed); curriculum development (M Ed); early childhood education (M Ed); educational foundations (M Ed); educational leadership (M Ed); literacy (M Ed); teaching K-8 (M Ed). *Program availability:* Part-time. *Degree requirements:* For master's, comprehensive exam. *Entrance requirements:* For master's, minimum GPA of 3.0. Additional exam requirements/recommendations for international students: Required—TOEFL (minimum score 580 paper-based; 92 iBT), IELTS (minimum score 7), PTE (minimum score 63). Electronic applications accepted.

East Stroudsburg University of Pennsylvania, Graduate and Extended Studies, College of Education, East Stroudsburg, PA 18301-2999. Offers M Ed, Ed D. *Program availability:* Part-time, evening/weekend, online learning. *Faculty:* 14 full-time (10 women), 6 part-time/adjunct (3 women). *Students:* 44 full-time (33 women), 281 part-time (222 women); includes 43 minority (14 Black or African American, non-Hispanic/Latino; 5 Asian, non-Hispanic/Latino; 19 Hispanic/Latino; 5 Two or more races, non-Hispanic/Latino; 1 international. Average age 36. 133 applicants, 81% accepted, 989 enrolled. In 2018, 45 master's, 5 doctorates awarded. *Degree requirements:* For master's, comprehensive exam, thesis (for some programs). *Entrance requirements:* For master's, Complete Act 34, 24, 151 and FBI Clearances; Disposition Self-Assessment, faculty interview and department recommendation, 2 letters of recommendation, resume, professional goals statement; for doctorate, 2 letters of recommendation, resume, professional goals statement. Additional exam requirements/recommendations for international students: Recommended—TOEFL (minimum score 560 paper-based; 83 iBT), IELTS. *Application deadline:* For fall admission, 7/31 priority date for domestic students, 6/30 priority date for international students; for spring admission, 11/30 for domestic students, 10/31 for international students. Applications are processed on a rolling basis. Application fee: $50. Electronic applications accepted. *Expenses: Tuition,* area resident: Full-time $9288; part-time $516 per credit. Tuition, state resident: full-time $9288. Tuition, nonresident: full-time $13,932; part-time $774 per credit. *International tuition:* $13,932 full-time. *Required fees:* $2059; $114 per credit. Tuition and fees vary according to course load and degree level. *Financial support:* Research assistantships with tuition reimbursements, career-related internships or fieldwork, Federal Work-Study, and unspecified assistantships available. Support available to part-time students. Financial award application deadline: 3/1; financial award applicants required to submit FAFSA. *Unit head:* Dr. Terry Barry, Dean, 570-422-3377, Fax: 570-

422-3506, E-mail: tbarry1@esu.edu. *Application contact:* Kevin Quintero, Associate Director, Graduate and Extended Studies, 570-422-3890, Fax: 570-422-3711, E-mail: kquintero@esu.edu. Website: https://www.esu.edu/college_education/index.cfm

East Tennessee State University, School of Graduate Studies, College of Education, Johnson City, TN 37614. Offers M Ed, MA, MAT, MS, Ed D, PhD, Ed S, Post-Master's Certificate, Postbaccalaureate Certificate. *Accreditation:* NCATE. *Entrance requirements:* Additional exam requirements/recommendations for international students: Required—TOEFL (minimum score 550 paper-based; 79 iBT). Electronic applications accepted.

East Texas Baptist University, Master of Education Program, Marshall, TX 75670-1498. Offers M Ed. *Program availability:* Part-time, evening/weekend, 100% online, blended/hybrid learning. *Faculty:* 2 full-time (1 woman), 5 part-time/adjunct (4 women). *Students:* 34 part-time (18 women); includes 14 minority (10 Black or African American, non-Hispanic/Latino; 1 American Indian or Alaska Native, non-Hispanic/Latino; 1 Hispanic/Latino; 2 Two or more races, non-Hispanic/Latino). Average age 29. 50 applicants, 50% accepted, 19 enrolled. In 2018, 18 master's awarded. *Entrance requirements:* Additional exam requirements/recommendations for international students: Recommended—TOEFL (minimum score 550 paper-based; 79 iBT). *Application deadline:* For fall admission, 8/15 for domestic students; for spring admission, 1/9 for domestic students; for summer admission, 5/11 for domestic students. Applications are processed on a rolling basis. Application fee: $50. Electronic applications accepted. *Expenses:* $700 per credit hour tuition; $150 per semester fees (6 or more hours enrolled); $75 per semester fees (1-5 hours enrolled). *Financial support:* In 2018–19, 12 students received support. Federal Work-Study, scholarships/grants, unspecified assistantships, and staff grants available. Financial award applicants required to submit FAFSA. *Unit head:* Dr. PJ Winters, Director, 903-923-2276, Fax: 903-935-4318, E-mail: med@etbu.edu. *Application contact:* Den Murley, Director of Graduate Admissions, 903-923-2079, Fax: 903-934-8115, E-mail: gradadmissions@etbu.edu. Website: https://www.etbu.edu/academics/academic-schools/school-education/department-teacher-education/programs/master-education-med

Edgewood College, School of Education, Madison, WI 53711-1997. Offers MA Ed, Ed D, Certificate. *Accreditation:* NCATE (one or more programs are accredited). *Program availability:* Part-time, evening/weekend. *Faculty:* 13 full-time (9 women), 15 part-time/adjunct (10 women). *Students:* 201 full-time (141 women), 141 part-time (97 women); includes 71 minority (24 Black or African American, non-Hispanic/Latino; 8 Asian, non-Hispanic/Latino; 31 Hispanic/Latino; 1 Native Hawaiian or other Pacific Islander, non-Hispanic/Latino; 7 Two or more races, non-Hispanic/Latino), 23 international. Average age 37. In 2018, 70 master's, 28 doctorates awarded. *Degree requirements:* For master's, practicum, research project; for doctorate, comprehensive exam, thesis/dissertation. *Entrance requirements:* For master's, minimum GPA of 2.75, 2 letters of recommendation, personal statement; for doctorate, resume, letter of intent, 2 letters of recommendation, interview, writing sample. Additional exam requirements/recommendations for international students: Required—TOEFL (minimum score 525 paper-based; 72 iBT). *Application deadline:* For fall admission, 8/15 for domestic students, 5/1 for international students; for spring admission, 1/8 for domestic students, 11/1 for international students. Applications are processed on a rolling basis. Application fee: $30. Electronic applications accepted. *Expenses: Tuition:* Part-time $963 per credit. *Financial support:* Applicants required to submit FAFSA. *Faculty research:* Urban high schools, transgender students, literacy pedagogy, funds of knowledge, English language learners. *Unit head:* Dr. Timothy D. Slekar, Dean, 608-663-2293, E-mail: tslekar@edgewood.edu. *Application contact:* Joann Eastman, Admissions Counselor, 608-663-3250, Fax: 608-663-2214, E-mail: gps@edgewood.edu. Website: https://www.edgewood.edu/academics/schools/school-of-education

Elizabeth City State University, Department of Education, Psychology and Health, Elizabeth City, NC 27909-7806. Offers M Ed, MSA. *Program availability:* Part-time, evening/weekend. *Degree requirements:* For master's, comprehensive exam (for some programs), thesis. Electronic applications accepted.

Elms College, Division of Education, Chicopee, MA 01013-2839. Offers early childhood education (MAT); education (M Ed, CAGS); elementary education (MAT); English as a second language (MAT); reading (MAT); secondary education (MAT), including biology education, English education, Spanish education; special education (MAT). *Program availability:* Part-time, evening/weekend. *Faculty:* 5 full-time (all women), 6 part-time/adjunct (5 women). *Students:* 3 full-time (all women), 117 part-time (94 women); includes 12 minority (1 Black or African American, non-Hispanic/Latino; 2 Asian, non-Hispanic/Latino; 9 Hispanic/Latino). Average age 34. 27 applicants, 96% accepted, 23 enrolled. In 2018, 34 master's, 3 other advanced degrees awarded. *Degree requirements:* For master's, thesis (for some programs). *Entrance requirements:* For master's, Massachusetts Educators Certification Test, minimum GPA of 3.0; for CAGS, master's degree in education. Additional exam requirements/recommendations for international students: Required—TOEFL. *Application deadline:* For fall admission, 7/1 priority date for domestic students; for spring admission, 11/1 priority date for domestic students. Applications are processed on a rolling basis. Application fee: $30. *Expenses: Tuition:* Full-time $14,328; part-time $796 per credit. *Required fees:* $200. Tuition and fees vary according to degree level and program. *Financial support:* In 2018–19, 2 teaching assistantships with partial tuition reimbursements were awarded. Financial award applicants required to submit FAFSA. *Unit head:* Dr. Mary Janeczek, Chair, Division of Education, 413-594-2761, Fax: 413-592-4871, E-mail: janeczeke@elms.edu. *Application contact:* Nancy Davis, Director, Office of Graduate and Continuing Education Admissions, 413-265-2239, E-mail: davisn@elms.edu.

Elon University, Program in Education, Elon, NC 27244-2010. Offers elementary education (M Ed). *Accreditation:* NCATE. *Program availability:* Part-time. *Faculty:* 7 full-time (4 women), 4 part-time/adjunct (all women). *Students:* 49 part-time (43 women); includes 20 minority (6 Black or African American, non-Hispanic/Latino; 2 Asian, non-Hispanic/Latino; 10 Hispanic/Latino; 2 Two or more races, non-Hispanic/Latino), 1 international. Average age 34. 51 applicants, 90% accepted, 37 enrolled. In 2018, 10 master's awarded. *Entrance requirements:* For master's, GRE, MAT. Additional exam requirements/recommendations for international students: Required—TOEFL (minimum score 550 paper-based; 79 iBT). *Application deadline:* For fall admission, 5/1 for domestic students. Applications are processed on a rolling basis. Application fee: $50. Electronic applications accepted. *Financial support:* Federal Work-Study and scholarships/grants available. Support available to part-time students. Financial award application deadline: 6/1; financial award applicants required to submit FAFSA. *Faculty research:* Teaching reading to low-achieving second and third graders, pre- and post-student teaching attitudes, children's writing, whole language methodology, critical creative thinking. *Unit head:* Dr. Ann Bullock, Dean of the School of Education/Professor, 336-278-5900, E-mail: abullock9@elon.edu. *Application contact:* Art Fadde, Director of Graduate Admissions, 800-334-8448 Ext. 3, Fax: 336-278-7699, E-mail: afadde@elon.edu. Website: http://www.elon.edu/med

Embry-Riddle Aeronautical University–Worldwide, Department of Aeronautics, Graduate Studies, Daytona Beach, FL 32114-3900. Offers aeronautics (MSA);

aeronautics and design (MS); aviation & aerospace sustainability (MS); aviation maintenance (MAM); aviation/aerospace research (MS); education (MS); human factors (MSHFS); occupational safety management (MS); operations (MS); safety/emergency response (MS); space systems (MS); unmanned systems (MS). *Program availability:* Part-time, evening/weekend, 100% online. *Faculty:* 30 full-time (11 women), 124 part-time/adjunct (19 women). *Students:* 663 full-time (149 women), 877 part-time (191 women); includes 420 minority (144 Black or African American, non-Hispanic/Latino; 6 American Indian or Alaska Native, non-Hispanic/Latino; 58 Asian, non-Hispanic/Latino; 168 Hispanic/Latino; 3 Native Hawaiian or other Pacific Islander, non-Hispanic/Latino; 41 Two or more races, non-Hispanic/Latino), 126 international. Average age 37. 602 applicants, 71% accepted, 272 enrolled. In 2018, 499 master's awarded. *Degree requirements:* For master's, comprehensive exam, thesis (for some programs), capstone or thesis dependent on degree program. *Entrance requirements:* For master's, GRE required for MSHF. Additional exam requirements/recommendations for international students: Required—TOEFL (minimum score 550 paper-based; 79 iBT), IELTS (minimum score 6), TOEFL or IELTS required for Applicants for whom English is not the primary language. *Application deadline:* Applications are processed on a rolling basis. Application fee: $50. Electronic applications accepted. *Expenses: Tuition:* Full-time $7980; part-time $665 per credit hour. Tuition and fees vary according to course load, degree level and program. *Financial support:* Career-related internships or fieldwork and scholarships/grants available. Financial award applicants required to submit FAFSA. *Unit head:* Kenneth Witcher, PhD, Associate Professor and Dean, College of Aeronautics, E-mail: kenneth.witcher@erau.edu. *Application contact:* Worldwide Campus, 800-522-6787, E-mail: worldwide@erau.edu. Website: http://worldwide.erau.edu/colleges/aeronautics/department-aeronautics-graduate-studies/

Emmanuel College, Graduate and Professional Programs, Graduate Programs in Education, Boston, MA 02115. Offers moderate learning disabilities (Certificate); urban education (M Ed). *Program availability:* Part-time, evening/weekend. *Degree requirements:* For master's, 36 credits, including 6-credit practicum. *Entrance requirements:* For master's, transcripts from all regionally-accredited institutions attended (showing proof of bachelor's degree completion), 2 letters of recommendation, essay, resume. Additional exam requirements/recommendations for international students: Required—TOEFL. Electronic applications accepted. *Expenses:* Contact institution.

Emory & Henry College, Graduate Programs, Emory, VA 24327. Offers American history (MA Ed); education professional studies (M Ed); occupational therapy (MOT); organizational leadership (MCOL); physical therapy (DPT); physician assistant studies (MPAS); reading specialist (MA Ed). *Program availability:* Part-time. *Degree requirements:* For master's, thesis optional; for doctorate, thesis/dissertation optional. *Entrance requirements:* For master's, GRE or PRAXIS I, official transcripts from all colleges previously attended, three professional recommendations, essay. Additional exam requirements/recommendations for international students: Recommended—TOEFL, IELTS (minimum score 6). Electronic applications accepted. *Expenses:* Contact institution.

Emory University, Laney Graduate School, Division of Educational Studies, Atlanta, GA 30322-1100. Offers educational studies (MA, PhD); middle grades teaching (MAT); secondary teaching (MAT). *Accreditation:* NCATE. Terminal master's awarded for partial completion of doctoral program. *Degree requirements:* For master's, thesis; for doctorate, comprehensive exam, thesis/dissertation. *Entrance requirements:* For master's and doctorate, GRE General Test, minimum GPA of 3.0. Additional exam requirements/recommendations for international students: Required—TOEFL. Electronic applications accepted. *Faculty research:* Educational policy, educational measurement, urban and multicultural education, mathematics and science education, comparative education.

Emporia State University, Program in Teaching, Emporia, KS 66801-5415. Offers M Ed. *Program availability:* Part-time, online learning. *Entrance requirements:* For master's, GRE or MAT, minimum GPA of 2.5 on last 60 undergraduate hours; two personal references.

Evangel University, Department of Education, Springfield, MO 65802. Offers curriculum and instruction (M Ed); educational leadership (M Ed); literacy (M Ed); secondary teaching (M Ed). *Accreditation:* NCATE. *Program availability:* Part-time, evening/weekend, 100% online, blended/hybrid learning. *Entrance requirements:* For master's, PRAXIS II (preferred) or GRE, minimum undergraduate GPA of 3.0. Additional exam requirements/recommendations for international students: Required—TOEFL (minimum score 550 paper-based). Electronic applications accepted. Application fee is waived when completed online.

The Evergreen State College, Graduate Programs, Program in Teaching, Olympia, WA 98505. Offers MIT. *Faculty:* 5 full-time (all women), 1 (woman) part-time/adjunct. *Students:* 63 full-time (44 women); includes 15 minority (1 Black or African American, non-Hispanic/Latino; 6 Hispanic/Latino; 1 Native Hawaiian or other Pacific Islander, non-Hispanic/Latino; 7 Two or more races, non-Hispanic/Latino). Average age 30. 51 applicants, 92% accepted, 43 enrolled. In 2018, 25 master's awarded. *Degree requirements:* For master's, project, 20-week teaching internship. *Entrance requirements:* For master's, Washington Educator Skills Test-Basic (WEST-B), Washington Educator Skills Test-Endorsements, minimum undergraduate GPA of 3.0 for last 90 quarter hours; official transcript; resume; 3 letters of recommendation; personal statement; thesis-based essay; Washington State Patrol and FBI background check; 4 quarter credits in college level math; 8 quarter credits in social sciences; 10 quarter credits of academic writing. Additional exam requirements/recommendations for international students: Required—TOEFL (minimum score 600 paper-based; 100 iBT). *Application deadline:* For fall admission, 4/2 priority date for domestic and international students. Applications are processed on a rolling basis. Application fee: $50. Electronic applications accepted. *Expenses:* Contact institution. *Financial support:* In 2018–19, 42 students received support, including 16 fellowships with partial tuition reimbursements available (averaging $705 per year); career-related internships or fieldwork, institutionally sponsored loans, scholarships/grants, and tuition waivers (partial) also available. Financial award application deadline: 2/1; financial award applicants required to submit FAFSA. *Faculty research:* Literacy, children's and adolescent literature, language/literacy acquisition, learning theory, developmental/social/personal psychology, multicultural education, qualitative research, critical pedagogy, feminist theory, education and equity, language acquisition, art and storytelling, community-based teacher education, democratic/public education, social and political foundations of education in the United States, typography and bookmaking, theories of learning and brain development, research a. *Unit head:* Dr. Sue Feldman, Director, 360-867-6909, E-mail: feldmans@evergreen.edu. *Application contact:* Jazminne Bailey, Associate Director, 360-867-6559, Fax: 360-867-6575, E-mail: baileyj@evergreen.edu. Website: http://www.evergreen.edu/mit/

Fairfield University, Graduate School of Education and Allied Professions, Fairfield, CT 06824. Offers applied behavior analysis (ATC); applied psychology (MA); clinical mental health counseling (MA, CAS); educational technology (MA); elementary education (MA, CAS); family studies (MA); integration of spirituality and religion in counseling (ATC); marriage and family therapy (MA); reading and language development (Sixth Year Certificate); school counseling (MA, CAS); school psychology (MA, CAS); school-based marriage and family therapy (ATC); secondary education (MA); special education (MA, CAS); substance abuse counseling (ATC); teaching (Certificate); teaching and foundations (MA, CAS); TESOL, world languages, and bilingual education (MA, CAS). *Accreditation:* NCATE. *Program availability:* Part-time, evening/weekend. *Degree requirements:* For master's, comprehensive exam. *Entrance requirements:* For master's, minimum GPA of 3.0, 2 recommendations, resume. Additional exam requirements/recommendations for international students: Required—TOEFL (minimum score 550 paper-based; 84 iBT) or IELTS (minimum score 7.5). Electronic applications accepted. *Expenses:* Contact institution. *Faculty research:* Reading and literacy, writing, social justice and inequality in education, addictions and mental health issues, therapeutic relationships and clinical supervision.

Fairleigh Dickinson University, Florham Campus, Maxwell Becton College of Arts and Sciences, Department of English, Communication and Philosophy, Program in Creative Writing and Literature for Educators, Madison, NJ 07940-1099. Offers MA.

Fairleigh Dickinson University, Florham Campus, University College: Arts, Sciences, and Professional Studies, Peter Sammartino School of Education, Madison, NJ 07940-1099. Offers education for certified teachers (MA, Certificate); educational leadership (MA); instructional technology (Certificate); literacy/reading (Certificate); teaching (MAT).

Fairleigh Dickinson University, Metropolitan Campus, University College: Arts, Sciences, and Professional Studies, Peter Sammartino School of Education, Teaneck, NJ 07666-1914. Offers dyslexia specialist (Certificate); education for certified teachers (MA); educational leadership (MA); instructional technology (Certificate); learning disabilities (MA); literacy/reading (Certificate); multilingual education (MA); teacher of the handicapped (Certificate); teaching (MAT). *Accreditation:* TEAC. *Program availability:* Part-time. *Degree requirements:* For master's, research project (MAT).

Fairmont State University, Programs in Education, Fairmont, WV 26554. Offers digital media, new literacies and learning (M Ed); education (MAT); exercise science, fitness and wellness (M Ed); professional studies (M Ed); reading (M Ed); special education (M Ed). *Accreditation:* NCATE. *Program availability:* Part-time, evening/weekend, 100% online. *Entrance requirements:* For master's, GRE. Additional exam requirements/recommendations for international students: Required—TOEFL (minimum score 80 iBT), IELTS (minimum score 6.5). Electronic applications accepted.

Faulkner University, College of Education, Montgomery, AL 36109-3398. Offers counseling (MS); curriculum and instruction (M Ed); elementary education (M Ed); school counseling (M Ed). *Program availability:* Part-time, evening/weekend, 100% online, blended/hybrid learning. *Degree requirements:* For master's, 5+ hours in clinical training (for MS, M Ed in school counseling). *Entrance requirements:* For master's, MAT (minimum score of 370) or GRE (minimum score of 280) taken within last five years, bachelor's degree from regionally-accredited college or university; official transcripts from all colleges and universities attended; 3 letters of recommendation; goal statement (approximately 600 words); minimum cumulative GPA of 2.75 in undergraduate courses, 3.0 in graduate courses. Additional exam requirements/recommendations for international students: Required—TOEFL (minimum score 500 paper-based). Electronic applications accepted. *Expenses:* Contact institution.

Felician University, Program in Education, Lodi, NJ 07644-2117. Offers education (MA); educational leadership (principal/supervision) (MA); educational supervision (PMC); principal (PMC). *Accreditation:* TEAC. *Program availability:* Part-time, evening/weekend. *Degree requirements:* For master's and PMC, thesis, presentation. *Entrance requirements:* For master's, PRAXIS Core (Reading/Writing/Math), minimum GPA of 3.0, two professional letters of recommendation, personal statement, personal interview. Additional exam requirements/recommendations for international students: Required—TOEFL (minimum score 550 paper-based; 79 iBT), IELTS (minimum score 6.5), PTE (minimum score 56). Electronic applications accepted. Application fee is waived when completed online. *Expenses:* Contact institution. *Faculty research:* Educational leadership, administration, supervision, curriculum.

Ferris State University, College of Education and Human Services, School of Education, Big Rapids, MI 49307. Offers curriculum and instruction (M Ed), including special education, subject area; training and development (MSCTE). *Program availability:* Part-time, evening/weekend, blended/hybrid learning. *Faculty:* 7 full-time (4 women), 1 (woman) part-time/adjunct. *Students:* 4 full-time (3 women), 39 part-time (23 women); includes 7 minority (3 Black or African American, non-Hispanic/Latino; 2 Hispanic/Latino; 2 Two or more races, non-Hispanic/Latino), 2 international. Average age 38. 14 applicants, 93% accepted, 7 enrolled. In 2018, 18 master's awarded. *Degree requirements:* For master's, thesis, Capstone project. *Entrance requirements:* For master's, minimum undergraduate GPA of 3.0. Additional exam requirements/recommendations for international students: Required—TOEFL (minimum score 550 paper-based; 79 iBT), IELTS (minimum score 6.5), TOEFL (minimum score 550 paper-based, 79 iBT) or IELTS 6.5. *Application deadline:* For fall admission, 7/1 priority date for domestic and international students; for spring admission, 11/1 priority date for domestic and international students; for summer admission, 3/1 priority date for domestic and international students. Applications are processed on a rolling basis. Application fee: $0 ($30 for international students). Electronic applications accepted. Application fee is waived when completed online. *Financial support:* In 2018–19, 7 students received support. Career-related internships or fieldwork and scholarships/grants available. Support available to part-time students. Financial award applicants required to submit FAFSA. *Faculty research:* Game based education, needs of students with disabilities in post-secondary education, elementary education students with reading difficulties. *Unit head:* Leonard Johnson, Interim Dean, 231-591-3648, Fax: 231-591-2043, E-mail: LeonardJohnson@ferris.edu. *Application contact:* Liza Ing, Graduate Program Coordinator, 231-591-5362, Fax: 231-591-2043, E-mail: lizaIng@ferris.edu. Website: http://www.ferris.edu/education/education/

Fielding Graduate University, Graduate Programs, School of Leadership Studies, Programs in Education, Santa Barbara, CA 93105-3814. Offers digital teaching and learning (MA); leadership for change (Ed D). *Program availability:* Part-time, evening/weekend. *Faculty:* 4 full-time (2 women), 10 part-time/adjunct (4 women). *Students:* 74 full-time (55 women), 4 part-time (1 woman); includes 49 minority (25 Black or African American, non-Hispanic/Latino; 13 American Indian or Alaska Native, non-Hispanic/Latino; 2 Asian, non-Hispanic/Latino; 5 Hispanic/Latino; 4 Two or more races, non-Hispanic/Latino), 1 international. Average age 51. 28 applicants, 64% accepted, 13 enrolled. In 2018, 4 master's, 17 doctorates awarded. *Degree requirements:* For doctorate, thesis/dissertation. *Entrance requirements:* For master's, bachelor's degree from regionally-accredited U.S. institution or equivalent, resume, statement of purpose, official transcript; for doctorate, bachelor's or master's degree from regionally-accredited U.S. institution or equivalent, resume, statement of purpose, reflexive essay, official transcript. *Application deadline:* For fall admission, 7/16 for domestic and international students; for spring admission, 10/24 for domestic and international students; for summer admission, 2/18 for domestic and international students. Application fee: $75. Electronic applications accepted. *Expenses:* Https://www.fielding.edu/how-to-apply/tuition-financial-aid/tuition-fees/. *Financial support:* In 2018–19, 32 students received support. Research assistantships, teaching assistantships, and scholarships/grants

available. Support available to part-time students. Financial award applicants required to submit FAFSA. *Faculty research:* Education, leadership, change. *Unit head:* Dr. Barbara Mink, E-mail: bmink@fielding.edu. *Application contact:* Enrollment Coordinator, 800-340-1099 Ext. 4098, Fax: 805-687-9793, E-mail: admissions@fielding.edu.
Website: http://www.fielding.edu/our-programs/school-of-leadership-studies/

Florida Agricultural and Mechanical University, Division of Graduate Studies, Research, and Continuing Education, College of Education, Tallahassee, FL 32307-3200. Offers M Ed, MBE, MS, MS Ed, PhD. *Accreditation:* NCATE. *Program availability:* Part-time, evening/weekend. *Degree requirements:* For master's, thesis (for some programs); for doctorate, thesis/dissertation. *Entrance requirements:* For master's, GRE General Test, minimum GPA of 3.0. Additional exam requirements/recommendations for international students: Required—TOEFL.

Florida Atlantic University, College of Education, Boca Raton, FL 33431-0991. Offers M Ed, MA, MS, Ed D, PhD, Ed S. *Accreditation:* NCATE. *Program availability:* Part-time, evening/weekend. *Faculty:* 85 full-time (50 women), 30 part-time/adjunct (15 women). *Students:* 315 full-time (236 women), 500 part-time (376 women); includes 353 minority (180 Black or African American, non-Hispanic/Latino; 15 Asian, non-Hispanic/Latino; 139 Hispanic/Latino; 19 Two or more races, non-Hispanic/Latino), 21 international. Average age 34. 927 applicants, 40% accepted, 288 enrolled. In 2018, 224 master's, 44 doctorates, 12 other advanced degrees awarded. *Degree requirements:* For doctorate, comprehensive exam, thesis/dissertation; for Ed S, departmental qualifying exam. *Entrance requirements:* For master's, doctorate, and Ed S, GRE General Test. Additional exam requirements/recommendations for international students: Required—TOEFL (minimum score 500 paper-based; 61 iBT), IELTS (minimum score 6). *Application deadline:* For fall admission, 5/1 for domestic students. Applications are processed on a rolling basis. Application fee: $30. Electronic applications accepted. *Expenses: Tuition, area resident:* Full-time $7400; part-time $369.82 per credit. Tuition, state resident: full-time $7400; part-time $369.82 per credit. Tuition, nonresident: full-time $20,496; part-time $1024.81 per credit. *Financial support:* Fellowships with partial tuition reimbursements, research assistantships with partial tuition reimbursements, teaching assistantships with partial tuition reimbursements, career-related internships or fieldwork, Federal Work-Study, and unspecified assistantships available. *Faculty research:* Marriage and family counseling, multicultural education, self-directed learning, assessment, reading. *Unit head:* Dr. Valerie Bristor, Dean, 561-297-3357, E-mail: bristor@fau.edu. *Application contact:* Dr. Valerie Bristor, Dean, 561-297-3357, E-mail: bristor@fau.edu.
Website: http://www.coe.fau.edu/

Florida Gulf Coast University, College of Education, Fort Myers, FL 33965-6565. Offers M Ed, MA. *Program availability:* Part-time, evening/weekend, online learning. *Entrance requirements:* For master's, GRE General Test, MAT, minimum GPA of 3.0. Additional exam requirements/recommendations for international students: Required—TOEFL (minimum score 550 paper-based). Electronic applications accepted. *Faculty research:* Inclusion, emergent literacy, pre-service and in-service teacher education, education policy.

Florida Memorial University, School of Education, Miami-Dade, FL 33054. Offers elementary education (MS); exceptional student education (MS); reading (MS). *Degree requirements:* For master's, comprehensive exam or thesis, field and clinical experiences, exit exam. *Entrance requirements:* For master's, GRE, CLAST, PRAXIS I, baccalaureate or graduate degree with minimum GPA of 3.0 in last 60 hours, 3 recommendations. Additional exam requirements/recommendations for international students: Recommended—TOEFL.

Florida Southern College, School of Education, Lakeland, FL 33801-5698. Offers M Ed, MAT, Ed D. *Program availability:* Part-time, evening/weekend, 100% online, blended/hybrid learning. *Faculty:* 11 full-time (8 women), 13 part-time/adjunct (8 women). *Students:* 127 full-time (96 women), 88 part-time (75 women); includes 67 minority (34 Black or African American, non-Hispanic/Latino; 1 American Indian or Alaska Native, non-Hispanic/Latino; 28 Hispanic/Latino; 2 Native Hawaiian or other Pacific Islander, non-Hispanic/Latino; 2 Two or more races, non-Hispanic/Latino), 1 international. Average age 41. 50 applicants, 100% accepted, 31 enrolled. In 2018, 36 master's, 10 doctorates awarded. *Degree requirements:* For master's, comprehensive exam (for some programs), thesis (for some programs), MAT in Transformational Curriculum and Instruction: FTCE General Knowledge test, Professional Education Exam, and Program includes thesis. MEd in Transformational Curriculum and Instruction: Program includes thesis. MEd in Educational Leadership - Florida Educational Leadership Exam (FELE); for doctorate, thesis/dissertation. *Entrance requirements:* For master's, entrance exam not required if GPA greater than 3.0, all programs: letter of reference, resume, personal statement, bachelor's degree; MAT in Transformational Curriculum and Instruction: Photo ID, Background Clearance, Personal Interview; MEd in Teaching Curriculum Instruction: FLDOE Certification; MEd in Educational Leadership: FLDOE Certification, FLDOE Teaching Requirement Form; for doctorate, entrance exam not required if GPA greater than 3.0, both programs: letter of reference, resume, personal statement, master's degree, personal interview; EdD Educational Leadership: Master of Education or FLDOE Certification. Additional exam requirements/recommendations for international students: Required—TOEFL (minimum score 550 paper-based; 79 iBT), IELTS (minimum score 6.5). *Application deadline:* For fall admission, 8/15 priority date for domestic and international students; for spring admission, 12/1 priority date for domestic and international students; for summer admission, 4/1 priority date for domestic and international students. Applications are processed on a rolling basis. Electronic applications accepted. Application fee is waived when completed online. *Expenses:* MAT and MED: Credit hrs needed: 34-47; Tuition per credit hr: $430; Technology fees per term: 5-8 Credit hrs: $50,8-12 Credit hrs: $100. EdD: Credit Hrs needed: 60; Tuition per credit hr: $474; Technology fee per term: 5-8 Credit Hrs: $50, 9-12 Credit Hrs: $100. *Financial support:* In 2018–19, 4 students received support. Application deadline: 8/21; applicants required to submit FAFSA. *Unit head:* Dr. Tracey Tedder, Dean, 863-680-4177, Fax: 863-680-4102, E-mail: ttedder@flsouthern.edu. *Application contact:* Kristen Pinner, Director of Adult and Graduate Admission, 863-680-3912, Fax: 863-680-3872, E-mail: kpinner@flsouthern.edu.
Website: www.flsouthern.edu/adult-graduate/graduate.aspx

Florida State University, The Graduate School, College of Education, Tallahassee, FL 32306. Offers MS, Ed D, PhD, Certificate, Ed S, MS/Ed S. *Accreditation:* NCATE. *Program availability:* Part-time, evening/weekend, blended/hybrid learning, asynchronous, minimal on-campus study. Terminal master's awarded for partial completion of doctoral program. *Degree requirements:* For master's and other advanced degree, comprehensive exam, thesis optional; for doctorate, comprehensive exam, thesis/dissertation, diagnostic exam, preliminary exam, prospectus defense, dissertation defense. *Entrance requirements:* For master's, doctorate, and other advanced degree, GRE General Test, minimum upper-division GPA of 3.0. Additional exam requirements/recommendations for international students: Required—TOEFL (minimum score 550 paper-based, 80 iBT), IELTS (minimum score 6.5), Michigan English Language Assessment Battery (minimum score 77), or PTE (minimum score 55). Electronic applications accepted. *Expenses: Tuition, area resident:* Part-time $479.32 per credit hour. Tuition and fees vary according to campus/location and program. *Faculty research:* Sport management and administration, educational psychology, instructional systems, teacher education, educational leadership and policy.

Fontbonne University, Graduate Programs, St. Louis, MO 63105-3098. Offers accounting (MBA, MS); art (MA); art (K-12) (MAT); business (MBA); computer science (MS); deaf education (MA); early intervention in deaf education (MA); education (MA), including autism spectrum disorders, curriculum and instruction, diverse learners, early childhood education, reading, special education; elementary education (MAT); family and consumer sciences (MA), including multidisciplinary health communication studies; fine arts (MFA); instructional design and technology (MS); management and leadership (MM); middle school education (MAT); secondary education (MAT); special education (MAT); speech-language pathology (MS); supply chain management (MS); theatre (MA). *Accreditation:* ASHA. *Program availability:* Part-time, evening/weekend, online learning. *Degree requirements:* For master's, comprehensive exam (for some programs), thesis (for some programs). *Entrance requirements:* Additional exam requirements/recommendations for international students: Required—TOEFL (minimum score 500 paper-based; 65 iBT). Electronic applications accepted.

Fordham University, Graduate School of Education, New York, NY 10023. Offers MSE, MST, Ed D, PhD, Adv C. *Accreditation:* NCATE. *Program availability:* Part-time, evening/weekend. Terminal master's awarded for partial completion of doctoral program. *Degree requirements:* For master's and Adv C, comprehensive exam (for some programs); for doctorate, comprehensive exam (for some programs), thesis/dissertation. *Entrance requirements:* For master's and Adv C, minimum GPA of 3.0; for doctorate, GRE or MAT. Additional exam requirements/recommendations for international students: Required—TOEFL (minimum score 577 paper-based, 90 iBT) or IELTS (minimum score 7.0). Electronic applications accepted. *Expenses:* Contact institution.

Fort Hays State University, Graduate School, College of Education, Hays, KS 67601-4099. Offers MS, MSE, Ed S. *Accreditation:* NCATE. *Program availability:* Part-time. *Degree requirements:* For master's, comprehensive exam, thesis or alternative. *Entrance requirements:* Additional exam requirements/recommendations for international students: Required—TOEFL (minimum score 550 paper-based). Electronic applications accepted.

Franciscan University of Steubenville, Graduate Programs, Department of Education, Steubenville, OH 43952-1763. Offers administration (MS Ed); teaching (MS Ed). *Accreditation:* NCATE. *Program availability:* Part-time, evening/weekend, online learning. *Degree requirements:* For master's, project. *Entrance requirements:* For master's, minimum undergraduate GPA of 2.5 or written exam. Additional exam requirements/recommendations for international students: Required—TOEFL. Electronic applications accepted. Application fee is waived when completed online. *Expenses:* Contact institution.

Francis Marion University, Graduate Programs, School of Education, Florence, SC 29502-0547. Offers learning disabilities (M Ed, MAT). *Accreditation:* NCATE. *Program availability:* Part-time. *Degree requirements:* For master's, comprehensive exam (for some programs), thesis (for some programs), supervised internship (for MAT). *Entrance requirements:* For master's, GRE General Test, MAT, NTE, or PRAXIS II, official transcripts; two letters of recommendation. Additional exam requirements/recommendations for international students: Required—TOEFL (minimum score 550 paper-based; 79 iBT). *Faculty research:* Identification and alternate assessment of at-risk students.

Freed-Hardeman University, Program in Education, Henderson, TN 38340-2399. Offers curriculum and instruction (M Ed); school counseling (M Ed), including administration and supervision, special education; school leadership (Ed S). *Accreditation:* NCATE. *Program availability:* Part-time, evening/weekend. *Degree requirements:* For master's, comprehensive exam, thesis optional; for Ed S, thesis. *Entrance requirements:* For master's, GRE General Test or NTE; for Ed S, 3 years of teaching experience. Additional exam requirements/recommendations for international students: Required—TOEFL (minimum score 500 paper-based).

Fresno Pacific University, Graduate Programs, School of Education, Fresno, CA 93702-4709. Offers MA, MA Ed, Certificate. *Program availability:* Part-time, evening/weekend. *Degree requirements:* For master's, thesis (for some programs). *Entrance requirements:* For master's, interview; GMAT, GRE, MAT, or 6 units of course work with a faculty recommendation. Additional exam requirements/recommendations for international students: Required—TOEFL (minimum score 550 paper-based). Electronic applications accepted.

Frostburg State University, College of Education, Frostburg, MD 21532-1099. Offers M Ed, MAT, MS, Ed D. *Accreditation:* NCATE. *Program availability:* Part-time, evening/weekend. *Faculty:* 14 full-time (8 women), 29 part-time/adjunct (22 women). *Students:* 90 full-time (62 women), 175 part-time (125 women); includes 30 minority (19 Black or African American, non-Hispanic/Latino; 2 Asian, non-Hispanic/Latino; 5 Hispanic/Latino; 4 Two or more races, non-Hispanic/Latino), 1 international. Average age 30. 164 applicants, 81% accepted, 100 enrolled. In 2018, 98 master's, 7 doctorates awarded. *Entrance requirements:* Additional exam requirements/recommendations for international students: Required—TOEFL. *Application deadline:* For fall admission, 7/15 priority date for domestic students. Applications are processed on a rolling basis. Application fee: $45. Electronic applications accepted. *Financial support:* In 2018–19, 29 research assistantships with full tuition reimbursements (averaging $5,000 per year) were awarded; career-related internships or fieldwork and Federal Work-Study also available. Financial award application deadline: 4/1; financial award applicants required to submit FAFSA. *Unit head:* Dr. Boyce Williams, Interim Dean, 301-687-4759, E-mail: bcwilliams@frostburg.edu. *Application contact:* Vickie Mazer, Director, Graduate Services, 301-687-7053, Fax: 301-687-4597, E-mail: vmmazer@frostburg.edu.

Furman University, Graduate Division, Department of Education, Greenville, SC 29613. Offers curriculum and instruction (MA); early childhood education (MA); educational leadership (Ed S); English as a second language (MA); literacy (MA); school leadership (MA); special education (MA). *Accreditation:* NCATE. *Program availability:* Part-time, online learning. *Degree requirements:* For master's, comprehensive exam (for some programs), thesis or alternative. *Entrance requirements:* For master's, PRAXIS II. *Expenses: Tuition:* Full-time $27,500; part-time $7290 per credit. Tuition and fees vary according to program. *Faculty research:* Literacy, pedagogy and practice, social justice, advanced leadership, achievement in high poverty schools.

Gallaudet University, The Graduate School, Washington, DC 20002-3625. Offers American Sign Language/English bilingual early childhood deaf education: birth to 5 (Certificate); audiology (Au D); clinical psychology (PhD); deaf and hard of hearing infants, toddlers, and their families (Certificate); deaf education (MA, Ed S); deaf history (Certificate); deaf studies (Certificate); educating deaf students with disabilities (Certificate); education: teacher preparation (MA), including deaf education, early childhood education and deaf education, elementary education and deaf education, secondary education and deaf education; educational neuroscience (PhD); hearing, speech and language sciences (MS, PhD); international development (MA); interpretation (MA, PhD), including combined interpreting practice and research (MA), interpreting research (MA); linguistics (MA, PhD); mental health counseling (MA); peer mentoring (Certificate); public administration (MPA); school counseling (MA); school

psychology (Psy S); sign language teaching (MA); social work (MSW); speech-language pathology (MS). *Program availability:* Part-time. Terminal master's awarded for partial completion of doctoral program. *Degree requirements:* For master's, comprehensive exam (for some programs), thesis optional; for doctorate, comprehensive exam, thesis/dissertation. *Entrance requirements:* For master's and doctorate, GRE General Test or MAT, letters of recommendation, interviews, goals statement, American Sign Language proficiency interview, written English competency. Additional exam requirements/recommendations for international students: Required—TOEFL. Electronic applications accepted. *Faculty research:* Signing math dictionaries, telecommunications access, cancer genetics, linguistics, visual language and visual learning, integrated quantum materials, deaf legal discourse, advance recruitment and retention in geosciences.

Gannon University, School of Graduate Studies, College of Humanities, Education, and Social Sciences, School of Education, Erie, PA 16541-0001. Offers curriculum and instruction (M Ed); curriculum supervisor (Certificate); English as a second language (Certificate); principal certification (Certificate); reading (M Ed); reading specialist (Certificate); superintendent letter of eligibility (Certificate). *Program availability:* Part-time, evening/weekend, 100% online. *Degree requirements:* For master's, thesis (for some programs), portfolio project. *Entrance requirements:* For master's, GRE, bachelor's degree from accredited institution, letters of recommendation, transcripts, teaching certificate (for some programs), minimum GPA of 3.0; for Certificate, GRE, master's degree (for some programs), teaching certificate, minimum GPA of 3.0, experience in field (for some programs). Additional exam requirements/recommendations for international students: Required—TOEFL (minimum score 79 iBT). Electronic applications accepted. Application fee is waived when completed online. *Expenses:* Contact institution.

Gardner-Webb University, Graduate School, School of Education, Boiling Springs, NC 28017. Offers curriculum and instruction (Ed D); educational leadership (Ed D); executive leadership studies (MA, Ed S); organizational leadership (Ed D); school administration (MA). *Accreditation:* NCATE. *Program availability:* Part-time, evening/weekend. *Degree requirements:* For master's, comprehensive exam. *Entrance requirements:* For master's, GRE General Test or NTE, PRAXIS, minimum GPA of 2.5. Electronic applications accepted. *Expenses:* Contact institution.

Geneva College, Master of Arts in Higher Education Program, Beaver Falls, PA 15010-3599. Offers campus ministry (MA); college teaching (MA); educational leadership (MA); student affairs administration (MA). *Program availability:* Part-time, evening/weekend, blended/hybrid learning. *Degree requirements:* For master's, 36 hours (27 in core courses) including a capstone research project. *Entrance requirements:* For master's, minimum GPA of 3.0, writing sample, 3 letters of recommendation, essay on motivation for participation in the program. Additional exam requirements/recommendations for international students: Required—TOEFL. Electronic applications accepted. *Expenses:* Contact institution. *Faculty research:* Learning theories, church-related higher education, organizational culture, sexual assault and transgender students at Christian colleges, emerging technology in higher education.

George Fox University, College of Education, Newberg, OR 97132-2697. Offers M Ed, MA, MAT, Ed D, Certificate, Ed S.

George Mason University, College of Education and Human Development, Fairfax, VA 22030. Offers M Ed, MS, PhD, Certificate. *Accreditation:* NCATE. *Program availability:* Part-time, evening/weekend, 100% online, blended/hybrid learning. *Faculty:* 129 full-time (91 women), 201 part-time/adjunct (133 women). *Students:* 486 full-time (379 women), 2,256 part-time (1,819 women); includes 804 minority (296 Black or African American, non-Hispanic/Latino; 4 American Indian or Alaska Native, non-Hispanic/Latino; 222 Asian, non-Hispanic/Latino; 226 Hispanic/Latino; 9 Native Hawaiian or other Pacific Islander, non-Hispanic/Latino; 47 Two or more races, non-Hispanic/Latino), 111 international. Average age 34. 1,402 applicants, 86% accepted, 884 enrolled. In 2018, 843 master's, 46 doctorates, 288 other advanced degrees awarded. *Degree requirements:* For doctorate, comprehensive exam, final project, internship. *Entrance requirements:* For master's, PRAXIS Core, GRE, or MAT (depending on program), minimum GPA of 3.0 in last 60 hours of course work, goals statement, interview or writing sample; for doctorate, GRE, appropriate master's degree, transcripts, resume, interview, 3 letters of recommendation, goals statement; 3 years of experience in educational, community, and human development settings (depending on program). Additional exam requirements/recommendations for international students: Required—TOEFL (minimum score 575 paper-based; 88 iBT), IELTS (minimum score 6.5), PTE (minimum score 59). *Application deadline:* For fall admission, 4/2 for domestic and international students; for spring admission, 11/1 for domestic and international students. Application fee: $75 ($80 for international students). Electronic applications accepted. *Expenses:* $489 per credit in-state tuition; $1,346.75 per credit out-of-state tuition (discounted to $689 per credit). *Financial support:* In 2018–19, 97 students received support, including 2 fellowships, 71 research assistantships with tuition reimbursements available (averaging $13,398 per year), 34 teaching assistantships with tuition reimbursements available (averaging $5,666 per year); career-related internships or fieldwork, Federal Work-Study, scholarships/grants, unspecified assistantships, and health care benefits (for full-time research or teaching assistantship recipients) also available. Support available to part-time students. Financial award application deadline: 3/1; financial award applicants required to submit FAFSA. *Faculty research:* Special education/human disabilities, mathematics/science/technology education, education leadership, school/community/agency/higher education, counseling and administration. *Total annual research expenditures:* $9.1 million. *Unit head:* Mark Ginsberg, Dean, 703-993-2004, Fax: 703-993-2001, E-mail: mginsber@gmu.edu. *Application contact:* Nicole Mariam, Graduate Admissions Coordinator, 703-993-3832, Fax: 703-993-2020, E-mail: nwhite5@gmu.edu.
Website: http://cehd.gmu.edu/

Georgetown College, Department of Education, Georgetown, KY 40324-1696. Offers reading and writing (MA Ed); special education (MA Ed); teaching (MA Ed). *Accreditation:* NCATE. *Program availability:* Part-time. *Degree requirements:* For master's, portfolio. *Entrance requirements:* For master's, teaching certificate, minimum GPA of 2.7 or GRE General Test.

The George Washington University, Graduate School of Education and Human Development, Washington, DC 20052. Offers M Ed, MA, MA Ed, MA Ed/HD, MAT, Ed D, PhD, Certificate, Ed S, Graduate Certificate, Teaching Certificate. *Accreditation:* NCATE. *Program availability:* Part-time, evening/weekend, online learning. *Students:* 384 full-time (312 women), 1,060 part-time (797 women); includes 497 minority (253 Black or African American, non-Hispanic/Latino; 5 American Indian or Alaska Native, non-Hispanic/Latino; 66 Asian, non-Hispanic/Latino; 126 Hispanic/Latino; 1 Native Hawaiian or other Pacific Islander, non-Hispanic/Latino; 46 Two or more races, non-Hispanic/Latino), 88 international. Average age 36. 1,625 applicants, 69% accepted, 567 enrolled. In 2018, 390 master's, 74 doctorates, 104 other advanced degrees awarded. *Degree requirements:* For master's and other advanced degree, comprehensive exam; for doctorate, comprehensive exam, thesis/dissertation. *Entrance requirements:* For master's, GRE General Test or MAT, minimum GPA of 2.75; for doctorate, GRE General Test or MAT, interview, minimum GPA of 3.3; for other advanced degree, GRE General Test or MAT, minimum GPA of 3.3. *Application deadline:* For fall admission, 1/15 priority date for domestic students; for spring admission, 10/1 for domestic students. Applications are processed on a rolling basis. Application fee: $75. Electronic applications accepted. *Financial support:* In 2018–19, 279 students received support. Fellowships, research assistantships, teaching assistantships, career-related internships or fieldwork, Federal Work-Study, and tuition waivers (full and partial) available. Support available to part-time students. Financial award application deadline: 1/15. *Faculty research:* Policy, special education, bilingual education, counseling, human resource development. *Total annual research expenditures:* $4.6 million. *Unit head:* Michael Feuer, Dean, 202-994-6161, Fax: 202-994-7207, E-mail: mjfeuer@gwu.edu. *Application contact:* Sarah Lang, Director of Graduate Admissions, 202-994-1447, Fax: 202-994-7207, E-mail: slang@gwu.edu.
Website: http://gsehd.gwu.edu/

Georgia College & State University, Graduate School, The John H. Lounsbury College of Education, Milledgeville, GA 31061. Offers M Ed, MAT, Ed S. *Accreditation:* NCATE. *Program availability:* Evening/weekend, 100% online, blended/hybrid learning. *Degree requirements:* For master's, minimum GPA of 3.0, complete program within 6 years; for Ed S, minimum GPA of 3.0, complete program within 4 years. Electronic applications accepted. *Expenses:* Contact institution.

Georgian Court University, School of Education, Lakewood, NJ 08701-2697. Offers administration and leadership (MA); autism spectrum disorders (Certificate); education (M Ed, MAT); instructional technology (M Mat SE, MA, Certificate). *Accreditation:* TEAC. *Program availability:* Part-time, evening/weekend. *Faculty:* 10 full-time (6 women), 28 part-time/adjunct (17 women). *Students:* 32 full-time (25 women), 396 part-time (324 women); includes 84 minority (35 Black or African American, non-Hispanic/Latino; 10 Asian, non-Hispanic/Latino; 36 Hispanic/Latino; 3 Two or more races, non-Hispanic/Latino). Average age 34. 323 applicants, 67% accepted, 148 enrolled. In 2018, 152 master's, 4 other advanced degrees awarded. *Degree requirements:* For master's, comprehensive exam (for some programs), thesis (for some programs). *Entrance requirements:* For master's, GRE, GMAT or NTE/PRAXIS, 3 letters of recommendation. Additional exam requirements/recommendations for international students: Required—TOEFL (minimum score 550 paper-based; 79 iBT). *Application deadline:* For fall admission, 8/15 priority date for domestic students, 5/1 for international students; for spring admission, 1/15 priority date for domestic students, 10/1 for international students. Applications are processed on a rolling basis. Application fee: $40. Electronic applications accepted. *Expenses: Tuition:* Full-time $856; part-time $856 per credit hour. *Required fees:* $968; $496 per unit. $248 per semester. Tuition and fees vary according to campus/location and program. *Financial support:* Scholarships/grants, health care benefits, and unspecified assistantships available. Financial award application deadline: 4/15; financial award applicants required to submit FAFSA. *Unit head:* Dr. Christopher Campisano, Dean of School of Education, 732-987-2729, E-mail: ccampisano@georgian.edu. *Application contact:* Patrick Givens, Director of Graduate and Professional Studies Admissions, 732-987-2736, Fax: 732-987-2000, E-mail: gps@georgian.edu.
Website: https://georgian.edu/academics/school-of-education/

Georgia Southern University, Jack N. Averitt College of Graduate Studies, College of Education, Statesboro, GA 30460. Offers M Ed, MAT, Ed D, Ed S. *Accreditation:* NCATE. *Program availability:* Part-time, evening/weekend, 100% online, blended/hybrid learning. *Degree requirements:* For master's, comprehensive exam (for some programs), thesis optional, portfolio or assessments; for doctorate, comprehensive exam, thesis/dissertation, exams; for Ed S, thesis (for some programs), assessments, field-based research projects. *Entrance requirements:* For doctorate, GRE General Test or MAT, minimum GPA of 3.5, letters of reference, writing sample; for Ed S, GRE General Test or MAT, minimum graduate GPA of 3.25. Additional exam requirements/recommendations for international students: Required—TOEFL (minimum score 550 paper-based; 80 iBT), IELTS (minimum score 6). Electronic applications accepted. *Expenses: Tuition, area resident:* Part-time $3324 per semester. Tuition, state resident: full-time $5814; part-time $3324 per semester. Tuition, nonresident: full-time $23,204; part-time $13,260 per semester. *Required fees:* $2092; $2092. Tuition and fees vary according to course load, degree level, campus/location and program. *Faculty research:* Scholarship of teaching and learning, curriculum studies, STEM education, social justice/multicultural education, teacher education best practices.

Georgia Southwestern State University, School of Education, Americus, GA 31709-4693. Offers early childhood education (M Ed, Ed S); middle grades education (Ed S); middle grades language arts (M Ed); middle grades mathematics (M Ed); special education (M Ed). *Accreditation:* NCATE. *Degree requirements:* For master's, minimum cumulative GPA of 3.0; maximum of 6 credit hours with C grade; no courses with D grade; degree completed within 7 calendar years; for Ed S, minimum GPA of 3.25 in all courses with no grade less than a B; degree must be completed within 7 calendar years from date of initial enrollment in graduate work. *Entrance requirements:* For master's, undergraduate degree from accredited institution; professional Georgia Teaching Certificate or eligibility; minimum undergraduate GPA of 2.75 as reported on official final transcripts from all accredited institutions attended; 2 confidential Administrative Recommendation Forms; for Ed S, master's degree from accredited college or university; professional Georgia Teaching Certificate or eligibility; minimum graduate GPA of 3.0 as reported on official final graduate transcripts from all accredited institutions attended; 2 confidential Administrative Recommendation Forms. Electronic applications accepted. *Expenses:* Contact institution.

Georgia State University, College of Education and Human Development, Atlanta, GA 30302-3083. Offers M Ed, MAT, MS, Ed D, PhD, Ed S. *Accreditation:* NCATE. *Program availability:* Part-time, evening/weekend, online learning. *Faculty:* 121 full-time (80 women), 52 part-time/adjunct (38 women). *Students:* 908 full-time (676 women), 553 part-time (388 women); includes 805 minority (568 Black or African American, non-Hispanic/Latino; 64 Asian, non-Hispanic/Latino; 109 Hispanic/Latino; 1 Native Hawaiian or other Pacific Islander, non-Hispanic/Latino; 63 Two or more races, non-Hispanic/Latino), 39 international. Average age 32. 1,209 applicants, 44% accepted, 399 enrolled. In 2018, 404 master's, 66 doctorates, 18 other advanced degrees awarded. Terminal master's awarded for partial completion of doctoral program. *Degree requirements:* For master's, comprehensive exam (for some programs), thesis (for some programs), minimum GPA of 3.0; for doctorate, comprehensive exam, thesis/dissertation, minimum GPA of 3.5; for Ed S, thesis or alternative, minimum GPA of 3.0. *Entrance requirements:* For master's, GRE, MAT (for some programs), minimum GPA of 2.5 on all undergraduate work attempted in which letter grades were awarded; for doctorate, GRE, MAT (for some programs), minimum GPA of 3.3 on all graduate coursework for which letter grades were awarded (for PhD); for Ed S, GRE, MAT (for some programs), graduate degree from regionally-accredited college or university unless specified otherwise by the program with minimum GPA of 3.25 on all graduate coursework for which letter grades were awarded. Application fee: $50. Electronic applications accepted. *Expenses: Tuition, area resident:* Full-time $9360; part-time $390 per credit hour. Tuition, state resident: full-time $9360; part-time $390 per credit hour. Tuition, nonresident: full-time $30,024; part-time $1251 per credit hour. *International tuition:* $30,024 full-time. *Required fees:* $2128. *Financial support:* In 2018–19, fellowships with full tuition reimbursements (averaging $25,000 per year), research assistantships with tuition reimbursements (averaging $4,867 per year), teaching assistantships with tuition reimbursements (averaging $4,683 per year) were awarded; career-related internships

or fieldwork, Federal Work-Study, scholarships/grants, tuition waivers (partial), and unspecified assistantships also available. Support available to part-time students. Financial award applicants required to submit FAFSA. *Faculty research:* Literacy: early, middle-secondary, adult and deaf/hard of hearing; teacher professional development, evaluation and urban education; STEM teacher education; health, physical activity and exercise science; school safety and counseling. *Unit head:* Dr. Paul A. Alberto, Dean, 404-413-8100, Fax: 404-413-8103, E-mail: palberto@gsu.edu. *Application contact:* Nancy Keita, Assistant Dean for Student Services, 404-413-8001, E-mail: nkeita@gsu.edu.
Website: https://education.gsu.edu/

Goddard College, Graduate Division, Master of Arts in Education Program, Plainfield, VT 05667-9432. Offers community education (MA); teacher licensure (MA). *Program availability:* Part-time, online learning. *Degree requirements:* For master's, thesis. *Entrance requirements:* For master's, PRAXIS, 3 letters of recommendation, statement of purpose, interview. Electronic applications accepted. *Faculty research:* Democratic curriculum leadership, service-learning and academic achievement, middle grades curriculum, community education, dual language.

Gonzaga University, School of Education, Spokane, WA 99258. Offers clinical mental health counseling (MA); educational leadership (M Ed, Ed D); elementary education (MIT); marriage and family counseling (MA); school counseling (MA); secondary education (MIT); special education (M Ed, MIT); sport and athletic administration (MA). *Accreditation:* NCATE. *Program availability:* Part-time, evening/weekend, 100% online, blended/hybrid learning. *Degree requirements:* For master's, comprehensive exam. *Entrance requirements:* For master's, GRE, MAT, and/or Washington Educator Skills Test-Basic (WEST-B), Washington Educator Skills Test-Endorsements (WEST-E), official transcripts from all colleges or universities attended, interview, two letters of recommendation, resume, essay, minimum GPA of 3.0. Additional exam requirements/recommendations for international students: Required—TOEFL (minimum score 580 paper-based, 88 iBT) or IELTS (minimum score 6.5). Electronic applications accepted. *Expenses:* Contact institution.

Gordon College, Graduate Education Program, Wenham, MA 01984-1899. Offers early childhood (M Ed); educational leadership (M Ed, Ed S); elementary education (M Ed); English as a second language (M Ed, Ed S); math specialist (M Ed); mathematics specialist (Ed S); middle school education (M Ed); moderate disabilities (M Ed); Montessori education (M Ed); reading (M Ed, Ed S); secondary education (M Ed). *Program availability:* Part-time, evening/weekend. *Degree requirements:* For master's, action research or clinical experience (for most programs); for Ed S, action research or clinical experience (for some programs). *Entrance requirements:* For master's, minimum undergraduate GPA of 3.0; 2 official undergraduate transcripts; professional resume; 3 recommendation letters (one professional reference, one academic reference, one personal reference); 500-700 word statement of purpose; for Ed S, minimum master's GPA of 3.3; 2 official transcripts from undergraduate and graduate schools; professional resume; 3 recommendation letters (one professional reference, one academic reference, one personal reference); 500-700 word statement of purpose. Additional exam requirements/recommendations for international students: Required—TOEFL (minimum score 550 paper-based, 80 iBT) or IELTS (minimum score 6.5). *Expenses:* Contact institution. *Faculty research:* Reading, early childhood development, English language learners, universal design for learning.

Goucher College, Graduate Programs in Education, Baltimore, MD 21204-2794. Offers at-risk and diverse learners (M Ed, Certificate); athletic program leadership and administration (M Ed, Certificate); elementary education (MAT); literacy strategies for content learning (M Ed); middle school (M Ed, Certificate); Montessori studies (M Ed); reading instruction (M Ed, Certificate); reducing student, classroom, and school disruption (M Ed); school improvement leadership (M Ed); secondary education (MAT); special education (MAT), including elementary education; special education for certified elementary and secondary teachers (M Ed); teacher as leader in technology (M Ed). *Program availability:* Part-time, evening/weekend. *Degree requirements:* For master's, thesis (M Ed), final presentation (MAT). *Entrance requirements:* For master's, minimum GPA of 3.0. Additional exam requirements/recommendations for international students: Required—TOEFL (minimum score 550 paper-based; 80 iBT), IELTS (minimum score 7). Electronic applications accepted. *Expenses:* Contact institution. *Faculty research:* Urban education, middle school, school improvement, teacher education, at-risk student achievement.

Governors State University, College of Education, Program in Education, University Park, IL 60484. Offers MA. *Program availability:* Part-time. *Faculty:* 19 full-time (12 women), 20 part-time/adjunct (13 women). *Students:* 15 part-time (12 women); includes 4 minority (all Hispanic/Latino). Average age 42. In 2018, 7 master's awarded. *Application deadline:* For fall admission, 4/1 for domestic students. Applications are processed on a rolling basis. Application fee: $50. Electronic applications accepted. *Financial support:* Application deadline: 5/1; applicants required to submit FAFSA. *Unit head:* Timothy Harrington, Chair, Division of Education, 708-534-5000 Ext. 4361, E-mail: tharrington2@govst.edu. *Application contact:* Timothy Harrington, Chair, Division of Education, 708-534-5000 Ext. 4361, E-mail: tharrington2@govst.edu.

Graceland University, Gleazer School of Education, Independence, MO 64050. Offers curriculum and instruction: collaborative learning and teaching (M Ed); differentiated instruction (M Ed); instructional leadership (M Ed); literacy instruction (M Ed); management in a quality classroom (M Ed); special education (M Ed); technology integration (M Ed). *Accreditation:* NCATE. *Program availability:* Part-time, 100% online. *Students:* 70 full-time (58 women), 36 part-time (34 women); includes 4 minority (1 Black or African American, non-Hispanic/Latino; 1 Asian, non-Hispanic/Latino; 1 Hispanic/Latino; 1 Two or more races, non-Hispanic/Latino). Average age 34. 29 applicants, 21% accepted, 1 enrolled. In 2018, 76 master's awarded. *Degree requirements:* For master's, action research capstone. *Entrance requirements:* For master's, minimum GPA of 3.0, teaching certificate, current teaching contract and license, two letters of reference, statement of professional goals, verification of ongoing access to computer technology, including email and Internet. Additional exam requirements/recommendations for international students: Required—TOEFL (minimum score 550 paper-based; 80 iBT). *Application deadline:* For winter admission, 11/1 for domestic students; for spring admission, 2/1 priority date for domestic students; for summer admission, 7/1 for domestic students. Applications are processed on a rolling basis. Application fee: $50. Electronic applications accepted. *Expenses:* Tuition, material fee, university tech fee, program support fee. *Financial support:* Tuition waivers (partial) available. Financial award applicants required to submit FAFSA. *Faculty research:* Literacy, technology, faculty mentoring, adult literacy, e-learning, online teaching. *Unit head:* Dr. Michele Dickey-Kotz, Dean, 641-784-5202, E-mail: dickey@graceland.edu. *Application contact:* Susan Freeze, Admissions Representative, 816-423-4676, Fax: 816-833-2990, E-mail: sfreeze1@graceland.edu.
Website: http://www.graceland.edu/education

Grambling State University, School of Graduate Studies and Research, College of Education, Grambling, LA 71245. Offers M Ed, MAT, MS, Ed D, PMC. *Accreditation:* NCATE. *Program availability:* Part-time, evening/weekend. *Degree requirements:* For master's, comprehensive exam, thesis (for some programs); for doctorate, comprehensive exam, thesis/dissertation. *Entrance requirements:* For master's, GRE; for doctorate, GRE (minimum score 1000, 500 on Verbal), master's degree, minimum GPA of 3.0 on last degree. Additional exam requirements/recommendations for international students: Required—TOEFL (minimum score 500 paper-based; 62 iBT). Electronic applications accepted.

Grand Canyon University, College of Education, Phoenix, AZ 85017-1097. Offers autism spectrum disorders (MA); curriculum and instruction (MA); early childhood education (M Ed); educational administration (M Ed); educational leadership (M Ed); elementary education (M Ed); gifted education (MA); instructional technology (MS); K-12 leadership (Ed S); reading (MA); secondary education (M Ed); secondary humanities education (M Ed); secondary STEM education (M Ed); special education (M Ed); teaching and learning (Ed D); teaching English to speakers of other languages (MA). *Program availability:* Part-time, evening/weekend, online learning. *Degree requirements:* For master's, publishable research paper (M Ed), e-portfolio. *Entrance requirements:* For master's, undergraduate degree from accredited, GCU-approved college, university, or program with minimum GPA 2.8. Additional exam requirements/recommendations for international students: Required—TOEFL (minimum score 550 paper-based; 79 iBT), IELTS (minimum score 6). Electronic applications accepted.

Grand Valley State University, College of Education, Programs in General Education, Allendale, MI 49401-9403. Offers adult and higher education (M Ed); early childhood education (M Ed); educational differentiation (M Ed); educational leadership (M Ed); educational technology integration (M Ed); elementary education (M Ed); middle level education (M Ed); school library media services (M Ed); secondary level education (M Ed); teaching English to speakers of other languages (M Ed). *Program availability:* Part-time, evening/weekend, 100% online, blended/hybrid learning. *Students:* 20 part-time (10 women); includes 1 minority (Black or African American, non-Hispanic/Latino). Average age 44. In 2018, 1 master's awarded. *Entrance requirements:* For master's, GRE General Test or minimum GPA of 3.0, last 60 credits from regionally-accredited college/university, 3 letters of recommendation. Additional exam requirements/recommendations for international students: Required—TOEFL (minimum iBT score of 80), IELTS (6.5), or Michigan English Language Assessment Battery (77). *Application deadline:* Applications are processed on a rolling basis. Application fee: $30. Electronic applications accepted. *Expenses:* $677 per credit hour, 33 credits. *Financial support:* In 2018–19, 1 student received support, including 1 fellowship; career-related internships or fieldwork, Federal Work-Study, scholarships/grants, and unspecified assistantships also available. *Faculty research:* Effectiveness of technology in education, parental involvement, effective teaching, effective schools research. *Unit head:* Dr. David Bair, Department Director, 616-331-6489, Fax: 616-331-6489, E-mail: baird@gvsu.edu. *Application contact:* Annukka Thelen, Director, Student Information and Services Center, 616-331-6205, Fax: 616-331-6217, E-mail: thelenan@gvsu.edu.
Website: http://www.gvsu.edu/coe/

Gratz College, Graduate Programs, Program in Education, Melrose Park, PA 19027. Offers MA. *Program availability:* Part-time. *Degree requirements:* For master's, one foreign language, project. *Entrance requirements:* For master's, teaching certificate.

Greensboro College, Program in Education, Greensboro, NC 27401-1875. Offers elementary education (M Ed); special education (M Ed). *Program availability:* Part-time, evening/weekend. *Degree requirements:* For master's, thesis. *Entrance requirements:* For master's, GRE, teacher license, 2 years of teaching experience, 2 letters of recommendation. Additional exam requirements/recommendations for international students: Required—TOEFL (minimum score 550 paper-based). Electronic applications accepted.

Greenville University, Program in Education, Greenville, IL 62246-0159. Offers education (MAT); elementary education (MAE); secondary education (MAE). *Degree requirements:* For master's, thesis (for some programs). *Entrance requirements:* For master's, GRE, Illinois Basic Skills Test, teacher certification. Electronic applications accepted.

Gwynedd Mercy University, School of Education, Gwynedd Valley, PA 19437-0901. Offers education (Ed D); educational administration (MS); master teacher (MS); school counseling (MS); special education (MS). *Program availability:* Part-time, evening/weekend, 100% online. *Degree requirements:* For master's, thesis, internship, practicum. *Entrance requirements:* For master's, GRE or MAT; PRAXIS I, minimum GPA of 3.0. *Expenses:* Contact institution. *Faculty research:* Learning and the brain, reading literacy, ethics and moral judgment, leadership, teaching and multicultural education.

Hamline University, School of Education, St. Paul, MN 55104-1284. Offers education (MA Ed, Ed D); English as a second language (MA); literacy education (MA); natural science and environmental education (MA Ed); teaching (MAT); teaching English to speakers of other languages (MA). *Accreditation:* NCATE (one or more programs are accredited). *Program availability:* Part-time, evening/weekend, 100% online, blended/hybrid learning. *Degree requirements:* For master's, thesis (for some programs), thesis or capstone project; for doctorate, comprehensive exam, thesis/dissertation. *Entrance requirements:* For master's, official transcripts, essay, letters of recommendation, minimum GPA of 3.0 from bachelor's work; resume and/or writing samples (for some programs); for doctorate, personal statement, master's degree with minimum GPA of 3.0, letters of recommendation, writing sample. Additional exam requirements/recommendations for international students: Required—TOEFL (minimum score 550 paper-based; 80 iBT), IELTS (minimum score 6.5). Electronic applications accepted. *Expenses:* Contact institution. *Faculty research:* Adult basic education, service-learning, teacher dispositions, diversity, technology.

Hampton University, School of Liberal Arts and Education, Hampton, VA 23668. Offers MA, MS, MT, PhD, Ed S. *Accreditation:* NCATE. *Program availability:* Part-time, evening/weekend. *Students:* 107 full-time (74 women), 39 part-time (30 women); includes 136 minority (135 Black or African American, non-Hispanic/Latino; 1 Asian, non-Hispanic/Latino). Average age 34. 71 applicants, 62% accepted, 33 enrolled. In 2018, 31 master's, 4 doctorates, 5 other advanced degrees awarded. *Degree requirements:* For master's, comprehensive exam, thesis (for some programs); for doctorate, comprehensive exam, thesis/dissertation. *Entrance requirements:* For master's, GRE General Test, PRAXIS; for doctorate, GRE General Test, GMAT. *Application deadline:* For fall admission, 6/1 priority date for domestic students, 4/1 priority date for international students; for winter admission, 9/1 priority date for international students; for spring admission, 11/1 for domestic students; for summer admission, 4/15 for domestic students, 2/1 priority date for international students. Applications are processed on a rolling basis. Application fee: $35. Electronic applications accepted. *Financial support:* Fellowships, research assistantships, teaching assistantships, career-related internships or fieldwork, Federal Work-Study, institutionally sponsored loans, and scholarships/grants available. Support available to part-time students. Financial award application deadline: 5/1; financial award applicants required to submit FAFSA. *Unit head:* Dr. Linda Malone-Colon, Dean, 757-727-5400. *Application contact:* Dr. Michelle Penn-Marshall, Dean, Graduate College, 757-727-5454, E-mail: hugrad@hamptonu.edu.
Website: http://edhd.hamptonu.edu/

Hannibal-LaGrange University, Program in Education, Hannibal, MO 63401-1999. Offers literacy (MS Ed); teaching and learning (MS Ed). *Program availability:* Part-time,

evening/weekend. *Degree requirements:* For master's, thesis, portfolio, documenting of program outcomes, public sharing of research. *Entrance requirements:* For master's, copy of current teaching certificate; minimum GPA of 2.75. *Faculty research:* Reading assessment, reading remediation, handwriting instruction, early childhood intervention.

Harding University, Cannon-Clary College of Education, Searcy, AR 72149-0001. Offers advanced studies in teaching and learning (M Ed); art (MSE); behavioral science (MSE); counseling (MS, Ed S); early childhood special education (M Ed, MSE); education (MSE); educational leadership (M Ed, Ed S); elementary education (M Ed); English (MSE); French (MSE); history/social science (MSE); kinesiology (MSE); math (MSE); reading (M Ed); secondary education (M Ed); Spanish (MSE); teaching (MAT); teaching English as a second language (MSE). *Accreditation:* NCATE. *Program availability:* Part-time, evening/weekend. *Degree requirements:* For master's, comprehensive exam (for some programs), thesis optional, portfolio(s); for Ed S, comprehensive exam, portfolio, project. *Entrance requirements:* For master's, GRE, MAT, PRAXIS; for Ed S, MAT or GRE. Additional exam requirements/recommendations for international students: Required—TOEFL (minimum score 550 paper-based; 79 iBT). *Faculty research:* Reading, comprehension, school violence, educational technology, behavior, college choice, differentiated instruction, brain-based teaching.

Hardin-Simmons University, Graduate School, College of Human Sciences and Educational Studies, Abilene, TX 79698-0001. Offers M Ed, Ed D. *Program availability:* Part-time. *Faculty:* 14 full-time (8 women), 2 part-time/adjunct (both women). *Students:* 12 full-time (7 women), 114 part-time (80 women); includes 33 minority (13 Black or African American, non-Hispanic/Latino; 1 Asian, non-Hispanic/Latino; 16 Hispanic/Latino; 3 Two or more races, non-Hispanic/Latino), 2 international. Average age 33. 51 applicants, 90% accepted, 38 enrolled. In 2018, 33 master's, 5 doctorates awarded. *Degree requirements:* For master's, comprehensive exam; for doctorate, comprehensive exam, thesis/dissertation. *Entrance requirements:* For master's, minimum undergraduate GPA of 3.0 in major, 2.7 overall. Additional exam requirements/recommendations for international students: Required—TOEFL (minimum score 550 paper-based; 79 iBT). *Application deadline:* For fall admission, 8/15 priority date for domestic students, 4/1 for international students; for spring admission, 1/5 priority date for domestic students, 9/1 for international students. Applications are processed on a rolling basis. Application fee: $50. Electronic applications accepted. *Expenses: Tuition:* Full-time $750; part-time $750 per credit hour. *Required fees:* $1300; $880 per credit. Tuition and fees vary according to degree level and program. *Financial support:* Fellowships, career-related internships or fieldwork, scholarships/grants, and coaching assistantships available. Support available to part-time students. Financial award application deadline: 6/30; financial award applicants required to submit FAFSA. *Unit head:* Dr. Perry Kay Brown, Dean, 325-670-1021, Fax: 325-670-5859, E-mail: pkbrown@hsutx.edu. *Application contact:* Dr. Nancy Kucinski, Dean of Graduate Studies, 325-670-1298, Fax: 325-670-1564, E-mail: gradoff@hsutx.edu.
Website: https://www.hsutx.edu/academics/schools-colleges/college-human-sciences-educational-studies/

Harrison Middleton University, Graduate Program, Tempe, AZ 85282. Offers education (MA, Ed D); humanities (MA); imaginative literature (MA); interdisciplinary studies (DA); jurisprudence (MA); natural science (MA); philosophy and religion (MA); social science (MA). *Program availability:* Part-time, evening/weekend, online learning. *Degree requirements:* For master's and doctorate, capstone project. *Entrance requirements:* For master's, interview; for doctorate, 2 academic letters of reference, interview, essay. Additional exam requirements/recommendations for international students: Required—TOEFL (minimum score 550 paper-based; 80 iBT). Electronic applications accepted. *Faculty research:* Japanese animation, educational leadership, war art, John Muir's wilderness.

Harvard University, Harvard Graduate School of Education, Cambridge, MA 02138. Offers Ed M, Ed L D, PhD. *Program availability:* Part-time. *Degree requirements:* For doctorate, thesis/dissertation (for some programs), capstone project or thesis (for Ed.L.D.). *Entrance requirements:* For master's, GRE General Test, statement of purpose, 3 letters of recommendation, resume, official transcripts; for doctorate, GRE General Test or GMAT (for Ed.L.D. only), statement of purpose, 3 letters of recommendation, resume, official transcripts, 2 short essay questions (for Ed.L.D. only). Additional exam requirements/recommendations for international students: Required—TOEFL (minimum score 613 paper-based; 104 iBT), TWE (minimum score 5). Electronic applications accepted. *Expenses:* Contact institution. *Faculty research:* Learning and development, educational leadership and organizations, education policy analysis.

Hastings College, Department of Teacher Education, Hastings, NE 68901. Offers MAT. *Accreditation:* NCATE. *Program availability:* Part-time. *Degree requirements:* For master's, comprehensive exam, thesis, or oral teaching presentation; digital portfolio. *Entrance requirements:* For master's, minimum GPA of 2.5, 2 letters of reference, interview. Additional exam requirements/recommendations for international students: Required—TOEFL. Electronic applications accepted. *Faculty research:* Assessments, performance competencies.

Hebrew College, Shoolman Graduate School of Jewish Education, Newton Centre, MA 02459. Offers early childhood Jewish education (Certificate); Jewish day school education (Certificate); Jewish education (MJ Ed); Jewish family education (Certificate); Jewish special education (Certificate); Jewish youth education, informal education and camping (Certificate). *Program availability:* Part-time, evening/weekend, online learning. *Degree requirements:* For master's, one foreign language. *Entrance requirements:* For master's, GRE, interview. Additional exam requirements/recommendations for international students: Required—TOEFL.

Hebrew Union College–Jewish Institute of Religion, School of Education, New York, NY 10012-1186. Offers MARE. *Program availability:* Part-time. *Degree requirements:* For master's, one foreign language, thesis. *Entrance requirements:* For master's, GRE, minimum 2 years of college-level Hebrew.

Heidelberg University, Master of Arts in Education Program, Tiffin, OH 44883-2462. Offers MAE. *Accreditation:* NCATE. *Program availability:* Part-time, evening/weekend. *Students:* 6 full-time (1 woman), 10 part-time (5 women). 10 applicants, 80% accepted, 6 enrolled. In 2018, 14 master's awarded. *Entrance requirements:* For master's, bachelor's degree with minimum cumulative GPA of 2.75; 3 letters of recommendation; goal statement. Additional exam requirements/recommendations for international students: Required—TOEFL (minimum score 550 paper-based, 79 iBT) or IELTS (minimum score 6.5). *Application deadline:* For fall admission, 8/15 for domestic students; for spring admission, 12/3 for domestic students; for summer admission, 5/1 for domestic students. Applications are processed on a rolling basis. Application fee: $0. Electronic applications accepted. Application fee is waived when completed online. *Expenses: Tuition:* Part-time $575 per semester hour. *Financial support:* Unspecified assistantships available. Financial award applicants required to submit FAFSA. *Unit head:* Dr. Karen Jones, Director of the School of Education, 419-448-2130, E-mail: kjones9@heidelberg.edu. *Application contact:* Katie Zeyen, Graduate Admissions Coordinator, 419-448-2602, Fax: 419-448-2565, E-mail: kzeyen@heidelberg.edu.
Website: https://www.heidelberg.edu/academics/programs/master-education

Henderson State University, Graduate Studies, Teachers College, Arkadelphia, AR 71999-0001. Offers MAT, MS, MSE, Ed S, Graduate Certificate. *Accreditation:* NCATE. *Program availability:* Part-time, 100% online. *Entrance requirements:* For master's, GRE General Test or MAT, minimum GPA of 2.7, teacher certification. Additional exam requirements/recommendations for international students: Required—TOEFL (minimum score 600 paper-based); Recommended—IELTS (minimum score 6.5).

Heritage University, Graduate Programs in Education, Toppenish, WA 98948-9599. Offers counseling (M Ed); educational administration (M Ed); professional studies (M Ed), including bilingual education/ESL, biology, English and literature, reading/literacy, special education; teaching (MIT). *Program availability:* Part-time, evening/weekend. *Degree requirements:* For master's, comprehensive exam, thesis (for some programs). *Entrance requirements:* For master's, interview, letters of recommendation, teaching certificate. Additional exam requirements/recommendations for international students: Recommended—TOEFL (minimum score 550 paper-based).

Hofstra University, School of Education, Hempstead, NY 11549. Offers MA, MS, MS Ed, Ed D, Advanced Certificate. *Accreditation:* TEAC. *Program availability:* Part-time, evening/weekend, blended/hybrid learning. *Degree requirements:* For master's, variable foreign language requirement, comprehensive exam (for some programs), thesis (for some programs), capstone, minimum GPA of 3.0, electronic portfolio, student teaching, practicum, internship, seminars, field work, curriculum project, clinical hours; for doctorate, variable foreign language requirement, comprehensive exam (for some programs), thesis/dissertation, qualifying hearing; for Advanced Certificate, comprehensive exam (for some programs), thesis optional, electronic portfolio, fieldwork, internship, state exams, exit project. *Entrance requirements:* For master's, GRE, letters of recommendation, interview, portfolio, resume, essay, certification; for doctorate, GRE, 3 letters of recommendation, essay, interview, 2 years' full-time teaching. Additional exam requirements/recommendations for international students: Required—TOEFL (minimum score 550 paper-based; 80 iBT). Electronic applications accepted. *Faculty research:* How children learn in contexts spanning from pre-school through high school and the learning needs of children with disabilities, the theory and practice of how teachers can effectively teach children in diverse contexts, educational leadership in K-12 and post secondary contexts.

Hollins University, Graduate Programs, Program in Teaching, Roanoke, VA 24020. Offers teaching (MAT); teaching and learning (MA). *Accreditation:* TEAC. *Program availability:* Part-time, evening/weekend, blended/hybrid learning. *Faculty:* 3 full-time (all women), 2 part-time/adjunct (1 woman). *Students:* 13 full-time (11 women), 19 part-time (18 women); includes 5 minority (1 Black or African American, non-Hispanic/Latino; 1 American Indian or Alaska Native, non-Hispanic/Latino; 1 Asian, non-Hispanic/Latino; 1 Hispanic/Latino; 1 Two or more races, non-Hispanic/Latino). Average age 34. 14 applicants, 93% accepted, 11 enrolled. In 2018, 13 master's awarded. *Degree requirements:* For master's, thesis or alternative. *Entrance requirements:* For master's, PRAXIS I or ACT/SAT, three letters of recommendation, bachelor's degree, official transcripts with minimum GPA of 2.5, personal statement. Additional exam requirements/recommendations for international students: Required—TOEFL (minimum score 550 paper-based; 80 iBT), IELTS (minimum score 6.5). *Application deadline:* For fall admission, 8/1 priority date for domestic and international students; for spring admission, 12/1 priority date for domestic and international students; for summer admission, 5/1 priority date for domestic and international students. Applications are processed on a rolling basis. Application fee: $40. Electronic applications accepted. *Expenses:* Contact institution. *Financial support:* Scholarships/grants available. Financial award application deadline: 7/15; financial award applicants required to submit FAFSA. *Faculty research:* Technology in the classroom, Classroom Management, Reading. *Unit head:* Dr. Lorraine Lange, Director, 540-362-7460, Fax: 540-362-6288, E-mail: hugrad@hollins.edu. *Application contact:* Donna Martin, Administrative Assistant, 540-362-7460, Fax: 540-362-6288, E-mail: dmartin@hollins.edu.
Website: http://www.hollins.edu/academics/graduate-degrees/teaching/

Holy Family University, Graduate and Professional Programs, School of Education, Philadelphia, PA 19114. Offers education (M Ed, Ed D), including early elementary education (PreK-Grade 4) (M Ed), education leadership (M Ed), educational leadership and professional studies (Ed D), general education (M Ed), reading specialist (M Ed), special education (M Ed), TESOL and literacy (M Ed). *Accreditation:* TEAC. *Program availability:* Part-time, evening/weekend. *Degree requirements:* For master's, comprehensive exam, thesis optional; for doctorate, comprehensive exam, thesis/dissertation. *Entrance requirements:* For master's, GRE or MAT (if GPA is below 3.0), interview, minimum GPA of 3.0, essay/personal statement, 2 letters of recommendation, official transcripts of all college or university work; for doctorate, GRE or MAT (taken within 5 years of application), minimum GPA of 3.5, 3 letters of recommendation, official transcripts of all college or university work, current resume, essay/personal statement, writing sample, interview. Additional exam requirements/recommendations for international students: Required—TOEFL (minimum score 550 paper-based; 79 iBT), IELTS (minimum score 6), or PTE (minimum score 54). Electronic applications accepted.

Holy Names University, Graduate Division, Department of Education, Oakland, CA 94619-1699. Offers educational therapy (Certificate); mild/moderate disabilities (Ed S); multiple subject teaching (Credential); single subject teaching (Credential); urban education: educational therapy (M Ed); urban education: K-12 education (M Ed); urban education: special education (M Ed). *Program availability:* Part-time. *Students:* 28 full-time (18 women), 63 part-time (45 women); includes 48 minority (22 Black or African American, non-Hispanic/Latino; 1 American Indian or Alaska Native, non-Hispanic/Latino; 3 Asian, non-Hispanic/Latino; 21 Hispanic/Latino; 1 Two or more races, non-Hispanic/Latino), 5 international. Average age 35. 69 applicants, 86% accepted, 34 enrolled. In 2018, 11 master's, 33 Certificates awarded. *Degree requirements:* For master's, comprehensive exam, research paper, thesis or project. *Entrance requirements:* For master's, minimum undergraduate GPA of 2.6 overall, 3.0 in major; personal statement; two recommendations; interview. Additional exam requirements/recommendations for international students: Required—TOEFL (minimum score 550 paper-based; 79 iBT). *Application deadline:* For fall admission, 8/1 priority date for domestic students, 7/15 for international students; for spring admission, 12/1 priority date for domestic students, 12/1 for international students; for summer admission, 5/1 priority date for domestic students, 5/1 for international students. Applications are processed on a rolling basis. Application fee: $65. Electronic applications accepted. Application fee is waived when completed online. *Expenses: Required fees:* $1003. *Financial support:* Career-related internships or fieldwork, Federal Work-Study, scholarships/grants, and unspecified assistantships available. Support available to part-time students. Financial award application deadline: 3/2; financial award applicants required to submit FAFSA. *Faculty research:* Cognitive development, language development, learning handicaps. *Unit head:* Dr. Kimberly Mayfield, Chair, 510-436-1396, Fax: 510-436-1325, E-mail: mayfield@hnu.edu. *Application contact:* Graduate Admission, 800-430-1321, Fax: 510-436-1325, E-mail: graduateadmissions@hnu.edu.
Website: http://www.hnu.edu/academics/graduatePrograms/education.html

Hood College, Graduate School, Department of Education, Frederick, MD 21701-8575. Offers curriculum and instruction (MS), including elementary education, elementary science and mathematics education, secondary education, special education; education, multidisciplinary studies (MS); educational leadership (MS, Certificate); reading specialization (MS); STEM education (Certificate). *Accreditation:* NCATE.

Education—General

Program availability: Part-time-only, evening/weekend. *Faculty:* 5 full-time (3 women), 32 part-time/adjunct (24 women). *Students:* 3 full-time (all women), 306 part-time (253 women); includes 65 minority (22 Black or African American, non-Hispanic/Latino; 9 Asian, non-Hispanic/Latino; 17 Hispanic/Latino; 17 Two or more races, non-Hispanic/Latino), 3 international. Average age 33. 80 applicants, 99% accepted, 45 enrolled. In 2018, 59 master's, 47 other advanced degrees awarded. *Degree requirements:* For master's, action research project, portfolio (for reading specialization); for Certificate, STEM capstone activity. *Entrance requirements:* For master's, minimum GPA of 2.75, teaching certification, writing sample during interview, letter of recommendation from principal (for educational leadership program only). Additional exam requirements/recommendations for international students: Required—TOEFL (minimum score 575 paper-based; 89 iBT), IELTS (minimum score 6.5). *Application deadline:* For fall admission, 8/15 priority date for domestic students, 8/5 for international students; for spring admission, 12/1 priority date for domestic students, 12/1 for international students; for summer admission, 5/1 priority date for domestic students, 4/15 for international students. Applications are processed on a rolling basis. Application fee: $50 ($100 for international students). Electronic applications accepted. *Expenses: Tuition:* Full-time $17,640; part-time $4410 per semester. *Required fees:* $125 per semester. Tuition and fees vary according to degree level and program. *Financial support:* Tuition waivers (partial) and unspecified assistantships available. Financial award applicants required to submit FAFSA. *Faculty research:* Leadership, action research, brain research, learning styles. *Unit head:* Dr. April M. Boulton, Dean of the Graduate School, 301-696-3612, E-mail: gofurther@hood.edu. *Application contact:* Tanith Fowler Corsi, Assistant Director of Graduate Admissions, 301-696-3603, E-mail: gofurther@hood.edu.
Website: https://www.hood.edu/academics/departments/department-education/programs-offered

Hope International University, School of Graduate and Professional Studies, Program in Education, Fullerton, CA 92831-3138. Offers education administration (MA); elementary education (ME); secondary education (ME). *Program availability:* Part-time, evening/weekend. *Degree requirements:* For master's, comprehensive exam (for some programs), thesis. *Entrance requirements:* For master's, minimum GPA of 3.0, 2 references. Additional exam requirements/recommendations for international students: Required—TOEFL (minimum score 550 paper-based; 86 iBT); Recommended—IELTS (minimum score 6.5). Electronic applications accepted. *Expenses:* Contact institution. *Faculty research:* Distance education.

Houston Baptist University, College of Education and Behavioral Sciences, Programs in Education, Houston, TX 77074-3298. Offers bilingual education (M Ed); counselor education (M Ed); curriculum and instruction (M Ed); curriculum and instruction (EC-6 bilingual) (M Ed); curriculum and instruction in all-level art, Spanish, music, or physical education (M Ed); curriculum and instruction in EC-6 and special education (EC-12) (M Ed); curriculum and instruction in instructional technology (M Ed); curriculum and instruction in mathematics, science, or social studies (4-8) (M Ed); curriculum and instruction with EC-6 generalist (M Ed); curriculum and instruction with English language arts and reading (4-8) (M Ed); educational administration (M Ed); educational diagnostician (M Ed); executive educational leadership (Ed D); higher education in business management (M Ed); higher education in Christian studies (M Ed); higher education in counseling (M Ed); higher education in educational technology (M Ed); reading (M Ed); special educational leadership (Ed D). *Program availability:* Part-time, evening/weekend, 100% online, blended/hybrid learning. *Degree requirements:* For master's, comprehensive exam; for doctorate, thesis/dissertation. *Entrance requirements:* For master's, minimum GPA of 2.75, two recommendations, resume, bachelor's degree conferred transcript; interview (for non-certified teachers); for doctorate, GRE, 5 letters of recommendation. Additional exam requirements/recommendations for international students: Required—TOEFL (minimum score 80 iBT), IELTS (minimum score 6.5). Electronic applications accepted. Application fee is waived when completed online. *Expenses:* Contact institution. *Faculty research:* Autism and inclusion, integrating technology into instruction, school change and leadership trust.

Houston Baptist University, School of Humanities, Program in Liberal Arts, Houston, TX 77074-3298. Offers education (EC-12 art, music, physical education, or Spanish) (MLA); education (EC-6 generalist) (MLA); general liberal arts (MLA); specialization in education (4-8 or 7-12) (MLA). *Program availability:* Part-time, evening/weekend. *Entrance requirements:* For master's, minimum GPA of 2.5, essay/personal statement, resume, bachelor's degree transcript. Additional exam requirements/recommendations for international students: Required—TOEFL (minimum score 80 iBT), IELTS (minimum score 6.5). Electronic applications accepted. Application fee is waived when completed online. *Expenses:* Contact institution.

Howard University, School of Education, Washington, DC 20059. Offers M Ed, Ed D, PhD, CAGS. *Accreditation:* NCATE. *Faculty:* 38 full-time (26 women), 9 part-time/adjunct (4 women). *Students:* 128 full-time (91 women), 48 part-time (32 women); includes 151 minority (150 Black or African American, non-Hispanic/Latino; 1 Hispanic/Latino), 23 international. Average age 31. 181 applicants, 39% accepted, 57 enrolled. In 2018, 17 master's, 23 doctorates awarded. *Degree requirements:* For master's, comprehensive exam, expository writing exam, practicum, PRAXIS II; for doctorate, one foreign language, comprehensive exam, thesis/dissertation, expository writing exam, internship. *Entrance requirements:* For master's, PRAXIS I or GRE General Test (for curriculum and instruction students only), minimum GPA of 3.0; for doctorate, GRE General Test, minimum GPA of 3.0. Additional exam requirements/recommendations for international students: Required—TOEFL (minimum score 550 paper-based; 79 iBT). *Application deadline:* For fall admission, 1/15 for domestic and international students. Application fee: $75. Electronic applications accepted. *Expenses:* Full-time tuition $29090 per year, Full-time fees $1575 per year; Part-time tuition $1700 per credit, Part-time fees $1575per year. *Financial support:* In 2018–19, 69 students received support, including 5 fellowships (averaging $49,000 per year), 17 research assistantships (averaging $24,500 per year); career-related internships or fieldwork, Federal Work-Study, institutionally sponsored loans, scholarships/grants, tuition waivers (full and partial), and unspecified assistantships also available. Financial award application deadline: 2/15; financial award applicants required to submit FAFSA. *Faculty research:* Policy and practice issues affecting education for African-Americans; information technology use in underserved school populations; increasing literacy skills for public school students; violence intervention and prevention; successes, problems, and needs of disabled African-Americans. *Total annual research expenditures:* $1.6 million. *Unit head:* Dr. Dawn G. Williams, Dean, School of Education, 202-806-7340, Fax: 202-806-7018, E-mail: dgwilliams@howard.edu. *Application contact:* Dr. Scott J. Dantley, Associate Dean for Academic Affairs, 202-806-7340, Fax: 202-806-7018, E-mail: scott.dantley@howard.edu.
Website: https://education.howard.edu/

Humboldt State University, Academic Programs, College of Professional Studies, School of Education, Arcata, CA 95521-8299. Offers MA. *Program availability:* Part-time, evening/weekend, online only, 100% online, blended/hybrid learning. *Faculty:* 7 full-time (3 women), 39 part-time/adjunct (27 women). *Students:* 5 full-time (4 women), 24 part-time (17 women); includes 9 minority (1 Asian, non-Hispanic/Latino; 6 Hispanic/Latino; 2 Two or more races, non-Hispanic/Latino). Average age 36. 16 applicants, 56% accepted, 5 enrolled. In 2018, 9 master's awarded. *Degree requirements:* For master's, thesis or alternative. *Entrance requirements:* For master's, minimum GPA of 3.0, 3 letters of recommendation. Additional exam requirements/recommendations for international students: Required—TOEFL (minimum score 500 paper-based). *Application deadline:* For fall admission, 4/1 for domestic and international students. Applications are processed on a rolling basis. Application fee: $55. Electronic applications accepted. *Expenses: Tuition:* Part-time $4649 per semester. *Required fees:* $2121; $1673. Tuition and fees vary according to program. *Financial support:* Application deadline: 3/1; applicants required to submit FAFSA. *Unit head:* Dr. Eric VanDuzer, Chair, School of Education, 707-826-5873, E-mail: evv1@humboldt.edu. *Application contact:* Dr. Eric VanDuzer, Chair, School of Education, 707-826-5873, E-mail: evv1@humboldt.edu.
Website: http://www.humboldt.edu/~educ/masters.html

Hunter College of the City University of New York, Graduate School, School of Education, New York, NY 10065-5085. Offers MA, MS, MS Ed, Ed D, AC. *Accreditation:* NCATE. *Program availability:* Part-time, evening/weekend. *Degree requirements:* For master's, comprehensive exam (for some programs), thesis (for some programs), minimum overall GPA of 3.0; portfolio review; for doctorate, thesis/dissertation; for AC, comprehensive exam (for some programs), minimum overall GPA of 3.0; portfolio review; valid and appropriate NY state certification. *Entrance requirements:* For master's, GRE (for teacher preparation programs), transcript review requiring BA with minimum GPA of 3.0; personal statement, letters of recommendation and/or writing sample; for doctorate, GRE (for teacher preparation programs), official transcripts; letters of recommendation; essay; resume; minimum GPA of 3.5 in a master's program; interview; for AC, GRE (for teacher preparation programs), transcript review requiring minimum B average in graduate course work; teaching certificate; minimum 3 years of full-time teaching experience; personal statement, letters of recommendation and/or writing sample. Additional exam requirements/recommendations for international students: Required—TOEFL. Electronic applications accepted. *Faculty research:* Multicultural and multiracial urban education; mentoring new teachers; mathematics and science education; bilingual, bi-cultural, and special education.

Idaho State University, Graduate School, College of Education, Pocatello, ID 83209-8059. Offers M Ed, MPE, Ed D, PhD, 5th Year Certificate, 6th Year Certificate, Ed S. *Accreditation:* NCATE. *Program availability:* Part-time. *Degree requirements:* For master's, comprehensive exam, thesis optional, oral exam, written exam; for doctorate, comprehensive exam, thesis/dissertation, written exam; for other advanced degree, comprehensive exam, oral exam, written exam, practicum or field project. *Entrance requirements:* For master's, GRE General Test or MAT, minimum undergraduate GPA of 3.0, interview, bachelor's degree or equivalent; for doctorate, GRE General Test or MAT, minimum undergraduate GPA of 3.0, 3.5 graduate; departmental interview; current curriculum vitae, computer skill competency checklist; for other advanced degree, GRE General Test, minimum graduate GPA of 3.0, master's degree, letter from supervisor attesting to school administration potential. Additional exam requirements/recommendations for international students: Required—TOEFL (minimum score 550 paper-based; 80 iBT). Electronic applications accepted. *Faculty research:* School reform, inclusion, students at risk, teacher education standards, teaching cases, education leadership.

Illinois College, Program in Education, Jacksonville, IL 62650-2299. Offers MA Ed. *Program availability:* Part-time-only, evening/weekend. *Degree requirements:* For master's, action research capstone experience. Electronic applications accepted. *Expenses:* Contact institution.

Indiana State University, College of Graduate and Professional Studies, Bayh College of Education, Terre Haute, IN 47809. Offers M Ed, MS, PhD, Ed S, MA/MS. *Accreditation:* NCATE. *Program availability:* Part-time, evening/weekend. *Degree requirements:* For doctorate, thesis/dissertation. *Entrance requirements:* For master's, minimum undergraduate GPA of 2.5; for doctorate, GRE General Test; for Ed S, GRE General Test, minimum graduate GPA of 3.25. Electronic applications accepted.

Indiana University Bloomington, School of Education, Bloomington, IN 47405-1006. Offers MS, Ed D, PhD, Ed S, Graduate Certificate. *Accreditation:* NCATE. *Program availability:* Part-time, 100% online, blended/hybrid learning. Terminal master's awarded for partial completion of doctoral program. *Degree requirements:* For master's, thesis optional; for doctorate, comprehensive exam, thesis/dissertation; for other advanced degree, comprehensive exam (for some programs), thesis (for some programs), comprehensive exam or project. *Entrance requirements:* For master's and other advanced degree, GRE General Test, minimum GPA of 3.0 (recommended), 3 letters of recommendation; for doctorate, GRE General Test, minimum GPA of 3.0, 3 letters of recommendation. Additional exam requirements/recommendations for international students: Required—TOEFL (minimum score 550 paper-based; 79 iBT). Electronic applications accepted.

Indiana University East, School of Education, Richmond, IN 47374-1289. Offers MS Ed. *Accreditation:* NCATE. *Entrance requirements:* For master's, 3 letters of recommendation, interview.

Indiana University Northwest, School of Education, Gary, IN 46408. Offers educational leadership (MS Ed); elementary education (MS Ed); K-12 online teaching (Graduate Certificate); secondary education (MS Ed). *Accreditation:* NCATE. *Program availability:* Part-time, evening/weekend. *Entrance requirements:* For master's, GRE General Test or MAT, minimum GPA of 3.0. Electronic applications accepted. *Expenses:* Contact institution.

Indiana University of Pennsylvania, School of Graduate Studies and Research, College of Education and Communications, Indiana, PA 15705. Offers M Ed, MA, MS, D Ed, PhD, Certificate. *Accreditation:* NCATE. *Program availability:* Part-time, evening/weekend. *Faculty:* 50 full-time (33 women), 11 part-time/adjunct (7 women). *Students:* 266 full-time (202 women), 405 part-time (277 women); includes 100 minority (54 Black or African American, non-Hispanic/Latino; 6 Asian, non-Hispanic/Latino; 18 Hispanic/Latino; 1 Native Hawaiian or other Pacific Islander, non-Hispanic/Latino; 21 Two or more races, non-Hispanic/Latino), 17 international. Average age 33. 690 applicants, 60% accepted, 258 enrolled. In 2018, 161 master's, 36 doctorates, 24 other advanced degrees awarded. Terminal master's awarded for partial completion of doctoral program. *Degree requirements:* For master's, thesis optional; for doctorate, comprehensive exam, thesis/dissertation. *Entrance requirements:* For master's and doctorate, 2 letters of recommendation. Additional exam requirements/recommendations for international students: Required—TOEFL (minimum score 540 paper-based; 76 iBT). *Application deadline:* Applications are processed on a rolling basis. Application fee: $50. Electronic applications accepted. *Expenses:* Tuition, state resident: full-time $12,384; part-time $516 per credit hour. Tuition, nonresident: full-time $18,576; part-time $774 per credit hour. *Required fees:* $4454; $186 per credit hour. $65 per semester. Tuition and fees vary according to program and reciprocity agreements. *Financial support:* In 2018–19, 21 fellowships (averaging $842 per year), 132 research assistantships with tuition reimbursements (averaging $4,244 per year), 9 teaching assistantships with tuition reimbursements (averaging $21,032 per year) were awarded; career-related internships or fieldwork, Federal Work-Study, scholarships/grants, and

unspecified assistantships also available. Support available to part-time students. Financial award application deadline: 4/15; financial award applicants required to submit FAFSA. *Unit head:* Dr. Lara Luetkehans, Dean, 724-357-2480, Fax: 724-357-5595. *Application contact:* Paula Stossel, Assistant Dean for Administration, 724-357-4511, Fax: 724-357-4862, E-mail: graduate-admissions@iup.edu.
Website: http://www.iup.edu/education

Indiana University–Purdue University Indianapolis, School of Education, Indianapolis, IN 46202-5155. Offers curriculum and instruction (MS); early childhood (MS); educational leadership (MS, Certificate); English as a second language (Certificate); kindergarten (Certificate); language education (MS); reading (Certificate); school counseling (MS); special education (MS, Certificate). *Program availability:* Part-time, evening/weekend. Terminal master's awarded for partial completion of doctoral program. *Degree requirements:* For master's, thesis optional. *Entrance requirements:* For master's, GRE General Test, minimum GPA of 2.5; for Certificate, official transcripts. Additional exam requirements/recommendations for international students: Required—TOEFL (minimum score 60 iBT), IELTS (minimum score 5.5). Electronic applications accepted. *Expenses:* Contact institution. *Faculty research:* Educational policies and school leaders' responses to these; issues of intersectionality in the experiences of African American lesbian, gay, and bisexual students attending historically black colleges and universities and those who belong to black Greek-letter organizations; students' experiential knowledge and their evolving disciplinary-specific literacy and understanding; innovative program development; urban ESL teacher preparation; target-based instructional coaching.

Indiana University South Bend, School of Education, South Bend, IN 46615. Offers addiction counseling (MS Ed); alcohol and drug counseling (Graduate Certificate); clinical mental health counseling (MS Ed); educational leadership (MS Ed); elementary education (MS Ed); marriage, couple, and family counseling (MS Ed); school counseling (MS Ed); secondary education (MS Ed); special education (MAT, MS Ed), including intense intervention (MS Ed), mild intervention (MS Ed). *Accreditation:* NCATE. *Program availability:* Part-time, evening/weekend. *Degree requirements:* For master's, thesis or alternative, exit project. *Entrance requirements:* For master's, letters of recommendation, GRE or minimum GPA of 3.0. Additional exam requirements/recommendations for international students: Required—TOEFL. Electronic applications accepted. *Expenses:* Contact institution. *Faculty research:* Professional dispositions, early childhood literacy, online learning, program assessments, problem-based learning.

Indiana University Southeast, School of Education, New Albany, IN 47150. Offers counselor education (MS Ed); elementary education (MS Ed); secondary education (MS Ed). *Accreditation:* NCATE. *Program availability:* Part-time, evening/weekend. *Entrance requirements:* For master's, minimum undergraduate GPA of 2.5, graduate 3.0. Electronic applications accepted. *Faculty research:* Learning styles, technology, constructivism, group process, innovative math strategies.

Institute for Christian Studies, Graduate Programs, Toronto, ON M5S 2E6, Canada. Offers education (M Phil F, PhD); history of philosophy (M Phil F, PhD); philosophical aesthetics (M Phil F, PhD); philosophy of religion (M Phil F, PhD); political theory (M Phil F, PhD); systematic philosophy (M Phil F, PhD); theology (M Phil F, PhD); worldview studies (MWS). *Program availability:* Part-time, online learning. *Degree requirements:* For master's, one foreign language, thesis; for doctorate, 2 foreign languages, thesis/dissertation. *Entrance requirements:* For master's and doctorate, philosophy background. Additional exam requirements/recommendations for international students: Required—TOEFL (minimum score 600 paper-based). *Faculty research:* Human rights, anthropology of self, medieval discourse, gender and body, post-modern thought; biblical hermeneutics, creational aesthetics, ecumenism, epistemology, political theory and public policy, relational psychotherapy.

Instituto Tecnologico de Santo Domingo, Graduate School, Area of Humanities and Social Sciences, Santo Domingo, Dominican Republic. Offers accounting (Certificate); adult education (Certificate); applied linguistics (MA); economics (MA); education (M Ed); educational psychology (MA, Certificate); gender and development (MA, Certificate); humanistic studies (MA); international marketing management (Certificate); international relations in the Caribbean basin (Certificate); intervention systems in family therapy (MA); linguistic and literary communication (Certificate); pedagogical support (MA); social science education (M Ed); sustainable human development (MA); terminal illness and death psychology (Certificate); youth and adult education (M Ed).

Instituto Tecnológico y de Estudios Superiores de Monterrey, Campus Central de Veracruz, Graduate Programs, Córdoba, Mexico. Offers administration (MA); administration of information technologies (MTI); computer sciences (MCC); education (MEE); educational institution administration (MAD); educational technology (MTE); electronic commerce (MCE); finance (MAF); humanistic studies (MEH); international business for Latin America (MNL); marketing (MMT); science (MCP). *Program availability:* Part-time, evening/weekend, online learning. *Degree requirements:* For master's, thesis (for some programs). *Entrance requirements:* For master's, PAEP College Board. Electronic applications accepted.

Instituto Tecnológico y de Estudios Superiores de Monterrey, Campus Ciudad de México, Virtual University Division, Ciudad de Mexico, Mexico. Offers administration of information technologies (MA); computer sciences (MA); education (MA, PhD); educational technology (MA); environmental engineering (MA); environmental systems (MA); humanistic studies (MA); industrial engineering (MA); international business for Latin America (MA); quality systems (MA); quality systems and productivity (MA). *Program availability:* Part-time, evening/weekend, online learning. *Entrance requirements:* For master's and doctorate, Instituto entrance exam. Additional exam requirements/recommendations for international students: Required—TOEFL.

Instituto Tecnológico y de Estudios Superiores de Monterrey, Campus Ciudad Juárez, Program in Education, Ciudad Juárez, Mexico. Offers M Ed.

Instituto Tecnológico y de Estudios Superiores de Monterrey, Campus Ciudad Obregón, Programs in Education, Ciudad Obregón, Mexico. Offers cognitive development (ME); communications (ME); mathematics (ME).

Instituto Tecnológico y de Estudios Superiores de Monterrey, Campus Estado de México, Professional and Graduate Division, Estado de Mexico, Mexico. Offers administration of information technologies (MITA); architecture (M Arch); business administration (GMBA, MBA); computer sciences (MCS, PhD); education (M Ed); educational institution administration (MAD); educational technology and innovation (PhD); electronic commerce (MEC); environmental systems (MS); finance (MAF); humanistic studies (MHS); information sciences and knowledge management (MISKM); information systems (MS); manufacturing systems (MS); marketing (MEM); quality systems and productivity (MS); science and materials engineering (PhD); telecommunications management (MTM). *Program availability:* Part-time, online learning. *Degree requirements:* For master's, one foreign language, thesis (for some programs); for doctorate, one foreign language, thesis/dissertation. *Entrance requirements:* For master's, E-PAEP 500, interview; for doctorate, E-PAEP 500, research proposal. Additional exam requirements/recommendations for international students: Required—TOEFL (minimum score 550 paper-based). *Faculty research:* Surface treatments by plasmas, mechanical properties, robotics, graphical computing, mechatronics security protocols.

Instituto Tecnológico y de Estudios Superiores de Monterrey, Campus Irapuato, Graduate Programs, Irapuato, Mexico. Offers administration (MBA); administration of information technology (MAIT); administration of telecommunications (MAT); architecture (M Arch); computer science (MCS); education (M Ed); educational administration (MEA); educational innovation and technology (DEIT); educational technology (MET); electronic commerce (MBA); environmental administration and planning (MEAP); environmental systems (MES); finances (MBA); humanistic studies (MHS); international management for Latin American executives (MIMLAE); library and information science (MLIS); manufacturing quality management (MMQM); marketing research (MBA).

Instituto Tecnológico y de Estudios Superiores de Monterrey, Campus Sonora Norte, Program in Education, Hermosillo, Mexico. Offers MA. *Entrance requirements:* For master's, MAT.

Inter American University of Puerto Rico, Arecibo Campus, Programs in Education, Arecibo, PR 00614-4050. Offers administration and educational supervision (MA Ed); counseling and guidance (MA Ed); curriculum and teaching (MA Ed), including biology education, English as a second language, history education, math education, Spanish; elementary education (MA Ed). *Accreditation:* TEAC. *Degree requirements:* For master's, comprehensive exam, thesis optional. *Entrance requirements:* For master's, GRE, EXADEP, bachelor's degree in education or teaching license (administration and supervision) or courses in education and psychology (counseling and guidance), minimum GPA of 2.5 in last 60 credits.

Inter American University of Puerto Rico, Barranquitas Campus, Program in Education, Barranquitas, PR 00794. Offers curriculum and teaching (M Ed), including biology, English as a second language, history, Spanish; educational leadership and management (MA); elementary education (M Ed); information and library service technology (M Ed); special education (MA). *Accreditation:* TEAC. *Program availability:* Part-time, evening/weekend. *Degree requirements:* For master's, 2 foreign languages, comprehensive exam, thesis (for some programs). *Entrance requirements:* For master's, GRE or EXADEP, bachelor's degree or its equivalent from accredited institution, official academic transcript from institution that conferred bachelor's degree, minimum GPA of 2.5, two recommendation letters, interview (for some programs), essay (for some programs). Electronic applications accepted. *Expenses:* Contact institution.

Inter American University of Puerto Rico, Metropolitan Campus, Graduate Programs, Program in Education, San Juan, PR 00919-1293. Offers curriculum and instruction (Ed D); educational administration (Ed D); guidance and counseling (MA, Ed D); special education administration (Ed D). *Accreditation:* TEAC. *Degree requirements:* For doctorate, comprehensive exam, thesis/dissertation. *Entrance requirements:* For doctorate, GRE, MAT, or EXADEP. Electronic applications accepted.

International Baptist College and Seminary, Program in Education, Chandler, AZ 85286. Offers M Ed. *Degree requirements:* For master's, research paper/thesis. *Entrance requirements:* For master's, letter of recommendation.

Iona College, School of Arts and Science, Department of Education, New Rochelle, NY 10801-1890. Offers adolescence education: biology (MS Ed, MST); adolescence education: English (MS Ed); adolescence education: mathematics (MST); adolescence education: social studies (MS Ed, MST); adolescence education: Spanish (MS Ed); adolescence special education 5-12 (MST); childhood and special education (MST); early childhood and childhood (MST); educational leadership (MS Ed). *Accreditation:* NCATE. *Program availability:* Part-time, evening/weekend. *Faculty:* 7 full-time (5 women), 9 part-time/adjunct (5 women). *Students:* 33 full-time (30 women), 26 part-time (20 women); includes 21 minority (6 Black or African American, non-Hispanic/Latino; 1 Asian, non-Hispanic/Latino; 13 Hispanic/Latino; 1 Two or more races, non-Hispanic/Latino). Average age 25. 39 applicants, 87% accepted, 14 enrolled. In 2018, 20 master's awarded. *Degree requirements:* For master's, thesis or alternative. *Entrance requirements:* For master's, minimum GPA of 3.0, NY State teaching certificate and bachelor's degree (for MS Ed). Additional exam requirements/recommendations for international students: Required—TOEFL (minimum score 550 paper-based; 80 iBT), IELTS (minimum score 6.5). *Application deadline:* For fall admission, 8/1 priority date for domestic students, 5/1 priority date for international students; for spring admission, 1/1 priority date for domestic students, 9/1 priority date for international students. Applications are processed on a rolling basis. Electronic applications accepted. *Expenses: Tuition:* Full-time $14,064; part-time $7032 per credit. *Required fees:* $245 per semester. One-time fee: $250. Tuition and fees vary according to program. *Financial support:* In 2018–19, 2 students received support. Unspecified assistantships available. Support available to part-time students. Financial award application deadline: 4/15; financial award applicants required to submit FAFSA. *Faculty research:* Engaging teacher educators in scientific process, cross-national comparisons of mathematics teaching, questioning strategies in the classroom, research methods, literacy development. *Unit head:* Malissa Scheuring Leipold, EdD, Chair, 914-633-2210, Fax: 914-633-2281, E-mail: mleipold@iona.edu. *Application contact:* Christopher Kash, Assistant Director of Graduate Admissions, 914-633-2403, E-mail: ckash@iona.edu.
Website: http://www.iona.edu/Academics/School-of-Arts-Science/Departments/Education/Graduate-Programs.aspx

Iowa State University of Science and Technology, Department of Education, Ames, IA 50011. Offers curriculum and instructional technology (M Ed, MS, PhD); elementary education (M Ed, MS); historical, philosophical, and comparative studies in education (M Ed, MS); special education (M Ed, MS, PhD). *Degree requirements:* For master's, thesis or alternative; for doctorate, thesis/dissertation. *Entrance requirements:* For master's and doctorate, GRE General Test. Additional exam requirements/recommendations for international students: Required—TOEFL (minimum score 560 paper-based; 83 iBT), IELTS (minimum score 6.5). Electronic applications accepted.

Jackson State University, Graduate School, College of Education and Human Development, Jackson, MS 39217. Offers MS, MS Ed, Ed D, PhD, Ed S. *Accreditation:* NCATE. *Program availability:* Part-time, evening/weekend, 100% online, blended/hybrid learning. Terminal master's awarded for partial completion of doctoral program. *Degree requirements:* For master's, comprehensive exam; for doctorate, comprehensive exam, thesis/dissertation. *Entrance requirements:* For master's, GRE General Test; for doctorate, MAT, teaching experience. Additional exam requirements/recommendations for international students: Required—TOEFL (minimum score 520 paper-based; 67 iBT). Electronic applications accepted. *Expenses:* Contact institution.

Jacksonville State University, Graduate Studies, School of Education, Jacksonville, AL 36265-1602. Offers MS, MS Ed, Ed S. *Accreditation:* NCATE. *Program availability:* Part-time, evening/weekend, 100% online, blended/hybrid learning. *Degree requirements:* For master's, comprehensive exam, thesis (for some programs). *Entrance requirements:* For master's, GRE General Test or MAT. Additional exam requirements/recommendations for international students: Required—TOEFL (minimum score 500 paper-based; 61 iBT). Electronic applications accepted.

John Brown University, Graduate Education Programs, Siloam Springs, AR 72761-2121. Offers curriculum and instruction (M Ed); secondary education (MAT). *Program availability:* Part-time, evening/weekend. *Entrance requirements:* For master's, GRE (minimum score of 300). Additional exam requirements/recommendations for international students: Required—TOEFL (minimum score 550 paper-based; 79 iBT). Electronic applications accepted.

Education—General

John Carroll University, Graduate Studies, Program in Professional Teacher Education, University Heights, OH 44118. Offers M Ed, MA. *Program availability:* Part-time, evening/weekend. *Entrance requirements:* Additional exam requirements/recommendations for international students: Required—TOEFL. *Application deadline:* Applications are processed on a rolling basis. Electronic applications accepted. *Expenses: Tuition:* Full-time $13,140; part-time $730 per credit hour. Tuition and fees vary according to program. *Financial support:* Scholarships/grants and unspecified assistantships available. Financial award applicants required to submit FAFSA. *Unit head:* Dr. Mark Storz, Coordinator, 216-397-3070, Fax: 216-397-3045, E-mail: mstorz@jcu.edu. *Application contact:* Colleen K. Sommerfeld, Assistant Dean for Graduate Admission & Retention, 216-397-4902, Fax: 216-397-1835, E-mail: csommerfeld@jcu.edu.
Website: http://sites.jcu.edu/graduatestudies/pages/graduate-programs/masters-programs/education/initial-teacher-license/

Johns Hopkins University, School of Education, Baltimore, MD 21218. Offers M Ed, MAT, MS, Ed D, PhD, Advanced Certificate, Graduate Certificate, Post-Master's Certificate. *Accreditation:* NCATE. *Program availability:* Part-time, evening/weekend, 100% online, blended/hybrid learning. *Faculty:* 118 full-time (86 women). *Students:* 593 full-time (454 women), 1,807 part-time (1,356 women). 1,541 applicants, 53% accepted, 625 enrolled. In 2018, 937 master's, 61 doctorates, 183 other advanced degrees awarded. *Degree requirements:* For master's, comprehensive exam (for some programs), portfolio, capstone project and/or internship; PRAXIS II (subject area assessments) for initial teacher preparation programs that lead to licensure, edTPA; for doctorate, comprehensive exam, thesis/dissertation. *Entrance requirements:* For master's, GRE (for full-time programs only); PRAXIS I/core or state-approved alternative (for initial teacher preparation programs that lead to licensure), minimum of bachelor's degree from regionally- or nationally-accredited institution; minimum GPA of 3.0 in all previous programs of study; official transcripts from all post-secondary institutions attended; essay; curriculum vitae/resume; letters of recommendation (3 for full-time programs, 2 for part-time programs); dispositions survey; for doctorate, GRE (for PhD only), master's degree from regionally- or nationally-accredited institution; minimum GPA of 3.0 in previous undergraduate and graduate studies (for Ed D only); official transcripts from all post-secondary institutions attended; three letters of recommendation; curriculum vitae/resume; personal statement; dispositions survey; for other advanced degree, minimum of bachelor's degree from regionally- or nationally-accredited institution (master's degree for some programs); minimum GPA of 3.0 in all previous programs of study; official transcripts from all post-secondary institutions attended; essay; curriculum vitae/resume; two letters of recommendation; dispositions survey. Additional exam requirements/recommendations for international students: Required—TOEFL (minimum score 600 paper-based; 100 iBT), IELTS (minimum score 7). *Application deadline:* For fall admission, 4/1 priority date for domestic students, 4/1 for international students; for spring admission, 10/1 priority date for domestic students, 10/1 for international students; for summer admission, 2/1 priority date for domestic students, 2/1 for international students. Applications are processed on a rolling basis. Application fee: $80. Electronic applications accepted. *Expenses:* Contact institution. *Financial support:* In 2018–19, 206 students received support, including 23 fellowships (averaging $25,500 per year); research assistantships, teaching assistantships, Federal Work-Study, and scholarships/grants also available. Support available to part-time students. Financial award application deadline: 4/1; financial award applicants required to submit FAFSA. *Faculty research:* Comprehensive school reform, dropout prevention, evidence-based decision making in education, neuro-education, entrepreneurial leadership. *Unit head:* Dr. Christopher C. Morphew, Dean, 410-516-7820, E-mail: soe.dean@jhu.edu. *Application contact:* Elisabeth Woodward, Director of Admissions, 410-516-9797, E-mail: admissions@jhu.edu.
Website: http://education.jhu.edu

Johnson & Wales University, Graduate Studies, MAT Program in Teacher Education, Providence, RI 02903-3703. Offers business education and secondary special education (MAT); culinary arts education (MAT); elementary education and elementary special education (MAT). *Program availability:* Part-time, evening/weekend. *Entrance requirements:* For master's, MAT, minimum GPA of 2.75. Additional exam requirements/recommendations for international students: Required—TOEFL (minimum score 550 paper-based) or IELTS (recommended). *Faculty research:* Secondary education, student teaching, educational reform, evaluation procedures.

Johnson & Wales University, Graduate Studies, M Ed Program in Teaching and Learning, Providence, RI 02903-3703. Offers M Ed. *Program availability:* Evening/weekend. *Entrance requirements:* For master's, bachelor's degree with minimum GPA of 2.75 from accredited institution of higher education, valid teaching license. Additional exam requirements/recommendations for international students: Required—TOEFL (minimum score 550 paper-based, 80 iBT) or Michigan English Language Assessment Battery (minimum score 77).

Johnson University, Graduate and Professional Programs, Knoxville, TN 37998-1001. Offers biblical interpretation (Graduate Certificate); business administration (MBA); Christian ministries (Graduate Certificate); clinical mental health counseling (MA); educational technology (MA); intercultural studies (MA); leadership (MBA); leadership studies (PhD); New Testament (MA); nonprofit management (MBA); school counseling (MA); spiritual formation and leadership (Graduate Certificate); strategic ministry (MA); teacher education (MA). *Program availability:* Part-time, evening/weekend, 100% online, blended/hybrid learning. *Degree requirements:* For master's, variable foreign language requirement, comprehensive exam, thesis (for some programs), internships; for doctorate, variable foreign language requirement, comprehensive exam, thesis/dissertation, internships. *Entrance requirements:* For master's, PRAXIS (for MA in teacher education); MAT (for counseling); GRE or GMAT (for MBA), interview, 3 references, transcripts, essay, minimum GPA of 2.5 or 3.0 (depending on program); for doctorate, GRE or MAT (taken not less than 5 years prior), interview, 3 references, transcripts, essay, minimum GPA of 3.0; for Graduate Certificate, interview, 3 references, transcripts, essay, minimum GPA of 3.0. Additional exam requirements/recommendations for international students: Required—TOEFL (minimum score 527 paper-based; 71 iBT). Electronic applications accepted. *Expenses:* Contact institution.

Kansas State University, Graduate School, College of Education, Manhattan, KS 66506. Offers MS, Ed D, PhD, Certificate. *Accreditation:* NCATE. *Program availability:* Part-time, evening/weekend, online learning. Terminal master's awarded for partial completion of doctoral program. *Degree requirements:* For master's, thesis or alternative, oral or comprehensive exam; for doctorate, thesis/dissertation, residency. *Entrance requirements:* For master's and doctorate, GRE or MAT. Additional exam requirements/recommendations for international students: Required—GRE General Test or TOEFL. Electronic applications accepted. *Faculty research:* Teacher preparation, program evaluation, science education, ESL-bilingual education, rural issues in education.

Kean University, College of Education, Union, NJ 07083. Offers MA, MS. *Accreditation:* NCATE. *Program availability:* Part-time. *Faculty:* 52 full-time (33 women). *Students:* 35 full-time (27 women), 126 part-time (89 women); includes 64 minority (20 Black or African American, non-Hispanic/Latino; 12 Asian, non-Hispanic/Latino; 30 Hispanic/Latino; 1 Native Hawaiian or other Pacific Islander, non-Hispanic/Latino; 1 Two or more races, non-Hispanic/Latino), 2 international. Average age 33. 73 applicants, 100% accepted, 58 enrolled. In 2018, 85 master's awarded. *Degree requirements:* For master's, comprehensive exam, thesis, practicum, portfolio, field experience. *Entrance requirements:* Additional exam requirements/recommendations for international students: Required—TOEFL (minimum score 550 paper-based; 79 iBT), IELTS (minimum score 6.5). *Application deadline:* For fall admission, 6/30 for domestic and international students; for spring admission, 12/1 for domestic and international students. Applications are processed on a rolling basis. Application fee: $75. Electronic applications accepted. *Expenses:* Tuition, state resident: full-time $15,025; part-time $733.50 per credit. Tuition, nonresident: full-time $19,890; part-time $884.50 per credit. *Required fees:* $2107.50; $89.50 per credit. Tuition and fees vary according to course level, course load, degree level and program. *Financial support:* Scholarships/grants and unspecified assistantships available. Financial award applicants required to submit FAFSA. *Application contact:* Brittany Gerstenhaber, Admissions Counselor, 908-737-7100, E-mail: gradadmissions@kean.edu.
Website: http://www.kean.edu/KU/College-of-Education

Keiser University, Master of Science in Education Program, Fort Lauderdale, FL 33309. Offers allied health teaching and leadership (MS Ed); career college administration (MS Ed); leadership (MS Ed); online teaching and learning (MS Ed); teaching and learning (MS Ed). *Program availability:* Part-time, online learning.

Kennesaw State University, Bagwell College of Education, Kennesaw, GA 30144. Offers M Ed, MAT, Ed D, Ed S. *Accreditation:* NCATE. *Program availability:* Part-time, 100% online, blended/hybrid learning. *Students:* 186 full-time (161 women), 909 part-time (701 women); includes 316 minority (236 Black or African American, non-Hispanic/Latino; 1 American Indian or Alaska Native, non-Hispanic/Latino; 22 Asian, non-Hispanic/Latino; 44 Hispanic/Latino; 2 Native Hawaiian or other Pacific Islander, non-Hispanic/Latino; 11 Two or more races, non-Hispanic/Latino), 1 international. Average age 36. 456 applicants, 72% accepted, 272 enrolled. In 2018, 197 master's, 27 doctorates, 191 other advanced degrees awarded. *Degree requirements:* For master's, thesis or alternative; for doctorate, comprehensive exam, thesis/dissertation or alternative. *Entrance requirements:* For master's, minimum GPA of 2.75, renewable teaching certificate. Additional exam requirements/recommendations for international students: Required—TOEFL (minimum score 550 paper-based; 80 iBT), IELTS (minimum score 6.5). *Application deadline:* For fall admission, 7/1 for domestic and international students; for spring admission, 11/1 for domestic and international students; for summer admission, 4/1 for domestic and international students. Applications are processed on a rolling basis. Application fee: $60. Electronic applications accepted. *Expenses: Tuition, area resident:* Full-time $6960; part-time $290 per credit hour. Tuition, state resident: full-time $6960; part-time $290 per credit hour. Tuition, nonresident: full-time $25,080; part-time $1045 per credit hour. *International tuition:* $25,080 full-time. *Required fees:* $2006; $1706 per semester. $853 per semester. *Financial support:* Research assistantships with tuition reimbursements, Federal Work-Study, and unspecified assistantships available. Support available to part-time students. Financial award application deadline: 4/1; financial award applicants required to submit FAFSA. *Unit head:* Cynthia Reed, Dean, 470-578-6117, Fax: 470-578-6567. *Application contact:* Admission Counselor, 470-578-4377, Fax: 470-578-9172, E-mail: ksugrad@kennesaw.edu.
Website: http://www.kennesaw.edu/education/

Kennesaw State University, University College, Kennesaw, GA 30144. Offers first-year studies (MS). *Students:* 3 full-time (all women), 7 part-time (4 women); includes 4 minority (3 Black or African American, non-Hispanic/Latino; 1 American Indian or Alaska Native, non-Hispanic/Latino). Average age 39. In 2018, 6 master's awarded. *Entrance requirements:* Additional exam requirements/recommendations for international students: Required—TOEFL (minimum score 550 paper-based; 80 iBT), IELTS (minimum score 6.5). Application fee: $60. *Expenses: Tuition, area resident:* Full-time $6960; part-time $290 per credit hour. Tuition, state resident: full-time $6960; part-time $290 per credit hour. Tuition, nonresident: full-time $25,080; part-time $1045 per credit hour. *International tuition:* $25,080 full-time. *Required fees:* $2006; $1706 per semester. $853 per semester. *Financial support:* Applicants required to submit FAFSA. *Application contact:* Admissions Counselor, 770-420-4377, Fax: 770-423-6885, E-mail: ksugrad@kennesaw.edu.
Website: http://uc.kennesaw.edu/

Kent State University, College of Education, Health and Human Services, Kent, OH 44242-0001. Offers M Ed, MA, MAT, MS, Au D, PhD, Ed S. *Accreditation:* NCATE. *Program availability:* Part-time, evening/weekend, online learning. *Faculty:* 188 full-time (116 women), 130 part-time/adjunct (87 women). *Students:* 865 full-time (619 women), 559 part-time (425 women); includes 199 minority (103 Black or African American, non-Hispanic/Latino; 9 American Indian or Alaska Native, non-Hispanic/Latino; 42 Asian, non-Hispanic/Latino; 15 Hispanic/Latino; 27 Native Hawaiian or other Pacific Islander, non-Hispanic/Latino; 3 Two or more races, non-Hispanic/Latino), 91 international. In 2018, 401 master's, 27 doctorates, 62 other advanced degrees awarded. *Degree requirements:* For master's, thesis (for some programs); for doctorate, comprehensive exam, thesis/dissertation. *Entrance requirements:* For doctorate and Ed S, GRE General Test. Additional exam requirements/recommendations for international students: Required—TOEFL (minimum score 550 paper-based; 80 iBT). *Application deadline:* Applications are processed on a rolling basis. Application fee: $45 ($60 for international students). Electronic applications accepted. *Expenses:* Tuition, state resident: full-time $11,766; part-time $536 per credit. Tuition, nonresident: full-time $21,952; part-time $999 per credit. *International tuition:* $21,952 full-time. Tuition and fees vary according to course load. *Financial support:* In 2018–19, 112 research assistantships with full tuition reimbursements (averaging $10,564 per year), 28 teaching assistantships (averaging $11,938 per year) were awarded; scholarships/grants, health care benefits, unspecified assistantships, and 30 administrative assistantships (averaging $10,406 per year) also available. Financial award application deadline: 4/1; financial award applicants required to submit FAFSA. *Unit head:* Dr. James Hannon, Dean, 330-672-0566, Fax: 330-672-3407, E-mail: jhannon5@kent.edu. *Application contact:* Cheryl Slusarczyk, Academic Program Director, Office of Graduate Student Services, 330-672-2576, Fax: 330-672-9162, E-mail: cslusarc@kent.edu.
Website: http://www.kent.edu/ehhs/

Kent State University at Stark, Graduate School of Education, Health and Human Services, Canton, OH 44720-7599. Offers curriculum and instruction studies (M Ed, MA).

King's College, Program in Education, Wilkes-Barre, PA 18711-0801. Offers M Ed. *Accreditation:* NCATE. *Program availability:* Part-time, evening/weekend. *Degree requirements:* For master's, thesis. *Entrance requirements:* Additional exam requirements/recommendations for international students: Required—TOEFL (minimum score 600 paper-based).

Kutztown University of Pennsylvania, College of Education, Kutztown, PA 19530-0730. Offers M Ed, MA, MLS, MS, Ed D. *Accreditation:* NCATE. *Program availability:* Part-time, evening/weekend, 100% online, blended/hybrid learning. *Faculty:* 34 full-time (26 women), 5 part-time/adjunct (1 woman). *Students:* 188 full-time (151 women), 413 part-time (323 women); includes 91 minority (27 Black or African American, non-Hispanic/Latino; 6 Asian, non-Hispanic/Latino; 43 Hispanic/Latino; 15 Two or more

races, non-Hispanic/Latino), 3 international. Average age 30. 416 applicants, 83% accepted, 206 enrolled. In 2018, 177 master's awarded. *Degree requirements:* For master's, comprehensive exam; for doctorate, thesis/dissertation. *Entrance requirements:* For master's, GRE; for doctorate, master's (or specialist) degree in education or related field from regionally-accredited institution of higher education with minimum graduate GPA of 3.25, significant educational experience, full- or part-time employment in educational setting (preferred), candidate statement, 3-5 letters of recommendation. Additional exam requirements/recommendations for international students: Required—TOEFL (minimum score 550 paper-based, 79 iBT), IELTS (minimum score 6.5), or PTE (minimum score 53). *Application deadline:* For fall admission, 8/1 for domestic and international students; for spring admission, 12/1 for domestic and international students. Application fee: $35. Electronic applications accepted. *Expenses:* Tuition, state resident: part-time $516 per credit. Tuition, nonresident: part-time $774 per credit. *Required fees:* $119 per credit. One-time fee: $50 part-time. Tuition and fees vary according to degree level. *Financial support:* Career-related internships or fieldwork, Federal Work-Study, and unspecified assistantships available. Financial award application deadline: 3/1; financial award applicants required to submit FAFSA. *Unit head:* Dr. Kenneth Teitelbaum, Dean, 610-683-4253, Fax: 610-683-4255, E-mail: teitelba@kutztown.edu. *Application contact:* Dr. Kenneth Teitelbaum, Dean, 610-683-4253, Fax: 610-683-4255, E-mail: teitelba@kutztown.edu.
Website: http://www.kutztown.edu/Education

LaGrange College, Graduate Programs, Department of Education, LaGrange, GA 30240-2999. Offers curriculum and instruction (M Ed, Ed S); middle grades (MAT); secondary education (MAT). *Program availability:* Part-time, evening/weekend. *Degree requirements:* For master's, comprehensive exam. *Entrance requirements:* For master's, GRE, MAT, minimum GPA of 2.5. Additional exam requirements/recommendations for international students: Required—TOEFL (minimum score 550 paper-based).

Lake Erie College, School of Education and Professional Studies, Painesville, OH 44077-3389. Offers M Ed. *Accreditation:* TEAC. *Program availability:* Part-time, evening/weekend. *Degree requirements:* For master's, comprehensive exam (for some programs), thesis optional, applied research project. *Entrance requirements:* For master's, GRE General Test (minimum score of 440 verbal or 500 quantitative) or minimum GPA of 2.75, bachelor's degree from accredited 4-year institution; references; essay. Additional exam requirements/recommendations for international students: Required—TOEFL (minimum score 550 paper-based; 79 iBT), IELTS (minimum score 6), STEP Eiken 1st and pre-1st grade level (for Japanese students). Electronic applications accepted. Application fee is waived when completed online. *Expenses:* Contact institution.

Lake Forest College, Master of Arts in Teaching Program, Lake Forest, IL 60045. Offers elementary education (MAT); K-12 French (MAT); K-12 music (MAT); K-12 Spanish (MAT); K-12 visual art (MAT); secondary biology (MAT); secondary chemistry (MAT); secondary English (MAT); secondary history (MAT); secondary mathematics (MAT). *Degree requirements:* For master's, comprehensive exam, portfolio. *Entrance requirements:* For master's, GRE.

Lakehead University, Graduate Studies, Faculty of Education, Thunder Bay, ON P7B 5E1, Canada. Offers educational studies (PhD); gerontology (M Ed); women's studies (M Ed). *Program availability:* Part-time, evening/weekend. *Degree requirements:* For master's, project or thesis. *Entrance requirements:* For master's, minimum B average. Additional exam requirements/recommendations for international students: Required—TOEFL. *Faculty research:* Art education, AIDS education, language arts education, gerontology, women's studies.

Lakeland University, Graduate Studies Division, Program in Education, Plymouth, WI 53073. Offers M Ed. *Accreditation:* TEAC. *Degree requirements:* For master's, thesis. *Expenses:* Contact institution.

Lamar University, College of Graduate Studies, College of Education and Human Development, Beaumont, TX 77710. Offers M Ed, MS, Ed D, Certificate. *Accreditation:* NCATE. *Program availability:* Part-time, evening/weekend, online learning. *Faculty:* 82 full-time (58 women), 48 part-time/adjunct (36 women). *Students:* 302 full-time (263 women), 4,473 part-time (3,437 women); includes 2,172 minority (1,038 Black or African American, non-Hispanic/Latino; 22 American Indian or Alaska Native, non-Hispanic/Latino; 70 Asian, non-Hispanic/Latino; 949 Hispanic/Latino; 4 Native Hawaiian or other Pacific Islander, non-Hispanic/Latino; 89 Two or more races, non-Hispanic/Latino), 17 international. Average age 37. 3,981 applicants, 85% accepted, 1092 enrolled. In 2018, 1,673 master's, 73 doctorates, 755 other advanced degrees awarded. *Degree requirements:* For master's, comprehensive exam, thesis optional; for doctorate, comprehensive exam, thesis/dissertation. *Entrance requirements:* For master's, GRE General Test, minimum GPA of 2.5; for doctorate, GRE, interview. Additional exam requirements/recommendations for international students: Required—TOEFL (minimum score 550 paper-based; 79 iBT), IELTS (minimum score 6.5). *Application deadline:* Applications are processed on a rolling basis. Application fee: $25 ($50 for international students). Electronic applications accepted. *Expenses:* Contact institution. *Financial support:* In 2018–19, 135 students received support. Fellowships, research assistantships, teaching assistantships, career-related internships or fieldwork, Federal Work-Study, institutionally sponsored loans, and scholarships/grants available. Support available to part-time students. Financial award applicants required to submit FAFSA. *Faculty research:* School dropouts, suicide prevention in public school students, school climate and gifted performance, teacher evaluation. *Total annual research expenditures:* $5,217. *Unit head:* Dr. Robert Spina, Dean, 409-880-8661. *Application contact:* Celeste Contreas, Director, Admissions and Academic Services, 409-880-8888, Fax: 409-880-7419, E-mail: gradmissions@lamar.edu.
Website: http://education.lamar.edu

Lander University, Graduate Studies, Greenwood, SC 29649-2099. Offers clinical nurse leader (MSN); emergency management (MS); Montessori education (M Ed); teaching and learning (M Ed). *Accreditation:* NCATE. *Program availability:* Part-time, online learning. *Degree requirements:* For master's, comprehensive exam, thesis or alternative. *Entrance requirements:* For master's, GRE General Test. Additional exam requirements/recommendations for international students: Required—TOEFL (minimum score 550 paper-based). Electronic applications accepted.

Langston University, School of Education and Behavioral Sciences, Langston, OK 73050. Offers bilingual/multicultural (M Ed); elementary education (M Ed); English as a second language (M Ed); rehabilitation counseling (M Sc); urban education (M Ed). *Accreditation:* CORE; NCATE (one or more programs are accredited). *Program availability:* Part-time. *Degree requirements:* For master's, comprehensive exam, thesis optional. *Entrance requirements:* For master's, GRE, writing skills test, minimum GPA of 2.5, 3 letters of recommendation. Additional exam requirements/recommendations for international students: Required—TOEFL, TWE. *Faculty research:* Bilingual/multicultural education, financing post-secondary education.

La Salle University, School of Arts and Sciences, Program in Education, Philadelphia, PA 19141-1199. Offers autism spectrum disorders (MA, Certificate); bilingual/bicultural studies (MA); classroom management (MA); dual early childhood and special education (MA); dual middle-level science and math and special education (MA); education (MA); English (MA); English as a second language (Certificate); history (MA); instructional coach (Certificate); instructional leadership (MA); reading specialist (MA, Certificate); secondary education (MA); special education (MA, Certificate). *Program availability:* Part-time, evening/weekend. *Degree requirements:* For master's, comprehensive exam. *Entrance requirements:* For master's, MAT or GRE, 2 letters of recommendation; for Certificate, GMAT or GRE, 2 letters of recommendation. Additional exam requirements/recommendations for international students: Required—TOEFL. Electronic applications accepted. Application fee is waived when completed online. *Expenses:* Contact institution.

Lasell College, Graduate and Professional Studies in Education, Newton, MA 02466-2709. Offers curriculum, leadership, and inclusion (M Ed); elementary education (M Ed); special education (M Ed), including moderate disabilities; teaching bilingual/English learners with disabilities (Graduate Certificate). *Program availability:* Part-time-only, evening/weekend, blended/hybrid learning. *Faculty:* 1 (woman) full-time, 5 part-time/adjunct (4 women). *Students:* 4 full-time (3 women), 45 part-time (37 women); includes 4 minority (3 Asian, non-Hispanic/Latino; 1 Hispanic/Latino). Average age 28. 23 applicants, 70% accepted, 10 enrolled. In 2018, 22 master's awarded. *Degree requirements:* For master's, minimum GPA of 3.0; practicum. *Entrance requirements:* For master's, Massachusetts Tests for Educator Licensure (MTEL) Curriculum and Literacy foundations of reading and writing subtest, one-page personal statement, 2 letters of recommendation, resume, bachelor's degree transcript. Additional exam requirements/recommendations for international students: Required—TOEFL (minimum score 550 paper-based, 79 iBT) or IELTS (minimum score 6). *Application deadline:* For fall admission, 8/31 priority date for domestic students, 6/30 priority date for international students; for spring admission, 12/31 priority date for domestic students, 10/31 priority date for international students. Applications are processed on a rolling basis. Electronic applications accepted. *Expenses: Tuition:* Part-time $600 per credit. *Required fees:* $40 per course. *Financial support:* Federal Work-Study, scholarships/grants, and tuition discounts available. Support available to part-time students. Financial award application deadline: 8/31; financial award applicants required to submit FAFSA. *Faculty research:* Inclusion, English language learners, literacy, and urban education; teacher inquiry; universal design for learning, deaf-blindness, and visual impairments; social and emotional learning; educational law, applied behavior analysis, and classroom management. *Unit head:* Eric Turner, Vice President of Graduate and Professional Studies, 617-243-2071, Fax: 617-243-2450, E-mail: gradinfo@lasell.edu. *Application contact:* Adrienne Franciosi, Director of Graduate Enrollment, 617-243-2214, Fax: 617-243-2450, E-mail: gradinfo@lasell.edu.
Website: http://www.lasell.edu/academics/graduate-and-professional-studies/programs-of-study/master-of-education.html

La Sierra University, School of Education, Riverside, CA 92505. Offers MA, MAT, Ed D, Ed S. *Program availability:* Part-time, evening/weekend. Terminal master's awarded for partial completion of doctoral program. *Degree requirements:* For doctorate, thesis/dissertation; for Ed S, thesis optional. *Entrance requirements:* For master's, minimum GPA of 3.0; for doctorate, GRE General Test, GRE Subject Test, minimum GPA of 3.3; for Ed S, minimum GPA of 3.3.

Lee University, Program in Education, Cleveland, TN 37320-3450. Offers art (MAT); curriculum and instruction (M Ed, Ed S); early childhood (MAT); educational leadership (M Ed, Ed S); elementary education (MAT); English and math (MAT); English and science (MAT); English and social studies (MAT); higher education administration (MS); history (MAT); history and economics (MAT); math and science (MAT); math and social studies (MAT); middle grades (MAT); science and social studies (MASW); secondary education (MAT); Spanish (MAT); special education (M Ed, MAT); TESOL (MAT). *Accreditation:* NCATE. *Program availability:* Part-time. *Faculty:* 13 full-time (5 women), 13 part-time/adjunct (7 women). *Students:* 32 full-time (26 women), 73 part-time (49 women); includes 13 minority (10 Black or African American, non-Hispanic/Latino; 3 Two or more races, non-Hispanic/Latino), 3 international. Average age 30. 56 applicants, 73% accepted, 34 enrolled. In 2018, 60 master's, 3 other advanced degrees awarded. *Degree requirements:* For master's, variable foreign language requirement, thesis optional, internship. *Entrance requirements:* For master's, MAT or GRE General Test, minimum undergraduate GPA of 2.75, 3 letters of recommendation, interview, writing sample, official transcripts, background check; for Ed S, minimum undergraduate and master's GPA of 2.75, official transcripts for undergraduate and master's degrees. Additional exam requirements/recommendations for international students: Required—TOEFL (minimum score 61 iBT). *Application deadline:* For fall admission, 6/1 priority date for domestic and international students; for spring admission, 11/1 priority date for domestic and international students; for summer admission, 4/1 priority date for domestic and international students. Applications are processed on a rolling basis. Application fee: $25. Electronic applications accepted. *Financial support:* In 2018–19, 43 students received support. Career-related internships or fieldwork, Federal Work-Study, institutionally sponsored loans, scholarships/grants, and unspecified assistantships available. Financial award application deadline: 3/1; financial award applicants required to submit FAFSA. *Unit head:* Dr. William Kamm, Director, 423-614-8544, E-mail: wkamm@leeuniversity.edu. *Application contact:* Jeffery McGirt, Director of Graduate Enrollment, 423-614-8691, Fax: 423-614-8317, E-mail: jmcgirt@leeuniversity.edu.
Website: http://www.leeuniversity.edu/academics/graduate/education

Lehigh University, College of Education, Bethlehem, PA 18015. Offers M Ed, MA, MS, Ed D, PhD, Certificate, Ed S, Graduate Certificate, M Ed/MA. *Program availability:* Part-time, evening/weekend, blended/hybrid learning. *Faculty:* 32 full-time (22 women), 34 part-time/adjunct (22 women). *Students:* 145 full-time (125 women), 251 part-time (168 women); includes 68 minority (17 Black or African American, non-Hispanic/Latino; 12 Asian, non-Hispanic/Latino; 36 Hispanic/Latino; 1 Native Hawaiian or other Pacific Islander, non-Hispanic/Latino; 2 Two or more races, non-Hispanic/Latino), 51 international. Average age 31. 322 applicants, 48% accepted, 70 enrolled. In 2018, 147 master's, 23 doctorates awarded. Terminal master's awarded for partial completion of doctoral program. *Degree requirements:* For master's, internship; for doctorate, comprehensive exam, thesis/dissertation, internship. *Entrance requirements:* For master's, essay, transcripts, 2 recommendation letters; for doctorate, GRE and/or MAT, GRE, essay, transcripts, 2 recommendation letters. Additional exam requirements/recommendations for international students: Required—TOEFL (minimum score 600 paper-based; 93 iBT), IELTS (minimum score 6.5). *Application deadline:* For fall admission, 1/1 for domestic and international students; for spring admission, 12/15 for domestic and international students; for summer admission, 4/15 for domestic and international students. Applications are processed on a rolling basis. Application fee: $65. Electronic applications accepted. *Expenses:* $565 per credit. Fees very per program. *Financial support:* In 2018–19, 127 students received support, including 3 fellowships with tuition reimbursements available (averaging $2,500 per year), 45 research assistantships with full and partial tuition reimbursements available (averaging $13,778 per year); career-related internships or fieldwork, scholarships/grants, and unspecified assistantships also available. Financial award application deadline: 3/1. *Faculty research:* Urban educational leadership, special education, instructional technology, school and counseling psychology, school psychology, counseling psychology. *Unit head:* Dr. William Gaudelli, Dean, 610-758-3221, Fax: 610-758-6223,

E-mail: wig318@lehigh.edu. *Application contact:* Donna M. Johnson, Manager of Admissions and Recruitment, 610-758-3231, Fax: 610-758-6223, E-mail: dmj4@lehigh.edu.
Website: https://ed.lehigh.edu

Lehman College of the City University of New York, School of Education, Bronx, NY 10468-1589. Offers MA, MS Ed. *Accreditation:* NCATE. *Program availability:* Part-time, evening/weekend.

Le Moyne College, Department of Education, Syracuse, NY 13214. Offers adolescent education (MS Ed, MST); adolescent education/special education (MS Ed, MST); adolescent English (MST), including grades 7-12; adolescent English/special education (MST), including grades 7-12; adolescent foreign language (MST), including grades 7-12; adolescent history (MST), including grades 7-12; childhood education (MS Ed); childhood education/special education (MS Ed); elementary education (MS Ed); general education (MS Ed); inclusive childhood education (MST); literacy education (MS Ed), including birth to grade 6, grades 5-12; school building leader (MS Ed); school building leadership (CAS); school district business leader (MS Ed, CAS); school district leader (MS Ed); school district leadership (CAS); secondary education (MS Ed); special education (MS Ed); teaching English to speakers of other languages (MS Ed); urban studies (MS Ed). *Accreditation:* TEAC. *Program availability:* Part-time, evening/weekend. *Faculty:* 7 full-time (5 women), 16 part-time/adjunct (11 women). *Students:* 35 full-time (28 women), 119 part-time (84 women); includes 14 minority (5 Black or African American, non-Hispanic/Latino; 1 Asian, non-Hispanic/Latino; 7 Hispanic/Latino; 1 Two or more races, non-Hispanic/Latino), 1 international. Average age 30. 123 applicants, 89% accepted, 96 enrolled. In 2018, 66 master's, 48 CASs awarded. Terminal master's awarded for partial completion of doctoral program. *Degree requirements:* For master's, thesis. *Entrance requirements:* For master's, bachelor's degree with minimum undergraduate GPA of 3.0, 2 letters of recommendation, transcripts. Additional exam requirements/recommendations for international students: Required—TOEFL (minimum score 79 iBT); Recommended—IELTS (minimum score 6.5). *Application deadline:* For fall admission, 4/1 priority date for domestic and international students; for spring admission, 10/1 priority date for domestic and international students; for summer admission, 3/1 priority date for domestic and international students. Applications are processed on a rolling basis. Electronic applications accepted. *Expenses:* $734 per credit hour; wellness fee $70 per semester for full-time graduate students taking 9+ credit hours; technology fee $75 per semester for full-time graduate students taking 9+ credit hours, $25 per semester for part-time students; $1,470 per credit hour (for ED.D.). *Financial support:* In 2018–19, 44 students received support. Career-related internships or fieldwork, scholarships/grants, and health care benefits available. Support available to part-time students. Financial award applicants required to submit FAFSA. *Faculty research:* Minority teachers, special education, multiculturalism, literacy, technology, media literacy learning, autism, school district organization, service-learning, higher level problem solving, teacher leadership. *Unit head:* Dr. Stephen C. Fleury, Chair, Department of Education, 315-445-4376, Fax: 315-445-4744, E-mail: fleurysc@lemoyne.edu. *Application contact:* Jody F Manning, Assistant Director for Graduate Admission, 315-445-5444, Fax: 315-445-6092, E-mail: manninjf@lemoyne.edu.
Website: http://www.lemoyne.edu/education

Lenoir-Rhyne University, Graduate Programs, School of Education, Hickory, NC 28601. Offers MA, MAT, MS. *Accreditation:* NCATE. *Program availability:* Part-time, evening/weekend, online learning. *Degree requirements:* For master's, comprehensive exam, thesis optional. *Entrance requirements:* Additional exam requirements/recommendations for international students: Required—TOEFL. Electronic applications accepted. *Expenses:* Contact institution.

Lesley University, Graduate School of Education, Cambridge, MA 02138-2790. Offers arts, community, and education (M Ed); autism studies (Certificate); curriculum and instruction (M Ed, CAGS); early childhood education (M Ed); ecological teaching and learning (MS); educational studies (PhD), including adult learning, educational leadership, individually designed; elementary education (M Ed); emergent technologies for educators (Certificate); ESLArts: language learning through the arts (M Ed); high school education (M Ed); individually designed (M Ed); integrated teaching through the arts (M Ed); literacy for K-8 classroom teachers (M Ed); mathematics education (M Ed); middle school education (M Ed); moderate disabilities (M Ed); online learning (Certificate); reading (CAGS); science in education (M Ed); severe disabilities (M Ed); special needs (CAGS); specialist teacher of reading (M Ed); teacher of visual art (M Ed); technology in education (M Ed, CAGS). *Accreditation:* TEAC. *Program availability:* Part-time, evening/weekend, online learning. *Degree requirements:* For master's, practicum; for doctorate, thesis/dissertation. *Entrance requirements:* For master's, Massachusetts Tests for Educator Licensure (MTEL), transcripts, statement of purpose, recommendations; interview (for special education); for doctorate, GRE General Test, transcripts, statement of purpose, recommendations, interview, master's degree, resume; for other advanced degree, interview, master's degree. Additional exam requirements/recommendations for international students: Required—TOEFL (minimum score 550 paper-based; 80 iBT). Electronic applications accepted. *Faculty research:* Assessment in literacy, mathematics and science; autism spectrum disorders; instructional technology and online learning; multicultural education and English language learners.

Lewis University, College of Education, Romeoville, IL 60446. Offers M Ed, MA, Ed D. *Accreditation:* NCATE. *Program availability:* Part-time, evening/weekend. *Students:* 76 full-time (56 women), 192 part-time (134 women); includes 74 minority (22 Black or African American, non-Hispanic/Latino; 7 Asian, non-Hispanic/Latino; 40 Hispanic/Latino; 5 Two or more races, non-Hispanic/Latino), 8 international. Average age 33. *Degree requirements:* For master's, thesis optional, departmental qualifying exam; for doctorate, thesis/dissertation. *Entrance requirements:* For master's, writing exam, minimum GPA of 2.75, 2 letters of recommendation, interview. Additional exam requirements/recommendations for international students: Required—TOEFL (minimum score 550 paper-based; 80 iBT), IELTS. *Application deadline:* For fall admission, 5/1 priority date for international students; for spring admission, 11/15 priority date for international students. Applications are processed on a rolling basis. Application fee: $40. Electronic applications accepted. *Financial support:* Career-related internships or fieldwork, Federal Work-Study, scholarships/grants, and unspecified assistantships available. Financial award application deadline: 5/1; financial award applicants required to submit FAFSA. *Total annual research expenditures:* $34. *Unit head:* Dr. Bonnie Bondavalli, Dean. *Application contact:* Kathy Lisak, Graduate Admission Counselor, 815-836-5610, E-mail: grad@lewisu.edu.

Liberty University, School of Education, Lynchburg, VA 24515. Offers reading specialist (M Ed). *Accreditation:* NCATE. *Program availability:* Part-time, online learning. *Students:* 2,922 full-time (2,241 women), 3,559 part-time (2,621 women); includes 1,770 minority (1,342 Black or African American, non-Hispanic/Latino; 38 American Indian or Alaska Native, non-Hispanic/Latino; 68 Asian, non-Hispanic/Latino; 177 Hispanic/Latino; 18 Native Hawaiian or other Pacific Islander, non-Hispanic/Latino; 127 Two or more races, non-Hispanic/Latino), 71 international. Average age 38. 9,077 applicants, 37% accepted, 1886 enrolled. In 2018, 1,020 master's, 173 doctorates, 402 other advanced degrees awarded. *Degree requirements:* For doctorate, comprehensive exam, thesis/dissertation. *Entrance requirements:* For master's, GRE General Test or MAT (if taken in or before 1999), 2 letters of recommendation, minimum undergraduate GPA of 3.0, curriculum vitae; for doctorate and other advanced degree, GRE General Test or MAT (if taken before 1999), minimum master's GPA of 3.0, 3 years of teaching experience. Additional exam requirements/recommendations for international students: Required—TOEFL (minimum score 600 paper-based; 100 iBT). *Application deadline:* For fall admission, 6/1 for domestic students; for spring admission, 11/1 for domestic students. Applications are processed on a rolling basis. Application fee: $50. Electronic applications accepted. *Expenses:* Contact institution. *Financial support:* In 2018–19, 265 students received support. Federal Work-Study and tuition waivers (partial) available. *Faculty research:* Self-determination, character education, bibliotherapy, learning styles, distance education. *Unit head:* Dr. Deanna Keith, Dean, 434-582-2417, E-mail: dkeith@liberty.edu. *Application contact:* Jay Bridge, Director of Graduate Admissions, 800-424-9595, Fax: 800-628-7977, E-mail: gradadmissions@liberty.edu.
Website: https://www.liberty.edu/education/

Lincoln Memorial University, Carter and Moyers School of Education, Harrogate, TN 37752-1901. Offers administration and supervision (M Ed, Ed S); counseling and guidance (M Ed); curriculum and instruction (M Ed, Ed D, Ed S); English (M Ed); executive leadership (Ed D); higher education administration (Ed D); human resource development (Ed D); leadership and administration (Ed D). *Program availability:* Part-time, evening/weekend, online learning. *Degree requirements:* For master's, comprehensive exam, thesis optional; for Ed S, comprehensive exam. *Entrance requirements:* For master's, PRAXIS, NTE, GRE, MAT, letters of recommendation; for Ed S, graduate transcripts. Additional exam requirements/recommendations for international students: Recommended—TOEFL. *Faculty research:* Brain compatible teaching and learning; poverty in Appalachia; leadership for change; ethics, moral responsibility and social justice; human and organizational learning.

Lindenwood University, Graduate Programs, School of Education, St. Charles, MO 63301-1695. Offers behavioral analysis (MA); education (MA), including autism spectrum disorders, character education, early intervention in autism and sensory impairment, gifted, technology; educational administration (MA, Ed D, Ed S); English to speakers of other languages (MA); instructional leadership (Ed D, Ed S); library media (MA); professional counseling (MA); school administration (MA, Ed S); school counseling (MA); teaching (MA). *Program availability:* Part-time, evening/weekend, 100% online, blended/hybrid learning. *Faculty:* 38 full-time (28 women), 111 part-time/adjunct (66 women). *Students:* 456 full-time (341 women), 1,107 part-time (851 women); includes 374 minority (296 Black or African American, non-Hispanic/Latino; 7 American Indian or Alaska Native, non-Hispanic/Latino; 8 Asian, non-Hispanic/Latino; 38 Hispanic/Latino; 1 Native Hawaiian or other Pacific Islander, non-Hispanic/Latino; 24 Two or more races, non-Hispanic/Latino), 17 international. Average age 36. 496 applicants, 72% accepted, 275 enrolled. In 2018, 454 master's, 64 doctorates, 66 other advanced degrees awarded. *Degree requirements:* For master's, thesis (for some programs), minimum GPA of 3.0; for doctorate, thesis/dissertation, minimum GPA of 3.0; for Ed S, comprehensive exam, project, minimum GPA of 3.0. *Entrance requirements:* For master's, interview, minimum undergraduate cumulative GPA of 3.0, writing sample, letter of recommendation; for doctorate, minimum graduate GPA of 3.4, resume, interview, writing sample, 4 letters of recommendation; for Ed S, master's degree in education, relevant work experience. Additional exam requirements/recommendations for international students: Required—TOEFL (minimum score 553 paper-based; 81 iBT); Recommended—IELTS (minimum score 6.5). *Application deadline:* For fall admission, 8/9 priority date for domestic students, 6/1 priority date for international students; for spring admission, 12/20 priority date for domestic students, 11/1 priority date for international students; for summer admission, 5/15 priority date for domestic students, 3/27 priority date for international students. Applications are processed on a rolling basis. Application fee: $0 ($100 for international students). Electronic applications accepted. *Expenses: Tuition:* Full-time $16,900; part-time $480 per credit hour. *Required fees:* $700; $350 per unit. Tuition and fees vary according to degree level. *Financial support:* In 2018–19, 316 students received support. Career-related internships or fieldwork, Federal Work-Study, institutionally sponsored loans, scholarships/grants, tuition waivers (partial), and unspecified assistantships available. Financial award application deadline: 6/30; financial award applicants required to submit FAFSA. *Unit head:* Dr. Anthony Scheffler, Dean, School of Education, 636-949-4618, Fax: 636-949-4197, E-mail: ascheffler@lindenwood.edu. *Application contact:* Kara Schilli, Assistant Vice President, University Admissions, 636-949-4349, Fax: 636-949-4109, E-mail: adultadmissions@lindenwood.edu.
Website: https://www.lindenwood.edu/academics/academic-schools/school-of-education/

Lindenwood University–Belleville, Graduate Programs, Belleville, IL 62226. Offers business administration (MBA); communications (MA), including digital and multimedia, media management, promotions, training and development; counseling (MA); criminal justice administration (MS); education (MA); healthcare administration (MS); human resource management (MS); school administration (MA); teaching (MAT).

Lipscomb University, College of Education, Nashville, TN 37204-3951. Offers applied behavior analysis (MS, Certificate); coaching for learning (M Ed, Certificate, Ed S); educational leadership (M Ed, Ed S); English language learning (M Ed, Ed S); instructional coaching (M Ed, Certificate, Ed S); instructional practice (M Ed); learning organizations and strategic change (Ed D); literacy coaching (Certificate, Ed S); reading specialty (M Ed, Ed S); school counseling (M Ed, Ed S); special education (M Ed); teaching, learning, and leading (M Ed); technology integration (M Ed, Ed S); technology integration specialist (Certificate). *Accreditation:* NCATE. *Program availability:* Part-time, evening/weekend, 100% online. *Degree requirements:* For master's, comprehensive exam, portfolio, research project and presentation; for doctorate, practical capstone project in experiential setting. *Entrance requirements:* For master's, MAT (minimum score 31) or GRE General Test (minimum score 294), 2 reference letters, goals statement, writing sample, interview; for doctorate, MAT or GRE General Test, 3 reference letters, artifact of demonstrated academic excellence, written personal statements, interview. Additional exam requirements/recommendations for international students: Required—TOEFL (minimum score 570 paper-based; 80 iBT). Electronic applications accepted. *Expenses:* Contact institution. *Faculty research:* Facilitative learning styles, leadership, student assessment, interactive multimedia inclusion, learning organizations and strategic change.

Lock Haven University of Pennsylvania, College of Liberal Arts and Education, Lock Haven, PA 17745-2390. Offers alternative education (M Ed); educational leadership (M Ed); teaching and learning (M Ed). *Accreditation:* NCATE. *Program availability:* Part-time, evening/weekend, online learning. *Degree requirements:* For master's, thesis. *Entrance requirements:* For master's, minimum undergraduate GPA of 3.0. Additional exam requirements/recommendations for international students: Required—TOEFL. Electronic applications accepted.

London Metropolitan University, Graduate Programs, London, United Kingdom. Offers applied psychology (M Sc); architecture (MA); biomedical science (M Sc); blood science (M Sc); cancer pharmacology (M Sc); computer networking and cyber security (M Sc); computing and information systems (M Sc); conference interpreting (MA); counter-terrorism studies (M Sc); creative, digital and professional writing (MA); crime, violence and prevention (M Sc); criminology (M Sc); curating contemporary art (MA);

data analytics (M Sc); digital media (MA); early childhood studies (MA); education (MA, Ed D); financial services law, regulation and compliance (LL M); food science (M Sc); forensic psychology (M Sc); health and social care management and policy (M Sc); human nutrition (M Sc); human resource management (MA); human rights and international conflict (MA); information technology (M Sc); intelligence and security studies (M Sc); international oil, gas and energy law (LL M); international relations (MA); interpreting (MA); learning and teaching in higher education (MA); legal practice (LL M); media and entertainment law (LL M); organizational and consumer psychology (M Sc); psychological therapy (M Sc); psychology of mental health (M Sc); public health (M Sc); public policy and management (MPA); security studies (M Sc); social work (M Sc); spatial planning and urban design (MA); sports therapy (M Sc); supporting older children and young people with dyslexia (MA); teaching languages (MA), including Arabic, English; translation (MA); woman and child abuse (MA).

Long Island University–LIU Brooklyn, School of Education, Brooklyn, NY 11201-8423. Offers adolescence urban education (MS Ed); applied behavior analysis (Advanced Certificate); bilingual education (Advanced Certificate); bilingual education in urban setting (MS Ed); bilingual school counselor (MS Ed, Advanced Certificate); childhood urban education (MS Ed); childhood/early childhood education (MS Ed); childhood/early childhood urban education (MS Ed); early childhood urban education (MS Ed, Advanced Certificate); educational leadership (Advanced Certificate); marriage and family therapy (MS, Advanced Certificate); mental health counseling (MS, Advanced Certificate); school building district leader (Advanced Certificate); school counselor (MS Ed, Advanced Certificate); school psychologist (MS Ed); teaching students with disabilities (MS Ed); teaching urban children with disabilities (MS Ed); TESOL (MS Ed, Advanced Certificate). *Accreditation:* TEAC. *Program availability:* Part-time, evening/weekend, 100% online. *Entrance requirements:* For master's, GRE. Additional exam requirements/recommendations for international students: Required—TOEFL (minimum score 527 paper-based, 75 iBT), IELTS, or PTE. Electronic applications accepted. *Faculty research:* Diversity issues in education and mental health care, inclusion - disability studies, sustainability, teacher professional development.

Long Island University–LIU Post, College of Education, Information and Technology, Brookville, NY 11548-1300. Offers adolescence education (MS); adolescence education 7-12 (MS); archives and records management (AC); art education (MS); childhood education (MS); childhood education/literacy B-6 (MS); childhood education/special education (MS); clinical mental health counseling (MS, AC); early childhood education (MS); early childhood education/childhood education (MS); educational leadership (AC); educational technology (MS); information studies (PhD); interdisciplinary educational studies (Ed D); middle childhood education (MS); music education (MS); public library administration (AC); school counselor (MS); special education (MS Ed); speech-language pathology (MA); students with disabilities, 7-12 generalist (AC); TESOL (MA). *Accreditation:* ASHA; TEAC. *Program availability:* Part-time, 100% online, blended/hybrid learning. Terminal master's awarded for partial completion of doctoral program. *Degree requirements:* For master's, variable foreign language requirement, comprehensive exam (for some programs), thesis optional; for doctorate, comprehensive exam, thesis/dissertation. *Entrance requirements:* For master's and AC, GRE (for some programs). Additional exam requirements/recommendations for international students: Required—TOEFL (minimum score 550 paper-based, 75 iBT), IELTS, or PTE. Electronic applications accepted. *Faculty research:* Sleep; use of technology to develop executive function by students with disabilities; early childhood literacy development through play; social justice through education; using a structured protocol to discuss Bad News.

Longwood University, College of Graduate and Professional Studies, College of Education and Human Services, Farmville, VA 23909. Offers education (MS), including algebra and middle school mathematics, counselor education, elementary and middle school mathematics, elementary education, elementary education initial licensure, health and physical education, special education general curriculum, special education initial licensure; reading, literacy and learning (M Ed); school librarianship (M Ed); social work and communication sciences and disorders (MS), including communication sciences and disorders. *Accreditation:* NCATE. *Program availability:* Part-time, evening/weekend. *Degree requirements:* For master's, comprehensive exam (for some programs), thesis optional, professional portfolio, internship, clinical experience, or practicum. *Entrance requirements:* For master's, PRAXIS I (for initial teaching licensure programs); GRE (for some programs), bachelor's degree from regionally-accredited institution, 2 recommendations (3 for some programs), minimum 500-word personal essay, official transcripts, minimum GPA of 2.75, valid teaching license (for some programs). Additional exam requirements/recommendations for international students: Required—TOEFL (minimum score 570 paper-based), IELTS (minimum score 6.5). Electronic applications accepted. *Expenses:* Contact institution.

Louisiana College, Graduate Programs, Pineville, LA 71359-0001. Offers clinical nurse leadership (MSN); educational leadership (M Ed); social work (MSW); teaching (MAT).

Louisiana State University and Agricultural & Mechanical College, Graduate School, College of Human Sciences and Education, Baton Rouge, LA 70803. Offers M Ed, MA, MAT, MLIS, MS, MSW, PhD, Ed S. *Accreditation:* NCATE.

Louisiana State University in Shreveport, College of Business, Education, and Human Development, Program in Education, Shreveport, LA 71115-2399. Offers curriculum and instruction (M Ed); leadership (M Ed); leadership studies (Ed D). *Accreditation:* NCATE. *Program availability:* Part-time. *Degree requirements:* For master's, orally-presented project, 200-hour internship (educational leadership). *Entrance requirements:* For master's, GRE, minimum GPA of 2.5; teacher certification; recommendations and interview (for educational leadership). Additional exam requirements/recommendations for international students: Required—TOEFL (minimum score 550 paper-based; 61 iBT). Electronic applications accepted.

Louisiana Tech University, Graduate School, College of Education, Ruston, LA 71272. Offers counseling and guidance (MA), including clinical mental health counseling, human services, orientation and mobility; counseling psychology (PhD); curriculum and instruction (M Ed); cyber education (Graduate Certificate); dynamics of domestic and family violence (Graduate Certificate); early childhood education - PreK-3 (MAT); educational leadership (M Ed, Ed D); elementary education and special education mild/moderate grades 1-5 (MAT); higher education administration (Graduate Certificate); industrial/organizational psychology (MA, PhD); kinesiology (MS); middle school education (MAT), including mathematics; orientation and mobility (Graduate Certificate); rehabilitation teaching for the blind (Graduate Certificate); secondary education (MAT), including agriculture, biology, business, chemistry, English; special education: visually impaired (MAT); teacher leader education (Graduate Certificate); visual impairments - blind education (Graduate Certificate). *Accreditation:* NCATE. *Program availability:* Part-time. *Degree requirements:* For master's, thesis; for doctorate, thesis/dissertation. *Entrance requirements:* For master's and doctorate, GRE General Test. Additional exam requirements/recommendations for international students: Required—TOEFL (minimum score 550 paper-based; 80 iBT), IELTS (minimum score 6.5). Electronic applications accepted. *Faculty research:* Blindness and the best methods for increasing independence for individuals who are blind or visually impaired; educating and investigating factors contributing to improvements in human performance across the lifespan and a reduction in injury rates during training.

Loyola Marymount University, School of Education, Los Angeles, CA 90045. Offers MA, Ed D, JD/MA. *Accreditation:* NCATE. *Program availability:* Part-time, evening/weekend. *Faculty:* 38 full-time (25 women), 114 part-time/adjunct (79 women). *Students:* 774 full-time (594 women), 136 part-time (97 women); includes 551 minority (65 Black or African American, non-Hispanic/Latino; 74 Asian, non-Hispanic/Latino; 387 Hispanic/Latino; 2 Native Hawaiian or other Pacific Islander, non-Hispanic/Latino; 23 Two or more races, non-Hispanic/Latino), 60 international. Average age 29. 544 applicants, 67% accepted, 276 enrolled. In 2018, 466 master's, 17 doctorates awarded. *Degree requirements:* For doctorate, thesis/dissertation. *Entrance requirements:* For master's, official transcripts, letters of recommendation. Additional exam requirements/recommendations for international students: Required—TOEFL, IELTS. Application fee: $50. Electronic applications accepted. *Financial support:* Research assistantships, teaching assistantships, institutionally sponsored loans, scholarships/grants, and unspecified assistantships available. Support available to part-time students. Financial award application deadline: 5/1; financial award applicants required to submit FAFSA. *Unit head:* Dr. Mary McCullough, Interim Dean, School of Education, 310-338-7312, E-mail: Mary.McCullough@lmu.edu. *Application contact:* Ammar Dalal, Assistant Vice Provost for Graduate Enrollment, 310-338-2721, Fax: 310-338-6086, E-mail: graduateinfo@lmu.edu.
Website: http://soe.lmu.edu

Loyola University Chicago, School of Education, Chicago, IL 60660. Offers M Ed, MA, Ed D, PhD, Certificate, Ed S. *Accreditation:* NCATE. *Program availability:* Part-time, evening/weekend. *Faculty:* 49 full-time (32 women), 69 part-time/adjunct (50 women). *Students:* 308 full-time (237 women), 182 part-time (135 women); includes 188 minority (71 Black or African American, non-Hispanic/Latino; 29 Asian, non-Hispanic/Latino; 73 Hispanic/Latino; 1 Native Hawaiian or other Pacific Islander, non-Hispanic/Latino; 14 Two or more races, non-Hispanic/Latino), 20 international. Average age 31. 608 applicants, 63% accepted, 146 enrolled. In 2018, 174 master's, 45 doctorates, 19 other advanced degrees awarded. *Degree requirements:* For master's, comprehensive exam (for some programs), thesis (for some programs); for doctorate, comprehensive exam, thesis/dissertation; for other advanced degree, comprehensive exam. *Entrance requirements:* For master's, minimum GPA of 3.0, 3 letters of recommendation, resume, transcripts; for doctorate, GRE, interview, minimum GPA of 3.0, 3 letters of recommendation, resume; for other advanced degree, GRE, interview, minimum GPA of 3.0, letters of recommendation, resume, transcripts. Additional exam requirements/recommendations for international students: Required—TOEFL (minimum score 550 paper-based; 79 iBT). Application fee: $50. Electronic applications accepted. Application fee is waived when completed online. *Expenses:* Contact institution. *Financial support:* In 2018–19, 293 students received support, including 120 fellowships with partial tuition reimbursements available, 80 research assistantships with full tuition reimbursements available (averaging $14,000 per year), 93 teaching assistantships (averaging $4,000 per year); career-related internships or fieldwork, Federal Work-Study, institutionally sponsored loans, scholarships/grants, traineeships, health care benefits, and unspecified assistantships also available. Support available to part-time students. Financial award application deadline: 2/1; financial award applicants required to submit FAFSA. *Faculty research:* Policy studies, historical foundations, teacher education, research methodologies, comparative education. *Total annual research expenditures:* $2.2 million. *Unit head:* Dr. Malik Henfield, Dean, 312-915-7002, E-mail: mhenfield@luc.edu. *Application contact:* Dr. Siobhan Cafferty, Program Chair, 312-915-7002, E-mail: scaffer@luc.edu.
Website: http://www.luc.edu/education

Loyola University Maryland, Graduate Programs, School of Education, Baltimore, MD 21210-2699. Offers M Ed, MA, MAT, CAS. *Accreditation:* NCATE. *Program availability:* Part-time, evening/weekend. *Degree requirements:* For master's, thesis. *Entrance requirements:* Additional exam requirements/recommendations for international students: Required—TOEFL (minimum score 550 paper-based), IELTS (minimum score 7). Electronic applications accepted. *Expenses:* Contact institution.

Loyola University New Orleans, College of Arts and Sciences, Master of Arts in Teaching Program, New Orleans, LA 70118-6195. Offers MAT. *Program availability:* Part-time. *Faculty:* 2 full-time (both women). *Students:* 21 part-time (15 women); includes 9 minority (8 Black or African American, non-Hispanic/Latino; 1 American Indian or Alaska Native, non-Hispanic/Latino). Average age 31. 17 applicants, 100% accepted, 13 enrolled. In 2018, 1 master's awarded. *Degree requirements:* For master's, comprehensive exam, Praxis II content-specific exam and Teaching (PLT). *Entrance requirements:* For master's, GRE; Praxis I (or have an ACT composite score of 22 or higher, an SAT combined verbal and math score of 1030, or a graduate degree), 3 professional references, a non-education baccalaureate degree from a regionally accredited institution with a 3.0 or higher GPA. *Application deadline:* Applications are processed on a rolling basis. Electronic applications accepted. *Expenses:* $409 per credit hour tuition, $733 per semester full-time fees, $376.50 per semester part-time fees. *Financial support:* Application deadline: 5/1; applicants required to submit FAFSA. *Unit head:* Dr. Glenda Hembree, Office of Teacher Education, 504-865-3081, E-mail: gghembre@loyno.edu. *Application contact:* Dr. Glenda Hembree, Office of Teacher Education, 504-865-3081, E-mail: gghembre@loyno.edu.
Website: http://cas.loyno.edu/teacher-education/mat

Lynn University, Donald E. and Helen L. Ross College of Education, Boca Raton, FL 33431-5598. Offers educational leadership (M Ed, Ed D), including K-12 (Ed D), school administration K-12 (M Ed); exceptional student education (M Ed), including school administration K-12. *Program availability:* Part-time, evening/weekend, online learning. *Faculty:* 6 full-time (4 women), 8 part-time/adjunct (7 women). *Students:* 38 full-time (30 women), 85 part-time (63 women); includes 50 minority (33 Black or African American, non-Hispanic/Latino; 1 Asian, non-Hispanic/Latino; 15 Hispanic/Latino; 1 Two or more races, non-Hispanic/Latino), 5 international. Average age 38. 78 applicants, 65% accepted, 41 enrolled. In 2018, 13 master's, 14 doctorates awarded. *Degree requirements:* For master's, comprehensive exam, thesis (for some programs), completion of degree in maximum of four calendar years; minimum cumulative GPA of 3.0 and B grade or higher in each course; orientation seminar (one credit); minimum of 40 credits; FTCE ESE K-12 Exam; for doctorate, thesis/dissertation, mid-program review; minimum cumulative GPA of 3.25 and B grade or higher in each course. *Entrance requirements:* For master's, bachelor's degree from accredited institution, minimum undergraduate GPA of 3.0, official undergraduate and graduate transcripts of all academic coursework attempted, current resume, statement of professional goals, writing sample, 2 recent letters of recommendation; for doctorate, professional practice statement that identifies applicant's goals and explains how Lynn's program will help attain them, official transcript showing conferral of master's degree, 2 letters of recommendation from previous professors or employers, current resume, interview. Additional exam requirements/recommendations for international students: Required—TOEFL (minimum score 550 paper-based; 80 iBT), IELTS (minimum score 6.5). *Application deadline:* For fall admission, 8/18 for domestic students, 8/4 for international students; for spring admission, 12/15 for domestic students, 12/1 for international students; for summer admission, 4/17 for domestic students, 4/3 for international students. Applications are processed on a rolling basis. Application fee: $45. Electronic applications accepted. *Expenses:* 850 per credit hour. *Financial support:* In 2018–19, 85 students received support. Career-related internships or fieldwork, Federal Work-

Study, scholarships/grants, tuition waivers (partial), and unspecified assistantships available. Support available to part-time students. Financial award application deadline: 3/1; financial award applicants required to submit FAFSA. *Faculty research:* Student achievement, students with learning differences, teacher and student retention, student motivation and cognition, neuroscience leadership and learning. *Unit head:* Dr. Kathleen Weigel, Dean, College of Education, 561-237-7441, E-mail: kweigel@lynn.edu. *Application contact:* Steven Pruitt, Director of Graduate and Undergraduate Evening Admission, 561-237-7834, Fax: 561-237-7100, E-mail: spruitt@lynn.edu.
Website: http://www.lynn.edu/academics/colleges/education

Madonna University, Programs in Education, Livonia, MI 48150-1173. Offers Catholic school leadership (MSA); educational leadership (MSA); learning disabilities (MAT); literacy education (MAT); teaching and learning (MAT). *Accreditation:* NCATE. *Program availability:* Part-time, evening/weekend. *Degree requirements:* For master's, thesis or alternative. Electronic applications accepted. *Expenses: Tuition:* Full-time $15,030; part-time $835 per credit hour. Tuition and fees vary according to degree level and program.

Malone University, Graduate Program in Education, Canton, OH 44709. Offers curriculum and instruction (MA); curriculum, instruction, and professional development (MA); educational leadership (principal license) (MA); intervention specialist (MA). *Accreditation:* NCATE. *Program availability:* Part-time, evening/weekend. *Degree requirements:* For master's, research project. *Entrance requirements:* For master's, minimum GPA of 3.0, teaching license. Additional exam requirements/recommendations for international students: Required—TOEFL (minimum score 550 paper-based; 79 iBT). *Faculty research:* Educational leadership styles: Jesus as master teacher, assessment accommodations for English language learners, preparing culturally proficient teachers, using naturally occurring text in the classroom to meet the syntactic needs of students with learning disabilities, using tablet instructional technology to meet the needs of students with disabilities.

Manhattan College, Graduate Programs, School of Education and Health, Riverdale, NY 10471. Offers MA, MS, MS Ed, Advanced Certificate, Certificate, Professional Diploma. *Accreditation:* TEAC. *Program availability:* Part-time, evening/weekend, online learning. *Degree requirements:* For master's and other advanced degree, thesis, internship. *Entrance requirements:* For master's and other advanced degree, minimum GPA of 3.0. Additional exam requirements/recommendations for international students: Required—TOEFL. *Faculty research:* Leadership, assessment, professional development, school improvement.

Manhattanville College, School of Education, Purchase, NY 10577-2132. Offers M Ed, MAT, MPS, Ed D, Advanced Certificate, Certificate, PD. *Accreditation:* NCATE. *Program availability:* Part-time, evening/weekend. *Faculty:* 28 full-time (17 women), 110 part-time/adjunct (75 women). *Students:* 235 full-time (148 women), 448 part-time (335 women); includes 119 minority (46 Black or African American, non-Hispanic/Latino; 1 American Indian or Alaska Native, non-Hispanic/Latino; 12 Asian, non-Hispanic/Latino; 53 Hispanic/Latino; 4 Native Hawaiian or other Pacific Islander, non-Hispanic/Latino; 3 Two or more races, non-Hispanic/Latino), 3 international. Average age 32. 304 applicants, 64% accepted, 153 enrolled. In 2018, 220 master's, 12 doctorates, 35 other advanced degrees awarded. *Degree requirements:* For master's, comprehensive exam (for some programs), thesis (for some programs), student teaching, research seminars, portfolios, internships, writing assessment; for doctorate, comprehensive exam (for some programs), thesis/dissertation. *Entrance requirements:* For master's, for programs that require certification, students must submit scores from GRE or MAT(Miller Analogies Test), minimum GPA of 3.0, 2 letters of recommendation, interview, essay (2-3 page personal statement that describes reasons for choosing teaching or educational leadership as profession and philosophy of education), proof of immunization (for those born after 1957); for doctorate, candidates must submit scores from GRE or MAT(Miller Analogies Test), GPA of 3.0+, 2 letters of recommendation, 1 letter of nomination, interview, writing sample(leadership experiences, your strengths in the role of educational leader, your interest in the doctoral program, and what knowledge and skills you hope to develop in the program), educator, leader, supervisor; proof of immunization for those born after 1957; for other advanced degree, art education candidates: art portfolio; music education candidates: exam and audition; Jump Start candidates: interview with the program coordinator; educational leadership candidates: interview with the program coordinator. Additional exam requirements/recommendations for international students: Required—TOEFL (minimum score 600 paper-based; 110 iBT); Recommended—IELTS (minimum score 8). *Application deadline:* For summer admission, 1/1 for domestic students. Applications are processed on a rolling basis. Application fee: $75. Electronic applications accepted. *Expenses:* 935 per credit; 1000 per credit for those who completed all degree requirements from another institution and just need to complete dissertation for doctorate. *Financial support:* In 2018–19, 86 students received support. Teaching assistantships, career-related internships or fieldwork, Federal Work-Study, institutionally sponsored loans, scholarships/grants, and unspecified assistantships available. Financial award application deadline: 3/15; financial award applicants required to submit FAFSA. *Faculty research:* Professional development schools, community schools, mindfulness, students with emotional difficulties, social capital, early childhood and physical education, story and happiness, early childhood and technology, diversity in higher education, education for sustainability, english learners, applied behavior analysis, leadership and longevity in administrative positions, and higher education and k-12 partnerships. *Total annual research expenditures:* $800. *Unit head:* Dr. Shelley Wepner, Dean, 914-323-3153, Fax: 914-323-5493, E-mail: Shelly.Wepner@mville.edu. *Application contact:* Alissa Wilson, Director, SOE Graduate Enrollment Management, 914-323-3150, E-mail: edschool@mville.edu.
Website: http://www.mville.edu/academics/school-education

Mansfield University of Pennsylvania, Graduate Studies, Department of Education and Special Education, Mansfield, PA 16933. Offers elementary education (M Ed); secondary education (MS); special education (M Ed). *Accreditation:* NCATE (one or more programs are accredited). *Program availability:* Part-time, evening/weekend, online learning. *Degree requirements:* For master's, comprehensive exam, thesis optional. *Entrance requirements:* For master's, minimum GPA of 3.0. Additional exam requirements/recommendations for international students: Required—TOEFL (minimum score 550 paper-based). Electronic applications accepted.

Maranatha Baptist University, Program in Teaching and Learning, Watertown, WI 53094. Offers M Ed. *Program availability:* Part-time, evening/weekend, 100% online. *Expenses:* Contact institution.

Marian University, Educators College, Indianapolis, IN 46222-1997. Offers MA, MAT. *Accreditation:* NCATE. *Program availability:* Part-time, evening/weekend, 100% online. *Degree requirements:* For master's, 2 classroom research courses, initial teacher licensure, final portfolio. *Entrance requirements:* For master's, Indiana CORE Academic Skills Assessment (or alternative). Additional exam requirements/recommendations for international students: Required—TOEFL (minimum score 69 iBT), IELTS. Electronic applications accepted. Application fee is waived when completed online. *Expenses:* Contact institution.

Marian University, School of Education, Fond du Lac, WI 54935-4699. Offers curriculum and instruction leadership (PhD); educational administration (PhD); educational leadership (MAE); educational technology (MAE); leadership studies (PhD); special education (MAE); teacher education (MAE). *Accreditation:* NCATE. *Program availability:* Part-time, evening/weekend, online learning. *Degree requirements:* For master's, exam, field-based experience project, portfolio; for doctorate, comprehensive exam, thesis/dissertation, field-based experience. *Entrance requirements:* For master's, minimum GPA of 3.0, BA in education or related field, teaching license; for doctorate, GRE, MAT, resume, 2 writing samples, interview. Additional exam requirements/recommendations for international students: Required—TOEFL (minimum score 525 paper-based; 70 iBT). *Faculty research:* At-risk youth, multicultural issues, values in education, teaching/learning strategies.

Marist College, Graduate Programs, School of Social and Behavioral Sciences, Poughkeepsie, NY 12601-1387. Offers education (M Ed, MA); mental health counseling (MA); school psychology (MA, Adv C). *Program availability:* Part-time, evening/weekend. *Degree requirements:* For master's, thesis optional. *Entrance requirements:* For master's, GRE General Test, letters of recommendation, minimum undergraduate GPA of 3.0, interview. Additional exam requirements/recommendations for international students: Required—TOEFL (minimum score 550 paper-based; 80 iBT); Recommended—IELTS (minimum score 6.5). Electronic applications accepted. *Faculty research:* AIDS prevention, educational intervention, humanistic counseling research, aging and development, neuroimaging.

Marquette University, Graduate School, College of Education, Milwaukee, WI 53201-1881. Offers M Ed, MA, MS, PhD, Certificate. *Accreditation:* NCATE. *Program availability:* Part-time. Terminal master's awarded for partial completion of doctoral program. *Degree requirements:* For master's, comprehensive exam, thesis (for some programs); for doctorate, thesis/dissertation, qualifying exam. *Entrance requirements:* For master's, GRE General Test or MAT, official transcripts from all current and previous colleges/universities except Marquette, three letters of recommendation, statement of purpose; for doctorate, GRE General Test, MAT, sample of written work, official transcripts from all current and previous colleges/universities except Marquette, three letters of recommendation, statement of purpose, resume/curriculum vitae; for Certificate, GRE General Test or MAT, master's degree. Additional exam requirements/recommendations for international students: Required—TOEFL (minimum score 530 paper-based). *Expenses:* Contact institution. *Faculty research:* Parenting, psychology of motivation, reading assessment, socialization of educational administrators, education philosophy of Cardinal Newman.

Marshall University, Academic Affairs Division, College of Education and Professional Development, Huntington, WV 25755. Offers MA, MAT, MS, Ed D, Certificate, Ed S. *Accreditation:* NCATE. *Program availability:* Part-time, evening/weekend. *Degree requirements:* For master's, thesis optional, comprehensive or oral assessment. *Entrance requirements:* Additional exam requirements/recommendations for international students: Required—TOEFL. Electronic applications accepted.

Martin Luther College, Graduate Studies, New Ulm, MN 56073. Offers early childhood director (MS Ed Admin); educational technology (MS Ed); instruction (MS Ed); leadership (MS Ed); principal (MS Ed Admin); special education (MS Ed). *Program availability:* Part-time, evening/weekend, online only, 100% online. *Faculty:* 13 full-time (2 women), 31 part-time/adjunct (10 women). *Students:* 1 full-time (0 women), 86 part-time (26 women); includes 1 minority (Two or more races, non-Hispanic/Latino), 1 international. Average age 38. 35 applicants, 100% accepted, 35 enrolled. In 2018, 26 master's awarded. *Degree requirements:* For master's, capstone project or comprehensive exam. *Entrance requirements:* For master's, undergraduate degree in education from an accredited college or university, minimum undergraduate GPA of 3.0. Additional exam requirements/recommendations for international students: Required—TOEFL (minimum score 550 paper-based; 80 iBT); Recommended—IELTS (minimum score 6.5). *Application deadline:* Applications are processed on a rolling basis. Application fee: $35. Electronic applications accepted. *Financial support:* In 2018–19, 1 student received support. Scholarships/grants available. Financial award application deadline: 9/1. *Faculty research:* Principal effectiveness, principal support, cognitive load in math instruction, reading strategies in multigrade classrooms, mentor provided professional development for new teachers. *Unit head:* John E. Meyer, Director of Graduate Studies, 507-354-8221 Ext. 398, E-mail: meyerjd@mlc-wels.edu. *Application contact:* John E. Meyer, Director of Graduate Studies, 507-354-8221 Ext. 398, E-mail: meyerjd@mlc-wels.edu.
Website: https://mlc-wels.edu/graduate-studies/

Mary Baldwin University, Graduate Studies, Programs in Education, Staunton, VA 24401-3610. Offers applied behavior analysis (MS); autism spectrum disorders (M Ed); elementary education (M Ed, MAT); English as a second language (M Ed); environment-based learning (M Ed); gifted education (M Ed); higher education (MS); leadership (M Ed); middle grades education (MAT); reading education (M Ed); special education (M Ed). *Accreditation:* TEAC.

Marymount University, School of Sciences, Mathematics, and Education, Program in Education, Arlington, VA 22207-4299. Offers curriculum and instruction (M Ed); elementary education (M Ed); professional studies (M Ed); secondary education (M Ed); special education: general curriculum (M Ed). *Accreditation:* NCATE. *Program availability:* Part-time, evening/weekend. *Faculty:* 7 full-time (all women), 8 part-time/adjunct (6 women). *Students:* 42 full-time (29 women), 103 part-time (80 women); includes 31 minority (8 Black or African American, non-Hispanic/Latino; 11 Asian, non-Hispanic/Latino; 10 Hispanic/Latino; 1 Native Hawaiian or other Pacific Islander, non-Hispanic/Latino; 1 Two or more races, non-Hispanic/Latino), 12 international. Average age 36. 44 applicants, 100% accepted, 30 enrolled. In 2018, 61 master's awarded. *Degree requirements:* For master's, thesis or alternative, capstone/internship. *Entrance requirements:* For master's, PRAXIS MATH or SAT/ACT, and Virginia Communication and Literacy Assessment (VCLA), 2 letters of recommendation, resume, interview, minimum undergraduate GPA of 2.75 or 3.25 in the last 60 hours. Additional exam requirements/recommendations for international students: Required—TOEFL (minimum score 600 paper-based; 96 iBT), IELTS (minimum score 6.5), PTE (minimum score 58). *Application deadline:* For fall admission, 7/16 priority date for domestic and international students; for spring admission, 11/16 priority date for domestic and international students. Applications are processed on a rolling basis. Application fee: $40. Electronic applications accepted. *Expenses:* $770 per credit. *Financial support:* In 2018–19, 3 students received support. Research assistantships, teaching assistantships, career-related internships or fieldwork, scholarships/grants, and unspecified assistantships available. Support available to part-time students. Financial award application deadline: 3/1; financial award applicants required to submit FAFSA. *Unit head:* Dr. Lisa Turissini, Chair, Education, 703-526-1668, E-mail: lisa.turissini@marymount.edu. *Application contact:* Rebecca Esposito, Senior Associate Director, Graduate Admissions, 703-284-5901, Fax: 703-527-3815, E-mail: grad.admissions@marymount.edu.
Website: https://www.marymount.edu/Academics/School-of-Sciences-Mathematics-and-Education/Graduate-Programs/Education-(M-Ed-)

Maryville University of Saint Louis, School of Education, St. Louis, MO 63141-7299. Offers early childhood education (MA Ed); educational leadership (Ed D); educational leadership w/principal certification (MA Ed); elementary education (MA Ed); gifted (MA Ed); higher education leadership (Ed D); middle grades education (MA Ed); reading/literacy specialist (MA Ed); teacher as leader (Ed D). *Accreditation:* NCATE.

Program availability: Part-time, 100% online, blended/hybrid learning. *Faculty:* 16 full-time (8 women), 18 part-time/adjunct (11 women). *Students:* 12 full-time (all women), 311 part-time (234 women); includes 99 minority (84 Black or African American, non-Hispanic/Latino; 2 Asian, non-Hispanic/Latino; 9 Hispanic/Latino; 4 Two or more races, non-Hispanic/Latino), 2 international. Average age 38. In 2018, 25 master's, 100 doctorates awarded. *Degree requirements:* For master's, thesis, project. *Entrance requirements:* For master's, minimum cumulative GPA of 3.0, 3 professional recommendations, essays, interview with program faculty; for doctorate, minimum GPA of 3.0, 3 professional recommendations, essay, interview, on-site writing sample. Additional exam requirements/recommendations for international students: Required— TOEFL (minimum score 550 paper-based; 79 iBT). *Application deadline:* Applications are processed on a rolling basis. Electronic applications accepted. *Expenses:* $449 per credit hour for master's programs; $897 per credit hour for doctoral programs. *Financial support:* Career-related internships or fieldwork, Federal Work-Study, tuition waivers (partial), and professional educator discounts available. Financial award application deadline: 4/1; financial award applicants required to submit FAFSA. *Faculty research:* Collaboration with public schools, pre-service program development, mathematics, diversity, literacy. *Unit head:* Dr. Maschael Schappe, Dean, 314-529-9670, Fax: 314-529-9921, E-mail: mschappe@maryville.edu. *Application contact:* Stacey Ruffin, Director of Clinical Experiences & Partnerships, 314-529-9542, Fax: 314-529-9921, E-mail: sruffin@maryville.edu.
Website: http://www.maryville.edu/ed/graduate-programs/

Marywood University, Academic Affairs, Reap College of Education and Human Development, Department of Education, Scranton, PA 18509-1598. Offers early childhood intervention (MS), including birth to age 9; higher education administration (MS); instructional leadership (M Ed); PK-4 education (MAT); reading education (MS); school leadership (MS); secondary/K-12 education (MAT); special education (MS); special education administration and supervision (MS). *Accreditation:* NCATE. *Program availability:* Part-time. Electronic applications accepted.

Massachusetts College of Liberal Arts, Graduate Programs, North Adams, MA 01247-4100. Offers business (MBA); educational administration (M Ed); educational leadership (CAGS); instruction and curriculum (M Ed); instructional technology (M Ed); physical education and health (M Ed); reading (M Ed); special education (M Ed). *Program availability:* Part-time, evening/weekend. *Degree requirements:* For master's, thesis. *Entrance requirements:* For master's, writing sample.

McGill University, Faculty of Graduate and Postdoctoral Studies, Faculty of Education, Department of Integrated Studies in Education, Montréal, QC H3A 2T5, Canada. Offers culture and values in education (MA, PhD); curriculum studies (MA); educational leadership (MA, Certificate); educational studies (PhD); integrated studies in education (M Ed); second language education (MA, PhD).

McKendree University, Graduate Programs, Programs in Education, Lebanon, IL 62254-1299. Offers curriculum design and instruction (Ed D, Ed S); educational administration and leadership (MA Ed); educational studies (MA Ed); higher education administrative services (MA Ed); music education (MA Ed); reading (MA Ed); special education (MA Ed); teacher leadership (MA Ed); teaching certification (MA Ed). *Accreditation:* NCATE. *Program availability:* Part-time, evening/weekend, online learning. *Entrance requirements:* For master's, official transcripts from all institutions previously attended, minimum GPA of 3.0, resume, references; for doctorate, GRE (within the past 5 years), master's degree in education and Ed S, or the equivalent, from regionally-accredited institution; official transcripts from all institutions previously attended; curriculum vitae/resume; essay/personal statement; two years of teaching/ professional experience; for Ed S, GRE (within the past 5 years), master's degree in education from regionally-accredited institution of higher education; official transcripts from all institutions previously attended; curriculum vitae/resume; essay/personal statement; two years of teaching/professional experience. Additional exam requirements/recommendations for international students: Required—TOEFL. Electronic applications accepted.

McNeese State University, Doré School of Graduate Studies, Burton College of Education, Department of Education Professions, Program in Multiple Levels Grades K-12, Lake Charles, LA 70609. Offers multiple levels grades K-12 (Postbaccalaureate Certificate), including art, health and physical education, music - instrumental, music - vocal. *Entrance requirements:* For degree, PRAXIS, 2 letters of recommendation, autobiography.

McPherson College, Program in Education, McPherson, KS 67460-1402. Offers M Ed. *Degree requirements:* For master's, project.

Medaille College, Program in Education, Buffalo, NY 14214-2695. Offers adolescent education (MS Ed); curriculum and instruction (MS Ed); education preparation (MS Ed); literacy (MS Ed); special education (MS). *Accreditation:* TEAC. *Program availability:* Part-time, evening/weekend. *Degree requirements:* For master's, comprehensive exam (for some programs), thesis or alternative. *Entrance requirements:* For master's, minimum undergraduate GPA of 2.7. Additional exam requirements/recommendations for international students: Required—TOEFL (minimum score 550 paper-based). Electronic applications accepted. *Faculty research:* Curriculum planning, truancy, tracking minority students, curriculum design, mentoring students.

Memorial University of Newfoundland, School of Graduate Studies, Faculty of Education, St. John's, NL A1C 5S7, Canada. Offers counseling psychology (M Ed); curriculum, teaching, and learning studies (M Ed); education (PhD); educational leadership studies (M Ed, Graduate Diploma); information technology (M Ed); post-secondary studies (M Ed, Diploma), including health professional education (Diploma). *Program availability:* Part-time. *Degree requirements:* For master's, thesis optional, internship, paper folio, project; for doctorate, comprehensive exam, thesis/dissertation, thesis seminar, oral defense of thesis. *Entrance requirements:* For master's, undergraduate degree with at least 2nd class standing, 1-2 years of work experience; for doctorate, minimum A average in graduate course work, MA in education, 2 years of professional experience; for other advanced degree, 2nd class degree, 2 years of work experience with adult learners, appropriate academic qualifications and work experience in a health-related field. Electronic applications accepted. *Faculty research:* Critical thinking, literacy, cognitive studies and counseling, educational change, technology in instruction.

Mercer University, Graduate Studies, Cecil B. Day Campus, Tift College of Education (Atlanta), Atlanta, GA 30341. Offers curriculum and instruction (PhD); early childhood education (M Ed, MAT, Ed S); educational leadership (PhD), including higher education leadership, P-12 school leadership; educational leadership P-12 (M Ed, Ed S); higher education leadership (M Ed); independent and charter school leadership (M Ed); middle grades education (M Ed, MAT); secondary education (M Ed, MAT); teacher leadership (Ed S). *Accreditation:* NCATE. *Program availability:* Part-time, evening/weekend. *Degree requirements:* For master's and Ed S, research project; for doctorate, comprehensive exam, thesis/dissertation. *Entrance requirements:* For master's, GRE or MAT, minimum undergraduate GPA of 2.75; for doctorate, GRE; for Ed S, GRE or MAT, minimum GPA of 3.25; 3 years of certified teaching experience (for educational leadership and teacher leadership). Additional exam requirements/recommendations for international students: Required—TOEFL (minimum score 80 iBT). Electronic

applications accepted. *Expenses:* Contact institution. *Faculty research:* Educational technology, multicultural and minority issues in education, educational leadership (P-12 and higher education), school discipline and school bullying, standards-based mathematics education.

Mercer University, Graduate Studies, Macon Campus, Tift College of Education (Macon), Macon, GA 31207. Offers curriculum and instruction (PhD); early childhood education (M Ed, Ed S); educational leadership (M Ed, PhD, Ed S), including higher education (PhD), P-12; higher education leadership (M Ed); independent and charter school leadership (M Ed); secondary education (MAT), including STEM; teacher leadership (Ed S). *Accreditation:* NCATE. *Program availability:* Part-time, evening/weekend, 100% online, blended/hybrid learning. *Degree requirements:* For master's, research project report; for doctorate, comprehensive exam, thesis/dissertation. *Entrance requirements:* For master's, GRE or MAT, minimum GPA of 2.75; for doctorate, GRE, minimum GPA of 3.5; interview; writing sample; 3 recommendations; for Ed S, GRE or MAT, minimum GPA of 3.5 (for teacher leadership), 3.0 (for educational leadership). Additional exam requirements/recommendations for international students: Required—TOEFL (minimum score 80 iBT). Electronic applications accepted. *Expenses:* Contact institution. *Faculty research:* Teacher effectiveness, specific learning disabilities, inclusion.

Mercy College, School of Education, Dobbs Ferry, NY 10522-1189. Offers MS, Advanced Certificate. *Program availability:* Part-time, evening/weekend, 100% online, blended/hybrid learning. *Students:* 176 full-time (143 women), 351 part-time (307 women); includes 267 minority (85 Black or African American, non-Hispanic/Latino; 1 American Indian or Alaska Native, non-Hispanic/Latino; 17 Asian, non-Hispanic/Latino; 154 Hispanic/Latino; 2 Native Hawaiian or other Pacific Islander, non-Hispanic/Latino; 8 Two or more races, non-Hispanic/Latino). Average age 33. 466 applicants, 53% accepted, 163 enrolled. In 2018, 185 master's, 26 other advanced degrees awarded. *Degree requirements:* For master's, Capstone project; clinical practice; passing scores on certification tests also required for some programs. *Entrance requirements:* For master's, GRE or PRAXIS, transcript(s); resume. Additional exam requirements/ recommendations for international students: Required—TOEFL (minimum score 600 paper-based; 71 iBT), IELTS (minimum score 8). *Application deadline:* Applications are processed on a rolling basis. Application fee: $40. Electronic applications accepted. *Expenses:* Tuition: Full-time $15,696; part-time $872 per credit. *Required fees:* $642; $161 per term. Tuition and fees vary according to course load, degree level and program. *Financial support:* Career-related internships or fieldwork, Federal Work-Study, scholarships/grants, and unspecified assistantships available. Support available to part-time students. Financial award applicants required to submit FAFSA. *Unit head:* Dr. Eric Martone, Interim Dean for the School of Education, 914-674-7618, Fax: 914-674-7352, E-mail: emartone@mercy.edu. *Application contact:* Allison Gurdineer, Executive Director of Admissions, 877-637-2946, Fax: 914-674-7382, E-mail: admissions@mercy.edu.
Website: https://www.mercy.edu/education/

Meredith College, School of Education, Health and Human Sciences, Raleigh, NC 27607-5298. Offers academically and intellectually gifted (M Ed); elementary education (M Ed, MAT); English as a second language (M Ed, MAT); health and physical education (MAT); nutrition, health and human performance (MS, Postbaccalaureate Certificate), including dietetic internship (Postbaccalaureate Certificate), nutrition (MS); psychology (MA), including industrial/organizational psychology; reading (M Ed); special education (MAT); special education (general curriculum) (M Ed). *Accreditation:* NCATE. *Program availability:* Part-time, evening/weekend. *Students:* 97 full-time (89 women), 76 part-time (73 women); includes 39 minority (17 Black or African American, non-Hispanic/ Latino; 1 American Indian or Alaska Native, non-Hispanic/Latino; 9 Asian, non-Hispanic/ Latino; 10 Hispanic/Latino; 2 Two or more races, non-Hispanic/Latino). Average age 28. In 2018, 56 master's, 36 other advanced degrees awarded. *Degree requirements:* For master's, thesis optional. *Entrance requirements:* For master's, GRE General Test or MAT, minimum GPA of 2.5, teaching license, recommendations. Additional exam requirements/recommendations for international students: Required—TOEFL. *Application deadline:* For fall admission, 7/1 priority date for domestic students; for spring admission, 11/1 priority date for domestic students. Applications are processed on a rolling basis. Application fee: $50. Electronic applications accepted. *Expenses:* $575 per credit hour for masters degree in education, $725 (for MS. PSY.IO degree), $20,295 (for pre-health post-baccalaureate certificate), $13,600 (for dietetic internship). *Financial support:* Career-related internships or fieldwork, institutionally sponsored loans, and tuition waivers (partial) available. Support available to part-time students. Financial award application deadline: 2/15; financial award applicants required to submit FAFSA. *Unit head:* Dr. Monica McKinney, Graduate Program Manager, 919-760-8056, Fax: 919-760-2303, E-mail: mckinneym@meredith.edu. *Application contact:* Dr. Monica McKinney, Graduate Program Manager, 919-760-8056, Fax: 919-760-2303, E-mail: mckinneym@meredith.edu.
Website: https://www.meredith.edu/school-of-education-health-and-human-sciences

Merrimack College, School of Education and Social Policy, North Andover, MA 01845-5800. Offers criminology and criminal justice (MS); educational leadership (CAGS); English as a second language (prek-6) (M Ed). *Program availability:* Part-time, evening/ weekend, 100% online courses with immersion events and in-classroom practicum close to home. *Faculty:* 11 full-time (7 women), 53 part-time/adjunct (39 women). *Students:* 324 full-time (274 women), 120 part-time (108 women); includes 48 minority (11 Black or African American, non-Hispanic/Latino; 2 Asian, non-Hispanic/Latino; 22 Hispanic/Latino; 1 Native Hawaiian or other Pacific Islander, non-Hispanic/Latino; 12 Two or more races, non-Hispanic/Latino), 3 international. Average age 27. 511 applicants, 85% accepted, 291 enrolled. In 2018, 177 master's awarded. *Degree requirements:* For master's, practicum, portfolio, and state test (for licensure track); capstone (for higher education, curriculum and instruction, and community engagement tracks); for CAGS, capstone. *Entrance requirements:* For master's, Massachusetts Teacher Education Licensure (MTEL), official transcripts from other colleges, resume, personal statement, 2 letters of recommendation. Additional exam requirements/ recommendations for international students: Required—TOEFL (minimum score 84 iBT), IELTS (minimum score 6.5), PTE (minimum score 56). *Application deadline:* For fall admission, 8/24 for domestic students, 7/30 for international students; for spring admission, 1/10 for domestic students, 12/10 for international students; for summer admission, 5/10 for domestic students, 4/10 for international students. Applications are processed on a rolling basis. Application fee: $0. Electronic applications accepted. Application fee is waived when completed online. *Expenses:* School Counseling $28,420; Master in Criminology $24,740; Master in Education $19,620; Master in Education (online) $16,000; Catholic School Leadership Certificate $3,660. *Financial support:* Fellowships with full tuition reimbursements, career-related internships or fieldwork, scholarships/grants, and health care benefits available. Support available to part-time students. Financial award application deadline: 5/1; financial award applicants required to submit FAFSA. *Unit head:* Dr. Isabelle Cherney, Dean, 978-837-5338, E-mail: cherneyi@merrimack.edu. *Application contact:* Alyssa Orlando, Graduate Admissions Counselor, 978-837-3563, E-mail: orlandoaf@merrimack.edu.
Website: http://www.merrimack.edu/academics/graduate/education/

Education—General

Metropolitan State University of Denver, School of Education, Denver, CO 80204. Offers elementary education (MAT); special education (MAT). *Expenses:* Contact institution.

Miami University, College of Education, Health and Society, Oxford, OH 45056. Offers M Ed, MA, MAT, MS, Ed D, PhD, Ed S. *Accreditation:* NCATE. *Faculty:* 90 full-time (50 women). *Students:* 267 full-time (187 women), 346 part-time (260 women); includes 102 minority (52 Black or African American, non-Hispanic/Latino; 11 Asian, non-Hispanic/Latino; 22 Hispanic/Latino; 17 Two or more races, non-Hispanic/Latino), 42 international. Average age 32. In 2018, 252 master's, 26 doctorates awarded. *Unit head:* Dr. Michael Dantley, Dean, 513-529-6317, E-mail: ehs@miamioh.edu. *Application contact:* Graduate Admission Coordinator, 513-529-3734, E-mail: applygrad@miamioh.edu.
Website: http://www.MiamiOH.edu/eap/

Michigan State University, The Graduate School, College of Education, East Lansing, MI 48824. Offers MA, MS, PhD, Ed S. *Accreditation:* TEAC. *Entrance requirements:* Additional exam requirements/recommendations for international students: Required—TOEFL. Electronic applications accepted.

MidAmerica Nazarene University, Professional and Graduate Studies in Education, Olathe, KS 66062-1899. Offers ESOL (M Ed); reading specialist (M Ed); technology enhanced teaching (M Ed). *Accreditation:* NCATE. *Program availability:* Part-time, evening/weekend, online only, 100% online. *Entrance requirements:* For master's, bachelor's degree from an accredited college or university, minimum undergraduate GPA of 3.0, valid teaching license. Additional exam requirements/recommendations for international students: Required—TOEFL (minimum score 81 iBT), IELTS (minimum score 6). Electronic applications accepted. *Expenses:* Contact institution.

Middle Tennessee State University, College of Graduate Studies, College of Education, Murfreesboro, TN 37132. Offers M Ed, PhD, Ed S. *Accreditation:* NCATE. *Program availability:* Part-time, evening/weekend, online learning. *Degree requirements:* For master's, comprehensive exam, thesis (for some programs); for doctorate, comprehensive exam, thesis/dissertation; for Ed S, comprehensive exam, thesis or alternative. *Entrance requirements:* For master's, doctorate, and Ed S, GRE, MAT, current teaching license or PRAXIS. Additional exam requirements/recommendations for international students: Required—TOEFL (minimum score 525 paper-based; 71 iBT) or IELTS (minimum score 6). Electronic applications accepted.

Midway University, Graduate Programs, Midway, KY 40347-1120. Offers education (MAT); leadership (MBA). *Degree requirements:* For master's, capstone course. *Entrance requirements:* For master's, GMAT (for MBA); GRE or PRAXIS I (for MAT), bachelor's degree; interview; minimum GPA of 3.0 (for MBA), 2.75 (for MAT); 3 years of professional work experience (for MBA). Additional exam requirements/recommendations for international students: Required—TOEFL (minimum score 550 paper-based; 80 iBT).

Midwestern State University, Billie Doris McAda Graduate School, West College of Education, Wichita Falls, TX 76308. Offers M Ed, MA. *Program availability:* Part-time, evening/weekend. *Degree requirements:* For master's, comprehensive exam, thesis (for some programs). *Entrance requirements:* For master's, GRE General Test or MAT. Additional exam requirements/recommendations for international students: Required—TOEFL (minimum score 550 paper-based). Electronic applications accepted. *Faculty research:* Assessment, reading education, vocabulary instruction, current role of the principal, educational research methodology.

Midwest University, Graduate Programs, Wentzville, MO 63385. Offers asset management/investment/real estate (MBA); Christian counseling (D Min); Christian education (D Min); counseling (MA), including marriage and family counseling, school counseling; divinity (M Div); education (MA), including brain and gifted education, Christian education; global business management (MBA); global leadership (MBA); leadership (PhD), including brain and gifted educational leadership, entrepreneurial leadership, international aviation leadership, organizational leadership, political leadership; mission studies (D Min); music (MM, DMA); pastoral theology (D Min); public policy/administration (MBA); teaching English to speakers of other languages (MA). *Program availability:* Part-time, online learning. *Degree requirements:* For master's, thesis (for some programs); for doctorate, thesis/dissertation. *Entrance requirements:* Additional exam requirements/recommendations for international students: Recommended—TOEFL (minimum score 550 paper-based).

Millersville University of Pennsylvania, College of Graduate Studies and Adult Learning, College of Education and Human Services, Millersville, PA 17551-0302. Offers assessment, curriculum, and teaching (M Ed), including integrative stem education; educational leadership (Ed D); social work (DSW). Doctor of Educational Leadership: Collaborative program with Shippensburg University; Doctor of Social Work: Collaborative program with Kutztown University; Master of Social Work: Collaborative program with Shippensburg University. *Accreditation:* NCATE. *Program availability:* Part-time, evening/weekend, 100% online, blended/hybrid learning, The DSW coursework is 100% online and students attend weekend residency at start of each semester. *Faculty:* 44 full-time (31 women), 30 part-time/adjunct (20 women). *Students:* 147 full-time (115 women), 390 part-time (311 women); includes 81 minority (33 Black or African American, non-Hispanic/Latino; 1 American Indian or Alaska Native, non-Hispanic/Latino; 6 Asian, non-Hispanic/Latino; 34 Hispanic/Latino; 7 Two or more races, non-Hispanic/Latino), 2 international. Average age 31. 304 applicants, 88% accepted, 179 enrolled. In 2018, 170 master's, 9 doctorates awarded. *Degree requirements:* For master's and Post-Master's Certificate, comprehensive exam (for some programs), thesis (for some programs); for doctorate, comprehensive exam, thesis/dissertation. *Entrance requirements:* For master's, GRE; MAT (not required with specific GPA's), teaching certificate, resume, letter of sponsorship, 3-5 years of professional experience as specified by PDE CSPG #96 for some programs, writing sample, clearances, completed MSW for some programs; for doctorate, teaching certificate, resume, letter of sponsorship, 3-5 years of professional experience as specified by PDE CSPG #96 for some programs, writing sample, clearances, completed MSW for some programs. Additional exam requirements/recommendations for international students: Required—TOEFL, IELTS (minimum score 6), PTE (minimum score 60). Application fee: $40. Electronic applications accepted. *Expenses:* Tuition, area resident: Full-time $9288; part-time $516 per credit. Tuition, state resident: Full-time $9288; part-time $516 per credit. Tuition, nonresident: full-time $13,932; part-time $774 per credit. *International tuition:* $13,932 full-time. *Required fees:* $2623.50; $145.75 per credit. Tuition and fees vary according to course load, degree level and program. *Financial support:* In 2018-19, 78 students received support. Unspecified assistantships available. Financial award application deadline: 3/15; financial award applicants required to submit FAFSA. *Faculty research:* Education, Social Work, Psychology, Wellness, Sport Sciences. *Unit head:* Dr. George Drake, Dean, 717-871-7333, E-mail: george.drake@millersville.edu. *Application contact:* Dr. James A. Delle, Acting Dean of College of Graduate Studies and Adult Learning/Associate Provost, Academic Administration, 717-871-7462, E-mail: James.Delle@millersville.edu.
Website: http://www.millersville.edu/education/

Milligan College, Area of Education, Milligan College, TN 37682. Offers combined preK-3/K-5 education (M Ed); educational leadership (Ed D); educational specialist (Ed S); K-5 education (M Ed); middle grades education (M Ed); preK-3 education (M Ed); preK-3 special education (M Ed); secondary education (M Ed). *Accreditation:* NCATE. *Program availability:* Part-time, 100% online, blended/hybrid learning. *Faculty:* 5 full-time (3 women), 6 part-time/adjunct (3 women). *Students:* 38 full-time (31 women), 8 part-time (4 women); includes 2 minority (1 Hispanic/Latino; 1 Two or more races, non-Hispanic/Latino), 1 international. Average age 35. 36 applicants, 97% accepted, 32 enrolled. In 2018, 18 master's awarded. *Degree requirements:* For master's, thesis, portfolio, research project; for doctorate, thesis/dissertation, portfolio, research project. *Entrance requirements:* For master's, MAT, GRE General Test, ACT, SAT, or PRAXIS, undergraduate degree and supporting transcripts, professional recommendations, interview; for doctorate, MAT or GRE, master's degree and supporting transcripts, demonstrated scholastic ability, recognized leadership role within education, professional recommendations, essay/personal statement, portfolio (professional development plan, evidence of ability, knowledge and qualities), interview. Additional exam requirements/recommendations for international students: Required—TOEFL (minimum score 550 paper-based, 79 iBT) or IELTS (6.5). *Application deadline:* For fall admission, 8/1 priority date for domestic students, 6/1 for international students; for spring admission, 11/15 priority date for domestic students, 12/1 for international students; for summer admission, 4/1 for domestic students. Applications are processed on a rolling basis. Application fee: $30. Electronic applications accepted. *Expenses:* $365 per hour (for masters); $485 per hour (for doctoral); $375 fees per semester; $75 one-time records fee. *Financial support:* Scholarships/grants available. Financial award application deadline: 12/1; financial award applicants required to submit FAFSA. *Faculty research:* Assessment; school mental health; literacy; technology; educator preparation. *Unit head:* Dr. Angela Hilton-Prillhart, Area Chair of Education, 423-461-8769, Fax: 423-461-3103, E-mail: anhilton-prillhart@milligan.edu. *Application contact:* Melissa Dillow, Graduate Admissions Recruiter, Education, 423-461-8306, Fax: 423-461-8982, E-mail: msdillow@milligan.edu.
Website: http://www.Milligan.edu/GPS

Mills College, Graduate Studies, School of Education, Oakland, CA 94613-1000. Offers MA, Ed D, Certificate. *Program availability:* Part-time, evening/weekend. Terminal master's awarded for partial completion of doctoral program. *Degree requirements:* For master's, comprehensive exam, thesis (for some programs); for doctorate, thesis/dissertation. *Entrance requirements:* For master's, statement of purpose, official transcript, 3 recommendations. Additional exam requirements/recommendations for international students: Required—TOEFL (minimum score 550 paper-based; 80 iBT) or IELTS (minimum score 6). Electronic applications accepted. *Expenses:* Contact institution. *Faculty research:* Early childhood education, teacher preparation, educational leadership.

Minnesota State University Mankato, College of Graduate Studies and Research, College of Education, Mankato, MN 56001. Offers MAT, MS, Ed D, Certificate. *Accreditation:* NCATE. *Program availability:* Part-time, evening/weekend. *Degree requirements:* For master's, comprehensive exam, thesis or alternative; for Certificate, thesis. *Entrance requirements:* For master's, GRE or MAT, minimum GPA of 3.0 during previous 2 years; for Certificate, minimum GPA of 3.0. Additional exam requirements/recommendations for international students: Required—TOEFL. Electronic applications accepted.

Minnesota State University Moorhead, Graduate and Extended Learning, College of Education and Human Services, Moorhead, MN 56563. Offers counseling and student affairs (MS); educational leadership (MS, Ed D, Ed S). *Accreditation:* ASHA; NCATE. *Program availability:* Part-time, evening/weekend, 100% online, blended/hybrid learning. *Students:* 129 full-time (105 women), 425 part-time (300 women); includes 32 minority (8 Black or African American, non-Hispanic/Latino; 4 American Indian or Alaska Native, non-Hispanic/Latino; 6 Asian, non-Hispanic/Latino; 7 Hispanic/Latino; 7 Two or more races, non-Hispanic/Latino), 1 international. Average age 33. 154 applicants, 77% accepted. In 2018, 198 master's, 29 other advanced degrees awarded. *Degree requirements:* For master's, comprehensive exam (for some programs), thesis, final oral defense; for doctorate, comprehensive exam (for some programs), thesis/dissertation, final oral defense. *Entrance requirements:* For master's, GRE, essay, letter of intent, letters of reference, teaching license, teaching verification, minimum cumulative GPA of 3.0; for doctorate, official transcripts; letter of intent; resume or curriculum vitae; master's degree; personal essay. Additional exam requirements/recommendations for international students: Required—TOEFL (minimum score 550 paper-based); Recommended—IELTS (minimum score 6.5). *Application deadline:* For fall admission, 7/1 priority date for domestic students; for spring admission, 11/15 priority date for domestic students. Applications are processed on a rolling basis. Application fee: $35. Electronic applications accepted. Tuition and fees vary according to course load, degree level, program and reciprocity agreements. *Financial support:* Federal Work-Study and unspecified assistantships available. Financial award application deadline: 10/1; financial award applicants required to submit FAFSA. *Unit head:* Dr. Ok-Hee Lee, Dean, 218-477-2095, E-mail: okheelee@mnstate.edu. *Application contact:* Karla Wenger, Office Manager, 218-477-2344, Fax: 218-477-2482, E-mail: wengerk@mnstate.edu.
Website: http://www.mnstate.edu/cehs

Misericordia University, College of Health Sciences and Education, Program in Education, Dallas, PA 18612-1098. Offers instructional technology (MS); reading specialist (MS); special education (MS). *Program availability:* Part-time, evening/weekend. *Entrance requirements:* For master's, minimum undergraduate GPA of 3.0. Additional exam requirements/recommendations for international students: Required—TOEFL. Electronic applications accepted.

Mississippi College, Graduate School, School of Education, Clinton, MS 39058. Offers M Ed, MS, Ed D, Ed S. *Accreditation:* NCATE. *Program availability:* Part-time, evening/weekend, online learning. *Degree requirements:* For master's, comprehensive exam, thesis optional. *Entrance requirements:* For master's, GRE or NTE, minimum GPA of 2.5, Class A Certificate (for some programs); for Ed S, NTE, minimum GPA of 3.0. Additional exam requirements/recommendations for international students: Recommended—TOEFL, IELTS. Electronic applications accepted.

Mississippi State University, College of Education, Mississippi State, MS 39762. Offers MAT, MS, MSIT, MST, PhD, Ed S. *Accreditation:* NCATE. *Program availability:* Part-time, evening/weekend, blended/hybrid learning. *Faculty:* 89 full-time (46 women), 3 part-time/adjunct (all women). *Students:* 252 full-time (170 women), 413 part-time (281 women); includes 226 minority (188 Black or African American, non-Hispanic/Latino; 5 American Indian or Alaska Native, non-Hispanic/Latino; 4 Asian, non-Hispanic/Latino; 18 Hispanic/Latino; 11 Two or more races, non-Hispanic/Latino), 19 international. Average age 32. 317 applicants, 67% accepted, 164 enrolled. In 2018, 168 master's, 29 doctorates, 22 other advanced degrees awarded. Terminal master's awarded for partial completion of doctoral program. *Degree requirements:* For master's, thesis optional, comprehensive oral or written exam; for doctorate, thesis/dissertation; for Ed S, thesis or alternative, final written or oral exam. *Entrance requirements:* For master's, doctorate, and Ed S, GRE. Additional exam requirements/recommendations for international students: Required—TOEFL (minimum score 550 paper-based; 79 iBT); Recommended—IELTS (minimum score 6.5). *Application deadline:* For fall admission, 7/1 for domestic students, 5/1 for international students; for spring admission, 11/1 for domestic students, 9/1 for international students. Applications are processed on a rolling

basis. Application fee: $60 ($80 for international students). Electronic applications accepted. *Expenses:* Tuition, state resident: full-time $8450; part-time $360.59 per credit hour. Tuition, nonresident: full-time $23,140; part-time $969.09 per credit hour. *Required fees:* $110. One-time fee: $55 full-time. Part-time tuition and fees vary according to course load, degree level, campus/location and reciprocity agreements. *Financial support:* In 2018–19, 13 research assistantships (averaging $10,862 per year), 22 teaching assistantships (averaging $9,923 per year) were awarded; career-related internships or fieldwork, Federal Work-Study, institutionally sponsored loans, scholarships/grants, and unspecified assistantships also available. Financial award application deadline: 4/1; financial award applicants required to submit FAFSA. *Faculty research:* Leadership behavior, creativity measures, early childhood education, employability of the blind, quality indicators of professional educators. *Total annual research expenditures:* $2.4 million. *Unit head:* Dr. Richard Blackbourn, Dean, 662-325-3717, Fax: 662-325-8784, E-mail: rlb277@msstate.edu. *Application contact:* Ryan King, Admissions and Enrollment Assistant, 662-325-8951, E-mail: rjk101@grad.msstate.edu.
Website: http://www.educ.msstate.edu/

Mississippi University for Women, Graduate School, College of Education and Human Sciences, Columbus, MS 39701-9998. Offers differentiated instruction (M Ed); educational leadership (M Ed); gifted studies (M Ed); reading/literacy (M Ed); teaching (MAT). *Accreditation:* ASHA; NCATE. *Program availability:* Part-time. *Degree requirements:* For master's, comprehensive exam, thesis optional. *Entrance requirements:* For master's, GRE General Test or NTE (M Ed in gifted education or MS in speech/language pathology), MAT (M Ed in instructional management), minimum QPA of 3.0.

Mississippi Valley State University, College of Education, Itta Bena, MS 38941-1400. Offers MAT, MS. *Accreditation:* NCATE. *Program availability:* Part-time, evening/weekend. *Faculty:* 6 full-time (5 women), 2 part-time/adjunct (both women). *Students:* 4 full-time (1 woman), 63 part-time (46 women); includes 65 minority (64 Black or African American, non-Hispanic/Latino; 1 Asian, non-Hispanic/Latino). Average age 35. In 2018, 12 master's awarded. *Degree requirements:* For master's, comprehensive exam, thesis (for some programs). *Entrance requirements:* Additional exam requirements/recommendations for international students: Required—TOEFL (minimum score 525 paper-based). *Application deadline:* Applications are processed on a rolling basis. Application fee: $0. *Expenses:* Contact institution. *Financial support:* Institutionally sponsored loans available. Financial award application deadline: 8/1; financial award applicants required to submit FAFSA. *Unit head:* Dr. Kalanya Moore, Interim Chair, 662-254-3619, Fax: 662-254-3623, E-mail: kalanya.moore@mvsu.edu. *Application contact:* Dr. Danisha Williams, Director of Admissions, 601-254-3344, Fax: 662-254-3759, E-mail: danisha.williams@mvsu.edu.

Missouri Baptist University, Graduate Programs, St. Louis, MO 63141-8660. Offers business administration (MBA); Christian ministries (MACM); counseling (MAC); education (MSE); education administration (MEA); educational leadership (MSE, Ed S); teaching (MAT).

Missouri Southern State University, Program in Teaching, Joplin, MO 64801-1595. Offers MAT. Program offered jointly with Missouri State University. *Accreditation:* NCATE. *Degree requirements:* For master's, research seminar.

Molloy College, Graduate Education Program, Rockville Centre, NY 11571-5002. Offers adolescent education in biology (MS); adolescent special education (Advanced Certificate); bilingual extension (Advanced Certificate); childhood education (MS); childhood special education (Advanced Certificate); early childhood education (MS); educational technology (MS); English (MS); mathematics (MS); social studies (MS); Spanish (MS); special education on both childhood and adolescent levels (MS); teaching English to speakers of other languages (TESOL) in grades pre-K to 12 (MS); TESOL (Advanced Certificate). *Accreditation:* NCATE. *Program availability:* Part-time, evening/weekend. *Faculty:* 24 full-time (22 women), 26 part-time/adjunct (19 women). *Students:* 106 full-time (78 women), 203 part-time (154 women); includes 65 minority (14 Black or African American, non-Hispanic/Latino; 5 Asian, non-Hispanic/Latino; 41 Hispanic/Latino; 5 Two or more races, non-Hispanic/Latino). Average age 41. 147 applicants, 63% accepted, 79 enrolled. In 2018, 120 master's, 1 other advanced degree awarded. *Entrance requirements:* Additional exam requirements/recommendations for international students: Required—TOEFL (minimum score 550 paper-based; 79 iBT). *Application deadline:* Applications are processed on a rolling basis. Application fee: $60. Electronic applications accepted. *Expenses: Tuition:* Full-time $20,790; part-time $1155 per credit. *Required fees:* $1060; $900. Tuition and fees vary according to course load and degree level. *Financial support:* Application deadline: 3/1; applicants required to submit FAFSA. *Faculty research:* English Language Learners; social emotional needs of students; gifted education; cultural diversity; collaborative teaching methods. *Unit head:* Joanne O'Brien, Dean, 516-323-3116, E-mail: jobrien@molloy.edu. *Application contact:* Faye Hood, Assistant Director for Admissions, 516-323-4009, E-mail: fhood@molloy.edu.

Monmouth University, Graduate Studies, School of Education, West Long Branch, NJ 07764-1898. Offers applied behavior analysis (Certificate); autism (Certificate); director of school counseling services (Post-Master's Certificate); early childhood (M Ed); educational leadership (Ed D); elementary education (MAT), including elementary level, secondary level; English as a second language (M Ed); learning disabilities teacher-consultant (Post-Master's Certificate); literacy (MS Ed); school counseling (MS Ed); special education (MS Ed), including autism, learning disabilities teacher-consultant, teacher of students with disabilities, teaching in inclusive settings; speech-language pathology (MS Ed); student affairs and college counseling (MS Ed); supervisor (Post-Master's Certificate); teaching English to speakers of other languages (Certificate). *Accreditation:* NCATE. *Program availability:* Part-time, evening/weekend, 100% online, blended/hybrid learning. *Faculty:* 29 full-time (23 women), 32 part-time/adjunct (24 women). *Students:* 214 full-time (187 women), 148 part-time (127 women); includes 60 minority (13 Black or African American, non-Hispanic/Latino; 2 Asian, non-Hispanic/Latino; 40 Hispanic/Latino; 5 Two or more races, non-Hispanic/Latino). Average age 27. In 2018, 108 master's, 9 other advanced degrees awarded. *Entrance requirements:* For master's, GRE taken within last 5 years (for MS Ed in speech-language pathology); SAT (minimum combined score of 1660 in 3 sections), ACT (23), GRE (minimum score of 4.0 on analytical writing section and minimum combined score of 310 on quantitative and verbal sections), or passing scores on 3 parts of Core Academic Skills Educators, minimum GPA of 3.0 in major; 2 letters of recommendation (for some programs); resume, personal statement or essay (depending on program). Additional exam requirements/recommendations for international students: Required—TOEFL (minimum score 550 paper-based; 79 iBT), IELTS (minimum score 6), Michigan English Language Assessment Battery (minimum score 77) or Certificate of Advanced English (minimum score 160). *Application deadline:* For fall admission, 7/15 priority date for domestic students, 7/1 for international students; for spring admission, 12/1 priority date for domestic students, 11/1 for international students; for summer admission, 5/1 for domestic students. Applications are processed on a rolling basis. Application fee: $50. Electronic applications accepted. *Expenses: Tuition:* Part-time $1233 per credit. *Required fees:* $178 per term. *Financial support:* In 2018–19, 290 students received support. Institutionally sponsored loans, scholarships/grants, and unspecified assistantships available. Support available to part-time students. Financial award applicants required to submit FAFSA. *Faculty research:* Multicultural literacy, science and mathematics teaching strategies, teacher as reflective practitioner, children with disabilities. *Unit head:* Dr. John E. Henning, Dean, 732-263-5513, Fax: 732-263-5277, E-mail: kodonnel@monmouth.edu. *Application contact:* Kirsten Sneeringer, Graduate Admission Counselor, 732-571-3452, Fax: 732-263-5123, E-mail: gradadm@monmouth.edu.
Website: http://www.monmouth.edu/academics/schools/education/default.asp

Montana State University, The Graduate School, College of Education, Health, and Human Development, Department of Education, Bozeman, MT 59717. Offers adult and higher education (Ed D); curriculum and instruction (M Ed, Ed D), including professional educator (M Ed), technology education (M Ed); education (M Ed), including adult and higher education, educational leadership, school counseling; educational leadership (Ed D, Ed S). *Accreditation:* TEAC. *Program availability:* Part-time, online learning. *Degree requirements:* For master's, comprehensive exam; for doctorate, comprehensive exam, thesis/dissertation. *Entrance requirements:* For master's, GRE, 3 letters of reference, essays, BA transcripts; for doctorate, GRE, MAT, 3 letters of reference, essay, BA and M Ed transcripts; for Ed S, PRAXIS. Additional exam requirements/recommendations for international students: Required—TOEFL (minimum score 550 paper-based). Electronic applications accepted. *Faculty research:* Critical literacy; standards-based education; school Improvement, organizational change, leadership in rural education, leadership in Indian education; student Learning; multicultural/culturally responsive education for social justice Native American indigenous education, community-centered education teacher preparation.

Montana State University Billings, College of Education, Billings, MT 59101. Offers M Ed, MS Sp Ed, Certificate. *Accreditation:* NCATE. *Program availability:* Part-time, 100% online, blended/hybrid learning. *Degree requirements:* For master's, thesis optional. *Entrance requirements:* For master's, GRE General Test, minimum GPA of 3.0. Additional exam requirements/recommendations for international students: Required—TOEFL (minimum score 79 iBT), IELTS (minimum score 6.5). Electronic applications accepted. *Faculty research:* Social studies education, science education.

Montana State University–Northern, Graduate Programs, Option in Instruction and Learning, Havre, MT 59501-7751. Offers MS Ed. *Program availability:* Part-time, blended/hybrid learning. *Degree requirements:* For master's, comprehensive exam, thesis optional, oral exams. *Entrance requirements:* For master's, GRE General Test or MAT, minimum GPA of 3.0. Electronic applications accepted. *Expenses:* Contact institution.

Montclair State University, The Graduate School, College of Education and Human Services, Montclair, NJ 07043-1624. Offers M Ed, MA, MAT, MPH, MS, Ed D, PhD, Certificate, Post Master's Certificate, Postbaccalaureate Certificate. *Accreditation:* NCATE. *Program availability:* Part-time, evening/weekend. *Degree requirements:* For master's, comprehensive exam (for some programs), thesis (for some programs); for doctorate, comprehensive exam, thesis/dissertation. *Entrance requirements:* For master's, GRE, GMAT, MAT, 2 letters of recommendation; for doctorate, GRE General Test, 3 letters of recommendation. Additional exam requirements/recommendations for international students: Required—TOEFL (minimum score 83 iBT) or IELTS. Electronic applications accepted. *Faculty research:* Key factors in the preparation of teachers for urban schools, factors affecting upper extremity motion patterns and injuries, implementation fidelity of instructional interventions, data-based decision-making in educational contexts, nutrition and physical activity of the aging population in the U.S.

Moravian College, Graduate and Continuing Studies, Education Programs, Bethlehem, PA 18018-6650. Offers curriculum and instruction (M Ed); education (MAT). *Program availability:* Part-time, evening/weekend. *Faculty:* 1 full-time (0 women), 4 part-time/adjunct (1 woman). *Students:* 6 full-time (4 women), 50 part-time (41 women); includes 5 minority (1 Black or African American, non-Hispanic/Latino; 4 Hispanic/Latino). Average age 29. 81 applicants, 83% accepted, 53 enrolled. In 2018, 20 master's awarded. *Degree requirements:* For master's, thesis. *Entrance requirements:* For master's, state teacher certification for Curriculum and Instruction. *Application deadline:* For fall admission, 8/1 priority date for domestic and international students; for spring admission, 1/1 priority date for domestic and international students; for summer admission, 5/1 priority date for domestic and international students. Applications are processed on a rolling basis. Electronic applications accepted. *Financial support:* Applicants required to submit FAFSA. *Faculty research:* Teacher action research, youth participatory research, practitioner inquiry, science education, deaf and hard of hearing education. *Unit head:* Scott Dams, Dean of Graduate and Adult Enrollment, 610-861-1400, Fax: 610-861-1466, E-mail: graduate@moravian.edu. *Application contact:* Jennifer Pagliaroli, Student Experience Mentor, 610-861-1400, Fax: 610-861-1466, E-mail: graduate@moravian.edu.
Website: https://www.moravian.edu/graduate/programs/education#/

Morehead State University, Graduate School, College of Education, Morehead, KY 40351. Offers MA, MA Ed, MAT, Ed S. *Accreditation:* NCATE. *Program availability:* Part-time, evening/weekend. *Degree requirements:* For master's, comprehensive exam, thesis or alternative; for Ed S, thesis. *Entrance requirements:* For master's, GRE General Test or PRAXIS, minimum overall undergraduate GPA of 2.5; for Ed S, GRE General Test, interview, master's degree, minimum GPA of 3.5, work experience. Additional exam requirements/recommendations for international students: Required—TOEFL (minimum score 500 paper-based). Electronic applications accepted. *Faculty research:* Regional economic development, computer applications for school administrators, effectiveness of teacher interns, perceptual processes, alcoholism.

Morgan State University, School of Graduate Studies, School of Education and Urban Studies, Baltimore, MD 21251. Offers MA, MAT, MS, Ed D, PhD. *Program availability:* Part-time. *Degree requirements:* For master's, comprehensive exam; for doctorate, comprehensive exam, thesis/dissertation. *Entrance requirements:* For doctorate, GRE General Test or MAT. Additional exam requirements/recommendations for international students: Required—TOEFL (minimum score 550 paper-based). *Faculty research:* Multicultural education, cooperative learning, psychology of cognition.

Morningside College, Graduate Programs, Sharon Walker School of Education, Sioux City, IA 51106. Offers professional educator (MAT); special education (MAT), including instructional strategist: mild/moderate (7-12), instructional strategist: mild/moderate (K-6), K-12 instructional strategist: behavior disorders/learning disabilities, K-12 instructional strategist: mental disabilities. *Program availability:* Part-time, online only, 100% online. *Entrance requirements:* For master's, writing sample. Electronic applications accepted. *Expenses:* Contact institution.

Mount Mary University, Graduate Programs, Programs in Education, Milwaukee, WI 53222-4597. Offers professional development (MA). *Program availability:* Part-time, evening/weekend. *Degree requirements:* For master's, action research project. *Entrance requirements:* For master's, minimum GPA of 2.75, teaching license. Additional exam requirements/recommendations for international students: Required—TOEFL (minimum score 550 paper-based; 80 iBT); Recommended—IELTS (minimum score 6.5). Electronic applications accepted. *Expenses:* Contact institution. *Faculty research:* Staff development, writing across the curriculum, effective schools, critical thinking skills, mathematics education.

Education—General

Mount Mercy University, Program in Education, Cedar Rapids, IA 52402-4797. Offers reading (MA Ed); special education (MA Ed); teacher leadership (MA Ed). *Entrance requirements:* For master's, minimum cumulative GPA of 3.0, 2 letters of recommendation, resume, valid teaching license. Additional exam requirements/recommendations for international students: Required—TOEFL (minimum score 570 paper-based; 88 iBT). Electronic applications accepted.

Mount St. Joseph University, Graduate Education Program, Cincinnati, OH 45233-1670. Offers adolescent to young adult education (MA); dyslexia (Certificate); inclusive early childhood education (MA); middle childhood education (MA); multicultural special education (MA); reading science (MA). *Accreditation:* TEAC. *Program availability:* Part-time, evening/weekend, 100% online, blended/hybrid learning. *Degree requirements:* For master's, comprehensive exam, thesis, research project, student teaching, clinical and field-based experiences. *Entrance requirements:* For master's, GRE (if GPA is below 3.0), letter of intent, 2 referrals, background check, interview, resume, minimum undergraduate GPA of 3.0. Additional exam requirements/recommendations for international students: Required—TOEFL (minimum score 560 paper-based; 83 iBT). Electronic applications accepted. *Expenses:* Contact institution. *Faculty research:* Foreign and second language learning problems/reading disabilities, multicultural/bilingual special education, science education, pedagogical content knowledge, early childhood, response to intervention.

Mount Saint Mary College, Division of Education, Newburgh, NY 12550-3494. Offers adolescence and special education (MS Ed); childhood education (MS Ed); literacy education (MS Ed); middle school (7-9) (MS Ed). *Accreditation:* NCATE. *Program availability:* Part-time, evening/weekend. *Faculty:* 7 full-time (6 women), 7 part-time/adjunct (all women). *Students:* 19 full-time (14 women), 78 part-time (64 women); includes 7 minority (5 Hispanic/Latino; 1 Native Hawaiian or other Pacific Islander, non-Hispanic/Latino; 1 Two or more races, non-Hispanic/Latino). Average age 28. 31 applicants, 61% accepted, 17 enrolled. In 2018, 28 master's awarded. *Entrance requirements:* Additional exam requirements/recommendations for international students: Required—TOEFL (minimum score 80 iBT). *Application deadline:* Applications are processed on a rolling basis. Application fee: $45. Electronic applications accepted. Application fee is waived when completed online. *Expenses: Tuition:* Full-time $14,454; part-time $803 per credit. *Required fees:* $172; $86 per semester. *Financial support:* In 2018–19, 17 students received support. Institutionally sponsored loans, scholarships/grants, and unspecified assistantships available. Financial award application deadline: 4/15; financial award applicants required to submit FAFSA. *Faculty research:* Learning and teaching styles, computers in special education, language development. *Unit head:* Dr. Vicki Caruana, Graduate Coordinator, 845-569-3530, Fax: 845-569-3551, E-mail: Victoria.caruana@msmc.edu. *Application contact:* Eileen Bardney, Director of Admissions, 845-569-3254, Fax: 845-569-3438, E-mail: Eileen.Bardney@msmc.edu. Website: http://www.msmc.edu/Academics/Graduate_Programs/Master_of_Science_in_Education

Mount Saint Mary's University, Graduate Division, Los Angeles, CA 90049. Offers business administration (MBA); counseling psychology (MS); creative writing (MFA); education (MS, Certificate); film and television (MFA); health policy and management (MS); humanities (MA); nursing (MSN, Certificate); physical therapy (DPT); religious studies (MA). *Program availability:* Part-time, evening/weekend. *Entrance requirements:* Additional exam requirements/recommendations for international students: Required—TOEFL. Electronic applications accepted. *Expenses: Tuition:* Full-time $45,260. *Required fees:* $170. Full-time tuition and fees vary according to course load and program.

Mount St. Mary's University, Program in Education, Emmitsburg, MD 21727-7799. Offers M Ed, MAT. *Accreditation:* NCATE. *Degree requirements:* For master's, thesis (for some programs), exit portfolio/presentation. *Entrance requirements:* For master's, PRAXIS I and II. Additional exam requirements/recommendations for international students: Required—TOEFL (minimum score 550 paper-based; 83 iBT). Electronic applications accepted. *Expenses:* Contact institution.

Mount Saint Vincent University, Graduate Programs, Faculty of Education, Halifax, NS B3M 2J6, Canada. Offers M Ed, MA, MA Ed, MA-R. *Program availability:* Part-time, evening/weekend, online learning. *Degree requirements:* For master's, thesis (for some programs), practicum. *Entrance requirements:* For master's, bachelor's degree in related field. Electronic applications accepted.

Mount Vernon Nazarene University, Department of Education, Mount Vernon, OH 43050-9500. Offers education (MA Ed); professional educator's license (MA Ed). *Accreditation:* NCATE. *Program availability:* Part-time, evening/weekend. *Degree requirements:* For master's, project.

Multnomah University, Graduate Programs, Portland, OR 97220-5898. Offers counseling (MA); global development and justice (MA); teaching (MA); TESOL (MA). *Program availability:* Part-time, evening/weekend. *Degree requirements:* For master's, variable foreign language requirement, comprehensive exam (for some programs), thesis (for some programs). *Entrance requirements:* For master's, interview; references; writing sample (for counseling). Additional exam requirements/recommendations for international students: Required—TOEFL (minimum score 550 paper-based). Electronic applications accepted. *Expenses: Tuition:* Full-time $13,440; part-time $6720 per semester hour. *Required fees:* $390; $250 per unit. Tuition and fees vary according to course load.

Murray State University, College of Education and Human Services, Murray, KY 42071. Offers MA Ed, MS, Ed D, Certificate, Ed S. PhD, EdD offered jointly with University of Kentucky. *Accreditation:* NCATE. *Program availability:* Part-time, evening/weekend, 100% online, blended/hybrid learning. Terminal master's awarded for partial completion of doctoral program. *Entrance requirements:* For master's, doctorate, and other advanced degree, GRE or GMAT, minimum university GPA of 2.75. Additional exam requirements/recommendations for international students: Required—TOEFL (minimum score 527 paper-based; 71 iBT). Electronic applications accepted.

Muskingum University, Graduate Programs in Education, New Concord, OH 43762. Offers MAE, MAT. *Accreditation:* NCATE. *Program availability:* Part-time. *Entrance requirements:* For master's, minimum GPA of 2.7, teaching license. *Faculty research:* Brain behavior relationships, school partnerships, staff development, school law, proficiency testing, multi-age groupings.

National Louis University, National College of Education, Chicago, IL 60603. Offers administration and supervision (M Ed, Ed D, CAS, Ed S); curriculum and instruction (M Ed, MS Ed, CAS); early childhood administration (M Ed, CAS); early childhood education (M Ed, MAT, MS Ed, CAS); education (Ed D); educational psychology/human learning and development (M Ed, MS Ed, CAS, Ed S); elementary education (MAT); interdisciplinary curriculum and instruction (M Ed); mathematics education (M Ed, MS Ed, CAS); middle grades education (MAT); reading and language (M Ed, MS Ed, CAS); school psychology (M Ed, Ed S); science education (M Ed, MS Ed, CAS); secondary education (MAT); special education (M Ed, MAT, CAS); technology in education (M Ed, CAS). *Accreditation:* NCATE. *Program availability:* Part-time, evening/weekend. *Degree requirements:* For doctorate, comprehensive exam, thesis/dissertation. *Entrance requirements:* For master's, MAT or GRE, minimum GPA of 3.0; for doctorate, GRE General Test, minimum GPA of 3.25, interview, resume, writing sample, 4 recommendations. Additional exam requirements/recommendations for international students: Required—TOEFL (minimum score 550 paper-based; 79 iBT).

National University, Sanford College of Education, La Jolla, CA 92037-1011. Offers advanced teaching practices (MS); applied behavior analysis (MS); applied school leadership (MS); e-teaching and learning (Certificate); education (MA); educational administration (MS); educational and instructional technology (MS); educational counseling (MS); higher education administration (MS); inspired teaching and learning (M Ed); school psychology (MS); special education (MA, MS). *Program availability:* Part-time, evening/weekend, 100% online, blended/hybrid learning. *Degree requirements:* For master's, thesis (for some programs). *Entrance requirements:* For master's, interview, minimum GPA of 2.5. Additional exam requirements/recommendations for international students: Required—TOEFL (minimum score 550 paper-based; 79 iBT), IELTS (minimum score 6). Electronic applications accepted. *Expenses: Tuition:* Full-time $10,320; part-time $430 per unit. Tuition and fees vary according to degree level. *Faculty research:* Teacher education, special education, educational effectiveness, teaching abroad, school counseling.

Nazareth College of Rochester, Graduate Studies, Department of Education, Rochester, NY 14618. Offers educational technology (MS Ed); inclusive adolescence education (MS Ed); inclusive childhood education (MS Ed); inclusive early childhood education (MS Ed); literacy education (MS Ed); teaching English to speakers of other languages (MS Ed). *Accreditation:* TEAC. *Program availability:* Part-time, evening/weekend. *Entrance requirements:* For master's, GRE or MAT (for education programs), minimum GPA of 3.0. Additional exam requirements/recommendations for international students: Required—TOEFL (minimum score 550 paper-based, 79 iBT) or IELTS (6.5). Electronic applications accepted.

Neumann University, Graduate Program in Education, Aston, PA 19014-1298. Offers education (MS), including administrative certification (school principal PK-12), autism, early elementary education, secondary education, special education. *Program availability:* Part-time, evening/weekend, 100% online, blended/hybrid learning. *Entrance requirements:* For master's, official transcripts from all institutions attended, letter of intent, three professional references, copy of any teaching certifications. Additional exam requirements/recommendations for international students: Required—TOEFL (minimum score 70 iBT). Electronic applications accepted. *Expenses:* Contact institution.

New England College, Program in Education, Henniker, NH 03242-3293. Offers higher education administration (MS, Ed D); K-12 leadership (Ed D); literacy and language arts (M Ed); meeting the needs of all learners/special education (M Ed); teacher leadership/school reform (M Ed). *Program availability:* Part-time, evening/weekend.

New Jersey City University, Debra Cannon Partridge Wolfe College of Education, Jersey City, NJ 07305-1597. Offers MA, MAT, Ed D. *Program availability:* Part-time, evening/weekend. *Entrance requirements:* Additional exam requirements/recommendations for international students: Required—TOEFL (minimum score 79 iBT).

Newman University, Master of Science in Education Program, Wichita, KS 67213-2097. Offers building leadership (MS Ed); curriculum and instruction (MS Ed), including English as a second language, reading specialist; organizational leadership (MS Ed). *Accreditation:* NCATE. *Program availability:* Part-time, evening/weekend, online learning. *Degree requirements:* For master's, thesis optional. *Entrance requirements:* For master's, 3 years' full-time teaching experience, minimum GPA of 3.0, writing sample, 2 letters of recommendation, evidence of teaching certification. Additional exam requirements/recommendations for international students: Required—TOEFL (minimum score 600 paper-based; 100 iBT). Electronic applications accepted. *Expenses:* Contact institution. *Faculty research:* Online course design and deliver, staff engagement, classroom action.

New Mexico Highlands University, Graduate Studies, School of Education, Las Vegas, NM 87701. Offers curriculum and instruction (MA); educational leadership (MA); professional counseling (MA); special education (MA). *Accreditation:* NCATE. *Program availability:* Part-time. *Degree requirements:* For master's, comprehensive exam, thesis or alternative. *Entrance requirements:* For master's, minimum undergraduate GPA of 3.0. Additional exam requirements/recommendations for international students: Required—TOEFL (minimum score 540 paper-based). *Faculty research:* Middle school curriculum, integrated computer applications for pre-service classroom teachers, adolescent literacy, narrative cognitive modes in New Mexico multicultural setting, math and math education.

New Mexico State University, College of Education, Las Cruces, NM 88003-8001. Offers education specialist (Ed S); teaching (MAT). *Accreditation:* NCATE. *Program availability:* Part-time-only, evening/weekend, blended/hybrid learning. *Faculty:* 66 full-time (47 women), 12 part-time/adjunct (9 women). *Students:* 257 full-time (190 women), 405 part-time (294 women); includes 367 minority (20 Black or African American, non-Hispanic/Latino; 14 American Indian or Alaska Native, non-Hispanic/Latino; 15 Asian, non-Hispanic/Latino; 302 Hispanic/Latino; 1 Native Hawaiian or other Pacific Islander, non-Hispanic/Latino; 15 Two or more races, non-Hispanic/Latino), 46 international. Average age 36. 404 applicants, 45% accepted, 128 enrolled. In 2018, 156 master's, 29 doctorates, 26 other advanced degrees awarded. Terminal master's awarded for partial completion of doctoral program. *Degree requirements:* For master's and other advanced degree, comprehensive exam (for some programs), thesis (for some programs); for doctorate, comprehensive exam (for some programs), thesis/dissertation (for some programs). *Entrance requirements:* Additional exam requirements/recommendations for international students: Required—TOEFL (minimum score 550 paper-based; 79 iBT), IELTS (minimum score 6.5). *Application deadline:* For fall admission, 3/15 for international students; for spring admission, 10/15 for international students. Applications are processed on a rolling basis. Application fee: $40 ($50 for international students). Electronic applications accepted. *Expenses: Tuition, area resident:* Full-time $4216.70; part-time $252.70 per credit hour. Tuition, state resident: full-time $4216.70; part-time $252.70 per credit hour. Tuition, nonresident: full-time $12,769; part-time $881.10 per credit hour. *International tuition:* $12,769.30 full-time. *Required fees:* $878.40; $48.80 per credit hour. Full-time tuition and fees vary according to course load and reciprocity agreements. *Financial support:* In 2018–19, 256 students received support, including 14 fellowships (averaging $4,548 per year), 26 research assistantships (averaging $11,172 per year), 48 teaching assistantships (averaging $12,418 per year); career-related internships or fieldwork, Federal Work-Study, scholarships/grants, traineeships, health care benefits, and unspecified assistantships also available. Support available to part-time students. Financial award application deadline: 3/1. *Faculty research:* Multicultural identity development, mindfulness, pediatric neuropsychology, multicultural training for teachers and school psychologists, counselor training and supervision, college student mental health, critical pedagogy, bilingual education, critical race feminisms, oral history, access to literacy, literacy comprehension strategies, early childhood education policy and reform, technology-based learning environments, family-school relations, immigrant parent involvement, language differences. *Total annual research expenditures:* $764,404. *Unit head:* Dr. Susan Brown, Interim Dean, 575-646-5858, Fax: 575-646-6032, E-mail: susanbro@nmsu.edu. *Application contact:* Dr. David Rutledge, Graduate Education Advising, 575-646-5411, Fax: 575-646-6032, E-mail: rutledge@nmsu.edu. Website: http://education.nmsu.edu/

New York University, Steinhardt School of Culture, Education, and Human Development, New York, NY 10003. Offers MA, MFA, MM, MPH, MS, DPS, DPT, Ed D, PhD, Advanced Certificate, Post Master's Certificate, Postbaccalaureate Certificate, Advanced Certificate/ MPH, MA/Advanced Certificate, MA/MA, MA/MS, MLIS/MA. *Accreditation:* TEAC. *Program availability:* Part-time. *Entrance requirements:* For doctorate, GRE General Test, interview. Additional exam requirements/recommendations for international students: Required—TOEFL (minimum score 100 iBT). Electronic applications accepted. *Expenses:* Contact institution. *Faculty research:* Equity, urban adolescents, arts in education, globalization, multivariate analysis, psychometrics.

Niagara University, Graduate Division of Education, Niagara University, NY 14109. Offers applied behavior analysis (Certificate); educational leadership (MS Ed, PhD, Certificate), including leadership and policy (PhD), school building leader (MS Ed), school district business leader (Certificate), school district leader (MS Ed, Certificate); literacy instruction (MS Ed); mental health counseling (MS, Certificate); school counseling (MS Ed, Certificate); school psychology (MS); teacher education (MS, MS Ed, Certificate), including early childhood and childhood education (MS Ed, Certificate), early childhood special education (MS), middle and adolescence education (Certificate), special education (MS Ed), special education (grades 1-6) (Certificate), special education (grades 7-12) (Certificate), teaching English to speakers of other languages (TESOL) (Certificate). *Accreditation:* NCATE (one or more programs are accredited). *Program availability:* Part-time, evening/weekend, 100% online, blended/ hybrid learning. *Students:* 241 full-time (181 women), 319 part-time (250 women); includes 73 minority (36 Black or African American, non-Hispanic/Latino; 3 American Indian or Alaska Native, non-Hispanic/Latino; 6 Asian, non-Hispanic/Latino; 19 Hispanic/ Latino; 9 Two or more races, non-Hispanic/Latino), 110 international. Average age 31. In 2018, 164 master's, 15 doctorates, 44 other advanced degrees awarded. *Entrance requirements:* For master's, GRE General Test or MAT. Additional exam requirements/ recommendations for international students: Required—TOEFL (minimum score 550 paper-based; 79 iBT), IELTS (minimum score 6). *Application deadline:* For fall admission, 8/1 for domestic students. Applications are processed on a rolling basis. Electronic applications accepted. *Expenses:* Contact institution. *Financial support:* Research assistantships with tuition reimbursements, teaching assistantships with tuition reimbursements, career-related internships or fieldwork, Federal Work-Study, scholarships/grants, and unspecified assistantships available. Support available to part-time students. Financial award application deadline: 4/15; financial award applicants required to submit FAFSA. *Faculty research:* Instructional supervision, appraisal and evaluation, career opportunities. *Unit head:* Dr. Chandra Foote, Dean, College of Education, 716-286-8549, Fax: 716-286-8561, E-mail: cjf@niagara.edu. *Application contact:* Evan Pierce, Associate Director for Graduate Recruitment, 716-286-8327, Fax: 716-286-8710, E-mail: epierce@niagara.edu.
Website: http://www.niagara.edu/advance/

Nicholls State University, Graduate Studies, College of Education, Department of Teacher Education, Thibodaux, LA 70310. Offers curriculum and instruction (M Ed); educational leadership (M Ed); elementary education (MAT); human performance education (MAT); middle school education (MAT); secondary education (MAT). *Accreditation:* NCATE. *Program availability:* Part-time, evening/weekend, online learning. *Degree requirements:* For master's, comprehensive exam, portfolio. *Entrance requirements:* For master's, GRE General Test, teaching license. Electronic applications accepted.

Nipissing University, Faculty of Education, North Bay, ON P1B 8L7, Canada. Offers M Ed, Certificate. *Program availability:* Part-time, evening/weekend. *Degree requirements:* For master's, comprehensive exam (for some programs), thesis (for some programs). *Entrance requirements:* For master's, 1 year of experience, letters of recommendation, minimum undergraduate GPA of 3.0. Additional exam requirements/ recommendations for international students: Required—TOEFL (minimum score 600 paper-based), IELTS (minimum score 7), TWE (minimum score 5).

Norfolk State University, School of Graduate Studies, School of Education, Norfolk, VA 23504. Offers MA, MAT. *Accreditation:* NCATE. *Program availability:* Part-time. *Degree requirements:* For master's, comprehensive exam. *Entrance requirements:* For master's, PRAXIS, GRE/GMAT, interview, teacher license. *Faculty research:* Urban, pre-elementary, and special education.

North Carolina Agricultural and Technical State University, The Graduate College, College of Education, Greensboro, NC 27411. Offers MA Ed, MAT, MS, MSA, PhD. *Accreditation:* NCATE. *Program availability:* Part-time, evening/weekend. *Degree requirements:* For master's, comprehensive exam, qualifying exam. *Entrance requirements:* For master's, GRE General Test.

North Carolina Central University, School of Education, Durham, NC 27707-3129. Offers M Ed, MA, MAT, MS, MSA. *Accreditation:* NCATE. *Program availability:* Part-time, evening/weekend. *Degree requirements:* For master's, comprehensive exam, thesis or alternative. *Entrance requirements:* For master's, minimum GPA of 3.0 in major, 2.5 overall. Additional exam requirements/recommendations for international students: Required—TOEFL.

North Carolina State University, Graduate School, College of Education, Raleigh, NC 27695. Offers M Ed, MS, MSA, Ed D, PhD, Certificate. *Accreditation:* NCATE. *Program availability:* Part-time. *Degree requirements:* For doctorate, thesis/dissertation. *Entrance requirements:* For master's, doctorate, and Certificate, GRE General Test or MAT, minimum GPA of 3.0 in major. Electronic applications accepted. *Faculty research:* Moral/ethical development, financial policy analysis, middle years education, adult education.

North Central College, School of Graduate and Professional Studies, Department of Education, Naperville, IL 60566-7063. Offers MA Ed. *Program availability:* Part-time, evening/weekend. *Degree requirements:* For master's, thesis optional, clinical practicum, project. *Entrance requirements:* For master's, interview. Additional exam requirements/ recommendations for international students: Required—TOEFL (minimum score 550 paper-based; 80 iBT), IELTS (minimum score 6.5). Electronic applications accepted. Application fee is waived when completed online. *Expenses:* Contact institution.

Northcentral University, Graduate Studies, San Diego, CA 92106. Offers business (MBA, DBA, PhD, Postbaccalaureate Certificate); education (M Ed, Ed D, PhD, Ed S, Post-Master's Certificate, Postbaccalaureate Certificate); marriage and family therapy (MA, DMFT, PhD, Post-Master's Certificate, Postbaccalaureate Certificate); psychology (MA, PhD, Post-Master's Certificate, Postbaccalaureate Certificate); technology (MS, PhD), including computer science, cybersecurity (MS), data science, technology and innovation management (PhD). *Program availability:* Part-time, evening/weekend, online only, 100% online. *Faculty:* 98 full-time (63 women), 385 part-time/adjunct (203 women). *Students:* 5,036 full-time (3,291 women), 5,747 part-time (3,977 women); includes 3,777 minority (2,550 Black or African American, non-Hispanic/Latino; 76 American Indian or Alaska Native, non-Hispanic/Latino; 192 Asian, non-Hispanic/Latino; 603 Hispanic/ Latino; 39 Native Hawaiian or other Pacific Islander, non-Hispanic/Latino; 317 Two or more races, non-Hispanic/Latino). Average age 45. In 2018, 929 master's, 782 doctorates, 278 other advanced degrees awarded. *Degree requirements:* For doctorate, comprehensive exam, thesis/dissertation. *Entrance requirements:* For master's, bachelor's degree from regionally- or nationally-accredited institution, current resume or

curriculum vitae, statement of intent, interview, and background check (for marriage and family therapy); for doctorate, post-baccalaureate master's degree and/or doctoral degree from nationally- or regionally-accredited academic institution; for other advanced degree, bachelor's-level or higher degree from accredited institution or university (for Post-Baccalaureate Certificate); master's and/or doctoral degree from regionally- or nationally-accredited academic institution (for Post-Master's Certificate). Additional exam requirements/recommendations for international students: Required—TOEFL (minimum score 550 paper-based; 79 iBT), IELTS (minimum score 6.5), PTE (minimum score 53). *Application deadline:* Applications are processed on a rolling basis. Application fee: $0. Electronic applications accepted. *Expenses: Tuition:* Full-time $893. *Required fees:* $95. Tuition and fees vary according to degree level and program. *Financial support:* Scholarships/grants available. *Faculty research:* Business management, curriculum and instruction, educational leadership, health psychology, organizational behavior. *Unit head:* Dr. David Harpool, Acting Provost, 888-327-2877 Ext. 8181, E-mail: provost@ncu.edu. *Application contact:* Ken Boutelle, Vice President, Enrollment Services, 888-628-4979, E-mail: enrollmentservices@ncu.edu.

North Dakota State University, College of Graduate and Interdisciplinary Studies, College of Human Development and Education, School of Education, Fargo, ND 58102. Offers agricultural education (M Ed, MS), including agricultural education; counselor education (M Ed, MS), including clinical mental health counseling, school counseling; counselor education and supervision (PhD), including counselor education and supervision; educational leadership (M Ed, MS, Ed S); family and consumer sciences education (M Ed, MS). *Accreditation:* NCATE. *Program availability:* Part-time, evening/ weekend, online learning. *Degree requirements:* For master's, comprehensive exam; for doctorate, thesis/dissertation; for Ed S, thesis. *Entrance requirements:* For degree, GRE General Test, master's degree, minimum GPA of 3.25. Additional exam requirements/ recommendations for international students: Required—TOEFL.

Northeastern Illinois University, College of Graduate Studies and Research, Daniel L. Goodwin College of Education, Chicago, IL 60625-4699. Offers MA, MAT, MS, MSI. *Program availability:* Part-time, evening/weekend. *Degree requirements:* For master's, comprehensive exam (for some programs), thesis (for some programs). *Entrance requirements:* For master's, minimum GPA of 2.75. Additional exam requirements/ recommendations for international students: Required—TOEFL (minimum score 550 paper-based; 79 iBT). Electronic applications accepted. *Faculty research:* Leadership, problem-based learning strategies, school improvement, bilingual education, use of technology.

Northeastern State University, College of Education, Tahlequah, OK 74464-2399. Offers M Ed, MS. *Accreditation:* NCATE. *Program availability:* Part-time, evening/ weekend. *Faculty:* 31 full-time (21 women), 9 part-time/adjunct (5 women). *Students:* 162 full-time (126 women), 299 part-time (239 women); includes 187 minority (19 Black or African American, non-Hispanic/Latino; 70 American Indian or Alaska Native, non-Hispanic/Latino; 5 Asian, non-Hispanic/Latino; 16 Hispanic/Latino; 77 Two or more races, non-Hispanic/Latino), 8 international. Average age 34. In 2018, 170 master's awarded. *Degree requirements:* For master's, thesis. *Entrance requirements:* For master's, GRE or MAT. Additional exam requirements/recommendations for international students: Required—TOEFL. *Application deadline:* For fall admission, 6/1 priority date for domestic students. Applications are processed on a rolling basis. Application fee: $25. Electronic applications accepted. *Expenses: Tuition, area resident:* Full-time $4500; part-time $250 per credit hour. Tuition, state resident: Full-time $4500; part-time $250 per credit hour. Tuition, nonresident: Full-time $9999; part-time $555.50 per credit hour. International tuition: $9999 full-time. *Required fees:* $601.20; $33.40 per credit hour. *Financial support:* Teaching assistantships, career-related internships or fieldwork, and Federal Work-Study available. Financial award application deadline: 3/1. *Unit head:* Dr. Vanessa Anton, Interim Dean of the College of Education, 918-444-3700, Fax: 918-458-2351, E-mail: anton@nsuok.edu. *Application contact:* Josh McCollum, Graduate Coordinator, 918-444-2093, E-mail: mccolluj@nsuok.edu.
Website: http://academics.nsuok.edu/education/EducationHome.aspx

Northern Arizona University, College of Education, Flagstaff, AZ 86011. Offers M Ed, MA, Ed D, PhD, Certificate, Ed S, Graduate Certificate. *Accreditation:* NCATE. *Program availability:* Part-time, 100% online, blended/hybrid learning. *Degree requirements:* For master's, variable foreign language requirement, comprehensive exam (for some programs), thesis (for some programs); for doctorate, variable foreign language requirement, comprehensive exam (for some programs), thesis/dissertation (for some programs); for other advanced degree, comprehensive exam (for some programs). *Entrance requirements:* Additional exam requirements/recommendations for international students: Required—TOEFL (minimum score 80 iBT), IELTS (minimum score 6.5). Electronic applications accepted.

Northern Illinois University, Graduate School, College of Education, De Kalb, IL 60115-2854. Offers MS, MS Ed, Ed D, Ed S. *Accreditation:* NCATE. *Program availability:* Part-time, evening/weekend, online learning. *Faculty:* 110 full-time (66 women), 5 part-time/adjunct (3 women). *Students:* 333 full-time (205 women), 888 part-time (629 women); includes 315 minority (125 Black or African American, non-Hispanic/ Latino; 2 American Indian or Alaska Native, non-Hispanic/Latino; 36 Asian, non-Hispanic/Latino; 111 Hispanic/Latino; 41 Two or more races, non-Hispanic/Latino), 74 international. Average age 36. 479 applicants, 77% accepted, 178 enrolled. In 2018, 308 master's, 61 doctorates, 2 other advanced degrees awarded. Terminal master's awarded for partial completion of doctoral program. *Degree requirements:* For master's and Ed S, comprehensive exam, thesis optional; for doctorate, thesis/dissertation, candidacy exam, dissertation defense. *Entrance requirements:* For master's, GRE General Test or MAT, minimum GPA of 2.75; for doctorate, GRE General Test or MAT, minimum GPA of 2.75 (undergraduate), 3.2 (graduate); for Ed S, GRE General Test, master's degree; minimum undergraduate GPA of 2.75, graduate 3.2. Additional exam requirements/recommendations for international students: Required—TOEFL (minimum score 550 paper-based). *Application deadline:* For fall admission, 6/1 for domestic students, 5/1 for international students; for spring admission, 11/1 for domestic students, 10/1 for international students. Applications are processed on a rolling basis. Application fee: $40. Electronic applications accepted. *Financial support:* In 2018–19, 1 research assistantship with full tuition reimbursement was awarded; fellowships with full tuition reimbursements, teaching assistantships with full tuition reimbursements, career-related internships or fieldwork, Federal Work-Study, scholarships/grants, tuition waivers (full), and staff assistantships also available. Support available to part-time students. Financial award applicants required to submit FAFSA. *Unit head:* Laurie Elish-Piper, Dean, 815-753-1949, Fax: 851-753-2100. *Application contact:* Graduate School Office, 815-753-0395, E-mail: gradsch@niu.edu.
Website: http://www.cedu.niu.edu/

Northern Kentucky University, Office of Graduate Programs, College of Education and Human Services, Highland Heights, KY 41099. Offers MA, MAT, MS, MSW, Ed D, Certificate, Ed S. *Accreditation:* NCATE. *Program availability:* Part-time, evening/ weekend. *Degree requirements:* For master's, comprehensive exam (for some programs), thesis (for some programs). *Entrance requirements:* For master's, GRE. Additional exam requirements/recommendations for international students: Required— TOEFL (minimum score 550 paper-based; 79 iBT); Recommended—IELTS (minimum score 6.5). Electronic applications accepted.

Education—General

Northern Michigan University, Office of Graduate Education and Research, College of Health Sciences and Professional Studies, School of Education, Leadership and Public Service, Marquette, MI 49855-5301. Offers administration and supervision (MAE); instruction (MAE); learning disabilities (MAE); postsecondary biology education (MS); reading education (MAE), including reading, reading specialist. *Accreditation:* TEAC. *Program availability:* Part-time, online learning. *Degree requirements:* For master's, thesis (for some programs). *Entrance requirements:* For master's, minimum GPA of 3.0. Additional exam requirements/recommendations for international students: Required—TOEFL (minimum score 550 paper-based; 79 iBT), IELTS (minimum score 6.5). Electronic applications accepted.

Northern State University, MS Ed Program in Educational Studies, Aberdeen, SD 57401-7198. Offers MS Ed. *Program availability:* Part-time, online learning. *Degree requirements:* For master's, comprehensive exam, thesis optional. *Entrance requirements:* For master's, minimum GPA of 2.75. Additional exam requirements/recommendations for international students: Required—TOEFL (minimum score 550 paper-based; 78 iBT), IELTS (minimum score 6). Electronic applications accepted.

Northern Vermont University–Johnson, Program in Education, Johnson, VT 05656. Offers applied behavior analysis (MA Ed); curriculum and instruction (MA Ed); foundations of education (MA Ed); special education (MA Ed). *Program availability:* Part-time. *Degree requirements:* For master's, thesis or alternative, exit interview. *Entrance requirements:* For master's, interview. Additional exam requirements/recommendations for international students: Required—TOEFL. Electronic applications accepted.

Northern Vermont University–Lyndon, Graduate Programs in Education, Lyndonville, VT 05851. Offers education (M Ed), including curriculum and instruction, reading specialist, special education, teaching and counseling; natural sciences (MST), including science education. *Program availability:* Part-time, evening/weekend. *Degree requirements:* For master's, exam or major field project. *Entrance requirements:* Additional exam requirements/recommendations for international students: Recommended—TOEFL (minimum score 500 paper-based). *Faculty research:* Impaired reading, cognitive style, counseling relationship.

North Greenville University, T. Walter Brashier Graduate School, Greer, SC 29651. Offers Christian ministry (MCM, D Min); education (M Ed, MAT); financial planning (MBA); human resources (MBA). *Program availability:* Part-time, evening/weekend, online learning. *Degree requirements:* For master's, comprehensive exam (for some programs), thesis or alternative, capstone course. *Entrance requirements:* For master's, minimum GPA of 2.25 overall, 2.5 in major; for doctorate, MAT. Additional exam requirements/recommendations for international students: Required—TOEFL (minimum score 550 paper-based). Electronic applications accepted. *Faculty research:* Organizational behavior, church growth, homiletics, human resources, business strategy.

North Park University, School of Education, Chicago, IL 60625-4895. Offers MA. *Degree requirements:* For master's, thesis. *Entrance requirements:* For master's, GRE General Test. *Faculty research:* Teacher leadership, research design, teacher education.

Northwest Christian University, School of Education and Counseling, Eugene, OR 97401-3745. Offers clinical mental health counseling (MA); elementary teaching (MAT); English for speakers of other languages (MAT); physical education (MAT); school counseling (MA); secondary teaching (MAT); special education (MAT). *Program availability:* Part-time, evening/weekend, online learning. *Degree requirements:* For master's, thesis (for some programs). *Entrance requirements:* For master's, GRE or MAT, minimum undergraduate GPA of 3.0, interview, 2-3 page statement of purpose, two letters of recommendation, resume, background check. Additional exam requirements/recommendations for international students: Required—TOEFL (minimum score 550 paper-based; 80 iBT). Electronic applications accepted. *Expenses:* Contact institution.

Northwestern College, Program in Education, Orange City, IA 51041-1996. Offers early childhood (M Ed); master teacher (M Ed); teacher leadership (M Ed, Graduate Certificate). *Program availability:* Online learning.

Northwestern Oklahoma State University, School of Professional Studies, Alva, OK 73717-2799. Offers adult education management and administration (M Ed); counseling psychology (MCP); curriculum and instruction (M Ed); educational leadership (M Ed); elementary education (M Ed); reading specialist (M Ed); school counseling (M Ed); secondary education (M Ed). *Accreditation:* NCATE (one or more programs are accredited). *Program availability:* Part-time. *Degree requirements:* For master's, comprehensive exam (for some programs), thesis optional, portfolio. *Entrance requirements:* For master's, GRE General Test or MAT, minimum GPA of 2.75.

Northwestern State University of Louisiana, Graduate Studies and Research, College of Education and Human Development, Natchitoches, LA 71497. Offers M Ed, MA, MAT, Ed S. *Accreditation:* NCATE. *Degree requirements:* For master's, comprehensive exam, thesis (for some programs); for Ed S, comprehensive exam, thesis. *Entrance requirements:* For master's, GRE General Test, GRE Subject Test, minimum undergraduate GPA of 2.5; for Ed S, GRE General Test. Additional exam requirements/recommendations for international students: Required—TOEFL. Electronic applications accepted. *Faculty research:* Teacher-parent-child-friendly physical activities for young children, Net generation and social media, positive emotion and multimedia learning, the effects of Web-based mathematics resources on the motivation and achievement of high school students with learning disabilities, educational leadership.

Northwestern University, The Graduate School, School of Education and Social Policy, Evanston, IL 60208. Offers education (MS), including elementary teaching, secondary teaching, teacher leadership; human development and social policy (PhD); learning and organizational change (MS); learning sciences (MA, PhD). MA and PhD admissions and degrees offered through The Graduate School. *Program availability:* Part-time, evening/weekend. *Degree requirements:* For doctorate, comprehensive exam, thesis/dissertation. *Entrance requirements:* For master's and doctorate, GRE General Test. Electronic applications accepted. *Expenses:* Contact institution. *Faculty research:* Technology, curriculum design, welfare, education reform, learning.

Northwest Missouri State University, Graduate School, School of Education, Maryville, MO 64468-6001. Offers early childhood education (MS Ed); education leadership (MS Ed), including elementary, K-12, secondary; educational leadership (Ed S), including elementary school principalship, secondary school principalship, superintendency; educational leadership and policy analysis (Ed D); elementary education (MS Ed); elementary mathematics (MS Ed); higher education leadership (MS); middle school education (MS Ed); reading (MS Ed); special education (MS Ed); teacher leadership (MS Ed); teaching English language learners (MS Ed). *Accreditation:* NCATE. *Program availability:* Part-time. *Faculty:* 26 full-time (16 women). *Students:* 109 full-time (87 women), 385 part-time (270 women); includes 30 minority (10 Black or African American, non-Hispanic/Latino; 2 American Indian or Alaska Native, non-Hispanic/Latino; 3 Asian, non-Hispanic/Latino; 12 Hispanic/Latino; 1 Native Hawaiian or other Pacific Islander, non-Hispanic/Latino; 2 Two or more races, non-Hispanic/Latino), 1 international. Average age 33. 210 applicants, 72% accepted, 142 enrolled. In 2018, 71 master's, 11 other advanced degrees awarded. *Degree requirements:* For master's, comprehensive exam; for Ed S, comprehensive exam, thesis. *Entrance requirements:* For master's, GRE General Test, writing sample; for Ed S, minimum graduate GPA of 3.25. Additional exam requirements/recommendations for international students: Required—TOEFL (minimum score 550 paper-based). *Application deadline:* For fall admission, 7/1 for domestic and international students; for spring admission, 11/15 for domestic and international students. Applications are processed on a rolling basis. Application fee: $0 ($75 for international students). Electronic applications accepted. *Expenses:* $389.11 in-state and $653.92 out-of-state per credit hour. *Financial support:* Research assistantships with full tuition reimbursements, teaching assistantships with full tuition reimbursements, and unspecified assistantships available. Financial award application deadline: 4/1; financial award applicants required to submit FAFSA. *Unit head:* Dr. Tim Wall, Director, 660-562-1179, E-mail: timwall@nwmissouri.edu. *Application contact:* Dr. Tim Wall, Director, 660-562-1179, E-mail: timwall@nwmissouri.edu.
Website: https://www.nwmissouri.edu/education/index.htm

Northwest Nazarene University, Graduate Education Program, Nampa, ID 83686-5897. Offers curriculum and instruction (M Ed); educational leadership (M Ed, Ed D, PhD, Ed S), including building administrator (M Ed, Ed S), director of special education (Ed S), leadership and organizational development (Ed S), superintendent (Ed S). *Accreditation:* ACA (one or more programs are accredited); NCATE. *Program availability:* Part-time, online only, 100% online, 2-week face-to-face residency (for doctoral programs). *Faculty:* 4 full-time (3 women), 18 part-time/adjunct (7 women). *Students:* 128 full-time (83 women), 59 part-time (37 women); includes 22 minority (3 Black or African American, non-Hispanic/Latino; 1 Asian, non-Hispanic/Latino; 3 Hispanic/Latino; 15 Two or more races, non-Hispanic/Latino), 1 international. Average age 44. 124 applicants, 84% accepted, 87 enrolled. In 2018, 37 master's, 18 doctorates, 28 other advanced degrees awarded. *Degree requirements:* For master's, comprehensive exam (for some programs), action research project; for doctorate, thesis/dissertation, Dissertation; for Ed S, comprehensive exam, research project. *Entrance requirements:* For master's, minimum undergraduate GPA of 3.0 overall or during final 30 semester credits, undergraduate degree, valid teaching certificate; for doctorate, Ed S or equivalent, minimum GPA of 3.5; for Ed S, undergraduate degree, valid teaching certificate. Additional exam requirements/recommendations for international students: Recommended—TOEFL. *Application deadline:* Applications are processed on a rolling basis. Application fee: $50. Electronic applications accepted. *Expenses:* Masters: $475 per credit, $95 technology fee per semester; EDS: $505 per credit, $95 technology fee per semester; PHD/EDD: $565 per credit, $520 dissertation fee, $95 technology fee per semester. *Financial support:* Application deadline: 1/15; applicants required to submit FAFSA. *Faculty research:* Action research, cooperative learning, accountability, institutional accreditation, personalized learning K-12. *Unit head:* Dr. Heidi Curtis, Chair, 208-467-8250, E-mail: hlcurtis@nnu.edu. *Application contact:* Charlene Brown, Admissions Counselor, 208-467-8492, Fax: 208-467-8384, E-mail: gradeducationinfo@nnu.edu.
Website: http://www.nnu.edu/graded/

Northwest University, School of Education, Kirkland, WA 98033. Offers education (M Ed); teaching (MIT). *Program availability:* Part-time, evening/weekend. *Degree requirements:* For master's, action research project. *Entrance requirements:* For master's, Washington Educator Skills Test-Basic (WEST-B)/Washington Educator Skills Test-Endorsements (WEST-E), minimum GPA of 3.3. Additional exam requirements/recommendations for international students: Recommended—TOEFL. Electronic applications accepted. *Expenses:* Contact institution.

Notre Dame de Namur University, Division of Academic Affairs, School of Education and Psychology, Program in Education, Belmont, CA 94002-1908. Offers curriculum and instruction (MA); disciplinary studies (MA). *Program availability:* Part-time, evening/weekend. *Students:* 2 full-time (both women), 36 part-time (29 women); includes 10 minority (4 Asian, non-Hispanic/Latino; 4 Hispanic/Latino; 2 Two or more races, non-Hispanic/Latino), 2 international. Average age 31. *Entrance requirements:* For master's, CBEST, CSET, valid teaching credential or substantial teaching experience. Additional exam requirements/recommendations for international students: Required—TOEFL (minimum score 550 paper-based; 79 iBT). *Application deadline:* For fall admission, 8/1 priority date for domestic students; for spring admission, 12/1 priority date for domestic students. Applications are processed on a rolling basis. Application fee: $60. Electronic applications accepted. *Expenses: Tuition:* Full-time $16,596; part-time $11,064 per semester. *Required fees:* $130; $130 per unit. $65 per semester. Tuition and fees vary according to program. *Financial support:* Career-related internships or fieldwork and scholarships/grants available. Financial award applicants required to submit FAFSA. *Unit head:* Kim Tolley, Program Director, Master of Arts in Education, 650-508-3464, E-mail: ktolley@ndnu.edu. *Application contact:* Kim Tolley, Program Director, Master of Arts in Education, 650-508-3464, E-mail: ktolley@ndnu.edu.
Website: https://www.ndnu.edu/education-and-leadership/graduate/education/

Notre Dame of Maryland University, Graduate Studies, Program in Teaching, Baltimore, MD 21210-2476. Offers MA. *Accreditation:* NCATE. *Entrance requirements:* For master's, Watson-Glaser Critical Thinking Appraisal, writing test, grammar test, interview. Additional exam requirements/recommendations for international students: Required—TOEFL (minimum score 500 paper-based; 61 iBT). Electronic applications accepted.

Nova Southeastern University, Abraham S. Fischler College of Education, Fort Lauderdale, FL 33314. Offers education (MS, Ed D, PhD, Ed S); instructional technology and distance education (MS); teaching and learning (MA). *Accreditation:* NCATE. *Program availability:* Part-time, evening/weekend, 100% online, blended/hybrid learning. *Degree requirements:* For master's, practicum, internship; for doctorate, thesis/dissertation; for Ed S, thesis, practicum, internship. *Entrance requirements:* For master's, MAT or GRE (for some programs), CLAST, PRAXIS I, CBEST, General Knowledge Test, teaching certification, minimum GPA of 2.5, verification of teaching, BS; for doctorate, MAT or GRE, master's degree, minimum cumulative GPA of 3.0; for Ed S, MAT or GRE, master's degree, teaching certificate, minimum GPA of 3.0. Additional exam requirements/recommendations for international students: Recommended—TOEFL (minimum score 550 paper-based; 79 iBT), IELTS (minimum score 6). Electronic applications accepted. *Expenses:* Contact institution. *Faculty research:* STEM education, educational technology, principal training, quality of life.

Oakland City University, School of Education, Oakland City, IN 47660-1099. Offers building level administration (MS Ed); curriculum and instruction (MS Ed, Ed D); education (MS Ed); elementary education (MAT); organizational management (Ed D); secondary education (MAT); superintendency (Ed D). *Accreditation:* NCATE. Terminal master's awarded for partial completion of doctoral program. *Degree requirements:* For master's, thesis; for doctorate, comprehensive exam, thesis/dissertation. *Entrance requirements:* For master's, MAT, minimum GPA of 3.0, interview, resume, letters of recommendation; for doctorate, MAT, GRE, minimum GPA of 3.2, interview, resume, letters of recommendation. *Expenses:* Contact institution. *Faculty research:* Assessment, cultural diversity, teacher education, education leadership.

Oakland University, Graduate Study and Lifelong Learning, School of Education and Human Services, Rochester, MI 48309-4401. Offers M Ed, MA, MAT, PhD, Certificate,

Ed S, Graduate Certificate, PMC. *Accreditation:* TEAC. *Program availability:* Part-time, evening/weekend. *Degree requirements:* For doctorate, thesis/dissertation. *Entrance requirements:* For master's and doctorate, minimum GPA of 3.0. Additional exam requirements/recommendations for international students: Required—TOEFL (minimum score 550 paper-based). Electronic applications accepted.

Ohio Dominican University, Division of Education, Columbus, OH 43219-2099. Offers curriculum and instruction (M Ed); educational leadership (M Ed); teaching English to speakers of other languages (MA). *Accreditation:* NCATE. *Program availability:* Part-time, evening/weekend, 100% online, blended/hybrid learning. *Faculty:* 7 full-time (4 women), 7 part-time/adjunct (4 women). *Students:* 6 full-time (5 women), 111 part-time (82 women); includes 12 minority (5 Black or African American, non-Hispanic/Latino; 3 Hispanic/Latino; 4 Two or more races, non-Hispanic/Latino), 8 international. Average age 34. 49 applicants, 53% accepted, 23 enrolled. In 2018, 64 master's awarded. *Degree requirements:* For master's, thesis (for some programs). *Entrance requirements:* For master's, minimum undergraduate GPA of 3.0, teaching certificate/license, teaching experience, 2 letters of recommendation, currently teaching or access to academic classroom. Additional exam requirements/recommendations for international students: Required—TOEFL (minimum score 550 paper-based), IELTS (minimum score 6.5). *Application deadline:* For fall admission, 8/15 for domestic students, 6/10 for international students; for spring admission, 1/4 for domestic students, 11/2 for international students. Applications are processed on a rolling basis. Application fee: $25. Electronic applications accepted. *Expenses:* $538/credit hour, $225/semester fees. *Financial support:* Tuition waivers and tuition discounts (for diocesan teachers) available. Financial award applicants required to submit FAFSA. *Unit head:* Dr. Marlissa Stauffer, Chair, Division of Education, 614-251-4621, E-mail: stauffem@ohiodominican.edu. *Application contact:* John W. Naughton, Vice President for Enrollment and Student Success, 614-251-4721, Fax: 614-251-6654, E-mail: grad@ohiodominican.edu.
Website: http://www.ohiodominican.edu/academics/graduate/master-of-education

The Ohio State University, Graduate School, College of Education and Human Ecology, Columbus, OH 43210. Offers M Ed, MA, MS, Ed D, PhD, Ed S. *Accreditation:* NCATE. *Faculty:* 160. *Students:* 770 full-time (519 women), 294 part-time (203 women). Average age 31. In 2018, 319 master's, 96 doctorates, 13 other advanced degrees awarded. Terminal master's awarded for partial completion of doctoral program. *Degree requirements:* For master's, comprehensive exam (for some programs), thesis optional; for doctorate, comprehensive exam, thesis/dissertation. *Entrance requirements:* For master's and doctorate, GRE or GMAT. Additional exam requirements/recommendations for international students: Required—TOEFL (minimum score 550 paper-based; 79 iBT), Michigan English Language Assessment Battery (minimum score 82); Recommended—IELTS (minimum score 7). *Application deadline:* Applications are processed on a rolling basis. Application fee: $60 ($70 for international students). Electronic applications accepted. *Financial support:* Fellowships with tuition reimbursements, research assistantships with tuition reimbursements, teaching assistantships with tuition reimbursements, career-related internships or fieldwork, Federal Work-Study, institutionally sponsored loans, scholarships/grants, traineeships, health care benefits, and unspecified assistantships available. Support available to part-time students. *Faculty research:* Math and science education; teaching professional development; issues related to urban education; health, well-being, and sports; literacy education. *Unit head:* Dr. Donald B. Pope-Davis, Dean, E-mail: pope-davis.1@osu.edu. *Application contact:* Graduate and Professional Admissions, 614-292-9444, Fax: 614-292-3895, E-mail: gpadmissions@osu.edu.
Website: http://ehe.osu.edu/

The Ohio State University at Mansfield, Graduate Programs, Mansfield, OH 44906-1599. Offers education (MA); social work (MSW). *Program availability:* Part-time. *Students:* 2. *Degree requirements:* For master's, comprehensive exam (for some programs), thesis (for some programs). *Entrance requirements:* For master's, GRE, minimum GPA of 3.0. Additional exam requirements/recommendations for international students: Required—TOEFL (minimum 550 paper-based, 79 iBT), IELTS (minimum score 7) or Michigan English Language Assessment Battery (minimum score 82). *Application deadline:* For fall admission, 4/1 for domestic students, 3/1 for international students; for spring admission, 10/15 for domestic and international students. Applications are processed on a rolling basis. Application fee: $60 ($70 for international students). Electronic applications accepted. *Financial support:* Teaching assistantships with full tuition reimbursements, Federal Work-Study, and scholarships/grants available. Support available to part-time students. Financial award application deadline: 2/15; financial award applicants required to submit FAFSA. *Unit head:* Dr. Norman W. Jones, Dean and Director, 419-755-4222, E-mail: jones.2376@osu.edu. *Application contact:* Graduate and Professional Admissions, 614-292-9444, Fax: 614-292-3895, E-mail: gpadmissions@osu.edu.

The Ohio State University at Marion, Graduate Programs, Marion, OH 43302-5695. Offers education (MA), including teaching and learning. *Program availability:* Part-time. *Degree requirements:* For master's, comprehensive exam (for some programs), thesis (for some programs). *Entrance requirements:* For master's, GRE, minimum undergraduate GPA of 3.0. Additional exam requirements/recommendations for international students: Required—TOEFL (minimum score 550 paper-based, 79 iBT), IELTS (minimum score 7) or Michigan English Language Assessment Battery (minimum score 82). *Application deadline:* Applications are processed on a rolling basis. Application fee: $60 ($70 for international students). Electronic applications accepted. *Financial support:* Application deadline: 2/15; applicants required to submit FAFSA. *Unit head:* Dr. Gregory S. Rose, Dean/Director, 740-725-6218, E-mail: rose.9@osu.edu. *Application contact:* Graduate and Professional Admissions, 614-292-9444, Fax: 614-292-3895, E-mail: gpadmissions@osu.edu.

The Ohio State University at Newark, Graduate Programs, Newark, OH 43055-1797. Offers education - teaching and learning (MA); social work (MSW). *Program availability:* Part-time. *Faculty:* 49. *Students:* 8 (5 women). Average age 37. Terminal master's awarded for partial completion of doctoral program. *Degree requirements:* For master's, comprehensive exam (for some programs), thesis (for some programs). *Entrance requirements:* For master's, GRE, minimum GPA of 3.0. Additional exam requirements/recommendations for international students: Required—TOEFL (minimum score 550 paper-based; 79 iBT), IELTS (minimum score 7), or Michigan English Language Assessment Battery (minimum score 82). *Application deadline:* For fall admission, 3/1 for domestic and international students. Applications are processed on a rolling basis. Application fee: $60 ($70 for international students). Electronic applications accepted. *Financial support:* Application deadline: 2/15. *Unit head:* Dr. William L. MacDonald, Dean and Director, 740-366-9333 Ext. 330, E-mail: macdonald.24@osu.edu. *Application contact:* Graduate and Professional Admissions, 614-292-9444, Fax: 614-292-3985, E-mail: gpadmissions@osu.edu.

Ohio University, Graduate College, Gladys W. and David H. Patton College of Education and Human Services, Athens, OH 45701-2979. Offers M Ed, MS, MSA, Ed D, PhD. *Accreditation:* NCATE. *Program availability:* Part-time, evening/weekend. *Degree requirements:* For master's, comprehensive exam (for some programs), thesis or alternative; for doctorate, comprehensive exam, thesis/dissertation. *Entrance requirements:* For master's, GRE General Test or MAT; for doctorate, GRE General

Test, MAT, master's degree. Additional exam requirements/recommendations for international students: Required—TOEFL (minimum score 550 paper-based; 80 iBT) or IELTS (minimum score 6.5). Electronic applications accepted. *Faculty research:* School improvement, partnerships, literacy, rural education.

Ohio Valley University, School of Graduate Education, Vienna, WV 26105-8000. Offers curriculum and instruction (M Ed). *Program availability:* Online learning. *Entrance requirements:* For master's, 2 letters of recommendation, official transcripts from all previous institutions, essay, bachelor's degree.

Oklahoma State University, College of Education, Health and Aviation, Stillwater, OK 74078. Offers MS, Ed D, PhD, Ed S. *Accreditation:* NCATE. *Program availability:* Part-time, online learning. *Degree requirements:* For master's, thesis or alternative; for doctorate, comprehensive exam, thesis/dissertation. *Entrance requirements:* For master's and doctorate, GRE or GMAT. Additional exam requirements/recommendations for international students: Required—TOEFL (minimum score 550 paper-based; 79 iBT). Electronic applications accepted. *Expenses:* Tuition, area resident: Full-time $4148. Tuition, state resident: full-time $4148. Tuition, nonresident: full-time $10,517. *International tuition:* $10,517 full-time. *Required fees:* $4394; $2929 per credit hour. Tuition and fees vary according to course load and program.

Old Dominion University, Darden College of Education, Norfolk, VA 23529. Offers MS, MS Ed, PhD, Ed S, Postbaccalaureate Certificate. *Program availability:* Part-time, evening/weekend, 100% online, blended/hybrid learning. *Degree requirements:* For master's, comprehensive exam (for some programs), thesis (for some programs); for doctorate, comprehensive exam, thesis/dissertation; for other advanced degree, comprehensive exam. *Entrance requirements:* For doctorate, GRE General Test, master's degree, minimum GPA of 3.25; for other advanced degree, GRE General Test or MAT. Additional exam requirements/recommendations for international students: Required—TOEFL (minimum score 550 paper-based). Electronic applications accepted. *Faculty research:* Effective urban teaching practices, curriculum theory, clinical practices, special education, instructional technology.

Olivet Nazarene University, Graduate School, Division of Education, Bourbonnais, IL 60914. Offers curriculum and instruction (MAE); elementary education (MAT); library information specialist (MAE); reading specialist (MAE); school leadership (MAE); secondary education (MAT). *Accreditation:* NCATE. *Program availability:* Evening/weekend. *Degree requirements:* For master's, thesis or alternative.

Open University, Graduate Programs, Milton Keynes, United Kingdom. Offers business (MBA); education (M Ed); engineering (M Eng); history (MA); music (MA); philosophy (MA).

Oral Roberts University, School of Education, Tulsa, OK 74171. Offers Christian school administration (K-12) (MA Ed, Ed D); college and higher education administration (Ed D); curriculum and instruction (MA Ed); initial teaching with alternative licensure (MAT); initial teaching with licensure (MAT); public school administration (K-12) (MA Ed, Ed D). *Accreditation:* NCATE. *Program availability:* Part-time, online learning. *Degree requirements:* For master's, comprehensive exam, thesis optional; for doctorate, comprehensive exam, thesis/dissertation. *Entrance requirements:* For master's, GRE General Test or MAT (minimum score in 80th percentile or higher); Oklahoma general education or subject area test (for MAT), minimum GPA of 3.0, bachelor's degree from regionally-accredited institution; for doctorate, minimum GPA of 3.0, master's degree from regionally-accredited institution. Electronic applications accepted. Application fee is waived when completed online. *Expenses:* Contact institution. *Faculty research:* Teacher effectiveness, college success in high achieving African-Americans, professional development practices.

Oregon State University, College of Education, Program in Education, Corvallis, OR 97331. Offers agricultural education (PhD); language equity and education policy (PhD); mathematics education (MS); science education (MS); science/mathematics education (PhD). *Program availability:* Part-time, 100% online, blended/hybrid learning. Terminal master's awarded for partial completion of doctoral program. *Degree requirements:* For master's, variable foreign language requirement, thesis (for some programs); for doctorate, variable foreign language requirement, thesis/dissertation. *Entrance requirements:* Additional exam requirements/recommendations for international students: Required—TOEFL (minimum score 575 paper-based). *Faculty research:* School administration, educational foundations, research methodology, education policy development, higher education administration.

Oregon State University, College of Education, Program in Teaching, Corvallis, OR 97331. Offers clinically based elementary education (MAT); elementary education (MAT); language arts (MAT); mathematics (MAT); music education (MAT); science (MAT); social studies (MAT). *Program availability:* Part-time, blended/hybrid learning. *Entrance requirements:* For master's, CBEST. Additional exam requirements/recommendations for international students: Required—TOEFL (minimum score 575 paper-based). *Expenses:* Contact institution.

Oregon State University–Cascades, Program in Education, Bend, OR 97701. Offers MAT.

Ottawa University, Graduate Studies-Arizona, Program in Education, Ottawa, KS 66067-3399. Offers community college counseling (MA); curriculum and instruction (MA); early childhood (MA); education intervention (MA); education leadership (MA); education technology (MA); Montessori early childhood education (MA); Montessori elementary education (MA); professional development (MA); school guidance counseling (MA); special education - cross categorical (MA). Programs offered in Mesa, Phoenix, Tempe and West Valley, AZ. *Accreditation:* NCATE. *Program availability:* Part-time. *Degree requirements:* For master's, thesis or alternative. *Entrance requirements:* For master's, minimum undergraduate GPA of 3.0, copy of current state certification or teaching license. Additional exam requirements/recommendations for international students: Required—TOEFL (minimum score 550 paper-based). Electronic applications accepted. *Expenses:* Contact institution.

Otterbein University, Department of Education, Westerville, OH 43081. Offers MAE, MAT. *Accreditation:* NCATE. *Degree requirements:* For master's, capstone project. *Entrance requirements:* For master's, 2 reference forms, essay, interview. Additional exam requirements/recommendations for international students: Required—TOEFL (minimum score 550 paper-based; 79 iBT). *Faculty research:* Computer technology middle level education, assessment, teacher leadership, multicultural education.

Pace University, School of Education, New York, NY 10038. Offers adolescent education (MST), including biology, chemistry, earth science, English, foreign languages, mathematics, physics, social studies; childhood education (MST); early childhood development, learning and intervention (MST); educational technology studies (MS); inclusive adolescent education (MST), including biology, chemistry, earth science, English, foreign languages, mathematics, physics, social studies; integrated instruction for educational technology (Certificate); integrated instruction for literacy and technology (Certificate); literacy (MS Ed); special education (MS Ed). *Accreditation:* NCATE. *Program availability:* Part-time, evening/weekend, 100% online, blended/hybrid learning. *Faculty:* 19 full-time (13 women), 86 part-time/adjunct (49 women). *Students:* 98 full-time (82 women), 542 part-time (391 women); includes 256 minority (116 Black or African American, non-Hispanic/Latino; 2 American Indian or Alaska Native, non-

Hispanic/Latino; 45 Asian, non-Hispanic/Latino; 83 Hispanic/Latino; 10 Two or more races, non-Hispanic/Latino, 4 international. Average age 30. 223 applicants, 89% accepted, 130 enrolled. In 2018, 269 master's, 12 other advanced degrees awarded. *Degree requirements:* For master's and Certificate, certification exams. *Entrance requirements:* For master's, GRE (for initial certification programs only), teaching certificate (for MS Ed in literacy and special education programs only). Additional exam requirements/recommendations for international students: Required—TOEFL (minimum score 88 iBT), IELTS or PTE. *Application deadline:* For fall admission, 8/1 priority date for domestic students, 6/1 for international students; for spring admission, 12/1 priority date for domestic students, 10/1 for international students. Applications are processed on a rolling basis. Application fee: $70. Electronic applications accepted. *Expenses:* Contact institution. *Financial support:* In 2018–19, 17 students received support, including 17 research assistantships with partial tuition reimbursements available (averaging $6,020 per year); career-related internships or fieldwork, Federal Work-Study, scholarships/grants, and unspecified assistantships also available. Financial award application deadline: 9/1; financial award applicants required to submit FAFSA. *Faculty research:* STEM education, TESOL, teacher education, special education, language and literary development. *Total annual research expenditures:* $1.4 million. *Unit head:* Dr. Harriet Feldman, Dean, School of Education, 914-773-3829, E-mail: hfeldman@pace.edu. *Application contact:* Susan Ford-Goldschein, Director of Graduate Admissions, 212-346-1531, Fax: 212-346-1585, E-mail: graduateadmission@pace.edu. Website: http://www.pace.edu/school-of-education

Pacific Lutheran University, School of Education and Kinesiology, Tacoma, WA 98447. Offers MAE. *Accreditation:* NCATE. *Program availability:* Part-time, evening/weekend. *Degree requirements:* For master's, comprehensive exam, thesis optional. *Entrance requirements:* For master's, WEST-B or WEST-B Exemption, interview. Additional exam requirements/recommendations for international students: Required—TOEFL (minimum score 550 paper-based; 88 iBT). Electronic applications accepted. *Expenses:* Contact institution.

Pacific Oaks College, Graduate School, Program in Education, Pasadena, CA 91103. Offers preliminary education specialist (MA); preliminary multiple subject (MA). *Program availability:* Online learning. *Degree requirements:* For master's, practicum. *Entrance requirements:* For master's, bachelor's degree from accredited college or university.

Pacific Union College, Education Department, Angwin, CA 94508-9707. Offers education (M Ed); elementary teaching (MAT); secondary teaching (MAT). *Program availability:* Part-time. *Faculty:* 3 full-time (1 woman), 1 (woman) part-time/adjunct. *Students:* 3 full-time (2 women). Average age 20. 4 applicants, 100% accepted, 4 enrolled. In 2018, 1 master's awarded. *Degree requirements:* For master's, thesis, action research project, field experiences. *Entrance requirements:* For master's, GRE General Test, two interviews, teaching credential, letters of recommendation, essay. *Application deadline:* For fall admission, 8/30 for domestic and international students; for summer admission, 6/1 for domestic and international students. Applications are processed on a rolling basis. Application fee: $0. *Expenses:* Contact institution. *Financial support:* Scholarships/grants available. Support available to part-time students. Financial award application deadline: 9/25. *Unit head:* Dr. Jean Buller, Department Chair, 707-965-7266, Fax: 707-965-6645, E-mail: jbuller@puc.edu. *Application contact:* Sarah Gitter, Credential Analyst, 707-965-6643, Fax: 707-965-6645, E-mail: teachingcredentials@puc.edu. Website: http://www.puc.edu/academics/departments/education/

Pacific University, College of Education, Forest Grove, OR 97116-1797. Offers early childhood education (MAT); education (MAE); elementary education (MAT); ESOL (MAT); high school education (MAT); middle school education (MAT); special education (MAT); speech-language pathology (MS); STEM education (MAT); talented and gifted (M Ed); visual function in learning (M Ed). *Accreditation:* ASHA; NCATE. *Program availability:* Part-time, evening/weekend. *Degree requirements:* For master's, research project. *Entrance requirements:* For master's, California Basic Educational Skills Test, PRAXIS II, minimum undergraduate GPA of 2.75, 3.0 graduate. Additional exam requirements/recommendations for international students: Required—TOEFL. Electronic applications accepted. *Expenses:* Contact institution. *Faculty research:* Defining a culturally competent classroom, technology in the K-12 classroom, Socratic seminars, social studies education.

Palm Beach Atlantic University, School of Education and Behavioral Studies, West Palm Beach, FL 33416-4708. Offers counseling psychology (MS), including addictions/mental health, general counseling, marriage and family therapy, mental health counseling, school guidance counseling. *Program availability:* Part-time, evening/weekend. *Faculty:* 9 full-time (2 women), 12 part-time/adjunct (9 women). *Students:* 182 full-time (149 women), 69 part-time (56 women); includes 130 minority (53 Black or African American, non-Hispanic/Latino; 3 Asian, non-Hispanic/Latino; 60 Hispanic/Latino; 14 Two or more races, non-Hispanic/Latino), 5 international. Average age 35. In 2018, 101 master's awarded. *Entrance requirements:* For master's, GRE or MAT, minimum GPA of 3.0; essay. Additional exam requirements/recommendations for international students: Required—TOEFL (minimum score 550 paper-based; 79 iBT). *Application deadline:* Applications are processed on a rolling basis. Application fee: $50. Electronic applications accepted. *Expenses: Tuition:* Part-time $767 per credit. Tuition and fees vary according to program. *Financial support:* In 2018–19, 63 students received support. Career-related internships or fieldwork, scholarships/grants, and employee education grants available. Financial award application deadline: 5/1; financial award applicants required to submit FAFSA. *Faculty research:* Group dynamics, phenomenology, spirituality, multicultural psychology. *Unit head:* Dr. Chelly Templeton, Dean, 561-803-2353. *Application contact:* Graduate Admissions, 888-468-6722, E-mail: grad@pba.edu. Website: http://learn-well.pba.edu/academics/ms-mental-health-counseling.html

Park University, School of Graduate and Professional Studies, Kansas City, MO 54105. Offers adult education (M Ed); business and government leadership (Graduate Certificate); business, government, and global society (MPA); communication and leadership (MA); creative and life writing (Graduate Certificate); disaster and emergency management (MPA, Graduate Certificate); educational leadership (M Ed); finance (MBA, Graduate Certificate); general business (MBA); global business (Graduate Certificate); healthcare administration (MHA); healthcare services management and leadership (Graduate Certificate); international business (MBA); language and literacy (M Ed), including English for speakers of other languages, special reading teacher/literacy coach; leadership of international healthcare organizations (Graduate Certificate); management information systems (MBA, Graduate Certificate); music performance (ADP, Graduate Certificate), including cello (MM, ADP), piano (MM, ADP), viola (MM, ADP), violin (MM, ADP); nonprofit and community services management (MPA); nonprofit leadership (Graduate Certificate); performance (MM), including cello (MM, ADP), piano (MM, ADP), viola (MM, ADP), violin (MM, ADP); public management (MPA); social work (MSW); teacher leadership (M Ed), including curriculum and assessment, instructional leader. *Program availability:* Part-time, evening/weekend, online learning. *Degree requirements:* For master's, comprehensive exam (for some programs), thesis (for some programs), internship (for some programs); exam (for some programs). *Entrance requirements:* For master's, GRE or GMAT (for some programs), teacher certification (for some M Ed programs), letters of recommendation, essay,

resume (for some programs). Additional exam requirements/recommendations for international students: Required—TOEFL (minimum score 550 paper-based; 79 iBT), IELTS (minimum score 6). Electronic applications accepted.

Penn State Harrisburg, Graduate School, School of Behavioral Sciences and Education, Middletown, PA 17057. Offers adult education in the health and medical professions (Certificate); applied behavior analysis (MA); applied clinical psychology (MA); applied psychological research (MA); community psychology and social change (MA); English as a second language (ESL) program specialist and leadership (Certificate); health education (M Ed); lifelong learning and adult education (M Ed, D Ed); literacy education (M Ed); literacy leadership (Certificate); psychology: applications in clinical psychology (Certificate); psychology: health psychology (Certificate); teaching and curriculum (M Ed); training and development (M Ed, Certificate). *Program availability:* Part-time, evening/weekend.

Penn State University Park, Graduate School, College of Education, University Park, PA 16802. Offers M Ed, MA, MS, D Ed, PhD, Certificate. *Accreditation:* NCATE. *Program availability:* Part-time, evening/weekend. *Entrance requirements:* Additional exam requirements/recommendations for international students: Required—TOEFL (minimum score 550 paper-based; 80 iBT), IELTS. Electronic applications accepted. *Expenses:* Contact institution.

Penn State York, Graduate School, York, PA 17403. Offers ESL specialist (Certificate); teaching and curriculum (M Ed). *Expenses:* Contact institution.

Peru State College, Graduate Programs, Program in Education, Peru, NE 68421. Offers curriculum and instruction (MS Ed). *Accreditation:* NCATE. *Program availability:* Part-time. *Degree requirements:* For master's, comprehensive exam (for some programs), thesis optional.

Piedmont College, School of Education, Demorest, GA 30535. Offers art education (MAT); curriculum and instruction (Ed D, Ed S); early childhood education (MA, MAT); middle grades education (MA, MAT); music education (MAT); secondary education (MA, MAT); special education (MA, MAT). *Program availability:* Part-time, evening/weekend. *Students:* 496 full-time (416 women), 650 part-time (560 women); includes 185 minority (137 Black or African American, non-Hispanic/Latino; 2 American Indian or Alaska Native, non-Hispanic/Latino; 13 Asian, non-Hispanic/Latino; 31 Hispanic/Latino; 1 Native Hawaiian or other Pacific Islander, non-Hispanic/Latino; 1 Two or more races, non-Hispanic/Latino). Average age 37. 483 applicants, 89% accepted, 372 enrolled. In 2018, 275 master's, 10 doctorates, 229 other advanced degrees awarded. *Degree requirements:* For master's, thesis, field experience in the classroom teaching; for doctorate, thesis/dissertation. *Entrance requirements:* For master's, GRE General Test, MAT; for Ed S, minimum graduate GPA of 3.5, valid teaching certificate. Additional exam requirements/recommendations for international students: Required—TOEFL (minimum score 550 paper-based). *Application deadline:* For fall admission, 7/15 for domestic students; for spring admission, 12/1 for domestic students. Applications are processed on a rolling basis. Electronic applications accepted. *Expenses: Tuition:* Full-time $9738; part-time $541 per credit. *Required fees:* $200 per semester. *Financial support:* Career-related internships or fieldwork, Federal Work-Study, and unspecified assistantships available. Support available to part-time students. Financial award applicants required to submit FAFSA. *Unit head:* Dr. R.D. Nordgren, Dean, 706-778-3000 Ext. 1201, Fax: 706-776-9608, E-mail: rdnordgren@piedmont.edu. *Application contact:* Kathleen Carter, Director of Graduate Enrollment Management, 706-778-8500 Ext. 1181, Fax: 706-778-0150, E-mail: kanderson@piedmont.edu.

Pittsburg State University, Graduate School, College of Education, Pittsburg, KS 66762. Offers MS, Ed S. *Accreditation:* NCATE. *Program availability:* Part-time, 100% online, blended/hybrid learning. Terminal master's awarded for partial completion of doctoral program. *Degree requirements:* For master's, thesis or alternative. *Entrance requirements:* For master's, GRE. Additional exam requirements/recommendations for international students: Required—TOEFL (minimum score 520 paper-based; 68 iBT), IELTS (minimum score 6), PTE (minimum score 47). Electronic applications accepted. *Expenses:* Contact institution.

Plymouth State University, College of Graduate Studies, Graduate Studies in Education, Certificate of Advanced Graduate Studies Programs, Plymouth, NH 03264-1595. Offers clinical mental health counseling (CAGS); educational leadership (CAGS); higher education (CAGS); school psychology (CAGS). *Program availability:* Part-time, evening/weekend.

Point Loma Nazarene University, School of Education, Program in Teaching, San Diego, CA 92106-2899. Offers MAT. *Program availability:* Part-time, evening/weekend. *Entrance requirements:* For master's, letters of recommendation, essay, interview. Electronic applications accepted. *Expenses:* Contact institution. *Faculty research:* Teaching preparation, the lives of teachers, co-teaching, teacher dispositions.

Point Park University, School of Arts and Sciences, Department of Education, Pittsburgh, PA 15222-1984. Offers adult learning and training (MA); athletic coaching (M Ed); curriculum and instruction (MA); educational administration (MA); leadership and administration (Ed D); secondary education (M Ed); special education grades 7-12 (M Ed); special education PreK-grade 8 (M Ed). *Program availability:* Part-time, evening/weekend, 100% online, blended/hybrid learning. *Degree requirements:* For master's, comprehensive exam (for some programs), thesis or alternative. *Entrance requirements:* For master's, minimum GPA of 3.0, resume, 2 letters of recommendation. Additional exam requirements/recommendations for international students: Required—TOEFL. Electronic applications accepted.

Pontifical Catholic University of Puerto Rico, College of Education, Ponce, PR 00717-0777. Offers M Ed, MA Ed, MRE, PhD. *Accreditation:* TEAC. *Program availability:* Part-time, evening/weekend. *Degree requirements:* For master's, comprehensive exam, thesis (for some programs). *Entrance requirements:* For master's, GRE General Test, 2 letters of recommendation, interview, minimum GPA of 2.75; for doctorate, EXADEP, GRE or MAT, 3 letters of recommendation. *Faculty research:* Teaching English as a second language, learning styles, leadership styles.

Portland State University, Graduate Studies, School of Education, Portland, OR 97207-0751. Offers M Ed, MA, MAT, MS, MST, Ed D. *Accreditation:* NCATE. *Program availability:* Part-time, evening/weekend. *Degree requirements:* For master's, variable foreign language requirement, comprehensive exam (for some programs), thesis (for some programs); for doctorate, variable foreign language requirement, comprehensive exam, thesis/dissertation. *Entrance requirements:* Additional exam requirements/recommendations for international students: Required—TOEFL (minimum score 550 paper-based; 80 iBT). Electronic applications accepted.

Post University, Program in Education, Waterbury, CT 06723-2540. Offers curriculum and instruction (M Ed); education (M Ed); educational technology (M Ed); higher education administration (MS); learning design and technology (M Ed); online teaching (M Ed); teaching English to speakers of other languages (TESOL) (M Ed). *Program availability:* Online learning. *Entrance requirements:* For master's, resume. *Expenses: Tuition:* Full-time $8300; part-time $570 per credit. *Required fees:* $140 per term. Tuition and fees vary according to course level, campus/location and program.

Prairie View A&M University, College of Education, Prairie View, TX 77446. Offers M Ed, MA, MA Ed, MS, MS Ed, PhD. *Accreditation:* NCATE. *Program availability:* Part-

time, evening/weekend, blended/hybrid learning. *Faculty:* 22 full-time (13 women), 3 part-time/adjunct (2 women). *Students:* 84 full-time (59 women), 185 part-time (141 women); includes 257 minority (242 Black or African American, non-Hispanic/Latino; 14 Hispanic/Latino; 1 Two or more races, non-Hispanic/Latino), 6 international. Average age 35. 86 applicants, 86% accepted, 58 enrolled. In 2018, 121 master's, 4 doctorates awarded. *Degree requirements:* For master's, comprehensive exam, thesis optional, minimum GPA of 3.0; for doctorate, comprehensive exam, thesis/dissertation. *Entrance requirements:* For master's, GRE, 3 letters of reference, minimum undergraduate GPA of 2.75; for doctorate, GRE General Test, 3 letters of reference, minimum undergraduate GPA of 3.0, essay. Additional exam requirements/recommendations for international students: Required—TOEFL (minimum score 550 paper-based; 79 iBT). *Application deadline:* For fall admission, 5/1 priority date for domestic and international students; for spring admission, 10/1 priority date for domestic students, 9/1 priority date for international students; for summer admission, 3/1 priority date for domestic students, 2/1 priority date for international students. Applications are processed on a rolling basis. Application fee: $50. Electronic applications accepted. *Expenses: Tuition, area resident:* Full-time $3172; part-time $317 per credit. Tuition, state resident: full-time $3172; part-time $317 per credit. Tuition, nonresident: full-time $7965; part-time $796 per credit. *Required fees:* $4847; $485 per credit. *Financial support:* Career-related internships or fieldwork, institutionally sponsored loans, scholarships/grants, and unspecified assistantships available. Support available to part-time students. Financial award application deadline: 4/1; financial award applicants required to submit FAFSA. *Faculty research:* Mentoring, assessment, humanistic education, diversity, literacy education, recruitment, student retention, school collaboration, leadership skills, structural equations. *Unit head:* Dr. Michael L McFrazier, Interim Dean, 936-261-3600 Ext. 2102, Fax: 936-261-3621, E-mail: mlmcFrazier@pvamu.edu. *Application contact:* Pauline Walker, Administrative Assistant II, Research and Graduate Studies, 936-261-3521, Fax: 936-261-3529, E-mail: gradadmissions@pvamu.edu.

Prescott College, Graduate Programs, Program in Education, Prescott, AZ 86301. Offers early childhood education (MA); early childhood special education (MA); education (MA); elementary education (MA); environmental education leadership and administration (MA); equine-assisted learning (MA); school guidance counseling (MA); secondary education (MA); special education: learning disabilities (MA); special education: mental retardation (MA); special education: serious emotional disabilities (MA); student-directed independent study (MA); sustainability education (PhD). *Program availability:* Part-time, online learning. *Degree requirements:* For master's, thesis, fieldwork or internship, practicum; for doctorate, thesis/dissertation. *Entrance requirements:* For master's, 2 letters of recommendation, resume; for doctorate, 3 letters of recommendation, resume, official transcripts, personal statement, program proposal. Additional exam requirements/recommendations for international students: Required—TOEFL (minimum score 500 paper-based). Electronic applications accepted.

Purdue University, Graduate School, College of Education, West Lafayette, IN 47907. Offers MS, MS Ed, PhD, Ed S. *Accreditation:* NCATE. *Program availability:* Part-time, evening/weekend. *Faculty:* 64 full-time (45 women), 5 part-time/adjunct (1 woman). *Students:* 147 full-time (107 women), 606 part-time (466 women); includes 132 minority (42 Black or African American, non-Hispanic/Latino; 1 American Indian or Alaska Native, non-Hispanic/Latino; 26 Asian, non-Hispanic/Latino; 45 Hispanic/Latino; 1 Native Hawaiian or other Pacific Islander, non-Hispanic/Latino; 17 Two or more races, non-Hispanic/Latino), 90 international. Average age 35. 402 applicants, 65% accepted, 139 enrolled. In 2018, 227 master's, 30 doctorates, 41 other advanced degrees awarded. *Degree requirements:* For master's, thesis optional; for doctorate, thesis/dissertation, oral and written exams; for Ed S, oral presentation, project. *Entrance requirements:* For master's, GRE General Test (if undergraduate GPA is below 3.0), minimum undergraduate GPA of 3.0 or equivalent; for doctorate, GRE General Test (minimum combined verbal and quantitative score of 1000, 300 for new scoring), minimum undergraduate GPA of 3.0 or equivalent; master's degree with minimum GPA of 3.0 or equivalent; for Ed S, GRE General Test (minimum combined verbal and quantitative score of 1000, 300 for new scoring), minimum undergraduate GPA of 3.0 or equivalent; master's degree. Additional exam requirements/recommendations for international students: Required—TOEFL (minimum score 550 paper-based; 77 iBT); Recommended—TWE. *Application deadline:* For fall admission, 12/15 for domestic students, 3/1 for international students; for spring admission, 9/15 for domestic students, 8/1 for international students. Application fee: $60 ($75 for international students). Electronic applications accepted. *Financial support:* Fellowships with full tuition reimbursements, research assistantships with full tuition reimbursements, teaching assistantships with full tuition reimbursements, career-related internships or fieldwork, and tuition waivers (full) available. Support available to part-time students. Financial award application deadline: 3/1; financial award applicants required to submit FAFSA. *Unit head:* Dr. Nancy Marchand-Martella, Dean, 765-494-2336, E-mail: nmarchand-martella@purdue.edu. *Application contact:* Graduate School Admissions, 765-494-2600, Fax: 765-494-0136, E-mail: gradinfo@purdue.edu.
Website: http://www.education.purdue.edu/

Purdue University Fort Wayne, College of Professional Studies, Fort Wayne, IN 46805-1499. Offers MPM, MS Ed, Certificate. *Accreditation:* NCATE. *Program availability:* Part-time. *Entrance requirements:* For master's, minimum GPA of 2.5, 3 professional letters of recommendation. Additional exam requirements/recommendations for international students: Required—TOEFL (minimum score 550 paper-based; 79 iBT). *Faculty research:* Alcoholism and sobriety, international faculty perceptions.

Purdue University Global, School of Teacher Education, Davenport, IA 52807. Offers education (M Ed); secondary education (M Ed); teaching and learning (MA); teaching literacy and language: grades 6-12 (MA); teaching literacy and language: grades K-6 (MA); teaching mathematics: grades 6-8 (MA); teaching mathematics: grades 9-12 (MA); teaching mathematics: grades K-5 (MA); teaching science: grades 6-12 (MA); teaching science: grades K-6 (MA); teaching students with special needs (MA); teaching with technology (MA). *Program availability:* Part-time, evening/weekend, online learning. *Entrance requirements:* Additional exam requirements/recommendations for international students: Required—TOEFL (minimum score 550 paper-based; 80 iBT).

Purdue University Northwest, Graduate Studies Office, School of Education, Hammond, IN 46323-2094. Offers counseling (MS Ed), including human services, mental health counseling, school counseling; educational administration (MS Ed); instructional technology (MS Ed); special education (MS Ed). *Accreditation:* NCATE. *Entrance requirements:* Additional exam requirements/recommendations for international students: Required—TOEFL.

Queens College of the City University of New York, Division of Education, Queens, NY 11367-1597. Offers MA, MAT, MS Ed, AC. *Accreditation:* NCATE. *Program availability:* Part-time, evening/weekend. *Faculty:* 67 full-time (47 women), 157 part-time/adjunct (115 women). *Students:* 240 full-time (204 women), 1,114 part-time (888 women); includes 2,763 minority (84 Black or African American, non-Hispanic/Latino; 1 American Indian or Alaska Native, non-Hispanic/Latino; 190 Asian, non-Hispanic/Latino; 359 Hispanic/Latino; 5 Native Hawaiian or other Pacific Islander, non-Hispanic/Latino; 2,124 Two or more races, non-Hispanic/Latino), 34 international. Average age 29. 1,255 applicants, 66% accepted, 643 enrolled. In 2018, 385 master's, 235 other advanced degrees awarded. *Degree requirements:* For master's, comprehensive exam (for some programs), thesis (for some programs), research project. *Entrance requirements:* For master's, minimum GPA of 3.0. Additional exam requirements/recommendations for international students: Required—TOEFL, IELTS. *Application deadline:* For fall admission, 4/1 for domestic students; for spring admission, 11/1 for domestic students. Applications are processed on a rolling basis. Application fee: $125. Electronic applications accepted. *Financial support:* Fellowships, career-related internships or fieldwork, and scholarships/grants available. Financial award application deadline: 4/1; financial award applicants required to submit FAFSA. *Unit head:* Dr. Craig Michaels, Dean, 718-997-5220, E-mail: craig.michaels@qc.cuny.edu. *Application contact:* Elizabeth D'Amico-Ramirez, Assistant Director of Graduate Admissions, 718-997-5203, E-mail: elizabeth.damicoramirez@qc.cuny.edu.

Queen's University at Kingston, School of Graduate Studies, Faculty of Education, Kingston, ON K7L 3N6, Canada. Offers M Ed, PhD. *Program availability:* Part-time. *Degree requirements:* For master's, thesis optional; for doctorate, comprehensive exam, thesis/dissertation. *Entrance requirements:* Additional exam requirements/recommendations for international students: Required—TOEFL (minimum score 580 paper-based); Recommended—TWE (minimum score 4). *Faculty research:* Literacy, assessment and evaluation, special needs, mathematics, science and technology education.

Queens University of Charlotte, Wayland H. Cato, Jr. School of Education, Charlotte, NC 28274-0002. Offers educational leadership (MA); K-6 (MAT); literacy K-12 (M Ed). *Accreditation:* NCATE. *Program availability:* Part-time, evening/weekend, online learning. *Degree requirements:* For master's, comprehensive exam. *Entrance requirements:* For master's, GRE General Test. *Expenses:* Contact institution.

Quincy University, Master of Science in Education Programs, Quincy, IL 62301-2699. Offers curriculum and instruction (MS Ed), including bilingual/English as a second language; education studies (MS Ed); leadership (MS Ed); reading education (MS Ed); teacher leader (MS Ed). *Program availability:* Part-time, evening/weekend, online learning. *Degree requirements:* For master's, comprehensive exam (for some programs), thesis optional. *Entrance requirements:* For master's, MAT or GRE, personal resume. Additional exam requirements/recommendations for international students: Required—TOEFL (minimum score 550 paper-based; 79 iBT). Electronic applications accepted. Application fee is waived when completed online.

Quinnipiac University, School of Education, Hamden, CT 06518-1940. Offers MAT, MS, Diploma. *Accreditation:* NCATE. Electronic applications accepted. *Faculty research:* Equity and excellence in education, school leadership.

Randolph College, Programs in Education, Lynchburg, VA 24503. Offers curriculum and instruction (MAT); special education-learning disabilities (M Ed, MAT). *Accreditation:* TEAC. *Entrance requirements:* For master's, minimum GPA of 3.0 in prerequisite education coursework, 2.7 in major or field of interest (MAT); teaching license (M Ed); 2 recommendations; interview.

Regent University, Graduate School, School of Education, Virginia Beach, VA 23464-9800. Offers education (M Ed, Ed D, PhD), including adult education (Ed D, PhD, Ed S), advanced educational leadership (Ed D, PhD, Ed S), character education (Ed D, PhD, Ed S), Christian education leadership (Ed D, PhD, Ed S), Christian school administration (M Ed), curriculum and instruction (Ed D, PhD, Ed S), curriculum and instruction - adult education (M Ed), curriculum and instruction - Christian school (M Ed), curriculum and instruction - gifted and talented (M Ed), curriculum and instruction - STEM education (M Ed), curriculum and instruction - teacher leader (M Ed), discipleship for ministry (M Ed), educational leadership (M Ed), educational psychology (Ed D, PhD, Ed S), educational technology and online learning (Ed D, PhD, Ed S), elementary education (M Ed), exceptional education executive leadership (Ed D, PhD, Ed S), higher education (Ed D, PhD, Ed S), higher education leadership and management (Ed D, PhD, Ed S), instructional design and technology (M Ed), K-12 school leadership (Ed D, PhD, Ed S), K-12 special education (M Ed), leadership in mathematics education (M Ed), reading specialist (M Ed), special education (Ed D, PhD, Ed S), student affairs (M Ed), TESOL - adult education (M Ed), TESOL - K-12 (M Ed); educational specialist (Ed S), including adult education (Ed D, PhD, Ed S), advanced educational leadership (Ed D, PhD, Ed S), character education (Ed D, PhD, Ed S), Christian education leadership (Ed D, PhD, Ed S), curriculum and instruction (Ed D, PhD, Ed S), educational psychology (Ed D, PhD, Ed S), educational technology and online learning (Ed D, PhD, Ed S), exceptional education executive leadership (Ed D, PhD, Ed S), higher education (Ed D, PhD, Ed S), higher education leadership and management (Ed D, PhD, Ed S), K-12 school leadership (Ed D, PhD, Ed S), special education (Ed D, PhD, Ed S). *Accreditation:* TEAC. *Program availability:* Part-time, evening/weekend, 100% online, blended/hybrid learning. *Degree requirements:* For master's, thesis or alternative; for doctorate, comprehensive exam, thesis/dissertation. *Entrance requirements:* For master's, Virginia Communication and Literacy Assessment (VCLA), PRAXIS, college transcripts, writing sample, interview; for doctorate, GRE, writing sample, resume, transcripts, interview. Additional exam requirements/recommendations for international students: Required—TOEFL (minimum score 577 paper-based). Electronic applications accepted. *Expenses:* Contact institution. *Faculty research:* Christian school administration, curriculum and instruction, educational technology and online learning, higher education, special education.

Regis College, Department of Education, Weston, MA 02493. Offers elementary teacher (M Ed); higher education leadership (Ed D); special education (M Ed). *Program availability:* Part-time, evening/weekend. *Degree requirements:* For doctorate, thesis/dissertation, capstone project. *Entrance requirements:* For master's, GRE or MAT, personal statement, recommendations, resume/curriculum vitae, official transcripts, interview; for doctorate, personal statement, recommendations, resume/curriculum vitae, official transcripts, presentation/interview. Additional exam requirements/recommendations for international students: Required—TOEFL (minimum score 560 paper-based; 79 iBT); Recommended—IELTS (minimum score 6.5). *Application deadline:* Applications are processed on a rolling basis. Application fee: $65. Electronic applications accepted. *Financial support:* Federal Work-Study, scholarships/grants, and unspecified assistantships available. Financial award applicants required to submit FAFSA. *Unit head:* Dr. Priscilla Boerger, Department Chair/Graduate Program Director, 781-768-7422, E-mail: priscilla.boerger@regiscollege.edu. *Application contact:* Dr. Priscilla Boerger, Department Chair/Graduate Program Director, 781-768-7422, E-mail: priscilla.boerger@regiscollege.edu.

Regis University, Regis College, Denver, CO 80221-1099. Offers biomedical sciences (MS); developmental practice (MDP); education (MA); environmental biology (MS). *Accreditation:* TEAC. *Program availability:* Part-time. *Degree requirements:* For master's, thesis (for some programs), capstone presentation. *Entrance requirements:* For master's, official transcript reflecting baccalaureate degree awarded from U.S.-based regionally-accredited college or university. Additional exam requirements/recommendations for international students: Required—TOEFL (minimum score 550 paper-based; 82 iBT). Electronic applications accepted. *Expenses:* Contact institution.

Reinhardt University, Price School of Education, Waleska, GA 30183-2981. Offers M Ed, MAT. *Program availability:* Part-time. *Faculty:* 2 full-time (both women), 3 part-time/adjunct (all women). *Students:* 17 full-time (14 women); includes 4 minority (3 Black

or African American, non-Hispanic/Latino; 1 Hispanic/Latino). Average age 33. In 2018, 54 master's awarded. *Entrance requirements:* For master's, GACE. Additional exam requirements/recommendations for international students: Required—TOEFL (minimum score 500 paper-based). *Application deadline:* Applications are processed on a rolling basis. Application fee: $50. Electronic applications accepted. Application fee is waived when completed online. *Expenses: Tuition:* Full-time $8732; part-time $495 per credit. *Required fees:* $200. Tuition and fees vary according to course load and program. *Financial support:* Application deadline: 7/1; applicants required to submit FAFSA. *Unit head:* Dr. Nancy Marsh, Dean, 770-720-5657, Fax: 770-720-9173, E-mail: njm@reinhardt.edu. *Application contact:* Graduate Admissions, 770-720-5760, E-mail: gradadmissions@reinhardt.edu.

Relay Graduate School of Education, Graduate Programs, New York, NY 10011. Offers MAT. Program also offered at Chicago, Delaware, Houston, Memphis, New Orleans, and Newark campuses. *Program availability:* Online learning.

Rhode Island College, School of Graduate Studies, Feinstein School of Education and Human Development, Program in Education, Providence, RI 02908-1991. Offers PhD. Program offered jointly with University of Rhode Island. *Accreditation:* NCATE. *Program availability:* Part-time, evening/weekend. *Faculty:* 1 (woman) full-time, 11 part-time/adjunct (8 women). *Students:* 53 part-time (33 women); includes 14 minority (5 Black or African American, non-Hispanic/Latino; 7 Asian, non-Hispanic/Latino; 2 Hispanic/Latino). Average age 41. In 2018, 5 doctorates awarded. *Degree requirements:* For doctorate, comprehensive exam, thesis/dissertation. *Entrance requirements:* For doctorate, GRE, two official transcripts from all colleges and universities attended, 3 letters of recommendation, personal statement, professional resume. Additional exam requirements/recommendations for international students: Required—TOEFL (minimum score 550 paper-based; 80 iBT). *Application deadline:* For fall admission, 1/29 for domestic students. Applications are processed on a rolling basis. Application fee: $65. Electronic applications accepted. *Expenses: Tuition, area resident:* Part-time $407 per credit. Tuition, nonresident: part-time $792 per credit. *Required fees:* $29 per credit. $100 per semester. *Financial support:* Health care benefits available. Support available to part-time students. Financial award application deadline: 5/15; financial award applicants required to submit FAFSA. *Unit head:* Dr. Patricia Cordeiro, Co-Director, 401-456-8626, E-mail: pcordeiro@ric.edu. *Application contact:* Dr. Patricia Cordeiro, Co-Director, 401-456-8626, E-mail: pcordeiro@ric.edu.
Website: http://www.ric.edu/feinsteinschooleducationhumandevelopment/Pages/Graduate-Programs-in-the-School-of-Education.aspx

Rice University, Graduate Programs, Programs in Education Certification, Houston, TX 77251-1892. Offers MAT. *Entrance requirements:* For master's, GRE General Test, minimum GPA of 3.0. Additional exam requirements/recommendations for international students: Required—TOEFL (minimum score 600 paper-based; 90 iBT). Electronic applications accepted. *Faculty research:* Assessment, integration of math and science.

Rider University, College of Education and Human Services, Lawrenceville, NJ 08648-3001. Offers MA, MAT, Certificate, Ed S. *Accreditation:* NCATE. *Program availability:* Part-time, evening/weekend. *Students:* 137 full-time (112 women), 292 part-time (226 women); includes 103 minority (49 Black or African American, non-Hispanic/Latino; 2 American Indian or Alaska Native, non-Hispanic/Latino; 11 Asian, non-Hispanic/Latino; 38 Hispanic/Latino; 3 Two or more races, non-Hispanic/Latino). Average age 33. 279 applicants, 67% accepted, 117 enrolled. In 2018, 144 master's, 137 other advanced degrees awarded. *Degree requirements:* For master's, comprehensive exam (for some programs), thesis or alternative, internship, portfolios; for other advanced degree, internship, professional portfolio. *Entrance requirements:* For master's, GRE (counseling, school psychology), MAT, interview, resume, letters of recommendation; for other advanced degree, PRAXIS. Additional exam requirements/recommendations for international students: Required—TOEFL (minimum score 540 paper-based; 79 iBT). *Application deadline:* For fall admission, 5/1 priority date for domestic students, 3/15 priority date for international students; for spring admission, 10/1 priority date for domestic students, 11/1 priority date for international students. Applications are processed on a rolling basis. Application fee: $50. Electronic applications accepted. *Expenses: Tuition:* Full-time $850; part-time $850 per credit hour. *Required fees:* $50; $50 per course. Tuition and fees vary according to program. *Financial support:* In 2018–19, 316 students received support. Applicants required to submit FAFSA. *Faculty research:* Gifted students, self-esteem, hope and mental health, conflicts in group work, cultural diversity and counseling assessment of special needs in children. *Unit head:* Dr. Sharon J. Sherman, Dean, 609-895-5048, E-mail: ssherman@rider.edu. *Application contact:* Jamie L. Mitchell, Director of Graduate Admissions, 609-896-5036, Fax: 609-895-5680, E-mail: jmitchell@rider.edu.

Rivier University, School of Graduate Studies, Department of Education, Nashua, NH 03060. Offers curriculum and instruction (M Ed); early childhood education (M Ed); educational administration (M Ed); educational studies (M Ed); elementary education (M Ed); elementary education and general special education (M Ed); emotional and behavioral disorders (M Ed); general social education (M Ed); leadership and learning (Ed D, CAGS); learning disabilities (M Ed); learning disabilities and reading (M Ed); mental health counseling (MA); reading (M Ed); school counseling (M Ed). *Program availability:* Part-time, evening/weekend. *Degree requirements:* For master's, comprehensive exam (for some programs), internships. *Entrance requirements:* For master's, GRE General Test or MAT.

Roberts Wesleyan College, Graduate Teacher Education Programs, Rochester, NY 14624-1997. Offers adolescence and special education (M Ed); childhood and special education (M Ed); literacy education (M Ed); special education (M Ed). *Program availability:* Part-time, evening/weekend. *Degree requirements:* For master's, thesis. Electronic applications accepted.

Rockford University, Graduate Studies, Department of Education, Rockford, IL 61108-2393. Offers early childhood education (MAT); elementary education (MAT); instructional strategies (MAT); reading (MAT); secondary education (MAT); special education (MAT). *Program availability:* Part-time, evening/weekend. *Degree requirements:* For master's, thesis optional, professional portfolio (for instructional strategies program). *Entrance requirements:* For master's, GRE General Test, basic skills test (for students seeking certification), 3 letters of recommendation. Additional exam requirements/recommendations for international students: Required—TOEFL (minimum score 550 paper-based; 79 iBT). Electronic applications accepted.

Rockhurst University, College of Health and Human Services, Program in Education, Kansas City, MO 64110-2561. Offers M Ed. *Accreditation:* TEAC. *Program availability:* Part-time, evening/weekend. *Entrance requirements:* For master's, minimum GPA of 2.5, 2 letters of recommendation. Additional exam requirements/recommendations for international students: Required—TOEFL (minimum score 550 paper-based; 79 iBT). Electronic applications accepted. *Expenses:* Contact institution. *Faculty research:* English language learners, urban literacy, online discussions, character education, teaching K-12 students about math and literacy.

Roger Williams University, Feinstein School of Humanities, Arts and Education, Bristol, RI 02809. Offers literacy education (MA); middle school certification (Certificate). *Program availability:* Part-time-only, evening/weekend. *Faculty:* 5 full-time (4 women), 5 part-time/adjunct (2 women). *Students:* 7 part-time (all women). Average age 36. 1 applicant, 100% accepted, 1 enrolled. In 2018, 6 master's awarded. *Entrance requirements:* For master's, resume, 2 letters of recommendation, college transcript, letter of intent, verification of active teaching license. Additional exam requirements/recommendations for international students: Required—TOEFL (minimum score 85 iBT), IELTS (minimum score 6.5). *Application deadline:* Applications are processed on a rolling basis. Application fee: $50. Electronic applications accepted. *Expenses:* $593 per credit hour for academic year 2018-2019 (for Master of Arts in Literacy, Middle School Endorsement Certificate), $267 graduation fee for all programs for academic year 2018-2019. *Financial support:* Application deadline: 3/15; applicants required to submit FAFSA. *Unit head:* Dr. Cynthia Scheinberg, Dean, 401-254-3828, E-mail: cscheinberg@rwu.edu. *Application contact:* Marcus Hanscom, Director of Graduate Admissions, 401-254-3345, Fax: 401-254-3557, E-mail: gradadmit@rwu.edu.
Website: http://www.rwu.edu/academics/schools-and-colleges/fshae

Rollins College, Hamilton Holt School, Graduate Education Programs, Winter Park, FL 32789-4499. Offers elementary education (M Ed, MAT). *Program availability:* Part-time, evening/weekend. *Degree requirements:* For master's, comprehensive exam, Professional Education Test (PED) and Subject Area Examination (SAE) of the Florida Teacher Certification Examinations (FTCE), successful review of the Expanded Teacher Education Portfolio (ETEP). *Entrance requirements:* For master's, General Knowledge Test of the Florida Teacher Certification Examination (FTCE), official transcripts, letter(s) of recommendation, essay. Additional exam requirements/recommendations for international students: Required—TOEFL (minimum score 550 paper-based; 80 iBT). *Expenses:* Contact institution.

Roosevelt University, Graduate Division, College of Education, Chicago, IL 60605. Offers MA. *Accreditation:* ACA; NCATE. *Program availability:* Part-time, evening/weekend. Electronic applications accepted.

Rosemont College, Schools of Graduate and Professional Studies, Graduate Education PreK-4 Program, Rosemont, PA 19010-1699. Offers elementary certification (MA); PreK-4 (MA). *Program availability:* Part-time, evening/weekend. *Degree requirements:* For master's, thesis optional. *Entrance requirements:* For master's, minimum college GPA of 3.0, 3 letters of recommendation. Additional exam requirements/recommendations for international students: Required—TOEFL. Electronic applications accepted. Application fee is waived when completed online.

Rowan University, Graduate School, College of Education, Glassboro, NJ 08028-1701. Offers M Ed, MA, MST, Ed D, CAGS, CGS, Ed S, Postbaccalaureate Certificate. *Accreditation:* NCATE. *Program availability:* Part-time, evening/weekend. *Degree requirements:* For master's, comprehensive exam, thesis; for doctorate, thesis/dissertation. *Entrance requirements:* For master's, GRE General Test, PRAXIS I, PRAXIS II; for doctorate, GRE, master's degree. Additional exam requirements/recommendations for international students: Required—TOEFL. Electronic applications accepted.

Rutgers University–New Brunswick, Graduate School of Education, New Brunswick, NJ 08901. Offers Ed M, Ed D, PhD. *Accreditation:* TEAC. *Program availability:* Part-time, evening/weekend. Terminal master's awarded for partial completion of doctoral program. *Degree requirements:* For master's, comprehensive exam (for some programs); for doctorate, thesis/dissertation. *Entrance requirements:* For master's and doctorate, GRE General Test. Additional exam requirements/recommendations for international students: Required—TOEFL (minimum score 575 paper-based; 83 iBT). Electronic applications accepted.

Sacred Heart University, Graduate Programs, Isabelle Farrington College of Education, Fairfield, CT 06825. Offers M Ed, MAT, Professional Certificate. *Accreditation:* NCATE. *Program availability:* Part-time, evening/weekend. *Degree requirements:* For master's, comprehensive exam (for some programs), thesis (for some programs). *Entrance requirements:* For master's, PRAXIS, minimum GPA of 2.67; for Professional Certificate, CT teacher certification. Electronic applications accepted. *Expenses:* Contact institution. *Faculty research:* Reading education, learning theory, teacher preparation, education of underachievers.

Sage Graduate School, Esteves School of Education, Troy, NY 12180-4115. Offers MS, MS Ed, Ed D, Post Master's Certificate. *Accreditation:* NCATE. *Program availability:* Part-time, evening/weekend. *Faculty:* 16 full-time (12 women), 24 part-time/adjunct (16 women). *Students:* 79 full-time (62 women), 332 part-time (255 women); includes 120 minority (54 Black or African American, non-Hispanic/Latino; 1 American Indian or Alaska Native, non-Hispanic/Latino; 16 Asian, non-Hispanic/Latino; 40 Hispanic/Latino; 1 Native Hawaiian or other Pacific Islander, non-Hispanic/Latino; 8 Two or more races, non-Hispanic/Latino). Average age 33. 482 applicants, 47% accepted, 138 enrolled. In 2018, 126 master's, 33 doctorates, 16 other advanced degrees awarded. *Entrance requirements:* Additional exam requirements/recommendations for international students: Required—TOEFL (minimum score 550 paper-based). *Application deadline:* Applications are processed on a rolling basis. Application fee: $30. Electronic applications accepted. *Financial support:* Fellowships, research assistantships, scholarships/grants, and unspecified assistantships available. Financial award application deadline: 3/1; financial award applicants required to submit FAFSA. *Faculty research:* Literacy development in at-risk children, effective behavior strategies for class instruction. *Unit head:* Dr. John Pelizza, Dean, Esteves School of Education, 518-244-2051, Fax: 518-244-2334, E-mail: pelizj@sage.edu. *Application contact:* Michael Jones, SR Associate Director of Graduate Enrollment Management, 518-292-8615, Fax: 518-292-1912, E-mail: jonesm4@sage.edu.

Saginaw Valley State University, College of Education, University Center, MI 48710. Offers M Ed, MA, MAT, Ed S. *Accreditation:* NCATE. *Program availability:* Part-time, evening/weekend, online learning. *Faculty:* 14 full-time (12 women), 14 part-time/adjunct (9 women). *Students:* 22 full-time (15 women), 192 part-time (155 women); includes 19 minority (6 Black or African American, non-Hispanic/Latino; 1 Asian, non-Hispanic/Latino; 6 Hispanic/Latino; 6 Two or more races, non-Hispanic/Latino), 12 international. Average age 35. 53 applicants, 94% accepted, 47 enrolled. In 2018, 20 master's, 28 other advanced degrees awarded. *Entrance requirements:* For master's, minimum GPA of 3.0, teaching certificate. Additional exam requirements/recommendations for international students: Required—TOEFL (minimum score 550 paper-based; 79 iBT). *Application deadline:* For fall admission, 7/15 for international students; for winter admission, 11/15 for international students; for spring admission, 4/15 for international students. Applications are processed on a rolling basis. Application fee: $30 ($90 for international students). Electronic applications accepted. *Expenses: Tuition, area resident:* Full-time $6225; part-time $623 per credit hour. Tuition, state resident: full-time $6225; part-time $623 per credit hour. Tuition, nonresident: full-time $14,215; part-time $1185 per credit hour. *International tuition:* $14,215 full-time. *Required fees:* $263; $14.60 per credit hour. Tuition and fees vary according to degree level. *Financial support:* Federal Work-Study and scholarships/grants available. Support available to part-time students. Financial award applicants required to submit FAFSA. *Unit head:* Dr. Craig Douglas, Dean, 989-964-4057, Fax: 989-964-4563, E-mail: coeconnect@svsu.edu. *Application contact:* Jenna Briggs, Director, Graduate and International Admissions, 989-964-6096, Fax: 989-964-2788, E-mail: gradadm@svsu.edu.
Website: http://www.svsu.edu/collegeofeducation

St. Ambrose University, School of Education, Davenport, IA 52803-2898. Offers early childhood education (M Ed); educational administration (M Ed). *Accreditation:* TEAC. *Program availability:* Part-time, evening/weekend, online learning. *Degree requirements:* For master's, comprehensive exam. *Entrance requirements:* For master's GRE General Test or MAT, minimum GPA of 2.75. Additional exam requirements/recommendations for international students: Required—TOEFL. Electronic applications accepted. *Faculty research:* Disabilities and postsecondary career avenues, self-determination.

St. Bonaventure University, School of Graduate School, School of Education, St. Bonaventure, NY 14778-2284. Offers MS Ed, Adv C. *Accreditation:* NCATE. *Program availability:* Part-time, evening/weekend, 100% online, blended/hybrid learning. *Faculty:* 11 full-time (9 women), 22 part-time/adjunct (14 women). *Students:* 44 full-time (34 women), 219 part-time (166 women); includes 43 minority (16 Black or African American, non-Hispanic/Latino; 1 American Indian or Alaska Native, non-Hispanic/Latino; 2 Asian, non-Hispanic/Latino; 16 Hispanic/Latino; 8 Two or more races, non-Hispanic/Latino). Average age 32. 156 applicants, 99% accepted, 88 enrolled. In 2018, 48 master's, 33 Adv Cs awarded. *Degree requirements:* For master's and Adv C, comprehensive exam, thesis optional, student teaching, electronic portfolio, internship, practicum. *Entrance requirements:* For master's, GRE or MAT, official transcripts, teacher certification, letters of recommendation, personal statement/writing sample. Additional exam requirements/recommendations for international students: Required—TOEFL (minimum score 550 paper-based; 79 iBT). *Application deadline:* For fall admission, 3/15 priority date for domestic students, 2/1 priority date for international students; for spring admission, 10/15 priority date for domestic students, 7/1 priority date for international students. Applications are processed on a rolling basis. Application fee: $0. Electronic applications accepted. *Financial support:* In 2018–19, 12 students received support. Career-related internships or fieldwork, scholarships/grants, health care benefits, and unspecified assistantships available. Financial award application deadline: 4/15; financial award applicants required to submit FAFSA. *Faculty research:* Interaction of education policy and practice, working with parents of children with exceptionalities, global competence. *Unit head:* Dr. Lisa Buenaventura, Dean, 716-375-2394, Fax: 716-375-2360, E-mail: lbuenave@sbu.edu. *Application contact:* Matthew Retchless, Director of Graduate Admissions, 716-375-2021, Fax: 716-375-4015, E-mail: gradsch@sbu.edu.

St. Catherine University, Graduate Programs, Program in Education - Initial Licensure, St. Paul, MN 55105. Offers MA, Certificate. *Program availability:* Part-time, evening/weekend. *Expenses:* Contact institution.

St. Cloud State University, School of Graduate Studies, School of Education, St. Cloud, MN 56301-4498. Offers MS, Ed D, Graduate Certificate. *Accreditation:* NCATE. *Program availability:* Part-time, evening/weekend, online learning. *Degree requirements:* For master's, comprehensive exam (for some programs), thesis or alternative; for doctorate, comprehensive exam, thesis/dissertation; for Graduate Certificate, thesis, field study. *Entrance requirements:* For master's, GRE General Test (for some programs), minimum GPA of 2.75; for doctorate, GRE; for Graduate Certificate, GRE General Test, minimum GPA of 3.25. Additional exam requirements/recommendations for international students: Required—Michigan English Language Assessment Battery; Recommended—TOEFL (minimum score 550 paper-based), IELTS (minimum score 6.5).

St. Edward's University, School of Education, Austin, TX 78704. Offers college student development (MA); counseling (MA); education (Certificate); liberal arts (MLA, Certificate), including humanities (MLA), liberal arts. *Program availability:* Part-time, evening/weekend. *Entrance requirements:* Additional exam requirements/recommendations for international students: Required—TOEFL, IELTS. Electronic applications accepted.

Saint Francis University, Graduate Education Program, Loretto, PA 15940-0600. Offers education (M Ed); leadership (M Ed); reading (M Ed). *Program availability:* Part-time, 100% online, blended/hybrid learning. *Degree requirements:* For master's, comprehensive exam, thesis optional. *Entrance requirements:* For master's, GRE or MAT (if undergraduate GPA less than 3.0). Additional exam requirements/recommendations for international students: Required—TOEFL (minimum score 550 paper-based; 75 iBT), IELTS (minimum score 6.5), International Test of English proficiency (minimum score 4). Electronic applications accepted. *Expenses:* Contact institution.

St. Francis Xavier University, Graduate Studies, Graduate Studies in Education, Antigonish, NS B2G 2W5, Canada. Offers curriculum and instruction (M Ed); educational administration and leadership (M Ed). *Program availability:* Part-time, online learning. *Degree requirements:* For master's, thesis. *Entrance requirements:* For master's, minimum undergraduate B average, 2 years of teaching experience. *Expenses: Tuition, area resident:* Full-time $7547 Canadian dollars. *Tuition, state resident:* full-time $7547 Canadian dollars; part-time $804.19 Canadian dollars per course. *Tuition, nonresident:* full-time $8839 Canadian dollars; part-time $932.49 Canadian dollars per course. *International tuition:* $932.49 Canadian dollars full-time. *Required fees:* $90.20 Canadian dollars; $90.20 Canadian dollars per course. One-time fee: $6 Canadian dollars. Tuition and fees vary according to course load, degree level and program. *Faculty research:* Inclusive education, qualitative research.

St. John Fisher College, Ralph C. Wilson Jr. School of Education, Rochester, NY 14618-3597. Offers MS, MS Ed, Ed D, Certificate. *Accreditation:* NCATE. *Program availability:* Part-time, evening/weekend. *Faculty:* 21 full-time (15 women), 7 part-time/adjunct (6 women). *Students:* 133 full-time (87 women), 70 part-time (55 women); includes 78 minority (64 Black or African American, non-Hispanic/Latino; 12 Hispanic/Latino; 2 Two or more races, non-Hispanic/Latino). Average age 40. 76 applicants, 72% accepted, 22 enrolled. In 2018, 69 master's, 60 doctorates awarded. *Degree requirements:* For doctorate, thesis/dissertation. *Entrance requirements:* For master's and doctorate, 2 letters of recommendation, current resume. Additional exam requirements/recommendations for international students: Required—TOEFL (minimum score 575 paper-based; 80 iBT). *Application deadline:* Applications are processed on a rolling basis. Application fee: $30. Electronic applications accepted. *Expenses:* Contact institution. *Financial support:* Scholarships/grants available. Financial award applicants required to submit FAFSA. *Unit head:* Dr. Michael Wischnowski, Dean, 585-385-7361, E-mail: mwischnowski@sjfc.edu. *Application contact:* Michelle Gosier, Director of Transfer and Graduate Admissions, 585-385-8064, E-mail: mgosier@sjfc.edu. Website: https://www.sjfc.edu/schools/school-of-education/

St. John's University, The School of Education, Queens, NY 11439. Offers MS Ed, Ed D, PhD, Adv C. *Accreditation:* TEAC. *Entrance requirements:* For master's, GRE, MAT, or PRAXIS, statement of goals (personal essay), official undergraduate transcripts, initial teaching certification (unless career change); for doctorate, GRE, resume, letters of recommendation, master's transcripts; for Adv C, initial teaching certification, first master's transcripts. Additional exam requirements/recommendations for international students: Required—TOEFL, IELTS. Electronic applications accepted.

St. Joseph's College, New York, Programs in Education, Brooklyn, NY 11205-3688. Offers educational leadership (MA), including critical consciousness; literacy and cognition (MA); special education (MA), including severe and multiple disabilities. *Program availability:* Part-time, evening/weekend. *Faculty:* 5 full-time (all women), 2 part-time/adjunct (both women). *Students:* 34 part-time (28 women); includes 11 minority (2 Black or African American, non-Hispanic/Latino; 9 Hispanic/Latino). Average age 24. 26 applicants, 77% accepted, 16 enrolled. In 2018, 16 master's awarded. *Entrance requirements:* For master's, GRE, PRAXIS or MAT, Application, $25 application fee, official transcripts, two letters of recommendation, current resume, copy of NYS teacher certifications. Additional exam requirements/recommendations for international students: Required—TOEFL (minimum score 80 iBT). *Application deadline:* Applications are processed on a rolling basis. Application fee: $25. Electronic applications accepted. *Expenses: Tuition:* Full-time $18,450; part-time $1025 per credit. *Required fees:* $414. *Financial support:* In 2018–19, 22 students received support. *Unit head:* Nancy Gilchriest, Associate Professor, Department Chair, 631-687-1472, E-mail: ngilchriest@sjcny.edu. *Application contact:* Nancy Gilchriest, Associate Professor, Department Chair, 631-687-1472, E-mail: ngilchriest@sjcny.edu. Website: https://www.sjcny.edu/brooklyn/admissions/graduate/graduate-education-programs-admissions-information

Saint Joseph's College of Maine, Master of Science in Education Program, Standish, ME 04084. Offers adult education and training (MS Ed); Catholic school leadership (MS Ed); health care educator (MS Ed); school educator (MS Ed). Program available by correspondence. *Program availability:* Part-time, online learning. Electronic applications accepted.

Saint Joseph's University, College of Arts and Sciences, Graduate Programs in Education, Philadelphia, PA 19131-1395. Offers curriculum supervisor (Certificate); educational leadership (MS, Ed D); elementary education (MS, Certificate); elementary/middle school education (Certificate); organizational development and leadership (MS); principal (Certificate); professional education (MS); reading specialist (MS, Certificate); reading supervisor (Certificate); secondary education (MS, Certificate); special education (MS); special education 7-12 (Certificate); special education PK-8 (Certificate); superintendent's letter of eligibility (Certificate); supervisor of special education (Certificate); teacher of the deaf and hard of hearing (Certificate). *Program availability:* Part-time, evening/weekend, blended/hybrid learning. *Degree requirements:* For master's, thesis or alternative; for doctorate, comprehensive exam, thesis/dissertation. *Entrance requirements:* For master's, 2 letters of recommendation, minimum GPA of 3.0, official transcripts, personal statement; for doctorate, GRE, master's degree from accredited institution, minimum graduate GPA of 3.5, computer competence, interview with program director. Additional exam requirements/recommendations for international students: Required—TOEFL (minimum score 550 paper-based; 80 iBT), IELTS (minimum score 6.5), PTE (minimum score 60). Electronic applications accepted. *Expenses:* Contact institution. *Faculty research:* Factors predicting early mathematics skills for low income children, early child care and development, preschool quality, parent communication and home-school collaboration issues, education of terminally ill children, preparing literacy teachers for urban schools.

Saint Leo University, Graduate Studies in Education, Saint Leo, FL 33574-6665. Offers school leadership (Ed D). *Program availability:* Part-time, evening/weekend, online only, 100% online. *Students:* Average age 37. 214 applicants, 69% accepted, 125 enrolled. In 2018, 139 master's, 9 other advanced degrees awarded. *Entrance requirements:* For master's, GRE (minimum score of 1000), MAT (minimum score of 410), or minimum undergraduate GPA of 3.0 in final 2 years, official transcripts, current resume, 2 professional recommendations, personal statement, bachelor's degree from regionally-accredited university, valid professional teaching certificate; for other advanced degree, valid professional teaching certificate (for Ed S). Additional exam requirements/recommendations for international students: Required—TOEFL (minimum score 550 paper-based; 78 iBT). *Application deadline:* For fall admission, 7/1 priority date for domestic students, 7/1 for international students; for winter admission, 7/1 for international students; for spring admission, 11/1 priority date for domestic students. Applications are processed on a rolling basis. Application fee: $80. Electronic applications accepted. *Expenses:* Contact institution. *Financial support:* In 2018–19, 17 students received support. Career-related internships or fieldwork, scholarships/grants, health care benefits, and tuition remission for Saint Leo employees and their dependents available. Financial award application deadline: 3/1; financial award applicants required to submit FAFSA. *Faculty research:* Impact of partnerships with K-12 school and university programs. *Unit head:* Dr. Fern Aefsky, Director of Graduate Studies in Education, 352-588-8309, Fax: 352-588-8861, E-mail: kara.winkler@saintleo.edu. *Application contact:* Mark Russum, Assistant Vice President, Enrollment, 800-707-8846, Fax: 352-588-7873, E-mail: grad.admissions@saintleo.edu. Website: https://www.saintleo.edu/education-master-degree

Saint Louis University, Graduate Programs, School of Education, Department of Educational Studies, St. Louis, MO 63103. Offers curriculum and instruction (MA, Ed D, PhD); educational foundations (MA, Ed D, PhD); special education (MA); teaching (MAT). *Accreditation:* NCATE. *Program availability:* Part-time. *Degree requirements:* For master's, comprehensive exam; for doctorate, comprehensive exam, thesis/dissertation, preliminary oral and written exams. *Entrance requirements:* For master's, GRE General Test or MAT, letters of recommendation, resume; for doctorate, GRE General Test, letters of recommendation, resumé, goal statement, transcripts. Additional exam requirements/recommendations for international students: Required—TOEFL (minimum score 525 paper-based). Electronic applications accepted. *Faculty research:* Teacher preparation, multicultural issues, children with special needs, qualitative research in education, inclusion.

Saint Martin's University, Office of Graduate Studies, College of Education, Lacey, WA 98503. Offers M Ed, MIT. *Accreditation:* TEAC. *Program availability:* Part-time, evening/weekend. *Faculty:* 9 full-time (6 women), 10 part-time/adjunct (6 women). *Students:* 34 full-time (18 women), 40 part-time (31 women); includes 16 minority (3 Black or African American, non-Hispanic/Latino; 5 Asian, non-Hispanic/Latino; 5 Hispanic/Latino; 3 Two or more races, non-Hispanic/Latino), 1 international. Average age 37. 28 applicants, 46% accepted, 11 enrolled. In 2018, 16 master's awarded. *Degree requirements:* For master's, comprehensive exam (for some programs), thesis or alternative, project or comprehensives. *Entrance requirements:* For master's, GRE General Test or MAT, three letters of recommendation; curriculum vitae. Additional exam requirements/recommendations for international students: Required—TOEFL (minimum score 550 paper-based; 79 iBT); Recommended—IELTS (minimum score 6.5). *Application deadline:* For fall admission, 4/1 priority date for domestic and international students; for spring admission, 11/1 priority date for domestic and international students. Applications are processed on a rolling basis. Application fee: $50. Electronic applications accepted. *Expenses: Tuition:* Full-time $22,950; part-time $1275 per credit. Tuition and fees vary according to course load, campus/location and program. *Financial support:* Career-related internships or fieldwork, Federal Work-Study, institutionally sponsored loans, and unspecified assistantships available. Support available to part-time students. Financial award application deadline: 3/1; financial award applicants required to submit FAFSA. *Faculty research:* Reader's theatre and reader/writer workshops, curriculum and assessment integration, gender and equity, classroom evaluations, organizational leadership. *Unit head:* Dr. Fumie Hashimoto, College of Education and Counseling, 360-438-4333, Fax: 360-438-4486, E-mail: fhashimoto@stmartin.edu. *Application contact:* Chantelle Petron Marker, Senior Recruiter, 360-412-6128, E-mail: cmarker@stmartin.edu. Website: https://www.stmartin.edu/directory/office-graduate-studies

Education—General

Saint Mary's College of California, Kalmanovitz School of Education, Moraga, CA 94575. Offers M Ed, MA, MA Ed, Ed D, Credential. *Program availability:* Part-time, evening/weekend. *Degree requirements:* For master's, thesis or alternative; for doctorate, thesis/dissertation. *Entrance requirements:* For master's, interview, minimum GPA of 3.0; for doctorate, GRE or MAT, interview, MA, minimum GPA of 3.0. *Expenses:* Contact institution. *Faculty research:* Teacher effectiveness, school-based management, multicultural teaching, language and literacy development.

St. Mary's College of Maryland, Department of Educational Studies, St. Mary's City, MD 20686-3001. Offers MAT. *Degree requirements:* For master's, internship, electronic portfolio, research projects, PRAXIS II. *Entrance requirements:* For master's, SAT, ACT, GRE or PRAXIS, 2 letters of recommendation, minimum GPA of 3.0. Additional exam requirements/recommendations for international students: Required—TOEFL. Electronic applications accepted. *Expenses:* Contact institution. *Faculty research:* Supporting English language learners across the curriculum, supporting women and minorities in math and science, instructional technology, multicultural young adult literature, educating teachers to be advocates for equity and social justice.

St. Mary's University, Graduate Studies, Program in Education, San Antonio, TX 78228. Offers MA. *Program availability:* Part-time, evening/weekend. *Students:* 1 (woman) part-time; minority (Hispanic/Latino). Average age 41. 2 applicants, 50% accepted, 1 enrolled. *Entrance requirements:* For master's, GRE, minimum undergraduate GPA of 2.7. Additional exam requirements/recommendations for international students: Required—TOEFL (minimum score 550 paper-based; 80 iBT), IELTS (minimum score 6). *Application deadline:* For fall admission, 7/1 for domestic students; for spring admission, 11/15 for domestic students; for summer admission, 4/1 for domestic students. Applications are processed on a rolling basis. Electronic applications accepted. *Expenses: Tuition:* Full-time $16,830; part-time $935 per credit hour. *Required fees:* $1055. Tuition and fees vary according to program. *Financial support:* Application deadline: 3/31; applicants required to submit FAFSA. *Faculty research:* Philosophy of education. *Unit head:* Dr. Dan Higgins, Program Director, 210-436-3121, E-mail: dhiggins@stmarytx.edu. *Application contact:* Kim Thornton, Director of Graduate Admission, 210-436-3101, E-mail: kthornton@stmarytx.edu.
Website: https://www.stmarytx.edu/academics/programs/master-of-education/

Saint Mary's University of Minnesota, Schools of Graduate and Professional Programs, Graduate School of Education, Education Program, Winona, MN 55987-1399. Offers MA, Certificate. *Unit head:* Lynn Albee, Director, 612-728-5128, Fax: 612-728-5121, E-mail: lalbee@smumn.edu. *Application contact:* Laurie Roy, Director of Admission of Schools of Graduate and Professional Programs, 507-457-8606, Fax: 612-728-5121, E-mail: lroy@smumn.edu.
Website: http://www.smumn.edu/graduate-home/areas-of-study/graduate-school-of-education/ma-in-education

Saint Mary's University of Minnesota, Schools of Graduate and Professional Programs, Graduate School of Education, Education-Wisconsin Program, Winona, MN 55987-1399. Offers MA. *Unit head:* Dr. Lynda Sullivan, Director, 877-442-4020, E-mail: lsulliva@smumn.edu. *Application contact:* Laurie Roy, Director of Admission of Schools of Graduate and Professional Programs, 507-457-8606, Fax: 612-728-5121, E-mail: lroy@smumn.edu.
Website: http://www.smumn.edu/graduate-home/areas-of-study/graduate-school-of-education/ma-in-education-wisconsin

Saint Mary's University of Minnesota, Schools of Graduate and Professional Programs, Graduate School of Education, Teaching and Learning Program, Winona, MN 55987-1399. Offers M Ed. *Unit head:* Tracy Lysne, Program Director, 612-238-4520, E-mail: tlysne@smumn.edu. *Application contact:* Laurie Roy, Director of Admission of Schools of Graduate and Professional Programs, 507-457-8606, Fax: 612-728-5121, E-mail: lroy@smumn.edu.
Website: http://www.smumn.edu/graduate-home/areas-of-study/graduate-school-of-education/med-in-teaching-learning

Saint Michael's College, Graduate Programs, Program in Education, Colchester, VT 05439. Offers arts in education (CAGS); literacy (M Ed); school leadership (CAGS); special education (M Ed). *Program availability:* Part-time, evening/weekend. *Degree requirements:* For master's, thesis. *Entrance requirements:* For master's, minimum GPA of 3.0, official transcripts, essay, interview. Electronic applications accepted. *Expenses: Tuition:* Part-time $590 per credit. *Faculty research:* Integrative curriculum, moral and spiritual dimensions of education, learning styles, multiple intelligences, integrating technology into the curriculum.

Saint Peter's University, Graduate Programs in Education, Jersey City, NJ 07306-5997. Offers director of school counseling services (Certificate); educational leadership (MA Ed, Ed D); higher education (MHE, Ed D), including educational leadership (Ed D), general administration (MHE); middle school mathematics (Certificate); professional/associate counselor (Certificate); reading (MA Ed); school business administrator (Certificate); school counseling (MA, Certificate); special education (MA Ed, Certificate), including applied behavioral analysis (MA Ed), literacy (MA Ed), teacher of students with disabilities (Certificate); teaching (MA Ed, Certificate), including 6-8 middle school education, K-12 secondary education, K-5 elementary education. *Accreditation:* TEAC. *Program availability:* Part-time, evening/weekend. *Degree requirements:* For master's, comprehensive exam; for doctorate, comprehensive exam, thesis/dissertation. *Entrance requirements:* For master's and doctorate, GRE or MAT. Additional exam requirements/recommendations for international students: Required—TOEFL. Electronic applications accepted.

St. Thomas Aquinas College, Division of Teacher Education, Sparkill, NY 10976. Offers adolescence education (MST); childhood and special education (MST); childhood education (MST); educational leadership (MS Ed); reading (MS Ed, PMC); special education (MS Ed, PMC); teaching (MS Ed), including elementary education, middle school education, secondary education. *Accreditation:* NCATE. *Program availability:* Part-time, evening/weekend. *Degree requirements:* For master's, comprehensive exam, comprehensive professional portfolio; for PMC, action research project. *Entrance requirements:* For master's, New York State Qualifying Exam, GRE General Test or minimum GPA of 3.0, teaching certificate; for PMC, GRE General Test or minimum GPA of 3.0. Electronic applications accepted. *Faculty research:* Computer applications in education, adolescent special education students, literacy development, inclusive practices for special education students.

St. Thomas University, School of Leadership Studies, Institute for Education, Miami Gardens, FL 33054-6459. Offers earth/space science (Certificate); educational administration (MS, Certificate); educational leadership (Ed D); elementary education (MS); ESOL (Certificate); gifted education (Certificate); instructional technology (MS, Certificate); professional/studies (Certificate); reading (MS, Certificate); special education (MS). *Program availability:* Part-time, evening/weekend. *Degree requirements:* For master's, comprehensive exam; for doctorate, comprehensive exam, thesis/dissertation. *Entrance requirements:* For master's, interview, minimum GPA of 3.0 or GRE; for doctorate, GRE or MAT. Additional exam requirements/recommendations for international students: Required—TOEFL (minimum score 550 paper-based; 79 iBT). Electronic applications accepted.

Saint Vincent College, Program in Education, Latrobe, PA 15650-2690. Offers curriculum and instruction (MS); instructional design and technology (MS); school administration and supervision (MS); special education (MS). *Program availability:* Part-time, evening/weekend. *Degree requirements:* For master's, comprehensive exam. *Entrance requirements:* For master's, GRE (if undergraduate GPA less than 3.0). Additional exam requirements/recommendations for international students: Required—TOEFL (minimum score 550 paper-based). *Faculty research:* Assessment and instructional technology.

Saint Xavier University, Graduate Studies, School of Education, Chicago, IL 60655-3105. Offers counseling (MA); curriculum and instruction (MA); early childhood education (MA); educational administration (MA); elementary education (MA); individualized studies (MA), including educational technology, English as a second language (ESL), ISTEM (integrative science, technology, engineering, and math), science education; music education (MA); reading (MA); secondary education (MA); Spanish education (MA); special education (MA); teaching and leadership (MA). *Accreditation:* NCATE. *Program availability:* Part-time, evening/weekend. *Degree requirements:* For master's, thesis or project. *Entrance requirements:* For master's, minimum GPA of 3.0. *Expenses:* Contact institution.

Salem College, Graduate Studies, Winston-Salem, NC 27101. Offers art education (MAT); elementary education (M Ed, MAT); language and literacy (M Ed); middle school education (MAT); organ (MM); piano (MM); school counseling (M Ed); second language studies (MAT); secondary education (MAT); special education (M Ed, MAT). *Accreditation:* NCATE. *Program availability:* Part-time, evening/weekend, online learning. *Degree requirements:* For master's, practicum (MAT), action research project (M Ed). *Entrance requirements:* For master's, minimum GPA of 3.0, two academic/professional recommendations, acceptable criminal background check. Additional exam requirements/recommendations for international students: Recommended—TOEFL. Electronic applications accepted. *Faculty research:* Teacher professional development, adolescent literacy, instructional technology.

Salem International University, School of Education, Salem, WV 26426-0500. Offers curriculum and instruction (M Ed); educational leadership (M Ed). *Program availability:* Part-time, evening/weekend, online learning. *Degree requirements:* For master's, comprehensive exam (for some programs), thesis (for some programs). *Entrance requirements:* For master's, GRE, MAT, NTE, 3 letters of recommendation. Additional exam requirements/recommendations for international students: Required—TOEFL (minimum score 550 paper-based). Electronic applications accepted. *Expenses:* Contact institution. *Faculty research:* Improved classroom effectiveness.

Samford University, Orlean Beeson School of Education, Birmingham, AL 35229. Offers educational leadership (MSE, Ed D); elementary education (MS Ed, MSE); gifted (MSE); instructional design and technology (MSE); instructional leadership (MSE, Ed S); secondary education (MSE); special education (MSE). *Accreditation:* NCATE. *Program availability:* Part-time, evening/weekend, 100% online, blended/hybrid learning. *Faculty:* 12 full-time (10 women), 16 part-time/adjunct (11 women). *Students:* 156 full-time (111 women), 101 part-time (73 women); includes 106 minority (100 Black or African American, non-Hispanic/Latino; 1 American Indian or Alaska Native, non-Hispanic/Latino; 5 Two or more races, non-Hispanic/Latino), 1 international. Average age 37. 107 applicants, 94% accepted, 65 enrolled. In 2018, 94 master's, 40 doctorates, 11 other advanced degrees awarded. *Degree requirements:* For master's and Ed S, comprehensive exam; for doctorate, comprehensive exam, thesis/dissertation. *Entrance requirements:* For master's, GRE, MAT, PRAXIS II, interview, transcripts, essay, recommendations, teaching certification; for doctorate, resume, transcripts, interview, essay, recommendations; for Ed S, teaching certification, transcripts, essay, interview, recommendations. Additional exam requirements/recommendations for international students: Required—TOEFL (minimum score 90 iBT); Recommended—IELTS (minimum score 6.5). *Application deadline:* For fall admission, 7/15 for domestic and international students; for winter admission, 11/15 for domestic and international students; for spring admission, 11/15 for domestic and international students; for summer admission, 4/15 for domestic and international students. Applications are processed on a rolling basis. Application fee: $35. Electronic applications accepted. *Expenses:* $862 Per Hour $100 School of Education $175 Technology Fee $100 Per Fully Online Class. *Financial support:* In 2018–19, 173 students received support. Scholarships/grants available. Financial award application deadline: 2/15; financial award applicants required to submit FAFSA. *Faculty research:* Principal leadership's and teacher organizational commitment mentoring, professional development, and middle grades leadership coaching and administrator effectiveness character development programs in schools teacher efficacy related STEM and professional growth. *Unit head:* Dr. Howard Finch, Interim Dean, 205-726-2745, E-mail: hfinch@samford.edu. *Application contact:* Brooke Karr, Graduate Admissions Office Coordinator, 205-729-2783, E-mail: kbgilrea@samford.edu.
Website: http://www.samford.edu/education

Sam Houston State University, College of Education, Huntsville, TX 77341. Offers M Ed, MA, MLS, Ed D, PhD. *Accreditation:* NCATE. *Program availability:* Part-time, evening/weekend, online learning. *Degree requirements:* For master's, comprehensive exam (for some programs), thesis optional, portfolio, internship; for doctorate, comprehensive exam (for some programs), thesis/dissertation. *Entrance requirements:* For master's, GRE General Test, references, essay, face-to-face interview, personal statement, resume; for doctorate, GRE General Test, on-site interview, on-site professional presentation, on-site writing prompt, personal statement, five references, master's degree, resume. Additional exam requirements/recommendations for international students: Required—TOEFL (minimum score 550 paper-based; 79 iBT), IELTS (minimum score 6.5). Electronic applications accepted.

San Diego Christian College, Graduate Programs, Santee, CA 92071. Offers education (MAT); organization (MSL).

San Diego State University, Graduate and Research Affairs, College of Education, San Diego, CA 92182. Offers MA, MS, Ed D, PhD. *Accreditation:* NCATE. *Program availability:* Part-time, evening/weekend. *Degree requirements:* For master's, thesis optional; for doctorate, thesis/dissertation. *Entrance requirements:* For master's, GRE General Test, letters of reference; for doctorate, GRE General Test, 3 letters of reference, resumé. Additional exam requirements/recommendations for international students: Required—TOEFL. Electronic applications accepted. *Faculty research:* Special education, rehabilitation counseling, educational psychology.

San Francisco State University, Division of Graduate Studies, College of Education, San Francisco, CA 94132-1722. Offers MA, MS, Ed D, PhD, AC, Certificate, Credential. *Accreditation:* NCATE.

San Ignacio University, Graduate Programs, Doral, FL 33178. Offers business administration (MBA), including human resources management, international business, marketing management; education (M Ed), including early childhood education, educational leadership, special education; hospitality management (MA), including gastronomy and restaurant management, tourism management.

Santa Clara University, School of Education and Counseling Psychology, Santa Clara, CA 95053. Offers alternative and correctional education (Certificate); counseling (MA); counseling psychology (MA); educational leadership (MA); interdisciplinary education

(MA); teaching + clear teaching certificate for catholic school teachers (MAT); teaching + teaching credential (mattc) - multiple subjects (MAT); teaching + teaching credential (mattc) - single subjects (MAT). *Program availability:* Part-time, online learning. *Faculty:* 31 full-time (19 women), 35 part-time/adjunct (24 women). *Students:* 291 full-time (235 women), 298 part-time (238 women); includes 301 minority (15 Black or African American, non-Hispanic/Latino; 1 American Indian or Alaska Native, non-Hispanic/Latino; 87 Asian, non-Hispanic/Latino; 146 Hispanic/Latino; 52 Two or more races, non-Hispanic/Latino), 44 international. Average age 31. 219 applicants, 79% accepted, 143 enrolled. In 2018, 223 master's awarded. *Entrance requirements:* For master's, Statement of purpose, resume or cv, official transcript; other requirements vary by degree. Additional exam requirements/recommendations for international students: Required—TOEFL (minimum score 90 iBT), IELTS (minimum score 6.5), A TOEFL score of 90 or above or IELTS score of 6.5 or above is required for international students. *Application deadline:* For fall admission, 9/23 for domestic students; for winter admission, 1/6 for domestic students. Applications are processed on a rolling basis. Application fee: $50. Electronic applications accepted. *Financial support:* Fellowships, Federal Work-Study, and scholarships/grants available. Support available to part-time students. Financial award applicants required to submit FAFSA. *Unit head:* Dr. Sabrina Zirkel, Dean, 408-551-3074, Fax: 408-554-4367, E-mail: szirkel@scu.edu. *Application contact:* Victoria Rodriguez, Graduate Admissions Advisor, 408-554-4723, Fax: 408-554-4367, E-mail: vlrodriguez@scu.edu.
Website: http://www.scu.edu/ecp/

Sarah Lawrence College, Graduate Studies, Program in the Art of Teaching, Bronxville, NY 10708-5999. Offers MS Ed. *Program availability:* Part-time. *Degree requirements:* For master's, thesis, fieldwork, oral presentation. *Entrance requirements:* For master's, minimum B average in undergraduate coursework. Additional exam requirements/recommendations for international students: Required—TOEFL (minimum score 600 paper-based). Electronic applications accepted. *Expenses:* Contact institution.

Schreiner University, Department of Education, Kerrville, TX 78028-5697. Offers education (M Ed); principal (Certificate). *Program availability:* Part-time, evening/weekend, online learning. *Entrance requirements:* For master's, GRE (waived if undergraduate cumulative GPA is 3.0 or above), 3 references; transcripts; interview. Additional exam requirements/recommendations for international students: Required—TOEFL. Electronic applications accepted.

Seattle Pacific University, Doctoral Program in Education, Seattle, WA 98119-1997. Offers Ed D, PhD. *Accreditation:* NCATE. *Students:* 11 part-time (7 women); includes 2 minority (1 Black or African American, non-Hispanic/Latino; 1 American Indian or Alaska Native, non-Hispanic/Latino), 2 international. Average age 50. 8 applicants, 50% accepted, 4 enrolled. In 2018, 14 doctorates awarded. *Degree requirements:* For doctorate, comprehensive exam, thesis/dissertation. *Entrance requirements:* For doctorate, GRE, MAT. Additional exam requirements/recommendations for international students: Required—TOEFL (minimum score 550 paper-based), IELTS (minimum score 7). *Application deadline:* For fall admission, 8/15 for domestic students; for winter admission, 11/15 for domestic students; for spring admission, 2/15 for domestic students; for summer admission, 5/15 for domestic students. Applications are processed on a rolling basis. Application fee: $50. *Expenses:* Contact institution. *Financial support:* Career-related internships or fieldwork available. Financial award applicants required to submit FAFSA. *Faculty research:* International education, curriculum and instruction, values and morals, school reform. *Unit head:* Nyaradzo Mvududu, Director of Doctoral Programs, 206-281-2551, E-mail: nyaradzo@spu.edu. *Application contact:* Nyaradzo Mvududu, Director of Doctoral Programs, 206-281-2551, E-mail: nyaradzo@spu.edu.
Website: http://spu.edu/academics/school-of-education/graduate-programs/doctoral-programs/doctor-of-philosophy-education-phd

Seattle University, College of Education, Seattle, WA 98122-1090. Offers M Ed, MA, MIT, Ed D, Certificate, Ed S, Post-Master's Certificate. *Accreditation:* NCATE. *Program availability:* Part-time, evening/weekend. *Faculty:* 30 full-time (17 women), 19 part-time/adjunct (12 women). *Students:* 255 full-time (208 women), 205 part-time (152 women); includes 163 minority (24 Black or African American, non-Hispanic/Latino; 3 American Indian or Alaska Native, non-Hispanic/Latino; 52 Asian, non-Hispanic/Latino; 61 Hispanic/Latino; 2 Native Hawaiian or other Pacific Islander, non-Hispanic/Latino; 21 Two or more races, non-Hispanic/Latino), 14 international. Average age 30. 465 applicants, 53% accepted, 148 enrolled. In 2018, 177 master's, 21 doctorates, 27 other advanced degrees awarded. *Degree requirements:* For master's and other advanced degree, comprehensive exam; for doctorate, comprehensive exam, thesis/dissertation. *Entrance requirements:* For doctorate, GRE General Test, MAT, interview, MA, minimum GPA of 3.5, 3 years of related experience. Additional exam requirements/recommendations for international students: Required—TOEFL. *Application deadline:* Applications are processed on a rolling basis. Application fee: $55. Electronic applications accepted. *Expenses:* Contact institution. *Financial support:* In 2018–19, 134 students received support. Career-related internships or fieldwork, Federal Work-Study, scholarships/grants, and unspecified assistantships available. Support available to part-time students. Financial award applicants required to submit FAFSA. *Faculty research:* Service-learning, learning and technology, assessment models of professional education, alternative delivery systems. *Unit head:* Dr. Deanna Sands, Dean, 206-296-5758, E-mail: sandsd@seattleu.edu. *Application contact:* Janet Shandley, Director of Graduate Admissions, 206-296-5900, Fax: 206-298-5656, E-mail: grad_admissions@seattleu.edu.
Website: https://www.seattleu.edu/education/

Seton Hall University, College of Education and Human Services, South Orange, NJ 07079-2697. Offers MA, MS, Ed D, Exec Ed D, PhD, Ed S. *Accreditation:* NCATE. *Program availability:* Part-time, evening/weekend, 100% online, blended/hybrid learning. *Degree requirements:* For master's, comprehensive exam (for some programs), internship; for doctorate, comprehensive exam, thesis/dissertation, internship. *Entrance requirements:* For master's, GRE or MAT, PRAXIS, letters of recommendation, interview, personal statement, curriculum vitae, transcript; for doctorate, GRE, interview, letters of recommendation, personal statement, curriculum vitae, transcript; for Ed S, GRE or MAT, PRAXIS, interview, letters of recommendation, personal statement, curriculum vitae, transcript. Additional exam requirements/recommendations for international students: Required—TOEFL. Electronic applications accepted. *Expenses:* Contact institution. *Faculty research:* Integration of technology, education leadership, educational media, special education, school district management.

Shawnee State University, Program in Curriculum and Instruction, Portsmouth, OH 45662. Offers M Ed. *Accreditation:* NCATE.

Shenandoah University, School of Education and Leadership, Winchester, VA 22601. Offers early childhood literacy (MS); reading licensure (MS); writing (MS). *Accreditation:* TEAC. *Program availability:* Part-time, evening/weekend. *Faculty:* 8 full-time (6 women), 26 part-time/adjunct (19 women). *Students:* 11 full-time (8 women), 211 part-time (163 women); includes 27 minority (14 Black or African American, non-Hispanic/Latino; 1 American Indian or Alaska Native, non-Hispanic/Latino; 4 Asian, non-Hispanic/Latino; 3 Hispanic/Latino; 1 Native Hawaiian or other Pacific Islander, non-Hispanic/Latino; 4 Two or more races, non-Hispanic/Latino), 2 international. Average age 38. 82 applicants, 96% accepted, 54 enrolled. In 2018, 62 master's, 11 doctorates, 34 other advanced degrees awarded. *Degree requirements:* For master's, comprehensive exam (for some programs), thesis (for some programs); for doctorate, comprehensive exam, thesis/dissertation. *Entrance requirements:* For degree, PRAXIS Academic Core, SAT/ACT, PRAXIS Academic Core Math, or VCLA, 3 letters of recommendation, writing sample, undergraduate degree; https://www.su.edu/admissions/graduate-students/education-application-information/. Additional exam requirements/recommendations for international students: Required—TOEFL (minimum score 550 paper-based; 79 iBT), IELTS (minimum score 6.5), TOEFL (minimum score 550 paper-based, 79 iBT) OR IELTS (6.5). *Application deadline:* For fall admission, 3/15 for domestic students, 3/17 for international students. Applications are processed on a rolling basis. Application fee: $30. Electronic applications accepted. *Expenses:* $525 per credit hour, $160 student services fee, $170 technology fee. *Financial support:* In 2018–19, 3 students received support. Scholarships/grants and unspecified assistantships available. Financial award application deadline: 1/15; financial award applicants required to submit FAFSA. *Faculty research:* Mentoring, behavior support for students, teacher change agency, educational technology in pedagogy, literacy education, leadership and pedagogy. *Total annual research expenditures:* $70,000. *Unit head:* Jill Lindsey, PhD, Director, School of Education and Leadership, 540-545-7324, Fax: 540-665-4726, E-mail: jlindsey@su.edu. *Application contact:* Andrew Woodall, Assistant Vice President for Admissions & Recruitment, 540-665-4581, Fax: 540-665-4627, E-mail: admit@su.edu.
Website: http://www.su.edu/education/

Shippensburg University of Pennsylvania, School of Graduate Studies, College of Education and Human Services, Shippensburg, PA 17257-2299. Offers M Ed, MAT, MS, MSW, Ed D. *Accreditation:* NCATE. *Program availability:* Part-time, evening/weekend, 100% online, blended/hybrid learning. *Faculty:* 40 full-time (22 women), 17 part-time/adjunct (12 women). *Students:* 150 full-time (123 women), 259 part-time (190 women); includes 62 minority (30 Black or African American, non-Hispanic/Latino; 4 Asian, non-Hispanic/Latino; 19 Hispanic/Latino; 9 Two or more races, non-Hispanic/Latino), 9 international. Average age 31. 376 applicants, 60% accepted, 156 enrolled. In 2018, 165 master's, 2 doctorates awarded. *Entrance requirements:* Additional exam requirements/recommendations for international students: Required—TOEFL (minimum score 550 paper-based; 68 iBT), IELTS (minimum score 6), TOEFL (minimum score 550 paper-based, 68 iBT) or IELTS (minimum score 6). *Application deadline:* For fall admission, 4/30 for international students; for spring admission, 9/30 for international students. Applications are processed on a rolling basis. Application fee: $45. Electronic applications accepted. *Expenses:* Tuition, state resident: part-time $516 per credit. Tuition, nonresident: part-time $750 per credit. *Required fees:* $149 per credit. *Financial support:* In 2018–19, 74 students received support. Career-related internships or fieldwork, scholarships/grants, unspecified assistantships, and resident hall director and student payroll positions available. Support available to part-time students. Financial award application deadline: 3/1; financial award applicants required to submit FAFSA. *Unit head:* Dr. Nicole R. Hill, Dean of the College of Education and Human Services, 717-477-1373, Fax: 717-477-4012, E-mail: nrhill@ship.edu. *Application contact:* Maya T. Mapp, Director of Admissions, 717-477-1231, Fax: 717-477-4016, E-mail: mtmapp@ship.edu.
Website: http://www.ship.edu/COEHS/

Siena Heights University, Graduate College, Adrian, MI 49221-1796. Offers clinical mental health counseling (MA); educational leadership (Specialist); leadership (MA), including health care leadership, organizational leadership; teacher education (MA), including early childhood education, early childhood education: Montessori, education leadership: principal, elementary education: reading K-12, leadership: higher education, secondary education: reading K-12, special education: cognitive impairment, special education: learning disabilities. *Program availability:* Part-time, evening/weekend. *Faculty:* 10 full-time (6 women), 16 part-time/adjunct (6 women). *Students:* 34 full-time (20 women), 183 part-time (126 women); includes 64 minority (38 Black or African American, non-Hispanic/Latino; 2 American Indian or Alaska Native, non-Hispanic/Latino; 4 Asian, non-Hispanic/Latino; 14 Hispanic/Latino; 6 Two or more races, non-Hispanic/Latino). Average age 36. 97 applicants, 41% accepted, 30 enrolled. In 2018, 72 master's awarded. *Degree requirements:* For master's, thesis, Presentation. *Entrance requirements:* For master's, Minimum GPA of 3.0, current resume, essay, all post-secondary transcripts, 3 letters of reference, conviction disclosure form; copy of teaching certificate (for some education programs); for Specialist, Master's degree, minimum GPA of 3.0, current resume, essay, all post-secondary transcripts, 3 letters of reference, conviction disclosure form; copy of teaching certificate (for some education programs). Additional exam requirements/recommendations for international students: Recommended—TOEFL, IELTS, TWE, TSE. *Application deadline:* Applications are processed on a rolling basis. Application fee: $50. Electronic applications accepted. *Expenses: Tuition:* Full-time $11,340; part-time $7560 per year. *Required fees:* $454; $454 per unit. $227 per semester. One-time fee: $100. Tuition and fees vary according to program. *Financial support:* In 2018–19, 55 students received support. Scholarships/grants, tuition waivers (full and partial), unspecified assistantships, and State of Michigan Scholarships/Grants available. Support available to part-time students. Financial award application deadline: 9/1; financial award applicants required to submit FAFSA. *Unit head:* Dr. Cheryl Betz, Dean, College for Professional Studies and Graduate College, 517-264-7234, Fax: 517-264-7714, E-mail: cbetz@sienaheights.edu. *Application contact:* Elizabeth Brooks, Assistant Director, 517-264-7165, Fax: 517-264-7714, E-mail: ebrooks@sienaheights.edu.
Website: http://www.sienaheights.edu

Sierra Nevada College, Teacher Education Program, Incline Village, NV 89451. Offers advanced teaching and leadership (M Ed); elementary education (MAT); secondary education (MAT). *Program availability:* Part-time, evening/weekend, online learning. *Degree requirements:* For master's, comprehensive exam, thesis, PRAXIS I and II. *Entrance requirements:* For master's, 2 letters of recommendation, minimum GPA of 3.0. Electronic applications accepted.

Silver Lake College of the Holy Family, Graduate School, Graduate Education Program, Manitowoc, WI 54220-9319. Offers administrative leadership (MA Ed); teacher leadership (MA Ed). *Program availability:* Part-time, evening/weekend, blended/hybrid learning. *Degree requirements:* For master's, comprehensive exam, thesis or alternative, capstone culminating project, comprehensive portfolio, or public presentation of project. *Entrance requirements:* For master's, ACT (preferred) or SAT, minimum undergraduate GPA of 3.0. Additional exam requirements/recommendations for international students: Required—TOEFL (minimum score 550 paper-based; 89 iBT). Electronic applications accepted. *Expenses:* Contact institution. *Faculty research:* Student development; school administration.

Simon Fraser University, Office of Graduate Studies and Postdoctoral Fellows, Faculty of Education, Burnaby, BC V5A 1S6, Canada. Offers M Ed, M Sc, MA, Ed D, PhD, Graduate Diploma. *Degree requirements:* For doctorate, thesis/dissertation. *Entrance requirements:* Additional exam requirements/recommendations for international students: Recommended—TOEFL (minimum score 580 paper-based; 93 iBT), IELTS (minimum score 7), TWE (minimum score 5). Electronic applications accepted.

Simpson College, Department of Education, Indianola, IA 50125-1297. Offers secondary education (MAT). *Degree requirements:* For master's, PRAXIS II, electronic portfolio. *Entrance requirements:* For master's, bachelor's degree; minimum cumulative GPA of 2.75, 3.0 in major; 3 letters of recommendation.

Education—General

Simpson University, School of Education, Redding, CA 96003-8606. Offers education (MA), including curriculum, education leadership; education and preliminary administrative services credential (MA); education and preliminary teaching credential (MA); teaching (MA). *Program availability:* Part-time, evening/weekend. *Degree requirements:* For master's, thesis optional. *Entrance requirements:* For master's, statement of purpose, 2 professional references, professional essay, interview. Additional exam requirements/recommendations for international students: Required—TOEFL (minimum score 550 paper-based). Electronic applications accepted. *Expenses:* Contact institution.

Sinte Gleska University, Graduate Education Program, Mission, SD 57555. Offers elementary education (M Ed). *Program availability:* Part-time, evening/weekend. *Degree requirements:* For master's, thesis. *Entrance requirements:* For master's, 2 years of experience in elementary education, minimum GPA of 2.5, South Dakota elementary education certification. *Faculty research:* American Indian graduate education, teaching of Native American students.

Slippery Rock University of Pennsylvania, Graduate Studies (Recruitment), College of Education, Slippery Rock, PA 16057-1383. Offers M Ed, MA, MS, Ed D. *Accreditation:* NCATE. *Program availability:* Part-time, evening/weekend, 100% online. *Faculty:* 101 full-time (55 women), 16 part-time/adjunct (12 women). *Students:* 186 full-time (141 women), 397 part-time (328 women); includes 31 minority (12 Black or African American, non-Hispanic/Latino; 1 American Indian or Alaska Native, non-Hispanic/Latino; 3 Asian, non-Hispanic/Latino; 9 Hispanic/Latino; 6 Two or more races, non-Hispanic/Latino), 3 international. Average age 30. 510 applicants, 76% accepted, 223 enrolled. In 2018, 231 master's, 12 doctorates awarded. *Degree requirements:* For master's, comprehensive exam (for some programs), thesis (for some programs), internship (depending on program). *Entrance requirements:* For master's, GRE General Test or MAT (depending on program), official transcripts, minimum GPA of 2.75 (depending on program). Additional exam requirements/recommendations for international students: Required—TOEFL (minimum score 550 paper-based; 80 iBT). *Application deadline:* For fall admission, 3/1 priority date for domestic students, 5/1 priority date for international students; for spring admission, 10/1 priority date for domestic students, 9/1 priority date for international students. Applications are processed on a rolling basis. Application fee: $25 ($30 for international students). Electronic applications accepted. *Expenses:* Contact institution. *Financial support:* In 2018–19, 91 students received support. Career-related internships or fieldwork, Federal Work-Study, institutionally sponsored loans, scholarships/grants, tuition waivers (partial), and unspecified assistantships available. Support available to part-time students. Financial award application deadline: 5/1; financial award applicants required to submit FAFSA. *Unit head:* Dr. A. Keith Dils, Dean, 724-738-2007, Fax: 724-738-2880, E-mail: keith.dils@sru.edu. *Application contact:* Brandi Weber-Mortimer, Director of Graduate Admissions, 724-738-2051, Fax: 724-738-2146, E-mail: graduate.admissions@sru.edu.
Website: http://www.sru.edu/academics/colleges-and-departments/coe

Smith College, Graduate and Special Programs, Department of Education and Child Study, Northampton, MA 01063. Offers elementary education (MAT), including elementary education, middle school education; secondary education (MAT), including secondary education. *Program availability:* Part-time. *Students:* 17 full-time (14 women), 9 part-time (6 women); includes 5 minority (2 Black or African American, non-Hispanic/Latino; 2 Asian, non-Hispanic/Latino; 1 Hispanic/Latino), 2 international. Average age 26. 44 applicants, 86% accepted, 23 enrolled. In 2018, 19 master's awarded. *Entrance requirements:* Additional exam requirements/recommendations for international students: Required—TOEFL (minimum score 595 paper-based; 97 iBT), IELTS (minimum score 7.5). *Application deadline:* For fall admission, 4/15 for domestic students, 1/15 for international students; for spring admission, 12/1 for domestic students. Applications are processed on a rolling basis. Application fee: $60. *Expenses:* The total tuition cost to each M.A.T. student (the full program fee, after 'built-in' scholarship award) is $18,500. *Financial support:* In 2018–19, 24 students received support, including 6 fellowships with full tuition reimbursements available; scholarships/grants and human resources employee benefit also available. Support available to part-time students. Financial award application deadline: 4/15; financial award applicants required to submit CSS PROFILE or FAFSA. *Unit head:* Lucy Mule, Department Chair, 413-585-3263, Fax: 413-585-3268, E-mail: lmule@smith.edu. *Application contact:* Ruth Morgan, Program Coordinator, 413-585-3050, Fax: 413-585-3054, E-mail: gradstdy@smith.edu.
Website: http://www.smith.edu/education

Sonoma State University, School of Education, Rohnert Park, CA 94928-3609. Offers administrative services (Credential); curriculum, teaching, and learning (MA); early childhood education (MA); education specialist (Credential); educational leadership (MA); multiple subject (Credential); reading and literacy (MA, Credential); single subject (Credential); special education (MA). *Accreditation:* NCATE. *Program availability:* Part-time, evening/weekend. *Entrance requirements:* For master's, minimum GPA of 2.5. Additional exam requirements/recommendations for international students: Required—TOEFL (minimum score 500 paper-based).

South Carolina State University, College of Graduate and Professional Studies, Department of Education, Orangeburg, SC 29117-0001. Offers early childhood education (MAT); education (M Ed); elementary education (M Ed, MAT); English (MAT); general science/biology (MAT); mathematics (MAT); secondary education (M Ed), including biology education, business education, counselor education, English education, home economics education, industrial education, mathematics education, science education, social studies education; special education (M Ed), including emotionally handicapped, learning disabilities, mentally handicapped. *Accreditation:* NCATE. *Program availability:* Part-time, evening/weekend. *Faculty:* 17 full-time (6 women), 12 part-time/adjunct (5 women). *Students:* 42 full-time (32 women), 93 part-time (64 women); includes 121 minority (119 Black or African American, non-Hispanic/Latino; 2 Asian, non-Hispanic/Latino), 2 international. Average age 40. 50 applicants, 98% accepted, 39 enrolled. In 2018, 9 master's awarded. *Degree requirements:* For master's, thesis optional, departmental qualifying exam. *Entrance requirements:* For master's, GRE General Test, NTE, interview, teaching certificate. *Application deadline:* For fall admission, 6/15 priority date for domestic students, 6/15 for international students; for spring admission, 11/1 for domestic and international students. Application fee: $25. Electronic applications accepted. *Expenses: Tuition, area resident:* Full-time $9928; part-time $552 per credit hour. Tuition, state resident: full-time $9928. Tuition, nonresident: full-time $21,038; part-time $1169 per credit hour. *Required fees:* $1532; $85 per credit hour. *Financial support:* Fellowships, career-related internships or fieldwork, Federal Work-Study, and scholarships/grants available. Financial award application deadline: 6/1. *Unit head:* Dr. Charlie Spell, Chair, Department of Education, 803-536-8963, Fax: 803-516-4568, E-mail: cspell@scsu.edu. *Application contact:* Curtis Foskey, Coordinator of Graduate Studies, 803-536-8419, Fax: 803-536-8812, E-mail: cfoskey@scsu.edu.

South Dakota State University, Graduate School, College of Education and Human Sciences, Brookings, SD 57007. Offers M Ed, MFCS, MS, PhD. *Degree requirements:* For master's, thesis, oral exam. *Entrance requirements:* Additional exam requirements/recommendations for international students: Required—TOEFL.

Southeastern Louisiana University, College of Education, Hammond, LA 70402. Offers M Ed, MAT, Ed D. *Accreditation:* NCATE. *Program availability:* Part-time, evening/weekend. *Faculty:* 19 full-time (13 women). *Students:* 34 full-time (29 women), 295 part-time (246 women); includes 95 minority (74 Black or African American, non-Hispanic/Latino; 9 Hispanic/Latino; 12 Two or more races, non-Hispanic/Latino), 1 international. Average age 38. 126 applicants, 73% accepted, 70 enrolled. In 2018, 33 master's, 14 doctorates awarded. *Degree requirements:* For master's, comprehensive exam (for some programs), thesis optional; for doctorate, thesis/dissertation. *Entrance requirements:* Additional exam requirements/recommendations for international students: Required—TOEFL (minimum score 500 paper-based; 61 iBT). *Application deadline:* For fall admission, 7/15 priority date for domestic students, 6/1 priority date for international students; for spring admission, 12/1 priority date for domestic students, 10/1 priority date for international students. Applications are processed on a rolling basis. Application fee: $20 ($30 for international students). Electronic applications accepted. *Expenses: Tuition, area resident:* Full-time $6684. Tuition, state resident: full-time $6684. Tuition, nonresident: full-time $19,162. *Required fees:* $2097. *Financial support:* In 2018–19, 8 students received support, including 1 fellowship with tuition reimbursement available (averaging $3,500 per year); career-related internships or fieldwork, Federal Work-Study, institutionally sponsored loans, scholarships/grants, and unspecified assistantships also available. Support available to part-time students. Financial award application deadline: 5/1; financial award applicants required to submit FAFSA. *Faculty research:* Principal preparation, early childhood education, school/industry partnership, literacy, math education. *Total annual research expenditures:* $404,225. *Unit head:* Dr. Paula Calderon, Dean, 985-549-2217, Fax: 985-549-2070, E-mail: collegeofeducation@southeastern.edu. *Application contact:* Dr. Paula Calderon, Dean, 985-549-2217, Fax: 985-549-2070, E-mail: collegeofeducation@southeastern.edu.
Website: http://www.southeastern.edu/acad_research/colleges/edu_hd/index.html

Southeastern Oklahoma State University, School of Education, Durant, OK 74701-0609. Offers math specialist (M Ed); reading specialist (M Ed); school administration (M Ed); school counseling (M Ed). *Accreditation:* NCATE. *Program availability:* Part-time, evening/weekend. *Degree requirements:* For master's, comprehensive exam, thesis optional, portfolio (M Ed). *Entrance requirements:* For master's, GRE General Test (for school counseling), minimum GPA of 3.0 in last 60 hours or 2.75 overall. Additional exam requirements/recommendations for international students: Required—TOEFL (minimum score 550 paper-based; 79 iBT). Electronic applications accepted.

Southeastern University, College of Education, Lakeland, FL 33801-6099. Offers curriculum and instruction (Ed D); educational leadership (M Ed); elementary education (M Ed); exceptional student education (M Ed); exceptional student education/educational therapy (M Ed); kinesiology (M Ed); organizational leadership (Ed D); reading education (M Ed); teaching English to speakers of other languages (M Ed). Electronic applications accepted.

Southern Adventist University, School of Education and Psychology, Collegedale, TN 37315-0370. Offers clinical mental health counseling (MS); instructional leadership (MS Ed); literacy education (MS Ed); outdoor education (MS Ed); professional school counseling (MS). *Accreditation:* NCATE. *Program availability:* Part-time, evening/weekend, 100% online, blended/hybrid learning. *Faculty:* 11 full-time (8 women), 11 part-time/adjunct (5 women). *Students:* 42 full-time (32 women), 40 part-time (29 women). 13 applicants, 38% accepted, 4 enrolled. *Degree requirements:* For master's, comprehensive exam (for some programs), thesis optional, portfolio (MS) portfolio (MS Ed in outdoor education). *Entrance requirements:* For master's, interview (MS); 9 semester hours of upper-division course work in psychology or related field, including 1 course in psychology research or statistics; 9 semester hours of education (MS Ed). Additional exam requirements/recommendations for international students: Required—TOEFL (minimum score 100 iBT). *Application deadline:* For fall admission, 7/1 priority date for domestic students, 6/1 priority date for international students; for winter admission, 11/1 priority date for domestic students, 10/1 priority date for international students; for spring admission, 4/1 priority date for domestic students, 3/1 priority date for international students. Applications are processed on a rolling basis. Application fee: $40. Electronic applications accepted. *Financial support:* Scholarships/grants and unspecified assistantships available. Support available to part-time students. Financial award application deadline: 4/1; financial award applicants required to submit FAFSA. *Faculty research:* Millennials, spiritual self-awareness, parenting styles, attitudes toward student mental health issues, reliance on social media. *Unit head:* Dr. Tammy Overstreet, Dean, 423-236-2444, Fax: 423-236-1765, E-mail: toverstreet@southern.edu. *Application contact:* Mikhaile Spence, Graduate Program Manager, 423-236-2496, Fax: 423-236-1765, E-mail: maspence@southern.edu.
Website: https://www.southern.edu/academics/edpsych.html

Southern Arkansas University–Magnolia, School of Graduate Studies, Magnolia, AR 71753. Offers agriculture (MS); business administration (MBA), including agribusiness, social entrepreneurship, supply chain management; clinical and mental health counseling (MS); computer and information sciences (MS), including cyber security and privacy, data science, information technology; gifted and talented (M Ed), including curriculum and instruction, educational administration and supervision, gifted and talented P-8/7-12, instructional specialist P-4; higher, adult and lifelong education (M Ed); kinesiology (M Ed), including coaching; library media and information specialist (M Ed); public administration (MPA); school counseling K-12 (M Ed); student affairs and college counseling (M Ed); teaching (MAT). *Accreditation:* NCATE. *Program availability:* Part-time, 100% online, blended/hybrid learning. *Faculty:* 36 full-time (21 women), 32 part-time/adjunct (15 women). *Students:* 164 full-time (77 women), 762 part-time (510 women); includes 192 minority (163 Black or African American, non-Hispanic/Latino; 7 American Indian or Alaska Native, non-Hispanic/Latino; 13 Asian, non-Hispanic/Latino; 1 Hispanic/Latino; 8 Two or more races, non-Hispanic/Latino), 213 international. Average age 28. 363 applicants, 100% accepted, 237 enrolled. In 2018, 716 master's awarded. *Degree requirements:* For master's, comprehensive exam (for some programs), thesis optional. *Entrance requirements:* For master's, GRE, MAT or GMAT, minimum GPA of 2.5. Additional exam requirements/recommendations for international students: Required—TOEFL (minimum score 550 paper-based), IELTS (minimum score 6). *Application deadline:* For fall admission, 8/1 for domestic and international students; for spring admission, 12/1 for domestic students, 11/15 for international students; for summer admission, 4/1 for domestic students, 5/10 for international students. Applications are processed on a rolling basis. Application fee: $25 ($90 for international students). Electronic applications accepted. *Expenses: Tuition, area resident:* Full-time $5130; part-time $3420 per year. Tuition, state resident: full-time $5130; part-time $3420 per year. Tuition, nonresident: full-time $7866; part-time $5244 per year. *International tuition:* $7866 full-time. *Required fees:* $1052; $710 per unit. Tuition and fees vary according to course load. *Financial support:* Career-related internships or fieldwork, Federal Work-Study, scholarships/grants, tuition waivers (full), and unspecified assistantships available. Financial award applicants required to submit FAFSA. *Faculty research:* Alternative certification for teachers, supervision of instruction, instructional leadership, counseling. *Unit head:* Dr. Kim Bloss, Dean, School of Graduate Studies, 870-235-4150, Fax: 870-235-5227, E-mail: kkbloss@saumag.edu. *Application contact:* Talia Jett, Admissions Coordinator, 870-2355450, Fax: 870-235-5227, E-mail: taliajett@saumag.edu.
Website: http://www.saumag.edu/graduate

Southern Connecticut State University, School of Graduate Studies, School of Education, New Haven, CT 06515-1355. Offers MLS, MS, MS Ed, Ed D, Diploma. *Accreditation:* NCATE. *Program availability:* Part-time. *Degree requirements:* For doctorate, comprehensive exam, thesis/dissertation. *Entrance requirements:* For degree, master's degree. Electronic applications accepted.

Southern Illinois University Carbondale, Graduate School, College of Education and Human Services, Carbondale, IL 62901-4701. Offers MPH, MS, MS Ed, MSW, PhD, JD/MSW. *Accreditation:* NCATE. *Program availability:* Part-time. Terminal master's awarded for partial completion of doctoral program. *Degree requirements:* For doctorate, thesis/dissertation. *Entrance requirements:* For master's, minimum GPA of 2.7. Additional exam requirements/recommendations for international students: Required—TOEFL (minimum score 550 paper-based; 80 iBT). Electronic applications accepted. *Faculty research:* Safety education, community health, curriculum development, gifted, effective schools.

Southern Illinois University Edwardsville, Graduate School, School of Education, Health, and Human Behavior, Edwardsville, IL 62062. Offers MA, MS, MS Ed, Ed D, Ed S, Post-Master's Certificate, Postbaccalaureate Certificate, SD. *Accreditation:* NCATE. *Program availability:* Part-time, evening/weekend. *Degree requirements:* For master's, comprehensive exam (for some programs), thesis (for some programs), final exam, portfolio. *Entrance requirements:* For master's, GRE. Additional exam requirements/recommendations for international students: Required—TOEFL (minimum score 550 paper-based; 79 iBT), IELTS (minimum score 6.5). Electronic applications accepted.

Southern Methodist University, Simmons School of Education and Human Development, Department of Teaching and Learning, Dallas, TX 75275. Offers bilingual education (MBE); education (M Ed, PhD); English as a second language (M Ed); gifted and talented (M Ed); literacy studies (M Ed); special education (M Ed). *Program availability:* Part-time, evening/weekend. Terminal master's awarded for partial completion of doctoral program. *Degree requirements:* For master's, comprehensive exam, minimum GPA of 3.0; for doctorate, thesis/dissertation, qualifying exams, major area paper, evidence of teaching competency, dissemination of research (e.g., conference presentation), professional portfolio. *Entrance requirements:* For master's, minimum GPA of 3.0 or GRE, 3 letters of recommendation; for doctorate, GRE, minimum GPA of 3.3, 3 years of full-time teaching, 3 letters of recommendation, interview. Additional exam requirements/recommendations for international students: Required—TOEFL. Electronic applications accepted. *Faculty research:* Reading intervention, mathematics intervention, bilingual education, new literacies.

Southern New Hampshire University, School of Education, Manchester, NH 03106-1045. Offers curriculum and instruction (M Ed), including dyslexia studies and language-based learning disabilities, educational leadership, reading, special education, technology integration; dyslexia studies and language-based learning disabilities (Certificate); early childhood and special education (M Ed); educational leadership (M Ed, Ed D); educational studies (M Ed); elementary and special education (M Ed); field based education (M Ed); higher education administration (MS); teaching English as a foreign language (MS). *Program availability:* Part-time, evening/weekend, online learning. *Degree requirements:* For master's, comprehensive exam (for some programs), thesis or alternative. *Entrance requirements:* For master's, PRAXIS I, minimum GPA of 2.75. Additional exam requirements/recommendations for international students: Required—TOEFL (minimum score 550 paper-based). Electronic applications accepted. *Expenses:* Contact institution.

Southern Oregon University, Graduate Studies, School of Education, Ashland, OR 97520. Offers elementary education (MA Ed, MS Ed), including classroom teacher, early childhood, handicapped learner, reading, supervision; secondary education (MA Ed, MS Ed), including classroom teacher, handicapped learner, reading, supervision; teaching (MAT). *Program availability:* Online learning. *Degree requirements:* For master's, thesis optional. *Entrance requirements:* For master's, GRE General Test, minimum cumulative GPA of 3.0 in the last 90 quarter credits (60 semester credits) of undergraduate coursework. Additional exam requirements/recommendations for international students: Required—TOEFL (minimum score 540 paper-based; 76 iBT), IELTS (minimum score 6), ELPT (minimum score 964) or ELS (minimum score 112). Electronic applications accepted.

Southern University and Agricultural and Mechanical College, Graduate School, College of Humanities and Interdisciplinary Studies, School of Education, Baton Rouge, LA 70813. Offers M Ed, MA, MS, PhD. *Accreditation:* NCATE. *Degree requirements:* For master's, comprehensive exam, thesis optional. *Entrance requirements:* For master's and doctorate, GRE General Test. Additional exam requirements/recommendations for international students: Required—TOEFL (minimum score 525 paper-based).

Southern Utah University, Program in Education, Cedar City, UT 84720-2498. Offers administrative licensure (Certificate); music education (MMus). *Accreditation:* TEAC. *Program availability:* Part-time, 100% online. *Faculty:* 13 full-time (6 women), 10 part-time/adjunct (4 women). *Students:* 7 full-time (all women), 346 part-time (240 women); includes 21 minority (3 Black or African American, non-Hispanic/Latino; 1 American Indian or Alaska Native, non-Hispanic/Latino; 5 Asian, non-Hispanic/Latino; 10 Hispanic/Latino; 2 Native Hawaiian or other Pacific Islander, non-Hispanic/Latino), 3 international. Average age 38. 78 applicants, 96% accepted, 55 enrolled. In 2018, 198 master's awarded. *Entrance requirements:* For master's, GRE (if GPA is less than 3.25), level 1 teaching license, minimum 2 full years of paid pre-K-20 teaching experience. Additional exam requirements/recommendations for international students: Required—TOEFL (minimum score 550 paper-based; 79 iBT), IELTS (minimum score 6), TOEFL (minimum score 550 paper-based, 79 iBT) or IELTS (minimum score 6). *Application deadline:* For fall admission, 7/15 for domestic and international students; for spring admission, 11/15 for domestic and international students; for summer admission, 4/15 for domestic and international students. Applications are processed on a rolling basis. Application fee: $60 ($65 for international students). Electronic applications accepted. *Expenses:* Contact institution. *Unit head:* Dr. Shawn Christiansen, Department Chair, 435-865-8171, Fax: 435-865-8485, E-mail: reynolds@suu.edu. *Application contact:* Tamara Lovell, Program Specialist, 435-865-8759, Fax: 435-865-8485, E-mail: tamaralovell@suu.edu.
Website: https://www.suu.edu/ed/graduate/master.html

Southern Wesleyan University, Program in Education, Central, SC 29630-1020. Offers M Ed. Program also offered at Greenville, S. C. site. *Accreditation:* NCATE. *Program availability:* Evening/weekend. *Entrance requirements:* For master's, GRE General Test or MAT, 1 year teaching experience, minimum undergraduate GPA of 3.0, teacher certification. Additional exam requirements/recommendations for international students: Required—TOEFL (minimum score 500 paper-based).

Southwest Baptist University, Program in Education, Bolivar, MO 65613-2597. Offers education (MS); educational administration (MS, Ed S). *Program availability:* Part-time. *Degree requirements:* For master's, comprehensive exam, thesis optional, 6-hour residency; for Ed S, comprehensive exam, 5-hour residency. *Entrance requirements:* For master's, GRE or PRAXIS II, interviews, minimum GPA of 2.75; for Ed S, master's degree. Additional exam requirements/recommendations for international students:

Required—TOEFL (minimum score 550 paper-based). *Faculty research:* At-risk programs, principal retention, mentoring beginning principals.

Southwestern Adventist University, Education Department, Keene, TX 76059. Offers curriculum and instruction with reading emphasis (M Ed); educational leadership (M Ed). *Program availability:* Part-time, evening/weekend. *Degree requirements:* For master's, thesis or alternative, professional paper. *Entrance requirements:* For master's, GRE General Test.

Southwestern Assemblies of God University, Thomas F. Harrison School of Graduate Studies, Program in Education, Waxahachie, TX 75165-5735. Offers Christian school administration (MS); curriculum development (MS); early education administration (M Ed); middle and secondary education (M Ed). *Degree requirements:* For master's, comprehensive written and oral exams. *Entrance requirements:* For master's, GRE General Test, minimum GPA of 2.5. Electronic applications accepted.

Southwestern College, Education Programs, Winfield, KS 67156-2499. Offers curriculum and instruction (M Ed); early childhood education (M Ed); educational leadership (Ed D), including higher education leadership, PK-12 education leadership; special education (M Ed), including high-incidence disabilities, low-incidence disabilities; teaching (MA). *Accreditation:* NCATE. *Program availability:* Part-time, evening/weekend, 100% online, blended/hybrid learning. *Faculty:* 7 full-time (5 women), 14 part-time/adjunct (12 women). *Students:* 6 full-time (5 women), 79 part-time (54 women); includes 11 minority (4 Black or African American, non-Hispanic/Latino; 2 American Indian or Alaska Native, non-Hispanic/Latino; 1 Asian, non-Hispanic/Latino; 3 Hispanic/Latino; 1 Two or more races, non-Hispanic/Latino), 4 international. Average age 38. 31 applicants, 74% accepted, 18 enrolled. In 2018, 24 master's, 8 doctorates awarded. *Degree requirements:* For master's, practicum, portfolio; for doctorate, thesis/dissertation, professional portfolio. *Entrance requirements:* For master's, baccalaureate degree, minimum GPA of 3.0, valid teaching certificate (for special education); for doctorate, GRE if no master's degree, baccalaureate degree with minimum GPA of 3.25 and current teaching experience, or master's degree with minimum GPA of 3.5. Additional exam requirements/recommendations for international students: Required—TOEFL (minimum score 60 paper-based; 70 iBT), IELTS (minimum score 5.5). *Application deadline:* Applications are processed on a rolling basis. Application fee: $40. Electronic applications accepted. *Expenses:* Masters programs are $606 per credit hour, $535 per online credit hour; doctorate program is $639 per credit hour. *Financial support:* In 2018–19, 13 students received support. Unspecified assistantships and employee tuition waivers available. Financial award applicants required to submit FAFSA. *Unit head:* J.K. Campbell, Education Division Chair, 620-229-6115, E-mail: JK.Campbell@sckans.edu. *Application contact:* Jen Caughron, Director of Enrollment Services & Marketing, 888-684-5335 Ext. 3312, Fax: 888-684-5218, E-mail: jennifer.caughron@sckans.edu.
Website: http://www.sckans.edu/graduate/education-med/

Southwestern Oklahoma State University, College of Professional and Graduate Studies, School of Behavioral Sciences and Education, Weatherford, OK 73096-3098. Offers biomedical science and microbiology (M Ed); community counseling (MS); early childhood education (M Ed); education administration (M Ed); elementary education (M Ed); kinesiology (M Ed), including health and physical education, sports management; mathematics (M Ed); natural sciences (M Ed); parks and recreation management (M Ed); school counseling (M Ed); school psychology (Ed S); school psychometry (M Ed); social sciences (M Ed); special education (M Ed). *Accreditation:* NCATE. *Program availability:* Part-time, evening/weekend, online learning. *Degree requirements:* For master's, exam. *Entrance requirements:* For master's, GRE General Test or minimum undergraduate GPA of 3.0. Additional exam requirements/recommendations for international students: Required—TOEFL (minimum score 550 paper-based), IELTS (minimum score 6.5).

Southwest Minnesota State University, Department of Education, Marshall, MN 56258. Offers ESL (MS); math (MS); reading (MS); special education (MS), including developmental disabilities, early childhood education, emotional behavioral disorders, learning disabilities; teaching, learning and leadership (MS). *Program availability:* Part-time, evening/weekend, online learning. *Entrance requirements:* Additional exam requirements/recommendations for international students: Required—TOEFL or IELTS; Recommended—TOEFL (minimum score 550 paper-based; 80 iBT), IELTS.

Spalding University, Graduate Studies, College of Education, Louisville, KY 40203-2188. Offers M Ed, MA, MAT, Ed D. *Accreditation:* NCATE. *Program availability:* Part-time, evening/weekend. *Degree requirements:* For doctorate, comprehensive exam, thesis/dissertation. *Entrance requirements:* For master's, GRE, GMAT, or MAT, transcripts, interview, letters of recommendation. Additional exam requirements/recommendations for international students: Required—TOEFL (minimum score 535 paper-based). Electronic applications accepted. Application fee is waived when completed online. *Expenses:* Contact institution. *Faculty research:* School leadership, assessment of student learning, classroom management.

Spring Arbor University, School of Education, Spring Arbor, MI 49283-9799. Offers education (MAE); reading (MAR); special education (MSE). *Accreditation:* TEAC. *Program availability:* Part-time, evening/weekend, online learning. *Degree requirements:* For master's, thesis. *Entrance requirements:* For master's, official transcripts from all institutions attended, including evidence of an earned bachelor's degree from regionally-accredited college or university with minimum cumulative GPA of 3.0 for the last two years of the bachelor's degree; two professional letters of recommendation. Additional exam requirements/recommendations for international students: Required—TOEFL (minimum score 600 paper-based). Electronic applications accepted.

Springfield College, Graduate Programs, Programs in Education, Springfield, MA 01109-3797. Offers early childhood education (M Ed); educational studies (M Ed); elementary education (M Ed); secondary education (M Ed); special education (M Ed, CAGS). *Program availability:* Part-time, evening/weekend. *Entrance requirements:* For master's, Massachusetts Tests for Educator Licensure (MTEL). Additional exam requirements/recommendations for international students: Required—TOEFL (minimum score 550 paper-based); Recommended—IELTS (minimum score 7). Electronic applications accepted. *Expenses:* Contact institution.

Spring Hill College, Graduate Programs, Program in Education, Mobile, AL 36608-1791. Offers early childhood education (MAT, MS Ed); educational theory (MS Ed); elementary education (MAT, MS Ed); secondary education (MAT, MS Ed). *Program availability:* Part-time. *Faculty:* 3 full-time (all women). *Students:* 1 full-time (0 women), 8 part-time (5 women); includes 2 minority (1 Hispanic/Latino; 1 Two or more races, non-Hispanic/Latino), 1 international. Average age 32. In 2018, 6 master's awarded. *Degree requirements:* For master's, comprehensive exam, completion of program within 6 calendar years of entrance into graduate studies at Spring Hill; documentation of course field assignments (MS) or completion of internship (MAT). *Entrance requirements:* For master's, GRE, MAT, or PRAXIS (varies by program), bachelor's degree with minimum undergraduate GPA of 3.0; class B certificate (for MS); minimum number of hours in specific fields (for MAT). Additional exam requirements/recommendations for international students: Required—TOEFL (minimum score 550 paper-based; 80 iBT), IELTS (minimum score 6.5), CPE or CAE (minimum score C), Michigan English Language Assessment Battery (minimum score 90). *Application deadline:* For fall

admission, 8/1 priority date for domestic and international students; for spring admission, 12/1 priority date for domestic and international students. Applications are processed on a rolling basis. Application fee: $25 ($35 for international students). Electronic applications accepted. *Expenses:* Contact institution. *Financial support:* Fellowships, research assistantships, teaching assistantships, and tuition waivers available. Financial award applicants required to submit FAFSA. *Unit head:* Dr. Lori P. Aultman, Chair of Education, 251-380-3473, Fax: 251-460-2184, E-mail: laultman@shc.edu. *Application contact:* Gary Bracken, Vice President of Enrollment Management, 251-380-3038, Fax: 251-460-2186, E-mail: gbracken@shc.edu.
Website: http://ug.shc.edu/graduate-degrees/master-science-education/

Stanford University, Graduate School of Education, Stanford, CA 94305-2004. Offers MA, MAE, PhD, MA/JD, MA/MBA, MPP/MA. *Accreditation:* NCATE. *Expenses: Tuition:* Full-time $50,703; part-time $32,970 per year. *Required fees:* $651.
Website: http://www.stanford.edu/group/SUSE/

State University of New York at Fredonia, College of Education, Fredonia, NY 14063-1136. Offers curriculum and instruction (MS Ed); literacy education (MS Ed), including birth-grade 12, grades 5-12; music education (M Mus), including k-12; TESOL (MS Ed). *Accreditation:* NCATE. *Program availability:* Part-time. *Faculty:* 16 full-time (14 women), 13 part-time/adjunct (11 women). *Students:* 39 full-time (33 women), 44 part-time (36 women); includes 5 minority (1 Asian, non-Hispanic/Latino; 3 Hispanic/Latino; 1 Two or more races, non-Hispanic/Latino), 4 international. Average age 27. 44 applicants, 89% accepted, 34 enrolled. In 2018, 25 master's awarded. *Degree requirements:* For master's, thesis. *Entrance requirements:* For master's, GRE, minimum undergraduate GPA of 3.0. Additional exam requirements/recommendations for international students: Required—TOEFL (minimum score 79 iBT), IELTS (minimum score 6.5). *Application deadline:* For fall admission, 4/1 priority date for domestic and international students; for spring admission, 11/1 priority date for domestic students, 11/1 for international students. Applications are processed on a rolling basis. Application fee: $75. Electronic applications accepted. *Expenses:* Tuition, state resident: full-time $6870; part-time $462 per credit hour. Tuition, nonresident: full-time $16,650; part-time $944 per credit hour. *International tuition:* $16,650 full-time. *Required fees:* $25; $2 per credit hour. $1 per semester. *Financial support:* In 2018–19, 13 students received support. Unspecified assistantships available. Financial award application deadline: 3/15; financial award applicants required to submit FAFSA. *Faculty research:* Positive behavioral intervention and support (PBIS), place-based science education, peer support for education, primary source material for social studies education, policies and practices in learning English language. *Unit head:* Dr. Christine Givner, Dean, 716-673-3311, E-mail: christine.givner@fredonia.edu. *Application contact:* Wendy S. Dunst, Interim Graduate Recruitment and Admissions Associate, 716-673-3808, Fax: 716-673-3712, E-mail: wendy.dunst@fredonia.edu.
Website: http://www.fredonia.edu/coe/

State University of New York at New Paltz, Graduate and Extended Learning School, School of Education, New Paltz, NY 12561. Offers MAT, MPS, MS Ed, MST, AC, CAS. *Accreditation:* NCATE. *Program availability:* Part-time, evening/weekend. *Faculty:* 26 full-time (19 women), 24 part-time/adjunct (19 women). *Students:* 147 full-time (104 women), 296 part-time (241 women); includes 72 minority (11 Black or African American, non-Hispanic/Latino; 2 Asian, non-Hispanic/Latino; 54 Hispanic/Latino; 5 Two or more races, non-Hispanic/Latino). 180 applicants, 83% accepted, 122 enrolled. In 2018, 169 master's, 45 other advanced degrees awarded. *Degree requirements:* For master's, comprehensive exam (for some programs), portfolio. *Entrance requirements:* For master's, GRE, MAT, minimum GPA of 3.0, New York State Teaching Certificate; for other advanced degree, minimum GPA of 3.0. Additional exam requirements/recommendations for international students: Required—TOEFL (minimum score 550 paper-based; 80 iBT), IELTS (minimum score 6.5). *Application deadline:* For fall admission, 3/1 for domestic and international students; for spring admission, 10/1 for domestic and international students. Application fee: $50. Electronic applications accepted. *Financial support:* Scholarships/grants available. Financial award application deadline: 8/1. *Faculty research:* Kindergarten readiness, translation learning experiences, assessment in mathematics education, long and short term outcomes of delayed school entry, parental involvement in children's education. *Unit head:* Dr. Michael Rosenberg, Dean, 845-257-2800, E-mail: schoolofed@newpaltz.edu. *Application contact:* Vika Shock, Director of Graduate Admissions, 845-257-3285, Fax: 845-257-3284, E-mail: gradstudies@newpaltz.edu.
Website: http://www.newpaltz.edu/schoolofed/

State University of New York at Oswego, Graduate Studies, School of Education, Oswego, NY 13126. Offers MAT, MS, MS Ed, MST, CAS, MS/CAS. *Accreditation:* NCATE. *Program availability:* Part-time. *Degree requirements:* For master's, comprehensive exam (for some programs), thesis optional. *Entrance requirements:* For degree, GRE General Test, interview, MA or MS, minimum GPA of 3.0. Additional exam requirements/recommendations for international students: Required—TOEFL (minimum score 560 paper-based).

State University of New York College at Cortland, Graduate Studies, School of Education, Cortland, NY 13045. Offers MS Ed, MST, CAS. *Accreditation:* NCATE. *Program availability:* Part-time, evening/weekend. *Entrance requirements:* Additional exam requirements/recommendations for international students: Required—TOEFL.

State University of New York College at Geneseo, Graduate Studies, School of Education, Geneseo, NY 14454-1401. Offers MS Ed. *Accreditation:* NCATE. *Program availability:* Part-time. *Degree requirements:* For master's, comprehensive exam (for some programs), thesis (for some programs). *Entrance requirements:* For master's, GRE, MAT, EAS, edTPA, PRAXIS, or another substantially equivalent test, proof of New York State initial certification or equivalent certification from another state. Additional exam requirements/recommendations for international students: Required—TOEFL (minimum score 525 paper-based; 71 iBT), IELTS (minimum score 6.5), PTE, iTEP. Electronic applications accepted. *Expenses:* Contact institution.

State University of New York College at Old Westbury, School of Education, Old Westbury, NY 11568-0210. Offers biology (MAT, MS); chemistry (MAT, MS); English language arts (MAT, MS); math (MAT, MS); social studies (MAT, MS); Spanish (MAT, MS). *Program availability:* Part-time, evening/weekend. *Entrance requirements:* For master's, Liberal Arts and Sciences Test, undergraduate degree with at least 30 semester hours of appropriate coursework as defined by the respective discipline; minimum cumulative undergraduate GPA of 3.0; two letters of recommendation (one from an academic source); essay. Additional exam requirements/recommendations for international students: Required—TOEFL (minimum score 550 paper-based); Recommended—IELTS.

State University of New York College at Oneonta, Graduate Programs, Division of Education, Oneonta, NY 13820-4015. Offers educational psychology, counseling and special education (MS Ed, CAS), including school counselor K-12, special education (MS Ed); elementary education and reading (MS Ed), including childhood education, literacy education. *Accreditation:* NCATE. *Program availability:* Part-time, evening/weekend. *Entrance requirements:* For master's, GRE General Test.

State University of New York Empire State College, School for Graduate Studies, Programs in Education, Saratoga Springs, NY 12866-4391. Offers adult learning (MA);

learning and emerging technologies (MA); teaching (MAT); teaching and learning (M Ed). *Program availability:* Online learning.

Stephen F. Austin State University, Graduate School, James I. Perkins College of Education, Nacogdoches, TX 75962. Offers M Ed, MA, MAT, MS, Ed D. *Accreditation:* NCATE. *Program availability:* Part-time, evening/weekend. *Degree requirements:* For master's, comprehensive exam; for doctorate, thesis/dissertation. *Entrance requirements:* For master's, GRE General Test; for doctorate, GRE General Test, interview, writing sample. Additional exam requirements/recommendations for international students: Required—TOEFL.

Stetson University, College of Arts and Sciences, Division of Education, DeLand, FL 32723. Offers M Ed, MS. *Accreditation:* NCATE (one or more programs are accredited). *Program availability:* Part-time, evening/weekend. *Faculty:* 12 full-time (8 women), 4 part-time/adjunct (3 women). *Students:* 141 full-time (113 women), 7 part-time (6 women); includes 50 minority (16 Black or African American, non-Hispanic/Latino; 3 American Indian or Alaska Native, non-Hispanic/Latino; 20 Hispanic/Latino; 11 Two or more races, non-Hispanic/Latino), 7 international. Average age 32. 103 applicants, 62% accepted, 52 enrolled. In 2018, 72 master's awarded. *Entrance requirements:* For master's, GRE or MAT. *Application deadline:* For fall admission, 8/1 priority date for domestic students; for spring admission, 1/1 priority date for domestic students; for summer admission, 5/1 priority date for domestic students. Applications are processed on a rolling basis. Application fee: $50. Electronic applications accepted. *Expenses:* $890 per credit hour (for MS Counselor Education), $938 per credit hour (for MED Educational Leadership). *Financial support:* In 2018–19, 53 students received support. Career-related internships or fieldwork, Federal Work-Study, institutionally sponsored loans, scholarships/grants, unspecified assistantships, and tuition waivers (for staff and dependents) available. Support available to part-time students. Financial award applicants required to submit FAFSA. *Unit head:* Dr. Elizabeth Skomp, Dean of the College of Arts and Sciences, 386-822-7515. *Application contact:* Jamie Vanderlip, Director of Admissions for Graduate, Transfer and Adult Programs, 386-822-7100, Fax: 386-822-7112, E-mail: jlvander@stetson.edu.

Stevenson University, Master of Arts in Teaching Program, Stevenson, MD 21153. Offers secondary biology (MAT); secondary chemistry (MAT); secondary mathematics (MAT). *Program availability:* Part-time, blended/hybrid learning. *Faculty:* 5 part-time/adjunct (all women). *Students:* 13 part-time (9 women); includes 5 minority (1 Black or African American, non-Hispanic/Latino; 2 Asian, non-Hispanic/Latino; 2 Hispanic/Latino). Average age 31. 8 applicants, 75% accepted, 6 enrolled. *Degree requirements:* For master's, internship, portfolio, action research project. *Entrance requirements:* For master's, PRAXIS, GRE, SAT, or ACT, official transcripts from each college or university attended verifying completion of baccalaureate degree in a science or math discipline from regionally-accredited institution. *Application deadline:* Applications are processed on a rolling basis. Electronic applications accepted. *Expenses:* Contact institution. *Financial support:* Unspecified assistantships available. Financial award applicants required to submit FAFSA. *Unit head:* Dr. Anne P. Davis, Dean, Stevenson University Online. *Application contact:* Amanda Millar, Director, Admissions, 443-352-4243, Fax: 443-352-4440, E-mail: amillar@stevenson.edu.
Website: http://www.stevenson.edu/online/academics/online-graduate-programs/master-arts-teaching/

Stockton University, Office of Graduate Studies, Program in Education, Galloway, NJ 08205-9441. Offers MA. *Accreditation:* TEAC. *Program availability:* Part-time, evening/weekend. *Faculty:* 8 full-time (6 women), 1 part-time/adjunct (0 women). *Students:* 12 full-time (11 women), 225 part-time (185 women); includes 30 minority (9 Black or African American, non-Hispanic/Latino; 2 Asian, non-Hispanic/Latino; 18 Hispanic/Latino; 1 Two or more races, non-Hispanic/Latino). Average age 34. 63 applicants, 83% accepted, 42 enrolled. In 2018, 23 master's awarded. *Entrance requirements:* For master's, GRE, MAT, minimum GPA of 2.75, teaching certificate. *Application deadline:* For fall admission, 7/1 for domestic students; for spring admission, 12/1 for domestic students. Applications are processed on a rolling basis. Application fee: $50. Electronic applications accepted. *Expenses:* Contact institution. *Financial support:* Fellowships, research assistantships, career-related internships or fieldwork, Federal Work-Study, scholarships/grants, and unspecified assistantships available. Support available to part-time students. Financial award application deadline: 3/1; financial award applicants required to submit FAFSA. *Faculty research:* Curriculum instruction, math, science, special education, language arts, literacy. *Unit head:* Dr. Kim LeBak, Program Director, 609-626-3640, E-mail: gradschool@stockton.edu. *Application contact:* Tara Williams, Assistant Director of Graduate Enrollment Management, 609-626-3640, Fax: 609-626-6050, E-mail: gradschool@stockton.edu.

Strayer University, Graduate Studies, Washington, DC 20005-2603. Offers accounting (MS); acquisition (MBA); business administration (MBA); communications technology (MS); educational management (M Ed); finance (MBA); health services administration (MHSA); hospitality and tourism management (MBA); human resource management (MBA); information systems (MS), including computer security management, decision support system management, enterprise resource management, network management, software engineering management, systems development management; management (MBA); management information systems (MS); marketing (MBA); professional accounting (MS), including accounting information systems, controllership, taxation; public administration (MPA); supply chain management (MBA); technology in education (M Ed). Programs also offered at campus locations in Birmingham, AL; Chamblee, GA; Cobb County, GA; Morrow, GA; White Marsh, MD; Charleston, SC; Columbia, SC; Greensboro, NC; Greenville, SC; Lexington, KY; Louisville, KY; Nashville, TN; North Raleigh, NC; Washington, DC. *Accreditation:* ACBSP. *Program availability:* Part-time, evening/weekend, online learning. *Degree requirements:* For master's, thesis. *Entrance requirements:* For master's, GMAT, GRE General Test, bachelor's degree from an accredited college or university, minimum undergraduate GPA of 2.75. Electronic applications accepted.

Sul Ross State University, College of Professional Studies, Department of Education, Alpine, TX 79832. Offers counseling (M Ed); educational diagnostics (M Ed); reading specialist (M Ed, Certificate), including master reading teacher (Certificate), Texas reading specialist (M Ed); school administration (M Ed). *Program availability:* Part-time, evening/weekend. *Degree requirements:* For master's, thesis optional. *Entrance requirements:* For master's, GMAT or GRE General Test, minimum GPA of 2.5 in last 60 hours of undergraduate work. *Faculty research:* Critical thinking skills, adolescent eating disorders, reading-based study skills, cross-cultural adaptations, educational leadership.

Sul Ross State University, Rio Grande College of Sul Ross State University, Alpine, TX 79832. Offers business administration (MBA); teacher education (M Ed), including bilingual education, counseling, educational diagnostics, elementary education, general education, reading, school administration, secondary education. *Program availability:* Part-time, evening/weekend, online learning. *Degree requirements:* For master's, comprehensive exam, thesis optional, minimum GPA of 3.0. *Entrance requirements:* For master's, GMAT or GRE General Test, minimum GPA of 2.5 in last 60 hours of undergraduate work. Additional exam requirements/recommendations for international students: Required—TOEFL.

Sweet Briar College, Department of Education, Sweet Briar, VA 24595. Offers M Ed, MAT. *Program availability:* Part-time. *Degree requirements:* For master's, comprehensive exam (for some programs), thesis. *Entrance requirements:* For master's, PRAXIS I and II; Virginia Communication and Literacy Assessment, Virginia Reading Assessment (MAT); GRE (M Ed), current teaching license (M Ed). Additional exam requirements/recommendations for international students: Required—TOEFL (minimum score 550 paper-based; 79 iBT), IELTS (minimum score 6.5). Electronic applications accepted. *Faculty research:* Differentiation of K-12 student achievement, mentoring and teacher retention, teaching science by inquiry.

Syracuse University, School of Education, Syracuse, NY 13244. Offers M Mus, MM, MS, Ed D, PhD, CAS, Ed D/PhD. *Accreditation:* NCATE. *Program availability:* Part-time. *Faculty:* 54 full-time (32 women), 51 part-time/adjunct (33 women). *Students:* 246 full-time (173 women), 216 part-time (152 women); includes 103 minority (47 Black or African American, non-Hispanic/Latino; 4 American Indian or Alaska Native, non-Hispanic/Latino; 4 Asian, non-Hispanic/Latino; 32 Hispanic/Latino; 16 Two or more races, non-Hispanic/Latino), 77 international. Average age 34. 480 applicants, 55% accepted, 114 enrolled. In 2018, 148 master's, 17 doctorates, 32 other advanced degrees awarded. *Degree requirements:* For master's, thesis or alternative; for doctorate, comprehensive exam, thesis/dissertation; for CAS, thesis. *Entrance requirements:* For master's, GRE (for some programs), baccalaureate degree from regionally-accredited college/university; for doctorate, GRE, master's degree. Additional exam requirements/recommendations for international students: Required—TOEFL (minimum score 100 iBT). *Application deadline:* Applications are processed on a rolling basis. Application fee: $75. Electronic applications accepted. *Financial support:* Fellowships with full tuition reimbursements, research assistantships, teaching assistantships, career-related internships or fieldwork, institutionally sponsored loans, scholarships/grants, health care benefits, tuition waivers (partial), and unspecified assistantships available. Financial award application deadline: 1/15; financial award applicants required to submit FAFSA. *Faculty research:* Literacy education, inclusive education, communication sciences and disorders, facilitated communication, school sustainability. *Unit head:* Dr. Joanna Masingila, Dean, 315-443-4751, E-mail: jomasing@syr.edu. *Application contact:* Speranza Migliore, Graduate Recruiter, School of Education, 315-443-2505, E-mail: gradrcrt@syr.edu.
Website: http://soeweb.syr.edu/

Taft University System, The Boyer Graduate School of Education, Denver, CO 80246. Offers M Ed.

Tarleton State University, College of Graduate Studies, College of Education, Stephenville, TX 76402. Offers M Ed, MS, Ed D, Certificate. *Program availability:* Part-time, evening/weekend, 100% online, blended/hybrid learning. *Faculty:* 32 full-time (19 women), 12 part-time/adjunct (8 women). *Students:* 74 full-time (54 women), 372 part-time (288 women); includes 134 minority (64 Black or African American, non-Hispanic/Latino; 3 American Indian or Alaska Native, non-Hispanic/Latino; 1 Asian, non-Hispanic/Latino; 57 Hispanic/Latino; 9 Two or more races, non-Hispanic/Latino), 3 international. Average age 38. 168 applicants, 84% accepted, 114 enrolled. In 2018, 172 master's, 28 doctorates awarded. *Degree requirements:* For master's, comprehensive exam, thesis (for some programs); for doctorate, thesis/dissertation. *Entrance requirements:* For master's, GRE General Test, minimum GPA of 3.0; for doctorate, GRE, 4 letters of reference, leadership portfolio. Additional exam requirements/recommendations for international students: Required—TOEFL (minimum score 520 paper-based; 69 iBT); Recommended—IELTS (minimum score 6), TSE (minimum score 50). *Application deadline:* For fall admission, 8/15 priority date for domestic students; for spring admission, 1/7 for domestic students. Applications are processed on a rolling basis. Application fee: $50 ($130 for international students). Electronic applications accepted. *Expenses:* Tuition, state resident: full-time $4200; part-time $652 per credit hour. Tuition, nonresident: full-time $11,750; part-time $652 per credit hour. *International tuition:* $11,750 full-time. *Required fees:* $1540. Tuition and fees vary according to degree level and program. *Financial support:* Research assistantships, teaching assistantships with partial tuition reimbursements, career-related internships or fieldwork, Federal Work-Study, institutionally sponsored loans, and tuition waivers (partial) available. Support available to part-time students. Financial award application deadline: 5/1; financial award applicants required to submit FAFSA. *Unit head:* Dr. Jordan Barkley, Dean, 254-968-9088, Fax: 254-968-9525, E-mail: jbarkley@tarleton.edu. *Application contact:* Wendy Weiss, Information Contact, 254-968-9104, Fax: 254-968-9670, E-mail: weiss@tarleton.edu.
Website: http://www.tarleton.edu/coe/index.html

Teachers College, Columbia University, Department of International and Transcultural Studies, New York, NY 10027-6696. Offers anthropology and education (MA, Ed D, PhD); applied anthropology (PhD); comparative and international education (MA, Ed D, PhD); international educational development (Ed M, MA, Ed D, PhD). *Program availability:* Part-time. *Students:* 94 full-time (79 women), 166 part-time (141 women); includes 90 minority (17 Black or African American, non-Hispanic/Latino; 32 Asian, non-Hispanic/Latino; 32 Hispanic/Latino; 9 Two or more races, non-Hispanic/Latino), 99 international. Average age 29. 389 applicants, 56% accepted, 99 enrolled. *Unit head:* Prof. Herve Varenne, Chair, 212-678-3190, E-mail: varenne@tc.columbia.edu. *Application contact:* Kelly Sutton Skinner, Director of Admission & New Student Enrollment, E-mail: kms2237@tc.columbia.edu.

Teachers College, Columbia University, Department of Mathematics, Science and Technology, New York, NY 10027-6696. Offers biology 7-12 (MA); chemistry 7-12 (MA); communication and education (MA, Ed D); computing in education (MA); earth science 7-12 (MA); instructional technology and media (Ed M, MA, Ed D); mathematics education (Ed M, MA, Ed D, Ed DCT, PhD); physics 7-12 (MA); science and dental education (MA); science education (Ed M, MS, Ed DCT, PhD); supervisor/teacher of science education (MA); technology specialist (MA). *Program availability:* Part-time, evening/weekend, online learning. *Students:* 155 full-time (114 women), 254 part-time (162 women); includes 136 minority (44 Black or African American, non-Hispanic/Latino; 1 American Indian or Alaska Native, non-Hispanic/Latino; 59 Asian, non-Hispanic/Latino; 23 Hispanic/Latino; 9 Two or more races, non-Hispanic/Latino), 140 international. Average age 31. 484 applicants, 60% accepted, 138 enrolled. Terminal master's awarded for partial completion of doctoral program. *Unit head:* Prof. Erica Walker, Chair, 212-678-8246, E-mail: ewalker@tc.columbia.edu. *Application contact:* Kelly Sutton Skinner, Director of Admission & New Student Enrollment, E-mail: kms2237@tc.columbia.edu.
Website: http://www.tc.columbia.edu/mathematics-science-and-technology/

Teachers College of San Joaquin, Master's Program in Education, Stockton, CA 95206. Offers early education (M Ed); educational inquiry (M Ed); educational leadership and school development (M Ed); science, technology, engineering, and mathematics (M Ed); special education (M Ed). *Expenses: Tuition:* Full-time $5520. Tuition and fees vary according to course load and program.

Temple University, College of Education, Philadelphia, PA 19122-6096. Offers Ed M, MS Ed, Ed D, PhD, Ed S. *Accreditation:* TEAC. *Program availability:* Part-time, evening/weekend. *Faculty:* 54 full-time (34 women), 93 part-time/adjunct (62 women). *Students:* 453 full-time (321 women), 373 part-time (259 women); includes 253 minority (145 Black or African American, non-Hispanic/Latino; 3 American Indian or Alaska Native, non-Hispanic/Latino; 37 Asian, non-Hispanic/Latino; 48 Hispanic/Latino; 1 Native Hawaiian or other Pacific Islander, non-Hispanic/Latino; 19 Two or more races, non-Hispanic/Latino), 33 international. 881 applicants, 53% accepted, 260 enrolled. In 2018, 291 master's, 59 doctorates, 70 other advanced degrees awarded. *Entrance requirements:* Additional exam requirements/recommendations for international students: Required—TOEFL, IELTS, PTE, one of three is required. Application fee: $60. Electronic applications accepted. *Financial support:* Fellowships, Federal Work-Study, scholarships/grants, health care benefits, and unspecified assistantships available. Financial award applicants required to submit FAFSA. *Faculty research:* Curriculum development, instruction, technology, learning, educational achievement. *Unit head:* Dr. Gregory Anderson, Dean, 215-204-8017, Fax: 215-204-5622, E-mail: gregory.anderson@temple.edu. *Application contact:* Joseph Paris, Assistant Dean of Marketing & Enrollment Management, 215-204-2810, E-mail: educate@temple.edu.
Website: http://education.temple.edu/

Tennessee State University, The School of Graduate Studies and Research, College of Education, Nashville, TN 37209-1561. Offers M Ed, MA Ed, MS, Ed D, PhD, Ed S. *Accreditation:* NCATE. *Program availability:* Part-time, evening/weekend. *Degree requirements:* For doctorate, thesis/dissertation. *Entrance requirements:* For doctorate, minimum GPA of 3.25. *Faculty research:* Class size, biobehavioral research, equity, dropout rate, K–12 teachers: first 5 years of employment.

Tennessee Technological University, College of Graduate Studies, College of Education, Cookeville, TN 38505. Offers MA, PhD, Ed S. *Accreditation:* NCATE. *Program availability:* Part-time, evening/weekend. *Faculty:* 58 full-time (16 women). *Students:* 123 full-time (96 women), 288 part-time (215 women); includes 32 minority (17 Black or African American, non-Hispanic/Latino; 3 Asian, non-Hispanic/Latino; 5 Hispanic/Latino; 7 Two or more races, non-Hispanic/Latino), 8 international. 221 applicants, 76% accepted, 120 enrolled. In 2018, 105 master's, 8 doctorates, 33 other advanced degrees awarded. *Degree requirements:* For master's and Ed S, comprehensive exam, thesis or alternative; for doctorate, comprehensive exam, thesis/dissertation. *Entrance requirements:* For master's, GRE or MAT; for doctorate, GRE; for Ed S, MAT or GRE. Additional exam requirements/recommendations for international students: Required—TOEFL (minimum score 527 paper-based; 71 iBT), IELTS (minimum score 5.5), PTE (minimum score 48), or TOEIC (Test of English as an International Communication). *Application deadline:* For fall admission, 8/1 for domestic students, 5/1 for international students; for spring admission, 12/1 for domestic students, 10/1 for international students; for summer admission, 5/1 for domestic students, 2/1 for international students. Applications are processed on a rolling basis. Application fee: $35 ($40 for international students). Electronic applications accepted. *Financial support:* Fellowships, research assistantships, teaching assistantships, and career-related internships or fieldwork available. Support available to part-time students. Financial award application deadline: 4/1. *Faculty research:* Teacher evaluation. *Unit head:* Dr. Lisa Zagumny, Dean, 931-372-3124, Fax: 931-372-6319, E-mail: lzagumny@tntech.edu. *Application contact:* Shelia K. Kendrick, Coordinator of Graduate Studies, 931-372-3808, Fax: 931-372-3497, E-mail: skendrick@tntech.edu.

Texas A&M International University, Office of Graduate Studies and Research, College of Education, Laredo, TX 78041. Offers MS, MS Ed. *Program availability:* Part-time, evening/weekend. *Degree requirements:* For master's, thesis (for some programs). *Entrance requirements:* For master's, GRE General Test. Additional exam requirements/recommendations for international students: Required—TOEFL (minimum score 550 paper-based; 79 iBT).

Texas A&M University, College of Education and Human Development, College Station, TX 77843. Offers M Ed, MS, Ed D, PhD. *Program availability:* Part-time, evening/weekend, blended/hybrid learning. *Faculty:* 183. *Students:* 721 full-time (531 women), 863 part-time (632 women); includes 560 minority (148 Black or African American, non-Hispanic/Latino; 6 American Indian or Alaska Native, non-Hispanic/Latino; 50 Asian, non-Hispanic/Latino; 328 Hispanic/Latino; 2 Native Hawaiian or other Pacific Islander, non-Hispanic/Latino; 26 Two or more races, non-Hispanic/Latino), 154 international. Average age 33. 589 applicants, 62% accepted, 283 enrolled. In 2018, 531 master's, 108 doctorates awarded. *Degree requirements:* For doctorate, thesis/dissertation. *Entrance requirements:* For master's and doctorate, GRE General Test. Additional exam requirements/recommendations for international students: Required—TOEFL (minimum score 550 paper-based; 80 iBT), IELTS (minimum score 6), PTE (minimum score 53). *Application deadline:* Applications are processed on a rolling basis. Application fee: $50 ($90 for international students). Electronic applications accepted. *Expenses:* Contact institution. *Financial support:* In 2018–19, 802 students received support, including 13 fellowships with tuition reimbursements available (averaging $22,861 per year), 221 research assistantships with tuition reimbursements available (averaging $10,462 per year), 132 teaching assistantships with tuition reimbursements available (averaging $9,872 per year); career-related internships or fieldwork, institutionally sponsored loans, scholarships/grants, traineeships, health care benefits, tuition waivers (full and partial), and unspecified assistantships also available. Support available to part-time students. Financial award application deadline: 3/15; financial award applicants required to submit FAFSA. *Unit head:* Dr. Joyce Alexander, Professor and Dean, 979-862-6649, E-mail: joycemalexander@tamu.edu. *Application contact:* Dr. Beverly Irby, Professor and Associate Dean for Academic Affairs, 979-845-5311, E-mail: beverly.irby@tamu.edu.
Website: http://education.tamu.edu/

Texas A&M University–Commerce, College of Education and Human Services, Commerce, TX 75429. Offers counseling (M Ed, MS, PhD); early childhood education (M Ed, MS); educational administration (M Ed, MS, Ed D); educational psychology (PhD); educational technology leadership (M Ed, MS); educational technology library science (M Ed, MS); elementary education (M Ed); health, kinesiology and sports studies (MS); higher education (MS, Ed D); psychology (MS); reading (M Ed, MS); school psychology (SSP); secondary education (M Ed, MS); social work (MSW); special education (M Ed, MS); supervision, curriculum and instruction-elementary education (Ed D); training and development (MS). *Program availability:* Part-time, evening/weekend, 100% online, blended/hybrid learning. *Faculty:* 95 full-time (59 women), 29 part-time/adjunct (22 women). *Students:* 356 full-time (295 women), 1,262 part-time (992 women); includes 683 minority (349 Black or African American, non-Hispanic/Latino; 9 American Indian or Alaska Native, non-Hispanic/Latino; 30 Asian, non-Hispanic/Latino; 238 Hispanic/Latino; 57 Two or more races, non-Hispanic/Latino), 9 international. Average age 37. 951 applicants, 42% accepted, 304 enrolled. In 2018, 532 master's, 51 doctorates awarded. *Degree requirements:* For master's, comprehensive exam, thesis optional, departmental qualifying exams (for some programs); for doctorate, comprehensive exam, thesis/dissertation, departmental qualifying exam; for SSP, comprehensive exam. *Entrance requirements:* For master's, GRE General Test, official transcripts, letters of recommendation, resume, statement of goals; for doctorate, GRE General Test, letters of recommendation, statement of goals, writing samples, writing sessions, resumes. Additional exam requirements/recommendations for international students: Required—TOEFL (minimum score 550 paper-based; 79 iBT), IELTS (minimum score 6), PTE (minimum score 53). *Application deadline:* For fall admission, 6/1 priority date for international students; for spring admission, 10/15 priority date for international students; for summer admission, 3/15 priority date for international

students. Applications are processed on a rolling basis. Application fee: $50 ($75 for international students). Electronic applications accepted. *Expenses: Tuition, area resident:* Full-time $3630. Tuition, state resident: full-time $3630. Tuition, nonresident: full-time $11,100. *International tuition:* $11,100 full-time. *Required fees:* $2794. Tuition and fees vary according to course load, degree level and program. *Financial support:* In 2018–19, 116 students received support, including 94 research assistantships with partial tuition reimbursements available (averaging $3,863 per year), 38 teaching assistantships with partial tuition reimbursements available (averaging $4,728 per year); career-related internships or fieldwork, Federal Work-Study, institutionally sponsored loans, scholarships/grants, health care benefits, and unspecified assistantships also available. Financial award application deadline: 5/1; financial award applicants required to submit FAFSA. *Faculty research:* Cognitive and bilingual education, positive behavioral intervention, literacy, math readiness. *Total annual research expenditures:* $1.1 million. *Unit head:* Dr. Madeline Justice, Interim Dean, 903-886-5181, Fax: 903-886-5905, E-mail: madeline.justice@tamuc.edu. *Application contact:* Vicky Turner, Doctoral Degree and Special Programs Coordinator, 903-886-5167, E-mail: vicky.turner@tamuc.edu.
Website: http://www.tamuc.edu/academics/graduateSchool/programs/education/default.aspx

Texas A&M University–Corpus Christi, College of Graduate Studies, College of Education and Human Development, Corpus Christi, TX 78412. Offers counseling (MS), including counseling; counselor education (PhD); curriculum and instruction (MS, PhD); early childhood education (MS); educational administration (MS); educational leadership (Ed D); elementary education (MS); instructional design and educational technology (MS); kinesiology (MS); reading (MS); secondary education (MS); special education (MS). *Program availability:* Part-time, evening/weekend, blended/hybrid learning. *Degree requirements:* For master's, comprehensive exam, capstone; for doctorate, thesis/dissertation. *Entrance requirements:* For master's, GRE General Test, essay (300 words); for doctorate, GRE, essay, resume, 3-4 reference forms. Electronic applications accepted.

Texas A&M University–Kingsville, College of Graduate Studies, College of Education and Human Performance, Kingsville, TX 78363. Offers M Ed, MA, MS, Ed D, Certificate. *Program availability:* 100% online, blended/hybrid learning. *Entrance requirements:* Additional exam requirements/recommendations for international students: Required—TOEFL (minimum score 550 paper-based; 79 iBT); Recommended—IELTS. Electronic applications accepted.

Texas A&M University–San Antonio, Department of Educator and Leadership Preparation, San Antonio, TX 78224. Offers bilingual education (MS); early childhood education (M Ed); educational administration (MA); reading specialization (MS); special education (M Ed), including educational diagnostician. *Program availability:* Part-time, evening/weekend, online learning. *Degree requirements:* For master's, comprehensive exam, thesis or alternative. *Entrance requirements:* For master's, GRE (Quantitative and Verbal) or MAT. Additional exam requirements/recommendations for international students: Required—TOEFL (minimum score 550 paper-based; 79 iBT), IELTS (minimum score 6). Electronic applications accepted. *Faculty research:* Equity in education, biliteracy practices among Latina and immigrants, academic achievement of low socio-economic students, equity practices in instruction and educational leadership in diverse settings, racial identity development and multicultural education.

Texas A&M University–Texarkana, Graduate Studies and Research, College of Education and Liberal Arts, Texarkana, TX 75503. Offers adult education (MS); curriculum and instruction (M Ed); education (MS); educational administration (M Ed); English (MA); instructional technology (MS); interdisciplinary studies (MA, MS); special education (MS). *Program availability:* Part-time, evening/weekend. *Degree requirements:* For master's, comprehensive exam (for some programs), thesis optional. *Entrance requirements:* For master's, minimum GPA of 2.5 on last 60 hours of bachelor's degree. Additional exam requirements/recommendations for international students: Required—TOEFL. Electronic applications accepted.

Texas Christian University, College of Education, Fort Worth, TX 76129-0002. Offers M Ed, MAT, Ed D, PhD, MBA/Ed D. *Program availability:* Part-time, evening/weekend. *Faculty:* 29 full-time (21 women), 3 part-time/adjunct (1 woman). *Students:* 204 full-time (151 women), 40 part-time (25 women); includes 93 minority (29 Black or African American, non-Hispanic/Latino; 2 American Indian or Alaska Native, non-Hispanic/Latino; 9 Asian, non-Hispanic/Latino; 45 Hispanic/Latino; 8 Two or more races, non-Hispanic/Latino), 7 international. Average age 33. 195 applicants, 72% accepted, 109 enrolled. In 2018, 62 master's, 12 doctorates awarded. *Degree requirements:* For master's, comprehensive exam (for some programs), thesis (for some programs); for doctorate, comprehensive exam, thesis/dissertation. *Entrance requirements:* For master's, GRE General Test; Pre-Admission Content Test; for doctorate, GRE General Test. Additional exam requirements/recommendations for international students: Required—TOEFL (minimum score 550 paper-based; 80 iBT), IELTS (minimum score 6.5). *Application deadline:* For fall admission, 2/1 for domestic and international students; for spring admission, 11/16 for domestic and international students; for summer admission, 2/1 for domestic and international students. Application fee: $60. Electronic applications accepted. *Financial support:* In 2018–19, 201 students received support, including 1 fellowship with full tuition reimbursement available (averaging $18,500 per year), 9 research assistantships with full tuition reimbursements available (averaging $18,500 per year), 39 teaching assistantships with full tuition reimbursements available (averaging $15,000 per year); career-related internships or fieldwork, scholarships/grants, health care benefits, and unspecified assistantships also available. Support available to part-time students. Financial award application deadline: 2/1. *Faculty research:* Science education, special education, literacy, educational leadership, higher education leadership, solution focused counseling. *Total annual research expenditures:* $1.4 million. *Unit head:* Dr. Jan Lacina, Interim Dean, 817-257-6786, Fax: 817-257-7466, E-mail: j.lacina@tcu.edu. *Application contact:* Lori Kimball, Graduate Coordinator, 817-257-7661, Fax: 817-257-7466, E-mail: l.kimball@tcu.edu.
Website: http://coe.tcu.edu/graduate-overview/

Texas Southern University, College of Education, Houston, TX 77004-4584. Offers M Ed, MS, Ed D. *Program availability:* Part-time, evening/weekend. *Degree requirements:* For master's, comprehensive exam; for doctorate, comprehensive exam, thesis/dissertation. *Entrance requirements:* For master's, GRE General Test, minimum GPA of 2.5; for doctorate, GRE General Test or MAT, master's degree, minimum B+ average. Additional exam requirements/recommendations for international students: Required—TOEFL. Electronic applications accepted.

Texas State University, The Graduate College, College of Education, San Marcos, TX 78666. Offers M Ed, MA, MS, MSRLS, Ed D, PhD, SSP. *Program availability:* Part-time, evening/weekend. *Faculty:* 129 full-time (85 women), 31 part-time/adjunct (21 women). *Students:* 541 full-time (413 women), 558 part-time (427 women); includes 486 minority (94 Black or African American, non-Hispanic/Latino; 1 American Indian or Alaska Native, non-Hispanic/Latino; 29 Asian, non-Hispanic/Latino; 338 Hispanic/Latino; 24 Two or more races, non-Hispanic/Latino), 26 international. Average age 31. 897 applicants, 56% accepted, 296 enrolled. In 2018, 363 master's, 27 doctorates awarded. *Degree requirements:* For master's, comprehensive exam, thesis (for some programs); for doctorate, comprehensive exam, thesis/dissertation. *Entrance requirements:* For master's, GRE (for some programs), baccalaureate degree from regionally-accredited institution; letters of recommendation, statement of purpose, resume, and/or interview (for some programs); for doctorate, GRE, baccalaureate and master's degrees from regionally-accredited institution; letters of recommendation, statement of purpose, resume, and/or interview (for some programs). Additional exam requirements/recommendations for international students: Required—TOEFL (minimum score 550 paper-based; 78 iBT). *Application deadline:* For fall admission, 1/15 priority date for domestic and international students; for spring admission, 10/1 priority date for domestic and international students. Applications are processed on a rolling basis. Application fee: $55 ($90 for international students). Electronic applications accepted. *Expenses:* Tuition, state resident: full-time $8102; part-time $4051 per semester. Tuition, nonresident: full-time $18,229; part-time $9115 per semester. *International tuition:* $18,229 full-time. *Required fees:* $2116; $120 per credit hour. Tuition and fees vary according to course load. *Financial support:* In 2018–19, 549 students received support, including 71 research assistantships (averaging $17,177 per year), 75 teaching assistantships (averaging $14,778 per year); fellowships, career-related internships or fieldwork, Federal Work-Study, institutionally sponsored loans, and scholarships/grants also available. Support available to part-time students. Financial award application deadline: 1/15; financial award applicants required to submit FAFSA. *Faculty research:* Improving writing instruction for children with disabilities; neuromuscular electrical stimulation; link between individual learning and organizational change; learning styles of the Autistic; Enhancing Physical Activity Programming for Employee Well-being; Adult student transition to postsecondary models; Biomechanics of sport and exercise. *Total annual research expenditures:* $6.1 million. *Unit head:* Dr. Michael O'Malley, Dean, 512-245-2150, Fax: 512-245-3158, E-mail: mo20@txstate.edu. *Application contact:* Dr. Andrea Golato, Dean of Graduate School, 512-245-2581, Fax: 512-245-8365, E-mail: gradcollege@txstate.edu.
Website: http://www.education.txstate.edu/

Texas Tech University, Graduate School, College of Education, Lubbock, TX 79409-1071. Offers M Ed, MS, Ed D, PhD. *Accreditation:* NCATE. *Program availability:* Part-time, evening/weekend. *Faculty:* 157 full-time (105 women), 5 part-time/adjunct (all women). *Students:* 309 full-time (225 women), 889 part-time (702 women); includes 428 minority (113 Black or African American, non-Hispanic/Latino; 3 American Indian or Alaska Native, non-Hispanic/Latino; 21 Asian, non-Hispanic/Latino; 256 Hispanic/Latino; 1 Native Hawaiian or other Pacific Islander, non-Hispanic/Latino; 34 Two or more races, non-Hispanic/Latino), 66 international. Average age 37. 538 applicants, 71% accepted, 303 enrolled. In 2018, 304 master's, 61 doctorates awarded. Terminal master's awarded for partial completion of doctoral program. *Degree requirements:* For master's, comprehensive exam (for some programs), thesis or alternative; for doctorate, thesis/dissertation. *Entrance requirements:* For master's and doctorate, GRE General Test. Additional exam requirements/recommendations for international students: Required—TOEFL (minimum score 550 paper-based; 79 iBT). *Application deadline:* For fall admission, 6/1 priority date for domestic students, 1/15 priority date for international students; for spring admission, 9/1 priority date for domestic students, 6/15 priority date for international students. Applications are processed on a rolling basis. Application fee: $65. Electronic applications accepted. *Expenses:* Contact institution. *Financial support:* In 2018–19, 635 students received support, including 625 fellowships (averaging $3,215 per year), 89 research assistantships (averaging $12,476 per year), 12 teaching assistantships (averaging $13,752 per year); career-related internships or fieldwork, Federal Work-Study, institutionally sponsored loans, scholarships/grants, traineeships, health care benefits, and unspecified assistantships also available. Support available to part-time students. Financial award application deadline: 2/1; financial award applicants required to submit FAFSA. *Faculty research:* Multicultural foundations of education, teacher education, psychological processes of teaching and learning, teaching populations with special needs, institutional technology, teacher preparation and educator quality, STEM education, blended and personalized learning using technology, autism and educational interventions around autism, partnerships for education and school reform. *Total annual research expenditures:* $9.5 million. *Unit head:* Dr. Jesse Perez Mendez, Dean, 806-742-2377, Fax: 806-742-2179, E-mail: jp.mendez@ttu.edu. *Application contact:* Beth Watson, Coordinator, 806-834-0429, Fax: 806-742-2179, E-mail: beth.watson@ttu.edu.
Website: www.educ.ttu.edu/

Texas Wesleyan University, Graduate Programs, Programs in Education, Fort Worth, TX 76105. Offers education (M Ed, Ed D). *Program availability:* Part-time, evening/weekend. *Degree requirements:* For master's, comprehensive exam (for some programs); for doctorate, thesis/dissertation. *Entrance requirements:* For master's and doctorate, GRE General Test. Additional exam requirements/recommendations for international students: Required—TOEFL (minimum score 550 paper-based; 79 iBT), IELTS (minimum score 6.5). Electronic applications accepted. *Expenses:* Contact institution. *Faculty research:* Teacher effectiveness, bilingual education, analytic teaching.

Texas Woman's University, Graduate School, College of Professional Education, Denton, TX 76204. Offers M Ed, MA, MAT, MLS, MS, PhD, Certificate. *Program availability:* Part-time, evening/weekend, 100% online, blended/hybrid learning. *Faculty:* 72 full-time (57 women), 64 part-time/adjunct (48 women). *Students:* 316 full-time (299 women), 931 part-time (875 women); includes 466 minority (140 Black or African American, non-Hispanic/Latino; 1 American Indian or Alaska Native, non-Hispanic/Latino; 23 Asian, non-Hispanic/Latino; 272 Hispanic/Latino; 30 Two or more races, non-Hispanic/Latino), 11 international. Average age 35. 481 applicants, 74% accepted, 257 enrolled. In 2018, 335 master's, 25 doctorates, 65 other advanced degrees awarded. *Degree requirements:* For master's, comprehensive exam (for some programs), thesis (for some programs); for doctorate, comprehensive exam, thesis/dissertation; for Certificate, comprehensive exam. *Entrance requirements:* For master's, minimum GPA of 3.0 on the last 60 hours; for doctorate, minimum GPA of 3.0. Additional exam requirements/recommendations for international students: Required—TOEFL (minimum score 550 paper-based; 79 iBT); Recommended—IELTS (minimum score 6.5), TSE (minimum score 53). *Application deadline:* For fall admission, 3/1 priority date for domestic and international students; for spring admission, 11/1 priority date for domestic students, 7/1 priority date for international students. Applications are processed on a rolling basis. Application fee: $50 ($75 for international students). Electronic applications accepted. *Expenses:* Contact institution. *Financial support:* In 2018–19, 257 students received support, including 3 research assistantships, 24 teaching assistantships (averaging $9,735 per year); career-related internships or fieldwork, Federal Work-Study, institutionally sponsored loans, scholarships/grants, traineeships, health care benefits, and unspecified assistantships also available. Support available to part-time students. Financial award application deadline: 3/1; financial award applicants required to submit FAFSA. *Unit head:* Dr. Lisa Huffman, Dean, 940-898-2202, Fax: 940-898-2209, E-mail: cope@twu.edu. *Application contact:* Korie Hawkins, Associate Director of Admissions, Graduate Recruitment, 940-898-3188, Fax: 940-898-3081, E-mail: admissions@twu.edu.
Website: http://www.twu.edu/college-professional-education/

Thomas More University, Program in Teaching, Crestview Hills, KY 41017-3495. Offers MAT. *Program availability:* Part-time. *Degree requirements:* For master's, comprehensive exam. *Entrance requirements:* For master's, GRE (minimum scores:

verbal 450, quantitative 490, and analytical 4.0) or PPST (minimum scores: math 174, reading 176, and writing 174), minimum undergraduate content GPA of 2.75, interview. Additional exam requirements/recommendations for international students: Required—TOEFL (minimum score 600 paper-based; 100 iBT). Electronic applications accepted. *Expenses:* Contact institution.

Thomas University, Department of Education, Thomasville, GA 31792-7499. Offers M Ed. *Program availability:* Part-time. *Entrance requirements:* For master's, resume, 3 academic/professional references. Additional exam requirements/recommendations for international students: Required—TOEFL (minimum score 600 paper-based). Electronic applications accepted.

Thompson Rivers University, Program in Education, Kamloops, BC V2C 0C8, Canada. Offers M Ed. *Program availability:* Part-time. *Entrance requirements:* For master's, 2 letters of reference, minimum GPA of 3.0 in final 2 years of undergraduate degree.

Tiffin University, Program in Education, Tiffin, OH 44883-2161. Offers educational technology management (M Ed); higher education administration (M Ed). *Program availability:* Part-time, evening/weekend, online only, 100% online, blended/hybrid learning. *Entrance requirements:* Additional exam requirements/recommendations for international students: Required—TOEFL. Electronic applications accepted. *Expenses:* Contact institution.

Touro College, Graduate School of Education, New York, NY 10010. Offers education and special education (MS); instructional technology (MS); mathematics education (MS); school leadership (MS); teaching English to speakers of other languages (MS); teaching literacy (MS). *Accreditation:* TEAC. *Program availability:* Part-time, evening/weekend, online learning. *Entrance requirements:* Additional exam requirements/recommendations for international students: Required—TOEFL (minimum score 83 iBT), IELTS (minimum score 6.5). *Faculty research:* Equity assistance, language development, scholarly communications, Latin American studies and cultural sensitivity, behavior management techniques and strategies in special education.

Touro University California, Graduate Programs, Vallejo, CA 94592. Offers education (MA); medical health sciences (MS); osteopathic medicine (DO); pharmacy (Pharm D); public health (MPH). *Accreditation:* ACPE; AOsA; ARC-PA; CEPH. *Program availability:* Part-time, evening/weekend. *Degree requirements:* For master's, comprehensive exam, thesis; for doctorate, comprehensive exam. *Entrance requirements:* For doctorate, BS/BA. Electronic applications accepted. *Faculty research:* Cancer, heart disease.

Towson University, College of Education, Program in Teaching, Towson, MD 21252-0001. Offers early childhood education (MAT); elementary education (MAT); secondary education (MAT); special education (MAT). *Entrance requirements:* For master's, ACT, GRE, PRAXIS I or SAT, 2 letters of reference, resume, minimum GPA of 3.0, essay. Electronic applications accepted. *Expenses: Tuition, area resident:* Full-time $9196; part-time $418 per unit. Tuition, state resident: Full-time $9196; part-time $418 per unit. Tuition, nonresident: full-time $19,030; part-time $865 per unit. *International tuition:* $19,030 full-time. *Required fees:* $3102; $141 per year. $423 per term. Tuition and fees vary according to campus/location and program.

Trevecca Nazarene University, Graduate Education Program, Nashville, TN 37210-2877. Offers accountability and instructional leadership (Ed S); curriculum and instruction for Christian school educators (M Ed); curriculum and instruction K-12 (M Ed); educational leadership (M Ed); English second language (M Ed); library and information science (MLI Sc); special education: visual impairments (M Ed); teaching (MAT), including teaching 6-12, teaching K-5. *Accreditation:* NCATE. *Program availability:* Part-time, evening/weekend, online learning. *Degree requirements:* For master's, comprehensive exam, exit assessment/e-portfolio. *Entrance requirements:* For master's, GRE or MAT; PRAXIS (for MAT), minimum GPA of 3.0, official transcript from regionally-accredited institution, references, interview, writing sample, at least 3 years' successful teaching experience (for M Ed in educational leadership); for Ed S, GRE or MAT, master's degree with minimum GPA of 3.0, official transcript from regionally accredited institution, at least 3 years' successful teaching experience, interview, writing sample, background and fingerprinting check, recommendations. Additional exam requirements/recommendations for international students: Required—TOEFL (minimum score 550 paper-based). Electronic applications accepted. *Expenses:* Contact institution.

Trident University International, College of Education, Cypress, CA 90630. Offers MA Ed, PhD. *Program availability:* Part-time, evening/weekend, online learning. *Degree requirements:* For doctorate, comprehensive exam, thesis/dissertation, defense of dissertation. *Entrance requirements:* For master's, minimum GPA of 2.5 (students with GPA 3.0 or greater may transfer up to 30% of graduate level credits); for doctorate, minimum GPA of 3.4, curriculum vitae, course work in research methods or statistics. Additional exam requirements/recommendations for international students: Required—TOEFL (minimum score 525 paper-based). Electronic applications accepted.

Trinity International University, Trinity Graduate School, Deerfield, IL 60015-1284. Offers athletic training (MA); bioethics (MA); counseling psychology (MA); diverse learning (M Ed); leadership (MA); teaching (MA). *Program availability:* Part-time, evening/weekend, online learning. *Degree requirements:* For master's, comprehensive exam. *Entrance requirements:* For master's, GRE General Test or MAT, minimum undergraduate GPA of 3.0. Additional exam requirements/recommendations for international students: Required—TOEFL (minimum score 580 paper-based), TWE (minimum score 4). Electronic applications accepted.

Trinity University, Department of Education, San Antonio, TX 78212-7200. Offers school leadership (M Ed); school psychology (MA); teaching (MAT). *Accreditation:* NCATE. *Program availability:* Part-time, evening/weekend. *Faculty:* 17 full-time (14 women), 12 part-time/adjunct (9 women). *Students:* 40 full-time (30 women); includes 24 minority (2 Black or African American, non-Hispanic/Latino; 21 Hispanic/Latino; 1 Two or more races, non-Hispanic/Latino), 2 international. Average age 31. In 2018, 42 master's awarded. Tuition and fees vary according to program and student level. *Financial support:* Application deadline: 5/1; applicants required to submit FAFSA. *Unit head:* Norvella Carter, Interim Chair, 210-999-7506, Fax: 210-999-7592, E-mail: ncarter1@trinity.edu. *Application contact:* Office of Admissions, 210-999-7207, Fax: 210-999-8164, E-mail: admissions@trinity.edu.

Trinity Washington University, School of Education, Washington, DC 20017-1094. Offers clinical mental health counseling (MA); early childhood education (MAT); educating for change (M Ed); educational administration (MSA); elementary education (MAT); reading (M Ed); school counseling (MA); secondary education (MAT), including English, social studies; special education (MAT). *Accreditation:* NCATE. *Program availability:* Part-time, evening/weekend. *Degree requirements:* For master's, thesis (for some programs), capstone project(s). *Entrance requirements:* For master's, PRAXIS I, minimum GPA of 2.8. Additional exam requirements/recommendations for international students: Required—TOEFL (minimum score 550 paper-based). *Faculty research:* Technology, literacy, special education, organizations, inclusion models.

Troy University, Graduate School, College of Education, Troy, AL 36082. Offers MS, MS Ed, Ed S. *Accreditation:* NCATE. *Program availability:* Part-time, evening/weekend. *Faculty:* 75 full-time (45 women), 26 part-time/adjunct (19 women). *Students:* 392 full-time (319 women), 560 part-time (463 women); includes 316 minority (284 Black or African American, non-Hispanic/Latino; 4 American Indian or Alaska Native, non-Hispanic/Latino; 3 Asian, non-Hispanic/Latino; 12 Hispanic/Latino; 1 Native Hawaiian or other Pacific Islander, non-Hispanic/Latino; 12 Two or more races, non-Hispanic/Latino), 17 international. Average age 35. 524 applicants, 86% accepted, 288 enrolled. In 2018, 338 master's, 30 other advanced degrees awarded. *Degree requirements:* For master's, comprehensive exam, thesis. *Entrance requirements:* For master's, GRE (minimum score of 850 on old exam or 290 on new exam), GMAT (minimum score of 380), or MAT (minimum score of 385), bachelor's degree; minimum undergraduate GPA of 2.5 or 3.0 on last 30 semester hours, letter of recommendation; for Ed S, GRE (minimum score of 850 on old exam or 290 on new exam), GMAT (minimum score of 380), or MAT (minimum score of 385), Alabama Class A certificate or equivalent, minimum graduate GPA of 3.0. Additional exam requirements/recommendations for international students: Required—TOEFL (minimum score 523 paper-based; 70 iBT), IELTS (minimum score 6). *Application deadline:* For fall admission, 1/1 for domestic students, 6/1 for international students; for spring admission, 10/15 for international students. Applications are processed on a rolling basis. Application fee: $50. Electronic applications accepted. *Expenses: Tuition, area resident:* Full-time $425; part-time $425 per credit hour. Tuition, state resident: full-time $425; part-time $425 per credit hour. Tuition, nonresident: full-time $850; part-time $850 per credit hour. *International tuition:* $850 full-time. *Required fees:* $50 per semester. Tuition and fees vary according to campus/location and program. *Financial support:* Fellowships, career-related internships or fieldwork, and scholarships/grants available. Support available to part-time students. Financial award applicants required to submit FAFSA. *Unit head:* Dr. Dionne Rosser-Mims, Dean, 334-670-3365, Fax: 334-670-3474, E-mail: drosser-mims@troy.edu. *Application contact:* Jessica A. Kimbro, Assistant Director of Graduate Programs, 334-670-3189, E-mail: jacord@troy.edu.
Website: https://www.troy.edu/academics/colleges-schools/education/index.html

Truman State University, Graduate School, School of Health Sciences and Education, Program in Education, Kirksville, MO 63501-4221. Offers MAE. *Accreditation:* NCATE. *Faculty:* 12 full-time (9 women). *Students:* 104 full-time (80 women), 6 part-time (4 women); includes 4 minority (1 Asian, non-Hispanic/Latino; 3 Hispanic/Latino). Average age 23. 18 applicants, 94% accepted, 17 enrolled. In 2018, 112 master's awarded. *Degree requirements:* For master's, comprehensive exam, thesis or alternative. *Entrance requirements:* For master's, GRE, minimum GPA of 2.75. Additional exam requirements/recommendations for international students: Required—TOEFL (minimum score 550 paper-based). *Application deadline:* For fall admission, 4/1 for domestic and international students; for spring admission, 11/1 for domestic and international students; for summer admission, 4/1 for domestic and international students. Application fee: $40. Electronic applications accepted. *Expenses:* Tuition, state resident: full-time $385.50; part-time $385.50 per credit hour. Tuition, nonresident: full-time $668; part-time $668 per credit hour. *International tuition:* $668 full-time. *Required fees:* $648. *Financial support:* In 2018–19, 5 teaching assistantships with full and partial tuition reimbursements (averaging $8,000 per year) were awarded; research assistantships with tuition reimbursements and career-related internships or fieldwork also available. Financial award application deadline: 5/1; financial award applicants required to submit FAFSA. *Unit head:* Dr. Wendy Miner, Director, 660-785-6074, E-mail: wsm@truman.edu. *Application contact:* Bethany Gibson, Graduate Office Secretary, 660-785-4109, Fax: 660-785-7460, E-mail: bethanyc@truman.edu.

Tufts University, Graduate School of Arts and Sciences, Department of Education, Medford, MA 02155. Offers art education (MAT); education (MA, MAT, MS, PhD), including educational studies (MA), elementary education (MAT), middle and secondary education (MAT), museum education (MA), secondary education (MA), STEM education (MS, PhD); school psychology (MA, Ed S). *Program availability:* Part-time. *Degree requirements:* For master's, thesis optional; for doctorate, thesis/dissertation. *Entrance requirements:* For master's and doctorate, GRE General Test. Additional exam requirements/recommendations for international students: Required—TOEFL (minimum score 550 paper-based; 80 iBT), IELTS (minimum score 6.5). Electronic applications accepted. *Expenses:* Contact institution.

Tusculum University, Program in Teaching, Greeneville, TN 37743-9997. Offers MAT. *Program availability:* Evening/weekend. *Entrance requirements:* For master's, PRAXIS I, GRE, MAT, minimum GPA of 3.0.

Union College, Graduate Programs, Department of Education, Barbourville, KY 40906-1499. Offers elementary education (MA); health and physical education (MA); middle grades (MA); music education (MA); principalship (MA); reading specialist (MA); secondary education (MA); special education (MA). *Degree requirements:* For master's, thesis optional. *Entrance requirements:* For master's, GRE General Test, NTE.

Union Institute & University, PhD Program in Interdisciplinary Studies, Cincinnati, OH 45206-1925. Offers educational studies (PhD), including Martin Luther King studies; ethical and creative leadership (PhD); humanities and culture (PhD); public policy and social change (PhD). Program requires participation in brief on-campus residencies twice each year (January and July). *Program availability:* Part-time, online only, blended/hybrid learning. *Degree requirements:* For doctorate, comprehensive exam, thesis/dissertation. *Entrance requirements:* For doctorate, master's degree, three letters of recommendation, statement of purpose. Additional exam requirements/recommendations for international students: Required—TOEFL. Electronic applications accepted. *Expenses:* Contact institution. *Faculty research:* Social responsibility, ethical leadership, Martin Luther King studies.

Union University, School of Education, Jackson, TN 38305-3697. Offers education (M Ed, MA Ed); education administration generalist (Ed S); educational leadership (Ed D); educational supervision (Ed S); higher education (Ed D). M Ed also available at Germantown campus. *Accreditation:* NCATE. *Program availability:* Part-time, evening/weekend, online learning. *Degree requirements:* For master's, thesis (for some programs), capstone research course (for MA Ed); performance exhibition (for M Ed); for doctorate, comprehensive exam, thesis/dissertation; for Ed S, thesis or alternative. *Entrance requirements:* For master's, MAT, PRAXIS II or GRE, minimum GPA of 3.0, teaching license (for M Ed only), writing sample; for doctorate, GRE, minimum graduate GPA of 3.2, writing sample; for Ed S, PRAXIS II, minimum graduate GPA of 3.2, writing sample. Additional exam requirements/recommendations for international students: Required—TOEFL (minimum score 560 paper-based; 80 iBT). Electronic applications accepted. *Expenses:* Contact institution. *Faculty research:* Mathematics education, brain compatible learning, transformational teaching, cognitive strategy development, instructional technology.

Universidad Autonoma de Guadalajara, Graduate Programs, Guadalajara, Mexico. Offers administrative law and justice (LL M); advertising and corporate communications (MA); architecture (M Arch); business (MBA); computational science (MCC); education (Ed M, Ed D); English-Spanish translation (MA); entrepreneurship and management (MBA); integrated management of digital animation (MA); international business (MIB); international corporate law (LL M); Internet technologies (MS); manufacturing systems (MMS); occupational health (MS); philosophy (MA, PhD); power electronics (MS); quality systems (MQS); renewable energy (MS); social evaluation of projects (MBA); strategic market research (MBA); tax law (MA); teaching mathematics (MA).

Education—General

Universidad de las Americas, A.C., Program in Education, Mexico City, Mexico. Offers M Ed. *Entrance requirements:* For master's, 2 years of professional experience; undergraduate degree in early childhood education, human communication, psychology, science of education, special education or related fields.

Universidad de las Américas Puebla, Division of Graduate Studies, School of Social Sciences, Program in Education, Puebla, Mexico. Offers MA. *Program availability:* Part-time, evening/weekend. *Degree requirements:* For master's, one foreign language, thesis. *Faculty research:* Curriculum development, curriculum evaluation, instructional technology, critical thinking.

Universidad del Turabo, Graduate Programs, Programs in Education, Gurabo, PR 00778-3030. Offers M Ed, MPHE, D Ed. *Program availability:* Part-time, evening/weekend. *Degree requirements:* For master's, thesis (for some programs). *Entrance requirements:* For master's, GRE, EXADEP, GMAT, interview, official transcript, essay, recommendation letter; for doctorate, GRE, EXADEP, GMAT, official transcript, recommendation letters, essay, curriculum vitae, interview. Electronic applications accepted.

Universidad Metropolitana, School of Education, San Juan, PR 00928-1150. Offers administration and supervision (M Ed); curriculum and teaching (M Ed); educational administration and supervision (M Ed); managing recreation and sports services (M Ed); pre-school centers administration (M Ed); special education (M Ed); teaching of physical education (M Ed), including teaching of adult physical education, teaching of elementary physical education, teaching of secondary physical education. *Program availability:* Part-time, evening/weekend. *Degree requirements:* For master's, thesis or alternative. Electronic applications accepted.

Université de Moncton, Faculty of Education, Graduate Studies in Education, Moncton, NB E1A 3E9, Canada. Offers educational psychology (M Ed, MA Ed); guidance (M Ed, MA Ed); school administration (M Ed, MA Ed); teaching (M Ed, MA Ed). *Program availability:* Part-time. *Degree requirements:* For master's, proficiency in English and French. *Entrance requirements:* For master's, minimum GPA of 3.0. *Faculty research:* Guidance, ethnolinguistic vitality, children's rights, ecological education, entrepreneurship.

Université de Montréal, Faculty of Education, Montréal, QC H3C 3J7, Canada. Offers M Ed, MA, PhD, DESS. *Program availability:* Part-time, evening/weekend. *Degree requirements:* For doctorate, thesis/dissertation, general exam. Electronic applications accepted.

Université de Saint-Boniface, Department of Education, Saint-Boniface, MB R2H 0H7, Canada. Offers M Ed.

Université de Sherbrooke, Faculty of Education, Sherbrooke, QC J1K 2R1, Canada. Offers M Ed, MA, Diploma. *Program availability:* Part-time, evening/weekend. *Degree requirements:* For master's, thesis. *Faculty research:* Career education, teaching, professional instruction.

Université du Québec à Chicoutimi, Graduate Programs, Program in Education, Chicoutimi, QC G7H 2B1, Canada. Offers M Ed, MA, PhD. PhD offered jointly with Université du Québec à Rimouski, Université du Québec à Trois-Rivières, Université du Québec èn Outaouais, Université du Québec en Abitibi-Témiscamingue. and Université du Québec à Montréal. *Program availability:* Part-time. *Degree requirements:* For doctorate, thesis/dissertation. *Entrance requirements:* For master's, appropriate bachelor's degree, proficiency in French; for doctorate, appropriate master's degree, proficiency in French.

Université du Québec à Montréal, Graduate Programs, Program in Education, Montréal, QC H3C 3P8, Canada. Offers education (M Ed, MA, PhD); education of the environmental sciences (Diploma). PhD offered jointly with Université du Québec à Chicoutimi, Université du Québec à Rimouski, Université du Québec à Trois-Rivières, Université du Québec en Outaouais, and Université du Québec en Abitibi-Témiscamingue. *Program availability:* Part-time. *Degree requirements:* For master's, thesis (for some programs); for doctorate, thesis/dissertation. *Entrance requirements:* For master's and Diploma, appropriate bachelor's degree or equivalent, proficiency in French; for doctorate, appropriate master's degree or equivalent, proficiency in French.

Université du Québec à Rimouski, Graduate Programs, Program in Education, Rimouski, QC G5L 3A1, Canada. Offers M Ed, MA, PhD, Diploma. M Ed and MA offered jointly with Université du Québec en Outaouais and Université du Québec en Abitibi-Témiscamingue; PhD with Université du Québec à Chicoutimi, Université du Québec à Trois-Rivières, Université du Québec en Outaouais, and Université du Québec en Abitibi-Témiscamingue. *Program availability:* Part-time. *Degree requirements:* For master's, thesis optional; for doctorate, thesis/dissertation. *Entrance requirements:* For master's, appropriate bachelor's degree, proficiency in French; for doctorate, appropriate master's degree, proficiency in French.

Université du Québec à Trois-Rivières, Graduate Programs, Program in Education, Trois-Rivières, QC G9A 5H7, Canada. Offers M Ed, PhD. *Program availability:* Part-time. *Degree requirements:* For master's, research report. *Entrance requirements:* For master's, appropriate bachelor's degree, proficiency in French.

Université du Québec en Abitibi-Témiscamingue, Graduate Programs, Program in Education, Rouyn-Noranda, QC J9X 5E4, Canada. Offers M Ed, MA, PhD, DESS. M Ed and MA offered jointly with Université du Québec à Rimouski and Université du Québec en Outaouais; PhD with Université du Québec à Chicoutimi, Université du Québec à Rimouski, Université du Québec à Trois-Rivières, Université du Québec en Outaouais, and Université du Québec à Montréal. *Program availability:* Part-time. *Degree requirements:* For master's, thesis optional; for doctorate, thesis/dissertation. *Entrance requirements:* For master's, appropriate bachelor's degree, proficiency in French; for doctorate, appropriate master's degree, proficiency in French.

Université du Québec en Outaouais, Graduate Programs, Program in Education, Gatineau, QC J8X 3X7, Canada. Offers M Ed, MA, PhD, DESS, Diploma. *Program availability:* Part-time. *Degree requirements:* For master's, thesis optional; for doctorate, thesis/dissertation. *Entrance requirements:* For master's, appropriate bachelor's degree, proficiency in French; for doctorate, appropriate master's degree, proficiency in French.

Université Laval, Faculty of Education, Québec, QC G1K 7P4, Canada. Offers MA, PhD, Diploma. *Program availability:* Part-time. *Degree requirements:* For doctorate, comprehensive exam, thesis/dissertation. Electronic applications accepted.

Université Sainte-Anne, Program in Education, Church Point, NS B0W 1M0, Canada. Offers M Ed. *Program availability:* Part-time.

University at Albany, State University of New York, School of Education, Albany, NY 12222-0001. Offers MS, PhD, Psy D, CAS. *Accreditation:* TEAC. *Program availability:* Part-time, evening/weekend, 100% online, blended/hybrid learning. *Faculty:* 68 full-time (39 women), 38 part-time/adjunct (24 women). *Students:* 348 full-time (271 women), 632 part-time (496 women); includes 184 minority (59 Black or African American, non-Hispanic/Latino; 33 Asian, non-Hispanic/Latino; 69 Hispanic/Latino; 1 Native Hawaiian or other Pacific Islander, non-Hispanic/Latino; 22 Two or more races, non-Hispanic/Latino), 82 international. Average age 31. 588 applicants, 64% accepted, 310 enrolled. In 2018, 192 master's, 18 doctorates, 24 other advanced degrees awarded. *Degree requirements:* For doctorate, thesis/dissertation. *Entrance requirements:* For doctorate, GRE General Test. Additional exam requirements/recommendations for international students: Required—TOEFL (minimum score 550 paper-based). Application fee: $75. Electronic applications accepted. *Financial support:* Fellowships, career-related internships or fieldwork, and Federal Work-Study available. *Unit head:* Jason Lane, Interim Dean, 518-442-4988, E-mail: jlane@albany.edu. *Application contact:* Jason Lane, Interim Dean, 518-442-4988, E-mail: jlane@albany.edu.
Website: http://www.albany.edu/education/

University at Buffalo, the State University of New York, Graduate School, Graduate School of Education, Buffalo, NY 14260. Offers Ed M, MA, MS, Ed D, PhD, Advanced Certificate, Certificate, Certificate/Ed M. *Accreditation:* TEAC. *Program availability:* Part-time, 100% online. *Faculty:* 74 full-time (45 women), 81 part-time/adjunct (53 women). *Students:* 467 full-time (343 women), 752 part-time (557 women); includes 182 minority (75 Black or African American, non-Hispanic/Latino; 4 American Indian or Alaska Native, non-Hispanic/Latino; 53 Asian, non-Hispanic/Latino; 40 Hispanic/Latino; 1 Native Hawaiian or other Pacific Islander, non-Hispanic/Latino; 9 Two or more races, non-Hispanic/Latino), 72 international. Average age 33. 981 applicants, 67% accepted, 451 enrolled. In 2018, 290 master's, 59 doctorates, 107 other advanced degrees awarded. Terminal master's awarded for partial completion of doctoral program. *Degree requirements:* For master's, comprehensive exam; for doctorate, thesis/dissertation. *Entrance requirements:* For master's, GRE General Test; for doctorate, GRE, MAT. Additional exam requirements/recommendations for international students: Required—TOEFL (minimum score 600 paper-based; 79 iBT), IELTS (minimum score 6.5), PTE (minimum score 55). *Application deadline:* Applications are processed on a rolling basis. Application fee: $50. Electronic applications accepted. *Financial support:* In 2018–19, 98 fellowships (averaging $5,401 per year), 125 research assistantships with tuition reimbursements (averaging $11,177 per year) were awarded; teaching assistantships, Federal Work-Study, institutionally sponsored loans, scholarships/grants, tuition waivers (full and partial), and unspecified assistantships also available. Support available to part-time students. Financial award applicants required to submit FAFSA. *Faculty research:* Early childhood mathematics education, finance and management of higher education, curricular policy, practice and reform, student behavior in small classes, psychological measurement and assessment. *Total annual research expenditures:* $3.8 million. *Unit head:* Dr. Suzanne Rosenblith, Dean, 716-645-1354, Fax: 716-645-2479, E-mail: gseinfo@buffalo.edu. *Application contact:* Cory Meyers, Assistant Dean for Enrollment Management, 716-645-2110, Fax: 716-645-7937, E-mail: gseinfo@buffalo.edu.
Website: http://www.gse.buffalo.edu/

The University of Akron, Graduate School, College of Education, Akron, OH 44325. Offers MA, MS. *Accreditation:* NCATE. *Program availability:* Part-time. Terminal master's awarded for partial completion of doctoral program. *Degree requirements:* For master's, comprehensive exam, thesis optional. *Entrance requirements:* For master's, GRE, letters of recommendation, resume, statement of purpose. Additional exam requirements/recommendations for international students: Required—TOEFL (minimum score 550 paper-based; 79 iBT), IELTS (minimum score 6.5). Electronic applications accepted. *Faculty research:* History, philosophy of education, ethnographic research in education, case study methodology in education, multiple linear regression.

The University of Alabama at Birmingham, School of Education, Birmingham, AL 35294. Offers MA, MA Ed, Ed D, PhD, Ed S. *Accreditation:* NCATE. *Program availability:* Part-time, evening/weekend, online learning. *Degree requirements:* For master's, thesis optional; for doctorate, thesis/dissertation; for Ed S, comprehensive exam, thesis optional. *Entrance requirements:* For master's, GRE General Test, MAT, or NTE, minimum GPA of 3.0; for doctorate, GRE General Test, MAT, minimum GPA of 3.25; for Ed S, GRE General Test, MAT, minimum GPA of 3.0, master's degree. Electronic applications accepted. *Expenses: Tuition, area resident:* Full-time $8100; part-time $8100 per year. Tuition, state resident: full-time $8100. Tuition, nonresident: full-time $19,188; part-time $19,188 per year. Tuition and fees vary according to program.

University of Alaska Anchorage, School of Education, Anchorage, AK 99508. Offers M Ed, Certificate. *Accreditation:* NCATE. *Program availability:* Part-time. *Degree requirements:* For master's, comprehensive exam, thesis or alternative, portfolio. *Entrance requirements:* For master's, interview, minimum GPA of 3.0. Additional exam requirements/recommendations for international students: Required—TOEFL (minimum score 550 paper-based).

University of Alaska Fairbanks, School of Education, Fairbanks, AK 99775. Offers M Ed, Graduate Certificate. *Accreditation:* NCATE. *Program availability:* 100% online, blended/hybrid learning. *Faculty:* 15 full-time (11 women), 1 part-time/adjunct (0 women). *Students:* 39 full-time (27 women), 105 part-time (89 women); includes 27 minority (8 American Indian or Alaska Native, non-Hispanic/Latino; 1 Asian, non-Hispanic/Latino; 9 Hispanic/Latino; 1 Native Hawaiian or other Pacific Islander, non-Hispanic/Latino; 8 Two or more races, non-Hispanic/Latino), 3 international. Average age 37. 63 applicants, 52% accepted, 29 enrolled. In 2018, 49 master's, 34 other advanced degrees awarded. *Degree requirements:* For master's, comprehensive exam, oral defense of project or thesis, student teaching. *Entrance requirements:* For master's and Graduate Certificate, bachelor's degree from accredited institution with minimum cumulative undergraduate and major GPA of 3.0. Additional exam requirements/recommendations for international students: Required—TOEFL (minimum score 550 paper-based; 79 iBT), IELTS (minimum score 6.5). *Application deadline:* For fall admission, 2/15 for domestic and international students; for spring admission, 10/1 for domestic students, 8/1 for international students. Application fee: $60. Electronic applications accepted. *Expenses: Tuition, area resident:* Full-time $8802; part-time $5868 per credit hour. Tuition, state resident: full-time $8802; part-time $5868 per credit hour. Tuition, nonresident: full-time $18,504; part-time $12,336 per credit hour. *International tuition:* $18,504 full-time. *Required fees:* $1416; $944 per credit hour. $472 per semester. Tuition and fees vary according to course load and program. *Financial support:* In 2018–19, 2 teaching assistantships with full tuition reimbursements (averaging $11,955 per year) were awarded; fellowships with full tuition reimbursements, research assistantships with full tuition reimbursements, career-related internships or fieldwork, Federal Work-Study, scholarships/grants, health care benefits, and unspecified assistantships also available. Support available to part-time students. Financial award application deadline: 6/1; financial award applicants required to submit FAFSA. *Faculty research:* Native ways of knowing, classroom research in methods of literacy instruction, multiple intelligence theory, geometry concept development, mathematics and science curriculum development. *Total annual research expenditures:* $92,000. *Unit head:* Dr. Amy Vinlove, Director, 907-474-7341, E-mail: uaf-soe-school@alaska.edu. *Application contact:* Samara Taber, Director of Admissions, 907-474-7500, E-mail: uaf-admissions@alaska.edu.
Website: http://www.uaf.edu/soe/

University of Alaska Southeast, Graduate Programs, Program in Education, Juneau, AK 99801. Offers educational leadership (M Ed); elementary education (MAT); learning design and technology (M Ed); mathematics education (M Ed); reading specialist (M Ed); secondary education (MAT); special education (M Ed, MAT). *Accreditation:* NCATE. *Program availability:* Part-time, evening/weekend, online learning. *Degree requirements:* For master's, comprehensive exam or project, portfolio. *Entrance requirements:* For master's, PRAXIS, minimum GPA of 3.0, writing sample, letters of

recommendation. Electronic applications accepted. *Faculty research:* Applied classroom research, culturally responsive practices, action research, teaching effectiveness.

The University of Arizona, College of Education, Tucson, AZ 85721. Offers M Ed, MA, MS, Ed D, PhD, Certificate, Ed S. *Program availability:* Part-time, online learning. Terminal master's awarded for partial completion of doctoral program. *Degree requirements:* For master's, comprehensive exam, thesis (for some programs); for doctorate, comprehensive exam, thesis/dissertation. *Entrance requirements:* For doctorate, GRE. Additional exam requirements/recommendations for international students: Required—TOEFL (minimum score 550 paper-based; 79 iBT). Electronic applications accepted. *Faculty research:* Teacher effectiveness, pupil achievement, learning skills, program evaluation, instructional method effects.

University of Arkansas, Graduate School, College of Education and Health Professions, Fayetteville, AR 72701. Offers M Ed, MAT, MAT, MS, MSN, Ed D, PhD, Ed S. *Accreditation:* NCATE. In 2018, 211 master's, 56 doctorates, 10 other advanced degrees awarded. *Application deadline:* For fall admission, 8/1 for domestic students, 4/1 for international students; for spring admission, 12/1 for domestic students, 10/1 for international students; for summer admission, 4/15 for domestic students, 3/1 for international students. Applications are processed on a rolling basis. Application fee: $60. Electronic applications accepted. *Financial support:* In 2018–19, 110 research assistantships, 15 teaching assistantships were awarded; fellowships with tuition reimbursements, career-related internships or fieldwork, and Federal Work-Study also available. Support available to part-time students. Financial award application deadline: 4/1; financial award applicants required to submit FAFSA. *Unit head:* Dr. Brian Primack, Dean, E-mail: bprimack@uark.edu. *Application contact:* Dr. Brian Primack, Dean, E-mail: bprimack@uark.edu.
Website: http://coehp.uark.edu/

University of Arkansas at Little Rock, Graduate School, College of Education and Health Professions, Little Rock, AR 72204-1099. Offers M Ed, MA, MS, MSW, Ed D, Ed S, Graduate Certificate. *Accreditation:* CORE; NCATE (one or more programs are accredited). *Program availability:* Part-time, evening/weekend. *Degree requirements:* For doctorate, comprehensive exam, oral defense of dissertation, residency; for other advanced degree, comprehensive exam. *Entrance requirements:* For master's, minimum GPA of 2.75; for doctorate, GRE General Test or MAT, minimum graduate GPA of 3.0, teaching certificate, work experience; for other advanced degree, GRE General Test or MAT, teaching certificate.

University of Arkansas at Monticello, School of Education, Monticello, AR 71656. Offers education (M Ed, MAT); educational leadership (M Ed). *Accreditation:* NCATE. *Program availability:* Part-time, evening/weekend, online learning. *Degree requirements:* For master's, comprehensive exam. *Entrance requirements:* For master's, minimum GPA of 3.0. Additional exam requirements/recommendations for international students: Required—TOEFL (minimum score 550 paper-based). Electronic applications accepted.

University of Arkansas at Pine Bluff, School of Education, Pine Bluff, AR 71601-2799. Offers elementary education (M Ed); secondary education (M Ed), including English education, mathematics education, science education, social studies education; teaching (MAT). *Accreditation:* NCATE. *Program availability:* Part-time, evening/weekend. *Degree requirements:* For master's, comprehensive exam. *Entrance requirements:* For master's, GRE, minimum GPA of 2.75, NTE or Standard Arkansas Teaching Certificate. *Faculty research:* Teacher certification, accreditation, assessment, standards, portfolio development, rehabilitation, technology.

University of Bridgeport, School of Education, Department of Education, Bridgeport, CT 06604. Offers education (MS); educational management (Ed D, Diploma), including intermediate administrator or supervisor (Diploma), leadership (Ed D); elementary education (MS, Diploma), including early childhood education, elementary education; middle school education (MS); music education (MS); remedial reading and language arts (Diploma); secondary education (MS, Diploma), including computer specialist (Diploma), international education (Diploma), reading specialist, secondary education. *Program availability:* Part-time, evening/weekend. *Degree requirements:* For master's, final exam, final project, or thesis; for doctorate, comprehensive exam, thesis/dissertation; for Diploma, thesis or alternative, final project. *Entrance requirements:* For master's, minimum undergraduate QPA of 2.67; for doctorate, GRE, MAT; for Diploma, GRE General Test or MAT, minimum graduate QPA of 3.0. Additional exam requirements/recommendations for international students: Recommended—TOEFL (minimum score 550 paper-based; 80 iBT), IELTS (minimum score 6.5). Electronic applications accepted. *Expenses:* Contact institution.

The University of British Columbia, Faculty of Education, Vancouver, BC V6T1Z4, Canada. Offers M Ed, M Kin, M Sc, MA, MET, MHPCTL, Ed D, PhD, Diploma. *Program availability:* Part-time, evening/weekend, online learning. Terminal master's awarded for partial completion of doctoral program. *Degree requirements:* For master's, thesis (for some programs); for doctorate, comprehensive exam, thesis/dissertation. *Entrance requirements:* Additional exam requirements/recommendations for international students: Required—TOEFL. Electronic applications accepted. *Expenses:* Contact institution. *Faculty research:* Curriculum and pedagogy; school counseling psychology; educational administration; human kinetics; language and literacy education.

University of California, Berkeley, Graduate Division, School of Education, Berkeley, CA 94720. Offers MA, PhD, MA/Credential, PhD/Credential, PhD/MA. Terminal master's awarded for partial completion of doctoral program. *Degree requirements:* For master's, exam or thesis; for doctorate, thesis/dissertation, oral qualifying exam (PhD). *Entrance requirements:* For master's and doctorate, GRE General Test, minimum undergraduate GPA of 3.0 during last 2 years, 3 letters of recommendation. Electronic applications accepted. *Faculty research:* Cognition and development; language, literacy and culture.

University of California, Berkeley, UC Berkeley Extension, Certificate Programs in Education, Berkeley, CA 94720. Offers college admissions and career planning (Certificate); teaching English as a second language (Certificate).

University of California, Davis, Graduate Studies, Graduate Group in Education, Davis, CA 95616. Offers education (MA, Ed D); instructional studies (PhD); psychological studies (PhD); sociocultural studies (PhD). Ed D offered jointly with California State University, Fresno. Terminal master's awarded for partial completion of doctoral program. *Degree requirements:* For master's, comprehensive exam (for some programs), thesis (for some programs); for doctorate, thesis/dissertation. *Entrance requirements:* For master's and doctorate, GRE. Additional exam requirements/recommendations for international students: Required—TOEFL (minimum score 550 paper-based). Electronic applications accepted. *Faculty research:* Language and literacy, mathematics education, science education, teacher development, school psychology.

University of California, Irvine, School of Education, Irvine, CA 92697. Offers educational administration (Ed D); educational administration and leadership (Ed D); elementary and secondary education (MAT). *Program availability:* Part-time, evening/weekend. *Students:* 213 full-time (155 women), 3 part-time (2 women); includes 107 minority (1 Black or African American, non-Hispanic/Latino; 51 Asian, non-Hispanic/Latino; 40 Hispanic/Latino; 15 Two or more races, non-Hispanic/Latino), 23 international. Average age 28. 482 applicants, 47% accepted, 148 enrolled. In 2018, 141 master's, 8 doctorates awarded. *Entrance requirements:* For master's, GRE, minimum GPA of 3.0; for doctorate, GRE General Test, minimum GPA of 3.0. Additional exam requirements/recommendations for international students: Required—TOEFL (minimum score 550 paper-based). *Application deadline:* For fall admission, 1/2 priority date for domestic students, 1/2 for international students. Application fee: $105 ($125 for international students). Electronic applications accepted. *Financial support:* Fellowships, research assistantships with full tuition reimbursements, institutionally sponsored loans, traineeships, health care benefits, and unspecified assistantships available. Financial award application deadline: 3/1; financial award applicants required to submit FAFSA. *Faculty research:* Education technology, learning theory, social theory, cultural diversity, postmodernism. *Unit head:* Richard Arum, Dean, 949-824-2534, E-mail: richard.arum@uci.edu. *Application contact:* Denise Earley, Assistant Director of Student Affairs, 949-824-4022, E-mail: denise.earley@uci.edu.
Website: http://education.uci.edu/

University of California, Los Angeles, Graduate Division, Graduate School of Education and Information Studies, Department of Education, Los Angeles, CA 90095. Offers M Ed, MA, Ed D, PhD. *Program availability:* Evening/weekend. *Degree requirements:* For master's, comprehensive exam; for doctorate, thesis/dissertation, oral and written qualifying exams. *Entrance requirements:* For master's, GRE General Test, minimum GPA of 3.0; for doctorate, GRE General Test, minimum undergraduate GPA of 3.0. Additional exam requirements/recommendations for international students: Required—TOEFL (minimum score 560 paper-based; 87 iBT). Electronic applications accepted.

University of California, Riverside, Graduate Division, Graduate School of Education, Riverside, CA 92521. Offers applied behavior analysis (M Ed); diversity and equity (M Ed); education policy analysis and leadership (PhD); education specialist (Credential); education, society, and culture (MA, PhD); educational psychology (MA, PhD); general education (M Ed); higher education administration and policy (M Ed, PhD); multiple subject (Credential); research, evaluation, measurement and statistics (MA); school psychology (PhD); single subject (Credential); special education (M Ed, PhD); special education and autism (MA); TESOL (M Ed). Terminal master's awarded for partial completion of doctoral program. *Degree requirements:* For master's, comprehensive exams or thesis (MA), case study or analytical report (M Ed); for doctorate, comprehensive exam, thesis/dissertation, written and oral qualifying exams, college teaching practicum. *Entrance requirements:* For master's, GRE General Test (for MA); CBEST and CSET (for M Ed in general education only), UCR Extension TESOL certificate (for M Ed with TESOL emphasis only); for doctorate, GRE General Test, writing sample; for Credential, CBEST, CSET. Additional exam requirements/recommendations for international students: Required—TOEFL (minimum score 550 paper-based; 80 iBT), IELTS (minimum score 7). Electronic applications accepted. *Faculty research:* Responsiveness to intervention, faculty core, response to intervention of English language learners, advanced modeling techniques, study on social capital, trust, and motivation.

University of California, San Diego, Graduate Division, Program in Education Studies, La Jolla, CA 92093. Offers education (M Ed, PhD); educational leadership (Ed D); teaching and learning (MA, Ed D), including bilingual education (MA), curriculum design (MA). Ed D offered jointly with California State University, San Marcos. *Students:* 100 full-time (78 women), 61 part-time (41 women). 262 applicants, 54% accepted, 81 enrolled. In 2018, 75 master's, 15 doctorates awarded. *Degree requirements:* For master's, thesis (for some programs), student teaching; for doctorate, comprehensive exam, thesis/dissertation. *Entrance requirements:* For master's, GRE General Test; CBEST and appropriate CSET exam (for select tracks), current teaching or educational assignment (for select tracks); for doctorate, GRE General Test, current teaching or educational assignment (for select tracks). Additional exam requirements/recommendations for international students: Required—TOEFL (minimum score 550 paper-based; 80 iBT), IELTS (minimum score 7). *Application deadline:* For fall admission, 12/6 for domestic students. Application fee: $105 ($125 for international students). Electronic applications accepted. *Financial support:* Fellowships, career-related internships or fieldwork, and scholarships/grants available. Financial award applicants required to submit FAFSA. *Faculty research:* Language, culture and literacy development of deaf/hard of hearing children; equity issues in education; educational reform; evaluation, assessment, and research methodologies; distributed learning. *Unit head:* Carolyn Hofstetter, Chair, 858-822-6688, E-mail: ajdaly@ucsd.edu. *Application contact:* Giselle Van Luit, Graduate Coordinator, 858-534-2958, E-mail: edsinfo@ucsd.edu.

University of California, Santa Barbara, Graduate Division, Gevirtz Graduate School of Education, Santa Barbara, CA 93106-9490. Offers counseling, clinical and school psychology (MA, PhD, Credential), including clinical psychology (PhD), counseling psychology (MA, PhD), pupil personnel services (Credential), school psychology (PhD); education (MA, PhD); teacher education (M Ed, Credential), including multiple subject teaching (Credential), single subject teaching (Credential), special education (Credential), teaching (M Ed); MA/PhD. *Accreditation:* APA (one or more programs are accredited). Terminal master's awarded for partial completion of doctoral program. *Degree requirements:* For master's, comprehensive exam (for some programs), thesis (for some programs); for doctorate, comprehensive exam (for some programs), thesis/dissertation. *Entrance requirements:* For master's and doctorate, GRE; for Credential, GRE or MAT, CSET, CBEST. Additional exam requirements/recommendations for international students: Required—TOEFL (minimum score 550 paper-based; 80 iBT), IELTS (minimum score 7). Electronic applications accepted. *Faculty research:* Needs of diverse students, school accountability and leadership, school violence, language learning and literacy, science/math education.

University of California, Santa Cruz, Division of Graduate Studies, Division of Social Sciences, Department of Education, Santa Cruz, CA 95064. Offers MA, PhD. Terminal master's awarded for partial completion of doctoral program. *Degree requirements:* For master's, thesis; for doctorate, thesis/dissertation. *Entrance requirements:* Additional exam requirements/recommendations for international students: Required—TOEFL (minimum score 550 paper-based; 83 iBT); Recommended—IELTS (minimum score 8). Electronic applications accepted. *Faculty research:* Bilingual/multicultural education, special education, curriculum and instruction, child development, gaps in the learning opportunities of underserved students, discovery of more effective practices.

University of Central Arkansas, Graduate School, College of Education, Conway, AR 72035-0001. Offers MAT, MS, MSE, Ed S, Graduate Certificate, PMC. *Accreditation:* NCATE. *Program availability:* Part-time, evening/weekend, online learning. Terminal master's awarded for partial completion of doctoral program. *Degree requirements:* For master's, comprehensive exam, thesis optional, portfolio. *Entrance requirements:* For master's, GRE General Test, minimum GPA of 2.7. Additional exam requirements/recommendations for international students: Required—TOEFL (minimum score 550 paper-based; 80 iBT). Electronic applications accepted.

University of Central Arkansas, Graduate School, College of Education, Department of Teaching and Learning, Graduate Program in Teaching, Conway, AR 72035-0001. Offers MAT. *Program availability:* Part-time, online learning. *Degree requirements:* For master's, comprehensive exam, thesis optional. *Entrance requirements:* For master's, GRE General Test, minimum GPA of 2.7. Additional exam requirements/recommendations for international students: Required—TOEFL (minimum score 550 paper-based). Electronic applications accepted.

Education—General

University of Central Arkansas, Graduate School, College of Education, Department of Teaching and Learning, Program in Advanced Studies of Teaching and Learning, Conway, AR 72035-0001. Offers MSE. *Program availability:* Evening/weekend, online learning. *Entrance requirements:* For master's, GRE General Test, minimum GPA of 2.7. Additional exam requirements/recommendations for international students: Required—TOEFL (minimum score 550 paper-based). Electronic applications accepted.

University of Central Missouri, The Graduate School, Warrensburg, MO 64093. Offers accountancy (MA); accounting (MBA); applied mathematics (MS); aviation safety (MA); biology (MS); business administration (MBA); career and technical education leadership (MS); college student personnel administration (MS); communication (MA); computer science (MS); counseling (MS); criminal justice (MS); educational leadership (Ed D); educational technology (MS); elementary and early childhood education (MSE); English (MA); environmental studies (MA); finance (MBA); history (MA); human services/educational technology (Ed S); human services/learning resources (Ed S); human services/professional counseling (Ed S); industrial hygiene (MS); industrial management (MS); information systems (MBA); information technology (MS); kinesiology (MS); library science and information services (MS); literacy education (MSE); marketing (MBA); mathematics (MS); music (MA); occupational safety management (MS); psychology (MS); rural family nursing (MS); school administration (MSE); social gerontology (MS); sociology (MA); special education (MSE); speech language pathology (MS); superintendency (Ed S); teaching (MAT); teaching English as a second language (MA); technology (MS); technology management (PhD); theatre (MA). *Accreditation:* ASHA. *Program availability:* Part-time, 100% online, blended/hybrid learning. *Degree requirements:* For master's and Ed S, comprehensive exam (for some programs), thesis (for some programs). *Entrance requirements:* Additional exam requirements/recommendations for international students: Required—TOEFL (minimum score 550 paper-based; 79 iBT). Electronic applications accepted.

University of Central Oklahoma, The Jackson College of Graduate Studies, College of Education and Professional Studies, Edmond, OK 73034-5209. Offers M Ed, MA, MS. *Accreditation:* NCATE. *Program availability:* Part-time. *Degree requirements:* For master's, comprehensive exam (for some programs), thesis (for some programs). *Entrance requirements:* For master's, GRE. Additional exam requirements/recommendations for international students: Required—TOEFL (minimum score 550 paper-based; 79 iBT), IELTS (minimum score 6.5). Electronic applications accepted.

University of Cincinnati, Graduate School, College of Education, Criminal Justice, and Human Services, Cincinnati, OH 45221. Offers M Ed, MA, MS, Ed D, PhD, CAGS, Certificate, Ed S, Graduate Certificate. *Accreditation:* NCATE. *Program availability:* Part-time, online learning. *Degree requirements:* For master's, comprehensive exam (for some programs), thesis (for some programs); for doctorate, comprehensive exam, thesis/dissertation. *Entrance requirements:* For master's and doctorate, GRE. Additional exam requirements/recommendations for international students: Required—TOEFL (minimum score 550 paper-based), OEPT 3. Electronic applications accepted. *Faculty research:* Alcohol and drug prevention, family-based prevention, criminal justice, literacy, urban education.

University of Colorado Boulder, Graduate School, School of Education, Boulder, CO 80309. Offers MA, PhD. *Accreditation:* NCATE. Terminal master's awarded for partial completion of doctoral program. *Degree requirements:* For master's, comprehensive exam, thesis or alternative; for doctorate, one foreign language, comprehensive exam, thesis/dissertation. *Entrance requirements:* For master's, GRE General Test or MAT, minimum undergraduate GPA of 2.75; for doctorate, GRE General Test. Electronic applications accepted. Application fee is waived when completed online. *Faculty research:* Teacher education; educational reform; literacy; equal educational opportunity; minority education.

University of Colorado Colorado Springs, College of Education, Colorado Springs, CO 80918. Offers counseling and human services (MA); curriculum and instruction (MA); educational leadership (MA); educational leadership, research and policy (PhD); special education (MA); teaching English to speakers of other languages (MA). *Accreditation:* ACA; NCATE. *Program availability:* Part-time, evening/weekend, 100% online, blended/hybrid learning. *Faculty:* 31 full-time (22 women), 61 part-time/adjunct (47 women). *Students:* 208 full-time (149 women), 351 part-time (256 women); includes 136 minority (30 Black or African American, non-Hispanic/Latino; 1 American Indian or Alaska Native, non-Hispanic/Latino; 12 Asian, non-Hispanic/Latino; 64 Hispanic/Latino; 29 Two or more races, non-Hispanic/Latino), 8 international. Average age 36. 230 applicants, 80% accepted, 101 enrolled. In 2018, 186 master's, 9 doctorates awarded. *Degree requirements:* For master's, comprehensive exam, thesis or alternative, microcomputer proficiency; for doctorate, comprehensive exam, thesis/dissertation, research lab. *Entrance requirements:* For master's, GRE General Test (recommended but not required), career goal statement, professional references; for doctorate, GRE General Test. Additional exam requirements/recommendations for international students: Recommended—TOEFL (minimum score 90 iBT), IELTS (minimum score 6.5). *Application deadline:* For fall admission, 1/28 priority date for domestic and international students; for spring admission, 11/1 priority date for domestic and international students. Applications are processed on a rolling basis. Application fee: $60 ($100 for international students). Electronic applications accepted. *Expenses:* Tuition and fees vary by program, course load, and residency type. Please visit the University of Colorado Colorado Springs Student Financial Services website to estimate current program costs: https://www.uccs.edu/bursar/index.php/estimate-your-bill. *Financial support:* In 2018–19, 15 students received support. Career-related internships or fieldwork, Federal Work-Study, scholarships/grants, and unspecified assistantships available. Support available to part-time students. Financial award application deadline: 3/1; financial award applicants required to submit FAFSA. *Faculty research:* Linguistically diverse education (LDE), educational policy, evidence-based reading and writing instruction, relational and social aggression, positive behavior supports, inclusive schooling, K-12 education policy. *Total annual research expenditures:* $607,967. *Unit head:* Dr. Valerie Martin Conley, Dean, 719-255-4133, E-mail: vmconley@uccs.edu. *Application contact:* The College of Education Student Resource Office, 719-255-4996, E-mail: education@uccs.edu.
Website: https://www.uccs.edu/coe/

University of Colorado Denver, School of Education and Human Development, Denver, CO 80217-3364. Offers MA, MS Ed, Ed D, PhD, Psy D, Ed S. *Accreditation:* NCATE. *Program availability:* Part-time, evening/weekend, online learning. *Students:* 896 full-time (724 women), 397 part-time (323 women); includes 323 minority (59 Black or African American, non-Hispanic/Latino; 5 American Indian or Alaska Native, non-Hispanic/Latino; 35 Asian, non-Hispanic/Latino; 190 Hispanic/Latino; 3 Native Hawaiian or other Pacific Islander, non-Hispanic/Latino; 31 Two or more races, non-Hispanic/Latino), 25 international. Average age 35. 803 applicants, 44% accepted, 275 enrolled. In 2018, 505 master's, 29 doctorates, 6 other advanced degrees awarded. *Degree requirements:* For master's and Ed S, comprehensive exam (for some programs); for doctorate, comprehensive exam, thesis/dissertation. *Entrance requirements:* Additional exam requirements/recommendations for international students: Required—TOEFL (minimum score 537 paper-based; 75 iBT); Recommended—IELTS (minimum score 6.5). Application fee: $0. Electronic applications accepted. *Expenses:* Tuition, state resident: full-time $6786; part-time $337 per credit hour. Tuition, nonresident: full-time $22,590; part-time $1255 per credit hour. *Required fees:* $1231; $137 per credit hour. Tuition and fees vary according to program and reciprocity agreements. *Financial support:* In 2018–19, 215 students received support. *Faculty research:* Educational equity: race, class, culture, power and privilege; analytic approaches to educational program effectiveness and measuring student learning; early childhood special education/early intervention policies; recruiting and retention of African-American teachers; secondary and postsecondary institutions; accountability systems to improve public education. *Total annual research expenditures:* $11.9 million. *Unit head:* Rebecca Kantor, Dean, 303-315-6343, E-mail: rebecca.kantor@ucdenver.edu. *Application contact:* Student Services Center, 303-315-6300, Fax: 303-315-6311, E-mail: education@ucdenver.edu.
Website: http://www.ucdenver.edu/academics/colleges/SchoolOfEducation/Pages/home.aspx

University of Connecticut, Graduate School, Neag School of Education, Storrs, CT 06269. Offers MA, PhD. *Accreditation:* NCATE. Terminal master's awarded for partial completion of doctoral program. *Degree requirements:* For master's, comprehensive exam, thesis or alternative; for doctorate, thesis/dissertation. *Entrance requirements:* For doctorate, GRE General Test. Additional exam requirements/recommendations for international students: Required—TOEFL (minimum score 550 paper-based). Electronic applications accepted.

University of Delaware, College of Education and Human Development, School of Education, Newark, DE 19716. Offers education (PhD); educational leadership (Ed D); higher education (M Ed); instruction (MI); reading (M Ed); school leadership (M Ed); school psychology (MA, Ed S); teaching English as a second language (TESL) (MA). *Accreditation:* NCATE. *Program availability:* Part-time, evening/weekend. Terminal master's awarded for partial completion of doctoral program. *Degree requirements:* For master's, comprehensive exam (for some programs), thesis (for some programs); for doctorate, comprehensive exam (for some programs), thesis/dissertation. *Entrance requirements:* For master's and doctorate, GRE, 3 letters of recommendation. Additional exam requirements/recommendations for international students: Required—TOEFL (minimum score 600 paper-based). Electronic applications accepted. *Faculty research:* Teacher education; curriculum theory and development; community based education models, educational leadership.

University of Denver, Morgridge College of Education, Denver, CO 80208. Offers child, family and school psychology (MA, PhD, Ed S); counseling psychology (MA, PhD); curriculum and instruction (MA, Ed D, PhD); curriculum instruction and teaching (Certificate); early childhood special education (MA, Certificate); educational leadership and policy studies (MA, Ed D, PhD, Certificate); higher education (Ed D, PhD); library and information science (MLIS); research methods and statistics (MA, PhD). *Accreditation:* ALA; APA (one or more programs are accredited). *Program availability:* Part-time, evening/weekend, online learning. *Faculty:* 49 full-time (35 women), 33 part-time/adjunct (20 women). *Students:* 509 full-time (400 women), 365 part-time (277 women); includes 236 minority (53 Black or African American, non-Hispanic/Latino; 6 American Indian or Alaska Native, non-Hispanic/Latino; 28 Asian, non-Hispanic/Latino; 116 Hispanic/Latino; 33 Two or more races, non-Hispanic/Latino), 56 international. Average age 31. 1,372 applicants, 57% accepted, 382 enrolled. In 2018, 258 master's, 41 doctorates, 162 other advanced degrees awarded. Terminal master's awarded for partial completion of doctoral program. *Degree requirements:* For master's, comprehensive exam (for some programs); for doctorate, comprehensive exam (for some programs), thesis/dissertation. *Entrance requirements:* For master's, GRE General Test or GMAT, bachelors degree; transcripts; two letters of recommendation; personal statement; resume; for doctorate, GRE General Test or GMAT, Masters degree; transcripts; two letters of recommendation; personal statement(s); resume. Additional exam requirements/recommendations for international students: Required—TOEFL (minimum score 550 paper-based; 80 iBT). *Application deadline:* Applications are processed on a rolling basis. Application fee: $65. Electronic applications accepted. *Expenses:* $33,183 per year full-time. *Financial support:* In 2018–19, 690 students received support, including 29 research assistantships with tuition reimbursements available (averaging $11,465 per year), 9 teaching assistantships with tuition reimbursements available (averaging $2,527 per year); career-related internships or fieldwork, Federal Work-Study, institutionally sponsored loans, scholarships/grants, and unspecified assistantships also available. Support available to part-time students. Financial award application deadline: 2/15; financial award applicants required to submit FAFSA. *Faculty research:* Early childhood education, educational leadership, access and opportunity to postsecondary education, marriage and family therapy, data management and archival research. *Total annual research expenditures:* $2.3 million. *Unit head:* Dr. Karen Riley, Dean, 303-871-3665, E-mail: karen.riley@du.edu. *Application contact:* Jodi Dye, Director of Admissions, 303-871-2510, E-mail: jodi.dye@du.edu.
Website: http://morgridge.du.edu

The University of Findlay, Office of Graduate Admissions, Findlay, OH 45840-3653. Offers applied security and analytics (MSAS); athletic training (MAT); business (MBA), including certified management accountant, certified public accountant, health care management, hospitality management; education (MA Ed, Ed D), including children's literature (MA Ed), curriculum and teaching (MA Ed), education (MA Ed), educational administration (MA Ed), human resource development (MA Ed), mathematics (MA Ed), reading (MA Ed), science education (MA Ed), superintendent (Ed D), teaching (Ed D), technology (MA Ed); environmental, safety, and health management (MSEM); health informatics (MS); occupational therapy (MOT); pharmacy (Pharm D); physical therapy (DPT); physician assistant (MPA); rhetoric and writing (MA); teaching English to speakers of other languages (TESOL) and applied linguistics (MA). *Program availability:* Part-time, evening/weekend, 100% online, blended/hybrid learning. *Degree requirements:* For master's, comprehensive exam (for some programs), thesis (for some programs), cumulative project, capstone project; for doctorate, thesis/dissertation (for some programs). *Entrance requirements:* For master's, GRE/GMAT, bachelor's degree from accredited institution, minimum undergraduate GPA of 2.5 in last 64 hours of course work; for doctorate, GRE, MAT, minimum cumulative GPA of 3.0. Additional exam requirements/recommendations for international students: Required—TOEFL (minimum score 79 iBT), IELTS (minimum score 7), PTE (minimum score 61). Electronic applications accepted.

University of Florida, Graduate School, College of Education, Gainesville, FL 32611. Offers M Ed, MAE, Ed D, PhD, Ed S, PhD/JD. *Accreditation:* NCATE. *Program availability:* Part-time, evening/weekend, online learning. Terminal master's awarded for partial completion of doctoral program. *Degree requirements:* For master's, comprehensive exam (for some programs), thesis (for some programs); for doctorate, comprehensive exam (for some programs), thesis/dissertation (for some programs), capstone project. *Entrance requirements:* For master's and doctorate, GRE General Test, minimum GPA of 3.0; for Ed S, GRE General Test. Additional exam requirements/recommendations for international students: Required—TOEFL (minimum score 550 paper-based; 80 iBT), IELTS (minimum score 6). Electronic applications accepted. *Faculty research:* Early childhood, teacher education, educator professional development, learning and intervention sciences, educational leadership and policy.

University of Georgia, College of Education, Athens, GA 30602. Offers M Ed, MA, MA Ed, MAT, MS, Ed D, PhD, Ed S. *Accreditation:* NCATE. *Degree requirements:* For doctorate, thesis/dissertation. *Entrance requirements:* For doctorate, GRE General Test. Electronic applications accepted.

University of Guam, Office of Graduate Studies, School of Education, Mangilao, GU 96923. Offers M Ed, MA. *Accreditation:* NCATE. *Program availability:* Part-time. *Degree requirements:* For master's, comprehensive oral and written exams. *Entrance requirements:* For master's, GRE General Test. Additional exam requirements/recommendations for international students: Required—TOEFL. *Faculty research:* Multicultural issues, computerized student advising.

University of Hartford, College of Education, Nursing, and Health Professions, West Hartford, CT 06117-1599. Offers M Ed, MS, MSN, MSPT, DPT, Ed D, CAGS, Sixth Year Certificate. *Accreditation:* NCATE. *Program availability:* Part-time, evening/weekend. *Degree requirements:* For doctorate, thesis/dissertation; for other advanced degree, comprehensive exam or research project. *Entrance requirements:* For doctorate, MAT. Additional exam requirements/recommendations for international students: Required—TOEFL (minimum score 550 paper-based). Electronic applications accepted. *Expenses:* Contact institution.

University of Hawaii at Hilo, Program in Education, Hilo, HI 96720-4091. Offers M Ed. *Program availability:* Part-time, evening/weekend. *Entrance requirements:* Additional exam requirements/recommendations for international students: Required—TOEFL, IELTS. Electronic applications accepted.

University of Hawaii at Hilo, Program in Teaching, Hilo, HI 96720-4091. Offers MA. *Entrance requirements:* Additional exam requirements/recommendations for international students: Required—TOEFL, IELTS. Electronic applications accepted.

University of Hawaii at Manoa, Office of Graduate Education, College of Education, Honolulu, HI 96822. Offers M Ed, M Ed T, MS, Ed D, PhD, Graduate Certificate. *Accreditation:* NCATE. *Program availability:* Part-time, evening/weekend. *Entrance requirements:* Additional exam requirements/recommendations for international students: Required—TOEFL or IELTS.

University of Holy Cross, Graduate Programs, New Orleans, LA 70131-7399. Offers biomedical sciences (MS); Catholic theology (MA); counseling (MA, PhD), including community counseling (MA), marriage and family counseling (MA), school counseling (MA); educational leadership (M Ed); executive leadership (Ed D); management (MS), including healthcare management, operations management; teaching and learning (M Ed). *Accreditation:* ACA; NCATE. *Program availability:* Part-time, evening/weekend, online learning. *Degree requirements:* For master's, thesis. *Entrance requirements:* For master's, GRE General Test, minimum GPA of 2.7.

University of Houston, College of Education, Houston, TX 77204-5023. Offers administration & supervision (M Ed); counseling psychology (PhD); professional leadership (Ed D), including health science education, k-12, literacy, mathematics, social studies, special populations. None. *Accreditation:* NCATE. *Program availability:* Part-time, evening/weekend, 100% online, blended/hybrid learning. *Faculty:* 89 full-time (64 women), 9 part-time/adjunct (5 women). *Students:* 388 full-time (314 women), 543 part-time (409 women); includes 535 minority (219 Black or African American, non-Hispanic/Latino; 5 American Indian or Alaska Native, non-Hispanic/Latino; 64 Asian, non-Hispanic/Latino; 225 Hispanic/Latino; 1 Native Hawaiian or other Pacific Islander, non-Hispanic/Latino; 21 Two or more races, non-Hispanic/Latino), 49 international. Average age 35. 614 applicants, 73% accepted, 227 enrolled. In 2018, 167 master's, 72 doctorates awarded. Terminal master's awarded for partial completion of doctoral program. *Degree requirements:* For master's, comprehensive exam or thesis; for doctorate, comprehensive exam, thesis/dissertation. *Entrance requirements:* For master's, GRE General Test, transcripts, 3 letters of recommendation, curriculum vita, goal statement; for doctorate, GRE General Test, transcripts, 3 letters of recommendation, curriculum vita, goal statement, writing sample, interview. Additional exam requirements/recommendations for international students: Required—TOEFL (minimum score 550 paper-based; 79 iBT). Application fee: $80 ($75 for international students). Electronic applications accepted. Application fee is waived when completed online. *Financial support:* In 2018–19, 34 students received support, including 2 fellowships with full tuition reimbursements available (averaging $2,000 per year), 17 research assistantships with full tuition reimbursements available (averaging $8,634 per year), 82 teaching assistantships with full tuition reimbursements available (averaging $8,697 per year); career-related internships or fieldwork, Federal Work-Study, institutionally sponsored loans, scholarships/grants, health care benefits, and unspecified assistantships also available. Support available to part-time students. Financial award application deadline: 2/1; financial award applicants required to submit FAFSA. *Faculty research:* Education policy, student access and success, school leadership, health disparities, mental health. *Total annual research expenditures:* $3.8 million. *Unit head:* Dr. Robert H. McPherson, Dean, 713-743-5003, Fax: 713-743-9870, E-mail: bmcph@uh.edu. *Application contact:* Bridgette Jones, Director of Student Affairs, 713-743-2978, E-mail: bajones5@uh.edu.
Website: http://www.coe.uh.edu

University of Houston–Clear Lake, School of Education, Houston, TX 77058-1002. Offers MS, Ed D. *Accreditation:* NCATE. *Program availability:* Part-time, evening/weekend. *Degree requirements:* For master's, thesis optional; for doctorate, comprehensive exam, thesis/dissertation. *Entrance requirements:* For master's, GRE or minimum GPA of 3.0 in last 60 hours; for doctorate, GRE, master's degree, letters of reference. Additional exam requirements/recommendations for international students: Required—TOEFL (minimum score 550 paper-based). Electronic applications accepted.

University of Houston–Victoria, School of Education, Health Professions and Human Development, Victoria, TX 77901-4450. Offers administration and supervision (M Ed); adult and higher education (M Ed); counselor education (M Ed); curriculum and instruction (M Ed); dyslexia education (Certificate); educational technology (M Ed); special education (M Ed). *Program availability:* Part-time, evening/weekend, online learning. *Degree requirements:* For master's, comprehensive exam, project or thesis. *Entrance requirements:* For master's, GRE General Test. Additional exam requirements/recommendations for international students: Required—TOEFL. Electronic applications accepted. *Expenses:* Tuition, area resident: Full-time $6154; part-time $3077 per semester. Tuition, state resident: full-time $6154; part-time $3077 per semester. Tuition, nonresident: full-time $13,624; part-time $6812 per semester. *International tuition:* $13,624 full-time. *Required fees:* $1405; $847 per semester. $423 per semester. Tuition and fees vary according to program. *Faculty research:* Reading and language arts education, evaluation and diagnosis of special children's abilities.

University of Idaho, College of Graduate Studies, College of Education, Health and Human Sciences, Moscow, ID 83844-3080. Offers M Ed, MS, MSAT, DAT, Ed D, PhD, Ed S. *Accreditation:* NCATE. *Faculty:* 57 full-time, 6 part-time/adjunct. *Students:* 175 full-time (102 women), 216 part-time (136 women). Average age 35. 221 applicants, 83% accepted, 130 enrolled. In 2018, 128 master's, 14 doctorates, 33 other advanced degrees awarded. *Degree requirements:* For doctorate, thesis/dissertation. *Entrance requirements:* For master's, minimum GPA of 3.0. Additional exam requirements/recommendations for international students: Required—TOEFL. *Application deadline:* For fall admission, 8/1 for domestic students; for spring admission, 12/15 for domestic

students. Applications are processed on a rolling basis. Application fee: $60. Electronic applications accepted. *Expenses:* Tuition, state resident: full-time $7266.44; part-time $474.50 per credit hour. Tuition, nonresident: full-time $24,902; part-time $1453.50 per credit hour. *Required fees:* $2085.56; $45.50 per credit hour. *Financial support:* Teaching assistantships and Federal Work-Study available. Support available to part-time students. Financial award applicants required to submit FAFSA. *Faculty research:* Technology integration, curricular development for cooperative environments, increasing science literacy, best practices for online pedagogy. *Unit head:* Dr. Alison Carr-Chellman, Dean, 208-885-6772, E-mail: ehhs@uidaho.edu. *Application contact:* Dr. Alison Carr-Chellman, Dean, 208-885-6772, E-mail: ehhs@uidaho.edu.
Website: http://www.uidaho.edu/ed/

University of Illinois at Chicago, College of Education, Chicago, IL 60607-7128. Offers M Ed, Ed D, PhD. *Program availability:* Part-time, evening/weekend. Terminal master's awarded for partial completion of doctoral program. *Degree requirements:* For doctorate, thesis/dissertation. *Entrance requirements:* For master's, minimum GPA of 2.75; for doctorate, GRE General Test, minimum GPA of 2.75. Additional exam requirements/recommendations for international students: Required—TOEFL. Electronic applications accepted. *Faculty research:* Teaching and learning, program design, school and classroom organization with emphasis on urban settings.

University of Illinois at Springfield, Graduate Programs, College of Education and Human Services, Springfield, IL 62703-5407. Offers MA, CAS, Certificate, Graduate Certificate. *Program availability:* Part-time, evening/weekend, 100% online, blended/hybrid learning. *Faculty:* 22 full-time (14 women), 12 part-time/adjunct (9 women). *Students:* 59 full-time (50 women), 204 part-time (155 women); includes 64 minority (42 Black or African American, non-Hispanic/Latino; 1 Asian, non-Hispanic/Latino; 12 Hispanic/Latino; 9 Two or more races, non-Hispanic/Latino), 5 international. Average age 32. 146 applicants, 42% accepted, 53 enrolled. In 2018, 72 master's, 4 other advanced degrees awarded. *Entrance requirements:* Additional exam requirements/recommendations for international students: Required—TOEFL (minimum score 500 paper-based; 61 iBT). *Application deadline:* Applications are processed on a rolling basis. Application fee: $60 ($75 for international students). Electronic applications accepted. *Financial support:* In 2018–19, research assistantships with full tuition reimbursements (averaging $10,384 per year), teaching assistantships with full tuition reimbursements (averaging $10,303 per year) were awarded; fellowships, career-related internships or fieldwork, Federal Work-Study, scholarships/grants, health care benefits, and unspecified assistantships also available. Support available to part-time students. Financial award application deadline: 11/15; financial award applicants required to submit FAFSA. *Unit head:* Dr. Hanfu Mi, Dean, 217-206-6784, Fax: 217-206-6775, E-mail: hmi2@uis.edu. *Application contact:* Dr. Hanfu Mi, Dean, 217-206-6784, Fax: 217-206-6775, E-mail: hmi2@uis.edu.
Website: cehs@uis.edu

University of Illinois at Urbana–Champaign, Graduate College, College of Education, Champaign, IL 61820. Offers Ed M, MA, MS, Ed D, PhD, CAS. *Program availability:* Part-time, online learning.

University of Indianapolis, Graduate Programs, School of Education, Indianapolis, IN 46227-3697. Offers art education (MAT); biology (MAT); chemistry (MAT); curriculum and instruction (MA); earth sciences (MAT); education (MA, MAT); educational leadership (MA); elementary education (MA); English (MAT); French (MAT); math (MAT); physical education (MAT); physics (MAT); secondary education (MA), including art education, education, English education, social studies education; social studies (MAT); Spanish (MAT). *Accreditation:* NCATE. *Program availability:* Part-time, evening/weekend. *Entrance requirements:* For master's, GRE Subject Test, PRAXIS I, minimum GPA of 2.5, 3 letters of recommendation, interview. Additional exam requirements/recommendations for international students: Required—TOEFL (minimum score 550 paper-based). *Faculty research:* Assessment of teacher education, perceptions of prospective teachers by parents.

The University of Iowa, Graduate College, College of Education, Iowa City, IA 52242-1316. Offers MA, MAT, MM, PhD, Ed S. *Degree requirements:* For master's and Ed S, exam; for doctorate, comprehensive exam, thesis/dissertation. *Entrance requirements:* For master's, doctorate, and Ed S, GRE General Test, minimum GPA of 3.0. Additional exam requirements/recommendations for international students: Required—TOEFL (minimum score 550 paper-based; 81 iBT). Electronic applications accepted. *Faculty research:* Computer-assisted instrumentation, testing and measurement, instructional design.

University of Jamestown, Program in Education, Jamestown, ND 58405. Offers curriculum and instruction (M Ed). *Degree requirements:* For master's, thesis or project.

The University of Kansas, Graduate Studies, School of Education, Lawrence, KS 66045-3101. Offers MA, MS, MS Ed, MSE, Ed D, PhD, Certificate, Ed S. *Accreditation:* NCATE. *Program availability:* Part-time, online learning. *Students:* 487 full-time (315 women), 745 part-time (576 women); includes 222 minority (79 Black or African American, non-Hispanic/Latino; 8 American Indian or Alaska Native, non-Hispanic/Latino; 31 Asian, non-Hispanic/Latino; 60 Hispanic/Latino; 1 Native Hawaiian or other Pacific Islander, non-Hispanic/Latino; 43 Two or more races, non-Hispanic/Latino), 104 international. Average age 33. 821 applicants, 71% accepted, 416 enrolled. In 2018, 446 master's, 77 doctorates, 110 other advanced degrees awarded. *Entrance requirements:* For master's and other advanced degree, minimum GPA of 3.0; for doctorate, GRE General Test. Additional exam requirements/recommendations for international students: Required—TOEFL, IELTS. Application fee: $65 ($85 for international students). Electronic applications accepted. *Financial support:* Fellowships, research assistantships, teaching assistantships, career-related internships or fieldwork, scholarships/grants, and unspecified assistantships available. Financial award application deadline: 2/1. *Unit head:* Dr. Rick J. Ginsberg, Dean, 785-864-4297, E-mail: ginsberg@ku.edu. *Application contact:* Kim Huggett, Graduate Student Services Manager, 785-864-4510, E-mail: khuggett@ku.edu.
Website: http://www.soe.ku.edu/

University of Kentucky, Graduate School, College of Education, Lexington, KY 40506-0032. Offers M Ed, MA Ed, MRC, MS, MS Ed, Ed D, PhD, Ed S. *Accreditation:* NCATE. *Program availability:* Part-time, evening/weekend. Terminal master's awarded for partial completion of doctoral program. *Degree requirements:* For master's and Ed S, comprehensive exam; for doctorate, comprehensive exam, thesis/dissertation. *Entrance requirements:* For master's, GRE General Test, minimum undergraduate GPA of 2.75; for doctorate, GRE General Test, minimum graduate GPA of 3.0; for Ed S, GRE General Test. Additional exam requirements/recommendations for international students: Required—TOEFL (minimum score 550 paper-based). Electronic applications accepted.

University of La Verne, LaFetra College of Education, Credential Program in Teacher Education, La Verne, CA 91750-4443. Offers multiple subject (Credential); single subject (Credential); teaching (Credential). *Accreditation:* NCATE. *Program availability:* Part-time. *Entrance requirements:* For degree, California Basic Educational Skills Test, minimum GPA of 3.0, interview, writing sample. Additional exam requirements/recommendations for international students: Required—TOEFL (minimum score 550 paper-based). *Expenses:* Contact institution.

Education—General

University of La Verne, LaFetra College of Education, Master of Arts in Teaching Program, La Verne, CA 91750-4443. Offers MA. *Entrance requirements:* Additional exam requirements/recommendations for international students: Required—TOEFL (minimum score 550 paper-based; 80 iBT), IELTS (minimum score 6.5). Electronic applications accepted.

University of La Verne, LaFetra College of Education, Master's Program in Education, La Verne, CA 91750-4443. Offers advanced teaching skills (M Ed); education (M Ed); educational leadership (M Ed); special emphasis (M Ed). *Accreditation:* NCATE. *Program availability:* Part-time. *Entrance requirements:* For master's, California Basic Educational Skills Test, interview, writing sample, minimum GPA of 3.0, 3 letters of recommendation. Additional exam requirements/recommendations for international students: Required—TOEFL (minimum score 550 paper-based). *Expenses:* Contact institution.

University of La Verne, Regional and Online Campuses, Graduate Credential Program in Education, California Statewide Campus, La Verne, CA 91750-4443. Offers administration services (preliminary) (Credential); education specialist: mild/moderate (Credential); English (Certificate); multiple subject teaching (Credential); pupil personnel services: school counseling (Credential); single subject teaching (Credential); special education (MS); special emphasis (M Ed). *Accreditation:* NCATE. *Program availability:* Part-time. *Entrance requirements:* For degree, California Basic Educational Skills Test, minimum undergraduate GPA of 2.75, 3 letters of recommendation, interview. *Expenses:* Contact institution.

University of La Verne, Regional and Online Campuses, Master's Programs in Education, California Statewide Campus, La Verne, CA 91750-4443. Offers administration services (preliminary) (Credential); education specialist: mild/moderate (Credential); educational counseling (MS); educational leadership (M Ed); multiple subject teaching (Credential); pupil personnel services: school counseling (Credential); single subject teaching (Credential); special education studies (MS); special emphasis (M Ed). *Accreditation:* NCATE. *Entrance requirements:* For master's, California Basic Educational Skills Test, 3 letters of recommendation, teaching credential. *Expenses:* Contact institution.

University of Lethbridge, School of Graduate Studies, Lethbridge, AB T1K 3M4, Canada. Offers addictions counseling (M Sc); agricultural biotechnology (M Sc); agricultural studies (M Sc, MA); anthropology (MA); archaeology (M Sc, MA); art (MA, MFA); biochemistry (M Sc); biological sciences (M Sc); biomolecular science (PhD); biosystems and biodiversity (PhD); Canadian studies (MA); chemistry (M Sc); computer science (M Sc); computer science and geographical information science (M Sc); counseling (MC); counseling psychology (M Ed); dramatic arts (MA); earth, space, and physical science (PhD); economics (MA); education (MA, PhD); educational leadership (M Ed); English (MA); environmental science (M Sc); evolution and behavior (PhD); exercise science (M Sc); French (MA); French/German (MA); French/Spanish (MA); general education (M Ed); geography (M Sc, MA); German (MA); health sciences (M Sc); individualized multidisciplinary (M Sc, MA); kinesiology (M Sc, MA); management (M Sc), including accounting, finance, human resource management and labor relations, information systems, international management, marketing, policy and strategy; mathematics (M Sc); music (M Mus, MA); Native American studies (MA); neuroscience (M Sc, PhD); new media (MA, MFA); nursing (M Sc, MN); philosophy (MA); physics (M Sc); political science (MA); psychology (M Sc, MA); religious studies (MA); sociology (MA); theatre and dramatic arts (MFA); theoretical and computational science (PhD); urban and regional studies (MA); women and gender studies (MA). *Program availability:* Part-time, evening/weekend. *Degree requirements:* For master's, thesis (for some programs); for doctorate, comprehensive exam, thesis/dissertation. *Entrance requirements:* For master's, GMAT (for M Sc in management), bachelor's degree in related field, minimum GPA of 3.0 during previous 20 graded semester courses, 2 years' teaching or related experience (M Ed); for doctorate, master's degree, minimum graduate GPA of 3.5. Additional exam requirements/recommendations for international students: Required—TOEFL (minimum score 580 paper-based; 93 iBT). Electronic applications accepted. *Faculty research:* Movement and brain plasticity, gibberellin physiology, photosynthesis, carbon cycling, molecular properties of main-group ring components.

University of Louisiana at Lafayette, College of Education, Lafayette, LA 70504. Offers M Ed, MS, Ed D. *Accreditation:* NCATE. *Program availability:* Part-time. *Entrance requirements:* For master's, GRE General Test, teaching certificate. Additional exam requirements/recommendations for international students: Required—TOEFL (minimum score 550 paper-based). Electronic applications accepted.

University of Louisiana at Monroe, Graduate School, College of Arts, Education, and Sciences, School of Education, Monroe, LA 71209-0001. Offers M Ed, MAT, Ed D. *Accreditation:* NCATE. *Program availability:* Part-time, evening/weekend, online learning. *Faculty:* 11 full-time (7 women). *Students:* 27 full-time (25 women), 116 part-time (95 women); includes 36 minority (25 Black or African American, non-Hispanic/Latino; 1 Asian, non-Hispanic/Latino; 5 Hispanic/Latino; 5 Two or more races, non-Hispanic/Latino). Average age 34. 67 applicants, 79% accepted, 37 enrolled. In 2018, 36 master's awarded. *Degree requirements:* For master's, thesis; for doctorate, comprehensive exam, thesis/dissertation. *Entrance requirements:* For master's, GRE General Test, PRAXIS, minimum GPA of 2.5; for doctorate, GRE General Test, minimum undergraduate GPA of 2.75, 3.25 graduate; 3 letters of recommendation; interview. Additional exam requirements/recommendations for international students: Required—TOEFL (minimum score 500 paper-based; 61 iBT). *Application deadline:* For fall admission, 8/24 priority date for domestic students, 7/1 for international students; for winter admission, 12/14 priority date for domestic students; for spring admission, 1/19 for domestic students, 11/1 for international students. Applications are processed on a rolling basis. Application fee: $20 ($30 for international students). Electronic applications accepted. *Financial support:* In 2018–19, 27 students received support. Research assistantships, career-related internships or fieldwork, Federal Work-Study, and unspecified assistantships available. Financial award application deadline: 4/1; financial award applicants required to submit FAFSA. Website: http://www.ulm.edu/education/index.html

University of Louisville, Graduate School, College of Education and Human Development, Louisville, KY 40292-0001. Offers M Ed, MA, MAT, MS, Ed D, PhD, Certificate, Ed S. *Accreditation:* NCATE. *Program availability:* Part-time, evening/weekend, 100% online, blended/hybrid learning. *Faculty:* 97 full-time (64 women), 131 part-time/adjunct (86 women). *Students:* 475 full-time (272 women), 669 part-time (389 women); includes 309 minority (178 Black or African American, non-Hispanic/Latino; 2 American Indian or Alaska Native, non-Hispanic/Latino; 25 Asian, non-Hispanic/Latino; 64 Hispanic/Latino; 2 Native Hawaiian or other Pacific Islander, non-Hispanic/Latino; 38 Two or more races, non-Hispanic/Latino), 18 international. Average age 33. 586 applicants, 66% accepted, 304 enrolled. In 2018, 235 master's, 10 doctorates, 22 other advanced degrees awarded. Terminal master's awarded for partial completion of doctoral program. *Degree requirements:* For master's, comprehensive exam (for some programs), thesis optional; for doctorate, comprehensive exam (for some programs), thesis/dissertation. *Entrance requirements:* For master's, GRE for most programs, PRAXIS for educator preparation programs, professional statement, recommendation letters, resume, transcripts; for doctorate and other advanced degree, GRE,

professional statement, recommendation letters, resume, transcripts. Additional exam requirements/recommendations for international students: Required—TOEFL (minimum score 550 paper-based; 79 iBT); Recommended—IELTS (minimum score 6.5). *Application deadline:* For fall admission, 6/1 priority date for domestic students, 5/1 priority date for international students; for spring admission, 10/1 priority date for domestic students, 11/1 priority date for international students; for summer admission, 3/1 priority date for domestic students, 4/1 priority date for international students. Application fee: $65. *Expenses:* Tuition, area resident: Full-time $6500; part-time $723 per credit hour. Tuition, state resident: full-time $6500. Tuition, nonresident: full-time $13,557; part-time $1507 per credit hour. Tuition and fees vary according to course load and program. *Financial support:* In 2018–19, 5 fellowships with full tuition reimbursements (averaging $21,024 per year), 32 research assistantships with full tuition reimbursements (averaging $21,024 per year), 18 teaching assistantships with full tuition reimbursements (averaging $21,024 per year) were awarded; Federal Work-Study, scholarships/grants, health care benefits, tuition waivers (full), and unspecified assistantships also available. Financial award application deadline: 3/1; financial award applicants required to submit FAFSA. *Faculty research:* Teacher preparation and P-12 school partnerships, Behavioral and psychological intervention and supports in P-20 settings, Teacher capacities in effective STEM instruction and assessment, Understanding workplace systems and cultures, trends in management of sport organizations and sport performance. *Total annual research expenditures:* $4.2 million. *Unit head:* Dr. Amy A. Lingo, Interim Dean, 502-852-3235, E-mail: cehdinfo@louisville.edu. *Application contact:* Margaret Penetcost, Assistant Dean for Graduate Student Success, 502-852-6437, Fax: 502-852-1417, E-mail: gedadm@louisville.edu. Website: http://www.louisville.edu/education

University of Maine, Graduate School, College of Education and Human Development, Orono, ME 04469. Offers M Ed, MA, MAT, MS, Ed D, PhD, CAS, CGS. *Accreditation:* NCATE. *Program availability:* Part-time, evening/weekend. *Faculty:* 35 full-time (19 women), 47 part-time/adjunct (34 women). *Students:* 194 full-time (154 women), 290 part-time (235 women); includes 21 minority (7 Black or African American, non-Hispanic/Latino; 4 American Indian or Alaska Native, non-Hispanic/Latino; 6 Asian, non-Hispanic/Latino; 3 Hispanic/Latino; 1 Two or more races, non-Hispanic/Latino), 4 international. Average age 37. 318 applicants, 93% accepted, 206 enrolled. In 2018, 103 master's, 6 doctorates, 59 other advanced degrees awarded. Terminal master's awarded for partial completion of doctoral program. *Degree requirements:* For master's, thesis (for some programs); for doctorate, comprehensive exam, thesis/dissertation. *Entrance requirements:* For master's, GRE General Test, MAT; for doctorate, GRE General Test; for other advanced degree, MA, M Ed, or MS. Additional exam requirements/recommendations for international students: Required—TOEFL (minimum score 550 paper-based; 80 iBT), IELTS (minimum score 6.5). *Application deadline:* For fall admission, 1/15 priority date for domestic students. Applications are processed on a rolling basis. Application fee: $65. Electronic applications accepted. *Financial support:* In 2018–19, 18 students received support, including 9 teaching assistantships with full tuition reimbursements available (averaging $15,200 per year); career-related internships or fieldwork, Federal Work-Study, institutionally sponsored loans, scholarships/grants, and unspecified assistantships also available. Support available to part-time students. Financial award application deadline: 3/1. *Faculty research:* Student hazing and hazing prevention epidemiology and birth defects prevention theories of science thinking and learning using writing to improve performance in athletics rural poverty and education. *Total annual research expenditures:* $3.5 million. *Unit head:* Dr. Timothy Reagan, Dean, 207-581-2441, Fax: 207-581-2423. *Application contact:* Scott G. Delcourt, Senior Associate Dean of the Graduate School, 207-581-3291, Fax: 207-581-3232, E-mail: graduate@maine.edu. Website: http://umaine.edu/edhd/

University of Maine at Farmington, Graduate Programs in Education, Farmington, ME 04938. Offers early childhood education (MS Ed); educational leadership (MS Ed); instructional technology (M Ed). M Ed offered in collaboration with University of Maine and University of Southern Maine. *Accreditation:* NCATE. *Program availability:* Part-time-only, evening/weekend, 100% online, blended/hybrid learning. *Degree requirements:* For master's, thesis, capstone research project. *Entrance requirements:* For master's, baccalaureate degree from accredited institution, valid teaching certificate or professional experience in education. Additional exam requirements/recommendations for international students: Required—TOEFL. Electronic applications accepted. *Expenses:* Contact institution. *Faculty research:* Teacher leadership, school improvement strategies, technology integration.

The University of Manchester, Manchester Institute of Education, Manchester, United Kingdom. Offers counseling (D Couns); counseling psychology (D Couns); education (M Phil, Ed D, PhD); educational and child psychology (Ed D); educational psychology (Ed D).

University of Manitoba, Faculty of Graduate Studies, College Universitaire de Saint Boniface, Education Program—Saint-Boniface, Winnipeg, MB R3T 2N2, Canada. Offers M Ed.

University of Manitoba, Faculty of Graduate Studies, Faculty of Education, Winnipeg, MB R3T 2N2, Canada. Offers M Ed, PhD. *Degree requirements:* For master's, thesis or alternative.

University of Mary, Liffrig Family School of Education and Behavioral Sciences, Department of Education, Bismarck, ND 58504-9652. Offers curriculum, instruction and assessment (M Ed); education (Ed D); elementary administration (M Ed); reading (M Ed); secondary administration (M Ed); special education strategist (M Ed). *Program availability:* Part-time. *Degree requirements:* For master's, portfolio or thesis. *Entrance requirements:* For master's, interview, letters of reference, minimum GPA of 2.5. Additional exam requirements/recommendations for international students: Required—TOEFL (minimum score 500 paper-based; 71 iBT). Electronic applications accepted.

University of Mary Hardin-Baylor, Graduate Studies in Education, Belton, TX 76513. Offers curriculum and instruction (M Ed); educational administration (M Ed, Ed D), including higher education (Ed D), leadership in nursing education (Ed D), P-12 (Ed D). *Program availability:* Part-time, evening/weekend. *Degree requirements:* For master's, comprehensive exam; for doctorate, thesis/dissertation. *Entrance requirements:* For master's, minimum GPA of 3.0, interview; for doctorate, minimum GPA of 3.5, interview, essay, resume, employment verification, 3 letters of recommendation. Additional exam requirements/recommendations for international students: Required—TOEFL (minimum score 60 iBT), IELTS (minimum score 4.5). Electronic applications accepted. *Expenses:* Contact institution. *Faculty research:* Motivational orientation of preservice teachers.

University of Maryland, Baltimore County, The Graduate School, College of Arts, Humanities and Social Sciences, Department of Education, Baltimore, MD 21250. Offers education (MAE, MAE), including K-8 mathematics instructional leadership (MAE), K-8 science education (MAE), K-8 STEM education (MAE), secondary science education (MAE), secondary STEM education (MAE); instructional systems development (MA, Graduate Certificate), including distance education (Graduate Certificate), instructional systems development, instructional technology (Graduate Certificate); teaching (MAT), including early childhood education, elementary education, teaching; teaching English to speakers of other languages (MA, Postbaccalaureate Certificate). *Accreditation:* NCATE.

Program availability: Part-time, evening/weekend, online learning. *Degree requirements:* For master's, comprehensive exam (for some programs), thesis (for some programs). *Entrance requirements:* For master's, GRE General Test, GRE Subject Test (for MA in TESOL); PRAXIS Core Examination or GRE with minimum score of 1000 (for MAT); PRAXIS II (for MAE), minimum GPA of 3.0. Additional exam requirements/recommendations for international students: Required—TOEFL. Electronic applications accepted. *Faculty research:* Teacher leadership; STEM education; ESOL/bilingual education; early childhood education; language, literacy and culture.

University of Maryland, College Park, Academic Affairs, College of Education, College Park, MD 20742. Offers M Ed, MA, Ed D, PhD, AGSC, CAGS. *Accreditation:* NCATE. *Program availability:* Part-time, evening/weekend, online learning. *Degree requirements:* For doctorate, thesis/dissertation. *Entrance requirements:* For master's, GRE General Test or MAT, minimum GPA of 3.0. Electronic applications accepted.

University of Maryland Eastern Shore, Graduate Programs, Department of Education, Program in Teaching, Princess Anne, MD 21853. Offers MAT. Program offered jointly with Salisbury University. *Accreditation:* NCATE. *Degree requirements:* For master's, comprehensive exam, internship, seminar paper, PRAXIS II. *Entrance requirements:* For master's, PRAXIS I, interview, minimum GPA of 3.0, writing sample. Additional exam requirements/recommendations for international students: Required—TOEFL (minimum score 80 iBT). Electronic applications accepted.

University of Maryland University College, The Graduate School, Master of Arts in Teaching Program, Adelphi, MD 20783. Offers MAT. *Program availability:* Part-time, evening/weekend. *Students:* 7 full-time (4 women), 102 part-time (59 women); includes 38 minority (16 Black or African American, non-Hispanic/Latino; 4 Asian, non-Hispanic/Latino; 13 Hispanic/Latino; 5 Two or more races, non-Hispanic/Latino), 2 international. Average age 33. 50 applicants, 100% accepted, 20 enrolled. In 2018, 36 master's awarded. *Degree requirements:* For master's, comprehensive exam, thesis or alternative. *Application deadline:* Applications are processed on a rolling basis. Application fee: $50. Electronic applications accepted. *Financial support:* Scholarships/grants available. Support available to part-time students. Financial award application deadline: 6/1; financial award applicants required to submit FAFSA. *Unit head:* Warna Gillies, Program Chair, 240-684-2400, E-mail: warna.gillies@umuc.edu. *Application contact:* Admissions, 800-888-8682, E-mail: studentsfirst@umuc.edu.
Website: https://www.umuc.edu/academic-programs/masters-degrees/teaching.cfm

University of Mary Washington, College of Education, Fredericksburg, VA 22401. Offers education (M Ed); elementary education (MS). *Program availability:* Part-time, evening/weekend. *Degree requirements:* For master's, one foreign language, comprehensive exam (for some programs). *Entrance requirements:* For master's, PRAXIS Core Academic Skills for Educators (Reading; Writing; Math or Virginia Department of Education accepted equivalent). Additional exam requirements/recommendations for international students: Required—TOEFL (minimum score 570 paper-based; 88 iBT), IELTS (minimum score 6.5). Electronic applications accepted. Application fee is waived when completed online. *Expenses:* Contact institution.

University of Massachusetts Amherst, Graduate School, College of Education, Amherst, MA 01003. Offers M Ed, Ed D, PhD, Ed S. *Accreditation:* NCATE. *Program availability:* Part-time, online learning. Terminal master's awarded for partial completion of doctoral program. *Degree requirements:* For doctorate, comprehensive exam, thesis/dissertation. *Entrance requirements:* Additional exam requirements/recommendations for international students: Required—TOEFL (minimum score 550 paper-based; 80 iBT), IELTS (minimum score 6.5). Electronic applications accepted.

University of Massachusetts Boston, College of Education and Human Development, Boston, MA 02125-3393. Offers M Ed, MS, Ed D, PhD, CAGS. *Program availability:* Part-time, evening/weekend. *Faculty:* 50 full-time (35 women), 42 part-time/adjunct (31 women). *Students:* 339 full-time (269 women), 384 part-time (280 women); includes 21 minority (10 Black or African American, non-Hispanic/Latino; 6 Asian, non-Hispanic/Latino; 5 Hispanic/Latino), 1 international. Average age 33. 779 applicants, 56% accepted, 300 enrolled. In 2018, 226 master's, 16 doctorates, 43 other advanced degrees awarded. *Degree requirements:* For master's, comprehensive exam; for doctorate, comprehensive exam, thesis/dissertation. *Entrance requirements:* For master's, GRE General Test or MAT; for doctorate, GRE General Test or MAT, minimum GPA of 2.75; for CAGS, minimum GPA of 2.75. *Application deadline:* For fall admission, 3/1 for domestic students. Application fee: $60 ($100 for international students). Electronic applications accepted. *Expenses: Tuition, area resident:* Full-time $17,896. Tuition, state resident: full-time $17,896. Tuition, nonresident: full-time $34,932. International tuition: $34,932 full-time. *Required fees:* $355. *Financial support:* Research assistantships, teaching assistantships, career-related internships or fieldwork, Federal Work-Study, and unspecified assistantships available. Support available to part-time students. Financial award application deadline: 3/1; financial award applicants required to submit FAFSA. *Faculty research:* Effects of ethnicity on applied psychology and education, enhancing equity and excellence in public schools, diversity and change in higher education, improving the functioning of individuals with disabilities. *Unit head:* Dr. Joseph B Berger, Dean, 617-287-7600, E-mail: Joseph.Berger@umb.edu. *Application contact:* Graduate Admissions Coordinator, 617-287-6400, Fax: 617-287-6236, E-mail: graduate.admissions@umb.edu.
Website: http://www.umb.edu/academics/cehd

University of Massachusetts Dartmouth, Graduate School, College of Arts and Sciences, School of Education, North Dartmouth, MA 02747-2300. Offers educational leadership (Ed D, PhD), including educational leadership and policy studies; STEM education and teacher development (MAT, PhD, Postbaccalaureate Certificate), including English as a second language (Postbaccalaureate Certificate), mathematics education (PhD), middle school education (MAT), secondary school education (MAT). *Program availability:* Part-time, online learning. *Faculty:* 13 full-time (6 women), 4 part-time/adjunct (3 women). *Students:* 28 full-time (24 women), 120 part-time (64 women); includes 32 minority (7 Black or African American, non-Hispanic/Latino; 1 American Indian or Alaska Native, non-Hispanic/Latino; 3 Asian, non-Hispanic/Latino; 15 Hispanic/Latino; 6 Two or more races, non-Hispanic/Latino), 4 international. Average age 39. 50 applicants, 88% accepted, 36 enrolled. In 2018, 77 master's, 6 doctorates, 1 other advanced degree awarded. *Degree requirements:* For doctorate, comprehensive exam, thesis/dissertation. *Entrance requirements:* For master's, Statement of Purpose, 2 letters of recommendation, Resume, Official transcripts, copy of MA MTELs, Professional Licensure Program (requires proof of license); for doctorate, GRE or GMAT, Statement of Purpose, Resume, Official Tanscripts, 3 letters of recommendation, Scholarly writing samples (min. 10 pages); for Postbaccalaureate Certificate, Statement of Purpose, Resume, Official Transcripts, 2 letters of recommendation, MTEL Score report. Additional exam requirements/recommendations for international students: Required—TOEFL (minimum score 550 paper-based; 79 iBT), IELTS (minimum score 6.5). Application fee: $60. Electronic applications accepted. *Financial support:* In 2018–19, 2 fellowships (averaging $21,000 per year), 3 research assistantships (averaging $10,692 per year), 6 teaching assistantships (averaging $8,017 per year) were awarded; tuition waivers (full) and doctoral support, dissertation writing support also available. *Faculty research:* Sociology of education, urban education, curriculum theory, mindfulness in education, literacies, assessment of teacher knowledge. *Total annual research expenditures:* $1.9 million. *Unit head:* Amy Shapiro, Associate Dean, College of Arts and Sciences, 508-910-9101, Fax:

508-999-9125, E-mail: ashapiro@umassd.edu. *Application contact:* Scott Webster, Director of Graduate Studies and Admissions, 508-999-8604, Fax: 508-999-8183, E-mail: graduate@umassd.edu.
Website: http://www.umassd.edu/cas/schoolofeducation

University of Massachusetts Lowell, Graduate School of Education, Lowell, MA 01854. Offers curriculum and instruction (M Ed). *Accreditation:* NCATE. *Program availability:* Part-time, evening/weekend, online learning. Terminal master's awarded for partial completion of doctoral program. *Entrance requirements:* For master's, GRE General Test. Additional exam requirements/recommendations for international students: Required—TOEFL. Electronic applications accepted.

University of Memphis, Graduate School, College of Education, Memphis, TN 38152. Offers M Ed, MAT, MS, Ed D, PhD, Graduate Certificate. *Accreditation:* NCATE. *Program availability:* Part-time, evening/weekend, 100% online, blended/hybrid learning. *Faculty:* 60 full-time (38 women), 28 part-time/adjunct (18 women). *Students:* 219 full-time (172 women), 689 part-time (521 women); includes 396 minority (337 Black or African American, non-Hispanic/Latino; 1 American Indian or Alaska Native, non-Hispanic/Latino; 13 Asian, non-Hispanic/Latino; 32 Hispanic/Latino; 13 Two or more races, non-Hispanic/Latino), 10 international. Average age 35. 344 applicants, 83% accepted, 240 enrolled. In 2018, 163 master's, 49 doctorates, 63 other advanced degrees awarded. Terminal master's awarded for partial completion of doctoral program. *Degree requirements:* For master's, comprehensive exam, thesis or alternative, practicum; for doctorate, comprehensive exam, thesis/dissertation, residency project, internship (for some). *Entrance requirements:* For master's, GRE General Test or MAT; for doctorate, GRE General Test, writing sample, interview, letters of reference; for Graduate Certificate, letters of reference. Additional exam requirements/recommendations for international students: Required—TOEFL (minimum score 550 paper-based; 79 iBT). *Application deadline:* Applications are processed on a rolling basis. Application fee: $35 ($60 for international students). Electronic applications accepted. *Expenses: Tuition, area resident:* Full-time $10,240; part-time $503 per credit hour. Tuition, state resident: full-time $10,464. Tuition, nonresident: full-time $20,224; part-time $991 per credit hour. *Required fees:* $850; $106 per credit hour. *Financial support:* Research assistantships with full tuition reimbursements, teaching assistantships with full tuition reimbursements, career-related internships or fieldwork, Federal Work-Study, scholarships/grants, tuition waivers (partial), and unspecified assistantships available. Financial award application deadline: 2/1; financial award applicants required to submit FAFSA. *Faculty research:* Urban school effectiveness, literacy development, teacher effectiveness, exercise physiology, crisis counseling. *Unit head:* Dr. Kandi Hill-Clarke, Dean, 901-678-5495, Fax: 901-678-4778, E-mail: k.hill-clarke@memphis.edu. *Application contact:* Stormey Warren, Graduate Programs, 901-678-2363, Fax: 901-678-4778, E-mail: shutsell@memphis.edu.
Website: https://www.memphis.edu/education/

University of Miami, Graduate School, School of Education and Human Development, Coral Gables, FL 33124. Offers MS Ed, Ed D, PhD, Certificate, Ed S. *Program availability:* Online only, 100% online. *Faculty:* 78 full-time (42 women), 38 part-time/adjunct (23 women). *Students:* 314 full-time (164 women), 131 part-time (88 women); includes 239 minority (84 Black or African American, non-Hispanic/Latino; 2 American Indian or Alaska Native, non-Hispanic/Latino; 11 Asian, non-Hispanic/Latino; 127 Hispanic/Latino; 15 Two or more races, non-Hispanic/Latino), 39 international. Average age 30. 560 applicants, 54% accepted, 177 enrolled. In 2018, 192 master's, 25 doctorates, 2 other advanced degrees awarded. Terminal master's awarded for partial completion of doctoral program. *Degree requirements:* For master's, comprehensive exam (for some programs), thesis optional, electronic portfolio, special project, personal growth experience; for doctorate, thesis/dissertation, qualifying exam, portfolio. *Entrance requirements:* For master's and doctorate, GRE General Test. Additional exam requirements/recommendations for international students: Required—TOEFL (minimum score 550 paper-based; 80 iBT); Recommended—IELTS (minimum score 6.5). *Application deadline:* For fall admission, 10/1 for international students. Application fee: $85. Electronic applications accepted. *Financial support:* Fellowships, research assistantships, teaching assistantships, career-related internships or fieldwork, institutionally sponsored loans, scholarships/grants, health care benefits, tuition waivers (full and partial), and unspecified assistantships available. Support available to part-time students. Financial award application deadline: 3/1; financial award applicants required to submit FAFSA. *Faculty research:* Social skills and learning disabilities, planning for mainstreamed pupils, alcohol and drug abuse, restructuring education for all learners, transition in special education and juvenile justice education, special education research and policy, family and multicultural issues. *Unit head:* Dr. Walter Secada, Vice Dean, 305-284-2102, Fax: 305-284-9395, E-mail: wsecada@miami.edu. *Application contact:* Lois Heffernan, Graduate Admissions Coordinator, 305-284-2167, Fax: 305-284-9395, E-mail: lheffernan@miami.edu.
Website: http://www.education.miami.edu

University of Michigan, Rackham Graduate School, Combined Program in Education and Psychology, Ann Arbor, MI 48109. Offers PhD. *Accreditation:* TEAC. *Faculty:* 21 part-time/adjunct (12 women). *Students:* 33 full-time (25 women); includes 20 minority (12 Black or African American, non-Hispanic/Latino; 2 Asian, non-Hispanic/Latino; 6 Hispanic/Latino). Average age 27. 98 applicants, 8% accepted, 7 enrolled. In 2018, 3 doctorates awarded. *Degree requirements:* For doctorate, thesis/dissertation, independent research project, preliminary exam, oral defense of dissertation. *Entrance requirements:* For doctorate, GRE General Test with Analytical Writing Test. Additional exam requirements/recommendations for international students: Required—TOEFL (minimum score 600 paper-based; 100 iBT). *Application deadline:* For fall admission, 12/1 for domestic and international students. Application fee: $75. Electronic applications accepted. *Expenses:* Tuition: precandidate level 3 years; candidate level 2 years; registration fees 10 terms total. *Financial support:* In 2018–19, 33 students received support, including 20 fellowships with full tuition reimbursements available (averaging $29,605 per year), 2 research assistantships with full tuition reimbursements available (averaging $27,737 per year), 44 teaching assistantships with full tuition reimbursements available (averaging $27,737 per year); institutionally sponsored loans, scholarships/grants, health care benefits, and unspecified assistantships also available. Financial award application deadline: 4/15. *Faculty research:* Human development in context of schools, families, communities; cognitive and learning sciences; motivation and self-regulated learning; culture, ethnicity, social and class influences on learning and motivation. *Unit head:* Dr. Allison Ryan, Chair, 734-647-0626, Fax: 734-615-2164, E-mail: aliryan@umich.edu. *Application contact:* Christina Zigulis, Program Coordinator, 734-763-0680, Fax: 734-615-2164, E-mail: cpep@umich.edu.
Website: http://www.soe.umich.edu/academics/doctoral_programs/ep/

University of Michigan, School of Education, Ann Arbor, MI 48109-1259. Offers MA, MS, PhD, MA/Certification, MBA/MA, MPP/MA, PhD/MA. *Accreditation:* TEAC. Terminal master's awarded for partial completion of doctoral program. *Degree requirements:* For master's, thesis optional; for doctorate, comprehensive exam, thesis/dissertation. *Entrance requirements:* For master's and doctorate, GRE General Test. Additional exam requirements/recommendations for international students: Required—TOEFL (minimum score 560 paper-based). Electronic applications accepted. *Faculty research:* Teaching, learning, policy, leadership, technology.

Education—General

University of Michigan–Dearborn, College of Education, Health, and Human Services, Master of Arts in Teaching Program, Dearborn, MI 48126-2638. Offers MAT. *Accreditation:* TEAC. *Program availability:* Part-time, evening/weekend. *Faculty:* 9 full-time (5 women), 8 part-time/adjunct (5 women). *Students:* 9 full-time (7 women), 3 part-time (all women); includes 2 minority (1 Black or African American, non-Hispanic/Latino; 1 Hispanic/Latino). Average age 33. 11 applicants, 45% accepted, 2 enrolled. In 2018, 2 master's awarded. *Entrance requirements:* For master's, minimum cumulative GPA of 3.0, 3 letters of recommendation, statement of purpose. Additional exam requirements/recommendations for international students: Required—TOEFL (minimum score 560 paper-based; 84 iBT), IELTS (minimum score 6.5). *Application deadline:* For fall admission, 8/1 priority date for domestic students, 5/1 priority date for international students; for winter admission, 12/1 priority date for domestic students, 9/1 priority date for international students; for spring admission, 4/1 priority date for domestic students, 1/1 priority date for international students. Applications are processed on a rolling basis. Application fee: $60. Electronic applications accepted. *Expenses:* $12,140 per academic year (typical full-time in-state); $20,708 per academic year (typical full-time out-of-state). *Financial support:* In 2018–19, 2 students received support. Career-related internships or fieldwork and scholarships/grants available. Financial award application deadline: 3/1; financial award applicants required to submit FAFSA. *Faculty research:* Technology and teaching, learning disabilities, pedagogy and interventions, literacy, multiculturalism. *Unit head:* Dr. Paul Fossum, Director, Master's Programs, 313-593-0982, E-mail: pfossum@umich.edu. *Application contact:* Office of Graduate Studies, 313-583-6321, E-mail: umd-graduatestudies@umich.edu.
Website: http://umdearborn.edu/cehhs/cehhs_mat/

University of Michigan–Dearborn, College of Education, Health, and Human Services, Master of Arts Program in Education, Dearborn, MI 48126-2638. Offers MA. *Accreditation:* TEAC. *Program availability:* Part-time, evening/weekend, 100% online. *Faculty:* 7 full-time (6 women), 8 part-time/adjunct (4 women). *Students:* 3 full-time (all women), 56 part-time (50 women); includes 7 minority (2 Black or African American, non-Hispanic/Latino; 3 Asian, non-Hispanic/Latino; 1 Hispanic/Latino; 1 Two or more races, non-Hispanic/Latino), 1 international. Average age 32. 20 applicants, 100% accepted, 13 enrolled. In 2018, 35 master's awarded. *Entrance requirements:* For master's, minimum GPA of 3.0, 3 letters of recommendation, statement of purpose, valid state of Michigan teaching certificate (if seeking an additional endorsement). Additional exam requirements/recommendations for international students: Required—TOEFL (minimum score 560 paper-based; 84 iBT), IELTS (minimum score 6.5). *Application deadline:* For fall admission, 8/1 for domestic students, 5/1 for international students; for winter admission, 12/1 for domestic students, 9/1 for international students; for spring admission, 4/1 for domestic students, 1/1 for international students. Applications are processed on a rolling basis. Application fee: $60. Electronic applications accepted. *Expenses:* $12,140 per academic year (typical full-time in-state); $20,708 per academic year (typical full-time out-of-state). *Financial support:* In 2018–19, 11 students received support. Career-related internships or fieldwork and scholarships/grants available. Financial award application deadline: 3/1; financial award applicants required to submit FAFSA. *Faculty research:* Urban education, literacy, curriculum development, pedagogy and interventions, language acquisition. *Unit head:* Dr. Paul Fossum, Director, Master's Programs, 313-593-0982, E-mail: pfossum@umich.edu. *Application contact:* Office of Graduate Studies, 313-583-6321, E-mail: umd-graduatestudies@umich.edu.
Website: http://umdearborn.edu/cehhs/cehhs_maed/

University of Michigan–Flint, School of Education and Human Services, Flint, MI 48502-1950. Offers MA, Ed D, Ed S. *Program availability:* Part-time, mixed mode format. *Faculty:* 16 full-time (10 women), 28 part-time/adjunct (14 women). *Students:* 31 full-time (23 women), 179 part-time (135 women); includes 54 minority (42 Black or African American, non-Hispanic/Latino; 3 Asian, non-Hispanic/Latino; 4 Hispanic/Latino; 1 Native Hawaiian or other Pacific Islander, non-Hispanic/Latino; 4 Two or more races, non-Hispanic/Latino), 1 international. Average age 39. 133 applicants, 72% accepted, 61 enrolled. In 2018, 60 master's awarded. *Degree requirements:* For master's, thesis optional; for doctorate, thesis/dissertation. *Entrance requirements:* For master's, bachelor's degree from regionally-accredited institution, minimum overall undergraduate GPA of 3.0 on 4.0 scale; for doctorate, completion of EdS from regionally accredited university, minimum GPA of 3.3 on 4.0 scale, or 6.0 on 9.0 scale, or equivalent, at least 3 years work experience in a P-16 educational institution or in an education-related position; for Ed S, MA or MS in an education-related field from accredited institution; minimum overall graduate GPA of 3.0 (6.0 on a 9.0 scale) or equivalent; at least 3 years of work experience in educational setting. Additional exam requirements/recommendations for international students: Required—TOEFL (minimum score 84 iBT), IELTS (minimum score 6.5). *Application deadline:* For fall admission, 7/1 for domestic students, 4/1 for international students; for winter admission, 11/15 for domestic students, 9/1 for international students; for spring admission, 3/15 for domestic students, 1/1 for international students. Applications are processed on a rolling basis. Application fee: $55. Electronic applications accepted. *Expenses:* Contact institution. *Financial support:* Federal Work-Study and unspecified assistantships available. Support available to part-time students. Financial award application deadline: 3/1; financial award applicants required to submit FAFSA. *Unit head:* Dr. Bob Barnett, Dean, 810-766-6878, Fax: 810-766-6891, E-mail: rbarnett@umflint.edu. *Application contact:* Matt Bohlen, Director of Graduate Admissions, 810-762-3171, Fax: 810-766-6789, E-mail: mbohlen@umflint.edu.
Website: http://www.umflint.edu/sehs

University of Minnesota, Duluth, Graduate School, College of Education and Human Service Professions, Department of Education, Duluth, MN 55812-2496. Offers M Ed, Ed D. *Program availability:* Part-time, evening/weekend. *Degree requirements:* For doctorate, comprehensive exam. *Entrance requirements:* For doctorate, GRE, MA (preferred) minimum GPA of 3.0, 3 letters of recommendation, 3 work samples. Additional exam requirements/recommendations for international students: Required—TOEFL (minimum score 550 paper-based).

University of Minnesota, Twin Cities Campus, Graduate School, College of Education and Human Development, Minneapolis, MN 55455-0213. Offers M Ed, MA, MS, MSW, Ed D, PhD, Certificate, Ed S. *Accreditation:* NCATE. *Program availability:* Part-time. *Faculty:* 167 full-time (89 women). *Students:* 1,485 full-time (1,079 women), 571 part-time (404 women); includes 458 minority (119 Black or African American, non-Hispanic/Latino; 12 American Indian or Alaska Native, non-Hispanic/Latino; 123 Asian, non-Hispanic/Latino; 115 Hispanic/Latino; 89 Two or more races, non-Hispanic/Latino), 221 international. Average age 32. 2,070 applicants, 58% accepted, 936 enrolled. In 2018, 765 master's, 113 doctorates, 124 other advanced degrees awarded. Application fee: $75 ($95 for international students). *Financial support:* In 2018–19, 108 fellowships, 249 research assistantships with full tuition reimbursements (averaging $12,642 per year), 223 teaching assistantships with full tuition reimbursements (averaging $12,068 per year) were awarded; scholarships/grants and tuition waivers (partial) also available. Financial award applicants required to submit FAFSA. *Faculty research:* Educational equity and achievement gap; living longer, living better - healthy aging across the lifespan; children's mental health, child welfare; autism spectrum disorders, neurodevelopment, developmental disability. *Total annual research expenditures:* $40.8 million. *Unit head:* Dr. Jean K. Quam, Dean, 612-626-9252, Fax: 612-626-7496, E-mail: jquam@umn.edu. *Application contact:* Schee Moua, Director of Graduate Education, 612-626-7356, E-mail: scmoua@umn.edu.
Website: http://www.cehd.umn.edu

University of Mississippi, Graduate School, School of Education, University, MS 38677. Offers counselor education (M Ed, PhD); counselor education - play therapy (Ed S); early childhood (M Ed); educational leadership K-12 (M Ed, Ed D, PhD, Ed S); elementary education (M Ed, Ed D, Ed S); higher education/student personnel (Ed D, PhD); literacy education (M Ed); math education (Ed D); secondary education (M Ed, PhD, Ed S); special education (M Ed, PhD, Ed S); teacher corporations (MA); teacher education (MA). *Accreditation:* NCATE. *Faculty:* 59 full-time (35 women), 34 part-time/adjunct (26 women). *Students:* 169 full-time (137 women), 461 part-time (329 women); includes 199 minority (185 Black or African American, non-Hispanic/Latino; 3 Asian, non-Hispanic/Latino; 7 Hispanic/Latino; 4 Two or more races, non-Hispanic/Latino), 5 international. Average age 33. In 2018, 180 master's, 57 doctorates, 37 other advanced degrees awarded. *Entrance requirements:* For master's, GRE General Test, minimum GPA of 3.0; for doctorate, GRE General Test. Additional exam requirements/recommendations for international students: Required—TOEFL. *Application deadline:* Applications are processed on a rolling basis. Application fee: $50. Electronic applications accepted. *Financial support:* Scholarships/grants available. Financial award application deadline: 3/1; financial award applicants required to submit FAFSA. *Unit head:* Dr. David Rock, Dean, 662-915-7063, Fax: 662-915-7249, E-mail: soe@olemiss.edu. *Application contact:* Temeka Smith, Graduate Activities Specialist for Admissions, 662-915-7474, Fax: 662-915-7577, E-mail: gschool@olemiss.edu.

University of Missouri, Office of Research and Graduate Studies, College of Education, Columbia, MO 65211. Offers M Ed, MA, Ed D, PhD, Ed S. *Accreditation:* TEAC. *Program availability:* Part-time, evening/weekend. Terminal master's awarded for partial completion of doctoral program. *Entrance requirements:* For master's, minimum GPA of 3.0; for doctorate, GRE General Test. Additional exam requirements/recommendations for international students: Required—TOEFL, IELTS.

University of Missouri–Kansas City, School of Education, Kansas City, MO 64110-2499. Offers administration (Ed D); counseling and guidance (MA, Ed S), including mental health counseling (Ed S), school counseling (Ed S); counseling psychology (PhD); curriculum and instruction (MA, Ed S), including language and literacy (Ed S); education (PhD), including higher education administration, PK-12 education administration; educational administration (MA, Ed S), including advanced principal (Ed S), beginning principal (Ed S), district-level administration (Ed S); reading education (MA); special education (MA). PhD in education offered through the School of Graduate Studies. *Accreditation:* NCATE. *Program availability:* Part-time, evening/weekend. *Degree requirements:* For doctorate, thesis/dissertation, internship, practicum. *Entrance requirements:* For master's, GRE, minimum GPA of 2.75, 2 letters of reference, written statement of purpose; for doctorate, GRE, minimum GPA of 3.0; for Ed S, minimum GPA of 3.0. Additional exam requirements/recommendations for international students: Required—TOEFL (minimum score 550 paper-based; 80 iBT). *Faculty research:* Urban education, inquiry-based field study, theories of counseling and psychotherapy, school literacy, educational technology.

University of Missouri–St. Louis, College of Education, St. Louis, MO 63121. Offers M Ed, Ed D, PhD, Certificate, Ed S. *Accreditation:* NCATE. *Program availability:* Part-time, evening/weekend. *Degree requirements:* For master's, comprehensive exam, thesis optional; for doctorate, thesis/dissertation. *Entrance requirements:* For doctorate, GRE General Test, 3 letters of recommendation. Additional exam requirements/recommendations for international students: Recommended—TOEFL (minimum score 550 paper-based; 79 iBT), IELTS (minimum score 6.5). Electronic applications accepted. *Faculty research:* Remedial reading, literacy, educational policy and research, science education.

University of Mobile, Graduate Studies, School of Education, Mobile, AL 36613. Offers education (MA); higher education leadership and policy (M Ed). *Program availability:* Part-time, 100% online, blended/hybrid learning. *Students:* 30 full-time (28 women); includes 16 minority (13 Black or African American, non-Hispanic/Latino; 2 American Indian or Alaska Native, non-Hispanic/Latino; 1 Asian, non-Hispanic/Latino). 23 applicants, 26% accepted, 12 enrolled. In 2018, 2 master's awarded. *Degree requirements:* For master's, comprehensive exam, thesis optional. *Entrance requirements:* For master's, Alabama teaching certificate if not seeking an Alternative Master's Degree. Additional exam requirements/recommendations for international students: Required—TOEFL (minimum score 550 paper-based; 80 iBT). *Application deadline:* For fall admission, 8/3 priority date for domestic students, 8/3 for international students; for spring admission, 12/23 priority date for domestic students, 12/3 priority date for international students. Applications are processed on a rolling basis. Application fee: $40 ($50 for international students). Electronic applications accepted. *Expenses: Tuition:* Full-time $453; part-time $453 per credit hour. *Required fees:* $320; $320. Tuition and fees vary according to degree level and program. *Financial support:* Application deadline: 8/1; applicants required to submit FAFSA. *Faculty research:* Retention, writing across the curriculum. *Unit head:* Dr. Carolyn D. Corliss, Dean, School of Education, 251-442-2276, Fax: 251-442-2523, E-mail: ccorliss@umobile.edu. *Application contact:* Brian Boyle, Director of Recruitment, 251-442-2727.
Website: http://umobile.edu/school-of-education/master-of-arts-in-education/

University of Montana, Graduate School, Phyllis J. Washington College of Education and Human Sciences, Missoula, MT 59812. Offers M Ed, MA, MS, Ed D, Ed S. *Accreditation:* NCATE. *Program availability:* Part-time. *Degree requirements:* For Ed S, thesis. *Entrance requirements:* For master's, GRE General Test, minimum GPA of 3.0; for Ed S, GRE General Test. Additional exam requirements/recommendations for international students: Required—TOEFL. *Faculty research:* Cooperative learning, administrative styles.

University of Montevallo, College of Education, Montevallo, AL 35115. Offers M Ed, Ed S. *Accreditation:* NCATE. *Program availability:* Part-time, evening/weekend. *Students:* 76 full-time (61 women), 151 part-time (113 women); includes 51 minority (41 Black or African American, non-Hispanic/Latino; 4 Hispanic/Latino; 6 Two or more races, non-Hispanic/Latino), 1 international. In 2018, 114 master's awarded. *Degree requirements:* For master's, comprehensive exam. *Entrance requirements:* For master's, GRE General Test, MAT, minimum undergraduate GPA of 2.5. Additional exam requirements/recommendations for international students: Required—TOEFL (minimum score 550 paper-based). *Application deadline:* For fall admission, 7/15 for domestic students; for spring admission, 11/15 for domestic students. Application fee: $30. *Expenses: Tuition, area resident:* Full-time $10,512. Tuition, state resident: full-time $10,512. Tuition, nonresident: full-time $22,464. *International tuition:* $22,464 full-time. *Financial support:* Federal Work-Study, scholarships/grants, and unspecified assistantships available. *Unit head:* Dr. Charlotte Daughhetee, Interim Dean, 205-665-6360, E-mail: daughc@montevallo.edu. *Application contact:* Colleen Kennedy, Graduate Program Assistant, 205-665-6350, E-mail: ckennedy@montevallo.edu.
Website: http://www.montevallo.edu/education/college-of-education/

University of Nebraska at Kearney, College of Education, Kearney, NE 68849-0001. Offers MA Ed, MS Ed, Ed S. *Accreditation:* NCATE. *Program availability:* Part-time, evening/weekend, 100% online. *Degree requirements:* For master's, comprehensive exam, thesis optional. *Entrance requirements:* Additional exam requirements/recommendations for international students: Recommended—TOEFL (minimum score 550 paper-based; 79 iBT), IELTS (minimum score 6.5). Electronic applications accepted.

University of Nebraska at Omaha, Graduate Studies, College of Education, Omaha, NE 68182. Offers MA, MS, Ed D, PhD, Certificate, Ed S. *Accreditation:* NCATE. *Program availability:* Part-time, evening/weekend. *Degree requirements:* For master's, comprehensive exam (for some programs), thesis (for some programs); for doctorate, comprehensive exam, thesis/dissertation. *Entrance requirements:* Additional exam requirements/recommendations for international students: Required—TOEFL, IELTS, PTE. Electronic applications accepted.

University of Nevada, Las Vegas, Graduate College, College of Education, Las Vegas, NV 89154-3001. Offers M Ed, MS, Ed D, PhD, Advanced Certificate, Certificate, Ed S, PhD/JD. *Program availability:* Part-time. *Degree requirements:* For master's, comprehensive exam (for some programs), thesis (for some programs); for doctorate, comprehensive exam, thesis/dissertation; for other advanced degree, comprehensive exam (for some programs). *Entrance requirements:* For master's and doctorate, GRE General Test. Additional exam requirements/recommendations for international students: Required—TOEFL (minimum score 550 paper-based; 80 iBT), IELTS (minimum score 7). Electronic applications accepted. *Expenses:* Contact institution. *Faculty research:* Technology integration in general and special education, assessment of behavioral and emotional disorders, teacher quality and student achievement, evidence-based practices in special education (autism and emotional and behavioral disorders), math and science education.

University of Nevada, Reno, Graduate School, College of Education, Reno, NV 89557. Offers M Ed, MA, MS, Ed D, PhD, Ed S. *Accreditation:* NCATE. Terminal master's awarded for partial completion of doctoral program. *Degree requirements:* For master's, thesis optional; for doctorate, thesis/dissertation. *Entrance requirements:* For master's, GRE, minimum GPA of 2.75; for doctorate, GRE, minimum GPA of 3.0. Additional exam requirements/recommendations for international students: Required—TOEFL (minimum score 500 paper-based; 61 iBT), IELTS (minimum score 6). Electronic applications accepted.

University of New Brunswick Fredericton, School of Graduate Studies, Faculty of Education, Fredericton, NB E3B 5A3, Canada. Offers M Ed, PhD. *Program availability:* Part-time, online learning. *Degree requirements:* For master's, variable foreign language requirement, thesis optional; for doctorate, variable foreign language requirement, comprehensive exam, thesis/dissertation. *Entrance requirements:* For master's, minimum GPA of 3.0. Additional exam requirements/recommendations for international students: Required—TOEFL (minimum score 650 paper-based); Recommended—TWE (minimum score 5.5). Electronic applications accepted. *Faculty research:* Adult education, educational administration and leadership, counseling, exceptional learners, critical studies.

University of New England, College of Graduate and Professional Studies, Portland, ME 04005-9526. Offers advanced educational leadership (CAGS); applied nutrition (MS); career and technical education (MS Ed); curriculum and instruction (MS Ed); education (CAGS, Post-Master's Certificate); educational leadership (MS Ed, Ed D); generalist (MS Ed); health informatics (MS, Graduate Certificate); inclusion education (MS Ed); literacy K-12 (MS Ed); medical education leadership (MMEL); public health (MPH, Graduate Certificate); reading specialist (MS Ed); social work (MSW). *Program availability:* Part-time, evening/weekend, online only, 100% online. *Faculty:* 109 part-time/adjunct (78 women). *Students:* 1,207 full-time (972 women), 561 part-time (450 women); includes 411 minority (280 Black or African American, non-Hispanic/Latino; 17 American Indian or Alaska Native, non-Hispanic/Latino; 74 Asian, non-Hispanic/Latino; 25 Hispanic/Latino; 9 Native Hawaiian or other Pacific Islander, non-Hispanic/Latino; 6 Two or more races, non-Hispanic/Latino). Average age 36. 740 applicants, 92% accepted, 494 enrolled. In 2018, 586 master's, 44 doctorates, 85 other advanced degrees awarded. *Application deadline:* Applications are processed on a rolling basis. Electronic applications accepted. *Financial support:* Application deadline: 5/1; applicants required to submit FAFSA. *Unit head:* Dr. Martha Wilson, Dean of the College of Graduate and Professional Studies, 207-221-4985, E-mail: mwilson13@une.edu. *Application contact:* Nicole Lindsay, Director of Online Admissions, 207-221-4966, E-mail: nlindsay1@une.edu.
Website: http://online.une.edu

University of New Hampshire, Graduate School, College of Liberal Arts, Department of Education, Durham, NH 03824. Offers assessment evaluation and policy (Postbaccalaureate Certificate); autism spectrum disorders (Postbaccalaureate Certificate); early childhood education (M Ed), including early childhood education, early childhood education: special needs; education (PhD, Postbaccalaureate Certificate), including children and youth in communities (PhD), curriculum and instruction leadership (Postbaccalaureate Certificate), education (PhD); educational administration and supervision (Ed S); educational studies (M Ed); elementary education (M Ed); mentoring teachers (Postbaccalaureate Certificate); secondary education (M Ed, MAT); special education (M Ed, Postbaccalaureate Certificate), including special education (M Ed), special education administration (Postbaccalaureate Certificate); technology integration (Postbaccalaureate Certificate). *Accreditation:* TEAC. *Program availability:* Part-time. *Entrance requirements:* For master's, doctorate, and other advanced degree, GRE General Test. Additional exam requirements/recommendations for international students: Required—TOEFL (minimum score 550 paper-based; 80 iBT). Electronic applications accepted.

University of New Hampshire, Graduate School Manchester Campus, Manchester, NH 03101. Offers business administration (MBA); cybersecurity policy and risk management (MS); educational administration and supervision (Ed S); educational studies (M Ed); elementary education (M Ed); information technology (MS); public administration (MPA); public health (MPH, Certificate); secondary education (M Ed, MAT); social work (MSW); substance use disorders (Certificate). *Program availability:* Part-time, evening/weekend. *Entrance requirements:* Additional exam requirements/recommendations for international students: Required—TOEFL (minimum score 550 paper-based; 80 iBT). Electronic applications accepted.

University of New Mexico, Graduate Studies, College of Education, Albuquerque, NM 87131-2039. Offers MA, MS, Ed D, PhD, Ed S, Graduate Certificate. *Accreditation:* NCATE. *Program availability:* Part-time, evening/weekend. *Students:* Average age 37. 398 applicants, 56% accepted, 212 enrolled. In 2018, 288 master's, 33 doctorates, 39 other advanced degrees awarded. *Degree requirements:* For master's, comprehensive exam (for some programs), thesis (for some programs); for doctorate, variable foreign language requirement, comprehensive exam, thesis/dissertation. *Entrance requirements:* Additional exam requirements/recommendations for international students: Required—TOEFL (minimum score 550 paper-based), IELTS (minimum score 7). *Application deadline:* For fall admission, 3/1 for international students; for spring admission, 8/1 for international students. Application fee: $50. Electronic applications accepted. *Financial support:* Career-related internships or fieldwork, Federal Work-Study, scholarships/grants, health care benefits, and unspecified assistantships available. Support available to part-time students. Financial award application deadline: 3/1; financial award applicants required to submit FAFSA. *Faculty research:* Best practices in pedagogy, quantitative analysis and assessment, socio-cultural issues, educational leadership, health and wellness across the lifespan. *Total annual research expenditures:* $578,105. *Unit head:* Dr. Richard Howell, Dean, 505-277-2231, Fax: 505-277-8427, E-mail: rhowell@unm.edu. *Application contact:* Academic Graduate Coordinator, 505-277-3190, E-mail: coeac@unm.edu.
Website: http://coe.unm.edu/

University of North Alabama, College of Education, Florence, AL 35632-0001. Offers MA, MA Ed, MS, Ed S. *Accreditation:* NCATE. *Program availability:* Part-time, 100% online, blended/hybrid learning. *Degree requirements:* For master's, comprehensive exam. *Entrance requirements:* For master's, GRE, MAT, PRAXIS II, or NTE, minimum GPA of 2.5, Alabama Class B Certificate or equivalent, teaching experience. Additional exam requirements/recommendations for international students: Required—TOEFL (minimum score 79 iBT), IELTS (minimum score 6), PTE (minimum score 54). Electronic applications accepted.

The University of North Carolina at Chapel Hill, Graduate School, School of Education, Chapel Hill, NC 27514-3500. Offers M Ed, MA, MAT, MSA, Ed D, PhD. *Accreditation:* NCATE. *Program availability:* Part-time. *Degree requirements:* For master's, comprehensive exam, thesis (for some programs); for doctorate, comprehensive exam, thesis/dissertation. *Entrance requirements:* For master's and doctorate, GRE General Test, minimum GPA of 3.0 during last 2 years of undergraduate course work. Additional exam requirements/recommendations for international students: Required—TOEFL (minimum score 550 paper-based). Electronic applications accepted. *Faculty research:* Curriculum development; school success and intervention; professional development, recruitment and retention; service-learning; evaluation.

The University of North Carolina at Charlotte, Cato College of Education, Charlotte, NC 28223-0001. Offers M Ed, MA, MAT, MSA, Ed D, PhD, Graduate Certificate, Post-Master's Certificate, Postbaccalaureate Certificate. *Accreditation:* ACA (one or more programs are accredited); NCATE. *Program availability:* Part-time, evening/weekend, 100% online, blended/hybrid learning. *Students:* 248 full-time (204 women), 1,051 part-time (846 women); includes 449 minority (327 Black or African American, non-Hispanic/Latino; 2 American Indian or Alaska Native, non-Hispanic/Latino; 20 Asian, non-Hispanic/Latino; 72 Hispanic/Latino; 28 Two or more races, non-Hispanic/Latino), 26 international. Average age 34. 918 applicants, 74% accepted, 487 enrolled. In 2018, 229 master's, 42 doctorates, 311 other advanced degrees awarded. *Entrance requirements:* For master's, bachelor's degree, or its U.S. equivalent, from regionally-accredited college or university; minimum overall GPA of 3.0 on all previous work beyond high school; statement of purpose (essay); at least three recommendation forms; for doctorate, bachelor's degree (or its U.S. equivalent) from regionally-accredited college or university; minimum overall GPA of 3.5 in master's degree program; for other advanced degree, bachelor's degree from regionally-accredited university; minimum GPA of 2.75 on all post-secondary work attempted; transcripts; personal statement outlining why the applicant seeks admission to the program. Additional exam requirements/recommendations for international students: Required—TOEFL (minimum score 523 paper-based; 70 iBT), IELTS (minimum score 6), TOEFL (minimum score 523 paper-based, 70 iBT) or IELTS (6). *Application deadline:* Applications are processed on a rolling basis. Application fee: $75. Electronic applications accepted. Tuition and fees vary according to course load and program. *Financial support:* Research assistantships, teaching assistantships, career-related internships or fieldwork, institutionally sponsored loans, scholarships/grants, unspecified assistantships, and administrative assistantships available. Support available to part-time students. Financial award application deadline: 3/1; financial award applicants required to submit FAFSA. *Faculty research:* Quality classroom instruction, culturally responsive instruction, teacher education policy and practice, early intervention, counseling practices. *Total annual research expenditures:* $6.3 million. *Unit head:* Dr. Ellen McIntyre, Dean, 704-687-8722, E-mail: ellen.mcintyre@uncc.edu. *Application contact:* Kathy B. Giddings, Director of Graduate Admissions, 704-687-5503, Fax: 704-687-1668, E-mail: gradadm@uncc.edu.
Website: https://education.uncc.edu/

The University of North Carolina at Greensboro, Graduate School, School of Education, Greensboro, NC 27412-5001. Offers M Ed, MLIS, MS, MSA, Ed D, PhD, Certificate, Ed S, PMC, MS/Ed S, MS/PhD. *Accreditation:* NCATE. *Program availability:* Part-time, evening/weekend. *Degree requirements:* For doctorate, thesis/dissertation. *Entrance requirements:* For master's, doctorate, and other advanced degree, GRE General Test. Additional exam requirements/recommendations for international students: Required—TOEFL. Electronic applications accepted. *Faculty research:* Effects of homogeneous grouping, women in higher education, assessment of student achievement.

The University of North Carolina at Pembroke, The Graduate School, School of Education, Pembroke, NC 28372-1510. Offers MA, MA Ed, MAT, MSA. *Accreditation:* NCATE. *Program availability:* Part-time, evening/weekend. *Degree requirements:* For master's, comprehensive exam (for some programs), thesis optional. *Entrance requirements:* For master's, GRE General Test or MAT, minimum GPA of 3.0 in major, 2.5 overall. Additional exam requirements/recommendations for international students: Required—TOEFL.

The University of North Carolina Wilmington, Watson College of Education, Wilmington, NC 28403-3297. Offers M Ed, MAT, MS, MSA, Ed D. *Accreditation:* NCATE. *Program availability:* Part-time. *Degree requirements:* For doctorate, comprehensive exam, thesis/dissertation. *Entrance requirements:* For doctorate, education statement of interest essay, master's degree in education field, 3 years of leadership experience. Additional exam requirements/recommendations for international students: Required—TOEFL (minimum score 550 paper-based; 79 iBT), IELTS (minimum score 6.5). Electronic applications accepted.

University of North Dakota, Graduate School, College of Education and Human Development, Grand Forks, ND 58202. Offers M Ed, MA, MS, MSW, Ed D, PhD, Ed S. *Accreditation:* NCATE. *Program availability:* Part-time, evening/weekend, online learning. *Degree requirements:* For master's, comprehensive exam, thesis or alternative; for doctorate, comprehensive exam, thesis/dissertation; for Ed S, comprehensive exam (for some programs), thesis (for some programs). *Entrance requirements:* For master's, GRE General Test, MAT, GRE Subject Test, minimum GPA of 3.0; for doctorate, GRE Subject Test, minimum GPA of 3.5. Additional exam requirements/recommendations for international students: Required—TOEFL (minimum score 550 paper-based; 79 iBT), IELTS (minimum score 6.5). Electronic applications accepted.

University of Northern British Columbia, Office of Graduate Studies, Prince George, BC V2N 4Z9, Canada. Offers business administration (Diploma); community health science (M Sc); disability management (MA); education (M Ed); first nations studies (MA); gender studies (MA); history (MA); interdisciplinary studies (MA); international studies (MA); mathematical, computer and physical sciences (M Sc); natural resources and environmental studies (M Sc, MA, MNRES, PhD); political science (MA); psychology (M Sc, PhD); social work (MSW). *Program availability:* Part-time, evening/weekend, online learning. *Degree requirements:* For master's, thesis; for doctorate, thesis/dissertation. *Entrance requirements:* For master's, GRE, minimum B average in undergraduate course work; for doctorate, candidacy exam, minimum A average in graduate course work.

University of Northern Colorado, Graduate School, College of Education and Behavioral Sciences, Greeley, CO 80639. Offers MA, MAT, MS, Ed D, PhD, Ed S. *Accreditation:* NCATE. *Program availability:* Part-time, online learning. *Degree requirements:* For master's, comprehensive exam, thesis optional; for doctorate, comprehensive exam, thesis/dissertation; for Ed S, comprehensive exam, thesis. *Entrance requirements:* For doctorate, GRE General Test.

Education—General

University of Northern Iowa, Graduate College, College of Education, Cedar Falls, IA 50614. Offers MA, MAE, MS, Ed D, Ed S. *Program availability:* Part-time, evening/weekend. *Degree requirements:* For Ed S, thesis or alternative. *Entrance requirements:* For master's, minimum GPA of 3.0; for doctorate, GRE, master's degree, minimum GPA of 3.5; for Ed S, GRE General Test, GRE Subject Test. Additional exam requirements/recommendations for international students: Required—TOEFL (minimum score 500 paper-based; 61 iBT). Electronic applications accepted.

University of North Florida, College of Education and Human Services, Jacksonville, FL 32224. Offers M Ed, MS, Ed D. *Accreditation:* NCATE. *Program availability:* Part-time, evening/weekend. *Faculty:* 53 full-time (33 women), 12 part-time/adjunct (7 women). *Students:* 110 full-time (92 women), 290 part-time (231 women); includes 138 minority (78 Black or African American, non-Hispanic/Latino; 8 Asian, non-Hispanic/Latino; 32 Hispanic/Latino; 1 Native Hawaiian or other Pacific Islander, non-Hispanic/Latino; 19 Two or more races, non-Hispanic/Latino), 15 international. Average age 36. 244 applicants, 59% accepted, 101 enrolled. In 2018, 115 master's, 20 doctorates awarded. Terminal master's awarded for partial completion of doctoral program. *Degree requirements:* For doctorate, thesis/dissertation. *Entrance requirements:* For master's, GRE General Test, minimum GPA of 3.0 in last 60 hours, interview, 3 letters of recommendation; for doctorate, GRE General Test, master's degree, interview, writing sample, 3 letters of recommendation. Additional exam requirements/recommendations for international students: Required—TOEFL (minimum score 500 paper-based). *Application deadline:* For fall admission, 7/1 priority date for domestic students, 5/1 for international students; for spring admission, 11/1 priority date for domestic students, 10/1 for international students. Application fee: $30. Electronic applications accepted. *Expenses: Tuition, area resident:* Part-time $408.10 per credit hour. Tuition, state resident: part-time $408.10 per credit hour. Tuition, nonresident: part-time $932.61 per credit hour. *Required fees:* $111.81 per credit hour. Tuition and fees vary according to course load, campus/location and program. *Financial support:* In 2018–19, 52 students received support, including 1 research assistantship (averaging $8,096 per year), 1 teaching assistantship (averaging $5,824 per year); career-related internships or fieldwork, Federal Work-Study, scholarships/grants, and tuition waivers (partial) also available. Support available to part-time students. Financial award application deadline: 4/1; financial award applicants required to submit FAFSA. *Faculty research:* Effective instruction, technology education, exceptional student education, multiculturalism. *Total annual research expenditures:* $482,034. *Unit head:* Dr. Diane Yendol-Hoppey, Dean, 904-620-2520, E-mail: diane.yendol-hoppey@unf.edu. *Application contact:* Dr. John Kemppainen, Director, Office of Student Services, 904-620-2530, Fax: 904-620-1135, E-mail: jkemppai@unf.edu.
Website: http://www.unf.edu/coehs/

University of North Georgia, Master of Arts in Teaching Program, Dahlonega, GA 30597. Offers physical education (MAT); secondary education - English (MAT); secondary education - history (MAT); secondary education - mathematics (MAT); secondary education - middle grades (MAT). *Degree requirements:* For master's, internship, capstone. *Entrance requirements:* For master's, GRE or MAT, GACE I and II, GA pre-service application, lawful presence verification, official transcripts, GA Educator Ethics Program entry assessment. Additional exam requirements/recommendations for international students: Required—TOEFL (minimum score 550 paper-based; 79 iBT), IELTS (minimum score 6.5). Electronic applications accepted. *Expenses:* Contact institution.

University of North Texas, Toulouse Graduate School, Denton, TX 76203-5459. Offers accounting (MS); applied anthropology (MA, MS); applied behavior analysis (Certificate); applied geography (MA); applied technology and performance improvement (M Ed, MS); art education (MA); art history (MA); arts leadership (Certificate); audiology (Au D); behavior analysis (MS); behavioral science (PhD); biochemistry and molecular biology (MS); biology (MA, MS); biomedical engineering (MS); business analysis (MS); chemistry (MS); clinical health psychology (PhD); communication studies (MA, MS); computer engineering (MS); computer science (MS); counseling (M Ed, MS), including clinical mental health counseling (MS), college and university counseling, elementary school counseling, secondary school counseling; creative writing (MA); criminal justice (MS); curriculum and instruction (M Ed); decision sciences (MBA); design (MA, MFA), including fashion design (MFA), innovation studies, interior design (MFA); early childhood studies (MS); economics (MS); educational leadership (M Ed, Ed D); educational psychology (MS, PhD), including family studies (MS), gifted and talented (MS), human development (MS), learning and cognition (MS), research, measurement and evaluation (MS); electrical engineering (MS); emergency management (MPA); engineering technology (MS); English (MA); English as a second language (MA); environmental science (MS); finance (MBA, MS); financial management (MPA); French (MA); health services management (MBA); higher education (M Ed, Ed D); history (MA, MS); hospitality management (MS); human resources management (MPA); information science (MS); information systems (PhD); information technologies (MBA); interdisciplinary studies (MA, MS); international studies (MA); international sustainable tourism (MS); jazz studies (MM); journalism (MA, MJ, Graduate Certificate), including interactive and virtual digital communication (Graduate Certificate), narrative journalism (Graduate Certificate), public relations (Graduate Certificate); kinesiology (MS); linguistics (MA); local government management (MPA); logistics (PhD); logistics and supply chain management (MBA); long-term care, senior housing, and aging services (MA); management (PhD); marketing (MBA); mathematics (MA, MS); mechanical and energy engineering (MS, PhD); music (MA), including ethnomusicology, music theory, musicology, performance; music composition (PhD); music education (MM Ed, PhD); nonprofit management (MPA); operations and supply chain management (MBA); performance (MM, DMA); philosophy (MA); political science (MA); professional and technical communication (MA); radio, television and film (MA, MFA); rehabilitation counseling (Certificate); sociology (MA); Spanish (MA); special education (M Ed); speech-language pathology (MA); strategic management (MBA); studio art (MFA); teaching (M Ed); MBA/MS. *Program availability:* Part-time, evening/weekend, online learning. Terminal master's awarded for partial completion of doctoral program. *Degree requirements:* For master's, variable foreign language requirement, comprehensive exam (for some programs), thesis (for some programs); for doctorate, variable foreign language requirement, comprehensive exam (for some programs), thesis/dissertation; for other advanced degree, variable foreign language requirement, comprehensive exam (for some programs). *Entrance requirements:* For master's and doctorate, GRE, GMAT. Additional exam requirements/recommendations for international students: Required—TOEFL (minimum score 550 paper-based; 79 iBT). Electronic applications accepted.

University of Northwestern–St. Paul, Master of Arts in Education Program, St. Paul, MN 55113-1598. Offers MA Ed. *Program availability:* Part-time, evening/weekend, online learning. Electronic applications accepted. *Expenses:* Contact institution.

University of Notre Dame, Institute for Educational Initiatives, Notre Dame, IN 46556. Offers M Ed, MA. Enrollment restricted to participants in the Alliance for Catholic Education (ACE) program. *Entrance requirements:* For master's, GRE General Test, acceptance into the Alliance for Catholic Education program. Electronic applications accepted. *Faculty research:* Effective teaching, motivation, social and ethical development, literacy.

University of Oklahoma, Jeannine Rainbolt College of Education, Norman, OK 73019. Offers communication, culture and pedagogy for Hispanic (ESL/ELL) populations in educational settings (Graduate Certificate). *Accreditation:* NCATE. *Program availability:* Part-time, evening/weekend. *Faculty:* 56 full-time (33 women), 4 part-time/adjunct (2 women). *Students:* 248 full-time (167 women), 443 part-time (332 women); includes 218 minority (66 Black or African American, non-Hispanic/Latino; 37 American Indian or Alaska Native, non-Hispanic/Latino; 17 Asian, non-Hispanic/Latino; 44 Hispanic/Latino; 1 Native Hawaiian or other Pacific Islander, non-Hispanic/Latino; 53 Two or more races, non-Hispanic/Latino), 26 international. Average age 34. 257 applicants, 72% accepted, 140 enrolled. In 2018, 175 master's, 42 doctorates, 42 other advanced degrees awarded. Terminal master's awarded for partial completion of doctoral program. *Degree requirements:* For master's, comprehensive exam (for some programs), thesis (for some programs); for doctorate, comprehensive exam (for some programs), thesis/dissertation (for some programs). *Entrance requirements:* Additional exam requirements/recommendations for international students: Required—TOEFL (minimum score 79 iBT) or IELTS (minimum score 6.5). Application fee: $50 ($100 for international students). Electronic applications accepted. *Expenses:* Tuition, state resident: full-time $5683.20; part-time $236.80 per credit hour. Tuition, nonresident: full-time $20,342; part-time $847.60 per credit hour. *International tuition:* $20,342.40 full-time. *Required fees:* $2894.20; $110.05 per credit hour. $126.50 per semester. Tuition and fees vary according to course load and program. *Financial support:* Fellowships, research assistantships, teaching assistantships, career-related internships or fieldwork, Federal Work-Study, institutionally sponsored loans, scholarships/grants, traineeships, health care benefits, and unspecified assistantships available. Support available to part-time students. Financial award application deadline: 6/1; financial award applicants required to submit FAFSA. *Unit head:* Dr. Gregg Garn, Dean, 405-325-1082, Fax: 405-325-7390, E-mail: garn@ou.edu. *Application contact:* Mike Jenkins, Graduate Programs Specialist, 405-325-4525, E-mail: mjenkins@ou.edu.
Website: http://www.ou.edu/education/

University of Oregon, Graduate School, College of Education, Eugene, OR 97403. Offers communication disorders and sciences (MA, MS, PhD); counseling psychology (PhD); couples and family therapy (MS); critical and sociocultural studies in education (PhD); curriculum and teacher education (MA, MS); educational leadership (MS, D Ed, PhD); prevention science (M Ed, MS, PhD); school psychology (MS, PhD); special education (M Ed, MA, MS, PhD). *Accreditation:* ASHA. *Program availability:* Part-time. Terminal master's awarded for partial completion of doctoral program. *Degree requirements:* For master's, exam, paper, or project; for doctorate, comprehensive exam, thesis/dissertation. *Entrance requirements:* Additional exam requirements/recommendations for international students: Required—TOEFL. *Faculty research:* Basic and applied research in teaching, learning and habilitation in all settings, schooling effectiveness.

University of Ottawa, Faculty of Graduate and Postdoctoral Studies, Faculty of Education, Ottawa, ON K1N 6N5, Canada. Offers M Ed, MA Ed, PhD, Certificate. *Program availability:* Online learning. *Degree requirements:* For master's, thesis or alternative; for doctorate, comprehensive exam, thesis/dissertation, seminar. *Entrance requirements:* For master's, honors degree or equivalent, minimum B average; for doctorate, master's degree, minimum B+ average. Electronic applications accepted. *Faculty research:* Teaching, learning and evaluation; second language education; organizational studies in education; society, culture and literacies; educational counseling.

University of Pennsylvania, Graduate School of Education, Philadelphia, PA 19104. Offers M Phil, MS, MS Ed, Ed D, PhD, Certificate. *Program availability:* Part-time, evening/weekend, online learning. *Students:* Average age 31. 3,105 applicants, 51% accepted, 888 enrolled. In 2018, 559 master's, 77 doctorates awarded. Terminal master's awarded for partial completion of doctoral program. Application fee: $80. Electronic applications accepted. *Unit head:* Dr. Pam Grossman, Dean, 215-898-7014, Fax: 215-746-6884, E-mail: admissions@gse.upenn.edu. *Application contact:* Dr. Pam Grossman, Dean, 215-898-7014, Fax: 215-746-6884, E-mail: admissions@gse.upenn.edu.
Website: http://www.gse.upenn.edu/

University of Pennsylvania, Graduate School of Education, Division of Teaching, Learning, and Leadership, Program in Teaching, Learning, and Teacher Education, Philadelphia, PA 19104. Offers Ed D, PhD.

University of Phoenix–Bay Area Campus, College of Education, San Jose, CA 95134-1805. Offers administration and supervision (MA Ed); adult education and training (MA Ed); early childhood education (MA Ed); education (Ed S); educational leadership (Ed D); elementary teacher education (MA Ed); higher education administration (PhD); secondary teacher education (MA Ed); special education (MA Ed); teacher leadership (MA Ed). *Program availability:* Evening/weekend, online learning. *Degree requirements:* For master's, thesis (for some programs). *Entrance requirements:* For master's, minimum undergraduate GPA of 2.5, 3 years of work experience. Additional exam requirements/recommendations for international students: Required—TOEFL (minimum score 550 paper-based; 79 iBT). Electronic applications accepted.

University of Phoenix–Central Valley Campus, College of Education, Fresno, CA 93720-1552. Offers curriculum and instruction (MA Ed); curriculum and instruction-computer education (MA Ed); elementary teacher education (MA Ed); secondary teacher education (MA Ed).

University of Phoenix–Dallas Campus, College of Education, Dallas, TX 75251. Offers curriculum and instruction (MA Ed).

University of Phoenix–Hawaii Campus, College of Education, Honolulu, HI 96813-3800. Offers administration and supervision (MA Ed); curriculum and instruction (MA Ed); elementary education (MA Ed); secondary education (MA Ed); special education (MA Ed); teacher education for elementary licensure (MA Ed). *Program availability:* Evening/weekend. *Degree requirements:* For master's, thesis (for some programs). *Entrance requirements:* For master's, minimum undergraduate GPA of 2.5, 3 years of work experience. Additional exam requirements/recommendations for international students: Required—TOEFL (minimum score 550 paper-based; 79 iBT). Electronic applications accepted.

University of Phoenix–Houston Campus, College of Education, Houston, TX 77079-2004. Offers curriculum and instruction (MA Ed).

University of Phoenix–Las Vegas Campus, College of Education, Las Vegas, NV 89135. Offers administration and supervision (MA Ed); curriculum and instruction (MA Ed); school counseling (MSC); teacher education-elementary licensure (MA Ed). *Program availability:* Evening/weekend. *Degree requirements:* For master's, thesis (for some programs). *Entrance requirements:* For master's, minimum undergraduate GPA of 2.5, 3 years of work experience. Additional exam requirements/recommendations for international students: Required—TOEFL (minimum score 550 paper-based; 79 iBT). Electronic applications accepted.

University of Phoenix–Online Campus, College of Education, Phoenix, AZ 85034-7209. Offers administration and supervision (MAEd, Certificate); adult education and training (MAEd); curriculum and instruction (MAEd), including computer education,

curriculum and instruction, English as a second language, language arts, mathematics, reading; early childhood education (MAEd); educational studies (MAEd); elementary teacher education (MAEd), including early childhood, elementary teacher education, high school middle level, middle level; principal licensure (Certificate); secondary teacher education (MAEd); special education (MAEd, Certificate); teacher education (MAEd), including middle level generalist; teacher education middle level mathematics (MAEd), including middle level mathematics; teacher education middle level science (MAEd), including middle level science; teacher education secondary mathematics (MAEd); teacher education secondary science (MAEd); teacher leadership (MAEd); teachers of English learners (Certificate); transition to teaching (Certificate), including elementary education, secondary education. *Program availability:* Evening/weekend, online learning. *Entrance requirements:* Additional exam requirements/recommendations for international students: Required—TOEFL, TOEIC (Test of English as an International Communication), Berlitz Online English Proficiency Exam, PTE, or IELTS. Electronic applications accepted. *Expenses:* Contact institution.

University of Phoenix–Phoenix Campus, College of Education, Tempe, AZ 85282-2371. Offers administration and supervision (MA Ed); adult education and training (MA Ed); curriculum and instruction reading (MA Ed); early childhood education (MA Ed); education studies (MA Ed); elementary teacher education (MA Ed); secondary teacher education (MA Ed); special education (MA Ed); teacher leadership (MA Ed). *Program availability:* Evening/weekend, online learning. *Entrance requirements:* Additional exam requirements/recommendations for international students: Required—TOEFL, TOEIC (Test of English as an International Communication), Berlitz Online English Proficiency Exam, PTE, or IELTS. Electronic applications accepted. *Expenses:* Contact institution.

University of Phoenix–Sacramento Valley Campus, College of Education, Sacramento, CA 95833-4334. Offers adult education (MA Ed); curriculum instruction (MA Ed); elementary teacher education (MA Ed); secondary teacher education (MA Ed); teacher education (Certificate). *Program availability:* Evening/weekend. *Degree requirements:* For master's, thesis (for some programs). *Entrance requirements:* For master's, 3 years of work experience, minimum undergraduate GPA of 2.5. Additional exam requirements/recommendations for international students: Required—TOEFL (minimum score 550 paper-based; 79 iBT). Electronic applications accepted.

University of Phoenix–San Diego Campus, College of Education, San Diego, CA 92123. Offers curriculum and instruction (MA Ed), including computer education, curriculum and instruction, English as a second language; elementary teacher education (MA Ed); secondary teacher education (MA Ed). *Program availability:* Evening/weekend. *Degree requirements:* For master's, thesis (for some programs). *Entrance requirements:* For master's, 3 years of work experience, minimum undergraduate GPA of 3.0. Additional exam requirements/recommendations for international students: Required—TOEFL (minimum score 550 paper-based; 79 iBT). Electronic applications accepted.

University of Pikeville, Patton College of Education, Pikeville, KY 41501. Offers teacher leader (MA). *Program availability:* Part-time, evening/weekend. *Degree requirements:* For master's, comprehensive exam. *Expenses:* Contact institution.

University of Pittsburgh, School of Education, Pittsburgh, PA 15260. Offers M Ed, MA, MAT, MS, Ed D, PhD. *Program availability:* Part-time, evening/weekend, online learning. Terminal master's awarded for partial completion of doctoral program. *Degree requirements:* For master's, comprehensive exam, thesis (for some programs); for doctorate, comprehensive exam, thesis/dissertation. *Entrance requirements:* For doctorate, GRE. Additional exam requirements/recommendations for international students: Required—TOEFL (minimum score 550 paper-based; 80 iBT). Electronic applications accepted.

University of Portland, School of Education, Portland, OR 97203-5798. Offers education (MA, MAT); educational leadership (M Ed); English for speakers of other languages (M Ed); initial administrator licensure (M Ed); neuroeducation (M Ed, Ed D); organizational leadership and development (Ed D); reading (M Ed); school leadership and development (Ed D); special education (M Ed). *Accreditation:* NCATE. *Program availability:* Part-time, evening/weekend. *Students:* 32 full-time (30 women), 239 part-time (187 women); includes 33 minority (7 Black or African American, non-Hispanic/Latino; 3 American Indian or Alaska Native, non-Hispanic/Latino; 13 Asian, non-Hispanic/Latino; 1 Native Hawaiian or other Pacific Islander, non-Hispanic/Latino; 9 Two or more races, non-Hispanic/Latino). Average age 34. 92 applicants, 60% accepted, 42 enrolled. In 2018, 57 master's, 16 doctorates awarded. *Degree requirements:* For doctorate, thesis/dissertation. *Entrance requirements:* For master's, minimum GPA of 3.0, teaching certificate, letters of recommendation, resume, statement of goals, official transcripts; for doctorate, 2 letters of recommendation, resume, essays, official transcripts. Additional exam requirements/recommendations for international students: Required—TOEFL (minimum score 550 paper-based; 80 iBT), IELTS (minimum score 7). *Application deadline:* For fall admission, 7/15 priority date for domestic and international students; for spring admission, 12/15 priority date for domestic and international students; for summer admission, 4/15 for domestic and international students. Applications are processed on a rolling basis. Electronic applications accepted. *Expenses:* MAT degree - $995/credit hour; EDD and Educational Specialist - $813/credit hour; all other degrees and certificates - $663/credit hour. *Financial support:* Fellowships, Federal Work-Study, and scholarships/grants available. Support available to part-time students. Financial award application deadline: 3/1; financial award applicants required to submit FAFSA. *Faculty research:* Multicultural education, supervision/leadership. *Unit head:* Dr. Bruce Weitzel, Associate Dean, 503-943-7135, E-mail: soed@up.edu. *Application contact:* Caitlin Biddulph, Graduate Programs and Admissions Specialist, 503-943-7107, E-mail: biddulph@up.edu.
Website: http://education.up.edu/default.aspx?cid-4318&pid-5590

University of Prince Edward Island, Faculty of Education, Charlottetown, PE C1A 4P3, Canada. Offers educational studies (PhD); leadership in learning (M Ed). *Program availability:* Part-time. *Degree requirements:* For master's, thesis. *Entrance requirements:* For master's, 2 years of professional experience, bachelor of education, professional certificate. Additional exam requirements/recommendations for international students: Required—TOEFL (minimum score 550 paper-based; 80 iBT), Canadian Academic English Language Assessment, Michigan English Language Assessment Battery, Canadian Test of English for Scholars and Trainees. *Faculty research:* Distance learning, aboriginal communities and education leadership development, international development, immersion language learning.

University of Puerto Rico–Río Piedras, College of Education, San Juan, PR 00931-3300. Offers M Ed, MS, Ed D. *Accreditation:* NCATE. *Program availability:* Part-time. *Degree requirements:* For master's, thesis; for doctorate, thesis/dissertation, internship. *Entrance requirements:* For master's, GRE or PAEG, minimum GPA of 3.0, letter of recommendation; for doctorate, GRE or PAEG, master's degree, minimum GPA of 3.0, letter of recommendation (2), interview. *Faculty research:* Curriculum, math teaching.

University of Puget Sound, School of Education, Tacoma, WA 98416. Offers M Ed, MAT. *Program availability:* Part-time. *Degree requirements:* For master's, capstone course (for M Ed); project (for MAT). *Entrance requirements:* For master's, GRE General Test, WEST-E or NES, WEST-B or ACT/SAT, two education foundation prerequisite courses (for MAT); interview (for M Ed). Additional exam requirements/recommendations for international students: Required—TOEFL (minimum score 550 paper-based; 90 iBT). Electronic applications accepted. *Expenses:* Contact institution. *Faculty research:* Pre-service teacher learning and public school partnerships, creating equitable classrooms, literacy development, teaching social studies, suicide prevention.

University of Redlands, School of Education, Redlands, CA 92373-0999. Offers MA, Ed D, Certificate. *Program availability:* Part-time, evening/weekend. *Entrance requirements:* For master's, minimum undergraduate GPA of 3.0, 2 letters of recommendation. Additional exam requirements/recommendations for international students: Required—TOEFL (minimum score 550 paper-based). *Expenses:* Contact institution.

University of Regina, Faculty of Graduate Studies and Research, Faculty of Education, Regina, SK S4S 0A2, Canada. Offers M Ed, MA Ed, MHRD, PhD, Master's Certificate. Joint with Gabriel Dumont Institute in Community Based Master program. *Program availability:* Part-time. *Faculty:* 52 full-time (36 women), 28 part-time/adjunct (15 women). *Students:* 98 full-time (72 women), 200 part-time (160 women). Average age 30. 88 applicants, 56% accepted, 26 enrolled. In 2018, 102 master's, 5 doctorates, 3 other advanced degrees awarded. *Degree requirements:* For master's, thesis (for some programs), practicum, project, or thesis; for doctorate, thesis/dissertation. *Entrance requirements:* For master's, 4-year B Ed or equivalent, two years of teaching or other relevant professional experience, post secondary transcripts and 2 letter of recommendations. Additional exam requirements/recommendations for international students: Required—TOEFL (minimum score 580 paper-based; 80 iBT), IELTS (minimum score 6.5), PTE (minimum score 59), other options are CAEL, MELAB, Cantest and U of R ESL. *Application deadline:* For fall admission, 2/15 for domestic and international students; for winter admission, 10/15 for domestic and international students; for spring admission, 2/15 for domestic and international students. Application fee: $100. Electronic applications accepted. *Expenses:* Estimated tuition and fees for one academic year is 6,702.90 for master's. The fee will vary base on your choice program. For doctoral program one academic year is estimated 14,129.40. International students will pay additional 1,191.75 for international surcharge per semester. *Financial support:* In 2018–19, 120 students received support, including 87 fellowships, 27 teaching assistantships (averaging $2,552 per year); research assistantships, career-related internships or fieldwork, Federal Work-Study, scholarships/grants, unspecified assistantships, and travel award and Graduate Scholarship Base funds also available. Support available to part-time students. Financial award application deadline: 9/30. *Faculty research:* Curriculum and instruction, educational leadership, educational psychology, human resource development, adult education. *Unit head:* Dr. Jarome Cranston, Dean, 306-585-4500, Fax: 306-585-5387, E-mail: Jerome.Cranston@uregina.ca. *Application contact:* Linda Jiang, Graduate Program Coordinator, 306-585-4506, Fax: 306-585-5387, E-mail: edgrad@uregina.ca.
Website: http://www.uregina.ca/education

University of Rhode Island, Graduate School, Alan Shawn Feinstein College of Education and Professional Studies, School of Education, Kingston, RI 02881. Offers education (PhD); reading (MA); special education (MA). *Accreditation:* NCATE. *Program availability:* Part-time, evening/weekend. *Faculty:* 19 full-time (13 women). *Students:* 53 full-time (35 women), 151 part-time (124 women); includes 28 minority (13 Black or African American, non-Hispanic/Latino; 3 American Indian or Alaska Native, non-Hispanic/Latino; 4 Asian, non-Hispanic/Latino; 5 Hispanic/Latino; 3 Two or more races, non-Hispanic/Latino), 6 international. 79 applicants, 71% accepted, 44 enrolled. In 2018, 54 master's, 6 doctorates awarded. *Entrance requirements:* For master's, 2 letters of recommendation; personal statement; two official transcripts; interview and minimum undergraduate GPA of 3.0 (for special education applicants); for doctorate, GRE, 3 letters of recommendation, resume, personal statement, two copies of official transcripts. Additional exam requirements/recommendations for international students: Required—TOEFL. Application fee: $65. Electronic applications accepted. *Expenses: Tuition, area resident:* Full-time $13,226; part-time $735 per credit. Tuition, state resident: full-time $13,226; part-time $735 per credit. Tuition, nonresident: full-time $25,854; part-time $1436 per credit. *International tuition:* $25,854 full-time. *Required fees:* $1698; $50 per credit. $35 per semester. One-time fee: $165. *Financial support:* In 2018–19, 1 research assistantship with tuition reimbursement (averaging $9,040 per year), 4 teaching assistantships with tuition reimbursements (averaging $15,776 per year) were awarded. Financial award applicants required to submit FAFSA. *Unit head:* Dr. David Byrd, Director, School of Education, 401-874-5484, Fax: 401-874-5471, E-mail: dbyrd@uri.edu. *Application contact:* Dr. David Byrd, Director, School of Education, 401-874-5484, Fax: 401-874-5471, E-mail: dbyrd@uri.edu.
Website: https://web.uri.edu/education/

University of Rio Grande, Graduate School, Rio Grande, OH 45674. Offers athletic coaching leadership (M Ed); educational leadership (M Ed); integrated arts (M Ed); intervention specialist in early childhood (M Ed); intervention specialist in mild/moderate (M Ed). *Accreditation:* NCATE. *Program availability:* Part-time. *Degree requirements:* For master's, final research project, portfolio. *Entrance requirements:* For master's, minimum GPA of 2.7 in major, 2.5 overall. Additional exam requirements/recommendations for international students: Required—TOEFL. *Faculty research:* Interagency collaboration, reading and mathematics, learning styles, college access, literacy.

University of Rochester, Margaret Warner Graduate School of Education and Human Development, Rochester, NY 14627. Offers MS, Ed D, PhD. *Accreditation:* ACA (one or more programs are accredited); NCATE. *Program availability:* Part-time, evening/weekend. Terminal master's awarded for partial completion of doctoral program. *Degree requirements:* For master's, thesis (for some programs); for doctorate, thesis/dissertation, qualifying exam. *Expenses: Tuition:* Full-time $52,974; part-time $1654 per credit hour. *Required fees:* $612. One-time fee: $30 part-time. Tuition and fees vary according to campus/location and program.

University of St. Francis, College of Education, Joliet, IL 60435-6169. Offers educational leadership (MS, Ed D); elementary education (M Ed); reading (MS); secondary education (M Ed), including English education, math education, science education, social studies education, visual arts education; special education (M Ed); teaching and learning (MS); TESOL (Certificate). *Accreditation:* NCATE. *Program availability:* Part-time, evening/weekend, 100% online, blended/hybrid learning. *Faculty:* 11 full-time (8 women), 58 part-time/adjunct (38 women). *Students:* 43 full-time (35 women), 453 part-time (354 women); includes 110 minority (48 Black or African American, non-Hispanic/Latino; 7 Asian, non-Hispanic/Latino; 52 Hispanic/Latino; 3 Two or more races, non-Hispanic/Latino), 3 international. Average age 37. 300 applicants, 66% accepted, 164 enrolled. In 2018, 151 master's, 42 doctorates, 4 other advanced degrees awarded. *Degree requirements:* For master's, comprehensive exam; for doctorate, thesis/dissertation. *Entrance requirements:* Additional exam requirements/recommendations for international students: Required—TOEFL (minimum score 550 paper-based; 79 iBT), IELTS (minimum score 6). *Application deadline:* Applications are processed on a rolling basis. Electronic applications accepted. Application fee is waived when completed online. *Expenses:* Contact institution. *Financial support:* In 2018–19, 33 students received support. Scholarships/grants and tuition waivers (partial) available. Support available to part-time students. Financial award applicants required to submit FAFSA. *Unit head:* Dr. John Gambro, Dean, 815-740-3456, E-mail: jgambro@

stfrancis.edu. *Application contact:* Sandee Sloka, Director Adult & Graduate Admissions, 800-735-7500, E-mail: ssloka@stfrancis.edu.
Website: https://www.stfrancis.edu/education/

University of Saint Francis, Graduate School, Department of Education, Fort Wayne, IN 46808-3994. Offers secondary education (MAT); special education (MS Ed), including intense intervention, mild intervention. *Accreditation:* NCATE. *Program availability:* Part-time, evening/weekend, online only, 100% online. *Faculty:* 2 full-time (1 woman), 3 part-time/adjunct (all women). *Students:* 3 full-time (2 women), 27 part-time (18 women); includes 3 minority (1 Black or African American, non-Hispanic/Latino; 1 Hispanic/Latino; 1 Two or more races, non-Hispanic/Latino). Average age 33. 19 applicants, 95% accepted, 18 enrolled. In 2018, 12 master's awarded. *Expenses: Tuition:* Full-time $22,440; part-time $935 per credit hour. *Required fees:* $330 per semester. Tuition and fees vary according to degree level, campus/location and program. *Unit head:* Mary Riepenhoff, Chair of the Department of Education, 260-399-7700 Ext. 8409, E-mail: mriepenhoff@sf.edu. *Application contact:* Kyle Richardson, Associate Director of Enrollment Services for Adult Learning, 260-399-7700 Ext. 6310, Fax: 260-399-8152, E-mail: krichardson@sf.edu.
Website: https://admissions.sf.edu/graduate/

University of Saint Joseph, Department of Education, West Hartford, CT 06117-2700. Offers curriculum and instruction (MA); elementary education (MAT); instructional technology (MA); literacy (MA); secondary education (MAT); TESOL (MA). *Program availability:* Part-time, evening/weekend. *Degree requirements:* For master's, comprehensive exam, thesis or alternative. *Entrance requirements:* For master's, 2 letters of recommendation. Electronic applications accepted. Application fee is waived when completed online.

University of Saint Mary, Graduate Programs, Program in Education, Leavenworth, KS 66048-5082. Offers MA. *Accreditation:* NCATE. *Program availability:* Part-time, evening/weekend, online learning. *Students:* 17 full-time (8 women), 3 part-time (2 women); includes 7 minority (4 Black or African American, non-Hispanic/Latino; 2 Hispanic/Latino; 1 Native Hawaiian or other Pacific Islander, non-Hispanic/Latino), 1 international. Average age 30. *Entrance requirements:* For master's, minimum undergraduate GPA of 2.75, bachelor's degree from accredited college, interview, official transcripts, two letters of recommendation, essay. *Application deadline:* Applications are processed on a rolling basis. Application fee: $25. Electronic applications accepted. *Expenses:* Contact institution. *Financial support:* Applicants required to submit FAFSA. *Unit head:* Dr. Cheryl Reding, Unit Head of Education, 913-758-6159, E-mail: cheryl.reding@stmary.edu. *Application contact:* Dr. Cheryl Reding, Unit Head of Education, 913-758-6159, E-mail: cheryl.reding@stmary.edu.
Website: http://www.stmary.edu/success/Grad-Program/Master-of-Arts-Education.aspx

University of St. Thomas, College of Education, Leadership and Counseling, St. Paul, MN 55105-1096. Offers MA, Ed D, Psy D, Certificate, Ed S. *Program availability:* Part-time, evening/weekend, 100% online, blended/hybrid learning. *Degree requirements:* For doctorate, thesis/dissertation. *Entrance requirements:* For master's, minimum GPA of 3.0 or MAT. Additional exam requirements/recommendations for international students: Required—TOEFL (minimum score 550 paper-based; 80 iBT). Electronic applications accepted. *Expenses:* Contact institution.

University of St. Thomas, School of Education and Human Services, Houston, TX 77006-4696. Offers all level education (M Ed); bilingual/dual language (M Ed); Catholic school teaching (M Ed); Catholic/private school leadership (M Ed); counselor education (M Ed); curriculum and instruction (M Ed); education (Ed D); educational leadership (M Ed); elementary teaching (M Ed); English as a second language (M Ed); exceptionality/educational diagnostician (M Ed); exceptionality/special education (M Ed); generalist (M Ed); reading (M Ed); secondary teaching (M Ed); teaching (MAT). *Accreditation:* TEAC. *Program availability:* Part-time, evening/weekend, online learning. *Degree requirements:* For master's, thesis, field experience. *Entrance requirements:* For master's, GRE or MAT if GPA is below 3.0, bachelor's degree; minimum GPA of 2.75 in bachelor's degree or last 60 credit hours; official transcripts from all institutions; goal statement of 250-300 words; 1 reference. Additional exam requirements/recommendations for international students: Required—TOEFL (minimum score 94 iBT), IELTS (minimum score 7), PTE (minimum score 53). Electronic applications accepted. *Expenses:* Contact institution. *Faculty research:* Leadership, diversity, personality traits, second language acquisition.

University of San Diego, School of Leadership and Education Sciences, San Diego, CA 92110-2492. Offers M Ed, MA, PhD, Certificate. *Accreditation:* NCATE. *Program availability:* Part-time, evening/weekend. *Faculty:* 30 full-time (17 women), 84 part-time/adjunct (54 women). *Students:* 361 full-time (290 women), 497 part-time (367 women); includes 373 minority (47 Black or African American, non-Hispanic/Latino; 66 Asian, non-Hispanic/Latino; 207 Hispanic/Latino; 3 Native Hawaiian or other Pacific Islander, non-Hispanic/Latino; 50 Two or more races, non-Hispanic/Latino), 32 international. Average age 31. In 2018, 365 master's, 17 doctorates awarded. *Degree requirements:* For master's, international experience; for doctorate, comprehensive exam (for some programs), thesis/dissertation (for some programs), international experience. *Entrance requirements:* For doctorate, master's degree. Additional exam requirements/recommendations for international students: Required—TOEFL (minimum score 580 paper-based; 83 iBT), TWE. Application fee: $45. *Financial support:* In 2018–19, 512 students received support. Career-related internships or fieldwork, Federal Work-Study, institutionally sponsored loans, scholarships/grants, unspecified assistantships, and stipends available. Support available to part-time students. Financial award application deadline: 4/1; financial award applicants required to submit FAFSA. *Unit head:* Dr. Nicholas Ladany, Dean, 619-260-4540, Fax: 619-260-6835, E-mail: nladany@sandiego.edu. *Application contact:* Erika Garwood, Associate Director of Graduate Admissions, 619-260-4524, Fax: 619-260-4158, E-mail: grads@sandiego.edu.
Website: http://www.sandiego.edu/soles/

University of San Francisco, School of Education, San Francisco, CA 94117. Offers MA, Ed D. *Program availability:* Part-time, evening/weekend. *Students:* 845 full-time (641 women), 199 part-time (151 women); includes 584 minority (91 Black or African American, non-Hispanic/Latino; 2 American Indian or Alaska Native, non-Hispanic/Latino; 150 Asian, non-Hispanic/Latino; 289 Hispanic/Latino; 7 Native Hawaiian or other Pacific Islander, non-Hispanic/Latino; 45 Two or more races, non-Hispanic/Latino), 64 international. Average age 31. 1,076 applicants, 73% accepted, 404 enrolled. In 2018, 355 master's, 37 doctorates awarded. *Degree requirements:* For doctorate, thesis/dissertation. *Entrance requirements:* For master's, CBEST, CSET, and/or CSET Writing Skills (depending on program); for doctorate, GRE or MAT. Additional exam requirements/recommendations for international students: Required—TOEFL (minimum score 580 paper-based; 92 iBT), IELTS (minimum score 7), PTE (minimum score 62). *Application deadline:* For fall admission, 3/1 priority date for domestic and international students; for spring admission, 10/15 priority date for domestic and international students. Applications are processed on a rolling basis. Application fee: $55. Electronic applications accepted. *Financial support:* Fellowships, research assistantships, and teaching assistantships available. Financial award application deadline: 3/2; financial award applicants required to submit FAFSA. *Unit head:* Dr. Shabnam Koirala-Azad, Dean, 415-422-6525. *Application contact:* Amy Fogliani, Director of Admission, 415-422-5467, E-mail: schoolofeducation@usfca.edu.

University of Saskatchewan, College of Graduate and Postdoctoral Studies, College of Education, Saskatoon, SK S7N 5A2, Canada. Offers M Ed, PhD, Diploma. *Program availability:* Part-time. *Degree requirements:* For master's, thesis (for some programs); for doctorate, comprehensive exam (for some programs), thesis/dissertation. *Entrance requirements:* Additional exam requirements/recommendations for international students: Required—TOEFL (minimum score 80 iBT); Recommended—IELTS (minimum score 6.5). Electronic applications accepted.

The University of Scranton, Panuska College of Professional Studies, Department of Education, Scranton, PA 18510. Offers curriculum and instruction (MS); educational administration (MS); reading education (MS); secondary education (MS). *Accreditation:* NCATE; TEAC. *Program availability:* Part-time, evening/weekend, online learning. *Faculty research:* Meta-analysis as a research tool, family involvement in school activities, effect of curriculum integration on student learning and attitude, the effects of inclusion on students, development of emotional intelligence of young children.

University of Sioux Falls, Fredrikson School of Education, Sioux Falls, SD 57105-1699. Offers educational administration (Ed S), including principal leadership, superintendent and district leadership; leadership in reading (M Ed); leadership in schools (M Ed); leadership in technology (M Ed); teaching (M Ed). Admission in summer only. *Accreditation:* NCATE. *Program availability:* Part-time, evening/weekend. *Degree requirements:* For master's, comprehensive exam (for some programs), research application project; for Ed S, comprehensive exam, portfolio. *Entrance requirements:* For master's, minimum GPA of 3.0, 1 year of teaching experience; for Ed S, minimum 3 years of teaching experience, minimum cumulative GPA of 3.5, 1 year of administrative experience. Additional exam requirements/recommendations for international students: Required—TOEFL. *Faculty research:* Reading, literacy, leadership.

University of South Africa, College of Human Sciences, Pretoria, South Africa. Offers adult education (M Ed); African languages (MA, PhD); African politics (MA, PhD); Afrikaans (MA, PhD); ancient history (MA, PhD); ancient Near Eastern studies (MA, PhD); anthropology (MA, PhD); applied linguistics (MA); Arabic (MA, PhD); archaeology (MA); art history (MA); Biblical archaeology (MA); Biblical studies (M Th, D Th, PhD); Christian spirituality (M Th, D Th); church history (M Th, D Th); classical studies (MA, PhD); clinical psychology (MA); communication (MA, PhD); comparative education (M Ed, Ed D); consulting psychology (D Admin, D Com, PhD); curriculum studies (M Ed, Ed D); development studies (M Admin, MA, D Admin, PhD); didactics (M Ed, Ed D); education (M Tech); education management (M Ed, Ed D); educational psychology (M Ed); English (MA); environmental education (M Ed); French (MA, PhD); German (MA, PhD); Greek (MA); guidance and counseling (M Ed); health studies (MA, PhD), including health sciences education (MA), health services management (MA), medical and surgical nursing science (critical care general) (MA), midwifery and neonatal nursing science (MA), trauma and emergency care (MA); history (MA, PhD); history of education (Ed D); inclusive education (M Ed, Ed D); information and communications technology policy and regulation (MA); information science (MA, MIS, PhD); international politics (MA, PhD); Islamic studies (MA, PhD); Italian (MA, PhD); Judaica (MA, PhD); linguistics (MA, PhD); mathematical education (M Ed); mathematics education (MA); missiology (M Th, D Th); modern Hebrew (MA, PhD); musicology (MA, MMus, D Mus, PhD); natural science education (M Ed); New Testament (M Th, D Th); Old Testament (D Th); pastoral therapy (M Th, D Th); philosophy (MA); philosophy of education (M Ed, Ed D); politics (MA, PhD); Portuguese (MA, PhD); practical theology (M Th, D Th); psychology (MA, MS, PhD); psychology of education (M Ed, Ed D); public health (MA); religious studies (MA, D Th, PhD); Romance languages (MA); Russian (MA, PhD); Semitic languages (MA, PhD); social behavior studies in HIV/AIDS (MA); social science (mental health) (MA); social science in development studies (MA); social science in psychology (MA); social science in social work (MA); social science in sociology (MA); social work (MSW, DSW, PhD); socio-education (M Ed, Ed D); sociolinguistics (MA); sociology (MA, PhD); Spanish (MA, PhD); systematic theology (M Th, D Th); TESOL (teaching English to speakers of other languages) (MA); theological ethics (M Th, D Th); theory of literature (MA, PhD); urban ministries (D Th); urban ministry (M Th).

University of South Alabama, College of Education and Professional Studies, Mobile, AL 36688. Offers M Ed, MS, Ed D, PhD, Ed S. *Accreditation:* NCATE. *Program availability:* Part-time, evening/weekend. *Degree requirements:* For master's, comprehensive exam; for doctorate, comprehensive exam, thesis/dissertation. *Entrance requirements:* For master's, GRE General Test or MAT; for doctorate, GRE, minimum graduate GPA of 3.25, 3 years of experience in field, 3 letters of recommendation, interview, official transcripts, statement of purpose; for Ed S, GRE, Class A certification, master's degree, two years of teaching experience, three letters of recommendation. Additional exam requirements/recommendations for international students: Required—TOEFL (minimum score 525 paper-based; 71 iBT). Electronic applications accepted. *Faculty research:* Mixed methods research and program evaluation.

University of South Carolina, The Graduate School, College of Education, Columbia, SC 29208. Offers IMA, M Ed, MAT, MS, MT, Ed D, PhD, Certificate, Ed S. *Accreditation:* NCATE. *Program availability:* Part-time, evening/weekend, online learning. *Degree requirements:* For master's, comprehensive exam, thesis (for some programs), foreign language (MA); for doctorate, one foreign language, comprehensive exam, thesis/dissertation. *Entrance requirements:* For master's, GRE General Test or MAT, official transcripts, letters of recommendation, letter of intent; for doctorate, GRE General Test or MAT/qualifying exams, letters of recommendation, letters of intent, interview. Electronic applications accepted. *Faculty research:* Inquiry learning, assessment of student learning, equity issues in education, multicultural education, cultural diversity.

University of South Carolina Upstate, Graduate Programs, Spartanburg, SC 29303-4999. Offers early childhood education (M Ed); elementary education (M Ed); informatics (MS); special education: visual impairment (M Ed). *Accreditation:* NCATE. *Program availability:* Part-time, evening/weekend. *Degree requirements:* For master's, professional portfolio. *Entrance requirements:* For master's, GRE General Test or MAT, interview, minimum undergraduate GPA of 2.5, teaching certificate, 2 letters of recommendation. *Faculty research:* Promoting university diversity awareness, rough and tumble play, social justice education, American Indian literatures and cultures, diversity and multicultural education, science teaching strategy.

University of South Dakota, Graduate School, School of Education, Vermillion, SD 57069. Offers MA, MS, Ed D, PhD, Certificate, Ed S. *Accreditation:* NCATE. *Program availability:* Part-time, evening/weekend, 100% online, blended/hybrid learning. *Degree requirements:* For master's and other advanced degree, comprehensive exam, thesis or alternative; for doctorate, comprehensive exam, thesis/dissertation. *Entrance requirements:* For master's and doctorate, GRE General Test or MAT, minimum GPA of 2.7. Additional exam requirements/recommendations for international students: Required—TOEFL (minimum score 550 paper-based; 79 iBT). Electronic applications accepted.

University of Southern California, Graduate School, Rossier School of Education, Los Angeles, CA 90089. Offers MAT, ME, MMFT, Ed D, PhD. *Degree requirements:* For master's, thesis optional; for doctorate, thesis/dissertation. *Entrance requirements:* For master's and doctorate, GRE. Additional exam requirements/recommendations for international students: Required—TOEFL (minimum score 100 iBT). Electronic applications accepted. *Faculty research:* Data-driven decision-making in K-12 schools

and districts; examination of college and university leadership and management in U. S. and Asia; studies in facilitating student learning; organizational change and the role of leaders; leadership, diversity, learning and accountability.

University of Southern Indiana, Graduate Studies, Pott College of Science, Engineering, and Education, Department of Teacher Education, Evansville, IN 47712-3590. Offers educational leadership (Ed D), including administrative leadership, pedagogical leadership; elementary education (MSE); school administration and leadership (MSE); secondary education (MSE), including secondary education. *Accreditation:* NCATE. *Program availability:* Part-time, evening/weekend. *Entrance requirements:* For master's, PRAXIS II, bachelor's degree with minimum cumulative GPA of 2.75 from college or university accredited by NCATE or comparable association; minimum GPA of 3.0 in all courses taken at graduate level at all schools attended; teaching license; for doctorate, GRE, master's degree transcript; essay; two letters of recommendation; resume/curriculum vitae. Additional exam requirements/recommendations for international students: Required—TOEFL (minimum score 550 paper-based; 79 iBT), IELTS (minimum score 6). Electronic applications accepted.

University of Southern Maine, College of Management and Human Service, School of Education and Human Development, Gorham, ME 04038. Offers MS, MS Ed, Psy D, CAS, CGS. *Accreditation:* TEAC. *Program availability:* Part-time, evening/weekend, online learning. Terminal master's awarded for partial completion of doctoral program. *Degree requirements:* For master's, comprehensive exam (for some programs), thesis or alternative; for doctorate, thesis/dissertation; for other advanced degree, thesis or alternative. *Entrance requirements:* For master's, GRE General Test or MAT, proof of teacher certification; for doctorate, GRE General Test; for other advanced degree, master's degree. Additional exam requirements/recommendations for international students: Required—TOEFL (minimum score 550 paper-based; 79 iBT). Electronic applications accepted. *Faculty research:* Teacher development, library technology outreach, literacy through literature, college-bound, multicultural education, school psychology, education policy and evaluation.

University of Southern Mississippi, College of Education and Human Sciences, Hattiesburg, MS 39406-0001. Offers M Ed, MA, MAT, MLIS, MS, MSW, Ed D, PhD, Ed S, Graduate Certificate. *Accreditation:* NCATE. *Program availability:* Part-time. Terminal master's awarded for partial completion of doctoral program. *Degree requirements:* For master's, comprehensive exam, thesis (for some programs); for doctorate, comprehensive exam, thesis/dissertation; for other advanced degree, comprehensive exam, thesis. *Entrance requirements:* For master's, GRE General Test, MAT, minimum GPA of 2.75 on last 60 hours; for doctorate, GRE General Test, minimum GPA of 3.5; for other advanced degree, GRE General Test. Additional exam requirements/recommendations for international students: Required—TOEFL, IELTS. Electronic applications accepted. *Faculty research:* Reading, sleep, animal cognition.

University of South Florida, College of Education, Tampa, FL 33620-9951. Offers M Ed, MA, MAT, Ed D, PhD, Ed S. *Accreditation:* NCATE. *Program availability:* Part-time, evening/weekend, online learning. *Faculty:* 87 full-time (54 women). *Students:* 486 full-time (368 women), 675 part-time (472 women); includes 349 minority (152 Black or African American, non-Hispanic/Latino; 4 American Indian or Alaska Native, non-Hispanic/Latino; 27 Asian, non-Hispanic/Latino; 144 Hispanic/Latino; 1 Native Hawaiian or other Pacific Islander, non-Hispanic/Latino; 21 Two or more races, non-Hispanic/Latino), 113 international. Average age 35. 824 applicants, 55% accepted, 289 enrolled. In 2018, 240 master's, 64 doctorates, 15 other advanced degrees awarded. *Degree requirements:* For master's, comprehensive exam, thesis (for some programs), project (for some programs); for doctorate, comprehensive exam, thesis/dissertation, philosophies of inquiry; multiple research methods. *Entrance requirements:* For master's, GRE General Test, minimum GPA of 3.5 in last 60 hours of course work; for doctorate, GRE General Test, minimum GPA of 3.5; for Ed S, GRE General Test. Additional exam requirements/recommendations for international students: Required—TOEFL (minimum score 550 paper-based). *Application deadline:* For fall admission, 2/15 for domestic students, 1/2 for international students; for spring admission, 10/15 for domestic students, 6/1 for international students. Application fee: $30. Electronic applications accepted. *Expenses:* Tuition, state resident: full-time $6350. Tuition, nonresident: full-time $19,048. *International tuition:* $19,048 full-time. *Required fees:* $2079. *Financial support:* In 2018–19, 260 students received support, including 9 fellowships with full tuition reimbursements available (averaging $15,000 per year), 2 research assistantships with full tuition reimbursements available (averaging $15,000 per year); career-related internships or fieldwork, Federal Work-Study, institutionally sponsored loans, scholarships/grants, health care benefits, and unspecified assistantships also available. Support available to part-time students. Financial award applicants required to submit FAFSA. *Faculty research:* Scholarship of teaching and learning, educator preparation, diversity issues as they relate to PK-20 education, urban education. *Total annual research expenditures:* $13.5 million. *Unit head:* Dr. Colleen S. Kennedy, Dean, 813-974-3400, Fax: 813-974-3826. *Application contact:* Dr. Diane Briscoe, Coordinator of Graduate Studies, 813-974-1804, Fax: 813-974-3391, E-mail: briscoe@usf.edu.
Website: http://www.coedu.usf.edu/

University of South Florida, St. Petersburg, College of Education, St. Petersburg, FL 33701. Offers educational leadership development (M Ed); elementary education (MA), including math/science; English education (MA); middle grades STEM education (MS); reading education (MA). *Program availability:* Part-time. *Degree requirements:* For master's, comprehensive exam, practicum, internship, comprehensive portfolio. *Entrance requirements:* For master's, State of Florida General Knowledge Test (GKT), Florida Teaching Certificate (for non-initial certification programs), letters of recommendation. Additional exam requirements/recommendations for international students: Required—TOEFL (minimum score 550 paper-based; 79 iBT); Recommended—IELTS. Electronic applications accepted.

The University of Tampa, Programs in Education, Tampa, FL 33606-1490. Offers curriculum and instruction (M Ed); educational leadership (M Ed); instructional design and technology (MS). *Program availability:* Part-time, evening/weekend. *Faculty:* 2 full-time (both women), 19 part-time/adjunct (15 women). *Students:* 52 full-time (38 women), 238 part-time (211 women); includes 86 minority (36 Black or African American, non-Hispanic/Latino; 1 American Indian or Alaska Native, non-Hispanic/Latino; 9 Asian, non-Hispanic/Latino; 32 Hispanic/Latino; 8 Two or more races, non-Hispanic/Latino), 15 international. Average age 33. 119 applicants, 71% accepted, 48 enrolled. In 2018, 37 master's awarded. *Degree requirements:* For master's, capstone. *Entrance requirements:* For master's, GMAT or GRE, current Florida Professional Teaching Certificate, statement of eligibility for Florida Professional Teaching Certificate, or professional teaching certificate from another state; bachelor's degree in an area of education. Additional exam requirements/recommendations for international students: Required—TOEFL (minimum score 577 paper-based; 90 iBT), IELTS (minimum score 7.5). *Application deadline:* Applications are processed on a rolling basis. Application fee: $40. Electronic applications accepted. *Expenses:* Contact institution. *Financial support:* In 2018–19, 28 students received support. Career-related internships or fieldwork, scholarships/grants, and unspecified assistantships available. Financial award applicants required to submit FAFSA. *Faculty research:* Diversity in the classroom, technology integration, assessment methodologies, complex and ill-structured problem

solving, communities of practice. *Unit head:* Dr. Antony Erben, Chair, 813-257-3414, E-mail: terben@ut.edu. *Application contact:* Ashley Russell, Staff Assistant, Admissions for Graduate and Continuing Studies, 813-253-6249, E-mail: arussell@ut.edu.
Website: http://www.ut.edu/graduate/education/

The University of Tennessee, Graduate School, College of Education, Health and Human Sciences, Knoxville, TN 37996. Offers MPH, MS, Ed D, PhD, Ed S, MS/MPH. *Accreditation:* NCATE. *Program availability:* Part-time, evening/weekend, online learning. Terminal master's awarded for partial completion of doctoral program. *Degree requirements:* For master's and Ed S, thesis optional; for doctorate, thesis/dissertation. *Entrance requirements:* For master's, minimum GPA of 2.7; for doctorate and Ed S, GRE General Test, minimum GPA of 2.7. Additional exam requirements/recommendations for international students: Required—TOEFL. Electronic applications accepted.

The University of Tennessee at Chattanooga, School of Education, Chattanooga, TN 37403. Offers counseling (M Ed), including community counseling, school counseling; education (M Ed, Post-Master's Certificate), including elementary education (M Ed); school leadership (Post-Master's Certificate); elementary education (M Ed); learning and leadership (Ed D), including educational leadership; school leadership (Post-Master's Certificate); school leadership: principal licensure (Ed S); secondary education (M Ed); special education (M Ed). *Accreditation:* ACA; NCATE. *Program availability:* Part-time. *Degree requirements:* For master's, comprehensive exam, thesis optional, culminating experience; for other advanced degree, internship. *Entrance requirements:* For master's, GRE General Test, PPST 1, teaching certificate; for other advanced degree, two letters of recommendation, graduate degree in education, teaching certificate with three years of experience. Additional exam requirements/recommendations for international students: Required—TOEFL (minimum score 550 paper-based; 79 iBT), IELTS (minimum score 6). Electronic applications accepted. *Expenses:* Contact institution. *Faculty research:* School counseling, community counseling, elementary and secondary education, school leadership and administration.

The University of Tennessee at Martin, Graduate Programs, College of Education, Health and Behavioral Sciences, Martin, TN 38238. Offers MS Ed. *Accreditation:* NCATE. *Program availability:* Part-time, online only, 100% online. *Faculty:* 42. *Students:* 42 full-time (36 women), 196 part-time (154 women); includes 32 minority (22 Black or African American, non-Hispanic/Latino; 5 Hispanic/Latino; 5 Two or more races, non-Hispanic/Latino). Average age 34. 135 applicants, 45% accepted, 40 enrolled. In 2018, 51 master's awarded. *Degree requirements:* For master's, comprehensive exam. *Entrance requirements:* For master's, GRE General Test, minimum GPA of 2.5. Additional exam requirements/recommendations for international students: Required—TOEFL (minimum score 525 paper-based; 71 iBT). *Application deadline:* For fall admission, 7/27 priority date for domestic and international students; for spring admission, 12/17 priority date for domestic and international students; for summer admission, 5/10 priority date for domestic and international students. Applications are processed on a rolling basis. Application fee: $30 ($130 for international students). Electronic applications accepted. *Expenses: Tuition,* area resident: Full-time $8918; part-time $495 per credit hour. Tuition, state resident: full-time $8918; part-time $485 per credit hour. Tuition, nonresident: full-time $14,958; part-time $831 per credit hour. *International tuition:* $22,862 full-time. *Required fees:* $1446; $81 per credit hour. Part-time tuition and fees vary according to course load. *Financial support:* In 2018–19, 50 students received support, including 1 research assistantship with full tuition reimbursement available (averaging $6,283 per year), 7 teaching assistantships with full tuition reimbursements available (averaging $7,126 per year); scholarships/grants and tuition waivers (full and partial) also available. Financial award application deadline: 2/1; financial award applicants required to submit FAFSA. *Faculty research:* Environmental education, self-concept, science education, attention deficit disorder, special education. *Unit head:* Cynthia West, Dean, 731-881-7127, Fax: 731-881-7975, E-mail: cwest@utm.edu. *Application contact:* Jolene L. Cunningham, Student Services Specialist, 731-881-7012, Fax: 731-881-7499, E-mail: jcunningham@utm.edu.
Website: http://www.utm.edu/departments/cehbs/

The University of Texas at Arlington, Graduate School, College of Education, Arlington, TX 76019. Offers M Ed, M Ed T, PhD.

The University of Texas at Austin, Graduate School, College of Education, Austin, TX 78712-1111. Offers M Ed, MA, MS, Ed D, PhD. *Program availability:* Part-time. *Entrance requirements:* For master's and doctorate, GRE General Test. Electronic applications accepted.

The University of Texas at El Paso, Graduate School, College of Education, El Paso, TX 79968-0001. Offers M Ed, MA, Ed D, PhD. *Program availability:* Part-time, evening/weekend, online learning. *Degree requirements:* For master's, thesis optional; for doctorate, thesis/dissertation. *Entrance requirements:* For master's, minimum GPA of 3.0, letter of intent, resume, letters of recommendation, copy of teaching certificate, district service record; for doctorate, GRE, resume, letters of recommendation, scholarly paper. Additional exam requirements/recommendations for international students: Required—TOEFL; Recommended—IELTS. Electronic applications accepted.

The University of Texas of the Permian Basin, Office of Graduate Studies, School of Education, Odessa, TX 79762-0001. Offers MA. *Accreditation:* NCATE. *Entrance requirements:* For master's, GRE General Test. Additional exam requirements/recommendations for international students: Required—TOEFL (minimum score 550 paper-based).

The University of Texas Rio Grande Valley, College of Education and P-16 Integration, Edinburg, TX 78539. Offers M Ed, MA, Ed D. *Program availability:* Part-time, evening/weekend. *Degree requirements:* For master's, comprehensive exam (for some programs), thesis optional; for doctorate, comprehensive exam, thesis/dissertation. *Entrance requirements:* Additional exam requirements/recommendations for international students: Required—TOEFL (minimum score 550 paper-based; 79 iBT), IELTS (minimum score 6.5). Electronic applications accepted. *Expenses: Tuition,* area resident: Full-time $6888. Tuition, state resident: full-time $6888. Tuition, nonresident: full-time $14,484. *International tuition:* $14,484 full-time. *Required fees:* $1468. *Faculty research:* Literacy development, bilingual education, special education, counseling, school leadership.

University of the Cumberlands, Graduate Programs in Education, Williamsburg, KY 40769-1372. Offers all grades (P-12) (M Ed); business and marketing (MA Ed, MAT); counselor education and supervision (Ed D); director of pupil personnel (Certificate); director of special education (Certificate); educational administration and supervision (Ed S); educational leadership (Ed D); elementary education (MA Ed, MAT); instructional leadership - principalship (MA Ed); instructional leadership - school principal (Certificate); middle school education (MA Ed, MAT); reading and writing (MA Ed); school counseling (MA Ed); school superintendent (Certificate); secondary education (MA Ed, MAT); special education (MAT); supervisor of instruction (Certificate); teacher leader (MA Ed). *Program availability:* Part-time, evening/weekend, online learning. *Degree requirements:* For master's, comprehensive exam. Electronic applications accepted.

University of the Incarnate Word, Dreeben School of Education, San Antonio, TX 78209-6397. Offers M Ed, MA, MAT, PhD. *Program availability:* Part-time, evening/

weekend. *Faculty:* 9 full-time (5 women), 3 part-time/adjunct (2 women). *Students:* 110 full-time (72 women), 101 part-time (59 women); includes 127 minority (23 Black or African American, non-Hispanic/Latino; 3 Asian, non-Hispanic/Latino; 97 Hispanic/Latino; 4 Two or more races, non-Hispanic/Latino), 29 international. 82 applicants, 96% accepted, 48 enrolled. In 2018, 21 master's, 12 doctorates awarded. *Degree requirements:* For master's, capstone course; for doctorate, thesis/dissertation, qualifying exam. *Entrance requirements:* For master's, baccalaureate degree, interview; for doctorate, master's degree, interview, supervised writing sample. Additional exam requirements/recommendations for international students: Required—TOEFL (minimum score 560 paper-based; 83 iBT). *Application deadline:* Applications are processed on a rolling basis. Application fee: $20. Electronic applications accepted. *Expenses: Tuition:* Full-time $22,560; part-time $940 per credit hour. *Required fees:* $2484; $94 per credit hour. Tuition and fees vary according to degree level, program and student level. *Financial support:* In 2018–19, 4 research assistantships were awarded; Federal Work-Study, scholarships/grants, tuition waivers (partial), and unspecified assistantships also available. Financial award applicants required to submit FAFSA. *Faculty research:* Political and social contexts of education, teaching children mathematics and science, thoughtfully adaptive teachers, college student success for underrepresented populations, technology integration in education. *Unit head:* Dr. Denise Staudt, Dean, 210-829-2761, Fax: 210-829-2765, E-mail: staudt@uiwtx.edu. *Application contact:* Jessica Delarosa, Associate Director of Admissions, 210-829-6005, Fax: 210-829-3921, E-mail: admis@uiwtx.edu.
Website: http://www.uiw.edu/education/index.htm

University of the Pacific, Gladys L. Benerd School of Education, Stockton, CA 95211-0197. Offers curriculum and instruction (MA, Ed D); education (M Ed); educational administration and leadership (MA, Ed D); educational and school psychology (MA, Ed D); educational entrepreneurship (MA); school psychology (Ed S); special education (MA); teacher education (MA). *Accreditation:* NCATE. *Degree requirements:* For doctorate, thesis/dissertation. *Entrance requirements:* For master's, GRE General Test; for doctorate, GRE General Test, GRE Subject Test. Additional exam requirements/recommendations for international students: Required—TOEFL.

University of the Sacred Heart, Graduate Programs, Department of Education, San Juan, PR 00914-0383. Offers early childhood education (M Ed); information technology and multimedia (Certificate); instruction systems and education technology (M Ed), including English, information technology and multimedia, instructional design, mathematics, Spanish. *Program availability:* Part-time, evening/weekend. *Degree requirements:* For master's, thesis. *Entrance requirements:* For master's, EXADEP, minimum undergraduate GPA of 2.75, interview.

University of the Southwest, Graduate Programs, Hobbs, NM 88240-9129. Offers business administration (MBA); curriculum and instruction (MSE); curriculum and instruction: bilingual (MSE); curriculum and instruction: TESOL (MSE); early childhood education (MSE); educational administration (MSE); mental health counseling (MSE); school counseling (MSE); special education (MSE); sports management (MBA). *Program availability:* Part-time, evening/weekend, online learning. *Degree requirements:* For master's, comprehensive exam, thesis (for some programs). *Entrance requirements:* Additional exam requirements/recommendations for international students: Recommended—TOEFL. Electronic applications accepted.

University of the Virgin Islands, School of Education, St. Thomas, VI 00802. Offers creative leadership for innovation and change (PhD); educational leadership (MA); school counseling (MA); school psychology (Ed S). *Program availability:* Part-time, evening/weekend. *Students:* 41 full-time (34 women), 95 part-time (75 women); includes 80 minority (79 Black or African American, non-Hispanic/Latino; 1 Hispanic/Latino), 24 international. Average age 43. In 2018, 6 master's, 7 doctorates awarded. *Degree requirements:* For master's, comprehensive exam, thesis or alternative; for doctorate, comprehensive exam, thesis/dissertation, qualifying examination; for Ed S, comprehensive exam. *Entrance requirements:* For master's, GRE, minimum GPA of 2.5, BA degree from accredited institution. Additional exam requirements/recommendations for international students: Required—TOEFL (minimum score 550 paper-based). *Application deadline:* For fall admission, 4/30 for domestic and international students; for spring admission, 10/30 for domestic and international students. Application fee: $25. Electronic applications accepted. *Expenses:* Contact institution. *Financial support:* Fellowships, research assistantships, teaching assistantships, and scholarships/grants available. Financial award application deadline: 4/15; financial award applicants required to submit FAFSA. *Unit head:* Dr. Karen Brown, Dean, 340-693-1321, Fax: 340-693-1335, E-mail: karen.brown@uvi.edu. *Application contact:* Charmaine M. Smith, Director of Admissions, 340-692-4070, E-mail: csmith@uvi.edu.

The University of Toledo, College of Graduate Studies, Judith Herb College of Education, Toledo, OH 43606-3390. Offers MAE, ME, MES, MME, DE, PhD, Certificate, Ed S. *Accreditation:* NCATE. *Program availability:* Part-time, evening/weekend. Terminal master's awarded for partial completion of doctoral program. *Degree requirements:* For master's, thesis; for doctorate, comprehensive exam (for some programs), thesis/dissertation (for some programs); for other advanced degree, thesis optional. *Entrance requirements:* For master's and other advanced degree, minimum cumulative GPA of 2.7 for all previous academic work, letters of recommendation, statement of purpose, transcripts from all prior institutions attended; for doctorate, GRE, minimum cumulative GPA of 2.7 for all previous academic work, 3.0 for occupational therapy and physical therapy; letters of recommendation; statement of purpose; transcripts from all prior institutions attended. Additional exam requirements/recommendations for international students: Required—TOEFL (minimum score 550 paper-based; 80 iBT). Electronic applications accepted.

University of Toronto, School of Graduate Studies, Ontario Institute for Studies in Education, Toronto, ON M5S 1A1, Canada. Offers M Ed, MA, MT, Ed D, PhD. *Program availability:* Part-time, evening/weekend. *Degree requirements:* For master's, thesis (for some programs); for doctorate, thesis/dissertation. *Entrance requirements:* For master's, minimum B average in final year, 1 year of professional experience in field (MA, M Ed); for doctorate, minimum B+ average, professional experience in education or a relevant field (Ed D). Additional exam requirements/recommendations for international students: Required—TOEFL (minimum score 580 paper-based; 93 iBT), TWE (minimum score 5). *Expenses:* Contact institution.

University of Utah, Graduate School, College of Education, Salt Lake City, UT 84112. Offers education, culture & society (MA); educational leadership & policy (Ed D); educational psychology (Ed S); educational psychology - statistics (M Stat); MPA/PhD. *Accreditation:* TEAC. *Faculty:* 48 full-time (31 women), 68 part-time/adjunct (48 women). *Students:* 304 full-time (221 women), 285 part-time (189 women); includes 153 minority (14 Black or African American, non-Hispanic/Latino; 1 American Indian or Alaska Native, non-Hispanic/Latino; 18 Asian, non-Hispanic/Latino; 98 Hispanic/Latino; 3 Native Hawaiian or other Pacific Islander, non-Hispanic/Latino; 19 Two or more races, non-Hispanic/Latino), 11 international. Average age 33. In 2018, 213 master's, 28 doctorates awarded. *Degree requirements:* For master's, comprehensive exam (for some programs), thesis (for some programs); for doctorate, comprehensive exam (for some programs), thesis/dissertation. *Entrance requirements:* For master's and doctorate, minimum GPA of 3.0. Additional exam requirements/recommendations for international students: Required—TOEFL. Electronic applications accepted. *Expenses:* Contact institution. *Financial support:* Application deadline: 2/1; applicants required to submit FAFSA. *Faculty research:* Sleep deprivation and stress, higher education in prison, cognitive disabilities, special education, behavior. *Unit head:* Elaine Clark, Dean, 801-581-8221, E-mail: el.clark@utah.edu. *Application contact:* Elaine Clark, Dean, 801-581-8221, E-mail: el.clark@utah.edu.
Website: http://education.utah.edu/

University of Vermont, Graduate College, College of Education and Social Services, Burlington, VT 05405. Offers M Ed, MAT, MS, MSW, Ed D, PhD. *Accreditation:* NCATE. *Program availability:* Part-time, evening/weekend. *Degree requirements:* For doctorate, thesis/dissertation. *Entrance requirements:* Additional exam requirements/recommendations for international students: Required—TOEFL (minimum score 550 paper-based, 90 iBT) or IELTS (6.5). Electronic applications accepted.

University of Victoria, Faculty of Graduate Studies, Faculty of Education, Victoria, BC V8W 2Y2, Canada. Offers M Ed, M Sc, MA, PhD.

University of Virginia, Curry School of Education, Charlottesville, VA 22903. Offers M Ed, MS, MT, Ed D, PhD, Ed S, MBA/M Ed, MPP/PhD. *Accreditation:* TEAC. *Degree requirements:* For master's, comprehensive exam (for some programs), thesis (for some programs); for doctorate, comprehensive exam (for some programs), thesis/dissertation. *Entrance requirements:* For master's, doctorate, and Ed S, GRE General Test, letters of recommendation. Additional exam requirements/recommendations for international students: Required—TOEFL (minimum score 600 paper-based; 90 iBT), IELTS (minimum score 7). Electronic applications accepted. *Expenses:* Contact institution.

University of Washington, Graduate School, College of Education, Seattle, WA 98195. Offers curriculum and instruction (M Ed, Ed D, PhD), including educational technology, general curriculum (Ed D, PhD), language, literacy, and culture, mathematics education, multicultural education, reading and language arts education (Ed D), science education, social studies education, teaching and curriculum (M Ed); educational leadership and policy studies (M Ed, Ed D, PhD), including administration (Ed D), educational policy, organization, and leadership (M Ed, PhD), higher education, leadership for learning (Ed D), social and cultural foundations of education (M Ed, PhD); educational psychology (M Ed, PhD), including educational psychology (PhD), human development and cognition (M Ed), learning sciences, measurement, statistics and research design (M Ed), school psychology (M Ed); instructional leadership (M Ed); intercollegiate athletic leadership (M Ed); special education (M Ed, Ed D, PhD), including early childhood special education (M Ed), emotional and behavioral disabilities (M Ed), learning disabilities (M Ed), low-incidence disabilities (M Ed), severe disabilities (M Ed), special education (Ed D, PhD); teacher education (MIT). *Accreditation:* APA. *Program availability:* Part-time, evening/weekend. *Degree requirements:* For master's, thesis optional; for doctorate, thesis/dissertation. *Entrance requirements:* For master's and doctorate, GRE General Test, minimum GPA of 3.0. Additional exam requirements/recommendations for international students: Required—TOEFL. Electronic applications accepted. *Faculty research:* School restructuring/effective schools, special education interventions, literacy and writing, technology, school partnerships, teacher preparation.

University of Washington, Bothell, Program in Education, Bothell, WA 98011. Offers education (M Ed); leadership development for educators (M Ed); secondary/middle level endorsement (M Ed). *Program availability:* Part-time, evening/weekend. *Degree requirements:* For master's, thesis. *Entrance requirements:* Additional exam requirements/recommendations for international students: Required—TOEFL. Electronic applications accepted. *Faculty research:* Multicultural education in citizenship education, intercultural education, knowledge and practice in the principalship, educational public policy, national board certification for teachers, teacher learning in literacy, technology and its impact on teaching and learning of mathematics, reading assessments, professional development in literacy education and mobility, digital media, education and class.

University of Washington, Tacoma, Graduate Programs, Program in Education, Tacoma, WA 98402-3100. Offers education (M Ed); educational administration (principal or program administrator certification) (M Ed); elementary education teacher certification (M Ed); elementary education/special education teacher certification (M Ed); secondary science or math teacher certification (M Ed). *Program availability:* Part-time, evening/weekend. *Degree requirements:* For master's, culminating project. *Entrance requirements:* For master's, WEST-B, WEST-E (teacher certification programs only), official sealed transcript from every college/university attended, personal goal statement, letters of recommendation, copy of valid teaching certificate. Additional exam requirements/recommendations for international students: Required—TOEFL (minimum score 580 paper-based; 92 iBT). Electronic applications accepted. *Faculty research:* Global learning communities for English/Chinese languages, evaluation of mathematics and reading intervention programs, response to intervention, school-wide behavioral and emotional support, mathematics education and culturally responsive mathematics education.

The University of West Alabama, School of Graduate Studies, College of Education, Livingston, AL 35470. Offers M Ed, MAT, MS, MSCE, Ed S. *Accreditation:* NCATE. *Program availability:* Part-time, evening/weekend, 100% online. *Faculty:* 46 full-time (27 women), 86 part-time/adjunct (49 women). *Students:* 2,601 full-time (2,202 women), 106 part-time (85 women); includes 953 minority (882 Black or African American, non-Hispanic/Latino; 15 American Indian or Alaska Native, non-Hispanic/Latino; 3 Asian, non-Hispanic/Latino; 21 Hispanic/Latino; 2 Native Hawaiian or other Pacific Islander, non-Hispanic/Latino; 30 Two or more races, non-Hispanic/Latino), 17 international. Average age 35. 891 applicants, 95% accepted, 645 enrolled. In 2018, 657 master's, 119 other advanced degrees awarded. *Degree requirements:* For master's, comprehensive exam, thesis optional; for Ed S, comprehensive exam. *Entrance requirements:* For master's, GRE, minimum GPA of 2.75. Additional exam requirements/recommendations for international students: Required—TOEFL (minimum score 500 paper-based; 61 iBT). *Application deadline:* Applications are processed on a rolling basis. Application fee: $40. Electronic applications accepted. *Expenses: Tuition, area resident:* Full-time $9100. Tuition, state resident: full-time $9100. Tuition, nonresident: full-time $19,200. *Required fees:* $1890; $130. *Financial support:* In 2018–19, 2 teaching assistantships (averaging $7,344 per year) were awarded; Federal Work-Study, scholarships/grants, and unspecified assistantships also available. Support available to part-time students. Financial award application deadline: 3/1; financial award applicants required to submit FAFSA. *Unit head:* Dr. B. J. Kimbrough, Dean of Graduate Studies, 205-652-3647, Fax: 205-652-3670, E-mail: bkimbrough@uwa.edu. *Application contact:* Dr. B. J. Kimbrough, Dean of Graduate Studies, 205-652-3647, Fax: 205-652-3670, E-mail: bkimbrough@uwa.edu.
Website: http://www.uwa.edu/academics/collegeofeducation

The University of Western Ontario, School of Graduate and Postdoctoral Studies, Faculty of Social Science, Faculty of Education, London, ON N6A 3K7, Canada. Offers M Ed. *Program availability:* Part-time. *Entrance requirements:* For master's, minimum B average.

University of West Georgia, College of Education, Carrollton, GA 30118. Offers business education (M Ed); early childhood education (M Ed, Ed S); educational leadership (M Ed, Ed S); media (M Ed, Ed S); professional counseling (M Ed, Ed S); professional counseling and supervision (Ed D); reading instruction (M Ed); school

improvement (Ed D); secondary education (M Ed); special education (M Ed, Ed S), including teaching (M Ed); speech language pathology (M Ed); teaching (MAT). *Accreditation:* NCATE. *Program availability:* Part-time, evening/weekend, 100% online, blended/hybrid learning. *Faculty:* 39 full-time (23 women). *Students:* 368 full-time (316 women), 1,140 part-time (960 women); includes 460 minority (376 Black or African American, non-Hispanic/Latino; 1 American Indian or Alaska Native, non-Hispanic/Latino; 11 Asian, non-Hispanic/Latino; 44 Hispanic/Latino; 28 Two or more races, non-Hispanic/Latino), 6 international. Average age 35. 625 applicants, 77% accepted, 401 enrolled. In 2018, 399 master's, 25 doctorates, 273 other advanced degrees awarded. *Entrance requirements:* Additional exam requirements/recommendations for international students: Required—TOEFL (minimum score 523 paper-based; 69 iBT); Recommended—IELTS (minimum score 6.5). *Application deadline:* For fall admission, 7/21 for domestic students, 6/1 for international students; for spring admission, 11/30 for domestic students, 10/15 for international students; for summer admission, 4/15 for domestic students, 3/30 for international students. Applications are processed on a rolling basis. Application fee: $40. Electronic applications accepted. Tuition and fees vary according to course load, degree level, campus/location and program. *Financial support:* Fellowships, research assistantships, teaching assistantships, career-related internships or fieldwork, Federal Work-Study, institutionally sponsored loans, scholarships/grants, and unspecified assistantships available. Support available to part-time students. Financial award application deadline: 4/1; financial award applicants required to submit FAFSA. *Unit head:* Dr. Diane Hoff, Dean, College of Education, 678-839-6570, Fax: 678-839-6098, E-mail: dhoff@westga.edu. *Application contact:* Dr. Toby Ziglar, Assistant Dean of the Graduate School, 678-839-1394, Fax: 678-839-1395, E-mail: graduate@westga.edu.
Website: http://www.westga.edu/education/

University of Windsor, Faculty of Graduate Studies, Faculty of Education, Windsor, ON N9B 3P4, Canada. Offers education (M Ed); educational studies (PhD). *Program availability:* Part-time, evening/weekend. *Degree requirements:* For master's, thesis or alternative; for doctorate, comprehensive exam, thesis/dissertation. *Entrance requirements:* For master's, minimum B average, teaching certificate; for doctorate, M Ed or MA in education, minimum A average, evidence of research competencies. Additional exam requirements/recommendations for international students: Required—TOEFL (minimum score 600 paper-based). Electronic applications accepted. *Faculty research:* School structures, teacher morale, cognitive deficits, new technologies in art education, internal and external factors that affect learning and teaching.

University of Wisconsin–Eau Claire, College of Education and Human Sciences, Eau Claire, WI 54702-4004. Offers ME-PD, MS, MSE, MST. *Degree requirements:* For master's, comprehensive exam. *Entrance requirements:* For master's, GRE (MAT, MST, MSE, MS); pre-professional skills test (MAT), minimum undergraduate GPA of 2.75 or 3.0 in the last half of undergraduate work. Additional exam requirements/recommendations for international students: Required—TOEFL (minimum score 79 iBT). Electronic applications accepted.

University of Wisconsin–Green Bay, Graduate Studies, Program in Applied Leadership for Teaching and Learning, Green Bay, WI 54311-7001. Offers MS Ed. *Program availability:* Part-time, evening/weekend. *Degree requirements:* For master's, thesis or alternative. *Entrance requirements:* For master's, minimum GPA of 3.0. Electronic applications accepted. *Faculty research:* Curriculum design, assessment.

University of Wisconsin–La Crosse, School of Education, La Crosse, WI 54601-3742. Offers English language arts elementary (Graduate Certificate); professional development in education (ME-PD); reading (MS Ed); special education (MS Ed). *Program availability:* Part-time, evening/weekend. *Entrance requirements:* For master's, GRE. Additional exam requirements/recommendations for international students: Required—TOEFL (minimum score 550 paper-based; 79 iBT). Electronic applications accepted.

University of Wisconsin–Madison, Graduate School, School of Education, Madison, WI 53706-1380. Offers MA, MFA, MS, PhD, Certificate. *Degree requirements:* For doctorate, thesis/dissertation. *Entrance requirements:* Additional exam requirements/recommendations for international students: Required—TOEFL (minimum score 580 paper-based; 92 iBT), IELTS (minimum score 7).

University of Wisconsin–Milwaukee, Graduate School, School of Education, Milwaukee, WI 53201. Offers MS, PhD, CAS, Ed S, Graduate Certificate. *Program availability:* Part-time. *Students:* 259 full-time (199 women), 361 part-time (279 women); includes 173 minority (64 Black or African American, non-Hispanic/Latino; 11 American Indian or Alaska Native, non-Hispanic/Latino; 18 Asian, non-Hispanic/Latino; 10 Hispanic/Latino; 1 Native Hawaiian or other Pacific Islander, non-Hispanic/Latino; 69 Two or more races, non-Hispanic/Latino), 11 international. Average age 34. 517 applicants, 43% accepted, 148 enrolled. In 2018, 129 master's, 16 doctorates, 24 other advanced degrees awarded. *Entrance requirements:* For doctorate, GRE General Test. *Application deadline:* For fall admission, 1/1 priority date for domestic students; for spring admission, 9/1 for domestic students. Application fee: $56 ($96 for international students). Electronic applications accepted. *Financial support:* Fellowships, teaching assistantships, career-related internships or fieldwork, Federal Work-Study, health care benefits, unspecified assistantships, and project assistantships available. Support available to part-time students. Financial award application deadline: 4/15; financial award applicants required to submit FAFSA. *Total annual research expenditures:* $1.8 million. *Unit head:* Alan Shoho, Dean, 414-229-4181, E-mail: shoho@uwm.edu. *Application contact:* Education Office of Student Services, 414-229-4721, E-mail: soeoss@uwm.edu.
Website: http://uwm.edu/education

University of Wisconsin–Oshkosh, Graduate Studies, College of Education and Human Services, Oshkosh, WI 54901. Offers MS, MSE. *Program availability:* Part-time, evening/weekend. *Degree requirements:* For master's, comprehensive exam (for some programs), thesis or alternative, field report, PPST, PRAXIS II. *Entrance requirements:* For master's, PPST, PRAXIS II, teaching license, letters of recommendation, interview. Additional exam requirements/recommendations for international students: Required—TOEFL (minimum score 550 paper-based; 79 iBT). Electronic applications accepted.

University of Wisconsin–Platteville, School of Graduate Studies, College of Liberal Arts and Education, School of Education, Platteville, WI 53818-3099. Offers adult education (MSE). *Accreditation:* NCATE. *Program availability:* Part-time, evening/weekend. *Degree requirements:* For master's, thesis or alternative. *Entrance requirements:* Additional exam requirements/recommendations for international students: Required—TOEFL (minimum score 550 paper-based; 79 iBT), IELTS (minimum score 6.5). Electronic applications accepted.

University of Wisconsin–River Falls, Outreach and Graduate Studies, College of Education and Professional Studies, Department of Teacher Education, River Falls, WI 54022. Offers elementary education (MSE); professional development shared inquiry communities (MSE); reading (MSE). *Program availability:* Part-time. *Degree requirements:* For master's, comprehensive exam, thesis or alternative. *Entrance requirements:* For master's, minimum GPA of 2.75. Additional exam requirements/recommendations for international students: Required—TOEFL (minimum score 500 paper-based; 65 iBT), IELTS (minimum score 5.5). Electronic applications accepted.

University of Wisconsin–Stevens Point, College of Professional Studies, School of Education, Stevens Point, WI 54481-3897. Offers education—general/reading (MSE); education—general/special (MSE); educational administration (MSE); educational sustainability (Ed D); elementary education (MSE). *Program availability:* Part-time. *Degree requirements:* For master's, comprehensive exam, thesis or alternative. *Entrance requirements:* For master's, teacher certification, minimum undergraduate GPA of 3.0, 2 years of teaching experience, letters of recommendation. Additional exam requirements/recommendations for international students: Required—TOEFL (minimum score 523 paper-based). *Faculty research:* Gifted education, early childhood special education, curriculum and instruction, standards-based education.

University of Wisconsin–Stout, Graduate School, College of Education, Health and Human Sciences, School of Education, Menomonie, WI 54751. Offers MS, MS Ed, Ed D, Ed S. *Accreditation:* NCATE. *Program availability:* Part-time, online learning. *Degree requirements:* For master's and Ed S, thesis. *Entrance requirements:* For degree, minimum GPA of 3.25. Additional exam requirements/recommendations for international students: Required—TOEFL (minimum score 500 paper-based; 61 iBT). Electronic applications accepted.

University of Wisconsin–Superior, Graduate Division, Department of Teacher Education, Superior, WI 54880-4500. Offers instruction (MSE); special education (MSE), including emotional/behavior disabilities, learning disabilities; teaching reading (MSE). *Program availability:* Part-time, evening/weekend, online learning. *Degree requirements:* For master's, research project. *Entrance requirements:* For master's, minimum GPA of 2.75, teaching certificate. Electronic applications accepted. *Faculty research:* Science teaching.

University of Wisconsin–Whitewater, School of Graduate Studies, College of Education and Professional Studies, Whitewater, WI 53190-1790. Offers MS, MSE, Postbaccalaureate Certificate. *Accreditation:* NCATE. *Program availability:* Part-time, evening/weekend, online learning. *Entrance requirements:* Additional exam requirements/recommendations for international students: Required—TOEFL (minimum score 550 paper-based). Electronic applications accepted.

Upper Iowa University, Master of Education Program, Fayette, IA 52142-1857. Offers early childhood (M Ed); English as a second language (M Ed); higher education (M Ed); instructional strategist (M Ed); reading (M Ed); teacher leadership (M Ed).

Urbana University–A Branch Campus of Franklin University, College of Education and Sports Studies, Urbana, OH 43078-2091. Offers classroom education (M Ed). *Program availability:* Part-time, evening/weekend. *Degree requirements:* For master's, comprehensive oral exam, capstone research project. *Entrance requirements:* For master's, minimum GPA of 2.7, teaching license. Additional exam requirements/recommendations for international students: Required—TOEFL (minimum score 550 paper-based). *Faculty research:* Best professional practices, reading/special education, classroom management, teaching models, school finance.

Utah State University, School of Graduate Studies, Emma Eccles Jones College of Education and Human Services, Logan, UT 84322. Offers M Ed, MA, MFHD, MRC, MS, Au D, Ed D, PhD, Ed S. *Accreditation:* TEAC. *Program availability:* Part-time, evening/weekend, online learning. *Degree requirements:* For doctorate, comprehensive exam, thesis/dissertation. *Entrance requirements:* For master's, GRE General Test, minimum GPA of 3.0; for doctorate, GRE General Test, master's degree; for Ed S, GRE General Test, GRE Subject Test. Additional exam requirements/recommendations for international students: Required—TOEFL (minimum score 550 paper-based). *Faculty research:* Literacy instruction, design and delivery of instruction, children at-risk and their families, hearing assessment and management, language and literacy development.

Utah Valley University, Program in Education, Orem, UT 84058-5999. Offers educational technology (M Ed); elementary mathematics (M Ed); elementary STEM (M Ed); English as a second language (M Ed); reading (M Ed); teachers as leaders (M Ed). *Accreditation:* TEAC. *Program availability:* Part-time. *Degree requirements:* For master's, project. *Entrance requirements:* For master's, GRE, 3 letters of recommendation, interview, essay. Additional exam requirements/recommendations for international students: Required—TOEFL (minimum score 83 iBT). Electronic applications accepted. *Expenses:* Contact institution.

Utica College, Teacher Education Programs, Utica, NY 13502-4892. Offers MS, MS Ed, CAS. *Accreditation:* TEAC. *Faculty:* 10 full-time (7 women). *Students:* 58 full-time (36 women), 20 part-time (13 women); includes 10 minority (3 Black or African American, non-Hispanic/Latino; 1 Asian, non-Hispanic/Latino; 4 Hispanic/Latino; 2 Two or more races, non-Hispanic/Latino). Average age 28. 85 applicants, 65% accepted, 46 enrolled. In 2018, 17 master's awarded. *Degree requirements:* For master's, comprehensive exam or thesis. *Entrance requirements:* For master's, CST, LAST, minimum GPA of 3.0. Additional exam requirements/recommendations for international students: Required—TOEFL (minimum score 525 paper-based). *Application deadline:* Applications are processed on a rolling basis. Application fee: $50. Electronic applications accepted. *Expenses:* Contact institution. *Financial support:* Career-related internships or fieldwork, scholarships/grants, tuition waivers (partial), and unspecified assistantships available. Support available to part-time students. Financial award application deadline: 3/15; financial award applicants required to submit FAFSA. *Unit head:* Dr. Patrice Hallock, Dean of Health Professions and Education, 315-792-3162, E-mail: phallock@utica.edu. *Application contact:* John D. Rowe, Director of Graduate Admissions, 315-792-3824, Fax: 315-792-3003, E-mail: jrowe@utica.edu.

Valley City State University, Online Graduate Programs, Valley City, ND 58072. Offers elementary education (M Ed); English education (M Ed); library and information technologies (M Ed); teaching (MAT); teaching and technology (M Ed); teaching English language learners (M Ed); technology education (M Ed). *Accreditation:* NCATE. *Program availability:* Part-time, evening/weekend, online only, 100% online. *Faculty:* 20 full-time (11 women), 13 part-time/adjunct (8 women). *Students:* 5 full-time (2 women), 133 part-time (100 women); includes 8 minority (1 Black or African American, non-Hispanic/Latino; 3 American Indian or Alaska Native, non-Hispanic/Latino; 2 Asian, non-Hispanic/Latino; 2 Hispanic/Latino). Average age 36. 23 applicants, 74% accepted, 12 enrolled. In 2018, 47 master's awarded. *Degree requirements:* For master's, action research report, comprehensive portfolio. *Entrance requirements:* For master's, GRE, MAT, PRAXIS II or National Teaching Board for Professional Standards (if GPA is less than 3.0). Additional exam requirements/recommendations for international students: Required—TOEFL (minimum score 525 paper-based; 71 iBT); Recommended—IELTS (minimum score 5.5). *Application deadline:* For fall admission, 7/26 for domestic and international students; for spring admission, 12/13 for domestic and international students; for summer admission, 5/18 for domestic and international students. Applications are processed on a rolling basis. Application fee: $35. Electronic applications accepted. *Expenses:* $396.39 per credit for all students regardless of residency. *Financial support:* In 2018–19, 16 students received support. Scholarships/grants, tuition waivers (full and partial), and unspecified assistantships available. Financial award applicants required to submit FAFSA. *Faculty research:* Universal accessibility, instructional design and technology, gender communication, STEM education in K-12, English language learners. *Unit head:* Dr. Sheri Okland, Dean, 701-845-7184, E-mail: sheri.l.okland@vcsu.edu. *Application contact:* Misty Lindgren, Graduate Studies, 701-845-7303, Fax: 701-845-7190, E-mail: misty.lindgren@vcsu.edu.
Website: http://www.vcsu.edu/graduate

Valparaiso University, Graduate School and Continuing Education, Programs in Education, Valparaiso, IN 46383. Offers initial licensure (M Ed), including Chinese teaching, elementary education, secondary education; instructional leadership (M Ed); school psychology (Ed S); secondary education (M Ed); M Ed/Ed S. *Accreditation:* NCATE. *Program availability:* Part-time, evening/weekend, online learning. *Entrance requirements:* For master's, GRE General Test, minimum GPA of 3.0. Additional exam requirements/recommendations for international students: Required—TOEFL (minimum score 550 paper-based; 80 iBT), IELTS (minimum score 6). Electronic applications accepted.

Vanderbilt University, Peabody College, Nashville, TN 37203-5721. Offers education policy (MPP). *Accreditation:* APA (one or more programs are accredited); NCATE. *Program availability:* Part-time, evening/weekend, online courses with semester immersions on campus. *Faculty:* 170 full-time (111 women), 83 part-time/adjunct (59 women). *Students:* 520 full-time (423 women), 442 part-time (312 women); includes 232 minority (132 Black or African American, non-Hispanic/Latino; 4 American Indian or Alaska Native, non-Hispanic/Latino; 37 Asian, non-Hispanic/Latino; 45 Hispanic/Latino; 14 Two or more races, non-Hispanic/Latino), 88 international. Average age 30. 1,878 applicants, 56% accepted, 561 enrolled. In 2018, 357 master's, 20 doctorates awarded. *Degree requirements:* For master's, comprehensive exam (for some programs), thesis optional; for doctorate, thesis/dissertation or alternative, qualifying examinations, doctoral/capstone projects. *Entrance requirements:* For master's and doctorate, GRE General Test. Additional exam requirements/recommendations for international students: Required—TOEFL (minimum score 550 paper-based; 80 iBT). *Application deadline:* For fall admission, 12/31 priority date for domestic and international students; for spring admission, 11/1 priority date for domestic and international students. Applications are processed on a rolling basis. Application fee: $0. Electronic applications accepted. *Expenses:* $1,828 per credit. *Financial support:* In 2018–19, 574 students received support. Fellowships with partial tuition reimbursements available, research assistantships with partial tuition reimbursements available, teaching assistantships with partial tuition reimbursements available, career-related internships or fieldwork, Federal Work-Study, institutionally sponsored loans, scholarships/grants, traineeships, tuition waivers (partial), and unspecified assistantships available. Support available to part-time students. Financial award application deadline: 1/15; financial award applicants required to submit FAFSA. *Total annual research expenditures:* $41.5 million. *Unit head:* Dr. Camilla P. Benbow, Dean, 615-322-8407, Fax: 615-322-8501, E-mail: camilla.benbow@vanderbilt.edu. *Application contact:* Kimberly Brazil, Director of Graduate and Professional Admissions, 615-332-8410, Fax: 615-343-3474, E-mail: kim.brazil@vanderbilt.edu.
Website: http://peabody.vanderbilt.edu/

See Display below and Close-Up on page 601.

Vanderbilt University, Program in Learning, Teaching and Diversity, Nashville, TN 37240-1001. Offers PhD. *Faculty:* 19 full-time (10 women), 2 part-time/adjunct (both women). *Students:* 38 full-time (31 women); includes 12 minority (3 Black or African American, non-Hispanic/Latino; 4 Asian, non-Hispanic/Latino; 1 Hispanic/Latino; 4 Two or more races, non-Hispanic/Latino), 3 international. Average age 32. 91 applicants, 12% accepted, 6 enrolled. In 2018, 8 doctorates awarded. *Degree requirements:* For doctorate, comprehensive exam, thesis/dissertation, qualifying examinations. *Entrance requirements:* For doctorate, GRE General Test. Additional exam requirements/recommendations for international students: Required—TOEFL (minimum score 570 paper-based; 88 iBT). *Application deadline:* For fall admission, 12/1 for domestic and international students. Application fee: $0. Electronic applications accepted. *Expenses:* Contact institution. *Financial support:* Fellowships with partial tuition reimbursements, research assistantships with full tuition reimbursements, teaching assistantships with full tuition reimbursements, Federal Work-Study, institutionally sponsored loans, scholarships/grants, traineeships, and health care benefits available. Financial award application deadline: 1/15; financial award applicants required to submit CSS PROFILE or FAFSA. *Faculty research:* New pedagogies for math, science, and language; the support of English language learners; the uses of new technology and media in the classroom; middle school mathematics and the institutional setting of teaching. *Unit head:* Dr. Deborah Rowe, Chair, 615-322-8044, Fax: 615-322-8014, E-mail: deborah.w.rowe@vanderbilt.edu. *Application contact:* Llana Horn, Director of Graduate Studies, 615-322-5884, Fax: 615-322-8014, E-mail: llana.horn@vanderbilt.edu.
Website: http://peabody.vanderbilt.edu/departments/tl/index.php

Vanguard University of Southern California, Graduate Programs in Education, Costa Mesa, CA 92626. Offers Christian education leadership (MA); curriculum and instruction (MA); teacher leadership (MA). *Program availability:* Evening/weekend. *Degree requirements:* For master's, thesis or alternative. *Entrance requirements:* For master's, California Basic Educational Skills Test, California Subject Examinations for Teachers, minimum GPA of 3.0. Additional exam requirements/recommendations for international students: Required—TOEFL (minimum score 550 paper-based; 79 iBT). Electronic applications accepted. *Expenses:* Contact institution. *Faculty research:* Reading, educational administration.

Villanova University, Graduate School of Liberal Arts and Sciences, Department of Education and Counseling, Villanova, PA 19085-1699. Offers elementary school counseling (MS), including counseling and human relations; teacher leadership (MA). *Program availability:* Part-time, evening/weekend. *Degree requirements:* For master's, comprehensive exam. *Entrance requirements:* For master's, GRE or MAT, minimum GPA of 3.0, statement of goals. Electronic applications accepted.

Virginia Commonwealth University, Graduate School, School of Education, Richmond, VA 23284-9005. Offers M Ed, MT, Ed D, PhD, Certificate. *Accreditation:* NCATE. *Program availability:* Part-time. *Degree requirements:* For doctorate, thesis/dissertation. *Entrance requirements:* For master's, GRE General Test or MAT; for doctorate, GRE (PhD only), MAT (Ed D only), interview, master's degree. Additional exam requirements/recommendations for international students: Required—TOEFL (minimum score 600 paper-based; 100 iBT); Recommended—IELTS (minimum score 6.5). Electronic applications accepted.

Virginia International University, School of Education, Fairfax, VA 22030. Offers applied linguistics (MS); education (M Ed); teaching English to speakers of other languages (MA). *Program availability:* Part-time, online learning. *Entrance requirements:* For master's, bachelor's degree. Additional exam requirements/recommendations for international students: Required—TOEFL (minimum score 550 paper-based; 80 iBT), IELTS (minimum score 6). Electronic applications accepted.

Virginia Polytechnic Institute and State University, VT Online, Blacksburg, VA 24061. Offers advanced transportation systems (Certificate); aerospace engineering (MS); agricultural and life sciences (MSLFS); business information systems (Graduate Certificate); career and technical education (MS); civil engineering (MS); computer engineering (M Eng, MS); decision support systems (Graduate Certificate); eLearning leadership (MA); electrical engineering (M Eng, MS); engineering administration (MEA); environmental engineering (Certificate); environmental politics and policy (Graduate Certificate); environmental sciences and engineering (MS); foundations of political analysis (Graduate Certificate); health product risk management (Graduate Certificate); industrial and systems engineering (MS); information policy and society (Graduate Certificate); information security (Graduate Certificate); information technology (MIT); instructional technology (MA); integrative STEM education (MA Ed); liberal arts (Graduate Certificate); life sciences: health product risk management (MS); natural resources (MNR, Graduate Certificate); networking (Graduate Certificate); nonprofit and

nongovernmental organization management (Graduate Certificate); ocean engineering (MS); political science (MA); security studies (Graduate Certificate); software development (Graduate Certificate). *Expenses:* Tuition, state resident: full-time $15,510; part-time $739.50 per credit hour. Tuition, nonresident: full-time $29,629; part-time $1490.25 per credit hour. *Required fees:* $2804; $550 per semester. Tuition and fees vary according to course load, campus/location and program. *Application contact:* Graduate Admissions and Academic Progress, 540-231-8636, E-mail: grads@vt.edu. Website: http://www.vto.vt.edu/

Virginia State University, College of Graduate Studies, College of Education, Petersburg, VA 23806-0001. Offers M Ed, MS, Ed D.

Virginia State University, College of Graduate Studies, College of Humanities and Social Sciences, Petersburg, VA 23806-0001. Offers M Ed, MA, MS. *Accreditation:* NCATE. *Program availability:* Part-time, evening/weekend.

Virginia Union University, Evelyn R. Syphax School of Education, Psychology and Interdisciplinary Studies, Richmond, VA 23220-1170. Offers curriculum and instruction (MA).

Virginia Wesleyan University, Graduate Studies, Virginia Beach, VA 23455. Offers business administration (MBA); secondary and PreK-12 education (MA Ed). *Program availability:* Online learning.

Viterbo University, Graduate Programs in Education, La Crosse, WI 54601-4797. Offers cross-categorical special education (Certificate); director of instruction (Certificate); director of special education and pupil services (Certificate); early childhood (Certificate); education (MAE); literacy coaching (Certificate); PreK-12 principal/supervisor of special education (Certificate); principal (Certificate); reading specialist endorsement (Certificate); reading teacher (Certificate); reading teacher 5-12 endorsement (Certificate); reading teacher K-8 endorsement (Certificate); superintendent (Certificate); talented and gifted endorsement (Certificate); Wisconsin school business administrator (Certificate). Weekend courses available in summer. *Accreditation:* NCATE. *Program availability:* Part-time, evening/weekend. *Degree requirements:* For master's, comprehensive exam, thesis, 30 credits of course work. *Entrance requirements:* For master's, BS, transcripts, teaching license, written narrative. Electronic applications accepted. *Expenses:* Contact institution.

Wagner College, Division of Graduate Studies, Education Department, Staten Island, NY 10301-4495. Offers childhood education/students with disabilities (MS Ed), including childhood education; early childhood education/students with disabilities (birth-grade 2) (MS Ed); higher education and learning organizations leadership (MA); secondary education/students with disabilities (MS Ed), including secondary education 7-12. *Accreditation:* NCATE. *Program availability:* Part-time, evening/weekend. *Degree requirements:* For master's, thesis (for some programs). *Entrance requirements:* For master's, GRE, minimum GPA of 3.0. Additional exam requirements/recommendations for international students: Required—TOEFL (minimum score 550 paper-based; 79 iBT), IELTS (minimum score 6.5). Electronic applications accepted. *Faculty research:* School-community partnerships, civic engagement, educational accountability, micro-aggression and bullying, cross-cultural pedagogy with students and families.

Wake Forest University, Graduate School of Arts and Sciences, Department of Education, Winston-Salem, NC 27109. Offers secondary education (MA Ed). *Accreditation:* ACA; NCATE. *Faculty:* 7 full-time (4 women). *Students:* 13 full-time (8 women); includes 1 minority (Black or African American, non-Hispanic/Latino). Average age 24. 20 applicants, 65% accepted, 11 enrolled. In 2018, 11 master's awarded. *Degree requirements:* For master's, thesis optional. *Entrance requirements:* For master's, GRE General Test. Additional exam requirements/recommendations for international students: Required—TOEFL (minimum score 550 paper-based). *Application deadline:* For fall admission, 1/15 for domestic students, 1/15 priority date for international students. Application fee: $75. Electronic applications accepted. *Expenses:* Contact institution. *Financial support:* In 2018–19, 11 students received support, including 11 fellowships with full tuition reimbursements available (averaging $49,000 per year), 3 teaching assistantships with full tuition reimbursements available (averaging $49,000 per year); scholarships/grants and tuition waivers (full and partial) also available. Financial award application deadline: 2/15. *Faculty research:* Teaching and learning. *Unit head:* Dr. Adam Friedman, Chair, 336-758-5507, Fax: 336-758-4591, E-mail: amfriedman@wfu.edu. *Application contact:* Dr. Leah McCoy, Program Director, 336-758-5498, Fax: 336-758-4591, E-mail: mccoy@wfu.edu.
Website: https://education.wfu.edu/graduate-program/overview-of-graduate-programs/

Walden University, Graduate Programs, Richard W. Riley College of Education and Leadership, Minneapolis, MN 55401. Offers adult education (Post-Master's Certificate); adult learning (Graduate Certificate); college teaching and learning (Graduate Certificate); community college leadership (Ed D); curriculum, instruction and assessment (Ed D, Ed S, Graduate Certificate); developmental education (Graduate Certificate); early childhood administration, management, and leadership (Graduate Certificate); early childhood education (Ed D, Ed S); early childhood public policy and advocacy (Graduate Certificate); early childhood studies (MS), including administration, management and leadership, early childhood public policy and advocacy, teaching adults in the early childhood field, teaching and diversity in early childhood education; education (MS, PhD), including adolescent literacy and learning (MS), curriculum, instruction, and assessment (grades K-12) (MS), curriculum, instruction, assessment, and evaluation (PhD), early childhood leadership and advocacy (PhD), early childhood special education (PhD), educational leadership (MS), educational leadership and administration (principal preparation) (MS), educational technology and design (PhD), elementary reading and literacy (PreK-6) (MS), elementary reading and mathematics (grades K-6) (MS), global and comparative education (PhD), higher education leadership management and policy (PhD), integrating technology in the classroom (grades K-12) (MS), learning, instruction and innovation (PhD), mathematics (grades 5-8) (MS), mathematics (grades K-6) (MS), mathematics and science (grades K-8) (MS), organizational research, assessment, and evaluation (PhD), reading and literacy with a reading K-12 endorsement (MS), reading literacy assessment and evaluation (PhD), science (grades K-8) (MS), special education (non-licensure) (grades K-12) (MS), teacher leadership (grades K-12) (MS), teaching English language learners (grades K-12) (MS); educational administration and leadership (Ed D); educational leadership and administration (principal preparation) (Ed S); educational technology (Ed D, Ed S, Post Master's Certificate); elementary reading and literacy (Graduate Certificate); engaging culturally diverse learners (Graduate Certificate); enrollment management and institutional marketing (Graduate Certificate); higher education (MS), including adult learning, college teaching and learning, enrollment management and institutional marketing, global higher education, leadership for student success, online and distance learning; higher education and adult learning (Ed D); higher education leadership and management (Ed D); higher education leadership for student success (Graduate Certificate); instructional design and technology (MS, Postbaccalaureate Certificate), including general program (MS), online learning (MS), training and performance improvement (MS); integrating technology in the classroom (Graduate Certificate); mathematics 5-8 (Graduate Certificate); mathematics K-6 (Graduate Certificate); online teaching for adult educators (Graduate Certificate); reading, literacy, and assessment (Ed D, Ed S); science K-8 (Graduate Certificate); special education (Ed D, Ed S, Graduate Certificate); special education (K-age 21) (MAT); teacher leadership (Graduate Certificate); teaching adults English as a second language (Graduate Certificate); teaching adults in the early childhood field (Graduate Certificate); teaching and diversity in early childhood education (Graduate Certificate); teaching English language learners (grades K-12) (Graduate Certificate); teaching K-12 students online (Graduate Certificate). *Accreditation:* NCATE. *Program availability:* Part-time, evening/weekend, online only, 100% online. *Degree requirements:* For doctorate, thesis/dissertation (for some programs), residency; for other advanced degree, residency (for some programs). *Entrance requirements:* For master's, bachelor's degree or higher; minimum GPA of 2.5; official transcripts; goal statement (for some programs); access to computer and Internet; for doctorate, master's degree or higher; three years of related professional or academic experience (preferred); minimum GPA of 3.0; goal statement and current resume (for select programs); official transcripts; access to computer and Internet; for other advanced degree, relevant work experience; access to computer and Internet. Additional exam requirements/recommendations for international students: Required—TOEFL (minimum score 550 paper-based, 79 iBT), IELTS (minimum score 6.5), Michigan English Language Assessment Battery (minimum score 82), or PTE (minimum score 53). Electronic applications accepted.

Walla Walla University, Graduate Studies, School of Education and Psychology, College Place, WA 99324. Offers curriculum and instruction (M Ed, MAT); educational leadership (M Ed, MAT); literacy instruction (M Ed, MAT); special education (M Ed, MAT). *Program availability:* Part-time. *Entrance requirements:* For master's, GRE General Test, minimum GPA of 2.75. Additional exam requirements/recommendations for international students: Required—TOEFL (minimum score 550 paper-based; 79 iBT). Electronic applications accepted. *Faculty research:* Admissions/retention, instructional psychology, moral development, teaching of reading.

Walsh University, Graduate Programs, Program in Education, North Canton, OH 44720-3396. Offers leadership with principal license (MA Ed); reading literacy (MA Ed). *Accreditation:* NCATE. *Program availability:* Part-time, evening/weekend. *Degree requirements:* For master's, comprehensive exam (for some programs), thesis optional, action research project or comprehensive exam. *Entrance requirements:* For master's, MAT (minimum score 396), GRE (minimum scores: verbal 145, quantitative 146, combined 291, writing 3.0), or minimum GPA of 3.0 on the baccalaureate transcript, interview, minimum GPA of 3.0, writing sample, 3 recommendation forms, notarized affidavit of good moral character. Additional exam requirements/recommendations for international students: Required—TOEFL (minimum score 500 paper-based; 61 iBT). Electronic applications accepted. Application fee is waived when completed online. *Expenses:* Contact institution. *Faculty research:* Learning and the brain, primary STEM, effective assessment practices, literacy.

Warner Pacific University, Graduate Programs, Portland, OR 97215-4099. Offers human services (MA); not-for-profit leadership (MS); organizational leadership (MS); teaching (MAT). *Program availability:* Part-time, evening/weekend. *Degree requirements:* For master's, thesis or alternative, presentation of defense. *Entrance requirements:* For master's, interview, minimum GPA of 2.5, letters of recommendation. *Faculty research:* New Testament studies, nineteenth-century Wesleyan theology, preaching and church growth, Christian ethics.

Warner University, School of Education, Lake Wales, FL 33859. Offers curriculum and instruction (MAEd); elementary education (MAEd); science, technology, engineering, and mathematics (STEM) (MAEd). *Program availability:* Part-time, evening/weekend, online learning. *Degree requirements:* For master's, thesis, accomplished practices portfolio. *Entrance requirements:* For master's, minimum GPA of 3.0 in last 60 hours of undergraduate coursework; 2 letters of recommendation. Additional exam requirements/recommendations for international students: Required—TOEFL (minimum score 550 paper-based). Electronic applications accepted.

Washburn University, College of Arts and Sciences, Department of Education, Topeka, KS 66621. Offers curriculum and instruction (M Ed); educational leadership (M Ed); reading (M Ed); special education (M Ed). *Accreditation:* NCATE. *Program availability:* Part-time. *Degree requirements:* For master's, comprehensive exam, thesis or alternative, portfolio, comprehensive paper, or action research project. *Entrance requirements:* For master's, department exam, GRE General Test, or MAT, minimum GPA of 3.0 in graduate coursework or last 60 hours of undergraduate coursework. Additional exam requirements/recommendations for international students: Required—TOEFL (minimum score 80 iBT). *Faculty research:* Reading/literature/literacy, foundations, special education, diversity, teaching and technology.

Washington State University, College of Education, Pullman, WA 99164-2114. Offers Ed M, MA, MIT, Ed D, PhD. *Degree requirements:* For master's, comprehensive exam (for some programs), thesis (for some programs), oral and written exams; for doctorate, comprehensive exam, thesis/dissertation, oral and written exams, internship. *Entrance requirements:* For master's, GRE General Test, minimum GPA of 3.0, 3 letters of recommendation, transcripts showing all college or university course work, statement of professional objectives, current curriculum vitae/resume; for doctorate, GRE General Test or MAT, minimum GPA of 3.0, 3 letters of recommendation, transcripts showing all college or university course work, statement of professional objectives, current curriculum vitae/resume. Additional exam requirements/recommendations for international students: Required—TOEFL (minimum score 550 paper-based; 80 iBT). Electronic applications accepted.

Washington University in St. Louis, The Graduate School, Department of Education, St. Louis, MO 63130-4899. Offers educational research (PhD); elementary education (MA Ed); secondary education (MAT). *Degree requirements:* For master's, thesis or alternative; for doctorate, thesis/dissertation. *Entrance requirements:* For master's and doctorate, GRE General Test. Additional exam requirements/recommendations for international students: Required—TOEFL. Electronic applications accepted. *Faculty research:* Teacher education, educational studies, urban education, policy studies, science and math education, second language research.

Wayland Baptist University, Graduate Programs, Program in Education, Plainview, TX 79072-6998. Offers education administration (M Ed); education diagnostics (M Ed); education literacy (M Ed); elementary certification (M Ed); English (M Ed); English as a second language (M Ed); higher education administration (M Ed); human resources (M Ed); instructional leadership (M Ed); instructional technology (M Ed); leadership training and development (M Ed); science education (M Ed); secondary certification (M Ed); social studies (M Ed); special education (M Ed); sports administration and management (M Ed). *Program availability:* Part-time, evening/weekend, 100% online. *Degree requirements:* For master's, comprehensive exam, capstone course. *Entrance requirements:* For master's, GRE, GMAT or MAT. Additional exam requirements/recommendations for international students: Required—TOEFL (minimum score 500 paper-based; 61 iBT). Electronic applications accepted.

Wayne State College, School of Education and Counseling, Wayne, NE 68787. Offers MSE, Ed S. *Accreditation:* NCATE. *Program availability:* Part-time, evening/weekend. *Degree requirements:* For master's, comprehensive exam, thesis (for some programs). *Entrance requirements:* For master's, GRE General Test, minimum cumulative GPA of 3.0; for Ed S, GRE General Test, minimum GPA of 3.2 in all program coursework. Additional exam requirements/recommendations for international students: Required—TOEFL (minimum score 550 paper-based).

Education—General

Wayne State University, College of Education, Detroit, MI 48202. Offers M Ed, MA, MAT, MSAT, Ed D, PhD, Certificate, Ed S, M Ed/MA. *Accreditation:* TEAC. *Program availability:* Part-time, evening/weekend, 100% online, blended/hybrid learning. *Faculty:* 46. *Students:* 426 full-time (307 women), 926 part-time (692 women); includes 511 minority (382 Black or African American, non-Hispanic/Latino; 3 American Indian or Alaska Native, non-Hispanic/Latino; 22 Asian, non-Hispanic/Latino; 44 Hispanic/Latino; 2 Native Hawaiian or other Pacific Islander, non-Hispanic/Latino; 58 Two or more races, non-Hispanic/Latino), 52 international. Average age 35. 919 applicants, 36% accepted, 228 enrolled. In 2018, 322 master's, 53 doctorates, 64 other advanced degrees awarded. *Degree requirements:* For master's, thesis (for some programs); for doctorate, thesis/dissertation, written exam. *Entrance requirements:* For master's, baccalaureate degree with minimum upper-division GPA of 2.75; teaching certificate (for some M Ed programs); for doctorate, written exam of writing ability, minimum undergraduate GPA of 3.0, 3 years of teaching experience (for some programs); master's degree (for most programs); for other advanced degree, minimum upper-division GPA of 2.75 or 3.4 in master's program (for Ed S); master's degree; 3 years of teaching experience (for some areas). Additional exam requirements/recommendations for international students: Required—TOEFL (minimum score 550 paper-based; 79 iBT), TWE (minimum score 5.5); Recommended—IELTS (minimum score 6.5). *Application deadline:* For fall admission, 6/1 priority date for domestic students, 5/1 for international students; for winter admission, 10/1 priority date for domestic students, 9/1 priority date for international students; for spring admission, 2/1 priority date for domestic students, 1/1 priority date for international students. Application fee: $50. Electronic applications accepted. *Financial support:* In 2018–19, 303 students received support, including 4 fellowships with tuition reimbursements available (averaging $13,500 per year), 13 research assistantships with tuition reimbursements available (averaging $18,339 per year), 5 teaching assistantships with tuition reimbursements available (averaging $18,534 per year); Federal Work-Study, scholarships/grants, traineeships, health care benefits, and unspecified assistantships also available. Support available to part-time students. Financial award applicants required to submit FAFSA. *Unit head:* Dr. R. Douglas Whitman, Dean, 313-577-1620, E-mail: dwhitman@wayne.edu. *Application contact:* Paul W. Johnson, Assistant Dean of Academic Services, 313-577-1606, E-mail: askcoe@wayne.edu.
Website: http://coe.wayne.edu/

Weber State University, Jerry and Vickie Moyes College of Education, Ogden, UT 84408-1001. Offers M Ed, MSAT. *Accreditation:* NCATE; TEAC. *Program availability:* Part-time, evening/weekend. *Faculty:* 27 full-time (15 women), 1 part-time/adjunct (0 women). *Students:* 43 full-time (30 women), 146 part-time (116 women); includes 13 minority (1 Black or African American, non-Hispanic/Latino; 2 American Indian or Alaska Native, non-Hispanic/Latino; 2 Asian, non-Hispanic/Latino; 7 Hispanic/Latino; 1 Two or more races, non-Hispanic/Latino), 8 international. Average age 35. In 2018, 50 master's awarded. *Degree requirements:* For master's, project presentation, exam. *Entrance requirements:* For master's, GRE. Additional exam requirements/recommendations for international students: Required—TOEFL (minimum score 525 paper-based). *Application deadline:* For fall admission, 5/15 for domestic students; for spring admission, 9/15 for domestic students; for summer admission, 1/15 for domestic students. Application fee: $60 ($90 for international students). *Expenses:* 6,626 per year. *Financial support:* In 2018–19, 33 students received support. Institutionally sponsored loans, scholarships/grants, tuition waivers (full and partial), and unspecified assistantships available. Support available to part-time students. Financial award application deadline: 4/1; financial award applicants required to submit FAFSA. *Unit head:* Dr. Jack Rasmussen, Dean, 801-626-6273, Fax: 801-626-7427, E-mail: jrasmussen@weber.edu. *Application contact:* Nathan Alexander, College of Education Recruiter, 801-626-8124, Fax: 801-626-7427, E-mail: nathanalexander@weber.edu.
Website: http://www.weber.edu/education/

Webster University, School of Education, St. Louis, MO 63119-3194. Offers MA, MAT, MET, Ed S. *Accreditation:* NCATE. *Program availability:* Part-time, online learning. *Degree requirements:* For master's, thesis (for some programs). *Entrance requirements:* For master's, minimum GPA of 2.5. Additional exam requirements/recommendations for international students: Required—TOEFL. *Expenses: Tuition:* Full-time $22,500; part-time $750 per credit hour. Tuition and fees vary according to degree level, campus/location and program.

Wesleyan College, Department of Education, Macon, GA 31210-4462. Offers early childhood education (MA). *Program availability:* Part-time. *Entrance requirements:* For master's, GRE or MAT, two letters of professional reference, official transcript from the institution in which a Bachelor's degree was earned with an undergraduate GPA of 3.0, a copy of a valid professional teaching certificate or evidence of having been the teacher of record in a classroom for at least two years. Additional exam requirements/recommendations for international students: Required—TOEFL (minimum score 550 paper-based). Electronic applications accepted. *Expenses:* Contact institution. *Unit head:* Dr. Virginia Wilcox, Associate Professor of Education, 478-7575279, E-mail: vwilcox@wesleyancollege.edu. *Application contact:* Mariana Furlin, Assessment Coordinator for Education Department, Program Assistant to the EMBA, 478-7572801, E-mail: mfurlin@wesleyancollege.edu.

Wesley College, Education Program, Dover, DE 19901-3875. Offers M Ed, MA Ed, MAT. *Accreditation:* NCATE. *Program availability:* Part-time, evening/weekend. *Degree requirements:* For master's, thesis optional. *Entrance requirements:* For master's, GRE. *Faculty research:* Learning styles, community-higher education partnerships, curriculum models, science learning and teaching, literacy development in early elementary.

West Chester University of Pennsylvania, College of Education and Social Work, West Chester, PA 19383. Offers M Ed, MS, MSW, Ed D, Certificate, Post Master's Certificate, Teaching Certificate. *Accreditation:* NCATE. *Program availability:* Part-time, evening/weekend, 100% online, blended/hybrid learning. *Degree requirements:* For master's, comprehensive exam (for some programs), thesis (for some programs). *Entrance requirements:* Additional exam requirements/recommendations for international students: Required—TOEFL or IELTS. Electronic applications accepted.

Westcliff University, College of Education, Irvine, CA 92606. Offers teaching English to speakers of other languages (MA).

Western Carolina University, Graduate School, College of Education and Allied Professions, Cullowhee, NC 28723. Offers MA. *Accreditation:* NCATE. *Program availability:* Part-time, evening/weekend, online learning. *Degree requirements:* For master's, comprehensive exam, thesis. *Entrance requirements:* For master's, GRE, appropriate undergraduate degree with minimum GPA of 3.0, 3 recommendations, writing sample, resume, interview. Additional exam requirements/recommendations for international students: Required—TOEFL (minimum score 550 paper-based; 79 iBT). *Expenses: Tuition, area resident:* Full-time $4435. Tuition, state resident: full-time $4435. Tuition, nonresident: full-time $14,842. *International tuition:* $14,842 full-time. *Required fees:* $2979. Part-time tuition and fees vary according to course load, degree level and program. *Faculty research:* Evolutionary psychology, marital and family development, program evaluation, rural education, special education, educational leadership, employee recruitment/retention.

Western Connecticut State University, Division of Graduate Studies, School of Professional Studies, Department of Education and Educational Psychology, Danbury, CT 06810-6885. Offers clinical mental health counseling (MS); curriculum (MS); instructional leadership (Ed D); instructional technology (MS); reading (MS); school counseling (MS); special education (MS). *Accreditation:* NCATE. *Program availability:* Part-time. *Students:* 14 full-time (12 women), 255 part-time (208 women). Average age 33. *Degree requirements:* For master's, thesis or alternative, completion of program in 6 years. *Entrance requirements:* For master's, MAT (if GPA is below 2.8), valid teaching certificate, letters of reference; for doctorate, GRE or MAT, resume, three recommendations (one in a supervisory capacity in an educational setting), satisfactory interview with WCSU representatives from the Ed D Admissions Committee. Additional exam requirements/recommendations for international students: Recommended—TOEFL (minimum score 550 paper-based; 79 iBT), IELTS (minimum score 6). *Application deadline:* For fall admission, 8/5 priority date for domestic students; for spring admission, 1/5 for domestic students. Applications are processed on a rolling basis. Application fee: $50. *Expenses:* Contact institution. *Financial support:* Scholarships/grants available. Financial award application deadline: 5/1; financial award applicants required to submit FAFSA. *Faculty research:* Cultural diversity in teacher and counselor education programs, African-American educational leaders, urban education and equity. *Unit head:* Dr. Catherine O'Callaghan, Chairperson, 203-837-3267, Fax: 203-837-8413. *Application contact:* Dr. Chris Shankle, Associate Director of Graduate Studies, 203-837-9005, Fax: 203-837-8326, E-mail: shanklec@wcsu.edu.
Website: http://www.wcsu.edu/education/

Western Governors University, Teachers College, Salt Lake City, UT 84107. Offers curriculum and instruction (MS); educational leadership (MS); elementary education (MAT, Postbaccalaureate Certificate); English education (5-12) (MAT); English language learning (PreK-12) (MA); instructional design (M Ed); learning and technology (M Ed); mathematics (5-12) (MAT); mathematics (5-9) (MAT); mathematics education (5-12) (MA); mathematics education (5-9) (MA); mathematics education (K-6) (MA); science (5-12) (MAT); science education (5-12) (MA), including biology, chemistry, earth science, physics; science education (5-9) (MA); special education (MS). *Accreditation:* NCATE. *Program availability:* Evening/weekend, online learning. *Degree requirements:* For master's, capstone project. *Entrance requirements:* For master's and Postbaccalaureate Certificate, transcripts. Additional exam requirements/recommendations for international students: Required—TOEFL (minimum score 450 paper-based; 80 iBT). Electronic applications accepted. Application fee is waived when completed online. *Expenses:* Contact institution.

Western Illinois University, School of Graduate Studies, College of Education and Human Services, Macomb, IL 61455-1390. Offers MA, MS, MS Ed, Ed D, Certificate, Ed S. *Accreditation:* NCATE. *Program availability:* Part-time, evening/weekend, online learning. *Degree requirements:* For master's, comprehensive exam (for some programs), thesis or alternative; for doctorate, comprehensive exam, thesis/dissertation, electronic portfolio. *Entrance requirements:* For master's, GRE and MAT (for selected programs); for doctorate, GRE. Additional exam requirements/recommendations for international students: Required—TOEFL. Electronic applications accepted.

Western Michigan University, Graduate College, College of Education and Human Development, Kalamazoo, MI 49008. Offers MA, MS, Ed D, PhD, Ed S, Graduate Certificate. *Accreditation:* NCATE. *Program availability:* Part-time. *Degree requirements:* For doctorate, thesis/dissertation; for other advanced degree, thesis.

Western New Mexico University, Graduate Division, School of Education, Silver City, NM 88062-0680. Offers bilingual education (MAT); educational leadership (MA); elementary education (MAT); reading (MAT); secondary education (MAT); special education (MAT); TESOL (teaching English to speakers of other languages) (MAT). *Accreditation:* NCATE. *Program availability:* Part-time, online learning. *Degree requirements:* For master's, comprehensive exam. *Entrance requirements:* For master's, minimum GPA of 3.0 in last 64 hours of undergraduate study. Additional exam requirements/recommendations for international students: Required—TOEFL (minimum score 550 paper-based; 79 iBT). Electronic applications accepted. *Faculty research:* International education, electronic reading assessment, developing STEM teachers.

Western Oregon University, Graduate Programs, College of Education, Monmouth, OR 97361. Offers MAT, MS, MS Ed. *Accreditation:* NCATE. *Program availability:* Part-time, evening/weekend, online learning. *Degree requirements:* For master's, comprehensive exam (for some programs), thesis optional, written exam. *Entrance requirements:* For master's, minimum GPA of 3.0. Additional exam requirements/recommendations for international students: Required—TOEFL (minimum score 550 paper-based; 79 iBT), IELTS (minimum score 6.5). *Faculty research:* Effectiveness of work, sample methodology, documentation of learning gains, appropriateness of advanced proficiency.

Western State Colorado University, Graduate Programs in Education, Gunnison, CO 81231. Offers education administrator leadership (MA); reading leadership (MA); teacher leadership (MA). *Program availability:* Online learning. *Degree requirements:* For master's, capstone.

Western Washington University, Graduate School, Woodring College of Education, Bellingham, WA 98225-5996. Offers M Ed, MA, MIT. *Accreditation:* NCATE. *Program availability:* Part-time, online learning. *Degree requirements:* For master's, comprehensive exam, thesis optional. *Entrance requirements:* For master's, GRE General Test or MAT, minimum GPA of 3.0 in last 60 semester hours or last 90 quarter hours. Additional exam requirements/recommendations for international students: Required—TOEFL (minimum score 567 paper-based). Electronic applications accepted.

Westfield State University, College of Graduate and Continuing Education, Department of Education, Westfield, MA 01086. Offers early childhood education (M Ed); elementary education (M Ed); reading specialist (M Ed); secondary education (M Ed), including biology teacher education, chemistry teacher education, general science teacher education, history teacher education, mathematics teacher education, physical education teacher education; special education (M Ed), including moderate disabilities, 5-12, moderate disabilities, preK-8; vocational technical education (M Ed). *Accreditation:* NCATE. *Program availability:* Part-time, evening/weekend. *Degree requirements:* For master's, comprehensive exam, practicum. *Entrance requirements:* For master's, GRE General Test or MAT, minimum undergraduate GPA of 2.8. Additional exam requirements/recommendations for international students: Recommended—TOEFL (minimum score 550 paper-based; 79 iBT). *Faculty research:* Collaborative teacher education, developmental early childhood education.

West Liberty University, College of Education and Human Performance, West Liberty, WV 26074. Offers community education research and leadership (MA Ed); innovative instruction (MA Ed); leadership in disability services (MA Ed); leadership studies (MA Ed); multi-categorical special education (MA Ed); reading specialist (MA Ed); sports leadership and coaching (MA Ed). *Accreditation:* NCATE. *Program availability:* Part-time, evening/weekend. *Degree requirements:* For master's, capstone experience. *Entrance requirements:* For master's, minimum GPA of 2.5 or 3.0 (depending on track). Additional exam requirements/recommendations for international students: Required—TOEFL. Electronic applications accepted.

Westminster College, School of Education, Salt Lake City, UT 84105-3697. Offers community leadership (MACL); education (M Ed); teaching (MAT). *Accreditation:* TEAC. *Program availability:* Part-time, evening/weekend. *Degree requirements:* For master's, thesis (for some programs), project or thesis. *Entrance requirements:* For master's, GRE, PRAXIS II, personal statement (2-pages), 2 letters of recommendation, personal resume, official transcript, minimum GPA of 3.0. Additional exam requirements/recommendations for international students: Required—TOEFL (minimum score 84 iBT), IELTS (minimum score 7). Electronic applications accepted. *Expenses:* Contact institution. *Faculty research:* Identity development, space among marginalized populations, adult education, Latin American studies and economic developments, educational travel, learning in social movements.

West Texas A&M University, College of Education and Social Sciences, Department of Education, Canyon, TX 79015. Offers counseling (MA); curriculum and instruction (M Ed); educational diagnostician (M Ed); educational leadership (M Ed); instructional design and technology (M Ed); reading education (M Ed); school counseling (M Ed); teaching (MAT). *Program availability:* Part-time, evening/weekend, online learning. *Degree requirements:* For master's, comprehensive exam, thesis optional. *Entrance requirements:* For master's, GRE General Test. Additional exam requirements/recommendations for international students: Required—TOEFL. Electronic applications accepted.

West Virginia University, College of Education and Human Services, Morgantown, WV 26506. Offers audiology (Au D); autism spectrum disorder (MA); clinical rehabilitation and mental health counseling (MS); communication science and disorders (PhD); counseling (MA); counseling psychology (PhD); curriculum and instruction (Ed D); early childhood education (MA); early intervention/ early childhood special education (MA); education (PhD); educational leadership (MA); educational leadership/ public school administration (Ed D); educational leadership/public school administration (MA); educational psychology (MA, Ed D); elementary education (MA); gifted education (MA); higher education administration (MA, Ed D); higher education curriculum and teaching (MA); institutional design and technology (MA); instructional design and technology (Ed D); literacy education (MA); secondary education (MA); secondary education/ English (MA); special education (Ed D); speech pathology (MS). *Accreditation:* ASHA; NCATE. *Program availability:* Part-time, evening/weekend, online learning. *Students:* 392 full-time (325 women), 337 part-time (285 women); includes 44 minority (16 Black or African American, non-Hispanic/Latino; 16 Hispanic/Latino; 12 Two or more races, non-Hispanic/Latino), 11 international. In 2018, 303 master's, 6 doctorates awarded. *Degree requirements:* For master's, content exams; for doctorate, comprehensive exam, thesis/dissertation. *Entrance requirements:* Additional exam requirements/recommendations for international students: Required—TOEFL (minimum score 500 paper-based; 61 iBT). *Application deadline:* For fall admission, 8/1 for domestic students; for spring admission, 1/1 for domestic students; for summer admission, 5/1 for domestic students. Application fee: $60. Electronic applications accepted. *Financial support:* Fellowships, research assistantships, teaching assistantships, career-related internships or fieldwork, Federal Work-Study, institutionally sponsored loans, health care benefits, tuition waivers (full and partial), and administrative assistantships available. Financial award applicants required to submit FAFSA. *Faculty research:* Internet training and integration for teachers, rural education, teacher preparation, organization of schools, evaluation of personnel. *Unit head:* Dr. Tracy L. Morris, Interim Dean, 304-293-0816, Fax: 304-293-7565, E-mail: Tracy.Morris@mail.wvu.edu. *Application contact:* Dr. Melissa Luna, Associate Dean for Research, 304-293-2174, Fax: 304-293-3802, E-mail: Melissa.Luna@mail.wvu.edu.
Website: http://cehs.wvu.edu/

Wheaton College, Graduate School, Department of Education, Wheaton, IL 60187-5593. Offers elementary education (MAT); secondary education (MAT). *Accreditation:* NCATE. *Faculty:* 1 full-time (0 women), 1 part-time/adjunct (0 women). *Students:* 18 full-time (13 women), 22 part-time (10 women); includes 7 minority (3 Asian, non-Hispanic/Latino; 3 Hispanic/Latino; 1 Two or more races, non-Hispanic/Latino), 1 international. Average age 24. 21 applicants, 86% accepted, 13 enrolled. In 2018, 14 master's awarded. *Degree requirements:* For master's, thesis or alternative. *Entrance requirements:* For master's, GRE General Test or MAT. Additional exam requirements/recommendations for international students: Required—TOEFL (minimum score 550 paper-based; 80 iBT), IELTS (minimum score 6.5). *Application deadline:* For fall admission, 5/1 for domestic students, 1/1 for international students; for spring admission, 11/1 for domestic students. Applications are processed on a rolling basis. Application fee: $30. Electronic applications accepted. *Expenses: Tuition:* Full-time $20,400; part-time $850 per credit hour. Tuition and fees vary according to degree level and program. *Financial support:* Career-related internships or fieldwork and Federal Work-Study available. Financial award application deadline: 3/1; financial award applicants required to submit FAFSA. *Unit head:* Dr. Paul Egeland, Chair, 630-752-5041, E-mail: education.dept@wheaton.edu. *Application contact:* Terrance Campbell, Director of Graduate Admissions, 630-752-5195, Fax: 630-752-7047, E-mail: graduate.admissions@wheaton.edu.
Website: https://www.wheaton.edu/graduate-school/degrees/ma-in-teaching/

Whittier College, Graduate Programs, Department of Education and Child Development, Whittier, CA 90608-0634. Offers educational administration (MA Ed); elementary education (MA Ed); secondary education (MA Ed). *Program availability:* Part-time, evening/weekend. *Degree requirements:* For master's, thesis. *Entrance requirements:* For master's, GRE General Test, MAT, minimum GPA of 3.5, academic writing sample.

Whitworth University, School of Education, Graduate Studies in Education, Spokane, WA 99251-0001. Offers administration (M Ed); counseling (M Ed), including school counselors, social agency/church setting; elementary education (M Ed); gifted and talented (MAT); secondary education (M Ed); special education (MAT); teaching (MIT). *Accreditation:* NCATE. *Program availability:* Part-time, evening/weekend. *Degree requirements:* For master's, comprehensive exam, thesis (for some programs). *Entrance requirements:* For master's, GRE General Test, MAT. Additional exam requirements/recommendations for international students: Required—TOEFL. *Faculty research:* Rural program development, mainstreaming, special needs learners.

Wichita State University, Graduate School, College of Applied Studies, Wichita, KS 67260. Offers M Ed, MAT, Ed D, Ed S. *Accreditation:* NCATE. *Program availability:* Part-time, evening/weekend, 100% online, blended/hybrid learning. *Unit head:* Dr. Shirley Lefever, Dean, 316-978-3301, Fax: 316-978-3302, E-mail: shirley.lefever@wichita.edu. *Application contact:* Jordan Oleson, Admissions Coordinator, 316-978-3095, Fax: 316-978-3253, E-mail: jordan.oleson@wichita.edu.
Website: http://www.wichita.edu/education

Widener University, School of Human Service Professions, Center for Education, Chester, PA 19013-5792. Offers adult education (M Ed); counseling in higher education (M Ed); counselor education (M Ed); early childhood education (M Ed); educational foundations (M Ed); educational leadership (M Ed); educational psychology (M Ed); elementary education (M Ed); English and language arts (M Ed); health education (M Ed); higher education leadership (Ed D); home and school visitor (M Ed); human sexuality (M Ed, PhD); mathematics education (M Ed); middle school education (M Ed); principalship (M Ed); reading and language arts (Ed D); reading education (M Ed); school administration (Ed D); science education (M Ed); social studies education (M Ed); special education (M Ed); technology education (M Ed). *Accreditation:* NCATE. *Program availability:* Part-time, evening/weekend. Terminal master's awarded for partial completion of doctoral program. *Degree requirements:* For doctorate, thesis/dissertation. *Entrance requirements:* For master's, minimum GPA of 2.5; for doctorate, GRE or MAT, minimum GPA of 2.0 (undergraduate), 3.5 (graduate). Electronic applications accepted. *Expenses:* Contact institution. *Faculty research:* Reading and cognition, adult education, technology education, educational leadership, special education.

Wilkes University, College of Graduate and Professional Studies, School of Education, Wilkes-Barre, PA 18766-0002. Offers educational development and strategies (MS Ed); educational leadership (MS Ed, Ed D); effective teaching (MS Ed); instructional media (MS Ed); instructional technology (MS Ed); international school leadership (MS Ed); international teaching and learning (MS Ed); literacy (MS Ed); middle level education (MS Ed); online teaching (MS Ed); school business leadership (MS Ed); special education (MS Ed); teaching English to speakers of other languages (MS Ed). *Program availability:* Part-time, evening/weekend, 100% online, blended/hybrid learning. *Students:* 87 full-time (67 women), 1,418 part-time (1,078 women); includes 87 minority (13 Black or African American, non-Hispanic/Latino; 1 American Indian or Alaska Native, non-Hispanic/Latino; 11 Asian, non-Hispanic/Latino; 40 Hispanic/Latino; 22 Two or more races, non-Hispanic/Latino). Average age 35. In 2018, 611 master's, 9 doctorates awarded. *Entrance requirements:* Additional exam requirements/recommendations for international students: Required—TOEFL (minimum score 550 paper-based; 79 iBT). *Application deadline:* Applications are processed on a rolling basis. Application fee: $45 ($65 for international students). Electronic applications accepted. *Expenses:* Contact institution. *Financial support:* Unspecified assistantships available. Financial award application deadline: 3/1; financial award applicants required to submit FAFSA. *Unit head:* Dr. Rhonda Rabbitt, Dean, 570-408-4680, Fax: 570-408-7872, E-mail: rhonda.rabbitt@wilkes.edu. *Application contact:* Stephanie Wasmanski, Associate Director of Graduate Admissions, 570-408-5535, Fax: 570-408-7846, E-mail: stephanie.wasmanski@wilkes.edu.
Website: http://www.wilkes.edu/academics/graduate-programs/masters-programs/graduate-education/index.aspx

William Carey University, School of Education, Hattiesburg, MS 39401. Offers art education (M Ed); art of teaching (M Ed); elementary education (M Ed, Ed S); English education (M Ed); gifted education (M Ed); history and social science (M Ed); mild/moderate disabilities (M Ed); secondary education (M Ed). *Accreditation:* NCATE. *Program availability:* Part-time. *Degree requirements:* For master's, comprehensive exam. *Entrance requirements:* For master's, GRE, MAT, minimum GPA of 2.5, Class A teacher's license. Additional exam requirements/recommendations for international students: Required—TOEFL (minimum score 550 paper-based).

William Jessup University, Program in Teaching, Rocklin, CA 95765. Offers single subject English (MAT); single subject math (MAT). *Program availability:* Evening/weekend.

William Jewell College, Department of Education, Liberty, MO 64068-1843. Offers differentiated instruction (MS Ed).

William Paterson University of New Jersey, College of Education, Wayne, NJ 07470-8420. Offers curriculum and learning (M Ed); early childhood education (Certificate); educational leadership (M Ed); educational media specialist (Certificate); elementary education (MAT, Certificate); elementary education subject area (Certificate); higher education administration (MA); learning disabilities consultant (Certificate); literacy (M Ed); middle level education (M Ed); middle school education subject area (Certificate); professional counseling (M Ed); reading specialist (Certificate); school library media specialist (Certificate); school principal (Certificate); school supervisor (Certificate); secondary education (MAT); special education (M Ed); teacher of students with disabilities (Certificate). *Accreditation:* NCATE. *Program availability:* Part-time, evening/weekend. *Students:* Average age 35. 347 applicants, 87% accepted, 226 enrolled. In 2018, 136 master's awarded. *Degree requirements:* For master's, comprehensive exam, thesis (for some programs), exit interview (for some programs); practicum/internship; minimum GPA of 3.0 (for some programs); exit portfolio (for some programs). *Entrance requirements:* For master's, GRE/MAT, minimum GPA of 2.75; teaching certificate; essay; interview; 2 letters of recommendation; personal statement. Additional exam requirements/recommendations for international students: Required—TOEFL (minimum score 550 paper-based; 79 iBT), IELTS (minimum score 6). *Application deadline:* For fall admission, 6/1 for domestic students, 3/1 for international students; for spring admission, 11/1 for domestic students, 10/1 for international students. Applications are processed on a rolling basis. Application fee: $50. Electronic applications accepted. *Expenses: Tuition, area resident:* Full-time $14,714; part-time $727 per credit. Tuition, state resident: full-time $14,714; part-time $727 per credit. Tuition, nonresident: full-time $22,952; part-time $727 per credit. *International tuition:* $22,952 full-time. *Required fees:* $4 per semester. Tuition and fees vary according to course load, degree level and program. *Financial support:* In 2018–19, 8,416 students received support. Career-related internships or fieldwork, Federal Work-Study, scholarships/grants, and unspecified assistantships available. Support available to part-time students. Financial award application deadline: 3/15; financial award applicants required to submit FAFSA. *Faculty research:* Code switching and creative writing, language instruction, teacher evaluation, preschools, history of educational theories. *Total annual research expenditures:* $311,226. *Unit head:* Dr. Dorothy Feola, Dean, 973-720-2138, Fax: 973-720-3647, E-mail: feolad@wpunj.edu. *Application contact:* Liana Fornarotto, Director of Education Enrollment and Certification, 973-720-2206, Fax: 973-720-2989, E-mail: fornarottol@wpunj.edu.
Website: http://www.wpunj.edu/coe

Williams Baptist College, Graduate Programs, Walnut Ridge, AR 72476. Offers teaching (MAT).

Wilmington College, Department of Education, Wilmington, OH 45177. Offers reading (M Ed); special education (M Ed). *Accreditation:* TEAC. *Program availability:* Part-time. *Degree requirements:* For master's, comprehensive exam. *Entrance requirements:* For master's, GRE or MAT, minimum GPA of 3.0, 2 letters of recommendation. Additional exam requirements/recommendations for international students: Required—TOEFL. *Faculty research:* Reading instruction, special education practices, conflict resolution in the schools, models of higher education for teachers.

Wilmington University, College of Education, New Castle, DE 19720-6491. Offers applied technology in education (M Ed); career and technical education (M Ed); educational leadership (Ed D); elementary and secondary school counseling (M Ed); elementary studies (M Ed); ESOL literacy (M Ed); higher education leadership (Ed D); instruction: gifted and talented (M Ed); instruction: teacher of reading (M Ed); instruction: teaching and learning (M Ed); organizational leadership (Ed D); school leadership (M Ed); secondary education (MAT); special education (M Ed). *Accreditation:* NCATE. *Program availability:* Part-time, evening/weekend. *Entrance requirements:* For master's, 2 letters of recommendation, interview. Additional exam requirements/recommendations for international students: Required—TOEFL (minimum score 500 paper-based). Electronic applications accepted.

Education—General

Wilson College, Graduate Programs, Chambersburg, PA 17201-1285. Offers accounting (M Acc); choreography and visual art (MFA); education (M Ed); educational technology (MET); healthcare administration (MHA); humanities (MA), including art and culture, critical/cultural theory, English language and literature, women's studies; management (MSM); nursing (MSN), including nursing education, nursing leadership and management; special education (MSE). *Program availability:* Evening/weekend. *Degree requirements:* For master's, project. *Entrance requirements:* For master's, PRAXIS, minimum undergraduate cumulative GPA of 3.0, 2 letters of recommendation, current certification for eligibility to teach in grades K-12, resume, personal interview. Electronic applications accepted.

Wingate University, Thayer School of Education, Wingate, NC 28174. Offers community college executive leadership (Ed D); educational leadership (MA Ed, Ed S); elementary education (MA Ed, MAT). *Accreditation:* NCATE. *Program availability:* Part-time, evening/weekend. *Degree requirements:* For master's, portfolio. *Entrance requirements:* For master's, GRE General Test or MAT, teaching certificate (MA Ed).

Winona State University, College of Education, Department of Education Studies, Winona, MN 55987. Offers multicultural education (Certificate). *Accreditation:* NCATE. *Program availability:* Part-time, evening/weekend.

Winston-Salem State University, MAT Program, Winston-Salem, NC 27110-0003. Offers middle grades education (MAT); special education (MAT). *Accreditation:* NCATE. *Program availability:* Part-time, evening/weekend, online learning. *Entrance requirements:* For master's, GRE, MAT, NC teacher licensure. Electronic applications accepted. *Faculty research:* Action research on issues in elementary classroom.

Winthrop University, College of Education, Rock Hill, SC 29733. Offers M Ed, MAT. *Accreditation:* NCATE. *Program availability:* Part-time. *Students:* 116 full-time (89 women), 271 part-time (224 women); includes 105 minority (85 Black or African American, non-Hispanic/Latino; 1 American Indian or Alaska Native, non-Hispanic/Latino; 1 Asian, non-Hispanic/Latino; 13 Hispanic/Latino; 5 Two or more races, non-Hispanic/Latino), 12 international. Average age 30. In 2018, 99 master's awarded. *Degree requirements:* For master's, comprehensive exam (for some programs). *Entrance requirements:* Additional exam requirements/recommendations for international students: Required—TOEFL (minimum paper-based score of 520, iBT 68) or IELTS (minimum score of 6). *Application deadline:* For fall admission, 7/15 priority date for domestic students; for spring admission, 12/1 for domestic students. Applications are processed on a rolling basis. Application fee: $50. Electronic applications accepted. *Expenses:* Tuition, state resident: full-time $15,166; part-time $635 per credit hour. Tuition, nonresident: full-time $29,214. *Required fees:* $500; $180 per semester. *Financial support:* Research assistantships with full tuition reimbursements, career-related internships or fieldwork, Federal Work-Study, scholarships/grants, and unspecified assistantships available. Support available to part-time students. Financial award application deadline: 2/1; financial award applicants required to submit FAFSA. *Unit head:* Dr. Jeannie Rakestraw, Dean, 803-323-2151, Fax: 803-323-4369, E-mail: rakestrawj@winthrop.edu. *Application contact:* 800-411-7041, Fax: 803-323-2292, E-mail: gradschool@winthrop.edu.
Website: http://www.winthrop.edu/coe

Wittenberg University, Graduate Program, Springfield, OH 45501-0720. Offers education (MA). *Accreditation:* NCATE.

Worcester State University, Graduate School, Department of Education, Worcester, MA 01602-2597. Offers adult English as a esl (Postbaccalaureate Certificate); curriculum and instruction (Ed S); early childhood education (M Ed); education (M Ed); elementary education (M Ed); English as a second language (M Ed, Postbaccalaureate Certificate); middle school education (M Ed); middle/secondary school education (Postbaccalaureate Certificate); moderate disabilities (M Ed, Postbaccalaureate Certificate); reading (M Ed, Postbaccalaureate Certificate); reading specialist (Postbaccalaureate Certificate); school leadership and education administration (M Ed); school psychology (M Ed, Ed S); secondary education (M Ed, Ed S, Postbaccalaureate Certificate). *Faculty:* 10 full-time (9 women), 23 part-time/adjunct (11 women). *Students:* 38 full-time (33 women), 281 part-time (212 women); includes 30 minority (4 Black or African American, non-Hispanic/Latino; 3 American Indian or Alaska Native, non-Hispanic/Latino; 2 Asian, non-Hispanic/Latino; 16 Hispanic/Latino; 5 Two or more races, non-Hispanic/Latino), 2 international. Average age 41. 102 applicants, 98% accepted, 88 enrolled. In 2018, 132 master's, 52 Ed Ss awarded. *Degree requirements:* For master's, comprehensive exam (for some programs), thesis (for some programs), For a detail list of degree completion requirements please see the graduate catalog at catalog.worcester.edu. *Entrance requirements:* For master's, GRE General Test, MAT or GMAT, teaching certificate. For a detail list of entrance requirements please see the graduate catalog at catalog.worcester.edu. Additional exam requirements/recommendations for international students: Required—TOEFL (minimum score 550 paper-based; 79 iBT), PTE. *Application deadline:* For fall admission, 3/1 for domestic and international students; for spring admission, 11/1 for domestic and international students; for summer admission, 3/1 for domestic and international students. Applications are processed on a rolling basis. Application fee: $50. Electronic applications accepted. *Expenses: Tuition, area resident:* Full-time $3042; part-time $169 per credit hour. Tuition, state resident: full-time $3042; part-time $169 per credit hour. Tuition, nonresident: full-time $3042; part-time $169 per credit hour. *International tuition:* $3042 full-time. *Required fees:* $2754; $153 per credit hour. *Financial support:* Career-related internships or fieldwork, scholarships/grants, and unspecified assistantships available. Support available to part-time students. Financial award application deadline: 3/1; financial award applicants required to submit FAFSA. *Unit head:* Dr. Sara Young, Graduate Program Coordinator, 508-929-8246, Fax: 508-929-8164, E-mail: syoung3@worcester.edu. *Application contact:* Sara Grady, Associate Dean of Graduate and Continuing Education, 508-929-8130, Fax: 508-929-8100, E-mail: sara.grady@worcester.edu.

Wright State University, Graduate School, College of Education and Human Services, Dayton, OH 45435. Offers M Ed, MA, MRC, MS, Ed S. *Accreditation:* NCATE. *Program availability:* Part-time, evening/weekend. *Degree requirements:* For Ed S, thesis. *Entrance requirements:* For master's, GRE General Test, MAT, PRAXIS II; for Ed S, GRE General Test, MAT. Additional exam requirements/recommendations for international students: Required—TOEFL.

Xavier University, College of Professional Sciences, School of Education, Cincinnati, OH 45207. Offers M Ed, MA, MS, Ed D. *Accreditation:* TEAC. *Entrance requirements:* Additional exam requirements/recommendations for international students: Required—TOEFL (minimum score 550 paper-based; 79 iBT). Electronic applications accepted. Application fee is waived when completed online. *Expenses:* Contact institution. *Faculty research:* Early childhood literacy, service-learning, family resiliency/special needs families, technology integration, leadership theory, Montessori methodology.

York College of Pennsylvania, Graduate Programs in Behavioral Sciences and Education, York, PA 17403-3651. Offers educational leadership (M Ed); educational technology (M Ed); reading specialist (M Ed). *Program availability:* Part-time-only, evening/weekend. *Faculty:* 1 full-time (0 women), 10 part-time/adjunct (8 women). *Students:* 1 full-time (0 women), 107 part-time (77 women); includes 3 minority (1 Hispanic/Latino; 2 Two or more races, non-Hispanic/Latino). Average age 34. 35 applicants, 69% accepted, 23 enrolled. In 2018, 10 master's awarded. *Degree requirements:* For master's, comprehensive exam (for some programs), thesis (for some programs). *Entrance requirements:* For master's, statement of applicant's professional and academic goals, 2 letters of recommendation, letter from current supervisor, official undergraduate and graduate transcript(s), copy of teaching certificate(s), current professional resume, interview. *Application deadline:* For fall admission, 7/15 priority date for domestic students; for spring admission, 11/15 priority date for domestic students; for summer admission, 4/15 priority date for domestic students. Applications are processed on a rolling basis. Application fee: $0. Electronic applications accepted. *Expenses:* $640 per credit; no general fee. *Financial support:* Scholarships/grants available. Financial award applicants required to submit FAFSA. *Faculty research:* Classroom technology, assessment, educational leadership, professional development, literacy. *Unit head:* Dr. Joshua D. DeSantis, Director, Graduate Programs in Behavioral Science and Education, 717-815-1936, E-mail: jdesant1@ycp.edu. *Application contact:* Dr. Joshua D. DeSantis, Director, Graduate Programs in Behavioral Science and Education, 717-815-1936, E-mail: jdesant1@ycp.edu.
Website: https://www.ycp.edu/med

York University, Faculty of Graduate Studies, Faculty of Education, Toronto, ON M3J 1P3, Canada. Offers M Ed, PhD. *Program availability:* Part-time. *Degree requirements:* For master's, thesis or alternative; for doctorate, comprehensive exam, thesis/dissertation. Electronic applications accepted.

Youngstown State University, College of Graduate Studies, Beeghly College of Education, Youngstown, OH 44555-0001. Offers MS Ed, Ed D, Ed S. *Accreditation:* NCATE. *Program availability:* Part-time, evening/weekend. *Degree requirements:* For master's, comprehensive exam; for doctorate, comprehensive exam, thesis/dissertation. *Entrance requirements:* For master's, minimum GPA of 2.7; for doctorate, GRE General Test, GRE Subject Test, interview, minimum GPA of 3.5. Additional exam requirements/recommendations for international students: Required—TOEFL. *Faculty research:* Euthanasia, psychometrics, ethical issues, community relations, educational law.

THE COLLEGE OF WILLIAM AND MARY
School of Education

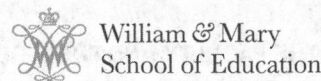

Programs of Study

Curriculum and Instruction—Teacher Education: The School of Education prepares tomorrow's educational leaders, because it attracts highly qualified students to its teacher education programs and then provides them with exemplary professional educational experiences. The School of Education offers one-year master's programs in elementary education, secondary education, special education, and ESL/bilingual education. (http://education.wm.edu/academics/ci/index.php)

Counseling and School Psychology: The school psychology and counseling programs at William and Mary prepare highly qualified professionals to practice in the public schools or in related educational and mental health settings. The School offers two-year master's programs in clinical mental health, couples, marriage and family, addictions, and school counseling. For students who want to study beyond the master's level, the School offers a Ph.D. in counselor education, which can be completed in three to four years of full-time enrollment. For students interested in school psychology, the School offers a three-year Ed.S. program that culminates in a year-long internship experience. For students who want to study online, William and Mary offers online counseling programs with concentrations in clinical mental health, military and veterans counseling, and school counseling. (http://education.wm.edu/academics/space/index.php)

Educational Policy, Planning and Leadership: The Educational Policy, Planning and Leadership department prepares students with the knowledge and skills necessary to guide, influence, and shape institutions at all levels of education, and to enhance the effectiveness of complex educational organizations through leadership, scholarship, and service. The School of Education offers master's degrees in K–12 administration and higher education administration. In addition, the School offers doctoral programs in K–12 leadership, gifted administration, curriculum and learning design, and higher education administration. Full-time students can expect to finish the doctorate in three to four years. (http://education.wm.edu/academics/eppl/index.php)

Research Facilities

The School of Education building was completed in May 2010. The facility houses W&M's nationally-ranked School of Education and brings all of its academic programs, outreach centers and research projects together in a highly professional setting designed to stimulate collaboration and innovation.

One such project, the Center for Gifted Education, provides services to educators, policy makers, graduate students, researchers, parents, and students in support of the needs of gifted and talented individuals. The center has established an international reputation for excellence in research, curriculum development, and service.

Another outreach center, the New Horizons Family Counseling Center, provides free services to families of children attending public schools in the local area. Families may be referred to the clinic by teachers, principals, counselors, school psychologists, or school social workers. Students in counseling programs complete clinical internships in the center. Under licensed faculty supervision, students serve as administrators, supervisors, and family counselors for the center.

Financial Aid

Financial assistance is available in the form of assistantships, fellowships, scholarships, and awards earmarked for School of Education students. Both full-time and part-time assistantships are available to full-time students. Awards and scholarships are merit based. Other forms of aid are available through the university's financial aid office. For more information about assistantships, prospective students should visit http://education.wm.edu/admissions/financialaid/assistantships/index.php. For more information about scholarships and awards, visit http://education.wm.edu/admissions/financialaid/soeawards/index.php.

Cost of Study

In 2019–20, the tuition and general fee for students is approximately $16,440 per year for residents of Virginia and $34,800 per year for nonresidents. Details about tuition can be found at http://education.wm.edu/admissions/graduate/tuition/index.php.

Living and Housing Costs

The College offers a limited number of graduate student housing spaces on campus, with costs averaging approximately $4,000 per semester. Application is made by submission of the housing request form after a student is admitted. In addition, the College maintains a website for off-campus student housing available in the Williamsburg community.

Student Group

The School of Education enrolls approximately 500 students each semester. Of those, 77 percent are degree-seeking students; 34 percent are pursuing doctorate degrees; 41 percent are enrolled full time; 18 percent are students of color; 19 percent are male; and 4 percent are international students. The average age is 28.

Admission is competitive. The average undergraduate GPA of admitted students is 3.4; the average GRE verbal score is the 69th percentile; the average GRE quantitative score is the 46th percentile.

Student Outcomes

Graduates of the School of Education find work in public and private K–12 schools, nonprofit organizations, clinical practices, and institutions of higher education, just to name a few.

Location

Williamsburg is on a Chesapeake Bay peninsula between the York and James rivers, 50 miles from Richmond and 150 miles from Washington, D.C. The College is located in a beautiful and historic city, constituting an integral part of Colonial Williamsburg. Williamsburg is serviced by Newport News, Norfolk, and Richmond airports; bus and railway services are also available.

The College

Although it retains the historic name under which it was chartered in 1693, the College of William and Mary in Virginia is a residential, full-time, coeducational, state-supported university. It is the second oldest college in the nation, but also a cutting-edge research university. It is selective, but also public, offering a world-class education without the sticker shock. It is a "Public Ivy"—one of only eight in the nation, which means it offers a superior education that's accessible to everyone.

Applying

Applications are available online at http://education.wm.edu/admissions/graduate/applying/index.php. The deadline for all application materials to be received, including transcripts, test scores, and letters of recommendation, is January 15 each year. The counseling and school psychology programs require the GRE (general test only); the educational leadership and administrative programs require either the GRE or the MAT. The initial teacher preparation programs require the Praxis Core Academic Skills for Educators exam. The school psychology program and doctorate in counselor education require admission interviews. Students are notified of admission decisions no later than mid-March.

Correspondence and Information

Dorothy Smith Osborne, Assistant Dean
School of Education—Office of Academic Programs
The College of William and Mary
P.O. Box 8795
Williamsburg, Virginia 23187-8795
United States
Phone: 757-221-2317
E-mail: graded@wm.edu
Website: https://education.wm.edu/
Request Information: http://education.wm.edu/admissions/graduate/requestinfo/index.php

The College of William and Mary

THE FACULTY AND THEIR RESEARCH

The School of Education has 42 tenure-line faculty members, of which 8 hold endowed professorships, combined with other personnel for a total of 90 faculty and staff members.

Spencer Niles, Dean and Professor—Ph.D., The Pennsylvania State University.

Virginia Ambler, Executive Assistant Professor, Ph.D., The College of William and Mary.

James Barber, Associate Professor, Ph.D., University of Michigan.

Katherine Barko-Alva, Instructor, Ph.D., University of Florida.

Stephanie Blackmon, Assistant Professor, Ph.D., University of Alabama, Tuscaloosa.

Brian Blouet, Professor, Ph.D., University of Hull.

Bruce Bracken, Professor, Ph.D., University of Georgia.

Johnston Brendel, Clinical Associate Professor, Ed.D., The College of William and Mary.

Jason Chen, Assistant Professor, Ph.D., Emory University.

Eddie Cole, Assistant Professor, Ph.D., Indiana University.

Kristen Conradi Smith, Assistant Professor, Ph.D., University of Virginia.

Margaret A. Constatino, Ph.D., University of Southern Mississippi.

Kristen Conradi, Assistant Professor, Ph.D., University of Virginia.

Tracy Cross, Professor, Ph.D., University of Tennessee, Knoxville.

Michael DiPaola, Professor, Ed.D., Rutgers, The State University of New Jersey.

Jamel Donnor, Associate Professor, Ph.D., University of Wisconsin–Madison.

Pamela Eddy, Associate Professor, Ph.D., Michigan State University.

Victoria Foster, Professor, Ed.D., North Carolina State University.

Christopher Gareis, Professor, Ed.D., The College of William and Mary.

W. Fanchon Glover, Executive Assistant Professor, Ed.D., The College of William and Mary.

Leslie Grant, Associate Professor, Ph.D., The College of William and Mary.

Charles Gressard, Professor, Ph.D., University of Iowa.

Daniel Gutierrez, Assistant Professor, Ph.D., University of Central Florida.

Judith Harris, Professor, Ph.D., University of Virginia.

Natoya Haskins, Assistant Professor, Ph.D., The College of William and Mary.

Judith Harris, Professor, Ph.D., University of Virginia.

Mark Hofer, Professor, Ph.D., University of Virginia.

Heartley Huber, Ph.D., Vanderbilt University.

C. Denise Johnson, Professor, Ph.D., University of Memphis.

Meredith Kier, Assistant Professor, Ph.D., North Carolina State University.

Kyung-Hee Kim, Associate Professor, Ph.D., Korea University; Ph.D., University of Georgia.

Gladys Krause, Assistant Professor, Ph.D., University of Texas at Austin.

Marguerite Mason, Professor, Ph.D., University of Iowa.

Charles McAdams, Professor, Ed.D., North Carolina State University.

Ryan J. McGill, Assistant Professor, Ph.D., Chapman University.

Virginia McLaughlin, Professor, Ed.D., Memphis State University.

Patrick R. Mullin, Assistant Professor, Ph.D., University of Central Florida.

Janise Parker, Assistant Professor, Ph.D., University of Florida.

Patricia Popp, Clinical Associate Professor, Ph.D., The College of William and Mary.

Deborah Ramer, Instructor, Ed.S., University of Virginia.

Stephen Staples, Executive Professor, Ed.D., Virginia Polytechnic Institute and State University

Drew Stelljis, Executive Assistant Professor, Ph.D., The College of William and Mary.

James Stronge, Professor, Ph.D., University of Alabama at Tuscaloosa.

Elizabeth Talbott, Professor, Ph.D., University of Virginia.
Carol Tieso, Professor, Ph.D., University of Connecticut.
Megan Tschannen-Moran, Professor, Ph.D., The Ohio State University.
Thomas Ward, Professor, The Pennsylvania State University.

VANDERBILT UNIVERSITY
Peabody College

VANDERBILT UNIVERSITY · Peabody College

Programs of Study

Vanderbilt University's Peabody College of Education and Human Development offers programs leading to the Master of Education (M.Ed.), Master of Public Policy (M.P.P.), and Doctor of Education (Ed.D.) degrees. The Vanderbilt Graduate School, through Peabody departments, offers the Doctor of Philosophy (Ph.D.) degree. Peabody is committed to preparing students to become research scholars or innovative practitioners in the field of education and human development. Students may attend full- or part-time. Weekend courses are offered in several programs for working professionals who want to earn an advanced degree.

Students may pursue the Master of Education (M.Ed.) in child studies; community development and action; elementary education; English language learners; higher education administration (including specializations in administration, student life, and service learning); human development counseling (with specializations in school and community counseling); independent school leadership; international education policy and management; leadership and organizational performance; learning, diversity, and urban studies; learning and design (including specializations in teaching and learning; digital literacies; language, culture, and international studies; science and mathematics; or an individualized program); quantitative methods; reading education; secondary education; and special education (including specializations in applied behavior analysis, early childhood, high-incidence disabilities, and low-incidence disabilities). A Master of Public Policy is available in education policy. Peabody also offers a joint M.P.P./J.D. program and a dual degree with the Vanderbilt Divinity School.

Students interested in doctoral study may enroll in educational leadership and policy (Ed.D.); educational neuroscience (Ph.D.); higher education leadership and policy (Ed.D.); community research and action (Ph.D.); leadership and learning in organizations (online Ed.D.); leadership and policy studies (Ph.D., with specializations in educational leadership and policy, higher education leadership and policy, and international education policy and management); learning, teaching, and diversity (Ph.D., with specializations in development, learning, and diversity; language, literacy, and culture; mathematics and science; and science and learning environment design); psychological sciences (Ph.D., with specializations in clinical science, cognitive science, developmental science, and quantitative methods and evaluation); and special education (Ph.D., with specializations in early childhood, high-incidence disabilities, and severe disabilities).

Peabody's teacher education and advanced certification programs are approved by the National Council for Accreditation of Teacher Education (NCATE). Programs in psychology and counseling are accredited by the American Psychological Association and the Council on Accreditation of Counseling and Related Educational Programs (CACREP), respectively.

Research Opportunities

In addition to the Vanderbilt University Library System, which has more than 2.6 million volumes, excellent research facilities and opportunities to conduct research are available through the Vanderbilt Kennedy Center for Research on Human Development, the Peabody Research Institute, the Susan Gray School, the National Center on School Choice, the National Center on Performance Initiatives, and the Center for Community Studies. The many local field sites available for research include hospitals, Metropolitan Nashville Public Schools, private schools, rehabilitation centers, schools for people with disabilities, government agencies, corporations, and nonprofit organizations.

Financial Aid

More than 70 percent of new students at Peabody receive financial aid. The College sponsors several substantial scholarship programs with offerings that range from partial to full tuition. In addition, assistantships, traineeships, loans, and part-time employment are available. Awards are made annually, and every attempt is made to meet a student's financial need. Application for financial aid does not affect the admission decision.

Cost of Study

Tuition for study at Peabody College for the 2019-2020 academic year is $1,938 per semester credit hour for the M.Ed., M.P.P., and Ed.D. programs, and $2,026 per semester credit hour for programs offered through the Graduate School.

Living and Housing Costs

Vanderbilt's location in Nashville offers students the advantage of a wide range of living choices. Costs for housing, food, and other living expenses are moderate when compared with other metropolitan areas nationwide.

Student Group

Vanderbilt has a diverse student body of about 12,000. Peabody has an enrollment of approximately 1,800 students, of whom about 700 are graduate students. Women make up about 65 percent of Peabody's graduate students, while students from underrepresented groups make up about 20 percent. Students have a broad range of academic backgrounds and include recent graduates of baccalaureate programs as well as men and women who have many years of professional experience. The median age of current students is 27.

Student Outcomes

Graduates who earn a master's or doctoral degree from Peabody are prepared to work for educational, corporate, government, and service organizations in a variety of roles. More than 10,000 alumni are practicing teachers, more than 175 are school superintendents, and more than 50 are current or former college or university presidents.

Location

Nashville, the capital of Tennessee, is a cosmopolitan city with a metropolitan area population of 1.7 million. Vanderbilt University is one of more than a dozen institutions of higher learning located in Nashville and the surrounding area, leading Nashville to be called the "Athens of the South."

Nashville offers residents and visitors much in the way of music, art, and recreation. More than 100 local venues provide a wide variety of music, while classical and contemporary music is performed by the Nashville Symphony Orchestra and the Nashville Chamber Orchestra. The Tennessee Performing Arts Center (TPAC) is home to two theater companies, a ballet company, and an opera company. Vanderbilt's own Great Performances series frequently brings the best in chamber music, new music, theater, and all forms of dance to the Vanderbilt campus. Outstanding exhibitions of fine art can be seen at the Frist Center for the Visual Arts and at Cheekwood Botanical Garden and Museum of Art. There are more than 6,000 acres of public parks in the city, and the surrounding region of rolling hills and lakes is dotted with state parks and recreation areas.

Nashville has been named one of the 15 best U.S. cities for work and family by *Fortune* magazine, was ranked as the most popular U.S. city for corporate relocations by *Expansion Management* magazine, and was named by *Forbes* magazine as one of the 25 cities most likely to have the country's highest job growth over the coming five years. More information on Nashville can be found online at http://www.vanderbilt.edu/nashville.

The University and The College

Vanderbilt University, founded in 1873, is a private nondenominational institution with a strong tradition of graduate and professional education. Peabody, recognized for more than a century as one of the nation's foremost independent colleges of education, merged with Vanderbilt University in 1979. Peabody seeks to create knowledge through research, to prepare leaders, to support practitioners, and to strengthen communities at all levels.

Applying

Admission to professional degree programs is based on an evaluation of the applicant's potential for academic success and professional service, with consideration given to transcripts of previous course work, GRE General Test or MAT scores, letters of reference, and a letter outlining personal goals. Additional supporting credentials, such as a sample of the applicant's scholarly writing or a personal interview, may also be required.

Applicants who apply after the deadline should know that admission and financial assistance depend upon the availability of space and funds in the department in which they seek to study. Deadlines are December 1 for the Ph.D. and Ed.D. programs and December 31 for the M.Ed. and M.P.P. programs.

Correspondence and Information

Graduate Admissions
Peabody College of Vanderbilt University
Peabody Station, Box 227
Nashville, Tennessee 37203
United States
Phone: 615-322-8410
Fax: 615-322-4029
E-mail: peabody.admissions@vanderbilt.edu
Website: http://peabody.vanderbilt.edu

THE FACULTY

Department of Human and Organizational Development
Sandra Barnes, Professor; Ph.D., Georgia State.
Kimberly D. Bess, Associate Professor of the Practice; Ph.D., Vanderbilt.
Mark D. Cannon, Associate Professor; Ph.D., Harvard.
Ashley Carse, Assistant Professor; Ph.D., North Carolina at Chapel Hill.
Gabrielle Chapman, Research Assistant Professor, Ph.D., Vanderbilt.
Brian Christens, Associate Professor; Ph.D., Vanderbilt.
Nicole Cobb, Senior Lecturer; Ed.D., Tennessee.
David K. Diehl, Assistant Professor; Ph.D., Stanford.
Kelly Duncan, Lecturer, Ph.D., University of South Dakota.
Karen Enyedy, Lecturer, Ph.D., University of Southern California
Bradley Erford, Professor; Ph.D., Virginia.
Andrew J. Finch, Associate Professor of the Practice; Ph.D., Vanderbilt.
Anjali Forber-Pratt, Assistant Professor; Ph.D., Illinois at Urbana-Champaign.
Gina Frieden, Assistant Professor of the Practice; Ph.D., Memphis State.
Susan K. Friedman, Lecturer; M.B.A., Arizona State.
Leigh Gilchrist, Assistant Professor of the Practice; Ed.D., Vanderbilt.
Leslie Kirby, Principal Senior Lecturer; Ph.D., Vanderbilt.
Heather Lefkowitz, Lecturer; M.Div., Vanderbilt.
Velma McBride Murry, University Professor; Ph.D., Missouri–Columbia.
Yolanda McDonald, Assistant Professor. Ph.D., Texas A&M University.
Maury Nation, Associate Professor; Ph.D., South Carolina.

Vanderbilt University

Nancy Nolan, Lecturer; M.Ed., Vanderbilt.
Jeremy Payne, Lecturer, Ed.D., Vanderbilt.
Michelle Perepiczka, Lecturer; Ph.D., Texas A&M University
Douglas Perkins, Professor; Ph.D., NYU.
Jessica Perkins, Assistant Professor; Ph.D., Harvard.
Sara Safransky, Assistant Professor; Ph.D., North Carolina at Chapel Hill.
Sharon Shields, Professor of the Practice; Ph.D., George Peabody.
Marybeth Shinn, Professor; Ph.D., Michigan.
Heather Smith, Assistant Professor of the Practice; Ph.D., Central Florida.
Paul Speer, Professor; Ph.D., Missouri–Kansas City.
Sarah V. Suiter, Assistant Professor of the Practice; Ph.D., Vanderbilt.
Kristen C. Tompkins, Lecturer; M.Ed., Vanderbilt.
Andrew Van Schaack, Principal Senior Lecturer; Ph.D., Utah State.

Department of Leadership, Policy, and Organizations
Tracey Armstrong, Lecturer; Ph.D., University of Virginia.
Jeremy Bolton, Lecturer; Ph.D., University of Florida.
Christopher Candelaria; Assistant Professor; Ph.D., Stanford.
Marisa A. Cannata, Research Assistant Professor; Ph.D., Michigan.
Sean Corcoran, Associate Professor.
Jose Cossa, Senior Lecturer; Ph.D., Chicago.
Xiu Cravens, Associate Professor of the Practice; Ph.D., Vanderbilt.
Shaun Dougherty, Associate Professor.
Susan Douglas, Assistant Professor of the Practice; Ph.D., Vanderbilt.
Corbette Doyle, Senior Lecturer; M.B.A., Vanderbilt.
William R. Doyle, Associate Professor; Ph.D., Stanford.
Brent Evans, Assistant Professor; Ph.D., Stanford.
Joanne Golann, Assistant Professor; Ph.D., Princeton.
Ellen Goldring, Professor; Ph.D., Chicago.
Jason Grissom, Associate Professor; Ph.D., Stanford.
Carolyn J. Heinrich, Professor; Ph.D., Chicago.
Brian L. Heuser, Assistant Professor; Ed.D., Vanderbilt.
David Laird, Assistant Professor of the Practice; Ed.D., Vanderbilt.
Daniel LeBreton; Lecturer.
Catherine Gavin Loss, Assistant Professor of the Practice; Ph.D., Virginia.
Christopher P. Loss, Associate Professor; Ph.D., Virginia.
Brenda McKenzie, Senior Lecturer; Ph.D., Kent.
Joseph Murphy, Professor; Ph.D., Ohio State.
Michael Neel, Lecturer; M.A., Samford.
Christine Quinn Trank, Associate Professor of the Practice; Ph.D., Iowa.
Mollie Rubin, Research Assistant Professor.
Patrick J. Schuermann, Assistant Professor; Ed.D., Vanderbilt.
Matthew Shaw, Assistant Professor; Ed.D., Harvard.
Claire Smrekar, Associate Professor; Ph.D., Stanford.
Adela Soliz, Assistant Professor; Ed.D., Harvard.
Deborah Tobey, Senior Lecturer; Ed.D., Vanderbilt.

Department of Psychology and Human Development
Camilla P. Benbow, Professor; Ed.D., Johns Hopkins.
Amy Booth, Professor; Ph.D., Pittsburgh.
James Booth, Professor; Ph.D., Maryland.
Sarah Brown-Schmidt, Associate Professor; Ph.D., Rochester.
Sun-Joo Cho, Associate Professor; Ph.D., Georgia.
David A. Cole, Professor; Ph.D., Houston.
Bruce E. Compas, Professor; Ph.D., UCLA.
Jenni Dunbar, Lecturer; Ph.D., Vanderbilt.
Elizabeth May Dykens, Professor; Ph.D., Kansas.
Lisa K. Fazio, Assistant Professor; Ph.D., Duke.
Judy Garber, Professor; Ph.D., Minnesota, Twin Cities.
Vicki S. Harris, Assistant Clinical Professor; Ph.D., Pennsylvania.
Kathryn Humphreys, Assistant Professor; Ph.D., California.
Shane Hutton, Lecturer; Ph.D., North Carolina–Chapel Hill.
Autumn Kujawa, Assistant Professor; Ph.D., SUNY.
Jonathan Lane, Assistant Professor; Ph.D., Michigan.
Daniel T. Levin, Professor; Ph.D., Cornell.
David Lubinski, Professor; Ph.D., Minnesota.
Nina Martin, Associate Clinical Professor; Ed.D., Harvard.
Amy Needham, Professor; Ph.D., Illinois.
Julia Noland, Senior Lecturer; Ph.D., Cornell.
Laura R. Novick, Associate Professor; Ph.D., Stanford.
Kristopher J. Preacher, Professor; Ph.D., Ohio.
Gavin Price, Assistant Professor; Ph.D., Jyväskylä (Finland).
Bethany Rittle-Johnson, Professor; Ph.D., Carnegie Mellon.
Joseph Lee Rodgers III, Professor; Ph.D., North Carolina.
Megan M. Saylor, Associate Professor; Ph.D., Oregon.
Craig A. Smith, Associate Professor; Ph.D., Stanford.
Sonya Sterba, Associate Professor; Ph.D., North Carolina–Chapel Hill.
Georgene Troseth, Associate Professor; Ph.D., Illinois at Urbana-Champaign.
Leigh Wadsworth, Senior Lecturer; Ph.D., Arizona State.
Tedra Ann Walden, Professor; Ph.D., Florida.
Duane Watson, Associate Professor; Ph.D., Rochester.
Bahr Weiss, Associate Professor; Ph.D., North Carolina–Chapel Hill.
Hao Wu, Associate Professor; Ph.D., Ohio State University.

Department of Special Education
Marcia Barnes, Professor; Ph.D., McMaster.
Erin Barton, Associate Professor; Ph.D., Vanderbilt.
Andrea Capizzi, Assistant Professor of the Practice; Ph.D., Vanderbilt.
Erik W. Carter, Professor; Ph.D., Vanderbilt.
Laurie Cutting, Professor; Ph.D., Northwestern.
Alex da Fonte, Assistant Professor of the Practice; M.S., Purdue.

Douglas Fuchs, Professor; Ph.D., Minnesota.
Lynn Fuchs, Professor; Ph.D., Minnesota.
Mary Louise Hemmeter, Professor; Ph.D., Vanderbilt.
Robert Hodapp, Professor; Ph.D., Boston University.
Nealetta J. Houchins-Juarez, Instructor of the Practice; M.A., Nevada.
Ann Kaiser, Professor; Ph.D., Kansas.
Joseph Lambert, Assistant Professor of the Practice; Ph.D., Utah State.
Jennifer Ledford, Assistant Professor; Ph.D., Vanderbilt.
Christopher Lemons, Associate Professor; Ph.D., Vanderbilt.
Blair Lloyd, Assistant Professor; Ph.D., Vanderbilt.
Kim Paulsen, Professor of the Practice; Ed.D., Nevada, Las Vegas.
Johanna Staubitz, Lecturer; Ph.D., Vanderbilt.
Naomi Tyler, Associate Professor of the Practice; Ph.D., New Mexico State.
Jeanne Wanzek, Associate Professor; Ph.D., University of Texas.
Joseph H. Wehby, Associate Professor; Ph.D., Vanderbilt.
Paul J. Yoder, Professor; Ph.D., North Carolina.

Department of Teaching and Learning
Corey Brady, Assistant Professor; Ph.D., Dartmouth.
Nicole Chaput-Guizani, Lecturer; M.Ed., David Lipscomb University.
Caroline Christopher, Research Assistant Professor.
Douglas Clark, Professor; Ph.D., Berkeley.
Paul A. Cobb, Research Professor; Ph.D., Georgia.
Molly F. Collins, Lecturer; Ed.D., Boston University. Shannon M. Daniel, Lecturer; Ph.D., Maryland.
Shannon Daniel, Senior Lecturer; Ph.D., University of Maryland.
Ana Christine DaSilva, Professor of the Practice; Ph.D., Nevada.
David Dickinson, Professor; Ed.D., Harvard.
Teresa Dunleavy, Assistant Professor of the Practice; Ph.D., Washington (Seattle).
Kelley Durkin, Research Assistant Professor.
Noel Enyedy, Professor.
Dale C. Farran, Research Professor; Ph.D., Bryn Mawr.
Emily Galloway, Assistant Professor; D.Ed., Harvard.
Kathy A. Ganske, Professor of the Practice; Ph.D., Virginia.
Amanda P. Goodwin, Associate Professor; Ph.D., Miami.
Melissa Sommerfield Gresalfi, Associate Professor; Ph.D., Stanford.
Rogers Hall, Professor; Ph.D., California, Irvine.
Andrea W. Henrie, Lecturer; Ph.D., Tennessee.
Ilana Horn, Associate Professor; Ph.D., Berkeley.
Andrew L. Hostetler, Assistant Professor of the Practice; Ph.D., Kent State.
Melanie K. Hundley, Associate Professor of the Practice; Ph.D., Georgia.
Robert T. Jimenez, Professor; Ph.D., Illinois at Urbana-Champaign.
Heather J. Johnson, Assistant Professor of the Practice; Ph.D., Northwestern.
Nicole Joseph, Assistant Professor; Ph.D., Washington.
Ocheze Joseph, Lecturer; Ed.D., Maryland.
Brian Kissel, Professor of the Practice; M.Ed., University of North Florida.
Kevin Leander, Associate Professor; Ph.D., Illinois.
Richard Lehrer, Professor; Ph.D., Chicago.
Luis Leyva, Assistant Professor; Ed.M., Rutgers.
Jeannette Mancilla-Martinez, Associate Professor; Ed.D., Harvard.
Ebony O. McGee, Assistant Professor; Ph.D., Illinois.
Catherine McTamaney, Senior Lecturer; Ed.D., Vanderbilt.
H. Rich Milner, Professor; Ph.D., Ohio State University.
Kristen W. Neal, Lecturer; Ph.D., Vanderbilt.
Ann M. Neely, Associate Professor of the Practice; Ed.D., Georgia.
Amy Palmeri, Assistant Professor of the Practice; Ph.D., Indiana Bloomington.
Emily Pendergrass, Senior Lecturer; Ph.D., Georgia.
Jeanne H. Peter, Lecturer; Ed.D., Vanderbilt.
Rebecca Peterson, Lecturer; M.Ed., Vanderbilt.
Lisa Pray, Professor of the Practice; Ph.D., Arizona State.
Deborah W. Rowe, Professor; Ph.D., Indiana.
Elizabeth Self, Lecturer; Ph.D., Vanderbilt.
Virginia L. Shepherd, Research Professor; Ph.D., Iowa.
Marcy Singer-Gabella, Professor; Ph.D., Stanford.
Barbara Stengel, Professor of the Practice; Ph.D., Pittsburgh.
Jennifer Ufnar, Research Assistant Professor; Ph.D., Vanderbilt.
Anita Wager, Professor of the Practice; Ph.D., Wisconsin.
Jessica Watkins, Assistant Professor; Ph.D., Harvard

The Faye and Joe Wyatt Center for Education.

Section 23
Administration, Instruction, and Theory

This section contains a directory of institutions offering graduate work in administration, instruction, and theory. Additional information about programs listed in the directory but not augmented by an in-depth entry may be obtained by writing directly to the dean of a graduate school or chair of a department at the address given in the directory.

For programs offering related work, see also in this book *Education, Instructional Levels, Leisure Studies and Recreation, Physical Education and Kinesiology, Special Focus,* and *Subject Areas.* In other guides in this series:

Graduate Programs in the Humanities, Arts & Social Sciences
See *Psychology and Counseling (School Psychology)*
Graduate Programs in the Biological/Biomedical Sciences and Health-Related Medical Professions
See *Health-Related Professions*

CONTENTS

Program Directories

Curriculum and Instruction

Acadia University, Faculty of Professional Studies, School of Education, Program in Curriculum Studies, Wolfville, NS B4P 2R6, Canada. Offers curriculum studies (M Ed); interprofessional health practice (M Ed); music education (M Ed). *Program availability:* Part-time. *Entrance requirements:* For master's, B Ed or the equivalent, minimum B average in undergraduate course work, 2 years of teaching experience. Additional exam requirements/recommendations for international students: Required—TOEFL (minimum score 580 paper-based; 93 iBT), IELTS (minimum score 6.5). *Faculty research:* Literacy development, postmodern philosophy and curriculum theory, historiography, philosophy of education, learning and technology.

Adams State University, Office of Graduate Studies, Department of Teacher Education, Alamosa, CO 81101. Offers teacher education (MA), including adaptive leadership, curriculum and instruction, curriculum and instruction-STEM, educational leadership. *Program availability:* Part-time, online learning. *Degree requirements:* For master's, qualifying exam. *Entrance requirements:* For master's, GRE General Test or MAT, minimum undergraduate GPA of 3.0.

American College of Education, Graduate Programs, Indianapolis, IN 46204. Offers curriculum and instruction (M Ed), including bilingual, ESL; educational leadership (M Ed); educational technology (M Ed).

American InterContinental University Online, Program in Education, Schaumburg, IL 60173. Offers curriculum and instruction (M Ed); educational assessment and evaluation (M Ed); instructional technology (M Ed); leadership of educational organizations (M Ed). *Accreditation:* TEAC. *Program availability:* Evening/weekend, online learning. *Entrance requirements:* Additional exam requirements/recommendations for international students: Required—TOEFL (minimum score 550 paper-based). Electronic applications accepted.

Andrews University, School of Graduate Studies, School of Education, Department of Teaching, Learning, and Curriculum, Program in Curriculum and Instruction, Berrien Springs, MI 49104. Offers MA, Ed D, PhD, Ed S. *Degree requirements:* For master's, thesis optional; for doctorate, thesis/dissertation. *Entrance requirements:* For master's, GRE Subject Test. Additional exam requirements/recommendations for international students: Required—TOEFL (minimum score 550 paper-based).

Angelo State University, College of Graduate Studies and Research, College of Education, Department of Curriculum and Instruction, San Angelo, TX 76909. Offers curriculum and instruction (MA); educational administration (M Ed); guidance and counseling (M Ed); student development and leadership in higher education (M Ed). *Program availability:* Part-time, evening/weekend, online learning. *Students:* 360 full-time (307 women), 456 part-time (364 women); includes 312 minority (93 Black or African American, non-Hispanic/Latino; 3 American Indian or Alaska Native, non-Hispanic/Latino; 7 Asian, non-Hispanic/Latino; 193 Hispanic/Latino; 1 Native Hawaiian or other Pacific Islander, non-Hispanic/Latino; 15 Two or more races, non-Hispanic/Latino). Average age 35. *Application deadline:* For fall admission, 7/15 priority date for domestic students, 6/10 for international students; for spring admission, 12/1 priority date for domestic students, 11/1 for international students. Application fee: $40 ($50 for international students). *Expenses: Tuition, area resident:* Full-time $3964; part-time $220 per credit hour. Tuition, state resident: full-time $3964; part-time $220 per credit hour. Tuition, nonresident: full-time $11,434; part-time $635 per credit hour. *International tuition:* $11,434 full-time. *Unit head:* Dr. Kim Livengood, Chair, 325-942-2647, Fax: 325-942-2039, E-mail: kim.livengood@angelo.edu. *Application contact:* Dr. Kim Livengood, Chair, 325-942-2647, Fax: 325-942-2039, E-mail: kim.livengood@angelo.edu.
Website: http://www.angelo.edu/dept/ci/

Appalachian State University, Cratis D. Williams School of Graduate Studies, Department of Curriculum and Instruction, Boone, NC 28608. Offers curriculum specialist (MA); educational media (MA); elementary education (MA); middle grades education (MA), including language arts, mathematics, science, social studies. *Accreditation:* NCATE. *Program availability:* Part-time, evening/weekend, online learning. *Degree requirements:* For master's, comprehensive exam, thesis or alternative. *Entrance requirements:* For master's, GRE General Test or MAT, 3 letters of recommendation. Additional exam requirements/recommendations for international students: Required—TOEFL (minimum score 570 paper-based; 79 iBT), IELTS (minimum score 6.5). Electronic applications accepted. *Expenses: Tuition, area resident:* Full-time $4839; part-time $237 per credit hour. Tuition, state resident: full-time $4839; part-time $237 per credit hour. Tuition, nonresident: full-time $18,271; part-time $895.50 per credit hour. *Faculty research:* Media literacy, elementary teaching, curriculum development, online learning environments.

Arcadia University, School of Education, Glenside, PA 19038-3295. Offers art education (M Ed); computer education (CAS); curriculum (CAS); curriculum studies (M Ed); early childhood education (M Ed), including individualized, master teacher, research in child development; educational leadership (M Ed, Ed D, CAS); elementary education (M Ed); English education (MA Ed); environmental education (MA Ed); instructional technology (M Ed); language arts (M Ed); library science (M Ed); mathematics education (M Ed, MA Ed); music education (MA Ed); psychology (MA Ed); reading (M Ed, CAS); science education (M Ed, CAS); secondary education (M Ed, CAS); special education (M Ed, Ed D, CAS); theater arts (MA Ed); written communication (MA Ed). *Accreditation:* NASAD. *Program availability:* Part-time, evening/weekend, online learning. *Faculty:* 14 full-time (10 women). *Students:* 35 full-time (24 women), 299 part-time (243 women); includes 72 minority (49 Black or African American, non-Hispanic/Latino; 1 American Indian or Alaska Native, non-Hispanic/Latino; 12 Asian, non-Hispanic/Latino; 8 Hispanic/Latino; 2 Two or more races, non-Hispanic/Latino), 5 international. In 2018, 152 master's, 8 doctorates awarded. *Entrance requirements:* Additional exam requirements/recommendations for international students: Required—Official results from the TOEFL or IELTS are required. *Application deadline:* Applications are processed on a rolling basis. Application fee: $25. Electronic applications accepted. *Expenses:* Contact institution. *Financial support:* Career-related internships or fieldwork, tuition waivers (partial), and unspecified assistantships available. *Unit head:* Kimberly Dean, Chair, 215-572-8629. *Application contact:* 215-572-2925, Fax: 215-572-2126, E-mail: grad@arcadia.edu.

Arizona State University at the Tempe campus, Mary Lou Fulton Teachers College, Program in Curriculum and Instruction, Phoenix, AZ 85069. Offers curriculum and instruction (M Ed, MA); elementary education (M Ed); physical education (MPE); secondary education (M Ed). *Program availability:* Part-time, evening/weekend, online learning. Terminal master's awarded for partial completion of doctoral program. *Degree requirements:* For master's, thesis or alternative, applied project, interactive Program of Study (iPOS) submitted before completing 50 percent of required credit hours. *Entrance requirements:* For master's, GRE or GMAT (for some programs), minimum GPA of 3.0 or equivalent in last 2 years of work leading to bachelor's degree, 3 letters of recommendation, personal statement describing research and career goals, curriculum vitae or resume, IVP fingerprint clearance card (for those seeking Arizona certification). Additional exam requirements/recommendations for international students: Required—TOEFL, IELTS, or PTE. Electronic applications accepted. *Expenses:* Contact institution. *Faculty research:* Early childhood, media and computers, elementary education, secondary education, English education, bilingual education, language and literacy, science education, engineering education, exercise and wellness education.

Arlington Baptist University, Program in Education, Arlington, TX 76012-3425. Offers curriculum and instruction (M Ed); educational leadership (M Ed). *Degree requirements:* For master's, professional portfolio; internship (for educational leadership). *Entrance requirements:* For master's, bachelor's degree from accredited college or university with minimum GPA of 3.0, minimum of 12 hours in Bible; minimum of three years' classroom teaching experience in an accredited K-12 public or private school (for educational leadership only).

Auburn University, Graduate School, College of Education, Department of Curriculum and Teaching, Auburn University, AL 36849. Offers curriculum and instruction (M Ed, MS, Ed S). *Accreditation:* NASM (one or more programs are accredited); NCATE. *Program availability:* Part-time. *Degree requirements:* For master's, thesis (for some programs); for doctorate, thesis/dissertation; for other advanced degree, field project. *Entrance requirements:* For master's, doctorate, and other advanced degree, GRE General Test. Electronic applications accepted. *Expenses:* Tuition, state resident: full-time $11,282; part-time $535 per credit hour. Tuition, nonresident: full-time $30,542; part-time $1605 per credit hour. *Required fees:* $826 per semester. Tuition and fees vary according to degree level and program. *Faculty research:* Emerging literacy, reading attitudes, music for at-risk youth, portfolio assessment.

Auburn University, Graduate School, College of Education, Department of Educational Foundations, Leadership, and Technology, Auburn University, AL 36849. Offers adult education (PhD, Ed S); curriculum supervision (M Ed, PhD); higher education administration (PhD); library media (Ed S); school administration (M Ed, PhD). *Accreditation:* NCATE. *Program availability:* Part-time. *Degree requirements:* For master's, thesis (for some programs); for doctorate, thesis/dissertation; for Ed S, field project. *Entrance requirements:* For master's, doctorate, and Ed S, GRE General Test. Electronic applications accepted. *Expenses:* Tuition, state resident: full-time $11,282; part-time $535 per credit hour. Tuition, nonresident: full-time $30,542; part-time $1605 per credit hour. *Required fees:* $826 per semester. Tuition and fees vary according to degree level and program.

Augusta University, College of Education, Program in Curriculum and Instruction, Augusta, GA 30912. Offers curriculum and instruction (Ed S); elementary education (MAT); foreign language education (MAT); instruction (M Ed); middle grades education (MAT); music education (MAT); secondary education (MAT); special education (MAT). *Degree requirements:* For master's, thesis, portfolio. *Entrance requirements:* For master's, GRE, MAT, minimum GPA of 2.5.

Aurora University, School of Education and Human Performance, Aurora, IL 60506-4892. Offers applied behavioral analysis (MS); bilingual-ESL education (MA); educational leadership with principal endorsement (MA); educational technology (MA); leadership in adult learning higher education (Ed D); leadership in curriculum and instruction (Ed D); leadership in educational administration (Ed D); reading instruction (MA); special education (MA). *Accreditation:* NCATE. *Program availability:* Part-time, evening/weekend, 100% online. *Faculty:* 14 full-time (6 women), 32 part-time/adjunct (17 women). *Students:* 28 full-time (25 women), 537 part-time (359 women); includes 101 minority (25 Black or African American, non-Hispanic/Latino; 8 Asian, non-Hispanic/Latino; 58 Hispanic/Latino; 2 Native Hawaiian or other Pacific Islander, non-Hispanic/Latino; 8 Two or more races, non-Hispanic/Latino), 2 international. Average age 38. 191 applicants, 98% accepted, 133 enrolled. In 2018, 213 master's, 16 doctorates awarded. *Degree requirements:* For master's, student teaching, research seminar, and practicum; for doctorate, comprehensive exam, thesis/dissertation. *Entrance requirements:* For master's, 2 years of teaching experience, valid teaching certificate, resume; for doctorate, appropriate master's degree, two references, curriculum vitae, personal statement, professional project, reflective essay. Additional exam requirements/recommendations for international students: Required—TOEFL (minimum score 550 paper-based; 79 iBT). *Application deadline:* For fall admission, 6/1 for international students; for spring admission, 10/1 for international students. Applications are processed on a rolling basis. Application fee: $0. Electronic applications accepted. *Expenses:* The reported tuition amount is for the program with the greatest enrollment, MA in Educational Leadership with Principal Endorsement. Other programs may require more semester hours, and thus have a greater total cost. The Education doctoral programs are roughly double the amount of the master's programs. *Financial support:* In 2018–19, 31 students received support. Federal Work-Study, scholarships/grants, and unspecified assistantships available. Financial award applicants required to submit FAFSA. *Unit head:* Dr. Jen Buckley, Dean, School of Education and Human Performance, 630-844-1542, Fax: 630-844-6155, E-mail: jbuckley@aurora.edu. *Application contact:* Center for Graduate Studies, 630-947-8955, E-mail: AUadmission@aurora.edu.
Website: http://aurora.edu/education

Averett University, Master in Education Program, Danville, VA 24541-3692. Offers administration and supervision (M Ed); curriculum and instruction (M Ed); special education with endorsement (M Ed); special education with licensure (M Ed). *Program availability:* Part-time, online only, 100% online. *Faculty:* 2 full-time (both women), 14 part-time/adjunct (11 women). *Students:* 141 full-time (108 women), 4 part-time (2 women); includes 31 minority (30 Black or African American, non-Hispanic/Latino; 1 Hispanic/Latino). Average age 37. 106 applicants, 58% accepted, 52 enrolled. In 2018, 52 master's awarded. *Degree requirements:* For master's, 30-credit core curriculum, minimum GPA of 3.0 throughout program, completion of degree requirements within six years from start of program. *Entrance requirements:* For master's, PRAXIS I, GRE, or MAT; writing proficiency test, minimum cumulative GPA of 3.0 over the last 60 hours of undergraduate study toward a baccalaureate degree, three letters of recommendation, Virginia teaching license (or eligibility). Additional exam requirements/recommendations for international students: Required—TOEFL (minimum score 600 paper-based; 100 iBT). *Application deadline:* Applications are processed on a rolling basis. Electronic applications accepted. *Expenses:* Contact institution. *Financial support:* Application deadline: 3/1; applicants required to submit FAFSA. *Unit head:* Dr. Nancy Riddell, Chair of the Education Department; Director of Teacher Education, 434-791-5741, Fax: 434-791-5020, E-mail: nriddell@averett.edu. *Application contact:* Christy Davis, Assistant Director of Admissions, 434-791-7133, E-mail: cdavis@averett.edu.
Website: http://gps.averett.edu/online/education/

Azusa Pacific University, School of Education, Department of Teacher Education, Program in Teaching, Azusa, CA 91702-7000. Offers MA Ed.

Ball State University, Graduate School, Teachers College, Department of Educational Studies, Program in Curriculum and Educational Technology, Muncie, IN 47306. Offers MA. *Accreditation:* NCATE. *Program availability:* Part-time, online only, 100% online. *Entrance requirements:* For master's, minimum baccalaureate GPA of 2.75 or 3.0 in latter half of baccalaureate. Additional exam requirements/recommendations for international students: Required—TOEFL (minimum score 550 paper-based; 79 iBT), IELTS (minimum score 6.5). Electronic applications accepted.

Ball State University, Graduate School, Teachers College, Department of Educational Studies, Program in Educational Studies, Muncie, IN 47306. Offers educational studies (PhD), including cultural and educational policy studies, curriculum, educational technology. *Program availability:* Part-time, blended/hybrid learning. *Degree requirements:* For doctorate, thesis/dissertation. *Entrance requirements:* For doctorate, GRE General Test, minimum graduate GPA of 3.2, curriculum vitae, writing sample, three letters of reference. Additional exam requirements/recommendations for international students: Required—TOEFL (minimum score 550 paper-based; 79 iBT), IELTS (minimum score 6.5). Electronic applications accepted. *Faculty research:* Emerging curriculum trends, secondary teacher preparation, issues of equity and social justice in education, teacher technology integration, teaching for transformative understanding, teacher leadership, history of educational policy and practices, ethics and education.

Barry University, School of Education, Program in Curriculum and Instruction, Miami Shores, FL 33161-6695. Offers accomplished teacher (Ed S); culture, language and literacy (TESOL) (PhD); curriculum evaluation and research (PhD); early childhood (Ed S); early childhood education (PhD); elementary (Ed S); elementary education (PhD); ESOL (Ed S); gifted (Ed S); Montessori (Ed S); PKP/elementary (Ed S); reading (Ed S); reading, language and cognition (PhD). *Entrance requirements:* For doctorate, GRE, minimum GPA of 3.25.

Baylor University, Graduate School, School of Education, Department of Curriculum and Instruction, Waco, TX 76798. Offers MA, MS Ed, Ed D, PhD. *Accreditation:* NCATE. *Program availability:* Part-time. *Students:* Average age 30. 26 applicants, 65% accepted, 14 enrolled. In 2018, 12 master's, 3 doctorates awarded. *Degree requirements:* For master's, comprehensive exam, thesis optional; for doctorate, comprehensive exam, thesis/dissertation. *Entrance requirements:* For master's, GRE General Test (including Analytic Writing), 3 letters of recommendation, personal statement, interview; for doctorate, GRE General Test (including Analytic Writing), 3 letters of recommendation, personal statement, interview, writing sample. Additional exam requirements/recommendations for international students: Required—TOEFL (minimum score 550 paper-based; 80 iBT). *Application deadline:* For fall admission, 3/15 priority date for domestic and international students; for spring admission, 10/15 priority date for domestic and international students. Applications are processed on a rolling basis. Application fee: $25. Electronic applications accepted. *Expenses:* Contact institution. *Financial support:* In 2018–19, 35 students received support, including 15 research assistantships with partial tuition reimbursements available (averaging $10,000 per year), 1 teaching assistantship with full tuition reimbursement available (averaging $19,000 per year); Federal Work-Study, institutionally sponsored loans, scholarships/grants, health care benefits, and unspecified assistantships also available. Support available to part-time students. Financial award application deadline: 3/15. *Faculty research:* Curriculum and pedagogy, elementary education, English language arts education, literacy and reading education, mathematics education, qualitative research, science education, social foundations and cultural studies, social studies education, secondary education, teacher education, technology education, media literacy, civics education, historically black colleges. *Total annual research expenditures:* $75,000. *Unit head:* Dr. Trena Wilkerson, Graduate Program Director, 254-710-6162, Fax: 254-710-3160, E-mail: trena_wilkerson@baylor.edu. *Application contact:* Carol Stukenbroeker, Administrative Assistant, 254-710-2410, Fax: 254-710-3160, E-mail: carol_stukenbroeker@baylor.edu.
Website: http://www.baylor.edu/soe/ci/

Berry College, Graduate Programs, Graduate Programs in Education, Program in Curriculum and Instruction, Mount Berry, GA 30149. Offers M Ed, Ed S. *Accreditation:* NCATE. *Faculty:* 2 part-time/adjunct (1 woman). *Students:* 29 full-time (25 women), 4 part-time (all women); includes 7 minority (3 Black or African American, non-Hispanic/Latino; 4 Hispanic/Latino). Average age 39. *Degree requirements:* For master's and Ed S, thesis, portfolio, oral exams. *Entrance requirements:* For master's, GRE or MAT, Baccalaureate degree in the filed of education from fully accredited institution of higher education, minimum GPA of 2.75.; for Ed S, Master's degree in the filed of education from fully accredited institution of higher education, minimum GPA 3.25. Additional exam requirements/recommendations for international students: Required—TOEFL (minimum score 550 paper-based). *Application deadline:* For fall admission, 7/26 for domestic students, 5/1 for international students; for spring admission, 12/1 for domestic students, 10/1 for international students. Applications are processed on a rolling basis. Application fee: $25 ($30 for international students). Electronic applications accepted. *Expenses:* $490 per credit hour. *Financial support:* In 2018–19, 1 student received support. Research assistantships, scholarships/grants, tuition waivers, and unspecified assistantships available. Support available to part-time students. Financial award application deadline: 3/1; financial award applicants required to submit FAFSA. *Unit head:* Dr. Jacqueline McDowell, Dean, 706-236-1717, Fax: 706-238-5827, E-mail: jmcdowell@berry.edu. *Application contact:* Admissions, 706-236-2215, Fax: 706-290-2178, E-mail: admissions@berry.edu.
Website: https://www.berry.edu/academics/graduate-studies/education/

Biola University, School of Education, La Mirada, CA 90639-0001. Offers curriculum and instruction (Certificate); early childhood (MA Ed, MAT); multiple subject (MAT); single subject (MAT); special education (MA Ed, MAT, Certificate). *Program availability:* Part-time, evening/weekend, online learning. *Entrance requirements:* For master's, CBEST, CSET, GRE (waived if cumulative GPA is 3.5 or above or if CBEST and all CSET subtests are passed). Additional exam requirements/recommendations for international students: Required—TOEFL (minimum score 100 iBT). Electronic applications accepted. *Faculty research:* Early childhood education, elementary education, special education, curriculum development, teacher preparation.

Black Hills State University, Graduate Studies, Program in Curriculum and Instruction, Spearfish, SD 57799. Offers MS. *Program availability:* Part-time. *Entrance requirements:* Additional exam requirements/recommendations for international students: Required—TOEFL (minimum score 500 paper-based; 60 iBT).

Bloomsburg University of Pennsylvania, School of Graduate Studies, College of Education, Department of Teaching and Learning, Program in Curriculum and Instruction, Bloomsburg, PA 17815-1301. Offers M Ed, Certificate. *Accreditation:* NCATE. *Degree requirements:* For master's, thesis. *Entrance requirements:* For master's, MAT, GRE, or PRAXIS, minimum QPA of 3.0, interview. Additional exam requirements/recommendations for international students: Required—TOEFL (minimum score 550 paper-based; 79 iBT), IELTS. Electronic applications accepted.

Bloomsburg University of Pennsylvania, School of Graduate Studies, College of Education, Department of Teaching and Learning, Program in Educational Leadership, Bloomsburg, PA 17815-1301. Offers college student affairs (M Ed); PreK-12 curriculum and instruction (M Ed); PreK-12 school counseling (M Ed); PreK-12 school principal (M Ed). *Degree requirements:* For master's, practicum. *Entrance requirements:* For master's, 3 letters of recommendation, resume, minimum QPA of 3.0, personal statement, interview. Additional exam requirements/recommendations for international students: Required—TOEFL, IELTS. Electronic applications accepted.

Bluffton University, Programs in Education, Bluffton, OH 45817. Offers intervention specialist (MA Ed); leadership (MA Ed); reading (MA Ed). *Accreditation:* NCATE. *Program availability:* Part-time, 100% online, blended/hybrid learning, videoconference. *Faculty:* 2 full-time (both women), 2 part-time/adjunct (1 woman). *Students:* 14 full-time (7 women), 7 part-time (all women). Average age 31. In 2018, 8 master's awarded. *Degree requirements:* For master's, action research project, public presentation. *Entrance requirements:* For master's, PRAXIS I, bachelor's degree, minimum GPA of 3.0. Additional exam requirements/recommendations for international students: Required—TOEFL. *Application deadline:* For fall admission, 8/15 priority date for domestic students, 6/15 priority date for international students; for spring admission, 12/15 priority date for domestic students, 9/15 priority date for international students. Applications are processed on a rolling basis. Electronic applications accepted. *Expenses:* Contact institution. *Financial support:* Unspecified assistantships available. Financial award application deadline: 9/15; financial award applicants required to submit FAFSA. *Unit head:* Dr. Amy K. Mullins, Director of Graduate Programs in Education, 419-358-3457, E-mail: mullinsa@bluffton.edu. *Application contact:* Shelby Koenig, Enrollment Counselor for Graduate Program, 419-358-3022, E-mail: koenigs@bluffton.edu.
Website: https://www.bluffton.edu/ags/index.aspx

Bob Jones University, Graduate Programs, Greenville, SC 29614. Offers accountancy (MS); Bible (MA); Bible translation (MA); Biblical studies (Certificate); business administration (MBA); church history (MA, PhD); church ministries (MA); church music (MM); cinema and video production (MA); counseling (MS); curriculum and instruction (Ed D); divinity (M Div); dramatic production (MA); educational leadership (MS, Ed D, Ed S); elementary education (M Ed, MAT); English (M Ed, MA, MAT); fine arts (MA); graphic design (MA); history (M Ed, MA); illustration (MA); interpretative speech (MA); mathematics (M Ed, MAT); medical missions (Certificate); ministry (MM, D Min); multi-categorical special education (M Ed, MAT); music (M Ed); New Testament interpretation (PhD); Old Testament interpretation (PhD); orchestral instrument performance (MM); organ performance (MM); pastoral studies (MA); personnel services (MS, Ed S); piano pedagogy (MM); piano performance (MM); platform arts (MA); rhetoric and public address (MA); secondary education (M Ed); studio art (MA); teaching Bible (MA); theology (MA, PhD); voice performance (MM); youth ministries (MA); M Div/MM.

Boise State University, College of Education, Department of Curriculum, Instruction and Foundational Studies, Boise, ID 83725-0399. Offers curriculum and instruction (MA Ed, Ed D); educational leadership (M Ed); executive educational leadership (Ed S). *Accreditation:* NCATE. *Program availability:* Part-time. *Degree requirements:* For master's, thesis optional. *Entrance requirements:* For master's, minimum GPA of 3.0. Additional exam requirements/recommendations for international students: Required—TOEFL (minimum score 550 paper-based; 80 iBT), IELTS (minimum score 6). Electronic applications accepted.

Boston College, Lynch School of Education and Human Development, Department of Teacher Education, Special Education and Curriculum and Instruction, Chestnut Hill, MA 02467-3800. Offers curriculum and instruction (M Ed, PhD, CAES); early childhood education (M Ed); elementary education (M Ed); law and curriculum and instruction (JD/M Ed); reading specialist (M Ed, CAES); religious education (M Ed, CAES); secondary education (M Ed, MAT, MST), including biology (MST), chemistry (MST), English (MAT), French (MAT), geology (MST), history (MAT), Latin and classical humanities (MAT), mathematics (MST), physics (MST), secondary teaching (M Ed), Spanish (MAT); special needs: moderate disabilities (M Ed, CAES); special needs: severe disabilities (M Ed); JD/M Ed. *Program availability:* Part-time, evening/weekend, 100% online. *Faculty:* 19 full-time (11 women). *Students:* 186 full-time (140 women), 92 part-time (74 women); includes 58 minority (20 Black or African American, non-Hispanic/Latino; 4 Asian, non-Hispanic/Latino; 29 Hispanic/Latino; 5 Two or more races, non-Hispanic/Latino), 33 international. Average age 28. In 2018, 132 master's, 13 doctorates awarded. Terminal master's awarded for partial completion of doctoral program. *Degree requirements:* For master's, comprehensive exam; for doctorate, comprehensive exam, thesis/dissertation. *Entrance requirements:* Additional exam requirements/recommendations for international students: Required—TOEFL. Application fee: $75. Electronic applications accepted. *Financial support:* Fellowships with full and partial tuition reimbursements, research assistantships with full and partial tuition reimbursements, teaching assistantships with full and partial tuition reimbursements, career-related internships or fieldwork, Federal Work-Study, institutionally sponsored loans, scholarships/grants, traineeships, health care benefits, tuition waivers (full and partial), and unspecified assistantships available. Support available to part-time students. Financial award applicants required to submit FAFSA. *Faculty research:* Teacher education, education research and policy, bilingual education, science education, disabilities, urban education. *Unit head:* Dr. Susan Bruce, Chairperson, 617-552-4214, Fax: 617-552-0812. *Application contact:* Jessica Rivers, Assistant Dean of Graduate Admission and Financial Aid, 617-552-4214, Fax: 617-552-0398, E-mail: riversja@bc.edu.
Website: http://www.bc.edu/education

Bowling Green State University, Graduate College, College of Education and Human Development, School of Teaching and Learning, Program in Curriculum and Teaching, Bowling Green, OH 43403. Offers M Ed. *Program availability:* Part-time, evening/weekend. *Degree requirements:* For master's, thesis or alternative. *Entrance requirements:* For master's, GRE General Test or PRAXIS. Additional exam requirements/recommendations for international students: Required—TOEFL. Electronic applications accepted. *Faculty research:* Cognitive development in cultural context, sociocultural and activity theory, philosophy in education, performance assessment.

Bradley University, The Graduate School, College of Education and Health Sciences, Department of Teacher Education, Peoria, IL 61625-0002. Offers curriculum and instruction (MA). *Accreditation:* NCATE. *Program availability:* Part-time, evening/weekend. *Faculty:* 13 full-time (9 women). *Students:* 1 (woman) full-time, 12 part-time (10 women); includes 3 minority (2 Black or African American, non-Hispanic/Latino; 1 Two or more races, non-Hispanic/Latino). Average age 33. 2 applicants, 100% accepted, 1 enrolled. In 2018, 3 master's awarded. *Degree requirements:* For master's, comprehensive exam, thesis optional. *Entrance requirements:* For master's, GRE General Test or MAT, 2 letters of recommendation. Additional exam requirements/recommendations for international students: Required—TOEFL (minimum score 550 paper-based; 79 iBT), IELTS (minimum score 6.5). *Application deadline:* For fall admission, 5/15 priority date for domestic and international students; for spring admission, 10/15 priority date for domestic and international students. Applications are processed on a rolling basis. Application fee: $40 ($50 for international students). Electronic applications accepted. *Expenses: Tuition:* Part-time $890 per credit. *Required*

fees: $50 per unit. *Financial support:* In 2018–19, 26 students received support. Career-related internships or fieldwork, scholarships/grants, tuition waivers (partial), and unspecified assistantships available. Financial award application deadline: 4/1. *Unit head:* Dr. Dean Cantu, Associate Dean and Director, Professor, 309-677-3190, E-mail: dcantu@bradley.edu. *Application contact:* Rachel Webb, Director of On-Campus Graduate Admissions & International Student and Scholar Services, 309-677-2375, E-mail: rkwebb@bradley.edu.
Website: http://www.bradley.edu/academic/departments/te/

Brandman University, School of Education, Irvine, CA 92618. Offers curriculum and instruction (MAE); educational administration (MAE); educational leadership (MAE); educational leadership and administration (MA); elementary education (MAT); instructional technology: teaching the 21st century learner (MAE); leadership in early childhood education (MAE); organizational leadership (Ed D); school counseling (MA); secondary education (MAT); special education (MA); teaching and learning (MAE).

Brandon University, Faculty of Education, Brandon, MB R7A 6A9, Canada. Offers curriculum and instruction (M Ed, Diploma); educational administration (M Ed, Diploma); guidance and counseling (M Ed, Diploma); special education (M Ed, Diploma). *Degree requirements:* For master's, thesis. *Entrance requirements:* For master's, minimum GPA of 3.0, teaching certificate or equivalent. Additional exam requirements/recommendations for international students: Required—TOEFL. *Faculty research:* Comparative education, environmental studies, parent/school council.

Brescia University, Program in Teacher Leadership, Owensboro, KY 42301-3023. Offers MSTL. *Program availability:* Part-time, evening/weekend. *Degree requirements:* For master's, action research project. *Entrance requirements:* For master's, PRAXIS II, NTE, or GRE, interview, minimum GPA of 2.75, BA or BS, two letters of reference, professional resume. Electronic applications accepted.

Buena Vista University, School of Education, Storm Lake, IA 50588. Offers curriculum and instruction (M Ed), including effective teaching, TESL; school guidance and counseling (MS Ed). Program offered in summer only. *Program availability:* Part-time, evening/weekend, online learning. *Degree requirements:* For master's, thesis, fieldwork/practicum, capstone portfolio. *Entrance requirements:* For master's, Analytical Writing Assessment (in-house), minimum undergraduate GPA of 2.75. Electronic applications accepted. *Faculty research:* Reading, curriculum, educational psychology, special education.

Cabrini University, Academic Affairs, Radnor, PA 19087. Offers accounting (M Acc); autism spectrum disorder (M Ed); biological sciences (MS), including civic leadership; criminology and criminal justice (MA); curriculum, instruction, and assessment (M Ed); educational leadership (M Ed, Ed D), including curriculum and instructional leadership (Ed D), preK-12 leadership (Ed D); English as a second language (M Ed); organizational leadership (DBA, PhD); preK to 4 (M Ed); reading specialist (M Ed); secondary education (M Ed), including biology, chemistry, English, English/communication, mathematics, social studies; special education grades 7-12 (M Ed); special education preK-8 (M Ed); teaching and learning (M Ed). *Program availability:* Part-time, evening/weekend. *Degree requirements:* For master's, comprehensive exam (for some programs), thesis (for some programs); for doctorate, comprehensive exam (for some programs), thesis/dissertation. *Entrance requirements:* For master's, professional resume, personal statement, two recommendations, official transcripts; for doctorate, official transcripts, minimum master's GPA of 3.0, two recommendations, interview with admissions committee. Additional exam requirements/recommendations for international students: Required—TOEFL (minimum score 80 iBT). Electronic applications accepted. Application fee is waived when completed online. *Expenses:* Contact institution.

California Baptist University, Program in Education, Riverside, CA 92504-3206. Offers educational leadership (MS); educational leadership for faith-based institutions (MS); educational leadership for public institutions (MS); educational technology (MS); instructional computer applications (MS); international education (MS); leadership and adult learning (MS); leadership and organizational studies (MS); online teaching and learning (MS); reading (MS); science education (MA); special education in mild/moderate disabilities (MS); special education in moderate/severe disabilities (MS); teacher leadership (MS); teaching (MS); teaching and learning (MS). *Program availability:* Part-time, evening/weekend, 100% online, blended/hybrid learning. *Faculty:* 26 full-time (13 women), 28 part-time/adjunct (21 women). *Students:* 201 full-time (164 women), 265 part-time (209 women); includes 226 minority (23 Black or African American, non-Hispanic/Latino; 4 American Indian or Alaska Native, non-Hispanic/Latino; 7 Asian, non-Hispanic/Latino; 169 Hispanic/Latino; 6 Native Hawaiian or other Pacific Islander, non-Hispanic/Latino; 17 Two or more races, non-Hispanic/Latino), 2 international. Average age 39. 145 applicants, 97% accepted, 141 enrolled. In 2018, 253 master's awarded. *Degree requirements:* For master's, comprehensive exam, project, or thesis. *Entrance requirements:* For master's, minimum undergraduate GPA of 2.75; 500-word essay; three letters of recommendation; two prerequisite courses completed with minimum C grade. Additional exam requirements/recommendations for international students: Required—TOEFL (minimum score 80 iBT). *Application deadline:* For fall admission, 8/1 priority date for domestic students, 7/1 for international students; for spring admission, 12/1 priority date for domestic students, 11/1 for international students. Applications are processed on a rolling basis. Application fee: $45. Electronic applications accepted. *Expenses:* $634 per unit. *Financial support:* In 2018–19, 312 students received support. Federal Work-Study and scholarships/grants available. Financial award applicants required to submit CSS PROFILE or FAFSA. *Faculty research:* Leadership development, complexity theory, faith and learning, special education, social and philosophical contexts of education. *Unit head:* Dr. Robin Duncan, Dean, School of Education, 951-552-8948, E-mail: rduncan@calbaptist.edu. *Application contact:* Dr. Shari Farris, Program Director, Online MS in Education, 951-343-2455, E-mail: sfarris@calbaptist.edu.
Website: http://www.calbaptist.edu/mastersined/

California Coast University, School of Education, Santa Ana, CA 92701. Offers administration (M Ed); curriculum and instruction (M Ed); educational administration (Ed D); educational psychology (Ed D); organizational leadership (Ed D). *Program availability:* Online learning.

California State Polytechnic University, Pomona, Master's Programs in Education, Pomona, CA 91768-2557. Offers education (MA). *Program availability:* Part-time, evening/weekend. *Students:* 34 full-time (20 women), 73 part-time (48 women); includes 75 minority (7 Black or African American, non-Hispanic/Latino; 13 Asian, non-Hispanic/Latino; 52 Hispanic/Latino; 1 Native Hawaiian or other Pacific Islander, non-Hispanic/Latino; 2 Two or more races, non-Hispanic/Latino), 3 international. Average age 34. 35 applicants, 54% accepted, 11 enrolled. In 2018, 39 master's awarded. *Entrance requirements:* Additional exam requirements/recommendations for international students: Required—TOEFL (minimum score 550 paper-based). *Application deadline:* Applications are processed on a rolling basis. Application fee: $55. Electronic applications accepted. *Expenses:* Contact institution. *Financial support:* Application deadline: 3/2; applicants required to submit FAFSA. *Unit head:* Dr. Richard A. Navarro, Professor/Graduate Coordinator, 909-869-2081, Fax: 909-869-4822, E-mail: ranavarro@cpp.edu. *Application contact:* Dr. Richard A. Navarro, Professor/Graduate Coordinator, 909-869-2081, Fax: 909-869-4822, E-mail: ranavarro@cpp.edu.
Website: http://www.cpp.edu/~ceis/education/masters-programs/index.shtml

California State University, Chico, Office of Graduate Studies, College of Communication and Education, School of Education, Chico, CA 95929-0722. Offers curriculum and instruction (MA); teaching English learners and special education advising patterns (MA), including special education, teaching English learners. *Program availability:* Part-time. *Faculty:* 8 full-time (5 women), 12 part-time/adjunct (10 women). *Students:* 15 applicants, 33% accepted, 5 enrolled. In 2018, 40 master's awarded. *Degree requirements:* For master's, thesis or project and comprehensive exam. *Entrance requirements:* For master's, 2 letters of recommendation, department letter of recommendation access waiver form, writing assessment: https://www.csuchico.edu/soe/_assets/documents/csu-chico-ma-educ-applicant-upload-instructions.pdf. Additional exam requirements/recommendations for international students: Required—TOEFL (minimum score 550 paper-based; 80 iBT), IELTS (minimum score 6.5), PTE (minimum score 59). *Application deadline:* For fall admission, 5/1 priority date for domestic and international students; for spring admission, 12/2 priority date for domestic and international students. Application fee: $55. Electronic applications accepted. *Expenses: Tuition, area resident:* Full-time $4622; part-time $3116 per unit. Tuition, state resident: full-time $4622; part-time $3116 per unit. Tuition, nonresident: full-time $10,634. *Required fees:* $2160; $1620 per year. Tuition and fees vary according to class time and program. *Financial support:* Fellowships, research assistantships, teaching assistantships, career-related internships or fieldwork, Federal Work-Study, scholarships/grants, traineeships, health care benefits, unspecified assistantships, and stipends available. Support available to part-time students. Financial award application deadline: 3/2; financial award applicants required to submit FAFSA. *Unit head:* Dr. Rebecca Justeson, Director, 530-898-6421, Fax: 530-898-6177, E-mail: educ@csuchico.edu. *Application contact:* Micah Lehner, Graduate Admission Coordinator, 530-898-5416, Fax: 530-898-3342, E-mail: mlehner@csuchico.edu.
Website: http://www.csuchico.edu/soe/

California State University, Fresno, Division of Research and Graduate Studies, Kremen School of Education and Human Development, Department of Curriculum and Instruction, Fresno, CA 93740-8027. Offers education (MA), including curriculum and instruction. *Accreditation:* NCATE. *Program availability:* Part-time, evening/weekend. *Degree requirements:* For master's, thesis or alternative. *Entrance requirements:* For master's, GRE General Test, MAT, minimum GPA of 2.75. Additional exam requirements/recommendations for international students: Required—TOEFL. Electronic applications accepted. *Faculty research:* Teacher excellence, teacher quality improvement, online assessment.

California State University, Los Angeles, Graduate Studies, Charter College of Education, Division of Curriculum and Instruction, Los Angeles, CA 90032-8530. Offers elementary teaching (MA). *Program availability:* Part-time, evening/weekend. *Entrance requirements:* For master's, minimum GPA of 2.75 in last 90 units of course work, teaching certificate. Additional exam requirements/recommendations for international students: Required—TOEFL (minimum score 500 paper-based). Electronic applications accepted. *Faculty research:* Media, language arts, mathematics, computers, drug-free schools.

California State University, Northridge, Graduate Studies, Michael D. Eisner College of Education, Department of Elementary Education, Northridge, CA 91330. Offers curriculum and instruction (MA); language and literacy (MA); multilingual/multicultural education (MA). *Accreditation:* NCATE. *Program availability:* Part-time, evening/weekend. *Degree requirements:* For master's, comprehensive exam. *Entrance requirements:* For master's, GRE General Test or minimum GPA of 3.0. Additional exam requirements/recommendations for international students: Required—TOEFL.

California State University, Sacramento, College of Education, Graduate and Professional Studies in Education, Sacramento, CA 95819. Offers behavioral science and gender equity (MA); child development (MA); counseling (MS); curriculum and instruction (MA); education (Ed D), including K-12 and community college; education leadership and policy studies (MA), including higher education, PreK-12; education specialist (Ed S), including school psychology; educational technology (MA); language and literacy (MA); multicultural education (MA); school psychology (MA); special education (MA); workforce development advocacy (MA). *Program availability:* Part-time, evening/weekend, blended/hybrid learning. *Degree requirements:* For master's, thesis or project; writing proficiency exam; for doctorate, thesis/dissertation. *Entrance requirements:* For master's and doctorate, GRE. Additional exam requirements/recommendations for international students: Required—TOEFL (minimum score 550 paper-based; 80 iBT); Recommended—IELTS (minimum score 7), TSE. Electronic applications accepted. *Expenses:* Contact institution.

California State University, Stanislaus, College of Education, Kinesiology and Social Work, MA Program in Education, Turlock, CA 95382. Offers curriculum and instruction (MA), including education technology, elementary education, multilingual education, physical education, reading, secondary education, special education; school administration (MA); school counseling (MA). *Program availability:* Part-time, evening/weekend. *Degree requirements:* For master's, comprehensive exam (for some programs), thesis (for some programs). *Entrance requirements:* For master's, MAT, GRE, or CBEST (varies by concentration), 3 letters of recommendation, personal statement. Additional exam requirements/recommendations for international students: Required—TOEFL (minimum score 550 paper-based). Electronic applications accepted. *Faculty research:* Children's perspectives on historical events, method elementary schools dual language education, K-12 reading programs.

Calvary University, Graduate School and Seminary, Kansas City, MO 64147. Offers Bible and theology (MS); Biblical counseling (MA); education (MS), including administration and leadership, Christian education, curriculum and instruction, elementary education; organizational development (MS); pastoral studies (M Div); worship arts (MS). *Program availability:* Part-time, evening/weekend. *Degree requirements:* For master's, variable foreign language requirement, comprehensive exam, thesis or alternative. *Entrance requirements:* For master's, minimum GPA of 2.5, BA or BS, doctrine agreement. Additional exam requirements/recommendations for international students: Required—TOEFL (minimum score 550 paper-based). Electronic applications accepted. *Expenses:* Contact institution.

Calvin College, Graduate Programs in Education, Grand Rapids, MI 49546-4388. Offers curriculum and instruction (M Ed). *Accreditation:* TEAC. *Program availability:* Part-time. *Degree requirements:* For master's, thesis or seminar. *Entrance requirements:* For master's, teaching certificate. Additional exam requirements/recommendations for international students: Required—TOEFL (minimum score 550 paper-based; 80 iBT). Electronic applications accepted. *Expenses:* Contact institution. *Faculty research:* Literacy, racialized gender and gendered identity, teacher learning, learning disabilities identification, leadership.

Cambridge College, School of Education, Boston, MA 02129. Offers autism specialist (M Ed); autism/behavior analyst (M Ed); behavior analyst (Post-Master's Certificate); curriculum and instruction (CAGS); early childhood teacher (M Ed); educational leadership (M Ed, Ed D); elementary teacher (M Ed); English as a second language (M Ed, Certificate); general science (M Ed); health education (Post-Master's Certificate);

interdisciplinary studies (M Ed); library teacher (M Ed); mathematics education (M Ed); mathematics specialist (Certificate); school administration (M Ed, CAGS); school nurse education (M Ed); teacher of students with moderate disabilities (M Ed); teaching skills and methodologies (M Ed). *Program availability:* Part-time, evening/weekend, online learning. *Degree requirements:* For master's, thesis, internship/practicum (licensure program only); for doctorate, thesis/dissertation; for other advanced degree, thesis. *Entrance requirements:* For master's, interview, resume, documentation of licensure, 2 professional references; for doctorate, official transcripts, interview, resume, written personal statement/essay, portfolio of scholarly and professional work, 2 professional references, health insurance, immunizations form; for other advanced degree, official transcripts, interview, resume, written personal statement/essay, 2 professional references, health insurance, immunizations form. Additional exam requirements/recommendations for international students: Required—TOEFL (minimum score 550 paper-based; 79 iBT), Michigan English Language Assessment Battery (minimum score 85); Recommended—IELTS (minimum score 6). *Application deadline:* Applications are processed on a rolling basis. Application fee: $30. Electronic applications accepted. *Expenses:* Contact institution. *Financial support:* Career-related internships or fieldwork, Federal Work-Study, and scholarships/grants available. Financial award applicants required to submit FAFSA. *Faculty research:* Adult education, accelerated learning, mathematics education, brain compatible learning, special education and law. *Unit head:* Dr. Mary Garrity, Interim Dean, 617-873-0168, E-mail: mary.garrity@cambridgecollege.edu. *Application contact:* Salvadore Liberto, Interim Assistant Vice President of Enrollment, 800-877-4723, E-mail: admissions@cambridgecollege.edu.
Website: https://www.cambridgecollege.edu/school/school-education

Capella University, School of Education, Doctoral Programs in Education, Minneapolis, MN 55402. Offers curriculum and instruction (PhD); educational leadership and management (Ed D); instructional design for online learning (PhD); K-12 studies in education (PhD); leadership for higher education (PhD); leadership in educational administration (PhD); postsecondary and adult education (PhD); professional studies in education (PhD); reading and literacy (Ed D); special education leadership (PhD); training and performance improvement (PhD).

Capella University, School of Education, Master's Programs in Education, Minneapolis, MN 55402. Offers adult education (MS); curriculum and instruction (MS); early childhood education (MS); enrollment management (MS); higher education leadership and management (MS); instructional design for online learning (MS); integrative studies (MS); K-12 studies in education (MS); leadership in educational administration (MS); reading and literacy (MS); special education teaching (MS).

Caribbean University, Graduate School, Bayamón, PR 00960-0493. Offers administration and supervision (MA Ed); criminal justice (MA); curriculum and instruction (MA Ed, PhD), including elementary education (MA Ed), English education (MA Ed), history education (MA Ed), mathematics education (MA Ed), primary education (MA Ed), science education (MA Ed), Spanish education (MA Ed); educational technology in instructional systems (MA Ed); gerontology (MSN); human resources (MBA); museology, archiving and art history (MA Ed); neonatal pediatrics (MSN); physical education (MA Ed); special education (MA Ed). *Entrance requirements:* For master's, interview, minimum GPA of 2.5.

Carlow University, College of Learning and Innovation, Program in Curriculum and Instruction, Pittsburgh, PA 15213-3165. Offers autism (M Ed); early childhood leadership (M Ed); online learning instructional design (M Ed); STEM (M Ed). *Program availability:* Part-time, evening/weekend. *Entrance requirements:* For master's, personal essay; resume or curriculum vitae; two recommendations; official transcripts; interview; minimum undergraduate GPA of 3.0. Additional exam requirements/recommendations for international students: Required—TOEFL (minimum score 550 paper-based). *Application deadline:* Applications are processed on a rolling basis. Electronic applications accepted. *Expenses: Tuition:* Full-time $13,090; part-time $5100 per semester. *Required fees:* $215; $84. Tuition and fees vary according to course load, degree level and program. *Financial support:* Application deadline: 4/1; applicants required to submit FAFSA. *Unit head:* Dr. Keeley Baronak, Chair, 412-578-6135, Fax: 412-578-6326, E-mail: kobaronak@carlow.edu. *Application contact:* Dr. Keeley Baronak, Chair, 412-578-6135, Fax: 412-578-6326, E-mail: kobaronak@carlow.edu.
Website: http://www.carlow.edu/Curriculum_and_Instruction_MEd.aspx

Carson-Newman University, Graduate Program in Education, Jefferson City, TN 37760. Offers curriculum and instruction (M Ed); educational leadership (M Ed); elementary education (MAT); school counseling (MS); secondary education (MAT); teaching English as a second language (MATESL). *Accreditation:* NCATE. *Program availability:* Part-time, evening/weekend, 100% online, blended/hybrid learning. *Faculty:* 20 full-time (11 women), 16 part-time/adjunct (13 women). *Students:* 14 full-time (8 women), 401 part-time (294 women); includes 45 minority (34 Black or African American, non-Hispanic/Latino; 1 American Indian or Alaska Native, non-Hispanic/Latino; 4 Hispanic/Latino; 1 Native Hawaiian or other Pacific Islander, non-Hispanic/Latino; 5 Two or more races, non-Hispanic/Latino). Average age 36. 223 applicants, 100% accepted, 199 enrolled. In 2018, 211 master's awarded. *Degree requirements:* For master's, thesis or alternative. *Entrance requirements:* For master's, PRAXIS II or GRE with minimum score of 290 on the verbal and quantitative components (for MAT), minimum GPA of 3.0 in major, 2.5 overall. Additional exam requirements/recommendations for international students: Recommended—TOEFL (minimum score 79 iBT), IELTS (minimum score 6.5), TSE (minimum score 53). *Application deadline:* For fall admission, 7/15 priority date for domestic students. Applications are processed on a rolling basis. Application fee: $50. *Expenses: Tuition:* Full-time $9036; part-time $502 per credit hour. *Required fees:* $900; $25 per credit hour. $300 per semester. One-time fee: $150. *Financial support:* Federal Work-Study and unspecified assistantships available. Financial award applicants required to submit FAFSA. *Unit head:* Dr. Kim Hawkins, Chair, 865-471-3314, E-mail: khawkins@cn.edu. *Application contact:* Nilma Stewart, Graduate Admissions and Services Adviser, 865-471-3230, Fax: 865-471-3875, E-mail: adults@cn.edu.
Website: http://www.cn.edu/adult-graduate-studies

Castleton University, Division of Graduate Studies, Department of Education, Program in Curriculum and Instruction, Castleton, VT 05735. Offers MA Ed. *Program availability:* Part-time, evening/weekend. *Degree requirements:* For master's, thesis or alternative. *Entrance requirements:* For master's, GRE General Test, MAT, interview, minimum undergraduate GPA of 3.0.

Central Michigan University, Central Michigan University Global Campus, Program in Education, Mount Pleasant, MI 48859. Offers college teaching (Graduate Certificate); community college (MA); curriculum and instruction (MA); educational technology (MA, DET); reading and literacy K-12 (MA); school principalship (MA), including charter school leadership; training and development (MA). *Accreditation:* TEAC. *Program availability:* Part-time, evening/weekend. *Entrance requirements:* For master's, minimum GPA of 2.7 in major. Additional exam requirements/recommendations for international students: Required—TOEFL. Electronic applications accepted.

Central Michigan University, College of Graduate Studies, College of Education and Human Services, Department of Educational Leadership, Mount Pleasant, MI 48859. Offers educational leadership (Ed D), including educational technology (Ed D, Ed S), higher education leadership, K-12 curriculum, K-12 leadership; general educational administration (Ed S), including administrative leadership K-12, educational technology (Ed D, Ed S), higher education administration, instructional leadership K-12; school principalship (MA), including charter school leadership, site-based leadership; student affairs administration (MA); teacher leadership (MA). *Program availability:* Part-time, evening/weekend. *Degree requirements:* For master's and Ed S, thesis or alternative; for doctorate, thesis/dissertation. *Entrance requirements:* For doctorate, GRE or MAT, master's degree, minimum GPA of 3.5, 3 years of professional education experience. Electronic applications accepted. *Faculty research:* Elementary administration, secondary administration, student achievement, in-service training, internships in administration.

Central Washington University, School of Graduate Studies and Research, College of Education and Professional Studies, Department of Curriculum, Supervision, and Educational Leadership, Program in Master Teacher, Ellensburg, WA 98926. Offers M Ed. *Program availability:* Part-time. *Degree requirements:* For master's, comprehensive exam (for some programs), thesis or alternative. *Entrance requirements:* For master's, minimum GPA of 3.0, 1 year of contracted teaching experience. Additional exam requirements/recommendations for international students: Required—TOEFL (minimum score 550 paper-based; 79 iBT), IELTS (minimum score 6.5). Electronic applications accepted.

Chapman University, Donna Ford Attallah College of Educational Studies, Orange, CA 92866. Offers counseling (MA), including school counseling (MA, Credential); curriculum and instruction (MA), including elementary education, secondary education; education (PhD), including cultural and curricular studies, disability studies, leadership studies, school psychology (PhD, Credential); educational psychology (MA); leadership development (MA); multiple subjects (Credential), including Spanish/English bilingual; pupil personnel services (Credential), including school counseling (MA, Credential), school psychology (PhD, Credential); school psychology (Ed S); single subject (Credential); special education (MA, Credential), including mild/moderate (Credential), moderate/severe (Credential); teaching (MA), including elementary education, secondary education, secondary music education. *Accreditation:* TEAC. *Program availability:* Part-time, evening/weekend. Electronic applications accepted. *Expenses:* Contact institution.

City University of Seattle, Graduate Division, Albright School of Education, Seattle, WA 98121. Offers administrator certification (Certificate); curriculum and instruction (M Ed); elementary education (MIT); guidance and counseling (M Ed); leadership (M Ed); reading and literacy (M Ed); school counseling (M Ed); special education (MIT); superintendent certification (Certificate). *Program availability:* Part-time, evening/weekend, online learning. *Degree requirements:* For master's, comprehensive exam (for some programs), thesis (for some programs). *Entrance requirements:* For master's, baccalaureate degree or equivalent from an accredited or otherwise recognized institution. Additional exam requirements/recommendations for international students: Required—TOEFL (minimum score 567 paper-based; 87 iBT); Recommended—IELTS. Electronic applications accepted. *Expenses:* Contact institution.

Clarion University of Pennsylvania, College of Arts, Education and Sciences, Master of Education Program, Clarion, PA 16214. Offers curriculum and instruction (M Ed); early childhood (M Ed); math education (M Ed); reading (M Ed); science education (M Ed); special education (M Ed); technology (M Ed). *Accreditation:* NCATE. *Program availability:* Part-time, evening/weekend, 100% online, blended/hybrid learning. *Faculty:* 6 full-time (3 women). *Students:* 5 full-time (all women), 85 part-time (73 women); includes 3 minority (2 Black or African American, non-Hispanic/Latino; 1 Two or more races, non-Hispanic/Latino). Average age 30. 57 applicants, 61% accepted, 26 enrolled. In 2018, 51 master's awarded. *Degree requirements:* For master's, comprehensive exam (for some programs), thesis or alternative. *Entrance requirements:* For master's, minimum QPA of 3.0. Additional exam requirements/recommendations for international students: Required—TOEFL (minimum score 550 paper-based; 80 iBT), Or IELTS. Satisfactory completion of a bachelor's degree from an accredited US college or university is also acceptable evidence of English language. *Application deadline:* For fall admission, 8/1 priority date for domestic students, 7/15 priority date for international students; for winter admission, 11/1 priority date for domestic students; for spring admission, 12/1 priority date for domestic students, 11/15 priority date for international students; for summer admission, 4/1 priority date for domestic students. Applications are processed on a rolling basis. Application fee: $40. Electronic applications accepted. *Expenses: Tuition, area resident:* Part-time $516 per credit hour. Tuition, state resident: part-time $516 per credit hour. Tuition, nonresident: part-time $774 per credit hour. *Required fees:* $159 per credit hour. One-time fee: $50 part-time. Tuition and fees vary according to degree level, campus/location and program. *Financial support:* Federal Work-Study, institutionally sponsored loans, and scholarships/grants available. Financial award application deadline: 3/1; financial award applicants required to submit FAFSA. *Unit head:* Dr. John McCullough, Chair, Department of Education, 814-393-2404, Fax: 814-393-2446, E-mail: gradstudies@clarion.edu. *Application contact:* Susan Staub, Graduate Admissions Counselor, 814-393-2337, Fax: 814-393-2722, E-mail: gradstudies@clarion.edu.

Clark Atlanta University, School of Education, Department of Curriculum and Instruction, Atlanta, GA 30314. Offers special education general curriculum (MA); teaching math and science (MAT). *Program availability:* Part-time. *Degree requirements:* For master's, one foreign language, comprehensive exam. *Entrance requirements:* For master's, GRE General Test, minimum undergraduate GPA of 2.6. Additional exam requirements/recommendations for international students: Required—TOEFL (minimum score 500 paper-based; 61 iBT).

Clarks Summit University, Online Master's Programs, South Abington Township, PA 18411. Offers Bible (MA); counseling (MA, MS); curriculum and instruction (M Ed); educational administration (M Ed); literature (MA); organizational leadership (MA). *Program availability:* Part-time, evening/weekend, online learning. *Entrance requirements:* Additional exam requirements/recommendations for international students: Required—TOEFL (minimum score 500 paper-based).

Clemson University, Graduate School, College of Education, Department of Teaching and Learning, Clemson, SC 29634. Offers curriculum and instruction (PhD); middle level education (MAT); secondary math and science (MAT); STEAM education (Certificate); teaching and learning (M Ed). *Program availability:* Part-time, evening/weekend, 100% online. *Faculty:* 16 full-time (13 women). *Students:* 40 full-time (36 women), 198 part-time (171 women); includes 32 minority (10 Black or African American, non-Hispanic/Latino; 1 American Indian or Alaska Native, non-Hispanic/Latino; 3 Asian, non-Hispanic/Latino; 12 Hispanic/Latino; 1 Native Hawaiian or other Pacific Islander, non-Hispanic/Latino; 5 Two or more races, non-Hispanic/Latino), 8 international. Average age 31. 257 applicants, 77% accepted, 163 enrolled. In 2018, 38 master's, 5 doctorates awarded. *Degree requirements:* For master's, comprehensive exam; for doctorate, comprehensive exam, thesis/dissertation. *Entrance requirements:* For master's, doctorate, and Certificate, GRE General Test, unofficial transcripts, letters of recommendation. Additional exam requirements/recommendations for international students: Required—TOEFL (minimum score 80 paper-based; 80 iBT); Recommended—IELTS (minimum score 6.5), TSE (minimum score 54). *Application deadline:* For fall admission, 4/15 for international students; for spring admission, 10/15

for international students. Applications are processed on a rolling basis. Application fee: $80 ($90 for international students). Electronic applications accepted. *Expenses:* $5198 per semester full-time resident, $10123 per semester full-time non-resident, $556 per credit hour part-time resident, $1109 per credit hour part-time non-resident, online $770 per credit hour, $4938 doctoral programs resident, $10405 doctoral programs non-resident, $1144 full-time graduate assistant, other fees may apply per session; MAT Programs: $5898 per semester full-time resident, $11623 per semester full-time non-resident, $724 per credit hour part-time resident, $1451 per credit hour part-time non-resident, online $955 per credit hour, $1144 full-time graduate assistant, other fees may apply per session. *Financial support:* In 2018–19, 8 students received support, including 9 fellowships with full and partial tuition reimbursements available (averaging $3,414 per year), 3 research assistantships with full and partial tuition reimbursements available (averaging $17,500 per year), 28 teaching assistantships with full and partial tuition reimbursements available (averaging $18,020 per year); career-related internships or fieldwork also available. *Faculty research:* STEAM education, inquiry-based instruction, cultural hegemony and mathematics, equity and ethics, teacher effectiveness. *Total annual research expenditures:* $1.3 million. *Unit head:* Dr. Jeff Marshall, Department Chair, 864-656-2059, E-mail: marsha9@clemson.edu. *Application contact:* Julie Jones, Student Services Manager, 864-656-5096, E-mail: jgambre@clemson.edu.
Website: http://www.clemson.edu/education/departments/teaching-learning/index.html

Coker College, Graduate Programs, Hartsville, SC 29550. Offers college athletic administration (MS); criminal and social justice policy (MS); curriculum and instructional technology (M Ed); literacy studies (M Ed); management and leadership (MS). *Program availability:* Part-time, 100% online. *Faculty:* 15 full-time (7 women), 7 part-time/adjunct (3 women). *Students:* 144 full-time (100 women), 6 part-time (2 women); includes 42 minority (33 Black or African American, non-Hispanic/Latino; 1 Asian, non-Hispanic/Latino; 4 Hispanic/Latino; 4 Two or more races, non-Hispanic/Latino). Average age 33. 120 applicants, 61% accepted, 65 enrolled. In 2018, 92 master's awarded. *Entrance requirements:* For master's, 1. Undergraduate overall gpa of 3.0 on 4.0 scale. 2. Official transcripts from all undergraduate institutions. 3. One-page personal statement. 4. Resume. 5. Two professional references. Additionally, for MEd in Literacy Studies - 1 year of teaching in PK-12 and letter of recommendation from principal/assistant principal. *Application deadline:* Applications are processed on a rolling basis. Application fee: $0. Electronic applications accepted. *Financial support:* Unspecified assistantships available. Financial award application deadline: 6/30; financial award applicants required to submit FAFSA. *Unit head:* Dr. Kathryn Flaherty, Dean of Graduate and Professional Programs, 843-857-4227, E-mail: kflaherty@coker.edu. *Application contact:* Lacey Rice-Serafin, Director of Graduate Programs, 843-857-4128, E-mail: lriceserafin@coker.edu.

The College at Brockport, State University of New York, School of Education, Health, and Human Services, Department of Education and Human Development, Brockport, NY 14420-2997. Offers adolescence education (MS Ed), including adolescence biology education, adolescence chemistry education, adolescence English, adolescence mathematics, adolescence physics, adolescence physics education, adolescence social studies education; bilingual education (MS Ed, AGC); childhood curriculum specialist (MS Ed); inclusive generalist education (MS Ed, AGC, Advanced Certificate), including biology (MS Ed, AGC), chemistry (MS Ed), English (MS Ed, Advanced Certificate), mathematics (MS Ed, Advanced Certificate), science (MS Ed, Advanced Certificate), social studies (MS Ed, Advanced Certificate); literacy education B-12 (MS Ed). *Accreditation:* NCATE. *Faculty:* 12 full-time (7 women), 10 part-time/adjunct (6 women). *Students:* 60 full-time (39 women), 227 part-time (157 women); includes 9 minority (1 Asian, non-Hispanic/Latino; 8 Hispanic/Latino). 135 applicants, 71% accepted, 59 enrolled. In 2018, 107 master's, 13 AGCs awarded. *Degree requirements:* For master's, thesis or alternative. *Entrance requirements:* For master's, minimum GPA of 3.0, letters of recommendation, interview (for some programs); statement of objectives, current resume. Additional exam requirements/recommendations for international students: Required—TOEFL (minimum score 550 paper-based; 79 iBT), IELTS (minimum score 6.5). *Application deadline:* For fall admission, 3/15 priority date for domestic and international students; for spring admission, 10/15 priority date for domestic and international students; for summer admission, 3/15 priority date for domestic and international students. Application fee: $80. Electronic applications accepted. *Expenses:* Tuition, state resident: part-time $471 per credit. Tuition, nonresident: part-time $963 per credit. *Financial support:* In 2018–19, 1 fellowship with full tuition reimbursement (averaging $7,500 per year), 1 teaching assistantship with full tuition reimbursement (averaging $6,000 per year) were awarded; Federal Work-Study, scholarships/grants, and unspecified assistantships also available. Support available to part-time students. Financial award application deadline: 3/15; financial award applicants required to submit FAFSA. *Faculty research:* Educational assessment, literacy education, inclusive education, teacher preparation, qualitative methodology. *Unit head:* Dr. Janka Szilagyi, Chairperson, 585-395-5945, Fax: 585-395-2172, E-mail: jszilagy@brockport.edu. *Application contact:* Buffie Edick, Graduate Program Director, 585-395-2326, Fax: 585-395-2172, E-mail: bedick@brockport.edu.
Website: https://www.brockport.edu/academics/education_human_development/department.html

The College of Idaho, Department of Education, Caldwell, ID 83605. Offers curriculum and instruction (M Ed); teaching (MAT). *Degree requirements:* For master's, thesis. *Entrance requirements:* For master's, GRE, portfolio, minimum undergraduate GPA of 3.0, interview. *Faculty research:* Discourse analysis, at-risk youth, children's literature, research design, program evaluation.

The College of Saint Rose, Graduate Studies, Thelma P. Lally School of Education, Teacher Education Programs, Albany, NY 12203-1419. Offers adolescence education (MS Ed, Advanced Certificate); adolescence education/special education (Advanced Certificate); childhood education (MS Ed); curriculum and instruction (MS Ed); early childhood education (MS Ed). *Students:* 49 full-time (39 women), 21 part-time (17 women); includes 3 minority (2 Black or African American, non-Hispanic/Latino; 1 Hispanic/Latino). Average age 27. 41 applicants, 66% accepted, 21 enrolled. In 2018, 48 master's, 1 Advanced Certificate awarded. *Entrance requirements:* For master's, minimum undergraduate GPA of 3.0. Additional exam requirements/recommendations for international students: Required—TOEFL (minimum score 550 paper-based; 80 iBT), IELTS (minimum score 6), PTE (minimum score 56). *Application deadline:* For fall admission, 4/1 priority date for domestic and international students; for spring admission, 10/15 priority date for domestic and international students; for summer admission, 3/15 priority date for domestic and international students. Applications are processed on a rolling basis. Application fee: $40. Electronic applications accepted. *Expenses: Tuition:* Full-time $14,382; part-time $799 per credit hour. *Required fees:* $924; $408 per credit. $286. *Financial support:* Career-related internships or fieldwork, scholarships/grants, tuition waivers (partial), and unspecified assistantships available. Support available to part-time students. Financial award application deadline: 4/15. *Unit head:* Dr. Drey Martone, Chair, 518-454-5262, E-mail: martoned@strose.edu. *Application contact:* Daniel Gallagher, Assistant Vice President for Graduate Recruitment and Enrollment, 518-485-3390, Fax: 518-458-5479, E-mail: grad@strose.edu.
Website: https://www.strose.edu/academics/schools/school-of-education/

The College of William and Mary, School of Education, Program in Curriculum and Instruction, Williamsburg, VA 23187-8795. Offers MA Ed. *Accreditation:* NCATE. *Program availability:* Part-time. *Faculty:* 17 full-time (12 women), 14 part-time/adjunct (12 women). *Students:* 63 full-time (44 women), 39 part-time (35 women); includes 24 minority (7 Black or African American, non-Hispanic/Latino; 1 Asian, non-Hispanic/Latino; 14 Hispanic/Latino; 2 Two or more races, non-Hispanic/Latino). Average age 31. 144 applicants, 78% accepted, 90 enrolled. In 2018, 67 master's awarded. *Degree requirements:* For master's, project. *Entrance requirements:* For master's, GRE, MAT, PRAXIS Core Academic Skills for Educators, minimum GPA of 2.5. Additional exam requirements/recommendations for international students: Required—TOEFL (minimum score 100 iBT), IELTS (minimum score 7). *Application deadline:* For fall admission, 1/15 for domestic and international students; for spring admission, 10/1 for domestic and international students. Application fee: $50. Electronic applications accepted. *Expenses:* Contact institution. *Financial support:* In 2018–19, 32 students received support, including 6 research assistantships with full tuition reimbursements available (averaging $7,791 per year); scholarships/grants and unspecified assistantships also available. Financial award application deadline: 1/15; financial award applicants required to submit FAFSA. *Faculty research:* Educational technology, professional development and evaluation, inclusive education, rural education, education policy. *Application contact:* Dorothy Smith Osborne, Assistant Dean for Academic Programs and Student Services, 757-221-2317, E-mail: dsosbo@wm.edu.
Website: http://education.wm.edu

Colorado Christian University, Program in Curriculum and Instruction, Lakewood, CO 80226. Offers corporate education (MACI); early childhood educator (MACI); elementary educator (MACI); instructional technology (MACI); master educator (MACI); online course developer (MACI); online teaching and learning (MACI); special education generalist (MACI). *Program availability:* Part-time, evening/weekend. *Degree requirements:* For master's, thesis optional, practicum. *Entrance requirements:* For master's, interviews, letters of recommendation. Additional exam requirements/recommendations for international students: Required—TOEFL. Electronic applications accepted. *Expenses:* Contact institution.

Columbia International University, Columbia Graduate School, Columbia, SC 29203. Offers Bible teaching (MABT); counseling (MACN); early childhood and elementary education (MAT); educational administration (M Ed); educational leadership (PhD); instruction and learning (M Ed); teaching English as a foreign language (Certificate); teaching English as a foreign language and intercultural studies (MATF). *Program availability:* Part-time, evening/weekend, online learning. *Degree requirements:* For master's, internships, professional project. *Entrance requirements:* For master's, MAT; GRE (for some programs), minimum GPA of 2.7. Additional exam requirements/recommendations for international students: Required—TOEFL. Electronic applications accepted.

Columbus State University, Graduate Studies, College of Education and Health Professions, Department of Counseling, Foundations, and Leadership, Columbus, GA 31907-5645. Offers clinical mental health counseling (MS); curriculum and leadership (Ed D), including curriculum, educational leadership, higher education (M Ed, Ed D); educational leadership (M Ed, Ed S), including higher education (M Ed, Ed D); school counseling (M Ed, Ed S). *Accreditation:* ACA; NCATE. *Program availability:* Part-time, evening/weekend, 100% online, blended/hybrid learning. *Faculty:* 13 full-time (5 women), 17 part-time/adjunct (8 women). *Students:* 66 full-time (50 women), 209 part-time (158 women); includes 145 minority (124 Black or African American, non-Hispanic/Latino; 5 Asian, non-Hispanic/Latino; 10 Hispanic/Latino; 6 Two or more races, non-Hispanic/Latino), 1 international. Average age 39. 168 applicants, 48% accepted, 54 enrolled. In 2018, 44 master's, 25 doctorates, 129 other advanced degrees awarded. *Degree requirements:* For master's, thesis, exit exam; for doctorate, comprehensive exam, thesis/dissertation; for Ed S, thesis or alternative. *Entrance requirements:* For master's, GRE General Test, minimum undergraduate GPA of 2.75; for doctorate, GRE General Test, minimum graduate GPA of 3.5, four years of professional service; for Ed S, GRE General Test, minimum undergraduate GPA of 2.75, graduate 3.0. Additional exam requirements/recommendations for international students: Required—TOEFL (minimum score 550 paper-based; 79 iBT). *Application deadline:* For fall admission, 6/30 for domestic and international students; for spring admission, 11/1 for domestic and international students; for summer admission, 3/1 for domestic and international students. Applications are processed on a rolling basis. Application fee: $50. Electronic applications accepted. *Expenses: Tuition, area resident:* Full-time $4924; part-time $618 per credit hour. Tuition, state resident: full-time $4924; part-time $618 per credit hour. Tuition, nonresident: full-time $19,218; part-time $2403 per credit hour. *International tuition:* $19,218 full-time. *Required fees:* $1870; $802. Tuition and fees vary according to course load, degree level and program. *Financial support:* In 2018–19, 30 students received support, including 6 research assistantships with partial tuition reimbursements available (averaging $3,000 per year); career-related internships or fieldwork, Federal Work-Study, institutionally sponsored loans, scholarships/grants, tuition waivers (partial), and unspecified assistantships also available. Support available to part-time students. Financial award application deadline: 5/1; financial award applicants required to submit FAFSA. *Unit head:* Dr. Tom Hackett, Department Chair, 706-507-8968, Fax: 706-569-3134, E-mail: hackett_paul@columbusstate.edu. *Application contact:* Catrina Smith-Edmond, Assistant Director for Graduate and Global Admission, 706-507-8824, Fax: 706-568-5091, E-mail: smithedmond_catrina@columbusstate.edu.
Website: http://cfl.columbusstate.edu/

Columbus State University, Graduate Studies, College of Education and Health Professions, Department of Teacher Education, Columbus, GA 31907-5645. Offers curriculum and instruction in accomplished teaching (M Ed); early childhood education (M Ed, MAT, Ed S); middle grades education (M Ed, MAT, Ed S); secondary education (M Ed, MAT, Ed S), including biology (MAT), chemistry (MAT), earth and space science (MAT), English/language arts, general science (M Ed), history (MAT), mathematics, science (Ed S), social science (M Ed, Ed S); special education (M Ed, MAT, Ed S), including general curriculum (M Ed, MAT); teacher leadership (M Ed). *Accreditation:* NCATE. *Program availability:* Part-time, evening/weekend, 100% online, blended/hybrid learning. *Faculty:* 20 full-time (12 women), 20 part-time/adjunct (15 women). *Students:* 110 full-time (84 women), 143 part-time (115 women); includes 105 minority (96 Black or African American, non-Hispanic/Latino; 4 Hispanic/Latino; 5 Two or more races, non-Hispanic/Latino). Average age 33. 147 applicants, 56% accepted, 62 enrolled. In 2018, 112 master's, 11 other advanced degrees awarded. *Degree requirements:* For Ed S, thesis or alternative. *Entrance requirements:* For master's, GRE General Test, minimum undergraduate GPA of 2.75; for Ed S, GRE General Test, minimum undergraduate GPA of 2.75, graduate 3.0. Additional exam requirements/recommendations for international students: Required—TOEFL (minimum score 550 paper-based; 79 iBT). *Application deadline:* For fall admission, 6/30 for domestic students, 5/1 for international students; for spring admission, 11/1 for domestic and international students; for summer admission, 3/1 for domestic and international students. Applications are processed on a rolling basis. Application fee: $50. Electronic applications accepted. *Expenses: Tuition, area resident:* Full-time $4924; part-time $618 per credit hour. Tuition, state resident: full-time $4924; part-time $618 per credit hour. Tuition, nonresident: full-time $19,218; part-time $2403 per credit hour. *International tuition:* $19,218 full-time. *Required fees:*

$1870; $802. Tuition and fees vary according to course load, degree level and program. *Financial support:* In 2018–19, 29 students received support, including 7 research assistantships with partial tuition reimbursements available (averaging $3,000 per year); career-related internships or fieldwork, Federal Work-Study, institutionally sponsored loans, scholarships/grants, tuition waivers (partial), and unspecified assistantships also available. Support available to part-time students. Financial award application deadline: 5/1; financial award applicants required to submit FAFSA. *Unit head:* Dr. Jan Burcham, Department Chair, 706-507-8519, Fax: 706-568-3134, E-mail: burcham_jan@columbusstate.edu. *Application contact:* Catrina Smith-Edmond, Assistant Director for Graduate and Global Admission, 706-507-8824, Fax: 706-568-5091, E-mail: smithedmond_catrina@columbusstate.edu.
Website: http://te.columbusstate.edu/

Concordia University, College of Education, Portland, OR 97211-6099. Offers administrative leadership (Ed D); career and technical education (M Ed); curriculum and instruction (M Ed), including adolescent literacy, early childhood education, educational technology leadership, English for speakers of other languages, environmental education, health and physical education, mathematics, methods and curriculum, reading interventionist, science, social studies, STEAM education, teacher leadership, the inclusive classroom, trauma and resilience in educational settings; educational administration (M Ed); educational leadership (M Ed); elementary education (MAT); higher education (Ed D); instructional leadership (Ed D); professional leadership, inquiry, and transformation (Ed D); secondary education (MAT); transformational leadership (Ed D). *Program availability:* Part-time, online learning. *Degree requirements:* For master's, comprehensive exam, work samples/portfolio. *Entrance requirements:* For master's, California Basic Educational Skills Test or PRAXIS I, minimum undergraduate GPA of 2.8, graduate 3.0; 2 letters of recommendation. Additional exam requirements/recommendations for international students: Required—TOEFL (minimum score 525 paper-based). Electronic applications accepted. *Faculty research:* Learner-centered classroom, brain-based learning, future of online learning.

Concordia University Ann Arbor, Graduate Programs, Ann Arbor, MI 48105-2797. Offers curriculum and instruction (MS); educational leadership (MS); organizational leadership and administration (MS). *Program availability:* Part-time, evening/weekend. *Degree requirements:* For master's, thesis. *Entrance requirements:* Additional exam requirements/recommendations for international students: Required—TOEFL (minimum score 80 iBT); Recommended—IELTS (minimum score 6.5). Electronic applications accepted.

Concordia University Chicago, College of Graduate Studies, Program in Curriculum and Instruction, River Forest, IL 60305-1499. Offers MA. *Accreditation:* NCATE. *Program availability:* Part-time, evening/weekend, online learning. *Degree requirements:* For master's, comprehensive exam, thesis. *Entrance requirements:* For master's, minimum GPA of 2.9. Additional exam requirements/recommendations for international students: Required—TOEFL (minimum score 550 paper-based). Electronic applications accepted. *Faculty research:* School discipline, school improvement, leadership.

Concordia University Chicago, College of Graduate Studies, Program in Educational Technology, River Forest, IL 60305-1499. Offers curriculum and instruction (MA); leadership (MA). *Program availability:* Online learning.

Concordia University Irvine, School of Education, Irvine, CA 92612-3299. Offers curriculum and instruction (MA); education and preliminary teaching credential (M Ed); educational administration and preliminary administrative services credential (MA); educational technology (MA); school counseling with pupil personnel services credential (MA). *Program availability:* Part-time, evening/weekend, online learning. *Degree requirements:* For master's, action research project. *Entrance requirements:* For master's, California Basic Educational Skills Test, California Subject Examinations for Teachers (M Ed and MA in educational administration and preliminary administrative services credential), official college transcript(s), signed statement of intent, two references, copy of credential. Additional exam requirements/recommendations for international students: Required—TOEFL. Electronic applications accepted. *Expenses:* Contact institution.

Concordia University, St. Paul, College of Education, St. Paul, MN 55104-5494. Offers classroom instruction (MA Ed), including K-12 reading; differentiated instruction (MA Ed); early childhood education (MA Ed); education (Ed D); educational leadership (MA Ed); educational technology (MA Ed, Certificate); K-12 principal licensure (Ed S); special education (MA Ed), including autism spectrum disorder, emotional and behavioral disorders, learning disabilities; superintendent (Ed S); teaching (MAT). *Accreditation:* NCATE. *Program availability:* Part-time, evening/weekend, 100% online, blended/hybrid learning. *Faculty:* 13 full-time (9 women), 82 part-time/adjunct (51 women). *Students:* 979 full-time (748 women), 40 part-time (28 women); includes 124 minority (49 Black or African American, non-Hispanic/Latino; 6 American Indian or Alaska Native, non-Hispanic/Latino; 34 Asian, non-Hispanic/Latino; 22 Hispanic/Latino; 1 Native Hawaiian or other Pacific Islander, non-Hispanic/Latino; 12 Two or more races, non-Hispanic/Latino), 11 international. Average age 34. 423 applicants, 99% accepted, 335 enrolled. In 2018, 358 master's, 3 doctorates, 119 other advanced degrees awarded. *Degree requirements:* For master's, thesis (for some programs); for doctorate, thesis/dissertation, capstone projects; for other advanced degree, e-folio review of competencies. *Entrance requirements:* For master's, official transcripts from regionally-accredited institution stating the conferral of a bachelor's degree with minimum cumulative GPA of 3.0; personal statement; professional resume; practitioner in field through work or volunteerism; resume; for doctorate, minimum master's or specialist degree GPA of 3.25; transcript; writing sample; three letters of recommendation; current resume; on-campus interview; for other advanced degree, minimum master's or specialist degree GPA of 3.25; transcript; statement covering employment history and long-term academic and professional goals; two letters of recommendation; interview with program director. Additional exam requirements/recommendations for international students: Recommended—TOEFL (minimum score 547 paper-based; 78 iBT), IELTS (minimum score 6). *Application deadline:* For fall admission, 8/1 for domestic and international students; for spring admission, 12/1 for domestic and international students; for summer admission, 5/1 for domestic and international students. Applications are processed on a rolling basis. Application fee: $0. Electronic applications accepted. *Expenses:* $395 per credit for 30 credits (for MA programs), $440 per credit for 42 credits (for MAT), $415 per credit for 30 credits (for EdS), $615 per credit for 64 credits (for EdD). *Financial support:* In 2018–19, 163 students received support. Federal Work-Study, scholarships/grants, and unspecified assistantships available. Financial award applicants required to submit FAFSA. *Faculty research:* School design for innovative learning practices, equine-assisted instruction, best practices for leadership in early childhood education, mental health needs in K-12 focusing on children of incarcerated parents, competency-based education. *Unit head:* Lonn Maly, Dean, 651-641-8203, E-mail: maly@csp.edu. *Application contact:* Amber Faletti, Director of Enrollment Management, 651-641-8838, Fax: 651-603-6320, E-mail: faletti@csp.edu.

Coppin State University, School of Graduate Studies, School of Education, Department of Instruction Leadership and Professional Development, Program in Curriculum and Instruction, Baltimore, MD 21216-3698. Offers M Ed. *Program availability:* Part-time, evening/weekend, online learning. *Degree requirements:* For master's, thesis. *Entrance requirements:* For master's, GRE or MAT, minimum GPA of 3.0, teacher certification.

Cornell University, Graduate School, Graduate Fields of Agriculture and Life Sciences, Field of Education, Ithaca, NY 14853. Offers adult and extension education (MPS, MS, PhD); learning, teaching, and social policy (MPS, MS, PhD); mathematics 7-12 (MS). Terminal master's awarded for partial completion of doctoral program. *Degree requirements:* For master's, thesis (MS); for doctorate, comprehensive exam, thesis/dissertation. *Entrance requirements:* For master's and doctorate, GRE General Test, sample of written work (recommended), 2 letters of recommendation. Additional exam requirements/recommendations for international students: Required—TOEFL (minimum score 550 paper-based; 77 iBT). Electronic applications accepted. *Faculty research:* Moral development and professional ethics, public issues education and community development, socio/political issues in public education, teacher education and curriculum in agricultural science and mathematics, extension research.

Dakota Wesleyan University, Program in Education, Mitchell, SD 57301. Offers curriculum and instruction (MA Ed); educational policy and administration (MA Ed); preK-12 principal certification (MA Ed); secondary certification (MA Ed). *Program availability:* Part-time, evening/weekend, online only, 100% online. *Faculty:* 5 part-time/adjunct (2 women). *Students:* 20 full-time (6 women), 4 part-time (1 woman); includes 8 minority (4 Black or African American, non-Hispanic/Latino; 3 Hispanic/Latino; 1 Two or more races, non-Hispanic/Latino). Average age 26. 12 applicants, 83% accepted, 8 enrolled. In 2018, 13 master's awarded. *Degree requirements:* For master's, comprehensive exam, thesis optional, electronic portfolio. *Entrance requirements:* For master's, minimum GPA of 2.7, elementary statistics course, statement of purpose, official transcripts, resume, three letters of recommendation. Additional exam requirements/recommendations for international students: Required—TOEFL (minimum score 500 paper-based), IELTS (minimum score 6.5). *Application deadline:* For fall admission, 8/1 priority date for domestic and international students; for winter admission, 12/1 priority date for domestic students; for spring admission, 4/1 priority date for domestic students, 12/1 priority date for international students. Applications are processed on a rolling basis. Application fee: $0. Electronic applications accepted. Application fee is waived when completed online. *Expenses:* Contact institution. *Financial support:* Applicants required to submit FAFSA. *Faculty research:* Technology in the classroom, current educational trends, higher education. *Unit head:* Dr. Melissa Weber, Director of Graduate Studies, 605-995-2630, Fax: 605-995-2609, E-mail: melissa.weber@dwu.edu. *Application contact:* Stacy Mock, Coordinator of Adult and Online Admissions, 605-995-2650, Fax: 605-995-2699, E-mail: admissions@dwu.edu.
Website: www.dwu.edu

Dallas Baptist University, Dorothy M. Bush College of Education, Program in Curriculum and Instruction, Dallas, TX 75211-9299. Offers Christian school administration (M Ed); distance learning (M Ed); English as a second language (M Ed); instructional technology (M Ed); professional life coaching (M Ed); special education (M Ed); supervision (M Ed). *Program availability:* Part-time, evening/weekend, online learning. *Application deadline:* Applications are processed on a rolling basis. Application fee: $25. Electronic applications accepted. Application fee is waived when completed online. *Expenses: Tuition:* Full-time $17,262; part-time $959 per credit hour. *Required fees:* $1000; $500 per semester. Tuition and fees vary according to course load and degree level. *Unit head:* Dr. Neil Dugger, Dean, 214-333-5202, E-mail: neil@dbu.edu. *Application contact:* Karla Hagan, Program Director, 214-333-5831, E-mail: karla@dbu.edu.
Website: http://www3.dbu.edu/graduate/curriculum_instruction.asp

Delaware State University, Graduate Programs, College of Education, Health and Public Policy, Program in Curriculum and Instruction, Dover, DE 19901-2277. Offers MA. *Program availability:* Part-time, evening/weekend. *Degree requirements:* For master's, comprehensive exam, thesis optional. *Entrance requirements:* For master's, GRE General Test, minimum GPA of 3.0 in major, 2.75 overall. Additional exam requirements/recommendations for international students: Required—TOEFL (minimum score 550 paper-based). Electronic applications accepted.

Delaware Valley University, Program in Educational Leadership, Doylestown, PA 18901-2697. Offers instruction, curriculum and technology (MS); school administration and leadership (MS). *Program availability:* Part-time, evening/weekend. *Entrance requirements:* For master's, minimum undergraduate GPA of 3.0.

DePaul University, College of Education, Chicago, IL 60614. Offers bilingual-bicultural education (M Ed, MA); counseling (M Ed, MA), including clinical mental health counseling, college student development, school counseling; curriculum studies (M Ed, MA, Ed D); early childhood education (M Ed, MA, Ed D); educational leadership (M Ed, MA, Ed D), including Catholic leadership (M Ed, MA), general (M Ed, MA), higher education (M Ed, MA), physical education (M Ed, MA), principal preparation (M Ed), teacher preparation (M Ed); elementary education (M Ed, MA); middle grades education (M Ed); middle school mathematics education (MS); reading specialist (M Ed, MA); secondary education (M Ed, MA); social and cultural foundations in education (M Ed, MA); special education (M Ed); sport, fitness and recreation leadership (MS); value-creating education for global citizenship (M Ed); world languages education (M Ed, MA). *Program availability:* Part-time, evening/weekend, online learning. *Degree requirements:* For doctorate, thesis/dissertation. Electronic applications accepted.

DeVry University–Folsom Campus, Graduate Programs, Folsom, CA 95630. Offers accounting (M Acc); accounting and financial management (MAFM); business administration (MBA); curriculum leadership (M Ed); educational leadership (M Ed); educational technology (M Ed); higher education leadership (M Ed); human resource management (MHRM); information systems management (MISM); network and communications management (MNCM); project management (MPM); public administration (MPA).

Doane University, Program in Education, Crete, NE 68333-2430. Offers curriculum and instruction (M Ed); education (Ed D); education specialist (Ed S); educational leadership (M Ed); school counseling (M Ed). *Accreditation:* NCATE. *Program availability:* Part-time, evening/weekend. *Faculty:* 10 full-time (7 women), 66 part-time/adjunct (50 women). *Students:* 287 full-time (235 women), 474 part-time (363 women); includes 57 minority (20 Black or African American, non-Hispanic/Latino; 1 American Indian or Alaska Native, non-Hispanic/Latino; 5 Asian, non-Hispanic/Latino; 22 Hispanic/Latino; 1 Native Hawaiian or other Pacific Islander, non-Hispanic/Latino; 8 Two or more races, non-Hispanic/Latino), 6 international. Average age 34. In 2018, 247 master's, 9 doctorates, 33 other advanced degrees awarded. *Degree requirements:* For master's, thesis; for doctorate, thesis/dissertation. *Entrance requirements:* For master's, minimum GPA of 2.5. Additional exam requirements/recommendations for international students: Required—TOEFL. *Application deadline:* Applications are processed on a rolling basis. Electronic applications accepted. *Expenses:* Contact institution. *Financial support:* Applicants required to submit FAFSA. *Unit head:* Dr. Lyn C. Forester, Dean, 402-826-8604, Fax: 402-826-8278. *Application contact:* Leah Schaber, Assistant Dean, 402-464-1223, Fax: 402-466-4228, E-mail: leah.schaber@doane.edu.
Website: http://www.doane.edu/masters-degrees

Drexel University, Goodwin College of Professional Studies, School of Education, Philadelphia, PA 19104-2875. Offers applied behavior analysis (MS); creativity and

innovation (MS); education improvement and transformation (MS); educational administration (MS); educational leadership and management (Ed D); educational leadership development and learning technologies (PhD); global and international education (MS); higher education (MS); human resources development (MS); learning technologies (MS); mathematics, learning and teaching (MS); special education (MS); teaching, learning and curriculum (MS). *Program availability:* Part-time, evening/weekend, online learning. *Degree requirements:* For doctorate, thesis/dissertation. *Entrance requirements:* For doctorate, GRE or GMAT. Additional exam requirements/recommendations for international students: Required—TOEFL, IELTS. Electronic applications accepted. Application fee is waived when completed online. *Expenses:* Contact institution. *Faculty research:* Leadership development, mathematics education, literacy, autism, educational technology.

Drury University, Master in Education Program, Springfield, MO 65802. Offers curriculum and instruction (M Ed), including elementary education, middle school education, secondary education; instructional leadership (M Ed); instructional technology (M Ed); integrated learning (M Ed); special education (M Ed); special reading (M Ed). *Accreditation:* NCATE. *Program availability:* Part-time, evening/weekend, 100% online, blended/hybrid learning. *Faculty:* 10 full-time (6 women), 8 part-time/adjunct (6 women). *Students:* 167 full-time (133 women). Average age 32. 92 applicants, 92% accepted, 69 enrolled. In 2018, 44 master's awarded. *Entrance requirements:* For master's, bachelor's degree with minimum GPA of 2.75. Additional exam requirements/recommendations for international students: Recommended—TOEFL (minimum score 80 iBT), IELTS (minimum score 6.5). *Application deadline:* For fall admission, 8/4 priority date for domestic and international students; for spring admission, 1/5 priority date for domestic and international students; for summer admission, 5/26 priority date for domestic and international students. Applications are processed on a rolling basis. Application fee: $25. Electronic applications accepted. *Expenses:* Tuition is $366 per credit hour. Fees are $7 per credit hour. Most M.Ed. degrees are 33 credit hours. *Financial support:* In 2018–19, 5 students received support. Career-related internships or fieldwork, scholarships/grants, and unspecified assistantships available. Financial award application deadline: 6/30; financial award applicants required to submit FAFSA. *Faculty research:* Instructional technology, autism, diversity, and social justice. *Unit head:* Dr. Asikaa Cosgrove, Director, Master in Education Program, 417-873-7806, E-mail: acosgrov@drury.edu. *Application contact:* Dr. Asikaa Cosgrove, Director, Master in Education Program, 417-873-7806, E-mail: acosgrov@drury.edu.
Website: http://www.drury.edu/education-masters

Duquesne University, School of Education, Department of Educational Foundations and Leadership, Program in School Administration and Supervision, Pittsburgh, PA 15282-0001. Offers curriculum and instruction (Post-Master's Certificate); school administration K-12 (MS Ed, Post-Master's Certificate); school supervision (MS Ed). *Program availability:* Part-time, evening/weekend. *Faculty:* 1 (woman) full-time. *Students:* 15 full-time (12 women), 2 part-time (both women); includes 1 minority (Black or African American, non-Hispanic/Latino), 2 international. Average age 34. 25 applicants, 68% accepted, 8 enrolled. In 2018, 8 master's awarded. *Entrance requirements:* For master's, bachelor's degree; minimum GPA of 3.0 overall or on most recent 48 credits, or minimum overall GPA of 2.8 and MAT (minimum score 396); resume that documents competence and effectiveness in professional work; 3 letters of professional reference; for Post-Master's Certificate, bachelor's degree. Additional exam requirements/recommendations for international students: Required—TOEFL (minimum score 550 paper-based), IELTS (minimum score 7). *Application deadline:* For fall admission, 9/1 for domestic students; for spring admission, 1/2 for domestic students. Applications are processed on a rolling basis. Application fee: $0. Electronic applications accepted. *Expenses: Tuition:* Full-time $23,112; part-time $1284 per credit. Tuition and fees vary according to program. *Financial support:* In 2018–19, 1 student received support, including 1 research assistantship (averaging $2,678 per year). Support available to part-time students. Financial award applicants required to submit FAFSA. *Faculty research:* Building culturally relevant systems of training for educational and helping professionals; preservice/in service teacher beliefs (self, content, equity); principal beliefs about teacher evaluation; beliefs about classroom assessment; school achievement and school effectiveness. *Unit head:* Dr. Fran Serenka, Associate Professor and Director, 412-396-5274, Fax: 412-396-1274, E-mail: serenkaf@duq.edu. *Application contact:* Kelly McGinley, Graduate Admissions Assistant, 412-396-1559, Fax: 412-396-5585, E-mail: mcginleyk@duq.edu.
Website: http://www.duq.edu/academics/schools/education/graduate-programs-education/school-admin-and-supervision

East Carolina University, Graduate School, College of Education, Department of Literacy Studies, English and History Education, Greenville, NC 27858-4353. Offers curriculum and instruction (MA Ed); English education (MAT); history education (MAT); reading education (MA Ed). *Accreditation:* NCATE. *Program availability:* Part-time, evening/weekend, online learning. *Application deadline:* For fall admission, 6/1 priority date for domestic students. *Expenses: Tuition, area resident:* Full-time $4749. Tuition, state resident: full-time $4749. Tuition, nonresident: full-time $17,898. *International tuition:* $17,898 full-time. *Required fees:* $2787. Part-time tuition and fees vary according to course load and program. *Financial support:* Application deadline: 6/1. *Unit head:* Dr. Kristin M Gesmann, Chair, 252-328-5670, E-mail: gaehsmannk18@ecu.edu. *Application contact:* Graduate School Admissions, 252-328-6012, Fax: 252-328-6071, E-mail: gradschool@ecu.edu.
Website: http://www.ecu.edu/cs-educ/libs/index.cfm

East Carolina University, Graduate School, College of Education, Department of Special Education, Foundations, and Research, Greenville, NC 27858-4353. Offers assistive technology (Certificate); autism (Certificate); special education (MA Ed, MAT), including behavioral-emotional disabilities (MA Ed), intellectual disabilities (MA Ed), learning disabilities (MA Ed), low-incidence disabilities (MA Ed). *Program availability:* Part-time, evening/weekend, online learning. *Application deadline:* For fall admission, 6/1 priority date for domestic students. *Expenses: Tuition, area resident:* Full-time $4749. Tuition, state resident: full-time $4749. Tuition, nonresident: full-time $17,898. *International tuition:* $17,898 full-time. *Required fees:* $2787. Part-time tuition and fees vary according to course load and program. *Financial support:* Application deadline: 6/1. *Unit head:* Dr. Guili Zhang, Interim Chair, 252-328-4989, E-mail: zhangg@ecu.edu. *Application contact:* Graduate School Admissions, 252-328-6012, Fax: 252-328-6071, E-mail: gradschool@ecu.edu.
Website: http://www.ecu.edu/cs-educ/sefr/index.cfm

Eastern Illinois University, Graduate School, College of Education, Department of Teaching, Learning, and Foundations, Charleston, IL 61920. Offers curriculum and instruction (MS Ed). *Accreditation:* NCATE. *Program availability:* Part-time, evening/weekend. *Degree requirements:* For master's, comprehensive exam (for some programs), thesis (for some programs). *Entrance requirements:* For master's, GMAT or GRE. Additional exam requirements/recommendations for international students: Required—TOEFL (minimum score 500 paper-based; 61 iBT), IELTS (minimum score 6). *Application deadline:* For fall admission, 5/15 for domestic and international students; for spring admission, 10/15 for domestic and international students. Applications are processed on a rolling basis. Application fee: $30. Electronic applications accepted. *Expenses:* Tuition, state resident: part-time $299 per credit hour. Tuition, nonresident: part-time $718 per credit hour. *Required fees:* $214.50 per credit hour. *Financial support:* Research assistantships with full tuition reimbursements, teaching assistantships with full tuition reimbursements, career-related internships or fieldwork, Federal Work-Study, scholarships/grants, and unspecified assistantships available. Support available to part-time students. Financial award application deadline: 3/1; financial award applicants required to submit FAFSA. *Unit head:* Jeanne E. Okrasinski, Ph.D., Chair, 217-581-5728, Fax: 217-581-6300, E-mail: jeokrasinski@eiu.edu. *Application contact:* Jeanne E. Okrasinski, Ph.D., Chair, 217-581-5728, Fax: 217-581-6300, E-mail: jeokrasinski@eiu.edu.
Website: http://www.eiu.edu/elegrad/

Eastern Kentucky University, The Graduate School, College of Education, Department of Curriculum and Instruction, Richmond, KY 40475-3102. Offers elementary education (MA Ed), including early elementary education, reading; library science (MA Ed); music education (MA Ed); secondary and higher education (MA Ed), including secondary education; teaching (MAT). *Accreditation:* NCATE. *Program availability:* Part-time. *Degree requirements:* For master's, portfolio is part of exam. *Entrance requirements:* For master's, GRE General Test, PRAXIS II (KY), minimum GPA of 2.5. *Faculty research:* Technology in education, reading instruction, e-portfolios, induction to teacher education, dispositions of teachers.

Eastern Mennonite University, Program in Teacher Education, Harrisonburg, VA 22802-2462. Offers curriculum and instruction (MA Ed); diverse needs (MA Ed); literacy (MA Ed); restorative justice in education (MA Ed). *Accreditation:* NCATE. *Program availability:* Part-time. *Degree requirements:* For master's, portfolio, research projects. *Entrance requirements:* For master's, 1 year of teaching experience, interview, minimum undergraduate GPA of 2.75. Additional exam requirements/recommendations for international students: Required—TOEFL (minimum score 550 paper-based). Electronic applications accepted. *Expenses:* Contact institution. *Faculty research:* Effective literacy instruction for middle school English language learners, beginning teacher's emotional experiences, constructivist learning environments, restorative discipline.

Eastern Michigan University, Graduate School, College of Education, Department of Teacher Education, Programs in Curriculum and Instruction, Ypsilanti, MI 48197. Offers advanced teaching and learning (MA); early literacy instruction (Graduate Certificate); instructional leadership (MA); learning, motivation and creativity (Graduate Certificate); literacy coaching (Graduate Certificate); online teaching (Certificate); secondary literacy instruction (Graduate Certificate); urban and diversity education (MA). *Students:* 1 (woman) full-time, 28 part-time (21 women); includes 11 minority (3 Black or African American, non-Hispanic/Latino; 1 Asian, non-Hispanic/Latino; 4 Hispanic/Latino; 3 Two or more races, non-Hispanic/Latino). Average age 31. 7 applicants, 71% accepted, 3 enrolled. In 2018, 5 master's awarded. Application fee: $45. *Application contact:* Dr. Virginia Harder, Graduate Coordinator/Advisor, 734-487-2729, Fax: 734-487-2101, E-mail: vharder1@emich.edu.

Eastern New Mexico University, Graduate School, College of Education and Technology, Department of Curriculum and Instruction, Portales, NM 88130. Offers alternative licensure in elementary education (M Ed); bilingual education (M Ed); career and technical education (M Ed); educational technology (M Ed); elementary education (M Ed); English as a second language (M Ed); pedagogy and learning (M Ed); reading/literacy (M Ed). *Program availability:* Part-time, online learning. *Degree requirements:* For master's, comprehensive exam, thesis optional. *Entrance requirements:* For master's, writing assessment, minimum GPA of 3.0, photocopy of teaching license, letter of recommendation. Additional exam requirements/recommendations for international students: Required—TOEFL (minimum score 550 paper-based; 79 iBT), IELTS (minimum score 6). Electronic applications accepted. *Expenses: Tuition, area resident:* Full-time $6776. Tuition, state resident: full-time $6776; part-time $282 per credit hour. Tuition, nonresident: full-time $8986; part-time $374 per credit hour. *Required fees:* $60 per semester. One-time fee: $25.

Eastern Washington University, Graduate Studies, College of Arts, Letters and Education, Department of Education, Program in Curriculum Development, Cheney, WA 99004-2431. Offers M Ed. *Degree requirements:* For master's, comprehensive exam. *Entrance requirements:* For master's, minimum GPA of 3.0. Additional exam requirements/recommendations for international students: Required—TOEFL (minimum score 580 paper-based; 92 iBT), IELTS (minimum score 7), PTE (minimum score 63). Electronic applications accepted.

East Tennessee State University, School of Graduate Studies, College of Education, Department of Curriculum and Instruction, Johnson City, TN 37614. Offers advanced studies in teaching and learning (M Ed), including childhood literacy; educational technology (M Ed), including educational communications and technology, school library media; elementary education (M Ed); reading (M Ed, MA), including reading education (MA), storytelling (MA); response to intervention (Post-Master's Certificate); school library professional (Post-Master's Certificate); secondary education (M Ed); STEAM K-12 education (Postbaccalaureate Certificate); storytelling (Postbaccalaureate Certificate); teacher education (MAT), including elementary education K-5, middle grades education 4-8, middle grades education 6-8, secondary education 6-12 and preK-12, secondary education K-12. *Accreditation:* NCATE. *Program availability:* Part-time, evening/weekend, online learning. *Degree requirements:* For master's, comprehensive exam, thesis optional, student teaching, practicum; for other advanced degree, field work (school library); culminating experience (storytelling). *Entrance requirements:* For master's, GRE, SAT, ACT, PRAXIS, minimum GPA of 3.0, interview, 3 letters of recommendation, background check; for other advanced degree, master's degree, TN teaching license. Additional exam requirements/recommendations for international students: Required—TOEFL (minimum score 550 paper-based; 79 iBT). Electronic applications accepted. *Faculty research:* Critical thinking; curriculum development in reading, math, and science education; cultural diversity; cognitive processes; effective teaching strategies.

Emporia State University, Program in Curriculum and Instruction, Emporia, KS 66801-5415. Offers curriculum leadership (MS); effective practitioner (MS); national board certification (MS). *Accreditation:* NCATE. *Program availability:* Part-time, online only, 100% online. *Degree requirements:* For master's, comprehensive exam or thesis, practicum. *Entrance requirements:* For master's, GRE or MAT, appropriate bachelor's degree, teacher certification, 1 year of teaching experience, letters of recommendation. Electronic applications accepted.

Emporia State University, Program in Instructional Specialist, Emporia, KS 66801-5415. Offers elementary subject matter (MS); reading (MS). *Accreditation:* NCATE. *Program availability:* Part-time. *Degree requirements:* For master's, comprehensive exam or thesis, practicum. *Entrance requirements:* For master's, GRE General Test or MAT, essay exam, appropriate bachelor's degree, letters of recommendation. Additional exam requirements/recommendations for international students: Required—TOEFL (minimum score 520 paper-based; 68 iBT). Electronic applications accepted.

Evangel University, Department of Education, Springfield, MO 65802. Offers curriculum and instruction (M Ed); educational leadership (M Ed); literacy (M Ed); secondary teaching (M Ed). *Accreditation:* NCATE. *Program availability:* Part-time, evening/weekend, 100% online, blended/hybrid learning. *Entrance requirements:* For master's, PRAXIS II (preferred) or GRE, minimum undergraduate GPA of 3.0. Additional

exam requirements/recommendations for international students: Required—TOEFL (minimum score 550 paper-based). Electronic applications accepted. Application fee is waived when completed online.

Evangel University, Doctor of Education in Educational Leadership, Curriculum, and Instruction Program, Springfield, MO 65802. Offers Ed D. *Program availability:* Part-time, evening/weekend. *Degree requirements:* For doctorate, thesis/dissertation. *Entrance requirements:* For doctorate, MA in education (preferred). Additional exam requirements/recommendations for international students: Required—TOEFL (minimum score 550 paper-based). Electronic applications accepted.

Fairleigh Dickinson University, Metropolitan Campus, University College: Arts, Sciences, and Professional Studies, Peter Sammartino School of Education, Teaneck, NJ 07666-1914. Offers dyslexia specialist (Certificate); education for certified teachers (MA); educational leadership (MA); instructional technology (Certificate); learning disabilities (MA); literacy/reading (Certificate); multilingual education (MA); teacher of the handicapped (Certificate); teaching (MAT). *Accreditation:* TEAC. *Program availability:* Part-time. *Degree requirements:* For master's, research project (MAT).

Faulkner University, College of Education, Montgomery, AL 36109-3398. Offers counseling (MS); curriculum and instruction (M Ed); elementary education (M Ed); school counseling (M Ed). *Program availability:* Part-time, evening/weekend, 100% online, blended/hybrid learning. *Degree requirements:* For master's, 5+ hours in clinical training (for MS, M Ed in school counseling). *Entrance requirements:* For master's, MAT (minimum score of 370) or GRE (minimum score of 280) taken within last five years, bachelor's degree from regionally-accredited college or university; official transcripts from all colleges and universities attended; 3 letters of recommendation; goal statement (approximately 600 words); minimum cumulative GPA of 2.75 in undergraduate courses, 3.0 in graduate courses. Additional exam requirements/recommendations for international students: Required—TOEFL (minimum score 500 paper-based). Electronic applications accepted. *Expenses:* Contact institution.

Ferris State University, College of Education and Human Services, School of Education, Big Rapids, MI 49307. Offers curriculum and instruction (M Ed), including special education, subject area; training and development (MSCTE). *Program availability:* Part-time, evening/weekend, blended/hybrid learning. *Faculty:* 7 full-time (4 women), 1 (woman) part-time/adjunct. *Students:* 4 full-time (3 women), 39 part-time (23 women); includes 7 minority (3 Black or African American, non-Hispanic/Latino; 2 Hispanic/Latino; 2 Two or more races, non-Hispanic/Latino), 2 international. Average age 38. 14 applicants, 93% accepted, 7 enrolled. In 2018, 18 master's awarded. *Degree requirements:* For master's, thesis, Capstone project. *Entrance requirements:* For master's, minimum undergraduate GPA of 3.0. Additional exam requirements/recommendations for international students: Required—TOEFL (minimum score 550 paper-based; 79 iBT), IELTS (minimum score 6.5), TOEFL (minimum score 550 paper-based, 79 iBT) or IELTS 6.5. *Application deadline:* For fall admission, 7/1 priority date for domestic and international students; for spring admission, 11/1 priority date for domestic and international students; for summer admission, 3/1 priority date for domestic and international students. Applications are processed on a rolling basis. Application fee: $0 ($30 for international students). Electronic applications accepted. Application fee is waived when completed online. *Financial support:* In 2018–19, 7 students received support. Career-related internships or fieldwork and scholarships/grants available. Support available to part-time students. Financial award applicants required to submit FAFSA. *Faculty research:* Game based education, needs of students with disabilities in post-secondary education, elementary education students with reading difficulties. *Unit head:* Leonard Johnson, Interim Dean, 231-591-3648, Fax: 231-591-2043, E-mail: LeonardJohnson@ferris.edu. *Application contact:* Liza Ing, Graduate Program Coordinator, 231-591-5362, Fax: 231-591-2043, E-mail: lizaIng@ferris.edu.
Website: http://www.ferris.edu/education/education/

Fitchburg State University, Division of Graduate and Continuing Education, Program in Curriculum and Teaching, Fitchburg, MA 01420-2697. Offers M Ed. *Program availability:* Part-time, evening/weekend. *Entrance requirements:* Additional exam requirements/recommendations for international students: Required—TOEFL (minimum score 550 paper-based; 79 iBT). Electronic applications accepted. *Expenses:* Contact institution.

Florida Atlantic University, College of Education, Department of Curriculum, Culture, and Educational Inquiry, Boca Raton, FL 33431-0991. Offers curriculum and instruction (M Ed, PhD, Ed S); early childhood education (M Ed); multicultural education (M Ed); TESOL and bilingual education (MA). *Program availability:* Part-time, evening/weekend. *Faculty:* 10 full-time (8 women), 2 part-time/adjunct (both women). *Students:* 15 full-time (11 women), 60 part-time (46 women); includes 24 minority (12 Black or African American, non-Hispanic/Latino; 2 Asian, non-Hispanic/Latino; 8 Hispanic/Latino; 2 Two or more races, non-Hispanic/Latino), 2 international. Average age 36. 45 applicants, 62% accepted, 21 enrolled. In 2018, 21 master's, 14 doctorates, 1 other advanced degree awarded. *Entrance requirements:* Additional exam requirements/recommendations for international students: Required—TOEFL (minimum score 500 paper-based; 61 iBT), IELTS (minimum score 6). *Application deadline:* For fall admission, 7/1 for domestic students, 2/15 for international students; for spring admission, 11/1 for domestic students, 7/15 for international students. Application fee: $30. *Expenses: Tuition, area resident:* Full-time $7400; part-time $369.82 per credit. Tuition, state resident: full-time $7400; part-time $369.82 per credit. Tuition, nonresident: full-time $20,496; part-time $1024.81 per credit. *Faculty research:* Multicultural education, early intervention strategies, family literacy, religious diversity in schools, early childhood curriculum. *Unit head:* Dr. Hanizah Zainuddin, Chair, 561-297-6594, E-mail: zainuddi@fau.edu. *Application contact:* Dr. Deborah Shepherd, Associate Dean, 561-297-3570, E-mail: dshep@fau.edu.
Website: http://www.coe.fau.edu/academicdepartments/ccei/

Florida Gulf Coast University, College of Education, Program in Curriculum and Instruction, Fort Myers, FL 33965-6565. Offers elementary education (M Ed); English education (M Ed); English speakers of other languages endorsement (M Ed); gifted education (M Ed); mathematics education (M Ed); middle school education (M Ed); reading education (M Ed); science education (M Ed); social science education (M Ed); special education (M Ed). *Program availability:* Part-time, evening/weekend, online learning. *Degree requirements:* For master's, final project or portfolio. *Entrance requirements:* For master's, GRE General Test, MAT, minimum undergraduate GPA of 3.0 in last 2 years. Additional exam requirements/recommendations for international students: Required—TOEFL (minimum score 550 paper-based). Electronic applications accepted. *Faculty research:* Internet in schools, technology in pre-service and in-service teacher training.

Florida International University, College of Arts, Sciences, and Education, Department of Teaching and Learning, Miami, FL 33199. Offers art education (MA, MS); curriculum and instruction (MS, Ed D, PhD, Ed S), including curriculum development (MS), elementary education (MS), English education (MS), learning technologies (MS), mathematics education (MS), modern language education (MS), physical education (MS), science education (MS), social studies education (MS), special education (MS); early childhood education (MS); exceptional student education (Ed D); foreign language education (MS), including foreign language education, teaching English to speakers of other languages (TESOL); language, literacy and culture (PhD); mathematics, science, and learning technologies (PhD); physical education (MS), including sport and fitness; reading education (MS). *Program availability:* Part-time, evening/weekend. *Faculty:* 64 full-time (43 women), 104 part-time/adjunct (76 women). *Students:* 169 full-time (144 women), 155 part-time (130 women); includes 260 minority (53 Black or African American, non-Hispanic/Latino; 7 Asian, non-Hispanic/Latino; 193 Hispanic/Latino; 7 Two or more races, non-Hispanic/Latino), 13 international. Average age 33. 184 applicants, 62% accepted, 87 enrolled. In 2018, 153 master's, 10 doctorates awarded. *Degree requirements:* For doctorate, comprehensive exam, thesis/dissertation. *Entrance requirements:* For master's, GRE General Test, Florida General Knowledge Test or Florida College Level Academic Skills Test; for doctorate and Ed S, GRE General Test. Additional exam requirements/recommendations for international students: Required—TOEFL (minimum score 550 paper-based; 80 iBT), IELTS (minimum score 6.3). *Application deadline:* For fall admission, 6/1 priority date for domestic students, 4/1 for international students; for winter admission, 10/1 priority date for domestic students, 9/1 for international students; for spring admission, 3/1 priority date for domestic students, 2/1 for international students. Applications are processed on a rolling basis. Application fee: $30. Electronic applications accepted. *Financial support:* Research assistantships and teaching assistantships available. *Unit head:* Dr. Maria Fernandez, Chair, 305-348-0193, Fax: 305-348-2086, E-mail: Maria.Fernandez9@fiu.edu. *Application contact:* Nanett Rojas, Manager, Admissions Operations, 305-348-7464, Fax: 305-348-7441, E-mail: gradadm@fiu.edu.
Website: https://tl.fiu.edu/

Florida State University, The Graduate School, College of Education, School of Teacher Education, Tallahassee, FL 32306. Offers curriculum and instruction (MS, PhD, Ed S), including reading and language arts (Ed S); teaching English to speakers of other languages (Certificate). *Program availability:* Part-time, evening/weekend, 100% online, blended/hybrid learning, asynchronous, minimal on-campus study. *Faculty:* 30 full-time (23 women), 8 part-time/adjunct (7 women). *Students:* 90 full-time (66 women), 66 part-time (51 women); includes 56 minority (12 Black or African American, non-Hispanic/Latino; 19 Asian, non-Hispanic/Latino; 15 Hispanic/Latino; 10 Two or more races, non-Hispanic/Latino), 32 international. Average age 32. 146 applicants, 56% accepted, 52 enrolled. In 2018, 50 master's, 15 doctorates, 2 other advanced degrees awarded. Terminal master's awarded for partial completion of doctoral program. *Degree requirements:* For master's and other advanced degree, comprehensive exam, thesis optional; for doctorate, comprehensive exam, thesis/dissertation, diagnostic exam, preliminary exam, prospectus defense, dissertation defense. *Entrance requirements:* For master's, doctorate, and other advanced degree, GRE General Test, minimum upper-division GPA of 3.0. Additional exam requirements/recommendations for international students: Required—TOEFL (minimum score 550 paper-based, 80 iBT), Michigan English Language Assessment Battery (minimum score 77), IELTS (minimum score 6.5) or PTE (minimum score 55). *Application deadline:* For fall admission, 6/17 for domestic students; for spring admission, 10/18 for domestic students; for summer admission, 2/11 for domestic students. Application fee: $30. Electronic applications accepted. *Expenses: Tuition, area resident:* Part-time $479.32 per credit hour. Tuition and fees vary according to campus/location and program. *Financial support:* Fellowships, research assistantships, teaching assistantships, scholarships/grants, tuition waivers (full and partial), and unspecified assistantships available. Financial award application deadline: 1/15; financial award applicants required to submit FAFSA. *Faculty research:* Identifying effective intervention strategies to improve reading skills; improving literacy teaching and learning through technology; understanding of student sense making, problem solving, the history and structure of STEM disciplines, and teacher education to support the development of ambitious instruction that supports the STEM learning of all students; examining practices of international education; identifying ways to support the professional development of teachers. *Unit head:* Dr. Sherry Southerland, Professor/Department Chair, 850-644-6885, Fax: 850-644-2725, E-mail: ssoutherland@admin.fsu.edu. *Application contact:* Britni DeZerga, Academic Program Specialist, 850-644-2122, Fax: 850-644-7736, E-mail: bpurvis@fsu.edu.
Website: http://education.fsu.edu

Fontbonne University, Graduate Programs, St. Louis, MO 63105-3098. Offers accounting (MBA, MS); art (MA); art (K-12) (MAT); business (MBA); computer science (MS); deaf education (MA); early intervention in deaf education (MA); education (MA), including autism spectrum disorders, curriculum and instruction, diverse learners, early childhood education, reading, special education; elementary education (MAT); family and consumer sciences (MA), including multidisciplinary health communication studies; fine arts (MFA); instructional design and technology (MS); management and leadership (MM); middle school education (MAT); secondary education (MAT); special education (MAT); speech-language pathology (MS); supply chain management (MS); theatre (MA). *Accreditation:* ASHA. *Program availability:* Part-time, evening/weekend, online learning. *Degree requirements:* For master's, comprehensive exam (for some programs), thesis (for some programs). *Entrance requirements:* Additional exam requirements/recommendations for international students: Required—TOEFL (minimum score 500 paper-based; 65 iBT). Electronic applications accepted.

Fordham University, Graduate School of Education, Division of Curriculum and Teaching, New York, NY 10023. Offers curriculum and teaching (MSE); early childhood education (MSE); elementary education (MST); special education (MSE, Adv C); teaching English as a second language (MSE). *Accreditation:* NCATE. *Program availability:* Part-time, evening/weekend. *Degree requirements:* For Adv C, thesis. *Entrance requirements:* Additional exam requirements/recommendations for international students: Required—TOEFL (minimum score 577 paper-based; 90 iBT), IELTS (minimum score 7). Electronic applications accepted.

Framingham State University, Graduate Studies, Program in Curriculum and Instructional Technology, Framingham, MA 01701-9101. Offers M Ed. *Program availability:* Online learning.

Franciscan University of Steubenville, Graduate Programs, Department of Education, Steubenville, OH 43952-1763. Offers administration (MS Ed); teaching (MS Ed). *Accreditation:* NCATE. *Program availability:* Part-time, evening/weekend, online learning. *Degree requirements:* For master's, project. *Entrance requirements:* For master's, minimum undergraduate GPA of 2.5 or written exam. Additional exam requirements/recommendations for international students: Required—TOEFL. Electronic applications accepted. Application fee is waived when completed online. *Expenses:* Contact institution.

Franklin Pierce University, Graduate and Professional Studies, Rindge, NH 03461-0060. Offers curriculum and instruction (M Ed); elementary education (MS Ed); emerging network technologies (Graduate Certificate); energy and sustainability studies (MBA, Graduate Certificate); health administration (MBA, Graduate Certificate); human resource management (MBA, Graduate Certificate); information technology (MBA); leadership (MBA); nursing education (MS); nursing leadership (MS); physical therapy (DPT); physician assistant studies (MPAS); special education (M Ed); sports management (MBA). *Accreditation:* APTA. *Program availability:* Part-time, 100% online, blended/hybrid learning. *Degree requirements:* For master's, concentrated original research projects; student teaching; fieldwork and/or internship; leadership project; PRAXIS I and II (for M Ed); for doctorate, concentrated original research projects,

clinical fieldwork and/or internship, leadership project. *Entrance requirements:* For master's, minimum GPA of 2.5, 3 letters of recommendation; competencies in accounting, economics, statistics, and computer skills through life experience or undergraduate coursework (for MBA); certification/e-portfolio, minimum C grade in all education courses (for M Ed); license to practice as RN (for MS); for doctorate, GRE, 80 hours of observation/work in PT settings; completion of anatomy, chemistry, physics, and statistics; minimum GPA of 3.0. Additional exam requirements/recommendations for international students: Required—TOEFL (minimum score 550 paper-based; 61 iBT). Electronic applications accepted. *Faculty research:* Evidence-based practice in sports physical therapy, human resource management in economic crisis, leadership in nursing, innovation in sports facility management, differentiated learning and understanding by design.

Freed-Hardeman University, Program in Education, Henderson, TN 38340-2399. Offers curriculum and instruction (M Ed); school counseling (M Ed), including administration and supervision, special education; school leadership (Ed S). *Accreditation:* NCATE. *Program availability:* Part-time, evening/weekend. *Degree requirements:* For master's, comprehensive exam, thesis optional; for Ed S, thesis. *Entrance requirements:* For master's, GRE General Test or NTE; for Ed S, 3 years of teaching experience. Additional exam requirements/recommendations for international students: Required—TOEFL (minimum score 500 paper-based).

Fresno Pacific University, Graduate Programs, School of Education, Program in Curriculum and Teaching, Fresno, CA 93702-4709. Offers MA. *Program availability:* Part-time, evening/weekend, online learning. *Degree requirements:* For master's, thesis or alternative. *Entrance requirements:* For master's, interview, statement of intent, three letters of recommendation, official transcript, BA/BS, minimum GPA of 2.75. Additional exam requirements/recommendations for international students: Required—TOEFL (minimum score 550 paper-based). Electronic applications accepted. *Expenses:* Contact institution.

Frostburg State University, College of Education, Department of Educational Professions, Program in Curriculum and Instruction, Frostburg, MD 21532-1099. Offers curriculum and instruction (Ed D); educational technology (M Ed); elementary education (M Ed); secondary education (M Ed). *Program availability:* Part-time, evening/weekend. *Degree requirements:* For master's, thesis or alternative. *Entrance requirements:* For master's, teaching certificate. Additional exam requirements/recommendations for international students: Required—TOEFL. Electronic applications accepted.

Furman University, Graduate Division, Department of Education, Greenville, SC 29613. Offers curriculum and instruction (MA); early childhood education (MA); educational leadership (Ed S); English as a second language (MA); literacy (MA); school leadership (MA); special education (MA). *Accreditation:* NCATE. *Program availability:* Part-time, online learning. *Degree requirements:* For master's, comprehensive exam (for some programs), thesis or alternative. *Entrance requirements:* For master's, PRAXIS II. *Expenses: Tuition:* Full-time $27,500; part-time $7290 per credit. Tuition and fees vary according to program. *Faculty research:* Literacy, pedagogy and practice, social justice, advanced leadership, achievement in high poverty schools.

Gannon University, School of Graduate Studies, College of Humanities, Education, and Social Sciences, School of Education, Program in Curriculum and Instruction, Erie, PA 16541-0001. Offers M Ed. *Program availability:* Part-time, evening/weekend, 100% online. *Degree requirements:* For master's, thesis or alternative, portfolio project. *Entrance requirements:* For master's, bachelor's degree from regionally-accredited college or university with minimum GPA of 3.0, official transcripts, 3 letters of recommendation. Additional exam requirements/recommendations for international students: Required—TOEFL (minimum score 79 iBT). Electronic applications accepted. Application fee is waived when completed online. *Expenses:* Contact institution.

Gannon University, School of Graduate Studies, College of Humanities, Education, and Social Sciences, School of Education, Program in Curriculum Supervisor, Erie, PA 16541-0001. Offers Certificate. *Program availability:* Part-time, evening/weekend, online learning. *Degree requirements:* For Certificate, internship. *Entrance requirements:* Additional exam requirements/recommendations for international students: Required—TOEFL (minimum score 79 iBT). Electronic applications accepted. Application fee is waived when completed online. *Expenses:* Contact institution.

Gardner-Webb University, Graduate School, School of Education, Boiling Springs, NC 28017. Offers curriculum and instruction (Ed D); educational leadership (Ed D); executive leadership studies (MA, Ed S); organizational leadership (Ed D); school administration (MA). *Accreditation:* NCATE. *Program availability:* Part-time, evening/weekend. *Degree requirements:* For master's, comprehensive exam. *Entrance requirements:* For master's, GRE General Test or NTE, PRAXIS, minimum GPA of 2.5. Electronic applications accepted. *Expenses:* Contact institution.

George Mason University, College of Education and Human Development, Programs in Curriculum and Instruction, Fairfax, VA 22030. Offers assistive technology (M Ed); designing digital learning in schools (M Ed); early childhood education (M Ed); early childhood education for diverse learners (M Ed); elementary education (M Ed); English as a second language (M Ed); gifted child education (M Ed); literacy (M Ed), including PK-12 classroom teachers, reading specialist; literacy leadership for diverse schools (M Ed), including K-12 reading; physical education (M Ed); science K-12 (M Ed); secondary education (M Ed), including biology, chemistry, earth science, English, history/social science, math, physics; special education (M Ed); teacher leadership (M Ed); transformative teaching (M Ed). *Program availability:* Part-time, evening/weekend, 100% online, blended/hybrid learning. *Faculty:* 48 full-time (40 women), 28 part-time/adjunct (20 women). *Students:* 165 full-time (147 women), 697 part-time (579 women); includes 243 minority (47 Black or African American, non-Hispanic/Latino; 3 American Indian or Alaska Native, non-Hispanic/Latino; 88 Asian, non-Hispanic/Latino; 85 Hispanic/Latino; 4 Native Hawaiian or other Pacific Islander, non-Hispanic/Latino; 16 Two or more races, non-Hispanic/Latino), 26 international. Average age 34. 450 applicants, 93% accepted, 315 enrolled. In 2018, 421 master's awarded. *Entrance requirements:* For master's, PRAXIS Core (for some programs), 2 letters of recommendation, interview, program goals statement; 9 hours of complete licensure endorsement requirements (for elementary education); minimum GPA of 3.0 in applicant's last 60 hours of undergraduate coursework (for secondary education); at least 1 year of teaching experience (for literacy). Additional exam requirements/recommendations for international students: Required—TOEFL (minimum score 575 paper-based; 88 iBT), IELTS (minimum score 6.5), PTE (minimum score 59). *Application deadline:* For fall admission, 4/2 priority date for domestic and international students; for spring admission, 11/1 for domestic and international students. Application fee: $75 ($80 for international students). Electronic applications accepted. *Financial support:* In 2018–19, 4 students received support, including 1 fellowship, 3 teaching assistantships (averaging $3,745 per year); career-related internships or fieldwork, Federal Work-Study, scholarships/grants, unspecified assistantships, and health care benefits (for full-time research or teaching assistantship recipients) also available. Support available to part-time students. Financial award application deadline: 3/1; financial award applicants required to submit FAFSA. *Faculty research:* Teacher preparation and professional development; adaptive teaching; wonder in science teacher preparation; literacy (digital, adolescent); site based course instruction. *Unit head:* Rebecca Fox, Professor and Academic Program Coordinator, 703-993-4123, E-mail: rfox@gmu.edu. *Application contact:* Rebecca Fox, Professor and Academic Program Coordinator, 703-993-4123, E-mail: rfox@gmu.edu.
Website: http://gse.gmu.edu/programs/gsemasters

The George Washington University, Graduate School of Education and Human Development, Department of Curriculum and Pedagogy, Program in Curriculum and Instruction, Washington, DC 20052. Offers MA Ed, Ed D, Ed S, Graduate Certificate. *Accreditation:* NCATE. *Program availability:* Evening/weekend. *Students:* 22 full-time (19 women), 40 part-time (32 women); includes 16 minority (9 Black or African American, non-Hispanic/Latino; 1 Asian, non-Hispanic/Latino; 6 Hispanic/Latino), 11 international. Average age 34. 92 applicants, 65% accepted, 27 enrolled. In 2018, 17 master's, 9 doctorates, 1 other advanced degree awarded. *Degree requirements:* For master's and other advanced degree, comprehensive exam; for doctorate, comprehensive exam, thesis/dissertation. *Entrance requirements:* For master's, GRE General Test or MAT, minimum GPA of 2.75, resume; for doctorate and other advanced degree, GRE General Test or MAT, interview, minimum GPA of 3.3. *Application deadline:* For fall admission, 1/15 priority date for domestic students; for spring admission, 10/1 for domestic students. Applications are processed on a rolling basis. Application fee: $75. *Financial support:* In 2018–19, 25 students received support. Fellowships, research assistantships, career-related internships or fieldwork, Federal Work-Study, and tuition waivers (partial) available. Financial award application deadline: 1/15; financial award applicants required to submit FAFSA. *Faculty research:* Cognitive skills-teaching, metacognitive strategies, adult basic literacy. *Unit head:* Dr. Sharon Lynch, Faculty Coordinator, 202-994-6174, E-mail: slynch@gwu.edu. *Application contact:* Sarah Lang, Director of Graduate Admissions, 202-994-1447, Fax: 202-994-7207, E-mail: slang@gwu.edu.

Georgia College & State University, Graduate School, The John H. Lounsbury College of Education, Program in Curriculum and Instruction, Milledgeville, GA 31061. Offers M Ed. *Program availability:* Part-time, evening/weekend, online only, 100% online. *Degree requirements:* For master's, minimum GPA of 3.0, complete program within 6 years. *Entrance requirements:* For master's, minimum GPA of 2.75; clear renewable level 4 Georgia Teacher Certificate or eligibility, two professional recommendations, official transcripts, verification of immunization. Additional exam requirements/recommendations for international students: Recommended—TOEFL. Electronic applications accepted. *Expenses:* Contact institution.

Georgia Southern University, Jack N. Averitt College of Graduate Studies, College of Education, Department of Curriculum, Foundations, and Reading, Program in Curriculum Studies, Statesboro, GA 30460. Offers curriculum studies (Ed D), including cultural curriculum, instructional improvement, multicultural studies, teaching and learning. *Program availability:* Part-time. *Degree requirements:* For doctorate, comprehensive exam, thesis/dissertation, exams; assessments. *Entrance requirements:* For doctorate, GRE or MAT, letters of reference, minimum GPA of 3.5, writing sample. Additional exam requirements/recommendations for international students: Required—TOEFL (minimum score 550 paper-based; 80 iBT), IELTS (minimum score 6). Electronic applications accepted. *Expenses: Tuition, area resident:* Part-time $3324 per semester. Tuition, state resident: full-time $5814; part-time $3324 per semester. Tuition, nonresident: full-time $23,204; part-time $13,260 per semester. *Required fees:* $2092; $2092. Tuition and fees vary according to course load, degree level, campus/location and program. *Faculty research:* Curriculum theory, cultural studies, narrative research, postmodern theory, critical race theory, international education, feminism, media literacy, documentary studies, post human condition, social and cultural foundations of education, democracy and education.

Georgia Southern University, Jack N. Averitt College of Graduate Studies, College of Education, Department of Elementary and Special Education, Program in Curriculum and Instruction - Accomplished Teaching, Statesboro, GA 30458. Offers M Ed. *Program availability:* Part-time, evening/weekend, 100% online. *Degree requirements:* For master's, key assessments. *Entrance requirements:* For master's, current Georgia teaching certificate. Additional exam requirements/recommendations for international students: Required—TOEFL (minimum score 550 paper-based; 80 iBT), IELTS (minimum score 6). Electronic applications accepted. *Expenses: Tuition, area resident:* Part-time $3324 per semester. Tuition, state resident: full-time $5814; part-time $3324 per semester. Tuition, nonresident: full-time $23,204; part-time $13,260 per semester. *Required fees:* $2092; $2092. Tuition and fees vary according to course load, degree level, campus/location and program. *Faculty research:* Teacher preparation, curriculum design, assessment for improved student outcomes, reflective practices of infield teachers, diversity responsive methods in instruction.

Georgia State University, College of Education and Human Development, Department of Middle and Secondary Education, Atlanta, GA 30302-3083. Offers curriculum and instruction (Ed D); English education (MAT); mathematics education (M Ed, MAT); middle level education (MAT); reading, language and literacy education (M Ed, MAT), including reading instruction (M Ed); science education (M Ed, MAT), including biology (MAT), broad field science (MAT), chemistry (MAT), earth science (MAT), physics (MAT); social studies education (M Ed, MAT), including economics (MAT), geography (MAT), history (MAT), political science (MAT); teaching and learning (PhD), including language and literacy, mathematics education, music education, science education, social studies education, teaching and teacher education. *Accreditation:* NCATE. *Program availability:* Part-time, evening/weekend, online learning. *Faculty:* 19 full-time (15 women), 9 part-time/adjunct (7 women). *Students:* 217 full-time (136 women), 203 part-time (140 women); includes 229 minority (156 Black or African American, non-Hispanic/Latino; 23 Asian, non-Hispanic/Latino; 31 Hispanic/Latino; 19 Two or more races, non-Hispanic/Latino), 3 international. Average age 34. 149 applicants, 60% accepted, 70 enrolled. In 2018, 112 master's, 23 doctorates awarded. *Entrance requirements:* For master's, GRE; GACE I (for initial teacher preparation programs), baccalaureate degree or equivalent, resume, goals statement, two letters of recommendation, minimum undergraduate GPA of 2.5; proof of initial teacher certification in the content area (for M Ed); for doctorate, GRE, resume, goals statement, writing sample, two letters of recommendation, minimum graduate GPA of 3.3, interview. *Application deadline:* For fall admission, 1/15 priority date for domestic and international students; for spring admission, 10/1 for domestic and international students. Application fee: $50. Electronic applications accepted. *Expenses: Tuition, area resident:* Full-time $9360; part-time $390 per credit hour. Tuition, state resident: full-time $9360; part-time $390 per credit hour. Tuition, nonresident: full-time $30,024; part-time $1251 per credit hour. *International tuition:* $30,024 full-time. *Required fees:* $2128. *Financial support:* In 2018–19, fellowships with full tuition reimbursements (averaging $19,667 per year), research assistantships with full tuition reimbursements (averaging $5,436 per year), teaching assistantships with full tuition reimbursements (averaging $2,779 per year) were awarded; career-related internships or fieldwork, Federal Work-Study, scholarships/grants, health care benefits, tuition waivers (full and partial), and unspecified assistantships also available. Financial award application deadline: 3/15. *Faculty research:* Teacher education in language and literacy, mathematics, science, and social studies in urban middle and secondary school settings; learning technologies in school, community, and corporate settings; multicultural education and education for social justice; urban education; international education. *Unit head:* Dr. Gertrude Marilyn

Tinker Sachs, Chair, 404-413-8384, Fax: 404-413-8063, E-mail: gtinkersachs@gsu.edu. *Application contact:* Shaleen Tibbs, Administrative Specialist, 404-413-8385, Fax: 404-413-8063, E-mail: stibbs@gsu.edu.
Website: http://mse.education.gsu.edu/

Graceland University, Gleazer School of Education, Independence, MO 64050. Offers curriculum and instruction: collaborative learning and teaching (M Ed); differentiated instruction (M Ed); instructional leadership (M Ed); literacy instruction (M Ed); management in a quality classroom (M Ed); special education (M Ed); technology integration (M Ed). *Accreditation:* NCATE. *Program availability:* Part-time, 100% online. *Students:* 70 full-time (58 women), 36 part-time (34 women); includes 4 minority (1 Black or African American, non-Hispanic/Latino; 1 Asian, non-Hispanic/Latino; 1 Hispanic/Latino; 1 Two or more races, non-Hispanic/Latino). Average age 34. 29 applicants, 21% accepted, 1 enrolled. In 2018, 76 master's awarded. *Degree requirements:* For master's, action research capstone. *Entrance requirements:* For master's, minimum GPA of 3.0, teaching certificate, current teaching contract and license, two letters of reference, statement of professional goals, verification of ongoing access to computer technology, including email and Internet. Additional exam requirements/recommendations for international students: Required—TOEFL (minimum score 550 paper-based; 80 iBT). *Application deadline:* For winter admission, 11/1 for domestic students; for spring admission, 2/1 priority date for domestic students; for summer admission, 7/1 for domestic students. Applications are processed on a rolling basis. Application fee: $50. Electronic applications accepted. *Expenses:* Tuition, material fee, university tech fee, program support fee. *Financial support:* Tuition waivers (partial) available. Financial award applicants required to submit FAFSA. *Faculty research:* Literacy, technology, faculty mentoring, adult literacy, e-learning, online teaching. *Unit head:* Dr. Michele Dickey-Kotz, Dean, 641-784-5202, E-mail: dickey@graceland.edu. *Application contact:* Susan Freeze, Admissions Representative, 816-423-4676, Fax: 816-833-2990, E-mail: sfreeze1@graceland.edu.
Website: http://www.graceland.edu/education

Grambling State University, School of Graduate Studies and Research, College of Education, Department of Curriculum and Instruction, Grambling, LA 71245. Offers curriculum and instruction (MS); special education (M Ed). *Program availability:* Part-time. *Degree requirements:* For master's, comprehensive exam, thesis (for some programs). *Entrance requirements:* Additional exam requirements/recommendations for international students: Required—TOEFL (minimum score 500 paper-based; 62 iBT).

Grambling State University, School of Graduate Studies and Research, College of Education, Department of Educational Leadership, Grambling, LA 71245. Offers developmental education (MS, Ed D, PMC), including curriculum and instructional design (Ed D), English (MS), guidance and counseling (MS), higher education administration and management (Ed D), mathematics (MS), reading (MS), science (MS), student development and personnel services (Ed D); educational leadership (M Ed). *Program availability:* Part-time, evening/weekend. *Degree requirements:* For master's, comprehensive exam, thesis (for some programs); for doctorate, comprehensive exam, thesis/dissertation. *Entrance requirements:* For master's, GRE, minimum GPA of 2.5 on last degree; for doctorate, GRE (minimum score 1000, 500 on Verbal), master's degree, minimum GPA of 3.0 on last degree. Additional exam requirements/recommendations for international students: Required—TOEFL (minimum score 500 paper-based; 62 iBT). Electronic applications accepted.

Grand Canyon University, College of Education, Phoenix, AZ 85017-1097. Offers autism spectrum disorders (MA); curriculum and instruction (MA); early childhood education (M Ed); educational administration (M Ed); educational leadership (M Ed); elementary education (M Ed); gifted education (MA); instructional technology (MS); K-12 leadership (Ed S); reading (MA); secondary education (M Ed); secondary humanities education (M Ed); secondary STEM education (M Ed); special education (M Ed); teaching and learning (Ed D); teaching English to speakers of other languages (MA). *Program availability:* Part-time, evening/weekend, online learning. *Degree requirements:* For master's, publishable research paper (M Ed), e-portfolio. *Entrance requirements:* For master's, undergraduate degree from accredited, GCU-approved college, university, or program with minimum GPA 2.8. Additional exam requirements/recommendations for international students: Required—TOEFL (minimum score 550 paper-based; 79 iBT), IELTS (minimum score 6). Electronic applications accepted.

Grand Valley State University, College of Education, Program in Instruction and Curriculum, Allendale, MI 49401-9403. Offers M Ed. *Program availability:* Part-time, evening/weekend. *Students:* 28 full-time (15 women), 115 part-time (97 women); includes 9 minority (4 Black or African American, non-Hispanic/Latino; 2 American Indian or Alaska Native, non-Hispanic/Latino; 3 Hispanic/Latino), 3 international. Average age 33. 43 applicants, 98% accepted, 16 enrolled. In 2018, 64 master's awarded. *Entrance requirements:* For master's, minimum GPA of 3.0 or GRE General Test, last 60 credits from a regionally-accredited college/university, 3 letters of recommendation. Additional exam requirements/recommendations for international students: Required—TOEFL (minimum iBT score of 80), IELTS (6.5), or Michigan English Language Assessment Battery (77). *Application deadline:* Applications are processed on a rolling basis. Application fee: $30. Electronic applications accepted. *Expenses:* $677 per credit hour, 33 credit hours. *Financial support:* In 2018–19, 35 students received support, including 35 fellowships; research assistantships and unspecified assistantships also available. *Unit head:* Dr. Paula Lancaster, Department Director, 616-331-6593, Fax: 616-331-6291, E-mail: lanscastp@gvsu.edu. *Application contact:* Annukka Thelen, Director, Student Information and Services Center, 616-331-6205, Fax: 616-331-6217, E-mail: thelenan@gvsu.edu.
Website: http://www.gvsu.edu/grad/instruction/

Harvard University, Harvard Graduate School of Education, Master's Programs in Education, Cambridge, MA 02138. Offers arts in education (Ed M); education policy and management (Ed M); higher education (Ed M); human development and psychology (Ed M); international education policy (Ed M); language and literacy (Ed M); learning and teaching (Ed M); mind, brain, and education (Ed M); prevention science and practice (Ed M); school leadership (Ed M); special studies (Ed M); teacher education (Ed M); technology, innovation, and education (Ed M). *Program availability:* Part-time. *Entrance requirements:* For master's, GRE General Test, statement of purpose, 3 letters of recommendation, resume, official transcripts. Additional exam requirements/recommendations for international students: Required—TOEFL (minimum score 613 paper-based; 104 iBT), TWE (minimum score 5). Electronic applications accepted. *Faculty research:* Learning and development, educational leadership and organizations, education policy analysis.

Henderson State University, Graduate Studies, Teachers College, Department of Advanced Instructional Studies, Arkadelphia, AR 71999-0001. Offers developmental therapy (MSE); dyslexia therapy (Graduate Certificate); education (MAT); educational technology leadership (Graduate Certificate); English as a second language (MSE, Graduate Certificate); instructional facilitator (MSE, Graduate Certificate); middle level education (MAT); special education (K-12) (MAT, MSE); special education/early childhood (MAT). *Accreditation:* NCATE. *Program availability:* Part-time. *Entrance requirements:* For master's, GRE General Test or MAT, minimum GPA of 2.7, teacher certification. Additional exam requirements/recommendations for international students:

Required—TOEFL (minimum score 600 paper-based); Recommended—IELTS (minimum score 6.5).

Hood College, Graduate School, Department of Education, Frederick, MD 21701-8575. Offers curriculum and instruction (MS), including elementary education, elementary science and mathematics education, secondary education, special education; education, multidisciplinary studies (MS); educational leadership (MS, Certificate); reading specialization (MS); STEM education (Certificate). *Accreditation:* NCATE. *Program availability:* Part-time-only, evening/weekend. *Faculty:* 5 full-time (3 women), 32 part-time/adjunct (24 women). *Students:* 3 full-time (all women), 306 part-time (253 women); includes 65 minority (22 Black or African American, non-Hispanic/Latino; 9 Asian, non-Hispanic/Latino; 17 Hispanic/Latino; 17 Two or more races, non-Hispanic/Latino), 3 international. Average age 33. 80 applicants, 99% accepted, 45 enrolled. In 2018, 59 master's, 47 other advanced degrees awarded. *Degree requirements:* For master's, action research project, portfolio (for reading specialization); for Certificate, STEM capstone activity. *Entrance requirements:* For master's, minimum GPA of 2.75, teaching certification, writing sample during interview, letter of recommendation from principal (for educational leadership program only). Additional exam requirements/recommendations for international students: Required—TOEFL (minimum score 575 paper-based; 89 iBT), IELTS (minimum score 6.5). *Application deadline:* For fall admission, 8/15 priority date for domestic students, 8/5 for international students; for spring admission, 12/1 priority date for domestic students, 12/1 for international students; for summer admission, 5/1 priority date for domestic students, 4/15 for international students. Applications are processed on a rolling basis. Application fee: $50 ($100 for international students). Electronic applications accepted. *Expenses:* Tuition: Full-time $17,640; part-time $4410 per semester. *Required fees:* $125 per semester. Tuition and fees vary according to degree level and program. *Financial support:* Tuition waivers (partial) and unspecified assistantships available. Financial award applicants required to submit FAFSA. *Faculty research:* Leadership, action research, brain research, learning styles. *Unit head:* Dr. April M. Boulton, Dean of the Graduate School, 301-696-3612, E-mail: gofurther@hood.edu. *Application contact:* Tanith Fowler Corsi, Assistant Director of Graduate Admissions, 301-696-3603, E-mail: gofurther@hood.edu.
Website: https://www.hood.edu/academics/departments/department-education/programs-offered

Houston Baptist University, College of Education and Behavioral Sciences, Programs in Education, Houston, TX 77074-3298. Offers bilingual education (M Ed); counselor education (M Ed); curriculum and instruction (M Ed); curriculum and instruction (EC-6 bilingual) (M Ed); curriculum and instruction in all-level art, Spanish, music, or physical education (M Ed); curriculum and instruction in EC-6 and special education (EC-12) (M Ed); curriculum and instruction in instructional technology (M Ed); curriculum and instruction in mathematics, science, or social studies (4-8) (M Ed); curriculum and instruction with EC-6 generalist (M Ed); curriculum and instruction with English language arts and reading (4-8) (M Ed); educational administration (M Ed); educational diagnostician (M Ed); executive educational leadership (Ed D); higher education in business management (M Ed); higher education in Christian studies (M Ed); higher education in counseling (M Ed); higher education in educational technology (M Ed); reading (M Ed); special educational leadership (Ed D). *Program availability:* Part-time, evening/weekend, 100% online, blended/hybrid learning. *Degree requirements:* For master's, comprehensive exam; for doctorate, thesis/dissertation. *Entrance requirements:* For master's, minimum GPA of 2.75, two recommendations, resume, bachelor's degree conferred transcript; interview (for non-certified teachers); for doctorate, GRE, 5 letters of recommendation. Additional exam requirements/recommendations for international students: Required—TOEFL (minimum score 80 iBT), IELTS (minimum score 6.5). Electronic applications accepted. Application fee is waived when completed online. *Expenses:* Contact institution. *Faculty research:* Autism and inclusion, integrating technology into instruction, school change and leadership trust.

Illinois State University, Graduate School, College of Education, Department of Curriculum and Instruction, Normal, IL 61790. Offers curriculum and instruction (MS, MS Ed, Ed D); educational policies (Ed D); postsecondary education (Ed D); reading (MS Ed); supervision (Ed D). *Accreditation:* NCATE. *Faculty:* 49 full-time (31 women), 80 part-time/adjunct (64 women). *Students:* 7 full-time (2 women), 21 part-time (18 women); includes 4 minority (2 Black or African American, non-Hispanic/Latino; 2 Hispanic/Latino), 5 international. Average age 33. 43 applicants, 93% accepted, 28 enrolled. In 2018, 51 master's, 7 doctorates awarded. *Degree requirements:* For master's, variable foreign language requirement, thesis or alternative; for doctorate, variable foreign language requirement, thesis/dissertation, 2 terms of residency, internship. *Entrance requirements:* For master's, GRE General Test, minimum GPA of 3.0 in last 60 hours of course work; for doctorate, GRE General Test. *Application deadline:* Applications are processed on a rolling basis. Application fee: $40. *Expenses:* Tuition, area resident: Full-time $7264.62. Tuition, state resident: full-time $9466. Tuition, nonresident: full-time $17,290. *International tuition:* $15,089.40 full-time. *Required fees:* $1481.04. *Financial support:* In 2018–19, 18 research assistantships were awarded; tuition waivers (full) and unspecified assistantships also available. Financial award application deadline: 4/1. *Faculty research:* In-service and pre-service teacher education for teachers of English language learners; teachers for all children: developing a model for alternative, bilingual elementary certification for paraprofessionals in Illinois; Illinois Geographic Alliance, Connections Project. *Unit head:* Dr. Alan Bates, Interim Director, 309-438-5425, E-mail: abates@ilstu.edu. *Application contact:* Dr. Ryan Brown, Graduate Coordinator, 309-438-3964, E-mail: rbrown@ilstu.edu.
Website: http://ci.illinoisstate.edu/

Indiana State University, College of Graduate and Professional Studies, Bayh College of Education, Department of Teaching and Learning, Terre Haute, IN 47809. Offers curriculum and instruction (M Ed, PhD); educational technology (MS). *Accreditation:* NCATE. *Degree requirements:* For doctorate, thesis/dissertation. *Entrance requirements:* For doctorate, GRE General Test. Electronic applications accepted. *Faculty research:* Discipline FERPA reading, teacher strengths and needs.

Indiana University Bloomington, School of Education, Department of Curriculum and Instruction, Bloomington, IN 47405-7000. Offers art education (MS, Ed D, PhD); curriculum studies (Ed D, PhD); elementary education (MS, Ed D, PhD, Ed S); mathematics education (MS, Ed D, PhD); science education (MS, Ed D, PhD); secondary education (MS, Ed D, PhD); social studies education (MS, PhD); special education (PhD, Ed S). *Accreditation:* NCATE. *Program availability:* Part-time, evening/weekend. Terminal master's awarded for partial completion of doctoral program. *Degree requirements:* For doctorate, thesis/dissertation; for Ed S, comprehensive exam or project. *Entrance requirements:* For master's, doctorate, and Ed S, GRE General Test. Electronic applications accepted.

Indiana University of Pennsylvania, School of Graduate Studies and Research, College of Education and Communications, Department of Professional Studies in Education, Program in Curriculum and Instruction, Indiana, PA 15705. Offers D Ed. *Accreditation:* NCATE. *Program availability:* Part-time, evening/weekend. *Faculty:* 11 full-time (8 women), 2 part-time/adjunct (1 woman). *Students:* 8 full-time (6 women), 69

part-time (49 women); includes 7 minority (3 Black or African American, non-Hispanic/Latino; 1 Asian, non-Hispanic/Latino; 1 Hispanic/Latino; 2 Two or more races, non-Hispanic/Latino), 9 international. Average age 42. 26 applicants, 50% accepted, 2 enrolled. In 2018, 9 doctorates awarded. *Degree requirements:* For doctorate, one foreign language, comprehensive exam, thesis/dissertation. *Entrance requirements:* For doctorate, 2 letters of recommendation; recorded five-minute, research-based presentation; 1.5 hour online writing task. Additional exam requirements/recommendations for international students: Required—TOEFL (minimum score 540 paper-based). *Application deadline:* Applications are processed on a rolling basis. Application fee: $50. Electronic applications accepted. *Expenses:* Contact institution. *Financial support:* In 2018–19, 10 fellowships with full tuition reimbursements (averaging $457 per year), 5 research assistantships with tuition reimbursements (averaging $3,465 per year), 2 teaching assistantships with partial tuition reimbursements (averaging $24,425 per year) were awarded; career-related internships or fieldwork, Federal Work-Study, scholarships/grants, and unspecified assistantships also available. Support available to part-time students. Financial award application deadline: 4/15; financial award applicants required to submit FAFSA. *Unit head:* Dr. Kelli Kerry-Moran, Graduate Coordinator, 724-357-4501, E-mail: kjkmoran@iup.edu. *Application contact:* Dr. Kelli Kerry-Moran, Graduate Coordinator, 724-357-4501, E-mail: kjkmoran@iup.edu.
Website: http://www.iup.edu/grad/CandI/default.aspx

Indiana University–Purdue University Indianapolis, School of Education, Indianapolis, IN 46202-5155. Offers curriculum and instruction (MS); early childhood (MS); educational leadership (MS, Certificate); English as a second language (Certificate); kindergarten (Certificate); language education (MS); reading (Certificate); school counseling (MS); special education (MS, Certificate). *Program availability:* Part-time, evening/weekend. Terminal master's awarded for partial completion of doctoral program. *Degree requirements:* For master's, thesis optional. *Entrance requirements:* For master's, GRE General Test, minimum GPA of 2.5; for Certificate, official transcripts. Additional exam requirements/recommendations for international students: Required—TOEFL (minimum score 60 iBT), IELTS (minimum score 5.5). Electronic applications accepted. *Expenses:* Contact institution. *Faculty research:* Educational policies and school leaders' responses to these; issues of intersectionality in the experiences of African American lesbian, gay, and bisexual students attending historically black colleges and universities and those who belong to black Greek-letter organizations; students' experiential knowledge and their evolving disciplinary-specific literacy and understanding; innovative program development; urban ESL teacher preparation; target-based instructional coaching.

Inter American University of Puerto Rico, Arecibo Campus, Programs in Education, Arecibo, PR 00614-4050. Offers administration and educational supervision (MA Ed); counseling and guidance (MA Ed); curriculum and teaching (MA Ed), including biology education, English as a second language, history education, math education, Spanish; elementary education (MA Ed). *Accreditation:* TEAC. *Degree requirements:* For master's, comprehensive exam, thesis optional. *Entrance requirements:* For master's, GRE, EXADEP, bachelor's degree in education or teaching license (administration and supervision) or courses in education and psychology (counseling and guidance), minimum GPA of 2.5 in last 60 credits.

Inter American University of Puerto Rico, Barranquitas Campus, Program in Education, Barranquitas, PR 00794. Offers curriculum and teaching (M Ed), including biology, English as a second language, history, Spanish; educational leadership and management (MA); elementary education (M Ed); information and library service technology (M Ed); special education (MA). *Accreditation:* TEAC. *Program availability:* Part-time, evening/weekend. *Degree requirements:* For master's, 2 foreign languages, comprehensive exam, thesis (for some programs). *Entrance requirements:* For master's, GRE or EXADEP, bachelor's degree or its equivalent from accredited institution, official academic transcript from institution that conferred bachelor's degree, minimum GPA of 2.5, two recommendation letters, interview (for some programs), essay (for some programs). Electronic applications accepted. *Expenses:* Contact institution.

Inter American University of Puerto Rico, Metropolitan Campus, Graduate Programs, Program in Education, San Juan, PR 00919-1293. Offers curriculum and instruction (Ed D); educational administration (Ed D); guidance and counseling (MA, Ed D); special education administration (Ed D). *Accreditation:* TEAC. *Degree requirements:* For doctorate, comprehensive exam, thesis/dissertation. *Entrance requirements:* For doctorate, GRE, MAT, or EXADEP. Electronic applications accepted.

Inter American University of Puerto Rico, San Germán Campus, Graduate Studies Center, Program in Curriculum and Instruction, San Germán, PR 00683-5008. Offers Ed D. *Program availability:* Part-time, evening/weekend. *Expenses: Tuition:* Full-time $212; part-time $212 per credit. *Required fees:* $366 per semester. One-time fee: $31. Tuition and fees vary according to degree level and program.

Iowa State University of Science and Technology, Department of Education, Ames, IA 50011. Offers curriculum and instructional technology (M Ed, MS, PhD); elementary education (M Ed, MS); historical, philosophical, and comparative studies in education (M Ed, MS); special education (M Ed, MS, PhD). *Degree requirements:* For master's, thesis or alternative; for doctorate, thesis/dissertation. *Entrance requirements:* For master's and doctorate, GRE General Test. Additional exam requirements/recommendations for international students: Required—TOEFL (minimum score 560 paper-based; 83 iBT), IELTS (minimum score 6.5). Electronic applications accepted.

Iowa Wesleyan University, Program in Curriculum and Instruction, Mount Pleasant, IA 52641-1398. Offers effective teaching and instruction (M Ed).

John Brown University, Graduate Education Programs, Siloam Springs, AR 72761-2121. Offers curriculum and instruction (M Ed); secondary education (MAT). *Program availability:* Part-time, evening/weekend. *Entrance requirements:* For master's, GRE (minimum score of 300). Additional exam requirements/recommendations for international students: Required—TOEFL (minimum score 550 paper-based; 79 iBT). Electronic applications accepted.

Kansas State University, Graduate School, College of Education, Department of Curriculum and Instruction, Manhattan, KS 66506. Offers curriculum and instruction (Ed D, PhD); digital teaching and learning (MS); educational computing, design and online learning (MS); elementary/middle level curriculum and instruction (MS); online learning (Certificate); reading specialist endorsement (MS); reading/language arts (MS); teacher leader/school improvement (MS); teaching and learning (Certificate). *Accreditation:* NCATE. *Program availability:* Part-time, online learning. *Degree requirements:* For master's, comprehensive exam, portfolio, project, report or thesis; for doctorate, comprehensive exam, thesis/dissertation, preliminary exam; for Certificate, comprehensive exam, portfolio. *Entrance requirements:* For master's, minimum GPA of 3.0, 3 letters of recommendation; for doctorate, GRE, minimum GPA of 3.0, 3 letters of recommendation, evidence of scholarly writing; for Certificate, minimum GPA of 3.0, letters of recommendation. Additional exam requirements/recommendations for international students: Required—TOEFL (minimum score 550 paper-based; 80 iBT) or IELTS. Electronic applications accepted. *Faculty research:* Literacy and technology, critical race theory and diversity, achievement gaps, school improvement, teacher education.

Kean University, College of Education, Program in Instruction and Curriculum, Union, NJ 07083. Offers bilingual/bicultural education (MA); teaching English as a second language (MA). *Accreditation:* NCATE. *Program availability:* Part-time. *Faculty:* 14 full-time (8 women). *Students:* 1 (woman) full-time, 14 part-time (11 women); includes 9 minority (all Hispanic/Latino), 1 international. Average age 33. 5 applicants, 100% accepted, 5 enrolled. In 2018, 19 master's awarded. *Degree requirements:* For master's, comprehensive exam (for some programs), thesis optional, two-semester advanced seminar. *Entrance requirements:* For master's, GRE General Test or MAT; PRAXIS (for some programs), minimum GPA of 3.0, personal statement, professional resume/curriculum vitae, commitment to working with children, certification (for some programs), two letters of recommendation. Additional exam requirements/recommendations for international students: Required—TOEFL (minimum score 550 paper-based; 79 iBT), IELTS (minimum score 6.5). *Application deadline:* For fall admission, 6/30 for domestic and international students; for spring admission, 12/1 for domestic and international students. Applications are processed on a rolling basis. Application fee: $75. Electronic applications accepted. *Expenses:* Tuition, state resident: full-time $15,025; part-time $733.50 per credit. Tuition, nonresident: full-time $19,890; part-time $884.50 per credit. *Required fees:* $2107.50; $89.50 per credit. Tuition and fees vary according to course level, course load, degree level and program. *Financial support:* Scholarships/grants and unspecified assistantships available. Financial award applicants required to submit FAFSA. *Unit head:* Dr. Gail Verdi, Program Coordinator, 908-737-3908, E-mail: gverdi@kean.edu. *Application contact:* Brittany Gerstenhaber, Admissions Counselor, 908-737-7100, E-mail: grad-adm@kean.edu.
Website: http://grad.kean.edu/masters-programs/bilingualbicultural-education-instruction-and-curriculum

Kennesaw State University, Bagwell College of Education, Program in Curriculum and Instruction, Kennesaw, GA 30144. Offers Ed S. *Program availability:* Part-time-only, online only, 100% online. *Students:* 1 (woman) full-time, 98 part-time (89 women); includes 36 minority (32 Black or African American, non-Hispanic/Latino; 1 American Indian or Alaska Native, non-Hispanic/Latino; 1 Asian, non-Hispanic/Latino; 2 Hispanic/Latino). Average age 37. 79 applicants, 86% accepted, 63 enrolled. In 2018, 31 Ed Ss awarded. *Degree requirements:* For Ed S, capstone seminar. *Entrance requirements:* For degree, official transcripts, interview. Additional exam requirements/recommendations for international students: Required—TOEFL (minimum score 80 iBT), IELTS (minimum score 6.5). *Application deadline:* For fall admission, 7/1 for domestic and international students. Application fee: $60. Electronic applications accepted. *Expenses: Tuition, area resident:* Full-time $6960; part-time $290 per credit hour. Tuition, state resident: full-time $6960; part-time $290 per credit hour. Tuition, nonresident: full-time $25,080; part-time $1045 per credit hour. *International tuition:* $25,080 full-time. *Required fees:* $2006; $1706 per semester. $853 per semester. *Application contact:* Admissions Counselor, 470-578-4377, Fax: 470-578-9172, E-mail: ksugrad@kennesaw.edu.
Website: http://bagwell.kennesaw.edu/majors-programs/specialist/curriculum-instruction.php

Kent State University, College of Education, Health and Human Services, School of Teaching, Learning and Curriculum Studies, Program in Curriculum and Instruction, Kent, OH 44242-0001. Offers M Ed, PhD, Ed S. *Accreditation:* NCATE. *Program availability:* Part-time, evening/weekend. *Faculty:* 21 full-time (11 women), 2 part-time/adjunct (both women). *Students:* 74 full-time (55 women), 39 part-time (30 women); includes 17 minority (4 Black or African American, non-Hispanic/Latino; 11 Asian, non-Hispanic/Latino; 1 Hispanic/Latino; 1 Native Hawaiian or other Pacific Islander, non-Hispanic/Latino), 15 international. 67 applicants, 28% accepted. In 2018, 16 master's, 13 doctorates, 2 other advanced degrees awarded. *Degree requirements:* For doctorate, comprehensive exam, thesis/dissertation. *Entrance requirements:* For master's, 2 letters of reference, goals statement; for doctorate, GRE General Test, 2 letters of reference, goals statement, writing sample, resume; for Ed S, GRE General Test, 2 letters of reference, goals statement. Additional exam requirements/recommendations for international students: Required—TOEFL (minimum score 550 paper-based; 80 iBT). *Application deadline:* Applications are processed on a rolling basis. Application fee: $45 ($60 for international students). Electronic applications accepted. *Expenses:* Tuition, state resident: full-time $11,766; part-time $536 per credit. Tuition, nonresident: full-time $21,952; part-time $999 per credit. *International tuition:* $21,952 full-time. Tuition and fees vary according to course load. *Financial support:* In 2018–19, 20 research assistantships with full tuition reimbursements (averaging $12,600 per year), 3 teaching assistantships with full tuition reimbursements (averaging $13,500 per year) were awarded; Federal Work-Study, scholarships/grants, unspecified assistantships, and 3 administrative assistantships (averaging $10,500 per year) also available. Financial award application deadline: 4/1; financial award applicants required to submit FAFSA. *Faculty research:* Gender equity issues in teaching, learning math and science, teaching as inquiry artistry, curriculum studies for democratic humanism. *Unit head:* Dr. Todd Hawley, Coordinator, 330-672-0670, E-mail: thawley1@kent.edu. *Application contact:* Cheryl Slusarczyk, Academic Program Director, Office of Graduate Student Services, 330-672-2576, Fax: 330-672-9162, E-mail: ogs@kent.edu.

Kent State University at Stark, Graduate School of Education, Health and Human Services, Canton, OH 44720-7599. Offers curriculum and instruction studies (M Ed, MA).

Kutztown University of Pennsylvania, College of Education, Program in Secondary Education, Kutztown, PA 19530-0730. Offers biology (M Ed); curriculum and instruction (M Ed); English (M Ed); mathematics (M Ed); middle level (M Ed); social studies (M Ed); teaching (M Ed); transformational teaching and learning (Ed D). *Accreditation:* NCATE. *Program availability:* Part-time, evening/weekend, 100% online, blended/hybrid learning. *Faculty:* 5 full-time (3 women), 3 part-time/adjunct (0 women). *Students:* 25 full-time (16 women), 80 part-time (51 women); includes 8 minority (1 Black or African American, non-Hispanic/Latino; 5 Hispanic/Latino; 2 Two or more races, non-Hispanic/Latino), 1 international. Average age 32. 86 applicants, 93% accepted, 45 enrolled. In 2018, 3,531 master's awarded. *Degree requirements:* For master's, comprehensive exam, thesis optional; for doctorate, thesis/dissertation. *Entrance requirements:* For master's, GRE General Test, minimum undergraduate major GPA of 3.0, 3 letters of recommendation, copy of PRAXIS II or valid instructional I or II teaching certificate; for doctorate, master's or specialist degree in education or related field from regionally-accredited institution of higher learning with minimum graduate GPA of 3.25, significant educational experience, employment in an education setting (preferred). Additional exam requirements/recommendations for international students: Required—TOEFL (minimum score 550 paper-based, 79 iBT), IELTS (minimum score 6.5), or PTE (minimum score 53). *Application deadline:* For fall admission, 8/1 for domestic and international students; for spring admission, 12/1 for domestic and international students. Application fee: $35. Electronic applications accepted. *Expenses:* Tuition, state resident: part-time $516 per credit. Tuition, nonresident: part-time $774 per credit. *Required fees:* $119 per credit. One-time fee: $50 part-time. Tuition and fees vary according to degree level. *Financial support:* Career-related internships or fieldwork, Federal Work-Study, scholarships/grants, and unspecified assistantships available. Financial award application deadline: 3/1; financial award applicants required to submit FAFSA. *Unit head:* Dr. Georgeos Sirrakos, Department Chair, 610-683-4279, Fax: 610-683-1338, E-mail: sirrakos@kutztown.edu. *Application contact:* Dr. Patricia Walsh Coates, Graduate Coordinator,

610-638-4289, Fax: 610-683-1338, E-mail: coates@kutztown.edu.
Website: https://www.kutztown.edu/academcs/graduate-programs/secondary-education.htm

LaGrange College, Graduate Programs, Department of Education, LaGrange, GA 30240-2999. Offers curriculum and instruction (M Ed, Ed S); middle grades (MAT); secondary education (MAT). *Program availability:* Part-time, evening/weekend. *Degree requirements:* For master's, comprehensive exam. *Entrance requirements:* For master's, GRE, MAT, minimum GPA of 2.5. Additional exam requirements/recommendations for international students: Required—TOEFL (minimum score 550 paper-based).

Lasell College, Graduate and Professional Studies in Education, Newton, MA 02466-2709. Offers curriculum, leadership, and inclusion (M Ed); elementary education (M Ed); special education (M Ed), including moderate disabilities; teaching bilingual/English learners with disabilities (Graduate Certificate). *Program availability:* Part-time-only, evening/weekend, blended/hybrid learning. *Faculty:* 1 (woman) full-time, 5 part-time/adjunct (4 women). *Students:* 4 full-time (3 women), 45 part-time (37 women); includes 4 minority (3 Asian, non-Hispanic/Latino; 1 Hispanic/Latino). Average age 28. 23 applicants, 70% accepted, 10 enrolled. In 2018, 22 master's awarded. *Degree requirements:* For master's, minimum GPA of 3.0; practicum. *Entrance requirements:* For master's, Massachusetts Tests for Educator Licensure (MTEL) Curriculum and Literacy foundations of reading and writing subtest, one-page personal statement, 2 letters of recommendation, resume, bachelor's degree transcript. Additional exam requirements/recommendations for international students: Required—TOEFL (minimum score 550 paper-based, 79 iBT) or IELTS (minimum score 6). *Application deadline:* For fall admission, 8/31 priority date for domestic students, 6/30 priority date for international students; for spring admission, 12/31 priority date for domestic students, 10/31 priority date for international students. Applications are processed on a rolling basis. Electronic applications accepted. *Expenses: Tuition:* Part-time $600 per credit. *Required fees:* $40 per course. *Financial support:* Federal Work-Study, scholarships/grants, and tuition discounts available. Support available to part-time students. Financial award application deadline: 8/31; financial award applicants required to submit FAFSA. *Faculty research:* Inclusion, English language learners, literacy, and urban education; teacher inquiry; universal design for learning, deaf-blindness, and visual impairments; social and emotional learning; educational law, applied behavior analysis, and classroom management. *Unit head:* Eric Turner, Vice President of Graduate and Professional Studies, 617-243-2071, Fax: 617-243-2450, E-mail: gradinfo@lasell.edu. *Application contact:* Adrienne Franciosi, Director of Graduate Enrollment, 617-243-2214, Fax: 617-243-2450, E-mail: gradinfo@lasell.edu.
Website: http://www.lasell.edu/academics/graduate-and-professional-studies/programs-of-study/master-of-education.html

La Sierra University, School of Education, Department of Curriculum and Instruction, Riverside, CA 92505. Offers curriculum and instruction (MA, Ed D, Ed S); teaching (MAT). *Program availability:* Part-time, evening/weekend. *Degree requirements:* For doctorate, thesis/dissertation; for Ed S, thesis optional. *Entrance requirements:* For master's, minimum GPA of 3.0; for doctorate, GRE General Test, GRE Subject Test, minimum GPA of 3.3; for Ed S, minimum GPA of 3.3. *Faculty research:* New teacher success, politics of knowledge, computer-assisted instruction, diversity issues.

Lee University, Program in Education, Cleveland, TN 37320-3450. Offers art (MAT); curriculum and instruction (M Ed, Ed S); early childhood (MAT); educational leadership (M Ed, Ed S); elementary education (MAT); English and math (MAT); English and science (MAT); English and social studies (MAT); higher education administration (MS); history (MAT); history and economics (MAT); math and science (MAT); math and social studies (MAT); middle grades (MAT); science and social studies (MASW); secondary education (MAT); Spanish (MAT); special education (M Ed, MAT); TESOL (MAT). *Accreditation:* NCATE. *Program availability:* Part-time. *Faculty:* 13 full-time (5 women), 13 part-time/adjunct (7 women). *Students:* 32 full-time (26 women), 73 part-time (49 women); includes 13 minority (10 Black or African American, non-Hispanic/Latino; 3 Two or more races, non-Hispanic/Latino), 3 international. Average age 30. 56 applicants, 73% accepted, 34 enrolled. In 2018, 60 master's, 3 other advanced degrees awarded. *Degree requirements:* For master's, variable foreign language requirement, thesis optional, internship. *Entrance requirements:* For master's, MAT or GRE General Test, minimum undergraduate GPA of 2.75, 3 letters of recommendation, interview, writing sample, official transcripts, background check; for Ed S, minimum undergraduate and master's GPA of 2.75, official transcripts for undergraduate and master's degrees. Additional exam requirements/recommendations for international students: Required—TOEFL (minimum score 61 iBT). *Application deadline:* For fall admission, 6/1 priority date for domestic and international students; for spring admission, 11/1 priority date for domestic and international students; for summer admission, 4/1 priority date for domestic and international students. Applications are processed on a rolling basis. Application fee: $25. Electronic applications accepted. *Financial support:* In 2018–19, 43 students received support. Career-related internships or fieldwork, Federal Work-Study, institutionally sponsored loans, scholarships/grants, and unspecified assistantships available. Financial award application deadline: 3/1; financial award applicants required to submit FAFSA. *Unit head:* Dr. William Kamm, Director, 423-614-8544, E-mail: wkamm@leeuniversity.edu. *Application contact:* Jeffery McGirt, Director of Graduate Enrollment, 423-614-8691, Fax: 423-614-8317, E-mail: jmcgirt@leeuniversity.edu.
Website: http://www.leeuniversity.edu/academics/graduate/education

Lehigh University, College of Education, Program in Educational Leadership, Bethlehem, PA 18015. Offers curriculum and instruction (Certificate); educational leadership (M Ed, Ed D); K-12 principal (Certificate); superintendent letter (Certificate). *Program availability:* Part-time, evening/weekend, online only, blended/hybrid learning. *Faculty:* 4 full-time (1 woman), 7 part-time/adjunct (2 women). *Students:* 11 full-time (7 women), 104 part-time (62 women); includes 24 minority (7 Black or African American, non-Hispanic/Latino; 2 Asian, non-Hispanic/Latino; 14 Hispanic/Latino; 1 Two or more races, non-Hispanic/Latino), 7 international. Average age 34. 42 applicants, 62% accepted, 14 enrolled. In 2018, 40 master's, 2 doctorates awarded. *Degree requirements:* For master's, thesis (for some programs); for doctorate, comprehensive exam, thesis/dissertation. *Entrance requirements:* For master's, minimum undergraduate GPA of 3.0, essay, transcripts, 2 letters of recommendation; for doctorate, GRE General Test or MAT, minimum graduate GPA of 3.6, 2 letters of recommendation, essay, transcript; for Certificate, minimum undergraduate GPA of 3.0. Additional exam requirements/recommendations for international students: Required—TOEFL (minimum score 600 paper-based; 93 iBT), IELTS (minimum score 6.5), Either TOEFL or IELTS is required. *Application deadline:* For fall admission, 1/15 for domestic and international students; for spring admission, 12/1 for domestic and international students; for summer admission, 5/8 for domestic and international students. Applications are processed on a rolling basis. Application fee: $65. Electronic applications accepted. *Expenses:* MBA/Educational Leadership $825 per credit. COE (per 3 credits) intern courses require a special supervision fee which varies from $225 to $350. *Financial support:* In 2018–19, 18 students received support, including 4 research assistantships (averaging $8,600 per year); fellowships, scholarships/grants, and unspecified assistantships also available. Financial award application deadline: 1/31; financial award applicants required to submit FAFSA. *Faculty research:* Supervision of instruction, middle-level education, organizational change, leadership preparation and development, international school leadership, urban school leadership, comparative education, social justice, education and human services, social network, principal leadership, policy implementation, teacher evaluation, teaching quality. *Total annual research expenditures:* $16,829. *Unit head:* Dr. Floyd D. Beachum, Director, 610-758-5955, Fax: 610-758-3227, E-mail: fdb209@lehigh.edu. *Application contact:* Lynn Spina, Coordinator, 610-758-3250, Fax: 610-758-6223, E-mail: lys218@lehigh.edu.
Website: https://ed.lehigh.edu/academics/programs/educational-leadership

Lesley University, Graduate School of Education, Cambridge, MA 02138-2790. Offers arts, community, and education (M Ed); autism studies (Certificate); curriculum and instruction (M Ed, CAGS); early childhood education (M Ed); ecological teaching and learning (MS); educational studies (PhD), including adult learning, educational leadership, individually designed; elementary education (M Ed); emergent technologies for educators (Certificate); ESLArts: language learning through the arts (M Ed); high school education (M Ed); individually designed (M Ed); integrated teaching through the arts (M Ed); literacy for K-8 classroom teachers (M Ed); mathematics education (M Ed); middle school education (M Ed); moderate disabilities (M Ed); online learning (Certificate); reading (CAGS); science in education (M Ed); severe disabilities (M Ed); special needs (CAGS); specialist teacher of reading (M Ed); teacher of visual art (M Ed); technology in education (M Ed, CAGS). *Accreditation:* TEAC. *Program availability:* Part-time, evening/weekend, online learning. *Degree requirements:* For master's, practicum; for doctorate, thesis/dissertation. *Entrance requirements:* For master's, Massachusetts Tests for Educator Licensure (MTEL), transcripts, statement of purpose, recommendations; interview (for special education); for doctorate, GRE General Test, transcripts, statement of purpose, recommendations, interview, master's degree, resume; for other advanced degree, interview, master's degree. Additional exam requirements/recommendations for international students: Required—TOEFL (minimum score 550 paper-based; 80 iBT). Electronic applications accepted. *Faculty research:* Assessment in literacy, mathematics and science; autism spectrum disorders; instructional technology and online learning; multicultural education and English language learners.

LeTourneau University, Graduate Programs, Longview, TX 75607-7001. Offers business administration (MBA); counseling (MA); curriculum and instruction (M Ed); educational administration (M Ed); engineering (ME, MS); engineering management (MEM); health care administration (MS); marriage and family therapy (MA); psychology (MA); strategic leadership (MSL); teacher leadership (M Ed); teaching and learning (M Ed). *Program availability:* Part-time, 100% online, blended/hybrid learning. *Students:* 61 full-time (47 women), 311 part-time (248 women); includes 184 minority (117 Black or African American, non-Hispanic/Latino; 3 American Indian or Alaska Native, non-Hispanic/Latino; 1 Asian, non-Hispanic/Latino; 35 Hispanic/Latino; 28 Two or more races, non-Hispanic/Latino), 2 international. Average age 37. In 2018, 97 master's awarded. *Entrance requirements:* Additional exam requirements/recommendations for international students: Required—TOEFL (minimum score 525 paper-based; 80 iBT), IELTS (minimum score 6), Either a TOEFL or IELTS is required for graduate students. One or the other. *Application deadline:* Applications are processed on a rolling basis. Electronic applications accepted. *Financial support:* Research assistantships, teaching assistantships, unspecified assistantships, and employee tuition waivers and institutionally sponsored loans available. Financial award applicants required to submit FAFSA.
Website: http://www.letu.edu

Lewis & Clark College, Graduate School of Education and Counseling, Department of Teacher Education, Program in Curriculum and Instruction, Portland, OR 97219-7899. Offers M Ed. *Program availability:* Part-time, evening/weekend. *Entrance requirements:* For master's, minimum GPA of 2.75. Additional exam requirements/recommendations for international students: Required—TOEFL (minimum score 575 paper-based). Electronic applications accepted.

Lewis University, College of Education, Program in Curriculum and Instruction: Technology Learning and Design, Romeoville, IL 60446. Offers M Ed. *Program availability:* Part-time, evening/weekend. *Students:* 5 part-time (all women); includes 1 minority (Black or African American, non-Hispanic/Latino). Average age 32. *Entrance requirements:* For master's, writing exam, bachelor's degree, minimum GPA of 2.75, two letters of recommendation, interview. Additional exam requirements/recommendations for international students: Required—TOEFL (minimum score 550 paper-based; 79 iBT), IELTS (minimum score 6). *Application deadline:* For fall admission, 5/1 priority date for international students; for spring admission, 11/15 priority date for international students. Applications are processed on a rolling basis. Application fee: $40. Electronic applications accepted. *Financial support:* Career-related internships or fieldwork, Federal Work-Study, institutionally sponsored loans, and unspecified assistantships available. Financial award application deadline: 5/1; financial award applicants required to submit FAFSA. *Unit head:* Dr. Seung Kim, Program Director, 815-838-0500, E-mail: kimse@lewisu.edu. *Application contact:* Kathy Lisak, Graduate Admission Counselor, 815-836-5610, E-mail: grad@lewisu.edu.

Lincoln Memorial University, Carter and Moyers School of Education, Harrogate, TN 37752-1901. Offers administration and supervision (M Ed, Ed S); counseling and guidance (M Ed); curriculum and instruction (M Ed, Ed D, Ed S); English (M Ed); executive leadership (Ed D); higher education administration (Ed D); human resource development (Ed D); leadership and administration (Ed D). *Program availability:* Part-time, evening/weekend, online learning. *Degree requirements:* For master's, comprehensive exam, thesis optional; for Ed S, comprehensive exam. *Entrance requirements:* For master's, PRAXIS, NTE, GRE, MAT, letters of recommendation; for Ed S, graduate transcripts. Additional exam requirements/recommendations for international students: Recommended—TOEFL. *Faculty research:* Brain compatible teaching and learning; poverty in Appalachia; leadership for change; ethics, moral responsibility and social justice; human and organizational learning.

Louisiana State University in Shreveport, College of Business, Education, and Human Development, Program in Education, Shreveport, LA 71115-2399. Offers curriculum and instruction (M Ed); leadership (M Ed); leadership studies (Ed D). *Accreditation:* NCATE. *Program availability:* Part-time. *Degree requirements:* For master's, orally-presented project, 200-hour internship (educational leadership). *Entrance requirements:* For master's, GRE, minimum GPA of 2.5; teacher certification; recommendations and interview (for educational leadership). Additional exam requirements/recommendations for international students: Required—TOEFL (minimum score 550 paper-based; 61 iBT). Electronic applications accepted.

Louisiana Tech University, Graduate School, College of Education, Ruston, LA 71272. Offers counseling and guidance (MA), including clinical mental health counseling, human services, orientation and mobility; counseling psychology (PhD); curriculum and instruction (M Ed); cyber education (Graduate Certificate); dynamics of domestic and family violence (Graduate Certificate); early childhood education - PreK-3 (MAT); educational leadership (M Ed, Ed D); elementary education and special education mild/moderate grades 1-5 (MAT); higher education administration (Graduate Certificate); industrial/organizational psychology (MA, PhD); kinesiology (MS); middle school education (MAT), including mathematics; orientation and mobility (Graduate Certificate);

rehabilitation teaching for the blind (Graduate Certificate); secondary education (MAT), including agriculture, biology, business, chemistry, English; special education: visually impaired (MAT); teacher leader education (Graduate Certificate); visual impairments - blind education (Graduate Certificate). *Accreditation:* NCATE. *Program availability:* Part-time. *Degree requirements:* For master's, thesis; for doctorate, thesis/dissertation. *Entrance requirements:* For master's and doctorate, GRE General Test. Additional exam requirements/recommendations for international students: Required—TOEFL (minimum score 550 paper-based; 80 iBT), IELTS (minimum score 6.5). Electronic applications accepted. *Faculty research:* Blindness and the best methods for increasing independence for individuals who are blind or visually impaired; educating and investigating factors contributing to improvements in human performance across the lifespan and a reduction in injury rates during training.

Lourdes University, Graduate School, Sylvania, OH 43560-2898. Offers business (MBA); leadership (M Ed); nurse anesthesia (MSN); nurse educator (MSN); nurse leader (MSN); organizational leadership (MOL); reading (M Ed); teaching and curriculum (M Ed); theology (MA). *Accreditation:* AANA/CANAEP. *Program availability:* Evening/weekend. *Entrance requirements:* Additional exam requirements/recommendations for international students: Required—TOEFL.

Loyola University Chicago, School of Education, Program in Curriculum and Instruction, Chicago, IL 60660. Offers M Ed, Ed D. *Program availability:* Part-time, evening/weekend. *Faculty:* 18 full-time (12 women), 33 part-time/adjunct (29 women). *Students:* 19 full-time (12 women), 13 part-time (11 women); includes 10 minority (5 Black or African American, non-Hispanic/Latino; 2 Asian, non-Hispanic/Latino; 2 Hispanic/Latino; 1 Two or more races, non-Hispanic/Latino), 5 international. Average age 38. 17 applicants, 12% accepted. In 2018, 4 master's, 9 doctorates awarded. *Degree requirements:* For master's, comprehensive exam; for doctorate, comprehensive exam, thesis/dissertation. *Entrance requirements:* For master's, 3 references, minimum GPA of 3.0, resume; for doctorate, GRE, 3 references, interview, minimum GPA of 3.0, resume. Additional exam requirements/recommendations for international students: Required—TOEFL (minimum score 550 paper-based; 79 iBT). *Application deadline:* For fall admission, 1/1 for domestic and international students. Applications are processed on a rolling basis. Application fee: $50. Electronic applications accepted. Application fee is waived when completed online. *Expenses:* Contact institution. *Financial support:* In 2018–19, 9 research assistantships with full tuition reimbursements (averaging $14,000 per year) were awarded; fellowships with partial tuition reimbursements, institutionally sponsored loans, scholarships/grants, and unspecified assistantships also available. Support available to part-time students. Financial award application deadline: 2/1; financial award applicants required to submit FAFSA. *Faculty research:* School improvement, technology, change, reading. *Unit head:* Dr. Hank Bohanon, Director, 312-915-7099, E-mail: hbohano@luc.edu. *Application contact:* Dr. Hank Bohanon, Director, 312-915-7099, E-mail: hbohano@luc.edu.

Loyola University Maryland, Graduate Programs, School of Education, Program in Curriculum and Instruction, Baltimore, MD 21210-2699. Offers MA. *Program availability:* Part-time. *Degree requirements:* For master's, thesis. *Entrance requirements:* For master's, essay, transcripts, resume. Additional exam requirements/recommendations for international students: Required—TOEFL (minimum score 550 paper-based), IELTS (minimum score 7). Electronic applications accepted. *Expenses:* Contact institution.

Malone University, Graduate Program in Education, Canton, OH 44709. Offers curriculum and instruction (MA); curriculum, instruction, and professional development (MA); educational leadership (principal license) (MA); intervention specialist (MA). *Accreditation:* NCATE. *Program availability:* Part-time, evening/weekend. *Degree requirements:* For master's, research project. *Entrance requirements:* For master's, minimum GPA of 3.0, teaching license. Additional exam requirements/recommendations for international students: Required—TOEFL (minimum score 550 paper-based; 79 iBT). *Faculty research:* Educational leadership styles: Jesus as master teacher, assessment accommodations for English language learners, preparing culturally proficient teachers, using naturally occurring text in the classroom to meet the syntactic needs of students with learning disabilities, using tablet instructional technology to meet the needs of students with disabilities.

Marian University, School of Education, Fond du Lac, WI 54935-4699. Offers curriculum and instruction leadership (PhD); educational administration (PhD); educational leadership (MAE); educational technology (MAE); leadership studies (PhD); special education (MAE); teacher education (MAE). *Accreditation:* NCATE. *Program availability:* Part-time, evening/weekend, online learning. *Degree requirements:* For master's, exam, field-based experience project, portfolio; for doctorate, comprehensive exam, thesis/dissertation, field-based experience. *Entrance requirements:* For master's, minimum GPA of 3.0, BA in education or related field, teaching license; for doctorate, GRE, MAT, resume, 2 writing samples, interview. Additional exam requirements/recommendations for international students: Required—TOEFL (minimum score 525 paper-based; 70 iBT). *Faculty research:* At-risk youth, multicultural issues, values in education, teaching/learning strategies.

Marquette University, Graduate School, College of Education, Department of Educational Policy and Leadership, Milwaukee, WI 53201-1881. Offers college student personnel administration (M Ed); curriculum and instruction (MA); education (MA); educational administration (M Ed); educational policy and foundations (MA); elementary education (Certificate); literacy (MA); principal (Certificate); reading specialist (Certificate); reading teacher (Certificate); secondary education (Certificate); superintendent (Certificate). *Program availability:* Part-time, evening/weekend. Terminal master's awarded for partial completion of doctoral program. *Degree requirements:* For master's, comprehensive exam, thesis (for some programs); for doctorate, thesis/dissertation, qualifying exam. *Entrance requirements:* For master's, GRE General Test or MAT, official transcripts from all current and previous colleges/universities except Marquette, three letters of recommendation, statement of purpose; for doctorate, GRE General Test, MAT, sample of written work, official transcripts from all current and previous colleges/universities except Marquette, three letters of recommendation, statement of purpose, resume/curriculum vitae; for Certificate, GRE General Test or MAT, master's degree. Additional exam requirements/recommendations for international students: Required—TOEFL (minimum score 530 paper-based). *Expenses:* Contact institution. *Faculty research:* Leadership; social justice in education; development of lifelong learners; race, class, and schooling in historical perspective; urban teacher education.

Martin Luther College, Graduate Studies, New Ulm, MN 56073. Offers early childhood director (MS Ed Admin); educational technology (MS Ed); instruction (MS Ed); leadership (MS Ed); principal (MS Ed Admin); special education (MS Ed). *Program availability:* Part-time, evening/weekend, online only, 100% online. *Faculty:* 13 full-time (2 women), 31 part-time/adjunct (10 women). *Students:* 1 full-time (0 women), 86 part-time (26 women); includes 1 minority (Two or more races, non-Hispanic/Latino), 1 international. Average age 38. 35 applicants, 100% accepted, 35 enrolled. In 2018, 26 master's awarded. *Degree requirements:* For master's, capstone project or comprehensive exam. *Entrance requirements:* For master's, undergraduate degree in education from an accredited college or university, minimum undergraduate GPA of 3.0. Additional exam requirements/recommendations for international students: Required—TOEFL (minimum score 550 paper-based; 80 iBT); Recommended—IELTS (minimum

score .6.5). *Application deadline:* Applications are processed on a rolling basis. Application fee: $35. Electronic applications accepted. *Financial support:* In 2018–19, 1 student received support. Scholarships/grants available. Financial award application deadline: 9/1. *Faculty research:* Principal effectiveness, principal support, cognitive load in math instruction, reading strategies in multigrade classrooms, mentor provided professional development for new teachers. *Unit head:* John E. Meyer, Director of Graduate Studies, 507-354-8221 Ext. 398, E-mail: meyerjd@mlc-wels.edu. *Application contact:* John E. Meyer, Director of Graduate Studies, 507-354-8221 Ext. 398, E-mail: meyerjd@mlc-wels.edu.
Website: https://mlc-wels.edu/graduate-studies/

Marygrove College, Graduate Studies, Detroit, MI 48221-2599. Offers autism spectrum disorders (M Ed, Certificate); curriculum instruction and assessment (MAT); educational leadership (MA); educational technology (M Ed); effective teaching in the 21st century-classroom focus (MAT); effective teaching in the 21st century-technology focus (MAT); human resource management (MA, Certificate); mathematics 6-8 (MAT); mathematics K-5 (MAT); reading and literacy K-6 (MAT); reading specialist (M Ed); school administrator (Certificate); social justice (MA); special education (MAT); special education - learning disabilities (M Ed); teaching - pre-elementary education (M Ed); teaching - pre-secondary education (M Ed). *Program availability:* Part-time, evening/weekend, 100% online, blended/hybrid learning. *Entrance requirements:* For master's, all official bachelor's transcripts. Additional exam requirements/recommendations for international students: Required—TOEFL (minimum score 550 paper-based; 80 iBT). Electronic applications accepted.

Marymount University, School of Sciences, Mathematics, and Education, Program in Education, Arlington, VA 22207-4299. Offers curriculum and instruction (M Ed); elementary education (M Ed); professional studies (M Ed); secondary education (M Ed); special education: general curriculum (M Ed). *Accreditation:* NCATE. *Program availability:* Part-time, evening/weekend. *Faculty:* 7 full-time (all women), 8 part-time/adjunct (6 women). *Students:* 42 full-time (29 women), 103 part-time (80 women); includes 31 minority (8 Black or African American, non-Hispanic/Latino; 11 Asian, non-Hispanic/Latino; 10 Hispanic/Latino; 1 Native Hawaiian or other Pacific Islander, non-Hispanic/Latino; 1 Two or more races, non-Hispanic/Latino), 12 international. Average age 36. 44 applicants, 100% accepted, 30 enrolled. In 2018, 61 master's awarded. *Degree requirements:* For master's, thesis or alternative, capstone/internship. *Entrance requirements:* For master's, PRAXIS MATH or SAT/ACT, and Virginia Communication and Literacy Assessment (VCLA), 2 letters of recommendation, resume, interview, minimum undergraduate GPA of 2.75 or 3.25 in the last 60 hours. Additional exam requirements/recommendations for international students: Required—TOEFL (minimum score 600 paper-based; 96 iBT), IELTS (minimum score 6.5), PTE (minimum score 58). *Application deadline:* For fall admission, 7/16 priority date for domestic and international students; for spring admission, 11/16 priority date for domestic and international students. Applications are processed on a rolling basis. Application fee: $40. Electronic applications accepted. *Expenses:* $770 per credit. *Financial support:* In 2018–19, 3 students received support. Research assistantships, teaching assistantships, career-related internships or fieldwork, scholarships/grants, and unspecified assistantships available. Support available to part-time students. Financial award application deadline: 3/1; financial award applicants required to submit FAFSA. *Unit head:* Dr. Lisa Turissini, Chair, Education, 703-526-1668, E-mail: lisa.turissini@marymount.edu. *Application contact:* Rebecca Esposito, Senior Associate Director, Graduate Admissions, 703-284-5901, Fax: 703-527-3815, E-mail: grad.admissions@marymount.edu.
Website: https://www.marymount.edu/Academics/School-of-Sciences-Mathematics-and-Education/Graduate-Programs/Education-(M-Ed-)

Massachusetts College of Liberal Arts, Graduate Programs, North Adams, MA 01247-4100. Offers business (MBA); educational administration (M Ed); educational leadership (CAGS); instruction and curriculum (M Ed); instructional technology (M Ed); physical education and health (M Ed); reading (M Ed); special education (M Ed). *Program availability:* Part-time, evening/weekend. *Degree requirements:* For master's, thesis. *Entrance requirements:* For master's, writing sample.

McDaniel College, Graduate and Professional Studies, Program in Curriculum and Instruction, Westminster, MD 21157-4390. Offers MS. *Program availability:* Part-time, evening/weekend, 100% online, blended/hybrid learning. *Degree requirements:* For master's, comprehensive exam (for some programs), thesis optional. *Entrance requirements:* For master's, one reference. Additional exam requirements/recommendations for international students: Required—TOEFL (minimum score 79 iBT), IELTS (minimum score 6). Electronic applications accepted.

McGill University, Faculty of Graduate and Postdoctoral Studies, Faculty of Education, Department of Integrated Studies in Education, Montréal, QC H3A 2T5, Canada. Offers culture and values in education (MA, PhD); curriculum studies (MA); educational leadership (MA, Certificate); educational studies (PhD); integrated studies in education (M Ed); second language education (MA, PhD).

McKendree University, Graduate Programs, Programs in Education, Lebanon, IL 62254-1299. Offers curriculum design and instruction (Ed D, Ed S); educational administration and leadership (MA Ed); educational studies (MA Ed); higher education administrative services (MA Ed); music education (MA Ed); reading (MA Ed); special education (MA Ed); teacher leadership (MA Ed); teaching certification (MA Ed). *Accreditation:* NCATE. *Program availability:* Part-time, evening/weekend, online learning. *Entrance requirements:* For master's, official transcripts from all institutions previously attended, minimum GPA of 3.0, resume, references; for doctorate, GRE (within the past 5 years), master's degree in education and Ed S, or the equivalent, from regionally-accredited institution; official transcripts from all institutions previously attended; curriculum vitae/resume; essay/personal statement; two years of teaching/professional experience; for Ed S, GRE (within the past 5 years), master's degree in education from regionally-accredited institution of higher education; official transcripts from all institutions previously attended; curriculum vitae/resume; essay/personal statement; two years of teaching/professional experience. Additional exam requirements/recommendations for international students: Required—TOEFL. Electronic applications accepted.

McNeese State University, Doré School of Graduate Studies, Burton College of Education, Department of Education Professions, Program in Curriculum and Instruction, Lake Charles, LA 70609. Offers academically gifted education (M Ed); elementary education (M Ed); reading (M Ed); secondary education (M Ed); special education (M Ed). *Program availability:* Evening/weekend. *Entrance requirements:* For master's, GRE, teaching certificate.

Medaille College, Program in Education, Buffalo, NY 14214-2695. Offers adolescent education (MS Ed); curriculum and instruction (MS Ed); education preparation (MS Ed); literacy (MS Ed); special education (MS). *Accreditation:* TEAC. *Program availability:* Part-time, evening/weekend. *Degree requirements:* For master's, comprehensive exam (for some programs), thesis or alternative. *Entrance requirements:* For master's, minimum undergraduate GPA of 2.7. Additional exam requirements/recommendations for international students: Required—TOEFL (minimum score 550 paper-based). Electronic applications accepted. *Faculty research:* Curriculum planning, truancy, tracking minority students, curriculum design, mentoring students.

Memorial University of Newfoundland, School of Graduate Studies, Faculty of Education, St. John's, NL A1C 5S7, Canada. Offers counseling psychology (M Ed); curriculum, teaching, and learning studies (M Ed); education (PhD); educational leadership studies (M Ed, Graduate Diploma); information technology (M Ed); post-secondary studies (M Ed, Diploma), including health professional education (Diploma). *Program availability:* Part-time. *Degree requirements:* For master's, thesis optional, internship, paper folio, project; for doctorate, comprehensive exam, thesis/dissertation, thesis seminar, oral defense of thesis. *Entrance requirements:* For master's, undergraduate degree with at least 2nd class standing, 1-2 years of work experience; for doctorate, minimum A average in graduate course work, MA in education, 2 years of professional experience; for other advanced degree, 2nd class degree, 2 years of work experience with adult learners, appropriate academic qualifications and work experience in a health-related field. Electronic applications accepted. *Faculty research:* Critical thinking, literacy, cognitive studies and counseling, educational change, technology in instruction.

Mercer University, Graduate Studies, Cecil B. Day Campus, Tift College of Education (Atlanta), Atlanta, GA 30341. Offers curriculum and instruction (PhD); early childhood education (M Ed, MAT, Ed S); educational leadership (PhD), including higher education leadership, P-12 school leadership; educational leadership P-12 (M Ed, Ed S); higher education leadership (M Ed); independent and charter school leadership (M Ed); middle grades education (M Ed, MAT); secondary education (M Ed, MAT); teacher leadership (Ed S). *Accreditation:* NCATE. *Program availability:* Part-time, evening/weekend. *Degree requirements:* For master's and Ed S, research project; for doctorate, comprehensive exam, thesis/dissertation. *Entrance requirements:* For master's, GRE or MAT, minimum undergraduate GPA of 2.75; for doctorate, GRE; for Ed S, GRE or MAT, minimum GPA of 3.25; 3 years of certified teaching experience (for educational leadership and teacher leadership). Additional exam requirements/recommendations for international students: Required—TOEFL (minimum score 80 iBT). Electronic applications accepted. *Expenses:* Contact institution. *Faculty research:* Educational technology, multicultural and minority issues in education, educational leadership (P-12 and higher education), school discipline and school bullying, standards-based mathematics education.

Mercer University, Graduate Studies, Macon Campus, Tift College of Education (Macon), Macon, GA 31207. Offers curriculum and instruction (PhD); early childhood education (M Ed, Ed S); educational leadership (M Ed, PhD, Ed S), including higher education (PhD), P-12; higher education leadership (M Ed); independent and charter school leadership (M Ed); secondary education (MAT), including STEM; teacher leadership (Ed S). *Accreditation:* NCATE. *Program availability:* Part-time, evening/weekend, 100% online, blended/hybrid learning. *Degree requirements:* For master's, research project report; for doctorate, comprehensive exam, thesis/dissertation. *Entrance requirements:* For master's, GRE or MAT, minimum GPA of 2.75; for doctorate, GRE, minimum GPA of 3.5; interview; writing sample; 3 recommendations; for Ed S, GRE or MAT, minimum GPA of 3.5 (for teacher leadership), 3.0 (for educational leadership). Additional exam requirements/recommendations for international students: Required—TOEFL (minimum score 80 iBT). Electronic applications accepted. *Expenses:* Contact institution. *Faculty research:* Teacher effectiveness, specific learning disabilities, inclusion.

Messiah College, Program in Education, Mechanicsburg, PA 17055. Offers curriculum and instruction (M Ed); special education (M Ed); teaching English to speakers of other languages (M Ed). *Program availability:* Part-time, online learning. Electronic applications accepted. *Faculty research:* Socio-cultural perspectives on education, TESOL, autism, special education.

Metropolitan State University, School of Urban Education, St. Paul, MN 55106-5000. Offers curriculum, pedagogy and schooling (MS); English as a second language (MS); secondary education (MS), including English teaching, life sciences teaching, mathematics teaching, social studies teaching; special education (MS).

Michigan State University, The Graduate School, College of Education, Department of Teacher Education, East Lansing, MI 48824. Offers curriculum, instruction and teacher education (PhD, Ed S); teaching and curriculum (MA). *Entrance requirements:* Additional exam requirements/recommendations for international students: Required—TOEFL. Electronic applications accepted.

Middle Tennessee State University, College of Graduate Studies, College of Education, Department of Educational Leadership, Program in Curriculum and Instruction, Murfreesboro, TN 37132. Offers curriculum and instruction (M Ed, Ed S); English as a second language (M Ed, Ed S); secondary education (M Ed); technology and curriculum design (Ed S). *Accreditation:* NCATE. *Program availability:* Part-time, evening/weekend, online learning. *Degree requirements:* For master's, comprehensive exam; for Ed S, comprehensive exam, thesis or alternative. *Entrance requirements:* For master's and Ed S, GRE, MAT or PRAXIS. Additional exam requirements/recommendations for international students: Required—TOEFL (minimum score 525 paper-based; 71 iBT) or IELTS (minimum score 6). Electronic applications accepted.

Midwestern State University, Billie Doris McAda Graduate School, West College of Education, Program in Curriculum and Instruction, Wichita Falls, TX 76308. Offers M Ed. *Program availability:* Part-time, evening/weekend. *Degree requirements:* For master's, comprehensive exam. *Entrance requirements:* For master's, GRE General Test, MAT, or GMAT. Additional exam requirements/recommendations for international students: Required—TOEFL (minimum score 550 paper-based). Electronic applications accepted. *Faculty research:* Role of the twenty-first century principal, instructional effectiveness, motivation, curriculum theory, educational research methodology.

Misericordia University, College of Health Sciences and Education, Program in Education, Dallas, PA 18612-1098. Offers instructional technology (MS); reading specialist (MS); special education (MS). *Program availability:* Part-time, evening/weekend. *Entrance requirements:* For master's, minimum undergraduate GPA of 3.0. Additional exam requirements/recommendations for international students: Required—TOEFL. Electronic applications accepted.

Mississippi College, Graduate School, School of Education, Department of Teacher Education and Leadership, Clinton, MS 39058. Offers art (M Ed); biological science (M Ed); business education (M Ed); computer science (M Ed); dyslexia therapy (M Ed); educational leadership (M Ed, Ed D, Ed S); elementary education (M Ed, Ed S); English (M Ed); higher education administration (MS); mathematics (M Ed); secondary education (M Ed); social studies (history) (M Ed); teaching arts (M Ed). *Program availability:* Part-time, online learning. *Degree requirements:* For master's, comprehensive exam, thesis optional. *Entrance requirements:* For master's, NTE. Additional exam requirements/recommendations for international students: Recommended—TOEFL, IELTS. Electronic applications accepted.

Mississippi State University, College of Education, Department of Curriculum, Instruction and Special Education, Mississippi State, MS 39762. Offers early childhood education (PhD); elementary education (MS, PhD, Ed S), including early childhood education (MS), general elementary education (MS); middle level education (MS); general curriculum and instruction (PhD); reading education (PhD); secondary education (MAT, MS, PhD, Ed S); special education (MAT, MS, PhD, Ed S). *Accreditation:* NCATE. *Program availability:* Part-time, evening/weekend. *Faculty:* 20 full-time (14

women), 1 (woman) part-time/adjunct. *Students:* 24 full-time (16 women), 151 part-time (109 women); includes 44 minority (38 Black or African American, non-Hispanic/Latino; 3 American Indian or Alaska Native, non-Hispanic/Latino; 1 Hispanic/Latino; 2 Two or more races, non-Hispanic/Latino), 3 international. Average age 32. 65 applicants, 65% accepted, 38 enrolled. In 2018, 57 master's, 3 doctorates, 1 other advanced degree awarded. *Degree requirements:* For master's, comprehensive exam; for doctorate, thesis/dissertation; for Ed S, comprehensive exam, thesis or alternative. *Entrance requirements:* For master's, GRE, minimum GPA of 2.75 in junior and senior year, eligibility for initial teacher certification; for doctorate, GRE, minimum GPA of 3.4 on previous graduate work; for Ed S, GRE, minimum GPA of 3.2 on master's degree. Additional exam requirements/recommendations for international students: Required—TOEFL (minimum score 550 paper-based; 79 iBT); Recommended—IELTS (minimum score 6.5). *Application deadline:* For fall admission, 3/1 priority date for domestic students, 5/1 for international students; for spring admission, 9/1 priority date for domestic students, 9/1 for international students. Applications are processed on a rolling basis. Application fee: $60 ($80 for international students). Electronic applications accepted. *Expenses: Tuition,* state resident: full-time $8450; part-time $360.59 per credit hour. Tuition, nonresident: full-time $23,140; part-time $969.09 per credit hour. *Required fees:* $110. One-time fee: $55 full-time. Part-time tuition and fees vary according to course load, degree level, campus/location and reciprocity agreements. *Financial support:* In 2018–19, 5 research assistantships with partial tuition reimbursements (averaging $11,453 per year), 1 teaching assistantship (averaging $11,700 per year) were awarded; Federal Work-Study, institutionally sponsored loans, scholarships/grants, and unspecified assistantships also available. Financial award application deadline: 4/1; financial award applicants required to submit FAFSA. *Faculty research:* Early childhood education, reading, rural schools, multicultural education, use of technology in instruction. *Unit head:* Dr. Linda Cornelious, Professor and Head, 662-325-3747, Fax: 662-325-7857, E-mail: lcornelious@colled.msstate.edu. *Application contact:* Robbie Salters, Admissions and Enrollment Assistant, 662-325-7400, E-mail: rsalters@grad.msstate.edu.
Website: http://www.cise.msstate.edu/

Mississippi University for Women, Graduate School, College of Education and Human Sciences, Columbus, MS 39701-9998. Offers differentiated instruction (M Ed); educational leadership (M Ed); gifted studies (M Ed); reading/literacy (M Ed); teaching (MAT). *Accreditation:* ASHA; NCATE. *Program availability:* Part-time. *Degree requirements:* For master's, comprehensive exam, thesis optional. *Entrance requirements:* For master's, GRE General Test or NTE (M Ed in gifted education or MS in speech/language pathology), MAT (M Ed in instructional management), minimum QPA of 3.0.

Montana State University, The Graduate School, College of Education, Health, and Human Development, Department of Education, Bozeman, MT 59717. Offers adult and higher education (Ed D); curriculum and instruction (M Ed, Ed D), including professional educator (M Ed), technology education (M Ed); education (M Ed), including adult and higher education, educational leadership, school counseling; educational leadership (Ed D, Ed S). *Accreditation:* TEAC. *Program availability:* Part-time, online learning. *Degree requirements:* For master's, comprehensive exam; for doctorate, comprehensive exam, thesis/dissertation. *Entrance requirements:* For master's, GRE, 3 letters of reference, essays, BA transcripts; for doctorate, GRE, MAT, 3 letters of reference, essay, BA and M Ed transcripts; for Ed S, PRAXIS. Additional exam requirements/recommendations for international students: Required—TOEFL (minimum score 550 paper-based). Electronic applications accepted. *Faculty research:* Critical literacy; standards-based education; school Improvement, organizational change, leadership in rural education, leadership in Indian education; student Learning; multicultural/culturally responsive education for social justice Native American indigenous education, community-centered education teacher preparation.

Montana State University Billings, College of Education, Department of Educational Theory and Practice, Option in Curriculum and Instruction, Billings, MT 59101. Offers K-8 elementary education (M Ed); secondary education (M Ed). *Accreditation:* NCATE. *Program availability:* Part-time. *Degree requirements:* For master's, thesis or professional paper and/or field experience. *Entrance requirements:* For master's, GRE General Test or MAT, minimum GPA of 3.0. Additional exam requirements/recommendations for international students: Required—TOEFL (minimum score 79 iBT), IELTS (minimum score 6.5). Electronic applications accepted. *Faculty research:* Social studies education, science education.

Montclair State University, The Graduate School, College of Education and Human Services, MAT Program in Teaching, Montclair, NJ 07043-1624. Offers art (MAT); biology (MAT); chemistry (MAT); earth science (MAT); English (MAT); French (MAT); health and physical education (MAT); health education (MAT); mathematics (MAT); music (MAT); physical education (MAT); physical science (MAT); social studies (MAT); Spanish (MAT); teacher of English as a second language (MAT). *Degree requirements:* For master's, comprehensive exam, thesis or alternative. *Entrance requirements:* For master's, interview, 2 letters of recommendation. Additional exam requirements/recommendations for international students: Required—TOEFL (minimum score 83 iBT), IELTS (minimum score 6.5). Electronic applications accepted.

Moravian College, Graduate and Continuing Studies, Education Programs, Bethlehem, PA 18018-6650. Offers curriculum and instruction (M Ed); education (MAT). *Program availability:* Part-time, evening/weekend. *Faculty:* 1 full-time (0 women), 4 part-time/adjunct (1 woman). *Students:* 6 full-time (4 women), 50 part-time (41 women); includes 5 minority (1 Black or African American, non-Hispanic/Latino; 4 Hispanic/Latino). Average age 29. 81 applicants, 83% accepted, 53 enrolled. In 2018, 20 master's awarded. *Degree requirements:* For master's, thesis. *Entrance requirements:* For master's, state teacher certification for Curriculum and Instruction. *Application deadline:* For fall admission, 8/1 priority date for domestic and international students; for spring admission, 1/1 priority date for domestic and international students; for summer admission, 5/1 priority date for domestic and international students. Applications are processed on a rolling basis. Electronic applications accepted. *Financial support:* Applicants required to submit FAFSA. *Faculty research:* Teacher action research, youth participatory research, practitioner inquiry, science education, deaf and hard of hearing education. *Unit head:* Scott Dams, Dean of Graduate and Adult Enrollment, 610-861-1400, Fax: 610-861-1466, E-mail: graduate@moravian.edu. *Application contact:* Jennifer Pagliaroli, Student Experience Mentor, 610-861-1400, Fax: 610-861-1466, E-mail: graduate@moravian.edu.
Website: https://www.moravian.edu/graduate/programs/education#/

Morehead State University, Graduate School, College of Education, Department of Foundational and Graduate Studies in Education, Morehead, KY 40351. Offers adult and higher education (MA, Ed S); certified professional counselor (Ed S); counseling P-12 (MA); curriculum and instruction (Ed S); educational technology (MA Ed); instructional leadership (Ed S); school administration (MA); school counseling (Ed S); teacher leader business and marketing content (MA Ed); teacher leader business and marketing technology (MA Ed); teacher leader educational technology (MA Ed); teacher leader English (MA Ed); teacher leader gifted education (MA Ed); teacher leader IECE certification (MA Ed); teacher leader interdisciplinary education P-5 (MA Ed); teacher leader middle grades (MA Ed); teacher leader non IECE certification (MA Ed); teacher

leader reading/writing - non-certification (MA Ed); teacher leader reading/writing certification (MA Ed); teacher leader school communication - certification (MA Ed); teacher leader school communication - non-certification (MA Ed); teacher leader social studies (MA Ed); teacher leader special education (MA Ed). *Accreditation:* NCATE. *Program availability:* Part-time, evening/weekend. *Degree requirements:* For master's, thesis optional, oral and/or written comprehensive exams; for Ed S, thesis, oral exam. *Entrance requirements:* For master's, GRE General Test, minimum overall undergraduate GPA of 2.5; for Ed S, GRE General Test, interview, master's degree, minimum GPA of 3.5, work experience. Additional exam requirements/recommendations for international students: Required—TOEFL (minimum score 500 paper-based). Electronic applications accepted. *Faculty research:* Character education, school accountability, computer applications for school administrators.

Mount Saint Vincent University, Graduate Programs, Faculty of Education, Program in Curriculum Studies, Halifax, NS B3M 2J6, Canada. Offers general curriculum studies (M Ed, MA Ed, MA-R); teaching English to speakers of other languages (M Ed, MA Ed, MA-R). *Program availability:* Part-time, evening/weekend, online learning. *Degree requirements:* For master's, thesis (for some programs). *Entrance requirements:* For master's, bachelor's degree in related field, minimum B average, 1 year of teaching experience. Electronic applications accepted. *Faculty research:* Science education, cultural studies, international education, curriculum development.

National Louis University, National College of Education, Chicago, IL 60603. Offers administration and supervision (M Ed, Ed D, CAS, Ed S); curriculum and instruction (M Ed, MS Ed, CAS); early childhood administration (M Ed, CAS); early childhood education (M Ed, MAT, MS Ed, CAS); education (Ed D); educational psychology/human learning and development (M Ed, MS Ed, CAS, Ed S); elementary education (MAT); interdisciplinary curriculum and instruction (M Ed); mathematics education (M Ed, MS Ed, CAS); middle grades education (MAT); reading and language (M Ed, MS Ed, CAS); school psychology (M Ed, Ed S); science education (M Ed, MS Ed, CAS); secondary education (MAT); special education (M Ed, MAT, CAS); technology in education (M Ed, CAS). *Accreditation:* NCATE. *Program availability:* Part-time, evening/weekend. *Degree requirements:* For doctorate, comprehensive exam, thesis/dissertation. *Entrance requirements:* For master's, MAT or GRE, minimum GPA of 3.0; for doctorate, GRE General Test, minimum GPA of 3.25, interview, resume, writing sample, 4 recommendations. Additional exam requirements/recommendations for international students: Required—TOEFL (minimum score 550 paper-based; 79 iBT).

Newman University, Master of Science in Education Program, Wichita, KS 67213-2097. Offers building leadership (MS Ed); curriculum and instruction (MS Ed), including English as a second language, reading specialist; organizational leadership (MS Ed). *Accreditation:* NCATE. *Program availability:* Part-time, evening/weekend, online learning. *Degree requirements:* For master's, thesis optional. *Entrance requirements:* For master's, 3 years' full-time teaching experience, minimum GPA of 3.0, writing sample, 2 letters of recommendation, evidence of teaching certification. Additional exam requirements/recommendations for international students: Required—TOEFL (minimum score 600 paper-based; 100 iBT). Electronic applications accepted. *Expenses:* Contact institution. *Faculty research:* Online course design and deliver, staff engagement, classroom action.

New Mexico Highlands University, Graduate Studies, School of Education, Las Vegas, NM 87701. Offers curriculum and instruction (MA); educational leadership (MA); professional counseling (MA); special education (MA). *Accreditation:* NCATE. *Program availability:* Part-time. *Degree requirements:* For master's, comprehensive exam, thesis or alternative. *Entrance requirements:* For master's, minimum undergraduate GPA of 3.0. Additional exam requirements/recommendations for international students: Required—TOEFL (minimum score 540 paper-based). *Faculty research:* Middle school curriculum, integrated computer applications for pre-service classroom teachers, adolescent literacy, narrative cognitive modes in New Mexico multicultural setting, math and math education.

Nicholls State University, Graduate Studies, College of Education, Department of Teacher Education, Thibodaux, LA 70310. Offers curriculum and instruction (M Ed); educational leadership (M Ed); elementary education (MAT); human performance education (MAT); middle school education (MAT); secondary education (MAT). *Accreditation:* NCATE. *Program availability:* Part-time, evening/weekend, online learning. *Degree requirements:* For master's, comprehensive exam, portfolio. *Entrance requirements:* For master's, GRE General Test, teaching license. Electronic applications accepted.

North Carolina State University, Graduate School, College of Education, Department of Teacher Education and Learning Sciences, Program in Curriculum and Instruction, Raleigh, NC 27695. Offers M Ed, MS, PhD. *Accreditation:* NCATE. *Degree requirements:* For master's, thesis (for some programs); for doctorate, thesis/dissertation. *Entrance requirements:* For master's, GRE General Test or MAT, minimum GPA of 3.0 in major; for doctorate, GRE General Test, minimum GPA of 3.0 in major. Electronic applications accepted. *Faculty research:* Curriculum development, teacher development, intervention for exceptional children, literacy development.

Northern Arizona University, College of Education, Department of Teaching and Learning, Flagstaff, AZ 86011. Offers curriculum and instruction (Ed D); early childhood education (M Ed); elementary education (M Ed); secondary education (M Ed). *Program availability:* Part-time, 100% online, blended/hybrid learning. *Degree requirements:* For master's, variable foreign language requirement, comprehensive exam (for some programs), thesis (for some programs); for doctorate, variable foreign language requirement, comprehensive exam (for some programs), thesis/dissertation (for some programs). *Entrance requirements:* Additional exam requirements/recommendations for international students: Required—TOEFL (minimum score 80 iBT), IELTS (minimum score 6.5). Electronic applications accepted.

Northern Illinois University, Graduate School, College of Education, Department of Curriculum and Instruction, De Kalb, IL 60115-2854. Offers curriculum and instruction (Ed D), including reading; literacy education (MS Ed). *Program availability:* Part-time, evening/weekend. *Faculty:* 12 full-time (10 women), 1 part-time/adjunct (0 women). *Students:* 14 full-time (12 women), 225 part-time (199 women); includes 40 minority (7 Black or African American, non-Hispanic/Latino; 6 Asian, non-Hispanic/Latino; 22 Hispanic/Latino; 5 Two or more races, non-Hispanic/Latino), 9 international. Average age 37. 64 applicants, 81% accepted, 30 enrolled. In 2018, 82 master's, 2 doctorates awarded. *Degree requirements:* For master's, comprehensive exam, thesis optional; for doctorate, thesis/dissertation, candidacy exam, dissertation defense. *Entrance requirements:* For master's, GRE General Test or MAT, minimum undergraduate GPA of 2.75; for doctorate, GRE General Test, minimum GPA of 2.75 (undergraduate), 3.2 (graduate). Additional exam requirements/recommendations for international students: Required—TOEFL (minimum score 550 paper-based). *Application deadline:* For fall admission, 3/1 priority date for domestic students, 5/1 for international students; for spring admission, 11/1 for domestic students, 10/1 for international students. Applications are processed on a rolling basis. Application fee: $40. Electronic applications accepted. *Financial support:* In 2018–19, 3 research assistantships with full tuition reimbursements, 13 teaching assistantships with full tuition reimbursements were awarded; fellowships with full tuition reimbursements, career-related internships or fieldwork, Federal Work-Study, scholarships/grants, tuition waivers (full), and staff assistantships also available. Support available to part-time students. Financial award applicants required to submit FAFSA. *Faculty research:* Early reading development, literacy for bilingual students, family literacy, expository writing, fluency. *Unit head:* Dr. Sally Blake, Chair, 815-753-8556, E-mail: sblake1@niu.edu. *Application contact:* Graduate School Office, 815-753-0395, E-mail: gradsch@niu.edu.
Website: http://cedu.niu.edu/leed/programs/masters1.shtml

Northern Illinois University, Graduate School, College of Education, Department of Special and Early Education, De Kalb, IL 60115-2854. Offers curriculum and instruction (MS Ed); early childhood education (MS Ed); elementary education (MS Ed); special education (MS Ed). *Program availability:* Part-time, evening/weekend. *Faculty:* 22 full-time (14 women), 2 part-time/adjunct (both women). *Students:* 43 full-time (33 women), 87 part-time (70 women); includes 22 minority (5 Black or African American, non-Hispanic/Latino; 1 Asian, non-Hispanic/Latino; 12 Hispanic/Latino; 4 Two or more races, non-Hispanic/Latino), 3 international. Average age 32. 75 applicants, 77% accepted, 37 enrolled. In 2018, 41 master's awarded. *Degree requirements:* For master's, comprehensive exam, thesis optional. *Entrance requirements:* For master's, GRE General Test or MAT, minimum undergraduate GPA of 2.75. Additional exam requirements/recommendations for international students: Required—TOEFL (minimum score 550 paper-based). *Application deadline:* For fall admission, 6/1 for domestic students, 5/1 for international students; for spring admission, 11/1 for domestic students, 10/1 for international students. Applications are processed on a rolling basis. Application fee: $40. Electronic applications accepted. *Financial support:* In 2018–19, 17 research assistantships with full tuition reimbursements were awarded; fellowships with full tuition reimbursements, teaching assistantships with full tuition reimbursements, career-related internships or fieldwork, Federal Work-Study, scholarships/grants, tuition waivers (full), and unspecified assistantships also available. Support available to part-time students. Financial award applicants required to submit FAFSA. *Faculty research:* Teacher certification, stress reduction during student teaching, teaching history, portfolios in student teaching. *Unit head:* Gregory Conderman, Chair, 815-753-1619, E-mail: seed@niu.edu. *Application contact:* Gail Myers, Clerk, Graduate Advising, 815-753-0381, E-mail: gmyers@niu.edu.
Website: http://www.cedu.niu.edu/seed/

Northern Michigan University, Office of Graduate Education and Research, College of Health Sciences and Professional Studies, School of Education, Leadership and Public Service, Marquette, MI 49855-5301. Offers administration and supervision (MAE); instruction (MAE); learning disabilities (MAE); postsecondary biology education (MS); reading education (MAE), including reading, reading specialist. *Accreditation:* TEAC. *Program availability:* Part-time, online learning. *Degree requirements:* For master's, thesis (for some programs). *Entrance requirements:* For master's, minimum GPA of 3.0. Additional exam requirements/recommendations for international students: Required—TOEFL (minimum score 550 paper-based; 79 iBT), IELTS (minimum score 6.5). Electronic applications accepted.

Northern State University, MS Ed Program in Teaching and Learning, Aberdeen, SD 57401-7198. Offers MS Ed. *Accreditation:* NCATE. *Program availability:* Part-time, evening/weekend, online learning. *Degree requirements:* For master's, comprehensive exam, thesis optional. *Entrance requirements:* For master's, minimum GPA of 2.75. Additional exam requirements/recommendations for international students: Required—TOEFL (minimum score 550 paper-based; 78 iBT), IELTS (minimum score 6). Electronic applications accepted.

Northern Vermont University–Johnson, Program in Education, Johnson, VT 05656. Offers applied behavior analysis (MA Ed); curriculum and instruction (MA Ed); foundations of education (MA Ed); special education (MA Ed). *Program availability:* Part-time. *Degree requirements:* For master's, thesis or alternative, exit interview. *Entrance requirements:* For master's, interview. Additional exam requirements/recommendations for international students: Required—TOEFL. Electronic applications accepted.

Northern Vermont University–Lyndon, Graduate Programs in Education, Department of Education, Lyndonville, VT 05851. Offers curriculum and instruction (M Ed); reading specialist (M Ed); special education (M Ed); teaching and counseling (M Ed). *Program availability:* Part-time, evening/weekend. *Degree requirements:* For master's, exam or major field project. *Entrance requirements:* Additional exam requirements/recommendations for international students: Recommended—TOEFL (minimum score 500 paper-based).

Northwestern Oklahoma State University, School of Professional Studies, Program in Curriculum and Instruction, Alva, OK 73717-2799. Offers M Ed. *Program availability:* Part-time. *Degree requirements:* For master's, thesis optional, portfolio. *Entrance requirements:* For master's, GRE General Test or MAT, minimum GPA of 2.75.

Northwestern State University of Louisiana, Graduate Studies and Research, College of Education and Human Development, Program in Curriculum and Instruction, Natchitoches, LA 71497. Offers M Ed. *Entrance requirements:* Additional exam requirements/recommendations for international students: Required—TOEFL. Electronic applications accepted.

Northwest Nazarene University, Graduate Education Program, Nampa, ID 83686-5897. Offers curriculum and instruction (M Ed); educational leadership (M Ed, Ed D, PhD, Ed S), including building administrator (M Ed, Ed S), director of special education (Ed S), leadership and organizational development (Ed S), superintendent (Ed S). *Accreditation:* ACA (one or more programs are accredited); NCATE. *Program availability:* Part-time, online only, 100% online, 2-week face-to-face residency (for doctoral programs). *Faculty:* 4 full-time (3 women), 18 part-time/adjunct (7 women). *Students:* 128 full-time (83 women), 59 part-time (37 women); includes 22 minority (3 Black or African American, non-Hispanic/Latino; 1 Asian, non-Hispanic/Latino; 3 Hispanic/Latino; 15 Two or more races, non-Hispanic/Latino), 1 international. Average age 44. 124 applicants, 84% accepted, 87 enrolled. In 2018, 37 master's, 18 doctorates, 28 other advanced degrees awarded. *Degree requirements:* For master's, comprehensive exam (for some programs), action research project; for doctorate, thesis/dissertation, Dissertation; for Ed S, comprehensive exam, research project. *Entrance requirements:* For master's, minimum undergraduate GPA of 3.0 overall or during final 30 semester credits, undergraduate degree, valid teaching certificate; for doctorate, Ed S or equivalent, minimum GPA of 3.5; for Ed S, undergraduate degree, valid teaching certificate. Additional exam requirements/recommendations for international students: Recommended—TOEFL. *Application deadline:* Applications are processed on a rolling basis. Application fee: $50. Electronic applications accepted. *Expenses:* Masters: $475 per credit, $95 technology fee per semester; EDS: $505 per credit, $95 technology fee per semester; PHD/EDD: $565 per credit, $520 dissertation fee, $95 technology fee per semester. *Financial support:* Application deadline: 1/15; applicants required to submit FAFSA. *Faculty research:* Action research, cooperative learning, accountability, institutional accreditation, personalized learning K-12. *Unit head:* Dr. Heidi Curtis, Chair, 208-467-8250, E-mail: hlcurtis@nnu.edu. *Application contact:* Charlene Brown, Admissions Counselor, 208-467-8492, Fax: 208-467-8384, E-mail: gradeducationinfo@nnu.edu.
Website: http://www.nnu.edu/graded/

Notre Dame de Namur University, Division of Academic Affairs, School of Education and Psychology, Program in Education, Belmont, CA 94002-1908. Offers curriculum and instruction (MA); disciplinary studies (MA). *Program availability:* Part-time, evening/weekend. *Students:* 2 full-time (both women), 36 part-time (29 women); includes 10 minority (4 Asian, non-Hispanic/Latino; 4 Hispanic/Latino; 2 Two or more races, non-Hispanic/Latino), 2 international. Average age 31. *Entrance requirements:* For master's, CBEST, CSET, valid teaching credential or substantial teaching experience. Additional exam requirements/recommendations for international students: Required—TOEFL (minimum score 550 paper-based; 79 iBT). *Application deadline:* For fall admission, 8/1 priority date for domestic students; for spring admission, 12/1 priority date for domestic students. Applications are processed on a rolling basis. Application fee: $60. Electronic applications accepted. *Expenses: Tuition:* Full-time $16,596; part-time $11,064 per semester. *Required fees:* $130; $130 per unit. $65 per semester. Tuition and fees vary according to program. *Financial support:* Career-related internships or fieldwork and scholarships/grants available. Financial award applicants required to submit FAFSA. *Unit head:* Kim Tolley, Program Director, Master of Arts in Education, 650-508-3464, E-mail: ktolley@ndnu.edu. *Application contact:* Kim Tolley, Program Director, Master of Arts in Education, 650-508-3464, E-mail: ktolley@ndnu.edu. Website: https://www.ndnu.edu/education-and-leadership/graduate/education/

Oakland City University, School of Education, Oakland City, IN 47660-1099. Offers building level administration (MS Ed); curriculum and instruction (MS Ed, Ed D); education (MS Ed); elementary education (MAT); organizational management (Ed D); secondary education (MAT); superintendency (Ed D). *Accreditation:* NCATE. Terminal master's awarded for partial completion of doctoral program. *Degree requirements:* For master's, thesis; for doctorate, comprehensive exam, thesis/dissertation. *Entrance requirements:* For master's, MAT, minimum GPA of 3.0, interview, resume, letters of recommendation; for doctorate, MAT, GRE, minimum GPA of 3.2, interview, resume, letters of recommendation. *Expenses:* Contact institution. *Faculty research:* Assessment, cultural diversity, teacher education, education leadership.

Ohio Dominican University, Division of Education, Program in Curriculum and Instruction, Columbus, OH 43219-2099. Offers M Ed. *Program availability:* Part-time, evening/weekend, online only, 100% online. *Faculty:* 6 full-time (4 women), 6 part-time/adjunct (3 women). *Students:* 1 (woman) full-time, 31 part-time (29 women); includes 3 minority (1 Black or African American, non-Hispanic/Latino; 2 Two or more races, non-Hispanic/Latino). Average age 33. 13 applicants, 54% accepted, 7 enrolled. In 2018, 17 master's awarded. *Entrance requirements:* For master's, bachelor's degree from regionally-accredited institution; teaching certificate/license; currently teaching or have access to an academic classroom; minimum undergraduate GPA of 3.0. Additional exam requirements/recommendations for international students: Required—TOEFL (minimum score 550 paper-based), IELTS (minimum score 6.5). *Application deadline:* For fall admission, 8/15 for domestic students, 6/10 for international students; for spring admission, 1/4 for domestic students, 11/2 for international students; for summer admission, 5/30 for domestic students. Applications are processed on a rolling basis. Application fee: $25. Electronic applications accepted. *Expenses:* $538/credit hour tuition, $225/semester fees. *Financial support:* Applicants required to submit FAFSA. *Unit head:* Dr. JoAnn Hohenbrink, Director of Graduate Education Programs, 614-251-4759, E-mail: hohenbrj@ohiodominican.edu. *Application contact:* John W. Naughton, Vice President for Enrollment and Student Success, 614-251-4721, Fax: 614-251-6654, E-mail: grad@ohiodominican.edu. Website: http://www.ohiodominican.edu/academics/graduate/master-of-education/curriculum-instruction

Ohio University, Graduate College, Gladys W. and David H. Patton College of Education and Human Services, Department of Teacher Education, Athens, OH 45701-2979. Offers adolescent to young adult education (M Ed); curriculum and instruction (M Ed, PhD); early childhood/special education (M Ed); intervention specialist/mild-moderate needs (M Ed); intervention specialist/moderate-intensive needs (M Ed); middle childhood education (M Ed); reading education (M Ed). *Program availability:* Part-time, evening/weekend. *Degree requirements:* For master's, thesis or alternative; for doctorate, comprehensive exam, thesis/dissertation. *Entrance requirements:* For master's, GRE General Test or MAT (if GPA is below 2.9); for doctorate, GRE General Test, minimum GPA of 3.4, work experience. Additional exam requirements/recommendations for international students: Required—TOEFL (minimum score 550 paper-based; 80 iBT) or IELTS (minimum score 6.5). Electronic applications accepted. *Faculty research:* Cognition literacy, character education, teacher's education reform, disabilities.

Ohio Valley University, School of Graduate Education, Vienna, WV 26105-8000. Offers curriculum and instruction (M Ed). *Program availability:* Online learning. *Entrance requirements:* For master's, 2 letters of recommendation, official transcripts from all previous institutions, essay, bachelor's degree.

Oklahoma State University, College of Education, Health and Aviation, School of Teaching and Curriculum Leadership, Stillwater, OK 74078. Offers MS, PhD. *Program availability:* Part-time. *Entrance requirements:* For master's and doctorate, GRE or GMAT. Additional exam requirements/recommendations for international students: Required—TOEFL (minimum score 550 paper-based; 79 iBT). Electronic applications accepted. *Expenses: Tuition,* area resident: Full-time $4148. Tuition, state resident: full-time $4148. Tuition, nonresident: full-time $10,517. *International tuition:* $10,517 full-time. *Required fees:* $4394; $2929 per credit hour. Tuition and fees vary according to course load and program.

Old Dominion University, Darden College of Education, Doctoral Program in Curriculum and Instruction, Norfolk, VA 23529. Offers PhD. *Program availability:* Part-time, evening/weekend. *Degree requirements:* For doctorate, comprehensive exam, thesis/dissertation. *Entrance requirements:* For doctorate, GRE, letters of recommendation; minimum undergraduate GPA of 2.8, graduate 3.2. Additional exam requirements/recommendations for international students: Required—TOEFL (minimum score 600 paper-based). Electronic applications accepted. *Faculty research:* Curriculum change, language arts, library science, multicultural education, foundations in education.

Old Dominion University, Darden College of Education, Program in Physical Education, Curriculum and Instruction Emphasis, Norfolk, VA 23529. Offers human movement sciences (PhD), including health and sport pedagogy; physical education (MS Ed), including adapted physical education, coaching education, curriculum and instruction. *Program availability:* Part-time, evening/weekend. *Degree requirements:* For master's, comprehensive exam (for some programs), thesis or alternative, internship, research project. *Entrance requirements:* For master's, GRE, PRAXIS tests (for licensure only), minimum GPA of 2.8 overall, 3.0 in major. Additional exam requirements/recommendations for international students: Required—TOEFL (minimum score 500 paper-based; 97 iBT). Electronic applications accepted. *Faculty research:* Motor development, physical activity and fitness, motivation and learning in physical education, curriculum and instruction, adapted physical education.

Olivet Nazarene University, Graduate School, Division of Education, Program in Curriculum and Instruction, Bourbonnais, IL 60914. Offers MAE. *Program availability:* Evening/weekend. *Degree requirements:* For master's, thesis or alternative.

Oral Roberts University, School of Education, Tulsa, OK 74171. Offers Christian school administration (K-12) (MA Ed, Ed D); college and higher education administration (Ed D); curriculum and instruction (MA Ed); initial teaching with alternative licensure (MAT); initial teaching with licensure (MAT); public school administration (K-12) (MA Ed, Ed D). *Accreditation:* NCATE. *Program availability:* Part-time, online learning. *Degree requirements:* For master's, comprehensive exam, thesis optional; for doctorate, comprehensive exam, thesis/dissertation. *Entrance requirements:* For master's, GRE General Test or MAT (minimum score in 80th percentile or higher); Oklahoma general education or subject area test (for MAT), minimum GPA of 3.0, bachelor's degree from regionally-accredited institution; for doctorate, minimum GPA of 3.0, master's degree from regionally-accredited institution. Electronic applications accepted. Application fee is waived when completed online. *Expenses:* Contact institution. *Faculty research:* Teacher effectiveness, college success in high achieving African-Americans, professional development practices.

Ottawa University, Graduate Studies-Arizona, Program in Education, Ottawa, KS 66067-3399. Offers community college counseling (MA); curriculum and instruction (MA); early childhood (MA); education intervention (MA); education leadership (MA); education technology (MA); Montessori early childhood education (MA); Montessori elementary education (MA); professional development (MA); school guidance counseling (MA); special education - cross categorical (MA). Programs offered in Mesa, Phoenix, Tempe and West Valley, AZ. *Accreditation:* NCATE. *Program availability:* Part-time. *Degree requirements:* For master's, thesis or alternative. *Entrance requirements:* For master's, minimum undergraduate GPA of 3.0, copy of current state certification or teaching license. Additional exam requirements/recommendations for international students: Required—TOEFL (minimum score 550 paper-based). Electronic applications accepted. *Expenses:* Contact institution.

Our Lady of the Lake University, College of Professional Studies, Program in Curriculum and Instruction, San Antonio, TX 78207-4689. Offers integrated science teaching (M Ed). *Program availability:* Part-time, evening/weekend. *Faculty:* 1 (woman) full-time, 1 (woman) part-time/adjunct. *Students:* 5 full-time (all women), 7 part-time (4 women); includes 10 minority (all Hispanic/Latino). Average age 34. 9 applicants, 100% accepted, 6 enrolled. In 2018, 1 master's awarded. *Degree requirements:* For master's, comprehensive exam. *Entrance requirements:* For master's, GRE General Test or MAT, official transcripts demonstrating bachelor's degree with minimum cumulative GPA of 2.75, personal statement, 2 references, completed FERPA Consent to Release Education Records and Information form, interview. Additional exam requirements/recommendations for international students: Required—TOEFL. *Application deadline:* For fall admission, 6/15 for domestic and international students; for spring admission, 11/15 for domestic and international students; for summer admission, 4/15 for domestic and international students. Applications are processed on a rolling basis. Application fee: $40 ($50 for international students). Electronic applications accepted. Application fee is waived when completed online. *Expenses: Tuition:* Full-time $16,326; part-time $907 per credit. *Financial support:* In 2018–19, 11 students received support. Federal Work-Study, scholarships/grants, unspecified assistantships, and tuition discounts available. Support available to part-time students. Financial award application deadline: 5/1; financial award applicants required to submit FAFSA. *Faculty research:* Multicultural Issues, technology integration, mentoring teachers, teacher retention. *Unit head:* Dr. Alycia Maurer, Chair, Education Department, 210-434-6711 Ext. 7152, E-mail: admaurer@ollusa.edu. *Application contact:* Office of Graduate Admissions, 210-431-3995, Fax: 210-431-3945, E-mail: gradadm@lake.ollusa.edu. Website: http://www.ollusa.edu/s/1190/hybrid/default-hybrid-ollu.aspx?sid-1190&gid-1&pgid-7883

Pacific Lutheran University, School of Education and Kinesiology, Program in Initial Teaching Certification, Tacoma, WA 98447. Offers MAE. *Accreditation:* NCATE. *Program availability:* Part-time, evening/weekend. *Degree requirements:* For master's, comprehensive exam, thesis optional. *Entrance requirements:* For master's, WEST-B or WEST-B Exemption (or CBEST and/or PRAXIS for out-of-state applicants), interview. Additional exam requirements/recommendations for international students: Required—TOEFL (minimum score 550 paper-based; 88 iBT), ACTFL (American Council on the Teaching of Foreign Languages) oral proficiency exam. Electronic applications accepted. *Expenses:* Contact institution.

Park University, School of Graduate and Professional Studies, Kansas City, MO 54105. Offers adult education (M Ed); business and government leadership (Graduate Certificate); business, government, and global society (MPA); communication and leadership (MA); creative and life writing (Graduate Certificate); disaster and emergency management (MPA, Graduate Certificate); educational leadership (M Ed); finance (MBA, Graduate Certificate); general business (MBA); global business (Graduate Certificate); healthcare administration (MHA); healthcare services management and leadership (Graduate Certificate); international business (MBA); language and literacy (M Ed), including English for speakers of other languages, special reading teacher/literacy coach; leadership of international healthcare organizations (Graduate Certificate); management information systems (MBA, Graduate Certificate); music performance (ADP, Graduate Certificate), including cello (MM, ADP), piano (MM, ADP), viola (MM, ADP), violin (MM, ADP); nonprofit and community services management (MPA); nonprofit leadership (Graduate Certificate); performance (MM), including cello (MM, ADP), piano (MM, ADP), viola (MM, ADP), violin (MM, ADP); public management (MPA); social work (MSW); teacher leadership (M Ed), including curriculum and assessment, instructional leader. *Program availability:* Part-time, evening/weekend, online learning. *Degree requirements:* For master's, comprehensive exam (for some programs), thesis (for some programs), internship (for some programs); exam (for some programs). *Entrance requirements:* For master's, GRE or GMAT (for some programs), teacher certification (for some M Ed programs), letters of recommendation, essay, resume (for some programs). Additional exam requirements/recommendations for international students: Required—TOEFL (minimum score 550 paper-based; 79 iBT), IELTS (minimum score 6). Electronic applications accepted.

Penn State Harrisburg, Graduate School, School of Behavioral Sciences and Education, Middletown, PA 17057. Offers adult education in the health and medical professions (Certificate); applied behavior analysis (MA); applied clinical psychology (MA); applied psychological research (MA); community psychology and social change (MA); English as a second language (ESL) program specialist and leadership (Certificate); health education (M Ed); lifelong learning and adult education (M Ed, D Ed); literacy education (M Ed); literacy leadership (Certificate); psychology: applications in clinical psychology (Certificate); psychology: health psychology (Certificate); teaching and curriculum (M Ed); training and development (M Ed, Certificate). *Program availability:* Part-time, evening/weekend.

Penn State University Park, Graduate School, College of Education, Department of Curriculum and Instruction, University Park, PA 16802. Offers M Ed, MS, PhD, Certificate. *Accreditation:* NCATE.

Penn State York, Graduate School, York, PA 17403. Offers ESL specialist (Certificate); teaching and curriculum (M Ed). *Expenses:* Contact institution.

Pensacola Christian College, Graduate Studies, Pensacola, FL 32503-2267. Offers business administration (MBA); curriculum and instruction (MS, Ed D, Ed S); dramatics

(MFA); educational leadership (MS, Ed D, Ed S); graphic design (MA, MFA); music (MA); nursing (MSN); performance studies (MA); studio art (MA, MFA).

Peru State College, Graduate Programs, Program in Education, Peru, NE 68421. Offers curriculum and instruction (MS Ed). *Accreditation:* NCATE. *Program availability:* Part-time. *Degree requirements:* For master's, comprehensive exam (for some programs), thesis optional.

Piedmont College, School of Education, Demorest, GA 30535. Offers art education (MAT); curriculum and instruction (Ed D, Ed S); early childhood education (MA, MAT); middle grades education (MA, MAT); music education (MAT); secondary education (MA, MAT); special education (MA, MAT). *Program availability:* Part-time, evening/weekend. *Students:* 496 full-time (416 women), 650 part-time (560 women); includes 185 minority (137 Black or African American, non-Hispanic/Latino; 2 American Indian or Alaska Native, non-Hispanic/Latino; 13 Asian, non-Hispanic/Latino; 31 Hispanic/Latino; 1 Native Hawaiian or other Pacific Islander, non-Hispanic/Latino; 1 Two or more races, non-Hispanic/Latino). Average age 37. 483 applicants, 89% accepted, 372 enrolled. In 2018, 275 master's, 10 doctorates, 229 other advanced degrees awarded. *Degree requirements:* For master's, thesis, field experience in the classroom teaching; for doctorate, thesis/dissertation. *Entrance requirements:* For master's, GRE General Test, MAT; for Ed S, minimum graduate GPA of 3.5, valid teaching certificate. Additional exam requirements/recommendations for international students: Required—TOEFL (minimum score 550 paper-based). *Application deadline:* For fall admission, 7/15 for domestic students; for spring admission, 12/1 for domestic students. Applications are processed on a rolling basis. Electronic applications accepted. *Expenses: Tuition:* Full-time $9738; part-time $541 per credit. *Required fees:* $200 per semester. *Financial support:* Career-related internships or fieldwork, Federal Work-Study, and unspecified assistantships available. Support available to part-time students. Financial award applicants required to submit FAFSA. *Unit head:* Dr. R.D. Nordgren, Dean, 706-778-3000 Ext. 1201, Fax: 706-776-9608, E-mail: rdnordgren@piedmont.edu. *Application contact:* Kathleen Carter, Director of Graduate Enrollment Management, 706-778-8500 Ext. 1181, Fax: 706-778-0150, E-mail: kanderson@piedmont.edu.

Piedmont International University, Graduate School, Winston-Salem, NC 27101-5197. Offers Biblical studies (PhD); curriculum and instruction (M Ed); divinity (M Div); educational leadership (M Ed); leadership (MA, PhD); ministry (MA Min, D Min); non-language track (MABS); PhD preparation track (MABS). *Program availability:* Part-time, online learning. Terminal master's awarded for partial completion of doctoral program. *Degree requirements:* For master's, 2 foreign languages, comprehensive exam, thesis or alternative; for doctorate, 2 foreign languages, comprehensive exam. *Entrance requirements:* For master's, GRE General Test; for doctorate, Hebrew and Greek proficiency, MA. Additional exam requirements/recommendations for international students: Required—TOEFL (minimum score 500 paper-based; 60 iBT). Electronic applications accepted. *Faculty research:* Theological and biblical studies.

Plymouth State University, College of Graduate Studies, Graduate Studies in Education, Program in Higher Education, Plymouth, NH 03264-1595. Offers administrative leadership (Ed D); curriculum and instruction (Ed D).

Point Park University, School of Arts and Sciences, Department of Education, Pittsburgh, PA 15222-1984. Offers adult learning and training (MA); athletic coaching (M Ed); curriculum and instruction (MA); educational administration (MA); leadership and administration (Ed D); secondary education (M Ed); special education grades 7-12 (M Ed); special education PreK-grade 8 (M Ed). *Program availability:* Part-time, evening/weekend, 100% online, blended/hybrid learning. *Degree requirements:* For master's, comprehensive exam (for some programs), thesis or alternative. *Entrance requirements:* For master's, minimum GPA of 3.0, resume, 2 letters of recommendation. Additional exam requirements/recommendations for international students: Required—TOEFL. Electronic applications accepted.

Pontifical Catholic University of Puerto Rico, College of Education, Doctoral Program in Curriculum and Instruction, Ponce, PR 00717-0777. Offers PhD. *Degree requirements:* For doctorate, thesis/dissertation. *Entrance requirements:* For doctorate, EXADEP, GRE General Test or MAT, 3 letters of recommendation.

Pontifical Catholic University of Puerto Rico, College of Education, Master's Program in Curriculum and Instruction, Ponce, PR 00717-0777. Offers M Ed. *Degree requirements:* For master's, comprehensive exam, thesis (for some programs). *Entrance requirements:* For master's, GRE, 2 letters of recommendation, interview, minimum GPA of 2.75.

Post University, Program in Education, Waterbury, CT 06723-2540. Offers curriculum and instruction (M Ed); education (M Ed); educational technology (M Ed); higher education administration (MS); learning design and technology (M Ed); online teaching (M Ed); teaching English to speakers of other languages (TESOL) (M Ed). *Program availability:* Online learning. *Entrance requirements:* For master's, resume. *Expenses: Tuition:* Full-time $8300; part-time $570 per credit. *Required fees:* $140 per term. Tuition and fees vary according to course level, campus/location and program.

Prairie View A&M University, College of Education, Department of Curriculum and Instruction, Prairie View, TX 77446. Offers M Ed, MA Ed, MS Ed. *Accreditation:* NCATE. *Program availability:* Part-time, evening/weekend. *Faculty:* 5 full-time (4 women), 1 (woman) part-time/adjunct. *Students:* 22 full-time (21 women), 11 part-time (10 women); includes 31 minority (30 Black or African American, non-Hispanic/Latino; 1 Hispanic/Latino), 2 international. Average age 31. 17 applicants, 94% accepted, 10 enrolled. In 2018, 24 master's awarded. *Degree requirements:* For master's, comprehensive exam, thesis optional. *Entrance requirements:* For master's, GRE, minimum GPA of 2.5, 3 references. Additional exam requirements/recommendations for international students: Required—TOEFL (minimum score 550 paper-based; 79 iBT). *Application deadline:* For fall admission, 5/1 priority date for domestic and international students; for spring admission, 10/1 priority date for domestic students, 9/1 priority date for international students; for summer admission, 3/1 priority date for domestic students, 2/1 priority date for international students. Applications are processed on a rolling basis. Application fee: $50. Electronic applications accepted. *Expenses: Tuition, area resident:* Full-time $3172; part-time $317 per credit. Tuition, state resident: full-time $3172; part-time $317 per credit. Tuition, nonresident: full-time $7965; part-time $796 per credit. *Required fees:* $4847; $485 per credit. *Financial support:* Career-related internships or fieldwork, institutionally sponsored loans, scholarships/grants, health care benefits, tuition waivers (full and partial), and unspecified assistantships available. Support available to part-time students. Financial award application deadline: 4/1; financial award applicants required to submit FAFSA. *Faculty research:* Metacognitive strategies, emotionally disturbed, language arts, teachers recruit, diversity, recruitment, retention, school collaboration. *Unit head:* Dr. Douglas Butler, Interim Department Head, 936-261-3410, Fax: 936-261-3419, E-mail: dmbutler@pvamu.edu. *Application contact:* Pauline Walker, Administrative Assistant II, Research and Graduate Studies, 936-261-3521, Fax: 936-261-3529, E-mail: gradadmissions@pvamu.edu.

Purdue University, Graduate School, College of Education, Department of Curriculum and Instruction, West Lafayette, IN 47907. Offers agricultural and extension education (MS, MS Ed, PhD, Ed S); art education (PhD); career and technical education (MS Ed, PhD, Ed S); curriculum studies (MS Ed, PhD, Ed S); educational technology (MS Ed, PhD, Ed S); elementary education (MS Ed); family and consumer sciences education (MS Ed, PhD, Ed S); foreign language education (MS Ed, PhD, Ed S); industrial technology (PhD, Ed S); language arts (MS Ed, PhD, Ed S); literacy (MS Ed, PhD, Ed S); mathematics education (MS, MS Ed, PhD, Ed S); science education (MS, MS Ed, PhD, Ed S); social studies education (MS Ed, PhD, Ed S). *Accreditation:* NCATE. *Program availability:* Part-time, evening/weekend, online learning. *Faculty:* 34 full-time (24 women), 3 part-time/adjunct (1 woman). *Students:* 75 full-time (52 women), 357 part-time (271 women); includes 83 minority (29 Black or African American, non-Hispanic/Latino; 1 American Indian or Alaska Native, non-Hispanic/Latino; 14 Asian, non-Hispanic/Latino; 29 Hispanic/Latino; 1 Native Hawaiian or other Pacific Islander, non-Hispanic/Latino; 9 Two or more races, non-Hispanic/Latino), 43 international. Average age 36. 169 applicants, 83% accepted, 102 enrolled. In 2018, 141 master's, 15 doctorates awarded. *Degree requirements:* For master's, thesis optional; for doctorate, thesis/dissertation, oral and written exams; for Ed S, oral presentation, project. *Entrance requirements:* For master's, GRE General Test (if undergraduate GPA is below 3.0), minimum undergraduate GPA of 3.0 or equivalent; for doctorate, GRE General Test (minimum combined verbal and quantitative score of 1000, 300 for new scoring), minimum undergraduate GPA of 3.0 or equivalent; master's degree with minimum GPA of 3.0 or equivalent; for Ed S, GRE General Test (minimum combined verbal and quantitative score of 1000, 300 for new scoring), minimum undergraduate GPA of 3.0 or equivalent; master's degree. Additional exam requirements/recommendations for international students: Required—TOEFL (minimum score 550 paper-based; 77 iBT). *Application deadline:* For fall admission, 12/15 for domestic students, 3/1 for international students; for spring admission, 9/15 for domestic students, 8/1 for international students. Application fee: $60 ($75 for international students). Electronic applications accepted. *Financial support:* Fellowships with full tuition reimbursements, research assistantships with full tuition reimbursements, teaching assistantships with full tuition reimbursements, career-related internships or fieldwork, and tuition waivers (full) available. Support available to part-time students. Financial award application deadline: 3/1; financial award applicants required to submit FAFSA. *Faculty research:* Literacy acquisition and development, teacher beliefs and knowledge, recruitment and retention of underrepresented students, economic education, literacy discourse. *Unit head:* Janet M. Alsup, Head, 765-494-9667, E-mail: alsupj@purdue.edu. *Application contact:* Heather Brinkman, Graduate Contact, 765-494-2345, E-mail: hbrinkma@purdue.edu. Website: http://www.edci.purdue.edu/

Quincy University, Master of Science in Education Programs, Quincy, IL 62301-2699. Offers curriculum and instruction (MS Ed), including bilingual/English as a second language; education studies (MS Ed); leadership (MS Ed); reading education (MS Ed); teacher leader (MS Ed). *Program availability:* Part-time, evening/weekend, online learning. *Degree requirements:* For master's, comprehensive exam (for some programs), thesis optional. *Entrance requirements:* For master's, MAT or GRE, personal resume. Additional exam requirements/recommendations for international students: Required—TOEFL (minimum score 550 paper-based; 79 iBT). Electronic applications accepted. Application fee is waived when completed online.

Randolph College, Programs in Education, Lynchburg, VA 24503. Offers curriculum and instruction (MAT); special education-learning disabilities (M Ed, MAT). *Accreditation:* TEAC. *Entrance requirements:* For master's, minimum GPA of 3.0 in prerequisite education coursework, 2.7 in major or field of interest (MAT); teaching license (M Ed); 2 recommendations; interview.

Regent University, Graduate School, School of Education, Virginia Beach, VA 23464-9800. Offers education (M Ed, Ed D, PhD), including adult education (Ed D, PhD, Ed S), advanced educational leadership (Ed D, PhD, Ed S), character education (Ed D, PhD, Ed S), Christian education leadership (Ed D, PhD, Ed S), Christian school administration (M Ed), curriculum and instruction (Ed D, PhD, Ed S), curriculum and instruction - adult education (M Ed), curriculum and instruction - Christian school (M Ed), curriculum and instruction - gifted and talented (M Ed), curriculum and instruction - STEM education (M Ed), curriculum and instruction - teacher leader (M Ed), discipleship for ministry (M Ed), educational leadership (M Ed), educational psychology (Ed D, PhD, Ed S), educational technology and online learning (Ed D, PhD, Ed S), elementary education (M Ed), exceptional education executive leadership (Ed D, PhD, Ed S), higher education (Ed D, PhD, Ed S), higher education leadership and management (Ed D, PhD, Ed S), instructional design and technology (M Ed), K-12 school leadership (Ed D, PhD, Ed S), K-12 special education (M Ed), leadership in mathematics education (M Ed), reading specialist (M Ed), special education (Ed D, PhD, Ed S), student affairs (M Ed), TESOL - adult education (M Ed), TESOL - K-12 (M Ed); educational specialist (Ed S), including adult education (Ed D, PhD, Ed S), advanced educational leadership (Ed D, PhD, Ed S), character education (Ed D, PhD, Ed S), Christian education leadership (Ed D, PhD, Ed S), curriculum and instruction (Ed D, PhD, Ed S), educational psychology (Ed D, PhD, Ed S), educational technology and online learning (Ed D, PhD, Ed S), exceptional education executive leadership (Ed D, PhD, Ed S), higher education (Ed D, PhD, Ed S), higher education leadership and management (Ed D, PhD, Ed S), K-12 school leadership (Ed D, PhD, Ed S), special education (Ed D, PhD, Ed S). *Accreditation:* TEAC. *Program availability:* Part-time, evening/weekend, 100% online, blended/hybrid learning. *Degree requirements:* For master's, thesis or alternative; for doctorate, comprehensive exam, thesis/dissertation. *Entrance requirements:* For master's, Virginia Communication and Literacy Assessment (VCLA), PRAXIS, college transcripts, writing sample, interview; for doctorate, GRE, writing sample, resume, transcripts, interview. Additional exam requirements/recommendations for international students: Required—TOEFL (minimum score 577 paper-based). Electronic applications accepted. *Expenses:* Contact institution. *Faculty research:* Christian school administration, curriculum and instruction, educational technology and online learning, higher education, special education.

Regis University, College of Contemporary Liberal Studies, Denver, CO 80221-1099. Offers creative writing (MFA); criminology (M Sc); curriculum, instruction and assessment (M Ed); education - teacher leadership (M Ed); educational leadership (M Ed); elementary education (M Ed); literacy (Certificate); reading (M Ed); secondary education (M Ed); special education (M Ed); teacher academic leadership (Certificate); teacher leadership (MA); teacher/educational leadership (M Ed); teaching the linguistically diverse (M Ed). *Program availability:* Part-time, evening/weekend, 100% online, blended/hybrid learning. *Degree requirements:* For master's, thesis (for some programs). *Entrance requirements:* For master's, official transcript reflecting baccalaureate degree awarded from regionally-accredited college or university, work experience, resume, letters of recommendation. Additional exam requirements/recommendations for international students: Required—TOEFL (minimum score 550 paper-based; 82 iBT). Electronic applications accepted. *Expenses:* Contact institution.

Rivier University, School of Graduate Studies, Department of Education, Nashua, NH 03060. Offers curriculum and instruction (M Ed); early childhood education (M Ed); educational administration (M Ed); educational studies (M Ed); elementary education (M Ed); elementary education and general special education (M Ed); emotional and behavioral disorders (M Ed); general social education (M Ed); leadership and learning (Ed D, CAGS); learning disabilities (M Ed); learning disabilities and reading (M Ed); mental health counseling (MA); reading (M Ed); school counseling (M Ed). *Program availability:* Part-time, evening/weekend. *Degree requirements:* For master's, comprehensive exam (for some programs), internships. *Entrance requirements:* For master's, GRE General Test or MAT.

St. Catherine University, Graduate Programs, Program in Education–Curriculum and Instruction, St. Paul, MN 55105. Offers MA. *Program availability:* Part-time, evening/weekend, online learning. *Degree requirements:* For master's, thesis. *Entrance requirements:* For master's, current teaching license, classroom experience, minimum GPA of 3.0. Additional exam requirements/recommendations for international students: Required—Michigan English Language Assessment Battery or TOEFL (minimum score 600 paper-based; 100 iBT). *Expenses:* Contact institution.

St. Francis Xavier University, Graduate Studies, Graduate Studies in Education, Antigonish, NS B2G 2W5, Canada. Offers curriculum and instruction (M Ed); educational administration and leadership (M Ed). *Program availability:* Part-time, online learning. *Degree requirements:* For master's, thesis. *Entrance requirements:* For master's, minimum undergraduate B average, 2 years of teaching experience. *Expenses:* Tuition, area resident: Full-time $7547 Canadian dollars. Tuition, state resident: full-time $7547 Canadian dollars; part-time $804.19 Canadian dollars per course. Tuition, nonresident: full-time $8839 Canadian dollars; part-time $932.49 Canadian dollars per course. *International tuition:* $932.49 Canadian dollars full-time. *Required fees:* $90.20 Canadian dollars; $90.20 Canadian dollars per course. One-time fee: $6 Canadian dollars. Tuition and fees vary according to course load, degree level and program. *Faculty research:* Inclusive education, qualitative research.

St. John's University, The School of Education, Department of Curriculum and Instruction, PhD in Curriculum and Instruction Program, Queens, NY 11439. Offers early childhood (PhD); global education (PhD); STEM education (PhD); teaching, learning, and knowing (PhD). *Program availability:* Part-time-only. *Degree requirements:* For doctorate, comprehensive exam, thesis/dissertation. *Entrance requirements:* For doctorate, teacher certification (or equivalent), at least three years' teaching experience or the equivalent in informal learning environments, master's degree. Additional exam requirements/recommendations for international students: Required—TOEFL. Electronic applications accepted. *Faculty research:* Literacies, early childhood, STEM, school culture, global education.

Saint Joseph's University, College of Arts and Sciences, Graduate Programs in Education, Philadelphia, PA 19131-1395. Offers curriculum supervisor (Certificate); educational leadership (MS, Ed D); elementary education (MS, Certificate); elementary/middle school education (Certificate); organizational development and leadership (MS); principal (Certificate); professional education (MS); reading specialist (MS, Certificate); reading supervisor (Certificate); secondary education (MS, Certificate); special education (MS); special education 7-12 (Certificate); special education PK-8 (Certificate); superintendent's letter of eligibility (Certificate); supervisor of special education (Certificate); teacher of the deaf and hard of hearing (Certificate). *Program availability:* Part-time, evening/weekend, blended/hybrid learning. *Degree requirements:* For master's, thesis or alternative; for doctorate, comprehensive exam, thesis/dissertation. *Entrance requirements:* For master's, 2 letters of recommendation, minimum GPA of 3.0, official transcripts, personal statement; for doctorate, GRE, master's degree from accredited institution, minimum graduate GPA of 3.5, computer competence, interview with program director. Additional exam requirements/recommendations for international students: Required—TOEFL (minimum score 550 paper-based; 80 iBT), IELTS (minimum score 6.5), PTE (minimum score 60). Electronic applications accepted. *Expenses:* Contact institution. *Faculty research:* Factors predicting early mathematics skills for low income children, early child care and development, preschool quality, parent communication and home-school collaboration issues, education of terminally ill children, preparing literacy teachers for urban schools.

Saint Louis University, Graduate Programs, School of Education, Department of Educational Studies, St. Louis, MO 63103. Offers curriculum and instruction (MA, Ed D, PhD); educational foundations (MA, Ed D, PhD); special education (MA); teaching (MAT). *Accreditation:* NCATE. *Program availability:* Part-time. *Degree requirements:* For master's, comprehensive exam; for doctorate, comprehensive exam, thesis/dissertation, preliminary oral and written exams. *Entrance requirements:* For master's, GRE General Test or MAT, letters of recommendation, resume; for doctorate, GRE General Test, letters of recommendation, resumé, goal statement, transcripts. Additional exam requirements/recommendations for international students: Required—TOEFL (minimum score 525 paper-based). Electronic applications accepted. *Faculty research:* Teacher preparation, multicultural issues, children with special needs, qualitative research in education, inclusion.

Saint Vincent College, Program in Education, Latrobe, PA 15650-2690. Offers curriculum and instruction (MS); instructional design and technology (MS); school administration and supervision (MS); special education (MS). *Program availability:* Part-time, evening/weekend. *Degree requirements:* For master's, comprehensive exam. *Entrance requirements:* For master's, GRE (if undergraduate GPA less than 3.0). Additional exam requirements/recommendations for international students: Required—TOEFL (minimum score 550 paper-based). *Faculty research:* Assessment and instructional technology.

Saint Xavier University, Graduate Studies, School of Education, Chicago, IL 60655-3105. Offers counseling (MA); curriculum and instruction (MA); early childhood education (MA); educational administration (MA); elementary education (MA); individualized studies (MA), including educational technology, English as a second language (ESL), ISTEM (integrative science, technology, engineering, and math), science education; music education (MA); reading (MA); secondary education (MA); Spanish education (MA); special education (MA); teaching and leadership (MA). *Accreditation:* NCATE. *Program availability:* Part-time, evening/weekend. *Degree requirements:* For master's, thesis or project. *Entrance requirements:* For master's, minimum GPA of 3.0. *Expenses:* Contact institution.

Salem International University, School of Education, Salem, WV 26426-0500. Offers curriculum and instruction (M Ed); educational leadership (M Ed). *Program availability:* Part-time, evening/weekend, online learning. *Degree requirements:* For master's, comprehensive exam (for some programs), thesis (for some programs). *Entrance requirements:* For master's, GRE, MAT, NTE, 3 letters of recommendation. Additional exam requirements/recommendations for international students: Required—TOEFL (minimum score 550 paper-based). Electronic applications accepted. *Expenses:* Contact institution. *Faculty research:* Improved classroom effectiveness.

Salisbury University, Program in Curriculum and Instruction, Salisbury, MD 21801-6837. Offers curriculum and instruction (M Ed). *Program availability:* Part-time, evening/weekend. *Faculty:* 10 full-time (7 women), 4 part-time/adjunct (3 women). *Students:* 11 full-time (2 women), 83 part-time (67 women); includes 14 minority (7 Black or African American, non-Hispanic/Latino; 1 Asian, non-Hispanic/Latino; 2 Hispanic/Latino; 4 Two or more races, non-Hispanic/Latino). Average age 29. 35 applicants, 80% accepted, 27 enrolled. In 2018, 27 master's awarded. *Entrance requirements:* For master's, transcripts from all colleges and universities attended; personal statement; minimum GPA of 3.0; resume; three letters of recommendation. Additional exam requirements/recommendations for international students: Required—TOEFL (minimum score 550 paper-based; 79 iBT), IELTS (minimum score 6.5). *Application deadline:* For fall admission, 4/1 priority date for domestic and international students; for spring admission, 10/1 priority date for domestic and international students; for summer admission, 4/1 priority date for domestic and international students. Applications are processed on a rolling basis. Application fee: $65. Electronic applications accepted. *Expenses:* Resident - $412 per credit hour; Non-resident - $746 per credit hour; Fees - $108. *Financial support:* In 2018–19, 8 students received support, including 11 teaching assistantships with full tuition reimbursements available (averaging $8,364 per year); career-related internships or fieldwork and scholarships/grants also available. Support available to part-time students. Financial award application deadline: 3/1; financial award applicants required to submit FAFSA. *Faculty research:* Leadership; organizational change; rural education; educational change; public school administration. *Unit head:* Dr. Douglas DeWitt, Graduate Program Director, 410-543-6286, E-mail: dmdewitt@salisbury.edu. *Application contact:* Dr. Douglas DeWitt, Graduate Program Director, 410-543-6286, E-mail: dmdewitt@salisbury.edu. Website: https://www.salisbury.edu/explore-academics/programs/graduate-degree-programs/med-programs/curriculum-instruction-masters/

Sam Houston State University, College of Education, Department of Curriculum and Instruction, Huntsville, TX 77341. Offers curriculum and instruction (M Ed). *Accreditation:* NCATE. *Program availability:* Part-time, evening/weekend. *Degree requirements:* For master's, comprehensive exam, thesis optional; for doctorate, comprehensive exam, thesis/dissertation. *Entrance requirements:* For master's, GRE General Test; for doctorate, GRE General Test, three letters of recommendation, sample of professional work, three years of working experience. Additional exam requirements/recommendations for international students: Required—TOEFL (minimum score 550 paper-based; 79 iBT), IELTS (minimum score 6.5). Electronic applications accepted.

San Diego State University, Graduate and Research Affairs, College of Education, School of Teacher Education, Program in Elementary Curriculum and Instruction, San Diego, CA 92182. Offers MA. *Accreditation:* NCATE. *Program availability:* Evening/weekend. *Entrance requirements:* For master's, GRE General Test, letters of reference. Additional exam requirements/recommendations for international students: Required—TOEFL. Electronic applications accepted.

San Diego State University, Graduate and Research Affairs, College of Education, School of Teacher Education, Program in Secondary Curriculum and Instruction, San Diego, CA 92182. Offers MA. *Accreditation:* NCATE. *Entrance requirements:* For master's, GRE General Test, letters of reference. Additional exam requirements/recommendations for international students: Required—TOEFL. Electronic applications accepted.

San Jose State University, Program in Elementary Education, San Jose, CA 95192-0001. Offers curriculum and instruction (MA); reading (Certificate). *Accreditation:* NCATE. *Degree requirements:* For master's, thesis or alternative. Electronic applications accepted.

Shawnee State University, Program in Curriculum and Instruction, Portsmouth, OH 45662. Offers M Ed. *Accreditation:* NCATE.

Shaw University, Department of Education & Child Development, Raleigh, NC 27601-2399. Offers early childhood education (MS). *Program availability:* Part-time, evening/weekend. *Faculty:* 1 (woman) full-time, 2 part-time/adjunct (both women). *Students:* 1 (woman) full-time, 8 part-time (6 women); includes 5 minority (4 Black or African American, non-Hispanic/Latino; 1 Hispanic/Latino), 1 international. Average age 33. 4 applicants, 100% accepted, 4 enrolled. In 2018, 9 master's awarded. *Degree requirements:* For master's, comprehensive exam, thesis, practicum/internship, PRAXIS II. *Entrance requirements:* For master's, GRE General Test, letters of recommendation. Additional exam requirements/recommendations for international students: Required—TOEFL (minimum score 500 paper-based). *Application deadline:* For fall admission, 4/1 priority date for domestic students, 1/30 priority date for international students; for spring admission, 10/31 priority date for domestic students, 8/30 priority date for international students. Applications are processed on a rolling basis. Application fee: $50. Electronic applications accepted. *Expenses:* Tuition: Full-time $10,404; part-time $578 per credit hour. *Required fees:* $2784; $408 per credit hour. $1023 per semester. *Financial support:* In 2018–19, 14 students received support. Career-related internships or fieldwork, Federal Work-Study, scholarships/grants, and tuition waivers (full) available. Support available to part-time students. Financial award applicants required to submit FAFSA. *Faculty research:* Multicultural education, instructional technology. *Unit head:* Dr. Lucy Wilson, Department Head, 919-546-8322, Fax: 919-546-8531, E-mail: lwilson@shawu.edu. *Application contact:* Dr. Paula Moten-Tolson, Program Coordinator/Asst. Professor, 919-546-8544, Fax: 919-546-8531, E-mail: pmoten@shawu.edu.

Shepherd University, Program in Curriculum and Instruction, Shepherdstown, WV 25443. Offers MA. *Accreditation:* NCATE.

Shippensburg University of Pennsylvania, School of Graduate Studies, College of Education and Human Services, Department of Teacher Education, Shippensburg, PA 17257-2299. Offers curriculum and instruction (M Ed), including biology, early childhood education, elementary education, geography/earth science, history, mathematics, middle school education, modern languages; reading (M Ed). *Accreditation:* NCATE. *Program availability:* Part-time, evening/weekend, 100% online, blended/hybrid learning. *Faculty:* 12 full-time (9 women), 2 part-time/adjunct (0 women). *Students:* 10 full-time (8 women), 68 part-time (64 women); includes 7 minority (2 Black or African American, non-Hispanic/Latino; 4 Hispanic/Latino; 1 Two or more races, non-Hispanic/Latino). Average age 31. 41 applicants, 73% accepted, 19 enrolled. In 2018, 34 master's awarded. *Degree requirements:* For master's, comprehensive exam (for some programs), thesis optional, practicum or internship; capstone seminar (for some programs). *Entrance requirements:* For master's, MAT or GRE (if GPA less than 2.75), interview, 3 letters of reference, questionnaire of teaching background and future goals, resume. Additional exam requirements/recommendations for international students: Required—TOEFL (minimum score 550 paper-based; 68 iBT), IELTS (minimum score 6), TOEFL (minimum score 550 paper-based, 68 iBT) or IELTS (minimum score 6). *Application deadline:* For fall admission, 4/1 priority date for domestic students, 4/30 for international students; for spring admission, 9/1 priority date for domestic students, 9/30 for international students; for summer admission, 2/1 priority date for domestic students. Applications are processed on a rolling basis. Application fee: $45. Electronic applications accepted. *Expenses:* Tuition, state resident: part-time $516 per credit. Tuition, nonresident: part-time $750 per credit. *Required fees:* $149 per credit. *Financial support:* In 2018–19, 5 students received support. Career-related internships or fieldwork, scholarships/grants, unspecified assistantships, and resident hall director and student payroll positions available. Support available to part-time students. Financial award application deadline: 3/1; financial award applicants required to submit FAFSA. *Unit head:* Dr. Christine A. Royce, Chairperson, 717-477-1688, Fax: 717-477-4046, E-mail: caroyc@ship.edu. *Application contact:* Maya T. Mapp, Director of Admissions, 717-477-1231, Fax: 717-477-4016, E-mail: mtmapp@ship.edu. Website: http://www.ship.edu/teacher/

Simon Fraser University, Office of Graduate Studies and Postdoctoral Fellows, Faculty of Education, Programs in Curriculum and Instruction, Burnaby, BC V5A 1S6, Canada. Offers curriculum and instruction (M Ed); curriculum and instruction foundations (M Ed, MA); curriculum theory and implementation (PhD); educational practice (M Ed); philosophy of education (PhD). *Degree requirements:* For master's, comprehensive

exam (for some programs), thesis (for some programs); for doctorate, comprehensive exam, thesis/dissertation. *Entrance requirements:* For master's, minimum GPA of 3.0 (on scale of 4.33) or 3.33 based on last 60 credits of undergraduate courses; for doctorate, minimum GPA of 3.5 (on scale of 4.33). Additional exam requirements/recommendations for international students: Recommended—TOEFL (minimum score 580 paper-based; 93 iBT), IELTS (minimum score 7), TWE (minimum score 5). Electronic applications accepted. *Faculty research:* Philosophy of education, applied and comparative epistemology, ethics and moral education, critical multicultural practices.

Simpson University, School of Education, Redding, CA 96003-8606. Offers education (MA), including curriculum, education leadership; education and preliminary administrative services credential (MA); education and preliminary teaching credential (MA); teaching (MA). *Program availability:* Part-time, evening/weekend. *Degree requirements:* For master's, thesis optional. *Entrance requirements:* For master's, statement of purpose, 2 professional references, professional essay, interview. Additional exam requirements/recommendations for international students: Required—TOEFL (minimum score 550 paper-based). Electronic applications accepted. *Expenses:* Contact institution.

Sitting Bull College, Graduate Programs, Fort Yates, ND 58538-9701. Offers curriculum and instruction (M Ed); environmental science (MS). *Entrance requirements:* For master's, GRE, official transcripts from all previous colleges and universities, three letters of recommendation, curriculum vitae, letter of intent.

Sonoma State University, School of Education, Rohnert Park, CA 94928-3609. Offers administrative services (Credential); curriculum, teaching, and learning (MA); early childhood education (MA); education specialist (Credential); educational leadership (MA); multiple subject (Credential); reading and literacy (MA, Credential); single subject (Credential); special education (MA). *Accreditation:* NCATE. *Program availability:* Part-time, evening/weekend. *Entrance requirements:* For master's, minimum GPA of 2.5. Additional exam requirements/recommendations for international students: Required—TOEFL (minimum score 500 paper-based).

South Dakota State University, Graduate School, College of Education and Human Sciences, Department of Teaching, Learning and Leadership, Brookings, SD 57007. Offers agricultural education (MS); curriculum and instruction (M Ed); educational administration (M Ed). *Program availability:* Part-time, evening/weekend, online learning. *Degree requirements:* For master's, portfolio, oral exam. *Entrance requirements:* For master's, minimum GPA of 2.75. Additional exam requirements/recommendations for international students: Required—TOEFL (minimum score 550 paper-based; 80 iBT). *Faculty research:* Inclusion school climate, K-12 reform and restructuring, rural development, ESL, leadership.

Southeastern Louisiana University, College of Education, Department of Teaching and Learning, Hammond, LA 70402. Offers curriculum and instruction (M Ed); elementary education (MAT); special education (M Ed); special education: early interventionist (MAT). *Accreditation:* NCATE. *Program availability:* Part-time. *Faculty:* 10 full-time (9 women). *Students:* 23 full-time (18 women), 118 part-time (102 women); includes 20 minority (14 Black or African American, non-Hispanic/Latino; 3 Hispanic/Latino; 3 Two or more races, non-Hispanic/Latino), 1 international. Average age 37. 78 applicants, 71% accepted, 40 enrolled. In 2018, 12 master's awarded. *Degree requirements:* For master's, comprehensive exam (for some programs), thesis (for some programs), action research project, oral defense of research project, portfolio, teaching certificate, minimum cumulative GPA of 3.0. *Entrance requirements:* For master's, GRE (verbal and quantitative), PRAXIS (for MAT), Prospective Education Candidate (PEC) self-assessment survey; competency on a technology performance assessment in education or three-hour graduate-level technology course; orientation seminar. Additional exam requirements/recommendations for international students: Required—TOEFL (minimum score 500 paper-based; 61 iBT). *Application deadline:* For fall admission, 7/15 priority date for domestic students, 6/1 priority date for international students; for spring admission, 12/1 priority date for domestic students, 10/1 priority date for international students. Applications are processed on a rolling basis. Application fee: $20 ($30 for international students). Electronic applications accepted. *Expenses: Tuition, area resident:* Full-time $6684. Tuition, state resident: full-time $6684. Tuition, nonresident: full-time $19,162. *Required fees:* $2097. *Financial support:* In 2018–19, 7 students received support, including 1 fellowship with tuition reimbursement available (averaging $3,500 per year); career-related internships or fieldwork, Federal Work-Study, institutionally sponsored loans, scholarships/grants, and unspecified assistantships also available. Support available to part-time students. Financial award application deadline: 5/1; financial award applicants required to submit FAFSA. *Faculty research:* Early childhood education, STEM education, literacy, special education early intervention, math education. *Total annual research expenditures:* $404,225. *Unit head:* Dr. Colleen Klein-Ezell, Department Head, 985-549-2221, Fax: 985-549-5009, E-mail: colleen.klein-ezell@southeastern.edu. *Application contact:* Dr. Colleen Klein-Ezell, Department Head, 985-549-2221, Fax: 985-549-5009, E-mail: colleen.klein-ezell@southeastern.edu.
Website: http://www.southeastern.edu/acad_research/depts/teach_lrn/index.html

Southeastern University, College of Education, Lakeland, FL 33801-6099. Offers curriculum and instruction (Ed D); educational leadership (M Ed); elementary education (M Ed); exceptional student education (M Ed); exceptional student education/educational therapy (M Ed); kinesiology (M Ed); organizational leadership (Ed D); reading education (M Ed); teaching English to speakers of other languages (M Ed). Electronic applications accepted.

Southern Arkansas University–Magnolia, School of Graduate Studies, Magnolia, AR 71753. Offers agriculture (MS); business administration (MBA), including agribusiness, social entrepreneurship, supply chain management; clinical and mental health counseling (MS); computer and information sciences (MS), including cyber security and privacy, data science, information technology; gifted and talented (M Ed), including curriculum and instruction, educational administration and supervision, gifted and talented P-8/7-12, instructional specialist P-4; higher, adult and lifelong education (M Ed); kinesiology (M Ed), including coaching; library media and information specialist (M Ed); public administration (MPA); school counseling K-12 (M Ed); student affairs and college counseling (M Ed); teaching (MAT). *Accreditation:* NCATE. *Program availability:* Part-time, 100% online, blended/hybrid learning. *Faculty:* 36 full-time (21 women), 32 part-time/adjunct (15 women). *Students:* 164 full-time (77 women), 762 part-time (510 women); includes 192 minority (163 Black or African American, non-Hispanic/Latino; 7 American Indian or Alaska Native, non-Hispanic/Latino; 13 Asian, non-Hispanic/Latino; 1 Hispanic/Latino; 8 Two or more races, non-Hispanic/Latino), 213 international. Average age 28. 363 applicants, 100% accepted, 237 enrolled. In 2018, 716 master's awarded. *Degree requirements:* For master's, comprehensive exam (for some programs), thesis optional. *Entrance requirements:* For master's, GRE, MAT or GMAT, minimum GPA of 2.5. Additional exam requirements/recommendations for international students: Required—TOEFL (minimum score 550 paper-based), IELTS (minimum score 6). *Application deadline:* For fall admission, 8/1 for domestic and international students; for spring admission, 12/1 for domestic students, 11/15 for international students; for summer admission, 4/1 for domestic students, 5/10 for international students. Applications are processed on a rolling basis. Application fee: $25 ($90 for international students). Electronic applications accepted. *Expenses: Tuition, area resident:* Full-time $5130; part-time $3420 per year. Tuition, state resident: full-time $5130; part-time $3420 per year. Tuition, nonresident: full-time $7866; part-time $5244 per year. *International tuition:* $7866 full-time. *Required fees:* $1052; $710 per unit. Tuition and fees vary according to course load. *Financial support:* Career-related internships or fieldwork, Federal Work-Study, scholarships/grants, tuition waivers (full), and unspecified assistantships available. Financial award applicants required to submit FAFSA. *Faculty research:* Alternative certification for teachers, supervision of instruction, instructional leadership, counseling. *Unit head:* Dr. Kim Bloss, Dean, School of Graduate Studies, 870-235-4150, Fax: 870-235-5227, E-mail: kkbloss@saumag.edu. *Application contact:* Talia Jett, Admissions Coordinator, 870-2355450, Fax: 870-235-5227, E-mail: taliajett@saumag.edu.
Website: http://www.saumag.edu/graduate

Southern Illinois University Carbondale, Graduate School, College of Education and Human Services, Department of Curriculum and Instruction, Carbondale, IL 62901-4701. Offers MS Ed, PhD. *Accreditation:* NCATE. *Program availability:* Part-time. *Degree requirements:* For doctorate, variable foreign language requirement, thesis/dissertation. *Entrance requirements:* For master's, minimum GPA of 2.7; for doctorate, GRE, minimum GPA of 3.25. Additional exam requirements/recommendations for international students: Required—TOEFL. *Faculty research:* Early childhood, science/environmental education, teacher education, instructional development/technology, reading.

Southern Illinois University Edwardsville, Graduate School, School of Education, Health, and Human Behavior, Department of Curriculum and Instruction, Program in Curriculum and Instruction, Edwardsville, IL 62026. Offers MS Ed. *Accreditation:* NCATE. *Program availability:* Part-time, evening/weekend. *Degree requirements:* For master's, thesis (for some programs), final exam/paper. *Entrance requirements:* For master's, teaching certificate. Additional exam requirements/recommendations for international students: Required—TOEFL (minimum score 550 paper-based; 79 iBT), IELTS (minimum score 6.5). Electronic applications accepted.

Southern New Hampshire University, School of Education, Manchester, NH 03106-1045. Offers curriculum and instruction (M Ed), including dyslexia studies and language-based learning disabilities, educational leadership, reading, special education, technology integration; dyslexia studies and language-based learning disabilities (Certificate); early childhood and special education (M Ed); educational leadership (M Ed, Ed D); educational studies (M Ed); elementary and special education (M Ed); field based education (M Ed); higher education administration (MS); teaching English as a foreign language (MS). *Program availability:* Part-time, evening/weekend, online learning. *Degree requirements:* For master's, comprehensive exam (for some programs), thesis or alternative. *Entrance requirements:* For master's, PRAXIS I, minimum GPA of 2.75. Additional exam requirements/recommendations for international students: Required—TOEFL (minimum score 550 paper-based). Electronic applications accepted. *Expenses:* Contact institution.

Southwestern Adventist University, Education Department, Keene, TX 76059. Offers curriculum and instruction with reading emphasis (M Ed); educational leadership (M Ed). *Program availability:* Part-time, evening/weekend. *Degree requirements:* For master's, thesis or alternative, professional paper. *Entrance requirements:* For master's, GRE General Test.

Southwestern Assemblies of God University, Thomas F. Harrison School of Graduate Studies, Program in Education, Waxahachie, TX 75165-5735. Offers Christian school administration (MS); curriculum development (MS); early education administration (M Ed); middle and secondary education (M Ed). *Degree requirements:* For master's, comprehensive written and oral exams. *Entrance requirements:* For master's, GRE General Test, minimum GPA of 2.5. Electronic applications accepted.

Southwestern College, Education Programs, Winfield, KS 67156-2499. Offers curriculum and instruction (M Ed); early childhood education (M Ed); educational leadership (Ed D), including higher education leadership, PK-12 education leadership; special education (M Ed), including high-incidence disabilities, low-incidence disabilities; teaching (MA). *Accreditation:* NCATE. *Program availability:* Part-time, evening/weekend, 100% online, blended/hybrid learning. *Faculty:* 7 full-time (5 women), 14 part-time/adjunct (12 women). *Students:* 6 full-time (5 women), 79 part-time (54 women); includes 11 minority (4 Black or African American, non-Hispanic/Latino; 2 American Indian or Alaska Native, non-Hispanic/Latino; 1 Asian, non-Hispanic/Latino; 3 Hispanic/Latino; 1 Two or more races, non-Hispanic/Latino), 4 international. Average age 38. 31 applicants, 74% accepted, 18 enrolled. In 2018, 24 master's, 8 doctorates awarded. *Degree requirements:* For master's, practicum, portfolio; for doctorate, thesis/dissertation, professional portfolio. *Entrance requirements:* For master's, baccalaureate degree, minimum GPA of 3.0, valid teaching certificate (for special education); for doctorate, GRE if no master's degree, baccalaureate degree with minimum GPA of 3.25 and current teaching experience, or master's degree with minimum GPA of 3.5. Additional exam requirements/recommendations for international students: Required—TOEFL (minimum score 60 paper-based; 70 iBT), IELTS (minimum score 5.5). *Application deadline:* Applications are processed on a rolling basis. Application fee: $40. Electronic applications accepted. *Expenses:* Masters programs are $606 per credit hour, $535 per online credit hour; doctorate program is $639 per credit hour. *Financial support:* In 2018–19, 13 students received support. Unspecified assistantships and employee tuition waivers available. Financial award applicants required to submit FAFSA. *Unit head:* J.K. Campbell, Education Division Chair, 620-229-6115, E-mail: JK.Campbell@sckans.edu. *Application contact:* Jen Caughron, Director of Enrollment Services & Marketing, 888-684-5335 Ext. 3312, Fax: 888-684-5218, E-mail: jennifer.caughron@sckans.edu.
Website: http://www.sckans.edu/graduate/education-med/

Stanford University, Graduate School of Education, Program in Curriculum and Teacher Education, Stanford, CA 94305-2004. Offers MA. *Expenses: Tuition:* Full-time $50,703; part-time $32,970 per year. *Required fees:* $651.

State University of New York at Fredonia, College of Education, Fredonia, NY 14063-1136. Offers curriculum and instruction (MS Ed); literacy education (MS Ed), including birth-grade 12, grades 5-12; music education (M Mus), including k-12; TESOL (MS Ed). *Accreditation:* NCATE. *Program availability:* Part-time. *Faculty:* 16 full-time (14 women), 13 part-time/adjunct (11 women). *Students:* 39 full-time (33 women), 44 part-time (36 women); includes 5 minority (1 Asian, non-Hispanic/Latino; 3 Hispanic/Latino; 1 Two or more races, non-Hispanic/Latino), 4 international. Average age 27. 44 applicants, 89% accepted, 34 enrolled. In 2018, 25 master's awarded. *Degree requirements:* For master's, thesis. *Entrance requirements:* For master's, GRE, minimum undergraduate GPA of 3.0. Additional exam requirements/recommendations for international students: Required—TOEFL (minimum score 79 iBT), IELTS (minimum score 6.5). *Application deadline:* For fall admission, 4/1 priority date for domestic and international students; for spring admission, 11/1 priority date for domestic students, 11/1 for international students. Applications are processed on a rolling basis. Application fee: $75. Electronic applications accepted. *Expenses:* Tuition, state resident: full-time $6870; part-time $462 per credit hour. Tuition, nonresident: full-time $16,650; part-time $944 per credit hour. *International tuition:* $16,650 full-time. *Required fees:* $25; $2 per credit hour. $1 per

semester. *Financial support:* In 2018–19, 13 students received support. Unspecified assistantships available. Financial award application deadline: 3/15; financial award applicants required to submit FAFSA. *Faculty research:* Positive behavioral intervention and support (PBIS), place-based science education, peer support for education, primary source material for social studies education, policies and practices in learning English language. *Unit head:* Dr. Christine Givner, Dean, 716-673-3311, E-mail: christine.givner@fredonia.edu. *Application contact:* Wendy S. Dunst, Interim Graduate Recruitment and Admissions Associate, 716-673-3808, Fax: 716-673-3712, E-mail: wendy.dunst@fredonia.edu.
Website: http://www.fredonia.edu/coe/

State University of New York at Oswego, Graduate Studies, School of Education, Department of Curriculum and Instruction, Oswego, NY 13126. Offers adolescence education (MST); art education (MAT); childhood education (MST); curriculum and instruction (MS Ed); literacy education (MS Ed); special education (MS Ed). *Program availability:* Part-time, evening/weekend. *Degree requirements:* For master's, comprehensive exam (for some programs), thesis optional. *Entrance requirements:* For master's, GRE General Test, minimum GPA of 2.7, provisional teaching certificate. Additional exam requirements/recommendations for international students: Required—TOEFL (minimum score 560 paper-based). *Faculty research:* Classroom applications for microcomputers; classroom questioning, wait-time, and achievement; values clarification and academic achievement.

State University of New York at Plattsburgh, School of Education, Health, and Human Services, Program in Teacher Education: Teaching and Learning, Plattsburgh, NY 12901-2681. Offers MS Ed. *Program availability:* Part-time, evening/weekend. *Entrance requirements:* For master's, minimum GPA of 2.5. Additional exam requirements/recommendations for international students: Required—TOEFL.

State University of New York College at Potsdam, School of Education and Professional Studies, Program in Curriculum and Instruction, Potsdam, NY 13676. Offers childhood education (MST); curriculum and instruction (MS Ed). *Accreditation:* NCATE. *Program availability:* Online learning. *Degree requirements:* For master's, thesis (for some programs). *Entrance requirements:* For master's, minimum GPA of 2.75 in last 60 credit hours of undergraduate study. Additional exam requirements/recommendations for international students: Required—TOEFL (minimum score 550 paper-based; 80 iBT), IELTS (minimum score 6). Electronic applications accepted.

Syracuse University, School of Education, Programs in Instructional Design, Development, and Evaluation, Syracuse, NY 13244. Offers MS, PhD, CAS. *Program availability:* Part-time. *Students:* Average age 34. *Degree requirements:* For master's, thesis or alternative; for doctorate, comprehensive exam, thesis/dissertation. *Entrance requirements:* For master's, GRE or MAT, baccalaureate degree from regionally-accredited college/university, statement of goals, three letters of recommendation, transcripts; for doctorate, GRE, master's degree in instructional design or equivalent, statement of goals, three letters of recommendation, transcripts; for CAS, GRE (recommended), master's degree in instructional design or equivalent, statement of goals, three letters of recommendation, transcripts. Additional exam requirements/recommendations for international students: Required—TOEFL (minimum score 100 iBT). *Application deadline:* For fall admission, 1/15 priority date for domestic and international students; for spring admission, 10/15 priority date for domestic and international students. Applications are processed on a rolling basis. Application fee: $75. Electronic applications accepted. *Financial support:* Fellowships with full tuition reimbursements, research assistantships, teaching assistantships, career-related internships or fieldwork, and scholarships/grants available. Financial award application deadline: 1/15. *Faculty research:* Digital media production, technologies for instructional settings, strategies in educational project management, educational technology in international settings. *Unit head:* Dr. Jing Lei, Chair, 315-443-3703, E-mail: jlei@syr.edu. *Application contact:* Speranza Migliore, Graduate Admissions Recruiter, 315-443-2505, E-mail: gradrcrt@syr.edu.
Website: http://soe.syr.edu/academic/Instructional_Design_Development_and_Evaluation/

Syracuse University, School of Education, Programs in Teaching and Curriculum, Syracuse, NY 13244. Offers MS, PhD. *Program availability:* Part-time. *Students:* Average age 37. *Degree requirements:* For master's, thesis or alternative; for doctorate, comprehensive exam, thesis/dissertation. *Entrance requirements:* For master's, baccalaureate degree from regionally-accredited college/university, relevant work experience, three letters of recommendation, personal statement, transcripts; for doctorate, GRE, master's degree, writing sample, three years of professional experience, resume, interview. Additional exam requirements/recommendations for international students: Required—TOEFL (minimum score 100 iBT). *Application deadline:* For fall admission, 1/15 priority date for domestic students, 5/15 priority date for international students; for spring admission, 10/15 priority date for domestic and international students; for summer admission, 1/15 priority date for domestic and international students. Applications are processed on a rolling basis. Application fee: $75. Electronic applications accepted. *Financial support:* Fellowships with full tuition reimbursements, research assistantships, teaching assistantships, scholarships/grants, and tuition waivers available. Financial award application deadline: 1/15. *Faculty research:* Theory and practice of curriculum, the lives and careers of teachers, policies and practices of teacher education, research design, implementation and analysis, forms of scholarly expression. *Unit head:* Dr. Benjamin Dotger, Chair of Teaching and Leadership/Professor, 315-443-2685, E-mail: bdotger@syr.edu. *Application contact:* Speranza Migliore, Graduate Admissions Recruiter, 315-443-2505, E-mail: gradrcrt@syr.edu.
Website: http://soe.syr.edu/academic/teaching_and_leadership/graduate/masters/teaching_and_curriculum/

Tarleton State University, College of Graduate Studies, College of Education, Department of Curriculum and Instruction, Stephenville, TX 76402. Offers curriculum and instruction (M Ed); educational diagnostician (M Ed); elementary education (M Ed); instructional design and technology (M Ed); instructional leadership (M Ed); secondary education (M Ed); special education (M Ed); technology applications (M Ed); technology director (M Ed). *Program availability:* Part-time, evening/weekend. *Faculty:* 11 full-time (10 women), 4 part-time/adjunct (1 woman). *Students:* 16 full-time (14 women), 158 part-time (143 women). Average age 40. 54 applicants, 87% accepted, 41 enrolled. In 2018, 46 master's awarded. *Degree requirements:* For master's, comprehensive exam, thesis (for some programs). *Entrance requirements:* For master's, GRE General Test, minimum GPA of 3.0. Additional exam requirements/recommendations for international students: Required—TOEFL (minimum score 520 paper-based; 69 iBT); Recommended—IELTS (minimum score 6), TSE (minimum score 50). *Application deadline:* For fall admission, 8/15 priority date for domestic students; for spring admission, 1/7 for domestic students. Applications are processed on a rolling basis. Application fee: $50 ($130 for international students). Electronic applications accepted. *Expenses:* Contact institution. *Financial support:* Research assistantships, teaching assistantships, career-related internships or fieldwork, Federal Work-Study, and institutionally sponsored loans available. Support available to part-time students. Financial award application deadline: 5/1; financial award applicants required to submit FAFSA. *Unit head:* Dr. Amber Lynn Diaz, Department Head, 254-968-0730, E-mail:

adiaz@tarleton.edu. *Application contact:* Information Contact, 254-968-9104, Fax: 254-968-9670, E-mail: gradoffice@tarleton.edu.
Website: http://www.tarleton.edu/cimasters/

Teachers College, Columbia University, Department of Curriculum and Teaching, New York, NY 10027-6696. Offers curriculum and teaching (Ed M, MA, Ed D); curriculum and teaching: elementary education (MA); curriculum and teaching: secondary education (MA); early childhood education (MA, Ed D); early childhood education: special education (MA); elementary education-gifted extension (MA); elementary inclusive education (MA); gifted education (MA); literacy specialist (MA); secondary inclusive education (MA); special inclusive elementary education (MA). *Program availability:* Part-time, evening/weekend. *Students:* 88 full-time (77 women), 264 part-time (239 women); includes 129 minority (45 Black or African American, non-Hispanic/Latino; 1 American Indian or Alaska Native, non-Hispanic/Latino; 41 Asian, non-Hispanic/Latino; 28 Hispanic/Latino; 14 Two or more races, non-Hispanic/Latino), 48 international. Average age 30. 460 applicants, 73% accepted, 149 enrolled. Terminal master's awarded for partial completion of doctoral program. *Unit head:* Prof. Daniel Friedrich, Chair, 212-678-3263, E-mail: friedrich@exchange.tc.columbia.edu. *Application contact:* Kelly Sutton-Skinner, Director of Admission & New Student Enrollment, E-mail: kms2237@tc.columbia.edu.

Tennessee State University, The School of Graduate Studies and Research, College of Education, Department of Teaching and Learning, Program in Curriculum and Instruction, Nashville, TN 37209-1561. Offers M Ed, Ed D. *Accreditation:* NCATE. *Degree requirements:* For master's, thesis optional; for doctorate, thesis/dissertation. *Entrance requirements:* For master's, GRE General Test or MAT, minimum GPA of 2.5; for doctorate, GRE General Test or MAT, minimum GPA of 3.25. Additional exam requirements/recommendations for international students: Required—TOEFL.

Tennessee Technological University, College of Graduate Studies, College of Education, Department of Curriculum and Instruction, Program in Curriculum, Cookeville, TN 38505. Offers MA, Ed S. *Accreditation:* NCATE. *Program availability:* Part-time, evening/weekend. *Faculty:* 2 full-time (1 woman). *Students:* 7 full-time (5 women), 26 part-time (22 women), 1 international. 16 applicants, 75% accepted, 9 enrolled. In 2018, 59 master's, 14 other advanced degrees awarded. *Degree requirements:* For master's and Ed S, comprehensive exam, thesis or alternative. *Entrance requirements:* For master's and Ed S, MAT or GRE. Additional exam requirements/recommendations for international students: Required—TOEFL (minimum score 527 paper-based; 71 iBT), IELTS (minimum score 5.5), PTE (minimum score 48), or TOEIC (Test of English as an International Communication). *Application deadline:* For fall admission, 8/1 for domestic students, 5/1 for international students; for spring admission, 12/1 for domestic students, 10/1 for international students; for summer admission, 5/1 for domestic students, 2/1 for international students. Applications are processed on a rolling basis. Application fee: $35 ($40 for international students). Electronic applications accepted. *Financial support:* Fellowships, research assistantships, and teaching assistantships available. Financial award application deadline: 4/1. *Unit head:* Dr. Jeremy Wendt, Chairperson, 931-372-3181, Fax: 931-372-6270, E-mail: jwendt@tntech.edu. *Application contact:* Shelia K. Kendrick, Coordinator of Graduate Studies, 931-372-3808, Fax: 931-372-3497, E-mail: skendrick@tntech.edu.

Texas A&M International University, Office of Graduate Studies and Research, College of Education, Department of Curriculum and Pedagogy, Laredo, TX 78041. Offers MS. *Degree requirements:* For master's, comprehensive exam. *Entrance requirements:* Additional exam requirements/recommendations for international students: Required—TOEFL (minimum score 550 paper-based; 79 iBT).

Texas A&M University, College of Education and Human Development, Department of Teaching, Learning, and Culture, College Station, TX 77843. Offers curriculum and instruction (M Ed, MS, Ed D, PhD). *Program availability:* Part-time. *Faculty:* 47. *Students:* 187 full-time (153 women), 277 part-time (222 women); includes 138 minority (44 Black or African American, non-Hispanic/Latino; 14 Asian, non-Hispanic/Latino; 74 Hispanic/Latino; 6 Two or more races, non-Hispanic/Latino), 50 international. Average age 33. 90 applicants, 70% accepted, 45 enrolled. In 2018, 182 master's, 42 doctorates awarded. *Degree requirements:* For master's, comprehensive exam, thesis (for some programs); for doctorate, comprehensive exam, thesis/dissertation. *Entrance requirements:* For master's, GRE General Test, minimum GPA of 3.0; for doctorate, GRE General Test, 3 years of teaching experience. Additional exam requirements/recommendations for international students: Required—TOEFL (minimum score 550 paper-based; 80 iBT), IELTS (minimum score 6), PTE (minimum score 53). *Application deadline:* For fall admission, 3/1 for domestic students, 1/1 for international students; for spring admission, 10/1 for domestic students, 8/1 for international students. Application fee: $50 ($90 for international students). Electronic applications accepted. *Expenses:* Contact institution. *Financial support:* In 2018–19, 90 students received support, including 2 fellowships with tuition reimbursements available (averaging $17,931 per year), 59 research assistantships with tuition reimbursements available (averaging $11,853 per year), 31 teaching assistantships with tuition reimbursements available (averaging $11,855 per year); career-related internships or fieldwork, institutionally sponsored loans, scholarships/grants, traineeships, health care benefits, tuition waivers (full and partial), and unspecified assistantships also available. Support available to part-time students. Financial award application deadline: 3/15; financial award applicants required to submit FAFSA. *Unit head:* Dr. Lynn Burlbaw, Professor and Interim Department Co-Head, 979-845-8384, Fax: 979-845-9663, E-mail: burlbaw@neo.tamu.edu. *Application contact:* Sarah Oakley, Academic Advisor II, 979-845-5063, Fax: 979-845-9663, E-mail: sarahoakley@tamu.edu.
Website: http://tlac.tamu.edu

Texas A&M University–Central Texas, Graduate Studies and Research, Killeen, TX 76549. Offers accounting (MS); business administration (MBA); clinical mental health counseling (MS); criminal justice (MCJ); curriculum and instruction (M Ed); educational administration (M Ed); educational psychology - experimental psychology (MS); history (MA); human resource management (MS); information systems (MS); liberal studies (MS); management and leadership (MS); marriage and family therapy (MS); mathematics (MS); political science (MA); school counseling (M Ed); school psychology (Ed S).

Texas A&M University–Commerce, College of Education and Human Services, Commerce, TX 75429. Offers counseling (M Ed, MS, PhD); early childhood education (M Ed, MS); educational administration (M Ed, MS, Ed D); educational psychology (PhD); educational technology leadership (M Ed, MS); educational technology library science (M Ed, MS); elementary education (M Ed); health, kinesiology and sports studies (MS); higher education (MS, Ed D); psychology (MS); reading (M Ed, MS); school psychology (SSP); secondary education (M Ed, MS); social work (MSW); special education (M Ed, MS); supervision, curriculum and instruction-elementary education (Ed D); training and development (MS). *Program availability:* Part-time, evening/weekend, 100% online, blended/hybrid learning. *Faculty:* 95 full-time (59 women), 29 part-time/adjunct (22 women). *Students:* 356 full-time (295 women), 1,262 part-time (992 women); includes 683 minority (349 Black or African American, non-Hispanic/Latino; 9 American Indian or Alaska Native, non-Hispanic/Latino; 30 Asian, non-Hispanic/Latino; 238 Hispanic/Latino; 57 Two or more races, non-Hispanic/Latino), 9 international. Average age 37. 951 applicants, 42% accepted, 304 enrolled. In 2018, 532

master's, 51 doctorates awarded. *Degree requirements:* For master's, comprehensive exam, thesis optional, departmental qualifying exams (for some programs); for doctorate, comprehensive exam, thesis/dissertation, departmental qualifying exam; for SSP, comprehensive exam. *Entrance requirements:* For master's, GRE General Test, official transcripts, letters of recommendation, resume, statement of goals; for doctorate, GRE General Test, letters of recommendation, statement of goals, writing samples, writing sessions, resumes. Additional exam requirements/recommendations for international students: Required—TOEFL (minimum score 550 paper-based; 79 iBT), IELTS (minimum score 6), PTE (minimum score 53). *Application deadline:* For fall admission, 6/1 priority date for international students; for spring admission, 10/15 priority date for international students; for summer admission, 3/15 priority date for international students. Applications are processed on a rolling basis. Application fee: $50 ($75 for international students). Electronic applications accepted. *Expenses: Tuition, area resident:* Full-time $3630. Tuition, state resident: full-time $3630. Tuition, nonresident: full-time $11,100. *International tuition:* $11,100 full-time. *Required fees:* $2794. Tuition and fees vary according to course load, degree level and program. *Financial support:* In 2018–19, 116 students received support, including 94 research assistantships with partial tuition reimbursements available (averaging $3,863 per year), 38 teaching assistantships with partial tuition reimbursements available (averaging $4,728 per year); career-related internships or fieldwork, Federal Work-Study, institutionally sponsored loans, scholarships/grants, health care benefits, and unspecified assistantships also available. Financial award application deadline: 5/1; financial award applicants required to submit FAFSA. *Faculty research:* Cognitive and bilingual education, positive behavioral intervention, literacy, math readiness. *Total annual research expenditures:* $1.1 million. *Unit head:* Dr. Madeline Justice, Interim Dean, 903-886-5181, Fax: 903-886-5905, E-mail: madeline.justice@tamuc.edu. *Application contact:* Vicky Turner, Doctoral Degree and Special Programs Coordinator, 903-886-5167, E-mail: vicky.turner@tamuc.edu.
Website: http://www.tamuc.edu/academics/graduateSchool/programs/education/default.aspx

Texas A&M University–Corpus Christi, College of Graduate Studies, College of Education and Human Development, Program in Curriculum and Instruction, Corpus Christi, TX 78412. Offers MS, PhD. *Program availability:* Part-time, evening/weekend. *Degree requirements:* For master's, comprehensive exam; for doctorate, thesis/dissertation. *Entrance requirements:* For master's, minimum GPA of 3.0 in last 60 hours; essay (approximately 300-400 words in length); for doctorate, GMAT/GRE (taken within 5 years), master's degree, minimum GPA of 3.0 in last 60 hours, 4 reference forms, 3 years' teaching experience, interview. Additional exam requirements/recommendations for international students: Required—TOEFL (minimum score 550 paper-based; 79 iBT), IELTS (minimum score 6.5). Electronic applications accepted.

Texas A&M University–Texarkana, Graduate Studies and Research, College of Education and Liberal Arts, Texarkana, TX 75503. Offers adult education (MS); curriculum and instruction (M Ed); education (MS); educational administration (M Ed); English (MA); instructional technology (MS); interdisciplinary studies (MA, MS); special education (MS). *Program availability:* Part-time, evening/weekend. *Degree requirements:* For master's, comprehensive exam (for some programs), thesis optional. *Entrance requirements:* For master's, minimum GPA of 2.5 on last 60 hours of bachelor's degree. Additional exam requirements/recommendations for international students: Required—TOEFL. Electronic applications accepted.

Texas Christian University, College of Education, Doctoral Programs in Education, Fort Worth, TX 76129-0002. Offers counseling and counselor education (PhD); curriculum studies (PhD); educational leadership (Ed D); higher educational leadership (Ed D); science education (PhD); MBA/Ed D. *Program availability:* Part-time, evening/weekend. *Faculty:* 29 full-time (21 women), 3 part-time/adjunct (1 woman). *Students:* 80 full-time (57 women), 26 part-time (13 women); includes 41 minority (15 Black or African American, non-Hispanic/Latino; 6 Asian, non-Hispanic/Latino; 17 Hispanic/Latino; 3 Two or more races, non-Hispanic/Latino), 6 international. Average age 39. 109 applicants, 50% accepted, 23 enrolled. In 2018, 12 doctorates awarded. *Degree requirements:* For doctorate, comprehensive exam, thesis/dissertation. *Entrance requirements:* For doctorate, GRE General Test. Additional exam requirements/recommendations for international students: Required—TOEFL (minimum score 550 paper-based; 80 iBT), IELTS (minimum score 6.5). *Application deadline:* For fall admission, 2/1 for domestic and international students; for winter admission, 2/1 for domestic and international students; for spring admission, 11/16 for domestic and international students. Application fee: $60. Electronic applications accepted. *Financial support:* In 2018–19, 66 students received support, including 1 fellowship with full tuition reimbursement available (averaging $18,500 per year), 8 research assistantships with full tuition reimbursements available (averaging $18,500 per year), 6 teaching assistantships with full tuition reimbursements available (averaging $18,500 per year); career-related internships or fieldwork, scholarships/grants, health care benefits, and unspecified assistantships also available. Support available to part-time students. Financial award application deadline: 2/1. *Unit head:* Dr. Jan Lacina, Interim Dean, 817-257-6786, Fax: 817-257-7466, E-mail: j.lacina@tcu.edu. *Application contact:* Lori Kimball, Graduate Studies Coordinator, 817-257-7661, Fax: 817-257-7466, E-mail: l.kimball@tcu.edu.
Website: http://coe.tcu.edu/graduate-overview/

Texas Christian University, College of Education, Master's Programs in Education, Fort Worth, TX 76129-0002. Offers counseling (M Ed); curriculum and instruction (M Ed), including curriculum studies, language and literacy, math education, science education; education (MAT); educational leadership (M Ed); special education (M Ed). *Program availability:* Part-time, evening/weekend. *Faculty:* 29 full-time (21 women), 3 part-time/adjunct (1 woman). *Students:* 124 full-time (94 women), 14 part-time (12 women); includes 52 minority (14 Black or African American, non-Hispanic/Latino; 2 American Indian or Alaska Native, non-Hispanic/Latino; 3 Asian, non-Hispanic/Latino; 28 Hispanic/Latino; 5 Two or more races, non-Hispanic/Latino), 1 international. Average age 28. 172 applicants, 69% accepted, 86 enrolled. In 2018, 62 master's awarded. *Degree requirements:* For master's, comprehensive exam (for some programs), thesis (for some programs). *Entrance requirements:* For master's, GRE General Test; Pre-Admission Content Test (for MAT). Additional exam requirements/recommendations for international students: Required—TOEFL (minimum score 550 paper-based; 80 iBT), IELTS (minimum score 6.5). *Application deadline:* For fall admission, 3/1 for domestic and international students; for spring admission, 11/16 for domestic and international students; for summer admission, 3/1 for domestic and international students. Application fee: $60. Electronic applications accepted. *Financial support:* In 2018–19, 135 students received support, including 3 research assistantships with full tuition reimbursements available (averaging $15,000 per year), 33 teaching assistantships with full tuition reimbursements available (averaging $15,000 per year); career-related internships or fieldwork, scholarships/grants, health care benefits, and unspecified assistantships also available. Support available to part-time students. Financial award application deadline: 3/1. *Unit head:* Dr. Jan Lacina, Interim Dean, 817-257-6786, Fax: 817-257-7466, E-mail: j.lacina@tcu.edu. *Application contact:* Lori Kimball, Graduate Studies Coordinator, 817-257-7661, Fax: 817-257-7466, E-mail: l.kimball@tcu.edu.
Website: http://coe.tcu.edu/graduate-overview/

Texas Southern University, College of Education, Area of Curriculum and Instruction, Houston, TX 77004-4584. Offers bilingual education (M Ed); curriculum and instruction (Ed D); secondary education (M Ed). *Program availability:* Part-time, evening/weekend. *Degree requirements:* For master's, comprehensive exam; for doctorate, comprehensive exam, thesis/dissertation. *Entrance requirements:* For master's, GRE General Test, minimum GPA of 2.5; for doctorate, GRE General Test or MAT, master's degree, minimum B+ average. Additional exam requirements/recommendations for international students: Required—TOEFL. Electronic applications accepted.

Texas Tech University, Graduate School, College of Education, Department of Curriculum and Instruction, Lubbock, TX 79409-1071. Offers bilingual education (M Ed); curriculum and instruction (M Ed, PhD); elementary education (M Ed); language/literacy education (M Ed); multidisciplinary science (MS); secondary education (M Ed). *Accreditation:* NCATE. *Program availability:* Part-time, evening/weekend, online learning. *Faculty:* 17 full-time (11 women), 1 (woman) part-time/adjunct. *Students:* 48 full-time (41 women), 265 part-time (220 women); includes 103 minority (25 Black or African American, non-Hispanic/Latino; 9 Asian, non-Hispanic/Latino; 64 Hispanic/Latino; 5 Two or more races, non-Hispanic/Latino), 27 international. Average age 40. 101 applicants, 65% accepted, 51 enrolled. In 2018, 26 master's, 21 doctorates awarded. Terminal master's awarded for partial completion of doctoral program. *Degree requirements:* For master's, comprehensive exam (for some programs), thesis optional; for doctorate, comprehensive exam, thesis/dissertation. *Entrance requirements:* For master's, bachelor's degree; resume; letter of intent; academic writing sample; 2 letters of recommendation; for doctorate, GRE, master's degree; resume; letter of intent; academic writing sample; 3 letters of recommendation. Additional exam requirements/recommendations for international students: Required—TOEFL (minimum score 550 paper-based; 79 iBT). *Application deadline:* For fall admission, 6/1 priority date for domestic students, 1/15 priority date for international students; for spring admission, 9/1 priority date for domestic students, 6/15 priority date for international students. Applications are processed on a rolling basis. Application fee: $65. Electronic applications accepted. *Expenses:* Contact institution. *Financial support:* In 2018–19, 142 students received support, including 136 fellowships (averaging $2,895 per year), 28 research assistantships (averaging $12,296 per year), 7 teaching assistantships (averaging $14,175 per year); Federal Work-Study, institutionally sponsored loans, scholarships/grants, health care benefits, and unspecified assistantships also available. Support available to part-time students. Financial award application deadline: 2/1; financial award applicants required to submit FAFSA. *Faculty research:* Teacher education, curriculum studies, bilingual education, science and math education, language and literacy education. *Total annual research expenditures:* $79,025. *Unit head:* Dr. Jerry Dwyer, Professor, Interim Department Chair, 806-834-7399, Fax: 806-742-2179, E-mail: jerry.dwyer@ttu.edu. *Application contact:* Brandi Stephens, Graduate Academic Advisor, 806-834-4554, Fax: 806-742-2179, E-mail: brandi.stephens@ttu.edu.
Website: www.educ.ttu.edu

Texas Woman's University, Graduate School, College of Professional Education, Department of Teacher Education, Denton, TX 76204. Offers educational administration (M Ed, MA); special education (M Ed, PhD), including educational diagnostician (M Ed), intervention specialist (M Ed); teaching, learning, and curriculum (M Ed, MA). *Program availability:* Part-time, 100% online, blended/hybrid learning. *Faculty:* 24 full-time (19 women), 24 part-time/adjunct (17 women). *Students:* 35 full-time (30 women), 170 part-time (153 women); includes 81 minority (18 Black or African American, non-Hispanic/Latino; 1 American Indian or Alaska Native, non-Hispanic/Latino; 4 Asian, non-Hispanic/Latino; 52 Hispanic/Latino; 6 Two or more races, non-Hispanic/Latino), 1 international. Average age 35. 79 applicants, 70% accepted, 43 enrolled. In 2018, 49 master's, 4 doctorates awarded. *Degree requirements:* For master's, comprehensive exam, thesis, professional paper (M Ed), internship for some; for doctorate, comprehensive exam, thesis/dissertation, residency, portfolio. *Entrance requirements:* For master's, minimum GPA of 3.0 on last 60 undergraduate hours, 2 letters of reference, resume, copy of certifications, teacher service record, statement of intent, interview (for MAT); for doctorate, minimum GPA of 3.0, 3 letters of reference, resume, copy of certifications, teacher service record, statement of intent, interview. Additional exam requirements/recommendations for international students: Required—TOEFL (minimum score 550 paper-based; 79 iBT); Recommended—IELTS (minimum score 6.5), TSE (minimum score 53). *Application deadline:* For fall admission, 7/15 priority date for domestic students, 3/1 priority date for international students; for spring admission, 11/1 priority date for domestic students, 7/1 priority date for international students; for summer admission, 4/1 priority date for domestic and international students. Application fee: $50 ($75 for international students). Electronic applications accepted. *Expenses:* $1,517 in-state resident per 3 hour course, $2,783 out-of-state resident per 3 hour course. *Financial support:* In 2018–19, 42 students received support, including 1 teaching assistantship; research assistantships, career-related internships or fieldwork, Federal Work-Study, institutionally sponsored loans, scholarships/grants, traineeships, health care benefits, and unspecified assistantships also available. Support available to part-time students. Financial award application deadline: 3/1; financial award applicants required to submit FAFSA. *Faculty research:* Experiential learning, classroom management, learning disabilities, staff and professional development, technology in the classroom. *Unit head:* Dr. Diane Myers, Chair, 940-898-2271, Fax: 940-898-2270, E-mail: teachereducation@twu.edu. *Application contact:* Korie Hawkins, Associate Director of Admissions, Graduate Recruitment, 940-898-3188, Fax: 940-898-3081, E-mail: admissions@twu.edu.
Website: http://www.twu.edu/teacher-education/

Trevecca Nazarene University, Graduate Education Program, Nashville, TN 37210-2877. Offers accountability and instructional leadership (Ed S); curriculum and instruction for Christian school educators (M Ed); curriculum and instruction K-12 (M Ed); educational leadership (M Ed); English second language (M Ed); library and information science (MLI Sc); special education: visual impairments (M Ed); teaching (MAT), including teaching 6-12, teaching K-5. *Accreditation:* NCATE. *Program availability:* Part-time, evening/weekend, online learning. *Degree requirements:* For master's, comprehensive exam, exit assessment/e-portfolio. *Entrance requirements:* For master's, GRE or MAT; PRAXIS (for MAT), minimum GPA of 3.0, official transcript from regionally-accredited institution, references, interview, writing sample, at least 3 years' successful teaching experience (for M Ed in educational leadership); for Ed S, GRE or MAT, master's degree with minimum GPA of 3.0, official transcript from regionally accredited institution, at least 3 years' successful teaching experience, interview, writing sample, background and fingerprinting check, recommendations. Additional exam requirements/recommendations for international students: Required—TOEFL (minimum score 550 paper-based). Electronic applications accepted. *Expenses:* Contact institution.

Trinity Baptist College, Graduate Programs, Jacksonville, FL 32221. Offers Bible (MA); curriculum and instruction (M Ed); educational leadership (M Ed); special education (M Ed). *Program availability:* Online learning. *Entrance requirements:* For master's, GRE (for M Ed), 2 letters of recommendation; minimum GPA of 2.5 (for M Min), 3.0 (for M Ed); goals essay; official transcripts.

Trinity Washington University, School of Education, Washington, DC 20017-1094. Offers clinical mental health counseling (MA); early childhood education (MAT); educating for change (M Ed); educational administration (MSA); elementary education (MAT); reading (M Ed); school counseling (MA); secondary education (MAT), including English, social studies; special education (MAT). *Accreditation:* NCATE. *Program availability:* Part-time, evening/weekend. *Degree requirements:* For master's, thesis (for some programs), capstone project(s). *Entrance requirements:* For master's, PRAXIS I, minimum GPA of 2.8. Additional exam requirements/recommendations for international students: Required—TOEFL (minimum score 550 paper-based). *Faculty research:* Technology, literacy, special education, organizations, inclusion models.

Tusculum University, Program in Curriculum and Instruction, Greeneville, TN 37743-9997. Offers special education (MA Ed). *Program availability:* Evening/weekend. *Degree requirements:* For master's, thesis or alternative. *Entrance requirements:* For master's, NTE, PRAXIS II, GRE, MAT, 3 years of work experience, minimum GPA of 3.0, bachelor's degree. Additional exam requirements/recommendations for international students: Required—TOEFL (minimum score 540 paper-based; 73 iBT).

Universidad Adventista de las Antillas, EGECED Department, Mayagüez, PR 00681-0118. Offers curriculum and instruction (M Ed); medical surgical nursing (MN); school administration and supervision (M Ed). *Degree requirements:* For master's, comprehensive exam (for some programs), thesis (for some programs). *Entrance requirements:* For master's, EXADEP or GRE General Test, recommendations. Electronic applications accepted.

Universidad del Turabo, Graduate Programs, Programs in Education, Program in Curriculum and Instruction and Appropriate Environment, Gurabo, PR 00778-3030. Offers D Ed. *Program availability:* Part-time, evening/weekend. *Entrance requirements:* For doctorate, EXADEP, GRE or GMAT, official transcript, recommendation letters, essay, curriculum vitae, interview. Electronic applications accepted.

Universidad del Turabo, Graduate Programs, Programs in Education, Program in Curriculum and Teaching, Gurabo, PR 00778-3030. Offers M Ed. *Program availability:* Part-time, evening/weekend. *Entrance requirements:* For master's, EXADEP, GRE or GMAT, interview, official transcript, essay, recommendation letter. Electronic applications accepted.

Universidad Metropolitana, School of Education, Program in Curriculum and Teaching, San Juan, PR 00928-1150. Offers M Ed. *Program availability:* Part-time, evening/weekend. *Degree requirements:* For master's, thesis or alternative. *Entrance requirements:* For master's, EXADEP, interview.

Université de Montréal, Faculty of Education, Department of Didactics, Montréal, QC H3C 3J7, Canada. Offers M Ed, MA, PhD, DESS. Terminal master's awarded for partial completion of doctoral program. *Degree requirements:* For master's, thesis (for some programs); for doctorate, thesis/dissertation, general exam. Electronic applications accepted. *Faculty research:* Teaching of French as a first or second language, teaching of science and technology, teaching of mathematics, teaching of arts.

Université Laval, Faculty of Education, Department of Teaching and Learning Studies, Programs in Didactics, Québec, QC G1K 7P4, Canada. Offers MA, PhD. Terminal master's awarded for partial completion of doctoral program. *Degree requirements:* For master's, thesis (for some programs); for doctorate, comprehensive exam, thesis/dissertation. *Entrance requirements:* For master's and doctorate, English exam (comprehension of written English), knowledge of French. Electronic applications accepted.

University at Albany, State University of New York, School of Education, Department of Educational Theory and Practice, Albany, NY 12222-0001. Offers curriculum and instruction (PhD, CAS); curriculum development and instructional technology (MS); general education studies (MS). *Program availability:* Part-time, evening/weekend, 100% online, blended/hybrid learning. *Faculty:* 16 full-time (8 women), 14 part-time/adjunct (8 women). *Students:* 93 full-time (66 women), 282 part-time (220 women); includes 69 minority (22 Black or African American, non-Hispanic/Latino; 15 Asian, non-Hispanic/Latino; 24 Hispanic/Latino; 1 Native Hawaiian or other Pacific Islander, non-Hispanic/Latino; 7 Two or more races, non-Hispanic/Latino), 30 international. Average age 31. 197 applicants, 68% accepted, 120 enrolled. In 2018, 83 master's, 4 doctorates, 8 other advanced degrees awarded. *Degree requirements:* For doctorate, one foreign language, thesis/dissertation. *Entrance requirements:* For doctorate, GRE General Test. Additional exam requirements/recommendations for international students: Required—TOEFL (minimum score 550 paper-based). *Application deadline:* For fall admission, 2/1 for domestic students, 1/31 for international students. Application fee: $75. Electronic applications accepted. *Financial support:* Fellowships available. *Unit head:* Jianwei Zhang, Chair, 518-442-5006, E-mail: jzhang@albany.edu. *Application contact:* Jianwei Zhang, Chair, 518-442-5006, E-mail: jzhang@albany.edu.

University at Buffalo, the State University of New York, Graduate School, Graduate School of Education, Department of Learning and Instruction, Buffalo, NY 14260. Offers biology education (Ed M, Certificate); chemistry education (Ed M, Certificate); childhood education (Ed M); childhood education with bilingual extension (Ed M); college teaching (Advanced Certificate); curriculum, instruction and the science of learning (PhD); early childhood education (Ed M); early childhood education with bilingual extension (Ed M); earth science education (Ed M, Certificate); education and technology (Ed M); education studies (Ed M); educational technology and new literacies (Certificate); educational technology and new literacies (Advanced Certificate); elementary education (Ed D); English education (Ed M, Certificate); English education studies (Ed M); English for speakers of other languages (Ed M); foreign and second language education (PhD); French education (Ed M, Certificate); German education (Ed M, Certificate); gifted education (Certificate); Latin education (Ed M, Certificate); literacy education studies (Ed M); literacy specialist (Ed M); literacy teaching and learning (Certificate); mathematics education (Ed M, Certificate); music education (Ed M, Certificate); music education studies (Ed M); music learning theory (Advanced Certificate); online education (Advanced Certificate); physics education (Ed M, Certificate); science and the public (Ed M); social studies education (Ed M, Certificate); Spanish education (Ed M, Certificate); special education (PhD); teaching English to speakers of other languages (Ed M). *Program availability:* Part-time, evening/weekend, 100% online. *Faculty:* 31 full-time (22 women), 41 part-time/adjunct (27 women). *Students:* 161 full-time (107 women), 369 part-time (260 women); includes 76 minority (26 Black or African American, non-Hispanic/Latino; 3 American Indian or Alaska Native, non-Hispanic/Latino; 30 Asian, non-Hispanic/Latino; 14 Hispanic/Latino; 3 Two or more races, non-Hispanic/Latino), 41 international. Average age 34. 368 applicants, 70% accepted, 179 enrolled. In 2018, 100 master's, 26 doctorates, 19 other advanced degrees awarded. *Degree requirements:* For master's, comprehensive exam; for doctorate, thesis/dissertation, research analysis exam, research experience. *Entrance requirements:* For master's, letters of reference; for doctorate, GRE General Test or MAT, interview, writing sample, letters of recommendation. Additional exam requirements/recommendations for international students: Required—TOEFL (minimum score 600 paper-based; 96 iBT), IELTS (minimum score 6.5), PTE (minimum score 55). *Application deadline:* For fall admission, 2/1 priority date for domestic and international students; for spring admission, 11/15 priority date for domestic students, 10/1 for international students. Applications are processed on a rolling basis. Application fee: $50. Electronic

applications accepted. *Financial support:* In 2018–19, 42 fellowships (averaging $5,181 per year), 44 research assistantships with tuition reimbursements (averaging $10,908 per year) were awarded; teaching assistantships, career-related internships or fieldwork, Federal Work-Study, institutionally sponsored loans, scholarships/grants, tuition waivers (full and partial), and unspecified assistantships also available. Financial award application deadline: 2/28; financial award applicants required to submit FAFSA. *Faculty research:* Science assessment, foreign language teaching and learning, early learning, new literacies, gender and education. *Total annual research expenditures:* $413,233. *Unit head:* Dr. Julie Gorlewski, Department Chair, 716-645-2455, Fax: 716-645-3161, E-mail: jgorlews@buffalo.edu. *Application contact:* Renad Aref, Assistant Director of Admission Recruitment, 716-645-2110, Fax: 716-645-7937, E-mail: gseinfo@buffalo.edu.
Website: http://ed.buffalo.edu/teaching.html

The University of Akron, Graduate School, College of Education, Department of Curricular and Instructional Studies, Program in Curriculum and Instruction with Licensure Options, Akron, OH 44325. Offers MS. *Entrance requirements:* For master's, minimum GPA of 3.0. Additional exam requirements/recommendations for international students: Required—TOEFL (minimum score 79 iBT), IELTS (minimum score 6.5).

The University of Alabama at Birmingham, School of Education, Program in Curriculum Education, Birmingham, AL 35294. Offers Ed S. *Program availability:* Part-time, online learning. *Degree requirements:* For Ed S, comprehensive exam, thesis optional. *Entrance requirements:* For degree, GRE General Test, MAT, minimum GPA of 3.0, master's degree. Electronic applications accepted. *Expenses: Tuition, area resident:* Full-time $8100; part-time $8100 per year. *Tuition, state resident:* full-time $8100. *Tuition, nonresident:* full-time $19,188; part-time $19,188 per year. Tuition and fees vary according to program.

University of Arkansas, Graduate School, College of Education and Health Professions, Department of Curriculum and Instruction, Program in Curriculum and Instruction, Fayetteville, AR 72701. Offers M Ed, PhD, Ed S. *Program availability:* Part-time. In 2018, 3 master's, 5 doctorates, 1 other advanced degree awarded. *Entrance requirements:* For doctorate, GRE General Test. *Application deadline:* For fall admission, 8/1 for domestic students, 4/1 for international students; for spring admission, 12/1 for domestic students, 10/1 for international students; for summer admission, 4/15 for domestic students, 3/1 for international students. Applications are processed on a rolling basis. Application fee: $60. Electronic applications accepted. *Financial support:* In 2018–19, 12 research assistantships, 2 teaching assistantships were awarded; fellowships with tuition reimbursements also available. Financial award application deadline: 4/1. *Unit head:* Dr. Cheryl A. Murphy, Department Head, 479-575-5111, Fax: 479-575-2492, E-mail: cmurphy@uark.edu. *Application contact:* Dr. Jason Endacott, Graduate Coordinator, 479-575-2657, Fax: 479-575-6676, E-mail: jendacot@uark.edu.
Website: http://cied.uark.edu/

University of Arkansas at Little Rock, Graduate School, College of Education and Health Professions, Department of Teacher Education, Program in Curriculum and Instruction, Little Rock, AR 72204-1099. Offers M Ed. *Entrance requirements:* For master's, teaching license.

The University of British Columbia, Faculty of Education, Department of Curriculum and Pedagogy, Vancouver, BC V6T 1Z4, Canada. Offers art education (M Ed, MA); curriculum studies (M Ed, MA, PhD); home economics education (M Ed, MA); mathematics education (M Ed, MA); media and technology studies education (M Ed, MA); music education (M Ed, MA); physical education (M Ed, MA); science education (M Ed, MA); social studies education (M Ed, MA). *Program availability:* Part-time, online learning. *Degree requirements:* For master's, thesis (MA); for doctorate, comprehensive exam, thesis/dissertation. *Entrance requirements:* Additional exam requirements/recommendations for international students: Required—TOEFL, IELTS. Electronic applications accepted. *Expenses:* Contact institution. *Faculty research:* School subjects, teaching and learning.

University of Calgary, Faculty of Graduate Studies, Werklund School of Education, Program in Educational Research, Calgary, AB T2N 1N4, Canada. Offers adult learning (M Ed, MA, Ed D, PhD); curriculum and learning (M Ed, MA, Ed D, PhD); educational leadership (M Ed, MA, Ed D, PhD); languages and diversity (M Ed, MA, Ed D, PhD); learning sciences (M Ed, MA, Ed D, PhD). Ed D in educational leadership offered via distance delivery. *Program availability:* Part-time, evening/weekend, online learning. *Degree requirements:* For master's, thesis (for some programs); for doctorate, thesis/dissertation, candidacy exam. *Entrance requirements:* For master's, minimum GPA of 3.0, 3 letters of reference; for doctorate, minimum GPA of 3.5, 3 letters of reference. Additional exam requirements/recommendations for international students: Required—TOEFL, IELTS. Electronic applications accepted. *Faculty research:* Curriculum, leadership, technology, contexts, gifted, second language teaching, work place and adult learning.

University of California, Davis, Graduate Studies, Graduate Group in Education, Davis, CA 95616. Offers education (MA, Ed D); instructional studies (PhD); psychological studies (PhD); sociocultural studies (PhD). Ed D offered jointly with California State University, Fresno. Terminal master's awarded for partial completion of doctoral program. *Degree requirements:* For master's, comprehensive exam (for some programs), thesis (for some programs); for doctorate, thesis/dissertation. *Entrance requirements:* For master's and doctorate, GRE. Additional exam requirements/recommendations for international students: Required—TOEFL (minimum score 550 paper-based). Electronic applications accepted. *Faculty research:* Language and literacy, mathematics education, science education, teacher development, school psychology.

University of California, San Diego, Graduate Division, Program in Education Studies, La Jolla, CA 92093. Offers education (M Ed, PhD); educational leadership (Ed D); teaching and learning (MA, Ed D), including bilingual education (MA), curriculum design (MA). Ed D offered jointly with California State University, San Marcos. *Students:* 100 full-time (78 women), 61 part-time (41 women). 262 applicants, 54% accepted, 81 enrolled. In 2018, 75 master's, 15 doctorates awarded. *Degree requirements:* For master's, thesis (for some programs), student teaching; for doctorate, comprehensive exam, thesis/dissertation. *Entrance requirements:* For master's, GRE General Test; CBEST and appropriate CSET exam (for select tracks), current teaching or educational assignment (for select tracks); for doctorate, GRE General Test, current teaching or educational assignment (for select tracks). Additional exam requirements/recommendations for international students: Required—TOEFL (minimum score 550 paper-based; 80 iBT), IELTS (minimum score 7). *Application deadline:* For fall admission, 12/6 for domestic students. Application fee: $105 ($125 for international students). Electronic applications accepted. *Financial support:* Fellowships, career-related internships or fieldwork, and scholarships/grants available. Financial award applicants required to submit FAFSA. *Faculty research:* Language, culture and literacy development of deaf/hard of hearing children; equity issues in education; educational reform; evaluation, assessment, and research methodologies; distributed learning. *Unit head:* Carolyn Hofstetter, Chair, 858-822-6688, E-mail: ajdaly@ucsd.edu. *Application contact:* Giselle Van Luit, Graduate Coordinator, 858-534-2958, E-mail: edsinfo@ucsd.edu.

Curriculum and Instruction

University of Central Arkansas, Graduate School, College of Education, Department of Leadership Studies, Conway, AR 72035-0001. Offers college student personnel (MS); district-level administration (PMC); educational leadership - district level (Ed S); instructional technology (MS); library media and information technology (MS); school counseling (MS); school leadership (MS); school-based leadership adult education program administration (PMC); school-based leadership building administration (PMC); school-based leadership curriculum administration (PMC); school-based leadership gifted and talented program administration (PMC); school-based leadership special education program administration (PMC). *Accreditation:* NCATE. *Program availability:* Part-time, evening/weekend, online learning. *Degree requirements:* For master's and other advanced degree, comprehensive exam. *Entrance requirements:* For master's, GRE. Additional exam requirements/recommendations for international students: Required—TOEFL (minimum score 80 iBT). Electronic applications accepted. *Expenses:* Contact institution.

University of Central Florida, College of Community Innovation and Education, Education Doctoral Programs, Program in Applied Learning and Instruction, Orlando, FL 32816. Offers MA. *Accreditation:* NCATE. *Program availability:* Part-time, evening/weekend. *Students:* 16 full-time (14 women), 45 part-time (38 women); includes 21 minority (6 Black or African American, non-Hispanic/Latino; 1 American Indian or Alaska Native, non-Hispanic/Latino; 1 Asian, non-Hispanic/Latino; 11 Hispanic/Latino; 2 Two or more races, non-Hispanic/Latino), 1 international. Average age 32. 62 applicants, 66% accepted, 25 enrolled. In 2018, 18 master's awarded. *Entrance requirements:* For master's, goal statement, writing sample. Additional exam requirements/recommendations for international students: Required—TOEFL. *Application deadline:* For fall admission, 7/15 for domestic students. Application fee: $30. Electronic applications accepted. *Financial support:* Career-related internships or fieldwork, Federal Work-Study, institutionally sponsored loans, health care benefits, and unspecified assistantships available. Financial award application deadline: 3/1; financial award applicants required to submit FAFSA. *Unit head:* Dr. Bobby Hoffman, Program Coordinator, 407-823-1770, E-mail: bobby.hoffman@ucf.edu. *Application contact:* Associate Director, Graduate Admissions, 407-823-2766, Fax: 407-823-6442, E-mail: gradadmissions@ucf.edu.
Website: https://edcollege.ucf.edu/academic-programs/graduate/applied-learning-instruction/

University of Central Florida, College of Community Innovation and Education, Education Doctoral Programs, Program in Curriculum and Instruction, Orlando, FL 32816. Offers M Ed. *Students:* 21 full-time (19 women), 65 part-time (59 women); includes 31 minority (10 Black or African American, non-Hispanic/Latino; 4 Asian, non-Hispanic/Latino; 16 Hispanic/Latino; 1 Two or more races, non-Hispanic/Latino). Average age 36. 53 applicants, 77% accepted, 31 enrolled. In 2018, 4 master's awarded. Application fee: $30. Electronic applications accepted. *Financial support:* In 2018–19, 5 students received support, including 1 fellowship with partial tuition reimbursement available (averaging $600 per year), 7 research assistantships with partial tuition reimbursements available (averaging $6,496 per year). *Unit head:* Dr. David Boote, Coordinator, 407-823-4160, E-mail: dboote@mail.ucf.edu. *Application contact:* Associate Director, Graduate Admissions, 407-823-2766, Fax: 407-823-6442, E-mail: gradadmissions@ucf.edu.

University of Central Florida, College of Community Innovation and Education, School of Teacher Education, Orlando, FL 32816. Offers applied learning and instruction (MA); curriculum and instruction (M Ed); elementary education (M Ed, MA); exceptional student education (M Ed, MA, Certificate), including autism spectrum disorders (Certificate), exceptional student education (M Ed), exceptional student education K-12 (MA), intervention specialist (Certificate), pre-kindergarten disabilities (Certificate), severe or profound disabilities (Certificate), special education (Certificate); K-8 mathematics and science education (M Ed, Certificate); reading education (M Ed, Certificate); teacher education (MAT), including art education, English language, mathematics education, middle school mathematics, middle school science, science education, social science education; world languages education - English for speakers of other languages (ESOL) (Certificate); world languages education - languages other than English (LOTE) (Certificate). *Program availability:* Part-time, evening/weekend. *Degree requirements:* For Certificate, thesis or alternative. *Entrance requirements:* For degree, GRE General Test, minimum GPA of 3.0. Additional exam requirements/recommendations for international students: Required—TOEFL. Electronic applications accepted.

University of Cincinnati, Graduate School, College of Education, Criminal Justice, and Human Services, School of Education, Program in Curriculum and Instruction, Cincinnati, OH 45221. Offers M Ed, Ed D. *Accreditation:* NCATE. *Program availability:* Part-time. *Degree requirements:* For master's, thesis; for doctorate, thesis/dissertation. *Entrance requirements:* For master's, GRE General Test; for doctorate, GRE General Test, GRE Subject Test. Additional exam requirements/recommendations for international students: Required—TOEFL (minimum score 550 paper-based), TWE (minimum score 4.5), OEPT. Electronic applications accepted.

University of Colorado Boulder, Graduate School, School of Education, Division of Curriculum and Instruction, Boulder, CO 80309. Offers MA, PhD. *Accreditation:* NCATE. Terminal master's awarded for partial completion of doctoral program. *Degree requirements:* For master's, comprehensive exam, thesis or alternative; for doctorate, one foreign language, comprehensive exam, thesis/dissertation. *Entrance requirements:* For master's, GRE General Test or MAT, minimum undergraduate GPA of 2.75; for doctorate, GRE General Test. Electronic applications accepted. Application fee is waived when completed online.

University of Colorado Colorado Springs, College of Education, Colorado Springs, CO 80918. Offers counseling and human services (MA); curriculum and instruction (MA); educational leadership (MA); educational leadership, research and policy (PhD); special education (MA); teaching English to speakers of other languages (MA). *Accreditation:* ACA; NCATE. *Program availability:* Part-time, evening/weekend, 100% online, blended/hybrid learning. *Faculty:* 31 full-time (22 women), 61 part-time/adjunct (47 women). *Students:* 208 full-time (149 women), 351 part-time (256 women); includes 136 minority (30 Black or African American, non-Hispanic/Latino; 1 American Indian or Alaska Native, non-Hispanic/Latino; 12 Asian, non-Hispanic/Latino; 64 Hispanic/Latino; 29 Two or more races, non-Hispanic/Latino), 8 international. Average age 36. 230 applicants, 80% accepted, 101 enrolled. In 2018, 186 master's, 9 doctorates awarded. *Degree requirements:* For master's, comprehensive exam, thesis or alternative, microcomputer proficiency; for doctorate, comprehensive exam, thesis/dissertation, research lab. *Entrance requirements:* For master's, GRE General Test (recommended but not required), career goal statement, professional references; for doctorate, GRE General Test. Additional exam requirements/recommendations for international students: Recommended—TOEFL (minimum score 90 iBT), IELTS (minimum score 6.5). *Application deadline:* For fall admission, 1/28 priority date for domestic and international students; for spring admission, 11/1 priority date for domestic and international students. Applications are processed on a rolling basis. Application fee: $60 ($100 for international students). Electronic applications accepted. *Expenses:* Tuition and fees vary by program, course load, and residency type. Please visit the University of Colorado Colorado Springs Student Financial Services website to estimate current program costs: https://www.uccs.edu/bursar/index.php/estimate-your-bill. *Financial support:* In 2018–19, 15 students received support. Career-related internships or fieldwork, Federal Work-Study, scholarships/grants, and unspecified assistantships available. Support available to part-time students. Financial award application deadline: 3/1; financial award applicants required to submit FAFSA. *Faculty research:* Linguistically diverse education (LDE), educational policy, evidence-based reading and writing instruction, relational and social aggression, positive behavior supports, inclusive schooling, K-12 education policy. *Total annual research expenditures:* $607,967. *Unit head:* Dr. Valerie Martin Conley, Dean, 719-255-4133, E-mail: vmconley@uccs.edu. *Application contact:* The College of Education Student Resource Office, 719-255-4996, E-mail: education@uccs.edu.
Website: https://www.uccs.edu/coe/

University of Connecticut, Graduate School, Neag School of Education, Department of Educational Psychology, Cognition, Instruction, and Learning Technology Program, Storrs, CT 06269. Offers MA, PhD. *Degree requirements:* For master's, comprehensive exam; for doctorate, thesis/dissertation. *Entrance requirements:* For doctorate, GRE General Test. Additional exam requirements/recommendations for international students: Required—TOEFL (minimum score 550 paper-based). Electronic applications accepted.

University of Delaware, College of Education and Human Development, School of Education, Newark, DE 19716. Offers education (PhD); educational leadership (Ed D); higher education (M Ed); instruction (MI); reading (M Ed); school leadership (M Ed); school psychology (MA, Ed S); teaching English as a second language (TESL) (MA). *Accreditation:* NCATE. *Program availability:* Part-time, evening/weekend. Terminal master's awarded for partial completion of doctoral program. *Degree requirements:* For master's, comprehensive exam (for some programs), thesis (for some programs); for doctorate, comprehensive exam (for some programs), thesis/dissertation. *Entrance requirements:* For master's and doctorate, GRE, 3 letters of recommendation. Additional exam requirements/recommendations for international students: Required—TOEFL (minimum score 600 paper-based). Electronic applications accepted. *Faculty research:* Teacher education; curriculum theory and development; community based education models, educational leadership.

University of Denver, Morgridge College of Education, Denver, CO 80208. Offers child, family and school psychology (MA, PhD, Ed S); counseling psychology (MA, PhD); curriculum and instruction (MA, Ed D, PhD); curriculum instruction and teaching (Certificate); early childhood special education (MA, Certificate); educational leadership and policy studies (MA, Ed D, PhD, Certificate); higher education (Ed D, PhD); library and information science (MLIS); research methods and statistics (MA, PhD). *Accreditation:* ALA; APA (one or more programs are accredited). *Program availability:* Part-time, evening/weekend, online learning. *Faculty:* 49 full-time (35 women), 33 part-time/adjunct (20 women). *Students:* 509 full-time (400 women), 365 part-time (277 women); includes 236 minority (53 Black or African American, non-Hispanic/Latino; 6 American Indian or Alaska Native, non-Hispanic/Latino; 28 Asian, non-Hispanic/Latino; 116 Hispanic/Latino; 33 Two or more races, non-Hispanic/Latino), 56 international. Average age 31. 1,372 applicants, 57% accepted, 382 enrolled. In 2018, 258 master's, 41 doctorates, 162 other advanced degrees awarded. Terminal master's awarded for partial completion of doctoral program. *Degree requirements:* For master's, comprehensive exam (for some programs); for doctorate, comprehensive exam (for some programs), thesis/dissertation. *Entrance requirements:* For master's, GRE General Test or GMAT, bachelors degree; transcripts; two letters of recommendation; personal statement; resume; for doctorate, GRE General Test or GMAT, Masters degree; transcripts; two letters of recommendation; personal statement(s); resume. Additional exam requirements/recommendations for international students: Required—TOEFL (minimum score 550 paper-based; 80 iBT). *Application deadline:* Applications are processed on a rolling basis. Application fee: $65. Electronic applications accepted. *Expenses:* $33,183 per year full-time. *Financial support:* In 2018–19, 690 students received support, including 29 research assistantships with tuition reimbursements available (averaging $11,465 per year), 9 teaching assistantships with tuition reimbursements available (averaging $2,527 per year); career-related internships or fieldwork, Federal Work-Study, institutionally sponsored loans, scholarships/grants, and unspecified assistantships also available. Support available to part-time students. Financial award application deadline: 2/15; financial award applicants required to submit FAFSA. *Faculty research:* Early childhood education, educational leadership, access and opportunity to postsecondary education, marriage and family therapy, data management and archival research. *Total annual research expenditures:* $2.3 million. *Unit head:* Dr. Karen Riley, Dean, 303-871-3665, E-mail: karen.riley@du.edu. *Application contact:* Jodi Dye, Director of Admissions, 303-871-2510, E-mail: jodi.dye@du.edu.
Website: http://morgridge.du.edu

University of Detroit Mercy, College of Liberal Arts and Education, Detroit, MI 48221. Offers addiction counseling (MA); addiction studies (Certificate); clinical mental health counseling (MA); clinical psychology (MA, PhD); computer and information systems (MS); criminal justice (MA); curriculum and instruction (MA); economics (MA); educational administration (MA); financial economics (MA); industrial/organizational psychology (MA); information assurance (MS); intelligence analysis (MA); liberal studies (MALS); religious studies (MA); school counseling (MA, Certificate); school psychology (Spec); security administration (MS); special education: emotionally impaired/behaviorally disordered (MA); special education: learning disabilities (MA). *Program availability:* Part-time, evening/weekend. *Degree requirements:* For doctorate, departmental qualifying exam. *Faculty research:* Psychology of aging, history of technology, Renaissance humanism, U.S. and Japanese economic relations.

University of Florida, Graduate School, College of Education, School of Teaching and Learning, Gainesville, FL 32611. Offers curriculum and instruction (M Ed, MAE, Ed D, PhD, Ed S); elementary education (M Ed, MAE); English education (M Ed, MAE); mathematics education (M Ed, MAE); reading education (M Ed, MAE); science education (M Ed, MAE); social studies education (M Ed, MAE). *Accreditation:* NCATE. *Program availability:* Part-time, evening/weekend, online learning. Terminal master's awarded for partial completion of doctoral program. *Degree requirements:* For master's, comprehensive exam (for some programs), thesis (for some programs); for doctorate, comprehensive exam (for some programs), thesis/dissertation (for some programs). *Entrance requirements:* For master's and doctorate, GRE General Test, minimum GPA of 3.0; for Ed S, GRE General Test. Additional exam requirements/recommendations for international students: Required—TOEFL (minimum score 550 paper-based; 80 iBT), IELTS (minimum score 6). Electronic applications accepted. *Faculty research:* STEM education; curriculum; teaching and teacher education; languages and literacy; schools, culture, and society; theories and processes of learning.

University of Hawaii at Manoa, Office of Graduate Education, College of Education, Department of Curriculum Studies, Honolulu, HI 96822. Offers curriculum studies (M Ed); early childhood education (M Ed). *Program availability:* Part-time. *Degree requirements:* For master's, thesis optional. *Entrance requirements:* Additional exam requirements/recommendations for international students: Required—TOEFL (minimum score 500 paper-based; 61 iBT), IELTS (minimum score 5).

University of Hawaii at Manoa, Office of Graduate Education, College of Education, PhD in Education Program, Honolulu, HI 96822. Offers curriculum and instruction (PhD); educational administration (PhD); educational foundations (PhD); educational policy studies (PhD); educational psychology (PhD); exceptionalities (PhD); kinesiology (PhD); learning design and technology (PhD). *Program availability:* Part-time, evening/ weekend. *Degree requirements:* For doctorate, thesis/dissertation. *Entrance requirements:* For doctorate, GRE General Test, sample of written work. Additional exam requirements/recommendations for international students: Required—TOEFL (minimum score 600 paper-based; 100 iBT), IELTS (minimum score 7).

University of Houston–Clear Lake, School of Education, Program in Curriculum and Instruction, Houston, TX 77058-1002. Offers curriculum and instruction (MS); early childhood education (MS); reading (MS); school library and information science (MS). *Program availability:* Part-time, evening/weekend. *Degree requirements:* For master's, thesis (for some programs). *Entrance requirements:* For master's, GRE or minimum GPA of 3.0 in last 60 hours. Additional exam requirements/recommendations for international students: Required—TOEFL (minimum score 550 paper-based). Electronic applications accepted.

University of Houston–Downtown, College of Public Service, Department of Urban Education, Houston, TX 77002. Offers curriculum and instruction (MAT). *Program availability:* Part-time, evening/weekend. *Degree requirements:* For master's, capstone course with completed project, position paper, grant proposal, empirical study, curriculum development/revision, or advanced technology project presented at annual Graduate Project Exhibition. *Entrance requirements:* For master's, GRE, personal statement, 3 recommendation forms. Additional exam requirements/recommendations for international students: Required—TOEFL (minimum score 550 paper-based; 80 iBT). Electronic applications accepted. *Expenses:* Contact institution.

University of Houston–Victoria, School of Education, Health Professions and Human Development, Victoria, TX 77901-4450. Offers administration and supervision (M Ed); adult and higher education (M Ed); counselor education (M Ed); curriculum and instruction (M Ed); dyslexia education (Certificate); educational technology (M Ed); special education (M Ed). *Program availability:* Part-time, evening/weekend, online learning. *Degree requirements:* For master's, comprehensive exam, project or thesis. *Entrance requirements:* For master's, GRE General Test. Additional exam requirements/ recommendations for international students: Required—TOEFL. Electronic applications accepted. *Expenses: Tuition, area resident:* Full-time $6154; part-time $3077 per semester. Tuition, state resident: full-time $6154; part-time $3077 per semester. Tuition, nonresident: full-time $13,624; part-time $6812 per semester. *International tuition:* $13,624 full-time. *Required fees:* $1405; $847 per semester. $423 per semester. Tuition and fees vary according to program. *Faculty research:* Reading and language arts education, evaluation and diagnosis of special children's abilities.

University of Idaho, College of Graduate Studies, College of Education, Health and Human Sciences, Department of Curriculum and Instruction, Moscow, ID 83844-3082. Offers career and technology education (M Ed); curriculum and instruction (M Ed, Ed S); special education (M Ed). *Faculty:* 28 full-time (19 women). *Students:* 30 full-time (24 women), 37 part-time (29 women). Average age 37. In 2018, 32 master's awarded. *Entrance requirements:* For master's, minimum GPA of 3.0. Additional exam requirements/recommendations for international students: Required—TOEFL (minimum score 79 iBT). *Application deadline:* For fall admission, 8/1 for domestic students; for spring admission, 12/15 for domestic students. Applications are processed on a rolling basis. Application fee: $60. Electronic applications accepted. *Expenses:* Tuition, state resident: full-time $7266.44; part-time $474.50 per credit hour. Tuition, nonresident: full-time $24,902; part-time $1453.50 per credit hour. *Required fees:* $2085.56; $45.50 per credit hour. *Financial support:* Research assistantships and teaching assistantships available. Financial award applicants required to submit FAFSA.
Website: http://www.uidaho.edu/ed/ci

University of Illinois at Chicago, College of Education, Department of Curriculum and Instruction, Chicago, IL 60607-7128. Offers curriculum studies (PhD); elementary education (M Ed); secondary education (M Ed). *Program availability:* Part-time, evening/ weekend. *Degree requirements:* For doctorate, thesis/dissertation. *Entrance requirements:* For master's, minimum GPA of 2.75; for doctorate, GRE General Test, minimum GPA of 2.75. Additional exam requirements/recommendations for international students: Required—TOEFL. Electronic applications accepted. *Faculty research:* Curriculum theory, curriculum development, research on teaching, curriculum and context, reading/literacy.

University of Illinois at Urbana–Champaign, Graduate College, College of Education, Department of Curriculum and Instruction, Champaign, IL 61820. Offers curriculum and instruction (Ed M, MA, MS, Ed D, PhD, CAS); early childhood education (Ed M); elementary education (Ed M); secondary education (Ed M). *Program availability:* Part-time, online learning.

University of Indianapolis, Graduate Programs, School of Education, Indianapolis, IN 46227-3697. Offers art education (MAT); biology (MAT); chemistry (MAT); curriculum and instruction (MA); earth sciences (MAT); education (MA, MAT); educational leadership (MA); elementary education (MA); English (MAT); French (MAT); math (MAT); physical education (MAT); physics (MAT); secondary education (MA), including art education, education, English education, social studies education; social studies (MAT); Spanish (MAT). *Accreditation:* NCATE. *Program availability:* Part-time, evening/ weekend. *Entrance requirements:* For master's, GRE Subject Test, PRAXIS I, minimum GPA of 2.5, 3 letters of recommendation, interview. Additional exam requirements/ recommendations for international students: Required—TOEFL (minimum score 550 paper-based). *Faculty research:* Assessment of teacher education, perceptions of prospective teachers by parents.

University of Jamestown, Program in Education, Jamestown, ND 58405. Offers curriculum and instruction (M Ed). *Degree requirements:* For master's, thesis or project.

The University of Kansas, Graduate Studies, School of Education, Department of Curriculum and Teaching, Lawrence, KS 66045-3101. Offers MA, MS Ed, PhD. *Program availability:* Part-time, evening/weekend, online learning. *Students:* 59 full-time (40 women), 243 part-time (192 women); includes 44 minority (15 Black or African American, non-Hispanic/Latino; 2 American Indian or Alaska Native, non-Hispanic/ Latino; 8 Asian, non-Hispanic/Latino; 10 Hispanic/Latino; 9 Two or more races, non-Hispanic/Latino), 18 international. Average age 34. 160 applicants, 83% accepted, 103 enrolled. In 2018, 180 master's, 16 doctorates awarded. *Entrance requirements:* For master's, minimum GPA of 3.0, official transcript(s), resume, statement of goals/ purpose, three letters of recommendation; for doctorate, GRE General Test, minimum graduate GPA of 3.5, official transcript(s), resume, statement of goals/purpose, three letters of recommendation, writing sample. Additional exam requirements/ recommendations for international students: Required—TOEFL, IELTS. *Application deadline:* For fall admission, 3/15 priority date for domestic and international students; for spring admission, 10/15 priority date for domestic and international students. Application fee: $65 ($85 for international students). Electronic applications accepted. *Financial support:* Fellowships, research assistantships, teaching assistantships, Federal Work-Study, scholarships/grants, and unspecified assistantships available. Financial award application deadline: 3/15; financial award applicants required to submit

FAFSA. *Faculty research:* Community-based field experiences in teacher education, vocabulary and narrative development of primary students, narrative inquiry, engaging students in critical thinking by using technology in the classroom, argumentation and evaluation intervention in science education. *Unit head:* Dr. Steven Hugh White, Chair of Curriculum and Teaching, 785-864-9662, E-mail: s-white@ku.edu. *Application contact:* Susan M. McGee, Graduate Admissions Coordinator, 785-864-4437, E-mail: smmcgee@ku.edu.
Website: http://ct.soe.ku.edu/

University of Kentucky, Graduate School, College of Education, Program in Curriculum and Instruction, Lexington, KY 40506-0032. Offers curriculum and instruction (Ed D, PhD); elementary education (MA Ed); instructional system design (MS Ed); literacy (MA Ed); middle school education (MA Ed, MS Ed); secondary education (MA Ed, MS Ed). *Accreditation:* NCATE. *Degree requirements:* For master's, comprehensive exam, thesis optional; for doctorate, comprehensive exam, thesis/ dissertation. *Entrance requirements:* For master's, GRE General Test, minimum undergraduate GPA of 2.75; for doctorate, GRE General Test, minimum graduate GPA of 3.0. Additional exam requirements/recommendations for international students: Required—TOEFL (minimum score 550 paper-based). Electronic applications accepted. *Faculty research:* Educational reform, multicultural education, classroom instructional practices, performance based assessment, primary school programs.

University of Louisiana at Lafayette, College of Education, Department of Educational Curriculum and Instruction, Program in Curriculum and Instruction, Lafayette, LA 70504. Offers instructional specialist (M Ed); K-8 mathematics education (M Ed); non-public school administration (M Ed); special education diagnostics (M Ed); teacher researcher (M Ed). *Accreditation:* NCATE. *Entrance requirements:* For master's, GRE General Test, teaching certificate. Additional exam requirements/recommendations for international students: Required—TOEFL (minimum score 550 paper-based). Electronic applications accepted.

University of Louisiana at Monroe, Graduate School, College of Arts, Education, and Sciences, School of Education, Program in Curriculum and Instruction, Monroe, LA 71209-0001. Offers M Ed, Ed D. *Accreditation:* NCATE. *Faculty:* 11 full-time (7 women). *Students:* 29 full-time (20 women), 91 part-time (73 women); includes 42 minority (33 Black or African American, non-Hispanic/Latino; 2 Asian, non-Hispanic/Latino; 3 Hispanic/Latino; 4 Two or more races, non-Hispanic/Latino). Average age 36. 32 applicants, 69% accepted, 18 enrolled. In 2018, 14 master's, 7 doctorates awarded. *Degree requirements:* For master's, comprehensive exam (for some programs), thesis; for doctorate, thesis/dissertation, internships. *Entrance requirements:* For master's, GRE General Test; for doctorate, GRE General Test, minimum undergraduate GPA of 2.75, graduate 3.25. Additional exam requirements/recommendations for international students: Required—TOEFL (minimum score 500 paper-based; 61 iBT). *Application deadline:* For fall admission, 8/24 priority date for domestic students, 7/1 for international students; for winter admission, 12/14 priority date for domestic students; for spring admission, 1/19 for domestic students, 11/1 for international students. Applications are processed on a rolling basis. Application fee: $20 ($30 for international students). Electronic applications accepted. *Financial support:* Research assistantships, career-related internships or fieldwork, Federal Work-Study, and unspecified assistantships available. Financial award application deadline: 4/1; financial award applicants required to submit FAFSA.

University of Louisville, Graduate School, College of Education and Human Development, Departments of Early Childhood and Elementary Education, Middle and Secondary Education, and Special Education, Louisville, KY 40292-0001. Offers art education (MAT); autism and applied behavior analysis (Certificate); curriculum and instruction (PhD); early elementary education (MAT); exercise physiology (MS); health and physical education (MAT); health professions education (Certificate); higher education (MA); human resources and organization development (MS); instructional technology (M Ed); interdisciplinary early childhood education (MAT); middle school education (MAT); music education (MAT); secondary education (MAT); special education (MAT); sport administration (MS); teacher leadership (M Ed). *Program availability:* Part-time, evening/weekend, 100% online, blended/hybrid learning. *Faculty:* 97 full-time (64 women), 131 part-time/adjunct (86 women). *Students:* 109 full-time (72 women), 139 part-time (87 women); includes 43 minority (18 Black or African American, non-Hispanic/Latino; 6 Asian, non-Hispanic/Latino; 10 Hispanic/Latino; 9 Two or more races, non-Hispanic/Latino), 9 international. Average age 29. 108 applicants, 75% accepted, 59 enrolled. In 2018, 64 master's awarded. Terminal master's awarded for partial completion of doctoral program. *Degree requirements:* For master's, comprehensive exam (for some programs), thesis optional; for doctorate, comprehensive exam (for some programs), thesis/dissertation. *Entrance requirements:* For master's, GRE (for most programs), PRAXIS (for educator preparation programs), professional statement, recommendation letters, resume, transcripts; for doctorate and Certificate, GRE, professional statement, recommendation letters, resume, transcripts. Additional exam requirements/recommendations for international students: Required— TOEFL (minimum score 550 paper-based; 79 iBT); Recommended—IELTS (minimum score 6.5). *Application deadline:* For fall admission, 6/1 priority date for domestic students, 5/1 priority date for international students; for spring admission, 10/1 for domestic students, 11/1 priority date for international students; for summer admission, 3/ 1 priority date for domestic students, 4/1 priority date for international students. Application fee: $65. *Expenses: Tuition, area resident:* Full-time $6500; part-time $723 per credit hour. Tuition, state resident: full-time $6500. Tuition, nonresident: full-time $13,557; part-time $1507 per credit hour. Tuition and fees vary according to course load and program. *Financial support:* In 2018–19, 144 students received support, including fellowships with full tuition reimbursements available (averaging $21,024 per year), research assistantships with full tuition reimbursements available (averaging $21,024 per year), teaching assistantships with full tuition reimbursements available (averaging $21,024 per year); Federal Work-Study, scholarships/grants, health care benefits, tuition waivers (full), and unspecified assistantships also available. Financial award application deadline: 3/1; financial award applicants required to submit FAFSA. *Faculty research:* Children's early reading and writing development, crelevance of basic facts in elementary mathematics instruction, clinical model of teacher education, cultural and linguistic context of diverse learners, and STEM-integrated curriculum design and development. STEM teaching and learning, content literacy for English language learners, social justice in teacher education, adolescent literacy, mathematics teacher development. Classroom and behavior management; moderate/severe disabilities, autism. *Unit head:* Dr. Amy Lingo, Interim Dean, 502-852-3235, Fax: 502-852-1464, E-mail: cehdinfo@louisville.edu. *Application contact:* Dr. Margaret Pentecost, Assistant Dean for Graduate Student Success, 502-852-6437, Fax: 502-852-1417, E-mail: gedadm@louisville.edu.
Website: http://louisville.edu/delphi

University of Lynchburg, Graduate Studies, M Ed Program in Curriculum and Instruction, Lynchburg, VA 24501-3199. Offers instructional leadership (M Ed); teacher licensure (M Ed). *Program availability:* Part-time, evening/weekend. *Degree requirements:* For master's, comprehensive exam, internship, state license exam. *Entrance requirements:* For master's, GRE, minimum GPA of 3.0 (preferred), official transcripts (bachelor's, others as relevant), three letters of recommendation, career

goals statement. Additional exam requirements/recommendations for international students: Required—TOEFL (minimum score 550 paper-based; 80 iBT), IELTS (minimum score 6). Electronic applications accepted. Application fee is waived when completed online. *Expenses:* Contact institution.

University of Manitoba, Faculty of Graduate Studies, Faculty of Education, Department of Curriculum, Teaching and Learning, Winnipeg, MB R3T 2N2, Canada. Offers language and literacy (M Ed); second language education (M Ed); studies in curriculum, teaching and learning (M Ed). *Degree requirements:* For master's, thesis or alternative.

University of Mary, Liffrig Family School of Education and Behavioral Sciences, Department of Education, Bismarck, ND 58504-9652. Offers curriculum, instruction and assessment (M Ed); education (Ed D); elementary administration (M Ed); reading (M Ed); secondary administration (M Ed); special education strategist (M Ed). *Program availability:* Part-time. *Degree requirements:* For master's, portfolio or thesis. *Entrance requirements:* For master's, interview, letters of reference, minimum GPA of 2.5. Additional exam requirements/recommendations for international students: Required—TOEFL (minimum score 500 paper-based; 71 iBT). Electronic applications accepted.

University of Mary Hardin-Baylor, Graduate Studies in Education, Belton, TX 76513. Offers curriculum and instruction (M Ed); educational administration (M Ed, Ed D), including higher education (Ed D); leadership in nursing education (Ed D); P-12 (Ed D). *Program availability:* Part-time, evening/weekend. *Degree requirements:* For master's, comprehensive exam; for doctorate, thesis/dissertation. *Entrance requirements:* For master's, minimum GPA of 3.0, interview; for doctorate, minimum GPA of 3.5, interview, essay, resume, employment verification, 3 letters of recommendation. Additional exam requirements/recommendations for international students: Required—TOEFL (minimum score 60 iBT), IELTS (minimum score 4.5). Electronic applications accepted. *Expenses:* Contact institution. *Faculty research:* Motivational orientation of preservice teachers.

University of Maryland, College Park, Academic Affairs, College of Education, Department of Teaching, Learning, Policy and Leadership, College Park, MD 20742. Offers reading (M Ed, MA, PhD, CAGS); secondary education (M Ed, MA, Ed D, PhD, CAGS); teaching English to speakers of other languages (M Ed). *Accreditation:* NCATE. *Program availability:* Part-time, evening/weekend, online learning. *Degree requirements:* For master's, comprehensive exam, seminar paper; for doctorate, comprehensive exam, thesis/dissertation, published paper, oral exam. *Entrance requirements:* For master's, GRE General Test or MAT, minimum GPA of 3.0, 3 letters of recommendation; for doctorate, GRE General Test or MAT, minimum undergraduate GPA of 3.0, graduate 3.5; 3 letters of recommendation. Electronic applications accepted. *Faculty research:* Teacher preparation, curriculum study, in-service education.

University of Massachusetts Lowell, Graduate School of Education, Lowell, MA 01854. Offers curriculum and instruction (M Ed). *Accreditation:* NCATE. *Program availability:* Part-time, evening/weekend, online learning. Terminal master's awarded for partial completion of doctoral program. *Entrance requirements:* For master's, GRE General Test. Additional exam requirements/recommendations for international students: Required—TOEFL. Electronic applications accepted.

University of Memphis, Graduate School, College of Education, Department of Instruction and Curriculum Leadership, Memphis, TN 38152. Offers advanced studies in teaching and learning (M Ed); applied behavior analysis (Graduate Certificate); autism studies (Graduate Certificate); early childhood education (MAT, MS, Ed D); elementary education (MAT); instruction and curriculum (MS, Ed D); instruction design and technology (MS, Ed D); instructional design and technology (Graduate Certificate); literacy, leadership, and coaching (Graduate Certificate); reading (MS, Ed D); school library information specialist (Graduate Certificate); secondary education (MAT); special education (MAT, MS, Ed D); STEM teacher leadership (Graduate Certificate); urban education (Graduate Certificate). *Accreditation:* NCATE (one or more programs are accredited). *Program availability:* Part-time. *Students:* 62 full-time (45 women), 412 part-time (326 women); includes 209 minority (179 Black or African American, non-Hispanic/Latino; 1 American Indian or Alaska Native, non-Hispanic/Latino; 5 Asian, non-Hispanic/Latino; 17 Hispanic/Latino; 7 Two or more races, non-Hispanic/Latino), 4 international. Average age 35. 195 applicants, 91% accepted, 143 enrolled. In 2018, 122 master's, 13 doctorates, 29 other advanced degrees awarded. Terminal master's awarded for partial completion of doctoral program. *Degree requirements:* For master's, comprehensive exam, thesis or alternative; for doctorate, comprehensive exam, thesis/dissertation. *Entrance requirements:* For master's, GRE General Test, PRAXIS, minimum GPA of 2.5, letters of reference; for doctorate, GRE General Test, GRE Subject Test, 2 years of teaching experience, letters of reference, statement of purpose, interview. Additional exam requirements/recommendations for international students: Required—TOEFL (minimum score 550 paper-based; 79 iBT). *Application deadline:* For fall admission, 4/1 priority date for domestic students; for spring admission, 10/1 priority date for domestic students; for summer admission, 2/1 priority date for domestic students. Applications are processed on a rolling basis. Application fee: $35 ($60 for international students). Electronic applications accepted. *Expenses: Tuition, area resident:* Full-time $10,240; part-time $503 per credit hour. *Tuition, state resident:* full-time $10,464. *Tuition, nonresident:* full-time $20,224; part-time $991 per credit hour. *Required fees:* $850; $106 per credit hour. *Financial support:* Research assistantships with full tuition reimbursements, teaching assistantships with full tuition reimbursements, career-related internships or fieldwork, Federal Work-Study, institutionally sponsored loans, scholarships/grants, traineeships, and unspecified assistantships available. Support available to part-time students. Financial award application deadline: 2/1; financial award applicants required to submit FAFSA. *Faculty research:* Effective urban teachers, preparation and retention of urban teachers, technology utilization in schools, field-based teacher preparation programs, effective use of online instruction. *Unit head:* Dr. Christian Mueller, Chair, 901-678-2365, E-mail: cemuellr@memphis.edu. *Application contact:* Dr. Lee Allen, Director of Graduate Programs, 901-678-4073, E-mail: allenlee@memphis.edu.
Website: http://www.memphis.edu/icl/

University of Michigan–Dearborn, College of Education, Health, and Human Services, Doctoral Program in Education, Dearborn, MI 48126. Offers curriculum and practice (Ed D); educational leadership (Ed D); metropolitan education (Ed D). *Program availability:* Part-time, evening/weekend. *Faculty:* 5 full-time (3 women), 1 part-time/adjunct (0 women). *Students:* 2 full-time (both women), 19 part-time (12 women); includes 9 minority (8 Black or African American, non-Hispanic/Latino; 1 Hispanic/Latino). Average age 44. 9 applicants, 44% accepted, 3 enrolled. In 2018, 5 doctorates awarded. *Degree requirements:* For doctorate, thesis/dissertation. *Entrance requirements:* For doctorate, GRE (taken within the last 5 years), master's degree with minimum GPA of 3.3, 3 letters of recommendation (1 from faculty), 3 years' professional and/or teaching experience. Additional exam requirements/recommendations for international students: Required—TOEFL (minimum score 560 paper-based; 84 iBT), IELTS (minimum score 6.5). *Application deadline:* For fall admission, 3/1 for domestic and international students. Application fee: $60. Electronic applications accepted. *Expenses:* $12,140 per academic year (typical full-time in-state); $20,708 per academic year (typical full-time out-of-state). *Financial support:* In 2018–19, 6 students received support. Scholarships/grants available. Financial award application deadline: 3/1; financial award applicants required to submit FAFSA. *Faculty research:* Urban education, educational leadership, assessment and evaluation, research methods,

science education. *Unit head:* Dr. Chris Burke, Director, 313-593-5319, E-mail: cjfburke@umich.edu. *Application contact:* Office of Graduate Studies, 313-583-6321, E-mail: umd-graduatestudies@umich.edu.
Website: http://umdearborn.edu/cehhs/cehhs_edd/

University of Michigan–Dearborn, College of Education, Health, and Human Services, Education Specialist Program, Dearborn, MI 48126. Offers curriculum and practice (Ed S); educational leadership (Ed S); metropolitan education (Ed S). *Program availability:* Part-time, evening/weekend. *Faculty:* 1 (woman) full-time, 1 part-time/adjunct (0 women). *Students:* 6 part-time (3 women); includes 1 minority (Black or African American, non-Hispanic/Latino). Average age 38. 3 applicants, 33% accepted, 1 enrolled. In 2018, 2 Ed Ss awarded. *Entrance requirements:* For degree, master's degree with minimum GPA of 3.3; at least 3 years' teaching experience or the equivalent experience working in a professional setting. Additional exam requirements/recommendations for international students: Required—TOEFL (minimum score 560 paper-based; 84 iBT), IELTS (minimum score 6.5). *Application deadline:* For fall admission, 8/1 for domestic students, 5/1 for international students; for winter admission, 12/1 for domestic students, 9/1 for international students; for spring admission, 4/1 for domestic students, 1/1 for international students. Applications are processed on a rolling basis. Application fee: $60. Electronic applications accepted. *Expenses:* $12,140 per academic year (typical full-time in-state); $20,708 per academic year (typical full-time out-of-state). *Financial support:* In 2018–19, 2 students received support. Scholarships/grants available. Financial award application deadline: 3/1; financial award applicants required to submit FAFSA. *Faculty research:* Educational leadership, curriculum development, education policy, organizational development, K-12 administration. *Unit head:* Dr. Chris Burke, Director, 313-593-5319, E-mail: cjfburke@umich.edu. *Application contact:* Office of Graduate Studies, 313-583-6321, E-mail: umd-graduatestudies@umich.edu.
Website: http://umdearborn.edu/cehhs/cehhs_eds/

University of Michigan–Flint, School of Education and Human Services, Department of Education, Flint, MI 48502-1950. Offers curriculum and instruction (Ed S); early childhood education (MA); education (Ed D); educational leadership (Ed S); educational technology (MA), including curriculum and instruction, developer; literacy education (MA); secondary education with certification (MA). *Program availability:* Part-time, evening/weekend, online only, 100% online, mixed mode format (for some programs). *Faculty:* 16 full-time (10 women), 28 part-time/adjunct (14 women). *Students:* 31 full-time (23 women), 179 part-time (135 women); includes 54 minority (42 Black or African American, non-Hispanic/Latino; 3 Asian, non-Hispanic/Latino; 4 Hispanic/Latino; 1 Native Hawaiian or other Pacific Islander, non-Hispanic/Latino; 4 Two or more races, non-Hispanic/Latino), 1 international. Average age 39. 133 applicants, 72% accepted, 61 enrolled. In 2018, 60 master's awarded. *Degree requirements:* For master's, thesis optional; for doctorate, thesis/dissertation. *Entrance requirements:* For master's, bachelor's degree from regionally-accredited institution, minimum overall undergraduate GPA of 3.0 on 4.0 scale; for doctorate, completion of Eds minimum overall graduate GPA of 3.3 (6.0 on a 9.0 scale) or equivalent; at least 3 years of work experience in a P-16 educational institution or in an education-related position; for Ed S, MA or MS in education-related field from accredited institution; minimum overall graduate GPA of 3.0 (6.0 on a 9.0 scale) or equivalent; at least 3 years of work experience in an educational setting. Additional exam requirements/recommendations for international students: Required—TOEFL (minimum score 84 iBT), IELTS (minimum score 6.5). *Application deadline:* For fall admission, 8/1 for domestic students, 5/1 for international students; for winter admission, 11/15 for domestic students, 9/15 for international students; for spring admission, 3/15 for domestic students, 1/15 for international students; for summer admission, 5/15 for domestic students. Applications are processed on a rolling basis. Application fee: $55. Electronic applications accepted. *Expenses:* Contact institution. *Financial support:* Federal Work-Study, scholarships/grants, and unspecified assistantships available. Financial award application deadline: 3/1; financial award applicants required to submit FAFSA. *Unit head:* Dr. Mary Jo Finney, Department Chair/Associate Professor, 810-766-6617, E-mail: mjfinney@umflint.edu. *Application contact:* Matt Bohlen, Director of Graduate Admissions, 810-762-3171, Fax: 810-766-6789, E-mail: mbohlen@umflint.edu.
Website: https://www.umflint.edu/education/graduate-programs

University of Minnesota, Twin Cities Campus, Graduate School, College of Education and Human Development, Department of Curriculum and Instruction, Program in Curriculum and Instruction, Minneapolis, MN 55455-0213. Offers M Ed, MA, PhD. *Students:* 165 full-time (111 women), 146 part-time (111 women); includes 72 minority (11 Black or African American, non-Hispanic/Latino; 3 American Indian or Alaska Native, non-Hispanic/Latino; 22 Asian, non-Hispanic/Latino; 22 Hispanic/Latino; 14 Two or more races, non-Hispanic/Latino), 45 international. Average age 36. 227 applicants, 52% accepted, 88 enrolled. In 2018, 46 master's, 21 doctorates awarded. Application fee: $75 ($95 for international students). *Unit head:* Dr. Mark Vagle, Chair, 612-625-4006, Fax: 612-624-8277, E-mail: mvagle@umn.edu. *Application contact:* Dr. Mark Vagle, Chair, 612-625-4006, Fax: 612-624-8277, E-mail: mvagle@umn.edu.
Website: http://www.cehd.umn.edu/ci

University of Missouri, Office of Research and Graduate Studies, College of Education, Department of Educational, School, and Counseling Psychology, Columbia, MO 65211. Offers counseling psychology (M Ed, MA, PhD, Ed S); educational psychology (M Ed, MA, PhD, Ed S); learning and instruction (M Ed); school psychology (M Ed, MA, PhD, Ed S). *Accreditation:* APA (one or more programs are accredited). *Program availability:* Part-time. *Entrance requirements:* For master's, doctorate, and Ed S, GRE General Test, minimum GPA of 3.0. Additional exam requirements/recommendations for international students: Required—TOEFL.

University of Missouri, Office of Research and Graduate Studies, College of Education, Department of Learning, Teaching and Curriculum, Columbia, MO 65211. Offers agricultural education (M Ed, PhD, Ed S); art education (M Ed, PhD, Ed S); business and office education (M Ed, PhD, Ed S); early childhood education (M Ed, PhD, Ed S); elementary education (M Ed, PhD, Ed S); English education (M Ed, PhD, Ed S); foreign language education (M Ed, PhD, Ed S); health education and promotion (M Ed, PhD); learning and instruction (M Ed); marketing education (M Ed, PhD, Ed S); mathematics education (M Ed, PhD, Ed S); music education (M Ed, PhD, Ed S); reading education (M Ed, PhD, Ed S); science education (M Ed, PhD, Ed S); social studies education (M Ed, PhD, Ed S); vocational education (M Ed, PhD, Ed S). *Program availability:* Part-time. Terminal master's awarded for partial completion of doctoral program. *Entrance requirements:* For master's and Ed S, GRE General Test or MAT, minimum GPA of 3.0; for doctorate, GRE General Test, minimum GPA of 3.0. Additional exam requirements/recommendations for international students: Required—TOEFL.

University of Missouri–Kansas City, School of Education, Kansas City, MO 64110-2499. Offers administration (Ed D); counseling and guidance (MA, Ed S), including mental health counseling (Ed S), school counseling (Ed S); counseling psychology (PhD); curriculum and instruction (MA, Ed S), including language and literacy (Ed S); education (PhD), including higher education administration, PK-12 education administration; educational administration (MA, Ed S), including advanced principal (Ed S), beginning principal (Ed S), district-level administration (Ed S); reading education (MA); special education (MA). PhD in education offered through the School of Graduate

Studies. *Accreditation:* NCATE. *Program availability:* Part-time, evening/weekend. *Degree requirements:* For doctorate, thesis/dissertation, internship, practicum. *Entrance requirements:* For master's, GRE, minimum GPA of 2.75, 2 letters of reference, written statement of purpose; for doctorate, GRE, minimum GPA of 3.0; for Ed S, minimum GPA of 3.0. Additional exam requirements/recommendations for international students: Required—TOEFL (minimum score 550 paper-based; 80 iBT). *Faculty research:* Urban education, inquiry-based field study, theories of counseling and psychotherapy, school literacy, educational technology.

University of Missouri–St. Louis, College of Education, Department of Educator Preparation, Innovation and Research, St. Louis, MO 63121. Offers elementary education (M Ed), including early childhood, general, reading; secondary education (M Ed), including curriculum and instruction, general, middle level education, reading, teaching English to speakers of other languages (TESOL); special education (M Ed), including autism and developmental disabilities, early childhood special education. *Program availability:* Part-time, evening/weekend. *Degree requirements:* For master's, comprehensive exam. *Entrance requirements:* Additional exam requirements/ recommendations for international students: Recommended—TOEFL (minimum score 550 paper-based; 79 iBT), IELTS (minimum score 6.5). Electronic applications accepted.

University of Montana, Graduate School, Phyllis J. Washington College of Education and Human Sciences, Department of Teaching and Learning, Missoula, MT 59812. Offers curriculum and instruction (M Ed, Ed D); early childhood education (M Ed); education (MA); teaching and learning (PhD). *Program availability:* Part-time. *Degree requirements:* For doctorate, thesis/dissertation. *Entrance requirements:* For master's, GRE General Test. Additional exam requirements/recommendations for international students: Required—TOEFL.

University of Nebraska at Kearney, College of Education, Department of Teacher Education, Kearney, NE 68849-0001. Offers curriculum and instruction (MA Ed), including early childhood education, elementary education, English as a second language, instructional effectiveness, reading/special education, secondary education; instructional technology (MS Ed), including information technology, instructional technology, school librarian; reading PK-12 (MA Ed); special education (MA Ed), including advanced practitioner: assistive technology specialist, advanced practitioner: behavioral interventionist, advanced practitioner: inclusive collaboration specialist, gifted, teacher education. *Program availability:* Part-time, evening/weekend, online only, 100% online. *Degree requirements:* For master's, comprehensive exam, thesis optional. *Entrance requirements:* For master's, portfolio or GRE. Additional exam requirements/ recommendations for international students: Recommended—TOEFL (minimum score 550 paper-based; 79 iBT), IELTS (minimum score 6.5). Electronic applications accepted. *Expenses:* Contact institution.

University of Nebraska–Lincoln, Graduate College, College of Education and Human Sciences, Department of Teaching, Learning and Teacher Education, Lincoln, NE 68588. Offers adult and continuing education (MA); educational studies (Ed D, PhD), including special education (Ed D); teaching, learning and teacher education (M Ed, MA, MST, Ed D, PhD); vocational and adult education (M Ed, MA). *Accreditation:* NCATE. *Degree requirements:* For master's, thesis optional. *Entrance requirements:* Additional exam requirements/recommendations for international students: Required—TOEFL (minimum score 550 paper-based). Electronic applications accepted. *Faculty research:* Teacher education, instructional leadership, literacy education, technology, improvement of school curriculum.

University of Nebraska–Lincoln, Graduate College, College of Education and Human Sciences, Interdepartmental Area of Administration, Curriculum and Instruction, Lincoln, NE 68588. Offers Ed D, PhD, JD/PhD. *Accreditation:* NCATE. *Program availability:* Online learning. *Degree requirements:* For doctorate, comprehensive exam, thesis/ dissertation. *Entrance requirements:* For doctorate, GRE, curriculum vitae. Additional exam requirements/recommendations for international students: Required—TOEFL (minimum score 550 paper-based). Electronic applications accepted.

University of Nevada, Las Vegas, Graduate College, College of Education, Department of Teaching and Learning, Las Vegas, NV 89154-3005. Offers curriculum and instruction (M Ed, MS, Ed D, PhD, Ed S), including teacher education (PhD); elementary teaching (Certificate); online teaching and training (Certificate); secondary teaching (Certificate); social justice studies (Certificate); teaching and learning (PhD). *Program availability:* Part-time, evening/weekend. *Faculty:* 25 full-time (12 women), 11 part-time/adjunct (8 women). *Students:* 304 full-time (212 women), 271 part-time (181 women); includes 255 minority (56 Black or African American, non-Hispanic/Latino; 1 American Indian or Alaska Native, non-Hispanic/Latino; 38 Asian, non-Hispanic/Latino; 124 Hispanic/Latino; 1 Native Hawaiian or other Pacific Islander, non-Hispanic/Latino; 35 Two or more races, non-Hispanic/Latino), 16 international. Average age 34. 228 applicants, 86% accepted, 164 enrolled. In 2018, 135 master's, 12 doctorates, 10 other advanced degrees awarded. *Degree requirements:* For master's, comprehensive exam (for some programs), thesis (for some programs); for doctorate, comprehensive exam, thesis/dissertation, defense of dissertation; for other advanced degree, comprehensive exam (for some programs), oral presentation of special project or professional paper. *Entrance requirements:* For master's, bachelor's degree with minimum GPA 2.75; for doctorate, GRE General Test, master's degree with minimum GPA of 3.0; statement of purpose; demonstration of oral communication skills; 3 letters of recommendation; for other advanced degree, PRAXIS Core (for some programs); PRAXIS II (for some programs), bachelor's degree (for some programs). Additional exam requirements/ recommendations for international students: Required—TOEFL (minimum score 550 paper-based; 80 iBT), IELTS (minimum score 7). *Application deadline:* For fall admission, 6/1 for domestic students, 5/1 for international students; for spring admission, 11/1 for domestic students, 10/1 for international students; for summer admission, 3/15 for domestic students. Application fee: $60 ($95 for international students). Electronic applications accepted. *Financial support:* In 2018–19, 31 students received support, including 7 research assistantships with full tuition reimbursements available (averaging $18,286 per year), 24 teaching assistantships with full tuition reimbursements available (averaging $19,271 per year); institutionally sponsored loans, scholarships/grants, health care benefits, and unspecified assistantships also available. Financial award application deadline: 3/15; financial award applicants required to submit FAFSA. *Faculty research:* Content area and critical literacy, education in content areas, teacher education, science, technology, engineering and mathematics education, immersive environments/simulations/games. *Total annual research expenditures:* $1.1 million. *Unit head:* Dr. P.G. Schrader, Chair/Professor, 702-895-3331, Fax: 702-895-4898, E-mail: tl.chair@unlv.edu. *Application contact:* Dr. Micah Stohlmann, Graduate Coordinator, 702-895-0836, Fax: 702-895-4898, E-mail: tl.gradcoord@unlv.edu. Website: http://tl.unlv.edu/

University of Nevada, Reno, Graduate School, College of Education, Department of Curriculum, Teaching and Learning, Program in Curriculum and Instruction, Reno, NV 89557. Offers PhD. *Degree requirements:* For doctorate, thesis/dissertation. *Entrance requirements:* For doctorate, GRE General Test, minimum GPA of 3.0. Additional exam requirements/recommendations for international students: Required—TOEFL (minimum score 500 paper-based; 61 iBT), IELTS (minimum score 6). Electronic applications accepted. *Faculty research:* Education, development, pedagogy.

University of Nevada, Reno, Graduate School, College of Education, Department of Curriculum, Teaching and Learning, Program in Curriculum, Teaching and Learning, Reno, NV 89557. Offers Ed D, PhD. *Degree requirements:* For doctorate, comprehensive exam, thesis/dissertation. *Entrance requirements:* For doctorate, GRE General Test, minimum GPA of 3.0. Additional exam requirements/recommendations for international students: Required—TOEFL (minimum score 500 paper-based; 61 iBT), IELTS (minimum score 6). Electronic applications accepted. *Faculty research:* Education, trends, pedagogy.

University of New England, College of Graduate and Professional Studies, Portland, ME 04005-9526. Offers advanced educational leadership (CAGS); applied nutrition (MS); career and technical education (MS Ed); curriculum and instruction (MS Ed); education (CAGS, Post-Master's Certificate); educational leadership (MS Ed, Ed D); generalist (MS Ed); health informatics (MS, Graduate Certificate); inclusion education (MS Ed); literacy K-12 (MS Ed); medical education leadership (MMEL); public health (MPH, Graduate Certificate); reading specialist (MS Ed); social work (MSW). *Program availability:* Part-time, evening/weekend, online only, 100% online. *Faculty:* 109 part-time/adjunct (78 women). *Students:* 1,207 full-time (972 women), 561 part-time (450 women); includes 411 minority (280 Black or African American, non-Hispanic/Latino; 17 American Indian or Alaska Native, non-Hispanic/Latino; 74 Asian, non-Hispanic/Latino; 25 Hispanic/Latino; 9 Native Hawaiian or other Pacific Islander, non-Hispanic/Latino; 6 Two or more races, non-Hispanic/Latino). Average age 36. 740 applicants, 92% accepted, 494 enrolled. In 2018, 586 master's, 44 doctorates, 85 other advanced degrees awarded. *Application deadline:* Applications are processed on a rolling basis. Electronic applications accepted. *Financial support:* Application deadline: 5/1; applicants required to submit FAFSA. *Unit head:* Dr. Martha Wilson, Dean of the College of Graduate and Professional Studies, 207-221-4985, E-mail: mwilson13@une.edu. *Application contact:* Nicole Lindsay, Director of Online Admissions, 207-221-4966, E-mail: nlindsay1@une.edu.
Website: http://online.une.edu

University of New Hampshire, Graduate School, College of Liberal Arts, Department of Education, Program in Education, Durham, NH 03824. Offers children and youth in communities (PhD); curriculum and instruction leadership (Postbaccalaureate Certificate); education (PhD). *Entrance requirements:* For doctorate, GRE General Test. Additional exam requirements/recommendations for international students: Required—TOEFL (minimum score 550 paper-based; 80 iBT). Electronic applications accepted.

University of New Orleans, Graduate School, College of Liberal Arts, Education and Human Development, Department of Curriculum, Instruction, and Special Education, New Orleans, LA 70148. Offers curriculum and instruction (M Ed); teaching (MAT). *Accreditation:* NCATE. *Program availability:* Evening/weekend. *Entrance requirements:* For master's, GRE General Test. Additional exam requirements/recommendations for international students: Required—TOEFL (minimum score 550 paper-based; 79 iBT). Electronic applications accepted. *Faculty research:* Inclusion, transition, early childhood, mild/moderate, severe/profound.

The University of North Carolina at Chapel Hill, Graduate School, School of Education, Program in Education, Chapel Hill, NC 27599. Offers culture, curriculum and change (MA, PhD); early childhood, intervention and literacy (MA, PhD); educational psychology, measurement and evaluation (MA, PhD). *Accreditation:* NCATE. *Degree requirements:* For master's, thesis; for doctorate, comprehensive exam, thesis/ dissertation. *Entrance requirements:* For master's, GRE General Test, minimum GPA of 3.0 during last 2 years of undergraduates course work; for doctorate, GRE General Test, minimum GPA of 3.0 during last 2 years of undergraduate course work. Additional exam requirements/recommendations for international students: Required—TOEFL (minimum score 550 paper-based). Electronic applications accepted.

The University of North Carolina at Charlotte, Cato College of Education, Interdisciplinary Education Programs, Charlotte, NC 28223-0001. Offers art education (Graduate Certificate); child and family development: early childhood education (MAT); curriculum and instruction (PhD); elementary education (MAT); foreign language education (MAT); middle grades education (MAT); secondary education (MAT); special education (MAT); teaching (Graduate Certificate); teaching English as a second language (MAT); theatre education (Graduate Certificate). *Program availability:* Part-time, 100% online, blended/hybrid learning. *Students:* 70 full-time (55 women), 511 part-time (414 women); includes 228 minority (160 Black or African American, non-Hispanic/ Latino; 1 American Indian or Alaska Native, non-Hispanic/Latino; 11 Asian, non-Hispanic/Latino; 38 Hispanic/Latino; 18 Two or more races, non-Hispanic/Latino), 8 international. Average age 34. 343 applicants, 92% accepted, 219 enrolled. In 2018, 69 master's, 13 doctorates, 161 other advanced degrees awarded. *Entrance requirements:* For master's, GRE or MAT, bachelor's degree, or its U.S. equivalent, from regionally-accredited college or university; minimum overall GPA of 3.0 on all previous work beyond high school; statement of purpose (essay); at least three recommendation forms; for doctorate, GRE or MAT, bachelor's degree (or its U.S. equivalent) from regionally-accredited college or university; minimum overall GPA of 3.5 in master's degree program; for Graduate Certificate, bachelor's degree from regionally-accredited university; minimum GPA of 2.75 on all post-secondary work attempted; transcripts; personal statement outlining why the applicant seeks admission to the program. Additional exam requirements/recommendations for international students: Required— TOEFL (minimum score 523 paper-based; 70 iBT), IELTS (minimum score 6), TOEFL (minimum score 523 paper-based, 70 iBT) or IELTS (6). *Application deadline:* Applications are processed on a rolling basis. Application fee: $75. Electronic applications accepted. Tuition and fees vary according to course load and program. *Financial support:* Career-related internships or fieldwork, institutionally sponsored loans, scholarships/grants, and unspecified assistantships available. Support available to part-time students. Financial award application deadline: 3/1; financial award applicants required to submit FAFSA. *Unit head:* Dr. Ellen McIntyre, Dean, 704-687-8722, E-mail: ellen.mcintyre@uncc.edu. *Application contact:* Kathy B. Giddings, Director of Graduate Admissions, 704-687-5503, Fax: 704-687-1668, E-mail: gradadm@uncc.edu.
Website: http://education.uncc.edu/academic-programs

The University of North Carolina at Greensboro, Graduate School, School of Education, Department of Educational Leadership and Cultural Foundations, Greensboro, NC 27412-5001. Offers curriculum and teaching (PhD), including cultural studies; educational leadership (Ed D, Ed S); school administration (MSA). *Accreditation:* NCATE. *Degree requirements:* For doctorate, thesis/dissertation. *Entrance requirements:* For master's, doctorate, and Ed S, GRE General Test. Additional exam requirements/recommendations for international students: Required— TOEFL. Electronic applications accepted.

The University of North Carolina at Greensboro, Graduate School, School of Education, Department of Teacher Education and Higher Education, Greensboro, NC 27412-5001. Offers college teaching and adult learning (Certificate); curriculum and instruction (M Ed), including chemistry education, elementary education, English as a second language, French education, instructional technology, mathematics education, middle grades education, reading education, science education, social studies education, Spanish education; curriculum and teaching (PhD), including higher education, teacher education and development; English as a second language

(Certificate); higher education (M Ed); supervision (M Ed). *Accreditation:* NCATE. *Program availability:* Part-time. *Degree requirements:* For doctorate, thesis/dissertation. *Entrance requirements:* For master's and doctorate, GRE General Test. Additional exam requirements/recommendations for international students: Required—TOEFL. Electronic applications accepted. *Faculty research:* Community college literacy program, middle school mathematics/computer mathematics.

The University of North Carolina Wilmington, Watson College of Education, Department of Educational Leadership, Wilmington, NC 28403-3297. Offers curriculum, instruction and supervision (M Ed); educational leadership and administration (Ed D), including curriculum and instruction; higher education (M Ed); school administration (MSA), including school administration. *Program availability:* Part-time, 100% online. *Degree requirements:* For master's, thesis or culminating project, e-Portfolio (for school administration); for doctorate, comprehensive exam, thesis/dissertation. *Entrance requirements:* For master's, GRE General Test, MAT, minimum B average in undergraduate work, 3 letters of recommendation, education statement of interest essay, autobiographical statement, NC Class A teacher licensure in related field, minimum of 3 years' teaching experience; for doctorate, education statement of interest essay, master's degree in education field, 3 years of leadership experience. Additional exam requirements/recommendations for international students: Required—TOEFL (minimum score 550 paper-based; 79 iBT), IELTS (minimum score 6.5). Electronic applications accepted.

University of Northern Colorado, Graduate School, College of Education and Behavioral Sciences, School of Teacher Education, Greeley, CO 80639. Offers curriculum studies (MAT); educational studies (Ed D); elementary education (MAT); English education (MAT); literacy (MA); multilingual education (MA), including TESOL, world languages; teaching diverse learners (MA). *Accreditation:* NCATE. *Program availability:* Part-time, evening/weekend. *Degree requirements:* For master's, comprehensive exam, thesis or alternative; for doctorate, comprehensive exam, thesis/dissertation. *Entrance requirements:* For master's and doctorate, GRE General Test, 3 letters of recommendation. Electronic applications accepted.

University of Northern Iowa, Graduate College, College of Education, Ed D Program in Education, Cedar Falls, IA 50614. Offers allied health, recreation, and community services (Ed D); curriculum and instruction (Ed D); educational leadership (Ed D). *Program availability:* Part-time, evening/weekend. *Degree requirements:* For doctorate, thesis/dissertation. *Entrance requirements:* For doctorate, GRE, minimum GPA of 3.0, master's degree. Additional exam requirements/recommendations for international students: Required—TOEFL (minimum score 500 paper-based; 61 iBT).

University of North Georgia, Program in Curriculum and Instruction, Dahlonega, GA 30597. Offers M Ed. *Program availability:* Part-time. *Entrance requirements:* For master's, GRE (minimum score 301 verbal and quantitative combined) or MAT (minimum score 391), baccalaureate degree with minimum GPA of 2.75, clear renewable teaching certificate. Additional exam requirements/recommendations for international students: Required—TOEFL (minimum score 550 paper-based; 79 iBT), IELTS (minimum score 6.5). Electronic applications accepted.

University of North Texas, Toulouse Graduate School, Denton, TX 76203-5459. Offers accounting (MS); applied anthropology (MA, MS); applied behavior analysis (Certificate); applied geography (MA); applied technology and performance improvement (M Ed, MS); art education (MA); art history (MA); arts leadership (Certificate); audiology (Au D); behavior analysis (MS); behavioral science (PhD); biochemistry and molecular biology (MS); biology (MA, MS); biomedical engineering (MS); business analysis (MS); chemistry (MS); clinical health psychology (PhD); communication studies (MA, MS); computer engineering (MS); computer science (MS); counseling (M Ed, MS), including clinical mental health counseling (MS), college and university counseling, elementary school counseling, secondary school counseling; creative writing (MA); criminal justice (MS); curriculum and instruction (M Ed); decision sciences (MBA); design (MA, MFA), including fashion design (MFA), innovation studies, interior design (MFA); early childhood studies (MS); economics (MS); educational leadership (M Ed, Ed D); educational psychology (MS, PhD), including family studies (MS), gifted and talented (MS), human development (MS), learning and cognition (MS), research, measurement and evaluation (MS); electrical engineering (MS); emergency management (MPA); engineering technology (MS); English (MA); English as a second language (MA); environmental science (MS); finance (MBA, MS); financial management (MPA); French (MA); health services management (MBA); higher education (M Ed, Ed D); history (MA, MS); hospitality management (MS); human resources management (MPA); information science (MS); information systems (PhD); information technologies (MBA); interdisciplinary studies (MA, MS); international studies (MA); international sustainable tourism (MS); jazz studies (MM); journalism (MA, MJ, Graduate Certificate), including interactive and virtual digital communication (Graduate Certificate), narrative journalism (Graduate Certificate), public relations (Graduate Certificate); kinesiology (MS); linguistics (MA); local government management (MPA); logistics (PhD); logistics and supply chain management (MBA); long-term care, senior housing, and aging services (MA); management (PhD); marketing (MBA); mathematics (MA, MS); mechanical and energy engineering (MS, PhD); music (MA), including ethnomusicology, music theory, musicology, performance; music composition (PhD); music education (MM Ed, PhD); nonprofit management (MPA); operations and supply chain management (MBA); performance (MM, DMA); philosophy (MA); political science (MA); professional and technical communication (MA); radio, television and film (MA, MFA); rehabilitation counseling (Certificate); sociology (MA); Spanish (MA); special education (M Ed); speech-language pathology (MA); strategic management (MBA); studio art (MFA); teaching (M Ed); MBA/MS. *Program availability:* Part-time, evening/weekend, online learning. Terminal master's awarded for partial completion of doctoral program. *Degree requirements:* For master's, variable foreign language requirement, comprehensive exam (for some programs), thesis (for some programs); for doctorate, variable foreign language requirement, comprehensive exam (for some programs), thesis/dissertation; for other advanced degree, variable foreign language requirement, comprehensive exam (for some programs). *Entrance requirements:* For master's and doctorate, GRE, GMAT. Additional exam requirements/recommendations for international students: Required—TOEFL (minimum score 550 paper-based; 79 iBT). Electronic applications accepted.

University of North Texas at Dallas, Graduate School, Dallas, TX 75241. Offers accounting (MBA); counseling (M Ed, MS); criminal justice (MS); curriculum and instruction (M Ed); educational administration (M Ed); human resources and organizational behavior (MBA); public leadership (MS); strategic management (MBA).

University of Oklahoma, Jeannine Rainbolt College of Education, Department of Educational Leadership and Policy Studies, Norman, OK 73019. Offers adult and higher education (M Ed, PhD), including adult and higher education; educational administration, curriculum and supervision (M Ed, Ed D, PhD); educational studies (M Ed, PhD). *Accreditation:* NCATE. *Program availability:* Part-time, evening/weekend, blended/hybrid learning. Terminal master's awarded for partial completion of doctoral program. *Degree requirements:* For master's, comprehensive exam, thesis (for some programs); for doctorate, comprehensive exam, thesis/dissertation. *Entrance requirements:* Additional exam requirements/recommendations for international students: Required—TOEFL (minimum score 79 iBT) or IELTS (minimum score 6.5). Electronic applications accepted. *Expenses:* Tuition, state resident: full-time $5683.20; part-time $236.80 per credit hour. Tuition, nonresident: full-time $20,342; part-time $847.60 per credit hour. *International tuition:* $20,342.40 full-time. *Required fees:* $2894.20; $110.05 per credit hour. $126.50 per semester. Tuition and fees vary according to course load and program. *Faculty research:* Improvement science, leadership and ethics, education and social policy, gender and equity, collegiate athletics.

University of Oregon, Graduate School, College of Education, Eugene, OR 97403. Offers communication disorders and sciences (MA, MS, PhD); counseling psychology (PhD); couples and family therapy (MS); critical and sociocultural studies in education (PhD); curriculum and teacher education (MA, MS); educational leadership (MS, D Ed, PhD); prevention science (M Ed, MS, PhD); school psychology (MS, PhD); special education (M Ed, MA, MS, PhD). *Accreditation:* ASHA. *Program availability:* Part-time. Terminal master's awarded for partial completion of doctoral program. *Degree requirements:* For master's, exam, paper, or project; for doctorate, comprehensive exam, thesis/dissertation. *Entrance requirements:* Additional exam requirements/recommendations for international students: Required—TOEFL. *Faculty research:* Basic and applied research in teaching, learning and habilitation in all settings, schooling effectiveness.

University of Phoenix–Central Valley Campus, College of Education, Fresno, CA 93720-1552. Offers curriculum and instruction (MA Ed); curriculum and instruction-computer education (MA Ed); elementary teacher education (MA Ed); secondary teacher education (MA Ed).

University of Phoenix–Dallas Campus, College of Education, Dallas, TX 75251. Offers curriculum and instruction (MA Ed).

University of Phoenix–Hawaii Campus, College of Education, Honolulu, HI 96813-3800. Offers administration and supervision (MA Ed); curriculum and instruction (MA Ed); elementary education (MA Ed); secondary education (MA Ed); special education (MA Ed); teacher education for elementary licensure (MA Ed). *Program availability:* Evening/weekend. *Degree requirements:* For master's, thesis (for some programs). *Entrance requirements:* For master's, minimum undergraduate GPA of 2.5, 3 years of work experience. Additional exam requirements/recommendations for international students: Required—TOEFL (minimum score 550 paper-based; 79 iBT). Electronic applications accepted.

University of Phoenix–Houston Campus, College of Education, Houston, TX 77079-2004. Offers curriculum and instruction (MA Ed).

University of Phoenix–Las Vegas Campus, College of Education, Las Vegas, NV 89135. Offers administration and supervision (MA Ed); curriculum and instruction (MA Ed); school counseling (MSC); teacher education-elementary licensure (MA Ed). *Program availability:* Evening/weekend. *Degree requirements:* For master's, thesis (for some programs). *Entrance requirements:* For master's, minimum undergraduate GPA of 2.5, 3 years of work experience. Additional exam requirements/recommendations for international students: Required—TOEFL (minimum score 550 paper-based; 79 iBT). Electronic applications accepted.

University of Phoenix–Online Campus, College of Education, Phoenix, AZ 85034-7209. Offers administration and supervision (MAEd, Certificate); adult education and training (MAEd); curriculum and instruction (MAEd), including computer education, curriculum and instruction, English as a second language, language arts, mathematics, reading; early childhood education (MAEd); educational studies (MAEd); elementary teacher education (MAEd), including early childhood, elementary teacher education, high school middle level, middle level; principal licensure (Certificate); secondary teacher education (MAEd); special education (MAEd, Certificate); teacher education (MAEd), including middle level generalist; teacher education middle level mathematics (MAEd), including middle level mathematics; teacher education middle level science (MAEd), including middle level science; teacher education secondary mathematics (MAEd); teacher education secondary science (MAEd); teacher leadership (MAEd); teachers of English learners (Certificate); transition to teaching (Certificate), including elementary education, secondary education. *Program availability:* Evening/weekend, online learning. *Entrance requirements:* Additional exam requirements/recommendations for international students: Required—TOEFL, TOEIC (Test of English as an International Communication), Berlitz Online English Proficiency Exam, PTE, or IELTS. Electronic applications accepted. *Expenses:* Contact institution.

University of Phoenix–Online Campus, School of Advanced Studies, Phoenix, AZ 85034-7209. Offers business administration (DBA); education (Ed S); educational leadership (Ed D), including curriculum and instruction, education technology, educational leadership; health administration (DHA); higher education administration (PhD); industrial/organizational psychology (PhD); nursing (PhD); organizational leadership (DM), including information systems and technology, organizational leadership. *Program availability:* Evening/weekend, online learning. *Degree requirements:* For doctorate, thesis/dissertation. *Entrance requirements:* Additional exam requirements/recommendations for international students: Required—TOEFL, TOEIC (Test of English as an International Communication), Berlitz Online English Proficiency Exam, PTE, or IELTS. Electronic applications accepted. *Expenses:* Contact institution.

University of Phoenix–Phoenix Campus, College of Education, Tempe, AZ 85282-2371. Offers administration and supervision (MA Ed); adult education and training (MA Ed); curriculum and instruction reading (MA Ed); early childhood education (MA Ed); education studies (MA Ed); elementary teacher education (MA Ed); secondary teacher education (MA Ed); special education (MA Ed); teacher leadership (MA Ed). *Program availability:* Evening/weekend, online learning. *Entrance requirements:* Additional exam requirements/recommendations for international students: Required—TOEFL, TOEIC (Test of English as an International Communication), Berlitz Online English Proficiency Exam, PTE, or IELTS. Electronic applications accepted. *Expenses:* Contact institution.

University of Phoenix–Sacramento Valley Campus, College of Education, Sacramento, CA 95833-4334. Offers adult education (MA Ed); curriculum instruction (MA Ed); elementary teacher education (MA Ed); secondary teacher education (MA Ed); teacher education (Certificate). *Program availability:* Evening/weekend. *Degree requirements:* For master's, thesis (for some programs). *Entrance requirements:* For master's, 3 years of work experience, minimum undergraduate GPA of 2.5. Additional exam requirements/recommendations for international students: Required—TOEFL (minimum score 550 paper-based; 79 iBT). Electronic applications accepted.

University of Phoenix–San Antonio Campus, College of Education, San Antonio, TX 78230. Offers curriculum and instruction (MA Ed).

University of Phoenix–San Diego Campus, College of Education, San Diego, CA 92123. Offers curriculum and instruction (MA Ed), including computer education, curriculum and instruction, English as a second language; elementary teacher education (MA Ed); secondary teacher education (MA Ed). *Program availability:* Evening/weekend. *Degree requirements:* For master's, thesis (for some programs). *Entrance requirements:* For master's, 3 years of work experience, minimum undergraduate GPA of 3.0.

Additional exam requirements/recommendations for international students: Required—TOEFL (minimum score 550 paper-based; 79 iBT). Electronic applications accepted.

University of Puerto Rico–Río Piedras, College of Education, Program in Curriculum and Teaching, San Juan, PR 00931-3300. Offers biology education (M Ed); chemistry education (M Ed); curriculum and teaching (Ed D); history education (M Ed); mathematics education (M Ed); physics education (M Ed); Spanish education (M Ed). *Program availability:* Part-time. *Degree requirements:* For master's, thesis; for doctorate, thesis/dissertation, internship. *Entrance requirements:* For master's, PAEG or GRE, minimum GPA of 3.0, letter of recommendation; for doctorate, GRE or PAEG, master's degree, minimum GPA of 3.0, letter of recommendation (2), interview. *Faculty research:* Curriculum, math teaching.

University of Regina, Faculty of Graduate Studies and Research, Faculty of Education, Department of Curriculum and Instruction, Regina, SK S4S 0A2, Canada. Offers M Ed. *Program availability:* Part-time. *Students:* 18 full-time (14 women), 74 part-time (65 women). Average age 30. 13 applicants, 92% accepted, 4 enrolled. In 2018, 41 master's awarded. *Degree requirements:* For master's, thesis (for some programs), practicum, project, or thesis. *Entrance requirements:* For master's, bachelor's degree in education, 2 years of teaching or other relevant professional experience. post secondary transcripts and 2 letter of recommendations. Additional exam requirements/recommendations for international students: Required—TOEFL (minimum score 580 paper-based; 80 iBT), IELTS (minimum score 6.5), PTE (minimum score 59), other options are CAEL, MELAB, Cantest and U of R ESL. *Application deadline:* For fall admission, 2/15 for domestic and international students; for winter admission, 10/15 for domestic and international students; for spring admission, 2/15 for domestic and international students. Application fee: $100. Electronic applications accepted. *Expenses:* Estimated tuition and fees for one academic year is 6,702.90 for master's. The fee will vary base on your choice program. For doctoral program one academic year is estimated 14,129.40. International students will pay additional 1,191.75 for international surcharge per semester. *Financial support:* Fellowships, research assistantships, teaching assistantships, career-related internships or fieldwork, Federal Work-Study, scholarships/grants, unspecified assistantships, and travel award and Graduate Scholarship Base funds available. Support available to part-time students. Financial award application deadline: 9/30. *Faculty research:* Writing process and pedagogy: the Saskatchewan Writing Project; second language reading, writing, and spoken acquisition; assessing experiential learning; multicultural and anti-racist relations issues in curriculum; social media and open education. *Unit head:* Dr. Twyla Salm, Associate Dean, Research & Graduate Programs, 306-585-54604, Fax: 306-585-4006, E-mail: Twyla.Salm@uregina.ca. *Application contact:* Linda Jiang, Graduate Program Coordinator, 306-585-4506, Fax: 306-585-5387, E-mail: edgrad@uregina.ca.
Website: http://www.uregina.ca/education/

University of Rochester, Eastman School of Music, Program in Music Theory Pedagogy, Rochester, NY 14627. Offers MA. *Expenses: Tuition:* Full-time $52,974; part-time $1654 per credit hour. *Required fees:* $612. One-time fee: $30 part-time. Tuition and fees vary according to campus/location and program.

University of Rochester, Margaret Warner Graduate School of Education and Human Development, Doctoral Programs in Education, Rochester, NY 14627. Offers counseling (Ed D); educational administration (Ed D); educational policy and theory (PhD); higher education (PhD); human development in educational context (PhD); teaching, curriculum, and change (PhD). *Expenses: Tuition:* Full-time $52,974; part-time $1654 per credit hour. *Required fees:* $612. One-time fee: $30 part-time. Tuition and fees vary according to campus/location and program.

University of Rochester, Margaret Warner Graduate School of Education and Human Development, Master's Program in Teaching and Curriculum, Rochester, NY 14627. Offers MS. *Expenses: Tuition:* Full-time $52,974; part-time $1654 per credit hour. *Required fees:* $612. One-time fee: $30 part-time. Tuition and fees vary according to campus/location and program.

University of St. Francis, College of Education, Joliet, IL 60435-6169. Offers educational leadership (MS, Ed D); elementary education (M Ed); reading (MS); secondary education (M Ed), including English education, math education, science education, social studies education, visual arts education; special education (M Ed); teaching and learning (MS); TESOL (Certificate). *Accreditation:* NCATE. *Program availability:* Part-time, evening/weekend, 100% online, blended/hybrid learning. *Faculty:* 11 full-time (8 women), 58 part-time/adjunct (38 women). *Students:* 43 full-time (35 women), 453 part-time (354 women); includes 110 minority (48 Black or African American, non-Hispanic/Latino; 7 Asian, non-Hispanic/Latino; 52 Hispanic/Latino; 3 Two or more races, non-Hispanic/Latino), 3 international. Average age 37. 300 applicants, 66% accepted, 164 enrolled. In 2018, 151 master's, 42 doctorates, 4 other advanced degrees awarded. *Degree requirements:* For master's, comprehensive exam; for doctorate, thesis/dissertation. *Entrance requirements:* Additional exam requirements/recommendations for international students: Required—TOEFL (minimum score 550 paper-based; 79 iBT), IELTS (minimum score 6). *Application deadline:* Applications are processed on a rolling basis. Electronic applications accepted. Application fee is waived when completed online. *Expenses:* Contact institution. *Financial support:* In 2018–19, 33 students received support. Scholarships/grants and tuition waivers (partial) available. Support available to part-time students. Financial award applicants required to submit FAFSA. *Unit head:* Dr. John Gambro, Dean, 815-740-3456, E-mail: jgambro@stfrancis.edu. *Application contact:* Sandee Sloka, Director Adult & Graduate Admissions, 800-735-7500, E-mail: ssloka@stfrancis.edu.
Website: https://www.stfrancis.edu/education/

University of Saint Joseph, Department of Education, West Hartford, CT 06117-2700. Offers curriculum and instruction (MA); elementary education (MAT); instructional technology (MA); literacy (MA); secondary education (MAT); TESOL (MA). *Program availability:* Part-time, evening/weekend. *Degree requirements:* For master's, comprehensive exam, thesis or alternative. *Entrance requirements:* For master's, 2 letters of recommendation. Electronic applications accepted. Application fee is waived when completed online.

University of St. Thomas, School of Education and Human Services, Houston, TX 77006-4696. Offers all level education (M Ed); bilingual/dual language (M Ed); Catholic school teaching (M Ed); Catholic/private school leadership (M Ed); counselor education (M Ed); curriculum and instruction (M Ed); education (Ed D); educational leadership (M Ed); elementary teaching (M Ed); English as a second language (M Ed); exceptionality/educational diagnostician (M Ed); exceptionality/special education (M Ed); generalist (M Ed); reading (M Ed); secondary teaching (M Ed); teaching (MAT). *Accreditation:* TEAC. *Program availability:* Part-time, evening/weekend, online learning. *Degree requirements:* For master's, thesis, field experience. *Entrance requirements:* For master's, GRE or MAT if GPA is below 3.0, bachelor's degree; minimum GPA of 2.75 in bachelor's degree or last 60 credit hours; official transcripts from all institutions; goal statement of 250-300 words; 1 reference. Additional exam requirements/recommendations for international students: Required—TOEFL (minimum score 94 iBT), IELTS (minimum score 7), PTE (minimum score 53). Electronic applications accepted. *Expenses:* Contact institution. *Faculty research:* Leadership, diversity, personality traits, second language acquisition.

University of San Diego, School of Leadership and Education Sciences, Department of Learning and Teaching, San Diego, CA 92110-2492. Offers curriculum and instruction (M Ed), including inclusive learning, literacy and digital learning, school leadership, steam (science, technology, engineering, arts, and mathematics); inclusive learning (M Ed); literacy and digital learning (M Ed); school leadership (M Ed); special education (M Ed); STEAM (science, technology, engineering, arts, and mathematics) (M Ed); TESOL, literacy and culture (M Ed). *Program availability:* Part-time, evening/weekend. *Faculty:* 9 full-time (7 women), 34 part-time/adjunct (26 women). *Students:* 136 full-time (102 women), 223 part-time (177 women); includes 130 minority (17 Black or African American, non-Hispanic/Latino; 21 Asian, non-Hispanic/Latino; 74 Hispanic/Latino; 3 Native Hawaiian or other Pacific Islander, non-Hispanic/Latino; 15 Two or more races, non-Hispanic/Latino), 10 international. Average age 33. 391 applicants, 85% accepted, 190 enrolled. In 2018, 201 master's awarded. *Degree requirements:* For master's, thesis (for some programs), international experience. *Entrance requirements:* For master's, California Basic Educational Skills Test, California Subject Examination for Teachers. Additional exam requirements/recommendations for international students: Required—TOEFL (minimum score 580 paper-based; 83 iBT), TWE. *Application deadline:* Applications are processed on a rolling basis. Application fee: $45. Electronic applications accepted. *Financial support:* In 2018–19, 127 students received support. Career-related internships or fieldwork, Federal Work-Study, institutionally sponsored loans, scholarships/grants, and stipends available. Financial award application deadline: 4/1; financial award applicants required to submit FAFSA. *Faculty research:* Action research methodology, cultural studies, instructional theories and practices, second language acquisition, school reform. *Unit head:* Dr. Reyes Quezada, Chair, 619-260-7655, E-mail: rquezada@sandiego.edu. *Application contact:* Erika Garwood, Associate Director of Graduate Admissions, 619-260-4524, Fax: 619-260-4158, E-mail: grads@sandiego.edu.
Website: http://www.sandiego.edu/soles/learning-and-teaching/

University of San Francisco, School of Education, Department of Learning and Instruction, San Francisco, CA 94117. Offers digital technologies for teaching and learning (MA); learning and instruction (MA, Ed D); special education (MA, Ed D); teaching reading (MA). *Program availability:* Part-time, evening/weekend. *Students:* 34 full-time (25 women), 11 part-time (8 women); includes 12 minority (4 Black or African American, non-Hispanic/Latino; 3 Asian, non-Hispanic/Latino; 5 Hispanic/Latino), 11 international. Average age 40. 24 applicants, 96% accepted, 16 enrolled. In 2018, 9 doctorates awarded. *Degree requirements:* For doctorate, thesis/dissertation. *Entrance requirements:* Additional exam requirements/recommendations for international students: Required—TOEFL, IELTS, PTE. *Application deadline:* For fall admission, 3/1 priority date for domestic and international students; for spring admission, 11/1 priority date for domestic and international students. Applications are processed on a rolling basis. Application fee: $55 ($65 for international students). Electronic applications accepted. *Financial support:* In 2018–19, 13 students received support. Fellowships, research assistantships, and teaching assistantships available. Financial award application deadline: 3/2; financial award applicants required to submit FAFSA. *Unit head:* Dr. Kevin Oh, Chair, 415-422-2099. *Application contact:* Peter Cole, Admission Coordinator, 415-422-5467, E-mail: schoolofeducation@usfca.edu.

University of Saskatchewan, College of Graduate and Postdoctoral Studies, College of Education, Department of Curriculum Studies, Saskatoon, SK S7N 5A2, Canada. Offers M Ed, PhD, Diploma. *Program availability:* Part-time. *Degree requirements:* For master's, thesis (for some programs); for doctorate, comprehensive exam (for some programs), thesis/dissertation. *Entrance requirements:* For master's, MAT. Additional exam requirements/recommendations for international students: Required—TOEFL (minimum score 80 iBT); Recommended—IELTS (minimum score 6.5). Electronic applications accepted.

The University of Scranton, Panuska College of Professional Studies, Department of Education, Program in Curriculum and Instruction, Scranton, PA 18510. Offers MS. *Program availability:* Part-time, evening/weekend, online only, 100% online.

University of South Africa, College of Human Sciences, Pretoria, South Africa. Offers adult education (M Ed); African languages (MA, PhD); African politics (MA, PhD); Afrikaans (MA, PhD); ancient history (MA, PhD); ancient Near Eastern studies (MA, PhD); anthropology (MA, PhD); applied linguistics (MA); Arabic (MA, PhD); archaeology (MA); art history (MA); Biblical archaeology (MA); Biblical studies (M Th, D Th, PhD); Christian spirituality (M Th, D Th); church history (M Th, D Th); classical studies (MA, PhD); clinical psychology (MA); communication (MA, PhD); comparative education (M Ed, Ed D); consulting psychology (D Admin, D Com, PhD); curriculum studies (M Ed, Ed D); development studies (M Admin, MA, D Admin, PhD); didactics (M Ed, Ed D); education (M Tech); education management (M Ed, Ed D); educational psychology (M Ed); English (MA); environmental education (M Ed); French (MA, PhD); German (MA, PhD); Greek (MA); guidance and counseling (M Ed); health studies (MA, PhD), including health sciences education (MA), health services management (MA), medical and surgical nursing science (critical care general) (MA), midwifery and neonatal nursing science (MA), trauma and emergency care (MA); history (MA, PhD); history of education (Ed D); inclusive education (M Ed, Ed D); information and communications technology policy and regulation (MA); information science (MA, MIS, PhD); international politics (MA, PhD); Islamic studies (MA, PhD); Italian (MA, PhD); Judaica (MA, PhD); linguistics (MA, PhD); mathematical education (M Ed); mathematics education (MA); missiology (M Th, D Th); modern Hebrew (MA, PhD); musicology (MA, MMus, D Mus, PhD); natural science education (M Ed); New Testament (M Th, D Th); Old Testament (D Th); pastoral therapy (M Th, D Th); philosophy (MA); philosophy of education (M Ed, Ed D); politics (MA, PhD); Portuguese (MA, PhD); practical theology (M Th, D Th); psychology (MA, MS, PhD); psychology of education (M Ed, Ed D); public health (MA); religious studies (MA, D Th, PhD); Romance languages (MA); Russian (MA, PhD); Semitic languages (MA, PhD); social behavior studies in HIV/AIDS (MA); social science (mental health) (MA); social science in development studies (MA); social science in psychology (MA); social science in social work (MA); social science in sociology (MA); social work (MSW, DSW, PhD); socio-education (M Ed, Ed D); sociolinguistics (MA); sociology (MA, PhD); Spanish (MA, PhD); systematic theology (M Th, D Th); TESOL (teaching English to speakers of other languages) (MA); theological ethics (M Th, D Th); theory of literature (MA, PhD); urban ministries (D Th); urban ministry (M Th).

University of South Carolina, The Graduate School, College of Education, Department of Instruction and Teacher Education, Program in Curriculum and Instruction, Columbia, SC 29208. Offers Ed D. This degree cuts across two departments and represents 6 different concentrations. *Accreditation:* NCATE. *Program availability:* Part-time, evening/weekend. *Degree requirements:* For doctorate, comprehensive exam, thesis/dissertation. *Entrance requirements:* For doctorate, GRE General Test or MAT, interview, resume, letter of intent, letters of reference. Electronic applications accepted. *Faculty research:* Teacher education, historian recording project, curriculum development in international areas, human sexuality.

University of South Dakota, Graduate School, School of Education, Division of Curriculum and Instruction, Vermillion, SD 57069. Offers American Indian education (Certificate); curriculum and instruction (Ed D, Ed S); elementary education (MA), including elementary education; English language learners (Certificate); literacy leadership and coaching (Certificate); reading interventionist (Certificate); science,

technology and math pedagogy (Certificate); secondary education (MA), including secondary education; special education (MA), including special education; technology for education and training (MS), including technology for education and training. *Accreditation:* NCATE. *Program availability:* Part-time, online learning. *Degree requirements:* For master's and other advanced degree, comprehensive exam, thesis or alternative; for doctorate, comprehensive exam, thesis/dissertation. *Entrance requirements:* For master's, doctorate, and other advanced degree, GRE General Test, MAT, minimum GPA of 2.7. Additional exam requirements/recommendations for international students: Required—TOEFL (minimum score 550 paper-based; 79 iBT). Electronic applications accepted.

University of Southern Mississippi, College of Education and Human Sciences, Department of Curriculum, Instruction and Special Education, Hattiesburg, MS 39406-0001. Offers elementary education (M Ed, PhD); instructional technology (MS); instructional technology and design (PhD); secondary education (MAT); special education (M Ed, PhD). *Program availability:* Part-time, online learning. *Degree requirements:* For master's, comprehensive exam, thesis (for some programs); for doctorate, comprehensive exam, thesis/dissertation. *Entrance requirements:* For master's, GRE General Test, MAT, minimum GPA of 3.0; for doctorate, GRE General Test, minimum GPA of 3.5. Additional exam requirements/recommendations for international students: Required—TOEFL, IELTS. *Faculty research:* Mathematical problem solving, integrative curriculum, writing process, teacher education models.

University of South Florida Sarasota-Manatee, College of Liberal Arts and Social Sciences, Sarasota, FL 34243. Offers criminal justice (MA); education (MA); educational leadership (M Ed), including curriculum leadership, K-12 public school leadership, non-public/charter school leadership; elementary education (MAT); English education (MA); social work (MSW). *Program availability:* Part-time, 100% online, blended/hybrid learning. *Faculty:* 14 full-time (9 women), 6 part-time/adjunct (5 women). *Students:* 10 full-time (8 women), 46 part-time (40 women); includes 17 minority (6 Black or African American, non-Hispanic/Latino; 7 Hispanic/Latino; 4 Two or more races, non-Hispanic/Latino). Average age 33. 57 applicants, 46% accepted, 24 enrolled. In 2018, 12 master's awarded. *Degree requirements:* For master's, comprehensive exam (for some programs). *Entrance requirements:* For master's, GRE. Additional exam requirements/recommendations for international students: Required—TOEFL (minimum score 550 paper-based; 79 iBT), IELTS (minimum score 6.5). *Application deadline:* For fall admission, 3/1 priority date for domestic students, 3/1 for international students; for spring admission, 10/1 priority date for domestic students, 10/1 for international students. Applications are processed on a rolling basis. Application fee: $30. Electronic applications accepted. *Expenses: Tuition, area resident:* Full-time $8350; part-time $348 per credit hour. Tuition, state resident: full-time $8350; part-time $348 per credit hour. Tuition, nonresident: full-time $19,048; part-time $794 per credit hour. *Required fees:* $1689; $70 per credit hour. $5 per semester. Tuition and fees vary according to program. *Financial support:* Career-related internships or fieldwork, institutionally sponsored loans, scholarships/grants, health care benefits, and unspecified assistantships available. Support available to part-time students. Financial award application deadline: 6/30; financial award applicants required to submit FAFSA. *Faculty research:* Educational leadership, secondary education, elementary education, and criminal justice. *Total annual research expenditures:* $97,764. *Unit head:* Dr. Jane Rose, Dean, 941-359-4469, Fax: 941-359-4778, E-mail: jane.rose@sar.usf.edu. *Application contact:* Brandon Avery, Assistant Director, Admissions, 941-359-4331, E-mail: bavery@sar.usf.edu.

The University of Tampa, Programs in Education, Tampa, FL 33606-1490. Offers curriculum and instruction (M Ed); educational leadership (M Ed); instructional design and technology (MS). *Program availability:* Part-time, evening/weekend. *Faculty:* 2 full-time (both women), 19 part-time/adjunct (15 women). *Students:* 52 full-time (38 women), 238 part-time (211 women); includes 86 minority (36 Black or African American, non-Hispanic/Latino; 1 American Indian or Alaska Native, non-Hispanic/Latino; 9 Asian, non-Hispanic/Latino; 32 Hispanic/Latino; 8 Two or more races, non-Hispanic/Latino), 15 international. Average age 33. 119 applicants, 71% accepted, 48 enrolled. In 2018, 37 master's awarded. *Degree requirements:* For master's, capstone. *Entrance requirements:* For master's, GMAT or GRE, current Florida Professional Teaching Certificate, statement of eligibility for Florida Professional Teaching Certificate, or professional teaching certificate from another state; bachelor's degree in an area of education. Additional exam requirements/recommendations for international students: Required—TOEFL (minimum score 577 paper-based; 90 iBT), IELTS (minimum score 7.5). *Application deadline:* Applications are processed on a rolling basis. Application fee: $40. Electronic applications accepted. *Expenses:* Contact institution. *Financial support:* In 2018–19, 28 students received support. Career-related internships or fieldwork, scholarships/grants, and unspecified assistantships available. Financial award applicants required to submit FAFSA. *Faculty research:* Diversity in the classroom, technology integration, assessment methodologies, complex and ill-structured problem solving, communities of practice. *Unit head:* Dr. Antony Erben, Chair, 813-257-3414, E-mail: terben@ut.edu. *Application contact:* Ashley Russell, Staff Assistant, Admissions for Graduate and Continuing Studies, 813-253-6249, E-mail: arussell@ut.edu.
Website: http://www.ut.edu/graduate/education/

The University of Tennessee, Graduate School, College of Education, Health and Human Sciences, Program in Education, Knoxville, TN 37996. Offers art education (MS); counseling education (PhD); cultural studies in education (PhD); curriculum (MS, Ed S); curriculum, educational research and evaluation (Ed D, PhD); early childhood education (PhD); early childhood special education (MS); education of deaf and hard of hearing (MS); educational administration and policy studies (Ed D, PhD); educational administration and supervision (Ed S); educational psychology (Ed D, PhD); elementary education (MS, Ed S); elementary teaching (MS); English education (MS, Ed S); exercise science (PhD); foreign language/ESL education (MS, Ed S); instructional technology (MS, Ed D, PhD, Ed S); literacy, language and ESL education (PhD); literacy, language education, and ESL education (Ed D); mathematics education (MS, Ed S); modified and comprehensive special education (MS); reading education (MS, Ed S); school counseling (Ed S); school psychology (PhD, Ed S); science education (MS, Ed S); secondary teaching (MS); social foundations (MS); social science education (MS, Ed S); socio-cultural foundations of sports and education (PhD); special education (Ed S); teacher education (Ed D, PhD). *Accreditation:* NCATE. *Program availability:* Part-time, evening/weekend. *Degree requirements:* For master's and Ed S, thesis optional; for doctorate, variable foreign language requirement, thesis/dissertation. *Entrance requirements:* For master's, minimum GPA of 2.7; for doctorate and Ed S, GRE General Test, minimum GPA of 2.7. Additional exam requirements/recommendations for international students: Required—TOEFL. Electronic applications accepted.

The University of Tennessee at Martin, Graduate Programs, College of Education, Health and Behavioral Sciences, Program in Teaching, Martin, TN 38238. Offers curriculum and instruction (MS Ed), including 7-12, K-6; initial licensure (MS Ed), including elementary education, secondary education; initial licensure k-8 (MS Ed), including library service, special education; interdisciplinary (MS Ed). *Program availability:* Part-time, online only, 100% online. *Students:* 24 full-time (20 women), 126 part-time (90 women); includes 19 minority (11 Black or African American, non-Hispanic/Latino; 3 Hispanic/Latino; 5 Two or more races, non-Hispanic/Latino). Average age 34. 69 applicants, 58% accepted, 21 enrolled. In 2018, 28 master's awarded. *Degree requirements:* For master's, comprehensive exam. *Entrance requirements:* For master's, GRE General Test, minimum GPA of 2.5, teaching license. Additional exam requirements/recommendations for international students: Required—TOEFL (minimum score 525 paper-based; 71 iBT). *Application deadline:* For fall admission, 7/27 for domestic and international students; for spring admission, 12/17 for domestic and international students; for summer admission, 5/10 for domestic and international students. Applications are processed on a rolling basis. Application fee: $30 ($130 for international students). Electronic applications accepted. *Expenses: Tuition, area resident:* Full-time $8918; part-time $495 per credit hour. Tuition, state resident: full-time $8918; part-time $485 per credit hour. Tuition, nonresident: full-time $14,958; part-time $831 per credit hour. *International tuition:* $22,862 full-time. *Required fees:* $1446; $81 per credit hour. Part-time tuition and fees vary according to course load. *Financial support:* In 2018–19, 26 students received support, including 1 research assistantship with full tuition reimbursement available (averaging $6,283 per year), 5 teaching assistantships with full tuition reimbursements available (averaging $7,464 per year); scholarships/grants and tuition waivers also available. Financial award application deadline: 2/1; financial award applicants required to submit FAFSA. *Faculty research:* Special education, science/math/technology, school reform, reading. *Unit head:* Cynthia West, Dean, 731-881-7125, Fax: 731-881-7975, E-mail: cwest@utm.edu. *Application contact:* Jolene L. Cunningham, Student Services Specialist, 731-881-7012, Fax: 731-881-7499, E-mail: jcunningham@utm.edu.

The University of Texas at Arlington, Graduate School, College of Education, Department of Curriculum and Instruction, Arlington, TX 76019. Offers curriculum and instruction (M Ed), including literacy studies, mathematics education, mind, brain, and education, science education; teaching (with certification) (M Ed T). *Accreditation:* NCATE. *Program availability:* Part-time, evening/weekend, online learning. *Degree requirements:* For master's, comprehensive exam (for some programs), comprehensive activity, research project. *Entrance requirements:* For master's, GRE General Test, minimum undergraduate GPA of 3.0 in last 60 hours of course work, writing sample, 3 letters of recommendation. Additional exam requirements/recommendations for international students: Required—TOEFL (minimum score 550 paper-based). Electronic applications accepted.

The University of Texas at Austin, Graduate School, College of Education, Department of Curriculum and Instruction, Austin, TX 78712-1111. Offers bilingual/bicultural education (M Ed, MA, PhD); cultural studies in education (M Ed, MA, PhD); early childhood education (M Ed, MA, PhD); language and literacy studies (M Ed, PhD); learning technologies (M Ed, MA, PhD); physical education (M Ed, MA, PhD). Terminal master's awarded for partial completion of doctoral program. *Degree requirements:* For doctorate, thesis/dissertation. *Entrance requirements:* For master's and doctorate, GRE General Test. Electronic applications accepted.

The University of Texas at El Paso, Graduate School, College of Education, Department of Teacher Education, El Paso, TX 79968-0001. Offers education (MA); instruction (M Ed); reading education (M Ed); teaching, learning, and culture (PhD). *Program availability:* Part-time, evening/weekend. *Degree requirements:* For master's, thesis optional. *Entrance requirements:* For master's, GRE General Test, minimum GPA of 3.0. Additional exam requirements/recommendations for international students: Required—TOEFL. Electronic applications accepted.

The University of Texas at San Antonio, College of Education and Human Development, Department of Interdisciplinary Learning and Teaching, San Antonio, TX 78249-0617. Offers education (MA), including curriculum and instruction, early childhood and elementary education, instructional technology, reading and literacy, special education; interdisciplinary learning and teaching (PhD). *Program availability:* Part-time, evening/weekend. *Degree requirements:* For master's, comprehensive exam, thesis optional, 36 hours of course work without thesis (33 with thesis); for doctorate, comprehensive exam, thesis/dissertation, minimum of 60 semester credit hours. *Entrance requirements:* For master's, bachelor's degree with minimum GPA of 3.0 in last 60 hours of coursework; 18 hours of undergraduate coursework in education or related field; for doctorate, GRE, transcripts from all colleges and universities attended, professional vitae demonstrating experience in work environment where education was primary professional emphasis, 3 letters of recommendation, statement of purpose, minimum GPA of 3.5. Additional exam requirements/recommendations for international students: Required—TOEFL (minimum score 550 paper-based; 79 iBT), IELTS (minimum score 6.5). Electronic applications accepted. *Faculty research:* Explorations of science, learning and teaching, family involvement in early childhood, culturally-responsive literacy instruction in diverse settings, STEM education, autism spectrum disorder.

The University of Texas Rio Grande Valley, College of Education and P-16 Integration, Department of Teaching and Learning, Edinburg, TX 78539. Offers curriculum and instruction (M Ed, Ed D); educational technology (M Ed). *Program availability:* Part-time, evening/weekend. *Degree requirements:* For master's, comprehensive exam, thesis optional; for doctorate, comprehensive exam, thesis/dissertation. *Entrance requirements:* For master's, minimum GPA of 3.0. Additional exam requirements/recommendations for international students: Required—TOEFL (minimum score 550 paper-based; 79 iBT), IELTS (minimum score 6.5). Electronic applications accepted. *Expenses: Tuition, area resident:* Full-time $6888. Tuition, state resident: full-time $6888. Tuition, nonresident: full-time $14,484. *International tuition:* $14,484 full-time. *Required fees:* $1468. *Faculty research:* Teacher education, mathematics education, science education, educational technology, pedagogy.

University of the Pacific, Gladys L. Benerd School of Education, Stockton, CA 95211-0197. Offers curriculum and instruction (MA, Ed D); education (M Ed); educational administration and leadership (MA, Ed D); educational and school psychology (MA, Ed D); educational entrepreneurship (MA); school psychology (Ed S); special education (MA); teacher education (MA). *Accreditation:* NCATE. *Degree requirements:* For doctorate, thesis/dissertation. *Entrance requirements:* For master's, GRE General Test; for doctorate, GRE General Test, GRE Subject Test. Additional exam requirements/recommendations for international students: Required—TOEFL.

University of the Southwest, Graduate Programs, Hobbs, NM 88240-9129. Offers business administration (MBA); curriculum and instruction (MSE); curriculum and instruction: bilingual (MSE); curriculum and instruction: TESOL (MSE); early childhood education (MSE); educational administration (MSE); mental health counseling (MSE); school counseling (MSE); special education (MSE); sports management (MBA). *Program availability:* Part-time, evening/weekend, online learning. *Degree requirements:* For master's, comprehensive exam, thesis (for some programs). *Entrance requirements:* Additional exam requirements/recommendations for international students: Recommended—TOEFL. Electronic applications accepted.

The University of Toledo, College of Graduate Studies, Judith Herb College of Education, Department of Curriculum and Instruction, Toledo, OH 43606-3390. Offers art education (ME); career and technical education (ME, Ed S); curriculum and instruction (ME, PhD, Ed S); early childhood education (Ed S); education and anthropology (MAE); education and biology (MES); education and chemistry (MES);

education and classics (MAE); education and economics (MAE); education and English (MAE); education and French (MAE); education and geology (MES); education and German (MAE); education and history (MAE); education and mathematics (MAE, MES); education and physics (MES); education and political science (MAE); education and sociology (MAE); education and Spanish (MAE); educational media (PhD); educational technology (ME); educational technology: virtual educator (Certificate); elementary education (PhD); English as a second language (MAE); gifted and talented education (PhD); middle childhood education (ME); secondary education (ME, PhD); special education (PhD). *Accreditation:* NCATE. *Program availability:* Part-time, evening/weekend. *Degree requirements:* For master's, comprehensive exam, thesis or alternative; for doctorate, comprehensive exam, thesis/dissertation; for other advanced degree, thesis optional. *Entrance requirements:* For master's, doctorate, and other advanced degree, minimum cumulative GPA of 2.7 for all previous academic work, letters of recommendation. Additional exam requirements/recommendations for international students: Required—TOEFL (minimum score 550 paper-based; 80 iBT). Electronic applications accepted.

University of Vermont, Graduate College, College of Education and Social Services, Program in Curriculum and Instruction, Burlington, VT 05405. Offers M Ed. *Accreditation:* NCATE. *Program availability:* Blended/hybrid learning. *Entrance requirements:* For master's, GRE General Test, VT PRAXIS II, or equivalent teacher examination scores from another state (e.g. Massachusetts Tests for Educator Licensure, MTEL), resume. Additional exam requirements/recommendations for international students: Required—TOEFL (minimum score 550 paper-based; 90 iBT), IELTS (minimum score 6.5). Electronic applications accepted.

University of Vermont, Graduate College, College of Education and Social Services, Program in Middle Level Education, Burlington, VT 05405. Offers curriculum and instruction (MAT), including middle level education. *Program availability:* Part-time. *Entrance requirements:* For master's, resume, writing sample. Additional exam requirements/recommendations for international students: Required—TOEFL (minimum iBT score of 90) or IELTS (6.5). Electronic applications accepted.

University of Vermont, Graduate College, College of Education and Social Services, Program in Secondary Education, Burlington, VT 05405. Offers curriculum and instruction (MAT), including secondary education. *Entrance requirements:* For master's, major or its equivalent in a state-approved licensing area. Additional exam requirements/recommendations for international students: Required—TOEFL (minimum iBT score of 90) or IELTS (6.5). Electronic applications accepted.

University of Victoria, Faculty of Graduate Studies, Faculty of Education, Department of Curriculum and Instruction, Victoria, BC V8W 2Y2, Canada. Offers art education (M Ed, PhD); curriculum studies (M Ed, MA, PhD); early childhood education (M Ed, PhD); educational studies (PhD); language and literacy (M Ed, MA, PhD); mathematics (M Ed, MA, PhD); music education (M Ed, MA, PhD); science (M Ed, MA, PhD); social studies (M Ed, MA); social, cultural and foundational studies (MA, PhD); technology and environmental education (PhD). *Program availability:* Part-time. *Degree requirements:* For master's, thesis, project (M Ed); for doctorate, comprehensive exam, thesis/dissertation. *Entrance requirements:* For master's, minimum B average. Additional exam requirements/recommendations for international students: Required—TOEFL (minimum score 575 paper-based), IELTS (minimum score 7). Electronic applications accepted. *Faculty research:* Elementary and secondary English, language arts, curriculum theory and practice, educational media and technology, educational administration and leadership, history and philosophy of education.

University of Virginia, Curry School of Education, Department of Curriculum, Instruction, and Special Education, Program in Curriculum and Instruction, Charlottesville, VA 22903. Offers curriculum and instruction (M Ed, Ed S); elementary education (M Ed, Ed D); English education (M Ed, Ed D); foreign language education (M Ed); mathematics education (M Ed, Ed D); science education (Ed D); social studies education (M Ed); MBA/M Ed. *Program availability:* 100% online. *Degree requirements:* For master's, comprehensive exam (for some programs); for doctorate, comprehensive exam, thesis/dissertation; for Ed S, comprehensive exam. *Entrance requirements:* For master's, doctorate, and Ed S, GRE General Test, 2 letters of recommendation. Additional exam requirements/recommendations for international students: Required—TOEFL (minimum score 600 paper-based; 90 iBT), IELTS (minimum score 7). Electronic applications accepted.

University of Virginia, Curry School of Education, Program in Education, Charlottesville, VA 22903. Offers administration and supervision (PhD); applied developmental science (PhD); counselor education (PhD); curriculum and instruction (PhD); early childhood special education (MT); education evaluation (PhD); educational psychology (PhD); educational research (PhD); elementary education (MT); English education (MT, PhD); foreign language education (MT); higher education (PhD); instructional technology (PhD); kinesiology (MT, PhD); math education (PhD); reading education (PhD); research, statistics and evaluation (PhD); school psychology (PhD); science education (PhD); social studies education (MT, PhD); special education (PhD); world languages education (MT). *Degree requirements:* For master's, comprehensive exam (for some programs), field project; for doctorate, comprehensive exam, thesis/dissertation. *Entrance requirements:* For doctorate, GRE General Test. Additional exam requirements/recommendations for international students: Required—TOEFL (minimum score 600 paper-based; 90 iBT), IELTS (minimum score 7). Electronic applications accepted.

University of Washington, Graduate School, College of Education, Seattle, WA 98195. Offers curriculum and instruction (M Ed, Ed D, PhD), including educational technology, general curriculum (Ed D, PhD), language, literacy, and culture, mathematics education, multicultural education, reading and language arts education (Ed D), science education, social studies education, teaching and curriculum (M Ed); educational leadership and policy studies (M Ed, Ed D, PhD), including administration (Ed D), educational policy, organization, and leadership (M Ed, PhD), higher education, leadership for learning (Ed D), social and cultural foundations of education (M Ed, PhD); educational psychology (M Ed, PhD), including educational psychology (PhD), human development and cognition (M Ed), learning sciences, measurement, statistics and research design (M Ed), school psychology (M Ed); instructional leadership (M Ed); intercollegiate athletic leadership (M Ed); special education (M Ed, Ed D, PhD), including early childhood special education (M Ed), emotional and behavioral disabilities (M Ed), learning disabilities (M Ed), low-incidence disabilities (M Ed), severe disabilities (M Ed), special education (Ed D, PhD); teacher education (MIT). *Accreditation:* APA. *Program availability:* Part-time, evening/weekend. *Degree requirements:* For master's, thesis optional; for doctorate, thesis/dissertation. *Entrance requirements:* For master's and doctorate, GRE General Test, minimum GPA of 3.0. Additional exam requirements/recommendations for international students: Required—TOEFL. Electronic applications accepted. *Faculty research:* School restructuring/effective schools, special education interventions, literacy and writing, technology, school partnerships, teacher preparation.

The University of Western Ontario, School of Graduate and Postdoctoral Studies, Faculty of Social Science, Faculty of Education, Program in Educational Studies, London, ON N6A 3K7, Canada. Offers curriculum studies (M Ed); educational policy studies (M Ed); educational psychology/special education (M Ed). *Program availability:*

Part-time. *Faculty research:* Reflective practice, gender and schooling, feminist pedagogy, narrative inquiry, second language, multiculturalism in Canada, education and law.

University of West Florida, College of Education and Professional Studies, Department of Research and Advanced Studies, Ed S Program in Curriculum and Instruction, Pensacola, FL 32514-5750. Offers Ed S. *Accreditation:* NCATE. *Program availability:* Evening/weekend. *Entrance requirements:* Additional exam requirements/recommendations for international students: Required—TOEFL (minimum score 550 paper-based).

University of West Florida, College of Education and Professional Studies, Department of Teacher Education and Educational Leadership, Program in Curriculum and Instruction, Pensacola, FL 32514-5750. Offers elementary education (M Ed); middle level education (M Ed); secondary education (M Ed). *Program availability:* Part-time, evening/weekend. *Entrance requirements:* For master's, GRE (minimum score 450 verbal) or MAT (minimum score 396) if bachelor's GPA less than 3.0, state teaching certification; letter of intent; two professional references. Additional exam requirements/recommendations for international students: Required—TOEFL (minimum score 550 paper-based).

University of Wisconsin–Madison, Graduate School, School of Education, Department of Curriculum and Instruction, Madison, WI 53706-1380. Offers curriculum and instruction (MS, PhD); English as a second language (MS). *Accreditation:* NASM (one or more programs are accredited). *Degree requirements:* For doctorate, thesis/dissertation.

University of Wisconsin–Milwaukee, Graduate School, School of Education, Department of Curriculum and Instruction, Milwaukee, WI 53201-0413. Offers curriculum and instruction (MS), including cross-curricular focus, early childhood education, English education, mathematics education, middle childhood/early adolescence education, reading education, science education, urban social studies education. *Program availability:* Part-time. *Students:* 19 full-time (15 women), 56 part-time (49 women); includes 15 minority (3 Black or African American, non-Hispanic/Latino; 1 American Indian or Alaska Native, non-Hispanic/Latino; 3 Asian, non-Hispanic/Latino; 1 Hispanic/Latino; 7 Two or more races, non-Hispanic/Latino), 2 international. Average age 33. 27 applicants, 44% accepted, 11 enrolled. In 2018, 20 master's awarded. *Entrance requirements:* Additional exam requirements/recommendations for international students: Required—TOEFL (minimum score 550 paper-based; 79 iBT), IELTS (minimum score 6.5). *Application deadline:* For fall admission, 1/1 priority date for domestic students; for spring admission, 9/1 for domestic students. Application fee: $56 ($96 for international students). Electronic applications accepted. *Financial support:* Fellowships, research assistantships, teaching assistantships, career-related internships or fieldwork, health care benefits, unspecified assistantships, and project assistantships available. Support available to part-time students. Financial award application deadline: 4/15; financial award applicants required to submit FAFSA. *Application contact:* General Information Contact, 414-229-4721, E-mail: soeinfo@uwm.edu.
Website: http://uwm.edu/education/academics/curriculum-instruction-department/

University of Wisconsin–Milwaukee, Graduate School, School of Education, Department of Exceptional Education, Milwaukee, WI 53201-0413. Offers autism spectrum disorders (Graduate Certificate); exceptional education (MS); transition for students with disabilities (Graduate Certificate); urban education (PhD), including adult, continuing and higher education leadership, art education, curriculum and instruction, exceptional education, mathematics education, multicultural studies, social foundations of education. *Program availability:* Part-time. *Students:* 38 full-time (29 women), 67 part-time (50 women); includes 39 minority (23 Black or African American, non-Hispanic/Latino; 1 American Indian or Alaska Native, non-Hispanic/Latino; 6 Asian, non-Hispanic/Latino; 1 Hispanic/Latino; 8 Two or more races, non-Hispanic/Latino), 2 international. Average age 40. 47 applicants, 40% accepted, 11 enrolled. In 2018, 13 master's, 14 doctorates, 4 other advanced degrees awarded. *Entrance requirements:* Additional exam requirements/recommendations for international students: Required—TOEFL (minimum score 550 paper-based; 79 iBT), IELTS (minimum score 6.5). *Application deadline:* For fall admission, 1/1 priority date for domestic students; for spring admission, 9/1 for domestic students. Application fee: $56 ($96 for international students). Electronic applications accepted. *Financial support:* Fellowships, research assistantships, teaching assistantships, career-related internships or fieldwork, health care benefits, and unspecified assistantships available. Support available to part-time students. Financial award application deadline: 4/15; financial award applicants required to submit FAFSA. *Faculty research:* Emotional disturbance, hearing impairment, learning disabilities, mental retardation. *Application contact:* General Information Contact, 414-229-4721, E-mail: soeinfo@uwm.edu.
Website: http://uwm.edu/education/academics/exceptional-edu-department/

University of Wisconsin–Oshkosh, Graduate Studies, College of Education and Human Services, Department of Curriculum and Instruction, Oshkosh, WI 54901. Offers MSE. *Program availability:* Part-time, evening/weekend. *Degree requirements:* For master's, thesis or alternative, seminar paper. *Entrance requirements:* For master's, teaching license, letters of recommendation. Additional exam requirements/recommendations for international students: Required—TOEFL (minimum score 550 paper-based; 79 iBT). Electronic applications accepted. *Faculty research:* Early childhood, middle school teaching, literacy, elementary teaching, bilingual education.

University of Wisconsin–Superior, Graduate Division, Department of Teacher Education, Program in Instruction, Superior, WI 54880-4500. Offers MSE. *Program availability:* Part-time, evening/weekend. *Degree requirements:* For master's, comprehensive exam, thesis or alternative, research project. *Entrance requirements:* For master's, minimum GPA of 2.75, teaching certificate. Electronic applications accepted.

University of Wyoming, College of Education, Programs in Curriculum and Instruction, Laramie, WY 82071. Offers MA, Ed D, PhD. *Program availability:* Part-time, online learning. Terminal master's awarded for partial completion of doctoral program. *Degree requirements:* For master's, comprehensive exam, thesis; for doctorate, comprehensive exam, thesis/dissertation. *Entrance requirements:* For master's, minimum GPA of 3.0, 3 letters of reference, writing samples; for doctorate, accredited master's degree, 3 letters of reference, 3 years of teaching experience, writing sample. Additional exam requirements/recommendations for international students: Required—TOEFL (minimum score 525 paper-based). *Expenses: Tuition, area resident:* Full-time $6504; part-time $271 per credit hour. Tuition, state resident: full-time $6504; part-time $271 per credit hour. Tuition, nonresident: full-time $19,464; part-time $811 per credit hour. *International tuition:* $19,464 full-time. *Required fees:* $1410.94; $343.82 per semester. $343.82 per semester. Tuition and fees vary according to course load, program and reciprocity agreements. *Faculty research:* Teaching and learning teacher education, multi-cultural education, early childhood, discipline-specific pedagogy.

Utah State University, School of Graduate Studies, Emma Eccles Jones College of Education and Human Services, Doctoral Program in Education, Logan, UT 84322. Offers business information systems (Ed D, PhD); curriculum and instruction (Ed D, PhD); research and evaluation (PhD). *Degree requirements:* For doctorate,

comprehensive exam, thesis/dissertation. *Entrance requirements:* For doctorate, GRE General Test, minimum GPA of 3.0, master's degree. Additional exam requirements/recommendations for international students: Required—TOEFL. Electronic applications accepted. *Faculty research:* Language and literacy development, math and science education, instructional technology, hearing problems/deafness, domestic violence and animal abuse.

Vanguard University of Southern California, Graduate Programs in Education, Costa Mesa, CA 92626. Offers Christian education leadership (MA); curriculum and instruction (MA); teacher leadership (MA). *Program availability:* Evening/weekend. *Degree requirements:* For master's, thesis or alternative. *Entrance requirements:* For master's, California Basic Educational Skills Test, California Subject Examinations for Teachers, minimum GPA of 3.0. Additional exam requirements/recommendations for international students: Required—TOEFL (minimum score 550 paper-based; 79 iBT). Electronic applications accepted. *Expenses:* Contact institution. *Faculty research:* Reading, educational administration.

Virginia Commonwealth University, Graduate School, School of Education, Doctoral Program in Education, Richmond, VA 23284-9005. Offers art education (PhD); counselor education and supervision (PhD); curriculum, culture and change (PhD); educational leadership (PhD); educational psychology (PhD); leadership (Ed D); research and evaluation (PhD); special education and disability leadership (PhD); sport leadership (PhD); urban services leadership (PhD). *Accreditation:* NCATE. *Program availability:* Part-time. *Degree requirements:* For doctorate, thesis/dissertation. *Entrance requirements:* For doctorate, GRE (for PhD), MAT (for Ed D), interview, master's degree, writing sample. Additional exam requirements/recommendations for international students: Required—TOEFL (minimum score 600 paper-based; 100 iBT). Electronic applications accepted.

Virginia Polytechnic Institute and State University, Graduate School, College of Liberal Arts and Human Sciences, Blacksburg, VA 24061. Offers career and technical education (MS Ed, Ed S); communication (MA); counselor education (MA); creative writing (MFA); curriculum and instruction (MA Ed, Ed S); educational leadership and policy studies (Ed S); educational research and evaluation (PhD); English (MA); social, political, ethical, and cultural thought (PhD); Ed D/PhD. *Faculty:* 420 full-time (221 women), 1 (woman) part-time/adjunct. *Students:* 603 full-time (428 women), 359 part-time (237 women); includes 189 minority (107 Black or African American, non-Hispanic/Latino; 4 American Indian or Alaska Native, non-Hispanic/Latino; 24 Asian, non-Hispanic/Latino; 27 Hispanic/Latino; 2 Native Hawaiian or other Pacific Islander, non-Hispanic/Latino; 25 Two or more races, non-Hispanic/Latino), 84 international. Average age 33. 856 applicants, 48% accepted, 262 enrolled. In 2018, 270 master's, 63 doctorates awarded. *Degree requirements:* For master's, comprehensive exam (for some programs), thesis (for some programs); for doctorate, comprehensive exam (for some programs), thesis/dissertation (for some programs). *Entrance requirements:* For master's and doctorate, GRE/GMAT. Additional exam requirements/recommendations for international students: Required—TOEFL (minimum score 90 iBT). *Application deadline:* For fall admission, 8/1 for domestic students, 4/1 for international students; for spring admission, 1/1 for domestic students, 9/1 for international students. Applications are processed on a rolling basis. Application fee: $75. Electronic applications accepted. *Expenses:* Tuition, state resident: full-time $15,510; part-time $739.50 per credit hour. Tuition, nonresident: full-time $29,629; part-time $1490.25 per credit hour. *Required fees:* $2804; $550 per semester. Tuition and fees vary according to course load, campus/location and program. *Financial support:* In 2018–19, 4 fellowships with full tuition reimbursements (averaging $23,122 per year), 28 research assistantships with full tuition reimbursements (averaging $15,605 per year), 245 teaching assistantships with full tuition reimbursements (averaging $16,046 per year) were awarded; scholarships/grants and unspecified assistantships also available. Financial award application deadline: 3/1; financial award applicants required to submit FAFSA. *Total annual research expenditures:* $7.5 million. *Unit head:* Dr. Laura Belmonte, Dean, 540-231-6779, Fax: 540-231-7157, E-mail: belmonte@vt.edu. *Application contact:* Chelsea Blanchet, Executive Assistant, 540-231-6779, Fax: 540-231-7157, E-mail: bchels1@vt.edu.
Website: http://www.liberalarts.vt.edu/

Virginia Union University, Evelyn R. Syphax School of Education, Psychology and Interdisciplinary Studies, Richmond, VA 23220-1170. Offers curriculum and instruction (MA).

Walden University, Graduate Programs, Richard W. Riley College of Education and Leadership, Minneapolis, MN 55401. Offers adult education (Post-Master's Certificate); adult learning (Graduate Certificate); college teaching and learning (Graduate Certificate); community college leadership (Ed D); curriculum, instruction and assessment (Ed D, Ed S, Graduate Certificate); developmental education (Graduate Certificate); early childhood administration, management, and leadership (Graduate Certificate); early childhood education (Ed D, Ed S); early childhood public policy and advocacy (Graduate Certificate); early childhood studies (MS), including administration, management and leadership, early childhood public policy and advocacy, teaching adults in the early childhood field, teaching and diversity in early childhood education; education (MS, PhD), including adolescent literacy and learning (MS), curriculum, instruction, and assessment (grades K-12) (MS), curriculum, instruction, assessment, and evaluation (PhD), early childhood leadership and advocacy (PhD), early childhood special education (PhD), educational leadership (MS), educational leadership and administration (principal preparation) (MS), educational technology and design (PhD), elementary reading and literacy (PreK-6) (MS), elementary reading and mathematics (grades K-6) (MS), global and comparative education (PhD), higher education leadership management and policy (PhD), integrating technology in the classroom (grades K-12) (MS), learning, instruction and innovation (PhD), mathematics (grades 5-8) (MS), mathematics (grades K-6) (MS), mathematics and science (grades K-8) (MS), organizational research, assessment, and evaluation (PhD), reading and literacy with a reading K-12 endorsement (MS), reading literacy assessment and evaluation (PhD), science (grades K-8) (MS), special education (non-licensure) (grades K-12) (MS), teacher leadership (grades K-12) (MS), teaching English language learners (grades K-12) (MS); educational administration and leadership (Ed D); educational leadership and administration (principal preparation) (Ed S); educational technology (Ed D, Ed S, Post Master's Certificate); elementary reading and literacy (Graduate Certificate); engaging culturally diverse learners (Graduate Certificate); enrollment management and institutional marketing (Graduate Certificate); higher education (MS), including adult learning, college teaching and learning, enrollment management and institutional marketing, global higher education, leadership for student success, online and distance learning; higher education and adult learning (Ed D); higher education leadership and management (Ed D); higher education leadership for student success (Graduate Certificate); instructional design and technology (MS, Postbaccalaureate Certificate), including general program (MS), online learning (MS), training and performance improvement (MS); integrating technology in the classroom (Graduate Certificate); mathematics 5-8 (Graduate Certificate); mathematics K-6 (Graduate Certificate); online teaching for adult educators (Graduate Certificate); reading, literacy, and assessment (Ed D, Ed S); science K-8 (Graduate Certificate); special education (Ed D, Ed S, Graduate Certificate); special education (K-age 21) (MAT); teacher leadership

(Graduate Certificate); teaching adults English as a second language (Graduate Certificate); teaching adults in the early childhood field (Graduate Certificate); teaching and diversity in early childhood education (Graduate Certificate); teaching English language learners (grades K-12) (Graduate Certificate); teaching K-12 students online (Graduate Certificate). *Accreditation:* NCATE. *Program availability:* Part-time, evening/weekend, online only, 100% online. *Degree requirements:* For doctorate, thesis/dissertation (for some programs), residency; for other advanced degree, residency (for some programs). *Entrance requirements:* For master's, bachelor's degree or higher; minimum GPA of 2.5; official transcripts; goal statement (for some programs); access to computer and Internet; for doctorate, master's degree or higher; three years of related professional or academic experience (preferred); minimum GPA of 3.0; goal statement and current resume (for select programs); official transcripts; access to computer and Internet; for other advanced degree, relevant work experience; access to computer and Internet. Additional exam requirements/recommendations for international students: Required—TOEFL (minimum score 550 paper-based, 79 iBT), IELTS (minimum score 6.5), Michigan English Language Assessment Battery (minimum score 82), or PTE (minimum score 53). Electronic applications accepted.

Walla Walla University, Graduate Studies, School of Education and Psychology, College Place, WA 99324. Offers curriculum and instruction (M Ed, MAT); educational leadership (M Ed, MAT); literacy instruction (M Ed, MAT); special education (M Ed, MAT). *Program availability:* Part-time. *Entrance requirements:* For master's, GRE General Test, minimum GPA of 2.75. Additional exam requirements/recommendations for international students: Required—TOEFL (minimum score 550 paper-based; 79 iBT). Electronic applications accepted. *Faculty research:* Admissions/retention, instructional psychology, moral development, teaching of reading.

Warner University, School of Education, Lake Wales, FL 33859. Offers curriculum and instruction (MAEd); elementary education (MAEd); science, technology, engineering, and mathematics (STEM) (MAEd). *Program availability:* Part-time, evening/weekend, online learning. *Degree requirements:* For master's, thesis, accomplished practices portfolio. *Entrance requirements:* For master's, minimum GPA of 3.0 in last 60 hours of undergraduate coursework; 2 letters of recommendation. Additional exam requirements/recommendations for international students: Required—TOEFL (minimum score 550 paper-based). Electronic applications accepted.

Washburn University, College of Arts and Sciences, Department of Education, Topeka, KS 66621. Offers curriculum and instruction (M Ed); educational leadership (M Ed); reading (M Ed); special education (M Ed). *Accreditation:* NCATE. *Program availability:* Part-time. *Degree requirements:* For master's, comprehensive exam, thesis or alternative, portfolio, comprehensive paper, or action research project. *Entrance requirements:* For master's, department exam, GRE General Test, or MAT, minimum GPA of 3.0 in graduate coursework or last 60 hours of undergraduate coursework. Additional exam requirements/recommendations for international students: Required—TOEFL (minimum score 80 iBT). *Faculty research:* Reading/literature/literacy, foundations, special education, diversity, teaching and technology.

Washington State University, College of Education, Department of Teaching and Learning, Pullman, WA 99164-2132. Offers cultural studies and social thought in education (PhD); curriculum and instruction (Ed M, MA); English language learners (Ed M, MA); language, literacy and technology (PhD); literacy education (Ed M, MA); mathematics education (PhD); special education (Ed M, MA, PhD); teacher leadership (Ed D); teaching (MIT), including elementary education, secondary education. Programs offered at the Pullman, Spokane, Tri-cities, Vancouver and Global (online) campuses. *Program availability:* Part-time, online learning. *Degree requirements:* For master's, comprehensive exam, thesis, oral or written exam; for doctorate, comprehensive exam, thesis/dissertation, oral and written exam. *Entrance requirements:* For master's, GRE General Test, minimum GPA of 3.0, 3 letters of recommendation, letter of intent, transcripts, resume/curriculum vitae; for doctorate, GRE General Test, minimum GPA of 3.0, 3 letters of recommendation, letter of intent, transcripts, writing sample, resume/curriculum vitae. Additional exam requirements/recommendations for international students: Required—TOEFL (minimum score 550 paper-based; 80 iBT). Electronic applications accepted. *Faculty research:* Intersection of gender, youth cultures and schooling; examination of ideology of power in children's literature; early childhood special education; analyzing pre-service and in-service teacher development; second language acquisition.

Waynesburg University, Graduate and Professional Studies, Canonsburg, PA 15370. Offers business (MBA), including energy management, finance, health systems, human resources, leadership, market development; counseling (MA), including addictions counseling, clinical mental health; counselor education and supervision (PhD); criminal investigation (MA); education (M Ed), including autism, curriculum and instruction, educational leadership, online teaching; nursing (MSN), including administration, education, informatics; nursing practice (DNP); special education (M Ed); technology (M Ed); MSN/MBA. *Accreditation:* AACN. *Program availability:* Part-time, evening/weekend. *Degree requirements:* For doctorate, thesis/dissertation. *Entrance requirements:* Additional exam requirements/recommendations for international students: Required—TOEFL. Electronic applications accepted.

Wayne State College, School of Education and Counseling, Department of Educational Foundations and Leadership, Program in Curriculum and Instruction, Wayne, NE 68787. Offers alternative education (MSE); business and information technology education (MSE); communication arts education (MSE); early childhood education (MSE); elementary education (MSE); English as a second language (MSE); English education (MSE); family and consumer sciences education (MSE); industrial technology and vocational education (MSE); learning communities (MSE); mathematics education (MSE); music education (MSE); science education (MSE); social science education (MSE). *Accreditation:* NCATE. *Program availability:* Part-time, evening/weekend. *Degree requirements:* For master's, comprehensive exam, thesis optional. *Entrance requirements:* For master's, GRE General Test. Additional exam requirements/recommendations for international students: Required—TOEFL (minimum score 550 paper-based).

Wayne State University, College of Education, Division of Teacher Education, Detroit, MI 48202. Offers art education (M Ed); bilingual/bicultural education (Certificate); curriculum and instruction (Ed D, PhD, Ed S), including English as a second language (MAT, Ed D, Ed S), K-12 curriculum (PhD); elementary education (MAT), including bilingual/bicultural education (M Ed, MAT), early childhood education (M Ed, MAT), English as a second language (MAT, Ed D, Ed S), foreign language education, science education (M Ed, MAT), special education (M Ed, MAT); elementary mathematics specialist (Certificate); English as a second language (Certificate); reading (M Ed, Ed S); reading, language and literature (Ed D); secondary education (MAT), including bilingual/bicultural education (M Ed, MAT), early childhood education (M Ed, MAT), English as a second language (MAT, Ed D, Ed S), English education, foreign language education, mathematics education (M Ed, MAT), science education (M Ed, MAT), social studies education (M Ed, MAT), special education (MAT), including career and technical education; teaching and learning (M Ed), including bilingual/bicultural education (M Ed, MAT), early childhood education (M Ed, MAT), elementary education, foreign language, mathematics education (M Ed, MAT), science education (M Ed, MAT), social studies education (M Ed, MAT), special education (M Ed, MAT). *Program availability:* Part-time,

evening/weekend. *Faculty:* 20. *Students:* 121 full-time (94 women), 251 part-time (209 women); includes 116 minority (83 Black or African American, non-Hispanic/Latino; 3 American Indian or Alaska Native, non-Hispanic/Latino; 3 Asian, non-Hispanic/Latino; 14 Hispanic/Latino; 13 Two or more races, non-Hispanic/Latino), 11 international. Average age 37. 171 applicants, 23% accepted, 32 enrolled. In 2018, 112 master's, 8 doctorates, 11 other advanced degrees awarded. *Degree requirements:* For master's, thesis (for some programs), essay or project (for some M Ed programs), professional field experience (for MAT programs); for doctorate, comprehensive exam, thesis/dissertation. *Entrance requirements:* For master's, undergraduate degree, verification of participation in group work with children, Michigan State Police criminal background check, negative tb test, personal statement (for MAT programs); for all other master's programs: undergraduate degree, personal statement; for doctorate, minimum undergraduate GPA of 3.0, graduate 3.5; interview; curriculum vitae; references; writing sample; letter of application; master's degree (for most programs); for other advanced degree, education specialist certificate: undergraduate with GPA of 2.5 or better and master's degree with GPA of 2.75 or better; personal statement. Additional exam requirements/recommendations for international students: Required—TOEFL (minimum score 550 paper-based; 79 iBT); Recommended—IELTS (minimum score 6.5), TWE (minimum score 5.5), TSE (minimum score 58). *Application deadline:* Applications are processed on a rolling basis. Application fee: $50. Electronic applications accepted. *Financial support:* In 2018–19, 85 students received support, including 3 fellowships (averaging $14,275 per year); research assistantships with tuition reimbursements available, Federal Work-Study, scholarships/grants, and unspecified assistantships also available. Support available to part-time students. Financial award applicants required to submit FAFSA. *Faculty research:* Improving students' skill achievement in mathematics, improving elementary children's understanding of informational text, teachers' use of their pedagogical and mathematical knowledge in the interactive work of teaching, the intersection of identity construction in teaching and learning, identifying effective methods of literacy instruction and assessments for bilingual students in elementary language arts classrooms. *Unit head:* Dr. Roland Coloma, Assistant Dean for Teacher Education, 313-577-0902, E-mail: rscoloma@wayne.edu. *Application contact:* Dr. Mary L. Waker, Graduate Admissions Officer, 313-577-1601, Fax: 313-577-7904, E-mail: m.waker@wayne.edu.
Website: http://coe.wayne.edu/ted/index.php

Weber State University, Jerry and Vickie Moyes College of Education, Program in Curriculum and Instruction, Ogden, UT 84408-1001. Offers M Ed. *Accreditation:* NCATE. *Program availability:* Part-time, evening/weekend. *Faculty:* 18 full-time (11 women). *Students:* 15 full-time (11 women), 145 part-time (116 women); includes 8 minority (1 Black or African American, non-Hispanic/Latino; 6 Hispanic/Latino; 1 Two or more races, non-Hispanic/Latino), 4 international. Average age 37. In 2018, 32 master's awarded. *Degree requirements:* For master's, thesis or alternative, project presentation, exam. *Entrance requirements:* For master's, MAT or GRE, minimum GPA of 3.0. Additional exam requirements/recommendations for international students: Required—TOEFL (minimum score 85 iBT). *Application deadline:* For fall admission, 5/15 for domestic students; for spring admission, 9/15 for domestic students; for summer admission, 1/15 for domestic students. Application fee: $60 ($90 for international students). Electronic applications accepted. *Expenses:* 6,626 per year. *Financial support:* In 2018–19, 11 students received support. Scholarships/grants available. Financial award application deadline: 4/1; financial award applicants required to submit FAFSA. *Unit head:* Dr. Peggy Saunders, Director, 801-626-7673, Fax: 801-626-7427, E-mail: psaunders@weber.edu. *Application contact:* Nathan Alexander, College of Education Recruiter, 801-626-8124, Fax: 801-626-7427, E-mail: nathanalexander@weber.edu.
Website: http://www.weber.edu/COE/med.html

Western Connecticut State University, Division of Graduate Studies, School of Professional Studies, Department of Education and Educational Psychology, Curriculum Option, Danbury, CT 06810-6885. Offers MS. *Program availability:* Part-time. *Students:* 11 full-time (9 women), 77 part-time (65 women). Average age 33. *Degree requirements:* For master's, thesis or alternative, thesis research project or 3 extra classes and comprehensive exam, completion of program in 6 years. *Entrance requirements:* For master's, minimum GPA of 2.8 or MAT, teaching certificate in elementary or secondary education. Additional exam requirements/recommendations for international students: Recommended—TOEFL (minimum score 550 paper-based; 79 iBT), IELTS (minimum score 6). *Application deadline:* For fall admission, 8/5 priority date for domestic students; for spring admission, 1/5 priority date for domestic students. Applications are processed on a rolling basis. Application fee: $50. *Financial support:* Application deadline: 5/1; applicants required to submit FAFSA. *Faculty research:* Teaching various methods of instruction that include class discussions, lectures, independent projects, cooperative learning, experiential learning and field studies, recitals, demonstrations, shows, group projects, and technology-enhanced instruction. *Unit head:* Dr. Catherine O'Callaghan, Graduate Coordinator, 203-837-3267, Fax: 203-837-8413, E-mail: ocallaghanc@wcsu.edu. *Application contact:* Dr. Chris Shankle, Associate Director of Graduate Studies, 203-837-9005, Fax: 203-837-8326, E-mail: shanklec@wcsu.edu.

Western Illinois University, School of Graduate Studies, College of Education and Human Services, Department of Curriculum and Instruction, Program in Curriculum and Instruction, Macomb, IL 61455-1390. Offers MS Ed. *Accreditation:* NCATE. *Program availability:* Part-time. *Students:* 95 part-time (87 women); includes 8 minority (2 Black or African American, non-Hispanic/Latino; 1 Asian, non-Hispanic/Latino; 4 Hispanic/Latino; 1 Two or more races, non-Hispanic/Latino). Average age 32. 29 applicants, 100% accepted, 25 enrolled. In 2018, 36 master's awarded. *Entrance requirements:* Additional exam requirements/recommendations for international students: Required—TOEFL (minimum score 550 paper-based; 80 iBT). *Application deadline:* Applications are processed on a rolling basis. Application fee: $30. Electronic applications accepted. *Financial support:* Applicants required to submit FAFSA. *Unit head:* Dr. Eric Sheffield, Chairperson, 309-298-1961. *Application contact:* Dr. Mark Mossman, Assistant Director of Graduate Studies, 309-298-1806, Fax: 309-298-2345, E-mail: grad-office@wiu.edu.
Website: http://wiu.edu/curriculum

Western New England University, College of Arts and Sciences, Program in Curriculum and Instruction, Springfield, MA 01119. Offers M Ed. *Program availability:* Part-time, evening/weekend, online learning. *Faculty:* 3 full-time (2 women). *Students:* 7 part-time (all women). Average age 30. 9 applicants, 100% accepted, 5 enrolled. In 2018, 10 master's awarded. *Entrance requirements:* For master's, initial license for elementary teaching, two letters of recommendation, official transcript, resume, personal statement. Additional exam requirements/recommendations for international students: Required—TOEFL (minimum score 79 iBT). *Application deadline:* Applications are processed on a rolling basis. Application fee: $30. Electronic applications accepted. *Expenses:* Contact institution. *Financial support:* Application deadline: 4/15; applicants required to submit FAFSA. *Unit head:* Dr. Saeed Ghahramani, Dean, 413-782-1218, Fax: 413-796-2118, E-mail: sghahram@wne.edu. *Application contact:* Matthew Fox, Executive Director of Graduate Admissions, 413-782-1410, Fax: 413-782-1777, E-mail: study@wne.edu.
Website: http://www1.wne.edu/academics/graduate/education-curriculum-and-instruction.cfm

West Texas A&M University, College of Education and Social Sciences, Department of Education, Program in Curriculum and Instruction, Canyon, TX 79015. Offers M Ed. *Program availability:* Part-time, evening/weekend, online learning. *Degree requirements:* For master's, comprehensive exam, thesis optional. *Entrance requirements:* For master's, GRE General Test, 18 semester hours of education course work. Additional exam requirements/recommendations for international students: Required—TOEFL (minimum score 550 paper-based). Electronic applications accepted.

West Virginia University, College of Education and Human Services, Morgantown, WV 26506. Offers audiology (Au D); autism spectrum disorder (MA); clinical rehabilitation and mental health counseling (MS); communication science and disorders (PhD); counseling (MA); counseling psychology (PhD); curriculum and instruction (Ed D); early childhood education (MA); early intervention/ early childhood special education (MA); education (PhD); educational leadership (MA); educational leadership/ public school administration (Ed D); educational leadership/public school administration (MA); educational psychology (MA, Ed D); elementary education (MA); gifted education (MA); higher education administration (MA, Ed D); higher education curriculum and teaching (MA); institutional design and technology (MA); instructional design and technology (Ed D); literacy education (MA); secondary education (MA); secondary education/English (MA); special education (Ed D); speech pathology (MS). *Accreditation:* ASHA; NCATE. *Program availability:* Part-time, evening/weekend, online learning. *Students:* 392 full-time (325 women), 337 part-time (285 women); includes 44 minority (16 Black or African American, non-Hispanic/Latino; 16 Hispanic/Latino; 12 Two or more races, non-Hispanic/Latino), 11 international. In 2018, 303 master's, 6 doctorates awarded. *Degree requirements:* For master's, content exams; for doctorate, comprehensive exam, thesis/dissertation. *Entrance requirements:* Additional exam requirements/recommendations for international students: Required—TOEFL (minimum score 500 paper-based; 61 iBT). *Application deadline:* For fall admission, 8/1 for domestic students; for spring admission, 1/1 for domestic students; for summer admission, 5/1 for domestic students. Application fee: $60. Electronic applications accepted. *Financial support:* Fellowships, research assistantships, teaching assistantships, career-related internships or fieldwork, Federal Work-Study, institutionally sponsored loans, health care benefits, tuition waivers (full and partial), and administrative assistantships available. Financial award applicants required to submit FAFSA. *Faculty research:* Internet training and integration for teachers, rural education, teacher preparation, organization of schools, evaluation of personnel. *Unit head:* Dr. Tracy L. Morris, Interim Dean, 304-293-0816, Fax: 304-293-7565, E-mail: Tracy.Morris@mail.wvu.edu. *Application contact:* Dr. Melissa Luna, Associate Dean for Research, 304-293-2174, Fax: 304-293-3802, E-mail: Melissa.Luna@mail.wvu.edu.
Website: http://cehs.wvu.edu/

Wichita State University, Graduate School, College of Applied Studies, School of Education, Wichita, KS 67260. Offers learning and instructional design (M Ed); special education (M Ed), including early childhood (M Ed, MAT), gifted, high incidence, low incidence; teaching (MAT), including early childhood (M Ed, MAT), middle level/secondary, transition to teaching. *Accreditation:* NCATE. *Program availability:* Part-time, evening/weekend, 100% online, blended/hybrid learning. *Entrance requirements:* For master's, MAT, minimum GPA of 2.75. *Unit head:* Dr. Edward Robeck, Department Head, 316-978-3322, E-mail: edward.robeck@wichita.edu. *Application contact:* Jordan Oleson, Admission Coordinator, 316-978-3095, Fax: 316-978-3253, E-mail: jordan.oleson@wichita.edu.

William Woods University, Graduate and Adult Studies, Fulton, MO 65251-1098. Offers administration (M Ed, Ed S); athletic/activities administration (M Ed); curriculum and instruction (M Ed, Ed S); educational leadership (Ed D); equestrian education (M Ed); health management (MBA); human resources (MBA); leadership (MBA); marketing, advertising, and public relations (MBA); teaching and technology (M Ed). *Program availability:* Part-time, evening/weekend. *Degree requirements:* For master's, capstone course (MBA), action research (M Ed); for Ed S, field experience. *Entrance requirements:* Additional exam requirements/recommendations for international students: Required—TOEFL (minimum score 550 paper-based). Electronic applications accepted. *Expenses:* Contact institution.

Wisconsin Lutheran College, College of Adult and Graduate Studies, Milwaukee, WI 53226-9942. Offers high performance instruction (MA Ed); instructional technology (MA Ed); leadership and innovation (MA Ed); science instruction (MA Ed).

Worcester State University, Graduate School, Department of Education, Worcester, MA 01602-2597. Offers adult English as a esl (Postbaccalaureate Certificate); curriculum and instruction (Ed S); early childhood education (M Ed); education (M Ed); elementary education (M Ed); English as a second language (M Ed, Postbaccalaureate Certificate); middle school education (M Ed); middle/secondary school education (Postbaccalaureate Certificate); moderate disabilities (M Ed, Postbaccalaureate Certificate); reading (M Ed, Postbaccalaureate Certificate); reading specialist (Postbaccalaureate Certificate); school leadership and education administration (M Ed); school psychology (M Ed, Ed S); secondary education (M Ed, Ed S, Postbaccalaureate Certificate). *Faculty:* 10 full-time (9 women), 23 part-time/adjunct (11 women). *Students:* 38 full-time (33 women), 281 part-time (212 women); includes 30 minority (4 Black or African American, non-Hispanic/Latino; 3 American Indian or Alaska Native, non-Hispanic/Latino; 2 Asian, non-Hispanic/Latino; 16 Hispanic/Latino; 5 Two or more races, non-Hispanic/Latino), 2 international. Average age 41. 102 applicants, 98% accepted, 88 enrolled. In 2018, 132 master's, 52 Ed Ss awarded. *Degree requirements:* For master's, comprehensive exam (for some programs), thesis (for some programs), For a detail list of degree completion requirements please see the graduate catalog at catalog.worcester.edu. *Entrance requirements:* For master's, GRE General Test, MAT or GMAT, teaching certificate. For a detail list of entrance requirements please see the graduate catalog at catalog.worcester.edu. Additional exam requirements/recommendations for international students: Required—TOEFL (minimum score 550 paper-based; 79 iBT), PTE. *Application deadline:* For fall admission, 3/1 for domestic and international students; for spring admission, 11/1 for domestic and international students; for summer admission, 3/1 for domestic and international students. Applications are processed on a rolling basis. Application fee: $50. Electronic applications accepted. *Expenses: Tuition, area resident:* Full-time $3042; part-time $169 per credit hour. Tuition, state resident: full-time $3042; part-time $169 per credit hour. Tuition, nonresident: full-time $3042; part-time $169 per credit hour. *International tuition:* $3042 full-time. *Required fees:* $2754; $153 per credit hour. *Financial support:* Career-related internships or fieldwork, scholarships/grants, and unspecified assistantships available. Support available to part-time students. Financial award application deadline: 3/1; financial award applicants required to submit FAFSA. *Unit head:* Dr. Sara Young, Graduate Program Coordinator, 508-929-8246, Fax: 508-929-8164, E-mail: syoung3@worcester.edu. *Application contact:* Sara Grady, Associate Dean of Graduate and Continuing Education, 508-929-8130, Fax: 508-929-8100, E-mail: sara.grady@worcester.edu.

Wright State University, Graduate School, College of Education and Human Services, Department of Educational Leadership, Program in Advanced Educational Leadership, Dayton, OH 45435. Offers advanced curriculum and instruction (Ed S). *Accreditation:* NCATE. *Degree requirements:* For Ed S, thesis. *Entrance requirements:* For degree, GRE General Test, MAT. Additional exam requirements/recommendations for international students: Required—TOEFL.

Curriculum and Instruction

Xavier University of Louisiana, Graduate School, Programs in Education, New Orleans, LA 70125. Offers counseling (MA); curriculum and instruction (MA), including special interest - non certification; educational leadership (MA). *Accreditation:* NCATE. *Program availability:* Part-time, evening/weekend. *Faculty:* 7 full-time (5 women), 2 part-time/adjunct (both women). *Students:* 96 full-time (84 women), 51 part-time (42 women); includes 139 minority (138 Black or African American, non-Hispanic/Latino; 1 Hispanic/Latino). Average age 31. 77 applicants, 100% accepted, 77 enrolled. In 2018, 70 master's awarded. *Degree requirements:* For master's, comprehensive exam, thesis or alternative. *Entrance requirements:* For master's, GRE General Test, MAT /Praxis I & II, minimum GPA of 2.5. Additional exam requirements/recommendations for international students: Required—TOEFL. *Application deadline:* For fall admission, 7/1 for domestic students, 3/1 priority date for international students; for spring admission, 12/1 for domestic students, 9/15 priority date for international students; for summer admission, 3/1 for domestic students. Applications are processed on a rolling basis. Application fee: $30. Electronic applications accepted. *Expenses: Tuition:* Full-time $2652; part-time $1326 per credit hour. *Required fees:* $531; $323 per semester. $258 per semester. Tuition and fees vary according to degree level and program. *Financial support:* Career-related internships or fieldwork and tuition waivers (partial) available. Support available to part-time students. Financial award application deadline: 6/30; financial award applicants required to submit FAFSA. *Unit head:* Dr. Judith Miranti, Chair, Division of Education, 504-520-7536, Fax: 504-520-7909, E-mail: jmiranti@xula.edu. *Application contact:* Yiraliz Beltran, Program Manager, 504-520-7487, Fax: 504-520-7896, E-mail: ybeltran@xula.edu.

Youngstown State University, College of Graduate Studies, Beeghly College of Education, Department of Teacher Education, Youngstown, OH 44555-0001. Offers content area concentration (MS Ed); curriculum and instruction (MS Ed); literacy (MS Ed); special education (MS Ed), including special education. *Accreditation:* NCATE. *Program availability:* Part-time, evening/weekend. *Degree requirements:* For master's, comprehensive exam. *Entrance requirements:* For master's, GRE, MAT, or teaching certificate; minimum GPA of 2.7. Additional exam requirements/recommendations for international students: Required—TOEFL. *Faculty research:* Multicultural literacy, hands-on mathematics teaching, integrated instruction, reading comprehension, emergent curriculum.

Distance Education Development

Athabasca University, Centre for Distance Education, Athabasca, AB T9S 3A3, Canada. Offers distance education (MDE, Ed D); distance education technology (Advanced Diploma). *Program availability:* Part-time, online learning. *Degree requirements:* For master's, thesis optional. *Entrance requirements:* For master's, 3- or 4-year baccalaureate degree. Electronic applications accepted. *Expenses:* Contact institution. *Faculty research:* Role development, interaction, educational technology, and communities of practice in distance education; instructional design.

Barry University, School of Education, Graduate Certificate Programs, Miami Shores, FL 33161-6695. Offers advanced teaching and learning with technology (Certificate); distance education (Certificate); higher education technology integration (Certificate); human resources: not for profit and religious organizations (Certificate); K-12 technology integration (Certificate).

Boise State University, College of Education, Department of Educational Technology, Boise, ID 83725-0399. Offers educational technology (MET, MS, Ed D); online teaching (Graduate Certificate); school technology coordination (Graduate Certificate); technology integration (Graduate Certificate). *Accreditation:* NCATE. *Program availability:* Part-time, 100% online, blended/hybrid learning. Terminal master's awarded for partial completion of doctoral program. *Degree requirements:* For master's, thesis optional; for doctorate, thesis/dissertation. *Entrance requirements:* For master's, minimum GPA of 3.0; for doctorate, GRE General Test. Additional exam requirements/recommendations for international students: Required—TOEFL (minimum score 550 paper-based; 80 iBT), IELTS (minimum score 6). Electronic applications accepted.

Brandeis University, Rabb School of Continuing Studies, Division of Graduate Professional Studies, Master of Science in Instructional Design and Technology Program, Waltham, MA 02454-9110. Offers MS. *Program availability:* Part-time-only. *Entrance requirements:* For master's, four-year bachelor's degree from regionally-accredited U.S. institution or equivalent; official transcript(s) from every college or university attended; resume or curriculum vitae; statement of goals; letter of recommendation. Additional exam requirements/recommendations for international students: Required—TWE (minimum score 4.5), TOEFL (minimum scores: 600 paper-based, 100 iBT), IELTS (7), or PTE (68). Electronic applications accepted. *Expenses:* Contact institution.

California Baptist University, Program in Education, Riverside, CA 92504-3206. Offers educational leadership (MS); educational leadership for faith-based institutions (MS); educational leadership for public institutions (MS); educational technology (MS); instructional computer applications (MS); international education (MS); leadership and adult learning (MS); leadership and organizational studies (MS); online teaching and learning (MS); reading (MS); science education (MA); special education in mild/moderate disabilities (MS); special education in moderate/severe disabilities (MS); teacher leadership (MS); teaching (MS); teaching and learning (MS). *Program availability:* Part-time, evening/weekend, 100% online, blended/hybrid learning. *Faculty:* 26 full-time (13 women), 28 part-time/adjunct (21 women). *Students:* 201 full-time (164 women), 265 part-time (209 women); includes 226 minority (23 Black or African American, non-Hispanic/Latino; 4 American Indian or Alaska Native, non-Hispanic/Latino; 7 Asian, non-Hispanic/Latino; 169 Hispanic/Latino; 6 Native Hawaiian or other Pacific Islander, non-Hispanic/Latino; 17 Two or more races, non-Hispanic/Latino), 2 international. Average age 39. 145 applicants, 97% accepted, 141 enrolled. In 2018, 253 master's awarded. *Degree requirements:* For master's, comprehensive exam, project, or thesis. *Entrance requirements:* For master's, minimum undergraduate GPA of 2.75; 500-word essay; three letters of recommendation; two prerequisite courses completed with minimum C grade. Additional exam requirements/recommendations for international students: Required—TOEFL (minimum score 80 iBT). *Application deadline:* For fall admission, 8/1 priority date for domestic students, 7/1 for international students; for spring admission, 12/1 priority date for domestic students, 11/1 for international students. Applications are processed on a rolling basis. Application fee: $45. Electronic applications accepted. *Expenses:* $634 per unit. *Financial support:* In 2018–19, 312 students received support. Federal Work-Study and scholarships/grants available. Financial award applicants required to submit CSS PROFILE or FAFSA. *Faculty research:* Leadership development, complexity theory, faith and learning, special education, social and philosophical contexts of education. *Unit head:* Dr. Robin Duncan, Dean, School of Education, 951-552-8948, E-mail: rduncan@calbaptist.edu. *Application contact:* Dr. Shari Farris, Program Director, Online MS in Education, 951-343-2455, E-mail: sfarris@calbaptist.edu.
Website: http://www.calbaptist.edu/mastersined/

Capella University, School of Education, Doctoral Programs in Education, Minneapolis, MN 55402. Offers curriculum and instruction (PhD); educational leadership and management (Ed D); instructional design for online learning (PhD); K-12 studies in education (PhD); leadership for higher education (PhD); leadership in educational administration (PhD); postsecondary and adult education (PhD); professional studies in education (PhD); reading and literacy (Ed D); special education leadership (PhD); training and performance improvement (PhD).

Capella University, School of Education, Master's Programs in Education, Minneapolis, MN 55402. Offers adult education (MS); curriculum and instruction (MS); early childhood education (MS); enrollment management (MS); higher education leadership and management (MS); instructional design for online learning (MS); integrative studies (MS); K-12 studies in education (MS); leadership in educational administration (MS); reading and literacy (MS); special education teaching (MS).

Carlow University, College of Learning and Innovation, Program in Education, Pittsburgh, PA 15213-3165. Offers early childhood education (M Ed); education (M Ed); online instructional design and technology (Certificate); special education (M Ed), including early childhood. *Program availability:* Part-time, evening/weekend, 100% online, blended/hybrid learning. *Students:* 41 full-time (33 women), 9 part-time (all women); includes 12 minority (10 Black or African American, non-Hispanic/Latino; 1 Asian, non-Hispanic/Latino; 1 Two or more races, non-Hispanic/Latino). Average age 32. 32 applicants, 100% accepted, 22 enrolled. In 2018, 24 master's, 5 Certificates awarded. *Entrance requirements:* For master's, personal essay; resume or curriculum vitae; two recommendations; official transcripts; interview; minimum undergraduate GPA of 3.0. Additional exam requirements/recommendations for international students: Required—TOEFL (minimum score 550 paper-based). *Application deadline:* Applications are processed on a rolling basis. Electronic applications accepted. *Expenses: Tuition:* Full-time $13,090; part-time $5100 per semester. *Required fees:* $215; $84. Tuition and fees vary according to course load, degree level and program. *Financial support:* Application deadline: 4/1; applicants required to submit FAFSA. *Unit head:* Dr. Keeley Baronak, Chair, Department of Education, 412-578-6135, Fax: 412-578-8816, E-mail: kobaronak@carlow.edu. *Application contact:* Dr. Keeley Baronak, Chair, Department of Education, 412-578-6135, Fax: 412-578-8816, E-mail: kobaronak@carlow.edu.
Website: http://www.carlow.edu/education.aspx

Clemson University, Graduate School, College of Behavioral, Social and Health Sciences, Department of Parks, Recreation, and Tourism Management, Clemson, SC 29634-0735. Offers international parks and tourism (Certificate); parks, recreation and tourism management (MS, PhD), including recreational therapy (PhD); public administration (MPA, Certificate); recreational therapy (MS); youth development leadership (MS, Certificate). *Program availability:* Part-time, evening/weekend, 100% online. *Faculty:* 31 full-time (10 women), 3 part-time/adjunct (0 women). *Students:* 84 full-time (58 women), 227 part-time (140 women); includes 62 minority (45 Black or African American, non-Hispanic/Latino; 1 American Indian or Alaska Native, non-Hispanic/Latino; 1 Asian, non-Hispanic/Latino; 9 Hispanic/Latino; 6 Two or more races, non-Hispanic/Latino), 18 international. Average age 31. 275 applicants, 80% accepted, 135 enrolled. In 2018, 72 master's, 9 doctorates, 26 other advanced degrees awarded. *Degree requirements:* For master's, comprehensive exam (for some programs), thesis (for some programs); for doctorate, comprehensive exam, thesis/dissertation; for Certificate, portfolio. *Entrance requirements:* For master's and doctorate, GRE General Test, unofficial transcripts, letter of intent, letters of reference; for Certificate, letter of recommendation, unofficial transcripts, personal statement, resume. Additional exam requirements/recommendations for international students: Required—TOEFL (minimum score 80 paper-based; 80 iBT); Recommended—IELTS (minimum score 6.5), TSE (minimum score 54). *Application deadline:* For fall admission, 4/15 priority date for international students; for spring admission, 10/15 priority date for international students. Applications are processed on a rolling basis. Application fee: $80 ($90 for international students). Electronic applications accepted. *Expenses: Tuition, area resident:* Full-time $11,270; part-time $8688 per credit hour. Tuition, state resident: full-time $11,796. Tuition, nonresident: full-time $23,802; part-time $17,412 per credit hour. *International tuition:* $23,246 full-time. *Required fees:* $1196; $497 per semester. Tuition and fees vary according to course load, degree level, campus/location and program. *Financial support:* In 2018–19, 59 students received support, including 1 research assistantship with full and partial tuition reimbursement available (averaging $4,324 per year), 55 teaching assistantships with full and partial tuition reimbursements available (averaging $10,318 per year); career-related internships or fieldwork and unspecified assistantships also available. *Faculty research:* Land use, recreational therapy, sustainability, tourism, public administration. *Total annual research expenditures:* $532,593. *Unit head:* Dr. Fran McGuire, Interim Chair, 864-656-3036, E-mail: lefty@clemson.edu. *Application contact:* Dr. Jeff Hallo, Graduate Coordinator, 864-656-3237, E-mail: jhallo@clemson.edu.
Website: http://www.clemson.edu/hehd/departments/prtm/

Coastal Carolina University, Spadoni College of Education, Conway, SC 29528-6054. Offers education (MAT); educational leadership (M Ed, Ed S); English for speakers of other languages (Certificate); instructional technology (M Ed, Ed S); language, literacy and culture (M Ed); learning and teaching (M Ed); online teaching and training (Certificate); special education (M Ed). *Accreditation:* NCATE. *Program availability:* Part-time, evening/weekend, 100% online, blended/hybrid learning. *Degree requirements:* For master's and other advanced degree, comprehensive exam. *Entrance requirements:* For master's, GRE, GMAT, 2 letters of recommendation, evidence of teacher certification, official transcripts; for other advanced degree, official transcripts, 3 letters of reference, master's degree in related field with minimum overall cumulative GPA of 3.0. Additional exam requirements/recommendations for international students: Required—TOEFL (minimum score 550 paper-based; 79 iBT), IELTS (minimum score 6.5). Electronic applications accepted.

College of Saint Elizabeth, Program in Education, Morristown, NJ 07960-6989. Offers assistive technology (Certificate); education (MA); ESL (Certificate); Holocaust/genocide education (Certificate); middle school science (Certificate); online teaching in the 21st

century (Certificate); teaching (Certificate), including K-12, K-6, teacher of students with disabilities. *Program availability:* Part-time. *Degree requirements:* For master's and Certificate, thesis. *Entrance requirements:* For master's, certification. Additional exam requirements/recommendations for international students: Required—TOEFL (minimum score 550 paper-based; 79 iBT), IELTS (minimum score 6.5). Electronic applications accepted. Application fee is waived when completed online.

Colorado Christian University, Program in Curriculum and Instruction, Lakewood, CO 80226. Offers corporate education (MACI); early childhood educator (MACI); elementary educator (MACI); instructional technology (MACI); master educator (MACI); online course developer (MACI); online teaching and learning (MACI); special education generalist (MACI). *Program availability:* Part-time, evening/weekend. *Degree requirements:* For master's, thesis optional, practicum. *Entrance requirements:* For master's, interviews, letters of recommendation. Additional exam requirements/recommendations for international students: Required—TOEFL. Electronic applications accepted. *Expenses:* Contact institution.

Dallas Baptist University, Dorothy M. Bush College of Education, Program in Curriculum and Instruction, Dallas, TX 75211-9299. Offers Christian school administration (M Ed); distance learning (M Ed); English as a second language (M Ed); instructional technology (M Ed); professional life coaching (M Ed); special education (M Ed); supervision (M Ed). *Program availability:* Part-time, evening/weekend, online learning. *Application deadline:* Applications are processed on a rolling basis. Application fee: $25. Electronic applications accepted. Application fee is waived when completed online. *Expenses: Tuition:* Full-time $17,262; part-time $959 per credit hour. *Required fees:* $1000; $500 per semester. Tuition and fees vary according to course load and degree level. *Unit head:* Dr. Neil Dugger, Dean, 214-333-5202, E-mail: neil@dbu.edu. *Application contact:* Karla Hagan, Program Director, 214-333-5831, E-mail: karla@dbu.edu.
Website: http://www3.dbu.edu/graduate/curriculum_instruction.asp

Dallas Baptist University, Dorothy M. Bush College of Education, Teaching Program, Dallas, TX 75211-9299. Offers distance learning (MAT); early childhood through grade 6 certification (MAT); early childhood-12 (MAT); elementary (MAT); English as a second language (MAT); Montessori (MAT); multisensory (MAT); secondary (MAT). *Program availability:* Part-time, evening/weekend, 100% online, blended/hybrid learning. *Application deadline:* Applications are processed on a rolling basis. Application fee: $25. Electronic applications accepted. Application fee is waived when completed online. *Expenses: Tuition:* Full-time $17,262; part-time $959 per credit hour. *Required fees:* $1000; $500 per semester. Tuition and fees vary according to course load and degree level. *Unit head:* Dr. Neil Dugger, Dean, 214-333-5202, E-mail: neil@dbu.edu. *Application contact:* Dr. DeAnna Jenkins, Program Director, 214-333-5402, E-mail: deannaj@dbu.edu.
Website: https://www.dbu.edu/graduate/degree-programs/ma-teaching

Dallas Baptist University, Gary Cook School of Leadership, Program in Higher Education, Dallas, TX 75211-9299. Offers leadership studies (M Ed); student affairs leadership (M Ed), including community college leadership, distance learning, interdisciplinary studies, student affairs leadership. *Program availability:* Part-time, evening/weekend, online learning. *Application deadline:* Applications are processed on a rolling basis. Application fee: $25. Electronic applications accepted. Application fee is waived when completed online. *Expenses: Tuition:* Full-time $17,262; part-time $959 per credit hour. *Required fees:* $1000; $500 per semester. Tuition and fees vary according to course load and degree level. *Unit head:* Dr. Jack Goodyear, Dean, 214-333-5595, Fax: 214-333-6809, E-mail: jackg@dbu.edu. *Application contact:* Dr. Jack Goodyear, Dean, 214-333-5595, Fax: 214-333-6809, E-mail: jackg@dbu.edu.
Website: https://www.dbu.edu/graduate/degree-programs/med-higher-education/

East Carolina University, Graduate School, College of Education, Department of Mathematics, Science, and Instructional Technology Education, Greenville, NC 27858-4353. Offers distance learning and administration (Certificate); elementary mathematics education (Certificate); instructional technology (MA Ed, MS); mathematics education (MA Ed); science education (MA Ed, MAT); special endorsement in computer education (Certificate). *Program availability:* Part-time, evening/weekend. *Application deadline:* For fall admission, 6/1 priority date for domestic students. *Expenses: Tuition, area resident:* Full-time $4749. Tuition, state resident: full-time $4749. Tuition, nonresident: full-time $17,898. *International tuition:* $17,898 full-time. *Required fees:* $2787. Part-time tuition and fees vary according to course load and program. *Financial support:* Application deadline: 6/1. *Unit head:* Dr. Ron Preston, Director of Students, 252-737-9355, E-mail: prestonr@ecu.edu. *Application contact:* Graduate School Admissions, 252-328-6012, Fax: 252-328-6071, E-mail: gradschool@ecu.edu.
Website: http://www.ecu.edu/cs-educ/msite/

Eastern Michigan University, Graduate School, College of Education, Department of Teacher Education, Programs in Curriculum and Instruction, Ypsilanti, MI 48197. Offers advanced teaching and learning (MA); early literacy instruction (Graduate Certificate); instructional leadership (MA); learning, motivation and creativity (Graduate Certificate); literacy coaching (Graduate Certificate); online teaching (Certificate); secondary literacy instruction (Graduate Certificate); urban and diversity education (MA). *Students:* 1 (woman) full-time, 28 part-time (21 women); includes 11 minority (3 Black or African American, non-Hispanic/Latino; 1 Asian, non-Hispanic/Latino; 4 Hispanic/Latino; 3 Two or more races, non-Hispanic/Latino). Average age 31. 7 applicants, 71% accepted, 3 enrolled. In 2018, 5 master's awarded. Application fee: $45. *Application contact:* Dr. Virginia Harder, Graduate Coordinator/Advisor, 734-487-2729, Fax: 734-487-2101, E-mail: vharder1@emich.edu.

Emporia State University, Department of Instructional Design and Technology, Emporia, KS 66801-5415. Offers elearning/online teaching (Certificate); teaching with technology (Certificate). *Accreditation:* NCATE. *Program availability:* Part-time, online only, 100% online. *Degree requirements:* For master's, comprehensive exam (for some programs), thesis (for some programs), project. *Entrance requirements:* For master's, appropriate bachelor's degree, letters of recommendation. Additional exam requirements/recommendations for international students: Required—TOEFL (minimum score 520 paper-based; 68 iBT). Electronic applications accepted.

Endicott College, Van Loan School of Graduate and Professional Studies, Program in Integrative Education, Beverly, MA 01915-2096. Offers M Ed. Program offered in conjunction with The Institute for Educational Studies (TIES). *Program availability:* Part-time, online only, 100% online. *Degree requirements:* For master's, thesis. *Entrance requirements:* For master's, undergraduate transcript. Additional exam requirements/recommendations for international students: Required—TOEFL. Electronic applications accepted. *Expenses:* Contact institution. *Faculty research:* Neurophenomenology, autopoiesis, systems view.

The George Washington University, Graduate School of Education and Human Development, Department of Educational Leadership, Program in E-Learning, Washington, DC 20052. Offers Graduate Certificate. *Students:* Average age 33. 2 applicants, 50% accepted. In 2018, 2 Graduate Certificates awarded. *Unit head:* Dr. Virginia Roach, Chair, 202-994-3094, E-mail: vroach@gwu.edu. *Application contact:* Sarah Lang, Director of Graduate Admissions, 202-994-1447, Fax: 202-994-7207, E-mail: slang@gwu.edu.
Website: http://gsehd.gwu.edu/e-learning-certificate

Kansas State University, Graduate School, College of Education, Department of Curriculum and Instruction, Manhattan, KS 66506. Offers curriculum and instruction (Ed D, PhD); digital teaching and learning (MS); educational computing, design and online learning (MS); elementary/middle level curriculum and instruction (MS); online learning (Certificate); reading specialist endorsement (MS); reading/language arts (MS); teacher leader/school improvement (MS); teaching and learning (Certificate). *Accreditation:* NCATE. *Program availability:* Part-time, online learning. *Degree requirements:* For master's, comprehensive exam, portfolio, project, report or thesis; for doctorate, comprehensive exam, thesis/dissertation, preliminary exam; for Certificate, comprehensive exam, portfolio. *Entrance requirements:* For master's, minimum GPA of 3.0, 3 letters of recommendation; for doctorate, GRE, minimum GPA of 3.0, 3 letters of recommendation, evidence of scholarly writing; for Certificate, minimum GPA of 3.0, letters of recommendation. Additional exam requirements/recommendations for international students: Required—TOEFL (minimum score 550 paper-based; 80 iBT) or IELTS. Electronic applications accepted. *Faculty research:* Literacy and technology, critical race theory and diversity, achievement gaps, school improvement, teacher education.

Keiser University, Master of Science in Education Program, Fort Lauderdale, FL 33309. Offers allied health teaching and leadership (MS Ed); career college administration (MS Ed); leadership (MS Ed); online teaching and learning (MS Ed); teaching and learning (MS Ed). *Program availability:* Part-time, online learning.

Lenoir-Rhyne University, Graduate Programs, School of Education, Program in Online Teaching and Instructional Design, Hickory, NC 28601. Offers MS. *Program availability:* Online learning. *Entrance requirements:* For master's, GRE or MAT, essay; minimum GPA of 2.7 undergraduate, 3.0 graduate. Additional exam requirements/recommendations for international students: Required—TOEFL (minimum score 600 paper-based). Electronic applications accepted. *Expenses:* Contact institution.

Lesley University, Graduate School of Education, Cambridge, MA 02138-2790. Offers arts, community, and education (M Ed); autism studies (Certificate); curriculum and instruction (M Ed, CAGS); early childhood education (M Ed); ecological teaching and learning (MS); educational studies (PhD), including adult learning, educational leadership, individually designed; elementary education (M Ed); emergent technologies for educators (Certificate); ESLArts: language learning through the arts (M Ed); high school education (M Ed); individually designed (M Ed); integrated teaching through the arts (M Ed); literacy for K-8 classroom teachers (M Ed); mathematics education (M Ed); middle school education (M Ed); moderate disabilities (M Ed); online learning (Certificate); reading (CAGS); science in education (M Ed); severe disabilities (M Ed); special needs (CAGS); specialist teacher of reading (M Ed); teacher of visual art (M Ed); technology in education (M Ed, CAGS). *Accreditation:* TEAC. *Program availability:* Part-time, evening/weekend, online learning. *Degree requirements:* For master's, practicum; for doctorate, thesis/dissertation. *Entrance requirements:* For master's, Massachusetts Tests for Educator Licensure (MTEL), transcripts, statement of purpose, recommendations; interview (for special education); for doctorate, GRE General Test, transcripts, statement of purpose, recommendations, interview, master's degree, resume; for other advanced degree, interview, master's degree. Additional exam requirements/recommendations for international students: Required—TOEFL (minimum score 550 paper-based; 80 iBT). Electronic applications accepted. *Faculty research:* Assessment in literacy, mathematics and science; autism spectrum disorders; instructional technology and online learning; multicultural education and English language learners.

Millersville University of Pennsylvania, College of Graduate Studies and Adult Learning, College of Education and Human Services, Department of Educational Foundations, Millersville, PA 17551-0302. Offers assessment, curriculum and teaching - online teaching (M Ed), including online instruction; assessment, curriculum and teaching - stem education (M Ed), including integrative stem education; educational leadership (Ed D); leadership for teaching and learning (M Ed). Doctor of Educational Leadership: Collaborative program with Shippensburg University. *Program availability:* Part-time, evening/weekend, 100% online, blended/hybrid learning. *Faculty:* 10 full-time (9 women), 10 part-time/adjunct (6 women). *Students:* 1 full-time (0 women), 78 part-time (53 women); includes 5 minority (3 Black or African American, non-Hispanic/Latino; 2 Hispanic/Latino). Average age 34. 42 applicants, 98% accepted, 21 enrolled. In 2018, 21 master's, 2 doctorates awarded. *Degree requirements:* For master's, comprehensive exam (for some programs), thesis (for some programs), graded portfolio and portfolio defense; for doctorate, comprehensive exam, thesis/dissertation. *Entrance requirements:* For master's, GRE or MAT, only if undergraduate cumulative GPA is lower than 2.8, Interview (Leadership for Teaching and Learning), Teaching Certificate; for doctorate, teaching certificate, resume, letter of sponsorship, 3-5 years of professional experience as specified by PDE CSPG #96. Additional exam requirements/recommendations for international students: Required—TOEFL, IELTS (minimum score 6), PTE (minimum score 60). *Application deadline:* Applications are processed on a rolling basis. Application fee: $40. Electronic applications accepted. *Expenses: Tuition, area resident:* Full-time $9288; part-time $516 per credit. Tuition, state resident: full-time $9288; part-time $516 per credit. Tuition, nonresident: full-time $13,932; part-time $774 per credit. *International tuition:* $13,932 full-time. *Required fees:* $2623.50; $145.75 per credit. Tuition and fees vary according to course load, degree level and program. *Financial support:* Unspecified assistantships available. Financial award application deadline: 3/15; financial award applicants required to submit FAFSA. *Faculty research:* Instructional technology, poverty research, support for LGBTQ educators and students, diversifying the teaching workforce, inclusive education. *Total annual research expenditures:* $741,634. *Unit head:* Dr. Timothy E. Mahoney, Chair, 717-871-7202, E-mail: timothy.mahoney@millersville.edu. *Application contact:* Dr. James A. Delle, Acting Dean of College of Graduate Studies and Adult Learning/Associate Provost, Academic Administration, 717-871-7462, E-mail: James.Delle@millersville.edu.
Website: http://www.millersville.edu/edfoundations/

National University, Sanford College of Education, La Jolla, CA 92037-1011. Offers advanced teaching practices (MS); applied behavior analysis (MS); applied school leadership (MS); e-teaching and learning (Certificate); education (MA); educational administration (MS); educational and instructional technology (MS); educational counseling (MS); higher education administration (MS); inspired teaching and learning (M Ed); school psychology (MS); special education (MA, MS). *Program availability:* Part-time, evening/weekend, 100% online, blended/hybrid learning. *Degree requirements:* For master's, thesis (for some programs). *Entrance requirements:* For master's, interview, minimum GPA of 2.5. Additional exam requirements/recommendations for international students: Required—TOEFL (minimum score 550 paper-based; 79 iBT), IELTS (minimum score 6). Electronic applications accepted. *Expenses: Tuition:* Full-time $10,320; part-time $430 per unit. Tuition and fees vary according to degree level. *Faculty research:* Teacher education, special education, educational effectiveness, teaching abroad, school counseling.

Nova Southeastern University, Abraham S. Fischler College of Education, Fort Lauderdale, FL 33314. Offers education (MS, Ed D, PhD, Ed S); instructional technology and distance education (MS); teaching and learning (MA). *Accreditation:* NCATE. *Program availability:* Part-time, evening/weekend, 100% online, blended/hybrid learning. *Degree requirements:* For master's, practicum, internship; for doctorate, thesis/

dissertation; for Ed S, thesis, practicum, internship. *Entrance requirements:* For master's, MAT or GRE (for some programs), CLAST, PRAXIS I, CBEST, General Knowledge Test, teaching certification, minimum GPA of 2.5, verification of teaching, BS; for doctorate, MAT or GRE, master's degree, minimum cumulative GPA of 3.0; for Ed S, MAT or GRE, master's degree, teaching certificate, minimum GPA of 3.0. Additional exam requirements/recommendations for international students: Recommended—TOEFL (minimum score 550 paper-based; 79 iBT), IELTS (minimum score 6). Electronic applications accepted. *Expenses:* Contact institution. *Faculty research:* STEM education, educational technology, principal training, quality of life.

Post University, Program in Education, Waterbury, CT 06723-2540. Offers curriculum and instruction (M Ed); education (M Ed); educational technology (M Ed); higher education administration (MS); learning design and technology (M Ed); online teaching (M Ed); teaching English to speakers of other languages (TESOL) (M Ed). *Program availability:* Online learning. *Entrance requirements:* For master's, resume. *Expenses: Tuition:* Full-time $8300; part-time $570 per credit. *Required fees:* $140 per term. Tuition and fees vary according to course level, campus/location and program.

Regent University, Graduate School, School of Education, Virginia Beach, VA 23464-9800. Offers education (M Ed, Ed D, PhD), including adult education (Ed D, PhD, Ed S), advanced educational leadership (Ed D, PhD, Ed S), character education (Ed D, PhD, Ed S), Christian education leadership (Ed D, PhD, Ed S), Christian school administration (M Ed), curriculum and instruction (Ed D, PhD, Ed S), curriculum and instruction - adult education (M Ed), curriculum and instruction - Christian school (M Ed), curriculum and instruction - gifted and talented (M Ed), curriculum and instruction - STEM education (M Ed), curriculum and instruction - teacher leader (M Ed), discipleship for ministry (M Ed), educational leadership (M Ed), educational psychology (Ed D, PhD, Ed S), educational technology and online learning (Ed D, PhD, Ed S), elementary education (M Ed), exceptional education executive leadership (Ed D, PhD, Ed S), higher education (Ed D, PhD, Ed S), higher education leadership and management (Ed D, PhD, Ed S), instructional design and technology (M Ed), K-12 school leadership (Ed D, PhD, Ed S), K-12 special education (M Ed), leadership in mathematics education (M Ed), reading specialist (M Ed), special education (Ed D, PhD, Ed S), student affairs (M Ed), TESOL - adult education (M Ed), TESOL - K-12 (M Ed); educational specialist (Ed S), including adult education (Ed D, PhD, Ed S), advanced educational leadership (Ed D, PhD, Ed S), character education (Ed D, PhD, Ed S), Christian education leadership (Ed D, PhD, Ed S), curriculum and instruction (Ed D, PhD, Ed S), educational psychology (Ed D, PhD, Ed S), educational technology and online learning (Ed D, PhD, Ed S), exceptional education executive leadership (Ed D, PhD, Ed S), higher education (Ed D, PhD, Ed S), higher education leadership and management (Ed D, PhD, Ed S), K-12 school leadership (Ed D, PhD, Ed S), special education (Ed D, PhD, Ed S). *Accreditation:* TEAC. *Program availability:* Part-time, evening/weekend, 100% online, blended/hybrid learning. *Degree requirements:* For master's, thesis or alternative; for doctorate, comprehensive exam, thesis/dissertation. *Entrance requirements:* For master's, Virginia Communication and Literacy Assessment (VCLA), PRAXIS, college transcripts, writing sample, interview; for doctorate, GRE, writing sample, resume, transcripts, interview. Additional exam requirements/recommendations for international students: Required—TOEFL (minimum score 577 paper-based). Electronic applications accepted. *Expenses:* Contact institution. *Faculty research:* Christian school administration, curriculum and instruction, educational technology and online learning, higher education, special education.

Télé-université, Graduate Programs, Québec, QC G1K 9H5, Canada. Offers computer science (PhD); corporate finance (MS); distance learning (MS). *Program availability:* Part-time.

Thomas Edison State University, Heavin School of Arts and Sciences, Program in Educational Technology and Online Learning, Trenton, NJ 08608. Offers educational technology and online learning (MA); online learning and teaching (Graduate Certificate). *Program availability:* Part-time, online learning. *Degree requirements:* For master's, practicum. *Entrance requirements:* Additional exam requirements/recommendations for international students: Required—TOEFL (minimum score 550 paper-based; 79 iBT). Electronic applications accepted.

University at Buffalo, the State University of New York, Graduate School, Graduate School of Education, Department of Learning and Instruction, Buffalo, NY 14260. Offers biology education (Ed M, Certificate); chemistry education (Ed M, Certificate); childhood education (Ed M); childhood education with bilingual extension (Ed M); college teaching (Advanced Certificate); curriculum, instruction and the science of learning (PhD); early childhood education (Ed M); early childhood education with bilingual extension (Ed M); earth science education (Ed M, Certificate); education and technology (Ed M); education studies (Ed M); educational technology and new literacies (Certificate); educational technology and new literacies (Advanced Certificate); elementary education (Ed D); English education (Ed M, Certificate); English education studies (Ed M); English for speakers of other languages (Ed M); foreign and second language education (PhD); French education (Ed M, Certificate); German education (Ed M, Certificate); gifted education (Certificate); Latin education (Ed M, Certificate); literacy education studies (Ed M); literacy specialist (Ed M); literacy teaching and learning (Certificate); mathematics education (Ed M, Certificate); music education (Ed M, Certificate); music education studies (Ed M); music learning theory (Advanced Certificate); online education (Advanced Certificate); physics education (Ed M, Certificate); science and the public (Ed M); social studies education (Ed M, Certificate); Spanish education (Ed M, Certificate); special education (PhD); teaching English to speakers of other languages (Ed M). *Program availability:* Part-time, evening/weekend, 100% online. *Faculty:* 31 full-time (22 women), 41 part-time/adjunct (27 women). *Students:* 161 full-time (107 women), 369 part-time (260 women); includes 76 minority (26 Black or African American, non-Hispanic/Latino; 3 American Indian or Alaska Native, non-Hispanic/Latino; 30 Asian, non-Hispanic/Latino; 14 Hispanic/Latino; 3 Two or more races, non-Hispanic/Latino), 41 international. Average age 34. 368 applicants, 70% accepted, 179 enrolled. In 2018, 100 master's, 26 doctorates, 19 other advanced degrees awarded. *Degree requirements:* For master's, comprehensive exam; for doctorate, thesis/dissertation, research analysis exam, research experience. *Entrance requirements:* For master's, letters of reference; for doctorate, GRE General Test or MAT, interview, writing sample, letters of recommendation. Additional exam requirements/recommendations for international students: Required—TOEFL (minimum score 600 paper-based; 96 iBT), IELTS (minimum score 6.5), PTE (minimum score 55). *Application deadline:* For fall admission, 2/1 priority date for domestic and international students; for spring admission, 11/15 priority date for domestic students, 10/1 for international students. Applications are processed on a rolling basis. Application fee: $50. Electronic applications accepted. *Financial support:* In 2018–19, 42 fellowships (averaging $5,181 per year), 44 research assistantships with tuition reimbursements (averaging $10,908 per year) were awarded; teaching assistantships, career-related internships or fieldwork, Federal Work-Study, institutionally sponsored loans, scholarships/grants, tuition waivers (full and partial), and unspecified assistantships also available. Financial award application deadline: 2/28; financial award applicants required to submit FAFSA. *Faculty research:* Science assessment, foreign language teaching and learning, early learning, new literacies, gender and education. *Total annual research expenditures:* $413,233. *Unit head:* Dr. Julie Gorlewski, Department Chair, 716-645-2455, Fax: 716-645-3161, E-mail: jgorlews@buffalo.edu. *Application contact:* Renad Aref, Assistant Director of Admission Recruitment, 716-645-2110, Fax: 716-645-7937, E-mail: gseinfo@buffalo.edu.
Website: http://ed.buffalo.edu/teaching.html

University of Colorado Denver, School of Education and Human Development, Information and Learning Technologies Program, Denver, CO 80217. Offers e-learning design and implementation (MA); instructional design and adult learning (MA); K-12 teaching (MA). *Program availability:* Part-time, evening/weekend, online learning. *Degree requirements:* For master's, comprehensive exam (for some programs), comprehensive exam or online portfolio; 30 credit hours. *Entrance requirements:* For master's, GRE or MAT (if GPA is below 2.75), resume, statement of intent, three letters of recommendation, transcripts from all colleges/universities previously attended. Additional exam requirements/recommendations for international students: Required—TOEFL (minimum score 537 paper-based; 75 iBT); Recommended—IELTS (minimum score 6.5). Electronic applications accepted. *Expenses:* Contact institution. *Faculty research:* Technology for educational management, instructional design foundations, e-learning, educational design.

University of Maryland, Baltimore County, The Graduate School, College of Arts, Humanities and Social Sciences, Department of Education, Program in Instructional Systems Development, Halethorpe, MD 21227. Offers distance education (Graduate Certificate); instructional systems development (MA, Graduate Certificate), including distance education (Graduate Certificate); instructional technology (Graduate Certificate). *Program availability:* Part-time, evening/weekend, 100% online, blended/hybrid learning. *Degree requirements:* For master's, comprehensive exam (for some programs), portfolio (for some programs). *Entrance requirements:* Additional exam requirements/recommendations for international students: Required—TOEFL (minimum score 99 iBT), GRE. Electronic applications accepted. *Faculty research:* E-learning, distance education, instructional design.

University of Maryland University College, The Graduate School, Program in Distance Education and E-learning, Adelphi, MD 20783. Offers MDE. *Program availability:* Part-time, evening/weekend, online learning. *Students:* 1 (woman) full-time, 102 part-time (75 women); includes 41 minority (27 Black or African American, non-Hispanic/Latino; 2 Asian, non-Hispanic/Latino; 9 Hispanic/Latino; 3 Two or more races, non-Hispanic/Latino), 6 international. Average age 44. 24 applicants, 100% accepted, 10 enrolled. In 2018, 23 master's awarded. *Degree requirements:* For master's, thesis or alternative. *Application deadline:* Applications are processed on a rolling basis. Application fee: $50. Electronic applications accepted. *Financial support:* Scholarships/grants available. Support available to part-time students. Financial award application deadline: 6/1; financial award applicants required to submit FAFSA. *Unit head:* Linda Smith, Program Chair, 240-684-2400, E-mail: Linda.J.Smith@umuc.edu. *Application contact:* Admissions, 800-888-8682, E-mail: studentfirst@umuc.edu.
Website: https://www.umuc.edu/academic-programs/masters-degrees/distance-education/index.cfm

University of Nevada, Las Vegas, Graduate College, College of Education, Department of Teaching and Learning, Las Vegas, NV 89154-3005. Offers curriculum and instruction (M Ed, MS, Ed D, PhD, Ed S), including teacher education (PhD); elementary teaching (Certificate); online teaching and training (Certificate); secondary teaching (Certificate); social justice studies (Certificate); teaching and learning (PhD). *Program availability:* Part-time, evening/weekend. *Faculty:* 25 full-time (12 women), 11 part-time/adjunct (8 women). *Students:* 304 full-time (212 women), 271 part-time (181 women); includes 255 minority (56 Black or African American, non-Hispanic/Latino; 1 American Indian or Alaska Native, non-Hispanic/Latino; 38 Asian, non-Hispanic/Latino; 124 Hispanic/Latino; 1 Native Hawaiian or other Pacific Islander, non-Hispanic/Latino; 35 Two or more races, non-Hispanic/Latino), 16 international. Average age 34. 228 applicants, 86% accepted, 164 enrolled. In 2018, 135 master's, 12 doctorates, 10 other advanced degrees awarded. *Degree requirements:* For master's, comprehensive exam (for some programs), thesis (for some programs); for doctorate, comprehensive exam, thesis/dissertation, defense of dissertation; for other advanced degree, comprehensive exam (for some programs), oral presentation of special project or professional paper. *Entrance requirements:* For master's, bachelor's degree with minimum GPA 2.75; for doctorate, GRE General Test, master's degree with minimum GPA of 3.0; statement of purpose; demonstration of oral communication skills; 3 letters of recommendation; for other advanced degree, PRAXIS Core (for some programs); PRAXIS II (for some programs), bachelor's degree (for some programs). Additional exam requirements/recommendations for international students: Required—TOEFL (minimum score 550 paper-based; 80 iBT), IELTS (minimum score 7). *Application deadline:* For fall admission, 6/1 for domestic students, 5/1 for international students; for spring admission, 11/1 for domestic students, 10/1 for international students; for summer admission, 3/15 for domestic students. Application fee: $60 ($95 for international students). Electronic applications accepted. *Financial support:* In 2018–19, 31 students received support, including 7 research assistantships with full tuition reimbursements available (averaging $18,286 per year), 24 teaching assistantships with full tuition reimbursements available (averaging $19,271 per year); institutionally sponsored loans, scholarships/grants, health care benefits, and unspecified assistantships also available. Financial award application deadline: 3/15; financial award applicants required to submit FAFSA. *Faculty research:* Content area and critical literacy, education in content areas, teacher education, science, technology, engineering and mathematics education, immersive environments/simulations/games. *Total annual research expenditures:* $1.1 million. *Unit head:* Dr. P.G. Schrader, Chair/Professor, 702-895-3331, Fax: 702-895-4898, E-mail: tl.chair@unlv.edu. *Application contact:* Dr. Micah Stohlmann, Graduate Coordinator, 702-895-0836, Fax: 702-895-4898, E-mail: tl.gradcoord@unlv.edu.
Website: http://tl.unlv.edu/

University of South Florida, Innovative Education, Tampa, FL 33620-9951. Offers adult, career and higher education (Graduate Certificate), including college teaching, leadership in developing human resources, leadership in higher education; Africana studies (Graduate Certificate), including diasporas and health disparities, genocide and human rights; aging studies (Graduate Certificate), including gerontology; art research (Graduate Certificate), including museum studies; business foundations (Graduate Certificate); chemical and biomedical engineering (Graduate Certificate), including materials science and engineering, water, health and sustainability; child and family studies (Graduate Certificate), including positive behavior support; civil and industrial engineering (Graduate Certificate), including transportation systems analysis; community and family health (Graduate Certificate), including maternal and child health, social marketing and public health, violence and injury: prevention and intervention, women's health; criminology (Graduate Certificate), including criminal justice administration; data science for public administration (Graduate Certificate); digital humanities (Graduate Certificate); educational measurement and research (Graduate Certificate), including evaluation; English (Graduate Certificate), including comparative literary studies, creative writing, professional and technical communication; entrepreneurship (Graduate Certificate); environmental health (Graduate Certificate), including safety management; epidemiology and biostatistics (Graduate Certificate), including applied biostatistics, biostatistics, concepts and tools of epidemiology, epidemiology, epidemiology of infectious diseases; geography, environment and

planning (Graduate Certificate), including community development, environmental policy and management, geographical information systems; geology (Graduate Certificate), including hydrogeology; global health (Graduate Certificate), including disaster management, global health and Latin American and Caribbean studies, global health practice, humanitarian assistance, infection control; government and international affairs (Graduate Certificate), including Cuban studies, globalization studies; health policy and management (Graduate Certificate), including health management and leadership, public health policy and programs; hearing specialist: early intervention (Graduate Certificate); industrial and management systems engineering (Graduate Certificate), including systems engineering, technology management; information studies (Graduate Certificate), including school library media specialist; information systems/decision sciences (Graduate Certificate), including analytics and business intelligence; instructional technology (Graduate Certificate), including distance education, Florida digital/virtual educator, instructional design, multimedia design, Web design; internal medicine, bioethics and medical humanities (Graduate Certificate), including biomedical ethics; Latin American and Caribbean studies (Graduate Certificate); leadership for coastal resiliency planning (Graduate Certificate); mass communications (Graduate Certificate), including multimedia journalism; mathematics and statistics (Graduate Certificate), including mathematics; medicine (Graduate Certificate), including aging and neuroscience, bioinformatics, biotechnology, brain fitness and memory management, clinical investigation, hand and upper limb rehabilitation, health informatics, health sciences, integrative weight management, intellectual property, medicine and gender, metabolic and nutritional medicine, metabolic cardiology, pharmacy sciences; national and competitive intelligence (Graduate Certificate); nursing (Graduate Certificate), including simulation based academic fellowship in advanced pain management; psychological and social foundations (Graduate Certificate), including career counseling, college teaching, diversity in education, mental health counseling, school counseling; public affairs (Graduate Certificate), including nonprofit management, public management, research administration; public health (Graduate Certificate), including assessing chemical toxicity and public health risks, health equity, pharmacoepidemiology, public health generalist, toxicology, translational research in adolescent behavioral health; public health practices (Graduate Certificate), including planning for healthy communities; rehabilitation and mental health counseling (Graduate Certificate), including integrative mental health care, marriage and family therapy, rehabilitation technology; secondary education (Graduate Certificate), including ESOL, foreign language education: culture and content, foreign language education: professional; social work (Graduate Certificate), including geriatric social work/clinical gerontology; special education (Graduate Certificate), including autism spectrum disorder, disabilities education: severe/profound; world languages (Graduate Certificate), including teaching English as a second language (TESL) or foreign language. *Expenses:* Tuition, state resident: full-time $6350. Tuition, nonresident: full-time $19,048. *International tuition:* $19,048 full-time. *Required fees:* $2079. *Unit head:* Dr. Cynthia DeLuca, Associate Vice President and Assistant Vice Provost, 813-974-3077, Fax: 813-974-7061, E-mail: deluca@usf.edu. *Application contact:* Owen Hooper, Director, Summer and Alternative Calendar Programs, 813-974-6917, E-mail: hooper@usf.edu.
Website: http://www.usf.edu/innovative-education/

Virginia Polytechnic Institute and State University, VT Online, Blacksburg, VA 24061. Offers advanced transportation systems (Certificate); aerospace engineering (MS); agricultural and life sciences (MSLFS); business information systems (Graduate Certificate); career and technical education (MS); civil engineering (MS); computer engineering (M Eng, MS); decision support systems (Graduate Certificate); eLearning leadership (MA); electrical engineering (M Eng, MS); engineering administration (MEA); environmental engineering (Certificate); environmental politics and policy (Graduate Certificate); environmental sciences and engineering (MS); foundations of political analysis (Graduate Certificate); health product risk management (Graduate Certificate); industrial and systems engineering (MS); information policy and society (Graduate Certificate); information security (Graduate Certificate); information technology (MIT); instructional technology (MA); integrative STEM education (MA Ed); liberal arts (Graduate Certificate); life sciences: health product risk management (MS); natural resources (MNR, Graduate Certificate); networking (Graduate Certificate); nonprofit and nongovernmental organization management (Graduate Certificate); ocean engineering (MS); political science (MA); security studies (Graduate Certificate); software development (Graduate Certificate). *Expenses:* Tuition, state resident: full-time $15,510; part-time $739.50 per credit hour. Tuition, nonresident: full-time $29,629; part-time $1490.25 per credit hour. *Required fees:* $2804; $550 per semester. Tuition and fees vary according to course load, campus/location and program. *Application contact:* Graduate Admissions and Academic Progress, 540-231-8636, E-mail: grads@vt.edu.
Website: http://www.vto.vt.edu/

Walden University, Graduate Programs, Richard W. Riley College of Education and Leadership, Minneapolis, MN 55401. Offers adult education (Post-Master's Certificate); adult learning (Graduate Certificate); college teaching and learning (Graduate Certificate); community college leadership (Ed D); curriculum, instruction and assessment (Ed D, Ed S, Graduate Certificate); developmental education (Graduate Certificate); early childhood administration, management, and leadership (Graduate Certificate); early childhood education (Ed D, Ed S); early childhood public policy and advocacy (Graduate Certificate); early childhood studies (MS), including administration, management and leadership, early childhood public policy and advocacy, teaching adults in the early childhood field, teaching and diversity in early childhood education; education (MS, PhD), including adolescent literacy and learning (MS), curriculum, instruction, and assessment (grades K-12) (MS), curriculum, instruction, assessment, and evaluation (PhD), early childhood leadership and advocacy (PhD), early childhood special education (PhD), educational leadership (MS), educational leadership and administration (principal preparation) (MS), educational technology and design (PhD), elementary reading and literacy (PreK-6) (MS), elementary reading and mathematics (grades K-6) (MS), global and comparative education (PhD), higher education leadership management and policy (PhD), integrating technology in the classroom (grades K-12) (MS), learning, instruction and innovation (PhD), mathematics (grades 5-8) (MS), mathematics (grades K-6) (MS), mathematics and science (grades K-8) (MS), organizational research, assessment, and evaluation (PhD), reading and literacy with a reading K-12 endorsement (MS), reading literacy assessment and evaluation (PhD), science (grades K-8) (MS), special education (non-licensure) (grades K-12) (MS), teacher leadership (grades K-12) (MS), teaching English language learners (grades K-12) (MS); educational administration and leadership (Ed D); educational leadership and administration (principal preparation) (Ed S); educational technology (Ed D, Ed S, Post Master's Certificate); elementary reading and literacy (Graduate Certificate); engaging culturally diverse learners (Graduate Certificate); enrollment management and institutional marketing (Graduate Certificate); higher education (MS), including adult learning, college teaching and learning, enrollment management and institutional marketing, global higher education, leadership for student success, online and distance learning; higher education and adult learning (Ed D); higher education leadership and management (Ed D); higher education leadership for student success (Graduate Certificate); instructional design and technology (MS, Postbaccalaureate Certificate), including general program (MS), online learning (MS), training and performance improvement (MS); integrating technology in the classroom (Graduate Certificate); mathematics 5-8 (Graduate Certificate); mathematics K-6 (Graduate Certificate); online teaching for adult educators (Graduate Certificate); reading, literacy, and assessment (Ed D, Ed S); science K-8 (Graduate Certificate); special education (Ed D, Ed S, Graduate Certificate); special education (K-age 21) (MAT); teacher leadership (Graduate Certificate); teaching adults English as a second language (Graduate Certificate); teaching adults in the early childhood field (Graduate Certificate); teaching and diversity in early childhood education (Graduate Certificate); teaching English language learners (grades K-12) (Graduate Certificate); teaching K-12 students online (Graduate Certificate). *Accreditation:* NCATE. *Program availability:* Part-time, evening/weekend, online only, 100% online. *Degree requirements:* For doctorate, thesis/dissertation (for some programs), residency; for other advanced degree, residency (for some programs). *Entrance requirements:* For master's, bachelor's degree or higher; minimum GPA of 2.5; official transcripts; goal statement (for some programs); access to computer and Internet; for doctorate, master's degree or higher; three years of related professional or academic experience (preferred); minimum GPA of 3.0; goal statement and current resume (for select programs); official transcripts; access to computer and Internet; for other advanced degree, relevant work experience; access to computer and Internet. Additional exam requirements/recommendations for international students: Required—TOEFL (minimum score 550 paper-based, 79 iBT), IELTS (minimum score 6.5), Michigan English Language Assessment Battery (minimum score 82), or PTE (minimum score 53). Electronic applications accepted.

Waynesburg University, Graduate and Professional Studies, Canonsburg, PA 15370. Offers business (MBA), including energy management, finance, health systems, human resources, leadership, market development; counseling (MA), including addictions counseling, clinical mental health; counselor education and supervision (PhD); criminal investigation (MA); education (M Ed), including autism, curriculum and instruction, educational leadership, online teaching; nursing (MSN), including administration, education, informatics; nursing practice (DNP); special education (M Ed); technology (M Ed); MSN/MBA. *Accreditation:* AACN. *Program availability:* Part-time, evening/weekend. *Degree requirements:* For doctorate, thesis/dissertation. *Entrance requirements:* Additional exam requirements/recommendations for international students: Required—TOEFL. Electronic applications accepted.

Wayne State University, College of Education, Division of Administrative and Organizational Studies, Detoit, MI 48202. Offers educational administration and supervision (Ed S); educational leadership (M Ed); educational leadership and policy studies (Ed D, PhD); educational technology (Certificate); learning design and technology (M Ed, Ed D, PhD, Ed S); online teaching (Certificate). *Program availability:* Part-time, evening/weekend. *Faculty:* 9. *Students:* 77 full-time (53 women), 223 part-time (160 women); includes 155 minority (126 Black or African American, non-Hispanic/Latino; 7 Asian, non-Hispanic/Latino; 11 Hispanic/Latino; 1 Native Hawaiian or other Pacific Islander, non-Hispanic/Latino; 10 Two or more races, non-Hispanic/Latino), 9 international. Average age 39. 239 applicants, 33% accepted, 58 enrolled. In 2018, 51 master's, 10 doctorates, 54 other advanced degrees awarded. *Degree requirements:* For master's, thesis (for some programs), GPA 3.0; for doctorate, comprehensive exam, thesis/dissertation, GPA 3.0; for other advanced degree, GPA 3.0. *Entrance requirements:* For master's, baccalaureate degree from accredited U.S. institution or equivalent from college or university of government-recognized standing; minimum undergraduate GPA of 2.75 in upper-division coursework; personal statement; for doctorate, GRE (instructional design and technology), interview; curriculum vitae; three to four recommendations; master's degree (for educational leadership and policy studies); minimum graduate GPA of 3.5; autobiographical statement; research experience (for PhD program); for other advanced degree, educational specialist certificate requirement include undergraduate and master's degrees (for both learning design and technology and administration and supervision); minimum graduate GPA of 3.4, and personal statement. Additional exam requirements/recommendations for international students: Required—TOEFL (minimum score 550 paper-based; 79 iBT); Recommended—IELTS (minimum score 6.5), TWE (minimum score 5.5), TSE (minimum score 58). *Application deadline:* Applications are processed on a rolling basis. Application fee: $50. Electronic applications accepted. *Financial support:* In 2018–19, 87 students received support, including 1 fellowship with tuition reimbursement available (averaging $20,000 per year), 4 research assistantships with tuition reimbursements available (averaging $19,267 per year); scholarships/grants and unspecified assistantships also available. Support available to part-time students. Financial award applicants required to submit FAFSA. *Faculty research:* Total quality management, participatory management, administering educational technology, school improvement, principalship. *Unit head:* Dr. William Hill, Assistant Dean, 313-577-9316, E-mail: ad2107@wayne.edu. *Application contact:* Dr. Mary L. Waker, Graduate Admissions Officer, 313-577-1601, Fax: 313-577-7904, E-mail: m.waker@wayne.edu.
Website: http://coe.wayne.edu/aos/index.php

Western Illinois University, School of Graduate Studies, College of Business and Technology, Program in Instructional Design and Technology, Macomb, IL 61455-1390. Offers educational technology specialist (Certificate); instructional design and technology (MS); instructional media development (Certificate); online and distance learning development (Certificate); technology integration in education (Certificate); workplace learning and performance (Certificate). *Program availability:* Part-time, online learning. *Students:* 13 full-time (6 women), 36 part-time (21 women); includes 5 minority (3 Black or African American, non-Hispanic/Latino; 1 Asian, non-Hispanic/Latino; 1 Hispanic/Latino), 6 international. Average age 34. 13 applicants, 92% accepted, 9 enrolled. In 2018, 30 master's, 8 other advanced degrees awarded. *Entrance requirements:* Additional exam requirements/recommendations for international students: Required—TOEFL (minimum score 550 paper-based; 80 iBT). *Application deadline:* Applications are processed on a rolling basis. Application fee: $30. Electronic applications accepted. *Financial support:* Teaching assistantships and unspecified assistantships available. Financial award applicants required to submit FAFSA. *Unit head:* Dr. Rafael Obregon, Chairperson, 309-298-1459. *Application contact:* Dr. Mark Mossman, Associate Provost and Director of Graduate Studies, 309-298-1806, Fax: 309-298-2345, E-mail: grad-office@wiu.edu.
Website: http://wiu.edu/idt

Wilkes University, College of Graduate and Professional Studies, School of Education, Wilkes-Barre, PA 18766-0002. Offers educational development and strategies (MS Ed); educational leadership (MS Ed, Ed D); effective teaching (MS Ed); instructional media (MS Ed); instructional technology (MS Ed); international school leadership (MS Ed); international teaching and learning (MS Ed); literacy (MS Ed); middle level education (MS Ed); online teaching (MS Ed); school business leadership (MS Ed); special education (MS Ed); teaching English to speakers of other languages (MS Ed). *Program availability:* Part-time, evening/weekend, 100% online, blended/hybrid learning. *Students:* 87 full-time (67 women), 1,418 part-time (1,078 women); includes 87 minority (13 Black or African American, non-Hispanic/Latino; 1 American Indian or Alaska Native, non-Hispanic/Latino; 11 Asian, non-Hispanic/Latino; 40 Hispanic/Latino; 22 Two or more races, non-Hispanic/Latino). Average age 35. In 2018, 611 master's, 9 doctorates awarded. *Entrance requirements:* Additional exam requirements/recommendations for international students: Required—TOEFL (minimum score 550 paper-based; 79 iBT). *Application deadline:* Applications are processed on a rolling basis. Application fee: $45

($65 for international students). Electronic applications accepted. *Expenses:* Contact institution. *Financial support:* Unspecified assistantships available. Financial award application deadline: 3/1; financial award applicants required to submit FAFSA. *Unit head:* Dr. Rhonda Rabbitt, Dean, 570-408-4680, Fax: 570-408-7872, E-mail: rhonda.rabbitt@wilkes.edu. *Application contact:* Stephanie Wasmanski, Associate Director of Graduate Admissions, 570-408-5535, Fax: 570-408-7846, E-mail: stephanie.wasmanski@wilkes.edu.
Website: http://www.wilkes.edu/academics/graduate-programs/masters-programs/graduate-education/index.aspx

Educational Leadership and Administration

Abilene Christian University, College of Graduate and Professional Studies, Instruction and Learning Program, Addison, TX 75001. Offers conflict management (M Ed); learning with emerging technologies (M Ed, Certificate). *Program availability:* Part-time, online only. *Faculty:* 2 full-time (1 woman), 1 part-time/adjunct (0 women). *Students:* 3 full-time (2 women). In 2018, 9 master's awarded. *Degree requirements:* For master's, comprehensive exam, practicum. *Entrance requirements:* Additional exam requirements/recommendations for international students: Required—TOEFL (minimum score 80 iBT), IELTS (minimum score 6), PTE. *Application deadline:* For fall admission, 10/7 for domestic students; for winter admission, 12/20 for domestic students; for spring admission, 2/24 for domestic students; for summer admission, 4/20 for domestic students. Applications are processed on a rolling basis. Application fee: $50. Electronic applications accepted. *Expenses:* $726 per hour. *Financial support:* Application deadline: 7/1; applicants required to submit FAFSA. *Unit head:* Dr. Brian Cole, Program Director, 214-721-0685, E-mail: bec15b@acu.edu. *Application contact:* Graduate Admissions, 855-219-7300, E-mail: onlineadmissions@acu.edu.
Website: http://www.acu.edu/online/academics/master-of-education-in-instructional-leadership.html

Abilene Christian University, College of Graduate and Professional Studies, Program in Organizational Leadership, Addison, TX 75001. Offers Ed D. *Program availability:* Part-time, online only, 100% online. *Faculty:* 12 full-time (9 women), 21 part-time/adjunct (10 women). *Students:* 293 full-time (198 women), 181 part-time (121 women); includes 257 minority (149 Black or African American, non-Hispanic/Latino; 2 American Indian or Alaska Native, non-Hispanic/Latino; 5 Asian, non-Hispanic/Latino; 86 Hispanic/Latino; 15 Two or more races, non-Hispanic/Latino), 5 international. 164 applicants, 77% accepted, 107 enrolled. In 2018, 2 doctorates awarded. *Degree requirements:* For doctorate, thesis/dissertation. *Entrance requirements:* Additional exam requirements/recommendations for international students: Required—TOEFL (minimum score 80 iBT), IELTS (minimum score 6). *Application deadline:* For fall admission, 10/7 for domestic students; for winter admission, 12/20 for domestic students; for spring admission, 2/24 for domestic students; for summer admission, 4/20 for domestic students. Applications are processed on a rolling basis. Application fee: $50. Electronic applications accepted. *Expenses:* $735 per hour. *Financial support:* In 2018–19, 53 students received support. Scholarships/grants available. Financial award application deadline: 7/1; financial award applicants required to submit FAFSA. *Unit head:* Dr. Sarah Lee, Interim Program Director, 214-305-9531, E-mail: sara.lee@acu.edu. *Application contact:* Graduate Advisor, 855-219-7300, E-mail: onlineadmissions@acu.edu.
Website: http://www.acu.edu/online/academics/organizational-leadership.html

Acacia University, American Graduate School of Education, Tempe, AZ 85284. Offers educational administration (M Ed); elementary education (MA); English as a second language (M Ed); secondary education (MA); special education (M Ed).

Acadia University, Faculty of Professional Studies, School of Education, Program in Leadership, Wolfville, NS B4P 2R6, Canada. Offers M Ed. *Program availability:* Part-time. *Degree requirements:* For master's, thesis optional. *Entrance requirements:* For master's, B Ed or the equivalent, 2 years of teaching or related experience. Additional exam requirements/recommendations for international students: Required—TOEFL (minimum score 580 paper-based; 93 iBT), IELTS (minimum score 6.5). *Faculty research:* Organizational theory and structural change, professionalism, sexuality education.

Adams State University, Office of Graduate Studies, Department of Teacher Education, Alamosa, CO 81101. Offers teacher education (MA), including adaptive leadership, curriculum and instruction, curriculum and instruction-STEM, educational leadership. *Program availability:* Part-time, online learning. *Degree requirements:* For master's, qualifying exam. *Entrance requirements:* For master's, GRE General Test or MAT, minimum undergraduate GPA of 3.0.

Alabama State University, College of Education, Department of Instructional Support Programs, Montgomery, AL 36101-0271. Offers counselor education (M Ed, MS, Ed S), including general counseling (MS, Ed S), school counseling (M Ed, Ed S); educational administration (M Ed), including instructional leadership; educational leadership, policy and law (PhD); library education media (Ed S). *Program availability:* Part-time, evening/weekend. *Faculty:* 11 full-time (6 women), 7 part-time/adjunct (5 women). *Students:* 27 full-time (17 women), 85 part-time (58 women); includes 182 minority (181 Black or African American, non-Hispanic/Latino; 1 Hispanic/Latino). Average age 41. 70 applicants, 54% accepted, 12 enrolled. In 2018, 14 master's, 6 doctorates, 1 other advanced degree awarded. Terminal master's awarded for partial completion of doctoral program. *Degree requirements:* For master's and Ed S, comprehensive exam; for doctorate, thesis/dissertation. *Entrance requirements:* For master's, GRE General Test, MAT, writing competency test, bachelor's degree or its equivalent from accredited college or university with minimum GPA of 2.5; for Ed S, GRE General Test, MAT, writing competency test, minimum GPA of 3.25. Additional exam requirements/recommendations for international students: Required—TOEFL (minimum score 500 paper-based). *Application deadline:* For fall admission, 4/15 for domestic and international students; for spring admission, 11/15 for domestic and international students; for summer admission, 3/15 for domestic and international students. Applications are processed on a rolling basis. Application fee: $25. Electronic applications accepted. *Expenses:* Contact institution. *Financial support:* In 2018–19, 3 students received support. Fellowships, research assistantships, teaching assistantships, Federal Work-Study, scholarships/grants, tuition waivers (partial), and unspecified assistantships available. Financial award application deadline: 6/30; financial award applicants required to submit FAFSA. *Unit head:* Dr. Kecia Asley, Chair, Instructional Leadership/Educational Leadership, Policy, & Law, 334-229-8828, Fax: 334-229-6831, E-mail: kashley@alasu.edu. *Application contact:* Dr. Ed Brown, Dean of Graduate Studies, 334-229-4275, Fax: 334-229-4928, E-mail: ebrown@alasu.edu.
Website: http://www.alasu.edu/academics/colleges—departments/college-of-education/instructional-support-programs/index.aspx

Albany State University, College of Education, Albany, GA 31705-2717. Offers early childhood education (M Ed); educational leadership (Ed S); health and physical education (M Ed); middle grades education (M Ed); school counseling (M Ed); special education (M Ed). *Accreditation:* NCATE. *Program availability:* Part-time, evening/weekend, online learning. *Degree requirements:* For master's, comprehensive exam, internship, GACE Content Exam. *Entrance requirements:* For master's, GRE or MAT. Electronic applications accepted. *Faculty research:* GACE preparation, STEM (science, technology, engineering, and mathematics), technology education, special education, professional teacher development, health implications liberation philosophy, NET-Q, learning community, disabled or at-risk students.

Alliant International University–San Diego, Shirley M. Hufstedler School of Education, Educational Leadership Programs, San Diego, CA 92131. Offers educational administration (MA); educational leadership and management (K-12) (Ed D); higher education (Ed D, Certificate); preliminary administrative services (Credential). *Program availability:* Part-time. *Degree requirements:* For doctorate, comprehensive exam, thesis/dissertation. *Entrance requirements:* For master's, minimum GPA of 2.5, letters of recommendation; for doctorate, minimum GPA of 3.0, letters of recommendation. Additional exam requirements/recommendations for international students: Required—TOEFL (minimum score 550 paper-based; 80 iBT), TWE (minimum score 5). Electronic applications accepted. *Faculty research:* Global education, women and international educational opportunities.

Alliant International University–San Francisco, Shirley M. Hufstedler School of Education, Educational Leadership Programs, San Francisco, CA 94133. Offers community college administration (Ed D); educational administration (MA); educational leadership and management (K-12) (Ed D); higher education (Ed D); preliminary administrative services (Credential). *Program availability:* Part-time. *Degree requirements:* For doctorate, comprehensive exam, thesis/dissertation. *Entrance requirements:* For master's and doctorate, minimum GPA of 3.0, letters of recommendation. Additional exam requirements/recommendations for international students: Required—TOEFL (minimum score 550 paper-based; 80 iBT), TWE (minimum score 5). Electronic applications accepted. *Faculty research:* Leadership in higher education, community colleges.

Alverno College, School of Professional Studies - Education Division, Milwaukee, WI 53234-3922. Offers adaptive education (MA); administrative leadership (MA); adult education and organizational development (MA); adult educational and instructional design (MA); adult educational and instructional technology (MA); global connections in the humanities (MA); instructional leadership (MA); instructional technology for K-12 settings (MA); professional development (MA); reading education (MA); reading education with adaptive education (MA); science education (MA); special education (MA); teaching in alternative schools (MA). *Accreditation:* NCATE. *Program availability:* Part-time, evening/weekend. *Degree requirements:* For master's, presentation/defense of proposal, conference presentation of inquiry projects. *Entrance requirements:* For master's, bachelor's degree in related field, communication samples from work setting, 3 letters of recommendation. Additional exam requirements/recommendations for international students: Required—TOEFL. Electronic applications accepted. *Expenses:* Contact institution. *Faculty research:* Student self-assessment, self-reflection, integration of curriculum, identifying needs of students in strategic situations and designing appropriate classroom strategies.

American College of Education, Graduate Programs, Indianapolis, IN 46204. Offers curriculum and instruction (M Ed), including bilingual, ESL; educational leadership (M Ed); educational technology (M Ed).

American InterContinental University Online, Program in Education, Schaumburg, IL 60173. Offers curriculum and instruction (M Ed); educational assessment and evaluation (M Ed); instructional technology (M Ed); leadership of educational organizations (M Ed). *Accreditation:* TEAC. *Program availability:* Evening/weekend, online learning. *Entrance requirements:* Additional exam requirements/recommendations for international students: Required—TOEFL (minimum score 550 paper-based). Electronic applications accepted.

American International College, School of Education, Low Residency Programs, Springfield, MA 01109-3189. Offers counseling psychology (MA); educational leadership and supervision (Ed D); professional counseling and supervision (Ed D); teaching and learning (Ed D). *Program availability:* Evening/weekend. *Degree requirements:* For doctorate, thesis/dissertation. *Entrance requirements:* For master's, minimum undergraduate GPA of 3.0, 2 letters of recommendation, personal goal statement, official transcript of all academic work (graduate and undergraduate); for doctorate, minimum master's GPA of 3.0, 3 letters of recommendation, personal goal statement/essay (6-8 pages), official transcript of all academic work (graduate and undergraduate). Additional exam requirements/recommendations for international students: Required—TOEFL. *Expenses:* Contact institution. *Faculty research:* Educational leadership, curriculum, program evaluation, educational policy.

American Public University System, AMU/APU Graduate Programs, Charles Town, WV 25414. Offers accounting (MS); applied business analytics (MS); business administration (MBA); criminal justice (MA); cybersecurity studies (MS); educational leadership (M Ed); environmental policy and management (MS); global security (DGS); health information management (MS); history (MA), including American military history, American Revolution, civil war, war since 1945, World War II; information technology (MS); international relations and conflict resolution (MA), including American politics and government, comparative government and development, general, international relations, public policy; national security studies (MA); nursing (MSN); political science (MA); public policy (MPP); reverse logistics management (MA), including comparative and security issues, conflict resolution, international and transnational security issues, peacekeeping; space studies (MS); sports management (MS); strategic intelligence (DSI); teaching (M Ed), including secondary social studies; transportation and logistics management (MA). *Program availability:* Part-time, evening/weekend, online only, 100% online. *Students:* 406 full-time (180 women), 7,826 part-time (3,329 women); includes 2,781 minority (1,438 Black or African American, non-Hispanic/Latino; 44 American Indian or Alaska Native, non-Hispanic/Latino; 193 Asian, non-Hispanic/Latino; 747 Hispanic/Latino; 53 Native Hawaiian or other Pacific Islander, non-Hispanic/Latino; 306 Two or more races, non-Hispanic/Latino), 121 international. Average age 38. In 2018, 2,717 master's awarded. *Degree requirements:* For master's, comprehensive exam or

practicum; for doctorate, practicum. *Entrance requirements:* For master's, official transcript showing earned bachelor's degree from institution accredited by recognized accrediting body. Additional exam requirements/recommendations for international students: Required—TOEFL (minimum score 550 paper-based), IELTS (minimum score 6.5). *Application deadline:* Applications are processed on a rolling basis. Application fee: $0. Electronic applications accepted. *Financial support:* Scholarships/grants available. Financial award applicants required to submit FAFSA. *Unit head:* Dr. Wallace Boston, President, 877-468-6268, Fax: 304-728-2348, E-mail: president@apus.edu. *Application contact:* Yoci Deal, Associate Vice President, Graduate and International Admissions, 877-468-6268, Fax: 304-724-3764, E-mail: info@apus.edu.
Website: http://www.apus.edu

American University, School of Education, Washington, DC 20016-8030. Offers education (Certificate); education policy and leadership (M Ed); international training and education (MA); special education (MA); teacher education (MAT); M Ed/MPA; M Ed/MPP; MAT/MA. *Accreditation:* NCATE. *Program availability:* Part-time, evening/weekend, 100% online. *Faculty:* 17 full-time (13 women), 33 part-time/adjunct (23 women). *Students:* 53 full-time (46 women), 246 part-time (191 women); includes 139 minority (97 Black or African American, non-Hispanic/Latino; 13 Asian, non-Hispanic/Latino; 23 Hispanic/Latino; 6 Two or more races, non-Hispanic/Latino), 5 international. Average age 29. 361 applicants, 88% accepted, 161 enrolled. In 2018, 73 master's, 2 other advanced degrees awarded. *Degree requirements:* For master's, comprehensive exam, thesis or alternative. *Entrance requirements:* For master's, Please visit website: https://www.american.edu/soe/, bachelor's degree, statement of purpose, transcripts, 2 letters of recommendation. Additional exam requirements/recommendations for international students: Required—TOEFL (minimum score 100 iBT). Application fee: $55. Electronic applications accepted. *Expenses: Tuition:* Full-time $30,744; part-time $1642 per credit hour. *Required fees:* $702; $200 per semester. Tuition and fees vary according to course load, degree level and program. *Financial support:* Research assistantships, teaching assistantships, institutionally sponsored loans, scholarships/grants, and unspecified assistantships available. Financial award application deadline: 2/1; financial award applicants required to submit FAFSA. *Unit head:* Dr. Cheryl Holcomb-McCoy, Dean, 202-885-3720, E-mail: educate@american.edu. *Application contact:* Ashleigh Huseth, Senior Coordinator, Admissions & Onboarding, E-mail: ahuseth@american.edu.
Website: https://www.american.edu/cas/education/

The American University in Cairo, Graduate School of Education, Cairo, Egypt. Offers educational leadership (MA); international and comparative education (MA). *Program availability:* Part-time, evening/weekend. *Degree requirements:* For master's, thesis. *Entrance requirements:* Additional exam requirements/recommendations for international students: Required—TOEFL (minimum score 450 paper-based; 45 iBT), IELTS (minimum score 5). Electronic applications accepted. *Faculty research:* Educational reform.

American University of Beirut, Graduate Programs, Faculty of Arts and Sciences, Beirut 1107 2020, Lebanon. Offers anthropology (MA); Arab and Middle Eastern history (PhD); Arabic language and literature (MA, PhD); archaeology (MA); art history and curating (MA); biology (MS); cell and molecular biology (PhD); chemistry (MS); clinical psychology (MA); computational sciences (MS); computer science (MS); economics (MA); education (MA), including administration and policy studies, elementary education, mathematics education, psychology school guidance, psychology test and measurements, science education, teaching English as a foreign language; English language (MA); English literature (MA); environmental policy planning (MS); financial economics (MAFE); general psychology (MA); geology (MS); history (MA); Islamic studies (MA); mathematics (MS); media studies (MA); Middle East studies (MA); philosophy (MA); physics (MS); political studies (MA); public administration (MA); public policy and international affairs (MA); sociology (MA); theoretical physics (PhD). *Program availability:* Part-time. *Faculty:* 187 full-time (64 women), 27 part-time/adjunct (15 women). *Students:* 292 full-time (215 women), 216 part-time (148 women). Average age 27. 422 applicants, 64% accepted, 124 enrolled. In 2018, 90 master's, 3 doctorates awarded. *Degree requirements:* For master's, comprehensive exam, thesis (for some programs), project; for doctorate, comprehensive exam, thesis/dissertation (for some programs). *Entrance requirements:* For master's, GRE General Test (for archaeology, clinical psychology, general psychology, economics, financial economics and biology); for doctorate, GRE General Test for all PhD programs, GRE Subject Test for theoretical physics. Additional exam requirements/recommendations for international students: Required—TOEFL (minimum score 583 paper-based; 97 iBT), IELTS (minimum score 7). *Application deadline:* For fall admission, 3/18 for domestic students; for spring admission, 11/5 for domestic students. Application fee: $50. Electronic applications accepted. *Expenses:* MA/MS: Humanities and social sciences=$912/credit. Sciences=$943/credit. Financial economics=$986/credit. Thesis: Humanities/social sciences=$6565 and sciences=$6865. *Financial support:* In 2018–19, 227 fellowships with full tuition reimbursements, 17 research assistantships with full tuition reimbursements, 83 teaching assistantships with full tuition reimbursements were awarded; scholarships/grants, tuition waivers (full and partial), and unspecified assistantships also available. Financial award application deadline: 3/18. *Faculty research:* Sciences: Physics: High energy, Particle, Polymer and Soft Matter, Thermal, Plasma; String Theory, Mathematical physics, Astrophysics (stellar evolution, planet and galaxy formation and evolution, astrophysical dynamics), Solid State physics/thin films, Spintronics, Magnetic properties of materials, Mineralogy, Petrology, and Geochemistry of Hard Rocks, Geophysics and Petrophysics, Hydrogeology, Micropaleontology, Sedimentology, and Stratigraphy, Structural Geology and Geotectonics, Renewable en. *Total annual research expenditures:* $4.3 million. *Unit head:* Dr. Nadia Maria El Cheikh, Dean, Faculty of Arts and Sciences, 961-1-350000 Ext. 3800, Fax: 961-1-744461, E-mail: nmcheikh@aub.edu.lb. *Application contact:* Adriana Michelle Zanaty, Curriculum and Graduate Studies Officer, 961-1-350000 Ext. 3833, Fax: 961-1-744461, E-mail: az48@aub.edu.lb.
Website: https://www.aub.edu.lb/fas/Pages/default.aspx

Anderson University, College of Education, Anderson, SC 29621-4035. Offers administration and supervision (M Ed); education (M Ed); elementary education (MAT). *Accreditation:* NCATE. *Program availability:* 100% online. *Expenses: Tuition:* Full-time $400; part-time $400 per credit. *Required fees:* $200; $200 per semester. Tuition and fees vary according to course load. *Financial support:* Scholarships/grants and tuition waivers available. Financial award application deadline: 3/1; financial award applicants required to submit FAFSA. *Unit head:* Dr. Mark Butler, Dean, 864-231-2042. *Application contact:* Dr. Mark Butler, Dean, 864-231-2042.
Website: https://www.andersonuniversity.edu/education

Andrews University, School of Graduate Studies, School of Education, Department of Leadership and Educational Administration, Program in Educational Administration and Leadership, Berrien Springs, MI 49104. Offers MA, Ed D, PhD, Ed S. *Degree requirements:* For master's, thesis or alternative; for doctorate, thesis/dissertation. *Entrance requirements:* For master's and doctorate, GRE Subject Test. Additional exam requirements/recommendations for international students: Required—TOEFL (minimum score 550 paper-based).

Andrews University, School of Graduate Studies, School of Education, Department of Leadership and Educational Administration, Program in Leadership, Berrien Springs, MI 49104. Offers MA, Ed D, PhD, Ed S. *Entrance requirements:* For master's, GRE. Additional exam requirements/recommendations for international students: Required—TOEFL (minimum score 550 paper-based).

Angelo State University, College of Graduate Studies and Research, College of Education, Department of Curriculum and Instruction, San Angelo, TX 76909. Offers curriculum and instruction (MA); educational administration (M Ed); guidance and counseling (M Ed); student development and leadership in higher education (M Ed). *Program availability:* Part-time, evening/weekend, online learning. *Students:* 360 full-time (307 women), 456 part-time (364 women); includes 312 minority (93 Black or African American, non-Hispanic/Latino; 3 American Indian or Alaska Native, non-Hispanic/Latino; 7 Asian, non-Hispanic/Latino; 193 Hispanic/Latino; 1 Native Hawaiian or other Pacific Islander, non-Hispanic/Latino; 15 Two or more races, non-Hispanic/Latino). Average age 35. *Application deadline:* For fall admission, 7/15 priority date for domestic students, 6/10 for international students; for spring admission, 12/1 priority date for domestic students, 11/1 for international students. Application fee: $40 ($50 for international students). *Expenses: Tuition, area resident:* Full-time $3964; part-time $220 per credit hour. Tuition, state resident: full-time $3964; part-time $220 per credit hour. Tuition, nonresident: full-time $11,434; part-time $635 per credit hour. *International tuition:* $11,434 full-time. *Unit head:* Dr. Kim Livengood, Chair, 325-942-2647, Fax: 325-942-2039, E-mail: kim.livengood@angelo.edu. *Application contact:* Dr. Kim Livengood, Chair, 325-942-2647, Fax: 325-942-2039, E-mail: kim.livengood@angelo.edu.
Website: http://www.angelo.edu/dept/ci/

Antioch University New England, Graduate School, Department of Education, Experienced Educators Program, Keene, NH 03431-3552. Offers foundations of education (M Ed), including applied behavioral analysis, autism spectrum disorders, educating for sustainability, next-generation learning using technology, problem-based learning using critical skills, teacher leadership; principal certification (PMC). *Degree requirements:* For master's, thesis, practicum. *Entrance requirements:* For master's, previous course work and work experience in education. Additional exam requirements/recommendations for international students: Required—TOEFL (minimum score 550 paper-based). Electronic applications accepted. *Expenses:* Contact institution. *Faculty research:* Classroom action research, school restructuring, problem-based learning, brain-based learning.

Appalachian State University, Cratis D. Williams School of Graduate Studies, Department of Leadership and Educational Studies, Boone, NC 28608. Offers educational administration (Ed S); educational media (MA); higher education (MA, Ed S); library science (MLS); school administration (MSA). *Program availability:* Part-time, evening/weekend, online learning. *Degree requirements:* For master's and Ed S, comprehensive exam, thesis optional. *Entrance requirements:* For master's and Ed S, GRE or MAT, 3 letters of recommendation. Additional exam requirements/recommendations for international students: Required—TOEFL (minimum score 570 paper-based; 79 iBT), IELTS (minimum score 6.5). Electronic applications accepted. *Expenses: Tuition, area resident:* Full-time $4839; part-time $237 per credit hour. Tuition, state resident: full-time $4839; part-time $237 per credit hour. Tuition, nonresident: full-time $18,271; part-time $895.50 per credit hour. *Faculty research:* Brain, learning and meditation; leadership of teaching and learning.

Arcadia University, School of Education, Glenside, PA 19038-3295. Offers art education (M Ed); computer education (CAS); curriculum (CAS); curriculum studies (M Ed); early childhood education (M Ed), including individualized, master teacher, research in child development; educational leadership (M Ed, Ed D, CAS); elementary education (M Ed); English education (MA Ed); environmental education (MA Ed); instructional technology (M Ed); language arts (M Ed); library science (M Ed); mathematics education (M Ed, MA Ed); music education (MA Ed); psychology (MA Ed); reading (M Ed, CAS); science education (M Ed, CAS); secondary education (M Ed, CAS); special education (M Ed, Ed D, CAS); theater arts (MA Ed); written communication (MA Ed). *Accreditation:* NASAD. *Program availability:* Part-time, evening/weekend, online learning. *Faculty:* 14 full-time (10 women). *Students:* 35 full-time (24 women), 299 part-time (243 women); includes 72 minority (49 Black or African American, non-Hispanic/Latino; 1 American Indian or Alaska Native, non-Hispanic/Latino; 12 Asian, non-Hispanic/Latino; 8 Hispanic/Latino; 2 Two or more races, non-Hispanic/Latino), 5 international. In 2018, 152 master's, 8 doctorates awarded. *Entrance requirements:* Additional exam requirements/recommendations for international students: Required—Official results from the TOEFL or IELTS are required. *Application deadline:* Applications are processed on a rolling basis. Application fee: $25. Electronic applications accepted. *Expenses:* Contact institution. *Financial support:* Career-related internships or fieldwork, tuition waivers (partial), and unspecified assistantships available. *Unit head:* Kimberly Dean, Chair, 215-572-8629. *Application contact:* 215-572-2925, Fax: 215-572-2126, E-mail: grad@arcadia.edu.

Argosy University, Atlanta, College of Education, Atlanta, GA 30328. Offers educational leadership (MAEd, Ed D, Ed S), including higher education administration (Ed D), K-12 education (Ed D); teaching and learning (MAEd, Ed D, Ed S), including education technology (Ed D), higher education (Ed D), K-12 education (Ed D).

Argosy University, Chicago, College of Education, Chicago, IL 60601. Offers adult education and training (MA Ed); community college executive leadership (Ed D); educational leadership (MA Ed, Ed D, Ed S), including district leadership (Ed D), higher education administration (Ed D), K-12 education (Ed D); instructional leadership (Ed D, Ed S), including higher education (Ed D), K-12 education (Ed D). *Program availability:* Online learning.

Argosy University, Hawai`i, College of Education, Honolulu, HI 96813. Offers adult education and training (MAEd); educational leadership (Ed D), including higher education administration, K-12 education; instructional leadership (Ed D), including higher education, K-12 education; school psychology (MA).

Argosy University, Los Angeles, College of Education, Los Angeles, CA 90045. Offers community college executive leadership (Ed D); educational leadership (MA Ed, Ed D), including higher education administration (Ed D), K-12 education (Ed D); instructional leadership (MA Ed, Ed D), including higher education (Ed D), K-12 education (Ed D), multiple subject teacher preparation (MA Ed), single subject teacher preparation (MA Ed).

Argosy University, Northern Virginia, College of Education, Arlington, VA 22209. Offers community college executive leadership (Ed D); educational leadership (MA Ed, Ed D, Ed S), including higher education administration (Ed D), K-12 education (Ed D); instructional leadership (MA Ed, Ed D, Ed S), including higher education (Ed D), K-12 education (Ed D).

Argosy University, Orange County, College of Education, Orange, CA 92868. Offers community college executive leadership (Ed D); educational leadership (MA Ed, Ed D), including higher education administration (Ed D), K-12 education (Ed D); instructional leadership (MA Ed, Ed D), including education technology (Ed D), higher education (Ed D), K-12 education (Ed D), multiple subject teacher preparation (MA Ed), single subject teacher preparation (MA Ed).

Educational Leadership and Administration

Argosy University, Phoenix, College of Education, Phoenix, AZ 85021. Offers adult education and training (MA Ed); advanced educational administration (Ed D, Ed S); community college executive leadership (Ed D); educational administration (MA Ed); educational leadership (MA Ed, Ed D, Ed S), including education technology (Ed D), higher education administration (Ed D), K-12 education (Ed D); higher and postsecondary education (MA Ed); initial educational administration (Ed D, Ed S); school psychology (MA); teaching and learning (MA Ed, Ed D, Ed S), including education technology (Ed D), higher education (Ed D), K-12 education (Ed D).

Argosy University, Seattle, College of Education, Seattle, WA 98121. Offers adult education and training (MA Ed); community college executive leadership (Ed D); educational leadership (MA Ed, Ed D), including higher education administration (Ed D), K-12 education (Ed D); higher and postsecondary education (MA Ed); instructional leadership (MA Ed, Ed D), including education technology (Ed D), higher education (Ed D), K-12 education (Ed D).

Argosy University, Tampa, College of Education, Tampa, FL 33607. Offers community college executive leadership (Ed D); educational leadership (MA Ed, Ed D, Ed S), including higher education administration (Ed D), K-12 education (Ed D); school counseling (MA); teaching and learning (MA Ed, Ed D, Ed S), including higher education (Ed D), K-12 education (Ed D).

Argosy University, Twin Cities, College of Education, Eagan, MN 55121. Offers advanced educational administration (Ed D, Ed S); educational leadership (MA Ed, Ed D, Ed S), including higher education administration (Ed D), K-12 education (Ed D); higher and postsecondary education (MA Ed); initial educational administration (Ed D, Ed S); instructional leadership (MA Ed, Ed D, Ed S), including education technology (Ed D), higher education (Ed D), K-12 education (Ed D).

Arizona State University at the Tempe campus, Mary Lou Fulton Teachers College, Program in Educational Leadership, Phoenix, AZ 85069. Offers educational leadership (M Ed); leadership and innovation (Ed D). *Program availability:* Part-time, evening/weekend, online learning. Terminal master's awarded for partial completion of doctoral program. *Degree requirements:* For master's, thesis or alternative, written portfolio, internship, interactive Program of Study (iPOS) submitted before completing 50 percent of required credit hours; for doctorate, thesis/dissertation, interactive Program of Study (iPOS) submitted before completing 50 percent of required credit hours. *Entrance requirements:* For master's, minimum GPA of 3.0 or equivalent in last 2 years of work leading to bachelor's degree, 1 year of teaching experience, 3 letters of recommendation, personal statement, writing sample, curriculum vitae or resume; for doctorate, master's degree in education or related field, resume, personal statement, writing samples based on short writing prompts, 3 letters of recommendation. Additional exam requirements/recommendations for international students: Required—TOEFL, IELTS, or PTE. Electronic applications accepted.

Arkansas State University, Graduate School, College of Education and Behavioral Science, School of Teacher Education and Leadership, State University, AR 72467. Offers community college administration (SCCT); curriculum and instruction (MSE); early childhood education (MSE); early childhood services (MS); educational leadership (MSE, Ed D, Ed S); educational theory and practice (MSE); middle level education (MAT, MSE); reading (MSE, Ed S); special education - gifted, talented, and creative (MSE); special education - instructional specialist grades 4-12 (MSE); special education - instructional specialist grades P-4 (MSE); special education, K-12 (MSE). *Accreditation:* NCATE. *Program availability:* Part-time, online learning. *Degree requirements:* For master's, comprehensive exam, thesis or alternative; for doctorate, comprehensive exam, thesis/dissertation; for other advanced degree, comprehensive exam. *Entrance requirements:* For master's, GRE General Test or MAT, appropriate bachelor's degree, official transcripts, immunization records, letters of reference, interview; for doctorate, GRE General Test or MAT, interview, master's degree, letters of reference, official transcript, personal statement, writing sample, immunization records; for other advanced degree, GRE General Test or MAT, interview, master's degree, official transcript, immunization records, letters of reference, 3 years of teaching experience, teaching license. Additional exam requirements/recommendations for international students: Required—TOEFL (minimum score 550 paper-based; 79 iBT), IELTS (minimum score 6), PTE (minimum score 56). Electronic applications accepted.

Arkansas Tech University, College of Education, Russellville, AR 72801. Offers college student personnel (MS); educational leadership (M Ed, Ed S); instructional technology (M Ed); school counseling and leadership (M Ed); school leadership (Ed D); special education K-12 (M Ed); strength and conditioning studies (MS); teaching (MAT); teaching, learning, and leadership (M Ed). *Accreditation:* NCATE. *Program availability:* Part-time, evening/weekend, 100% online, blended/hybrid learning. *Students:* 90 full-time (52 women), 450 part-time (359 women); includes 100 minority (63 Black or African American, non-Hispanic/Latino; 6 American Indian or Alaska Native, non-Hispanic/Latino; 1 Asian, non-Hispanic/Latino; 15 Hispanic/Latino; 15 Two or more races, non-Hispanic/Latino), 4 international. Average age 34. In 2018, 130 master's, 14 doctorates, 1 other advanced degree awarded. *Degree requirements:* For master's, comprehensive exam, thesis optional, action research project; for doctorate, thesis/dissertation. *Entrance requirements:* Additional exam requirements/recommendations for international students: Required—TOEFL (minimum score 550 paper-based; 79 iBT), IELTS (minimum score 6.5), PTE (minimum score 58). *Application deadline:* For fall admission, 3/1 priority date for domestic students, 5/1 priority date for international students; for spring admission, 10/1 priority date for domestic and international students. Applications are processed on a rolling basis. Application fee: $40 ($90 for international students). Electronic applications accepted. *Expenses: Tuition,* area resident: Full-time $6816; part-time $284 per credit hour. Tuition, state resident: full-time $6816; part-time $284 per credit hour. Tuition, nonresident: full-time $13,632; part-time $568 per credit hour. *International tuition:* $13,632 full-time. *Required fees:* $457.50 per semester. Tuition and fees vary according to course load and degree level. *Financial support:* In 2018–19, research assistantships with full and partial tuition reimbursements (averaging $4,800 per year), teaching assistantships with full and partial tuition reimbursements (averaging $4,800 per year) were awarded; career-related internships or fieldwork, Federal Work-Study, scholarships/grants, health care benefits, and unspecified assistantships also available. Support available to part-time students. Financial award application deadline: 4/15; financial award applicants required to submit FAFSA. *Unit head:* Dr. Linda Bean, Dean, 479-964-3217, E-mail: lbean@atu.edu. *Application contact:* Dr. Jeff Robertson, Interim Dean of Graduate College, 479-968-0398, Fax: 479-964-0542, E-mail: gradcollege@atu.edu.
Website: http://www.atu.edu/education/

Arlington Baptist University, Program in Education, Arlington, TX 76012-3425. Offers curriculum and instruction (M Ed); educational leadership (M Ed). *Degree requirements:* For master's, professional portfolio; internship (for educational leadership). *Entrance requirements:* For master's, bachelor's degree from accredited college or university with minimum GPA of 3.0, minimum of 12 hours in Bible; minimum of three years' classroom teaching experience in an accredited K-12 public or private school (for educational leadership only).

Asbury University, School of Graduate and Professional Studies, Wilmore, KY 40390-1198. Offers biology: alternative certificate (MA Ed); chemistry: alternative certificate (MA Ed); English (MA Ed); English as a second language (MA Ed); ESL (MA Ed); French (MA Ed); Latin: alternative certificate (MA Ed); mathematics: alternative certificate (MA Ed); reading/writing endorsement (MA Ed); social studies (MA Ed); social work (MSW), including child and family services; Spanish (MA Ed); special education (MA Ed); special education: alternative certificate (MA Ed); teacher as leader endorsement (MA Ed). *Accreditation:* NCATE. *Program availability:* Part-time. *Degree requirements:* For master's, action research project, portfolio. *Entrance requirements:* For master's, PRAXIS/NTE, minimum GPA of 2.75, letters of recommendation. Additional exam requirements/recommendations for international students: Required—TOEFL (minimum score 550 paper-based). Electronic applications accepted.

Ashland University, Dwight Schar College of Education, Doctoral Program in Educational Leadership Studies, Ashland, OH 44805-3702. Offers executive leadership studies (Ed D); leadership studies (Ed D). *Degree requirements:* For doctorate, comprehensive exam, thesis/dissertation. *Entrance requirements:* For doctorate, master's degree, minimum GPA of 3.3, writing sample, letters of recommendation, leadership statement, resume. Additional exam requirements/recommendations for international students: Recommended—TOEFL, IELTS, TSE. Electronic applications accepted. *Expenses:* Contact institution. *Faculty research:* School funding, charter schools, administrative jobs, continuous improvement, marginalized groups, school finance, minority superintendent trends, teacher salaries, minority recruiting, women's issues.

Ashland University, Dwight Schar College of Education, Program in Educational Leadership and Administration, Ashland, OH 44805-3702. Offers educational leadership and administration (M Ed). *Program availability:* Part-time. *Degree requirements:* For master's, thesis or alternative, internship. *Entrance requirements:* For master's, teaching certificate or license, bachelor's degree, minimum cumulative GPA of 2.75. Additional exam requirements/recommendations for international students: Recommended—TOEFL, IELTS, TSE. Electronic applications accepted. *Expenses: Tuition:* Full-time $6660; part-time $3330 per credit hour. *Required fees:* $360; $180 per credit hour. Tuition and fees vary according to program. *Faculty research:* Gender and religious considerations in employment, Interstate School Leaders Licensure Consortium (ISLLC) standards, adjunct faculty training, politics of school finance, ethnicity and employment.

Auburn University, Graduate School, College of Education, Department of Educational Foundations, Leadership, and Technology, Auburn University, AL 36849. Offers adult education (PhD, Ed S); curriculum supervision (M Ed, PhD); higher education administration (PhD); library media (Ed S); school administration (M Ed, PhD). *Accreditation:* NCATE. *Program availability:* Part-time. *Degree requirements:* For master's, thesis (for some programs); for doctorate, thesis/dissertation; for Ed S, field project. *Entrance requirements:* For master's, doctorate, and Ed S, GRE General Test. Electronic applications accepted. *Expenses:* Tuition, state resident: full-time $11,282; part-time $535 per credit hour. Tuition, nonresident: full-time $30,542; part-time $1605 per credit hour. *Required fees:* $826 per semester. Tuition and fees vary according to degree level and program.

Auburn University at Montgomery, College of Education, Department of Counselor, Leadership, and Special Education, Montgomery, AL 36124-4023. Offers counselor education (M Ed, Ed S), including clinical mental health counseling, school counseling; early childhood special education (M Ed); instructional leadership (M Ed, Ed S); special education/collaborative teacher (M Ed, Ed S). *Accreditation:* ACA; NCATE. *Program availability:* Part-time, evening/weekend. *Students:* Average age 34. 76 applicants, 72% accepted, 26 enrolled. In 2018, 37 master's awarded. *Entrance requirements:* For master's, GRE General Test or MAT, certification, BS in teaching; for Ed S, GRE General Test or MAT, certification. Additional exam requirements/recommendations for international students: Recommended—TOEFL (minimum score 500 paper-based; 61 iBT), IELTS (minimum score 5.5), TSE (minimum score 44). *Application deadline:* For fall admission, 7/15 for international students; for spring admission, 11/15 for international students; for summer admission, 4/15 for international students. Applications are processed on a rolling basis. Electronic applications accepted. *Expenses: Tuition,* area resident: Full-time $7146; part-time $4764 per credit hour. Tuition, state resident: full-time $7146; part-time $4764 per credit hour. Tuition, nonresident: full-time $16,056; part-time $10,704 per credit hour. *International tuition:* $16,056 full-time. *Required fees:* $766. One-time fee: $25 full-time. *Financial support:* Career-related internships or fieldwork and scholarships/grants available. Support available to part-time students. Financial award application deadline: 3/1; financial award applicants required to submit FAFSA. *Unit head:* Dr. Samuel Flynt, Head, 334-244-3835, Fax: 334-244-3101, E-mail: sflynt@aum.edu. *Application contact:* Dr. Rhonda Morton, Associate Dean/Graduate Coordinator, 334-244-3287, Fax: 334-244-3978, E-mail: rmorton@aum.edu.
Website: http://education.aum.edu/academic-departments/counselor-leadership-and-special-education

Augusta University, College of Education, Department of Counselor Education, Leadership, and Research, Augusta, GA 30912. Offers counselor education (M Ed, Ed S), including clinical mental health counseling (M Ed), school counselor (M Ed). *Accreditation:* ACA; NCATE. *Program availability:* Part-time, evening/weekend. *Degree requirements:* For master's, comprehensive exam; for Ed S, comprehensive exam, thesis. *Entrance requirements:* For master's, GRE, MAT, minimum GPA of 2.5; for Ed S, GRE, MAT. *Faculty research:* Restructuring schools, financing education, student transition.

Augusta University, College of Education, Program in Leadership, Augusta, GA 30912. Offers leadership (Ed S); school administration (M Ed); teacher leadership (M Ed). *Entrance requirements:* For master's, GRE or MAT, minimum baccalaureate GPA of 2.5.

Aurora University, School of Education and Human Performance, Aurora, IL 60506-4892. Offers applied behavioral analysis (MS); bilingual-ESL education (MA); educational leadership with principal endorsement (MA); educational technology (MA); leadership in adult learning higher education (Ed D); leadership in curriculum and instruction (Ed D); leadership in educational administration (Ed D); reading instruction (MA); special education (MA). *Accreditation:* NCATE. *Program availability:* Part-time, evening/weekend, 100% online. *Faculty:* 14 full-time (6 women), 32 part-time/adjunct (17 women). *Students:* 28 full-time (25 women), 537 part-time (359 women); includes 101 minority (25 Black or African American, non-Hispanic/Latino; 8 Asian, non-Hispanic/Latino; 58 Hispanic/Latino; 2 Native Hawaiian or other Pacific Islander, non-Hispanic/Latino; 8 Two or more races, non-Hispanic/Latino), 2 international. Average age 38. 191 applicants, 98% accepted, 133 enrolled. In 2018, 213 master's, 16 doctorates awarded. *Degree requirements:* For master's, student teaching, research seminar, and practicum; for doctorate, comprehensive exam, thesis/dissertation. *Entrance requirements:* For master's, 2 years of teaching experience, valid teaching certificate, resume; for doctorate, appropriate master's degree, two references, curriculum vitae, personal statement, professional project, reflective essay. Additional exam requirements/recommendations for international students: Required—TOEFL (minimum score 550 paper-based; 79 iBT). *Application deadline:* For fall admission, 6/1 for international students; for spring admission, 10/1 for international students. Applications are processed on a rolling basis. Application fee: $0. Electronic applications accepted. *Expenses:* The reported tuition amount is for the program with the greatest enrollment, MA in Educational Leadership with Principal

Endorsement. Other programs may require more semester hours, and thus have a greater total cost. The Education doctoral programs are roughly double the amount of the master's programs. *Financial support:* In 2018–19, 31 students received support. Federal Work-Study, scholarships/grants, and unspecified assistantships available. Financial award applicants required to submit FAFSA. *Unit head:* Dr. Jen Buckley, Dean, School of Education and Human Performance, 630-844-1542, Fax: 630-844-6155, E-mail: jbuckley@aurora.edu. *Application contact:* Center for Graduate Studies, 630-947-8955, E-mail: AUadmission@aurora.edu.
Website: http://aurora.edu/education

Averett University, Master in Education Program, Danville, VA 24541-3692. Offers administration and supervision (M Ed); curriculum and instruction (M Ed); special education with endorsement (M Ed); special education with licensure (M Ed). *Program availability:* Part-time, online only, 100% online. *Faculty:* 2 full-time (both women), 14 part-time/adjunct (11 women). *Students:* 141 full-time (108 women), 4 part-time (2 women); includes 31 minority (30 Black or African American, non-Hispanic/Latino; 1 Hispanic/Latino). Average age 37. 106 applicants, 58% accepted, 52 enrolled. In 2018, 52 master's awarded. *Degree requirements:* For master's, 30-credit core curriculum, minimum GPA of 3.0 throughout program, completion of degree requirements within six years from start of program. *Entrance requirements:* For master's, PRAXIS I, GRE, or MAT; writing proficiency test, minimum cumulative GPA of 3.0 over the last 60 hours of undergraduate study toward a baccalaureate degree, three letters of recommendation, Virginia teaching license (or eligibility). Additional exam requirements/recommendations for international students: Required—TOEFL (minimum score 600 paper-based; 100 iBT). *Application deadline:* Applications are processed on a rolling basis. Electronic applications accepted. *Expenses:* Contact institution. *Financial support:* Application deadline: 3/1; applicants required to submit FAFSA. *Unit head:* Dr. Nancy Riddell, Chair of the Education Department; Director of Teacher Education, 434-791-5741, Fax: 434-791-5020, E-mail: nriddell@averett.edu. *Application contact:* Christy Davis, Assistant Director of Admissions, 434-791-7133, E-mail: cdavis@averett.edu.
Website: http://gps.averett.edu/online/education/

Azusa Pacific University, School of Behavioral and Applied Sciences, Department of Higher Education, Azusa, CA 91702-7000. Offers college counseling and student development (MS); higher education (PhD); higher education leadership (Ed D).

Azusa Pacific University, School of Education, Department of Educational Leadership, Azusa, CA 91702-7000. Offers MA, Ed D. *Program availability:* Part-time, evening/weekend. *Degree requirements:* For doctorate, oral defense of dissertation, qualifying exam. *Entrance requirements:* For doctorate, GRE General Test or MAT, 5 years of experience, writing sample. Additional exam requirements/recommendations for international students: Required—TOEFL. *Expenses:* Contact institution. *Faculty research:* Ethics in educational administration.

Baldwin Wallace University, Graduate Programs, School of Education, Leadership in Higher Education Program, Berea, OH 44017-2088. Offers MA Ed. *Program availability:* Part-time, evening/weekend. *Students:* 22 full-time (16 women), 2 part-time (both women); includes 6 minority (5 Black or African American, non-Hispanic/Latino; 1 Asian, non-Hispanic/Latino). Average age 30. 55 applicants, 27% accepted, 12 enrolled. In 2018, 16 master's awarded. *Degree requirements:* For master's, comprehensive exam (for some programs), capstone project, portfolio. *Entrance requirements:* For master's, bachelor's degree, MAT or minimum GPA of 3.0. Additional exam requirements/recommendations for international students: Required—TOEFL (minimum score 550 paper-based; 79 iBT). *Application deadline:* For fall admission, 8/15 for domestic students; for spring admission, 12/15 for domestic students. Applications are processed on a rolling basis. Application fee: $25. Electronic applications accepted. Application fee is waived when completed online. *Expenses:* $545 per credit hour part-time (for LHE students who are employed by a partnership college or university), $742 per credit hour part-time (for LHE non-partnership students). *Financial support:* Paid internships (for full-time students) available. Financial award applicants required to submit FAFSA. *Faculty research:* Program development in higher education, leadership styles, the psychology of leadership and learning in higher education. *Unit head:* Dr. Ken Schneck, Director, 440-826-8062, Fax: 440-826-3779, E-mail: kschneck@bw.edu. *Application contact:* Kate Glaser, Associate Director of Admission, 440-826-8016, Fax: 440-826-3830, E-mail: kglaser@bw.edu.
Website: https://www.bw.edu/academics/master-of-arts-in-education/maed-school-leadership/

Baldwin Wallace University, Graduate Programs, School of Education, Specialization in School Leadership, Berea, OH 44017-2088. Offers MA Ed. *Program availability:* Part-time, evening/weekend, 100% online. *Students:* 16 full-time (10 women), 18 part-time (13 women); includes 3 minority (1 Black or African American, non-Hispanic/Latino; 2 Two or more races, non-Hispanic/Latino). Average age 32. 15 applicants, 93% accepted, 11 enrolled. In 2018, 11 master's awarded. *Degree requirements:* For master's, 2-semester internship. *Entrance requirements:* For master's, bachelor's degree in field, MAT or minimum GPA of 3.0. Additional exam requirements/recommendations for international students: Required—TOEFL (minimum score 550 paper-based; 79 iBT). *Application deadline:* For fall admission, 8/15 priority date for domestic students; for spring admission, 12/15 priority date for domestic students. Applications are processed on a rolling basis. Application fee: $25. Electronic applications accepted. Application fee is waived when completed online. *Expenses:* Partnership tuition - $545 per credit; Non-partnership tuition - $721 per credit. *Financial support:* Career-related internships or fieldwork available. Financial award applicants required to submit FAFSA. *Faculty research:* Leadership styles, instructional strategies, formative assessment. *Unit head:* Dr. Joseph Hruby, Coordinator, 440-826-8539, Fax: 440-826-3779, E-mail: jhruby@bw.edu. *Application contact:* Amirya Alveranga, Admission Counselor, 440-826-8005, Fax: 440-826-3830, E-mail: aalveran@bw.edu.
Website: http://www.bw.edu/academics/master-of-arts-in-education/maed-school-leadership/

Ball State University, Graduate School, Teachers College, Department of Educational Leadership, Program in Educational Administration and Supervision, Muncie, IN 47306. Offers MA, Ed D. *Accreditation:* NCATE. *Program availability:* Part-time, 100% online, blended/hybrid learning. *Degree requirements:* For doctorate, thesis/dissertation. *Entrance requirements:* For master's, minimum baccalaureate GPA of 2.75 or 3.0 in latter half of baccalaureate; for doctorate, GRE General Test, interview, minimum graduate GPA of 3.2. Additional exam requirements/recommendations for international students: Required—TOEFL (minimum score 550 paper-based; 79 iBT), IELTS (minimum score 6.5). Electronic applications accepted.

Ball State University, Graduate School, Teachers College, Department of Educational Leadership, Program in School Superintendency, Muncie, IN 47306. Offers Ed S. *Accreditation:* NCATE. *Program availability:* Part-time, online only, 100% online. *Degree requirements:* For Ed S, thesis. *Entrance requirements:* For degree, GRE General Test, minimum graduate GPA of 3.2, professional portfolio including platform statement, writing sample, curriculum vitae, five references. Additional exam requirements/recommendations for international students: Required—TOEFL (minimum score 550 paper-based; 79 iBT), IELTS (minimum score 6.5). Electronic applications accepted.

Ball State University, Graduate School, Teachers College, Department of Educational Studies, Program in Executive Development for Public Service, Muncie, IN 47306.

Offers MA. *Program availability:* Part-time, online only, 100% online, blended/hybrid learning. *Entrance requirements:* For master's, minimum baccalaureate GPA of 2.75 or 3.0 in latter half of baccalaureate. Additional exam requirements/recommendations for international students: Required—TOEFL (minimum score 550 paper-based; 79 iBT), IELTS (minimum score 6.5). Electronic applications accepted.

Ball State University, Graduate School, Teachers College, Department of Educational Studies, Program in Student Affairs Administration in Higher Education, Muncie, IN 47306. Offers MA. *Accreditation:* NCATE. *Entrance requirements:* For master's, GRE General Test, minimum baccalaureate GPA of 2.75 or 3.0 in latter half of baccalaureate, resume, three professional references. Additional exam requirements/recommendations for international students: Required—TOEFL (minimum score 550 paper-based; 79 iBT), IELTS (minimum score 6.5). Electronic applications accepted.

Bank Street College of Education, Graduate School, Programs in Educational Leadership, New York, NY 10025. Offers early childhood leadership (MS Ed); educational leadership (MS Ed); leadership for educational change (Ed M, MS Ed); leadership in community-based learning (MS Ed); leadership in mathematics education (MS Ed); leadership in museum education (MS Ed); leadership in the arts: creative writing (MS Ed); leadership in the arts: visual arts (MS Ed). *Degree requirements:* For master's, thesis. *Entrance requirements:* For master's, interview, essays, minimum of 2 years experience as a classroom teacher. Additional exam requirements/recommendations for international students: Required—TOEFL (minimum score 600 paper-based; 100 iBT), IELTS (minimum score 7). Electronic applications accepted. *Faculty research:* Leadership in urban schools, leadership in small schools, mathematics in elementary schools, professional development in early childhood, leadership in arts education, leadership in special education, museum leadership, community-based leadership.

Barry University, School of Education, Program in Educational Leadership, Miami Shores, FL 33161-6695. Offers MS, Ed D, Certificate, Ed S. *Program availability:* Part-time, evening/weekend. *Degree requirements:* For master's and other advanced degree, comprehensive exam. *Entrance requirements:* For master's, GRE General Test or MAT, minimum GPA of 3.0; for other advanced degree, GRE General Test, minimum GPA of 3.0. Electronic applications accepted.

Barry University, School of Education, Program in Higher Education Administration, Miami Shores, FL 33161-6695. Offers MS. *Program availability:* Part-time, evening/weekend. *Degree requirements:* For master's, comprehensive exam. *Entrance requirements:* For master's, GRE General Test or MAT, minimum GPA of 3.0. Electronic applications accepted.

Barry University, School of Education, Program in Leadership and Education, Miami Shores, FL 33161-6695. Offers educational technology (PhD); exceptional student education (PhD); higher education administration (PhD); human resource development (PhD); leadership (PhD). *Program availability:* Part-time, evening/weekend. *Degree requirements:* For doctorate, thesis/dissertation. *Entrance requirements:* For doctorate, GRE General Test, minimum GPA of 3.25. Electronic applications accepted.

Baruch College of the City University of New York, Austin W. Marxe School of Public and International Affairs, Program in Educational Leadership, New York, NY 10010-5585. Offers educational leadership (MS Ed); school building leadership (Advanced Certificate); school district leadership (Advanced Certificate). *Program availability:* Part-time, evening/weekend. *Degree requirements:* For master's, internship. *Entrance requirements:* For master's, GRE or master's degree. Additional exam requirements/recommendations for international students: Required—TOEFL. Electronic applications accepted. *Faculty research:* School administration, program development, school leadership, violence in schools, school leadership development, school reform, school discipline policy, program development.

Baruch College of the City University of New York, Austin W. Marxe School of Public and International Affairs, Program in Higher Education Administration, New York, NY 10010-5585. Offers MS Ed. *Program availability:* Part-time, evening/weekend. *Entrance requirements:* For master's, GRE General Test. Additional exam requirements/recommendations for international students: Required—TOEFL. Electronic applications accepted. *Expenses:* Contact institution.

Bayamón Central University, Graduate Programs, Program in Education, Bayamón, PR 00960-1725. Offers administration and supervision (MA Ed); commercial education (MA Ed); elementary education (K–3) (MA Ed); family counseling (Graduate Certificate); guidance and counseling (MA Ed); pre-elementary teacher (MA Ed); rehabilitation counseling (MA Ed); special education (MA Ed), including attention deficit disorder, education of the autistic, learning disabilities. *Program availability:* Part-time, evening/weekend. *Degree requirements:* For master's, comprehensive exam. *Entrance requirements:* For master's, EXADEP, bachelor's degree in education or related field.

Baylor University, Graduate School, School of Education, Department of Educational Leadership, Waco, TX 76798. Offers MS Ed, Ed S. *Accreditation:* NCATE. *Students:* 80 full-time (44 women), 28 part-time (18 women); includes 26 minority (5 Black or African American, non-Hispanic/Latino; 1 American Indian or Alaska Native, non-Hispanic/Latino; 2 Asian, non-Hispanic/Latino; 12 Hispanic/Latino; 6 Two or more races, non-Hispanic/Latino), 2 international. 90 applicants, 44% accepted, 14 enrolled. In 2018, 1 master's awarded. *Entrance requirements:* For master's, GRE General Test. *Application deadline:* Applications are processed on a rolling basis. Application fee: $25. *Financial support:* In 2018–19, 20 students received support, including 2 research assistantships; teaching assistantships, Federal Work-Study, institutionally sponsored loans, and scholarships/grants also available. *Faculty research:* Christian higher education sport management marketing and impact. *Total annual research expenditures:* $69,060. *Unit head:* Dr. Robert Cloud, Graduate Program Director, 254-710-6110, Fax: 254-710-3265, E-mail: robert_cloud@baylor.edu. *Application contact:* Julie Baker, Administrative Assistant, 254-710-3050, Fax: 254-710-3870, E-mail: julie_l_baker@baylor.edu.
Website: http://www.baylor.edu/soe/edl/

Bay Path University, Program in Higher Education Administration, Longmeadow, MA 01106-2292. Offers enrollment management (MS); general administration (MS); institutional advancement (MS); online teaching and program administration (MS). *Program availability:* Part-time, online only, 100% online. *Students:* 2 full-time (both women), 34 part-time (25 women); includes 11 minority (6 Black or African American, non-Hispanic/Latino; 1 Asian, non-Hispanic/Latino; 3 Hispanic/Latino; 1 Two or more races, non-Hispanic/Latino). Average age 34. *Entrance requirements:* For master's, completed application; official undergraduate and graduate transcripts (a GPA of 3.0 or higher is preferred); original essay of at least 250 words on the topic: "Why the MS in Higher Education Administration is important to my personal and professional goals"; current resume; 2 recommendations. *Application deadline:* Applications are processed on a rolling basis. Electronic applications accepted. Application fee is waived when completed online. *Expenses:* Contact institution. *Financial support:* Unspecified assistantships available. Financial award applicants required to submit FAFSA. *Unit head:* Dr. Lauren Way, Program Director, 413-565-1193, E-mail: lway@baypath.edu. *Application contact:* Jennifer Palma, Director of Graduate Admissions, 413-565-1181, Fax: 413-565-1250, E-mail: jpalma@baypath.edu.
Website: https://www.baypath.edu/academics/graduate-programs/higher-education-administration-ms/

Educational Leadership and Administration

Belhaven University, School of Education, Jackson, MS 39202-1789. Offers education (M Ed, MAT); educational leadership (Ed D, Ed S); reading literacy (M Ed). *Program availability:* Part-time, evening/weekend, 100% online, blended/hybrid learning. *Faculty:* 8 full-time (6 women), 24 part-time/adjunct (20 women). *Students:* 11 full-time (7 women), 452 part-time (360 women); includes 262 minority (244 Black or African American, non-Hispanic/Latino; 1 American Indian or Alaska Native, non-Hispanic/Latino; 3 Asian, non-Hispanic/Latino; 3 Hispanic/Latino; 11 Two or more races, non-Hispanic/Latino), 1 international. Average age 36. 299 applicants, 49% accepted, 103 enrolled. In 2018, 65 master's, 5 other advanced degrees awarded. *Degree requirements:* For master's, comprehensive exam, portfolio; for doctorate, thesis/dissertation. *Entrance requirements:* For master's, PRAXIS I and II, minimum GPA of 2.8; for doctorate, MAT or GRE, master's degree in education or related field with minimum GPA of 3.0; essay; three professional letters of recommendation; minimum three years' experience in a PK-12 education context. *Application deadline:* Applications are processed on a rolling basis. Application fee: $25. Electronic applications accepted. *Expenses:* $525 per credit hour, $75 technology fee per course. *Financial support:* Applicants required to submit FAFSA. *Unit head:* Dr. David Hand, Dean, 601-965-7020, E-mail: dhand@belhaven.edu. *Application contact:* Sean Kirnan, Assistant Vice President for Adult and Graduate Enrollment and Student Services, 601-968-8727, Fax: 601-968-5953, E-mail: gradadmission@belhaven.edu.

Bellarmine University, Annsley Frazier Thornton School of Education, Louisville, KY 40205. Offers education and district leadership (Ed D); education and social change (PhD); elementary education (MA Ed, MAT); leadership in higher education (PhD); middle school education (MA Ed, MAT); principalship (Ed S); reading and writing (MA Ed); secondary education (MAT); teacher leadership (MA Ed). *Accreditation:* NCATE. *Program availability:* Part-time, evening/weekend. *Faculty:* 14 full-time (7 women), 17 part-time/adjunct (11 women). *Students:* 27 full-time (19 women), 205 part-time (156 women); includes 74 minority (53 Black or African American, non-Hispanic/Latino; 6 Asian, non-Hispanic/Latino; 7 Hispanic/Latino; 8 Two or more races, non-Hispanic/Latino). Average age 34. 155 applicants, 71% accepted, 95 enrolled. In 2018, 69 master's, 10 doctorates, 30 other advanced degrees awarded. *Degree requirements:* For master's, comprehensive exam (for some programs), thesis (for some programs); for doctorate, comprehensive exam (for some programs), thesis/dissertation; for Ed S, comprehensive exam (for some programs). *Entrance requirements:* For master's, GRE, baccalaureate degree from accredited institution; minimum cumulative GPA of 2.75; recommendations from employers, supervisors, or professors attesting to applicant's potential as graduate student; statement of intent to pursue graduate degree; for doctorate, GRE, minimum GPA of 3.5 in all graduate coursework; baccalaureate and master's degrees in education or fields directly relevant to education; three letters of recommendation; two essays (no more than 1,000 words each); resume or curriculum vitae; interview; for Ed S, master's degree in education; valid teaching certificate; three years of experience in teaching; three recommendations; minimum GPA of 3.0 in all graduate work; interview; essays; personal goal statement. Additional exam requirements/recommendations for international students: Required—TOEFL (minimum score 80 iBT), IELTS (minimum score 6), TOEFL (minimum score 550 paper-based, 68 iBT), IELTS (minimum score 6), or Michigan English Language Assessment Battery. *Application deadline:* For fall admission, 8/1 priority date for domestic and international students; for spring admission, 12/1 priority date for domestic and international students; for summer admission, 4/10 priority date for domestic and international students. Applications are processed on a rolling basis. Application fee: $40. Electronic applications accepted. *Expenses:* Doctor of Education: $855 per credit hour; Educational Specialist: $410 per credit hour; Master of Arts in Education: $410 per credit hour; Master of Arts in Teaching: $665 per credit hour; Master of Arts in Teaching, undergraduate content courses: $410 per credit hour; Master of Education in Higher Education Leadership and Social Justice: $665 per credit hour; Ph.D., Social Change: $855 per credit hour; Ph.D., Leadership in Higher Education: $855 per credit hour; Rank I Programs: $410 per credit hour. *Financial support:* Scholarships/grants available. Financial award applicants required to submit FAFSA. *Faculty research:* Literacy, service-learning, dispositions, educational technology, special education. *Unit head:* Dr. Elizabeth Dinkins, Dean, 502-272-7958, Fax: 502-272-8189, E-mail: edinkins@bellarmine.edu. *Application contact:* Sarah Schuble, Assistant Director of Graduate Student Enrollment, 502-272-8271, Fax: 502-272-8002, E-mail: sschuble@bellarmine.edu.
Website: http://www.bellarmine.edu/education/graduate

Benedictine College, Master of Arts in School Leadership Program, Atchison, KS 66002-1499. Offers MA. *Accreditation:* NCATE. *Program availability:* Part-time, evening/weekend. *Degree requirements:* For master's, comprehensive exam, practicum. *Entrance requirements:* For master's, minimum GPA of 3.0. Additional exam requirements/recommendations for international students: Recommended—TOEFL, IELTS. Electronic applications accepted. Application fee is waived when completed online. *Expenses:* Contact institution. *Faculty research:* Teacher leadership, special education issues, diversity in schools, Catholic school leadership, professional development.

Berry College, Graduate Programs, Graduate Programs in Education, Program in Educational Leadership, Mount Berry, GA 30149. Offers Ed S. *Faculty:* 1 full-time (0 women), 2 part-time/adjunct (1 woman). *Students:* 4 part-time (3 women). Average age 44. In 2018, 48 Ed Ss awarded. *Degree requirements:* For Ed S, thesis, portfolio, oral exams. *Entrance requirements:* For degree, M Ed from accredited school, minimum GPA of 3.25. Additional exam requirements/recommendations for international students: Required—TOEFL (minimum score 550 paper-based). *Application deadline:* For fall admission, 7/26 for domestic students, 5/1 for international students; for spring admission, 12/1 for domestic students, 10/1 for international students. Applications are processed on a rolling basis. Application fee: $25 ($30 for international students). Electronic applications accepted. *Expenses:* $490 per credit hour. *Financial support:* In 2018–19, 2 students received support. Research assistantships, scholarships/grants, traineeships, and unspecified assistantships available. Support available to part-time students. Financial award application deadline: 3/1; financial award applicants required to submit FAFSA. *Unit head:* Dr. Jacqueline McDowell, Dean, Charter School of Education and Human Sciences, 706-236-1717, Fax: 706-238-5827, E-mail: jmcdowell@berry.edu. *Application contact:* Admissions, 706-236-2215, Fax: 706-290-2178, E-mail: admissions@berry.edu.
Website: https://www.berry.edu/academics/graduate-studies/education/

Bethel University, Graduate Programs, McKenzie, TN 38201. Offers administration and supervision (MA Ed); business administration (MBA); conflict resolution (MA); physician assistant studies (MS). *Program availability:* Part-time, evening/weekend. *Degree requirements:* For master's, thesis (for some programs). *Entrance requirements:* For master's, GRE General Test or MAT, minimum undergraduate GPA of 2.5.

Bethel University, Graduate School, St. Paul, MN 55112-6999. Offers business administration (MBA); classroom management (Certificate); counseling (MA); K-12 education (MA); leadership (Ed D); leadership foundations (Certificate); nurse educator (MS, Certificate); nurse-midwifery (MS); physician assistant (MS); special education (MA); strategic leadership (MA); teaching (MA); teaching and learning (Certificate). *Program availability:* Part-time, evening/weekend, 100% online, blended/hybrid learning. *Faculty:* 23 full-time (17 women), 73 part-time/adjunct (45 women). *Students:* 586 full-time (426 women), 372 part-time (244 women); includes 141 minority (49 Black or African American, non-Hispanic/Latino; 6 American Indian or Alaska Native, non-Hispanic/Latino; 19 Asian, non-Hispanic/Latino; 40 Hispanic/Latino; 2 Native Hawaiian or other Pacific Islander, non-Hispanic/Latino; 25 Two or more races, non-Hispanic/Latino), 25 international. Average age 35. 642 applicants, 39% accepted, 194 enrolled. In 2018, 312 master's, 28 doctorates, 134 other advanced degrees awarded. *Degree requirements:* For master's, comprehensive exam (for some programs), thesis (for some programs); for doctorate, comprehensive exam, thesis/dissertation. *Entrance requirements:* Additional exam requirements/recommendations for international students: Required—TOEFL (minimum score 550 paper-based; 80 iBT), TOEFL (minimum score 550 paper-based, 80 iBT) or IELTS. *Application deadline:* Applications are processed on a rolling basis. Application fee: $0. Electronic applications accepted. *Expenses:* Contact institution. *Financial support:* Teaching assistantships, career-related internships or fieldwork, and scholarships/grants available. Support available to part-time students. Financial award applicants required to submit FAFSA. *Unit head:* Dr. Randy Bergen, Associate Provost, 651-635-8000, Fax: 651-635-8004, E-mail: r-bergen@bethel.edu. *Application contact:* Director of Admissions, 651-635-8000, Fax: 651-635-8004, E-mail: gs@bethel.edu.
Website: https://www.bethel.edu/graduate/

Binghamton University, State University of New York, Graduate School, College of Community and Public Affairs, Department of Student Affairs Administration, Binghamton, NY 13902-6000. Offers MS. *Program availability:* Part-time. *Degree requirements:* For master's, comprehensive exam. *Entrance requirements:* For master's, GRE General Test. Additional exam requirements/recommendations for international students: Required—TOEFL (minimum score 80 iBT). Electronic applications accepted.

Binghamton University, State University of New York, Graduate School, College of Community and Public Affairs, Department of Teaching, Learning and Educational Leadership, Binghamton, NY 13902-6000. Offers adolescence education (MAT, MS Ed), including biology education, chemistry education, earth science education, English education, French education, mathematical sciences education, physics, social studies, Spanish education; childhood and early childhood education (MS Ed); educational leadership (Certificate); educational studies (MS); educational theory and practice (Ed D); literacy education (MS Ed); special education (MS Ed); TESOL education (MA, MS Ed). *Accreditation:* TEAC. *Program availability:* Part-time, evening/weekend. *Degree requirements:* For doctorate, thesis/dissertation. *Entrance requirements:* For master's, GRE General Test, teaching certification; for doctorate, GRE General Test, writing sample. Additional exam requirements/recommendations for international students: Required—TOEFL (minimum score 550 paper-based; 80 iBT). Electronic applications accepted.

Bloomsburg University of Pennsylvania, School of Graduate Studies, College of Education, Department of Teaching and Learning, Program in Educational Leadership, Bloomsburg, PA 17815-1301. Offers college student affairs (M Ed); PreK-12 curriculum and instruction (M Ed); PreK-12 school counseling (M Ed); PreK-12 school principal (M Ed). *Degree requirements:* For master's, practicum. *Entrance requirements:* For master's, 3 letters of recommendation, resume, minimum QPA of 3.0, personal statement, interview. Additional exam requirements/recommendations for international students: Required—TOEFL, IELTS. Electronic applications accepted.

Bluffton University, Programs in Education, Bluffton, OH 45817. Offers intervention specialist (MA Ed); leadership (MA Ed); reading (MA Ed). *Accreditation:* NCATE. *Program availability:* Part-time, 100% online, blended/hybrid learning, videoconference. *Faculty:* 2 full-time (both women), 2 part-time/adjunct (1 woman). *Students:* 14 full-time (7 women), 7 part-time (all women). Average age 31. In 2018, 8 master's awarded. *Degree requirements:* For master's, action research project, public presentation. *Entrance requirements:* For master's, PRAXIS I, bachelor's degree, minimum GPA of 3.0. Additional exam requirements/recommendations for international students: Required—TOEFL. *Application deadline:* For fall admission, 8/15 priority date for domestic students, 6/15 priority date for international students; for spring admission, 12/15 priority date for domestic students, 9/15 priority date for international students. Applications are processed on a rolling basis. Electronic applications accepted. *Expenses:* Contact institution. *Financial support:* Unspecified assistantships available. Financial award application deadline: 9/15; financial award applicants required to submit FAFSA. *Unit head:* Dr. Amy K. Mullins, Director of Graduate Programs in Education, 419-358-3457, E-mail: mullinsa@bluffton.edu. *Application contact:* Shelby Koenig, Enrollment Counselor for Graduate Program, 419-358-3022, E-mail: koenigs@bluffton.edu.
Website: https://www.bluffton.edu/ags/index.aspx

Bob Jones University, Graduate Programs, Greenville, SC 29614. Offers accountancy (MS); Bible (MA); Bible translation (MA); Biblical studies (Certificate); business administration (MBA); church history (MA, PhD); church ministries (MA); church music (MM); cinema and video production (MA); counseling (MS); curriculum and instruction (Ed D); divinity (M Div); dramatic production (MA); educational leadership (MS, Ed D, Ed S); elementary education (M Ed, MAT); English (M Ed, MA, MAT); fine arts (MA); graphic design (MA); history (M Ed, MA); illustration (MA); interpretative speech (MA); mathematics (M Ed, MAT); medical missions (Certificate); ministry (MM, D Min); multi-categorical special education (M Ed, MAT); music (M Ed); New Testament interpretation (PhD); Old Testament interpretation (PhD); orchestral instrument performance (MM); organ performance (MM); pastoral studies (MA); personnel services (MS, Ed S); piano pedagogy (MM); piano performance (MM); platform arts (MA); rhetoric and public address (MA); secondary education (M Ed); studio art (MA); teaching Bible (MA); theology (MA, PhD); voice performance (MM); youth ministries (MA); M Div/MM.

Boise State University, College of Education, Department of Curriculum, Instruction and Foundational Studies, Boise, ID 83725-0399. Offers curriculum and instruction (MA Ed, Ed D); educational leadership (M Ed); executive educational leadership (Ed S). *Accreditation:* NCATE. *Program availability:* Part-time. *Degree requirements:* For master's, thesis optional. *Entrance requirements:* For master's, minimum GPA of 3.0. Additional exam requirements/recommendations for international students: Required—TOEFL (minimum score 550 paper-based; 80 iBT), IELTS (minimum score 6). Electronic applications accepted.

Bowie State University, Graduate Programs, Program in Educational Leadership/Executive Fellows, Bowie, MD 20715-9465. Offers Ed D. *Program availability:* Part-time, evening/weekend. *Degree requirements:* For doctorate, comprehensive exam, thesis/dissertation. Electronic applications accepted.

Bowie State University, Graduate Programs, Program in Elementary and Secondary School Administration, Bowie, MD 20715-9465. Offers M Ed. *Program availability:* Part-time, evening/weekend. *Degree requirements:* For master's, comprehensive exam. *Entrance requirements:* For master's, copy of teaching certificate, 3 years of teaching experience, letter of recommendation from current supervisor. Electronic applications accepted.

Bowie State University, Graduate Programs, Program in School Administration and Supervision, Bowie, MD 20715-9465. Offers M Ed. *Program availability:* Part-time,

evening/weekend. *Degree requirements:* For master's, comprehensive exam, thesis optional, research paper. *Entrance requirements:* For master's, minimum undergraduate GPA of 3.0, 3 years of teaching experience, teaching certificate.

Bowling Green State University, Graduate College, College of Education and Human Development, Department of Higher Education and Student Affairs, Program in Higher Education Administration, Bowling Green, OH 43403. Offers PhD. *Accreditation:* NCATE. *Program availability:* Part-time. *Degree requirements:* For doctorate, comprehensive exam, thesis/dissertation. *Entrance requirements:* For doctorate, GRE General Test. Additional exam requirements/recommendations for international students: Required—TOEFL. Electronic applications accepted. *Faculty research:* Adult learners, legal issues, intellectual development.

Bowling Green State University, Graduate College, College of Education and Human Development, School of Educational Foundations, Leadership and Policy, Program in Educational Administration and Supervision, Bowling Green, OH 43403. Offers educational leadership (M Ed, Ed S); leadership studies (Ed D). *Accreditation:* NCATE. *Program availability:* Part-time, evening/weekend. *Degree requirements:* For master's, thesis or alternative; for doctorate, comprehensive exam, thesis/dissertation; for Ed S, thesis or alternative, field experience or internship. *Entrance requirements:* For master's, doctorate, and Ed S, GRE General Test. Additional exam requirements/recommendations for international students: Required—TOEFL. Electronic applications accepted. *Faculty research:* Professional development for school leaders, organizational development, school finance, legal challenges to school decision making, administering urban schools.

Bradley University, The Graduate School, College of Education and Health Sciences, Department of Leadership in Education, Nonprofits and Counseling, Peoria, IL 61625-0002. Offers counseling (MA), including clinical mental health counseling, professional school counseling; leadership in educational administration (MA); nonprofit leadership (MA). *Accreditation:* ACA; NCATE. *Program availability:* Part-time, evening/weekend, blended/hybrid learning. *Faculty:* 11 full-time (6 women), 10 part-time/adjunct (6 women). *Students:* 83 full-time (68 women), 166 part-time (137 women); includes 50 minority (26 Black or African American, non-Hispanic/Latino; 2 American Indian or Alaska Native, non-Hispanic/Latino; 4 Asian, non-Hispanic/Latino; 14 Hispanic/Latino; 4 Two or more races, non-Hispanic/Latino), 3 international. Average age 33. 181 applicants, 97% accepted, 54 enrolled. In 2018, 58 master's awarded. *Degree requirements:* For master's, comprehensive exam, thesis optional. *Entrance requirements:* For master's, GRE General Test or MAT, interview, 3 letters of recommendation. Additional exam requirements/recommendations for international students: Required—TOEFL (minimum score 550 paper-based; 79 iBT), IELTS (minimum score 6.5). *Application deadline:* For fall admission, 5/15 priority date for domestic and international students; for spring admission, 10/15 priority date for domestic and international students. Applications are processed on a rolling basis. Application fee: $40 ($50 for international students). Electronic applications accepted. *Expenses: Tuition:* Part-time $890 per credit. *Required fees:* $50 per unit. *Financial support:* In 2018–19, 67 students received support, including 1 fellowship with full tuition reimbursement available (averaging $16,020 per year), 12 research assistantships with full tuition reimbursements available (averaging $14,388 per year); career-related internships or fieldwork, scholarships/grants, tuition waivers (partial), and unspecified assistantships also available. Support available to part-time students. Financial award application deadline: 4/1. *Unit head:* Dean Cantu, Associate Dean and Director, Professor, 309-677-3190, E-mail: dcantu@bradley.edu. *Application contact:* Rachel Webb, Director of On-Campus Graduate Admissions & International Student and Scholar Services, 309-677-2375, E-mail: rkwebb@bradley.edu.
Website: http://www.bradley.edu/academic/departments/lenc/

Brandeis University, Graduate School of Arts and Sciences, Department of Education, Waltham, MA 02454-9110. Offers Jewish day schools (MAT); public elementary education (MAT); secondary education (MAT), including Bible, biology, chemistry, Chinese, English, history, Jewish day schools, math, physics; teacher leadership (Ed M, AGC). *Faculty:* 5 full-time (3 women), 9 part-time/adjunct (all women). *Students:* 17 full-time (13 women), 36 part-time (33 women); includes 9 minority (1 Black or African American, non-Hispanic/Latino; 6 Asian, non-Hispanic/Latino; 1 Hispanic/Latino; 1 Two or more races, non-Hispanic/Latino). Average age 36. 90 applicants, 79% accepted, 50 enrolled. In 2018, 44 master's, 18 other advanced degrees awarded. *Degree requirements:* For master's, thesis or alternative, internship, research project, capstone. *Entrance requirements:* For master's, GRE or MAT, transcripts, letters of recommendation, resume, statement of purpose; for AGC, transcripts, letters of recommendation, resume, statement of purpose, interview. Additional exam requirements/recommendations for international students: Required—TOEFL, IELTS, PTE. *Application deadline:* For fall admission, 3/15 priority date for domestic students. Applications are processed on a rolling basis. Application fee: $75. Electronic applications accepted. *Financial support:* Scholarships/grants available. *Faculty research:* Teacher education, education, teaching, elementary education, secondary education, Jewish education, English, history, biology, chemistry, physics, math, Chinese, Bible/Tanakh. *Unit head:* Danielle Igra, Director of Graduate Study, 781-736-8519, E-mail: digra@brandeis.edu. *Application contact:* Manuel Tuan, Administrator, 781-736-2002, E-mail: tuan@brandeis.edu.
Website: http://www.brandeis.edu/gsas/programs/education.html

Brandman University, School of Education, Irvine, CA 92618. Offers curriculum and instruction (MAE); educational administration (MAE); educational leadership (MAE); educational leadership and administration (MA); elementary education (MAT); instructional technology: teaching the 21st century learner (MAE); leadership in early childhood education (MAE); organizational leadership (Ed D); school counseling (MA); secondary education (MAT); special education (MA); teaching and learning (MAE).

Brandon University, Faculty of Education, Brandon, MB R7A 6A9, Canada. Offers curriculum and instruction (M Ed, Diploma); educational administration (M Ed, Diploma); guidance and counseling (M Ed, Diploma); special education (M Ed, Diploma). *Degree requirements:* For master's, thesis. *Entrance requirements:* For master's, minimum GPA of 3.0, teaching certificate or equivalent. Additional exam requirements/recommendations for international students: Required—TOEFL. *Faculty research:* Comparative education, environmental studies, parent/school council.

Bridgewater State University, College of Graduate Studies, College of Education and Allied Studies, Department of Secondary Education and Professional Programs, Program in Educational Leadership, Bridgewater, MA 02325. Offers M Ed, CAGS. *Accreditation:* NCATE. *Program availability:* Part-time, evening/weekend. *Degree requirements:* For master's and CAGS, comprehensive exam. *Entrance requirements:* For master's, GRE General Test or Massachusetts Test for Educator Licensure, work experience; for CAGS, master's degree.

Brooklyn College of the City University of New York, School of Education, Program in Educational Leadership, Brooklyn, NY 11210-2889. Offers school building leader (MS Ed); school district leader (MS Ed). *Program availability:* Part-time, evening/weekend. *Entrance requirements:* For master's, 2 supervisory letters of recommendation, essay, resume, teaching certificate, interview. Additional exam requirements/recommendations for international students: Required—TOEFL (minimum score 500 paper-based; 61 iBT). Electronic applications accepted.

Buffalo State College, State University of New York, The Graduate School, School of Education, Department of Elementary Education, Literacy, and Educational Leadership, Program in Educational Leadership, Buffalo, NY 14222-1095. Offers CAS. *Accreditation:* NCATE. *Program availability:* Part-time, evening/weekend. *Degree requirements:* For CAS, internship. *Entrance requirements:* For degree, master's degree, New York teaching certificate, 3 years of teaching experience. Additional exam requirements/recommendations for international students: Required—TOEFL (minimum score 550 paper-based).

Butler University, College of Education, Indianapolis, IN 46208-3485. Offers educational administration (MS). *Accreditation:* ACA; NCATE. *Program availability:* Part-time. *Faculty:* 12 full-time (8 women), 12 part-time/adjunct (all women). *Students:* 11 full-time (8 women), 169 part-time (140 women); includes 27 minority (11 Black or African American, non-Hispanic/Latino; 3 Asian, non-Hispanic/Latino; 7 Hispanic/Latino; 6 Two or more races, non-Hispanic/Latino). Average age 34. 74 applicants, 85% accepted, 63 enrolled. In 2018, 51 master's, 32 other advanced degrees awarded. *Degree requirements:* For master's, thesis. *Entrance requirements:* For master's, GRE (minimum score 291) or MAT (minimum score 396) unless undergraduate GPA is a 3.0 or higher, two letters of recommendation, transcripts, interview, professional resume. Additional exam requirements/recommendations for international students: Required—TOEFL (minimum score 550 paper-based; 79 iBT), IELTS (minimum score 6). *Application deadline:* For fall admission, 2/1 for domestic and international students; for spring admission, 11/1 for domestic and international students; for summer admission, 4/1 for domestic and international students. Applications are processed on a rolling basis. Application fee: $0. Electronic applications accepted. Application fee is waived when completed online. *Expenses:* Contact institution. *Financial support:* In 2018–19, 64 students received support. Scholarships/grants, tuition waivers (full and partial), and unspecified assistantships available. Financial award application deadline: 7/15; financial award applicants required to submit FAFSA. *Faculty research:* Educational neuroscience, transformational adult learning, culture and leadership, educational leadership. *Unit head:* Dr. Ena Shelley, Dean, 317-940-9752, Fax: 317-940-6481. *Application contact:* Diane Dubord, Graduate Student Services Specialist, 317-940-8100, Fax: 317-940-8250, E-mail: ddubord@butler.edu.
Website: https://www.butler.edu/coe/graduate-programs

Cabrini University, Academic Affairs, Radnor, PA 19087. Offers accounting (M Acc); autism spectrum disorder (M Ed); biological sciences (MS), including civic leadership; criminology and criminal justice (MA); curriculum, instruction, and assessment (M Ed); educational leadership (M Ed, Ed D), including curriculum and instructional leadership (Ed D), preK-12 leadership (Ed D); English as a second language (M Ed); organizational leadership (DBA, PhD); preK to 4 (M Ed); reading specialist (M Ed); secondary education (M Ed), including biology, chemistry, English, English/communication, mathematics, social studies; special education grades 7-12 (M Ed); special education preK-8 (M Ed); teaching and learning (M Ed). *Program availability:* Part-time, evening/weekend. *Degree requirements:* For master's, comprehensive exam (for some programs), thesis (for some programs); for doctorate, comprehensive exam (for some programs), thesis/dissertation. *Entrance requirements:* For master's, professional resume, personal statement, two recommendations, official transcripts; for doctorate, official transcripts, minimum master's GPA of 3.0, two recommendations, interview with admissions committee. Additional exam requirements/recommendations for international students: Required—TOEFL (minimum score 80 iBT). Electronic applications accepted. Application fee is waived when completed online. *Expenses:* Contact institution.

Cairn University, School of Education, Langhorne, PA 19047-2990. Offers applied behavior analysis (MS Sp Ed, Certificate); educational leadership and administration (MS El); instruction (MS Sp Ed); teacher education (MS Ed). *Program availability:* Part-time, evening/weekend, 100% online, blended/hybrid learning. *Entrance requirements:* Additional exam requirements/recommendations for international students: Required—TOEFL (minimum score 550 paper-based). Electronic applications accepted. Application fee is waived when completed online. *Expenses:* Contact institution.

Caldwell University, School of Education, Caldwell, NJ 07006-6195. Offers elementary, secondary or preschool endorsement, special ed, ESL (Postbaccalaureate Certificate). *Program availability:* Part-time, evening/weekend. *Faculty:* 9 full-time (6 women), 18 part-time/adjunct (10 women). *Students:* 35 full-time (29 women), 170 part-time (125 women); includes 45 minority (22 Black or African American, non-Hispanic/Latino; 1 American Indian or Alaska Native, non-Hispanic/Latino; 5 Asian, non-Hispanic/Latino; 14 Hispanic/Latino; 3 Two or more races, non-Hispanic/Latino). Average age 36. 75 applicants, 93% accepted, 42 enrolled. In 2018, 40 master's, 8 doctorates awarded. *Degree requirements:* For master's, comprehensive exam (for some programs), thesis (for some programs); for doctorate, thesis/dissertation. *Entrance requirements:* For master's, PRAXIS, 3 years of work experience (for some programs), prior teaching certification (for some programs); one to two professional references; writing sample (for some programs); personal statement (for some programs); interview (for some programs); bachelor's or graduate degree (for some programs); minimum 3.0 GPA (for some programs); for doctorate, GRE or MAT, 3 years of work experience, prior teaching certification; two letters of recommendation; copy of completed research paper/thesis (or other sample of some type of research writing); resume; interview; master's degree in education or related field; minimum 3.6 GPA in graduate courses; for other advanced degree, PRAXIS (for some programs), bachelor's degree (for some programs); master's degree (for some programs); minimum 3.0 GPA (for some programs); 2 professional references (for some programs); 2 letters of recommendation (for some programs); personal statement; interview; work experience (for some programs); prior certification (for some programs). Additional exam requirements/recommendations for international students: Required—The TOEFL or IELTS is required of international students who were not educated at the Bachelors level in English. Recommended—TOEFL (minimum score 580 paper-based; 92 iBT), IELTS (minimum score 7.5). *Application deadline:* For fall admission, 7/15 for domestic students. Applications are processed on a rolling basis. Application fee: $50. Electronic applications accepted. *Expenses:* $63,450 for full EdD tuition; $77,550 for full PhD tuition; $24,300 for full MA online tuition; $35,820 for full MA tuition. *Financial support:* Unspecified assistantships available. Financial award applicants required to submit FAFSA. *Faculty research:* Curriculum and instruction, secondary education, special education, education and technology, literacy instruction, higher education administration, education leadership. *Unit head:* Dr. Joan Moriarity, Associate Dean, 973-618-3626, E-mail: jmoriarity@caldwell.edu. *Application contact:* Tom Disch, Senior Admissions Counselor, 973-618-3544, E-mail: graduate@caldwell.edu.

California Baptist University, Program in Education, Riverside, CA 92504-3206. Offers educational leadership (MS); educational leadership for faith-based institutions (MS); educational leadership for public institutions (MS); educational technology (MS); instructional computer applications (MS); international education (MS); leadership and adult learning (MS); leadership and organizational studies (MS); online teaching and learning (MS); reading (MS); science education (MA); special education in mild/moderate disabilities (MS); special education in moderate/severe disabilities (MS);

teacher leadership (MS); teaching (MS); teaching and learning (MS). *Program availability:* Part-time, evening/weekend, 100% online, blended/hybrid learning. *Faculty:* 26 full-time (13 women), 28 part-time/adjunct (21 women). *Students:* 201 full-time (164 women), 265 part-time (209 women); includes 226 minority (23 Black or African American, non-Hispanic/Latino; 4 American Indian or Alaska Native, non-Hispanic/Latino; 7 Asian, non-Hispanic/Latino; 169 Hispanic/Latino; 6 Native Hawaiian or other Pacific Islander, non-Hispanic/Latino; 17 Two or more races, non-Hispanic/Latino), 2 international. Average age 39. 145 applicants, 97% accepted, 141 enrolled. In 2018, 253 master's awarded. *Degree requirements:* For master's, comprehensive exam, project, or thesis. *Entrance requirements:* For master's, minimum undergraduate GPA of 2.75; 500-word essay; three letters of recommendation; two prerequisite courses completed with minimum C grade. Additional exam requirements/recommendations for international students: Required—TOEFL (minimum score 80 iBT). *Application deadline:* For fall admission, 8/1 priority date for domestic students, 7/1 for international students; for spring admission, 12/1 priority date for domestic students, 11/1 for international students. Applications are processed on a rolling basis. Application fee: $45. Electronic applications accepted. *Expenses:* $634 per unit. *Financial support:* In 2018–19, 312 students received support. Federal Work-Study and scholarships/grants available. Financial award applicants required to submit CSS PROFILE or FAFSA. *Faculty research:* Leadership development, complexity theory, faith and learning, special education, social and philosophical contexts of education. *Unit head:* Dr. Robin Duncan, Dean, School of Education, 951-552-8948, E-mail: rduncan@calbaptist.edu. *Application contact:* Dr. Shari Farris, Program Director, Online MS in Education, 951-343-2455, E-mail: sfarris@calbaptist.edu.
Website: http://www.calbaptist.edu/mastersined/

California Coast University, School of Education, Santa Ana, CA 92701. Offers administration (M Ed); curriculum and instruction (M Ed); educational administration (Ed D); educational psychology (Ed D); organizational leadership (Ed D). *Program availability:* Online learning.

California Lutheran University, Graduate Studies, Graduate School of Education, Thousand Oaks, CA 91360-2787. Offers counseling and guidance (MS), including college student personnel, counseling and guidance; educational leadership (MA, Ed D), including educational leadership (K-12) (Ed D), higher education leadership (Ed D); special education (MS); teacher leadership (M Ed); teaching (M Ed). *Accreditation:* NCATE. *Program availability:* Part-time, evening/weekend. *Degree requirements:* For master's, comprehensive exam or thesis; for doctorate, thesis/dissertation. *Entrance requirements:* For master's, GRE General Test, interview, minimum GPA of 3.0. Electronic applications accepted.

California State Polytechnic University, Pomona, Ed D Program in Educational Leadership, Pomona, CA 91768-2557. Offers educational leadership (Ed D). *Program availability:* Part-time, evening/weekend. *Students:* 2 full-time (0 women), 42 part-time (31 women); includes 29 minority (8 Black or African American, non-Hispanic/Latino; 4 Asian, non-Hispanic/Latino; 16 Hispanic/Latino; 1 Two or more races, non-Hispanic/Latino), 3 international. Average age 43. 2 applicants, 100% accepted, 2 enrolled. In 2018, 18 doctorates awarded. *Entrance requirements:* Additional exam requirements/recommendations for international students: Required—TOEFL (minimum score 550 paper-based). *Application deadline:* Applications are processed on a rolling basis. Application fee: $55. Electronic applications accepted. *Expenses:* Contact institution. *Financial support:* Applicants required to submit FAFSA. *Unit head:* Dr. Betty T Alford, Professor/Doctoral Program Co-Director, 909-869-5369, Fax: 909-869-4822, E-mail: btalford@cpp.edu. *Application contact:* Dr. Betty T Alford, Professor/Doctoral Program Co-Director, 909-869-5369, Fax: 909-869-4822, E-mail: btalford@cpp.edu.
Website: http://www.cpp.edu/~doctoralstudies/

California State University, Bakersfield, Division of Graduate Studies, School of Social Sciences and Education, Program in Educational Administration, Bakersfield, CA 93311. Offers MA. *Faculty:* 3 full-time (0 women), 3 part-time/adjunct (all women). *Students:* 21 full-time (11 women), 1 (woman) part-time; includes 8 minority (1 Asian, non-Hispanic/Latino; 7 Hispanic/Latino). Average age 40. 29 applicants, 62% accepted, 13 enrolled. In 2018, 24 master's awarded. *Degree requirements:* For master's, thesis or alternative, project or culminating exam. *Application deadline:* Applications are processed on a rolling basis. Application fee: $55. *Unit head:* Dr. Michael Szolowicz, Director, 661-664-2663, Fax: 661-664-2479, E-mail: mszolocwicz@csub.edu. *Application contact:* Martha Manriquez, Graduate Student Center Coordinator, 661-654-2786, Fax: 661-654-2791, E-mail: gsc@csub.edu.
Website: https://www.csub.edu/sse/departments/advancededucationalstudies/educational_administration/index.html

California State University, Bakersfield, Division of Graduate Studies, School of Social Sciences and Education, Program in Educational Leadership, Bakersfield, CA 93311. Offers Ed D. *Faculty:* 8 full-time (0 women), 3 part-time/adjunct (1 woman). *Students:* 22 full-time (16 women), 10 part-time (3 women); includes 22 minority (4 Black or African American, non-Hispanic/Latino; 1 American Indian or Alaska Native, non-Hispanic/Latino; 3 Asian, non-Hispanic/Latino; 10 Hispanic/Latino; 4 Two or more races, non-Hispanic/Latino). Average age 40. 20 applicants, 65% accepted, 11 enrolled. In 2018, 2 doctorates awarded. *Degree requirements:* For doctorate, thesis/dissertation. *Financial support:* In 2018–19, fellowships (averaging $1,850 per year) were awarded; Federal Work-Study, scholarships/grants, and tuition waivers (full and partial) also available. Financial award application deadline: 3/2; financial award applicants required to submit FAFSA. *Unit head:* Dr. John Stark, Director, 661-654-3140, E-mail: jstark@csub.edu. *Application contact:* Martha Manriquez, Graduate Student Center Coordinator, 661-654-2786, Fax: 661-654-2791, E-mail: gsc@csub.edu.
Website: https://www.csub.edu/edd/index.html

California State University, East Bay, Office of Graduate Studies, College of Education and Allied Studies, Department of Educational Leadership, Hayward, CA 94542-3000. Offers MS, Ed D. *Accreditation:* NCATE. *Program availability:* Part-time, evening/weekend, online learning. *Degree requirements:* For master's, comprehensive exam, project or thesis; for doctorate, thesis/dissertation. *Entrance requirements:* For master's, CBEST, teaching or services credential and experience; minimum GPA of 3.0; for doctorate, GRE, MA with minimum GPA of 3.0; PK-12 leadership position; portfolio of work samples; employer/district support agreement. Additional exam requirements/recommendations for international students: Required—TOEFL (minimum score 550 paper-based). Electronic applications accepted.

California State University, East Bay, Office of Graduate Studies, College of Education and Allied Studies, Department of Teacher Education, Hayward, CA 94542-3000. Offers education (MS), including curriculum, early childhood education, educational technology and leadership, reading instruction. *Program availability:* Online learning. *Degree requirements:* For master's, project or thesis. *Entrance requirements:* For master's, minimum GPA of 3.0 in field, 2.5 overall; teaching experience; baccalaureate degree; 3 letters of recommendation. Additional exam requirements/recommendations for international students: Required—TOEFL (minimum score 550 paper-based), IELTS. Electronic applications accepted. *Faculty research:* Online, pedagogy, writing, learning, teaching.

California State University, Fresno, Division of Research and Graduate Studies, Kremen School of Education and Human Development, Department of Educational Leadership, Fresno, CA 93740-8027. Offers education (MA), including educational leadership and administration. *Accreditation:* NCATE. *Program availability:* Part-time, evening/weekend. *Degree requirements:* For master's, thesis or alternative. *Entrance requirements:* For master's, GRE General Test, MAT, minimum GPA of 2.75. Additional exam requirements/recommendations for international students: Required—TOEFL. Electronic applications accepted. *Faculty research:* Substance abuse on youth education.

California State University, Fresno, Division of Research and Graduate Studies, Kremen School of Education and Human Development, Doctoral Program in Educational Leadership, Fresno, CA 93740-8027. Offers Ed D. *Program availability:* Part-time. *Degree requirements:* For doctorate, thesis/dissertation. *Entrance requirements:* For doctorate, GRE, minimum GPA of 3.0, master's degree, personal interview, written statement of purpose. Additional exam requirements/recommendations for international students: Required—TOEFL. Electronic applications accepted. *Expenses:* Contact institution. *Faculty research:* Minority special education leadership, literacy, ethics of leadership, organizational planning, language development.

California State University, Fullerton, Graduate Studies, College of Education, Department of Educational Leadership, Fullerton, CA 92831-3599. Offers educational administration (MS); educational leadership (Ed D). *Accreditation:* NCATE. *Program availability:* Part-time. *Degree requirements:* For master's, thesis or alternative, project. *Entrance requirements:* For master's, minimum GPA of 2.5. *Faculty research:* Creation of a substance abuse prevention training and demonstration program.

California State University, Long Beach, Graduate Studies, College of Education, Department of Advanced Studies in Education and Counseling, Long Beach, CA 90840. Offers counseling (MS), including marriage and family therapy, school counseling, student development in higher education; education (MA, Ed D); educational administration (MA, Ed D); educational psychology (MA); special education (MS). *Program availability:* Part-time, evening/weekend. *Entrance requirements:* For master's, GRE General Test, minimum GPA of 2.75. *Application deadline:* For fall admission, 3/1 for domestic students. Applications are processed on a rolling basis. Application fee: $55. Electronic applications accepted. *Expenses: Required fees:* $2628 per term. Tuition and fees vary according to class time, course level, course load, degree level, campus/location and program. *Financial support:* Federal Work-Study, institutionally sponsored loans, and scholarships/grants available. Financial award application deadline: 3/2; financial award applicants required to submit FAFSA. *Unit head:* Dr. Hiromi Masunaga, Chair, 562-985-4517, E-mail: asec@csulb.edu. *Application contact:* Dr. Hiromi Masunaga, Chair, 562-985-4517, E-mail: asec@csulb.edu.
Website: http://www.csulb.edu/college-of-education/advanced-studies-education-and-counseling

California State University, Northridge, Graduate Studies, Michael D. Eisner College of Education, Department of Educational Leadership and Policy Studies, Northridge, CA 91330. Offers education (MA); educational administration (MA); educational leadership (Ed D). *Accreditation:* NCATE. *Program availability:* Part-time, evening/weekend. *Entrance requirements:* For master's, 2 letters of recommendation. Additional exam requirements/recommendations for international students: Required—TOEFL. *Faculty research:* Bilingual educational training.

California State University, Sacramento, College of Education, Graduate and Professional Studies in Education, Sacramento, CA 95819. Offers behavioral science and gender equity (MA); child development (MA); counseling (MS); curriculum and instruction (MA); education (Ed D), including K-12 and community college; education leadership and policy studies (MA), including higher education, PreK-12; education specialist (Ed S), including school psychology; educational technology (MA); language and literacy (MA); multicultural education (MA); school psychology (MA); special education (MA); workforce development advocacy (MA). *Program availability:* Part-time, evening/weekend, blended/hybrid learning. *Degree requirements:* For master's, thesis or project; writing proficiency exam; for doctorate, thesis/dissertation. *Entrance requirements:* For master's and doctorate, GRE. Additional exam requirements/recommendations for international students: Required—TOEFL (minimum score 550 paper-based; 80 iBT); Recommended—IELTS (minimum score 7), TSE. Electronic applications accepted. *Expenses:* Contact institution.

California State University, San Bernardino, Graduate Studies, College of Education, Program in Educational Administration, San Bernardino, CA 92407. Offers MA. *Program availability:* Part-time, evening/weekend. *Faculty:* 24 full-time (14 women), 37 part-time/adjunct (27 women). *Students:* 29 full-time (20 women), 21 part-time (15 women); includes 27 minority (5 Black or African American, non-Hispanic/Latino; 22 Hispanic/Latino). Average age 41. 28 applicants, 86% accepted, 18 enrolled. In 2018, 51 master's awarded. *Degree requirements:* For master's, thesis or alternative. *Entrance requirements:* Additional exam requirements/recommendations for international students: Required—TOEFL. *Application deadline:* For fall admission, 7/16 for domestic students; for winter admission, 10/16 for domestic students; for spring admission, 2/5 for domestic students. Application fee: $55. *Unit head:* Susan Jindra, Program Coordinator, 909-537-5674, E-mail: sjindra@csusb.edu. *Application contact:* Dr. Dorota Huizinga, Dean of Graduate Studies, 909-537-3064, E-mail: dorota.huizinga@csusb.edu.

California State University, San Bernardino, Graduate Studies, College of Education, Program in Educational Leadership: Community College Specialization, San Bernardino, CA 92407. Offers MA. *Program availability:* Part-time, evening/weekend. *Students:* 12 full-time (8 women), 21 part-time (11 women); includes 21 minority (3 Black or African American, non-Hispanic/Latino; 3 Asian, non-Hispanic/Latino; 14 Hispanic/Latino; 1 Two or more races, non-Hispanic/Latino), 2 international. Average age 43. 24 applicants, 67% accepted, 11 enrolled. *Degree requirements:* For master's, thesis optional. *Entrance requirements:* Additional exam requirements/recommendations for international students: Required—TOEFL. *Application deadline:* For fall admission, 7/17 for domestic students. Application fee: $55. *Unit head:* Dr. Lynne Diaz- Rico, Co-Director, 909-537-5651, E-mail: diazrico@csusb.edu. *Application contact:* Dr. Dorota Huizinga, Dean of Graduate Studies, 909-537-3064, E-mail: dorota.huizinga@csusb.edu.

California State University, San Bernardino, Graduate Studies, College of Education, Program in Educational Leadership: P-12 Specialization, San Bernardino, CA 92407. Offers Ed D. *Students:* 1 full-time (0 women), 34 part-time (29 women); includes 24 minority (3 Black or African American, non-Hispanic/Latino; 3 Asian, non-Hispanic/Latino; 17 Hispanic/Latino; 1 Two or more races, non-Hispanic/Latino). Average age 43. 9 applicants, 67% accepted, 6 enrolled. In 2018, 10 doctorates awarded. *Entrance requirements:* Additional exam requirements/recommendations for international students: Required—TOEFL. *Application deadline:* For fall admission, 7/16 for domestic students. Application fee: $55. *Unit head:* Dr. Lynne Diaz-Rico, Co-Director, 909-537-5651, E-mail: diaz-rico@csusb.edu. *Application contact:* Dr. Dorota Huizinga, Dean of Graduate Studies, 909-537-3064, E-mail: dorota.huizinga@csusb.edu.

California State University, San Marcos, College of Education, Health and Human Services, School of Education, San Marcos, CA 92096-0001. Offers education (MA);

educational administration (MA); educational leadership (Ed D); literacy education (MA); special education (MA). *Accreditation:* NCATE (one or more programs are accredited). *Program availability:* Part-time, evening/weekend. *Entrance requirements:* For master's, minimum GPA of 3.0, teaching credentials, 1 year of teaching experience. *Application deadline:* For fall admission, 2/1 priority date for domestic students. Applications are processed on a rolling basis. Application fee: $55. *Financial support:* Applicants required to submit FAFSA. *Faculty research:* Multicultural literature, art as knowledge, poetry and second language acquisition, restructuring K–12 education and improving the training of K–8 science teachers. *Unit head:* Pat Stall, Director, 760-750-4386, E-mail: pstall@csusm.edu. *Application contact:* Dr. Wesley Schultz, Dean of Office of Graduate Studies and Research, 760-750-8045, Fax: 760-750-8045, E-mail: apply@csusm.edu.
Website: http://www.csusm.edu/education/

California State University, Stanislaus, College of Education, Kinesiology and Social Work, Doctor of Education in Educational Leadership Programs, Turlock, CA 95382. Offers community college leadership (Ed D); P-12 leadership (Ed D). *Program availability:* Part-time, evening/weekend. *Degree requirements:* For doctorate, thesis/dissertation. *Entrance requirements:* For doctorate, GRE, minimum GPA of 3.0, 3 letters of reference, interview, personal statement. Additional exam requirements/recommendations for international students: Required—TOEFL (minimum score 550 paper-based). Electronic applications accepted.

California State University, Stanislaus, College of Education, Kinesiology and Social Work, MA Program in Education, Turlock, CA 95382. Offers curriculum and instruction (MA), including education technology, elementary education, multilingual education, physical education, reading, secondary education, special education; school administration (MA); school counseling (MA). *Program availability:* Part-time, evening/weekend. *Degree requirements:* For master's, comprehensive exam (for some programs), thesis (for some programs). *Entrance requirements:* For master's, MAT, GRE, or CBEST (varies by concentration), 3 letters of recommendation, personal statement. Additional exam requirements/recommendations for international students: Required—TOEFL (minimum score 550 paper-based). Electronic applications accepted. *Faculty research:* Children's perspectives on historical events, method elementary schools dual language education, K-12 reading programs.

California University of Pennsylvania, School of Graduate Studies and Research, College of Education and Human Services, Program in School Administration, California, PA 15419-1394. Offers education administration and leadership (Ed D); educational leadership (M Ed), including educational studies, weather and climatology. *Accreditation:* NCATE. *Program availability:* Part-time, evening/weekend, online learning. *Degree requirements:* For master's, comprehensive exam, thesis optional. *Entrance requirements:* For master's, MAT, interview, minimum GPA of 3.0, teaching certificate, 2 years of teaching experience. Additional exam requirements/recommendations for international students: Required—TOEFL (minimum score 550 paper-based; 80 iBT). Electronic applications accepted. *Faculty research:* Educational leadership, peer coaching, online education-effective teaching strategies, instruction strategies, school law.

Calumet College of Saint Joseph, Program in Leadership in Teaching, Whiting, IN 46394-2195. Offers MS Ed.

Calvary University, Graduate School and Seminary, Kansas City, MO 64147. Offers Bible and theology (MS); Biblical counseling (MA); education (MS), including administration and leadership, Christian education, curriculum and instruction, elementary education; organizational development (MS); pastoral studies (M Div); worship arts (MS). *Program availability:* Part-time, evening/weekend. *Degree requirements:* For master's, variable foreign language requirement, comprehensive exam, thesis or alternative. *Entrance requirements:* For master's, minimum GPA of 2.5, BA or BS, doctrine agreement. Additional exam requirements/recommendations for international students: Required—TOEFL (minimum score 550 paper-based). Electronic applications accepted. *Expenses:* Contact institution.

Cambridge College, School of Education, Boston, MA 02129. Offers autism specialist (M Ed); autism/behavior analyst (M Ed); behavior analyst (Post-Master's Certificate); curriculum and instruction (CAGS); early childhood teacher (M Ed); educational leadership (M Ed, Ed D); elementary teacher (M Ed); English as a second language (M Ed, Certificate); general science (M Ed); health education (Post-Master's Certificate); interdisciplinary studies (M Ed); library teacher (M Ed); mathematics education (M Ed); mathematics specialist (Certificate); school administration (M Ed, CAGS); school nurse education (M Ed); teacher of students with moderate disabilities (M Ed); teaching skills and methodologies (M Ed). *Program availability:* Part-time, evening/weekend, online learning. *Degree requirements:* For master's, thesis, internship/practicum (licensure program only); for doctorate, thesis/dissertation; for other advanced degree, thesis. *Entrance requirements:* For master's, interview, resume, documentation of licensure, 2 professional references; for doctorate, official transcripts, interview, resume, written personal statement/essay, portfolio of scholarly and professional work, 2 professional references, health insurance, immunizations form; for other advanced degree, official transcripts, interview, resume, written personal statement/essay, 2 professional references, health insurance, immunizations form. Additional exam requirements/recommendations for international students: Required—TOEFL (minimum score 550 paper-based; 79 iBT), Michigan English Language Assessment Battery (minimum score 85); Recommended—IELTS (minimum score 6). *Application deadline:* Applications are processed on a rolling basis. Application fee: $30. Electronic applications accepted. *Expenses:* Contact institution. *Financial support:* Career-related internships or fieldwork, Federal Work-Study, and scholarships/grants available. Financial award applicants required to submit FAFSA. *Faculty research:* Adult education, accelerated learning, mathematics education, brain compatible learning, special education and law. *Unit head:* Dr. Mary Garrity, Interim Dean, 617-873-0168, E-mail: mary.garrity@cambridgecollege.edu. *Application contact:* Salvadore Liberto, Interim Assistant Vice President of Enrollment, 800-877-4723, E-mail: admissions@cambridgecollege.edu.
Website: https://www.cambridgecollege.edu/school/school-education

Cameron University, Office of Graduate Studies, Program in Educational Leadership, Lawton, OK 73505-6377. Offers MS. *Program availability:* Part-time, evening/weekend. *Degree requirements:* For master's, portfolio.

Campbellsville University, School of Education, Campbellsville, KY 42718-2799. Offers education (MA); school counseling (MA); school improvement (MA); special education (MASE); special education-teacher leader (MA); teacher leader (MA); teaching (MAT), including middle grades biology, middle grades chemistry, middle grades English. *Accreditation:* NCATE. *Program availability:* Part-time, evening/weekend, 100% online, blended/hybrid learning. *Faculty:* 16 full-time (10 women), 13 part-time/adjunct (7 women). *Students:* 154 full-time (122 women), 44 part-time (36 women); includes 18 minority (16 Black or African American, non-Hispanic/Latino; 1 Hispanic/Latino; 1 Two or more races, non-Hispanic/Latino), 1 international. Average age 34. 280 applicants, 30% accepted, 72 enrolled. In 2018, 66 master's awarded. *Degree requirements:* For master's, comprehensive exam (for some programs), thesis, research paper. *Entrance requirements:* For master's, GRE or PRAXIS, minimum undergraduate GPA of 2.75, teaching certificate, professional growth plan, letters of recommendation, interview. Additional exam requirements/recommendations for international students: Recommended—TOEFL (minimum score 550 paper-based; 79 iBT), IELTS (minimum score 6). *Application deadline:* Applications are processed on a rolling basis. Application fee: $25. Electronic applications accepted. Application fee is waived when completed online. *Expenses:* $299/credit hour. *Financial support:* Unspecified assistantships available. Financial award applicants required to submit FAFSA. *Faculty research:* Professional development, curriculum development, school governance, assessment, special education. *Unit head:* Dr. Lisa Allen, Dean of School of Education, 270-789-5344, Fax: 270-789-5206, E-mail: lsallen@campbellsville.edu. *Application contact:* Monica Bamwine, Director of Graduate Admissions, 270-789-5221, Fax: 270-789-5071, E-mail: mkbamwine@campbellsville.edu.

Campbell University, Graduate and Professional Programs, School of Education, Buies Creek, NC 27506. Offers elementary education (M Ed); interdisciplinary studies (M Ed); middle grades education (M Ed); physical education (M Ed); school administration (MSA); school counseling (M Ed); secondary education (M Ed). *Accreditation:* NCATE. *Program availability:* Part-time, evening/weekend. *Degree requirements:* For master's, comprehensive exam. *Entrance requirements:* For master's, GRE General Test, minimum GPA of 2.7. *Faculty research:* Spiritual values and wellness issues in counseling, stress and professional burnout among counselors, thinking strategies, leadership, adaptive technology.

Canisius College, Graduate Division, School of Education and Human Services, Department of Graduate Education and Leadership, Buffalo, NY 14208-1098. Offers business and marketing education (MS Ed); college student personnel (MS Ed); deaf education (MS Ed); deaf/adolescent education, grades 7-12 (MS Ed); deaf/childhood education, grades 1-6 (MS Ed); differentiated instruction (MS Ed); education administration (MS); educational administration (MS Ed); educational technologies (Certificate); gifted education extension (Certificate); literacy (MS Ed); reading (Certificate); school building leadership (MS Ed, Certificate); school district leadership (Certificate); teacher leader (Certificate); TESOL (MS Ed). *Accreditation:* NCATE. *Program availability:* Part-time, evening/weekend, 100% online, blended/hybrid learning. *Faculty:* 5 full-time (all women), 21 part-time/adjunct (16 women). *Students:* 79 full-time (66 women), 135 part-time (106 women); includes 45 minority (27 Black or African American, non-Hispanic/Latino; 1 American Indian or Alaska Native, non-Hispanic/Latino; 3 Asian, non-Hispanic/Latino; 9 Hispanic/Latino; 5 Two or more races, non-Hispanic/Latino), 1 international. Average age 32. 83 applicants, 96% accepted, 74 enrolled. In 2018, 94 master's, 47 other advanced degrees awarded. *Entrance requirements:* For master's, GRE (if cumulative GPA less than 2.7), transcripts, two letters of recommendation. Additional exam requirements/recommendations for international students: Required—TOEFL (minimum score 550 paper-based, 79 iBT), IELTS (minimum score 6.5), or CAEL (minimum score 70). *Application deadline:* Applications are processed on a rolling basis. Application fee: $0. Electronic applications accepted. *Expenses: Tuition:* Part-time $820 per credit hour. *Required fees:* $25 per semester. One-time fee: $65 part-time. Tuition and fees vary according to program. *Financial support:* In 2018–19, 206 students received support. Career-related internships or fieldwork, Federal Work-Study, scholarships/grants, tuition waivers (partial), and unspecified assistantships available. Support available to part-time students. Financial award application deadline: 4/30; financial award applicants required to submit FAFSA. *Faculty research:* Asperger's disease, autism, private higher education, reading strategies. *Unit head:* Dr. Anne Marie Tryjankowski, Chair/Associate Professor of Graduate Education and Leadership, 716-888-3715, Fax: 716-888-3142, E-mail: tryjanka@canisius.edu. *Application contact:* Dr. Anne Marie Tryjankowski, Chair/Associate Professor of Graduate Education and Leadership, 716-888-3715, Fax: 716-888-3142, E-mail: tryjanka@canisius.edu.

Capella University, School of Education, Doctoral Programs in Education, Minneapolis, MN 55402. Offers curriculum and instruction (PhD); educational leadership and management (Ed D); instructional design for online learning (PhD); K-12 studies in education (PhD); leadership for higher education (PhD); leadership in educational administration (PhD); postsecondary and adult education (PhD); professional studies in education (PhD); reading and literacy (Ed D); special education leadership (PhD); training and performance improvement (PhD).

Capella University, School of Education, Master's Programs in Education, Minneapolis, MN 55402. Offers adult education (MS); curriculum and instruction (MS); early childhood education (MS); enrollment management (MS); higher education leadership and management (MS); instructional design for online learning (MS); integrative studies (MS); K-12 studies in education (MS); leadership in educational administration (MS); reading and literacy (MS); special education teaching (MS).

Cardinal Stritch University, College of Education and Leadership, Department of Education, Milwaukee, WI 53217-3985. Offers educational leadership (MS); higher education student affairs leadership (MS); leadership for the advancement of learning and service (Ed D, PhD); leadership for the advancement of learning and service in higher education (Ed D, PhD); teaching (MAT); urban education (MA). *Accreditation:* NCATE. *Program availability:* Part-time, evening/weekend, 100% online, blended/hybrid learning. *Degree requirements:* For master's, comprehensive exam, thesis (for some programs), research project, faculty recommendation; for doctorate, thesis/dissertation, practica, field experience. *Entrance requirements:* For master's, 2 letters of recommendation, minimum GPA of 3.0; for doctorate, minimum GPA of 3.5 in master's coursework, 3 letters of recommendation. Additional exam requirements/recommendations for international students: Required—TOEFL (minimum score 550 paper-based; 79 iBT), IELTS (minimum score 6.5). Electronic applications accepted. *Expenses:* Contact institution.

Caribbean University, Graduate School, Bayamón, PR 00960-0493. Offers administration and supervision (MA Ed); criminal justice (MA); curriculum and instruction (MA Ed, PhD), including elementary education (MA Ed), English education (MA Ed), history education (MA Ed), mathematics education (MA Ed), primary education (MA Ed), science education (MA Ed), Spanish education (MA Ed); educational technology in instructional systems (MA Ed); gerontology (MSN); human resources (MBA); museology, archiving and art history (MA Ed); neonatal pediatrics (MSN); physical education (MA Ed); special education (MA Ed). *Entrance requirements:* For master's, interview, minimum GPA of 2.5.

Carroll University, Graduate Programs in Education, Waukesha, WI 53186-5593. Offers adult and continuing education (M Ed); educational leadership (MS); PK-12 (M Ed). *Program availability:* Part-time, evening/weekend. *Degree requirements:* For master's, thesis. *Entrance requirements:* For master's, minimum undergraduate GPA of 2.5 in related field. Additional exam requirements/recommendations for international students: Required—TOEFL. Electronic applications accepted. *Faculty research:* Qualitative research methods, whole language approaches to teaching, the writing process, multicultural education, gifted/talented learners.

Carson-Newman University, Graduate Program in Education, Jefferson City, TN 37760. Offers curriculum and instruction (M Ed); educational leadership (M Ed); elementary education (MAT); school counseling (MS); secondary education (MAT); teaching English as a second language (MATESL). *Accreditation:* NCATE. *Program availability:* Part-time, evening/weekend, 100% online, blended/hybrid learning. *Faculty:*

20 full-time (11 women), 16 part-time/adjunct (13 women). *Students:* 14 full-time (8 women), 401 part-time (294 women); includes 45 minority (34 Black or African American, non-Hispanic/Latino; 1 American Indian or Alaska Native, non-Hispanic/Latino; 4 Hispanic/Latino; 1 Native Hawaiian or other Pacific Islander, non-Hispanic/Latino; 5 Two or more races, non-Hispanic/Latino). Average age 36. 223 applicants, 100% accepted, 199 enrolled. In 2018, 211 master's awarded. *Degree requirements:* For master's, thesis or alternative. *Entrance requirements:* For master's, PRAXIS II or GRE with minimum score of 290 on the verbal and quantitative components (for MAT), minimum GPA of 3.0 in major, 2.5 overall. Additional exam requirements/recommendations for international students: Recommended—TOEFL (minimum score 79 iBT), IELTS (minimum score 6.5), TSE (minimum score 53). *Application deadline:* For fall admission, 7/15 priority date for domestic students. Applications are processed on a rolling basis. Application fee: $50. *Expenses: Tuition:* Full-time $9036; part-time $502 per credit hour. *Required fees:* $900; $25 per credit hour. $300 per semester. One-time fee: $150. *Financial support:* Federal Work-Study and unspecified assistantships available. Financial award applicants required to submit FAFSA. *Unit head:* Dr. Kim Hawkins, Chair, 865-471-3314, E-mail: khawkins@cn.edu. *Application contact:* Nilma Stewart, Graduate Admissions and Services Adviser, 865-471-3230, Fax: 865-471-3875, E-mail: adults@cn.edu.
Website: http://www.cn.edu/adult-graduate-studies

Carthage College, Division of Teacher Education, Kenosha, WI 53140. Offers classroom guidance and counseling (M Ed); creative arts (M Ed); gifted and talented children (M Ed); language arts (M Ed); modern language (M Ed); natural sciences (M Ed); reading (M Ed, Certificate); social sciences (M Ed); teacher leadership (M Ed). *Program availability:* Part-time, evening/weekend. *Degree requirements:* For master's, thesis optional. *Entrance requirements:* For master's, MAT, minimum B average, letters of reference.

Castleton University, Division of Graduate Studies, Department of Education, Program in Educational Leadership, Castleton, VT 05735. Offers MA Ed, CAGS. *Program availability:* Part-time, evening/weekend. *Degree requirements:* For master's, thesis or alternative; for CAGS, publishable paper. *Entrance requirements:* For master's, GRE General Test, MAT, interview, minimum undergraduate GPA of 3.0; for CAGS, educational research, master's degree, minimum undergraduate GPA of 3.0.

The Catholic University of America, School of Arts and Sciences, Department of Education, Washington, DC 20064. Offers Catholic school leadership (MA); education (Certificate); secondary education (MA); special education (MA), including early childhood, non-categorical. *Accreditation:* NCATE. *Program availability:* Part-time. *Faculty:* 7 full-time (6 women), 7 part-time/adjunct (5 women). *Students:* 12 full-time (11 women), 15 part-time (6 women); includes 3 minority (2 Hispanic/Latino; 1 Two or more races, non-Hispanic/Latino), 2 international. Average age 37. 12 applicants, 75% accepted, 8 enrolled. In 2018, 14 master's awarded. *Degree requirements:* For master's, comprehensive exam, thesis or alternative; for Certificate, action research project. *Entrance requirements:* For master's, GRE General Test or MAT, statement of purpose, official copies of academic transcripts, three letters of recommendation, interview; for Certificate, PRAXIS I, statement of purpose, official copies of academic transcripts, three letters of recommendation, interview. Additional exam requirements/recommendations for international students: Required—TOEFL (minimum score 550 paper-based; 80 iBT). *Application deadline:* For fall admission, 7/15 priority date for domestic students, 7/1 for international students; for spring admission, 11/15 priority date for domestic students, 11/1 for international students. Applications are processed on a rolling basis. Application fee: $55. Electronic applications accepted. *Expenses:* Contact institution. *Financial support:* Fellowships, research assistantships, teaching assistantships, Federal Work-Study, scholarships/grants, tuition waivers (full and partial), and unspecified assistantships available. Financial award application deadline: 2/1; financial award applicants required to submit FAFSA. *Faculty research:* Special education, early childhood education, educational psychology, Catholic school administration, leadership and policy studies, counseling, curriculum and instruction. *Unit head:* Dr. Agnes Cave, Chair, 202-319-5805, Fax: 202-319-5815, E-mail: cave@cua.edu. *Application contact:* Dr. Steven Brown, Director of Graduate Admissions, 202-319-5057, Fax: 202-319-6533, E-mail: cua-admissions@cua.edu.
Website: http://education.cua.edu/

Centenary University, Program in Education, Hackettstown, NJ 07840-2100. Offers education practice (M Ed); educational leadership (MA, Ed D); instructional leadership (MA); reading (M Ed); special education (MA). *Accreditation:* TEAC. *Program availability:* Part-time, evening/weekend, online learning. *Degree requirements:* For master's, thesis. *Entrance requirements:* For master's, interview, minimum undergraduate GPA of 2.8.

Central Connecticut State University, School of Graduate Studies, School of Education and Professional Studies, Department of Educational Leadership, Policy and Instructional Technology, New Britain, CT 06050-4010. Offers MS, Ed D, AC, Sixth Year Certificate. *Program availability:* Part-time, evening/weekend. *Faculty:* 14 full-time (6 women), 19 part-time/adjunct (8 women). *Students:* 2 full-time (1 woman), 380 part-time (270 women); includes 67 minority (24 Black or African American, non-Hispanic/Latino; 1 American Indian or Alaska Native, non-Hispanic/Latino; 4 Asian, non-Hispanic/Latino; 34 Hispanic/Latino; 4 Two or more races, non-Hispanic/Latino), 1 international. Average age 37. 48 applicants, 85% accepted, 32 enrolled. In 2018, 53 master's, 6 doctorates, 81 other advanced degrees awarded. *Degree requirements:* For master's, thesis or alternative; for doctorate, thesis/dissertation or alternative; for other advanced degree, thesis or alternative, qualifying exam. *Entrance requirements:* For master's, minimum undergraduate GPA of 2.7; for doctorate, GRE, master's degree, minimum GPA of 3.0 on all graduate coursework, essay, interview, resume, letters of recommendation; for other advanced degree, master's degree with minimum GPA of 3.0, essay, portfolio, letters of recommendation. Additional exam requirements/recommendations for international students: Required—TOEFL (minimum score 550 paper-based; 79 iBT); Recommended—IELTS (minimum score 6.5). *Application deadline:* For summer admission, 11/1 for domestic and international students. Applications are processed on a rolling basis. Application fee: $50. Electronic applications accepted. *Expenses: Tuition, area resident:* Full-time $7027; part-time $388 per credit. Tuition, state resident: full-time $9750; part-time $388 per credit. Tuition, nonresident: full-time $18,102; part-time $388 per credit. *International tuition:* $18,102 full-time. *Required fees:* $266 per semester. *Financial support:* In 2018–19, 18 students received support. Career-related internships or fieldwork, Federal Work-Study, scholarships/grants, and unspecified assistantships available. Support available to part-time students. Financial award application deadline: 3/1; financial award applicants required to submit FAFSA. *Faculty research:* Curriculum development, organizational leadership in educational settings, educational planning and development. *Unit head:* Dr. Ethan Heinen, Chair, 860-832-2130, E-mail: heineneth@ccsu.edu. *Application contact:* Patricia Gardner, Associate Director of Graduate Studies, 860-832-2350, Fax: 860-832-2362.
Website: http://www.ccsu.edu/elpit/

Central Connecticut State University, School of Graduate Studies, School of Engineering, Science and Technology, Department of Mathematical Sciences, New Britain, CT 06050-4010. Offers data mining (MS, Certificate); mathematics (MA, MS), including actuarial science (MA), computer science (MA), statistics (MA); mathematics education leadership (Sixth Year Certificate); mathematics for secondary education (Certificate). *Program availability:* Part-time, evening/weekend, 100% online. *Faculty:* 13 full-time (4 women). *Students:* 14 full-time (9 women), 70 part-time (39 women); includes 21 minority (8 Black or African American, non-Hispanic/Latino; 9 Asian, non-Hispanic/Latino; 3 Hispanic/Latino; 1 Two or more races, non-Hispanic/Latino), 2 international. Average age 33. 57 applicants, 70% accepted, 20 enrolled. In 2018, 20 master's, 3 other advanced degrees awarded. *Degree requirements:* For master's, comprehensive exam, thesis or alternative, special project; for other advanced degree, qualifying exam. *Entrance requirements:* For master's, minimum undergraduate GPA of 2.7; for other advanced degree, minimum undergraduate GPA of 3.0, essay, letters of recommendation. Additional exam requirements/recommendations for international students: Required—TOEFL (minimum score 550 paper-based; 79 iBT); Recommended—IELTS (minimum score 6.5). *Application deadline:* For fall admission, 6/1 for domestic students, 5/1 for international students; for spring admission, 11/1 for domestic and international students. Applications are processed on a rolling basis. Application fee: $50. Electronic applications accepted. *Expenses: Tuition, area resident:* Full-time $7027; part-time $388 per credit. Tuition, state resident: full-time $9750; part-time $388 per credit. Tuition, nonresident: full-time $18,102; part-time $388 per credit. *International tuition:* $18,102 full-time. *Required fees:* $266 per semester. *Financial support:* In 2018–19, 22 students received support. Career-related internships or fieldwork, Federal Work-Study, scholarships/grants, and unspecified assistantships available. Support available to part-time students. Financial award application deadline: 3/1; financial award applicants required to submit FAFSA. *Faculty research:* Statistics, actuarial mathematics, computer systems and engineering, computer programming techniques, operations research. *Unit head:* Dr. Robin Kalder, Chair, 860-832-2835, E-mail: kalderr@ccsu.edu. *Application contact:* Patricia Gardner, Associate Director of Graduate Studies, 860-832-2350, Fax: 860-832-2362.
Website: http://www.ccsu.edu/mathematics/

Central Michigan University, Central Michigan University Global Campus, Program in Education, Mount Pleasant, MI 48859. Offers college teaching (Graduate Certificate); community college (MA); curriculum and instruction (MA); educational technology (MA, DET); reading and literacy K-12 (MA); school principalship (MA), including charter school leadership; training and development (MA). *Accreditation:* TEAC. *Program availability:* Part-time, evening/weekend. *Entrance requirements:* For master's, minimum GPA of 2.7 in major. Additional exam requirements/recommendations for international students: Required—TOEFL. Electronic applications accepted.

Central Michigan University, Central Michigan University Global Campus, Program in Educational Leadership, Mount Pleasant, MI 48859. Offers K-12 leadership (Ed D). *Program availability:* Part-time, evening/weekend. *Entrance requirements:* Additional exam requirements/recommendations for international students: Required—TOEFL. Electronic applications accepted.

Central Michigan University, College of Graduate Studies, College of Education and Human Services, Department of Educational Leadership, Mount Pleasant, MI 48859. Offers educational leadership (Ed D), including educational technology (Ed D, Ed S), higher education leadership, K-12 curriculum, K-12 leadership; general educational administration (Ed S), including administrative leadership K-12, educational technology (Ed D, Ed S), higher education administration, instructional leadership K-12; school principalship (MA), including charter school leadership, site-based leadership; student affairs administration (MA); teacher leadership (MA). *Program availability:* Part-time, evening/weekend. *Degree requirements:* For master's and Ed S, thesis or alternative; for doctorate, thesis/dissertation. *Entrance requirements:* For doctorate, GRE or MAT, master's degree, minimum GPA of 3.5, 3 years of professional education experience. Electronic applications accepted. *Faculty research:* Elementary administration, secondary administration, student achievement, in-service training, internships in administration.

Central Washington University, School of Graduate Studies and Research, College of Education and Professional Studies, Department of Curriculum, Supervision, and Educational Leadership, Ellensburg, WA 98926. Offers higher education (M Ed); master teacher (M Ed). *Program availability:* Part-time. *Degree requirements:* For master's, comprehensive exam (for some programs), thesis or alternative. *Entrance requirements:* For master's, 1 year of contracted teaching experience. Additional exam requirements/recommendations for international students: Required—TOEFL (minimum score 550 paper-based; 79 iBT), IELTS (minimum score 6.5). Electronic applications accepted.

Chadron State College, School of Professional and Graduate Studies, Department of Education, Chadron, NE 69337. Offers business (MA Ed); community counseling (MA Ed); educational administration (MS Ed, Sp Ed); elementary education (MS Ed); history (MA Ed); language and literature (MA Ed); secondary administration (MS Ed); secondary education (MS Ed). *Accreditation:* NCATE. *Program availability:* Part-time, evening/weekend, online learning. *Degree requirements:* For master's, thesis optional. *Entrance requirements:* For master's, GRE General Test, GRE Writing Test, minimum GPA of 2.75 or 12 graduate hours at CSC with minimum GPA of 3.25. Additional exam requirements/recommendations for international students: Required—TOEFL. Electronic applications accepted. *Faculty research:* Rural education, technology, mental health.

Chaminade University of Honolulu, Graduate, Program in Education, Honolulu, HI 96816-1578. Offers child development (M Ed); early childhood education (Montessori) (MAT); early childhood education (PK-3) (MAT); educational leadership (M Ed); elementary education (MAT); instructional leadership (M Ed); Montessori (M Ed); secondary education (MAT); special education (MAT); teacher leader (M Ed). *Program availability:* Part-time, evening/weekend, 100% online, blended/hybrid learning. *Faculty:* 8 full-time (3 women), 11 part-time/adjunct (8 women). *Students:* 80 full-time (57 women), 100 part-time (77 women); includes 113 minority (6 Black or African American, non-Hispanic/Latino; 4 American Indian or Alaska Native, non-Hispanic/Latino; 45 Asian, non-Hispanic/Latino; 6 Hispanic/Latino; 50 Native Hawaiian or other Pacific Islander, non-Hispanic/Latino; 2 Two or more races, non-Hispanic/Latino), 2 international. Average age 35. 53 applicants, 92% accepted, 40 enrolled. In 2018, 92 master's awarded. *Degree requirements:* For master's, thesis or alternative. *Entrance requirements:* For master's, PRAXIS (for MAT), official transcripts, writing sample (for MAT). Additional exam requirements/recommendations for international students: Required—TOEFL (minimum score 550 paper-based; 79 iBT). *Application deadline:* Applications are processed on a rolling basis. Application fee: $40. Electronic applications accepted. *Expenses:* $780 per credit; $93 fee per online course. *Financial support:* Applicants required to submit FAFSA. *Unit head:* Dr. Dale Fryxell, Dean, 808-739-4652, Fax: 808-739-4607, E-mail: edu-office@chaminade.edu. *Application contact:* 808-739-7478, E-mail: gradserv@chaminade.edu.
Website: https://chaminade.edu/academics/education-behavioral-sciences/

Chapman University, Donna Ford Attallah College of Educational Studies, Orange, CA 92866. Offers counseling (MA), including school counseling (MA, Credential); curriculum and instruction (MA), including elementary education, secondary education; education (PhD), including cultural and curricular studies, disability studies, leadership studies, school psychology (PhD, Credential); educational psychology (MA); leadership development (MA); multiple subjects (Credential), including Spanish/English bilingual; pupil personnel services (Credential), including school counseling (MA, Credential),

school psychology (PhD, Credential); school psychology (Ed S); single subject (Credential); special education (MA, Credential), including mild/moderate (Credential), moderate/severe (Credential); teaching (MA), including elementary education, secondary education, secondary music education. *Accreditation:* TEAC. *Program availability:* Part-time, evening/weekend. Electronic applications accepted. *Expenses:* Contact institution.

Charleston Southern University, College of Education, Charleston, SC 29423-8087. Offers elementary administration and supervision (M Ed); elementary education (M Ed); secondary administration and supervision (M Ed). *Accreditation:* NCATE. *Program availability:* Part-time, evening/weekend. *Degree requirements:* For master's, thesis optional. *Entrance requirements:* For master's, GRE or MAT. Additional exam requirements/recommendations for international students: Required—TOEFL (minimum score 550 paper-based; 79 iBT). Electronic applications accepted. *Expenses:* Contact institution.

Chestnut Hill College, School of Graduate Studies, Department of Education, Program in Educational Leadership, Philadelphia, PA 19118-2693. Offers M Ed. *Program availability:* Part-time, evening/weekend. *Degree requirements:* For master's, thesis optional. *Entrance requirements:* For master's, PRAXIS I or proof of teaching certification, letters of recommendation, writing sample, 6 graduate credits with minimum B grade if undergraduate GPA less than 3.0. Additional exam requirements/recommendations for international students: Required—TOEFL (minimum score 500 paper-based), IELTS (minimum score 6.0), or TWE (minimum score 22). Electronic applications accepted. *Expenses:* Contact institution. *Faculty research:* Mentoring and induction program.

Cheyney University of Pennsylvania, Graduate Programs, Principal Certification Program (K-12), Cheyney, PA 19319. Offers Certificate. Program also offered on campus of West Chester University of Pennsylvania. *Entrance requirements:* For degree, five years of professional school experience.

Cheyney University of Pennsylvania, Graduate Programs, Program in Educational Leadership, Cheyney, PA 19319. Offers M Ed, Certificate. *Program availability:* Part-time, evening/weekend. *Degree requirements:* For master's, thesis or alternative; for Certificate, internship. *Entrance requirements:* For master's, minimum GPA of 3.0, writing sample. Electronic applications accepted. *Faculty research:* Teacher motivation, critical thinking.

Chicago State University, School of Graduate and Professional Studies, College of Education, Department of Educational Leadership, Curriculum and Foundations, Program in Educational Leadership, Chicago, IL 60628. Offers educational leadership (Ed D); higher education administration (MA); principal preparation (MA). *Accreditation:* NCATE. *Degree requirements:* For master's, comprehensive exam, thesis optional. *Entrance requirements:* For master's, minimum GPA of 2.75.

Christian Brothers University, School of Arts, Memphis, TN 38104-5581. Offers Catholic studies (MACS); educational leadership (MSEL); teacher-leadership (M Ed); teaching (MAT). *Program availability:* Part-time, evening/weekend. *Entrance requirements:* For master's, GRE, GMAT, PRAXIS II. *Expenses:* Contact institution.

The Citadel, The Military College of South Carolina, Citadel Graduate College, Zucker Family School of Education, Charleston, SC 29409. Offers elementary/secondary school administration and supervision (M Ed); elementary/secondary school counseling (M Ed); interdisciplinary STEM education (M Ed); literacy education (M Ed, Graduate Certificate); middle grades (MAT), including English, mathematics, science, social studies; physical education (grades K-12) (MAT); school superintendency (Ed S); secondary education (MAT), including biology, English, mathematics, social studies; student affairs (Graduate Certificate); student affairs and college counseling (M Ed). *Accreditation:* NCATE. *Program availability:* Part-time, evening/weekend, 100% online, blended/hybrid learning. *Degree requirements:* For master's, comprehensive exam (for some programs). *Entrance requirements:* For master's, GRE (minimum combined verbal and quantitative score of 290) or MAT (minimum score 396). Additional exam requirements/recommendations for international students: Required—TOEFL (minimum score 550 paper-based; 79 iBT). Electronic applications accepted. *Expenses:* Tuition, state resident: part-time $595 per credit hour. Tuition, nonresident: part-time $1020 per credit hour. *Required fees:* $90 per term.

City College of the City University of New York, Graduate School, School of Education, Department of Leadership and Special Education, New York, NY 10031-9198. Offers educational leadership (MS, AC); teacher of students with disabilities in adolescent education (MS Ed); teacher of students with disabilities in childhood education (MS Ed). *Degree requirements:* For master's, thesis, research paper. *Entrance requirements:* For master's, Liberal Arts and Sciences Test (LAST), Content Specialty Test (CST), interview; minimum GPA of 3.0 in major, 2.5 overall. Additional exam requirements/recommendations for international students: Required—TOEFL. *Faculty research:* Dynamics of organizational change, impact of laws on educational policy, leadership development in schools.

City University of Seattle, Graduate Division, Albright School of Education, Seattle, WA 98121. Offers administrator certification (Certificate); curriculum and instruction (M Ed); elementary education (MIT); guidance and counseling (M Ed); leadership (M Ed); reading and literacy (M Ed); school counseling (M Ed); special education (MIT); superintendent certification (Certificate). *Program availability:* Part-time, evening/weekend, online learning. *Degree requirements:* For master's, comprehensive exam (for some programs), thesis (for some programs). *Entrance requirements:* For master's, baccalaureate degree or equivalent from an accredited or otherwise recognized institution. Additional exam requirements/recommendations for international students: Required—TOEFL (minimum score 567 paper-based; 87 iBT); Recommended—IELTS. Electronic applications accepted. *Expenses:* Contact institution.

City University of Seattle, Graduate Division, Division of Doctoral Studies, Seattle, WA 98121. Offers leadership (Ed D). *Program availability:* Online learning. *Entrance requirements:* For doctorate, master's degree from an accredited or otherwise recognized institution; resume/curriculum vitae that demonstrates two or more years in a leadership capacity; interview with a member of the program faculty.

Claremont Graduate University, Graduate Programs, School of Educational Studies, Claremont, CA 91711-6160. Offers Africana education (Certificate); education and policy (MA, PhD); higher education/student affairs (MA, PhD); human development (MA, PhD); public school administration (MA, PhD); quantitative evaluation (MA, PhD); special education (MA, PhD); teacher education (MA); teaching and learning (MA, PhD); urban leadership (PhD); MBA/PhD. PhD program offered jointly with San Diego State University. *Program availability:* Part-time. Terminal master's awarded for partial completion of doctoral program. *Entrance requirements:* For master's and doctorate, GRE General Test. Additional exam requirements/recommendations for international students: Required—TOEFL (minimum score 75 iBT). Electronic applications accepted. *Faculty research:* Education administration, K-12 and higher education, multicultural education, education policy, diversity in higher education, faculty issues.

Clark Atlanta University, School of Education, Department of Educational Leadership, Atlanta, GA 30314. Offers MA, Ed D, Ed S. *Program availability:* Part-time, evening/weekend. *Degree requirements:* For master's and Ed S, comprehensive exam; for doctorate, comprehensive exam, thesis/dissertation. *Entrance requirements:* For master's, GRE General Test, minimum undergraduate GPA of 2.6; for doctorate and Ed S, GRE General Test, minimum graduate GPA of 3.0. Additional exam requirements/recommendations for international students: Required—TOEFL (minimum score 500 paper-based; 61 iBT). Electronic applications accepted.

Clarke University, Program in Education, Dubuque, IA 52001-3198. Offers instructional leadership (MAE). *Program availability:* Part-time, 100% online, blended/hybrid learning. *Degree requirements:* For master's, thesis optional. *Entrance requirements:* For master's, official transcripts documenting completion of undergraduate degree from accredited college or university, copy of teaching certificates and licenses, two recommendation forms, statement of goals and career plans, minimum GPA of 2.75. Additional exam requirements/recommendations for international students: Required—TOEFL (minimum score 550 paper-based; 80 iBT), IELTS (minimum score 6.5). Electronic applications accepted. *Expenses:* Contact institution.

Clarks Summit University, Online Master's Programs, South Abington Township, PA 18411. Offers Bible (MA); counseling (MA, MS); curriculum and instruction (M Ed); educational administration (M Ed); literature (MA); organizational leadership (MA). *Program availability:* Part-time, evening/weekend, online learning. *Entrance requirements:* Additional exam requirements/recommendations for international students: Required—TOEFL (minimum score 500 paper-based).

Clemson University, Graduate School, College of Education, Department of Educational and Organizational Leadership Development, Clemson, SC 29634. Offers administration and supervision (M Ed, Ed S); athletic leadership (MS, Certificate); education systems improvement science (Ed D); educational leadership (PhD), including higher education, P-12; human resource development (MHRD), including human resource development; leadership (Certificate); student affairs (M Ed). *Program availability:* Part-time, evening/weekend, 100% online. *Faculty:* 17 full-time (11 women). *Students:* 105 full-time (64 women), 265 part-time (170 women); includes 76 minority (61 Black or African American, non-Hispanic/Latino; 1 American Indian or Alaska Native, non-Hispanic/Latino; 3 Asian, non-Hispanic/Latino; 5 Hispanic/Latino; 6 Two or more races, non-Hispanic/Latino). Average age 32. 204 applicants, 83% accepted, 123 enrolled. In 2018, 93 master's, 17 doctorates, 28 other advanced degrees awarded. *Degree requirements:* For master's, thesis (for some programs); for doctorate, comprehensive exam, thesis/dissertation. *Entrance requirements:* For master's, doctorate, and other advanced degree, GRE General Test, unofficial transcripts, letters of recommendation. Additional exam requirements/recommendations for international students: Required—TOEFL (minimum score 80 paper-based; 80 iBT); Recommended—IELTS (minimum score 6.5), TSE (minimum score 54). *Application deadline:* For fall admission, 4/15 priority date for international students; for spring admission, 10/15 priority date for international students. Applications are processed on a rolling basis. Application fee: $80 ($90 for international students). Electronic applications accepted. *Expenses:* $5198 per semester full-time resident, $10123 per semester full-time non-resident, $556 per credit hour part-time resident, $1109 per credit hour part-time non-resident, online $770 per credit hour, $4938 doctoral programs resident, $10405 doctoral programs non-resident, $1144 full-time graduate assistant, other fees may apply per session. *Financial support:* In 2018–19, 30 students received support, including 8 fellowships with full and partial tuition reimbursements available (averaging $4,525 per year), 3 research assistantships with full and partial tuition reimbursements available (averaging $7,500 per year); career-related internships or fieldwork and unspecified assistantships also available. *Faculty research:* Leadership, ethics, policy development, performance improvement. *Total annual research expenditures:* $79,638. *Unit head:* Dr. Roy Jones, Interim Department Chair, 864-656-7915, E-mail: royj@clemson.edu. *Application contact:* Alison Search, Student Services Program Coordinator, 864-250-8880, E-mail: alisonp@clemson.edu.
Website: http://www.clemson.edu/education/departments/educational-organizational-leadership-development/index.html

Cleveland State University, College of Graduate Studies, College of Education and Human Services, Department of Counseling, Administration, Supervision and Adult Learning (CASAL), Cleveland, OH 44115. Offers adult learning and development (M Ed); counselor education (PhD); early childhood mental health counseling (Certificate); educational administration and supervision (M Ed). *Accreditation:* ACA (one or more programs are accredited). *Program availability:* Part-time, evening/weekend. *Faculty:* 15 full-time (8 women), 19 part-time/adjunct (10 women). *Students:* 134 full-time (118 women), 259 part-time (195 women); includes 131 minority (93 Black or African American, non-Hispanic/Latino; 2 American Indian or Alaska Native, non-Hispanic/Latino; 4 Asian, non-Hispanic/Latino; 23 Hispanic/Latino; 9 Two or more races, non-Hispanic/Latino), 11 international. Average age 33. 57 applicants, 93% accepted, 51 enrolled. In 2018, 119 master's, 1 other advanced degree awarded. *Degree requirements:* For master's, comprehensive exam (for some programs), thesis optional, internship. *Entrance requirements:* For master's, GRE General Test or MAT, letter of recommendation and minimum GPA of 2.75 (for counseling); 2 letters of recommendation and interviews (for organizational leadership). Additional exam requirements/recommendations for international students: Required—TOEFL (minimum score 550 paper-based; 78 iBT), IELTS (minimum score 6). *Application deadline:* For fall admission, 6/21 for domestic students, 5/15 for international students; for spring admission, 8/31 for domestic students, 11/1 for international students. Application fee: $40. Electronic applications accepted. *Expenses:* Tuition, state resident: full-time $7232.55; part-time $6676 per credit hour. Tuition, nonresident: full-time $12,375. *International tuition:* $18,914 full-time. *Required fees:* $80; $80 $40. Tuition and fees vary according to program. *Financial support:* In 2018–19, 19 students received support, including 10 research assistantships with tuition reimbursements available (averaging $11,882 per year), 5 teaching assistantships with tuition reimbursements available (averaging $11,882 per year); scholarships/grants and unspecified assistantships also available. Support available to part-time students. *Faculty research:* Education law, career development, bullying, psychopharmacology, counseling and spirituality. *Total annual research expenditures:* $225,821. *Unit head:* Dr. R. Elliott Ingersoll, Chair/Professor, 216-687-4582, Fax: 216-687-5378, E-mail: r.ingersoll@csuohio.edu. *Application contact:* Deborah L. Brown, Interim Assistant Director, Graduate Admissions, 216-523-7572, Fax: 216-687-5400, E-mail: d.l.brown@csuohio.edu.
Website: http://www.csuohio.edu/cehs/departments/CASAL/casal_dept.html

Cleveland State University, College of Graduate Studies, College of Education and Human Services, Program in Urban Education, Specialization in School Administration, Cleveland, OH 44115. Offers PhD. *Program availability:* Part-time. *Faculty:* 4 full-time (0 women). *Students:* 3 full-time (2 women), 8 part-time (2 women); includes 5 minority (4 Black or African American, non-Hispanic/Latino; 1 Hispanic/Latino). Average age 40. 10 applicants, 40% accepted. In 2018, 2 doctorates awarded. *Entrance requirements:* For doctorate, GRE General Test (minimum score of 297 for combined Verbal and Quantitative exams, 4.0 preferred for Analytical Writing), minimum graduate GPA of 3.25, curriculum vitae or resume, personal statement, 2 letters of recommendation. Additional exam requirements/recommendations for international students: Required—TOEFL (minimum score 550 paper-based; 78 iBT), IELTS (minimum score 6). Application fee: $40. Electronic applications accepted. *Expenses:* Tuition, state

resident: full-time $7232.55; part-time $6676 per credit hour. Tuition, nonresident: full-time $12,375. *International tuition:* $18,914 full-time. *Required fees:* $80; $80 $40. Tuition and fees vary according to program. *Financial support:* In 2018–19, 1 student received support. Teaching assistantships and tuition waivers available. Support available to part-time students. Financial award application deadline: 4/1; financial award applicants required to submit FAFSA. *Faculty research:* Theory and practice of management and leadership in educational, government, human resource development, and social service settings. *Unit head:* Dr. Graham Stead, Director, Doctoral Studies, 216-687-3828, E-mail: g.b.stead@csuohio.edu. *Application contact:* Rita M. Grabowski, Administrative Coordinator, 216-687-4697, Fax: 216-875-9697, E-mail: r.grabowski@csuohio.edu.
Website: http://www.csuohio.edu/cehs/casal/programs-1

Coastal Carolina University, Spadoni College of Education, Conway, SC 29528-6054. Offers education (MAT); educational leadership (M Ed, Ed S); English for speakers of other languages (Certificate); instructional technology (M Ed, Ed S); language, literacy and culture (M Ed); learning and teaching (M Ed); online teaching and training (Certificate); special education (M Ed). *Accreditation:* NCATE. *Program availability:* Part-time, evening/weekend, 100% online, blended/hybrid learning. *Degree requirements:* For master's and other advanced degree, comprehensive exam. *Entrance requirements:* For master's, GRE, GMAT, 2 letters of recommendation, evidence of teacher certification, official transcripts; for other advanced degree, official transcripts, 3 letters of reference, master's degree in related field with minimum overall cumulative GPA of 3.0. Additional exam requirements/recommendations for international students: Required—TOEFL (minimum score 550 paper-based; 79 iBT), IELTS (minimum score 6.5). Electronic applications accepted.

The College at Brockport, State University of New York, School of Education, Health, and Human Services, Department of Counselor Education, Brockport, NY 14420-2997. Offers college counseling (MS Ed, CAS); mental health counseling (MS, CAS); school counseling (MS Ed, CAS); school counselor supervision (CAS). *Accreditation:* ACA (one or more programs are accredited). *Program availability:* Part-time. *Faculty:* 7 full-time (3 women), 4 part-time/adjunct (all women). *Students:* 26 full-time (22 women), 104 part-time (73 women); includes 8 minority (7 Black or African American, non-Hispanic/Latino; 1 Hispanic/Latino). 91 applicants, 45% accepted, 25 enrolled. In 2018, 39 master's, 6 other advanced degrees awarded. *Degree requirements:* For master's, thesis, internship. *Entrance requirements:* For master's, group interview, letters of recommendation, written objectives, audio response; for CAS, master's degree, New York state school counselor certificate. Additional exam requirements/recommendations for international students: Required—TOEFL (minimum score 550 paper-based; 79 iBT), IELTS (minimum score 6.5). *Application deadline:* For fall admission, 2/1 priority date for domestic and international students; for spring admission, 9/1 priority date for domestic and international students; for summer admission, 2/1 priority date for domestic and international students. Application fee: $80. Electronic applications accepted. *Expenses:* Tuition, state resident: part-time $471 per credit. Tuition, nonresident: part-time $963 per credit. *Financial support:* In 2018–19, 1 fellowship with full tuition reimbursement (averaging $7,500 per year), 1 teaching assistantship with full tuition reimbursement (averaging $6,000 per year) were awarded; Federal Work-Study, scholarships/grants, and unspecified assistantships also available. Support available to part-time students. Financial award application deadline: 3/15; financial award applicants required to submit FAFSA. *Faculty research:* Gender and diversity issues; counseling outcomes; spirituality; school, college and mental health counseling; obesity. *Unit head:* Dr. Robert Dobmeier, Chair, 585-395-5090, Fax: 585-395-2366, E-mail: rdobmeie@brockport.edu. *Application contact:* Danielle A. Welch, Graduate Admissions Counselor, 585-395-5465, Fax: 585-395-2515.
Website: https://www.brockport.edu/academics/counselor_education/

The College at Brockport, State University of New York, School of Education, Health, and Human Services, Department of Educational Administration, Brockport, NY 14420-2997. Offers school building leader (CAS); school building leader/school district leader (CAS); school district business leader (CAS); school district leader (CAS); teacher leadership (Graduate Certificate). *Program availability:* Part-time. *Faculty:* 1 full-time (0 women), 10 part-time/adjunct (6 women). *Students:* 123 part-time (89 women); includes 11 minority (5 Black or African American, non-Hispanic/Latino; 6 Hispanic/Latino). 48 applicants, 83% accepted, 31 enrolled. In 2018, 63 CASs awarded. *Degree requirements:* For other advanced degree, thesis or alternative, internship. *Entrance requirements:* For degree, minimum GPA of 3.0, letter of recommendation. Additional exam requirements/recommendations for international students: Required—TOEFL (minimum score 550 paper-based; 79 iBT), IELTS (minimum score 6.5). *Application deadline:* For fall admission, 7/15 priority date for domestic and international students; for spring admission, 11/15 priority date for domestic and international students. Application fee: $80. Electronic applications accepted. *Expenses:* Tuition, state resident: part-time $471 per credit. Tuition, nonresident: part-time $963 per credit. *Financial support:* Federal Work-Study, scholarships/grants, and unspecified assistantships available. Support available to part-time students. Financial award application deadline: 3/15; financial award applicants required to submit FAFSA. *Faculty research:* Superintendency, budgeting, school business administration, leadership, special education administration. *Unit head:* Jeffrey Linn, Graduate Director, 585-395-2661, Fax: 585-395-2172, E-mail: jlinn@brockport.edu. *Application contact:* Danielle A. Welch, Graduate Admissions Counselor, 585-395-2525, Fax: 585-395-2515.
Website: https://www.brockport.edu/academics/educational_administration/

The College of New Jersey, Office of Graduate and Advancing Education, School of Education, Department of Educational Administration and Secondary Education, Program in Educational Leadership, Ewing, NJ 08628. Offers M Ed, Certificate. *Program availability:* Part-time, evening/weekend. *Degree requirements:* For master's, comprehensive exam. *Entrance requirements:* For master's, GRE, minimum GPA of 3.0 in field or 2.75 overall; for Certificate, previous master's degree or higher. Additional exam requirements/recommendations for international students: Required—TOEFL. Electronic applications accepted.

The College of New Rochelle, Graduate School, Division of Education, Program in Educational Leadership, New Rochelle, NY 10805-2308. Offers school building leader (MS, Advanced Certificate); school district leader (MS, Advanced Diploma). *Degree requirements:* For master's, internship. *Entrance requirements:* For master's, interview, minimum GPA of 3.0 in field, 2.7 overall, minimum 3 years teaching or education administration experience.

College of Saint Elizabeth, Department of Educational Leadership, Morristown, NJ 07960-6989. Offers educational leadership (MA, Ed D), including higher education (Ed D), Pre-K to 12th grade (Ed D); supervisor (Certificate). *Program availability:* Part-time. *Degree requirements:* For master's, thesis or alternative; for doctorate, thesis/dissertation. *Entrance requirements:* For master's, baccalaureate degree with minimum GPA of 2.75, standard teaching certificate, three years of exemplary certified teaching experience, writing sample, two letters of recommendation from school(s) of employment, personal interview (for educational leadership); for doctorate, MA in educational leadership or related field; leadership experience including certification as principal and/or supervisor; letter of recommendation from college/university professor attesting to candidate's ability to perform a high level of academic work in the program; for Certificate, MA in education; certification; baccalaureate degree with minimum GPA of 2.75; personal written statement; two letters of recommendation; official transcripts from all colleges attended. Additional exam requirements/recommendations for international students: Required—TOEFL (minimum score 550 paper-based; 79 iBT), IELTS (minimum score 6.5). Electronic applications accepted. Application fee is waived when completed online. *Expenses:* Contact institution.

College of Saint Mary, Program in Education, Omaha, NE 68106. Offers assessment leadership (MSE); English as a second language (MSE). *Program availability:* Part-time. *Entrance requirements:* For master's, technology competency test or equivalent, minimum cumulative GPA of 3.0, teaching certificate, 2 letters of reference, resume.

The College of Saint Rose, Graduate Studies, Thelma P. Lally School of Education, Programs in Educational Leadership and Administration, Albany, NY 12203-1419. Offers educational leadership (MS Ed); school building leader (Certificate); school district business leader (Certificate); school district leader (Certificate). *Program availability:* Part-time, evening/weekend. *Students:* 24 full-time (21 women), 854 part-time (672 women); includes 369 minority (150 Black or African American, non-Hispanic/Latino; 1 American Indian or Alaska Native, non-Hispanic/Latino; 27 Asian, non-Hispanic/Latino; 107 Hispanic/Latino; 84 Two or more races, non-Hispanic/Latino), 1 international. Average age 37. 397 applicants, 71% accepted, 251 enrolled. In 2018, 101 master's, 733 Certificates awarded. *Degree requirements:* For master's, comprehensive exam or thesis. *Entrance requirements:* For master's, minimum undergraduate GPA of 3.0, timed writing sample, interview, permanent certification or 3 years of teaching experience. Additional exam requirements/recommendations for international students: Required—TOEFL (minimum score 550 paper-based; 80 iBT), IELTS (minimum score 6), PTE (minimum score 56). *Application deadline:* For fall admission, 4/1 priority date for domestic and international students; for spring admission, 10/15 priority date for domestic and international students; for summer admission, 3/15 priority date for domestic students, 3/14 priority date for international students. Applications are processed on a rolling basis. Application fee: $40. Electronic applications accepted. *Expenses: Tuition:* Full-time $14,382; part-time $799 per credit hour. *Required fees:* $924; $408 per credit. $286. *Financial support:* Career-related internships or fieldwork, scholarships/grants, tuition waivers (partial), and unspecified assistantships available. Support available to part-time students. Financial award application deadline: 4/15. *Application contact:* Cris Murray, Assistant Vice President for Graduate Recruitment and Enrollment, 518-485-3390, Fax: 518-458-5479, E-mail: grad@strose.edu.
Website: https://www.strose.edu/educational-leadership-and-administration/

The College of Saint Rose, Graduate Studies, Thelma P. Lally School of Education, Programs in Higher Education Leadership and Administration, Albany, NY 12203-1419. Offers MS Ed, Advanced Certificate. *Program availability:* Part-time, evening/weekend. *Students:* 3 full-time (1 woman), 10 part-time (5 women); includes 2 minority (1 Hispanic/Latino; 1 Two or more races, non-Hispanic/Latino), 2 international. Average age 30. 6 applicants, 67% accepted, 2 enrolled. In 2018, 6 master's awarded. *Degree requirements:* For master's, capstone seminar. *Entrance requirements:* For master's, resume, letter of recommendation. Additional exam requirements/recommendations for international students: Required—TOEFL (minimum score 550 paper-based; 80 iBT), IELTS (minimum score 6), PTE (minimum score 56). *Application deadline:* For fall admission, 4/1 priority date for domestic and international students; for spring admission, 10/15 priority date for domestic and international students; for summer admission, 3/15 priority date for domestic and international students. Applications are processed on a rolling basis. Application fee: $40. Electronic applications accepted. *Expenses: Tuition:* Full-time $14,382; part-time $799 per credit hour. *Required fees:* $924; $408 per credit. $286. *Financial support:* Scholarships/grants, tuition waivers (partial), and unspecified assistantships available. Support available to part-time students. Financial award application deadline: 4/15. *Unit head:* Dr. Margaret McLane, Institutional Strategist, 518-485-3334, E-mail: mclanem@strose.edu. *Application contact:* Daniel Gallagher, Assistant Vice President for Graduate Recruitment and Enrollment, 518-454-5136, Fax: 518-458-5479, E-mail: grad@strose.edu.
Website: https://www.strose.edu/higher-education-leadership-and-administration/

College of Staten Island of the City University of New York, Graduate Programs, School of Education, Program in Leadership in Education, Staten Island, NY 10314-6600. Offers leadership in education (Post-Master's Certificate), including school building leader/school district leader, school district leader. *Program availability:* Part-time, evening/weekend. *Students:* 37. 39 applicants, 72% accepted, 22 enrolled. In 2018, 19 Post-Master's Certificates awarded. *Degree requirements:* For Post-Master's Certificate, 30 credits: 24 credits in supervision, administration, curriculum, policy analysis, human relations; theory, research, and practice in educational leadership. *Entrance requirements:* For degree, master's degree with minimum GPA of 3.0, 3 professional recommendations, letter of intent, interview with faculty; evidence of 4 years teaching experience (school building leader and school district leader track); 3 years full-time teaching or pupil personnel services experiences (school district leader track). *Application deadline:* For fall admission, 4/25 for domestic students, 4/25 priority date for international students. Applications are processed on a rolling basis. Application fee: $75. Electronic applications accepted. *Expenses: Tuition, area resident:* Full-time $10,770; part-time $455 per credit. Tuition, state resident: full-time $10,770; part-time $455 per credit. Tuition, nonresident: full-time $19,920; part-time $830 per credit. *International tuition:* $19,920 full-time. *Required fees:* $559.20; $181.10 per semester. Tuition and fees vary according to program. *Faculty research:* Supervision of instruction, school-community partnerships, education reform, history of education, organizational theory. *Unit head:* Dr. Susan Sullivan, Program Coordinator, 718-982-3744, E-mail: susan.sullivan@csi.cuny.edu. *Application contact:* Sasha Spence, Associate Director for Graduate Admissions, 718-982-2019, Fax: 718-982-2500, E-mail: sasha.spence@csi.cuny.edu.
Website: https://www.csi.cuny.edu/sites/default/files/pdf/admissions/grad/pdf/PostMasters%20in%20Leadership%20Fact%20Sheet.pdf

The College of William and Mary, School of Education, Program in Education Policy, Planning, and Leadership, Williamsburg, VA 23187-8795. Offers M Ed, Ed D, PhD. *Accreditation:* NCATE. *Program availability:* Part-time, evening/weekend. *Faculty:* 17 full-time (7 women), 6 part-time/adjunct (4 women). *Students:* 59 full-time (45 women), 174 part-time (116 women); includes 70 minority (39 Black or African American, non-Hispanic/Latino; 4 Asian, non-Hispanic/Latino; 19 Hispanic/Latino; 8 Two or more races, non-Hispanic/Latino), 5 international. Average age 40. 114 applicants, 71% accepted, 58 enrolled. In 2018, 36 master's, 34 doctorates awarded. *Degree requirements:* For doctorate, comprehensive exam, thesis/dissertation. *Entrance requirements:* For master's, GRE or MAT, minimum GPA of 2.5; for doctorate, GRE or MAT, minimum GPA of 3.0. Additional exam requirements/recommendations for international students: Required—TOEFL (minimum score 100 iBT), IELTS (minimum score 7). *Application deadline:* For fall admission, 1/15 for domestic and international students. Application fee: $50. Electronic applications accepted. *Expenses:* Contact institution. *Financial support:* In 2018–19, 52 students received support, including 1 fellowship (averaging $20,000 per year), 43 research assistantships with full tuition reimbursements available (averaging $20,151 per year); scholarships/grants and unspecified assistantships also available. Support available to part-time students. Financial award application deadline: 1/15; financial award applicants required to submit FAFSA. *Faculty research:* Higher

education policy, evaluation of teachers, program evaluation, civil rights and higher education, program evaluation. *Unit head:* Dr. Pamela Eddy, Department Chair, 757-221-2349, E-mail: pamela.eddy@wm.edu. *Application contact:* Dorothy Smith Osborne, Assistant Dean for Academic Programs and Student Services, 757-221-2317, E-mail: dsosbo@wm.edu.
Website: http://education.wm.edu

Colorado Mesa University, Center for Teacher Education, Grand Junction, CO 81501-3122. Offers educational leadership (MAEd); English for speakers of other languages (MAEd); exceptional learner/special education (MAEd); teacher education (Graduate Certificate); teacher leader (MAEd). *Accreditation:* NCATE. *Program availability:* Part-time. *Degree requirements:* For master's, comprehensive exam (for some programs), capstone presentation. *Entrance requirements:* For master's, 3 professional letters of recommendation, Colorado teaching license, minimum baccalaureate GPA of 3.0; for Graduate Certificate, minimum baccalaureate GPA of 3.0. Additional exam requirements/recommendations for international students: Required—TOEFL (minimum score 550 paper-based). Electronic applications accepted. *Expenses:* Contact institution. *Faculty research:* K-8 STEM instruction, special education inclusion, elementary math literacy, secondary literacy, elementary/early childhood education literacy.

Colorado State University, College of Health and Human Sciences, School of Education, Fort Collins, CO 80523-1588. Offers adult education and training (M Ed); counseling and career development (MA); education and human resources (M Ed); education, equity, and transformation (PhD); higher education leadership (PhD); organizational learning, performance, and change (M Ed, PhD); student affairs in higher education (MS). *Accreditation:* ACA; TEAC. *Program availability:* Part-time, online only, 100% online, blended/hybrid learning. *Degree requirements:* For master's, thesis optional, professional portfolio or capstone project; for doctorate, comprehensive exam, thesis/dissertation. *Entrance requirements:* For master's, bachelor's degree; minimum GPA of 3.0 in last degree earned; for doctorate, GRE; GRE or GMAT (for organizational learning, performance and change only), master's degree; minimum GPA of 3.0 in last degree earned. Additional exam requirements/recommendations for international students: Required—TOEFL (minimum score 550 paper-based; 80 iBT), IELTS (minimum score 6.5), PTE (minimum score 58). Electronic applications accepted. *Expenses:* Contact institution. *Faculty research:* Diversity, equity, and inclusion; STEM education; higher education; occupational learning, performance and change; teacher education.

Colorado State University–Global Campus, Graduate Programs, Greenwood Village, CO 80111. Offers criminal justice and law enforcement administration (MS); education leadership (MS); finance (MS); healthcare administration and management (MS); human resource management (MHRM); information technology management (MITM); international management (MS); management (MS); organizational leadership (MS); professional accounting (MPA); project management (MS); teaching and learning (MS). *Accreditation:* ACBSP. *Program availability:* Online learning.

Columbia College, Graduate Programs, Education Division, Columbia, SC 29203-5998. Offers divergent learning (M Ed); higher education administration (M Ed). *Accreditation:* NCATE. *Program availability:* Part-time, evening/weekend, online learning. *Degree requirements:* For master's, thesis. *Entrance requirements:* For master's, GRE General Test, MAT, 2 recommendations, current South Carolina teaching certificate, minimum GPA of 3.2. Electronic applications accepted. *Expenses:* Contact institution.

Columbia College, Master of Education in Educational Leadership Program, Columbia, MO 65216-0002. Offers M Ed. *Program availability:* Part-time, evening/weekend, 100% online, blended/hybrid learning. *Faculty:* 5 full-time (3 women), 18 part-time/adjunct (12 women). *Students:* 5 full-time (all women), 36 part-time (27 women); includes 8 minority (5 Black or African American, non-Hispanic/Latino; 2 Hispanic/Latino; 1 Two or more races, non-Hispanic/Latino). Average age 38. 29 applicants, 90% accepted, 17 enrolled. In 2018, 25 master's awarded. *Entrance requirements:* For master's, bachelor degree, 3.0 or higher GPA, goal statement, resume, application, valid teaching certificate. Additional exam requirements/recommendations for international students: Required—TOEFL (minimum score 550 paper-based; 79 iBT). *Application deadline:* For fall admission, 8/9 priority date for domestic and international students; for spring admission, 12/27 priority date for domestic and international students. Applications are processed on a rolling basis. Application fee: $0. Electronic applications accepted. *Expenses:* 17640 all fees are included with tuition. *Financial support:* In 2018–19, 30 students received support. Scholarships/grants, tuition waivers (full and partial), and unspecified assistantships available. Financial award application deadline: 3/1; financial award applicants required to submit FAFSA. *Unit head:* Dr. Lisa Ford-Brown, Dean of the School of Humanities, Arts and Social Sciences, 573-875-7570, E-mail: labrown@ccis.edu. *Application contact:* Stephanie Johnson, Associate Vice President for Recruiting & Admissions Division, 573-875-7352, Fax: 573-875-7506, E-mail: sjohnson@ccis.edu.

Columbia International University, Columbia Graduate School, Columbia, SC 29203. Offers Bible teaching (MABT); counseling (MACN); early childhood and elementary education (MAT); educational administration (M Ed); educational leadership (PhD); instruction and learning (M Ed); teaching English as a foreign language (Certificate); teaching English as a foreign language and intercultural studies (MATF). *Program availability:* Part-time, evening/weekend, online learning. *Degree requirements:* For master's, internships, professional project. *Entrance requirements:* For master's, MAT; GRE (for some programs), minimum GPA of 2.7. Additional exam requirements/recommendations for international students: Required—TOEFL. Electronic applications accepted.

Columbus State University, Graduate Studies, College of Education and Health Professions, Department of Counseling, Foundations, and Leadership, Columbus, GA 31907-5645. Offers clinical mental health counseling (MS); curriculum and leadership (Ed D), including curriculum, educational leadership, higher education (M Ed, Ed D); educational leadership (M Ed, Ed S), including higher education (M Ed, Ed D); school counseling (M Ed, Ed S). *Accreditation:* ACA; NCATE. *Program availability:* Part-time, evening/weekend, 100% online, blended/hybrid learning. *Faculty:* 13 full-time (5 women), 17 part-time/adjunct (8 women). *Students:* 66 full-time (50 women), 209 part-time (158 women); includes 145 minority (124 Black or African American, non-Hispanic/Latino; 5 Asian, non-Hispanic/Latino; 10 Hispanic/Latino; 6 Two or more races, non-Hispanic/Latino), 1 international. Average age 39. 168 applicants, 48% accepted, 54 enrolled. In 2018, 44 master's, 25 doctorates, 129 other advanced degrees awarded. *Degree requirements:* For master's, thesis, exit exam; for doctorate, comprehensive exam, thesis/dissertation; for Ed S, thesis or alternative. *Entrance requirements:* For master's, GRE General Test, minimum undergraduate GPA of 2.75; for doctorate, GRE General Test, minimum graduate GPA of 3.5, four years of professional service; for Ed S, GRE General Test, minimum undergraduate GPA of 2.75, graduate 3.0. Additional exam requirements/recommendations for international students: Required—TOEFL (minimum score 550 paper-based; 79 iBT). *Application deadline:* For fall admission, 6/30 for domestic and international students; for spring admission, 11/1 for domestic and international students; for summer admission, 3/1 for domestic and international students. Applications are processed on a rolling basis. Application fee:

$50. Electronic applications accepted. *Expenses: Tuition, area resident:* Full-time $4924; part-time $618 per credit hour. Tuition, state resident: full-time $4924; part-time $618 per credit hour. Tuition, nonresident: full-time $19,218; part-time $2403 per credit hour. *International tuition:* $19,218 full-time. *Required fees:* $1870; $802. Tuition and fees vary according to course load, degree level and program. *Financial support:* In 2018–19, 30 students received support, including 6 research assistantships with partial tuition reimbursements available (averaging $3,000 per year); career-related internships or fieldwork, Federal Work-Study, institutionally sponsored loans, scholarships/grants, tuition waivers (partial), and unspecified assistantships also available. Support available to part-time students. Financial award application deadline: 5/1; financial award applicants required to submit FAFSA. *Unit head:* Dr. Tom Hackett, Department Chair, 706-507-8968, Fax: 706-569-3134, E-mail: hackett_paul@columbusstate.edu. *Application contact:* Catrina Smith-Edmond, Assistant Director for Graduate and Global Admission, 706-507-8824, Fax: 706-568-5091, E-mail: smithedmond_catrina@columbusstate.edu.
Website: http://cfl.columbusstate.edu/

Columbus State University, Graduate Studies, College of Education and Health Professions, Department of Teacher Education, Columbus, GA 31907-5645. Offers curriculum and instruction in accomplished teaching (M Ed); early childhood education (M Ed, MAT, Ed S); middle grades education (M Ed, MAT, Ed S); secondary education (M Ed, MAT, Ed S), including biology (MAT), chemistry (MAT), earth and space science (MAT), English/language arts, general science (M Ed), history (MAT), mathematics, science (Ed S), social science (M Ed, Ed S); special education (M Ed, MAT, Ed S), including general curriculum (M Ed, MAT); teacher leadership (M Ed). *Accreditation:* NCATE. *Program availability:* Part-time, evening/weekend, 100% online, blended/hybrid learning. *Faculty:* 20 full-time (12 women), 20 part-time/adjunct (15 women). *Students:* 110 full-time (84 women), 143 part-time (115 women); includes 105 minority (96 Black or African American, non-Hispanic/Latino; 4 Hispanic/Latino; 5 Two or more races, non-Hispanic/Latino). Average age 33. 147 applicants, 56% accepted, 62 enrolled. In 2018, 112 master's, 11 other advanced degrees awarded. *Degree requirements:* For Ed S, thesis or alternative. *Entrance requirements:* For master's, GRE General Test, minimum undergraduate GPA of 2.75; for Ed S, GRE General Test, minimum undergraduate GPA of 2.75, graduate 3.0. Additional exam requirements/recommendations for international students: Required—TOEFL (minimum score 550 paper-based; 79 iBT). *Application deadline:* For fall admission, 6/30 for domestic students, 5/1 for international students; for spring admission, 11/1 for domestic and international students; for summer admission, 3/1 for domestic and international students. Applications are processed on a rolling basis. Application fee: $50. Electronic applications accepted. *Expenses: Tuition, area resident:* Full-time $4924; part-time $618 per credit hour. Tuition, state resident: full-time $4924; part-time $618 per credit hour. Tuition, nonresident: full-time $19,218; part-time $2403 per credit hour. *International tuition:* $19,218 full-time. *Required fees:* $1870; $802. Tuition and fees vary according to course load, degree level and program. *Financial support:* In 2018–19, 29 students received support, including 7 research assistantships with partial tuition reimbursements available (averaging $3,000 per year); career-related internships or fieldwork, Federal Work-Study, institutionally sponsored loans, scholarships/grants, tuition waivers (partial), and unspecified assistantships also available. Support available to part-time students. Financial award application deadline: 5/1; financial award applicants required to submit FAFSA. *Unit head:* Dr. Jan Burcham, Department Chair, 706-507-8519, Fax: 706-568-3134, E-mail: burcham_jan@columbusstate.edu. *Application contact:* Catrina Smith-Edmond, Assistant Director for Graduate and Global Admission, 706-507-8824, Fax: 706-568-5091, E-mail: smithedmond_catrina@columbusstate.edu.
Website: http://te.columbusstate.edu/

Concordia University, College of Education, Portland, OR 97211-6099. Offers administrative leadership (Ed D); career and technical education (M Ed); curriculum and instruction (M Ed), including adolescent literacy, early childhood education, educational technology leadership, English for speakers of other languages, environmental education, health and physical education, mathematics, methods and curriculum, reading interventionist, science, social studies, STEAM education, teacher leadership, the inclusive classroom, trauma and resilience in educational settings; educational administration (M Ed); educational leadership (M Ed); elementary education (MAT); higher education (Ed D); instructional leadership (Ed D); professional leadership, inquiry, and transformation (Ed D); secondary education (MAT); transformational leadership (Ed D). *Program availability:* Part-time, online learning. *Degree requirements:* For master's, comprehensive exam, work samples/portfolio. *Entrance requirements:* For master's, California Basic Educational Skills Test or PRAXIS I, minimum undergraduate GPA of 2.8, graduate 3.0; 2 letters of recommendation. Additional exam requirements/recommendations for international students: Required—TOEFL (minimum score 525 paper-based). Electronic applications accepted. *Faculty research:* Learner-centered classroom, brain-based learning, future of online learning.

Concordia University Ann Arbor, Graduate Programs, Ann Arbor, MI 48105-2797. Offers curriculum and instruction (MS); educational leadership (MS); organizational leadership and administration (MS). *Program availability:* Part-time, evening/weekend. *Degree requirements:* For master's, thesis. *Entrance requirements:* Additional exam requirements/recommendations for international students: Required—TOEFL (minimum score 80 iBT); Recommended—IELTS (minimum score 6.5). Electronic applications accepted.

Concordia University Chicago, College of Graduate Studies, Program in Educational Technology, River Forest, IL 60305-1499. Offers curriculum and instruction (MA); leadership (MA). *Program availability:* Online learning.

Concordia University Chicago, College of Graduate Studies, Program in Leadership, River Forest, IL 60305-1499. Offers educational administration (MA); leadership (Ed D, PhD); teacher leadership (MA). *Accreditation:* NCATE. *Program availability:* Part-time, evening/weekend. *Degree requirements:* For master's, comprehensive exam, thesis optional. *Entrance requirements:* For master's, minimum GPA of 2.9. Additional exam requirements/recommendations for international students: Required—TOEFL (minimum score 550 paper-based). Electronic applications accepted. *Faculty research:* Effectiveness of urban Lutheran schools in impacting children's faith development, effectiveness of centers for urban ministries in supporting urban ministry and teaching science.

Concordia University Irvine, School of Education, Irvine, CA 92612-3299. Offers curriculum and instruction (MA); education and preliminary teaching credential (M Ed); educational administration and preliminary administrative services credential (MA); educational technology (MA); school counseling with pupil personnel services credential (MA). *Program availability:* Part-time, evening/weekend, online learning. *Degree requirements:* For master's, action research project. *Entrance requirements:* For master's, California Basic Educational Skills Test, California Subject Examinations for Teachers (M Ed and MA in educational administration and preliminary administrative services credential), official college transcript(s), signed statement of intent, two references, copy of credential. Additional exam requirements/recommendations for international students: Required—TOEFL. Electronic applications accepted. *Expenses:* Contact institution.

Educational Leadership and Administration

Concordia University, Nebraska, Graduate Programs in Education, Program in Educational Administration, Seward, NE 68434. Offers elementary and secondary education (M Ed); elementary education (M Ed); secondary education (M Ed). *Accreditation:* NCATE. *Program availability:* Part-time. *Degree requirements:* For master's, thesis or alternative. *Entrance requirements:* For master's, GRE, MAT, or NTE, BS in education or equivalent, minimum GPA of 3.0.

Concordia University, St. Paul, College of Education, St. Paul, MN 55104-5494. Offers classroom instruction (MA Ed), including K-12 reading; differentiated instruction (MA Ed); early childhood education (MA Ed); education (Ed D); educational leadership (MA Ed); educational technology (MA Ed, Certificate); K-12 principal licensure (Ed S); special education (MA Ed), including autism spectrum disorder, emotional and behavioral disorders, learning disabilities; superintendent (Ed S); teaching (MAT). *Accreditation:* NCATE. *Program availability:* Part-time, evening/weekend, 100% online, blended/hybrid learning. *Faculty:* 13 full-time (9 women), 82 part-time/adjunct (51 women). *Students:* 979 full-time (748 women), 40 part-time (28 women); includes 124 minority (49 Black or African American, non-Hispanic/Latino; 6 American Indian or Alaska Native, non-Hispanic/Latino; 34 Asian, non-Hispanic/Latino; 22 Hispanic/Latino; 1 Native Hawaiian or other Pacific Islander, non-Hispanic/Latino; 12 Two or more races, non-Hispanic/Latino), 11 international. Average age 34. 423 applicants, 99% accepted, 335 enrolled. In 2018, 358 master's, 3 doctorates, 119 other advanced degrees awarded. *Degree requirements:* For master's, thesis (for some programs); for doctorate, thesis/dissertation, capstone projects; for other advanced degree, e-folio review of competencies. *Entrance requirements:* For master's, official transcripts from regionally-accredited institution stating the conferral of a bachelor's degree with minimum cumulative GPA of 3.0; personal statement; professional resume; practitioner in field through work or volunteerism; resume; for doctorate, minimum master's or specialist degree GPA of 3.25; transcript; writing sample; three letters of recommendation; current resume; on-campus interview; for other advanced degree, minimum master's or specialist degree GPA of 3.25; transcript; statement covering employment history and long-term academic and professional goals; two letters of recommendation; interview with program director. Additional exam requirements/recommendations for international students: Recommended—TOEFL (minimum score 547 paper-based; 78 iBT), IELTS (minimum score 6). *Application deadline:* For fall admission, 8/1 for domestic and international students; for spring admission, 12/1 for domestic and international students; for summer admission, 5/1 for domestic and international students. Applications are processed on a rolling basis. Application fee: $0. Electronic applications accepted. *Expenses:* $395 per credit for 30 credits (for MA programs), $440 per credit for 42 credits (for MAT), $415 per credit for 30 credits (for EdS), $615 per credit for 64 credits (for EdD). *Financial support:* In 2018–19, 163 students received support. Federal Work-Study, scholarships/grants, and unspecified assistantships available. Financial award applicants required to submit FAFSA. *Faculty research:* School design for innovative learning practices, equine-assisted instruction, best practices for leadership in early childhood education, mental health needs in K-12 focusing on children of incarcerated parents, competency-based education. *Unit head:* Lonn Maly, Dean, 651-641-8203, E-mail: maly@csp.edu. *Application contact:* Amber Faletti, Director of Enrollment Management, 651-641-8838, Fax: 651-603-6320, E-mail: faletti@csp.edu.

Concordia University Wisconsin, Graduate Programs, School of Education, Program in Educational Administration, Mequon, WI 53097-2402. Offers MS Ed. *Program availability:* Part-time, evening/weekend, online learning. *Degree requirements:* For master's, comprehensive exam, thesis or alternative. *Entrance requirements:* For master's, minimum GPA of 3.0. Additional exam requirements/recommendations for international students: Required—TOEFL.

Concord University, Graduate Studies, Athens, WV 24712-1000. Offers educational leadership and supervision (M Ed); health promotion (MA); reading specialist (M Ed); social work (MSW); special education (M Ed); teaching (MAT). *Program availability:* Part-time, evening/weekend, 100% online. *Degree requirements:* For master's, thesis (for some programs). *Entrance requirements:* For master's, GRE or MAT, baccalaureate degree with minimum GPA of 2.5 from regionally-accredited institution; teaching license; 2 letters of recommendation; completed disposition assessment form. Electronic applications accepted.

Converse College, Education Specialist Program, Spartanburg, SC 29302. Offers administration and leadership (Ed S); administration and supervision (Ed S); literacy (Ed S). *Accreditation:* AAMFT/COAMFTE. *Program availability:* Part-time. *Entrance requirements:* For degree, GRE or MAT (marriage and family therapy), minimum GPA of 3.0. Electronic applications accepted.

Converse College, Program in Educational Administration and Supervision, Spartanburg, SC 29302. Offers administration and supervision (M Ed). *Degree requirements:* For master's, capstone paper. *Entrance requirements:* For master's, NTE, minimum GPA of 2.75, nomination by school district, 3 recommendations. Electronic applications accepted.

Creighton University, Graduate School, College of Arts and Sciences, Department of Education, Program in Educational Leadership, Omaha, NE 68178-0001. Offers MS. *Program availability:* Part-time, online only, 100% online, blended/hybrid learning. *Faculty:* 10 full-time (5 women). *Students:* 108 part-time (75 women); includes 4 minority (1 Black or African American, non-Hispanic/Latino; 2 Asian, non-Hispanic/Latino; 1 Hispanic/Latino), 2 international. Average age 36. In 2018, 52 master's awarded. *Degree requirements:* For master's, portfolio. *Entrance requirements:* For master's, 2 writing samples, 3 letters of recommendation. Additional exam requirements/recommendations for international students: Required—TOEFL (minimum score 90 iBT). *Application deadline:* For fall admission, 7/1 for domestic students, 3/1 for international students; for winter admission, 10/1 for domestic students, 5/1 for international students; for spring admission, 3/1 for domestic students, 10/1 for international students. Applications are processed on a rolling basis. Application fee: $50. Electronic applications accepted. *Financial support:* Scholarships/grants and tuition waivers (partial) available. Support available to part-time students. Financial award application deadline: 5/1; financial award applicants required to submit FAFSA. *Faculty research:* Catholic school leadership, early childhood education. *Unit head:* Dr. Ann Mausbach, Assistant Professor of Education, 402-280-2889, E-mail: AnnMausbach@creighton.edu. *Application contact:* Lindsay Johnson, Director of Graduate and Adult Recruitment, 402-280-2703, Fax: 402-280-2423, E-mail: gradschool@creighton.edu.

Creighton University, Graduate School, Department of Interdisciplinary Studies, Interdisciplinary Ed D Program in Leadership, Omaha, NE 68178-0001. Offers Ed D. *Program availability:* Part-time, online only, blended/hybrid learning. *Degree requirements:* For doctorate, thesis/dissertation. *Entrance requirements:* For doctorate, master's or equivalent professional degree, current resume, official transcripts, three recommendations. Additional exam requirements/recommendations for international students: Required—TOEFL (minimum score 90 iBT). Electronic applications accepted. *Expenses:* Contact institution.

Dakota Wesleyan University, Program in Education, Mitchell, SD 57301. Offers curriculum and instruction (MA Ed); educational policy and administration (MA Ed); preK-12 principal certification (MA Ed); secondary certification (MA Ed). *Program availability:* Part-time, evening/weekend, online only, 100% online. *Faculty:* 5 part-time/adjunct (2 women). *Students:* 20 full-time (6 women), 4 part-time (1 woman); includes 8 minority (4 Black or African American, non-Hispanic/Latino; 3 Hispanic/Latino; 1 Two or more races, non-Hispanic/Latino). Average age 26. 12 applicants, 83% accepted, 8 enrolled. In 2018, 13 master's awarded. *Degree requirements:* For master's, comprehensive exam, thesis optional, electronic portfolio. *Entrance requirements:* For master's, minimum GPA of 2.7, elementary statistics course, statement of purpose, official transcripts, resume, three letters of recommendation. Additional exam requirements/recommendations for international students: Required—TOEFL (minimum score 500 paper-based), IELTS (minimum score 6.5). *Application deadline:* For fall admission, 8/1 priority date for domestic and international students; for winter admission, 12/1 priority date for domestic students; for spring admission, 4/1 priority date for domestic students, 12/1 priority date for international students. Applications are processed on a rolling basis. Application fee: $0. Electronic applications accepted. Application fee is waived when completed online. *Expenses:* Contact institution. *Financial support:* Applicants required to submit FAFSA. *Faculty research:* Technology in the classroom, current educational trends, higher education. *Unit head:* Dr. Melissa Weber, Director of Graduate Studies, 605-995-2630, Fax: 605-995-2609, E-mail: melissa.weber@dwu.edu. *Application contact:* Stacy Mock, Coordinator of Adult and Online Admissions, 605-995-2650, Fax: 605-995-2699, E-mail: admissions@dwu.edu.
Website: www.dwu.edu

Dallas Baptist University, Dorothy M. Bush College of Education, Program in Curriculum and Instruction, Dallas, TX 75211-9299. Offers Christian school administration (M Ed); distance learning (M Ed); English as a second language (M Ed); instructional technology (M Ed); professional life coaching (M Ed); special education (M Ed); supervision (M Ed). *Program availability:* Part-time, evening/weekend, online learning. *Application deadline:* Applications are processed on a rolling basis. Application fee: $25. Electronic applications accepted. Application fee is waived when completed online. *Expenses: Tuition:* Full-time $17,262; part-time $959 per credit hour. *Required fees:* $1000; $500 per semester. Tuition and fees vary according to course load and degree level. *Unit head:* Dr. Neil Dugger, Dean, 214-333-5202, E-mail: neil@dbu.edu. *Application contact:* Karla Hagan, Program Director, 214-333-5831, E-mail: karla@dbu.edu.
Website: http://www3.dbu.edu/graduate/curriculum_instruction.asp

Dallas Baptist University, Dorothy M. Bush College of Education, Program in Educational Leadership, Dallas, TX 75211-9299. Offers charter school administration (M Ed); educational leadership (M Ed); educational leadership K-12 (Ed D). *Program availability:* Part-time, evening/weekend, online learning. *Application deadline:* Applications are processed on a rolling basis. Application fee: $25. Electronic applications accepted. Application fee is waived when completed online. *Expenses: Tuition:* Full-time $17,262; part-time $959 per credit hour. *Required fees:* $1000; $500 per semester. Tuition and fees vary according to course load and degree level. *Unit head:* Dr. Neil Dugger, Dean, 214-333-5202, E-mail: neil@dbu.edu. *Application contact:* Dr. Carolyn Spain, Program Director, 214-333-5217, E-mail: carolyns@dbu.edu.
Website: http://www3.dbu.edu/graduate/education.asp

Dallas Baptist University, Gary Cook School of Leadership, Program in Educational Leadership, Dallas, TX 75211-9299. Offers higher education leadership (Ed D), including educational ministry leadership, general leadership, higher education leadership. *Program availability:* Part-time. *Degree requirements:* For doctorate, thesis/dissertation. *Application deadline:* Applications are processed on a rolling basis. Application fee: $25. Electronic applications accepted. Application fee is waived when completed online. *Expenses: Tuition:* Full-time $17,262; part-time $959 per credit hour. *Required fees:* $1000; $500 per semester. Tuition and fees vary according to course load and degree level. *Unit head:* Dr. Jack Goodyear, Dean, 214-333-5595, E-mail: jackg@dbu.edu. *Application contact:* Dr. Ozzie Ingram, Program Director, 214-333-6875, E-mail: ozzie@dbu.edu.
Website: http://www4.dbu.edu/leadership/education-leadership-ed-d

Dallas Theological Seminary, Graduate Programs, Dallas, TX 75204-6499. Offers adult education (Th M); apologetics (Th M); Bible backgrounds (Th M); Bible translation (Th M); Biblical and theological studies (Certificate); biblical counseling (MA); biblical exegesis and linguistics (MA); biblical exposition (PhD); biblical studies (MA); Biblical theology (Th M); children's education (Th M); Christian education (MA, D Min); Christian leadership (MA); cross-cultural ministries (MA); educational administration (Th M); educational leadership (Th M); evangelism and discipleship (Th M); exposition of Biblical books (Th M); family life education (Th M); general studies (Th M); Hebrew and cognate studies (Th M); hermeneutics (Th M); historical theology (Th M); homiletics (Th M); intercultural ministries (Th M); Jesus studies (Th M); leadership studies (Th M); media and communication (MA); media arts (Th M); ministry (D Min); ministry with women (Th M); New Testament studies (Th M, PhD); Old Testament studies (Th M, PhD); parachurch ministries (Th M); pastoral care and counseling (Th M); pastoral theology and practice (Th M); philosophy (Th M); sacred theology (STM); spiritual formation (Th M); systematic theology (Th M); teaching in Christian institutions (Th M); theological studies (PhD); urban ministries (Th M); worship studies (Th M); youth education (Th M). *Program availability:* Part-time, online learning. *Degree requirements:* For master's, variable foreign language requirement, thesis (for some programs); for doctorate, 2 foreign languages, thesis/dissertation. *Entrance requirements:* For master's, GRE or MAT (if minimum undergraduate cumulative GPA is below 2.5 or undergraduate degree is unaccredited). Additional exam requirements/recommendations for international students: Required—TOEFL (minimum score 575 paper-based; 85 iBT), TWE. Electronic applications accepted.

Delaware State University, Graduate Programs, College of Education, Health and Public Policy, Program in Educational Leadership, Dover, DE 19901-2277. Offers MA, Ed D. *Entrance requirements:* Additional exam requirements/recommendations for international students: Required—TOEFL (minimum score 550 paper-based).

Delaware Valley University, Program in Educational Leadership, Doylestown, PA 18901-2697. Offers instruction, curriculum and technology (MS); school administration and leadership (MS). *Program availability:* Part-time, evening/weekend. *Entrance requirements:* For master's, minimum undergraduate GPA of 3.0.

Delta State University, Graduate Programs, College of Education, Division of Teacher Education, Leadership, and Research, Program in Professional Studies, Cleveland, MS 38733-0001. Offers counselor education (Ed D); elementary education (Ed D); higher education (Ed D). *Program availability:* Part-time, evening/weekend. *Degree requirements:* For doctorate, thesis/dissertation. *Entrance requirements:* For doctorate, GRE General Test. *Expenses: Tuition, area resident:* Full-time $7076; part-time $393 per credit hour. Tuition, state resident: full-time $7076; part-time $393 per credit hour. Tuition, nonresident: full-time $7076; part-time $393 per credit hour. *International tuition:* $7076 full-time. *Required fees:* $170; $18.90 per credit hour. $9.45 per semester. Part-time tuition and fees vary according to program.

Delta State University, Graduate Programs, College of Education, Division of Teacher Education, Leadership, and Research, Programs in Educational Administration and Supervision, Cleveland, MS 38733-0001. Offers M Ed, Ed S. *Accreditation:* NCATE.

Program availability: Part-time, evening/weekend. *Degree requirements:* For master's, thesis optional. *Entrance requirements:* For master's, GRE General Test or MAT; for Ed S, master's degree, teaching certificate. *Expenses: Tuition, area resident:* Full-time $7076; part-time $393 per credit hour. Tuition, state resident: full-time $7076; part-time $393 per credit hour. Tuition, nonresident: full-time $7076; part-time $393 per credit hour. *International tuition:* $7076 full-time. *Required fees:* $170; $18.90 per credit hour. $9.45 per semester. Part-time tuition and fees vary according to program.

DePaul University, College of Education, Chicago, IL 60614. Offers bilingual-bicultural education (M Ed, MA); counseling (M Ed, MA), including clinical mental health counseling, college student development, school counseling; curriculum studies (M Ed, MA, Ed D); early childhood education (M Ed, MA, Ed D); educational leadership (M Ed, MA, Ed D), including Catholic leadership (M Ed, MA), general (M Ed, MA), higher education (M Ed, MA), physical education (M Ed, MA), principal preparation (M Ed), teacher preparation (M Ed); elementary education (M Ed, MA); middle grades education (M Ed); middle school mathematics education (MS); reading specialist (M Ed, MA); secondary education (M Ed, MA); social and cultural foundations in education (M Ed, MA); special education (M Ed); sport, fitness and recreation leadership (MS); value-creating education for global citizenship (M Ed); world languages education (M Ed, MA). *Program availability:* Part-time, evening/weekend, online learning. *Degree requirements:* For doctorate, thesis/dissertation. Electronic applications accepted.

DeVry University–Folsom Campus, Graduate Programs, Folsom, CA 95630. Offers accounting (M Acc); accounting and financial management (MAFM); business administration (MBA); curriculum leadership (M Ed); educational leadership (M Ed); educational technology (M Ed); higher education leadership (M Ed); human resource management (MHRM); information systems management (MISM); network and communications management (MNCM); project management (MPM); public administration (MPA).

Doane University, Program in Education, Crete, NE 68333-2430. Offers curriculum and instruction (M Ed); education (Ed D); education specialist (Ed S); educational leadership (M Ed); school counseling (M Ed). *Accreditation:* NCATE. *Program availability:* Part-time, evening/weekend. *Faculty:* 10 full-time (7 women), 66 part-time/adjunct (50 women). *Students:* 287 full-time (235 women), 474 part-time (363 women); includes 57 minority (20 Black or African American, non-Hispanic/Latino; 1 American Indian or Alaska Native, non-Hispanic/Latino; 5 Asian, non-Hispanic/Latino; 22 Hispanic/Latino; 1 Native Hawaiian or other Pacific Islander, non-Hispanic/Latino; 8 Two or more races, non-Hispanic/Latino), 6 international. Average age 34. In 2018, 247 master's, 9 doctorates, 33 other advanced degrees awarded. *Degree requirements:* For master's, thesis; for doctorate, thesis/dissertation. *Entrance requirements:* For master's, minimum GPA of 2.5. Additional exam requirements/recommendations for international students: Required—TOEFL. *Application deadline:* Applications are processed on a rolling basis. Electronic applications accepted. *Expenses:* Contact institution. *Financial support:* Applicants required to submit FAFSA. *Unit head:* Dr. Lyn C. Forester, Dean, 402-826-8604, Fax: 402-826-8278. *Application contact:* Leah Schaber, Assistant Dean, 402-464-1223, Fax: 402-466-4228, E-mail: leah.schaber@doane.edu.
Website: http://www.doane.edu/masters-degrees

Drake University, School of Education, Des Moines, IA 50311-4516. Offers applied behavior analysis (MS); counseling (MS); education (PhD); education administration (Ed D); educational leadership (MSE, Ed D); effective teaching (MSE); leadership development (MS); literacy (Ed S); literacy education (MSE); rehabilitation administration (MS); rehabilitation placement (MS); special education (MSE); STEM education (MSE); teacher education (5-12) (MAT); teacher education (K-8) (MST); teacher effectiveness and professional development (MSE). *Program availability:* Part-time, evening/weekend, 100% online, blended/hybrid learning. *Students:* 90 full-time (74 women), 690 part-time (532 women); includes 69 minority (30 Black or African American, non-Hispanic/Latino; 1 American Indian or Alaska Native, non-Hispanic/Latino; 9 Asian, non-Hispanic/Latino; 16 Hispanic/Latino; 13 Two or more races, non-Hispanic/Latino). Average age 34. In 2018, 253 master's, 30 doctorates awarded. *Degree requirements:* For master's and Ed S, comprehensive exam, internships (for some programs); for doctorate, comprehensive exam, thesis/dissertation, internships (for some programs). *Entrance requirements:* For master's, GRE General Test, MAT, or Drake Writing Assessment, resume, 2 letters of recommendation; for doctorate, GRE General Test or MAT, master's degree, 3 letters of recommendation; for Ed S, GRE General Test or MAT. Additional exam requirements/recommendations for international students: Required—TOEFL (minimum score 550 paper-based). *Application deadline:* For fall admission, 7/1 priority date for domestic students, 6/1 priority date for international students; for spring admission, 11/1 priority date for domestic students, 10/1 priority date for international students. Applications are processed on a rolling basis. Application fee: $25. Electronic applications accepted. *Expenses:* Contact institution. *Financial support:* Research assistantships, career-related internships or fieldwork, and unspecified assistantships available. Support available to part-time students. *Faculty research:* Counseling and rehabilitation, behavioral supports, inquiry-based science methods, teacher quality enhancement. *Unit head:* Dr. Janet McMahill, Dean, 515-271-3829, E-mail: janet.mcmahill@drake.edu. *Application contact:* Dr. Janet McMahill, Dean, 515-271-3829, E-mail: janet.mcmahill@drake.edu.
Website: http://www.drake.edu/soe/

Drexel University, Goodwin College of Professional Studies, School of Education, Philadelphia, PA 19104-2875. Offers applied behavior analysis (MS); creativity and innovation (MS); education improvement and transformation (MS); educational administration (MS); educational leadership and management (Ed D); educational leadership development and learning technologies (PhD); global and international education (MS); higher education (MS); human resources development (MS); learning technologies (MS); mathematics, learning and teaching (MS); special education (MS); teaching, learning and curriculum (MS). *Program availability:* Part-time, evening/weekend, online learning. *Degree requirements:* For doctorate, thesis/dissertation. *Entrance requirements:* For doctorate, GRE or GMAT. Additional exam requirements/recommendations for international students: Required—TOEFL, IELTS. Electronic applications accepted. Application fee is waived when completed online. *Expenses:* Contact institution. *Faculty research:* Leadership development, mathematics education, literacy, autism, educational technology.

Drury University, Master in Education Program, Springfield, MO 65802. Offers curriculum and instruction (M Ed), including elementary education, middle school education, secondary education; instructional leadership (M Ed); instructional technology (M Ed); integrated learning (M Ed); special education (M Ed); special reading (M Ed). *Accreditation:* NCATE. *Program availability:* Part-time, evening/weekend, 100% online, blended/hybrid learning. *Faculty:* 10 full-time (6 women), 8 part-time/adjunct (6 women). *Students:* 167 full-time (133 women). Average age 32. 92 applicants, 92% accepted, 69 enrolled. In 2018, 44 master's awarded. *Entrance requirements:* For master's, bachelor's degree with minimum GPA of 2.75. Additional exam requirements/recommendations for international students: Recommended—TOEFL (minimum score 80 iBT), IELTS (minimum score 6.5). *Application deadline:* For fall admission, 8/4 priority date for domestic and international students; for spring admission, 1/5 priority date for domestic and international students; for summer admission, 5/26 priority date for domestic and international students. Applications are processed on a rolling basis. Application fee: $25. Electronic applications accepted. *Expenses:* Tuition is $366 per credit hour. Fees are $7 per credit hour. Most M.Ed. degrees are 33 credit hours. *Financial support:* In 2018–19, 5 students received support. Career-related internships or fieldwork, scholarships/grants, and unspecified assistantships available. Financial award application deadline: 6/30; financial award applicants required to submit FAFSA. *Faculty research:* Instructional technology, autism, diversity, and social justice. *Unit head:* Dr. Asikaa Cosgrove, Director, Master in Education Program, 417-873-7806, E-mail: acosgrov@drury.edu. *Application contact:* Dr. Asikaa Cosgrove, Director, Master in Education Program, 417-873-7806, E-mail: acosgrov@drury.edu.
Website: http://www.drury.edu/education-masters

Duquesne University, School of Education, Department of Educational Foundations and Leadership, Ed D in Educational Leadership Program, Pittsburgh, PA 15282-0001. Offers Ed D. *Program availability:* Part-time, evening/weekend. *Faculty:* 7 full-time (3 women). *Students:* 46 full-time (32 women); includes 14 minority (all Black or African American, non-Hispanic/Latino), 3 international. Average age 40. 19 applicants, 84% accepted, 10 enrolled. In 2018, 7 doctorates awarded. *Entrance requirements:* For doctorate, GRE, current curriculum vitae or resume; minimum GPA of 3.0 on last 30 hours of graduate work; master's degree in education or related field from accredited institution; 2 written essays; 3 letters of recommendation. Additional exam requirements/recommendations for international students: Required—TOEFL (minimum score 550 paper-based), IELTS (minimum score 7). *Application deadline:* For fall admission, 1/23 for domestic students. Application fee: $0. Electronic applications accepted. *Expenses: Tuition:* Full-time $23,112; part-time $1284 per credit. Tuition and fees vary according to program. *Financial support:* In 2018–19, 5 students received support, including 5 research assistantships with full and partial tuition reimbursements available (averaging $2,101 per year). Financial award applicants required to submit FAFSA. *Faculty research:* Effective school leadership; classroom assessment and social justice; evidence-based decision making; c-engaged educational improvement; scholarship of teaching. *Unit head:* Dr. Connie Moss, Associate Professor, 412-396-4433, Fax: 412-396-6017, E-mail: moss@duq.edu. *Application contact:* Kelly McGinley, Graduate Admissions Assistant, 412-396-1559, Fax: 412-396-5585, E-mail: mcginleyk@duq.edu.
Website: http://wwwtest.duq.edu/academics/schools/education/graduate-programs-education/educational-leadership

Duquesne University, School of Education, Department of Educational Foundations and Leadership, Program in School Administration and Supervision, Pittsburgh, PA 15282-0001. Offers curriculum and instruction (Post-Master's Certificate); school administration K-12 (MS Ed, Post-Master's Certificate); school supervision (MS Ed). *Program availability:* Part-time, evening/weekend. *Faculty:* 1 (woman) full-time. *Students:* 15 full-time (12 women), 2 part-time (both women); includes 1 minority (Black or African American, non-Hispanic/Latino), 2 international. Average age 34. 25 applicants, 68% accepted, 8 enrolled. In 2018, 8 master's awarded. *Entrance requirements:* For master's, bachelor's degree; minimum GPA of 3.0 overall or on most recent 48 credits, or minimum overall GPA of 2.8 and MAT (minimum score 396); resume that documents competence and effectiveness in professional work; 3 letters of professional reference; for Post-Master's Certificate, bachelor's degree. Additional exam requirements/recommendations for international students: Required—TOEFL (minimum score 550 paper-based), IELTS (minimum score 7). *Application deadline:* For fall admission, 9/1 for domestic students; for spring admission, 1/2 for domestic students. Applications are processed on a rolling basis. Application fee: $0. Electronic applications accepted. *Expenses: Tuition:* Full-time $23,112; part-time $1284 per credit. Tuition and fees vary according to program. *Financial support:* In 2018–19, 1 student received support, including 1 research assistantship (averaging $2,678 per year). Support available to part-time students. Financial award applicants required to submit FAFSA. *Faculty research:* Building culturally relevant systems of training for educational and helping professionals; preservice/in service teacher beliefs (self, content, equity); principal beliefs about teacher evaluation; beliefs about classroom assessment; school achievement and school effectiveness. *Unit head:* Dr. Fran Serenka, Associate Professor and Director, 412-396-5274, Fax: 412-396-1274, E-mail: serenkaf@duq.edu. *Application contact:* Kelly McGinley, Graduate Admissions Assistant, 412-396-1559, Fax: 412-396-5585, E-mail: mcginleyk@duq.edu.
Website: http://www.duq.edu/academics/schools/education/graduate-programs-education/school-admin-and-supervision

D'Youville College, Department of Education, Buffalo, NY 14201-1084. Offers educational leadership (Ed D); elementary education (MS Ed); secondary education (MS Ed); special education (MS Ed). *Program availability:* Part-time, evening/weekend. *Degree requirements:* For master's, one foreign language, comprehensive exam, project or thesis. *Entrance requirements:* For master's, GRE (if GPA less than 2.75), minimum GPA of 3.0. Additional exam requirements/recommendations for international students: Required—TOEFL (minimum score 500 paper-based). Electronic applications accepted. *Faculty research:* Developmental disabilities, multiculturalism, early childhood education.

East Carolina University, Graduate School, College of Education, Department of Educational Leadership, Greenville, NC 27858-4353. Offers educational administration and supervision (Ed S); educational leadership (Ed D); school administration (MSA). *Accreditation:* NCATE. *Program availability:* Part-time, evening/weekend, online learning. *Application deadline:* For fall admission, 6/1 priority date for domestic students. *Expenses: Tuition, area resident:* Full-time $4749. Tuition, state resident: full-time $4749. Tuition, nonresident: full-time $17,898. *International tuition:* $17,898 full-time. *Required fees:* $2787. Part-time tuition and fees vary according to course load and program. *Financial support:* Application deadline: 6/1. *Unit head:* Dr. Majorie Ringler, Chair, 252-328-4825, E-mail: ringlerm@ecu.edu. *Application contact:* Graduate School Admissions, 252-328-6012, Fax: 252-328-6071, E-mail: gradschool@ecu.edu.
Website: http://www.ecu.edu/cs-educ/leed/index.cfm

Eastern Illinois University, Graduate School, College of Education, Department of Educational Leadership, Charleston, IL 61920. Offers educational administration (Ed S); educational leadership (MS Ed). *Accreditation:* NCATE. *Program availability:* Part-time, evening/weekend. *Degree requirements:* For master's, comprehensive exam; for Ed S, comprehensive exam, thesis. *Entrance requirements:* For master's and Ed S, GMAT or GRE. Additional exam requirements/recommendations for international students: Required—TOEFL (minimum score 500 paper-based; 61 iBT), IELTS (minimum score 6). *Application deadline:* For fall admission, 5/15 for domestic and international students; for spring admission, 10/15 for domestic and international students. Applications are processed on a rolling basis. Application fee: $30. Electronic applications accepted. *Expenses:* Tuition, state resident: part-time $299 per credit hour. Tuition, nonresident: part-time $718 per credit hour. *Required fees:* $214.50 per credit hour. *Financial support:* Research assistantships with tuition reimbursements, teaching assistantships with tuition reimbursements, career-related internships or fieldwork, Federal Work-Study, scholarships/grants, and unspecified assistantships available. Support available to part-time students. Financial award application deadline: 3/1; financial award applicants required to submit FAFSA. *Unit head:* Cliff Karnes, Ed.D., Chair, 217-581-2919, Fax: 217-581-6673, E-mail: cdkarnes@eiu.edu. *Application contact:* Cliff Karnes, Ed.D., Chair, 217-581-2919, Fax: 217-581-6673, E-mail: cdkarnes@eiu.edu.
Website: http://www.eiu.edu/~edadmin/

Educational Leadership and Administration

Eastern Kentucky University, The Graduate School, College of Education, Department of Counseling and Educational Leadership, Richmond, KY 40475-3102. Offers human services (MA); instructional leadership (MA Ed); mental health counseling (MA); school counseling (MA Ed). *Accreditation:* ACA (one or more programs are accredited); NCATE. *Program availability:* Part-time, online learning. *Entrance requirements:* For master's, GRE General Test, minimum GPA of 2.5.

Eastern Michigan University, Graduate School, College of Education, Department of Leadership and Counseling, Programs in Educational Leadership, Ypsilanti, MI 48197. Offers community college leadership (Graduate Certificate); educational leadership (MA, Ed D, SPA); higher education/general administration (MA); higher education/student affairs (MA); K-12 administration (MA); K-12 basic administration (Post Master's Certificate). *Program availability:* Part-time, evening/weekend, online learning. *Students:* 39 full-time (29 women), 283 part-time (195 women); includes 92 minority (67 Black or African American, non-Hispanic/Latino; 2 Asian, non-Hispanic/Latino; 12 Hispanic/Latino; 11 Two or more races, non-Hispanic/Latino), 2 international. Average age 36. 192 applicants, 74% accepted, 80 enrolled. In 2018, 98 master's, 18 doctorates, 22 other advanced degrees awarded. *Entrance requirements:* For doctorate, GRE. Additional exam requirements/recommendations for international students: Required—TOEFL. *Application deadline:* For winter admission, 2/1 for domestic and international students. Applications are processed on a rolling basis. Application fee: $45. *Financial support:* Fellowships, research assistantships with full tuition reimbursements, teaching assistantships with full tuition reimbursements, career-related internships or fieldwork, Federal Work-Study, institutionally sponsored loans, scholarships/grants, tuition waivers (partial), and unspecified assistantships available. Support available to part-time students. *Application contact:* Dr. Jaclynn Tracy, Coordinator of Advising, Programs in Educational Leadership, 734-487-0255, Fax: 734-487-4608, E-mail: jtracy@emich.edu.

Eastern Michigan University, Graduate School, College of Education, Department of Special Education & Communication Sciences and Disorders, Ypsilanti, MI 48197. Offers autism spectrum disorders (MA); cognitive impairment (M Ed); emotional impairment (M Ed); learning disabilities (MA); physical/other health impairment (M Ed); special education (MA, SPA), including administration and supervision (SPA), special education (MA); speech-language pathology (MA); visual impairment (M Ed). *Accreditation:* NCATE. *Program availability:* Part-time, evening/weekend, online learning. *Faculty:* 19 full-time (15 women). *Students:* 95 full-time (82 women), 132 part-time (110 women); includes 33 minority (13 Black or African American, non-Hispanic/Latino; 6 Asian, non-Hispanic/Latino; 10 Hispanic/Latino; 4 Two or more races, non-Hispanic/Latino), 5 international. Average age 32. 244 applicants, 32% accepted, 57 enrolled. In 2018, 74 master's, 2 other advanced degrees awarded. *Entrance requirements:* For master's, GRE General Test. Additional exam requirements/recommendations for international students: Required—TOEFL. *Application deadline:* Applications are processed on a rolling basis. Application fee: $45. *Financial support:* Fellowships, research assistantships with full tuition reimbursements, teaching assistantships with full tuition reimbursements, career-related internships or fieldwork, Federal Work-Study, institutionally sponsored loans, scholarships/grants, tuition waivers (partial), and unspecified assistantships available. Support available to part-time students. Financial award applicants required to submit FAFSA. *Unit head:* Dr. David Winters, Department Head, 734-487-3300, Fax: 734-487-2473, E-mail: david.winters@emich.edu. *Application contact:* Dr. Derrick Fries, Graduate Coordinator, 734-487-3300, Fax: 734-487-2473, E-mail: dfries@emich.edu.
Website: http://www.emich.edu/coe/sped/

Eastern Michigan University, Graduate School, College of Education, Department of Teacher Education, Programs in Curriculum and Instruction, Ypsilanti, MI 48197. Offers advanced teaching and learning (MA); early literacy instruction (Graduate Certificate); instructional leadership (MA); learning, motivation and creativity (Graduate Certificate); literacy coaching (Graduate Certificate); online teaching (Certificate); secondary literacy instruction (Graduate Certificate); urban and diversity education (MA). *Students:* 1 (woman) full-time, 28 part-time (21 women); includes 11 minority (3 Black or African American, non-Hispanic/Latino; 1 Asian, non-Hispanic/Latino; 4 Hispanic/Latino; 3 Two or more races, non-Hispanic/Latino). Average age 31. 7 applicants, 71% accepted, 3 enrolled. In 2018, 5 master's awarded. Application fee: $45. *Application contact:* Dr. Virginia Harder, Graduate Coordinator/Advisor, 734-487-2729, Fax: 734-487-2101, E-mail: vharder1@emich.edu.

Eastern Nazarene College, Adult and Graduate Studies, Division of Teacher Education, Quincy, MA 02170. Offers administration (M Ed); early childhood education (M Ed, Certificate); elementary education (M Ed, Certificate); English as a second language (Certificate); instructional enrichment and development (Certificate); middle school education (M Ed, Certificate); moderate special needs education (Certificate); principal (Certificate); program development and supervision (Certificate); secondary education (M Ed, Certificate); special education administrator (Certificate); special needs (M Ed); supervisor (Certificate); teacher of reading (M Ed, Certificate). M Ed also available through weekend program for administration, special needs, and teacher of reading only. *Program availability:* Part-time, evening/weekend. *Entrance requirements:* Additional exam requirements/recommendations for international students: Required—TOEFL (minimum score 550 paper-based).

Eastern New Mexico University, Graduate School, College of Education and Technology, Department of Educational Studies, Portales, NM 88130. Offers counseling (MA); education (M Ed), including educational administration, secondary education; school counseling (M Ed); special education (M Ed, M Sp Ed), including early childhood special education (M Sp Ed), general special education (M Sp Ed), gifted education pedagogy (M Ed), special education pedagogy (M Ed). *Accreditation:* NCATE. *Program availability:* Part-time, evening/weekend, online learning. *Degree requirements:* For master's, comprehensive exam, thesis optional. *Entrance requirements:* For master's, writing assessment, minimum GPA of 3.0, letter of recommendation, photocopy of teaching license; Level II teaching license (for M Ed in educational administration). Additional exam requirements/recommendations for international students: Required—TOEFL (minimum score 550 paper-based; 79 iBT), IELTS (minimum score 6). Electronic applications accepted. *Expenses: Tuition, area resident:* Full-time $6776. Tuition, state resident: full-time $6776; part-time $282 per credit hour. Tuition, nonresident: full-time $8986; part-time $374 per credit hour. *Required fees:* $60 per semester. One-time fee: $25.

Eastern University, Graduate Education Programs, St. Davids, PA 19087-3696. Offers ESL program specialist (K-12) (Certificate); general supervisor (PreK-12) (Certificate); health and physical education (K-12) (Certificate); middle level (4-8) (Certificate); multicultural education (M Ed); music (K-12) (Certificate); Pre K-4 (Certificate); Pre K-4 with special education (Certificate); reading (M Ed); reading specialist (K-12) (Certificate); reading supervisor (K-12) (Certificate); school counseling (MA, CAGS); school principalship (preK-12) (Certificate); school psychology (MS, CAGS); secondary biology education (7-12) (Certificate); secondary chemistry education (7-12) (Certificate); secondary communication education (7-12) (Certificate); secondary English education (7-12) (Certificate); secondary math education (7-12) (Certificate); secondary social studies education (7-12) (Certificate); special education (M Ed); special education (7-12) (Certificate); special education (Pre K-8) (Certificate); special education supervisor (K-12) (Certificate); TESOL (M Ed); world language (Certificate), including Spanish. *Program availability:* Part-time, evening/weekend, online learning. *Entrance requirements:* Additional exam requirements/recommendations for international students: Required—TOEFL. Electronic applications accepted. Application fee is waived when completed online. *Expenses:* Contact institution.

Eastern University, Program in Organizational Leadership, St. Davids, PA 19087-3696. Offers leadership studies (CAGS); organizational leadership (PhD), including business management, educational administration, public and nonprofit administration. Electronic applications accepted. *Expenses:* Contact institution.

Eastern Washington University, Graduate Studies, College of Arts, Letters and Education, Department of Education, Cheney, WA 99004-2431. Offers adult education (M Ed); curriculum development (M Ed); early childhood education (M Ed); educational foundations (M Ed); educational leadership (M Ed); literacy (M Ed); teaching K-8 (M Ed). *Program availability:* Part-time. *Degree requirements:* For master's, comprehensive exam. *Entrance requirements:* For master's, minimum GPA of 3.0. Additional exam requirements/recommendations for international students: Required—TOEFL (minimum score 580 paper-based; 92 iBT), IELTS (minimum score 7), PTE (minimum score 63). Electronic applications accepted.

East Tennessee State University, School of Graduate Studies, College of Education, Department of Educational Leadership and Policy Analysis, Johnson City, TN 37614. Offers administrative endorsement (Ed D, Ed S); classroom leadership (Ed D); community college leadership (Postbaccalaureate Certificate); counselor leadership (Ed S); postsecondary and private sector leadership (Ed D); school and administrator leadership (M Ed); school system leadership (Ed D, Ed S); student personnel leadership (M Ed); teacher leadership (M Ed, Ed S). *Accreditation:* NCATE. *Program availability:* Part-time, online learning. *Degree requirements:* For master's, comprehensive exam, portfolio development and presentation, performance assessment; for doctorate, comprehensive exam, thesis/dissertation, residency, internship; for other advanced degree, comprehensive exam, field experience; internship (for some programs). *Entrance requirements:* For master's, writing assessment, minimum GPA of 2.75, professional resume, teaching certificate, 3 years of teaching experience, interview, four letters of recommendation; for doctorate, GRE General Test, writing assessment, professional resume, teaching certificate (for some programs), interview, four letters of recommendation; for other advanced degree, writing assessment, professional resume, teaching certificate (for some programs), four letters of recommendation. Additional exam requirements/recommendations for international students: Required—TOEFL (minimum score 550 paper-based; 79 iBT). Electronic applications accepted. *Faculty research:* Assessment and evaluation; examining school leadership, management, and accountability systems that limit learning; college and university enrollment and retention issues.

Edinboro University of Pennsylvania, Department of Middle and Secondary Education and Educational Leadership, Edinboro, PA 16444. Offers educational leadership (M Ed); middle and secondary instruction (M Ed). *Program availability:* Part-time, evening/weekend. *Degree requirements:* For master's, comprehensive exam, thesis or alternative, project. *Entrance requirements:* For master's, GRE or MAT, minimum QPA of 2.5. Electronic applications accepted.

Elizabeth City State University, Department of Education, Psychology and Health, Master of School Administration Program, Elizabeth City, NC 27909-7806. Offers MSA. *Program availability:* Part-time, evening/weekend. *Degree requirements:* For master's, thesis or alternative, electronic portfolio. *Entrance requirements:* For master's, MAT, GRE, minimum GPA of 3.0, 3 years of teaching experience, 3 letters of recommendation, two official transcripts from all undergraduate/graduate schools attended, teacher license, 3-4 page statement of purpose. Additional exam requirements/recommendations for international students: Required—TOEFL (minimum score 550 paper-based, 80 iBT) or IELTS (minimum score 6.5). Electronic applications accepted. *Faculty research:* Mentoring, assessment, professional learning communities, common core standards, Interstate School Leaders Licensure Consortium (ISLLC), differentiating instruction.

Elmhurst College, Graduate Programs, Program in Teacher Leadership, Elmhurst, IL 60126-3296. Offers M Ed. *Program availability:* Part-time, evening/weekend. *Faculty:* 3 full-time (all women), 3 part-time/adjunct (2 women). *Students:* 31 part-time (26 women); includes 5 minority (1 Black or African American, non-Hispanic/Latino; 1 American Indian or Alaska Native, non-Hispanic/Latino; 1 Asian, non-Hispanic/Latino; 2 Hispanic/Latino). Average age 32. 30 applicants, 73% accepted, 21 enrolled. In 2018, 12 master's awarded. *Entrance requirements:* For master's, 3 recommendations, resume, statement of purpose. Additional exam requirements/recommendations for international students: Required—TOEFL (minimum score 550 paper-based; 79 iBT), IELTS (minimum score 6.5). *Application deadline:* Applications are processed on a rolling basis. Application fee: $0. Electronic applications accepted. *Expenses:* $490 per semester hour. *Financial support:* In 2018–19, 10 students received support. Scholarships/grants available. Support available to part-time students. Financial award applicants required to submit FAFSA. *Unit head:* Jeanne White, Director, 630-617-6485, E-mail: whitej521@elmhurst.edu. *Application contact:* Timothy J. Panfil, Senior Director of Graduate Admission and Enrollment Management, 630-617-3300 Ext. 3256, Fax: 630-617-6471, E-mail: panfilt@elmhurst.edu.
Website: http://www.elmhurst.edu/tl

Emporia State University, Program in Curriculum and Instruction, Emporia, KS 66801-5415. Offers curriculum leadership (MS); effective practitioner (MS); national board certification (MS). *Accreditation:* NCATE. *Program availability:* Part-time, online only, 100% online. *Degree requirements:* For master's, comprehensive exam or thesis, practicum. *Entrance requirements:* For master's, GRE or MAT, appropriate bachelor's degree, teacher certification, 1 year of teaching experience, letters of recommendation. Electronic applications accepted.

Emporia State University, Program in Educational Administration, Emporia, KS 66801-5415. Offers elementary administration (MS); elementary/secondary administration (MS); secondary administration (MS). *Accreditation:* NCATE. *Program availability:* Part-time. *Degree requirements:* For master's, comprehensive exam or thesis, practicum. *Entrance requirements:* For master's, GRE or MAT, appropriate bachelor's degree, letters of recommendation, teacher certification, 1 year of teaching experience. Electronic applications accepted.

Endicott College, Van Loan School of Graduate and Professional Studies, Program in Administrative Leadership, Beverly, MA 01915-2096. Offers M Ed. *Program availability:* Part-time, evening/weekend. *Entrance requirements:* For master's, Massachusetts Tests for Educator Licensure (MTEL) Communication and Literacy Test; MAT or GRE, baccalaureate degree, at least three years of school-based employment. Additional exam requirements/recommendations for international students: Required—TOEFL. Electronic applications accepted. *Expenses:* Contact institution.

Endicott College, Van Loan School of Graduate and Professional Studies, Program in Educational Leadership, Beverly, MA 01915-2096. Offers Ed D. *Program availability:* Part-time, evening/weekend. *Degree requirements:* For doctorate, comprehensive exam, thesis/dissertation, apprenticeship. *Entrance requirements:* For doctorate, GRE or MAT, official undergraduate and graduate transcripts, three letters of recommendation, personal statement, resume or curriculum vitae, writing sample,

interview. Additional exam requirements/recommendations for international students: Required—TOEFL. *Expenses:* Contact institution. *Faculty research:* Learning styles in post-secondary education, leadership in the professoriate, collapsing boundaries PreK-PhD.

Evangel University, Department of Education, Springfield, MO 65802. Offers curriculum and instruction (M Ed); educational leadership (M Ed); literacy (M Ed); secondary teaching (M Ed). *Accreditation:* NCATE. *Program availability:* Part-time, evening/weekend, 100% online, blended/hybrid learning. *Entrance requirements:* For master's, PRAXIS II (preferred) or GRE, minimum undergraduate GPA of 3.0. Additional exam requirements/recommendations for international students: Required—TOEFL (minimum score 550 paper-based). Electronic applications accepted. Application fee is waived when completed online.

Evangel University, Doctor of Education in Educational Leadership, Curriculum, and Instruction Program, Springfield, MO 65802. Offers Ed D. *Program availability:* Part-time, evening/weekend. *Degree requirements:* For doctorate, thesis/dissertation. *Entrance requirements:* For doctorate, MA in education (preferred). Additional exam requirements/recommendations for international students: Required—TOEFL (minimum score 550 paper-based). Electronic applications accepted.

Fairleigh Dickinson University, Florham Campus, University College: Arts, Sciences, and Professional Studies, Peter Sammartino School of Education, Program in Educational Leadership, Madison, NJ 07940-1099. Offers MA.

Fairleigh Dickinson University, Metropolitan Campus, University College: Arts, Sciences, and Professional Studies, Peter Sammartino School of Education, Program in Educational Leadership, Teaneck, NJ 07666-1914. Offers MA.

Fayetteville State University, Graduate School, Programs in Educational Leadership and School Administration, Fayetteville, NC 28301-4298. Offers school administration (MSA). *Accreditation:* NCATE (one or more programs are accredited). *Program availability:* Part-time, evening/weekend. *Faculty:* 7 full-time (3 women), 3 part-time/adjunct (1 woman). *Students:* 66 full-time (46 women), 47 part-time (32 women); includes 89 minority (80 Black or African American, non-Hispanic/Latino; 1 American Indian or Alaska Native, non-Hispanic/Latino; 6 Hispanic/Latino; 2 Two or more races, non-Hispanic/Latino), 1 international. Average age 42. 40 applicants, 90% accepted, 28 enrolled. In 2018, 13 master's, 8 doctorates awarded. *Degree requirements:* For master's, internship, written and oral exams; for doctorate, thesis/dissertation. *Entrance requirements:* For master's, GRE or MAT, minimum GPA of 2.5. Additional exam requirements/recommendations for international students: Required—TOEFL. *Application deadline:* For fall admission, 4/1 for domestic students. Applications are processed on a rolling basis. Application fee: $40. Electronic applications accepted. *Financial support:* Application deadline: 3/1; applicants required to submit FAFSA. *Faculty research:* First-generation college students and academic successes, educational law and higher education, educational policy and K-12/higher education. *Unit head:* Dr. Abul Pitre, Chair and Professor, Department of Educational Leadership, 910-672-1731, Fax: 910-672-2075, E-mail: apetri@uncfsu.edu. *Application contact:* Dr. Paris Jones, Professor and Director, Master of School Administration, 910-672-1262, Fax: 910-672-2075, E-mail: pjones@uncfsu.edu.

Felician University, Program in Education, Lodi, NJ 07644-2117. Offers education (MA); educational leadership (principal/supervision) (MA); educational supervision (PMC); principal (PMC). *Accreditation:* TEAC. *Program availability:* Part-time, evening/weekend. *Degree requirements:* For master's and PMC, thesis, presentation. *Entrance requirements:* For master's, PRAXIS Core (Reading/Writing/Math), minimum GPA of 3.0, two professional letters of recommendation, personal statement, personal interview. Additional exam requirements/recommendations for international students: Required—TOEFL (minimum score 550 paper-based; 79 iBT), IELTS (minimum score 6.5), PTE (minimum score 56). Electronic applications accepted. Application fee is waived when completed online. *Expenses:* Contact institution. *Faculty research:* Educational leadership, administration, supervision, curriculum.

Ferris State University, Extended and International Operations, Big Rapids, MI 49307. Offers community college leadership (Ed D). *Program availability:* Evening/weekend, blended/hybrid learning. *Faculty:* 27 part-time/adjunct (18 women). *Students:* 119 full-time (79 women), 2 part-time (1 woman); includes 46 minority (31 Black or African American, non-Hispanic/Latino; 1 American Indian or Alaska Native, non-Hispanic/Latino; 1 Asian, non-Hispanic/Latino; 12 Hispanic/Latino; 1 Two or more races, non-Hispanic/Latino). Average age 45. 40 applicants, 75% accepted, 26 enrolled. In 2018, 17 doctorates awarded. *Degree requirements:* For doctorate, thesis/dissertation, course work completed (minimum GPA of 2.7), e-portfolio demonstration of program & additional comprehensive requirements, successful dissertation. *Entrance requirements:* For doctorate, master's degree with minimum GPA of 3.25, fierce commitment to the mission of community colleges, essay, writing samples. *Application deadline:* For spring admission, 10/31 for domestic and international students; for summer admission, 4/15 for domestic and international students. Applications are processed on a rolling basis. Application fee: $0. Electronic applications accepted. *Expenses:* $690 per credit hour with no additional fees. Total is $42,090. *Financial support:* In 2018–19, 15 students received support, including 6 teaching assistantships (averaging $690 per year). Financial award applicants required to submit FAFSA. *Faculty research:* Community college leadership. *Unit head:* Dr. Roberta Teahen, Director, 231-591-3805, E-mail: robertateahen@ferris.edu. *Application contact:* Megan Biller, Coordinator, 231-591-2710, Fax: 231-591-3539, E-mail: meganbiller@ferris.edu.

Fitchburg State University, Division of Graduate and Continuing Education, Program in Educational Leadership and Management, Fitchburg, MA 01420-2697. Offers education technology (Certificate); educational leadership and management (M Ed, CAGS); higher education administration (CAGS); school principal (M Ed, CAGS); supervisor/director (M Ed, CAGS). *Accreditation:* NCATE. *Program availability:* Part-time, evening/weekend. *Entrance requirements:* Additional exam requirements/recommendations for international students: Required—TOEFL (minimum score 550 paper-based; 79 iBT). Electronic applications accepted. *Expenses:* Contact institution.

Florida Agricultural and Mechanical University, Division of Graduate Studies, Research, and Continuing Education, College of Education, Department of Educational Leadership and Human Services, Tallahassee, FL 32307-3200. Offers administration and supervision (M Ed, MS, PhD); adult education (M Ed, MS); educational leadership (PhD); guidance and counseling (M Ed, MS). *Accreditation:* NCATE. *Degree requirements:* For master's, thesis (for some programs); for doctorate, thesis/dissertation. *Entrance requirements:* For master's, GRE General Test, minimum GPA of 3.0. Additional exam requirements/recommendations for international students: Required—TOEFL.

Florida Atlantic University, College of Education, Department of Educational Leadership and Research Methodology, Boca Raton, FL 33431-0991. Offers adult and community education (M Ed, PhD, Ed S); educational leadership (M Ed, PhD, Ed S); higher education (M Ed, PhD); K-12 school leadership (M Ed, PhD, Ed S). *Accreditation:* NCATE. *Program availability:* Part-time, evening/weekend, online learning. *Faculty:* 22 full-time (12 women), 22 part-time/adjunct (11 women). *Students:* 91 full-time (56 women), 260 part-time (177 women); includes 172 minority (107 Black or African American, non-Hispanic/Latino; 5 Asian, non-Hispanic/Latino; 53 Hispanic/Latino; 7 Two

or more races, non-Hispanic/Latino), 8 international. Average age 37. 226 applicants, 68% accepted, 131 enrolled. In 2018, 96 master's, 19 doctorates, 2 other advanced degrees awarded. *Degree requirements:* For doctorate, comprehensive exam, thesis/dissertation, departmental qualifying exam; for Ed S, departmental qualifying exam. *Entrance requirements:* For master's, GRE General Test, minimum GPA of 3.0 during previous 2 years; for doctorate, GRE General Test, minimum GPA of 3.5; for Ed S, GRE General Test. Additional exam requirements/recommendations for international students: Required—TOEFL (minimum score 500 paper-based; 61 iBT), IELTS (minimum score 6). *Application deadline:* For fall admission, 7/1 for domestic students, 2/15 for international students; for spring admission, 9/15 for domestic students, 7/15 for international students. Applications are processed on a rolling basis. Application fee: $30. Electronic applications accepted. *Expenses: Tuition, area resident:* Full-time $7400; part-time $369.82 per credit. Tuition, state resident: full-time $7400; part-time $369.82 per credit. Tuition, nonresident: full-time $20,496; part-time $1024.81 per credit. *Financial support:* Fellowships, research assistantships, teaching assistantships, career-related internships or fieldwork, and tuition waivers (partial) available. *Faculty research:* Self-directed learning, school reform issues, legal issues, mentoring, school leadership. *Unit head:* Dr. Robert E. Shockley, Chair, 561-297-3551, Fax: 561-297-3618, E-mail: shockley@fau.edu. *Application contact:* Kathy DuBois, Senior Secretary, 561-297-6551, Fax: 561-297-3618, E-mail: edleadership@fau.edu.
Website: http://www.coe.fau.edu/academicdepartments/el/

Florida Gulf Coast University, College of Education, Program in Educational Leadership, Fort Myers, FL 33965-6565. Offers M Ed, MA. *Program availability:* Part-time, evening/weekend. *Degree requirements:* For master's, thesis or alternative, learning and professional portfolios. *Entrance requirements:* For master's, GRE General Test, MAT, minimum GPA of 3.0. Additional exam requirements/recommendations for international students: Required—TOEFL (minimum score 550 paper-based). Electronic applications accepted. *Faculty research:* Inclusion, technology in teaching, curriculum development in educational leadership, education policy and law.

Florida International University, College of Arts, Sciences, and Education, Department of Leadership and Professional Studies, Miami, FL 33199. Offers adult education and human resource development (MS, Ed D); counseling (MS), including rehabilitation counseling, school counseling; counselor education (MS), including clinical mental health counseling; educational administration and supervision (Ed D); educational leadership (MS, Certificate, Ed S); higher education (Ed D); higher education administration (MS); international and comparative education (MS); recreation and sport management (MS), including recreation and sport management, recreational therapy; school psychology (Ed S); urban education (MS), including instruction in urban settings, learning technologies, multicultural/bilingual, multicultural/TESOL, urban education. *Program availability:* Part-time, evening/weekend. *Faculty:* 64 full-time (43 women), 104 part-time/adjunct (76 women). *Students:* 258 full-time (196 women), 217 part-time (155 women); includes 387 minority (118 Black or African American, non-Hispanic/Latino; 8 Asian, non-Hispanic/Latino; 249 Hispanic/Latino; 12 Two or more races, non-Hispanic/Latino), 11 international. Average age 31. 345 applicants, 57% accepted, 126 enrolled. In 2018, 172 master's, 11 doctorates awarded. *Entrance requirements:* For master's, minimum GPA of 3.0; for doctorate and other advanced degree, GRE General Test. Additional exam requirements/recommendations for international students: Required—TOEFL (minimum score 550 paper-based; 80 iBT), IELTS (minimum score 6.3). *Application deadline:* For fall admission, 6/1 priority date for domestic students, 4/1 for international students; for winter admission, 10/1 priority date for domestic students, 9/1 for international students; for spring admission, 3/1 priority date for domestic students, 2/1 for international students. Applications are processed on a rolling basis. Application fee: $30. Electronic applications accepted. *Financial support:* Fellowships, research assistantships, teaching assistantships, Federal Work-Study, and tuition waivers (full and partial) available. Support available to part-time students. Financial award applicants required to submit FAFSA. *Unit head:* Dr. Benjamin Baez, Chair, 305-348-3214, Fax: 305-348-1515, E-mail: benjamin.baez@fiu.edu. *Application contact:* Nanett Rojas, Manager, Admissions Operations, 305-348-7464, Fax: 305-348-7441, E-mail: gradadm@fiu.edu
Website: http://education.fiu.edu

Florida State University, The Graduate School, College of Education, Department of Educational Leadership and Policy Studies, Tallahassee, FL 32306. Offers educational leadership and administration (Certificate); educational leadership and policy (MS, Ed D, PhD, Ed S), including education policy and evaluation (MS, Ed D, PhD), educational leadership and administration; foundations of education (MS, PhD), including history and philosophy of education, international and multicultural education; higher education (MS, PhD); institutional research (Certificate); program evaluation (Certificate). *Program availability:* Part-time, evening/weekend, 100% online, blended/hybrid learning, asynchronous, minimal on-campus study. *Degree requirements:* For master's, comprehensive exam, thesis optional; for doctorate, comprehensive exam, thesis/dissertation, diagnostic exam, preliminary exam, prospectus defense, dissertation defense. *Entrance requirements:* For master's, doctorate, and other advanced degree, GRE General Test, minimum GPA of 3.0. Additional exam requirements/recommendations for international students: Required—TOEFL (minimum score 550 paper-based, 80 iBT), IELTS (minimum score 6.5), Michigan English Language Assessment Battery (minimum score 77), or PTE (minimum score 55). Electronic applications accepted. *Expenses: Tuition, area resident:* Part-time $479.32 per credit hour. Tuition and fees vary according to campus/location and program. *Faculty research:* Post-secondary success; leadership education; education policy; international education; multicultural education.

Fordham University, Graduate School of Education, Division of Educational Leadership, Administration and Policy, New York, NY 10023. Offers administration and supervision (MSE, Adv C); administration and supervision for church leaders (PhD); educational administration and supervision (Ed D, PhD). *Accreditation:* NCATE. *Program availability:* Part-time, evening/weekend. *Degree requirements:* For master's, comprehensive exam (for some programs); for doctorate, comprehensive exam (for some programs), thesis/dissertation. *Entrance requirements:* For doctorate, MAT, GRE General Test. Electronic applications accepted.

Fort Hays State University, Graduate School, College of Education, Department of Educational Administration and Counseling, Program in Educational Administration, Hays, KS 67601-4099. Offers MS, Ed S. *Accreditation:* NCATE. *Degree requirements:* For master's and Ed S, comprehensive exam, thesis or alternative. *Entrance requirements:* For master's, GRE General Test or MAT. Additional exam requirements/recommendations for international students: Required—TOEFL (minimum score 550 paper-based). Electronic applications accepted. *Faculty research:* Guide to negotiations, nutrition program for disadvantaged, accountability, student insurance practices, student liability.

Fort Lewis College, Program in Teacher Leadership, Durango, CO 81301-3999. Offers MA, Certificate. *Degree requirements:* For master's, culminating research project. *Entrance requirements:* For master's and Certificate, baccalaureate degree from regionally-accredited college or university; minimum cumulative undergraduate and graduate GPA of 3.0; one year of full-time teaching experience in P-12 schools.

Educational Leadership and Administration

Framingham State University, Graduate Studies, Program in Educational Leadership, Framingham, MA 01701-9101. Offers MA. *Program availability:* Part-time, evening/weekend. *Entrance requirements:* For master's, MAT.

Franciscan University of Steubenville, Graduate Programs, Department of Education, Steubenville, OH 43952-1763. Offers administration (MS Ed); teaching (MS Ed). *Accreditation:* NCATE. *Program availability:* Part-time, evening/weekend, online learning. *Degree requirements:* For master's, project. *Entrance requirements:* For master's, minimum undergraduate GPA of 2.5 or written exam. Additional exam requirements/recommendations for international students: Required—TOEFL. Electronic applications accepted. Application fee is waived when completed online. *Expenses:* Contact institution.

Freed-Hardeman University, Program in Education, Henderson, TN 38340-2399. Offers curriculum and instruction (M Ed); school counseling (M Ed), including administration and supervision, special education; school leadership (Ed S). *Accreditation:* NCATE. *Program availability:* Part-time, evening/weekend. *Degree requirements:* For master's, comprehensive exam, thesis optional; for Ed S, thesis. *Entrance requirements:* For master's, GRE General Test or NTE; for Ed S, 3 years of teaching experience. Additional exam requirements/recommendations for international students: Required—TOEFL (minimum score 500 paper-based).

Fresno Pacific University, Graduate Programs, School of Education, Division of Administrative Services, Fresno, CA 93702-4709. Offers MA. *Program availability:* Part-time, evening/weekend. *Degree requirements:* For master's, thesis or alternative, 4 practica. *Entrance requirements:* Additional exam requirements/recommendations for international students: Required—TOEFL (minimum score 550 paper-based). Electronic applications accepted. *Expenses:* Contact institution.

Frostburg State University, College of Education, Department of Educational Professions, Program in Educational Administration and Supervision, Frostburg, MD 21532-1099. Offers educational administration and supervision (Ed D); elementary (M Ed); secondary (M Ed). *Program availability:* Part-time, evening/weekend. *Degree requirements:* For master's, thesis or alternative. *Entrance requirements:* For master's, teaching certificate. Additional exam requirements/recommendations for international students: Required—TOEFL. Electronic applications accepted. *Faculty research:* Practicum experience in schools.

Furman University, Graduate Division, Department of Education, Greenville, SC 29613. Offers curriculum and instruction (MA); early childhood education (MA); educational leadership (Ed S); English as a second language (MA); literacy (MA); school leadership (MA); special education (MA). *Accreditation:* NCATE. *Program availability:* Part-time, online learning. *Degree requirements:* For master's, comprehensive exam (for some programs), thesis or alternative. *Entrance requirements:* For master's, PRAXIS II. *Expenses: Tuition:* Full-time $27,500; part-time $7290 per credit. Tuition and fees vary according to program. *Faculty research:* Literacy, pedagogy and practice, social justice, advanced leadership, achievement in high poverty schools.

Gannon University, School of Graduate Studies, College of Humanities, Education, and Social Sciences, School of Education, Program in Principal Certification, Erie, PA 16541-0001. Offers Certificate. *Program availability:* Part-time, evening/weekend. *Degree requirements:* For Certificate, internship, portfolio. *Entrance requirements:* For degree, transcripts, master's degree in education or related field from regionally-accredited college or university with minimum GPA of 3.0, 3 letters of recommendation, documentation of 3 years of educational experience working under a certificate. Additional exam requirements/recommendations for international students: Required—TOEFL (minimum score 79 iBT). Electronic applications accepted. Application fee is waived when completed online. *Expenses:* Contact institution.

Gannon University, School of Graduate Studies, College of Humanities, Education, and Social Sciences, School of Education, Program in Superintendent Letter of Eligibility Certification, Erie, PA 16541-0001. Offers Certificate. *Program availability:* Part-time, evening/weekend. *Degree requirements:* For Certificate, thesis or alternative, superintendent internship, portfolio. *Entrance requirements:* For degree, transcripts, master's degree in education or related field from regionally-accredited college or university with minimum GPA of 3.0, 3 letters of recommendation, documentation of 6 years of educational experience working under a certificate. Additional exam requirements/recommendations for international students: Required—TOEFL (minimum score 79 iBT). Electronic applications accepted. Application fee is waived when completed online. *Expenses:* Contact institution.

Gannon University, School of Graduate Studies, College of Humanities, Education, and Social Sciences, School of Humanities, Program in Organizational Learning and Leadership, Erie, PA 16541-0001. Offers PhD. *Program availability:* Part-time, evening/weekend. *Degree requirements:* For doctorate, thesis/dissertation. *Entrance requirements:* For doctorate, GRE, master's or other post-baccalaureate professional graduate-level degree from regionally-accredited institution of higher education with minimum GPA of 3.5; 2 years of post-baccalaureate work experience; 3 letters of recommendation; transcripts; resume; statement of purpose. Additional exam requirements/recommendations for international students: Required—TOEFL (minimum score 79 iBT). Electronic applications accepted. Application fee is waived when completed online.

Gardner-Webb University, Graduate School, School of Education, Boiling Springs, NC 28017. Offers curriculum and instruction (Ed D); educational leadership (Ed D); executive leadership studies (MA, Ed S); organizational leadership (Ed D); school administration (MA). *Accreditation:* NCATE. *Program availability:* Part-time, evening/weekend. *Degree requirements:* For master's, comprehensive exam. *Entrance requirements:* For master's, GRE General Test or NTE, PRAXIS, minimum GPA of 2.5. Electronic applications accepted. *Expenses:* Contact institution.

Gateway Seminary, Graduate and Professional Programs, Ontario, CA 91761-8642. Offers divinity (M Div); early childhood education (Certificate); education leadership (MAEL, Diploma); ministry (D Min); theological studies (MTS); theology (Th M); youth ministry (Certificate). *Accreditation:* ACIPE; ATS. *Program availability:* Part-time, evening/weekend. *Degree requirements:* For master's, thesis (for some programs); for doctorate, 2 foreign languages, thesis/dissertation. *Entrance requirements:* For doctorate, MAT. Additional exam requirements/recommendations for international students: Required—TOEFL (minimum score 550 paper-based). Electronic applications accepted.

Geneva College, Master of Arts in Higher Education Program, Beaver Falls, PA 15010-3599. Offers campus ministry (MA); college teaching (MA); educational leadership (MA); student affairs administration (MA). *Program availability:* Part-time, evening/weekend, blended/hybrid learning. *Degree requirements:* For master's, 36 hours (27 in core courses) including a capstone research project. *Entrance requirements:* For master's, minimum GPA of 3.0, writing sample, 3 letters of recommendation, essay on motivation for participation in the program. Additional exam requirements/recommendations for international students: Required—TOEFL. Electronic applications accepted. *Expenses:* Contact institution. *Faculty research:* Learning theories, church-related higher education, organizational culture, sexual assault and transgender students at Christian colleges, emerging technology in higher education.

George Fox University, College of Education, Doctor of Education in Educational Leadership Program, Newberg, OR 97132-2697. Offers Ed D. *Program availability:* Online learning.

George Fox University, College of Education, Graduate Teaching and Leading Program, Newberg, OR 97132-2697. Offers administrative leadership (Ed S); continuing administrator license (Certificate); educational leadership (M Ed); educational technology (M Ed); English for speakers of other languages (M Ed); ESOL (Certificate); initial administrator license (Certificate); reading (M Ed, Certificate); special education (M Ed); teaching (MAT). *Accreditation:* NCATE. *Program availability:* Part-time, evening/weekend, online learning. *Degree requirements:* For master's, thesis (for some programs). *Entrance requirements:* For master's, minimum undergraduate GPA of 3.0 during previous 2 years of course work, resume, 3 professional recommendations on university forms, official transcripts. Additional exam requirements/recommendations for international students: Required—TOEFL (minimum score 577 paper-based; 90 iBT). Electronic applications accepted. *Expenses:* Contact institution.

George Mason University, College of Education and Human Development, Program in Education Leadership, Fairfax, VA 22030. Offers M Ed, Certificate. *Accreditation:* NCATE. *Program availability:* Part-time, evening/weekend, 100% online, blended/hybrid learning. *Faculty:* 6 full-time (3 women), 8 part-time/adjunct (1 woman). *Students:* 4 full-time (2 women), 341 part-time (263 women); includes 72 minority (40 Black or African American, non-Hispanic/Latino; 9 Asian, non-Hispanic/Latino; 17 Hispanic/Latino; 1 Native Hawaiian or other Pacific Islander, non-Hispanic/Latino; 5 Two or more races, non-Hispanic/Latino), 1 international. Average age 35. 162 applicants, 81% accepted, 106 enrolled. In 2018, 117 master's, 37 Certificates awarded. *Entrance requirements:* For master's, bachelor's degree from regionally-accredited institution with minimum GPA of 3.0 overall or in last 60 credit hours; 2 official transcripts; expanded goals statement; 3 letters of recommendation; 3 years of documented teaching experience. Additional exam requirements/recommendations for international students: Required—TOEFL (minimum score 575 paper-based; 88 iBT), IELTS (minimum score 6.5), PTE (minimum score 59). *Application deadline:* For fall admission, 3/1 priority date for domestic and international students; for spring admission, 10/1 for domestic and international students. Application fee: $75 ($80 for international students). Electronic applications accepted. *Financial support:* Federal Work-Study, scholarships/grants, unspecified assistantships, and health care benefits (for full-time research or teaching assistantship recipients) available. Financial award application deadline: 3/1; financial award applicants required to submit FAFSA. *Faculty research:* Understanding of the complexities of change in schools, communities, and organizations; education law; foundations of education leadership, history and leadership. *Unit head:* Farnoosh Shahrokhi, Academic Program Coordinator, 703-993-2009, E-mail: fshahrok@gmu.edu. *Application contact:* Farnoosh Shahrokhi, Academic Program Coordinator, 703-993-2009, E-mail: fshahrok@gmu.edu.
Website: http://gse.gmu.edu/programs/edleadership/

George Mason University, College of Education and Human Development, Programs in Curriculum and Instruction, Fairfax, VA 22030. Offers assistive technology (M Ed); designing digital learning in schools (M Ed); early childhood education (M Ed); early childhood education for diverse learners (M Ed); elementary education (M Ed); English as a second language (M Ed); gifted child education (M Ed); literacy (M Ed), including PK-12 classroom teachers, reading specialist; literacy leadership for diverse schools (M Ed), including K-12 reading; physical education (M Ed); science K-12 (M Ed); secondary education (M Ed), including biology, chemistry, earth science, English, history/social science, math, physics; special education (M Ed); teacher leadership (M Ed); transformative teaching (M Ed). *Program availability:* Part-time, evening/weekend, 100% online, blended/hybrid learning. *Faculty:* 48 full-time (40 women), 28 part-time/adjunct (20 women). *Students:* 165 full-time (147 women), 697 part-time (579 women); includes 243 minority (47 Black or African American, non-Hispanic/Latino; 3 American Indian or Alaska Native, non-Hispanic/Latino; 88 Asian, non-Hispanic/Latino; 85 Hispanic/Latino; 4 Native Hawaiian or other Pacific Islander, non-Hispanic/Latino; 16 Two or more races, non-Hispanic/Latino), 26 international. Average age 34. 450 applicants, 93% accepted, 315 enrolled. In 2018, 421 master's awarded. *Entrance requirements:* For master's, PRAXIS Core (for some programs), 2 letters of recommendation, interview, program goals statement; 9 hours of complete licensure endorsement requirements (for elementary education); minimum GPA of 3.0 in applicant's last 60 hours of undergraduate coursework (for secondary education); at least 1 year of teaching experience (for literacy). Additional exam requirements/recommendations for international students: Required—TOEFL (minimum score 575 paper-based; 88 iBT), IELTS (minimum score 6.5), PTE (minimum score 59). *Application deadline:* For fall admission, 4/2 priority date for domestic and international students; for spring admission, 11/1 for domestic and international students. Application fee: $75 ($80 for international students). Electronic applications accepted. *Financial support:* In 2018–19, 4 students received support, including 1 fellowship, 3 teaching assistantships (averaging $3,745 per year); career-related internships or fieldwork, Federal Work-Study, scholarships/grants, unspecified assistantships, and health care benefits (for full-time research or teaching assistantship recipients) also available. Support available to part-time students. Financial award application deadline: 3/1; financial award applicants required to submit FAFSA. *Faculty research:* Teacher preparation and professional development; adaptive teaching; wonder in science teacher preparation; literacy (digital, adolescent); site based course instruction. *Unit head:* Rebecca Fox, Professor and Academic Program Coordinator, 703-993-4123, E-mail: rfox@gmu.edu. *Application contact:* Rebecca Fox, Professor and Academic Program Coordinator, 703-993-4123, E-mail: rfox@gmu.edu.
Website: http://gse.gmu.edu/programs/gsemasters

The George Washington University, Graduate School of Education and Human Development, Department of Educational Leadership, Program in Educational Administration and Policy Studies, Washington, DC 20052. Offers education policy (Ed D); educational administration (Ed D). Ed D in educational administration offered at Newport News and Alexandria, VA. *Accreditation:* NCATE. *Students:* 91 part-time (64 women); includes 42 minority (32 Black or African American, non-Hispanic/Latino; 5 Asian, non-Hispanic/Latino; 3 Hispanic/Latino; 2 Two or more races, non-Hispanic/Latino), 1 international. Average age 42. In 2018, 15 doctorates awarded. *Degree requirements:* For doctorate, comprehensive exam, thesis/dissertation. *Entrance requirements:* For doctorate, GRE General Test or MAT, interview, minimum GPA of 3.3. *Application deadline:* For fall admission, 1/15 priority date for domestic students; for spring admission, 10/1 for domestic students. Applications are processed on a rolling basis. Application fee: $75. *Financial support:* In 2018–19, 9 students received support. Fellowships, research assistantships, teaching assistantships, career-related internships or fieldwork, Federal Work-Study, and tuition waivers (partial) available. Financial award application deadline: 1/15; financial award applicants required to submit FAFSA. *Unit head:* Michael Feuer, Dean, 202-994-6161, E-mail: mjfeuer@gwu.edu. *Application contact:* Sarah Lang, Director, Admissions and Marketing, 202-994-1447, Fax: 202-994-7207, E-mail: slang@gwu.edu.

The George Washington University, Graduate School of Education and Human Development, Department of Educational Leadership, Program in Educational Leadership and Administration, Washington, DC 20052. Offers MA Ed, Certificate, Ed S.

Programs offered at Newport News and Alexandria, VA. *Accreditation:* NCATE. *Program availability:* Evening/weekend. *Students:* 4 full-time (2 women), 206 part-time (155 women); includes 98 minority (62 Black or African American, non-Hispanic/Latino; 5 Asian, non-Hispanic/Latino; 21 Hispanic/Latino; 10 Two or more races, non-Hispanic/Latino), 4 international. Average age 38. 246 applicants, 71% accepted, 127 enrolled. In 2018, 27 master's, 36 Certificates awarded. *Entrance requirements:* For master's, GRE General Test or MAT, interview, minimum GPA of 2.75. *Application deadline:* For fall admission, 1/15 priority date for domestic students; for spring admission, 10/1 for domestic students. Applications are processed on a rolling basis. Application fee: $75. *Financial support:* Fellowships, teaching assistantships, career-related internships or fieldwork, and Federal Work-Study available. Financial award application deadline: 1/15; financial award applicants required to submit FAFSA. *Faculty research:* Organizational learning. *Unit head:* Michael Feuer, Dean, 202-994-6161, E-mail: mjfeuer@gwu.edu. *Application contact:* Sarah Lang, Director of Graduate Admissions, 202-994-1447, Fax: 202-994-7207, E-mail: slang@gwu.edu.

The George Washington University, Graduate School of Education and Human Development, Department of Educational Leadership, Program in Higher Education Administration, Washington, DC 20052. Offers college teaching and academic leadership (MA Ed/HD, Ed S); general administration (MA Ed/HD, Ed S); higher education administration (Ed D); higher education finance (MA Ed/HD, Ed S); international education (MA Ed/HD, Ed S); policy (MA Ed/HD, Ed S); student affairs administration (MA Ed/HD, Ed S). *Accreditation:* NCATE. *Students:* 27 full-time (19 women), 55 part-time (41 women); includes 37 minority (21 Black or African American, non-Hispanic/Latino; 5 Asian, non-Hispanic/Latino; 8 Hispanic/Latino; 3 Two or more races, non-Hispanic/Latino), 4 international. Average age 32. 131 applicants, 85% accepted, 37 enrolled. In 2018, 15 master's, 4 doctorates, 1 other advanced degree awarded. *Degree requirements:* For master's and Ed S, comprehensive exam; for doctorate, comprehensive exam, thesis/dissertation. *Entrance requirements:* For master's, GRE General Test or MAT, minimum GPA of 2.75; for doctorate, GRE General Test or MAT, interview, minimum GPA of 3.3; for Ed S, GRE General Test or MAT, minimum GPA of 3.3. *Application deadline:* For fall admission, 1/15 priority date for domestic students; for spring admission, 10/1 for domestic students. Applications are processed on a rolling basis. Application fee: $75. *Financial support:* In 2018–19, 17 students received support. Fellowships, research assistantships, career-related internships or fieldwork, Federal Work-Study, and tuition waivers (partial) available. Financial award application deadline: 1/15; financial award applicants required to submit FAFSA. *Faculty research:* Technology in higher education administration. *Unit head:* Michael Feuer, Dean, 202-994-6161, E-mail: mjfeuer@gwu.edu. *Application contact:* Sarah Lang, Director of Graduate Admissions, 202-994-1447, Fax: 202-994-7207, E-mail: slang@gwu.edu.

The George Washington University, Graduate School of Education and Human Development, Department of Educational Leadership, Program in Leadership in Educational Technology, Washington, DC 20052. Offers Graduate Certificate. *Students:* 1 (woman) part-time. Average age 45. *Unit head:* Dr. Natalie Milman, Coordinator, 202-994-1884, E-mail: nmilman@gwu.edu. *Application contact:* Sarah Lang, Director of Graduate Admissions, 202-994-1447, Fax: 202-994-7207, E-mail: slang@gwu.edu.
Website: http://gsehd.gwu.edu/

Georgia College & State University, Graduate School, The John H. Lounsbury College of Education, Program in Educational Leadership, Milledgeville, GA 31061. Offers M Ed, Ed S. *Accreditation:* NCATE. *Program availability:* Part-time, evening/weekend, online only, 100% online. *Degree requirements:* For master's, comprehensive exam, electronic portfolio presentation; for Ed S, comprehensive exam, minimum GPA of 3.0, electronic portfolio presentation. *Entrance requirements:* For master's, GACE, 2 professional recommendations, transcript, documentation of completing coursework for the identification and education of children with special needs, verification of immunization, minimum GPA of 2.5; for Ed S, GACE, certification in educational leadership, leadership position at P-12 school or local unit of administration, 2 professional recommendations, transcripts, minimum GPA of 3.25, verification of immunization. Electronic applications accepted. *Expenses:* Contact institution.

Georgian Court University, School of Education, Lakewood, NJ 08701-2697. Offers administration and leadership (MA); autism spectrum disorders (Certificate); education (M Ed, MAT); instructional technology (M Mat SE, MA, Certificate). *Accreditation:* TEAC. *Program availability:* Part-time, evening/weekend. *Faculty:* 10 full-time (6 women), 28 part-time/adjunct (17 women). *Students:* 32 full-time (25 women), 396 part-time (324 women); includes 84 minority (35 Black or African American, non-Hispanic/Latino; 10 Asian, non-Hispanic/Latino; 36 Hispanic/Latino; 3 Two or more races, non-Hispanic/Latino). Average age 34. 323 applicants, 67% accepted, 148 enrolled. In 2018, 152 master's, 4 other advanced degrees awarded. *Degree requirements:* For master's, comprehensive exam (for some programs), thesis (for some programs). *Entrance requirements:* For master's, GRE, GMAT or NTE/PRAXIS, 3 letters of recommendation. Additional exam requirements/recommendations for international students: Required—TOEFL (minimum score 550 paper-based; 79 iBT). *Application deadline:* For fall admission, 8/15 priority date for domestic students, 5/1 for international students; for spring admission, 1/15 priority date for domestic students, 10/1 for international students. Applications are processed on a rolling basis. Application fee: $40. Electronic applications accepted. *Expenses: Tuition:* Full-time $856; part-time $856 per credit hour. *Required fees:* $968; $496 per unit. $248 per semester. Tuition and fees vary according to campus/location and program. *Financial support:* Scholarships/grants, health care benefits, and unspecified assistantships available. Financial award application deadline: 4/15; financial award applicants required to submit FAFSA. *Unit head:* Dr. Christopher Campisano, Dean of School of Education, 732-987-2729, E-mail: ccampisano@georgian.edu. *Application contact:* Patrick Givens, Director of Graduate and Professional Studies Admissions, 732-987-2736, Fax: 732-987-2000, E-mail: gps@georgian.edu.
Website: https://georgian.edu/academics/school-of-education/

Georgia Southern University, Jack N. Averitt College of Graduate Studies, College of Education, Department of Leadership, Technology, and Human Development, Ed D Program in Educational Leadership, Statesboro, GA 30460. Offers educational leadership (Ed S); higher education leadership (Ed D); P-12 leadership (Ed D). *Program availability:* Part-time, evening/weekend, 100% online, blended/hybrid learning. *Degree requirements:* For doctorate, comprehensive exam, thesis/dissertation, exams. *Entrance requirements:* For doctorate, GRE General Test or MAT, minimum GPA of 3.5, letters of reference, resume. Additional exam requirements/recommendations for international students: Required—TOEFL (minimum score 550 paper-based; 80 iBT), IELTS (minimum score 6). Electronic applications accepted. *Expenses: Tuition, area resident:* Part-time $3324 per semester. Tuition, state resident: full-time $5814; part-time $3324 per semester. Tuition, nonresident: full-time $23,204; part-time $13,260 per semester. *Required fees:* $2092; $2092. Tuition and fees vary according to course load, degree level, campus/location and program. *Faculty research:* National and local policies regarding school renewal, student achievement, and university leadership; development of an instrument to measure student dispositions; the impact of cultural context on leadership practices and behaviors; technology leadership preparation.

Georgia Southern University, Jack N. Averitt College of Graduate Studies, College of Education, Department of Leadership, Technology, and Human Development, M Ed Program in Educational Leadership, Statesboro, GA 30460. Offers M Ed, Ed S. *Accreditation:* NCATE. *Program availability:* Part-time, evening/weekend. *Degree requirements:* For master's, comprehensive exam, transition point assessments; for Ed S, transition point assessments. *Entrance requirements:* For master's, GRE General Test or MAT, minimum GPA of 2.5, 3 years of teaching experience; for Ed S, GRE General Test or MAT, minimum graduate GPA of 3.25. Additional exam requirements/recommendations for international students: Required—TOEFL (minimum score 550 paper-based; 80 iBT), IELTS (minimum score 6). Electronic applications accepted. *Expenses: Tuition, area resident:* Part-time $3324 per semester. Tuition, state resident: full-time $5814; part-time $3324 per semester. Tuition, nonresident: full-time $23,204; part-time $13,260 per semester. *Required fees:* $2092; $2092. Tuition and fees vary according to course load, degree level, campus/location and program. *Faculty research:* Principalship, performance-based leadership preparation, instructional technology for school leaders, dispositions of educational leaders, school/system-wide support services, student-oriented support services, universal vs. cultural contextuality of international educational leadership characteristics and behaviors.

Georgia Southern University, Jack N. Averitt College of Graduate Studies, College of Education, Department of Leadership, Technology, and Human Development, Program in Higher Education, Statesboro, GA 30460. Offers educational leadership (Ed D); higher education administration (M Ed). *Accreditation:* NCATE. *Program availability:* Part-time, evening/weekend. *Degree requirements:* For master's, portfolio, practicum, transition point assessments; for doctorate, comprehensive exam, thesis/dissertation. *Entrance requirements:* For master's, minimum GPA of 2.5. Additional exam requirements/recommendations for international students: Required—TOEFL (minimum score 550 paper-based; 80 iBT), IELTS (minimum score 6). Electronic applications accepted. *Expenses: Tuition, area resident:* Part-time $3324 per semester. Tuition, state resident: full-time $5814; part-time $3324 per semester. Tuition, nonresident: full-time $23,204; part-time $13,260 per semester. *Required fees:* $2092; $2092. Tuition and fees vary according to course load, degree level, campus/location and program. *Faculty research:* Global issues in higher education, leadership and identity development in higher education, student affairs.

Georgia Southern University, Jack N. Averitt College of Graduate Studies, College of Education, Department of Leadership, Technology, and Human Development, Program in Higher Education Administration, Statesboro, GA 30458. Offers M Ed. *Program availability:* Part-time, evening/weekend. *Entrance requirements:* For master's, GRE, minimum GPA of 2.5. Additional exam requirements/recommendations for international students: Required—TOEFL (minimum score 550 paper-based; 80 iBT), IELTS (minimum score 6). Electronic applications accepted. *Expenses: Tuition, area resident:* Part-time $3324 per semester. Tuition, state resident: full-time $5814; part-time $3324 per semester. Tuition, nonresident: full-time $23,204; part-time $13,260 per semester. *Required fees:* $2092; $2092. Tuition and fees vary according to course load, degree level, campus/location and program. *Faculty research:* Higher education administration, student affairs.

Georgia State University, College of Education and Human Development, Department of Educational Policy Studies, Program in Educational Leadership, Atlanta, GA 30302-3083. Offers educational leadership (M Ed, Ed D, Ed S); urban teacher leadership (M Ed). *Accreditation:* NCATE. *Program availability:* Part-time. *Entrance requirements:* For master's, GRE; for doctorate and Ed S, GRE, MAT. *Application deadline:* Applications are processed on a rolling basis. Application fee: $50. Electronic applications accepted. *Expenses: Tuition, area resident:* Full-time $9360; part-time $390 per credit hour. Tuition, state resident: full-time $9360; part-time $390 per credit hour. Tuition, nonresident: full-time $30,024; part-time $1251 per credit hour. *International tuition:* $30,024 full-time. *Required fees:* $2128. *Financial support:* Fellowships, research assistantships, teaching assistantships, career-related internships or fieldwork, scholarships/grants, health care benefits, tuition waivers, and unspecified assistantships available. Support available to part-time students. Financial award application deadline: 3/15. *Faculty research:* Practices with diverse populations, leadership and success, the cohort model of instruction, technology in the schools, instructional supervision and academic coaching. *Unit head:* Dr. Jennifer Esposito, Interim Department Chair, 404-413-8281, Fax: 404-413-8003, E-mail: jesposito@gsu.edu. *Application contact:* Aishah Cowan, Administrative Academic Specialist, 404-413-8273, Fax: 404-413-8033, E-mail: acowan@gsu.edu.
Website: https://education.gsu.edu/program/med-educational-leadership/

Gonzaga University, School of Education, Spokane, WA 99258. Offers clinical mental health counseling (MA); educational leadership (M Ed, Ed D); elementary education (MIT); marriage and family counseling (MA); school counseling (MA); secondary education (MIT); special education (M Ed, MIT); sport and athletic administration (MA). *Accreditation:* NCATE. *Program availability:* Part-time, evening/weekend, 100% online, blended/hybrid learning. *Degree requirements:* For master's, comprehensive exam. *Entrance requirements:* For master's, GRE, MAT, and/or Washington Educator Skills Test-Basic (WEST-B), Washington Educator Skills Test-Endorsements (WEST-E), official transcripts from all colleges or universities attended, interview, two letters of recommendation, resume, essay, minimum GPA of 3.0. Additional exam requirements/recommendations for international students: Required—TOEFL (minimum score 580 paper-based, 88 iBT) or IELTS (minimum score 6.5). Electronic applications accepted. *Expenses:* Contact institution.

Gordon College, Graduate Education Program, Wenham, MA 01984-1899. Offers early childhood (M Ed); educational leadership (M Ed, Ed S); elementary education (M Ed); English as a second language (M Ed, Ed S); math specialist (M Ed); mathematics specialist (Ed S); middle school education (M Ed); moderate disabilities (M Ed); Montessori education (M Ed); reading (M Ed, Ed S); secondary education (M Ed). *Program availability:* Part-time, evening/weekend. *Degree requirements:* For master's, action research or clinical experience (for most programs); for Ed S, action research or clinical experience (for some programs). *Entrance requirements:* For master's, minimum undergraduate GPA of 3.0; 2 official undergraduate transcripts; professional resume; 3 recommendation letters (one professional reference, one academic reference, one personal reference); 500-700 word statement of purpose; for Ed S, minimum master's GPA of 3.3; 2 official transcripts from undergraduate and graduate schools; professional resume; 3 recommendation letters (one professional reference, one academic reference, one personal reference); 500-700 word statement of purpose. Additional exam requirements/recommendations for international students: Required—TOEFL (minimum score 550 paper-based, 80 iBT) or IELTS (minimum score 6.5). *Expenses:* Contact institution. *Faculty research:* Reading, early childhood development, English language learners, universal design for learning.

Gordon College, Graduate Leadership Program, Wenham, MA 01984-1899. Offers leadership (MA, Ed S). *Degree requirements:* For master's, capstone research. *Entrance requirements:* For master's, official transcripts of all degrees from undergraduate schools; professional resume; 3 references (one academic, one personal, one professional); 500-700 word statement of purpose; minimum undergraduate GPA of 3.0; for Ed S, official transcript of master's degree from accredited school; minimum GPA of 3.3 in master's program; statement of purpose essay, generally 500-700 words; professional resume; professional reference. *Expenses:* Contact institution.

Educational Leadership and Administration

Goucher College, Graduate Programs in Education, Baltimore, MD 21204-2794. Offers at-risk and diverse learners (M Ed, Certificate); athletic program leadership and administration (M Ed, Certificate); elementary education (MAT); literacy strategies for content learning (M Ed); middle school (M Ed, Certificate); Montessori studies (M Ed); reading instruction (M Ed, Certificate); reducing student, classroom, and school disruption (M Ed); school improvement leadership (M Ed); secondary education (MAT); special education (MAT), including elementary education; special education for certified elementary and secondary teachers (M Ed); teacher as leader in technology (M Ed). *Program availability:* Part-time, evening/weekend. *Degree requirements:* For master's, thesis (M Ed), final presentation (MAT). *Entrance requirements:* For master's, minimum GPA of 3.0. Additional exam requirements/recommendations for international students: Required—TOEFL (minimum score 550 paper-based; 80 iBT), IELTS (minimum score 7). Electronic applications accepted. *Expenses:* Contact institution. *Faculty research:* Urban education, middle school, school improvement, teacher education, at-risk student achievement.

Governors State University, College of Education, Program in Educational Administration and Supervision, University Park, IL 60484. Offers MA. *Program availability:* Part-time. *Faculty:* 19 full-time (12 women), 20 part-time/adjunct (13 women). *Students:* 58 part-time (37 women); includes 24 minority (22 Black or African American, non-Hispanic/Latino; 1 Hispanic/Latino; 1 Two or more races, non-Hispanic/Latino). Average age 37. 42 applicants, 88% accepted, 33 enrolled. In 2018, 27 master's awarded. *Application deadline:* For fall admission, 4/1 for domestic students. Applications are processed on a rolling basis. Application fee: $50. Electronic applications accepted. *Financial support:* Application deadline: 5/1; applicants required to submit FAFSA. *Unit head:* Timothy Harrington, Chair, Division of Education, 708-534-5000 Ext. 4361, E-mail: tharrington2@govst.edu. *Application contact:* Timothy Harrington, Chair, Division of Education, 708-534-5000 Ext. 4361, E-mail: tharrington2@govst.edu.

Governors State University, College of Education, Program in Interdisciplinary Leadership, University Park, IL 60484. Offers higher education administration (Ed D). *Program availability:* Part-time. *Faculty:* 19 full-time (12 women), 20 part-time/adjunct (13 women). *Students:* 38 full-time (29 women), 14 part-time (9 women); includes 34 minority (28 Black or African American, non-Hispanic/Latino; 5 Hispanic/Latino; 1 Two or more races, non-Hispanic/Latino). Average age 43. 27 applicants, 70% accepted, 19 enrolled. In 2018, 7 doctorates awarded. *Application deadline:* For fall admission, 4/1 for domestic students. Applications are processed on a rolling basis. Application fee: $75. Electronic applications accepted. *Expenses:* $477/credit hour; $5,724 in tuition/term; $6,854 in tuition and fees/term; $13,708/year. *Financial support:* Application deadline: 5/1; applicants required to submit FAFSA. *Unit head:* Timothy Harrington, Chair, Division of Education, 708-534-5000 Ext. 4361, E-mail: tharrington2@govst.edu. *Application contact:* Timothy Harrington, Chair, Division of Education, 708-534-5000 Ext. 4361, E-mail: tharrington2@govst.edu.

Graceland University, Gleazer School of Education, Independence, MO 64050. Offers curriculum and instruction: collaborative learning and teaching (M Ed); differentiated instruction (M Ed); instructional leadership (M Ed); literacy instruction (M Ed); management in a quality classroom (M Ed); special education (M Ed); technology integration (M Ed). *Accreditation:* NCATE. *Program availability:* Part-time, 100% online. *Students:* 70 full-time (58 women), 36 part-time (34 women); includes 4 minority (1 Black or African American, non-Hispanic/Latino; 1 Asian, non-Hispanic/Latino; 1 Hispanic/Latino; 1 Two or more races, non-Hispanic/Latino). Average age 34. 29 applicants, 21% accepted, 1 enrolled. In 2018, 76 master's awarded. *Degree requirements:* For master's, action research capstone. *Entrance requirements:* For master's, minimum GPA of 3.0, teaching certificate, current teaching contract and license, two letters of reference, statement of professional goals, verification of ongoing access to computer technology, including email and Internet. Additional exam requirements/recommendations for international students: Required—TOEFL (minimum score 550 paper-based; 80 iBT). *Application deadline:* For winter admission, 11/1 for domestic students; for spring admission, 2/1 priority date for domestic students; for summer admission, 7/1 for domestic students. Applications are processed on a rolling basis. Application fee: $50. Electronic applications accepted. *Expenses:* Tuition, material fee, university tech fee, program support fee. *Financial support:* Tuition waivers (partial) available. Financial award applicants required to submit FAFSA. *Faculty research:* Literacy, technology, faculty mentoring, adult literacy, e-learning, online teaching. *Unit head:* Dr. Michele Dickey-Kotz, Dean, 641-784-5202, E-mail: dickey@graceland.edu. *Application contact:* Susan Freeze, Admissions Representative, 816-423-4676, Fax: 816-833-2990, E-mail: sfreeze1@graceland.edu.
Website: http://www.graceland.edu/education

Grambling State University, School of Graduate Studies and Research, College of Education, Department of Educational Leadership, Grambling, LA 71245. Offers developmental education (MS, Ed D, PMC), including curriculum and instructional design (Ed D), English (MS), guidance and counseling (MS), higher education administration and management (Ed D), mathematics (MS), reading (MS), science (MS), student development and personnel services (Ed D); educational leadership (M Ed). *Program availability:* Part-time, evening/weekend. *Degree requirements:* For master's, comprehensive exam, thesis (for some programs); for doctorate, comprehensive exam, thesis/dissertation. *Entrance requirements:* For master's, GRE, minimum GPA of 2.5 on last degree; for doctorate, GRE (minimum score 1000, 500 on Verbal), master's degree, minimum GPA of 3.0 on last degree. Additional exam requirements/recommendations for international students: Required—TOEFL (minimum score 500 paper-based; 62 iBT). Electronic applications accepted.

Grand Canyon University, College of Education, Phoenix, AZ 85017-1097. Offers autism spectrum disorders (MA); curriculum and instruction (MA); early childhood education (M Ed); educational administration (M Ed); educational leadership (M Ed); elementary education (M Ed); gifted education (MA); instructional technology (MS); K-12 leadership (Ed S); reading (MA); secondary education (M Ed); secondary humanities education (M Ed); secondary STEM education (M Ed); special education (M Ed); teaching and learning (Ed D); teaching English to speakers of other languages (MA). *Program availability:* Part-time, evening/weekend, online learning. *Degree requirements:* For master's, publishable research paper (M Ed), e-portfolio. *Entrance requirements:* For master's, undergraduate degree from accredited, GCU-approved college, university, or program with minimum GPA 2.8. Additional exam requirements/recommendations for international students: Required—TOEFL (minimum score 550 paper-based; 79 iBT), IELTS (minimum score 6). Electronic applications accepted.

Grand Valley State University, College of Education, Program in Educational Leadership, Allendale, MI 49401-9403. Offers M Ed. *Program availability:* Part-time. *Students:* 4 full-time (2 women), 230 part-time (162 women); includes 37 minority (20 Black or African American, non-Hispanic/Latino; 4 Asian, non-Hispanic/Latino; 9 Hispanic/Latino; 4 Two or more races, non-Hispanic/Latino; 1 international). Average age 35. 71 applicants, 99% accepted, 24 enrolled. In 2018, 57 master's awarded. *Degree requirements:* For master's, thesis or project. *Entrance requirements:* For master's, minimum undergraduate GPA of 3.0 or GRE General Test, last 60 credits from regionally-accredited college/university, 3 letters of recommendation. Additional exam requirements/recommendations for international students: Required—TOEFL (minimum

iBT score of 80), IELTS (6.5), or Michigan English Language Assessment Battery (77). *Application deadline:* Applications are processed on a rolling basis. Electronic applications accepted. *Expenses:* $652 per credit hour, 33 credit hours. *Financial support:* In 2018–19, 64 students received support, including 63 fellowships, 1 research assistantship; unspecified assistantships also available. *Unit head:* Dr. John Shinsky, Director, 616-331-6682, Fax: 616-331-6515, E-mail: shinskjoj@gvsu.edu. *Application contact:* Dr. Rick Vandermolen, Graduate Program Director, 616-331-6272, Fax: 616-331-6422, E-mail: vanderri@gvsu.edu.
Website: http://www.gvsu.edu/grad/eduleadership/

Grand Valley State University, College of Education, Program in Leadership, Allendale, MI 49401-9403. Offers Ed S. *Program availability:* Part-time, evening/weekend. *Students:* 15 part-time (10 women); includes 4 minority (all Black or African American, non-Hispanic/Latino). Average age 41. 4 applicants, 100% accepted, 2 enrolled. In 2018, 9 Ed Ss awarded. *Entrance requirements:* For degree, GRE, master's degree with minimum GPA of 3.0, resume, 3 recommendations. Additional exam requirements/recommendations for international students: Required—TOEFL (minimum iBT score of 80), IELTS (6.5), or Michigan English Language Assessment Battery (77). *Application deadline:* Applications are processed on a rolling basis. Application fee: $30. Electronic applications accepted. *Expenses:* $677 per credit hour, 33 credit hours. *Financial support:* In 2018–19, 2 students received support, including 2 fellowships; research assistantships and unspecified assistantships also available. *Unit head:* Dr. John Shinsky, Department Director, 616-331-6682, Fax: 616-331-6515, E-mail: shinskjo@gvsu.edu. *Application contact:* Annukka Thelen, Director, Student Information and Services Center, 616-331-6205, Fax: 616-331-6217, E-mail: thelenan@gvsu.edu.

Grand Valley State University, College of Education, Programs in General Education, Allendale, MI 49401-9403. Offers adult and higher education (M Ed); early childhood education (M Ed); educational differentiation (M Ed); educational leadership (M Ed); educational technology integration (M Ed); elementary education (M Ed); middle level education (M Ed); school library media services (M Ed); secondary level education (M Ed); teaching English to speakers of other languages (M Ed). *Program availability:* Part-time, evening/weekend, 100% online, blended/hybrid learning. *Students:* 20 part-time (10 women); includes 1 minority (Black or African American, non-Hispanic/Latino). Average age 44. In 2018, 1 master's awarded. *Entrance requirements:* For master's, GRE General Test or minimum GPA of 3.0, last 60 credits from regionally-accredited college/university, 3 letters of recommendation. Additional exam requirements/recommendations for international students: Required—TOEFL (minimum iBT score of 80), IELTS (6.5), or Michigan English Language Assessment Battery (77). *Application deadline:* Applications are processed on a rolling basis. Application fee: $30. Electronic applications accepted. *Expenses:* $677 per credit hour, 33 credits. *Financial support:* In 2018–19, 1 student received support, including 1 fellowship; career-related internships or fieldwork, Federal Work-Study, scholarships/grants, and unspecified assistantships also available. *Faculty research:* Effectiveness of technology in education, parental involvement, effective teaching, effective schools research. *Unit head:* Dr. David Bair, Department Director, 616-331-6489, Fax: 616-331-6489, E-mail: baird@gvsu.edu. *Application contact:* Annukka Thelen, Director, Student Information and Services Center, 616-331-6205, Fax: 616-331-6217, E-mail: thelenan@gvsu.edu.
Website: http://www.gvsu.edu/coe/

Grand View University, Graduate Studies, Des Moines, IA 50316-1599. Offers athletic training (MS); clinical nurse leader (MSN, Post Master's Certificate); nursing education (MSN, Post Master's Certificate); organizational leadership (MS); sport management (MS); teacher leadership (M Ed); urban education (M Ed). *Program availability:* Part-time, evening/weekend. *Degree requirements:* For master's, completion of all required coursework in common core and selected track with minimum cumulative GPA of 3.0 and no more than two grades of C. *Entrance requirements:* For master's, GRE, GMAT, or essay, minimum undergraduate GPA of 3.0, professional resume, 3 letters of recommendation, interview. Additional exam requirements/recommendations for international students: Required—TOEFL (minimum score 550 paper-based). Electronic applications accepted.

Granite State College, MS in Instruction and Leadership Program, Concord, NH 03301. Offers MS. *Program availability:* Part-time, evening/weekend. *Degree requirements:* For master's, capstone. *Entrance requirements:* For master's, bachelor's degree with minimum GPA of 3.0 on last 60 credit hours, 500-1000 word statement of purpose, two letters of professional or academic reference, resume, official transcripts. Post-Baccalaureate Teacher Certification. Additional exam requirements/recommendations for international students: Required—TOEFL (minimum score 80 iBT), IELTS (minimum score 6.5). Electronic applications accepted.

Gratz College, Graduate Programs, Program in Jewish Education, Melrose Park, PA 19027. Offers education leadership (Ed D); Jewish instructional education (MA); MA/MA. *Program availability:* Part-time, evening/weekend, online learning. *Degree requirements:* For master's, one foreign language, internship. *Entrance requirements:* For master's, interview.

Gwynedd Mercy University, School of Education, Gwynedd Valley, PA 19437-0901. Offers education (Ed D); educational administration (MS); master teacher (MS); school counseling (MS); special education (MS). *Program availability:* Part-time, evening/weekend, 100% online. *Degree requirements:* For master's, thesis, internship, practicum. *Entrance requirements:* For master's, GRE or MAT; PRAXIS I, minimum GPA of 3.0. *Expenses:* Contact institution. *Faculty research:* Learning and the brain, reading literacy, ethics and moral judgment, leadership, teaching and multicultural education.

Hampton University, School of Liberal Arts and Education, Program in Educational Management, Hampton, VA 23668. Offers PhD. *Faculty:* 2. *Students:* 26 full-time (20 women), 20 part-time (14 women); includes 47 minority (46 Black or African American, non-Hispanic/Latino; 1 Asian, non-Hispanic/Latino). Average age 43. 3 applicants, 100% accepted, 3 enrolled. In 2018, 3 doctorates awarded. *Degree requirements:* For doctorate, comprehensive exam, thesis/dissertation. *Entrance requirements:* Additional exam requirements/recommendations for international students: Required—TOEFL (minimum score 525 paper-based), IELTS (minimum score 6.5). *Application deadline:* For summer admission, 1/15 for domestic students. Applications are processed on a rolling basis. Application fee: $50. Electronic applications accepted. *Financial support:* Application deadline: 6/30; applicants required to submit FAFSA. *Unit head:* Dr. Martha Jallim-Hall, Graduate Program Coordinator, 757-727-5793. *Application contact:* Dr. Martha Jallim-Hall, Graduate Program Coordinator, 757-727-5793.

Hampton University, School of Liberal Arts and Education, Program in Master of Divinity, Hampton, VA 23668. Offers MA. *Students:* 3 part-time (0 women); all minorities (all Black or African American, non-Hispanic/Latino). Average age 41. 3 applicants, 100% accepted, 3 enrolled. *Entrance requirements:* For master's, GRE. Additional exam requirements/recommendations for international students: Required—TOEFL (minimum score 525 paper-based) or IELTS (6.5). *Application deadline:* For fall admission, 6/1 priority date for domestic students, 4/1 priority date for international students; for spring admission, 11/1 priority date for domestic students, 9/1 priority date for international students; for summer admission, 4/1 priority date for domestic students, 2/1 priority date for international students. Applications are processed on a rolling basis. Application fee: $35. Electronic applications accepted.

Harding University, Cannon-Clary College of Education, Searcy, AR 72149-0001. Offers advanced studies in teaching and learning (M Ed); art (MSE); behavioral science (MSE); counseling (MS, Ed S); early childhood special education (M Ed, MSE); education (MSE); educational leadership (M Ed, Ed S); elementary education (M Ed); English (MSE); French (MSE); history/social science (MSE); kinesiology (MSE); math (MSE); reading (M Ed); secondary education (M Ed); Spanish (MSE); teaching (MAT); teaching English as a second language (MSE). *Accreditation:* NCATE. *Program availability:* Part-time, evening/weekend. *Degree requirements:* For master's, comprehensive exam (for some programs), thesis optional, portfolio(s); for Ed S, comprehensive exam, portfolio, project. *Entrance requirements:* For master's, GRE, MAT, PRAXIS; for Ed S, MAT or GRE. Additional exam requirements/recommendations for international students: Required—TOEFL (minimum score 550 paper-based; 79 iBT). *Faculty research:* Reading, comprehension, school violence, educational technology, behavior, college choice, differentiated instruction, brain-based teaching.

Hardin-Simmons University, Graduate School, College of Human Sciences and Educational Studies, Program in Education Leadership, Abilene, TX 79698-0001. Offers educational leadership in superintendency (Ed D); higher education leadership (Ed D). *Program availability:* Part-time. *Students:* 32 part-time (26 women); includes 3 minority (all Hispanic/Latino). Average age 41. 10 applicants, 70% accepted, 6 enrolled. In 2018, 5 doctorates awarded. *Entrance requirements:* For doctorate, minimum master's GPA of 3.5; resume or curriculum vitae; three recommendations from doctoral degree holder, employer/supervisor, and professional colleague. Additional exam requirements/recommendations for international students: Required—TOEFL (minimum score 550 paper-based; 79 iBT), TWE (minimum score 5). *Application deadline:* For fall admission, 7/15 priority date for domestic students, 4/1 for international students; for spring admission, 1/5 priority date for domestic students, 8/1 for international students. Applications are processed on a rolling basis. Application fee: $50. Electronic applications accepted. *Expenses: Tuition:* Full-time $750; part-time $750 per credit hour. *Required fees:* $1300; $880 per credit. Tuition and fees vary according to degree level and program. *Financial support:* Fellowships and scholarships/grants available. Support available to part-time students. Financial award application deadline: 6/30; financial award applicants required to submit FAFSA. *Unit head:* Dr. Mary Christopher, Program Director, 325-670-1510, Fax: 325-670-5859, E-mail: leadership@hsutx.edu. *Application contact:* Dr. Nancy Kucinski, Dean of Graduate Studies, 325-670-1298, Fax: 325-670-1564, E-mail: gradoff@hsutx.edu.
Website: http://www.hsutx.edu/doctorateinleadership

Harvard University, Harvard Graduate School of Education, Doctor of Education Leadership (Ed.L.D.) Program, Cambridge, MA 02138. Offers Ed L D. *Degree requirements:* For doctorate, thesis/dissertation, capstone project. *Entrance requirements:* For doctorate, GRE or GMAT, statement of purpose, 3 letters of recommendation, resume, official transcripts, 2 short essay questions. Additional exam requirements/recommendations for international students: Required—TOEFL (minimum score 613 paper-based; 104 iBT), TWE (minimum score 5). Electronic applications accepted. *Expenses:* Contact institution. *Faculty research:* System level leadership in education.

Harvard University, Harvard Graduate School of Education, Master's Programs in Education, Cambridge, MA 02138. Offers arts in education (Ed M); education policy and management (Ed M); higher education (Ed M); human development and psychology (Ed M); international education policy (Ed M); language and literacy (Ed M); learning and teaching (Ed M); mind, brain, and education (Ed M); prevention science and practice (Ed M); school leadership (Ed M); special studies (Ed M); teacher education (Ed M); technology, innovation, and education (Ed M). *Program availability:* Part-time. *Entrance requirements:* For master's, GRE General Test, statement of purpose, 3 letters of recommendation, resume, official transcripts. Additional exam requirements/recommendations for international students: Required—TOEFL (minimum score 613 paper-based; 104 iBT), TWE (minimum score 5). Electronic applications accepted. *Faculty research:* Learning and development, educational leadership and organizations, education policy analysis.

Hawai'i Pacific University, College of Professional Studies, Program in Educational Leadership, Honolulu, HI 96813. Offers M Ed. *Program availability:* Evening/weekend, online only, 100% online, blended/hybrid learning. *Entrance requirements:* For master's, transcripts, personal statement, interview, two letters of recommendation. Additional exam requirements/recommendations for international students: Recommended—TOEFL (minimum score 550 paper-based; 80 iBT), IELTS (minimum score 6), TWE (minimum score 5). Electronic applications accepted.

Henderson State University, Graduate Studies, Teachers College, Department of Advanced Instructional Studies, Arkadelphia, AR 71999-0001. Offers developmental therapy (MSE); dyslexia therapy (Graduate Certificate); education (MAT); educational technology leadership (Graduate Certificate); English as a second language (MSE, Graduate Certificate); instructional facilitator (MSE, Graduate Certificate); middle level education (MAT); special education (K-12) (MAT, MSE); special education/early childhood (MAT). *Accreditation:* NCATE. *Program availability:* Part-time. *Entrance requirements:* For master's, GRE General Test or MAT, minimum GPA of 2.7, teacher certification. Additional exam requirements/recommendations for international students: Required—TOEFL (minimum score 600 paper-based); Recommended—IELTS (minimum score 6.5).

Henderson State University, Graduate Studies, Teachers College, Department of Educational Leadership, Arkadelphia, AR 71999-0001. Offers curriculum leadership (Ed S); educational leadership (MSE, Ed S, Graduate Certificate). *Program availability:* Part-time, 100% online. *Entrance requirements:* For master's, GRE or MAT, minimum GPA of 2.7, teacher licensure. Additional exam requirements/recommendations for international students: Required—TOEFL (minimum score 600 paper-based); Recommended—IELTS (minimum score 6.5).

Heritage University, Graduate Programs in Education, Program in Educational Administration, Toppenish, WA 98948-9599. Offers M Ed. *Program availability:* Part-time, evening/weekend. *Degree requirements:* For master's, comprehensive exam, thesis optional, special project. *Entrance requirements:* For master's, valid teaching certificate, 3 years of teaching experience, interview, letters of recommendation.

High Point University, Norcross Graduate School, High Point, NC 27268. Offers athletic training (MSAT); business administration (MBA); educational leadership (M Ed, Ed D); elementary education (M Ed, MAT); pharmacy (Pharm D); physical therapy (DPT); physician assistant studies (MPAS); secondary mathematics (M Ed, MAT); special education (M Ed); strategic communication (MA). *Accreditation:* NCATE. *Program availability:* Part-time, evening/weekend. *Degree requirements:* For master's, comprehensive exam (for some programs), thesis (for some programs). *Entrance requirements:* For master's, GMAT (MBA), GRE, MAT, minimum GPA of 3.0. Additional exam requirements/recommendations for international students: Required—TOEFL (minimum score 550 paper-based). Electronic applications accepted.

High Tech High Graduate School of Education, Program in Educational Leadership, San Diego, CA 92106. Offers M Ed. *Program availability:* Part-time. *Degree requirements:* For master's, project, leadership fieldwork.

Hofstra University, School of Education, Specialized Programs in Education, Hempstead, NY 11549. Offers applied behavior analysis (Advanced Certificate); childhood special education (MS Ed); early childhood special education (MS Ed, Advanced Certificate); educational and policy leadership (Ed D); educational leadership (Advanced Certificate); educational leadership and policy studies (MS Ed), including K-12; elementary special education (MS Ed); gifted education (Advanced Certificate); health education (MS); health professions pedagogy and leadership (MS); higher education leadership and policy studies (MS Ed); inclusive early childhood special education (MS Ed); inclusive elementary special education (MS Ed); inclusive secondary special education (MS Ed); literacy studies (MA, MS Ed, Ed D, Advanced Certificate); pedagogy for health professions (Advanced Certificate); physical education (MS); school district business leader (Advanced Certificate); secondary education generalist - students with disabilities 7-12 (MS Ed); secondary special education generalist - secondary education (MS Ed); special education (MS Ed, Advanced Certificate); special education assessment and diagnosis (Advanced Certificate); special education early childhood intervention (MS Ed); special education: international perspectives (MS Ed); teaching students with severe or multiple disabilities (Advanced Certificate). *Program availability:* Part-time, evening/weekend, blended/hybrid learning. *Students:* 126 full-time (91 women), 230 part-time (175 women); includes 90 minority (40 Black or African American, non-Hispanic/Latino; 4 American Indian or Alaska Native, non-Hispanic/Latino; 11 Asian, non-Hispanic/Latino; 32 Hispanic/Latino; 3 Two or more races, non-Hispanic/Latino), 4 international. Average age 32. 215 applicants, 90% accepted, 117 enrolled. In 2018, 130 master's, 9 doctorates, 23 other advanced degrees awarded. *Degree requirements:* For master's, one foreign language, comprehensive exam (for some programs), thesis (for some programs), electronic portfolio, capstone course, internship, practicum, student teaching, seminars, minimum GPA of 3.0; for doctorate, one foreign language, comprehensive exam, thesis/dissertation, qualifying hearing. *Entrance requirements:* For master's, GRE, interview, letters of recommendation, portfolio, essay, certification; for doctorate, GRE or MAT, interview, resume, essay, master's degree, 3 letters of recommendation, writing sample; for Advanced Certificate, GRE, interview, letters of recommendation, essay, professional experience, resume, master's degree. Additional exam requirements/recommendations for international students: Required—TOEFL (minimum score 550 paper-based; 80 iBT). *Application deadline:* Applications are processed on a rolling basis. Application fee: $75. Electronic applications accepted. *Financial support:* In 2018–19, 208 students received support, including 105 fellowships with full and partial tuition reimbursements available (averaging $3,948 per year), 12 research assistantships with full and partial tuition reimbursements available (averaging $6,573 per year); career-related internships or fieldwork, Federal Work-Study, institutionally sponsored loans, scholarships/grants, traineeships, tuition waivers (full and partial), unspecified assistantships, and scholarships and endowed scholarships also available. Support available to part-time students. Financial award applicants required to submit FAFSA. *Faculty research:* Water quality and income inequality; girls and stem; new media literacies; applied behavior analysis; k-12 leadership development. *Unit head:* Dr. Alan Flurkey, Chairperson, 516-463-5237, E-mail: alan.d.flurkey@hofstra.edu. *Application contact:* Sunil Samuel, Assistant Vice President of Admissions, 516-463-4723, Fax: 516-463-4664, E-mail: graduateadmission@hofstra.edu.
Website: http://www.hofstra.edu/education/

Holy Family University, Graduate and Professional Programs, School of Education, Doctor of Education Programs, Philadelphia, PA 19114. Offers educational leadership and professional studies (Ed D). *Degree requirements:* For doctorate, thesis/dissertation. Electronic applications accepted.

Holy Family University, Graduate and Professional Programs, School of Education, Master of Education Programs, Philadelphia, PA 19114. Offers early elementary education (PreK-Grade 4) (M Ed); education leadership (M Ed); general education (M Ed); reading specialist (M Ed); special education (M Ed); TESOL and literacy (M Ed). *Program availability:* Part-time. *Degree requirements:* For master's, thesis optional. Electronic applications accepted.

Hood College, Graduate School, Department of Education, Frederick, MD 21701-8575. Offers curriculum and instruction (MS), including elementary education, elementary science and mathematics education, secondary education, special education; education, multidisciplinary studies (MS); educational leadership (MS, Certificate); reading specialization (MS); STEM education (Certificate). *Accreditation:* NCATE. *Program availability:* Part-time-only, evening/weekend. *Faculty:* 5 full-time (3 women), 32 part-time/adjunct (24 women). *Students:* 3 full-time (all women), 306 part-time (253 women); includes 65 minority (22 Black or African American, non-Hispanic/Latino; 9 Asian, non-Hispanic/Latino; 17 Hispanic/Latino; 17 Two or more races, non-Hispanic/Latino), 3 international. Average age 33. 80 applicants, 99% accepted, 45 enrolled. In 2018, 59 master's, 47 other advanced degrees awarded. *Degree requirements:* For master's, action research project, portfolio (for reading specialization); for Certificate, STEM capstone activity. *Entrance requirements:* For master's, minimum GPA of 2.75, teaching certification, writing sample during interview, letter of recommendation from principal (for educational leadership program only). Additional exam requirements/recommendations for international students: Required—TOEFL (minimum score 575 paper-based; 89 iBT), IELTS (minimum score 6.5). *Application deadline:* For fall admission, 8/15 priority date for domestic students, 8/5 for international students; for spring admission, 12/1 priority date for domestic students, 12/1 for international students; for summer admission, 5/1 priority date for domestic students, 4/15 for international students. Applications are processed on a rolling basis. Application fee: $50 ($100 for international students). Electronic applications accepted. *Expenses: Tuition:* Full-time $17,640; part-time $4410 per semester. *Required fees:* $125 per semester. Tuition and fees vary according to degree level and program. *Financial support:* Tuition waivers (partial) and unspecified assistantships available. Financial award applicants required to submit FAFSA. *Faculty research:* Leadership, action research, brain research, learning styles. *Unit head:* Dr. April M. Boulton, Dean of the Graduate School, 301-696-3612, E-mail: gofurther@hood.edu. *Application contact:* Tanith Fowler Corsi, Assistant Director of Graduate Admissions, 301-696-3603, E-mail: gofurther@hood.edu.
Website: https://www.hood.edu/academics/departments/department-education/programs-offered

Hope International University, School of Graduate and Professional Studies, Program in Education, Fullerton, CA 92831-3138. Offers education administration (MA); elementary education (ME); secondary education (ME). *Program availability:* Part-time, evening/weekend. *Degree requirements:* For master's, comprehensive exam (for some programs), thesis. *Entrance requirements:* For master's, minimum GPA of 3.0, 2 references. Additional exam requirements/recommendations for international students: Required—TOEFL (minimum score 550 paper-based; 86 iBT); Recommended—IELTS (minimum score 6.5). Electronic applications accepted. *Expenses:* Contact institution. *Faculty research:* Distance education.

Houston Baptist University, College of Education and Behavioral Sciences, Programs in Education, Houston, TX 77074-3298. Offers bilingual education (M Ed); counselor education (M Ed); curriculum and instruction (M Ed); curriculum and instruction (EC-6 bilingual) (M Ed); curriculum and instruction in all-level art, Spanish, music, or physical

education (M Ed); curriculum and instruction in EC-6 and special education (EC-12) (M Ed); curriculum and instruction in instructional technology (M Ed); curriculum and instruction in mathematics, science, or social studies (4-8) (M Ed); curriculum and instruction with EC-6 generalist (M Ed); curriculum and instruction with English language arts and reading (4-8) (M Ed); educational administration (M Ed); educational diagnostician (M Ed); executive educational leadership (Ed D); higher education in business management (M Ed); higher education in Christian studies (M Ed); higher education in counseling (M Ed); higher education in educational technology (M Ed); reading (M Ed); special educational leadership (Ed D). *Program availability:* Part-time, evening/weekend, 100% online, blended/hybrid learning. *Degree requirements:* For master's, comprehensive exam; for doctorate, thesis/dissertation. *Entrance requirements:* For master's, minimum GPA of 2.75, two recommendations, resume, bachelor's degree conferred transcript; interview (for non-certified teachers); for doctorate, GRE, 5 letters of recommendation. Additional exam requirements/recommendations for international students: Required—TOEFL (minimum score 80 iBT), IELTS (minimum score 6.5). Electronic applications accepted. Application fee is waived when completed online. *Expenses:* Contact institution. *Faculty research:* Autism and inclusion, integrating technology into instruction, school change and leadership trust.

Howard Payne University, Program in Instructional Leadership, Brownwood, TX 76801-2715. Offers M Ed. *Program availability:* Part-time, evening/weekend, online only. *Degree requirements:* For master's, comprehensive exam (for some programs), thesis or alternative. *Entrance requirements:* For master's, undergraduate degree, valid teaching certificate. Additional exam requirements/recommendations for international students: Required—TOEFL (minimum score 79 iBT). Electronic applications accepted. *Expenses:* Contact institution.

Howard University, School of Education, Department of Educational Leadership and Policy Studies, Washington, DC 20059. Offers educational administration (Ed D); educational administration and supervision (M Ed, CAGS). *Program availability:* Part-time. *Degree requirements:* For master's, comprehensive exam, School Leaders Licensure Assessment, practicum; for doctorate, comprehensive exam, thesis/dissertation, internship; for CAGS, thesis. *Entrance requirements:* For master's, minimum GPA of 2.7; for doctorate, minimum GPA of 3.0. Additional exam requirements/recommendations for international students: Required—TOEFL (minimum score 550 paper-based; 79 iBT). Electronic applications accepted.

Hunter College of the City University of New York, Graduate School, School of Education, Department of Curriculum and Teaching, Program in Educational Supervision and Administration, New York, NY 10065-5085. Offers administration and supervision (AC); instructional leadership (Ed D). *Degree requirements:* For AC, portfolio review. *Entrance requirements:* For degree, minimum B average in graduate course work, teaching certificate, minimum 3 years of full-time teaching experience, interview, 2 letters of support. Additional exam requirements/recommendations for international students: Required—TOEFL. *Faculty research:* Supervision of instruction, theory in action, human relations and leadership.

Husson University, Graduate Nursing Program, Bangor, ME 04401-2999. Offers educational leadership (MSN); family and community nurse practitioner (MSN, PMC); psychiatric mental health nurse practitioner (MSN, PMC). *Accreditation:* AACN. *Program availability:* Part-time, evening/weekend. *Degree requirements:* For master's, comprehensive exam (for some programs), research project. *Entrance requirements:* For master's, proof of RN licensure. Additional exam requirements/recommendations for international students: Required—TOEFL (minimum score 550 paper-based; 80 iBT), IELTS (minimum score 6.5). Electronic applications accepted. *Expenses:* Contact institution. *Faculty research:* Health disparities and methods to better identify and provide healthcare services to those most in need.

Huston-Tillotson University, Graduate Programs, Austin, TX 78702-2795. Offers educational leadership (M Ed).

Idaho State University, Graduate School, College of Education, Department of School Psychology and Educational Leadership, Pocatello, ID 83209-8059. Offers educational administration (M Ed, 6th Year Certificate, Ed S); educational leadership (Ed D), including higher education administration, K-12 school administration; school psychology (M Ed, Ed S). *Program availability:* Part-time. *Degree requirements:* For master's, comprehensive exam, thesis optional, internship, oral exam or deferred thesis; for doctorate, comprehensive exam, thesis/dissertation, written exam; for other advanced degree, comprehensive exam, thesis (for some programs), written and oral exam. *Entrance requirements:* For master's, MAT, bachelor's degree, minimum GPA of 3.0, 1 year of training experience; for doctorate, GRE General Test or MAT, minimum GPA of 3.0 (undergraduate), 3.5 (graduate); departmental interview; for other advanced degree, GRE General Test, minimum GPA of 3.0, master's degree. Additional exam requirements/recommendations for international students: Required—TOEFL (minimum score 550 paper-based; 80 iBT). Electronic applications accepted. *Faculty research:* Educational leadership, gender issues in education and sport, staff development.

Illinois State University, Graduate School, College of Education, Department of Educational Administration and Foundations, Normal, IL 61790. Offers college student personnel administration (MS); educational administration (MS, MS Ed, Ed D, PhD). *Accreditation:* NCATE. *Faculty:* 18 full-time (12 women), 19 part-time/adjunct (13 women). *Students:* 44 full-time (34 women), 217 part-time (128 women); includes 92 minority (60 Black or African American, non-Hispanic/Latino; 1 American Indian or Alaska Native, non-Hispanic/Latino; 1 Asian, non-Hispanic/Latino; 26 Hispanic/Latino; 4 Two or more races, non-Hispanic/Latino), 5 international. Average age 37. 104 applicants, 69% accepted, 49 enrolled. In 2018, 31 master's, 9 doctorates awarded. *Degree requirements:* For master's, thesis or alternative; for doctorate, variable foreign language requirement, thesis/dissertation, 2 terms of residency. *Entrance requirements:* For master's, GRE General Test, minimum GPA of 2.6 in last 60 hours of course work; for doctorate, GRE General Test, master's degree or equivalent, minimum GPA of 3.5. *Application deadline:* Applications are processed on a rolling basis. Application fee: $40. *Expenses: Tuition, area resident:* Full-time $7264.62. Tuition, state resident: full-time $9466. Tuition, nonresident: full-time $17,290. *International tuition:* $15,089.40 full-time. *Required fees:* $1481.04. *Financial support:* Research assistantships, teaching assistantships, tuition waivers (full), and unspecified assistantships available. Financial award application deadline: 4/1. *Faculty research:* Illinois Principals Association, special populations professional development and technical assistance project, Illinois state action for education leadership project. *Unit head:* Dr. Kevin Laudner, Dean, 309-438-2453, E-mail: klaudne@ilstu.edu. *Application contact:* Brad Hutchinson, Graduate Coordinator, 309-438-1301, E-mail: bkhutch@ilstu.edu.
Website: http://eaf.illinoisstate.edu/

Immaculata University, College of Graduate Studies, Program in Educational Leadership, Immaculata, PA 19345. Offers educational leadership (MA, Ed D); principal (Certificate); secondary education (Certificate); supervisor of special education (Certificate). *Program availability:* Part-time, evening/weekend. *Degree requirements:* For master's, comprehensive exam, thesis optional; for doctorate, comprehensive exam, thesis/dissertation. *Entrance requirements:* For master's, GRE or MAT, minimum GPA of 3.0; for doctorate, GRE General Test or MAT, minimum GPA of 3.5. Additional exam requirements/recommendations for international students: Required—TOEFL. Electronic applications accepted. *Faculty research:* Cooperative learning, school-based management, whole language, performance assessment.

Indiana State University, College of Graduate and Professional Studies, Bayh College of Education, Department of Educational Leadership, Terre Haute, IN 47809. Offers educational administration (PhD); higher education leadership (PhD); K-12 district leadership (PhD); school administration (Ed S); school administration and supervision (M Ed); student affairs and higher education (MS). *Accreditation:* NCATE. *Program availability:* Part-time, evening/weekend. Terminal master's awarded for partial completion of doctoral program. *Degree requirements:* For master's, thesis; for doctorate, thesis/dissertation. *Entrance requirements:* For master's, GRE General Test, minimum undergraduate GPA of 2.5; for doctorate, GRE General Test, minimum undergraduate GPA of 3.5; for Ed S, GRE General Test, minimum graduate GPA of 3.25. Electronic applications accepted.

Indiana University Bloomington, School of Education, Department of Educational Leadership and Policy Studies, Bloomington, IN 47405. Offers educational leadership (MS, Ed D, Ed S); higher education (Ed D, PhD); higher education and student affairs (MS); history and philosophy of education (MS); history, philosophy, and policy in education (PhD), including education policy studies, history of education, philosophy of education; international and comparative education (MS). *Accreditation:* NCATE. *Degree requirements:* For master's, thesis optional; for doctorate, comprehensive exam, thesis/dissertation; for Ed S, comprehensive exam or project. *Entrance requirements:* For master's, doctorate, and Ed S, GRE General Test. Additional exam requirements/recommendations for international students: Required—TOEFL (minimum score 79 iBT). Electronic applications accepted. *Faculty research:* Culturally engaging campus environments, school choice policy analysis, democracy and education in the national and international context, and principal leadership.

Indiana University Northwest, School of Education, Gary, IN 46408. Offers educational leadership (MS Ed); elementary education (MS Ed); K-12 online teaching (Graduate Certificate); secondary education (MS Ed). *Accreditation:* NCATE. *Program availability:* Part-time, evening/weekend. *Entrance requirements:* For master's, GRE General Test or MAT, minimum GPA of 3.0. Electronic applications accepted. *Expenses:* Contact institution.

Indiana University of Pennsylvania, School of Graduate Studies and Research, College of Education and Communications, Department of Professional Studies in Education, Doctoral Program in Administration and Leadership Studies, Indiana, PA 15705. Offers D Ed. Program also offered jointly with East Stroudsburg University of Pennsylvania. *Program availability:* Part-time, evening/weekend. *Faculty:* 11 full-time (8 women), 2 part-time/adjunct (1 woman). *Students:* 1 (woman) full-time, 97 part-time (54 women); includes 13 minority (10 Black or African American, non-Hispanic/Latino; 1 American Indian or Alaska Native, non-Hispanic/Latino; 2 Asian, non-Hispanic/Latino), 6 international. Average age 44. 23 applicants, 96% accepted, 11 enrolled. In 2018, 22 doctorates awarded. *Degree requirements:* For doctorate, one foreign language, comprehensive exam, thesis/dissertation, written exam. *Entrance requirements:* For doctorate, 2 letters of recommendation, interview. *Application deadline:* Applications are processed on a rolling basis. Application fee: $50. Electronic applications accepted. *Expenses:* Tuition, state resident: full-time $12,384; part-time $516 per credit hour. Tuition, nonresident: full-time $18,576; part-time $774 per credit hour. *Required fees:* $4454; $186 per credit hour. $65 per semester. Tuition and fees vary according to program and reciprocity agreements. *Financial support:* In 2018–19, 7 fellowships with full tuition reimbursements (averaging $1,168 per year), 5 research assistantships with tuition reimbursements (averaging $3,488 per year) were awarded; teaching assistantships, career-related internships or fieldwork, Federal Work-Study, scholarships/grants, and unspecified assistantships also available. Support available to part-time students. Financial award application deadline: 4/15; financial award applicants required to submit FAFSA. *Unit head:* Dr. Deanna Laverick, Graduate Coordinator, 724-357-2400, E-mail: D.M.Laverick@iup.edu. *Application contact:* Dr. Deanna Laverick, Graduate Coordinator, 724-357-2400, E-mail: D.M.Laverick@iup.edu.
Website: http://www.iup.edu/pse/grad/administration-leadership-studies-ded/default.aspx

Indiana University of Pennsylvania, School of Graduate Studies and Research, College of Education and Communications, Department of Professional Studies in Education, Principal Certification Program, Indiana, PA 15705. Offers Certificate. *Program availability:* Part-time, evening/weekend. *Faculty:* 11 full-time (8 women), 2 part-time/adjunct (1 woman). *Students:* 22 part-time (15 women); includes 1 minority (Hispanic/Latino). Average age 36. 24 applicants, 100% accepted, 18 enrolled. *Entrance requirements:* For degree, 2 letters of recommendation. Additional exam requirements/recommendations for international students: Required—TOEFL (minimum score 540 paper-based). *Application deadline:* For fall admission, 7/1 priority date for domestic students; for spring admission, 11/1 for domestic students. Applications are processed on a rolling basis. Application fee: $50. Electronic applications accepted. *Expenses:* Tuition, state resident: full-time $12,384; part-time $516 per credit hour. Tuition, nonresident: full-time $18,576; part-time $774 per credit hour. *Required fees:* $4454; $186 per credit hour. $65 per semester. Tuition and fees vary according to program and reciprocity agreements. *Financial support:* Career-related internships or fieldwork, Federal Work-Study, and scholarships/grants available. Support available to part-time students. Financial award application deadline: 4/15; financial award applicants required to submit FAFSA. *Unit head:* Dr. Susan Sibert, Graduate Coordinator, 724-357-3023, E-mail: susan.sibert@iup.edu. *Application contact:* Dr. Susan Sibert, Graduate Coordinator, 724-357-3023, E-mail: susan.sibert@iup.edu.
Website: http://www.iup.edu/pse/programs/principalcert/default.aspx

Indiana University–Purdue University Indianapolis, School of Education, Indianapolis, IN 46202-5155. Offers curriculum and instruction (MS); early childhood (MS); educational leadership (MS, Certificate); English as a second language (Certificate); kindergarten (Certificate); language education (MS); reading (Certificate); school counseling (MS); special education (MS, Certificate). *Program availability:* Part-time, evening/weekend. Terminal master's awarded for partial completion of doctoral program. *Degree requirements:* For master's, thesis optional. *Entrance requirements:* For master's, GRE General Test, minimum GPA of 2.5; for Certificate, official transcripts. Additional exam requirements/recommendations for international students: Required—TOEFL (minimum score 60 iBT), IELTS (minimum score 5.5). Electronic applications accepted. *Expenses:* Contact institution. *Faculty research:* Educational policies and school leaders' responses to these; issues of intersectionality in the experiences of African American lesbian, gay, and bisexual students attending historically black colleges and universities and those who belong to black Greek-letter organizations; students' experiential knowledge and their evolving disciplinary-specific literacy and understanding; innovative program development; urban ESL teacher preparation; target-based instructional coaching.

Indiana University South Bend, School of Education, South Bend, IN 46615. Offers addiction counseling (MS Ed); alcohol and drug counseling (Graduate Certificate); clinical mental health counseling (MS Ed); educational leadership (MS Ed); elementary education (MS Ed); marriage, couple, and family counseling (MS Ed); school counseling (MS Ed); secondary education (MS Ed); special education (MAT, MS Ed), including

intense intervention (MS Ed), mild intervention (MS Ed). *Accreditation:* NCATE. *Program availability:* Part-time, evening/weekend. *Degree requirements:* For master's, thesis or alternative, exit project. *Entrance requirements:* For master's, letters of recommendation, GRE or minimum GPA of 3.0. Additional exam requirements/recommendations for international students: Required—TOEFL. Electronic applications accepted. *Expenses:* Contact institution. *Faculty research:* Professional dispositions, early childhood literacy, online learning, program assessments, problem-based learning.

Indiana Wesleyan University, College of Adult and Professional Studies, School of Educational Leadership, Marion, IN 46953. Offers M Ed, Ed S. *Accreditation:* NCATE. *Program availability:* Part-time, evening/weekend, online learning. *Degree requirements:* For master's, portfolio. *Entrance requirements:* For master's, minimum GPA of 2.75, teaching experience, teaching license. Additional exam requirements/recommendations for international students: Required—TOEFL (minimum score 550 paper-based). Electronic applications accepted. *Faculty research:* Mentoring, performance-based assessments, faith integration, integration of technology, program assessment.

Instituto Tecnologico de Santo Domingo, Graduate School, Area of Humanities and Social Sciences, Santo Domingo, Dominican Republic. Offers accounting (Certificate); adult education (Certificate); applied linguistics (MA); economics (MA); education (M Ed); educational psychology (MA, Certificate); gender and development (MA, Certificate); humanistic studies (MA); international marketing management (Certificate); international relations in the Caribbean basin (Certificate); intervention systems in family therapy (MA); linguistic and literary communication (Certificate); pedagogical support (MA); social science education (M Ed); sustainable human development (MA); terminal illness and death psychology (Certificate); youth and adult education (M Ed).

Instituto Tecnológico y de Estudios Superiores de Monterrey, Campus Central de Veracruz, Graduate Programs, Córdoba, Mexico. Offers administration (MA); administration of information technologies (MTI); computer sciences (MCC); education (MEE); educational institution administration (MAD); educational technology (MTE); electronic commerce (MCE); finance (MAF); humanistic studies (MEH); international business for Latin America (MNL); marketing (MMT); science (MCP). *Program availability:* Part-time, evening/weekend, online learning. *Degree requirements:* For master's, thesis (for some programs). *Entrance requirements:* For master's, PAEP College Board. Electronic applications accepted.

Instituto Tecnológico y de Estudios Superiores de Monterrey, Campus Ciudad Juárez, Program in Educational Administration, Ciudad Juárez, Mexico. Offers MEA.

Instituto Tecnológico y de Estudios Superiores de Monterrey, Campus Estado de México, Professional and Graduate Division, Estado de Mexico, Mexico. Offers administration of information technologies (MITA); architecture (M Arch); business administration (GMBA, MBA); computer sciences (MCS, PhD); education (M Ed); educational institution administration (MAD); educational technology and innovation (PhD); electronic commerce (MEC); environmental systems (MS); finance (MAF); humanistic studies (MHS); information sciences and knowledge management (MISKM); information systems (MS); manufacturing systems (MS); marketing (MEM); quality systems and productivity (MS); science and materials engineering (PhD); telecommunications management (MTM). *Program availability:* Part-time, online learning. *Degree requirements:* For master's, one foreign language, thesis (for some programs); for doctorate, one foreign language, thesis/dissertation. *Entrance requirements:* For master's, E-PAEP 500, interview; for doctorate, E-PAEP 500, research proposal. Additional exam requirements/recommendations for international students: Required—TOEFL (minimum score 550 paper-based). *Faculty research:* Surface treatments by plasmas, mechanical properties, robotics, graphical computing, mechatronics security protocols.

Instituto Tecnológico y de Estudios Superiores de Monterrey, Campus Irapuato, Graduate Programs, Irapuato, Mexico. Offers administration (MBA); administration of information technology (MAIT); administration of telecommunications (MAT); architecture (M Arch); computer science (MCS); education (M Ed); educational administration (MEA); educational innovation and technology (DEIT); educational technology (MET); electronic commerce (MBA); environmental administration and planning (MEAP); environmental systems (MES); finances (MBA); humanistic studies (MHS); international management for Latin American executives (MIMLAE); library and information science (MLIS); manufacturing quality management (MMQM); marketing research (MBA).

Inter American University of Puerto Rico, Aguadilla Campus, Graduate School, Aguadilla, PR 00605. Offers accounting (MBA); counseling psychology specializing in family (MS); criminal justice (MA); educative management and leadership (MA); elementary education (M Ed); finance (MBA); human resources (MBA); industrial management (MBA); management information systems (MBA); marketing (MBA). *Program availability:* Part-time, evening/weekend. *Degree requirements:* For master's, comprehensive exam. *Entrance requirements:* For master's, EXADEP, 2 letters of recommendation, minimum GPA of 2.5. Electronic applications accepted.

Inter American University of Puerto Rico, Arecibo Campus, Programs in Education, Arecibo, PR 00614-4050. Offers administration and educational supervision (MA Ed); counseling and guidance (MA Ed); curriculum and teaching (MA Ed), including biology education, English as a second language, history education, math education, Spanish; elementary education (MA Ed). *Accreditation:* TEAC. *Degree requirements:* For master's, comprehensive exam, thesis optional. *Entrance requirements:* For master's, GRE, EXADEP, bachelor's degree in education or teaching license (administration and supervision) or courses in education and psychology (counseling and guidance), minimum GPA of 2.5 in last 60 credits.

Inter American University of Puerto Rico, Barranquitas Campus, Program in Education, Barranquitas, PR 00794. Offers curriculum and teaching (M Ed), including biology, English as a second language, history, Spanish; educational leadership and management (MA); elementary education (M Ed); information and library service technology (M Ed); special education (MA). *Accreditation:* TEAC. *Program availability:* Part-time, evening/weekend. *Degree requirements:* For master's, 2 foreign languages, comprehensive exam, thesis (for some programs). *Entrance requirements:* For master's, GRE or EXADEP, bachelor's degree or its equivalent from accredited institution, official academic transcript from institution that conferred bachelor's degree, minimum GPA of 2.5, two recommendation letters, interview (for some programs), essay (for some programs). Electronic applications accepted. *Expenses:* Contact institution.

Inter American University of Puerto Rico, Fajardo Campus, Graduate Programs, Fajardo, PR 00738-7003. Offers computer science (MS); educational management and leadership (MA Ed); general business (MBA); human resources (MBA); management information systems (MBA); marketing (MBA); special education (MA Ed). *Program availability:* Online learning.

Inter American University of Puerto Rico, Metropolitan Campus, Graduate Programs, Program in Education, San Juan, PR 00919-1293. Offers curriculum and instruction (Ed D); educational administration (Ed D); guidance and counseling (MA, Ed D); special education administration (Ed D). *Accreditation:* TEAC. *Degree requirements:* For doctorate, comprehensive exam, thesis/dissertation. *Entrance requirements:* For doctorate, GRE, MAT, or EXADEP. Electronic applications accepted.

Iona College, School of Arts and Science, Department of Education, New Rochelle, NY 10801-1890. Offers adolescence education: biology (MS Ed, MST); adolescence education: English (MS Ed); adolescence education: mathematics (MST); adolescence education: social studies (MS Ed, MST); adolescence education: Spanish (MS Ed); adolescence special education 5-12 (MST); childhood and special education (MST); early childhood and childhood (MST); educational leadership (MS Ed). *Accreditation:* NCATE. *Program availability:* Part-time, evening/weekend. *Faculty:* 7 full-time (5 women), 9 part-time/adjunct (5 women). *Students:* 33 full-time (30 women), 26 part-time (20 women); includes 21 minority (6 Black or African American, non-Hispanic/Latino; 1 Asian, non-Hispanic/Latino; 13 Hispanic/Latino; 1 Two or more races, non-Hispanic/Latino). Average age 25. 39 applicants, 87% accepted, 14 enrolled. In 2018, 20 master's awarded. *Degree requirements:* For master's, thesis or alternative. *Entrance requirements:* For master's, minimum GPA of 3.0, NY State teaching certificate and bachelor's degree (for MS Ed). Additional exam requirements/recommendations for international students: Required—TOEFL (minimum score 550 paper-based; 80 iBT), IELTS (minimum score 6.5). *Application deadline:* For fall admission, 8/1 priority date for domestic students, 5/1 priority date for international students; for spring admission, 1/1 priority date for domestic students, 9/1 priority date for international students. Applications are processed on a rolling basis. Electronic applications accepted. *Expenses: Tuition:* Full-time $14,064; part-time $7032 per credit. *Required fees:* $245 per semester. One-time fee: $250. Tuition and fees vary according to program. *Financial support:* In 2018–19, 2 students received support. Unspecified assistantships available. Support available to part-time students. Financial award application deadline: 4/15; financial award applicants required to submit FAFSA. *Faculty research:* Engaging teacher educators in scientific process, cross-national comparisons of mathematics teaching, questioning strategies in the classroom, research methods, literacy development. *Unit head:* Malissa Scheuring Leipold, EdD, Chair, 914-633-2210, Fax: 914-633-2281, E-mail: mleipold@iona.edu. *Application contact:* Christopher Kash, Assistant Director of Graduate Admissions, 914-633-2403, E-mail: ckash@iona.edu. Website: http://www.iona.edu/Academics/School-of-Arts-Science/Departments/Education/Graduate-Programs.aspx

Iowa State University of Science and Technology, Department of Educational Leadership and Policy Studies, Ames, IA 50011. Offers counselor education (M Ed, MS); educational administration (M Ed, MS); educational leadership (PhD); higher education (M Ed, MS); organizational learning and human resource development (M Ed, MS); research and evaluation (MS); student affairs (MS). *Degree requirements:* For master's, thesis or alternative; for doctorate, thesis/dissertation. *Entrance requirements:* For master's and doctorate, GRE General Test. Additional exam requirements/recommendations for international students: Required—TOEFL (minimum score 560 paper-based; 83 iBT), IELTS (minimum score 6.5). Electronic applications accepted.

Jackson State University, Graduate School, College of Education and Human Development, Department of Educational Leadership, Jackson, MS 39217. Offers education administration and supervision (Ed S); educational administration and supervision (MS Ed, PhD); higher education (Ed S). *Accreditation:* NCATE. *Program availability:* Part-time, evening/weekend, online only, 100% online, blended/hybrid learning. *Degree requirements:* For master's and Ed S, comprehensive exam, thesis; for doctorate, comprehensive exam, thesis/dissertation. *Entrance requirements:* For master's, GRE General Test; for doctorate, MAT, GRE, teaching experience. Additional exam requirements/recommendations for international students: Required—TOEFL (minimum score 520 paper-based; 67 iBT). Electronic applications accepted. *Expenses:* Contact institution.

Jacksonville State University, Graduate Studies, School of Education, Program in Instructional Leadership, Jacksonville, AL 36265-1602. Offers MS Ed, Ed S. *Accreditation:* NCATE. *Program availability:* Part-time, evening/weekend. *Degree requirements:* For master's, comprehensive exam, thesis (for some programs). *Entrance requirements:* For master's, GRE General Test or MAT. Additional exam requirements/recommendations for international students: Required—TOEFL (minimum score 500 paper-based; 61 iBT). Electronic applications accepted.

Jacksonville University, College of Arts and Sciences, MS in Education Leadership Program, Jacksonville, FL 32211. Offers leadership and learning (MS). *Program availability:* Part-time, evening/weekend. *Degree requirements:* For master's, comprehensive exam, practicum. *Entrance requirements:* For master's, GRE or minimum cumulative GPA of 3.3 and 3 years' relative work experience, baccalaureate degree from regionally-accredited institution with minimum GPA of 3.3; official transcripts; 2 letters of recommendation (1 from school principal); statement of professional goals (250-word minimum); resume. Additional exam requirements/recommendations for international students: Required—TOEFL. Electronic applications accepted. *Expenses:* Contact institution.

James Madison University, The Graduate School, College of Education, Program in Education, Harrisonburg, VA 22807. Offers early childhood education (preK-3) (MAT); educational leadership (M Ed); educational technology (M Ed); elementary education (MAT); equity and cultural diversity (M Ed); inclusive early childhood education (MAT); K-8 mathematics specialist (M Ed); middle education (MAT); reading education (M Ed); secondary education (MAT); Spanish language and culture for educators (M Ed); TESOL (MAT). *Accreditation:* NCATE. *Program availability:* Part-time, evening/weekend. *Students:* 255 full-time (224 women), 200 part-time (140 women); includes 56 minority (13 Black or African American, non-Hispanic/Latino; 8 Asian, non-Hispanic/Latino; 21 Hispanic/Latino; 14 Two or more races, non-Hispanic/Latino), 1 international. Average age 30. In 2018, 295 master's awarded. Application fee: $60. Electronic applications accepted. *Expenses:* Tuition, state resident: full-time $10,848. Tuition, nonresident: full-time $27,888. *Required fees:* $1128. *Financial support:* In 2018–19, 22 students received support. Teaching assistantships, career-related internships or fieldwork, Federal Work-Study, and assistantships (averaging $7911) available. Financial award application deadline: 3/1; financial award applicants required to submit FAFSA. *Unit head:* Dr. Phillip M. Wishon, Dean, 540-568-6572, E-mail: wishonpm@jmu.edu. *Application contact:* Lynette D. Michael, Director of Graduate Admissions, 540-568-6131 Ext. 6395, Fax: 540-568-7860, E-mail: michaeld@jmu.edu. Website: http://www.jmu.edu/coe/index.shtml

Johnson & Wales University, Graduate Studies, Ed D Program in Educational Leadership, Providence, RI 02903-3703. Offers Ed D. *Program availability:* Part-time. *Degree requirements:* For doctorate, thesis/dissertation. *Entrance requirements:* For doctorate, MAT, minimum GPA of 3.25; master's degree in appropriate field from accredited institution. Additional exam requirements/recommendations for international students: Required—TOEFL (minimum score 550 paper-based); Recommended—IELTS, TWE. *Faculty research:* Site-based management, collaborative learning, technology and education, K-16 education.

Kansas State University, Graduate School, College of Education, Department of Curriculum and Instruction, Manhattan, KS 66506. Offers curriculum and instruction (Ed D, PhD); digital teaching and learning (MS); educational computing, design and online learning (MS); elementary/middle level curriculum and instruction (MS); online learning (Certificate); reading specialist endorsement (MS); reading/language arts (MS); teacher leader/school improvement (MS); teaching and learning (Certificate). *Accreditation:* NCATE. *Program availability:* Part-time, online learning. *Degree*

requirements: For master's, comprehensive exam, portfolio, project, report or thesis; for doctorate, comprehensive exam, thesis/dissertation, preliminary exam; for Certificate, comprehensive exam, portfolio. *Entrance requirements:* For master's, minimum GPA of 3.0, 3 letters of recommendation; for doctorate, GRE, minimum GPA of 3.0, 3 letters of recommendation, evidence of scholarly writing; for Certificate, minimum GPA of 3.0, letters of recommendation. Additional exam requirements/recommendations for international students: Required—TOEFL (minimum score 550 paper-based; 80 iBT) or IELTS. Electronic applications accepted. *Faculty research:* Literacy and technology, critical race theory and diversity, achievement gaps, school improvement, teacher education.

Kansas State University, Graduate School, College of Education, Department of Educational Leadership, Manhattan, KS 66506. Offers adult learning (Certificate); educational leadership (MS, Ed D, PhD); leadership dynamics for adult learners (Certificate); qualitative research (Certificate); social justice education (Certificate); teaching English as a second language for adult learners (Certificate). *Accreditation:* NCATE. *Program availability:* Online learning. *Degree requirements:* For master's, comprehensive exam; for doctorate, comprehensive exam, thesis/dissertation. *Entrance requirements:* For master's, minimum undergraduate GPA of 3.0; for doctorate, MAT (for educational administration); GRE General Test (for adult education), minimum GPA of 3.0 in last 60 hours. Additional exam requirements/recommendations for international students: Required—TOEFL. Electronic applications accepted. *Faculty research:* Educational law, school finance, school facilities, organizational leadership, adult learning, distance learning/education.

Kean University, Nathan Weiss Graduate College, Doctorate Program in Educational Leadership, Union, NJ 07083. Offers Ed D. *Program availability:* Part-time. *Faculty:* 4 full-time (2 women). *Students:* 2 full-time (1 woman), 35 part-time (29 women); includes 20 minority (13 Black or African American, non-Hispanic/Latino; 1 Asian, non-Hispanic/Latino; 6 Hispanic/Latino), 2 international. Average age 45. 17 applicants, 94% accepted, 11 enrolled. In 2018, 5 doctorates awarded. *Degree requirements:* For doctorate, comprehensive exam, thesis/dissertation. *Entrance requirements:* For doctorate, GRE or MAT, master's degree from accredited college or university, minimum GPA of 3.0 in last degree attained, substantial experience working in education or family support agencies, 2 letters of recommendation, personal interview, transcripts, leadership portfolio, resume, letter of endorsement from superintendent or agency director. Additional exam requirements/recommendations for international students: Required—TOEFL (minimum score 550 paper-based; 79 iBT), IELTS (minimum score 6.5). *Application deadline:* For fall admission, 6/30 for domestic and international students. Applications are processed on a rolling basis. Application fee: $75. Electronic applications accepted. *Expenses:* Contact institution. *Financial support:* Scholarships/grants and unspecified assistantships available. Financial award applicants required to submit FAFSA. *Unit head:* Dr. Soundaram Ramaswami, Program Coordinator, 908-737-5979, E-mail: sramaswa@kean.edu. *Application contact:* Brittany Gerstenhaber, Admissions Counselor, 908-737-7100, E-mail: grad-adm@kean.edu.
Website: http://grad.kean.edu/edleadership/edd

Kean University, Nathan Weiss Graduate College, Program in Educational Administration, Union, NJ 07083. Offers school business administrator (MA); supervisor and principal (MA); supervisors, principals, and school business administrators (MA). *Accreditation:* NCATE. *Program availability:* Part-time, 100% online. *Faculty:* 4 full-time (2 women). *Students:* 5 full-time (3 women), 84 part-time (54 women); includes 33 minority (16 Black or African American, non-Hispanic/Latino; 2 Asian, non-Hispanic/Latino; 13 Hispanic/Latino; 2 Two or more races, non-Hispanic/Latino). Average age 36. 41 applicants, 88% accepted, 23 enrolled. In 2018, 24 master's awarded. *Degree requirements:* For master's, comprehensive exam (for some programs), portfolio, field experience, research component, internship, teaching experience. *Entrance requirements:* For master's, GRE General Test or MAT, minimum GPA of 3.0; New Jersey or out-of-state Standard Instructional or Educational Services Certificate; one year of experience under the appropriate certificate; official transcripts from all institutions attended; two letters of recommendation; personal statement; professional resume/curriculum vitae. Additional exam requirements/recommendations for international students: Required—TOEFL (minimum score 550 paper-based; 79 iBT), IELTS (minimum score 6.5). *Application deadline:* For fall admission, 6/30 for domestic and international students; for spring admission, 12/1 for domestic and international students; for summer admission, 5/15 for domestic and international students. Applications are processed on a rolling basis. Application fee: $75. Electronic applications accepted. *Expenses:* Tuition, state resident: full-time $15,025; part-time $733.50 per credit. Tuition, nonresident: full-time $19,890; part-time $884.50 per credit. *Required fees:* $2107.50; $89.50 per credit. Tuition and fees vary according to course level, course load, degree level and program. *Financial support:* Scholarships/grants and unspecified assistantships available. Financial award applicants required to submit FAFSA. *Unit head:* Dr. Steven Locasio, Program Coordinator, 908-737-5977, E-mail: locascst@kean.edu. *Application contact:* Brittany Gerstenhaber, Admissions Counselor, 908-737-7100, E-mail: gradadmissions@kean.edu.
Website: http://grad.kean.edu/edleadership/ma-combined

Keiser University, Ed S in Educational Leadership Program, Fort Lauderdale, FL 33309. Offers Ed S.

Keiser University, Joint MS Ed/MBA Program, Fort Lauderdale, FL 33309. Offers MS Ed/MBA.

Keiser University, Master of Science in Education Program, Fort Lauderdale, FL 33309. Offers allied health teaching and leadership (MS Ed); career college administration (MS Ed); leadership (MS Ed); online teaching and learning (MS Ed); teaching and learning (MS Ed). *Program availability:* Part-time, online learning.

Keiser University, PhD in Educational Leadership Program, Fort Lauderdale, FL 33309. Offers PhD.

Kennesaw State University, Bagwell College of Education, Program in Educational Leadership, Kennesaw, GA 30144. Offers M Ed. *Program availability:* Part-time-only, evening/weekend, 100% online, blended/hybrid learning. *Students:* 1 (woman) full-time, 58 part-time (40 women); includes 26 minority (24 Black or African American, non-Hispanic/Latino; 1 Hispanic/Latino; 1 Native Hawaiian or other Pacific Islander, non-Hispanic/Latino). Average age 37. 49 applicants, 43% accepted, 18 enrolled. In 2018, 16 master's awarded. *Entrance requirements:* For master's, GACE, GRE or MAT, minimum GPA of 2.75, transcripts, bachelor's degree. Additional exam requirements/recommendations for international students: Required—TOEFL (minimum score 80 iBT), IELTS (minimum score 6.5). *Application deadline:* For fall admission, 7/1 for domestic students; for spring admission, 11/1 for domestic students; for summer admission, 4/1 for domestic students. Applications are processed on a rolling basis. Application fee: $60. Electronic applications accepted. *Expenses: Tuition, area resident:* Full-time $6960; part-time $290 per credit hour. Tuition, state resident: full-time $6960; part-time $290 per credit hour. Tuition, nonresident: full-time $25,080; part-time $1045 per credit hour. *International tuition:* $25,080 full-time. *Required fees:* $2006; $1706 per semester. $853 per semester. *Unit head:* Dr. Ugena Whitlock, Department Chair, 470-578-6888, E-mail: uwhitloc@kennesaw.edu. *Application contact:* Admission Counselor, 470-578-4377, Fax: 470-578-9172, E-mail: ksugrad@kennesaw.edu.
Website: http://bagwell.kennesaw.edu/departments/edl/programs/med/

Kennesaw State University, Bagwell College of Education, Program in Teacher Leadership, Kennesaw, GA 30144. Offers M Ed, Ed D, Ed S. *Program availability:* Part-time-only, evening/weekend, online only, 100% online, blended/hybrid learning. *Students:* 46 part-time (31 women); includes 22 minority (18 Black or African American, non-Hispanic/Latino; 2 Hispanic/Latino; 2 Two or more races, non-Hispanic/Latino). Average age 38. 2 applicants, 100% accepted, 2 enrolled. In 2018, 6 master's, 13 doctorates, 2 other advanced degrees awarded. *Entrance requirements:* Additional exam requirements/recommendations for international students: Required—TOEFL (minimum score 80 iBT), IELTS (minimum score 6.5). *Application deadline:* For summer admission, 4/1 for domestic students. Applications are processed on a rolling basis. Application fee: $60. Electronic applications accepted. *Expenses: Tuition, area resident:* Full-time $6960; part-time $290 per credit hour. Tuition, state resident: full-time $6960; part-time $290 per credit hour. Tuition, nonresident: full-time $25,080; part-time $1045 per credit hour. *International tuition:* $25,080 full-time. *Required fees:* $2006; $1706 per semester. $853 per semester. *Application contact:* Admission Counselor, 470-578-4377, Fax: 470-578-9172, E-mail: ksugrad@kennesaw.edu.

Kent State University, College of Education, Health and Human Services, School of Foundations, Leadership and Administration, Program in Educational Leadership K-12, Kent, OH 44242-0001. Offers M Ed, PhD, Ed S. *Faculty:* 3 full-time (all women), 3 part-time/adjunct (2 women). *Students:* 16 full-time (9 women), 24 part-time (17 women); includes 3 minority (1 Black or African American, non-Hispanic/Latino; 1 American Indian or Alaska Native, non-Hispanic/Latino; 1 Asian, non-Hispanic/Latino), 2 international. 42 applicants, 40% accepted. In 2018, 2 master's, 4 doctorates, 3 other advanced degrees awarded. *Degree requirements:* For master's, thesis optional; for doctorate, comprehensive exam, thesis/dissertation. *Entrance requirements:* For master's, GRE if GPA is below 3.0, 2 letters of reference, goals statement; for doctorate, minimum master's-level GPA of 3.5, interview, resume, 2 letters of reference, goals statement; for Ed S, GRE if GPA is below 3.0. Additional exam requirements/recommendations for international students: Required—TOEFL (minimum score 550 paper-based; 80 iBT). *Application deadline:* Applications are processed on a rolling basis. Application fee: $45 ($60 for international students). Electronic applications accepted. *Expenses:* Tuition, state resident: full-time $11,766; part-time $536 per credit. Tuition, nonresident: full-time $21,952; part-time $999 per credit. *International tuition:* $21,952 full-time. Tuition and fees vary according to course load. *Financial support:* In 2018–19, 2 research assistantships (averaging $12,000 per year) were awarded; teaching assistantships, Federal Work-Study, scholarships/grants, health care benefits, and unspecified assistantships also available. *Unit head:* Natasha Levinson, Coordinator, 330-672-0592, E-mail: nlevinso@kent.edu. *Application contact:* Cheryl Slusarczyk, Academic Program Director, Office of Graduate Student Services, 330-672-2576, Fax: 330-672-9162, E-mail: ogs@kent.edu.

Keystone College, Master's in Early Childhood Education Leadership, La Plume, PA 18440. Offers M Ed. *Program availability:* Part-time, blended/hybrid learning. *Faculty:* 1 (woman) full-time, 4 part-time/adjunct (all women). *Students:* 48. 22 applicants, 100% accepted, 18 enrolled. In 2018, 20 master's awarded. *Degree requirements:* For master's, thesis or alternative. *Entrance requirements:* For master's, GRE, college transcripts, resume or curriculum vitae, current clearances. Additional exam requirements/recommendations for international students: Required—TOEFL (minimum score 80 iBT), IELTS (minimum score 6.5), TOEFL (minimum score 80 iBT) or IELTS (minimum score 6.5). *Application deadline:* For fall admission, 8/1 for domestic students; for spring admission, 1/1 for domestic students; for summer admission, 5/1 for domestic students. Applications are processed on a rolling basis. Application fee: $0. Electronic applications accepted. *Expenses:* Contact institution. *Financial support:* Unspecified assistantships available. Financial award application deadline: 5/1; financial award applicants required to submit FAFSA. *Unit head:* Heather Shanks-McElroy, PhD, Professor, 570-945-8475, E-mail: heather.mcelroy@keystone.edu. *Application contact:* Jennifer Sekol, Director of Admissions, 570-945-8117, Fax: 570-945-7916, E-mail: jennifer.sekol@keystone.edu.

Kutztown University of Pennsylvania, College of Education, Program in Student Affairs in Higher Education, Kutztown, PA 19530-0730. Offers M Ed. *Accreditation:* NCATE. *Program availability:* Part-time, evening/weekend. *Faculty:* 1 (woman) full-time. *Students:* 27 full-time (15 women), 9 part-time (5 women); includes 14 minority (6 Black or African American, non-Hispanic/Latino; 1 Asian, non-Hispanic/Latino; 4 Hispanic/Latino; 3 Two or more races, non-Hispanic/Latino). Average age 25. 36 applicants, 78% accepted, 20 enrolled. In 2018, 15 master's awarded. *Entrance requirements:* For master's, GRE General Test, 3 letters of recommendation, minimum undergraduate GPA of 3.0, department interview, statement of knowledge and experience in student affairs. Additional exam requirements/recommendations for international students: Required—TOEFL (minimum score 550 paper-based, 79 iBT), IELTS (minimum score 6.5), or PTE (minimum score 53). *Application deadline:* For fall admission, 3/1 for domestic and international students; for spring admission, 10/1 for domestic and international students. Application fee: $35. Electronic applications accepted. *Expenses:* Tuition, state resident: part-time $516 per credit. Tuition, nonresident: part-time $774 per credit. *Required fees:* $119 per credit. One-time fee: $50 part-time. Tuition and fees vary according to degree level. *Financial support:* Career-related internships or fieldwork, Federal Work-Study, and unspecified assistantships available. Financial award application deadline: 3/1; financial award applicants required to submit FAFSA. *Unit head:* Dr. Kelley Kenney, Professor, 610-683-4223, E-mail: kenney@kutztown.edu. *Application contact:* Dr. Kelley Kenney, Professor, 610-683-4223, E-mail: kenney@kutztown.edu.
Website: https://www.kutztown.edu/academics/graduate-programs/counseling.htm

Lamar University, College of Graduate Studies, College of Education and Human Development, Department of Educational Leadership, Beaumont, TX 77710. Offers digital learning and leading (M Ed); education administration (M Ed); educational leadership (Ed D); educational technology (M Ed). *Program availability:* Part-time, evening/weekend. *Faculty:* 24 full-time (14 women), 16 part-time/adjunct (11 women). *Students:* 2,691 part-time (1,904 women); includes 1,217 minority (571 Black or African American, non-Hispanic/Latino; 10 American Indian or Alaska Native, non-Hispanic/Latino; 36 Asian, non-Hispanic/Latino; 559 Hispanic/Latino; 2 Native Hawaiian or other Pacific Islander, non-Hispanic/Latino; 39 Two or more races, non-Hispanic/Latino), 1 international. Average age 37. 2,445 applicants, 90% accepted, 578 enrolled. In 2018, 882 master's, 73 doctorates awarded. Terminal master's awarded for partial completion of doctoral program. *Degree requirements:* For master's, comprehensive exam, thesis optional; for doctorate, thesis/dissertation. *Entrance requirements:* For master's, GRE General Test, minimum GPA of 2.5; for doctorate, GRE. Additional exam requirements/recommendations for international students: Required—TOEFL (minimum score 550 paper-based; 79 iBT), IELTS (minimum score 6.5). *Application deadline:* Applications are processed on a rolling basis. Application fee: $25 ($50 for international students). Electronic applications accepted. *Expenses:* Contact institution. *Financial support:* In 2018–19, 79 students received support, including 3 fellowships (averaging $20,000 per year), 1 research assistantship with tuition reimbursement available (averaging $6,500 per year); teaching assistantships with tuition reimbursements available, career-related

internships or fieldwork, and scholarships/grants also available. Support available to part-time students. Financial award applicants required to submit FAFSA. *Faculty research:* School dropouts, suicide prevention in public school students, school climate and gifted performance, teacher evaluation. *Total annual research expenditures:* $2,026. *Unit head:* Dr. Diane Mason, Department Chair, 409-880-8689, Fax: 409-880-8685. *Application contact:* Celeste Contreas, Director, Admissions and Academic Services, 409-880-8888, Fax: 409-880-7419, E-mail: gradmissions@lamar.edu.
Website: http://education.lamar.edu/educational-leadership

Lamar University, College of Graduate Studies, College of Education and Human Development, Department of Teacher Education, Beaumont, TX 77710. Offers M Ed. *Faculty:* 10 full-time (9 women), 3 part-time/adjunct (2 women). *Students:* 1 (woman) full-time, 246 part-time (214 women); includes 99 minority (42 Black or African American, non-Hispanic/Latino; 1 American Indian or Alaska Native, non-Hispanic/Latino; 5 Asian, non-Hispanic/Latino; 47 Hispanic/Latino; 4 Two or more races, non-Hispanic/Latino). Average age 36. 199 applicants, 94% accepted, 75 enrolled. In 2018, 114 master's awarded. *Entrance requirements:* Additional exam requirements/recommendations for international students: Required—TOEFL (minimum score 550 paper-based; 79 iBT), IELTS (minimum score 6.5). *Expenses:* Tuition, state resident: full-time $6234; part-time $346 per credit hour. Tuition, nonresident: full-time $6852; part-time $761 per credit hour. *International tuition:* $6852 full-time. *Required fees:* $1940; $327 per credit hour. Tuition and fees vary according to course load, campus/location, program and reciprocity agreements. *Financial support:* In 2018–19, 4 students received support. Fellowships, research assistantships, teaching assistantships, scholarships/grants, and unspecified assistantships available. Financial award applicants required to submit FAFSA. *Unit head:* Dr. Debbie Troxclair, Interim Department Chair, 409-880-8217, Fax: 409-880-7788. *Application contact:* Celeste Contreas, Director, Admissions and Academic Services, 409-880-8888, Fax: 409-880-7419, E-mail: gradmissions@lamar.edu.
Website: http://education.lamar.edu/teacher-education

La Salle University, School of Arts and Sciences, Program in Education, Philadelphia, PA 19141-1199. Offers autism spectrum disorders (MA, Certificate); bilingual/bicultural studies (MA); classroom management (MA); dual early childhood and special education (MA); dual middle-level science and math and special education (MA); education (MA); English (MA); English as a second language (Certificate); history (MA); instructional coach (Certificate); instructional leadership (MA); reading specialist (MA, Certificate); secondary education (MA); special education (MA, Certificate). *Program availability:* Part-time, evening/weekend. *Degree requirements:* For master's, comprehensive exam. *Entrance requirements:* For master's, MAT or GRE, 2 letters of recommendation; for Certificate, GMAT or GRE, 2 letters of recommendation. Additional exam requirements/recommendations for international students: Required—TOEFL. Electronic applications accepted. Application fee is waived when completed online. *Expenses:* Contact institution.

Lasell College, Graduate and Professional Studies in Education, Newton, MA 02466-2709. Offers curriculum, leadership, and inclusion (M Ed); elementary education (M Ed); special education (M Ed), including moderate disabilities; teaching bilingual/English learners with disabilities (Graduate Certificate). *Program availability:* Part-time-only, evening/weekend, blended/hybrid learning. *Faculty:* 1 (woman) full-time, 5 part-time/adjunct (4 women). *Students:* 4 full-time (3 women), 45 part-time (37 women); includes 4 minority (3 Asian, non-Hispanic/Latino; 1 Hispanic/Latino). Average age 28. 23 applicants, 70% accepted, 10 enrolled. In 2018, 22 master's awarded. *Degree requirements:* For master's, minimum GPA of 3.0; practicum. *Entrance requirements:* For master's, Massachusetts Tests for Educator Licensure (MTEL) Curriculum and Literacy foundations of reading and writing subtest, one-page personal statement, 2 letters of recommendation, resume, bachelor's degree transcript. Additional exam requirements/recommendations for international students: Required—TOEFL (minimum score 550 paper-based, 79 iBT) or IELTS (minimum score 6). *Application deadline:* For fall admission, 8/31 priority date for domestic students, 6/30 priority date for international students; for spring admission, 12/31 priority date for domestic students, 10/31 priority date for international students. Applications are processed on a rolling basis. Electronic applications accepted. *Expenses: Tuition:* Part-time $600 per credit. *Required fees:* $40 per course. *Financial support:* Federal Work-Study, scholarships/grants, and tuition discounts available. Support available to part-time students. Financial award application deadline: 8/31; financial award applicants required to submit FAFSA. *Faculty research:* Inclusion, English language learners, literacy, and urban education; teacher inquiry; universal design for learning, deaf-blindness, and visual impairments; social and emotional learning; educational law, applied behavior analysis, and classroom management. *Unit head:* Eric Turner, Vice President of Graduate and Professional Studies, 617-243-2071, Fax: 617-243-2450, E-mail: gradinfo@lasell.edu. *Application contact:* Adrienne Franciosi, Director of Graduate Enrollment, 617-243-2214, Fax: 617-243-2450, E-mail: gradinfo@lasell.edu.
Website: http://www.lasell.edu/academics/graduate-and-professional-studies/programs-of-study/master-of-education.html

La Sierra University, School of Education, Department of Administration and Leadership, Riverside, CA 92505. Offers MA, Ed D, Ed S. *Program availability:* Part-time, evening/weekend. Terminal master's awarded for partial completion of doctoral program. *Degree requirements:* For master's, thesis optional; for doctorate, thesis/dissertation, fieldwork, qualifying exam; for Ed S, thesis optional, fieldwork. *Entrance requirements:* For master's, minimum GPA of 3.0; for doctorate, GRE General Test, GRE Subject Test, minimum GPA of 3.3, Ed S; for Ed S, master's degree, minimum GPA of 3.3.

Lee University, Program in Education, Cleveland, TN 37320-3450. Offers art (MAT); curriculum and instruction (M Ed, Ed S); early childhood (MAT); educational leadership (M Ed, Ed S); elementary education (MAT); English and math (MAT); English and science (MAT); English and social studies (MAT); higher education administration (MS); history (MAT); history and economics (MAT); math and science (MAT); math and social studies (MAT); middle grades (MAT); science and social studies (MASW); secondary education (MAT); Spanish (MAT); special education (M Ed, MAT); TESOL (MAT). *Accreditation:* NCATE. *Program availability:* Part-time. *Faculty:* 13 full-time (5 women), 13 part-time/adjunct (7 women). *Students:* 32 full-time (26 women), 73 part-time (49 women); includes 13 minority (10 Black or African American, non-Hispanic/Latino; 3 Two or more races, non-Hispanic/Latino), 3 international. Average age 30. 56 applicants, 73% accepted, 34 enrolled. In 2018, 60 master's, 3 other advanced degrees awarded. *Degree requirements:* For master's, variable foreign language requirement, thesis optional, internship. *Entrance requirements:* For master's, MAT or GRE General Test, minimum undergraduate GPA of 2.75, 3 letters of recommendation, interview, writing sample, official transcripts, background check; for Ed S, minimum undergraduate and master's GPA of 2.75, official transcripts for undergraduate and master's degrees. Additional exam requirements/recommendations for international students: Required—TOEFL (minimum score 61 iBT). *Application deadline:* For fall admission, 6/1 priority date for domestic and international students; for spring admission, 11/1 priority date for domestic and international students; for summer admission, 4/1 priority date for domestic and international students. Applications are processed on a rolling basis. Application fee: $25. Electronic applications accepted. *Financial support:* In 2018–19, 43 students received support. Career-related internships or fieldwork, Federal Work-Study, institutionally sponsored loans, scholarships/grants, and unspecified assistantships available. Financial award application deadline: 3/1; financial award applicants required to submit FAFSA. *Unit head:* Dr. William Kamm, Director, 423-614-8544, E-mail: wkamm@leeuniversity.edu. *Application contact:* Jeffery McGirt, Director of Graduate Enrollment, 423-614-8691, Fax: 423-614-8317, E-mail: jmcgirt@leeuniversity.edu.
Website: http://www.leeuniversity.edu/academics/graduate/education

Lehigh University, College of Education, Program in Educational Leadership, Bethlehem, PA 18015. Offers curriculum and instruction (Certificate); educational leadership (M Ed, Ed D); K-12 principal (Certificate); superintendent letter (Certificate). *Program availability:* Part-time, evening/weekend, online only, blended/hybrid learning. *Faculty:* 4 full-time (1 woman), 7 part-time/adjunct (2 women). *Students:* 11 full-time (7 women), 104 part-time (62 women); includes 24 minority (7 Black or African American, non-Hispanic/Latino; 2 Asian, non-Hispanic/Latino; 14 Hispanic/Latino; 1 Two or more races, non-Hispanic/Latino), 7 international. Average age 34. 42 applicants, 62% accepted, 14 enrolled. In 2018, 40 master's, 2 doctorates awarded. *Degree requirements:* For master's, thesis (for some programs); for doctorate, comprehensive exam, thesis/dissertation. *Entrance requirements:* For master's, minimum undergraduate GPA of 3.0, essay, transcripts, 2 letters of recommendation; for doctorate, GRE General Test or MAT, minimum graduate GPA of 3.6, 2 letters of recommendation, essay, transcript; for Certificate, minimum undergraduate GPA of 3.0. Additional exam requirements/recommendations for international students: Required—TOEFL (minimum score 600 paper-based; 93 iBT), IELTS (minimum score 6.5), Either TOEFL or IELTS is required. *Application deadline:* For fall admission, 1/15 for domestic and international students; for spring admission, 12/1 for domestic and international students; for summer admission, 5/8 for domestic and international students. Applications are processed on a rolling basis. Application fee: $65. Electronic applications accepted. *Expenses:* MBA/Educational Leadership $825 per credit. COE (per 3 credits) intern courses require a special supervision fee which varies from $225 to $350. *Financial support:* In 2018–19, 18 students received support, including 4 research assistantships (averaging $8,600 per year); fellowships, scholarships/grants, and unspecified assistantships also available. Financial award application deadline: 1/31; financial award applicants required to submit FAFSA. *Faculty research:* Supervision of instruction, middle-level education, organizational change, leadership preparation and development, international school leadership, urban school leadership, comparative education, social justice, education and human services, social network, principal leadership, policy implementation, teacher evaluation, teaching quality. *Total annual research expenditures:* $16,829. *Unit head:* Dr. Floyd D. Beachum, Director, 610-758-5955, Fax: 610-758-3227, E-mail: fdb209@lehigh.edu. *Application contact:* Lynn Spina, Coordinator, 610-758-3250, Fax: 610-758-6223, E-mail: lys218@lehigh.edu.
Website: https://ed.lehigh.edu/academics/programs/educational-leadership

Le Moyne College, Department of Education, Syracuse, NY 13214. Offers adolescent education (MS Ed, MST); adolescent education/special education (MS Ed, MST); adolescent English (MST), including grades 7-12; adolescent English/special education (MST), including grades 7-12; adolescent foreign language (MST), including grades 7-12; adolescent history (MST), including grades 7-12; childhood education (MS Ed); childhood education/special education (MS Ed); elementary education (MS Ed); general education (MS Ed); inclusive childhood education (MST); literacy education (MS Ed), including birth to grade 6, grades 5-12; school building leader (MS Ed); school building leadership (CAS); school district business leader (MS Ed, CAS); school district leader (MS Ed); school district leadership (CAS); secondary education (MS Ed); special education (MS Ed); teaching English to speakers of other languages (MS Ed); urban studies (MS Ed). *Accreditation:* TEAC. *Program availability:* Part-time, evening/weekend. *Faculty:* 7 full-time (5 women), 16 part-time/adjunct (11 women). *Students:* 35 full-time (28 women), 119 part-time (84 women); includes 14 minority (5 Black or African American, non-Hispanic/Latino; 1 Asian, non-Hispanic/Latino; 7 Hispanic/Latino; 1 Two or more races, non-Hispanic/Latino), 1 international. Average age 30. 123 applicants, 89% accepted, 96 enrolled. In 2018, 66 master's, 48 CASs awarded. Terminal master's awarded for partial completion of doctoral program. *Degree requirements:* For master's, thesis. *Entrance requirements:* For master's, bachelor's degree with minimum undergraduate GPA of 3.0, 2 letters of recommendation, transcripts. Additional exam requirements/recommendations for international students: Required—TOEFL (minimum score 79 iBT); Recommended—IELTS (minimum score 6.5). *Application deadline:* For fall admission, 4/1 priority date for domestic and international students; for spring admission, 10/1 priority date for domestic and international students; for summer admission, 3/1 priority date for domestic and international students. Applications are processed on a rolling basis. Electronic applications accepted. *Expenses:* $734 per credit hour; wellness fee $70 per semester for full-time graduate students taking 9+ credit hours; technology fee $75 per semester for full-time graduate students taking 9+ credit hours, $25 per semester for part-time students; $1,470 per credit hour (for ED.D.). *Financial support:* In 2018–19, 44 students received support. Career-related internships or fieldwork, scholarships/grants, and health care benefits available. Support available to part-time students. Financial award applicants required to submit FAFSA. *Faculty research:* Minority teachers, special education, multiculturalism, literacy, technology, media literacy learning, autism, school district organization, service-learning, higher level problem solving, teacher leadership. *Unit head:* Dr. Stephen C. Fleury, Chair, Department of Education, 315-445-4376, Fax: 315-445-4744, E-mail: fleurysc@lemoyne.edu. *Application contact:* Jody F Manning, Assistant Director for Graduate Admission, 315-445-5444, Fax: 315-445-6092, E-mail: manninjf@lemoyne.edu.
Website: http://www.lemoyne.edu/education

Lenoir-Rhyne University, Graduate Programs, School of Education, Program in Leadership, Hickory, NC 28601. Offers community and nonprofit leadership (MA); general management (MA); higher education leadership (MA); second language community services (MA). *Program availability:* Online learning. *Entrance requirements:* Additional exam requirements/recommendations for international students: Required—TOEFL (minimum score 600 paper-based). Electronic applications accepted. *Expenses:* Contact institution.

Lesley University, Graduate School of Education, Cambridge, MA 02138-2790. Offers arts, community, and education (M Ed); autism studies (Certificate); curriculum and instruction (M Ed, CAGS); early childhood education (M Ed); ecological teaching and learning (MS); educational studies (PhD), including adult learning, educational leadership, individually designed; elementary education (M Ed); emergent technologies for educators (Certificate); ESLArts: language learning through the arts (M Ed); high school education (M Ed); individually designed (M Ed); integrated teaching through the arts (M Ed); literacy for K-8 classroom teachers (M Ed); mathematics education (M Ed); middle school education (M Ed); moderate disabilities (M Ed); online learning (Certificate); reading (CAGS); science in education (M Ed); severe disabilities (M Ed); special needs (CAGS); specialist teacher of reading (M Ed); teacher of visual art (M Ed); technology in education (M Ed, CAGS). *Accreditation:* TEAC. *Program availability:* Part-time, evening/weekend, online learning. *Degree requirements:* For master's, practicum; for doctorate, thesis/dissertation. *Entrance requirements:* For master's, Massachusetts Tests for Educator Licensure (MTEL), transcripts, statement of purpose, recommendations; interview (for special education); for doctorate, GRE General Test,

transcripts, statement of purpose, recommendations, interview, master's degree, resume; for other advanced degree, interview, master's degree. Additional exam requirements/recommendations for international students: Required—TOEFL (minimum score 550 paper-based; 80 iBT). Electronic applications accepted. *Faculty research:* Assessment in literacy, mathematics and science; autism spectrum disorders; instructional technology and online learning; multicultural education and English language learners.

LeTourneau University, Graduate Programs, Longview, TX 75607-7001. Offers business administration (MBA); counseling (MA); curriculum and instruction (M Ed); educational administration (M Ed); engineering (ME, MS); engineering management (MEM); health care administration (MS); marriage and family therapy (MA); psychology (MA); strategic leadership (MSL); teacher leadership (M Ed); teaching and learning (M Ed). *Program availability:* Part-time, 100% online, blended/hybrid learning. *Students:* 61 full-time (47 women), 311 part-time (248 women); includes 184 minority (117 Black or African American, non-Hispanic/Latino; 3 American Indian or Alaska Native, non-Hispanic/Latino; 1 Asian, non-Hispanic/Latino; 35 Hispanic/Latino; 28 Two or more races, non-Hispanic/Latino), 2 international. Average age 37. In 2018, 97 master's awarded. *Entrance requirements:* Additional exam requirements/recommendations for international students: Required—TOEFL (minimum score 525 paper-based; 80 iBT), IELTS (minimum score 6), Either a TOEFL or IELTS is required for graduate students. One or the other. *Application deadline:* Applications are processed on a rolling basis. Electronic applications accepted. *Financial support:* Research assistantships, teaching assistantships, unspecified assistantships, and employee tuition waivers and institutionally sponsored loans available. Financial award applicants required to submit FAFSA.
Website: http://www.letu.edu

Lewis & Clark College, Graduate School of Education and Counseling, Department of Educational Leadership, Program in Educational Leadership, Portland, OR 97219-7899. Offers educational administration (M Ed, Ed S); educational leadership (Ed D); student affairs administration (MA). *Program availability:* Part-time, evening/weekend. *Degree requirements:* For doctorate, thesis/dissertation. *Entrance requirements:* For master's, minimum undergraduate GPA of 2.75, Oregon teaching or personnel service license, three years of successful teaching and/or personnel service experience in the public schools or regionally-accredited private schools; for doctorate, master's degree plus minimum of 14 degree-applicable, post-master's semester credits; minimum undergraduate GPA of 2.75. Additional exam requirements/recommendations for international students: Required—TOEFL (minimum score 575 paper-based). Electronic applications accepted.

Lewis University, College of Education, Program in Educational Leadership for Teaching and Learning, Romeoville, IL 60446. Offers Ed D. *Program availability:* Part-time-only, evening/weekend. *Students:* 45 part-time (26 women); includes 16 minority (11 Black or African American, non-Hispanic/Latino; 1 Asian, non-Hispanic/Latino; 4 Hispanic/Latino), 2 international. Average age 43. *Degree requirements:* For doctorate, thesis/dissertation. *Entrance requirements:* For doctorate, master's degree, letters of recommendation, personal statement, academic and scholarly work, interview. Additional exam requirements/recommendations for international students: Required—TOEFL (minimum score 550 paper-based; 79 iBT), IELTS (minimum score 6). *Application deadline:* For fall admission, 5/1 priority date for international students; for spring admission, 11/1 priority date for international students. Application fee: $40. Electronic applications accepted. *Financial support:* Federal Work-Study, institutionally sponsored loans, scholarships/grants, and unspecified assistantships available. Financial award application deadline: 5/1; financial award applicants required to submit FAFSA. *Unit head:* Dr. Lauren Hoffman, Program Director. *Application contact:* Kathy Lisak, Graduate Admission Counselor, 815-836-5610, E-mail: grad@lewisu.edu.

Lewis University, College of Education, Program in Educational Leadership with Principal Preparation Endorsement, Romeoville, IL 60446. Offers M Ed, MA. *Program availability:* Part-time, evening/weekend. *Students:* 3 full-time (all women), 28 part-time (19 women); includes 10 minority (3 Black or African American, non-Hispanic/Latino; 1 Asian, non-Hispanic/Latino; 5 Hispanic/Latino; 1 Two or more races, non-Hispanic/Latino). Average age 36. *Entrance requirements:* For master's, bachelor's degree, minimum GPA of 2.75, two letters of recommendation, resume, interview, four years' teaching experience, portfolio. Additional exam requirements/recommendations for international students: Required—TOEFL (minimum score 550 paper-based; 79 iBT), IELTS (minimum score 6). *Application deadline:* For fall admission, 5/1 priority date for international students; for spring admission, 11/15 priority date for international students. Applications are processed on a rolling basis. Application fee: $40. Electronic applications accepted. *Financial support:* Career-related internships or fieldwork, Federal Work-Study, scholarships/grants, and unspecified assistantships available. Financial award application deadline: 5/1; financial award applicants required to submit FAFSA. *Unit head:* Dr. Lauren Hoffman, Program Director. *Application contact:* Kathy Lisak, Graduate Admission Counselor, 815-836-5610, E-mail: grad@lewisu.edu.

Lewis University, College of Education, Program in Educational Leadership with Teacher Leader Endorsement, Romeoville, IL 60446. Offers M Ed. *Program availability:* Part-time, evening/weekend. *Students:* 4 full-time (2 women), 7 part-time (3 women), 3 international. Average age 32. *Degree requirements:* For master's, comprehensive exam. *Entrance requirements:* For master's, bachelor's degree, minimum GPA of 2.75, two letters of recommendation, resume, interview, three years' teaching experience, portfolio. Additional exam requirements/recommendations for international students: Required—TOEFL (minimum score 550 paper-based; 79 iBT), IELTS (minimum score 6). *Application deadline:* For fall admission, 5/1 priority date for international students; for spring admission, 11/1 priority date for international students. Application fee: $40. Electronic applications accepted. *Financial support:* Federal Work-Study and unspecified assistantships available. Financial award application deadline: 5/1; financial award applicants required to submit FAFSA. *Unit head:* Dr. Lauren Hoffman, Program Director. *Application contact:* Kathy Lisak, Graduate Admission Counselor, 815-836-5610, E-mail: grad@lewisu.edu.
Website: http://www.lewisu.edu/academics/grad-education/teacherleadership/index.htm

Lincoln Memorial University, Carter and Moyers School of Education, Harrogate, TN 37752-1901. Offers administration and supervision (M Ed, Ed S); counseling and guidance (M Ed); curriculum and instruction (M Ed, Ed D, Ed S); English (M Ed); executive leadership (Ed D); higher education administration (Ed D); human resource development (Ed D); leadership and administration (Ed D). *Program availability:* Part-time, evening/weekend, online learning. *Degree requirements:* For master's, comprehensive exam, thesis optional; for Ed S, comprehensive exam. *Entrance requirements:* For master's, PRAXIS, NTE, GRE, MAT, letters of recommendation; for Ed S, graduate transcripts. Additional exam requirements/recommendations for international students: Recommended—TOEFL. *Faculty research:* Brain compatible teaching and learning; poverty in Appalachia; leadership for change; ethics, moral responsibility and social justice; human and organizational learning.

Lincoln University, The School of Adult & Continuing Education, Philadelphia, PA 19104. Offers counseling (MSC); early childhood education (M Ed), including PreK-4; early childhood education and special education (M Ed); educational leadership (M Ed), including principal certification; finance (MBA); human resources management (MBA);

human services delivery (MAHS). *Program availability:* Part-time, evening/weekend. *Faculty:* 8 full-time (3 women), 22 part-time/adjunct (12 women). *Students:* 192 full-time (154 women), 62 part-time (40 women); includes 230 minority (218 Black or African American, non-Hispanic/Latino; 9 Hispanic/Latino; 3 Two or more races, non-Hispanic/Latino), 3 international. Average age 33. 278 applicants, 58% accepted, 94 enrolled. In 2018, 105 master's awarded. *Degree requirements:* For master's, comprehensive exam, thesis or alternative, capstone, grant proposal. *Entrance requirements:* For master's, GRE/GMAT (Optional), Official academic transcript(s), letters of recommendation, personal statement, resume, supervisor's evaluation form, Application fee. Additional exam requirements/recommendations for international students: Required—TOEFL (minimum score 500 paper-based; 71 iBT); Recommended—IELTS (minimum score 6.5). *Application deadline:* For fall admission, 8/19 for domestic and international students; for spring admission, 12/30 for domestic and international students. Applications are processed on a rolling basis. Application fee: $50. Electronic applications accepted. *Financial support:* Scholarships/grants available. Financial award application deadline: 4/1; financial award applicants required to submit FAFSA. *Unit head:* Dr. Patricia Joseph, Dean of Faculty, 484-365-7659, E-mail: joseph@lincoln.edu. *Application contact:* Jernice Lea, Director, Student Services and Admissions, 215-590-8231, Fax: 215-387-3859, E-mail: jlea@lincoln.edu.
Website: http://www.lincoln.edu/admissions/graduate-admissions

Lindenwood University, Graduate Programs, School of Education, St. Charles, MO 63301-1695. Offers behavioral analysis (MA); education (MA), including autism spectrum disorders, character education, early intervention in autism and sensory impairment, gifted, technology; educational administration (MA, Ed D, Ed S); English to speakers of other languages (MA); instructional leadership (Ed D, Ed S); library media (MA); professional counseling (MA); school administration (MA, Ed S); school counseling (MA); teaching (MA). *Program availability:* Part-time, evening/weekend, 100% online, blended/hybrid learning. *Faculty:* 38 full-time (28 women), 111 part-time/adjunct (66 women). *Students:* 456 full-time (341 women), 1,107 part-time (851 women); includes 374 minority (296 Black or African American, non-Hispanic/Latino; 7 American Indian or Alaska Native, non-Hispanic/Latino; 8 Asian, non-Hispanic/Latino; 38 Hispanic/Latino; 1 Native Hawaiian or other Pacific Islander, non-Hispanic/Latino; 24 Two or more races, non-Hispanic/Latino), 17 international. Average age 36. 496 applicants, 72% accepted, 275 enrolled. In 2018, 454 master's, 64 doctorates, 66 other advanced degrees awarded. *Degree requirements:* For master's, thesis (for some programs), minimum GPA of 3.0; for doctorate, thesis/dissertation, minimum GPA of 3.0; for Ed S, comprehensive exam, project, minimum GPA of 3.0. *Entrance requirements:* For master's, interview, minimum undergraduate cumulative GPA of 3.0, writing sample, letter of recommendation; for doctorate, minimum graduate GPA of 3.4, resume, interview, writing sample, 4 letters of recommendation; for Ed S, master's degree in education, relevant work experience. Additional exam requirements/recommendations for international students: Required—TOEFL (minimum score 553 paper-based; 81 iBT); Recommended—IELTS (minimum score 6.5). *Application deadline:* For fall admission, 8/9 priority date for domestic students, 6/1 priority date for international students; for spring admission, 12/20 priority date for domestic students, 11/1 priority date for international students; for summer admission, 5/15 priority date for domestic students, 3/27 priority date for international students. Applications are processed on a rolling basis. Application fee: $0 ($100 for international students). Electronic applications accepted. *Expenses:* Tuition: Full-time $16,900; part-time $480 per credit hour. *Required fees:* $700; $350 per unit. Tuition and fees vary according to degree level. *Financial support:* In 2018–19, 316 students received support. Career-related internships or fieldwork, Federal Work-Study, institutionally sponsored loans, scholarships/grants, tuition waivers (partial), and unspecified assistantships available. Financial award application deadline: 6/30; financial award applicants required to submit FAFSA. *Unit head:* Dr. Anthony Scheffler, Dean, School of Education, 636-949-4618, Fax: 636-949-4197, E-mail: ascheffler@lindenwood.edu. *Application contact:* Kara Schilli, Assistant Vice President, University Admissions, 636-949-4349, Fax: 636-949-4109, E-mail: adultadmissions@lindenwood.edu.
Website: https://www.lindenwood.edu/academics/academic-schools/school-of-education/

Lindenwood University–Belleville, Graduate Programs, Belleville, IL 62226. Offers business administration (MBA); communications (MA), including digital and multimedia, media management, promotions, training and development; counseling (MA); criminal justice administration (MS); education (MA); healthcare administration (MS); human resource management (MS); school administration (MA); teaching (MAT).

Lindsey Wilson College, Division of Education, Columbia, KY 42728. Offers teacher as leader (M Ed). *Program availability:* Online learning. *Entrance requirements:* For master's, bachelor's degree from accredited institution, minimum undergraduate GPA of 3.0, letters of recommendation.

Lipscomb University, College of Education, Nashville, TN 37204-3951. Offers applied behavior analysis (MS, Certificate); coaching for learning (M Ed, Certificate, Ed S); educational leadership (M Ed, Ed S); English language learning (M Ed, Ed S); instructional coaching (M Ed, Certificate, Ed S); instructional practice (M Ed); learning organizations and strategic change (Ed D); literacy coaching (Certificate, Ed S); reading specialty (M Ed, Ed S); school counseling (M Ed, Ed S); special education (M Ed); teaching, learning, and leading (M Ed); technology integration (M Ed, Ed S); technology integration specialist (Certificate). *Accreditation:* NCATE. *Program availability:* Part-time, evening/weekend, 100% online. *Degree requirements:* For master's, comprehensive exam, portfolio, research project and presentation; for doctorate, practical capstone project in experiential setting. *Entrance requirements:* For master's, MAT (minimum score 31) or GRE General Test (minimum score 294), 2 reference letters, goals statement, writing sample, interview; for doctorate, MAT or GRE General Test, 3 reference letters, artifact of demonstrated academic excellence, written personal statements, interview. Additional exam requirements/recommendations for international students: Required—TOEFL (minimum score 570 paper-based; 80 iBT). Electronic applications accepted. *Expenses:* Contact institution. *Faculty research:* Facilitative learning styles, leadership, student assessment, interactive multimedia inclusion, learning organizations and strategic change.

Lock Haven University of Pennsylvania, College of Liberal Arts and Education, Lock Haven, PA 17745-2390. Offers alternative education (M Ed); educational leadership (M Ed); teaching and learning (M Ed). *Accreditation:* NCATE. *Program availability:* Part-time, evening/weekend, online learning. *Degree requirements:* For master's, thesis. *Entrance requirements:* For master's, minimum undergraduate GPA of 3.0. Additional exam requirements/recommendations for international students: Required—TOEFL. Electronic applications accepted.

Long Island University–Brentwood Campus, Graduate Programs, Brentwood, NY 11717. Offers childhood education (MS), including grades 1-6; childhood education/literacy B-6 (MS); childhood education/special education (grades 1-6) (MS); clinical mental health counseling (MS, Advanced Certificate); criminal justice (MS); early childhood education (MS); educational leadership (MS Ed); family nurse practitioner (MS, Advanced Certificate); health administration (MPA); library and information science (MS); literacy (B-6) (MS Ed); school counselor (MS, Advanced Certificate); social work (MSW); special education (MS Ed); students with disabilities generalist (grades 7-12)

(Advanced Certificate). *Program availability:* Part-time. *Entrance requirements:* For master's and Advanced Certificate, GRE. Additional exam requirements/recommendations for international students: Required—TOEFL or IELTS. Electronic applications accepted.

Long Island University–Hudson, Graduate School, Purchase, NY 10577. Offers autism (Advanced Certificate); bilingual education (Advanced Certificate); childhood education (MS Ed); crisis management (Advanced Certificate); early childhood education (MS Ed); educational leadership (MS Ed); health administration (MPA); literacy (MS Ed); marriage and family therapy (MS); mental health counseling (MS, Advanced Certificate), including credentialed alcoholism and substance abuse counselor (MS); middle childhood and adolescence education (MS Ed); pharmaceutics (MS), including cosmetic science, industrial pharmacy; public administration (MPA); school counseling (MS Ed, Advanced Certificate); school psychology (MS Ed); special education (MS Ed); TESOL (MS Ed); TESOL (all grades) (Advanced Certificate). *Program availability:* Part-time, evening/weekend. *Entrance requirements:* Additional exam requirements/recommendations for international students: Required—TOEFL. Electronic applications accepted. *Expenses:* Contact institution.

Long Island University–LIU Brooklyn, School of Education, Brooklyn, NY 11201-8423. Offers adolescence urban education (MS Ed); applied behavior analysis (Advanced Certificate); bilingual education (Advanced Certificate); bilingual education in urban setting (MS Ed); bilingual school counselor (MS Ed, Advanced Certificate); childhood urban education (MS Ed); childhood/early childhood education (MS Ed); childhood/early childhood urban education (MS Ed); early childhood urban education (MS Ed, Advanced Certificate); educational leadership (Advanced Certificate); marriage and family therapy (MS, Advanced Certificate); mental health counseling (MS, Advanced Certificate); school building district leader (Advanced Certificate); school counselor (MS Ed, Advanced Certificate); school psychologist (MS Ed); teaching students with disabilities (MS Ed); teaching urban children with disabilities (MS Ed); TESOL (MS Ed, Advanced Certificate). *Accreditation:* TEAC. *Program availability:* Part-time, evening/weekend, 100% online. *Entrance requirements:* For master's, GRE. Additional exam requirements/recommendations for international students: Required—TOEFL (minimum score 527 paper-based, 75 iBT), IELTS, or PTE. Electronic applications accepted. *Faculty research:* Diversity issues in education and mental health care, inclusion - disability studies, sustainability, teacher professional development.

Long Island University–LIU Post, College of Education, Information and Technology, Brookville, NY 11548-1300. Offers adolescence education (MS); adolescence education 7-12 (MS); archives and records management (AC); art education (MS); childhood education (MS); childhood education/literacy B-6 (MS); childhood education/special education (MS); clinical mental health counseling (MS, AC); early childhood education (MS); early childhood education/childhood education (MS); educational leadership (AC); educational technology (MS); information studies (PhD); interdisciplinary educational studies (Ed D); middle childhood education (MS); music education (MS); public library administration (AC); school counselor (MS); special education (MS Ed); speech-language pathology (MA); students with disabilities, 7-12 generalist (AC); TESOL (MA). *Accreditation:* ASHA; TEAC. *Program availability:* Part-time, 100% online, blended/hybrid learning. Terminal master's awarded for partial completion of doctoral program. *Degree requirements:* For master's, variable foreign language requirement, comprehensive exam (for some programs), thesis optional; for doctorate, comprehensive exam, thesis/dissertation. *Entrance requirements:* For master's and AC, GRE (for some programs). Additional exam requirements/recommendations for international students: Required—TOEFL (minimum score 550 paper-based, 75 iBT), IELTS, or PTE. Electronic applications accepted. *Faculty research:* Sleep; use of technology to develop executive function by students with disabilities; early childhood literacy development through play; social justice through education; using a structured protocol to discuss Bad News.

Loras College, Graduate Division, Program in Educational Leadership, Dubuque, IA 52004-0178. Offers MA. *Program availability:* Part-time, evening/weekend. *Degree requirements:* For master's, comprehensive exam, thesis optional. *Entrance requirements:* For master's, minimum cumulative undergraduate GPA of 3.0.

Louisiana College, Graduate Programs, Pineville, LA 71359-0001. Offers clinical nurse leadership (MSN); educational leadership (M Ed); social work (MSW); teaching (MAT).

Louisiana State University and Agricultural & Mechanical College, Graduate School, College of Human Sciences and Education, Department of Educational Theory, Policy and Practice, Baton Rouge, LA 70803. Offers counseling (M Ed, MA, Ed S); educational administration (M Ed, MA, PhD, Ed S); educational technology (MA); elementary education (M Ed, MAT); higher education (PhD); research methodology (PhD); secondary education (M Ed, MAT). *Accreditation:* ACA (one or more programs are accredited); NCATE.

Louisiana State University in Shreveport, College of Business, Education, and Human Development, Program in Education, Shreveport, LA 71115-2399. Offers curriculum and instruction (M Ed); leadership (M Ed); leadership studies (Ed D). *Accreditation:* NCATE. *Program availability:* Part-time. *Degree requirements:* For master's, orally-presented project, 200-hour internship (educational leadership). *Entrance requirements:* For master's, GRE, minimum GPA of 2.5; teacher certification; recommendations and interview (for educational leadership). Additional exam requirements/recommendations for international students: Required—TOEFL (minimum score 550 paper-based; 61 iBT). Electronic applications accepted.

Louisiana Tech University, Graduate School, College of Education, Ruston, LA 71272. Offers counseling and guidance (MA), including clinical mental health counseling, human services, orientation and mobility; counseling psychology (PhD); curriculum and instruction (M Ed); cyber education (Graduate Certificate); dynamics of domestic and family violence (Graduate Certificate); early childhood education - PreK-3 (MAT); educational leadership (M Ed, Ed D); elementary education and special education mild/moderate grades 1-5 (MAT); higher education administration (Graduate Certificate); industrial/organizational psychology (MA, PhD); kinesiology (MS); middle school education (MAT), including mathematics; orientation and mobility (Graduate Certificate); rehabilitation teaching for the blind (Graduate Certificate); secondary education (MAT), including agriculture, biology, business, chemistry, English; special education: visually impaired (MAT); teacher leader education (Graduate Certificate); visual impairments - blind education (Graduate Certificate). *Accreditation:* NCATE. *Program availability:* Part-time. *Degree requirements:* For master's, thesis; for doctorate, thesis/dissertation. *Entrance requirements:* For master's and doctorate, GRE General Test. Additional exam requirements/recommendations for international students: Required—TOEFL (minimum score 550 paper-based; 80 iBT), IELTS (minimum score 6.5). Electronic applications accepted. *Faculty research:* Blindness and the best methods for increasing independence for individuals who are blind or visually impaired; educating and investigating factors contributing to improvements in human performance across the lifespan and a reduction in injury rates during training.

Lourdes University, Graduate School, Sylvania, OH 43560-2898. Offers business (MBA); leadership (M Ed); nurse anesthesia (MSN); nurse educator (MSN); nurse leader (MSN); organizational leadership (MOL); reading (M Ed); teaching and curriculum (M Ed); theology (MA). *Accreditation:* AANA/CANAEP. *Program availability:* Evening/

weekend. *Entrance requirements:* Additional exam requirements/recommendations for international students: Required—TOEFL.

Loyola Marymount University, School of Education, Doctorate in Educational Leadership for Social Justice Program, Los Angeles, CA 90045. Offers Ed D. *Unit head:* Dr. Jill Bickett, Director, Doctorate in Educational Leadership for Social Justice, 310-338-3777, E-mail: jbickett@lmu.edu. *Application contact:* Chake H. Kouyoumjian, Associate Dean of Graduate Studies, 310-338-2721, Fax: 310-338-6086, E-mail: graduateinfo@lmu.edu. Website: http://soe.lmu.edu/academics/doctoral

Loyola Marymount University, School of Education, Program in School Administration, Los Angeles, CA 90045. Offers MA. *Unit head:* Dr. Manuel Ponce, Jr., Director, Institute of School Leadership and Administration, 310-568-7165, E-mail: mponce8@lmu.edu. *Application contact:* Chake H. Kouyoumjian, Associate Dean of Graduate Studies, 310-338-2721, Fax: 310-338-6086, E-mail: graduateinfo@lmu.edu. Website: http://soe.lmu.edu/academics/isla

Loyola University Chicago, School of Education, Program in Administration and Supervision, Chicago, IL 60660. Offers M Ed, Ed D, Certificate. *Program availability:* Part-time, evening/weekend. *Faculty:* 5 full-time (4 women), 8 part-time/adjunct (3 women). *Students:* 36 full-time (27 women); includes 18 minority (9 Black or African American, non-Hispanic/Latino; 3 Asian, non-Hispanic/Latino; 6 Hispanic/Latino). Average age 42. 4 applicants, 25% accepted. In 2018, 3 master's, 10 doctorates, 5 Certificates awarded. *Degree requirements:* For master's, comprehensive exam; for doctorate, comprehensive exam, thesis/dissertation. *Entrance requirements:* For master's, minimum GPA of 3.0, letters of recommendation, resume, transcripts; for doctorate, GRE General Test, interview, minimum GPA of 3.0, letters of recommendation, resume. Additional exam requirements/recommendations for international students: Required—TOEFL (minimum score 550 paper-based; 79 iBT). *Application deadline:* For fall admission, 2/15 for domestic and international students. Applications are processed on a rolling basis. Application fee: $50. Electronic applications accepted. Application fee is waived when completed online. *Expenses:* Contact institution. *Financial support:* In 2018–19, 40 fellowships, 1 research assistantship (averaging $14,000 per year) were awarded; career-related internships or fieldwork, institutionally sponsored loans, scholarships/grants, and unspecified assistantships also available. Support available to part-time students. Financial award application deadline: 2/1; financial award applicants required to submit FAFSA. *Faculty research:* Leadership, school law, school administration, supervision, ethics. *Unit head:* Dr. Siobhan Cafferty, Director, 312-915-7002, Fax: 312-915-6980, E-mail: scaffer@luc.edu. *Application contact:* Dr. Siobhan Cafferty, Director, 312-915-7002, Fax: 312-915-6980, E-mail: scaffer@luc.edu.

Loyola University Maryland, Graduate Programs, School of Education, Program in Educational Leadership, Baltimore, MD 21210-2699. Offers M Ed, CAS. *Program availability:* Part-time. *Entrance requirements:* For master's, transcripts, essay, resume. Additional exam requirements/recommendations for international students: Required—TOEFL (minimum score 550 paper-based), IELTS (minimum score 7). Electronic applications accepted. *Expenses:* Contact institution.

Lynn University, Donald E. and Helen L. Ross College of Education, Boca Raton, FL 33431-5598. Offers educational leadership (M Ed, Ed D), including K-12 (Ed D); school administration K-12 (M Ed); exceptional student education (M Ed), including school administration K-12. *Program availability:* Part-time, evening/weekend, online learning. *Faculty:* 6 full-time (4 women), 8 part-time/adjunct (7 women). *Students:* 38 full-time (30 women), 85 part-time (63 women); includes 50 minority (33 Black or African American, non-Hispanic/Latino; 1 Asian, non-Hispanic/Latino; 15 Hispanic/Latino; 1 Two or more races, non-Hispanic/Latino), 5 international. Average age 38. 78 applicants, 65% accepted, 41 enrolled. In 2018, 13 master's, 14 doctorates awarded. *Degree requirements:* For master's, comprehensive exam, thesis (for some programs), completion of degree in maximum of four calendar years; minimum cumulative GPA of 3.0 and B grade or higher in each course; orientation seminar (one credit); minimum of 40 credits; FTCE ESE K-12 Exam; for doctorate, thesis/dissertation, mid-program review; minimum cumulative GPA of 3.25 and B grade or higher in each course. *Entrance requirements:* For master's, bachelor's degree from accredited institution, minimum undergraduate GPA of 3.0, official undergraduate and graduate transcripts of all academic coursework attempted, current resume, statement of professional goals, writing sample, 2 recent letters of recommendation; for doctorate, professional practice statement that identifies applicant's goals and explains how Lynn's program will help attain them, official transcript showing conferral of master's degree, 2 letters of recommendation from previous professors or employers, current resume, interview. Additional exam requirements/recommendations for international students: Required—TOEFL (minimum score 550 paper-based; 80 iBT), IELTS (minimum score 6.5). *Application deadline:* For fall admission, 8/18 for domestic students, 8/4 for international students; for spring admission, 12/15 for domestic students, 12/1 for international students; for summer admission, 4/17 for domestic students, 4/3 for international students. Applications are processed on a rolling basis. Application fee: $45. Electronic applications accepted. *Expenses:* 850 per credit hour. *Financial support:* In 2018–19, 85 students received support. Career-related internships or fieldwork, Federal Work-Study, scholarships/grants, tuition waivers (partial), and unspecified assistantships available. Support available to part-time students. Financial award application deadline: 3/1; financial award applicants required to submit FAFSA. *Faculty research:* Student achievement, students with learning differences, teacher and student retention, student motivation and cognition, neuroscience leadership and learning. *Unit head:* Dr. Kathleen Weigel, Dean, College of Education, 561-237-7441, E-mail: kweigel@lynn.edu. *Application contact:* Steven Pruitt, Director of Graduate and Undergraduate Evening Admission, 561-237-7834, Fax: 561-237-7100, E-mail: spruitt@lynn.edu. Website: http://www.lynn.edu/academics/colleges/education

Madonna University, Programs in Education, Livonia, MI 48150-1173. Offers Catholic school leadership (MSA); educational leadership (MSA); learning disabilities (MAT); literacy education (MAT); teaching and learning (MAT). *Accreditation:* NCATE. *Program availability:* Part-time, evening/weekend. *Degree requirements:* For master's, thesis or alternative. Electronic applications accepted. *Expenses: Tuition:* Full-time $15,030; part-time $835 per credit hour. Tuition and fees vary according to degree level and program.

Malone University, Graduate Program in Education, Canton, OH 44709. Offers curriculum and instruction (MA); curriculum, instruction, and professional development (MA); educational leadership (principal license) (MA); intervention specialist (MA). *Accreditation:* NCATE. *Program availability:* Part-time, evening/weekend. *Degree requirements:* For master's, research project. *Entrance requirements:* For master's, minimum GPA of 3.0, teaching license. Additional exam requirements/recommendations for international students: Required—TOEFL (minimum score 550 paper-based; 79 iBT). *Faculty research:* Educational leadership styles: Jesus as master teacher, assessment accommodations for English language learners, preparing culturally proficient teachers, using naturally occurring text in the classroom to meet the syntactic needs of students with learning disabilities, using tablet instructional technology to meet the needs of students with disabilities.

Educational Leadership and Administration

Manhattan College, Graduate Programs, School of Education and Health, Program in Educational Leadership, Riverdale, NY 10471. Offers advanced leadership studies (MS Ed, Advanced Certificate), including school district leadership; school building leadership (MS Ed, Advanced Certificate). *Program availability:* Part-time, evening/weekend, blended/hybrid learning. *Degree requirements:* For master's, thesis, internship; for Advanced Certificate, internship. *Entrance requirements:* For master's, GRE (for the first graduate course), baccalaureate degree, minimum GPA of 3.0, 3 years of pupil personnel service, professional recommendation; for Advanced Certificate, New York State certification examination, master's degree; 3 years of personnel service; minimum GPA of 3.0; professional recommendations. Additional exam requirements/recommendations for international students: Required—TOEFL (minimum score 550 paper-based). Electronic applications accepted. *Expenses:* Contact institution. *Faculty research:* Distance learning and teacher efficacy, leadership and student achievement, professional development and student achievement, leadership development, professional development for teachers, authentic assessment strategies, curriculum development and adaptation.

Manhattanville College, School of Education, Program in Educational Leadership, Purchase, NY 10577-2132. Offers education leadership (Ed D); educational leadership (MPS); educational leadership - school building leader (PD); educational leadership - school building leader and school district leader (PD); higher education leadership (Ed D); school district leader (Advanced Certificate). *Program availability:* Part-time, evening/weekend. *Faculty:* 6 full-time (2 women), 14 part-time/adjunct (9 women). *Students:* 100 full-time (65 women), 47 part-time (32 women); includes 38 minority (20 Black or African American, non-Hispanic/Latino; 5 Asian, non-Hispanic/Latino; 13 Hispanic/Latino), 1 international. Average age 43. 59 applicants, 64% accepted, 33 enrolled. In 2018, 2 master's, 12 doctorates, 12 Advanced Certificates awarded. *Degree requirements:* For master's, comprehensive exam (for some programs), thesis (for some programs), student teaching, research seminars, portfolios, internships, writing assessment; for doctorate, thesis/dissertation, professional portfolio; for other advanced degree, comprehensive exam (for some programs). *Entrance requirements:* For master's, for programs leading to certification, candidates must submit scores from GRE or MAT(Miller Analogies Test), minimum undergraduate GPA of 3.0, all transcripts from all colleges and universities attended, 2 letters of recommendation, interview, essay (2-3 page personal statement that describes reasons for choosing education as profession and personal philosophy of education), proof of immunization (for those born after 1957); for doctorate, for programs leading to certification, candidates must submit scores from GRE or MAT(Miller Analogies Test), GPA of 3.0+, 2 letters of recommendation, 1 letter of nomination, interview, writing sample(leadership experiences, your strengths in the role of educational leader, your interest in the doctoral program, and what knowledge and skills you hope to develop in the program), educator, leader, supervisor; proof of immunization for those born after 1957. Additional exam requirements/recommendations for international students: Required—TOEFL (minimum score 600 paper-based; 110 iBT); Recommended—IELTS (minimum score 8). *Application deadline:* Applications are processed on a rolling basis. Application fee: $75. Electronic applications accepted. *Expenses:* 935 per credit; 1000 per credit for those who completed all degree requirements from another institution and just need to complete dissertation for doctorate. *Financial support:* Teaching assistantships, career-related internships or fieldwork, Federal Work-Study, institutionally sponsored loans, scholarships/grants, and unspecified assistantships available. Financial award application deadline: 3/15; financial award applicants required to submit FAFSA. *Faculty research:* Social capital, diversity in higher education, school leadership. *Unit head:* Dr. Shelley Wepner, Dean, 914-323-3153, Fax: 914-323-5493, E-mail: Shelley.Wepner@mville.edu. *Application contact:* Lenora Boehlert, Department Chair, 914-323-5443, E-mail: Lenora.Boehlert@mville.edu.
Website: http://www.mville.edu/programs/educational-leadership

Marconi International University, Graduate Programs, Miami, FL 33132. Offers business administration (DBA); education leadership (Ed D); education leadership, management and emerging technologies (M Ed); international business administration (IMBA).

Marian University, School of Education, Fond du Lac, WI 54935-4699. Offers curriculum and instruction leadership (PhD); educational administration (PhD); educational leadership (MAE); educational technology (MAE); leadership studies (PhD); special education (MAE); teacher education (MAE). *Accreditation:* NCATE. *Program availability:* Part-time, evening/weekend, online learning. *Degree requirements:* For master's, exam, field-based experience project, portfolio; for doctorate, comprehensive exam, thesis/dissertation, field-based experience. *Entrance requirements:* For master's, minimum GPA of 3.0, BA in education or related field, teaching license; for doctorate, GRE, MAT, resume, 2 writing samples, interview. Additional exam requirements/recommendations for international students: Required—TOEFL (minimum score 525 paper-based; 70 iBT). *Faculty research:* At-risk youth, multicultural issues, values in education, teaching/learning strategies.

Marquette University, Graduate School, College of Education, Department of Educational Policy and Leadership, Milwaukee, WI 53201-1881. Offers college student personnel administration (M Ed); curriculum and instruction (MA); education (MA); educational administration (M Ed); educational policy and foundations (MA); elementary education (Certificate); literacy (MA); principal (Certificate); reading specialist (Certificate); reading teacher (Certificate); secondary education (Certificate); superintendent (Certificate). *Program availability:* Part-time, evening/weekend. Terminal master's awarded for partial completion of doctoral program. *Degree requirements:* For master's, comprehensive exam, thesis (for some programs); for doctorate, thesis/dissertation, qualifying exam. *Entrance requirements:* For master's, GRE General Test or MAT, official transcripts from all current and previous colleges/universities except Marquette, three letters of recommendation, statement of purpose; for doctorate, GRE General Test, MAT, sample of written work, official transcripts from all current and previous colleges/universities except Marquette, three letters of recommendation, statement of purpose, resume/curriculum vitae; for Certificate, GRE General Test or MAT, master's degree. Additional exam requirements/recommendations for international students: Required—TOEFL (minimum score 530 paper-based). *Expenses:* Contact institution. *Faculty research:* Leadership; social justice in education; development of lifelong learners; race, class, and schooling in historical perspective; urban teacher education.

Marshall University, Academic Affairs Division, College of Education and Professional Development, Program in Leadership Studies, Huntington, WV 25755. Offers MA. *Program availability:* Part-time, evening/weekend. *Degree requirements:* For master's, thesis optional, comprehensive or oral assessment. *Entrance requirements:* For master's, GRE General Test or MAT.

Martin Luther College, Graduate Studies, New Ulm, MN 56073. Offers early childhood director (MS Ed Admin); educational technology (MS Ed); instruction (MS Ed); leadership (MS Ed); principal (MS Ed Admin); special education (MS Ed). *Program availability:* Part-time, evening/weekend, online only, 100% online. *Faculty:* 13 full-time (2 women), 31 part-time/adjunct (10 women). *Students:* 1 full-time (0 women), 86 part-time (26 women); includes 1 minority (Two or more races, non-Hispanic/Latino), 1 international. Average age 38. 35 applicants, 100% accepted, 35 enrolled. In 2018, 26 master's awarded. *Degree requirements:* For master's, capstone project or comprehensive exam. *Entrance requirements:* For master's, undergraduate degree in education from an accredited college or university, minimum undergraduate GPA of 3.0. Additional exam requirements/recommendations for international students: Required—TOEFL (minimum score 550 paper-based; 80 iBT); Recommended—IELTS (minimum score 6.5). *Application deadline:* Applications are processed on a rolling basis. Application fee: $35. Electronic applications accepted. *Financial support:* In 2018–19, 1 student received support. Scholarships/grants available. Financial award application deadline: 9/1. *Faculty research:* Principal effectiveness, principal support, cognitive load in math instruction, reading strategies in multigrade classrooms, mentor provided professional development for new teachers. *Unit head:* John E. Meyer, Director of Graduate Studies, 507-354-8221 Ext. 398, E-mail: meyerjd@mlc-wels.edu. *Application contact:* John E. Meyer, Director of Graduate Studies, 507-354-8221 Ext. 398, E-mail: meyerjd@mlc-wels.edu.
Website: https://mlc-wels.edu/graduate-studies/

Mary Baldwin University, Graduate Studies, Programs in Education, Staunton, VA 24401-3610. Offers applied behavior analysis (MS); autism spectrum disorders (M Ed); elementary education (M Ed, MAT); English as a second language (M Ed); environment-based learning (M Ed); gifted education (M Ed); higher education (MS); leadership (M Ed); middle grades education (MAT); reading education (M Ed); special education (M Ed). *Accreditation:* TEAC.

Marygrove College, Graduate Studies, Detroit, MI 48221-2599. Offers autism spectrum disorders (M Ed, Certificate); curriculum instruction and assessment (MAT); educational leadership (MA); educational technology (M Ed); effective teaching in the 21st century-classroom focus (MAT); effective teaching in the 21st century-technology focus (MAT); human resource management (MA, Certificate); mathematics 6-8 (MAT); mathematics K-5 (MAT); reading and literacy K-6 (MAT); reading specialist (M Ed); school administrator (Certificate); social justice (MA); special education (MAT); special education - learning disabilities (M Ed); teaching - pre-elementary education (M Ed); teaching - pre-secondary education (M Ed). *Program availability:* Part-time, evening/weekend, 100% online, blended/hybrid learning. *Entrance requirements:* For master's, all official bachelor's transcripts. Additional exam requirements/recommendations for international students: Required—TOEFL (minimum score 550 paper-based; 80 iBT). Electronic applications accepted.

Maryville University of Saint Louis, School of Education, St. Louis, MO 63141-7299. Offers early childhood education (MA Ed); educational leadership (Ed D); educational leadership w/principal certification (MA Ed); elementary education (MA Ed); gifted (MA Ed); higher education leadership (Ed D); middle grades education (MA Ed); reading/literacy specialist (MA Ed); teacher as leader (Ed D). *Accreditation:* NCATE. *Program availability:* Part-time, 100% online, blended/hybrid learning. *Faculty:* 16 full-time (8 women), 18 part-time/adjunct (11 women). *Students:* 12 full-time (all women), 311 part-time (234 women); includes 99 minority (84 Black or African American, non-Hispanic/Latino; 2 Asian, non-Hispanic/Latino; 9 Hispanic/Latino; 4 Two or more races, non-Hispanic/Latino), 2 international. Average age 38. In 2018, 25 master's, 100 doctorates awarded. *Degree requirements:* For master's, thesis, project. *Entrance requirements:* For master's, minimum cumulative GPA of 3.0, 3 professional recommendations, essays, interview with program faculty; for doctorate, minimum GPA of 3.0, 3 professional recommendations, essay, interview, on-site writing sample. Additional exam requirements/recommendations for international students: Required—TOEFL (minimum score 550 paper-based; 79 iBT). *Application deadline:* Applications are processed on a rolling basis. Electronic applications accepted. *Expenses:* $449 per credit hour for master's programs; $897 per credit hour for doctoral programs. *Financial support:* Career-related internships or fieldwork, Federal Work-Study, tuition waivers (partial), and professional educator discounts available. Financial award application deadline: 4/1; financial award applicants required to submit FAFSA. *Faculty research:* Collaboration with public schools, pre-service program development, mathematics, diversity, literacy. *Unit head:* Dr. Maschael Schappe, Dean, 314-529-9670, Fax: 314-529-9921, E-mail: mschappe@maryville.edu. *Application contact:* Stacey Ruffin, Director of Clinical Experiences & Partnerships, 314-529-9542, Fax: 314-529-9921, E-mail: sruffin@maryville.edu.
Website: http://www.maryville.edu/ed/graduate-programs/

Marywood University, Academic Affairs, Center for Interdisciplinary Studies, Scranton, PA 18509-1598. Offers human development (PhD), including educational administration, health promotion, higher education administration, instructional leadership, social work. *Program availability:* Part-time. Electronic applications accepted. *Expenses:* Contact institution.

Marywood University, Academic Affairs, Reap College of Education and Human Development, Department of Education, Program in Higher Education Administration, Scranton, PA 18509-1598. Offers MS. *Program availability:* Part-time, evening/weekend. Electronic applications accepted. *Faculty research:* Integrated thematic instruction.

Marywood University, Academic Affairs, Reap College of Education and Human Development, Department of Education, Program in Instructional Leadership, Scranton, PA 18509-1598. Offers M Ed. *Program availability:* Part-time. Electronic applications accepted.

Marywood University, Academic Affairs, Reap College of Education and Human Development, Department of Education, Program in School Leadership, Scranton, PA 18509-1598. Offers MS. *Accreditation:* NCATE. *Program availability:* Part-time. Electronic applications accepted.

Marywood University, Academic Affairs, Reap College of Education and Human Development, Department of Education, Program in Special Education Administration and Supervision, Scranton, PA 18509-1598. Offers MS. *Accreditation:* NCATE. *Program availability:* Part-time. Electronic applications accepted.

Massachusetts College of Liberal Arts, Graduate Programs, North Adams, MA 01247-4100. Offers business (MBA); educational administration (M Ed); educational leadership (CAGS); instruction and curriculum (M Ed); instructional technology (M Ed); physical education and health (M Ed); reading (M Ed); special education (M Ed). *Program availability:* Part-time, evening/weekend. *Degree requirements:* For master's, thesis. *Entrance requirements:* For master's, writing sample.

McDaniel College, Graduate and Professional Studies, Program in Educational Leadership, Westminster, MD 21157-4390. Offers MS. *Program availability:* Part-time-only, evening/weekend. *Degree requirements:* For master's, comprehensive exam (for some programs), thesis optional, portfolio. *Entrance requirements:* For master's, 3 recommendations, Principal Mentor Form. Additional exam requirements/recommendations for international students: Required—TOEFL (minimum score 79 iBT), IELTS (minimum score 6). Electronic applications accepted.

McGill University, Faculty of Graduate and Postdoctoral Studies, Faculty of Education, Department of Integrated Studies in Education, Montréal, QC H3A 2T5, Canada. Offers culture and values in education (MA, PhD); curriculum studies (MA); educational leadership (MA, Certificate); educational studies (PhD); integrated studies in education (M Ed); second language education (MA, PhD).

McKendree University, Graduate Programs, Programs in Education, Lebanon, IL 62254-1299. Offers curriculum design and instruction (Ed D, Ed S); educational administration and leadership (MA Ed); educational studies (MA Ed); higher education administrative services (MA Ed); music education (MA Ed); reading (MA Ed); special education (MA Ed); teacher leadership (MA Ed); teaching certification (MA Ed). *Accreditation:* NCATE. *Program availability:* Part-time, evening/weekend, online learning. *Entrance requirements:* For master's, official transcripts from all institutions previously attended, minimum GPA of 3.0, resume, references; for doctorate, GRE (within the past 5 years), master's degree in education and Ed S, or the equivalent, from regionally-accredited institution; official transcripts from all institutions previously attended; curriculum vitae/resume; essay/personal statement; two years of teaching/professional experience; for Ed S, GRE (within the past 5 years), master's degree in education from regionally-accredited institution of higher education; official transcripts from all institutions previously attended; curriculum vitae/resume; essay/personal statement; two years of teaching/professional experience. Additional exam requirements/recommendations for international students: Required—TOEFL. Electronic applications accepted.

McNeese State University, Doré School of Graduate Studies, Burton College of Education, Department of Education Professions, Program in Educational Leadership, Lake Charles, LA 70609. Offers educational leadership (M Ed, Ed S); educational technology (Ed S). *Program availability:* Evening/weekend. *Entrance requirements:* For master's, GRE, teaching certificate, 3 years of full-time teaching experience; for Ed S, teaching certificate, 3 years of teaching experience, 1 year of administration or supervision experience, master's degree with 12 semester hours in education.

Memorial University of Newfoundland, School of Graduate Studies, Faculty of Education, St. John's, NL A1C 5S7, Canada. Offers counseling psychology (M Ed); curriculum, teaching, and learning studies (M Ed); education (PhD); educational leadership studies (M Ed, Graduate Diploma); information technology (M Ed); post-secondary studies (M Ed, Diploma), including health professional education (Diploma). *Program availability:* Part-time. *Degree requirements:* For master's, thesis optional, internship, paper folio, project; for doctorate, comprehensive exam, thesis/dissertation, thesis seminar, oral defense of thesis. *Entrance requirements:* For master's, undergraduate degree with at least 2nd class standing, 1-2 years of work experience; for doctorate, minimum A average in graduate course work, MA in education, 2 years of professional experience; for other advanced degree, 2nd class degree, 2 years of work experience with adult learners, appropriate academic qualifications and work experience in a health-related field. Electronic applications accepted. *Faculty research:* Critical thinking, literacy, cognitive studies and counseling, educational change, technology in instruction.

Mercer University, Graduate Studies, Cecil B. Day Campus, Tift College of Education (Atlanta), Atlanta, GA 30341. Offers curriculum and instruction (PhD); early childhood education (M Ed, MAT, Ed S); educational leadership (PhD), including higher education leadership, P-12 school leadership; educational leadership P-12 (M Ed, Ed S); higher education leadership (M Ed); independent and charter school leadership (M Ed); middle grades education (M Ed, MAT); secondary education (M Ed, MAT); teacher leadership (Ed S). *Accreditation:* NCATE. *Program availability:* Part-time, evening/weekend. *Degree requirements:* For master's and Ed S, research project; for doctorate, comprehensive exam, thesis/dissertation. *Entrance requirements:* For master's, GRE or MAT, minimum undergraduate GPA of 2.75; for doctorate, GRE; for Ed S, GRE or MAT, minimum GPA of 3.25; 3 years of certified teaching experience (for educational leadership and teacher leadership). Additional exam requirements/recommendations for international students: Required—TOEFL (minimum score 80 iBT). Electronic applications accepted. *Expenses:* Contact institution. *Faculty research:* Educational technology, multicultural and minority issues in education, educational leadership (P-12 and higher education), school discipline and school bullying, standards-based mathematics education.

Mercer University, Graduate Studies, Macon Campus, Tift College of Education (Macon), Macon, GA 31207. Offers curriculum and instruction (PhD); early childhood education (M Ed, Ed S); educational leadership (M Ed, PhD, Ed S), including higher education (PhD), P-12; higher education leadership (M Ed); independent and charter school leadership (M Ed); secondary education (MAT), including STEM; teacher leadership (Ed S). *Accreditation:* NCATE. *Program availability:* Part-time, evening/weekend, 100% online, blended/hybrid learning. *Degree requirements:* For master's, research project report; for doctorate, comprehensive exam, thesis/dissertation. *Entrance requirements:* For master's, GRE or MAT, minimum GPA of 2.75; for doctorate, GRE, minimum GPA of 3.5; interview; writing sample; 3 recommendations; for Ed S, GRE or MAT, minimum GPA of 3.5 (for teacher leadership), 3.0 (for educational leadership). Additional exam requirements/recommendations for international students: Required—TOEFL (minimum score 80 iBT). Electronic applications accepted. *Expenses:* Contact institution. *Faculty research:* Teacher effectiveness, specific learning disabilities, inclusion.

Mercy College, School of Education, Advanced Certificate Program in Educational Leadership, Dobbs Ferry, NY 10522-1189. Offers educational leadership (Advanced Certificate). *Program availability:* Part-time, evening/weekend. *Students:* 3 part-time (1 woman). Average age 41. 10 applicants, 90% accepted, 3 enrolled. In 2018, 4 Advanced Certificates awarded. *Entrance requirements:* For degree, GRE or PRAXIS; passing grade on the School District Leader Assessment, transcript(s); resume; three years of teaching or pupil-personnel experience; master's degree from accredited institution. Additional exam requirements/recommendations for international students: Required—TOEFL (minimum score 600 paper-based; 71 iBT), IELTS (minimum score 8). *Application deadline:* Applications are processed on a rolling basis. Application fee: $40. Electronic applications accepted. *Expenses: Tuition:* Full-time $15,696; part-time $872 per credit. *Required fees:* $642; $161 per term. Tuition and fees vary according to course load, degree level and program. *Financial support:* Career-related internships or fieldwork, Federal Work-Study, scholarships/grants, and unspecified assistantships available. Support available to part-time students. Financial award applicants required to submit FAFSA. *Unit head:* Dr. Eric Martone, Interim Dean, School of Education, 914-674-7618, Fax: 914-674-7352, E-mail: emartone@mercy.edu. *Application contact:* Mary Ellen Hoffman, Director, Graduate Education Programs, 914-674-7334, E-mail: mehoffman@mercy.edu.
Website: https://www.mercy.edu/education/educational-leadership

Mercy College, School of Education, Program in Educational Leadership, Dobbs Ferry, NY 10522-1189. Offers MS. *Program availability:* Part-time, evening/weekend, blended/hybrid learning. *Students:* 11 full-time (9 women), 82 part-time (69 women); includes 49 minority (26 Black or African American, non-Hispanic/Latino; 1 American Indian or Alaska Native, non-Hispanic/Latino; 20 Hispanic/Latino; 1 Native Hawaiian or other Pacific Islander, non-Hispanic/Latino; 1 Two or more races, non-Hispanic/Latino). Average age 39. 73 applicants, 66% accepted, 30 enrolled. In 2018, 33 master's awarded. *Degree requirements:* For master's, Passing scores on the New York State School District Leadership Examination and the Educating All Students exam required for certification. *Entrance requirements:* For master's, GRE or PRAXIS, transcript(s); resume; initial or professional teacher or pupil personnel certification; two years of paid teaching or specialty area experience; master's degree from an accredited institution

required for some programs. Additional exam requirements/recommendations for international students: Required—TOEFL (minimum score 600 paper-based; 71 iBT), IELTS (minimum score 8). *Application deadline:* Applications are processed on a rolling basis. Application fee: $40. Electronic applications accepted. *Expenses: Tuition:* Full-time $15,696; part-time $872 per credit. *Required fees:* $642; $161 per term. Tuition and fees vary according to course load, degree level and program. *Financial support:* Career-related internships or fieldwork, Federal Work-Study, scholarships/grants, and unspecified assistantships available. Support available to part-time students. Financial award applicants required to submit FAFSA. *Unit head:* Dr. Eric Martone, Interim Dean, School of Education, 914-674-7618, Fax: 914-674-7352, E-mail: emartone@mercy.edu. *Application contact:* Allison Gurdineer, Executive Director of Admissions, 877-637-2946, Fax: 914-674-7382, E-mail: admissions@mercy.edu.
Website: https://www.mercy.edu/education/educational-leadership

Mercyhurst University, Graduate Studies, Program in Organizational Leadership, Erie, PA 16546. Offers accounting (MS); higher education administration (MS); human resources (MS); organizational leadership (MS, Certificate); sports leadership (MS); strategy and innovation (MS). *Program availability:* Part-time, evening/weekend. *Degree requirements:* For master's, thesis. *Entrance requirements:* For master's, GRE General Test or MAT, interview, resume, essay, three professional references, transcripts. Additional exam requirements/recommendations for international students: Required—TOEFL (minimum score 80 iBT), IELTS (minimum score 6.5). Electronic applications accepted. *Faculty research:* Leadership training, organizational communication, leadership pedagogy.

Miami University, College of Education, Health and Society, Department of Educational Leadership, Oxford, OH 45056. Offers educational leadership (Ed D, PhD); school leadership (M Ed); student affairs in higher education (MS, PhD); transformative education (M Ed). *Accreditation:* NCATE. *Faculty:* 14 full-time (8 women). *Students:* 70 full-time (46 women), 163 part-time (116 women); includes 45 minority (24 Black or African American, non-Hispanic/Latino; 4 Asian, non-Hispanic/Latino; 9 Hispanic/Latino; 8 Two or more races, non-Hispanic/Latino), 15 international. Average age 35. In 2018, 27 master's, 26 doctorates awarded. *Unit head:* Dr. Thomas Poetter, Chair and Director of Graduate Studies, 513-529-6848, E-mail: poettets@miamioh.edu. *Application contact:* Dr. Thomas Poetter, Professor and Director of Graduate Studies, 513-529-6825, E-mail: poettets@miamioh.edu.
Website: http://www.MiamiOH.edu/EDL

Michigan State University, The Graduate School, College of Education, Department of Educational Administration, East Lansing, MI 48824. Offers higher, adult and lifelong education (MA, PhD); K–12 educational administration (MA, PhD, Ed S); student affairs administration (MA). *Program availability:* Part-time. *Entrance requirements:* Additional exam requirements/recommendations for international students: Required—TOEFL. Electronic applications accepted.

Middle Tennessee State University, College of Graduate Studies, College of Education, Department of Educational Leadership, Program in Administration and Supervision, Murfreesboro, TN 37132. Offers M Ed, Ed S. *Program availability:* Part-time, evening/weekend, online learning. *Degree requirements:* For master's, comprehensive exam; for Ed S, comprehensive exam, thesis or alternative. *Entrance requirements:* For master's and Ed S, GRE, MAT or current teaching license. Additional exam requirements/recommendations for international students: Required—TOEFL (minimum score 525 paper-based; 71 iBT) or IELTS (minimum score 6). Electronic applications accepted.

Midwestern State University, Billie Doris McAda Graduate School, West College of Education, Programs in Educational Leadership and Technology, Wichita Falls, TX 76308. Offers educational leadership (M Ed); educational technology (M Ed). *Program availability:* Part-time, evening/weekend. *Degree requirements:* For master's, comprehensive exam. *Entrance requirements:* For master's, GRE General Test or MAT. Additional exam requirements/recommendations for international students: Required—TOEFL (minimum score 550 paper-based). Electronic applications accepted. *Faculty research:* Role of the principal in the twenty-first century, culturally proficient leadership, human diversity, immigration, teacher collaboration.

Millersville University of Pennsylvania, College of Graduate Studies and Adult Learning, College of Education and Human Services, Department of Educational Foundations, Millersville, PA 17551-0302. Offers assessment, curriculum and teaching - online teaching (M Ed), including online instruction; assessment, curriculum and teaching - stem education (M Ed), including integrative stem education; educational leadership (Ed D); leadership for teaching and learning (M Ed). Doctor of Educational Leadership: Collaborative program with Shippensburg University. *Program availability:* Part-time, evening/weekend, 100% online, blended/hybrid learning. *Faculty:* 10 full-time (9 women), 10 part-time/adjunct (6 women). *Students:* 1 full-time (0 women), 78 part-time (53 women); includes 5 minority (3 Black or African American, non-Hispanic/Latino; 2 Hispanic/Latino). Average age 34. 42 applicants, 98% accepted, 21 enrolled. In 2018, 21 master's, 2 doctorates awarded. *Degree requirements:* For master's, comprehensive exam (for some programs), thesis (for some programs), graded portfolio and portfolio defense; for doctorate, comprehensive exam, thesis/dissertation. *Entrance requirements:* For master's, GRE or MAT, only if undergraduate cumulative GPA is lower than 2.8, Interview (Leadership for Teaching and Learning), Teaching Certificate; for doctorate, teaching certificate, resume, letter of sponsorship, 3-5 years of professional experience as specified by PDE CSPG #96. Additional exam requirements/recommendations for international students: Required—TOEFL, IELTS (minimum score 6), PTE (minimum score 60). *Application deadline:* Applications are processed on a rolling basis. Application fee: $40. Electronic applications accepted. *Expenses: Tuition, area resident:* Full-time $9288; part-time $516 per credit. Tuition, state resident: full-time $9288; part-time $516 per credit. Tuition, nonresident: full-time $13,932; part-time $774 per credit. *International tuition:* $13,932 full-time. *Required fees:* $2623.50; $145.75 per credit. Tuition and fees vary according to course load, degree level and program. *Financial support:* Unspecified assistantships available. Financial award application deadline: 3/15; financial award applicants required to submit FAFSA. *Faculty research:* Instructional technology, poverty research, support for LGBTQ educators and students, diversifying the teaching workforce, inclusive education. *Total annual research expenditures:* $741,634. *Unit head:* Dr. Timothy E. Mahoney, Chair, 717-871-7202, E-mail: timothy.mahoney@millersville.edu. *Application contact:* Dr. James A. Delle, Acting Dean of College of Graduate Studies and Adult Learning/Associate Provost, Academic Administration, 717-871-7462, E-mail: James.Delle@millersville.edu.
Website: http://www.millersville.edu/edfoundations/

Milligan College, Area of Education, Milligan College, TN 37682. Offers combined preK-3/K-5 education (M Ed); educational leadership (Ed D); educational specialist (Ed S); K-5 education (M Ed); middle grades education (M Ed); preK-3 education (M Ed); preK-3 special education (M Ed); secondary education (M Ed). *Accreditation:* NCATE. *Program availability:* Part-time, 100% online, blended/hybrid learning. *Faculty:* 5 full-time (3 women), 6 part-time/adjunct (3 women). *Students:* 38 full-time (31 women), 8 part-time (4 women); includes 2 minority (1 Hispanic/Latino; 1 Two or more races, non-Hispanic/Latino), 1 international. Average age 35. 36 applicants, 97% accepted, 32 enrolled. In 2018, 18 master's awarded. *Degree requirements:* For master's, thesis, portfolio, research project; for doctorate, thesis/dissertation, portfolio, research project.

Entrance requirements: For master's, MAT, GRE General Test, ACT, SAT, or PRAXIS, undergraduate degree and supporting transcripts, professional recommendations, interview; for doctorate, MAT or GRE, master's degree and supporting transcripts, demonstrated scholastic ability, recognized leadership role within education, professional recommendations, essay/personal statement, portfolio (professional development plan, evidence of ability, knowledge and qualities), interview. Additional exam requirements/recommendations for international students: Required—TOEFL (minimum score 550 paper-based, 79 iBT) or IELTS (6.5). *Application deadline:* For fall admission, 8/1 priority date for domestic students, 6/1 for international students; for spring admission, 11/15 priority date for domestic students, 12/1 for international students; for summer admission, 4/1 for domestic students. Applications are processed on a rolling basis. Application fee: $30. Electronic applications accepted. *Expenses:* $365 per hour (for masters); $485 per hour (for doctoral); $375 fees per semester; $75 one-time records fee. *Financial support:* Scholarships/grants available. Financial award application deadline: 12/1; financial award applicants required to submit FAFSA. *Faculty research:* Assessment; school mental health; literacy; technology; educator preparation. *Unit head:* Dr. Angela Hilton-Prillhart, Area Chair of Education, 423-461-8769, Fax: 423-461-3103, E-mail: anhilton-prillhart@milligan.edu. *Application contact:* Melissa Dillow, Graduate Admissions Recruiter, Education, 423-461-8306, Fax: 423-461-8982, E-mail: msdillow@milligan.edu.
Website: http://www.Milligan.edu/GPS

Mills College, Graduate Studies, MBA/MA Program in Educational Leadership, Oakland, CA 94613-1000. Offers MBA/MA. Program offered jointly between School of Education and Lorry I. Lokey Graduate School of Business. *Entrance requirements:* Additional exam requirements/recommendations for international students: Required—TOEFL (minimum score 550 paper-based; 80 iBT) or IELTS (minimum score 6). Electronic applications accepted.

Minnesota State University Mankato, College of Graduate Studies and Research, College of Education, Department of Educational Leadership, Program in Experiential Education, Mankato, MN 56001. Offers MS. *Accreditation:* NCATE. *Program availability:* Part-time, evening/weekend. *Degree requirements:* For master's, thesis or alternative. *Entrance requirements:* For master's, minimum GPA of 3.0 during previous 2 years. Additional exam requirements/recommendations for international students: Required—TOEFL. Electronic applications accepted.

Minnesota State University Moorhead, Graduate and Extended Learning, College of Education and Human Services, Moorhead, MN 56563. Offers counseling and student affairs (MS); educational leadership (MS, Ed D, Ed S). *Accreditation:* ASHA; NCATE. *Program availability:* Part-time, evening/weekend, 100% online, blended/hybrid learning. *Students:* 129 full-time (105 women), 425 part-time (300 women); includes 32 minority (8 Black or African American, non-Hispanic/Latino; 4 American Indian or Alaska Native, non-Hispanic/Latino; 6 Asian, non-Hispanic/Latino; 7 Hispanic/Latino; 7 Two or more races, non-Hispanic/Latino), 1 international. Average age 33. 154 applicants, 77% accepted. In 2018, 198 master's, 29 other advanced degrees awarded. *Degree requirements:* For master's, comprehensive exam (for some programs), thesis, final oral defense; for doctorate, comprehensive exam (for some programs), thesis/dissertation, final oral defense. *Entrance requirements:* For master's, GRE, essay, letter of intent, letters of reference, teaching license, teaching verification, minimum cumulative GPA of 3.0; for doctorate, official transcripts; letter of intent; resume or curriculum vitae; master's degree; personal essay. Additional exam requirements/recommendations for international students: Required—TOEFL (minimum score 550 paper-based); Recommended—IELTS (minimum score 6.5). *Application deadline:* For fall admission, 7/1 priority date for domestic students; for spring admission, 11/15 priority date for domestic students. Applications are processed on a rolling basis. Application fee: $35. Electronic applications accepted. Tuition and fees vary according to course load, degree level, program and reciprocity agreements. *Financial support:* Federal Work-Study and unspecified assistantships available. Financial award application deadline: 10/1; financial award applicants required to submit FAFSA. *Unit head:* Dr. Ok-Hee Lee, Dean, 218-477-2095, E-mail: okheelee@mnstate.edu. *Application contact:* Karla Wenger, Office Manager, 218-477-2344, Fax: 218-477-2482, E-mail: wengerk@mnstate.edu.
Website: http://www.mnstate.edu/cehs/

Mississippi College, Graduate School, School of Education, Department of Teacher Education and Leadership, Clinton, MS 39058. Offers art (M Ed); biological science (M Ed); business education (M Ed); computer science (M Ed); dyslexia therapy (M Ed); educational leadership (M Ed, Ed D, Ed S); elementary education (M Ed, Ed S); English (M Ed); higher education administration (MS); mathematics (M Ed); secondary education (M Ed); social studies (history) (M Ed); teaching arts (M Ed). *Program availability:* Part-time, online learning. *Degree requirements:* For master's, comprehensive exam, thesis optional. *Entrance requirements:* For master's, NTE. Additional exam requirements/recommendations for international students: Recommended—TOEFL, IELTS. Electronic applications accepted.

Mississippi College, Graduate School, School of Education, Program in Higher Education Administration, Clinton, MS 39058. Offers MS. *Program availability:* Part-time, online learning. *Degree requirements:* For master's, comprehensive exam, thesis optional. *Entrance requirements:* For master's, GRE or GMAT, minimum GPA of 3.0. Additional exam requirements/recommendations for international students: Recommended—TOEFL, IELTS.

Mississippi State University, College of Agriculture and Life Sciences, School of Human Sciences, Mississippi State, MS 39762. Offers agriculture and extension education (MS), including communication, leadership; agriculture science (PhD), including agriculture and extension education; fashion design and merchandising (MS), including design and product development, merchandising; human development and family studies (MS, PhD). *Accreditation:* NCATE (one or more programs are accredited). *Program availability:* Part-time. *Faculty:* 21 full-time (12 women). *Students:* 30 full-time (28 women), 51 part-time (35 women); includes 17 minority (13 Black or African American, non-Hispanic/Latino; 1 Hispanic/Latino; 3 Two or more races, non-Hispanic/Latino), 4 international. Average age 34. 26 applicants, 62% accepted, 16 enrolled. In 2018, 8 master's, 12 doctorates awarded. *Degree requirements:* For master's, thesis optional, comprehensive oral or written exam. *Entrance requirements:* For master's, GRE, minimum GPA of 2.75 in last 4 semesters of course work; for doctorate, minimum GPA of 3.0 on prior graduate work. Additional exam requirements/recommendations for international students: Required—TOEFL (minimum score 477 paper-based; 53 iBT); Recommended—IELTS (minimum score 4.5). *Application deadline:* For fall admission, 7/1 for domestic students, 5/1 for international students; for spring admission, 11/1 for domestic students, 9/1 for international students. Applications are processed on a rolling basis. Application fee: $60 ($80 for international students). Electronic applications accepted. *Expenses:* Tuition, state resident: full-time $8450; part-time $360.59 per credit hour. Tuition, nonresident: full-time $23,140; part-time $969.09 per credit hour. *Required fees:* $110. One-time fee: $55 full-time. Part-time tuition and fees vary according to course load, degree level, campus/location and reciprocity agreements. *Financial support:* In 2018–19, 14 research assistantships (averaging $12,575 per year) were awarded; Federal Work-Study, institutionally sponsored loans, and unspecified assistantships also available. Financial award application deadline: 4/1; financial award applicants required to submit FAFSA. *Faculty research:* Animal welfare, agroscience, information technology, learning styles, problem solving. *Unit head:* Dr. Michael Newman, Professor and Director, 662-325-2950, E-mail: mnewman@humansci.msstate.edu. *Application contact:* Ryan King, Admissions and Enrollment Assistant, 662-325-8951, E-mail: rjk101@grad.msstate.edu.
Website: http://www.humansci.msstate.edu

Mississippi State University, College of Education, Educational Leadership Program, Mississippi State, MS 39762. Offers community college education (MAT); community college leadership (PhD); higher education leadership (PhD); P-12 school leadership (PhD); school administration (MS, Ed S); student affairs and higher education (MS); workforce education leadership (MS). MS in workforce education leadership held jointly with Alcorn State University. *Faculty:* 12 full-time (9 women). *Students:* 74 full-time (43 women), 145 part-time (89 women); includes 86 minority (75 Black or African American, non-Hispanic/Latino; 1 American Indian or Alaska Native, non-Hispanic/Latino; 6 Hispanic/Latino; 4 Two or more races, non-Hispanic/Latino). Average age 35. 83 applicants, 82% accepted, 55 enrolled. In 2018, 48 master's, 12 doctorates, 13 other advanced degrees awarded. *Degree requirements:* For master's and Ed S, comprehensive exam, thesis; for doctorate, comprehensive exam, thesis/dissertation. *Entrance requirements:* For master's, GRE, minimum GPA of 2.75 in junior and senior courses; for doctorate, GRE, minimum GPA of 3.4 on previous graduate work; for Ed S, GRE, minimum GPA of 3.2, master's degree. Additional exam requirements/recommendations for international students: Required—TOEFL (minimum score 550 paper-based; 79 iBT); Recommended—IELTS (minimum score 6.5). *Application deadline:* For fall admission, 7/1 for domestic students, 5/1 for international students; for spring admission, 11/1 for domestic students, 9/1 for international students. Application fee: $60 ($80 for international students). Electronic applications accepted. *Expenses:* Tuition, state resident: full-time $8450; part-time $360.59 per credit hour. Tuition, nonresident: full-time $23,140; part-time $969.09 per credit hour. *Required fees:* $110. One-time fee: $55 full-time. Part-time tuition and fees vary according to course load, degree level, campus/location and reciprocity agreements. *Financial support:* In 2018–19, 1 research assistantship with full tuition reimbursement (averaging $11,861 per year) was awarded; Federal Work-Study, institutionally sponsored loans, and unspecified assistantships also available. Financial award application deadline: 4/1; financial award applicants required to submit FAFSA. *Unit head:* Dr. Eric Moyen, Associate Professor and Head, 662-325-0969, Fax: 662-325-0975, E-mail: em1621@msstate.edu. *Application contact:* Nathan Drake, Admissions and Enrollment Assistant, 662-325-3804, E-mail: ndrake@grad.msstate.edu.
Website: http://www.educationalleadership.msstate.edu/

Mississippi University for Women, Graduate School, College of Education and Human Sciences, Columbus, MS 39701-9998. Offers differentiated instruction (M Ed); educational leadership (M Ed); gifted studies (M Ed); reading/literacy (M Ed); teaching (MAT). *Accreditation:* ASHA; NCATE. *Program availability:* Part-time. *Degree requirements:* For master's, comprehensive exam, thesis optional. *Entrance requirements:* For master's, GRE General Test or NTE (M Ed in gifted education or MS in speech/language pathology), MAT (M Ed in instructional management), minimum QPA of 3.0.

Missouri Baptist University, Graduate Programs, St. Louis, MO 63141-8660. Offers business administration (MBA); Christian ministries (MACM); counseling (MAC); education (MSE); education administration (MEA); educational leadership (MSE, Ed S); teaching (MAT).

Missouri State University, Graduate College, College of Education, Department of Counseling, Leadership, and Special Education, Program in Educational Administration, Springfield, MO 65897. Offers elementary principal (MS Ed, Ed S); secondary principal (MS Ed, Ed S); superintendent (Ed S). *Program availability:* Part-time, evening/weekend. *Faculty:* 5 full-time (2 women), 1 part-time/adjunct (0 women). *Students:* 6 full-time (all women), 84 part-time (56 women); includes 9 minority (1 Black or African American, non-Hispanic/Latino; 1 American Indian or Alaska Native, non-Hispanic/Latino; 4 Hispanic/Latino; 3 Two or more races, non-Hispanic/Latino). Average age 26. 46 applicants, 98% accepted. In 2018, 10 master's, 3 Ed Ss awarded. *Degree requirements:* For master's and Ed S, comprehensive exam, thesis or alternative. *Entrance requirements:* For master's, minimum GPA of 2.75; for Ed S, GRE General Test, MAT, minimum GPA of 2.75. Additional exam requirements/recommendations for international students: Required—TOEFL (minimum score 550 paper-based; 79 iBT), IELTS (minimum score 6). *Application deadline:* For fall admission, 7/20 priority date for domestic students, 5/1 for international students; for spring admission, 12/20 priority date for domestic students, 9/1 for international students; for summer admission, 5/20 priority date for domestic students. Applications are processed on a rolling basis. Application fee: $55 ($60 for international students). Electronic applications accepted. Tuition and fees vary according to class time, course level, course load, degree level, campus/location, program and student level. *Financial support:* Career-related internships or fieldwork, Federal Work-Study, institutionally sponsored loans, scholarships/grants, and unspecified assistantships available. Financial award application deadline: 1/31; financial award applicants required to submit FAFSA. *Unit head:* Dr. James Satterfield, Department Head, 417-836-5392, Fax: 417-836-4918, E-mail: clse@missouristate.edu. *Application contact:* Lakan Drinker, Director, Graduate Enrollment Management, 417-836-5330, Fax: 417-836-6200, E-mail: lakandrinker@missouristate.edu.
Website: http://education.missouristate.edu/edadmin/

Missouri State University, Graduate College, College of Education, Department of Reading, Foundations, and Technology, Springfield, MO 65897. Offers educational technology (MS Ed); literacy (MS Ed, Certificate, Graduate Certificate); teacher leadership (Certificate, Ed S); teaching (MAT); teaching and learning (MA, Certificate). *Program availability:* Part-time, evening/weekend, 100% online, blended/hybrid learning. *Faculty:* 13 full-time (6 women), 8 part-time/adjunct (7 women). *Students:* 17 full-time (11 women), 180 part-time (151 women); includes 15 minority (2 Black or African American, non-Hispanic/Latino; 1 Asian, non-Hispanic/Latino; 8 Hispanic/Latino; 4 Two or more races, non-Hispanic/Latino), 3 international. Average age 26. 67 applicants, 79% accepted. In 2018, 74 master's, 3 other advanced degrees awarded. *Degree requirements:* For master's, comprehensive exam, thesis or alternative. *Entrance requirements:* Additional exam requirements/recommendations for international students: Required—TOEFL (minimum score 550 paper-based; 79 iBT), IELTS (minimum score 6). *Application deadline:* For fall admission, 7/20 priority date for domestic students, 5/1 for international students; for spring admission, 12/20 priority date for domestic students, 9/1 for international students; for summer admission, 5/20 priority date for domestic students. Applications are processed on a rolling basis. Application fee: $55 ($60 for international students). Electronic applications accepted. Tuition and fees vary according to class time, course level, course load, degree level, campus/location, program and student level. *Financial support:* Federal Work-Study, institutionally sponsored loans, scholarships/grants, and unspecified assistantships available. Financial award application deadline: 1/31; financial award applicants required to submit FAFSA. *Faculty research:* Literacy and technology, struggling readers, community service learning. *Unit head:* Dr. Emmett Sawyer, Interim Department Head, 417-836-6769, Fax: 417-836-6252, E-mail: rft@missouristate.edu. *Application contact:* Lakan Drinker, Director, Graduate Enrollment Management, 417-836-5330, Fax: 417-836-6200, E-mail: lakandrinker@missouristate.edu.
Website: http://education.missouristate.edu/rft/

Monmouth University, Graduate Studies, School of Education, West Long Branch, NJ 07764-1898. Offers applied behavior analysis (Certificate); autism (Certificate); director of school counseling services (Post-Master's Certificate); early childhood (M Ed); educational leadership (Ed D); elementary education (MAT), including elementary level, secondary level; English as a second language (M Ed); learning disabilities teacher-consultant (Post-Master's Certificate); literacy (MS Ed); school counseling (MS Ed); special education (MS Ed), including autism, learning disabilities teacher-consultant, teacher of students with disabilities, teaching in inclusive settings; speech-language pathology (MS Ed); student affairs and college counseling (MS Ed); supervisor (Post-Master's Certificate); teaching English to speakers of other languages (Certificate). *Accreditation:* NCATE. *Program availability:* Part-time, evening/weekend, 100% online, blended/hybrid learning. *Faculty:* 29 full-time (23 women), 32 part-time/adjunct (24 women). *Students:* 214 full-time (187 women), 148 part-time (127 women); includes 60 minority (13 Black or African American, non-Hispanic/Latino; 2 Asian, non-Hispanic/Latino; 40 Hispanic/Latino; 5 Two or more races, non-Hispanic/Latino). Average age 27. In 2018, 108 master's, 9 other advanced degrees awarded. *Entrance requirements:* For master's, GRE taken within last 5 years (for MS Ed in speech-language pathology); SAT (minimum combined score of 1660 in 3 sections), ACT (23), GRE (minimum score of 4.0 on analytical writing section and minimum combined score of 310 on quantitative and verbal sections), or passing scores on 3 parts of Core Academic Skills Educators, minimum GPA of 3.0 in major; 2 letters of recommendation (for some programs); resume, personal statement or essay (depending on program). Additional exam requirements/recommendations for international students: Required—TOEFL (minimum score 550 paper-based; 79 iBT), IELTS (minimum score 6), Michigan English Language Assessment Battery (minimum score 77) or Certificate of Advanced English (minimum score 160). *Application deadline:* For fall admission, 7/15 priority date for domestic students, 7/1 for international students; for spring admission, 12/1 priority date for domestic students, 11/1 for international students; for summer admission, 5/1 for domestic students. Applications are processed on a rolling basis. Application fee: $50. Electronic applications accepted. *Expenses: Tuition:* Part-time $1233 per credit. *Required fees:* $178 per term. *Financial support:* In 2018–19, 290 students received support. Institutionally sponsored loans, scholarships/grants, and unspecified assistantships available. Support available to part-time students. Financial award applicants required to submit FAFSA. *Faculty research:* Multicultural literacy, science and mathematics teaching strategies, teacher as reflective practitioner, children with disabilities. *Unit head:* Dr. John E. Henning, Dean, 732-263-5513, Fax: 732-263-5277, E-mail: kodonnel@monmouth.edu. *Application contact:* Kirsten Sneeringer, Graduate Admission Counselor, 732-571-3452, Fax: 732-263-5123, E-mail: gradadm@monmouth.edu.
Website: http://www.monmouth.edu/academics/schools/education/default.asp

Montana State University, The Graduate School, College of Education, Health, and Human Development, Department of Education, Bozeman, MT 59717. Offers adult and higher education (Ed D); curriculum and instruction (M Ed, Ed D), including professional educator (M Ed), technology education (M Ed); education (M Ed), including adult and higher education, educational leadership, school counseling; educational leadership (Ed D, Ed S). *Accreditation:* TEAC. *Program availability:* Part-time, online learning. *Degree requirements:* For master's, comprehensive exam; for doctorate, comprehensive exam, thesis/dissertation. *Entrance requirements:* For master's, GRE, 3 letters of reference, essays, BA transcripts; for doctorate, GRE, MAT, 3 letters of reference, essay, BA and M Ed transcripts; for Ed S, PRAXIS. Additional exam requirements/recommendations for international students: Required—TOEFL (minimum score 550 paper-based). Electronic applications accepted. *Faculty research:* Critical literacy; standards-based education; school Improvement, organizational change, leadership in rural education, leadership in Indian education; student Learning; multicultural/culturally responsive education for social justice Native American indigenous education, community-centered education teacher preparation.

Montclair State University, The Graduate School, College of Education and Human Services, Doctoral Program in Teacher Education and Teacher Development, Montclair, NJ 07043-1624. Offers PhD. *Program availability:* Part-time, evening/weekend. *Degree requirements:* For doctorate, comprehensive exam (for some programs), thesis/dissertation. *Entrance requirements:* For doctorate, GRE General Test, interview, 3 letters of recommendation, essay. Additional exam requirements/recommendations for international students: Required—TOEFL (minimum score 83 iBT), IELTS (minimum score 6.5). Electronic applications accepted.

Montclair State University, The Graduate School, College of Education and Human Services, Program in Educational Leadership, Montclair, NJ 07043-1624. Offers MA. *Program availability:* Part-time, evening/weekend. *Degree requirements:* For master's, comprehensive exam, thesis or alternative. *Entrance requirements:* For master's, GRE General Test, interview, 2 letters of recommendation. Additional exam requirements/recommendations for international students: Required—TOEFL (minimum score 83 iBT), IELTS (minimum score 6.5). Electronic applications accepted.

Morehead State University, Graduate School, College of Education, Department of Foundational and Graduate Studies in Education, Morehead, KY 40351. Offers adult and higher education (MA, Ed S); certified professional counselor (Ed S); counseling P-12 (MA); curriculum and instruction (Ed S); educational technology (MA Ed); instructional leadership (Ed S); school administration (MA); school counseling (Ed S); teacher leader business and marketing content (MA Ed); teacher leader business and marketing technology (MA Ed); teacher leader educational technology (MA Ed); teacher leader English (MA Ed); teacher leader gifted education (MA Ed); teacher leader IECE certification (MA Ed); teacher leader interdisciplinary education P-5 (MA Ed); teacher leader middle grades (MA Ed); teacher leader non IECE certification (MA Ed); teacher leader reading/writing - non-certification (MA Ed); teacher leader reading/writing certification (MA Ed); teacher leader school communication - certification (MA Ed); teacher leader school communication - non-certification (MA Ed); teacher leader social studies (MA Ed); teacher leader special education (MA Ed). *Accreditation:* NCATE. *Program availability:* Part-time, evening/weekend. *Degree requirements:* For master's, thesis optional, oral and/or written comprehensive exams; for Ed S, thesis, oral exam. *Entrance requirements:* For master's, GRE General Test, minimum overall undergraduate GPA of 2.5; for Ed S, GRE General Test, interview, master's degree, minimum GPA of 3.5, work experience. Additional exam requirements/recommendations for international students: Required—TOEFL (minimum score 500 paper-based). Electronic applications accepted. *Faculty research:* Character education, school accountability, computer applications for school administrators.

Morgan State University, School of Graduate Studies, School of Education and Urban Studies, Department of Advanced Studies, Leadership and Policy, Program in Community College Leadership, Baltimore, MD 21251. Offers Ed D. *Accreditation:* NCATE. *Program availability:* Part-time, evening/weekend. *Degree requirements:* For doctorate, comprehensive exam, thesis/dissertation. *Entrance requirements:* For doctorate, GRE General Test or MAT. Additional exam requirements/recommendations for international students: Required—TOEFL (minimum score 550 paper-based). *Faculty research:* Multicultural education, cooperative learning, psychology of cognition.

Morgan State University, School of Graduate Studies, School of Education and Urban Studies, Department of Advanced Studies, Leadership and Policy, Program in Higher Education Administration, Baltimore, MD 21251. Offers higher education (PhD); higher education and student affairs administration (MA). *Degree requirements:* For doctorate, comprehensive exam, thesis/dissertation. *Entrance requirements:* For doctorate, GRE General Test or MAT, minimum GPA of 3.0.

Mount Holyoke College, Professional and Graduate Education (PaGE), South Hadley, MA 01075. Offers initial teacher licensure (MAT); mathematics teaching (MAMT); teacher leadership (MATL). *Program availability:* Part-time, evening/weekend, blended/hybrid learning. *Faculty:* 48 part-time/adjunct (38 women). *Students:* 16 full-time (15 women), 111 part-time (91 women); includes 23 minority (5 Black or African American, non-Hispanic/Latino; 2 Asian, non-Hispanic/Latino; 10 Hispanic/Latino; 6 Two or more races, non-Hispanic/Latino), 7 international. Average age 36. 86 applicants, 91% accepted, 50 enrolled. In 2018, 32 master's awarded. *Degree requirements:* For master's, practicum (for MAT); capstone project (for MATL); capstone portfolio (for MAMT); internship required for some programs. *Entrance requirements:* For master's, Communication & Literacy (both subtests) MTEL for Initial Licensure students, bachelor's degree; subject area knowledge in desired teaching discipline; personal statement; essay; official transcripts; two letters of recommendation; history of effective classroom teaching (for MATL). Additional exam requirements/recommendations for international students: Required—TOEFL (minimum score 100 paper-based), IELTS (minimum score 7). *Application deadline:* For fall admission, 8/1 for domestic and international students; for winter admission, 12/1 for domestic and international students; for spring admission, 1/15 for domestic and international students; for summer admission, 5/15 for domestic and international students. Applications are processed on a rolling basis. Application fee: $50. Electronic applications accepted. Application fee is waived when completed online. *Expenses: Tuition:* Full-time $27,900; part-time $775 per credit hour. One-time fee: $150. Tuition and fees vary according to course level, course load, program and student level. *Financial support:* In 2018–19, 134 students received support, including 5 fellowships with partial tuition reimbursements available (averaging $3,390 per year); scholarships/grants and unspecified assistantships also available. Financial award applicants required to submit FAFSA. *Faculty research:* Mathematics education; educational leadership; special education and inclusivity; equity and advocacy in education; professional development for teachers. *Unit head:* Dr. Tiffany Espinosa, Executive Director of Professional and Graduate Education, 413-538-3478, Fax: 413-538-3098, E-mail: tespinos@mtholyoke.edu. *Application contact:* Dr. Tiffany Espinosa, Executive Director of Professional and Graduate Education, 413-538-3478, Fax: 413-538-3098, E-mail: tespinos@mtholyoke.edu.
Website: https://www.mtholyoke.edu/professional-graduate

Mount Mercy University, Program in Education, Cedar Rapids, IA 52402-4797. Offers reading (MA Ed); special education (MA Ed); teacher leadership (MA Ed). *Entrance requirements:* For master's, minimum cumulative GPA of 3.0, 2 letters of recommendation, resume, valid teaching license. Additional exam requirements/recommendations for international students: Required—TOEFL (minimum score 570 paper-based; 88 iBT). Electronic applications accepted.

Murray State University, College of Education and Human Services, Department of Adolescent, Career, and Special Education, Murray, KY 42071. Offers career and technical education (MS); middle school teacher leader (MA Ed); secondary teacher leader (MA Ed); special education (MA Ed), including mild learning and behavior disorders, moderate to severe disabilities (P-12), teacher leader in special education learning and behavior disorders; teacher education and professional development (Ed S). *Accreditation:* NCATE. *Program availability:* Part-time. *Entrance requirements:* For master's and Ed S, GRE or GMAT, minimum university GPA of 2.75. Additional exam requirements/recommendations for international students: Required—TOEFL (minimum score 527 paper-based; 71 iBT). Electronic applications accepted.

Murray State University, College of Education and Human Services, Department of Early Childhood and Elementary Education, Murray, KY 42071. Offers elementary teacher leader (MA Ed); interdisciplinary early childhood education (MA Ed), including elementary education (MA Ed, Ed S), reading and writing; teacher education and professional development (Ed S), including elementary education (MA Ed, Ed S). *Accreditation:* NCATE. *Program availability:* Part-time. *Entrance requirements:* For master's and Ed S, GRE or GMAT, minimum university GPA of 2.75. Additional exam requirements/recommendations for international students: Required—TOEFL (minimum score 527 paper-based; 71 iBT). Electronic applications accepted.

Murray State University, College of Education and Human Services, Department of Educational Studies, Leadership and Counseling, Murray, KY 42071. Offers college advising (Certificate); education administration (MA Ed); human development and leadership (MS, Certificate); library media (MA Ed); middle school teacher leader (MA Ed); P-20 and community leadership (Ed D); postsecondary education administration (MA Ed); school counseling (MA Ed); school guidance and counseling (Ed S); secondary teacher leader (MA Ed). *Program availability:* Part-time, evening/weekend, 100% online, blended/hybrid learning. *Entrance requirements:* For master's and other advanced degree, GRE or GMAT, minimum university GPA of 2.75. Additional exam requirements/recommendations for international students: Required—TOEFL (minimum score 527 paper-based; 71 iBT). Electronic applications accepted.

National American University, Roueche Graduate Center, Austin, TX 78731. Offers accounting (MBA); aviation management (MBA, MM); care coordination (MSN); community college leadership (Ed D); criminal justice (MM); e-marketing (MBA, MM); health care administration (MBA, MM); higher education (MM); human resources management (MBA, MM); information technology management (MBA, MM); international business (MBA); leadership (EMBA); management (MBA); nursing administration (MSN); nursing education (MSN); nursing informatics (MSN); operations and configuration management (MBA, MM); project and process management (MBA, MM). Master's programs offered online through the Harold D. Buckingham Graduate School. *Program availability:* Part-time, evening/weekend, online learning. *Entrance requirements:* For master's, minimum undergraduate GPA of 2.75. Additional exam requirements/recommendations for international students: Required—TOEFL, TWE. Electronic applications accepted. *Faculty research:* Tourism, finance, marketing.

National Louis University, National College of Education, Chicago, IL 60603. Offers administration and supervision (M Ed, Ed D, CAS, Ed S); curriculum and instruction (M Ed, MS Ed, CAS); early childhood administration (M Ed, CAS); early childhood education (M Ed, MAT, MS Ed, CAS); education (Ed D); educational psychology/human learning and development (M Ed, MS Ed, CAS, Ed S); elementary education (MAT); interdisciplinary curriculum and instruction (M Ed); mathematics education (M Ed, MS Ed, CAS); middle grades education (MAT); reading and language (M Ed, MS Ed, CAS); school psychology (M Ed, Ed S); science education (M Ed, MS Ed, CAS); secondary education (MAT); special education (M Ed, MAT, CAS); technology in education (M Ed, CAS). *Accreditation:* NCATE. *Program availability:* Part-time, evening/weekend. *Degree requirements:* For doctorate, comprehensive exam, thesis/dissertation. *Entrance requirements:* For master's, MAT or GRE, minimum GPA of 3.0; for doctorate, GRE General Test, minimum GPA of 3.25, interview, resume, writing sample, 4 recommendations. Additional exam requirements/recommendations for international students: Required—TOEFL (minimum score 550 paper-based; 79 iBT).

Educational Leadership and Administration

National University, Sanford College of Education, La Jolla, CA 92037-1011. Offers advanced teaching practices (MS); applied behavior analysis (MS); applied school leadership (MS); e-teaching and learning (Certificate); education (MA); educational administration (MS); educational and instructional technology (MS); educational counseling (MS); higher education administration (MS); inspired teaching and learning (M Ed); school psychology (MS); special education (MA, MS). *Program availability:* Part-time, evening/weekend, 100% online, blended/hybrid learning. *Degree requirements:* For master's, thesis (for some programs). *Entrance requirements:* For master's, interview, minimum GPA of 2.5. Additional exam requirements/recommendations for international students: Required—TOEFL (minimum score 550 paper-based; 79 iBT), IELTS (minimum score 6). Electronic applications accepted. *Expenses: Tuition:* Full-time $10,320; part-time $430 per unit. Tuition and fees vary according to degree level. *Faculty research:* Teacher education, special education, educational effectiveness, teaching abroad, school counseling.

Nebraska Christian College of Hope International University, Graduate Programs, Papillion, NE 68046. Offers biblical studies (M Div); business as mission/social entrepreneurship (MBA); children, youth, and family (M Div); church planting (M Div); counseling psychology (MS); educational administration (MA); elementary education (M Ed); general management (MBA); gifted and talented education (M Ed); intercultural studies (M Div); international development (MBA); marketing management (MBA); ministry (MA); ministry and leadership (M Div); music education (M Ed); non-profit management (MBA); pastoral care (M Div); secondary education (M Ed); spiritual formation (M Div); worship ministry (M Div).

Neumann University, Graduate Program in Education, Aston, PA 19014-1298. Offers education (MS), including administrative certification (school principal PK-12), autism, early elementary education, secondary education, special education. *Program availability:* Part-time, evening/weekend, 100% online, blended/hybrid learning. *Entrance requirements:* For master's, official transcripts from all institutions attended, letter of intent, three professional references, copy of any teaching certifications. Additional exam requirements/recommendations for international students: Required—TOEFL (minimum score 70 iBT). Electronic applications accepted. *Expenses:* Contact institution.

Neumann University, Program in Educational Leadership, Aston, PA 19014-1298. Offers educational leadership (Ed D), including PreK-12, superintendent's letter of eligibility. *Program availability:* Part-time, evening/weekend. *Degree requirements:* For doctorate, comprehensive exam, thesis/dissertation. *Entrance requirements:* For doctorate, master's degree, official transcripts from all institutions attended, resume or curriculum vitae, three official letters of recommendation, two essays. Additional exam requirements/recommendations for international students: Required—TOEFL (minimum score 70 iBT). Electronic applications accepted. *Expenses:* Contact institution.

New England College, Program in Education, Henniker, NH 03242-3293. Offers higher education administration (MS, Ed D); K-12 leadership (Ed D); literacy and language arts (M Ed); meeting the needs of all learners/special education (M Ed); teacher leadership/school reform (M Ed). *Program availability:* Part-time, evening/weekend.

New Jersey City University, Debra Cannon Partridge Wolfe College of Education, Department of Educational Leadership and Counseling, Jersey City, NJ 07305-1597. Offers counselor education (MA); educational administration and supervision (MA); urban education (MA). *Accreditation:* TEAC. *Program availability:* Part-time, evening/weekend. *Entrance requirements:* Additional exam requirements/recommendations for international students: Required—TOEFL (minimum score 79 iBT).

Newman University, Master of Science in Education Program, Wichita, KS 67213-2097. Offers building leadership (MS Ed); curriculum and instruction (MS Ed), including English as a second language, reading specialist; organizational leadership (MS Ed). *Accreditation:* NCATE. *Program availability:* Part-time, evening/weekend, online learning. *Degree requirements:* For master's, thesis optional. *Entrance requirements:* For master's, 3 years' full-time teaching experience, minimum GPA of 3.0, writing sample, 2 letters of recommendation, evidence of teaching certification. Additional exam requirements/recommendations for international students: Required—TOEFL (minimum score 600 paper-based; 100 iBT). Electronic applications accepted. *Expenses:* Contact institution. *Faculty research:* Online course design and deliver, staff engagement, classroom action.

New Mexico Highlands University, Graduate Studies, School of Education, Las Vegas, NM 87701. Offers curriculum and instruction (MA); educational leadership (MA); professional counseling (MA); special education (MA). *Accreditation:* NCATE. *Program availability:* Part-time. *Degree requirements:* For master's, comprehensive exam, thesis or alternative. *Entrance requirements:* For master's, minimum undergraduate GPA of 3.0. Additional exam requirements/recommendations for international students: Required—TOEFL (minimum score 540 paper-based). *Faculty research:* Middle school curriculum, integrated computer applications for pre-service classroom teachers, adolescent literacy, narrative cognitive modes in New Mexico multicultural setting, math and math education.

New York Institute of Technology, School of Interdisciplinary Studies and Education, Department of School Leadership and Technology, Old Westbury, NY 11568-8000. Offers Advanced Diploma. *Program availability:* Part-time, evening/weekend, online only, 100% online, blended/hybrid learning. *Faculty:* 1 full-time (0 women), 5 part-time/adjunct (3 women). *Students:* 1 (woman) full-time, 42 part-time (24 women); includes 7 minority (2 Black or African American, non-Hispanic/Latino; 2 Asian, non-Hispanic/Latino; 3 Hispanic/Latino). Average age 37. 27 applicants, 93% accepted, 17 enrolled. In 2018, 29 Advanced Diplomas awarded. *Degree requirements:* For Advanced Diploma, internship. *Entrance requirements:* For degree, master's degree with minimum cumulative GPA of 3.0; personal statement; at least 3 years of full-time teaching experience; professional NY state teacher certification; demonstration of computer competency; two letters of reference from school building or district administrator. Additional exam requirements/recommendations for international students: Required—TOEFL (minimum score 79 iBT), IELTS (minimum score 6), PTE (minimum score 53). *Application deadline:* Applications are processed on a rolling basis. Application fee: $50. Electronic applications accepted. *Expenses:* $1285 per credit plus $215 fees per year (full-time) or $175 fees per year (part-time); $1395 per 3-credit education UFT or off-site graduate course. *Financial support:* Career-related internships or fieldwork, scholarships/grants, and unspecified assistantships available. Support available to part-time students. Financial award application deadline: 2/15; financial award applicants required to submit FAFSA. *Faculty research:* College readiness; school-community partnerships; administrator-school counselor relationships. *Unit head:* Dr. Robert Feirsen, Chair, 516-686-1169, E-mail: rfeirsen@nyit.edu. *Application contact:* Alice Dolitsky, Director, Graduate Admissions, 516-686-7520, Fax: 516-686-1116, E-mail: admissions@nyit.edu.
Website: https://www.nyit.edu/departments/school_leadership_and_technology

New York University, Steinhardt School of Culture, Education, and Human Development, Department of Administration, Leadership, and Technology, Program in Educational Leadership, New York, NY 10012. Offers educational leadership (Ed D, PhD); educational leadership, politics and advocacy (MA); school building leader (MA); school district leader (Advanced Certificate). *Program availability:* Part-time, evening/weekend. *Entrance requirements:* For doctorate, GRE General Test, interview; for Advanced Certificate, master's degree. Additional exam requirements/recommendations for international students: Required—TOEFL (minimum score 100 iBT). Electronic applications accepted. *Faculty research:* Schools and communities; critical theories of race, class and gender; school restructuring; educational reform; social organization of schools, educational advocacy.

New York University, Steinhardt School of Culture, Education, and Human Development, Department of Administration, Leadership, and Technology, Program in Higher Education, New York, NY 10012. Offers higher and postsecondary education (PhD); higher education administration (Ed D); higher education and student affairs (MA). *Accreditation:* TEAC. *Program availability:* Part-time. *Entrance requirements:* For master's, interview, 2 letters of recommendation; for doctorate, GRE General Test, interview. Additional exam requirements/recommendations for international students: Required—TOEFL (minimum score 100 iBT). Electronic applications accepted. *Faculty research:* Organizational theory and culture, systemic change, leadership development, access, equity and diversity.

Niagara University, Graduate Division of Education, Concentration in Educational Leadership, Niagara University, NY 14109. Offers leadership and policy (PhD); school building leader (MS Ed); school district business leader (Certificate); school district leader (MS Ed, Certificate). *Program availability:* Part-time, evening/weekend, 100% online. *Students:* 50 full-time (29 women), 157 part-time (110 women); includes 33 minority (20 Black or African American, non-Hispanic/Latino; 2 Asian, non-Hispanic/Latino; 8 Hispanic/Latino; 3 Two or more races, non-Hispanic/Latino), 51 international. Average age 39. In 2018, 27 master's, 15 doctorates, 20 other advanced degrees awarded. *Entrance requirements:* For master's, GRE General Test or MAT; for Certificate, GRE General Test and GRE Subject Test or MAT. Additional exam requirements/recommendations for international students: Required—TOEFL (minimum score 550 paper-based; 79 iBT), IELTS (minimum score 6). *Application deadline:* For fall admission, 8/1 for domestic students. Applications are processed on a rolling basis. Electronic applications accepted. *Expenses:* Contact institution. *Financial support:* Research assistantships with tuition reimbursements, teaching assistantships with tuition reimbursements, career-related internships or fieldwork, Federal Work-Study, scholarships/grants, and unspecified assistantships available. Support available to part-time students. Financial award application deadline: 4/15; financial award applicants required to submit FAFSA. *Unit head:* Dr. James Mills, Coordinator of Educational Leadership, 716-286-8553, E-mail: jmills@niagara.edu. *Application contact:* Evan Pierce, Associate Director, Graduate Studies, 716-286-8327, E-mail: epierce@niagara.edu.
Website: http://www.niagara.edu/educational-leadership-online

Nicholls State University, Graduate Studies, College of Education, Department of Teacher Education, Thibodaux, LA 70310. Offers curriculum and instruction (M Ed); educational leadership (M Ed); elementary education (MAT); human performance education (MAT); middle school education (MAT); secondary education (MAT). *Accreditation:* NCATE. *Program availability:* Part-time, evening/weekend, online learning. *Degree requirements:* For master's, comprehensive exam, portfolio. *Entrance requirements:* For master's, GRE General Test, teaching license. Electronic applications accepted.

Norfolk State University, School of Graduate Studies, School of Education, Department of Secondary Education and School Leadership, Norfolk, VA 23504. Offers principal preparation (MA); secondary education (MAT); urban education/administration (MA), including teaching. *Accreditation:* NCATE. *Program availability:* Part-time. *Entrance requirements:* For master's, GRE General Test, PRAXIS I, minimum GPA of 3.0 in major, 2.5 overall. Additional exam requirements/recommendations for international students: Required—TOEFL (minimum score 500 paper-based).

North American University, Program in Educational Leadership, Stafford, TX 77477. Offers M Ed.

North Carolina Agricultural and Technical State University, The Graduate College, College of Education, Department of Administration and Instructional Services, Greensboro, NC 27411. Offers instructional technology (MS); reading education (MA Ed); school administration (MSA). *Accreditation:* NCATE. *Program availability:* Part-time, evening/weekend. *Degree requirements:* For master's, comprehensive exam, qualifying exam. *Entrance requirements:* For master's, GRE General Test, minimum GPA of 3.0.

North Carolina Agricultural and Technical State University, The Graduate College, College of Education, Department of Leadership Studies and Adult Education, Greensboro, NC 27411. Offers adult education (MS); interdisciplinary leadership studies (PhD). *Accreditation:* NCATE. *Program availability:* Part-time, evening/weekend. *Degree requirements:* For master's, comprehensive exam, comprehensive portfolio. *Entrance requirements:* For master's, GRE General Test, minimum GPA of 3.0.

North Carolina Central University, School of Education, Program in School Administration, Durham, NC 27707-3129. Offers MSA.

North Carolina State University, Graduate School, College of Education, Department of Educational Leadership, Policy, and Human Development, Program in Educational Administration and Supervision, Raleigh, NC 27695. Offers Ed D. *Degree requirements:* For doctorate, thesis/dissertation. *Entrance requirements:* For doctorate, GRE General Test or MAT, minimum GPA of 3.0, interview, sample of work. Electronic applications accepted.

North Carolina State University, Graduate School, College of Education, Department of Educational Leadership, Policy, and Human Development, Program in School Administration, Raleigh, NC 27695. Offers MSA. *Degree requirements:* For master's, comprehensive exam, thesis optional. *Entrance requirements:* For master's, GRE General Test or MAT, minimum GPA of 3.0 in major, 3 years of teaching experience. Electronic applications accepted. *Faculty research:* State and national policy, educational evaluation, cohort preparation programs.

North Central College, School of Graduate and Professional Studies, Program in Leadership Studies, Naperville, IL 60566-7063. Offers MLD. *Program availability:* Part-time, evening/weekend. *Degree requirements:* For master's, thesis optional, project. *Entrance requirements:* For master's, interview. Additional exam requirements/recommendations for international students: Required—TOEFL (minimum score 550 paper-based; 80 iBT), IELTS (minimum score 6.5). Electronic applications accepted. Application fee is waived when completed online. *Expenses:* Contact institution.

North Dakota State University, College of Graduate and Interdisciplinary Studies, College of Human Development and Education, School of Education, Program in Educational Leadership, Fargo, ND 58102. Offers M Ed, MS, Ed S. MS and Ed S offered jointly with Minnesota State University Moorhead. *Accreditation:* NCATE. *Program availability:* Part-time, evening/weekend, online learning. *Entrance requirements:* For degree, GRE General Test, master's degree, minimum GPA of 3.25. Additional exam requirements/recommendations for international students: Required—TOEFL. *Faculty research:* Organizational change and development, goal setting and systematic planning, beginning teacher assistance.

Northeastern Illinois University, College of Graduate Studies and Research, Daniel L. Goodwin College of Education, Program in School Leadership, Chicago, IL 60625. Offers educational administration and supervision (MA), including chief school business official. *Program availability:* Part-time, evening/weekend. *Degree requirements:* For master's, comprehensive exam, practicum. *Entrance requirements:* For master's, 2 years of teaching experience, minimum GPA of 2.75. Additional exam requirements/recommendations for international students: Required—TOEFL (minimum score 550 paper-based; 79 iBT). Electronic applications accepted. *Faculty research:* Student motivation, leadership, teacher expectation, educational partnerships, community/school relations.

Northeastern State University, College of Education, Department of Educational Leadership, Program in Higher Education Leadership, Tahlequah, OK 74464-2399. Offers MS. *Faculty:* 13 full-time (9 women), 2 part-time/adjunct (0 women). *Students:* 7 full-time (all women), 18 part-time (16 women); includes 10 minority (2 Black or African American, non-Hispanic/Latino; 7 American Indian or Alaska Native, non-Hispanic/Latino; 1 Two or more races, non-Hispanic/Latino), 3 international. Average age 28. In 2018, 15 master's awarded. *Degree requirements:* For master's, thesis. *Entrance requirements:* For master's, MAT or GRE. Additional exam requirements/recommendations for international students: Required—TOEFL. *Application deadline:* For fall admission, 6/1 priority date for domestic students. Applications are processed on a rolling basis. Application fee: $25. Electronic applications accepted. *Expenses: Tuition, area resident:* Full-time $4500; part-time $250 per credit hour. Tuition, state resident: full-time $4500; part-time $250 per credit hour. Tuition, nonresident: full-time $9999; part-time $555.50 per credit hour. *International tuition:* $9999 full-time. *Required fees:* $601.20; $33.40 per credit hour. *Financial support:* Application deadline: 3/1. *Unit head:* Dr. Renee Cambiano, Program Chair, 918-444-3741, E-mail: cambiare@nsuok.edu. *Application contact:* Josh McCollum, Graduate Coordinator, 918-444-2093, E-mail: mccolluj@nsuok.edu.
Website: http://academics.nsuok.edu/education/DegreePrograms/GraduatePrograms/HigherEducationLeadership.aspx

Northeastern State University, College of Education, Department of Educational Leadership, Program in Instructional Leadership, Tahlequah, OK 74464-2399. Offers M Ed. *Program availability:* Part-time, evening/weekend. *Faculty:* 12 full-time (9 women), 2 part-time/adjunct (1 woman). *Students:* 10 full-time (all women), 16 part-time (11 women); includes 15 minority (2 Black or African American, non-Hispanic/Latino; 4 American Indian or Alaska Native, non-Hispanic/Latino; 1 Asian, non-Hispanic/Latino; 1 Hispanic/Latino; 7 Two or more races, non-Hispanic/Latino). Average age 33. In 2018, 9 master's awarded. *Degree requirements:* For master's, thesis. *Entrance requirements:* For master's, MAT or GRE. Additional exam requirements/recommendations for international students: Required—TOEFL. *Application deadline:* For fall admission, 7/1 priority date for domestic and international students; for spring admission, 10/1 priority date for domestic and international students. Applications are processed on a rolling basis. Application fee: $25. Electronic applications accepted. *Expenses: Tuition, area resident:* Full-time $4500; part-time $250 per credit hour. Tuition, state resident: full-time $4500; part-time $250 per credit hour. Tuition, nonresident: full-time $9999; part-time $555.50 per credit hour. *International tuition:* $9999 full-time. *Required fees:* $601.20; $33.40 per credit hour. *Financial support:* Federal Work-Study available. Financial award application deadline: 3/1. *Unit head:* Dr. Renee Cambiano, Program Chair, 918-444-3741, E-mail: cambiare@nsuok.edu. *Application contact:* Josh McCollum, Graduate Coordinator, 918-444-2093, E-mail: mccolluj@nsuok.edu.

Northeastern State University, College of Education, Department of Educational Leadership, Program in School Administration, Tahlequah, OK 74464-2399. Offers M Ed. *Program availability:* Part-time, evening/weekend. *Faculty:* 13 full-time (9 women), 2 part-time/adjunct (0 women). *Students:* 20 full-time (12 women), 57 part-time (38 women); includes 26 minority (1 Black or African American, non-Hispanic/Latino; 8 American Indian or Alaska Native, non-Hispanic/Latino; 3 Hispanic/Latino; 14 Two or more races, non-Hispanic/Latino). Average age 38. In 2018, 31 master's awarded. *Degree requirements:* For master's, thesis. *Entrance requirements:* For master's, MAT or GRE, minimum GPA of 3.0. Additional exam requirements/recommendations for international students: Required—TOEFL. *Application deadline:* For fall admission, 6/1 priority date for domestic students. Applications are processed on a rolling basis. Application fee: $25. Electronic applications accepted. *Expenses: Tuition, area resident:* Full-time $4500; part-time $250 per credit hour. Tuition, state resident: full-time $4500; part-time $250 per credit hour. Tuition, nonresident: full-time $9999; part-time $555.50 per credit hour. *International tuition:* $9999 full-time. *Required fees:* $601.20; $33.40 per credit hour. *Financial support:* Teaching assistantships and Federal Work-Study available. Financial award application deadline: 3/1. *Unit head:* Dr. Jim Ferrell, Department Chair, 918-444-3722, E-mail: ferrellj@nsuok.edu. *Application contact:* Josh McCollum, Graduate Coordinator, 918-444-2093, E-mail: mccolluj@nsuok.edu.
Website: http://academics.nsuok.edu/education/DegreePrograms/GraduatePrograms/SchoolAdministration.aspx

Northeastern University, College of Professional Studies, Boston, MA 02115-5096. Offers applied nutrition (MS); college athletics administration (MSL); commerce and economic development (MS); corporate and organizational communication (MS); criminal justice (MS); digital media (MPS); elearning and instructional design (M Ed); elementary education (MAT); geographic information technology (MPS); global studies and international relations (MS); higher education administration (M Ed); homeland security (MA); human services (MS); informatics (MPS); leadership (MS); learning analytics (M Ed); learning and instruction (M Ed); nonprofit management (MS); professional sports administration (MSL); project management (MS); regulatory affairs for drugs, biologics, and medical devices (MS); respiratory care leadership (MS); special education (M Ed); technical communication (MS). *Program availability:* Part-time, evening/weekend, 100% online, blended/hybrid learning. Electronic applications accepted. *Expenses:* Contact institution.

Northern Arizona University, College of Education, Department of Educational Leadership, Flagstaff, AZ 86011. Offers community college teaching and learning (Graduate Certificate); educational leadership (M Ed, Ed D), including community college/higher education (M Ed), educational foundations (M Ed), instructional leadership K-12 school leadership (M Ed), principal certification K-12 (M Ed); principal (Graduate Certificate); superintendent (Graduate Certificate). *Program availability:* Part-time. *Degree requirements:* For master's, comprehensive exam, thesis (for some programs); for doctorate, comprehensive exam, thesis/dissertation; for Graduate Certificate, comprehensive exam (for some programs). *Entrance requirements:* Additional exam requirements/recommendations for international students: Required—TOEFL (minimum score 80 iBT), IELTS (minimum score 6.5). Electronic applications accepted.

Northern Illinois University, Graduate School, College of Education, Department of Leadership, Educational Psychology and Foundations, De Kalb, IL 60115-2854. Offers educational administration (MS Ed, Ed D, Ed S); educational psychology (MS Ed, Ed D); foundations of education (MS Ed); school business management (MS Ed). *Program availability:* Part-time, evening/weekend, online learning. *Faculty:* 23 full-time (12 women). *Students:* 9 full-time (4 women), 170 part-time (98 women); includes 45 minority (16 Black or African American, non-Hispanic/Latino; 6 Asian, non-Hispanic/Latino; 15 Hispanic/Latino; 8 Two or more races, non-Hispanic/Latino), 2 international. Average age 39. 78 applicants, 86% accepted, 34 enrolled. In 2018, 52 master's, 28 doctorates, 2 other advanced degrees awarded. *Degree requirements:* For master's, comprehensive exam, thesis optional; for doctorate, thesis/dissertation, candidacy exam, dissertation defense. *Entrance requirements:* For master's, minimum undergraduate GPA of 2.75; for doctorate, GRE General Test, minimum undergraduate GPA of 2.75, 3.2 graduate; for Ed S, GRE General Test, minimum GPA of 2.75 (undergraduate), 3.2 (graduate). Additional exam requirements/recommendations for international students: Required—TOEFL (minimum score 550 paper-based). *Application deadline:* For fall admission, 6/1 for domestic students, 5/1 for international students; for spring admission, 11/1 for domestic students, 10/1 for international students. Applications are processed on a rolling basis. Application fee: $40. Electronic applications accepted. *Financial support:* In 2018–19, 1 research assistantship with full tuition reimbursement, 2 teaching assistantships with full tuition reimbursements were awarded; fellowships with full tuition reimbursements, career-related internships or fieldwork, Federal Work-Study, scholarships/grants, tuition waivers (full), and staff assistantships also available. Support available to part-time students. Financial award applicants required to submit FAFSA. *Faculty research:* Interpersonal forgiveness, learner-centered education, psychedelic studies, senior theory, professional growth. *Unit head:* Carolyn V. Schee, Chair, 815-753-4404, E-mail: lepf@niu.edu. *Application contact:* Graduate School Office, 815-753-0395, E-mail: gradsch@niu.edu.
Website: http://cedu.niu.edu/LEPF/

Northern Kentucky University, Office of Graduate Programs, College of Education and Human Services, Doctor of Education in Educational Leadership Program, Highland Heights, KY 41099. Offers Ed D. *Program availability:* Part-time, evening/weekend. *Entrance requirements:* For doctorate, master's (or specialist) degree in education or a related field; minimum GPA of 3.25; five or more years of educational leadership experience; letter describing educational and leadership background, goals, style, and philosophy; professional vitae; leadership situation account; 3 letters of recommendation; interview. Additional exam requirements/recommendations for international students: Required—TOEFL (minimum score 79 iBT); Recommended—IELTS (minimum score 6.5). Electronic applications accepted. *Faculty research:* Educator dispositions, civic engagement and service-learning in education, school leadership, technology in education, professional development.

Northern Kentucky University, Office of Graduate Programs, College of Education and Human Services, Education Program: Teacher as a Leader, Highland Heights, KY 41099. Offers MA, Certificate. *Program availability:* Part-time, evening/weekend, online learning. *Degree requirements:* For master's, thesis optional, portfolio. *Entrance requirements:* For master's, GRE, teacher certification, bachelor's degree in appropriate subject area, minimum GPA of 2.5, 3 letters of recommendation, 1 year of teaching experience, statement of personal goals. Additional exam requirements/recommendations for international students: Required—TOEFL (minimum score 79 iBT); Recommended—IELTS (minimum score 6.5). Electronic applications accepted. *Faculty research:* Teaching with technology, middle school education, children with disabilities, teaching in the content areas, diversifying faculty.

Northern Kentucky University, Office of Graduate Programs, College of Education and Human Services, Education Specialist in Educational Leadership Program, Highland Heights, KY 41099. Offers Ed S. *Degree requirements:* For Ed S, capstone and two presentations. *Entrance requirements:* For degree, copy of valid teaching certificate showing successful completion of 3 years' full-time documented classroom teaching experience, official transcripts, 3 letters of recommendation, minimum GPA of 3.5, 3 essays, professional folio, interview. Additional exam requirements/recommendations for international students: Required—TOEFL (minimum score 79 iBT); Recommended—IELTS (minimum score 6.5). Electronic applications accepted.

Northern Michigan University, Office of Graduate Education and Research, College of Health Sciences and Professional Studies, School of Education, Leadership and Public Service, Marquette, MI 49855-5301. Offers administration and supervision (MAE); instruction (MAE); learning disabilities (MAE); postsecondary biology education (MS); reading education (MAE), including reading, reading specialist. *Accreditation:* TEAC. *Program availability:* Part-time, online learning. *Degree requirements:* For master's, thesis (for some programs). *Entrance requirements:* For master's, minimum GPA of 3.0. Additional exam requirements/recommendations for international students: Required—TOEFL (minimum score 550 paper-based; 79 iBT), IELTS (minimum score 6.5). Electronic applications accepted.

Northern State University, MS Ed Program in Leadership and Administration, Aberdeen, SD 57401-7198. Offers MS Ed. *Accreditation:* NCATE. *Program availability:* Part-time, evening/weekend, online learning. *Degree requirements:* For master's, comprehensive exam, thesis optional. *Entrance requirements:* For master's, minimum GPA of 2.75. Additional exam requirements/recommendations for international students: Required—TOEFL (minimum score 550 paper-based; 78 iBT), IELTS (minimum score 6). Electronic applications accepted.

Northwestern College, Program in Education, Orange City, IA 51041-1996. Offers early childhood (M Ed); master teacher (M Ed); teacher leadership (M Ed, Graduate Certificate). *Program availability:* Online learning.

Northwestern Oklahoma State University, School of Professional Studies, Program in Educational Leadership, Alva, OK 73717-2799. Offers M Ed. *Program availability:* Part-time. *Degree requirements:* For master's, thesis optional, portfolio. *Entrance requirements:* For master's, GRE General Test or MAT, minimum GPA of 2.75.

Northwestern State University of Louisiana, Graduate Studies and Research, College of Education and Human Development, Programs in Educational Leadership and Instruction, Natchitoches, LA 71497. Offers counseling (Ed S); educational leadership (M Ed, Ed S); educational technology (Ed S); elementary teaching (Ed S); reading (Ed S); secondary teaching (Ed S); special education (Ed S). *Accreditation:* NASAD. *Degree requirements:* For master's, comprehensive exam, thesis (for some programs). *Entrance requirements:* For master's and Ed S, GRE General Test. Additional exam requirements/recommendations for international students: Required—TOEFL. Electronic applications accepted.

Northwestern University, The Graduate School, School of Education and Social Policy, Education and Social Policy Program, Evanston, IL 60035. Offers elementary teaching (MS); secondary teaching (MS); teacher leadership (MS). *Program availability:* Part-time, evening/weekend. *Degree requirements:* For master's, research project. *Entrance requirements:* For master's, GRE General Test, Illinois State Board of Education Basic Skills Exam (secondary and elementary), bachelor's degree. Additional exam requirements/recommendations for international students: Recommended—TOEFL. Electronic applications accepted. *Faculty research:* Cultural context and literacy, philosophy of education and interpretive discussion, productivity, enhancing research and teaching, motivation, new and junior faculty issues, professional development for K-12 teachers to improve math and science teaching, female/underrepresented students/faculty in STEM disciplines.

Northwest Missouri State University, Graduate School, School of Education, Maryville, MO 64468-6001. Offers early childhood education (MS Ed); education leadership (MS Ed), including elementary, K-12, secondary; educational leadership

(Ed S), including elementary school principalship, secondary school principalship, superintendency; educational leadership and policy analysis (Ed D); elementary education (MS Ed); elementary mathematics (MS Ed); higher education leadership (MS); middle school education (MS Ed); reading (MS Ed); special education (MS Ed); teacher leadership (MS Ed); teaching English language learners (MS Ed). *Accreditation:* NCATE. *Program availability:* Part-time. *Faculty:* 26 full-time (16 women). *Students:* 109 full-time (87 women), 385 part-time (270 women); includes 30 minority (10 Black or African American, non-Hispanic/Latino; 2 American Indian or Alaska Native, non-Hispanic/Latino; 3 Asian, non-Hispanic/Latino; 12 Hispanic/Latino; 1 Native Hawaiian or other Pacific Islander, non-Hispanic/Latino; 2 Two or more races, non-Hispanic/Latino), 1 international. Average age 33. 210 applicants, 72% accepted, 142 enrolled. In 2018, 71 master's, 11 other advanced degrees awarded. *Degree requirements:* For master's, comprehensive exam; for Ed S, comprehensive exam, thesis. *Entrance requirements:* For master's, GRE General Test, writing sample; for Ed S, minimum graduate GPA of 3.25. Additional exam requirements/recommendations for international students: Required—TOEFL (minimum score 550 paper-based). *Application deadline:* For fall admission, 7/1 for domestic and international students; for spring admission, 11/15 for domestic and international students. Applications are processed on a rolling basis. Application fee: $0 ($75 for international students). Electronic applications accepted. *Expenses:* $389.11 in-state and $653.92 out-of-state per credit hour. *Financial support:* Research assistantships with full tuition reimbursements, teaching assistantships with full tuition reimbursements, and unspecified assistantships available. Financial award application deadline: 4/1; financial award applicants required to submit FAFSA. *Unit head:* Dr. Tim Wall, Director, 660-562-1179, E-mail: timwall@nwmissouri.edu. *Application contact:* Dr. Tim Wall, Director, 660-562-1179, E-mail: timwall@nwmissouri.edu.
Website: https://www.nwmissouri.edu/education/index.htm

Northwest Nazarene University, Graduate Education Program, Nampa, ID 83686-5897. Offers curriculum and instruction (M Ed); educational leadership (M Ed, Ed D, PhD, Ed S), including building administrator (M Ed, Ed S), director of special education (Ed S), leadership and organizational development (Ed S), superintendent (Ed S). *Accreditation:* ACA (one or more programs are accredited); NCATE. *Program availability:* Part-time, online only, 100% online, 2-week face-to-face residency (for doctoral programs). *Faculty:* 4 full-time (3 women), 18 part-time/adjunct (7 women). *Students:* 128 full-time (83 women), 59 part-time (37 women); includes 22 minority (3 Black or African American, non-Hispanic/Latino; 1 Asian, non-Hispanic/Latino; 3 Hispanic/Latino; 15 Two or more races, non-Hispanic/Latino), 1 international. Average age 44. 124 applicants, 84% accepted, 87 enrolled. In 2018, 37 master's, 18 doctorates, 28 other advanced degrees awarded. *Degree requirements:* For master's, comprehensive exam (for some programs), action research project; for doctorate, thesis/dissertation, Dissertation; for Ed S, comprehensive exam, research project. *Entrance requirements:* For master's, minimum undergraduate GPA of 3.0 overall or during final 30 semester credits, undergraduate degree, valid teaching certificate; for doctorate, Ed S or equivalent, minimum GPA of 3.5; for Ed S, undergraduate degree, valid teaching certificate. Additional exam requirements/recommendations for international students: Recommended—TOEFL. *Application deadline:* Applications are processed on a rolling basis. Application fee: $50. Electronic applications accepted. *Expenses:* Masters: $475 per credit, $95 technology fee per semester; EDS: $505 per credit, $95 technology fee per semester; PHD/EDD: $565 per credit, $520 dissertation fee, $95 technology fee per semester. *Financial support:* Application deadline: 1/15; applicants required to submit FAFSA. *Faculty research:* Action research, cooperative learning, accountability, institutional accreditation, personalized learning K-12. *Unit head:* Dr. Heidi Curtis, Chair, 208-467-8250, E-mail: hlcurtis@nnu.edu. *Application contact:* Charlene Brown, Admissions Counselor, 208-467-8492, Fax: 208-467-8384, E-mail: gradeducationinfo@nnu.edu.
Website: http://www.nnu.edu/graded/

Notre Dame de Namur University, Division of Academic Affairs, School of Education and Psychology, Program in School Administration, Belmont, CA 94002-1908. Offers MA. *Program availability:* Part-time, evening/weekend. *Students:* 13 part-time (7 women); includes 5 minority (1 Asian, non-Hispanic/Latino; 3 Hispanic/Latino; 1 Native Hawaiian or other Pacific Islander, non-Hispanic/Latino). Average age 37. *Degree requirements:* For master's, thesis optional, capstone course. *Entrance requirements:* For master's, interview, valid teaching credential, minimum 1 year of classroom teaching experience. Additional exam requirements/recommendations for international students: Required—TOEFL (minimum score 550 paper-based; 79 iBT). *Application deadline:* For fall admission, 8/1 priority date for domestic students; for spring admission, 12/1 priority date for domestic students. Applications are processed on a rolling basis. Application fee: $60. Electronic applications accepted. *Expenses: Tuition:* Full-time $16,596; part-time $11,064 per semester. *Required fees:* $130; $130 per unit. $65 per semester. Tuition and fees vary according to program. *Financial support:* Career-related internships or fieldwork and scholarships/grants available. Financial award applicants required to submit FAFSA. *Application contact:* Susan Charles, Program Director, Master's in School Administration, 650-508-3473, E-mail: scharles@ndnu.edu.

Notre Dame of Maryland University, Graduate Studies, Leadership in Teaching Program, Baltimore, MD 21210-2476. Offers MA. *Entrance requirements:* For master's, interview, 1 year of teaching experience, minimum GPA of 3.0. Additional exam requirements/recommendations for international students: Required—TOEFL (minimum score 500 paper-based; 61 iBT). Electronic applications accepted.

Notre Dame of Maryland University, Graduate Studies, Program in Instructional Leadership for Changing Populations, Baltimore, MD 21210-2476. Offers PhD. *Entrance requirements:* Additional exam requirements/recommendations for international students: Required—TOEFL (minimum score 500 paper-based; 61 iBT).

Oakland City University, School of Education, Oakland City, IN 47660-1099. Offers building level administration (MS Ed); curriculum and instruction (MS Ed, Ed D); education (MS Ed); elementary education (MAT); organizational management (Ed D); secondary education (MAT); superintendency (Ed D). *Accreditation:* NCATE. Terminal master's awarded for partial completion of doctoral program. *Degree requirements:* For master's, thesis; for doctorate, comprehensive exam, thesis/dissertation. *Entrance requirements:* For master's, MAT, minimum GPA of 3.0, interview, resume, letters of recommendation; for doctorate, MAT, GRE, minimum GPA of 3.2, interview, resume, letters of recommendation. *Expenses:* Contact institution. *Faculty research:* Assessment, cultural diversity, teacher education, education leadership.

Oakland University, Graduate Study and Lifelong Learning, School of Education and Human Services, Department of Organizational Leadership, Rochester, MI 48309-4401. Offers educational leadership (M Ed, PhD); higher education (Certificate); school administration (Ed S). *Entrance requirements:* Additional exam requirements/recommendations for international students: Required—TOEFL (minimum score 550 paper-based).

Oakland University, Graduate Study and Lifelong Learning, School of Education and Human Services, Department of Teacher Development and Educational Studies, Rochester, MI 48309-4401. Offers educational studies (M Ed); elementary education (MAT); secondary education (MAT); teaching and learning (Graduate Certificate). *Entrance requirements:* For master's, minimum GPA of 3.0. Electronic applications accepted.

Oglala Lakota College, Graduate Studies, Program in Educational Administration, Kyle, SD 57752-0490. Offers MA. *Program availability:* Part-time, evening/weekend. *Entrance requirements:* For master's, minimum GPA of 2.5.

Ohio Dominican University, Division of Education, Program in Educational Leadership, Columbus, OH 43219-2099. Offers M Ed. *Program availability:* Part-time, evening/weekend, 100% online, blended/hybrid learning. *Faculty:* 6 full-time (4 women), 6 part-time/adjunct (3 women). *Students:* 3 full-time (2 women), 62 part-time (41 women); includes 6 minority (4 Black or African American, non-Hispanic/Latino; 2 Hispanic/Latino), 2 international. Average age 35. 25 applicants, 48% accepted, 11 enrolled. In 2018, 39 master's awarded. *Entrance requirements:* For master's, bachelor's degree from regionally-accredited institution; teaching certificate/license; currently teaching or have access to an academic classroom. Additional exam requirements/recommendations for international students: Required—TOEFL (minimum score 550 paper-based), IELTS (minimum score 6.5). *Application deadline:* For fall admission, 8/15 for domestic students, 6/10 for international students; for spring admission, 1/4 for domestic students, 11/2 for international students; for summer admission, 5/30 for domestic students. Applications are processed on a rolling basis. Application fee: $25. Electronic applications accepted. *Expenses:* $538/credit hour tuition, $225/semester fees. *Financial support:* Applicants required to submit FAFSA. *Unit head:* Dr. JoAnn Hohenbrink, Director of Graduate Education Programs, 614-251-4759, E-mail: hohenbrj@ohiodominican.edu. *Application contact:* John W. Naughton, Vice President for Enrollment and Student Success, 614-251-4721, Fax: 614-251-6654, E-mail: grad@ohiodominican.edu.
Website: http://www.ohiodominican.edu/academics/graduate/master-of-education/educational-leadership

The Ohio State University, Graduate School, College of Education and Human Ecology, Department of Educational Studies, Columbus, OH 43210. Offers M Ed, MA, PhD, Ed S. *Accreditation:* NCATE. *Program availability:* Part-time. *Faculty:* 57. *Students:* 331 full-time (219 women), 199 part-time (135 women); includes 130 minority (83 Black or African American, non-Hispanic/Latino; 11 Asian, non-Hispanic/Latino; 17 Hispanic/Latino; 19 Two or more races, non-Hispanic/Latino), 53 international. Average age 32. In 2018, 129 master's, 39 doctorates, 10 other advanced degrees awarded. *Degree requirements:* For master's, thesis optional; for doctorate, thesis/dissertation. *Entrance requirements:* For master's and doctorate, GRE General Test. Additional exam requirements/recommendations for international students: Required—TOEFL (minimum score 550 paper-based; 79 iBT), Michigan English Language Assessment Battery (minimum score 82); Recommended—IELTS (minimum score 7). *Application deadline:* For fall admission, 12/1 priority date for domestic and international students; for spring admission, 11/1 for domestic and international students; for summer admission, 3/1 for domestic and international students. Applications are processed on a rolling basis. Application fee: $60 ($70 for international students). Electronic applications accepted. *Financial support:* Fellowships with tuition reimbursements, research assistantships with tuition reimbursements, teaching assistantships with tuition reimbursements, Federal Work-Study, institutionally sponsored loans, and unspecified assistantships available. Support available to part-time students. *Unit head:* Dr. Antoinette Miranda, Interim Chair, 614-292-5909, E-mail: miranda.2@osu.edu. *Application contact:* Graduate and Professional Admissions, 614-292-9444, E-mail: gpadmissions@osu.edu.
Website: http://ehe.osu.edu/educational-studies/

Ohio University, Graduate College, Gladys W. and David H. Patton College of Education and Human Services, Department of Educational Studies, Athens, OH 45701-2979. Offers computer education and technology (M Ed); educational administration (M Ed, Ed D); educational research and evaluation (M Ed, PhD); instructional technology (PhD). *Program availability:* Part-time, evening/weekend, online learning. *Degree requirements:* For master's, thesis or alternative; for doctorate, comprehensive exam, thesis/dissertation. *Entrance requirements:* For master's, GRE General Test (if GPA less than 2.9); for doctorate, GRE General Test, GRE Subject Test, minimum GPA of 2.9, work experience, 3 letters of reference, autobiography. Additional exam requirements/recommendations for international students: Required—TOEFL (minimum score 550 paper-based; 80 iBT) or IELTS (minimum score 6.5). Electronic applications accepted. *Faculty research:* Race, class and gender; computer programs; development and organization theory; evaluation/development of instruments, leadership.

Oklahoma State University, College of Education, Health and Aviation, School of Teaching and Curriculum Leadership, Stillwater, OK 74078. Offers MS, PhD. *Program availability:* Part-time. *Entrance requirements:* For master's and doctorate, GRE or GMAT. Additional exam requirements/recommendations for international students: Required—TOEFL (minimum score 550 paper-based; 79 iBT). Electronic applications accepted. *Expenses: Tuition, area resident:* Full-time $4148. Tuition, state resident: full-time $4148. Tuition, nonresident: full-time $10,517. *International tuition:* $10,517 full-time. *Required fees:* $4394; $2929 per credit hour. Tuition and fees vary according to course load and program.

Old Dominion University, Darden College of Education, Educational Leadership Services Programs, Norfolk, VA 23529. Offers educational leadership (MS Ed, PhD, Ed S). *Accreditation:* NCATE. *Program availability:* Part-time, evening/weekend, 100% online, blended/hybrid learning. *Degree requirements:* For master's and Ed S, comprehensive exam, thesis optional, internship, portfolio, school leadership licensure assessment; for doctorate, comprehensive exam, thesis/dissertation. *Entrance requirements:* For master's, minimum GPA of 3.0 in major, letters of recommendation, resume, 2 essays; for doctorate, GRE, minimum graduate GPA of 3.5, 3 letters of recommendation, essays, resume; for Ed S, minimum GPA of 3.0 in major, 2 letters of recommendation, essays, resume. Additional exam requirements/recommendations for international students: Required—TOEFL (minimum score 550 paper-based). Electronic applications accepted. *Faculty research:* Leadership preparation, supervision, policy studies, finance, learning sciences.

Olivet Nazarene University, Graduate School, Division of Education, Program in School Leadership, Bourbonnais, IL 60914. Offers MAE.

Oral Roberts University, School of Education, Tulsa, OK 74171. Offers Christian school administration (K-12) (MA Ed, Ed D); college and higher education administration (Ed D); curriculum and instruction (MA Ed); initial teaching with alternative licensure (MAT); initial teaching with licensure (MAT); public school administration (K-12) (MA Ed, Ed D). *Accreditation:* NCATE. *Program availability:* Part-time, online learning. *Degree requirements:* For master's, comprehensive exam, thesis optional; for doctorate, comprehensive exam, thesis/dissertation. *Entrance requirements:* For master's, GRE General Test or MAT (minimum score in 80th percentile or higher); Oklahoma general education or subject area test (for MAT), minimum GPA of 3.0, bachelor's degree from regionally-accredited institution; for doctorate, minimum GPA of 3.0, master's degree from regionally-accredited institution. Electronic applications accepted. Application fee is waived when completed online. *Expenses:* Contact institution. *Faculty research:* Teacher effectiveness, college success in high achieving African-Americans, professional development practices.

Oregon State University, College of Education, Program in Adult and Higher Education, Corvallis, OR 97331. Offers Ed M, Ed D, PhD. *Accreditation:* NCATE. *Program availability:* Part-time, blended/hybrid learning. *Entrance requirements:* For master's, minimum GPA of 3.0 in last 90 hours. Additional exam requirements/ recommendations for international students: Required—TOEFL (minimum score 575 paper-based).

Ottawa University, Graduate Studies-Arizona, Program in Education, Ottawa, KS 66067-3399. Offers community college counseling (MA); curriculum and instruction (MA); early childhood (MA); education intervention (MA); education leadership (MA); education technology (MA); Montessori early childhood education (MA); Montessori elementary education (MA); professional development (MA); school guidance counseling (MA); special education - cross categorical (MA). Programs offered in Mesa, Phoenix, Tempe and West Valley, AZ. *Accreditation:* NCATE. *Program availability:* Part-time. *Degree requirements:* For master's, thesis or alternative. *Entrance requirements:* For master's, minimum undergraduate GPA of 3.0, copy of current state certification or teaching license. Additional exam requirements/recommendations for international students: Required—TOEFL (minimum score 550 paper-based). Electronic applications accepted. *Expenses:* Contact institution.

Park University, School of Graduate and Professional Studies, Kansas City, MO 54105. Offers adult education (M Ed); business and government leadership (Graduate Certificate); business, government, and global society (MPA); communication and leadership (MA); creative and life writing (Graduate Certificate); disaster and emergency management (MPA, Graduate Certificate); educational leadership (M Ed); finance (MBA, Graduate Certificate); general business (MBA); global business (Graduate Certificate); healthcare administration (MHA); healthcare services management and leadership (Graduate Certificate); international business (MBA); language and literacy (M Ed), including English for speakers of other languages, special reading teacher/ literacy coach; leadership of international healthcare organizations (Graduate Certificate); management information systems (MBA, Graduate Certificate); music performance (ADP, Graduate Certificate), including cello (MM, ADP), piano (MM, ADP), viola (MM, ADP), violin (MM, ADP); nonprofit and community services management (MPA); nonprofit leadership (Graduate Certificate); performance (MM), including cello (MM, ADP), piano (MM, ADP), viola (MM, ADP), violin (MM, ADP); public management (MPA); social work (MSW); teacher leadership (M Ed), including curriculum and assessment, instructional leader. *Program availability:* Part-time, evening/weekend, online learning. *Degree requirements:* For master's, comprehensive exam (for some programs), thesis (for some programs), internship (for some programs); exam (for some programs). *Entrance requirements:* For master's, GRE or GMAT (for some programs), teacher certification (for some M Ed programs), letters of recommendation, essay, resume (for some programs). Additional exam requirements/recommendations for international students: Required—TOEFL (minimum score 550 paper-based; 79 iBT), IELTS (minimum score 6). Electronic applications accepted.

Penn State University Park, Graduate School, College of Education, Department of Education Policy Studies, University Park, PA 16802. Offers educational leadership (M Ed, D Ed, PhD, Certificate); educational theory and policy (MA, PhD); higher education (M Ed, D Ed, PhD). *Accreditation:* NCATE. *Program availability:* Online learning.

Pensacola Christian College, Graduate Studies, Pensacola, FL 32503-2267. Offers business administration (MBA); curriculum and instruction (MS, Ed D, Ed S); dramatics (MFA); educational leadership (MS, Ed D, Ed S); graphic design (MA, MFA); music (MA); nursing (MSN); performance studies (MA); studio art (MA, MFA).

Piedmont International University, Graduate School, Winston-Salem, NC 27101-5197. Offers Biblical studies (PhD); curriculum and instruction (M Ed); divinity (M Div); educational leadership (M Ed); leadership (MA, PhD); ministry (MA Min, D Min); non-language track (MABS); PhD preparation track (MABS). *Program availability:* Part-time, online learning. Terminal master's awarded for partial completion of doctoral program. *Degree requirements:* For master's, 2 foreign languages, comprehensive exam, thesis or alternative; for doctorate, 2 foreign languages, comprehensive exam. *Entrance requirements:* For master's, GRE General Test; for doctorate, Hebrew and Greek proficiency, MA. Additional exam requirements/recommendations for international students: Required—TOEFL (minimum score 500 paper-based; 60 iBT). Electronic applications accepted. *Faculty research:* Theological and biblical studies.

Pittsburg State University, Graduate School, College of Education, Department of Teaching and Leadership, Advanced Studies in Leadership Program, Pittsburg, KS 66762. Offers advanced studies in leadership (Ed S), including general school administration, special education. *Program availability:* Part-time, online only, 100% online. *Degree requirements:* For Ed S, thesis optional. *Entrance requirements:* Additional exam requirements/recommendations for international students: Required—TOEFL (minimum score 520 paper-based; 68 iBT), IELTS (minimum score 6), PTE (minimum score 47). Electronic applications accepted. *Expenses:* Contact institution.

Pittsburg State University, Graduate School, College of Education, Department of Teaching and Leadership, Program in Educational Leadership, Pittsburg, KS 66762. Offers MS. *Program availability:* Part-time-only, online only, 100% online. Terminal master's awarded for partial completion of doctoral program. *Degree requirements:* For master's, thesis optional. *Entrance requirements:* Additional exam requirements/ recommendations for international students: Required—TOEFL (minimum score 520 paper-based; 68 iBT), IELTS (minimum score 6), PTE (minimum score 47). Electronic applications accepted. *Expenses:* Contact institution.

Plymouth State University, College of Graduate Studies, Graduate Studies in Education, Certificate of Advanced Graduate Studies Programs, Plymouth, NH 03264-1595. Offers clinical mental health counseling (CAGS); educational leadership (CAGS); higher education (CAGS); school psychology (CAGS). *Program availability:* Part-time, evening/weekend.

Plymouth State University, College of Graduate Studies, Graduate Studies in Education, Program in Educational Leadership, Plymouth, NH 03264-1595. Offers M Ed. *Accreditation:* NCATE. *Program availability:* Part-time, evening/weekend. *Degree requirements:* For master's, thesis optional, PRAXIS. *Entrance requirements:* For master's, MAT, minimum GPA of 3.0.

Plymouth State University, College of Graduate Studies, Graduate Studies in Education, Program in Higher Education, Plymouth, NH 03264-1595. Offers administrative leadership (Ed D); curriculum and instruction (Ed D).

Point Loma Nazarene University, School of Education, Program in Education, San Diego, CA 92106-2899. Offers counseling and guidance (MA); educational administration (MA); leadership in learning (MA). *Program availability:* Part-time, evening/weekend. *Entrance requirements:* For master's, interview, letters of recommendation, essay. Additional exam requirements/recommendations for international students: Required—TOEFL. Electronic applications accepted. *Expenses:* Contact institution.

Point Park University, Center for Innovative Learning, Pittsburgh, PA 15222-1984. Offers community engagement (PhD). *Expenses:* Contact institution.

Point Park University, School of Arts and Sciences, Department of Education, Pittsburgh, PA 15222-1984. Offers adult learning and training (MA); athletic coaching (M Ed); curriculum and instruction (MA); educational administration (MA); leadership and administration (Ed D); secondary education (M Ed); special education grades 7-12 (M Ed); special education PreK-grade 8 (M Ed). *Program availability:* Part-time, evening/ weekend, 100% online, blended/hybrid learning. *Degree requirements:* For master's, comprehensive exam (for some programs), thesis or alternative. *Entrance requirements:* For master's, minimum GPA of 3.0, resume, 2 letters of recommendation. Additional exam requirements/recommendations for international students: Required—TOEFL. Electronic applications accepted.

Pontifical Catholic University of Puerto Rico, College of Education, Program in Educational Leadership and Administration, Ponce, PR 00717-0777. Offers PhD.

Post University, Program in Education, Waterbury, CT 06723-2540. Offers curriculum and instruction (M Ed); education (M Ed); educational technology (M Ed); higher education administration (MS); learning design and technology (M Ed); online teaching (M Ed); teaching English to speakers of other languages (TESOL) (M Ed). *Program availability:* Online learning. *Entrance requirements:* For master's, resume. *Expenses: Tuition:* Full-time $8300; part-time $570 per credit. *Required fees:* $140 per term. Tuition and fees vary according to course level, campus/location and program.

Prairie View A&M University, College of Education, Department of Educational Leadership and Counseling, Prairie View, TX 77446. Offers M Ed, MA, MS Ed, PhD. *Accreditation:* NCATE. *Program availability:* Part-time, evening/weekend. *Faculty:* 13 full-time (5 women), 2 part-time/adjunct (1 woman). *Students:* 31 full-time (19 women), 167 part-time (129 women); includes 188 minority (177 Black or African American, non-Hispanic/Latino; 11 Hispanic/Latino), 4 international. Average age 37. 46 applicants, 83% accepted, 30 enrolled. In 2018, 87 master's, 4 doctorates awarded. *Degree requirements:* For master's, thesis optional; for doctorate, comprehensive exam, thesis/ dissertation. *Entrance requirements:* For master's, GRE General Test, 3 letters of reference, minimum undergraduate GPA of 2.5; for doctorate, GRE General Test, 3 letters of reference. Additional exam requirements/recommendations for international students: Required—TOEFL (minimum score 550 paper-based; 79 iBT). *Application deadline:* For fall admission, 5/1 priority date for domestic students, 5/1 for international students; for spring admission, 10/1 priority date for domestic students, 9/1 for international students; for summer admission, 3/1 for domestic students, 2/1 for international students. Applications are processed on a rolling basis. Application fee: $50. Electronic applications accepted. *Expenses: Tuition, area resident:* Full-time $3172; part-time $317 per credit. Tuition, state resident: full-time $3172; part-time $317 per credit. Tuition, nonresident: full-time $7965; part-time $796 per credit. *Required fees:* $4847; $485 per credit. *Financial support:* Career-related internships or fieldwork available. Support available to part-time students. Financial award application deadline: 4/1; financial award applicants required to submit FAFSA. *Faculty research:* Mentoring, personality assessment, holistic/humanistic education. *Unit head:* Dr. Maduakolam Ireh, Department Head, 936-261-3565, Fax: 936-261-3617, E-mail: maireh@pvamu.edu. *Application contact:* Pauline Walker, Administrative Assistant II, Research and Graduate Studies, 936-261-3521, Fax: 936-261-3529, E-mail: gradadmissions@pvamu.edu.

Prescott College, Graduate Programs, Program in Education, Prescott, AZ 86301. Offers early childhood education (MA); early childhood special education (MA); education (MA); elementary education (MA); environmental education leadership and administration (MA); equine-assisted learning (MA); school guidance counseling (MA); secondary education (MA); special education: learning disabilities (MA); special education: mental retardation (MA); special education: serious emotional disabilities (MA); student-directed independent study (MA); sustainability education (PhD). *Program availability:* Part-time, online learning. *Degree requirements:* For master's, thesis, fieldwork or internship, practicum; for doctorate, thesis/dissertation. *Entrance requirements:* For master's, 2 letters of recommendation, resume; for doctorate, 3 letters of recommendation, resume, official transcripts, personal statement, program proposal. Additional exam requirements/recommendations for international students: Required—TOEFL (minimum score 500 paper-based). Electronic applications accepted.

Providence College, Programs in Administration, Providence, RI 02918. Offers elementary administration (M Ed); secondary administration (M Ed). *Program availability:* Part-time, evening/weekend. *Degree requirements:* For master's, comprehensive exam, portfolio. *Entrance requirements:* Additional exam requirements/ recommendations for international students: Required—TOEFL (minimum score 577 paper-based; 90 iBT).

Purdue University, Graduate School, College of Education, Department of Educational Studies, West Lafayette, IN 47907. Offers administration (MS Ed, Ed S); foundations of education (MS Ed); higher education administration (PhD). *Accreditation:* ACA (one or more programs are accredited); NCATE (one or more programs are accredited). *Program availability:* Part-time, evening/weekend. *Faculty:* 30 full-time (21 women), 2 part-time/adjunct (0 women). *Students:* 72 full-time (55 women), 240 part-time (186 women); includes 46 minority (13 Black or African American, non-Hispanic/Latino; 12 Asian, non-Hispanic/Latino; 14 Hispanic/Latino; 7 Two or more races, non-Hispanic/ Latino), 47 international. Average age 32. 218 applicants, 51% accepted, 83 enrolled. In 2018, 86 master's, 15 doctorates awarded. *Degree requirements:* For master's, thesis optional; for doctorate, thesis/dissertation, oral and written exams; for Ed S, oral presentation, project. *Entrance requirements:* For master's, GRE General Test (except for special education if undergraduate GPA is higher than a 3.0), minimum undergraduate GPA of 3.0; for doctorate and Ed S, GRE General Test (minimum combined score of 1000, 300 for new scoring), minimum undergraduate GPA of 3.0. Additional exam requirements/recommendations for international students: Required—TOEFL (minimum score 550 paper-based; 77 iBT), TWE (minimum score 5). *Application deadline:* Applications are processed on a rolling basis. Application fee: $60 ($75 for international students). Electronic applications accepted. *Financial support:* Fellowships with full tuition reimbursements, research assistantships with full tuition reimbursements, teaching assistantships with full tuition reimbursements, career-related internships or fieldwork, and tuition waivers (full) available. Support available to part-time students. Financial award application deadline: 3/1; financial award applicants required to submit FAFSA. *Faculty research:* Motivation, learning disabilities, school learning, group processes, cognitive development. *Unit head:* F. Richard Olenchak, Head, 765-494-9170, E-mail: olenchak@purdue.edu. *Application contact:* Heather Brinkman, Graduate Contact, 765-494-2345, Fax: 765-494-5832, E-mail: hbrinkma@purdue.edu.
Website: http://www.edst.purdue.edu/

Purdue University Fort Wayne, College of Professional Studies, School of Education, Fort Wayne, IN 46805-1499. Offers couple and family counseling (MS Ed); educational leadership (MS Ed); elementary education (MS Ed); school counseling (MS Ed); secondary education (MS Ed); special education (MS Ed, Certificate). *Accreditation:* NCATE. *Program availability:* Part-time. *Entrance requirements:* For master's, minimum GPA of 2.5, three professional letters of recommendation. Additional exam requirements/recommendations for international students: Required—TOEFL (minimum score 550 paper-based; 79 iBT). *Faculty research:* International faculty, gender in Burmese refugee narratives, planning effective instruction.

Educational Leadership and Administration

Purdue University Global, School of Higher Education Studies, Davenport, IA 52807. Offers college administration and leadership (MS); college teaching and learning (MS); student services (MS). *Program availability:* Part-time, evening/weekend, online learning. *Entrance requirements:* Additional exam requirements/recommendations for international students: Required—TOEFL (minimum score 550 paper-based; 80 iBT).

Purdue University Northwest, Graduate Studies Office, School of Education, Program in Educational Administration, Hammond, IN 46323-2094. Offers MS Ed. *Entrance requirements:* Additional exam requirements/recommendations for international students: Required—TOEFL.

Queens College of the City University of New York, Division of Education, Department of Educational and Community Programs, Queens, NY 11367-1597. Offers bilingual pupil personnel (AC); counselor education (MS Ed); mental health counseling (MS); school building leader (AC); school district leader (AC); school psychologist (MS Ed); special education-childhood education (AC); special education-early childhood (MS Ed); teacher of special education 1-6 (MS Ed); teacher of special education birth-2 (MS Ed); teaching students with disabilities, grades 7-12 (MS Ed, AC). *Program availability:* Part-time. *Faculty:* 19 full-time (13 women), 53 part-time/adjunct (31 women). *Students:* 90 full-time (83 women), 380 part-time (316 women); includes 217 minority (42 Black or African American, non-Hispanic/Latino; 1 American Indian or Alaska Native, non-Hispanic/Latino; 53 Asian, non-Hispanic/Latino; 114 Hispanic/Latino; 7 Two or more races, non-Hispanic/Latino), 6 international. Average age 29. 470 applicants, 65% accepted, 236 enrolled. In 2018, 164 master's, 59 other advanced degrees awarded. *Degree requirements:* For master's, Research project; for AC, internship, research project. *Entrance requirements:* For master's, minimum GPA of 3.0. Additional exam requirements/recommendations for international students: Required—TOEFL, IELTS. *Application deadline:* For fall admission, 3/1 for domestic students. Applications are processed on a rolling basis. Application fee: $125. Electronic applications accepted. *Financial support:* Fellowships available. Financial award application deadline: 4/1; financial award applicants required to submit FAFSA. *Unit head:* Dr. Emilia Lopez, Chair, 718-997-5250, E-mail: emilia.lopez@qc.cuny.edu. *Application contact:* Elizabeth D'Amico-Ramirez, Assistant Director of Graduate Admissions, 718-997-5203, E-mail: elizabeth.damicoramirez@qc.cuny.edu.

Queens University of Charlotte, Wayland H. Cato, Jr. School of Education, Charlotte, NC 28274-0002. Offers educational leadership (MA); K-6 (MAT); literacy K-12 (M Ed). *Accreditation:* NCATE. *Program availability:* Part-time, evening/weekend, online learning. *Degree requirements:* For master's, comprehensive exam. *Entrance requirements:* For master's, GRE General Test. *Expenses:* Contact institution.

Quincy University, Master of Science in Education Programs, Quincy, IL 62301-2699. Offers curriculum and instruction (MS Ed), including bilingual/English as a second language; education studies (MS Ed); leadership (MS Ed); reading education (MS Ed); teacher leader (MS Ed). *Program availability:* Part-time, evening/weekend, online learning. *Degree requirements:* For master's, comprehensive exam (for some programs), thesis optional. *Entrance requirements:* For master's, MAT or GRE, personal resume. Additional exam requirements/recommendations for international students: Required—TOEFL (minimum score 550 paper-based; 79 iBT). Electronic applications accepted. Application fee is waived when completed online.

Quinnipiac University, School of Education, Program in Educational Leadership, Hamden, CT 06518-1940. Offers Diploma. *Program availability:* Part-time-only, evening/weekend. *Entrance requirements:* For degree, 3 years of experience in pre K-12 setting, interview, 3 credits in special education course. Electronic applications accepted. *Expenses:* Contact institution. *Faculty research:* Leadership and teacher quality, leadership and student achievement.

Quinnipiac University, School of Education, Program in Teacher Leadership, Hamden, CT 06518-1940. Offers MS. *Program availability:* Part-time-only, evening/weekend, online only, 100% online. *Degree requirements:* For master's, capstone experience. Electronic applications accepted. *Expenses:* Contact institution. *Faculty research:* Leadership and school climate, distributed leadership, teacher retention.

Radford University, College of Graduate Studies and Research, Program in Educational Leadership, Radford, VA 24142. Offers MS. *Accreditation:* NCATE. *Program availability:* Part-time, evening/weekend, 100% online, blended/hybrid learning. *Faculty:* 2 full-time (1 woman), 2 part-time/adjunct (1 woman). *Students:* 1 full-time (0 women), 39 part-time (26 women); includes 3 minority (2 Black or African American, non-Hispanic/Latino; 1 Hispanic/Latino). Average age 35. 23 applicants, 96% accepted, 19 enrolled. In 2018, 21 master's awarded. *Degree requirements:* For master's, comprehensive exam. *Entrance requirements:* For master's, GRE or MAT (waived for any applicant with advanced degree), minimum GPA of 2.75, 3 years of K-12 classroom experience, writing sample, 3 letters of reference, resume, official transcripts. Additional exam requirements/recommendations for international students: Required—TOEFL (minimum score 550 paper-based; 79 iBT), IELTS (minimum score 6.5). *Application deadline:* For fall admission, 2/15 priority date for domestic students, 12/1 for international students; for spring admission, 7/1 for international students. Applications are processed on a rolling basis. Application fee: $50. Electronic applications accepted. *Expenses: Tuition, area resident:* Full-time $8915; part-time $371 per credit hour. Tuition, state resident: full-time $8915; part-time $371 per credit hour. Tuition, nonresident: full-time $17,441. *Required fees:* $3288; $138 per credit hour. *Financial support:* Career-related internships or fieldwork, scholarships/grants, and unspecified assistantships available. Support available to part-time students. Financial award application deadline: 3/1; financial award applicants required to submit FAFSA. *Unit head:* Dr. Brad Bizzell, Coordinator, 540-831-5140, E-mail: bbizzell@radford.edu. *Application contact:* Dr. Brad Bizzell, Coordinator, 540-831-5140, E-mail: bbizzell@radford.edu.
Website: http://www.radford.edu/content/cehd/home/teacher-ed/programs/education-leadership.html

Ramapo College of New Jersey, Master of Arts in Educational Leadership Program, Mahwah, NJ 07430-1680. Offers MA. *Program availability:* Part-time. *Faculty:* 1 full-time (0 women), 11 part-time/adjunct (1 woman). *Students:* 31 full-time (23 women), 30 part-time (18 women); includes 5 minority (2 Black or African American, non-Hispanic/Latino; 1 Asian, non-Hispanic/Latino; 2 Hispanic/Latino). Average age 33. 57 applicants, 93% accepted, 38 enrolled. In 2018, 37 master's awarded. *Degree requirements:* For master's, capstone project. *Entrance requirements:* For master's, PRAXIS, official transcripts of baccalaureate degree from accredited institution with minimum GPA of 3.0; letter of recommendation; resume. Additional exam requirements/recommendations for international students: Required—TOEFL (minimum score 550 paper-based; 79 iBT); Recommended—IELTS (minimum score 6). *Application deadline:* For fall admission, 5/1 for domestic and international students; for spring admission, 12/1 for domestic and international students; for summer admission, 5/1 for domestic and international students. Applications are processed on a rolling basis. Application fee: $65. Electronic applications accepted. *Expenses:* Tuition, state resident: part-time $706.15 per credit. Tuition, nonresident: part-time $706.15 per credit. *Required fees:* $57.50 per credit. *Financial support:* Career-related internships or fieldwork available. Financial award application deadline: 3/1; financial award applicants required to submit FAFSA. *Faculty research:* Elements and indicators of effective modern learning organizations and application of systems thinking to guide contemporary educational leaders. *Unit head:* Dr. Brian P. Chinni, Assistant Dean, Teacher Education, 201-684-7613, E-mail: bchinni@ramapo.edu. *Application contact:* Karen Viviani, Graduate Program Assistant, 201-684-7638, Fax: 201-684-7983, E-mail: kdroubi@ramapo.edu.
Website: http://www.ramapo.edu/mael/

Regent University, Graduate School, School of Education, Virginia Beach, VA 23464-9800. Offers education (M Ed, Ed D, PhD), including adult education (Ed D, PhD, Ed S), advanced educational leadership (Ed D, PhD, Ed S), character education (Ed D, PhD, Ed S), Christian education leadership (Ed D, PhD, Ed S), Christian school administration (M Ed), curriculum and instruction (Ed D, PhD, Ed S), curriculum and instruction - adult education (M Ed), curriculum and instruction - Christian school (M Ed), curriculum and instruction - gifted and talented (M Ed), curriculum and instruction - STEM education (M Ed), curriculum and instruction - teacher leader (M Ed), discipleship for ministry (M Ed), educational leadership (M Ed), educational psychology (Ed D, PhD, Ed S), educational technology and online learning (Ed D, PhD, Ed S), elementary education (M Ed), exceptional education executive leadership (Ed D, PhD, Ed S), higher education (Ed D, PhD, Ed S), higher education leadership and management (Ed D, PhD, Ed S), instructional design and technology (M Ed), K-12 school leadership (Ed D, PhD, Ed S), K-12 special education (M Ed), leadership in mathematics education (M Ed), reading specialist (M Ed), special education (Ed D, PhD, Ed S), student affairs (M Ed), TESOL - adult education (M Ed), TESOL - K-12 (M Ed); educational specialist (Ed S), including adult education (Ed D, PhD, Ed S), advanced educational leadership (Ed D, PhD, Ed S), character education (Ed D, PhD, Ed S), Christian education leadership (Ed D, PhD, Ed S), curriculum and instruction (Ed D, PhD, Ed S), educational psychology (Ed D, PhD, Ed S), educational technology and online learning (Ed D, PhD, Ed S), exceptional education executive leadership (Ed D, PhD, Ed S), higher education (Ed D, PhD, Ed S), higher education leadership and management (Ed D, PhD, Ed S), K-12 school leadership (Ed D, PhD, Ed S), special education (Ed D, PhD, Ed S). *Accreditation:* TEAC. *Program availability:* Part-time, evening/weekend, 100% online, blended/hybrid learning. *Degree requirements:* For master's, thesis or alternative; for doctorate, comprehensive exam, thesis/dissertation. *Entrance requirements:* For master's, Virginia Communication and Literacy Assessment (VCLA), PRAXIS, college transcripts, writing sample, interview; for doctorate, GRE, writing sample, resume, transcripts, interview. Additional exam requirements/recommendations for international students: Required—TOEFL (minimum score 577 paper-based). Electronic applications accepted. *Expenses:* Contact institution. *Faculty research:* Christian school administration, curriculum and instruction, educational technology and online learning, higher education, special education.

Regis College, Department of Education, Weston, MA 02493. Offers elementary teacher (M Ed); higher education leadership (Ed D); special education (M Ed). *Program availability:* Part-time, evening/weekend. *Degree requirements:* For doctorate, thesis/dissertation, capstone project. *Entrance requirements:* For master's, GRE or MAT, personal statement, recommendations, resume/curriculum vitae, official transcripts, interview; for doctorate, personal statement, recommendations, resume/curriculum vitae, official transcripts, presentation/interview. Additional exam requirements/recommendations for international students: Required—TOEFL (minimum score 560 paper-based; 79 iBT); Recommended—IELTS (minimum score 6.5). *Application deadline:* Applications are processed on a rolling basis. Application fee: $65. Electronic applications accepted. *Financial support:* Federal Work-Study, scholarships/grants, and unspecified assistantships available. Financial award applicants required to submit FAFSA. *Unit head:* Dr. Priscilla Boerger, Department Chair/Graduate Program Director, 781-768-7422, E-mail: priscilla.boerger@regiscollege.edu. *Application contact:* Dr. Priscilla Boerger, Department Chair/Graduate Program Director, 781-768-7422, E-mail: priscilla.boerger@regiscollege.edu.

Regis University, College of Contemporary Liberal Studies, Denver, CO 80221-1099. Offers creative writing (MFA); criminology (M Sc); curriculum, instruction and assessment (M Ed); education - teacher leadership (M Ed); educational leadership (M Ed); elementary education (M Ed); literacy (Certificate); reading (M Ed); secondary education (M Ed); special education (M Ed); teacher academic leadership (Certificate); teacher leadership (MA); teacher/educational leadership (M Ed); teaching the linguistically diverse (M Ed). *Program availability:* Part-time, evening/weekend, 100% online, blended/hybrid learning. *Degree requirements:* For master's, thesis (for some programs). *Entrance requirements:* For master's, official transcript reflecting baccalaureate degree awarded from regionally-accredited college or university, work experience, resume, letters of recommendation. Additional exam requirements/recommendations for international students: Required—TOEFL (minimum score 550 paper-based; 82 iBT). Electronic applications accepted. *Expenses:* Contact institution.

Rhode Island College, School of Graduate Studies, Feinstein School of Education and Human Development, Department of Counseling, Educational Leadership, and School Psychology, Providence, RI 02908-1991. Offers advanced counseling (CGS); agency counseling (MA); clinical mental health counseling (MS); co-occurring disorders (MA, CGS); educational leadership (M Ed); mental health counseling (CAGS); school counseling (MA); school psychology (CAGS); teacher leadership (CGS). *Accreditation:* ACA; NCATE. *Program availability:* Part-time, evening/weekend. *Faculty:* 12 full-time (9 women), 5 part-time/adjunct (4 women). *Students:* 45 full-time (35 women), 47 part-time (39 women); includes 12 minority (2 Black or African American, non-Hispanic/Latino; 10 Hispanic/Latino). Average age 30. In 2018, 13 master's, 27 other advanced degrees awarded. *Degree requirements:* For master's and other advanced degree, comprehensive exam (for some programs), thesis (for some programs). *Entrance requirements:* For master's, GRE General Test or MAT, undergraduate transcripts; minimum undergraduate GPA of 3.0; for other advanced degree, GRE or MAT (for most programs), undergraduate transcripts; minimum undergraduate GPA of 3.0; 3 letters of recommendation; current resume. Additional exam requirements/recommendations for international students: Required—TOEFL (minimum score 550 paper-based; 80 iBT). *Application deadline:* For fall admission, 3/1 for domestic students; for spring admission, 11/1 for domestic students. Applications are processed on a rolling basis. Application fee: $50. Electronic applications accepted. *Expenses: Tuition, area resident:* Part-time $407 per credit. Tuition, nonresident: part-time $792 per credit. *Required fees:* $29 per credit. $100 per semester. *Financial support:* Teaching assistantships, career-related internships or fieldwork, Federal Work-Study, scholarships/grants, health care benefits, and unspecified assistantships available. Support available to part-time students. Financial award application deadline: 5/15; financial award applicants required to submit FAFSA. *Unit head:* Dr. John Eagle, Chair, 401-456-8023. *Application contact:* Dr. John Eagle, Chair, 401-456-8023.
Website: http://www.ric.edu/counselingEducationalLeadershipSchoolPsychology/index.php

Rivier University, School of Graduate Studies, Department of Education, Nashua, NH 03060. Offers curriculum and instruction (M Ed); early childhood education (M Ed); educational administration (M Ed); educational studies (M Ed); elementary education (M Ed); elementary education and general special education (M Ed); emotional and behavioral disorders (M Ed); general social education (M Ed); leadership and learning (Ed D, CAGS); learning disabilities (M Ed); learning disabilities and reading (M Ed); mental health counseling (MA); reading (M Ed); school counseling (M Ed). *Program*

availability: Part-time, evening/weekend. *Degree requirements:* For master's, comprehensive exam (for some programs), internships. *Entrance requirements:* For master's, GRE General Test or MAT.

Robert Morris University Illinois, Morris Graduate School of Management, Chicago, IL 60605. Offers accounting (MBA); accounting/finance (MBA); business analytics (MIS); health care administration (MM); higher education administration (MM); human performance (MS); human resource management (MBA); information security (MIS); information systems management (MIS); law enforcement administration (MM); management (MBA); management/finance (MBA); management/human resource management (MBA); sports administration (MM). *Program availability:* Part-time, evening/weekend. *Entrance requirements:* For master's, official transcripts and letters of recommendation (for some programs); written personal statement. Additional exam requirements/recommendations for international students: Required—TOEFL (minimum score 550 paper-based). Electronic applications accepted.

Rocky Mountain College, Program in Educational Leadership, Billings, MT 59102-1796. Offers M Ed. *Faculty:* 2 full-time (both women). *Students:* 17 full-time (9 women), 1 (woman) part-time; includes 1 minority (Hispanic/Latino). Average age 33. In 2018, 18 master's awarded. *Entrance requirements:* For master's, valid (current) teaching certificate. Additional exam requirements/recommendations for international students: Required—TOEFL (minimum score 570 paper-based; 88 iBT), IELTS (minimum score 6.5). *Application deadline:* Applications are processed on a rolling basis. Application fee: $35 ($40 for international students). Electronic applications accepted. Application fee is waived when completed online. *Expenses:* Contact institution. *Financial support:* In 2018–19, 17 students received support. Scholarships/grants available. Financial award applicants required to submit FAFSA. *Unit head:* Dr. Stevie Schmitz, Director of Educational Leadership and Distance Education, 406-657-1134, E-mail: schmitzs@rocky.edu. *Application contact:* Austin Mapston, Dean of Enrollment Services, 406-657-1026, Fax: 406-657-1189, E-mail: admissions@rocky.edu.
Website: https://www.rocky.edu/mel

Roosevelt University, Graduate Division, College of Education, Program in Instructional Leadership, Chicago, IL 60605. Offers MA. Electronic applications accepted.

Rowan University, Graduate School, College of Education, Department of Educational Services and Leadership, Program in Educational Leadership, Glassboro, NJ 08028-1701. Offers Ed D, CAGS. *Accreditation:* NCATE. *Program availability:* Part-time, evening/weekend. *Degree requirements:* For doctorate, thesis/dissertation. *Entrance requirements:* For doctorate, GMAT or GRE General Test, master's degree. Additional exam requirements/recommendations for international students: Required—TOEFL.

Rowan University, Graduate School, College of Education, Department of Educational Services and Leadership, Program in Higher Education Administration, Glassboro, NJ 08028-1701. Offers MA. *Accreditation:* NCATE. *Program availability:* Part-time, evening/weekend. *Degree requirements:* For master's, comprehensive exam, thesis. *Entrance requirements:* For master's, GRE General Test, minimum GPA of 2.8, 2 years of teaching experience. Additional exam requirements/recommendations for international students: Required—TOEFL. Electronic applications accepted.

Rowan University, Graduate School, College of Education, Department of Educational Services and Leadership, Program in Principal Preparation, Glassboro, NJ 08028-1701. Offers CAGS. *Program availability:* Part-time, evening/weekend. *Degree requirements:* For CAGS, comprehensive exam, thesis, internship. *Entrance requirements:* For degree, GRE General Test, minimum GPA of 2.81, 1 year of teaching experience. Additional exam requirements/recommendations for international students: Required—TOEFL. Electronic applications accepted.

Rowan University, Graduate School, College of Education, Department of Educational Services and Leadership, Program in School Administration, Glassboro, NJ 08028-1701. Offers MA. Electronic applications accepted.

Rowan University, Graduate School, College of Education, Department of Educational Services and Leadership, Program in Supervisor Certification, Glassboro, NJ 08028-1701. Offers CAGS. Electronic applications accepted.

Rowan University, Graduate School, College of Education, Department of Interdisciplinary and Inclusive Education, Program in Teacher Leadership, Glassboro, NJ 08028-1701. Offers M Ed. *Program availability:* Part-time, evening/weekend. *Degree requirements:* For master's, thesis. *Entrance requirements:* For master's, GRE General Test, minimum GPA of 2.8, 1 year of teaching experience. Additional exam requirements/recommendations for international students: Required—TOEFL. Electronic applications accepted.

Rutgers University–Camden, Graduate School of Arts and Sciences, Department of Public Policy and Administration, Camden, NJ 08102. Offers education policy and leadership (MPA); international public service and development (MPA); public management (MPA); JD/MPA; MPA/MA. *Accreditation:* NASPAA. *Program availability:* Part-time, evening/weekend. *Degree requirements:* For master's, directed study, research workshop, 42 credits. *Entrance requirements:* For master's, GRE General Test, GMAT or LSAT, 3 letters of recommendation; resume. Additional exam requirements/recommendations for international students: Required—TOEFL (minimum score 550 paper-based), IELTS. Electronic applications accepted. *Faculty research:* Nonprofit management, county and municipal administration, health and human services, government communication, administrative law, educational finance.

Rutgers University–New Brunswick, Graduate School of Education, Department of Educational Theory, Policy and Administration, Programs in Educational Administration and Supervision, Piscataway, NJ 08854-8097. Offers Ed M, Ed D. *Program availability:* Part-time, evening/weekend. *Degree requirements:* For doctorate, thesis/dissertation, qualifying exam. *Entrance requirements:* For master's, GRE General Test, minimum GPA of 3.0; for doctorate, GRE General Test, minimum GPA of 3.0, master's degree in educational administration. Additional exam requirements/recommendations for international students: Required—TOEFL. Electronic applications accepted. *Faculty research:* Leadership of education, finance, law, schools as organizations.

Sacred Heart University, Graduate Programs, Isabelle Farrington College of Education, Department of Leadership/Literacy, Fairfield, CT 06825. Offers advanced studies in administration (Professional Certificate); advanced studies in literacy (Professional Certificate). *Program availability:* Part-time, evening/weekend. *Degree requirements:* For Professional Certificate, thesis or alternative. *Entrance requirements:* For degree, CT teacher certification. Electronic applications accepted. *Expenses:* Contact institution.

Sage Graduate School, Esteves School of Education, Program in Educational Leadership, Troy, NY 12180-4115. Offers Ed D. *Program availability:* Part-time-only. *Faculty:* 8 full-time (5 women), 7 part-time/adjunct (3 women). *Students:* 115 part-time (83 women); includes 63 minority (39 Black or African American, non-Hispanic/Latino; 5 Asian, non-Hispanic/Latino; 17 Hispanic/Latino; 1 Native Hawaiian or other Pacific Islander, non-Hispanic/Latino; 1 Two or more races, non-Hispanic/Latino). Average age 45. 122 applicants, 39% accepted, 33 enrolled. In 2018, 33 doctorates awarded. *Degree requirements:* For doctorate, comprehensive exam. *Entrance requirements:* For doctorate, Completed application, graduate transcripts totaling at least 60 credits with a

cumulative GPA of 3.5 or above; three letters of professional reference that address candidate's potential in relationship to New York State Education Department's nine essential characteristics of effective school leader; current resume; statement of career goals. Additional exam requirements/recommendations for international students: Required—TOEFL (minimum score 550 paper-based). *Application deadline:* Applications are processed on a rolling basis. Application fee: $30. Electronic applications accepted. *Expenses:* Contact institution. *Financial support:* Applicants required to submit FAFSA. *Unit head:* Dr. John Pelizza, Dean, Esteves School of Education, 518-244-2051, Fax: 518-244-2334, E-mail: pelizj@sage.edu. *Application contact:* Jerome Steele, Assistant Professor and Chair, Doctoral Program in Educational Leadership, 518-244-2070, Fax: 518-266-1391, E-mail: steelj2@sage.edu.

Saginaw Valley State University, College of Education, Program in Educational Leadership, University Center, MI 48710. Offers M Ed, Ed S. *Accreditation:* NCATE. *Program availability:* Part-time, evening/weekend, online learning. *Students:* 2 full-time (1 woman), 57 part-time (36 women); includes 9 minority (5 Black or African American, non-Hispanic/Latino; 1 Asian, non-Hispanic/Latino; 1 Hispanic/Latino; 2 Two or more races, non-Hispanic/Latino). Average age 38. 11 applicants, 100% accepted, 15 enrolled. In 2018, 1 master's, 8 Ed Ss awarded. *Degree requirements:* For master's, capstone course. *Entrance requirements:* For master's, minimum GPA of 3.0, teaching certificate; for Ed S, master's degree with minimum GPA of 3.3. Additional exam requirements/recommendations for international students: Required—TOEFL (minimum score 550 paper-based; 79 iBT). *Application deadline:* For fall admission, 7/15 for international students; for winter admission, 11/15 for international students; for spring admission, 4/15 for international students. Applications are processed on a rolling basis. Application fee: $30 ($90 for international students). Electronic applications accepted. *Expenses: Tuition, area resident:* Full-time $6225; part-time $623 per credit hour. Tuition, state resident: full-time $6225; part-time $623 per credit hour. Tuition, nonresident: full-time $14,215; part-time $1185 per credit hour. International tuition: $14,215 full-time. *Required fees:* $263; $14.60 per credit hour. Tuition and fees vary according to degree level. *Financial support:* Federal Work-Study and scholarships/grants available. Support available to part-time students. Financial award applicants required to submit FAFSA. *Unit head:* Dr. Jonathan Gould, Associate Professor of Teacher Education, 989-964-4978, Fax: 989-964-4981, E-mail: jagould@svsu.edu. *Application contact:* Jenna Briggs, Director, Graduate and International Admissions, 989-964-6096, Fax: 989-964-2788, E-mail: gradadm@svsu.edu.

St. Ambrose University, School of Education, Davenport, IA 52803-2898. Offers early childhood education (M Ed); educational administration (M Ed). *Accreditation:* TEAC. *Program availability:* Part-time, evening/weekend, online learning. *Degree requirements:* For master's, comprehensive exam. *Entrance requirements:* For master's, GRE General Test or MAT, minimum GPA of 2.75. Additional exam requirements/recommendations for international students: Required—TOEFL. Electronic applications accepted. *Faculty research:* Disabilities and postsecondary career avenues, self-determination.

St. Bonaventure University, School of Graduate School, School of Education, Program in Educational Leadership, St. Bonaventure, NY 14778-2284. Offers educational leadership (MS Ed); school building leader (Adv C); school district leader (Adv C). *Program availability:* Part-time, evening/weekend, online learning. *Faculty:* 1 (woman) full-time, 6 part-time/adjunct (3 women). *Students:* 2 full-time (1 woman), 69 part-time (49 women); includes 5 minority (2 Black or African American, non-Hispanic/Latino; 2 Hispanic/Latino; 1 Two or more races, non-Hispanic/Latino). Average age 37. 29 applicants, 97% accepted, 17 enrolled. In 2018, 4 master's, 26 Adv Cs awarded. *Degree requirements:* For master's, comprehensive exam, thesis optional, minimum cumulative GPA of 3.0, practicum, internship, electronic portfolio; for Adv C, comprehensive exam, minimum cumulative GPA of 3.0, practicum, internship, electronic portfolio. *Entrance requirements:* For master's, teaching, counseling or other school certification; three years of K-12 school experience; transcripts from all colleges previously attended; two references (one from supervising principal or superintendent); interview; writing sample (academic or professional); for Adv C, master's degree in education or certification-related area; three years of K-12 school experience; teaching or counseling certification; transcripts from all colleges previously attended; two references (one from supervising principal or superintendent); interview; writing sample. Additional exam requirements/recommendations for international students: Required—TOEFL (minimum score 550 paper-based; 79 iBT). *Application deadline:* For fall admission, 3/15 priority date for domestic students, 2/1 priority date for international students; for spring admission, 10/1 for domestic students. Applications are processed on a rolling basis. Application fee: $0. Electronic applications accepted. *Expenses:* $755.00 per credit hour, $100 one time fee. *Financial support:* Scholarships/grants, health care benefits, and unspecified assistantships available. Financial award application deadline: 4/15; financial award applicants required to submit FAFSA. *Faculty research:* Global competence, teacher leadership. *Unit head:* Dr. Lisa Buenaventura, Director, 716-375-2394, Fax: 716-375-2360, E-mail: lbuenave@sbu.edu. *Application contact:* Matthew Retchless Campbell, Director of Graduate Admissions, 716-375-2021, Fax: 716-375-4015, E-mail: gradsch@sbu.edu.
Website: http://www.sbu.edu/academics/schools/education/graduate-degrees-certificates/msed-in-educational-leadership

St. Cloud State University, School of Graduate Studies, School of Education, Department of Educational Leadership and Higher Education, Program in Higher Education Administration, St. Cloud, MN 56301-4498. Offers Ed D.

St. Cloud State University, School of Graduate Studies, School of Health and Human Services, Department of Counseling and Community Psychology, Program in Educational Administration and Leadership, St. Cloud, MN 56301-4498. Offers MS. *Program availability:* Part-time. *Degree requirements:* For master's, comprehensive exam (for some programs), thesis or alternative. *Entrance requirements:* For master's, GRE General Test, minimum GPA of 2.75. Additional exam requirements/recommendations for international students: Required—Michigan English Language Assessment Battery; Recommended—TOEFL (minimum score 550 paper-based), IELTS (minimum score 6.5). Electronic applications accepted.

Saint Francis University, Graduate Education Program, Loretto, PA 15940-0600. Offers education (M Ed); leadership (M Ed); reading (M Ed). *Program availability:* Part-time, 100% online, blended/hybrid learning. *Degree requirements:* For master's, comprehensive exam, thesis optional. *Entrance requirements:* For master's, GRE or MAT (if undergraduate GPA less than 3.0). Additional exam requirements/recommendations for international students: Required—TOEFL (minimum score 550 paper-based; 75 iBT), IELTS (minimum score 6.5), International Test of English proficiency (minimum score 4). Electronic applications accepted. *Expenses:* Contact institution.

St. Francis Xavier University, Graduate Studies, Graduate Studies in Education, Antigonish, NS B2G 2W5, Canada. Offers curriculum and instruction (M Ed); educational administration and leadership (M Ed). *Program availability:* Part-time, online learning. *Degree requirements:* For master's, thesis. *Entrance requirements:* For master's, minimum undergraduate B average, 2 years of teaching experience. *Expenses: Tuition, area resident:* Full-time $7547 Canadian dollars. Tuition, state resident: full-time $7547 Canadian dollars; part-time $804.19 Canadian dollars per course. Tuition, nonresident: full-time $8839 Canadian dollars; part-time $932.49

Canadian dollars per course. *International tuition:* $932.49 Canadian dollars full-time. *Required fees:* $90.20 Canadian dollars; $90.20 Canadian dollars per course. One-time fee: $6 Canadian dollars. Tuition and fees vary according to course load, degree level and program. *Faculty research:* Inclusive education, qualitative research.

St. John Fisher College, Ralph C. Wilson Jr. School of Education, Educational Leadership Program, Rochester, NY 14618-3597. Offers MS Ed. *Program availability:* Part-time, evening/weekend. *Faculty:* 3 full-time (2 women), 2 part-time/adjunct (both women). *Students:* 23 part-time (21 women); includes 3 minority (2 Black or African American, non-Hispanic/Latino; 1 Hispanic/Latino). Average age 38. 18 applicants, 94% accepted, 12 enrolled. In 2018, 10 master's awarded. *Degree requirements:* For master's, capstone project, internship. *Entrance requirements:* For master's, teacher certification, minimum 2 years of teaching experience, 2 letters of recommendation, current resume. Additional exam requirements/recommendations for international students: Required—TOEFL (minimum score 575 paper-based; 80 iBT). *Application deadline:* Applications are processed on a rolling basis. Application fee: $30. Electronic applications accepted. *Expenses:* Contact institution. *Financial support:* Scholarships/grants available. Financial award applicants required to submit FAFSA. *Faculty research:* Urban school leadership, assessment, effective school leadership. *Unit head:* Dr. Diane Reed, Director, 585-385-7257, E-mail: dreed@sjfc.edu. *Application contact:* Michelle Gosier, Director of Transfer and Graduate Admissions, 585-385-8064, E-mail: mgosier@sjfc.edu.
Website: https://www.sjfc.edu/graduate-programs/ms-in-educational-leadership/

St. John Fisher College, Ralph C. Wilson Jr. School of Education, Executive Leadership Program, Rochester, NY 14618-3597. Offers Ed D. *Program availability:* Evening/weekend. *Faculty:* 11 full-time (7 women), 2 part-time/adjunct (1 woman). *Students:* 89 full-time (55 women), 34 part-time (24 women); includes 72 minority (61 Black or African American, non-Hispanic/Latino; 10 Hispanic/Latino; 1 Two or more races, non-Hispanic/Latino). Average age 45. 69 applicants, 83% accepted, 48 enrolled. In 2018, 60 doctorates awarded. *Degree requirements:* For doctorate, comprehensive exam, thesis/dissertation, field experiences. *Entrance requirements:* For doctorate, 3 professional writing samples, 2 letters of reference, interview, minimum of 3 years' management experience, master's degree. Additional exam requirements/recommendations for international students: Required—TOEFL (minimum score 575 paper-based; 80 iBT). *Application deadline:* For fall admission, 3/1 for domestic and international students. Applications are processed on a rolling basis. Electronic applications accepted. *Expenses:* Contact institution. *Financial support:* Fellowships and scholarships/grants available. Financial award applicants required to submit FAFSA. *Faculty research:* Leadership, organizational development. *Unit head:* Dr. Jeannine Dingus-Eason, Program Director, 585-385-8002, E-mail: jdingus@sjfc.edu. *Application contact:* Michelle Gosier, Director of Transfer and Graduate Admissions, 585-385-8064, E-mail: mgosier@sjfc.edu.
Website: https://www.sjfc.edu/graduate-programs/executive-leadership-edd/

St. John's University, The School of Education, Department of Administrative and Instructional Leadership, Program in Administration and Supervision, Queens, NY 11439. Offers Ed D. *Program availability:* Part-time, blended/hybrid learning. *Degree requirements:* For doctorate, comprehensive exam, thesis/dissertation. *Entrance requirements:* For doctorate, GRE, official master's transcript, statement of purpose. Additional exam requirements/recommendations for international students: Required—TOEFL, IELTS. Electronic applications accepted. *Faculty research:* School administrators' accountability in response to New York state and federal regulations and reforms; budgetary and expenditure decision-making among school district administrators; compliance, and changing demographics; twenty-first century technological tools in today's schools; teacher decision-making models based on decision theory.

St. John's University, The School of Education, Department of Administrative and Instructional Leadership, Program in Instructional Leadership, Queens, NY 11439. Offers gifted education (Adv C); instructional leadership (Ed D, Adv C). *Program availability:* Part-time, blended/hybrid learning. *Degree requirements:* For doctorate, comprehensive exam, thesis/dissertation. *Entrance requirements:* For doctorate, GRE, official master's transcript, statement of purpose; for Adv C, statement of purpose, official master's transcripts, teaching certification. Additional exam requirements/recommendations for international students: Required—TOEFL, IELTS. Electronic applications accepted. *Faculty research:* Mathematics learning disabilities and difficulties with students identified as learning disabled or students who are English language learners, identification of mathematical giftedness in students who are English language learners, effects of parental participation and parenting behaviors on the science and mathematics academic achievement of school-age students, analysis of major theoretical perspectives in curriculum design and implementation.

St. John's University, The School of Education, Department of Administrative and Instructional Leadership, Program in School Building Leadership, Queens, NY 11439. Offers MS Ed, Adv C. *Program availability:* Part-time, evening/weekend. *Degree requirements:* For master's, internship. *Entrance requirements:* For master's, GRE, MAT, or PRAXIS, statement of goals (personal essay), official undergraduate transcripts, initial teaching certification; for Adv C, initial teaching certification, first master's transcripts, statement of purpose. Additional exam requirements/recommendations for international students: Required—TOEFL, IELTS. Electronic applications accepted. *Faculty research:* Analysis of non-public school graduate student outcomes in programs and certification, Catholic school parents' perceptions of school and after school programs, issues in school business leadership from a financial management perspective.

St. John's University, The School of Education, Department of Administrative and Instructional Leadership, Program in School District Leadership, Queens, NY 11439. Offers Adv C. *Program availability:* Part-time, evening/weekend, blended/hybrid learning. *Degree requirements:* For Adv C, internship. *Entrance requirements:* For degree, initial teaching certification, first master's transcripts, statement of purpose. Additional exam requirements/recommendations for international students: Required—TOEFL, IELTS. Electronic applications accepted. *Faculty research:* Analysis of school district finances related to resource allocation and decision-making, responsiveness of districts to New York State Proposition 13 (property tax caps), implementation of technology planning for the twenty-first century at the school district level.

St. Joseph's College, New York, Programs in Education, Field in Educational Leadership, Brooklyn, NY 11205-3688. Offers MA. *Program availability:* Part-time, evening/weekend. *Students:* 7 part-time (4 women); includes 3 minority (2 Black or African American, non-Hispanic/Latino; 1 Hispanic/Latino). Average age 29. 3 applicants, 100% accepted, 2 enrolled. *Entrance requirements:* For master's, GRE, PRAXIS, or MAT, Application, $25 application fee, official transcripts, two letters of recommendation, current resume, copy of NYS teacher certifications, personal statement, minimum three years of teaching. Additional exam requirements/recommendations for international students: Required—TOEFL (minimum score 80 iBT). *Application deadline:* Applications are processed on a rolling basis. Application fee: $25. Electronic applications accepted. *Expenses: Tuition:* Full-time $18,450; part-time $1025 per credit. *Required fees:* $414. *Financial support:* In 2018–19, 4 students received support. Alumni grants and/or alumni excellence awards available. *Unit head:* Nancy Gilchriest, Associate Professor/Department Chair, 631-687-1472, E-mail: ngilchriest@sjcny.edu. *Application contact:* Nancy Gilchriest, Associate Professor/Department Chair, 631-687-1472, E-mail: ngilchriest@sjcny.edu.
Website: https://www.sjcny.edu

Saint Joseph's College of Maine, Master of Science in Education Program, Standish, ME 04084. Offers adult education and training (MS Ed); Catholic school leadership (MS Ed); health care educator (MS Ed); school educator (MS Ed). Program available by correspondence. *Program availability:* Part-time, online learning. Electronic applications accepted.

Saint Joseph's University, College of Arts and Sciences, Graduate Programs in Education, Philadelphia, PA 19131-1395. Offers curriculum supervisor (Certificate); educational leadership (MS, Ed D); elementary education (MS, Certificate); elementary/middle school education (Certificate); organizational development and leadership (MS); principal (Certificate); professional education (MS); reading specialist (MS, Certificate); reading supervisor (Certificate); secondary education (MS, Certificate); special education (MS); special education 7-12 (Certificate); special education PK-8 (Certificate); superintendent's letter of eligibility (Certificate); supervisor of special education (Certificate); teacher of the deaf and hard of hearing (Certificate). *Program availability:* Part-time, evening/weekend, blended/hybrid learning. *Degree requirements:* For master's, thesis or alternative; for doctorate, comprehensive exam, thesis/dissertation. *Entrance requirements:* For master's, 2 letters of recommendation, minimum GPA of 3.0, official transcripts, personal statement; for doctorate, GRE, master's degree from accredited institution, minimum graduate GPA of 3.5, computer competence, interview with program director. Additional exam requirements/recommendations for international students: Required—TOEFL (minimum score 550 paper-based; 80 iBT), IELTS (minimum score 6.5), PTE (minimum score 60). Electronic applications accepted. *Expenses:* Contact institution. *Faculty research:* Factors predicting early mathematics skills for low income children, early child care and development, preschool quality, parent communication and home-school collaboration issues, education of terminally ill children, preparing literacy teachers for urban schools.

Saint Leo University, Graduate Studies in Education, Saint Leo, FL 33574-6665. Offers school leadership (Ed D). *Program availability:* Part-time, evening/weekend, online only, 100% online. *Students:* Average age 37. 214 applicants, 69% accepted, 125 enrolled. In 2018, 139 master's, 9 other advanced degrees awarded. *Entrance requirements:* For master's, GRE (minimum score of 1000), MAT (minimum score of 410), or minimum undergraduate GPA of 3.0 in final 2 years, official transcripts, current resume, 2 professional recommendations, personal statement, bachelor's degree from regionally-accredited university, valid professional teaching certificate; for other advanced degree, valid professional teaching certificate (for Ed S). Additional exam requirements/recommendations for international students: Required—TOEFL (minimum score 550 paper-based; 78 iBT). *Application deadline:* For fall admission, 7/1 priority date for domestic students, 7/1 for international students; for winter admission, 7/1 for international students; for spring admission, 11/1 priority date for domestic students. Applications are processed on a rolling basis. Application fee: $80. Electronic applications accepted. *Expenses:* Contact institution. *Financial support:* In 2018–19, 17 students received support. Career-related internships or fieldwork, scholarships/grants, health care benefits, and tuition remission for Saint Leo employees and their dependents available. Financial award application deadline: 3/1; financial award applicants required to submit FAFSA. *Faculty research:* Impact of partnerships with K-12 school and university programs. *Unit head:* Dr. Fern Aefsky, Director of Graduate Studies in Education, 352-588-8309, Fax: 352-588-8861, E-mail: kara.winkler@saintleo.edu. *Application contact:* Mark Russum, Assistant Vice President, Enrollment, 800-707-8846, Fax: 352-588-7873, E-mail: grad.admissions@saintleo.edu.
Website: https://www.saintleo.edu/education-master-degree

Saint Louis University, Graduate Programs, School of Education, Department of Educational Leadership and Higher Education, St. Louis, MO 63103. Offers Catholic school leadership (MA); educational administration (MA, Ed D, PhD, Ed S); higher education (MA, Ed D, PhD); student personnel administration (MA). *Accreditation:* NCATE. *Program availability:* Part-time. *Degree requirements:* For master's, comprehensive written and oral exam; for doctorate, comprehensive exam, thesis/dissertation, preliminary oral and written exams. *Entrance requirements:* For master's, GRE General Test, MAT, LSAT, GMAT or MCAT, letters of recommendation, resume; for doctorate and Ed S, GRE General Test, LSAT, GMAT or MCAT, letters of recommendation, resumé, goal statement, transcripts. Additional exam requirements/recommendations for international students: Required—TOEFL (minimum score 525 paper-based). Electronic applications accepted. *Faculty research:* Superintendent of schools, school finance, school facilities, student personal administration, building leadership.

Saint Mary's College of California, Kalmanovitz School of Education, Program in Early Childhood Education, Moraga, CA 94575. Offers supervision and leadership (MA). *Program availability:* Part-time, evening/weekend. *Degree requirements:* For master's, thesis or alternative. *Entrance requirements:* For master's, interview, minimum GPA of 3.0.

Saint Mary's College of California, Kalmanovitz School of Education, Program in Educational Leadership, Moraga, CA 94575. Offers educational administration (MA); educational leadership (Ed D); preliminary administrative services (Credential). *Program availability:* Part-time, evening/weekend. *Degree requirements:* For master's, thesis or alternative; for doctorate, thesis/dissertation. *Entrance requirements:* For master's, interview, minimum GPA of 3.0, teaching credential; for doctorate, GRE or MAT, interview, MA, minimum GPA of 3.0. *Faculty research:* Building communities, programs in educational leadership, alignment of curriculum to standards.

Saint Mary's College of California, Kalmanovitz School of Education, Teaching Leadership Program, Moraga, CA 94575. Offers MA.

St. Mary's University, Graduate Studies, Program in Catholic School Leadership, San Antonio, TX 78228. Offers MA. *Program availability:* Part-time, evening/weekend, online learning. *Students:* 7 part-time (5 women); includes 4 minority (all Hispanic/Latino). Average age 45. In 2018, 3 master's awarded. *Degree requirements:* For master's, comprehensive exam. *Entrance requirements:* For master's, GRE, minimum undergraduate GPA of 2.7. Additional exam requirements/recommendations for international students: Required—TOEFL (minimum score 550 paper-based; 80 iBT), IELTS (minimum score 6). *Application deadline:* For fall admission, 7/1 for domestic students; for spring admission, 11/15 for domestic students; for summer admission, 4/1 for domestic students. Applications are processed on a rolling basis. Application fee: $0. Electronic applications accepted. *Expenses: Tuition:* Full-time $16,830; part-time $935 per credit hour. *Required fees:* $1055. Tuition and fees vary according to program. *Financial support:* Career-related internships or fieldwork, Federal Work-Study, institutionally sponsored loans, scholarships/grants, health care benefits, and unspecified assistantships available. Financial award application deadline: 3/31; financial award applicants required to submit FAFSA. *Faculty research:* Classical American philosophy, philosophy of education. *Unit head:* Dr. Dan Higgins, Program Director, 210-436-3121, E-mail: dhiggins@stmarytx.edu. *Application contact:* Kim Thornton, Director of Graduate Admission, 210-436-3101, E-mail: kthornton@stmarytx.edu.
Website: https://www.stmarytx.edu/academics/programs/master-catholic-school-leadership/

St. Mary's University, Graduate Studies, Program in Educational Leadership, San Antonio, TX 78228. Offers MA. *Program availability:* Part-time, evening/weekend. *Students:* 10 full-time (7 women), 7 part-time (5 women); includes 9 minority (2 Black or African American, non-Hispanic/Latino; 7 Hispanic/Latino), 1 international. Average age 26. 14 applicants, 86% accepted, 10 enrolled. In 2018, 5 master's awarded. *Entrance requirements:* For master's, GRE, minimum undergraduate GPA of 2.7. Additional exam requirements/recommendations for international students: Required—TOEFL (minimum score 550 paper-based; 80 iBT), IELTS (minimum score 6). *Application deadline:* For fall admission, 7/1 for domestic students; for spring admission, 11/15 for domestic students; for summer admission, 4/1 for domestic students. Applications are processed on a rolling basis. Application fee: $0. Electronic applications accepted. *Expenses: Tuition:* Full-time $16,830; part-time $935 per credit hour. *Required fees:* $1055. Tuition and fees vary according to program. *Financial support:* Fellowships, career-related internships or fieldwork, Federal Work-Study, institutionally sponsored loans, scholarships/grants, health care benefits, and unspecified assistantships available. Financial award application deadline: 3/31; financial award applicants required to submit FAFSA. *Faculty research:* Philosophy of education. *Unit head:* Dr. Dan Higgins, Program Director, 210-436-3121, E-mail: dhiggins@stmarytx.edu. *Application contact:* Kim Thornton, Director of Graduate Admission, 210-436-3101, E-mail: kthornton@stmarytx.edu.
Website: https://www.stmarytx.edu/academics/programs/master-educational-leadership/

Saint Mary's University of Minnesota, Schools of Graduate and Professional Programs, Graduate School of Education, Educational Administration Program, Winona, MN 55987-1399. Offers educational administration (Certificate, Ed S), including director of special education, K-12 principal, superintendent. *Unit head:* Dr. William Bjorum, Director, 612-728-5126, Fax: 612-728-5121, E-mail: wbjorum@smumn.edu. *Application contact:* Laurie Roy, Director of Admissions for Graduate and Professional Programs, 612-728-5158, Fax: 612-728-5121, E-mail: lroy@smumn.edu.
Website: https://www.smumn.edu/academics/graduate/education/programs/ed.s.-in-educational-administration

Saint Mary's University of Minnesota, Schools of Graduate and Professional Programs, Graduate School of Education, Educational Leadership Program, Winona, MN 55987-1399. Offers MA, Ed D. *Program availability:* Online learning. *Unit head:* Dr. John McClure, Director, 612-728-5216, Fax: 612-728-5121, E-mail: jmcclure@smumn.edu. *Application contact:* Laurie Roy, Director of Admission of Schools of Graduate and Professional Programs, 507-457-8606, Fax: 612-728-5121, E-mail: lroy@smumn.edu.
Website: http://www.smumn.edu/graduate-home/areas-of-study/graduate-school-of-education/edd-in-leadership

Saint Mary's University of Minnesota, Schools of Graduate and Professional Programs, Graduate School of Education, Institute for LaSallian Studies, Winona, MN 55987-1399. Offers LaSallian leadership (MA); LaSallian studies (MA). *Unit head:* Dr. Roxanne Eubank, Director, 612-728-5217, E-mail: reubank@smumn.edu. *Application contact:* Laurie Roy, Director of Admission of Schools of Graduate and Professional Programs, 507-457-8606, Fax: 612-728-5121, E-mail: lroy@smumn.edu.
Website: https://www.smumn.edu/about/institutes-affiliates/institute-for-lasallian-studies

Saint Michael's College, Graduate Programs, Program in Education, Colchester, VT 05439. Offers arts in education (CAGS); literacy (M Ed); school leadership (CAGS); special education (M Ed). *Program availability:* Part-time, evening/weekend. *Degree requirements:* For master's, thesis. *Entrance requirements:* For master's, minimum GPA of 3.0, official transcripts, essay, interview. Electronic applications accepted. *Expenses: Tuition:* Part-time $590 per credit. *Faculty research:* Integrative curriculum, moral and spiritual dimensions of education, learning styles, multiple intelligences, integrating technology into the curriculum.

Saint Peter's University, Graduate Programs in Education, Program in Educational Leadership, Jersey City, NJ 07306-5997. Offers MA Ed, Ed D. *Program availability:* Part-time, evening/weekend. *Degree requirements:* For master's, comprehensive exam; for doctorate, comprehensive exam, thesis/dissertation. *Entrance requirements:* For master's and doctorate, GRE or MAT. Additional exam requirements/recommendations for international students: Required—TOEFL. Electronic applications accepted.

Saint Peter's University, Graduate Programs in Education, Program in Higher Education, Jersey City, NJ 07306-5997. Offers educational leadership (Ed D); general administration (MHE). *Degree requirements:* For doctorate, comprehensive exam, thesis/dissertation, qualifying examination, internship. *Entrance requirements:* For doctorate, GRE or MAT (taken within the last 5 years), official transcripts from all previously attended postsecondary institutions; bachelor's degree; master's degree; three letters of recommendation; essay; current resume; personal interview.

St. Thomas Aquinas College, Division of Teacher Education, Sparkill, NY 10976. Offers adolescence education (MST); childhood and special education (MST); childhood education (MST); educational leadership (MS Ed); reading (MS Ed, PMC); special education (MS Ed, PMC); teaching (MS Ed), including elementary education, middle school education, secondary education. *Accreditation:* NCATE. *Program availability:* Part-time, evening/weekend. *Degree requirements:* For master's, comprehensive exam, comprehensive professional portfolio; for PMC, action research project. *Entrance requirements:* For master's, New York State Qualifying Exam, GRE General Test or minimum GPA of 3.0, teaching certificate; for PMC, GRE General Test or minimum GPA of 3.0. Electronic applications accepted. *Faculty research:* Computer applications in education, adolescent special education students, literacy development, inclusive practices for special education students.

St. Thomas University, School of Leadership Studies, Institute for Education, Miami Gardens, FL 33054-6459. Offers earth/space science (Certificate); educational administration (MS, Certificate); educational leadership (Ed D); elementary education (MS); ESOL (Certificate); gifted education (Certificate); instructional technology (MS, Certificate); professional/studies (Certificate); reading (MS, Certificate); special education (MS). *Program availability:* Part-time, evening/weekend. *Degree requirements:* For master's, comprehensive exam; for doctorate, comprehensive exam, thesis/dissertation. *Entrance requirements:* For master's, interview, minimum GPA of 3.0 or GRE; for doctorate, GRE or MAT. Additional exam requirements/recommendations for international students: Required—TOEFL (minimum score 550 paper-based; 79 iBT). Electronic applications accepted.

Saint Vincent College, Program in Education, Latrobe, PA 15650-2690. Offers curriculum and instruction (MS); instructional design and technology (MS); school administration and supervision (MS); special education (MS). *Program availability:* Part-time, evening/weekend. *Degree requirements:* For master's, comprehensive exam. *Entrance requirements:* For master's, GRE (if undergraduate GPA less than 3.0). Additional exam requirements/recommendations for international students: Required—TOEFL (minimum score 550 paper-based). *Faculty research:* Assessment and instructional technology.

Saint Xavier University, Graduate Studies, School of Education, Chicago, IL 60655-3105. Offers counseling (MA); curriculum and instruction (MA); early childhood education (MA); educational administration (MA); elementary education (MA); individualized studies (MA), including educational technology, English as a second language (ESL), ISTEM (integrative science, technology, engineering, and math), science education; music education (MA); reading (MA); secondary education (MA); Spanish education (MA); special education (MA); teaching and leadership (MA). *Accreditation:* NCATE. *Program availability:* Part-time, evening/weekend. *Degree requirements:* For master's, thesis or project. *Entrance requirements:* For master's, minimum GPA of 3.0. *Expenses:* Contact institution.

Salem International University, School of Education, Salem, WV 26426-0500. Offers curriculum and instruction (M Ed); educational leadership (M Ed). *Program availability:* Part-time, evening/weekend, online learning. *Degree requirements:* For master's, comprehensive exam (for some programs), thesis (for some programs). *Entrance requirements:* For master's, GRE, MAT, NTE, 3 letters of recommendation. Additional exam requirements/recommendations for international students: Required—TOEFL (minimum score 550 paper-based). Electronic applications accepted. *Expenses:* Contact institution. *Faculty research:* Improved classroom effectiveness.

Salem State University, School of Graduate Studies, Program in Higher Education in Student Affairs, Salem, MA 01970-5353. Offers M Ed. *Program availability:* Part-time, evening/weekend. *Entrance requirements:* For master's, GRE or MAT. Additional exam requirements/recommendations for international students: Required—TOEFL (minimum score 550 paper-based; 80 iBT) or IELTS (minimum score 5.5).

Salisbury University, Program in Educational Leadership, Salisbury, MD 21801-6837. Offers educational leadership (M Ed). *Program availability:* Part-time, evening/weekend. *Faculty:* 3 full-time (0 women), 1 (woman) part-time/adjunct. *Students:* 2 full-time (both women), 46 part-time (29 women); includes 8 minority (7 Black or African American, non-Hispanic/Latino; 1 Two or more races, non-Hispanic/Latino). Average age 31. 22 applicants, 86% accepted, 15 enrolled. In 2018, 8 master's awarded. *Degree requirements:* For master's, comprehensive exam, SLLA exam. *Entrance requirements:* For master's, transcripts from all colleges and universities attended; evidence of at least 18 months of satisfactory teaching performance; three letters of recommendation; minimum GPA of 3.0;. Additional exam requirements/recommendations for international students: Required—TOEFL (minimum score 550 paper-based; 79 iBT), IELTS (minimum score 6.5). *Application deadline:* For fall admission, 4/1 priority date for domestic and international students; for spring admission, 10/1 priority date for domestic and international students; for summer admission, 4/1 priority date for domestic and international students. Applications are processed on a rolling basis. Application fee: $65. Electronic applications accepted. *Expenses:* Resident - $412 per credit hour; Non-resident - $746 per credit hour; Fees - $108. *Financial support:* Career-related internships or fieldwork and scholarships/grants available. Support available to part-time students. Financial award application deadline: 3/1; financial award applicants required to submit FAFSA. *Faculty research:* Leadership; organizational change; rural education leadership; educational change; public school administration. *Unit head:* Dr. Douglas DeWitt, Graduate Program Director, 410-543-6286, E-mail: dmdewitt@salisbury.edu. *Application contact:* Dr. Douglas DeWitt, Graduate Program Director, 410-543-6286, E-mail: dmdewitt@salisbury.edu.
Website: https://www.salisbury.edu/explore-academics/programs/graduate-degree-programs/med-programs/educational-leadership-masters/

Samford University, Orlean Beeson School of Education, Birmingham, AL 35229. Offers educational leadership (MSE, Ed D); elementary education (MS Ed, MSE); gifted (MSE); instructional design and technology (MSE); instructional leadership (MSE, Ed S); secondary education (MSE); special education (MSE). *Accreditation:* NCATE. *Program availability:* Part-time, evening/weekend, 100% online, blended/hybrid learning. *Faculty:* 12 full-time (10 women), 16 part-time/adjunct (11 women). *Students:* 156 full-time (111 women), 101 part-time (73 women); includes 106 minority (100 Black or African American, non-Hispanic/Latino; 1 American Indian or Alaska Native, non-Hispanic/Latino; 5 Two or more races, non-Hispanic/Latino), 1 international. Average age 37. 107 applicants, 94% accepted, 65 enrolled. In 2018, 94 master's, 40 doctorates, 11 other advanced degrees awarded. *Degree requirements:* For master's and Ed S, comprehensive exam; for doctorate, comprehensive exam, thesis/dissertation. *Entrance requirements:* For master's, GRE, MAT, PRAXIS II, interview, transcripts, essay, recommendations, teaching certification; for doctorate, resume, transcripts, interview, essay, recommendations; for Ed S, teaching certification, transcripts, essay, interview, recommendations. Additional exam requirements/recommendations for international students: Required—TOEFL (minimum score 90 iBT); Recommended—IELTS (minimum score 6.5). *Application deadline:* For fall admission, 7/15 for domestic and international students; for winter admission, 11/15 for domestic and international students; for spring admission, 11/15 for domestic and international students; for summer admission, 4/15 for domestic and international students. Applications are processed on a rolling basis. Application fee: $35. Electronic applications accepted. *Expenses:* $862 Per Hour $100 School of Education $175 Technology Fee $100 Per Fully Online Class. *Financial support:* In 2018–19, 173 students received support. Scholarships/grants available. Financial award application deadline: 2/15; financial award applicants required to submit FAFSA. *Faculty research:* Principal leadership's and teacher organizational commitment mentoring, professional development, and middle grades leadership coaching and administrator effectiveness character development programs in schools teacher efficacy related STEM and professional growth. *Unit head:* Dr. Howard Finch, Interim Dean, 205-726-2745, E-mail: hfinch@samford.edu. *Application contact:* Brooke Karr, Graduate Admissions Office Coordinator, 205-729-2783, E-mail: kbgilrea@samford.edu.
Website: http://www.samford.edu/education

Sam Houston State University, College of Education, Department of Educational Leadership, Huntsville, TX 77341. Offers administration (M Ed); developmental education administration (Ed D); educational leadership (Ed D); higher education administration (MA); higher education leadership (Ed D); instructional leadership (M Ed, MA). *Program availability:* Part-time, evening/weekend, online learning. *Degree requirements:* For master's, comprehensive exam (for some programs), thesis (for some programs); for doctorate, comprehensive exam, thesis/dissertation. *Entrance requirements:* For master's, GRE General Test, references, personal essay, resume, professional statement; for doctorate, GRE General Test, master's degree, references, personal essay, resume. Additional exam requirements/recommendations for international students: Required—TOEFL (minimum score 550 paper-based; 79 iBT), IELTS (minimum score 6.5). Electronic applications accepted.

San Diego State University, Graduate and Research Affairs, College of Education, Department of Administration, Rehabilitation and Post-Secondary Education, San Diego, CA 92182. Offers educational leadership in post-secondary education (MA); rehabilitation counseling (MS), including deafness. *Program availability:* Evening/weekend, online learning. *Degree requirements:* For master's, comprehensive exam (for some programs), thesis (for some programs). *Entrance requirements:* For master's, GRE General Test, letters of reference. Additional exam requirements/recommendations for international students: Required—TOEFL. Electronic applications accepted. *Faculty research:* Rehabilitation in cultural diversity, distance learning technology.

San Diego State University, Graduate and Research Affairs, College of Education, Department of Educational Leadership, San Diego, CA 92182. Offers MA. *Accreditation:*

NCATE. *Program availability:* Evening/weekend. *Entrance requirements:* For master's, GRE General Test, letters of reference. Additional exam requirements/recommendations for international students: Required—TOEFL. Electronic applications accepted.

San Francisco State University, Division of Graduate Studies, College of Education, Department of Equity, Leadership Studies, and Instructional Technologies, Program in Educational Administration, San Francisco, CA 94132-1722. Offers MA, Credential. *Accreditation:* NCATE. *Application deadline:* Applications are processed on a rolling basis. *Unit head:* Dr. Doris Flowers, Chair, 415-338-2614, Fax: 415-338-0568, E-mail: dflowers@sfsu.edu. *Application contact:* Dr. Irina Okhremtchouk, Advisor, 415-338-3462, Fax: 415-338-0568, E-mail: irinao@sfsu.edu.
Website: http://elsit.sfsu.edu/

San Francisco State University, Division of Graduate Studies, College of Education, Program in Educational Leadership, San Francisco, CA 94132-1722. Offers Ed D. *Unit head:* Dr. Barbara Henderson, Interim Director, 415-405-4103, Fax: 415-338-7019, E-mail: barbarah@sfsu.edu. *Application contact:* Dr. Andrea Goldfien, Graduate Coordinator, 415-338-7873, Fax: 415-338-7019, E-mail: goldfien@sfsu.edu.
Website: http://edd.sfsu.edu/

San Ignacio University, Graduate Programs, Doral, FL 33178. Offers business administration (MBA), including human resources management, international business, marketing management; education (M Ed), including early childhood education, educational leadership, special education; hospitality management (MA), including gastronomy and restaurant management, tourism management.

San Jose State University, Program in Educational Leadership, San Jose, CA 95192-0001. Offers educational administration (K-12) (MA); educational leadership (Ed D); higher education administration (MA). *Accreditation:* NCATE. *Degree requirements:* For master's, thesis or alternative. Electronic applications accepted.

Santa Clara University, School of Education and Counseling Psychology, Santa Clara, CA 95053. Offers alternative and correctional education (Certificate); counseling (MA); counseling psychology (MA); educational leadership (MA); interdisciplinary education (MA); teaching + clear teaching certificate for catholic school teachers (MAT); teaching + teaching credential (mattc) - multiple subjects (MAT); teaching + teaching credential (mattc) - single subjects (MAT). *Program availability:* Part-time, online learning. *Faculty:* 31 full-time (19 women), 35 part-time/adjunct (24 women). *Students:* 291 full-time (235 women), 298 part-time (238 women); includes 301 minority (15 Black or African American, non-Hispanic/Latino; 1 American Indian or Alaska Native, non-Hispanic/Latino; 87 Asian, non-Hispanic/Latino; 146 Hispanic/Latino; 52 Two or more races, non-Hispanic/Latino), 44 international. Average age 31. 219 applicants, 79% accepted, 143 enrolled. In 2018, 223 master's awarded. *Entrance requirements:* For master's, Statement of purpose, resume or cv, official transcript; other requirements vary by degree. Additional exam requirements/recommendations for international students: Required—TOEFL (minimum score 90 iBT), IELTS (minimum score 6.5), A TOEFL score of 90 or above or IELTS score of 6.5 or above is required for international students. *Application deadline:* For fall admission, 9/23 for domestic students; for winter admission, 1/6 for domestic students. Applications are processed on a rolling basis. Application fee: $50. Electronic applications accepted. *Financial support:* Fellowships, Federal Work-Study, and scholarships/grants available. Support available to part-time students. Financial award applicants required to submit FAFSA. *Unit head:* Dr. Sabrina Zirkel, Dean, 408-551-3074, Fax: 408-554-4367, E-mail: szirkel@scu.edu. *Application contact:* Victoria Rodriguez, Graduate Admissions Advisor, 408-554-4723, Fax: 408-554-4367, E-mail: vlrodriguez@scu.edu.
Website: http://www.scu.edu/ecp/

Schreiner University, Department of Education, Kerrville, TX 78028-5697. Offers education (M Ed); principal (Certificate). *Program availability:* Part-time, evening/weekend, online learning. *Entrance requirements:* For master's, GRE (waived if undergraduate cumulative GPA is 3.0 or above), 3 references; transcripts; interview. Additional exam requirements/recommendations for international students: Required—TOEFL. Electronic applications accepted.

Seattle Pacific University, Educational Leadership Programs, Seattle, WA 98119-1997. Offers educational leadership (M Ed, Ed D); principal (Certificate); program administrator (Certificate); superintendent (Certificate). *Accreditation:* NCATE. *Program availability:* Part-time, evening/weekend. *Students:* 2 full-time (1 woman), 55 part-time (33 women); includes 8 minority (3 Black or African American, non-Hispanic/Latino; 1 Asian, non-Hispanic/Latino; 3 Hispanic/Latino; 1 Two or more races, non-Hispanic/Latino). Average age 41. 20 applicants, 90% accepted, 18 enrolled. In 2018, 15 master's awarded. *Degree requirements:* For master's, comprehensive exam; for doctorate, comprehensive exam, thesis/dissertation. *Entrance requirements:* For master's, GRE (preferred minimum scores of Verbal: 148 and Quantitative: 147), MAT (preferred minimum scaled score of 400), or minimum GPA of 3.0, copy of Residency Teacher certificate or Educational Staff Associate (ESA) certificate; Career Tech Educator (CTE) certificate (for principal certificate candidates only); official transcript; resume; personal statement; minimum GPA of 3.0 in last 45 quarter credits of coursework completed; two letters of recommendation; for doctorate, GRE General Test or MAT, minimum GPA of 3.0, formal interview. Additional exam requirements/recommendations for international students: Required—TOEFL (minimum score 550 paper-based), IELTS (minimum score 7). *Application deadline:* For fall admission, 8/15 priority date for domestic students; for winter admission, 11/15 for domestic students; for spring admission, 2/15 priority date for domestic students; for summer admission, 5/15 for domestic students. Applications are processed on a rolling basis. Application fee: $50. Electronic applications accepted. *Financial support:* Career-related internships or fieldwork available. Financial award applicants required to submit FAFSA. *Unit head:* Dr. William Prenevost, Chair, 206-281-2370, Fax: 206-281-2756, E-mail: prenew@spu.edu. *Application contact:* The Graduate Center, 206-281-2091.
Website: http://spu.edu/academics/school-of-education/graduate-programs/masters-programs/educational-leadership-med

Seattle Pacific University, Master of Education in Teacher Leadership Program, Seattle, WA 98119-1997. Offers M Ed. *Accreditation:* NCATE. *Program availability:* Part-time, evening/weekend. *Students:* 1 (woman) full-time, 35 part-time (27 women); includes 5 minority (2 Black or African American, non-Hispanic/Latino; 2 Asian, non-Hispanic/Latino; 1 Hispanic/Latino), 1 international. Average age 36. 14 applicants, 93% accepted, 11 enrolled. In 2018, 21 master's awarded. *Degree requirements:* For master's, comprehensive exam. *Entrance requirements:* For master's, GRE General Test or MAT, copy of teaching certificate, official transcript(s), resume, personal statement, two letters of recommendation. Additional exam requirements/recommendations for international students: Required—TOEFL (minimum score 550 paper-based). *Application deadline:* For fall admission, 8/15 priority date for domestic students, 7/1 for international students; for winter admission, 11/15 for domestic students; for spring admission, 2/15 for domestic students, 3/1 for international students; for summer admission, 5/15 for domestic students. Applications are processed on a rolling basis. Application fee: $50. Electronic applications accepted. *Expenses:* Contact institution. *Financial support:* Applicants required to submit FAFSA. *Faculty research:* Educational technology, classroom environments, character education. *Unit head:* Robin Henrikson, Chair, 206-281-2186, E-mail: henrir@spu.edu. *Application contact:* The Graduate Center, 206-281-2091.
Website: http://spu.edu/academics/school-of-education/graduate-programs/masters-programs/teacher-leadership

Seattle University, College of Education, Program in Educational Administration, Seattle, WA 98122-1090. Offers M Ed, MA, Certificate, Ed S. *Accreditation:* NCATE. *Program availability:* Part-time, evening/weekend. *Faculty:* 3 full-time (1 woman), 3 part-time/adjunct (all women). *Students:* 10 part-time (5 women); includes 1 minority (Hispanic/Latino). Average age 39. 1 applicant, 100% accepted. In 2018, 4 master's awarded. *Degree requirements:* For master's and other advanced degree, comprehensive exam. *Entrance requirements:* For master's, GRE, MAT, or minimum GPA of 3.0; interview; 1 year of related experience. Additional exam requirements/recommendations for international students: Required—TOEFL. *Application deadline:* For fall admission, 8/20 priority date for domestic students; for winter admission, 11/20 for domestic students; for spring admission, 2/20 for domestic students. Applications are processed on a rolling basis. Application fee: $55. *Financial support:* In 2018–19, 3 students received support. Career-related internships or fieldwork and Federal Work-Study available. Support available to part-time students. Financial award applicants required to submit FAFSA. *Unit head:* Dr. Michael Silver, Director, 206-296-5798, E-mail: silverm@seattleu.edu. *Application contact:* Janet Shandley, Associate Dean of Graduate Admissions, 206-296-5900, Fax: 206-298-5656, E-mail: grad_admissions@seattleu.edu.
Website: https://www.seattleu.edu/education/edadmin/

Seattle University, College of Education, Program in Educational Leadership, Seattle, WA 98122-1090. Offers Ed D. *Accreditation:* NCATE. *Program availability:* Part-time, evening/weekend. *Faculty:* 15 full-time (8 women), 13 part-time/adjunct (8 women). *Students:* 13 full-time (8 women), 34 part-time (20 women); includes 17 minority (10 Black or African American, non-Hispanic/Latino; 3 Asian, non-Hispanic/Latino; 4 Hispanic/Latino), 6 international. Average age 38. In 2018, 21 doctorates awarded. *Degree requirements:* For doctorate, comprehensive exam, thesis/dissertation. *Entrance requirements:* For doctorate, GRE General Test, MAT, interview, MA, minimum GPA of 3.5, 3 years of related experience. Additional exam requirements/recommendations for international students: Required—TOEFL. *Application deadline:* For fall admission, 4/1 for domestic students. Application fee: $55. *Expenses:* Contact institution. *Financial support:* In 2018–19, 19 students received support. Career-related internships or fieldwork and Federal Work-Study available. Support available to part-time students. Financial award applicants required to submit FAFSA. *Unit head:* Dr. Laurie Stevahn, Chair, 206-296-5750, E-mail: stevahnl@seattleu.edu. *Application contact:* Janet Shandley, Associate Dean of Graduate Admissions, 206-296-5900, Fax: 206-298-5656, E-mail: grad_admissions@seattleu.edu.
Website: https://www.seattleu.edu/education/edlr/

Seattle University, College of Education, Program in Student Development Administration, Seattle, WA 98122-1090. Offers M Ed, MA. *Program availability:* Part-time, evening/weekend. *Faculty:* 4 full-time (3 women). *Students:* 40 full-time (28 women), 24 part-time (18 women); includes 41 minority (1 Black or African American, non-Hispanic/Latino; 20 Asian, non-Hispanic/Latino; 15 Hispanic/Latino; 5 Two or more races, non-Hispanic/Latino). Average age 25. 74 applicants, 85% accepted, 32 enrolled. In 2018, 26 master's awarded. *Degree requirements:* For master's, comprehensive exam. *Entrance requirements:* For master's, GRE, MAT, or minimum GPA of 3.0; two recommendations; resume; self-assessment form; autobiography. Additional exam requirements/recommendations for international students: Required—TOEFL. *Application deadline:* For fall admission, 1/15 priority date for domestic students; for winter admission, 11/20 for domestic students; for spring admission, 2/20 for domestic students. Applications are processed on a rolling basis. Application fee: $55. *Financial support:* In 2018–19, 30 students received support. Career-related internships or fieldwork, Federal Work-Study, and unspecified assistantships available. Support available to part-time students. Financial award applicants required to submit FAFSA. *Unit head:* Dr. Jeremy Stringer, Coordinator, 206-296-6170, E-mail: stringer@seattleu.edu. *Application contact:* Janet Shandley, Associate Dean of Graduate Admissions, 206-296-5900, Fax: 206-298-5656, E-mail: grad_admissions@seattleu.edu.
Website: https://www.seattleu.edu/education/sda/

Seton Hall University, College of Education and Human Services, Department of Education Leadership, Management and Policy, Program in Higher Education Administration, South Orange, NJ 07079-2697. Offers Ed D, PhD. *Accreditation:* NCATE. *Program availability:* Part-time, evening/weekend. *Degree requirements:* For doctorate, comprehensive exam, thesis/dissertation, internship. *Entrance requirements:* For doctorate, GRE or MAT, interview, minimum GPA of 3.5. Additional exam requirements/recommendations for international students: Required—TOEFL.

Seton Hall University, College of Education and Human Services, Department of Education Leadership, Management and Policy, Program in K–12 Leadership, Management and Policy, South Orange, NJ 07079-2697. Offers Ed D, Exec Ed D, Ed S. *Program availability:* Part-time, evening/weekend. *Degree requirements:* For doctorate, comprehensive exam, thesis/dissertation. *Entrance requirements:* For doctorate, MAT or GRE, interview. Additional exam requirements/recommendations for international students: Required—TOEFL.

Shasta Bible College, Program in School and Church Administration, Redding, CA 96002. Offers MS. *Program availability:* Part-time, evening/weekend. *Degree requirements:* For master's, comprehensive exam (for some programs), thesis or alternative. *Entrance requirements:* For master's, cumulative GPA of 3.0, 9 semester hours of education or psychology courses. Additional exam requirements/recommendations for international students: Required—TOEFL (minimum score 550 paper-based).

Shippensburg University of Pennsylvania, School of Graduate Studies, College of Education and Human Services, Department of Educational Leadership and Special Education, Shippensburg, PA 17257-2299. Offers educational leadership (M Ed, Ed D); special education (M Ed). *Accreditation:* NCATE. *Program availability:* Part-time, evening/weekend, blended/hybrid learning. *Faculty:* 5 full-time (0 women), 4 part-time/adjunct (3 women). *Students:* 8 full-time (7 women), 101 part-time (60 women); includes 8 minority (4 Black or African American, non-Hispanic/Latino; 1 Asian, non-Hispanic/Latino; 3 Two or more races, non-Hispanic/Latino), 5 international. Average age 35. 81 applicants, 64% accepted, 40 enrolled. In 2018, 31 master's, 2 doctorates awarded. *Degree requirements:* For master's, candidacy, thesis, or practicum; for doctorate, comprehensive exam, thesis/dissertation, candidacy exam; 24 credits (six 4-credit residencies) of field-based courses leading to the superintendent's letter of eligibility. *Entrance requirements:* For master's, GRE or MAT (if GPA is less than 2.75), 2 years of successful teaching experience; 3 letters of reference; interview; statement of purpose; writing sample; personal goals statement; resume; two recommendation forms; Education Leadership Certification as a teacher with at least 2 years of teaching experience.; for doctorate, resume; three letters of recommendation; 500-1000 word goals statement; teaching certifications and endorsements currently held; experience as public school administrator or supervisor that requires an administrative/supervisory certificate. Additional exam requirements/recommendations for international students:

Required—TOEFL (minimum score 550 paper-based; 68 iBT), IELTS (minimum score 6), TOEFL (minimum score 550 paper-based, 68 iBT) or IELTS (minimum score 6). *Application deadline:* For fall admission, 2/1 for domestic students, 4/30 for international students; for spring admission, 7/1 for domestic students, 9/30 for international students. Applications are processed on a rolling basis. Application fee: $45. Electronic applications accepted. *Expenses:* Tuition, state resident: part-time $516 per credit. Tuition, nonresident: part-time $750 per credit. *Required fees:* $149 per credit. *Financial support:* In 2018–19, 2 students received support. Career-related internships or fieldwork, scholarships/grants, unspecified assistantships, and resident hall director and student payroll positions available. Support available to part-time students. Financial award application deadline: 3/1; financial award applicants required to submit FAFSA. *Unit head:* Dr. Thomas C. Gibbon, Departmental Chair, 717-477-1498, Fax: 717-477-4036, E-mail: tcgibb@ship.edu. *Application contact:* Maya T. Mapp, Director of Admissions, 717-477-1231, Fax: 717-477-4016, E-mail: mtmap@ship.edu.
Website: http://www.ship.edu/else/

Siena Heights University, Graduate College, Adrian, MI 49221-1796. Offers clinical mental health counseling (MA); educational leadership (Specialist); leadership (MA), including health care leadership, organizational leadership; teacher education (MA), including early childhood education, early childhood education: Montessori, education leadership: principal, elementary education: reading K-12, leadership: higher education, secondary education: reading K-12, special education: cognitive impairment, special education: learning disabilities. *Program availability:* Part-time, evening/weekend. *Faculty:* 10 full-time (6 women), 16 part-time/adjunct (6 women). *Students:* 34 full-time (20 women), 183 part-time (126 women); includes 64 minority (38 Black or African American, non-Hispanic/Latino; 2 American Indian or Alaska Native, non-Hispanic/Latino; 4 Asian, non-Hispanic/Latino; 14 Hispanic/Latino; 6 Two or more races, non-Hispanic/Latino). Average age 36. 97 applicants, 41% accepted, 30 enrolled. In 2018, 72 master's awarded. *Degree requirements:* For master's, thesis, Presentation. *Entrance requirements:* For master's, Minimum GPA of 3.0, current resume, essay, all post-secondary transcripts, 3 letters of reference, conviction disclosure form; copy of teaching certificate (for some education programs); for Specialist, Master's degree, minimum GPA of 3.0, current resume, essay, all post-secondary transcripts, 3 letters of reference, conviction disclosure form; copy of teaching certificate (for some education programs). Additional exam requirements/recommendations for international students: Recommended—TOEFL, IELTS, TWE, TSE. *Application deadline:* Applications are processed on a rolling basis. Application fee: $50. Electronic applications accepted. *Expenses: Tuition:* Full-time $11,340; part-time $7560 per year. *Required fees:* $454; $454 per unit. $227 per semester. One-time fee: $100. Tuition and fees vary according to program. *Financial support:* In 2018–19, 55 students received support. Scholarships/grants, tuition waivers (full and partial), unspecified assistantships, and State of Michigan Scholarships/Grants available. Support available to part-time students. Financial award application deadline: 9/1; financial award applicants required to submit FAFSA. *Unit head:* Dr. Cheryl Betz, Dean, College for Professional Studies and Graduate College, 517-264-7234, Fax: 517-264-7714, E-mail: cbetz@sienaheights.edu. *Application contact:* Elizabeth Brooks, Assistant Director, 517-264-7165, Fax: 517-264-7714, E-mail: ebrooks@sienaheights.edu.
Website: http://www.sienaheights.edu

Sierra Nevada College, Teacher Education Program, Incline Village, NV 89451. Offers advanced teaching and leadership (M Ed); elementary education (MAT); secondary education (MAT). *Program availability:* Part-time, evening/weekend, online learning. *Degree requirements:* For master's, comprehensive exam, thesis, PRAXIS I and II. *Entrance requirements:* For master's, 2 letters of recommendation, minimum GPA of 3.0. Electronic applications accepted.

Silver Lake College of the Holy Family, Graduate School, Graduate Education Program, Manitowoc, WI 54220-9319. Offers administrative leadership (MA Ed); teacher leadership (MA Ed). *Program availability:* Part-time, evening/weekend, blended/hybrid learning. *Degree requirements:* For master's, comprehensive exam, thesis or alternative, capstone culminating project, comprehensive portfolio, or public presentation of project. *Entrance requirements:* For master's, ACT (preferred) or SAT, minimum undergraduate GPA of 3.0. Additional exam requirements/recommendations for international students: Required—TOEFL (minimum score 550 paper-based; 89 iBT). Electronic applications accepted. *Expenses:* Contact institution. *Faculty research:* Student development; school administration.

Simon Fraser University, Office of Graduate Studies and Postdoctoral Fellows, Faculty of Education, Program in Educational Leadership, Burnaby, BC V5A 1S6, Canada. Offers M Ed, MA, Ed D. *Program availability:* Part-time, evening/weekend. *Degree requirements:* For master's, comprehensive exam (for some programs), thesis (for some programs); for doctorate, comprehensive exam, thesis/dissertation. *Entrance requirements:* For master's, minimum GPA of 3.0 (on scale of 4.33) or 3.33 based on last 60 credits of undergraduate courses; for doctorate, minimum GPA of 3.5 (on scale of 4.33). Additional exam requirements/recommendations for international students: Recommended—TOEFL (minimum score 580 paper-based; 93 iBT), IELTS (minimum score 7), TWE (minimum score 5). Electronic applications accepted. *Faculty research:* Language learning, assessment and accountability policy, intersections between student affairs and services, recruitment and retention, indigenous peoples, student success in post-secondary education.

Simpson University, School of Education, Redding, CA 96003-8606. Offers education (MA), including curriculum, education leadership; education and preliminary administrative services credential (MA); education and preliminary teaching credential (MA); teaching (MA). *Program availability:* Part-time, evening/weekend. *Degree requirements:* For master's, thesis optional. *Entrance requirements:* For master's, statement of purpose, 2 professional references, professional essay, interview. Additional exam requirements/recommendations for international students: Required—TOEFL (minimum score 550 paper-based). Electronic applications accepted. *Expenses:* Contact institution.

SIT Graduate Institute, Graduate Programs, Master of Education Program in Global Youth Development and Leadership, Brattleboro, VT 05302-0676. Offers M Ed.

Slippery Rock University of Pennsylvania, Graduate Studies (Recruitment), College of Education, Department of Special Education, Slippery Rock, PA 16057-1383. Offers autism (M Ed); master teacher (M Ed), including birth to grade 8, grades 7 to 12; special education (Ed D); supervision (M Ed); technology for online instruction (M Ed). *Accreditation:* NCATE. *Program availability:* Part-time, evening/weekend, 100% online. *Faculty:* 12 full-time (6 women). *Students:* 45 full-time (36 women), 232 part-time (191 women); includes 12 minority (2 Black or African American, non-Hispanic/Latino; 1 American Indian or Alaska Native, non-Hispanic/Latino; 1 Asian, non-Hispanic/Latino; 2 Hispanic/Latino; 6 Two or more races, non-Hispanic/Latino). Average age 30. 197 applicants, 84% accepted, 96 enrolled. In 2018, 108 master's, 12 doctorates awarded. *Degree requirements:* For master's, thesis optional. *Entrance requirements:* For master's, minimum GPA of 3.0, official transcripts, teaching certification. Additional exam requirements/recommendations for international students: Required—TOEFL (minimum score 550 paper-based; 80 iBT). *Application deadline:* For fall admission, 3/1 priority date for domestic students, 5/1 priority date for international students; for spring admission, 10/1 priority date for domestic students, 9/1 priority date for international students. Applications are processed on a rolling basis. Application fee: $25 ($30 for international students). Electronic applications accepted. *Expenses:* Contact institution. *Financial support:* In 2018–19, 15 students received support. Career-related internships or fieldwork, Federal Work-Study, institutionally sponsored loans, scholarships/grants, tuition waivers (partial), and unspecified assistantships available. Support available to part-time students. Financial award application deadline: 5/1; financial award applicants required to submit FAFSA. *Unit head:* Dr. Rachel Barger-Anderson, Graduate Coordinator, 724-738-2873, Fax: 724-738-4395, E-mail: rachel.barger-ander@sru.edu. *Application contact:* Brandi Weber-Mortimer, Director of Graduate Admissions, 724-738-2051, Fax: 724-738-2146, E-mail: graduate.admissions@sru.edu.
Website: http://www.sru.edu/academics/colleges-and-departments/coe/departments/special-education/graduate-programs

Soka University of America, Graduate School, Aliso Viejo, CA 92656. Offers educational leadership and societal change (MA). *Program availability:* Evening/weekend. *Entrance requirements:* For master's, GRE. Additional exam requirements/recommendations for international students: Required—TOEFL (minimum score 600 paper-based; 100 iBT).

Sonoma State University, School of Education, Rohnert Park, CA 94928-3609. Offers administrative services (Credential); curriculum, teaching, and learning (MA); early childhood education (MA); education specialist (Credential); educational leadership (MA); multiple subject (Credential); reading and literacy (MA, Credential); single subject (Credential); special education (MA). *Accreditation:* NCATE. *Program availability:* Part-time, evening/weekend. *Entrance requirements:* For master's, minimum GPA of 2.5. Additional exam requirements/recommendations for international students: Required—TOEFL (minimum score 500 paper-based).

South Dakota State University, Graduate School, College of Education and Human Sciences, Department of Teaching, Learning and Leadership, Brookings, SD 57007. Offers agricultural education (MS); curriculum and instruction (M Ed); educational administration (M Ed). *Program availability:* Part-time, evening/weekend, online learning. *Degree requirements:* For master's, portfolio, oral exam. *Entrance requirements:* For master's, minimum GPA of 2.75. Additional exam requirements/recommendations for international students: Required—TOEFL (minimum score 550 paper-based; 80 iBT). *Faculty research:* Inclusion school climate, K-12 reform and restructuring, rural development, ESL, leadership.

Southeastern Louisiana University, College of Education, Department of Educational Leadership and Technology, Hammond, LA 70402. Offers educational leadership (M Ed, Ed D). *Program availability:* Part-time, evening/weekend. *Faculty:* 9 full-time (4 women). *Students:* 11 full-time (all women), 177 part-time (144 women); includes 75 minority (60 Black or African American, non-Hispanic/Latino; 6 Hispanic/Latino; 9 Two or more races, non-Hispanic/Latino). Average age 39. 48 applicants, 77% accepted, 30 enrolled. In 2018, 21 master's, 14 doctorates awarded. *Degree requirements:* For doctorate, thesis/dissertation. *Entrance requirements:* For master's, GRE, copy of valid teaching certificate, verification of minimum of 1 successful year of teaching experience in either public or private schools, completed recommendation form from school official who can attest to applicant's leadership potential and likelihood of success in program, minimum score of 500 based on the formula (GPA x 85 + GRE = 500); for doctorate, GRE (minimum scores: Verbal 145; Quantitative 145), 3 letters of recommendation, verification of at least 3 years of appropriate professional experience, minimum GPA 3.0 on all graduate-level course work, master's degree from an accredited university. Additional exam requirements/recommendations for international students: Required—TOEFL (minimum score 500 paper-based; 61 iBT). *Application deadline:* For fall admission, 4/1 for domestic and international students; for spring admission, 11/1 for domestic and international students. Application fee: $20 ($30 for international students). Electronic applications accepted. *Expenses: Tuition, area resident:* Full-time $6684. Tuition, state resident: full-time $6684. Tuition, nonresident: full-time $19,162. *Required fees:* $2097. *Financial support:* In 2018–19, 1 student received support. Career-related internships or fieldwork, Federal Work-Study, institutionally sponsored loans, scholarships/grants, and unspecified assistantships available. Support available to part-time students. Financial award application deadline: 5/1; financial award applicants required to submit FAFSA. *Faculty research:* Principal preparation, data literacy, school/industry partnership, research methods in educational leadership, college persistence. *Unit head:* Dr. Thomas Devaney, Department Head, 985-549-5713, Fax: 985-549-5712, E-mail: tdevaney@southeastern.edu. *Application contact:* Office of Admissions, 985-549-5637, Fax: 985-549-5632, E-mail: admissions@southeastern.edu.
Website: http://www.southeastern.edu/acad_research/depts/edlt

Southeastern Oklahoma State University, School of Education, Durant, OK 74701-0609. Offers math specialist (M Ed); reading specialist (M Ed); school administration (M Ed); school counseling (M Ed). *Accreditation:* NCATE. *Program availability:* Part-time, evening/weekend. *Degree requirements:* For master's, comprehensive exam, thesis optional, portfolio (M Ed). *Entrance requirements:* For master's, GRE General Test (for school counseling), minimum GPA of 3.0 in last 60 hours or 2.75 overall. Additional exam requirements/recommendations for international students: Required—TOEFL (minimum score 550 paper-based; 79 iBT). Electronic applications accepted.

Southeastern University, College of Education, Lakeland, FL 33801-6099. Offers curriculum and instruction (Ed D); educational leadership (M Ed); elementary education (M Ed); exceptional student education (M Ed); exceptional student education/educational therapy (M Ed); kinesiology (M Ed); organizational leadership (Ed D); reading education (M Ed); teaching English to speakers of other languages (M Ed). Electronic applications accepted.

Southeast Missouri State University, School of Graduate Studies, Leadership, Middle and Secondary Education, Program in Educational Administration, Cape Girardeau, MO 63701-4799. Offers educational leadership (Ed D); higher education administration (MA); secondary administration (MA); teacher leadership (MA, Ed S). *Accreditation:* NCATE. *Program availability:* Part-time, evening/weekend, online only, 100% online, blended/hybrid learning. *Faculty:* 7 full-time (4 women), 4 part-time/adjunct (1 woman). *Students:* 45 full-time (28 women), 210 part-time (135 women); includes 22 minority (16 Black or African American, non-Hispanic/Latino; 2 American Indian or Alaska Native, non-Hispanic/Latino; 1 Asian, non-Hispanic/Latino; 3 Two or more races, non-Hispanic/Latino), 13 international. Average age 32. 111 applicants, 100% accepted, 111 enrolled. In 2018, 63 master's, 26 other advanced degrees awarded. *Degree requirements:* For master's and Ed S, comprehensive exam, thesis or alternative, paper; for doctorate, comprehensive exam, thesis/dissertation. *Entrance requirements:* For master's, minimum GPA of 3.5; for doctorate, GRE, interview; for Ed S, minimum GPA of 3.7. Additional exam requirements/recommendations for international students: Required—TOEFL (minimum score 550 paper-based; 79 iBT), IELTS (minimum score 6), PTE (minimum score 53). *Application deadline:* For fall admission, 8/1 for domestic students, 6/1 for international students; for spring admission, 11/21 for domestic students, 10/1 for international students; for summer admission, 5/15 for domestic students. Applications are processed on a rolling basis. Application fee: $30 ($40 for international students). Electronic applications accepted. *Expenses:* Contact institution. *Financial support:* In 2018–19, 22 students received support. Career-related internships or fieldwork, Federal Work-Study, scholarships/grants, traineeships, tuition waivers (full), and unspecified assistantships available. Financial award application deadline: 6/30; financial award

applicants required to submit FAFSA. *Faculty research:* Learning and technology; leadership, equity and social justice in P-12 schools and higher education; school culture; leadership and academic achievement; school leadership and student success. *Unit head:* Dr. C. P. Gause, Professor/Chair, 573-651-2137, Fax: 573-986-6512, E-mail: cgause@semo.edu. *Application contact:* Dr. Lisa Bertrand, Professor/Coordinator, 573-651-5080, Fax: 573-986-6512, E-mail: lbertrand@semo.edu. Website: http://www.semo.edu/eduleadcounsel/

Southern Adventist University, School of Education and Psychology, Collegedale, TN 37315-0370. Offers clinical mental health counseling (MS); instructional leadership (MS Ed); literacy education (MS Ed); outdoor education (MS Ed); professional school counseling (MS). *Accreditation:* NCATE. *Program availability:* Part-time, evening/weekend, 100% online, blended/hybrid learning. *Faculty:* 11 full-time (8 women), 11 part-time/adjunct (5 women). *Students:* 42 full-time (32 women), 40 part-time (29 women). 13 applicants, 38% accepted, 4 enrolled. *Degree requirements:* For master's, comprehensive exam (for some programs), thesis optional, portfolio (MS) portfolio (MS Ed in outdoor education). *Entrance requirements:* For master's, interview (MS); 9 semester hours of upper-division course work in psychology or related field, including 1 course in psychology research or statistics; 9 semester hours of education (MS Ed). Additional exam requirements/recommendations for international students: Required—TOEFL (minimum score 100 iBT). *Application deadline:* For fall admission, 7/1 priority date for domestic students, 6/1 priority date for international students; for winter admission, 11/1 priority date for domestic students, 10/1 priority date for international students; for spring admission, 4/1 priority date for domestic students, 3/1 priority date for international students. Applications are processed on a rolling basis. Application fee: $40. Electronic applications accepted. *Financial support:* Scholarships/grants and unspecified assistantships available. Support available to part-time students. Financial award application deadline: 4/1; financial award applicants required to submit FAFSA. *Faculty research:* Millennials, spiritual self-awareness, parenting styles, attitudes toward student mental health issues, reliance on social media. *Unit head:* Dr. Tammy Overstreet, Dean, 423-236-2444, Fax: 423-236-1765, E-mail: toverstreet@southern.edu. *Application contact:* Mikhaile Spence, Graduate Program Manager, 423-236-2496, Fax: 423-236-1765, E-mail: maspence@southern.edu. Website: https://www.southern.edu/academics/edpsych.html

Southern Arkansas University–Magnolia, School of Graduate Studies, Magnolia, AR 71753. Offers agriculture (MS); business administration (MBA), including agribusiness, social entrepreneurship, supply chain management; clinical and mental health counseling (MS); computer and information sciences (MS), including cyber security and privacy, data science, information technology; gifted and talented (M Ed), including curriculum and instruction, educational administration and supervision, gifted and talented P-8/7-12, instructional specialist P-4; higher, adult and lifelong education (M Ed); kinesiology (M Ed), including coaching; library media and information specialist (M Ed); public administration (MPA); school counseling K-12 (M Ed); student affairs and college counseling (M Ed); teaching (MAT). *Accreditation:* NCATE. *Program availability:* Part-time, 100% online, blended/hybrid learning. *Faculty:* 36 full-time (21 women), 32 part-time/adjunct (15 women). *Students:* 164 full-time (77 women), 762 part-time (510 women); includes 192 minority (163 Black or African American, non-Hispanic/Latino; 7 American Indian or Alaska Native, non-Hispanic/Latino; 13 Asian, non-Hispanic/Latino; 1 Hispanic/Latino; 8 Two or more races, non-Hispanic/Latino), 213 international. Average age 28. 363 applicants, 100% accepted, 237 enrolled. In 2018, 716 master's awarded. *Degree requirements:* For master's, comprehensive exam (for some programs), thesis optional. *Entrance requirements:* For master's, GRE, MAT or GMAT, minimum GPA of 2.5. Additional exam requirements/recommendations for international students: Required—TOEFL (minimum score 550 paper-based), IELTS (minimum score 6). *Application deadline:* For fall admission, 8/1 for domestic and international students; for spring admission, 12/1 for domestic students, 11/15 for international students; for summer admission, 4/1 for domestic students, 5/10 for international students. Applications are processed on a rolling basis. Application fee: $25 ($90 for international students). Electronic applications accepted. *Expenses: Tuition, area resident:* Full-time $5130; part-time $3420 per year. Tuition, state resident: full-time $5130; part-time $3420 per year. Tuition, nonresident: full-time $7866; part-time $5244 per year. *International tuition:* $7866 full-time. *Required fees:* $1052; $710 per unit. Tuition and fees vary according to course load. *Financial support:* Career-related internships or fieldwork, Federal Work-Study, scholarships/grants, tuition waivers (full), and unspecified assistantships available. Financial award applicants required to submit FAFSA. *Faculty research:* Alternative certification for teachers, supervision of instruction, instructional leadership, counseling. *Unit head:* Dr. Kim Bloss, Dean, School of Graduate Studies, 870-235-4150, Fax: 870-235-5227, E-mail: kkbloss@saumag.edu. *Application contact:* Talia Jett, Admissions Coordinator, 870-2355450, Fax: 870-235-5227, E-mail: taliajett@saumag.edu. Website: http://www.saumag.edu/graduate

Southern Connecticut State University, School of Graduate Studies, School of Education, Department of Educational Leadership, New Haven, CT 06515-1355. Offers educational leadership (Ed D, Diploma); research, statistics, and measurement (MS). *Program availability:* Part-time, evening/weekend. *Entrance requirements:* For degree, master's degree, minimum GPA of 3.0, writing sample. Electronic applications accepted.

Southern Illinois University Carbondale, Graduate School, College of Education and Human Services, Department of Educational Administration and Higher Education, Program in Educational Administration, Carbondale, IL 62901-4701. Offers MS Ed, PhD. PhD offered jointly with Southeast Missouri State University. *Accreditation:* NCATE. *Program availability:* Part-time. *Degree requirements:* For master's, thesis or alternative; for doctorate, thesis/dissertation. *Entrance requirements:* For master's, minimum GPA of 2.7; for doctorate, GRE General Test, MAT, minimum GPA of 3.5. Additional exam requirements/recommendations for international students: Required—TOEFL. *Faculty research:* School principalship, history and philosophy of education, supervision.

Southern Illinois University Edwardsville, Graduate School, School of Education, Health, and Human Behavior, Department of Educational Leadership, Program in Educational Administration, Edwardsville, IL 62026. Offers MS Ed, Ed S. *Accreditation:* NCATE. *Program availability:* Part-time, evening/weekend. *Degree requirements:* For master's, thesis or alternative, portfolio. *Entrance requirements:* Additional exam requirements/recommendations for international students: Required—TOEFL (minimum score 550 paper-based; 79 iBT), IELTS (minimum score 6.5). Electronic applications accepted.

Southern Illinois University Edwardsville, Graduate School, School of Education, Health, and Human Behavior, Department of Educational Leadership, Program in Educational Leadership, Edwardsville, IL 62026. Offers Ed D. *Program availability:* Part-time, evening/weekend. *Degree requirements:* For doctorate, thesis/dissertation or alternative, project. *Entrance requirements:* For doctorate, GRE. Additional exam requirements/recommendations for international students: Required—TOEFL (minimum score 550 paper-based; 79 iBT), IELTS (minimum score 6.5). Electronic applications accepted.

Southern Methodist University, Simmons School of Education and Human Development, Department of Education Policy and Leadership, Dallas, TX 75275. Offers higher education (M Ed, Ed D); PK-12 school leadership (M Ed, Ed D).

Southern New Hampshire University, School of Education, Manchester, NH 03106-1045. Offers curriculum and instruction (M Ed), including dyslexia studies and language-based learning disabilities, educational leadership, reading, special education, technology integration; dyslexia studies and language-based learning disabilities (Certificate); early childhood and special education (M Ed); educational leadership (M Ed, Ed D); educational studies (M Ed); elementary and special education (M Ed); field based education (M Ed); higher education administration (MS); teaching English as a foreign language (MS). *Program availability:* Part-time, evening/weekend, online learning. *Degree requirements:* For master's, comprehensive exam (for some programs), thesis or alternative. *Entrance requirements:* For master's, PRAXIS I, minimum GPA of 2.75. Additional exam requirements/recommendations for international students: Required—TOEFL (minimum score 550 paper-based). Electronic applications accepted. *Expenses:* Contact institution.

Southern Oregon University, Graduate Studies, School of Education, Ashland, OR 97520. Offers elementary education (MA Ed, MS Ed), including classroom teacher, early childhood, handicapped learner, reading, supervision; secondary education (MA Ed, MS Ed), including classroom teacher, handicapped learner, reading, supervision; teaching (MAT). *Program availability:* Online learning. *Degree requirements:* For master's, thesis optional. *Entrance requirements:* For master's, GRE General Test, minimum cumulative GPA of 3.0 in the last 90 quarter credits (60 semester credits) of undergraduate coursework. Additional exam requirements/recommendations for international students: Required—TOEFL (minimum score 540 paper-based; 76 iBT), IELTS (minimum score 6), ELPT (minimum score 964) or ELS (minimum score 112). Electronic applications accepted.

Southern University and Agricultural and Mechanical College, Graduate School, College of Humanities and Interdisciplinary Studies, School of Education, Department of Counseling and Educational Leadership, Program in Administration and Supervision, Baton Rouge, LA 70813. Offers M Ed.

Southern University and Agricultural and Mechanical College, Graduate School, College of Humanities and Interdisciplinary Studies, School of Education, Department of Counseling and Educational Leadership, Program in Educational Leadership, Baton Rouge, LA 70813. Offers M Ed. *Entrance requirements:* For master's, GRE General Test.

Southwest Baptist University, Program in Education, Bolivar, MO 65613-2597. Offers education (MS); educational administration (MS, Ed S). *Program availability:* Part-time. *Degree requirements:* For master's, comprehensive exam, thesis optional, 6-hour residency; for Ed S, comprehensive exam, 5-hour residency. *Entrance requirements:* For master's, GRE or PRAXIS II, interviews, minimum GPA of 2.75; for Ed S, master's degree. Additional exam requirements/recommendations for international students: Required—TOEFL (minimum score 550 paper-based). *Faculty research:* At-risk programs, principal retention, mentoring beginning principals.

Southwestern Adventist University, Education Department, Keene, TX 76059. Offers curriculum and instruction with reading emphasis (M Ed); educational leadership (M Ed). *Program availability:* Part-time, evening/weekend. *Degree requirements:* For master's, thesis or alternative, professional paper. *Entrance requirements:* For master's, GRE General Test.

Southwestern Assemblies of God University, Thomas F. Harrison School of Graduate Studies, Program in Education, Waxahachie, TX 75165-5735. Offers Christian school administration (MS); curriculum development (MS); early education administration (M Ed); middle and secondary education (M Ed). *Degree requirements:* For master's, comprehensive written and oral exams. *Entrance requirements:* For master's, GRE General Test, minimum GPA of 2.5. Electronic applications accepted.

Southwestern College, Education Programs, Winfield, KS 67156-2499. Offers curriculum and instruction (M Ed); early childhood education (M Ed); educational leadership (Ed D), including higher education leadership, PK-12 education leadership; special education (M Ed), including high-incidence disabilities, low-incidence disabilities; teaching (MA). *Accreditation:* NCATE. *Program availability:* Part-time, evening/weekend, 100% online, blended/hybrid learning. *Faculty:* 7 full-time (5 women), 14 part-time/adjunct (12 women). *Students:* 6 full-time (5 women), 79 part-time (54 women); includes 11 minority (4 Black or African American, non-Hispanic/Latino; 2 American Indian or Alaska Native, non-Hispanic/Latino; 1 Asian, non-Hispanic/Latino; 3 Hispanic/Latino; 1 Two or more races, non-Hispanic/Latino), 4 international. Average age 38. 31 applicants, 74% accepted, 18 enrolled. In 2018, 24 master's, 8 doctorates awarded. *Degree requirements:* For master's, practicum, portfolio; for doctorate, thesis/dissertation, professional portfolio. *Entrance requirements:* For master's, baccalaureate degree, minimum GPA of 3.0, valid teaching certificate (for special education); for doctorate, GRE if no master's degree, baccalaureate degree with minimum GPA of 3.25 and current teaching experience, or master's degree with minimum GPA of 3.5. Additional exam requirements/recommendations for international students: Required—TOEFL (minimum score 60 paper-based; 70 iBT), IELTS (minimum score 5.5). *Application deadline:* Applications are processed on a rolling basis. Application fee: $40. Electronic applications accepted. *Expenses:* Masters programs are $606 per credit hour, $535 per online credit hour; doctorate program is $639 per credit hour. *Financial support:* In 2018–19, 13 students received support. Unspecified assistantships and employee tuition waivers available. Financial award applicants required to submit FAFSA. *Unit head:* J.K. Campbell, Education Division Chair, 620-229-6115, E-mail: JK.Campbell@sckans.edu. *Application contact:* Jen Caughron, Director of Enrollment Services & Marketing, 888-684-5335 Ext. 3312, Fax: 888-684-5218, E-mail: jennifer.caughron@sckans.edu. Website: http://www.sckans.edu/graduate/education-med/

Southwestern Oklahoma State University, College of Professional and Graduate Studies, School of Behavioral Sciences and Education, Specialization in Education Administration, Weatherford, OK 73096-3098. Offers M Ed. *Accreditation:* NCATE. *Program availability:* Part-time, evening/weekend, online learning. *Degree requirements:* For master's, exam. *Entrance requirements:* For master's, GRE General Test or minimum undergraduate GPA of 3.0, portfolio. Additional exam requirements/recommendations for international students: Required—TOEFL (minimum score 550 paper-based), IELTS (minimum score 6.5).

Southwest Minnesota State University, Department of Education, Marshall, MN 56258. Offers ESL (MS); math (MS); reading (MS); special education (MS), including developmental disabilities, early childhood education, emotional behavioral disorders, learning disabilities; teaching, learning and leadership (MS). *Program availability:* Part-time, evening/weekend, online learning. *Entrance requirements:* Additional exam requirements/recommendations for international students: Required—TOEFL or IELTS; Recommended—TOEFL (minimum score 550 paper-based; 80 iBT), IELTS.

Spalding University, Graduate Studies, College of Education, Program in Leadership Education, Louisville, KY 40203-2188. Offers executive (Ed D); scholar-practitioner (Ed D). *Accreditation:* NCATE. *Program availability:* Part-time, evening/weekend. *Degree requirements:* For doctorate, comprehensive exam, thesis/dissertation. *Entrance requirements:* For doctorate, GRE General Test or MAT, interview, letters of recommendation, resume, transcripts. Additional exam requirements/recommendations for international students: Required—TOEFL (minimum score 535 paper-based). Electronic applications accepted. *Faculty research:* Leadership of schools, achievement gap, women in leadership.

Spalding University, Graduate Studies, College of Education, Programs in Education, Louisville, KY 40203-2188. Offers art teacher education (MAT); business teacher education (MAT); elementary school education (MAT); foreign language (MAT); high school education (MAT); middle school education (MAT); secondary education (MAT); special education (learning and behavioral disorders) (MAT); student guidance counselor (MA); teacher leader (M Ed). *Accreditation:* NCATE. *Program availability:* Part-time, evening/weekend. *Entrance requirements:* For master's, GRE General Test or MAT, interview, letters of recommendation, resume. Additional exam requirements/recommendations for international students: Required—TOEFL (minimum score 535 paper-based). Electronic applications accepted. *Faculty research:* Instructional technology, achievement gap, classroom management, assessment.

Springfield College, Graduate Programs, Programs in Physical Education, Springfield, MA 01109-3797. Offers adapted physical education (MS); advanced-level coaching (M Ed); athletic administration (MS); exercise physiology (PhD); health promotion and disease prevention (MS); physical education initial licensure (CAGS); sport and exercise psychology (PhD); teaching and administration (PhD). *Program availability:* Part-time. *Degree requirements:* For master's, comprehensive exam, thesis (for some programs). *Entrance requirements:* For master's and doctorate, GRE General Test. Additional exam requirements/recommendations for international students: Required—TOEFL (minimum score 550 paper-based); Recommended—IELTS (minimum score 7). Electronic applications accepted.

Stanford University, Graduate School of Education, Program in Policy, Organization, and Leadership Studies, Stanford, CA 94305-2004. Offers MA, MA/MBA. *Expenses: Tuition:* Full-time $50,703; part-time $32,970 per year. *Required fees:* $651.

State University of New York at New Paltz, Graduate and Extended Learning School, School of Education, Department of Educational Foundations and Leadership, New Paltz, NY 12561. Offers school building leader (CAS); school district leader alternate route: transition d (CAS); school leadership (MS Ed, CAS). *Program availability:* Part-time, evening/weekend. *Faculty:* 5 full-time (3 women), 9 part-time/adjunct (7 women). *Students:* 20 full-time (13 women), 125 part-time (92 women); includes 24 minority (6 Black or African American, non-Hispanic/Latino; 17 Hispanic/Latino; 1 Two or more races, non-Hispanic/Latino). 22 applicants, 95% accepted, 18 enrolled. In 2018, 12 master's, 40 CASs awarded. *Entrance requirements:* For master's, GRE General Test or MAT, minimum GPA of 3.0, New York state teaching certificate; for CAS, minimum GPA of 3.0, proof of 3 years' teaching experience, New York state teaching certificate. Additional exam requirements/recommendations for international students: Required—TOEFL (minimum score 550 paper-based; 80 iBT), IELTS (minimum score 6.5). *Application deadline:* Applications are processed on a rolling basis. Application fee: $50. Electronic applications accepted. *Financial support:* Application deadline: 8/1. *Faculty research:* Time management of administrators, social justice, women in educational leadership, diversity in educational leadership, superintendency. *Unit head:* Arthur Gould, Program Coordinator, 845-257-2958, E-mail: gouldaj@newpaltz.edu. *Application contact:* Vika Shock, Director of Graduate Admissions, 845-257-3286, Fax: 845-257-3284, E-mail: gradstudies@newpaltz.edu.
Website: http://www.newpaltz.edu/edadmin/

State University of New York at New Paltz, Graduate and Extended Learning School, School of Education, Program of Educational Administration, New Paltz, NY 12561. Offers humanistic/multicultural education (MPS, AC), including humanistic/multicultural education (MPS), multicultural education (AC); special education (MS Ed), including adolescence special education (7-12), adolescence special education and literacy, childhood special education (1-6), childhood special education and literacy, early childhood special education (B-2). *Program availability:* Part-time, evening/weekend. *Faculty:* 1 full-time (0 women), 8 part-time/adjunct (6 women). *Students:* 18 full-time (11 women), 93 part-time (67 women); includes 15 minority (4 Black or African American, non-Hispanic/Latino; 11 Hispanic/Latino). 15 applicants, 100% accepted, 13 enrolled. In 2018, 1 master's, 39 ACs awarded. *Entrance requirements:* For master's, minimum GPA of 3.0, New York state teaching certificate (MS Ed). Additional exam requirements/recommendations for international students: Required—TOEFL (minimum score 550 paper-based; 80 iBT), IELTS (minimum score 6.5). *Application deadline:* For fall admission, 3/15 priority date for domestic students, 3/15 for international students; for spring admission, 10/15 for domestic and international students. Application fee: $50. Electronic applications accepted. *Financial support:* Scholarships/grants available. Financial award application deadline: 8/1. *Unit head:* Dr. Gowri Parameswaran, Chair, 845-257-2834, E-mail: paramesg@newpaltz.edu. *Application contact:* Vika Shock, Director of Graduate Admissions, 845-257-3286, E-mail: gradstudies@newpaltz.edu.
Website: http://www.newpaltz.edu/edstudies/

State University of New York at Oswego, Graduate Studies, School of Education, Department of Educational Administration, Oswego, NY 13126. Offers educational administration (CAS); school building leadership (CAS). *Program availability:* Part-time. *Degree requirements:* For CAS, comprehensive exam, internship. *Entrance requirements:* For degree, interview, MA or MS, minimum GPA of 3.0, teaching certificate. Additional exam requirements/recommendations for international students: Required—TOEFL (minimum score 560 paper-based). *Faculty research:* Professional growth and development, leadership, governance, strategic planning, shared decision-making.

State University of New York at Plattsburgh, School of Education, Health, and Human Services, Program in Educational Leadership, Plattsburgh, NY 12901-2681. Offers CAS. *Program availability:* Part-time, evening/weekend. *Entrance requirements:* Additional exam requirements/recommendations for international students: Required—TOEFL.

State University of New York College at Cortland, Graduate Studies, School of Education, Program in Educational Leadership, Cortland, NY 13045. Offers school building leader (CAS); school building leader and school district leader (CAS); school district business leader (CAS); school district leader (CAS). *Program availability:* Part-time, evening/weekend. *Degree requirements:* For CAS, one foreign language. *Entrance requirements:* For degree, MS in education, permanent New York teaching certificate. Additional exam requirements/recommendations for international students: Required—TOEFL.

Stephen F. Austin State University, Graduate School, James I. Perkins College of Education, Department of Secondary Education and Educational Leadership, Nacogdoches, TX 75962. Offers educational leadership (Ed D); secondary education (M Ed); secondary education leadership (MAT). *Accreditation:* NCATE. *Degree requirements:* For master's, comprehensive exam; for doctorate, thesis/dissertation. *Entrance requirements:* For master's, GRE General Test; for doctorate, GRE General Test, interview, writing sample. Additional exam requirements/recommendations for international students: Required—TOEFL. Electronic applications accepted.

Stetson University, College of Arts and Sciences, Division of Education, Department of Teacher Education, Program in Educational Leadership, DeLand, FL 32723. Offers M Ed. *Accreditation:* NCATE. *Program availability:* Evening/weekend. *Faculty:* 6 full-time (3 women). *Students:* 51 full-time (41 women), 1 (woman) part-time; includes 19 minority (11 Black or African American, non-Hispanic/Latino; 7 Hispanic/Latino; 1 Two or more races, non-Hispanic/Latino), 1 international. Average age 36. 51 applicants, 67% accepted, 31 enrolled. In 2018, 46 master's awarded. *Degree requirements:* For master's, comprehensive exam. *Entrance requirements:* For master's, GRE or MAT, transcripts, three letters of recommendation, copy of professional teaching certificate. Additional exam requirements/recommendations for international students: Required—TOEFL (minimum score 90 iBT), IELTS (minimum score 7). *Application deadline:* For fall admission, 8/1 priority date for domestic students; for spring admission, 1/1 priority date for domestic students; for summer admission, 5/1 priority date for domestic students. Applications are processed on a rolling basis. Application fee: $50. Electronic applications accepted. *Expenses:* $938 per credit hour. *Financial support:* In 2018–19, 23 students received support. Career-related internships or fieldwork, Federal Work-Study, scholarships/grants, unspecified assistantships, and tuition waivers (for staff and dependents) available. Support available to part-time students. Financial award applicants required to submit FAFSA. *Faculty research:* Mission Driven Leadership, Leadership and Charisma, Children's Literature, Reading and Writing Instruction, Social Justice, K-6 Pedagogy, Succession Planning, Leadership Pathways, Educational Reform, Assessment and Data Analysis, Single Gender Education, Teacher Collaboration, Comparative Education, Social Justice, Women in Leadership. *Unit head:* Dr. Debra Touchton, Director, 386-822-7075. *Application contact:* Jamie Vanderlip, Director of Admissions for Graduate, Transfer and Adult Programs, 386-822-7100, Fax: 386-822-7112, E-mail: jlvander@stetson.edu.

Stevenson University, Program in Community-Based Education and Leadership, Stevenson, MD 21153. Offers MS. *Program availability:* Part-time, evening/weekend. *Faculty:* 1 (woman) full-time, 2 part-time/adjunct (both women). *Students:* 6 full-time (5 women), 27 part-time (23 women); includes 14 minority (11 Black or African American, non-Hispanic/Latino; 1 Asian, non-Hispanic/Latino; 1 Hispanic/Latino; 1 Two or more races, non-Hispanic/Latino). Average age 32. 25 applicants, 68% accepted, 13 enrolled. In 2018, 10 master's awarded. *Degree requirements:* For master's, capstone. *Entrance requirements:* For master's, bachelor's degree from regionally-accredited institution, official college transcript from degree-granting institution, minimum cumulative GPA of 3.0 in past acadmeic work, two letters of recommendation, resume of professional experience, personal statement. *Application deadline:* Applications are processed on a rolling basis. Electronic applications accepted. *Expenses: Tuition:* Part-time $695 per credit. Tuition and fees vary according to program. *Financial support:* Unspecified assistantships available. Financial award applicants required to submit FAFSA. *Unit head:* Lisa Moyer, Program Coordinator. *Application contact:* Amanda Millar, Director, Admissions, 443-334-3334, Fax: 443-394-0538, E-mail: amillar@stevenson.edu.
Website: http://www.stevenson.edu/online/academics/online-graduate-programs/community-based-education-leadership/

Stony Brook University, State University of New York, School of Professional Development, Stony Brook, NY 11794. Offers coaching (Graduate Certificate); environmental management (MPS); German (MAT); higher education administration (MA, Certificate); human resource management (MS, Graduate Certificate); Italian (MAT); liberal studies (MA); mathematics (MAT); school district business leadership (Advanced Certificate); social studies (MAT); Spanish (MAT). *Program availability:* Part-time, evening/weekend, online learning. *Faculty:* 3 full-time (2 women), 94 part-time/adjunct (40 women). *Students:* 214 full-time (138 women), 1,100 part-time (813 women); includes 313 minority (117 Black or African American, non-Hispanic/Latino; 2 American Indian or Alaska Native, non-Hispanic/Latino; 32 Asian, non-Hispanic/Latino; 140 Hispanic/Latino; 3 Native Hawaiian or other Pacific Islander, non-Hispanic/Latino; 19 Two or more races, non-Hispanic/Latino), 7 international. Average age 33. 483 applicants, 89% accepted, 337 enrolled. In 2018, 315 master's, 178 other advanced degrees awarded. *Entrance requirements:* Additional exam requirements/recommendations for international students: Required—TOEFL (minimum score 85 iBT). *Application deadline:* For fall admission, 1/15 for domestic students, 6/1 for international students; for spring admission, 10/1 for domestic and international students. Applications are processed on a rolling basis. Application fee: $100. *Expenses:* Contact institution. *Financial support:* Fellowships, research assistantships, teaching assistantships, and career-related internships or fieldwork available. Support available to part-time students. *Unit head:* Patricia Malone, Associate Vice President for Professional Education and Assistant Provost for Engaged Learning, 631-632-7512, Fax: 631-632-9046, E-mail: patricia.malone@stonybrook.edu. *Application contact:* Melissa Jordan, Assistant Dean, 631-632-7751, E-mail: melissa.jordan@stonybrook.edu.
Website: http://www.stonybrook.edu/spd/

Suffolk University, College of Arts and Sciences, Department of Philosophy, Boston, MA 02108-2770. Offers administration of higher education (M Ed, CAGS); disability services (Certificate); ethics and public policy (MS). *Program availability:* Part-time, evening/weekend. *Faculty:* 3 full-time (all women), 2 part-time/adjunct (0 women). *Students:* 14 full-time (8 women), 28 part-time (18 women); includes 10 minority (7 Black or African American, non-Hispanic/Latino; 2 Hispanic/Latino; 1 Two or more races, non-Hispanic/Latino), 1 international. Average age 30. 32 applicants, 81% accepted, 9 enrolled. In 2018, 24 master's awarded. *Degree requirements:* For master's, internship or thesis; practicum (for M Ed). *Entrance requirements:* For master's, GRE General Test, MAT, GMAT, statement of professional goals, official transcripts, 2 letters of recommendation, resume. Additional exam requirements/recommendations for international students: Required—TOEFL (minimum score 550 paper-based; 80 iBT). *Application deadline:* For fall admission, 3/15 priority date for domestic and international students; for spring admission, 10/15 priority date for domestic and international students. Applications are processed on a rolling basis. Application fee: $50. Electronic applications accepted. *Expenses:* Contact institution. *Financial support:* In 2018–19, 18 students received support, including 12 fellowships (averaging $3,450 per year); career-related internships or fieldwork, Federal Work-Study, institutionally sponsored loans, and unspecified assistantships also available. Support available to part-time students. Financial award application deadline: 4/1; financial award applicants required to submit FAFSA. *Faculty research:* Predicting competent Head Start preschoolers, cultural differences, school counseling technology, sibling attachment in divorce cases, consequences of ethical breaches by human resource professionals. *Unit head:* Dr. Evgenia Cherkasova, Chair of Philosophy Department, 617-573-1970, E-mail: echerkasova@suffolk.edu. *Application contact:* Mara Marzocchi, Associate Director of Graduate Admissions, 617-573-8302, Fax: 617-305-1733, E-mail: grad.admission@suffolk.edu.
Website: http://www.suffolk.edu/college/graduate/69296.php

Sul Ross State University, College of Professional Studies, Department of Education, Program in School Administration, Alpine, TX 79832. Offers M Ed. *Program availability:* Part-time, evening/weekend. *Degree requirements:* For master's, thesis optional. *Entrance requirements:* For master's, GMAT or GRE General Test, minimum GPA of 2.5 in last 60 hours of undergraduate work.

Sul Ross State University, Rio Grande College of Sul Ross State University, Alpine, TX 79832. Offers business administration (MBA); teacher education (M Ed), including bilingual education, counseling, educational diagnostics, elementary education, general education, reading, school administration, secondary education. *Program availability:* Part-time, evening/weekend, online learning. *Degree requirements:* For master's, comprehensive exam, thesis optional, minimum GPA of 3.0. *Entrance requirements:* For

master's, GMAT or GRE General Test, minimum GPA of 2.5 in last 60 hours of undergraduate work. Additional exam requirements/recommendations for international students: Required—TOEFL.

Syracuse University, School of Education, CAS Program in School District Business Leadership, Syracuse, NY 13244. Offers CAS. *Program availability:* Part-time. *Degree requirements:* For CAS, thesis or alternative, internship. *Entrance requirements:* For degree, master's degree, transcripts, resume. Additional exam requirements/recommendations for international students: Required—TOEFL (minimum score 100 iBT). *Application deadline:* For fall admission, 1/15 priority date for domestic and international students; for spring admission, 10/15 priority date for domestic and international students; for summer admission, 4/15 priority date for domestic and international students. Applications are processed on a rolling basis. Electronic applications accepted. *Financial support:* Fellowships, research assistantships, teaching assistantships, career-related internships or fieldwork, and scholarships/grants available. Financial award application deadline: 1/15. *Faculty research:* Education management, procurement, human resource management, educational leadership and administration, long-term strategic planning. *Unit head:* Dr. Benjamin Dotger, Chair of Teaching and Leadership/Professor, 315-443-2685, E-mail: bdotger@syr.edu. *Application contact:* Speranza Migliore, Graduate Admissions Recruiter, 315-443-2505, E-mail: gradrcrt@syr.edu.
Website: http://soeweb.syr.edu/academic/teaching_and_leadership/graduate/CAS/school_district_business_leadership/default.aspx

Syracuse University, School of Education, Programs in Educational Leadership, Syracuse, NY 13244. Offers MS, Ed D, CAS. *Program availability:* Part-time. In 2018, 1 master's, 1 doctorate, 22 other advanced degrees awarded. *Degree requirements:* For master's, thesis or alternative; for doctorate, comprehensive exam, thesis/dissertation; for CAS, thesis. *Entrance requirements:* For master's, personal statement, transcripts, three letters of recommendation, resume; for doctorate, GRE, master's degree, writing sample, resume, three letters of recommendation, transcripts; for CAS, master's degree, minimum three years of teaching experience, resume, personal statement, three letters of reference. Additional exam requirements/recommendations for international students: Required—TOEFL (minimum score 100 iBT). *Application deadline:* For fall admission, 6/15 for domestic and international students; for spring admission, 12/1 for domestic students, 10/15 for international students; for summer admission, 3/1 for domestic and international students. Applications are processed on a rolling basis. Application fee: $75. Electronic applications accepted. *Financial support:* Fellowships with full tuition reimbursements, research assistantships, teaching assistantships, career-related internships or fieldwork, and scholarships/grants available. Financial award application deadline: 1/15; financial award applicants required to submit FAFSA. *Faculty research:* Curriculum and instruction leadership for equity and excellence, information management in school, supervision of instruction, leadership for literacy development, assessment of teaching. *Unit head:* Dr. Benjamin Dotger, Chair of Teaching and Leadership/Professor, 315-443-2685, E-mail: bdotger@syr.edu. *Application contact:* Speranza Migliore, Graduate Admissions Recruiter, 315-443-2505, E-mail: gradrcrt@syr.edu.
Website: http://soe.syr.edu/academic/teaching_and_leadership/graduate/CAS/educational_leadership/default.aspx

Tarleton State University, College of Graduate Studies, College of Education, Department of Curriculum and Instruction, Stephenville, TX 76402. Offers curriculum and instruction (M Ed); educational diagnostician (M Ed); elementary education (M Ed); instructional design and technology (M Ed); instructional leadership (M Ed); secondary education (M Ed); special education (M Ed); technology applications (M Ed); technology director (M Ed). *Program availability:* Part-time, evening/weekend. *Faculty:* 11 full-time (10 women), 4 part-time/adjunct (1 woman). *Students:* 16 full-time (14 women), 158 part-time (143 women). Average age 40. 54 applicants, 87% accepted, 41 enrolled. In 2018, 46 master's awarded. *Degree requirements:* For master's, comprehensive exam, thesis (for some programs). *Entrance requirements:* For master's, GRE General Test, minimum GPA of 3.0. Additional exam requirements/recommendations for international students: Required—TOEFL (minimum score 520 paper-based; 69 iBT); Recommended—IELTS (minimum score 6), TSE (minimum score 50). *Application deadline:* For fall admission, 8/15 priority date for domestic students; for spring admission, 1/7 for domestic students. Applications are processed on a rolling basis. Application fee: $50 ($130 for international students). Electronic applications accepted. *Expenses:* Contact institution. *Financial support:* Research assistantships, teaching assistantships, career-related internships or fieldwork, Federal Work-Study, and institutionally sponsored loans available. Support available to part-time students. Financial award application deadline: 5/1; financial award applicants required to submit FAFSA. *Unit head:* Dr. Amber Lynn Diaz, Department Head, 254-968-0730, E-mail: adiaz@tarleton.edu. *Application contact:* Information Contact, 254-968-9104, Fax: 254-968-9670, E-mail: gradoffice@tarleton.edu.
Website: http://www.tarleton.edu/cimasters/

Tarleton State University, College of Graduate Studies, College of Education, Department of Educational Leadership and Technology, Stephenville, TX 76402. Offers educational administration (M Ed); educational leadership (Ed D, Certificate). *Program availability:* Part-time, evening/weekend, 100% online, blended/hybrid learning. *Faculty:* 9 full-time (3 women), 7 part-time/adjunct (6 women). *Students:* 18 full-time (12 women), 40 part-time (32 women). Average age 33. 50 applicants, 80% accepted, 18 enrolled. In 2018, 32 master's, 28 doctorates awarded. *Degree requirements:* For master's, comprehensive exam, thesis optional; for doctorate, thesis/dissertation. *Entrance requirements:* For master's, GRE General Test, minimum GPA of 3.0; for doctorate, GRE, 4 letters of reference, leadership portfolio. Additional exam requirements/recommendations for international students: Required—TOEFL (minimum score 520 paper-based; 69 iBT); Recommended—IELTS (minimum score 6), TSE (minimum score 50). *Application deadline:* For fall admission, 8/15 priority date for domestic students; for spring admission, 1/7 for domestic students. Applications are processed on a rolling basis. Application fee: $50 ($130 for international students). Electronic applications accepted. *Expenses:* Contact institution. *Financial support:* Teaching assistantships, career-related internships or fieldwork, Federal Work-Study, and institutionally sponsored loans available. Support available to part-time students. Financial award application deadline: 5/1; financial award applicants required to submit FAFSA. *Unit head:* Dr. Randall Bowden, Department Head, 254-968-1936, E-mail: rbowden@tarleton.edu. *Application contact:* Information Contact, 254-968-9104, Fax: 254-968-9670, E-mail: gradoffice@tarleton.edu.
Website: http://www.tarleton.edu/edlps/

Teachers College, Columbia University, Department of Organization and Leadership, New York, NY 10027-6696. Offers adult education guided intensive study (Ed D); adult learning and leadership (Ed M, MA, Ed D); educational leadership (Ed D); higher and postsecondary education (MA, Ed D); leadership, policy and politics (Ed D); nurse executive (MA, Ed D), including administration studies (MA), professorial studies (MA); private school leadership (Ed M, MA); public school building leadership (Ed M, MA); social and organizational psychology (MA); urban education leaders (Ed D); MA/MBA. *Program availability:* Part-time, evening/weekend. *Students:* 249 full-time (165 women), 427 part-time (299 women); includes 275 minority (99 Black or African American, non-Hispanic/Latino; 75 Asian, non-Hispanic/Latino; 82 Hispanic/Latino; 1 Native Hawaiian or other Pacific Islander, non-Hispanic/Latino; 18 Two or more races, non-Hispanic/Latino), 84 international. Average age 34. 770 applicants, 59% accepted, 267 enrolled. *Unit head:* Prof. Bill Baldwin, Chair, 212-678-3043, E-mail: wjb12@tc.columbia.edu. *Application contact:* Kelly Sutton-Skinner, Director of Admission & New Student Enrollment, E-mail: kms2237@tc.columbia.edu.

Teachers College of San Joaquin, Master's Program in Education, Stockton, CA 95206. Offers early education (M Ed); educational inquiry (M Ed); educational leadership and school development (M Ed); science, technology, engineering, and mathematics (M Ed); special education (M Ed). *Expenses: Tuition:* Full-time $5520. Tuition and fees vary according to course load and program.

Temple University, College of Education, Department of Policy, Organizational & Leadership Studies, Philadelphia, PA 19122-6096. Offers Ed M, Ed D. *Program availability:* Part-time, evening/weekend. *Faculty:* 11 full-time (6 women), 5 part-time/adjunct (1 woman). *Students:* 118 full-time (80 women), 186 part-time (132 women); includes 115 minority (82 Black or African American, non-Hispanic/Latino; 2 American Indian or Alaska Native, non-Hispanic/Latino; 6 Asian, non-Hispanic/Latino; 18 Hispanic/Latino; 7 Two or more races, non-Hispanic/Latino), 12 international. 227 applicants, 69% accepted, 82 enrolled. In 2018, 73 master's, 27 doctorates awarded. *Entrance requirements:* For master's, 2 letters of recommendation, goal statement, resume; for doctorate, GRE (PhD programs), statement of goals, academic writing sample. Additional exam requirements/recommendations for international students: Required—TOEFL (minimum score 79 iBT), IELTS, PTE, one of three is required. Application fee: $60. Electronic applications accepted. *Financial support:* Fellowships, research assistantships, teaching assistantships, career-related internships or fieldwork, Federal Work-Study, scholarships/grants, health care benefits, and unspecified assistantships available. Financial award applicants required to submit FAFSA. *Faculty research:* School leadership, urban education, higher education. *Unit head:* Christopher McGinley, Associate Professor Teaching/Instruction of School Leadership and Department Chairperson, E-mail: christopher.mcginley@temple.edu. *Application contact:* Belinda McLeod, Academic Coordinator, 215-204-6795, E-mail: belinda.mcleod@temple.edu.
Website: https://education.temple.edu/pols

Tennessee Technological University, College of Graduate Studies, College of Education, Department of Curriculum and Instruction, Program in Instructional Leadership, Cookeville, TN 38505. Offers MA, Ed S. *Accreditation:* NCATE. *Program availability:* Part-time, evening/weekend. *Faculty:* 9 full-time (3 women). *Students:* 3 full-time (2 women), 38 part-time (25 women); includes 5 minority (all Black or African American, non-Hispanic/Latino). 11 applicants, 91% accepted, 7 enrolled. In 2018, 8 master's, 14 other advanced degrees awarded. *Degree requirements:* For master's and Ed S, comprehensive exam, thesis or alternative. *Entrance requirements:* For master's and Ed S, MAT or GRE. Additional exam requirements/recommendations for international students: Required—TOEFL (minimum score 527 paper-based; 71 iBT), IELTS (minimum score 5.5), PTE (minimum score 48), or TOEIC (Test of English as an International Communication). *Application deadline:* For fall admission, 8/1 for domestic students, 5/1 for international students; for spring admission, 12/1 for domestic students, 10/1 for international students; for summer admission, 5/1 for domestic students, 2/1 for international students. Applications are processed on a rolling basis. Application fee: $35 ($40 for international students). Electronic applications accepted. *Financial support:* Fellowships, research assistantships, teaching assistantships, and career-related internships or fieldwork available. Financial award application deadline: 4/1. *Faculty research:* School board member training, community school education. *Unit head:* Dr. Jeremy Wendt, Chairperson, 931-372-3181, Fax: 931-372-6270, E-mail: jwendt@tntech.edu. *Application contact:* Shelia K. Kendrick, Coordinator of Graduate Studies, 931-372-3808, Fax: 931-372-3497, E-mail: skendrick@tntech.edu.

Texas A&M International University, Office of Graduate Studies and Research, College of Education, Department of Professional Programs, Laredo, TX 78041. Offers educational administration (MS Ed); generic special education (MS Ed); school counseling (MS). *Entrance requirements:* Additional exam requirements/recommendations for international students: Required—TOEFL (minimum score 550 paper-based; 79 iBT).

Texas A&M University, College of Education and Human Development, Department of Educational Administration and Human Resource Development, College Station, TX 77843. Offers educational administration (M Ed, MS, Ed D); educational human resource development (PhD). *Program availability:* Part-time. *Faculty:* 33. *Students:* 177 full-time (143 women), 262 part-time (165 women); includes 182 minority (47 Black or African American, non-Hispanic/Latino; 1 American Indian or Alaska Native, non-Hispanic/Latino; 13 Asian, non-Hispanic/Latino; 118 Hispanic/Latino; 1 Native Hawaiian or other Pacific Islander, non-Hispanic/Latino; 2 Two or more races, non-Hispanic/Latino), 30 international. Average age 36. 261 applicants, 57% accepted, 129 enrolled. In 2018, 85 master's, 29 doctorates awarded. *Degree requirements:* For master's, thesis optional; for doctorate, thesis/dissertation. *Entrance requirements:* For master's, GRE General Test, writing exam, interview, professional experience; for doctorate, GRE General Test, writing exam, interview/presentation, professional experience. Additional exam requirements/recommendations for international students: Required—TOEFL (minimum score 550 paper-based; 80 iBT), IELTS (minimum score 6), PTE (minimum score 53). *Application deadline:* For fall admission, 12/1 for domestic and international students; for spring admission, 8/15 for domestic and international students. Application fee: $50 ($90 for international students). Electronic applications accepted. *Expenses:* Contact institution. *Financial support:* In 2018–19, 77 students received support, including 6 fellowships with tuition reimbursements available (averaging $2,583 per year), 55 research assistantships with tuition reimbursements available (averaging $12,390 per year), 22 teaching assistantships with tuition reimbursements available (averaging $14,003 per year); career-related internships or fieldwork, institutionally sponsored loans, scholarships/grants, traineeships, health care benefits, tuition waivers (full and partial), and unspecified assistantships also available. Support available to part-time students. Financial award application deadline: 3/15; financial award applicants required to submit FAFSA. *Faculty research:* Higher education administration, public school administration, student affairs. *Unit head:* Dr. Fred M. Nafukho, Head, 979-862-3395, Fax: 979-862-4347, E-mail: fnafukho@tamu.edu. *Application contact:* Joyce Nelson, Director of Academic Advising, 979-845-3017, Fax: 979-862-4347, E-mail: eahradvisor@tamu.edu.
Website: http://eahr.tamu.edu

Texas A&M University–Central Texas, Graduate Studies and Research, Killeen, TX 76549. Offers accounting (MS); business administration (MBA); clinical mental health counseling (MS); criminal justice (MCJ); curriculum and instruction (M Ed); educational administration (M Ed); educational psychology - experimental psychology (MS); history (MA); human resource management (MS); information systems (MS); liberal studies (MS); management and leadership (MS); marriage and family therapy (MS); mathematics (MS); political science (MA); school counseling (M Ed); school psychology (Ed S).

Texas A&M University–Commerce, College of Education and Human Services, Commerce, TX 75429. Offers counseling (M Ed, MS, PhD); early childhood education (M Ed, MS); educational administration (M Ed, MS, Ed D); educational psychology

(PhD); educational technology leadership (M Ed, MS); educational technology library science (M Ed, MS); elementary education (M Ed); health, kinesiology and sports studies (MS); higher education (MS, Ed D); psychology (MS); reading (M Ed, MS); school psychology (SSP); secondary education (M Ed, MS); social work (MSW); special education (M Ed, MS); supervision, curriculum and instruction-elementary education (Ed D); training and development (MS). *Program availability:* Part-time, evening/weekend, 100% online, blended/hybrid learning. *Faculty:* 95 full-time (59 women), 29 part-time/adjunct (22 women). *Students:* 356 full-time (295 women), 1,262 part-time (992 women); includes 683 minority (349 Black or African American, non-Hispanic/Latino; 9 American Indian or Alaska Native, non-Hispanic/Latino; 30 Asian, non-Hispanic/Latino; 238 Hispanic/Latino; 57 Two or more races, non-Hispanic/Latino), 9 international. Average age 37. 951 applicants, 42% accepted, 304 enrolled. In 2018, 532 master's, 51 doctorates awarded. *Degree requirements:* For master's, comprehensive exam, thesis optional, departmental qualifying exams (for some programs); for doctorate, comprehensive exam, thesis/dissertation, departmental qualifying exam; for SSP, comprehensive exam. *Entrance requirements:* For master's, GRE General Test, official transcripts, letters of recommendation, resume, statement of goals; for doctorate, GRE General Test, letters of recommendation, statement of goals, writing samples, writing sessions, resumes. Additional exam requirements/recommendations for international students: Required—TOEFL (minimum score 550 paper-based; 79 iBT), IELTS (minimum score 6), PTE (minimum score 53). *Application deadline:* For fall admission, 6/1 priority date for international students; for spring admission, 10/15 priority date for international students; for summer admission, 3/15 priority date for international students. Applications are processed on a rolling basis. Application fee: $50 ($75 for international students). Electronic applications accepted. *Expenses: Tuition, area resident:* Full-time $3630. Tuition, state resident: full-time $3630. Tuition, nonresident: full-time $11,100. *International tuition:* $11,100 full-time. *Required fees:* $2794. Tuition and fees vary according to course load, degree level and program. *Financial support:* In 2018–19, 116 students received support, including 94 research assistantships with partial tuition reimbursements available (averaging $3,863 per year), 38 teaching assistantships with partial tuition reimbursements available (averaging $4,728 per year); career-related internships or fieldwork, Federal Work-Study, institutionally sponsored loans, scholarships/grants, health care benefits, and unspecified assistantships also available. Financial award application deadline: 5/1; financial award applicants required to submit FAFSA. *Faculty research:* Cognitive and bilingual education, positive behavioral intervention, literacy, math readiness. *Total annual research expenditures:* $1.1 million. *Unit head:* Dr. Madeline Justice, Interim Dean, 903-886-5181, Fax: 903-886-5905, E-mail: madeline.justice@tamuc.edu. *Application contact:* Vicky Turner, Doctoral Degree and Special Programs Coordinator, 903-886-5167, E-mail: vicky.turner@tamuc.edu.
Website: http://www.tamuc.edu/academics/graduateSchool/programs/education/default.aspx

Texas A&M University–Corpus Christi, College of Graduate Studies, College of Education and Human Development, Program in Educational Administration, Corpus Christi, TX 78412. Offers MS. *Program availability:* Part-time, evening/weekend. *Degree requirements:* For master's, comprehensive exam. *Entrance requirements:* For master's, minimum GPA of 3.0 in last 60 hours; essay (approximately 300-400 words in length). Additional exam requirements/recommendations for international students: Required—TOEFL (minimum score 550 paper-based; 79 iBT), IELTS (minimum score 6.5). Electronic applications accepted.

Texas A&M University–Corpus Christi, College of Graduate Studies, College of Education and Human Development, Program in Educational Leadership, Corpus Christi, TX 78412. Offers Ed D. *Program availability:* Part-time, evening/weekend. *Degree requirements:* For doctorate, thesis/dissertation. *Entrance requirements:* For doctorate, GMAT/GRE (taken within 5 years), master's degree, minimum graduate GPA of 3.0 in last 60 hours, essay (300-400 words in length), 4 reference forms, resume or curriculum vitae. Additional exam requirements/recommendations for international students: Required—TOEFL (minimum score 550 paper-based; 79 iBT), IELTS (minimum score 6.5). Electronic applications accepted.

Texas A&M University–Kingsville, College of Graduate Studies, College of Education and Human Performance, Department of Educational Leadership and Counseling, Program in Educational Administration, Kingsville, TX 78363. Offers MA, MS. *Program availability:* Part-time, evening/weekend, online only, 100% online, blended/hybrid learning. *Entrance requirements:* Additional exam requirements/recommendations for international students: Required—TOEFL (minimum score 550 paper-based; 79 iBT); Recommended—IELTS. Electronic applications accepted.

Texas A&M University–Kingsville, College of Graduate Studies, College of Education and Human Performance, Department of Educational Leadership and Counseling, Program in Educational Leadership, Kingsville, TX 78363. Offers PhD. Program offered jointly with Texas A&M University. *Program availability:* Part-time, evening/weekend. *Degree requirements:* For doctorate, variable foreign language requirement, comprehensive exam, thesis/dissertation (for some programs). *Entrance requirements:* For doctorate, GRE, MAT, GMAT, two-page statement of desire to pursue doctoral degree in educational leadership; 3 letters of recommendation; curriculum vitae listing accomplishments or any other evidence of scholarship, leadership, and/or professionalism. Additional exam requirements/recommendations for international students: Required—TOEFL (minimum score 550 paper-based; 79 iBT). Electronic applications accepted.

Texas A&M University–San Antonio, Department of Educator and Leadership Preparation, San Antonio, TX 78224. Offers bilingual education (MS); early childhood education (M Ed); educational administration (MA); reading specialization (MS); special education (M Ed), including educational diagnostician. *Program availability:* Part-time, evening/weekend, online learning. *Degree requirements:* For master's, comprehensive exam, thesis or alternative. *Entrance requirements:* For master's, GRE (Quantitative and Verbal) or MAT. Additional exam requirements/recommendations for international students: Required—TOEFL (minimum score 550 paper-based; 79 iBT), IELTS (minimum score 6). Electronic applications accepted. *Faculty research:* Equity in education, biliteracy practices among Latina and immigrants, academic achievement of low socio-economic students, equity practices in instruction and educational leadership in diverse settings, racial identity development and multicultural education.

Texas A&M University–Texarkana, Graduate Studies and Research, College of Education and Liberal Arts, Texarkana, TX 75503. Offers adult education (MS); curriculum and instruction (M Ed); education (MS); educational administration (M Ed); English (MA); instructional technology (MS); interdisciplinary studies (MA, MS); special education (MS). *Program availability:* Part-time, evening/weekend. *Degree requirements:* For master's, comprehensive exam (for some programs), thesis optional. *Entrance requirements:* For master's, minimum GPA of 2.5 on last 60 hours of bachelor's degree. Additional exam requirements/recommendations for international students: Required—TOEFL. Electronic applications accepted.

Texas Christian University, College of Education, Doctoral Programs in Education, Fort Worth, TX 76129-0002. Offers counseling and counselor education (PhD); curriculum studies (PhD); educational leadership (Ed D); higher educational leadership (Ed D); science education (PhD); MBA/Ed D. *Program availability:* Part-time, evening/

weekend. *Faculty:* 29 full-time (21 women), 3 part-time/adjunct (1 woman). *Students:* 80 full-time (57 women), 26 part-time (13 women); includes 41 minority (15 Black or African American, non-Hispanic/Latino; 6 Asian, non-Hispanic/Latino; 17 Hispanic/Latino; 3 Two or more races, non-Hispanic/Latino), 6 international. Average age 39. 109 applicants, 50% accepted, 23 enrolled. In 2018, 12 doctorates awarded. *Degree requirements:* For doctorate, comprehensive exam, thesis/dissertation. *Entrance requirements:* For doctorate, GRE General Test. Additional exam requirements/recommendations for international students: Required—TOEFL (minimum score 550 paper-based; 80 iBT), IELTS (minimum score 6.5). *Application deadline:* For fall admission, 2/1 for domestic and international students; for winter admission, 2/1 for domestic and international students; for spring admission, 11/16 for domestic and international students. Application fee: $60. Electronic applications accepted. *Financial support:* In 2018–19, 66 students received support, including 1 fellowship with full tuition reimbursement available (averaging $18,500 per year), 8 research assistantships with full tuition reimbursements available (averaging $18,500 per year), 6 teaching assistantships with full tuition reimbursements available (averaging $18,500 per year); career-related internships or fieldwork, scholarships/grants, health care benefits, and unspecified assistantships also available. Support available to part-time students. Financial award application deadline: 2/1. *Unit head:* Dr. Jan Lacina, Interim Dean, 817-257-6786, Fax: 817-257-7466, E-mail: j.lacina@tcu.edu. *Application contact:* Lori Kimball, Graduate Studies Coordinator, 817-257-7661, Fax: 817-257-7466, E-mail: l.kimball@tcu.edu.
Website: http://coe.tcu.edu/graduate-overview/

Texas Christian University, College of Education, Master's Programs in Education, Fort Worth, TX 76129-0002. Offers counseling (M Ed); curriculum and instruction (M Ed), including curriculum studies, language and literacy, math education, science education; education (MAT); educational leadership (M Ed); special education (M Ed). *Program availability:* Part-time, evening/weekend. *Faculty:* 29 full-time (21 women), 3 part-time/adjunct (1 woman). *Students:* 124 full-time (94 women), 14 part-time (12 women); includes 52 minority (14 Black or African American, non-Hispanic/Latino; 2 American Indian or Alaska Native, non-Hispanic/Latino; 3 Asian, non-Hispanic/Latino; 28 Hispanic/Latino; 5 Two or more races, non-Hispanic/Latino), 1 international. Average age 28. 172 applicants, 69% accepted, 86 enrolled. In 2018, 62 master's awarded. *Degree requirements:* For master's, comprehensive exam (for some programs), thesis (for some programs). *Entrance requirements:* For master's, GRE General Test; Pre-Admission Content Test (for MAT). Additional exam requirements/recommendations for international students: Required—TOEFL (minimum score 550 paper-based; 80 iBT), IELTS (minimum score 6.5). *Application deadline:* For fall admission, 3/1 for domestic and international students; for spring admission, 11/16 for domestic and international students; for summer admission, 3/1 for domestic and international students. Application fee: $60. Electronic applications accepted. *Financial support:* In 2018–19, 135 students received support, including 3 research assistantships with full tuition reimbursements available (averaging $15,000 per year), 33 teaching assistantships with full tuition reimbursements available (averaging $15,000 per year); career-related internships or fieldwork, scholarships/grants, health care benefits, and unspecified assistantships also available. Support available to part-time students. Financial award application deadline: 3/1. *Unit head:* Dr. Jan Lacina, Interim Dean, 817-257-6786, Fax: 817-257-7466, E-mail: j.lacina@tcu.edu. *Application contact:* Lori Kimball, Graduate Studies Coordinator, 817-257-7661, Fax: 817-257-7466, E-mail: l.kimball@tcu.edu.
Website: http://coe.tcu.edu/graduate-overview/

Texas Southern University, College of Education, Department of Educational Administration and Foundation, Houston, TX 77004-4584. Offers educational administration (M Ed, Ed D). *Program availability:* Part-time, evening/weekend. *Degree requirements:* For master's, comprehensive exam; for doctorate, comprehensive exam, thesis/dissertation. *Entrance requirements:* For master's, GRE General Test, minimum GPA of 2.5; for doctorate, GRE General Test or MAT, master's degree, minimum B+ average. Additional exam requirements/recommendations for international students: Required—TOEFL. Electronic applications accepted.

Texas State University, The Graduate College, College of Education, Program in Educational Leadership, San Marcos, TX 78666. Offers educational leadership (M Ed); instructional leadership (MA). *Program availability:* Part-time, evening/weekend. *Faculty:* 1 full-time, 10 part-time/adjunct (8 women). *Students:* 1 full-time, 97 part-time (79 women); includes 46 minority (8 Black or African American, non-Hispanic/Latino; 1 Asian, non-Hispanic/Latino; 35 Hispanic/Latino; 2 Two or more races, non-Hispanic/Latino). Average age 35. 37 applicants, 62% accepted, 15 enrolled. In 2018, 34 master's awarded. *Degree requirements:* For master's, comprehensive exam, thesis (for some programs). *Entrance requirements:* For master's, baccalaureate degree from regionally-accredited institution with minimum GPA of 2.75 in last 60 hours of undergraduate course work; copy of official teaching certificate; copy of official teaching record documenting at least 1 year of teaching experience. Additional exam requirements/recommendations for international students: Required—TOEFL (minimum score 550 paper-based; 78 iBT), IELTS (minimum score 6.5). *Application deadline:* For fall admission, 2/1 priority date for domestic and international students; for summer admission, 5/1 for domestic students, 3/15 for international students. Applications are processed on a rolling basis. Application fee: $55 ($90 for international students). Electronic applications accepted. *Expenses:* Tuition, state resident: full-time $8102; part-time $4051 per semester. Tuition, nonresident: full-time $18,229; part-time $9115 per semester. *International tuition:* $18,229 full-time. *Required fees:* $2116; $120 per credit hour. Tuition and fees vary according to course load. *Financial support:* In 2018–19, 18 students received support. Research assistantships, teaching assistantships, career-related internships or fieldwork, Federal Work-Study, institutionally sponsored loans, and scholarships/grants available. Support available to part-time students. Financial award application deadline: 1/15; financial award applicants required to submit FAFSA. *Faculty research:* Neurofeedback in the mitigation of ADHD symptoms; addressing anxiety and self-doubt as a counselor; promoting resilience in children of alcoholics; experiences of practicum students in a school-based mental health counseling clinic. *Unit head:* Dr. Bergeron Harris, Graduate Advisor, 512-245-9909, E-mail: bh26@txstate.edu. *Application contact:* Dr. Andrea Golato, Dean of Graduate School, 512-245-2581, Fax: 512-245-8365, E-mail: gradcollege@txstate.edu.
Website: http://www.txstate.edu/clas/Educational-Leadership.html

Texas State University, The Graduate College, College of Education, Program in School Improvement, San Marcos, TX 78666. Offers PhD. *Program availability:* Part-time. *Faculty:* 15 full-time (7 women), 1 (woman) part-time/adjunct. *Students:* 15 full-time (11 women), 69 part-time (36 women); includes 44 minority (8 Black or African American, non-Hispanic/Latino; 36 Hispanic/Latino), 2 international. Average age 42. 31 applicants, 52% accepted, 12 enrolled. In 2018, 5 doctorates awarded. *Degree requirements:* For doctorate, comprehensive exam, thesis/dissertation. *Entrance requirements:* For doctorate, baccalaureate and master's degrees from regionally-accredited university (master's degree in an area related to proposed studies with minimum graduate GPA of 3.5); resume/CV; statement of purpose (500 words); 3 letters of reference addressing professional and academic background; possible interview with program faculty;. Additional exam requirements/recommendations for international students: Required—TOEFL (minimum score 78 iBT), IELTS (minimum score 6.5). *Application deadline:* For fall admission, 2/1 for domestic and international students. Applications are processed on a rolling basis. Application fee: $55 ($90 for international

students). Electronic applications accepted. *Expenses:* Tuition, state resident: full-time $8102; part-time $4051 per semester. Tuition, nonresident: full-time $18,229; part-time $9115 per semester. *International tuition:* $18,229 full-time. *Required fees:* $2116; $120 per credit hour. Tuition and fees vary according to course load. *Financial support:* In 2018–19, 22 students received support, including 8 research assistantships (averaging $26,691 per year); teaching assistantships, scholarships/grants, and unspecified assistantships also available. Financial award application deadline: 1/15; financial award applicants required to submit FAFSA. *Faculty research:* Social and emotional learning at the middle level; community building, community youth development, race and ethnicity, university and community partnerships, and Latino youth and families; Assistant principal dilemma: Walking the line between compliance and leadership; Photography, visual culture, and the (re)definition of the male gaze; Examining intersectionalities among male faculty of color on the tenure-track; Public educational policy as performance; Developing new psychometric and statis. *Total annual research expenditures:* $40,246. *Unit head:* Dr. James Koschoreck, PhD Program Director, 512-245-9909, Fax: 512-245-9923, E-mail: j_k266@txstate.edu. *Application contact:* Dr. Andrea Golato, Dean of Graduate School, 512-245-2581, Fax: 512-245-8365, E-mail: gradcollege@txstate.edu.
Website: http://si.education.txstate.edu

Texas Tech University, Graduate School, College of Education, Department of Educational Psychology and Leadership, Lubbock, TX 79409-1071. Offers counselor education (M Ed, PhD); educational leadership (M Ed, Ed D, PhD); educational psychology (M Ed, PhD); higher education administration (M Ed, Ed D); higher education research (PhD); instructional technology (M Ed, Ed D); special education (M Ed, Ed D, PhD). *Accreditation:* ACA; NCATE. *Program availability:* Part-time, evening/weekend, 100% online, blended/hybrid learning. *Faculty:* 65 full-time (29 women), 3 part-time/adjunct (all women). *Students:* 261 full-time (184 women), 624 part-time (482 women); includes 325 minority (88 Black or African American, non-Hispanic/Latino; 3 American Indian or Alaska Native, non-Hispanic/Latino; 12 Asian, non-Hispanic/Latino; 192 Hispanic/Latino; 1 Native Hawaiian or other Pacific Islander, non-Hispanic/Latino; 29 Two or more races, non-Hispanic/Latino), 39 international. Average age 36. 437 applicants, 73% accepted, 252 enrolled. In 2018, 278 master's, 40 doctorates awarded. Terminal master's awarded for partial completion of doctoral program. *Degree requirements:* For master's, comprehensive exam, thesis optional; for doctorate, comprehensive exam, thesis/dissertation. *Entrance requirements:* For master's, GRE (for some programs); for doctorate, GRE. Additional exam requirements/recommendations for international students: Required—TOEFL (minimum score 550 paper-based; 79 iBT). *Application deadline:* For fall admission, 6/1 priority date for domestic students, 1/15 priority date for international students; for spring admission, 9/1 priority date for domestic students, 6/15 priority date for international students. Applications are processed on a rolling basis. Application fee: $65. Electronic applications accepted. *Expenses:* Contact institution. *Financial support:* In 2018–19, 493 students received support, including 489 fellowships (averaging $3,305 per year), 61 research assistantships (averaging $12,558 per year), 5 teaching assistantships (averaging $13,161 per year); scholarships/grants and unspecified assistantships also available. Support available to part-time students. Financial award application deadline: 1/3; financial award applicants required to submit FAFSA. *Faculty research:* Cognitive, motivational, and developmental processes in learning; counseling education; instructional technology; generic special education and sensory impairment; community college administration; K-12 school administration. *Total annual research expenditures:* $204,930. *Unit head:* Dr. Hansel Burley, Professor, Department Chair, 806-834-5135, Fax: 806-742-2179, E-mail: hansel.burley@ttu.edu. *Application contact:* Pam Smith, Admissions Advisor, 806-834-2969, Fax: 806-742-2179, E-mail: pam.smith@ttu.edu.
Website: www.educ.ttu.edu/

Texas Woman's University, Graduate School, College of Professional Education, Department of Teacher Education, Denton, TX 76204. Offers educational administration (M Ed, MA); special education (M Ed, PhD), including educational diagnostician (M Ed), intervention specialist (M Ed); teaching, learning, and curriculum (M Ed, MA). *Program availability:* Part-time, 100% online, blended/hybrid learning. *Faculty:* 24 full-time (19 women), 24 part-time/adjunct (17 women). *Students:* 35 full-time (30 women), 170 part-time (153 women); includes 81 minority (18 Black or African American, non-Hispanic/Latino; 1 American Indian or Alaska Native, non-Hispanic/Latino; 4 Asian, non-Hispanic/Latino; 52 Hispanic/Latino; 6 Two or more races, non-Hispanic/Latino), 1 international. Average age 35. 79 applicants, 70% accepted, 43 enrolled. In 2018, 49 master's, 4 doctorates awarded. *Degree requirements:* For master's, comprehensive exam, thesis, professional paper (M Ed), internship for some; for doctorate, comprehensive exam, thesis/dissertation, residency, portfolio. *Entrance requirements:* For master's, minimum GPA of 3.0 on last 60 undergraduate hours, 2 letters of reference, resume, copy of certifications, teacher service record, statement of intent, interview (for MAT); for doctorate, minimum GPA of 3.0, 3 letters of reference, resume, copy of certifications, teacher service record, statement of intent, interview. Additional exam requirements/recommendations for international students: Required—TOEFL (minimum score 550 paper-based; 79 iBT); Recommended—IELTS (minimum score 6.5), TSE (minimum score 53). *Application deadline:* For fall admission, 7/15 priority date for domestic students, 3/1 priority date for international students; for spring admission, 11/1 priority date for domestic students, 7/1 priority date for international students; for summer admission, 4/1 priority date for domestic and international students. Application fee: $50 ($75 for international students). Electronic applications accepted. *Expenses:* $1,517 in-state resident per 3 hour course, $2,783 out-of-state resident per 3 hour course. *Financial support:* In 2018–19, 42 students received support, including 1 teaching assistantship; research assistantships, career-related internships or fieldwork, Federal Work-Study, institutionally sponsored loans, scholarships/grants, traineeships, health care benefits, and unspecified assistantships also available. Support available to part-time students. Financial award application deadline: 3/1; financial award applicants required to submit FAFSA. *Faculty research:* Experiential learning, classroom management, learning disabilities, staff and professional development, technology in the classroom. *Unit head:* Dr. Diane Myers, Chair, 940-898-2271, Fax: 940-898-2270, E-mail: teachereducation@twu.edu. *Application contact:* Korie Hawkins, Associate Director of Admissions, Graduate Recruitment, 940-898-3188, Fax: 940-898-3081, E-mail: admissions@twu.edu.
Website: http://www.twu.edu/teacher-education/

Thomas Edison State University, Heavin School of Arts and Sciences, Program in Educational Leadership, Trenton, NJ 08608. Offers MAEL, Graduate Certificate. *Program availability:* Part-time, online learning. *Degree requirements:* For master's, field-based practicum, professional portfolio development. *Entrance requirements:* For master's, at least 3 years of teaching experience; valid teacher's certification; letter of recommendation from a building-level administrator; school setting and on-site mentor available to conduct site-based fieldwork and inquiry projects successfully for each course; statement of goals and objectives. Additional exam requirements/recommendations for international students: Required—TOEFL (minimum score 550 paper-based; 79 iBT). Electronic applications accepted.

Thomas More University, Program in Teacher Leader, Crestview Hills, KY 41017-3495. Offers M Ed. *Program availability:* Part-time, evening/weekend. *Degree requirements:* For master's, comprehensive exam. *Entrance requirements:* For master's, GRE, minimum undergraduate cumulative GPA of 2.7. Additional exam requirements/recommendations for international students: Required—TOEFL (minimum score 100 iBT). Electronic applications accepted.

Tiffin University, Program in Education, Tiffin, OH 44883-2161. Offers educational technology management (M Ed); higher education administration (M Ed). *Program availability:* Part-time, evening/weekend, online only, 100% online, blended/hybrid learning. *Entrance requirements:* Additional exam requirements/recommendations for international students: Required—TOEFL. Electronic applications accepted. *Expenses:* Contact institution.

Touro College, Graduate School of Education, New York, NY 10010. Offers education and special education (MS); instructional technology (MS); mathematics education (MS); school leadership (MS); teaching English to speakers of other languages (MS); teaching literacy (MS). *Accreditation:* TEAC. *Program availability:* Part-time, evening/weekend, online learning. *Entrance requirements:* Additional exam requirements/recommendations for international students: Required—TOEFL (minimum score 83 iBT), IELTS (minimum score 6.5). *Faculty research:* Equity assistance, language development, scholarly communications, Latin American studies and cultural sensitivity, behavior management techniques and strategies in special education.

Towson University, College of Education, Program in Instructional Leadership and Professional Development, Towson, MD 21252-0001. Offers CAS, Postbaccalaureate Certificate. Electronic applications accepted. *Expenses: Tuition, area resident:* Full-time $9196; part-time $418 per unit. Tuition, state resident: full-time $9196; part-time $418 per unit. Tuition, nonresident: full-time $19,030; part-time $865 per unit. *International tuition:* $19,030 full-time. *Required fees:* $3102; $141 per year. $423 per term. Tuition and fees vary according to campus/location and program.

Towson University, College of Education, Program in Special Education, Towson, MD 21252-0001. Offers special education (M Ed); teacher as leader in autism spectrum disorder (M Ed). *Accreditation:* NCATE. *Program availability:* Part-time, evening/weekend. *Degree requirements:* For master's, thesis optional. *Entrance requirements:* For master's, letter of recommendation, bachelor's degree, professional teacher certification, minimum GPA of 3.0. Electronic applications accepted. *Expenses: Tuition, area resident:* Full-time $9196; part-time $418 per unit. Tuition, state resident: full-time $9196; part-time $418 per unit. Tuition, nonresident: full-time $19,030; part-time $865 per unit. *International tuition:* $19,030 full-time. *Required fees:* $3102; $141 per year. $423 per term. Tuition and fees vary according to campus/location and program.

Towson University, College of Liberal Arts, Program in Human Resource Development, Towson, MD 21252-0001. Offers education leadership (MS); general human resource management (MS). *Program availability:* Part-time, evening/weekend. *Degree requirements:* For master's, comprehensive exam. *Entrance requirements:* For master's, bachelor's degree, 2 letters of recommendation, minimum GPA of 3.0, essay, resume. Additional exam requirements/recommendations for international students: Required—TOEFL. Electronic applications accepted. *Expenses: Tuition, area resident:* Full-time $9196; part-time $418 per unit. Tuition, state resident: full-time $9196; part-time $418 per unit. Tuition, nonresident: full-time $19,030; part-time $865 per unit. *International tuition:* $19,030 full-time. *Required fees:* $3102; $141 per year. $423 per term. Tuition and fees vary according to campus/location and program.

Towson University, Jess and Mildred Fisher College of Science and Mathematics, Program in Integrated STEM Instructional Leadership, Towson, MD 21252-0001. Offers Postbaccalaureate Certificate. *Entrance requirements:* For degree, bachelor's degree, two years of teaching experience, minimum GPA of 3.0, two letters of recommendation, one-page personal statement, resume. Electronic applications accepted. *Expenses: Tuition, area resident:* Full-time $9196; part-time $418 per unit. Tuition, state resident: full-time $9196; part-time $418 per unit. Tuition, nonresident: full-time $19,030; part-time $865 per unit. *International tuition:* $19,030 full-time. *Required fees:* $3102; $141 per year. $423 per term. Tuition and fees vary according to campus/location and program.

Trevecca Nazarene University, Graduate Education Program, Nashville, TN 37210-2877. Offers accountability and instructional leadership (Ed S); curriculum and instruction for Christian school educators (M Ed); curriculum and instruction K-12 (M Ed); educational leadership (M Ed); English second language (M Ed); library and information science (MLI Sc); special education: visual impairments (M Ed); teaching (MAT), including teaching 6-12, teaching K-5. *Accreditation:* NCATE. *Program availability:* Part-time, evening/weekend, online learning. *Degree requirements:* For master's, comprehensive exam, exit assessment/e-portfolio. *Entrance requirements:* For master's, GRE or MAT; PRAXIS (for MAT), minimum GPA of 3.0, official transcript from regionally-accredited institution, references, interview, writing sample, at least 3 years' successful teaching experience (for M Ed in educational leadership); for Ed S, GRE or MAT, master's degree with minimum GPA of 3.0, official transcript from regionally accredited institution, at least 3 years' successful teaching experience, interview, writing sample, background and fingerprinting check, recommendations. Additional exam requirements/recommendations for international students: Required—TOEFL (minimum score 550 paper-based). Electronic applications accepted. *Expenses:* Contact institution.

Trevecca Nazarene University, Graduate Leadership Programs, Nashville, TN 37210-2877. Offers leadership and professional practice (Ed D); organizational leadership (MOL). *Program availability:* Online learning. *Degree requirements:* For master's, capstone course; for doctorate, thesis/dissertation, proposal study, symposium presentation. *Entrance requirements:* For master's, minimum GPA of 2.5, official transcript from regionally accredited institution; for doctorate, minimum GPA of 3.4, official transcript from regionally accredited institution, resume, writing sample, references. Additional exam requirements/recommendations for international students: Required—TOEFL (minimum score 550 paper-based; 80 iBT). Electronic applications accepted. *Expenses:* Contact institution.

Trident University International, College of Education, Program in Educational Leadership, Cypress, CA 90630. Offers e-learning leadership (MA Ed, PhD); educational leadership (MA Ed); higher education leadership (PhD); K-12 leadership (PhD). *Program availability:* Part-time, evening/weekend, online learning. *Degree requirements:* For doctorate, comprehensive exam, thesis/dissertation, defense of dissertation. *Entrance requirements:* For master's, minimum GPA of 2.5 (students with GPA 3.0 or greater may transfer up to 30% of graduate level credits); for doctorate, minimum GPA of 3.4, course work in research methods or statistics. Additional exam requirements/recommendations for international students: Required—TOEFL. Electronic applications accepted.

Trinity Baptist College, Graduate Programs, Jacksonville, FL 32221. Offers Bible (MA); curriculum and instruction (M Ed); educational leadership (M Ed); special education (M Ed). *Program availability:* Online learning. *Entrance requirements:* For master's, GRE (for M Ed), 2 letters of recommendation; minimum GPA of 2.5 (for M Min), 3.0 (for M Ed); goals essay; official transcripts.

Trinity University, Department of Education, San Antonio, TX 78212-7200. Offers school leadership (M Ed); school psychology (MA); teaching (MAT). *Accreditation:* NCATE. *Program availability:* Part-time, evening/weekend. *Faculty:* 17 full-time (14

women), 12 part-time/adjunct (9 women). *Students:* 40 full-time (30 women); includes 24 minority (2 Black or African American, non-Hispanic/Latino; 21 Hispanic/Latino; 1 Two or more races, non-Hispanic/Latino), 2 international. Average age 31. In 2018, 42 master's awarded. Tuition and fees vary according to program and student level. *Financial support:* Application deadline: 5/1; applicants required to submit FAFSA. *Unit head:* Norvella Carter, Interim Chair, 210-999-7506, Fax: 210-999-7592, E-mail: ncarter1@trinity.edu. *Application contact:* Office of Admissions, 210-999-7207, Fax: 210-999-8164, E-mail: admissions@trinity.edu.

Trinity Washington University, School of Education, Washington, DC 20017-1094. Offers clinical mental health counseling (MA); early childhood education (MAT); educating for change (M Ed); educational administration (MSA); elementary education (MAT); reading (M Ed); school counseling (MA); secondary education (MAT), including English, social studies; special education (MAT). *Accreditation:* NCATE. *Program availability:* Part-time, evening/weekend. *Degree requirements:* For master's, thesis (for some programs), capstone project(s). *Entrance requirements:* For master's, PRAXIS I, minimum GPA of 2.8. Additional exam requirements/recommendations for international students: Required—TOEFL (minimum score 550 paper-based). *Faculty research:* Technology, literacy, special education, organizations, inclusion models.

Trinity Western University, School of Graduate Studies, Program in Leadership, Langley, BC V2Y 1Y1, Canada. Offers business (MA, Certificate); Christian ministry (MA); education (MA, Certificate); healthcare (MA, Certificate); non-profit (MA, Certificate). *Program availability:* Online learning. *Degree requirements:* For master's, major project. *Entrance requirements:* For master's, minimum GPA of 2.7. Additional exam requirements/recommendations for international students: Required—TOEFL (minimum score 620 paper-based; 105 iBT). Electronic applications accepted. *Expenses:* Contact institution. *Faculty research:* Servant leadership.

Troy University, Graduate School, College of Education, Program in Educational Administration/Leadership, Troy, AL 36082. Offers MS, Ed S. *Accreditation:* NCATE. *Program availability:* Part-time, evening/weekend. *Faculty:* 3 full-time (2 women), 2 part-time/adjunct (both women). *Students:* 10 full-time (7 women), 18 part-time (15 women); includes 11 minority (all Black or African American, non-Hispanic/Latino). Average age 36. 27 applicants, 81% accepted, 17 enrolled. In 2018, 12 master's, 6 other advanced degrees awarded. *Degree requirements:* For master's, comprehensive exam, thesis, internship. *Entrance requirements:* For master's, GRE (minimum score of 850 on old exam or 290 on new exam), GMAT (minimum score of 380), or MAT (minimum score of 385), bachelor's degree; minimum undergraduate GPA of 2.5 or 3.0 on last 30 semester hours, letter of recommendation; 3 years of teaching experience; for Ed S, GRE (minimum score of 850 on old exam or 290 on new exam), GMAT (minimum score of 380), or MAT (minimum score of 380), master's degree. Additional exam requirements/recommendations for international students: Required—TOEFL (minimum score 523 paper-based; 70 iBT), IELTS (minimum score 6). *Application deadline:* Applications are processed on a rolling basis. Application fee: $50. Electronic applications accepted. *Expenses: Tuition, area resident:* Full-time $425; part-time $425 per credit hour. Tuition, state resident: full-time $425; part-time $425 per credit hour. Tuition, nonresident: full-time $850; part-time $850 per credit hour. *International tuition:* $850 full-time. *Required fees:* $50 per semester. Tuition and fees vary according to campus/location and program. *Financial support:* Available to part-time students. Applicants required to submit FAFSA. *Unit head:* Dr. Trellys Riley, Associate Professor, Assistant Dean, Chair, Ed. Admin & Leadership, 334-241-9575, E-mail: tariley@troy.edu. *Application contact:* Jessica A. Kimbro, Assistant Director of Graduate Programs, 334-670-3189, E-mail: jacord@troy.edu.

Union College, Graduate Programs, Department of Education, Barbourville, KY 40906-1499. Offers elementary education (MA); health and physical education (MA); middle grades (MA); music education (MA); principalship (MA); reading specialist (MA); secondary education (MA); special education (MA). *Degree requirements:* For master's, thesis optional. *Entrance requirements:* For master's, GRE General Test, NTE.

Union College, Graduate Programs, Educational Leadership Program, Barbourville, KY 40906-1499. Offers principalship (MA).

Union University, School of Education, Jackson, TN 38305-3697. Offers education (M Ed, MA Ed); education administration generalist (Ed S); educational leadership (Ed D); educational supervision (Ed S); higher education (Ed D). M Ed also available at Germantown campus. *Accreditation:* NCATE. *Program availability:* Part-time, evening/weekend, online learning. *Degree requirements:* For master's, thesis (for some programs), capstone research course (for MA Ed); performance exhibition (for M Ed); for doctorate, comprehensive exam, thesis/dissertation; for Ed S, thesis or alternative. *Entrance requirements:* For master's, MAT, PRAXIS II or GRE, minimum GPA of 3.0, teaching license (for M Ed only), writing sample; for doctorate, GRE, minimum graduate GPA of 3.2, writing sample; for Ed S, PRAXIS II, minimum graduate GPA of 3.2, writing sample. Additional exam requirements/recommendations for international students: Required—TOEFL (minimum score 560 paper-based; 80 iBT). Electronic applications accepted. *Expenses:* Contact institution. *Faculty research:* Mathematics education, brain compatible learning, transformational teaching, cognitive strategy development, instructional technology.

Universidad Adventista de las Antillas, EGECED Department, Mayagüez, PR 00681-0118. Offers curriculum and instruction (M Ed); medical surgical nursing (MN); school administration and supervision (M Ed). *Degree requirements:* For master's, comprehensive exam (for some programs), thesis (for some programs). *Entrance requirements:* For master's, EXADEP or GRE General Test, recommendations. Electronic applications accepted.

Universidad del Turabo, Graduate Programs, Programs in Education, Program in Educational Administration, Gurabo, PR 00778-3030. Offers M Ed. *Program availability:* Part-time, evening/weekend. *Entrance requirements:* For master's, GRE, EXADEP, GMAT, interview, official transcript, essay, recommendation letters. Electronic applications accepted.

Universidad del Turabo, Graduate Programs, Programs in Education, Program in Educational Leadership, Gurabo, PR 00778-3030. Offers D Ed. *Program availability:* Part-time, evening/weekend. *Entrance requirements:* For doctorate, GRE, EXADEP, GMAT, official transcript, recommendation letters, essay, curriculum vitae, interview. Electronic applications accepted.

Universidad Iberoamericana, Graduate School, Santo Domingo D.N., Dominican Republic. Offers business administration (MBA, PMBA); constitutional law (LL M); dentistry (DMD); educational management (MA); integrated marketing communication (MA); psychopedagogical intervention (M Ed); real estate law (LL M); strategic management of human talent (MM).

Universidad Metropolitana, School of Education, Program in Educational Administration and Supervision, San Juan, PR 00928-1150. Offers M Ed. *Program availability:* Part-time. *Degree requirements:* For master's, thesis or alternative. *Entrance requirements:* For master's, EXADEP, interview. Electronic applications accepted.

Universidad Metropolitana, School of Education, Program in Pre-School Centers Administration, San Juan, PR 00928-1150. Offers M Ed. *Program availability:* Part-time.

Degree requirements: For master's, thesis or alternative. *Entrance requirements:* For master's, EXADEP, interview. Electronic applications accepted.

Université de Moncton, Faculty of Education, Graduate Studies in Education, Moncton, NB E1A 3E9, Canada. Offers educational psychology (M Ed, MA Ed); guidance (M Ed, MA Ed); school administration (M Ed, MA Ed); teaching (M Ed, MA Ed). *Program availability:* Part-time. *Degree requirements:* For master's, proficiency in English and French. *Entrance requirements:* For master's, minimum GPA of 3.0. *Faculty research:* Guidance, ethnolinguistic vitality, children's rights, ecological education, entrepreneurship.

Université de Montréal, Faculty of Education, Department of Administration and Foundations of Education, Montréal, QC H3C 3J7, Canada. Offers M Ed, MA, PhD, DESS. *Program availability:* Part-time. *Degree requirements:* For master's, thesis; for doctorate, thesis/dissertation, general exam. *Entrance requirements:* For master's and DESS, bachelor's degree in related field with minimum B average; for doctorate, master's degree in related field with minimum B average. Electronic applications accepted. *Faculty research:* Pluriethnicity, formative education, comparative education, diagnostic evaluation.

Université de Sherbrooke, Faculty of Education, Program in School Administration, Sherbrooke, QC J1K 2R1, Canada. Offers M Ed. *Program availability:* Part-time, evening/weekend. *Degree requirements:* For master's, thesis.

Université du Québec à Trois-Rivières, Graduate Programs, Program in Educational Administration, Trois-Rivières, QC G9A 5H7, Canada. Offers DESS.

Université Laval, Faculty of Education, Department of Foundations and Interventions in Education, Programs in Educational Administration and Evaluation, Québec, QC G1K 7P4, Canada. Offers MA, PhD. Terminal master's awarded for partial completion of doctoral program. *Degree requirements:* For master's, thesis (for some programs); for doctorate, comprehensive exam, thesis/dissertation. *Entrance requirements:* For master's and doctorate, English exam (comprehension of written English), knowledge of French and English. Electronic applications accepted.

Université Laval, Faculty of Education, Department of Foundations and Interventions in Education, Programs in Educational Practice, Québec, QC G1K 7P4, Canada. Offers educational pedagogy (Diploma); pedagogy management and development (Diploma); school adaptation (Diploma). *Program availability:* Part-time. *Entrance requirements:* For degree, English exam (comprehension of written English), knowledge of French and English. Electronic applications accepted.

University at Albany, State University of New York, School of Education, Department of Educational Policy and Leadership, Albany, NY 12222-0001. Offers educational policy and leadership (MS, PhD); higher education (MS); international education management (CAS). *Program availability:* Evening/weekend. *Faculty:* 12 full-time (5 women), 3 part-time/adjunct (2 women). *Students:* 42 full-time (31 women), 132 part-time (84 women); includes 47 minority (21 Black or African American, non-Hispanic/Latino; 4 Asian, non-Hispanic/Latino; 20 Hispanic/Latino; 2 Two or more races, non-Hispanic/Latino), 23 international. Average age 32. 72 applicants, 71% accepted, 48 enrolled. In 2018, 11 master's, 7 doctorates, 12 other advanced degrees awarded. *Degree requirements:* For doctorate, one foreign language, thesis/dissertation. *Entrance requirements:* For doctorate, GRE General Test, GRE Subject Test. Additional exam requirements/recommendations for international students: Required—TOEFL (minimum score 550 paper-based). *Application deadline:* For fall admission, 2/1 for domestic students, 5/1 for international students; for spring admission, 9/1 for domestic students, 11/1 for international students. Applications are processed on a rolling basis. Application fee: $75. Electronic applications accepted. *Financial support:* Fellowships and career-related internships or fieldwork available. Financial award application deadline: 3/15. *Unit head:* Jason Lane, Chair, 518-442-5092, E-mail: jlane@albany.edu. *Application contact:* Jason Lane, Chair, 518-442-5092, E-mail: jlane@albany.edu. Website: http://www.albany.edu/epl/

University at Buffalo, the State University of New York, Graduate School, Graduate School of Education, Department of Educational Leadership and Policy, Buffalo, NY 14260. Offers economics and education policy analysis (MA); education studies (Ed M); educational administration (Ed M, Ed D, PhD); educational culture, policy and society (PhD); higher education administration (Ed M, PhD); school building leadership (Certificate); school business and human resource administration (Certificate); school district business leadership (Certificate); school district leadership (Certificate). *Program availability:* Part-time, evening/weekend. *Faculty:* 16 full-time (10 women), 11 part-time/adjunct (4 women). *Students:* 73 full-time (50 women), 128 part-time (82 women); includes 40 minority (21 Black or African American, non-Hispanic/Latino; 7 Asian, non-Hispanic/Latino; 11 Hispanic/Latino; 1 Two or more races, non-Hispanic/Latino), 19 international. Average age 34. 136 applicants, 69% accepted, 53 enrolled. In 2018, 39 master's, 20 doctorates, 25 other advanced degrees awarded. *Degree requirements:* For master's, comprehensive exam (for some programs), thesis optional; for doctorate, comprehensive exam, thesis/dissertation. *Entrance requirements:* For master's, interview, letters of reference; for doctorate, GRE General Test or MAT, writing sample, letters of reference. Additional exam requirements/recommendations for international students: Required—TOEFL (minimum score 600 paper-based; 79 iBT), IELTS (minimum score 6.5), PTE (minimum score 55). *Application deadline:* For fall admission, 2/1 priority date for domestic students, 2/1 for international students; for spring admission, 11/15 priority date for domestic students, 10/1 for international students. Applications are processed on a rolling basis. Application fee: $50. Electronic applications accepted. *Financial support:* In 2018–19, 18 fellowships (averaging $5,673 per year), 34 research assistantships with tuition reimbursements (averaging $12,055 per year) were awarded; career-related internships or fieldwork, Federal Work-Study, institutionally sponsored loans, scholarships/grants, health care benefits, tuition waivers (full and partial), and unspecified assistantships also available. Financial award application deadline: 3/15; financial award applicants required to submit FAFSA. *Faculty research:* College access and choice, school leadership preparation and practice, public policy, curriculum and pedagogy, comparative and international education. *Total annual research expenditures:* $637,951. *Unit head:* Dr. Nathan Daun-Barnett, Department Chair, 716-645-1096, Fax: 716-645-2481, E-mail: nbarnett@buffalo.edu. *Application contact:* Renad Aref, Assistant Director of Admission Recruitment, 716-645-2110, Fax: 716-645-7937, E-mail: gseinfo@buffalo.edu. Website: http://gse.buffalo.edu/elp

The University of Akron, Graduate School, College of Education, Department of Educational Foundations and Leadership, Akron, OH 44325. Offers principalship (MA, MS). *Accreditation:* NCATE. Terminal master's awarded for partial completion of doctoral program. *Degree requirements:* For master's, comprehensive exam (for some programs), thesis optional, written comprehensive exam or portfolio assessment. *Entrance requirements:* For master's, GRE, minimum GPA of 2.75, statement of purpose. Additional exam requirements/recommendations for international students: Required—TOEFL (minimum score 79 iBT), IELTS (minimum score 6.5). Electronic applications accepted. *Faculty research:* K-12 education law, K-12 education leadership, higher education leadership, postsecondary technical education, diversity of learned (K-16 U.S. and international).

Educational Leadership and Administration

The University of Alabama, Graduate School, College of Education, Department of Educational Leadership, Policy, and Technology Studies, Educational Administration Program, Tuscaloosa, AL 35487. Offers Ed D, PhD. *Program availability:* Part-time, evening/weekend. *Degree requirements:* For doctorate, comprehensive exam, thesis/dissertation. *Entrance requirements:* For doctorate, GRE or MAT, master's degree in field, minimum GPA of 3.0. Additional exam requirements/recommendations for international students: Recommended—TOEFL. Electronic applications accepted. *Faculty research:* Organizational theory, instructional supervision, data-based decision-making.

The University of Alabama, Graduate School, College of Education, Department of Educational Leadership, Policy, and Technology Studies, Educational Leadership Program, Tuscaloosa, AL 35487. Offers MA, Ed S. *Program availability:* Part-time, evening/weekend. *Degree requirements:* For master's, comprehensive exam, internship. *Entrance requirements:* For master's, MAT or GRE, 3 years of teaching experience, teaching certification, interview, portfolio, minimum GPA of 3.0; for Ed S, MAT or GRE, master's degree, minimum GPA of 3.0. Additional exam requirements/recommendations for international students: Required—TOEFL. Electronic applications accepted. *Faculty research:* Instructional supervision, school effectiveness, organizational theory, politics of education, educational law.

The University of Alabama, Graduate School, College of Education, Department of Educational Leadership, Policy, and Technology Studies, Higher Education Administration Program, Tuscaloosa, AL 35487. Offers MA, Ed D, PhD. *Program availability:* Evening/weekend, 100% online. Terminal master's awarded for partial completion of doctoral program. *Degree requirements:* For master's, capstone seminar; for doctorate, comprehensive exam, thesis/dissertation. *Entrance requirements:* For master's, GRE or MAT, minimum GPA of 3.0; for doctorate, GRE (for PhD), GRE or MAT (for Ed D), master's degree, minimum GPA of 3.0. Additional exam requirements/recommendations for international students: Required—TOEFL. Electronic applications accepted. *Faculty research:* College teaching and learning, faculty-administration relations, community colleges, organizational change, student affairs.

The University of Alabama, Graduate School, College of Education, Department of Educational Leadership, Policy, and Technology Studies, Instructional Leadership Program, Tuscaloosa, AL 35487. Offers Ed D, PhD. *Program availability:* Part-time, evening/weekend. *Degree requirements:* For doctorate, comprehensive exam, thesis/dissertation. *Entrance requirements:* Additional exam requirements/recommendations for international students: Recommended—TOEFL. Electronic applications accepted.

The University of Alabama at Birmingham, School of Education, Program in Educational Leadership, Birmingham, AL 35294. Offers MA Ed, Ed D, Ed S. Ed D, PhD offered jointly with The University of Alabama (Tuscaloosa). *Accreditation:* NCATE. *Program availability:* Part-time. *Degree requirements:* For master's, thesis optional; for doctorate, thesis/dissertation; for Ed S, comprehensive exam, thesis optional. *Entrance requirements:* For master's, MAT, minimum GPA of 3.0, 3 years' teaching, interview; for doctorate, MAT (at or above 50th percentile), minimum GPA of 3.0, Ed S in educational leadership, school leadership experience, references, writing sample; for Ed S, MAT (minimum score of 388), minimum GPA of 3.0, master's degree or Class A certification, references. Electronic applications accepted. *Expenses: Tuition, area resident:* Full-time $8100; part-time $8100 per year. Tuition, state resident: full-time $8100. Tuition, nonresident: full-time $19,188; part-time $19,188 per year. Tuition and fees vary according to program. *Faculty research:* Roles of assistant principals; mission, vision, and values of K-12; bullying.

University of Alaska Anchorage, School of Education, Program in Educational Leadership, Anchorage, AK 99508. Offers educational leadership (M Ed); principal (Certificate). *Program availability:* Part-time. *Entrance requirements:* For master's, GRE or MAT, interview, minimum GPA of 3.0. Additional exam requirements/recommendations for international students: Required—TOEFL (minimum score 550 paper-based).

University of Alaska Southeast, Graduate Programs, Program in Education, Juneau, AK 99801. Offers educational leadership (M Ed); elementary education (MAT); learning design and technology (M Ed); mathematics education (M Ed); reading specialist (M Ed); secondary education (MAT); special education (M Ed, MAT). *Accreditation:* NCATE. *Program availability:* Part-time, evening/weekend, online learning. *Degree requirements:* For master's, comprehensive exam or project, portfolio. *Entrance requirements:* For master's, PRAXIS, minimum GPA of 3.0, writing sample, letters of recommendation. Electronic applications accepted. *Faculty research:* Applied classroom research, culturally responsive practices, action research, teaching effectiveness.

University of Alberta, Faculty of Graduate Studies and Research, Department of Educational Policy Studies, Edmonton, AB T6G 2E1, Canada. Offers adult education (M Ed, Ed D, PhD); educational administration and leadership (M Ed, Ed D, PhD, Postgraduate Diploma); First Nations education (M Ed, Ed D, PhD); theoretical, cultural and international studies in education (M Ed, Ed D, PhD). *Degree requirements:* For master's, thesis (for some programs); for doctorate, thesis/dissertation. *Entrance requirements:* For master's, minimum GPA of 6.5 on a 9.0 scale; for doctorate, minimum GPA of 7.5 on a 9.0 scale. Additional exam requirements/recommendations for international students: Required—TOEFL (minimum score 580 paper-based). Electronic applications accepted.

The University of Arizona, College of Education, Department of Educational Policy Studies and Practice, Program of Educational Leadership, Tucson, AZ 85721. Offers M Ed, Ed D, Ed S. *Program availability:* Part-time. *Degree requirements:* For master's and Ed S, capstone experience; for doctorate, comprehensive exam, thesis/dissertation. *Entrance requirements:* For master's, leadership experience; for doctorate, GRE General Test, minimum GPA of 3.5, 3 letters of recommendation, curriculum vitae, writing sample. Additional exam requirements/recommendations for international students: Required—TOEFL (minimum score 550 paper-based; 79 iBT). Electronic applications accepted. *Faculty research:* School governance, higher order thinking, restructuring schools, bilingual education policy, authority in education.

University of Arkansas, Graduate School, College of Education and Health Professions, Department of Curriculum and Instruction, Program in Educational Leadership, Fayetteville, AR 72701. Offers M Ed, Ed D, Ed S. *Accreditation:* NCATE. *Program availability:* Part-time, evening/weekend. In 2018, 19 master's, 9 doctorates, 9 other advanced degrees awarded. *Entrance requirements:* For master's, GRE General Test, MAT or minimum GPA of 3.0; for doctorate, GRE General Test or MAT. *Application deadline:* For fall admission, 8/1 for domestic students, 4/1 for international students; for spring admission, 12/1 for domestic students, 10/1 for international students; for summer admission, 4/15 for domestic students, 3/1 for international students. Applications are processed on a rolling basis. Application fee: $60. Electronic applications accepted. *Financial support:* Fellowships with tuition reimbursements, research assistantships, teaching assistantships, career-related internships or fieldwork, and Federal Work-Study available. Support available to part-time students. Financial award application deadline: 4/1; financial award applicants required to submit FAFSA. *Unit head:* Dr. Cheryl Murphy, Department Head, 479-575-5111, Fax: 479-575-2492, E-mail: cmurphy@uark.edu. *Application contact:* Dr. Ed Bengston, Graduate Coordinator, 479-575-5092, Fax: 479-575-2492, E-mail: egbengst@uark.edu. Website: https://edle.uark.edu

University of Arkansas at Little Rock, Graduate School, College of Education and Health Professions, Department of Educational Leadership, Program in Educational Administration and Supervision, Little Rock, AR 72204-1099. Offers M Ed, Ed D, Ed S. *Program availability:* Part-time, evening/weekend. *Degree requirements:* For master's, comprehensive exam; for doctorate, comprehensive exam, oral defense of dissertation, residency; for Ed S, comprehensive exam, professional project. *Entrance requirements:* For master's, GRE General Test or MAT, 4 years of work experience (minimum 3 in teaching), interview, minimum GPA of 2.75, teaching certificate; for doctorate, GRE General Test or MAT, 4 years of work experience, minimum graduate GPA of 3.0, teaching certificate; for Ed S, GRE General Test or MAT, 4 years of work experience, minimum GPA of 2.75, teaching certificate.

University of Arkansas at Little Rock, Graduate School, College of Education and Health Professions, Department of Educational Leadership, Program in Higher Education, Little Rock, AR 72204-1099. Offers administration (MA); college student affairs (MA); health professions teaching and learning (MA); higher education (Ed D); two-year college teaching (MA). *Degree requirements:* For doctorate, comprehensive exam, oral defense of dissertation, residency. *Entrance requirements:* For master's, GRE General Test or MAT, interview, minimum graduate GPA of 3.0; for doctorate, GRE General Test, interview, minimum graduate GPA of 3.5, teaching certificate, three years of work experience.

University of Arkansas at Monticello, School of Education, Monticello, AR 71656. Offers education (M Ed, MAT); educational leadership (M Ed). *Accreditation:* NCATE. *Program availability:* Part-time, evening/weekend, online learning. *Degree requirements:* For master's, comprehensive exam. *Entrance requirements:* For master's, minimum GPA of 3.0. Additional exam requirements/recommendations for international students: Required—TOEFL (minimum score 550 paper-based). Electronic applications accepted.

University of Bridgeport, School of Education, Department of Education, Bridgeport, CT 06604. Offers education (MS); educational management (Ed D, Diploma), including intermediate administrator or supervisor (Diploma), leadership (Ed D); elementary education (MS, Diploma), including early childhood education, elementary education; middle school education (MS); music education (MS); remedial reading and language arts (Diploma); secondary education (MS, Diploma), including computer specialist (Diploma), international education (Diploma), reading specialist, secondary education. *Program availability:* Part-time, evening/weekend. *Degree requirements:* For master's, final exam, final project, or thesis; for doctorate, comprehensive exam, thesis/dissertation; for Diploma, thesis or alternative, final project. *Entrance requirements:* For master's, minimum undergraduate QPA of 2.67; for doctorate, GRE, MAT; for Diploma, GRE General Test or MAT, minimum graduate QPA of 3.0. Additional exam requirements/recommendations for international students: Recommended—TOEFL (minimum score 550 paper-based; 80 iBT), IELTS (minimum score 6.5). Electronic applications accepted. *Expenses:* Contact institution.

University of Bridgeport, School of Education, Department of Educational Leadership, Bridgeport, CT 06604. Offers intermediate administrator or supervisor (Diploma); leadership (Ed D). *Degree requirements:* For doctorate, comprehensive exam, thesis/dissertation; for Diploma, thesis or alternative, final project. *Entrance requirements:* For doctorate, GRE, MAT; for Diploma, GRE General Test or MAT, minimum graduate QPA of 3.0. Additional exam requirements/recommendations for international students: Recommended—TOEFL (minimum score 550 paper-based; 80 iBT), IELTS (minimum score 6.5). Electronic applications accepted. *Expenses:* Contact institution.

The University of British Columbia, Faculty of Education, Department of Educational Studies, Vancouver, BC V6T 1Z1, Canada. Offers adult learning and education (M Ed); adult learning and global change (M Ed); curriculum and leadership (M Ed); educational administration and leadership (M Ed); educational leadership and policy (Ed D); educational studies (M Ed, MA, PhD); higher education (M Ed); society, culture and politics in education (M Ed). *Program availability:* Part-time, evening/weekend. Terminal master's awarded for partial completion of doctoral program. *Degree requirements:* For master's, thesis; for doctorate, comprehensive exam, thesis/dissertation. *Entrance requirements:* For master's, minimum B+ average, 4-year undergraduate degree, field-related experience; for doctorate, minimum B+ average, 4-year undergraduate degree, master's degree, field-related experience. Additional exam requirements/recommendations for international students: Required—TOEFL (minimum score 600 paper-based; 100 iBT) or IELTS (minimum score 6.5). Electronic applications accepted. *Expenses:* Contact institution. *Faculty research:* Educational leadership educational administration adult education politics in education, global change and adult learning.

University of Calgary, Faculty of Graduate Studies, Werklund School of Education, Program in Educational Research, Calgary, AB T2N 1N4, Canada. Offers adult learning (M Ed, MA, Ed D, PhD); curriculum and learning (M Ed, MA, Ed D, PhD); educational leadership (M Ed, MA, Ed D, PhD); languages and diversity (M Ed, MA, Ed D, PhD); learning sciences (M Ed, MA, Ed D, PhD). Ed D in educational leadership offered via distance delivery. *Program availability:* Part-time, evening/weekend, online learning. *Degree requirements:* For master's, thesis (for some programs); for doctorate, thesis/dissertation, candidacy exam. *Entrance requirements:* For master's, minimum GPA of 3.0, 3 letters of reference; for doctorate, minimum GPA of 3.5, 3 letters of reference. Additional exam requirements/recommendations for international students: Required—TOEFL, IELTS. Electronic applications accepted. *Faculty research:* Curriculum, leadership, technology, contexts, gifted, second language teaching, work place and adult learning.

University of California, Berkeley, Graduate Division, School of Education, Programs in Education, Berkeley, CA 94720. Offers development in mathematics and science (MA); education in mathematics, science, and technology (MA, PhD); human development and education (MA, PhD); leadership education (MA); special education (PhD); teacher education (MA); MA/Credential; PhD/Credential; PhD/MA. Terminal master's awarded for partial completion of doctoral program. *Degree requirements:* For master's, exam or thesis; for doctorate, thesis/dissertation, oral qualifying exam. *Entrance requirements:* For master's and doctorate, GRE General Test, minimum GPA of 3.0 during last 2 years of undergraduate course work. Electronic applications accepted. *Faculty research:* Human development, social and moral educational psychology, developmental teacher preparation.

University of California, Irvine, School of Education, Irvine, CA 92697. Offers educational administration (Ed D); educational administration and leadership (Ed D); elementary and secondary education (MAT). *Program availability:* Part-time, evening/weekend. *Students:* 213 full-time (155 women), 3 part-time (2 women); includes 107 minority (1 Black or African American, non-Hispanic/Latino; 51 Asian, non-Hispanic/Latino; 40 Hispanic/Latino; 15 Two or more races, non-Hispanic/Latino), 23 international. Average age 28. 482 applicants, 47% accepted, 148 enrolled. In 2018, 141 master's, 8 doctorates awarded. *Entrance requirements:* For master's, GRE, minimum GPA of 3.0; for doctorate, GRE General Test, minimum GPA of 3.0. Additional exam requirements/recommendations for international students: Required—TOEFL (minimum score 550 paper-based). *Application deadline:* For fall admission, 1/2 priority date for domestic students, 1/2 for international students. Application fee: $105 ($125 for

international students). Electronic applications accepted. *Financial support:* Fellowships, research assistantships with full tuition reimbursements, institutionally sponsored loans, traineeships, health care benefits, and unspecified assistantships available. Financial award application deadline: 3/1; financial award applicants required to submit FAFSA. *Faculty research:* Education technology, learning theory, social theory, cultural diversity, postmodernism. *Unit head:* Richard Arum, Dean, 949-824-2534, E-mail: richard.arum@uci.edu. *Application contact:* Denise Earley, Assistant Director of Student Affairs, 949-824-4022, E-mail: denise.earley@uci.edu.
Website: http://education.uci.edu/

University of California, Los Angeles, Graduate Division, Graduate School of Education and Information Studies, Program in Educational Leadership, Los Angeles, CA 90095. Offers Ed D. *Program availability:* Evening/weekend. *Degree requirements:* For doctorate, thesis/dissertation, oral and written qualifying exams. *Entrance requirements:* For doctorate, GRE General Test, minimum undergraduate GPA of 3.0, resume. Electronic applications accepted.

University of California, Riverside, Graduate Division, Graduate School of Education, Riverside, CA 92521. Offers applied behavior analysis (M Ed); diversity and equity (M Ed); education policy analysis and leadership (PhD); education specialist (Credential); education, society, and culture (MA, PhD); educational psychology (MA, PhD); general education (M Ed); higher education administration and policy (M Ed, PhD); multiple subject (Credential); research, evaluation, measurement and statistics (MA); school psychology (PhD); single subject (Credential); special education (M Ed, PhD); special education and autism (MA); TESOL (M Ed). Terminal master's awarded for partial completion of doctoral program. *Degree requirements:* For master's, comprehensive exams or thesis (MA), case study or analytical report (M Ed); for doctorate, comprehensive exam, thesis/dissertation, written and oral qualifying exams, college teaching practicum. *Entrance requirements:* For master's, GRE General Test (for MA); CBEST and CSET (for M Ed in general education only), UCR Extension TESOL certificate (for M Ed with TESOL emphasis only); for doctorate, GRE General Test, writing sample; for Credential, CBEST, CSET. Additional exam requirements/recommendations for international students: Required—TOEFL (minimum score 550 paper-based; 80 iBT), IELTS (minimum score 7). Electronic applications accepted. *Faculty research:* Responsiveness to intervention, faculty core, response to intervention of English language learners, advanced modeling techniques, study on social capital, trust, and motivation.

University of California, San Diego, Graduate Division, Program in Education Studies, La Jolla, CA 92093. Offers education (M Ed, PhD); educational leadership (Ed D); teaching and learning (MA, Ed D), including bilingual education (MA), curriculum design (MA). Ed D offered jointly with California State University, San Marcos. *Students:* 100 full-time (78 women), 61 part-time (41 women). 262 applicants, 54% accepted, 81 enrolled. In 2018, 75 master's, 15 doctorates awarded. *Degree requirements:* For master's, thesis (for some programs), student teaching; for doctorate, comprehensive exam, thesis/dissertation. *Entrance requirements:* For master's, GRE General Test; CBEST and appropriate CSET exam (for select tracks), current teaching or educational assignment (for select tracks); for doctorate, GRE General Test, current teaching or educational assignment (for select tracks). Additional exam requirements/recommendations for international students: Required—TOEFL (minimum score 550 paper-based; 80 iBT), IELTS (minimum score 7). *Application deadline:* For fall admission, 12/6 for domestic students. Application fee: $105 ($125 for international students). Electronic applications accepted. *Financial support:* Fellowships, career-related internships or fieldwork, and scholarships/grants available. Financial award applicants required to submit FAFSA. *Faculty research:* Language, culture and literacy development of deaf/hard of hearing children; equity issues in education; educational reform; evaluation, assessment, and research methodologies; distributed learning. *Unit head:* Carolyn Hofstetter, Chair, 858-822-6688, E-mail: ajdaly@ucsd.edu. *Application contact:* Giselle Van Luit, Graduate Coordinator, 858-534-2958, E-mail: edsinfo@ucsd.edu.

University of Central Arkansas, Graduate School, College of Education, Department of Leadership Studies, Conway, AR 72035-0001. Offers college student personnel (MS); district-level administration (PMC); educational leadership - district level (Ed S); instructional technology (MS); library media and information technology (MS); school counseling (MS); school leadership (MS); school-based leadership adult education program administration (PMC); school-based leadership building administration (PMC); school-based leadership curriculum administration (PMC); school-based leadership gifted and talented program administration (PMC); school-based leadership special education program administration (PMC). *Accreditation:* NCATE. *Program availability:* Part-time, evening/weekend, online learning. *Degree requirements:* For master's and other advanced degree, comprehensive exam. *Entrance requirements:* For master's, GRE. Additional exam requirements/recommendations for international students: Required—TOEFL (minimum score 80 iBT). Electronic applications accepted. *Expenses:* Contact institution.

University of Central Florida, College of Community Innovation and Education, Department of Educational Leadership and Higher Education, Orlando, FL 32816. Offers career and technical education (MA); educational leadership (M Ed, MA, Ed S); higher education/college teaching and leadership (MA); higher education/student personnel (MA). *Program availability:* Part-time, evening/weekend. *Degree requirements:* For master's, thesis or alternative; for Ed S, thesis or alternative, final exam. *Entrance requirements:* For master's, GRE General Test; for Ed S, GRE General Test, minimum GPA of 3.0, resume, letters of recommendation. Additional exam requirements/recommendations for international students: Required—TOEFL. Electronic applications accepted.

University of Central Missouri, The Graduate School, Warrensburg, MO 64093. Offers accountancy (MA); accounting (MBA); applied mathematics (MS); aviation safety (MA); biology (MS); business administration (MBA); career and technical education leadership (MS); college student personnel administration (MS); communication (MA); computer science (MS); counseling (MS); criminal justice (MS); educational leadership (Ed D); educational technology (MS); elementary and early childhood education (MSE); English (MA); environmental studies (MA); finance (MBA); history (MA); human services/educational technology (Ed S); human services/learning resources (Ed S); human services/professional counseling (Ed S); industrial hygiene (MS); industrial management (MS); information systems (MBA); information technology (MS); kinesiology (MS); library science and information services (MS); literacy education (MSE); marketing (MBA); mathematics (MS); music (MA); occupational safety management (MS); psychology (MS); rural family nursing (MS); school administration (MSE); social gerontology (MS); sociology (MA); special education (MSE); speech language pathology (MS); superintendency (Ed S); teaching (MAT); teaching English as a second language (MA); technology (MS); technology management (PhD); theatre (MA). *Accreditation:* ASHA. *Program availability:* Part-time, 100% online, blended/hybrid learning. *Degree requirements:* For master's and Ed S, comprehensive exam (for some programs), thesis (for some programs). *Entrance requirements:* Additional exam requirements/recommendations for international students: Required—TOEFL (minimum score 550 paper-based; 79 iBT). Electronic applications accepted.

University of Central Oklahoma, The Jackson College of Graduate Studies, College of Education and Professional Studies, Donna Nigh Department of Advanced Professional and Special Services, Edmond, OK 73034-5209. Offers educational leadership (M Ed); library media education (M Ed); reading (M Ed); school counseling (M Ed); special education (M Ed), including mild/moderate disabilities, severe-profound/multiple disabilities; speech-language pathology (MS). *Accreditation:* ASHA. *Program availability:* Part-time. *Degree requirements:* For master's, comprehensive exam (for some programs), thesis (for some programs). *Entrance requirements:* Additional exam requirements/recommendations for international students: Required—TOEFL (minimum score 550 paper-based; 79 iBT), IELTS (minimum score 6.5). Electronic applications accepted.

University of Cincinnati, Graduate School, College of Education, Criminal Justice, and Human Services, School of Education, Program in Educational Leadership, Cincinnati, OH 45221. Offers M Ed, Ed S. *Accreditation:* NCATE. *Program availability:* Part-time, online learning. *Degree requirements:* For master's, thesis or alternative. *Entrance requirements:* For master's, GRE General Test, 3 letters of reference, resume, minimum GPA of 2.8; for Ed S, references, interview. Additional exam requirements/recommendations for international students: Required—TOEFL (minimum score 550 paper-based). Electronic applications accepted.

University of Cincinnati, Graduate School, College of Education, Criminal Justice, and Human Services, School of Education, Program in Urban Educational Leadership, Cincinnati, OH 45221. Offers Ed D. *Degree requirements:* For doctorate, thesis/dissertation. *Entrance requirements:* For doctorate, GRE General Test, GRE Subject Test. Additional exam requirements/recommendations for international students: Required—TOEFL (minimum score 550 paper-based), OEPT.

University of Colorado Colorado Springs, College of Education, Colorado Springs, CO 80918. Offers counseling and human services (MA); curriculum and instruction (MA); educational leadership (MA); educational leadership, research and policy (PhD); special education (MA); teaching English to speakers of other languages (MA). *Accreditation:* ACA; NCATE. *Program availability:* Part-time, evening/weekend, 100% online, blended/hybrid learning. *Faculty:* 31 full-time (22 women), 61 part-time/adjunct (47 women). *Students:* 208 full-time (149 women), 351 part-time (256 women); includes 136 minority (30 Black or African American, non-Hispanic/Latino; 1 American Indian or Alaska Native, non-Hispanic/Latino; 12 Asian, non-Hispanic/Latino; 64 Hispanic/Latino; 29 Two or more races, non-Hispanic/Latino), 8 international. Average age 36. 230 applicants, 80% accepted, 101 enrolled. In 2018, 186 master's, 9 doctorates awarded. *Degree requirements:* For master's, comprehensive exam, thesis or alternative, microcomputer proficiency; for doctorate, comprehensive exam, thesis/dissertation, research lab. *Entrance requirements:* For master's, GRE General Test (recommended but not required), career goal statement, professional references; for doctorate, GRE General Test. Additional exam requirements/recommendations for international students: Recommended—TOEFL (minimum score 90 iBT), IELTS (minimum score 6.5). *Application deadline:* For fall admission, 1/28 priority date for domestic and international students; for spring admission, 11/1 priority date for domestic and international students. Applications are processed on a rolling basis. Application fee: $60 ($100 for international students). Electronic applications accepted. *Expenses:* Tuition and fees vary by program, course load, and residency type. Please visit the University of Colorado Colorado Springs Student Financial Services website to estimate current program costs: https://www.uccs.edu/bursar/index.php/estimate-your-bill. *Financial support:* In 2018–19, 15 students received support. Career-related internships or fieldwork, Federal Work-Study, scholarships/grants, and unspecified assistantships available. Support available to part-time students. Financial award application deadline: 3/1; financial award applicants required to submit FAFSA. *Faculty research:* Linguistically diverse education (LDE), educational policy, evidence-based reading and writing instruction, relational and social aggression, positive behavior supports, inclusive schooling, K-12 education policy. *Total annual research expenditures:* $607,967. *Unit head:* Dr. Valerie Martin Conley, Dean, 719-255-4133, E-mail: vmconley@uccs.edu. *Application contact:* The College of Education Student Resource Office, 719-255-4996, E-mail: education@uccs.edu.
Website: https://www.uccs.edu/coe/

University of Colorado Denver, School of Education and Human Development, Administrative Leadership and Policy Studies Program, Denver, CO 80217. Offers MA, Ed S. *Accreditation:* NCATE. *Program availability:* Part-time, evening/weekend. *Degree requirements:* For master's, comprehensive exam, 9 credit hours beyond the 32 required for principal-administrator licensure; for Ed S, comprehensive exam, 9 credit hours beyond the 32 required for principal-administrator licensure (for those already holding MA). *Entrance requirements:* For master's and Ed S, GRE or MAT (if GPA is below 2.75), minimum GPA of 2.75, interview, 3 letters of recommendation, resume. Additional exam requirements/recommendations for international students: Required—TOEFL (minimum score 525 paper-based; 71 iBT); Recommended—IELTS (minimum score 6.3). Electronic applications accepted. *Expenses:* Tuition, state resident: full-time $6786; part-time $337 per credit hour. Tuition, nonresident: full-time $22,590; part-time $1255 per credit hour. *Required fees:* $1231; $137 per credit hour. Tuition and fees vary according to program and reciprocity agreements. *Faculty research:* Learning cultures, teaching and learning in educational administration.

University of Colorado Denver, School of Education and Human Development, Program in Educational Leadership and Innovation, Denver, CO 80217. Offers educational studies and research (PhD), including administrative leadership and policy, early childhood special education, math education, research, assessment and evaluation, science education, urban ecologies. *Program availability:* Part-time, evening/weekend. *Degree requirements:* For doctorate, comprehensive exam, thesis/dissertation, 75 credit hours (for PhD). *Entrance requirements:* For doctorate, GRE or equivalent, resume or curriculum vitae, letters of recommendation, master's degree or equivalent, completion of basic or advanced statistics course with minimum B grade. Additional exam requirements/recommendations for international students: Required—TOEFL (minimum score 537 paper-based; 75 iBT); Recommended—IELTS (minimum score 6.5). Electronic applications accepted. *Expenses:* Tuition, state resident: full-time $6786; part-time $337 per credit hour. Tuition, nonresident: full-time $22,590; part-time $1255 per credit hour. *Required fees:* $1231; $137 per credit hour. Tuition and fees vary according to program and reciprocity agreements. *Faculty research:* Administrative leadership and policy studies, early childhood education, research in diversity, paraprofessionals in education, urban schools lab.

University of Colorado Denver, School of Education and Human Development, Program in Education and Human Development, Denver, CO 80217. Offers administrative leadership and policy (PhD); assessment (MA); early childhood special education/early childhood education (PhD); family science and human development (PhD); human development and family relations (MA); learning (MA); mathematics education (PhD); research and evaluation methods (MA); research, assessment and evaluation (PhD); science education (PhD); urban ecologies (PhD). MA program also offered in partnership with Boulder Journey School, Friends School and Stanley British Primary School. *Program availability:* Part-time, evening/weekend. *Degree requirements:* For master's, comprehensive exam, 9 hours of core courses embedded within a minimum of 36 to 38 hours of relevant coursework, including an educational

psychology practicum, independent study project or thesis (recommended). *Entrance requirements:* For master's, GRE if undergraduate GPA below 2.75, resume, three letters of recommendation, transcripts. Additional exam requirements/recommendations for international students: Required—TOEFL (minimum score 537 paper-based; 75 iBT); Recommended—IELTS (minimum score 6.5). Electronic applications accepted. *Expenses:* Contact institution. *Faculty research:* Crisis response and intervention, school violence prevention, immigrant experience, educational environments for English language learners, culturally competent assessment and intervention, child and youth suicide.

University of Colorado Denver, School of Education and Human Development, Program in Leadership for Educational Equity, Denver, CO 80217. Offers executive leadership (Ed D); instructional leadership (Ed D). *Entrance requirements:* For doctorate, GRE General Test, resume with minimum of 5 years experience in an educational background, 2-3 professional artifacts illuminating leadership experiences, three professional letters of recommendation, master's degree with recommended minimum GPA of 3.2. *Expenses:* Tuition, state resident: full-time $6786; part-time $337 per credit hour. Tuition, nonresident: full-time $22,590; part-time $1255 per credit hour. *Required fees:* $1231; $137 per credit hour. Tuition and fees vary according to program and reciprocity agreements.

University of Connecticut, Graduate School, Neag School of Education, Department of Educational Leadership, Field of Educational Administration, Storrs, CT 06269. Offers MA. *Accreditation:* NCATE. *Entrance requirements:* Additional exam requirements/recommendations for international students: Required—TOEFL (minimum score 550 paper-based). Electronic applications accepted.

University of Dayton, Department of Counselor Education and Human Services, Dayton, OH 45469. Offers clinical mental health counseling (MS Ed); college student personnel (MS Ed); higher education administration (MS Ed); human services (MS Ed); school counseling (MS Ed); school psychology (MS Ed, Ed S). *Accreditation:* ACA; NCATE. *Program availability:* Part-time. *Degree requirements:* For master's, thesis (for some programs); for Ed S, thesis (for some programs), professional portfolio. *Entrance requirements:* For master's, MAT or GRE (if GPA less than 2.75), essays (for some programs). Additional exam requirements/recommendations for international students: Required—TOEFL (minimum score 550 paper-based; 80 iBT). Electronic applications accepted. *Expenses:* Contact institution. *Faculty research:* Student school bonding, traumatic brain injuries, wellness and counseling, creativity in education.

University of Dayton, Department of Educational Administration, Dayton, OH 45469. Offers Catholic school leadership (MS Ed); educational leadership (MS Ed, Ed S); leadership for educational systems (MS Ed). Ed S program in educational leadership offered jointly by the Graduate Schools of the University of Dayton and Wright State University. *Program availability:* Part-time, blended/hybrid learning. *Degree requirements:* For master's, thesis optional; for Ed S, thesis. *Entrance requirements:* For master's, MAT or GRE if undergraduate GPA is below 2.75. Additional exam requirements/recommendations for international students: Required—TOEFL (minimum score 550 paper-based; 80 iBT). Electronic applications accepted. *Expenses:* Contact institution. *Faculty research:* Data use for equity, school law, religion in education.

University of Dayton, Department of Teacher Education, Dayton, OH 45469. Offers adolescence to young adult education (MS Ed); early childhood leadership and advocacy (MS Ed); interdisciplinary education (MS Ed), including visual arts; interdisciplinary education studies (MS Ed); leadership in educational systems (MS Ed); literacy (MS Ed); mathematics education (MS Ed); middle childhood education (MS Ed); multi-age education (MS Ed), including world languages; music education (MS Ed); teacher as leader (MS Ed); teacher education (MS Ed); technology-enhanced learning (MS Ed); trans-disciplinary early childhood education (MS Ed). *Program availability:* Part-time, 100% online. *Degree requirements:* For master's, variable foreign language requirement, thesis or alternative, internship (for teaching licensure or endorsement). *Entrance requirements:* For master's, GRE (minimum score of 149 verbal, 4 on writing) or MAT (minimum score of 396) if undergraduate GPA was under 2.75, minimum GPA of 2.75, 3 letters of recommendation, personal statement or resume, official transcripts. Additional exam requirements/recommendations for international students: Required—TOEFL (minimum score 550 paper-based; 80 iBT); Recommended—IELTS (minimum score 6.5). Electronic applications accepted. *Expenses:* Contact institution. *Faculty research:* Social emotional learning, culturally responsive teaching, urban teaching, literacy, instructional strategies, pre-service teacher education preparation.

University of Dayton, PhD Program in Educational Leadership, Dayton, OH 45469. Offers educational leadership (PhD). *Program availability:* Part-time. *Degree requirements:* For doctorate, comprehensive exam, thesis/dissertation. *Entrance requirements:* For doctorate, GRE (minimum score of 149 verbal, 4.0 writing), official transcripts, 3 letters of recommendation, 500-700 word essay, current resume, interview. Additional exam requirements/recommendations for international students: Required—TOEFL (minimum score 550 paper-based; 80 iBT), GRE. Electronic applications accepted. *Expenses:* Contact institution. *Faculty research:* School law; school finance; leadership, diversity, research methodology.

University of Delaware, College of Education and Human Development, School of Education, Newark, DE 19716. Offers education (PhD); educational leadership (Ed D); higher education (M Ed); instruction (MI); reading (M Ed); school leadership (M Ed); school psychology (MA, Ed S); teaching English as a second language (TESL) (MA). *Accreditation:* NCATE. *Program availability:* Part-time, evening/weekend. Terminal master's awarded for partial completion of doctoral program. *Degree requirements:* For master's, comprehensive exam (for some programs), thesis (for some programs); for doctorate, comprehensive exam (for some programs), thesis/dissertation. *Entrance requirements:* For master's and doctorate, GRE, 3 letters of recommendation. Additional exam requirements/recommendations for international students: Required—TOEFL (minimum score 600 paper-based). Electronic applications accepted. *Faculty research:* Teacher education; curriculum theory and development; community based education models, educational leadership.

University of Denver, Morgridge College of Education, Denver, CO 80208. Offers child, family and school psychology (MA, PhD, Ed S); counseling psychology (MA, PhD); curriculum and instruction (MA, Ed D, PhD); curriculum instruction and teaching (Certificate); early childhood special education (MA, Certificate); educational leadership and policy studies (MA, Ed D, PhD, Certificate); higher education (Ed D, PhD); library and information science (MLIS); research methods and statistics (MA, PhD). *Accreditation:* ALA; APA (one or more programs are accredited). *Program availability:* Part-time, evening/weekend, online learning. *Faculty:* 49 full-time (35 women), 33 part-time/adjunct (20 women). *Students:* 509 full-time (400 women), 365 part-time (277 women); includes 236 minority (53 Black or African American, non-Hispanic/Latino; 6 American Indian or Alaska Native, non-Hispanic/Latino; 28 Asian, non-Hispanic/Latino; 116 Hispanic/Latino; 33 Two or more races, non-Hispanic/Latino), 56 international. Average age 31. 1,372 applicants, 57% accepted, 382 enrolled. In 2018, 258 master's, 41 doctorates, 162 other advanced degrees awarded. Terminal master's awarded for partial completion of doctoral program. *Degree requirements:* For master's, comprehensive exam (for some programs); for doctorate, comprehensive exam (for some programs), thesis/dissertation. *Entrance requirements:* For master's, GRE General Test or GMAT, bachelors degree; transcripts; two letters of recommendation; personal statement; resume; for doctorate, GRE General Test or GMAT, Masters degree; transcripts; two letters of recommendation; personal statement(s); resume. Additional exam requirements/recommendations for international students: Required—TOEFL (minimum score 550 paper-based; 80 iBT). *Application deadline:* Applications are processed on a rolling basis. Application fee: $65. Electronic applications accepted. *Expenses:* $33,183 per year full-time. *Financial support:* In 2018–19, 690 students received support, including 29 research assistantships with tuition reimbursements available (averaging $11,465 per year), 9 teaching assistantships with tuition reimbursements available (averaging $2,527 per year); career-related internships or fieldwork, Federal Work-Study, institutionally sponsored loans, scholarships/grants, and unspecified assistantships also available. Support available to part-time students. Financial award application deadline: 2/15; financial award applicants required to submit FAFSA. *Faculty research:* Early childhood education, educational leadership, access and opportunity to postsecondary education, marriage and family therapy, data management and archival research. *Total annual research expenditures:* $2.3 million. *Unit head:* Dr. Karen Riley, Dean, 303-871-3665, E-mail: karen.riley@du.edu. *Application contact:* Jodi Dye, Director of Admissions, 303-871-2510, E-mail: jodi.dye@du.edu.
Website: http://morgridge.du.edu

University of Detroit Mercy, College of Liberal Arts and Education, Detroit, MI 48221. Offers addiction counseling (MA); addiction studies (Certificate); clinical mental health counseling (MA); clinical psychology (MA, PhD); computer and information systems (MS); criminal justice (MA); curriculum and instruction (MA); economics (MA); educational administration (MA); financial economics (MA); industrial/organizational psychology (MA); information assurance (MS); intelligence analysis (MA); liberal studies (MALS); religious studies (MA); school counseling (MA, Certificate); school psychology (Spec); security administration (MS); special education: emotionally impaired/behaviorally disordered (MA); special education: learning disabilities (MA). *Program availability:* Part-time, evening/weekend. *Degree requirements:* For doctorate, departmental qualifying exam. *Faculty research:* Psychology of aging, history of technology, Renaissance humanism, U.S. and Japanese economic relations.

The University of Findlay, Office of Graduate Admissions, Findlay, OH 45840-3653. Offers applied security and analytics (MSAS); athletic training (MAT); business (MBA), including certified management accountant, certified public accountant, health care management, hospitality management; education (MA Ed, Ed D), including children's literature (MA Ed), curriculum and teaching (MA Ed), education (MA Ed), educational administration (MA Ed), human resource development (MA Ed), mathematics (MA Ed), reading (MA Ed), science education (MA Ed), superintendent (Ed D), teaching (Ed D), technology (MA Ed); environmental, safety, and health management (MSEM); health informatics (MS); occupational therapy (MOT); pharmacy (Pharm D); physical therapy (DPT); physician assistant (MPA); rhetoric and writing (MA); teaching English to speakers of other languages (TESOL) and applied linguistics (MA). *Program availability:* Part-time, evening/weekend, 100% online, blended/hybrid learning. *Degree requirements:* For master's, comprehensive exam (for some programs), thesis (for some programs), cumulative project, capstone project; for doctorate, thesis/dissertation (for some programs). *Entrance requirements:* For master's, GRE/GMAT, bachelor's degree from accredited institution, minimum undergraduate GPA of 2.5 in last 64 hours of course work; for doctorate, GRE, MAT, minimum cumulative GPA of 3.0. Additional exam requirements/recommendations for international students: Required—TOEFL (minimum score 79 iBT), IELTS (minimum score 7), PTE (minimum score 61). Electronic applications accepted.

University of Florida, Graduate School, College of Education, School of Human Development and Organizational Studies in Education, Gainesville, FL 32611. Offers counseling and counselor education (Ed D, PhD), including counseling and counselor education, marriage and family counseling, mental health counseling, school counseling and guidance; educational leadership (M Ed, MAE, Ed D, PhD, Ed S), including educational leadership (Ed D, PhD), educational policy (Ed D, PhD); higher education administration (Ed D, PhD), including education policy (Ed D), educational policy, higher education administration; marriage and family counseling (M Ed, MAE, Ed D, PhD, Ed S); mental health counseling (M Ed, MAE, Ed D, PhD, Ed S); research and evaluation methodology (M Ed, MAE, Ed D, PhD); school counseling and guidance (M Ed, MAE, Ed D, PhD, Ed S); student personnel in higher education (M Ed, MAE). *Accreditation:* ACA (one or more programs are accredited); NCATE. *Program availability:* Part-time, online learning. Terminal master's awarded for partial completion of doctoral program. *Degree requirements:* For master's, thesis optional; for doctorate, comprehensive exam, thesis/dissertation. *Entrance requirements:* For master's and doctorate, GRE General Test, minimum GPA of 3.0 (undergraduate), 3.5 (graduate); for Ed S, GRE General Test. Additional exam requirements/recommendations for international students: Required—TOEFL (minimum score 550 paper-based; 80 iBT), IELTS (minimum score 6). Electronic applications accepted.

University of Georgia, College of Education, Department of Lifelong Education, Administration and Policy, Athens, GA 30602. Offers adult education (Ed D, Ed S); lifelong education, administration and policy (PhD). *Accreditation:* NCATE. *Entrance requirements:* For doctorate, GRE General Test; for Ed S, GRE General Test or MAT. Electronic applications accepted.

University of Guam, Office of Graduate Studies, School of Education, Program in Administration and Supervision, Mangilao, GU 96923. Offers M Ed. *Degree requirements:* For master's, comprehensive oral and written exams, special project or thesis. *Entrance requirements:* For master's, GRE General Test. Additional exam requirements/recommendations for international students: Required—TOEFL.

University of Hartford, College of Education, Nursing, and Health Professions, Doctoral Program in Educational Leadership, West Hartford, CT 06117-1599. Offers Ed D. *Accreditation:* NCATE. *Program availability:* Part-time, evening/weekend. *Degree requirements:* For doctorate, thesis/dissertation. *Entrance requirements:* For doctorate, MAT, 3 letters of recommendation, writing samples, interview, resume, letter of support from employer. *Expenses:* Contact institution.

University of Hawaii at Manoa, Office of Graduate Education, College of Education, Department of Educational Administration, Honolulu, HI 96822. Offers M Ed. *Program availability:* Part-time. *Degree requirements:* For master's, thesis optional. *Entrance requirements:* Additional exam requirements/recommendations for international students: Required—TOEFL (minimum score 600 paper-based; 100 iBT), IELTS (minimum score 7). *Faculty research:* Leadership, educational policy, organizational processes, finance.

University of Hawaii at Manoa, Office of Graduate Education, College of Education, Ed D in Professional Practice Program, Honolulu, HI 96822. Offers Ed D. *Entrance requirements:* Additional exam requirements/recommendations for international students: Required—TOEFL (minimum score 600 paper-based; 100 iBT).

University of Hawaii at Manoa, Office of Graduate Education, College of Education, PhD in Education Program, Honolulu, HI 96822. Offers curriculum and instruction (PhD); educational administration (PhD); educational foundations (PhD); educational policy studies (PhD); educational psychology (PhD); exceptionalities (PhD); kinesiology (PhD);

learning design and technology (PhD). *Program availability:* Part-time, evening/weekend. *Degree requirements:* For doctorate, thesis/dissertation. *Entrance requirements:* For doctorate, GRE General Test, sample of written work. Additional exam requirements/recommendations for international students: Required—TOEFL (minimum score 600 paper-based; 100 iBT), IELTS (minimum score 7).

University of Holy Cross, Graduate Programs, New Orleans, LA 70131-7399. Offers biomedical sciences (MS); Catholic theology (MA); counseling (MA, PhD), including community counseling (MA), marriage and family counseling (MA), school counseling (MA); educational leadership (M Ed); executive leadership (Ed D); management (MS), including healthcare management, operations management; teaching and learning (M Ed). *Accreditation:* ACA; NCATE. *Program availability:* Part-time, evening/weekend, online learning. *Degree requirements:* For master's, thesis. *Entrance requirements:* For master's, GRE General Test, minimum GPA of 2.7.

University of Houston, College of Education, Department of Curriculum and Instruction, Houston, TX 77204. Offers administration and supervision (M Ed); curriculum and instruction (M Ed, Ed D), including art education (M Ed); professional leadership (Ed D), including health science education. None. *Accreditation:* NCATE. *Program availability:* Part-time-only, evening/weekend, 100% online, blended/hybrid learning. *Faculty:* 35 full-time (26 women), 2 part-time/adjunct (1 woman). *Students:* 126 full-time (103 women), 266 part-time (207 women); includes 222 minority (81 Black or African American, non-Hispanic/Latino; 2 American Indian or Alaska Native, non-Hispanic/Latino; 36 Asian, non-Hispanic/Latino; 95 Hispanic/Latino; 1 Native Hawaiian or other Pacific Islander, non-Hispanic/Latino; 7 Two or more races, non-Hispanic/Latino), 27 international. Average age 36. 185 applicants, 85% accepted, 80 enrolled. In 2018, 50 master's, 36 doctorates awarded. Terminal master's awarded for partial completion of doctoral program. *Degree requirements:* For master's, comprehensive exam, thesis optional; for doctorate, comprehensive exam, thesis/dissertation. *Entrance requirements:* For master's and doctorate, GRE, minimum cumulative undergraduate GPA of 2.6, 3 letters of recommendation, resume/vita, goal statement. Additional exam requirements/recommendations for international students: Required—TOEFL (minimum score 550 paper-based; 79 iBT). *Application deadline:* For fall admission, 3/1 for domestic and international students; for spring admission, 10/1 for domestic and international students. Application fee: $80 ($75 for international students). Electronic applications accepted. Application fee is waived when completed online. *Financial support:* In 2018–19, 14 students received support, including 9 research assistantships with full tuition reimbursements available (averaging $8,608 per year), 26 teaching assistantships with full tuition reimbursements available (averaging $8,560 per year); career-related internships or fieldwork, Federal Work-Study, institutionally sponsored loans, scholarships/grants, health care benefits, and unspecified assistantships also available. Support available to part-time students. Financial award application deadline: 2/1; financial award applicants required to submit FAFSA. *Faculty research:* Teaching-learning process, instructional technology in schools, teacher education, classroom management, at-risk students. *Total annual research expenditures:* $1.7 million. *Unit head:* Dr. Margaret A. Hale, Interim Department Chair, 713-743-5037, E-mail: mhale@uh.edu. *Application contact:* Bridget D. Jones, Director of Student Affairs, 713-743-2978, E-mail: bajones5@uh.edu.
Website: http://www.coe.uh.edu/academic-departments/cuin/index.php

University of Houston, College of Education, Department of Psychological, Health and Learning Sciences, Houston, TX 77204. Offers administration and supervision - higher education (M Ed); counseling (M Ed); counseling psychology (PhD); educational psychology (M Ed); school psychology (PhD); school psychology and individual differences (PhD); special education (M Ed). None. *Accreditation:* NCATE. *Program availability:* Part-time, evening/weekend, 100% online, blended/hybrid learning. *Faculty:* 31 full-time (23 women), 3 part-time/adjunct (1 woman). *Students:* 163 full-time (135 women), 51 part-time (43 women); includes 106 minority (35 Black or African American, non-Hispanic/Latino; 1 American Indian or Alaska Native, non-Hispanic/Latino; 18 Asian, non-Hispanic/Latino; 46 Hispanic/Latino; 6 Two or more races, non-Hispanic/Latino), 17 international. Average age 29. 216 applicants, 58% accepted, 60 enrolled. In 2018, 39 master's, 18 doctorates awarded. Terminal master's awarded for partial completion of doctoral program. *Degree requirements:* For master's, comprehensive exam or thesis; for doctorate, comprehensive exam, thesis/dissertation. *Entrance requirements:* For master's, GRE, transcripts, 3 letters of recommendation, curriculum vita, goal statement; for doctorate, GRE, transcripts, 3 letters of recommendation, curriculum vita, goal statement, writing sample, interview. Additional exam requirements/recommendations for international students: Required—TOEFL (minimum score 550 paper-based; 79 iBT). *Application deadline:* For fall admission, 1/15 for domestic and international students; for spring admission, 9/15 for domestic and international students. Applications are processed on a rolling basis. Application fee: $80 ($75 for international students). Electronic applications accepted. Application fee is waived when completed online. *Financial support:* In 2018–19, 10 students received support, including 5 fellowships with full tuition reimbursements available (averaging $2,000 per year), 8 research assistantships with full tuition reimbursements available (averaging $8,664 per year), 56 teaching assistantships with full tuition reimbursements available (averaging $8,760 per year); career-related internships or fieldwork, Federal Work-Study, institutionally sponsored loans, scholarships/grants, health care benefits, and unspecified assistantships also available. Support available to part-time students. Financial award application deadline: 2/1. *Faculty research:* Evidence-based assessment and intervention, multicultural issues in psychology, social and cultural context of learning, systemic barriers to college, motivational aspects of self-regulated learning. *Total annual research expenditures:* $1.9 million. *Unit head:* Dr. Nathan Grant Smith, Interim Department Chair, 713-743-7648, Fax: 713-743-4996, E-mail: ngsmith@uh.edu. *Application contact:* Bridgette Jones, Director of Student Affairs, 713-743-2978, E-mail: bajones5@uh.edu.
Website: http://www.uh.edu/education/departments/phls/

University of Houston–Clear Lake, School of Education, Program in Educational Leadership, Houston, TX 77058-1002. Offers educational leadership (Ed D); educational management (MS). *Degree requirements:* For master's, thesis optional; for doctorate, comprehensive exam, thesis/dissertation.

University of Houston–Victoria, School of Education, Health Professions and Human Development, Victoria, TX 77901-4450. Offers administration and supervision (M Ed); adult and higher education (M Ed); counselor education (M Ed); curriculum and instruction (M Ed); dyslexia education (Certificate); educational technology (M Ed); special education (M Ed). *Program availability:* Part-time, evening/weekend, online learning. *Degree requirements:* For master's, comprehensive exam, project or thesis. *Entrance requirements:* For master's, GRE General Test. Additional exam requirements/recommendations for international students: Required—TOEFL. Electronic applications accepted. *Expenses: Tuition, area resident:* Full-time $6154; part-time $3077 per semester. Tuition, state resident: full-time $6154; part-time $3077 per semester. Tuition, nonresident: full-time $13,624; part-time $6812 per semester. *International tuition:* $13,624 full-time. *Required fees:* $1405; $847 per semester. $423 per semester. Tuition and fees vary according to program. *Faculty research:* Reading and language arts education, evaluation and diagnosis of special children's abilities.

University of Idaho, College of Graduate Studies, College of Education, Health and Human Sciences, Department of Leadership and Counseling, Boise, ID 83702. Offers adult/organizational learning and leadership (Ed S); educational leadership (Ed S); rehabilitation counseling and human services (M Ed); school counseling (M Ed, MS). *Faculty:* 14. *Students:* 32 full-time (19 women), 123 part-time (68 women). Average age 37. In 2018, 53 master's, 22 other advanced degrees awarded. *Entrance requirements:* For master's, minimum GPA of 3.0, writing sample. Additional exam requirements/recommendations for international students: Required—TOEFL (minimum score 79 iBT). *Application deadline:* Applications are processed on a rolling basis. Application fee: $60. Electronic applications accepted. *Expenses:* Tuition, state resident: full-time $7266.44; part-time $474.50 per credit hour. Tuition, nonresident: full-time $24,902; part-time $1453.50 per credit hour. *Required fees:* $2085.56; $45.50 per credit hour. *Financial support:* Applicants required to submit FAFSA. *Unit head:* Dr. Kathy Canfield-Davis, Chair, 208-364-4047, E-mail: lead@uidaho.edu. *Application contact:* Dr. Kathy Canfield-Davis, Chair, 208-364-4047, E-mail: lead@uidaho.edu.
Website: https://www.uidaho.edu/ed/lc

University of Illinois at Chicago, College of Education, Department of Educational Policy Studies, Chicago, IL 60607-7128. Offers policy studies (M Ed); policy studies in urban education (PhD); urban education leadership (Ed D). *Faculty research:* Social foundations of education, educational organizations and leadership, education policy analysis, understanding and addressing educational problems in urban contexts.

University of Illinois at Springfield, Graduate Programs, College of Education and Human Services, Department of Educational Leadership, Springfield, IL 62703-5407. Offers MA, CAS, Graduate Certificate. *Program availability:* Part-time, evening/weekend, 100% online, blended/hybrid learning. *Faculty:* 5 full-time (1 woman), 10 part-time/adjunct (8 women). *Students:* 2 full-time (both women), 93 part-time (56 women); includes 9 minority (6 Black or African American, non-Hispanic/Latino; 1 Asian, non-Hispanic/Latino; 1 Hispanic/Latino; 1 Two or more races, non-Hispanic/Latino). Average age 35. 52 applicants, 40% accepted, 18 enrolled. In 2018, 25 master's, 4 other advanced degrees awarded. *Degree requirements:* For master's, capstone course. *Entrance requirements:* For master's, minimum undergraduate GPA of 3.0, valid Illinois Teaching License, current resume, minimum of two years of successful teaching experience, portfolio that includes letters of recommendation, interview. Additional exam requirements/recommendations for international students: Required—TOEFL (minimum score 500 paper-based; 61 iBT). *Application deadline:* Applications are processed on a rolling basis. Application fee: $60 ($75 for international students). Electronic applications accepted. *Financial support:* In 2018–19, research assistantships with full tuition reimbursements (averaging $10,384 per year), teaching assistantships with full tuition reimbursements (averaging $10,303 per year) were awarded; fellowships, career-related internships or fieldwork, Federal Work-Study, scholarships/grants, health care benefits, and unspecified assistantships also available. Support available to part-time students. Financial award application deadline: 11/15; financial award applicants required to submit FAFSA. *Unit head:* Dr. Vickie Cook, Interim Program Administrator, 217-206-7520, Fax: 217-206-6775, E-mail: vcook02s@uis.edu. *Application contact:* Dr. Vickie Cook, Interim Program Administrator, 217-206-7520, Fax: 217-206-6775, E-mail: vcook02s@uis.edu.
Website: http://www.uis.edu/edl/

University of Illinois at Urbana–Champaign, Graduate College, College of Education, Department of Education Policy, Organization, and Leadership, Champaign, IL 61820. Offers educational organization and leadership (Ed M, MS, Ed D, PhD, CAS); educational policy studies (Ed M, MA, PhD); human resource education (Ed M, MS, Ed D, PhD, CAS). *Program availability:* Part-time, online learning.

University of Indianapolis, Graduate Programs, School of Education, Indianapolis, IN 46227-3697. Offers art education (MAT); biology (MAT); chemistry (MAT); curriculum and instruction (MA); earth sciences (MAT); education (MA, MAT); educational leadership (MA); elementary education (MA); English (MAT); French (MAT); math (MAT); physical education (MAT); physics (MAT); secondary education (MA), including art education, education, English education, social studies education; social studies (MAT); Spanish (MAT). *Accreditation:* NCATE. *Program availability:* Part-time, evening/weekend. *Entrance requirements:* For master's, GRE Subject Test, PRAXIS I, minimum GPA of 2.5, 3 letters of recommendation, interview. Additional exam requirements/recommendations for international students: Required—TOEFL (minimum score 550 paper-based). *Faculty research:* Assessment of teacher education, perceptions of prospective teachers by parents.

The University of Iowa, Graduate College, College of Education, Department of Educational Policy and Leadership Studies, Program in Educational Leadership, Iowa City, IA 52242-1316. Offers MA, PhD, Ed S. *Degree requirements:* For master's and Ed S, exam; for doctorate, comprehensive exam, thesis/dissertation. *Entrance requirements:* For master's, doctorate, and Ed S, GRE General Test, minimum GPA of 3.0. Additional exam requirements/recommendations for international students: Required—TOEFL (minimum score 550 paper-based; 81 iBT). Electronic applications accepted.

The University of Kansas, Graduate Studies, School of Education, Department of Educational Leadership and Policy Studies, Education Leadership and Policy Program, Lawrence, KS 66045-3101. Offers policy studies (PhD); social and cultural studies in education (MSE, PhD). *Program availability:* Part-time, evening/weekend. *Students:* 131 full-time (74 women), 52 part-time (25 women); includes 44 minority (18 Black or African American, non-Hispanic/Latino; 2 American Indian or Alaska Native, non-Hispanic/Latino; 3 Asian, non-Hispanic/Latino; 9 Hispanic/Latino; 12 Two or more races, non-Hispanic/Latino), 32 international. Average age 38. 58 applicants, 76% accepted, 32 enrolled. In 2018, 29 doctorates awarded. *Entrance requirements:* For master's, minimum GPA of 3.0, resume or curriculum vitae, statement of purpose, official academic transcripts, three letters of recommendation; for doctorate, GRE General Test, minimum graduate GPA of 3.5, resume or curriculum vitae, statement of purpose, official academic transcripts, three letters of recommendation, writing sample. Additional exam requirements/recommendations for international students: Required—TOEFL, IELTS. *Application deadline:* For fall admission, 7/1 for domestic and international students; for spring admission, 11/1 for domestic and international students; for summer admission, 4/1 for domestic and international students. Application fee: $65 ($85 for international students). Electronic applications accepted. *Financial support:* Fellowships, research assistantships, teaching assistantships, scholarships/grants, and unspecified assistantships available. Financial award application deadline: 3/15. *Faculty research:* Historical and philosophical issues in education, education policy and leadership, higher education faculty, research on college students, education technology. *Unit head:* Dr. Susan B. Twombly, Chair, 785-864-9721, E-mail: stwombly@ku.edu. *Application contact:* Denise Brubaker, Admissions Coordinator, 785-864-7973, E-mail: brubaker@ku.edu.
Website: http://elps.soe.ku.edu/

The University of Kansas, Graduate Studies, School of Education, Department of Educational Leadership and Policy Studies, Program in Educational Administration, Lawrence, KS 66045-3101. Offers MSE, Ed D, PhD. Program begins in summer semester only. *Program availability:* Part-time, evening/weekend, online learning. *Students:* 4 full-time (0 women), 85 part-time (60 women); includes 14 minority (8 Black

or African American, non-Hispanic/Latino; 1 American Indian or Alaska Native, non-Hispanic/Latino; 3 Hispanic/Latino; 2 Two or more races, non-Hispanic/Latino), 1 international. Average age 32. 41 applicants, 93% accepted, 33 enrolled. In 2018, 66 master's awarded. *Entrance requirements:* For master's, minimum GPA of 3.0, resume, statement of purpose, official transcript, three letters of recommendation; for doctorate, GRE General Test, minimum graduate GPA of 3.5, resume, statement of purpose, academic transcripts, three letters of recommendation, writing sample. Additional exam requirements/recommendations for international students: Required—TOEFL, IELTS. *Application deadline:* For fall admission, 8/7 for domestic students; for spring admission, 12/20 for domestic students; for summer admission, 4/17 for domestic students. Application fee: $65 ($85 for international students). Electronic applications accepted. *Financial support:* Research assistantships, teaching assistantships, Federal Work-Study, scholarships/grants, and unspecified assistantships available. Financial award application deadline: 3/1. *Unit head:* Dr. Susan B. Twombly, Chair, 785-864-9721, Fax: 785-864-4697, E-mail: stwombly@ku.edu. *Application contact:* Denise Brubaker, Admissions Coordinator, 785-864-7973, Fax: 785-864-4697, E-mail: brubaker@ku.edu.
Website: http://elps.soe.ku.edu/academics/edadmin/mse

University of Kentucky, Graduate School, College of Education, Program in Educational Leadership Studies, Lexington, KY 40506-0032. Offers educational leadership (M Ed, Ed D, PhD, Ed S); educational sciences (PhD); family resource and youth services (M Ed, Ed S); principalship (Ed D, Ed S); school technology leadership (M Ed, PhD, Ed S); teacher leadership (M Ed, Ed S). *Degree requirements:* For master's and Ed S, comprehensive exam; for doctorate, comprehensive exam, thesis/dissertation. *Entrance requirements:* For master's, GRE General Test, minimum undergraduate GPA of 2.75; for doctorate, GRE General Test, minimum graduate GPA of 3.0. Additional exam requirements/recommendations for international students: Required—TOEFL (minimum score 550 paper-based). Electronic applications accepted. *Faculty research:* School governance, teacher empowerment, planned change, systemic reform, issues of equity and fairness.

University of La Verne, LaFetra College of Education, Doctoral Program in Organizational Leadership, La Verne, CA 91750-4443. Offers Ed D. *Program availability:* Part-time. *Entrance requirements:* For doctorate, GRE or MAT, minimum graduate GPA of 3.0, resume or curriculum vitae, 2 endorsement forms. Additional exam requirements/recommendations for international students: Required—TOEFL (minimum score 550 paper-based). *Expenses:* Contact institution.

University of La Verne, LaFetra College of Education, Master's Program in Education, La Verne, CA 91750-4443. Offers advanced teaching skills (M Ed); education (M Ed); educational leadership (M Ed); special emphasis (M Ed). *Accreditation:* NCATE. *Program availability:* Part-time. *Entrance requirements:* For master's, California Basic Educational Skills Test, interview, writing sample, minimum GPA of 3.0, 3 letters of recommendation. Additional exam requirements/recommendations for international students: Required—TOEFL (minimum score 550 paper-based). *Expenses:* Contact institution.

University of La Verne, Regional and Online Campuses, Graduate Credential Program in Education, California Statewide Campus, La Verne, CA 91750-4443. Offers administration services (preliminary) (Credential); education specialist: mild/moderate (Credential); English (Certificate); multiple subject teaching (Credential); pupil personnel services: school counseling (Credential); single subject teaching (Credential); special education (MS); special emphasis (M Ed). *Accreditation:* NCATE. *Program availability:* Part-time. *Entrance requirements:* For degree, California Basic Educational Skills Test, minimum undergraduate GPA of 2.75, 3 letters of recommendation, interview. *Expenses:* Contact institution.

University of La Verne, Regional and Online Campuses, Graduate Programs, High Desert Campus, Victorville, CA 92392. Offers business administration for experienced professionals (MBA); educational (special emphasis) (M Ed); educational counseling (MS); leadership and management (MS); multiple subject (elementary) (Credential); preliminary administrative services (Credential); pupil personnel services (Credential); single subject (secondary) (Credential). *Expenses:* Contact institution.

University of La Verne, Regional and Online Campuses, Graduate Programs, Kern County Campus, Bakersfield, CA 93301. Offers business administration for experienced professionals (MBA-EP); education (special emphasis) (M Ed); educational counseling (MS); educational leadership (M Ed); health administration (MHA); leadership and management (MS); mild/moderate education specialist (Credential); multiple subject (elementary) (Credential); organizational leadership (Ed D); preliminary administrative services (Credential); single subject (secondary) (Credential); special education studies (MS). *Program availability:* Part-time, evening/weekend. *Expenses:* Contact institution.

University of La Verne, Regional and Online Campuses, Graduate Programs, Orange County Campus, Irvine, CA 92840. Offers business administration for experienced professionals (MBA); educational counseling (MS); educational leadership (M Ed); health administration (MHA); leadership and management (MS); preliminary administrative services (Credential); pupil personnel services (Credential). *Program availability:* Part-time. *Expenses:* Contact institution.

University of La Verne, Regional and Online Campuses, Graduate Programs, San Fernando Valley Campus, Burbank, CA 91505. Offers business administration for experienced professionals (MBA-EP); educational counseling (MS); educational leadership (M Ed); leadership and management (MS); preliminary administrative services (Credential); pupil personnel services (Credential). *Program availability:* Part-time, evening/weekend. *Expenses:* Contact institution.

University of La Verne, Regional and Online Campuses, Graduate Programs, Ventura County/Point Mugu Naval Air Station Campuses, Oxnard, CA 93036. Offers business administration for experienced professionals (MS); educational counseling (MS); educational leadership (M Ed); leadership and management (MS); multiple subject (elementary) (Credential); pupil personnel services (Credential); single subject (secondary) (Credential). *Program availability:* Part-time, evening/weekend. *Expenses:* Contact institution.

University of La Verne, Regional and Online Campuses, Master's Programs in Education, California Statewide Campus, La Verne, CA 91750-4443. Offers administration services (preliminary) (Credential); education specialist: mild/moderate (Credential); educational counseling (MS); educational leadership (M Ed); multiple subject teaching (Credential); pupil personnel services: school counseling (Credential); single subject teaching (Credential); special education studies (MS); special emphasis (M Ed). *Accreditation:* NCATE. *Entrance requirements:* For master's, California Basic Educational Skills Test, 3 letters of recommendation, teaching credential. *Expenses:* Contact institution.

University of Lethbridge, School of Graduate Studies, Lethbridge, AB T1K 3M4, Canada. Offers addictions counseling (M Sc); agricultural biotechnology (M Sc); agricultural studies (M Sc, MA); anthropology (MA); archaeology (M Sc, MA); art (MA, MFA); biochemistry (M Sc); biological sciences (M Sc); biomolecular science (PhD); biosystems and biodiversity (PhD); Canadian studies (MA); chemistry (M Sc); computer science (M Sc); computer science and geographical information science (M Sc); counseling (MC); counseling psychology (M Ed); dramatic arts (MA); earth, space, and physical science (PhD); economics (MA); education (MA, PhD); educational leadership (M Ed); English (MA); environmental science (M Sc); evolution and behavior (PhD); exercise science (M Sc); French (MA); French/German (MA); French/Spanish (MA); general education (M Ed); geography (M Sc, MA); German (MA); health sciences (M Sc); individualized multidisciplinary (M Sc, MA); kinesiology (M Sc, MA); management (M Sc), including accounting, finance, human resource management and labor relations, information systems, international management, marketing, policy and strategy; mathematics (M Sc); music (M Mus, MA); Native American studies (MA); neuroscience (M Sc, PhD); new media (MA, MFA); nursing (M Sc, MN); philosophy (MA); physics (M Sc); political science (MA); psychology (M Sc, MA); religious studies (MA); sociology (MA); theatre and dramatic arts (MFA); theoretical and computational science (PhD); urban and regional studies (MA); women and gender studies (MA). *Program availability:* Part-time, evening/weekend. *Degree requirements:* For master's, thesis (for some programs); for doctorate, comprehensive exam, thesis/dissertation. *Entrance requirements:* For master's, GMAT (for M Sc in management), bachelor's degree in related field, minimum GPA of 3.0 during previous 20 graded semester courses, 2 years' teaching or related experience (M Ed); for doctorate, master's degree, minimum graduate GPA of 3.5. Additional exam requirements/recommendations for international students: Required—TOEFL (minimum score 580 paper-based; 93 iBT). Electronic applications accepted. *Faculty research:* Movement and brain plasticity, gibberellin physiology, photosynthesis, carbon cycling, molecular properties of main-group ring components.

University of Louisiana at Lafayette, College of Education, Department of Educational Curriculum and Instruction, Program in Curriculum and Instruction, Lafayette, LA 70504. Offers instructional specialist (M Ed); K-8 mathematics education (M Ed); non-public school administration (M Ed); special education diagnostics (M Ed); teacher researcher (M Ed). *Accreditation:* NCATE. *Entrance requirements:* For master's, GRE General Test, teaching certificate. Additional exam requirements/recommendations for international students: Required—TOEFL (minimum score 550 paper-based). Electronic applications accepted.

University of Louisiana at Lafayette, College of Education, Department of Educational Foundations and Leadership, Lafayette, LA 70504. Offers M Ed, Ed D. *Entrance requirements:* Additional exam requirements/recommendations for international students: Required—TOEFL (minimum score 550 paper-based).

University of Louisville, Graduate School, College of Education and Human Development, Department of Educational Leadership, Evaluation and Organizational Development, Louisville, KY 40292-0001. Offers educational leadership and organizational development (Ed D, PhD), including evaluation (PhD), human resource development (PhD), P-12 administration (PhD), post-secondary administration (PhD), sport administration (MA, PhD); health professions education (Certificate); higher education administration (MA), including sport administration (MA, PhD); human resources and organization development (MS), including health professions education, human resource leadership, workplace learning and performance; P-12 educational administration (Ed S), including principalship, supervisor of instruction. *Accreditation:* NCATE. *Program availability:* Part-time, evening/weekend, 100% online, blended/hybrid learning. *Students:* 200 full-time (82 women), 474 part-time (262 women); includes 218 minority (127 Black or African American, non-Hispanic/Latino; 1 American Indian or Alaska Native, non-Hispanic/Latino; 18 Asian, non-Hispanic/Latino; 46 Hispanic/Latino; 2 Native Hawaiian or other Pacific Islander, non-Hispanic/Latino; 24 Two or more races, non-Hispanic/Latino), 5 international. Average age 36. 257 applicants, 77% accepted, 170 enrolled. In 2018, 111 master's, 10 doctorates, 22 other advanced degrees awarded. Terminal master's awarded for partial completion of doctoral program. *Degree requirements:* For master's, comprehensive exam (for some programs), thesis (for some programs); for doctorate, comprehensive exam (for some programs), thesis/dissertation. *Entrance requirements:* For master's, GRE (for most programs), PRAXIS (for educator preparation programs), professional statement, recommendation letters, resume, transcripts; for doctorate and other advanced degree, GRE, professional statement, recommendation letters, resume, transcripts. Additional exam requirements/recommendations for international students: Required—TOEFL (minimum score 550 paper-based; 79 iBT); Recommended—IELTS (minimum score 6.5). *Application deadline:* For fall admission, 6/1 priority date for domestic students, 5/1 priority date for international students; for spring admission, 10/1 priority date for domestic students, 11/1 priority date for international students; for summer admission, 3/1 for domestic students, 4/1 priority date for international students. Application fee: $65. *Expenses: Tuition, area resident:* Full-time $6500; part-time $723 per credit hour. Tuition, state resident: full-time $6500. Tuition, nonresident: full-time $13,557; part-time $1507 per credit hour. Tuition and fees vary according to course load and program. *Financial support:* In 2018–19, 144 students received support, including fellowships (averaging $21,024 per year), research assistantships with full tuition reimbursements available (averaging $21,024 per year), teaching assistantships with full tuition reimbursements available (averaging $21,024 per year); Federal Work-Study, scholarships/grants, health care benefits, tuition waivers (full), and unspecified assistantships also available. Financial award application deadline: 3/1; financial award applicants required to submit FAFSA. *Faculty research:* Human resources and organizational development; career, technical, health professions, and economic education; health professions education; community and military partnerships; higher education. *Unit head:* Dr. Sharron Kerrick, Chair, 502-852-6475, E-mail: lead@louisville.edu. *Application contact:* Dr. Margaret Pentecost, Assistant Dean for Graduate Student Success, 502-852-6437, Fax: 502-852-1417, E-mail: gedadm@louisville.edu.
Website: http://louisville.edu/education/departments/eleod

University of Louisville, Graduate School, College of Education and Human Development, Departments of Early Childhood and Elementary Education, Middle and Secondary Education, and Special Education, Louisville, KY 40292-0001. Offers art education (MAT); autism and applied behavior analysis (Certificate); curriculum and instruction (PhD); early elementary education (MAT); exercise physiology (MS); health and physical education (MAT); health professions education (Certificate); higher education (MA); human resources and organization development (MS); instructional technology (M Ed); interdisciplinary early childhood education (MAT); middle school education (MAT); music education (MAT); secondary education (MAT); special education (MAT); sport administration (MS); teacher leadership (M Ed). *Program availability:* Part-time, evening/weekend, 100% online, blended/hybrid learning. *Faculty:* 97 full-time (64 women), 131 part-time/adjunct (86 women). *Students:* 109 full-time (72 women), 139 part-time (87 women); includes 43 minority (18 Black or African American, non-Hispanic/Latino; 6 Asian, non-Hispanic/Latino; 10 Hispanic/Latino; 9 Two or more races, non-Hispanic/Latino), 9 international. Average age 29. 108 applicants, 75% accepted, 59 enrolled. In 2018, 64 master's awarded. Terminal master's awarded for partial completion of doctoral program. *Degree requirements:* For master's, comprehensive exam (for some programs), thesis optional; for doctorate, comprehensive exam (for some programs), thesis/dissertation. *Entrance requirements:* For master's, GRE (for most programs), PRAXIS (for educator preparation programs), professional statement, recommendation letters, resume, transcripts; for doctorate and Certificate, GRE, professional statement, recommendation letters, resume, transcripts. Additional exam requirements/recommendations for international students: Required—TOEFL (minimum score 550 paper-based; 79 iBT); Recommended—IELTS (minimum

score 6.5). *Application deadline:* For fall admission, 6/1 priority date for domestic students, 5/1 priority date for international students; for spring admission, 10/1 for domestic students, 11/1 priority date for international students; for summer admission, 3/1 priority date for domestic students, 4/1 priority date for international students. Application fee: $65. *Expenses: Tuition, area resident:* Full-time $6500; part-time $723 per credit hour. Tuition, state resident: full-time $6500. Tuition, nonresident: full-time $13,557; part-time $1507 per credit hour. Tuition and fees vary according to course load and program. *Financial support:* In 2018–19, 144 students received support, including fellowships with full tuition reimbursements available (averaging $21,024 per year), research assistantships with full tuition reimbursements available (averaging $21,024 per year), teaching assistantships with full tuition reimbursements available (averaging $21,024 per year); Federal Work-Study, scholarships/grants, health care benefits, tuition waivers (full), and unspecified assistantships also available. Financial award application deadline: 3/1; financial award applicants required to submit FAFSA. *Faculty research:* Children's early reading and writing development, crelevance of basic facts in elementary mathematics instruction, clinical model of teacher education, cultural and linguistic context of diverse learners, and STEM-integrated curriculum design and development. STEM teaching and learning, content literacy for English language learners, social justice in teacher education, adolescent literacy, mathematics teacher development. Classroom and behavior management; moderate/severe disabilities, autism. *Unit head:* Dr. Amy Lingo, Interim Dean, 502-852-3235, Fax: 502-852-1464, E-mail: cehdinfo@louisville.edu. *Application contact:* Dr. Margaret Pentecost, Assistant Dean for Graduate Student Success, 502-852-6437, Fax: 502-852-1417, E-mail: gedadm@louisville.edu.
Website: http://louisville.edu/delphi

University of Lynchburg, Graduate Studies, Ed D in Leadership Studies Program, Lynchburg, VA 24501-3199. Offers educational leadership (Ed D). *Program availability:* Part-time, evening/weekend. *Degree requirements:* For doctorate, comprehensive exam, thesis/dissertation. *Entrance requirements:* For doctorate, GRE or GMAT, current resume or curriculum vitae, career goals statement, master's degree, official transcripts (bachelor's, master's, others of relevance), master's-level research course, three letters of recommendation, evidence of strong writing skills. Additional exam requirements/recommendations for international students: Required—TOEFL (minimum score 550 paper-based; 80 iBT), IELTS (minimum score 6). Electronic applications accepted. Application fee is waived when completed online. *Expenses:* Contact institution.

University of Lynchburg, Graduate Studies, M Ed Program in Educational Leadership, Lynchburg, VA 24501-3199. Offers higher education (M Ed); PK-12 administrative and supervisory (M Ed). *Program availability:* Part-time, evening/weekend. *Degree requirements:* For master's, comprehensive exam (for some programs), internship; SLLC exam or comprehensive exam. *Entrance requirements:* For master's, GRE, minimum GPA of 3.0 (preferred), official transcripts (bachelor's, others as relevant), three letters of recommendation, career goals statement. Additional exam requirements/recommendations for international students: Required—TOEFL (minimum score 550 paper-based; 80 iBT), IELTS (minimum score 6). Electronic applications accepted. Application fee is waived when completed online. *Expenses:* Contact institution.

University of Maine, Graduate School, College of Education and Human Development, School of Educational Leadership, Higher Education, and Human Development, Orono, ME 04469. Offers educational leadership (M Ed, CAS); higher education (CAS); human development (MS). *Program availability:* Part-time. *Faculty:* 11 full-time (7 women), 10 part-time/adjunct (5 women). *Students:* 72 full-time (53 women), 64 part-time (44 women); includes 11 minority (3 Black or African American, non-Hispanic/Latino; 4 Asian, non-Hispanic/Latino; 4 Hispanic/Latino), 1 international. Average age 37. 101 applicants, 85% accepted, 49 enrolled. In 2018, 18 master's, 4 doctorates, 10 other advanced degrees awarded. *Degree requirements:* For master's, thesis (for some programs); for doctorate, comprehensive exam, thesis/dissertation. *Entrance requirements:* For master's, GRE General Test, MAT; for doctorate, GRE. Additional exam requirements/recommendations for international students: Required—TOEFL (minimum score 550 paper-based; 80 iBT), IELTS (minimum score 6.5). *Application deadline:* For fall admission, 2/1 priority date for domestic students. Applications are processed on a rolling basis. Application fee: $65. Electronic applications accepted. *Financial support:* In 2018–19, 39 students received support, including 3 teaching assistantships with full tuition reimbursements available (averaging $15,600 per year); career-related internships or fieldwork, Federal Work-Study, institutionally sponsored loans, tuition waivers (full and partial), and unspecified assistantships also available. Financial award application deadline: 3/1. *Faculty research:* Student hazing and hazing prevention, sexuality education, cross cultural perspectives on family, early childhood development, fatherhood/parenting, campus climate, social justice, rural higher education, gender in higher education, discourse, rural sociology, school-community relationships, instructional supervision, rural educational leadership. *Unit head:* Dr. Jim Artesani, Associate Dean of Accreditation and Graduate Affairs, 207-581-4061, Fax: 207-581-3120. *Application contact:* Scott G. Delcourt, Senior Associate Dean of the Graduate School, 207-581-3291, Fax: 207-581-3232, E-mail: graduate@maine.edu.
Website: http://www.umaine.edu/edhd/

University of Maine at Farmington, Graduate Programs in Education, Farmington, ME 04938. Offers early childhood education (MS Ed); educational leadership (MS Ed); instructional technology (M Ed). M Ed offered in collaboration with University of Maine and University of Southern Maine. *Accreditation:* NCATE. *Program availability:* Part-time-only, evening/weekend, 100% online, blended/hybrid learning. *Degree requirements:* For master's, thesis, capstone research project. *Entrance requirements:* For master's, baccalaureate degree from accredited institution, valid teaching certificate or professional experience in education. Additional exam requirements/recommendations for international students: Required—TOEFL. Electronic applications accepted. *Expenses:* Contact institution. *Faculty research:* Teacher leadership, school improvement strategies, technology integration.

University of Manitoba, Faculty of Graduate Studies, Faculty of Education, Department of Educational Administration, Foundations and Psychology, Winnipeg, MB R3T 2N2, Canada. Offers adult and post-secondary education (M Ed); educational administration (M Ed); guidance and counseling (M Ed); inclusive special education (M Ed); social foundations of education (M Ed). *Degree requirements:* For master's, thesis or alternative.

University of Mary, Liffrig Family School of Education and Behavioral Sciences, Department of Education, Bismarck, ND 58504-9652. Offers curriculum, instruction and assessment (M Ed); education (Ed D); elementary administration (M Ed); reading (M Ed); secondary administration (M Ed); special education strategist (M Ed). *Program availability:* Part-time. *Degree requirements:* For master's, portfolio or thesis. *Entrance requirements:* For master's, interview, letters of reference, minimum GPA of 2.5. Additional exam requirements/recommendations for international students: Required—TOEFL (minimum score 500 paper-based; 71 iBT). Electronic applications accepted.

University of Mary Hardin-Baylor, Graduate Studies in Education, Belton, TX 76513. Offers curriculum and instruction (M Ed); educational administration (M Ed, Ed D), including higher education (Ed D), leadership in nursing education (Ed D), P-12 (Ed D). *Program availability:* Part-time, evening/weekend. *Degree requirements:* For master's, comprehensive exam; for doctorate, thesis/dissertation. *Entrance requirements:* For master's, minimum GPA of 3.0, interview; for doctorate, minimum GPA of 3.5, interview, essay, resume, employment verification, 3 letters of recommendation. Additional exam requirements/recommendations for international students: Required—TOEFL (minimum score 60 iBT), IELTS (minimum score 4.5). Electronic applications accepted. *Expenses:* Contact institution. *Faculty research:* Motivational orientation of preservice teachers.

University of Maryland, College Park, Academic Affairs, College of Education, Department of Counseling, Higher Education and Special Education, College Park, MD 20742. Offers college student personnel (M Ed, MA); college student personnel administration (PhD); community counseling (CAGS); community/career counseling (M Ed, MA); counseling and personnel services (M Ed, MA, PhD), including art therapy (M Ed), college student personnel (M Ed), counseling and personnel services (PhD), counseling psychology (M Ed), mental health counseling (M Ed), school counseling (M Ed); counseling psychology (PhD); counselor education (PhD); rehabilitation counseling (M Ed, MA, AGSC); school counseling (M Ed, MA); school psychology (M Ed, MA, PhD). *Accreditation:* APA (one or more programs are accredited); NCATE. *Program availability:* Part-time, evening/weekend, online learning. *Degree requirements:* For master's, thesis (for some programs); for doctorate, thesis/dissertation. *Entrance requirements:* For master's, GRE General Test or MAT, minimum GPA of 3.0, 3 letters of recommendation; for doctorate, GRE General Test or MAT, minimum GPA of 3.5, 3 letters of recommendation. Additional exam requirements/recommendations for international students: Required—TOEFL. Electronic applications accepted. *Faculty research:* Educational psychology, counseling, health.

University of Maryland, College Park, Academic Affairs, College of Education, Department of Education Policy and Leadership, College Park, MD 20742. Offers curriculum and educational communications (M Ed, MA, Ed D, PhD); social foundations of education (M Ed, MA, Ed D, PhD, CAGS). *Accreditation:* NCATE. *Program availability:* Part-time, evening/weekend, online learning. *Degree requirements:* For master's, thesis or alternative, internship and/or field experience; for doctorate, comprehensive exam, thesis/dissertation, practicum or internship. *Entrance requirements:* For master's, GRE General Test or MAT, minimum GPA of 3.0, scholarly writing sample, 3 letters of recommendation; for doctorate, GRE General Test or MAT, scholarly writing sample; minimum undergraduate GPA of 3.0, graduate 3.5. *Faculty research:* Educational technology, adult and higher education.

University of Maryland Eastern Shore, Graduate Programs, Department of Education, Program in Education Leadership, Princess Anne, MD 21853. Offers Ed D. *Program availability:* Evening/weekend. *Degree requirements:* For doctorate, comprehensive exam, thesis/dissertation, internship. *Entrance requirements:* For doctorate, interview, writing sample, state certification in a standard area, 3 years of recent teaching or successful professional experience in K-12 school setting. Additional exam requirements/recommendations for international students: Required—TOEFL (minimum score 80 iBT). Electronic applications accepted.

University of Massachusetts Amherst, Graduate School, College of Education, Program in Education, Amherst, MA 01003. Offers bilingual, English as a second language, and multicultural education (M Ed, Ed S); child study and early education (M Ed); children, families and schools (Ed D, Ed S); early childhood and elementary teacher education (M Ed); educational leadership (M Ed); educational policy and leadership (Ed D); higher education (M Ed); international education (M Ed); language, literacy and culture (Ed D); learning, media and technology (M Ed, Ed S); mathematics, science, and learning technologies (Ed D); reading and writing (M Ed); research, educational measurement and psychometrics (Ed D); school counselor education (M Ed, Ed S); school psychology (Ed S); science education (Ed S); secondary teacher education (M Ed); social justice education (M Ed, Ed D, Ed S); special education (M Ed, Ed D, Ed S); teacher education and school improvement (Ed D, Ed S). *Accreditation:* NCATE. *Program availability:* Part-time, online learning. Terminal master's awarded for partial completion of doctoral program. *Degree requirements:* For doctorate, comprehensive exam, thesis/dissertation. *Entrance requirements:* Additional exam requirements/recommendations for international students: Required—TOEFL (minimum score 550 paper-based; 80 iBT), IELTS (minimum score 6.5). Electronic applications accepted.

University of Massachusetts Boston, College of Education and Human Development, Program in Educational Administration, Boston, MA 02125-3393. Offers M Ed, CAGS. *Program availability:* Part-time, evening/weekend. *Students:* 13 part-time (7 women); includes 6 minority (3 Black or African American, non-Hispanic/Latino; 3 Hispanic/Latino), 2 international. Average age 34. 20 applicants, 60% accepted, 7 enrolled. In 2018, 7 master's, 26 CAGSs awarded. *Application deadline:* For fall admission, 3/12 for domestic students. Application fee: $60 ($100 for international students). Electronic applications accepted. *Expenses: Tuition, area resident:* Full-time $17,896. Tuition, state resident: full-time $17,896. Tuition, nonresident: full-time $34,932. *International tuition:* $34,932 full-time. *Required fees:* $355. *Financial support:* Research assistantships, teaching assistantships, career-related internships or fieldwork, Federal Work-Study, and unspecified assistantships available. Support available to part-time students. Financial award application deadline: 3/1; financial award applicants required to submit FAFSA. *Faculty research:* Power in the classroom, teacher leadership, professional development schools. *Unit head:* Casel Walker, Graduate Program Director, 617-287.4848, E-mail: casel.walker@umb.edu. *Application contact:* Graduate Admissions Coordinator, 617-287-6400, Fax: 617-287-6236, E-mail: graduate.admissions@umb.edu.

University of Massachusetts Boston, College of Education and Human Development, Program in Urban Education, Leadership, and Policy Studies, Boston, MA 02125-3393. Offers Ed D, PhD. *Program availability:* Part-time, evening/weekend. *Faculty:* 11 full-time (7 women), 10 part-time/adjunct (6 women). *Students:* 1 (woman) full-time, 43 part-time (29 women); includes 19 minority (8 Black or African American, non-Hispanic/Latino; 10 Hispanic/Latino; 1 Two or more races, non-Hispanic/Latino), 3 international. Average age 38. 18 applicants, 33% accepted, 3 enrolled. In 2018, 3 doctorates awarded. *Entrance requirements:* For doctorate, GRE General Test or MAT, minimum GPA of 2.75. *Application deadline:* For summer admission, 3/1 for domestic students. Application fee: $60 ($100 for international students). Electronic applications accepted. *Expenses: Tuition, area resident:* Full-time $17,896. Tuition, state resident: full-time $17,896. Tuition, nonresident: full-time $34,932. *International tuition:* $34,932 full-time. *Required fees:* $355. *Financial support:* Research assistantships, teaching assistantships, career-related internships or fieldwork, Federal Work-Study, and unspecified assistantships available. Support available to part-time students. Financial award application deadline: 3/1; financial award applicants required to submit FAFSA. *Faculty research:* School reform, race and culture in schools, race and higher education, language, literacy and writing. *Unit head:* Dr. Wenfan Yan, Graduate Program Director, 617-287.4873, E-mail: WenFan.Yan@umb.edu. *Application contact:* Graduate Admissions Coordinator, 617-287-6400, Fax: 617-287-6236, E-mail: graduate.admissions@umb.edu.

University of Massachusetts Dartmouth, Graduate School, College of Arts and Sciences, School of Education, Department of Educational Leadership, North Dartmouth, MA 02747-2300. Offers educational leadership and policy studies (Ed D, PhD). *Program availability:* Part-time. *Faculty:* 4 full-time (0 women), 1 (woman) part-time/adjunct. *Students:* 7 full-time (6 women), 20 part-time (11 women); includes 12

minority (4 Black or African American, non-Hispanic/Latino; 1 American Indian or Alaska Native, non-Hispanic/Latino; 1 Asian, non-Hispanic/Latino; 4 Hispanic/Latino; 2 Two or more races, non-Hispanic/Latino), 1 international. Average age 44. In 2018, 5 doctorates awarded. *Degree requirements:* For doctorate, comprehensive exam, thesis/dissertation. *Entrance requirements:* For doctorate, GRE or GMAT, statement of purpose (minimum of 300 words), resume, 3 letters of recommendation, official transcripts (from all post secondary institutions), scholarly writing sample (minimum of 10 pages of writing). Additional exam requirements/recommendations for international students: Required—TOEFL (minimum score 550 paper-based; 79 iBT), IELTS (minimum score 6.5). *Application deadline:* For fall admission, 4/30 priority date for domestic students, 3/30 priority date for international students. Application fee: $60. Electronic applications accepted. *Financial support:* In 2018–19, 1 fellowship (averaging $24,000 per year) was awarded; tuition waivers (full) and doctoral support, dissertation writing support also available. Financial award application deadline: 3/1; financial award applicants required to submit FAFSA. *Faculty research:* Sociology of education, critical theory, curriculum theory, globalization and education, urban education, teacher education. *Total annual research expenditures:* $162,000. *Unit head:* Amy Shapiro, Interim Dean, College of Arts and Sciences, 508-999-8352, Fax: 508-999-9125, E-mail: ashapiro@umassd.edu. *Application contact:* Scott Webster, Director of Graduate Studies and Admissions, 508-999-8604, Fax: 508-999-8183, E-mail: graduate@umassd.edu.
Website: http://www.umassd.edu/educationalleadership

University of Memphis, Graduate School, College of Education, Department of Instruction and Curriculum Leadership, Memphis, TN 38152. Offers advanced studies in teaching and learning (M Ed); applied behavior analysis (Graduate Certificate); autism studies (Graduate Certificate); early childhood education (MAT, MS, Ed D); elementary education (MAT); instruction and curriculum (MS, Ed D); instruction design and technology (MS, Ed D); instructional design and technology (Graduate Certificate); literacy, leadership, and coaching (Graduate Certificate); reading (MS, Ed D); school library information specialist (Graduate Certificate); secondary education (MAT); special education (MAT, MS, Ed D); STEM teacher leadership (Graduate Certificate); urban education (Graduate Certificate). *Accreditation:* NCATE (one or more programs are accredited). *Program availability:* Part-time. *Students:* 62 full-time (45 women), 412 part-time (326 women); includes 209 minority (179 Black or African American, non-Hispanic/Latino; 1 American Indian or Alaska Native, non-Hispanic/Latino; 5 Asian, non-Hispanic/Latino; 17 Hispanic/Latino; 7 Two or more races, non-Hispanic/Latino), 4 international. Average age 35. 195 applicants, 91% accepted, 143 enrolled. In 2018, 122 master's, 13 doctorates, 29 other advanced degrees awarded. Terminal master's awarded for partial completion of doctoral program. *Degree requirements:* For master's, comprehensive exam, thesis or alternative; for doctorate, comprehensive exam, thesis/dissertation. *Entrance requirements:* For master's, GRE General Test, PRAXIS, minimum GPA of 2.5, letters of reference; for doctorate, GRE General Test, GRE Subject Test, 2 years of teaching experience, letters of reference, statement of purpose, interview. Additional exam requirements/recommendations for international students: Required—TOEFL (minimum score 550 paper-based; 79 iBT). *Application deadline:* For fall admission, 4/1 priority date for domestic students; for spring admission, 10/1 priority date for domestic students; for summer admission, 2/1 priority date for domestic students. Applications are processed on a rolling basis. Application fee: $35 ($60 for international students). Electronic applications accepted. *Expenses: Tuition, area resident:* Full-time $10,240; part-time $503 per credit hour. Tuition, state resident: full-time $10,464. Tuition, nonresident: full-time $20,224; part-time $991 per credit hour. *Required fees:* $850; $106 per credit hour. *Financial support:* Research assistantships with full tuition reimbursements, teaching assistantships with full tuition reimbursements, career-related internships or fieldwork, Federal Work-Study, institutionally sponsored loans, scholarships/grants, traineeships, and unspecified assistantships available. Support available to part-time students. Financial award application deadline: 2/1; financial award applicants required to submit FAFSA. *Faculty research:* Effective urban teachers, preparation and retention of urban teachers, technology utilization in schools, field-based teacher preparation programs, effective use of online instruction. *Unit head:* Dr. Christian Mueller, Chair, 901-678-2365, E-mail: cemuellr@memphis.edu. *Application contact:* Dr. Lee Allen, Director of Graduate Programs, 901-678-4073, E-mail: allenlee@memphis.edu.
Website: http://www.memphis.edu/icl/

University of Memphis, Graduate School, College of Education, Department of Leadership, Memphis, TN 38152. Offers adult education (Ed D); community college teaching and leadership (Graduate Certificate); community education (Ed D); educational leadership (Ed D); higher education (Ed D); leadership (MS); policy studies (Ed D); school administration and supervision (MS); student personnel (MS). *Accreditation:* NCATE. *Program availability:* Part-time, evening/weekend, online learning. *Students:* 19 full-time (12 women), 137 part-time (90 women); includes 87 minority (80 Black or African American, non-Hispanic/Latino; 2 Asian, non-Hispanic/Latino; 4 Hispanic/Latino; 1 Two or more races, non-Hispanic/Latino), 1 international. Average age 41. 44 applicants, 98% accepted, 37 enrolled. In 2018, 11 master's, 17 doctorates, 2 other advanced degrees awarded. *Degree requirements:* For master's, comprehensive exam, thesis optional; for doctorate, comprehensive exam, thesis/dissertation. *Entrance requirements:* For master's, GRE, resume, letters of reference, statement of professional goals, current teacher certification, sample work, interview; for doctorate, GRE, resume, letters of reference, statement of professional goals, interview. Additional exam requirements/recommendations for international students: Required—TOEFL (minimum score 550 paper-based; 79 iBT). *Application deadline:* For fall admission, 6/15 for domestic students; for spring admission, 9/15 for domestic students; for summer admission, 2/15 for domestic students. Application fee: $35 ($60 for international students). Electronic applications accepted. *Expenses: Tuition, area resident:* Full-time $10,240; part-time $503 per credit hour. Tuition, state resident: full-time $10,464. Tuition, nonresident: full-time $20,224; part-time $991 per credit hour. *Required fees:* $850; $106 per credit hour. *Financial support:* Research assistantships with full tuition reimbursements, teaching assistantships, Federal Work-Study, scholarships/grants, and unspecified assistantships available. Financial award application deadline: 2/1; financial award applicants required to submit FAFSA. *Faculty research:* School improvement, social justice, online learning, adult learning, diversity. *Unit head:* Dr. R Eric Platt, Interim Chair, 901-678-4229, E-mail: replatt@memphis.edu. *Application contact:* Dr. R Eric Platt, Interim Chair, 901-678-4229, E-mail: replatt@memphis.edu.
Website: http://www.memphis.edu/lead

University of Michigan–Dearborn, College of Education, Health, and Human Services, Doctoral Program in Education, Dearborn, MI 48126. Offers curriculum and practice (Ed D); educational leadership (Ed D); metropolitan education (Ed D). *Program availability:* Part-time, evening/weekend. *Faculty:* 5 full-time (3 women), 1 part-time/adjunct (0 women). *Students:* 2 full-time (both women), 19 part-time (12 women); includes 9 minority (8 Black or African American, non-Hispanic/Latino; 1 Hispanic/Latino). Average age 44. 9 applicants, 44% accepted, 3 enrolled. In 2018, 5 doctorates awarded. *Degree requirements:* For doctorate, thesis/dissertation. *Entrance requirements:* For doctorate, GRE (taken within the last 5 years), master's degree with minimum GPA of 3.3, 3 letters of recommendation (1 from faculty), 3 years' professional

and/or teaching experience. Additional exam requirements/recommendations for international students: Required—TOEFL (minimum score 560 paper-based; 84 iBT), IELTS (minimum score 6.5). *Application deadline:* For fall admission, 3/1 for domestic and international students. Application fee: $60. Electronic applications accepted. *Expenses:* $12,140 per academic year (typical full-time in-state); $20,708 per academic year (typical full-time out-of-state). *Financial support:* In 2018–19, 6 students received support. Scholarships/grants available. Financial award application deadline: 3/1; financial award applicants required to submit FAFSA. *Faculty research:* Urban education, educational leadership, assessment and evaluation, research methods, science education. *Unit head:* Dr. Chris Burke, Director, 313-593-5319, E-mail: cjfburke@umich.edu. *Application contact:* Office of Graduate Studies, 313-583-6321, E-mail: umd-graduatestudies@umich.edu.
Website: http://umdearborn.edu/cehhs/cehhs_edd/

University of Michigan–Dearborn, College of Education, Health, and Human Services, Education Specialist Program, Dearborn, MI 48126. Offers curriculum and practice (Ed S); educational leadership (Ed S); metropolitan education (Ed S). *Program availability:* Part-time, evening/weekend. *Faculty:* 1 (woman) full-time, 1 part-time/adjunct (0 women). *Students:* 6 part-time (3 women); includes 1 minority (Black or African American, non-Hispanic/Latino). Average age 38. 3 applicants, 33% accepted, 1 enrolled. In 2018, 2 Ed Ss awarded. *Entrance requirements:* For degree, master's degree with minimum GPA of 3.3; at least 3 years' teaching experience or the equivalent experience working in a professional setting. Additional exam requirements/recommendations for international students: Required—TOEFL (minimum score 560 paper-based; 84 iBT), IELTS (minimum score 6.5). *Application deadline:* For fall admission, 8/1 for domestic students, 5/1 for international students; for winter admission, 12/1 for domestic students, 9/1 for international students; for spring admission, 4/1 for domestic students, 1/1 for international students. Applications are processed on a rolling basis. Application fee: $60. Electronic applications accepted. *Expenses:* $12,140 per academic year (typical full-time in-state); $20,708 per academic year (typical full-time out-of-state). *Financial support:* In 2018–19, 2 students received support. Scholarships/grants available. Financial award application deadline: 3/1; financial award applicants required to submit FAFSA. *Faculty research:* Educational leadership, curriculum development, education policy, organizational development, K-12 administration. *Unit head:* Dr. Chris Burke, Director, 313-593-5319, E-mail: cjfburke@umich.edu. *Application contact:* Office of Graduate Studies, 313-583-6321, E-mail: umd-graduatestudies@umich.edu.
Website: http://umdearborn.edu/cehhs/cehhs_eds/

University of Michigan–Dearborn, College of Education, Health, and Human Services, Master of Arts Program in Educational Leadership, Dearborn, MI 48126. Offers MA. *Program availability:* Part-time, evening/weekend. *Faculty:* 1 (woman) full-time, 2 part-time/adjunct (0 women). *Students:* 18 part-time (12 women); includes 2 minority (1 Black or African American, non-Hispanic/Latino; 1 Hispanic/Latino). Average age 32. 9 applicants, 100% accepted, 7 enrolled. In 2018, 13 master's awarded. *Entrance requirements:* Additional exam requirements/recommendations for international students: Required—TOEFL (minimum score 560 paper-based; 84 iBT), IELTS (minimum score 6.5). *Application deadline:* For fall admission, 8/1 priority date for domestic students, 5/1 for international students; for winter admission, 12/1 priority date for domestic students, 9/1 for international students; for spring admission, 4/1 priority date for domestic students, 1/1 for international students. Applications are processed on a rolling basis. Application fee: $60. Electronic applications accepted. *Expenses:* $12,140 per academic year (typical full-time in-state); $20,708 per academic year (typical full-time out-of-state). *Financial support:* Scholarships/grants available. Financial award application deadline: 3/1; financial award applicants required to submit FAFSA. *Faculty research:* Educational leadership, curriculum development, education policy, organizational development, K-12 administration. *Unit head:* Dr. Paul Fossum, Director, Master's Programs, 313-593-0982, E-mail: pfossum@umich.edu. *Application contact:* Office of Graduate Studies, 313-583-6321, E-mail: umd-graduatestudies@umich.edu.
Website: http://umdearborn.edu/cehhs/cehhs_mael/

University of Michigan–Flint, Graduate Programs, Program in Public Administration, Flint, MI 48502-1950. Offers administration of non-profit agencies (MPA); criminal justice administration (MPA); educational administration (MPA); general public administration (MPA); healthcare administration (MPA). *Program availability:* Part-time. *Faculty:* 2 part-time/adjunct (1 woman). *Students:* 10 full-time (8 women), 98 part-time (63 women); includes 39 minority (30 Black or African American, non-Hispanic/Latino; 3 American Indian or Alaska Native, non-Hispanic/Latino; 1 Asian, non-Hispanic/Latino; 2 Hispanic/Latino; 3 Two or more races, non-Hispanic/Latino), 3 international. Average age 36. 75 applicants, 69% accepted, 34 enrolled. In 2018, 40 master's awarded. *Degree requirements:* For master's, thesis or alternative, internship. *Entrance requirements:* For master's, bachelor's degree from regionally-accredited institution, minimum overall undergraduate GPA of 3.0 on 4.0 scale. Additional exam requirements/recommendations for international students: Required—TOEFL (minimum score 84 iBT), IELTS (minimum score 6.5). *Application deadline:* For fall admission, 8/1 for domestic students, 5/1 for international students; for winter admission, 11/15 for domestic students, 9/1 for international students; for spring admission, 3/15 for domestic students, 1/1 for international students; for summer admission, 5/15 for domestic students. Applications are processed on a rolling basis. Application fee: $55. Electronic applications accepted. *Expenses:* Contact institution. *Financial support:* Career-related internships or fieldwork, Federal Work-Study, and scholarships/grants available. Support available to part-time students. Financial award application deadline: 3/1; financial award applicants required to submit FAFSA. *Unit head:* Dr. Kim Sacks McManaway, Director, 810-766-6628, E-mail: kimsaks@umflint.edu. *Application contact:* Matt Bohlen, Director of Graduate Admissions, 810-762-3171, Fax: 810-766-6789, E-mail: mbohlen@umflint.edu.
Website: http://www.umflint.edu/graduateprograms/public-administration-mpa

University of Michigan–Flint, School of Education and Human Services, Department of Education, Flint, MI 48502-1950. Offers curriculum and instruction (Ed S); early childhood education (MA); education (Ed D); educational leadership (Ed S); educational technology (MA), including curriculum and instruction, developer; literacy education (MA); secondary education with certification (MA). *Program availability:* Part-time, evening/weekend, online only, 100% online, mixed mode format (for some programs). *Faculty:* 16 full-time (10 women), 28 part-time/adjunct (14 women). *Students:* 31 full-time (23 women), 179 part-time (135 women); includes 54 minority (42 Black or African American, non-Hispanic/Latino; 3 Asian, non-Hispanic/Latino; 4 Hispanic/Latino; 1 Native Hawaiian or other Pacific Islander, non-Hispanic/Latino; 4 Two or more races, non-Hispanic/Latino), 1 international. Average age 39. 133 applicants, 72% accepted, 61 enrolled. In 2018, 60 master's awarded. *Degree requirements:* For master's, thesis optional; for doctorate, thesis/dissertation. *Entrance requirements:* For master's, bachelor's degree from regionally-accredited institution, minimum overall undergraduate GPA of 3.0 on 4.0 scale; for doctorate, completion of Eds minimum overall graduate GPA of 3.3 (6.0 on a 9.0 scale) or equivalent; at least 3 years of work experience in a P-16 educational institution or in an education-related position; for Ed S, MA or MS in education-related field from accredited institution; minimum overall graduate GPA of 3.0 (6.0 on a 9.0 scale) or equivalent; at least 3 years of work experience in an educational

setting. Additional exam requirements/recommendations for international students: Required—TOEFL (minimum score 84 iBT), IELTS (minimum score 6.5). *Application deadline:* For fall admission, 8/1 for domestic students, 5/1 for international students; for winter admission, 11/15 for domestic students, 9/15 for international students; for spring admission, 3/15 for domestic students, 1/15 for international students; for summer admission, 5/15 for domestic students. Applications are processed on a rolling basis. Application fee: $55. Electronic applications accepted. *Expenses:* Contact institution. *Financial support:* Federal Work-Study, scholarships/grants, and unspecified assistantships available. Financial award application deadline: 3/1; financial award applicants required to submit FAFSA. *Unit head:* Dr. Mary Jo Finney, Department Chair/Associate Professor, 810-766-6617, E-mail: mjfinney@umflint.edu. *Application contact:* Matt Bohlen, Director of Graduate Admissions, 810-762-3171, Fax: 810-766-6789, E-mail: mbohlen@umflint.edu.
Website: https://www.umflint.edu/education/graduate-programs

University of Minnesota, Twin Cities Campus, Graduate School, College of Education and Human Development, Department of Organizational Leadership, Policy and Development, Program in Education Policy and Leadership, Minneapolis, MN 55455-0213. Offers educational policy and leadership (MA, Ed D, PhD); leadership in education (M Ed). *Students:* 114 full-time (72 women), 43 part-time (27 women); includes 37 minority (20 Black or African American, non-Hispanic/Latino; 6 Asian, non-Hispanic/Latino; 5 Hispanic/Latino; 6 Two or more races, non-Hispanic/Latino), 2 international. Average age 38. 146 applicants, 82% accepted, 85 enrolled. In 2018, 13 master's, 5 doctorates awarded. Application fee: $75 ($95 for international students). *Unit head:* Dr. Kenneth Bartlett, Chair, 612-624-1006, E-mail: bartlett@umn.edu. *Application contact:* Dr. Jeremy J. Hernandez, Director of Graduate Studies, 612-626-9377, E-mail: olpd@umn.edu.
Website: http://www.cehd.umn.edu/OLPD/grad-programs/EPL/

University of Mississippi, Graduate School, School of Education, University, MS 38677. Offers counselor education (M Ed, PhD); counselor education - play therapy (Ed S); early childhood (M Ed); educational leadership K-12 (M Ed, Ed D, PhD, Ed S); elementary education (M Ed, Ed D, Ed S); higher education/student personnel (Ed D, PhD); literacy education (M Ed); math education (Ed D); secondary education (M Ed, PhD, Ed S); special education (M Ed, PhD, Ed S); teacher corporations (MA); teacher education (MA). *Accreditation:* NCATE. *Faculty:* 59 full-time (35 women), 34 part-time/adjunct (26 women). *Students:* 169 full-time (137 women), 461 part-time (329 women); includes 199 minority (185 Black or African American, non-Hispanic/Latino; 3 Asian, non-Hispanic/Latino; 7 Hispanic/Latino; 4 Two or more races, non-Hispanic/Latino), 5 international. Average age 33. In 2018, 180 master's, 57 doctorates, 37 other advanced degrees awarded. *Entrance requirements:* For master's, GRE General Test, minimum GPA of 3.0; for doctorate, GRE General Test. Additional exam requirements/recommendations for international students: Required—TOEFL. *Application deadline:* Applications are processed on a rolling basis. Application fee: $50. Electronic applications accepted. *Financial support:* Scholarships/grants available. Financial award application deadline: 3/1; financial award applicants required to submit FAFSA. *Unit head:* Dr. David Rock, Dean, 662-915-7063, Fax: 662-915-7249, E-mail: soe@olemiss.edu. *Application contact:* Temeka Smith, Graduate Activities Specialist for Admissions, 662-915-7474, Fax: 662-915-7577, E-mail: gschool@olemiss.edu.

University of Missouri, Office of Research and Graduate Studies, College of Education, Department of Educational Leadership and Policy Analysis, Columbia, MO 65211. Offers education administration (M Ed, MA, Ed D, PhD, Ed S); higher and adult education (M Ed, MA, Ed D, PhD, Ed S). *Program availability:* Part-time. *Entrance requirements:* For master's, doctorate, and Ed S, minimum GPA of 3.0.

University of Missouri–Kansas City, School of Education, Kansas City, MO 64110-2499. Offers administration (Ed D); counseling and guidance (MA, Ed S), including mental health counseling (Ed S), school counseling (Ed S); counseling psychology (PhD); curriculum and instruction (MA, Ed S), including language and literacy (Ed S); education (PhD), including higher education administration, PK-12 education administration; educational administration (MA, Ed S), including advanced principal (Ed S), beginning principal (Ed S), district-level administration (Ed S); reading education (MA); special education (MA). PhD in education offered through the School of Graduate Studies. *Accreditation:* NCATE. *Program availability:* Part-time, evening/weekend. *Degree requirements:* For doctorate, thesis/dissertation, internship, practicum. *Entrance requirements:* For master's, GRE, minimum GPA of 2.75, 2 letters of reference, written statement of purpose; for doctorate, GRE, minimum GPA of 3.0; for Ed S, minimum GPA of 3.0. Additional exam requirements/recommendations for international students: Required—TOEFL (minimum score 550 paper-based; 80 iBT). *Faculty research:* Urban education, inquiry-based field study, theories of counseling and psychotherapy, school literacy, educational technology.

University of Missouri–St. Louis, College of Education, Interdisciplinary Doctoral Programs, St. Louis, MO 63121. Offers counseling (PhD); educational leadership and policy studies (PhD); educational psychology (PhD); leadership in educational practice (Ed D); teaching-learning processes (PhD). *Degree requirements:* For doctorate, thesis/dissertation. *Entrance requirements:* For doctorate, GRE General Test, 3 letters of recommendation; personal interview. Additional exam requirements/recommendations for international students: Recommended—TOEFL (minimum score 550 paper-based; 79 iBT), IELTS (minimum score 6.5). Electronic applications accepted. *Faculty research:* Higher education law and policy, gender and higher education, student retention, lifelong learning orientation, school counselor's role in violence prevention.

University of Mobile, Graduate Studies, School of Education, Mobile, AL 36613. Offers education (MA); higher education leadership and policy (M Ed). *Program availability:* Part-time, 100% online, blended/hybrid learning. *Students:* 30 full-time (28 women); includes 16 minority (13 Black or African American, non-Hispanic/Latino; 2 American Indian or Alaska Native, non-Hispanic/Latino; 1 Asian, non-Hispanic/Latino). 23 applicants, 26% accepted, 12 enrolled. In 2018, 2 master's awarded. *Degree requirements:* For master's, comprehensive exam, thesis optional. *Entrance requirements:* For master's, Alabama teaching certificate if not seeking an Alternative Master's Degree. Additional exam requirements/recommendations for international students: Required—TOEFL (minimum score 550 paper-based; 80 iBT). *Application deadline:* For fall admission, 8/3 priority date for domestic students, 8/3 for international students; for spring admission, 12/23 priority date for domestic students, 12/3 priority date for international students. Applications are processed on a rolling basis. Application fee: $40 ($50 for international students). Electronic applications accepted. *Expenses: Tuition:* Full-time $453; part-time $453 per credit hour. *Required fees:* $320; $320. Tuition and fees vary according to degree level and program. *Financial support:* Application deadline: 8/1; applicants required to submit FAFSA. *Faculty research:* Retention, writing across the curriculum. *Unit head:* Dr. Carolyn D. Corliss, Dean, School of Education, 251-442-2276, Fax: 251-442-2523, E-mail: ccorliss@umobile.edu. *Application contact:* Brian Boyle, Director of Recruitment, 251-442-2727.
Website: http://umobile.edu/school-of-education/master-of-arts-in-education/

University of Montana, Graduate School, Phyllis J. Washington College of Education and Human Sciences, Department of Educational Leadership, Missoula, MT 59812. Offers M Ed, Ed D, Ed S. *Degree requirements:* For doctorate, thesis/dissertation; for

Ed S, thesis. *Entrance requirements:* For master's and Ed S, GRE General Test. Additional exam requirements/recommendations for international students: Required—TOEFL.

University of Montevallo, College of Education, Program in Educational Administration, Montevallo, AL 35115. Offers M Ed, Ed S. *Accreditation:* NCATE. *Program availability:* Part-time, evening/weekend. *Students:* 34 part-time (27 women); includes 7 minority (6 Black or African American, non-Hispanic/Latino; 1 Two or more races, non-Hispanic/Latino). In 2018, 24 master's awarded. *Entrance requirements:* For master's, GRE General Test or MAT. Additional exam requirements/recommendations for international students: Required—TOEFL (minimum score 550 paper-based). *Application deadline:* For fall admission, 7/15 for domestic students; for spring admission, 11/15 for domestic students. Application fee: $30. *Expenses: Tuition, area resident:* Full-time $10,512. Tuition, state resident: full-time $10,512. Tuition, nonresident: full-time $22,464. *International tuition:* $22,464 full-time. *Financial support:* Federal Work-Study, scholarships/grants, and unspecified assistantships available. *Unit head:* Dr. Charlotte Daughhetee, Interim Dean, 205-665-6360, E-mail: daughc@montevallo.edu. *Application contact:* Colleen Kennedy, Graduate Program Assistant, 205-665-6350, E-mail: ckennedy@montevallo.edu.
Website: http://www.montevallo.edu/education/college-of-education/traditional-masters-degrees/leadership/

University of Mount Union, Program in Educational Leadership, Alliance, OH 44601-3993. Offers MA. *Program availability:* Part-time, online only, 100% online. *Entrance requirements:* For master's, two recommendations, official transcript from each college or university previously attended, curriculum vitae or resume, personal statement. Additional exam requirements/recommendations for international students: Required—TOEFL (minimum score 100 iBT). Electronic applications accepted. *Expenses:* Contact institution.

University of Nebraska at Kearney, College of Education, Department of Educational Administration, Kearney, NE 68849-0001. Offers curriculum supervisor of academic area (MA Ed); school principalship 7-12 (MA Ed); school principalship PK-8 (MA Ed); school superintendent (Ed S); supervisor of special education (MA Ed). *Accreditation:* NCATE. *Program availability:* Part-time, evening/weekend, online only, 100% online. *Degree requirements:* For master's and Ed S, comprehensive exam, thesis optional. *Entrance requirements:* For master's, letters of recommendation, resume, letter of interest; for Ed S, letters of recommendation, resume, essay. Additional exam requirements/recommendations for international students: Recommended—TOEFL (minimum score 550 paper-based; 79 iBT), IELTS (minimum score 6.5). Electronic applications accepted. *Faculty research:* Leadership and organizational behavior.

University of Nebraska at Omaha, Graduate Studies, College of Education, Department of Educational Leadership, Omaha, NE 68182. Offers educational administration and supervision (Ed D); educational leadership (MS, Ed S). *Accreditation:* NCATE. *Program availability:* Part-time, evening/weekend. *Degree requirements:* For master's, comprehensive exam, thesis (for some programs); for doctorate, comprehensive exam, thesis/dissertation; for Ed S, comprehensive exam, thesis. *Entrance requirements:* For master's, minimum GPA of 3.0, transcripts, resume, copy of teaching certificate, 3 letters of recommendation, statement of purpose; for doctorate, GRE General Test, resume, 3 samples of research/written work, 3 letters of recommendation, statement of purpose, transcripts. Additional exam requirements/recommendations for international students: Required—TOEFL, IELTS, PTE. Electronic applications accepted.

University of Nebraska–Lincoln, Graduate College, College of Education and Human Sciences, Department of Educational Administration, Lincoln, NE 68588. Offers M Ed, MA, Ed D, Certificate. Ed D offered jointly with University of Nebraska at Omaha. *Accreditation:* NCATE. *Degree requirements:* For master's, thesis optional; for doctorate, comprehensive exam, thesis/dissertation. *Entrance requirements:* For master's, GRE or MAT; for doctorate, GRE General Test, administrative certification. Additional exam requirements/recommendations for international students: Required—TOEFL (minimum score 550 paper-based). Electronic applications accepted. *Faculty research:* Educational policy, school finance, school law, school restructuring, leadership behavior.

University of Nebraska–Lincoln, Graduate College, College of Education and Human Sciences, Interdepartmental Area of Administration, Curriculum and Instruction, Lincoln, NE 68588. Offers Ed D, PhD, JD/PhD. *Accreditation:* NCATE. *Program availability:* Online learning. *Degree requirements:* For doctorate, comprehensive exam, thesis/dissertation. *Entrance requirements:* For doctorate, GRE, curriculum vitae. Additional exam requirements/recommendations for international students: Required—TOEFL (minimum score 550 paper-based). Electronic applications accepted.

University of Nevada, Las Vegas, Graduate College, College of Education, Department of Educational Psychology and Higher Education, Las Vegas, NV 89154-3002. Offers chief diversity officer in higher education (Certificate); college sport leadership (Certificate); educational policy and leadership (M Ed); educational psychology (MS, PhD, Ed S); educational psychology/law (PhD/JD); higher education (M Ed, PhD, Certificate); psychology/learning and technology (PhD), including learning and technology; workforce development/educational leadership (PhD); PhD/JD. *Program availability:* Part-time, evening/weekend, 100% online, blended/hybrid learning. *Faculty:* 20 full-time (12 women), 6 part-time/adjunct (5 women). *Students:* 74 full-time (50 women), 95 part-time (61 women); includes 64 minority (20 Black or African American, non-Hispanic/Latino; 9 Asian, non-Hispanic/Latino; 26 Hispanic/Latino; 9 Two or more races, non-Hispanic/Latino), 10 international. Average age 36. 106 applicants, 49% accepted, 40 enrolled. In 2018, 57 master's, 4 doctorates, 12 other advanced degrees awarded. *Degree requirements:* For master's, comprehensive exam (for some programs), thesis (for some programs); for doctorate, comprehensive exam, thesis/dissertation. *Entrance requirements:* For master's, GRE General Test or GMAT (for some programs), letters of recommendation; writing sample; bachelor's degree; for doctorate, GMAT or GRE General Test, writing exam; for other advanced degree, GRE General Test (for some programs). Additional exam requirements/recommendations for international students: Required—TOEFL (minimum score 550 paper-based; 80 iBT), IELTS (minimum score 7). Application fee: $60 ($95 for international students). Electronic applications accepted. *Financial support:* In 2018–19, 43 students received support, including 28 research assistantships with full tuition reimbursements available (averaging $14,674 per year), 15 teaching assistantships with full tuition reimbursements available (averaging $18,733 per year); institutionally sponsored loans, scholarships/grants, health care benefits, and unspecified assistantships also available. Financial award application deadline: 3/15; financial award applicants required to submit FAFSA. *Faculty research:* Innovation and change in educational settings; educational policy, finance, and marketing; psycho-educational assessment; student retention, persistence, development, language, and culture; statistical modeling, program evaluation, qualitative and quantitative research methods. *Total annual research expenditures:* $426,511. *Unit head:* Dr. Alice Corkill, Chair/Professor, 702-895-4164, E-mail: ephe.chair@unlv.edu. *Application contact:* Dr. Nancy Lough, Graduate Coordinator, 702-895-5392, E-mail: highered.gradcoord@unlv.edu.
Website: http://education.unlv.edu/ephe/

Educational Leadership and Administration

University of Nevada, Reno, Graduate School, College of Education, Department of Educational Leadership, Reno, NV 89557. Offers M Ed, MA, MS, Ed D, PhD, Ed S. *Accreditation:* NCATE. Terminal master's awarded for partial completion of doctoral program. *Degree requirements:* For master's, comprehensive exam, thesis optional; for doctorate, comprehensive exam, thesis/dissertation. *Entrance requirements:* For master's, minimum GPA of 2.75; for doctorate, GRE General Test, minimum GPA of 3.0. Additional exam requirements/recommendations for international students: Required—TOEFL (minimum score 500 paper-based; 61 iBT), IELTS (minimum score 6). Electronic applications accepted. *Faculty research:* Law, finance, supervision, organizational theory, principalship.

University of New England, College of Graduate and Professional Studies, Portland, ME 04005-9526. Offers advanced educational leadership (CAGS); applied nutrition (MS); career and technical education (MS Ed); curriculum and instruction (MS Ed); education (CAGS, Post-Master's Certificate); educational leadership (MS Ed, Ed D); generalist (MS Ed); health informatics (MS, Graduate Certificate); inclusion education (MS Ed); literacy K-12 (MS Ed); medical education leadership (MMEL); public health (MPH, Graduate Certificate); reading specialist (MS Ed); social work (MSW). *Program availability:* Part-time, evening/weekend, online only, 100% online. *Faculty:* 109 part-time/adjunct (78 women). *Students:* 1,207 full-time (972 women), 561 part-time (450 women); includes 411 minority (280 Black or African American, non-Hispanic/Latino; 17 American Indian or Alaska Native, non-Hispanic/Latino; 74 Asian, non-Hispanic/Latino; 25 Hispanic/Latino; 9 Native Hawaiian or other Pacific Islander, non-Hispanic/Latino; 6 Two or more races, non-Hispanic/Latino). Average age 36. 740 applicants, 92% accepted, 494 enrolled. In 2018, 586 master's, 44 doctorates, 85 other advanced degrees awarded. *Application deadline:* Applications are processed on a rolling basis. Electronic applications accepted. *Financial support:* Application deadline: 5/1; applicants required to submit FAFSA. *Unit head:* Dr. Martha Wilson, Dean of the College of Graduate and Professional Studies, 207-221-4985, E-mail: mwilson13@une.edu. *Application contact:* Nicole Lindsay, Director of Online Admissions, 207-221-4966, E-mail: nlindsay1@une.edu.
Website: http://online.une.edu

University of New Hampshire, Graduate School, College of Liberal Arts, Department of Education, Program in Educational Administration and Supervision, Durham, NH 03824. Offers Ed S. *Program availability:* Part-time. *Entrance requirements:* For degree, master's degree in educational administration or equivalent. Additional exam requirements/recommendations for international students: Required—TOEFL (minimum score 550 paper-based; 80 iBT). Electronic applications accepted.

University of New Hampshire, Graduate School, College of Liberal Arts, Department of Education, Program in Special Education, Durham, NH 03824. Offers special education (M Ed); special education administration (Postbaccalaureate Certificate). *Program availability:* Part-time. *Entrance requirements:* For master's, PRAXIS, Department of Education background check. Additional exam requirements/recommendations for international students: Required—TOEFL (minimum score 550 paper-based; 80 iBT). Electronic applications accepted.

University of New Hampshire, Graduate School Manchester Campus, Manchester, NH 03101. Offers business administration (MBA); cybersecurity policy and risk management (MS); educational administration and supervision (Ed S); educational studies (M Ed); elementary education (M Ed); information technology (MS); public administration (MPA); public health (MPH, Certificate); secondary education (M Ed, MAT); social work (MSW); substance use disorders (Certificate). *Program availability:* Part-time, evening/weekend. *Entrance requirements:* Additional exam requirements/recommendations for international students: Required—TOEFL (minimum score 550 paper-based; 80 iBT). Electronic applications accepted.

University of New Mexico, Graduate Studies, College of Education, Program in Educational Leadership, Albuquerque, NM 87131-2039. Offers MA, Ed D, Ed S. *Accreditation:* NCATE. *Program availability:* Part-time, evening/weekend, online learning. *Students:* Average age 41. 57 applicants, 72% accepted, 41 enrolled. In 2018, 13 master's, 5 doctorates, 17 other advanced degrees awarded. *Degree requirements:* For master's, comprehensive exam; for doctorate, comprehensive exam, thesis/dissertation. *Entrance requirements:* For master's, bachelor's degree; for doctorate, GRE, master's degree. *Application deadline:* For fall admission, 6/1 for domestic students; for spring admission, 10/1 for domestic students. Applications are processed on a rolling basis. Application fee: $50. Electronic applications accepted. *Financial support:* Research assistantships, career-related internships or fieldwork, and scholarships/grants available. Financial award application deadline: 3/1; financial award applicants required to submit FAFSA. *Faculty research:* K-20 educational and organizational leadership, individual and organizational learning, policy, legal and political contexts. *Unit head:* Dr. Patricia Boverie, Head, 505-277-2408, Fax: 505-277-5553, E-mail: pboverie@unm.edu. *Application contact:* Linda Wood, Information Contact, 505-277-0441, Fax: 505-277-5553, E-mail: woodl@unm.edu.
Website: http://coe.unm.edu/departments-programs/teelp/education-leadership-program/index.html

University of New Orleans, Graduate School, College of Liberal Arts, Education and Human Development, Department of Educational Leadership, Counseling, and Foundations, Program in Educational Leadership, New Orleans, LA 70148. Offers educational administration (PhD); educational leadership (M Ed); higher education (M Ed). *Accreditation:* NCATE. *Program availability:* Evening/weekend. Terminal master's awarded for partial completion of doctoral program. *Degree requirements:* For doctorate, variable foreign language requirement, thesis/dissertation. *Entrance requirements:* For master's and doctorate, GRE General Test. Additional exam requirements/recommendations for international students: Required—TOEFL (minimum score 550 paper-based; 79 iBT). Electronic applications accepted.

University of North Alabama, College of Arts and Sciences, Department of Interdisciplinary and Professional Studies, Florence, AL 35632-0001. Offers professional studies (MPS), including community development, higher education administration, information technology, security and safety leadership. *Program availability:* Part-time, 100% online. *Degree requirements:* For master's, thesis optional. *Entrance requirements:* For master's, ETS PPI, personal statement; three letters of recommendation. Additional exam requirements/recommendations for international students: Required—TOEFL (minimum score 79 iBT), IELTS (minimum score 6), PTE (minimum score 54). Electronic applications accepted.

University of North Alabama, College of Education, Department of Secondary Education, Program in Instructional Leadership, Florence, AL 35632-0001. Offers instructional leadership (MA Ed, Ed S); teacher leader (Ed S). *Accreditation:* NCATE. *Program availability:* Part-time, 100% online, blended/hybrid learning. *Entrance requirements:* Additional exam requirements/recommendations for international students: Required—TOEFL (minimum score 79 iBT), IELTS (minimum score 6), PTE (minimum score 54). Electronic applications accepted.

The University of North Carolina at Chapel Hill, Graduate School, School of Education, Programs in Educational Leadership and School Administration, Chapel Hill, NC 27599. Offers educational leadership (Ed D); school administration (MSA). *Accreditation:* NCATE. *Program availability:* Part-time. *Degree requirements:* For master's, comprehensive exam; for doctorate, comprehensive exam, thesis/dissertation. *Entrance requirements:* For master's, GRE General Test or MAT, minimum GPA of 3.2 during last 2 years of undergraduate course work, 3 years of school-based professional experience; for doctorate, GRE General Test, minimum GPA of 3.2 during last 2 years of undergraduate course work, 3 years of school-based professional experience. Additional exam requirements/recommendations for international students: Required—TOEFL (minimum score 550 paper-based). *Faculty research:* Gender, race, and class issues; school leadership; school finance and reform.

The University of North Carolina at Charlotte, Cato College of Education, Department of Educational Leadership, Charlotte, NC 28223-0001. Offers education research, measurement, and evaluation (PhD); educational leadership (Ed D); instructional systems technology (M Ed, Graduate Certificate); quantitative analysis (Graduate Certificate); school administration (MSA, Post-Master's Certificate); university and college teaching (Graduate Certificate). *Program availability:* Part-time, evening/weekend, 100% online, blended/hybrid learning. *Students:* 38 full-time (30 women), 234 part-time (160 women); includes 99 minority (79 Black or African American, non-Hispanic/Latino; 4 Asian, non-Hispanic/Latino; 13 Hispanic/Latino; 3 Two or more races, non-Hispanic/Latino), 8 international. Average age 37. 172 applicants, 71% accepted, 99 enrolled. In 2018, 45 master's, 13 doctorates, 69 other advanced degrees awarded. *Entrance requirements:* For master's, GRE or MAT, bachelor's degree, or its U.S. equivalent, from regionally-accredited college or university; minimum overall GPA of 3.5 on all previous work beyond high school; statement of purpose (essay); at least three recommendation forms; for doctorate, GRE or MAT, bachelor's degree (or its U.S. equivalent) from regionally-accredited college or university; minimum overall GPA of 3.5 in master's degree program; for other advanced degree, bachelor's degree from regionally-accredited university; minimum GPA of 2.75 on all post-secondary work attempted; transcripts; personal statement outlining why the applicant seeks admission to the program. Additional exam requirements/recommendations for international students: Required—TOEFL (minimum score 523 paper-based; 70 iBT), IELTS (minimum score 6), TOEFL (minimum score 523 paper-based, 70 iBT) or IELTS (6). *Application deadline:* Applications are processed on a rolling basis. Application fee: $75. Electronic applications accepted. Tuition and fees vary according to course load and program. *Financial support:* Research assistantships, career-related internships or fieldwork, institutionally sponsored loans, scholarships/grants, and unspecified assistantships available. Support available to part-time students. Financial award application deadline: 3/1; financial award applicants required to submit FAFSA. *Total annual research expenditures:* $1.8 million. *Unit head:* Dr. Claudia Flowers, Chair, 704-687-8862, E-mail: cpflower@uncc.edu. *Application contact:* Kathy B. Giddings, Director of Graduate Admissions, 704-687-5503, Fax: 704-687-1668, E-mail: gradadm@uncc.edu.
Website: http://edld.uncc.edu/

The University of North Carolina at Charlotte, Cato College of Education, Interdisciplinary Education Programs, Charlotte, NC 28223-0001. Offers art education (Graduate Certificate); child and family development: early childhood education (MAT); curriculum and instruction (PhD); elementary education (MAT); foreign language education (MAT); middle grades education (MAT); secondary education (MAT); special education (MAT); teaching (Graduate Certificate); teaching English as a second language (MAT); theatre education (Graduate Certificate). *Program availability:* Part-time, 100% online, blended/hybrid learning. *Students:* 70 full-time (55 women), 511 part-time (414 women); includes 228 minority (160 Black or African American, non-Hispanic/Latino; 1 American Indian or Alaska Native, non-Hispanic/Latino; 11 Asian, non-Hispanic/Latino; 38 Hispanic/Latino; 18 Two or more races, non-Hispanic/Latino), 8 international. Average age 34. 343 applicants, 92% accepted, 219 enrolled. In 2018, 69 master's, 13 doctorates, 161 other advanced degrees awarded. *Entrance requirements:* For master's, GRE or MAT, bachelor's degree, or its U.S. equivalent, from regionally-accredited college or university; minimum overall GPA of 3.0 on all previous work beyond high school; statement of purpose (essay); at least three recommendation forms; for doctorate, GRE or MAT, bachelor's degree (or its U.S. equivalent) from regionally-accredited college or university; minimum overall GPA of 3.5 in master's degree program; for Graduate Certificate, bachelor's degree from regionally-accredited university; minimum GPA of 2.75 on all post-secondary work attempted; transcripts; personal statement outlining why the applicant seeks admission to the program. Additional exam requirements/recommendations for international students: Required—TOEFL (minimum score 523 paper-based; 70 iBT), IELTS (minimum score 6), TOEFL (minimum score 523 paper-based, 70 iBT) or IELTS (6). *Application deadline:* Applications are processed on a rolling basis. Application fee: $75. Electronic applications accepted. Tuition and fees vary according to course load and program. *Financial support:* Career-related internships or fieldwork, institutionally sponsored loans, scholarships/grants, and unspecified assistantships available. Support available to part-time students. Financial award application deadline: 3/1; financial award applicants required to submit FAFSA. *Unit head:* Dr. Ellen McIntyre, Dean, 704-687-8722, E-mail: ellen.mcintyre@uncc.edu. *Application contact:* Kathy B. Giddings, Director of Graduate Admissions, 704-687-5503, Fax: 704-687-1668, E-mail: gradadm@uncc.edu.
Website: http://education.uncc.edu/academic-programs

The University of North Carolina at Greensboro, Graduate School, School of Education, Department of Educational Leadership and Cultural Foundations, Greensboro, NC 27412-5001. Offers curriculum and teaching (PhD), including cultural studies; educational leadership (Ed D, Ed S); school administration (MSA). *Accreditation:* NCATE. *Degree requirements:* For doctorate, thesis/dissertation. *Entrance requirements:* For master's, doctorate, and Ed S, GRE General Test. Additional exam requirements/recommendations for international students: Required—TOEFL. Electronic applications accepted.

The University of North Carolina at Greensboro, Graduate School, School of Education, Department of Teacher Education and Higher Education, Greensboro, NC 27412-5001. Offers college teaching and adult learning (Certificate); curriculum and instruction (M Ed), including chemistry education, elementary education, English as a second language, French education, instructional technology, mathematics education, middle grades education, reading education, science education, social studies education, Spanish education; curriculum and teaching (PhD), including higher education, teacher education and development; English as a second language (Certificate); higher education (M Ed); supervision (M Ed). *Accreditation:* NCATE. *Program availability:* Part-time. *Degree requirements:* For doctorate, thesis/dissertation. *Entrance requirements:* For master's and doctorate, GRE General Test. Additional exam requirements/recommendations for international students: Required—TOEFL. Electronic applications accepted. *Faculty research:* Community college literacy program, middle school mathematics/computer mathematics.

The University of North Carolina at Pembroke, The Graduate School, School of Education, Program in School Administration, Pembroke, NC 28372-1510. Offers MSA. *Program availability:* Part-time, evening/weekend. *Entrance requirements:* For master's, GRE General Test or MAT, minimum GPA of 3.0 in major, 2.5 overall; 3 years of teaching experience; two recommendations. Additional exam requirements/recommendations for international students: Required—TOEFL.

The University of North Carolina Wilmington, Watson College of Education, Department of Early Childhood, Elementary, Middle, Literacy and Special Education, Wilmington, NC 28403-3297. Offers educational leadership, policy, and advocacy (M Ed); elementary education (M Ed, MAT); language and literacy (M Ed); middle grades education (MAT). *Accreditation:* NCATE. *Program availability:* Part-time, blended/hybrid learning. *Degree requirements:* For master's, thesis or alternative, exit portfolio, oral presentation, internship, research project (depending on specialization). *Entrance requirements:* For master's, 3 letters of recommendations, NC Class A teacher license in related field, education statement of interest essay. Additional exam requirements/recommendations for international students: Required—TOEFL (minimum score 550 paper-based; 79 iBT), IELTS (minimum score 6.5). Electronic applications accepted.

The University of North Carolina Wilmington, Watson College of Education, Department of Educational Leadership, Wilmington, NC 28403-3297. Offers curriculum, instruction and supervision (M Ed); educational leadership and administration (Ed D), including curriculum and instruction; higher education (M Ed); school administration (MSA), including school administration. *Program availability:* Part-time, 100% online. *Degree requirements:* For master's, thesis or culminating project, e-Portfolio (for school administration); for doctorate, comprehensive exam, thesis/dissertation. *Entrance requirements:* For master's, GRE General Test, MAT, minimum B average in undergraduate work, 3 letters of recommendation, education statement of interest essay, autobiographical statement, NC Class A teacher licensure in related field, minimum of 3 years' teaching experience; for doctorate, education statement of interest essay, master's degree in education field, 3 years of leadership experience. Additional exam requirements/recommendations for international students: Required—TOEFL (minimum score 550 paper-based; 79 iBT), IELTS (minimum score 6.5). Electronic applications accepted.

University of North Dakota, Graduate School, College of Education and Human Development, Department of Educational Leadership, Grand Forks, ND 58202. Offers M Ed, Ed D, PhD, Ed S. *Accreditation:* NCATE. *Program availability:* Part-time, evening/weekend, online learning. *Degree requirements:* For master's and Ed S, comprehensive exam, thesis or alternative; for doctorate, comprehensive exam, thesis/dissertation, final exam. *Entrance requirements:* For master's, minimum GPA of 3.0; for doctorate, minimum GPA of 3.5. Additional exam requirements/recommendations for international students: Required—TOEFL (minimum score 550 paper-based; 79 iBT), IELTS (minimum score 6.5). Electronic applications accepted.

University of Northern Colorado, Graduate School, College of Education and Behavioral Sciences, Department of Leadership, Policy and Development: Higher Education and P-12 Education, Educational Leadership and Policy Studies Program, Greeley, CO 80639. Offers educational leadership (MA, Ed S); educational leadership and policy studies (Ed D). *Accreditation:* NCATE. *Program availability:* Part-time, evening/weekend, online learning. *Degree requirements:* For master's, comprehensive exam, thesis or alternative; for doctorate, comprehensive exam, thesis/dissertation; for Ed S, comprehensive exam, thesis. *Entrance requirements:* For master's, resume, interview; for doctorate, GRE General Test, resume, interview; for Ed S, resume. Electronic applications accepted.

University of Northern Colorado, Graduate School, College of Education and Behavioral Sciences, School of Teacher Education, Program in Educational Studies, Greeley, CO 80639. Offers Ed D. *Program availability:* Part-time, evening/weekend. Electronic applications accepted.

University of Northern Iowa, Graduate College, College of Education, Department of Educational Leadership and Postsecondary Education, MAE Program in Principalship, Cedar Falls, IA 50614. Offers MAE. *Program availability:* Part-time, evening/weekend. *Degree requirements:* For master's, comprehensive exam (for some programs), thesis or alternative, minimum of 1 year of successful teaching appropriate to the major. *Entrance requirements:* For master's, minimum GPA of 3.0. Additional exam requirements/recommendations for international students: Required—TOEFL (minimum score 500 paper-based; 61 iBT). Electronic applications accepted.

University of Northern Iowa, Graduate College, College of Education, Ed D Program in Education, Cedar Falls, IA 50614. Offers allied health, recreation, and community services (Ed D); curriculum and instruction (Ed D); educational leadership (Ed D). *Program availability:* Part-time, evening/weekend. *Degree requirements:* For doctorate, thesis/dissertation. *Entrance requirements:* For doctorate, GRE, minimum GPA of 3.0, master's degree. Additional exam requirements/recommendations for international students: Required—TOEFL (minimum score 500 paper-based; 61 iBT).

University of North Florida, College of Education and Human Services, Department of Leadership, School Counseling and Sport Management, Jacksonville, FL 32224. Offers counselor education (M Ed), including school counseling; educational leadership (M Ed, Ed D), including athletic administration (M Ed), educational leadership, educational technology (M Ed), instructional leadership (M Ed). *Program availability:* Part-time, evening/weekend. *Faculty:* 19 full-time (13 women), 3 part-time/adjunct (1 woman). *Students:* 73 full-time (58 women), 228 part-time (179 women); includes 111 minority (66 Black or African American, non-Hispanic/Latino; 7 Asian, non-Hispanic/Latino; 26 Hispanic/Latino; 1 Native Hawaiian or other Pacific Islander, non-Hispanic/Latino; 11 Two or more races, non-Hispanic/Latino), 8 international. Average age 38. 184 applicants, 58% accepted, 74 enrolled. In 2018, 77 master's, 20 doctorates awarded. *Degree requirements:* For doctorate, thesis/dissertation. *Entrance requirements:* For master's, GRE General Test, minimum GPA of 3.0 in last 60 hours, interview, 3 letters of recommendation; for doctorate, GRE General Test, master's degree, interview, 3 letters of recommendation, writing sample. Additional exam requirements/recommendations for international students: Required—TOEFL (minimum score 500 paper-based). *Application deadline:* For fall admission, 5/1 priority date for domestic students, 5/1 for international students. Application fee: $30. Electronic applications accepted. *Expenses: Tuition, area resident:* Part-time $408.10 per credit hour. Tuition, state resident: part-time $408.10 per credit hour. Tuition, nonresident: part-time $932.61 per credit hour. *Required fees:* $111.81 per credit hour. Tuition and fees vary according to course load, campus/location and program. *Financial support:* In 2018–19, 42 students received support, including 1 research assistantship (averaging $8,096 per year), 1 teaching assistantship (averaging $5,824 per year); career-related internships or fieldwork, Federal Work-Study, scholarships/grants, tuition waivers (partial), and unspecified assistantships also available. Support available to part-time students. Financial award application deadline: 4/1; financial award applicants required to submit FAFSA. *Faculty research:* Counseling: ethics; lesbian, bisexual and transgender issues; educational leadership: school culture and climate; educational assessment and accountability; school safety and student discipline. *Total annual research expenditures:* $12,024. *Unit head:* Dr. Liz Gregg, Chair, 904-620-5199, E-mail: liz.gregg@unf.edu. *Application contact:* Dr. Amanda Pascale, Director, The Graduate School, 904-620-1360, Fax: 904-620-1362, E-mail: graduateschool@unf.edu.
Website: http://www.unf.edu/coehs/lscsm/

University of North Georgia, Doctor of Education Program in Higher Education Leadership and Practice, Dahlonega, GA 30597. Offers Ed D. *Program availability:* Part-time, evening/weekend, online only, 100% online. *Degree requirements:* For doctorate, thesis/dissertation. *Entrance requirements:* Additional exam requirements/recommendations for international students: Required—TOEFL (minimum score 550 paper-based; 79 iBT), IELTS (minimum score 6.5). Electronic applications accepted. *Expenses:* Contact institution.

University of North Georgia, Ed S in Educational Leadership Program, Dahlonega, GA 30597. Offers Certificate, Ed S. *Program availability:* Part-time, evening/weekend, blended/hybrid learning. *Entrance requirements:* Additional exam requirements/recommendations for international students: Required—TOEFL (minimum score 550 paper-based; 79 iBT), IELTS (minimum score 6.5). Electronic applications accepted. *Expenses:* Contact institution.

University of North Texas, Toulouse Graduate School, Denton, TX 76203-5459. Offers accounting (MS); applied anthropology (MA, MS); applied behavior analysis (Certificate); applied geography (MA); applied technology and performance improvement (M Ed, MS); art education (MA); art history (MA); arts leadership (Certificate); audiology (Au D); behavior analysis (MS); behavioral science (PhD); biochemistry and molecular biology (MS); biology (MA, MS); biomedical engineering (MS); business analysis (MS); chemistry (MS); clinical health psychology (PhD); communication studies (MA, MS); computer engineering (MS); computer science (MS); counseling (M Ed, MS), including clinical mental health counseling (MS), college and university counseling, elementary school counseling, secondary school counseling; creative writing (MA); criminal justice (MS); curriculum and instruction (M Ed); decision sciences (MBA); design (MA, MFA), including fashion design (MFA), innovation studies, interior design (MFA); early childhood studies (MS); economics (MS); educational leadership (M Ed, Ed D); educational psychology (MS, PhD), including family studies (MS), gifted and talented (MS), human development (MS), learning and cognition (MS), research, measurement and evaluation (MS); electrical engineering (MS); emergency management (MPA); engineering technology (MS); English (MA); English as a second language (MA); environmental science (MS); finance (MBA, MS); financial management (MPA); French (MA); health services management (MBA); higher education (M Ed, Ed D); history (MA, MS); hospitality management (MS); human resources management (MPA); information science (MS); information systems (PhD); information technologies (MBA); interdisciplinary studies (MA, MS); international studies (MA); international sustainable tourism (MS); jazz studies (MM); journalism (MA, MJ, Graduate Certificate), including interactive and virtual digital communication (Graduate Certificate), narrative journalism (Graduate Certificate), public relations (Graduate Certificate); kinesiology (MS); linguistics (MA); local government management (MPA); logistics (PhD); logistics and supply chain management (MBA); long-term care, senior housing, and aging services (MA); management (PhD); marketing (MBA); mathematics (MA, MS); mechanical and energy engineering (MS, PhD); music (MA), including ethnomusicology, music theory, musicology, performance; music composition (PhD); music education (MM Ed, PhD); nonprofit management (MPA); operations and supply chain management (MBA); performance (MM, DMA); philosophy (MA); political science (MA); professional and technical communication (MA); radio, television and film (MA, MFA); rehabilitation counseling (Certificate); sociology (MA); Spanish (MA); special education (M Ed); speech-language pathology (MA); strategic management (MBA); studio art (MFA); teaching (M Ed); MBA/MS. *Program availability:* Part-time, evening/weekend, online learning. Terminal master's awarded for partial completion of doctoral program. *Degree requirements:* For master's, variable foreign language requirement, comprehensive exam (for some programs), thesis (for some programs); for doctorate, variable foreign language requirement, comprehensive exam (for some programs), thesis/dissertation; for other advanced degree, variable foreign language requirement, comprehensive exam (for some programs). *Entrance requirements:* For master's and doctorate, GRE, GMAT. Additional exam requirements/recommendations for international students: Required—TOEFL (minimum score 550 paper-based; 79 iBT). Electronic applications accepted.

University of North Texas at Dallas, Graduate School, Dallas, TX 75241. Offers accounting (MBA); counseling (M Ed, MS); criminal justice (MS); curriculum and instruction (M Ed); educational administration (M Ed); human resources and organizational behavior (MBA); public leadership (MS); strategic management (MBA).

University of Oklahoma, Jeannine Rainbolt College of Education, Department of Educational Leadership and Policy Studies, Norman, OK 73019. Offers adult and higher education (M Ed, PhD), including adult and higher education; educational administration, curriculum and supervision (M Ed, Ed D, PhD); educational studies (M Ed, PhD). *Accreditation:* NCATE. *Program availability:* Part-time, evening/weekend, blended/hybrid learning. Terminal master's awarded for partial completion of doctoral program. *Degree requirements:* For master's, comprehensive exam, thesis (for some programs); for doctorate, comprehensive exam, thesis/dissertation. *Entrance requirements:* Additional exam requirements/recommendations for international students: Required—TOEFL (minimum score 79 iBT) or IELTS (minimum score 6.5). Electronic applications accepted. *Expenses:* Tuition, state resident: full-time $5683.20; part-time $236.80 per credit hour. Tuition, nonresident: full-time $20,342; part-time $847.60 per credit hour. *International tuition:* $20,342.40 full-time. *Required fees:* $2894.20; $110.05 per credit hour. $126.50 per semester. Tuition and fees vary according to course load and program. *Faculty research:* Improvement science, leadership and ethics, education and social policy, gender and equity, collegiate athletics.

University of Oregon, Graduate School, College of Education, Eugene, OR 97403. Offers communication disorders and sciences (MA, MS, PhD); counseling psychology (PhD); couples and family therapy (MS); critical and sociocultural studies in education (PhD); curriculum and teacher education (MA, MS); educational leadership (MS, D Ed, PhD); prevention science (M Ed, MS, PhD); school psychology (MS, PhD); special education (M Ed, MA, MS, PhD). *Accreditation:* ASHA. *Program availability:* Part-time. Terminal master's awarded for partial completion of doctoral program. *Degree requirements:* For master's, exam, paper, or project; for doctorate, comprehensive exam, thesis/dissertation. *Entrance requirements:* Additional exam requirements/recommendations for international students: Required—TOEFL. *Faculty research:* Basic and applied research in teaching, learning and habilitation in all settings, schooling effectiveness.

University of Pennsylvania, Graduate School of Education, Division of Teaching, Learning, and Leadership, Program in Educational Leadership, Philadelphia, PA 19104. Offers MS Ed, Ed D, PhD. *Program availability:* Part-time. *Students:* 12 full-time (8 women), 4 part-time (0 women); includes 6 minority (1 Black or African American, non-Hispanic/Latino; 1 Asian, non-Hispanic/Latino; 4 Two or more races, non-Hispanic/Latino). Average age 36. 49 applicants, 4% accepted, 2 enrolled. In 2018, 2 doctorates awarded. *Entrance requirements:* For master's, GRE or MAT; for doctorate, GRE. Application fee: $80.

University of Pennsylvania, Graduate School of Education, Division of Teaching, Learning, and Leadership, Program in School Leadership, Philadelphia, PA 19104. Offers MS Ed. *Program availability:* Part-time, evening/weekend. *Students:* 32 full-time (16 women), 7 part-time (6 women); includes 13 minority (5 Black or African American, non-Hispanic/Latino; 3 Asian, non-Hispanic/Latino; 5 Two or more races, non-Hispanic/Latino). Average age 35. 102 applicants, 49% accepted, 40 enrolled. In 2018, 33 master's awarded. *Entrance requirements:* For master's, bachelor's degree. Additional

exam requirements/recommendations for international students: Required—TOEFL, IELTS. *Application deadline:* Applications are processed on a rolling basis. Application fee: $80. Electronic applications accepted. *Financial support:* In 2018–19, 27 students received support. Scholarships/grants available. *Faculty research:* Governance issues in schools, teacher professional development, independent schools, leadership identification and development, curriculum innovation and design. *Unit head:* Dr. Earl Ball, Director, 215-573-7499. *Application contact:* Amara Rockar, Administrative Coordinator, 215-746-2718, E-mail: arockar@upenn.edu.
Website: http://www.gse.upenn.edu/tll/slp

University of Pennsylvania, Graduate School of Education, Division of Teaching, Learning, and Leadership, Program in Teaching, Learning, and Leadership, Philadelphia, PA 19104. Offers educational leadership (MS Ed); teaching and learning (MS Ed). *Program availability:* Part-time. *Students:* 77 full-time (54 women), 46 part-time (32 women); includes 46 minority (22 Black or African American, non-Hispanic/Latino; 9 Asian, non-Hispanic/Latino; 7 Hispanic/Latino; 8 Two or more races, non-Hispanic/Latino), 17 international. Average age 35. 349 applicants, 58% accepted, 130 enrolled. In 2018, 42 master's awarded. Application fee: $80.

University of Pennsylvania, Graduate School of Education, Mid-Career Doctoral Program in Educational Leadership, Philadelphia, PA 19104. Offers Ed D. *Program availability:* Evening/weekend. *Students:* 85 full-time (47 women), 2 part-time (both women); includes 43 minority (25 Black or African American, non-Hispanic/Latino; 1 American Indian or Alaska Native, non-Hispanic/Latino; 6 Asian, non-Hispanic/Latino; 5 Hispanic/Latino; 6 Two or more races, non-Hispanic/Latino), 1 international. Average age 42. 102 applicants, 32% accepted, 27 enrolled. In 2018, 22 doctorates awarded. *Degree requirements:* For doctorate, comprehensive exam, thesis/dissertation. *Entrance requirements:* For doctorate, master's degree. *Application deadline:* For summer admission, 2/1 priority date for domestic and international students. Application fee: $80. Electronic applications accepted. *Faculty research:* Educational leadership, district reform, team effectiveness, identity development and social identification, racial/ethnic socialization and negotiation. *Unit head:* Martha Williams, Program Coordinator, 215-746-6573, E-mail: marthaw@upenn.edu. *Application contact:* Martha Williams, Program Coordinator, 215-746-6573, E-mail: marthaw@upenn.edu.
Website: http://www2.gse.upenn.edu/midcareer/

University of Pennsylvania, Graduate School of Education, Penn Chief Learning Officer (CLO) Executive Doctoral Program, Philadelphia, PA 19104. Offers Ed D. *Program availability:* Evening/weekend. *Students:* 70 full-time (30 women), 1 part-time (0 women); includes 29 minority (18 Black or African American, non-Hispanic/Latino; 6 Asian, non-Hispanic/Latino; 4 Hispanic/Latino; 1 Two or more races, non-Hispanic/Latino), 5 international. Average age 48. 54 applicants, 33% accepted, 18 enrolled. In 2018, 10 doctorates awarded. Terminal master's awarded for partial completion of doctoral program. *Degree requirements:* For doctorate, comprehensive exam, thesis/dissertation. *Entrance requirements:* For doctorate, bachelor's degree. *Application deadline:* For fall admission, 7/1 priority date for domestic and international students; for spring admission, 10/1 priority date for domestic and international students; for summer admission, 3/2 priority date for domestic and international students. Applications are processed on a rolling basis. Application fee: $80. Electronic applications accepted. *Faculty research:* Strategic leadership, workplace learning, business acumen, evidenced-best decision making, technology in the work place. *Unit head:* Associate Director, 215-573-0591. *Application contact:* Associate Director, 215-573-0591.
Website: http://www.pennclo.com/

University of Phoenix–Bay Area Campus, College of Education, San Jose, CA 95134-1805. Offers administration and supervision (MA Ed); adult education and training (MA Ed); early childhood education (MA Ed); education (Ed S); educational leadership (Ed D); elementary teacher education (MA Ed); higher education administration (PhD); secondary teacher education (MA Ed); special education (MA Ed); teacher leadership (MA Ed). *Program availability:* Evening/weekend, online learning. *Degree requirements:* For master's, thesis (for some programs). *Entrance requirements:* For master's, minimum undergraduate GPA of 2.5, 3 years of work experience. Additional exam requirements/recommendations for international students: Required—TOEFL (minimum score 550 paper-based; 79 iBT). Electronic applications accepted.

University of Phoenix–Hawaii Campus, College of Education, Honolulu, HI 96813-3800. Offers administration and supervision (MA Ed); curriculum and instruction (MA Ed); elementary education (MA Ed); secondary education (MA Ed); special education (MA Ed); teacher education for elementary licensure (MA Ed). *Program availability:* Evening/weekend. *Degree requirements:* For master's, thesis (for some programs). *Entrance requirements:* For master's, minimum undergraduate GPA of 2.5, 3 years of work experience. Additional exam requirements/recommendations for international students: Required—TOEFL (minimum score 550 paper-based; 79 iBT). Electronic applications accepted.

University of Phoenix–Las Vegas Campus, College of Education, Las Vegas, NV 89135. Offers administration and supervision (MA Ed); curriculum and instruction (MA Ed); school counseling (MSC); teacher education-elementary licensure (MA Ed). *Program availability:* Evening/weekend. *Degree requirements:* For master's, thesis (for some programs). *Entrance requirements:* For master's, minimum undergraduate GPA of 2.5, 3 years of work experience. Additional exam requirements/recommendations for international students: Required—TOEFL (minimum score 550 paper-based; 79 iBT). Electronic applications accepted.

University of Phoenix–Online Campus, College of Education, Phoenix, AZ 85034-7209. Offers administration and supervision (MAEd, Certificate); adult education and training (MAEd); curriculum and instruction (MAEd), including computer education, curriculum and instruction, English as a second language, language arts, mathematics, reading; early childhood education (MAEd); educational studies (MAEd); elementary teacher education (MAEd), including early childhood, elementary teacher education, high school middle level, middle level; principal licensure (Certificate); secondary teacher education (MAEd); special education (MAEd, Certificate); teacher education (MAEd), including middle level generalist; teacher education middle level mathematics (MAEd), including middle level mathematics; teacher education middle level science (MAEd), including middle level science; teacher education secondary mathematics (MAEd); teacher education secondary science (MAEd); teacher leadership (MAEd); teachers of English learners (Certificate); transition to teaching (Certificate), including elementary education, secondary education. *Program availability:* Evening/weekend, online learning. *Entrance requirements:* Additional exam requirements/recommendations for international students: Required—TOEFL, TOEIC (Test of English as an International Communication), Berlitz Online English Proficiency Exam, PTE, or IELTS. Electronic applications accepted. *Expenses:* Contact institution.

University of Phoenix–Online Campus, School of Advanced Studies, Phoenix, AZ 85034-7209. Offers business administration (DBA); education (Ed S); educational leadership (Ed D), including curriculum and instruction, education technology, educational leadership; health administration (DHA); higher education administration (PhD); industrial/organizational psychology (PhD); nursing (PhD); organizational leadership (DM), including information systems and technology, organizational leadership. *Program availability:* Evening/weekend, online learning. *Degree requirements:* For doctorate, thesis/

dissertation. *Entrance requirements:* Additional exam requirements/recommendations for international students: Required—TOEFL, TOEIC (Test of English as an International Communication), Berlitz Online English Proficiency Exam, PTE, or IELTS. Electronic applications accepted. *Expenses:* Contact institution.

University of Phoenix–Phoenix Campus, College of Education, Tempe, AZ 85282-2371. Offers administration and supervision (MA Ed); adult education and training (MA Ed); curriculum and instruction reading (MA Ed); early childhood education (MA Ed); education studies (MA Ed); elementary teacher education (MA Ed); secondary teacher education (MA Ed); special education (MA Ed); teacher leadership (MA Ed). *Program availability:* Evening/weekend, online learning. *Entrance requirements:* Additional exam requirements/recommendations for international students: Required—TOEFL, TOEIC (Test of English as an International Communication), Berlitz Online English Proficiency Exam, PTE, or IELTS. Electronic applications accepted. *Expenses:* Contact institution.

University of Pikeville, Patton College of Education, Pikeville, KY 41501. Offers teacher leader (MA). *Program availability:* Part-time, evening/weekend. *Degree requirements:* For master's, comprehensive exam. *Expenses:* Contact institution.

University of Pittsburgh, School of Education, Department of Administrative and Policy Studies, Program in School Leadership, Pittsburgh, PA 15260. Offers M Ed, Ed D, PhD. *Program availability:* Part-time, evening/weekend. *Degree requirements:* For master's, thesis; for doctorate, thesis/dissertation. *Entrance requirements:* For doctorate, GRE General Test. Additional exam requirements/recommendations for international students: Required—TOEFL (minimum score 80 iBT). Electronic applications accepted.

University of Portland, School of Education, Portland, OR 97203-5798. Offers education (MA, MAT); educational leadership (M Ed); English for speakers of other languages (M Ed); initial administrator licensure (M Ed); neuroeducation (M Ed, Ed D); organizational leadership and development (Ed D); reading (M Ed); school leadership and development (Ed D); special education (M Ed). *Accreditation:* NCATE. *Program availability:* Part-time, evening/weekend. *Students:* 32 full-time (30 women), 239 part-time (187 women); includes 33 minority (7 Black or African American, non-Hispanic/Latino; 3 American Indian or Alaska Native, non-Hispanic/Latino; 13 Asian, non-Hispanic/Latino; 1 Native Hawaiian or other Pacific Islander, non-Hispanic/Latino; 9 Two or more races, non-Hispanic/Latino). Average age 34. 92 applicants, 60% accepted, 42 enrolled. In 2018, 57 master's, 16 doctorates awarded. *Degree requirements:* For doctorate, thesis/dissertation. *Entrance requirements:* For master's, minimum GPA of 3.0, teaching certificate, letters of recommendation, resume, statement of goals, official transcripts; for doctorate, 2 letters of recommendation, resume, essays, official transcripts. Additional exam requirements/recommendations for international students: Required—TOEFL (minimum score 550 paper-based; 80 iBT), IELTS (minimum score 7). *Application deadline:* For fall admission, 7/15 priority date for domestic and international students; for spring admission, 12/15 priority date for domestic and international students; for summer admission, 4/15 for domestic and international students. Applications are processed on a rolling basis. Electronic applications accepted. *Expenses:* MAT degree - $995/credit hour; EDD and Educational Specialist - $813/credit hour; all other degrees and certificates - $663/credit hour. *Financial support:* Fellowships, Federal Work-Study, and scholarships/grants available. Support available to part-time students. Financial award application deadline: 3/1; financial award applicants required to submit FAFSA. *Faculty research:* Multicultural education, supervision/leadership. *Unit head:* Dr. Bruce Weitzel, Associate Dean, 503-943-7135, E-mail: soed@up.edu. *Application contact:* Caitlin Biddulph, Graduate Programs and Admissions Specialist, 503-943-7107, E-mail: biddulph@up.edu.
Website: http://education.up.edu/default.aspx?cid-4318&pid-5590

University of Prince Edward Island, Faculty of Education, Charlottetown, PE C1A 4P3, Canada. Offers educational studies (PhD); leadership in learning (M Ed). *Program availability:* Part-time. *Degree requirements:* For master's, thesis. *Entrance requirements:* For master's, 2 years of professional experience, bachelor of education, professional certificate. Additional exam requirements/recommendations for international students: Required—TOEFL (minimum score 550 paper-based; 80 iBT), Canadian Academic English Language Assessment, Michigan English Language Assessment Battery, Canadian Test of English for Scholars and Trainees. *Faculty research:* Distance learning, aboriginal communities and education leadership development, international development, immersion language learning.

University of Puerto Rico–Río Piedras, College of Education, Program in School Administration and Supervision, San Juan, PR 00931-3300. Offers M Ed, Ed D. *Program availability:* Part-time. *Degree requirements:* For master's, thesis; for doctorate, thesis/dissertation, internship. *Entrance requirements:* For master's, PAEG or GRE, minimum GPA of 3.0, letter of recommendation; for doctorate, GRE or PAEG, interview, master's degree, minimum GPA of 3.0, letter of recommendation.

University of Regina, Faculty of Graduate Studies and Research, Faculty of Education, Department of Educational Leadership, Regina, SK S4S 0A2, Canada. Offers M Ed. *Program availability:* Part-time. *Students:* 8 full-time (7 women), 32 part-time (15 women). Average age 30. 11 applicants, 100% accepted, 9 enrolled. In 2018, 12 master's awarded. *Degree requirements:* For master's, thesis (for some programs), practicum, project, or thesis. *Entrance requirements:* For master's, bachelor's degree in education, 2 years of teaching or other relevant professional experience. Additional exam requirements/recommendations for international students: Required—TOEFL (minimum score 580 paper-based; 80 iBT), IELTS (minimum score 6.5), PTE (minimum score 59), other options are CAEL, MELAB, Cantest and U of R ESL. *Application deadline:* For fall admission, 2/15 for domestic and international students; for winter admission, 10/15 for domestic and international students; for spring admission, 2/15 for domestic and international students. Application fee: $100. Electronic applications accepted. Tuition and fees vary according to course level, course load, degree level and program. *Financial support:* Fellowships, research assistantships, teaching assistantships, career-related internships or fieldwork, Federal Work-Study, scholarships/grants, unspecified assistantships, and travel award and Graduate Scholarship Base funds available. Support available to part-time students. Financial award application deadline: 9/30. *Faculty research:* Legal aspects of school administration, economics of education, education planning, politics of education, administrative behavior in education. *Unit head:* Dr. Twyla Salm, Associate Dean, Research and Graduate Programs in Education, 306-585-4604, Fax: 306-585-5330, E-mail: Twyla.Salm@uregina.ca. *Application contact:* Linda Jiang, Graduate Program Coordinator, 306-585-4506, Fax: 306-585-4880, E-mail: linda.jiang@uregina.ca.
Website: http://www.uregina.ca/education/

University of Rio Grande, Graduate School, Rio Grande, OH 45674. Offers athletic coaching leadership (M Ed); educational leadership (M Ed); integrated arts (M Ed); intervention specialist in early childhood (M Ed); intervention specialist in mild/moderate (M Ed). *Accreditation:* NCATE. *Program availability:* Part-time. *Degree requirements:* For master's, final research project, portfolio. *Entrance requirements:* For master's, minimum GPA of 2.7 in major, 2.5 overall. Additional exam requirements/recommendations for international students: Required—TOEFL. *Faculty research:* Interagency collaboration, reading and mathematics, learning styles, college access, literacy.

University of Rochester, Margaret Warner Graduate School of Education and Human Development, Doctoral Programs in Education, Rochester, NY 14627. Offers counseling (Ed D); educational administration (Ed D); educational policy and theory (PhD); higher education (PhD); human development in educational context (PhD); teaching, curriculum, and change (PhD). *Expenses: Tuition:* Full-time $52,974; part-time $1654 per credit hour. *Required fees:* $612. One-time fee: $30 part-time. Tuition and fees vary according to campus/location and program.

University of Rochester, Margaret Warner Graduate School of Education and Human Development, Master's Program in School Leadership, Rochester, NY 14627. Offers MS. *Expenses: Tuition:* Full-time $52,974; part-time $1654 per credit hour. *Required fees:* $612. One-time fee: $30 part-time. Tuition and fees vary according to campus/location and program.

University of St. Francis, College of Education, Joliet, IL 60435-6169. Offers educational leadership (MS, Ed D); elementary education (M Ed); reading (MS); secondary education (M Ed), including English education, math education, science education, social studies education, visual arts education; special education (M Ed); teaching and learning (MS); TESOL (Certificate). *Accreditation:* NCATE. *Program availability:* Part-time, evening/weekend, 100% online, blended/hybrid learning. *Faculty:* 11 full-time (8 women), 58 part-time/adjunct (38 women). *Students:* 43 full-time (35 women), 453 part-time (354 women); includes 110 minority (48 Black or African American, non-Hispanic/Latino; 7 Asian, non-Hispanic/Latino; 52 Hispanic/Latino; 3 Two or more races, non-Hispanic/Latino). 3 international. Average age 37. 300 applicants, 66% accepted, 164 enrolled. In 2018, 151 master's, 42 doctorates, 4 other advanced degrees awarded. *Degree requirements:* For master's, comprehensive exam; for doctorate, thesis/dissertation. *Entrance requirements:* Additional exam requirements/recommendations for international students: Required—TOEFL (minimum score 550 paper-based; 79 iBT), IELTS (minimum score 6). *Application deadline:* Applications are processed on a rolling basis. Electronic applications accepted. Application fee is waived when completed online. *Expenses:* Contact institution. *Financial support:* In 2018–19, 33 students received support. Scholarships/grants and tuition waivers (partial) available. Support available to part-time students. Financial award applicants required to submit FAFSA. *Unit head:* Dr. John Gambro, Dean, 815-740-3456, E-mail: jgambro@stfrancis.edu. *Application contact:* Sandee Sloka, Director Adult & Graduate Admissions, 800-735-7500, E-mail: ssloka@stfrancis.edu.
Website: https://www.stfrancis.edu/education/

University of St. Thomas, College of Education, Leadership and Counseling, Department of Leadership, Policy and Administration, St. Paul, MN 55105-1096. Offers education leadership and administration (MA); educational leadership and learning (Ed D); executive coaching (Certificate); K-12 administration (Ed S); leadership in student affairs (MA). *Program availability:* Part-time, evening/weekend. Terminal master's awarded for partial completion of doctoral program. *Degree requirements:* For master's, thesis (for some programs); for doctorate, thesis/dissertation; for other advanced degree, thesis or alternative. *Entrance requirements:* For master's, minimum GPA of 3.0 or MAT; for doctorate, MAT, minimum graduate GPA of 3.5; for other advanced degree, minimum graduate GPA of 3.25 or MAT. Additional exam requirements/recommendations for international students: Required—TOEFL (minimum score 550 paper-based). Electronic applications accepted. *Expenses:* Contact institution.

University of St. Thomas, School of Education and Human Services, Houston, TX 77006-4696. Offers all level education (M Ed); bilingual/dual language (M Ed); Catholic school teaching (M Ed); Catholic/private school leadership (M Ed); counselor education (M Ed); curriculum and instruction (M Ed); education (Ed D); educational leadership (M Ed); elementary teaching (M Ed); English as a second language (M Ed); exceptionality/educational diagnostician (M Ed); exceptionality/special education (M Ed); generalist (M Ed); reading (M Ed); secondary teaching (M Ed); teaching (MAT). *Accreditation:* TEAC. *Program availability:* Part-time, evening/weekend, online learning. *Degree requirements:* For master's, thesis, field experience. *Entrance requirements:* For master's, GRE or MAT if GPA is below 3.0, bachelor's degree; minimum GPA of 2.75 in bachelor's degree or last 60 credit hours; official transcripts from all institutions; goal statement of 250-300 words; 1 reference. Additional exam requirements/recommendations for international students: Required—TOEFL (minimum score 94 iBT), IELTS (minimum score 7), PTE (minimum score 53). Electronic applications accepted. *Expenses:* Contact institution. *Faculty research:* Leadership, diversity, personality traits, second language acquisition.

University of San Diego, School of Leadership and Education Sciences, Department of Leadership Studies, San Diego, CA 92110-2492. Offers higher education leadership (MA); leadership studies (MA, PhD, Certificate); nonprofit leadership and management (MA). *Program availability:* Part-time, evening/weekend. *Faculty:* 8 full-time (3 women), 24 part-time/adjunct (11 women). *Students:* 46 full-time (28 women), 225 part-time (147 women); includes 124 minority (19 Black or African American, non-Hispanic/Latino; 25 Asian, non-Hispanic/Latino; 66 Hispanic/Latino; 14 Two or more races, non-Hispanic/Latino), 17 international. Average age 34. 299 applicants, 67% accepted, 105 enrolled. In 2018, 93 master's, 17 doctorates awarded. *Degree requirements:* For master's, thesis (for some programs), international experience; for doctorate, comprehensive exam, thesis/dissertation, international experience. *Entrance requirements:* For master's, GRE (recommended with GPA less than 3.25); for doctorate, GRE (less than 5 years old) strongly encouraged, master's degree, minimum GPA of 3.5 (graduate coursework), resume. Additional exam requirements/recommendations for international students: Required—TOEFL (minimum score 580 paper-based; 83 iBT), TWE. Application fee: $45. Electronic applications accepted. *Financial support:* In 2018–19, 190 students received support. Career-related internships or fieldwork, Federal Work-Study, institutionally sponsored loans, unspecified assistantships, and stipends available. Support available to part-time students. Financial award application deadline: 4/1; financial award applicants required to submit FAFSA. *Faculty research:* Higher education administration policy and relations, organizational leadership, nonprofits and philanthropy, student affairs leadership. *Unit head:* Dr. Lea Hubbard, Graduate Program Director, 619-260-7818, E-mail: lhubbard@sandiego.edu. *Application contact:* Erika Garwood, Associate Director of Graduate Admissions, 619-260-4524, Fax: 619-260-4158, E-mail: grads@sandiego.edu.
Website: https://www.sandiego.edu/soles/leadership-studies/

University of San Diego, School of Leadership and Education Sciences, Department of Learning and Teaching, San Diego, CA 92110-2492. Offers curriculum and instruction (M Ed), including inclusive learning, literacy and digital learning, school leadership, steam (science, technology, engineering, arts, and mathematics); inclusive learning (M Ed); literacy and digital learning (M Ed); school leadership (M Ed); special education (M Ed); STEAM (science, technology, engineering, arts, and mathematics) (M Ed); TESOL, literacy and culture (M Ed). *Program availability:* Part-time, evening/weekend. *Faculty:* 9 full-time (7 women), 34 part-time/adjunct (26 women). *Students:* 136 full-time (102 women), 223 part-time (177 women); includes 130 minority (17 Black or African American, non-Hispanic/Latino; 21 Asian, non-Hispanic/Latino; 74 Hispanic/Latino; 3 Native Hawaiian or other Pacific Islander, non-Hispanic/Latino; 15 Two or more races, non-Hispanic/Latino), 10 international. Average age 33. 391 applicants, 85% accepted, 190 enrolled. In 2018, 201 master's awarded. *Degree requirements:* For master's, thesis

(for some programs), international experience. *Entrance requirements:* For master's, California Basic Educational Skills Test, California Subject Examination for Teachers. Additional exam requirements/recommendations for international students: Required—TOEFL (minimum score 580 paper-based; 83 iBT), TWE. *Application deadline:* Applications are processed on a rolling basis. Application fee: $45. Electronic applications accepted. *Financial support:* In 2018–19, 127 students received support. Career-related internships or fieldwork, Federal Work-Study, institutionally sponsored loans, scholarships/grants, and stipends available. Financial award application deadline: 4/1; financial award applicants required to submit FAFSA. *Faculty research:* Action research methodology, cultural studies, instructional theories and practices, second language acquisition, school reform. *Unit head:* Dr. Reyes Quezada, Chair, 619-260-7655, E-mail: rquezada@sandiego.edu. *Application contact:* Erika Garwood, Associate Director of Graduate Admissions, 619-260-4524, Fax: 619-260-4158, E-mail: grads@sandiego.edu.
Website: http://www.sandiego.edu/soles/learning-and-teaching/

University of San Francisco, School of Education, Catholic Educational Leadership Program, San Francisco, CA 94117. Offers Catholic school leadership (Ed D). *Program availability:* Part-time, evening/weekend. *Students:* 14 full-time (5 women), 11 part-time (4 women); includes 8 minority (4 Asian, non-Hispanic/Latino; 2 Hispanic/Latino; 1 Native Hawaiian or other Pacific Islander, non-Hispanic/Latino; 1 Two or more races, non-Hispanic/Latino), 6 international. Average age 38. 14 applicants, 86% accepted, 7 enrolled. In 2018, 16 master's, 5 doctorates awarded. *Degree requirements:* For doctorate, thesis/dissertation. *Entrance requirements:* Additional exam requirements/recommendations for international students: Required—TOEFL, IELTS, PTE. Application fee: $55 ($65 for international students). Electronic applications accepted. *Financial support:* Fellowships, research assistantships, and teaching assistantships available. Financial award application deadline: 3/2; financial award applicants required to submit FAFSA. *Unit head:* Dr. Patricia Mitchell, Chair, 415-422-6226. *Application contact:* Peter Cole, Admission Coordinator, 415-422-5467, E-mail: schoolofeducation@usfca.edu.
Website: https://www.usfca.edu/catalog/graduate/school-of-education/programs-catholic-educational-leadership

University of San Francisco, School of Education, Leadership Studies Program, San Francisco, CA 94117. Offers MA, Ed D. *Program availability:* Part-time, evening/weekend. *Students:* 76 full-time (45 women), 32 part-time (18 women); includes 71 minority (22 Black or African American, non-Hispanic/Latino; 16 Asian, non-Hispanic/Latino; 21 Hispanic/Latino; 3 Native Hawaiian or other Pacific Islander, non-Hispanic/Latino; 9 Two or more races, non-Hispanic/Latino), 11 international. Average age 36. 75 applicants, 75% accepted, 32 enrolled. In 2018, 20 master's, 11 doctorates awarded. *Degree requirements:* For doctorate, thesis/dissertation. *Entrance requirements:* Additional exam requirements/recommendations for international students: Required—TOEFL, IELTS, PTE. *Application deadline:* For fall admission, 3/1 priority date for domestic and international students; for spring admission, 10/15 priority date for domestic and international students. Applications are processed on a rolling basis. Application fee: $55 ($65 for international students). Electronic applications accepted. *Financial support:* Fellowships, research assistantships, and teaching assistantships available. Financial award application deadline: 3/2; financial award applicants required to submit FAFSA. *Unit head:* Dr. Patricia Mitchell, Chair, 415-422-6551. *Application contact:* Peter Cole, Admission Coordinator, 415-422-5467, E-mail: schoolofeducation@usfca.edu.
Website: https://www.usfca.edu/catalog/graduate/school-of-education/programs-organization-and-leadership

University of Saskatchewan, College of Graduate and Postdoctoral Studies, College of Education, Department of Educational Administration, Saskatoon, SK S7N 5A2, Canada. Offers M Ed, PhD, Diploma. *Program availability:* Part-time. *Degree requirements:* For master's, thesis (for some programs); for doctorate, comprehensive exam (for some programs), thesis/dissertation. *Entrance requirements:* Additional exam requirements/recommendations for international students: Required—TOEFL (minimum score 80 iBT); Recommended—IELTS (minimum score 6.5). Electronic applications accepted.

The University of Scranton, Panuska College of Professional Studies, Department of Education, Program in Educational Administration, Scranton, PA 18510. Offers MS. *Accreditation:* NCATE. *Program availability:* Part-time, evening/weekend, online only, 100% online.

University of Sioux Falls, Fredrikson School of Education, Sioux Falls, SD 57105-1699. Offers educational administration (Ed S), including principal leadership, superintendent and district leadership; leadership in reading (M Ed); leadership in schools (M Ed); leadership in technology (M Ed); teaching (M Ed). Admission in summer only. *Accreditation:* NCATE. *Program availability:* Part-time, evening/weekend. *Degree requirements:* For master's, comprehensive exam (for some programs), research application project; for Ed S, comprehensive exam, portfolio. *Entrance requirements:* For master's, minimum GPA of 3.0, 1 year of teaching experience; for Ed S, minimum 3 years of teaching experience, minimum cumulative GPA of 3.5, 1 year of administrative experience. Additional exam requirements/recommendations for international students: Required—TOEFL. *Faculty research:* Reading, literacy, leadership.

University of South Africa, College of Human Sciences, Pretoria, South Africa. Offers adult education (M Ed); African languages (MA, PhD); African politics (MA, PhD); Afrikaans (MA, PhD); ancient history (MA, PhD); ancient Near Eastern studies (MA, PhD); anthropology (MA, PhD); applied linguistics (MA); Arabic (MA, PhD); archaeology (MA); art history (MA); Biblical archaeology (MA); Biblical studies (M Th, D Th, PhD); Christian spirituality (M Th, D Th); church history (M Th, D Th); classical studies (MA, PhD); clinical psychology (MA); communication (MA, PhD); comparative education (M Ed, Ed D); consulting psychology (D Admin, D Com, PhD); curriculum studies (M Ed, Ed D); development studies (M Admin, MA, D Admin, PhD); didactics (M Ed, Ed D); education (M Tech); education management (M Ed, Ed D); educational psychology (M Ed); English (MA); environmental education (M Ed); French (MA, PhD); German (MA, PhD); Greek (MA); guidance and counseling (M Ed); health studies (MA, PhD), including health sciences education (MA), health services management (MA), medical and surgical nursing science (critical care general) (MA), midwifery and neonatal nursing science (MA), trauma and emergency care (MA); history (MA, PhD); history of education (Ed D); inclusive education (M Ed, Ed D); information and communications technology policy and regulation (MA); information science (MA, MIS, PhD); international politics (MA, PhD); Islamic studies (MA, PhD); Italian (MA, PhD); Judaica (MA, PhD); linguistics (MA, PhD); mathematical education (M Ed); mathematics education (MA); missiology (M Th, D Th); modern Hebrew (MA, PhD); musicology (MA, MMus, D Mus, PhD); natural science education (M Ed); New Testament (M Th, D Th); Old Testament (D Th); pastoral therapy (M Th, D Th); philosophy (MA); philosophy of education (M Ed, Ed D); politics (MA, PhD); Portuguese (MA, PhD); practical theology (M Th, D Th); psychology (MA, MS, PhD); psychology of education (M Ed, Ed D); public health (MA); religious studies (MA, D Th, PhD); Romance languages (MA); Russian (MA, PhD); Semitic languages (MA, PhD); social behavior studies in HIV/AIDS (MA); social science (mental health) (MA); social science in development studies (MA); social science in psychology (MA); social science in social work (MA); social science in sociology (MA); social work

(MSW, DSW, PhD); socio-education (M Ed, Ed D); sociolinguistics (MA); sociology (MA, PhD); Spanish (MA, PhD); systematic theology (M Th, D Th); TESOL (teaching English to speakers of other languages) (MA); theological ethics (M Th, D Th); theory of literature (MA, PhD); urban ministries (D Th); urban ministry (M Th).

University of South Alabama, College of Education and Professional Studies, Department of Leadership and Teacher Education, Mobile, AL 36688. Offers art education (M Ed); early childhood education (M Ed); educational leadership (M Ed, Ed D); elementary education (M Ed); reading education (M Ed); science education (M Ed); secondary education (M Ed); special education (M Ed). *Accreditation:* NCATE. *Program availability:* Part-time. *Degree requirements:* For master's, comprehensive exam, thesis (for some programs); for doctorate, comprehensive exam, thesis/dissertation. *Entrance requirements:* For master's, GRE General Test or MAT, minimum GPA of 3.0; for doctorate, GRE, minimum graduate GPA of 3.25, 3 years of experience in field, 3 letters of recommendation, interview, official transcripts. Additional exam requirements/recommendations for international students: Required—TOEFL. Electronic applications accepted.

University of South Carolina, The Graduate School, College of Education, Department of Educational Leadership and Policies, Program in Educational Administration, Columbia, SC 29208. Offers M Ed, PhD, Ed S. *Accreditation:* NCATE. *Program availability:* Part-time, evening/weekend, online learning. *Degree requirements:* For master's, comprehensive exam, thesis (for some programs), foreign language (MA); for doctorate, comprehensive exam, thesis/dissertation. *Entrance requirements:* For master's, GRE General Test or MAT, letter of reference, resume; for doctorate and Ed S, GRE General Test or MAT, interview, letter of intent, letter of reference, transcripts, resum&e. Electronic applications accepted.

University of South Dakota, Graduate School, School of Education, Division of Curriculum and Instruction, Vermillion, SD 57069. Offers American Indian education (Certificate); curriculum and instruction (Ed D, Ed S); elementary education (MA), including elementary education; English language learners (Certificate); literacy leadership and coaching (Certificate); reading interventionist (Certificate); science, technology and math pedagogy (Certificate); secondary education (MA), including secondary education; special education (MA), including special education; technology for education and training (MS), including technology for education and training. *Accreditation:* NCATE. *Program availability:* Part-time, online learning. *Degree requirements:* For master's and other advanced degree, comprehensive exam, thesis or alternative; for doctorate, comprehensive exam, thesis/dissertation. *Entrance requirements:* For master's, doctorate, and other advanced degree, GRE General Test, MAT, minimum GPA of 2.7. Additional exam requirements/recommendations for international students: Required—TOEFL (minimum score 550 paper-based; 79 iBT). Electronic applications accepted.

University of South Dakota, Graduate School, School of Education, Division of Educational Leadership, Vermillion, SD 57069. Offers educational administration (MA, Ed D, Ed S), including adult and higher education (MA, Ed D), curriculum director, director of special education (Ed D, Ed S), preK-12 principal, school district superintendent (Ed D, Ed S). *Accreditation:* NCATE. *Program availability:* Part-time, evening/weekend, 100% online, blended/hybrid learning. *Degree requirements:* For master's and Ed S, comprehensive exam, thesis or alternative; for doctorate, comprehensive exam, thesis/dissertation. *Entrance requirements:* For master's, GRE General Test, MAT, minimum GPA of 2.7; for doctorate, minimum GPA of 2.7. Additional exam requirements/recommendations for international students: Required—TOEFL (minimum score 550 paper-based; 79 iBT). Electronic applications accepted.

University of Southern California, Graduate School, Rossier School of Education, Doctor of Education Programs, Los Angeles, CA 90089. Offers educational psychology (Ed D); higher education administration (Ed D); K-12 leadership in urban school settings (Ed D); teacher education in multicultural societies (Ed D). *Program availability:* Part-time, evening/weekend. *Degree requirements:* For doctorate, thesis/dissertation. *Entrance requirements:* For doctorate, GRE. Additional exam requirements/recommendations for international students: Required—TOEFL (minimum score 100 iBT). Electronic applications accepted. *Faculty research:* Data-driven decision-making in K-12 schools and districts; examination of college and university leadership and management in U. S. and Asia; studies in facilitating student learning; organizational change and the role of leaders; leadership, diversity, learning and accountability.

University of Southern California, Graduate School, Rossier School of Education, Doctor of Philosophy in Education Programs, Los Angeles, CA 90089. Offers educational psychology (PhD); higher education administration and policy (PhD); K-12 policy and practice (PhD). *Degree requirements:* For doctorate, thesis/dissertation, 63 units; qualifying exam; dissertation proposal and defense. *Entrance requirements:* For doctorate, GRE. Additional exam requirements/recommendations for international students: Required—TOEFL (minimum score 100 iBT). Electronic applications accepted. *Faculty research:* Diversity in higher education, organizational change, educational psychology, policy and politics of educational reform, economics of education and education policy.

University of Southern Indiana, Graduate Studies, Pott College of Science, Engineering, and Education, Department of Teacher Education, Program in Educational Leadership, Evansville, IN 47712-3590. Offers administrative leadership (Ed D); pedagogical leadership (Ed D). *Program availability:* Part-time, evening/weekend. *Entrance requirements:* For doctorate, GRE, master's degree transcript, essay, two letters of recommendation, resume/curriculum vitae. Additional exam requirements/recommendations for international students: Required—TOEFL (minimum score 550 paper-based; 79 iBT), IELTS (minimum score 6).

University of Southern Indiana, Graduate Studies, Pott College of Science, Engineering, and Education, Department of Teacher Education, Program in School Administration and Leadership, Evansville, IN 47712-3590. Offers MSE. *Program availability:* Part-time, evening/weekend. *Entrance requirements:* For master's, PRAXIS II, bachelor's degree with minimum cumulative GPA of 2.75 from college or university accredited by NCATE or comparable association; minimum GPA of 3.0 in all courses taken at graduate level at all schools attended; teaching license. Additional exam requirements/recommendations for international students: Required—TOEFL (minimum score 550 paper-based; 79 iBT), IELTS (minimum score 6). Electronic applications accepted.

University of Southern Maine, College of Management and Human Service, School of Education and Human Development, Educational Leadership Program, Portland, ME 04103. Offers assistant principal (CGS); educational leadership (MS Ed, CAS). *Program availability:* Part-time, evening/weekend, online learning. *Degree requirements:* For master's, thesis or alternative, practicum, internship; for other advanced degree, thesis or alternative. *Entrance requirements:* For master's, three years of documented teaching; for other advanced degree, master's degree. Additional exam requirements/recommendations for international students: Required—TOEFL (minimum score 550 paper-based; 79 iBT). Electronic applications accepted. *Faculty research:* Teaching strategies, technology-enhanced leadership, school-community partnerships, workforce development, higher education.

University of Southern Mississippi, College of Education and Human Sciences, Department of Educational Research and Administration, Hattiesburg, MS 39406-0001. Offers educational administration (M Ed, Ed D, PhD, Ed S); educational administration and supervision (M Ed); educational studies and research (MS); higher education (Ed D); higher education administration (PhD); higher education: student affairs (M Ed); research, evaluation, statistics, assessment (PhD). *Degree requirements:* For master's and Ed S, comprehensive exam, thesis (for some programs); for doctorate, comprehensive exam, thesis/dissertation. *Entrance requirements:* For master's and doctorate, GRE General Test, minimum GPA of 2.75. Additional exam requirements/recommendations for international students: Required—TOEFL.

University of South Florida, College of Education, Department of Leadership, Counseling, Adult, Career and Higher Education, Tampa, FL 33620-9951. Offers adult education (MA, Ed D, PhD, Ed S); career and technical education (MA); career and workforce education (PhD); higher education/community college teaching (MA, Ed D, PhD); vocational education (Ed S). *Faculty:* 19 full-time (11 women). *Students:* 107 full-time (81 women), 275 part-time (185 women); includes 143 minority (67 Black or African American, non-Hispanic/Latino; 2 American Indian or Alaska Native, non-Hispanic/Latino; 10 Asian, non-Hispanic/Latino; 56 Hispanic/Latino; 8 Two or more races, non-Hispanic/Latino), 14 international. Average age 36. 188 applicants, 54% accepted, 73 enrolled. In 2018, 51 master's, 8 doctorates, 3 other advanced degrees awarded. *Entrance requirements:* For master's, GRE may be required, goals statement; letters of recommendation; proof of educational or professional experience; prerequisites, if needed; for doctorate, GRE may be required, letters of recommendation; masters degree in appropriate field; optional interview; evidence of professional experience; personal statement. Additional exam requirements/recommendations for international students: Required—TOEFL. Application fee: $30. *Expenses:* Tuition, state resident: full-time $6350. Tuition, nonresident: full-time $19,048. *International tuition:* $19,048 full-time. *Required fees:* $2079. *Financial support:* In 2018–19, 19 students received support. *Total annual research expenditures:* $40,520. *Unit head:* Dr. Judith Ponticell, Chair, 813-974-4897, Fax: 813-974-5423, E-mail: jponticell@usf.edu. *Application contact:* Dr. Judith Ponticell, Chair, 813-974-4897, Fax: 813-974-5423, E-mail: jponticell@usf.edu.
Website: http://www.coedu.usf.edu/main/departments/ache/ache.html

University of South Florida, Innovative Education, Tampa, FL 33620-9951. Offers adult, career and higher education (Graduate Certificate), including college teaching, leadership in developing human resources, leadership in higher education; Africana studies (Graduate Certificate), including diasporas and health disparities, genocide and human rights; aging studies (Graduate Certificate), including gerontology; art research (Graduate Certificate), including museum studies; business foundations (Graduate Certificate); chemical and biomedical engineering (Graduate Certificate), including materials science and engineering, water, health and sustainability; child and family studies (Graduate Certificate), including positive behavior support; civil and industrial engineering (Graduate Certificate), including transportation systems analysis; community and family health (Graduate Certificate), including maternal and child health, social marketing and public health, violence and injury: prevention and intervention, women's health; criminology (Graduate Certificate), including criminal justice administration; data science for public administration (Graduate Certificate); digital humanities (Graduate Certificate); educational measurement and research (Graduate Certificate), including evaluation; English (Graduate Certificate), including comparative literary studies, creative writing, professional and technical communication; entrepreneurship (Graduate Certificate); environmental health (Graduate Certificate), including safety management; epidemiology and biostatistics (Graduate Certificate), including applied biostatistics, biostatistics, concepts and tools of epidemiology, epidemiology, epidemiology of infectious diseases; geography, environment and planning (Graduate Certificate), including community development, environmental policy and management, geographical information systems; geology (Graduate Certificate), including hydrogeology; global health (Graduate Certificate), including disaster management, global health and Latin American and Caribbean studies, global health practice, humanitarian assistance, infection control; government and international affairs (Graduate Certificate), including Cuban studies, globalization studies; health policy and management (Graduate Certificate), including health management and leadership, public health policy and programs; hearing specialist: early intervention (Graduate Certificate); industrial and management systems engineering (Graduate Certificate), including systems engineering, technology management; information studies (Graduate Certificate), including school library media specialist; information systems/decision sciences (Graduate Certificate), including analytics and business intelligence; instructional technology (Graduate Certificate), including distance education, Florida digital/virtual educator, instructional design, multimedia design, Web design; internal medicine, bioethics and medical humanities (Graduate Certificate), including biomedical ethics; Latin American and Caribbean studies (Graduate Certificate); leadership for coastal resiliency planning (Graduate Certificate); mass communications (Graduate Certificate), including multimedia journalism; mathematics and statistics (Graduate Certificate), including mathematics; medicine (Graduate Certificate), including aging and neuroscience, bioinformatics, biotechnology, brain fitness and memory management, clinical investigation, hand and upper limb rehabilitation, health informatics, health sciences, integrative weight management, intellectual property, medicine and gender, metabolic and nutritional medicine, metabolic cardiology, pharmacy sciences; national and competitive intelligence (Graduate Certificate); nursing (Graduate Certificate), including simulation based academic fellowship in advanced pain management; psychological and social foundations (Graduate Certificate), including career counseling, college teaching, diversity in education, mental health counseling, school counseling; public affairs (Graduate Certificate), including nonprofit management, public management, research administration; public health (Graduate Certificate), including assessing chemical toxicity and public health risks, health equity, pharmacoepidemiology, public health generalist, toxicology, translational research in adolescent behavioral health; public health practices (Graduate Certificate), including planning for healthy communities; rehabilitation and mental health counseling (Graduate Certificate), including integrative mental health care, marriage and family therapy, rehabilitation technology; secondary education (Graduate Certificate), including ESOL, foreign language education: culture and content, foreign language education: professional; social work (Graduate Certificate), including geriatric social work/clinical gerontology; special education (Graduate Certificate), including autism spectrum disorder, disabilities education: severe/profound; world languages (Graduate Certificate), including teaching English as a second language (TESL) or foreign language. *Expenses:* Tuition, state resident: full-time $6350. Tuition, nonresident: full-time $19,048. *International tuition:* $19,048 full-time. *Required fees:* $2079. *Unit head:* Dr. Cynthia DeLuca, Associate Vice President and Assistant Vice Provost, 813-974-3077, Fax: 813-974-7061, E-mail: deluca@usf.edu. *Application contact:* Owen Hooper, Director, Summer and Alternative Calendar Programs, 813-974-6917, E-mail: hooper@usf.edu.
Website: http://www.usf.edu/innovative-education/

University of South Florida, St. Petersburg, College of Education, St. Petersburg, FL 33701. Offers educational leadership development (M Ed); elementary education (MA), including math/science; English education (MA); middle grades STEM education (MS);

reading education (MA). *Program availability:* Part-time. *Degree requirements:* For master's, comprehensive exam, practicum, internship, comprehensive portfolio. *Entrance requirements:* For master's, State of Florida General Knowledge Test (GKT), Florida Teaching Certificate (for non-initial certification programs), letters of recommendation. Additional exam requirements/recommendations for international students: Required—TOEFL (minimum score 550 paper-based; 79 iBT); Recommended—IELTS. Electronic applications accepted.

University of South Florida Sarasota-Manatee, College of Liberal Arts and Social Sciences, Sarasota, FL 34243. Offers criminal justice (MA); education (MA); educational leadership (M Ed), including curriculum leadership, K-12 public school leadership, non-public/charter school leadership; elementary education (MAT); English education (MA); social work (MSW). *Program availability:* Part-time, 100% online, blended/hybrid learning. *Faculty:* 14 full-time (9 women), 6 part-time/adjunct (5 women). *Students:* 10 full-time (8 women), 46 part-time (40 women); includes 17 minority (6 Black or African American, non-Hispanic/Latino; 7 Hispanic/Latino; 4 Two or more races, non-Hispanic/Latino). Average age 33. 57 applicants, 46% accepted, 24 enrolled. In 2018, 12 master's awarded. *Degree requirements:* For master's, comprehensive exam (for some programs). *Entrance requirements:* For master's, GRE. Additional exam requirements/recommendations for international students: Required—TOEFL (minimum score 550 paper-based; 79 iBT), IELTS (minimum score 6.5). *Application deadline:* For fall admission, 3/1 priority date for domestic students, 3/1 for international students; for spring admission, 10/1 priority date for domestic students, 10/1 for international students. Applications are processed on a rolling basis. Application fee: $30. Electronic applications accepted. *Expenses: Tuition, area resident:* Full-time $8350; part-time $348 per credit hour. Tuition, state resident: full-time $8350; part-time $348 per credit hour. Tuition, nonresident: full-time $19,048; part-time $794 per credit hour. *Required fees:* $1689; $70 per credit hour. $5 per semester. Tuition and fees vary according to program. *Financial support:* Career-related internships or fieldwork, institutionally sponsored loans, scholarships/grants, health care benefits, and unspecified assistantships available. Support available to part-time students. Financial award application deadline: 6/30; financial award applicants required to submit FAFSA. *Faculty research:* Educational leadership, secondary education, elementary education, and criminal justice. *Total annual research expenditures:* $97,764. *Unit head:* Dr. Jane Rose, Dean, 941-359-4469, Fax: 941-359-4778, E-mail: jane.rose@sar.usf.edu. *Application contact:* Brandon Avery, Assistant Director, Admissions, 941-359-4331, E-mail: bavery@sar.usf.edu.

The University of Tampa, Programs in Education, Tampa, FL 33606-1490. Offers curriculum and instruction (M Ed); educational leadership (M Ed); instructional design and technology (MS). *Program availability:* Part-time, evening/weekend. *Faculty:* 2 full-time (both women), 19 part-time/adjunct (15 women). *Students:* 52 full-time (38 women), 238 part-time (211 women); includes 86 minority (36 Black or African American, non-Hispanic/Latino; 1 American Indian or Alaska Native, non-Hispanic/Latino; 9 Asian, non-Hispanic/Latino; 32 Hispanic/Latino; 8 Two or more races, non-Hispanic/Latino), 15 international. Average age 33. 119 applicants, 71% accepted, 48 enrolled. In 2018, 37 master's awarded. *Degree requirements:* For master's, capstone. *Entrance requirements:* For master's, GMAT or GRE, current Florida Professional Teaching Certificate, statement of eligibility for Florida Professional Teaching Certificate, or professional teaching certificate from another state; bachelor's degree in an area of education. Additional exam requirements/recommendations for international students: Required—TOEFL (minimum score 577 paper-based; 90 iBT), IELTS (minimum score 7.5). *Application deadline:* Applications are processed on a rolling basis. Application fee: $40. Electronic applications accepted. *Expenses:* Contact institution. *Financial support:* In 2018–19, 28 students received support. Career-related internships or fieldwork, scholarships/grants, and unspecified assistantships available. Financial award applicants required to submit FAFSA. *Faculty research:* Diversity in the classroom, technology integration, assessment methodologies, complex and ill-structured problem solving, communities of practice. *Unit head:* Dr. Antony Erben, Chair, 813-257-3414, E-mail: terben@ut.edu. *Application contact:* Ashley Russell, Staff Assistant, Admissions for Graduate and Continuing Studies, 813-253-6249, E-mail: arussell@ut.edu.
Website: http://www.ut.edu/graduate/education/

The University of Tennessee, Graduate School, College of Education, Health and Human Sciences, Program in Education, Knoxville, TN 37996. Offers art education (MS); counseling education (PhD); cultural studies in education (PhD); curriculum (MS, Ed S); curriculum, educational research and evaluation (Ed D, PhD); early childhood education (PhD); early childhood special education (MS); education of deaf and hard of hearing (MS); educational administration and policy studies (Ed D, PhD); educational administration and supervision (Ed S); educational psychology (Ed D, PhD); elementary education (MS, Ed S); elementary teaching (MS); English education (MS, Ed S); exercise science (PhD); foreign language/ESL education (MS, Ed S); instructional technology (MS, Ed D, PhD, Ed S); literacy, language and ESL education (PhD); literacy, language education, and ESL education (Ed D); mathematics education (MS, Ed S); modified and comprehensive special education (MS); reading education (MS, Ed S); school counseling (Ed S); school psychology (PhD, Ed S); science education (MS, Ed S); secondary teaching (MS); social foundations (MS); social science education (MS, Ed S); socio-cultural foundations of sports and education (PhD); special education (Ed S); teacher education (Ed D, PhD). *Accreditation:* NCATE. *Program availability:* Part-time, evening/weekend. *Degree requirements:* For master's and Ed S, thesis optional; for doctorate, variable foreign language requirement, thesis/dissertation. *Entrance requirements:* For master's, minimum GPA of 2.7; for doctorate and Ed S, GRE General Test, minimum GPA of 2.7. Additional exam requirements/recommendations for international students: Required—TOEFL. Electronic applications accepted.

The University of Tennessee, Graduate School, College of Education, Health and Human Sciences, Program in Educational Administration and Policy Studies, Knoxville, TN 37996. Offers educational administration and policy studies (Ed D); educational administration and supervision (MS). *Accreditation:* NCATE. *Program availability:* Part-time, evening/weekend, online learning. *Degree requirements:* For master's, thesis optional. *Entrance requirements:* For master's, minimum GPA of 2.7. Additional exam requirements/recommendations for international students: Required—TOEFL. Electronic applications accepted.

The University of Tennessee at Chattanooga, Program in Learning and Leadership, Chattanooga, TN 37403. Offers educational leadership (Ed D, PhD). *Degree requirements:* For doctorate, thesis/dissertation, portfolio. *Entrance requirements:* For doctorate, GRE General Test, master's degree with minimum cumulative GPA of 3.0, two years of practical work experience in organizational environment. Additional exam requirements/recommendations for international students: Required—TOEFL (minimum score 550 paper-based; 79 iBT), IELTS (minimum score 6). Electronic applications accepted. *Faculty research:* Instructional design and development, curriculum inquiry/mapping, program evaluation, professional development and teacher training, fostering student diligence.

The University of Tennessee at Chattanooga, School of Education, Chattanooga, TN 37403. Offers counseling (M Ed), including community counseling, school counseling; education (M Ed, Post-Master's Certificate), including elementary education (M Ed), school leadership (Post-Master's Certificate); elementary education (M Ed); learning and leadership (Ed D), including educational leadership; school leadership (Post-Master's Certificate); school leadership: principal licensure (Ed S); secondary education (M Ed); special education (M Ed). *Accreditation:* ACA; NCATE. *Program availability:* Part-time. *Degree requirements:* For master's, comprehensive exam, thesis optional, culminating experience; for other advanced degree, internship. *Entrance requirements:* For master's, GRE General Test, PPST 1, teaching certificate; for other advanced degree, two letters of recommendation, graduate degree in education, teaching certificate with three years of experience. Additional exam requirements/recommendations for international students: Required—TOEFL (minimum score 550 paper-based; 79 iBT), IELTS (minimum score 6). Electronic applications accepted. *Expenses:* Contact institution. *Faculty research:* School counseling, community counseling, elementary and secondary education, school leadership and administration.

The University of Tennessee at Martin, Graduate Programs, College of Education, Health and Behavioral Sciences, Program in Educational Leadership, Martin, TN 38238. Offers MS Ed. *Program availability:* Part-time, online only, 100% online. *Students:* 14 part-time (11 women); includes 1 minority (Hispanic/Latino). Average age 39. 10 applicants, 10% accepted, 1 enrolled. In 2018, 7 master's awarded. *Degree requirements:* For master's, comprehensive exam. *Entrance requirements:* For master's, GRE General Test, minimum GPA of 2.5, letters of reference, teaching license, resume, teaching experience. Additional exam requirements/recommendations for international students: Required—TOEFL (minimum score 525 paper-based; 71 iBT). *Application deadline:* For fall admission, 7/27 priority date for domestic and international students; for spring admission, 12/17 priority date for domestic and international students; for summer admission, 5/10 priority date for domestic and international students. Applications are processed on a rolling basis. Application fee: $30 ($130 for international students). Electronic applications accepted. *Expenses: Tuition, area resident:* Full-time $8918; part-time $495 per credit hour. Tuition, state resident: full-time $8918; part-time $485 per credit hour. Tuition, nonresident: full-time $14,958; part-time $831 per credit hour. *International tuition:* $22,862 full-time. *Required fees:* $1446; $81 per credit hour. Part-time tuition and fees vary according to course load. *Financial support:* In 2018–19, 1 student received support. Research assistantships with full tuition reimbursements available, teaching assistantships with full tuition reimbursements available, scholarships/grants, and tuition waivers (full and partial) available. Financial award application deadline: 2/1; financial award applicants required to submit FAFSA. *Unit head:* Cynthia West, Dean, 731-881-7125, Fax: 731-881-7975, E-mail: cwest@utm.edu. *Application contact:* Jolene L. Cunningham, Student Services Specialist, 731-881-7012, Fax: 731-881-7499, E-mail: jcunningham@utm.edu.

The University of Texas at Arlington, Graduate School, College of Education, Department of Educational Leadership and Policy Studies, Arlington, TX 76019. Offers educational leadership (PhD); higher education (M Ed); principal certification (M Ed). *Program availability:* Part-time, evening/weekend, online learning. *Degree requirements:* For master's, 2 field-based practica; for doctorate, comprehensive exam, thesis/dissertation, 2 research-based practica. *Entrance requirements:* For master's, GRE, 3 references, minimum undergraduate GPA of 3.0 in last 60 hours of course work; for doctorate, GRE, resume, statement of intent, 3 reference forms, applicable master's degree. *Faculty research:* Lived realities of students of color in K-16 contexts, K-16 faculty, K-16 policy and law, K-16 student access, K-16 student success.

The University of Texas at Austin, Graduate School, College of Education, Department of Educational Administration, Austin, TX 78712-1111. Offers M Ed, Ed D, PhD. *Degree requirements:* For doctorate, thesis/dissertation. *Entrance requirements:* For master's and doctorate, GRE General Test. Electronic applications accepted.

The University of Texas at Austin, Graduate School, College of Education, Department of Special Education, Austin, TX 78712-1111. Offers autism and developmental disabilities (Ed D, PhD); autism and developmental disability (M Ed, MA); early childhood special education (M Ed, MA, Ed D, PhD); learning disabilities (Ed D, PhD); learning disabilities/behavior disorders (M Ed, MA); multicultural special education (M Ed, MA, Ed D, PhD); rehabilitation counselor (M Ed); rehabilitation counselor education (Ed D, PhD); special education administration (Ed D, PhD). *Accreditation:* CORE. *Program availability:* Part-time, evening/weekend, online learning. *Degree requirements:* For master's, thesis or alternative; for doctorate, thesis/dissertation. *Entrance requirements:* For master's and doctorate, GRE General Test. *Faculty research:* Anchored instruction, reading disabilities, multicultural/bilingual.

The University of Texas at El Paso, Graduate School, College of Education, Department of Educational Leadership and Foundations, El Paso, TX 79968-0001. Offers educational administration (M Ed); educational leadership and administration (Ed D). *Program availability:* Part-time, evening/weekend. *Degree requirements:* For master's, thesis optional; for doctorate, thesis/dissertation. *Entrance requirements:* For doctorate, GRE General Test, minimum graduate GPA of 3.0. Additional exam requirements/recommendations for international students: Required—TOEFL. Electronic applications accepted.

The University of Texas at San Antonio, College of Education and Human Development, Department of Educational Leadership and Policy Studies, San Antonio, TX 78249-0617. Offers educational leadership (Ed D); educational leadership and policy studies (M Ed), including educational leadership, higher education administration. *Program availability:* Part-time. *Degree requirements:* For master's, comprehensive exam, thesis or alternative; for doctorate, comprehensive exam, thesis/dissertation. *Entrance requirements:* For master's, transcripts, statement of purpose, resume or curriculum vitae; for doctorate, GRE General Test, minimum GPA of 3.5 in a master's program, resume, three letters of recommendation, statement of purpose. Additional exam requirements/recommendations for international students: Required—TOEFL (minimum score 550 paper-based; 79 iBT), IELTS (minimum score 6.5). Electronic applications accepted. *Faculty research:* Urban and international school leadership, student success, college access, higher education policy, multiculturalism, minority student achievement.

The University of Texas of the Permian Basin, Office of Graduate Studies, School of Education, Program in Educational Leadership, Odessa, TX 79762-0001. Offers MA. *Degree requirements:* For master's, comprehensive exam (for some programs), thesis (for some programs). *Entrance requirements:* For master's, GRE General Test. Additional exam requirements/recommendations for international students: Required—TOEFL (minimum score 550 paper-based).

The University of Texas Rio Grande Valley, College of Education and P-16 Integration, Department of Organization and School Leadership, Edinburg, TX 78539. Offers educational leadership (M Ed, Ed D). *Program availability:* Part-time, evening/weekend. *Degree requirements:* For master's, comprehensive exam, thesis optional; for doctorate, comprehensive exam, thesis/dissertation. *Entrance requirements:* For master's, GRE, minimum GPA of 3.0 on undergraduate coursework; for doctorate, master's degree. Additional exam requirements/recommendations for international students: Required—TOEFL (minimum score 550 paper-based; 79 iBT), IELTS (minimum score 6.5). Electronic applications accepted. *Expenses: Tuition, area resident:* Full-time $6888. Tuition, state resident: full-time $6888. Tuition, nonresident: full-time $14,484. *International tuition:* $14,484 full-time. *Required fees:* $1468. *Faculty research:* Leadership and gender studies, continuous improvement processes, leadership.

Educational Leadership and Administration

University of the Cumberlands, Graduate Programs in Education, Williamsburg, KY 40769-1372. Offers all grades (P-12) (M Ed); business and marketing (MA Ed, MAT); counselor education and supervision (Ed D); director of pupil personnel (Certificate); director of special education (Certificate); educational administration and supervision (Ed S); educational leadership (Ed D); elementary education (MA Ed, MAT); instructional leadership - principalship (MA Ed); instructional leadership - school principal (Certificate); middle school education (MA Ed, MAT); reading and writing (MA Ed); school counseling (MA Ed); school superintendent (Certificate); secondary education (MA Ed, MAT); special education (MAT); supervisor of instruction (Certificate); teacher leader (MA Ed). *Program availability:* Part-time, evening/weekend, online learning. *Degree requirements:* For master's, comprehensive exam. Electronic applications accepted.

University of the Pacific, Gladys L. Benerd School of Education, Stockton, CA 95211-0197. Offers curriculum and instruction (MA, Ed D); education (M Ed); educational administration and leadership (MA, Ed D); educational and school psychology (MA, Ed D); educational entrepreneurship (MA); school psychology (Ed S); special education (MA); teacher education (MA). *Accreditation:* NCATE. *Degree requirements:* For doctorate, thesis/dissertation. *Entrance requirements:* For master's, GRE General Test; for doctorate, GRE General Test, GRE Subject Test. Additional exam requirements/recommendations for international students: Required—TOEFL.

University of the Southwest, Graduate Programs, Hobbs, NM 88240-9129. Offers business administration (MBA); curriculum and instruction (MSE); curriculum and instruction: bilingual (MSE); curriculum and instruction: TESOL (MSE); early childhood education (MSE); educational administration (MSE); mental health counseling (MSE); school counseling (MSE); special education (MSE); sports management (MBA). *Program availability:* Part-time, evening/weekend, online learning. *Degree requirements:* For master's, comprehensive exam, thesis (for some programs). *Entrance requirements:* Additional exam requirements/recommendations for international students: Recommended—TOEFL. Electronic applications accepted.

University of the Virgin Islands, School of Education, St. Thomas, VI 00802. Offers creative leadership for innovation and change (PhD); educational leadership (MA); school counseling (MA); school psychology (Ed S). *Program availability:* Part-time, evening/weekend. *Students:* 41 full-time (34 women), 95 part-time (75 women); includes 80 minority (79 Black or African American, non-Hispanic/Latino; 1 Hispanic/Latino), 24 international. Average age 43. In 2018, 6 master's, 7 doctorates awarded. *Degree requirements:* For master's, comprehensive exam, thesis or alternative; for doctorate, comprehensive exam, thesis/dissertation, qualifying examination; for Ed S, comprehensive exam. *Entrance requirements:* For master's, GRE, minimum GPA of 2.5, BA degree from accredited institution. Additional exam requirements/recommendations for international students: Required—TOEFL (minimum score 550 paper-based). *Application deadline:* For fall admission, 4/30 for domestic and international students; for spring admission, 10/30 for domestic and international students. Application fee: $25. Electronic applications accepted. *Expenses:* Contact institution. *Financial support:* Fellowships, research assistantships, teaching assistantships, and scholarships/grants available. Financial award application deadline: 4/15; financial award applicants required to submit FAFSA. *Unit head:* Dr. Karen Brown, Dean, 340-693-1321, Fax: 340-693-1335, E-mail: karen.brown@uvi.edu. *Application contact:* Charmaine M. Smith, Director of Admissions, 340-692-4070, E-mail: csmith@uvi.edu.

The University of Toledo, College of Graduate Studies, Judith Herb College of Education, Department of Educational Foundations and Leadership, Toledo, OH 43606-3390. Offers educational administration and supervision (ME, DE, Ed S); educational psychology (ME, PhD); educational research and measurement (ME, PhD); educational sociology (PhD); educational theory and social foundations (ME); foundations of education (DE, PhD); history of education (PhD); philosophy of education (PhD). *Accreditation:* NCATE. *Program availability:* Part-time, evening/weekend. *Degree requirements:* For master's, comprehensive exam, thesis or alternative; for doctorate, comprehensive exam, thesis/dissertation; for Ed S, thesis optional. *Entrance requirements:* For master's, doctorate, and Ed S, minimum cumulative GPA of 2.7 for all previous academic work, letters of recommendation. Additional exam requirements/recommendations for international students: Required—TOEFL (minimum score 550 paper-based; 80 iBT). Electronic applications accepted.

University of Vermont, Graduate College, College of Education and Social Services, Ed D Program in Educational Leadership and Policy Studies, Burlington, VT 05405-0160. Offers Ed D. *Accreditation:* NCATE. *Degree requirements:* For doctorate, thesis/dissertation. *Entrance requirements:* For doctorate, resume, writing sample. Additional exam requirements/recommendations for international students: Required—TOEFL (minimum score 550 paper-based, 90 iBT) or IELTS (6.5). Electronic applications accepted.

University of Vermont, Graduate College, College of Education and Social Services, PhD Program in Educational Leadership and Policy Studies, Burlington, VT 05405. Offers PhD. *Degree requirements:* For doctorate, thesis/dissertation. *Entrance requirements:* For doctorate, GRE General Test, resume, writing sample. Additional exam requirements/recommendations for international students: Required—TOEFL (minimum iBT score of 90) or IELTS (6.5). Electronic applications accepted.

University of Vermont, Graduate College, College of Education and Social Services, Program in Educational Leadership, Burlington, VT 05405. Offers educational leadership (M Ed), including community and organizational leadership, school leader with administrative endorsement. *Accreditation:* NCATE. *Degree requirements:* For master's, thesis or alternative. *Entrance requirements:* Additional exam requirements/recommendations for international students: Required—TOEFL (minimum score 550 paper-based, 90 iBT) or IELTS (6.5). Electronic applications accepted.

University of Vermont, Graduate College, College of Education and Social Services, Program in Higher Education and Student Affairs Administration, Burlington, VT 05405-0305. Offers M Ed. *Accreditation:* NCATE. *Program availability:* Part-time. *Degree requirements:* For master's, thesis or alternative. *Entrance requirements:* For master's, resume. Additional exam requirements/recommendations for international students: Required—TOEFL (minimum score 550 paper-based, 90 iBT) or IELTS (6.5). Electronic applications accepted.

University of Victoria, Faculty of Graduate Studies, Faculty of Education, Department of Educational Psychology and Leadership Studies, Victoria, BC V8W 2Y2, Canada. Offers aboriginal communities counseling (M Ed); counseling (M Ed, MA); educational psychology (M Ed, MA, PhD), including counseling psychology (M Ed, MA), leadership studies (PhD), learning and development (MA, PhD), measurement and evaluation, special education (M Ed, MA); leadership studies (M Ed, MA). *Program availability:* Part-time. *Degree requirements:* For master's, thesis (for some programs), comprehensive exam (M Ed); for doctorate, comprehensive exam, thesis/dissertation, candidacy exam. *Entrance requirements:* For master's, 2 years of work experience in a relevant field; for doctorate, GRE, 2 years of work experience in a relevant field, minimum B average. Additional exam requirements/recommendations for international students: Required—TOEFL (minimum score 575 paper-based), IELTS (minimum score 7). *Faculty research:* Learning and development (child, adolescent and adult), special education and exceptional children.

University of Virginia, Curry School of Education, Department of Leadership, Foundations and Policy, Program in Administration and Supervision, Charlottesville, VA 22903. Offers M Ed, Ed D, Ed S. *Entrance requirements:* For master's, doctorate, and Ed S, GRE General Test, letters of recommendation. Electronic applications accepted.

University of Virginia, Curry School of Education, Program in Education, Charlottesville, VA 22903. Offers administration and supervision (PhD); applied developmental science (PhD); counselor education (PhD); curriculum and instruction (PhD); early childhood special education (MT); education evaluation (PhD); educational psychology (PhD); educational research (PhD); elementary education (MT); English education (MT, PhD); foreign language education (MT); higher education (PhD); instructional technology (PhD); kinesiology (MT, PhD); math education (PhD); reading education (PhD); research, statistics and evaluation (PhD); school psychology (PhD); science education (PhD); social studies education (MT, PhD); special education (PhD); world languages education (MT). *Degree requirements:* For master's, comprehensive exam (for some programs), field project; for doctorate, comprehensive exam, thesis/dissertation. *Entrance requirements:* For doctorate, GRE General Test. Additional exam requirements/recommendations for international students: Required—TOEFL (minimum score 600 paper-based; 90 iBT), IELTS (minimum score 7). Electronic applications accepted.

University of Washington, Graduate School, College of Education, Seattle, WA 98195. Offers curriculum and instruction (M Ed, Ed D, PhD), including educational technology, general curriculum (Ed D, PhD), language, literacy, and culture, mathematics education, multicultural education, reading and language arts education (Ed D), science education, social studies education, teaching and curriculum (M Ed); educational leadership and policy studies (M Ed, Ed D, PhD), including administration (Ed D), educational policy, organization, and leadership (M Ed, PhD), higher education, leadership for learning (Ed D), social and cultural foundations of education (M Ed, PhD); educational psychology (M Ed, PhD), including educational psychology (PhD), human development and cognition (M Ed), learning sciences, measurement, statistics and research design (M Ed), school psychology (M Ed); instructional leadership (M Ed); intercollegiate athletic leadership (M Ed); special education (M Ed, Ed D, PhD), including early childhood special education (M Ed), emotional and behavioral disabilities (M Ed), learning disabilities (M Ed), low-incidence disabilities (M Ed), severe disabilities (M Ed), special education (Ed D, PhD); teacher education (MIT). *Accreditation:* APA. *Program availability:* Part-time, evening/weekend. *Degree requirements:* For master's, thesis optional; for doctorate, thesis/dissertation. *Entrance requirements:* For master's and doctorate, GRE General Test, minimum GPA of 3.0. Additional exam requirements/recommendations for international students: Required—TOEFL. Electronic applications accepted. *Faculty research:* School restructuring/effective schools, special education interventions, literacy and writing, technology, school partnerships, teacher preparation.

University of Washington, Bothell, Program in Education, Bothell, WA 98011. Offers education (M Ed); leadership development for educators (M Ed); secondary/middle level endorsement (M Ed). *Program availability:* Part-time, evening/weekend. *Degree requirements:* For master's, thesis. *Entrance requirements:* Additional exam requirements/recommendations for international students: Required—TOEFL. Electronic applications accepted. *Faculty research:* Multicultural education in citizenship education, intercultural education, knowledge and practice in the principalship, educational public policy, national board certification for teachers, teacher learning in literacy, technology and its impact on teaching and learning of mathematics, reading assessments, professional development in literacy education and mobility, digital media, education and class.

University of Washington, Tacoma, Graduate Programs, Program in Education, Tacoma, WA 98402-3100. Offers education (M Ed); educational administration (principal or program administrator certification) (M Ed); elementary education teacher certification (M Ed); elementary education/special education teacher certification (M Ed); secondary science or math teacher certification (M Ed). *Program availability:* Part-time, evening/weekend. *Degree requirements:* For master's, culminating project. *Entrance requirements:* For master's, WEST-B, WEST-E (teacher certification programs only), official sealed transcript from every college/university attended, personal goal statement, letters of recommendation, copy of valid teaching certificate. Additional exam requirements/recommendations for international students: Required—TOEFL (minimum score 580 paper-based; 92 iBT). Electronic applications accepted. *Faculty research:* Global learning communities for English/Chinese languages, evaluation of mathematics and reading intervention programs, response to intervention, school-wide behavioral and emotional support, mathematics education and culturally responsive mathematics education.

The University of West Alabama, School of Graduate Studies, College of Education, Program in Instructional Leadership, Livingston, AL 35470. Offers instructional leadership (M Ed, Ed S); teacher leader (Ed S). *Accreditation:* NCATE. *Program availability:* Part-time, evening/weekend, 100% online. *Faculty:* 6 full-time (5 women), 17 part-time/adjunct (10 women). *Students:* 501 full-time (349 women), 5 part-time (4 women); includes 154 minority (139 Black or African American, non-Hispanic/Latino; 2 American Indian or Alaska Native, non-Hispanic/Latino; 1 Asian, non-Hispanic/Latino; 4 Hispanic/Latino; 8 Two or more races, non-Hispanic/Latino). Average age 38. 213 applicants, 96% accepted, 128 enrolled. In 2018, 57 master's, 29 Ed Ss awarded. *Degree requirements:* For master's, comprehensive exam, thesis optional; for Ed S, comprehensive exam. *Entrance requirements:* For master's, GRE, valid Class B Professional Educator Certificate in a teaching field; verification of background clearance/fingerprints; transcripts documenting completion of bachelor's degree from regionally-accredited college or university with minimum GPA of 2.75. Additional exam requirements/recommendations for international students: Required—TOEFL (minimum score 500 paper-based; 61 iBT). *Application deadline:* Applications are processed on a rolling basis. Application fee: $40. Electronic applications accepted. *Expenses: Tuition, area resident:* Full-time $9100. *Tuition, state resident:* full-time $9100. *Tuition, nonresident:* full-time $19,200. *Required fees:* $1890; $130. *Financial support:* Teaching assistantships, Federal Work-Study, scholarships/grants, and unspecified assistantships available. Support available to part-time students. Financial award application deadline: 3/1; financial award applicants required to submit FAFSA. *Unit head:* Dr. Jodie Winship, Chair of College of Education, 205-652-5415, Fax: 205-652-3706, E-mail: jwinship@uwa.edu. *Application contact:* Dr. B. J. Kimbrough, Dean of Graduate Studies, 205-652-3647, Fax: 205-652-3670, E-mail: bkimbrough@uwa.edu. Website: http://www.uwa.edu/medinstructionalleadership.aspx

University of West Florida, College of Education and Professional Studies, Department of Teacher Education and Educational Leadership, Program in Educational Leadership, Pensacola, FL 32514-5750. Offers M Ed. *Accreditation:* NCATE. *Program availability:* Part-time, evening/weekend, online learning. *Degree requirements:* For master's, thesis optional. *Entrance requirements:* For master's, GRE General Test or minimum GPA of 3.0. Additional exam requirements/recommendations for international students: Required—TOEFL (minimum score 550 paper-based).

University of West Florida, College of Education and Professional Studies, Ed D Programs, Specialization in Administrative and Leadership Studies, Pensacola, FL 32514-5750. Offers Ed D. *Degree requirements:* For doctorate, comprehensive exam, thesis/dissertation. *Entrance requirements:* For doctorate, GRE, MAT, or GMAT, letter of

intent; writing sample; three letters of recommendation; two completed disposition assessment forms; written statement of goals; interview with admissions committee. Additional exam requirements/recommendations for international students: Required—TOEFL (minimum score 550 paper-based).

University of West Georgia, College of Education, Carrollton, GA 30118. Offers business education (M Ed); early childhood education (M Ed, Ed S); educational leadership (M Ed, Ed S); media (M Ed, Ed S); professional counseling (M Ed, Ed S); professional counseling and supervision (Ed D); reading instruction (M Ed); school improvement (Ed D); secondary education (M Ed); special education (M Ed, Ed S), including teaching (M Ed); speech language pathology (M Ed); teaching (MAT). *Accreditation:* NCATE. *Program availability:* Part-time, evening/weekend, 100% online, blended/hybrid learning. *Faculty:* 39 full-time (23 women). *Students:* 368 full-time (316 women), 1,140 part-time (960 women); includes 460 minority (376 Black or African American, non-Hispanic/Latino; 1 American Indian or Alaska Native, non-Hispanic/Latino; 11 Asian, non-Hispanic/Latino; 44 Hispanic/Latino; 28 Two or more races, non-Hispanic/Latino), 6 international. Average age 35. 625 applicants, 77% accepted, 401 enrolled. In 2018, 399 master's, 25 doctorates, 273 other advanced degrees awarded. *Entrance requirements:* Additional exam requirements/recommendations for international students: Required—TOEFL (minimum score 523 paper-based; 69 iBT); Recommended—IELTS (minimum score 6.5). *Application deadline:* For fall admission, 7/21 for domestic students, 6/1 for international students; for spring admission, 11/30 for domestic students, 10/15 for international students; for summer admission, 4/15 for domestic students, 3/30 for international students. Applications are processed on a rolling basis. Application fee: $40. Electronic applications accepted. Tuition and fees vary according to course load, degree level, campus/location and program. *Financial support:* Fellowships, research assistantships, teaching assistantships, career-related internships or fieldwork, Federal Work-Study, institutionally sponsored loans, scholarships/grants, and unspecified assistantships available. Support available to part-time students. Financial award application deadline: 4/1; financial award applicants required to submit FAFSA. *Unit head:* Dr. Diane Hoff, Dean, College of Education, 678-839-6570, Fax: 678-839-6098, E-mail: dhoff@westga.edu. *Application contact:* Dr. Toby Ziglar, Assistant Dean of the Graduate School, 678-839-1394, Fax: 678-839-1395, E-mail: graduate@westga.edu.
Website: http://www.westga.edu/education/

University of Wisconsin–Madison, Graduate School, School of Education, Department of Educational Leadership and Policy Analysis, Madison, WI 53706-1380. Offers administration (Certificate); educational policy (MS, PhD); global higher education (MS). *Degree requirements:* For doctorate, thesis/dissertation. *Entrance requirements:* For master's and doctorate, GRE General Test. Electronic applications accepted.

University of Wisconsin–Milwaukee, Graduate School, School of Education, Department of Administrative Leadership, Milwaukee, WI 53201-0413. Offers administrative leadership (MS), including adult and continuing education leadership, educational administration and supervision, higher education administration; support services for online students in higher education (Graduate Certificate); teaching and learning in higher education (Graduate Certificate). *Program availability:* Part-time. *Students:* 12 full-time (10 women), 163 part-time (124 women); includes 51 minority (19 Black or African American, non-Hispanic/Latino; 5 American Indian or Alaska Native, non-Hispanic/Latino; 4 Asian, non-Hispanic/Latino; 3 Hispanic/Latino; 20 Two or more races, non-Hispanic/Latino). Average age 35. 98 applicants, 70% accepted, 43 enrolled. In 2018, 43 master's, 3 other advanced degrees awarded. *Degree requirements:* For master's, comprehensive exam, thesis or alternative. *Entrance requirements:* For master's, GRE General Test. Additional exam requirements/recommendations for international students: Required—TOEFL (minimum score 550 paper-based; 79 iBT), IELTS (minimum score 6.5). *Application deadline:* For fall admission, 1/1 priority date for domestic students; for spring admission, 9/1 for domestic students. Application fee: $56 ($96 for international students). Electronic applications accepted. *Financial support:* In 2018–19, 2 fellowships were awarded; research assistantships, teaching assistantships, career-related internships or fieldwork, health care benefits, unspecified assistantships, and project assistantships also available. Support available to part-time students. Financial award application deadline: 4/15; financial award applicants required to submit FAFSA. *Unit head:* Alan Shoho, Dean, 414-229-4181, E-mail: shoho@uwm.edu. *Application contact:* General Information Contact, 414-229-4721, E-mail: soeinfo@uwm.edu.
Website: http://uwm.edu/education/academics/administrative-leadership-department/

University of Wisconsin–Milwaukee, Graduate School, School of Education, Department of Exceptional Education, Milwaukee, WI 53201-0413. Offers autism spectrum disorders (Graduate Certificate); exceptional education (MS); transition for students with disabilities (Graduate Certificate); urban education (PhD), including adult, continuing and higher education leadership, art education, curriculum and instruction, exceptional education, mathematics education, multicultural studies, social foundations of education. *Program availability:* Part-time. *Students:* 38 full-time (29 women), 67 part-time (50 women); includes 39 minority (23 Black or African American, non-Hispanic/Latino; 1 American Indian or Alaska Native, non-Hispanic/Latino; 6 Asian, non-Hispanic/Latino; 1 Hispanic/Latino; 8 Two or more races, non-Hispanic/Latino), 2 international. Average age 40. 47 applicants, 40% accepted, 11 enrolled. In 2018, 13 master's, 14 doctorates, 4 other advanced degrees awarded. *Entrance requirements:* Additional exam requirements/recommendations for international students: Required—TOEFL (minimum score 550 paper-based; 79 iBT), IELTS (minimum score 6.5). *Application deadline:* For fall admission, 1/1 priority date for domestic students; for spring admission, 9/1 for domestic students. Application fee: $56 ($96 for international students). Electronic applications accepted. *Financial support:* Fellowships, research assistantships, teaching assistantships, career-related internships or fieldwork, health care benefits, and unspecified assistantships available. Support available to part-time students. Financial award application deadline: 4/15; financial award applicants required to submit FAFSA. *Faculty research:* Emotional disturbance, hearing impairment, learning disabilities, mental retardation. *Application contact:* General Information Contact, 414-229-4721, E-mail: soeinfo@uwm.edu.
Website: http://uwm.edu/education/academics/exceptional-edu-department/

University of Wisconsin–Oshkosh, Graduate Studies, College of Education and Human Services, Department of Educational Leadership and Human Services, Oshkosh, WI 54901. Offers educational leadership (MS). *Program availability:* Part-time, evening/weekend. *Degree requirements:* For master's, comprehensive exam, thesis optional. *Entrance requirements:* For master's, bachelor's degree in education or related field. Additional exam requirements/recommendations for international students: Required—TOEFL (minimum score 550 paper-based; 79 iBT). Electronic applications accepted. *Faculty research:* Supervision models, learning styles, total quality management, cooperative learning, school choice.

University of Wisconsin–Stevens Point, College of Professional Studies, School of Education, Stevens Point, WI 54481-3897. Offers education—general/reading (MSE); education—general/special (MSE); educational administration (MSE); educational sustainability (Ed D); elementary education (MSE). *Program availability:* Part-time. *Degree requirements:* For master's, comprehensive exam, thesis or alternative. *Entrance requirements:* For master's, teacher certification, minimum undergraduate

GPA of 3.0, 2 years of teaching experience, letters of recommendation. Additional exam requirements/recommendations for international students: Required—TOEFL (minimum score 523 paper-based). *Faculty research:* Gifted education, early childhood special education, curriculum and instruction, standards-based education.

University of Wisconsin–Superior, Graduate Division, Department of Educational Administration, Superior, WI 54880-4500. Offers MSE, Ed S. Programs offered jointly with University of Wisconsin - Eau Claire, University of Wisconsin - Stevens Point. *Program availability:* Part-time, evening/weekend, online learning. *Degree requirements:* For master's, thesis or alternative, research project or position paper, written exam; for Ed S, thesis, internship, oral and written exams. *Entrance requirements:* For master's, GRE General Test or MAT, minimum GPA of 2.75, teaching license, 3 years of teaching experience; for Ed S, MAT, GRE, master's degree, 3 years of teaching experience, teaching license. *Faculty research:* Postsecondary disabilities, educational partnerships, K-12.

University of Wisconsin–Whitewater, School of Graduate Studies, College of Business and Economics, Program in School Business Management, Whitewater, WI 53190-1790. Offers MSE. *Program availability:* Part-time, evening/weekend, online learning. *Entrance requirements:* For master's, minimum GPA of 2.75. Additional exam requirements/recommendations for international students: Required—TOEFL (minimum score 550 paper-based; 80 iBT), IELTS (minimum score 6). Electronic applications accepted.

University of Wyoming, College of Education, Programs in Educational Leadership, Laramie, WY 82071. Offers MA, Ed D, Certificate. *Program availability:* Part-time, online learning. *Degree requirements:* For master's, thesis; for doctorate, comprehensive exam, thesis/dissertation; for Certificate, comprehensive exam, thesis, residency. *Entrance requirements:* For master's and Certificate, GRE; for doctorate, MA, 3 years' teaching experience. Additional exam requirements/recommendations for international students: Required—TOEFL (minimum score 520 paper-based). *Expenses: Tuition, area resident:* Full-time $6504; part-time $271 per credit hour. Tuition, state resident: full-time $6504; part-time $271 per credit hour. Tuition, nonresident: full-time $19,464; part-time $811 per credit hour. *International tuition:* $19,464 full-time. *Required fees:* $1410.94; $343.82 per semester. $343.82 per semester. Tuition and fees vary according to course load, program and reciprocity agreements. *Faculty research:* School leadership, leadership preparation, leadership skills.

Upper Iowa University, Master of Education Program, Fayette, IA 52142-1857. Offers early childhood (M Ed); English as a second language (M Ed); higher education (M Ed); instructional strategist (M Ed); reading (M Ed); teacher leadership (M Ed).

Ursuline College, School of Graduate and Professional Studies, Program in Educational Administration, Pepper Pike, OH 44124-4398. Offers MA. *Program availability:* Part-time. *Faculty:* 2 full-time (0 women), 6 part-time/adjunct (1 woman). *Students:* 14 full-time (9 women), 40 part-time (26 women); includes 13 minority (all Black or African American, non-Hispanic/Latino). Average age 37. 31 applicants, 100% accepted, 5 enrolled. In 2018, 9 master's awarded. *Degree requirements:* For master's, thesis or alternative. *Entrance requirements:* For master's, minimum undergraduate GPA of 3.0, teaching certificate, professional experience. Additional exam requirements/recommendations for international students: Required—TOEFL (minimum score 500 paper-based; 80 iBT). *Application deadline:* For fall admission, 8/1 priority date for domestic students. Applications are processed on a rolling basis. Application fee: $25. Electronic applications accepted. *Expenses:* 30 hours at $702 per for MA, certificates vary. *Financial support:* In 2018–19, 8 students received support. Scholarships/grants and tuition waivers (partial) available. Support available to part-time students. Financial award application deadline: 3/1; financial award applicants required to submit FAFSA. *Faculty research:* Qualities of successful teachers, longevity of female superintendents. *Unit head:* Dr. James Connell, Director, 440-449-3413, Fax: 440-646-8328, E-mail: jconnell@ursuline.edu. *Application contact:* Melanie Steele, Director, Graduate Admission, 440-646-8146, Fax: 440-684-6138, E-mail: graduateadmissions@ursuline.edu.

Utah Valley University, Program in Education, Orem, UT 84058-5999. Offers educational technology (M Ed); elementary mathematics (M Ed); elementary STEM (M Ed); English as a second language (M Ed); reading (M Ed); teachers as leaders (M Ed). *Accreditation:* TEAC. *Program availability:* Part-time. *Degree requirements:* For master's, project. *Entrance requirements:* For master's, GRE, 3 letters of recommendation, interview, essay. Additional exam requirements/recommendations for international students: Required—TOEFL (minimum score 83 iBT). Electronic applications accepted. *Expenses:* Contact institution.

Valdosta State University, Department of Curriculum, Leadership, and Technology, Valdosta, GA 31698. Offers leadership (Ed D); P-12 school leadership (M Ed); performance-based leadership (Ed S). *Accreditation:* NCATE. *Program availability:* 100% online, blended/hybrid learning. *Degree requirements:* For master's, thesis (for some programs), comprehensive written and/or oral exams; for doctorate, thesis/dissertation, comprehensive written and/or oral exams; for Ed S, thesis. *Entrance requirements:* For master's and Ed S, GRE General Test or MAT; for doctorate, GRE General Test, minimum GPA of 3.5. Additional exam requirements/recommendations for international students: Required—TOEFL (minimum score 523 paper-based); Recommended—IELTS. Electronic applications accepted. *Expenses:* Contact institution. *Faculty research:* Mentoring in higher education, contemporary issues in higher education.

Valparaiso University, Graduate School and Continuing Education, Programs in Education, Valparaiso, IN 46383. Offers initial licensure (M Ed), including Chinese teaching, elementary education, secondary education; instructional leadership (M Ed); school psychology (Ed S); secondary education (M Ed); M Ed/Ed S. *Accreditation:* NCATE. *Program availability:* Part-time, evening/weekend, online learning. *Entrance requirements:* For master's, GRE General Test, minimum GPA of 3.0. Additional exam requirements/recommendations for international students: Required—TOEFL (minimum score 550 paper-based; 80 iBT), IELTS (minimum score 6). Electronic applications accepted.

Vanderbilt University, Program in Leadership and Policy Studies, Nashville, TN 37240-1001. Offers higher education leadership and policy (PhD); K-12 educational leadership and policy (PhD). *Faculty:* 14 full-time (7 women). *Students:* 31 full-time (19 women), 2 part-time (both women); includes 12 minority (4 Black or African American, non-Hispanic/Latino; 5 Asian, non-Hispanic/Latino; 1 Hispanic/Latino; 2 Two or more races, non-Hispanic/Latino). Average age 30. 73 applicants, 14% accepted, 6 enrolled. In 2018, 5 doctorates awarded. *Degree requirements:* For doctorate, comprehensive exam, thesis/dissertation, qualifying examinations. *Entrance requirements:* For doctorate, GRE General Test. Additional exam requirements/recommendations for international students: Required—TOEFL (minimum score 570 paper-based; 88 iBT). *Application deadline:* For fall admission, 12/1 for domestic and international students. Application fee: $0. Electronic applications accepted. *Expenses:* Contact institution. *Financial support:* Fellowships with full tuition reimbursements, research assistantships with full tuition reimbursements, teaching assistantships with full tuition reimbursements, Federal Work-Study, institutionally sponsored loans, scholarships/grants, traineeships, and health care benefits available. Financial award application deadline: 1/15; financial

award applicants required to submit CSS PROFILE or FAFSA. *Faculty research:* Charter schooling, pay for performance, access and equity for immigrant and at-risk students, higher-education policy, race and ethnic relations, college student departure, college student success, and international comparisons. *Unit head:* Carolyn Heinrich, Chair, 615-322-1169, Fax: 615-343-7094, E-mail: carolyn.j.heinrich@vanderbilt.edu. *Application contact:* Sean Corcoran, Director of Graduate Studies, 615-322-8021, Fax: 615-343-7094, E-mail: sean.corcoran@vanderbilt.edu.
Website: http://peabody.vanderbilt.edu/departments/lpo/
graduate_and_professional_programs/phd/index.php

Vanguard University of Southern California, Graduate Programs in Education, Costa Mesa, CA 92626. Offers Christian education leadership (MA); curriculum and instruction (MA); teacher leadership (MA). *Program availability:* Evening/weekend. *Degree requirements:* For master's, thesis or alternative. *Entrance requirements:* For master's, California Basic Educational Skills Test, California Subject Examinations for Teachers, minimum GPA of 3.0. Additional exam requirements/recommendations for international students: Required—TOEFL (minimum score 550 paper-based; 79 iBT). Electronic applications accepted. *Expenses:* Contact institution. *Faculty research:* Reading, educational administration.

Villanova University, Graduate School of Liberal Arts and Sciences, Department of Education and Counseling, Villanova, PA 19085-1699. Offers elementary school counseling (MS), including counseling and human relations; teacher leadership (MA). *Program availability:* Part-time, evening/weekend. *Degree requirements:* For master's, comprehensive exam. *Entrance requirements:* For master's, GRE or MAT, minimum GPA of 3.0, statement of goals. Electronic applications accepted.

Virginia Commonwealth University, Graduate School, School of Education, Doctoral Program in Education, Richmond, VA 23284-9005. Offers art education (PhD); counselor education and supervision (PhD); curriculum, culture and change (PhD); educational leadership (PhD); educational psychology (PhD); leadership (Ed D); research and evaluation (PhD); special education and disability leadership (PhD); sport leadership (PhD); urban services leadership (PhD). *Accreditation:* NCATE. *Program availability:* Part-time. *Degree requirements:* For doctorate, thesis/dissertation. *Entrance requirements:* For doctorate, GRE (for PhD), MAT (for Ed D), interview, master's degree, writing sample. Additional exam requirements/recommendations for international students: Required—TOEFL (minimum score 600 paper-based; 100 iBT). Electronic applications accepted.

Virginia Commonwealth University, Graduate School, School of Education, Program in Educational Leadership, Richmond, VA 23284-9005. Offers M Ed. *Entrance requirements:* Additional exam requirements/recommendations for international students: Required—TOEFL (minimum score 600 paper-based; 100 iBT); Recommended—IELTS. Electronic applications accepted.

Virginia Polytechnic Institute and State University, Graduate School, College of Liberal Arts and Human Sciences, Blacksburg, VA 24061. Offers career and technical education (MS Ed, Ed S); communication (MA); counselor education (MA); creative writing (MFA); curriculum and instruction (MA Ed, Ed S); educational leadership and policy studies (Ed S); educational research and evaluation (PhD); English (MA); social, political, ethical, and cultural thought (PhD); Ed D/PhD. *Faculty:* 420 full-time (221 women), 1 (woman) part-time/adjunct. *Students:* 603 full-time (428 women), 359 part-time (237 women); includes 189 minority (107 Black or African American, non-Hispanic/Latino; 4 American Indian or Alaska Native, non-Hispanic/Latino; 24 Asian, non-Hispanic/Latino; 27 Hispanic/Latino; 2 Native Hawaiian or other Pacific Islander, non-Hispanic/Latino; 25 Two or more races, non-Hispanic/Latino), 84 international. Average age 33. 856 applicants, 48% accepted, 262 enrolled. In 2018, 270 master's, 63 doctorates awarded. *Degree requirements:* For master's, comprehensive exam (for some programs), thesis (for some programs); for doctorate, comprehensive exam (for some programs), thesis/dissertation (for some programs). *Entrance requirements:* For master's and doctorate, GRE/GMAT. Additional exam requirements/recommendations for international students: Required—TOEFL (minimum score 90 iBT). *Application deadline:* For fall admission, 8/1 for domestic students, 4/1 for international students; for spring admission, 1/1 for domestic students, 9/1 for international students. Applications are processed on a rolling basis. Application fee: $75. Electronic applications accepted. *Expenses:* Tuition, state resident: full-time $15,510; part-time $739.50 per credit hour. Tuition, nonresident: full-time $29,629; part-time $1490.25 per credit hour. *Required fees:* $2804; $550 per semester. Tuition and fees vary according to course load, campus/location and program. *Financial support:* In 2018–19, 4 fellowships with full tuition reimbursements (averaging $23,122 per year), 28 research assistantships with full tuition reimbursements (averaging $15,605 per year), 245 teaching assistantships with full tuition reimbursements (averaging $16,046 per year) were awarded; scholarships/grants and unspecified assistantships also available. Financial award application deadline: 3/1; financial award applicants required to submit FAFSA. *Total annual research expenditures:* $7.5 million. *Unit head:* Dr. Laura Belmonte, Dean, 540-231-6779, Fax: 540-231-7157, E-mail: belmonte@vt.edu. *Application contact:* Chelsea Blanchet, Executive Assistant, 540-231-6779, Fax: 540-231-7157, E-mail: bchels1@vt.edu.
Website: http://www.liberalarts.vt.edu/

Virginia State University, College of Graduate Studies, College of Education, Department of Educational Leadership, Petersburg, VA 23806-0001. Offers administration and supervision (M Ed). *Accreditation:* NCATE. *Degree requirements:* For master's, thesis optional.

Virginia Theological Seminary, Graduate and Professional Programs, Alexandria, VA 22304. Offers Christian spirituality (D Min); educational leadership (D Ed Min, D Min); ministry development (D Min); theology (M Div, MA). *Accreditation:* ATS. *Program availability:* Part-time. *Degree requirements:* For master's, 2 foreign languages, thesis; for doctorate, thesis/dissertation. *Entrance requirements:* For master's and doctorate, GRE General Test.

Viterbo University, Graduate Programs in Education, La Crosse, WI 54601-4797. Offers cross-categorical special education (Certificate); director of instruction (Certificate); director of special education and pupil services (Certificate); early childhood (Certificate); education (MAE); literacy coaching (Certificate); PreK-12 principal/supervisor of special education (Certificate); principal (Certificate); reading specialist endorsement (Certificate); reading teacher (Certificate); reading teacher 5-12 endorsement (Certificate); reading teacher K-8 endorsement (Certificate); superintendent (Certificate); talented and gifted endorsement (Certificate); Wisconsin school business administrator (Certificate). Weekend courses available in summer. *Accreditation:* NCATE. *Program availability:* Part-time, evening/weekend. *Degree requirements:* For master's, comprehensive exam, thesis, 30 credits of course work. *Entrance requirements:* For master's, BS, transcripts, teaching license, written narrative. Electronic applications accepted. *Expenses:* Contact institution.

Walden University, Graduate Programs, Richard W. Riley College of Education and Leadership, Minneapolis, MN 55401. Offers adult education (Post-Master's Certificate); adult learning (Graduate Certificate); college teaching and learning (Graduate Certificate); community college leadership (Ed D); curriculum, instruction and assessment (Ed D, Ed S, Graduate Certificate); developmental education (Graduate Certificate); early childhood administration, management, and leadership (Graduate Certificate); early childhood education (Ed D, Ed S); early childhood public policy and advocacy (Graduate Certificate); early childhood studies (MS), including administration, management and leadership, early childhood public policy and advocacy, teaching adults in the early childhood field, teaching and diversity in early childhood education; education (MS, PhD), including adolescent literacy and learning (MS); curriculum, instruction, and assessment (grades K-12) (MS), curriculum, instruction, assessment, and evaluation (PhD), early childhood leadership and advocacy (PhD), early childhood special education (PhD), educational leadership (MS), educational leadership and administration (principal preparation) (MS), educational technology and design (PhD), elementary reading and literacy (PreK-6) (MS), elementary reading and mathematics (grades K-6) (MS), global and comparative education (PhD), higher education leadership management and policy (PhD), integrating technology in the classroom (grades K-12) (MS), learning, instruction and innovation (PhD), mathematics (grades 5-8) (MS), mathematics (grades K-6) (MS), mathematics and science (grades K-8) (MS), organizational research, assessment, and evaluation (PhD), reading and literacy with a reading K-12 endorsement (MS), reading literacy assessment and evaluation (PhD), science (grades K-8) (MS), special education (non-licensure) (grades K-12) (MS), teacher leadership (grades K-12) (MS), teaching English language learners (grades K-12) (MS); educational administration and leadership (Ed D); educational leadership and administration (principal preparation) (Ed S); educational technology (Ed D, Ed S, Post Master's Certificate); elementary reading and literacy (Graduate Certificate); engaging culturally diverse learners (Graduate Certificate); enrollment management and institutional marketing (Graduate Certificate); higher education (MS), including adult learning, college teaching and learning, enrollment management and institutional marketing, global higher education, leadership for student success, online and distance learning; higher education and adult learning (Ed D); higher education leadership and management (Ed D); higher education leadership for student success (Graduate Certificate); instructional design and technology (MS, Postbaccalaureate Certificate), including general program (MS), online learning (MS), training and performance improvement (MS); integrating technology in the classroom (Graduate Certificate); mathematics 5-8 (Graduate Certificate); mathematics K-6 (Graduate Certificate); online teaching for adult educators (Graduate Certificate); reading, literacy, and assessment (Ed D, Ed S); science K-8 (Graduate Certificate); special education (Ed D, Ed S, Graduate Certificate); special education (K-age 21) (MAT); teacher leadership (Graduate Certificate); teaching adults English as a second language (Graduate Certificate); teaching adults in the early childhood field (Graduate Certificate); teaching and diversity in early childhood education (Graduate Certificate); teaching English language learners (grades K-12) (Graduate Certificate); teaching K-12 students online (Graduate Certificate). *Accreditation:* NCATE. *Program availability:* Part-time, evening/weekend, online only, 100% online. *Degree requirements:* For doctorate, thesis/dissertation (for some programs), residency; for other advanced degree, residency (for some programs). *Entrance requirements:* For master's, bachelor's degree or higher; minimum GPA of 2.5; official transcripts; goal statement (for some programs); access to computer and Internet; for doctorate, master's degree or higher; three years of related professional or academic experience (preferred); minimum GPA of 3.0; goal statement and current resume (for select programs); official transcripts; access to computer and Internet; for other advanced degree, relevant work experience; access to computer and Internet. Additional exam requirements/recommendations for international students: Required—TOEFL (minimum score 550 paper-based, 79 iBT), IELTS (minimum score 6.5), Michigan English Language Assessment Battery (minimum score 82), or PTE (minimum score 53). Electronic applications accepted.

Waldorf University, Program in Organizational Leadership, Forest City, IA 50436. Offers criminal justice leadership (MA); emergency management leadership (MA); fire/rescue executive leadership (MA); human resource development (MA); public administration (MA); sport management (MA); teacher leader (MA).

Walla Walla University, Graduate Studies, School of Education and Psychology, College Place, WA 99324. Offers curriculum and instruction (M Ed, MAT); educational leadership (M Ed, MAT); literacy instruction (M Ed, MAT); special education (M Ed, MAT). *Program availability:* Part-time. *Entrance requirements:* For master's, GRE General Test, minimum GPA of 2.75. Additional exam requirements/recommendations for international students: Required—TOEFL (minimum score 550 paper-based; 79 iBT). Electronic applications accepted. *Faculty research:* Admissions/retention, instructional psychology, moral development, teaching of reading.

Washburn University, College of Arts and Sciences, Department of Education, Topeka, KS 66621. Offers curriculum and instruction (M Ed); educational leadership (M Ed); reading (M Ed); special education (M Ed). *Accreditation:* NCATE. *Program availability:* Part-time. *Degree requirements:* For master's, comprehensive exam, thesis or alternative, portfolio, comprehensive paper, or action research project. *Entrance requirements:* For master's, department exam, GRE General Test, or MAT, minimum GPA of 3.0 in graduate coursework or last 60 hours of undergraduate coursework. Additional exam requirements/recommendations for international students: Required—TOEFL (minimum score 80 iBT). *Faculty research:* Reading/literature/literacy, foundations, special education, diversity, teaching and technology.

Washington State University, College of Education, Department of Educational Leadership, Sports Studies, and Educational/Counseling Psychology, Pullman, WA 99164-2136. Offers counseling psychology (PhD); educational leadership (Ed M, MA, Ed D, PhD); educational psychology (MA, PhD); sport management (MA). Programs also offered at the Spokane, Tri-Cities, Vancouver and Global (online) campuses. *Program availability:* Part-time, online learning. *Degree requirements:* For master's, comprehensive exam (for some programs), thesis (for some programs), oral or written exam; for doctorate, comprehensive exam, thesis/dissertation, oral and written exam, internship. *Entrance requirements:* For master's and doctorate, GRE General Test, minimum GPA of 3.0, 3 letters of recommendation, transcripts showing all college or university course work, statement of professional objectives, current curriculum vitae/resume. Additional exam requirements/recommendations for international students: Required—TOEFL (minimum score 550 paper-based; 80 iBT). Electronic applications accepted. *Faculty research:* Multicultural counseling and career development, educational and psychological measurement issues, business decision-making process and power relationships, leadership practices and processes as suffused with and constituted by emotion work.

Washington State University, College of Education, Department of Teaching and Learning, Pullman, WA 99164-2132. Offers cultural studies and social thought in education (PhD); curriculum and instruction (Ed M, MA); English language learners (Ed M, MA); language, literacy and technology (PhD); literacy education (Ed M, MA); mathematics education (PhD); special education (Ed M, MA, PhD); teacher leadership (Ed D); teaching (MIT), including elementary education, secondary education. Programs offered at the Pullman, Spokane, Tri-cities, Vancouver and Global (online) campuses. *Program availability:* Part-time, online learning. *Degree requirements:* For master's, comprehensive exam, thesis, oral or written exam; for doctorate, comprehensive exam, thesis/dissertation, oral and written exam. *Entrance requirements:* For master's, GRE General Test, minimum GPA of 3.0, 3 letters of recommendation, letter of intent, transcripts, resume/curriculum vitae; for doctorate, GRE General Test, minimum GPA of

3.0, 3 letters of recommendation, letter of intent, transcripts, writing sample, resume/curriculum vitae. Additional exam requirements/recommendations for international students: Required—TOEFL (minimum score 550 paper-based; 80 iBT). Electronic applications accepted. *Faculty research:* Intersection of gender, youth cultures and schooling; examination of ideology of power in children's literature; early childhood special education; analyzing pre-service and in-service teacher development; second language acquisition.

Wayland Baptist University, Graduate Programs, Program in Education, Plainview, TX 79072-6998. Offers education administration (M Ed); education diagnostics (M Ed); education literacy (M Ed); elementary certification (M Ed); English (M Ed); English as a second language (M Ed); higher education administration (M Ed); human resources (M Ed); instructional leadership (M Ed); instructional technology (M Ed); leadership training and development (M Ed); science education (M Ed); secondary certification (M Ed); social studies (M Ed); special education (M Ed); sports administration and management (M Ed). *Program availability:* Part-time, evening/weekend, 100% online. *Degree requirements:* For master's, comprehensive exam, capstone course. *Entrance requirements:* For master's, GRE, GMAT or MAT. Additional exam requirements/recommendations for international students: Required—TOEFL (minimum score 500 paper-based; 61 iBT). Electronic applications accepted.

Waynesburg University, Graduate and Professional Studies, Canonsburg, PA 15370. Offers business (MBA), including energy management, finance, health systems, human resources, leadership, market development; counseling (MA), including addictions counseling, clinical mental health; counselor education and supervision (PhD); criminal investigation (MA); education (M Ed), including autism, curriculum and instruction, educational leadership, online teaching; nursing (MSN), including administration, education, informatics; nursing practice (DNP); special education (M Ed); technology (M Ed); MSN/MBA. *Accreditation:* AACN. *Program availability:* Part-time, evening/weekend. *Degree requirements:* For doctorate, thesis/dissertation. *Entrance requirements:* Additional exam requirements/recommendations for international students: Required—TOEFL. Electronic applications accepted.

Wayne State College, School of Education and Counseling, Department of Educational Foundations and Leadership, Program in Educational Administration, Wayne, NE 68787. Offers educational administration (Ed S); elementary administration (MSE); elementary and secondary administration (MSE); secondary administration (MSE). *Accreditation:* NCATE. *Program availability:* Part-time, evening/weekend. *Degree requirements:* For master's, comprehensive exam, thesis optional, research paper. *Entrance requirements:* For master's, GRE General Test, minimum GPA of 2.5; for Ed S, GRE General Test, minimum GPA of 3.2. Additional exam requirements/recommendations for international students: Required—TOEFL (minimum score 550 paper-based). Electronic applications accepted.

Wayne State University, College of Education, Division of Administrative and Organizational Studies, Detoit, MI 48202. Offers educational administration and supervision (Ed S); educational leadership (M Ed); educational leadership and policy studies (Ed D, PhD); educational technology (Certificate); learning design and technology (M Ed, Ed D, PhD, Ed S); online teaching (Certificate). *Program availability:* Part-time, evening/weekend. *Faculty:* 9. *Students:* 77 full-time (53 women), 223 part-time (160 women); includes 155 minority (126 Black or African American, non-Hispanic/Latino; 7 Asian, non-Hispanic/Latino; 11 Hispanic/Latino; 1 Native Hawaiian or other Pacific Islander, non-Hispanic/Latino; 10 Two or more races, non-Hispanic/Latino), 9 international. Average age 39. 239 applicants, 33% accepted, 58 enrolled. In 2018, 51 master's, 10 doctorates, 54 other advanced degrees awarded. *Degree requirements:* For master's, thesis (for some programs), GPA 3.0; for doctorate, comprehensive exam, thesis/dissertation, GPA 3.0; for other advanced degree, GPA 3.0. *Entrance requirements:* For master's, baccalaureate degree from accredited U.S. institution or equivalent from college or university of government-recognized standing; minimum undergraduate GPA of 2.75 in upper-division coursework; personal statement; for doctorate, GRE (instructional design and technology), interview; curriculum vitae; three to four recommendations; master's degree (for educational leadership and policy studies); minimum graduate GPA of 3.5; autobiographical statement; research experience (for PhD program); for other advanced degree, educational specialist certificate requirement include undergraduate and master's degrees (for both learning design and technology and administration and supervision); minimum graduate GPA of 3.4, and personal statement. Additional exam requirements/recommendations for international students: Required—TOEFL (minimum score 550 paper-based; 79 iBT); Recommended—IELTS (minimum score 6.5), TWE (minimum score 5.5), TSE (minimum score 58). *Application deadline:* Applications are processed on a rolling basis. Application fee: $50. Electronic applications accepted. *Financial support:* In 2018–19, 87 students received support, including 1 fellowship with tuition reimbursement available (averaging $20,000 per year), 4 research assistantships with tuition reimbursements available (averaging $19,267 per year); scholarships/grants and unspecified assistantships also available. Support available to part-time students. Financial award applicants required to submit FAFSA. *Faculty research:* Total quality management, participatory management, administering educational technology, school improvement, principalship. *Unit head:* Dr. William Hill, Assistant Dean, 313-577-9316, E-mail: ad2107@wayne.edu. *Application contact:* Dr. Mary L. Waker, Graduate Admissions Officer, 313-577-1601, Fax: 313-577-7904, E-mail: m.waker@wayne.edu.
Website: http://coe.wayne.edu/aos/index.php

West Chester University of Pennsylvania, College of Education and Social Work, Department of Early and Middle Grades Education, West Chester, PA 19383. Offers applied studies in teaching and learning (M Ed); early childhood education (M Ed), including accomplished teacher, program administrator; grades 4-8 (Teaching Certificate); grades preK-4 (Teaching Certificate). *Accreditation:* NCATE. *Program availability:* Part-time, 100% online. *Degree requirements:* For master's, teacher research project, portfolio. *Entrance requirements:* For master's, certification (for applied studies in teaching and learning track); one year of full time teaching; minimum GPA of 3.0; for Teaching Certificate, math, social studies, or science concentration exams (for middle grades preparation), minimum GPA of 3.0. Additional exam requirements/recommendations for international students: Required—TOEFL or IELTS. Electronic applications accepted. *Faculty research:* Cooperative learning, creative expression and critical thinking, teacher research, learning styles, middle school education.

West Chester University of Pennsylvania, College of Education and Social Work, Program in Policy, Planning, and Administration, West Chester, PA 19383. Offers Ed D. *Program availability:* Part-time, evening/weekend, online only, 100% online. *Degree requirements:* For doctorate, comprehensive exam. *Entrance requirements:* For doctorate, GRE if master's GPA lower than 3.85, master's degree from regionally-accredited college or university, three letters of recommendation from education professionals, professional writing demonstration at time of application (waived for applicants who present GRE analytical writing score of 4.5 or higher), resume or curriculum vitae, interview (upon committee request). Additional exam requirements/recommendations for international students: Required—TOEFL or IELTS. Electronic applications accepted. *Expenses:* Contact institution. *Faculty research:* Literacy, special education, critical pedagogy, social and cultural foundations of education, educational technology.

Western Connecticut State University, Division of Graduate Studies, School of Professional Studies, Department of Education and Educational Psychology, Program in Instructional Leadership, Danbury, CT 06810-6885. Offers Ed D. *Program availability:* Part-time. *Students:* 43 part-time (26 women). Average age 39. *Degree requirements:* For doctorate, comprehensive exam, thesis/dissertation, completion of program in 6 years. *Entrance requirements:* For doctorate, GRE or MAT, resume, three recommendations (one in a supervisory capacity in an educational setting), satisfactory interview with WCSU representatives from the Ed D Admissions Committee. Additional exam requirements/recommendations for international students: Recommended—TOEFL (minimum score 550 paper-based; 79 iBT), IELTS (minimum score 6). *Application deadline:* For fall admission, 3/30 priority date for domestic students. Application fee: $100. *Expenses:* Contact institution. *Faculty research:* Differentiated instruction, the transition of teacher learning, teacher retention, relationship building through the evaluation process, leadership development. *Unit head:* Dr. Marcy Delcourt, Coordinator, 203-837-9121, Fax: 203-837-8413, E-mail: delcourtm@wcsu.edu. *Application contact:* Dr. Chris Shankle, Associate Director of Graduate Studies, 203-837-9005, Fax: 203-837-8326, E-mail: shanklec@wcsu.edu.

Western Governors University, Teachers College, Salt Lake City, UT 84107. Offers curriculum and instruction (MS); educational leadership (MS); elementary education (MAT, Postbaccalaureate Certificate); English education (5-12) (MAT); English language learning (PreK-12) (MA); instructional design (M Ed); learning and technology (M Ed); mathematics (5-12) (MAT); mathematics (5-9) (MAT); mathematics education (5-12) (MA); mathematics education (5-9) (MA); mathematics education (K-6) (MA); science (5-12) (MAT); science education (5-12) (MA), including biology, chemistry, earth science, physics; science education (5-9) (MA); special education (MS). *Accreditation:* NCATE. *Program availability:* Evening/weekend, online learning. *Degree requirements:* For master's, capstone project. *Entrance requirements:* For master's and Postbaccalaureate Certificate, transcripts. Additional exam requirements/recommendations for international students: Required—TOEFL (minimum score 450 paper-based; 80 iBT). Electronic applications accepted. Application fee is waived when completed online. *Expenses:* Contact institution.

Western Illinois University, School of Graduate Studies, College of Education and Human Services, Department of Educational Studies, Program in College Student Personnel, Macomb, IL 61455-1390. Offers college student personnel (MS), including higher education leadership, student affairs. *Accreditation:* NCATE. *Program availability:* Part-time. *Students:* 54 full-time (37 women), 12 part-time (8 women); includes 21 minority (5 Black or African American, non-Hispanic/Latino; 11 Hispanic/Latino; 5 Two or more races, non-Hispanic/Latino), 2 international. Average age 25. 56 applicants, 77% accepted, 22 enrolled. In 2018, 46 master's awarded. *Entrance requirements:* For master's, interview. Additional exam requirements/recommendations for international students: Required—TOEFL (minimum score 550 paper-based; 80 iBT). *Application deadline:* For fall admission, 1/5 priority date for domestic students. Application fee: $30. Electronic applications accepted. *Financial support:* Unspecified assistantships available. Financial award applicants required to submit FAFSA. *Unit head:* Dr. Tracy Davis, Coordinator, 309-298-1183. *Application contact:* Dr. Mark Mossman, Associate Provost and Director of Graduate Studies, 309-298-1806, Fax: 309-298-2345, E-mail: grad-office@wiu.edu.
Website: http://wiu.edu/csp/

Western Illinois University, School of Graduate Studies, College of Education and Human Services, Department of Educational Studies, Program in Educational Leadership, Macomb, IL 61455-1390. Offers MS Ed, Ed D, Ed S. *Accreditation:* NCATE. *Program availability:* Part-time, evening/weekend. *Students:* 13 full-time (6 women), 160 part-time (90 women); includes 20 minority (9 Black or African American, non-Hispanic/Latino; 10 Hispanic/Latino; 1 Two or more races, non-Hispanic/Latino). Average age 39. 35 applicants, 97% accepted, 27 enrolled. In 2018, 32 master's, 17 doctorates, 5 other advanced degrees awarded. *Degree requirements:* For master's, thesis or alternative; for doctorate, comprehensive exam, thesis/dissertation, electronic portfolio. *Entrance requirements:* For master's and Ed S, interview; for doctorate, GRE General Test. Additional exam requirements/recommendations for international students: Required—TOEFL (minimum score 575 paper-based; 88 iBT). *Application deadline:* Applications are processed on a rolling basis. Application fee: $30. Electronic applications accepted. *Financial support:* Unspecified assistantships available. Financial award applicants required to submit FAFSA. *Unit head:* Dr. Eric Sheffield, Chairperson, 309-298-1183. *Application contact:* Dr. Mark Mossman, Associate Provost and Director of Graduate Studies, 309-298-1806, Fax: 309-298-2345, E-mail: grad-office@wiu.edu.

Western Kentucky University, Graduate School, College of Education and Behavioral Sciences, Department of Educational Administration, Leadership, and Research, Bowling Green, KY 42101. Offers adult education (MAE); educational leadership (Ed D); school administration (Ed S); school principal (MAE). *Accreditation:* NCATE. *Program availability:* Part-time, evening/weekend. *Degree requirements:* For master's, comprehensive exam, thesis or applied project and oral defense; for Ed S, thesis. *Entrance requirements:* For master's, GRE General Test, minimum GPA of 2.75. Additional exam requirements/recommendations for international students: Required—TOEFL (minimum score 555 paper-based; 79 iBT). *Faculty research:* Principal internship, superintendent assessment, administrative leadership, group training for residential workers.

Western Michigan University, Graduate College, College of Education and Human Development, Department of Educational Leadership, Research and Technology, Kalamazoo, MI 49008. Offers educational leadership (MA, PhD, Ed S), including educational leadership (MA); educational technology (MA, Graduate Certificate); evaluation, measurement and research (MA, PhD); organizational learning and performance (MA).

Western New Mexico University, Graduate Division, School of Education, Silver City, NM 88062-0680. Offers bilingual education (MAT); educational leadership (MA); elementary education (MAT); reading (MAT); secondary education (MAT); special education (MAT); TESOL (teaching English to speakers of other languages) (MAT). *Accreditation:* NCATE. *Program availability:* Part-time, online learning. *Degree requirements:* For master's, comprehensive exam. *Entrance requirements:* For master's, minimum GPA of 3.0 in last 64 hours of undergraduate study. Additional exam requirements/recommendations for international students: Required—TOEFL (minimum score 550 paper-based; 79 iBT). Electronic applications accepted. *Faculty research:* International education, electronic reading assessment, developing STEM teachers.

Western State Colorado University, Graduate Programs in Education, Gunnison, CO 81231. Offers education administrator leadership (MA); reading leadership (MA); teacher leadership (MA). *Program availability:* Online learning. *Degree requirements:* For master's, capstone.

Western Washington University, Graduate School, Woodring College of Education, Department of Educational Leadership, Educational Administration Program, Bellingham, WA 98225-5996. Offers M Ed. *Accreditation:* NCATE. *Program availability:* Part-time. *Degree requirements:* For master's, comprehensive exam, thesis optional. *Entrance requirements:* For master's, GRE General Test or MAT, minimum GPA of 3.0 in last 60 semester hours or last 90 quarter hours, certification. Additional exam

requirements/recommendations for international students: Required—TOEFL (minimum score 567 paper-based). Electronic applications accepted. *Faculty research:* Principal efficacy, collaborative school leadership, school/university partnerships, case study methodology, ethical leadership.

Western Washington University, Graduate School, Woodring College of Education, Department of Educational Leadership, Program in Student Affairs Administration, Bellingham, WA 98225-5996. Offers M Ed. *Accreditation:* NCATE. *Program availability:* Part-time. *Degree requirements:* For master's, comprehensive exam, thesis optional, research project. *Entrance requirements:* For master's, GRE General Test or MAT, minimum GPA of 3.0 in last 60 semester hours or last 90 quarter hours. Additional exam requirements/recommendations for international students: Required—TOEFL (minimum score 567 paper-based). Electronic applications accepted. *Faculty research:* Outcomes assessment, adult learning, best practices/student affairs, college health promotion, cultural pluralism.

West Liberty University, College of Education and Human Performance, West Liberty, WV 26074. Offers community education research and leadership (MA Ed); innovative instruction (MA Ed); leadership in disability services (MA Ed); leadership studies (MA Ed); multi-categorical special education (MA Ed); reading specialist (MA Ed); sports leadership and coaching (MA Ed). *Accreditation:* NCATE. *Program availability:* Part-time, evening/weekend. *Degree requirements:* For master's, capstone experience. *Entrance requirements:* For master's, minimum GPA of 2.5 or 3.0 (depending on track). Additional exam requirements/recommendations for international students: Required—TOEFL. Electronic applications accepted.

Westminster College, Graduate School, Program in Educational Administration, New Wilmington, PA 16172-0001. Offers school principal K-12 (M Ed); school superintendent (M Ed).

West Texas A&M University, College of Education and Social Sciences, Department of Education, Program in Educational Leadership, Canyon, TX 79015. Offers M Ed. *Program availability:* Part-time, evening/weekend, online learning. *Degree requirements:* For master's, comprehensive exam, thesis optional. *Entrance requirements:* For master's, GRE General Test. Additional exam requirements/recommendations for international students: Required—TOEFL (minimum score 550 paper-based). Electronic applications accepted. *Faculty research:* Teacher quality, leadership, recruitment, retention.

West Virginia University, College of Education and Human Services, Morgantown, WV 26506. Offers audiology (Au D); autism spectrum disorder (MA); clinical rehabilitation and mental health counseling (MS); communication science and disorders (PhD); counseling (MA); counseling psychology (PhD); curriculum and instruction (Ed D); early childhood education (MA); early intervention/ early childhood special education (MA); education (PhD); educational leadership (MA); educational leadership/ public school administration (Ed D); educational leadership/public school administration (MA); educational psychology (MA, Ed D); elementary education (MA); gifted education (MA); higher education administration (MA, Ed D); higher education curriculum and teaching (MA); institutional design and technology (MA); instructional design and technology (Ed D); literacy education (MA); secondary education (MA); secondary education/ English (MA); special education (Ed D); speech pathology (MS). *Accreditation:* ASHA; NCATE. *Program availability:* Part-time, evening/weekend, online learning. *Students:* 392 full-time (325 women), 337 part-time (285 women); includes 44 minority (16 Black or African American, non-Hispanic/Latino; 16 Hispanic/Latino; 12 Two or more races, non-Hispanic/Latino), 11 international. In 2018, 303 master's, 6 doctorates awarded. *Degree requirements:* For master's, content exams; for doctorate, comprehensive exam, thesis/dissertation. *Entrance requirements:* Additional exam requirements/recommendations for international students: Required—TOEFL (minimum score 500 paper-based; 61 iBT). *Application deadline:* For fall admission, 8/1 for domestic students; for spring admission, 1/1 for domestic students; for summer admission, 5/1 for domestic students. Application fee: $60. Electronic applications accepted. *Financial support:* Fellowships, research assistantships, teaching assistantships, career-related internships or fieldwork, Federal Work-Study, institutionally sponsored loans, health care benefits, tuition waivers (full and partial), and administrative assistantships available. Financial award applicants required to submit FAFSA. *Faculty research:* Internet training and integration for teachers, rural education, teacher preparation, organization of schools, evaluation of personnel. *Unit head:* Dr. Tracy L. Morris, Interim Dean, 304-293-0816, Fax: 304-293-7565, E-mail: Tracy.Morris@mail.wvu.edu. *Application contact:* Dr. Melissa Luna, Associate Dean for Research, 304-293-2174, Fax: 304-293-3802, E-mail: Melissa.Luna@mail.wvu.edu.
Website: http://cehs.wvu.edu/

Wheeling Jesuit University, Department of Education, Wheeling, WV 26003-6295. Offers MEL. *Program availability:* Part-time, evening/weekend, online learning. *Degree requirements:* For master's, thesis. *Entrance requirements:* For master's, GRE or MAT, minimum GPA of 2.5, professional teaching certificate. Additional exam requirements/recommendations for international students: Required—TOEFL (minimum score 600 paper-based; 100 iBT). Electronic applications accepted. Application fee is waived when completed online. *Faculty research:* Education leadership, school improvement, student achievement, leadership in special education.

Whittier College, Graduate Programs, Department of Education and Child Development, Program in Educational Administration, Whittier, CA 90608-0634. Offers MA Ed. *Program availability:* Part-time, evening/weekend. *Degree requirements:* For master's, thesis. *Entrance requirements:* For master's, GRE General Test, MAT. *Faculty research:* Candidate leadership development.

Whitworth University, School of Education, Graduate Studies in Education, Program in Administration, Spokane, WA 99251-0001. Offers M Ed. *Accreditation:* NCATE. *Program availability:* Part-time, evening/weekend. *Degree requirements:* For master's, comprehensive exam, internship, practicum, research project, or thesis. *Entrance requirements:* For master's, GRE General Test, MAT. *Faculty research:* Rural staff development.

Wichita State University, Graduate School, College of Applied Studies, Department of Counseling, Educational Leadership, Educational and School Psychology, Wichita, KS 67260. Offers counseling (M Ed); educational leadership (M Ed, Ed D); educational psychology (M Ed); school psychology (Ed S). *Accreditation:* NCATE. *Program availability:* Part-time, evening/weekend. Application fee: $50 ($65 for international students). *Unit head:* Dr. Jody Fiorini, Department Head, 316-978-3325, Fax: 316-978-3102, E-mail: jody.fiorini@wichita.edu. *Application contact:* Jordan Oleson, Admissions Coordinator, 316-978-3095, Fax: 316-978-3253, E-mail: jordan.oleson@wichita.edu.
Website: http://www.wichita.edu/cles

Widener University, School of Human Service Professions, Center for Education, Chester, PA 19013-5792. Offers adult education (M Ed); counseling in higher education (M Ed); counselor education (M Ed); early childhood education (M Ed); educational foundations (M Ed); educational leadership (M Ed); educational psychology (M Ed); elementary education (M Ed); English and language arts (M Ed); health education (M Ed); higher education leadership (Ed D); home and school visitor (M Ed); human sexuality (M Ed, PhD); mathematics education (M Ed); middle school education (M Ed); principalship (M Ed); reading and language arts (Ed D); reading education (M Ed);

school administration (Ed D); science education (M Ed); social studies education (M Ed); special education (M Ed); technology education (M Ed). *Accreditation:* NCATE. *Program availability:* Part-time, evening/weekend. Terminal master's awarded for partial completion of doctoral program. *Degree requirements:* For doctorate, thesis/dissertation. *Entrance requirements:* For master's, minimum GPA of 2.5; for doctorate, GRE or MAT, minimum GPA of 2.0 (undergraduate), 3.5 (graduate). Electronic applications accepted. *Expenses:* Contact institution. *Faculty research:* Reading and cognition, adult education, technology education, educational leadership, special education.

Wilkes University, College of Graduate and Professional Studies, School of Education, Wilkes-Barre, PA 18766-0002. Offers educational development and strategies (MS Ed); educational leadership (MS Ed, Ed D); effective teaching (MS Ed); instructional media (MS Ed); instructional technology (MS Ed); international school leadership (MS Ed); international teaching and learning (MS Ed); literacy (MS Ed); middle level education (MS Ed); online teaching (MS Ed); school business leadership (MS Ed); special education (MS Ed); teaching English to speakers of other languages (MS Ed). *Program availability:* Part-time, evening/weekend, 100% online, blended/hybrid learning. *Students:* 87 full-time (67 women), 1,418 part-time (1,078 women); includes 87 minority (13 Black or African American, non-Hispanic/Latino; 1 American Indian or Alaska Native, non-Hispanic/Latino; 11 Asian, non-Hispanic/Latino; 40 Hispanic/Latino; 22 Two or more races, non-Hispanic/Latino). Average age 35. In 2018, 611 master's, 9 doctorates awarded. *Entrance requirements:* Additional exam requirements/recommendations for international students: Required—TOEFL (minimum score 550 paper-based; 79 iBT). *Application deadline:* Applications are processed on a rolling basis. Application fee: $45 ($65 for international students). Electronic applications accepted. *Expenses:* Contact institution. *Financial support:* Unspecified assistantships available. Financial award application deadline: 3/1; financial award applicants required to submit FAFSA. *Unit head:* Dr. Rhonda Rabbitt, Dean, 570-408-4680, Fax: 570-408-7872, E-mail: rhonda.rabbitt@wilkes.edu. *Application contact:* Stephanie Wasmanski, Associate Director of Graduate Admissions, 570-408-5535, Fax: 570-408-7846, E-mail: stephanie.wasmanski@wilkes.edu.
Website: http://www.wilkes.edu/academics/graduate-programs/masters-programs/graduate-education/index.aspx

William Paterson University of New Jersey, College of Education, Wayne, NJ 07470-8420. Offers curriculum and learning (M Ed); early childhood education (Certificate); educational leadership (M Ed); educational media specialist (Certificate); elementary education (MAT, Certificate); elementary education subject area (Certificate); higher education administration (MA); learning disabilities consultant (Certificate); literacy (M Ed); middle level education (M Ed); middle school education subject area (Certificate); professional counseling (M Ed); reading specialist (Certificate); school library media specialist (Certificate); school principal (Certificate); school supervisor (Certificate); secondary education (MAT); special education (M Ed); teacher of students with disabilities (Certificate). *Accreditation:* NCATE. *Program availability:* Part-time, evening/weekend. *Students:* Average age 35. 347 applicants, 87% accepted, 226 enrolled. In 2018, 136 master's awarded. *Degree requirements:* For master's, comprehensive exam, thesis (for some programs), exit interview (for some programs); practicum/internship; minimum GPA of 3.0 (for some programs); exit portfolio (for some programs). *Entrance requirements:* For master's, GRE/MAT, minimum GPA of 2.75; teaching certificate; essay; interview; 2 letters of recommendation; personal statement. Additional exam requirements/recommendations for international students: Required—TOEFL (minimum score 550 paper-based; 79 iBT), IELTS (minimum score 6). *Application deadline:* For fall admission, 6/1 for domestic students, 3/1 for international students; for spring admission, 11/1 for domestic students, 10/1 for international students. Applications are processed on a rolling basis. Application fee: $50. Electronic applications accepted. *Expenses:* Tuition, area resident: Full-time $14,714; part-time $727 per credit. Tuition, state resident: full-time $14,714; part-time $727 per credit. Tuition, nonresident: full-time $22,952; part-time $727 per credit. *International tuition:* $22,952 full-time. *Required fees:* $4 per semester. Tuition and fees vary according to course load, degree level and program. *Financial support:* In 2018–19, 8,416 students received support. Career-related internships or fieldwork, Federal Work-Study, scholarships/grants, and unspecified assistantships available. Support available to part-time students. Financial award application deadline: 3/15; financial award applicants required to submit FAFSA. *Faculty research:* Code switching and creative writing, language instruction, teacher evaluation, preschools, history of educational theories. *Total annual research expenditures:* $311,226. *Unit head:* Dr. Dorothy Feola, Dean, 973-720-2138, Fax: 973-720-3647, E-mail: feolad@wpunj.edu. *Application contact:* Liana Fornarotto, Director of Education Enrollment and Certification, 973-720-2206, Fax: 973-720-2989, E-mail: fornarottol@wpunj.edu.
Website: http://www.wpunj.edu/coe

William Woods University, Graduate and Adult Studies, Fulton, MO 65251-1098. Offers administration (M Ed, Ed S); athletic/activities administration (M Ed); curriculum and instruction (M Ed, Ed S); educational leadership (Ed D); equestrian education (M Ed); health management (MBA); human resources (MBA); leadership (MBA); marketing, advertising, and public relations (MBA); teaching and technology (M Ed). *Program availability:* Part-time, evening/weekend. *Degree requirements:* For master's, capstone course (MBA), action research (M Ed); for Ed S, field experience. *Entrance requirements:* Additional exam requirements/recommendations for international students: Required—TOEFL (minimum score 550 paper-based). Electronic applications accepted. *Expenses:* Contact institution.

Wilmington University, College of Education, New Castle, DE 19720-6491. Offers applied technology in education (M Ed); career and technical education (M Ed); educational leadership (Ed D); elementary and secondary school counseling (M Ed); elementary studies (M Ed); ESOL literacy (M Ed); higher education leadership (Ed D); instruction: gifted and talented (M Ed); instruction: teacher of reading (M Ed); instruction: teaching and learning (M Ed); organizational leadership (Ed D); school leadership (M Ed); secondary education (MAT); special education (M Ed). *Accreditation:* NCATE. *Program availability:* Part-time, evening/weekend. *Entrance requirements:* For master's, 2 letters of recommendation, interview. Additional exam requirements/recommendations for international students: Required—TOEFL (minimum score 500 paper-based). Electronic applications accepted.

Wingate University, Thayer School of Education, Wingate, NC 28174. Offers community college executive leadership (Ed D); educational leadership (MA Ed, Ed S); elementary education (MA Ed, MAT). *Accreditation:* NCATE. *Program availability:* Part-time, evening/weekend. *Degree requirements:* For master's, portfolio. *Entrance requirements:* For master's, GRE General Test or MAT, teaching certificate (MA Ed).

Winona State University, College of Education, Department of Leadership Education, Winona, MN 55987. Offers education leadership (MS, Ed S), including k-12 principal (Ed S), superintendent (Ed S); organizational leadership (MS); professional leadership (MS); sport management (MS). MS in sport management offered in cooperation with Department of Physical Education and Sport Science. *Accreditation:* NCATE. *Program availability:* Part-time, evening/weekend. *Degree requirements:* For master's, comprehensive exam, thesis optional; for Ed S, thesis optional.

Winthrop University, College of Education, Program in Educational Leadership, Rock Hill, SC 29733. Offers M Ed. *Students:* 58 part-time (45 women); includes 26 minority (20 Black or African American, non-Hispanic/Latino; 6 Hispanic/Latino), 1 international. Average age 37. In 2018, 13 master's awarded. *Entrance requirements:* For master's, GRE General Test or MAT, 3 years of experience, South Carolina Class III Teaching Certificate, recommendations from current principal and district-level administrator. Additional exam requirements/recommendations for international students: Required—TOEFL (minimum score 550 paper-based; 79 iBT), IELTS (minimum score 6). *Application deadline:* For fall admission, 7/15 priority date for domestic students; for spring admission, 12/1 for domestic students. Applications are processed on a rolling basis. Application fee: $50. Electronic applications accepted. *Expenses:* Tuition, state resident: full-time $15,166; part-time $635 per credit hour. Tuition, nonresident: full-time $29,214. *Required fees:* $500; $180 per semester. *Financial support:* Application deadline: 2/1; applicants required to submit FAFSA. *Unit head:* Dr. Walter Hart, Graduate Program Director, 803-323-4710, E-mail: hartw@winthrop.edu. *Application contact:* 800-411-7041, Fax: 803-323-2204, E-mail: gradschool@winthrop.edu. Website: http://www.winthrop.edu/coe/edleadership

Wisconsin Lutheran College, College of Adult and Graduate Studies, Milwaukee, WI 53226-9942. Offers high performance instruction (MA Ed); instructional technology (MA Ed); leadership and innovation (MA Ed); science instruction (MA Ed).

Worcester State University, Graduate School, Department of Education, Worcester, MA 01602-2597. Offers adult English as a esl (Postbaccalaureate Certificate); curriculum and instruction (Ed S); early childhood education (M Ed); education (M Ed); elementary education (M Ed); English as a second language (M Ed, Postbaccalaureate Certificate); middle school education (M Ed); middle/secondary school education (Postbaccalaureate Certificate); moderate disabilities (M Ed, Postbaccalaureate Certificate); reading (M Ed, Postbaccalaureate Certificate); reading specialist (Postbaccalaureate Certificate); school leadership and education administration (M Ed); school psychology (M Ed, Ed S); secondary education (M Ed, Ed S, Postbaccalaureate Certificate). *Faculty:* 10 full-time (9 women), 23 part-time/adjunct (11 women). *Students:* 38 full-time (33 women), 281 part-time (212 women); includes 30 minority (4 Black or African American, non-Hispanic/Latino; 3 American Indian or Alaska Native, non-Hispanic/Latino; 2 Asian, non-Hispanic/Latino; 16 Hispanic/Latino; 5 Two or more races, non-Hispanic/Latino), 2 international. Average age 41. 102 applicants, 98% accepted, 88 enrolled. In 2018, 132 master's, 52 Ed Ss awarded. *Degree requirements:* For master's, comprehensive exam (for some programs), thesis (for some programs), For a detail list of degree completion requirements please see the graduate catalog at catalog.worcester.edu. *Entrance requirements:* For master's, GRE General Test, MAT or GMAT, teaching certificate. For a detail list of entrance requirements please see the graduate catalog at catalog.worcester.edu. Additional exam requirements/recommendations for international students: Required—TOEFL (minimum score 550 paper-based; 79 iBT), PTE. *Application deadline:* For fall admission, 3/1 for domestic and international students; for spring admission, 11/1 for domestic and international students; for summer admission, 3/1 for domestic and international students. Applications are processed on a rolling basis. Application fee: $50. Electronic applications accepted. *Expenses: Tuition, area resident:* Full-time $3042; part-time $169 per credit hour. Tuition, state resident: full-time $3042; part-time $169 per credit hour. Tuition, nonresident: full-time $3042; part-time $169 per credit hour. *International tuition:* $3042 full-time. *Required fees:* $2754; $153 per credit hour. *Financial support:* Career-related internships or fieldwork, scholarships/grants, and unspecified assistantships available. Support available to part-time students. Financial award application deadline: 3/1; financial award applicants required to submit FAFSA. *Unit head:* Dr. Sara Young, Graduate Program Coordinator, 508-929-8246, Fax: 508-929-8164, E-mail: syoung3@worcester.edu. *Application contact:* Sara Grady, Associate Dean of Graduate and Continuing Education, 508-929-8130, Fax: 508-929-8100, E-mail: sara.grady@worcester.edu.

Wright State University, Graduate School, College of Education and Human Services, Department of Educational Leadership, Program in Advanced Educational Leadership, Dayton, OH 45435. Offers advanced curriculum and instruction (Ed S). *Accreditation:* NCATE. *Degree requirements:* For Ed S, thesis. *Entrance requirements:* For degree, GRE General Test, MAT. Additional exam requirements/recommendations for international students: Required—TOEFL.

Xavier University, College of Professional Sciences, School of Education, Department of Educational Leadership and Human Resource Development, Cincinnati, OH 45207. Offers educational administration (M Ed); human resource development (MS). *Program availability:* Part-time, evening/weekend. *Degree requirements:* For master's, internship; for doctorate, comprehensive exam, thesis/dissertation. *Entrance requirements:* For master's, GRE or MAT, resume; 2 letters of recommendation; goal statement; official transcript; for doctorate, GRE, GMAT, LSAT or MAT, official transcript; 1,000-word goal statement; resume; 3 letters of recommendation. Additional exam requirements/recommendations for international students: Required—TOEFL (minimum score 550

paper-based; 79 iBT). Electronic applications accepted. Application fee is waived when completed online. *Expenses:* Contact institution.

Xavier University of Louisiana, Graduate School, Programs in Education, New Orleans, LA 70125. Offers counseling (MA); curriculum and instruction (MA), including special interest - non certification; educational leadership (MA). *Accreditation:* NCATE. *Program availability:* Part-time, evening/weekend. *Faculty:* 7 full-time (5 women), 2 part-time/adjunct (both women). *Students:* 96 full-time (84 women), 51 part-time (42 women); includes 139 minority (138 Black or African American, non-Hispanic/Latino; 1 Hispanic/Latino). Average age 31. 77 applicants, 100% accepted, 77 enrolled. In 2018, 70 master's awarded. *Degree requirements:* For master's, comprehensive exam, thesis or alternative. *Entrance requirements:* For master's, GRE General Test, MAT /Praxis I & II, minimum GPA of 2.5. Additional exam requirements/recommendations for international students: Required—TOEFL. *Application deadline:* For fall admission, 7/1 for domestic students, 3/1 priority date for international students; for spring admission, 12/1 for domestic students, 9/15 priority date for international students; for summer admission, 3/1 for domestic students. Applications are processed on a rolling basis. Application fee: $30. Electronic applications accepted. *Expenses: Tuition:* Full-time $2652; part-time $1326 per credit hour. *Required fees:* $531; $323 per semester. $258 per semester. Tuition and fees vary according to degree level and program. *Financial support:* Career-related internships or fieldwork and tuition waivers (partial) available. Support available to part-time students. Financial award application deadline: 6/30; financial award applicants required to submit FAFSA. *Unit head:* Dr. Judith Miranti, Chair, Division of Education, 504-520-7536, Fax: 504-520-7909, E-mail: jmiranti@xula.edu. *Application contact:* Yiraliz Beltran, Program Manager, 504-520-7487, Fax: 504-520-7896, E-mail: ybeltran@xula.edu.

Yeshiva University, Azrieli Graduate School of Jewish Education and Administration, New York, NY 10033-4391. Offers MS, Ed D, Specialist. *Accreditation:* TEAC. *Program availability:* Part-time, evening/weekend. Terminal master's awarded for partial completion of doctoral program. *Degree requirements:* For master's, one foreign language, student teaching experience, comprehensive exam or thesis; for doctorate, one foreign language, comprehensive exam, thesis/dissertation, certifying exams, internship; for Specialist, one foreign language, comprehensive exam, certifying exams, internship. *Entrance requirements:* For master's, GRE General Test, BA in Jewish studies or equivalent; for doctorate and Specialist, GRE General Test, master's degree in Jewish education, 2 years of teaching experience. *Expenses:* Contact institution. *Faculty research:* Social patterns of American and Israeli Jewish population, special education, adult education, technology in education, return to religious values.

York College of Pennsylvania, Graduate Programs in Behavioral Sciences and Education, York, PA 17403-3651. Offers educational leadership (M Ed); educational technology (M Ed); reading specialist (M Ed). *Program availability:* Part-time-only, evening/weekend. *Faculty:* 1 full-time (0 women), 10 part-time/adjunct (8 women). *Students:* 1 full-time (0 women), 107 part-time (77 women); includes 3 minority (1 Hispanic/Latino; 2 Two or more races, non-Hispanic/Latino). Average age 34. 35 applicants, 69% accepted, 23 enrolled. In 2018, 10 master's awarded. *Degree requirements:* For master's, comprehensive exam (for some programs), thesis (for some programs). *Entrance requirements:* For master's, statement of applicant's professional and academic goals, 2 letters of recommendation, letter from current supervisor, official undergraduate and graduate transcript(s), copy of teaching certificate(s), current professional resume, interview. *Application deadline:* For fall admission, 7/15 priority date for domestic students; for spring admission, 11/15 priority date for domestic students; for summer admission, 4/15 priority date for domestic students. Applications are processed on a rolling basis. Application fee: $0. Electronic applications accepted. *Expenses:* $640 per credit; no general fee. *Financial support:* Scholarships/grants available. Financial award applicants required to submit FAFSA. *Faculty research:* Classroom technology, assessment, educational leadership, professional development, literacy. *Unit head:* Dr. Joshua D. DeSantis, Director, Graduate Programs in Behavioral Science and Education, 717-815-1936, E-mail: jdesant1@ycp.edu. *Application contact:* Dr. Joshua D. DeSantis, Director, Graduate Programs in Behavioral Science and Education, 717-815-1936, E-mail: jdesant1@ycp.edu. Website: https://www.ycp.edu/med

Youngstown State University, College of Graduate Studies, Beeghly College of Education, Department of Counseling, School Psychology and Educational Leadership, Youngstown, OH 44555-0001. Offers counseling (MS Ed); educational administration (MS Ed); educational leadership (Ed D); school psychology (Ed S). *Accreditation:* NCATE. *Program availability:* Part-time, evening/weekend. *Degree requirements:* For master's, comprehensive exam; for doctorate, comprehensive exam, thesis/dissertation. *Entrance requirements:* For master's, GRE, MAT, or teaching certificate; minimum GPA of 2.7; for doctorate, GRE General Test, GRE Subject Test, interview, minimum GPA of 3.5. Additional exam requirements/recommendations for international students: Required—TOEFL. *Faculty research:* Administrative theory, computer applications, education law, school and community relations, finance principalship.

Educational Measurement and Evaluation

American InterContinental University Online, Program in Education, Schaumburg, IL 60173. Offers curriculum and instruction (M Ed); educational assessment and evaluation (M Ed); instructional technology (M Ed); leadership of educational organizations (M Ed). *Accreditation:* TEAC. *Program availability:* Evening/weekend, online learning. *Entrance requirements:* Additional exam requirements/recommendations for international students: Required—TOEFL (minimum score 550 paper-based). Electronic applications accepted.

American University, School of Professional and Extended Studies, Washington, DC 20016. Offers agile project management (MS); healthcare management (MS, Graduate Certificate); human resource analytics and management (MS, Graduate Certificate); instructional design and learning analytics (MS); measurement and evaluation (MS); project monitoring and evaluation (Graduate Certificate); sports analytics and management (MS, Graduate Certificate). *Program availability:* Part-time, evening/weekend, 100% online, blended/hybrid learning. *Faculty:* 27 full-time (14 women), 33 part-time/adjunct (20 women). *Students:* 2 full-time (both women), 113 part-time (68 women); includes 6 minority (4 Black or African American, non-Hispanic/Latino; 1 Asian, non-Hispanic/Latino; 1 Hispanic/Latino). Average age 31. 156 applicants, 93% accepted, 66 enrolled. In 2018, 1 master's, 6 other advanced degrees awarded. *Entrance requirements:* For master's, Please visit website: https://www.american.edu/spexs/, official transcript(s), resume. Additional exam requirements/recommendations for international students: Required—TOEFL. *Application deadline:* Applications are processed on a rolling basis. Application fee: $55. Electronic applications accepted.

Expenses: Contact institution. *Financial support:* Applicants required to submit FAFSA. *Unit head:* Jill Klein, Dean, 202-895-4900, E-mail: spexs@american.edu. *Application contact:* Emily Emily, Assistant Director for Recruitment and Admission, 202-885-4910, E-mail: aronoff@american.edu. Website: http://www.american.edu/spexs

Arizona State University at the Tempe campus, Mary Lou Fulton Teachers College, Program in Educational Policy and Evaluation, Phoenix, AZ 85069. Offers PhD. Fall admission only. *Degree requirements:* For doctorate, comprehensive exam, thesis/dissertation, interactive Program of Study (iPOS) submitted before completing 50 percent of required credit hours. *Entrance requirements:* For doctorate, GRE, minimum GPA of 3.0 or equivalent in last 2 years of work leading to bachelor's degree, 3 letters of recommendation, personal statement, writing sample, curriculum vitae or resume. Additional exam requirements/recommendations for international students: Required—TOEFL, IELTS, or PTE. Electronic applications accepted. *Expenses:* Contact institution. *Faculty research:* Education policy analysis, school finance and quantitative methods, school improvement in ethnically, linguistically and economically diverse communities, parent/teacher engagement, school choice, accountability polices, school finance litigation, school segregation.

Ball State University, Graduate School, Teachers College, Department of Educational Psychology, Muncie, IN 47306. Offers educational psychology (MA, MS), including educational psychology (MA, MS, PhD); educational psychology (PhD), including educational psychology (MA, MS, PhD); gifted and talented education (Certificate);

human development and learning (Certificate); instructional design and assessment (Certificate); neuropsychology (Certificate); quantitative psychology (MS); response to intervention (Certificate); school psychology (MA, PhD), including school psychology (MA, PhD, Ed S); school psychology (Ed S), including school psychology (MA, PhD, Ed S). *Program availability:* 100% online. *Degree requirements:* For doctorate, thesis/dissertation; for other advanced degree, thesis. *Entrance requirements:* For master's, GRE General Test, minimum baccalaureate GPA of 2.75 or 3.0 in latter half of baccalaureate, professional goals and self-assessment; for doctorate, GRE General Test, minimum graduate GPA of 3.2; for other advanced degree, GRE General Test. Additional exam requirements/recommendations for international students: Required—TOEFL (minimum score 550 paper-based; 79 iBT), IELTS (minimum score 6.5). Electronic applications accepted.

Brandeis University, Rabb School of Continuing Studies, Division of Graduate Professional Studies, Graduate Certificate in Learning Analytics Program, Waltham, MA 02454-9110. Offers Graduate Certificate. *Program availability:* Part-time-only, online only, 100% online. *Entrance requirements:* For degree, three years of work experience; master's or doctoral degree in analytics, instructional design or a related field; master's degree from regionally-accredited U.S. institution or equivalent; official transcript(s) from every college or university attended; resume or curriculum vitae; statement of goals; letter of recommendation. Additional exam requirements/recommendations for international students: Required—TWE (minimum score 4.5), TOEFL (minimum scores: 600 paper-based, 100 iBT), IELTS (7), or PTE (68). Electronic applications accepted. *Expenses:* Contact institution.

Cambridge College, School of Education, Boston, MA 02129. Offers autism specialist (M Ed); autism/behavior analyst (M Ed); behavior analyst (Post-Master's Certificate); curriculum and instruction (CAGS); early childhood teacher (M Ed); educational leadership (M Ed, Ed D); elementary teacher (M Ed); English as a second language (M Ed, Certificate); general science (M Ed); health education (Post-Master's Certificate); interdisciplinary studies (M Ed); library teacher (M Ed); mathematics education (M Ed); mathematics specialist (Certificate); school administration (M Ed, CAGS); school nurse education (M Ed); teacher of students with moderate disabilities (M Ed); teaching skills and methodologies (M Ed). *Program availability:* Part-time, evening/weekend, online learning. *Degree requirements:* For master's, thesis, internship/practicum (licensure program only); for doctorate, thesis/dissertation; for other advanced degree, thesis. *Entrance requirements:* For master's, interview, resume, documentation of licensure, 2 professional references; for doctorate, official transcripts, interview, resume, written personal statement/essay, portfolio of scholarly and professional work, 2 professional references, health insurance, immunizations form; for other advanced degree, official transcripts, interview, resume, written personal statement/essay, 2 professional references, health insurance, immunizations form. Additional exam requirements/recommendations for international students: Required—TOEFL (minimum score 550 paper-based; 79 iBT), Michigan English Language Assessment Battery (minimum score 85); Recommended—IELTS (minimum score 6). *Application deadline:* Applications are processed on a rolling basis. Application fee: $30. Electronic applications accepted. *Expenses:* Contact institution. *Financial support:* Career-related internships or fieldwork, Federal Work-Study, and scholarships/grants available. Financial award applicants required to submit FAFSA. *Faculty research:* Adult education, accelerated learning, mathematics education, brain compatible learning, special education and law. *Unit head:* Dr. Mary Garrity, Interim Dean, 617-873-0168, E-mail: mary.garrity@cambridgecollege.edu. *Application contact:* Salvadore Liberto, Interim Assistant Vice President of Enrollment, 800-877-4723, E-mail: admissions@cambridgecollege.edu.
Website: https://www.cambridgecollege.edu/school/school-education

Claremont Graduate University, Graduate Programs, School of Educational Studies, Claremont, CA 91711-6160. Offers Africana education (Certificate); education and policy (MA, PhD); higher education/student affairs (MA, PhD); human development (MA, PhD); public school administration (MA, PhD); quantitative evaluation (MA, PhD); special education (MA, PhD); teacher education (MA); teaching and learning (MA, PhD); urban leadership (PhD); MBA/PhD. PhD program offered jointly with San Diego State University. *Program availability:* Part-time. Terminal master's awarded for partial completion of doctoral program. *Entrance requirements:* For master's and doctorate, GRE General Test. Additional exam requirements/recommendations for international students: Required—TOEFL (minimum score 75 iBT). Electronic applications accepted. *Faculty research:* Education administration, K-12 and higher education, multicultural education, education policy, diversity in higher education, faculty issues.

Clemson University, Graduate School, College of Education, Department of Education and Human Development, Clemson, SC 29634. Offers counselor education (M Ed, Ed S), including mental health counseling, school counseling, student affairs (M Ed); learning sciences (PhD); literacy (M Ed); literacy, language and culture (PhD); special education (M Ed, MAT, PhD). *Program availability:* Part-time, evening/weekend, 100% online. *Faculty:* 35 full-time (24 women). *Students:* 103 full-time (87 women), 132 part-time (123 women); includes 37 minority (11 Black or African American, non-Hispanic/Latino; 1 American Indian or Alaska Native, non-Hispanic/Latino; 3 Asian, non-Hispanic/Latino; 11 Hispanic/Latino; 11 Two or more races, non-Hispanic/Latino), 5 international. Average age 29. 435 applicants, 67% accepted, 180 enrolled. In 2018, 51 master's, 3 doctorates, 34 other advanced degrees awarded. *Degree requirements:* For master's, thesis (for some programs); for doctorate, comprehensive exam (for some programs), thesis/dissertation. *Entrance requirements:* For master's and doctorate, GRE General Test, unofficial transcripts, letters of recommendation. Additional exam requirements/recommendations for international students: Required—TOEFL (minimum score 80 paper-based; 80 iBT); Recommended—IELTS (minimum score 6.5), TSE (minimum score 54). *Application deadline:* For fall admission, 4/15 priority date for international students; for spring admission, 10/15 priority date for international students. Applications are processed on a rolling basis. Application fee: $80 ($90 for international students). Electronic applications accepted. *Expenses:* $5198 per semester full-time resident, $10123 per semester full-time non-resident, $556 per credit hour part-time resident, $1109 per credit hour part-time non-resident, online $770 per credit hour, $4938 doctoral programs resident, $10405 doctoral programs non-resident, $1144 full-time graduate assistant, other fees may apply per session. *Financial support:* In 2018–19, 78 students received support, including 5 teaching assistantships with full and partial tuition reimbursements available (averaging $8,759 per year); career-related internships or fieldwork and unspecified assistantships also available. *Faculty research:* Literacy, reading recovery, exceptional children, policy development. *Total annual research expenditures:* $1.3 million. *Unit head:* Dr. Debi Switzer, Department Chair, 864-656-5098, E-mail: debi@clemson.edu. *Application contact:* Julie Jones, Student Services Program Coordinator, 864-656-5096, E-mail: jgambre@clemson.edu.
Website: http://www.clemson.edu/education/departments/education-human-development/index.html

College of Saint Mary, Program in Education, Omaha, NE 68106. Offers assessment leadership (MSE); English as a second language (MSE). *Program availability:* Part-time. *Entrance requirements:* For master's, technology competency test or equivalent, minimum cumulative GPA of 3.0, teaching certificate, 2 letters of reference, resume.

Duquesne University, School of Education, Department of Educational Foundations and Leadership, Program in Educational Studies, Pittsburgh, PA 15282-0001. Offers educational studies (MS Ed); program evaluation (MS Ed). *Program availability:* Part-time, evening/weekend, 100% online. *Faculty:* 1 full-time (0 women). *Students:* 3 full-time (1 woman), 4 part-time (1 woman); includes 1 minority (Black or African American, non-Hispanic/Latino), 2 international. Average age 34. 12 applicants, 92% accepted, 2 enrolled. In 2018, 15 master's awarded. *Entrance requirements:* For master's, bachelor's degree. Additional exam requirements/recommendations for international students: Required—TOEFL (minimum score 550 paper-based), IELTS (minimum score 7). *Application deadline:* For fall admission, 8/15 for domestic students; for spring admission, 1/2 for domestic students. Applications are processed on a rolling basis. Application fee: $0. Electronic applications accepted. *Expenses: Tuition:* Full-time $23,112; part-time $1284 per credit. Tuition and fees vary according to program. *Financial support:* Research assistantships available. Support available to part-time students. Financial award applicants required to submit FAFSA. *Faculty research:* Online learning; impact of trauma on childhood and adolescent development; evaluation of educational programs; research in mathematics education; beliefs about classroom assessment. *Unit head:* Dr. Gibbs Kanyongo, Associate Professor, 412-396-5190, Fax: 412-396-5454, E-mail: kanyongog@duq.edu. *Application contact:* Kelly McGinley, Graduate Admissions Assistant, 412-396-1559, Fax: 412-396-5585, E-mail: mcginleyk@duq.edu.

Eastern Michigan University, Graduate School, College of Education, Department of Teacher Education, Programs in Educational Psychology and Assessment, Ypsilanti, MI 48197. Offers educational assessment (Graduate Certificate); learning technology and design (MA). *Accreditation:* NCATE. *Program availability:* Part-time, evening/weekend, online learning. *Students:* 35 part-time (29 women); includes 6 minority (1 Black or African American, non-Hispanic/Latino; 3 Hispanic/Latino; 2 Two or more races, non-Hispanic/Latino). Average age 30. 22 applicants, 86% accepted, 9 enrolled. In 2018, 7 master's, 1 other advanced degree awarded. *Entrance requirements:* For master's, GRE. Additional exam requirements/recommendations for international students: Required—TOEFL. *Application deadline:* Applications are processed on a rolling basis. Application fee: $45. *Financial support:* Fellowships, research assistantships with full tuition reimbursements, teaching assistantships with full tuition reimbursements, career-related internships or fieldwork, Federal Work-Study, institutionally sponsored loans, scholarships/grants, tuition waivers (partial), and unspecified assistantships available. Support available to part-time students. Financial award applicants required to submit FAFSA. *Application contact:* Dr. Alane Starko, Coordinator, 734-487-2789, Fax: 734-487-2101, E-mail: astarko@emich.edu.

Florida State University, The Graduate School, College of Education, Department of Educational Leadership and Policy Studies, Tallahassee, FL 32306. Offers educational leadership and administration (Certificate); educational leadership and policy (MS, Ed D, PhD, Ed S), including education policy and evaluation (MS, Ed D, PhD), educational leadership and administration; foundations of education (MS, PhD), including history and philosophy of education, international and multicultural education; higher education (MS, PhD); institutional research (Certificate); program evaluation (Certificate). *Program availability:* Part-time, evening/weekend, 100% online, blended/hybrid learning, asynchronous, minimal on-campus study. *Degree requirements:* For master's, comprehensive exam, thesis optional; for doctorate, comprehensive exam, thesis/dissertation, diagnostic exam, preliminary exam, prospectus defense, dissertation defense. *Entrance requirements:* For master's, doctorate, and other advanced degree, GRE General Test, minimum GPA of 3.0. Additional exam requirements/recommendations for international students: Required—TOEFL (minimum score 550 paper-based, 80 iBT), IELTS (minimum score 6.5), Michigan English Language Assessment Battery (minimum score 77), or PTE (minimum score 55). Electronic applications accepted. *Expenses: Tuition, area resident:* Part-time $479.32 per credit hour. Tuition and fees vary according to campus/location and program. *Faculty research:* Post-secondary success; leadership education; education policy; international education; multicultural education.

Florida State University, The Graduate School, College of Education, Department of Educational Psychology and Learning Systems, Tallahassee, FL 32306. Offers counseling and human systems (PhD, MS/Ed S), including mental health counseling (MS/Ed S), school psychology (MS/Ed S); educational psychology (MS, PhD); human performance and technology (Certificate); instructional systems and learning technologies (MS, PhD); measurement and statistics (MS, PhD, Certificate); online instructional development (Certificate); MS/Ed S. *Program availability:* Part-time, evening/weekend, 100% online, blended/hybrid learning, asynchronous, minimal on-campus study. *Faculty:* 27 full-time (17 women), 8 part-time/adjunct (4 women). *Students:* 210 full-time (145 women), 122 part-time (89 women); includes 146 minority (39 Black or African American, non-Hispanic/Latino; 1 American Indian or Alaska Native, non-Hispanic/Latino; 51 Asian, non-Hispanic/Latino; 36 Hispanic/Latino; 19 Two or more races, non-Hispanic/Latino), 68 international. Average age 32. 419 applicants, 39% accepted, 82 enrolled. In 2018, 84 master's, 27 doctorates, 38 other advanced degrees awarded. Terminal master's awarded for partial completion of doctoral program. *Degree requirements:* For master's and Certificate, comprehensive exam, thesis optional; for doctorate, comprehensive exam, thesis/dissertation, diagnostic exam, preliminary exam, prospectus defense. *Entrance requirements:* For master's, doctorate, and Certificate, GRE General Test, minimum GPA of 3.0. Additional exam requirements/recommendations for international students: Required—TOEFL (minimum score 550 paper-based, 80 iBT), IELTS (minimum score 6.5) or Michigan English Language Assessment Battery (minimum score 77). Application fee: $30. Electronic applications accepted. *Expenses: Tuition, area resident:* Part-time $479.32 per credit hour. Tuition and fees vary according to campus/location and program. *Financial support:* In 2018–19, 8 research assistantships with partial tuition reimbursements (averaging $6,640 per year), 42 teaching assistantships with partial tuition reimbursements (averaging $6,740 per year) were awarded. Financial award application deadline: 1/15; financial award applicants required to submit FAFSA. *Faculty research:* Learning and cognition, counseling and school psychology, instructional systems, measurement and evaluation. *Unit head:* Dr. James Klein, Chair, 850-644-4592, Fax: 850-644-8776, E-mail: jklein@fsu.edu. *Application contact:* Mary Kate McKee, Academic Program Specialist, 850-644-8046, Fax: 850-644-8781, E-mail: mmckee@campus.fsu.edu.

Georgetown University, Master of Arts in Learning and Design Program, Washington, DC 20007. Offers MA. *Program availability:* Part-time, evening/weekend. *Degree requirements:* For master's, design studio/capstone project, ePortfolio. *Entrance requirements:* For master's, GRE (recommended), personal/academic statement, writing sample, resume, 3 letters of recommendation (at least one professional and one faculty/professor). Additional exam requirements/recommendations for international students: Required—TOEFL (minimum score 550 paper-based; 80 iBT), IELTS (minimum score 7). Electronic applications accepted.

Georgia Southern University, Jack N. Averitt College of Graduate Studies, College of Education, Department of Curriculum, Foundations, and Reading, Statesboro, GA 30460. Offers curriculum studies (Ed D), including curriculum studies; evaluation, assessment, research, and learning (M Ed); reading education (M Ed, Ed S). *Accreditation:* NCATE. *Program availability:* Part-time, evening/weekend. *Degree requirements:* For master's, comprehensive exam; for doctorate, comprehensive exam, thesis/dissertation, exams. *Entrance requirements:* For master's, GRE General Test or

MAT, minimum GPA of 2.5; for doctorate, GRE General Test or MAT, minimum GPA of 3.5, letters of reference, writing sample. Additional exam requirements/recommendations for international students: Required—TOEFL (minimum score 550 paper-based; 80 iBT), IELTS (minimum score 6). Electronic applications accepted. *Expenses: Tuition, area resident:* Part-time $3324 per semester. Tuition, state resident: full-time $5814; part-time $3324 per semester. Tuition, nonresident: full-time $23,204; part-time $13,260 per semester. *Required fees:* $2092; $2092. Tuition and fees vary according to course load, degree level, campus/location and program. *Faculty research:* Curriculum theories, at-risk students, gifted female adolescents, cognitive mapping, faculty evaluation, learning environments, research methodology, social and cultural conditions of learning, preservice teacher education.

Georgia State University, College of Education and Human Development, Department of Educational Policy Studies, Program in Educational Research, Atlanta, GA 30302-3083. Offers MS, PhD. MS offered jointly with Department of Counseling and Psychological Services. *Accreditation:* NCATE. *Program availability:* Part-time. *Entrance requirements:* For master's and doctorate, GRE. *Application deadline:* Applications are processed on a rolling basis. Application fee: $50. Electronic applications accepted. *Expenses: Tuition, area resident:* Full-time $9360; part-time $390 per credit hour. Tuition, state resident: full-time $9360; part-time $390 per credit hour. Tuition, nonresident: full-time $30,024; part-time $1251 per credit hour. *International tuition:* $30,024 full-time. *Required fees:* $2128. *Financial support:* Fellowships, research assistantships, teaching assistantships, career-related internships or fieldwork, scholarships/grants, health care benefits, tuition waivers (full), and unspecified assistantships available. Support available to part-time students. Financial award application deadline: 3/15. *Faculty research:* Program evaluation, item response theory, quantitative research methodology, qualitative research methodology, gender and identity studies. *Unit head:* Dr. Jennifer Esposito, Interim Department Chair, 404-413-8281, Fax: 404-413-8003, E-mail: jesposito@gsu.edu. *Application contact:* Aishah Cowan, Administrative Academic Specialist, 404-413-8273, Fax: 404-413-8003, E-mail: acowan@gsu.edu.
Website: https://education.gsu.edu/eps/

Houston Baptist University, College of Education and Behavioral Sciences, Programs in Education, Houston, TX 77074-3298. Offers bilingual education (M Ed); counselor education (M Ed); curriculum and instruction (M Ed); curriculum and instruction (EC-6 bilingual) (M Ed); curriculum and instruction in all-level art, Spanish, music, or physical education (M Ed); curriculum and instruction in EC-6 and special education (EC-12) (M Ed); curriculum and instruction in instructional technology (M Ed); curriculum and instruction in mathematics, science, or social studies (4-8) (M Ed); curriculum and instruction with EC-6 generalist (M Ed); curriculum and instruction with English language arts and reading (4-8) (M Ed); educational administration (M Ed); educational diagnostician (M Ed); executive educational leadership (Ed D); higher education in business management (M Ed); higher education in Christian studies (M Ed); higher education in counseling (M Ed); higher education in educational technology (M Ed); reading (M Ed); special educational leadership (Ed D). *Program availability:* Part-time, evening/weekend, 100% online, blended/hybrid learning. *Degree requirements:* For master's, comprehensive exam; for doctorate, thesis/dissertation. *Entrance requirements:* For master's, minimum GPA of 2.75, two recommendations, resume, bachelor's degree conferred transcript; interview (for non-certified teachers); for doctorate, GRE, 5 letters of recommendation. Additional exam requirements/recommendations for international students: Required—TOEFL (minimum score 80 iBT), IELTS (minimum score 6.5). Electronic applications accepted. Application fee is waived when completed online. *Expenses:* Contact institution. *Faculty research:* Autism and inclusion, integrating technology into instruction, school change and leadership trust.

Indiana University Bloomington, School of Education, Department of Counseling and Educational Psychology, Bloomington, IN 47405-1006. Offers counseling (MS, PhD, Ed S); counselor education (MS, Ed S); educational psychology (MS, PhD); inquiry methodology (PhD); learning and developmental sciences (MS, PhD); school psychology (PhD, Ed S). *Accreditation:* ACA (one or more programs are accredited); APA (one or more programs are accredited); NCATE. Terminal master's awarded for partial completion of doctoral program. *Degree requirements:* For master's, thesis optional; for doctorate, thesis/dissertation; for Ed S, comprehensive exam or project. *Entrance requirements:* For master's, doctorate, and Ed S, GRE General Test. Additional exam requirements/recommendations for international students: Required—TOEFL. Electronic applications accepted. *Faculty research:* Counseling psychology, inquiry methodology, school psychology, learning sciences, human development, educational psychology.

Indiana University Bloomington, School of Education, Program in Inquiry Methodology, Bloomington, IN 47405-7000. Offers PhD.

Iowa State University of Science and Technology, Department of Educational Leadership and Policy Studies, Ames, IA 50011. Offers counselor education (M Ed, MS); educational administration (M Ed, MS); educational leadership (PhD); higher education (M Ed, MS); organizational learning and human resource development (M Ed, MS); research and evaluation (MS); student affairs (MS). *Degree requirements:* For master's, thesis or alternative; for doctorate, thesis/dissertation. *Entrance requirements:* For master's and doctorate, GRE General Test. Additional exam requirements/recommendations for international students: Required—TOEFL (minimum score 560 paper-based; 83 iBT), IELTS (minimum score 6.5). Electronic applications accepted.

James Madison University, The Graduate School, College of Education, Program in Adult Education and Human Resource Development, Harrisonburg, VA 22807. Offers higher education (MS Ed); human resource management (MS Ed); individualized (MS Ed); instructional design (MS Ed); leadership and facilitation (MS Ed); program evaluation and measurement (MS Ed). *Accreditation:* NCATE. *Program availability:* Part-time, evening/weekend. *Students:* 10 full-time (7 women), 11 part-time (8 women); includes 8 minority (5 Black or African American, non-Hispanic/Latino; 1 American Indian or Alaska Native, non-Hispanic/Latino; 1 Hispanic/Latino; 1 Two or more races, non-Hispanic/Latino), 1 international. Average age 30. In 2018, 10 master's awarded. Application fee: $60. Electronic applications accepted. *Expenses:* Tuition, state resident: full-time $10,848. Tuition, nonresident: full-time $27,888. *Required fees:* $1128. *Financial support:* In 2018–19, 8 students received support. Teaching assistantships, Federal Work-Study, and assistantships (averaging $7911) available. Financial award application deadline: 3/1; financial award applicants required to submit FAFSA. *Unit head:* Dr. Jane B. Thall, Department Head, 540-568-5531, E-mail: thalljb@jmu.edu. *Application contact:* Lynette D. Michael, Director of Graduate Admissions, 540-568-6131 Ext. 6395, Fax: 540-568-7860, E-mail: michaeld@jmu.edu.

James Madison University, The Graduate School, College of Health and Behavioral Studies, Program in Assessment and Measurement, Harrisonburg, VA 22807. Offers PhD. *Program availability:* Part-time. *Students:* 8 full-time (4 women), 2 part-time (both women); includes 3 minority (1 Black or African American, non-Hispanic/Latino; 2 Asian, non-Hispanic/Latino). Average age 30. In 2018, 3 doctorates awarded. Electronic applications accepted. *Expenses:* Tuition, state resident: full-time $10,848. Tuition, nonresident: full-time $27,888. *Required fees:* $1128. *Financial support:* In 2018–19, 7 students received support. Fellowships, Federal Work-Study, unspecified assistantships, and doctoral assistantships (stipend varies) available. Financial award application deadline: 3/1; financial award applicants required to submit FAFSA. *Unit head:* Dr. Deborah L. Bandalos, Graduate Program Director, 540-568-7132, E-mail: bandaldl@jmu.edu. *Application contact:* Lynette D. Michael, Director of Graduate Admissions and Student Records, 540-568-6131 Ext. 6395, Fax: 540-568-7860, E-mail: michaeld@jmu.edu.
Website: http://www.psyc.jmu.edu/assessment/

Kent State University, College of Education, Health and Human Services, School of Foundations, Leadership and Administration, Program in Evaluation and Measurement, Kent, OH 44242-0001. Offers M Ed, PhD. *Faculty:* 5 full-time (4 women), 4 part-time/adjunct (1 woman). *Students:* 24 full-time (9 women), 12 part-time (7 women); includes 7 minority (1 American Indian or Alaska Native, non-Hispanic/Latino; 4 Asian, non-Hispanic/Latino; 2 Native Hawaiian or other Pacific Islander, non-Hispanic/Latino), 9 international. 42 applicants, 40% accepted. In 2018, 3 master's, 2 doctorates awarded. *Degree requirements:* For doctorate, comprehensive exam, thesis/dissertation. *Entrance requirements:* For master's, minimum GPA of 2.75, 2 letters of reference, goals statement; for doctorate, GRE, minimum GPA of 3.5 from master's degree, resume, 2 letters of reference, goal statement. Additional exam requirements/recommendations for international students: Required—TOEFL (minimum score 550 paper-based; 80 iBT). *Application deadline:* For fall admission, 3/15 priority date for domestic and international students; for spring admission, 10/15 priority date for domestic and international students; for summer admission, 3/15 priority date for domestic and international students. Application fee: $45 ($60 for international students). Electronic applications accepted. *Expenses:* Tuition, state resident: full-time $11,766; part-time $536 per credit. Tuition, nonresident: full-time $21,952; part-time $999 per credit. *International tuition:* $21,952 full-time. Tuition and fees vary according to course load. *Financial support:* In 2018–19, 4 research assistantships (averaging $12,000 per year), 1 teaching assistantship (averaging $12,000 per year) were awarded; fellowships, career-related internships or fieldwork, Federal Work-Study, institutionally sponsored loans, scholarships/grants, health care benefits, and unspecified assistantships also available. Support available to part-time students. *Unit head:* Dr. Tricia Niesz, Coordinator, 330-672-0591, E-mail: tniesz@kent.edu. *Application contact:* Cheryl Slusarczyk, Academic Program Director, Office of Graduate Student Services, 330-672-2576, Fax: 330-672-9162, E-mail: ogs@kent.edu.
Website: http://www.kent.edu/ehhs/eval/

Louisiana State University and Agricultural & Mechanical College, Graduate School, College of Human Sciences and Education, Department of Educational Theory, Policy and Practice, Baton Rouge, LA 70803. Offers counseling (M Ed, MA, Ed S); educational administration (M Ed, MA, PhD, Ed S); educational technology (MA); elementary education (M Ed, MAT); higher education (PhD); research methodology (PhD); secondary education (M Ed, MAT). *Accreditation:* ACA (one or more programs are accredited); NCATE.

Loyola University Chicago, School of Education, Program in Research Methods, Chicago, IL 60660. Offers measurement $ quantitative methods (Certificate); research methodology (PhD). PhD offered through the Graduate School. *Program availability:* Part-time, evening/weekend. *Faculty:* 4 full-time (3 women), 1 part-time/adjunct (0 women). *Students:* 7 full-time (6 women), 8 part-time (4 women); includes 4 minority (1 Black or African American, non-Hispanic/Latino; 1 Asian, non-Hispanic/Latino; 2 Hispanic/Latino), 1 international. Average age 38. 18 applicants, 39% accepted, 4 enrolled. In 2018, 5 doctorates, 2 other advanced degrees awarded. *Degree requirements:* For master's, comprehensive exam (M Ed), thesis (MA); for doctorate, comprehensive exam, thesis/dissertation. *Entrance requirements:* For master's, GRE General Test, letters of recommendation, resume, minimum GPA of 3.0; for doctorate, GRE General Test, interview. Additional exam requirements/recommendations for international students: Required—TOEFL (minimum score 550 paper-based; 79 iBT). *Application deadline:* For fall admission, 12/1 for domestic and international students. Applications are processed on a rolling basis. Application fee: $50. Electronic applications accepted. Application fee is waived when completed online. *Expenses:* Contact institution. *Financial support:* In 2018–19, 2 research assistantships with full tuition reimbursements (averaging $14,000 per year), 10 teaching assistantships (averaging $4,000 per year) were awarded; institutionally sponsored loans, scholarships/grants, health care benefits, and unspecified assistantships also available. Support available to part-time students. Financial award application deadline: 2/1; financial award applicants required to submit FAFSA. *Faculty research:* Circular statistics, program evaluation, psychological measurement, infant attachment, adolescent development. *Unit head:* Dr. Leanne Kallemeyn, Program Chair, 312-915-6909, E-mail: lkallemeyn@luc.edu. *Application contact:* Dr. Leanne Kallemeyn, Program Chair, 312-915-6909, E-mail: lkallemeyn@luc.edu.

McNeese State University, Doré School of Graduate Studies, Burton College of Education, Department of Education Professions, Lake Charles, LA 70609. Offers curriculum and instruction (M Ed), including academically gifted education, elementary education, reading, secondary education, special education; early childhood education grades PK-3 (Postbaccalaureate Certificate); educational leadership (M Ed, Ed S), including educational leadership, educational technology (Ed S); educational technology leadership (M Ed); elementary education (MAT); elementary education grades 1-5 (Postbaccalaureate Certificate); instructional technology (MS); middle school education grades 4-8 (Postbaccalaureate Certificate), including middle school education grades 4-8; multiple levels grades K-12 (Postbaccalaureate Certificate), including multiple levels grades K-12; school counseling (M Ed); school librarian (Postbaccalaureate Certificate); secondary education (MAT); secondary education grades 6-12 (Postbaccalaureate Certificate); special education (M Ed), including advanced professional, autism, educational diagnostician; special education - mild/moderate grades 1-12 (MAT); special education, mild/moderate for elementary education grades 1-5 (Postbaccalaureate Certificate). *Program availability:* Evening/weekend. *Entrance requirements:* For master's, GRE.

Michigan State University, The Graduate School, College of Education, Department of Counseling, Educational Psychology and Special Education, East Lansing, MI 48824. Offers counseling (MA); educational psychology and educational technology (PhD); educational technology (MA); measurement and quantitative methods (PhD); rehabilitation counseling (MA); rehabilitation counselor education (PhD); school psychology (MA, PhD, Ed S); special education (MA, PhD). *Accreditation:* APA (one or more programs are accredited); CORE (one or more programs are accredited). *Program availability:* Part-time. *Entrance requirements:* Additional exam requirements/recommendations for international students: Required—TOEFL. Electronic applications accepted.

Missouri State University, Graduate College, College of Education, Department of Counseling, Leadership, and Special Education, Program in Counseling and Assessment, Springfield, MO 65897. Offers Ed S. *Program availability:* Part-time. *Faculty:* 8 full-time (5 women), 2 part-time/adjunct (both women). *Students:* 3 part-time (2 women). Average age 35. 5 applicants. In 2018, 4 Ed Ss awarded. *Degree requirements:* For Ed S, comprehensive exam. *Entrance requirements:* For degree, GRE. Additional exam requirements/recommendations for international students: Required—TOEFL (minimum score 550 paper-based; 79 iBT), IELTS (minimum score

6). *Application deadline:* For fall admission, 2/1 for domestic and international students. Application fee: $55 ($60 for international students). Electronic applications accepted. Tuition and fees vary according to class time, course level, course load, degree level, campus/location, program and student level. *Financial support:* Federal Work-Study, institutionally sponsored loans, scholarships/grants, and unspecified assistantships available. Financial award application deadline: 1/31; financial award applicants required to submit FAFSA. *Unit head:* Dr. James Satterfield, Department Head, 417-836-5392, Fax: 417-836-4918, E-mail: clse@missouristate.edu. *Application contact:* Lakan Drinker, Director, Graduate Enrollment Management, 417-836-5330, Fax: 417-836-6200, E-mail: lakandrinker@missouristate.edu.
Website: http://education.missouristate.edu/assessment/

Missouri Western State University, Program in Assessment, St. Joseph, MO 64507-2294. Offers K-12 cross-categorical special education (MAS); TESOL (Graduate Certificate). *Program availability:* Part-time. *Students:* 1 (woman) full-time, 33 part-time (32 women); includes 3 minority (2 American Indian or Alaska Native, non-Hispanic/Latino; 1 Asian, non-Hispanic/Latino). Average age 40. 16 applicants, 100% accepted, 8 enrolled. In 2018, 12 master's, 4 other advanced degrees awarded. *Entrance requirements:* For master's, minimum GPA of 2.75. Additional exam requirements/recommendations for international students: Recommended—TOEFL (minimum score 79 iBT), IELTS (minimum score 6). *Application deadline:* For fall admission, 7/15 for domestic and international students; for spring admission, 11/1 for domestic and international students; for summer admission, 4/29 for domestic and international students. Applications are processed on a rolling basis. Application fee: $45 ($50 for international students). Electronic applications accepted. *Expenses: Tuition, area resident:* Part-time $359.39 per credit hour. Tuition, state resident: part-time $359.39 per credit hour. Tuition, nonresident: part-time $643.39 per credit hour. Tuition and fees vary according to program. *Financial support:* Scholarships/grants and unspecified assistantships available. Support available to part-time students. *Unit head:* Dr. Susan Bashinski, Dean of Graduate Programs, 816-271-4394, E-mail: graduate@missouriwestern.edu. *Application contact:* Dr. Susan Bashinski, Dean of Graduate Programs, 816-271-4394, Fax: 816-271-4525, E-mail: graduate@missouriwestern.edu.
Website: https://www.missouriwestern.edu/graduate/

Montclair State University, The Graduate School, College of Education and Human Services, Program Evaluation Certificate Program, Montclair, NJ 07043-1624. Offers Certificate.

Mount Saint Vincent University, Graduate Programs, Faculty of Education, Program in Educational Psychology, Halifax, NS B3M 2J6, Canada. Offers education of the blind or visually impaired (M Ed); education of the deaf or hard of hearing (M Ed); educational psychology (MA-R); evaluation (M Ed); human relations (M Ed). *Program availability:* Part-time, evening/weekend, online learning. *Degree requirements:* For master's, thesis (for some programs). *Entrance requirements:* For master's, bachelor's degree in related field, 1 year of teaching experience. Electronic applications accepted. *Faculty research:* Personality measurement, values reasoning, aggression and sexuality, power and control, quantitative and qualitative research methodologies.

New Mexico State University, College of Education, Department of Counseling and Educational Psychology, Las Cruces, NM 88003-8001. Offers counseling psychology (PhD); educational diagnostics (MA), including clinical mental health counseling, educational diagnostics; school psychology (Ed S). *Accreditation:* ACA; APA (one or more programs are accredited); NCATE. *Program availability:* Part-time, evening/weekend. *Faculty:* 13 full-time (10 women), 3 part-time/adjunct (2 women). *Students:* 80 full-time (61 women), 33 part-time (24 women); includes 70 minority (4 Black or African American, non-Hispanic/Latino; 4 American Indian or Alaska Native, non-Hispanic/Latino; 5 Asian, non-Hispanic/Latino; 53 Hispanic/Latino; 4 Two or more races, non-Hispanic/Latino), 1 international. Average age 31. 118 applicants, 44% accepted, 32 enrolled. In 2018, 21 master's, 8 doctorates, 6 other advanced degrees awarded. *Degree requirements:* For master's, comprehensive exam, thesis optional, internship; for doctorate, comprehensive exam, thesis/dissertation, internship; for Ed S, comprehensive exam, thesis or alternative, internship as alternate. *Entrance requirements:* For master's, doctorate, and Ed S, GRE General Test, minimum GPA of 3.0. Additional exam requirements/recommendations for international students: Required—TOEFL (minimum score 550 paper-based; 79 iBT), IELTS (minimum score 6.5). *Application deadline:* For fall admission, 12/15 for domestic and international students; for spring admission, 2/1 priority date for domestic students, 2/1 for international students. Application fee: $40 ($50 for international students). Electronic applications accepted. *Expenses: Tuition, area resident:* Full-time $4216.70; part-time $252.70 per credit hour. Tuition, state resident: full-time $4216.70; part-time $252.70 per credit hour. Tuition, nonresident: full-time $12,769; part-time $881.10 per credit hour. *International tuition:* $12,769.30 full-time. *Required fees:* $878.40; $48.80 per credit hour. Full-time tuition and fees vary according to course load and reciprocity agreements. *Financial support:* In 2018–19, 71 students received support, including 9 fellowships (averaging $4,548 per year), 4 research assistantships (averaging $12,396 per year), 23 teaching assistantships (averaging $13,755 per year); career-related internships or fieldwork, Federal Work-Study, scholarships/grants, traineeships, health care benefits, and unspecified assistantships also available. Support available to part-time students. Financial award application deadline: 3/1. *Faculty research:* Multicultural counseling and training, school and counseling psychology, social justice, integrated primary care behavioral health training, mental health disparities. *Total annual research expenditures:* $30,427. *Unit head:* Dr. Barbara Gormley, Department Head, 575-646-2121, Fax: 575-646-8035, E-mail: bgormley@nmsu.edu. *Application contact:* Norma Arrieta, Student Program Coordinator, 575-646-2121, Fax: 575-646-8035, E-mail: cep@nmsu.edu.
Website: http://cep.education.nmsu.edu

New Mexico State University, College of Education, Department of Curriculum and Instruction, Las Cruces, NM 88003-8001. Offers bilingual education (MA); curriculum and instruction (Ed D, PhD); early childhood education (MA); educational diagnostics (Ed S); language, literacy and culture (MA); learning design and technologies (MA); teaching (MAT); teaching English to speakers of other languages (MA). *Accreditation:* NCATE. *Program availability:* Part-time, evening/weekend, 100% online. *Faculty:* 22 full-time (17 women), 7 part-time/adjunct (5 women). *Students:* 82 full-time (49 women), 186 part-time (134 women); includes 153 minority (13 Black or African American, non-Hispanic/Latino; 2 American Indian or Alaska Native, non-Hispanic/Latino; 3 Asian, non-Hispanic/Latino; 129 Hispanic/Latino; 6 Two or more races, non-Hispanic/Latino), 33 international. Average age 37. 110 applicants, 79% accepted, 60 enrolled. In 2018, 75 master's, 13 doctorates, 16 other advanced degrees awarded. *Degree requirements:* For master's, comprehensive exam, thesis; for doctorate, comprehensive exam, thesis/dissertation. *Entrance requirements:* For master's, minimum cumulative GPA of 3.0; for doctorate, portfolio, minimum cumulative GPA of 3.0. Additional exam requirements/recommendations for international students: Required—TOEFL (minimum score 550 paper-based; 79 iBT), IELTS (minimum score 6.5). *Application deadline:* For fall admission, 12/15 priority date for domestic and international students. Applications are processed on a rolling basis. Application fee: $40 ($50 for international students). Electronic applications accepted. *Expenses: Tuition, area resident:* Full-time $4216.70; part-time $252.70 per credit hour. Tuition, state resident: full-time $4216.70; part-time $252.70 per credit hour. Tuition, nonresident: full-time $12,769; part-time $881.10 per credit hour. *International tuition:* $12,769.30 full-time. *Required fees:* $878.40; $48.80 per credit hour. Full-time tuition and fees vary according to course load and reciprocity agreements. *Financial support:* In 2018–19, 111 students received support, including 2 fellowships (averaging $4,548 per year), 11 research assistantships (averaging $11,673 per year), 10 teaching assistantships (averaging $10,582 per year); career-related internships or fieldwork, Federal Work-Study, scholarships/grants, traineeships, health care benefits, and unspecified assistantships also available. Support available to part-time students. Financial award application deadline: 3/1. *Faculty research:* STEM education, bilingual and English as a second language education, critical pedagogy/multicultural education, learning design and technology, early childhood education. *Total annual research expenditures:* $10,685. *Unit head:* Dr. David Rutledge, Department Head, 575-646-5411, Fax: 575-646-5436, E-mail: rutledge@nmsu.edu. *Application contact:* Dr. David Rutledge, Associate Department Head for Graduate Programs, 575-646-5411, Fax: 575-646-5436, E-mail: rutledge@nmsu.edu.
Website: http://ci.education.nmsu.edu

North Carolina State University, Graduate School, College of Education, Department of Educational Leadership, Policy, and Human Development, Program in Educational Research and Policy Analysis, Raleigh, NC 27695. Offers PhD. *Degree requirements:* For doctorate, thesis/dissertation. *Entrance requirements:* For doctorate, GRE General Test, minimum GPA of 3.0, interview, sample of work. Electronic applications accepted.

Ohio University, Graduate College, Gladys W. and David H. Patton College of Education and Human Services, Department of Educational Studies, Athens, OH 45701-2979. Offers computer education and technology (M Ed); educational administration (M Ed, Ed D); educational research and evaluation (M Ed, PhD); instructional technology (PhD). *Program availability:* Part-time, evening/weekend, online learning. *Degree requirements:* For master's, thesis or alternative; for doctorate, comprehensive exam, thesis/dissertation. *Entrance requirements:* For master's, GRE General Test (if GPA less than 2.9); for doctorate, GRE General Test, GRE Subject Test, minimum GPA of 2.9, work experience, 3 letters of reference, autobiography. Additional exam requirements/recommendations for international students: Required—TOEFL (minimum score 550 paper-based; 80 iBT) or IELTS (minimum score 6.5). Electronic applications accepted. *Faculty research:* Race, class and gender; computer programs; development and organization theory; evaluation/development of instruments, leadership.

Old Dominion University, Darden College of Education, Program in Educational Psychology and Program Evaluation, Norfolk, VA 23529. Offers education (PhD), including educational psychology, program evaluation. *Program availability:* Part-time, evening/weekend. *Degree requirements:* For doctorate, comprehensive exam, thesis/dissertation. *Entrance requirements:* Additional exam requirements/recommendations for international students: Required—TOEFL. Electronic applications accepted. *Expenses:* Contact institution. *Faculty research:* Motivation, self-regulated learning, distance learning, calibration, STEM.

Rutgers University–New Brunswick, Graduate School of Education, Department of Educational Psychology, Program in Educational Statistics, Measurement and Evaluation, Piscataway, NJ 08854-8097. Offers Ed M. *Program availability:* Part-time, evening/weekend. *Entrance requirements:* For master's, GRE General Test, 3 letters of recommendation. Additional exam requirements/recommendations for international students: Required—TOEFL (minimum score 550 paper-based; 83 iBT). Electronic applications accepted. *Faculty research:* Program evaluation of student assessment, Type I error and power comparisons, test performance factors, theory building in participatory program evaluation, test validity in higher education admissions.

Seton Hall University, College of Education and Human Services, Department of Education Leadership, Management and Policy, South Orange, NJ 07079-2697. Offers college student personnel administration (MA); education research, assessment and program evaluation (PhD); higher education administration (Ed D, PhD); human resource training and development (MA); K–12 administration and supervision (Ed D, Exec Ed D, Ed S); K–12 leadership, management and policy (Ed D, Exec Ed D, Ed S). *Program availability:* Part-time, evening/weekend, blended/hybrid learning. *Degree requirements:* For master's, comprehensive exam, thesis or alternative; for doctorate, thesis/dissertation, oral exam, written exam; for Ed S, internship, research project. *Entrance requirements:* For master's, GRE or MAT, minimum GPA of 3.0; for doctorate, GRE or MAT, interview, minimum GPA of 3.5; for Ed S, GRE or MAT, minimum GPA of 3.5. Additional exam requirements/recommendations for international students: Required—TOEFL. *Expenses:* Contact institution.

Southern Connecticut State University, School of Graduate Studies, School of Education, Department of Educational Leadership, New Haven, CT 06515-1355. Offers educational leadership (Ed D, Diploma); research, statistics, and measurement (MS). *Program availability:* Part-time, evening/weekend. *Entrance requirements:* For degree, master's degree, minimum GPA of 3.0, writing sample. Electronic applications accepted.

Southwestern Oklahoma State University, College of Professional and Graduate Studies, School of Behavioral Sciences and Education, Specialization in School Psychometry, Weatherford, OK 73096-3098. Offers M Ed. M Ed distance learning degree program offered to Oklahoma residents only. *Accreditation:* NCATE. *Program availability:* Part-time, evening/weekend. *Degree requirements:* For master's, exam. *Entrance requirements:* For master's, GRE General Test or minimum undergraduate GPA of 3.0, portfolio. Additional exam requirements/recommendations for international students: Required—TOEFL (minimum score 550 paper-based), IELTS (minimum score 6.5).

Sul Ross State University, College of Professional Studies, Department of Education, Program in Educational Diagnostics, Alpine, TX 79832. Offers M Ed, Certificate. *Program availability:* Part-time, evening/weekend. *Degree requirements:* For master's, thesis optional. *Entrance requirements:* For master's, GMAT or GRE General Test, minimum GPA of 2.5 in last 60 hours of undergraduate work.

Sul Ross State University, Rio Grande College of Sul Ross State University, Alpine, TX 79832. Offers business administration (MBA); teacher education (M Ed), including bilingual education, counseling, educational diagnostics, elementary education, general education, reading, school administration, secondary education. *Program availability:* Part-time, evening/weekend, online learning. *Degree requirements:* For master's, comprehensive exam, thesis optional, minimum GPA of 3.0. *Entrance requirements:* For master's, GMAT or GRE General Test, minimum GPA of 2.5 in last 60 hours of undergraduate work. Additional exam requirements/recommendations for international students: Required—TOEFL.

Syracuse University, School of Education, Programs in Instructional Design, Development, and Evaluation, Syracuse, NY 13244. Offers MS, PhD, CAS. *Program availability:* Part-time. *Students:* Average age 34. *Degree requirements:* For master's, thesis or alternative; for doctorate, comprehensive exam, thesis/dissertation. *Entrance requirements:* For master's, GRE or MAT, baccalaureate degree from regionally-accredited college/university, statement of goals, three letters of recommendation, transcripts; for doctorate, GRE, master's degree in instructional design or equivalent, statement of goals, three letters of recommendation, transcripts; for CAS, GRE (recommended), master's degree in instructional design or equivalent, statement of

goals, three letters of recommendation, transcripts. Additional exam requirements/recommendations for international students: Required—TOEFL (minimum score 100 iBT). *Application deadline:* For fall admission, 1/15 priority date for domestic and international students; for spring admission, 10/15 priority date for domestic and international students. Applications are processed on a rolling basis. Application fee: $75. Electronic applications accepted. *Financial support:* Fellowships with full tuition reimbursements, research assistantships, teaching assistantships, career-related internships or fieldwork, and scholarships/grants available. Financial award application deadline: 1/15. *Faculty research:* Digital media production, technologies for instructional settings, strategies in educational project management, educational technology in international settings. *Unit head:* Dr. Jing Lei, Chair, 315-443-3703, E-mail: jlei@syr.edu. *Application contact:* Speranza Migliore, Graduate Admissions Recruiter, 315-443-2505, E-mail: gradrcrt@syr.edu.
Website: http://soe.syr.edu/academic/Instructional_Design_Development_and_Evaluation/

Teachers College, Columbia University, Department of Human Development, New York, NY 10027-6696. Offers applied statistics (MS); cognitive studies in education (MA, Ed D, PhD); developmental psychology (MA, Ed D, PhD); educational psychology-human cognition and learning (Ed M, MA, Ed D, PhD); learning analytics (MS); measurement and evaluation (ME, Ed D, PhD); measurement, evaluation, and statistics (MA, MS, Ed D, PhD). *Program availability:* Part-time. *Students:* 114 full-time (89 women), 168 part-time (119 women); includes 75 minority (19 Black or African American, non-Hispanic/Latino; 36 Asian, non-Hispanic/Latino; 18 Hispanic/Latino; 2 Two or more races, non-Hispanic/Latino), 132 international. Average age 29. 401 applicants, 56% accepted, 109 enrolled. *Unit head:* Jim Corter, Chair, 212-678-3843, E-mail: jec34@tc.columbia.edu. *Application contact:* Kelly Sutton-Skinner, Director of Admission & New Student Enrollment, E-mail: kms2237@tc.columbia.edu.
Website: http://www.tc.columbia.edu/human-development/

Teachers College of San Joaquin, Master's Program in Education, Stockton, CA 95206. Offers early education (M Ed); educational inquiry (M Ed); educational leadership and school development (M Ed); science, technology, engineering, and mathematics (M Ed); special education (M Ed). *Expenses: Tuition:* Full-time $5520. Tuition and fees vary according to course load and program.

Tennessee Technological University, College of Graduate Studies, College of Education, Department of Curriculum and Instruction, Program in Exceptional Learning, Cookeville, TN 38505. Offers applied behavior analysis (PhD); literacy (PhD); program planning and evaluation (PhD); STEM education (PhD). *Program availability:* Part-time, evening/weekend. *Students:* 14 full-time (8 women), 20 part-time (12 women); includes 2 minority (1 Black or African American, non-Hispanic/Latino; 1 Two or more races, non-Hispanic/Latino), 3 international. 16 applicants, 56% accepted, 2 enrolled. In 2018, 8 doctorates awarded. *Degree requirements:* For doctorate, comprehensive exam, thesis/dissertation. *Entrance requirements:* For doctorate, GRE, minimum GPA of 3.0. Additional exam requirements/recommendations for international students: Required—TOEFL (minimum score 550 paper-based; 79 iBT), IELTS (minimum score 5.5), PTE (minimum score 53), or TOEIC (Test of English as an International Communication). *Application deadline:* For fall admission, 8/1 for domestic students, 5/1 for international students; for spring admission, 12/1 for domestic students, 10/1 for international students; for summer admission, 5/1 for domestic students, 2/1 for international students. Applications are processed on a rolling basis. Application fee: $35 ($40 for international students). Electronic applications accepted. *Financial support:* Fellowships, research assistantships, and teaching assistantships available. Financial award application deadline: 4/1. *Unit head:* Dr. Lisa Zagumny, Dean, College of Education, 931-372-3078, Fax: 931-372-3517, E-mail: lzagumny@tntech.edu. *Application contact:* Shelia K. Kendrick, Coordinator of Graduate Studies, 931-372-3808, Fax: 931-372-3497, E-mail: skendrick@tntech.edu.
Website: https://www.tntech.edu/education/elphd/

Texas A&M University–San Antonio, Department of Educator and Leadership Preparation, San Antonio, TX 78224. Offers bilingual education (MS); early childhood education (M Ed); educational administration (MA); reading specialization (MS); special education (M Ed), including educational diagnostician. *Program availability:* Part-time, evening/weekend, online learning. *Degree requirements:* For master's, comprehensive exam, thesis or alternative. *Entrance requirements:* For master's, GRE (Quantitative and Verbal) or MAT. Additional exam requirements/recommendations for international students: Required—TOEFL (minimum score 550 paper-based; 79 iBT), IELTS (minimum score 6). Electronic applications accepted. *Faculty research:* Equity in education, biliteracy practices among Latina and immigrants, academic achievement of low socio-economic students, equity practices in instruction and educational leadership in diverse settings, racial identity development and multicultural education.

Université Laval, Faculty of Education, Department of Foundations and Interventions in Education, Québec, QC G1K 7P4, Canada. Offers educational administration and evaluation (MA, PhD); educational practice (Diploma), including educational pedagogy, pedagogy management and development, school adaptation; orientation sciences (MA, PhD). *Degree requirements:* For doctorate, comprehensive exam, thesis/dissertation. Electronic applications accepted.

University of Arkansas, Graduate School, College of Education and Health Professions, Department of Rehabilitation, Human Resources and Communication Disorders, Program in Educational Statistics and Research Methods, Fayetteville, AR 72701. Offers MS, PhD. In 2018, 1 doctorate awarded. *Application deadline:* For fall admission, 8/1 for domestic students, 4/1 for international students; for spring admission, 12/1 for domestic students, 10/1 for international students; for summer admission, 4/15 for domestic students, 3/1 for international students. Applications are processed on a rolling basis. Application fee: $60. Electronic applications accepted. *Financial support:* In 2018–19, 14 research assistantships were awarded; fellowships and teaching assistantships also available. *Unit head:* Dr. Matthew Ganio, Department Head, 479-575-2956, E-mail: msganio@uark.edu. *Application contact:* Dr. Paul Calleja, Assistant Dept. head - HHPR, Graduate Coordinator, 479-575-2854, Fax: 479-575-5778, E-mail: pcallej@uark.edu.
Website: https://esrm.uark.edu

The University of British Columbia, Faculty of Education, Department of Educational and Counseling Psychology, and Special Education, Vancouver, BC V6T 1Z4, Canada. Offers counseling psychology (M Ed, MA, PhD); guidance studies (Diploma); human development, learning and culture (M Ed, MA, PhD); measurement, evaluation, and research methodology (M Ed, MA, PhD); school psychology (M Ed, MA, PhD); special education (M Ed, MA, PhD, Diploma). *Program availability:* Part-time. *Degree requirements:* For master's, thesis (for some programs); for doctorate, comprehensive exam, thesis/dissertation. *Entrance requirements:* For master's, GRE General Test (for MA in counseling psychology); for doctorate, GRE General Test. Additional exam requirements/recommendations for international students: Required—TOEFL. Electronic applications accepted. *Expenses:* Contact institution. *Faculty research:* Women, family, social problems, career transition, stress and coping problems.

University of Calgary, Faculty of Graduate Studies, Werklund School of Education, Program in Educational Research, Calgary, AB T2N 1N4, Canada. Offers adult learning (M Ed, MA, Ed D, PhD); curriculum and learning (M Ed, MA, Ed D, PhD); educational leadership (M Ed, MA, Ed D, PhD); languages and diversity (M Ed, MA, Ed D, PhD); learning sciences (M Ed, MA, Ed D, PhD). Ed D in educational leadership offered via distance delivery. *Program availability:* Part-time, evening/weekend, online learning. *Degree requirements:* For master's, thesis (for some programs); for doctorate, thesis/dissertation, candidacy exam. *Entrance requirements:* For master's, minimum GPA of 3.0, 3 letters of reference; for doctorate, minimum GPA of 3.5, 3 letters of reference. Additional exam requirements/recommendations for international students: Required—TOEFL, IELTS. Electronic applications accepted. *Faculty research:* Curriculum, leadership, technology, contexts, gifted, second language teaching, work place and adult learning.

University of California, Riverside, Graduate Division, Graduate School of Education, Riverside, CA 92521. Offers applied behavior analysis (M Ed); diversity and equity (M Ed); education policy analysis and leadership (PhD); education specialist (Credential); education, society, and culture (MA, PhD); educational psychology (MA, PhD); general education (M Ed); higher education administration and policy (M Ed, PhD); multiple subject (Credential); research, evaluation, measurement and statistics (MA); school psychology (PhD); single subject (Credential); special education (M Ed, PhD); special education and autism (MA); TESOL (M Ed). Terminal master's awarded for partial completion of doctoral program. *Degree requirements:* For master's, comprehensive exams or thesis (MA), case study or analytical report (M Ed); for doctorate, comprehensive exam, thesis/dissertation, written and oral qualifying exams, college teaching practicum. *Entrance requirements:* For master's, GRE General Test (for MA); CBEST and CSET (for M Ed in general education only), UCR Extension TESOL certificate (for M Ed with TESOL emphasis only); for doctorate, GRE General Test, writing sample; for Credential, CBEST, CSET. Additional exam requirements/recommendations for international students: Required—TOEFL (minimum score 550 paper-based; 80 iBT), IELTS (minimum score 7). Electronic applications accepted. *Faculty research:* Responsiveness to intervention, faculty core, response to intervention of English language learners, advanced modeling techniques, study on social capital, trust, and motivation.

University of Colorado Boulder, Graduate School, School of Education, Division of Research and Evaluation Methodology, Boulder, CO 80309. Offers PhD. *Accreditation:* NCATE. *Degree requirements:* For doctorate, one foreign language, comprehensive exam, thesis/dissertation. *Entrance requirements:* For doctorate, GRE General Test, minimum undergraduate GPA of 2.75. Electronic applications accepted. Application fee is waived when completed online.

University of Colorado Denver, School of Education and Human Development, Program in Educational Leadership and Innovation, Denver, CO 80217. Offers educational studies and research (PhD), including administrative leadership and policy, early childhood special education, math education, research, assessment and evaluation, science education, urban ecologies. *Program availability:* Part-time, evening/weekend. *Degree requirements:* For doctorate, comprehensive exam, thesis/dissertation, 75 credit hours (for PhD). *Entrance requirements:* For doctorate, GRE or equivalent, resume or curriculum vitae, letters of recommendation, master's degree or equivalent, completion of basic or advanced statistics course with minimum B grade. Additional exam requirements/recommendations for international students: Required—TOEFL (minimum score 537 paper-based; 75 iBT); Recommended—IELTS (minimum score 6.5). Electronic applications accepted. *Expenses:* Tuition, state resident: full-time $6786; part-time $337 per credit hour. Tuition, nonresident: full-time $22,590; part-time $1255 per credit hour. *Required fees:* $1231; $137 per credit hour. Tuition and fees vary according to program and reciprocity agreements. *Faculty research:* Administrative leadership and policy studies, early childhood education, research in diversity, paraprofessionals in education, urban schools lab.

University of Colorado Denver, School of Education and Human Development, Program in Education and Human Development, Denver, CO 80217. Offers administrative leadership and policy (PhD); assessment (MA); early childhood special education/early childhood education (PhD); family science and human development (PhD); human development and family relations (MA); learning (MA); mathematics education (PhD); research and evaluation methods (MA); research, assessment and evaluation (PhD); science education (PhD); urban ecologies (PhD). MA program also offered in partnership with Boulder Journey School, Friends School and Stanley British Primary School. *Program availability:* Part-time, evening/weekend. *Degree requirements:* For master's, comprehensive exam, 9 hours of core courses embedded within a minimum of 36 to 38 hours of relevant coursework, including an educational psychology practicum, independent study project or thesis (recommended). *Entrance requirements:* For master's, GRE if undergraduate GPA below 2.75, resume, three letters of recommendation, transcripts. Additional exam requirements/recommendations for international students: Required—TOEFL (minimum score 537 paper-based; 75 iBT); Recommended—IELTS (minimum score 6.5). Electronic applications accepted. *Expenses:* Contact institution. *Faculty research:* Crisis response and intervention, school violence prevention, immigrant experience, educational environments for English language learners, culturally competent assessment and intervention, child and youth suicide.

University of Denver, Morgridge College of Education, Denver, CO 80208. Offers child, family and school psychology (MA, PhD, Ed S); counseling psychology (MA, PhD); curriculum and instruction (MA, Ed D, PhD); curriculum instruction and teaching (Certificate); early childhood special education (MA, Certificate); educational leadership and policy studies (MA, Ed D, PhD, Certificate); higher education (Ed D, PhD); library and information science (MLIS); research methods and statistics (MA, PhD). *Accreditation:* ALA; APA (one or more programs are accredited). *Program availability:* Part-time, evening/weekend, online learning. *Faculty:* 49 full-time (35 women), 33 part-time/adjunct (20 women). *Students:* 509 full-time (400 women), 365 part-time (277 women); includes 236 minority (53 Black or African American, non-Hispanic/Latino; 6 American Indian or Alaska Native, non-Hispanic/Latino; 28 Asian, non-Hispanic/Latino; 116 Hispanic/Latino; 33 Two or more races, non-Hispanic/Latino), 56 international. Average age 31. 1,372 applicants, 57% accepted, 382 enrolled. In 2018, 258 master's, 41 doctorates, 162 other advanced degrees awarded. Terminal master's awarded for partial completion of doctoral program. *Degree requirements:* For master's, comprehensive exam (for some programs); for doctorate, comprehensive exam (for some programs), thesis/dissertation. *Entrance requirements:* For master's, GRE General Test or GMAT, bachelors degree; transcripts; two letters of recommendation; personal statement; resume; for doctorate, GRE General Test or GMAT, Masters degree; transcripts; two letters of recommendation; personal statement(s); resume. Additional exam requirements/recommendations for international students: Required—TOEFL (minimum score 550 paper-based; 80 iBT). *Application deadline:* Applications are processed on a rolling basis. Application fee: $65. Electronic applications accepted. *Expenses:* $33,183 per year full-time. *Financial support:* In 2018–19, 690 students received support, including 29 research assistantships with tuition reimbursements available (averaging $11,465 per year), 9 teaching assistantships with tuition reimbursements available (averaging $2,527 per year); career-related internships or fieldwork, Federal Work-Study, institutionally sponsored loans, scholarships/grants, and unspecified assistantships also available. Support available to part-time students.

Financial award application deadline: 2/15; financial award applicants required to submit FAFSA. *Faculty research:* Early childhood education, educational leadership, access and opportunity to postsecondary education, marriage and family therapy, data management and archival research. *Total annual research expenditures:* $2.3 million. *Unit head:* Dr. Karen Riley, Dean, 303-871-3665, E-mail: karen.riley@du.edu. *Application contact:* Jodi Dye, Director of Admissions, 303-871-2510, E-mail: jodi.dye@du.edu.
Website: http://morgridge.du.edu

University of Florida, Graduate School, College of Education, School of Human Development and Organizational Studies in Education, Gainesville, FL 32611. Offers counseling and counselor education (Ed D, PhD), including counseling and counselor education, marriage and family counseling, mental health counseling, school counseling and guidance; educational leadership (M Ed, MAE, Ed D, PhD, Ed S), including educational leadership (Ed D, PhD), educational policy (Ed D, PhD); higher education administration (Ed D, PhD), including education policy (Ed D), educational policy, higher education administration; marriage and family counseling (M Ed, MAE, Ed D, PhD, Ed S); mental health counseling (M Ed, MAE, Ed D, PhD, Ed S); research and evaluation methodology (M Ed, MAE, Ed D, PhD); school counseling and guidance (M Ed, MAE, Ed D, PhD, Ed S); student personnel in higher education (M Ed, MAE). *Accreditation:* ACA (one or more programs are accredited); NCATE. *Program availability:* Part-time, online learning. Terminal master's awarded for partial completion of doctoral program. *Degree requirements:* For master's, thesis optional; for doctorate, comprehensive exam, thesis/dissertation. *Entrance requirements:* For master's and doctorate, GRE General Test, minimum GPA of 3.0 (undergraduate), 3.5 (graduate); for Ed S, GRE General Test. Additional exam requirements/recommendations for international students: Required—TOEFL (minimum score 550 paper-based; 80 iBT), IELTS (minimum score 6). Electronic applications accepted.

University of Illinois at Chicago, College of Education, Department of Educational Psychology, Chicago, IL 60607-7128. Offers early childhood education (M Ed); educational psychology (PhD); measurement, evaluation, statistics, and assessment (M Ed); youth development (M Ed). *Program availability:* Part-time, online learning. *Faculty research:* Children's construction of morality, development of resilience in the face of enduring economical difficulties, cognition and cognitive development, test fairness.

The University of Iowa, Graduate College, College of Education, Department of Psychological and Quantitative Foundations, Iowa City, IA 52242-1316. Offers counseling psychology (PhD); educational measurement and statistics (MA, PhD); educational psychology (MA, PhD); school psychology (PhD, Ed S). *Accreditation:* APA. *Degree requirements:* For master's, thesis optional, exam; for doctorate, comprehensive exam, thesis/dissertation; for Ed S, exam. *Entrance requirements:* For master's, doctorate, and Ed S, GRE General Test, minimum GPA of 3.0. Additional exam requirements/recommendations for international students: Required—TOEFL (minimum score 550 paper-based; 81 iBT). Electronic applications accepted.

The University of Kansas, Graduate Studies, School of Education, Department of Educational Psychology, Program in Educational Psychology and Research, Lawrence, KS 66045. Offers MS Ed, PhD. *Program availability:* Part-time. *Students:* 40 full-time (24 women), 6 part-time (5 women); includes 6 minority (2 Black or African American, non-Hispanic/Latino; 3 Asian, non-Hispanic/Latino; 1 Hispanic/Latino), 21 international. Average age 31. 27 applicants, 74% accepted, 11 enrolled. In 2018, 3 master's, 7 doctorates awarded. *Entrance requirements:* For master's, GRE General Test, minimum GPA of 3.0, resume, statement of purpose, official transcripts, three recommendation letters; for doctorate, GRE General Test, resume, statement of purpose, official transcripts, three recommendation letters. Additional exam requirements/recommendations for international students: Required—TOEFL, IELTS. *Application deadline:* For fall admission, 12/15 for domestic and international students. Application fee: $65 ($85 for international students). Electronic applications accepted. *Financial support:* Fellowships, research assistantships, teaching assistantships, career-related internships or fieldwork, institutionally sponsored loans, scholarships/grants, traineeships, health care benefits, tuition waivers (full and partial), and unspecified assistantships available. Support available to part-time students. Financial award application deadline: 12/15. *Faculty research:* Educational measurement, applied statistics, research design, program evaluation, learning and development. *Unit head:* David M Hansen, Chair, 785-864-1874, E-mail: dhansen1@ku.edu. *Application contact:* Penny Fritts, Admissions Coordinator, 785-864-9645, E-mail: fritts@ku.edu.
Website: http://www.soe.ku.edu/PRE/

University of Kentucky, Graduate School, College of Education, Program in Educational Policy Studies and Evaluation, Lexington, KY 40506-0032. Offers educational policy studies and evaluation (Ed D); higher education (MS Ed, PhD); social and philosophical studies (MS Ed). *Accreditation:* NCATE. Terminal master's awarded for partial completion of doctoral program. *Degree requirements:* For master's, comprehensive exam, thesis optional; for doctorate, comprehensive exam, thesis/dissertation. *Entrance requirements:* For master's, GRE General Test, minimum undergraduate GPA of 2.75; for doctorate, GRE General Test, minimum graduate GPA of 3.0. Additional exam requirements/recommendations for international students: Required—TOEFL (minimum score 550 paper-based). Electronic applications accepted. *Faculty research:* Studies in higher education; comparative and international education; evaluation of educational programs, policies, and reform; student, teacher, and faculty cultures; gender and education.

University of Louisville, Graduate School, College of Education and Human Development, Department of Counseling and Human Development, Louisville, KY 40292-0001. Offers counseling and personnel services (M Ed, PhD), including art therapy (M Ed), college student personnel, counseling psychology, counselor education and supervision (PhD), educational psychology, measurement, and evaluation (PhD), mental health counseling (M Ed), school counseling (M Ed). *Accreditation:* APA; NCATE. *Program availability:* Part-time, evening/weekend, 100% online, blended/hybrid learning. *Students:* 136 full-time (109 women), 53 part-time (38 women); includes 40 minority (26 Black or African American, non-Hispanic/Latino; 1 American Indian or Alaska Native, non-Hispanic/Latino; 1 Asian, non-Hispanic/Latino; 8 Hispanic/Latino; 4 Two or more races, non-Hispanic/Latino), 4 international. Average age 29. 180 applicants, 47% accepted, 54 enrolled. In 2018, 39 master's awarded. Terminal master's awarded for partial completion of doctoral program. *Degree requirements:* For master's, comprehensive exam (for some programs), thesis optional; for doctorate, comprehensive exam (for some programs), thesis/dissertation. *Entrance requirements:* For master's, GRE (for most programs), PRAXIS (for educator preparation programs), professional statement, recommendation letters, resume, transcripts; for doctorate, GRE, professional statement, recommendation letters, resume, transcripts. Additional exam requirements/recommendations for international students: Required—TOEFL (minimum score 550 paper-based; 79 iBT); Recommended—IELTS (minimum score 6.5). *Application deadline:* For fall admission, 6/1 priority date for domestic students, 5/1 priority date for international students; for spring admission, 10/1 priority date for domestic students, 11/1 priority date for international students; for summer admission, 3/1 priority date for domestic students, 4/1 priority date for international students. Application fee: $65. *Expenses: Tuition, area resident:* Full-time $6500; part-time $723

per credit hour. Tuition, state resident: full-time $6500. Tuition, nonresident: full-time $13,557; part-time $1507 per credit hour. Tuition and fees vary according to course load and program. *Financial support:* In 2018–19, 95 students received support, including 5 fellowships with full tuition reimbursements available (averaging $21,024 per year), 32 research assistantships with full tuition reimbursements available (averaging $21,024 per year), 18 teaching assistantships with full tuition reimbursements available (averaging $21,024 per year); Federal Work-Study, scholarships/grants, health care benefits, and unspecified assistantships also available. Financial award application deadline: 3/1; financial award applicants required to submit FAFSA. *Faculty research:* Mental health services and under-served populations; health disparities and outcomes; well-being identity development; measurement and evaluation; college student personnel. *Unit head:* Dr. Mark M. Leach, Chair and Professor, 502-852-6884, E-mail: ecpy@louisville.edu. *Application contact:* Dr. Margaret Pentecost, Assistant Dean for Graduate Student Success, 502-852-2628, Fax: 502-852-1417, E-mail: gedadm@louisville.edu.
Website: http://www.louisville.edu/education/departments/ecpy

University of Maryland, College Park, Academic Affairs, College of Education, Department of Human Development and Quantitative Methodology, College Park, MD 20742. Offers MA, Ed D, PhD. *Entrance requirements:* Additional exam requirements/recommendations for international students: Required—TOEFL.

University of Massachusetts Amherst, Graduate School, College of Education, Program in Education, Amherst, MA 01003. Offers bilingual, English as a second language, and multicultural education (M Ed, Ed S); child study and early education (M Ed); children, families and schools (Ed D, Ed S); early childhood and elementary teacher education (M Ed); educational leadership (M Ed); educational policy and leadership (Ed D); higher education (M Ed); international education (M Ed); language, literacy and culture (Ed D); learning, media and technology (M Ed, Ed S); mathematics, science, and learning technologies (Ed D); reading and writing (M Ed); research, educational measurement and psychometrics (Ed D); school counselor education (M Ed, Ed S); school psychology (Ed S); science education (Ed S); secondary teacher education (M Ed); social justice education (M Ed, Ed D, Ed S); special education (M Ed, Ed D, Ed S); teacher education and school improvement (Ed D, Ed S). *Accreditation:* NCATE. *Program availability:* Part-time, online learning. Terminal master's awarded for partial completion of doctoral program. *Degree requirements:* For doctorate, comprehensive exam, thesis/dissertation. *Entrance requirements:* Additional exam requirements/recommendations for international students: Required—TOEFL (minimum score 550 paper-based; 80 iBT), IELTS (minimum score 6.5). Electronic applications accepted.

University of Memphis, Graduate School, College of Education, Department of Counseling, Educational Psychology and Research, Memphis, TN 38152. Offers counseling (MS, Ed D), including clinical mental health counseling (MS), clinical rehabilitation counseling (MS), rehabilitation counseling (MS), school counseling (MS); counseling psychology (PhD); educational psychology and research (MS, PhD), including educational psychology, educational research. *Accreditation:* ACA (one or more programs are accredited); APA (one or more programs are accredited); CORE (one or more programs are accredited); NCATE. *Program availability:* Blended/hybrid learning. *Students:* 137 full-time (114 women), 126 part-time (96 women); includes 96 minority (75 Black or African American, non-Hispanic/Latino; 6 Asian, non-Hispanic/Latino; 10 Hispanic/Latino; 5 Two or more races, non-Hispanic/Latino), 5 international. Average age 33. 103 applicants, 61% accepted, 59 enrolled. In 2018, 30 master's, 19 doctorates awarded. *Degree requirements:* For master's, comprehensive exam, thesis or alternative, internship; for doctorate, comprehensive exam, thesis/dissertation, practicum, internship, residency, scholarly work. *Entrance requirements:* For master's, GRE General Test or MAT, minimum GPA of 2.5, letters of reference, interview; for doctorate, GRE General Test, master's degree or equivalent, letters of reference, interview, curriculum vitae, personal statement. Additional exam requirements/recommendations for international students: Required—TOEFL (minimum score 550 paper-based; 79 iBT). *Application deadline:* For fall admission, 10/1 priority date for domestic students; for spring admission, 4/1 priority date for domestic students. Applications are processed on a rolling basis. Application fee: $35 ($60 for international students). Electronic applications accepted. *Expenses: Tuition, area resident:* Full-time $10,240; part-time $503 per credit hour. Tuition, state resident: full-time $10,464. Tuition, nonresident: full-time $20,224; part-time $991 per credit hour. *Required fees:* $850; $106 per credit hour. *Financial support:* Fellowships with full tuition reimbursements, research assistantships with full tuition reimbursements, teaching assistantships with full tuition reimbursements, career-related internships or fieldwork, Federal Work-Study, scholarships/grants, and unspecified assistantships available. Financial award application deadline: 2/1; financial award applicants required to submit FAFSA. *Faculty research:* Anger management, aging and disability, supervision, multicultural counseling. *Unit head:* Dr. Steve West, Chair, 901-678-2841, Fax: 901-678-5114, E-mail: slwest@memphis.edu. *Application contact:* Stormey Warren, Graduate Programs, 901-678-2363, Fax: 901-678-4778, E-mail: shutsell@memphis.edu.
Website: http://www.memphis.edu/cepr/

University of Miami, Graduate School, School of Education and Human Development, Department of Educational and Psychological Studies, Program in Research, Measurement, and Evaluation, Coral Gables, FL 33124. Offers MS Ed, PhD. *Faculty:* 2 full-time (1 woman). *Students:* 3 full-time (2 women), 6 part-time (3 women); includes 3 minority (all Hispanic/Latino), 3 international. Average age 31. 6 applicants, 33% accepted, 1 enrolled. In 2018, 3 master's, 1 doctorate awarded. Terminal master's awarded for partial completion of doctoral program. *Degree requirements:* For master's, comprehensive exam; for doctorate, thesis/dissertation, qualifying exam. *Entrance requirements:* For master's and doctorate, GRE General Test. Additional exam requirements/recommendations for international students: Required—TOEFL (minimum score 550 paper-based; 80 iBT); Recommended—IELTS (minimum score 6.5). *Application deadline:* For fall admission, 1/2 for domestic students, 10/1 for international students; for winter admission, 5/1 for domestic students, 10/1 for international students. Application fee: $75. Electronic applications accepted. *Financial support:* Fellowships, research assistantships, teaching assistantships, institutionally sponsored loans, scholarships/grants, health care benefits, tuition waivers (full and partial), and unspecified assistantships available. Support available to part-time students. Financial award application deadline: 3/1; financial award applicants required to submit FAFSA. *Faculty research:* Psychometric theory, computer-based testing, quantitative research methods. *Unit head:* Dr. Cenguz Zopluoglu, Associate Professor and Program Director, 305-284-5102, E-mail: c.zopluoglu@miami.edu. *Application contact:* Lois Heffernan, Graduate Admissions Coordinator, 305-284-2167, Fax: 305-284-9395, E-mail: lheffernan@miami.edu.
Website: http://www.education.miami.edu

University of Michigan–Dearborn, College of Education, Health, and Human Services, Master of Arts Program in Program Evaluation and Assessment, Dearborn, MI 48126. Offers MA. *Program availability:* Part-time, evening/weekend. *Faculty:* 4 full-time (3 women). *Students:* 3 part-time (all women); includes 1 minority (Two or more races, non-Hispanic/Latino). Average age 33. 1 applicant. *Degree requirements:* For master's, essay. *Entrance requirements:* Additional exam requirements/recommendations for

international students: Required—TOEFL (minimum score 560 paper-based; 84 iBT), IELTS (minimum score 6.5). *Application deadline:* For fall admission, 8/1 for domestic students, 5/1 for international students; for winter admission, 12/1 for domestic students, 9/1 for international students; for spring admission, 4/1 for domestic students, 1/1 for international students. Applications are processed on a rolling basis. Application fee: $60. Electronic applications accepted. *Expenses:* $12,140 per academic year (typical full-time in-state); $20,708 per academic year (typical full-time out-of-state). *Financial support:* In 2018–19, 1 student received support. Scholarships/grants available. Financial award application deadline: 3/1; financial award applicants required to submit FAFSA. *Faculty research:* Assessment and evaluation, research methodology, multiculturalism, urban education, pedagogy and interventions. *Unit head:* Dr. Paul Fossum, Director, Master's Degree Programs, 313-593-0982, E-mail: pfossum@umich.edu. *Application contact:* Office of Graduate Studies, 313-583-6321, E-mail: umd-graduatestudies@umich.edu.
Website: https://umdearborn.edu/cehhs/graduate-programs/areas-study/ma-program-evaluation-and-assessment

University of Minnesota, Twin Cities Campus, Graduate School, College of Education and Human Development, Department of Educational Psychology, Program in Quantitative Methods in Education, Minneapolis, MN 55455-0213. Offers MA, PhD. *Students:* 25 full-time (10 women), 8 part-time (6 women); includes 10 minority (1 Black or African American, non-Hispanic/Latino; 4 Asian, non-Hispanic/Latino; 4 Hispanic/Latino; 1 Two or more races, non-Hispanic/Latino), 9 international. Average age 33. 28 applicants, 25% accepted, 5 enrolled. In 2018, 3 master's, 3 doctorates awarded. *Financial support:* Fellowships, scholarships/grants, and unspecified assistantships available. Financial award application deadline: 12/1. *Unit head:* Dr. Kristen McMaster, Chair, 612-624-6083, Fax: 612-624-8241, E-mail: mcmas004@umn.edu. *Application contact:* Dr. Panayiota Kendeou, Director of Graduate Studies, 612-626-7814, E-mail: kend0040@umn.edu.
Website: http://www.cehd.umn.edu/edpsych/programs/qme/

University of Minnesota, Twin Cities Campus, Graduate School, College of Education and Human Development, Department of Organizational Leadership, Policy and Development, Program in Evaluation Studies, Minneapolis, MN 55455-0213. Offers MA, PhD. *Students:* 21 full-time (16 women), 21 part-time (19 women); includes 11 minority (1 Black or African American, non-Hispanic/Latino; 2 American Indian or Alaska Native, non-Hispanic/Latino; 3 Asian, non-Hispanic/Latino; 2 Hispanic/Latino; 3 Two or more races, non-Hispanic/Latino), 7 international. Average age 40. 24 applicants, 71% accepted, 12 enrolled. In 2018, 3 master's, 4 doctorates awarded. Application fee: $75 ($95 for international students). *Unit head:* Dr. Kenneth Bartlett, Chair, 612-624-1006, E-mail: bartlett@umn.edu. *Application contact:* Dr. Jeremy J. Hernandez, Director of Graduate Studies, 612-626-9377, E-mail: olpd@umn.edu.
Website: http://www.cehd.umn.edu/OLPD/grad-programs/ES/

University of Missouri–St. Louis, College of Education, Department of Education Sciences and Professional Programs, St. Louis, MO 63121. Offers adult and higher education (M Ed); educational psychology (M Ed), including character and citizenship education, research and program evaluation; program evaluation (Certificate); school psychology (Ed S). *Degree requirements:* For other advanced degree, comprehensive exam, thesis or alternative, internship. *Entrance requirements:* For degree, GRE General Test, 2-4 letters of recommendation, personal interview. Additional exam requirements/recommendations for international students: Required—IELTS (minimum score 6.5); Recommended—TOEFL (minimum score 550 paper-based; 79 iBT). Electronic applications accepted. *Faculty research:* Child/adolescent psychology, quantitative and qualitative methodology, evaluation processes, measurement and assessment.

University of Missouri–St. Louis, Graduate School, Program in Public Policy Administration, St. Louis, MO 63121. Offers local government management (MPPA, Certificate); nonprofit management and leadership (MPPA, Certificate); policy and program evaluation (MPPA, Certificate). *Accreditation:* NASPAA. *Program availability:* Part-time, evening/weekend. *Degree requirements:* For master's, exit project. *Entrance requirements:* For master's, 3 letters of recommendation, personal statement. Additional exam requirements/recommendations for international students: Recommended—TOEFL (minimum score 550 paper-based), IELTS (minimum score 6.5). Electronic applications accepted. *Faculty research:* Urban policy, public finance, evaluation.

University of Nebraska–Lincoln, Graduate College, College of Education and Human Sciences, Department of Educational Psychology, Lincoln, NE 68588. Offers cognition, learning and development (MA); counseling psychology (MA); educational psychology (MA, Ed S); psychological studies in education (PhD), including cognition, learning and development, counseling psychology, quantitative, qualitative, and psychometric methods, school psychology; quantitative, qualitative, and psychometric methods (MA); school psychology (MA, Ed S). *Accreditation:* APA (one or more programs are accredited); NCATE. *Degree requirements:* For master's, thesis optional. *Entrance requirements:* For master's, GRE General Test. Additional exam requirements/recommendations for international students: Required—TOEFL (minimum score 500 paper-based). Electronic applications accepted. *Faculty research:* Measurement and assessment, metacognition, academic skills, child development, multicultural education and counseling.

The University of North Carolina at Chapel Hill, Graduate School, School of Education, Program in Education, Chapel Hill, NC 27599. Offers culture, curriculum and change (MA, PhD); early childhood, intervention and literacy (MA, PhD); educational psychology, measurement and evaluation (MA, PhD). *Accreditation:* NCATE. *Degree requirements:* For master's, thesis; for doctorate, comprehensive exam, thesis/dissertation. *Entrance requirements:* For master's, GRE General Test, minimum GPA of 3.0 during last 2 years of undergraduates course work; for doctorate, GRE General Test, minimum GPA of 3.0 during last 2 years of undergraduate course work. Additional exam requirements/recommendations for international students: Required—TOEFL (minimum score 550 paper-based). Electronic applications accepted.

The University of North Carolina at Greensboro, Graduate School, School of Education, Department of Educational Research Methodology, Greensboro, NC 27412-5001. Offers educational research, measurement and evaluation (PhD); MS/PhD. *Accreditation:* NCATE. *Degree requirements:* For doctorate, thesis/dissertation. *Entrance requirements:* For doctorate, GRE General Test. Additional exam requirements/recommendations for international students: Required—TOEFL. Electronic applications accepted.

University of Northern Colorado, Graduate School, College of Education and Behavioral Sciences, Department of Applied Statistics and Research Methods, Greeley, CO 80639. Offers MS, PhD. *Program availability:* Part-time. *Degree requirements:* For master's, comprehensive exam; for doctorate, comprehensive exam, thesis/dissertation. *Entrance requirements:* For master's, 3 letters of reference; for doctorate, GRE General Test, 3 letters of reference. Electronic applications accepted.

University of Northern Iowa, Graduate College, College of Education, Department of Educational Psychology and Foundations, MAE Program in Educational Psychology: Context and Techniques of Assessment, Cedar Falls, IA 50614. Offers MAE. *Entrance requirements:* For master's, GRE, official transcripts, statement of purpose, three reference letters, writing sample.

University of North Texas, Toulouse Graduate School, Denton, TX 76203-5459. Offers accounting (MS); applied anthropology (MA, MS); applied behavior analysis (Certificate); applied geography (MA); applied technology and performance improvement (M Ed, MS); art education (MA); art history (MA); arts leadership (Certificate); audiology (Au D); behavior analysis (MS); behavioral science (PhD); biochemistry and molecular biology (MS); biology (MA, MS); biomedical engineering (MS); business analysis (MS); chemistry (MS); clinical health psychology (PhD); communication studies (MA, MS); computer engineering (MS); computer science (MS); counseling (M Ed, MS), including clinical mental health counseling (MS), college and university counseling, elementary school counseling, secondary school counseling; creative writing (MA); criminal justice (MS); curriculum and instruction (M Ed); decision sciences (MBA); design (MA, MFA), including fashion design (MFA), innovation studies, interior design (MFA); early childhood studies (MS); economics (MS); educational leadership (M Ed, Ed D); educational psychology (MS, PhD), including family studies (MS), gifted and talented (MS), human development (MS), learning and cognition (MS), research, measurement and evaluation (MS); electrical engineering (MS); emergency management (MPA); engineering technology (MS); English (MA); English as a second language (MA); environmental science (MS); finance (MBA, MS); financial management (MPA); French (MA); health services management (MBA); higher education (M Ed, Ed D); history (MA, MS); hospitality management (MS); human resources management (MPA); information science (MS); information systems (PhD); information technologies (MBA); interdisciplinary studies (MA, MS); international studies (MA); international sustainable tourism (MS); jazz studies (MM); journalism (MA, MJ, Graduate Certificate), including interactive and virtual digital communication (Graduate Certificate), narrative journalism (Graduate Certificate), public relations (Graduate Certificate); kinesiology (MS); linguistics (MA); local government management (MPA); logistics (PhD); logistics and supply chain management (MBA); long-term care, senior housing, and aging services (MA); management (PhD); marketing (MBA); mathematics (MA, MS); mechanical and energy engineering (MS, PhD); music (MA), including ethnomusicology, music theory, musicology, performance; music composition (PhD); music education (MM Ed, PhD); nonprofit management (MPA); operations and supply chain management (MBA); performance (MM, DMA); philosophy (MA); political science (MA); professional and technical communication (MA); radio, television and film (MA, MFA); rehabilitation counseling (Certificate); sociology (MA); Spanish (MA); special education (M Ed); speech-language pathology (MA); strategic management (MBA); studio art (MFA); teaching (M Ed); MBA/MS. *Program availability:* Part-time, evening/weekend, online learning. Terminal master's awarded for partial completion of doctoral program. *Degree requirements:* For master's, variable foreign language requirement, comprehensive exam (for some programs), thesis (for some programs); for doctorate, variable foreign language requirement, comprehensive exam (for some programs), thesis/dissertation; for other advanced degree, variable foreign language requirement, comprehensive exam (for some programs). *Entrance requirements:* For master's and doctorate, GRE, GMAT. Additional exam requirements/recommendations for international students: Required—TOEFL (minimum score 550 paper-based; 79 iBT). Electronic applications accepted.

University of Pennsylvania, Graduate School of Education, Division of Human Development and Quantitative Methods, Program in Quantitative Methods, Philadelphia, PA 19104. Offers M Phil, MS, PhD. *Program availability:* Part-time. *Students:* 12 full-time (9 women), 2 part-time (1 woman); includes 2 minority (1 Asian, non-Hispanic/Latino; 1 Two or more races, non-Hispanic/Latino), 5 international. Average age 30. 39 applicants, 15% accepted, 4 enrolled. In 2018, 2 master's awarded. *Entrance requirements:* For master's, bachelor's degree. Application fee: $80. *Financial support:* In 2018–19, 20 students received support. Applicants required to submit FAFSA.

University of Pennsylvania, Graduate School of Education, Division of Human Development and Quantitative Methods, Program in Statistics, Measurement, Assessment, and Research Technology (SMART), Philadelphia, PA 19104. Offers MS. *Students:* 19 full-time (12 women), 21 part-time (15 women); includes 3 minority (all Asian, non-Hispanic/Latino), 34 international. Average age 24. 197 applicants, 29% accepted, 24 enrolled. In 2018, 27 master's awarded. Application fee: $80.

University of Pittsburgh, School of Education, Department of Psychology in Education, Program in Research Methodology, Pittsburgh, PA 15260. Offers M Ed, MA, PhD. *Program availability:* Part-time, evening/weekend. Terminal master's awarded for partial completion of doctoral program. *Degree requirements:* For master's, thesis; for doctorate, thesis/dissertation. *Entrance requirements:* For doctorate, GRE General Test. Additional exam requirements/recommendations for international students: Required—TOEFL. Electronic applications accepted.

University of Puerto Rico–Río Piedras, College of Education, Program in Educational Research and Evaluation, San Juan, PR 00931-3300. Offers M Ed. *Program availability:* Part-time. *Degree requirements:* For master's, thesis. *Entrance requirements:* For master's, PAEG or GRE, interview, minimum GPA of 3.0, letter of recommendation.

University of St. Thomas, School of Education and Human Services, Houston, TX 77006-4696. Offers all level education (M Ed); bilingual/dual language (M Ed); Catholic school teaching (M Ed); Catholic/private school leadership (M Ed); counselor education (M Ed); curriculum and instruction (M Ed); education (Ed D); educational leadership (M Ed); elementary teaching (M Ed); English as a second language (M Ed); exceptionality/educational diagnostician (M Ed); exceptionality/special education (M Ed); generalist (M Ed); reading (M Ed); secondary teaching (M Ed); teaching (MAT). *Accreditation:* TEAC. *Program availability:* Part-time, evening/weekend, online learning. *Degree requirements:* For master's, thesis, field experience. *Entrance requirements:* For master's, GRE or MAT if GPA is below 3.0, bachelor's degree; minimum GPA of 2.75 in bachelor's degree or last 60 credit hours; official transcripts from all institutions; goal statement of 250-300 words; 1 reference. Additional exam requirements/recommendations for international students: Required—TOEFL (minimum score 94 iBT), IELTS (minimum score 7), PTE (minimum score 53). Electronic applications accepted. *Expenses:* Contact institution. *Faculty research:* Leadership, diversity, personality traits, second language acquisition.

University of Saskatchewan, College of Graduate and Postdoctoral Studies, College of Education, Department of Educational Psychology and Special Education, Saskatoon, SK S7N 5A2, Canada. Offers measurement and evaluation (M Ed, PhD); school and counseling psychology (M Ed, PhD); special education (M Ed, PhD). *Degree requirements:* For master's, thesis (for some programs); for doctorate, comprehensive exam (for some programs), thesis/dissertation. *Entrance requirements:* Additional exam requirements/recommendations for international students: Required—TOEFL (minimum score 80 iBT); Recommended—IELTS (minimum score 6.5). Electronic applications accepted.

University of South Carolina, The Graduate School, College of Education, Department of Educational Studies, Program in Educational Psychology, Research, Columbia, SC 29208. Offers M Ed, PhD. *Accreditation:* NCATE. *Program availability:* Part-time. *Degree requirements:* For master's, comprehensive exam, thesis (for some programs); for doctorate, comprehensive exam, thesis/dissertation. *Entrance requirements:* For

master's, GRE General Test; for doctorate, GRE General Test, interview. Electronic applications accepted. *Faculty research:* Problem solving, higher order thinking skills, psychometric research, methodology.

University of Southern Mississippi, College of Education and Human Sciences, Department of Educational Research and Administration, Hattiesburg, MS 39406-0001. Offers educational administration (M Ed, Ed D, PhD, Ed S); educational administration and supervision (M Ed); educational studies and research (MS); higher education (Ed D); higher education administration (PhD); higher education: student affairs (M Ed); research, evaluation, statistics, assessment (PhD). *Degree requirements:* For master's and Ed S, comprehensive exam, thesis (for some programs); for doctorate, comprehensive exam, thesis/dissertation. *Entrance requirements:* For master's and doctorate, GRE General Test, minimum GPA of 2.75. Additional exam requirements/recommendations for international students: Required—TOEFL.

University of South Florida, Innovative Education, Tampa, FL 33620-9951. Offers adult, career and higher education (Graduate Certificate), including college teaching, leadership in developing human resources, leadership in higher education; Africana studies (Graduate Certificate), including diasporas and health disparities, genocide and human rights; aging studies (Graduate Certificate), including gerontology; art research (Graduate Certificate), including museum studies; business foundations (Graduate Certificate); chemical and biomedical engineering (Graduate Certificate), including materials science and engineering, water, health and sustainability; child and family studies (Graduate Certificate), including positive behavior support; civil and industrial engineering (Graduate Certificate), including transportation systems analysis; community and family health (Graduate Certificate), including maternal and child health, social marketing and public health, violence and injury: prevention and intervention, women's health; criminology (Graduate Certificate), including criminal justice administration; data science for public administration (Graduate Certificate); digital humanities (Graduate Certificate); educational measurement and research (Graduate Certificate), including evaluation; English (Graduate Certificate), including comparative literary studies, creative writing, professional and technical communication; entrepreneurship (Graduate Certificate); environmental health (Graduate Certificate), including safety management; epidemiology and biostatistics (Graduate Certificate), including applied biostatistics, biostatistics, concepts and tools of epidemiology, epidemiology, epidemiology of infectious diseases; geography, environment and planning (Graduate Certificate), including community development, environmental policy and management, geographical information systems; geology (Graduate Certificate), including hydrogeology; global health (Graduate Certificate), including disaster management, global health and Latin American and Caribbean studies, global health practice, humanitarian assistance, infection control; government and international affairs (Graduate Certificate), including Cuban studies, globalization studies; health policy and management (Graduate Certificate), including health management and leadership, public health policy and programs; hearing specialist: early intervention (Graduate Certificate); industrial and management systems engineering (Graduate Certificate), including systems engineering, technology management; information studies (Graduate Certificate), including school library media specialist; information systems/decision sciences (Graduate Certificate), including analytics and business intelligence; instructional technology (Graduate Certificate), including distance education, Florida digital/virtual educator, instructional design, multimedia design, Web design; internal medicine, bioethics and medical humanities (Graduate Certificate), including biomedical ethics; Latin American and Caribbean studies (Graduate Certificate); leadership for coastal resiliency planning (Graduate Certificate); mass communications (Graduate Certificate), including multimedia journalism; mathematics and statistics (Graduate Certificate), including mathematics; medicine (Graduate Certificate), including aging and neuroscience, bioinformatics, biotechnology, brain fitness and memory management, clinical investigation, hand and upper limb rehabilitation, health informatics, health sciences, integrative weight management, intellectual property, medicine and gender, metabolic and nutritional medicine, metabolic cardiology, pharmacy sciences; national and competitive intelligence (Graduate Certificate); nursing (Graduate Certificate), including simulation based academic fellowship in advanced pain management; psychological and social foundations (Graduate Certificate), including career counseling, college teaching, diversity in education, mental health counseling, school counseling; public affairs (Graduate Certificate), including nonprofit management, public management, research administration; public health (Graduate Certificate), including assessing chemical toxicity and public health risks, health equity, pharmacoepidemiology, public health generalist, toxicology, translational research in adolescent behavioral health; public health practices (Graduate Certificate), including planning for healthy communities; rehabilitation and mental health counseling (Graduate Certificate), including integrative mental health care, marriage and family therapy, rehabilitation technology; secondary education (Graduate Certificate), including ESOL, foreign language education: culture and content, foreign language education: professional; social work (Graduate Certificate), including geriatric social work/clinical gerontology; special education (Graduate Certificate), including autism spectrum disorder, disabilities education: severe/profound; world languages (Graduate Certificate), including teaching English as a second language (TESL) or foreign language. *Expenses:* Tuition, state resident: full-time $6350. Tuition, nonresident: full-time $19,048. *International tuition:* $19,048 full-time. *Required fees:* $2079. *Unit head:* Dr. Cynthia DeLuca, Associate Vice President and Assistant Vice Provost, 813-974-3077, Fax: 813-974-7061, E-mail: deluca@usf.edu. *Application contact:* Owen Hooper, Director, Summer and Alternative Calendar Programs, 813-974-6917, E-mail: hooper@usf.edu.
Website: http://www.usf.edu/innovative-education/

The University of Tennessee, Graduate School, College of Education, Health and Human Sciences, Program in Education, Knoxville, TN 37996. Offers art education (MS); counseling education (PhD); cultural studies in education (PhD); curriculum (MS, Ed S); curriculum, educational research and evaluation (Ed D, PhD); early childhood education (PhD); early childhood special education (MS); education of deaf and hard of hearing (MS); educational administration and policy studies (Ed D, PhD); educational administration and supervision (Ed S); educational psychology (Ed D, PhD); elementary education (MS, Ed S); elementary teaching (MS); English education (MS, Ed S); exercise science (PhD); foreign language/ESL education (MS, Ed S); instructional technology (MS, Ed D, PhD, Ed S); literacy, language and ESL education (PhD); literacy, language education, and ESL education (Ed D); mathematics education (MS, Ed S); modified and comprehensive special education (MS); reading education (MS, Ed S); school counseling (Ed S); school psychology (PhD, Ed S); science education (MS, Ed S); secondary teaching (MS); social foundations (MS); social science education (MS, Ed S); socio-cultural foundations of sports and education (PhD); special education (Ed S); teacher education (Ed D, PhD). *Accreditation:* NCATE. *Program availability:* Part-time, evening/weekend. *Degree requirements:* For master's and Ed S, thesis optional; for doctorate, variable foreign language requirement, thesis/dissertation. *Entrance requirements:* For master's, minimum GPA of 2.7; for doctorate and Ed S, GRE General Test, minimum GPA of 2.7. Additional exam requirements/recommendations for international students: Required—TOEFL. Electronic applications accepted.

The University of Texas at El Paso, Graduate School, College of Education, Department of Educational Psychology and Special Services, El Paso, TX 79968-0001. Offers educational diagnostics (M Ed); guidance and counseling (M Ed); special education (M Ed). *Program availability:* Part-time, evening/weekend. *Degree requirements:* For master's, thesis optional. *Entrance requirements:* For master's, minimum GPA of 3.0. Additional exam requirements/recommendations for international students: Required—TOEFL. Electronic applications accepted.

The University of Texas at San Antonio, College of Education and Human Development, Department of Educational Psychology, San Antonio, TX 78207. Offers applied behavior analysis (Certificate); educational psychology (MA), including applied educational psychology, behavior assessment and intervention, general educational psychology, program evaluation; language acquisition and bilingual psychoeducational assessment (Certificate); school psychology (MA). *Program availability:* Part-time. *Degree requirements:* For master's, comprehensive exam, thesis (for some programs). *Entrance requirements:* For master's, GRE, bachelor's degree with 18 credit hours in field of study or in another appropriate field of study, two letters of recommendation, statement of purpose; for Certificate, 18 hours in psychology, sociology, education, or anything related (for applied behavioral analysis); minimum GPA of 2.7 in last 30 hours (for language acquisition and bilingual psychoeducational assessment). Additional exam requirements/recommendations for international students: Required—TOEFL (minimum score 550 paper-based; 79 iBT), IELTS (minimum score 6.5). Electronic applications accepted. *Faculty research:* Teacher consultation and culturally responsive school psychology practices, youth mentoring, cross-age peer mentoring, adolescent connectedness, pair counseling.

The University of Toledo, College of Graduate Studies, Judith Herb College of Education, Department of Educational Foundations and Leadership, Toledo, OH 43606-3390. Offers educational administration and supervision (ME, DE, Ed S); educational psychology (ME, PhD); educational research and measurement (ME, PhD); educational sociology (PhD); educational theory and social foundations (ME); foundations of education (DE, PhD); history of education (PhD); philosophy of education (PhD). *Accreditation:* NCATE. *Program availability:* Part-time, evening/weekend. *Degree requirements:* For master's, comprehensive exam, thesis or alternative; for doctorate, comprehensive exam, thesis/dissertation; for Ed S, thesis optional. *Entrance requirements:* For master's, doctorate, and Ed S, minimum cumulative GPA of 2.7 for all previous academic work, letters of recommendation. Additional exam requirements/recommendations for international students: Required—TOEFL (minimum score 550 paper-based; 80 iBT). Electronic applications accepted.

University of Victoria, Faculty of Graduate Studies, Faculty of Education, Department of Educational Psychology and Leadership Studies, Victoria, BC V8W 2Y2, Canada. Offers aboriginal communities counseling (M Ed); counseling (M Ed, MA); educational psychology (M Ed, MA, PhD), including counseling psychology (M Ed, MA), leadership studies (PhD), learning and development (MA, PhD), measurement and evaluation, special education (M Ed, MA); leadership studies (M Ed, MA). *Program availability:* Part-time. *Degree requirements:* For master's, thesis (for some programs), comprehensive exam (M Ed); for doctorate, comprehensive exam, thesis/dissertation, candidacy exam. *Entrance requirements:* For master's, 2 years of work experience in a relevant field; for doctorate, GRE, 2 years of work experience in a relevant field, minimum B average. Additional exam requirements/recommendations for international students: Required—TOEFL (minimum score 575 paper-based), IELTS (minimum score 7). *Faculty research:* Learning and development (child, adolescent and adult), special education and exceptional children.

University of Virginia, Curry School of Education, Department of Leadership, Foundations and Policy, Program in Educational Psychology, Charlottesville, VA 22903. Offers applied developmental science (M Ed); educational evaluation (M Ed); educational psychology (M Ed, Ed D, Ed S); educational research (Ed D); gifted education (M Ed); instructional technology (M Ed, Ed S); research statistics and evaluation (Ed D); school psychology (Ed D). *Degree requirements:* For master's, comprehensive exam. *Entrance requirements:* For master's and doctorate, GRE General Test, 2 letters of recommendation. Additional exam requirements/recommendations for international students: Required—TOEFL (minimum score 600 paper-based; 90 iBT), IELTS (minimum score 7). Electronic applications accepted.

University of Virginia, Curry School of Education, Program in Education, Charlottesville, VA 22903. Offers administration and supervision (PhD); applied developmental science (PhD); counselor education (PhD); curriculum and instruction (PhD); early childhood special education (MT); education evaluation (PhD); educational psychology (PhD); educational research (PhD); elementary education (MT); English education (MT, PhD); foreign language education (MT); higher education (PhD); instructional technology (PhD); kinesiology (MT, PhD); math education (PhD); reading education (PhD); research, statistics and evaluation (PhD); school psychology (PhD); science education (PhD); social studies education (MT, PhD); special education (PhD); world languages education (MT). *Degree requirements:* For master's, comprehensive exam (for some programs), field project; for doctorate, comprehensive exam, thesis/dissertation. *Entrance requirements:* For doctorate, GRE General Test. Additional exam requirements/recommendations for international students: Required—TOEFL (minimum score 600 paper-based; 90 iBT), IELTS (minimum score 7). Electronic applications accepted.

University of Washington, Graduate School, College of Education, Program in Educational Psychology, Seattle, WA 98195. Offers educational psychology (PhD); human development and cognition (M Ed); learning sciences (M Ed, PhD); measurement, statistics and research design (M Ed); school psychology (M Ed). *Accreditation:* APA. *Degree requirements:* For master's, thesis optional; for doctorate, thesis/dissertation. *Entrance requirements:* For master's and doctorate, GRE General Test, minimum GPA of 3.0. Additional exam requirements/recommendations for international students: Required—TOEFL.

University of Wisconsin–Milwaukee, Graduate School, School of Education, Department of Educational Psychology, Milwaukee, WI 53201-0413. Offers children's mental health for school professionals (Graduate Certificate); counseling psychology (PhD); educational statistics and measurement (MS, PhD); learning and development (MS, PhD); multicultural knowledge of mental health practices (Graduate Certificate); school counseling (MS, Graduate Certificate); school psychology (MS, PhD, Ed S). *Accreditation:* APA. *Program availability:* Part-time. *Students:* 181 full-time (137 women), 45 part-time (31 women); includes 50 minority (11 Black or African American, non-Hispanic/Latino; 1 American Indian or Alaska Native, non-Hispanic/Latino; 5 Asian, non-Hispanic/Latino; 5 Hispanic/Latino; 1 Native Hawaiian or other Pacific Islander, non-Hispanic/Latino; 27 Two or more races, non-Hispanic/Latino), 7 international. Average age 31. 320 applicants, 35% accepted, 78 enrolled. In 2018, 41 master's, 2 doctorates, 16 other advanced degrees awarded. *Degree requirements:* For master's, comprehensive exam, thesis; for doctorate, thesis/dissertation. *Entrance requirements:* For master's, minimum GPA of 3.0; for doctorate, GRE General Test, minimum GPA of 3.0. Additional exam requirements/recommendations for international students: Required—TOEFL (minimum score 550 paper-based; 79 iBT), IELTS (minimum score 6.5). *Application deadline:* For fall admission, 1/1 priority date for domestic students; for spring admission, 9/1 for domestic students. Application fee: $56 ($96 for international

students). Electronic applications accepted. *Financial support:* Fellowships, research assistantships, teaching assistantships, career-related internships or fieldwork, health care benefits, unspecified assistantships, and project assistantships available. Support available to part-time students. Financial award application deadline: 4/15; financial award applicants required to submit FAFSA. *Application contact:* General Information Contact, 414-229-4721, E-mail: soeinfo@uwm.edu.
Website: http://uwm.edu/education/academics/educational-psychology-department/

Utah State University, School of Graduate Studies, Emma Eccles Jones College of Education and Human Services, Department of Psychology, Logan, UT 84322. Offers clinical/counseling/school psychology (PhD); research and evaluation methodology (PhD); school counseling (MS); school psychology (MS). *Accreditation:* APA (one or more programs are accredited). *Program availability:* Part-time, evening/weekend, online learning. Terminal master's awarded for partial completion of doctoral program. *Degree requirements:* For master's, thesis (for some programs); for doctorate, thesis/dissertation. *Entrance requirements:* For master's, GRE General Test (school psychology), MAT (school counseling), minimum GPA of 3.5; for doctorate, GRE General Test, minimum GPA of 3.5. Additional exam requirements/recommendations for international students: Required—TOEFL. *Faculty research:* Hearing loss detection in infancy, ADHD, eating disorders, domestic violence, neuropsychology, bilingual/Spanish speaking students/parents.

Utah State University, School of Graduate Studies, Emma Eccles Jones College of Education and Human Services, Doctoral Program in Education, Logan, UT 84322. Offers business information systems (Ed D, PhD); curriculum and instruction (Ed D, PhD); research and evaluation (PhD). *Degree requirements:* For doctorate, comprehensive exam, thesis/dissertation. *Entrance requirements:* For doctorate, GRE General Test, minimum GPA of 3.0, master's degree. Additional exam requirements/recommendations for international students: Required—TOEFL. Electronic applications accepted. *Faculty research:* Language and literacy development, math and science education, instructional technology, hearing problems/deafness, domestic violence and animal abuse.

Virginia Commonwealth University, Graduate School, School of Education, Doctoral Program in Education, Richmond, VA 23284-9005. Offers art education (PhD); counselor education and supervision (PhD); curriculum, culture and change (PhD); educational leadership (PhD); educational psychology (PhD); leadership (Ed D); research and evaluation (PhD); special education and disability leadership (PhD); sport leadership (PhD); urban services leadership (PhD). *Accreditation:* NCATE. *Program availability:* Part-time. *Degree requirements:* For doctorate, thesis/dissertation. *Entrance requirements:* For doctorate, GRE (for PhD), MAT (for Ed D), interview, master's degree, writing sample. Additional exam requirements/recommendations for international students: Required—TOEFL (minimum score 600 paper-based; 100 iBT). Electronic applications accepted.

Virginia Polytechnic Institute and State University, Graduate School, College of Liberal Arts and Human Sciences, Blacksburg, VA 24061. Offers career and technical education (MS Ed, Ed S); communication (MA); counselor education (MA); creative writing (MFA); curriculum and instruction (MA Ed, Ed S); educational leadership and policy studies (Ed S); educational research and evaluation (PhD); English (MA); social, political, ethical, and cultural thought (PhD); Ed D/PhD. *Faculty:* 420 full-time (221 women), 1 (woman) part-time/adjunct. *Students:* 603 full-time (428 women), 359 part-time (237 women); includes 189 minority (107 Black or African American, non-Hispanic/Latino; 4 American Indian or Alaska Native, non-Hispanic/Latino; 24 Asian, non-Hispanic/Latino; 27 Hispanic/Latino; 2 Native Hawaiian or other Pacific Islander, non-Hispanic/Latino; 25 Two or more races, non-Hispanic/Latino), 84 international. Average age 33. 856 applicants, 48% accepted, 262 enrolled. In 2018, 270 master's, 63 doctorates awarded. *Degree requirements:* For master's, comprehensive exam (for some programs), thesis (for some programs); for doctorate, comprehensive exam (for some programs), thesis/dissertation (for some programs). *Entrance requirements:* For master's and doctorate, GRE/GMAT. Additional exam requirements/recommendations for international students: Required—TOEFL (minimum score 90 iBT). *Application deadline:* For fall admission, 8/1 for domestic students, 4/1 for international students; for spring admission, 1/1 for domestic students, 9/1 for international students. Applications are processed on a rolling basis. Application fee: $75. Electronic applications accepted. *Expenses:* Tuition, state resident: full-time $15,510; part-time $739.50 per credit hour. Tuition, nonresident: full-time $29,629; part-time $1490.25 per credit hour. *Required fees:* $2804; $550 per semester. Tuition and fees vary according to course load, campus/location and program. *Financial support:* In 2018–19, 4 fellowships with full tuition reimbursements (averaging $23,122 per year), 28 research assistantships with full tuition reimbursements (averaging $15,605 per year), 245 teaching assistantships with full tuition reimbursements (averaging $16,046 per year) were awarded; scholarships/grants and unspecified assistantships also available. Financial award application deadline: 3/1; financial award applicants required to submit FAFSA. *Total annual research expenditures:* $7.5 million. *Unit head:* Dr. Laura Belmonte, Dean, 540-231-6779, Fax: 540-231-7157, E-mail: belmonte@vt.edu. *Application contact:* Chelsea Blanchet, Executive Assistant, 540-231-6779, Fax: 540-231-7157, E-mail: bchels1@vt.edu.
Website: http://www.liberalarts.vt.edu/

Walden University, Graduate Programs, Richard W. Riley College of Education and Leadership, Minneapolis, MN 55401. Offers adult education (Post-Master's Certificate); adult learning (Graduate Certificate); college teaching and learning (Graduate Certificate); community college leadership (Ed D); curriculum, instruction and assessment (Ed D, Ed S, Graduate Certificate); developmental education (Graduate Certificate); early childhood administration, management, and leadership (Graduate Certificate); early childhood education (Ed D, Ed S); early childhood public policy and advocacy (Graduate Certificate); early childhood studies (MS), including administration, management and leadership, early childhood public policy and advocacy, teaching adults in the early childhood field, teaching and diversity in early childhood education; education (MS, PhD), including adolescent literacy and learning (MS), curriculum, instruction, and assessment (grades K-12) (MS), curriculum, instruction, assessment, and evaluation (PhD), early childhood leadership and advocacy (PhD), early childhood special education (PhD), educational leadership (MS), educational leadership and administration (principal preparation) (MS), educational technology and design (PhD), elementary reading and literacy (PreK-6) (MS), elementary reading and mathematics (grades K-6) (MS), global and comparative education (PhD), higher education leadership management and policy (PhD), integrating technology in the classroom (grades K-12) (MS), learning, instruction and innovation (PhD), mathematics (grades 5-8) (MS), mathematics (grades K-6) (MS), mathematics and science (grades K-8) (MS), organizational research, assessment, and evaluation (PhD), reading and literacy with a reading K-12 endorsement (MS), reading literacy assessment and evaluation (PhD), science (grades K-8) (MS), special education (non-licensure) (grades K-12) (MS), teacher leadership (grades K-12) (MS), teaching English language learners (grades K-12) (MS); educational administration and leadership (Ed D); educational leadership and administration (principal preparation) (Ed S); educational technology (Ed D, Ed S, Post Master's Certificate); elementary reading and literacy (Graduate Certificate); engaging culturally diverse learners (Graduate Certificate); enrollment management and institutional marketing (Graduate Certificate); higher education (MS), including adult learning, college teaching and learning, enrollment management and institutional marketing, global higher education, leadership for student success, online and distance learning; higher education and adult learning (Ed D); higher education leadership and management (Ed D); higher education leadership for student success (Graduate Certificate); instructional design and technology (MS, Postbaccalaureate Certificate), including general program (MS), online learning (MS), training and performance improvement (MS); integrating technology in the classroom (Graduate Certificate); mathematics 5-8 (Graduate Certificate); mathematics K-6 (Graduate Certificate); online teaching for adult educators (Graduate Certificate); reading, literacy, and assessment (Ed D, Ed S); science K-8 (Graduate Certificate); special education (Ed D, Ed S, Graduate Certificate); special education (K-age 21) (MAT); teacher leadership (Graduate Certificate); teaching adults English as a second language (Graduate Certificate); teaching adults in the early childhood field (Graduate Certificate); teaching and diversity in early childhood education (Graduate Certificate); teaching English language learners (grades K-12) (Graduate Certificate); teaching K-12 students online (Graduate Certificate). *Accreditation:* NCATE. *Program availability:* Part-time, evening/weekend, online only, 100% online. *Degree requirements:* For doctorate, thesis/dissertation (for some programs), residency; for other advanced degree, residency (for some programs). *Entrance requirements:* For master's, bachelor's degree or higher; minimum GPA of 2.5; official transcripts; goal statement (for some programs); access to computer and Internet; for doctorate, master's degree or higher; three years of related professional or academic experience (preferred); minimum GPA of 3.0; goal statement and current resume (for select programs); official transcripts; access to computer and Internet; for other advanced degree, relevant work experience; access to computer and Internet. Additional exam requirements/recommendations for international students: Required—TOEFL (minimum score 550 paper-based, 79 iBT), IELTS (minimum score 6.5), Michigan English Language Assessment Battery (minimum score 82), or PTE (minimum score 53). Electronic applications accepted.

Washington University in St. Louis, The Graduate School, Department of Education, Program in Educational Research, St. Louis, MO 63130-4899. Offers PhD. *Entrance requirements:* For doctorate, GRE General Test. Additional exam requirements/recommendations for international students: Required—TOEFL. Electronic applications accepted.

Wayland Baptist University, Graduate Programs, Program in Education, Plainview, TX 79072-6998. Offers education administration (M Ed); education diagnostics (M Ed); education literacy (M Ed); elementary certification (M Ed); English (M Ed); English as a second language (M Ed); higher education administration (M Ed); human resources (M Ed); instructional leadership (M Ed); instructional technology (M Ed); leadership training and development (M Ed); science education (M Ed); secondary certification (M Ed); social studies (M Ed); special education (M Ed); sports administration and management (M Ed). *Program availability:* Part-time, evening/weekend, 100% online. *Degree requirements:* For master's, comprehensive exam, capstone course. *Entrance requirements:* For master's, GRE, GMAT or MAT. Additional exam requirements/recommendations for international students: Required—TOEFL (minimum score 500 paper-based; 61 iBT). Electronic applications accepted.

Wayne State University, College of Education, Division of Theoretical and Behavioral Foundations, Detroit, MI 48202. Offers applied behavior analysis (Certificate); counseling (M Ed, MA, Ed D, Ed S); counseling psychology (MA, PhD); education evaluation and research (M Ed, Ed D); educational psychology (M Ed, PhD), including learning and instruction sciences (PhD); rehabilitation counseling and community inclusion (MA); school and community psychology (MA, Certificate). *Accreditation:* ACA (one or more programs are accredited); CORE (one or more programs are accredited). *Program availability:* Part-time, evening/weekend. *Faculty:* 9. *Students:* 168 full-time (136 women), 200 part-time (171 women); includes 128 minority (82 Black or African American, non-Hispanic/Latino; 2 American Indian or Alaska Native, non-Hispanic/Latino; 8 Asian, non-Hispanic/Latino; 12 Hispanic/Latino; 24 Two or more races, non-Hispanic/Latino), 14 international. Average age 32. 340 applicants, 24% accepted, 66 enrolled. In 2018, 103 master's, 6 doctorates, 18 other advanced degrees awarded. *Degree requirements:* For master's, thesis (for some programs); for doctorate, comprehensive exam, thesis/dissertation. *Entrance requirements:* For master's, GRE, interview, personal statement, portfolio (only art therapy); references; program application; for doctorate, GRE, departmental writing exam, interview, curriculum vitae, references, master's degree in closely-related field with minimum GPA of 3.5, demonstration of counseling skills (for Ed D in counseling); autobiographical statement; letter of application; personal statement; for other advanced degree, education specialist certificate: GRE, education specialist certificate: master's degree in counseling or closely related field and licensure; personal statement; recommendations; autobiographical statement; interview. Additional exam requirements/recommendations for international students: Required—TOEFL (minimum score 550 paper-based; 79 iBT); Recommended—IELTS (minimum score 6.5), TWE (minimum score 5.5), TSE (minimum score 58). *Application deadline:* Applications are processed on a rolling basis. Application fee: $50. Electronic applications accepted. *Expenses:* Contact institution. *Financial support:* In 2018–19, 86 students received support, including 2 research assistantships with tuition reimbursements available (averaging $19,267 per year); fellowships, teaching assistantships, Federal Work-Study, scholarships/grants, health care benefits, and unspecified assistantships also available. Support available to part-time students. Financial award applicants required to submit FAFSA. *Faculty research:* Adolescents at risk, supervision of counseling. *Unit head:* Dr. Cheryl Somers, Assistant Dean, 313-577-1670, E-mail: c.somers@wayne.edu. *Application contact:* Dr. Mary L Waker, Graduate Admissions Officer, 313-577-1601, Fax: 313-577-7904, E-mail: m.waker@wayne.edu.
Website: http://coe.wayne.edu/tbf/index.php

Western Michigan University, Graduate College, College of Education and Human Development, Department of Educational Leadership, Research and Technology, Kalamazoo, MI 49008. Offers educational leadership (MA, PhD, Ed S), including educational leadership (MA); educational technology (MA, Graduate Certificate); evaluation, measurement and research (MA, PhD); organizational learning and performance (MA).

Western Michigan University, Graduate College, College of Education and Human Development, Department of Interdisciplinary Education, Kalamazoo, MI 49008. Offers PhD.

West Texas A&M University, College of Education and Social Sciences, Department of Education, Program in Educational Diagnostician, Canyon, TX 79015. Offers M Ed. *Program availability:* Part-time, online learning. *Degree requirements:* For master's, comprehensive exam, thesis optional. *Entrance requirements:* For master's, GRE General Test, 3 years' teaching experience, competency in diagnosis and prescription. Additional exam requirements/recommendations for international students: Required—TOEFL (minimum score 550 paper-based). Electronic applications accepted. *Faculty research:* Teacher preparation through web-based instruction, developmental disabilities.

Wilkes University, College of Graduate and Professional Studies, School of Education, Wilkes-Barre, PA 18766-0002. Offers educational development and strategies (MS Ed);

educational leadership (MS Ed, Ed D); effective teaching (MS Ed); instructional media (MS Ed); instructional technology (MS Ed); international school leadership (MS Ed); international teaching and learning (MS Ed); literacy (MS Ed); middle level education (MS Ed); online teaching (MS Ed); school business leadership (MS Ed); special education (MS Ed); teaching English to speakers of other languages (MS Ed). *Program availability:* Part-time, evening/weekend, 100% online, blended/hybrid learning. *Students:* 87 full-time (67 women), 1,418 part-time (1,078 women); includes 87 minority (13 Black or African American, non-Hispanic/Latino; 1 American Indian or Alaska Native, non-Hispanic/Latino; 11 Asian, non-Hispanic/Latino; 40 Hispanic/Latino; 22 Two or more races, non-Hispanic/Latino). Average age 35. In 2018, 611 master's, 9 doctorates awarded. *Entrance requirements:* Additional exam requirements/recommendations for

international students: Required—TOEFL (minimum score 550 paper-based; 79 iBT). *Application deadline:* Applications are processed on a rolling basis. Application fee: $45 ($65 for international students). Electronic applications accepted. *Expenses:* Contact institution. *Financial support:* Unspecified assistantships available. Financial award application deadline: 3/1; financial award applicants required to submit FAFSA. *Unit head:* Dr. Rhonda Rabbitt, Dean, 570-408-4680, Fax: 570-408-7872, E-mail: rhonda.rabbitt@wilkes.edu. *Application contact:* Stephanie Wasmanski, Associate Director of Graduate Admissions, 570-408-5535, Fax: 570-408-7846, E-mail: stephanie.wasmanski@wilkes.edu.
Website: http://www.wilkes.edu/academics/graduate-programs/masters-programs/graduate-education/index.aspx

Educational Media/Instructional Technology

Adelphi University, College of Education & Health Sciences, College of Education and Health Services, Garden City, NY 11530-0701. Offers MA. *Program availability:* Online learning. *Students:* 8 full-time (0 women), 24 part-time (6 women); includes 8 minority (5 Black or African American, non-Hispanic/Latino; 1 Asian, non-Hispanic/Latino; 2 Hispanic/Latino), 6 international. Average age 32. 37 applicants, 65% accepted, 18 enrolled. In 2018, 7 master's awarded. *Entrance requirements:* For master's, personal statement, two letters of reference, current resume or curriculum vitae. Additional exam requirements/recommendations for international students: Required—TOEFL (minimum score 550 paper-based; 80 iBT), IELTS (minimum score 6.5). *Application deadline:* Applications are processed on a rolling basis. Application fee: $50. Electronic applications accepted. *Unit head:* Aaron Chia Yuan Hung, Dean, 516-877-8159, E-mail: hung@adelphi.edu. *Application contact:* Aaron Chia Yuan Hung, Dean, 516-877-8159, E-mail: hung@adelphi.edu.
Website: http://education-ci.adelphi.edu/educational-technology/

Alabama Agricultural and Mechanical University, School of Graduate Studies, College of Education, Humanities, and Behavioral Sciences, Department of Educational Leadership and Secondary Education, Huntsville, AL 35811. Offers biology (M Ed); business/marketing education (M Ed, Ed S); chemistry (M Ed); collaborative teacher secondary education (M Ed, Ed S); education (M Ed, Ed S); English language arts (M Ed); family/consumer science education (M Ed, Ed S); general science (M Ed); general social science (M Ed); mathematics (M Ed, Ed S); physics (M Ed, Ed S); technology education (M Ed). *Accreditation:* NCATE. *Program availability:* Evening/weekend. *Degree requirements:* For master's, comprehensive exam; for Ed S, thesis. *Entrance requirements:* For master's, GRE General Test. Additional exam requirements/recommendations for international students: Required—TOEFL (minimum score 500 paper-based; 61 iBT). Electronic applications accepted. *Faculty research:* World peace through education, computer-assisted instruction.

Alabama State University, College of Education, Department of Instructional Support Programs, Montgomery, AL 36101-0271. Offers counselor education (M Ed, MS, Ed S), including general counseling (MS, Ed S), school counseling (M Ed, Ed S); educational administration (M Ed), including instructional leadership; educational leadership, policy and law (PhD); library education media (Ed S). *Program availability:* Part-time, evening/weekend. *Faculty:* 11 full-time (6 women), 7 part-time/adjunct (5 women). *Students:* 27 full-time (17 women), 85 part-time (58 women); includes 182 minority (181 Black or African American, non-Hispanic/Latino; 1 Hispanic/Latino). Average age 41. 70 applicants, 54% accepted, 12 enrolled. In 2018, 14 master's, 6 doctorates, 1 other advanced degree awarded. Terminal master's awarded for partial completion of doctoral program. *Degree requirements:* For master's and Ed S, comprehensive exam; for doctorate, thesis/dissertation. *Entrance requirements:* For master's, GRE General Test, MAT, writing competency test, bachelor's degree or its equivalent from accredited college or university with minimum GPA of 2.5; for Ed S, GRE General Test, MAT, writing competency test, minimum GPA of 3.25. Additional exam requirements/recommendations for international students: Required—TOEFL (minimum score 500 paper-based). *Application deadline:* For fall admission, 4/15 for domestic and international students; for spring admission, 11/15 for domestic and international students; for summer admission, 3/15 for domestic and international students. Applications are processed on a rolling basis. Application fee: $25. Electronic applications accepted. *Expenses:* Contact institution. *Financial support:* In 2018–19, 3 students received support. Fellowships, research assistantships, teaching assistantships, Federal Work-Study, scholarships/grants, tuition waivers (partial), and unspecified assistantships available. Financial award application deadline: 6/30; financial award applicants required to submit FAFSA. *Unit head:* Dr. Kecia Asley, Chair, Instructional Leadership/Educational Leadership, Policy, & Law, 334-229-8828, Fax: 334-229-6831, E-mail: kashley@alasu.edu. *Application contact:* Dr. Ed Brown, Dean of Graduate Studies, 334-229-4275, Fax: 334-229-4928, E-mail: ebrown@alasu.edu.
Website: http://www.alasu.edu/academics/colleges—departments/college-of-education/instructional-support-programs/index.aspx

Alverno College, School of Professional Studies - Education Division, Milwaukee, WI 53234-3922. Offers adaptive education (MA); administrative leadership (MA); adult education and organizational development (MA); adult educational and instructional design (MA); adult educational and instructional technology (MA); global connections in the humanities (MA); instructional leadership (MA); instructional technology for K-12 settings (MA); professional development (MA); reading education (MA); reading education with adaptive education (MA); science education (MA); special education (MA); teaching in alternative schools (MA). *Accreditation:* NCATE. *Program availability:* Part-time, evening/weekend. *Degree requirements:* For master's, presentation/defense of proposal, conference presentation of inquiry projects. *Entrance requirements:* For master's, bachelor's degree in related field, communication samples from work setting, 3 letters of recommendation. Additional exam requirements/recommendations for international students: Required—TOEFL. Electronic applications accepted. *Expenses:* Contact institution. *Faculty research:* Student self-assessment, self-reflection, integration of curriculum, identifying needs of students in strategic situations and designing appropriate classroom strategies.

American College of Education, Graduate Programs, Indianapolis, IN 46204. Offers curriculum and instruction (M Ed), including bilingual, ESL; educational leadership (M Ed); educational technology (M Ed).

American InterContinental University Online, Program in Education, Schaumburg, IL 60173. Offers curriculum and instruction (M Ed); educational assessment and evaluation (M Ed); instructional technology (M Ed); leadership of educational organizations (M Ed). *Accreditation:* TEAC. *Program availability:* Evening/weekend, online learning. *Entrance requirements:* Additional exam requirements/recommendations for international

students: Required—TOEFL (minimum score 550 paper-based). Electronic applications accepted.

American University, School of Professional and Extended Studies, Washington, DC 20016. Offers agile project management (MS); healthcare management (MS, Graduate Certificate); human resource analytics and management (MS, Graduate Certificate); instructional design and learning analytics (MS); measurement and evaluation (MS); project monitoring and evaluation (Graduate Certificate); sports analytics and management (MS, Graduate Certificate). *Program availability:* Part-time, evening/weekend, 100% online, blended/hybrid learning. *Faculty:* 27 full-time (14 women), 33 part-time/adjunct (20 women). *Students:* 2 full-time (both women), 113 part-time (68 women); includes 6 minority (4 Black or African American, non-Hispanic/Latino; 1 Asian, non-Hispanic/Latino; 1 Hispanic/Latino). Average age 31. 156 applicants, 93% accepted, 66 enrolled. In 2018, 1 master's, 6 other advanced degrees awarded. *Entrance requirements:* For master's, Please visit website: https://www.american.edu/spexs/, official transcript(s), resume. Additional exam requirements/recommendations for international students: Required—TOEFL. *Application deadline:* Applications are processed on a rolling basis. Application fee: $55. Electronic applications accepted. *Expenses:* Contact institution. *Financial support:* Applicants required to submit FAFSA. *Unit head:* Jill Klein, Dean, 202-895-4900, E-mail: spexs@american.edu. *Application contact:* Emily Emily, Assistant Director for Recruitment and Admission, 202-885-4910, E-mail: aronoff@american.edu.
Website: http://www.american.edu/spexs/

Antioch University New England, Graduate School, Department of Education, Experienced Educators Program, Keene, NH 03431-3552. Offers foundations of education (M Ed), including applied behavioral analysis, autism spectrum disorders, educating for sustainability, next-generation learning using technology, problem-based learning using critical skills, teacher leadership; principal certification (PMC). *Degree requirements:* For master's, thesis, practicum. *Entrance requirements:* For master's, previous course work and work experience in education. Additional exam requirements/recommendations for international students: Required—TOEFL (minimum score 550 paper-based). Electronic applications accepted. *Expenses:* Contact institution. *Faculty research:* Classroom action research, school restructuring, problem-based learning, brain-based learning.

Appalachian State University, Cratis D. Williams School of Graduate Studies, Department of Curriculum and Instruction, Boone, NC 28608. Offers curriculum specialist (MA); educational media (MA); elementary education (MA); middle grades education (MA), including language arts, mathematics, science, social studies. *Accreditation:* NCATE. *Program availability:* Part-time, evening/weekend, online learning. *Degree requirements:* For master's, comprehensive exam, thesis or alternative. *Entrance requirements:* For master's, GRE General Test or MAT, 3 letters of recommendation. Additional exam requirements/recommendations for international students: Required—TOEFL (minimum score 570 paper-based; 79 iBT), IELTS (minimum score 6.5). Electronic applications accepted. *Expenses: Tuition, area resident:* Full-time $4839; part-time $237 per credit hour. *Tuition, state resident:* full-time $4839; part-time $237 per credit hour. *Tuition, nonresident:* full-time $18,271; part-time $895.50 per credit hour. *Faculty research:* Media literacy, elementary teaching, curriculum development, online learning environments.

Appalachian State University, Cratis D. Williams School of Graduate Studies, Department of Leadership and Educational Studies, Boone, NC 28608. Offers educational administration (Ed S); educational media (MA); higher education (MA, Ed S); library science (MLS); school administration (MSA). *Program availability:* Part-time, evening/weekend, online learning. *Degree requirements:* For master's and Ed S, comprehensive exam, thesis optional. *Entrance requirements:* For master's and Ed S, GRE or MAT, 3 letters of recommendation. Additional exam requirements/recommendations for international students: Required—TOEFL (minimum score 570 paper-based; 79 iBT), IELTS (minimum score 6.5). Electronic applications accepted. *Expenses: Tuition, area resident:* Full-time $4839; part-time $237 per credit hour. *Tuition, state resident:* full-time $4839; part-time $237 per credit hour. *Tuition, nonresident:* full-time $18,271; part-time $895.50 per credit hour. *Faculty research:* Brain, learning and meditation; leadership of teaching and learning.

Arcadia University, School of Education, Glenside, PA 19038-3295. Offers art education (M Ed); computer education (CAS); curriculum (CAS); curriculum studies (M Ed); early childhood education (M Ed), including individualized, master teacher, research in child development; educational leadership (M Ed, Ed D, CAS); elementary education (M Ed); English education (MA Ed); environmental education (MA Ed); instructional technology (M Ed); language arts (M Ed); library science (M Ed); mathematics education (M Ed, MA Ed); music education (MA Ed); psychology (MA Ed); reading (M Ed, CAS); science education (M Ed, CAS); secondary education (M Ed, CAS); special education (M Ed, Ed D, CAS); theater arts (MA Ed); written communication (MA Ed). *Accreditation:* NASAD. *Program availability:* Part-time, evening/weekend, online learning. *Faculty:* 14 full-time (10 women). *Students:* 35 full-time (24 women), 299 part-time (243 women); includes 72 minority (49 Black or African American, non-Hispanic/Latino; 1 American Indian or Alaska Native, non-Hispanic/Latino; 12 Asian, non-Hispanic/Latino; 8 Hispanic/Latino; 2 Two or more races, non-Hispanic/Latino), 5 international. In 2018, 152 master's, 8 doctorates awarded. *Entrance requirements:* Additional exam requirements/recommendations for international students: Required—Official results from the TOEFL or IELTS are required. *Application deadline:* Applications are processed on a rolling basis. Application fee: $25. Electronic applications accepted. *Expenses:* Contact institution. *Financial support:* Career-related internships or fieldwork, tuition waivers (partial), and unspecified assistantships available. *Unit head:* Kimberly Dean, Chair, 215-572-8629. *Application contact:* 215-572-2925, Fax: 215-572-2126, E-mail: grad@arcadia.edu.

Argosy University, Atlanta, College of Education, Atlanta, GA 30328. Offers educational leadership (MAEd, Ed D, Ed S), including higher education administration (Ed D), K-12 education (Ed D); teaching and learning (MAEd, Ed D, Ed S), including education technology (Ed D), higher education (Ed D), K-12 education (Ed D).

Argosy University, Orange County, College of Education, Orange, CA 92868. Offers community college executive leadership (Ed D); educational leadership (MA Ed, Ed D), including higher education administration (Ed D), K-12 education (Ed D); instructional leadership (MA Ed, Ed D), including education technology (Ed D), higher education (Ed D), K-12 education (Ed D), multiple subject teacher preparation (MA Ed), single subject teacher preparation (MA Ed).

Argosy University, Phoenix, College of Education, Phoenix, AZ 85021. Offers adult education and training (MA Ed); advanced educational administration (Ed D, Ed S); community college executive leadership (Ed D); educational administration (MA Ed); educational leadership (MA Ed, Ed D, Ed S), including education technology (Ed D), higher education administration (Ed D), K-12 education (Ed D); higher and postsecondary education (MA Ed); initial educational administration (Ed D, Ed S); school psychology (MA); teaching and learning (MA Ed, Ed D, Ed S), including education technology (Ed D), higher education (Ed D), K-12 education (Ed D).

Argosy University, Seattle, College of Education, Seattle, WA 98121. Offers adult education and training (MA Ed); community college executive leadership (Ed D); educational leadership (MA Ed, Ed D), including higher education administration (Ed D), K-12 education (Ed D); higher and postsecondary education (MA Ed); instructional leadership (MA Ed, Ed D), including education technology (Ed D), higher education (Ed D), K-12 education (Ed D).

Argosy University, Twin Cities, College of Education, Eagan, MN 55121. Offers advanced educational administration (Ed D, Ed S); educational leadership (MA Ed, Ed D, Ed S), including higher education administration (Ed D), K-12 education (Ed D); higher and postsecondary education (MA Ed); initial educational administration (Ed D, Ed S); instructional leadership (MA Ed, Ed D, Ed S), including education technology (Ed D), higher education (Ed D), K-12 education (Ed D).

Arizona State University at the Tempe campus, Mary Lou Fulton Teachers College, Program in Educational Technology, Phoenix, AZ 85069. Offers educational technology (M Ed); instructional design and performance improvement (Graduate Certificate); online teaching for grades K-12 (Graduate Certificate). *Program availability:* Part-time, evening/weekend, online learning. Terminal master's awarded for partial completion of doctoral program. *Degree requirements:* For master's, thesis or alternative, applied project, interactive Program of Study (iPOS) submitted before completing 50 percent of required credit hours. *Entrance requirements:* For master's, GRE (Verbal section) or MAT (for students with less than 3 years of professional experience as teacher, trainer or instructional designer), minimum GPA of 3.0 or equivalent in last 2 years of work leading to bachelor's degree, 3 letters of recommendation, personal statement, curriculum vitae or resume. Additional exam requirements/recommendations for international students: Required—TOEFL (minimum score 600 paper-based; 100 iBT). Electronic applications accepted. *Faculty research:* Virtual environments; innovative technologies; theory, design, and implementation of computer-based learning environments; impact of technology into curricula on student achievement/attitude; electronic portfolios for learning and assessment.

Arkansas Tech University, College of Education, Russellville, AR 72801. Offers college student personnel (MS); educational leadership (M Ed, Ed S); instructional technology (M Ed); school counseling and leadership (M Ed); school leadership (Ed D); special education K-12 (M Ed); strength and conditioning studies (MS); teaching (MAT); teaching, learning, and leadership (M Ed). *Accreditation:* NCATE. *Program availability:* Part-time, evening/weekend, 100% online, blended/hybrid learning. *Students:* 90 full-time (52 women), 450 part-time (359 women); includes 100 minority (63 Black or African American, non-Hispanic/Latino; 6 American Indian or Alaska Native, non-Hispanic/Latino; 1 Asian, non-Hispanic/Latino; 15 Hispanic/Latino; 15 Two or more races, non-Hispanic/Latino), 4 international. Average age 34. In 2018, 130 master's, 14 doctorates, 1 other advanced degree awarded. *Degree requirements:* For master's, comprehensive exam, thesis optional, action research project; for doctorate, thesis/dissertation. *Entrance requirements:* Additional exam requirements/recommendations for international students: Required—TOEFL (minimum score 550 paper-based; 79 iBT), IELTS (minimum score 6.5), PTE (minimum score 58). *Application deadline:* For fall admission, 3/1 priority date for domestic students, 5/1 priority date for international students; for spring admission, 10/1 priority date for domestic and international students. Applications are processed on a rolling basis. Application fee: $40 ($90 for international students). Electronic applications accepted. *Expenses:* Tuition, area resident: Full-time $6816; part-time $284 per credit hour. Tuition, state resident: full-time $6816; part-time $284 per credit hour. Tuition, nonresident: full-time $13,632; part-time $568 per credit hour. *International tuition:* $13,632 full-time. *Required fees:* $457.50 per semester. Tuition and fees vary according to course load and degree level. *Financial support:* In 2018–19, research assistantships with full and partial tuition reimbursements (averaging $4,800 per year), teaching assistantships with full and partial tuition reimbursements (averaging $4,800 per year) were awarded; career-related internships or fieldwork, Federal Work-Study, scholarships/grants, health care benefits, and unspecified assistantships also available. Support available to part-time students. Financial award application deadline: 4/15; financial award applicants required to submit FAFSA. *Unit head:* Dr. Linda Bean, Dean, 479-964-3217, E-mail: lbean@atu.edu. *Application contact:* Dr. Jeff Robertson, Interim Dean of Graduate College, 479-968-0398, Fax: 479-964-0542, E-mail: gradcollege@atu.edu.
Website: http://www.atu.edu/education/

Auburn University, Graduate School, College of Education, Department of Educational Foundations, Leadership, and Technology, Auburn University, AL 36849. Offers adult education (PhD, Ed S); curriculum supervision (M Ed, PhD); higher education administration (PhD); library media (Ed S); school administration (M Ed, PhD). *Accreditation:* NCATE. *Program availability:* Part-time. *Degree requirements:* For master's, thesis (for some programs); for doctorate, thesis/dissertation; for Ed S, field project. *Entrance requirements:* For master's, doctorate, and Ed S, GRE General Test. Electronic applications accepted. *Expenses:* Tuition, state resident: full-time $11,282; part-time $535 per credit hour. Tuition, nonresident: full-time $30,542; part-time $1605 per credit hour. *Required fees:* $826 per semester. Tuition and fees vary according to degree level and program.

Auburn University at Montgomery, College of Education, Department of Counselor, Leadership, and Special Education, Montgomery, AL 36124-4023. Offers counselor education (M Ed, Ed S), including clinical mental health counseling, school counseling; early childhood special education (M Ed); instructional leadership (M Ed, Ed S); special education/collaborative teacher (M Ed, Ed S). *Accreditation:* ACA; NCATE. *Program availability:* Part-time, evening/weekend. *Students:* Average age 34. 76 applicants, 72% accepted, 26 enrolled. In 2018, 37 master's awarded. *Entrance requirements:* For master's, GRE General Test or MAT, certification, BS in teaching; for Ed S, GRE General Test or MAT, certification. Additional exam requirements/recommendations for international students: Recommended—TOEFL (minimum score 500 paper-based; 61 iBT), IELTS (minimum score 5.5), TSE (minimum score 44). *Application deadline:* For fall admission, 7/15 for international students; for spring admission, 11/15 for international students; for summer admission, 4/15 for international students. Applications are processed on a rolling basis. Electronic applications accepted. *Expenses: Tuition, area resident:* Full-time $7146; part-time $4764 per credit hour. Tuition, state resident: full-time $7146; part-time $4764 per credit hour. Tuition, nonresident: full-time $16,056; part-time $10,704 per credit hour. *International tuition:* $16,056 full-time. *Required fees:* $766. One-time fee: $25 full-time. *Financial support:* Career-related internships or fieldwork and scholarships/grants available. Support available to part-time students. Financial award application deadline: 3/1; financial award applicants required to submit FAFSA. *Unit head:* Dr. Samuel Flynt, Head, 334-244-3835, Fax: 334-244-3101, E-mail: sflynt@aum.edu. *Application contact:* Dr. Rhonda Morton, Associate Dean/Graduate Coordinator, 334-244-3287, Fax: 334-244-3978, E-mail: rmorton@aum.edu.
Website: http://education.aum.edu/academic-departments/counselor-leadership-and-special-education

Auburn University at Montgomery, College of Education, Department of Curriculum, Instruction, and Technology, Montgomery, AL 36124-4023. Offers elementary education (M Ed, Ed S); instructional technology (Ed S); secondary education (M Ed). *Faculty:* 12 full-time (8 women), 8 part-time/adjunct (all women). *Students:* 43 full-time (34 women), 81 part-time (65 women); includes 39 minority (38 Black or African American, non-Hispanic/Latino; 1 Hispanic/Latino), 2 international. Average age 33. 99 applicants, 70% accepted, 37 enrolled. In 2018, 47 master's awarded. *Degree requirements:* For master's, comprehensive exam, thesis (for some programs). *Entrance requirements:* For master's, GRE or MAT. Additional exam requirements/recommendations for international students: Recommended—TOEFL (minimum score 500 paper-based; 61 iBT), IELTS (minimum score 5.5), TSE (minimum score 44). *Application deadline:* For fall admission, 7/15 for international students; for spring admission, 11/15 for international students; for summer admission, 4/15 for international students. Applications are processed on a rolling basis. Application fee: $25. Electronic applications accepted. *Expenses: Tuition, area resident:* Full-time $7146; part-time $4764 per credit hour. Tuition, state resident: full-time $7146; part-time $4764 per credit hour. Tuition, nonresident: full-time $16,056; part-time $10,704 per credit hour. *International tuition:* $16,056 full-time. *Required fees:* $766. One-time fee: $25 full-time. *Financial support:* Application deadline: 3/1; applicants required to submit FAFSA. *Unit head:* Dr. Kellie Shumack, Head, 334-244-3737, Fax: 334-244-3835, E-mail: kshumack@aum.edu. *Application contact:* Dr. Rhonda Morton, Associate Dean/Graduate Coordinator, 334-224-3287, Fax: 334-244-3978, E-mail: rmorton@aum.edu.
Website: http://education.aum.edu/academic-departments/curriculum-instruction-technology

Augustana University, MA in Education Program, Sioux Falls, SD 57197. Offers instructional strategies (MA); reading (MA); special populations (MA); STEM (MA); technology (MA). *Accreditation:* NCATE. *Program availability:* Part-time-only, evening/weekend, online only, 100% online. *Degree requirements:* For master's, thesis. *Entrance requirements:* For master's, appropriate bachelor's degree, minimum GPA of 3.0, teaching certificate. Additional exam requirements/recommendations for international students: Required—TOEFL (minimum score 550 paper-based). Electronic applications accepted. *Expenses:* Contact institution. *Faculty research:* Multicultural education, education of students with autism, well-being in school settings, factors that predict academic hopefulness.

Augusta University, College of Education, Program in Educational Innovation, Augusta, GA 30912. Offers educational innovation (Ed D).

Aurora University, School of Education and Human Performance, Aurora, IL 60506-4892. Offers applied behavioral analysis (MS); bilingual-ESL education (MA); educational leadership with principal endorsement (MA); educational technology (MA); leadership in adult learning higher education (Ed D); leadership in curriculum and instruction (Ed D); leadership in educational administration (Ed D); reading instruction (MA); special education (MA). *Accreditation:* NCATE. *Program availability:* Part-time, evening/weekend, 100% online. *Faculty:* 14 full-time (6 women), 32 part-time/adjunct (17 women). *Students:* 28 full-time (25 women), 537 part-time (359 women); includes 101 minority (25 Black or African American, non-Hispanic/Latino; 8 Asian, non-Hispanic/Latino; 58 Hispanic/Latino; 2 Native Hawaiian or other Pacific Islander, non-Hispanic/Latino; 8 Two or more races, non-Hispanic/Latino), 2 international. Average age 38. 191 applicants, 98% accepted, 133 enrolled. In 2018, 213 master's, 16 doctorates awarded. *Degree requirements:* For master's, student teaching, research seminar, and practicum; for doctorate, comprehensive exam, thesis/dissertation. *Entrance requirements:* For master's, 2 years of teaching experience, valid teaching certificate, resume; for doctorate, appropriate master's degree, two references, curriculum vitae, personal statement, professional project, reflective essay. Additional exam requirements/recommendations for international students: Required—TOEFL (minimum score 550 paper-based; 79 iBT). *Application deadline:* For fall admission, 6/1 for international students; for spring admission, 10/1 for international students. Applications are processed on a rolling basis. Application fee: $0. Electronic applications accepted. *Expenses:* The reported tuition amount is for the program with the greatest enrollment, MA in Educational Leadership with Principal Endorsement. Other programs may require more semester hours, and thus have a greater total cost. The Education doctoral programs are roughly double the amount of the master's programs. *Financial support:* In 2018–19, 31 students received support. Federal Work-Study, scholarships/grants, and unspecified assistantships available. Financial award applicants required to submit FAFSA. *Unit head:* Dr. Jen Buckley, Dean, School of Education and Human Performance, 630-844-1542, Fax: 630-844-6155, E-mail: jbuckley@aurora.edu. *Application contact:* Center for Graduate Studies, 630-947-8955, E-mail: AUadmission@aurora.edu.
Website: http://aurora.edu/education

Avila University, School of Professional Studies, Kansas City, MO 64145-1698. Offers executive leadership (MS); fundraising (MA); instructional design and technology (MA, MS); leadership coaching (MS); project management (MA); strategic human resources (MS). *Program availability:* Part-time-only, evening/weekend, 100% online, blended/hybrid learning. *Faculty:* 14 part-time/adjunct (8 women). *Students:* 69 full-time (49 women), 48 part-time (42 women); includes 45 minority (38 Black or African American, non-Hispanic/Latino; 5 Hispanic/Latino; 2 Two or more races, non-Hispanic/Latino), 5 international. Average age 39. 63 applicants, 60% accepted, 29 enrolled. In 2018, 34 master's awarded. *Degree requirements:* For master's, thesis optional. *Entrance requirements:* For master's, 2 letters of recommendation, minimum GPA of 3.0 during last 60 hours, resume, statement of intent. Additional exam requirements/recommendations for international students: Required—TOEFL (minimum score 550 paper-based; 79 iBT). *Application deadline:* Applications are processed on a rolling basis. Application fee: $0. Electronic applications accepted. *Expenses:* Contact institution. *Financial support:* In 2018–19, 12 students received support. Unspecified assistantships available. Support available to part-time students. Financial award applicants required to submit FAFSA. *Unit head:* Sarah Sullivan, Coordinator, 816-501-0429, Fax: 816-941-4650, E-mail: advantage@avila.edu. *Application contact:* Jessica Burson, Graduate Admission Advisor, 816-501-2482, Fax: 816-941-4650, E-mail: advantage@avila.edu.
Website: https://www.avila.edu/mrk/advantage-3

Educational Media/Instructional Technology

Azusa Pacific University, School of Education, Department of Teacher Education, Program in Educational Technology, Azusa, CA 91702-7000. Offers MA. *Program availability:* Part-time, evening/weekend, 100% online. *Degree requirements:* For master's, comprehensive exam, core exam, oral presentation. *Entrance requirements:* For master's, 12 units of course work in education, minimum GPA of 3.0. *Expenses:* Contact institution.

Azusa Pacific University, School of Education, Department of Teacher Education, Program in Learning and Technology, Azusa, CA 91702-7000. Offers MA Ed. *Program availability:* Online learning.

Baldwin Wallace University, Graduate Programs, School of Education, Leadership in Technology for Teaching and Learning Program, Berea, OH 44017-2088. Offers MA Ed. *Program availability:* Part-time, evening/weekend, 100% online. *Students:* 13 full-time (10 women), 15 part-time (9 women); includes 3 minority (2 Black or African American, non-Hispanic/Latino; 1 Two or more races, non-Hispanic/Latino). Average age 32. 11 applicants, 91% accepted, 9 enrolled. In 2018, 3 master's awarded. *Degree requirements:* For master's, capstone project. *Entrance requirements:* For master's, bachelor's degree in field, MAT or minimum GPA of 3.0. Additional exam requirements/recommendations for international students: Required—TOEFL (minimum score 550 paper-based; 79 iBT). *Application deadline:* For fall admission, 8/15 priority date for domestic students; for spring admission, 12/15 priority date for domestic students. Applications are processed on a rolling basis. Application fee: $25. Electronic applications accepted. Application fee is waived when completed online. *Expenses:* Partnership tuition - $545 per credit hour; non-partnership tuition - $721 per credit hour. *Financial support:* Career-related internships or fieldwork available. Financial award applicants required to submit FAFSA. *Faculty research:* No-cost software, online resources for building a classroom learning management system. *Unit head:* Dr. Susan Finelli-Genovese, Coordinator, 440-826-8064, Fax: 440-826-3779, E-mail: sfinelli@bw.edu. *Application contact:* Amiyra Alveranga, Admission Counselor, 440-826-8005, Fax: 440-826-3830, E-mail: aalveran@bw.edu.
Website: http://www.bw.edu/academics/master-of-arts-in-education/maed-technology-leadership/

Ball State University, Graduate School, Teachers College, Department of Educational Studies, Program in Curriculum and Educational Technology, Muncie, IN 47306. Offers MA. *Accreditation:* NCATE. *Program availability:* Part-time, online only, 100% online. *Entrance requirements:* For master's, minimum baccalaureate GPA of 2.75 or 3.0 in latter half of baccalaureate. Additional exam requirements/recommendations for international students: Required—TOEFL (minimum score 550 paper-based; 79 iBT), IELTS (minimum score 6.5). Electronic applications accepted.

Ball State University, Graduate School, Teachers College, Department of Educational Studies, Program in Educational Studies, Muncie, IN 47306. Offers educational studies (PhD), including cultural and educational policy studies, curriculum, educational technology. *Program availability:* Part-time, blended/hybrid learning. *Degree requirements:* For doctorate, thesis/dissertation. *Entrance requirements:* For doctorate, GRE General Test, minimum graduate GPA of 3.2, curriculum vitae, writing sample, three letters of reference. Additional exam requirements/recommendations for international students: Required—TOEFL (minimum score 550 paper-based; 79 iBT), IELTS (minimum score 6.5). Electronic applications accepted. *Faculty research:* Emerging curriculum trends, secondary teacher preparation, issues of equity and social justice in education, teacher technology integration, teaching for transformative understanding, teacher leadership, history of educational policy and practices, ethics and education.

Barry University, School of Education, Graduate Certificate Programs, Miami Shores, FL 33161-6695. Offers advanced teaching and learning with technology (Certificate); distance education (Certificate); higher education technology integration (Certificate); human resources: not for profit and religious organizations (Certificate); K-12 technology integration (Certificate).

Barry University, School of Education, Program in Educational Technology Applications, Miami Shores, FL 33161-6695. Offers educational computing and technology (MS, Ed S). *Program availability:* Part-time, evening/weekend, online learning. *Degree requirements:* For master's and Ed S, comprehensive exam. *Entrance requirements:* For master's, GRE General Test or MAT, minimum GPA of 3.0; for Ed S, GRE General Test, minimum GPA of 3.0.

Barry University, School of Education, Program in Leadership and Education, Miami Shores, FL 33161-6695. Offers educational technology (PhD); exceptional student education (PhD); higher education administration (PhD); human resource development (PhD); leadership (PhD). *Program availability:* Part-time, evening/weekend. *Degree requirements:* For doctorate, thesis/dissertation. *Entrance requirements:* For doctorate, GRE General Test, minimum GPA of 3.25. Electronic applications accepted.

Barry University, School of Education, Program in Technology and TESOL, Miami Shores, FL 33161-6695. Offers MS, Ed S.

Bay Path University, Program in Higher Education Administration, Longmeadow, MA 01106-2292. Offers enrollment management (MS); general administration (MS); institutional advancement (MS); online teaching and program administration (MS). *Program availability:* Part-time, online only, 100% online. *Students:* 2 full-time (both women), 34 part-time (25 women); includes 11 minority (6 Black or African American, non-Hispanic/Latino; 1 Asian, non-Hispanic/Latino; 3 Hispanic/Latino; 1 Two or more races, non-Hispanic/Latino). Average age 34. *Entrance requirements:* For master's, completed application; official undergraduate and graduate transcripts (a GPA of 3.0 or higher is preferred); original essay of at least 250 words on the topic: "Why the MS in Higher Education Administration is important to my personal and professional goals"; current resume; 2 recommendations. *Application deadline:* Applications are processed on a rolling basis. Electronic applications accepted. Application fee is waived when completed online. *Expenses:* Contact institution. *Financial support:* Unspecified assistantships available. Financial award applicants required to submit FAFSA. *Unit head:* Dr. Lauren Way, Program Director, 413-565-1193, E-mail: lway@baypath.edu. *Application contact:* Jennifer Palma, Director of Graduate Admissions, 413-565-1181, Fax: 413-565-1250, E-mail: jpalma@baypath.edu.
Website: https://www.baypath.edu/academics/graduate-programs/higher-education-administration-ms/

Bellevue University, Graduate School, College of Professional Studies, Bellevue, NE 68005-3098. Offers instructional design and development (MS); justice administration and criminal management (MS); leadership (MA); organizational performance (MS); public administration (MPA); security management (MS).

Bloomsburg University of Pennsylvania, School of Graduate Studies, College of Science and Technology, Department of Instructional Technology, Bloomsburg, PA 17815-1301. Offers corporate instructional technology (MS); eLearning developer (Certificate). *Program availability:* Online learning. *Degree requirements:* For master's, thesis optional. *Entrance requirements:* For master's, minimum QPA of 2.8, 3 letters of recommendation, personal statement. Additional exam requirements/recommendations for international students: Required—TOEFL (minimum score 550 paper-based), IELTS. Electronic applications accepted.

Boise State University, College of Education, Department of Educational Technology, Boise, ID 83725-0399. Offers educational technology (MET, MS, Ed D); online teaching (Graduate Certificate); school technology coordination (Graduate Certificate); technology integration (Graduate Certificate). *Accreditation:* NCATE. *Program availability:* Part-time, 100% online, blended/hybrid learning. Terminal master's awarded for partial completion of doctoral program. *Degree requirements:* For master's, thesis optional; for doctorate, thesis/dissertation. *Entrance requirements:* For master's, minimum GPA of 3.0; for doctorate, GRE General Test. Additional exam requirements/recommendations for international students: Required—TOEFL (minimum score 550 paper-based; 80 iBT), IELTS (minimum score 6). Electronic applications accepted.

Bowling Green State University, Graduate College, College of Education and Human Development, School of Teaching and Learning, Program in Classroom Technology, Bowling Green, OH 43403. Offers M Ed. *Accreditation:* NCATE. *Program availability:* Part-time, evening/weekend. *Degree requirements:* For master's, thesis or alternative. *Entrance requirements:* For master's, GRE General Test. Additional exam requirements/recommendations for international students: Required—TOEFL. Electronic applications accepted.

Brandman University, School of Education, Irvine, CA 92618. Offers curriculum and instruction (MAE); educational administration (MAE); educational leadership (MAE); educational leadership and administration (MA); elementary education (MAT); instructional technology: teaching the 21st century learner (MAE); leadership in early childhood education (MAE); organizational leadership (Ed D); school counseling (MA); secondary education (MAT); special education (MA); teaching and learning (MAE).

Bridgewater State University, College of Graduate Studies, College of Education and Allied Studies, Department of Secondary Education and Professional Programs, Program in Instructional Technology, Bridgewater, MA 02325. Offers M Ed. *Program availability:* Part-time, evening/weekend. *Entrance requirements:* For master's, GRE General Test or Massachusetts Test for Educator Licensure.

Brigham Young University, Graduate Studies, Ira A. Fulton College of Engineering, School of Technology, Provo, UT 84602. Offers construction management (MS); information technology (MS); manufacturing engineering technology (MS); technology and engineering education (MS). *Faculty:* 30 full-time (1 woman), 2 part-time/adjunct (0 women). *Students:* 30 full-time (4 women); includes 6 minority (1 Asian, non-Hispanic/Latino; 1 Hispanic/Latino; 1 Native Hawaiian or other Pacific Islander, non-Hispanic/Latino; 3 Two or more races, non-Hispanic/Latino), 2 international. Average age 28. 14 applicants, 79% accepted, 11 enrolled. In 2018, 29 master's awarded. *Degree requirements:* For master's, thesis. *Entrance requirements:* For master's, GRE General Test; GMAT or GRE (for construction management emphasis), Minimum GPA of 3.0 in last 60 hours of course work. Additional exam requirements/recommendations for international students: Required—TOEFL (minimum score 580 paper-based; 85 iBT). *Application deadline:* For fall admission, 2/15 for domestic and international students; for winter admission, 9/10 for domestic and international students; for spring admission, 2/15 for domestic and international students; for summer admission, 2/15 for domestic and international students. Application fee: $50. Electronic applications accepted. *Financial support:* In 2018–19, 28 students received support, including 9 research assistantships (averaging $3,496 per year), 11 teaching assistantships (averaging $4,755 per year); scholarships/grants also available. Financial award application deadline: 1/15; financial award applicants required to submit FAFSA. *Faculty research:* Information assurance and security, HEI and databases, manufacturing materials, processes and systems, innovation in construction management scheduling and delivery methods. *Total annual research expenditures:* $67,118. *Unit head:* Dr. Barry M. Lunt, Director, 801-422-6300, Fax: 801-422-0490, E-mail: blunt@byu.edu. *Application contact:* Clifton Farnsworth, Graduate Coordinator, 801-422-6494, Fax: 801-422-0490, E-mail: clifton_farnsworth@byu.edu.
Website: http://www.et.byu.edu/sot/

Buffalo State College, State University of New York, The Graduate School, School of Education, Department of Career and Technical Education, Buffalo, NY 14222-1095. Offers business and marketing education (MS Ed); career and technical education (MS Ed); technology education (MS Ed). *Accreditation:* NCATE. *Program availability:* Part-time, evening/weekend. *Degree requirements:* For master's, thesis or project. *Entrance requirements:* For master's, minimum GPA of 2.5 in last 60 hours, New York teaching certificate. Additional exam requirements/recommendations for international students: Required—TOEFL (minimum score 550 paper-based).

California Baptist University, Program in Education, Riverside, CA 92504-3206. Offers educational leadership (MS); educational leadership for faith-based institutions (MS); educational leadership for public institutions (MS); educational technology (MS); instructional computer applications (MS); international education (MS); leadership and adult learning (MS); leadership and organizational studies (MS); online teaching and learning (MS); reading (MS); science education (MA); special education in mild/moderate disabilities (MS); special education in moderate/severe disabilities (MS); teacher leadership (MS); teaching (MS); teaching and learning (MS). *Program availability:* Part-time, evening/weekend, 100% online, blended/hybrid learning. *Faculty:* 26 full-time (13 women), 28 part-time/adjunct (21 women). *Students:* 201 full-time (164 women), 265 part-time (209 women); includes 226 minority (23 Black or African American, non-Hispanic/Latino; 4 American Indian or Alaska Native, non-Hispanic/Latino; 7 Asian, non-Hispanic/Latino; 169 Hispanic/Latino; 6 Native Hawaiian or other Pacific Islander, non-Hispanic/Latino; 17 Two or more races, non-Hispanic/Latino), 2 international. Average age 39. 145 applicants, 97% accepted, 141 enrolled. In 2018, 253 master's awarded. *Degree requirements:* For master's, comprehensive exam, project, or thesis. *Entrance requirements:* For master's, minimum undergraduate GPA of 2.75; 500-word essay; three letters of recommendation; two prerequisite courses completed with minimum C grade. Additional exam requirements/recommendations for international students: Required—TOEFL (minimum score 80 iBT). *Application deadline:* For fall admission, 8/1 priority date for domestic students, 7/1 for international students; for spring admission, 12/1 priority date for domestic students, 11/1 for international students. Applications are processed on a rolling basis. Application fee: $45. Electronic applications accepted. *Expenses:* $634 per unit. *Financial support:* In 2018–19, 312 students received support. Federal Work-Study and scholarships/grants available. Financial award applicants required to submit CSS PROFILE or FAFSA. *Faculty research:* Leadership development, complexity theory, faith and learning, special education, social and philosophical contexts of education. *Unit head:* Dr. Robin Duncan, Dean, School of Education, 951-552-8948, E-mail: rduncan@calbaptist.edu. *Application contact:* Dr. Shari Farris, Program Director, Online MS in Education, 951-343-2455, E-mail: sfarris@calbaptist.edu.
Website: http://www.calbaptist.edu/mastersined/

California State University, East Bay, Office of Graduate Studies, College of Education and Allied Studies, Department of Teacher Education, Hayward, CA 94542-3000. Offers education (MS), including curriculum, early childhood education, educational technology and leadership, reading instruction. *Program availability:* Online learning. *Degree requirements:* For master's, project or thesis. *Entrance requirements:* For master's, minimum GPA of 3.0 in field, 2.5 overall; teaching experience; baccalaureate degree; 3 letters of recommendation. Additional exam requirements/recommendations for international students: Required—TOEFL (minimum score 550 paper-based), IELTS. Electronic applications accepted. *Faculty research:* Online, pedagogy, writing, learning, teaching.

California State University, Fullerton, Graduate Studies, College of Education, Department of Elementary and Bilingual Education, Fullerton, CA 92831-3599. Offers bilingual/bicultural education (MS); educational technology (MS); elementary curriculum and instruction (MS). *Accreditation:* NCATE. *Program availability:* Part-time. *Degree requirements:* For master's, comprehensive exam, project or thesis. *Entrance requirements:* For master's, minimum GPA of 2.5, teaching certificate. *Faculty research:* Teacher training and tracking, model for improvement of teaching.

California State University, Fullerton, Graduate Studies, College of Education, Program in Instructional Design and Technology, Fullerton, CA 92831-3599. Offers MS. *Program availability:* Part-time, online learning.

California State University, Northridge, Graduate Studies, Michael D. Eisner College of Education, Department of Secondary Education, Northridge, CA 91330. Offers educational technology (MA); English education (MA); mathematics education (MA); secondary science education (MA); teaching and learning (MA). *Accreditation:* NCATE. *Program availability:* Part-time. *Degree requirements:* For master's, thesis optional. *Entrance requirements:* For master's, GRE General Test or minimum GPA of 3.0. Additional exam requirements/recommendations for international students: Required—TOEFL.

California State University, Sacramento, College of Education, Graduate and Professional Studies in Education, Sacramento, CA 95819. Offers behavioral science and gender equity (MA); child development (MA); counseling (MS); curriculum and instruction (MA); education (Ed D), including K-12 and community college; education leadership and policy studies (MA), including higher education, PreK-12; education specialist (Ed S), including school psychology; educational technology (MA); language and literacy (MA); multicultural education (MA); school psychology (MA); special education (MA); workforce development advocacy (MA). *Program availability:* Part-time, evening/weekend, blended/hybrid learning. *Degree requirements:* For master's, thesis or project; writing proficiency exam; for doctorate, thesis/dissertation. *Entrance requirements:* For master's and doctorate, GRE. Additional exam requirements/recommendations for international students: Required—TOEFL (minimum score 550 paper-based; 80 iBT); Recommended—IELTS (minimum score 7), TSE. Electronic applications accepted. *Expenses:* Contact institution.

California State University, Stanislaus, College of Education, Kinesiology and Social Work, MA Program in Education, Turlock, CA 95382. Offers curriculum and instruction (MA), including education technology, elementary education, multilingual education, physical education, reading, secondary education, special education; school administration (MA); school counseling (MA). *Program availability:* Part-time, evening/weekend. *Degree requirements:* For master's, comprehensive exam (for some programs), thesis (for some programs). *Entrance requirements:* For master's, MAT, GRE, or CBEST (varies by concentration), 3 letters of recommendation, personal statement. Additional exam requirements/recommendations for international students: Required—TOEFL (minimum score 550 paper-based). Electronic applications accepted. *Faculty research:* Children's perspectives on historical events, method elementary schools dual language education, K-12 reading programs.

Cambridge College, School of Education, Boston, MA 02129. Offers autism specialist (M Ed); autism/behavior analyst (M Ed); behavior analyst (Post-Master's Certificate); curriculum and instruction (CAGS); early childhood teacher (M Ed); educational leadership (M Ed, Ed D); elementary teacher (M Ed); English as a second language (M Ed, Certificate); general science (M Ed); health education (Post-Master's Certificate); interdisciplinary studies (M Ed); library teacher (M Ed); mathematics education (M Ed); mathematics specialist (Certificate); school administration (M Ed, CAGS); school nurse education (M Ed); teacher of students with moderate disabilities (M Ed); teaching skills and methodologies (M Ed). *Program availability:* Part-time, evening/weekend, online learning. *Degree requirements:* For master's, thesis, internship/practicum (licensure program only); for doctorate, thesis/dissertation; for other advanced degree, thesis. *Entrance requirements:* For master's, interview, resume, documentation of licensure, 2 professional references; for doctorate, official transcripts, interview, resume, written personal statement/essay, portfolio of scholarly and professional work, 2 professional references, health insurance, immunizations form; for other advanced degree, official transcripts, interview, resume, written personal statement/essay, 2 professional references, health insurance, immunizations form. Additional exam requirements/recommendations for international students: Required—TOEFL (minimum score 550 paper-based; 79 iBT), Michigan English Language Assessment Battery (minimum score 85); Recommended—IELTS (minimum score 6). *Application deadline:* Applications are processed on a rolling basis. Application fee: $30. Electronic applications accepted. *Expenses:* Contact institution. *Financial support:* Career-related internships or fieldwork, Federal Work-Study, and scholarships/grants available. Financial award applicants required to submit FAFSA. *Faculty research:* Adult education, accelerated learning, mathematics education, brain compatible learning, special education and law. *Unit head:* Dr. Mary Garrity, Interim Dean, 617-873-0168, E-mail: mary.garrity@cambridgecollege.edu. *Application contact:* Salvadore Liberto, Interim Assistant Vice President of Enrollment, 800-877-4723, E-mail: admissions@cambridgecollege.edu.
Website: https://www.cambridgecollege.edu/school/school-education

Canisius College, Graduate Division, School of Education and Human Services, Department of Graduate Education and Leadership, Buffalo, NY 14208-1098. Offers business and marketing education (MS Ed); college student personnel (MS Ed); deaf education (MS Ed); deaf/adolescent education, grades 7-12 (MS Ed); deaf/childhood education, grades 1-6 (MS Ed); differentiated instruction (MS Ed); education administration (MS); educational administration (MS Ed); educational technologies (Certificate); gifted education extension (Certificate); literacy (MS Ed); reading (Certificate); school building leadership (MS Ed, Certificate); school district leadership (Certificate); teacher leader (Certificate); TESOL (MS Ed). *Accreditation:* NCATE. *Program availability:* Part-time, evening/weekend, 100% online, blended/hybrid learning. *Faculty:* 5 full-time (all women), 21 part-time/adjunct (16 women). *Students:* 79 full-time (66 women), 135 part-time (106 women); includes 45 minority (27 Black or African American, non-Hispanic/Latino; 1 American Indian or Alaska Native, non-Hispanic/Latino; 3 Asian, non-Hispanic/Latino; 9 Hispanic/Latino; 5 Two or more races, non-Hispanic/Latino), 1 international. Average age 32. 83 applicants, 96% accepted, 74 enrolled. In 2018, 94 master's, 47 other advanced degrees awarded. *Entrance requirements:* For master's, GRE (if cumulative GPA less than 2.7), transcripts, two letters of recommendation. Additional exam requirements/recommendations for international students: Required—TOEFL (minimum score 550 paper-based, 79 iBT), IELTS (minimum score 6.5), or CAEL (minimum score 70). *Application deadline:* Applications are processed on a rolling basis. Application fee: $0. Electronic applications accepted. *Expenses: Tuition:* Part-time $820 per credit hour. *Required fees:* $25 per semester. One-time fee: $65 part-time. Tuition and fees vary according to program. *Financial support:* In 2018–19, 206 students received support. Career-related internships or fieldwork, Federal Work-Study, scholarships/grants, tuition waivers (partial), and unspecified assistantships available. Support available to part-time students. Financial award application deadline: 4/30; financial award applicants required to submit FAFSA. *Faculty research:* Asperger's disease, autism, private higher education, reading strategies. *Unit head:* Dr. Anne Marie Tryjankowski, Chair/Associate Professor of Graduate Education and Leadership, 716-888-3715, Fax: 716-888-3142, E-mail: tryjanka@canisius.edu. *Application contact:* Dr. Anne Marie Tryjankowski, Chair/Associate Professor of Graduate Education and Leadership, 716-888-3715, Fax: 716-888-3142, E-mail: tryjanka@canisius.edu.

Capella University, School of Education, Doctoral Programs in Education, Minneapolis, MN 55402. Offers curriculum and instruction (PhD); educational leadership and management (Ed D); instructional design for online learning (PhD); K-12 studies in education (PhD); leadership for higher education (PhD); leadership in educational administration (PhD); postsecondary and adult education (PhD); professional studies in education (PhD); reading and literacy (Ed D); special education leadership (PhD); training and performance improvement (PhD).

Capella University, School of Education, Master's Programs in Education, Minneapolis, MN 55402. Offers adult education (MS); curriculum and instruction (MS); early childhood education (MS); enrollment management (MS); higher education leadership and management (MS); instructional design for online learning (MS); integrative studies (MS); K-12 studies in education (MS); leadership in educational administration (MS); reading and literacy (MS); special education teaching (MS).

Caribbean University, Graduate School, Bayamón, PR 00960-0493. Offers administration and supervision (MA Ed); criminal justice (MA); curriculum and instruction (MA Ed, PhD), including elementary education (MA Ed), English education (MA Ed), history education (MA Ed), mathematics education (MA Ed), primary education (MA Ed), science education (MA Ed), Spanish education (MA Ed); educational technology in instructional systems (MA Ed); gerontology (MSN); human resources (MBA); museology, archiving and art history (MA Ed); neonatal pediatrics (MSN); physical education (MA Ed); special education (MA Ed). *Entrance requirements:* For master's, interview, minimum GPA of 2.5.

Central Michigan University, Central Michigan University Global Campus, Program in Education, Mount Pleasant, MI 48859. Offers college teaching (Graduate Certificate); community college (MA); curriculum and instruction (MA); educational technology (MA, DET); reading and literacy K-12 (MA); school principalship (MA), including charter school leadership; training and development (MA). *Accreditation:* TEAC. *Program availability:* Part-time, evening/weekend. *Entrance requirements:* For master's, minimum GPA of 2.7 in major. Additional exam requirements/recommendations for international students: Required—TOEFL. Electronic applications accepted.

Central Michigan University, College of Graduate Studies, College of Education and Human Services, Department of Educational Leadership, Mount Pleasant, MI 48859. Offers educational leadership (Ed D), including educational technology (Ed D, Ed S), higher education leadership, K-12 curriculum, K-12 leadership; general educational administration (Ed S), including administrative leadership K-12, educational technology (Ed D, Ed S), higher education administration, instructional leadership K-12; school principalship (MA), including charter school leadership, site-based leadership; student affairs administration (MA); teacher leadership (MA). *Program availability:* Part-time, evening/weekend. *Degree requirements:* For master's and Ed S, thesis or alternative; for doctorate, thesis/dissertation. *Entrance requirements:* For doctorate, GRE or MAT, master's degree, minimum GPA of 3.5, 3 years of professional education experience. Electronic applications accepted. *Faculty research:* Elementary administration, secondary administration, student achievement, in-service training, internships in administration.

Central Michigan University, College of Graduate Studies, College of Education and Human Services, Department of Teacher Education and Professional Development, Mount Pleasant, MI 48859. Offers educational technology (MA, Graduate Certificate); elementary education (MA), including classroom teaching, early childhood; reading and literacy K-12 (MA); secondary education (MA). *Program availability:* Part-time, evening/weekend. *Degree requirements:* For master's, thesis or alternative. Electronic applications accepted. *Faculty research:* Integrating literacy across the curriculum, science teaching and aesthetic learning in science, diversity education, educational technology, educational psychology and child development.

Chestnut Hill College, School of Graduate Studies, Program in Instructional Technology, Philadelphia, PA 19118-2693. Offers instructional technology (MS, CAS), including instructional design and e-learning, instructional design and e-learning with instructional technology specialist certification preparation. *Program availability:* Part-time, evening/weekend. *Degree requirements:* For master's, special project/internship. *Entrance requirements:* For master's, GRE General Test or MAT, letters of recommendation, writing sample. Additional exam requirements/recommendations for international students: Required—TOEFL (minimum score 500 paper-based), IELTS (minimum score 6.0), or TWE (minimum score 22). Electronic applications accepted. *Expenses:* Contact institution. *Faculty research:* Instructional design, learning management systems and related technologies, video as a teaching and learning tool, Web 2.0 technologies and virtual worlds as a learning tool, utilization of laptops and iPads in the classroom.

Clarion University of Pennsylvania, College of Business Administration and Information Sciences, MSLS Program in Information and Library Science, Clarion, PA 16214. Offers information and library science (MSLS); school library media (MSLS). *Accreditation:* ALA. *Program availability:* Part-time, evening/weekend, online only, 100% online. *Faculty:* 5 full-time (4 women), 5 part-time/adjunct (3 women). *Students:* 117 full-time (97 women), 247 part-time (206 women); includes 55 minority (23 Black or African American, non-Hispanic/Latino; 7 Asian, non-Hispanic/Latino; 19 Hispanic/Latino; 6 Two or more races, non-Hispanic/Latino), 2 international. Average age 33. 239 applicants, 62% accepted, 139 enrolled. In 2018, 129 master's awarded. *Entrance requirements:* For master's, Overall GPA for the bacc degree of at least 3.00 on a 4.00 scale; Or a 3.00 GPA for the last 60 credits of the bacc degree with an overall QPA of at least 2.75; or a 2.75 to 2.99 overall GPA for the bacc degree with a score of at least 412 on the MAT or score of at least 300 on the GRE; or a graduate degree with at least a GPA of 3.00. Additional exam requirements/recommendations for international students: Required—TOEFL (minimum score 80 iBT), International students are required to achieve a minimum score of 213 computer-based or 80 internet-based on the TOEFL MSLS with Pennsylvania. *Application deadline:* For fall admission, 8/1 priority date for domestic students, 7/15 priority date for international students; for winter admission, 11/1 priority date for domestic students; for spring admission, 12/1 priority date for domestic students, 11/15 priority date for international students; for summer admission, 4/1 priority date for domestic students. Applications are processed on a rolling basis. Application fee: $40. Electronic applications accepted. *Expenses:* $675.60 per credit including fees in state. *Financial support:* Career-related internships or fieldwork, institutionally sponsored loans, scholarships/grants, and unspecified assistantships available. Financial award application deadline: 3/1; financial award applicants required to submit FAFSA. *Unit head:* Dr. Linda Lillard, Department Chair, 814-393-2383, E-mail: llillard@clarion.edu. *Application contact:* Susan Staub, Graduate Admissions Counselor, 814-393-2337, Fax: 814-393-2722, E-mail: gradstudies@clarion.edu.
Website: http://www.clarion.edu/academics/colleges-and-schools/college-of-business-administration-and-information-sciences/library-science/

Cleveland State University, College of Graduate Studies, College of Education and Human Services, Program in Urban Education, Specialization in Learning and Development, Cleveland, OH 44115. Offers PhD. *Program availability:* Part-time.

Faculty: 17 full-time (9 women). *Students:* 5 full-time (all women), 16 part-time (13 women); includes 10 minority (9 Black or African American, non-Hispanic/Latino; 1 Asian, non-Hispanic/Latino), 1 international. Average age 47. 18 applicants, 28% accepted. In 2018, 1 doctorate awarded. *Entrance requirements:* For doctorate, GRE General Test (minimum score of 297 for combined Verbal and Quantitative exams, 4.0 preferred for Analytical Writing), minimum graduate GPA of 3.25 in educational psychology, school psychology and/or special education; curriculum vitae or resume; personal statement; 2 letters of recommendation. Additional exam requirements/recommendations for international students: Required—TOEFL (minimum score 550 paper-based; 78 iBT), IELTS (minimum score 6). Application fee: $40. Electronic applications accepted. *Expenses:* Tuition, state resident: full-time $7232.55; part-time $6676 per credit hour. Tuition, nonresident: full-time $12,375. *International tuition:* $18,914 full-time. *Required fees:* $80; $80 $40. Tuition and fees vary according to program. *Financial support:* In 2018–19, 5 students received support. Research assistantships, teaching assistantships, and tuition waivers available. Support available to part-time students. Financial award application deadline: 4/1; financial award applicants required to submit FAFSA. *Faculty research:* Implications of human variability to instruction service delivery in educational and social agencies. *Unit head:* Dr. Graham Stead, Director, Doctoral Studies, 216-875-9869, E-mail: g.b.stead@csuohio.edu. *Application contact:* Rita M. Grabowski, Administrative Coordinator, 216-687-4697, Fax: 216-875-9697, E-mail: r.grabowski@csuohio.edu.
Website: http://www.csuohio.edu/cehs/casal/programs-0

Coastal Carolina University, Spadoni College of Education, Conway, SC 29528-6054. Offers education (MAT); educational leadership (M Ed, Ed S); English for speakers of other languages (Certificate); instructional technology (M Ed, Ed S); language, literacy and culture (M Ed); learning and teaching (M Ed); online teaching and training (Certificate); special education (M Ed). *Accreditation:* NCATE. *Program availability:* Part-time, evening/weekend, 100% online, blended/hybrid learning. *Degree requirements:* For master's and other advanced degree, comprehensive exam. *Entrance requirements:* For master's, GRE, GMAT, 2 letters of recommendation, evidence of teacher certification, official transcripts; for other advanced degree, official transcripts, 3 letters of reference, master's degree in related field with minimum overall cumulative GPA of 3.0. Additional exam requirements/recommendations for international students: Required—TOEFL (minimum score 550 paper-based; 79 iBT), IELTS (minimum score 6.5). Electronic applications accepted.

Coker College, Graduate Programs, Hartsville, SC 29550. Offers college athletic administration (MS); criminal and social justice policy (MS); curriculum and instructional technology (M Ed); literacy studies (M Ed); management and leadership (MS). *Program availability:* Part-time, 100% online. *Faculty:* 15 full-time (7 women), 7 part-time/adjunct (3 women). *Students:* 144 full-time (100 women), 6 part-time (2 women); includes 42 minority (33 Black or African American, non-Hispanic/Latino; 1 Asian, non-Hispanic/Latino; 4 Hispanic/Latino; 4 Two or more races, non-Hispanic/Latino). Average age 33. 120 applicants, 61% accepted, 65 enrolled. In 2018, 92 master's awarded. *Entrance requirements:* For master's, undergraduate overall gpa of 3.0 on 4.0 scale, official transcripts from all undergraduate institutions, 1 page personal statement, resume, 2 professional references. Additionally, for MEd in Literacy Studies: 1 year of teaching in PK-12 and letter of recommendation from principal/assistant principal. *Application deadline:* Applications are processed on a rolling basis. Application fee: $0. Electronic applications accepted. *Financial support:* Unspecified assistantships available. Financial award application deadline: 6/30; financial award applicants required to submit FAFSA. *Unit head:* Dr. Kathryn Flaherty, Dean of Graduate and Professional Programs, 843-857-4227, E-mail: kflaherty@coker.edu. *Application contact:* Lacey Rice-Serafin, Director of Graduate Programs, 843-857-4128, E-mail: lriceserafin@coker.edu.

College of Mount Saint Vincent, School of Professional and Graduate Studies, Department of Teacher Education, Riverdale, NY 10471-1093. Offers instructional technology and global perspectives (Certificate); middle level education (Certificate); multicultural studies (Certificate); teaching English to speakers of other languages (MS Ed); urban and multicultural education (MS Ed). *Accreditation:* TEAC. *Program availability:* Part-time. *Degree requirements:* For master's, comprehensive exam. *Entrance requirements:* For master's, interview, New York teaching certificate. Additional exam requirements/recommendations for international students: Required—TOEFL.

Colorado Christian University, Program in Curriculum and Instruction, Lakewood, CO 80226. Offers corporate education (MACI); early childhood educator (MACI); elementary educator (MACI); instructional technology (MACI); master educator (MACI); online course developer (MACI); online teaching and learning (MACI); special education generalist (MACI). *Program availability:* Part-time, evening/weekend. *Degree requirements:* For master's, thesis optional, practicum. *Entrance requirements:* For master's, interviews, letters of recommendation. Additional exam requirements/recommendations for international students: Required—TOEFL. Electronic applications accepted. *Expenses:* Contact institution.

Colorado State University–Pueblo, College of Education, Engineering and Professional Studies, Education Program, Pueblo, CO 81001-4901. Offers art education (M Ed); foreign language education (M Ed); health and physical education (M Ed); instructional technology (M Ed); linguistically diverse education (M Ed); music education (M Ed); special education (M Ed). *Accreditation:* TEAC. *Program availability:* Part-time. *Degree requirements:* For master's, portfolio. *Entrance requirements:* For master's, 3 recommendations, teaching license. Additional exam requirements/recommendations for international students: Required—TOEFL (minimum score 500 paper-based). Electronic applications accepted. *Faculty research:* Portfolio assessment, math education, science education.

Concordia University, College of Education, Portland, OR 97211-6099. Offers administrative leadership (Ed D); career and technical education (M Ed); curriculum and instruction (M Ed), including adolescent literacy, early childhood education, educational technology leadership, English for speakers of other languages, environmental education, health and physical education, mathematics, methods and curriculum, reading interventionist, science, social studies, STEAM education, teacher leadership, the inclusive classroom, trauma and resilience in educational settings; educational administration (M Ed); educational leadership (M Ed); elementary education (MAT); higher education (Ed D); instructional leadership (Ed D); professional leadership, inquiry, and transformation (Ed D); secondary education (MAT); transformational leadership (Ed D). *Program availability:* Part-time, online learning. *Degree requirements:* For master's, comprehensive exam, work samples/portfolio. *Entrance requirements:* For master's, California Basic Educational Skills Test or PRAXIS I, minimum undergraduate GPA of 2.8, graduate 3.0; 2 letters of recommendation. Additional exam requirements/recommendations for international students: Required—TOEFL (minimum score 525 paper-based). Electronic applications accepted. *Faculty research:* Learner-centered classroom, brain-based learning, future of online learning.

Concordia University, School of Graduate Studies, Faculty of Arts and Science, Department of Education, Program in Educational Technology, Montréal, QC H3G 1M8, Canada. Offers MA. *Degree requirements:* For master's, one foreign language, thesis optional, internship. *Faculty research:* Instructional design and tele-education, educational cybernetics and systems analysis, media research and theory development, distance education.

Concordia University, School of Graduate Studies, Faculty of Arts and Science, Department of Education, Program in Instructional Technology, Montréal, QC H3G 1M8, Canada. Offers Diploma. *Entrance requirements:* For degree, BA in related field.

Concordia University Chicago, College of Graduate Studies, Program in Educational Technology, River Forest, IL 60305-1499. Offers curriculum and instruction (MA); leadership (MA). *Program availability:* Online learning.

Concordia University Irvine, School of Education, Irvine, CA 92612-3299. Offers curriculum and instruction (MA); education and preliminary teaching credential (M Ed); educational administration and preliminary administrative services credential (MA); educational technology (MA); school counseling with pupil personnel services credential (MA). *Program availability:* Part-time, evening/weekend, online learning. *Degree requirements:* For master's, action research project. *Entrance requirements:* For master's, California Basic Educational Skills Test, California Subject Examinations for Teachers (M Ed and MA in educational administration and preliminary administrative services credential), official college transcript(s), signed statement of intent, two references, copy of credential. Additional exam requirements/recommendations for international students: Required—TOEFL. Electronic applications accepted. *Expenses:* Contact institution.

Concordia University, St. Paul, College of Education, St. Paul, MN 55104-5494. Offers classroom instruction (MA Ed), including K-12 reading; differentiated instruction (MA Ed); early childhood education (MA Ed); education (Ed D); educational leadership (MA Ed); educational technology (MA Ed, Certificate); K-12 principal licensure (Ed S); special education (MA Ed), including autism spectrum disorder, emotional and behavioral disorders, learning disabilities; superintendent (Ed S); teaching (MAT). *Accreditation:* NCATE. *Program availability:* Part-time, evening/weekend, 100% online, blended/hybrid learning. *Faculty:* 13 full-time (9 women), 82 part-time/adjunct (51 women). *Students:* 979 full-time (748 women), 40 part-time (28 women); includes 124 minority (49 Black or African American, non-Hispanic/Latino; 6 American Indian or Alaska Native, non-Hispanic/Latino; 34 Asian, non-Hispanic/Latino; 22 Hispanic/Latino; 1 Native Hawaiian or other Pacific Islander, non-Hispanic/Latino; 12 Two or more races, non-Hispanic/Latino), 11 international. Average age 34. 423 applicants, 99% accepted, 335 enrolled. In 2018, 358 master's, 3 doctorates, 119 other advanced degrees awarded. *Degree requirements:* For master's, thesis (for some programs); for doctorate, thesis/dissertation, capstone projects; for other advanced degree, e-folio review of competencies. *Entrance requirements:* For master's, official transcripts from regionally-accredited institution stating the conferral of a bachelor's degree with minimum cumulative GPA of 3.0; personal statement; professional resume; practitioner in field through work or volunteerism; resume; for doctorate, minimum master's or specialist degree GPA of 3.25; transcript; writing sample; three letters of recommendation; current resume; on-campus interview; for other advanced degree, minimum master's or specialist degree GPA of 3.25; transcript; statement covering employment history and long-term academic and professional goals; two letters of recommendation; interview with program director. Additional exam requirements/recommendations for international students: Recommended—TOEFL (minimum score 547 paper-based; 78 iBT), IELTS (minimum score 6). *Application deadline:* For fall admission, 8/1 for domestic and international students; for spring admission, 12/1 for domestic and international students; for summer admission, 5/1 for domestic and international students. Applications are processed on a rolling basis. Application fee: $0. Electronic applications accepted. *Expenses:* $395 per credit for 30 credits (for MA programs), $440 per credit for 42 credits (for MAT), $415 per credit for 30 credits (for EdS), $615 per credit for 64 credits (for EdD). *Financial support:* In 2018–19, 163 students received support. Federal Work-Study, scholarships/grants, and unspecified assistantships available. Financial award applicants required to submit FAFSA. *Faculty research:* School design for innovative learning practices, equine-assisted instruction, best practices for leadership in early childhood education, mental health needs in K-12 focusing on children of incarcerated parents, competency-based education. *Unit head:* Lonn Maly, Dean, 651-641-8203, E-mail: maly@csp.edu. *Application contact:* Amber Faletti, Director of Enrollment Management, 651-641-8838, Fax: 651-603-6320, E-mail: faletti@csp.edu.

Dakota State University, College of Education, Madison, SD 57042-1799. Offers educational technology (MSET). *Accreditation:* NCATE. *Program availability:* Part-time-only, evening/weekend, online only, 100% online. *Faculty:* 4 full-time (0 women). *Students:* 20 part-time (15 women); includes 1 minority (American Indian or Alaska Native, non-Hispanic/Latino). Average age 34. 12 applicants, 100% accepted, 10 enrolled. In 2018, 8 master's awarded. *Degree requirements:* For master's, thesis optional, portfolio. *Entrance requirements:* For master's, GRE General Test, demonstration of technology skills, minimum GPA of 2.7. *Application deadline:* For fall admission, 6/15 for domestic students; for spring admission, 11/15 for domestic students; for summer admission, 4/15 for domestic students. Applications are processed on a rolling basis. Application fee: $35. Electronic applications accepted. *Expenses: Tuition, area resident:* Full-time $7666. Tuition, state resident: full-time $7666. Tuition, nonresident: full-time $14,311. *International tuition:* $14,311 full-time. *Required fees:* $953. *Financial support:* In 2018–19, 3 students received support. Career-related internships or fieldwork, Federal Work-Study, scholarships/grants, unspecified assistantships, and administrative assistantships available. Support available to part-time students. Financial award applicants required to submit FAFSA. *Faculty research:* Educational technology evaluation, computer-supported collaborative learning, cognitive theory and visual representation of the effects of ubiquitous wireless computing on student learning and productivity, accessible learning, pedagogies for exceptional children. *Unit head:* Dr. Crystal Pauli, Dean of College of Education, 605-256-5799. *Application contact:* Dr. Kevin Smith, MSET Program Coordinator, 605-256-5175, Fax: 605-256-7300, E-mail: kevin.smith@dsu.edu.
Website: http://dsu.edu/graduate-students/mset

Dallas Baptist University, Dorothy M. Bush College of Education, Program in Curriculum and Instruction, Dallas, TX 75211-9299. Offers Christian school administration (M Ed); distance learning (M Ed); English as a second language (M Ed); instructional technology (M Ed); professional life coaching (M Ed); special education (M Ed); supervision (M Ed). *Program availability:* Part-time, evening/weekend, online learning. *Application deadline:* Applications are processed on a rolling basis. Application fee: $25. Electronic applications accepted. Application fee is waived when completed online. *Expenses: Tuition:* Full-time $17,262; part-time $959 per credit hour. *Required fees:* $1000; $500 per semester. Tuition and fees vary according to course load and degree level. *Unit head:* Dr. Neil Dugger, Dean, 214-333-5202, E-mail: neil@dbu.edu. *Application contact:* Karla Hagan, Program Director, 214-333-5831, E-mail: karla@dbu.edu.
Website: http://www3.dbu.edu/graduate/curriculum_instruction.asp

Delaware Valley University, Program in Educational Leadership, Doylestown, PA 18901-2697. Offers instruction, curriculum and technology (MS); school administration and leadership (MS). *Program availability:* Part-time, evening/weekend. *Entrance requirements:* For master's, minimum undergraduate GPA of 3.0.

DeSales University, Division of Liberal Arts and Social Sciences, Center Valley, PA 18034-9568. Offers criminal justice (MCJ); digital forensics (MCJ, Postbaccalaureate Certificate); education (M Ed), including instructional technology, secondary education, special education, teaching English to speakers of other languages; investigative forensics (MCJ, Postbaccalaureate Certificate). *Program availability:* Part-time, 100% online, blended/hybrid learning. *Entrance requirements:* For master's, bachelor's degree from accredited institution, minimum undergraduate GPA of 3.0, personal statement showing potential of graduate work, three letters of recommendation, professional goal statement. Additional exam requirements/recommendations for international students: Required—TOEFL. Electronic applications accepted.

DeVry University–Folsom Campus, Graduate Programs, Folsom, CA 95630. Offers accounting (M Acc); accounting and financial management (MAFM); business administration (MBA); curriculum leadership (M Ed); educational leadership (M Ed); educational technology (M Ed); higher education leadership (M Ed); human resource management (MHRM); information systems management (MISM); network and communications management (MNCM); project management (MPM); public administration (MPA).

Drexel University, Goodwin College of Professional Studies, School of Education, Philadelphia, PA 19104-2875. Offers applied behavior analysis (MS); creativity and innovation (MS); education improvement and transformation (MS); educational administration (MS); educational leadership and management (Ed D); educational leadership development and learning technologies (PhD); global and international education (MS); higher education (MS); human resources development (MS); learning technologies (MS); mathematics, learning and teaching (MS); special education (MS); teaching, learning and curriculum (MS). *Program availability:* Part-time, evening/weekend, online learning. *Degree requirements:* For doctorate, thesis/dissertation. *Entrance requirements:* For doctorate, GRE or GMAT. Additional exam requirements/recommendations for international students: Required—TOEFL, IELTS. Electronic applications accepted. Application fee is waived when completed online. *Expenses:* Contact institution. *Faculty research:* Leadership development, mathematics education, literacy, autism, educational technology.

Drexel University, Goodwin College of Professional Studies, School of Technology and Professional Studies, Philadelphia, PA 19104-2875. Offers construction management (MS); creativity and innovation (MS); engineering technology (MS); food science (MS); hospitality management (MS); professional studies: creativity studies (MS); professional studies: e-learning leadership (MS); professional studies: homeland security management (MS); project management (MS); property management (MS); sport management (MS). *Program availability:* Part-time, evening/weekend. *Entrance requirements:* Additional exam requirements/recommendations for international students: Required—TOEFL, IELTS. Electronic applications accepted. Application fee is waived when completed online.

Drury University, Master in Education Program, Springfield, MO 65802. Offers curriculum and instruction (M Ed), including elementary education, middle school education, secondary education; instructional leadership (M Ed); instructional technology (M Ed); integrated learning (M Ed); special education (M Ed); special reading (M Ed). *Accreditation:* NCATE. *Program availability:* Part-time, evening/weekend, 100% online, blended/hybrid learning. *Faculty:* 10 full-time (6 women), 8 part-time/adjunct (6 women). *Students:* 167 full-time (133 women). Average age 32. 92 applicants, 92% accepted, 69 enrolled. In 2018, 44 master's awarded. *Entrance requirements:* For master's, bachelor's degree with minimum GPA of 2.75. Additional exam requirements/recommendations for international students: Recommended—TOEFL (minimum score 80 iBT), IELTS (minimum score 6.5). *Application deadline:* For fall admission, 8/4 priority date for domestic and international students; for spring admission, 1/5 priority date for domestic and international students; for summer admission, 5/26 priority date for domestic and international students. Applications are processed on a rolling basis. Application fee: $25. Electronic applications accepted. *Expenses:* Tuition is $366 per credit hour. Fees are $7 per credit hour. Most M.Ed. degrees are 33 credit hours. *Financial support:* In 2018–19, 5 students received support. Career-related internships or fieldwork, scholarships/grants, and unspecified assistantships available. Financial award application deadline: 6/30; financial award applicants required to submit FAFSA. *Faculty research:* Instructional technology, autism, diversity, and social justice. *Unit head:* Dr. Asikaa Cosgrove, Director, Master in Education Program, 417-873-7806, E-mail: acosgrov@drury.edu. *Application contact:* Dr. Asikaa Cosgrove, Director, Master in Education Program, 417-873-7806, E-mail: acosgrov@drury.edu. Website: http://www.drury.edu/education-masters

Duquesne University, Graduate School of Liberal Arts, Department of Media, Pittsburgh, PA 15282-0001. Offers MS, Certificate. *Program availability:* Part-time, evening/weekend, blended/hybrid learning. *Faculty:* 9 full-time (2 women), 3 part-time/adjunct (0 women). *Students:* 21 full-time (9 women); includes 2 minority (1 Black or African American, non-Hispanic/Latino; 1 Hispanic/Latino), 7 international. Average age 26. 12 applicants, 92% accepted, 7 enrolled. In 2018, 12 master's awarded. *Entrance requirements:* For master's, portfolio, writing sample. Additional exam requirements/recommendations for international students: Required—TOEFL. *Application deadline:* For fall admission, 8/1 for domestic students, 5/1 for international students; for spring admission, 11/1 for domestic students. Applications are processed on a rolling basis. Application fee: $0. Electronic applications accepted. *Expenses:* Tuition: Full-time $23,112; part-time $1284 per credit. Tuition and fees vary according to program. *Financial support:* In 2018–19, 10 students received support, including 10 teaching assistantships with full tuition reimbursements available (averaging $8,000 per year); Federal Work-Study also available. Support available to part-time students. Financial award application deadline: 5/1. *Unit head:* James Vota, Director, 412-396-1727, E-mail: vota@duq.edu. *Application contact:* Linda Rendulic, Assistant to the Dean, 412-396-6400, Fax: 412-396-5265, E-mail: rendulic@duq.edu. Website: http://www.duq.edu/academics/schools/liberal-arts/graduate-school/programs/media-arts-and-technology

Duquesne University, School of Education, Department of Instruction and Leadership, Program in Instructional Technology, Pittsburgh, PA 15282-0001. Offers MS Ed, Ed D, Post-Master's Certificate. *Program availability:* Part-time, evening/weekend, minimal on-campus study. *Faculty:* 3 full-time (1 woman). *Students:* 52 full-time (39 women), 15 part-time (10 women); includes 7 minority (2 Black or African American, non-Hispanic/Latino; 4 Asian, non-Hispanic/Latino; 1 Hispanic/Latino), 10 international. Average age 36. 39 applicants, 74% accepted, 15 enrolled. In 2018, 8 master's, 7 doctorates awarded. *Entrance requirements:* For master's, bachelor's degree; minimum GPA of 3.0 overall or on most recent 48 credits; for doctorate, GRE, master's degree; letter of interest; three letters of recommendation; electronic portfolio; for Post-Master's Certificate, bachelor's/master's degree. Additional exam requirements/recommendations for international students: Required—TOEFL (minimum score 550 paper-based), IELTS (minimum score 7). *Application deadline:* For fall admission, 9/1 for domestic students; for spring admission, 1/2 for domestic students. Applications are processed on a rolling basis. Application fee: $0. Electronic applications accepted. *Expenses:* Tuition: Full-time $23,112; part-time $1284 per credit. Tuition and fees vary according to program. *Financial support:* In 2018–19, 2 students received support, including 2 teaching assistantships with full and partial tuition reimbursements available (averaging $2,307 per year). Support available to part-time students. Financial award applicants required to submit FAFSA. *Faculty research:* Instructional technology in STEM; computational thinking; drag and drop programming; the advantages of individuals' processing speeds in different learning settings; different cognitive styles of problem solving. *Unit head:* Dr. David Carbonara, Assistant Professor/Director, 412-396-4039, Fax: 412-396-1997, E-mail: carbonara@duq.edu. *Application contact:* Kelly McGinley, Graduate Admissions Assistant, 412-396-1559, Fax: 412-396-5585, E-mail: mcginleyk@duq.edu. Website: http://www.duq.edu/academics/schools/education/graduate-programs/instructional-technology

East Carolina University, Graduate School, College of Education, Department of Mathematics, Science, and Instructional Technology Education, Greenville, NC 27858-4353. Offers distance learning and administration (Certificate); elementary mathematics education (Certificate); instructional technology (MA Ed, MS); mathematics education (MA Ed); science education (MA Ed, MAT); special endorsement in computer education (Certificate). *Program availability:* Part-time, evening/weekend. *Application deadline:* For fall admission, 6/1 priority date for domestic students. *Expenses:* Tuition, area resident: Full-time $4749. Tuition, state resident: full-time $4749. Tuition, nonresident: full-time $17,898. *International tuition:* $17,898 full-time. *Required fees:* $2787. Part-time tuition and fees vary according to course load and program. *Financial support:* Application deadline: 6/1. *Unit head:* Dr. Ron Preston, Director of Students, 252-737-9355, E-mail: prestonr@ecu.edu. *Application contact:* Graduate School Admissions, 252-328-6012, Fax: 252-328-6071, E-mail: gradschool@ecu.edu. Website: http://www.ecu.edu/cs-educ/msite/

East Carolina University, Graduate School, College of Education, Department of Special Education, Foundations, and Research, Greenville, NC 27858-4353. Offers assistive technology (Certificate); autism (Certificate); special education (MA Ed, MAT), including behavioral-emotional disabilities (MA Ed), intellectual disabilities (MA Ed), learning disabilities (MA Ed), low-incidence disabilities (MA Ed). *Program availability:* Part-time, evening/weekend, online learning. *Application deadline:* For fall admission, 6/1 priority date for domestic students. *Expenses:* Tuition, area resident: Full-time $4749. Tuition, state resident: full-time $4749. Tuition, nonresident: full-time $17,898. *International tuition:* $17,898 full-time. *Required fees:* $2787. Part-time tuition and fees vary according to course load and program. *Financial support:* Application deadline: 6/1. *Unit head:* Dr. Guili Zhang, Interim Chair, 252-328-4989, E-mail: zhangg@ecu.edu. *Application contact:* Graduate School Admissions, 252-328-6012, Fax: 252-328-6071, E-mail: gradschool@ecu.edu. Website: http://www.ecu.edu/cs-educ/sefr/index.cfm

Eastern Connecticut State University, School of Education and Professional Studies/Graduate Division, Program in Educational Technology, Willimantic, CT 06226-2295. Offers MS. *Program availability:* Part-time, evening/weekend, 100% online, blended/hybrid learning. *Degree requirements:* For master's, comprehensive exam, thesis or alternative, culminating portfolio. *Entrance requirements:* For master's, minimum GPA of 2.7, bachelor's degree from accredited institution. Additional exam requirements/recommendations for international students: Required—TOEFL (minimum score 550 paper-based; 79 iBT); Recommended—IELTS (minimum score 6). Electronic applications accepted.

Eastern Michigan University, Graduate School, College of Education, Department of Teacher Education, Programs in Curriculum and Instruction, Ypsilanti, MI 48197. Offers advanced teaching and learning (MA); early literacy instruction (Graduate Certificate); instructional leadership (MA); learning, motivation and creativity (Graduate Certificate); literacy coaching (Graduate Certificate); online teaching (Certificate); secondary literacy instruction (Graduate Certificate); urban and diversity education (MA). *Students:* 1 (woman) full-time, 28 part-time (21 women); includes 11 minority (3 Black or African American, non-Hispanic/Latino; 1 Asian, non-Hispanic/Latino; 4 Hispanic/Latino; 3 Two or more races, non-Hispanic/Latino). Average age 31. 7 applicants, 71% accepted, 3 enrolled. In 2018, 5 master's awarded. Application fee: $45. *Application contact:* Dr. Virginia Harder, Graduate Coordinator/Advisor, 734-487-2729, Fax: 734-487-2101, E-mail: vharder1@emich.edu.

Eastern Michigan University, Graduate School, College of Education, Department of Teacher Education, Programs in Learning Technology and Design, Ypsilanti, MI 48197. Offers MA, Graduate Certificate. *Program availability:* Part-time, evening/weekend, online learning. *Students:* 1 (woman) full-time, 12 part-time (6 women); includes 2 minority (1 Black or African American, non-Hispanic/Latino; 1 Hispanic/Latino). Average age 35. 1 applicant. In 2018, 12 master's awarded. *Entrance requirements:* Additional exam requirements/recommendations for international students: Required—TOEFL. *Application deadline:* Applications are processed on a rolling basis. Application fee: $45. *Financial support:* Fellowships, research assistantships with full tuition reimbursements, teaching assistantships with full tuition reimbursements, career-related internships or fieldwork, Federal Work-Study, institutionally sponsored loans, scholarships/grants, tuition waivers (partial), and unspecified assistantships available. Support available to part-time students. Financial award applicants required to submit FAFSA. *Application contact:* Dr. Toni Stokes Jones, Coordinator, 734-487-3260, Fax: 734-487-2101, E-mail: tjones1@emich.edu.

Eastern New Mexico University, Graduate School, College of Education and Technology, Department of Curriculum and Instruction, Portales, NM 88130. Offers alternative licensure in elementary education (M Ed); bilingual education (M Ed); career and technical education (M Ed); educational technology (M Ed); elementary education (M Ed); English as a second language (M Ed); pedagogy and learning (M Ed); reading/literacy (M Ed). *Program availability:* Part-time, online learning. *Degree requirements:* For master's, comprehensive exam, thesis optional. *Entrance requirements:* For master's, writing assessment, minimum GPA of 3.0, photocopy of teaching license, letter of recommendation. Additional exam requirements/recommendations for international students: Required—TOEFL (minimum score 550 paper-based; 79 iBT), IELTS (minimum score 6). Electronic applications accepted. *Expenses:* Tuition, area resident: Full-time $6776. Tuition, state resident: full-time $6776; part-time $282 per credit hour. Tuition, nonresident: full-time $8986; part-time $374 per credit hour. *Required fees:* $60 per semester. One-time fee: $25.

East Stroudsburg University of Pennsylvania, Graduate and Extended Studies, College of Education, Department of Digital Media Technologies, East Stroudsburg, PA 18301-2999. Offers M Ed. *Program availability:* Part-time, evening/weekend, online learning. *Faculty:* 1 full-time (0 women), 3 part-time/adjunct (1 woman). *Students:* 3 full-time (0 women), 22 part-time (14 women); includes 3 minority (1 Hispanic/Latino; 2 Two or more races, non-Hispanic/Latino), 2 international. Average age 33. 10 applicants, 100% accepted, 6 enrolled. In 2018, 9 master's awarded. *Degree requirements:* For master's, comprehensive exam, comprehensive portfolio, internship. *Entrance requirements:* For master's, two letters of recommendation, portfolio or interview, minimum overall undergraduate QPA of 2.5. Additional exam requirements/recommendations for international students: Recommended—TOEFL (minimum score 560 paper-based; 83 iBT), IELTS. *Application deadline:* For fall admission, 7/31 priority date for domestic students, 6/30 priority date for international students; for spring admission, 11/30 for domestic students, 10/31 for international students. Applications are processed on a rolling basis. Application fee: $50. Electronic applications accepted.

Expenses: Tuition, area resident: Full-time $9288; part-time $516 per credit. Tuition, state resident: full-time $9288. Tuition, nonresident: full-time $13,932; part-time $774 per credit. *International tuition:* $13,932 full-time. *Required fees:* $2059; $114 per credit. Tuition and fees vary according to course load and degree level. *Financial support:* Research assistantships with tuition reimbursements, career-related internships or fieldwork, Federal Work-Study, and unspecified assistantships available. Support available to part-time students. Financial award application deadline: 3/1; financial award applicants required to submit FAFSA. *Unit head:* Dr. Richard Otto, Chair, 570-422-3763, Fax: 570-422-3876, E-mail: rotto@esu.edu. *Application contact:* Kevin Quintero, Associate Director, Graduate and Extended Studies, 570-422-3890, Fax: 570-422-2711, E-mail: kquintero@esu.edu.

East Tennessee State University, School of Graduate Studies, College of Education, Department of Curriculum and Instruction, Johnson City, TN 37614. Offers advanced studies in teaching and learning (M Ed), including childhood literacy; educational technology (M Ed), including educational communications and technology, school library media; elementary education (M Ed); reading (M Ed, MA), including reading education (MA), storytelling (MA); response to intervention (Post-Master's Certificate); school library professional (Post-Master's Certificate); secondary education (M Ed); STEAM K-12 education (Postbaccalaureate Certificate); storytelling (Postbaccalaureate Certificate); teacher education (MAT), including elementary education K-5, middle grades education 4-8, middle grades education 6-8, secondary education 6-12 and preK-12, secondary education K-12. *Accreditation:* NCATE. *Program availability:* Part-time, evening/weekend, online learning. *Degree requirements:* For master's, comprehensive exam, thesis optional, student teaching, practicum; for other advanced degree, field work (school library); culminating experience (storytelling). *Entrance requirements:* For master's, GRE, SAT, ACT, PRAXIS, minimum GPA of 3.0, interview, 3 letters of recommendation, background check; for other advanced degree, master's degree, TN teaching license. Additional exam requirements/recommendations for international students: Required—TOEFL (minimum score 550 paper-based; 79 iBT). Electronic applications accepted. *Faculty research:* Critical thinking; curriculum development in reading, math, and science education; cultural diversity; cognitive processes; effective teaching strategies.

Emporia State University, Department of Instructional Design and Technology, Emporia, KS 66801-5415. Offers elearning/online teaching (Certificate); teaching with technology (Certificate). *Accreditation:* NCATE. *Program availability:* Part-time, online only, 100% online. *Degree requirements:* For master's, comprehensive exam (for some programs), thesis (for some programs), project. *Entrance requirements:* For master's, appropriate bachelor's degree, letters of recommendation. Additional exam requirements/recommendations for international students: Required—TOEFL (minimum score 520 paper-based; 68 iBT). Electronic applications accepted.

Fairfield University, Graduate School of Education and Allied Professions, Fairfield, CT 06824. Offers applied behavior analysis (ATC); applied psychology (MA); clinical mental health counseling (MA, CAS); educational technology (MA); elementary education (MA, CAS); family studies (MA); integration of spirituality and religion in counseling (ATC); marriage and family therapy (MA); reading and language development (Sixth Year Certificate); school counseling (MA, CAS); school psychology (MA, CAS); school-based marriage and family therapy (ATC); secondary education (MA); special education (MA, CAS); substance abuse counseling (ATC); teaching (Certificate); teaching and foundations (MA, CAS); TESOL, world languages, and bilingual education (MA, CAS). *Accreditation:* NCATE. *Program availability:* Part-time, evening/weekend. *Degree requirements:* For master's, comprehensive exam. *Entrance requirements:* For master's, minimum GPA of 3.0, 2 recommendations, resume. Additional exam requirements/recommendations for international students: Required—TOEFL (minimum score 550 paper-based; 84 iBT) or IELTS (minimum score 7.5). Electronic applications accepted. *Expenses:* Contact institution. *Faculty research:* Reading and literacy, writing, social justice and inequality in education, addictions and mental health issues, therapeutic relationships and clinical supervision.

Fairleigh Dickinson University, Florham Campus, University College: Arts, Sciences, and Professional Studies, Peter Sammartino School of Education, Madison, NJ 07940-1099. Offers education for certified teachers (MA, Certificate); educational leadership (MA); instructional technology (Certificate); literacy/reading (Certificate); teaching (MAT).

Fairleigh Dickinson University, Metropolitan Campus, University College: Arts, Sciences, and Professional Studies, Peter Sammartino School of Education, Teaneck, NJ 07666-1914. Offers dyslexia specialist (Certificate); education for certified teachers (MA); educational leadership (MA); instructional technology (Certificate); learning disabilities (MA); literacy/reading (Certificate); multilingual education (MA); teacher of the handicapped (Certificate); teaching (MAT). *Accreditation:* TEAC. *Program availability:* Part-time. *Degree requirements:* For master's, research project (MAT).

Fairmont State University, Programs in Education, Fairmont, WV 26554. Offers digital media, new literacies and learning (M Ed); education (MAT); exercise science, fitness and wellness (M Ed); professional studies (M Ed); reading (M Ed); special education (M Ed). *Accreditation:* NCATE. *Program availability:* Part-time, evening/weekend, 100% online. *Entrance requirements:* For master's, GRE. Additional exam requirements/recommendations for international students: Required—TOEFL (minimum score 80 iBT), IELTS (minimum score 6.5). Electronic applications accepted.

Florida Atlantic University, College of Education, Department of Teaching and Learning, Boca Raton, FL 33431-0991. Offers elementary education (M Ed); environmental education (M Ed); instructional technology (M Ed); reading education (M Ed); secondary education (M Ed). *Accreditation:* NCATE. *Program availability:* Part-time, evening/weekend. *Faculty:* 16 full-time (12 women), 1 part-time/adjunct (0 women). *Students:* 30 full-time (21 women), 45 part-time (36 women); includes 27 minority (14 Black or African American, non-Hispanic/Latino; 3 Asian, non-Hispanic/Latino; 8 Hispanic/Latino; 2 Two or more races, non-Hispanic/Latino), 6 international. Average age 30. 71 applicants, 58% accepted, 28 enrolled. In 2018, 23 master's awarded. *Entrance requirements:* For master's, GRE General Test, minimum GPA of 3.0 in last 2 years of undergraduate course work. Additional exam requirements/recommendations for international students: Required—TOEFL (minimum score 500 paper-based; 61 iBT), IELTS (minimum score 6). *Application deadline:* For fall admission, 7/1 for domestic students, 2/15 for international students; for spring admission, 11/1 for domestic students, 7/15 for international students. Applications are processed on a rolling basis. Application fee: $30. *Expenses: Tuition, area resident:* Full-time $7400; part-time $369.82 per credit. Tuition, state resident: full-time $7400; part-time $369.82 per credit. Tuition, nonresident: full-time $20,496; part-time $1024.81 per credit. *Financial support:* Fellowships with partial tuition reimbursements, research assistantships with partial tuition reimbursements, teaching assistantships with partial tuition reimbursements, career-related internships or fieldwork, scholarships/grants, and unspecified assistantships available. *Faculty research:* Technology, teaching English to speakers of other languages, math teaching, electronic portfolio assessment, global perspectives through social studies. *Unit head:* Dr. Barbara Ridener, Chairperson, 561-297-3588, E-mail: bridener@fau.edu. *Application contact:* Dr. Debora Shepherd, Associate Dean, 561-296-3570, E-mail: dshep@fau.edu. Website: http://www.coe.fau.edu/academicdepartments/tl/

Florida International University, College of Arts, Sciences, and Education, Department of Leadership and Professional Studies, Miami, FL 33199. Offers adult education and human resource development (MS, Ed D); counseling (MS), including rehabilitation counseling, school counseling; counselor education (MS), including clinical mental health counseling; educational administration and supervision (Ed D); educational leadership (MS, Certificate, Ed S); higher education (Ed D); higher education administration (MS); international and comparative education (MS); recreation and sport management (MS), including recreation and sport management, recreational therapy; school psychology (Ed S); urban education (MS), including instruction in urban settings, learning technologies, multicultural/bilingual, multicultural/TESOL, urban education. *Program availability:* Part-time, evening/weekend. *Faculty:* 64 full-time (43 women), 104 part-time/adjunct (76 women). *Students:* 258 full-time (196 women), 217 part-time (155 women); includes 387 minority (118 Black or African American, non-Hispanic/Latino; 8 Asian, non-Hispanic/Latino; 249 Hispanic/Latino; 12 Two or more races, non-Hispanic/Latino), 11 international. Average age 31. 345 applicants, 57% accepted, 126 enrolled. In 2018, 172 master's, 11 doctorates awarded. *Entrance requirements:* For master's, minimum GPA of 3.0; for doctorate and other advanced degree, GRE General Test. Additional exam requirements/recommendations for international students: Required—TOEFL (minimum score 550 paper-based; 80 iBT), IELTS (minimum score 6.3). *Application deadline:* For fall admission, 6/1 priority date for domestic students, 4/1 for international students; for winter admission, 10/1 priority date for domestic students, 9/1 for international students; for spring admission, 3/1 priority date for domestic students, 2/1 for international students. Applications are processed on a rolling basis. Application fee: $30. Electronic applications accepted. *Financial support:* Fellowships, research assistantships, teaching assistantships, Federal Work-Study, and tuition waivers (full and partial) available. Support available to part-time students. Financial award applicants required to submit FAFSA. *Unit head:* Dr. Benjamin Baez, Chair, 305-348-3214, Fax: 305-348-1515, E-mail: benjamin.baez@fiu.edu. *Application contact:* Nanett Rojas, Manager, Admissions Operations, 305-348-7464, Fax: 305-348-7441, E-mail: gradadm@fiu.edu. Website: http://education.fiu.edu

Florida International University, College of Arts, Sciences, and Education, Department of Teaching and Learning, Miami, FL 33199. Offers art education (MA, MS); curriculum and instruction (MS, Ed D, PhD, Ed S), including curriculum development (MS), elementary education (MS), English education (MS), learning technologies (MS), mathematics education (MS), modern language education (MS), physical education (MS), science education (MS), social studies education (MS), special education (MS); early childhood education (MS); exceptional student education (Ed D); foreign language education (MS), including foreign language education, teaching English to speakers of other languages (TESOL); language, literacy and culture (PhD); mathematics, science, and learning technologies (PhD); physical education (MS), including sport and fitness; reading education (MS). *Program availability:* Part-time, evening/weekend. *Faculty:* 64 full-time (43 women), 104 part-time/adjunct (76 women). *Students:* 169 full-time (144 women), 155 part-time (130 women); includes 260 minority (53 Black or African American, non-Hispanic/Latino; 7 Asian, non-Hispanic/Latino; 193 Hispanic/Latino; 7 Two or more races, non-Hispanic/Latino), 13 international. Average age 33. 184 applicants, 62% accepted, 87 enrolled. In 2018, 153 master's, 10 doctorates awarded. *Degree requirements:* For doctorate, comprehensive exam, thesis/dissertation. *Entrance requirements:* For master's, GRE General Test, Florida General Knowledge Test or Florida College Level Academic Skills Test; for doctorate and Ed S, GRE General Test. Additional exam requirements/recommendations for international students: Required—TOEFL (minimum score 550 paper-based; 80 iBT), IELTS (minimum score 6.3). *Application deadline:* For fall admission, 6/1 priority date for domestic students, 4/1 for international students; for winter admission, 10/1 priority date for domestic students, 9/1 for international students; for spring admission, 3/1 priority date for domestic students, 2/1 for international students. Applications are processed on a rolling basis. Application fee: $30. Electronic applications accepted. *Financial support:* Research assistantships and teaching assistantships available. *Unit head:* Dr. Maria Fernandez, Chair, 305-348-0193, Fax: 305-348-2086, E-mail: Maria.Fernandez9@fiu.edu. *Application contact:* Nanett Rojas, Manager, Admissions Operations, 305-348-7464, Fax: 305-348-7441, E-mail: gradadm@fiu.edu. Website: https://tl.fiu.edu/

Florida State University, The Graduate School, College of Education, Department of Educational Psychology and Learning Systems, Tallahassee, FL 32306. Offers counseling and human systems (PhD, MS/Ed S), including mental health counseling (MS/Ed S), school psychology (MS/Ed S); educational psychology (MS, PhD); human performance and technology (Certificate); instructional systems and learning technologies (MS, PhD); measurement and statistics (MS, PhD, Certificate); online instructional development (Certificate); MS/Ed S. *Program availability:* Part-time, evening/weekend, 100% online, blended/hybrid learning, asynchronous, minimal on-campus study. *Faculty:* 27 full-time (17 women), 8 part-time/adjunct (4 women). *Students:* 210 full-time (145 women), 122 part-time (89 women); includes 146 minority (39 Black or African American, non-Hispanic/Latino; 1 American Indian or Alaska Native, non-Hispanic/Latino; 51 Asian, non-Hispanic/Latino; 36 Hispanic/Latino; 19 Two or more races, non-Hispanic/Latino), 68 international. Average age 32. 419 applicants, 39% accepted, 82 enrolled. In 2018, 84 master's, 27 doctorates, 38 other advanced degrees awarded. Terminal master's awarded for partial completion of doctoral program. *Degree requirements:* For master's and Certificate, comprehensive exam, thesis optional; for doctorate, comprehensive exam, thesis/dissertation, diagnostic exam, preliminary exam, prospectus defense. *Entrance requirements:* For master's, doctorate, and Certificate, GRE General Test, minimum GPA of 3.0. Additional exam requirements/recommendations for international students: Required—TOEFL (minimum score 550 paper-based, 80 iBT), IELTS (minimum score 6.5) or Michigan English Language Assessment Battery (minimum score 77). Application fee: $30. Electronic applications accepted. *Expenses: Tuition, area resident:* Part-time $479.32 per credit hour. Tuition and fees vary according to campus/location and program. *Financial support:* In 2018–19, 8 research assistantships with partial tuition reimbursements (averaging $6,640 per year), 42 teaching assistantships with partial tuition reimbursements (averaging $6,740 per year) were awarded. Financial award application deadline: 1/15; financial award applicants required to submit FAFSA. *Faculty research:* Learning and cognition, counseling and school psychology, instructional systems, measurement and evaluation. *Unit head:* Dr. James Klein, Chair, 850-644-4592, Fax: 850-644-8776, E-mail: jklein@fsu.edu. *Application contact:* Mary Kate McKee, Academic Program Specialist, 850-644-8046, Fax: 850-644-8781, E-mail: mmckee@campus.fsu.edu.

Fontbonne University, Graduate Programs, St. Louis, MO 63105-3098. Offers accounting (MBA, MS); art (MA); art (K-12) (MAT); business (MBA); computer science (MS); deaf education (MA); early intervention in deaf education (MA); education (MA), including autism spectrum disorders, curriculum and instruction, diverse learners, early childhood education, reading, special education; elementary education (MAT); family and consumer sciences (MA), including multidisciplinary health communication studies; fine arts (MFA); instructional design and technology (MS); management and leadership (MM); middle school education (MAT); secondary education (MAT); special education (MAT); speech-language pathology (MS); supply chain management (MS); theatre (MA). *Accreditation:* ASHA. *Program availability:* Part-time, evening/weekend, online

learning. *Degree requirements:* For master's, comprehensive exam (for some programs), thesis (for some programs). *Entrance requirements:* Additional exam requirements/recommendations for international students: Required—TOEFL (minimum score 500 paper-based; 65 iBT). Electronic applications accepted.

Fort Hays State University, Graduate School, College of Education, Department of Technology Studies, Hays, KS 67601-4099. Offers instructional technology (MS). *Degree requirements:* For master's, comprehensive exam, thesis or alternative. *Entrance requirements:* Additional exam requirements/recommendations for international students: Required—TOEFL (minimum score 550 paper-based). Electronic applications accepted.

Framingham State University, Graduate Studies, Program in Curriculum and Instructional Technology, Framingham, MA 01701-9101. Offers M Ed. *Program availability:* Online learning.

Franklin University, Instructional Design and Learning Technology Program, Columbus, OH 43215-5399. Offers MS.

Fresno Pacific University, Graduate Programs, School of Education, Program in Educational Technology, Fresno, CA 93702-4709. Offers MA. *Program availability:* Part-time, evening/weekend, online learning. *Degree requirements:* For master's, thesis or alternative. *Entrance requirements:* For master's, three references. Additional exam requirements/recommendations for international students: Required—TOEFL (minimum score 550 paper-based). *Expenses:* Contact institution.

Fresno Pacific University, Graduate Programs, School of Education, Program in School Library and Information Technology, Fresno, CA 93702-4709. Offers MA Ed. *Program availability:* Part-time, evening/weekend, online learning. *Degree requirements:* For master's, thesis or alternative. *Entrance requirements:* For master's, CBEST. Additional exam requirements/recommendations for international students: Required—TOEFL (minimum score 550 paper-based). Electronic applications accepted. *Expenses:* Contact institution.

Frostburg State University, College of Education, Department of Educational Professions, Program in Curriculum and Instruction, Frostburg, MD 21532-1099. Offers curriculum and instruction (Ed D); educational technology (M Ed); elementary education (M Ed); secondary education (M Ed). *Program availability:* Part-time, evening/weekend. *Degree requirements:* For master's, thesis or alternative. *Entrance requirements:* For master's, teaching certificate. Additional exam requirements/recommendations for international students: Required—TOEFL. Electronic applications accepted.

Full Sail University, Education Media Design and Technology Master of Science Program - Online, Winter Park, FL 32792-7437. Offers MS. *Program availability:* Online learning. *Entrance requirements:* Additional exam requirements/recommendations for international students: Required—TOEFL (minimum score 550 paper-based; 79 iBT).

George Fox University, College of Education, Graduate Teaching and Leading Program, Newberg, OR 97132-2697. Offers administrative leadership (Ed S); continuing administrator license (Certificate); educational leadership (M Ed); educational technology (M Ed); English for speakers of other languages (M Ed); ESOL (Certificate); initial administrator license (Certificate); reading (M Ed, Certificate); special education (M Ed); teaching (MAT). *Accreditation:* NCATE. *Program availability:* Part-time, evening/weekend, online learning. *Degree requirements:* For master's, thesis (for some programs). *Entrance requirements:* For master's, minimum undergraduate GPA of 3.0 during previous 2 years of course work, resume, 3 professional recommendations on university forms, official transcripts. Additional exam requirements/recommendations for international students: Required—TOEFL (minimum score 577 paper-based; 90 iBT). Electronic applications accepted. *Expenses:* Contact institution.

George Mason University, College of Education and Human Development, Programs in Curriculum and Instruction, Fairfax, VA 22030. Offers assistive technology (M Ed); designing digital learning in schools (M Ed); early childhood education (M Ed); early childhood education for diverse learners (M Ed); elementary education (M Ed); English as a second language (M Ed); gifted child education (M Ed); literacy (M Ed), including PK-12 classroom teachers, reading specialist; literacy leadership for diverse schools (M Ed), including K-12 reading; physical education (M Ed); science K-12 (M Ed); secondary education (M Ed), including biology, chemistry, earth science, English, history/social science, math, physics; special education (M Ed); teacher leadership (M Ed); transformative teaching (M Ed). *Program availability:* Part-time, evening/weekend, 100% online, blended/hybrid learning. *Faculty:* 48 full-time (40 women), 28 part-time/adjunct (20 women). *Students:* 165 full-time (147 women), 697 part-time (579 women); includes 243 minority (47 Black or African American, non-Hispanic/Latino; 3 American Indian or Alaska Native, non-Hispanic/Latino; 88 Asian, non-Hispanic/Latino; 85 Hispanic/Latino; 4 Native Hawaiian or other Pacific Islander, non-Hispanic/Latino; 16 Two or more races, non-Hispanic/Latino), 26 international. Average age 34. 450 applicants, 93% accepted, 315 enrolled. In 2018, 421 master's awarded. *Entrance requirements:* For master's, PRAXIS Core (for some programs), 2 letters of recommendation, interview, program goals statement; 9 hours of complete licensure endorsement requirements (for elementary education); minimum GPA of 3.0 in applicant's last 60 hours of undergraduate coursework (for secondary education); at least 1 year of teaching experience (for literacy). Additional exam requirements/recommendations for international students: Required—TOEFL (minimum score 575 paper-based; 88 iBT), IELTS (minimum score 6.5), PTE (minimum score 59). *Application deadline:* For fall admission, 4/2 priority date for domestic and international students; for spring admission, 11/1 for domestic and international students. Application fee: $75 ($80 for international students). Electronic applications accepted. *Financial support:* In 2018–19, 4 students received support, including 1 fellowship, 3 teaching assistantships (averaging $3,745 per year); career-related internships or fieldwork, Federal Work-Study, scholarships/grants, unspecified assistantships, and health care benefits (for full-time research or teaching assistantship recipients) also available. Support available to part-time students. Financial award application deadline: 3/1; financial award applicants required to submit FAFSA. *Faculty research:* Teacher preparation and professional development; adaptive teaching; wonder in science teacher preparation; literacy (digital, adolescent); site based course instruction. *Unit head:* Rebecca Fox, Professor and Academic Program Coordinator, 703-993-4123, E-mail: rfox@gmu.edu. *Application contact:* Rebecca Fox, Professor and Academic Program Coordinator, 703-993-4123, E-mail: rfox@gmu.edu.
Website: http://gse.gmu.edu/programs/gsemasters

The George Washington University, Graduate School of Education and Human Development, Department of Educational Leadership, Program in Educational Technology Leadership, Washington, DC 20052. Offers MA Ed. *Accreditation:* NCATE. *Program availability:* Part-time, evening/weekend. *Students:* 4 full-time (3 women), 59 part-time (38 women); includes 20 minority (9 Black or African American, non-Hispanic/Latino; 1 American Indian or Alaska Native, non-Hispanic/Latino; 3 Asian, non-Hispanic/Latino; 6 Hispanic/Latino; 1 Two or more races, non-Hispanic/Latino), 1 international. Average age 36. 33 applicants, 85% accepted, 19 enrolled. In 2018, 24 master's awarded. *Degree requirements:* For master's, comprehensive exam, thesis or alternative. *Entrance requirements:* For master's, GRE General Test or MAT, minimum GPA of 2.75. *Application deadline:* For fall admission, 1/15 priority date for domestic students; for spring admission, 10/1 for domestic students. Applications are processed on a rolling basis. Application fee: $75. *Expenses:* Contact institution. *Financial support:* Fellowships, research assistantships, teaching assistantships, and career-related internships or fieldwork available. Financial award application deadline: 1/15. *Faculty research:* Interactive multimedia, distance education, federal technology policy. *Unit head:* Dr. Natalie Milman, Coordinator, 202-994-1884, E-mail: milman@gwu.edu. *Application contact:* Sarah Lang, Director of Graduate Admissions, 202-994-1447, Fax: 202-994-7207, E-mail: slang@gwu.edu.

The George Washington University, Graduate School of Education and Human Development, Department of Educational Leadership, Program in Instructional Design, Washington, DC 20052. Offers Graduate Certificate. *Students:* 9 part-time (all women); includes 1 minority (Hispanic/Latino). Average age 41. 12 applicants, 83% accepted, 6 enrolled. In 2018, 4 Graduate Certificates awarded. *Unit head:* Michael Feuer, Dean, 202-994-6161, E-mail: mjfeuer@gwu.edu. *Application contact:* Sarah Lang, Director of Graduate Admissions, 202-994-1447, Fax: 202-994-7207, E-mail: slang@gwu.edu.
Website: http://gsehd.gwu.edu/instructional-design-certificate

The George Washington University, Graduate School of Education and Human Development, Department of Educational Leadership, Program in Integrating Technology into Education, Washington, DC 20052. Offers Graduate Certificate. *Students:* 1 (woman) part-time; minority (Hispanic/Latino). Average age 35. 4 applicants, 50% accepted, 1 enrolled. In 2018, 1 Graduate Certificate awarded. *Unit head:* Dr. Natalie Milman, Coordinator, 202-994-1884, E-mail: nmilman@gwu.edu. *Application contact:* Sarah Lang, Director of Graduate Admissions, 202-994-1447, Fax: 202-994-7207, E-mail: slang@gwu.edu.
Website: http://gsehd.gwu.edu/integrating-technology-education-certificate

The George Washington University, Graduate School of Education and Human Development, Department of Educational Leadership, Program in Leadership in Educational Technology, Washington, DC 20052. Offers Graduate Certificate. *Students:* 1 (woman) part-time. Average age 45. *Unit head:* Dr. Natalie Milman, Coordinator, 202-994-1884, E-mail: nmilman@gwu.edu. *Application contact:* Sarah Lang, Director of Graduate Admissions, 202-994-1447, Fax: 202-994-7207, E-mail: slang@gwu.edu.
Website: http://gsehd.gwu.edu/

The George Washington University, Graduate School of Education and Human Development, Department of Educational Leadership, Program in Training and Educational Technology, Washington, DC 20052. Offers Graduate Certificate. *Students:* Average age 36. 3 applicants, 67% accepted. In 2018, 1 Graduate Certificate awarded. *Unit head:* Dr. Natalie Milman, Coordinator, 202-994-1884, E-mail: nmilman@gwu.edu. *Application contact:* Sarah Lang, Director of Graduate Admissions, 202-994-1447, Fax: 202-994-7207, E-mail: slang@gwu.edu.
Website: http://gsehd.gwu.edu/training-and-educational-technology-certificate

Georgia College & State University, Graduate School, The John H. Lounsbury College of Education, Program in Instructional Technology, Milledgeville, GA 31061. Offers M Ed. *Program availability:* Part-time, evening/weekend, online only, 100% online. *Degree requirements:* For master's, comprehensive exam, minimum GPA of 3.0, complete program within 6 years. *Entrance requirements:* For master's, minimum GPA of 2.75, level 4 Georgia Teacher certificate or eligibility, 2 professional recommendations, transcripts, proof of immunization. Additional exam requirements/recommendations for international students: Recommended—TOEFL. Electronic applications accepted. *Expenses:* Contact institution.

Georgia College & State University, Graduate School, The John H. Lounsbury College of Education, Program in Library Media, Milledgeville, GA 31061. Offers M Ed. *Program availability:* Part-time, evening/weekend, online only, 100% online. *Degree requirements:* For master's, comprehensive exam, minimum GPA of 3.0, complete program within 4 years, electronic portfolio presentation. *Entrance requirements:* For master's, 2 professional recommendations, transcripts, proof of immunization, minimum GPA of 2.75, 2 years' teaching experience with clear and renewable certificate. Electronic applications accepted. *Expenses:* Contact institution.

Georgian Court University, School of Arts and Sciences, Lakewood, NJ 08701-2697. Offers applied behavior analysis (MA); autism spectrum disorders (Certificate); clinical mental health counseling (MA); criminal justice and human rights (MS); holistic health studies (MA, Certificate); homeland security (Certificate); instructional technology (CPC); mercy spirituality (Certificate); parish business management (Certificate); professional counselor (Certificate); school psychology (MA, Certificate); theology (MA, Certificate). *Program availability:* Part-time, evening/weekend. *Faculty:* 15 full-time (9 women), 11 part-time/adjunct (9 women). *Students:* 90 full-time (84 women), 99 part-time (67 women); includes 28 minority (9 Black or African American, non-Hispanic/Latino; 1 Asian, non-Hispanic/Latino; 14 Hispanic/Latino; 4 Two or more races, non-Hispanic/Latino), 2 international. Average age 34. 138 applicants, 59% accepted, 60 enrolled. In 2018, 68 master's, 19 other advanced degrees awarded. *Degree requirements:* For master's, comprehensive exam (for some programs), thesis (for some programs). *Entrance requirements:* For master's, GRE, GMAT, or NTE/PRAXIS, 3 letters of recommendation. Additional exam requirements/recommendations for international students: Required—TOEFL (minimum score 550 paper-based; 79 iBT). *Application deadline:* For fall admission, 8/15 for domestic students, 5/1 for international students; for spring admission, 1/15 for domestic students, 10/1 for international students. Applications are processed on a rolling basis. Application fee: $40. Electronic applications accepted. *Expenses: Tuition:* Full-time $856; part-time $856 per credit hour. *Required fees:* $968; $496 per unit. $248 per semester. Tuition and fees vary according to campus/location and program. *Financial support:* Scholarships/grants, health care benefits, and unspecified assistantships available. Financial award application deadline: 4/15; financial award applicants required to submit FAFSA. *Unit head:* Dr. Mary Chinery, Dean, 732-987-2493, Fax: 732-987-2007, E-mail: mchinery@georgian.edu. *Application contact:* Patrick Givens, Director of Graduate and Professional Studies Admissions, 732-987-2736, Fax: 732-987-2000, E-mail: gps@georgian.edu.
Website: https://georgian.edu/academics/school-of-arts-sciences/

Georgian Court University, School of Education, Lakewood, NJ 08701-2697. Offers administration and leadership (MA); autism spectrum disorders (Certificate); education (M Ed, MAT); instructional technology (M Mat SE, MA, Certificate). *Accreditation:* TEAC. *Program availability:* Part-time, evening/weekend. *Faculty:* 10 full-time (6 women), 28 part-time/adjunct (17 women). *Students:* 32 full-time (25 women), 396 part-time (324 women); includes 84 minority (35 Black or African American, non-Hispanic/Latino; 10 Asian, non-Hispanic/Latino; 36 Hispanic/Latino; 3 Two or more races, non-Hispanic/Latino). Average age 34. 323 applicants, 67% accepted, 148 enrolled. In 2018, 152 master's, 4 other advanced degrees awarded. *Degree requirements:* For master's, comprehensive exam (for some programs), thesis (for some programs). *Entrance requirements:* For master's, GRE, GMAT or NTE/PRAXIS, 3 letters of recommendation. Additional exam requirements/recommendations for international students: Required—TOEFL (minimum score 550 paper-based; 79 iBT). *Application deadline:* For fall admission, 8/15 priority date for domestic students, 5/1 for international students; for spring admission, 1/15 priority date for domestic students, 10/1 for international students. Applications are processed on a rolling basis. Application fee: $40. Electronic applications accepted. *Expenses: Tuition:* Full-time $856; part-time $856 per credit hour. *Required fees:* $968; $496 per unit. $248 per semester. Tuition and fees vary according

to campus/location and program. *Financial support:* Scholarships/grants, health care benefits, and unspecified assistantships available. Financial award application deadline: 4/15; financial award applicants required to submit FAFSA. *Unit head:* Dr. Christopher Campisano, Dean of School of Education, 732-987-2729, E-mail: ccampisano@georgian.edu. *Application contact:* Patrick Givens, Director of Graduate and Professional Studies Admissions, 732-987-2736, Fax: 732-987-2000, E-mail: gps@georgian.edu.
Website: https://georgian.edu/academics/school-of-education/

Georgia Southern University, Jack N. Averitt College of Graduate Studies, College of Education, Department of Leadership, Technology, and Human Development, Program in Instructional Technology, Statesboro, GA 30460. Offers instructional technology (M Ed, Ed S); school library media (M Ed, Ed S). *Program availability:* Part-time, evening/weekend, online only, 100% online. *Degree requirements:* For master's, portfolio, transition point assessments. *Entrance requirements:* For master's, minimum GPA of 2.5. Additional exam requirements/recommendations for international students: Required—TOEFL (minimum score 550 paper-based; 80 iBT), IELTS (minimum score 6). Electronic applications accepted. *Expenses: Tuition, area resident:* Part-time $3324 per semester. Tuition, state resident: full-time $5814; part-time $3324 per semester. Tuition, nonresident: full-time $23,204; part-time $13,260 per semester. *Required fees:* $2092; $2092. Tuition and fees vary according to course load, degree level, campus/location and program. *Faculty research:* Online learning in higher education and K-12, instructional technology leadership, school library media programs, twenty-first century skills, instructional technology in the content areas.

Georgia State University, College of Education and Human Development, Learning Technologies Division, Atlanta, GA 30302-3083. Offers instructional design and technology (MS); instructional technology (PhD). *Program availability:* Part-time, evening/weekend. *Faculty:* 7 full-time (3 women). In 2018, 6 master's, 3 doctorates awarded. *Entrance requirements:* For master's, GRE General Test, minimum GPA of 2.5; for doctorate, GRE General Test or MAT, minimum GPA of 3.3. Additional exam requirements/recommendations for international students: Required—TOEFL. *Application deadline:* For fall admission, 1/15 for domestic and international students; for summer admission, 1/15 for domestic and international students. Application fee: $50. Electronic applications accepted. *Expenses: Tuition, area resident:* Full-time $9360; part-time $390 per credit hour. Tuition, state resident: full-time $9360; part-time $390 per credit hour. Tuition, nonresident: full-time $30,024; part-time $1251 per credit hour. *International tuition:* $30,024 full-time. *Required fees:* $2128. *Financial support:* Federal Work-Study and institutionally sponsored loans available. *Unit head:* Dr. Brendan Calandra, 404-413-8420, Fax: 404-413-8420, E-mail: bcalandra@gsu.edu. *Application contact:* Nancy Keita, Director, Office of Academic Assistance and Graduate Admissions, 404-413-8001, E-mail: nkeita@gsu.edu.
Website: http://ltd.education.gsu.edu/

Goucher College, Graduate Programs in Education, Baltimore, MD 21204-2794. Offers at-risk and diverse learners (M Ed, Certificate); athletic program leadership and administration (M Ed, Certificate); elementary education (MAT); literacy strategies for content learning (M Ed); middle school (M Ed, Certificate); Montessori studies (M Ed); reading instruction (M Ed, Certificate); reducing student, classroom, and school disruption (M Ed); school improvement leadership (M Ed); secondary education (MAT); special education (MAT), including elementary education; special education for certified elementary and secondary teachers (M Ed); teacher as leader in technology (M Ed). *Program availability:* Part-time, evening/weekend. *Degree requirements:* For master's, thesis (M Ed), final presentation (MAT). *Entrance requirements:* For master's, minimum GPA of 3.0. Additional exam requirements/recommendations for international students: Required—TOEFL (minimum score 550 paper-based; 80 iBT), IELTS (minimum score 7). Electronic applications accepted. *Expenses:* Contact institution. *Faculty research:* Urban education, middle school, school improvement, teacher education, at-risk student achievement.

Graceland University, Gleazer School of Education, Independence, MO 64050. Offers curriculum and instruction: collaborative learning and teaching (M Ed); differentiated instruction (M Ed); instructional leadership (M Ed); literacy instruction (M Ed); management in a quality classroom (M Ed); special education (M Ed); technology integration (M Ed). *Accreditation:* NCATE. *Program availability:* Part-time, 100% online. *Students:* 70 full-time (58 women), 36 part-time (34 women); includes 4 minority (1 Black or African American, non-Hispanic/Latino; 1 Asian, non-Hispanic/Latino; 1 Hispanic/Latino; 1 Two or more races, non-Hispanic/Latino). Average age 34. 29 applicants, 21% accepted, 1 enrolled. In 2018, 76 master's awarded. *Degree requirements:* For master's, action research capstone. *Entrance requirements:* For master's, minimum GPA of 3.0, teaching certificate, current teaching contract and license, two letters of reference, statement of professional goals, verification of ongoing access to computer technology, including email and Internet. Additional exam requirements/recommendations for international students: Required—TOEFL (minimum score 550 paper-based; 80 iBT). *Application deadline:* For winter admission, 11/1 for domestic students; for spring admission, 2/1 priority date for domestic students; for summer admission, 7/1 for domestic students. Applications are processed on a rolling basis. Application fee: $50. Electronic applications accepted. *Expenses:* Tuition, material fee, university tech fee, program support fee. *Financial support:* Tuition waivers (partial) available. Financial award applicants required to submit FAFSA. *Faculty research:* Literacy, technology, faculty mentoring, adult literacy, e-learning, online teaching. *Unit head:* Dr. Michele Dickey-Kotz, Dean, 641-784-5202, E-mail: dickey@graceland.edu. *Application contact:* Susan Freeze, Admissions Representative, 816-423-4676, Fax: 816-833-2990, E-mail: sfreeze1@graceland.edu.
Website: http://www.graceland.edu/education

Grambling State University, School of Graduate Studies and Research, College of Education, Department of Educational Leadership, Grambling, LA 71245. Offers developmental education (MS, Ed D, PMC), including curriculum and instructional design (Ed D), English (MS), guidance and counseling (MS), higher education administration and management (Ed D), mathematics (MS), reading (MS), science (MS), student development and personnel services (Ed D); educational leadership (M Ed). *Program availability:* Part-time, evening/weekend. *Degree requirements:* For master's, comprehensive exam, thesis (for some programs); for doctorate, comprehensive exam, thesis/dissertation. *Entrance requirements:* For master's, GRE, minimum GPA of 2.5 on last degree; for doctorate, GRE (minimum score 1000, 500 on Verbal), master's degree, minimum GPA of 3.0 on last degree. Additional exam requirements/recommendations for international students: Required—TOEFL (minimum score 500 paper-based; 62 iBT). Electronic applications accepted.

Grand Canyon University, College of Education, Phoenix, AZ 85017-1097. Offers autism spectrum disorders (MA); curriculum and instruction (MA); early childhood education (M Ed); educational administration (M Ed); educational leadership (M Ed); elementary education (M Ed); gifted education (MA); instructional technology (MS); K-12 leadership (Ed S); reading (MA); secondary education (M Ed); secondary humanities education (M Ed); secondary STEM education (M Ed); special education (M Ed); teaching and learning (Ed D); teaching English to speakers of other languages (MA). *Program availability:* Part-time, evening/weekend, online learning. *Degree requirements:* For master's, publishable research paper (M Ed), e-portfolio. *Entrance requirements:* For master's, undergraduate degree from accredited, GCU-approved college, university, or program with minimum GPA 2.8. Additional exam requirements/recommendations for international students: Required—TOEFL (minimum score 550 paper-based; 79 iBT), IELTS (minimum score 6). Electronic applications accepted.

Grand Valley State University, College of Education, Program in Educational Technology, Allendale, MI 49401-9403. Offers M Ed. *Accreditation:* NCATE. *Program availability:* Part-time, evening/weekend, 100% online. *Students:* 1 (woman) full-time, 23 part-time (17 women); includes 2 minority (1 Asian, non-Hispanic/Latino; 1 Hispanic/Latino). Average age 34. 7 applicants, 100% accepted, 3 enrolled. In 2018, 19 master's awarded. *Degree requirements:* For master's, project or thesis. *Entrance requirements:* For master's, GRE General Test or minimum GPA of 3.0, last 60 credits from regionally-accredited college/university, 3 letters of recommendation. Additional exam requirements/recommendations for international students: Required—TOEFL (minimum iBT score of 80), IELTS (6.5), or Michigan English Language Assessment Battery (77). *Application deadline:* Applications are processed on a rolling basis. Application fee: $30. Electronic applications accepted. *Expenses:* $677 per credit hour, 33 credit hours. *Financial support:* In 2018–19, 6 students received support, including 5 fellowships with full and partial tuition reimbursements available (averaging $8,000 per year), 1 research assistantship; unspecified assistantships also available. *Unit head:* Dr. Sean Lancaster, Department Director, 616-331-6802, Fax: 616-331-6285, E-mail: lancasts@gvsu.edu. *Application contact:* Annukka Thelen, Director, Student Information and Services Center, 616-331-6205, Fax: 616-331-6217, E-mail: thelenan@gvsu.edu.

Grand Valley State University, College of Education, Programs in General Education, Allendale, MI 49401-9403. Offers adult and higher education (M Ed); early childhood education (M Ed); educational differentiation (M Ed); educational leadership (M Ed); educational technology integration (M Ed); elementary education (M Ed); middle level education (M Ed); school library media services (M Ed); secondary level education (M Ed); teaching English to speakers of other languages (M Ed). *Program availability:* Part-time, evening/weekend, 100% online, blended/hybrid learning. *Students:* 20 part-time (10 women); includes 1 minority (Black or African American, non-Hispanic/Latino). Average age 44. In 2018, 1 master's awarded. *Entrance requirements:* For master's, GRE General Test or minimum GPA of 3.0, last 60 credits from regionally-accredited college/university, 3 letters of recommendation. Additional exam requirements/recommendations for international students: Required—TOEFL (minimum iBT score of 80), IELTS (6.5), or Michigan English Language Assessment Battery (77). *Application deadline:* Applications are processed on a rolling basis. Application fee: $30. Electronic applications accepted. *Expenses:* $677 per credit hour, 33 credits. *Financial support:* In 2018–19, 1 student received support, including 1 fellowship; career-related internships or fieldwork, Federal Work-Study, scholarships/grants, and unspecified assistantships also available. *Faculty research:* Effectiveness of technology in education, parental involvement, effective teaching, effective schools research. *Unit head:* Dr. David Bair, Department Director, 616-331-6489, Fax: 616-331-6489, E-mail: baird@gvsu.edu. *Application contact:* Annukka Thelen, Director, Student Information and Services Center, 616-331-6205, Fax: 616-331-6217, E-mail: thelenan@gvsu.edu.
Website: http://www.gvsu.edu/coe/

Harrisburg University of Science and Technology, Learning Technologies and Media Systems Program, Harrisburg, PA 17101. Offers games and simulations (MS); instructional design (MS); instructional development (MS); instructional technology (MS); integration and leadership (MS). *Program availability:* Part-time, evening/weekend. *Degree requirements:* For master's, thesis optional. *Entrance requirements:* Additional exam requirements/recommendations for international students: Required—TOEFL (minimum score 520 paper-based; 80 iBT); Recommended—IELTS (minimum score 6). Electronic applications accepted. *Faculty research:* User compatibility with technology, teaching and training, curriculum development, instructional design, gamification.

Harvard University, Extension School, Cambridge, MA 02138-3722. Offers applied sciences (CAS); biotechnology (ALM); educational technologies (ALM); educational technology (CET); English for graduate and professional studies (DGP); environmental management (ALM, CEM); information technology (ALM); journalism (ALM); liberal arts (ALM); management (ALM, CM); mathematics for teaching (ALM); museum studies (ALM); premedical studies (Diploma); publication and communication (CPC). *Program availability:* Part-time, evening/weekend. *Degree requirements:* For master's, thesis. *Entrance requirements:* For master's, 3 completed graduate courses with grade of B or higher. Additional exam requirements/recommendations for international students: Required—TOEFL (minimum score 600 paper-based), TWE (minimum score 5). *Expenses:* Contact institution.

Harvard University, Harvard Graduate School of Education, Master's Programs in Education, Cambridge, MA 02138. Offers arts in education (Ed M); education policy and management (Ed M); higher education (Ed M); human development and psychology (Ed M); international education policy (Ed M); language and literacy (Ed M); learning and teaching (Ed M); mind, brain, and education (Ed M); prevention science and practice (Ed M); school leadership (Ed M); special studies (Ed M); teacher education (Ed M); technology, innovation, and education (Ed M). *Program availability:* Part-time. *Entrance requirements:* For master's, GRE General Test, statement of purpose, 3 letters of recommendation, resume, official transcripts. Additional exam requirements/recommendations for international students: Required—TOEFL (minimum score 613 paper-based; 104 iBT), TWE (minimum score 5). Electronic applications accepted. *Faculty research:* Learning and development, educational leadership and organizations, education policy analysis.

Hofstra University, School of Education, Programs in Teacher Education, Hempstead, NY 11549. Offers bilingual education (MA); bilingual extension (Advanced Certificate); business education (MS Ed); curriculum studies (MS Ed); early childhood and childhood education (MS Ed); early childhood education (MA, MS Ed); educational technology (Advanced Certificate); elementary education (MA, MS Ed); English education (MS Ed); family and consumer science (MS Ed); fine arts and music education (Advanced Certificate); fine arts education (MS Ed); foreign language and TESOL (MS Ed); foreign language education (MA, MS Ed); languages other than English and teaching English as a second language (MA); learning and teaching (Ed D); mathematics education (MA, MS Ed); middle childhood extension (Advanced Certificate); music education (MA, MS Ed); science education (MA); secondary education (Advanced Certificate); social studies education (MA, MS Ed); teaching languages other than English and TESOL (MS Ed); technology for learning (MA); TESOL (MS Ed, Advanced Certificate); TESOL with specialization in STEM (MA); work based learning extension (Advanced Certificate). *Program availability:* Part-time, evening/weekend, blended/hybrid learning. *Students:* 138 full-time (94 women), 109 part-time (78 women); includes 66 minority (16 Black or African American, non-Hispanic/Latino; 17 Asian, non-Hispanic/Latino; 31 Hispanic/Latino; 2 Native Hawaiian or other Pacific Islander, non-Hispanic/Latino), 6 international. Average age 29. 217 applicants, 86% accepted, 113 enrolled. In 2018, 105 master's, 11 doctorates, 25 other advanced degrees awarded. *Degree requirements:* For master's, comprehensive exam, thesis (for some programs), exit project, student teaching, fieldwork, electronic portfolio, curriculum project, minimum GPA of 3.0; for doctorate, dissertation; for Advanced Certificate, 3 foreign languages, comprehensive exam (for some programs), thesis project. *Entrance requirements:* For master's, GRE, 2

letters of recommendation, portfolio, teacher certification (MA), interview, essay; for doctorate, GMAT, GRE, LSAT, or MAT; for Advanced Certificate, 2 letters of recommendation, essay, interview and/or portfolio, teaching certificate. Additional exam requirements/recommendations for international students: Required—TOEFL (minimum score 550 paper-based; 80 iBT). *Application deadline:* Applications are processed on a rolling basis. Application fee: $75. Electronic applications accepted. *Financial support:* In 2018–19, 86 students received support, including 51 fellowships with full and partial tuition reimbursements available (averaging $5,080 per year), 2 research assistantships with full and partial tuition reimbursements available (averaging $3,470 per year); career-related internships or fieldwork, Federal Work-Study, institutionally sponsored loans, scholarships/grants, traineeships, tuition waivers (full and partial), unspecified assistantships, and scholarships and endowed scholarships also available. Support available to part-time students. Financial award applicants required to submit FAFSA. *Faculty research:* Impact of memory on learning; brain function, cognitive-development, learning, and achievement; student activism and civic education; using children's literature to promote diversity; 2nd language acquisition. *Unit head:* Dr. Alan Singer, Chairperson, 516-463-5853, Fax: 516-463-6275, E-mail: alan.j.singer@hofstra.edu. *Application contact:* Sunil Samuel, Assistant Vice President of Admissions, 516-463-4723, Fax: 516-463-4664, E-mail: graduateadmission@hofstra.edu. Website: http://www.hofstra.edu/education/

Houston Baptist University, College of Education and Behavioral Sciences, Programs in Education, Houston, TX 77074-3298. Offers bilingual education (M Ed); counselor education (M Ed); curriculum and instruction (M Ed); curriculum and instruction (EC-6 bilingual) (M Ed); curriculum and instruction in all-level art, Spanish, music, or physical education (M Ed); curriculum and instruction in EC-6 and special education (EC-12) (M Ed); curriculum and instruction in instructional technology (M Ed); curriculum and instruction in mathematics, science, or social studies (4-8) (M Ed); curriculum and instruction with EC-6 generalist (M Ed); curriculum and instruction with English language arts and reading (4-8) (M Ed); educational administration (M Ed); educational diagnostician (M Ed); executive educational leadership (Ed D); higher education in business management (M Ed); higher education in Christian studies (M Ed); higher education in counseling (M Ed); higher education in educational technology (M Ed); reading (M Ed); special educational leadership (Ed D). *Program availability:* Part-time, evening/weekend, 100% online, blended/hybrid learning. *Degree requirements:* For master's, comprehensive exam; for doctorate, thesis/dissertation. *Entrance requirements:* For master's, minimum GPA of 2.75, two recommendations, resume, bachelor's degree conferred transcript; interview (for non-certified teachers); for doctorate, GRE, 5 letters of recommendation. Additional exam requirements/recommendations for international students: Required—TOEFL (minimum score 80 iBT), IELTS (minimum score 6.5). Electronic applications accepted. Application fee is waived when completed online. *Expenses:* Contact institution. *Faculty research:* Autism and inclusion, integrating technology into instruction, school change and leadership trust.

Idaho State University, Graduate School, College of Education, Department of Organizational Learning and Performance, Pocatello, ID 83209. Offers human resource development (MS); instructional design (PhD); instructional technology (M Ed). *Program availability:* Part-time. *Degree requirements:* For master's, comprehensive exam, thesis optional, minimum 36 credits; for doctorate, comprehensive exam, thesis/dissertation (for some programs). *Entrance requirements:* For master's, GRE or MAT, bachelor's degree; for doctorate, GRE or MAT, master's degree. Additional exam requirements/recommendations for international students: Required—TOEFL (minimum score 550 paper-based; 80 iBT). Electronic applications accepted.

Indiana State University, College of Graduate and Professional Studies, Bayh College of Education, Department of Teaching and Learning, Terre Haute, IN 47809. Offers curriculum and instruction (M Ed, PhD); educational technology (MS). *Accreditation:* NCATE. *Degree requirements:* For doctorate, thesis/dissertation. *Entrance requirements:* For doctorate, GRE General Test. Electronic applications accepted. *Faculty research:* Discipline FERPA reading, teacher strengths and needs.

Indiana University Bloomington, School of Education, Department of Instructional Systems Technology, Bloomington, IN 47405-1006. Offers MS, PhD. *Program availability:* Online learning. Terminal master's awarded for partial completion of doctoral program. *Degree requirements:* For master's, thesis optional, portfolio; for doctorate, comprehensive exam, thesis/dissertation, dossier review. *Entrance requirements:* For master's and doctorate, GRE General Test, minimum GPA of 2.75. Additional exam requirements/recommendations for international students: Required—TOEFL. Electronic applications accepted. *Faculty research:* Instructional design and theory development, e-learning and distance education, systemic change, serious simulations and games, human performance improvement, technology integration in education.

Indiana University of Pennsylvania, School of Graduate Studies and Research, College of Education and Communications, Department of Adult and Community Education, Program in Adult and Community Education/Communications Technology, Indiana, PA 15705. Offers MA. *Program availability:* Part-time, evening/weekend. *Faculty:* 2 full-time (both women). *Students:* 1 (woman) full-time. Average age 38. 16 applicants, 81% accepted, 7 enrolled. In 2018, 15 master's awarded. *Degree requirements:* For master's, thesis optional. *Entrance requirements:* For master's, 2 letters of recommendation, resume. Additional exam requirements/recommendations for international students: Required—TOEFL (minimum score 540 paper-based; 76 iBT). *Application deadline:* Applications are processed on a rolling basis. Application fee: $50. Electronic applications accepted. *Expenses:* Tuition, state resident: full-time $12,384; part-time $516 per credit hour. Tuition, nonresident: full-time $18,576; part-time $774 per credit hour. *Required fees:* $4454; $186 per credit hour. $65 per semester. Tuition and fees vary according to program and reciprocity agreements. *Financial support:* Fellowships, research assistantships with tuition reimbursements, teaching assistantships, career-related internships or fieldwork, Federal Work-Study, scholarships/grants, and unspecified assistantships available. Support available to part-time students. Financial award application deadline: 4/15; financial award applicants required to submit FAFSA. *Unit head:* Prof. Jacqueline McGinty, Coordinator, 724-357-2470, E-mail: jacqueline.mcginty@iup.edu. *Application contact:* Prof. Jacqueline McGinty, Coordinator, 724-357-2470, E-mail: jacqueline.mcginty@iup.edu. Website: http://www.iup.edu/aec

Indiana University of Pennsylvania, School of Graduate Studies and Research, College of Education and Communications, Department of Communications Media, Program in Communications Media and Instructional Technology, Indiana, PA 15705. Offers PhD. *Faculty:* 8 full-time (2 women). *Students:* 10 full-time (4 women), 33 part-time (13 women); includes 8 minority (4 Black or African American, non-Hispanic/Latino; 1 Asian, non-Hispanic/Latino; 2 Hispanic/Latino; 1 Two or more races, non-Hispanic/Latino), 6 international. Average age 38. 36 applicants, 36% accepted, 7 enrolled. In 2018, 6 doctorates awarded. Application fee: $50. *Expenses:* Contact institution. *Financial support:* In 2018–19, 2 fellowships with full tuition reimbursements (averaging $2,049 per year), 6 research assistantships with tuition reimbursements (averaging $4,957 per year), 3 teaching assistantships with partial tuition reimbursements (averaging $24,425 per year) were awarded. *Unit head:* Dr. Zachary Stiegler, Coordinator, 724-357-3219, E-mail: zachary.stiegler@iup.edu. *Application contact:* Dr.

Zachary Stiegler, Coordinator, 724-357-3219, E-mail: zachary.stiegler@iup.edu. Website: http://www.iup.edu/commmedia/programs/phdcmit/

Indiana University South Bend, College of Liberal Arts and Sciences, South Bend, IN 46615. Offers advanced computer programming (Graduate Certificate); applied informatics (Graduate Certificate); applied mathematics and computer science (MS); behavior modification (Graduate Certificate); computer applications (Graduate Certificate); computer programming (Graduate Certificate); correctional management and supervision (Graduate Certificate); English (MA); health systems management (Graduate Certificate); international studies (Graduate Certificate); liberal studies (MLS); nonprofit management (Graduate Certificate); paralegal studies (Graduate Certificate); professional writing (Graduate Certificate); public affairs (MPA); public management (Graduate Certificate); social and cultural diversity (Graduate Certificate); strategic sustainability leadership (Graduate Certificate); technology for administration (Graduate Certificate). *Program availability:* Part-time, evening/weekend. *Degree requirements:* For master's, variable foreign language requirement, thesis (for some programs). *Entrance requirements:* For master's, minimum GPA of 3.0. Additional exam requirements/recommendations for international students: Required—TOEFL (minimum score 550 paper-based; 80 iBT). *Expenses:* Contact institution. *Faculty research:* Artificial intelligence, bioinformatics, English language and literature, creative writing, computer networks.

Instituto Tecnológico y de Estudios Superiores de Monterrey, Campus Central de Veracruz, Graduate Programs, Córdoba, Mexico. Offers administration (MA); administration of information technologies (MTI); computer sciences (MCC); education (MEE); educational institution administration (MAD); educational technology (MTE); electronic commerce (MCE); finance (MAF); humanistic studies (MEH); international business for Latin America (MNL); marketing (MMT); science (MCP). *Program availability:* Part-time, evening/weekend, online learning. *Degree requirements:* For master's, thesis (for some programs). *Entrance requirements:* For master's, PAEP College Board. Electronic applications accepted.

Instituto Tecnológico y de Estudios Superiores de Monterrey, Campus Ciudad de México, Virtual University Division, Ciudad de Mexico, Mexico. Offers administration of information technologies (MA); computer sciences (MA); education (MA, PhD); educational technology (MA); environmental engineering (MA); environmental systems (MA); humanistic studies (MA); industrial engineering (MA); international business for Latin America (MA); quality systems (MA); quality systems and productivity (MA). *Program availability:* Part-time, evening/weekend, online learning. *Entrance requirements:* For master's and doctorate, Instituto entrance exam. Additional exam requirements/recommendations for international students: Required—TOEFL.

Instituto Tecnológico y de Estudios Superiores de Monterrey, Campus Ciudad Juárez, Program in Educational Innovation, Ciudad Juárez, Mexico. Offers DE.

Instituto Tecnológico y de Estudios Superiores de Monterrey, Campus Ciudad Juárez, Program in Educational Technology, Ciudad Juárez, Mexico. Offers MTE.

Instituto Tecnológico y de Estudios Superiores de Monterrey, Campus Estado de México, Professional and Graduate Division, Estado de Mexico, Mexico. Offers administration of information technologies (MITA); architecture (M Arch); business administration (GMBA, MBA); computer sciences (MCS, PhD); education (M Ed); educational institution administration (MAD); educational technology and innovation (PhD); electronic commerce (MEC); environmental systems (MS); finance (MAF); humanistic studies (MHS); information sciences and knowledge management (MISKM); information systems (MS); manufacturing systems (MS); marketing (MEM); quality systems and productivity (MS); science and materials engineering (PhD); telecommunications management (MTM). *Program availability:* Part-time, online learning. *Degree requirements:* For master's, one foreign language, thesis (for some programs); for doctorate, one foreign language, thesis/dissertation. *Entrance requirements:* For master's, E-PAEP 500, interview; for doctorate, E-PAEP 500, research proposal. Additional exam requirements/recommendations for international students: Required—TOEFL (minimum score 550 paper-based). *Faculty research:* Surface treatments by plasmas, mechanical properties, robotics, graphical computing, mechatronics security protocols.

Instituto Tecnológico y de Estudios Superiores de Monterrey, Campus Irapuato, Graduate Programs, Irapuato, Mexico. Offers administration (MBA); administration of information technology (MAIT); administration of telecommunications (MAT); architecture (M Arch); computer science (MCS); education (M Ed); educational administration (MEA); educational innovation and technology (DEIT); educational technology (MET); electronic commerce (MBA); environmental administration and planning (MEAP); environmental systems (MES); finances (MBA); humanistic studies (MHS); international management for Latin American executives (MIMLAE); library and information science (MLIS); manufacturing quality management (MMQM); marketing research (MBA).

Inter American University of Puerto Rico, Metropolitan Campus, Graduate Programs, Program in Educational Computing, San Juan, PR 00919-1293. Offers MA. *Degree requirements:* For master's, comprehensive exam, portfolio. *Entrance requirements:* For master's, GRE or EXADEP, minimum GPA of 2.5. Electronic applications accepted. *Faculty research:* Effectiveness of multimedia, World Wide Web for distance learning.

Iowa State University of Science and Technology, Department of Education, Ames, IA 50011. Offers curriculum and instructional technology (M Ed, MS, PhD); elementary education (M Ed, MS); historical, philosophical, and comparative studies in education (M Ed, MS); special education (M Ed, MS, PhD). *Degree requirements:* For master's, thesis or alternative; for doctorate, thesis/dissertation. *Entrance requirements:* For master's and doctorate, GRE General Test. Additional exam requirements/recommendations for international students: Required—TOEFL (minimum score 560 paper-based; 83 iBT), IELTS (minimum score 6.5). Electronic applications accepted.

Jacksonville State University, Graduate Studies, School of Education, Program in Library Media, Jacksonville, AL 36265-1602. Offers MS Ed. *Program availability:* Part-time, evening/weekend. *Degree requirements:* For master's, comprehensive exam, thesis (for some programs). *Entrance requirements:* For master's, GRE General Test or MAT. Additional exam requirements/recommendations for international students: Required—TOEFL (minimum score 500 paper-based; 61 iBT). Electronic applications accepted.

James Madison University, The Graduate School, College of Education, Program in Education, Harrisonburg, VA 22807. Offers early childhood education (preK-3) (MAT); educational leadership (M Ed); educational technology (M Ed); elementary education (MAT); equity and cultural diversity (M Ed); inclusive early childhood education (MAT); K-8 mathematics specialist (M Ed); middle education (MAT); reading education (M Ed); secondary education (MAT); Spanish language and culture for educators (M Ed); TESOL (MAT). *Accreditation:* NCATE. *Program availability:* Part-time, evening/weekend. *Students:* 255 full-time (224 women), 200 part-time (140 women); includes 56 minority (13 Black or African American, non-Hispanic/Latino; 8 Asian, non-Hispanic/Latino; 21 Hispanic/Latino; 14 Two or more races, non-Hispanic/Latino), 1 international. Average age 30. In 2018, 295 master's awarded. Application fee: $60. Electronic

applications accepted. *Expenses:* Tuition, state resident: full-time $10,848. Tuition, nonresident: full-time $27,888. *Required fees:* $1128. *Financial support:* In 2018–19, 22 students received support. Teaching assistantships, career-related internships or fieldwork, Federal Work-Study, and assistantships (averaging $7911) available. Financial award application deadline: 3/1; financial award applicants required to submit FAFSA. *Unit head:* Dr. Phillip M. Wishon, Dean, 540-568-6572, E-mail: wishonpm@jmu.edu. *Application contact:* Lynette D. Michael, Director of Graduate Admissions, 540-568-6131 Ext. 6395, Fax: 540-568-7860, E-mail: michaeld@jmu.edu.
Website: http://www.jmu.edu/coe/index.shtml

Johnson University, Graduate and Professional Programs, Knoxville, TN 37998-1001. Offers biblical interpretation (Graduate Certificate); business administration (MBA); Christian ministries (Graduate Certificate); clinical mental health counseling (MA); educational technology (MA); intercultural studies (MA); leadership (MBA); leadership studies (PhD); New Testament (MA); nonprofit management (MBA); school counseling (MA); spiritual formation and leadership (Graduate Certificate); strategic ministry (MA); teacher education (MA). *Program availability:* Part-time, evening/weekend, 100% online, blended/hybrid learning. *Degree requirements:* For master's, variable foreign language requirement, comprehensive exam, thesis (for some programs), internships; for doctorate, variable foreign language requirement, comprehensive exam, thesis/dissertation, internships. *Entrance requirements:* For master's, PRAXIS (for MA in teacher education); MAT (for counseling); GRE or GMAT (for MBA), interview, 3 references, transcripts, essay, minimum GPA of 2.5 or 3.0 (depending on program); for doctorate, GRE or MAT (taken not less than 5 years prior), interview, 3 references, transcripts, essay, minimum GPA of 3.0; for Graduate Certificate, interview, 3 references, transcripts, essay, minimum GPA of 3.0. Additional exam requirements/recommendations for international students: Required—TOEFL (minimum score 527 paper-based; 71 iBT). Electronic applications accepted. *Expenses:* Contact institution.

Kansas State University, Graduate School, College of Education, Department of Curriculum and Instruction, Manhattan, KS 66506. Offers curriculum and instruction (Ed D, PhD); digital teaching and learning (MS); educational computing, design and online learning (MS); elementary/middle level curriculum and instruction (MS); online learning (Certificate); reading specialist endorsement (MS); reading/language arts (MS); teacher leader/school improvement (MS); teaching and learning (Certificate). *Accreditation:* NCATE. *Program availability:* Part-time, online learning. *Degree requirements:* For master's, comprehensive exam, portfolio, project, report or thesis; for doctorate, comprehensive exam, thesis/dissertation, preliminary exam; for Certificate, comprehensive exam, portfolio. *Entrance requirements:* For master's, minimum GPA of 3.0, 3 letters of recommendation; for doctorate, GRE, minimum GPA of 3.0, 3 letters of recommendation, evidence of scholarly writing; for Certificate, minimum GPA of 3.0, letters of recommendation. Additional exam requirements/recommendations for international students: Required—TOEFL (minimum score 550 paper-based; 80 iBT) or IELTS. Electronic applications accepted. *Faculty research:* Literacy and technology, critical race theory and diversity, achievement gaps, school improvement, teacher education.

Keiser University, Ed S in Instructional Design and Technology Program, Fort Lauderdale, FL 33309. Offers Ed S.

Keiser University, PhD in Instructional Design and Technology Program, Fort Lauderdale, FL 33309. Offers PhD.

Kennesaw State University, Bagwell College of Education, Program in Instructional Technology, Kennesaw, GA 30144. Offers M Ed, Ed D, Ed S. *Program availability:* Part-time-only, evening/weekend, online only, 100% online. *Students:* 6 full-time (5 women), 363 part-time (283 women); includes 109 minority (75 Black or African American, non-Hispanic/Latino; 11 Asian, non-Hispanic/Latino; 20 Hispanic/Latino; 1 Native Hawaiian or other Pacific Islander, non-Hispanic/Latino; 2 Two or more races, non-Hispanic/Latino). Average age 36. 169 applicants, 63% accepted, 90 enrolled. In 2018, 41 master's, 79 other advanced degrees awarded. *Entrance requirements:* Additional exam requirements/recommendations for international students: Required—TOEFL (minimum score 80 iBT), IELTS (minimum score 6.5). *Application deadline:* For fall admission, 7/1 for domestic students; for spring admission, 11/1 for domestic students; for summer admission, 4/1 for domestic students. Applications are processed on a rolling basis. Application fee: $60. Electronic applications accepted. *Expenses: Tuition, area resident:* Full-time $6960; part-time $290 per credit hour. Tuition, state resident: full-time $6960; part-time $290 per credit hour. Tuition, nonresident: full-time $25,080; part-time $1045 per credit hour. *International tuition:* $25,080 full-time. *Required fees:* $2006; $1706 per semester. $853 per semester. *Application contact:* Admission Counselor, 470-578-4377, Fax: 470-578-9172, E-mail: ksugrad@kennesaw.edu.

Kent State University, College of Education, Health and Human Services, School of Lifespan Development and Educational Sciences, Kent, OH 44242-0001. Offers clinical mental health counseling (M Ed); counseling (Ed S); counseling and human development services (PhD); educational psychology (M Ed, MA); human development and family studies (MA); instructional technology (M Ed, PhD), including computer technology (M Ed), educational psychology (PhD), general instructional technology (M Ed); rehabilitation counseling (M Ed); school counseling (M Ed); school psychology (PhD, Ed S); special education (M Ed, PhD, Ed S), including deaf education (M Ed), early childhood education (M Ed), educational interpreter K-12 (M Ed), general special education (M Ed), gifted education (M Ed), mild/moderate intervention (M Ed), moderate/intensive intervention (M Ed), special education (PhD, Ed S), transition to work (M Ed). *Program availability:* Part-time, evening/weekend. *Faculty:* 71 full-time (37 women), 80 part-time/adjunct (61 women). *Students:* 341 full-time (272 women), 238 part-time (193 women); includes 66 minority (40 Black or African American, non-Hispanic/Latino; 5 American Indian or Alaska Native, non-Hispanic/Latino; 5 Asian, non-Hispanic/Latino; 8 Hispanic/Latino; 7 Native Hawaiian or other Pacific Islander, non-Hispanic/Latino; 1 Two or more races, non-Hispanic/Latino), 16 international. 461 applicants, 35% accepted. In 2018, 162 master's, 21 doctorates, 14 other advanced degrees awarded. *Degree requirements:* For master's, thesis optional; for doctorate, comprehensive exam, thesis/dissertation. *Entrance requirements:* For master's, doctorate, and Ed S, GRE General Test. Additional exam requirements/recommendations for international students: Required—TOEFL (minimum score 550 paper-based; 80 iBT). *Application deadline:* Applications are processed on a rolling basis. Application fee: $45 ($60 for international students). Electronic applications accepted. *Expenses:* Tuition, state resident: full-time $11,766; part-time $536 per credit. Tuition, nonresident: full-time $21,952; part-time $999 per credit. *International tuition:* $21,952 full-time. Tuition and fees vary according to course load. *Financial support:* In 2018–19, 35 research assistantships with full tuition reimbursements (averaging $10,000 per year), 8 teaching assistantships with full tuition reimbursements (averaging $12,000 per year) were awarded; Federal Work-Study, scholarships/grants, unspecified assistantships, and 16 administrative assistantships (averaging $9,594 per year) also available. Financial award application deadline: 4/1. *Unit head:* Dr. Mary Dellmann-Jenkins, Director, 330-672-6958, E-mail: mdellman@kent.edu. *Application contact:* Cheryl Slusarczyk, Academic Program Director, Office of Graduate Student Services, 330-672-2576, Fax: 330-672-9162, E-mail: ogs@kent.edu.
Website: http://www.kent.edu/ehhs/lde s/

Kutztown University of Pennsylvania, College of Education, Program in Instructional Technology, Kutztown, PA 19530-0730. Offers M Ed. *Program availability:* Part-time, evening/weekend, 100% online, blended/hybrid learning. *Faculty:* 4 full-time (3 women). *Students:* 1 (woman) full-time, 75 part-time (57 women); includes 5 minority (2 Black or African American, non-Hispanic/Latino; 2 Hispanic/Latino; 1 Two or more races, non-Hispanic/Latino). Average age 31. 36 applicants, 97% accepted, 18 enrolled. In 2018, 22 master's awarded. *Entrance requirements:* For master's, GRE or valid PA teaching certificate, 3 letters of recommendation. Additional exam requirements/recommendations for international students: Required—TOEFL (minimum score 550 paper-based, 79 iBT), IELTS (minimum score 6.5), or PTE (minimum score 53). *Application deadline:* For fall admission, 8/1 for domestic and international students; for spring admission, 12/1 for domestic and international students. Application fee: $35. Electronic applications accepted. *Expenses:* Tuition, state resident: part-time $516 per credit. Tuition, nonresident: part-time $774 per credit. *Required fees:* $119 per credit. One-time fee: $50 part-time. Tuition and fees vary according to degree level. *Financial support:* Career-related internships or fieldwork, Federal Work-Study, and unspecified assistantships available. Financial award application deadline: 3/1; financial award applicants required to submit FAFSA. *Unit head:* Dr. Andrea Harmer, Chairperson, 610-683-4301, Fax: 610-683-1326, E-mail: harmer@kutztown.edu. *Application contact:* Dr. Andrea Harmer, Chairperson, 610-683-4301, Fax: 610-683-1326, E-mail: harmer@kutztown.edu.
Website: https://www.kutztown.edu/academics/graduate-programs/instructional-technology.htm

Lamar University, College of Graduate Studies, College of Education and Human Development, Department of Educational Leadership, Beaumont, TX 77710. Offers digital learning and leading (M Ed); education administration (M Ed); educational leadership (Ed D); educational technology (M Ed). *Program availability:* Part-time, evening/weekend. *Faculty:* 24 full-time (14 women), 16 part-time/adjunct (11 women). *Students:* 2,691 part-time (1,904 women); includes 1,217 minority (571 Black or African American, non-Hispanic/Latino; 10 American Indian or Alaska Native, non-Hispanic/Latino; 36 Asian, non-Hispanic/Latino; 559 Hispanic/Latino; 2 Native Hawaiian or other Pacific Islander, non-Hispanic/Latino; 39 Two or more races, non-Hispanic/Latino), 1 international. Average age 37. 2,445 applicants, 90% accepted, 578 enrolled. In 2018, 882 master's, 73 doctorates awarded. Terminal master's awarded for partial completion of doctoral program. *Degree requirements:* For master's, comprehensive exam, thesis optional; for doctorate, thesis/dissertation. *Entrance requirements:* For master's, GRE General Test, minimum GPA of 2.5; for doctorate, GRE. Additional exam requirements/recommendations for international students: Required—TOEFL (minimum score 550 paper-based; 79 iBT), IELTS (minimum score 6.5). *Application deadline:* Applications are processed on a rolling basis. Application fee: $25 ($50 for international students). Electronic applications accepted. *Expenses:* Contact institution. *Financial support:* In 2018–19, 79 students received support, including 3 fellowships (averaging $20,000 per year), 1 research assistantship with tuition reimbursement available (averaging $6,500 per year); teaching assistantships with tuition reimbursements available, career-related internships or fieldwork, and scholarships/grants also available. Support available to part-time students. Financial award applicants required to submit FAFSA. *Faculty research:* School dropouts, suicide prevention in public school students, school climate and gifted performance, teacher evaluation. *Total annual research expenditures:* $2,026. *Unit head:* Dr. Diane Mason, Department Chair, 409-880-8689, Fax: 409-880-8685. *Application contact:* Celeste Contreas, Director, Admissions and Academic Services, 409-880-8888, Fax: 409-880-7419, E-mail: gradmissions@lamar.edu.
Website: http://education.lamar.edu/educational-leadership

La Salle University, School of Arts and Sciences, Program in Instructional Technology Management, Philadelphia, PA 19141-1199. Offers MS, Certificate. *Program availability:* Part-time, evening/weekend, online only, 100% online. *Degree requirements:* For master's, capstone project. *Entrance requirements:* For master's and Certificate, baccalaureate degree; two letters of recommendation; 3 years of professional experience in corporate training, human resources, information technology or business. Additional exam requirements/recommendations for international students: Required—TOEFL. Electronic applications accepted. Application fee is waived when completed online. *Expenses:* Contact institution.

Lawrence Technological University, College of Arts and Sciences, Southfield, MI 48075-1058. Offers bioinformatics (Graduate Certificate); computer science (MS), including data science, big data, and data mining, intelligent systems; educational technology (MA), including robotics; instructional design, communication, and presentation (Graduate Certificate); integrated science (MA); science education (MA); technical and professional communication (MS, Graduate Certificate); writing for the digital age (Graduate Certificate). *Program availability:* Part-time, evening/weekend. *Degree requirements:* For master's, thesis (for some programs). *Entrance requirements:* Additional exam requirements/recommendations for international students: Required—TOEFL (minimum score 550 paper-based; 79 iBT), IELTS (minimum score 6.5). Electronic applications accepted. *Faculty research:* Computer analysis of music, machine learning of literature and lyrics, customer sentiments and response analysis through social media, peta-scale computing in astronomical databases, early detection of diseases with pattern recognition.

Lehigh University, College of Education, Program in Teaching, Learning and Technology, Bethlehem, PA 18015. Offers elementary education (M Ed); instructional technology (MS); teaching, learning and technology (PhD); M Ed/MA. *Program availability:* Part-time. *Faculty:* 6 full-time (4 women), 8 part-time/adjunct (5 women). *Students:* 18 full-time (12 women), 55 part-time (32 women); includes 9 minority (1 Asian, non-Hispanic/Latino; 7 Hispanic/Latino; 1 Native Hawaiian or other Pacific Islander, non-Hispanic/Latino), 6 international. Average age 32. 50 applicants, 70% accepted, 9 enrolled. In 2018, 28 master's, 4 doctorates awarded. Terminal master's awarded for partial completion of doctoral program. *Degree requirements:* For doctorate, comprehensive exam, thesis/dissertation, qualifying exam. *Entrance requirements:* For master's, minimum GPA of 3.0, 2 letters of recommendation, essay, transcript; for doctorate, GRE General Test, minimum graduate GPA of 3.0, writing sample, 2 letters of recommendation, essay, transcript. Additional exam requirements/recommendations for international students: Required—TOEFL (minimum score 93 iBT), IELTS (minimum score 6.5), TOEFL or IELTS is required. *Application deadline:* For fall admission, 7/15 for domestic and international students; for spring admission, 12/15 for domestic and international students; for summer admission, 4/15 for domestic and international students. Application fee: $65. Electronic applications accepted. *Expenses:* $565 per credit. *Financial support:* In 2018–19, 11 students received support, including 3 research assistantships with full and partial tuition reimbursements available (averaging $15,778 per year); fellowships, scholarships/grants, and unspecified assistantships also available. Financial award application deadline: 1/31. *Faculty research:* Teaching and learning, K-16 curriculum development, web-based learning, teaching and technology, language and literacy, teaching, learning with spatial technologies, visual instructional technologies, environmental science curriculum, multicultural issues, English language education, educational access and equity, elLs with disabilities, integrated curriculum, augmented. *Total annual research expenditures:* $786,227. *Unit head:* Dr. Lynn Columba, Director, 610-758-3237, Fax: 610-758-3243, E-mail: hlc0@lehigh.edu. *Application contact:* Donna Toothman, Coordinator, 610-758-3230, Fax: 610-758-3243, E-mail: djt2@lehigh.edu.
Website: https://ed.lehigh.edu/academics/programs/teacher-education

Lenoir-Rhyne University, Graduate Programs, School of Education, Program in Online Teaching and Instructional Design, Hickory, NC 28601. Offers MS. *Program availability:* Online learning. *Entrance requirements:* For master's, GRE or MAT, essay; minimum GPA of 2.7 undergraduate, 3.0 graduate. Additional exam requirements/recommendations for international students: Required—TOEFL (minimum score 600 paper-based). Electronic applications accepted. *Expenses:* Contact institution.

Lesley University, Graduate School of Education, Cambridge, MA 02138-2790. Offers arts, community, and education (M Ed); autism studies (Certificate); curriculum and instruction (M Ed, CAGS); early childhood education (M Ed); ecological teaching and learning (MS); educational studies (PhD), including adult learning, educational leadership, individually designed; elementary education (M Ed); emergent technologies for educators (Certificate); ESLArts: language learning through the arts (M Ed); high school education (M Ed); individually designed (M Ed); integrated teaching through the arts (M Ed); literacy for K-8 classroom teachers (M Ed); mathematics education (M Ed); middle school education (M Ed); moderate disabilities (M Ed); online learning (Certificate); reading (CAGS); science in education (M Ed); severe disabilities (M Ed); special needs (CAGS); specialist teacher of reading (M Ed); teacher of visual art (M Ed); technology in education (M Ed, CAGS). *Accreditation:* TEAC. *Program availability:* Part-time, evening/weekend, online learning. *Degree requirements:* For master's, practicum; for doctorate, thesis/dissertation. *Entrance requirements:* For master's, Massachusetts Tests for Educator Licensure (MTEL), transcripts, statement of purpose, recommendations; interview (for special education); for doctorate, GRE General Test, transcripts, statement of purpose, recommendations, interview, master's degree, resume; for other advanced degree, interview, master's degree. Additional exam requirements/recommendations for international students: Required—TOEFL (minimum score 550 paper-based; 80 iBT). Electronic applications accepted. *Faculty research:* Assessment in literacy, mathematics and science; autism spectrum disorders; instructional technology and online learning; multicultural education and English language learners.

Lewis University, College of Education, Program in Curriculum and Instruction: Technology Learning and Design, Romeoville, IL 60446. Offers M Ed. *Program availability:* Part-time, evening/weekend. *Students:* 5 part-time (all women); includes 1 minority (Black or African American, non-Hispanic/Latino). Average age 32. *Entrance requirements:* For master's, writing exam, bachelor's degree, minimum GPA of 2.75, two letters of recommendation, interview. Additional exam requirements/recommendations for international students: Required—TOEFL (minimum score 550 paper-based; 79 iBT), IELTS (minimum score 6). *Application deadline:* For fall admission, 5/1 priority date for international students; for spring admission, 11/15 priority date for international students. Applications are processed on a rolling basis. Application fee: $40. Electronic applications accepted. *Financial support:* Career-related internships or fieldwork, Federal Work-Study, institutionally sponsored loans, and unspecified assistantships available. Financial award application deadline: 5/1; financial award applicants required to submit FAFSA. *Unit head:* Dr. Seung Kim, Program Director, 815-838-0500, E-mail: kimse@lewisu.edu. *Application contact:* Kathy Lisak, Graduate Admission Counselor, 815-836-5610, E-mail: grad@lewisu.edu.

Lindenwood University, Graduate Programs, School of Education, St. Charles, MO 63301-1695. Offers behavioral analysis (MA); education (MA), including autism spectrum disorders, character education, early intervention in autism and sensory impairment, gifted, technology; educational administration (MA, Ed D, Ed S); English to speakers of other languages (MA); instructional leadership (Ed D, Ed S); library media (MA); professional counseling (MA); school administration (MA, Ed S); school counseling (MA); teaching (MA). *Program availability:* Part-time, evening/weekend, 100% online, blended/hybrid learning. *Faculty:* 38 full-time (28 women), 111 part-time/adjunct (66 women). *Students:* 456 full-time (341 women), 1,107 part-time (851 women); includes 374 minority (296 Black or African American, non-Hispanic/Latino; 7 American Indian or Alaska Native, non-Hispanic/Latino; 8 Asian, non-Hispanic/Latino; 38 Hispanic/Latino; 1 Native Hawaiian or other Pacific Islander, non-Hispanic/Latino; 24 Two or more races, non-Hispanic/Latino), 17 international. Average age 36. 496 applicants, 72% accepted, 275 enrolled. In 2018, 454 master's, 64 doctorates, 66 other advanced degrees awarded. *Degree requirements:* For master's, thesis (for some programs), minimum GPA of 3.0; for doctorate, thesis/dissertation, minimum GPA of 3.0; for Ed S, comprehensive exam, project, minimum GPA of 3.0. *Entrance requirements:* For master's, interview, minimum undergraduate cumulative GPA of 3.0, writing sample, letter of recommendation; for doctorate, minimum graduate GPA of 3.4, resume, interview, writing sample, 4 letters of recommendation; for Ed S, master's degree in education, relevant work experience. Additional exam requirements/recommendations for international students: Required—TOEFL (minimum score 553 paper-based; 81 iBT); Recommended—IELTS (minimum score 6.5). *Application deadline:* For fall admission, 8/9 priority date for domestic students, 6/1 priority date for international students; for spring admission, 12/20 priority date for domestic students, 11/1 priority date for international students; for summer admission, 5/15 priority date for domestic students, 3/27 priority date for international students. Applications are processed on a rolling basis. Application fee: $0 ($100 for international students). Electronic applications accepted. *Expenses: Tuition:* Full-time $16,900; part-time $480 per credit hour. *Required fees:* $700; $350 per unit. Tuition and fees vary according to degree level. *Financial support:* In 2018–19, 316 students received support. Career-related internships or fieldwork, Federal Work-Study, institutionally sponsored loans, scholarships/grants, tuition waivers (partial), and unspecified assistantships available. Financial award application deadline: 6/30; financial award applicants required to submit FAFSA. *Unit head:* Dr. Anthony Scheffler, Dean, School of Education, 636-949-4618, Fax: 636-949-4197, E-mail: ascheffler@lindenwood.edu. *Application contact:* Kara Schilli, Assistant Vice President, University Admissions, 636-949-4349, Fax: 636-949-4109, E-mail: adultadmissions@lindenwood.edu.
Website: https://www.lindenwood.edu/academics/academic-schools/school-of-education/

Lipscomb University, College of Education, Nashville, TN 37204-3951. Offers applied behavior analysis (MS, Certificate); coaching for learning (M Ed, Certificate, Ed S); educational leadership (M Ed, Ed S); English language learning (M Ed, Ed S); instructional coaching (M Ed, Certificate, Ed S); instructional practice (M Ed); learning organizations and strategic change (Ed D); literacy coaching (Certificate, Ed S); reading specialty (M Ed, Ed S); school counseling (M Ed, Ed S); special education (M Ed); teaching, learning, and leading (M Ed); technology integration (M Ed, Ed S); technology integration specialist (Certificate). *Accreditation:* NCATE. *Program availability:* Part-time, evening/weekend, 100% online. *Degree requirements:* For master's, comprehensive exam, portfolio, research project and presentation; for doctorate, practical capstone project in experiential setting. *Entrance requirements:* For master's, MAT (minimum score 31) or GRE General Test (minimum score 294), 2 reference letters, goals statement, writing sample, interview; for doctorate, MAT or GRE General Test, 3 reference letters, artifact of demonstrated academic excellence, written personal statements, interview. Additional exam requirements/recommendations for international students: Required—TOEFL (minimum score 570 paper-based; 80 iBT). Electronic applications accepted. *Expenses:* Contact institution. *Faculty research:* Facilitative learning styles, leadership, student assessment, interactive multimedia inclusion, learning organizations and strategic change.

Long Island University–LIU Post, College of Education, Information and Technology, Brookville, NY 11548-1300. Offers adolescence education (MS); adolescence education 7-12 (MS); archives and records management (AC); art education (MS); childhood education (MS); childhood education/literacy B-6 (MS); childhood education/special education (MS); clinical mental health counseling (MS, AC); early childhood education (MS); early childhood education/childhood education (MS); educational leadership (AC); educational technology (MS); information studies (PhD); interdisciplinary educational studies (Ed D); middle childhood education (MS); music education (MS); public library administration (AC); school counselor (MS); special education (MS Ed); speech-language pathology (MA); students with disabilities, 7-12 generalist (AC); TESOL (MA). *Accreditation:* ASHA; TEAC. *Program availability:* Part-time, 100% online, blended/hybrid learning. Terminal master's awarded for partial completion of doctoral program. *Degree requirements:* For master's, variable foreign language requirement, comprehensive exam (for some programs), thesis optional; for doctorate, comprehensive exam, thesis/dissertation. *Entrance requirements:* For master's and AC, GRE (for some programs). Additional exam requirements/recommendations for international students: Required—TOEFL (minimum score 550 paper-based, 75 iBT), IELTS, or PTE. Electronic applications accepted. *Faculty research:* Sleep; use of technology to develop executive function by students with disabilities; early childhood literacy development through play; social justice through education; using a structured protocol to discuss Bad News.

Longwood University, College of Graduate and Professional Studies, College of Education and Human Services, Program in School Librarianship, Farmville, VA 23909. Offers M Ed. *Program availability:* Part-time, evening/weekend. *Degree requirements:* For master's, professional portfolio. *Entrance requirements:* For master's, PRAXIS I (for initial teaching licensure track), bachelor's degree from regionally-accredited institution, 2 recommendations, minimum 500-word personal essay, official transcripts, minimum GPA of 2.75, valid teaching license. Additional exam requirements/recommendations for international students: Required—TOEFL (minimum score 570 paper-based; 80 iBT), IELTS (minimum score 6.5). Electronic applications accepted. *Expenses:* Contact institution.

Louisiana State University and Agricultural & Mechanical College, Graduate School, College of Human Sciences and Education, Department of Educational Theory, Policy and Practice, Baton Rouge, LA 70803. Offers counseling (M Ed, MA, Ed S); educational administration (M Ed, MA, PhD, Ed S); educational technology (MA); elementary education (M Ed, MAT); higher education (PhD); research methodology (PhD); secondary education (M Ed, MAT). *Accreditation:* ACA (one or more programs are accredited); NCATE.

Loyola University Maryland, Graduate Programs, School of Education, Program in Educational Technology, Baltimore, MD 21210-2699. Offers M Ed, MA. *Program availability:* Part-time. *Degree requirements:* For master's, thesis. *Entrance requirements:* For master's, transcript, essay. Additional exam requirements/recommendations for international students: Required—TOEFL (minimum score 550 paper-based), IELTS (minimum score 7). Electronic applications accepted. *Expenses:* Contact institution.

Manhattan College, Graduate Programs, School of Education and Health, Program in Instructional Design and Delivery, Riverdale, NY 10471. Offers MS. *Program availability:* Part-time, evening/weekend. *Degree requirements:* For master's, thesis. *Entrance requirements:* For master's, GRE. Electronic applications accepted. *Expenses:* Contact institution. *Faculty research:* Simulations, gaming, adult technology integration, pre-service training, STEM integration into curriculum, Web 2.0 tool development.

Marconi International University, Graduate Programs, Miami, FL 33132. Offers business administration (DBA); education leadership (Ed D); education leadership, management and emerging technologies (M Ed); international business administration (IMBA).

Marian University, School of Education, Fond du Lac, WI 54935-4699. Offers curriculum and instruction leadership (PhD); educational administration (PhD); educational leadership (MAE); educational technology (MAE); leadership studies (PhD); special education (MAE); teacher education (MAE). *Accreditation:* NCATE. *Program availability:* Part-time, evening/weekend, online learning. *Degree requirements:* For master's, exam, field-based experience project, portfolio; for doctorate, comprehensive exam, thesis/dissertation, field-based experience. *Entrance requirements:* For master's, minimum GPA of 3.0, BA in education or related field, teaching license; for doctorate, GRE, MAT, resume, 2 writing samples, interview. Additional exam requirements/recommendations for international students: Required—TOEFL (minimum score 525 paper-based; 70 iBT). *Faculty research:* At-risk youth, multicultural issues, values in education, teaching/learning strategies.

Marlboro College, Graduate and Professional Studies, Program in Learning Design and Technology, Marlboro, VT 05344. Offers educational technology (Certificate); teaching with technology (MAT). *Program availability:* Part-time, evening/weekend, blended/hybrid learning. *Degree requirements:* For master's, 36 credits including capstone project. *Entrance requirements:* For master's, statement of intent, 2 letters of recommendation, transcripts. Electronic applications accepted. *Expenses:* Contact institution.

Martin Luther College, Graduate Studies, New Ulm, MN 56073. Offers early childhood director (MS Ed Admin); educational technology (MS Ed); instruction (MS Ed); leadership (MS Ed); principal (MS Ed Admin); special education (MS Ed). *Program availability:* Part-time, evening/weekend, online only, 100% online. *Faculty:* 13 full-time (2 women), 31 part-time/adjunct (10 women). *Students:* 1 full-time (0 women), 86 part-time (26 women); includes 1 minority (Two or more races, non-Hispanic/Latino), 1 international. Average age 38. 35 applicants, 100% accepted, 35 enrolled. In 2018, 26 master's awarded. *Degree requirements:* For master's, capstone project or comprehensive exam. *Entrance requirements:* For master's, undergraduate degree in education from an accredited college or university, minimum undergraduate GPA of 3.0. Additional exam requirements/recommendations for international students: Required—TOEFL (minimum score 550 paper-based; 80 iBT); Recommended—IELTS (minimum score 6.5). *Application deadline:* Applications are processed on a rolling basis. Application fee: $35. Electronic applications accepted. *Financial support:* In 2018–19, 1 student received support. Scholarships/grants available. Financial award application deadline: 9/1. *Faculty research:* Principal effectiveness, principal support, cognitive load in math instruction, reading strategies in multigrade classrooms, mentor provided professional development for new teachers. *Unit head:* John E. Meyer, Director of Graduate Studies, 507-354-8221 Ext. 398, E-mail: meyerjd@mlc-wels.edu. *Application contact:* John E. Meyer, Director of Graduate Studies, 507-354-8221 Ext. 398, E-mail: meyerjd@mlc-wels.edu.
Website: https://mlc-wels.edu/graduate-studies/

Marygrove College, Graduate Studies, Detroit, MI 48221-2599. Offers autism spectrum disorders (M Ed, Certificate); curriculum instruction and assessment (MAT); educational leadership (MA); educational technology (M Ed); effective teaching in the 21st century-classroom focus (MAT); effective teaching in the 21st century-technology focus (MAT); human resource management (MA, Certificate); mathematics 6-8 (MAT); mathematics K-5 (MAT); reading and literacy K-6 (MAT); reading specialist (M Ed); school

administrator (Certificate); social justice (MA); special education (MAT); special education - learning disabilities (M Ed); teaching - pre-elementary education (M Ed); teaching - pre-secondary education (M Ed). *Program availability:* Part-time, evening/weekend, 100% online, blended/hybrid learning. *Entrance requirements:* For master's, all official bachelor's transcripts. Additional exam requirements/recommendations for international students: Required—TOEFL (minimum score 550 paper-based; 80 iBT). Electronic applications accepted.

Massachusetts College of Liberal Arts, Graduate Programs, North Adams, MA 01247-4100. Offers business (MBA); educational administration (M Ed); educational leadership (CAGS); instruction and curriculum (M Ed); instructional technology (M Ed); physical education and health (M Ed); reading (M Ed); special education (M Ed). *Program availability:* Part-time, evening/weekend. *Degree requirements:* For master's, thesis. *Entrance requirements:* For master's, writing sample.

McDaniel College, Graduate and Professional Studies, Program in School Librarianship, Westminster, MD 21157-4390. Offers MS. *Program availability:* Part-time, evening/weekend, online only, 100% online. *Degree requirements:* For master's, comprehensive exam, thesis optional. *Entrance requirements:* For master's, PRAXIS, 3 recommendations, essay. Additional exam requirements/recommendations for international students: Required—TOEFL (minimum score 79 iBT), IELTS (minimum score 6). Electronic applications accepted.

McNeese State University, Doré School of Graduate Studies, Burton College of Education, Department of Education Professions, Program in Educational Leadership, Lake Charles, LA 70609. Offers educational leadership (M Ed, Ed S); educational technology (Ed S). *Program availability:* Evening/weekend. *Entrance requirements:* For master's, GRE, teaching certificate, 3 years of full-time teaching experience; for Ed S, teaching certificate, 3 years of teaching experience, 1 year of administration or supervision experience, master's degree with 12 semester hours in education.

McNeese State University, Doré School of Graduate Studies, Burton College of Education, Department of Education Professions, Program in Educational Technology Leadership, Lake Charles, LA 70609. Offers M Ed. *Program availability:* Evening/weekend. *Entrance requirements:* For master's, GRE, teaching certificate.

McNeese State University, Doré School of Graduate Studies, Burton College of Education, Department of Education Professions, Program in Instructional Technology, Lake Charles, LA 70609. Offers MS. *Program availability:* Evening/weekend. *Entrance requirements:* For master's, GRE.

Memorial University of Newfoundland, School of Graduate Studies, Faculty of Education, St. John's, NL A1C 5S7, Canada. Offers counseling psychology (M Ed); curriculum, teaching, and learning studies (M Ed); education (PhD); educational leadership studies (M Ed, Graduate Diploma); information technology (M Ed); post-secondary studies (M Ed, Diploma), including health professional education (Diploma). *Program availability:* Part-time. *Degree requirements:* For master's, thesis optional, internship, paper folio, project; for doctorate, comprehensive exam, thesis/dissertation, thesis seminar, oral defense of thesis. *Entrance requirements:* For master's, undergraduate degree with at least 2nd class standing, 1-2 years of work experience; for doctorate, minimum A average in graduate course work, MA in education, 2 years of professional experience; for other advanced degree, 2nd class degree, 2 years of work experience with adult learners, appropriate academic qualifications and work experience in a health-related field. Electronic applications accepted. *Faculty research:* Critical thinking, literacy, cognitive studies and counseling, educational change, technology in instruction.

Michigan State University, The Graduate School, College of Education, Department of Counseling, Educational Psychology and Special Education, East Lansing, MI 48824. Offers counseling (MA); educational psychology and educational technology (PhD); educational technology (MA); measurement and quantitative methods (PhD); rehabilitation counseling (MA); rehabilitation counselor education (PhD); school psychology (MA, PhD, Ed S); special education (MA, PhD). *Accreditation:* APA (one or more programs are accredited); CORE (one or more programs are accredited). *Program availability:* Part-time. *Entrance requirements:* Additional exam requirements/recommendations for international students: Required—TOEFL. Electronic applications accepted.

MidAmerica Nazarene University, Professional and Graduate Studies in Education, Olathe, KS 66062-1899. Offers ESOL (M Ed); reading specialist (M Ed); technology enhanced teaching (M Ed). *Accreditation:* NCATE. *Program availability:* Part-time, evening/weekend, online only, 100% online. *Entrance requirements:* For master's, bachelor's degree from an accredited college or university, minimum undergraduate GPA of 3.0, valid teaching license. Additional exam requirements/recommendations for international students: Required—TOEFL (minimum score 81 iBT), IELTS (minimum score 6). Electronic applications accepted. *Expenses:* Contact institution.

Middle Tennessee State University, College of Graduate Studies, College of Education, Department of Educational Leadership, Program in Curriculum and Instruction, Murfreesboro, TN 37132. Offers curriculum and instruction (M Ed, Ed S); English as a second language (M Ed, Ed S); secondary education (M Ed); technology and curriculum design (Ed S). *Accreditation:* NCATE. *Program availability:* Part-time, evening/weekend, online learning. *Degree requirements:* For master's, comprehensive exam; for Ed S, comprehensive exam, thesis or alternative. *Entrance requirements:* For master's and Ed S, GRE, MAT or PRAXIS. Additional exam requirements/recommendations for international students: Required—TOEFL (minimum score 525 paper-based; 71 iBT) or IELTS (minimum score 6). Electronic applications accepted.

Midwestern State University, Billie Doris McAda Graduate School, West College of Education, Programs in Educational Leadership and Technology, Wichita Falls, TX 76308. Offers educational leadership (M Ed); educational technology (M Ed). *Program availability:* Part-time, evening/weekend. *Degree requirements:* For master's, comprehensive exam. *Entrance requirements:* For master's, GRE General Test or MAT. Additional exam requirements/recommendations for international students: Required—TOEFL (minimum score 550 paper-based). Electronic applications accepted. *Faculty research:* Role of the principal in the twenty-first century, culturally proficient leadership, human diversity, immigration, teacher collaboration.

Misericordia University, College of Health Sciences and Education, Program in Education, Dallas, PA 18612-1098. Offers instructional technology (MS); reading specialist (MS); special education (MS). *Program availability:* Part-time, evening/weekend. *Entrance requirements:* For master's, minimum undergraduate GPA of 3.0. Additional exam requirements/recommendations for international students: Required—TOEFL. Electronic applications accepted.

Mississippi State University, College of Education, Department of Instructional Systems and Workforce Development, Mississippi State, MS 39762. Offers instructional systems and workforce development (MSIT, PhD); technology (MST, Ed S). *Faculty:* 9 full-time (5 women). *Students:* 11 full-time (5 women), 45 part-time (34 women); includes 32 minority (31 Black or African American, non-Hispanic/Latino; 1 Two or more races, non-Hispanic/Latino). Average age 36. 11 applicants, 36% accepted, 3 enrolled. In 2018, 3 master's, 6 doctorates, 2 other advanced degrees awarded. *Degree requirements:* For master's, thesis optional, comprehensive oral or written exam; for doctorate, thesis/dissertation, comprehensive oral and written exam; for Ed S, thesis, comprehensive written exam. *Entrance requirements:* For master's, GRE, minimum GPA of 2.75 on undergraduate work, 3.0 graduate; for doctorate, GRE, minimum GPA of 3.4 on graduate work; for Ed S, GRE, minimum GPA of 3.2, master's degree. Additional exam requirements/recommendations for international students: Required—TOEFL (minimum score 550 paper-based; 79 iBT); Recommended—IELTS (minimum score 6.5). *Application deadline:* For fall admission, 7/1 for domestic students, 5/1 for international students; for spring admission, 11/1 for domestic students, 9/1 for international students. Applications are processed on a rolling basis. Application fee: $60 ($80 for international students). Electronic applications accepted. *Expenses:* Tuition, state resident: full-time $8450; part-time $360.59 per credit hour. Tuition, nonresident: full-time $23,140; part-time $969.09 per credit hour. *Required fees:* $110. One-time fee: $55 full-time. Part-time tuition and fees vary according to course load, degree level, campus/location and reciprocity agreements. *Financial support:* In 2018–19, 1 teaching assistantship with full tuition reimbursement (averaging $10,800 per year) was awarded; Federal Work-Study, institutionally sponsored loans, scholarships/grants, and unspecified assistantships also available. Financial award application deadline: 4/1; financial award applicants required to submit FAFSA. *Faculty research:* Computer technology, nontraditional students, interactive video, instructional technology, educational leadership. *Unit head:* Dr. Trey Martindale, Associate Professor and Head, 662-325-7258, Fax: 662-325-7599, E-mail: tmartindale@colled.msstate.edu. *Application contact:* Angie Campbell, Admissions and Enrollment Assistant, 662-325-9514, E-mail: acampbell@grad.msstate.edu.
Website: http://www.iswd.msstate.edu

Missouri Southern State University, Program in Instructional Technology, Joplin, MO 64801-1595. Offers MS Ed. Program offered jointly with Northwest Missouri State University. *Degree requirements:* For master's, comprehensive exam, research paper. *Entrance requirements:* For master's, GRE (minimum combined score of 700), writing assessment, minimum overall undergraduate GPA of 3.0.

Missouri State University, Graduate College, College of Education, Department of Reading, Foundations, and Technology, Program in Educational Technology, Springfield, MO 65897. Offers MS Ed. *Program availability:* Part-time. *Faculty:* 16 full-time (11 women), 14 part-time/adjunct (13 women). *Students:* 2 full-time (1 woman), 34 part-time (24 women); includes 3 minority (1 Black or African American, non-Hispanic/Latino; 1 Asian, non-Hispanic/Latino; 1 Hispanic/Latino), 3 international. Average age 27. 13 applicants, 85% accepted. In 2018, 20 master's awarded. *Degree requirements:* For master's, comprehensive exam, thesis or alternative. *Entrance requirements:* Additional exam requirements/recommendations for international students: Required—TOEFL (minimum score 550 paper-based; 79 iBT), IELTS (minimum score 6). *Application deadline:* For fall admission, 7/20 priority date for domestic students, 5/1 for international students; for spring admission, 12/20 priority date for domestic students, 9/1 for international students; for summer admission, 5/20 priority date for domestic students. Applications are processed on a rolling basis. Application fee: $55 ($60 for international students). Electronic applications accepted. Tuition and fees vary according to class time, course level, course load, degree level, campus/location, program and student level. *Financial support:* Federal Work-Study, institutionally sponsored loans, scholarships/grants, and unspecified assistantships available. Financial award application deadline: 1/31; financial award applicants required to submit FAFSA. *Unit head:* Dr. Emmett Sawyer, Interim Department Head, 417-836-6769, E-mail: rft@missouristate.edu. *Application contact:* Lakan Drinker, Director, Graduate Enrollment Management, 417-836-5330, Fax: 417-836-6200, E-mail: lakandrinker@missouristate.edu.
Website: http://education.missouristate.edu/rft/

Molloy College, Graduate Education Program, Rockville Centre, NY 11571-5002. Offers adolescent education in biology (MS); adolescent special education (Advanced Certificate); bilingual extension (Advanced Certificate); childhood education (MS); childhood special education (Advanced Certificate); early childhood education (MS); educational technology (MS); English (MS); mathematics (MS); social studies (MS); Spanish (MS); special education on both childhood and adolescent levels (MS); teaching English to speakers of other languages (TESOL) in grades pre-K to 12 (MS); TESOL (Advanced Certificate). *Accreditation:* NCATE. *Program availability:* Part-time, evening/weekend. *Faculty:* 24 full-time (22 women), 26 part-time/adjunct (19 women). *Students:* 106 full-time (78 women), 203 part-time (154 women); includes 65 minority (14 Black or African American, non-Hispanic/Latino; 5 Asian, non-Hispanic/Latino; 41 Hispanic/Latino; 5 Two or more races, non-Hispanic/Latino). Average age 41. 147 applicants, 63% accepted, 79 enrolled. In 2018, 120 master's, 1 other advanced degree awarded. *Entrance requirements:* Additional exam requirements/recommendations for international students: Required—TOEFL (minimum score 550 paper-based; 79 iBT). *Application deadline:* Applications are processed on a rolling basis. Application fee: $60. Electronic applications accepted. *Expenses: Tuition:* Full-time $20,790; part-time $1155 per credit. *Required fees:* $1060; $900. Tuition and fees vary according to course load and degree level. *Financial support:* Application deadline: 3/1; applicants required to submit FAFSA. *Faculty research:* English Language Learners; social emotional needs of students; gifted education; cultural diversity; collaborative teaching methods. *Unit head:* Joanne O'Brien, Dean, 516-323-3116, E-mail: jobrien@molloy.edu. *Application contact:* Faye Hood, Assistant Director for Admissions, 516-323-4009, E-mail: fhood@molloy.edu.

Montana State University Billings, College of Education, Department of Educational Theory and Practice, Option in Online Instructional Technologies, Billings, MT 59101. Offers M Ed. *Accreditation:* NCATE. *Program availability:* Part-time. *Degree requirements:* For master's, professional paper or thesis. *Entrance requirements:* For master's, GRE General Test or MAT, minimum GPA of 3.0. Additional exam requirements/recommendations for international students: Required—TOEFL (minimum score 79 iBT), IELTS (minimum score 6.5). Electronic applications accepted.

Morehead State University, Graduate School, College of Education, Department of Foundational and Graduate Studies in Education, Morehead, KY 40351. Offers adult and higher education (MA, Ed S); certified professional counselor (Ed S); counseling P-12 (MA); curriculum and instruction (Ed S); educational technology (MA Ed); instructional leadership (Ed S); school administration (MA); school counseling (Ed S); teacher leader business and marketing content (MA Ed); teacher leader business and marketing technology (MA Ed); teacher leader educational technology (MA Ed); teacher leader English (MA Ed); teacher leader gifted education (MA Ed); teacher leader IECE certification (MA Ed); teacher leader interdisciplinary education P-5 (MA Ed); teacher leader middle grades (MA Ed); teacher leader non IECE certification (MA Ed); teacher leader reading/writing - non-certification (MA Ed); teacher leader reading/writing certification (MA Ed); teacher leader school communication - certification (MA Ed); teacher leader school communication - non-certification (MA Ed); teacher leader social studies (MA Ed); teacher leader special education (MA Ed). *Accreditation:* NCATE. *Program availability:* Part-time, evening/weekend. *Degree requirements:* For master's, thesis optional, oral and/or written comprehensive exams; for Ed S, thesis, oral exam. *Entrance requirements:* For master's, GRE General Test, minimum overall undergraduate GPA of 2.5; for Ed S, GRE General Test, interview, master's degree, minimum GPA of 3.5, work experience. Additional exam requirements/

recommendations for international students: Required—TOEFL (minimum score 500 paper-based). Electronic applications accepted. *Faculty research:* Character education, school accountability, computer applications for school administrators.

Murray State University, College of Education and Human Services, Department of Educational Studies, Leadership and Counseling, Murray, KY 42071. Offers college advising (Certificate); education administration (MA Ed); human development and leadership (MS, Certificate); library media (MA Ed); middle school teacher leader (MA Ed); P-20 and community leadership (Ed D); postsecondary education administration (MA Ed); school counseling (MA Ed); school guidance and counseling (Ed S); secondary teacher leader (MA Ed). *Program availability:* Part-time, evening/weekend, 100% online, blended/hybrid learning. *Entrance requirements:* For master's and other advanced degree, GRE or GMAT, minimum university GPA of 2.75. Additional exam requirements/recommendations for international students: Required—TOEFL (minimum score 527 paper-based; 71 iBT). Electronic applications accepted.

National Louis University, National College of Education, Chicago, IL 60603. Offers administration and supervision (M Ed, Ed D, CAS, Ed S); curriculum and instruction (M Ed, MS Ed, CAS); early childhood administration (M Ed, CAS); early childhood education (M Ed, MAT, MS Ed, CAS); education (Ed D); educational psychology/human learning and development (M Ed, MS Ed, CAS, Ed S); elementary education (MAT); interdisciplinary curriculum and instruction (M Ed); mathematics education (M Ed, MS Ed, CAS); middle grades education (MAT); reading and language (M Ed, MS Ed, CAS); school psychology (M Ed, Ed S); science education (M Ed, MS Ed, CAS); secondary education (MAT); special education (M Ed, MAT, CAS); technology in education (M Ed, CAS). *Accreditation:* NCATE. *Program availability:* Part-time, evening/weekend. *Degree requirements:* For doctorate, comprehensive exam, thesis/dissertation. *Entrance requirements:* For master's, MAT or GRE, minimum GPA of 3.0; for doctorate, GRE General Test, minimum GPA of 3.25, interview, resume, writing sample, 4 recommendations. Additional exam requirements/recommendations for international students: Required—TOEFL (minimum score 550 paper-based; 79 iBT).

National University, Sanford College of Education, La Jolla, CA 92037-1011. Offers advanced teaching practices (MS); applied behavior analysis (MS); applied school leadership (MS); e-teaching and learning (Certificate); education (MA); educational administration (MS); educational and instructional technology (MS); educational counseling (MS); higher education administration (MS); inspired teaching and learning (M Ed); school psychology (MS); special education (MA, MS). *Program availability:* Part-time, evening/weekend, 100% online, blended/hybrid learning. *Degree requirements:* For master's, thesis (for some programs). *Entrance requirements:* For master's, interview, minimum GPA of 2.5. Additional exam requirements/recommendations for international students: Required—TOEFL (minimum score 550 paper-based; 79 iBT), IELTS (minimum score 6). Electronic applications accepted. *Expenses: Tuition:* Full-time $10,320; part-time $430 per unit. Tuition and fees vary according to degree level. *Faculty research:* Teacher education, special education, educational effectiveness, teaching abroad, school counseling.

Nazareth College of Rochester, Graduate Studies, Department of Education, Program of Educational Technology, Rochester, NY 14618. Offers MS Ed. *Program availability:* Part-time, evening/weekend. *Entrance requirements:* For master's, minimum GPA of 3.0. Additional exam requirements/recommendations for international students: Required—TOEFL or IELTS.

New Jersey City University, Debra Cannon Partridge Wolfe College of Education, Department of Educational Technology, Jersey City, NJ 07305-1597. Offers educational technology (MA); educational technology leadership (Ed D). *Accreditation:* NCATE. *Program availability:* Part-time, evening/weekend, online learning. *Degree requirements:* For master's, internship. *Entrance requirements:* Additional exam requirements/recommendations for international students: Required—TOEFL (minimum score 79 iBT).

New York Institute of Technology, School of Interdisciplinary Studies and Education, Department of Instructional Technology, Old Westbury, NY 11568-8000. Offers emerging technologies for trainers (Advanced Certificate); instructional design for global e-learning (Advanced Certificate); instructional technology (MS), including educators, trainers; STEM education (Advanced Certificate). *Program availability:* Part-time, evening/weekend, 100% online, blended/hybrid learning. *Faculty:* 2 full-time (1 woman), 13 part-time/adjunct (5 women). *Students:* 1 full-time (0 women), 80 part-time (51 women); includes 22 minority (8 Black or African American, non-Hispanic/Latino; 5 Asian, non-Hispanic/Latino; 7 Hispanic/Latino; 2 Two or more races, non-Hispanic/Latino). Average age 33. 56 applicants, 63% accepted, 25 enrolled. In 2018, 54 master's, 6 other advanced degrees awarded. *Entrance requirements:* For master's, bachelor's degree; minimum undergraduate GPA of 3.0; demonstrated proficiency in basic uses of instructional technologies; initial/provisional or permanent/professional NY state certification in any teaching area; for Advanced Certificate, BS; minimum undergraduate GPA of 3.0; demonstrated proficiency in basic uses of instructional technologies. Additional exam requirements/recommendations for international students: Required—TOEFL (minimum score 79 iBT), IELTS (minimum score 6), PTE (minimum score 53). *Application deadline:* Applications are processed on a rolling basis. Application fee: $50. Electronic applications accepted. *Expenses:* $1285 per credit plus $215 fees per year (full-time) or $175 fees per year (part-time); $1395 per three-credit education UFT or off-site graduate course. *Financial support:* Career-related internships or fieldwork, scholarships/grants, health care benefits, tuition waivers (full and partial), and unspecified assistantships available. Support available to part-time students. Financial award application deadline: 2/15; financial award applicants required to submit FAFSA. *Faculty research:* Integration of information and communication technologies (ICTs) and media literacy education into learning environments; urban K-12 teachers' effective use of technology to enhance student achievement; instructional design and transdisciplinary curriculum studies for online instruction; STEM and computing partnerships for K-12 teachers; experiential, collaborative, and performance-based approaches to pedagogy and technology integration in the K-12 classroom. *Unit head:* Dr. Melda Yildiz, Department Chair, 516-686-1053, Fax: 516-686-7655, E-mail: myildiz@nyit.edu. *Application contact:* Alice Dolitsky, Director, Graduate Admissions, 516-686-7520, Fax: 516-686-1116, E-mail: admissions@nyit.edu.
Website: http://www.nyit.edu/departments_instructional_technology

New York Institute of Technology, School of Interdisciplinary Studies and Education, Department of School Leadership and Technology, Old Westbury, NY 11568-8000. Offers Advanced Diploma. *Program availability:* Part-time, evening/weekend, online only, 100% online, blended/hybrid learning. *Faculty:* 1 full-time (0 women), 5 part-time/adjunct (3 women). *Students:* 1 (woman) full-time, 42 part-time (24 women); includes 7 minority (2 Black or African American, non-Hispanic/Latino; 2 Asian, non-Hispanic/Latino; 3 Hispanic/Latino). Average age 37. 27 applicants, 93% accepted, 17 enrolled. In 2018, 29 Advanced Diplomas awarded. *Degree requirements:* For Advanced Diploma, internship. *Entrance requirements:* For degree, master's degree with minimum cumulative GPA of 3.0; personal statement; at least 3 years of full-time teaching experience; professional NY state teacher certification; demonstration of computer competency; two letters of reference from school building or district administrator. Additional exam requirements/recommendations for international students: Required—TOEFL (minimum score 79 iBT), IELTS (minimum score 6), PTE (minimum score 53). *Application deadline:* Applications are processed on a rolling basis. Application fee: $50. Electronic applications accepted. *Expenses:* $1285 per credit plus $215 fees per year (full-time) or $175 fees per year (part-time); $1395 per 3-credit education UFT or off-site graduate course. *Financial support:* Career-related internships or fieldwork, scholarships/grants, and unspecified assistantships available. Support available to part-time students. Financial award application deadline: 2/15; financial award applicants required to submit FAFSA. *Faculty research:* College readiness; school-community partnerships; administrator-school counselor relationships. *Unit head:* Dr. Robert Feirsen, Chair, 516-686-1169, E-mail: rfeirsen@nyit.edu. *Application contact:* Alice Dolitsky, Director, Graduate Admissions, 516-686-7520, Fax: 516-686-1116, E-mail: admissions@nyit.edu.
Website: https://www.nyit.edu/departments/school_leadership_and_technology

New York University, Steinhardt School of Culture, Education, and Human Development, Department of Administration, Leadership, and Technology, Programs in Educational Communication and Technology, Brooklyn, NY 11201. Offers digital media design for learning (MA, Advanced Certificate); educational communication and technology (PhD); games for learning (MS). *Program availability:* Part-time. *Entrance requirements:* For doctorate, GRE General Test, interview; for Advanced Certificate, master's degree. Additional exam requirements/recommendations for international students: Required—TOEFL (minimum score 100 iBT). Electronic applications accepted. *Faculty research:* Digital design for learning, critical evaluation of games, multimedia, cognitive science, individual differences in multimedia learning, serious games.

North Carolina Agricultural and Technical State University, The Graduate College, College of Education, Department of Administration and Instructional Services, Greensboro, NC 27411. Offers instructional technology (MS); reading education (MA Ed); school administration (MSA). *Accreditation:* NCATE. *Program availability:* Part-time, evening/weekend. *Degree requirements:* For master's, comprehensive exam, qualifying exam. *Entrance requirements:* For master's, GRE General Test, minimum GPA of 3.0.

North Carolina Central University, School of Education, Program in Educational Technology, Durham, NC 27707-3129. Offers MA. *Accreditation:* NCATE. *Program availability:* Part-time, evening/weekend. *Degree requirements:* For master's, comprehensive exam, thesis or alternative. *Entrance requirements:* For master's, GRE, minimum GPA of 3.0 in major, 2.5 overall. Additional exam requirements/recommendations for international students: Required—TOEFL.

North Carolina State University, Graduate School, College of Education, Department of Science, Technology, Engineering, and Mathematics Education, Program in Technology Education, Raleigh, NC 27695. Offers M Ed, MS, Ed D. *Degree requirements:* For master's, thesis (for some programs); for doctorate, thesis/dissertation. *Entrance requirements:* For master's, GRE or MAT; for doctorate, GRE General Test or MAT, minimum GPA of 3.0, interview. Electronic applications accepted.

Northeastern State University, College of Education, Department of Curriculum and Instruction, Program in Library Media and Information Technology, Tahlequah, OK 74464-2399. Offers MS. *Faculty:* 15 full-time (11 women), 2 part-time/adjunct (0 women). *Students:* 7 full-time (5 women), 37 part-time (36 women); includes 16 minority (3 Black or African American, non-Hispanic/Latino; 9 American Indian or Alaska Native, non-Hispanic/Latino; 1 Asian, non-Hispanic/Latino; 3 Two or more races, non-Hispanic/Latino). Average age 36. In 2018, 14 master's awarded. *Entrance requirements:* Additional exam requirements/recommendations for international students: Required—TOEFL. *Application deadline:* For fall admission, 7/1 for domestic and international students; for spring admission, 11/1 for domestic and international students. Applications are processed on a rolling basis. Application fee: $25. Electronic applications accepted. *Expenses: Tuition, area resident:* Full-time $4500; part-time $250 per credit hour. Tuition, state resident: full-time $4500; part-time $250 per credit hour. Tuition, nonresident: full-time $9999; part-time $555.50 per credit hour. *International tuition:* $9999 full-time. *Required fees:* $601.20; $33.40 per credit hour. *Unit head:* Dr. Kelli Carney, Program Chair, 918-449-6365, E-mail: carneyka@nsuok.edu. *Application contact:* Josh McCollum, Graduate Coordinator, 918-444-2093, E-mail: mccolluj@nsuok.edu.
Website: http://academics.nsuok.edu/education/DegreePrograms/GraduatePrograms/LibraryMediaInformationTechnology.aspx

Northern Arizona University, College of Education, Department of Educational Specialties, Flagstaff, AZ 86011. Offers autism spectrum disorders (Certificate); bilingual/multicultural education (M Ed), including bilingual, ESL; career and technical education (M Ed, Certificate); educational technology (M Ed, Certificate); English as a second language (Certificate); positive behavior support (Certificate); special education (M Ed), including early childhood special education, mild/moderate disabilities. *Program availability:* Part-time, 100% online, blended/hybrid learning. *Degree requirements:* For master's, variable foreign language requirement, comprehensive exam (for some programs), thesis (for some programs); for Certificate, comprehensive exam (for some programs). *Entrance requirements:* Additional exam requirements/recommendations for international students: Required—TOEFL (minimum score 80 iBT), IELTS (minimum score 6.5). Electronic applications accepted.

Northern Illinois University, Graduate School, College of Education, Department of Educational Technology, Research and Assessment, De Kalb, IL 60115-2854. Offers educational research and evaluation (MS); instructional technology (MS Ed, Ed D). *Program availability:* Part-time, evening/weekend. *Faculty:* 13 full-time (7 women). *Students:* 57 full-time (32 women), 133 part-time (84 women); includes 35 minority (13 Black or African American, non-Hispanic/Latino; 9 Asian, non-Hispanic/Latino; 8 Hispanic/Latino; 5 Two or more races, non-Hispanic/Latino), 47 international. Average age 39. 48 applicants, 77% accepted, 26 enrolled. In 2018, 39 master's, 10 doctorates awarded. Terminal master's awarded for partial completion of doctoral program. *Degree requirements:* For master's, comprehensive exam, thesis optional; for doctorate, thesis/dissertation, candidacy exam, dissertation defense. *Entrance requirements:* For master's, GRE General Test or MAT, minimum GPA of 2.75; for doctorate, GRE General Test or MAT, minimum undergraduate GPA of 2.75, 3.2 graduate. Additional exam requirements/recommendations for international students: Required—TOEFL (minimum score 550 paper-based). *Application deadline:* For fall admission, 6/1 for domestic students, 5/1 for international students; for spring admission, 11/1 for domestic students, 10/1 for international students. Applications are processed on a rolling basis. Application fee: $40. Electronic applications accepted. *Financial support:* In 2018–19, 1 research assistantship with full tuition reimbursement, 39 teaching assistantships with full tuition reimbursements were awarded; fellowships with full tuition reimbursements, career-related internships or fieldwork, Federal Work-Study, scholarships/grants, tuition waivers (full), and unspecified assistantships also available. Support available to part-time students. Financial award applicants required to submit FAFSA. *Faculty research:* Distance education, Web-based training, copyright assessment during student teaching, instructional software. *Unit head:* Dr. Wei-Chen Hung, Chair, 815-753-9339, E-mail: etra@niu.edu. *Application contact:* Graduate School Office, 815-753-0395, E-mail: gradsch@niu.edu.
Website: http://www.cedu.niu.edu/etra/index.html

Educational Media/Instructional Technology

Northern State University, MS Ed Program in Instructional Design in E-learning, Aberdeen, SD 57401-7198. Offers MS Ed. *Program availability:* Part-time, online learning. *Degree requirements:* For master's, comprehensive exam, thesis optional. *Entrance requirements:* For master's, minimum GPA of 2.75. Additional exam requirements/recommendations for international students: Required—TOEFL (minimum score 550 paper-based; 78 iBT), IELTS (minimum score 6). Electronic applications accepted.

Northern State University, MS Program in Training and Development in E-learning, Aberdeen, SD 57401-7198. Offers MS. *Program availability:* Part-time, online learning. *Degree requirements:* For master's, comprehensive exam, thesis optional. *Entrance requirements:* For master's, minimum GPA of 2.75. Additional exam requirements/recommendations for international students: Required—TOEFL (minimum score 550 paper-based; 78 iBT), IELTS (minimum score 6). Electronic applications accepted.

Northwestern State University of Louisiana, Graduate Studies and Research, College of Education and Human Development, Program in Educational Technology Leadership, Natchitoches, LA 71497. Offers M Ed. *Degree requirements:* For master's, comprehensive exam, thesis (for some programs). *Entrance requirements:* For master's, GRE General Test. Additional exam requirements/recommendations for international students: Required—TOEFL. Electronic applications accepted.

Northwestern State University of Louisiana, Graduate Studies and Research, College of Education and Human Development, Programs in Educational Leadership and Instruction, Natchitoches, LA 71497. Offers counseling (Ed S); educational leadership (M Ed, Ed S); educational technology (Ed S); elementary teaching (Ed S); reading (Ed S); secondary teaching (Ed S); special education (Ed S). *Accreditation:* NASAD. *Degree requirements:* For master's, comprehensive exam, thesis (for some programs). *Entrance requirements:* For master's and Ed S, GRE General Test. Additional exam requirements/recommendations for international students: Required—TOEFL. Electronic applications accepted.

Northwestern University, The Graduate School, School of Education and Social Policy, Program in Learning Sciences, Evanston, IL 60208. Offers MA, PhD. Admissions and degrees offered through The Graduate School. Terminal master's awarded for partial completion of doctoral program. *Degree requirements:* For master's, thesis or alternative, portfolio; for doctorate, thesis/dissertation, qualifying exam. *Entrance requirements:* For doctorate, GRE General Test. Additional exam requirements/recommendations for international students: Required—TOEFL (minimum score 600 paper-based; 100 iBT). Electronic applications accepted. *Expenses:* Contact institution. *Faculty research:* Technologically supported learning environments; inquiry-based learning in mathematics, science, and literacy; learning social contexts; cognitive models of learning and problem solving; changing roles for teachers involved in innovative design and practice.

Northwest Missouri State University, Graduate School, School of Computer Science and Information Systems, Maryville, MO 64468-6001. Offers applied computer science (MS); information systems (MS); instructional technology (MS). *Program availability:* Part-time. *Faculty:* 13 full-time (5 women). *Students:* 205 full-time (82 women), 36 part-time (14 women); includes 1 minority (Two or more races, non-Hispanic/Latino), 233 international. Average age 24. 459 applicants, 79% accepted, 116 enrolled. In 2018, 185 master's awarded. *Degree requirements:* For master's, comprehensive exam. *Entrance requirements:* For master's, GRE General Test, minimum GPA of 3.0. Additional exam requirements/recommendations for international students: Required—TOEFL (minimum score 550 paper-based). *Application deadline:* Applications are processed on a rolling basis. Application fee: $0 ($75 for international students). *Expenses: Tuition, area resident:* Full-time $4551; part-time $252.86 per credit hour. Tuition, state resident: full-time $4551; part-time $252.86 per credit hour. Tuition, nonresident: full-time $9103; part-time $505.72 per credit hour. International tuition: $9103 full-time. Required fees: $2668; $148.20 per credit hour. Tuition and fees vary according to program. *Financial support:* Research assistantships, teaching assistantships with full tuition reimbursements, and unspecified assistantships available. Financial award application deadline: 4/1; financial award applicants required to submit FAFSA. *Unit head:* Dr. Douglas Hawley, Director of School of Computer Science and Information Systems, 660-562-1200, Fax: 660-562-1963, E-mail: hawley@nwmissouri.edu. *Application contact:* Dr. Gregory Haddock, Dean of Graduate School, 660-562-1145, Fax: 660-562-1096, E-mail: gradsch@nwmissouri.edu.
Website: http://www.nwmissouri.edu/csis/

Nova Southeastern University, Abraham S. Fischler College of Education, Fort Lauderdale, FL 33314. Offers education (MS, Ed D, PhD, Ed S); instructional technology and distance education (MS); teaching and learning (MA). *Accreditation:* NCATE. *Program availability:* Part-time, evening/weekend, 100% online, blended/hybrid learning. *Degree requirements:* For master's, practicum, internship; for doctorate, thesis/dissertation; for Ed S, thesis, practicum, internship. *Entrance requirements:* For master's, MAT or GRE (for some programs), CLAST, PRAXIS I, CBEST, General Knowledge Test, teaching certification, minimum GPA of 2.5, verification of teaching, BS; for doctorate, MAT or GRE, master's degree, minimum cumulative GPA of 3.0; for Ed S, MAT or GRE, master's degree, teaching certificate, minimum GPA of 3.0. Additional exam requirements/recommendations for international students: Recommended—TOEFL (minimum score 550 paper-based; 79 iBT), IELTS (minimum score 6). Electronic applications accepted. *Expenses:* Contact institution. *Faculty research:* STEM education, educational technology, principal training, quality of life.

Ohio University, Graduate College, Gladys W. and David H. Patton College of Education and Human Services, Department of Educational Studies, Athens, OH 45701-2979. Offers computer education and technology (M Ed); educational administration (M Ed, Ed D); educational research and evaluation (M Ed, PhD); instructional technology (PhD). *Program availability:* Part-time, evening/weekend, online learning. *Degree requirements:* For master's, thesis or alternative; for doctorate, comprehensive exam, thesis/dissertation. *Entrance requirements:* For master's, GRE General Test (if GPA less than 2.9); for doctorate, GRE General Test, GRE Subject Test, minimum GPA of 2.9, work experience, 3 letters of reference, autobiography. Additional exam requirements/recommendations for international students: Required—TOEFL (minimum score 550 paper-based; 80 iBT) or IELTS (minimum score 6.5). Electronic applications accepted. *Faculty research:* Race, class and gender; computer programs; development and organization theory; evaluation/development of instruments, leadership.

Old Dominion University, Darden College of Education, Program in Elementary/Middle Education, Norfolk, VA 23529. Offers elementary education (Postbaccalaureate Certificate); instructional technology (MS Ed); library science (MS Ed). *Accreditation:* NCATE. *Program availability:* Part-time, evening/weekend, 100% online, blended/hybrid learning. *Degree requirements:* For master's, comprehensive exam. *Entrance requirements:* For master's, GRE General Test or MAT; PRAXIS I, SAT or ACT, minimum GPA of 2.8. Additional exam requirements/recommendations for international students: Required—TOEFL (minimum score 600 paper-based). Electronic applications accepted. *Expenses:* Contact institution. *Faculty research:* Education pre-K to 6, school librarianship, reading, TESOL, literacy.

Old Dominion University, Darden College of Education, Program in Instructional Design and Technology, Norfolk, VA 23529. Offers PhD. *Program availability:* Part-time, evening/weekend, 100% online, blended/hybrid learning. *Degree requirements:* For doctorate, comprehensive exam, thesis/dissertation. *Entrance requirements:* For doctorate, GRE, references, interview, essay of 500 words. Additional exam requirements/recommendations for international students: Required—TOEFL (minimum score 550 paper-based). Electronic applications accepted. *Faculty research:* Instructional design, distance education, instructional strategies, human performance technology, simulation design.

Ottawa University, Graduate Studies-Arizona, Program in Education, Ottawa, KS 66067-3399. Offers community college counseling (MA); curriculum and instruction (MA); early childhood (MA); education intervention (MA); education leadership (MA); education technology (MA); Montessori early childhood education (MA); Montessori elementary education (MA); professional development (MA); school guidance counseling (MA); special education - cross categorical (MA). Programs offered in Mesa, Phoenix, Tempe and West Valley, AZ. *Accreditation:* NCATE. *Program availability:* Part-time. *Degree requirements:* For master's, thesis or alternative. *Entrance requirements:* For master's, minimum undergraduate GPA of 3.0, copy of current state certification or teaching license. Additional exam requirements/recommendations for international students: Required—TOEFL (minimum score 550 paper-based). Electronic applications accepted. *Expenses:* Contact institution.

Pace University, School of Education, New York, NY 10038. Offers adolescent education (MST), including biology, chemistry, earth science, English, foreign languages, mathematics, physics, social studies; childhood education (MST); early childhood development, learning and intervention (MST); educational technology studies (MS); inclusive adolescent education (MST), including biology, chemistry, earth science, English, foreign languages, mathematics, physics, social studies; integrated instruction for educational technology (Certificate); integrated instruction for literacy and technology (Certificate); literacy (MS Ed); special education (MS Ed). *Accreditation:* NCATE. *Program availability:* Part-time, evening/weekend, 100% online, blended/hybrid learning. *Faculty:* 19 full-time (13 women), 86 part-time/adjunct (49 women). *Students:* 98 full-time (82 women), 542 part-time (391 women); includes 256 minority (116 Black or African American, non-Hispanic/Latino; 2 American Indian or Alaska Native, non-Hispanic/Latino; 45 Asian, non-Hispanic/Latino; 83 Hispanic/Latino; 10 Two or more races, non-Hispanic/Latino), 4 international. Average age 30. 223 applicants, 89% accepted, 130 enrolled. In 2018, 269 master's, 12 other advanced degrees awarded. *Degree requirements:* For master's and Certificate, certification exams. *Entrance requirements:* For master's, GRE (for initial certification programs only), teaching certificate (for MS Ed in literacy and special education programs only). Additional exam requirements/recommendations for international students: Required—TOEFL (minimum score 88 iBT), IELTS or PTE. *Application deadline:* For fall admission, 8/1 priority date for domestic students, 6/1 for international students; for spring admission, 12/1 priority date for domestic students, 10/1 for international students. Applications are processed on a rolling basis. Application fee: $70. Electronic applications accepted. *Expenses:* Contact institution. *Financial support:* In 2018–19, 17 students received support, including 17 research assistantships with partial tuition reimbursements available (averaging $6,020 per year); career-related internships or fieldwork, Federal Work-Study, scholarships/grants, and unspecified assistantships also available. Financial award application deadline: 9/1; financial award applicants required to submit FAFSA. *Faculty research:* STEM education, TESOL, teacher education, special education, language and literary development. *Total annual research expenditures:* $1.4 million. *Unit head:* Dr. Harriet Feldman, Dean, School of Education, 914-773-3829, E-mail: hfeldman@pace.edu. *Application contact:* Susan Ford-Goldschein, Director of Graduate Admissions, 212-346-1531, Fax: 212-346-1585, E-mail: graduateadmission@pace.edu. Website: http://www.pace.edu/school-of-education

Penn State University Park, Graduate School, College of Education, Department of Learning and Performance Systems, University Park, PA 16802. Offers learning, design, and technology (M Ed, MS, PhD, Certificate); lifelong learning and adult education (M Ed, D Ed, PhD, Certificate); workforce education and development (M Ed, MS, PhD).

Pittsburg State University, Graduate School, College of Education, Department of Teaching and Leadership, Program in Educational Technology, Pittsburg, KS 66762. Offers MS. *Accreditation:* NCATE. *Program availability:* Part-time, online only, 100% online. *Degree requirements:* For master's, thesis or alternative. *Entrance requirements:* For master's, PPST. Additional exam requirements/recommendations for international students: Required—TOEFL (minimum score 520 paper-based; 68 iBT), IELTS (minimum score 6), PTE (minimum score 47). Electronic applications accepted. *Expenses:* Contact institution.

Post University, Program in Education, Waterbury, CT 06723-2540. Offers curriculum and instruction (M Ed); education (M Ed); educational technology (M Ed); higher education administration (MS); learning design and technology (M Ed); online teaching (M Ed); teaching English to speakers of other languages (TESOL) (M Ed). *Program availability:* Online learning. *Entrance requirements:* For master's, resume. *Expenses: Tuition:* Full-time $8300; part-time $570 per credit. Required fees: $140 per term. Tuition and fees vary according to course level, campus/location and program.

Purdue University, Graduate School, College of Education, Department of Curriculum and Instruction, West Lafayette, IN 47907. Offers agricultural and extension education (MS, MS Ed, PhD, Ed S); art education (PhD); career and technical education (MS Ed, PhD, Ed S); curriculum studies (MS Ed, PhD, Ed S); educational technology (MS Ed, PhD, Ed S); elementary education (MS Ed); family and consumer sciences education (MS Ed, PhD, Ed S); foreign language education (MS Ed, PhD, Ed S); industrial technology (PhD, Ed S); language arts (MS Ed, PhD, Ed S); literacy (MS Ed, PhD, Ed S); mathematics education (MS, MS Ed, PhD, Ed S); science education (MS, MS Ed, PhD, Ed S); social studies education (MS Ed, PhD, Ed S). *Accreditation:* NCATE. *Program availability:* Part-time, evening/weekend, online learning. *Faculty:* 34 full-time (24 women), 3 part-time/adjunct (1 woman). *Students:* 75 full-time (52 women), 357 part-time (271 women); includes 83 minority (29 Black or African American, non-Hispanic/Latino; 1 American Indian or Alaska Native, non-Hispanic/Latino; 14 Asian, non-Hispanic/Latino; 29 Hispanic/Latino; 1 Native Hawaiian or other Pacific Islander, non-Hispanic/Latino; 9 Two or more races, non-Hispanic/Latino), 43 international. Average age 36. 169 applicants, 83% accepted, 102 enrolled. In 2018, 141 master's, 15 doctorates awarded. *Degree requirements:* For master's, thesis optional; for doctorate, thesis/dissertation, oral and written exams; for Ed S, oral presentation, project. *Entrance requirements:* For master's, GRE General Test (if undergraduate GPA is below 3.0), minimum undergraduate GPA of 3.0 or equivalent; for doctorate, GRE General Test (minimum combined verbal and quantitative score of 1000, 300 for new scoring), minimum undergraduate GPA of 3.0 or equivalent; master's degree with minimum GPA of 3.0 or equivalent; for Ed S, GRE General Test (minimum combined verbal and quantitative score of 1000, 300 for new scoring), minimum undergraduate GPA of 3.0 or equivalent; master's degree. Additional exam requirements/recommendations for international students: Required—TOEFL (minimum score 550 paper-based; 77 iBT). *Application deadline:* For fall admission, 12/15 for domestic students, 3/1 for international students; for spring admission, 9/15 for domestic students, 8/1 for international students. Application fee: $60 ($75 for international students). Electronic

applications accepted. *Financial support:* Fellowships with full tuition reimbursements, research assistantships with full tuition reimbursements, teaching assistantships with full tuition reimbursements, career-related internships or fieldwork, and tuition waivers (full) available. Support available to part-time students. Financial award application deadline: 3/1; financial award applicants required to submit FAFSA. *Faculty research:* Literacy acquisition and development, teacher beliefs and knowledge, recruitment and retention of underrepresented students, economic education, literacy discourse. *Unit head:* Janet M. Alsup, Head, 765-494-9667, E-mail: alsupj@purdue.edu. *Application contact:* Heather Brinkman, Graduate Contact, 765-494-2345, E-mail: hbrinkma@purdue.edu.
Website: http://www.edci.purdue.edu/

Purdue University Global, School of Teacher Education, Davenport, IA 52807. Offers education (M Ed); secondary education (M Ed); teaching and learning (MA); teaching literacy and language: grades 6-12 (MA); teaching literacy and language: grades K-6 (MA); teaching mathematics: grades 6-8 (MA); teaching mathematics: grades 9-12 (MA); teaching mathematics: grades K-5 (MA); teaching science: grades 6-12 (MA); teaching science: grades K-6 (MA); teaching students with special needs (MA); teaching with technology (MA). *Program availability:* Part-time, evening/weekend, online learning. *Entrance requirements:* Additional exam requirements/recommendations for international students: Required—TOEFL (minimum score 550 paper-based; 80 iBT).

Purdue University Northwest, Graduate Studies Office, School of Education, Program in Instructional Technology, Hammond, IN 46323-2094. Offers MS Ed. *Entrance requirements:* Additional exam requirements/recommendations for international students: Required—TOEFL.

Quinnipiac University, School of Education, Program in Instructional Design, Hamden, CT 06518-1940. Offers MS. *Program availability:* Part-time-only, evening/weekend, online only, 100% online. Electronic applications accepted. *Expenses:* Contact institution.

Ramapo College of New Jersey, Master of Science in Educational Technology Program, Mahwah, NJ 07430. Offers MS. *Program availability:* Part-time, evening/weekend. *Faculty:* 8 part-time/adjunct (3 women). *Students:* 5 full-time (all women), 104 part-time (76 women); includes 14 minority (6 Black or African American, non-Hispanic/Latino; 2 Asian, non-Hispanic/Latino; 6 Hispanic/Latino), 1 international. Average age 35. 73 applicants, 95% accepted, 59 enrolled. In 2018, 75 master's awarded. *Degree requirements:* For master's, capstone course. *Entrance requirements:* For master's, official transcript of baccalaureate degree from accredited institution with minimum recommended GPA of 3.0; personal statement; letter of recommendation; resume. Additional exam requirements/recommendations for international students: Required—TOEFL (minimum score 550 paper-based; 79 iBT); Recommended—IELTS (minimum score 6). *Application deadline:* For fall admission, 5/1 for domestic and international students; for spring admission, 12/1 for domestic and international students. Applications are processed on a rolling basis. Application fee: $65. Electronic applications accepted. *Expenses:* Tuition, state resident: part-time $706.15 per credit. Tuition, nonresident: part-time $706.15 per credit. *Required fees:* $57.50 per credit. *Financial support:* Career-related internships or fieldwork available. Financial award application deadline: 3/1; financial award applicants required to submit FAFSA. *Faculty research:* Integrating technology in the curriculum of K-12 learning environment. *Unit head:* Dr. Richard Russo, Director of the Master in Educational Technology Program, 201-684-7899, Fax: 201-684-6699, E-mail: rrusso@ramapo.edu. *Application contact:* Karen Viviani, Graduate Program Assistant, 201-684-7638, Fax: 201-684-7983, E-mail: kdroubi@ramapo.edu.
Website: http://www.ramapo.edu/mset/

Regent University, Graduate School, School of Education, Virginia Beach, VA 23464-9800. Offers education (M Ed, Ed D, PhD), including adult education (Ed D, PhD, Ed S), advanced educational leadership (Ed D, PhD, Ed S), character education (Ed D, PhD, Ed S), Christian education leadership (Ed D, PhD, Ed S), Christian school administration (M Ed), curriculum and instruction (Ed D, PhD, Ed S), curriculum and instruction - adult education (M Ed), curriculum and instruction - Christian school (M Ed), curriculum and instruction - gifted and talented (M Ed), curriculum and instruction - STEM education (M Ed), curriculum and instruction - teacher leader (M Ed), discipleship for ministry (M Ed), educational leadership (M Ed), educational psychology (Ed D, PhD, Ed S), educational technology and online learning (Ed D, PhD, Ed S), elementary education (M Ed), exceptional education executive leadership (Ed D, PhD, Ed S), higher education (Ed D, PhD, Ed S), higher education leadership and management (Ed D, PhD, Ed S), instructional design and technology (M Ed), K-12 school leadership (Ed D, PhD, Ed S), K-12 special education (M Ed), leadership in mathematics education (M Ed), reading specialist (M Ed), special education (Ed D, PhD, Ed S), student affairs (M Ed), TESOL - adult education (M Ed), TESOL - K-12 (M Ed); educational specialist (Ed S), including adult education (Ed D, PhD, Ed S), advanced educational leadership (Ed D, PhD, Ed S), character education (Ed D, PhD, Ed S), Christian education leadership (Ed D, PhD, Ed S), curriculum and instruction (Ed D, PhD, Ed S), educational psychology (Ed D, PhD, Ed S), educational technology and online learning (Ed D, PhD, Ed S), exceptional education executive leadership (Ed D, PhD, Ed S), higher education (Ed D, PhD, Ed S), higher education leadership and management (Ed D, PhD, Ed S), K-12 school leadership (Ed D, PhD, Ed S), special education (Ed D, PhD, Ed S). *Accreditation:* TEAC. *Program availability:* Part-time, evening/weekend, 100% online, blended/hybrid learning. *Degree requirements:* For master's, thesis or alternative; for doctorate, comprehensive exam, thesis/dissertation. *Entrance requirements:* For master's, Virginia Communication and Literacy Assessment (VCLA), PRAXIS, college transcripts, writing sample, interview; for doctorate, GRE, writing sample, resume, transcripts, interview. Additional exam requirements/recommendations for international students: Required—TOEFL (minimum score 577 paper-based). Electronic applications accepted. *Expenses:* Contact institution. *Faculty research:* Christian school administration, curriculum and instruction, educational technology and online learning, higher education, special education.

Rockford University, Graduate Studies, Department of Education, Program in Instructional Strategies, Rockford, IL 61108-2393. Offers MAT. *Program availability:* Part-time, evening/weekend, online learning. *Degree requirements:* For master's, professional portfolio. *Entrance requirements:* For master's, GRE General Test, official transcripts, three letter of recommendation forms, essay. Additional exam requirements/recommendations for international students: Required—TOEFL (minimum score 550 paper-based; 79 iBT). Electronic applications accepted. *Expenses:* Contact institution.

Rowan University, Graduate School, College of Education, Department of Science, Technology, Engineering, Art and Math Education, Glassboro, NJ 08028-1701. Offers educational technology (CGS); STEM education (MA). *Program availability:* Part-time, evening/weekend. *Degree requirements:* For master's, thesis. *Entrance requirements:* For master's, GRE General Test. Additional exam requirements/recommendations for international students: Required—TOEFL. Electronic applications accepted.

Saginaw Valley State University, College of Education, Program in Instructional Technology, University Center, MI 48710. Offers MA. *Program availability:* Part-time, evening/weekend. *Students:* 1 full-time (0 women), 10 part-time (7 women); includes 2 minority (1 Hispanic/Latino; 1 Two or more races, non-Hispanic/Latino). Average age 33. 3 applicants, 100% accepted, 2 enrolled. *Degree requirements:* For master's, capstone course or thesis. *Entrance requirements:* For master's, minimum GPA of 3.0. Additional exam requirements/recommendations for international students: Required—TOEFL (minimum score 550 paper-based; 79 iBT). *Application deadline:* For fall admission, 7/15 for international students; for winter admission, 11/15 for international students; for spring admission, 4/15 for international students. Applications are processed on a rolling basis. Application fee: $30 ($90 for international students). Electronic applications accepted. *Expenses: Tuition, area resident:* Full-time $6225; part-time $623 per credit hour. Tuition, state resident: full-time $6225; part-time $623 per credit hour. Tuition, nonresident: full-time $14,215; part-time $1185 per credit hour. *International tuition:* $14,215 full-time. *Required fees:* $263; $14.60 per credit hour. Tuition and fees vary according to degree level. *Financial support:* Federal Work-Study and scholarships/grants available. Support available to part-time students. Financial award applicants required to submit FAFSA. *Unit head:* Dr. Carolyn Gilbreath, Associate Professor of Teaching Education, 989-749-4772, Fax: 989-964-4563, E-mail: cagilbre@svsu.edu. *Application contact:* Jenna Briggs, Director, Graduate and International Admissions, 989-964-6096, Fax: 989-964-2788, E-mail: gradadm@svsu.edu.

St. Cloud State University, School of Graduate Studies, College of Science and Engineering, Department of Computer Science and Information Technology, St. Cloud, MN 56301-4498. Offers computer science (MS); instructional technology (Graduate Certificate). *Degree requirements:* For master's, thesis or alternative. *Entrance requirements:* For master's, GRE General Test, minimum GPA of 2.75. Additional exam requirements/recommendations for international students: Required—Michigan English Language Assessment Battery; Recommended—TOEFL (minimum score 550 paper-based), IELTS (minimum score 6.5). Electronic applications accepted.

St. Cloud State University, School of Graduate Studies, School of Education, Center for Information Media, St. Cloud, MN 56301-4498. Offers MS, Graduate Certificate. *Program availability:* Part-time, evening/weekend, online learning. *Degree requirements:* For master's, comprehensive exam, thesis or alternative. *Entrance requirements:* For master's, minimum overall GPA of 2.75 in previous undergraduate and graduate records or in last half of undergraduate work. Additional exam requirements/recommendations for international students: Required—Michigan English Language Assessment Battery; Recommended—TOEFL (minimum score 550 paper-based; 79 iBT), IELTS (minimum score 6.5). Electronic applications accepted.

St. John Fisher College, Ralph C. Wilson Jr. School of Education, Program in Library Media, Rochester, NY 14618-3597. Offers MS. *Program availability:* Evening/weekend, online only, 100% online. *Faculty:* 1 (woman) full-time, 1 (woman) part-time/adjunct. *Students:* 12 full-time (all women), 2 part-time (both women). Average age 33. 21 applicants, 81% accepted, 13 enrolled. In 2018, 21 master's awarded. *Degree requirements:* For master's, practicum. *Entrance requirements:* For master's, teacher certification, 2 letters of recommendation, personal statement, current resume. Additional exam requirements/recommendations for international students: Required—TOEFL (minimum score 575 paper-based; 80 iBT). *Application deadline:* Applications are processed on a rolling basis. Application fee: $30. Electronic applications accepted. *Expenses:* Contact institution. *Financial support:* Scholarships/grants available. Financial award applicants required to submit FAFSA. *Unit head:* Dr. Michael Wischnowski, Dean, 585-385-7361, E-mail: mwischnowski@sjfc.edu. *Application contact:* Michelle Gosier, Associate Director of Transfer and Graduate Admissions, 585-385-8064, E-mail: mgosier@sjfc.edu.
Website: https://www.sjfc.edu/graduate-programs/ms-in-library-media/

Saint Mary's University of Minnesota, Schools of Graduate and Professional Programs, Graduate School of Education, Learning Design and Technology Program, Winona, MN 55987-1399. Offers M Ed. *Program availability:* Online learning. *Unit head:* Nancy Van Erp, Associate Program Director, 320-260-5116, E-mail: nvanerp@smumn.edu. *Application contact:* Laurie Roy, Director of Admission of Schools of Graduate and Professional Programs, 507-457-8606, Fax: 612-728-5121, E-mail: lroy@smumn.edu.
Website: https://onlineprograms.smumn.edu/meldt/masters-of-education-in-learning-design-and-technology?_ga=2.33053374.1013844339.1562589332-1359115499.15151709

St. Thomas University, School of Leadership Studies, Institute for Education, Miami Gardens, FL 33054-6459. Offers earth/space science (Certificate); educational administration (MS, Certificate); educational leadership (Ed D); elementary education (MS); ESOL (Certificate); gifted education (Certificate); instructional technology (MS, Certificate); professional/studies (Certificate); reading (MS, Certificate); special education (MS). *Program availability:* Part-time, evening/weekend. *Degree requirements:* For master's, comprehensive exam; for doctorate, comprehensive exam, thesis/dissertation. *Entrance requirements:* For master's, interview, minimum GPA of 3.0 or GRE; for doctorate, GRE or MAT. Additional exam requirements/recommendations for international students: Required—TOEFL (minimum score 550 paper-based; 79 iBT). Electronic applications accepted.

Saint Vincent College, Program in Education, Latrobe, PA 15650-2690. Offers curriculum and instruction (MS); instructional design and technology (MS); school administration and supervision (MS); special education (MS). *Program availability:* Part-time, evening/weekend. *Degree requirements:* For master's, comprehensive exam. *Entrance requirements:* For master's, GRE (if undergraduate GPA less than 3.0). Additional exam requirements/recommendations for international students: Required—TOEFL (minimum score 550 paper-based). *Faculty research:* Assessment and instructional technology.

Saint Xavier University, Graduate Studies, School of Education, Chicago, IL 60655-3105. Offers counseling (MA); curriculum and instruction (MA); early childhood education (MA); educational administration (MA); elementary education (MA); individualized studies (MA), including educational technology, English as a second language (ESL), ISTEM (integrative science, technology, engineering, and math), science education; music education (MA); reading (MA); secondary education (MA); Spanish education (MA); special education (MA); teaching and leadership (MA). *Accreditation:* NCATE. *Program availability:* Part-time, evening/weekend. *Degree requirements:* For master's, thesis or project. *Entrance requirements:* For master's, minimum GPA of 3.0. *Expenses:* Contact institution.

Salem State University, School of Graduate Studies, Program in Library Media Studies, Salem, MA 01970-5353. Offers M Ed. *Accreditation:* NCATE. *Program availability:* Part-time, evening/weekend. *Entrance requirements:* For master's, GRE or MAT. Additional exam requirements/recommendations for international students: Required—TOEFL (minimum score 550 paper-based; 80 iBT) or IELTS (minimum score 5.5).

Samford University, Orlean Beeson School of Education, Birmingham, AL 35229. Offers educational leadership (MSE, Ed D); elementary education (MS Ed, MSE); gifted (MSE); instructional design and technology (MSE); instructional leadership (MSE, Ed S); secondary education (MSE); special education (MSE). *Accreditation:* NCATE. *Program availability:* Part-time, evening/weekend, 100% online, blended/hybrid learning. *Faculty:* 12 full-time (10 women), 16 part-time/adjunct (11 women). *Students:* 156 full-time (111 women), 101 part-time (73 women); includes 106 minority (100 Black or African American, non-Hispanic/Latino; 1 American Indian or Alaska Native, non-Hispanic/

Latino; 5 Two or more races, non-Hispanic/Latino), 1 international. Average age 37. 107 applicants, 94% accepted, 65 enrolled. In 2018, 94 master's, 40 doctorates, 11 other advanced degrees awarded. *Degree requirements:* For master's and Ed S, comprehensive exam; for doctorate, comprehensive exam, thesis/dissertation. *Entrance requirements:* For master's, GRE, MAT, PRAXIS II, interview, transcripts, essay, recommendations, teaching certification; for doctorate, resume, transcripts, interview, essay, recommendations; for Ed S, teaching certification, transcripts, essay, interview, recommendations. Additional exam requirements/recommendations for international students: Required—TOEFL (minimum score 90 iBT); Recommended—IELTS (minimum score 6.5). *Application deadline:* For fall admission, 7/15 for domestic and international students; for winter admission, 11/15 for domestic and international students; for spring admission, 11/15 for domestic and international students; for summer admission, 4/15 for domestic and international students. Applications are processed on a rolling basis. Application fee: $35. Electronic applications accepted. *Expenses:* $862 Per Hour $100 School of Education $175 Technology Fee $100 Per Fully Online Class. *Financial support:* In 2018–19, 173 students received support. Scholarships/grants available. Financial award application deadline: 2/15; financial award applicants required to submit FAFSA. *Faculty research:* Principal leadership's and teacher organizational commitment mentoring, professional development, and middle grades leadership coaching and administrator effectiveness character development programs in schools teacher efficacy related STEM and professional growth. *Unit head:* Dr. Howard Finch, Interim Dean, 205-726-2745, E-mail: hfinch@samford.edu. *Application contact:* Brooke Karr, Graduate Admissions Office Coordinator, 205-729-2783, E-mail: kbgilrea@samford.edu.
Website: http://www.samford.edu/education

San Diego State University, Graduate and Research Affairs, College of Education, Department of Educational Technology, San Diego, CA 92182. Offers educational technology (MA); educational technology and teaching and learning (Ed D). *Accreditation:* NCATE. *Program availability:* Evening/weekend. *Entrance requirements:* For master's, GRE General Test, letters of reference. Additional exam requirements/recommendations for international students: Required—TOEFL. Electronic applications accepted.

San Francisco State University, Division of Graduate Studies, College of Education, Department of Equity, Leadership Studies, and Instructional Technologies, Program in Instructional Technologies, San Francisco, CA 94132-1722. Offers MA. *Unit head:* Dr. Doris Flowers, Chair, 415-338-2614, Fax: 415-338-0568, E-mail: dflowers@sfsu.edu. *Application contact:* Dr. Patricia Donohue, Program Coordinator, 415-338-7833, Fax: 415-338-0568, E-mail: pdonohue@sfsu.edu.
Website: http://elsit.sfsu.edu/

Seattle Pacific University, Program in Digital Education Leadership, Seattle, WA 98119-1997. Offers M Ed. *Students:* 1 (woman) full-time, 14 part-time (12 women); includes 3 minority (1 American Indian or Alaska Native, non-Hispanic/Latino; 1 Asian, non-Hispanic/Latino; 1 Hispanic/Latino). Average age 36. 11 applicants, 91% accepted, 8 enrolled. In 2018, 9 master's awarded. *Application deadline:* For fall admission, 9/8 for domestic students. *Unit head:* Rick Eigenbrood, Dean, 206-281-2710, E-mail: eigend@spu.edu. *Application contact:* Graduate Center, 206-281-2091.
Website: http://spu.edu/academics/school-of-education/graduate-programs/masters-programs/digital-education

Seton Hall University, College of Education and Human Services, Department of Educational Studies, South Orange, NJ 07079-2697. Offers instructional design and technology (MA); special education (MA). *Program availability:* Part-time, evening/weekend, blended/hybrid learning. *Degree requirements:* For master's, comprehensive exam, capstone project. *Entrance requirements:* For master's, GRE or MAT, PRAXIS (for certification candidates), minimum GPA of 2.75. Electronic applications accepted. *Expenses:* Contact institution. *Faculty research:* Special education, applied behavioral analysis, educational technology.

Seton Hill University, Program in Innovative Instruction, Greensburg, PA 15601. Offers M Ed. *Program availability:* Part-time, evening/weekend. *Students:* Average age 34. 21 applicants, 48% accepted, 9 enrolled. In 2018, 5 master's awarded. *Entrance requirements:* For master's, minimum GPA of 3.0. Additional exam requirements/recommendations for international students: Required—TOEFL. *Application deadline:* Applications are processed on a rolling basis. Application fee: $35. Electronic applications accepted. *Financial support:* In 2018–19, 7 students received support. Scholarships/grants, tuition waivers (partial), and unspecified assistantships available. Support available to part-time students. Financial award application deadline: 8/15; financial award applicants required to submit FAFSA. *Faculty research:* Use of technology for teaching and learning, problem-based theories in education and instruction.
Website: https://www.setonhill.edu/academics/graduate-programs/innovative-instruction/

Simon Fraser University, Office of Graduate Studies and Postdoctoral Fellows, Faculty of Education, Program in Educational Technology and Learning Design, Burnaby, BC V5A 1S6, Canada. Offers M Ed, MA, PhD. *Program availability:* Part-time, evening/weekend. *Degree requirements:* For master's, comprehensive exam (for some programs), thesis (for some programs); for doctorate, comprehensive exam, thesis/dissertation. *Entrance requirements:* For master's, minimum GPA of 3.0 (on scale of 4.33) or 3.33 based on last 60 credits of undergraduate courses; for doctorate, minimum GPA of 3.5 (on scale of 4.33). Additional exam requirements/recommendations for international students: Recommended—TOEFL (minimum score 580 paper-based; 93 iBT), IELTS (minimum score 7), TWE (minimum score 5). *Faculty research:* Integration of technological applications in post-secondary education, problems in learning and teaching science, gaming and simulation for learning, adaptive software for researching and promoting self-regulated learning, design and use of online environments for learning.

Slippery Rock University of Pennsylvania, Graduate Studies (Recruitment), College of Education, Department of Special Education, Slippery Rock, PA 16057-1383. Offers autism (M Ed); master teacher (M Ed), including birth to grade 8, grades 7 to 12; special education (Ed D); supervision (M Ed); technology for online instruction (M Ed). *Accreditation:* NCATE. *Program availability:* Part-time, evening/weekend, 100% online. *Faculty:* 12 full-time (6 women). *Students:* 45 full-time (36 women), 232 part-time (191 women); includes 12 minority (2 Black or African American, non-Hispanic/Latino; 1 American Indian or Alaska Native, non-Hispanic/Latino; 1 Asian, non-Hispanic/Latino; 2 Hispanic/Latino; 6 Two or more races, non-Hispanic/Latino). Average age 30. 197 applicants, 84% accepted, 96 enrolled. In 2018, 108 master's, 12 doctorates awarded. *Degree requirements:* For master's, thesis optional. *Entrance requirements:* For master's, minimum GPA of 3.0, official transcripts, teaching certification. Additional exam requirements/recommendations for international students: Required—TOEFL (minimum score 550 paper-based; 80 iBT). *Application deadline:* For fall admission, 3/1 priority date for domestic students, 5/1 priority date for international students; for spring admission, 10/1 priority date for domestic students, 9/1 priority date for international students. Applications are processed on a rolling basis. Application fee: $25 ($30 for international students). Electronic applications accepted. *Expenses:* Contact institution. *Financial support:* In 2018–19, 15 students received support. Career-related internships or fieldwork, Federal Work-Study, institutionally sponsored loans, scholarships/grants, tuition waivers (partial), and unspecified assistantships available. Support available to part-time students. Financial award application deadline: 5/1; financial award applicants required to submit FAFSA. *Unit head:* Dr. Rachel Barger-Anderson, Graduate Coordinator, 724-738-2873, Fax: 724-738-4395, E-mail: rachel.barger-ander@sru.edu. *Application contact:* Brandi Weber-Mortimer, Director of Graduate Admissions, 724-738-2051, Fax: 724-738-2146, E-mail: graduate.admissions@sru.edu.
Website: http://www.sru.edu/academics/colleges-and-departments/coe/departments/special-education/graduate-programs

Southern Illinois University Edwardsville, Graduate School, School of Education, Health, and Human Behavior, Department of Educational Leadership, Program in Instructional Technology, Edwardsville, IL 62026. Offers MS Ed. *Accreditation:* NCATE. *Program availability:* Part-time, evening/weekend. *Degree requirements:* For master's, thesis or alternative, portfolio. *Entrance requirements:* Additional exam requirements/recommendations for international students: Required—TOEFL (minimum score 550 paper-based; 79 iBT), IELTS (minimum score 6.5). Electronic applications accepted.

Southern Illinois University Edwardsville, Graduate School, School of Education, Health, and Human Behavior, Department of Educational Leadership, Program in Web-Based Learning, Edwardsville, IL 62026. Offers Postbaccalaureate Certificate. *Program availability:* Part-time. *Entrance requirements:* Additional exam requirements/recommendations for international students: Required—TOEFL (minimum score 550 paper-based; 79 iBT), IELTS (minimum score 6.5). Electronic applications accepted.

Southern New Hampshire University, School of Education, Manchester, NH 03106-1045. Offers curriculum and instruction (M Ed), including dyslexia studies and language-based learning disabilities, educational leadership, reading, special education, technology integration; dyslexia studies and language-based learning disabilities (Certificate); early childhood and special education (M Ed); educational leadership (M Ed, Ed D); educational studies (M Ed); elementary and special education (M Ed); field based education (M Ed); higher education administration (MS); teaching English as a foreign language (MS). *Program availability:* Part-time, evening/weekend, online learning. *Degree requirements:* For master's, comprehensive exam (for some programs), thesis or alternative. *Entrance requirements:* For master's, PRAXIS I, minimum GPA of 2.75. Additional exam requirements/recommendations for international students: Required—TOEFL (minimum score 550 paper-based). Electronic applications accepted. *Expenses:* Contact institution.

Southern University and Agricultural and Mechanical College, Graduate School, College of Humanities and Interdisciplinary Studies, School of Education, Department of Curriculum and Instruction, Baton Rouge, LA 70813. Offers elementary education (M Ed); media (M Ed); secondary education (M Ed). *Degree requirements:* For master's, comprehensive exam, thesis optional. *Entrance requirements:* For master's, GMAT or GRE General Test. Additional exam requirements/recommendations for international students: Required—TOEFL (minimum score 525 paper-based).

Stanford University, Graduate School of Education, Program in Learning, Design, and Technology, Stanford, CA 94305-2004. Offers MA. *Expenses: Tuition:* Full-time $50,703; part-time $32,970 per year. *Required fees:* $651.

State University of New York College at Potsdam, School of Education and Professional Studies, Program in Information and Communication Technology, Potsdam, NY 13676. Offers educational technology specialist (MS Ed); organizational performance and technology (MS). *Program availability:* Part-time, evening/weekend. *Degree requirements:* For master's, culminating experience. *Entrance requirements:* For master's, minimum GPA of 3.0 in last 60 hours of course work. Additional exam requirements/recommendations for international students: Required—TOEFL (minimum score 550 paper-based; 80 iBT), IELTS (minimum score 6). Electronic applications accepted.

State University of New York Empire State College, School for Graduate Studies, Programs in Education, Saratoga Springs, NY 12866-4391. Offers adult learning (MA); learning and emerging technologies (MA); teaching (MAT); teaching and learning (M Ed). *Program availability:* Online learning.

Stockton University, Office of Graduate Studies, Program in Instructional Technology, Galloway, NJ 08205-9441. Offers MA. *Program availability:* Part-time, evening/weekend. *Faculty:* 4 full-time (2 women), 2 part-time/adjunct (both women). *Students:* 7 full-time (3 women), 38 part-time (28 women); includes 9 minority (6 Black or African American, non-Hispanic/Latino; 1 Asian, non-Hispanic/Latino; 2 Hispanic/Latino). Average age 36. 19 applicants, 89% accepted, 14 enrolled. In 2018, 23 master's awarded. *Entrance requirements:* For master's, GRE or MAT, minimum GPA of 3.0. Additional exam requirements/recommendations for international students: Required—TOEFL. *Application deadline:* For fall admission, 7/1 priority date for domestic students, 7/1 for international students; for spring admission, 12/1 for domestic students, 11/1 for international students. Applications are processed on a rolling basis. Application fee: $50. Electronic applications accepted. *Expenses:* Contact institution. *Financial support:* Fellowships, research assistantships, career-related internships or fieldwork, Federal Work-Study, scholarships/grants, and unspecified assistantships available. Support available to part-time students. Financial award application deadline: 3/1; financial award applicants required to submit FAFSA. *Faculty research:* Ethics, digital imaging, virtual reality in the classroom, 3D art in multimedia, technology projects for job-skills training, community computing networks. *Unit head:* Dr. Doug Harvey, Director, 609-626-3640, E-mail: mait@stockton.edu. *Application contact:* Tara Williams, Assistant Director of Graduate Enrollment, 609-626-3640, Fax: 609-626-6050, E-mail: gradschool@stockton.edu.
Website: http://www.stockton.edu/grad

Strayer University, Graduate Studies, Washington, DC 20005-2603. Offers accounting (MS); acquisition (MBA); business administration (MBA); communications technology (MS); educational management (M Ed); finance (MBA); health services administration (MHSA); hospitality and tourism management (MBA); human resource management (MBA); information systems (MS), including computer security management, decision support system management, enterprise resource management, network management, software engineering management, systems development management; management (MBA); management information systems (MS); marketing (MBA); professional accounting (MS), including accounting information systems, controllership, taxation; public administration (MPA); supply chain management (MBA); technology in education (M Ed). Programs also offered at campus locations in Birmingham, AL; Chamblee, GA; Cobb County, GA; Morrow, GA; White Marsh, MD; Charleston, SC; Columbia, SC; Greensboro, NC; Greenville, SC; Lexington, KY; Louisville, KY; Nashville, TN; North Raleigh, NC; Washington, DC. *Accreditation:* ACBSP. *Program availability:* Part-time, evening/weekend, online learning. *Degree requirements:* For master's, thesis. *Entrance requirements:* For master's, GMAT, GRE General Test, bachelor's degree from an accredited college or university, minimum undergraduate GPA of 2.75. Electronic applications accepted.

Syracuse University, School of Education, CAS Program in Educational Technology, Syracuse, NY 13244. Offers CAS. *Accreditation:* ACA. *Program availability:* Part-time. *Entrance requirements:* For degree, baccalaureate degree from regionally-accredited college/university, statement of goals, three recommendation letters, transcripts. Additional exam requirements/recommendations for international students: Required—

TOEFL (minimum score 100 iBT). *Application deadline:* Applications are processed on a rolling basis. Application fee: $75. Electronic applications accepted. *Financial support:* Fellowships, research assistantships, teaching assistantships, career-related internships or fieldwork, and scholarships/grants available. Financial award application deadline: 1/15. *Faculty research:* Instructional design, learning with digital technologies, training and professional development, designing effective and efficient instruction, designing digital instruction. *Unit head:* Dr. Jing Lei, Chair, 315-443-3703, E-mail: takoszal@syr.edu. *Application contact:* Speranza Migliore, Graduate Admissions Recruiter, 315-443-2505, E-mail: gradrcrt@syr.edu.
Website: http://soe.syr.edu/academic/
Instructional_Design_Development_and_Evaluation/graduate/certificates/default.aspx

Syracuse University, School of Education, MS Program in Instructional Technology, Syracuse, NY 13244. Offers MS. *Program availability:* Part-time. *Students:* Average age 25. In 2018, 2 master's awarded. *Entrance requirements:* For master's, GRE, baccalaureate degree from regionally-accredited college/university, initial New York State teaching certification, statement of goals, three letters of recommendation, transcripts. Additional exam requirements/recommendations for international students: Required—TOEFL (minimum score 100 iBT). *Application deadline:* For fall admission, 1/15 for domestic students, 1/15 priority date for international students. Application fee: $75. Electronic applications accepted. *Financial support:* Fellowships with full tuition reimbursements, research assistantships, teaching assistantships, career-related internships or fieldwork, and scholarships/grants available. Financial award application deadline: 1/15. *Unit head:* Dr. Jing Lei, Chair, 315-443-3703, E-mail: takoszal@syr.edu. *Application contact:* Speranza Migliore, Graduate Admissions Recruiter, 315-443-2505, E-mail: gradrcrt@syr.edu.
Website: http://soeweb.syr.edu/academic/
Instructional_Design_Development_and_Evaluation/graduate/masters/
instructional_technology/default.aspx

Syracuse University, School of Information Studies, CAS Program in School Media, Syracuse, NY 13244. Offers CAS. *Program availability:* Part-time, evening/weekend, online learning. *Entrance requirements:* For degree, MS in library and information science, letter of recommendation, personal statement, resume, official transcripts. Additional exam requirements/recommendations for international students: Required—TOEFL (minimum score 100 iBT). *Application deadline:* For fall admission, 1/1 priority date for domestic and international students; for spring admission, 10/15 priority date for domestic and international students; for summer admission, 2/1 priority date for domestic and international students. Applications are processed on a rolling basis. Application fee: $75. Electronic applications accepted. *Financial support:* Application deadline: 1/1. *Faculty research:* Managing a school library, literacy through school libraries, information technologies in educational organizations, information services to students with disabilities. *Unit head:* Prof. Caroline Haythornthwaite, Program Director, 315-443-2911, E-mail: igrad@syr.edu. *Application contact:* Susan Corieri, Director of Enrollment Management, 315-443-2575, E-mail: igrad@syr.edu.
Website: https://ischool.syr.edu/academics/graduate/cas/cas-school-media/

Syracuse University, School of Information Studies, MS Program in Library and Information Science: School Media, Syracuse, NY 13244. Offers MS. *Program availability:* Part-time, evening/weekend, online learning. *Students:* Average age 34. *Entrance requirements:* For master's, GRE General Test, personal statement, two letters of recommendation, resume. Additional exam requirements/recommendations for international students: Required—TOEFL (minimum score 100 iBT). *Application deadline:* For fall admission, 1/1 priority date for domestic and international students; for spring admission, 10/15 priority date for domestic and international students. Applications are processed on a rolling basis. Application fee: $75. Electronic applications accepted. *Financial support:* Fellowships with full tuition reimbursements, research assistantships with partial tuition reimbursements, and teaching assistantships with partial tuition reimbursements available. Financial award application deadline: 1/1. *Faculty research:* Collection management based on a unified media concept, use of information resources from a problem-solving perspective, digital literacy, curriculum consultation and technology innovation. *Unit head:* Prof. Caroline Haythornthwaite, Program Director, 315-443-2911, E-mail: igrad@syr.edu. *Application contact:* Susan Corieri, Director of Enrollment Management, 315-443-2575, E-mail: ischool@syr.edu.
Website: https://ischool.syr.edu/academics/graduate/masters-degrees/ms-library-information-science-school-media/

Tarleton State University, College of Graduate Studies, College of Education, Department of Curriculum and Instruction, Stephenville, TX 76402. Offers curriculum and instruction (M Ed); educational diagnostician (M Ed); elementary education (M Ed); instructional design and technology (M Ed); instructional leadership (M Ed); secondary education (M Ed); special education (M Ed); technology applications (M Ed); technology director (M Ed). *Program availability:* Part-time, evening/weekend. *Faculty:* 11 full-time (10 women), 4 part-time/adjunct (1 woman). *Students:* 16 full-time (14 women), 158 part-time (143 women). Average age 40. 54 applicants, 87% accepted, 41 enrolled. In 2018, 46 master's awarded. *Degree requirements:* For master's, comprehensive exam, thesis (for some programs). *Entrance requirements:* For master's, GRE General Test, minimum GPA of 3.0. Additional exam requirements/recommendations for international students: Required—TOEFL (minimum score 520 paper-based; 69 iBT); Recommended—IELTS (minimum score 6), TSE (minimum score 50). *Application deadline:* For fall admission, 8/15 priority date for domestic students; for spring admission, 1/7 for domestic students. Applications are processed on a rolling basis. Application fee: $50 ($130 for international students). Electronic applications accepted. *Expenses:* Contact institution. *Financial support:* Research assistantships, teaching assistantships, career-related internships or fieldwork, Federal Work-Study, and institutionally sponsored loans available. Support available to part-time students. Financial award application deadline: 5/1; financial award applicants required to submit FAFSA. *Unit head:* Dr. Amber Lynn Diaz, Department Head, 254-968-0730, E-mail: adiaz@tarleton.edu. *Application contact:* Information Contact, 254-968-9104, Fax: 254-968-9670, E-mail: gradoffice@tarleton.edu.
Website: http://www.tarleton.edu/cimasters/

Teachers College, Columbia University, Department of Mathematics, Science and Technology, New York, NY 10027-6696. Offers biology 7-12 (MA); chemistry 7-12 (MA); communication and education (MA, Ed D); computing in education (MA); earth science 7-12 (MA); instructional technology and media (Ed M, MA, Ed D); mathematics education (Ed M, MA, Ed D, Ed DCT, PhD); physics 7-12 (MA); science and dental education (MA); science education (Ed M, MS, Ed DCT, PhD); supervisor/teacher of science education (MA); technology specialist (MA). *Program availability:* Part-time, evening/weekend, online learning. *Students:* 155 full-time (114 women), 254 part-time (162 women); includes 136 minority (44 Black or African American, non-Hispanic/Latino; 1 American Indian or Alaska Native, non-Hispanic/Latino; 59 Asian, non-Hispanic/Latino; 23 Hispanic/Latino; 9 Two or more races, non-Hispanic/Latino), 140 international. Average age 31. 484 applicants, 60% accepted, 138 enrolled. Terminal master's awarded for partial completion of doctoral program. *Unit head:* Prof. Erica Walker, Chair, 212-678-8246, E-mail: ewalker@tc.columbia.edu. *Application contact:* Kelly Sutton Skinner, Director of Admission & New Student Enrollment, E-mail: kms2237@tc.columbia.edu.
Website: http://www.tc.columbia.edu/mathematics-science-and-technology/

Tennessee Technological University, College of Graduate Studies, College of Education, Department of Curriculum and Instruction, Program in Educational Technology, Cookeville, TN 38505. Offers MA, Ed S. *Program availability:* Part-time, evening/weekend. *Students:* 3 full-time (2 women), 17 part-time (16 women); includes 1 minority (Two or more races, non-Hispanic/Latino). 8 applicants, 75% accepted, 5 enrolled. *Degree requirements:* For master's, comprehensive exam, thesis or alternative. *Entrance requirements:* For master's, MAT or GRE. Additional exam requirements/recommendations for international students: Required—TOEFL (minimum score 527 paper-based; 71 iBT), IELTS (minimum score 5.5), PTE (minimum score 48), or TOEIC (Test of English as an International Communication). *Application deadline:* For fall admission, 8/1 for domestic students, 5/1 for international students; for spring admission, 12/1 for domestic students, 10/1 for international students; for summer admission, 5/1 for domestic students, 2/1 for international students. Application fee: $35 ($40 for international students). Electronic applications accepted. *Unit head:* Dr. Jeremy Wendt, Chairperson, 931-372-3181, Fax: 931-372-6270, E-mail: jwendt@tntech.edu. *Application contact:* Shelia K. Kendrick, Coordinator of Graduate Studies, 931-372-3808, Fax: 931-372-3497, E-mail: skendrick@tntech.edu.

Texas A&M University, College of Education and Human Development, Department of Educational Psychology, College Station, TX 77843. Offers bilingual education (M Ed, MS); counseling psychology (PhD); educational psychology (M Ed, MS, PhD); educational technology (M Ed); school psychology (PhD); special education (M Ed, MS). *Accreditation:* APA (one or more programs are accredited). *Program availability:* Part-time, evening/weekend, blended/hybrid learning. *Faculty:* 47. *Students:* 146 full-time (118 women), 244 part-time (204 women); includes 146 minority (22 Black or African American, non-Hispanic/Latino; 2 American Indian or Alaska Native, non-Hispanic/Latino; 18 Asian, non-Hispanic/Latino; 92 Hispanic/Latino; 1 Native Hawaiian or other Pacific Islander, non-Hispanic/Latino; 11 Two or more races, non-Hispanic/Latino), 50 international. Average age 33. 142 applicants, 50% accepted, 49 enrolled. In 2018, 152 master's, 23 doctorates awarded. *Degree requirements:* For master's, thesis optional; for doctorate, thesis/dissertation. *Entrance requirements:* For master's and doctorate, GRE General Test. Additional exam requirements/recommendations for international students: Required—TOEFL (minimum score 550 paper-based; 80 iBT), IELTS (minimum score 6), PTE (minimum score 53). *Application deadline:* For fall admission, 12/1 for domestic students; for spring admission, 10/15 for domestic students. Application fee: $50 ($90 for international students). Electronic applications accepted. *Expenses:* Contact institution. *Financial support:* In 2018–19, 125 students received support, including 3 fellowships with tuition reimbursements available (averaging $19,520 per year), 106 research assistantships with tuition reimbursements available (averaging $15,181 per year), 19 teaching assistantships with tuition reimbursements available (averaging $9,322 per year); career-related internships or fieldwork, institutionally sponsored loans, scholarships/grants, traineeships, health care benefits, tuition waivers (full and partial), and unspecified assistantships also available. Support available to part-time students. Financial award application deadline: 3/15; financial award applicants required to submit FAFSA. *Unit head:* Dr. Victor Willson, Department Head, 979-845-1394, E-mail: v-willson@tamu.edu. *Application contact:* Kristie Stramaski, Senior Academic Advisor, 979-845-1833, E-mail: epsyadvisor@tamu.edu.
Website: http://epsy.tamu.edu

Texas A&M University–Commerce, College of Education and Human Services, Commerce, TX 75429. Offers counseling (M Ed, MS, PhD); early childhood education (M Ed, MS); educational administration (M Ed, MS, Ed D); educational psychology (PhD); educational technology leadership (M Ed, MS); educational technology library science (M Ed, MS); elementary education (M Ed); health, kinesiology and sports studies (MS); higher education (MS, Ed D); psychology (MS); reading (M Ed, MS); school psychology (SSP); secondary education (M Ed, MS); social work (MSW); special education (M Ed, MS); supervision, curriculum and instruction-elementary education (Ed D); training and development (MS). *Program availability:* Part-time, evening/weekend, 100% online, blended/hybrid learning. *Faculty:* 95 full-time (59 women), 29 part-time/adjunct (22 women). *Students:* 356 full-time (295 women), 1,262 part-time (992 women); includes 683 minority (349 Black or African American, non-Hispanic/Latino; 9 American Indian or Alaska Native, non-Hispanic/Latino; 30 Asian, non-Hispanic/Latino; 238 Hispanic/Latino; 57 Two or more races, non-Hispanic/Latino), 9 international. Average age 37. 951 applicants, 42% accepted, 304 enrolled. In 2018, 532 master's, 51 doctorates awarded. *Degree requirements:* For master's, comprehensive exam, thesis optional, departmental qualifying exams (for some programs); for doctorate, comprehensive exam, thesis/dissertation, departmental qualifying exam; for SSP, comprehensive exam. *Entrance requirements:* For master's, GRE General Test, official transcripts, letters of recommendation, resume, statement of goals; for doctorate, GRE General Test, letters of recommendation, statement of goals, writing samples, writing sessions, resumes. Additional exam requirements/recommendations for international students: Required—TOEFL (minimum score 550 paper-based; 79 iBT), IELTS (minimum score 6), PTE (minimum score 53). *Application deadline:* For fall admission, 6/1 priority date for international students; for spring admission, 10/15 priority date for international students; for summer admission, 3/15 priority date for international students. Applications are processed on a rolling basis. Application fee: $50 ($75 for international students). Electronic applications accepted. *Expenses: Tuition, area resident:* Full-time $3630. Tuition, state resident: full-time $3630. Tuition, nonresident: full-time $11,100. *International tuition:* $11,100 full-time. *Required fees:* $2794. Tuition and fees vary according to course load, degree level and program. *Financial support:* In 2018–19, 116 students received support, including 94 research assistantships with partial tuition reimbursements available (averaging $3,863 per year), 38 teaching assistantships with partial tuition reimbursements available (averaging $4,728 per year); career-related internships or fieldwork, Federal Work-Study, institutionally sponsored loans, scholarships/grants, health care benefits, and unspecified assistantships also available. Financial award application deadline: 5/1; financial award applicants required to submit FAFSA. *Faculty research:* Cognitive and bilingual education, positive behavioral intervention, literacy, math readiness. *Total annual research expenditures:* $1.1 million. *Unit head:* Dr. Madeline Justice, Interim Dean, 903-886-5181, Fax: 903-886-5905, E-mail: madeline.justice@tamuc.edu. *Application contact:* Vicky Turner, Doctoral Degree and Special Programs Coordinator, 903-886-5167, E-mail: vicky.turner@tamuc.edu.
Website: http://www.tamuc.edu/academics/graduateSchool/programs/education/default.aspx

Texas A&M University–Corpus Christi, College of Graduate Studies, College of Education and Human Development, Corpus Christi, TX 78412. Offers counseling (MS), including counseling; counselor education (PhD); curriculum and instruction (MS, PhD); early childhood education (MS); educational administration (MS); educational leadership (Ed D); elementary education (MS); instructional design and educational technology (MS); kinesiology (MS); reading (MS); secondary education (MS); special education (MS). *Program availability:* Part-time, evening/weekend, blended/hybrid learning. *Degree requirements:* For master's, comprehensive exam, capstone; for doctorate, thesis/dissertation. *Entrance requirements:* For master's, GRE General Test, essay (300 words); for doctorate, GRE, essay, resume, 3-4 reference forms. Electronic applications accepted.

Educational Media/Instructional Technology

Texas A&M University–Kingsville, College of Graduate Studies, College of Education and Human Performance, Department of Educational Leadership and Counseling, Program in Instructional Technology, Kingsville, TX 78363. Offers MS. *Program availability:* Part-time, evening/weekend. *Degree requirements:* For master's, variable foreign language requirement, comprehensive exam, thesis (for some programs). *Entrance requirements:* For master's, GRE, MAT, GMAT. Additional exam requirements/recommendations for international students: Required—TOEFL (minimum score 550 paper-based; 79 iBT). Electronic applications accepted.

Texas A&M University–Texarkana, Graduate Studies and Research, College of Education and Liberal Arts, Texarkana, TX 75503. Offers adult education (MS); curriculum and instruction (M Ed); education (MS); educational administration (M Ed); English (MA); instructional technology (MS); interdisciplinary studies (MA, MS); special education (MS). *Program availability:* Part-time, evening/weekend. *Degree requirements:* For master's, comprehensive exam (for some programs), thesis optional. *Entrance requirements:* For master's, minimum GPA of 2.5 on last 60 hours of bachelor's degree. Additional exam requirements/recommendations for international students: Required—TOEFL. Electronic applications accepted.

Texas State University, The Graduate College, College of Education, Program in Educational Technology, San Marcos, TX 78666. Offers M Ed. *Program availability:* Part-time, evening/weekend. *Faculty:* 3 full-time (1 woman). *Students:* 2 full-time (both women), 11 part-time (6 women); includes 4 minority (3 Hispanic/Latino; 1 Two or more races, non-Hispanic/Latino), 1 international. Average age 38. 1 applicant, 100% accepted. In 2018, 3 master's awarded. *Degree requirements:* For master's, comprehensive exam. *Entrance requirements:* For master's, baccalaureate degree from regionally-accredited institution with minimum GPA of 2.75 in undergraduate work, statement of purpose. Additional exam requirements/recommendations for international students: Required—TOEFL (minimum score 550 paper-based; 78 iBT), IELTS (minimum score 6.5), TOEFL (minimum iBT scores: 22 listening, 22 reading, 24 speaking, 21 writing). *Application deadline:* For fall admission, 6/15 for domestic students, 6/1 for international students; for spring admission, 10/15 for domestic students, 10/1 for international students; for summer admission, 4/15 for domestic students, 3/15 for international students. Applications are processed on a rolling basis. Application fee: $55 ($90 for international students). Electronic applications accepted. *Expenses:* Tuition, state resident: full-time $8102; part-time $4051 per semester. Tuition, nonresident: full-time $18,229; part-time $9115 per semester. *International tuition:* $18,229 full-time. *Required fees:* $2116; $120 per credit hour. Tuition and fees vary according to course load. *Financial support:* In 2018–19, 5 students received support. Research assistantships, teaching assistantships, scholarships/grants, and unspecified assistantships available. Financial award application deadline: 1/15; financial award applicants required to submit FAFSA. *Unit head:* Dr. Douglas Holschuh, Graduate Advisor, 512-245-3701, Fax: 512-245-7911, E-mail: dh61@txstate.edu. *Application contact:* Dr. Andrea Golato, Dean of Graduate School, 512-245-2581, Fax: 512-245-8365, E-mail: gradcollege@txstate.edu.
Website: http://www.education.txstate.edu/ci/degrees-programs/graduate/edtech.html

Texas Tech University, Graduate School, College of Education, Department of Educational Psychology and Leadership, Lubbock, TX 79409-1071. Offers counselor education (M Ed, PhD); educational leadership (M Ed, Ed D, PhD); educational psychology (M Ed, PhD); higher education administration (M Ed, Ed D); higher education research (PhD); instructional technology (M Ed, Ed D); special education (M Ed, Ed D, PhD). *Accreditation:* ACA; NCATE. *Program availability:* Part-time, evening/weekend, 100% online, blended/hybrid learning. *Faculty:* 65 full-time (29 women), 3 part-time/adjunct (all women). *Students:* 261 full-time (184 women), 624 part-time (482 women); includes 325 minority (88 Black or African American, non-Hispanic/Latino; 3 American Indian or Alaska Native, non-Hispanic/Latino; 12 Asian, non-Hispanic/Latino; 192 Hispanic/Latino; 1 Native Hawaiian or other Pacific Islander, non-Hispanic/Latino; 29 Two or more races, non-Hispanic/Latino), 39 international. Average age 36. 437 applicants, 73% accepted, 252 enrolled. In 2018, 278 master's, 40 doctorates awarded. Terminal master's awarded for partial completion of doctoral program. *Degree requirements:* For master's, comprehensive exam, thesis optional; for doctorate, comprehensive exam, thesis/dissertation. *Entrance requirements:* For master's, GRE (for some programs); for doctorate, GRE. Additional exam requirements/recommendations for international students: Required—TOEFL (minimum score 550 paper-based; 79 iBT). *Application deadline:* For fall admission, 6/1 priority date for domestic students, 1/15 priority date for international students; for spring admission, 9/1 priority date for domestic students, 6/15 priority date for international students. Applications are processed on a rolling basis. Application fee: $65. Electronic applications accepted. *Expenses:* Contact institution. *Financial support:* In 2018–19, 493 students received support, including 489 fellowships (averaging $3,305 per year), 61 research assistantships (averaging $12,558 per year), 5 teaching assistantships (averaging $13,161 per year); scholarships/grants and unspecified assistantships also available. Support available to part-time students. Financial award application deadline: 1/3; financial award applicants required to submit FAFSA. *Faculty research:* Cognitive, motivational, and developmental processes in learning; counseling education; instructional technology; generic special education and sensory impairment; community college administration; K-12 school administration. *Total annual research expenditures:* $204,930. *Unit head:* Dr. Hansel Burley, Professor, Department Chair, 806-834-5135, Fax: 806-742-2179, E-mail: hansel.burley@ttu.edu. *Application contact:* Pam Smith, Admissions Advisor, 806-834-2969, Fax: 806-742-2179, E-mail: pam.smith@ttu.edu.
Website: www.educ.ttu.edu/

Thomas Edison State University, Heavin School of Arts and Sciences, Program in Educational Technology and Online Learning, Trenton, NJ 08608. Offers educational technology and online learning (MA); online learning and teaching (Graduate Certificate). *Program availability:* Part-time, online learning. *Degree requirements:* For master's, practicum. *Entrance requirements:* Additional exam requirements/recommendations for international students: Required—TOEFL (minimum score 550 paper-based; 79 iBT). Electronic applications accepted.

Tiffin University, Program in Education, Tiffin, OH 44883-2161. Offers educational technology management (M Ed); higher education administration (M Ed). *Program availability:* Part-time, evening/weekend, online only, 100% online, blended/hybrid learning. *Entrance requirements:* Additional exam requirements/recommendations for international students: Required—TOEFL. Electronic applications accepted. *Expenses:* Contact institution.

Touro College, Graduate School of Education, New York, NY 10010. Offers education and special education (MS); instructional technology (MS); mathematics education (MS); school leadership (MS); teaching English to speakers of other languages (MS); teaching literacy (MS). *Accreditation:* TEAC. *Program availability:* Part-time, evening/weekend, online learning. *Entrance requirements:* Additional exam requirements/recommendations for international students: Required—TOEFL (minimum score 83 iBT), IELTS (minimum score 6.5). *Faculty research:* Equity assistance, language development, scholarly communications, Latin American studies and cultural sensitivity, behavior management techniques and strategies in special education.

Touro College, Graduate School of Technology, New York, NY 10010. Offers information systems (MS); instructional technology (MS); Web and multimedia design

(MA). *Entrance requirements:* Additional exam requirements/recommendations for international students: Required—TOEFL (minimum score 83 iBT), IELTS (minimum score 6.5), PTE (minimum score 58).

Towson University, College of Education, Program in Instructional Technology, Towson, MD 21252-0001. Offers educational technology (MS); instructional design and development (MS); school library media (MS). *Program availability:* Part-time, evening/weekend. *Degree requirements:* For master's, thesis optional. *Entrance requirements:* For master's, minimum GPA of 3.0, technological literacy. Additional exam requirements/recommendations for international students: Required—TOEFL. Electronic applications accepted. *Expenses: Tuition, area resident:* Full-time $9196; part-time $418 per unit. Tuition, state resident: full-time $9196; part-time $418 per unit. Tuition, nonresident: full-time $19,030; part-time $865 per unit. *International tuition:* $19,030 full-time. *Required fees:* $3102; $141 per year. $423 per term. Tuition and fees vary according to campus/location and program.

Trevecca Nazarene University, Graduate Instructional Design and Technology Program, Nashville, TN 37210-2877. Offers MS. *Program availability:* Online only. *Degree requirements:* For master's, capstone. *Entrance requirements:* For master's, minimum GPA of 2.75, minimum math grade of C, minimum English composition grade of C. Additional exam requirements/recommendations for international students: Required—TOEFL (minimum score 550 paper-based; 80 iBT). Electronic applications accepted. *Expenses:* Contact institution.

Trident University International, College of Education, Program in Educational Leadership, Cypress, CA 90630. Offers e-learning leadership (MA Ed, PhD); educational leadership (MA Ed); higher education leadership (PhD); K-12 leadership (PhD). *Program availability:* Part-time, evening/weekend, online learning. *Degree requirements:* For doctorate, comprehensive exam, thesis/dissertation, defense of dissertation. *Entrance requirements:* For master's, minimum GPA of 2.5 (students with GPA 3.0 or greater may transfer up to 30% of graduate level credits); for doctorate, minimum GPA of 3.4, course work in research methods or statistics. Additional exam requirements/recommendations for international students: Required—TOEFL. Electronic applications accepted.

Université Laval, Faculty of Education, Department of Teaching and Learning Studies, Programs in Teaching Technology, Québec, QC G1K 7P4, Canada. Offers MA, PhD. Terminal master's awarded for partial completion of doctoral program. *Degree requirements:* For master's, thesis (for some programs); for doctorate, comprehensive exam, thesis/dissertation. *Entrance requirements:* For master's and doctorate, English exam (comprehension of written English), knowledge of French. Electronic applications accepted.

University at Albany, State University of New York, School of Education, Department of Educational Theory and Practice, Albany, NY 12222-0001. Offers curriculum and instruction (PhD, CAS); curriculum development and instructional technology (MS); general education studies (MS). *Program availability:* Part-time, evening/weekend, 100% online, blended/hybrid learning. *Faculty:* 16 full-time (8 women), 14 part-time/adjunct (8 women). *Students:* 93 full-time (66 women), 282 part-time (220 women); includes 69 minority (22 Black or African American, non-Hispanic/Latino; 15 Asian, non-Hispanic/Latino; 24 Hispanic/Latino; 1 Native Hawaiian or other Pacific Islander, non-Hispanic/Latino; 7 Two or more races, non-Hispanic/Latino), 30 international. Average age 31. 197 applicants, 68% accepted, 120 enrolled. In 2018, 83 master's, 4 doctorates, 8 other advanced degrees awarded. *Degree requirements:* For doctorate, one foreign language, thesis/dissertation. *Entrance requirements:* For doctorate, GRE General Test. Additional exam requirements/recommendations for international students: Required—TOEFL (minimum score 550 paper-based). *Application deadline:* For fall admission, 2/1 for domestic students, 1/31 for international students. Application fee: $75. Electronic applications accepted. *Financial support:* Fellowships available. *Unit head:* Jianwei Zhang, Chair, 518-442-5006, E-mail: jzhang@albany.edu. *Application contact:* Jianwei Zhang, Chair, 518-442-5006, E-mail: jzhang@albany.edu.

University at Buffalo, the State University of New York, Graduate School, Graduate School of Education, Department of Information Science, Buffalo, NY 14260. Offers information and library science (MS); library and information studies (Certificate); school librarianship (MS). *Accreditation:* ALA (one or more programs are accredited). *Program availability:* Part-time, 100% online. *Faculty:* 11 full-time (6 women), 6 part-time/adjunct (4 women). *Students:* 75 full-time (58 women), 130 part-time (109 women); includes 14 minority (4 Black or African American, non-Hispanic/Latino; 1 American Indian or Alaska Native, non-Hispanic/Latino; 5 Asian, non-Hispanic/Latino; 2 Hispanic/Latino; 1 Native Hawaiian or other Pacific Islander, non-Hispanic/Latino; 1 Two or more races, non-Hispanic/Latino). Average age 33. 122 applicants, 87% accepted, 72 enrolled. In 2018, 85 master's, 1 other advanced degree awarded. *Degree requirements:* For master's, thesis optional; for Certificate, thesis. *Entrance requirements:* For master's, letters of recommendation. Additional exam requirements/recommendations for international students: Required—TOEFL (minimum score 600 paper-based; 79 iBT), IELTS (minimum score 6.5), PTE (minimum score 55). *Application deadline:* For fall admission, 4/1 priority date for domestic and international students; for spring admission, 10/15 priority date for domestic students, 10/15 for international students. Applications are processed on a rolling basis. Application fee: $50. Electronic applications accepted. *Financial support:* In 2018–19, 16 fellowships (averaging $2,345 per year), 6 research assistantships with tuition reimbursements (averaging $10,222 per year) were awarded; teaching assistantships, Federal Work-Study, scholarships/grants, tuition waivers (full and partial), and unspecified assistantships also available. Support available to part-time students. Financial award application deadline: 2/1; financial award applicants required to submit FAFSA. *Faculty research:* Information-seeking behavior, thesauri, impact of technology, questioning behaviors, educational informatics. *Total annual research expenditures:* $56,553. *Unit head:* Dr. Heidi Julien, Chair, 716-645-1474, Fax: 716-645-3775, E-mail: heidijul@buffalo.edu. *Application contact:* Renad Aref, Assistant Director of Admission Recruitment, 716-645-2110, Fax: 716-645-7937, E-mail: gseinfo@buffalo.edu.
Website: http://www.gse.buffalo.edu/lis/

University at Buffalo, the State University of New York, Graduate School, Graduate School of Education, Department of Learning and Instruction, Buffalo, NY 14260. Offers biology education (Ed M, Certificate); chemistry education (Ed M, Certificate); childhood education (Ed M); childhood education with bilingual extension (Ed M); college teaching (Advanced Certificate); curriculum, instruction and the science of learning (PhD); early childhood education (Ed M); early childhood education with bilingual extension (Ed M); earth science education (Ed M, Certificate); education and technology (Ed M); education studies (Ed M); educational technology and new literacies (Certificate); educational technology and new literacies (Advanced Certificate); elementary education (Ed D); English education (Ed M, Certificate); English education studies (Ed M); English for speakers of other languages (Ed M); foreign and second language education (PhD); French education (Ed M, Certificate); German education (Ed M, Certificate); gifted education (Certificate); Latin education (Ed M, Certificate); literacy education studies (Ed M); literacy specialist (Ed M); literacy teaching and learning (Certificate); mathematics education (Ed M, Certificate); music education (Ed M, Certificate); music education studies (Ed M); music learning theory (Advanced Certificate); online education (Advanced Certificate); physics education (Ed M, Certificate); science and the

public (Ed M); social studies education (Ed M, Certificate); Spanish education (Ed M, Certificate); special education (PhD); teaching English to speakers of other languages (Ed M). *Program availability:* Part-time, evening/weekend, 100% online. *Faculty:* 31 full-time (22 women), 41 part-time/adjunct (27 women). *Students:* 161 full-time (107 women), 369 part-time (260 women); includes 76 minority (26 Black or African American, non-Hispanic/Latino; 3 American Indian or Alaska Native, non-Hispanic/Latino; 30 Asian, non-Hispanic/Latino; 14 Hispanic/Latino; 3 Two or more races, non-Hispanic/Latino), 41 international. Average age 34. 368 applicants, 70% accepted, 179 enrolled. In 2018, 100 master's, 26 doctorates, 19 other advanced degrees awarded. *Degree requirements:* For master's, comprehensive exam; for doctorate, thesis/dissertation, research analysis exam, research experience. *Entrance requirements:* For master's, letters of reference; for doctorate, GRE General Test or MAT, interview, writing sample, letters of recommendation. Additional exam requirements/recommendations for international students: Required—TOEFL (minimum score 600 paper-based; 96 iBT), IELTS (minimum score 6.5), PTE (minimum score 55). *Application deadline:* For fall admission, 2/1 priority date for domestic and international students; for spring admission, 11/15 priority date for domestic students, 10/1 for international students. Applications are processed on a rolling basis. Application fee: $50. Electronic applications accepted. *Financial support:* In 2018–19, 42 fellowships (averaging $5,181 per year), 44 research assistantships with tuition reimbursements (averaging $10,908 per year) were awarded; teaching assistantships, career-related internships or fieldwork, Federal Work-Study, institutionally sponsored loans, scholarships/grants, tuition waivers (full and partial), and unspecified assistantships also available. Financial award application deadline: 2/28; financial award applicants required to submit FAFSA. *Faculty research:* Science assessment, foreign language teaching and learning, early learning, new literacies, gender and education. *Total annual research expenditures:* $413,233. *Unit head:* Dr. Julie Gorlewski, Department Chair, 716-645-2455, Fax: 716-645-3161, E-mail: jgorlews@buffalo.edu. *Application contact:* Renad Aref, Assistant Director of Admission Recruitment, 716-645-2110, Fax: 716-645-7937, E-mail: gseinfo@buffalo.edu.
Website: http://ed.buffalo.edu/teaching.html

University of Alaska Southeast, Graduate Programs, Program in Education, Juneau, AK 99801. Offers educational leadership (M Ed); elementary education (MAT); learning design and technology (M Ed); mathematics education (M Ed); reading specialist (M Ed); secondary education (MAT); special education (M Ed, MAT). *Accreditation:* NCATE. *Program availability:* Part-time, evening/weekend, online learning. *Degree requirements:* For master's, comprehensive exam or project, portfolio. *Entrance requirements:* For master's, PRAXIS, minimum GPA of 3.0, writing sample, letters of recommendation. Electronic applications accepted. *Faculty research:* Applied classroom research, culturally responsive practices, action research, teaching effectiveness.

University of Alberta, Faculty of Graduate Studies and Research, Department of Educational Psychology, Edmonton, AB T6G 2E1, Canada. Offers counseling psychology (M Ed, PhD); educational psychology (M Ed, PhD); instructional technology (M Ed); school counseling (M Ed); school psychology (M Ed, PhD); special education (M Ed, PhD); special education-deafness studies (M Ed); teaching English as a second language (M Ed). *Program availability:* Part-time. *Degree requirements:* For master's, thesis optional; for doctorate, comprehensive exam, thesis/dissertation. *Entrance requirements:* For master's and doctorate, minimum GPA of 3.0. Additional exam requirements/recommendations for international students: Required—TOEFL. *Faculty research:* Human learning, development and assessment.

University of Arkansas, Graduate School, College of Education and Health Professions, Department of Curriculum and Instruction, Program in Educational Technology, Fayetteville, AR 72701. Offers M Ed. *Accreditation:* NCATE. *Program availability:* Part-time, evening/weekend. In 2018, 10 master's awarded. *Entrance requirements:* For master's, GRE General Test, MAT or minimum GPA of 3.0. *Application deadline:* For fall admission, 8/1 for domestic students, 4/1 for international students; for spring admission, 12/1 for domestic students, 10/1 for international students; for summer admission, 4/15 for domestic students, 3/1 for international students. Applications are processed on a rolling basis. Application fee: $60. Electronic applications accepted. *Financial support:* Fellowships with tuition reimbursements, research assistantships, teaching assistantships, career-related internships or fieldwork, and Federal Work-Study available. Support available to part-time students. Financial award application deadline: 4/1; financial award applicants required to submit FAFSA. *Unit head:* Dr. Cheryl Murphy, Department Head, 479-575-5111, Fax: 479-575-6676, E-mail: cmurphy@uark.edu. *Application contact:* Dr. Derrick Mears, Graduate Coordinator, 479-575-5439, Fax: 479-575-6676, E-mail: dmears@uark.edu.
Website: https://etec.uark.edu

University of Arkansas at Little Rock, Graduate School, College of Education and Health Professions, Department of Educational Leadership, Program in Learning Systems Technology Education, Little Rock, AR 72204-1099. Offers M Ed. *Degree requirements:* For master's, comprehensive exam or defense of portfolio. *Faculty research:* Instructional program development, educational technology product development, educational technology management.

University of Central Arkansas, Graduate School, College of Education, Department of Leadership Studies, Program in Library Media and Information Technology, Conway, AR 72035-0001. Offers MS. *Program availability:* Part-time, evening/weekend, online learning. *Degree requirements:* For master's, comprehensive exam. *Entrance requirements:* For master's, GRE General Test, minimum GPA of 2.7. Additional exam requirements/recommendations for international students: Required—TOEFL (minimum score 550 paper-based). Electronic applications accepted.

University of Central Florida, College of Community Innovation and Education, Education Doctoral Programs, Program in Instructional Design and Technology, Orlando, FL 32816. Offers e-learning (Certificate); educational technology (Certificate); instructional design (Certificate); instructional design and technology (MA), including e-learning, educational technology, instructional systems; instructional design for simulations (Certificate). *Program availability:* Part-time. *Students:* 25 full-time (20 women), 127 part-time (93 women); includes 56 minority (19 Black or African American, non-Hispanic/Latino; 1 American Indian or Alaska Native, non-Hispanic/Latino; 6 Asian, non-Hispanic/Latino; 27 Hispanic/Latino; 3 Two or more races, non-Hispanic/Latino), 1 international. Average age 36. 93 applicants, 89% accepted, 57 enrolled. In 2018, 35 master's, 16 other advanced degrees awarded. *Entrance requirements:* For master's, letters of recommendation, resume. Additional exam requirements/recommendations for international students: Required—TOEFL. *Application deadline:* For fall admission, 7/15 for domestic students; for spring admission, 12/1 for domestic students. Application fee: $30. Electronic applications accepted. *Financial support:* In 2018–19, 5 students received support, including 5 research assistantships with partial tuition reimbursements available (averaging $14,317 per year); health care benefits also available. Financial award application deadline: 3/1; financial award applicants required to submit FAFSA. *Unit head:* Dr. Richard Hartshorne, Program Coordinator, 407-823-1861, E-mail: richard.hartshorne@ucf.edu. *Application contact:* Associate Director, Graduate Admissions, 407-823-2766, Fax: 407-823-6442, E-mail: gradadmissions@ucf.edu.
Website: https://edcollege.ucf.edu/insttech/

University of Central Missouri, The Graduate School, Warrensburg, MO 64093. Offers accountancy (MA); accounting (MBA); applied mathematics (MS); aviation safety (MA); biology (MS); business administration (MBA); career and technical education leadership (MS); college student personnel administration (MS); communication (MA); computer science (MS); counseling (MS); criminal justice (MS); educational leadership (Ed D); educational technology (MS); elementary and early childhood education (MSE); English (MA); environmental studies (MA); finance (MBA); history (MA); human services/educational technology (Ed S); human services/learning resources (Ed S); human services/professional counseling (Ed S); industrial hygiene (MS); industrial management (MS); information systems (MBA); information technology (MS); kinesiology (MS); library science and information services (MS); literacy education (MSE); marketing (MBA); mathematics (MS); music (MA); occupational safety management (MS); psychology (MS); rural family nursing (MS); school administration (MSE); social gerontology (MS); sociology (MA); special education (MSE); speech language pathology (MS); superintendency (Ed S); teaching (MAT); teaching English as a second language (MA); technology (MS); technology management (PhD); theatre (MA). *Accreditation:* ASHA. *Program availability:* Part-time, 100% online, blended/hybrid learning. *Degree requirements:* For master's and Ed S, comprehensive exam (for some programs), thesis (for some programs). *Entrance requirements:* Additional exam requirements/recommendations for international students: Required—TOEFL (minimum score 550 paper-based; 79 iBT). Electronic applications accepted.

University of Central Oklahoma, The Jackson College of Graduate Studies, College of Education and Professional Studies, Donna Nigh Department of Advanced Professional and Special Services, Edmond, OK 73034-5209. Offers educational leadership (M Ed); library media education (M Ed); reading (M Ed); school counseling (M Ed); special education (M Ed), including mild/moderate disabilities, severe-profound/multiple disabilities; speech-language pathology (MS). *Accreditation:* ASHA. *Program availability:* Part-time. *Degree requirements:* For master's, comprehensive exam (for some programs), thesis (for some programs). *Entrance requirements:* Additional exam requirements/recommendations for international students: Required—TOEFL (minimum score 550 paper-based; 79 iBT), IELTS (minimum score 6.5). Electronic applications accepted.

University of Colorado Denver, School of Education and Human Development, Information and Learning Technologies Program, Denver, CO 80217. Offers e-learning design and implementation (MA); instructional design and adult learning (MA); K-12 teaching (MA). *Program availability:* Part-time, evening/weekend, online learning. *Degree requirements:* For master's, comprehensive exam (for some programs), comprehensive exam or online portfolio; 30 credit hours. *Entrance requirements:* For master's, GRE or MAT (if GPA is below 2.75), resume, statement of intent, three letters of recommendation, transcripts from all colleges/universities previously attended. Additional exam requirements/recommendations for international students: Required—TOEFL (minimum score 537 paper-based; 75 iBT); Recommended—IELTS (minimum score 6.5). Electronic applications accepted. *Expenses:* Contact institution. *Faculty research:* Technology for educational management, instructional design foundations, e-learning, educational design.

University of Connecticut, Graduate School, Neag School of Education, Department of Educational Psychology, Cognition, Instruction, and Learning Technology Program, Storrs, CT 06269. Offers MA, PhD. *Degree requirements:* For master's, comprehensive exam; for doctorate, thesis/dissertation. *Entrance requirements:* For doctorate, GRE General Test. Additional exam requirements/recommendations for international students: Required—TOEFL (minimum score 550 paper-based). Electronic applications accepted.

University of Dayton, Department of Teacher Education, Dayton, OH 45469. Offers adolescence to young adult education (MS Ed); early childhood leadership and advocacy (MS Ed); interdisciplinary education (MS Ed), including visual arts; interdisciplinary education studies (MS Ed); leadership in educational systems (MS Ed); literacy (MS Ed); mathematics education (MS Ed); middle childhood education (MS Ed); multi-age education (MS Ed), including world languages; music education (MS Ed); teacher as leader (MS Ed); teacher education (MS Ed); technology-enhanced learning (MS Ed); trans-disciplinary early childhood education (MS Ed). *Program availability:* Part-time, 100% online. *Degree requirements:* For master's, variable foreign language requirement, thesis or alternative, internship (for teaching licensure or endorsement). *Entrance requirements:* For master's, GRE (minimum score of 149 verbal, 4 on writing) or MAT (minimum score of 396) if undergraduate GPA was under 2.75, minimum GPA of 2.75, 3 letters of recommendation, personal statement or resume, official transcripts. Additional exam requirements/recommendations for international students: Required—TOEFL (minimum score 550 paper-based; 80 iBT); Recommended—IELTS (minimum score 6.5). Electronic applications accepted. *Expenses:* Contact institution. *Faculty research:* Social emotional learning, culturally responsive teaching, urban teaching, literacy, instructional strategies, pre-service teacher education preparation.

The University of Findlay, Office of Graduate Admissions, Findlay, OH 45840-3653. Offers applied security and analytics (MSAS); athletic training (MAT); business (MBA), including certified management accountant, certified public accountant, health care management, hospitality management; education (MA Ed, Ed D), including children's literature (MA Ed), curriculum and teaching (MA Ed), education (MA Ed), educational administration (MA Ed), human resource development (MA Ed), mathematics (MA Ed), reading (MA Ed), science education (MA Ed), superintendent (Ed D), teaching (Ed D), technology (MA Ed); environmental, safety, and health management (MSEM); health informatics (MS); occupational therapy (MOT); pharmacy (Pharm D); physical therapy (DPT); physician assistant (MPA); rhetoric and writing (MA); teaching English to speakers of other languages (TESOL) and applied linguistics (MA). *Program availability:* Part-time, evening/weekend, 100% online, blended/hybrid learning. *Degree requirements:* For master's, comprehensive exam (for some programs), thesis (for some programs), cumulative project, capstone project; for doctorate, thesis/dissertation (for some programs). *Entrance requirements:* For master's, GRE/GMAT, bachelor's degree from accredited institution, minimum undergraduate GPA of 2.5 in last 64 hours of course work; for doctorate, GRE, MAT, minimum cumulative GPA of 3.0. Additional exam requirements/recommendations for international students: Required—TOEFL (minimum score 79 iBT), IELTS (minimum score 7), PTE (minimum score 61). Electronic applications accepted.

University of Georgia, College of Education, Department of Career and Information Studies, Athens, GA 30602. Offers learning, design, and technology (M Ed, PhD, Ed S), including instructional design and development (M Ed, Ed S); workforce education (MAT, Ed D), including business education (MAT). *Accreditation:* NCATE. *Entrance requirements:* For master's, GRE General Test, MAT; for doctorate, GRE General Test; for Ed S, GRE General Test or MAT. Electronic applications accepted.

University of Hawaii at Manoa, Office of Graduate Education, College of Education, Department of Educational Technology, Honolulu, HI 96822. Offers M Ed. *Program availability:* Part-time. *Degree requirements:* For master's, thesis optional. *Entrance requirements:* Additional exam requirements/recommendations for international students: Required—TOEFL (minimum score 650 paper-based; 114 iBT), IELTS (minimum score 7). *Faculty research:* Distance education-interaction via electronic means.

Educational Media/Instructional Technology

University of Hawaii at Manoa, Office of Graduate Education, College of Education, PhD in Education Program, Honolulu, HI 96822. Offers curriculum and instruction (PhD); educational administration (PhD); educational foundations (PhD); educational policy studies (PhD); educational psychology (PhD); exceptionalities (PhD); kinesiology (PhD); learning design and technology (PhD). *Program availability:* Part-time, evening/weekend. *Degree requirements:* For doctorate, thesis/dissertation. *Entrance requirements:* For doctorate, GRE General Test, sample of written work. Additional exam requirements/recommendations for international students: Required—TOEFL (minimum score 600 paper-based; 100 iBT), IELTS (minimum score 7).

University of Houston–Clear Lake, School of Education, Program in Curriculum and Instruction, Houston, TX 77058-1002. Offers curriculum and instruction (MS); early childhood education (MS); reading (MS); school library and information science (MS). *Program availability:* Part-time, evening/weekend. *Degree requirements:* For master's, thesis (for some programs). *Entrance requirements:* For master's, GRE or minimum GPA of 3.0 in last 60 hours. Additional exam requirements/recommendations for international students: Required—TOEFL (minimum score 550 paper-based). Electronic applications accepted.

University of Houston–Clear Lake, School of Education, Program in Foundations and Professional Studies, Houston, TX 77058-1002. Offers counseling (MS); instructional technology (MS); multicultural studies (MS). *Program availability:* Part-time, evening/weekend. *Degree requirements:* For master's, thesis optional. *Entrance requirements:* For master's, GRE or minimum GPA of 3.0 in last 60 hours. Additional exam requirements/recommendations for international students: Required—TOEFL (minimum score 550 paper-based). Electronic applications accepted.

University of Houston–Victoria, School of Education, Health Professions and Human Development, Victoria, TX 77901-4450. Offers administration and supervision (M Ed); adult and higher education (M Ed); counselor education (M Ed); curriculum and instruction (M Ed); dyslexia education (Certificate); educational technology (M Ed); special education (M Ed). *Program availability:* Part-time, evening/weekend, online learning. *Degree requirements:* For master's, comprehensive exam, project or thesis. *Entrance requirements:* For master's, GRE General Test. Additional exam requirements/recommendations for international students: Required—TOEFL. Electronic applications accepted. *Expenses: Tuition, area resident:* Full-time $6154; part-time $3077 per semester. Tuition, state resident: full-time $6154; part-time $3077 per semester. Tuition, nonresident: full-time $13,624; part-time $6812 per semester. *International tuition:* $13,624 full-time. *Required fees:* $1405; $847 per semester. $423 per semester. Tuition and fees vary according to program. *Faculty research:* Reading and language arts education, evaluation and diagnosis of special children's abilities.

The University of Kansas, Graduate Studies, School of Education, Department of Educational Leadership and Policy Studies, Program in Educational Technology, Lawrence, KS 66045. Offers MS Ed, PhD. *Program availability:* Part-time, evening/weekend. *Students:* 4 full-time (2 women), 8 part-time (7 women); includes 4 minority (1 Black or African American, non-Hispanic/Latino; 2 Asian, non-Hispanic/Latino; 1 Hispanic/Latino), 3 international. Average age 38. 10 applicants, 40% accepted, 4 enrolled. In 2018, 5 master's awarded. *Entrance requirements:* For master's, resume or electronic portfolio, official transcripts, statement of purpose, three letters of recommendation; for doctorate, GRE, resume or electronic portfolio, official transcripts, statement of purpose, three letters of recommendation, sample of academic writing. Additional exam requirements/recommendations for international students: Required—TOEFL, IELTS. *Application deadline:* For fall admission, 6/1 priority date for domestic and international students; for spring admission, 11/1 for domestic and international students; for summer admission, 4/1 for domestic and international students. Application fee: $65 ($85 for international students). Electronic applications accepted. *Financial support:* Research assistantships, teaching assistantships, and unspecified assistantships available. Financial award application deadline: 2/21. *Unit head:* Dr. Susan B. Twombly, Chair, 785-864-9721, E-mail: stwombly@ku.edu. *Application contact:* Denise Brubaker, Admissions Coordinator, 785-864-7973, Fax: 785-864-4697, E-mail: brubaker@ku.edu.
Website: http://edtech.ku.edu/

University of Kentucky, Graduate School, College of Education, Program in Curriculum and Instruction, Lexington, KY 40506-0032. Offers curriculum and instruction (Ed D, PhD); elementary education (MA Ed); instructional system design (MS Ed); literacy (MA Ed); middle school education (MA Ed, MS Ed); secondary education (MA Ed, MS Ed). *Accreditation:* NCATE. *Degree requirements:* For master's, comprehensive exam, thesis optional; for doctorate, comprehensive exam, thesis/dissertation. *Entrance requirements:* For master's, GRE General Test, minimum undergraduate GPA of 2.75; for doctorate, GRE General Test, minimum graduate GPA of 3.0. Additional exam requirements/recommendations for international students: Required—TOEFL (minimum score 550 paper-based). Electronic applications accepted. *Faculty research:* Educational reform, multicultural education, classroom instructional practices, performance based assessment, primary school programs.

University of Louisiana at Lafayette, College of Engineering, Department of Industrial Technology, Lafayette, LA 70504. Offers systems technology (MRE). *Program availability:* Part-time, evening/weekend. *Degree requirements:* For master's, comprehensive exam, thesis or alternative. *Entrance requirements:* For master's, GRE General Test, minimum GPA of 2.85. Additional exam requirements/recommendations for international students: Required—TOEFL (minimum score 550 paper-based). Electronic applications accepted. *Faculty research:* Mathematical programming, production management forecasting.

University of Maine, Graduate School, College of Education and Human Development, School of Kinesiology, Physical Education and Athletic Training, Orono, ME 04469. Offers classroom technology integrationist (CGS); education data specialist (CGS); educational technology coordinator (CGS); kinesiology and physical education (M Ed, MS); science education (M Ed, MS); STEM education (PhD). *Program availability:* Part-time, evening/weekend. *Faculty:* 3 full-time (0 women). *Students:* 9 full-time (5 women), 2 part-time (0 women); includes 2 minority (1 Black or African American, non-Hispanic/Latino; 1 Asian, non-Hispanic/Latino). Average age 24. 8 applicants, 75% accepted, 3 enrolled. In 2018, 3 master's awarded. *Degree requirements:* For master's, thesis (for some programs); for doctorate, comprehensive exam, thesis/dissertation. *Entrance requirements:* For master's, GRE General Test, MAT; for doctorate, GRE General Test. Additional exam requirements/recommendations for international students: Required—TOEFL. *Application deadline:* For fall admission, 1/15 for domestic students. Applications are processed on a rolling basis. Application fee: $65. Electronic applications accepted. *Financial support:* In 2018–19, 7 students received support, including 6 teaching assistantships with full tuition reimbursements available (averaging $15,600 per year); Federal Work-Study, scholarships/grants, and unspecified assistantships also available. Financial award application deadline: 3/1. *Faculty research:* Geriatric equilibrium, physical activity and technology, muscle cell metabolism, hormonal response to exercise. *Unit head:* Dr. Jim Artesani, Associate Dean of Accreditation and Graduate Affairs, 207-581-4061, Fax: 207-581-2423. *Application contact:* Scott G. Delcourt, Assistant Vice President for Graduate Studies and Senior Associate Dean, 207-581-3291, Fax: 207-581-3232, E-mail: graduate@maine.edu.
Website: http://umaine.edu/edhd/

University of Maine at Farmington, Graduate Programs in Education, Farmington, ME 04938. Offers early childhood education (MS Ed); educational leadership (MS Ed); instructional technology (M Ed). M Ed offered in collaboration with University of Maine and University of Southern Maine. *Accreditation:* NCATE. *Program availability:* Part-time-only, evening/weekend, 100% online, blended/hybrid learning. *Degree requirements:* For master's, thesis, capstone research project. *Entrance requirements:* For master's, baccalaureate degree from accredited institution, valid teaching certificate or professional experience in education. Additional exam requirements/recommendations for international students: Required—TOEFL. Electronic applications accepted. *Expenses:* Contact institution. *Faculty research:* Teacher leadership, school improvement strategies, technology integration.

University of Maryland, Baltimore County, The Graduate School, College of Arts, Humanities and Social Sciences, Department of Education, Program in Instructional Systems Development, Halethorpe, MD 21227. Offers distance education (Graduate Certificate); instructional systems development (MA, Graduate Certificate), including distance education (Graduate Certificate); instructional technology (Graduate Certificate). *Program availability:* Part-time, evening/weekend, 100% online, blended/hybrid learning. *Degree requirements:* For master's, comprehensive exam (for some programs), portfolio (for some programs). *Entrance requirements:* Additional exam requirements/recommendations for international students: Required—TOEFL (minimum score 99 iBT), GRE. Electronic applications accepted. *Faculty research:* E-learning, distance education, instructional design.

University of Maryland, College Park, Academic Affairs, College of Education, Department of Education Policy and Leadership, College Park, MD 20742. Offers curriculum and educational communications (M Ed, MA, Ed D, PhD); social foundations of education (M Ed, MA, Ed D, PhD, CAGS). *Accreditation:* NCATE. *Program availability:* Part-time, evening/weekend, online learning. *Degree requirements:* For master's, thesis or alternative, internship and/or field experience; for doctorate, comprehensive exam, thesis/dissertation, practicum or internship. *Entrance requirements:* For master's, GRE General Test or MAT, minimum GPA of 3.0, scholarly writing sample, 3 letters of recommendation; for doctorate, GRE General Test or MAT, scholarly writing sample; minimum undergraduate GPA of 3.0, graduate 3.5. *Faculty research:* Educational technology, adult and higher education.

University of Maryland University College, The Graduate School, Program in Instructional Technology, Adelphi, MD 20783. Offers M Ed.

University of Maryland University College, The Graduate School, Program in Learning Design and Technology, Adelphi, MD 20783. Offers MS. *Program availability:* Part-time, evening/weekend. *Students:* 87 part-time (63 women); includes 34 minority (22 Black or African American, non-Hispanic/Latino; 2 Asian, non-Hispanic/Latino; 5 Hispanic/Latino; 5 Two or more races, non-Hispanic/Latino), 2 international. Average age 42. 54 applicants, 100% accepted, 23 enrolled. In 2018, 26 master's awarded. *Application deadline:* Applications are processed on a rolling basis. Application fee: $50. Electronic applications accepted. *Financial support:* Scholarships/grants available. Financial award application deadline: 6/1; financial award applicants required to submit FAFSA. *Unit head:* Randy Hansen, Acting Vice Dean and Program Chair, 240-6842962, E-mail: Randy.Hansen@umuc.edu. *Application contact:* Admissions, 800-888-8682, E-mail: studentfirst@umuc.edu.
Website: https://www.umuc.edu/academic-programs/masters-degrees/learning-design-technology-ms.cfm

University of Massachusetts Amherst, Graduate School, College of Education, Program in Education, Amherst, MA 01003. Offers bilingual, English as a second language, and multicultural education (M Ed, Ed S); child study and early education (M Ed); children, families and schools (Ed D, Ed S); early childhood and elementary teacher education (M Ed); educational leadership (M Ed); educational policy and leadership (Ed D); higher education (M Ed); international education (M Ed); language, literacy and culture (Ed D); learning, media and technology (M Ed, Ed S); mathematics, science, and learning technologies (Ed D); reading and writing (M Ed); research, educational measurement and psychometrics (Ed D); school counselor education (M Ed, Ed S); school psychology (Ed S); science education (Ed S); secondary teacher education (M Ed); social justice education (M Ed, Ed D, Ed S); special education (M Ed, Ed D, Ed S); teacher education and school improvement (Ed D, Ed S). *Accreditation:* NCATE. *Program availability:* Part-time, online learning. Terminal master's awarded for partial completion of doctoral program. *Degree requirements:* For doctorate, comprehensive exam, thesis/dissertation. *Entrance requirements:* Additional exam requirements/recommendations for international students: Required—TOEFL (minimum score 550 paper-based; 80 iBT), IELTS (minimum score 6.5). Electronic applications accepted.

University of Massachusetts Boston, College of Advancing and Professional Studies, Program in Instructional Design, Boston, MA 02125-3393. Offers M Ed, Certificate. *Program availability:* Part-time, evening/weekend. *Students:* 6 full-time (4 women), 65 part-time (52 women); includes 7 minority (2 Black or African American, non-Hispanic/Latino; 1 Asian, non-Hispanic/Latino; 4 Hispanic/Latino), 2 international. Average age 42. 22 applicants, 100% accepted, 18 enrolled. In 2018, 24 master's, 17 Certificates awarded. *Entrance requirements:* For master's, MAT, minimum GPA of 2.75. *Application deadline:* For fall admission, 6/1 for domestic students; for spring admission, 11/15 for domestic students. Application fee: $60 ($100 for international students). Electronic applications accepted. *Expenses: Tuition, area resident:* Full-time $17,896. Tuition, state resident: full-time $17,896. Tuition, nonresident: full-time $34,932. *International tuition:* $34,932 full-time. *Required fees:* $355. *Financial support:* Research assistantships, teaching assistantships, career-related internships or fieldwork, Federal Work-Study, and unspecified assistantships available. Support available to part-time students. Financial award application deadline: 3/1; financial award applicants required to submit FAFSA. *Faculty research:* Distance education, adult education. *Unit head:* Judith Erdman, 617-287-7749, E-mail: instructionaldesign@umb.edu. *Application contact:* Graduate Admissions Coordinator, 617-287-6400, Fax: 617-287-6236, E-mail: graduate.admissions@umb.edu.

University of Memphis, Graduate School, College of Education, Department of Instruction and Curriculum Leadership, Memphis, TN 38152. Offers advanced studies in teaching and learning (M Ed); applied behavior analysis (Graduate Certificate); autism studies (Graduate Certificate); early childhood education (MAT, MS, Ed D); elementary education (MAT); instruction and curriculum (MS, Ed D); instruction design and technology (MS, Ed D); instructional design and technology (Graduate Certificate); literacy, leadership, and coaching (Graduate Certificate); reading (MS, Ed D); school library information specialist (Graduate Certificate); secondary education (MAT); special education (MAT, MS, Ed D); STEM teacher leadership (Graduate Certificate); urban education (Graduate Certificate). *Accreditation:* NCATE (one or more programs are accredited). *Program availability:* Part-time. *Students:* 62 full-time (45 women), 412 part-time (326 women); includes 209 minority (179 Black or African American, non-Hispanic/Latino; 1 American Indian or Alaska Native, non-Hispanic/Latino; 5 Asian, non-Hispanic/Latino; 17 Hispanic/Latino; 7 Two or more races, non-Hispanic/Latino), 4 international. Average age 35. 195 applicants, 91% accepted, 143 enrolled. In 2018, 122 master's, 13 doctorates, 29 other advanced degrees awarded. Terminal master's awarded for partial completion of doctoral program. *Degree requirements:* For master's, comprehensive

exam, thesis or alternative; for doctorate, comprehensive exam, thesis/dissertation. *Entrance requirements:* For master's, GRE General Test, PRAXIS, minimum GPA of 2.5, letters of reference; for doctorate, GRE General Test, GRE Subject Test, 2 years of teaching experience, letters of reference, statement of purpose, interview. Additional exam requirements/recommendations for international students: Required—TOEFL (minimum score 550 paper-based; 79 iBT). *Application deadline:* For fall admission, 4/1 priority date for domestic students; for spring admission, 10/1 priority date for domestic students; for summer admission, 2/1 priority date for domestic students. Applications are processed on a rolling basis. Application fee: $35 ($60 for international students). Electronic applications accepted. *Expenses:* Tuition, area resident: Full-time $10,240; part-time $503 per credit hour. Tuition, state resident: full-time $10,464. Tuition, nonresident: full-time $20,224; part-time $991 per credit hour. *Required fees:* $850; $106 per credit hour. *Financial support:* Research assistantships with full tuition reimbursements, teaching assistantships with full tuition reimbursements, career-related internships or fieldwork, Federal Work-Study, institutionally sponsored loans, scholarships/grants, traineeships, and unspecified assistantships available. Support available to part-time students. Financial award application deadline: 2/1; financial award applicants required to submit FAFSA. *Faculty research:* Effective urban teachers, preparation and retention of urban teachers, technology utilization in schools, field-based teacher preparation programs, effective use of online instruction. *Unit head:* Dr. Christian Mueller, Chair, 901-678-2365, E-mail: cemuellr@memphis.edu. *Application contact:* Dr. Lee Allen, Director of Graduate Programs, 901-678-4073, E-mail: allenlee@memphis.edu.
Website: http://www.memphis.edu/icl/

University of Michigan–Dearborn, College of Education, Health, and Human Services, Master of Arts Program in Educational Technology, Dearborn, MI 48126. Offers MA. *Program availability:* Part-time, evening/weekend, online only, 100% online. *Faculty:* 2 full-time (0 women), 2 part-time/adjunct (0 women). *Students:* 24 part-time (20 women); includes 5 minority (3 Black or African American, non-Hispanic/Latino; 2 Hispanic/Latino). Average age 32. 5 applicants, 100% accepted, 3 enrolled. In 2018, 18 master's awarded. *Entrance requirements:* Additional exam requirements/recommendations for international students: Required—TOEFL (minimum score 560 paper-based; 84 iBT), IELTS (minimum score 6.5). *Application deadline:* For fall admission, 8/1 priority date for domestic students; 5/1 priority date for international students; for winter admission, 12/1 priority date for domestic students, 9/1 priority date for international students; for spring admission, 4/1 priority date for domestic students, 1/1 priority date for international students. Applications are processed on a rolling basis. Application fee: $60. Electronic applications accepted. *Expenses:* $12,140 per academic year (typical full-time in-state); $20,708 per academic year (typical full-time out-of-state). *Financial support:* In 2018–19, 5 students received support. Scholarships/grants available. Financial award application deadline: 3/1; financial award applicants required to submit FAFSA. *Faculty research:* Technology integration, gamified learning, mobile technologies, instructional design, impact of technology on academic achievement. *Unit head:* Dr. Paul Fossum, Director, Master's Programs, 313-593-0982, E-mail: pfossum@umich.edu. *Application contact:* Office of Graduate Studies, 313-583-6321, E-mail: umd-graduatestudies@umich.edu.
Website: http://umdearborn.edu/cehhs/cehhs_ma_ed_tech/

University of Michigan–Flint, School of Education and Human Services, Department of Education, Flint, MI 48502-1950. Offers curriculum and instruction (Ed S); early childhood education (MA); education (Ed D); educational leadership (Ed S); educational technology (MA), including curriculum and instruction, developer; literacy education (MA); secondary education with certification (MA). *Program availability:* Part-time, evening/weekend, online only, 100% online, mixed mode format (for some programs). *Faculty:* 16 full-time (10 women), 28 part-time/adjunct (14 women). *Students:* 31 full-time (23 women), 179 part-time (135 women); includes 54 minority (42 Black or African American, non-Hispanic/Latino; 3 Asian, non-Hispanic/Latino; 4 Hispanic/Latino; 1 Native Hawaiian or other Pacific Islander, non-Hispanic/Latino; 4 Two or more races, non-Hispanic/Latino), 1 international. Average age 39. 133 applicants, 72% accepted, 61 enrolled. In 2018, 60 master's awarded. *Degree requirements:* For master's, thesis optional; for doctorate, thesis/dissertation. *Entrance requirements:* For master's, bachelor's degree from regionally-accredited institution, minimum overall undergraduate GPA of 3.0 on 4.0 scale; for doctorate, completion of Eds minimum overall graduate GPA of 3.3 (6.0 on a 9.0 scale) or equivalent; at least 3 years of work experience in a P-16 educational institution or in an education-related position; for Ed S, MA or MS in education-related field from accredited institution; minimum overall graduate GPA of 3.0 (6.0 on a 9.0 scale) or equivalent; at least 3 years of work experience in an educational setting. Additional exam requirements/recommendations for international students: Required—TOEFL (minimum score 84 iBT), IELTS (minimum score 6.5). *Application deadline:* For fall admission, 8/1 for domestic students, 5/1 for international students; for winter admission, 11/15 for domestic students, 9/15 for international students; for spring admission, 3/15 for domestic students, 1/15 for international students; for summer admission, 5/15 for domestic students. Applications are processed on a rolling basis. Application fee: $55. Electronic applications accepted. *Expenses:* Contact institution. *Financial support:* Federal Work-Study, scholarships/grants, and unspecified assistantships available. Financial award application deadline: 3/1; financial award applicants required to submit FAFSA. *Unit head:* Dr. Mary Jo Finney, Department Chair/Associate Professor, 810-766-6617, E-mail: mjfinney@umflint.edu. *Application contact:* Matt Bohlen, Director of Graduate Admissions, 810-762-3171, Fax: 810-766-6789, E-mail: mbohlen@umflint.edu.
Website: https://www.umflint.edu/education/graduate-programs

University of Minnesota, Twin Cities Campus, Graduate School, College of Education and Human Development, Department of Curriculum and Instruction, Minneapolis, MN 55455-0213. Offers art education (M Ed, MA, PhD); curriculum and instruction (M Ed, MA, PhD); elementary education (MA, PhD); English education (PhD); language and immersion education (Certificate); learning technologies (MA, PhD); literacy education (MA, PhD); second language education (MA, PhD); social studies education (MA, PhD); STEM education (MA, PhD); teaching (M Ed), including mathematics, science, social studies, teaching; teaching English to speakers of other languages (MA); technology enhanced learning (Certificate). *Faculty:* 33 full-time (18 women). *Students:* 414 full-time (293 women), 247 part-time (170 women); includes 129 minority (16 Black or African American, non-Hispanic/Latino; 3 American Indian or Alaska Native, non-Hispanic/Latino; 38 Asian, non-Hispanic/Latino; 47 Hispanic/Latino; 25 Two or more races, non-Hispanic/Latino), 57 international. Average age 31. 610 applicants, 69% accepted, 349 enrolled. In 2018, 338 master's, 21 doctorates, 41 other advanced degrees awarded. Application fee: $75 ($95 for international students). *Financial support:* In 2018–19, 9 fellowships, 35 research assistantships with full tuition reimbursements (averaging $11,380 per year), 85 teaching assistantships with full tuition reimbursements (averaging $11,180 per year) were awarded. *Faculty research:* Teaching and learning; influence of cultural, linguistic, social, political, and technological factors on teaching, learning and educational research; relationship between educational practice and a democratic and just society; urban education; immigrant education, racial justice and education. *Total annual research expenditures:* $3.9 million. *Unit head:* Dr. Mark Vagle, Chair, 612-625-4006, E-mail: mvagle@umn.edu. *Application*

contact: Dr. Mark Vagle, Chair, 612-625-4006, E-mail: mvagle@umn.edu.
Website: http://www.cehd.umn.edu/ci

University of Missouri, Office of Research and Graduate Studies, College of Education, School of Information Science and Learning Technologies, Columbia, MO 65211. Offers information science and learning technology (PhD). *Accreditation:* ALA. *Program availability:* Part-time, evening/weekend. *Entrance requirements:* Additional exam requirements/recommendations for international students: Required—TOEFL. Electronic applications accepted.

University of Nebraska at Kearney, College of Education, Department of Teacher Education, Kearney, NE 68849-0001. Offers curriculum and instruction (MA Ed), including early childhood education, elementary education, English as a second language, instructional effectiveness, reading/special education, secondary education; instructional technology (MS Ed), including information technology, instructional technology, school librarian; reading PK-12 (MA Ed); special education (MA Ed), including advanced practitioner: assistive technology specialist, advanced practitioner: behavioral interventionist, advanced practitioner: inclusive collaboration specialist, gifted, teacher education. *Program availability:* Part-time, evening/weekend, online only, 100% online. *Degree requirements:* For master's, comprehensive exam, thesis optional. *Entrance requirements:* For master's, portfolio or GRE. Additional exam requirements/recommendations for international students: Recommended—TOEFL (minimum score 550 paper-based; 79 iBT), IELTS (minimum score 6.5). Electronic applications accepted. *Expenses:* Contact institution.

University of Nevada, Las Vegas, Graduate College, College of Education, Department of Educational Psychology and Higher Education, Las Vegas, NV 89154-3002. Offers chief diversity officer in higher education (Certificate); college sport leadership (Certificate); educational policy and leadership (M Ed); educational psychology (MS, PhD, Ed S); educational psychology/law (PhD/JD); higher education (M Ed, PhD, Certificate); psychology/learning and technology (PhD), including learning and technology; workforce development/educational leadership (PhD); PhD/JD. *Program availability:* Part-time, evening/weekend, 100% online, blended/hybrid learning. *Faculty:* 20 full-time (12 women), 6 part-time/adjunct (5 women). *Students:* 74 full-time (50 women), 95 part-time (61 women); includes 64 minority (20 Black or African American, non-Hispanic/Latino; 9 Asian, non-Hispanic/Latino; 26 Hispanic/Latino; 9 Two or more races, non-Hispanic/Latino), 10 international. Average age 36. 106 applicants, 49% accepted, 40 enrolled. In 2018, 57 master's, 4 doctorates, 12 other advanced degrees awarded. *Degree requirements:* For master's, comprehensive exam (for some programs), thesis (for some programs); for doctorate, comprehensive exam, thesis/dissertation. *Entrance requirements:* For master's, GRE General Test or GMAT (for some programs), letters of recommendation; writing sample; bachelor's degree; for doctorate, GMAT or GRE General Test, writing exam; for other advanced degree, GRE General Test (for some programs). Additional exam requirements/recommendations for international students: Required—TOEFL (minimum score 550 paper-based; 80 iBT), IELTS (minimum score 7). Application fee: $60 ($95 for international students). Electronic applications accepted. *Financial support:* In 2018–19, 43 students received support, including 28 research assistantships with full tuition reimbursements available (averaging $14,674 per year), 15 teaching assistantships with full tuition reimbursements available (averaging $18,733 per year); institutionally sponsored loans, scholarships/grants, health care benefits, and unspecified assistantships also available. Financial award application deadline: 3/15; financial award applicants required to submit FAFSA. *Faculty research:* Innovation and change in educational settings; educational policy, finance, and marketing; psycho-educational assessment; student retention, persistence, development, language, and culture; statistical modeling, program evaluation, qualitative and quantitative research methods. *Total annual research expenditures:* $426,511. *Unit head:* Dr. Alice Corkill, Chair/Professor, 702-895-4164, E-mail: ephe.chair@unlv.edu. *Application contact:* Dr. Nancy Lough, Graduate Coordinator, 702-895-5392, E-mail: highered.gradcoord@unlv.edu.
Website: http://education.unlv.edu/ephe/

University of New Hampshire, Graduate School, College of Health and Human Services, Department of Occupational Therapy, Durham, NH 03824. Offers assistive technology (Postbaccalaureate Certificate); occupational therapy (MS). *Accreditation:* AOTA. *Program availability:* Part-time. *Entrance requirements:* For master's, OT Course Prerequisite Verification Form. Additional exam requirements/recommendations for international students: Required—TOEFL (minimum score 550 paper-based; 80 iBT). Electronic applications accepted.

University of New Mexico, Graduate Studies, College of University Libraries and Learning Sciences, Albuquerque, NM 87131-2039. Offers organization, information and learning sciences (MA, PhD, Ed S). *Accreditation:* NCATE. *Program availability:* Part-time, evening/weekend, online learning. *Students:* Average age 45. 30 applicants, 80% accepted, 21 enrolled. In 2018, 19 master's, 4 doctorates awarded. *Degree requirements:* For master's, comprehensive exam, thesis or alternative; for doctorate, comprehensive exam, thesis/dissertation. *Entrance requirements:* For master's, minimum GPA of 3.0 in last 60 hours of course work, bachelor's degree; for doctorate, GRE General Test, MAT, master's degree, minimum GPA of 3.5. Additional exam requirements/recommendations for international students: Required—TOEFL. *Application deadline:* For fall admission, 3/15 for domestic and international students; for spring admission, 10/15 for domestic and international students. Application fee: $50. Electronic applications accepted. *Financial support:* Fellowships, research assistantships, teaching assistantships, and career-related internships or fieldwork available. Financial award application deadline: 3/1; financial award applicants required to submit FAFSA. *Faculty research:* Adult learning, distance education, instructional multimedia, organizational learning and development, transformational learning, workplace and learning environment factors that enhance learning and productivity, program and organization evaluation and reform, effects of technology on learning and problem solving. *Total annual research expenditures:* $50,371. *Unit head:* Dr. Charlotte Gunawardens, Program Director, 505-277-5046, Fax: 505-277-1427, E-mail: lani@unm.edu. *Application contact:* Linda Wood, Program Coordinator, 505-277-4131, Fax: 505-277-1427, E-mail: woodl@unm.edu.
Website: http://oils.unm.edu/

The University of North Carolina at Charlotte, Cato College of Education, Department of Educational Leadership, Charlotte, NC 28223-0001. Offers education research, measurement, and evaluation (PhD); educational leadership (Ed D); instructional systems technology (M Ed, Graduate Certificate); quantitative analysis (Graduate Certificate); school administration (MSA, Post-Master's Certificate); university and college teaching (Graduate Certificate). *Program availability:* Part-time, evening/weekend, 100% online, blended/hybrid learning. *Students:* 38 full-time (30 women), 234 part-time (160 women); includes 99 minority (79 Black or African American, non-Hispanic/Latino; 4 Asian, non-Hispanic/Latino; 13 Hispanic/Latino; 3 Two or more races, non-Hispanic/Latino), 8 international. Average age 37. 172 applicants, 71% accepted, 99 enrolled. In 2018, 45 master's, 13 doctorates, 69 other advanced degrees awarded. *Entrance requirements:* For master's, GRE or MAT, bachelor's degree, or its U.S. equivalent, from regionally-accredited college or university; minimum overall GPA of 3.5 on all previous work beyond high school; statement of purpose (essay); at least three recommendation forms; for doctorate, GRE or MAT, bachelor's degree (or its U.S.

equivalent) from regionally-accredited college or university; minimum overall GPA of 3.5 in master's degree program; for other advanced degree, bachelor's degree from regionally-accredited university; minimum GPA of 2.75 on all post-secondary work attempted; transcripts; personal statement outlining why the applicant seeks admission to the program. Additional exam requirements/recommendations for international students: Required—TOEFL (minimum score 523 paper-based; 70 iBT), IELTS (minimum score 6), TOEFL (minimum score 523 paper-based, 70 iBT) or IELTS (6). *Application deadline:* Applications are processed on a rolling basis. Application fee: $75. Electronic applications accepted. Tuition and fees vary according to course load and program. *Financial support:* Research assistantships, career-related internships or fieldwork, institutionally sponsored loans, scholarships/grants, and unspecified assistantships available. Support available to part-time students. Financial award application deadline: 3/1; financial award applicants required to submit FAFSA. *Total annual research expenditures:* $1.8 million. *Unit head:* Dr. Claudia Flowers, Chair, 704-687-8862, E-mail: cpflower@uncc.edu. *Application contact:* Kathy B. Giddings, Director of Graduate Admissions, 704-687-5503, Fax: 704-687-1668, E-mail: gradadm@uncc.edu.
Website: http://edld.uncc.edu/

The University of North Carolina at Greensboro, Graduate School, School of Education, Department of Teacher Education and Higher Education, Greensboro, NC 27412-5001. Offers college teaching and adult learning (Certificate); curriculum and instruction (M Ed), including chemistry education, elementary education, English as a second language, French education, instructional technology, mathematics education, middle grades education, reading education, science education, social studies education, Spanish education; curriculum and teaching (PhD), including higher education, teacher education and development; English as a second language (Certificate); higher education (M Ed); supervision (M Ed). *Accreditation:* NCATE. *Program availability:* Part-time. *Degree requirements:* For doctorate, thesis/dissertation. *Entrance requirements:* For master's and doctorate, GRE General Test. Additional exam requirements/recommendations for international students: Required—TOEFL. Electronic applications accepted. *Faculty research:* Community college literacy program, middle school mathematics/computer mathematics.

The University of North Carolina Wilmington, Watson College of Education, Department of Instructional Technology, Foundations and Secondary Education, Wilmington, NC 28403-3297. Offers English as a second language (M Ed, MAT); instructional technology (MS); secondary education (M Ed, MAT). *Program availability:* Part-time, blended/hybrid learning. *Degree requirements:* For master's, thesis or research project/portfolio. *Entrance requirements:* For master's, GRE or MAT, education statement of interest essay, 3 letters of recommendation. Additional exam requirements/recommendations for international students: Required—TOEFL (minimum score 550 paper-based; 79 iBT), IELTS (minimum score 6.5). Electronic applications accepted.

University of North Dakota, Graduate School, College of Education and Human Development, Program in Instructional Design and Technology, Grand Forks, ND 58202. Offers M Ed, MS. *Degree requirements:* For master's, comprehensive exam, thesis or alternative. *Entrance requirements:* For master's, minimum GPA of 3.0. Additional exam requirements/recommendations for international students: Required—TOEFL (minimum score 550 paper-based; 79 iBT), IELTS (minimum score 6.5). Electronic applications accepted.

University of Northern Iowa, Graduate College, College of Education, Department of Curriculum and Instruction, MA Program in Instructional Technology, Cedar Falls, IA 50614. Offers instructional technology (MA); performance and training technology (MA); school library endorsement (MA). *Degree requirements:* For master's, comprehensive exam, thesis or alternative. *Entrance requirements:* For master's, minimum GPA of 3.0. Additional exam requirements/recommendations for international students: Required—TOEFL (minimum score 500 paper-based; 61 iBT). Electronic applications accepted.

University of Northern Iowa, Graduate College, College of Education, Department of Curriculum and Instruction, MA Program in School Library Studies, Cedar Falls, IA 50614. Offers MA. *Program availability:* Part-time, evening/weekend. *Degree requirements:* For master's, comprehensive exam (for some programs), thesis or alternative, comprehensive portfolio. *Entrance requirements:* For master's, minimum GPA of 3.0. Additional exam requirements/recommendations for international students: Required—TOEFL (minimum score 500 paper-based; 61 iBT). Electronic applications accepted.

University of North Florida, College of Education and Human Services, Department of Leadership, School Counseling and Sport Management, Jacksonville, FL 32224. Offers counselor education (M Ed), including school counseling; educational leadership (M Ed, Ed D), including athletic administration (M Ed), educational leadership, educational technology (M Ed), instructional leadership (M Ed). *Program availability:* Part-time, evening/weekend. *Faculty:* 19 full-time (13 women), 3 part-time/adjunct (1 woman). *Students:* 73 full-time (58 women), 228 part-time (179 women); includes 111 minority (66 Black or African American, non-Hispanic/Latino; 7 Asian, non-Hispanic/Latino; 26 Hispanic/Latino; 1 Native Hawaiian or other Pacific Islander, non-Hispanic/Latino; 11 Two or more races, non-Hispanic/Latino), 8 international. Average age 38. 184 applicants, 58% accepted, 74 enrolled. In 2018, 77 master's, 20 doctorates awarded. *Degree requirements:* For doctorate, thesis/dissertation. *Entrance requirements:* For master's, GRE General Test, minimum GPA of 3.0 in last 60 hours, interview, 3 letters of recommendation; for doctorate, GRE General Test, master's degree, interview, 3 letters of recommendation, writing sample. Additional exam requirements/recommendations for international students: Required—TOEFL (minimum score 500 paper-based). *Application deadline:* For fall admission, 5/1 priority date for domestic students, 5/1 for international students. Application fee: $30. Electronic applications accepted. *Expenses: Tuition, area resident:* Part-time $408.10 per credit hour. Tuition, state resident: part-time $408.10 per credit hour. Tuition, nonresident: part-time $932.61 per credit hour. *Required fees:* $111.81 per credit hour. Tuition and fees vary according to course load, campus/location and program. *Financial support:* In 2018–19, 42 students received support, including 1 research assistantship (averaging $8,096 per year), 1 teaching assistantship (averaging $5,824 per year); career-related internships or fieldwork, Federal Work-Study, scholarships/grants, tuition waivers (partial), and unspecified assistantships also available. Support available to part-time students. Financial award application deadline: 4/1; financial award applicants required to submit FAFSA. *Faculty research:* Counseling: ethics; lesbian, bisexual and transgender issues; educational leadership: school culture and climate; educational assessment and accountability; school safety and student discipline. *Total annual research expenditures:* $12,024. *Unit head:* Dr. Liz Gregg, Chair, 904-620-5199, E-mail: liz.gregg@unf.edu. *Application contact:* Dr. Amanda Pascale, Director, The Graduate School, 904-620-1360, Fax: 904-620-1362, E-mail: graduateschool@unf.edu.
Website: http://www.unf.edu/coehs/lscsm/

University of Oklahoma, Jeannine Rainbolt College of Education, Department of Educational Psychology, Norman, OK 73019. Offers instructional psychology and technology (M Ed, PhD), including educational psychology (M Ed), instructional design and technology (M Ed), instructional psychology and technology (PhD), integrating technology in teaching (M Ed); professional counseling (M Ed), including professional counseling; special education (M Ed, PhD), including applied behavior analysis (M Ed), higher education and community support (PhD), higher education professor (PhD), school instruction and leadership (PhD), secondary transition education (M Ed). *Accreditation:* NCATE. *Program availability:* Part-time, 100% online, blended/hybrid learning. Terminal master's awarded for partial completion of doctoral program. *Degree requirements:* For master's, comprehensive exam (for some programs), thesis (for some programs); for doctorate, comprehensive exam (for some programs), thesis/dissertation. *Entrance requirements:* For doctorate, GRE. Additional exam requirements/recommendations for international students: Required—TOEFL (minimum score 79 iBT) or IELTS (minimum score 6.5). Electronic applications accepted. *Expenses:* Tuition, state resident: full-time $5683.20; part-time $236.80 per credit hour. Tuition, nonresident: full-time $20,342; part-time $847.60 per credit hour. *International tuition:* $20,342.40 full-time. *Required fees:* $2894.20; $110.05 per credit hour. $126.50 per semester. Tuition and fees vary according to course load and program. *Faculty research:* Diversity Issues in counseling; qualitative and mixed-methods research; high-stakes assessments and related educational policy; self-determination and post-secondary outcomes; reading, writing, spelling, and mathematics interventions.

University of Oklahoma, Price College of Business, Division of Management Information Systems, Norman, OK 73019. Offers digital technologies (Graduate Certificate); management of information technology (MS), including business analytics. *Program availability:* Part-time, evening/weekend. *Faculty:* 9 full-time (6 women), 3 part-time/adjunct (0 women). *Students:* 23 full-time (8 women), 15 part-time (8 women); includes 8 minority (1 Black or African American, non-Hispanic/Latino; 2 Asian, non-Hispanic/Latino; 2 Hispanic/Latino; 3 Two or more races, non-Hispanic/Latino), 10 international. Average age 27. 28 applicants, 25% accepted, 5 enrolled. In 2018, 17 master's, 4 other advanced degrees awarded. *Degree requirements:* For master's, thesis optional. *Entrance requirements:* For master's and Graduate Certificate, GMAT or GRE, resume, statement of goals, 3 letters of recommendation. Additional exam requirements/recommendations for international students: Required—TOEFL (minimum score 100 iBT) or IELTS (minimum score 7). *Application deadline:* For fall admission, 6/15 for domestic students, 3/1 for international students; for spring admission, 10/1 for domestic students, 8/1 for international students. Applications are processed on a rolling basis. Application fee: $50 ($100 for international students). Electronic applications accepted. *Expenses:* Tuition, state resident: full-time $5683.20; part-time $236.80 per credit hour. Tuition, nonresident: full-time $20,342; part-time $847.60 per credit hour. *International tuition:* $20,342.40 full-time. *Required fees:* $2894.20; $110.05 per credit hour. $126.50 per semester. Tuition and fees vary according to course load and program. *Financial support:* Research assistantships, teaching assistantships, career-related internships or fieldwork, scholarships/grants, and unspecified assistantships available. Support available to part-time students. Financial award application deadline: 6/1; financial award applicants required to submit FAFSA. *Faculty research:* Human-computer interaction and cognition; deception detection in IT-mediated contexts; social media use; computer-mediated collaboration and communication; meaning in discourse about IT and discourse through IT. *Unit head:* Radhika Santhanam, Chair/Division Director, 405-325-0791, E-mail: radhika@ou.edu. *Application contact:* Jennifer Aragon, Academic Advisor, 405-325-2074, Fax: 405-325-7118, E-mail: jhardman@ou.edu.
Website: http://www.ou.edu/content/price/mis/mis_ms_in_mis.html

University of Pennsylvania, Graduate School of Education, Division of Teaching, Learning, and Leadership, Program in Learning Sciences and Technologies, Philadelphia, PA 19104. Offers MS Ed. *Students:* 28 full-time (24 women), 9 part-time (6 women); includes 3 minority (1 Black or African American, non-Hispanic/Latino; 1 Asian, non-Hispanic/Latino; 1 Hispanic/Latino), 28 international. Average age 30. 106 applicants, 80% accepted, 38 enrolled. In 2018, 14 master's awarded. Application fee: $80.

University of Phoenix–Online Campus, School of Advanced Studies, Phoenix, AZ 85034-7209. Offers business administration (DBA); education (Ed S); educational leadership (Ed D), including curriculum and instruction, education technology, educational leadership; health administration (DHA); higher education administration (PhD); industrial/organizational psychology (PhD); nursing (PhD); organizational leadership (DM), including information systems and technology, organizational leadership. *Program availability:* Evening/weekend, online learning. *Degree requirements:* For doctorate, thesis/dissertation. *Entrance requirements:* Additional exam requirements/recommendations for international students: Required—TOEFL, TOEIC (Test of English as an International Communication), Berlitz Online English Proficiency Exam, PTE, or IELTS. Electronic applications accepted. *Expenses:* Contact institution.

University of Saint Joseph, Department of Education, West Hartford, CT 06117-2700. Offers curriculum and instruction (MA); elementary education (MAT); instructional technology (MA); literacy (MA); secondary education (MAT); TESOL (MA). *Program availability:* Part-time, evening/weekend. *Degree requirements:* For master's, comprehensive exam, thesis or alternative. *Entrance requirements:* For master's, 2 letters of recommendation. Electronic applications accepted. Application fee is waived when completed online.

University of San Francisco, School of Education, Department of Learning and Instruction, San Francisco, CA 94117. Offers digital technologies for teaching and learning (MA); learning and instruction (MA, Ed D); special education (MA, Ed D); teaching reading (MA). *Program availability:* Part-time, evening/weekend. *Students:* 34 full-time (25 women), 11 part-time (8 women); includes 12 minority (4 Black or African American, non-Hispanic/Latino; 3 Asian, non-Hispanic/Latino; 5 Hispanic/Latino), 11 international. Average age 40. 24 applicants, 96% accepted, 16 enrolled. In 2018, 9 doctorates awarded. *Degree requirements:* For doctorate, thesis/dissertation. *Entrance requirements:* Additional exam requirements/recommendations for international students: Required—TOEFL, IELTS, PTE. *Application deadline:* For fall admission, 3/1 priority date for domestic and international students; for spring admission, 11/1 priority date for domestic and international students. Applications are processed on a rolling basis. Application fee: $55 ($65 for international students). Electronic applications accepted. *Financial support:* In 2018–19, 13 students received support. Fellowships, research assistantships, and teaching assistantships available. Financial award application deadline: 3/2; financial award applicants required to submit FAFSA. *Unit head:* Dr. Kevin Oh, Chair, 415-422-2099. *Application contact:* Peter Cole, Admission Coordinator, 415-422-5467, E-mail: schoolofeducation@usfca.edu.

University of San Francisco, School of Education, Department of Teacher Education, San Francisco, CA 94117. Offers digital media and learning (MA); teaching (MA); teaching reading (MA); teaching urban education and social justice (MA). *Program availability:* Part-time. *Students:* 377 full-time (280 women), 51 part-time (43 women); includes 228 minority (28 Black or African American, non-Hispanic/Latino; 62 Asian, non-Hispanic/Latino; 121 Hispanic/Latino; 1 Native Hawaiian or other Pacific Islander, non-Hispanic/Latino; 16 Two or more races, non-Hispanic/Latino), 22 international. Average age 29. 536 applicants, 70% accepted, 182 enrolled. In 2018, 212 master's awarded. *Entrance requirements:* Additional exam requirements/recommendations for international students: Required—TOEFL, IELTS, PTE. *Application deadline:* For fall admission, 3/1 priority date for domestic and international students; for spring admission, 10/15 priority date for domestic students, 10/1 for international students. Applications are processed on a rolling basis. Electronic applications accepted.

Financial support: Applicants required to submit FAFSA. *Unit head:* Dr. Noah Borrero, Chair, 415-422-6481. *Application contact:* Peter Cole, Admission Coordinator, 415-422-5467, E-mail: schoolofeducation@usfca.edu.
Website: https://www.usfca.edu/catalog/graduate/school-of-education/programs-teacher-education

University of Sioux Falls, Fredrikson School of Education, Sioux Falls, SD 57105-1699. Offers educational administration (Ed S), including principal leadership; superintendent and district leadership; leadership in reading (M Ed); leadership in schools (M Ed); leadership in technology (M Ed); teaching (M Ed). Admission in summer only. *Accreditation:* NCATE. *Program availability:* Part-time, evening/weekend. *Degree requirements:* For master's, comprehensive exam (for some programs), research application project; for Ed S, comprehensive exam, portfolio. *Entrance requirements:* For master's, minimum GPA of 3.0, 1 year of teaching experience; for Ed S, minimum 3 years of teaching experience, minimum cumulative GPA of 3.5, 1 year of administrative experience. Additional exam requirements/recommendations for international students: Required—TOEFL. *Faculty research:* Reading, literacy, leadership.

University of South Africa, College of Human Sciences, Pretoria, South Africa. Offers adult education (M Ed); African languages (MA, PhD); African politics (MA, PhD); Afrikaans (MA, PhD); ancient history (MA, PhD); ancient Near Eastern studies (MA, PhD); anthropology (MA, PhD); applied linguistics (MA); Arabic (MA, PhD); archaeology (MA); art history (MA); Biblical archaeology (MA); Biblical studies (M Th, D Th, PhD); Christian spirituality (M Th, D Th); church history (M Th, D Th); classical studies (MA, PhD); clinical psychology (MA); communication (MA, PhD); comparative education (M Ed, Ed D); consulting psychology (D Admin, D Com, PhD); curriculum studies (M Ed, Ed D); development studies (M Admin, MA, D Admin, PhD); didactics (M Ed, Ed D); education (M Tech); education management (M Ed, Ed D); educational psychology (M Ed); English (MA); environmental education (M Ed); French (MA, PhD); German (MA, PhD); Greek (MA); guidance and counseling (M Ed); health studies (MA, PhD), including health sciences education (MA), health services management (MA), medical and surgical nursing science (critical care general) (MA), midwifery and neonatal nursing science (MA), trauma and emergency care (MA); history (MA, PhD); history of education (Ed D); inclusive education (M Ed, Ed D); information and communications technology policy and regulation (MA); information science (MA, MIS, PhD); international politics (MA, PhD); Islamic studies (MA, PhD); Italian (MA, PhD); Judaica (MA, PhD); linguistics (MA, PhD); mathematical education (M Ed); mathematics education (MA); missiology (M Th, D Th); modern Hebrew (MA, PhD); musicology (MA, MMus, D Mus, PhD); natural science education (M Ed); New Testament (M Th, D Th); Old Testament (D Th); pastoral therapy (M Th, D Th); philosophy (MA); philosophy of education (M Ed, Ed D); politics (MA, PhD); Portuguese (MA, PhD); practical theology (M Th, D Th); psychology (MA, MS, PhD); psychology of education (M Ed, Ed D); public health (MA); religious studies (MA, D Th, PhD); Romance languages (MA); Russian (MA, PhD); Semitic languages (MA, PhD); social behavior studies in HIV/AIDS (MA); social science (mental health) (MA); social science in development studies (MA); social science in psychology (MA); social science in social work (MA); social science in sociology (MA); social work (MSW, DSW, PhD); socio-education (M Ed, Ed D); sociolinguistics (MA); sociology (MA, PhD); Spanish (MA, PhD); systematic theology (M Th, D Th); TESOL (teaching English to speakers of other languages) (MA); theological ethics (M Th, D Th); theory of literature (MA, PhD); urban ministries (D Th); urban ministry (M Th).

University of South Alabama, College of Education and Professional Studies, Department of Counseling and Instructional Sciences, Mobile, AL 36688. Offers clinical mental health counseling (MS); educational media (M Ed); educational media and technology (MS); instructional design and development (MS, PhD); instructional leadership (Ed S); school counseling (M Ed). *Accreditation:* NCATE. *Program availability:* Part-time. *Degree requirements:* For master's, comprehensive exam; for doctorate, comprehensive exam, thesis/dissertation. *Entrance requirements:* For master's, GRE General Test or MAT, minimum GPA of 3.0, three letters of recommendation; for doctorate, GRE, three letters of recommendation, master's degree in field or completion of prerequisites, resume. Additional exam requirements/recommendations for international students: Required—TOEFL (minimum score 525 paper-based; 71 iBT). Electronic applications accepted. *Faculty research:* Agency counseling, rehabilitation counseling, school psychometry, juvenile delinquency, mixed methods research.

University of South Carolina, The Graduate School, College of Education, Department of Educational Studies, Program in Educational Technology, Columbia, SC 29208. Offers M Ed. *Accreditation:* NCATE. *Program availability:* Part-time, online learning. *Degree requirements:* For master's, comprehensive exam. *Entrance requirements:* For master's, GRE or MAT, interview, letters of intent and reference.

University of South Carolina Aiken, Program in Educational Technology, Aiken, SC 29801. Offers M Ed. Program offered with University of South Carolina in Columbia. *Program availability:* Part-time, evening/weekend, online only, 100% online. *Faculty:* 2 full-time (1 woman), 1 (woman) part-time/adjunct. *Students:* 9 part-time (5 women); includes 1 minority (Hispanic/Latino). Average age 37. 9 applicants, 67% accepted, 5 enrolled. In 2018, 4 master's awarded. *Degree requirements:* For master's, culminating electronic portfolio, professional conference presentations. *Entrance requirements:* For master's, GRE or MAT. Additional exam requirements/recommendations for international students: Required—TOEFL (minimum score 551 paper-based; 80 iBT), IELTS (minimum score 6), PTE (minimum score 53), USC Aiken accepts the TOEFL, IELTS, or PTE exams to demonstrate English proficiency. *Application deadline:* Applications are processed on a rolling basis. Application fee: $45 ($100 for international students). Electronic applications accepted. *Expenses:* Tuition, state resident: full-time $13,650; part-time $568.75 per credit hour. Tuition, nonresident: full-time $29,196; part-time $1216.50 per credit hour. *Required fees:* $13 per credit hour. $25 per semester. Full-time tuition and fees vary according to course load and program. *Financial support:* In 2018–19, 5 students received support. Fellowships with partial tuition reimbursements available, career-related internships or fieldwork, Federal Work-Study, scholarships/grants, tuition waivers (partial), and unspecified assistantships available. Support available to part-time students. Financial award application deadline: 3/1; financial award applicants required to submit FAFSA. *Faculty research:* Educational technology, instructional design, digital badges, e-learning, and technology-enhanced learning environments. *Total annual research expenditures:* $159,395. *Unit head:* Dr. Erin Besser, Educational Technology Program Coordinator, 803-641-3712, E-mail: erinbe@usca.edu. *Application contact:* Dan Robb, Associate Vice Chancellor for Enrollment Management, 803-641-3487, Fax: 803-641-3727, E-mail: danr@usca.edu.
Website: https://www.usca.edu/majors-programs/graduate/edtech

University of South Dakota, Graduate School, School of Education, Division of Curriculum and Instruction, Program in Technology for Education and Training, Vermillion, SD 57069. Offers MS. *Program availability:* Part-time, evening/weekend, 100% online, blended/hybrid learning. *Degree requirements:* For master's, comprehensive exam, thesis or alternative. *Entrance requirements:* For master's, GRE, minimum GPA of 2.7. Additional exam requirements/recommendations for international students: Required—TOEFL (minimum score 550 paper-based; 79 iBT). Electronic applications accepted.

University of Southern Mississippi, College of Education and Human Sciences, Department of Curriculum, Instruction and Special Education, Hattiesburg, MS 39406-0001. Offers elementary education (M Ed, PhD); instructional technology (MS); instructional technology and design (PhD); secondary education (MAT); special education (M Ed, PhD). *Program availability:* Part-time, online learning. *Degree requirements:* For master's, comprehensive exam, thesis (for some programs); for doctorate, comprehensive exam, thesis/dissertation. *Entrance requirements:* For master's, GRE General Test, MAT, minimum GPA of 3.0; for doctorate, GRE General Test, minimum GPA of 3.5. Additional exam requirements/recommendations for international students: Required—TOEFL, IELTS. *Faculty research:* Mathematical problem solving, integrative curriculum, writing process, teacher education models.

University of South Florida, Innovative Education, Tampa, FL 33620-9951. Offers adult, career and higher education (Graduate Certificate), including college teaching, leadership in developing human resources, leadership in higher education; Africana studies (Graduate Certificate), including diasporas and health disparities, genocide and human rights; aging studies (Graduate Certificate), including gerontology; art research (Graduate Certificate), including museum studies; business foundations (Graduate Certificate); chemical and biomedical engineering (Graduate Certificate), including materials science and engineering, water, health and sustainability; child and family studies (Graduate Certificate), including positive behavior support; civil and industrial engineering (Graduate Certificate), including transportation systems analysis; community and family health (Graduate Certificate), including maternal and child health, social marketing and public health, violence and injury: prevention and intervention, women's health; criminology (Graduate Certificate), including criminal justice administration; data science for public administration (Graduate Certificate); digital humanities (Graduate Certificate); educational measurement and research (Graduate Certificate), including evaluation; English (Graduate Certificate), including comparative literary studies, creative writing, professional and technical communication; entrepreneurship (Graduate Certificate); environmental health (Graduate Certificate), including safety management; epidemiology and biostatistics (Graduate Certificate), including applied biostatistics, biostatistics, concepts and tools of epidemiology, epidemiology, epidemiology of infectious diseases; geography, environment and planning (Graduate Certificate), including community development, environmental policy and management, geographical information systems; geology (Graduate Certificate), including hydrogeology; global health (Graduate Certificate), including disaster management, global health and Latin American and Caribbean studies, global health practice, humanitarian assistance, infection control; government and international affairs (Graduate Certificate), including Cuban studies, globalization studies; health policy and management (Graduate Certificate), including health management and leadership, public health policy and programs; hearing specialist: early intervention (Graduate Certificate); industrial and management systems engineering (Graduate Certificate), including systems engineering, technology management; information studies (Graduate Certificate), including school library media specialist; information systems/decision sciences (Graduate Certificate), including analytics and business intelligence; instructional technology (Graduate Certificate), including distance education, Florida digital/virtual educator, instructional design, multimedia design, Web design; internal medicine, bioethics and medical humanities (Graduate Certificate), including biomedical ethics; Latin American and Caribbean studies (Graduate Certificate); leadership for coastal resiliency planning (Graduate Certificate); mass communications (Graduate Certificate), including multimedia journalism; mathematics and statistics (Graduate Certificate), including mathematics; medicine (Graduate Certificate), including aging and neuroscience, bioinformatics, biotechnology, brain fitness and memory management, clinical investigation, hand and upper limb rehabilitation, health informatics, health sciences, integrative weight management, intellectual property, medicine and gender, metabolic and nutritional medicine, metabolic cardiology, pharmacy sciences; national and competitive intelligence (Graduate Certificate); nursing (Graduate Certificate), including simulation based academic fellowship in advanced pain management; psychological and social foundations (Graduate Certificate), including career counseling, college teaching, diversity in education, mental health counseling, school counseling; public affairs (Graduate Certificate), including nonprofit management, public management, research administration; public health (Graduate Certificate), including assessing chemical toxicity and public health risks, health equity, pharmacoepidemiology, public health generalist, toxicology, translational research in adolescent behavioral health; public health practices (Graduate Certificate), including planning for healthy communities; rehabilitation and mental health counseling (Graduate Certificate), including integrative mental health care, marriage and family therapy, rehabilitation technology; secondary education (Graduate Certificate), including ESOL, foreign language education: culture and content, foreign language education: professional; social work (Graduate Certificate), including geriatric social work/clinical gerontology; special education (Graduate Certificate), including autism spectrum disorder, disabilities education: severe/profound; world languages (Graduate Certificate), including teaching English as a second language (TESL) or foreign language. *Expenses:* Tuition, state resident: full-time $6350. Tuition, nonresident: full-time $19,048. *International tuition:* $19,048 full-time. *Required fees:* $2079. *Unit head:* Dr. Cynthia DeLuca, Associate Vice President and Assistant Vice Provost, 813-974-3077, Fax: 813-974-7061, E-mail: deluca@usf.edu. *Application contact:* Owen Hooper, Director, Summer and Alternative Calendar Programs, 813-974-6917, E-mail: hooper@usf.edu.
Website: http://www.usf.edu/innovative-education/

The University of Tampa, Programs in Education, Tampa, FL 33606-1490. Offers curriculum and instruction (M Ed); educational leadership (M Ed); instructional design and technology (MS). *Program availability:* Part-time, evening/weekend. *Faculty:* 2 full-time (both women), 19 part-time/adjunct (15 women). *Students:* 52 full-time (38 women), 238 part-time (211 women); includes 86 minority (36 Black or African American, non-Hispanic/Latino; 1 American Indian or Alaska Native, non-Hispanic/Latino; 9 Asian, non-Hispanic/Latino; 32 Hispanic/Latino; 8 Two or more races, non-Hispanic/Latino), 15 international. Average age 33. 119 applicants, 71% accepted, 48 enrolled. In 2018, 37 master's awarded. *Degree requirements:* For master's, capstone. *Entrance requirements:* For master's, GMAT or GRE, current Florida Professional Teaching Certificate, statement of eligibility for Florida Professional Teaching Certificate, or professional teaching certificate from another state; bachelor's degree in an area of education. Additional exam requirements/recommendations for international students: Required—TOEFL (minimum score 577 paper-based; 90 iBT), IELTS (minimum score 7.5). *Application deadline:* Applications are processed on a rolling basis. Application fee: $40. Electronic applications accepted. *Expenses:* Contact institution. *Financial support:* In 2018–19, 28 students received support. Career-related internships or fieldwork, scholarships/grants, and unspecified assistantships available. Financial award applicants required to submit FAFSA. *Faculty research:* Diversity in the classroom, technology integration, assessment methodologies, complex and ill-structured problem solving, communities of practice. *Unit head:* Dr. Antony Erben, Chair, 813-257-3414, E-mail: terben@ut.edu. *Application contact:* Ashley Russell, Staff Assistant, Admissions for Graduate and Continuing Studies, 813-253-6249, E-mail: arussell@ut.edu.
Website: http://www.ut.edu/graduate/education/

The University of Tennessee, Graduate School, College of Education, Health and Human Sciences, Program in Education, Knoxville, TN 37996. Offers art education (MS); counseling education (PhD); cultural studies in education (PhD); curriculum (MS, Ed S); curriculum, educational research and evaluation (Ed D, PhD); early childhood education (PhD); early childhood special education (MS); education of deaf and hard of hearing (MS); educational administration and policy studies (Ed D, PhD); educational administration and supervision (Ed S); educational psychology (Ed D, PhD); elementary education (MS, Ed S); elementary teaching (MS); English education (MS, Ed S); exercise science (PhD); foreign language/ESL education (MS, Ed S); instructional technology (MS, Ed D, PhD, Ed S); literacy, language and ESL education (PhD); literacy, language education, and ESL education (Ed D); mathematics education (MS, Ed S); modified and comprehensive special education (MS); reading education (MS, Ed S); school counseling (Ed S); school psychology (PhD, Ed S); science education (MS, Ed S); secondary teaching (MS); social foundations (MS); social science education (MS, Ed S); socio-cultural foundations of sports and education (PhD); special education (Ed S); teacher education (Ed D, PhD). *Accreditation:* NCATE. *Program availability:* Part-time, evening/weekend. *Degree requirements:* For master's and Ed S, thesis optional; for doctorate, variable foreign language requirement, thesis/dissertation. *Entrance requirements:* For master's, minimum GPA of 2.7; for doctorate and Ed S, GRE General Test, minimum GPA of 2.7. Additional exam requirements/recommendations for international students: Required—TOEFL. Electronic applications accepted.

The University of Texas at Austin, Graduate School, College of Education, Department of Curriculum and Instruction, Austin, TX 78712-1111. Offers bilingual/bicultural education (M Ed, MA, PhD); cultural studies in education (M Ed, MA, PhD); early childhood education (M Ed, MA, PhD); language and literacy studies (M Ed, PhD); learning technologies (M Ed, MA, PhD); physical education (M Ed, MA, PhD). Terminal master's awarded for partial completion of doctoral program. *Degree requirements:* For doctorate, thesis/dissertation. *Entrance requirements:* For master's and doctorate, GRE General Test. Electronic applications accepted.

The University of Texas at San Antonio, College of Education and Human Development, Department of Interdisciplinary Learning and Teaching, San Antonio, TX 78249-0617. Offers education (MA), including curriculum and instruction, early childhood and elementary education, instructional technology, reading and literacy, special education; interdisciplinary learning and teaching (PhD). *Program availability:* Part-time, evening/weekend. *Degree requirements:* For master's, comprehensive exam, thesis optional, 36 hours of course work without thesis (33 with thesis); for doctorate, comprehensive exam, thesis/dissertation, minimum of 60 semester credit hours. *Entrance requirements:* For master's, bachelor's degree with minimum GPA of 3.0 in last 60 hours of coursework; 18 hours of undergraduate coursework in education or related field; for doctorate, GRE, transcripts from all colleges and universities attended, professional vitae demonstrating experience in work environment where education was primary professional emphasis, 3 letters of recommendation, statement of purpose, minimum GPA of 3.5. Additional exam requirements/recommendations for international students: Required—TOEFL (minimum score 550 paper-based; 79 iBT), IELTS (minimum score 6.5). Electronic applications accepted. *Faculty research:* Explorations of science, learning and teaching, family involvement in early childhood, culturally-responsive literacy instruction in diverse settings, STEM education, autism spectrum disorder.

The University of Texas Rio Grande Valley, College of Education and P-16 Integration, Department of Teaching and Learning, Edinburg, TX 78539. Offers curriculum and instruction (M Ed, Ed D); educational technology (M Ed). *Program availability:* Part-time, evening/weekend. *Degree requirements:* For master's, comprehensive exam, thesis optional; for doctorate, comprehensive exam, thesis/dissertation. *Entrance requirements:* For master's, minimum GPA of 3.0. Additional exam requirements/recommendations for international students: Required—TOEFL (minimum score 550 paper-based; 79 iBT), IELTS (minimum score 6.5). Electronic applications accepted. *Expenses: Tuition, area resident:* Full-time $6888. Tuition, state resident: full-time $6888. Tuition, nonresident: full-time $14,484. *International tuition:* $14,484 full-time. *Required fees:* $1468. *Faculty research:* Teacher education, mathematics education, science education, educational technology, pedagogy.

University of the Sacred Heart, Graduate Programs, Department of Education, Program in Instruction Systems and Education Technology, San Juan, PR 00914-0383. Offers M Ed. *Program availability:* Part-time, evening/weekend. *Degree requirements:* For master's, thesis. *Entrance requirements:* For master's, EXADEP, interview, minimum undergraduate GPA of 2.75.

The University of Toledo, College of Graduate Studies, Judith Herb College of Education, Department of Curriculum and Instruction, Toledo, OH 43606-3390. Offers art education (ME); career and technical education (ME, Ed S); curriculum and instruction (ME, PhD, Ed S); early childhood education (Ed S); education and anthropology (MAE); education and biology (MES); education and chemistry (MES); education and classics (MAE); education and economics (MAE); education and English (MAE); education and French (MAE); education and geology (MES); education and German (MAE); education and history (MAE); education and mathematics (MAE, MES); education and physics (MES); education and political science (MAE); education and sociology (MAE); education and Spanish (MAE); educational media (PhD); educational technology (ME); educational technology: virtual educator (Certificate); elementary education (PhD); English as a second language (MAE); gifted and talented education (PhD); middle childhood education (ME); secondary education (ME, PhD); special education (PhD). *Accreditation:* NCATE. *Program availability:* Part-time, evening/weekend. *Degree requirements:* For master's, comprehensive exam, thesis or alternative; for doctorate, comprehensive exam, thesis/dissertation; for other advanced degree, thesis optional. *Entrance requirements:* For master's, doctorate, and other advanced degree, minimum cumulative GPA of 2.7 for all previous academic work, letters of recommendation. Additional exam requirements/recommendations for international students: Required—TOEFL (minimum score 550 paper-based; 80 iBT). Electronic applications accepted.

University of Utah, Graduate School, College of Education, Department of Educational Psychology, Salt Lake City, UT 84112. Offers clinical mental health counseling (M Ed); counseling psychology (PhD); elementary education (M Ed); instructional design and educational technology (M Ed); instructional design and technology (MS); learning and cognition (MS, PhD); reading and literacy (M Ed, PhD); school counseling (M Ed); school psychology (M Ed, PhD, Ed S); statistics (M Stat). *Accreditation:* APA (one or more programs are accredited). *Faculty:* 20 full-time (12 women), 50 part-time/adjunct (34 women). *Students:* 127 full-time (93 women), 92 part-time (63 women); includes 33 minority (1 Black or African American, non-Hispanic/Latino; 7 Asian, non-Hispanic/Latino; 18 Hispanic/Latino; 1 Native Hawaiian or other Pacific Islander, non-Hispanic/Latino; 6 Two or more races, non-Hispanic/Latino), 5 international. Average age 32. 296 applicants, 27% accepted, 73 enrolled. In 2018, 68 master's, 10 doctorates, 3 other advanced degrees awarded. Terminal master's awarded for partial completion of doctoral program. *Degree requirements:* For master's, thesis (for some programs); for doctorate, thesis/dissertation. *Entrance requirements:* For master's and doctorate, GRE General Test, minimum GPA of 3.0. Additional exam requirements/recommendations for international students: Required—TOEFL (minimum score 80 iBT). *Application deadline:* For fall admission, 12/15 for domestic and international students; for winter admission, 11/1 for domestic and international students; for spring admission, 3/15 for domestic and international students. Application fee: $55 ($65 for international students). Electronic applications accepted. *Expenses:* Contact institution. *Financial support:* In 2018–19, 72 students received support, including 6 fellowships with full and partial tuition reimbursements available (averaging $17,000 per year), 14 research assistantships with full and partial tuition reimbursements available (averaging $15,750 per year), 27 teaching assistantships with full and partial tuition reimbursements available (averaging $15,500 per year); career-related internships or fieldwork, scholarships/grants, traineeships, health care benefits, and unspecified assistantships also available. Financial award application deadline: 4/1; financial award applicants required to submit FAFSA. *Faculty research:* Autism, computer technology and instruction, cognitive behavior, aging, group counseling. *Total annual research expenditures:* $620,935. *Unit head:* Dr. Anne E. Cook, Chair, 801-581-7148, Fax: 801-581-5566, E-mail: anne.cook@utah.edu. *Application contact:* JoLynn N. Yates, Academic Coordinator, 801-581-7148, Fax: 801-581-5566, E-mail: jo.yates@utah.edu.
Website: http://www.ed.utah.edu/edps/

University of Virginia, Curry School of Education, Department of Leadership, Foundations and Policy, Program in Educational Psychology, Charlottesville, VA 22903. Offers applied developmental science (M Ed); educational evaluation (M Ed); educational psychology (M Ed, Ed D, Ed S); educational research (Ed D); gifted education (M Ed); instructional technology (M Ed, Ed S); research statistics and evaluation (Ed D); school psychology (Ed D). *Degree requirements:* For master's, comprehensive exam. *Entrance requirements:* For master's and doctorate, GRE General Test, 2 letters of recommendation. Additional exam requirements/recommendations for international students: Required—TOEFL (minimum score 600 paper-based; 90 iBT), IELTS (minimum score 7). Electronic applications accepted.

University of Virginia, Curry School of Education, Program in Education, Charlottesville, VA 22903. Offers administration and supervision (PhD); applied developmental science (PhD); counselor education (PhD); curriculum and instruction (PhD); early childhood special education (MT); education evaluation (PhD); educational psychology (PhD); educational research (PhD); elementary education (MT); English education (MT, PhD); foreign language education (MT); higher education (PhD); instructional technology (PhD); kinesiology (MT, PhD); math education (PhD); reading education (PhD); research, statistics and evaluation (PhD); school psychology (PhD); science education (PhD); social studies education (MT, PhD); special education (PhD); world languages education (MT). *Degree requirements:* For master's, comprehensive exam (for some programs), field project; for doctorate, comprehensive exam, thesis/dissertation. *Entrance requirements:* For doctorate, GRE General Test. Additional exam requirements/recommendations for international students: Required—TOEFL (minimum score 600 paper-based; 90 iBT), IELTS (minimum score 7). Electronic applications accepted.

University of Washington, Graduate School, College of Education, Seattle, WA 98195. Offers curriculum and instruction (M Ed, Ed D, PhD), including educational technology, general curriculum (Ed D, PhD), language, literacy, and culture, mathematics education, multicultural education, reading and language arts education (Ed D), science education, social studies education, teaching and curriculum (M Ed); educational leadership and policy studies (M Ed, Ed D, PhD), including administration (Ed D), educational policy, organization, and leadership (M Ed, PhD), higher education, leadership for learning (Ed D), social and cultural foundations of education (M Ed, PhD); educational psychology (M Ed, PhD), including educational psychology (PhD), human development and cognition (M Ed), learning sciences, measurement, statistics and research design (M Ed), school psychology (M Ed); instructional leadership (M Ed); intercollegiate athletic leadership (M Ed); special education (M Ed, Ed D, PhD), including early childhood special education (M Ed), emotional and behavioral disabilities (M Ed), learning disabilities (M Ed), low-incidence disabilities (M Ed), severe disabilities (M Ed), special education (Ed D, PhD); teacher education (MIT). *Accreditation:* APA. *Program availability:* Part-time, evening/weekend. *Degree requirements:* For master's, thesis optional; for doctorate, thesis/dissertation. *Entrance requirements:* For master's and doctorate, GRE General Test, minimum GPA of 3.0. Additional exam requirements/recommendations for international students: Required—TOEFL. Electronic applications accepted. *Faculty research:* School restructuring/effective schools, special education interventions, literacy and writing, technology, school partnerships, teacher preparation.

The University of West Alabama, School of Graduate Studies, College of Education, Program in Continuing Education, Livingston, AL 35470. Offers counseling and psychology (MSCE); general (MSCE); library media (MSCE). *Accreditation:* NCATE. *Program availability:* Part-time, evening/weekend, 100% online. *Faculty:* 10 full-time (8 women), 53 part-time/adjunct (35 women). *Students:* 157 full-time (133 women), 2 part-time (both women); includes 105 minority (102 Black or African American, non-Hispanic/Latino; 1 Hispanic/Latino; 2 Two or more races, non-Hispanic/Latino), 2 international. Average age 35. 44 applicants, 98% accepted, 35 enrolled. In 2018, 57 master's awarded. *Degree requirements:* For master's, comprehensive exam, thesis optional. *Entrance requirements:* For master's, GRE, minimum GPA of 2.75. Additional exam requirements/recommendations for international students: Required—TOEFL (minimum score 500 paper-based; 61 iBT). *Application deadline:* Applications are processed on a rolling basis. Application fee: $40. Electronic applications accepted. *Expenses: Tuition, area resident:* Full-time $9100. Tuition, state resident: full-time $9100. Tuition, nonresident: full-time $19,200. *Required fees:* $1890; $130. *Financial support:* Teaching assistantships, Federal Work-Study, scholarships/grants, and unspecified assistantships available. Support available to part-time students. Financial award application deadline: 3/1; financial award applicants required to submit FAFSA. *Unit head:* Dr. Jodie Winship, Chair of College of Education, 205-652-5415, E-mail: jwinship@uwa.edu. *Application contact:* Dr. B. J. Kimbrough, Dean of Graduate Studies, 205-652-3647, Fax: 205-652-3670, E-mail: bkimbrough@uwa.edu.

The University of West Alabama, School of Graduate Studies, College of Education, Program in Library Media, Livingston, AL 35470. Offers learning, design, and technology (M Ed); library media (M Ed, Ed S). *Program availability:* Part-time, evening/weekend, 100% online. *Faculty:* 6 part-time/adjunct (4 women). *Students:* 159 full-time (152 women); includes 37 minority (30 Black or African American, non-Hispanic/Latino; 1 American Indian or Alaska Native, non-Hispanic/Latino; 1 Asian, non-Hispanic/Latino; 1 Hispanic/Latino; 4 Two or more races, non-Hispanic/Latino), 1 international. Average age 37. 42 applicants, 100% accepted, 35 enrolled. In 2018, 83 master's, 19 Ed Ss awarded. *Degree requirements:* For master's, comprehensive exam, thesis optional; for Ed S, comprehensive exam. *Entrance requirements:* For master's, GRE, minimum GPA of 2.75, verification of background clearance/fingerprints, valid bachelor's-level Professional Educator Certificate in same teaching field. Additional exam requirements/recommendations for international students: Required—TOEFL (minimum score 500 paper-based; 61 iBT). *Application deadline:* Applications are processed on a rolling basis. Application fee: $40. Electronic applications accepted. *Expenses: Tuition, area resident:* Full-time $9100. Tuition, state resident: full-time $9100. Tuition, nonresident: full-time $19,200. *Required fees:* $1890; $130. *Financial support:* Teaching assistantships, Federal Work-Study, scholarships/grants, and unspecified

assistantships available. Support available to part-time students. Financial award application deadline: 3/1; financial award applicants required to submit FAFSA. *Unit head:* Dr. Jodie Winship, Chair of College of Education, 205-652-5415, Fax: 205-652-3706, E-mail: jwinship@uwa.edu. *Application contact:* Dr. B. J. Kimbrough, Dean of Graduate Studies, 205-652-3647, Fax: 205-652-3670, E-mail: bkimbrough@uwa.edu.

University of West Florida, College of Education and Professional Studies, Department of Instructional, Workforce and Applied Technology, Pensacola, FL 32514-5750. Offers instructional design and technology (M Ed, Ed D), including instructional design and technology (M Ed), technology leadership (M Ed); network operations, performance and security (M Ed). *Entrance requirements:* For master's, GRE, GMAT, or MAT, letter of intent, names of references. Additional exam requirements/recommendations for international students: Required—TOEFL (minimum score 550 paper-based). Electronic applications accepted.

University of West Florida, College of Education and Professional Studies, Ed D Programs, Specialization in Instructional Design and Technology, Pensacola, FL 32514-5750. Offers Ed D. *Degree requirements:* For doctorate, comprehensive exam, thesis/dissertation. *Entrance requirements:* For doctorate, GRE, MAT, or GMAT, letter of intent; writing sample; three letters of recommendation; two completed disposition assessment forms; written statement of goals; interview with admissions committee. Additional exam requirements/recommendations for international students: Required—TOEFL (minimum score 550 paper-based).

University of West Georgia, College of Education, Carrollton, GA 30118. Offers business education (M Ed); early childhood education (M Ed, Ed S); educational leadership (M Ed, Ed S); media (M Ed, Ed S); professional counseling (M Ed, Ed S); professional counseling and supervision (Ed D); reading instruction (M Ed); school improvement (Ed D); secondary education (M Ed); special education (M Ed, Ed S), including teaching (M Ed); speech language pathology (M Ed); teaching (MAT). *Accreditation:* NCATE. *Program availability:* Part-time, evening/weekend, 100% online, blended/hybrid learning. *Faculty:* 39 full-time (23 women). *Students:* 368 full-time (316 women), 1,140 part-time (960 women); includes 460 minority (376 Black or African American, non-Hispanic/Latino; 1 American Indian or Alaska Native, non-Hispanic/Latino; 11 Asian, non-Hispanic/Latino; 44 Hispanic/Latino; 28 Two or more races, non-Hispanic/Latino), 6 international. Average age 35. 625 applicants, 77% accepted, 401 enrolled. In 2018, 399 master's, 25 doctorates, 273 other advanced degrees awarded. *Entrance requirements:* Additional exam requirements/recommendations for international students: Required—TOEFL (minimum score 523 paper-based; 69 iBT); Recommended—IELTS (minimum score 6.5). *Application deadline:* For fall admission, 7/21 for domestic students, 6/1 for international students; for spring admission, 11/30 for domestic students, 10/15 for international students; for summer admission, 4/15 for domestic students, 3/30 for international students. Applications are processed on a rolling basis. Application fee: $40. Electronic applications accepted. Tuition and fees vary according to course load, degree level, campus/location and program. *Financial support:* Fellowships, research assistantships, teaching assistantships, career-related internships or fieldwork, Federal Work-Study, institutionally sponsored loans, scholarships/grants, and unspecified assistantships available. Support available to part-time students. Financial award application deadline: 4/1; financial award applicants required to submit FAFSA. *Unit head:* Dr. Diane Hoff, Dean, College of Education, 678-839-6570, Fax: 678-839-6098, E-mail: dhoff@westga.edu. *Application contact:* Dr. Toby Ziglar, Assistant Dean of the Graduate School, 678-839-1394, Fax: 678-839-1395, E-mail: graduate@westga.edu.
Website: http://www.westga.edu/education/

University of Wisconsin–Milwaukee, Graduate School, College of Health Sciences, Department of Occupational Science and Technology, Milwaukee, WI 53201-0413. Offers assistive technology and design (MS); disability and occupation (MS); ergonomics (MS); therapeutic recreation (MS). *Accreditation:* AOTA. *Students:* 96 full-time (85 women), 2 part-time (both women); includes 13 minority (4 Asian, non-Hispanic/Latino; 2 Hispanic/Latino; 7 Two or more races, non-Hispanic/Latino), 2 international. Average age 28. 131 applicants, 28% accepted, 33 enrolled. In 2018, 34 master's awarded. *Entrance requirements:* Additional exam requirements/recommendations for international students: Required—TOEFL (minimum score 550 paper-based; 79 iBT), IELTS (minimum score 6.5). *Application deadline:* For fall admission, 1/1 priority date for domestic students; for spring admission, 9/1 for domestic students. Applications are processed on a rolling basis. Application fee: $56 ($75 for international students). *Financial support:* Fellowships, research assistantships, teaching assistantships, and unspecified assistantships available. Support available to part-time students. Financial award application deadline: 4/15. *Unit head:* Jay Kapellusch, PhD, Department Chair, 414-229-5292, Fax: 414-229-2619, E-mail: kap@uwm.edu. *Application contact:* Bhagwant S. Sindhu, PhD, Graduate Program Coordinator, 414-229-1180, Fax: 414-229-5100, E-mail: sindhu@uwm.edu.
Website: http://uwm.edu/healthsciences/academics/occupational-science-technology/

University of Wyoming, College of Education, Program in Instructional Technology, Laramie, WY 82071. Offers MS, Ed D, PhD. *Program availability:* Part-time, online learning. *Degree requirements:* For master's, thesis or alternative; for doctorate, comprehensive exam, thesis/dissertation. *Entrance requirements:* For master's, GRE, minimum GPA of 3.0; for doctorate, MS or MA, minimum GPA of 3.0. Additional exam requirements/recommendations for international students: Required—TOEFL. Electronic applications accepted. *Expenses: Tuition, area resident:* Full-time $6504; part-time $271 per credit hour. Tuition, state resident: full-time $6504; part-time $271 per credit hour. Tuition, nonresident: full-time $19,464; part-time $811 per credit hour. *International tuition:* $19,464 full-time. *Required fees:* $1410.94; $343.82 per semester. $343.82 per semester. Tuition and fees vary according to course load, program and reciprocity agreements. *Faculty research:* Web based instruction, instructional decision, adult education history, literacy in adults, international distance education.

Utah State University, School of Graduate Studies, Emma Eccles Jones College of Education and Human Services, Department of Instructional Technology and Learning Sciences, Logan, UT 84322. Offers M Ed, MS, PhD, Ed S. *Program availability:* Part-time, evening/weekend, online learning. Terminal master's awarded for partial completion of doctoral program. *Degree requirements:* For master's, thesis (for some programs); for doctorate, comprehensive exam, thesis/dissertation. *Entrance requirements:* For master's, GRE General Test or MAT, minimum GPA of 3.0, 3 recommendation letters; for doctorate, GRE General Test, minimum GPA of 3.0, 3 recommendation letters, transcripts, letter of intent; for Ed S, GRE General Test, GRE Subject Test, minimum GPA of 3.0. Additional exam requirements/recommendations for international students: Required—TOEFL (minimum score 550 paper-based). Electronic applications accepted. *Faculty research:* Interactive learning environments, computer-assisted instruction, learning, distance education, corporate training.

Utah Valley University, Program in Education, Orem, UT 84058-5999. Offers educational technology (M Ed); elementary mathematics (M Ed); elementary STEM (M Ed); English as a second language (M Ed); reading (M Ed); teachers as leaders (M Ed). *Accreditation:* TEAC. *Program availability:* Part-time. *Degree requirements:* For master's, project. *Entrance requirements:* For master's, GRE, 3 letters of recommendation, interview, essay. Additional exam requirements/recommendations for international students: Required—TOEFL (minimum score 83 iBT). Electronic applications accepted. *Expenses:* Contact institution.

Valley City State University, Online Graduate Programs, Valley City, ND 58072. Offers elementary education (M Ed); English education (M Ed); library and information technologies (M Ed); teaching (MAT); teaching and technology (M Ed); teaching English language learners (M Ed); technology education (M Ed). *Accreditation:* NCATE. *Program availability:* Part-time, evening/weekend, online only, 100% online. *Faculty:* 20 full-time (11 women), 13 part-time/adjunct (8 women). *Students:* 5 full-time (2 women), 133 part-time (100 women); includes 8 minority (1 Black or African American, non-Hispanic/Latino; 3 American Indian or Alaska Native, non-Hispanic/Latino; 2 Asian, non-Hispanic/Latino; 2 Hispanic/Latino). Average age 36. 23 applicants, 74% accepted, 12 enrolled. In 2018, 47 master's awarded. *Degree requirements:* For master's, action research report, comprehensive portfolio. *Entrance requirements:* For master's, GRE, MAT, PRAXIS II or National Teaching Board for Professional Standards (if GPA is less than 3.0). Additional exam requirements/recommendations for international students: Required—TOEFL (minimum score 525 paper-based; 71 iBT); Recommended—IELTS (minimum score 5.5). *Application deadline:* For fall admission, 7/26 for domestic and international students; for spring admission, 12/13 for domestic and international students; for summer admission, 5/18 for domestic and international students. Applications are processed on a rolling basis. Application fee: $35. Electronic applications accepted. *Expenses:* $396.39 per credit for all students regardless of residency. *Financial support:* In 2018–19, 16 students received support. Scholarships/grants, tuition waivers (full and partial), and unspecified assistantships available. Financial award applicants required to submit FAFSA. *Faculty research:* Universal accessibility, instructional design and technology, gender communication, STEM education in K-12, English language learners. *Unit head:* Dr. Sheri Okland, Dean, 701-845-7184, E-mail: sheri.l.okland@vcsu.edu. *Application contact:* Misty Lindgren, Graduate Studies, 701-845-7303, Fax: 701-845-7190, E-mail: misty.lindgren@vcsu.edu.
Website: http://www.vcsu.edu/graduate

Virginia Commonwealth University, Graduate School, School of Education, Program in Adult Learning, Richmond, VA 23284-9005. Offers adult literacy (M Ed); human resource development (M Ed); teaching and learning with technology (M Ed). *Accreditation:* NCATE. *Program availability:* Part-time. *Entrance requirements:* For master's, GRE General Test or MAT. Additional exam requirements/recommendations for international students: Required—TOEFL (minimum score 600 paper-based; 100 iBT). Electronic applications accepted. *Faculty research:* Adult development and learning, program planning and evaluation.

Virginia Polytechnic Institute and State University, VT Online, Blacksburg, VA 24061. Offers advanced transportation systems (Certificate); aerospace engineering (MS); agricultural and life sciences (MSLFS); business information systems (Graduate Certificate); career and technical education (MS); civil engineering (MS); computer engineering (M Eng, MS); decision support systems (Graduate Certificate); eLearning leadership (MA); electrical engineering (M Eng, MS); engineering administration (MEA); environmental engineering (Certificate); environmental politics and policy (Graduate Certificate); environmental sciences and engineering (MS); foundations of political analysis (Graduate Certificate); health product risk management (Graduate Certificate); industrial and systems engineering (MS); information policy and society (Graduate Certificate); information security (Graduate Certificate); information technology (MIT); instructional technology (MA); integrative STEM education (MA Ed); liberal arts (Graduate Certificate); life sciences: health product risk management (MS); natural resources (MNR, Graduate Certificate); networking (Graduate Certificate); nonprofit and nongovernmental organization management (Graduate Certificate); ocean engineering (MS); political science (MA); security studies (Graduate Certificate); software development (Graduate Certificate). *Expenses:* Tuition, state resident: full-time $15,510; part-time $739.50 per credit hour. Tuition, nonresident: full-time $29,629; part-time $1490.25 per credit hour. *Required fees:* $2804; $550 per semester. Tuition and fees vary according to course load, campus/location and program. *Application contact:* Graduate Admissions and Academic Progress, 540-231-8636, E-mail: grads@vt.edu.
Website: http://www.vto.vt.edu/

Walden University, Graduate Programs, Richard W. Riley College of Education and Leadership, Minneapolis, MN 55401. Offers adult education (Post-Master's Certificate); adult learning (Graduate Certificate); college teaching and learning (Graduate Certificate); community college leadership (Ed D); curriculum, instruction and assessment (Ed D, Ed S, Graduate Certificate); developmental education (Graduate Certificate); early childhood administration, management, and leadership (Graduate Certificate); early childhood education (Ed D, Ed S); early childhood public policy and advocacy (Graduate Certificate); early childhood studies (MS), including administration, management and leadership, early childhood public policy and advocacy, teaching adults in the early childhood field, teaching and diversity in early childhood education; education (MS, PhD), including adolescent literacy and learning (MS), curriculum, instruction, and assessment (grades K-12) (MS), curriculum, instruction, assessment, and evaluation (PhD), early childhood leadership and advocacy (PhD), early childhood special education (PhD), educational leadership (MS), educational leadership and administration (principal preparation) (MS), educational technology and design (PhD), elementary reading and literacy (PreK-6) (MS), elementary reading and mathematics (grades K-6) (MS), global and comparative education (PhD), higher education leadership management and policy (PhD), integrating technology in the classroom (grades K-12) (MS), learning, instruction and innovation (PhD), mathematics (grades 5-8) (MS), mathematics (grades K-6) (MS), mathematics and science (grades K-8) (MS), organizational research, assessment, and evaluation (PhD), reading and literacy with a reading K-12 endorsement (MS), reading literacy assessment and evaluation (PhD), science (grades K-8) (MS), special education (non-licensure) (grades K-12) (MS), teacher leadership (grades K-12) (MS), teaching English language learners (grades K-12) (MS); educational administration and leadership (Ed D); educational leadership and administration (principal preparation) (Ed S); educational technology (Ed D, Ed S, Post Master's Certificate); elementary reading and literacy (Graduate Certificate); engaging culturally diverse learners (Graduate Certificate); enrollment management and institutional marketing (Graduate Certificate); higher education (MS), including adult learning, college teaching and learning, enrollment management and institutional marketing, global higher education, leadership for student success, online and distance learning; higher education and adult learning (Ed D); higher education leadership and management (Ed D); higher education leadership for student success (Graduate Certificate); instructional design and technology (MS, Postbaccalaureate Certificate), including general program (MS), online learning (MS), training and performance improvement (MS); integrating technology in the classroom (Graduate Certificate); mathematics 5-8 (Graduate Certificate); mathematics K-6 (Graduate Certificate); online teaching for adult educators (Graduate Certificate); reading, literacy, and assessment (Ed D, Ed S); science K-8 (Graduate Certificate); special education (Ed D, Ed S, Graduate Certificate); special education (K-age 21) (MAT); teacher leadership (Graduate Certificate); teaching adults English as a second language (Graduate Certificate); teaching adults in the early childhood field (Graduate Certificate); teaching and diversity in early childhood education (Graduate Certificate); teaching English language learners (grades K-12) (Graduate Certificate); teaching K-12 students online (Graduate Certificate). *Accreditation:* NCATE. *Program availability:* Part-time, evening/

weekend, online only, 100% online. *Degree requirements:* For doctorate, thesis/dissertation (for some programs), residency; for other advanced degree, residency (for some programs). *Entrance requirements:* For master's, bachelor's degree or higher; minimum GPA of 2.5; official transcripts; goal statement (for some programs); access to computer and Internet; for doctorate, master's degree or higher; three years of related professional or academic experience (preferred); minimum GPA of 3.0; goal statement and current resume (for select programs); official transcripts; access to computer and Internet; for other advanced degree, relevant work experience; access to computer and Internet. Additional exam requirements/recommendations for international students: Required—TOEFL (minimum score 550 paper-based, 79 iBT), IELTS (minimum score 6.5), Michigan English Language Assessment Battery (minimum score 82), or PTE (minimum score 53). Electronic applications accepted.

Walden University, Graduate Programs, School of Psychology, Minneapolis, MN 55401. Offers clinical psychology (MS), including counseling, general program; forensic psychology (MS), including forensic psychology in the community, general program, mental health applications, program planning and evaluation in forensic settings, psychology and legal systems; industrial organizational (MS, PhD), including consulting psychology, forensic (MS), forensic psychology (PhD), general practice, leadership development and coaching (MS), organizational diversity and social change, research evaluation (PhD); online teaching in psychology (Post-Master's Certificate); organizational psychology and development (Postbaccalaureate Certificate); psychology (MS, PhD), including applied psychology (MS), clinical psychology (PhD), crisis management and response (MS), educational psychology, forensic psychology (PhD), general psychology (MS), general psychology research (PhD), general psychology teaching (PhD), health psychology, leadership development and coaching (MS), psychology of culture (MS), psychology, public administration, and social change (MS), social psychology, terrorism and security (MS); psychology respecialization (Post-Doctoral Certificate). *Program availability:* Part-time, evening/weekend, online only, 100% online. Terminal master's awarded for partial completion of doctoral program. *Degree requirements:* For master's, thesis optional; for doctorate, thesis/dissertation, residency. *Entrance requirements:* For master's, bachelor's degree or higher; minimum GPA of 2.5; official transcripts; goal statement (for some programs); access to computer and Internet; for doctorate, master's degree or higher; three years of related professional or academic experience (preferred); minimum GPA of 3.0; goal statement and current resume (for select programs); official transcripts; access to computer and Internet; for other advanced degree, relevant work experience; access to computer and Internet. Additional exam requirements/recommendations for international students: Required—TOEFL (minimum score 550 paper-based, 79 iBT), IELTS (minimum score 6.5), Michigan English Language Assessment Battery (minimum score 82), or PTE (minimum score 53). Electronic applications accepted.

Warner University, School of Education, Lake Wales, FL 33859. Offers curriculum and instruction (MAEd); elementary education (MAEd); science, technology, engineering, and mathematics (STEM) (MAEd). *Program availability:* Part-time, evening/weekend, online learning. *Degree requirements:* For master's, thesis, accomplished practices portfolio. *Entrance requirements:* For master's, minimum GPA of 3.0 in last 60 hours of undergraduate coursework; 2 letters of recommendation. Additional exam requirements/recommendations for international students: Required—TOEFL (minimum score 550 paper-based). Electronic applications accepted.

Wayland Baptist University, Graduate Programs, Program in Education, Plainview, TX 79072-6998. Offers education administration (M Ed); education diagnostics (M Ed); education literacy (M Ed); elementary certification (M Ed); English (M Ed); English as a second language (M Ed); higher education administration (M Ed); human resources (M Ed); instructional leadership (M Ed); instructional technology (M Ed); leadership training and development (M Ed); science education (M Ed); secondary certification (M Ed); social studies (M Ed); special education (M Ed); sports administration and management (M Ed). *Program availability:* Part-time, evening/weekend, 100% online. *Degree requirements:* For master's, comprehensive exam, capstone course. *Entrance requirements:* For master's, GRE, GMAT or MAT. Additional exam requirements/recommendations for international students: Required—TOEFL (minimum score 500 paper-based; 61 iBT). Electronic applications accepted.

Waynesburg University, Graduate and Professional Studies, Canonsburg, PA 15370. Offers business (MBA), including energy management, finance, health systems, human resources, leadership, market development; counseling (MA), including addictions counseling, clinical mental health; counselor education and supervision (PhD); criminal investigation (MA); education (M Ed), including autism, curriculum and instruction, educational leadership, online teaching; nursing (MSN), including administration, education, informatics; nursing practice (DNP); special education (M Ed); technology (M Ed); MSN/MBA. *Accreditation:* AACN. *Program availability:* Part-time, evening/weekend. *Degree requirements:* For doctorate, thesis/dissertation. *Entrance requirements:* Additional exam requirements/recommendations for international students: Required—TOEFL. Electronic applications accepted.

Wayne State University, College of Education, Division of Administrative and Organizational Studies, Detoit, MI 48202. Offers educational administration and supervision (Ed S); educational leadership (M Ed); educational leadership and policy studies (Ed D, PhD); educational technology (Certificate); learning design and technology (M Ed, Ed D, PhD, Ed S); online teaching (Certificate). *Program availability:* Part-time, evening/weekend. *Faculty:* 9. *Students:* 77 full-time (53 women), 223 part-time (160 women); includes 155 minority (126 Black or African American, non-Hispanic/Latino; 7 Asian, non-Hispanic/Latino; 11 Hispanic/Latino; 1 Native Hawaiian or other Pacific Islander, non-Hispanic/Latino; 10 Two or more races, non-Hispanic/Latino), 9 international. Average age 39. 239 applicants, 33% accepted, 58 enrolled. In 2018, 51 master's, 10 doctorates, 54 other advanced degrees awarded. *Degree requirements:* For master's, thesis (for some programs), GPA 3.0; for doctorate, comprehensive exam, thesis/dissertation, GPA 3.0; for other advanced degree, GPA 3.0. *Entrance requirements:* For master's, baccalaureate degree from accredited U.S. institution or equivalent from college or university of government-recognized standing; minimum undergraduate GPA of 2.75 in upper-division coursework; personal statement; for doctorate, GRE (instructional design and technology), interview; curriculum vitae; three to four recommendations; master's degree (for educational leadership and policy studies); minimum graduate GPA of 3.5; autobiographical statement; research experience (for PhD program); for other advanced degree, educational specialist certificate requirement include undergraduate and master's degrees (for both learning design and technology and administration and supervision); minimum graduate GPA of 3.4, and personal statement. Additional exam requirements/recommendations for international students: Required—TOEFL (minimum score 550 paper-based; 79 iBT); Recommended—IELTS (minimum score 6.5), TWE (minimum score 5.5), TSE (minimum score 58). *Application deadline:* Applications are processed on a rolling basis. Application fee: $50. Electronic applications accepted. *Financial support:* In 2018–19, 87 students received support, including 1 fellowship with tuition reimbursement available (averaging $20,000 per year), 4 research assistantships with tuition reimbursements available (averaging $19,267 per year); scholarships/grants and unspecified assistantships also available. Support available to part-time students. Financial award applicants required to submit FAFSA. *Faculty research:* Total quality management, participatory management, administering educational technology, school improvement, principalship. *Unit head:* Dr. William Hill, Assistant Dean, 313-577-9316, E-mail: ad2107@wayne.edu. *Application contact:* Dr. Mary L. Waker, Graduate Admissions Officer, 313-577-1601, Fax: 313-577-7904, E-mail: m.waker@wayne.edu.
Website: http://coe.wayne.edu/aos/index.php

Webster University, School of Education, Department of Multidisciplinary Studies, St. Louis, MO 63119-3194. Offers applied educational psychology (MA, Ed S); communication arts (MA); early childhood education (MA, MAT); education and innovation (MA); educational technology (MET); elementary education (MAT); mathematics for educators (MA); middle school education (MAT); multidisciplinary studies (MAT); multimodal literacy for global impact (MA); reading (MA); secondary school education (MAT); special education (MA, MAT); teaching English as a second language (MA); transformative learning in the global community (Ed S). *Program availability:* Part-time. *Entrance requirements:* For master's, minimum GPA of 2.5. Additional exam requirements/recommendations for international students: Required—TOEFL. *Expenses: Tuition:* Full-time $22,500; part-time $750 per credit hour. Tuition and fees vary according to degree level, campus/location and program.

West Chester University of Pennsylvania, College of Education and Social Work, Department of Educational Foundations and Policy Studies, West Chester, PA 19383. Offers education for sustainability (Certificate); educational technology (Certificate); higher education policy and student affairs (MS); transformative education and social change (MS). *Program availability:* Part-time. *Degree requirements:* For master's, comprehensive exam (for some programs), thesis, 36 credits (42 credits for MS in higher education policy and student affairs). *Entrance requirements:* For master's, teaching certification (strongly recommended); for Certificate, minimum GPA of 3.0. Additional exam requirements/recommendations for international students: Required—TOEFL or IELTS. Electronic applications accepted. *Faculty research:* Technology integration: preparing our teachers for the twenty-first century, critical pedagogy, education for sustainability.

West Chester University of Pennsylvania, College of Education and Social Work, Department of Special Education, West Chester, PA 19383. Offers autism (Certificate); special education (Teaching Certificate); special education (M Ed); universal design for learning and assistive technology (Certificate). *Accreditation:* NCATE. *Program availability:* Part-time, 100% online. *Degree requirements:* For master's, minimum GPA of 3.0, action research; for other advanced degree, minimum GPA of 3.0; modified student teaching. *Entrance requirements:* For master's, GRE if GPA is below 3.0, two letters of recommendation; for other advanced degree, GRE if GPA is below 3.0. Additional exam requirements/recommendations for international students: Required—TOEFL or IELTS. Electronic applications accepted. *Faculty research:* Instructional strategies for students with moderate to severe disabilities; family involvement for families of students with disabilities; instructional strategies for students with autism; math instruction for students with learning disabilities; transitions for students with disabilities; behavior management for students with behavior disorders.

Western Connecticut State University, Division of Graduate Studies, School of Professional Studies, Department of Education and Educational Psychology, Instructional Technology Option, Danbury, CT 06810-6885. Offers MS. *Program availability:* Part-time. *Entrance requirements:* For master's, minimum GPA of 2.8, teaching certificate. Additional exam requirements/recommendations for international students: Recommended—TOEFL (minimum score 550 paper-based; 79 iBT), IELTS (minimum score 6). *Application deadline:* For fall admission, 8/5 priority date for domestic students; for spring admission, 1/5 priority date for domestic students. Applications are processed on a rolling basis. Application fee: $50. *Financial support:* Application deadline: 5/1; applicants required to submit FAFSA. *Faculty research:* Connectivism in education. *Application contact:* Dr. Chris Shankle, Associate Director of Graduate Studies, 203-837-9005, Fax: 203-837-8326, E-mail: shanklec@wcsu.edu.

Western Governors University, Teachers College, Salt Lake City, UT 84107. Offers curriculum and instruction (MS); educational leadership (MS); elementary education (MAT, Postbaccalaureate Certificate); English education (5-12) (MAT); English language learning (PreK-12) (MA); instructional design (M Ed); learning and technology (M Ed); mathematics (5-12) (MAT); mathematics (5-9) (MAT); mathematics education (5-12) (MA); mathematics education (5-9) (MA); mathematics education (K-6) (MA); science (5-12) (MAT); science education (5-12) (MA), including biology, chemistry, earth science, physics; science education (5-9) (MA); special education (MS). *Accreditation:* NCATE. *Program availability:* Evening/weekend, online learning. *Degree requirements:* For master's, capstone project. *Entrance requirements:* For master's and Postbaccalaureate Certificate, transcripts. Additional exam requirements/recommendations for international students: Required—TOEFL (minimum score 450 paper-based; 80 iBT). Electronic applications accepted. Application fee is waived when completed online. *Expenses:* Contact institution.

Western Illinois University, School of Graduate Studies, College of Business and Technology, Program in Instructional Design and Technology, Macomb, IL 61455-1390. Offers educational technology specialist (Certificate); instructional design and technology (MS); instructional media development (Certificate); online and distance learning development (Certificate); technology integration in education (Certificate); workplace learning and performance (Certificate). *Program availability:* Part-time, online learning. *Students:* 13 full-time (6 women), 36 part-time (21 women); includes 5 minority (3 Black or African American, non-Hispanic/Latino; 1 Asian, non-Hispanic/Latino; 1 Hispanic/Latino), 6 international. Average age 34. 13 applicants, 92% accepted, 9 enrolled. In 2018, 30 master's, 8 other advanced degrees awarded. *Entrance requirements:* Additional exam requirements/recommendations for international students: Required—TOEFL (minimum score 550 paper-based; 80 iBT). *Application deadline:* Applications are processed on a rolling basis. Application fee: $30. Electronic applications accepted. *Financial support:* Teaching assistantships and unspecified assistantships available. Financial award applicants required to submit FAFSA. *Unit head:* Dr. Rafael Obregon, Chairperson, 309-298-1459. *Application contact:* Dr. Mark Mossman, Associate Provost and Director of Graduate Studies, 309-298-1806, Fax: 309-298-2345, E-mail: grad-office@wiu.edu.
Website: http://wiu.edu/idt

Western Kentucky University, Graduate School, College of Education and Behavioral Sciences, School of Teacher Education, Bowling Green, KY 42101. Offers elementary education (MAE, Ed S); exceptional education: learning and behavioral disorders (MAE); instructional design (MS); interdisciplinary early childhood education (MAE); library media education (MS); literacy education (MAE); middle grades education (MAE); secondary education (MAE, Ed S); special education: moderate and severe disabilities (MAE). *Program availability:* Part-time, evening/weekend, online learning. *Degree requirements:* For master's, comprehensive exam. *Entrance requirements:* For master's, GRE General Test. Additional exam requirements/recommendations for international students: Required—TOEFL (minimum score 555 paper-based; 79 iBT). *Faculty research:* Teacher preparation in moderate/severe disabilities.

Western Michigan University, Graduate College, College of Education and Human Development, Department of Educational Leadership, Research and Technology, Kalamazoo, MI 49008. Offers educational leadership (MA, PhD, Ed S), including

educational leadership (MA); educational technology (MA, Graduate Certificate); evaluation, measurement and research (MA, PhD); organizational learning and performance (MA).

Western Oregon University, Graduate Programs, College of Education, Division of Teacher Education, Program in Information Technology, Monmouth, OR 97361. Offers MS Ed. *Accreditation:* NCATE. *Program availability:* Part-time, evening/weekend, online learning. *Degree requirements:* For master's, written exams. *Entrance requirements:* For master's, interview, minimum GPA of 3.0, teaching license. Additional exam requirements/recommendations for international students: Required—TOEFL (minimum score 550 paper-based; 79 iBT), IELTS (minimum score 6.5). *Faculty research:* Impact of technology on teaching and learning.

West Texas A&M University, College of Education and Social Sciences, Department of Education, Program in Instructional Design and Technology, Canyon, TX 79015. Offers M Ed. *Program availability:* Part-time, evening/weekend, 100% online. *Degree requirements:* For master's, comprehensive exam, thesis optional. *Entrance requirements:* For master's, GRE General Test, approval from the instructional technology admissions committee. Additional exam requirements/recommendations for international students: Required—TOEFL (minimum score 550 paper-based). Electronic applications accepted. *Faculty research:* Mathematics and science instruction, technology, developing online courses for freshmen, integrity of online courses.

West Virginia University, College of Education and Human Services, Morgantown, WV 26506. Offers audiology (Au D); autism spectrum disorder (MA); clinical rehabilitation and mental health counseling (MS); communication science and disorders (PhD); counseling (MA); counseling psychology (PhD); curriculum and instruction (Ed D); early childhood education (MA); early intervention/ early childhood special education (MA); education (PhD); educational leadership (MA); educational leadership/ public school administration (Ed D); educational leadership/public school administration (MA); educational psychology (MA, Ed D); elementary education (MA); gifted education (MA); higher education administration (MA, Ed D); higher education curriculum and teaching (MA); institutional design and technology (MA); instructional design and technology (Ed D); literacy education (MA); secondary education (MA); secondary education/ English (MA); special education (Ed D); speech pathology (MS). *Accreditation:* ASHA; NCATE. *Program availability:* Part-time, evening/weekend, online learning. *Students:* 392 full-time (325 women), 337 part-time (285 women); includes 44 minority (16 Black or African American, non-Hispanic/Latino; 16 Hispanic/Latino; 12 Two or more races, non-Hispanic/Latino), 11 international. In 2018, 303 master's, 6 doctorates awarded. *Degree requirements:* For master's, content exams; for doctorate, comprehensive exam, thesis/ dissertation. *Entrance requirements:* Additional exam requirements/recommendations for international students: Required—TOEFL (minimum score 500 paper-based; 61 iBT). *Application deadline:* For fall admission, 8/1 for domestic students; for spring admission, 1/1 for domestic students; for summer admission, 5/1 for domestic students. Application fee: $60. Electronic applications accepted. *Financial support:* Fellowships, research assistantships, teaching assistantships, career-related internships or fieldwork, Federal Work-Study, institutionally sponsored loans, health care benefits, tuition waivers (full and partial), and administrative assistantships available. Financial award applicants required to submit FAFSA. *Faculty research:* Internet training and integration for teachers, rural education, teacher preparation, organization of schools, evaluation of personnel. *Unit head:* Dr. Tracy L. Morris, Interim Dean, 304-293-0816, Fax: 304-293-7565, E-mail: Tracy.Morris@mail.wvu.edu. *Application contact:* Dr. Melissa Luna, Associate Dean for Research, 304-293-2174, Fax: 304-293-3802, E-mail: Melissa.Luna@mail.wvu.edu.
Website: http://cehs.wvu.edu/

Widener University, School of Human Service Professions, Center for Education, Chester, PA 19013-5792. Offers adult education (M Ed); counseling in higher education (M Ed); counselor education (M Ed); early childhood education (M Ed); educational foundations (M Ed); educational leadership (M Ed); educational psychology (M Ed); elementary education (M Ed); English and language arts (M Ed); health education (M Ed); higher education leadership (Ed D); home and school visitor (M Ed); human sexuality (M Ed, PhD); mathematics education (M Ed); middle school education (M Ed); principalship (M Ed); reading and language arts (Ed D); reading education (M Ed); school administration (Ed D); science education (M Ed); social studies education (M Ed); special education (M Ed); technology education (M Ed). *Accreditation:* NCATE. *Program availability:* Part-time, evening/weekend. Terminal master's awarded for partial completion of doctoral program. *Degree requirements:* For doctorate, thesis/ dissertation. *Entrance requirements:* For master's, minimum GPA of 2.5; for doctorate, GRE or MAT, minimum GPA of 2.0 (undergraduate), 3.5 (graduate). Electronic applications accepted. *Expenses:* Contact institution. *Faculty research:* Reading and cognition, adult education, technology education, educational leadership, special education.

Wilkes University, College of Graduate and Professional Studies, School of Education, Wilkes-Barre, PA 18766-0002. Offers educational development and strategies (MS Ed); educational leadership (MS Ed, Ed D); effective teaching (MS Ed); instructional media (MS Ed); instructional technology (MS Ed); international school leadership (MS Ed); international teaching and learning (MS Ed); literacy (MS Ed); middle level education (MS Ed); online teaching (MS Ed); school business leadership (MS Ed); special education (MS Ed); teaching English to speakers of other languages (MS Ed). *Program availability:* Part-time, evening/weekend, 100% online, blended/hybrid learning. *Students:* 87 full-time (67 women), 1,418 part-time (1,078 women); includes 87 minority (13 Black or African American, non-Hispanic/Latino; 1 American Indian or Alaska Native, non-Hispanic/Latino; 11 Asian, non-Hispanic/Latino; 40 Hispanic/Latino; 22 Two or more races, non-Hispanic/Latino). Average age 35. In 2018, 611 master's, 9 doctorates awarded. *Entrance requirements:* Additional exam requirements/recommendations for international students: Required—TOEFL (minimum score 550 paper-based; 79 iBT). *Application deadline:* Applications are processed on a rolling basis. Application fee: $45 ($65 for international students). Electronic applications accepted. *Expenses:* Contact institution. *Financial support:* Unspecified assistantships available. Financial award application deadline: 3/1; financial award applicants required to submit FAFSA. *Unit head:* Dr. Rhonda Rabbitt, Dean, 570-408-4680, Fax: 570-408-7872, E-mail: rhonda.rabbitt@wilkes.edu. *Application contact:* Stephanie Wasmanski, Associate Director of Graduate Admissions, 570-408-5535, Fax: 570-408-7846, E-mail: stephanie.wasmanski@wilkes.edu.
Website: http://www.wilkes.edu/academics/graduate-programs/masters-programs/graduate-education/index.aspx

William Paterson University of New Jersey, College of Education, Wayne, NJ 07470-8420. Offers curriculum and learning (M Ed); early childhood education (Certificate); educational leadership (M Ed); educational media specialist (Certificate); elementary education (MAT, Certificate); elementary education subject area (Certificate); higher education administration (MA); learning disabilities consultant (Certificate); literacy (M Ed); middle level education (M Ed); middle school education subject area (Certificate); professional counseling (M Ed); reading specialist (Certificate); school library media specialist (Certificate); school principal (Certificate); school supervisor (Certificate); secondary education (MAT); special education (M Ed); teacher of students with disabilities (Certificate). *Accreditation:* NCATE. *Program availability:* Part-time, evening/weekend. *Students:* Average age 35. 347 applicants, 87% accepted, 226 enrolled. In 2018, 136 master's awarded. *Degree requirements:* For master's, comprehensive exam, thesis (for some programs), exit interview (for some programs), practicum/internship; minimum GPA of 3.0 (for some programs); exit portfolio (for some programs). *Entrance requirements:* For master's, GRE/MAT, minimum GPA of 2.75; teaching certificate; essay; interview; 2 letters of recommendation; personal statement. Additional exam requirements/recommendations for international students: Required—TOEFL (minimum score 550 paper-based; 79 iBT), IELTS (minimum score 6). *Application deadline:* For fall admission, 6/1 for domestic students, 3/1 for international students; for spring admission, 11/1 for domestic students, 10/1 for international students. Applications are processed on a rolling basis. Application fee: $50. Electronic applications accepted. *Expenses: Tuition, area resident:* Full-time $14,714; part-time $727 per credit. Tuition, state resident: full-time $14,714; part-time $727 per credit. Tuition, nonresident: full-time $22,952; part-time $727 per credit. *International tuition:* $22,952 full-time. *Required fees:* $4 per semester. Tuition and fees vary according to course load, degree level and program. *Financial support:* In 2018–19, 8,416 students received support. Career-related internships or fieldwork, Federal Work-Study, scholarships/grants, and unspecified assistantships available. Support available to part-time students. Financial award application deadline: 3/15; financial award applicants required to submit FAFSA. *Faculty research:* Code switching and creative writing, language instruction, teacher evaluation, preschools, history of educational theories. *Total annual research expenditures:* $311,226. *Unit head:* Dr. Dorothy Feola, Dean, 973-720-2138, Fax: 973-720-3647, E-mail: feolad@wpunj.edu. *Application contact:* Liana Fornarotto, Director of Education Enrollment and Certification, 973-720-2206, Fax: 973-720-2989, E-mail: fornarottol@wpunj.edu.
Website: http://www.wpunj.edu/coe

William Woods University, Graduate and Adult Studies, Fulton, MO 65251-1098. Offers administration (M Ed, Ed S); athletic/activities administration (M Ed); curriculum and instruction (M Ed, Ed S); educational leadership (Ed D); equestrian education (M Ed); health management (MBA); human resources (MBA); leadership (MBA); marketing, advertising, and public relations (MBA); teaching and technology (M Ed). *Program availability:* Part-time, evening/weekend. *Degree requirements:* For master's, capstone course (MBA), action research (M Ed); for Ed S, field experience. *Entrance requirements:* Additional exam requirements/recommendations for international students: Required—TOEFL (minimum score 550 paper-based). Electronic applications accepted. *Expenses:* Contact institution.

Wilmington University, College of Education, New Castle, DE 19720-6491. Offers applied technology in education (M Ed); career and technical education (M Ed); educational leadership (Ed D); elementary and secondary school counseling (M Ed); elementary studies (M Ed); ESOL literacy (M Ed); higher education leadership (Ed D); instruction: gifted and talented (M Ed); instruction: teacher of reading (M Ed); instruction: teaching and learning (M Ed); organizational leadership (Ed D); school leadership (M Ed); secondary education (MAT); special education (M Ed). *Accreditation:* NCATE. *Program availability:* Part-time, evening/weekend. *Entrance requirements:* For master's, 2 letters of recommendation, interview. Additional exam requirements/recommendations for international students: Required—TOEFL (minimum score 500 paper-based). Electronic applications accepted.

Wilson College, Graduate Programs, Chambersburg, PA 17201-1285. Offers accounting (M Acc); choreography and visual art (MFA); education (M Ed); educational technology (MET); healthcare administration (MHA); humanities (MA), including art and culture, critical/cultural theory, English language and literature, women's studies; management (MSM); nursing (MSN), including nursing education, nursing leadership and management; special education (MSE). *Program availability:* Evening/weekend. *Degree requirements:* For master's, project. *Entrance requirements:* For master's, PRAXIS, minimum undergraduate cumulative GPA of 3.0, 2 letters of recommendation, current certification for eligibility to teach in grades K-12, resume, personal interview. Electronic applications accepted.

Wisconsin Lutheran College, College of Adult and Graduate Studies, Milwaukee, WI 53226-9942. Offers high performance instruction (MA Ed); instructional technology (MA Ed); leadership and innovation (MA Ed); science instruction (MA Ed).

Worcester Polytechnic Institute, Graduate Admissions, Program in Learning Sciences and Technologies, Worcester, MA 01609-2280. Offers learning sciences & technologies (PhD). Program offered jointly between Department of Social Science and Policy Studies and Department of Computer Science. *Program availability:* Part-time, evening/ weekend. *Students:* 6 full-time (3 women), 4 part-time (3 women); includes 2 minority (1 Hispanic/Latino; 1 Two or more races, non-Hispanic/Latino), 1 international. Average age 32. 5 applicants, 80% accepted, 1 enrolled. In 2018, 4 master's, 3 doctorates awarded. *Entrance requirements:* For master's and doctorate, GRE (strongly recommended), statement of purpose, brief sample of scholarly writing. Additional exam requirements/recommendations for international students: Required—TOEFL (minimum score 563 paper-based; 84 iBT), IELTS (minimum score 7). *Application deadline:* For fall admission, 1/1 for domestic and international students; for spring admission, 10/1 for domestic and international students. Applications are processed on a rolling basis. Application fee: $70. Electronic applications accepted. *Financial support:* Fellowships, research assistantships, teaching assistantships, career-related internships or fieldwork, health care benefits, and unspecified assistantships available. Financial award application deadline: 1/1. *Unit head:* Neil Heffernan, Director, 508-831-5296, Fax: 508-831-5776, E-mail: nth@wpi.edu. *Application contact:* Tricia Desmarais, Administrative Assistant, 508-831-5569, Fax: 508-831-5776, E-mail: td@wpi.edu.
Website: https://www.wpi.edu/academics/departments/learning-sciences-technologies

York College of Pennsylvania, Graduate Programs in Behavioral Sciences and Education, York, PA 17403-3651. Offers educational leadership (M Ed); educational technology (M Ed); reading specialist (M Ed). *Program availability:* Part-time-only, evening/weekend. *Faculty:* 1 full-time (0 women), 10 part-time/adjunct (8 women). *Students:* 1 full-time (0 women), 107 part-time (77 women); includes 3 minority (1 Hispanic/Latino; 2 Two or more races, non-Hispanic/Latino). Average age 34. 35 applicants, 69% accepted, 23 enrolled. In 2018, 10 master's awarded. *Degree requirements:* For master's, comprehensive exam (for some programs), thesis (for some programs). *Entrance requirements:* For master's, statement of applicant's professional and academic goals, 2 letters of recommendation, letter from current supervisor, official undergraduate and graduate transcript(s), copy of teaching certificate(s), current professional resume, interview. *Application deadline:* For fall admission, 7/15 priority date for domestic students; for spring admission, 11/15 priority date for domestic students; for summer admission, 4/15 priority date for domestic students. Applications are processed on a rolling basis. Application fee: $0. Electronic applications accepted. *Expenses:* $640 per credit; no general fee. *Financial support:* Scholarships/grants available. Financial award applicants required to submit FAFSA. *Faculty research:* Classroom technology, assessment, educational leadership, professional development, literacy. *Unit head:* Dr. Joshua D. DeSantis, Director, Graduate Programs in Behavioral Science and Education, 717-815-1936, E-mail: jdesant1@ycp.edu. *Application contact:* Dr. Joshua D. DeSantis, Director, Graduate Programs in Behavioral Science and Education, 717-815-1936, E-mail: jdesant1@ycp.edu.
Website: https://www.ycp.edu/med

Educational Policy

American University, School of Education, Washington, DC 20016-8030. Offers education (Certificate); education policy and leadership (M Ed); international training and education (MA); special education (MA); teacher education (MAT); M Ed/MPA; M Ed/MPP; MAT/MA. *Accreditation:* NCATE. *Program availability:* Part-time, evening/weekend, 100% online. *Faculty:* 17 full-time (13 women), 33 part-time/adjunct (23 women). *Students:* 53 full-time (46 women), 246 part-time (191 women); includes 139 minority (97 Black or African American, non-Hispanic/Latino; 13 Asian, non-Hispanic/Latino; 23 Hispanic/Latino; 6 Two or more races, non-Hispanic/Latino), 5 international. Average age 29. 361 applicants, 88% accepted, 161 enrolled. In 2018, 73 master's, 2 other advanced degrees awarded. *Degree requirements:* For master's, comprehensive exam, thesis or alternative. *Entrance requirements:* For master's, Please visit website: https://www.american.edu/soe/, bachelor's degree, statement of purpose, transcripts, 2 letters of recommendation. Additional exam requirements/recommendations for international students: Required—TOEFL (minimum score 100 iBT). Application fee: $55. Electronic applications accepted. *Expenses: Tuition:* Full-time $30,744; part-time $1642 per credit hour. *Required fees:* $702; $200 per semester. Tuition and fees vary according to course load, degree level and program. *Financial support:* Research assistantships, teaching assistantships, institutionally sponsored loans, scholarships/grants, and unspecified assistantships available. Financial award application deadline: 2/1; financial award applicants required to submit FAFSA. *Unit head:* Dr. Cheryl Holcomb-McCoy, Dean, 202-885-3720, E-mail: educate@american.edu. *Application contact:* Ashleigh Huseth, Senior Coordinator, Admissions & Onboarding, E-mail: ahuseth@american.edu.
Website: https://www.american.edu/cas/education/

American University of Beirut, Graduate Programs, Faculty of Arts and Sciences, Beirut 1107 2020, Lebanon. Offers anthropology (MA); Arab and Middle Eastern history (PhD); Arabic language and literature (MA, PhD); archaeology (MA); art history and curating (MA); biology (MS); cell and molecular biology (PhD); chemistry (MS); clinical psychology (MA); computational sciences (MS); computer science (MS); economics (MA); education (MA), including administration and policy studies, elementary education, mathematics education, psychology school guidance, psychology test and measurements, science education, teaching English as a foreign language; English language (MA); English literature (MA); environmental policy planning (MS); financial economics (MAFE); general psychology (MA); geology (MS); history (MA); Islamic studies (MA); mathematics (MS); media studies (MA); Middle East studies (MA); philosophy (MA); physics (MS); political studies (MA); public administration (MA); public policy and international affairs (MA); sociology (MA); theoretical physics (PhD). *Program availability:* Part-time. *Faculty:* 187 full-time (64 women), 27 part-time/adjunct (15 women). *Students:* 292 full-time (215 women), 216 part-time (148 women). Average age 27. 422 applicants, 64% accepted, 124 enrolled. In 2018, 90 master's, 3 doctorates awarded. *Degree requirements:* For master's, comprehensive exam, thesis (for some programs), project; for doctorate, comprehensive exam, thesis/dissertation (for some programs). *Entrance requirements:* For master's, GRE General Test (for archaeology, clinical psychology, general psychology, economics, financial economics and biology); for doctorate, GRE General Test for all PhD programs, GRE Subject Test for theoretical physics. Additional exam requirements/recommendations for international students: Required—TOEFL (minimum score 583 paper-based; 97 iBT), IELTS (minimum score 7). *Application deadline:* For fall admission, 3/18 for domestic students; for spring admission, 11/5 for domestic students. Application fee: $50. Electronic applications accepted. *Expenses:* MA/MS: Humanities and social sciences=$912/credit. Sciences=$943/credit. Financial economics=$986/credit. Thesis: Humanities/social sciences=$6565 and sciences=$6865. *Financial support:* In 2018–19, 227 fellowships with full tuition reimbursements, 17 research assistantships with full tuition reimbursements, 83 teaching assistantships with full tuition reimbursements were awarded; scholarships/grants, tuition waivers (full and partial), and unspecified assistantships also available. Financial award application deadline: 3/18. *Faculty research:* Sciences: Physics: High energy, Particle, Polymer and Soft Matter, Thermal, Plasma; String Theory, Mathematical physics, Astrophysics (stellar evolution, planet and galaxy formation and evolution, astrophysical dynamics), Solid State physics/thin films, Spintronics, Magnetic properties of materials, Mineralogy, Petrology, and Geochemistry of Hard Rocks, Geophysics and Petrophysics, Hydrogeology, Micropaleontology, Sedimentology, and Stratigraphy, Structural Geology and Geotectonics, Renewable en. *Total annual research expenditures:* $4.3 million. *Unit head:* Dr. Nadia Maria El Cheikh, Dean, Faculty of Arts and Sciences, 961-1-350000 Ext. 3800, Fax: 961-1-744461, E-mail: nmcheikh@aub.edu.lb. *Application contact:* Adriana Michelle Zanaty, Curriculum and Graduate Studies Officer, 961-1-350000 Ext. 3833, Fax: 961-1-744461, E-mail: az48@aub.edu.lb.
Website: https://www.aub.edu.lb/fas/Pages/default.aspx

Arizona State University at the Tempe campus, Mary Lou Fulton Teachers College, Program in Educational Policy and Evaluation, Phoenix, AZ 85069. Offers PhD. Fall admission only. *Degree requirements:* For doctorate, comprehensive exam, thesis/dissertation, interactive Program of Study (iPOS) submitted before completing 50 percent of required credit hours. *Entrance requirements:* For doctorate, GRE, minimum GPA of 3.0 or equivalent in last 2 years of work leading to bachelor's degree, 3 letters of recommendation, personal statement, writing sample, curriculum vitae or resume. Additional exam requirements/recommendations for international students: Required—TOEFL, IELTS, or PTE. Electronic applications accepted. *Expenses:* Contact institution. *Faculty research:* Education policy analysis, school finance and quantitative methods, school improvement in ethnically, linguistically and economically diverse communities, parent/teacher engagement, school choice, accountability polices, school finance litigation, school segregation.

Ball State University, Graduate School, Teachers College, Department of Educational Studies, Program in Educational Studies, Muncie, IN 47306. Offers educational studies (PhD), including cultural and educational policy studies, curriculum, educational technology. *Program availability:* Part-time, blended/hybrid learning. *Degree requirements:* For doctorate, thesis/dissertation. *Entrance requirements:* For doctorate, GRE General Test, minimum graduate GPA of 3.2, curriculum vitae, writing sample, three letters of reference. Additional exam requirements/recommendations for international students: Required—TOEFL (minimum score 550 paper-based; 79 iBT), IELTS (minimum score 6.5). Electronic applications accepted. *Faculty research:* Emerging curriculum trends, secondary teacher preparation, issues of equity and social justice in education, teacher technology integration, teaching for transformative understanding, teacher leadership, history of educational policy and practices, ethics and education.

Brigham Young University, Graduate Studies, David O. McKay School of Education, Department of Educational Leadership and Foundations, Provo, UT 84602. Offers doctorate of education (Ed D); education policy studies (M Ed); school leadership (M Ed). *Program availability:* Part-time, evening/weekend. *Faculty:* 12 full-time (1 woman), 1 part-time/adjunct (0 women). *Students:* 19 full-time (15 women), 54 part-time (20 women); includes 12 minority (2 Black or African American, non-Hispanic/Latino; 1 American Indian or Alaska Native, non-Hispanic/Latino; 3 Asian, non-Hispanic/Latino; 6 Hispanic/Latino). Average age 42. 32 applicants, 91% accepted, 26 enrolled. In 2018, 17 master's, 2 doctorates awarded. *Degree requirements:* For master's, comprehensive exam, thesis optional, Administrative Internship; Thesis; for doctorate, comprehensive exam, thesis/dissertation. *Entrance requirements:* For master's, GRE, or GMAT, or LSAT, or MAT, Resume; for doctorate, GRE, or GMAT, or LSAT, Master's degree or equivalent; Three years' professional experience in leadership position related to education; Resume. Additional exam requirements/recommendations for international students: Required—E3PT and Cambridge English Proficiency Exam are also options. Only one assessment is required.; Recommended—TOEFL (minimum score 580 paper-based; 85 iBT), IELTS (minimum score 7). *Application deadline:* For fall admission, 5/1 for domestic and international students; for spring admission, 1/15 for domestic and international students. Application fee: $50. Electronic applications accepted. *Financial support:* In 2018–19, 57 students received support, including 37 research assistantships (averaging $1,175 per year); scholarships/grants also available. Financial award application deadline: 5/31. *Faculty research:* Role of trust in education leadership; inequality of educational opportunity; educational law; educational policy; education and globalization. *Unit head:* Dr. Pamela Hallam, Department Chair, 801-422-3600, Fax: 801-422-0196, E-mail: pam_hallam@byu.edu. *Application contact:* Michele Price, Department Secretary, 801-422-3813, Fax: 801-422-0196, E-mail: michele_price@byu.edu.
Website: https://education.byu.edu/edlf/

California State University, Sacramento, College of Education, Graduate and Professional Studies in Education, Sacramento, CA 95819. Offers behavioral science and gender equity (MA); child development (MA); counseling (MS); curriculum and instruction (MA); education (Ed D), including K-12 and community college; education leadership and policy studies (MA), including higher education, PreK-12; education specialist (Ed S), including school psychology; educational technology (MA); language and literacy (MA); multicultural education (MA); school psychology (MA); special education (MA); workforce development advocacy (MA). *Program availability:* Part-time, evening/weekend, blended/hybrid learning. *Degree requirements:* For master's, thesis or project; writing proficiency exam; for doctorate, thesis/dissertation. *Entrance requirements:* For master's and doctorate, GRE. Additional exam requirements/recommendations for international students: Required—TOEFL (minimum score 550 paper-based; 80 iBT); Recommended—IELTS (minimum score 7), TSE. Electronic applications accepted. *Expenses:* Contact institution.

Cleveland State University, College of Graduate Studies, College of Education and Human Services, Program in Urban Education, Specialization in Policy Studies, Cleveland, OH 44115. Offers PhD. *Program availability:* Part-time. *Faculty:* 6 full-time (1 woman). *Students:* 3 full-time (all women), 15 part-time (11 women); includes 8 minority (6 Black or African American, non-Hispanic/Latino; 2 Hispanic/Latino). Average age 46. 6 applicants, 33% accepted, 2 enrolled. In 2018, 2 doctorates awarded. *Entrance requirements:* For doctorate, GRE General Test (minimum score of 297 for combined Verbal and Quantitative exams, 4.0 preferred for Analytical Writing), minimum graduate GPA of 3.25, curriculum vitae or resume, personal statement, 2 letters of recommendation. Additional exam requirements/recommendations for international students: Required—TOEFL (minimum score 550 paper-based; 78 iBT), IELTS (minimum score 6). Application fee: $40. Electronic applications accepted. *Expenses:* Tuition, state resident: full-time $7232.55; part-time $6676 per credit hour. Tuition, nonresident: full-time $12,375. *International tuition:* $18,914 full-time. *Required fees:* $80; $80 $40. Tuition and fees vary according to program. *Financial support:* In 2018–19, 5 students received support. Research assistantships, teaching assistantships, and tuition waivers (full and partial) available. Support available to part-time students. Financial award application deadline: 4/1; financial award applicants required to submit FAFSA. *Faculty research:* Historical, theoretical and practical aspects of educational policy formation; relationship of educational policy within the larger context of urban affairs, public policy, and school reform. *Unit head:* Dr. Graham Stead, Director, 216-875-9869, Fax: 216-875-9697, E-mail: g.b.stead@csuohio.edu. *Application contact:* Rita M. Grabowski, Administrative Coordinator, 216-687-4697, Fax: 216-875-9697, E-mail: r.grabowski@csuohio.edu.
Website: http://www.csuohio.edu/cehs/departments/DOC/ep_doc.html

Cornell University, Graduate School, Graduate Fields of Agriculture and Life Sciences, Field of Education, Ithaca, NY 14853. Offers adult and extension education (MPS, MS, PhD); learning, teaching, and social policy (MPS, MS, PhD); mathematics 7-12 (MS). Terminal master's awarded for partial completion of doctoral program. *Degree requirements:* For master's, thesis (MS); for doctorate, comprehensive exam, thesis/dissertation. *Entrance requirements:* For master's and doctorate, GRE General Test, sample of written work (recommended), 2 letters of recommendation. Additional exam requirements/recommendations for international students: Required—TOEFL (minimum score 550 paper-based; 77 iBT). Electronic applications accepted. *Faculty research:* Moral development and professional ethics, public issues education and community development, socio/political issues in public education, teacher education and curriculum in agricultural science and mathematics, extension research.

Eastern Michigan University, Graduate School, College of Arts and Sciences, Department of Sociology, Anthropology and Criminology, Program in Schools, Society and Violence, Ypsilanti, MI 48197. Offers MA. *Students:* 2 part-time (1 woman); includes 1 minority (Black or African American, non-Hispanic/Latino). Average age 45. 1 applicant. Application fee: $45. *Application contact:* Dr. Solage Simoes, Coordinator, 734-487-0012, Fax: 734-487-9666, E-mail: ssimoes@emich.edu.
Website: http://www.emich.edu/sac/

Florida State University, The Graduate School, College of Education, Department of Educational Leadership and Policy Studies, Tallahassee, FL 32306. Offers educational leadership and administration (Certificate); educational leadership and policy (MS, Ed D, PhD, Ed S), including education policy and evaluation (MS, Ed D, PhD), educational leadership and administration; foundations of education (MS, PhD), including history and philosophy of education, international and multicultural education; higher education (MS, PhD); institutional research (Certificate); program evaluation (Certificate). *Program availability:* Part-time, evening/weekend, 100% online, blended/hybrid learning, asynchronous, minimal on-campus study. *Degree requirements:* For master's, comprehensive exam, thesis optional; for doctorate, comprehensive exam, thesis/dissertation, diagnostic exam, preliminary exam, prospectus defense, dissertation defense. *Entrance requirements:* For master's, doctorate, and other advanced degree, GRE General Test, minimum GPA of 3.0. Additional exam requirements/recommendations for international students: Required—TOEFL (minimum score 550

paper-based, 80 iBT), IELTS (minimum score 6.5), Michigan English Language Assessment Battery (minimum score 77), or PTE (minimum score 55). Electronic applications accepted. *Expenses: Tuition, area resident:* Part-time $479.32 per credit hour. Tuition and fees vary according to campus/location and program. *Faculty research:* Post-secondary success; leadership education; education policy; international education; multicultural education.

The George Washington University, Graduate School of Education and Human Development, Department of Educational Leadership, Program in Educational Administration and Policy Studies, Washington, DC 20052. Offers education policy (Ed D); educational administration (Ed D). Ed D in educational administration offered at Newport News and Alexandria, VA. *Accreditation:* NCATE. *Students:* 91 part-time (64 women); includes 42 minority (32 Black or African American, non-Hispanic/Latino; 5 Asian, non-Hispanic/Latino; 3 Hispanic/Latino; 2 Two or more races, non-Hispanic/Latino), 1 international. Average age 42. In 2018, 15 doctorates awarded. *Degree requirements:* For doctorate, comprehensive exam, thesis/dissertation. *Entrance requirements:* For doctorate, GRE General Test or MAT, interview, minimum GPA of 3.3. *Application deadline:* For fall admission, 1/15 priority date for domestic students; for spring admission, 10/1 for domestic students. Applications are processed on a rolling basis. Application fee: $75. *Financial support:* In 2018–19, 9 students received support. Fellowships, research assistantships, teaching assistantships, career-related internships or fieldwork, Federal Work-Study, and tuition waivers (partial) available. Financial award application deadline: 1/15; financial award applicants required to submit FAFSA. *Unit head:* Michael Feuer, Dean, 202-994-6161, E-mail: mjfeuer@gwu.edu. *Application contact:* Sarah Lang, Director, Admissions and Marketing, 202-994-1447, Fax: 202-994-7207, E-mail: slang@gwu.edu.

The George Washington University, Graduate School of Education and Human Development, Department of Educational Leadership, Program in Education Policy Studies, Washington, DC 20052. Offers MA Ed. *Accreditation:* NCATE. *Students:* 18 full-time (13 women), 6 part-time (5 women); includes 5 minority (3 Black or African American, non-Hispanic/Latino; 2 Hispanic/Latino). Average age 27. 49 applicants, 78% accepted, 12 enrolled. In 2018, 11 master's awarded. *Entrance requirements:* For master's, GRE General Test or MAT, interview, minimum GPA of 2.75. *Application deadline:* For fall admission, 1/15 priority date for domestic students; for spring admission, 10/1 for domestic students. Applications are processed on a rolling basis. Application fee: $75. *Financial support:* In 2018–19, 10 students received support. Fellowships, career-related internships or fieldwork, Federal Work-Study, and tuition waivers (partial) available. Financial award application deadline: 1/15. *Unit head:* Michael Feuer, Dean, 202-994-6161, E-mail: mjfeuer@gwu.edu. *Application contact:* Sarah Lang, Director of Graduate Admissions, 202-994-1447, Fax: 202-994-7207, E-mail: slang@gwu.edu.

The George Washington University, Graduate School of Education and Human Development, Department of Educational Leadership, Program in Higher Education Administration, Washington, DC 20052. Offers college teaching and academic leadership (MA Ed/HD, Ed S); general administration (MA Ed/HD, Ed S); higher education administration (Ed D); higher education finance (MA Ed/HD, Ed S); international education (MA Ed/HD, Ed S); policy (MA Ed/HD, Ed S); student affairs administration (MA Ed/HD, Ed S). *Accreditation:* NCATE. *Students:* 27 full-time (19 women), 55 part-time (41 women); includes 37 minority (21 Black or African American, non-Hispanic/Latino; 5 Asian, non-Hispanic/Latino; 8 Hispanic/Latino; 3 Two or more races, non-Hispanic/Latino), 4 international. Average age 32. 131 applicants, 85% accepted, 37 enrolled. In 2018, 15 master's, 4 doctorates, 1 other advanced degree awarded. *Degree requirements:* For master's and Ed S, comprehensive exam; for doctorate, comprehensive exam, thesis/dissertation. *Entrance requirements:* For master's, GRE General Test or MAT, minimum GPA of 2.75; for doctorate, GRE General Test or MAT, interview, minimum GPA of 3.3; for Ed S, GRE General Test or MAT, minimum GPA of 3.3. *Application deadline:* For fall admission, 1/15 priority date for domestic students; for spring admission, 10/1 for domestic students. Applications are processed on a rolling basis. Application fee: $75. *Financial support:* In 2018–19, 17 students received support. Fellowships, research assistantships, career-related internships or fieldwork, Federal Work-Study, and tuition waivers (partial) available. Financial award application deadline: 1/15; financial award applicants required to submit FAFSA. *Faculty research:* Technology in higher education administration. *Unit head:* Michael Feuer, Dean, 202-994-6161, E-mail: mjfeuer@gwu.edu. *Application contact:* Sarah Lang, Director of Graduate Admissions, 202-994-1447, Fax: 202-994-7207, E-mail: slang@gwu.edu.

Georgia State University, College of Education and Human Development, Department of Educational Policy Studies, Atlanta, GA 30302-3083. Offers educational leadership (M Ed, Ed D, Ed S), including educational leadership, urban teacher leadership (M Ed); educational research (MS, PhD); social foundations of education (MS, PhD). *Program availability:* Part-time. *Faculty:* 20 full-time (12 women), 11 part-time/adjunct (6 women). *Students:* 44 full-time (31 women), 99 part-time (58 women); includes 81 minority (67 Black or African American, non-Hispanic/Latino; 2 Asian, non-Hispanic/Latino; 10 Hispanic/Latino; 2 Two or more races, non-Hispanic/Latino), 1 international. Average age 37. 84 applicants, 63% accepted, 38 enrolled. In 2018, 12 master's, 17 doctorates, 13 other advanced degrees awarded. *Entrance requirements:* For master's, GRE; for doctorate and Ed S, GRE, MAT. *Application deadline:* For fall admission, 1/15 for domestic and international students; for winter admission, 2/1 for domestic and international students; for spring admission, 10/1 for domestic and international students. Applications are processed on a rolling basis. Application fee: $50. Electronic applications accepted. *Expenses: Tuition, area resident:* Full-time $9360; part-time $390 per credit hour. Tuition, state resident: full-time $9360; part-time $390 per credit hour. Tuition, nonresident: full-time $30,024; part-time $1251 per credit hour. *International tuition:* $30,024 full-time. *Required fees:* $2128. *Financial support:* In 2018–19, fellowships with full tuition reimbursements (averaging $23,000 per year), research assistantships with full tuition reimbursements (averaging $27,671 per year), teaching assistantships with full tuition reimbursements (averaging $2,300 per year) were awarded; career-related internships or fieldwork, institutionally sponsored loans, scholarships/grants, health care benefits, tuition waivers (full), and unspecified assistantships also available. Support available to part-time students. Financial award application deadline: 3/15. *Faculty research:* Social and cultural influences on schools, equity and social justice, research methodology, program evaluation, leadership and instruction in schools. *Unit head:* Dr. Jennifer Esposito, Interim Chair, 404-413-8281, Fax: 404-413-8003, E-mail: jesposito@gsu.edu. *Application contact:* Aishah Cowan, Administrative Academic Specialist, 404-413-8273, Fax: 404-413-8033, E-mail: acowan@gsu.edu.
Website: http://eps.education.gsu.edu/

Harvard University, Harvard Graduate School of Education, Master's Programs in Education, Cambridge, MA 02138. Offers arts in education (Ed M); education policy and management (Ed M); higher education (Ed M); human development and psychology (Ed M); international education policy (Ed M); language and literacy (Ed M); learning and teaching (Ed M); mind, brain, and education (Ed M); prevention science and practice (Ed M); school leadership (Ed M); special studies (Ed M); teacher education (Ed M); technology, innovation, and education (Ed M). *Program availability:* Part-time. *Entrance requirements:* For master's, GRE General Test, statement of purpose, 3 letters of recommendation, resume, official transcripts. Additional exam requirements/recommendations for international students: Required—TOEFL (minimum score 613 paper-based; 104 iBT), TWE (minimum score 5). Electronic applications accepted. *Faculty research:* Learning and development, educational leadership and organizations, education policy analysis.

Howard University, School of Education, Department of Educational Leadership and Policy Studies, Washington, DC 20059. Offers educational administration (Ed D); educational administration and supervision (M Ed, CAGS). *Program availability:* Part-time. *Degree requirements:* For master's, comprehensive exam, School Leaders Licensure Assessment, practicum; for doctorate, comprehensive exam, thesis/dissertation, internship; for CAGS, thesis. *Entrance requirements:* For master's, minimum GPA of 2.7; for doctorate, minimum GPA of 3.0. Additional exam requirements/recommendations for international students: Required—TOEFL (minimum score 550 paper-based; 79 iBT). Electronic applications accepted.

Illinois State University, Graduate School, College of Education, Department of Curriculum and Instruction, Normal, IL 61790. Offers curriculum and instruction (MS, MS Ed, Ed D); educational policies (Ed D); postsecondary education (Ed D); reading (MS Ed); supervision (Ed D). *Accreditation:* NCATE. *Faculty:* 49 full-time (31 women), 80 part-time/adjunct (64 women). *Students:* 7 full-time (2 women), 21 part-time (18 women); includes 4 minority (2 Black or African American, non-Hispanic/Latino; 2 Hispanic/Latino), 5 international. Average age 33. 43 applicants, 93% accepted, 28 enrolled. In 2018, 51 master's, 7 doctorates awarded. *Degree requirements:* For master's, variable foreign language requirement, thesis or alternative; for doctorate, variable foreign language requirement, thesis/dissertation, 2 terms of residency, internship. *Entrance requirements:* For master's, GRE General Test, minimum GPA of 3.0 in last 60 hours of course work; for doctorate, GRE General Test. *Application deadline:* Applications are processed on a rolling basis. Application fee: $40. *Expenses: Tuition, area resident:* Full-time $7264.62. Tuition, state resident: full-time $9466. Tuition, nonresident: full-time $17,290. *International tuition:* $15,089.40 full-time. *Required fees:* $1481.04. *Financial support:* In 2018–19, 18 research assistantships were awarded; tuition waivers (full) and unspecified assistantships also available. Financial award application deadline: 4/1. *Faculty research:* In-service and pre-service teacher education for teachers of English language learners; teachers for all children: developing a model for alternative, bilingual elementary certification for paraprofessionals in Illinois; Illinois Geographic Alliance, Connections Project. *Unit head:* Dr. Alan Bates, Interim Director, 309-438-5425, E-mail: abates@ilstu.edu. *Application contact:* Dr. Ryan Brown, Graduate Coordinator, 309-438-3964, E-mail: rbrown@ilstu.edu.
Website: http://ci.illinoisstate.edu/

Indiana University Bloomington, School of Education, Department of Educational Leadership and Policy Studies, Bloomington, IN 47405. Offers educational leadership (MS, Ed D, Ed S); higher education (Ed D, PhD); higher education and student affairs (MS); history and philosophy of education (MS); history, philosophy, and policy in education (PhD), including education policy studies, history of education, philosophy of education; international and comparative education (MS). *Accreditation:* NCATE. *Degree requirements:* For master's, thesis optional; for doctorate, comprehensive exam, thesis/dissertation; for Ed S, comprehensive exam or project. *Entrance requirements:* For master's, doctorate, and Ed S, GRE General Test. Additional exam requirements/recommendations for international students: Required—TOEFL (minimum score 79 iBT). Electronic applications accepted. *Faculty research:* Culturally engaging campus environments, school choice policy analysis, democracy and education in the national and international context, and principal leadership.

Loyola University Chicago, School of Education, Program in Cultural and Educational Policy Studies, Chicago, IL 60660. Offers M Ed, MA, PhD. PhD offered through the Graduate School. *Program availability:* Part-time, evening/weekend. *Faculty:* 4 full-time (2 women), 3 part-time/adjunct (0 women). *Students:* 37 full-time (23 women), 34 part-time (25 women); includes 28 minority (16 Black or African American, non-Hispanic/Latino; 2 Asian, non-Hispanic/Latino; 7 Hispanic/Latino; 3 Two or more races, non-Hispanic/Latino), 4 international. Average age 32. 65 applicants, 45% accepted, 14 enrolled. In 2018, 19 master's, 3 doctorates awarded. *Degree requirements:* For master's, comprehensive exam (M Ed), thesis (MA); for doctorate, comprehensive exam, thesis/dissertation, oral candidacy exam. *Entrance requirements:* For master's, letters of recommendation, minimum GPA of 3.0; for doctorate, GRE General Test, interview, letter of recommendation, resume, minimum GPA of 3.0. Additional exam requirements/recommendations for international students: Required—TOEFL (minimum score 550 paper-based; 79 iBT). *Application deadline:* For fall admission, 12/1 for domestic and international students; for spring admission, 11/1 for domestic and international students. Applications are processed on a rolling basis. Application fee: $50. Electronic applications accepted. Application fee is waived when completed online. *Expenses:* Contact institution. *Financial support:* In 2018–19, 8 research assistantships with full tuition reimbursements (averaging $14,000 per year), 22 teaching assistantships (averaging $4,000 per year) were awarded; career-related internships or fieldwork, institutionally sponsored loans, scholarships/grants, health care benefits, and unspecified assistantships also available. Support available to part-time students. Financial award application deadline: 2/1; financial award applicants required to submit FAFSA. *Faculty research:* Politics of education, cultural foundations, policy studies, qualitative research methods, multicultural diversity. *Unit head:* Dr. Noah Sobe, Director, 312-915-6954, E-mail: nsobe@luc.edu. *Application contact:* Dr. Noah Sobe, Director, 312-915-6954, E-mail: nsobe@luc.edu.

Marquette University, Graduate School, College of Education, Department of Educational Policy and Leadership, Milwaukee, WI 53201-1881. Offers college student personnel administration (M Ed); curriculum and instruction (MA); education (MA); educational administration (M Ed); educational policy and foundations (MA); elementary education (Certificate); literacy (MA); principal (Certificate); reading specialist (Certificate); reading teacher (Certificate); secondary education (Certificate); superintendent (Certificate). *Program availability:* Part-time, evening/weekend. Terminal master's awarded for partial completion of doctoral program. *Degree requirements:* For master's, comprehensive exam, thesis (for some programs); for doctorate, thesis/dissertation, qualifying exam. *Entrance requirements:* For master's, GRE General Test or MAT, official transcripts from all current and previous colleges/universities except Marquette, three letters of recommendation, statement of purpose; for doctorate, GRE General Test, MAT, sample of written work, official transcripts from all current and previous colleges/universities except Marquette, three letters of recommendation, statement of purpose, resume/curriculum vitae; for Certificate, GRE General Test or MAT, master's degree. Additional exam requirements/recommendations for international students: Required—TOEFL (minimum score 530 paper-based). *Expenses:* Contact institution. *Faculty research:* Leadership; social justice in education; development of lifelong learners; race, class, and schooling in historical perspective; urban teacher education.

Michigan State University, The Graduate School, College of Education, Program in Educational Policy, East Lansing, MI 48824. Offers PhD. *Entrance requirements:* Additional exam requirements/recommendations for international students: Required—TOEFL. Electronic applications accepted.

Educational Policy

New York University, Steinhardt School of Culture, Education, and Human Development, Applied Statistics, Social Science, and Humanities, Program in Sociology of Education, New York, NY 10012. Offers education policy (MA); social and cultural studies of education (MA); sociology of education (PhD). *Program availability:* Part-time. *Entrance requirements:* For master's, letters of recommendation; for doctorate, GRE General Test, interview. Additional exam requirements/recommendations for international students: Required—TOEFL (minimum score 100 iBT). Electronic applications accepted. *Faculty research:* Legal and institutional environments of schools; social inequality; high school reform and achievement; urban schooling, economics and education, educational policy.

Niagara University, Graduate Division of Education, Concentration in Educational Leadership, Niagara University, NY 14109. Offers leadership and policy (PhD); school building leader (MS Ed); school district business leader (Certificate); school district leader (MS Ed, Certificate). *Program availability:* Part-time, evening/weekend, 100% online. *Students:* 50 full-time (29 women), 157 part-time (110 women); includes 33 minority (20 Black or African American, non-Hispanic/Latino; 2 Asian, non-Hispanic/Latino; 8 Hispanic/Latino; 3 Two or more races, non-Hispanic/Latino), 51 international. Average age 39. In 2018, 27 master's, 15 doctorates, 20 other advanced degrees awarded. *Entrance requirements:* For master's, GRE General Test or MAT; for Certificate, GRE General Test and GRE Subject Test or MAT. Additional exam requirements/recommendations for international students: Required—TOEFL (minimum score 550 paper-based; 79 iBT), IELTS (minimum score 6). *Application deadline:* For fall admission, 8/1 for domestic students. Applications are processed on a rolling basis. Electronic applications accepted. *Expenses:* Contact institution. *Financial support:* Research assistantships with tuition reimbursements, teaching assistantships with tuition reimbursements, career-related internships or fieldwork, Federal Work-Study, scholarships/grants, and unspecified assistantships available. Support available to part-time students. Financial award application deadline: 4/15; financial award applicants required to submit FAFSA. *Unit head:* Dr. James Mills, Coordinator of Educational Leadership, 716-286-8553, E-mail: jmills@niagara.edu. *Application contact:* Evan Pierce, Associate Director, Graduate Studies, 716-286-8327, E-mail: epierce@niagara.edu.
Website: http://www.niagara.edu/educational-leadership-online

Northwest Missouri State University, Graduate School, School of Education, Maryville, MO 64468-6001. Offers early childhood education (MS Ed); education leadership (MS Ed), including elementary, K-12, secondary; educational leadership (Ed S), including elementary school principalship, secondary school principalship, superintendency; educational leadership and policy analysis (Ed D); elementary education (MS Ed); elementary mathematics (MS Ed); higher education leadership (MS); middle school education (MS Ed); reading (MS Ed); special education (MS Ed); teacher leadership (MS Ed); teaching English language learners (MS Ed). *Accreditation:* NCATE. *Program availability:* Part-time. *Faculty:* 26 full-time (16 women). *Students:* 109 full-time (87 women), 385 part-time (270 women); includes 30 minority (10 Black or African American, non-Hispanic/Latino; 2 American Indian or Alaska Native, non-Hispanic/Latino; 3 Asian, non-Hispanic/Latino; 12 Hispanic/Latino; 1 Native Hawaiian or other Pacific Islander, non-Hispanic/Latino; 2 Two or more races, non-Hispanic/Latino), 1 international. Average age 33. 210 applicants, 72% accepted, 142 enrolled. In 2018, 71 master's, 11 other advanced degrees awarded. *Degree requirements:* For master's, comprehensive exam; for Ed S, comprehensive exam, thesis. *Entrance requirements:* For master's, GRE General Test, writing sample; for Ed S, minimum graduate GPA of 3.25. Additional exam requirements/recommendations for international students: Required—TOEFL (minimum score 550 paper-based). *Application deadline:* For fall admission, 7/1 for domestic and international students; for spring admission, 11/15 for domestic and international students. Applications are processed on a rolling basis. Application fee: $0 ($75 for international students). Electronic applications accepted. *Expenses:* $389.11 in-state and $653.92 out-of-state per credit hour. *Financial support:* Research assistantships with full tuition reimbursements, teaching assistantships with full tuition reimbursements, and unspecified assistantships available. Financial award application deadline: 4/1; financial award applicants required to submit FAFSA. *Unit head:* Dr. Tim Wall, Director, 660-562-1179, E-mail: timwall@nwmissouri.edu. *Application contact:* Dr. Tim Wall, Director, 660-562-1179, E-mail: timwall@nwmissouri.edu.
Website: https://www.nwmissouri.edu/education/index.htm

The Ohio State University, Graduate School, College of Education and Human Ecology, Department of Educational Studies, Columbus, OH 43210. Offers M Ed, MA, PhD, Ed S. *Accreditation:* NCATE. *Program availability:* Part-time. *Faculty:* 57. *Students:* 331 full-time (219 women), 199 part-time (135 women); includes 130 minority (83 Black or African American, non-Hispanic/Latino; 11 Asian, non-Hispanic/Latino; 17 Hispanic/Latino; 19 Two or more races, non-Hispanic/Latino), 53 international. Average age 32. In 2018, 129 master's, 39 doctorates, 10 other advanced degrees awarded. *Degree requirements:* For master's, thesis optional; for doctorate, thesis/dissertation. *Entrance requirements:* For master's and doctorate, GRE General Test. Additional exam requirements/recommendations for international students: Required—TOEFL (minimum score 550 paper-based; 79 iBT), Michigan English Language Assessment Battery (minimum score 82); Recommended—IELTS (minimum score 7). *Application deadline:* For fall admission, 12/1 priority date for domestic and international students; for spring admission, 11/1 for domestic and international students; for summer admission, 3/1 for domestic and international students. Applications are processed on a rolling basis. Application fee: $60 ($70 for international students). Electronic applications accepted. *Financial support:* Fellowships with tuition reimbursements, research assistantships with tuition reimbursements, teaching assistantships with tuition reimbursements, Federal Work-Study, institutionally sponsored loans, and unspecified assistantships available. Support available to part-time students. *Unit head:* Dr. Antoinette Miranda, Interim Chair, 614-292-5909, E-mail: miranda.2@osu.edu. *Application contact:* Graduate and Professional Admissions, 614-292-9444, E-mail: gpadmissions@osu.edu.
Website: http://ehe.osu.edu/educational-studies/

Oregon State University, College of Education, Program in Education, Corvallis, OR 97331. Offers agricultural education (PhD); language equity and education policy (PhD); mathematics education (MS); science education (MS); science/mathematics education (PhD). *Program availability:* Part-time, 100% online, blended/hybrid learning. Terminal master's awarded for partial completion of doctoral program. *Degree requirements:* For master's, variable foreign language requirement, thesis (for some programs); for doctorate, variable foreign language requirement, thesis/dissertation. *Entrance requirements:* Additional exam requirements/recommendations for international students: Required—TOEFL (minimum score 575 paper-based). *Faculty research:* School administration, educational foundations, research methodology, education policy development, higher education administration.

Penn State University Park, Graduate School, College of Education, Department of Education Policy Studies, University Park, PA 16802. Offers educational leadership (M Ed, D Ed, PhD, Certificate); educational theory and policy (MA, PhD); higher education (M Ed, D Ed, PhD). *Accreditation:* NCATE. *Program availability:* Online learning.

Rutgers University–Camden, Graduate School of Arts and Sciences, Department of Public Policy and Administration, Camden, NJ 08102. Offers education policy and leadership (MPA); international public service and development (MPA); public management (MPA); JD/MPA; MPA/MA. *Accreditation:* NASPAA. *Program availability:* Part-time, evening/weekend. *Degree requirements:* For master's, directed study, research workshop, 42 credits. *Entrance requirements:* For master's, GRE General Test, GMAT or LSAT, 3 letters of recommendation; resume. Additional exam requirements/recommendations for international students: Required—TOEFL (minimum score 550 paper-based), IELTS. Electronic applications accepted. *Faculty research:* Nonprofit management, county and municipal administration, health and human services, government communication, administrative law, educational finance.

Rutgers University–New Brunswick, Graduate School of Education, Doctoral Program in Education, New Brunswick, NJ 08901. Offers educational policy (PhD); educational psychology (PhD); literacy education (PhD); mathematics education (PhD). *Program availability:* Part-time. *Degree requirements:* For doctorate, thesis/dissertation, qualifying exam. *Entrance requirements:* For doctorate, GRE General Test, GRE Subject Test (mathematics education). Additional exam requirements/recommendations for international students: Required—TOEFL (minimum score 575 paper-based; 83 iBT). Electronic applications accepted. *Faculty research:* Literacy education, math education, educational psychology, educational policy, learning sciences.

Stanford University, Graduate School of Education, Program in Policy, Organization, and Leadership Studies, Stanford, CA 94305-2004. Offers MA, MA/MBA. *Expenses: Tuition:* Full-time $50,703; part-time $32,970 per year. *Required fees:* $651.

Teachers College, Columbia University, Department of Education Policy and Social Analysis, New York, NY 10027-6696. Offers economics and education (Ed M, MA, PhD); education policy (Ed M, MA, Ed D, PhD); politics and education (Ed M, MA, Ed D, PhD); sociology and education (Ed M, MA, Ed D, PhD). *Students:* 82 full-time (67 women), 181 part-time (140 women); includes 91 minority (39 Black or African American, non-Hispanic/Latino; 1 American Indian or Alaska Native, non-Hispanic/Latino; 19 Asian, non-Hispanic/Latino; 27 Hispanic/Latino; 5 Two or more races, non-Hispanic/Latino), 79 international. Average age 28. 497 applicants, 54% accepted, 110 enrolled. *Unit head:* Dr. Aaron Pallas, Chair, 212-678-8119, E-mail: amp155@tc.columbia.edu. *Application contact:* Kelly Sutton-Skinner, Director of Admissions & New Student Enrollment, E-mail: kms2237@tc.columbia.edu.
Website: http://www.tc.columbia.edu/education-policy-and-social-analysis/

Teachers College, Columbia University, Department of Organization and Leadership, New York, NY 10027-6696. Offers adult education guided intensive study (Ed D); adult learning and leadership (Ed M, MA, Ed D); educational leadership (Ed D); higher and postsecondary education (MA, Ed D); leadership, policy and politics (Ed D); nurse executive (MA, Ed D), including administration studies (MA), professorial studies (MA); private school leadership (Ed M, MA); public school building leadership (Ed M, MA); social and organizational psychology (MA); urban education leaders (Ed D); MA/MBA. *Program availability:* Part-time, evening/weekend. *Students:* 249 full-time (165 women), 427 part-time (299 women); includes 275 minority (99 Black or African American, non-Hispanic/Latino; 75 Asian, non-Hispanic/Latino; 82 Hispanic/Latino; 1 Native Hawaiian or other Pacific Islander, non-Hispanic/Latino; 18 Two or more races, non-Hispanic/Latino), 84 international. Average age 34. 770 applicants, 59% accepted, 267 enrolled. *Unit head:* Prof. Bill Baldwin, Chair, 212-678-3043, E-mail: wjb12@tc.columbia.edu. *Application contact:* Kelly Sutton-Skinner, Director of Admission & New Student Enrollment, E-mail: kms2237@tc.columbia.edu.

University at Albany, State University of New York, School of Education, Department of Educational Policy and Leadership, Albany, NY 12222-0001. Offers educational policy and leadership (MS, PhD); higher education (MS); international education management (CAS). *Program availability:* Evening/weekend. *Faculty:* 12 full-time (5 women), 3 part-time/adjunct (2 women). *Students:* 42 full-time (31 women), 132 part-time (84 women); includes 47 minority (21 Black or African American, non-Hispanic/Latino; 4 Asian, non-Hispanic/Latino; 20 Hispanic/Latino; 2 Two or more races, non-Hispanic/Latino), 23 international. Average age 32. 72 applicants, 71% accepted, 48 enrolled. In 2018, 11 master's, 7 doctorates, 12 other advanced degrees awarded. *Degree requirements:* For doctorate, one foreign language, thesis/dissertation. *Entrance requirements:* For doctorate, GRE General Test, GRE Subject Test. Additional exam requirements/recommendations for international students: Required—TOEFL (minimum score 550 paper-based). *Application deadline:* For fall admission, 2/1 for domestic students, 5/1 for international students; for spring admission, 9/1 for domestic students, 11/1 for international students. Applications are processed on a rolling basis. Application fee: $75. Electronic applications accepted. *Financial support:* Fellowships and career-related internships or fieldwork available. Financial award application deadline: 3/15. *Unit head:* Jason Lane, Chair, 518-442-5092, E-mail: jlane@albany.edu. *Application contact:* Jason Lane, Chair, 518-442-5092, E-mail: jlane@albany.edu.
Website: http://www.albany.edu/epl/

University of Alberta, Faculty of Graduate Studies and Research, Department of Educational Policy Studies, Edmonton, AB T6G 2E1, Canada. Offers adult education (M Ed, Ed D, PhD); educational administration and leadership (M Ed, Ed D, PhD, Postgraduate Diploma); First Nations education (M Ed, Ed D, PhD); theoretical, cultural and international studies in education (M Ed, Ed D, PhD). *Degree requirements:* For master's, thesis (for some programs); for doctorate, thesis/dissertation. *Entrance requirements:* For master's, minimum GPA of 6.5 on a 9.0 scale; for doctorate, minimum GPA of 7.5 on a 9.0 scale. Additional exam requirements/recommendations for international students: Required—TOEFL (minimum score 580 paper-based). Electronic applications accepted.

University of Arkansas, Graduate School, College of Education and Health Professions, Department of Education Reform, Fayettevillee, AR 72701. Offers education policy (PhD). In 2018, 3 doctorates awarded. *Application deadline:* For fall admission, 8/1 for domestic students, 4/1 for international students; for spring admission, 12/1 for domestic students, 10/1 for international students; for summer admission, 4/15 for domestic students, 3/1 for international students. Applications are processed on a rolling basis. Application fee: $60. Electronic applications accepted. *Financial support:* In 2018–19, 14 research assistantships were awarded; fellowships and teaching assistantships also available. *Unit head:* Dr. Jay Greene, Department Head, 479-575-3162, Fax: 479-575-3196, E-mail: jpg@uark.edu. *Application contact:* Dr. Dirk C. VanRaemdonck, Chief of Staff and Graduate Coordinator, 479-575-5597, Fax: 479-575-3196, E-mail: dvanraem@uark.edu.
Website: http://edre.uark.edu/

The University of British Columbia, Faculty of Education, Department of Educational Studies, Vancouver, BC V6T 1Z1, Canada. Offers adult learning and education (M Ed); adult learning and global change (M Ed); curriculum and leadership (M Ed); educational administration and leadership (M Ed); educational leadership and policy (Ed D); educational studies (M Ed, MA, PhD); higher education (M Ed); society, culture and politics in education (M Ed). *Program availability:* Part-time, evening/weekend. Terminal master's awarded for partial completion of doctoral program. *Degree requirements:* For master's, thesis; for doctorate, comprehensive exam, thesis/dissertation. *Entrance requirements:* For master's, minimum B+ average, 4-year undergraduate degree, field-

related experience; for doctorate, minimum B+ average, 4-year undergraduate degree, master's degree, field-related experience. Additional exam requirements/ recommendations for international students: Required—TOEFL (minimum score 600 paper-based; 100 iBT) or IELTS (minimum score 6.5). Electronic applications accepted. *Expenses:* Contact institution. *Faculty research:* Educational leadership educational administration adult education politics in education, global change and adult learning.

University of California, Riverside, Graduate Division, Graduate School of Education, Riverside, CA 92521. Offers applied behavior analysis (M Ed); diversity and equity (M Ed); education policy analysis and leadership (PhD); education specialist (Credential); education, society, and culture (MA, PhD); educational psychology (MA, PhD); general education (M Ed); higher education administration and policy (M Ed, PhD); multiple subject (Credential); research, evaluation, measurement and statistics (MA); school psychology (PhD); single subject (Credential); special education (M Ed, PhD); special education and autism (MA); TESOL (M Ed). Terminal master's awarded for partial completion of doctoral program. *Degree requirements:* For master's, comprehensive exams or thesis (MA), case study or analytical report (M Ed); for doctorate, comprehensive exam, thesis/dissertation, written and oral qualifying exams, college teaching practicum. *Entrance requirements:* For master's, GRE General Test (for MA); CBEST and CSET (for M Ed in general education only), UCR Extension TESOL certificate (for M Ed with TESOL emphasis only); for doctorate, GRE General Test, writing sample; for Credential, CBEST, CSET. Additional exam requirements/ recommendations for international students: Required—TOEFL (minimum score 550 paper-based; 80 iBT), IELTS (minimum score 7). Electronic applications accepted. *Faculty research:* Responsiveness to intervention, faculty core, response to intervention of English language learners, advanced modeling techniques, study on social capital, trust, and motivation.

University of Colorado Boulder, Graduate School, School of Education, Division of Educational Foundations, Policy, and Practice, Boulder, CO 80309. Offers MA, PhD. *Entrance requirements:* For master's, minimum undergraduate GPA of 2.75. Electronic applications accepted. Application fee is waived when completed online.

University of Colorado Denver, School of Education and Human Development, Administrative Leadership and Policy Studies Program, Denver, CO 80217. Offers MA, Ed S. *Accreditation:* NCATE. *Program availability:* Part-time, evening/weekend. *Degree requirements:* For master's, comprehensive exam, 9 credit hours beyond the 32 required for principal-administrator licensure; for Ed S, comprehensive exam, 9 credit hours beyond the 32 required for principal-administrator licensure (for those already holding MA). *Entrance requirements:* For master's and Ed S, GRE or MAT (if GPA is below 2.75), minimum GPA of 2.75, interview, 3 letters of recommendation, resume. Additional exam requirements/recommendations for international students: Required—TOEFL (minimum score 525 paper-based; 71 iBT); Recommended—IELTS (minimum score 6.3). Electronic applications accepted. *Expenses:* Tuition, state resident: full-time $6786; part-time $337 per credit hour. Tuition, nonresident: full-time $22,590; part-time $1255 per credit hour. *Required fees:* $1231; $137 per credit hour. Tuition and fees vary according to program and reciprocity agreements. *Faculty research:* Learning cultures, teaching and learning in educational administration.

University of Colorado Denver, School of Education and Human Development, Program in Educational Leadership and Innovation, Denver, CO 80217. Offers educational studies and research (PhD), including administrative leadership and policy, early childhood special education, math education, research, assessment and evaluation, science education, urban ecologies. *Program availability:* Part-time, evening/ weekend. *Degree requirements:* For doctorate, comprehensive exam, thesis/ dissertation, 75 credit hours (for PhD). *Entrance requirements:* For doctorate, GRE or equivalent, resume or curriculum vitae, letters of recommendation, master's degree or equivalent, completion of basic or advanced statistics course with minimum B grade. Additional exam requirements/recommendations for international students: Required—TOEFL (minimum score 537 paper-based; 75 iBT); Recommended—IELTS (minimum score 6.5). Electronic applications accepted. *Expenses:* Tuition, state resident: full-time $6786; part-time $337 per credit hour. Tuition, nonresident: full-time $22,590; part-time $1255 per credit hour. *Required fees:* $1231; $137 per credit hour. Tuition and fees vary according to program and reciprocity agreements. *Faculty research:* Administrative leadership and policy studies, early childhood education, research in diversity, paraprofessionals in education, urban schools lab.

University of Colorado Denver, School of Education and Human Development, Program in Education and Human Development, Denver, CO 80217. Offers administrative leadership and policy (PhD); assessment (MA); early childhood special education/early childhood education (PhD); family science and human development (PhD); human development and family relations (MA); learning (MA); mathematics education (PhD); research and evaluation methods (MA); research, assessment and evaluation (PhD); science education (PhD); urban ecologies (PhD). MA program also offered in partnership with Boulder Journey School, Friends School and Stanley British Primary School. *Program availability:* Part-time, evening/weekend. *Degree requirements:* For master's, comprehensive exam, 9 hours of core courses embedded within a minimum of 36 to 38 hours of relevant coursework, including an educational psychology practicum, independent study project or thesis (recommended). *Entrance requirements:* For master's, GRE if undergraduate GPA below 2.75, resume, three letters of recommendation, transcripts. Additional exam requirements/recommendations for international students: Required—TOEFL (minimum score 537 paper-based; 75 iBT); Recommended—IELTS (minimum score 6.5). Electronic applications accepted. *Expenses:* Contact institution. *Faculty research:* Crisis response and intervention, school violence prevention, immigrant experience, educational environments for English language learners, culturally competent assessment and intervention, child and youth suicide.

University of Denver, Morgridge College of Education, Denver, CO 80208. Offers child, family and school psychology (MA, PhD, Ed S); counseling psychology (MA, PhD); curriculum and instruction (MA, Ed D, PhD); curriculum instruction and teaching (Certificate); early childhood special education (MA, Certificate); educational leadership and policy studies (MA, Ed D, PhD, Certificate); higher education (Ed D, PhD); library and information science (MLIS); research methods and statistics (MA, PhD). *Accreditation:* ALA; APA (one or more programs are accredited). *Program availability:* Part-time, evening/weekend, online learning. *Faculty:* 49 full-time (35 women), 33 part-time/adjunct (20 women). *Students:* 509 full-time (400 women), 365 part-time (277 women); includes 236 minority (53 Black or African American, non-Hispanic/Latino; 6 American Indian or Alaska Native, non-Hispanic/Latino; 28 Asian, non-Hispanic/Latino; 116 Hispanic/Latino; 33 Two or more races, non-Hispanic/Latino), 56 international. Average age 31. 1,372 applicants, 57% accepted, 382 enrolled. In 2018, 258 master's, 41 doctorates, 162 other advanced degrees awarded. Terminal master's awarded for partial completion of doctoral program. *Degree requirements:* For master's, comprehensive exam (for some programs); for doctorate, comprehensive exam (for some programs), thesis/dissertation. *Entrance requirements:* For master's, GRE General Test or GMAT, bachelors degree; transcripts; two letters of recommendation; personal statement; resume; for doctorate, GRE General Test or GMAT, Masters degree; transcripts; two letters of recommendation; personal statement(s); resume. Additional exam requirements/recommendations for international students: Required—TOEFL (minimum score 550 paper-based; 80 iBT). *Application deadline:* Applications are processed on a rolling basis. Application fee: $65. Electronic applications accepted. *Expenses:* $33,183 per year full-time. *Financial support:* In 2018–19, 690 students received support, including 29 research assistantships with tuition reimbursements available (averaging $11,465 per year), 9 teaching assistantships with tuition reimbursements available (averaging $2,527 per year); career-related internships or fieldwork, Federal Work-Study, institutionally sponsored loans, scholarships/grants, and unspecified assistantships also available. Support available to part-time students. Financial award application deadline: 2/15; financial award applicants required to submit FAFSA. *Faculty research:* Early childhood education, educational leadership, access and opportunity to postsecondary education, marriage and family therapy, data management and archival research. *Total annual research expenditures:* $2.3 million. *Unit head:* Dr. Karen Riley, Dean, 303-871-3665, E-mail: karen.riley@du.edu. *Application contact:* Jodi Dye, Director of Admissions, 303-871-2510, E-mail: jodi.dye@du.edu.
Website: http://morgridge.du.edu

University of Florida, Graduate School, College of Education, School of Human Development and Organizational Studies in Education, Gainesville, FL 32611. Offers counseling and counselor education (Ed D, PhD), including counseling and counselor education, marriage and family counseling, mental health counseling, school counseling and guidance; educational leadership (M Ed, MAE, Ed D, PhD, Ed S), including educational leadership (Ed D, PhD), educational policy (Ed D, PhD); higher education administration (Ed D, PhD), including education policy (Ed D), educational policy, higher education administration; marriage and family counseling (M Ed, MAE, Ed D, PhD, Ed S); mental health counseling (M Ed, MAE, Ed D, PhD, Ed S); research and evaluation methodology (M Ed, MAE, Ed D, PhD); school counseling and guidance (M Ed, MAE, Ed D, PhD, Ed S); student personnel in higher education (M Ed, MAE). *Accreditation:* ACA (one or more programs are accredited); NCATE. *Program availability:* Part-time, online learning. Terminal master's awarded for partial completion of doctoral program. *Degree requirements:* For master's, thesis optional; for doctorate, comprehensive exam, thesis/dissertation. *Entrance requirements:* For master's and doctorate, GRE General Test, minimum GPA of 3.0 (undergraduate), 3.5 (graduate); for Ed S, GRE General Test. Additional exam requirements/recommendations for international students: Required—TOEFL (minimum score 550 paper-based; 80 iBT), IELTS (minimum score 6). Electronic applications accepted.

University of Florida, Graduate School, College of Liberal Arts and Sciences, Department of Political Science, Gainesville, FL 32611. Offers educational policy (PhD); international development policy and administration (MA, Certificate); international relations (MA, MAT); political campaigning (MA, Certificate); political science (MA, PhD); public affairs (MA, Certificate); tropical conservation and development (MA, PhD); JD/MA. Terminal master's awarded for partial completion of doctoral program. *Degree requirements:* For master's, variable foreign language requirement, comprehensive exam (for some programs), thesis or alternative, internship (for some programs); for doctorate, variable foreign language requirement, comprehensive exam, thesis/ dissertation. *Entrance requirements:* For master's and doctorate, GRE General Test (minimum score: 308 combined verbal/quantitative), minimum GPA of 3.5. Additional exam requirements/recommendations for international students: Required—TOEFL (minimum score 550 paper-based; 80 iBT), IELTS (minimum score 6). Electronic applications accepted. *Faculty research:* American electoral politics and political institutions, comparative democratization and development, theories of international relation, and political theory.

University of Georgia, College of Education, Department of Lifelong Education, Administration and Policy, Athens, GA 30602. Offers adult education (Ed D, Ed S); lifelong education, administration and policy (PhD). *Accreditation:* NCATE. *Entrance requirements:* For doctorate, GRE General Test; for Ed S, GRE General Test or MAT. Electronic applications accepted.

University of Hawaii at Manoa, Office of Graduate Education, College of Education, PhD in Education Program, Honolulu, HI 96822. Offers curriculum and instruction (PhD); educational administration (PhD); educational foundations (PhD); educational policy studies (PhD); educational psychology (PhD); exceptionalities (PhD); kinesiology (PhD); learning design and technology (PhD). *Program availability:* Part-time, evening/ weekend. *Degree requirements:* For doctorate, thesis/dissertation. *Entrance requirements:* For doctorate, GRE General Test, sample of written work. Additional exam requirements/recommendations for international students: Required—TOEFL (minimum score 600 paper-based; 100 iBT), IELTS (minimum score 7).

University of Illinois at Chicago, College of Education, Department of Educational Policy Studies, Chicago, IL 60607-7128. Offers policy studies (M Ed); policy studies in urban education (PhD); urban education leadership (Ed D). *Faculty research:* Social foundations of education, educational organizations and leadership, education policy analysis, understanding and addressing educational problems in urban contexts.

University of Illinois at Urbana–Champaign, Graduate College, College of Education, Department of Education Policy, Organization, and Leadership, Champaign, IL 61820. Offers educational organization and leadership (Ed M, MS, Ed D, PhD, CAS); educational policy studies (Ed M, MA, PhD); human resource education (Ed M, MS, Ed D, PhD, CAS). *Program availability:* Part-time, online learning.

The University of Iowa, Graduate College, College of Education, Department of Educational Policy and Leadership Studies, Iowa City, IA 52242-1316. Offers educational leadership (MA, PhD, Ed S); higher education and student affairs (MA, PhD); schools, culture, and society (MA, PhD). *Degree requirements:* For master's and Ed S, exam; for doctorate, comprehensive exam, thesis/dissertation. *Entrance requirements:* For master's, doctorate, and Ed S, GRE General Test, minimum GPA of 3.0. Additional exam requirements/recommendations for international students: Required—TOEFL (minimum score 550 paper-based; 81 iBT). Electronic applications accepted.

The University of Kansas, Graduate Studies, School of Education, Department of Educational Leadership and Policy Studies, Education Leadership and Policy Program, Lawrence, KS 66045-3101. Offers policy studies (PhD); social and cultural studies in education (MSE, PhD). *Program availability:* Part-time, evening/weekend. *Students:* 131 full-time (74 women), 52 part-time (25 women); includes 44 minority (18 Black or African American, non-Hispanic/Latino; 2 American Indian or Alaska Native, non-Hispanic/ Latino; 3 Asian, non-Hispanic/Latino; 9 Hispanic/Latino; 12 Two or more races, non-Hispanic/Latino), 32 international. Average age 38. 58 applicants, 76% accepted, 32 enrolled. In 2018, 29 doctorates awarded. *Entrance requirements:* For master's, minimum GPA of 3.0, resume or curriculum vitae, statement of purpose, official academic transcripts, three letters of recommendation; for doctorate, GRE General Test, minimum graduate GPA of 3.5, resume or curriculum vitae, statement of purpose, official academic transcripts, three letters of recommendation, writing sample. Additional exam requirements/recommendations for international students: Required—TOEFL, IELTS. *Application deadline:* For fall admission, 7/1 for domestic and international students; for spring admission, 11/1 for domestic and international students; for summer admission, 4/1 for domestic and international students. Application fee: $65 ($85 for international students). Electronic applications accepted. *Financial support:* Fellowships, research

assistantships, teaching assistantships, scholarships/grants, and unspecified assistantships available. Financial award application deadline: 3/15. *Faculty research:* Historical and philosophical issues in education, education policy and leadership, higher education faculty, research on college students, education technology. *Unit head:* Dr. Susan B. Twombly, Chair, 785-864-9721, E-mail: stwombly@ku.edu. *Application contact:* Denise Brubaker, Admissions Coordinator, 785-864-7973, E-mail: brubaker@ku.edu.
Website: http://elps.soe.ku.edu/

University of Kentucky, Graduate School, College of Education, Program in Educational Policy Studies and Evaluation, Lexington, KY 40506-0032. Offers educational policy studies and evaluation (Ed D); higher education (MS Ed, PhD); social and philosophical studies (MS Ed). *Accreditation:* NCATE. Terminal master's awarded for partial completion of doctoral program. *Degree requirements:* For master's, comprehensive exam, thesis optional; for doctorate, comprehensive exam, thesis/dissertation. *Entrance requirements:* For master's, GRE General Test, minimum undergraduate GPA of 2.75; for doctorate, GRE General Test, minimum graduate GPA of 3.0. Additional exam requirements/recommendations for international students: Required—TOEFL (minimum score 550 paper-based). Electronic applications accepted. *Faculty research:* Studies in higher education; comparative and international education; evaluation of educational programs, policies, and reform; student, teacher, and faculty cultures; gender and education.

University of Maryland, Baltimore County, The Graduate School, College of Arts, Humanities and Social Sciences, School of Public Policy, Baltimore, MD 21250. Offers public policy (MPP, PhD), including economics (PhD), educational policy, emergency services (PhD), environmental policy (MPP), evaluation and analytical methods, health policy, policy history (PhD), public management, urban policy. *Program availability:* Part-time, evening/weekend. Terminal master's awarded for partial completion of doctoral program. *Degree requirements:* For master's, thesis, policy analysis paper, internship for pre-service; for doctorate, comprehensive exam, thesis/dissertation, comprehensive and field qualifying exams. *Entrance requirements:* For master's, GRE General Test, 3 academic letters of reference, resume, official transcripts; for doctorate, GRE General Test, 3 academic letters of reference, resume, research paper, official transcripts. Additional exam requirements/recommendations for international students: Required—TOEFL (minimum score 550 paper-based; 80 iBT), IELTS (minimum score 6.5). Electronic applications accepted. *Expenses:* Contact institution. *Faculty research:* Education policy, health policy, urban and environmental policy, public management, evaluation and analytical method.

University of Massachusetts Amherst, Graduate School, College of Education, Program in Education, Amherst, MA 01003. Offers bilingual, English as a second language, and multicultural education (M Ed, Ed S); child study and early education (M Ed); children, families and schools (Ed D, Ed S); early childhood and elementary teacher education (M Ed); educational leadership (M Ed); educational policy and leadership (Ed D); higher education (M Ed); international education (M Ed); language, literacy and culture (Ed D); learning, media and technology (M Ed, Ed S); mathematics, science, and learning technologies (Ed D); reading and writing (M Ed); research, educational measurement and psychometrics (Ed D); school counselor education (M Ed, Ed S); school psychology (Ed S); science education (Ed S); secondary teacher education (M Ed); social justice education (M Ed, Ed D, Ed S); special education (M Ed, Ed D, Ed S); teacher education and school improvement (Ed D, Ed S). *Accreditation:* NCATE. *Program availability:* Part-time, online learning. Terminal master's awarded for partial completion of doctoral program. *Degree requirements:* For doctorate, comprehensive exam, thesis/dissertation. *Entrance requirements:* Additional exam requirements/recommendations for international students: Required—TOEFL (minimum score 550 paper-based; 80 iBT), IELTS (minimum score 6.5). Electronic applications accepted.

University of Massachusetts Boston, College of Education and Human Development, Program in Urban Education, Leadership, and Policy Studies, Boston, MA 02125-3393. Offers Ed D, PhD. *Program availability:* Part-time, evening/weekend. *Faculty:* 11 full-time (7 women), 10 part-time/adjunct (6 women). *Students:* 1 (woman) full-time, 43 part-time (29 women); includes 19 minority (8 Black or African American, non-Hispanic/Latino; 10 Hispanic/Latino; 1 Two or more races, non-Hispanic/Latino), 3 international. Average age 38. 18 applicants, 33% accepted, 3 enrolled. In 2018, 3 doctorates awarded. *Entrance requirements:* For doctorate, GRE General Test or MAT, minimum GPA of 2.75. *Application deadline:* For summer admission, 3/1 for domestic students. Application fee: $60 ($100 for international students). Electronic applications accepted. *Expenses: Tuition, area resident:* Full-time $17,896. Tuition, state resident: full-time $17,896. Tuition, nonresident: full-time $34,932. *International tuition:* $34,932 full-time. *Required fees:* $355. *Financial support:* Research assistantships, teaching assistantships, career-related internships or fieldwork, Federal Work-Study, and unspecified assistantships available. Support available to part-time students. Financial award application deadline: 3/1; financial award applicants required to submit FAFSA. *Faculty research:* School reform, race and culture in schools, race and higher education, language, literacy and writing. *Unit head:* Dr. Wenfan Yan, Graduate Program Director, 617-287.4873, E-mail: WenFan.Yan@umb.edu. *Application contact:* Graduate Admissions Coordinator, 617-287-6400, Fax: 617-287-6236, E-mail: graduate.admissions@umb.edu.

University of Massachusetts Dartmouth, Graduate School, College of Arts and Sciences, Department of Public Policy, North Dartmouth, MA 02747-2300. Offers educational policy (Graduate Certificate); environmental policy (Graduate Certificate); public management (Graduate Certificate); public policy (MPP). *Program availability:* Part-time, 100% online, blended/hybrid learning. *Faculty:* 4 full-time (0 women), 1 part-time/adjunct (0 women). *Students:* 11 full-time (10 women), 60 part-time (37 women); includes 16 minority (6 Black or African American, non-Hispanic/Latino; 2 Asian, non-Hispanic/Latino; 7 Hispanic/Latino; 1 Two or more races, non-Hispanic/Latino). Average age 35. 55 applicants, 95% accepted, 33 enrolled. In 2018, 16 master's, 24 other advanced degrees awarded. *Degree requirements:* For master's, e-portfolio. *Entrance requirements:* For master's, GRE or GMAT (waived if applicant has already earned a graduate degree from accredited school or if applicant has successfully completed the educational, environmental or public management certificate program), statement of purpose (minimum of 300 words), resume, 2 letters of recommendation, official transcripts; for Graduate Certificate, statement of purpose (minimum of 300 words), resume, official transcripts. Additional exam requirements/recommendations for international students: Required—TOEFL (minimum score 600 paper-based; 100 iBT). *Application deadline:* Applications are processed on a rolling basis. Application fee: $60. Electronic applications accepted. *Financial support:* Health care benefits available. Financial award application deadline: 3/1; financial award applicants required to submit FAFSA. *Faculty research:* Environmental justice, sustainability, international trade and finance, corporate social responsibility, global governance. *Total annual research expenditures:* $9,000. *Unit head:* Chad McGuire, Graduate Program Director, Public Policy, 508-999-8520, E-mail: cmcguire@umassd.edu. *Application contact:* Scott Webster, Director of Graduate Studies & Admissions, 508-999-8604, Fax: 508-999-8183, E-mail: graduate@umassd.edu.
Website: http://www.umassd.edu/cas/departmentsanddegreeprograms/publicpolicy/

University of Massachusetts Dartmouth, Graduate School, College of Arts and Sciences, School of Education, Department of Educational Leadership, North Dartmouth, MA 02747-2300. Offers educational leadership and policy studies (Ed D, PhD). *Program availability:* Part-time. *Faculty:* 4 full-time (0 women), 1 (woman) part-time/adjunct. *Students:* 7 full-time (6 women), 20 part-time (11 women); includes 12 minority (4 Black or African American, non-Hispanic/Latino; 1 American Indian or Alaska Native, non-Hispanic/Latino; 1 Asian, non-Hispanic/Latino; 4 Hispanic/Latino; 2 Two or more races, non-Hispanic/Latino), 1 international. Average age 44. In 2018, 5 doctorates awarded. *Degree requirements:* For doctorate, comprehensive exam, thesis/dissertation. *Entrance requirements:* For doctorate, GRE or GMAT, statement of purpose (minimum of 300 words), resume, 3 letters of recommendation, official transcripts (from all post secondary institutions), scholarly writing sample (minimum of 10 pages of writing). Additional exam requirements/recommendations for international students: Required—TOEFL (minimum score 550 paper-based; 79 iBT), IELTS (minimum score 6.5). *Application deadline:* For fall admission, 4/30 priority date for domestic students, 3/30 priority date for international students. Application fee: $60. Electronic applications accepted. *Financial support:* In 2018–19, 1 fellowship (averaging $24,000 per year) was awarded; tuition waivers (full) and doctoral support, dissertation writing support also available. Financial award application deadline: 3/1; financial award applicants required to submit FAFSA. *Faculty research:* Sociology of education, critical theory, curriculum theory, globalization and education, urban education, teacher education. *Total annual research expenditures:* $162,000. *Unit head:* Amy Shapiro, Interim Dean, College of Arts and Sciences, 508-999-8352, Fax: 508-999-9125, E-mail: ashapiro@umassd.edu. *Application contact:* Scott Webster, Director of Graduate Studies and Admissions, 508-999-8604, Fax: 508-999-8183, E-mail: graduate@umassd.edu.
Website: http://www.umassd.edu/educationalleadership

University of Minnesota, Twin Cities Campus, Graduate School, College of Education and Human Development, Department of Organizational Leadership, Policy and Development, Program in Education Policy and Leadership, Minneapolis, MN 55455-0213. Offers educational policy and leadership (MA, Ed D, PhD); leadership in education (M Ed). *Students:* 114 full-time (72 women), 43 part-time (27 women); includes 37 minority (20 Black or African American, non-Hispanic/Latino; 6 Asian, non-Hispanic/Latino; 5 Hispanic/Latino; 6 Two or more races, non-Hispanic/Latino), 2 international. Average age 38. 146 applicants, 82% accepted, 85 enrolled. In 2018, 13 master's, 5 doctorates awarded. Application fee: $75 ($95 for international students). *Unit head:* Dr. Kenneth Bartlett, Chair, 612-624-1006, E-mail: bartlett@umn.edu. *Application contact:* Dr. Jeremy J. Hernandez, Director of Graduate Studies, 612-626-9377, E-mail: olpd@umn.edu.
Website: http://www.cehd.umn.edu/OLPD/grad-programs/EPL/

University of Missouri–St. Louis, College of Education, Interdisciplinary Doctoral Programs, St. Louis, MO 63121. Offers counseling (PhD); educational leadership and policy studies (PhD); educational psychology (PhD); leadership in educational practice (Ed D); teaching-learning processes (PhD). *Degree requirements:* For doctorate, thesis/dissertation. *Entrance requirements:* For doctorate, GRE General Test, 3 letters of recommendation; personal interview. Additional exam requirements/recommendations for international students: Recommended—TOEFL (minimum score 550 paper-based; 79 iBT), IELTS (minimum score 6.5). Electronic applications accepted. *Faculty research:* Higher education law and policy, gender and higher education, student retention, lifelong learning orientation, school counselor's role in violence prevention.

University of Mobile, Graduate Studies, School of Education, Mobile, AL 36613. Offers education (MA); higher education leadership and policy (M Ed). *Program availability:* Part-time, 100% online, blended/hybrid learning. *Students:* 30 full-time (28 women); includes 16 minority (13 Black or African American, non-Hispanic/Latino; 2 American Indian or Alaska Native, non-Hispanic/Latino; 1 Asian, non-Hispanic/Latino). 23 applicants, 26% accepted, 12 enrolled. In 2018, 2 master's awarded. *Degree requirements:* For master's, comprehensive exam, thesis optional. *Entrance requirements:* For master's, Alabama teaching certificate if not seeking an Alternative Master's Degree. Additional exam requirements/recommendations for international students: Required—TOEFL (minimum score 550 paper-based; 80 iBT). *Application deadline:* For fall admission, 8/3 priority date for domestic students, 8/3 for international students; for spring admission, 12/23 priority date for domestic students, 12/3 priority date for international students. Applications are processed on a rolling basis. Application fee: $40 ($50 for international students). Electronic applications accepted. *Expenses: Tuition:* Full-time $453; part-time $453 per credit hour. *Required fees:* $320; $320. Tuition and fees vary according to degree level and program. *Financial support:* Application deadline: 8/1; applicants required to submit FAFSA. *Faculty research:* Retention, writing across the curriculum. *Unit head:* Dr. Carolyn D. Corliss, Dean, School of Education, 251-442-2276, Fax: 251-442-2523, E-mail: ccorliss@umobile.edu. *Application contact:* Brian Boyle, Director of Recruitment, 251-442-2727.
Website: http://umobile.edu/school-of-education/master-of-arts-in-education/

The University of North Carolina Wilmington, Watson College of Education, Department of Early Childhood, Elementary, Middle, Literacy and Special Education, Wilmington, NC 28403-3297. Offers educational leadership, policy, and advocacy (M Ed); elementary education (M Ed, MAT); language and literacy (M Ed); middle grades education (MAT). *Accreditation:* NCATE. *Program availability:* Part-time, blended/hybrid learning. *Degree requirements:* For master's, thesis or alternative, exit portfolio, oral presentation, internship, research project (depending on specialization). *Entrance requirements:* For master's, 3 letters of recommendations, NC Class A teacher license in related field, education statement of interest essay. Additional exam requirements/recommendations for international students: Required—TOEFL (minimum score 550 paper-based; 79 iBT), IELTS (minimum score 6.5). Electronic applications accepted.

University of Northern Colorado, Graduate School, College of Education and Behavioral Sciences, Department of Leadership, Policy and Development: Higher Education and P-12 Education, Educational Leadership and Policy Studies Program, Greeley, CO 80639. Offers educational leadership (MA, Ed S); educational leadership and policy studies (Ed D). *Accreditation:* NCATE. *Program availability:* Part-time, evening/weekend, online learning. *Degree requirements:* For master's, comprehensive exam, thesis or alternative; for doctorate, comprehensive exam, thesis/dissertation; for Ed S, comprehensive exam, thesis. *Entrance requirements:* For master's, resume, interview; for doctorate, GRE General Test, resume, interview; for Ed S, resume. Electronic applications accepted.

University of Pennsylvania, Graduate School of Education, Division of Education Policy, Philadelphia, PA 19104. Offers MS Ed, PhD. *Program availability:* Part-time. *Students:* Average age 28. 250 applicants, 50% accepted, 34 enrolled. In 2018, 16 master's, 2 doctorates awarded. *Degree requirements:* For master's, thesis or alternative, research practicum; for doctorate, comprehensive exam, thesis/dissertation. *Entrance requirements:* For master's, GRE, bachelor's degree; for doctorate, GRE, bachelor's degree; master's degree (preferred). Additional exam requirements/recommendations for international students: Required—TOEFL, IELTS. *Application deadline:* For fall admission, 12/8 priority date for domestic and international students. Applications are processed on a rolling basis. Application fee: $75. Electronic

applications accepted. *Financial support:* In 2018–19, 13 students received support. Fellowships, research assistantships, teaching assistantships, Federal Work-Study, scholarships/grants, and health care benefits available. *Faculty research:* Teachers and teaching policy, school reform, standards, and assessment, early childhood education, program evaluation and policy analysis, career and college readiness. *Unit head:* Krista Featherstone, Program Manager, 215-573-8075, E-mail: kfeat@upenn.edu. *Application contact:* Krista Featherstone, Program Manager, 215-573-8075, E-mail: kfeat@upenn.edu.
Website: http://www.gse.upenn.edu/ep

University of Pittsburgh, School of Education, Learning Sciences and Policy Program, Pittsburgh, PA 15260. Offers PhD. *Program availability:* Part-time, evening/weekend. *Degree requirements:* For doctorate, comprehensive exam, thesis/dissertation. *Entrance requirements:* Additional exam requirements/recommendations for international students: Required—TOEFL (minimum score 550 paper-based; 80 iBT).

University of Rochester, Margaret Warner Graduate School of Education and Human Development, Doctoral Programs in Education, Rochester, NY 14627. Offers counseling (Ed D); educational administration (Ed D); educational policy and theory (PhD); higher education (PhD); human development in educational context (PhD); teaching, curriculum, and change (PhD). *Expenses: Tuition:* Full-time $52,974; part-time $1654 per credit hour. *Required fees:* $612. One-time fee: $30 part-time. Tuition and fees vary according to campus/location and program.

University of Rochester, Margaret Warner Graduate School of Education and Human Development, Master's Program in Educational Policy, Rochester, NY 14627. Offers MS. *Expenses: Tuition:* Full-time $52,974; part-time $1654 per credit hour. *Required fees:* $612. One-time fee: $30 part-time. Tuition and fees vary according to campus/location and program.

University of Southern California, Graduate School, Rossier School of Education, Doctor of Philosophy in Education Programs, Los Angeles, CA 90089. Offers educational psychology (PhD); higher education administration and policy (PhD); K-12 policy and practice (PhD). *Degree requirements:* For doctorate, thesis/dissertation, 63 units; qualifying exam; dissertation proposal and defense. *Entrance requirements:* For doctorate, GRE. Additional exam requirements/recommendations for international students: Required—TOEFL (minimum score 100 iBT). Electronic applications accepted. *Faculty research:* Diversity in higher education, organizational change, educational psychology, policy and politics of educational reform, economics of education and education policy.

The University of Texas at Arlington, Graduate School, College of Education, Department of Educational Leadership and Policy Studies, Arlington, TX 76019. Offers educational leadership (PhD); higher education (M Ed); principal certification (M Ed). *Program availability:* Part-time, evening/weekend, online learning. *Degree requirements:* For master's, 2 field-based practica; for doctorate, comprehensive exam, thesis/dissertation, 2 research-based practica. *Entrance requirements:* For master's, GRE, 3 references, minimum undergraduate GPA of 3.0 in last 60 hours of course work; for doctorate, GRE, resume, statement of intent, 3 reference forms, applicable master's degree. *Faculty research:* Lived realities of students of color in K-16 contexts, K-16 faculty, K-16 policy and law, K-16 student access, K-16 student success.

University of Vermont, Graduate College, College of Education and Social Services, PhD Program in Educational Leadership and Policy Studies, Burlington, VT 05405. Offers PhD. *Degree requirements:* For doctorate, thesis/dissertation. *Entrance requirements:* For doctorate, GRE General Test, resume, writing sample. Additional exam requirements/recommendations for international students: Required—TOEFL (minimum iBT score of 90) or IELTS (6.5). Electronic applications accepted.

University of Virginia, Curry School of Education, Department of Leadership, Foundations and Policy, Program in Educational Policy, Charlottesville, VA 22903. Offers PhD, PhD/MPP. *Entrance requirements:* For doctorate, GRE General Test, 2 letters of recommendation. Additional exam requirements/recommendations for international students: Required—TOEFL (minimum score 600 paper-based; 90 iBT), IELTS (minimum score 7). Electronic applications accepted.

University of Washington, Graduate School, College of Education, Seattle, WA 98195. Offers curriculum and instruction (M Ed, Ed D, PhD), including educational technology, general curriculum (Ed D, PhD), language, literacy, and culture, mathematics education, multicultural education, reading and language arts education (Ed D), science education, social studies education, teaching and curriculum (M Ed); educational leadership and policy studies (M Ed, Ed D, PhD), including administration (Ed D), educational policy, organization, and leadership (M Ed, PhD), higher education, leadership for learning (Ed D), social and cultural foundations of education (M Ed, PhD); educational psychology (M Ed, PhD), including educational psychology (PhD), human development and cognition (M Ed), learning sciences, measurement, statistics and research design (M Ed), school psychology (M Ed); instructional leadership (M Ed); intercollegiate athletic leadership (M Ed); special education (M Ed, Ed D, PhD), including early childhood special education (M Ed), emotional and behavioral disabilities (M Ed), learning disabilities (M Ed), low-incidence disabilities (M Ed), severe disabilities (M Ed), special education (Ed D, PhD); teacher education (MIT). *Accreditation:* APA. *Program availability:* Part-time, evening/weekend. *Degree requirements:* For master's, thesis optional; for doctorate, thesis/dissertation. *Entrance requirements:* For master's and doctorate, GRE General Test, minimum GPA of 3.0. Additional exam requirements/recommendations for international students: Required—TOEFL. Electronic applications accepted. *Faculty research:* School restructuring/effective schools, special education interventions, literacy and writing, technology, school partnerships, teacher preparation.

The University of Western Ontario, School of Graduate and Postdoctoral Studies, Faculty of Social Science, Faculty of Education, Program in Educational Studies, London, ON N6A 3K7, Canada. Offers curriculum studies (M Ed); educational policy studies (M Ed); educational psychology/special education (M Ed). *Program availability:* Part-time. *Faculty research:* Reflective practice, gender and schooling, feminist pedagogy, narrative inquiry, second language, multiculturalism in Canada, education and law.

University of Wisconsin–Madison, Graduate School, School of Education, Department of Educational Leadership and Policy Analysis, Madison, WI 53706-1380. Offers administration (Certificate); educational policy (MS, PhD); global higher education (MS). *Degree requirements:* For doctorate, thesis/dissertation. *Entrance requirements:* For master's and doctorate, GRE General Test. Electronic applications accepted.

University of Wisconsin–Madison, Graduate School, School of Education, Department of Educational Policy Studies, Madison, WI 53706-1380. Offers MA, PhD. *Degree requirements:* For doctorate, thesis/dissertation. *Entrance requirements:* For master's and doctorate, GRE General Test. Electronic applications accepted.

University of Wisconsin–Milwaukee, Graduate School, School of Education, Department of Educational Policy and Community Studies, Milwaukee, WI 53201-0413. Offers cultural foundations of community engagement and education (MS), including alternative education, community engagement and partnerships, educational policy, race relations, youth work; educational policy (Graduate Certificate). *Program availability:* Part-time. *Students:* 8 full-time (7 women), 30 part-time (25 women); includes 18 minority (8 Black or African American, non-Hispanic/Latino; 3 American Indian or Alaska Native, non-Hispanic/Latino; 7 Two or more races, non-Hispanic/Latino). Average age 35. 25 applicants, 44% accepted, 5 enrolled. In 2018, 12 master's awarded. *Entrance requirements:* Additional exam requirements/recommendations for international students: Required—TOEFL (minimum score 550 paper-based; 79 iBT), IELTS (minimum score 6.5). *Application deadline:* For fall admission, 1/1 priority date for domestic students; for spring admission, 9/1 for domestic students. Application fee: $56 ($96 for international students). Electronic applications accepted. *Financial support:* Fellowships with full tuition reimbursements, research assistantships, teaching assistantships, career-related internships or fieldwork, health care benefits, and unspecified assistantships available. Support available to part-time students. Financial award application deadline: 4/15; financial award applicants required to submit FAFSA. *Application contact:* General Information Contact, 414-229-4721, E-mail: soeinfo@uwm.edu.
Website: http://uwm.edu/education/academics/edu-policy-community-studies-department/

Virginia Polytechnic Institute and State University, Graduate School, College of Liberal Arts and Human Sciences, Blacksburg, VA 24061. Offers career and technical education (MS Ed, Ed S); communication (MA); counselor education (MA); creative writing (MFA); curriculum and instruction (MA Ed, Ed S); educational leadership and policy studies (Ed S); educational research and evaluation (PhD); English (MA); social, political, ethical, and cultural thought (PhD); Ed D/PhD. *Faculty:* 420 full-time (221 women), 1 (woman) part-time/adjunct. *Students:* 603 full-time (428 women), 359 part-time (237 women); includes 189 minority (107 Black or African American, non-Hispanic/Latino; 4 American Indian or Alaska Native, non-Hispanic/Latino; 24 Asian, non-Hispanic/Latino; 27 Hispanic/Latino; 2 Native Hawaiian or other Pacific Islander, non-Hispanic/Latino; 25 Two or more races, non-Hispanic/Latino), 84 international. Average age 33. 856 applicants, 48% accepted, 262 enrolled. In 2018, 270 master's, 63 doctorates awarded. *Degree requirements:* For master's, comprehensive exam (for some programs), thesis (for some programs); for doctorate, comprehensive exam (for some programs), thesis/dissertation (for some programs). *Entrance requirements:* For master's and doctorate, GRE/GMAT. Additional exam requirements/recommendations for international students: Required—TOEFL (minimum score 90 iBT). *Application deadline:* For fall admission, 8/1 for domestic students, 4/1 for international students; for spring admission, 1/1 for domestic students, 9/1 for international students. Applications are processed on a rolling basis. Application fee: $75. Electronic applications accepted. *Expenses:* Tuition, state resident: full-time $15,510; part-time $739.50 per credit hour. Tuition, nonresident: full-time $29,629; part-time $1490.25 per credit hour. *Required fees:* $2804; $550 per semester. Tuition and fees vary according to course load, campus/location and program. *Financial support:* In 2018–19, 4 fellowships with full tuition reimbursements (averaging $23,122 per year), 28 research assistantships with full tuition reimbursements (averaging $15,605 per year), 245 teaching assistantships with full tuition reimbursements (averaging $16,046 per year) were awarded; scholarships/grants and unspecified assistantships also available. Financial award application deadline: 3/1; financial award applicants required to submit FAFSA. *Total annual research expenditures:* $7.5 million. *Unit head:* Dr. Laura Belmonte, Dean, 540-231-6779, Fax: 540-231-7157, E-mail: belmonte@vt.edu. *Application contact:* Chelsea Blanchet, Executive Assistant, 540-231-6779, Fax: 540-231-7157, E-mail: bchels1@vt.edu.
Website: http://www.liberalarts.vt.edu/

Wayne State University, College of Education, Division of Administrative and Organizational Studies, Detoit, MI 48202. Offers educational administration and supervision (Ed S); educational leadership (M Ed); educational leadership and policy studies (Ed D, PhD); educational technology (Certificate); learning design and technology (M Ed, Ed D, PhD, Ed S); online teaching (Certificate). *Program availability:* Part-time, evening/weekend. *Faculty:* 9. *Students:* 77 full-time (53 women), 223 part-time (160 women); includes 155 minority (126 Black or African American, non-Hispanic/Latino; 7 Asian, non-Hispanic/Latino; 11 Hispanic/Latino; 1 Native Hawaiian or other Pacific Islander, non-Hispanic/Latino; 10 Two or more races, non-Hispanic/Latino), 9 international. Average age 39. 239 applicants, 33% accepted, 58 enrolled. In 2018, 51 master's, 10 doctorates, 54 other advanced degrees awarded. *Degree requirements:* For master's, thesis (for some programs), GPA 3.0; for doctorate, comprehensive exam, thesis/dissertation, GPA 3.0; for other advanced degree, GPA 3.0. *Entrance requirements:* For master's, baccalaureate degree from accredited U.S. institution or equivalent from college or university of government-recognized standing; minimum undergraduate GPA of 2.75 in upper-division coursework; personal statement; for doctorate, GRE (instructional design and technology), interview; curriculum vitae; three to four recommendations; master's degree (for educational leadership and policy studies); minimum graduate GPA of 3.5; autobiographical statement; research experience (for PhD program); for other advanced degree, educational specialist certificate requirement include undergraduate and master's degrees (for both learning design and technology and administration and supervision); minimum graduate GPA of 3.4, and personal statement. Additional exam requirements/recommendations for international students: Required—TOEFL (minimum score 550 paper-based; 79 iBT); Recommended—IELTS (minimum score 6.5), TWE (minimum score 5.5), TSE (minimum score 58). *Application deadline:* Applications are processed on a rolling basis. Application fee: $50. Electronic applications accepted. *Financial support:* In 2018–19, 87 students received support, including 1 fellowship with tuition reimbursement available (averaging $20,000 per year), 4 research assistantships with tuition reimbursements available (averaging $19,267 per year); scholarships/grants and unspecified assistantships also available. Support available to part-time students. Financial award applicants required to submit FAFSA. *Faculty research:* Total quality management, participatory management, administering educational technology, school improvement, principalship. *Unit head:* Dr. William Hill, Assistant Dean, 313-577-9316, E-mail: ad2107@wayne.edu. *Application contact:* Dr. Mary L. Waker, Graduate Admissions Officer, 313-577-1601, Fax: 313-577-7904, E-mail: m.waker@wayne.edu.
Website: http://coe.wayne.edu/aos/index.php

West Chester University of Pennsylvania, College of Education and Social Work, Department of Educational Foundations and Policy Studies, West Chester, PA 19383. Offers education for sustainability (Certificate); educational technology (Certificate); higher education policy and student affairs (MS); transformative education and social change (MS). *Program availability:* Part-time. *Degree requirements:* For master's, comprehensive exam (for some programs), thesis, 36 credits (42 credits for MS in higher education policy and student affairs). *Entrance requirements:* For master's, teaching certification (strongly recommended); for Certificate, minimum GPA of 3.0. Additional exam requirements/recommendations for international students: Required—TOEFL or IELTS. Electronic applications accepted. *Faculty research:* Technology integration: preparing our teachers for the twenty-first century, critical pedagogy, education for sustainability.

West Chester University of Pennsylvania, College of Education and Social Work, Program in Policy, Planning, and Administration, West Chester, PA 19383. Offers Ed D. *Program availability:* Part-time, evening/weekend, online only, 100% online. *Degree requirements:* For doctorate, comprehensive exam. *Entrance requirements:* For doctorate, GRE if master's GPA lower than 3.85, master's degree from regionally-

accredited college or university, three letters of recommendation from education professionals, professional writing demonstration at time of application (waived for applicants who present GRE analytical writing score of 4.5 or higher), resume or curriculum vitae, interview (upon committee request). Additional exam requirements/

recommendations for international students: Required—TOEFL or IELTS. Electronic applications accepted. *Expenses:* Contact institution. *Faculty research:* Literacy, special education, critical pedagogy, social and cultural foundations of education, educational technology.

Educational Psychology

Alliant International University–Irvine, Shirley M. Hufstedler School of Education, Educational Psychology Programs, Irvine, CA 92606. Offers educational psychology (Psy D); pupil personnel services (Credential); school psychology (MA). *Program availability:* Part-time. *Degree requirements:* For doctorate, thesis/dissertation. *Entrance requirements:* For master's, minimum GPA of 2.5, letters of recommendation; for doctorate, interview, minimum GPA of 3.0, letters of recommendation. Additional exam requirements/recommendations for international students: Required—TOEFL (minimum score 550 paper-based; 80 iBT), TWE (minimum score 5). *Faculty research:* School-based mental health.

Alliant International University–Los Angeles, Shirley M. Hufstedler School of Education, Educational Psychology Programs, Alhambra, CA 91803. Offers educational psychology (Psy D); pupil personnel services (Credential); school psychology (MA). *Program availability:* Part-time. *Degree requirements:* For doctorate, comprehensive exam, thesis/dissertation. *Entrance requirements:* For master's, minimum GPA of 2.5, letters of recommendation; for doctorate, interview, minimum GPA of 3.0, letters of recommendation. Additional exam requirements/recommendations for international students: Required—TOEFL (minimum score 550 paper-based), TWE (minimum score 5). Electronic applications accepted. *Faculty research:* Early identification and intervention with high-risk preschoolers, pediatric neuropsychology, interpersonal violence, ADHD, learning theories.

Alliant International University–San Diego, Shirley M. Hufstedler School of Education, Educational Psychology Programs, San Diego, CA 92131. Offers educational psychology (Psy D); pupil personnel services (Credential); school neuropsychology (Certificate); school psychology (MA); school-based mental health (Certificate). *Program availability:* Part-time. *Degree requirements:* For doctorate, comprehensive exam, thesis/dissertation, internship. *Entrance requirements:* For master's, minimum GPA of 2.5, letters of recommendation; for doctorate, minimum GPA of 3.0, letters of recommendation. Additional exam requirements/recommendations for international students: Required—TOEFL (minimum score 550 paper-based; 80 iBT), TWE (minimum score 5). Electronic applications accepted. *Faculty research:* School-based mental health, pupil personnel services, childhood mood, school-based assessment.

Alliant International University–San Francisco, Shirley M. Hufstedler School of Education, Educational Psychology Programs, San Francisco, CA 94133. Offers educational psychology (Psy D); pupil personnel services (Credential); school psychology (MA). *Program availability:* Part-time. Terminal master's awarded for partial completion of doctoral program. *Degree requirements:* For doctorate, thesis/dissertation. *Entrance requirements:* For master's, minimum GPA of 3.0, letters of recommendation; for doctorate, interview, minimum GPA of 3.0, letters of recommendation. Additional exam requirements/recommendations for international students: Required—TOEFL (minimum score 550 paper-based), TWE (minimum score 5). Electronic applications accepted. *Faculty research:* Social skills, ADHD, cognitive functioning and learning, innovative teaching methods.

American International College, School of Business, Arts and Sciences, Springfield, MA 01109-3189. Offers accounting and taxation (MS); business administration (MBA); clinical psychology (MA); educational psychology (Ed D); forensic psychology (MS); general psychology (MA, CAGS); management (CAGS); resort and casino management (MBA, CAGS). *Program availability:* Part-time, evening/weekend. *Degree requirements:* For master's, practicum; for doctorate, comprehensive exam, thesis/dissertation, practicum. *Entrance requirements:* For master's, BS or BA, minimum undergraduate GPA of 2.75, 2 letters of recommendation, official transcripts, personal goal statement or essay; for doctorate, 3 letters of recommendation; BS or BA; minimum undergraduate GPA of 3.0 (3.25 recommended); official transcripts; personal goal statement or essay. Additional exam requirements/recommendations for international students: Required—TOEFL (minimum score 550 paper-based; 80 iBT). *Expenses:* Contact institution. *Faculty research:* Substance abuse, forensic psychology, special education.

Andrews University, School of Graduate Studies, School of Education, Department of Graduate Psychology and Counseling, Program in Educational and Developmental Psychology, Berrien Springs, MI 49104. Offers educational and developmental psychology (MA); educational psychology (Ed D, PhD). *Degree requirements:* For master's, thesis optional. *Entrance requirements:* For master's, GRE. Additional exam requirements/recommendations for international students: Required—TOEFL (minimum score 550 paper-based).

Ball State University, Graduate School, Teachers College, Department of Educational Psychology, Program in Educational Psychology, Muncie, IN 47306. Offers MA, MS, PhD. *Accreditation:* NCATE. *Program availability:* Part-time, 100% online. *Entrance requirements:* For master's, GRE General Test (for MS only), minimum baccalaureate GPA of 2.75 or 3.0 in latter half of baccalaureate; for doctorate, GRE General Test, minimum graduate GPA of 3.2. Additional exam requirements/recommendations for international students: Required—TOEFL (minimum score 550 paper-based; 79 iBT), IELTS (minimum score 6.5). Electronic applications accepted.

Ball State University, Graduate School, Teachers College, Department of Educational Psychology, Program in Quantitative Psychology, Muncie, IN 47306. Offers MS. *Program availability:* Online learning. *Entrance requirements:* For master's, official transcripts, minimum GPA of 2.75. Electronic applications accepted.

Baylor University, Graduate School, School of Education, Department of Educational Psychology, Waco, TX 76798. Offers educational psychology (MS Ed); exceptionalities (PhD); learning and development (PhD); quantitative methods (MA); school psychology (Ed S). *Accreditation:* NCATE. *Students:* 51 full-time (46 women), 9 part-time (8 women); includes 18 minority (1 Black or African American, non-Hispanic/Latino; 3 Asian, non-Hispanic/Latino; 11 Hispanic/Latino; 3 Two or more races, non-Hispanic/Latino), 4 international. Average age 29. 90 applicants, 33% accepted, 30 enrolled. In 2018, 21 master's, 1 doctorate, 9 other advanced degrees awarded. Terminal master's awarded for partial completion of doctoral program. *Degree requirements:* For master's, thesis optional; for doctorate, comprehensive exam, thesis/dissertation; for Ed S, comprehensive exam, thesis or alternative. *Entrance requirements:* For master's, GRE, minimum GPA of 3.0; for doctorate, GRE General Test, master's degree; for Ed S, GRE General Test. Additional exam requirements/recommendations for international

students: Required—TOEFL (minimum score 550 paper-based; 80 iBT), IELTS (minimum score 6.5). *Application deadline:* For fall admission, 2/1 priority date for domestic and international students. Application fee: $80. Electronic applications accepted. *Financial support:* In 2018–19, 42 students received support, including 20 fellowships with full and partial tuition reimbursements available, 22 research assistantships with full and partial tuition reimbursements available; career-related internships or fieldwork, Federal Work-Study, institutionally sponsored loans, scholarships/grants, health care benefits, tuition waivers (full and partial), unspecified assistantships, and stipends also available. Financial award application deadline: 2/1; financial award applicants required to submit FAFSA. *Faculty research:* Individual differences, quantitative methods, gifted and talented, special education, school psychology, autism, applied behavior analysis, learning, human development. *Total annual research expenditures:* $300,000. *Unit head:* Dr. Susan K. Johnsen, Professor and Interim Chair, 254-710-6116, E-mail: susan_johnsen@baylor.edu. *Application contact:* Heather Tindle, Office Manager, 254-710-3112, E-mail: heather_tindle@baylor.edu.
Website: http://www.baylor.edu/soe/EDP/

Boston College, Lynch School of Education and Human Development, Department of Counseling, Developmental, and Educational Psychology, Chestnut Hill, MA 02467-3800. Offers applied developmental and education psychology (MA, PhD); counseling psychology (PhD); mental health counseling (MA); school counseling (MA); theology and ministry and counseling (MA/MA); MA/MA. *Accreditation:* APA (one or more programs are accredited). *Program availability:* Part-time, evening/weekend. *Faculty:* 27 full-time (20 women). *Students:* 219 full-time (167 women), 23 part-time (19 women); includes 70 minority (17 Black or African American, non-Hispanic/Latino; 1 American Indian or Alaska Native, non-Hispanic/Latino; 18 Asian, non-Hispanic/Latino; 25 Hispanic/Latino; 9 Two or more races, non-Hispanic/Latino), 41 international. Average age 26. In 2018, 71 master's, 10 doctorates awarded. Terminal master's awarded for partial completion of doctoral program. *Degree requirements:* For master's, comprehensive exam; for doctorate, comprehensive exam, thesis/dissertation. Application fee: $75. Electronic applications accepted. *Financial support:* Fellowships with full and partial tuition reimbursements, research assistantships with full and partial tuition reimbursements, teaching assistantships with full and partial tuition reimbursements, career-related internships or fieldwork, Federal Work-Study, scholarships/grants, traineeships, health care benefits, tuition waivers (full and partial), and unspecified assistantships available. Support available to part-time students. Financial award applicants required to submit FAFSA. *Faculty research:* Gender, racial and social class differences; psychopathological disorders; impact of violence, community well-being and social justice, psychology of working; child development within impoverished and dangerous contexts. *Unit head:* Dr. Rebekah Levine Coley, Chairperson, 617-552-4214, Fax: 617-552-0812. *Application contact:* Jessica Rivers, Assistant Dean, Graduate Admissions and Financial Aid, 617-552-4214, Fax: 617-552-0398, E-mail: riversja@bc.edu.
Website: http://www.bc.edu/education

California Coast University, School of Education, Santa Ana, CA 92701. Offers administration (M Ed); curriculum and instruction (M Ed); educational administration (Ed D); educational psychology (Ed D); organizational leadership (Ed D). *Program availability:* Online learning.

California State University, Long Beach, Graduate Studies, College of Education, Department of Advanced Studies in Education and Counseling, Long Beach, CA 90840. Offers counseling (MS), including marriage and family therapy, school counseling, student development in higher education; education (MA, Ed D); educational administration (MA, Ed D); educational psychology (MA); special education (MS). *Program availability:* Part-time, evening/weekend. *Entrance requirements:* For master's, GRE General Test, minimum GPA of 2.75. *Application deadline:* For fall admission, 3/1 for domestic students. Applications are processed on a rolling basis. Application fee: $55. Electronic applications accepted. *Expenses: Required fees:* $2628 per term. Tuition and fees vary according to class time, course level, course load, degree level, campus/location and program. *Financial support:* Federal Work-Study, institutionally sponsored loans, and scholarships/grants available. Financial award application deadline: 3/2; financial award applicants required to submit FAFSA. *Unit head:* Dr. Hiromi Masunaga, Chair, 562-985-4517, E-mail: asec@csulb.edu. *Application contact:* Dr. Hiromi Masunaga, Chair, 562-985-4517, E-mail: asec@csulb.edu.
Website: http://www.csulb.edu/college-of-education/advanced-studies-education-and-counseling

California State University, Northridge, Graduate Studies, Michael D. Eisner College of Education, Department of Educational Psychology and Counseling, Northridge, CA 91330. Offers counseling (MS), including career counseling, college counseling and student services, marriage and family therapy, school counseling, school psychology; educational psychology (MA Ed), including development, learning, and instruction, early childhood education. *Accreditation:* ACA (one or more programs are accredited); NCATE. *Program availability:* Part-time, evening/weekend. *Entrance requirements:* For master's, GRE General Test or minimum GPA of 3.0. Additional exam requirements/recommendations for international students: Required—TOEFL.

Capella University, Harold Abel School of Social and Behavioral Science, Doctoral Programs in Psychology, Minneapolis, MN 55402. Offers addiction psychology (PhD); clinical psychology (Psy D); educational psychology (PhD); general advanced studies in human behavior (PhD); general psychology (PhD); industrial/organizational psychology (PhD); school psychology (Psy D).

Capella University, Harold Abel School of Social and Behavioral Science, Master's Programs in Psychology, Minneapolis, MN 55402. Offers applied behavior analysis (MS); clinical psychology (MS); counseling psychology (MS); educational psychology (MS); evaluation, research, and measurement (MS); general advanced studies in human behavior (MS); general psychology (MS); industrial/organizational psychology (MS); leadership coaching psychology (MS); school psychology (MS); sport psychology (MS).

Chapman University, Donna Ford Attallah College of Educational Studies, Orange, CA 92866. Offers counseling (MA), including school counseling (MA, Credential); curriculum

and instruction (MA), including elementary education, secondary education; education (PhD), including cultural and curricular studies, disability studies, leadership studies, school psychology (PhD, Credential); educational psychology (MA); leadership development (MA); multiple subjects (Credential), including Spanish/English bilingual; pupil personnel services (Credential), including school counseling (MA, Credential); school psychology (PhD, Credential); school psychology (Ed S); single subject (Credential); special education (MA, Credential), including mild/moderate (Credential), moderate/severe (Credential); teaching (MA), including elementary education, secondary education, secondary music education. *Accreditation:* TEAC. *Program availability:* Part-time, evening/weekend. Electronic applications accepted. *Expenses:* Contact institution.

Clark Atlanta University, School of Education, Department of Counseling and Psychological Studies, Atlanta, GA 30314. Offers MA. *Accreditation:* ACA. *Program availability:* Part-time. *Degree requirements:* For master's, comprehensive exam. *Entrance requirements:* For master's, GRE General Test, minimum undergraduate GPA of 2.6. Additional exam requirements/recommendations for international students: Required—TOEFL (minimum score 500 paper-based; 61 iBT). Electronic applications accepted.

The College of Saint Rose, Graduate Studies, Thelma P. Lally School of Education, Educational and School Psychology Programs, Albany, NY 12203-1419. Offers educational psychology (MS Ed, Certificate); school psychology (MS Ed). *Students:* 44 full-time (40 women), 14 part-time (13 women); includes 5 minority (1 Black or African American, non-Hispanic/Latino; 1 Asian, non-Hispanic/Latino; 1 Hispanic/Latino; 2 Two or more races, non-Hispanic/Latino). Average age 24. 66 applicants, 70% accepted, 24 enrolled. In 2018, 23 master's, 16 Certificates awarded. *Entrance requirements:* For master's, minimum undergraduate GPA of 3.0. Additional exam requirements/ recommendations for international students: Required—TOEFL (minimum score 550 paper-based; 80 iBT), IELTS (minimum score 6), PTE (minimum score 56). *Application deadline:* For fall admission, 2/15 priority date for domestic and international students. Applications are processed on a rolling basis. Application fee: $40. Electronic applications accepted. *Expenses:* Tuition: Full-time $14,382; part-time $799 per credit hour. *Required fees:* $924; $408 per credit. $286. *Financial support:* Career-related internships or fieldwork, scholarships/grants, tuition waivers (partial), and unspecified assistantships available. Support available to part-time students. Financial award application deadline: 4/15. *Unit head:* Dr. Andrew Shanock, Chair, 518-337-5694, E-mail: shanocka@strose.edu. *Application contact:* Daniel Gallagher, Assistant Vice President for Graduate Recruitment and Enrollment, 518-485-3390, Fax: 518-458-5479, E-mail: grad@strose.edu.
Website: https://www.strose.edu/school-psychology/

Eastern Michigan University, Graduate School, College of Education, Department of Teacher Education, Programs in Educational Psychology and Assessment, Ypsilanti, MI 48197. Offers educational assessment (Graduate Certificate); learning technology and design (MA). *Accreditation:* NCATE. *Program availability:* Part-time, evening/weekend, online learning. *Students:* 35 part-time (29 women); includes 6 minority (1 Black or African American, non-Hispanic/Latino; 3 Hispanic/Latino; 2 Two or more races, non-Hispanic/Latino). Average age 30. 22 applicants, 86% accepted, 9 enrolled. In 2018, 7 master's, 1 other advanced degree awarded. *Entrance requirements:* For master's, GRE. Additional exam requirements/recommendations for international students: Required—TOEFL. *Application deadline:* Applications are processed on a rolling basis. Application fee: $45. *Financial support:* Fellowships, research assistantships with full tuition reimbursements, teaching assistantships with full tuition reimbursements, career-related internships or fieldwork, Federal Work-Study, institutionally sponsored loans, scholarships/grants, tuition waivers (partial), and unspecified assistantships available. Support available to part-time students. Financial award applicants required to submit FAFSA. *Application contact:* Dr. Alane Starko, Coordinator, 734-487-2789, Fax: 734-487-2101, E-mail: astarko@emich.edu.

Edinboro University of Pennsylvania, Department of Counseling, School Psychology and Special Education, Edinboro, PA 16444. Offers counseling (MA), including art therapy, clinical mental health counseling, college counseling, rehabilitation counseling, school counseling; educational psychology (M Ed); school psychology (Ed S); special education (M Ed), including autism, behavior management. *Accreditation:* ACA. *Program availability:* Part-time, evening/weekend. *Degree requirements:* For master's, thesis or alternative, competency exam; for Ed S, thesis or alternative. *Entrance requirements:* For master's and Ed S, GRE or MAT, minimum QPA of 2.5. Electronic applications accepted.

Florida State University, The Graduate School, College of Education, Department of Educational Psychology and Learning Systems, Tallahassee, FL 32306. Offers counseling and human systems (PhD, MS/Ed S), including mental health counseling (MS/Ed S), school psychology (MS/Ed S); educational psychology (MS, PhD); human performance and technology (Certificate); instructional systems and learning technologies (MS, PhD); measurement and statistics (MS, PhD, Certificate); online instructional development (Certificate); MS/Ed S. *Program availability:* Part-time, evening/weekend, 100% online, blended/hybrid learning, asynchronous, minimal on-campus study. *Faculty:* 27 full-time (17 women), 8 part-time/adjunct (4 women). *Students:* 210 full-time (145 women), 122 part-time (89 women); includes 146 minority (39 Black or African American, non-Hispanic/Latino; 1 American Indian or Alaska Native, non-Hispanic/Latino; 51 Asian, non-Hispanic/Latino; 36 Hispanic/Latino; 19 Two or more races, non-Hispanic/Latino), 68 international. Average age 32. 419 applicants, 39% accepted, 82 enrolled. In 2018, 84 master's, 27 doctorates, 38 other advanced degrees awarded. Terminal master's awarded for partial completion of doctoral program. *Degree requirements:* For master's and Certificate, comprehensive exam, thesis optional; for doctorate, comprehensive exam, thesis/dissertation, diagnostic exam, preliminary exam, prospectus defense. *Entrance requirements:* For master's, doctorate, and Certificate, GRE General Test, minimum GPA of 3.0. Additional exam requirements/recommendations for international students: Required—TOEFL (minimum score 550 paper-based, 80 iBT), IELTS (minimum score 6.5) or Michigan English Language Assessment Battery (minimum score 77). Application fee: $30. Electronic applications accepted. *Expenses: Tuition, area resident:* Part-time $479.32 per credit hour. Tuition and fees vary according to campus/location and program. *Financial support:* In 2018–19, 8 research assistantships with partial tuition reimbursements (averaging $6,640 per year), 42 teaching assistantships with partial tuition reimbursements (averaging $6,740 per year) were awarded. Financial award application deadline: 1/15; financial award applicants required to submit FAFSA. *Faculty research:* Learning and cognition, counseling and school psychology, instructional systems, measurement and evaluation. *Unit head:* Dr. James Klein, Chair, 850-644-4592, Fax: 850-644-8776, E-mail: jklein@fsu.edu. *Application contact:* Mary Kate McKee, Academic Program Specialist, 850-644-8046, Fax: 850-644-8781, E-mail: mmckee@campus.fsu.edu.

Fordham University, Graduate School of Arts and Sciences, Department of Psychology, Program in Psychometrics and Quantitative Psychology, New York, NY 10458. Offers PhD. *Students:* 10 full-time (8 women), 2 part-time (both women); includes 4 minority (1 Black or African American, non-Hispanic/Latino; 3 Asian, non-Hispanic/Latino), 7 international. Average age 33. 21 applicants, 43% accepted, 2 enrolled. In 2018, 1 doctorate awarded. *Degree requirements:* For doctorate,

comprehensive exam, thesis/dissertation. *Entrance requirements:* For doctorate, GRE General Test. Additional exam requirements/recommendations for international students: Required—TOEFL (minimum score 600 paper-based). *Application deadline:* For fall admission, 12/14 for domestic students. Application fee: $70. Electronic applications accepted. *Financial support:* In 2018–19, 16 students received support, including 3 fellowships with tuition reimbursements available (averaging $25,870 per year), 1 research assistantship with tuition reimbursement available (averaging $24,130 per year), 2 teaching assistantships with tuition reimbursements available (averaging $7,950 per year); career-related internships or fieldwork, institutionally sponsored loans, tuition waivers (full and partial), and unspecified assistantships also available. Financial award application deadline: 12/14; financial award applicants required to submit FAFSA. *Faculty research:* Applications of Bayesian statistics, ethnic identity, hierarchical linear models. *Unit head:* Dr. Barry Rosenfeld, Department Chair, 718-817-3794, Fax: 718-817-3785, E-mail: rosenfeld@fordham.edu. *Application contact:* Garrett Marino, Director of Graduate Admissions, 718-817-4419, Fax: 718-817-3566, E-mail: gmarino10@fordham.edu.

Fordham University, Graduate School of Education, Division of Psychological and Educational Services, New York, NY 10023. Offers counseling and personnel services (MSE); counseling psychology (PhD); school psychology (PhD). *Accreditation:* APA (one or more programs are accredited); NCATE. *Program availability:* Part-time, evening/weekend. Terminal master's awarded for partial completion of doctoral program. *Degree requirements:* For master's, comprehensive exam (for some programs); for doctorate, comprehensive exam (for some programs), thesis/dissertation. *Entrance requirements:* For doctorate, GRE General Test. Additional exam requirements/recommendations for international students: Required—TOEFL (minimum score 577 paper-based; 90 iBT), IELTS (minimum score 7). Electronic applications accepted.

George Mason University, College of Education and Human Development, Program in Educational Psychology, Fairfax, VA 22030. Offers assessment, evaluation, and testing (MS); learning and decision-making in leadership (MS); learning, cognition, and motivation (MS); teacher preparation (MS). *Program availability:* Part-time. *Faculty:* 6 full-time (5 women), 2 part-time/adjunct (both women). *Students:* 27 full-time (19 women), 36 part-time (30 women); includes 18 minority (10 Black or African American, non-Hispanic/Latino; 4 Asian, non-Hispanic/Latino; 3 Hispanic/Latino; 1 Native Hawaiian or other Pacific Islander, non-Hispanic/Latino), 16 international. Average age 29. 29 applicants, 86% accepted, 16 enrolled. In 2018, 11 master's awarded. *Entrance requirements:* For master's, GRE, official transcripts; 3 letters of recommendation; expanded goals statement. Additional exam requirements/recommendations for international students: Required—TOEFL (minimum score 575 paper-based; 80 iBT), IELTS (minimum score 6.5), PTE (minimum score 59). *Application deadline:* For fall admission, 4/2 priority date for domestic and international students; for spring admission, 11/1 priority date for domestic and international students. Application fee: $75 ($80 for international students). Electronic applications accepted. *Expenses:* $489 per credit in-state tuition; $1,346.75 per credit out-of-state tuition (discounted to $689 per credit). *Financial support:* In 2018–19, 1 student received support, including 1 research assistantship with tuition reimbursement available; career-related internships or fieldwork, Federal Work-Study, scholarships/grants, unspecified assistantships, and health care benefits (for full-time research or teaching assistantship recipients) also available. Support available to part-time students. Financial award application deadline: 3/1; financial award applicants required to submit FAFSA. *Faculty research:* Learning, cognition, motivation measurement, evaluation assessment, educational policy. *Unit head:* Erin Peters-Burton, Academic Program Coordinator, 703-993-9695, Fax: 703-993-3678, E-mail: epeters1@gmu.edu. *Application contact:* Kim Howe, Office Manager, 703-993-3679, Fax: 703-993-3678, E-mail: khowe1@gmu.edu.
Website: http://gse.gmu.edu/programs/edpsych/

Georgia State University, College of Education and Human Development, Department of Learning Sciences, Program in Educational Psychology, Atlanta, GA 30302-3083. Offers MS, PhD. *Accreditation:* NCATE. *Program availability:* Part-time, evening/weekend, online learning. *Entrance requirements:* For master's and doctorate, GRE. *Application deadline:* Applications are processed on a rolling basis. Application fee: $50. Electronic applications accepted. *Expenses: Tuition, area resident:* Full-time $9360; part-time $390 per credit hour. Tuition, state resident: full-time $9360; part-time $390 per credit hour. Tuition, nonresident: full-time $30,024; part-time $1251 per credit hour. *International tuition:* $30,024 full-time. *Required fees:* $2128. *Financial support:* Fellowships, research assistantships, teaching assistantships, institutionally sponsored loans, scholarships/grants, tuition waivers, and unspecified assistantships available. Financial award applicants required to submit FAFSA. *Faculty research:* Language and literacy, social emotional development, cognitive development, applied behavior analysis, motivation and metacognition. *Unit head:* Dr. Miles Anthony Irving, Program Coordinator, 404-413-3808, E-mail: iam@gsu.edu. *Application contact:* Sandy Vaughn, Senior Administrative Coordinator, 404-413-8318, E-mail: svaughn@gsu.edu.
Website: https://education.gsu.edu/program/ms-educational-psychology/

The Graduate Center, City University of New York, Graduate Studies, Program in Educational Psychology, New York, NY 10016-4039. Offers PhD. *Accreditation:* APA. *Degree requirements:* For doctorate, 2 foreign languages, thesis/dissertation. *Entrance requirements:* For doctorate, GRE General Test, interview, minimum GPA of 3.0. Additional exam requirements/recommendations for international students: Required—TOEFL. Electronic applications accepted.

Harvard University, Harvard Graduate School of Education, Master's Programs in Education, Cambridge, MA 02138. Offers arts in education (Ed M); education policy and management (Ed M); higher education (Ed M); human development and psychology (Ed M); international education policy (Ed M); language and literacy (Ed M); learning and teaching (Ed M); mind, brain, and education (Ed M); prevention science and practice (Ed M); school leadership (Ed M); special studies (Ed M); teacher education (Ed M); technology, innovation, and education (Ed M). *Program availability:* Part-time. *Entrance requirements:* For master's, GRE General Test, statement of purpose, 3 letters of recommendation, resume, official transcripts. Additional exam requirements/recommendations for international students: Required—TOEFL (minimum score 613 paper-based; 104 iBT), TWE (minimum score 5). Electronic applications accepted. *Faculty research:* Learning and development, educational leadership and organizations, education policy analysis.

Holy Names University, Graduate Division, Department of Education, Oakland, CA 94619-1699. Offers educational therapy (Certificate); mild/moderate disabilities (Ed S); multiple subject teaching (Credential); single subject teaching (Credential); urban education: educational therapy (M Ed); urban education: K-12 education (M Ed); urban education: special education (M Ed). *Program availability:* Part-time. *Students:* 28 full-time (18 women), 63 part-time (45 women); includes 48 minority (22 Black or African American, non-Hispanic/Latino; 1 American Indian or Alaska Native, non-Hispanic/Latino; 3 Asian, non-Hispanic/Latino; 21 Hispanic/Latino; 1 Two or more races, non-Hispanic/Latino), 5 international. Average age 35. 69 applicants, 86% accepted, 34 enrolled. In 2018, 11 master's, 33 Certificates awarded. *Degree requirements:* For master's, comprehensive exam, research paper, thesis or project. *Entrance requirements:* For master's, minimum undergraduate GPA of 2.6 overall, 3.0 in major;

personal statement; two recommendations; interview. Additional exam requirements/recommendations for international students: Required—TOEFL (minimum score 550 paper-based; 79 iBT). *Application deadline:* For fall admission, 8/1 priority date for domestic students, 7/15 for international students; for spring admission, 12/1 priority date for domestic students, 12/1 for international students; for summer admission, 5/1 priority date for domestic students, 5/1 for international students. Applications are processed on a rolling basis. Application fee: $65. Electronic applications accepted. Application fee is waived when completed online. *Expenses: Required fees:* $1003. *Financial support:* Career-related internships or fieldwork, Federal Work-Study, scholarships/grants, and unspecified assistantships available. Support available to part-time students. Financial award application deadline: 3/2; financial award applicants required to submit FAFSA. *Faculty research:* Cognitive development, language development, learning handicaps. *Unit head:* Dr. Kimberly Mayfield, Chair, 510-436-1396, Fax: 510-436-1325, E-mail: mayfield@hnu.edu. *Application contact:* Graduate Admission, 800-430-1321, Fax: 510-436-1325, E-mail: graduateadmissions@hnu.edu. Website: http://www.hnu.edu/academics/graduatePrograms/education.html

Howard University, School of Education, Department of Human Development and Psychoeducational Studies, Program in Educational Psychology, Washington, DC 20059-0002. Offers PhD. *Program availability:* Part-time. *Degree requirements:* For doctorate, one foreign language, comprehensive exam, thesis/dissertation, expository writing exam, internship. *Entrance requirements:* For doctorate, GRE General Test, minimum GPA of 3.4. Additional exam requirements/recommendations for international students: Required—TOEFL (minimum score 550 paper-based; 79 iBT). Electronic applications accepted.

Immaculata University, College of Graduate Studies, Department of Psychology, Immaculata, PA 19345. Offers clinical mental health counseling (MA); clinical psychology (Psy D); forensic psychology (Graduate Certificate); integrative psychotherapy (Graduate Certificate); neuropsychology (Graduate Certificate); psychodynamic psychotherapy (Graduate Certificate); psychological testing (Graduate Certificate); school counseling (MA, Graduate Certificate); school psychology (MA). *Accreditation:* APA. *Program availability:* Part-time, evening/weekend. Terminal master's awarded for partial completion of doctoral program. *Degree requirements:* For master's, comprehensive exam, thesis optional; for doctorate, comprehensive exam, thesis/dissertation. *Entrance requirements:* For master's, GRE General Test or MAT, minimum GPA of 3.0; for doctorate, GRE General Test or MAT, minimum GPA of 3.5. Additional exam requirements/recommendations for international students: Required—TOEFL, IELTS. Electronic applications accepted. *Faculty research:* Supervision ethics, psychology of teaching, gender.

Indiana University Bloomington, School of Education, Department of Counseling and Educational Psychology, Bloomington, IN 47405-1006. Offers counseling (MS, PhD, Ed S); counselor education (MS, Ed S); educational psychology (MS, PhD); inquiry methodology (PhD); learning and developmental sciences (MS, PhD); school psychology (PhD, Ed S). *Accreditation:* ACA (one or more programs are accredited); APA (one or more programs are accredited); NCATE. Terminal master's awarded for partial completion of doctoral program. *Degree requirements:* For master's, thesis optional; for doctorate, thesis/dissertation; for Ed S, comprehensive exam or project. *Entrance requirements:* For master's, doctorate, and Ed S, GRE General Test. Additional exam requirements/recommendations for international students: Required—TOEFL. Electronic applications accepted. *Faculty research:* Counseling psychology, inquiry methodology, school psychology, learning sciences, human development, educational psychology.

Indiana University of Pennsylvania, School of Graduate Studies and Research, College of Education and Communications, Department of Educational and School Psychology, Program in Educational Psychology, Indiana, PA 15705. Offers M Ed, Certificate. *Accreditation:* NCATE. *Program availability:* Part-time. *Faculty:* 6 full-time (2 women). *Students:* 7 full-time (6 women). Average age 23. 21 applicants, 57% accepted, 7 enrolled. In 2018, 10 master's awarded. *Degree requirements:* For master's, thesis optional. *Entrance requirements:* For master's, GRE General Test, 2 letters of recommendation. Additional exam requirements/recommendations for international students: Required—TOEFL (minimum score 540 paper-based; 76 iBT). *Application deadline:* For fall admission, 2/1 priority date for domestic students. Application fee: $50. Electronic applications accepted. *Expenses:* Tuition, state resident: full-time $12,384; part-time $516 per credit hour. Tuition, nonresident: full-time $18,576; part-time $774 per credit hour. *Required fees:* $4454; $186 per credit hour. $65 per semester. Tuition and fees vary according to program and reciprocity agreements. *Financial support:* In 2018–19, 6 research assistantships with tuition reimbursements (averaging $3,330 per year) were awarded; fellowships with full tuition reimbursements, teaching assistantships with partial tuition reimbursements, career-related internships or fieldwork, Federal Work-Study, scholarships/grants, and unspecified assistantships also available. Support available to part-time students. Financial award application deadline: 4/15; financial award applicants required to submit FAFSA. *Unit head:* Dr. Mark R. McGowan, Graduate Coordinator, 724-357-2174, E-mail: mmcgowan@iup.edu. *Application contact:* Dr. Mark R. McGowan, Graduate Coordinator, 724-357-2174, E-mail: mmcgowan@iup.edu. Website: http://www.iup.edu/schoolpsychology/grad/educational-psychology-med/default.aspx

Instituto Tecnologico de Santo Domingo, Graduate School, Area of Humanities and Social Sciences, Santo Domingo, Dominican Republic. Offers accounting (Certificate); adult education (Certificate); applied linguistics (MA); economics (MA); education (M Ed); educational psychology (MA, Certificate); gender and development (MA, Certificate); humanistic studies (MA); international marketing management (Certificate); international relations in the Caribbean basin (Certificate); intervention systems in family therapy (MA); linguistic and literary communication (Certificate); pedagogical support (MA); social science education (M Ed); sustainable human development (MA); terminal illness and death psychology (Certificate); youth and adult education (M Ed).

John Carroll University, Graduate Studies, Programs in Educational and School Psychology, University Heights, OH 44118. Offers educational psychology (M Ed, Ed S); school psychology (Ed S). *Accreditation:* NCATE. *Program availability:* Part-time, evening/weekend. *Entrance requirements:* Additional exam requirements/recommendations for international students: Required—TOEFL. *Application deadline:* For fall admission, 2/15 priority date for domestic students. Applications are processed on a rolling basis. Electronic applications accepted. *Expenses:* Tuition: Full-time $13,140; part-time $730 per credit hour. Tuition and fees vary according to program. *Financial support:* Scholarships/grants and unspecified assistantships available. Financial award applicants required to submit FAFSA. *Unit head:* Dr. Annie Moses, Chair, 216-397-1900, Fax: 216-397-3045, E-mail: education@jcu.edu. *Application contact:* Colleen K. Sommerfeld, Assistant Dean for Graduate Admission & Retention, 216-397-4902, Fax: 216-397-1835, E-mail: csommerfeld@jcu.edu. Website: http://sites.jcu.edu/education/pages/programs-of-study/graduate-programs/

Kent State University, College of Education, Health and Human Services, School of Lifespan Development and Educational Sciences, Program in Educational Psychology, Kent, OH 44242-0001. Offers M Ed, MA. *Faculty:* 3 full-time (1 woman). *Students:* 34 full-time (19 women), 19 part-time (12 women). 47 applicants, 38% accepted. In 2018, 3

master's awarded. *Degree requirements:* For master's, thesis optional. *Entrance requirements:* For master's, 2 letters of reference, minimum GPA of 3.5, goals statement. Additional exam requirements/recommendations for international students: Required—TOEFL (minimum score 550 paper-based; 80 iBT). *Application deadline:* For fall admission, 1/1 priority date for domestic and international students. Applications are processed on a rolling basis. Application fee: $45 ($60 for international students). Electronic applications accepted. *Expenses:* Tuition, state resident: full-time $11,766; part-time $536 per credit. Tuition, nonresident: full-time $21,952; part-time $999 per credit. *International tuition:* $21,952 full-time. Tuition and fees vary according to course load. *Financial support:* In 2018–19, 8 research assistantships (averaging $11,417 per year), 2 teaching assistantships (averaging $12,000 per year) were awarded; Federal Work-Study, scholarships/grants, health care benefits, and unspecified assistantships also available. *Unit head:* Dr. Brad Morris, Coordinator, 330-672-0590, Fax: 330-672-2512, E-mail: bmorri20@kent.edu. *Application contact:* Cheryl Slusarczyk, Academic Program Director, Office of Graduate Student Services, 330-672-2576, Fax: 330-672-9162, E-mail: ogs@kent.edu. Website: http://www.kent.edu/ehhs/ldes/epsy

La Sierra University, School of Education, Department of School Psychology and Counseling, Riverside, CA 92505. Offers counseling (MA); educational psychology (Ed S); school psychology (Ed S). *Program availability:* Part-time, evening/weekend. *Degree requirements:* For master's, thesis optional; for Ed S, practicum (educational psychology). *Entrance requirements:* For master's, California Basic Educational Skills Test, NTE, minimum GPA of 3.0; for Ed S, minimum GPA of 3.3. *Faculty research:* Equivalent score scales, self perception.

McGill University, Faculty of Graduate and Postdoctoral Studies, Faculty of Education, Department of Educational and Counseling Psychology, Montréal, QC H3A 2T5, Canada. Offers counseling psychology (MA, PhD); educational psychology (M Ed, MA, PhD); school/applied child psychology and applied developmental psychology (M Ed, MA, PhD, Diploma), including school psychology. *Accreditation:* APA.

Memorial University of Newfoundland, School of Graduate Studies, Faculty of Education, St. John's, NL A1C 5S7, Canada. Offers counseling psychology (M Ed); curriculum, teaching, and learning studies (M Ed); education (PhD); educational leadership studies (M Ed, Graduate Diploma); information technology (M Ed); post-secondary studies (M Ed, Diploma), including health professional education (Diploma). *Program availability:* Part-time. *Degree requirements:* For master's, thesis optional, internship, paper folio, project; for doctorate, comprehensive exam, thesis/dissertation, thesis seminar, oral defense of thesis. *Entrance requirements:* For master's, undergraduate degree with at least 2nd class standing, 1-2 years of work experience; for doctorate, minimum A average in graduate course work, MA in education, 2 years of professional experience; for other advanced degree, 2nd class degree, 2 years of work experience with adult learners, appropriate academic qualifications and work experience in a health-related field. Electronic applications accepted. *Faculty research:* Critical thinking, literacy, cognitive studies and counseling, educational change, technology in instruction.

Miami University, College of Education, Health and Society, Department of Educational Psychology, Oxford, OH 45056. Offers M Ed, MA, MS, Ed S. *Accreditation:* NCATE. *Faculty:* 12 full-time (7 women). *Students:* 58 full-time (44 women), 125 part-time (99 women); includes 25 minority (11 Black or African American, non-Hispanic/Latino; 5 Asian, non-Hispanic/Latino; 8 Hispanic/Latino; 1 Two or more races, non-Hispanic/Latino), 16 international. Average age 31. In 2018, 82 master's awarded. *Unit head:* Dr. Amity Noltemeyer, Interim Chair and Professor, 513-529-6621, E-mail: anoltemeyer@miamioh.edu. *Application contact:* Dr. Amity Noltemeyer, Interim Chair and Professor, 513-529-6621, E-mail: anoltemeyer@miamioh.edu. Website: http://www.MiamiOH.edu/EDP

Michigan School of Psychology, MA and Psy D Programs in Clinical Psychology, Farmington Hills, MI 48334. Offers MA, Psy D. *Accreditation:* APA. *Program availability:* Part-time, evening/weekend. *Degree requirements:* For master's, practicum; for doctorate, comprehensive exam, thesis/dissertation, internship, practicum. *Entrance requirements:* For master's, undergraduate degree from accredited institution with minimum GPA of 2.5; major in psychology, social work, or counseling; for doctorate, GRE General Test, undergraduate degree from accredited institution with minimum GPA of 2.5; graduate degree in psychology, social work, or counseling from accredited institution with minimum GPA of 3.25; graduate-level practicum. Additional exam requirements/recommendations for international students: Required—TOEFL (minimum score 550 paper-based; 79 iBT). Electronic applications accepted. *Expenses:* Contact institution. *Faculty research:* Health psychology, trauma, multicultural, humanistic, applied behavior analysis.

Michigan State University, The Graduate School, College of Education, Department of Counseling, Educational Psychology and Special Education, East Lansing, MI 48824. Offers counseling (MA); educational psychology and educational technology (PhD); educational technology (MA); measurement and quantitative methods (PhD); rehabilitation counseling (MA); rehabilitation counselor education (PhD); school psychology (MA, PhD, Ed S); special education (MA, PhD). *Accreditation:* APA (one or more programs are accredited); CORE (one or more programs are accredited). *Program availability:* Part-time. *Entrance requirements:* Additional exam requirements/recommendations for international students: Required—TOEFL. Electronic applications accepted.

Mississippi State University, College of Education, Department of Counseling, Educational Psychology, and Foundations, Mississippi State, MS 39762. Offers clinical mental health (MS); college counseling (MS); counseling/mental health (PhD); counseling/school psychology (PhD); counselor education (Ed S); educational psychology/general educational psychology (PhD); educational psychology/school psychology (PhD); general educational psychology (MS); psychometry (MS); rehabilitation counseling (MS); school counseling (MS); school psychology (Ed S); student affairs (MS). *Accreditation:* ACA (one or more programs are accredited); APA; CORE (one or more programs are accredited); NCATE. *Program availability:* Part-time, blended/hybrid learning. *Faculty:* 17 full-time (12 women), 2 part-time/adjunct (both women). *Students:* 94 full-time (81 women), 54 part-time (44 women); includes 50 minority (39 Black or African American, non-Hispanic/Latino; 2 Asian, non-Hispanic/Latino; 8 Hispanic/Latino; 1 Two or more races, non-Hispanic/Latino), 6 international. Average age 29. 90 applicants, 63% accepted, 45 enrolled. In 2018, 33 master's, 6 doctorates, 6 other advanced degrees awarded. Terminal master's awarded for partial completion of doctoral program. *Degree requirements:* For master's, comprehensive exam, thesis optional; for doctorate, thesis/dissertation, comprehensive oral and written exam. *Entrance requirements:* For master's, GRE (taken within the last five years), BS with minimum GPA of 2.75 on last 60 hours; for doctorate, GRE, MS from CACREP- or CORE-accredited program in counseling; for Ed S, GRE, MS in counseling or related field, minimum GPA of 3.3 on all graduate work. Additional exam requirements/recommendations for international students: Required—TOEFL (minimum score 550 paper-based; 79 iBT); Recommended—IELTS (minimum score 6.5). *Application deadline:* For fall admission, 2/1 priority date for domestic and international students. Applications are processed on a rolling basis. Application fee: $60 ($80 for international students). Electronic applications accepted. *Expenses:* Tuition, state resident: full-time

$8450; part-time $360.59 per credit hour. Tuition, nonresident: full-time $23,140; part-time $969.09 per credit hour. *Required fees:* $110. One-time fee: $55 full-time. Part-time tuition and fees vary according to course load, degree level, campus/location and reciprocity agreements. *Financial support:* In 2018–19, 6 research assistantships (averaging $10,050 per year), 6 teaching assistantships with full tuition reimbursements (averaging $8,401 per year) were awarded; career-related internships or fieldwork, Federal Work-Study, institutionally sponsored loans, and unspecified assistantships also available. Financial award application deadline: 2/1; financial award applicants required to submit FAFSA. *Faculty research:* HIV/AIDS in college population, substance abuse in youth and college students, ADHD and conduct disorders in youth, assessment and identification of early childhood disabilities, assessment and vocational transition of the disabled. *Unit head:* Dr. Daniel Gadke, Professor and Interim Head, 662-325-3426, Fax: 662-325-3263, E-mail: dgadke@colled.msstate.edu. *Application contact:* Ryan King, Admissions and Enrollment Assistant, 662-325-8951, E-mail: rjk101@grad.msstate.edu. Website: http://www.cep.msstate.edu/

Mount Saint Vincent University, Graduate Programs, Faculty of Education, Program in Educational Psychology, Halifax, NS B3M 2J6, Canada. Offers education of the blind or visually impaired (M Ed); education of the deaf or hard of hearing (M Ed); educational psychology (MA-R); evaluation (M Ed); human relations (M Ed). *Program availability:* Part-time, evening/weekend, online learning. *Degree requirements:* For master's, thesis (for some programs). *Entrance requirements:* For master's, bachelor's degree in related field, 1 year of teaching experience. Electronic applications accepted. *Faculty research:* Personality measurement, values reasoning, aggression and sexuality, power and control, quantitative and qualitative research methodologies.

National Louis University, National College of Education, Chicago, IL 60603. Offers administration and supervision (M Ed, Ed D, CAS, Ed S); curriculum and instruction (M Ed, MS Ed, CAS); early childhood administration (M Ed, CAS); early childhood education (M Ed, MAT, MS Ed, CAS); education (Ed D); educational psychology/human learning and development (M Ed, MS Ed, CAS, Ed S); elementary education (MAT); interdisciplinary curriculum and instruction (M Ed); mathematics education (M Ed, MS Ed, CAS); middle grades education (MAT); reading and language (M Ed, MS Ed, CAS); school psychology (M Ed, Ed S); science education (M Ed, MS Ed, CAS); secondary education (MAT); special education (M Ed, MAT, CAS); technology in education (M Ed, CAS). *Accreditation:* NCATE. *Program availability:* Part-time, evening/weekend. *Degree requirements:* For doctorate, comprehensive exam, thesis/dissertation. *Entrance requirements:* For master's, MAT or GRE, minimum GPA of 3.0; for doctorate, GRE General Test, minimum GPA of 3.25, interview, resume, writing sample, 4 recommendations. Additional exam requirements/recommendations for international students: Required—TOEFL (minimum score 550 paper-based; 79 iBT).

New York University, Steinhardt School of Culture, Education, and Human Development, Department of Applied Psychology, Programs in Educational and Developmental Psychology, New York, NY 10012. Offers developmental psychology (PhD); human development and social intervention (MA); psychology and social intervention (PhD). *Accreditation:* APA (one or more programs are accredited). *Program availability:* Part-time. *Entrance requirements:* For doctorate, GRE General Test, interview. Additional exam requirements/recommendations for international students: Required—TOEFL. Electronic applications accepted. *Faculty research:* Schools and communities, self-regulation and academic achievement, intervention and social change, trauma and resilience, cognition.

Northern Arizona University, College of Education, Department of Educational Psychology, Flagstaff, AZ 86011. Offers clinical mental health counseling (MA); combined counseling/school psychology (PhD), including counseling psychology; counseling (M Ed), including school counseling, student affairs; human relations (M Ed); psychology of human development and learning (Graduate Certificate); school psychology (Ed S). *Program availability:* Part-time, 100% online, blended/hybrid learning. Terminal master's awarded for partial completion of doctoral program. *Degree requirements:* For master's, variable foreign language requirement, comprehensive exam (for some programs), thesis (for some programs); for doctorate, variable foreign language requirement, comprehensive exam (for some programs), thesis/dissertation (for some programs); for other advanced degree, comprehensive exam (for some programs). *Entrance requirements:* Additional exam requirements/recommendations for international students: Required—TOEFL (minimum score 80 iBT), IELTS (minimum score 6.5). Electronic applications accepted.

Northern Illinois University, Graduate School, College of Education, Department of Leadership, Educational Psychology and Foundations, De Kalb, IL 60115-2854. Offers educational administration (MS Ed, Ed D, Ed S); educational psychology (MS Ed, Ed D); foundations of education (MS Ed); school business management (MS Ed). *Program availability:* Part-time, evening/weekend, online learning. *Faculty:* 23 full-time (12 women). *Students:* 9 full-time (4 women), 170 part-time (98 women); includes 45 minority (16 Black or African American, non-Hispanic/Latino; 6 Asian, non-Hispanic/Latino; 15 Hispanic/Latino; 8 Two or more races, non-Hispanic/Latino), 2 international. Average age 39. 78 applicants, 86% accepted, 34 enrolled. In 2018, 52 master's, 28 doctorates, 2 other advanced degrees awarded. *Degree requirements:* For master's, comprehensive exam, thesis optional; for doctorate, thesis/dissertation, candidacy exam, dissertation defense. *Entrance requirements:* For master's, minimum undergraduate GPA of 2.75; for doctorate, GRE General Test, minimum undergraduate GPA of 2.75, 3.2 graduate; for Ed S, GRE General Test, minimum GPA of 2.75 (undergraduate), 3.2 (graduate). Additional exam requirements/recommendations for international students: Required—TOEFL (minimum score 550 paper-based). *Application deadline:* For fall admission, 6/1 for domestic students, 5/1 for international students; for spring admission, 11/1 for domestic students, 10/1 for international students. Applications are processed on a rolling basis. Application fee: $40. Electronic applications accepted. *Financial support:* In 2018–19, 1 research assistantship with full tuition reimbursement, 2 teaching assistantships with full tuition reimbursements were awarded; fellowships with full tuition reimbursements, career-related internships or fieldwork, Federal Work-Study, scholarships/grants, tuition waivers (full), and staff assistantships also available. Support available to part-time students. Financial award applicants required to submit FAFSA. *Faculty research:* Interpersonal forgiveness, learner-centered education, psychedelic studies, senior theory, professional growth. *Unit head:* Carolyn V. Schee, Chair, 815-753-4404, E-mail: lepf@niu.edu. *Application contact:* Graduate School Office, 815-753-0395, E-mail: gradsch@niu.edu. Website: http://cedu.niu.edu/LEPF/

Oklahoma State University, College of Education, Health and Aviation, School of Applied Health and Educational Psychology, Stillwater, OK 74078. Offers applied behavioral studies (Ed D); applied health and educational psychology (MS, PhD, Ed S). *Accreditation:* APA (one or more programs are accredited). *Program availability:* Part-time. *Entrance requirements:* For master's and doctorate, GRE or GMAT. Additional exam requirements/recommendations for international students: Required—TOEFL (minimum score 550 paper-based; 79 iBT). Electronic applications accepted. *Expenses: Tuition, area resident:* Full-time $4148. Tuition, state resident: full-time $4148. Tuition, nonresident: full-time $10,517. *International tuition:* $10,517 full-time. *Required fees:* $4394; $2929 per credit hour. Tuition and fees vary according to course load and program.

Old Dominion University, Darden College of Education, Program in Educational Psychology and Program Evaluation, Norfolk, VA 23529. Offers education (PhD), including educational psychology, program evaluation. *Program availability:* Part-time, evening/weekend. *Degree requirements:* For doctorate, comprehensive exam, thesis/dissertation. *Entrance requirements:* Additional exam requirements/recommendations for international students: Required—TOEFL. Electronic applications accepted. *Expenses:* Contact institution. *Faculty research:* Motivation, self-regulated learning, distance learning, calibration, STEM.

Penn State University Park, Graduate School, College of Education, Department of Educational Psychology, Counseling, and Special Education, University Park, PA 16802. Offers counselor education (M Ed, D Ed, PhD, Certificate); educational psychology (MS, PhD, Certificate); school psychology (M Ed, MS, PhD, Certificate); special education (M Ed, MS, PhD).

Philadelphia College of Osteopathic Medicine, Graduate and Professional Programs, Department of Psychology, Philadelphia, PA 19131-1694. Offers applied behavior analysis (Certificate); clinical health psychology (Post-Doctoral Certificate); clinical neuropsychology (Post-Doctoral Certificate); clinical psychology (Psy D); educational psychology (PhD); mental health counseling (MS); organizational development and leadership (MS); psychology (Certificate); public health management and administration (MS); school psychology (MS, Psy D, Ed S). *Accreditation:* APA. *Faculty:* 19 full-time (11 women), 122 part-time/adjunct (58 women). *Students:* 342 (285 women); includes 108 minority (65 Black or African American, non-Hispanic/Latino; 1 American Indian or Alaska Native, non-Hispanic/Latino; 10 Asian, non-Hispanic/Latino; 14 Hispanic/Latino; 18 Two or more races, non-Hispanic/Latino). 357 applicants, 51% accepted, 113 enrolled. In 2018, 79 master's, 38 doctorates, 16 other advanced degrees awarded. Terminal master's awarded for partial completion of doctoral program. *Degree requirements:* For master's, comprehensive exam (for some programs), thesis (for some programs); for doctorate, comprehensive exam, thesis/dissertation. *Entrance requirements:* For master's, GRE or MAT, minimum GPA of 3.0; bachelor's degree from regionally-accredited college or university; for doctorate, PRAXIS II (for Psy D in school psychology), minimum undergraduate GPA of 3.0; for other advanced degree, GRE (for Ed S). Additional exam requirements/recommendations for international students: Required—TOEFL (minimum score 79 iBT). *Application deadline:* Applications are processed on a rolling basis. Application fee: $50. Electronic applications accepted. Tuition and fees vary according to course load, degree level and program. *Financial support:* In 2018–19, 28 teaching assistantships were awarded; Federal Work-Study, institutionally sponsored loans, and scholarships/grants also available. Financial award application deadline: 3/15; financial award applicants required to submit FAFSA. *Faculty research:* Adult and childhood anxiety and ADHD; coping with chronic illness; primary care psychology/integrated health care; applied behavior analysis; psychological, educational, and neuropsychological assessment. *Total annual research expenditures:* $533,489. *Unit head:* Dr. Robert DiTomasso, Chairman, 215-871-6442, Fax: 215-871-6458, E-mail: robertd@pcom.edu. *Application contact:* Johnathan Cox, Associate Director of Admissions, 215-871-6700, Fax: 215-871-6719, E-mail: johnathancox@pcom.edu.

Pontifical Catholic University of Puerto Rico, College of Education, Program in Educational Psychology, Ponce, PR 00717-0777. Offers M Ed. *Degree requirements:* For master's, comprehensive exam, thesis (for some programs). *Entrance requirements:* For master's, GRE, 2 letters of recommendation, interview, minimum GPA of 2.75.

Regent University, Graduate School, School of Education, Virginia Beach, VA 23464-9800. Offers education (M Ed, Ed D, PhD), including adult education (Ed D, PhD, Ed S), advanced educational leadership (Ed D, PhD, Ed S), character education (Ed D, PhD, Ed S), Christian education leadership (Ed D, PhD, Ed S), Christian school administration (M Ed), curriculum and instruction (Ed D, PhD, Ed S), curriculum and instruction - adult education (M Ed), curriculum and instruction - Christian school (M Ed), curriculum and instruction - gifted and talented (M Ed), curriculum and instruction - STEM education (M Ed), curriculum and instruction - teacher leader (M Ed), discipleship for ministry (M Ed), educational leadership (M Ed), educational psychology (Ed D, PhD, Ed S), educational technology and online learning (Ed D, PhD, Ed S), elementary education (M Ed), exceptional education executive leadership (Ed D, PhD, Ed S), higher education (Ed D, PhD, Ed S), higher education leadership and management (Ed D, PhD, Ed S), instructional design and technology (M Ed), K-12 school leadership (Ed D, PhD, Ed S), K-12 special education (M Ed), leadership in mathematics education (M Ed), reading specialist (M Ed), special education (Ed D, PhD, Ed S), student affairs (M Ed), TESOL - adult education (M Ed), TESOL - K-12 (M Ed); educational specialist (Ed S), including adult education (Ed D, PhD, Ed S), advanced educational leadership (Ed D, PhD, Ed S), character education (Ed D, PhD, Ed S), Christian education leadership (Ed D, PhD, Ed S), curriculum and instruction (Ed D, PhD, Ed S), educational psychology (Ed D, PhD, Ed S), educational technology and online learning (Ed D, PhD, Ed S), exceptional education executive leadership (Ed D, PhD, Ed S), higher education (Ed D, PhD, Ed S), higher education leadership and management (Ed D, PhD, Ed S), K-12 school leadership (Ed D, PhD, Ed S), special education (Ed D, PhD, Ed S). *Accreditation:* TEAC. *Program availability:* Part-time, evening/weekend, 100% online, blended/hybrid learning. *Degree requirements:* For master's, thesis or alternative; for doctorate, comprehensive exam, thesis/dissertation. *Entrance requirements:* For master's, Virginia Communication and Literacy Assessment (VCLA), PRAXIS, college transcripts, writing sample, interview; for doctorate, GRE, writing sample, resume, transcripts, interview. Additional exam requirements/recommendations for international students: Required—TOEFL (minimum score 577 paper-based). Electronic applications accepted. *Expenses:* Contact institution. *Faculty research:* Christian school administration, curriculum and instruction, educational technology and online learning, higher education, special education.

Rutgers University–New Brunswick, Graduate School of Education, Department of Educational Psychology, Program in Learning, Cognition and Development, Piscataway, NJ 08854-8097. Offers Ed M. *Program availability:* Part-time, evening/weekend. *Entrance requirements:* For master's, GRE General Test, 3 letters of recommendation. Additional exam requirements/recommendations for international students: Required—TOEFL (minimum score 550 paper-based; 83 iBT). Electronic applications accepted. *Faculty research:* Cognitive development, gender roles, cognition and instruction, peer learning, infancy and early childhood.

Rutgers University–New Brunswick, Graduate School of Education, Doctoral Program in Education, New Brunswick, NJ 08901. Offers educational policy (PhD); educational psychology (PhD); literacy education (PhD); mathematics education (PhD). *Program availability:* Part-time. *Degree requirements:* For doctorate, thesis/dissertation, qualifying exam. *Entrance requirements:* For doctorate, GRE General Test, GRE Subject Test (mathematics education). Additional exam requirements/recommendations for international students: Required—TOEFL (minimum score 575 paper-based; 83 iBT). Electronic applications accepted. *Faculty research:* Literacy education, math education, educational psychology, educational policy, learning sciences.

Simon Fraser University, Office of Graduate Studies and Postdoctoral Fellows, Faculty of Education, Program in Educational Psychology, Burnaby, BC V5A 1S6, Canada. Offers M Ed, MA, PhD. *Program availability:* Part-time, evening/weekend. *Degree requirements:* For master's, comprehensive exam (for some programs), thesis (for some

programs), project or thesis; for doctorate, comprehensive exam, thesis/dissertation. *Entrance requirements:* For master's, minimum GPA of 3.0 (on scale of 4.33) or 3.33 based on last 60 credits of undergraduate courses; for doctorate, GRE, minimum GPA of 3.5 (on scale of 4.33). Additional exam requirements/recommendations for international students: Recommended—TOEFL (minimum score 580 paper-based; 93 iBT), IELTS (minimum score 7), TWE (minimum score 5). Electronic applications accepted. *Faculty research:* Autism and social interaction; cultural and personal dimensions in psychological development; early childhood education; social and emotional development; historical emergence, practice, and ongoing development of the constructs of learning disabilities.

Southern Illinois University Carbondale, Graduate School, College of Education and Human Services, Department of Educational Psychology and Special Education, Program in Educational Psychology, Carbondale, IL 62901-4701. Offers MS Ed, PhD. *Accreditation:* NCATE. *Degree requirements:* For master's, thesis; for doctorate, thesis/dissertation. *Entrance requirements:* For master's, GRE General Test, minimum GPA of 2.7; for doctorate, minimum GPA of 3.25. Additional exam requirements/recommendations for international students: Required—TOEFL. *Faculty research:* Career development, problem-solving, learning and instruction, cognitive development, family assessment.

State University of New York College at Oneonta, Graduate Programs, Division of Education, Department of Educational Psychology, Counseling and Special Education, Oneonta, NY 13820-4015. Offers school counselor K-12 (MS Ed, CAS); special education (MS Ed). *Accreditation:* NCATE. *Program availability:* Part-time, evening/weekend. *Degree requirements:* For master's, comprehensive exam. *Entrance requirements:* For master's, GRE General Test.

Teachers College, Columbia University, Department of Health and Behavior Studies, New York, NY 10027-6696. Offers applied behavior analysis (MA, PhD); applied educational psychology: school psychology (Ed M, PhD); behavioral nutrition (PhD), including nutrition (Ed D, PhD); community health education (MS); community nutrition education (Ed M), including community nutrition education; education of deaf and hard of hearing (MA, PhD); health education (MA, Ed D); hearing impairment (Ed D); intellectual disability/autism (MA, Ed D, PhD); nursing education (Ed D, Advanced Certificate); nutrition and education (MS); nutrition and exercise physiology (MS); nutrition and public health (MS); nutrition education (Ed D), including nutrition (Ed D, PhD); physical disabilities (Ed D); reading specialist (MA); severe or multiple disabilities (MA); special education (Ed M, MA, Ed D); teaching of sign language (MA). *Program availability:* Part-time, evening/weekend. *Students:* 157 full-time (145 women), 344 part-time (310 women); includes 169 minority (46 Black or African American, non-Hispanic/Latino; 2 American Indian or Alaska Native, non-Hispanic/Latino; 55 Asian, non-Hispanic/Latino; 57 Hispanic/Latino; 9 Two or more races, non-Hispanic/Latino), 64 international. Average age 31. 495 applicants, 64% accepted, 171 enrolled. Terminal master's awarded for partial completion of doctoral program. *Unit head:* Prof. Dolores Perin, Chair, 212-678-3091, E-mail: dp111@tc.columbia.edu. *Application contact:* Kelly Sutton-Skinner, Director of Admission & New Student Enrollment, E-mail: kms2237@tc.columbia.edu.
Website: http://www.tc.columbia.edu/health-and-behavior-studies/

Teachers College, Columbia University, Department of Human Development, New York, NY 10027-6696. Offers applied statistics (MS); cognitive studies in education (MA, Ed D, PhD); developmental psychology (MA, Ed D, PhD); educational psychology-human cognition and learning (Ed M, MA, Ed D, PhD); learning analytics (MS); measurement and evaluation (ME, Ed D, PhD); measurement, evaluation, and statistics (MA, MS, Ed D, PhD). *Program availability:* Part-time. *Students:* 114 full-time (89 women), 168 part-time (119 women); includes 75 minority (19 Black or African American, non-Hispanic/Latino; 36 Asian, non-Hispanic/Latino; 18 Hispanic/Latino; 2 Two or more races, non-Hispanic/Latino), 132 international. Average age 29. 401 applicants, 56% accepted, 109 enrolled. *Unit head:* Jim Corter, Chair, 212-678-3843, E-mail: jec34@tc.columbia.edu. *Application contact:* Kelly Sutton-Skinner, Director of Admission & New Student Enrollment, E-mail: kms2237@tc.columbia.edu.
Website: http://www.tc.columbia.edu/human-development/

Temple University, College of Education, Department of Psychological Studies in Education, Philadelphia, PA 19122-6096. Offers applied behavior analysis (MS Ed); counseling psychology (Ed M), including agency counseling, school counseling; educational psychology (Ed M); school psychology (PhD, Ed S). *Accreditation:* APA (one or more programs are accredited). *Program availability:* Part-time, evening/weekend. *Faculty:* 16 full-time (9 women), 17 part-time/adjunct (10 women). *Students:* 154 full-time (115 women), 59 part-time (49 women); includes 67 minority (38 Black or African American, non-Hispanic/Latino; 11 Asian, non-Hispanic/Latino; 11 Hispanic/Latino; 7 Two or more races, non-Hispanic/Latino), 9 international. 420 applicants, 37% accepted, 75 enrolled. In 2018, 70 master's, 6 doctorates, 13 other advanced degrees awarded. *Degree requirements:* For master's, comprehensive exam (for some programs); for doctorate, thesis/dissertation. *Entrance requirements:* For master's, statement of goals, 2 recommendation letters; for doctorate, GRE, statement of goals, academic writing sample, 2 recommendation letters. Additional exam requirements/recommendations for international students: Required—TOEFL (minimum score 79 iBT), IELTS, PTE, one of three is required. Application fee: $60. Electronic applications accepted. *Financial support:* Fellowships, research assistantships, teaching assistantships, career-related internships or fieldwork, Federal Work-Study, health care benefits, and unspecified assistantships available. Financial award applicants required to submit FAFSA. *Faculty research:* Educational psychology, counseling psychology, school psychology. *Unit head:* Renée Tobin, Prof. of Counseling Psychology and Dept. Chairperson, 215-204-7884, E-mail: renee.tobin@temple.edu. *Application contact:* Remy Van Wyk, Academic Coordinator, 215-204-1474, E-mail: remy.van.wyk@temple.edu.
Website: http://education.temple.edu/pse

Tennessee Technological University, College of Graduate Studies, College of Education, Department of Counseling and Psychology, Cookeville, TN 38505. Offers MA, Ed S. *Accreditation:* NCATE (one or more programs are accredited). *Program availability:* Part-time, evening/weekend. *Faculty:* 24 full-time (6 women). *Students:* 39 full-time (35 women), 33 part-time (31 women); includes 7 minority (3 Black or African American, non-Hispanic/Latino; 2 Asian, non-Hispanic/Latino; 1 Hispanic/Latino; 1 Two or more races, non-Hispanic/Latino). 48 applicants, 73% accepted, 25 enrolled. In 2018, 21 master's, 5 other advanced degrees awarded. *Degree requirements:* For master's and Ed S, comprehensive exam, thesis or alternative. *Entrance requirements:* For master's and Ed S, GRE. Additional exam requirements/recommendations for international students: Required—FLS International (completion of Level 18). *Application deadline:* For fall admission, 8/1 for domestic students, 5/1 for international students; for spring admission, 12/1 for domestic students, 10/1 for international students; for summer admission, 5/1 for domestic students, 2/1 for international students. Applications are processed on a rolling basis. Application fee: $35 ($40 for international students). Electronic applications accepted. *Financial support:* Fellowships, research assistantships, teaching assistantships, and career-related internships or fieldwork available. Financial award application deadline: 4/1. *Unit head:* Dr. Barry Stein, Chairperson, 931-372-3457, Fax: 931-372-6319, E-mail: bstein@tntech.edu. *Application contact:* Shelia K. Kendrick, Coordinator of Graduate Studies, 931-372-3808, Fax: 931-372-3497, E-mail: skendrick@tntech.edu.

Texas A&M University, College of Education and Human Development, Department of Educational Psychology, College Station, TX 77843. Offers bilingual education (M Ed, MS); counseling psychology (PhD); educational psychology (M Ed, MS, PhD); educational technology (M Ed); school psychology (PhD); special education (M Ed, MS). *Accreditation:* APA (one or more programs are accredited). *Program availability:* Part-time, evening/weekend, blended/hybrid learning. *Faculty:* 47. *Students:* 146 full-time (118 women), 244 part-time (204 women); includes 146 minority (22 Black or African American, non-Hispanic/Latino; 2 American Indian or Alaska Native, non-Hispanic/Latino; 18 Asian, non-Hispanic/Latino; 92 Hispanic/Latino; 1 Native Hawaiian or other Pacific Islander, non-Hispanic/Latino; 11 Two or more races, non-Hispanic/Latino), 50 international. Average age 33. 142 applicants, 50% accepted, 49 enrolled. In 2018, 152 master's, 23 doctorates awarded. *Degree requirements:* For master's, thesis optional; for doctorate, thesis/dissertation. *Entrance requirements:* For master's and doctorate, GRE General Test. Additional exam requirements/recommendations for international students: Required—TOEFL (minimum score 550 paper-based; 80 iBT), IELTS (minimum score 6), PTE (minimum score 53). *Application deadline:* For fall admission, 12/1 for domestic students; for spring admission, 10/15 for domestic students. Application fee: $50 ($90 for international students). Electronic applications accepted. *Expenses:* Contact institution. *Financial support:* In 2018–19, 125 students received support, including 3 fellowships with tuition reimbursements available (averaging $19,520 per year), 106 research assistantships with tuition reimbursements available (averaging $15,181 per year), 19 teaching assistantships with tuition reimbursements available (averaging $9,322 per year); career-related internships or fieldwork, institutionally sponsored loans, scholarships/grants, traineeships, health care benefits, tuition waivers (full and partial), and unspecified assistantships also available. Support available to part-time students. Financial award application deadline: 3/15; financial award applicants required to submit FAFSA. *Unit head:* Dr. Victor Willson, Department Head, 979-845-1394, E-mail: v-willson@tamu.edu. *Application contact:* Kristie Stramaski, Senior Academic Advisor, 979-845-1833, E-mail: epsyadvisor@tamu.edu.
Website: http://epsy.tamu.edu

Texas A&M University–Central Texas, Graduate Studies and Research, Killeen, TX 76549. Offers accounting (MS); business administration (MBA); clinical mental health counseling (MS); criminal justice (MCJ); curriculum and instruction (M Ed); educational administration (M Ed); educational psychology - experimental psychology (MS); history (MA); human resource management (MS); information systems (MS); liberal studies (MS); management and leadership (MS); marriage and family therapy (MS); mathematics (MS); political science (MA); school counseling (M Ed); school psychology (Ed S).

Texas A&M University–Commerce, College of Education and Human Services, Commerce, TX 75429. Offers counseling (M Ed, MS, PhD); early childhood education (M Ed, MS); educational administration (M Ed, MS, Ed D); educational psychology (PhD); educational technology leadership (M Ed, MS); educational technology library science (M Ed, MS); elementary education (M Ed); health, kinesiology and sports studies (MS); higher education (MS, Ed D); psychology (MS); reading (M Ed, MS); school psychology (SSP); secondary education (M Ed, MS); social work (MSW); special education (M Ed, MS); supervision, curriculum and instruction-elementary education (Ed D); training and development (MS). *Program availability:* Part-time, evening/weekend, 100% online, blended/hybrid learning. *Faculty:* 95 full-time (59 women), 29 part-time/adjunct (22 women). *Students:* 356 full-time (295 women), 1,262 part-time (992 women); includes 683 minority (349 Black or African American, non-Hispanic/Latino; 9 American Indian or Alaska Native, non-Hispanic/Latino; 30 Asian, non-Hispanic/Latino; 238 Hispanic/Latino; 57 Two or more races, non-Hispanic/Latino), 9 international. Average age 37. 951 applicants, 42% accepted, 304 enrolled. In 2018, 532 master's, 51 doctorates awarded. *Degree requirements:* For master's, comprehensive exam, thesis optional, departmental qualifying exams (for some programs); for doctorate, comprehensive exam, thesis/dissertation, departmental qualifying exam; for SSP, comprehensive exam. *Entrance requirements:* For master's, GRE General Test, official transcripts, letters of recommendation, resume, statement of goals; for doctorate, GRE General Test, letters of recommendation, statement of goals, writing samples, writing sessions, resumes. Additional exam requirements/recommendations for international students: Required—TOEFL (minimum score 550 paper-based; 79 iBT), IELTS (minimum score 6), PTE (minimum score 53). *Application deadline:* For fall admission, 6/1 priority date for international students; for spring admission, 10/15 priority date for international students; for summer admission, 3/15 priority date for international students. Applications are processed on a rolling basis. Application fee: $50 ($75 for international students). Electronic applications accepted. *Expenses: Tuition, area resident:* Full-time $3630. Tuition, state resident: full-time $3630. Tuition, nonresident: full-time $11,100. *International tuition:* $11,100 full-time. *Required fees:* $2794. Tuition and fees vary according to course load, degree level and program. *Financial support:* In 2018–19, 116 students received support, including 94 research assistantships with partial tuition reimbursements available (averaging $3,863 per year), 38 teaching assistantships with partial tuition reimbursements available (averaging $4,728 per year); career-related internships or fieldwork, Federal Work-Study, institutionally sponsored loans, scholarships/grants, health care benefits, and unspecified assistantships also available. Financial award application deadline: 5/1; financial award applicants required to submit FAFSA. *Faculty research:* Cognitive and bilingual education, positive behavioral intervention, literacy, math readiness. *Total annual research expenditures:* $1.1 million. *Unit head:* Dr. Madeline Justice, Interim Dean, 903-886-5181, Fax: 903-886-5905, E-mail: madeline.justice@tamuc.edu. *Application contact:* Vicky Turner, Doctoral Degree and Special Programs Coordinator, 903-886-5167, E-mail: vicky.turner@tamuc.edu.
Website: http://www.tamuc.edu/academics/graduateSchool/programs/education/default.aspx

Texas Tech University, Graduate School, College of Education, Department of Educational Psychology and Leadership, Lubbock, TX 79409-1071. Offers counselor education (M Ed, PhD); educational leadership (M Ed, Ed D, PhD); educational psychology (M Ed, PhD); higher education administration (M Ed, Ed D); higher education research (PhD); instructional technology (M Ed, Ed D); special education (M Ed, Ed D, PhD). *Accreditation:* ACA; NCATE. *Program availability:* Part-time, evening/weekend, 100% online, blended/hybrid learning. *Faculty:* 65 full-time (29 women), 3 part-time/adjunct (all women). *Students:* 261 full-time (184 women), 624 part-time (482 women); includes 325 minority (88 Black or African American, non-Hispanic/Latino; 3 American Indian or Alaska Native, non-Hispanic/Latino; 12 Asian, non-Hispanic/Latino; 192 Hispanic/Latino; 1 Native Hawaiian or other Pacific Islander, non-Hispanic/Latino; 29 Two or more races, non-Hispanic/Latino), 39 international. Average age 36. 437 applicants, 73% accepted, 252 enrolled. In 2018, 278 master's, 40 doctorates awarded. Terminal master's awarded for partial completion of doctoral program. *Degree requirements:* For master's, comprehensive exam, thesis optional; for doctorate, comprehensive exam, thesis/dissertation. *Entrance requirements:* For master's, GRE (for some programs); for doctorate, GRE. Additional exam requirements/recommendations for international students: Required—TOEFL (minimum score 550 paper-based; 79 iBT). *Application deadline:* For fall admission, 6/1 priority date for

domestic students, 1/15 priority date for international students; for spring admission, 9/1 priority date for domestic students, 6/15 priority date for international students. Applications are processed on a rolling basis. Application fee: $65. Electronic applications accepted. *Expenses:* Contact institution. *Financial support:* In 2018–19, 493 students received support, including 489 fellowships (averaging $3,305 per year), 61 research assistantships (averaging $12,558 per year), 5 teaching assistantships (averaging $13,161 per year); scholarships/grants and unspecified assistantships also available. Support available to part-time students. Financial award application deadline: 1/3; financial award applicants required to submit FAFSA. *Faculty research:* Cognitive, motivational, and developmental processes in learning; counseling education; instructional technology; generic special education and sensory impairment; community college administration; K-12 school administration. *Total annual research expenditures:* $204,930. *Unit head:* Dr. Hansel Burley, Professor, Department Chair, 806-834-5135, Fax: 806-742-2179, E-mail: hansel.burley@ttu.edu. *Application contact:* Pam Smith, Admissions Advisor, 806-834-2969, Fax: 806-742-2179, E-mail: pam.smith@ttu.edu. Website: www.educ.ttu.edu/

Universidad de Iberoamerica, Graduate School, San Jose, Costa Rica. Offers clinical neuropsychology (PhD); clinical psychology (M Psych); educational psychology (M Psych); forensic psychology (M Psych); hospital management (MHA); intensive care nursing (MN); medicine (MD).

Université de Moncton, Faculty of Education, Graduate Studies in Education, Moncton, NB E1A 3E9, Canada. Offers educational psychology (M Ed, MA Ed); guidance (M Ed, MA Ed); school administration (M Ed, MA Ed); teaching (M Ed, MA Ed). *Program availability:* Part-time. *Degree requirements:* For master's, proficiency in English and French. *Entrance requirements:* For master's, minimum GPA of 3.0. *Faculty research:* Guidance, ethnolinguistic vitality, children's rights, ecological education, entrepreneurship.

Université de Montréal, Faculty of Education, Department of Psychopedagogy and Andragogy, Montréal, QC H3C 3J7, Canada. Offers M Ed, MA, PhD, DESS. *Program availability:* Part-time, evening/weekend. Terminal master's awarded for partial completion of doctoral program. *Degree requirements:* For master's, thesis (for some programs); for doctorate, thesis/dissertation, general exam. *Entrance requirements:* For doctorate, MA or M Ed. Electronic applications accepted.

Université du Québec à Trois-Rivières, Graduate Programs, Program in Psychoeducation, Trois-Rivières, QC G9A 5H7, Canada. Offers M Ed, PhD. M Ed offered jointly with Université du Québec en Outaouais. *Entrance requirements:* For master's, appropriate bachelor's degree, proficiency in French. *Faculty research:* Troubled youth intervention.

Université du Québec en Outaouais, Graduate Programs, Program in Psychoeducation, Gatineau, QC J8X 3X7, Canada. Offers M Ed, MA. *Program availability:* Part-time. *Degree requirements:* For master's, thesis (for some programs). *Entrance requirements:* For master's, appropriate bachelor's degree, proficiency in French.

Université Laval, Faculty of Education, Department of Teaching and Learning Studies, Programs in Educational Psychology, Québec, QC G1K 7P4, Canada. Offers MA, PhD. Terminal master's awarded for partial completion of doctoral program. *Degree requirements:* For master's, thesis (for some programs); for doctorate, comprehensive exam, thesis/dissertation. *Entrance requirements:* For master's and doctorate, English exam (comprehension of written English), knowledge of French. Electronic applications accepted. *Faculty research:* Emotional, social, and cognitive development; learning and motivation in school; language development; reading acquisition; computer and learning strategies.

University at Buffalo, the State University of New York, Graduate School, Graduate School of Education, Department of Counseling, School, and Educational Psychology, Buffalo, NY 14260. Offers applied statistical analysis (Advanced Certificate); counseling/school psychology (PhD); counselor education (PhD); education studies (Ed M); educational psychology (MA, PhD); mental health counseling (MS, Certificate); mindful counseling for wellness and engagement (Advanced Certificate); rehabilitation counseling (MS, Advanced Certificate); school counseling (Ed M, Certificate). *Accreditation:* CORE (one or more programs are accredited). *Program availability:* Part-time, 100% online. *Faculty:* 21 full-time (11 women), 23 part-time/adjunct (18 women). *Students:* 163 full-time (132 women), 137 part-time (111 women); includes 55 minority (25 Black or African American, non-Hispanic/Latino; 11 Asian, non-Hispanic/Latino; 15 Hispanic/Latino; 4 Two or more races, non-Hispanic/Latino), 15 international. Average age 32. 355 applicants, 57% accepted, 147 enrolled. In 2018, 66 master's, 13 doctorates, 62 other advanced degrees awarded. *Degree requirements:* For master's, comprehensive exam (for some programs), thesis (for some programs); for doctorate, comprehensive exam, thesis/dissertation. *Entrance requirements:* For master's, GRE General Test, interview, letters of reference; for doctorate, GRE General Test, interview, letters of reference, writing sample. Additional exam requirements/recommendations for international students: Required—TOEFL (minimum score 600 paper-based; 79 iBT), IELTS (minimum score 6.5), PTE (minimum score 55). *Application deadline:* For fall admission, 2/1 priority date for domestic and international students. Application fee: $50. Electronic applications accepted. *Financial support:* In 2018–19, 22 fellowships (averaging $7,823 per year), 41 research assistantships with tuition reimbursements (averaging $10,876 per year) were awarded; teaching assistantships, career-related internships or fieldwork, Federal Work-Study, institutionally sponsored loans, scholarships/grants, tuition waivers (full and partial), and unspecified assistantships also available. Financial award application deadline: 2/1; financial award applicants required to submit FAFSA. *Faculty research:* Multicultural counseling, class size effects, good work in counseling, eating disorders, outcome assessment, change agents and therapeutic factors in group counseling. *Total annual research expenditures:* $1.3 million. *Unit head:* Dr. Myles Faith, Department Chair, 716-645-1124, Fax: 716-645-6616, E-mail: mfaith@buffalo.edu. *Application contact:* Renad Aref, Assistant Director of Admission Recruitment, 716-645-2110, Fax: 716-645-7937, E-mail: gseinfo@buffalo.edu. Website: http://gse.buffalo.edu/csep

University of Alberta, Faculty of Graduate Studies and Research, Department of Educational Psychology, Edmonton, AB T6G 2E1, Canada. Offers counseling psychology (M Ed, PhD); educational psychology (M Ed, PhD); instructional technology (M Ed); school counseling (M Ed); school psychology (M Ed, PhD); special education (M Ed, PhD); special education-deafness studies (M Ed); teaching English as a second language (M Ed). *Program availability:* Part-time. *Degree requirements:* For master's, thesis optional; for doctorate, comprehensive exam, thesis/dissertation. *Entrance requirements:* For master's and doctorate, minimum GPA of 3.0. Additional exam requirements/recommendations for international students: Required—TOEFL. *Faculty research:* Human learning, development and assessment.

The University of Arizona, College of Education, Department of Educational Psychology, Tucson, AZ 85721. Offers educational psychology (MA, PhD); educational research methodology (Certificate); motivating learning environments (Certificate). *Accreditation:* APA (one or more programs are accredited). *Program availability:* Part-time. Terminal master's awarded for partial completion of doctoral program. *Degree*

requirements: For master's, comprehensive exam (for some programs), thesis optional; for doctorate, comprehensive exam, thesis/dissertation. *Entrance requirements:* For master's, minimum GPA of 3.0, 3 letters of recommendation, 500-word professional writing sample; for doctorate, GRE General Test, minimum GPA of 3.0, 3 letters of recommendation, statement of purpose, 500-word professional writing sample. Additional exam requirements/recommendations for international students: Required—TOEFL (minimum score 600 paper-based). Electronic applications accepted. *Faculty research:* School reform, motivational learning in classroom settings, measurement and evaluation of learning outcomes, student resilience, preadolescent and adolescent development.

University of California, Davis, Graduate Studies, Graduate Group in Education, Davis, CA 95616. Offers education (MA, Ed D); instructional studies (PhD); psychological studies (PhD); sociocultural studies (PhD). Ed D offered jointly with California State University, Fresno. Terminal master's awarded for partial completion of doctoral program. *Degree requirements:* For master's, comprehensive exam (for some programs), thesis (for some programs); for doctorate, thesis/dissertation. *Entrance requirements:* For master's and doctorate, GRE. Additional exam requirements/recommendations for international students: Required—TOEFL (minimum score 550 paper-based). Electronic applications accepted. *Faculty research:* Language and literacy, mathematics education, science education, teacher development, school psychology.

University of California, Riverside, Graduate Division, Graduate School of Education, Riverside, CA 92521. Offers applied behavior analysis (M Ed); diversity and equity (M Ed); education policy analysis and leadership (PhD); education specialist (Credential); education, society, and culture (MA, PhD); educational psychology (MA, PhD); general education (M Ed); higher education administration and policy (M Ed, PhD); multiple subject (Credential); research, evaluation, measurement and statistics (MA); school psychology (PhD); single subject (Credential); special education (M Ed, PhD); special education and autism (MA); TESOL (M Ed). Terminal master's awarded for partial completion of doctoral program. *Degree requirements:* For master's, comprehensive exams or thesis (MA), case study or analytical report (M Ed); for doctorate, comprehensive exam, thesis/dissertation, written and oral qualifying exams, college teaching practicum. *Entrance requirements:* For master's, GRE General Test (for MA), CBEST and CSET (for M Ed in general education only), UCR Extension TESOL certificate (for M Ed with TESOL emphasis only); for doctorate, GRE General Test, writing sample; for Credential, CBEST, CSET. Additional exam requirements/recommendations for international students: Required—TOEFL (minimum score 550 paper-based; 80 iBT), IELTS (minimum score 7). Electronic applications accepted. *Faculty research:* Responsiveness to intervention, faculty core, response to intervention of English language learners, advanced modeling techniques, study on social capital, trust, and motivation.

University of Colorado Boulder, Graduate School, School of Education, Division of Educational and Psychological Studies, Boulder, CO 80309. Offers MA, PhD. *Accreditation:* NCATE. Terminal master's awarded for partial completion of doctoral program. *Degree requirements:* For master's, comprehensive exam, thesis or alternative; for doctorate, one foreign language, comprehensive exam, thesis/dissertation. *Entrance requirements:* For master's, GRE General Test or MAT, minimum undergraduate GPA of 2.75; for doctorate, GRE General Test. Electronic applications accepted. Application fee is waived when completed online.

University of Connecticut, Graduate School, Neag School of Education, Department of Educational Psychology, Storrs, CT 06269. Offers cognition and instruction (MA, PhD). *Degree requirements:* For master's, comprehensive exam; for doctorate, thesis/dissertation. *Entrance requirements:* For doctorate, GRE General Test. Additional exam requirements/recommendations for international students: Required—TOEFL (minimum score 550 paper-based). Electronic applications accepted.

University of Georgia, College of Education, Department of Educational Psychology, Athens, GA 30602. Offers educational psychology (Ed S). *Accreditation:* NCATE. *Entrance requirements:* For degree, GRE General Test or MAT. Electronic applications accepted.

University of Hawaii at Manoa, Office of Graduate Education, College of Education, Department of Educational Psychology, Honolulu, HI 96822. Offers M Ed, PhD. *Program availability:* Part-time. *Degree requirements:* For master's, thesis optional; for doctorate, comprehensive exam, thesis/dissertation. *Entrance requirements:* Additional exam requirements/recommendations for international students: Required—TOEFL (minimum score 600 paper-based; 100 iBT), IELTS (minimum score 7). *Faculty research:* Human learning and development, measurement, research methods, statistics.

University of Hawaii at Manoa, Office of Graduate Education, College of Education, PhD in Education Program, Honolulu, HI 96822. Offers curriculum and instruction (PhD); educational administration (PhD); educational foundations (PhD); educational policy studies (PhD); educational psychology (PhD); exceptionalities (PhD); kinesiology (PhD); learning design and technology (PhD). *Program availability:* Part-time, evening/weekend. *Degree requirements:* For doctorate, thesis/dissertation. *Entrance requirements:* For doctorate, GRE General Test, sample of written work. Additional exam requirements/recommendations for international students: Required—TOEFL (minimum score 600 paper-based; 100 iBT), IELTS (minimum score 7).

University of Illinois at Chicago, College of Education, Department of Educational Psychology, Chicago, IL 60607-7128. Offers early childhood education (M Ed); educational psychology (PhD); measurement, evaluation, statistics, and assessment (M Ed); youth development (M Ed). *Program availability:* Part-time, online learning. *Faculty research:* Children's construction of morality, development of resilience in the face of enduring economical difficulties, cognition and cognitive development, test fairness.

University of Illinois at Urbana–Champaign, Graduate College, College of Education, Department of Educational Psychology, Champaign, IL 61820. Offers Ed M, MA, MS, PhD, CAS. *Accreditation:* APA (one or more programs are accredited). *Program availability:* Part-time, online learning.

The University of Iowa, Graduate College, College of Education, Department of Psychological and Quantitative Foundations, Iowa City, IA 52242-1316. Offers counseling psychology (PhD); educational measurement and statistics (MA, PhD); educational psychology (MA, PhD); school psychology (PhD, Ed S). *Accreditation:* APA. *Degree requirements:* For master's, thesis optional, exam; for doctorate, comprehensive exam, thesis/dissertation; for Ed S, exam. *Entrance requirements:* For master's, doctorate, and Ed S, GRE General Test, minimum GPA of 3.0. Additional exam requirements/recommendations for international students: Required—TOEFL (minimum score 550 paper-based; 81 iBT). Electronic applications accepted.

The University of Kansas, Graduate Studies, School of Education, Department of Educational Psychology, Program in Educational Psychology and Research, Lawrence, KS 66045. Offers MS Ed, PhD. *Program availability:* Part-time. *Students:* 40 full-time (24 women), 6 part-time (5 women); includes 6 minority (2 Black or African American, non-Hispanic/Latino; 3 Asian, non-Hispanic/Latino; 1 Hispanic/Latino), 21 international.

Average age 31. 27 applicants, 74% accepted, 11 enrolled. In 2018, 3 master's, 7 doctorates awarded. *Entrance requirements:* For master's, GRE General Test, minimum GPA of 3.0, resume, statement of purpose, official transcripts, three recommendation letters; for doctorate, GRE General Test, resume, statement of purpose, official transcripts, three recommendation letters. Additional exam requirements/recommendations for international students: Required—TOEFL, IELTS. *Application deadline:* For fall admission, 12/15 for domestic and international students. Application fee: $65 ($85 for international students). Electronic applications accepted. *Financial support:* Fellowships, research assistantships, teaching assistantships, career-related internships or fieldwork, institutionally sponsored loans, scholarships/grants, traineeships, health care benefits, tuition waivers (full and partial), and unspecified assistantships available. Support available to part-time students. Financial award application deadline: 12/15. *Faculty research:* Educational measurement, applied statistics, research design, program evaluation, learning and development. *Unit head:* David M Hansen, Chair, 785-864-1874, E-mail: dhansen1@ku.edu. *Application contact:* Penny Fritts, Admissions Coordinator, 785-864-9645, E-mail: fritts@ku.edu.
Website: http://www.soe.ku.edu/PRE/

University of Kentucky, Graduate School, College of Education, Program in Educational and Counseling Psychology, Lexington, KY 40506-0032. Offers counseling psychology (MS, PhD, Ed S); educational psychology (MS, PhD); school psychology (PhD, Ed S). *Accreditation:* APA (one or more programs are accredited); NCATE. *Degree requirements:* For doctorate, comprehensive exam, thesis/dissertation; for Ed S, comprehensive exam. *Entrance requirements:* For doctorate, GRE General Test, minimum graduate GPA of 3.0; for Ed S, GRE General Test. Additional exam requirements/recommendations for international students: Required—TOEFL (minimum score 550 paper-based). Electronic applications accepted.

University of Louisville, Graduate School, College of Education and Human Development, Department of Counseling and Human Development, Louisville, KY 40292-0001. Offers counseling and personnel services (M Ed, PhD), including art therapy (M Ed), college student personnel, counseling psychology, counselor education and supervision (PhD), educational psychology, measurement, and evaluation (PhD), mental health counseling (M Ed), school counseling (M Ed). *Accreditation:* APA; NCATE. *Program availability:* Part-time, evening/weekend, 100% online, blended/hybrid learning. *Students:* 136 full-time (109 women), 53 part-time (38 women); includes 40 minority (26 Black or African American, non-Hispanic/Latino; 1 American Indian or Alaska Native, non-Hispanic/Latino; 1 Asian, non-Hispanic/Latino; 8 Hispanic/Latino; 4 Two or more races, non-Hispanic/Latino), 4 international. Average age 29. 180 applicants, 47% accepted, 54 enrolled. In 2018, 39 master's awarded. Terminal master's awarded for partial completion of doctoral program. *Degree requirements:* For master's, comprehensive exam (for some programs), thesis optional; for doctorate, comprehensive exam (for some programs), thesis/dissertation. *Entrance requirements:* For master's, GRE (for most programs), PRAXIS (for educator preparation programs), professional statement, recommendation letters, resume, transcripts; for doctorate, GRE, professional statement, recommendation letters, resume, transcripts. Additional exam requirements/recommendations for international students: Required—TOEFL (minimum score 550 paper-based; 79 iBT); Recommended—IELTS (minimum score 6.5). *Application deadline:* For fall admission, 6/1 priority date for domestic students, 5/1 priority date for international students; for spring admission, 10/1 priority date for domestic students, 11/1 priority date for international students; for summer admission, 3/1 priority date for domestic students, 4/1 priority date for international students. Application fee: $65. *Expenses: Tuition, area resident:* Full-time $6500; part-time $723 per credit hour. Tuition, state resident: full-time $6500. Tuition, nonresident: full-time $13,557; part-time $1507 per credit hour. Tuition and fees vary according to course load and program. *Financial support:* In 2018–19, 95 students received support, including 5 fellowships with full tuition reimbursements available (averaging $21,024 per year), 32 research assistantships with full tuition reimbursements available (averaging $21,024 per year), 18 teaching assistantships with full tuition reimbursements available (averaging $21,024 per year); Federal Work-Study, scholarships/grants, health care benefits, and unspecified assistantships also available. Financial award application deadline: 3/1; financial award applicants required to submit FAFSA. *Faculty research:* Mental health services and under-served populations; health disparities and outcomes; well-being identity development; measurement and evaluation; college student personnel. *Unit head:* Dr. Mark M. Leach, Chair and Professor, 502-852-6884, E-mail: ecpy@louisville.edu. *Application contact:* Dr. Margaret Pentecost, Assistant Dean for Graduate Student Success, 502-852-2628, Fax: 502-852-1417, E-mail: gedadm@louisville.edu.
Website: http://www.louisville.edu/education/departments/ecpy

The University of Manchester, Manchester Institute of Education, Manchester, United Kingdom. Offers counseling (D Couns); counseling psychology (D Couns); education (M Phil, Ed D, PhD); educational and child psychology (Ed D); educational psychology (Ed D).

University of Manitoba, Faculty of Graduate Studies, Faculty of Education, Department of Educational Administration, Foundations and Psychology, Winnipeg, MB R3T 2N2, Canada. Offers adult and post-secondary education (M Ed); educational administration (M Ed); guidance and counseling (M Ed); inclusive special education (M Ed); social foundations of education (M Ed). *Degree requirements:* For master's, thesis or alternative.

University of Memphis, Graduate School, College of Education, Department of Counseling, Educational Psychology and Research, Memphis, TN 38152. Offers counseling (MS, Ed D), including clinical mental health counseling (MS), clinical rehabilitation counseling (MS), rehabilitation counseling (MS), school counseling (MS); counseling psychology (PhD); educational psychology and research (MS, PhD), including educational psychology, educational research. *Accreditation:* ACA (one or more programs are accredited); APA (one or more programs are accredited); CORE (one or more programs are accredited); NCATE. *Program availability:* Blended/hybrid learning. *Students:* 137 full-time (114 women), 126 part-time (96 women); includes 96 minority (75 Black or African American, non-Hispanic/Latino; 6 Asian, non-Hispanic/Latino; 10 Hispanic/Latino; 5 Two or more races, non-Hispanic/Latino), 5 international. Average age 33. 103 applicants, 61% accepted, 59 enrolled. In 2018, 30 master's, 19 doctorates awarded. *Degree requirements:* For master's, comprehensive exam, thesis or alternative, internship; for doctorate, comprehensive exam, thesis/dissertation, practicum, internship, residency, scholarly work. *Entrance requirements:* For master's, GRE General Test or MAT, minimum GPA of 2.5, letters of reference, interview; for doctorate, GRE General Test, master's degree or equivalent, letters of reference, interview, curriculum vitae, personal statement. Additional exam requirements/recommendations for international students: Required—TOEFL (minimum score 550 paper-based; 79 iBT). *Application deadline:* For fall admission, 10/1 priority date for domestic students; for spring admission, 4/1 priority date for domestic students. Applications are processed on a rolling basis. Application fee: $35 ($60 for international students). Electronic applications accepted. *Expenses: Tuition, area resident:* Full-time $10,240; part-time $503 per credit hour. Tuition, state resident: full-time $10,464. Tuition, nonresident: full-time $20,224; part-time $991 per credit hour. *Required fees:* $850; $106 per credit hour. *Financial support:* Fellowships with full tuition reimbursements, research assistantships with full tuition reimbursements, teaching assistantships with full tuition reimbursements, career-related internships or fieldwork, Federal Work-Study, scholarships/grants, and unspecified assistantships available. Financial award application deadline: 2/1; financial award applicants required to submit FAFSA. *Faculty research:* Anger management, aging and disability, supervision, multicultural counseling. *Unit head:* Dr. Steve West, Chair, 901-678-2841, Fax: 901-678-5114, E-mail: slwest@memphis.edu. *Application contact:* Stormey Warren, Graduate Programs, 901-678-2363, Fax: 901-678-4778, E-mail: shutsell@memphis.edu.
Website: http://www.memphis.edu/cepr/

University of Minnesota, Twin Cities Campus, Graduate School, College of Education and Human Development, Department of Educational Psychology, Minneapolis, MN 55455-0213. Offers autism spectrum disorder (Certificate); counseling and student personnel psychology (MA); early childhood special education (M Ed); psychological foundations of education (MA, PhD); quantitative methods in education (MA, PhD); school psychology (MA, PhD, Ed S); special education (M Ed, MA, PhD); talent development and gifted education (Certificate). *Accreditation:* APA (one or more programs are accredited). *Faculty:* 29 full-time (13 women). *Students:* 243 full-time (181 women), 38 part-time (31 women); includes 45 minority (6 Black or African American, non-Hispanic/Latino; 17 Asian, non-Hispanic/Latino; 12 Hispanic/Latino; 10 Two or more races, non-Hispanic/Latino), 42 international. Average age 29. 278 applicants, 46% accepted, 95 enrolled. In 2018, 100 master's, 21 doctorates, 16 other advanced degrees awarded. Application fee: $75 ($95 for international students). *Financial support:* In 2018–19, 16 fellowships, 65 research assistantships (averaging $13,491 per year), 37 teaching assistantships (averaging $11,583 per year) were awarded. *Faculty research:* Achievement gap; autism; behavioral and social-emotional development; improving skills in mathematics, reading, and comprehension; measuring and analyzing student change. *Total annual research expenditures:* $6.9 million. *Unit head:* Dr. Kristen McMaster, Chair, 612-624-6083, Fax: 612-624-8241, E-mail: mcmas004@umn.edu. *Application contact:* Dr. Panayiota Kendeou, Director of Graduate Studies, 612-626-7814, E-mail: kend0040@umn.edu.
Website: http://www.cehd.umn.edu/EdPsych

University of Missouri, Office of Research and Graduate Studies, College of Education, Department of Educational, School, and Counseling Psychology, Columbia, MO 65211. Offers counseling psychology (M Ed, MA, PhD, Ed S); educational psychology (M Ed, MA, PhD, Ed S); learning and instruction (M Ed); school psychology (M Ed, MA, PhD, Ed S). *Accreditation:* APA (one or more programs are accredited). *Program availability:* Part-time. *Entrance requirements:* For master's, doctorate, and Ed S, GRE General Test, minimum GPA of 3.0. Additional exam requirements/recommendations for international students: Required—TOEFL.

University of Missouri–St. Louis, College of Education, Interdisciplinary Doctoral Programs, St. Louis, MO 63121. Offers counseling (PhD); educational leadership and policy studies (PhD); educational psychology (PhD); leadership in educational practice (Ed D); teaching-learning processes (PhD). *Degree requirements:* For doctorate, thesis/dissertation. *Entrance requirements:* For doctorate, GRE General Test, 3 letters of recommendation; personal interview. Additional exam requirements/recommendations for international students: Recommended—TOEFL (minimum score 550 paper-based; 79 iBT), IELTS (minimum score 6.5). Electronic applications accepted. *Faculty research:* Higher education law and policy, gender and higher education, student retention, lifelong learning orientation, school counselor's role in violence prevention.

University of Nebraska–Lincoln, Graduate College, College of Education and Human Sciences, Department of Educational Psychology, Lincoln, NE 68588. Offers cognition, learning and development (MA); counseling psychology (MA); educational psychology (MA, Ed S); psychological studies in education (PhD), including cognition, learning and development, counseling psychology, quantitative, qualitative, and psychometric methods, school psychology; quantitative, qualitative, and psychometric methods (MA); school psychology (MA, Ed S). *Accreditation:* APA (one or more programs are accredited); NCATE. *Degree requirements:* For master's, thesis optional. *Entrance requirements:* For master's, GRE General Test. Additional exam requirements/recommendations for international students: Required—TOEFL (minimum score 500 paper-based). Electronic applications accepted. *Faculty research:* Measurement and assessment, metacognition, academic skills, child development, multicultural education and counseling.

University of Nevada, Reno, Graduate School, College of Education, Department of Counseling and Educational Psychology, Reno, NV 89557. Offers M Ed, MA, MS, Ed D, PhD, Ed S. *Accreditation:* ACA (one or more programs are accredited); NCATE. Terminal master's awarded for partial completion of doctoral program. *Degree requirements:* For master's, comprehensive exam, thesis optional; for doctorate, comprehensive exam, thesis/dissertation, qualifying exam. *Entrance requirements:* For master's, GRE, minimum GPA of 2.75; for doctorate, GRE, minimum GPA of 3.0. Additional exam requirements/recommendations for international students: Required—TOEFL (minimum score 500 paper-based; 61 iBT), IELTS (minimum score 6). Electronic applications accepted. *Faculty research:* Marriage and family counseling, substance abuse attitudes of teachers, current supply of counseling educators, HIV-positive services for patients, family counseling for youth at risk.

University of New Mexico, Graduate Studies, College of Education, Program in Educational Psychology, Albuquerque, NM 87131-2039. Offers MA, PhD. *Accreditation:* NCATE. *Program availability:* Part-time, evening/weekend. *Students:* Average age 37. 1 applicant, 100% accepted, 1 enrolled. In 2018, 4 master's, 4 doctorates awarded. Terminal master's awarded for partial completion of doctoral program. *Degree requirements:* For master's, comprehensive exam (for some programs), thesis (for some programs); for doctorate, comprehensive exam, thesis/dissertation. *Entrance requirements:* For master's, GRE General Test or MAT, minimum GPA of 3.0 in last 2 years of undergraduate study, 3 letters of reference, interview with 3 faculty; for doctorate, GRE General Test or MAT, minimum GPA of 3.0 in last 2 years of undergraduate study, 3 letters of reference, interview with 3 faculty, writing sample. Additional exam requirements/recommendations for international students: Required—TOEFL. *Application deadline:* For fall admission, 3/1 for domestic and international students; for spring admission, 10/1 for domestic and international students. Application fee: $50. Electronic applications accepted. *Financial support:* Teaching assistantships and unspecified assistantships available. Financial award application deadline: 3/1; financial award applicants required to submit FAFSA. *Faculty research:* Measurement and assessment, cognitive strategies, accountability, motivation, instructional technology, educational research, human lifespan development, beliefs. *Unit head:* Dr. Jay Parkes, Department Chair, 505-277-3320, Fax: 505-277-8361, E-mail: edpsy@unm.edu. *Application contact:* Cynthia Salas, Department Administrator, 505-277-4535, Fax: 505-277-8361, E-mail: divbse@unm.edu.
Website: https://coe.unm.edu/departments-programs/ifce/educational-psychology/

The University of North Carolina at Chapel Hill, Graduate School, School of Education, Program in Education, Chapel Hill, NC 27599. Offers culture, curriculum and change (MA, PhD); early childhood, intervention and literacy (MA, PhD); educational psychology, measurement and evaluation (MA, PhD). *Accreditation:* NCATE. *Degree requirements:* For master's, thesis; for doctorate, comprehensive exam, thesis/dissertation. *Entrance requirements:* For master's, GRE General Test, minimum GPA of

3.0 during last 2 years of undergraduates course work; for doctorate, GRE General Test, minimum GPA of 3.0 during last 2 years of undergraduate course work. Additional exam requirements/recommendations for international students: Required—TOEFL (minimum score 550 paper-based). Electronic applications accepted.

University of Northern Colorado, Graduate School, College of Education and Behavioral Sciences, School of Psychological Sciences, Greeley, CO 80639. Offers educational psychology (MA, PhD). *Program availability:* Part-time. *Degree requirements:* For master's, comprehensive exam, thesis or alternative; for doctorate, comprehensive exam, thesis/dissertation. *Entrance requirements:* For master's and doctorate, GRE General Test, letters of recommendation. Electronic applications accepted.

University of Northern Iowa, Graduate College, College of Education, Department of Educational Psychology and Foundations, MAE Program in Educational Psychology: Professional Development for Teachers, Cedar Falls, IA 50614. Offers MAE. *Program availability:* Online learning.

University of North Texas, Toulouse Graduate School, Denton, TX 76203-5459. Offers accounting (MS); applied anthropology (MA, MS); applied behavior analysis (Certificate); applied geography (MA); applied technology and performance improvement (M Ed, MS); art education (MA); art history (MA); arts leadership (Certificate); audiology (Au D); behavior analysis (MS); behavioral science (PhD); biochemistry and molecular biology (MS); biology (MA, MS); biomedical engineering (MS); business analysis (MS); chemistry (MS); clinical health psychology (PhD); communication studies (MA, MS); computer engineering (MS); computer science (MS); counseling (M Ed, MS), including clinical mental health counseling (MS), college and university counseling, elementary school counseling, secondary school counseling; creative writing (MA); criminal justice (MS); curriculum and instruction (M Ed); decision sciences (MBA); design (MA, MFA), including fashion design (MFA), innovation studies, interior design (MFA); early childhood studies (MS); economics (MS); educational leadership (M Ed, Ed D); educational psychology (MS, PhD), including family studies (MS), gifted and talented (MS), human development (MS), learning and cognition (MS), research, measurement and evaluation (MS); electrical engineering (MS); emergency management (MPA); engineering technology (MS); English (MA); English as a second language (MA); environmental science (MS); finance (MBA, MS); financial management (MPA); French (MA); health services management (MBA); higher education (M Ed, Ed D); history (MA, MS); hospitality management (MS); human resources management (MPA); information science (MS); information systems (PhD); information technologies (MBA); interdisciplinary studies (MA, MS); international studies (MA); international sustainable tourism (MS); jazz studies (MM); journalism (MA, MJ, Graduate Certificate), including interactive and virtual digital communication (Graduate Certificate), narrative journalism (Graduate Certificate), public relations (Graduate Certificate); kinesiology (MS); linguistics (MA); local government management (MPA); logistics (PhD); logistics and supply chain management (MBA); long-term care, senior housing, and aging services (MA); management (PhD); marketing (MBA); mathematics (MA, MS); mechanical and energy engineering (MS, PhD); music (MA), including ethnomusicology, music theory, musicology, performance; music composition (PhD); music education (MM Ed, PhD); nonprofit management (MPA); operations and supply chain management (MBA); performance (MM, DMA); philosophy (MA); political science (MA); professional and technical communication (MA); radio, television and film (MA, MFA); rehabilitation counseling (Certificate); sociology (MA); Spanish (MA); special education (M Ed); speech-language pathology (MA); strategic management (MBA); studio art (MFA); teaching (M Ed); MBA/MS. *Program availability:* Part-time, evening/weekend, online learning. Terminal master's awarded for partial completion of doctoral program. *Degree requirements:* For master's, variable foreign language requirement, comprehensive exam (for some programs), thesis (for some programs); for doctorate, variable foreign language requirement, comprehensive exam (for some programs), thesis/dissertation; for other advanced degree, variable foreign language requirement, comprehensive exam (for some programs). *Entrance requirements:* For master's and doctorate, GRE, GMAT. Additional exam requirements/recommendations for international students: Required—TOEFL (minimum score 550 paper-based; 79 iBT). Electronic applications accepted.

University of Oklahoma, Jeannine Rainbolt College of Education, Department of Educational Psychology, Norman, OK 73019. Offers instructional psychology and technology (M Ed, PhD), including educational psychology (M Ed), instructional design and technology (M Ed), instructional psychology and technology (PhD), integrating technology in teaching (M Ed); professional counseling (M Ed), including professional counseling; special education (M Ed, PhD), including applied behavior analysis (M Ed), higher education and community support (PhD), higher education professor (PhD), school instruction and leadership (PhD), secondary transition education (M Ed). *Accreditation:* NCATE. *Program availability:* Part-time, 100% online, blended/hybrid learning. Terminal master's awarded for partial completion of doctoral program. *Degree requirements:* For master's, comprehensive exam (for some programs), thesis (for some programs); for doctorate, comprehensive exam (for some programs), thesis/dissertation. *Entrance requirements:* For doctorate, GRE. Additional exam requirements/recommendations for international students: Required—TOEFL (minimum score 79 iBT) or IELTS (minimum score 6.5). Electronic applications accepted. *Expenses:* Tuition, state resident: full-time $5683.20; part-time $236.80 per credit hour. Tuition, nonresident: full-time $20,342; part-time $847.60 per credit hour. *International tuition:* $20,342.40 full-time. *Required fees:* $2894.20; $110.05 per credit hour. $126.50 per semester. Tuition and fees vary according to course load and program. *Faculty research:* Diversity Issues in counseling; qualitative and mixed-methods research; high-stakes assessments and related educational policy; self-determination and post-secondary outcomes; reading, writing, spelling, and mathematics interventions.

University of Regina, Faculty of Graduate Studies and Research, Faculty of Education, Department of Educational Psychology, Regina, SK S4S 0A2, Canada. Offers M Ed. *Program availability:* Part-time. *Students:* 12 full-time (10 women), 60 part-time (54 women). Average age 35. 14 applicants. In 2018, 29 master's awarded. *Degree requirements:* For master's, thesis (for some programs), practicum, project, or thesis. *Entrance requirements:* For master's, four-year degree applicable to the program (normally a B.Ed., B.H.R.D., or B.A.Ed., or equivalent); 2 years of teaching or other relevant professional experience preferred; grade point average of 70 percent. Additional exam requirements/recommendations for international students: Required—TOEFL (minimum score 580 paper-based; 80 iBT), IELTS (minimum score 6.5), PTE (minimum score 59), other options are CAEL, MELAB, Cantest and U of R ESL. *Application deadline:* For fall admission, 2/15 for domestic and international students; for winter admission, 10/15 for domestic and international students; for spring admission, 2/15 for domestic and international students. Application fee: $100. Electronic applications accepted. *Expenses:* Estimated tuition and fees for one academic year is 6,702.90 for master's. The fee will vary base on your choice program. For doctoral program one academic year is estimated 14,129.40. International students will pay additional 1,191.75 for international surcharge per semester. *Financial support:* Fellowships, research assistantships, teaching assistantships, career-related internships or fieldwork, Federal Work-Study, scholarships/grants, unspecified assistantships, and travel award and Graduate Scholarship Base Funds available. Support available to part-time students. Financial award application deadline: 9/30. *Faculty research:* Theories of counseling, psychology of learning, aptitude and achievement analysis, education and vocational guidance, resilience: re-conceptualizing PRAXIS. *Unit head:* Dr. Twyla Salm, Associate Dean, Research & Graduate Programs, 306-585-4604, Fax: 306-585-4006, E-mail: Twyla.Salm@uregina.ca. *Application contact:* Linda Jiang, Graduate Program Coordinator, 306-585-4506, Fax: 306-585-5387, E-mail: edgrad@uregina.ca. Website: http://www.uregina.ca/education/

University of Saskatchewan, College of Graduate and Postdoctoral Studies, College of Education, Department of Educational Psychology and Special Education, Saskatoon, SK S7N 5A2, Canada. Offers measurement and evaluation (M Ed, PhD); school and counseling psychology (M Ed, PhD); special education (M Ed, PhD). *Degree requirements:* For master's, thesis (for some programs); for doctorate, comprehensive exam (for some programs), thesis/dissertation. *Entrance requirements:* Additional exam requirements/recommendations for international students: Required—TOEFL (minimum score 80 iBT); Recommended—IELTS (minimum score 6.5). Electronic applications accepted.

University of South Africa, College of Human Sciences, Pretoria, South Africa. Offers adult education (M Ed); African languages (MA, PhD); African politics (MA, PhD); Afrikaans (MA, PhD); ancient history (MA, PhD); ancient Near Eastern studies (MA, PhD); anthropology (MA, PhD); applied linguistics (MA); Arabic (MA, PhD); archaeology (MA); art history (MA); Biblical archaeology (MA); Biblical studies (M Th, D Th, PhD); Christian spirituality (M Th, D Th); church history (M Th, D Th); classical studies (MA, PhD); clinical psychology (MA); communication (MA, PhD); comparative education (M Ed, Ed D); consulting psychology (D Admin, D Com, PhD); curriculum studies (M Ed, Ed D); development studies (M Admin, MA, D Admin, PhD); didactics (M Ed, Ed D); education (M Tech); education management (M Ed, Ed D); educational psychology (M Ed); English (MA); environmental education (M Ed); French (MA, PhD); German (MA, PhD); Greek (MA); guidance and counseling (M Ed); health studies (MA, PhD), including health sciences education (MA), health services management (MA), medical and surgical nursing science (critical care general) (MA), midwifery and neonatal nursing science (MA), trauma and emergency care (MA); history (MA, PhD); history of education (Ed D); inclusive education (M Ed, Ed D); information and communications technology policy and regulation (MA); information science (MA, MIS, PhD); international politics (MA, PhD); Islamic studies (MA, PhD); Italian (MA, PhD); Judaica (MA, PhD); linguistics (MA, PhD); mathematical education (M Ed); mathematics education (MA); missiology (M Th, D Th); modern Hebrew (MA, PhD); musicology (MA, MMus, D Mus, PhD); natural science education (M Ed); New Testament (M Th, D Th); Old Testament (D Th); pastoral therapy (M Th, D Th); philosophy (MA); philosophy of education (M Ed, Ed D); politics (MA, PhD); Portuguese (MA, PhD); practical theology (M Th, D Th); psychology (MA, MS, PhD); psychology of education (M Ed, Ed D); public health (MA); religious studies (MA, D Th, PhD); Romance languages (MA); Russian (MA, PhD); Semitic languages (MA, PhD); social behavior studies in HIV/AIDS (MA); social science (mental health) (MA); social science in development studies (MA); social science in psychology (MA); social science in social work (MA); social science in sociology (MA); social work (MSW, DSW, PhD); socio-education (M Ed, Ed D); sociolinguistics (MA); sociology (MA, PhD); Spanish (MA, PhD); systematic theology (M Th, D Th); TESOL (teaching English to speakers of other languages) (MA); theological ethics (M Th, D Th); theory of literature (MA, PhD); urban ministries (D Th); urban ministry (M Th).

University of South Carolina, The Graduate School, College of Education, Department of Educational Studies, Program in Educational Psychology, Research, Columbia, SC 29208. Offers M Ed, PhD. *Accreditation:* NCATE. *Program availability:* Part-time. *Degree requirements:* For master's, comprehensive exam, thesis (for some programs); for doctorate, comprehensive exam, thesis/dissertation. *Entrance requirements:* For master's, GRE General Test; for doctorate, GRE General Test, interview. Electronic applications accepted. *Faculty research:* Problem solving, higher order thinking skills, psychometric research, methodology.

University of South Dakota, Graduate School, School of Education, Division of Counseling and Psychology in Education, Vermillion, SD 57069. Offers counseling (MA, PhD, Ed S); human development and educational psychology (MA, PhD, Ed S); mental health counseling (Certificate); school psychology (PhD, Ed S). *Accreditation:* ACA (one or more programs are accredited); NCATE. *Program availability:* Part-time. *Degree requirements:* For master's and other advanced degree, comprehensive exam, thesis or alternative; for doctorate, comprehensive exam, thesis/dissertation. *Entrance requirements:* For master's and doctorate, GRE General Test, minimum GPA of 3.0. Additional exam requirements/recommendations for international students: Required—TOEFL (minimum score 550 paper-based; 79 iBT). Electronic applications accepted.

University of Southern California, Graduate School, Rossier School of Education, Doctor of Education Programs, Los Angeles, CA 90089. Offers educational psychology (Ed D); higher education administration (Ed D); K-12 leadership in urban school settings (Ed D); teacher education in multicultural societies (Ed D). *Program availability:* Part-time, evening/weekend. *Degree requirements:* For doctorate, thesis/dissertation. *Entrance requirements:* For doctorate, GRE. Additional exam requirements/recommendations for international students: Required—TOEFL (minimum score 100 iBT). Electronic applications accepted. *Faculty research:* Data-driven decision-making in K-12 schools and districts; examination of college and university leadership and management in U. S. and Asia; studies in facilitating student learning; organizational change and the role of leaders; leadership, diversity, learning and accountability.

University of Southern California, Graduate School, Rossier School of Education, Doctor of Philosophy in Education Programs, Los Angeles, CA 90089. Offers educational psychology (PhD); higher education administration and policy (PhD); K-12 policy and practice (PhD). *Degree requirements:* For doctorate, thesis/dissertation, 63 units; qualifying exam; dissertation proposal and defense. *Entrance requirements:* For doctorate, GRE. Additional exam requirements/recommendations for international students: Required—TOEFL (minimum score 100 iBT). Electronic applications accepted. *Faculty research:* Diversity in higher education, organizational change, educational psychology, policy and politics of educational reform, economics of education and education policy.

University of Southern Maine, College of Management and Human Service, School of Education and Human Development, Program in Educational Psychology, Portland, ME 04103. Offers applied behavior analysis (MS, CGS). *Program availability:* Part-time, evening/weekend. *Entrance requirements:* For master's, GRE or MAT. Additional exam requirements/recommendations for international students: Required—TOEFL (minimum score 550 paper-based; 79 iBT). Electronic applications accepted. *Faculty research:* Applied behavior analysis, functional behavioral analysis, positive behavioral interventions and supports.

University of South Florida, College of Education, Department of Educational and Psychological Studies, Tampa, FL 33620-9951. Offers college student affairs (M Ed); counselor education (MA, PhD, Ed S); interdisciplinary education (PhD, Ed S); school psychology (PhD, Ed S). *Faculty:* 27 full-time (14 women). *Students:* 133 full-time (92 women), 113 part-time (81 women); includes 64 minority (23 Black or African American, non-Hispanic/Latino; 6 Asian, non-Hispanic/Latino; 27 Hispanic/Latino; 1 Native Hawaiian or other Pacific Islander, non-Hispanic/Latino; 7 Two or more races, non-

Hispanic/Latino), 29 international. Average age 32. 205 applicants, 57% accepted, 85 enrolled. In 2018, 49 master's, 11 doctorates awarded. *Degree requirements:* For master's, comprehensive exam, thesis (for some programs); for doctorate, comprehensive exam, thesis/dissertation (for some programs). *Entrance requirements:* For master's, GRE may be required, Letters of recommendation, personal statement, interview, resume; CLAST/GKT may be required; for doctorate, GRE may be required, 3.5 master's GPA; letter of intent; resume; letters of reference. Additional exam requirements/recommendations for international students: Required—TOEFL. Application fee: $30. *Expenses:* Tuition, state resident: full-time $6350. Tuition, nonresident: full-time $19,048. *International tuition:* $19,048 full-time. *Required fees:* $2079. *Financial support:* In 2018–19, 1 student received support. *Faculty research:* College student affairs, counselor education, educational psychology, school psychology, social foundations. *Total annual research expenditures:* $10.8 million. *Unit head:* Dr. Barabara Shircliff, Chair, 813-974-4001, E-mail: shirclif@usf.edu. *Application contact:* Dr. Barabara Shircliff, Chair, 813-974-4001, E-mail: shirclif@usf.edu.

The University of Tennessee, Graduate School, College of Education, Health and Human Sciences, Department of Educational Psychology and Counseling, Knoxville, TN 37996. Offers adult education (MS); applied educational psychology (MS); collaborative learning (Ed D); college student personnel (MS); mental health counseling (MS); rehabilitation counseling (MS); school counseling (MS). *Accreditation:* ACA (one or more programs are accredited); CORE (one or more programs are accredited); NCATE. *Program availability:* Part-time, evening/weekend. *Degree requirements:* For master's, thesis optional. *Entrance requirements:* For master's, GRE General Test, minimum GPA of 2.7. Additional exam requirements/recommendations for international students: Required—TOEFL. Electronic applications accepted.

The University of Tennessee, Graduate School, College of Education, Health and Human Sciences, Program in Education, Knoxville, TN 37996. Offers art education (MS); counseling education (PhD); cultural studies in education (PhD); curriculum (MS, Ed S); curriculum, educational research and evaluation (Ed D, PhD); early childhood education (PhD); early childhood special education (MS); education of deaf and hard of hearing (MS); educational administration and policy studies (Ed D, PhD); educational administration and supervision (Ed S); educational psychology (Ed D, PhD); elementary education (MS, Ed S); elementary teaching (MS); English education (MS, Ed S); exercise science (PhD); foreign language/ESL education (MS, Ed S); instructional technology (MS, Ed D, PhD, Ed S); literacy, language and ESL education (PhD); literacy, language education, and ESL education (Ed D); mathematics education (MS, Ed S); modified and comprehensive special education (MS); reading education (MS, Ed S); school counseling (Ed S); school psychology (PhD, Ed S); science education (MS, Ed S); secondary teaching (MS); social foundations (MS); social science education (MS, Ed S); socio-cultural foundations of sports and education (PhD); special education (Ed S); teacher education (Ed D, PhD). *Accreditation:* NCATE. *Program availability:* Part-time, evening/weekend. *Degree requirements:* For master's and Ed S, thesis optional; for doctorate, variable foreign language requirement, thesis/dissertation. *Entrance requirements:* For master's, minimum GPA of 2.7; for doctorate and Ed S, GRE General Test, minimum GPA of 2.7. Additional exam requirements/recommendations for international students: Required—TOEFL. Electronic applications accepted.

The University of Texas at Austin, Graduate School, College of Education, Department of Educational Psychology, Austin, TX 78712-1111. Offers academic educational psychology (M Ed, MA); counseling psychology (PhD); counselor education (M Ed); human development, culture and learning sciences (PhD); program evaluation (MA); quantitative methods (M Ed, MA, PhD); school psychology (MA, PhD). *Accreditation:* APA (one or more programs are accredited). *Degree requirements:* For master's, thesis optional; for doctorate, thesis/dissertation. *Entrance requirements:* For master's and doctorate, GRE General Test, 3 letters of recommendation. Additional exam requirements/recommendations for international students: Required—TOEFL.

The University of Texas at El Paso, Graduate School, College of Education, Department of Educational Psychology and Special Services, El Paso, TX 79968-0001. Offers educational diagnostics (M Ed); guidance and counseling (M Ed); special education (M Ed). *Program availability:* Part-time, evening/weekend. *Degree requirements:* For master's, thesis optional. *Entrance requirements:* For master's, minimum GPA of 3.0. Additional exam requirements/recommendations for international students: Required—TOEFL. Electronic applications accepted.

The University of Texas at San Antonio, College of Education and Human Development, Department of Educational Psychology, San Antonio, TX 78207. Offers applied behavior analysis (Certificate); educational psychology (MA), including applied educational psychology, behavior assessment and intervention, general educational psychology, program evaluation; language acquisition and bilingual psychoeducational assessment (Certificate); school psychology (MA). *Program availability:* Part-time. *Degree requirements:* For master's, comprehensive exam, thesis (for some programs). *Entrance requirements:* For master's, GRE, bachelor's degree with 18 credit hours in field of study or in another appropriate field of study, two letters of recommendation, statement of purpose; for Certificate, 18 hours in psychology, sociology, education, or anything related (for applied behavioral analysis); minimum GPA of 2.7 in last 30 hours (for language acquisition and bilingual psychoeducational assessment). Additional exam requirements/recommendations for international students: Required—TOEFL (minimum score 550 paper-based; 79 iBT), IELTS (minimum score 6.5). Electronic applications accepted. *Faculty research:* Teacher consultation and culturally responsive school psychology practices, youth mentoring, cross-age peer mentoring, adolescent connectedness, pair counseling.

The University of Texas Rio Grande Valley, College of Education and P-16 Integration, Department of Human Development and School Services, Edinburg, TX 78539. Offers early childhood education (M Ed); early childhood special education (M Ed); school psychology (MA); special education (M Ed). *Program availability:* Part-time, evening/weekend. *Degree requirements:* For master's, comprehensive exam (for some programs). *Entrance requirements:* For master's, minimum GPA of 3.0. Additional exam requirements/recommendations for international students: Required—TOEFL (minimum score 550 paper-based; 79 iBT), IELTS (minimum score 6.5). Electronic applications accepted. *Expenses: Tuition, area resident:* Full-time $6888. Tuition, state resident: full-time $6888. Tuition, nonresident: full-time $14,484. *International tuition:* $14,484 full-time. *Required fees:* $1468. *Faculty research:* Special education, assessment practice, behavior interventions, mental retardation, early childhood.

University of the Pacific, Gladys L. Benerd School of Education, Stockton, CA 95211-0197. Offers curriculum and instruction (MA, Ed D); education (M Ed); educational administration and leadership (MA, Ed D); educational and school psychology (MA, Ed D); educational entrepreneurship (MA); school psychology (Ed S); special education (MA); teacher education (MA). *Accreditation:* NCATE. *Degree requirements:* For doctorate, thesis/dissertation. *Entrance requirements:* For master's, GRE General Test; for doctorate, GRE General Test, GRE Subject Test. Additional exam requirements/recommendations for international students: Required—TOEFL.

The University of Toledo, College of Graduate Studies, Judith Herb College of Education, Department of Educational Foundations and Leadership, Toledo, OH 43606-3390. Offers educational administration and supervision (ME, DE, Ed S); educational psychology (ME, PhD); educational research and measurement (ME, PhD); educational sociology (PhD); educational theory and social foundations (ME); foundations of education (DE, PhD); history of education (PhD); philosophy of education (PhD). *Accreditation:* NCATE. *Program availability:* Part-time, evening/weekend. *Degree requirements:* For master's, comprehensive exam, thesis or alternative; for doctorate, comprehensive exam, thesis/dissertation; for Ed S, thesis optional. *Entrance requirements:* For master's, doctorate, and Ed S, minimum cumulative GPA of 2.7 for all previous academic work, letters of recommendation. Additional exam requirements/recommendations for international students: Required—TOEFL (minimum score 550 paper-based; 80 iBT). Electronic applications accepted.

University of Victoria, Faculty of Graduate Studies, Faculty of Education, Department of Educational Psychology and Leadership Studies, Victoria, BC V8W 2Y2, Canada. Offers aboriginal communities counseling (M Ed); counseling (M Ed, MA); educational psychology (M Ed, MA, PhD), including counseling psychology (M Ed, MA), leadership studies (PhD), learning and development (MA, PhD), measurement and evaluation, special education (M Ed, MA); leadership studies (M Ed, MA). *Program availability:* Part-time. *Degree requirements:* For master's, thesis (for some programs), comprehensive exam (M Ed); for doctorate, comprehensive exam, thesis/dissertation, candidacy exam. *Entrance requirements:* For master's, 2 years of work experience in a relevant field; for doctorate, GRE, 2 years of work experience in a relevant field, minimum B average. Additional exam requirements/recommendations for international students: Required—TOEFL (minimum score 575 paper-based), IELTS (minimum score 7). *Faculty research:* Learning and development (child, adolescent and adult), special education and exceptional children.

University of Virginia, Curry School of Education, Department of Leadership, Foundations and Policy, Program in Educational Psychology, Charlottesville, VA 22903. Offers applied developmental science (M Ed); educational evaluation (M Ed); educational psychology (M Ed, Ed D, Ed S); educational research (Ed D); gifted education (M Ed); instructional technology (M Ed, Ed S); research statistics and evaluation (Ed D); school psychology (Ed D). *Degree requirements:* For master's, comprehensive exam. *Entrance requirements:* For master's and doctorate, GRE General Test, 2 letters of recommendation. Additional exam requirements/recommendations for international students: Required—TOEFL (minimum score 600 paper-based; 90 iBT), IELTS (minimum score 7). Electronic applications accepted.

University of Virginia, Curry School of Education, Program in Education, Charlottesville, VA 22903. Offers administration and supervision (PhD); applied developmental science (PhD); counselor education (PhD); curriculum and instruction (PhD); early childhood special education (MT); education evaluation (PhD); educational psychology (PhD); educational research (PhD); elementary education (MT); English education (MT, PhD); foreign language education (MT); higher education (PhD); instructional technology (PhD); kinesiology (MT, PhD); math education (PhD); reading education (PhD); research, statistics and evaluation (PhD); school psychology (PhD); science education (PhD); social studies education (MT, PhD); special education (PhD); world languages education (MT). *Degree requirements:* For master's, comprehensive exam (for some programs), field project; for doctorate, comprehensive exam, thesis/dissertation. *Entrance requirements:* For doctorate, GRE General Test. Additional exam requirements/recommendations for international students: Required—TOEFL (minimum score 600 paper-based; 90 iBT), IELTS (minimum score 7). Electronic applications accepted.

University of Washington, Graduate School, College of Education, Program in Educational Psychology, Seattle, WA 98195. Offers educational psychology (PhD); human development and cognition (M Ed); learning sciences (M Ed, PhD); measurement, statistics and research design (M Ed); school psychology (M Ed). *Accreditation:* APA. *Degree requirements:* For master's, thesis optional; for doctorate, thesis/dissertation. *Entrance requirements:* For master's and doctorate, GRE General Test, minimum GPA of 3.0. Additional exam requirements/recommendations for international students: Required—TOEFL.

The University of Western Ontario, School of Graduate and Postdoctoral Studies, Faculty of Social Science, Faculty of Education, Program in Educational Studies, London, ON N6A 3K7, Canada. Offers curriculum studies (M Ed); educational policy studies (M Ed); educational psychology/special education (M Ed). *Program availability:* Part-time. *Faculty research:* Reflective practice, gender and schooling, feminist pedagogy, narrative inquiry, second language, multiculturalism in Canada, education and law.

University of Wisconsin–Madison, Graduate School, School of Education, Department of Educational Psychology, Madison, WI 53706-1380. Offers MS, PhD. *Accreditation:* APA (one or more programs are accredited). *Degree requirements:* For doctorate, thesis/dissertation. *Entrance requirements:* For master's and doctorate, GRE General Test. Electronic applications accepted.

University of Wisconsin–Milwaukee, Graduate School, School of Education, Department of Educational Psychology, Milwaukee, WI 53201-0413. Offers children's mental health for school professionals (Graduate Certificate); counseling psychology (PhD); educational statistics and measurement (MS, PhD); learning and development (MS, PhD); multicultural knowledge of mental health practices (Graduate Certificate); school counseling (MS, Graduate Certificate); school psychology (MS, PhD, Ed S). *Accreditation:* APA. *Program availability:* Part-time. *Students:* 181 full-time (137 women), 45 part-time (31 women); includes 50 minority (11 Black or African American, non-Hispanic/Latino; 1 American Indian or Alaska Native, non-Hispanic/Latino; 5 Asian, non-Hispanic/Latino; 5 Hispanic/Latino; 1 Native Hawaiian or other Pacific Islander, non-Hispanic/Latino; 27 Two or more races, non-Hispanic/Latino), 7 international. Average age 31. 320 applicants, 35% accepted, 78 enrolled. In 2018, 41 master's, 2 doctorates, 16 other advanced degrees awarded. *Degree requirements:* For master's, comprehensive exam, thesis; for doctorate, thesis/dissertation. *Entrance requirements:* For master's, minimum GPA of 3.0; for doctorate, GRE General Test, minimum GPA of 3.0. Additional exam requirements/recommendations for international students: Required—TOEFL (minimum score 550 paper-based; 79 iBT), IELTS (minimum score 6.5). *Application deadline:* For fall admission, 1/1 priority date for domestic students; for spring admission, 9/1 for domestic students. Application fee: $56 ($96 for international students). Electronic applications accepted. *Financial support:* Fellowships, research assistantships, teaching assistantships, career-related internships or fieldwork, health care benefits, unspecified assistantships, and project assistantships available. Support available to part-time students. Financial award application deadline: 4/15; financial award applicants required to submit FAFSA. *Application contact:* General Information Contact, 414-229-4721, E-mail: soeinfo@uwm.edu.
Website: http://uwm.edu/education/academics/educational-psychology-department/

Virginia Commonwealth University, Graduate School, School of Education, Doctoral Program in Education, Richmond, VA 23284-9005. Offers art education (PhD); counselor education and supervision (PhD); curriculum, culture and change (PhD); educational leadership (PhD); educational psychology (PhD); leadership (Ed D); research and evaluation (PhD); special education and disability leadership (PhD); sport leadership (PhD); urban services leadership (PhD). *Accreditation:* NCATE. *Program*

availability: Part-time. *Degree requirements:* For doctorate, thesis/dissertation. *Entrance requirements:* For doctorate, GRE (for PhD), MAT (for Ed D), interview, master's degree, writing sample. Additional exam requirements/recommendations for international students: Required—TOEFL (minimum score 600 paper-based; 100 iBT). Electronic applications accepted.

Walden University, Graduate Programs, School of Psychology, Minneapolis, MN 55401. Offers clinical psychology (MS), including counseling, general program; forensic psychology (MS), including forensic psychology in the community, general program, mental health applications, program planning and evaluation in forensic settings, psychology and legal systems; industrial organizational (MS, PhD), including consulting psychology, forensic (MS), forensic psychology (PhD), general practice, leadership development and coaching (MS), organizational diversity and social change, research evaluation (PhD); online teaching in psychology (Post-Master's Certificate); organizational psychology and development (Postbaccalaureate Certificate); psychology (MS, PhD), including applied psychology (MS), clinical psychology (PhD), crisis management and response (MS), educational psychology, forensic psychology (PhD), general psychology (MS), general psychology research (PhD), general psychology teaching (PhD), health psychology, leadership development and coaching (MS), psychology of culture (MS), psychology, public administration, and social change (MS), social psychology, terrorism and security (MS); psychology respecialization (Post-Doctoral Certificate). *Program availability:* Part-time, evening/weekend, online only, 100% online. Terminal master's awarded for partial completion of doctoral program. *Degree requirements:* For master's, thesis optional; for doctorate, thesis/dissertation, residency. *Entrance requirements:* For master's, bachelor's degree or higher; minimum GPA of 2.5; official transcripts; goal statement (for some programs); access to computer and Internet; for doctorate, master's degree or higher; three years of related professional or academic experience (preferred); minimum GPA of 3.0; goal statement and current resume (for select programs); official transcripts; access to computer and Internet; for other advanced degree, relevant work experience; access to computer and Internet. Additional exam requirements/recommendations for international students: Required— TOEFL (minimum score 550 paper-based, 79 iBT), IELTS (minimum score 6.5), Michigan English Language Assessment Battery (minimum score 82), or PTE (minimum score 53). Electronic applications accepted.

Washington State University, College of Education, Department of Educational Leadership, Sports Studies, and Educational/Counseling Psychology, Pullman, WA 99164-2136. Offers counseling psychology (PhD); educational leadership (Ed M, MA, Ed D, PhD); educational psychology (MA, PhD); sport management (MA). Programs also offered at the Spokane, Tri-Cities, Vancouver and Global (online) campuses. *Program availability:* Part-time, online learning. *Degree requirements:* For master's, comprehensive exam (for some programs), thesis (for some programs), oral or written exam; for doctorate, comprehensive exam, thesis/dissertation, oral and written exam, internship. *Entrance requirements:* For master's and doctorate, GRE General Test, minimum GPA of 3.0, 3 letters of recommendation, transcripts showing all college or university course work, statement of professional objectives, current curriculum vitae/ resume. Additional exam requirements/recommendations for international students: Required—TOEFL (minimum score 550 paper-based; 80 iBT). Electronic applications accepted. *Faculty research:* Multicultural counseling and career development, educational and psychological measurement issues, business decision-making process and power relationships, leadership practices and processes as suffused with and constituted by emotion work.

Wayne State University, College of Education, Division of Theoretical and Behavioral Foundations, Detroit, MI 48202. Offers applied behavior analysis (Certificate); counseling (M Ed, MA, Ed D, Ed S); counseling psychology (MA, PhD); education evaluation and research (M Ed, Ed D); educational psychology (M Ed, PhD), including learning and instruction sciences (PhD); rehabilitation counseling and community inclusion (MA); school and community psychology (MA, Certificate). *Accreditation:* ACA (one or more programs are accredited); CORE (one or more programs are accredited). *Program availability:* Part-time, evening/weekend. *Faculty:* 9. *Students:* 168 full-time (136 women), 200 part-time (171 women); includes 128 minority (82 Black or African American, non-Hispanic/Latino; 2 American Indian or Alaska Native, non-Hispanic/ Latino; 8 Asian, non-Hispanic/Latino; 12 Hispanic/Latino; 24 Two or more races, non-Hispanic/Latino), 14 international. Average age 32. 340 applicants, 24% accepted, 66 enrolled. In 2018, 103 master's, 6 doctorates, 18 other advanced degrees awarded. *Degree requirements:* For master's, thesis (for some programs); for doctorate, comprehensive exam, thesis/dissertation. *Entrance requirements:* For master's, GRE, interview, personal statement, portfolio (only art therapy); references; program application; for doctorate, GRE, departmental writing exam, interview, curriculum vitae, references, master's degree in closely-related field with minimum GPA of 3.5, demonstration of counseling skills (for Ed D in counseling); autobiographical statement; letter of application; personal statement; for other advanced degree, education specialist certificate: GRE, education specialist certificate: master's degree in counseling or closely related field and licensure; personal statement; recommendations; autobiographical statement; interview. Additional exam requirements/recommendations for international students: Required—TOEFL (minimum score 550 paper-based; 79 iBT); Recommended—IELTS (minimum score 6.5), TWE (minimum score 5.5), TSE (minimum score 58). *Application deadline:* Applications are processed on a rolling basis. Application fee: $50. Electronic applications accepted. *Expenses:* Contact institution. *Financial support:* In 2018–19, 86 students received support, including 2 research

assistantships with tuition reimbursements available (averaging $19,267 per year); fellowships, teaching assistantships, Federal Work-Study, scholarships/grants, health care benefits, and unspecified assistantships also available. Support available to part-time students. Financial award applicants required to submit FAFSA. *Faculty research:* Adolescents at risk, supervision of counseling. *Unit head:* Dr. Cheryl Somers, Assistant Dean, 313-577-1670, E-mail: c.somers@wayne.edu. *Application contact:* Dr. Mary L Waker, Graduate Admissions Officer, 313-577-1601, Fax: 313-577-7904, E-mail: m.waker@wayne.edu.
Website: http://coe.wayne.edu/tbf/index.php

Webster University, School of Education, Department of Multidisciplinary Studies, St. Louis, MO 63119-3194. Offers applied educational psychology (MA, Ed S); communication arts (MA); early childhood education (MA, MAT); education and innovation (MA); educational technology (MET); elementary education (MAT); mathematics for educators (MA); middle school education (MAT); multidisciplinary studies (MAT); multimodal literacy for global impact (MA); reading (MA); secondary school education (MAT); special education (MA, MAT); teaching English as a second language (MA); transformative learning in the global community (Ed S). *Program availability:* Part-time. *Entrance requirements:* For master's, minimum GPA of 2.5. Additional exam requirements/recommendations for international students: Required— TOEFL. *Expenses:* Tuition: Full-time $22,500; part-time $750 per credit hour. Tuition and fees vary according to degree level, campus/location and program.

West Virginia University, College of Education and Human Services, Morgantown, WV 26506. Offers audiology (Au D); autism spectrum disorder (MA); clinical rehabilitation and mental health counseling (MS); communication science and disorders (PhD); counseling (MA); counseling psychology (PhD); curriculum and instruction (Ed D); early childhood education (MA); early intervention/ early childhood special education (MA); education (PhD); educational leadership (MA); educational leadership/ public school administration (Ed D); educational leadership/public school administration (MA); educational psychology (MA, Ed D); elementary education (MA); gifted education (MA); higher education administration (MA, Ed D); higher education curriculum and teaching (MA); institutional design and technology (MA); instructional design and technology (Ed D); literacy education (MA); secondary education (MA); secondary education/English (MA); special education (Ed D); speech pathology (MS). *Accreditation:* ASHA; NCATE. *Program availability:* Part-time, evening/weekend, online learning. *Students:* 392 full-time (325 women), 337 part-time (285 women); includes 44 minority (16 Black or African American, non-Hispanic/Latino; 16 Hispanic/Latino; 12 Two or more races, non-Hispanic/Latino), 11 international. In 2018, 303 master's, 6 doctorates awarded. *Degree requirements:* For master's, content exams; for doctorate, comprehensive exam, thesis/dissertation. *Entrance requirements:* Additional exam requirements/recommendations for international students: Required—TOEFL (minimum score 500 paper-based; 61 iBT). *Application deadline:* For fall admission, 8/1 for domestic students; for spring admission, 1/1 for domestic students; for summer admission, 5/1 for domestic students. Application fee: $60. Electronic applications accepted. *Financial support:* Fellowships, research assistantships, teaching assistantships, career-related internships or fieldwork, Federal Work-Study, institutionally sponsored loans, health care benefits, tuition waivers (full and partial), and administrative assistantships available. Financial award applicants required to submit FAFSA. *Faculty research:* Internet training and integration for teachers, rural education, teacher preparation, organization of schools, evaluation of personnel. *Unit head:* Dr. Tracy L. Morris, Interim Dean, 304-293-0816, Fax: 304-293-7565, E-mail: Tracy.Morris@mail.wvu.edu. *Application contact:* Dr. Melissa Luna, Associate Dean for Research, 304-293-2174, Fax: 304-293-3802, E-mail: Melissa.Luna@mail.wvu.edu.
Website: http://cehs.wvu.edu/

Wichita State University, Graduate School, College of Applied Studies, Department of Counseling, Educational Leadership, Educational and School Psychology, Wichita, KS 67260. Offers counseling (M Ed); educational leadership (M Ed, Ed D); educational psychology (M Ed); school psychology (Ed S). *Accreditation:* NCATE. *Program availability:* Part-time, evening/weekend. Application fee: $50 ($65 for international students). *Unit head:* Dr. Jody Fiorini, Department Head, 316-978-3325, Fax: 316-978-3102, E-mail: jody.fiorini@wichita.edu. *Application contact:* Jordan Oleson, Admissions Coordinator, 316-978-3095, Fax: 316-978-3253, E-mail: jordan.oleson@wichita.edu.
Website: http://www.wichita.edu/cles

Widener University, School of Human Service Professions, Center for Education, Chester, PA 19013-5792. Offers adult education (M Ed); counseling in higher education (M Ed); counselor education (M Ed); early childhood education (M Ed); educational foundations (M Ed); educational leadership (M Ed); educational psychology (M Ed); elementary education (M Ed); English and language arts (M Ed); health education (M Ed); higher education leadership (Ed D); home and school visitor (M Ed); human sexuality (M Ed, PhD); mathematics education (M Ed); middle school education (M Ed); principalship (M Ed); reading and language arts (Ed D); reading education (M Ed); school administration (Ed D); science education (M Ed); social studies education (M Ed); special education (M Ed); technology education (M Ed). *Accreditation:* NCATE. *Program availability:* Part-time, evening/weekend. Terminal master's awarded for partial completion of doctoral program. *Degree requirements:* For doctorate, thesis/dissertation. *Entrance requirements:* For master's, minimum GPA of 2.5; for doctorate, GRE or MAT, minimum GPA of 2.0 (undergraduate), 3.5 (graduate). Electronic applications accepted. *Expenses:* Contact institution. *Faculty research:* Reading and cognition, adult education, technology education, educational leadership, special education.

Foundations and Philosophy of Education

Antioch University New England, Graduate School, Department of Education, Experienced Educators Program, Keene, NH 03431-3552. Offers foundations of education (M Ed), including applied behavioral analysis, autism spectrum disorders, educating for sustainability, next-generation learning using technology, problem-based learning using critical skills, teacher leadership; principal certification (PMC). *Degree requirements:* For master's, thesis, practicum. *Entrance requirements:* For master's, previous course work and work experience in education. Additional exam requirements/recommendations for international students: Required—TOEFL (minimum score 550 paper-based). Electronic applications accepted. *Expenses:* Contact institution. *Faculty research:* Classroom action research, school restructuring, problem-based learning, brain-based learning.

Arkansas State University, Graduate School, College of Education and Behavioral Science, School of Teacher Education and Leadership, State University, AR 72467. Offers community college administration (SCCT); curriculum and instruction (MSE); early childhood education (MSE); early childhood services (MS); educational leadership

(MSE, Ed D, Ed S); educational theory and practice (MSE); middle level education (MAT, MSE); reading (MSE, Ed S); special education - gifted, talented, and creative (MSE); special education - instructional specialist grades 4-12 (MSE); special education - instructional specialist grades P-4 (MSE); special education, K-12 (MSE). *Accreditation:* NCATE. *Program availability:* Part-time, online learning. *Degree requirements:* For master's, comprehensive exam, thesis or alternative; for doctorate, comprehensive exam, thesis/dissertation; for other advanced degree, comprehensive exam. *Entrance requirements:* For master's, GRE General Test or MAT, appropriate bachelor's degree, official transcripts, immunization records, letters of reference, interview; for doctorate, GRE General Test or MAT, interview, master's degree, letters of reference, official transcript, personal statement, writing sample, immunization records; for other advanced degree, GRE General Test or MAT, interview, master's degree, official transcript, immunization records, letters of reference, 3 years of teaching experience, teaching license. Additional exam requirements/recommendations for international students: Required—TOEFL (minimum score 550 paper-based; 79 iBT), IELTS (minimum score 6), PTE (minimum score 56). Electronic applications accepted.

Foundations and Philosophy of Education

Ball State University, Graduate School, Teachers College, Department of Educational Studies, Program in Educational Studies, Muncie, IN 47306. Offers educational studies (PhD), including cultural and educational policy studies, curriculum, educational technology. *Program availability:* Part-time, blended/hybrid learning. *Degree requirements:* For doctorate, thesis/dissertation. *Entrance requirements:* For doctorate, GRE General Test, minimum graduate GPA of 3.2, curriculum vitae, writing sample, three letters of reference. Additional exam requirements/recommendations for international students: Required—TOEFL (minimum score 550 paper-based; 79 iBT), IELTS (minimum score 6.5). Electronic applications accepted. *Faculty research:* Emerging curriculum trends, secondary teacher preparation, issues of equity and social justice in education, teacher technology integration, teaching for transformative understanding, teacher leadership, history of educational policy and practices, ethics and education.

Bank Street College of Education, Graduate School, Studies in Education Program, New York, NY 10025. Offers Ed M, MS Ed. *Degree requirements:* For master's, thesis. *Entrance requirements:* For master's, interview, essays. Additional exam requirements/recommendations for international students: Required—TOEFL (minimum score 600 paper-based; 100 iBT), IELTS (minimum score 7). Electronic applications accepted.

Binghamton University, State University of New York, Graduate School, College of Community and Public Affairs, Department of Teaching, Learning and Educational Leadership, Program in Educational Theory and Practice, Binghamton, NY 13902-6000. Offers Ed D. *Program availability:* Part-time. *Degree requirements:* For doctorate, thesis/dissertation. *Entrance requirements:* For doctorate, GRE General Test. Additional exam requirements/recommendations for international students: Required—TOEFL (minimum score 550 paper-based; 80 iBT). Electronic applications accepted.

Chicago State University, School of Graduate and Professional Studies, College of Education, Department of Educational Leadership, Curriculum and Foundations, Program in Curriculum and Instruction, Chicago, IL 60628. Offers instructional foundations (MS Ed), including adult education, elementary education, secondary education. *Degree requirements:* For master's, comprehensive exam, thesis optional. *Entrance requirements:* For master's, minimum GPA of 2.75.

Columbia University, Graduate School of Arts and Sciences, New York, NY 10027. Offers African-American studies (MA); American studies (MA); anthropology (MA, PhD); art history and archaeology (MA, PhD); astronomy (PhD); biological sciences (PhD); biotechnology (MA); chemical physics (PhD); chemistry (PhD); classical studies (MA, PhD); classics (MA, PhD); climate and society (MA); conservation biology (MA); earth and environmental sciences (PhD); East Asia: regional studies (MA); East Asian languages and cultures (MA, PhD); ecology, evolution and environmental biology (MA), including conservation biology; ecology, evolution, and environmental biology (PhD), including ecology and evolutionary biology, evolutionary primatology; economics (MA, PhD); English and comparative literature (MA, PhD); French and Romance philology (MA, PhD); Germanic languages (MA, PhD); global French studies (MA); global thought (MA); Hispanic cultural studies (MA); history (PhD); history and literature (MA); human rights studies (MA); Islamic studies (MA); Italian (MA, PhD); Japanese pedagogy (MA); Jewish studies (MA); Latin America and the Caribbean: regional studies (MA); Latin American and Iberian cultures (PhD); mathematics (MA, PhD), including finance (MA); medieval and Renaissance studies (MA); Middle Eastern, South Asian, and African studies (MA, PhD); modern art: critical and curatorial studies (MA); modern European studies (MA); museum anthropology (MA); music (DMA, PhD); oral history (MA); philosophical foundations of physics (MA); philosophy (MA, PhD); physics (PhD); political science (MA, PhD); psychology (PhD); quantitative methods in the social sciences (MA); religion (MA, PhD); Russia, Eurasia and East Europe: regional studies (MA); Russian translation (MA); Slavic cultures (MA); Slavic languages (MA, PhD); sociology (MA, PhD); South Asian studies (MA); statistics (MA, PhD); theatre (PhD). Dual-degree programs require admission to both Graduate School of Arts and Sciences and another Columbia school. *Program availability:* Part-time. Terminal master's awarded for partial completion of doctoral program. *Degree requirements:* For master's, variable foreign language requirement, comprehensive exam (for some programs), thesis (for some programs); for doctorate, variable foreign language requirement, comprehensive exam (for some programs), thesis/dissertation. *Entrance requirements:* For master's and doctorate, GRE General Test, GRE Subject Test (for some programs). Additional exam requirements/recommendations for international students: Required—TOEFL, IELTS. Electronic applications accepted.

Curry College, Graduate Studies, Program in Education, Milton, MA 02186-9984. Offers elementary education (M Ed); foundations (non-license) (M Ed); reading (M Ed, Certificate); special education (M Ed). *Program availability:* Part-time, evening/weekend. *Degree requirements:* For master's, project or thesis. *Entrance requirements:* For master's, interview, recommendations, resume, written statement. Additional exam requirements/recommendations for international students: Required—TOEFL (minimum score 550 paper-based; 80 iBT). *Expenses:* Contact institution. *Faculty research:* Classroom trauma, therapeutic writing, inclusionary practices.

DePaul University, College of Education, Chicago, IL 60614. Offers bilingual-bicultural education (M Ed, MA); counseling (M Ed, MA), including clinical mental health counseling, college student development, school counseling; curriculum studies (M Ed, MA, Ed D); early childhood education (M Ed, MA, Ed D); educational leadership (M Ed, MA, Ed D), including Catholic leadership (M Ed, MA), general (M Ed, MA), higher education (M Ed, MA), physical education (M Ed, MA), principal preparation (M Ed), teacher preparation (M Ed); elementary education (M Ed, MA); middle grades education (M Ed); middle school mathematics education (MS); reading specialist (M Ed, MA); secondary education (M Ed, MA); social and cultural foundations in education (M Ed, MA); special education (M Ed); sport, fitness and recreation leadership (MS); value-creating education for global citizenship (M Ed); world languages education (M Ed, MA). *Program availability:* Part-time, evening/weekend, online learning. *Degree requirements:* For doctorate, thesis/dissertation. Electronic applications accepted.

Duquesne University, School of Education, Department of Educational Foundations and Leadership, Program in Educational Studies, Pittsburgh, PA 15282-0001. Offers educational studies (MS Ed); program evaluation (MS Ed). *Program availability:* Part-time, evening/weekend, 100% online. *Faculty:* 1 full-time (0 women). *Students:* 3 full-time (1 woman), 4 part-time (1 woman); includes 1 minority (Black or African American, non-Hispanic/Latino), 2 international. Average age 34. 12 applicants, 92% accepted, 2 enrolled. In 2018, 15 master's awarded. *Entrance requirements:* For master's, bachelor's degree. Additional exam requirements/recommendations for international students: Required—TOEFL (minimum score 550 paper-based), IELTS (minimum score 7). *Application deadline:* For fall admission, 8/15 for domestic students; for spring admission, 1/2 for domestic students. Applications are processed on a rolling basis. Application fee: $0. Electronic applications accepted. *Expenses: Tuition:* Full-time $23,112; part-time $1284 per credit. Tuition and fees vary according to program. *Financial support:* Research assistantships available. Support available to part-time students. Financial award applicants required to submit FAFSA. *Faculty research:* Online learning; impact of trauma on childhood and adolescent development; evaluation of educational programs; research in mathematics education; beliefs about classroom assessment. *Unit head:* Dr. Gibbs Kanyongo, Associate Professor, 412-396-5190, Fax: 412-396-5454, E-mail: kanyongog@duq.edu. *Application contact:* Kelly McGinley, Graduate Admissions Assistant, 412-396-1559, Fax: 412-396-5585, E-mail: mcginleyk@duq.edu.

Eastern Michigan University, Graduate School, College of Education, Department of Teacher Education, Program in Social Foundations, Ypsilanti, MI 48197. Offers MA. *Accreditation:* NCATE. *Program availability:* Part-time, evening/weekend, online learning. *Students:* 2 full-time (both women), 11 part-time (9 women); includes 4 minority (3 Black or African American, non-Hispanic/Latino; 1 Two or more races, non-Hispanic/Latino), 1 international. Average age 35. 2 applicants, 100% accepted, 1 enrolled. In 2018, 3 master's awarded. *Entrance requirements:* For master's, GRE. Additional exam requirements/recommendations for international students: Required—TOEFL. *Application deadline:* Applications are processed on a rolling basis. Application fee: $45. *Financial support:* Fellowships, research assistantships with full tuition reimbursements, teaching assistantships with full tuition reimbursements, career-related internships or fieldwork, Federal Work-Study, institutionally sponsored loans, scholarships/grants, tuition waivers (partial), and unspecified assistantships available. Support available to part-time students. Financial award applicants required to submit FAFSA. *Application contact:* Dr. Paul (Joe) Ramsey, Coordinator, 734-487-3260, Fax: 734-487-2101, E-mail: pramsey1@emich.edu.

Eastern Washington University, Graduate Studies, College of Arts, Letters and Education, Department of Education, Program in Educational Foundations, Cheney, WA 99004-2431. Offers M Ed. *Degree requirements:* For master's, comprehensive exam. *Entrance requirements:* For master's, minimum GPA of 3.0. Additional exam requirements/recommendations for international students: Required—TOEFL (minimum score 580 paper-based; 92 iBT), IELTS (minimum score 7).

Fairfield University, Graduate School of Education and Allied Professions, Fairfield, CT 06824. Offers applied behavior analysis (ATC); applied psychology (MA); clinical mental health counseling (MA, CAS); educational technology (MA); elementary education (MA, CAS); family studies (MA); integration of spirituality and religion in counseling (ATC); marriage and family therapy (MA); reading and language development (Sixth Year Certificate); school counseling (MA, CAS); school psychology (MA, CAS); school-based marriage and family therapy (ATC); secondary education (MA); special education (MA, CAS); substance abuse counseling (ATC); teaching (Certificate); teaching and foundations (MA, CAS); TESOL, world languages, and bilingual education (MA, CAS). *Accreditation:* NCATE. *Program availability:* Part-time, evening/weekend. *Degree requirements:* For master's, comprehensive exam. *Entrance requirements:* For master's, minimum GPA of 3.0, 2 recommendations, resume. Additional exam requirements/recommendations for international students: Required—TOEFL (minimum score 550 paper-based; 84 iBT) or IELTS (minimum score 7.5). Electronic applications accepted. *Expenses:* Contact institution. *Faculty research:* Reading and literacy, writing, social justice and inequality in education, addictions and mental health issues, therapeutic relationships and clinical supervision.

Fairleigh Dickinson University, Metropolitan Campus, University College: Arts, Sciences, and Professional Studies, School of Computer Sciences and Engineering, Program in Mathematical Foundation, Teaneck, NJ 07666-1914. Offers MS.

Florida State University, The Graduate School, College of Education, Department of Educational Leadership and Policy Studies, Tallahassee, FL 32306. Offers educational leadership and administration (Certificate); educational leadership and policy (MS, Ed D, PhD, Ed S), including education policy and evaluation (MS, Ed D, PhD), educational leadership and administration; foundations of education (MS, PhD), including history and philosophy of education, international and multicultural education; higher education (MS, PhD); institutional research (Certificate); program evaluation (Certificate). *Program availability:* Part-time, evening/weekend, 100% online, blended/hybrid learning, asynchronous, minimal on-campus study. *Degree requirements:* For master's, comprehensive exam, thesis optional; for doctorate, comprehensive exam, thesis/dissertation, diagnostic exam, preliminary exam, prospectus defense, dissertation defense. *Entrance requirements:* For master's, doctorate, and other advanced degree, GRE General Test, minimum GPA of 3.0. Additional exam requirements/recommendations for international students: Required—TOEFL (minimum score 550 paper-based, 80 iBT), IELTS (minimum score 6.5), Michigan English Language Assessment Battery (minimum score 77), or PTE (minimum score 55). Electronic applications accepted. *Expenses: Tuition, area resident:* Part-time $479.32 per credit hour. Tuition and fees vary according to campus/location and program. *Faculty research:* Post-secondary success; leadership education; education policy; international education; multicultural education.

Georgia State University, College of Education and Human Development, Department of Educational Policy Studies, Program in Social Foundations of Education, Atlanta, GA 30302-3083. Offers MS, PhD. *Accreditation:* NCATE. *Program availability:* Part-time. *Entrance requirements:* For master's and doctorate, GRE. *Application deadline:* Applications are processed on a rolling basis. Application fee: $50. Electronic applications accepted. *Expenses: Tuition, area resident:* Full-time $9360; part-time $390 per credit hour. Tuition, state resident: full-time $9360; part-time $390 per credit hour. Tuition, nonresident: full-time $30,024; part-time $1251 per credit hour. *International tuition:* $30,024 full-time. *Required fees:* $2128. *Financial support:* Fellowships, research assistantships, teaching assistantships, career-related internships or fieldwork, institutionally sponsored loans, scholarships/grants, health care benefits, tuition waivers, and unspecified assistantships available. Financial award application deadline: 3/15. *Faculty research:* Social and cultural influences on schools, globalization and the workforce, history of women teachers in the U.S., school-corporate nexus, curriculum transformation for equity and inclusion. *Unit head:* Dr. Jennifer Esposito, Interim Department Chair, 404-413-8281, Fax: 404-413-8003, E-mail: jesposito@gsu.edu. *Application contact:* Aishah Cowan, Administrative Academic Specialist, 404-413-8273, Fax: 404-413-8033, E-mail: acowan@gsu.edu.
Website: https://education.gsu.edu/eps/

Harvard University, Extension School, Cambridge, MA 02138-3722. Offers applied sciences (CAS); biotechnology (ALM); educational technologies (ALM); educational technology (CET); English for graduate and professional studies (DGP); environmental management (ALM, CEM); information technology (ALM); journalism (ALM); liberal arts (ALM); management (ALM, CM); mathematics for teaching (ALM); museum studies (ALM); premedical studies (Diploma); publication and communication (CPC). *Program availability:* Part-time, evening/weekend. *Degree requirements:* For master's, thesis. *Entrance requirements:* For master's, 3 completed graduate courses with grade of B or higher. Additional exam requirements/recommendations for international students: Required—TOEFL (minimum score 600 paper-based), TWE (minimum score 5). *Expenses:* Contact institution.

Indiana University Bloomington, School of Education, Department of Educational Leadership and Policy Studies, Bloomington, IN 47405. Offers educational leadership (MS, Ed D, Ed S); higher education (Ed D, PhD); higher education and student affairs (MS); history and philosophy of education (MS); history, philosophy, and policy in education (PhD), including education policy studies, history of education, philosophy of education; international and comparative education (MS). *Accreditation:* NCATE. *Degree requirements:* For master's, thesis optional; for doctorate, comprehensive exam, thesis/dissertation; for Ed S, comprehensive exam or project. *Entrance requirements:*

For master's, doctorate, and Ed S, GRE General Test. Additional exam requirements/ recommendations for international students: Required—TOEFL (minimum score 79 iBT). Electronic applications accepted. *Faculty research:* Culturally engaging campus environments, school choice policy analysis, democracy and education in the national and international context, and principal leadership.

Indiana University Bloomington, University Graduate School, College of Arts and Sciences, School of Global and International Studies, Department of East Asian Languages and Cultures, Bloomington, IN 47408. Offers Chinese (MA, PhD); Chinese language pedagogy (MA); East Asian studies (MA); Japanese (MA, PhD); Japanese language pedagogy (MA). *Program availability:* Part-time. *Degree requirements:* For master's, one foreign language, thesis; for doctorate, 2 foreign languages, comprehensive exam, thesis/dissertation. *Entrance requirements:* Additional exam requirements/recommendations for international students: Required—TOEFL (minimum score 93 iBT). Electronic applications accepted. *Faculty research:* Modern East Asian history; politics and society; traditional Chinese thought and society; medieval and premodern Japanese history, literature and society; modern Chinese and Japanese film and literature; Chinese, Japanese, Korean language and linguistics.

Iowa State University of Science and Technology, Department of Education, Ames, IA 50011. Offers curriculum and instructional technology (M Ed, MS, PhD); elementary education (M Ed, MS); historical, philosophical, and comparative studies in education (M Ed, MS); special education (M Ed, MS, PhD). *Degree requirements:* For master's, thesis or alternative; for doctorate, thesis/dissertation. *Entrance requirements:* For master's and doctorate, GRE General Test. Additional exam requirements/ recommendations for international students: Required—TOEFL (minimum score 560 paper-based; 83 iBT), IELTS (minimum score 6.5). Electronic applications accepted.

Kent State University, College of Education, Health and Human Services, School of Foundations, Leadership and Administration, Program in Cultural Foundations, Kent, OH 44242-0001. Offers M Ed, MA, PhD. *Accreditation:* NCATE. *Faculty:* 5 full-time (4 women), 4 part-time/adjunct (1 woman). *Students:* 30 full-time (22 women), 26 part-time (21 women); includes 28 minority (16 Black or African American, non-Hispanic/Latino; 5 Asian, non-Hispanic/Latino; 3 Hispanic/Latino; 4 Native Hawaiian or other Pacific Islander, non-Hispanic/Latino), 5 international. 42 applicants, 40% accepted. In 2018, 3 master's, 2 doctorates awarded. *Degree requirements:* For master's, thesis optional; for doctorate, comprehensive exam, thesis/dissertation. *Entrance requirements:* For master's, minimum GPA of 2.75, 2 letters of reference, goal statement; for doctorate, GRE General Test, minimum GPA of 3.5, master's degree, resume, interview, goal statement, 2 letters of reference. Additional exam requirements/recommendations for international students: Required—TOEFL (minimum score 550 paper-based; 80 iBT). *Application deadline:* Applications are processed on a rolling basis. Application fee: $30 ($60 for international students). Electronic applications accepted. *Expenses:* Tuition, state resident: full-time $11,766; part-time $536 per credit. Tuition, nonresident: full-time $21,952; part-time $999 per credit. *International tuition:* $21,952 full-time. Tuition and fees vary according to course load. *Financial support:* In 2018–19, 4 research assistantships with full tuition reimbursements (averaging $12,000 per year), 1 teaching assistantship with full tuition reimbursement (averaging $12,000 per year) were awarded; career-related internships or fieldwork, Federal Work-Study, institutionally sponsored loans, scholarships/grants, health care benefits, and unspecified assistantships also available. Support available to part-time students. Financial award application deadline: 4/1; financial award applicants required to submit FAFSA. *Faculty research:* Public politics, intercultural communication and training, research paradigms, comparative and international education. *Unit head:* Dr. Natasha Levinson, Coordinator, 330-672-0594, E-mail: nlevinso@kent.edu. *Application contact:* Cheryl Slusarczyk, Academic Program Director, Office of Graduate Student Services, 330-672-2576, Fax: 330-672-9162, E-mail: ogs@kent.edu.
Website: http://www.kent.edu/ehhs/cult/

Marquette University, Graduate School, College of Education, Department of Educational Policy and Leadership, Milwaukee, WI 53201-1881. Offers college student personnel administration (M Ed); curriculum and instruction (MA); education (MA); educational administration (M Ed); educational policy and foundations (MA); elementary education (Certificate); literacy (MA); principal (Certificate); reading specialist (Certificate); reading teacher (Certificate); secondary education (Certificate); superintendent (Certificate). *Program availability:* Part-time, evening/weekend. Terminal master's awarded for partial completion of doctoral program. *Degree requirements:* For master's, comprehensive exam, thesis (for some programs); for doctorate, thesis/ dissertation, qualifying exam. *Entrance requirements:* For master's, GRE General Test or MAT, official transcripts from all current and previous colleges/universities except Marquette, three letters of recommendation, statement of purpose; for doctorate, GRE General Test, MAT, sample of written work, official transcripts from all current and previous colleges/universities except Marquette, three letters of recommendation, statement of purpose, resume/curriculum vitae; for Certificate, GRE General Test or MAT, master's degree. Additional exam requirements/recommendations for international students: Required—TOEFL (minimum score 530 paper-based). *Expenses:* Contact institution. *Faculty research:* Leadership; social justice in education; development of lifelong learners; race, class, and schooling in historical perspective; urban teacher education.

McGill University, Faculty of Graduate and Postdoctoral Studies, Faculty of Education, Department of Integrated Studies in Education, Montréal, QC H3A 2T5, Canada. Offers culture and values in education (MA, PhD); curriculum studies (MA); educational leadership (MA, Certificate); educational studies (PhD); integrated studies in education (M Ed); second language education (MA, PhD).

Mount Saint Vincent University, Graduate Programs, Faculty of Education, Program in Educational Foundations, Halifax, NS B3M 2J6, Canada. Offers M Ed, MA Ed, MA-R. *Program availability:* Part-time, evening/weekend. *Degree requirements:* For master's, thesis (for some programs). *Entrance requirements:* For master's, bachelor's degree in related field, minimum B average. Electronic applications accepted. *Faculty research:* Research paradigms, moral aspects of education and teaching, private/independent schools, theory of critical thinking, teachers as workers and as agents of social change.

New York University, Steinhardt School of Culture, Education, and Human Development, Applied Statistics, Social Science, and Humanities, Program in History of Education, New York, NY 10012. Offers MA, PhD. *Program availability:* Part-time. *Entrance requirements:* For doctorate, GRE General Test, interview. Additional exam requirements/recommendations for international students: Required—TOEFL (minimum score 100 iBT). Electronic applications accepted. *Faculty research:* American educational thought, democratic community and education, twentieth century history of education, Jewish history.

Northern Arizona University, College of Education, Department of Educational Leadership, Flagstaff, AZ 86011. Offers community college teaching and learning (Graduate Certificate); educational leadership (M Ed, Ed D), including community college/higher education (M Ed), educational foundations (M Ed), instructional leadership K-12 school leadership (M Ed), principal certification K-12 (M Ed); principal (Graduate Certificate); superintendent (Graduate Certificate). *Program availability:* Part-time. *Degree requirements:* For master's, comprehensive exam, thesis (for some programs); for doctorate, comprehensive exam, thesis/dissertation; for Graduate Certificate, comprehensive exam (for some programs). *Entrance requirements:* Additional exam requirements/recommendations for international students: Required—TOEFL (minimum score 80 iBT), IELTS (minimum score 6.5). Electronic applications accepted.

Northern Illinois University, Graduate School, College of Education, Department of Leadership, Educational Psychology and Foundations, De Kalb, IL 60115-2854. Offers educational administration (MS Ed, Ed D, Ed S); educational psychology (MS Ed, Ed D); foundations of education (MS Ed); school business management (MS Ed). *Program availability:* Part-time, evening/weekend, online learning. *Faculty:* 23 full-time (12 women). *Students:* 9 full-time (4 women), 170 part-time (98 women); includes 45 minority (16 Black or African American, non-Hispanic/Latino; 6 Asian, non-Hispanic/ Latino; 15 Hispanic/Latino; 8 Two or more races, non-Hispanic/Latino), 2 international. Average age 39. 78 applicants, 86% accepted, 34 enrolled. In 2018, 52 master's, 28 doctorates, 2 other advanced degrees awarded. *Degree requirements:* For master's, comprehensive exam, thesis optional; for doctorate, thesis/dissertation, candidacy exam, dissertation defense. *Entrance requirements:* For master's, minimum undergraduate GPA of 2.75; for doctorate, GRE General Test, minimum undergraduate GPA of 2.75, 3.2 graduate; for Ed S, GRE General Test, minimum GPA of 2.75 (undergraduate), 3.2 (graduate). Additional exam requirements/recommendations for international students: Required—TOEFL (minimum score 550 paper-based). *Application deadline:* For fall admission, 6/1 for domestic students, 5/1 for international students; for spring admission, 11/1 for domestic students, 10/1 for international students. Applications are processed on a rolling basis. Application fee: $40. Electronic applications accepted. *Financial support:* In 2018–19, 1 research assistantship with full tuition reimbursement, 2 teaching assistantships with full tuition reimbursements were awarded; fellowships with full tuition reimbursements, career-related internships or fieldwork, Federal Work-Study, scholarships/grants, tuition waivers (full), and staff assistantships also available. Support available to part-time students. Financial award applicants required to submit FAFSA. *Faculty research:* Interpersonal forgiveness, learner-centered education, psychedelic studies, senior theory, professional growth. *Unit head:* Carolyn V. Schee, Chair, 815-753-4404, E-mail: lepf@niu.edu. *Application contact:* Graduate School Office, 815-753-0395, E-mail: gradsch@niu.edu.
Website: http://cedu.niu.edu/LEPF/

Northern Vermont University–Johnson, Program in Education, Johnson, VT 05656. Offers applied behavior analysis (MA Ed); curriculum and instruction (MA Ed); foundations of education (MA Ed); special education (MA Ed). *Program availability:* Part-time. *Degree requirements:* For master's, thesis or alternative, exit interview. *Entrance requirements:* For master's, interview. Additional exam requirements/recommendations for international students: Required—TOEFL. Electronic applications accepted.

Penn State University Park, Graduate School, College of Education, Department of Education Policy Studies, University Park, PA 16802. Offers educational leadership (M Ed, D Ed, PhD, Certificate); educational theory and policy (MA, PhD); higher education (M Ed, D Ed, PhD). *Accreditation:* NCATE. *Program availability:* Online learning.

Purdue University, Graduate School, College of Education, Department of Educational Studies, West Lafayette, IN 47907. Offers administration (MS Ed, Ed S); foundations of education (MS Ed); higher education administration (PhD). *Accreditation:* ACA (one or more programs are accredited); NCATE (one or more programs are accredited). *Program availability:* Part-time, evening/weekend. *Faculty:* 30 full-time (21 women), 2 part-time/adjunct (0 women). *Students:* 72 full-time (55 women), 240 part-time (186 women); includes 46 minority (13 Black or African American, non-Hispanic/Latino; 12 Asian, non-Hispanic/Latino; 14 Hispanic/Latino; 7 Two or more races, non-Hispanic/ Latino), 47 international. Average age 32. 218 applicants, 51% accepted, 83 enrolled. In 2018, 86 master's, 15 doctorates awarded. *Degree requirements:* For master's, thesis optional; for doctorate, thesis/dissertation, oral and written exams; for Ed S, oral presentation, project. *Entrance requirements:* For master's, GRE General Test (except for special education if undergraduate GPA is higher than a 3.0), minimum undergraduate GPA of 3.0; for doctorate and Ed S, GRE General Test (minimum combined score of 1000, 300 for new scoring), minimum undergraduate GPA of 3.0. Additional exam requirements/recommendations for international students: Required—TOEFL (minimum score 550 paper-based; 77 iBT), TWE (minimum score 5). *Application deadline:* Applications are processed on a rolling basis. Application fee: $60 ($75 for international students). Electronic applications accepted. *Financial support:* Fellowships with full tuition reimbursements, research assistantships with full tuition reimbursements, teaching assistantships with full tuition reimbursements, career-related internships or fieldwork, and tuition waivers (full) available. Support available to part-time students. Financial award application deadline: 3/1; financial award applicants required to submit FAFSA. *Faculty research:* Motivation, learning disabilities, school learning, group processes, cognitive development. *Unit head:* F. Richard Olenchak, Head, 765-494-9170, E-mail: olenchak@purdue.edu. *Application contact:* Heather Brinkman, Graduate Contact, 765-494-2345, Fax: 765-494-5832, E-mail: hbrinkma@purdue.edu.
Website: http://www.edst.purdue.edu/

Rutgers University–New Brunswick, Graduate School of Education, Department of Educational Theory, Policy and Administration, Program in Social and Philosophical Foundations of Education, Piscataway, NJ 08854-8097. Offers Ed M, Ed D. *Program availability:* Part-time, evening/weekend. *Degree requirements:* For doctorate, thesis/ dissertation, qualifying exam. *Entrance requirements:* For master's, GRE General Test; for doctorate, GRE General Test, writing sample. Additional exam requirements/ recommendations for international students: Required—TOEFL. Electronic applications accepted. *Faculty research:* Anthropology, history, sociology, philosophy, comparative education.

Saint Louis University, Graduate Programs, School of Education, Department of Educational Studies, St. Louis, MO 63103. Offers curriculum and instruction (MA, Ed D, PhD); educational foundations (MA, Ed D, PhD); special education (MA); teaching (MAT). *Accreditation:* NCATE. *Program availability:* Part-time. *Degree requirements:* For master's, comprehensive exam; for doctorate, comprehensive exam, thesis/dissertation, preliminary oral and written exams. *Entrance requirements:* For master's, GRE General Test or MAT, letters of recommendation, resume; for doctorate, GRE General Test, letters of recommendation, resumé, goal statement, transcripts. Additional exam requirements/recommendations for international students: Required—TOEFL (minimum score 525 paper-based). Electronic applications accepted. *Faculty research:* Teacher preparation, multicultural issues, children with special needs, qualitative research in education, inclusion.

Simon Fraser University, Office of Graduate Studies and Postdoctoral Fellows, Faculty of Education, Programs in Curriculum and Instruction, Burnaby, BC V5A 1S6, Canada. Offers curriculum and instruction (M Ed); curriculum and instruction foundations (M Ed, MA); curriculum theory and implementation (PhD); educational practice (M Ed); philosophy of education (PhD). *Degree requirements:* For master's, comprehensive exam (for some programs), thesis (for some programs); for doctorate, comprehensive exam, thesis/dissertation. *Entrance requirements:* For master's, minimum GPA of 3.0 (on scale of 4.33) or 3.33 based on last 60 credits of undergraduate courses; for doctorate, minimum GPA of 3.5 (on scale of 4.33). Additional exam requirements/recommendations for

international students: Recommended—TOEFL (minimum score 580 paper-based; 93 iBT), IELTS (minimum score 7), TWE (minimum score 5). Electronic applications accepted. *Faculty research:* Philosophy of education, applied and comparative epistemology, ethics and moral education, critical multicultural practices.

Southern Illinois University Edwardsville, Graduate School, School of Education, Health, and Human Behavior, Department of Educational Leadership, Program in Learning, Culture, and Society, Edwardsville, IL 62026. Offers MS Ed. *Program availability:* Part-time, evening/weekend. *Degree requirements:* For master's, thesis or alternative, project, oral defense. *Entrance requirements:* Additional exam requirements/recommendations for international students: Required—TOEFL (minimum score 550 paper-based; 79 iBT), IELTS (minimum score 6.5). Electronic applications accepted.

Spring Hill College, Graduate Programs, Program in Education, Mobile, AL 36608-1791. Offers early childhood education (MAT, MS Ed); educational theory (MS Ed); elementary education (MAT, MS Ed); secondary education (MAT, MS Ed). *Program availability:* Part-time. *Faculty:* 3 full-time (all women). *Students:* 1 full-time (0 women), 8 part-time (5 women); includes 2 minority (1 Hispanic/Latino; 1 Two or more races, non-Hispanic/Latino), 1 international. Average age 32. In 2018, 6 master's awarded. *Degree requirements:* For master's, comprehensive exam, completion of program within 6 calendar years of entrance into graduate studies at Spring Hill; documentation of course field assignments (MS) or completion of internship (MAT). *Entrance requirements:* For master's, GRE, MAT, or PRAXIS (varies by program), bachelor's degree with minimum undergraduate GPA of 3.0; class B certificate (for MS); minimum number of hours in specific fields (for MAT). Additional exam requirements/recommendations for international students: Required—TOEFL (minimum score 550 paper-based; 80 iBT), IELTS (minimum score 6.5), CPE or CAE (minimum score C), Michigan English Language Assessment Battery (minimum score 90). *Application deadline:* For fall admission, 8/1 priority date for domestic and international students; for spring admission, 12/1 priority date for domestic and international students. Applications are processed on a rolling basis. Application fee: $25 ($35 for international students). Electronic applications accepted. *Expenses:* Contact institution. *Financial support:* Fellowships, research assistantships, teaching assistantships, and tuition waivers available. Financial award applicants required to submit FAFSA. *Unit head:* Dr. Lori P. Aultman, Chair of Education, 251-380-3473, Fax: 251-460-2184, E-mail: laultman@shc.edu. *Application contact:* Gary Bracken, Vice President of Enrollment Management, 251-380-3038, Fax: 251-460-2186, E-mail: gbracken@shc.edu.
Website: http://ug.shc.edu/graduate-degrees/master-science-education/

Syracuse University, School of Education, CAS Program in Instructional Design Foundations, Syracuse, NY 13244. Offers CAS. *Program availability:* Part-time. *Entrance requirements:* For degree, baccalaureate degree from regionally-accredited college/university, statement of goals, three recommendation letters, transcripts. *Application deadline:* Applications are processed on a rolling basis. Application fee: $75. Electronic applications accepted. *Financial support:* Fellowships, research assistantships, teaching assistantships, career-related internships or fieldwork, and scholarships/grants available. Financial award application deadline: 1/15. *Unit head:* Dr. Jing Lei, Chair, 315-443-3703, E-mail: takoszal@syr.edu. *Application contact:* Speranza Migliore, Graduate Admissions Recruiter, 315-443-2505, E-mail: gradrcrt@syr.edu.
Website: http://soe.syr.edu/academic/Instructional_Design_Development_and_Evaluation/graduate/certificates/default.aspx

Syracuse University, School of Education, Programs in Cultural Foundations of Education, Syracuse, NY 13244. Offers MS, PhD, CAS. *Program availability:* Part-time. In 2018, 4 master's, 4 doctorates awarded. *Degree requirements:* For master's, thesis or alternative; for doctorate, comprehensive exam, thesis/dissertation. *Entrance requirements:* For master's, baccalaureate degree from regionally-accredited college/university, writing sample; for doctorate, GRE, master's degree (preferred); writing sample; interview (recommended); personal statement. Additional exam requirements/recommendations for international students: Required—TOEFL (minimum score 100 iBT). *Application deadline:* For fall admission, 1/15 priority date for domestic and international students. Applications are processed on a rolling basis. Application fee: $75. Electronic applications accepted. *Financial support:* Fellowships with full tuition reimbursements, research assistantships, teaching assistantships, career-related internships or fieldwork, and scholarships/grants available. Financial award application deadline: 1/15; financial award applicants required to submit FAFSA. *Faculty research:* Gender and education, history of women's education, the role of science in liberal education, student attrition, inequality in education. *Unit head:* Dr. Barbara Applebaum, Chair, 315-443-3343, E-mail: bappleba@syr.edu. *Application contact:* Speranza Migliore, Graduate Admissions Recruiter, 315-443-2505, E-mail: gradrcrt@syr.edu.
Website: http://soe.syr.edu/academic/cultural_foundations_of_education/

Teachers College, Columbia University, Department of Arts and Humanities, New York, NY 10027. Offers applied linguistics (MA, Ed D); art and art education (Ed M, MA, Ed D, Ed DCT); arts administration (MA); bilingual and bicultural education (MA); global competence (Certificate); history and education (Ed D, PhD); music and music education (Ed DCT); philosophy and education (MA, Ed D, PhD); social studies education (Ed M, PhD); teaching English to speakers of other languages (Ed M); teaching of English and English education (Ed M, MA, Ed D, PhD), including English education (Ed M, Ed D, PhD), teaching of English (MA); teaching of social studies (MA); TESOL (MA, Ed D). *Program availability:* Part-time, evening/weekend. *Students:* 267 full-time (216 women), 569 part-time (400 women); includes 235 minority (62 Black or African American, non-Hispanic/Latino; 2 American Indian or Alaska Native, non-Hispanic/Latino; 88 Asian, non-Hispanic/Latino; 69 Hispanic/Latino; 14 Two or more races, non-Hispanic/Latino), 229 international. Average age 31. 1,075 applicants, 56% accepted, 342 enrolled. Terminal master's awarded for partial completion of doctoral program. *Financial support:* Fellowships, research assistantships, teaching assistantships, career-related internships or fieldwork, Federal Work-Study, institutionally sponsored loans, tuition waivers (full and partial), and unspecified assistantships available. Support available to part-time students. *Unit head:* Prof. ZhaoHong Han, Department Chair, E-mail: zhh2@tc.columbia.edu. *Application contact:* Kelly Sutton-Skinner, Director of Admissions & New Student Enrollment, E-mail: kms2237@tc.columbia.edu.

University at Buffalo, the State University of New York, Graduate School, Graduate School of Education, Department of Educational Leadership and Policy, Buffalo, NY 14260. Offers economics and education policy analysis (MA); education studies (Ed M); educational administration (Ed M, Ed D, PhD); educational culture, policy and society (PhD); higher education administration (Ed M, PhD); school building leadership (Certificate); school business and human resource administration (Certificate); school district business leadership (Certificate); school district leadership (Certificate). *Program availability:* Part-time, evening/weekend. *Faculty:* 16 full-time (10 women), 11 part-time/adjunct (4 women). *Students:* 73 full-time (50 women), 128 part-time (82 women); includes 40 minority (21 Black or African American, non-Hispanic/Latino; 7 Asian, non-Hispanic/Latino; 11 Hispanic/Latino; 1 Two or more races, non-Hispanic/Latino), 19 international. Average age 34. 136 applicants, 69% accepted, 53 enrolled. In 2018, 39 master's, 20 doctorates, 25 other advanced degrees awarded. *Degree requirements:* For master's, comprehensive exam (for some programs), thesis optional; for doctorate,

comprehensive exam, thesis/dissertation. *Entrance requirements:* For master's, interview, letters of reference; for doctorate, GRE General Test or MAT, writing sample, letters of reference. Additional exam requirements/recommendations for international students: Required—TOEFL (minimum score 600 paper-based; 79 iBT), IELTS (minimum score 6.5), PTE (minimum score 55). *Application deadline:* For fall admission, 2/1 priority date for domestic students, 2/1 for international students; for spring admission, 11/15 priority date for domestic students, 10/1 for international students. Applications are processed on a rolling basis. Application fee: $50. Electronic applications accepted. *Financial support:* In 2018–19, 18 fellowships (averaging $5,673 per year), 34 research assistantships with tuition reimbursements (averaging $12,055 per year) were awarded; career-related internships or fieldwork, Federal Work-Study, institutionally sponsored loans, scholarships/grants, health care benefits, tuition waivers (full and partial), and unspecified assistantships also available. Financial award application deadline: 3/15; financial award applicants required to submit FAFSA. *Faculty research:* College access and choice, school leadership preparation and practice, public policy, curriculum and pedagogy, comparative and international education. *Total annual research expenditures:* $637,951. *Unit head:* Dr. Nathan Daun-Barnett, Department Chair, 716-645-1096, Fax: 716-645-2481, E-mail: nbarnett@buffalo.edu. *Application contact:* Renad Aref, Assistant Director of Admission Recruitment, 716-645-2110, Fax: 716-645-7937, E-mail: gseinfo@buffalo.edu.
Website: http://gse.buffalo.edu/elp

The University of British Columbia, Faculty of Education, Department of Educational Studies, Vancouver, BC V6T 1Z1, Canada. Offers adult learning and education (M Ed); adult learning and global change (M Ed); curriculum and leadership (M Ed); educational administration and leadership (M Ed); educational leadership and policy (Ed D); educational studies (M Ed, MA, PhD); higher education (M Ed); society, culture and politics in education (M Ed). *Program availability:* Part-time, evening/weekend. Terminal master's awarded for partial completion of doctoral program. *Degree requirements:* For master's, thesis; for doctorate, comprehensive exam, thesis/dissertation. *Entrance requirements:* For master's, minimum B+ average, 4-year undergraduate degree, field-related experience; for doctorate, minimum B+ average, 4-year undergraduate degree, master's degree, field-related experience. Additional exam requirements/recommendations for international students: Required—TOEFL (minimum score 600 paper-based; 100 iBT) or IELTS (minimum score 6.5). Electronic applications accepted. *Expenses:* Contact institution. *Faculty research:* Educational leadership educational administration adult education politics in education, global change and adult learning.

University of California, Riverside, Graduate Division, Graduate School of Education, Riverside, CA 92521. Offers applied behavior analysis (M Ed); diversity and equity (M Ed); education policy analysis and leadership (PhD); education specialist (Credential); education, society, and culture (MA, PhD); educational psychology (MA, PhD); general education (M Ed); higher education administration and policy (M Ed, PhD); multiple subject (Credential); research, evaluation, measurement and statistics (MA); school psychology (PhD); single subject (Credential); special education (M Ed, PhD); special education and autism (MA); TESOL (M Ed). Terminal master's awarded for partial completion of doctoral program. *Degree requirements:* For master's, comprehensive exams or thesis (MA), case study or analytical report (M Ed); for doctorate, comprehensive exam, thesis/dissertation, written and oral qualifying exams, college teaching practicum. *Entrance requirements:* For master's, GRE General Test (for MA), CBEST and CSET (for M Ed in general education only), UCR Extension TESOL certificate (for M Ed with TESOL emphasis only); for doctorate, GRE General Test, writing sample; for Credential, CBEST, CSET. Additional exam requirements/recommendations for international students: Required—TOEFL (minimum score 550 paper-based; 80 iBT), IELTS (minimum score 7). Electronic applications accepted. *Faculty research:* Responsiveness to intervention, faculty core, response to intervention of English language learners, advanced modeling techniques, study on social capital, trust, and motivation.

University of Central Oklahoma, The Jackson College of Graduate Studies, College of Liberal Arts, Department of Political Science, Edmond, OK 73034-5209. Offers political science (MA), including international affairs; public administration (MPA), including public and nonprofit management, urban management. *Program availability:* Part-time. *Degree requirements:* For master's, comprehensive exam (for some programs), thesis (for some programs). *Entrance requirements:* For master's, 18 undergraduate hours in political science. Additional exam requirements/recommendations for international students: Required—TOEFL (minimum score 550 paper-based; 79 iBT), IELTS (minimum score 6.5). Electronic applications accepted.

University of Cincinnati, Graduate School, College of Education, Criminal Justice, and Human Services, School of Education, Program in Educational Studies, Cincinnati, OH 45221. Offers M Ed, PhD. *Accreditation:* NCATE. *Program availability:* Part-time. *Degree requirements:* For master's, thesis optional; for doctorate, comprehensive exam, thesis/dissertation. *Entrance requirements:* For master's, GRE General Test; for doctorate, GRE General Test, GRE Subject Test. Additional exam requirements/recommendations for international students: Required—TOEFL (minimum score 520 paper-based), OEPT 3. Electronic applications accepted.

University of Hawaii at Manoa, Office of Graduate Education, College of Education, Department of Educational Foundations, Honolulu, HI 96822. Offers M Ed. *Program availability:* Part-time, evening/weekend. *Degree requirements:* For master's, thesis optional. *Entrance requirements:* Additional exam requirements/recommendations for international students: Required—TOEFL (minimum score 580 paper-based; 92 iBT), IELTS (minimum score 5). *Faculty research:* Multicultural-ethnic education, comparative education, educational policy, interdisciplinary inquiry, moral/political education.

University of Hawaii at Manoa, Office of Graduate Education, College of Education, PhD in Education Program, Honolulu, HI 96822. Offers curriculum and instruction (PhD); educational administration (PhD); educational foundations (PhD); educational policy studies (PhD); educational psychology (PhD); exceptionalities (PhD); kinesiology (PhD); learning design and technology (PhD). *Program availability:* Part-time, evening/weekend. *Degree requirements:* For doctorate, thesis/dissertation. *Entrance requirements:* For doctorate, GRE General Test, sample of written work. Additional exam requirements/recommendations for international students: Required—TOEFL (minimum score 600 paper-based; 100 iBT), IELTS (minimum score 7).

University of Houston–Clear Lake, School of Education, Program in Foundations and Professional Studies, Houston, TX 77058-1002. Offers counseling (MS); instructional technology (MS); multicultural studies (MS). *Program availability:* Part-time, evening/weekend. *Degree requirements:* For master's, thesis optional. *Entrance requirements:* For master's, GRE or minimum GPA of 3.0 in last 60 hours. Additional exam requirements/recommendations for international students: Required—TOEFL (minimum score 550 paper-based). Electronic applications accepted.

The University of Iowa, Graduate College, College of Education, Department of Educational Policy and Leadership Studies, Program in Schools, Culture, and Society, Iowa City, IA 52242-1316. Offers MA, PhD. *Degree requirements:* For master's, thesis optional, exam; for doctorate, comprehensive exam, thesis/dissertation. *Entrance requirements:* For master's and doctorate, GRE General Test, minimum GPA of 3.0. Additional exam requirements/recommendations for international students: Required—TOEFL (minimum score 550 paper-based; 81 iBT). Electronic applications accepted.

The University of Iowa, Graduate College, College of Education, Department of Psychological and Quantitative Foundations, Iowa City, IA 52242-1316. Offers counseling psychology (PhD); educational measurement and statistics (MA, PhD); educational psychology (MA, PhD); school psychology (PhD, Ed S). *Accreditation:* APA. *Degree requirements:* For master's, thesis optional, exam; for doctorate, comprehensive exam, thesis/dissertation; for Ed S, exam. *Entrance requirements:* For master's, doctorate, and Ed S, GRE General Test, minimum GPA of 3.0. Additional exam requirements/recommendations for international students: Required—TOEFL (minimum score 550 paper-based; 81 iBT). Electronic applications accepted.

University of Manitoba, Faculty of Graduate Studies, Faculty of Education, Department of Educational Administration, Foundations and Psychology, Winnipeg, MB R3T 2N2, Canada. Offers adult and post-secondary education (M Ed); educational administration (M Ed); guidance and counseling (M Ed); inclusive special education (M Ed); social foundations of education (M Ed). *Degree requirements:* For master's, thesis or alternative.

University of Maryland, College Park, Academic Affairs, College of Education, Department of Education Policy and Leadership, College Park, MD 20742. Offers curriculum and educational communications (M Ed, MA, Ed D, PhD); social foundations of education (M Ed, MA, Ed D, PhD, CAGS). *Accreditation:* NCATE. *Program availability:* Part-time, evening/weekend, online learning. *Degree requirements:* For master's, thesis or alternative, internship and/or field experience; for doctorate, comprehensive exam, thesis/dissertation, practicum or internship. *Entrance requirements:* For master's, GRE General Test or MAT, minimum GPA of 3.0, scholarly writing sample, 3 letters of recommendation; for doctorate, GRE General Test or MAT, scholarly writing sample; minimum undergraduate GPA of 3.0, graduate 3.5. *Faculty research:* Educational technology, adult and higher education.

University of Minnesota, Twin Cities Campus, Graduate School, College of Education and Human Development, Department of Educational Psychology, Program in Psychological Foundations of Education, Minneapolis, MN 55455-0213. Offers MA, PhD. *Students:* 22 full-time (15 women); includes 5 minority (3 Asian, non-Hispanic/Latino; 2 Two or more races, non-Hispanic/Latino), 8 international. Average age 22. 45 applicants, 16% accepted, 4 enrolled. In 2018, 2 master's, 2 doctorates awarded. Application fee: $75 ($95 for international students). *Unit head:* Dr. Kristen McMaster, Chair, 612-624-6083, Fax: 612-624-8241, E-mail: mcmas004@umn.edu. *Application contact:* Dr. Panayiota Kendeou, Director of Graduate Studies, 612-626-7814, E-mail: kend0040@umn.edu.
Website: http://www.cehd.umn.edu/EdPsych/programs/Foundations/

University of New Mexico, Graduate Studies, College of Education, Program in Language, Literacy and Sociocultural Studies, Albuquerque, NM 87131-2039. Offers American Indian education (MA); bilingual education (MA, PhD); educational linguistics (PhD); educational thought and sociocultural studies (MA, PhD); literacy/language arts (MA, PhD); social studies (MA); TESOL (MA, PhD). *Students:* Average age 40. 61 applicants, 38% accepted, 23 enrolled. In 2018, 36 master's, 4 doctorates awarded. *Degree requirements:* For master's, comprehensive exam, thesis optional; for doctorate, comprehensive exam, thesis/dissertation, research skills. *Entrance requirements:* For master's, letter of intent, 3 letters of recommendation, resume, BA/BS, department demographic form, transcripts; for doctorate, writing sample, letter of intent, 3 letters of recommendation, resume, BA/BS, MA, department demographic form, transcripts. Additional exam requirements/recommendations for international students: Required—TOEFL. *Application deadline:* For fall admission, 12/1 for domestic and international students; for spring admission, 9/15 for domestic and international students. Application fee: $50. Electronic applications accepted. *Financial support:* Fellowships, research assistantships, teaching assistantships, career-related internships or fieldwork, institutionally sponsored loans, scholarships/grants, and unspecified assistantships available. Support available to part-time students. Financial award application deadline: 3/1; financial award applicants required to submit FAFSA. *Faculty research:* School reform, professional development, history of education, Native American education, politics of education, feminism and issues of sexual identity, critical race theory, bilingualism, literacy reading, adolescent literature, second language acquisition, critical theory and schooling, indigenous languages. *Unit head:* Dr. Lois M. Meyer, Chair, 505-277-7244, Fax: 505-277-8362, E-mail: lsmeyer@unm.edu. *Application contact:* Debra Schaffer, Administrative Assistant, 505-277-0437, Fax: 505-277-8362, E-mail: schaffer@unm.edu.
Website: http://coe.unm.edu/departments-programs/llss/index.html

University of Pennsylvania, Graduate School of Education, Division of Literacy, Culture, and International Education, Program in Education, Culture and Society, Philadelphia, PA 19104. Offers MS Ed, PhD. *Students:* 34 full-time (29 women), 10 part-time (9 women); includes 17 minority (6 Black or African American, non-Hispanic/Latino; 3 Asian, non-Hispanic/Latino; 4 Hispanic/Latino; 4 Two or more races, non-Hispanic/Latino), 4 international. Average age 27. 235 applicants, 38% accepted, 34 enrolled. In 2018, 19 master's, 1 doctorate awarded. Application fee: $80.

University of Pittsburgh, School of Education, Department of Administrative and Policy Studies, Program in Social and Comparative Analysis in Education, Pittsburgh, PA 15260. Offers M Ed, MA, Ed D, PhD. *Program availability:* Evening/weekend. *Degree requirements:* For master's, thesis; for doctorate, thesis/dissertation. *Entrance requirements:* For doctorate, GRE General Test. Additional exam requirements/recommendations for international students: Required—TOEFL (minimum score 80 iBT). Electronic applications accepted.

University of Rochester, Margaret Warner Graduate School of Education and Human Development, Doctoral Programs in Education, Rochester, NY 14627. Offers counseling (Ed D); educational administration (Ed D); educational policy and theory (PhD); higher education (PhD); human development in educational context (PhD); teaching, curriculum, and change (PhD). *Expenses: Tuition:* Full-time $52,974; part-time $1654 per credit hour. *Required fees:* $612. One-time fee: $30 part-time. Tuition and fees vary according to campus/location and program.

University of Saskatchewan, College of Graduate and Postdoctoral Studies, College of Education, Department of Educational Foundations, Saskatoon, SK S7N 5A2, Canada. Offers M Ed, PhD, Diploma. *Program availability:* Part-time. *Degree requirements:* For master's, thesis (for some programs); for doctorate, comprehensive exam (for some programs), thesis/dissertation. *Entrance requirements:* Additional exam requirements/recommendations for international students: Required—TOEFL (minimum score 80 iBT); Recommended—IELTS (minimum score 6.5). Electronic applications accepted. *Faculty research:* Indian and northern education, adult and continuing education, international education.

University of South Africa, College of Human Sciences, Pretoria, South Africa. Offers adult education (M Ed); African languages (MA, PhD); African politics (MA, PhD); Afrikaans (MA, PhD); ancient history (MA, PhD); ancient Near Eastern studies (MA, PhD); anthropology (MA, PhD); applied linguistics (MA); Arabic (MA, PhD); archaeology (MA); art history (MA); Biblical archaeology (MA); Biblical studies (M Th, D Th, PhD); Christian spirituality (M Th, D Th); church history (M Th, D Th); classical studies (MA, PhD); clinical psychology (MA); communication (MA, PhD); comparative education (M Ed, Ed D); consulting psychology (D Admin, D Com, PhD); curriculum studies (M Ed, Ed D); development studies (M Admin, MA, D Admin, PhD); didactics (M Ed, Ed D); education (M Tech); education management (M Ed, Ed D); educational psychology (M Ed); English (MA); environmental education (M Ed); French (MA, PhD); German (MA, PhD); Greek (MA); guidance and counseling (M Ed); health studies (MA, PhD), including health sciences education (MA), health services management (MA), medical and surgical nursing science (critical care general) (MA), midwifery and neonatal nursing science (MA), trauma and emergency care (MA); history (MA, PhD); history of education (Ed D); inclusive education (M Ed, Ed D); information and communications technology policy and regulation (MA); information science (MA, MIS, PhD); international politics (MA, PhD); Islamic studies (MA, PhD); Italian (MA, PhD); Judaica (MA, PhD); linguistics (MA, PhD); mathematical education (M Ed); mathematics education (MA); missiology (M Th, D Th); modern Hebrew (MA, PhD); musicology (MA, MMus, D Mus, PhD); natural science education (M Ed); New Testament (M Th, D Th); Old Testament (D Th); pastoral therapy (M Th, D Th); philosophy (MA); philosophy of education (M Ed, Ed D); politics (MA, PhD); Portuguese (MA, PhD); practical theology (M Th, D Th); psychology (MA, MS, PhD); psychology of education (M Ed, Ed D); public health (MA); religious studies (MA, D Th, PhD); Romance languages (MA); Russian (MA, PhD); Semitic languages (MA, PhD); social behavior studies in HIV/AIDS (MA); social science (mental health) (MA); social science in development studies (MA); social science in psychology (MA); social science in social work (MA); social science in sociology (MA); social work (MSW, DSW, PhD); socio-education (M Ed, Ed D); sociolinguistics (MA); sociology (MA, PhD); Spanish (MA, PhD); systematic theology (M Th, D Th); TESOL (teaching English to speakers of other languages) (MA); theological ethics (M Th, D Th); theory of literature (MA, PhD); urban ministries (D Th); urban ministry (M Th).

University of South Carolina, The Graduate School, College of Education, Department of Educational Studies, Program in Foundations in Education, Columbia, SC 29208. Offers PhD. *Accreditation:* NCATE. *Program availability:* Part-time. *Degree requirements:* For doctorate, comprehensive exam, thesis/dissertation. *Entrance requirements:* For doctorate, GRE General Test or MAT, interview. Electronic applications accepted. *Faculty research:* Oral history, educational biography, home schooling, international education.

The University of Tennessee, Graduate School, College of Education, Health and Human Sciences, Program in Education, Knoxville, TN 37996. Offers art education (MS); counseling education (PhD); cultural studies in education (PhD); curriculum (MS, Ed S); curriculum, educational research and evaluation (Ed D, PhD); early childhood education (PhD); early childhood special education (MS); education of deaf and hard of hearing (MS); educational administration and policy studies (Ed D, PhD); educational administration and supervision (Ed S); educational psychology (Ed D, PhD); elementary education (MS, Ed S); elementary teaching (MS); English education (MS, Ed S); exercise science (PhD); foreign language/ESL education (MS, Ed S); instructional technology (MS, Ed D, PhD, Ed S); literacy, language and ESL education (PhD); literacy, language education, and ESL education (Ed D); mathematics education (MS, Ed S); modified and comprehensive special education (MS); reading education (MS, Ed S); school counseling (Ed S); school psychology (PhD, Ed S); science education (MS, Ed S); secondary teaching (MS); social foundations (MS); social science education (MS, Ed S); socio-cultural foundations of sports and education (PhD); special education (Ed S); teacher education (Ed D, PhD). *Accreditation:* NCATE. *Program availability:* Part-time, evening/weekend. *Degree requirements:* For master's and Ed S, thesis optional; for doctorate, variable foreign language requirement, thesis/dissertation. *Entrance requirements:* For master's, minimum GPA of 2.7; for doctorate and Ed S, GRE General Test, minimum GPA of 2.7. Additional exam requirements/recommendations for international students: Required—TOEFL. Electronic applications accepted.

The University of Texas of the Permian Basin, Office of Graduate Studies, School of Education, Program in Professional Education, Odessa, TX 79762-0001. Offers MA. *Degree requirements:* For master's, comprehensive exam (for some programs), thesis (for some programs). *Entrance requirements:* For master's, GRE General Test. Additional exam requirements/recommendations for international students: Required—TOEFL (minimum score 550 paper-based).

The University of Toledo, College of Graduate Studies, Judith Herb College of Education, Department of Educational Foundations and Leadership, Toledo, OH 43606-3390. Offers educational administration and supervision (ME, DE, Ed S); educational psychology (ME, PhD); educational research and measurement (ME, PhD); educational sociology (PhD); educational theory and social foundations (ME); foundations of education (DE, PhD); history of education (PhD); philosophy of education (PhD). *Accreditation:* NCATE. *Program availability:* Part-time, evening/weekend. *Degree requirements:* For master's, comprehensive exam, thesis or alternative; for doctorate, comprehensive exam, thesis/dissertation; for Ed S, thesis optional. *Entrance requirements:* For master's, doctorate, and Ed S, minimum cumulative GPA of 2.7 for all previous academic work, letters of recommendation. Additional exam requirements/recommendations for international students: Required—TOEFL (minimum score 550 paper-based; 80 iBT). Electronic applications accepted.

University of Victoria, Faculty of Graduate Studies, Faculty of Education, Department of Curriculum and Instruction, Victoria, BC V8W 2Y2, Canada. Offers art education (M Ed, PhD); curriculum studies (M Ed, MA, PhD); early childhood education (M Ed, PhD); educational studies (PhD); language and literacy (M Ed, MA, PhD); mathematics (M Ed, MA, PhD); music education (M Ed, MA, PhD); science (M Ed, MA, PhD); social studies (M Ed, MA); social, cultural and foundational studies (MA, PhD); technology and environmental education (PhD). *Program availability:* Part-time. *Degree requirements:* For master's, thesis, project (M Ed); for doctorate, comprehensive exam, thesis/dissertation. *Entrance requirements:* For master's, minimum B average. Additional exam requirements/recommendations for international students: Required—TOEFL (minimum score 575 paper-based), IELTS (minimum score 7). Electronic applications accepted. *Faculty research:* Elementary and secondary English, language arts, curriculum theory and practice, educational media and technology, educational administration and leadership, history and philosophy of education.

University of Washington, Graduate School, College of Education, Seattle, WA 98195. Offers curriculum and instruction (M Ed, Ed D, PhD), including educational technology, general curriculum (Ed D, PhD), language, literacy, and culture, mathematics education, multicultural education, reading and language arts education (Ed D), science education, social studies education, teaching and curriculum (M Ed); educational leadership and policy studies (M Ed, Ed D, PhD), including administration (Ed D), educational policy, organization, and leadership (M Ed, PhD), higher education, leadership for learning (Ed D), social and cultural foundations of education (M Ed, PhD); educational psychology (M Ed, PhD), including educational psychology (PhD), human development and cognition (M Ed), learning sciences, measurement, statistics and research design (M Ed), school psychology (M Ed); instructional leadership (M Ed); intercollegiate athletic leadership (M Ed); special education (M Ed, Ed D, PhD), including early childhood special education (M Ed), emotional and behavioral disabilities (M Ed), learning disabilities (M Ed), low-incidence disabilities (M Ed), severe disabilities (M Ed), special education (Ed D, PhD); teacher education (MIT). *Accreditation:* APA. *Program availability:* Part-time, evening/weekend. *Degree requirements:* For master's, thesis optional; for doctorate, thesis/dissertation. *Entrance requirements:* For master's and

doctorate, GRE General Test, minimum GPA of 3.0. Additional exam requirements/recommendations for international students: Required—TOEFL. Electronic applications accepted. *Faculty research:* School restructuring/effective schools, special education interventions, literacy and writing, technology, school partnerships, teacher preparation.

University of Wisconsin–Milwaukee, Graduate School, School of Education, Department of Educational Policy and Community Studies, Milwaukee, WI 53201-0413. Offers cultural foundations of community engagement and education (MS), including alternative education, community engagement and partnerships, educational policy, race relations, youth work; educational policy (Graduate Certificate). *Program availability:* Part-time. *Students:* 8 full-time (7 women), 30 part-time (25 women); includes 18 minority (8 Black or African American, non-Hispanic/Latino; 3 American Indian or Alaska Native, non-Hispanic/Latino; 7 Two or more races, non-Hispanic/Latino). Average age 35. 25 applicants, 44% accepted, 5 enrolled. In 2018, 12 master's awarded. *Entrance requirements:* Additional exam requirements/recommendations for international students: Required—TOEFL (minimum score 550 paper-based; 79 iBT), IELTS (minimum score 6.5). *Application deadline:* For fall admission, 1/1 priority date for domestic students; for spring admission, 9/1 for domestic students. Application fee: $56 ($96 for international students). Electronic applications accepted. *Financial support:* Fellowships with full tuition reimbursements, research assistantships, teaching assistantships, career-related internships or fieldwork, health care benefits, and unspecified assistantships available. Support available to part-time students. Financial award application deadline: 4/15; financial award applicants required to submit FAFSA. *Application contact:* General Information Contact, 414-229-4721, E-mail: soeinfo@uwm.edu.
Website: http://uwm.edu/education/academics/edu-policy-community-studies-department/

University of Wisconsin–Milwaukee, Graduate School, School of Education, Department of Exceptional Education, Milwaukee, WI 53201-0413. Offers autism spectrum disorders (Graduate Certificate); exceptional education (MS); transition for students with disabilities (Graduate Certificate); urban education (PhD), including adult, continuing and higher education leadership, art education, curriculum and instruction, exceptional education, mathematics education, multicultural studies, social foundations of education. *Program availability:* Part-time. *Students:* 38 full-time (29 women), 67 part-time (50 women); includes 39 minority (23 Black or African American, non-Hispanic/Latino; 1 American Indian or Alaska Native, non-Hispanic/Latino; 6 Asian, non-Hispanic/Latino; 1 Hispanic/Latino; 8 Two or more races, non-Hispanic/Latino), 2 international. Average age 40. 47 applicants, 40% accepted, 11 enrolled. In 2018, 13 master's, 14 doctorates, 4 other advanced degrees awarded. *Entrance requirements:* Additional exam requirements/recommendations for international students: Required—TOEFL (minimum score 550 paper-based; 79 iBT), IELTS (minimum score 6.5). *Application deadline:* For fall admission, 1/1 priority date for domestic students; for spring admission, 9/1 for domestic students. Application fee: $56 ($96 for international students). Electronic applications accepted. *Financial support:* Fellowships, research assistantships, teaching assistantships, career-related internships or fieldwork, health care benefits, and unspecified assistantships available. Support available to part-time students. Financial award application deadline: 4/15; financial award applicants required to submit FAFSA. *Faculty research:* Emotional disturbance, hearing impairment, learning disabilities, mental retardation. *Application contact:* General Information Contact, 414-229-4721, E-mail: soeinfo@uwm.edu.
Website: http://uwm.edu/education/academics/exceptional-edu-department/

Wayne State University, College of Education, Division of Theoretical and Behavioral Foundations, Detroit, MI 48202. Offers applied behavior analysis (Certificate); counseling (M Ed, MA, Ed D, Ed S); counseling psychology (MA, PhD); education evaluation and research (M Ed, Ed D); educational psychology (M Ed, PhD), including learning and instruction sciences (PhD); rehabilitation counseling and community inclusion (MA); school and community psychology (MA, Certificate). *Accreditation:* ACA (one or more programs are accredited); CORE (one or more programs are accredited). *Program availability:* Part-time, evening/weekend. *Faculty:* 9. *Students:* 168 full-time (136 women), 200 part-time (171 women); includes 128 minority (82 Black or African American, non-Hispanic/Latino; 2 American Indian or Alaska Native, non-Hispanic/Latino; 8 Asian, non-Hispanic/Latino; 12 Hispanic/Latino; 24 Two or more races, non-Hispanic/Latino), 14 international. Average age 32. 340 applicants, 24% accepted, 66 enrolled. In 2018, 103 master's, 6 doctorates, 18 other advanced degrees awarded. *Degree requirements:* For master's, thesis (for some programs); for doctorate, comprehensive exam, thesis/dissertation. *Entrance requirements:* For master's, GRE, interview, personal statement, portfolio (only art therapy); references; program application; for doctorate, GRE, departmental writing exam, interview, curriculum vitae, references, master's degree in closely-related field with minimum GPA of 3.5, demonstration of counseling skills (for Ed D in counseling); autobiographical statement; letter of application; personal statement; for other advanced degree, education specialist certificate: GRE, education specialist certificate: master's degree in counseling or closely related field and licensure; personal statement; recommendations; autobiographical statement; interview. Additional exam requirements/recommendations for international students: Required—TOEFL (minimum score 550 paper-based; 79 iBT); Recommended—IELTS (minimum score 6.5), TWE (minimum score 5.5), TSE (minimum score 58). *Application deadline:* Applications are processed on a rolling basis. Application fee: $50. Electronic applications accepted. *Expenses:* Contact institution. *Financial support:* In 2018–19, 86 students received support, including 2 research assistantships with tuition reimbursements available (averaging $19,267 per year); fellowships, teaching assistantships, Federal Work-Study, scholarships/grants, health care benefits, and unspecified assistantships also available. Support available to part-time students. Financial award applicants required to submit FAFSA. *Faculty research:* Adolescents at risk, supervision of counseling. *Unit head:* Dr. Cheryl Somers, Assistant Dean, 313-577-1670, E-mail: c.somers@wayne.edu. *Application contact:* Dr. Mary L Waker, Graduate Admissions Officer, 313-577-1601, Fax: 313-577-7904, E-mail: m.waker@wayne.edu.
Website: http://coe.wayne.edu/tbf/index.php

West Chester University of Pennsylvania, College of Education and Social Work, Department of Educational Foundations and Policy Studies, West Chester, PA 19383. Offers education for sustainability (Certificate); educational technology (Certificate); higher education policy and student affairs (MS); transformative education and social change (MS). *Program availability:* Part-time. *Degree requirements:* For master's, comprehensive exam (for some programs), thesis, 36 credits (42 credits for MS in higher education policy and student affairs). *Entrance requirements:* For master's, teaching certification (strongly recommended); for Certificate, minimum GPA of 3.0. Additional exam requirements/recommendations for international students: Required—TOEFL or IELTS. Electronic applications accepted. *Faculty research:* Technology integration: preparing our teachers for the twenty-first century, critical pedagogy, education for sustainability.

Western Illinois University, School of Graduate Studies, College of Education and Human Services, Department of Educational Studies, Educational Studies, Macomb, IL 61455-1390. Offers educational and interdisciplinary studies (MS Ed); teaching English to speakers of other languages (Certificate). *Accreditation:* NCATE. *Program availability:* Part-time. *Students:* 5 full-time (all women), 26 part-time (24 women); includes 3 minority (1 Asian, non-Hispanic/Latino; 1 Hispanic/Latino; 1 Two or more races, non-Hispanic/Latino), 2 international. Average age 35. 9 applicants, 89% accepted, 5 enrolled. In 2018, 7 master's, 1 Certificate awarded. *Entrance requirements:* For master's, minimum GPA of 2.75, interview. Additional exam requirements/recommendations for international students: Required—TOEFL (minimum score 550 paper-based; 80 iBT). *Application deadline:* Applications are processed on a rolling basis. Application fee: $30. Electronic applications accepted. *Financial support:* In 2018–19, 1 research assistantship with full tuition reimbursement (averaging $7,544 per year) was awarded; unspecified assistantships also available. Financial award applicants required to submit FAFSA. *Unit head:* Dr. Eric Sheffield, Chairperson, 309-298-1183. *Application contact:* Dr. Mark Mossman, Associate Provost and Director of Graduate Studies, 309-298-1806, Fax: 309-298-2345, E-mail: grad-office@wiu.edu.
Website: http://www.wiu.edu/coehs/es/programs/eis/eis.php

Widener University, School of Human Service Professions, Center for Education, Chester, PA 19013-5792. Offers adult education (M Ed); counseling in higher education (M Ed); counselor education (M Ed); early childhood education (M Ed); educational foundations (M Ed); educational leadership (M Ed); educational psychology (M Ed); elementary education (M Ed); English and language arts (M Ed); health education (M Ed); higher education leadership (Ed D); home and school visitor (M Ed); human sexuality (M Ed, PhD); mathematics education (M Ed); middle school education (M Ed); principalship (M Ed); reading and language arts (Ed D); reading education (M Ed); school administration (Ed D); science education (M Ed); social studies education (M Ed); special education (M Ed); technology education (M Ed). *Accreditation:* NCATE. *Program availability:* Part-time, evening/weekend. Terminal master's awarded for partial completion of doctoral program. *Degree requirements:* For doctorate, thesis/dissertation. *Entrance requirements:* For master's, minimum GPA of 2.5; for doctorate, GRE or MAT, minimum GPA of 2.0 (undergraduate), 3.5 (graduate). Electronic applications accepted. *Expenses:* Contact institution. *Faculty research:* Reading and cognition, adult education, technology education, educational leadership, special education.

William Paterson University of New Jersey, College of Humanities and Social Sciences, Wayne, NJ 07470-8420. Offers applied sociology (MA); assessment and evaluation research (Certificate); bilingual education (Certificate); clinical and counseling psychology (MA); clinical psychology (Psy D); creative and professional writing (MFA); English (MA); history (MA); public policy and international affairs (MA); teaching English as a second language (Certificate). *Program availability:* Part-time. *Faculty:* 41 full-time (25 women), 7 part-time/adjunct (5 women). *Students:* 69 full-time (49 women), 65 part-time (42 women); includes 55 minority (6 Black or African American, non-Hispanic/Latino; 2 Asian, non-Hispanic/Latino; 41 Hispanic/Latino; 6 Two or more races, non-Hispanic/Latino), 3 international. Average age 32. 152 applicants, 47% accepted, 44 enrolled. In 2018, 46 master's awarded. *Degree requirements:* For master's, Programs Differ see: https://academiccatalog.wpunj.edu/content.php?catoid=1&navoid=68. *Entrance requirements:* For master's, program details: https://www.wpunj.edu/admissions/graduate/admission-deadlines-and-requirements/. Additional exam requirements/recommendations for international students: Required—TOEFL (minimum score 550 paper-based; 79 iBT), IELTS (minimum score 6). *Application deadline:* For fall admission, 6/1 for domestic students, 3/1 for international students; for spring admission, 11/1 for domestic students, 10/1 for international students. Applications are processed on a rolling basis. Application fee: $50. Electronic applications accepted. *Expenses: Tuition, area resident:* Full-time $14,714; part-time $727 per credit. Tuition, state resident: full-time $14,714; part-time $727 per credit. Tuition, nonresident: full-time $22,952; part-time $727 per credit. *International tuition:* $22,952 full-time. *Required fees:* $4 per semester. Tuition and fees vary according to course load, degree level and program. *Financial support:* In 2018–19, 16 students received support. Career-related internships or fieldwork, Federal Work-Study, scholarships/grants, tuition waivers, and unspecified assistantships available. Support available to part-time students. Financial award application deadline: 3/15; financial award applicants required to submit FAFSA. *Faculty research:* Relationship violence, work-family balance, social development of Japan, theories justifying war, reactions to trauma. *Total annual research expenditures:* $119,089. *Unit head:* Dr. Kara Rabbitt, Dean, 973-720-2180, Fax: 973-720-2955, E-mail: rabbittk@wpunj.edu. *Application contact:* Tinu Adeniran, Associate Director, Graduate Admissions, 973-720-2764, Fax: 973-720-2035, E-mail: adenirant@wpunj.edu.
Website: http://www.wpunj.edu/cohss

International and Comparative Education

American University, School of Education, Washington, DC 20016-8030. Offers education (Certificate); education policy and leadership (M Ed); international training and education (MA); special education (MA); teacher education (MAT); M Ed/MPA; M Ed/MPP; MAT/MA. *Accreditation:* NCATE. *Program availability:* Part-time, evening/weekend, 100% online. *Faculty:* 17 full-time (13 women), 33 part-time/adjunct (23 women). *Students:* 53 full-time (46 women), 246 part-time (191 women); includes 139 minority (97 Black or African American, non-Hispanic/Latino; 13 Asian, non-Hispanic/Latino; 23 Hispanic/Latino; 6 Two or more races, non-Hispanic/Latino), 5 international. Average age 29. 361 applicants, 88% accepted, 161 enrolled. In 2018, 73 master's, 2 other advanced degrees awarded. *Degree requirements:* For master's, comprehensive exam, thesis or alternative. *Entrance requirements:* For master's, Please visit website: https://www.american.edu/soe/, bachelor's degree, statement of purpose, transcripts, 2 letters of recommendation. Additional exam requirements/recommendations for international students: Required—TOEFL (minimum score 100 iBT). Application fee: $55. Electronic applications accepted. *Expenses: Tuition:* Full-time $30,744; part-time $1642 per credit hour. *Required fees:* $702; $200 per semester. Tuition and fees vary according to course load, degree level and program. *Financial support:* Research assistantships, teaching assistantships, institutionally sponsored loans, scholarships/grants, and unspecified assistantships available. Financial award application deadline: 2/1; financial award applicants required to submit FAFSA. *Unit head:* Dr. Cheryl

Holcomb-McCoy, Dean, 202-885-3720, E-mail: educate@american.edu. *Application contact:* Ashleigh Huseth, Senior Coordinator, Admissions & Onboarding, E-mail: ahuseth@american.edu.
Website: https://www.american.edu/cas/education/

The American University in Cairo, Graduate School of Education, Cairo, Egypt. Offers educational leadership (MA); international and comparative education (MA). *Program availability:* Part-time, evening/weekend. *Degree requirements:* For master's, thesis. *Entrance requirements:* Additional exam requirements/recommendations for international students: Required—TOEFL (minimum score 450 paper-based; 45 iBT), IELTS (minimum score 5). Electronic applications accepted. *Faculty research:* Educational reform.

Andrews University, School of Graduate Studies, College of Arts and Sciences, Department of Behavioral Science, Berrien Springs, MI 49104. Offers international development (MSCID), including community and international development. *Entrance requirements:* For master's, GRE. Additional exam requirements/recommendations for international students: Required—TOEFL (minimum score 550 paper-based). *Faculty research:* Risk behaviors.

Bowling Green State University, Graduate College, College of Education and Human Development, School of Educational Foundations, Leadership and Policy, Program in Cross-Cultural and International Education, Bowling Green, OH 43403. Offers MA. *Program availability:* Part-time. *Degree requirements:* For master's, thesis or alternative. *Entrance requirements:* For master's, GRE General Test. Additional exam requirements/ recommendations for international students: Required—TOEFL.

California Baptist University, Program in Education, Riverside, CA 92504-3206. Offers educational leadership (MS); educational leadership for faith-based institutions (MS); educational leadership for public institutions (MS); educational technology (MS); instructional computer applications (MS); international education (MS); leadership and adult learning (MS); leadership and organizational studies (MS); online teaching and learning (MS); reading (MS); science education (MA); special education in mild/ moderate disabilities (MS); special education in moderate/severe disabilities (MS); teacher leadership (MS); teaching (MS); teaching and learning (MS). *Program availability:* Part-time, evening/weekend, 100% online, blended/hybrid learning. *Faculty:* 26 full-time (13 women), 28 part-time/adjunct (21 women). *Students:* 201 full-time (164 women), 265 part-time (209 women); includes 226 minority (23 Black or African American, non-Hispanic/Latino; 4 American Indian or Alaska Native, non-Hispanic/ Latino; 7 Asian, non-Hispanic/Latino; 169 Hispanic/Latino; 6 Native Hawaiian or other Pacific Islander, non-Hispanic/Latino; 17 Two or more races, non-Hispanic/Latino), 2 international. Average age 39. 145 applicants, 97% accepted, 141 enrolled. In 2018, 253 master's awarded. *Degree requirements:* For master's, comprehensive exam, project, or thesis. *Entrance requirements:* For master's, minimum undergraduate GPA of 2.75; 500-word essay; three letters of recommendation; two prerequisite courses completed with minimum C grade. Additional exam requirements/recommendations for international students: Required—TOEFL (minimum score 80 iBT). *Application deadline:* For fall admission, 8/1 priority date for domestic students, 7/1 for international students; for spring admission, 12/1 priority date for domestic students, 11/1 for international students. Applications are processed on a rolling basis. Application fee: $45. Electronic applications accepted. *Expenses:* $634 per unit. *Financial support:* In 2018–19, 312 students received support. Federal Work-Study and scholarships/grants available. Financial award applicants required to submit CSS PROFILE or FAFSA. *Faculty research:* Leadership development, complexity theory, faith and learning, special education, social and philosophical contexts of education. *Unit head:* Dr. Robin Duncan, Dean, School of Education, 951-552-8948, E-mail: rduncan@calbaptist.edu. *Application contact:* Dr. Shari Farris, Program Director, Online MS in Education, 951-343-2455, E-mail: sfarris@calbaptist.edu.
Website: http://www.calbaptist.edu/mastersined/

California State University, Dominguez Hills, College of Extended and International Education, Carson, CA 90747-0001. Offers MA, MS. *Program availability:* Part-time, evening/weekend, online learning. *Degree requirements:* For master's, thesis. *Entrance requirements:* Additional exam requirements/recommendations for international students: Required—TOEFL. Electronic applications accepted. *Expenses:* Contact institution.

The College of New Jersey, Office of Graduate and Advancing Education, Office of Global Programs, Program in Overseas Education, Ewing, NJ 08628. Offers M Ed, Certificate. *Program availability:* Part-time. *Degree requirements:* For master's, comprehensive exam. *Entrance requirements:* For master's, GRE, minimum GPA of 3.0 in field or 2.75 overall; for Certificate, previous master's degree or higher. Additional exam requirements/recommendations for international students: Required—TOEFL. Electronic applications accepted.

Drexel University, Goodwin College of Professional Studies, School of Education, Philadelphia, PA 19104-2875. Offers applied behavior analysis (MS); creativity and innovation (MS); education improvement and transformation (MS); educational administration (MS); educational leadership and management (Ed D); educational leadership development and learning technologies (PhD); global and international education (MS); higher education (MS); human resources development (MS); learning technologies (MS); mathematics, learning and teaching (MS); special education (MS); teaching, learning and curriculum (MS). *Program availability:* Part-time, evening/ weekend, online learning. *Degree requirements:* For doctorate, thesis/dissertation. *Entrance requirements:* For doctorate, GRE or GMAT. Additional exam requirements/ recommendations for international students: Required—TOEFL, IELTS. Electronic applications accepted. Application fee is waived when completed online. *Expenses:* Contact institution. *Faculty research:* Leadership development, mathematics education, literacy, autism, educational technology.

East Carolina University, Graduate School, Thomas Harriot College of Arts and Sciences, Program in International Studies, Greenville, NC 27858-4353. Offers international studies (MA); international teaching (Certificate). *Program availability:* Part-time. *Application deadline:* For fall admission, 7/1 priority date for domestic and international students; for spring admission, 11/15 priority date for domestic and international students; for summer admission, 3/15 priority date for domestic and international students. *Expenses: Tuition, area resident:* Full-time $4749. Tuition, state resident: full-time $4749. Tuition, nonresident: full-time $17,898. *International tuition:* $17,898 full-time. *Required fees:* $2787. Part-time tuition and fees vary according to course load and program. *Financial support:* Application deadline: 3/1. *Unit head:* Dr. David L. Smith, Director, 252-328-5524, E-mail: smithdav@ecu.edu. *Application contact:* Graduate School Admissions, 252-328-6012, Fax: 252-328-6071, E-mail: gradschool@ecu.edu.
Website: http://www.ecu.edu/cs-cas/international/maisindex.cfm

Florida International University, College of Arts, Sciences, and Education, Department of Leadership and Professional Studies, Miami, FL 33199. Offers adult education and human resource development (MS, Ed D); counseling (MS), including rehabilitation counseling, school counseling; counselor education (MS), including clinical mental health counseling; educational administration and supervision (Ed D); educational leadership (MS, Certificate, Ed S); higher education (Ed D); higher education administration (MS); international and comparative education (MS); recreation and sport management (MS), including recreation and sport management, recreational therapy; school psychology (Ed S); urban education (MS), including instruction in urban settings, learning technologies, multicultural/bilingual, multicultural/TESOL, urban education. *Program availability:* Part-time, evening/weekend. *Faculty:* 64 full-time (43 women), 104 part-time/adjunct (76 women). *Students:* 258 full-time (196 women), 217 part-time (155 women); includes 387 minority (118 Black or African American, non-Hispanic/Latino; 8 Asian, non-Hispanic/Latino; 249 Hispanic/Latino; 12 Two or more races, non-Hispanic/Latino), 11 international. Average age 31. 345 applicants, 57% accepted, 126 enrolled. In 2018, 172 master's, 11 doctorates awarded. *Entrance requirements:* For master's, minimum GPA of 3.0; for doctorate and other advanced degree, GRE General Test. Additional exam requirements/recommendations for international students: Required—TOEFL (minimum score 550 paper-based; 80 iBT), IELTS (minimum score 6.3). *Application deadline:* For fall admission, 6/1 priority date for domestic students, 4/1 for international students; for winter admission, 10/1 priority date for domestic students, 9/1 for international students; for spring admission, 3/1 priority date for domestic students, 2/1 for international students. Applications are processed on a rolling basis. Application fee: $30. Electronic applications accepted. *Financial support:* Fellowships, research assistantships, teaching assistantships, Federal Work-Study, and tuition waivers (full and partial) available. Support available to part-time students. Financial award applicants required to submit FAFSA. *Unit head:* Dr. Benjamin Baez, Chair, 305-348-3214, Fax: 305-348-1515, E-mail: benjamin.baez@fiu.edu. *Application contact:* Nanett Rojas, Manager, Admissions Operations, 305-348-7464, Fax: 305-348-7441, E-mail: gradadm@fiu.edu.
Website: http://education.fiu.edu

Florida State University, The Graduate School, College of Education, Department of Educational Leadership and Policy Studies, Tallahassee, FL 32306. Offers educational leadership and administration (Certificate); educational leadership and policy (MS, Ed D, PhD, Ed S), including education policy and evaluation (MS, Ed D, PhD), educational leadership and administration; foundations of education (MS, PhD), including history and philosophy of education, international and multicultural education; higher education (MS, PhD); institutional research (Certificate); program evaluation (Certificate). *Program availability:* Part-time, evening/weekend, 100% online, blended/hybrid learning, asynchronous, minimal on-campus study. *Degree requirements:* For master's, comprehensive exam, thesis optional; for doctorate, comprehensive exam, thesis/ dissertation, diagnostic exam, preliminary exam, prospectus defense, dissertation defense. *Entrance requirements:* For master's, doctorate, and other advanced degree, GRE General Test, minimum GPA of 3.0. Additional exam requirements/ recommendations for international students: Required—TOEFL (minimum score 550 paper-based, 80 iBT), IELTS (minimum score 6.5), Michigan English Language Assessment Battery (minimum score 77), or PTE (minimum score 55). Electronic applications accepted. *Expenses: Tuition, area resident:* Part-time $479.32 per credit hour. Tuition and fees vary according to campus/location and program. *Faculty research:* Post-secondary success; leadership education; education policy; international education; multicultural education.

Gallaudet University, The Graduate School, Washington, DC 20002-3625. Offers American Sign Language/English bilingual early childhood deaf education: birth to 5 (Certificate); audiology (Au D); clinical psychology (PhD); deaf and hard of hearing infants, toddlers, and their families (Certificate); deaf education (MA, Ed S); deaf history (Certificate); deaf studies (Certificate); educating deaf students with disabilities (Certificate); education: teacher preparation (MA), including deaf education, early childhood education and deaf education, elementary education and deaf education, secondary education and deaf education; educational neuroscience (PhD); hearing, speech and language sciences (MS, PhD); international development (MA); interpretation (MA, PhD), including combined interpreting practice and research (MA), interpreting research (MA); linguistics (MA, PhD); mental health counseling (MA); peer mentoring (Certificate); public administration (MPA); school counseling (MA); school psychology (Psy S); sign language teaching (MA); social work (MSW); speech-language pathology (MS). *Program availability:* Part-time. Terminal master's awarded for partial completion of doctoral program. *Degree requirements:* For master's, comprehensive exam (for some programs), thesis optional; for doctorate, comprehensive exam, thesis/ dissertation. *Entrance requirements:* For master's and doctorate, GRE General Test or MAT, letters of recommendation, interviews, goals statement, American Sign Language proficiency interview, written English competency. Additional exam requirements/ recommendations for international students: Required—TOEFL. Electronic applications accepted. *Faculty research:* Signing math dictionaries, telecommunications access, cancer genetics, linguistics, visual language and visual learning, integrated quantum materials, deaf legal discourse, advance recruitment and retention in geosciences.

The George Washington University, Graduate School of Education and Human Development, Department of Educational Leadership, Program in Higher Education Administration, Washington, DC 20052. Offers college teaching and academic leadership (MA Ed/HD, Ed S); general administration (MA Ed/HD, Ed S); higher education administration (Ed D); higher education finance (MA Ed/HD, Ed S); international education (MA Ed/HD, Ed S); policy (MA Ed/HD, Ed S); student affairs administration (MA Ed/HD, Ed S). *Accreditation:* NCATE. *Students:* 27 full-time (19 women), 55 part-time (41 women); includes 37 minority (21 Black or African American, non-Hispanic/Latino; 5 Asian, non-Hispanic/Latino; 8 Hispanic/Latino; 3 Two or more races, non-Hispanic/Latino), 4 international. Average age 32. 131 applicants, 85% accepted, 37 enrolled. In 2018, 15 master's, 4 doctorates, 1 other advanced degree awarded. *Degree requirements:* For master's and Ed S, comprehensive exam; for doctorate, comprehensive exam, thesis/dissertation. *Entrance requirements:* For master's, GRE General Test or MAT, minimum GPA of 2.75; for doctorate, GRE General Test or MAT, interview, minimum GPA of 3.3; for Ed S, GRE General Test or MAT, minimum GPA of 3.3. *Application deadline:* For fall admission, 1/15 priority date for domestic students; for spring admission, 10/1 for domestic students. Applications are processed on a rolling basis. Application fee: $75. *Financial support:* In 2018–19, 17 students received support. Fellowships, research assistantships, career-related internships or fieldwork, Federal Work-Study, and tuition waivers (partial) available. Financial award application deadline: 1/15; financial award applicants required to submit FAFSA. *Faculty research:* Technology in higher education administration. *Unit head:* Michael Feuer, Dean, 202-994-6161, E-mail: mjfeuer@gwu.edu. *Application contact:* Sarah Lang, Director of Graduate Admissions, 202-994-1447, Fax: 202-994-7207, E-mail: slang@gwu.edu.

The George Washington University, Graduate School of Education and Human Development, Department of Educational Leadership, Program in International Education, Washington, DC 20052. Offers MA Ed. *Accreditation:* NCATE. *Students:* 50 full-time (40 women), 40 part-time (34 women); includes 28 minority (7 Black or African American, non-Hispanic/Latino; 9 Asian, non-Hispanic/Latino; 9 Hispanic/Latino; 3 Two or more races, non-Hispanic/Latino), 16 international. Average age 28. 147 applicants, 88% accepted, 44 enrolled. In 2018, 44 master's awarded. *Entrance requirements:* For master's, GRE General Test or MAT, minimum GPA of 2.75. *Application deadline:* For fall admission, 1/15 priority date for domestic students; for spring admission, 10/1 for domestic students. Applications are processed on a rolling basis. Application fee: $75. *Financial support:* In 2018–19, 13 students received support. Fellowships, research

assistantships, career-related internships or fieldwork, Federal Work-Study, and tuition waivers available. Financial award application deadline: 1/15; financial award applicants required to submit FAFSA. *Faculty research:* Education and development. *Unit head:* Dr. William K. Cummings, Coordinator, 202-994-4698, E-mail: wkcum@gwu.edu. *Application contact:* Sarah Lang, Director of Graduate Admissions, 202-994-1447, Fax: 202-994-7207, E-mail: slang@gwu.edu.

Harvard University, Harvard Graduate School of Education, Master's Programs in Education, Cambridge, MA 02138. Offers arts in education (Ed M); education policy and management (Ed M); higher education (Ed M); human development and psychology (Ed M); international education policy (Ed M); language and literacy (Ed M); learning and teaching (Ed M); mind, brain, and education (Ed M); prevention science and practice (Ed M); school leadership (Ed M); special studies (Ed M); teacher education (Ed M); technology, innovation, and education (Ed M). *Program availability:* Part-time. *Entrance requirements:* For master's, GRE General Test, statement of purpose, 3 letters of recommendation, resume, official transcripts. Additional exam requirements/recommendations for international students: Required—TOEFL (minimum score 613 paper-based; 104 iBT), TWE (minimum score 5). Electronic applications accepted. *Faculty research:* Learning and development, educational leadership and organizations, education policy analysis.

Indiana University Bloomington, School of Education, Department of Educational Leadership and Policy Studies, Bloomington, IN 47405. Offers educational leadership (MS, Ed D, Ed S); higher education (Ed D, PhD); higher education and student affairs (MS); history and philosophy of education (MS); history, philosophy, and policy in education (PhD), including education policy studies, history of education, philosophy of education; international and comparative education (MS). *Accreditation:* NCATE. *Degree requirements:* For master's, thesis optional; for doctorate, comprehensive exam, thesis/dissertation; for Ed S, comprehensive exam or project. *Entrance requirements:* For master's, doctorate, and Ed S, GRE General Test. Additional exam requirements/recommendations for international students: Required—TOEFL (minimum score 79 iBT). Electronic applications accepted. *Faculty research:* Culturally engaging campus environments, school choice policy analysis, democracy and education in the national and international context, and principal leadership.

Louisiana State University and Agricultural & Mechanical College, Graduate School, College of Human Sciences and Education, School of Human Resource Education and Workforce Development, Baton Rouge, LA 70803. Offers agriculture and extension education and youth development (MS, PhD); career and technical education (MS, PhD); comprehensive vocational education (MS, PhD); extension and international education (MS, PhD); human resource and leadership development (MS, PhD); industrial education (MS); vocational agriculture education (MS, PhD); vocational business education (MS); vocational home economics education (MS). *Accreditation:* NCATE.

Loyola University Chicago, School of Education, Program in Higher Education, Chicago, IL 60660. Offers higher education (M Ed, PhD); international higher education (M Ed). PhD offered through the Graduate School. *Accreditation:* NCATE. *Program availability:* Part-time, blended/hybrid learning. *Faculty:* 4 full-time (2 women), 10 part-time/adjunct (9 women). *Students:* 49 full-time (30 women), 63 part-time (50 women); includes 51 minority (17 Black or African American, non-Hispanic/Latino; 8 Asian, non-Hispanic/Latino; 21 Hispanic/Latino; 5 Two or more races, non-Hispanic/Latino). Average age 30. 172 applicants, 83% accepted, 39 enrolled. In 2018, 70 master's, 5 doctorates awarded. *Degree requirements:* For master's, comprehensive exam; for doctorate, comprehensive exam, thesis/dissertation. *Entrance requirements:* For master's, letters of recommendation, minimum GPA of 3.0, resume, transcripts; for doctorate, GMAT, GRE General Test, or MAT, 5 years of higher education work experience, interview. Additional exam requirements/recommendations for international students: Required—TOEFL (minimum score 550 paper-based; 79 iBT). *Application deadline:* For fall admission, 12/1 for domestic and international students. Applications are processed on a rolling basis. Application fee: $50. Electronic applications accepted. Application fee is waived when completed online. *Expenses:* Contact institution. *Financial support:* In 2018–19, 37 fellowships with partial tuition reimbursements, 42 research assistantships with full tuition reimbursements (averaging $14,000 per year), 23 teaching assistantships with full tuition reimbursements (averaging $4,000 per year) were awarded; career-related internships or fieldwork, institutionally sponsored loans, scholarships/grants, traineeships, health care benefits, and unspecified assistantships also available. Support available to part-time students. Financial award application deadline: 2/1; financial award applicants required to submit FAFSA. *Faculty research:* Church-affiliated higher education, enrollment management, academic programs, program evaluation/quality. *Unit head:* Dr. Bridget Kelly, Director, 312-915-6855, Fax: 312-915-6660, E-mail: bkelly4@luc.edu. *Application contact:* Dr. Bridget Kelly, Director, 312-915-6855, Fax: 312-915-6660, E-mail: bkelly4@luc.edu.

Middlebury Institute of International Studies at Monterey, Graduate School of International Policy and Management, Program in International Education Management, Monterey, CA 93940-2691. Offers MA. *Degree requirements:* For master's, one foreign language, practicum. *Entrance requirements:* For master's, minimum GPA of 3.0, proficiency in a foreign language. Additional exam requirements/recommendations for international students: Required—TOEFL (minimum score 550 paper-based; 80 iBT). Electronic applications accepted. Application fee is waived when completed online.

New York University, Steinhardt School of Culture, Education, and Human Development, Applied Statistics, Social Science, and Humanities, Program in International Education, New York, NY 10012. Offers MA, PhD, Advanced Certificate. *Program availability:* Part-time. *Entrance requirements:* For doctorate, GRE General Test, interview; for Advanced Certificate, master's degree. Additional exam requirements/recommendations for international students: Required—TOEFL (minimum score 100 iBT). Electronic applications accepted. *Faculty research:* Civic education, ethnic identity among students and teachers, comparative education, education during emergencies, cross-cultural exchange.

St. John's University, The School of Education, Department of Curriculum and Instruction, PhD in Curriculum and Instruction Program, Queens, NY 11439. Offers early childhood (PhD); global education (PhD); STEM education (PhD); teaching, learning, and knowing (PhD). *Program availability:* Part-time-only. *Degree requirements:* For doctorate, comprehensive exam, thesis/dissertation. *Entrance requirements:* For doctorate, teacher certification (or equivalent), at least three years' teaching experience or the equivalent in informal learning environments, master's degree. Additional exam requirements/recommendations for international students: Required—TOEFL. Electronic applications accepted. *Faculty research:* Literacies, early childhood, STEM, school culture, global education.

SIT Graduate Institute, Graduate Programs, Master's Programs in Intercultural Service, Leadership, and Management, Master's Program in International Education, Brattleboro, VT 05302-0676. Offers MA.

Stanford University, Graduate School of Education, Program in International Comparative Education, Stanford, CA 94305-2004. Offers MA, PhD. *Expenses: Tuition:* Full-time $50,703; part-time $32,970 per year. *Required fees:* $651.

Teachers College, Columbia University, Department of International and Transcultural Studies, New York, NY 10027-6696. Offers anthropology and education (MA, Ed D, PhD); applied anthropology (PhD); comparative and international education (MA, Ed D, PhD); international educational development (Ed M, MA, Ed D, PhD). *Program availability:* Part-time. *Students:* 94 full-time (79 women), 166 part-time (141 women); includes 90 minority (17 Black or African American, non-Hispanic/Latino; 32 Asian, non-Hispanic/Latino; 32 Hispanic/Latino; 9 Two or more races, non-Hispanic/Latino), 99 international. Average age 29. 389 applicants, 56% accepted, 99 enrolled. *Unit head:* Prof. Herve Varenne, Chair, 212-678-3190, E-mail: varenne@tc.columbia.edu. *Application contact:* Kelly Sutton Skinner, Director of Admission & New Student Enrollment, E-mail: kms2237@tc.columbia.edu.

University at Albany, State University of New York, School of Education, Department of Educational Policy and Leadership, Albany, NY 12222-0001. Offers educational policy and leadership (MS, PhD); higher education (MS); international education management (CAS). *Program availability:* Evening/weekend. *Faculty:* 12 full-time (5 women), 3 part-time/adjunct (2 women). *Students:* 42 full-time (31 women), 132 part-time (84 women); includes 47 minority (21 Black or African American, non-Hispanic/Latino; 4 Asian, non-Hispanic/Latino; 20 Hispanic/Latino; 2 Two or more races, non-Hispanic/Latino), 23 international. Average age 32. 72 applicants, 71% accepted, 48 enrolled. In 2018, 11 master's, 7 doctorates, 12 other advanced degrees awarded. *Degree requirements:* For doctorate, one foreign language, thesis/dissertation. *Entrance requirements:* For doctorate, GRE General Test, GRE Subject Test. Additional exam requirements/recommendations for international students: Required—TOEFL (minimum score 550 paper-based). *Application deadline:* For fall admission, 2/1 for domestic students, 5/1 for international students; for spring admission, 9/1 for domestic students, 11/1 for international students. Applications are processed on a rolling basis. Application fee: $75. Electronic applications accepted. *Financial support:* Fellowships and career-related internships or fieldwork available. Financial award application deadline: 3/15. *Unit head:* Jason Lane, Chair, 518-442-5092, E-mail: jlane@albany.edu. *Application contact:* Jason Lane, Chair, 518-442-5092, E-mail: jlane@albany.edu.
Website: http://www.albany.edu/epl/

University of Bridgeport, School of Education, Department of Education, Bridgeport, CT 06604. Offers education (MS); educational management (Ed D, Diploma), including intermediate administrator or supervisor (Diploma), leadership (Ed D); elementary education (MS, Diploma), including early childhood education, elementary education; middle school education (MS); music education (MS); remedial reading and language arts (Diploma); secondary education (MS, Diploma), including computer specialist (Diploma), international education (Diploma), reading specialist, secondary education. *Program availability:* Part-time, evening/weekend. *Degree requirements:* For master's, final exam, final project, or thesis; for doctorate, comprehensive exam, thesis/dissertation; for Diploma, thesis or alternative, final project. *Entrance requirements:* For master's, minimum undergraduate QPA of 2.67; for doctorate, GRE, MAT; for Diploma, GRE General Test or MAT, minimum graduate QPA of 3.0. Additional exam requirements/recommendations for international students: Recommended—TOEFL (minimum score 550 paper-based; 80 iBT), IELTS (minimum score 6.5). Electronic applications accepted. *Expenses:* Contact institution.

University of Massachusetts Amherst, Graduate School, College of Education, Program in Education, Amherst, MA 01003. Offers bilingual, English as a second language, and multicultural education (M Ed, Ed S); child study and early education (M Ed); children, families and schools (Ed D, Ed S); early childhood and elementary teacher education (M Ed); educational leadership (M Ed); educational policy and leadership (Ed D); higher education (M Ed); international education (M Ed); language, literacy and culture (Ed D); learning, media and technology (M Ed, Ed S); mathematics, science, and learning technologies (Ed D); reading and writing (M Ed); research, educational measurement and psychometrics (Ed D); school counselor education (M Ed, Ed S); school psychology (Ed S); science education (Ed S); secondary teacher education (M Ed); social justice education (M Ed, Ed D, Ed S); special education (M Ed, Ed D, Ed S); teacher education and school improvement (Ed D, Ed S). *Accreditation:* NCATE. *Program availability:* Part-time, online learning. Terminal master's awarded for partial completion of doctoral program. *Degree requirements:* For doctorate, comprehensive exam, thesis/dissertation. *Entrance requirements:* Additional exam requirements/recommendations for international students: Required—TOEFL (minimum score 550 paper-based; 80 iBT), IELTS (minimum score 6.5). Electronic applications accepted.

University of Minnesota, Twin Cities Campus, Graduate School, College of Education and Human Development, Department of Organizational Leadership, Policy and Development, Program in Comparative and International Development Education, Minneapolis, MN 55455-0213. Offers MA, PhD. *Students:* 56 full-time (43 women), 39 part-time (29 women); includes 18 minority (5 Black or African American, non-Hispanic/Latino; 7 Asian, non-Hispanic/Latino; 4 Hispanic/Latino; 2 Two or more races, non-Hispanic/Latino), 20 international. Average age 36. 63 applicants, 41% accepted, 17 enrolled. In 2018, 10 master's, 13 doctorates awarded. Application fee: $75 ($95 for international students). *Unit head:* Dr. Kenneth Bartlett, Chair, 612-624-1006, Fax: 612-624-3377, E-mail: bartlett@umn.edu. *Application contact:* Dr. Jeremy J. Hernandez, Director of Graduate Studies, 612-626-9377, E-mail: olpd@umn.edu.
Website: http://www.cehd.umn.edu/OLPD/grad-programs/CIDE/

University of Pennsylvania, Graduate School of Education, Division of Literacy, Culture, and International Education, Program in International Educational Development, Philadelphia, PA 19104. Offers MS Ed. *Students:* 46 full-time (39 women), 6 part-time (4 women); includes 11 minority (6 Asian, non-Hispanic/Latino; 3 Hispanic/Latino; 2 Two or more races, non-Hispanic/Latino), 26 international. Average age 27. 179 applicants, 53% accepted, 41 enrolled. In 2018, 29 master's awarded. Application fee: $80.

University of Pittsburgh, School of Education, Department of Administrative and Policy Studies, Program in Social and Comparative Analysis in Education, Pittsburgh, PA 15260. Offers M Ed, MA, Ed D, PhD. *Program availability:* Evening/weekend. *Degree requirements:* For master's, thesis; for doctorate, thesis/dissertation. *Entrance requirements:* For doctorate, GRE General Test. Additional exam requirements/recommendations for international students: Required—TOEFL (minimum score 80 iBT). Electronic applications accepted.

University of San Francisco, School of Education, Department of International and Multicultural Education, San Francisco, CA 94117. Offers MA, Ed D. *Program availability:* Part-time, evening/weekend. *Students:* 50 full-time (43 women), 34 part-time (27 women); includes 52 minority (9 Black or African American, non-Hispanic/Latino; 11 Asian, non-Hispanic/Latino; 25 Hispanic/Latino; 2 Native Hawaiian or other Pacific Islander, non-Hispanic/Latino; 5 Two or more races, non-Hispanic/Latino), 10 international. Average age 35. 74 applicants, 85% accepted, 21 enrolled. In 2018, 15 master's, 10 doctorates awarded. *Degree requirements:* For doctorate, thesis/dissertation. *Entrance requirements:* Additional exam requirements/recommendations for international students: Required—TOEFL, IELTS, PTE. *Application deadline:* For fall admission, 3/1 priority date for domestic students, 3/1 for international students; for spring admission, 10/15 priority date for domestic and international students. Applications are processed on a rolling basis. Application fee: $55 ($65 for international

students). Electronic applications accepted. *Financial support:* Fellowships, research assistantships, and teaching assistantships available. Financial award application deadline: 3/2; financial award applicants required to submit FAFSA. *Unit head:* Dr. Emma Fuentes, Chair, 415-422-6878. *Application contact:* Peter Cole, Admission Coordinator, 415-422-5467, E-mail: schoolofeducation@usfca.edu.

University of South Africa, College of Human Sciences, Pretoria, South Africa. Offers adult education (M Ed); African languages (MA, PhD); African politics (MA, PhD); Afrikaans (MA, PhD); ancient history (MA, PhD); ancient Near Eastern studies (MA, PhD); anthropology (MA, PhD); applied linguistics (MA); Arabic (MA, PhD); archaeology (MA); art history (MA); Biblical archaeology (MA); Biblical studies (M Th, D Th, PhD); Christian spirituality (M Th, D Th); church history (M Th, D Th); classical studies (MA, PhD); clinical psychology (MA); communication (MA, PhD); comparative education (M Ed, Ed D); consulting psychology (D Admin, D Com, PhD); curriculum studies (M Ed, Ed D); development studies (M Admin, MA, D Admin, PhD); didactics (M Ed, Ed D); education (M Tech); education management (M Ed, Ed D); educational psychology (M Ed); English (MA); environmental education (M Ed); French (MA, PhD); German (MA, PhD); Greek (MA); guidance and counseling (M Ed); health studies (MA, PhD), including health sciences education (MA), health services management (MA), medical and surgical nursing science (critical care general) (MA), midwifery and neonatal nursing science (MA), trauma and emergency care (MA); history (MA, PhD); history of education (Ed D); inclusive education (M Ed, Ed D); information and communications technology policy and regulation (MA); information science (MA, MIS, PhD); international politics (MA, PhD); Islamic studies (MA, PhD); Italian (MA, PhD); Judaica (MA, PhD); linguistics (MA, PhD); mathematical education (M Ed); mathematics education (MA); missiology (M Th, D Th); modern Hebrew (MA, PhD); musicology (MA, MMus, D Mus, PhD); natural science education (M Ed); New Testament (M Th, D Th); Old Testament (D Th); pastoral therapy (M Th, D Th); philosophy (MA); philosophy of education (M Ed, Ed D); politics (MA, PhD); Portuguese (MA, PhD); practical theology (M Th, D Th); psychology (MA, MS, PhD); psychology of education (M Ed, Ed D); public health (MA); religious studies (MA, D Th, PhD); Romance languages (MA); Russian (MA, PhD); Semitic languages (MA, PhD); social behavior studies in HIV/AIDS (MA); social science (mental health) (MA); social science in development studies (MA); social science in psychology (MA); social science in social work (MA); social science in sociology (MA); social work (MSW, DSW, PhD); socio-education (M Ed, Ed D); sociolinguistics (MA); sociology (MA, PhD); Spanish (MA, PhD); systematic theology (M Th, D Th); TESOL (teaching English to speakers of other languages) (MA); theological ethics (M Th, D Th); theory of literature (MA, PhD); urban ministries (D Th); urban ministry (M Th).

University of Wisconsin–Madison, Graduate School, School of Education, Department of Educational Leadership and Policy Analysis, Madison, WI 53706-1380. Offers administration (Certificate); educational policy (MS, PhD); global higher education (MS). *Degree requirements:* For doctorate, thesis/dissertation. *Entrance requirements:* For master's and doctorate, GRE General Test. Electronic applications accepted.

Walden University, Graduate Programs, Richard W. Riley College of Education and Leadership, Minneapolis, MN 55401. Offers adult education (Post-Master's Certificate); adult learning (Graduate Certificate); college teaching and learning (Graduate Certificate); community college leadership (Ed D); curriculum, instruction and assessment (Ed D, Ed S, Graduate Certificate); developmental education (Graduate Certificate); early childhood administration, management, and leadership (Graduate Certificate); early childhood education (Ed D, Ed S); early childhood public policy and advocacy (Graduate Certificate); early childhood studies (MS), including administration, management and leadership, early childhood public policy and advocacy, teaching adults in the early childhood field, teaching and diversity in early childhood education; education (MS, PhD), including adolescent literacy and learning (MS), curriculum, instruction, and assessment (grades K-12) (MS); curriculum, instruction, assessment, and evaluation (PhD), early childhood leadership and advocacy (PhD), early childhood special education (PhD), educational leadership (MS), educational leadership and administration (principal preparation) (MS), educational technology and design (PhD), elementary reading and literacy (PreK-6) (MS), elementary reading and mathematics (grades K-6) (MS), global and comparative education (PhD), higher education leadership management and policy (PhD), integrating technology in the classroom (grades K-12) (MS), learning, instruction and innovation (PhD), mathematics (grades 5-8) (MS), mathematics (grades K-6) (MS), mathematics and science (grades K-8) (MS),

organizational research, assessment, and evaluation (PhD), reading and literacy with a reading K-12 endorsement (MS), reading literacy assessment and evaluation (PhD), science (grades K-8) (MS), special education (non-licensure) (grades K-12) (MS), teacher leadership (grades K-12) (MS), teaching English language learners (grades K-12) (MS); educational administration and leadership (Ed D); educational leadership and administration (principal preparation) (Ed S); educational technology (Ed D, Ed S, Post Master's Certificate); elementary reading and literacy (Graduate Certificate); engaging culturally diverse learners (Graduate Certificate); enrollment management and institutional marketing (Graduate Certificate); higher education (MS), including adult learning, college teaching and learning, enrollment management and institutional marketing, global higher education, leadership for student success, online and distance learning; higher education and adult learning (Ed D); higher education leadership and management (Ed D); higher education leadership for student success (Graduate Certificate); instructional design and technology (MS, Postbaccalaureate Certificate), including general program (MS), online learning (MS), training and performance improvement (MS); integrating technology in the classroom (Graduate Certificate); mathematics 5-8 (Graduate Certificate); mathematics K-6 (Graduate Certificate); online teaching for adult educators (Graduate Certificate); reading, literacy, and assessment (Ed D, Ed S); science K-8 (Graduate Certificate); special education (Ed D, Ed S, Graduate Certificate); special education (K-age 21) (MAT); teacher leadership (Graduate Certificate); teaching adults English as a second language (Graduate Certificate); teaching adults in the early childhood field (Graduate Certificate); teaching and diversity in early childhood education (Graduate Certificate); teaching English language learners (grades K-12) (Graduate Certificate); teaching K-12 students online (Graduate Certificate). *Accreditation:* NCATE. *Program availability:* Part-time, evening/weekend, online only, 100% online. *Degree requirements:* For doctorate, thesis/dissertation (for some programs), residency; for other advanced degree, residency (for some programs). *Entrance requirements:* For master's, bachelor's degree or higher; minimum GPA of 2.5; official transcripts; goal statement (for some programs); access to computer and Internet; for doctorate, master's degree or higher; three years of related professional or academic experience (preferred); minimum GPA of 3.0; goal statement and current resume (for select programs); official transcripts; access to computer and Internet; for other advanced degree, relevant work experience; access to computer and Internet. Additional exam requirements/recommendations for international students: Required—TOEFL (minimum score 550 paper-based, 79 iBT), IELTS (minimum score 6.5), Michigan English Language Assessment Battery (minimum score 82), or PTE (minimum score 53). Electronic applications accepted.

Wilkes University, College of Graduate and Professional Studies, School of Education, Wilkes-Barre, PA 18766-0002. Offers educational development and strategies (MS Ed); educational leadership (MS Ed, Ed D); effective teaching (MS Ed); instructional media (MS Ed); instructional technology (MS Ed); international school leadership (MS Ed); international teaching and learning (MS Ed); literacy (MS Ed); middle level education (MS Ed); online teaching (MS Ed); school business leadership (MS Ed); special education (MS Ed); teaching English to speakers of other languages (MS Ed). *Program availability:* Part-time, evening/weekend, 100% online, blended/hybrid learning. *Students:* 87 full-time (67 women), 1,418 part-time (1,078 women); includes 87 minority (13 Black or African American, non-Hispanic/Latino; 1 American Indian or Alaska Native, non-Hispanic/Latino; 11 Asian, non-Hispanic/Latino; 40 Hispanic/Latino; 22 Two or more races, non-Hispanic/Latino). Average age 35. In 2018, 611 master's, 9 doctorates awarded. *Entrance requirements:* Additional exam requirements/recommendations for international students: Required—TOEFL (minimum score 550 paper-based; 79 iBT). *Application deadline:* Applications are processed on a rolling basis. Application fee: $45 ($65 for international students). Electronic applications accepted. *Expenses:* Contact institution. *Financial support:* Unspecified assistantships available. Financial award application deadline: 3/1; financial award applicants required to submit FAFSA. *Unit head:* Dr. Rhonda Rabbitt, Dean, 570-408-4680, Fax: 570-408-7872, E-mail: rhonda.rabbitt@wilkes.edu. *Application contact:* Stephanie Wasmanski, Associate Director of Graduate Admissions, 570-408-5535, Fax: 570-408-7846, E-mail: stephanie.wasmanski@wilkes.edu.
Website: http://www.wilkes.edu/academics/graduate-programs/masters-programs/graduate-education/index.aspx

Student Affairs

Alfred University, Graduate School, Division of Education, Alfred, NY 14802-1205. Offers college student development (MS Ed); literacy (MS Ed). *Accreditation:* TEAC. *Program availability:* Part-time. *Entrance requirements:* For master's, Liberal Arts and Sciences Test (LAST), Assessment of Teaching Skills (written) (ATS-W), Content Specialty Test (CST). Additional exam requirements/recommendations for international students: Required—TOEFL (minimum score 590 paper-based; 90 iBT), IELTS (minimum score 6.5). Electronic applications accepted.

Alliant International University–Los Angeles, Shirley M. Hufstedler School of Education, Educational Psychology Programs, Alhambra, CA 91803. Offers educational psychology (Psy D); pupil personnel services (Credential); school psychology (MA). *Program availability:* Part-time. *Degree requirements:* For doctorate, comprehensive exam, thesis/dissertation. *Entrance requirements:* For master's, minimum GPA of 2.5, letters of recommendation; for doctorate, interview, minimum GPA of 3.0, letters of recommendation. Additional exam requirements/recommendations for international students: Required—TOEFL (minimum score 550 paper-based), TWE (minimum score 5). Electronic applications accepted. *Faculty research:* Early identification and intervention with high-risk preschoolers, pediatric neuropsychology, interpersonal violence, ADHD, learning theories.

Alliant International University–San Diego, Shirley M. Hufstedler School of Education, Educational Psychology Programs, San Diego, CA 92131. Offers educational psychology (Psy D); pupil personnel services (Credential); school neuropsychology (Certificate); school psychology (MA); school-based mental health (Certificate). *Program availability:* Part-time. *Degree requirements:* For doctorate, comprehensive exam, thesis/dissertation, internship. *Entrance requirements:* For master's, minimum GPA of 2.5, letters of recommendation; for doctorate, minimum GPA of 3.0, letters of recommendation. Additional exam requirements/recommendations for international students: Required—TOEFL (minimum score 550 paper-based; 80 iBT), TWE (minimum score 5). Electronic applications accepted. *Faculty research:* School-based mental health, pupil personnel services, childhood mood, school-based assessment.

Appalachian State University, Cratis D. Williams School of Graduate Studies, Department of Human Development and Psychological Counseling, Boone, NC 28608. Offers clinical mental health counseling (MA); college student development (MA); marriage and family therapy (MA); school counseling (MA). *Accreditation:* AAMFT/COAMFTE; ACA; NCATE. *Program availability:* Part-time. *Degree requirements:* For master's, comprehensive exam (for some programs), thesis optional, internships. *Entrance requirements:* For master's, GRE General Test, 3 letters of recommendation. Additional exam requirements/recommendations for international students: Required—TOEFL (minimum score 570 paper-based; 79 iBT), IELTS (minimum score 6.5). Electronic applications accepted. *Expenses: Tuition, area resident:* Full-time $4839; part-time $237 per credit hour. *Tuition, state resident:* full-time $4839; part-time $237 per credit hour. *Tuition, nonresident:* full-time $18,271; part-time $895.50 per credit hour. *Faculty research:* Multicultural counseling, addictions counseling, play therapy, expressive arts, child and adolescent therapy, sexual abuse counseling.

Arkansas State University, Graduate School, College of Education and Behavioral Science, Department of Psychology and Counseling, State University, AR 72467. Offers clinical mental health counseling (Graduate Certificate); college student personnel services (MS); dyslexia therapy (Graduate Certificate); psychological science (MS); psychology and counseling (Ed S); rehabilitation counseling (MRC); school counseling (MSE); student affairs (Graduate Certificate). *Accreditation:* ACA (one or more programs are accredited); CORE (one or more programs are accredited); NCATE. *Program availability:* Part-time. *Degree requirements:* For master's and other advanced degree, comprehensive exam, thesis or alternative. *Entrance requirements:* For master's, GRE General Test or MAT (for MSE), appropriate bachelor's degree, interview, letters of reference, official transcripts, immunization records, written statement, 2-3 page autobiography; for other advanced degree, GRE General Test, interview, master's degree, letters of reference, official transcript, personal statement, immunization records. Additional exam requirements/recommendations for international students: Required—TOEFL (minimum score 550 paper-based; 79 iBT), IELTS (minimum score 6), PTE (minimum score 56). Electronic applications accepted.

Student Affairs

Arkansas Tech University, College of Education, Russellville, AR 72801. Offers college student personnel (MS); educational leadership (M Ed, Ed S); instructional technology (M Ed); school counseling and leadership (M Ed); school leadership (Ed D); special education K-12 (M Ed); strength and conditioning studies (MS); teaching (MAT); teaching, learning, and leadership (M Ed). *Accreditation:* NCATE. *Program availability:* Part-time, evening/weekend, 100% online, blended/hybrid learning. *Students:* 90 full-time (52 women), 450 part-time (359 women); includes 100 minority (63 Black or African American, non-Hispanic/Latino; 6 American Indian or Alaska Native, non-Hispanic/Latino; 1 Asian, non-Hispanic/Latino; 15 Hispanic/Latino; 15 Two or more races, non-Hispanic/Latino), 4 international. Average age 34. In 2018, 130 master's, 14 doctorates, 1 other advanced degree awarded. *Degree requirements:* For master's, comprehensive exam, thesis optional, action research project; for doctorate, thesis/dissertation. *Entrance requirements:* Additional exam requirements/recommendations for international students: Required—TOEFL (minimum score 550 paper-based; 79 iBT), IELTS (minimum score 6.5), PTE (minimum score 58). *Application deadline:* For fall admission, 3/1 priority date for domestic students, 5/1 priority date for international students; for spring admission, 10/1 priority date for domestic and international students. Applications are processed on a rolling basis. Application fee: $40 ($90 for international students). Electronic applications accepted. *Expenses: Tuition, area resident:* Full-time $6816; part-time $284 per credit hour. Tuition, state resident: full-time $6816; part-time $284 per credit hour. Tuition, nonresident: full-time $13,632; part-time $568 per credit hour. *International tuition:* $13,632 full-time. *Required fees:* $457.50 per semester. Tuition and fees vary according to course load and degree level. *Financial support:* In 2018–19, research assistantships with full and partial tuition reimbursements (averaging $4,800 per year), teaching assistantships with full and partial tuition reimbursements (averaging $4,800 per year) were awarded; career-related internships or fieldwork, Federal Work-Study, scholarships/grants, health care benefits, and unspecified assistantships also available. Support available to part-time students. Financial award application deadline: 4/15; financial award applicants required to submit FAFSA. *Unit head:* Dr. Linda Bean, Dean, 479-964-3217, E-mail: lbean@atu.edu. *Application contact:* Dr. Jeff Robertson, Interim Dean of Graduate College, 479-968-0398, Fax: 479-964-0542, E-mail: gradcollege@atu.edu.
Website: http://www.atu.edu/education/

Binghamton University, State University of New York, Graduate School, College of Community and Public Affairs, Department of Student Affairs Administration, Binghamton, NY 13902-6000. Offers MS. *Program availability:* Part-time. *Degree requirements:* For master's, comprehensive exam. *Entrance requirements:* For master's, GRE General Test. Additional exam requirements/recommendations for international students: Required—TOEFL (minimum score 80 iBT). Electronic applications accepted.

Bloomsburg University of Pennsylvania, School of Graduate Studies, College of Education, Department of Teaching and Learning, Program in Educational Leadership, Bloomsburg, PA 17815-1301. Offers college student affairs (M Ed); PreK-12 curriculum and instruction (M Ed); PreK-12 school counseling (M Ed); PreK-12 school principal (M Ed). *Degree requirements:* For master's, practicum. *Entrance requirements:* For master's, 3 letters of recommendation, resume, minimum QPA of 3.0, personal statement, interview. Additional exam requirements/recommendations for international students: Required—TOEFL, IELTS. Electronic applications accepted.

Bob Jones University, Graduate Programs, Greenville, SC 29614. Offers accountancy (MS); Bible (MA); Bible translation (MA); Biblical studies (Certificate); business administration (MBA); church history (MA, PhD); church ministries (MA); church music (MM); cinema and video production (MA); counseling (MS); curriculum and instruction (Ed D); divinity (M Div); dramatic production (MA); educational leadership (MS, Ed D, Ed S); elementary education (M Ed, MAT); English (M Ed, MA, MAT); fine arts (MA); graphic design (MA); history (M Ed, MA); illustration (MA); interpretative speech (MA); mathematics (M Ed, MAT); medical missions (Certificate); ministry (MM, D Min); multi-categorical special education (M Ed, MAT); music (M Ed); New Testament interpretation (PhD); Old Testament interpretation (PhD); orchestral instrument performance (MM); organ performance (MM); pastoral studies (MA); personnel services (MS, Ed S); piano pedagogy (MM); piano performance (MM); platform arts (MA); rhetoric and public address (MA); secondary education (M Ed); studio art (MA); teaching Bible (MA); theology (MA, PhD); voice performance (MM); youth ministries (MA); M Div/MM.

Bowling Green State University, Graduate College, College of Education and Human Development, Department of Higher Education and Student Affairs, Program in College Student Personnel, Bowling Green, OH 43403. Offers MA. *Program availability:* Part-time. *Degree requirements:* For master's, thesis or alternative. *Entrance requirements:* For master's, GRE General Test, interview. Additional exam requirements/recommendations for international students: Required—TOEFL. Electronic applications accepted. *Faculty research:* Adult learning, legal issues, moral and ethical development.

Bucknell University, Graduate Studies, College of Arts and Sciences, Department of Education, Lewisburg, PA 17837. Offers college student personnel (MS Ed). *Program availability:* Part-time. *Degree requirements:* For master's, comprehensive exam (for some programs), thesis or alternative. *Entrance requirements:* For master's, GRE General Test, minimum GPA of 3.0. Additional exam requirements/recommendations for international students: Required—TOEFL (minimum score 600 paper-based).

California State University, Bakersfield, Division of Graduate Studies, School of Social Sciences and Education, Program in Counseling, Bakersfield, CA 93311. Offers school counseling (MS); student affairs (MS). *Accreditation:* NCATE. *Faculty:* 1 (woman) full-time, 7 part-time/adjunct (5 women). *Students:* 69 full-time (53 women), 3 part-time (2 women); includes 59 minority (2 Black or African American, non-Hispanic/Latino; 1 American Indian or Alaska Native, non-Hispanic/Latino; 1 Asian, non-Hispanic/Latino; 55 Hispanic/Latino), 4 international. Average age 28. 81 applicants, 47% accepted, 37 enrolled. In 2018, 31 master's awarded. *Degree requirements:* For master's, thesis or alternative, culminating projects. *Entrance requirements:* For master's, CBEST (for school counseling). *Application deadline:* Applications are processed on a rolling basis. Application fee: $55. *Financial support:* In 2018–19, fellowships (averaging $1,850 per year) were awarded; Federal Work-Study, scholarships/grants, and tuition waivers (full and partial) also available. Financial award application deadline: 3/2; financial award applicants required to submit FAFSA. *Unit head:* Dr. Yvonne Oritz-Bush, Director, 661-654-3193, Fax: 661-654-2479, E-mail: yortiz_bush@csub.edu. *Application contact:* Martha Manriquez, Graduate Student Center Coordinator, 661-654-2786, Fax: 661-654-2791, E-mail: gsc@csub.edu.
Website: https://www.csub.edu/sse/departments/advancededucationalstudies/educational_counseling/index.html

California State University, Fresno, Division of Research and Graduate Studies, Kremen School of Education and Human Development, Department of Counselor Education and Rehabilitation, Program in Student Affairs and College Counseling, Fresno, CA 93740-8027. Offers MS. *Accreditation:* NCATE. *Program availability:* Part-time, evening/weekend. *Degree requirements:* For master's, thesis or alternative. *Entrance requirements:* For master's, GRE General Test, MAT, minimum GPA of 3.0. Additional exam requirements/recommendations for international students: Required—TOEFL. Electronic applications accepted.

California State University, Long Beach, Graduate Studies, College of Education, Department of Advanced Studies in Education and Counseling, Long Beach, CA 90840. Offers counseling (MS), including marriage and family therapy, school counseling, student development in higher education; education (MA, Ed D); educational administration (MA, Ed D); educational psychology (MA); special education (MS). *Program availability:* Part-time, evening/weekend. *Entrance requirements:* For master's, GRE General Test, minimum GPA of 2.75. *Application deadline:* For fall admission, 3/1 for domestic students. Applications are processed on a rolling basis. Application fee: $55. Electronic applications accepted. *Expenses: Required fees:* $2628 per term. Tuition and fees vary according to class time, course level, course load, degree level, campus/location and program. *Financial support:* Federal Work-Study, institutionally sponsored loans, and scholarships/grants available. Financial award application deadline: 3/2; financial award applicants required to submit FAFSA. *Unit head:* Dr. Hiromi Masunaga, Chair, 562-985-4517, E-mail: asec@csulb.edu. *Application contact:* Dr. Hiromi Masunaga, Chair, 562-985-4517, E-mail: asec@csulb.edu.
Website: http://www.csulb.edu/college-of-education/advanced-studies-education-and-counseling

Canisius College, Graduate Division, School of Education and Human Services, Department of Graduate Education and Leadership, Buffalo, NY 14208-1098. Offers business and marketing education (MS Ed); college student personnel (MS Ed); deaf education (MS Ed); deaf/adolescent education, grades 7-12 (MS Ed); deaf/childhood education, grades 1-6 (MS Ed); differentiated instruction (MS Ed); education administration (MS); educational administration (MS Ed); educational technologies (Certificate); gifted education extension (Certificate); literacy (MS Ed); reading (Certificate); school building leadership (MS Ed, Certificate); school district leadership (Certificate); teacher leader (Certificate); TESOL (MS Ed). *Accreditation:* NCATE. *Program availability:* Part-time, evening/weekend, 100% online, blended/hybrid learning. *Faculty:* 5 full-time (all women), 21 part-time/adjunct (16 women). *Students:* 79 full-time (66 women), 135 part-time (106 women); includes 45 minority (27 Black or African American, non-Hispanic/Latino; 1 American Indian or Alaska Native, non-Hispanic/Latino; 3 Asian, non-Hispanic/Latino; 9 Hispanic/Latino; 5 Two or more races, non-Hispanic/Latino), 1 international. Average age 32. 83 applicants, 96% accepted, 74 enrolled. In 2018, 94 master's, 47 other advanced degrees awarded. *Entrance requirements:* For master's, GRE (if cumulative GPA less than 2.7), transcripts, two letters of recommendation. Additional exam requirements/recommendations for international students: Required—TOEFL (minimum score 550 paper-based, 79 iBT), IELTS (minimum score 6.5), or CAEL (minimum score 70). *Application deadline:* Applications are processed on a rolling basis. Application fee: $0. Electronic applications accepted. *Expenses: Tuition:* Part-time $820 per credit hour. *Required fees:* $25 per semester. One-time fee: $65 part-time. Tuition and fees vary according to program. *Financial support:* In 2018–19, 206 students received support. Career-related internships or fieldwork, Federal Work-Study, scholarships/grants, tuition waivers (partial), and unspecified assistantships available. Support available to part-time students. Financial award application deadline: 4/30; financial award applicants required to submit FAFSA. *Faculty research:* Asperger's disease, autism, private higher education, reading strategies. *Unit head:* Dr. Anne Marie Tryjankowski, Chair/Associate Professor of Graduate Education and Leadership, 716-888-3715, Fax: 716-888-3142, E-mail: tryjanka@canisius.edu. *Application contact:* Dr. Anne Marie Tryjankowski, Chair/Associate Professor of Graduate Education and Leadership, 716-888-3715, Fax: 716-888-3142, E-mail: tryjanka@canisius.edu.

Cardinal Stritch University, College of Education and Leadership, Department of Education, Milwaukee, WI 53217-3985. Offers educational leadership (MS); higher education student affairs leadership (MS); leadership for the advancement of learning and service (Ed D, PhD); leadership for the advancement of learning and service in higher education (Ed D, PhD); teaching (MAT); urban education (MA). *Accreditation:* NCATE. *Program availability:* Part-time, evening/weekend, 100% online, blended/hybrid learning. *Degree requirements:* For master's, comprehensive exam, thesis (for some programs), research project, faculty recommendation; for doctorate, thesis/dissertation, practica, field experience. *Entrance requirements:* For master's, 2 letters of recommendation, minimum GPA of 3.0; for doctorate, minimum GPA of 3.5 in master's coursework, 3 letters of recommendation. Additional exam requirements/recommendations for international students: Required—TOEFL (minimum score 550 paper-based; 79 iBT), IELTS (minimum score 6.5). Electronic applications accepted. *Expenses:* Contact institution.

Carlow University, College of Leadership and Social Change, Program in Student Affairs, Pittsburgh, PA 15213-3165. Offers MA. *Program availability:* Part-time, evening/weekend. *Students:* 4 full-time (3 women); includes 1 minority (Black or African American, non-Hispanic/Latino). Average age 34. 4 applicants, 100% accepted. In 2018, 2 master's awarded. *Entrance requirements:* For master's, personal essay; resume or curriculum vitae; two recommendations; official transcripts; interview; minimum undergraduate GPA of 3.0. Additional exam requirements/recommendations for international students: Required—TOEFL (minimum score 550 paper-based). *Application deadline:* Applications are processed on a rolling basis. Electronic applications accepted. *Expenses: Tuition:* Full-time $13,090; part-time $5100 per semester. *Required fees:* $215; $84. Tuition and fees vary according to course load, degree level and program. *Financial support:* Application deadline: 4/1; applicants required to submit FAFSA. *Unit head:* Dr. Harriet Schwartz, Chair, 412-578-8720, E-mail: hlschwartz@carlow.edu. *Application contact:* Dr. Harriet Schwartz, Chair, 412-578-8720, E-mail: hlschwartz@carlow.edu.
Website: http://www.carlow.edu/MA_studentaffairs.aspx

Carlow University, College of Leadership and Social Change, Student Affairs/Professional Counseling Dual Degree Program, Pittsburgh, PA 15213-3165. Offers MA/MS. *Program availability:* Part-time, evening/weekend. *Students:* 9 full-time (8 women), 9 part-time (all women); includes 6 minority (5 Black or African American, non-Hispanic/Latino; 1 Two or more races, non-Hispanic/Latino). Average age 29. 8 applicants, 100% accepted, 2 enrolled. *Entrance requirements:* Additional exam requirements/recommendations for international students: Required—TOEFL (minimum score 550 paper-based). *Application deadline:* Applications are processed on a rolling basis. Electronic applications accepted. *Expenses: Tuition:* Full-time $13,090; part-time $5100 per semester. *Required fees:* $215; $84. Tuition and fees vary according to course load, degree level and program. *Financial support:* Application deadline: 4/1; applicants required to submit FAFSA. *Unit head:* Dr. Harriet Schwartz, Chair, 412-578-8720, E-mail: hlschwartz@carlow.edu. *Application contact:* Dr. Harriet Schwartz, Chair, 412-578-8720, E-mail: hlschwartz@carlow.edu.
Website: https://www.carlow.edu/MA_studentaffairs.aspx

Central Michigan University, College of Graduate Studies, College of Education and Human Services, Department of Educational Leadership, Mount Pleasant, MI 48859. Offers educational leadership (Ed D), including educational technology (Ed D, Ed S), higher education leadership, K-12 curriculum, K-12 leadership; general educational administration (Ed S), including administrative leadership K-12, educational technology (Ed D, Ed S), higher education administration, instructional leadership K-12; school principalship (MA), including charter school leadership, site-based leadership; student affairs administration (MA); teacher leadership (MA). *Program availability:* Part-time,

evening/weekend. *Degree requirements:* For master's and Ed S, thesis or alternative; for doctorate, thesis/dissertation. *Entrance requirements:* For doctorate, GRE or MAT, master's degree, minimum GPA of 3.5, 3 years of professional education experience. Electronic applications accepted. *Faculty research:* Elementary administration, secondary administration, student achievement, in-service training, internships in administration.

The Citadel, The Military College of South Carolina, Citadel Graduate College, Zucker Family School of Education, Charleston, SC 29409. Offers elementary/secondary school administration and supervision (M Ed); elementary/secondary school counseling (M Ed); interdisciplinary STEM education (M Ed); literacy education (M Ed, Graduate Certificate); middle grades (MAT), including English, mathematics, science, social studies; physical education (grades K-12) (MAT); school superintendency (Ed S); secondary education (MAT), including biology, English, mathematics, social studies; student affairs (Graduate Certificate); student affairs and college counseling (M Ed). *Accreditation:* NCATE. *Program availability:* Part-time, evening/weekend, 100% online, blended/hybrid learning. *Degree requirements:* For master's, comprehensive exam (for some programs). *Entrance requirements:* For master's, GRE (minimum combined verbal and quantitative score of 290) or MAT (minimum score 396). Additional exam requirements/recommendations for international students: Required—TOEFL (minimum score 550 paper-based; 79 iBT). Electronic applications accepted. *Expenses:* Tuition, state resident: part-time $595 per credit hour. Tuition, nonresident: part-time $1020 per credit hour. *Required fees:* $90 per term.

Claremont Graduate University, Graduate Programs, School of Educational Studies, Claremont, CA 91711-6160. Offers Africana education (Certificate); education and policy (MA, PhD); higher education/student affairs (MA, PhD); human development (MA, PhD); public school administration (MA, PhD); quantitative evaluation (MA, PhD); special education (MA, PhD); teacher education (MA); teaching and learning (MA, PhD); urban leadership (PhD); MBA/PhD. PhD program offered jointly with San Diego State University. *Program availability:* Part-time. Terminal master's awarded for partial completion of doctoral program. *Entrance requirements:* For master's and doctorate, GRE General Test. Additional exam requirements/recommendations for international students: Required—TOEFL (minimum score 75 iBT). Electronic applications accepted. *Faculty research:* Education administration, K-12 and higher education, multicultural education, education policy, diversity in higher education, faculty issues.

Clemson University, Graduate School, College of Education, Department of Educational and Organizational Leadership Development, Clemson, SC 29634. Offers administration and supervision (M Ed, Ed S); athletic leadership (MS, Certificate); education systems improvement science (Ed D); educational leadership (PhD), including higher education, P-12; human resource development (MHRD), including human resource development; leadership (Certificate); student affairs (M Ed). *Program availability:* Part-time, evening/weekend, 100% online. *Faculty:* 17 full-time (11 women). *Students:* 105 full-time (64 women), 265 part-time (170 women); includes 76 minority (61 Black or African American, non-Hispanic/Latino; 1 American Indian or Alaska Native, non-Hispanic/Latino; 3 Asian, non-Hispanic/Latino; 5 Hispanic/Latino; 6 Two or more races, non-Hispanic/Latino). Average age 32. 204 applicants, 83% accepted, 123 enrolled. In 2018, 93 master's, 17 doctorates, 28 other advanced degrees awarded. *Degree requirements:* For master's, thesis (for some programs); for doctorate, comprehensive exam, thesis/dissertation. *Entrance requirements:* For master's, doctorate, and other advanced degree, GRE General Test, unofficial transcripts, letters of recommendation. Additional exam requirements/recommendations for international students: Required—TOEFL (minimum score 80 paper-based; 80 iBT); Recommended—IELTS (minimum score 6.5), TSE (minimum score 54). *Application deadline:* For fall admission, 4/15 priority date for international students; for spring admission, 10/15 priority date for international students. Applications are processed on a rolling basis. Application fee: $80 ($90 for international students). Electronic applications accepted. *Expenses:* $5198 per semester full-time resident, $10123 per semester full-time non-resident, $556 per credit hour part-time resident, $1109 per credit hour part-time non-resident, online $770 per credit hour, $4938 doctoral programs resident, $10405 doctoral programs non-resident, $1144 full-time graduate assistant, other fees may apply per session. *Financial support:* In 2018–19, 30 students received support, including 8 fellowships with full and partial tuition reimbursements available (averaging $4,525 per year), 3 research assistantships with full and partial tuition reimbursements available (averaging $7,500 per year); career-related internships or fieldwork and unspecified assistantships also available. *Faculty research:* Leadership, ethics, policy development, performance improvement. *Total annual research expenditures:* $79,638. *Unit head:* Dr. Roy Jones, Interim Department Chair, 864-656-7915, E-mail: royj@clemson.edu. *Application contact:* Alison Search, Student Services Program Coordinator, 864-250-8880, E-mail: alisonp@clemson.edu.
Website: http://www.clemson.edu/education/departments/educational-organizational-leadership-development/index.html

Clemson University, Graduate School, College of Education, Department of Education and Human Development, Clemson, SC 29634. Offers counselor education (M Ed, Ed S), including mental health counseling, school counseling, student affairs (M Ed); learning sciences (PhD); literacy (M Ed); literacy, language and culture (PhD); special education (M Ed, MAT, PhD). *Program availability:* Part-time, evening/weekend, 100% online. *Faculty:* 35 full-time (24 women). *Students:* 103 full-time (87 women), 132 part-time (123 women); includes 37 minority (11 Black or African American, non-Hispanic/Latino; 1 American Indian or Alaska Native, non-Hispanic/Latino; 3 Asian, non-Hispanic/Latino; 11 Hispanic/Latino; 11 Two or more races, non-Hispanic/Latino), 5 international. Average age 29. 435 applicants, 67% accepted, 180 enrolled. In 2018, 51 master's, 3 doctorates, 34 other advanced degrees awarded. *Degree requirements:* For master's, thesis (for some programs); for doctorate, comprehensive exam (for some programs), thesis/dissertation. *Entrance requirements:* For master's and doctorate, GRE General Test, unofficial transcripts, letters of recommendation. Additional exam requirements/recommendations for international students: Required—TOEFL (minimum score 80 paper-based; 80 iBT); Recommended—IELTS (minimum score 6.5), TSE (minimum score 54). *Application deadline:* For fall admission, 4/15 priority date for international students; for spring admission, 10/15 priority date for international students. Applications are processed on a rolling basis. Application fee: $80 ($90 for international students). Electronic applications accepted. *Expenses:* $5198 per semester full-time resident, $10123 per semester full-time non-resident, $556 per credit hour part-time resident, $1109 per credit hour part-time non-resident, online $770 per credit hour, $4938 doctoral programs resident, $10405 doctoral programs non-resident, $1144 full-time graduate assistant, other fees may apply per session. *Financial support:* In 2018–19, 78 students received support, including 5 teaching assistantships with full and partial tuition reimbursements available (averaging $8,759 per year); career-related internships or fieldwork and unspecified assistantships also available. *Faculty research:* Literacy, reading recovery, exceptional children, policy development. *Total annual research expenditures:* $1.3 million. *Unit head:* Dr. Debi Switzer, Department Chair, 864-656-5098, E-mail: debi@clemson.edu. *Application contact:* Julie Jones, Student Services Program Coordinator, 864-656-5096, E-mail: jgambre@clemson.edu.
Website: http://www.clemson.edu/education/departments/education-human-development/index.html

The College of Saint Rose, Graduate Studies, Thelma P. Lally School of Education, Program in College Student Services Administration, Albany, NY 12203-1419. Offers MS Ed. *Accreditation:* NCATE. *Program availability:* Part-time, evening/weekend. *Students:* 5 full-time (3 women), 2 part-time (1 woman); includes 3 minority (2 Black or African American, non-Hispanic/Latino; 1 Hispanic/Latino). Average age 26. 3 applicants. In 2018, 5 master's awarded. *Degree requirements:* For master's, comprehensive exam or thesis. *Entrance requirements:* For master's, interview, minimum undergraduate GPA of 3.0, 9 hours of psychology coursework. Additional exam requirements/recommendations for international students: Required—TOEFL (minimum score 550 paper-based; 80 iBT), IELTS (minimum score 6), PTE (minimum score 56). *Application deadline:* For fall admission, 4/1 for domestic and international students; for spring admission, 10/15 priority date for domestic and international students; for summer admission, 3/15 for domestic and international students. Applications are processed on a rolling basis. Application fee: $40. Electronic applications accepted. *Expenses: Tuition:* Full-time $14,382; part-time $799 per credit hour. *Required fees:* $924; $408 per credit. $286. *Financial support:* Career-related internships or fieldwork, scholarships/grants, tuition waivers (partial), and unspecified assistantships available. Support available to part-time students. Financial award application deadline: 4/15. *Unit head:* Claudia Lingertat-Putnam, Department Chair, 518-337-4311, E-mail: lingertc@strose.edu. *Application contact:* Daniel Gallagher, Assistant Vice President for Graduate Recruitment and Enrollment, 518-485-3390, Fax: 518-458-5479, E-mail: grad@strose.edu.
Website: https://www.strose.edu/academics/agraduate-programs/college-student-services-administration-ms/

Colorado State University, College of Health and Human Sciences, School of Education, Fort Collins, CO 80523-1588. Offers adult education and training (M Ed); counseling and career development (MA); education and human resources (M Ed); education, equity, and transformation (PhD); higher education leadership (PhD); organizational learning, performance, and change (M Ed, PhD); student affairs in higher education (MS). *Accreditation:* ACA; TEAC. *Program availability:* Part-time, online only, 100% online, blended/hybrid learning. *Degree requirements:* For master's, thesis optional, professional portfolio or capstone project; for doctorate, comprehensive exam, thesis/dissertation. *Entrance requirements:* For master's, bachelor's degree; minimum GPA of 3.0 in last degree earned; for doctorate, GRE; GRE or GMAT (for organizational learning, performance and change only), master's degree; minimum GPA of 3.0 in last degree earned. Additional exam requirements/recommendations for international students: Required—TOEFL (minimum score 550 paper-based; 80 iBT), IELTS (minimum score 6.5), PTE (minimum score 58). Electronic applications accepted. *Expenses:* Contact institution. *Faculty research:* Diversity, equity, and inclusion; STEM education; higher education; occupational learning, performance, and change; teacher education.

Dallas Baptist University, Gary Cook School of Leadership, Program in Higher Education, Dallas, TX 75211-9299. Offers leadership studies (M Ed); student affairs leadership (M Ed), including community college leadership, distance learning, interdisciplinary studies, student affairs leadership. *Program availability:* Part-time, evening/weekend, online learning. *Application deadline:* Applications are processed on a rolling basis. Application fee: $25. Electronic applications accepted. Application fee is waived when completed online. *Expenses: Tuition:* Full-time $17,262; part-time $959 per credit hour. *Required fees:* $1000; $500 per semester. Tuition and fees vary according to course load and degree level. *Unit head:* Dr. Jack Goodyear, Dean, 214-333-5595, Fax: 214-333-6809, E-mail: jackg@dbu.edu. *Application contact:* Dr. Jack Goodyear, Dean, 214-333-5595, Fax: 214-333-6809, E-mail: jackg@dbu.edu.
Website: https://www.dbu.edu/graduate/degree-programs/med-higher-education/

DePaul University, College of Education, Chicago, IL 60614. Offers bilingual-bicultural education (M Ed, MA); counseling (M Ed, MA), including clinical mental health counseling, college student development, school counseling; curriculum studies (M Ed, MA, Ed D); early childhood education (M Ed, MA, Ed D); educational leadership (M Ed, MA, Ed D), including Catholic leadership (M Ed, MA), general (M Ed, MA), higher education (M Ed, MA), physical education (M Ed, MA), principal preparation (M Ed), teacher preparation (M Ed); elementary education (M Ed, MA); middle grades education (M Ed); middle school mathematics education (MS); reading specialist (M Ed, MA); secondary education (M Ed, MA); social and cultural foundations in education (M Ed, MA); special education (M Ed); sport, fitness and recreation leadership (MS); value-creating education for global citizenship (M Ed); world languages education (M Ed, MA). *Program availability:* Part-time, evening/weekend, online learning. *Degree requirements:* For doctorate, thesis/dissertation. Electronic applications accepted.

Eastern Illinois University, Graduate School, College of Education, Department of Counseling and Higher Education, Charleston, IL 61920. Offers college student affairs (MS); counseling (MS). *Accreditation:* ACA; NCATE. *Program availability:* Part-time, evening/weekend, online learning. *Degree requirements:* For master's, comprehensive exam (for some programs), thesis (for some programs). *Entrance requirements:* For master's, GMAT or GRE. Additional exam requirements/recommendations for international students: Required—TOEFL (minimum score 500 paper-based; 61 iBT), IELTS (minimum score 6). *Application deadline:* For fall admission, 5/15 for domestic and international students; for spring admission, 10/15 for domestic and international students. Applications are processed on a rolling basis. Application fee: $30. Electronic applications accepted. *Expenses:* Tuition, state resident: part-time $299 per credit hour. Tuition, nonresident: part-time $718 per credit hour. *Required fees:* $214.50 per credit hour. *Financial support:* Research assistantships with full tuition reimbursements, career-related internships or fieldwork, Federal Work-Study, scholarships/grants, and unspecified assistantships available. Support available to part-time students. Financial award application deadline: 3/1; financial award applicants required to submit FAFSA. *Unit head:* Richard Roberts, Ph.D., Chair, 217-581-2400, Fax: 217-581-7800, E-mail: rlroberts@eiu.edu. *Application contact:* Richard Roberts, Ph.D., Chair, 217-581-2400, Fax: 217-581-7800, E-mail: rlroberts@eiu.edu.
Website: https://www.eiu.edu/che/

Eastern Michigan University, Graduate School, Academic and Student Affairs Division, Ypsilanti, MI 48197. Offers individualized studies (MA, MS); integrated marketing communications (MS). *Faculty:* 1 full-time (0 women). *Students:* 1 part-time (0 women). Average age 33. 40 applicants, 90% accepted, 13 enrolled. In 2018, 1 master's awarded. *Entrance requirements:* Additional exam requirements/recommendations for international students: Required—TOEFL. Application fee: $45. *Unit head:* Dr. Wade Tornquist, Interim Dean, 734-487-0042, Fax: 734-487-0050, E-mail: wade.tornquist@emich.edu. *Application contact:* Graduate Admissions, 734-487-2400, Fax: 734-487-6559, E-mail: graduate.admissions@emich.edu.

Eastern Michigan University, Graduate School, College of Education, Department of Leadership and Counseling, Programs in Educational Leadership, Ypsilanti, MI 48197. Offers community college leadership (Graduate Certificate); educational leadership (MA, Ed D, SPA); higher education/general administration (MA); higher education/student affairs (MA); K-12 administration (MA); K-12 basic administration (Post Master's Certificate). *Program availability:* Part-time, evening/weekend, online learning. *Students:* 39 full-time (29 women), 283 part-time (195 women); includes 92 minority (67 Black or African American, non-Hispanic/Latino; 2 Asian, non-Hispanic/Latino; 12 Hispanic/

Latino; 11 Two or more races, non-Hispanic/Latino), 2 international. Average age 36. 192 applicants, 74% accepted, 80 enrolled. In 2018, 98 master's, 18 doctorates, 22 other advanced degrees awarded. *Entrance requirements:* For doctorate, GRE. Additional exam requirements/recommendations for international students: Required—TOEFL. *Application deadline:* For winter admission, 2/1 for domestic and international students. Applications are processed on a rolling basis. Application fee: $45. *Financial support:* Fellowships, research assistantships with full tuition reimbursements, teaching assistantships with full tuition reimbursements, career-related internships or fieldwork, Federal Work-Study, institutionally sponsored loans, scholarships/grants, tuition waivers (partial), and unspecified assistantships available. Support available to part-time students. *Application contact:* Dr. Jaclynn Tracy, Coordinator of Advising, Programs in Educational Leadership, 734-487-0255, Fax: 734-487-4608, E-mail: jtracy@emich.edu.

Fresno Pacific University, Graduate Programs, School of Education, Division of Pupil Personnel Services, Fresno, CA 93702-4709. Offers board certified associate behavior analyst (Certificate); school counseling (MA); school psychology (MA). *Program availability:* Part-time. *Degree requirements:* For master's, thesis or alternative. *Entrance requirements:* Additional exam requirements/recommendations for international students: Required—TOEFL (minimum score 550 paper-based).

The George Washington University, Graduate School of Education and Human Development, Department of Educational Leadership, Program in Higher Education Administration, Washington, DC 20052. Offers college teaching and academic leadership (MA Ed/HD, Ed S); general administration (MA Ed/HD, Ed S); higher education administration (Ed D); higher education finance (MA Ed/HD, Ed S); international education (MA Ed/HD, Ed S); policy (MA Ed/HD, Ed S); student affairs administration (MA Ed/HD, Ed S). *Accreditation:* NCATE. *Students:* 27 full-time (19 women), 55 part-time (41 women); includes 37 minority (21 Black or African American, non-Hispanic/Latino; 5 Asian, non-Hispanic/Latino; 8 Hispanic/Latino; 3 Two or more races, non-Hispanic/Latino), 4 international. Average age 32. 131 applicants, 85% accepted, 37 enrolled. In 2018, 15 master's, 4 doctorates, 1 other advanced degree awarded. *Degree requirements:* For master's and Ed S, comprehensive exam; for doctorate, comprehensive exam, thesis/dissertation. *Entrance requirements:* For master's, GRE General Test or MAT, minimum GPA of 2.75; for doctorate, GRE General Test or MAT, interview, minimum GPA of 3.3; for Ed S, GRE General Test or MAT, minimum GPA of 3.3. *Application deadline:* For fall admission, 1/15 priority date for domestic students; for spring admission, 10/1 for domestic students. Applications are processed on a rolling basis. Application fee: $75. *Financial support:* In 2018–19, 17 students received support. Fellowships, research assistantships, career-related internships or fieldwork, Federal Work-Study, and tuition waivers (partial) available. Financial award application deadline: 1/15; financial award applicants required to submit FAFSA. *Faculty research:* Technology in higher education administration. *Unit head:* Michael Feuer, Dean, 202-994-6161, E-mail: mjfeuer@gwu.edu. *Application contact:* Sarah Lang, Director of Graduate Admissions, 202-994-1447, Fax: 202-994-7207, E-mail: slang@gwu.edu.

Grambling State University, School of Graduate Studies and Research, College of Education, Department of Educational Leadership, Grambling, LA 71245. Offers developmental education (MS, Ed D, PMC), including curriculum and instructional design (Ed D), English (MS), guidance and counseling (MS), higher education administration and management (Ed D), mathematics (MS), reading (MS), science (MS), student development and personnel services (Ed D); educational leadership (M Ed). *Program availability:* Part-time, evening/weekend. *Degree requirements:* For master's, comprehensive exam, thesis (for some programs); for doctorate, comprehensive exam, thesis/dissertation. *Entrance requirements:* For master's, GRE, minimum GPA of 2.5 on last degree; for doctorate, GRE (minimum score 1000, 500 on Verbal), master's degree, minimum GPA of 3.0 on last degree. Additional exam requirements/recommendations for international students: Required—TOEFL (minimum score 500 paper-based; 62 iBT). Electronic applications accepted.

Hampton University, School of Liberal Arts and Education, Program in Counseling, Hampton, VA 23668. Offers college student development (MA); community agency counseling (MA); counseling (Ed S); counselor education and supervision (PhD); pastoral counseling (MA); school counseling (MA). *Accreditation:* ACA; NCATE. *Program availability:* Part-time, evening/weekend, online learning. *Students:* 42 full-time (35 women), 12 part-time (11 women); includes 49 minority (48 Black or African American, non-Hispanic/Latino; 1 Asian, non-Hispanic/Latino). Average age 35. 35 applicants, 63% accepted, 17 enrolled. In 2018, 9 master's, 1 doctorate, 5 other advanced degrees awarded. *Degree requirements:* For master's, comprehensive exam; for doctorate, comprehensive exam, thesis/dissertation. *Entrance requirements:* For master's, GRE General Test, personal statement, two letters of recommendation; for doctorate, GRE General Test, personal statement, writing sample, three letters of recommendation; for Ed S, personal statement, two letters of recommendation. Additional exam requirements/recommendations for international students: Required—TOEFL, TOEFL (minimum score 525 paper-based) or IELTS (6.5). *Application deadline:* For fall admission, 6/1 priority date for domestic students, 4/1 priority date for international students; for winter admission, 9/1 priority date for international students; for spring admission, 11/1 priority date for domestic students, 9/1 for international students; for summer admission, 4/1 priority date for domestic students, 2/1 priority date for international students. Applications are processed on a rolling basis. Application fee: $35. Electronic applications accepted. *Financial support:* Fellowships, research assistantships, teaching assistantships, career-related internships or fieldwork, Federal Work-Study, institutionally sponsored loans, scholarships/grants, tuition waivers, unspecified assistantships, and grant funding provided 10k when students enrolled in the required internships available. Support available to part-time students. Financial award application deadline: 6/30; financial award applicants required to submit FAFSA. *Faculty research:* Personality development, temperament, post-traumatic stress disorder, continuum of normal to abnormal personality. *Unit head:* Dr. Richard Mason, Chairperson, 757-728-6160, E-mail: richard.mason@hamptonu.edu. *Application contact:* Dr. Richard Mason, Chairperson, 757-728-6160, E-mail: richard.mason@hamptonu.edu.
Website: http://edhd.hamptonu.edu/counseling/

Illinois State University, Graduate School, College of Education, Department of Educational Administration and Foundations, Program in College Student Personnel Administration, Normal, IL 61790. Offers MS. *Faculty:* 18 full-time (12 women), 19 part-time/adjunct (13 women). *Students:* 17 full-time (12 women), 32 part-time (20 women); includes 6 minority (3 Black or African American, non-Hispanic/Latino; 3 Hispanic/Latino), 1 international. Average age 37. 51 applicants, 61% accepted, 21 enrolled. In 2018, 15 master's awarded. *Degree requirements:* For master's, thesis or alternative. *Entrance requirements:* For master's, GMAT. Application fee: $40. *Expenses: Tuition, area resident:* Full-time $7264.62. Tuition, state resident: full-time $9466. Tuition, nonresident: full-time $17,290. *International tuition:* $15,089.40 full-time. *Required fees:* $1481.04. *Financial support:* In 2018–19, 5 research assistantships were awarded. Financial award application deadline: 4/1. *Unit head:* Dr. Kevin Laudner, Dean, 309-438-2453, E-mail: klaudne@ilstu.edu. *Application contact:* Dr. Gavin Weiser, Graduate Coordinator, 309-438-5422, E-mail: smweis1@ilstu.edu.
Website: http://www.coe.ilstu.edu/eafdept/programs/cspa/cspa.shtml

Indiana State University, College of Graduate and Professional Studies, Bayh College of Education, Department of Educational Leadership, Terre Haute, IN 47809. Offers educational administration (PhD); higher education leadership (PhD); K-12 district leadership (PhD); school administration (Ed S); school administration and supervision (M Ed); student affairs and higher education (MS). *Accreditation:* NCATE. *Program availability:* Part-time, evening/weekend. Terminal master's awarded for partial completion of doctoral program. *Degree requirements:* For master's, thesis; for doctorate, thesis/dissertation. *Entrance requirements:* For master's, GRE General Test, minimum undergraduate GPA of 2.5; for doctorate, GRE General Test, minimum undergraduate GPA of 3.5; for Ed S, GRE General Test, minimum graduate GPA of 3.25. Electronic applications accepted.

Indiana University Bloomington, School of Education, Department of Educational Leadership and Policy Studies, Bloomington, IN 47405. Offers educational leadership (MS, Ed D, Ed S); higher education (Ed D, PhD); higher education and student affairs (MS); history and philosophy of education (MS); history, philosophy, and policy in education (PhD), including education policy studies, history of education, philosophy of education; international and comparative education (MS). *Accreditation:* NCATE. *Degree requirements:* For master's, thesis optional; for doctorate, comprehensive exam, thesis/dissertation; for Ed S, comprehensive exam or project. *Entrance requirements:* For master's, doctorate, and Ed S, GRE General Test. Additional exam requirements/recommendations for international students: Required—TOEFL (minimum score 79 iBT). Electronic applications accepted. *Faculty research:* Culturally engaging campus environments, school choice policy analysis, democracy and education in the national and international context, and principal leadership.

Indiana University of Pennsylvania, School of Graduate Studies and Research, College of Education and Communications, Department of Student Affairs in Higher Education, Indiana, PA 15705. Offers MA. *Accreditation:* NCATE. *Program availability:* Part-time. *Faculty:* 3 full-time (1 woman), 1 (woman) part-time/adjunct. *Students:* 47 full-time (24 women), 1 part-time (0 women); includes 11 minority (5 Black or African American, non-Hispanic/Latino; 2 Asian, non-Hispanic/Latino; 4 Hispanic/Latino), 1 international. Average age 23. 76 applicants, 84% accepted, 28 enrolled. In 2018, 25 master's awarded. *Degree requirements:* For master's, comprehensive exam, thesis optional. *Entrance requirements:* For master's, resume, interview, 2 letters of recommendation, writing sample, minimum GPA of 2.8. Additional exam requirements/recommendations for international students: Required—TOEFL (minimum score 540 paper-based). *Application deadline:* For fall admission, 1/15 priority date for domestic students. Application fee: $50. Electronic applications accepted. *Expenses:* Contact institution. *Financial support:* In 2018–19, 21 research assistantships with tuition reimbursements (averaging $5,129 per year) were awarded; fellowships, career-related internships or fieldwork, Federal Work-Study, scholarships/grants, and unspecified assistantships also available. Support available to part-time students. Financial award application deadline: 4/15; financial award applicants required to submit FAFSA. *Unit head:* Dr. John Wesley Lowery, Chairperson, 724-357-4545, Fax: 724-357-7821, E-mail: jlowery@iup.edu. *Application contact:* Dr. John Wesley Lowery, Chairperson, 724-357-4545, Fax: 724-357-7821, E-mail: jlowery@iup.edu.
Website: http://www.iup.edu/sahe

Iowa State University of Science and Technology, Department of Educational Leadership and Policy Studies, Ames, IA 50011. Offers counselor education (M Ed, MS); educational administration (M Ed, MS); educational leadership (PhD); higher education (M Ed, MS); organizational learning and human resource development (M Ed, MS); research and evaluation (MS); student affairs (MS). *Degree requirements:* For master's, thesis or alternative; for doctorate, thesis/dissertation. *Entrance requirements:* For master's and doctorate, GRE General Test. Additional exam requirements/recommendations for international students: Required—TOEFL (minimum score 560 paper-based; 83 iBT), IELTS (minimum score 6.5). Electronic applications accepted.

Kansas State University, Graduate School, College of Education, Department of Special Education, Counseling and Student Affairs, Manhattan, KS 66506. Offers academic advising (MS, Certificate); counseling and student development (MS), including college student development, school counseling; special education (MS, Ed D); special education, counseling, and student affairs (PhD). *Accreditation:* ACA; NCATE. *Program availability:* Part-time, online learning. *Degree requirements:* For master's, comprehensive exam; for doctorate, comprehensive exam, thesis/dissertation. *Entrance requirements:* For master's, minimum undergraduate GPA of 3.0; for doctorate, GRE General Test, minimum GPA of 3.0 in last 60 hours. Additional exam requirements/recommendations for international students: Required—TOEFL. Electronic applications accepted. *Faculty research:* Counseling supervision, academic advising, career development, student development, universal design for learning, autism, learning disabilities.

Kent State University, College of Education, Health and Human Services, School of Foundations, Leadership and Administration, Program in Higher Education Administration and Student Affairs, Kent, OH 44242-0001. Offers M Ed. *Accreditation:* NCATE. *Program availability:* Part-time, evening/weekend. *Faculty:* 5 full-time (3 women), 2 part-time/adjunct (1 woman). *Students:* 75 full-time (49 women), 24 part-time (20 women); includes 21 minority (13 Black or African American, non-Hispanic/Latino; 1 American Indian or Alaska Native, non-Hispanic/Latino; 1 Asian, non-Hispanic/Latino; 6 Native Hawaiian or other Pacific Islander, non-Hispanic/Latino), 3 international. 164 applicants, 30% accepted. In 2018, 56 master's awarded. *Degree requirements:* For master's, thesis. *Entrance requirements:* For master's, GRE if undergraduate GPA is below 3.0, resume, interview, 2 letters of recommendation, goals statement. Additional exam requirements/recommendations for international students: Required—TOEFL (minimum score 550 paper-based; 80 iBT). *Application deadline:* For fall admission, 1/5 priority date for domestic and international students. Applications are processed on a rolling basis. Application fee: $45 ($60 for international students). Electronic applications accepted. *Expenses:* Tuition, state resident: full-time $11,766; part-time $536 per credit. Tuition, nonresident: full-time $21,952; part-time $999 per credit. *International tuition:* $21,952 full-time. Tuition and fees vary according to course load. *Financial support:* In 2018–19, 4 research assistantships with full tuition reimbursements (averaging $8,500 per year) were awarded; teaching assistantships with full tuition reimbursements, Federal Work-Study, scholarships/grants, unspecified assistantships, and 8 administrative assistantships (averaging $8,500 per year) also available. Financial award application deadline: 4/1; financial award applicants required to submit FAFSA. *Faculty research:* History/sociology of higher education, organization and administration in higher education. *Unit head:* Dr. Mark Kretovics, Coordinator, 330-672-0642, E-mail: mkretov1@kent.edu. *Application contact:* Cheryl Slusarczyk, Academic Program Director, Office of Graduate Student Services, 330-672-2576, Fax: 330-672-9162, E-mail: ogs@kent.edu.

Lewis & Clark College, Graduate School of Education and Counseling, Department of Educational Leadership, Program in Educational Leadership, Portland, OR 97219-7899. Offers educational administration (M Ed, Ed S); educational leadership (Ed D); student affairs administration (MA). *Program availability:* Part-time, evening/weekend. *Degree requirements:* For doctorate, thesis/dissertation. *Entrance requirements:* For master's, minimum undergraduate GPA of 2.75, Oregon teaching or personnel service license, three years of successful teaching and/or personnel service experience in the public

schools or regionally-accredited private schools; for doctorate, master's degree plus minimum of 14 degree-applicable, post-master's semester credits; minimum undergraduate GPA of 2.75. Additional exam requirements/recommendations for international students: Required—TOEFL (minimum score 575 paper-based). Electronic applications accepted.

Lewis University, College of Arts and Sciences, Program in Organizational Leadership, Romeoville, IL 60446. Offers higher education/student services (MA); organizational and leadership coaching (MA); training and development (MA). *Program availability:* Part-time, evening/weekend, 100% online, blended/hybrid learning. *Students:* 13 full-time (9 women), 150 part-time (115 women); includes 45 minority (28 Black or African American, non-Hispanic/Latino; 3 Asian, non-Hispanic/Latino; 10 Hispanic/Latino; 4 Two or more races, non-Hispanic/Latino), 2 international. Average age 38. *Entrance requirements:* For master's, bachelor's degree, personal statement, minimum GPA of 3.0, letters of recommendation. Additional exam requirements/recommendations for international students: Required—TOEFL (minimum score 550 paper-based; 79 iBT), IELTS (minimum score 6). *Application deadline:* For fall admission, 5/1 priority date for international students; for spring admission, 11/15 priority date for international students. Applications are processed on a rolling basis. Application fee: $40. Electronic applications accepted. *Financial support:* Federal Work-Study, tuition waivers, and unspecified assistantships available. Financial award application deadline: 5/1; financial award applicants required to submit FAFSA. *Unit head:* Dr. Lesley Page, Chair, Organizational Leadership. *Application contact:* Kathy Lisak, Graduate Admission Counselor, 815-836-5610, E-mail: grad@lewisu.edu.

Manhattan College, Graduate Programs, School of Education and Health, Program in School Counseling, Riverdale, NY 10471. Offers bilingual pupil personnel services (Professional Diploma); school counseling (MA, Professional Diploma). *Program availability:* Part-time, evening/weekend. *Degree requirements:* For master's, thesis, internship. *Entrance requirements:* For master's, minimum GPA of 3.0. Additional exam requirements/recommendations for international students: Required—TOEFL. Electronic applications accepted. *Expenses:* Contact institution. *Faculty research:* Cognitive development, college and career readiness, group counseling, cultural attitudes, bullying, family social environments.

Marquette University, Graduate School, College of Education, Department of Educational Policy and Leadership, Milwaukee, WI 53201-1881. Offers college student personnel administration (M Ed); curriculum and instruction (MA); education (MA); educational administration (M Ed); educational policy and foundations (MA); elementary education (Certificate); literacy (MA); principal (Certificate); reading specialist (Certificate); reading teacher (Certificate); secondary education (Certificate); superintendent (Certificate). *Program availability:* Part-time, evening/weekend. Terminal master's awarded for partial completion of doctoral program. *Degree requirements:* For master's, comprehensive exam, thesis (for some programs); for doctorate, thesis/dissertation, qualifying exam. *Entrance requirements:* For master's, GRE General Test or MAT, official transcripts from all current and previous colleges/universities except Marquette, three letters of recommendation, statement of purpose; for doctorate, GRE General Test, MAT, sample of written work, official transcripts from all current and previous colleges/universities except Marquette, three letters of recommendation, statement of purpose, resume/curriculum vitae; for Certificate, GRE General Test or MAT, master's degree. Additional exam requirements/recommendations for international students: Required—TOEFL (minimum score 530 paper-based). *Expenses:* Contact institution. *Faculty research:* Leadership; social justice in education; development of lifelong learners; race, class, and schooling in historical perspective; urban teacher education.

Messiah College, Program in Higher Education, Mechanicsburg, PA 17055. Offers college athletics management (MA); self-designed concentration (MA); student affairs (MA). *Program availability:* Part-time. Electronic applications accepted. *Faculty research:* College athletics management, assessment and student learning outcomes, the life and legacy of Ernest L. Boyer, common learning, student affairs practice.

Miami University, College of Education, Health and Society, Department of Educational Leadership, Oxford, OH 45056. Offers educational leadership (Ed D, PhD); school leadership (M Ed); student affairs in higher education (MS, PhD); transformative education (M Ed). *Accreditation:* NCATE. *Faculty:* 14 full-time (8 women). *Students:* 70 full-time (46 women), 163 part-time (116 women); includes 45 minority (24 Black or African American, non-Hispanic/Latino; 4 Asian, non-Hispanic/Latino; 9 Hispanic/Latino; 8 Two or more races, non-Hispanic/Latino), 15 international. Average age 35. In 2018, 27 master's, 26 doctorates awarded. *Unit head:* Dr. Thomas Poetter, Chair and Director of Graduate Studies, 513-529-6848, E-mail: poettets@miamioh.edu. *Application contact:* Dr. Thomas Poetter, Professor and Director of Graduate Studies, 513-529-6825, E-mail: poettets@miamioh.edu.
Website: http://www.MiamiOH.edu/EDL

Minnesota State University Mankato, College of Graduate Studies and Research, College of Education, Department of Counseling and Student Personnel, Mankato, MN 56001. Offers college student affairs (MS); counselor education and supervision (Ed D); mental health counseling (MS); professional school counseling (K-12) (MS). *Accreditation:* ACA (one or more programs are accredited); NCATE. *Degree requirements:* For master's, comprehensive exam, thesis or alternative. *Entrance requirements:* For master's, GRE General Test or MAT (if GPA less than 3.0 for last 2 years), minimum GPA of 3.0 during previous 2 years, 3 letters of reference. Additional exam requirements/recommendations for international students: Required—TOEFL. Electronic applications accepted.

Mississippi State University, College of Education, Department of Counseling, Educational Psychology, and Foundations, Mississippi State, MS 39762. Offers clinical mental health (MS); college counseling (MS); counseling/mental health (PhD); counseling/school psychology (PhD); counselor education (Ed S); educational psychology/general educational psychology (PhD); educational psychology/school psychology (PhD); general educational psychology (MS); psychometry (MS); rehabilitation counseling (MS); school counseling (MS); school psychology (Ed S); student affairs (MS). *Accreditation:* ACA (one or more programs are accredited); APA; CORE (one or more programs are accredited); NCATE. *Program availability:* Part-time, blended/hybrid learning. *Faculty:* 17 full-time (12 women), 2 part-time/adjunct (both women). *Students:* 94 full-time (81 women), 54 part-time (44 women); includes 50 minority (39 Black or African American, non-Hispanic/Latino; 2 Asian, non-Hispanic/Latino; 8 Hispanic/Latino; 1 Two or more races, non-Hispanic/Latino), 6 international. Average age 29. 90 applicants, 63% accepted, 45 enrolled. In 2018, 33 master's, 6 doctorates, 6 other advanced degrees awarded. Terminal master's awarded for partial completion of doctoral program. *Degree requirements:* For master's, comprehensive exam, thesis optional; for doctorate, thesis/dissertation, comprehensive oral and written exam. *Entrance requirements:* For master's, GRE (taken within the last five years), BS with minimum GPA of 2.75 on last 60 hours; for doctorate, GRE, MS from CACREP- or CORE-accredited program in counseling; for Ed S, GRE, MS in counseling or related field, minimum GPA of 3.3 on all graduate work. Additional exam requirements/recommendations for international students: Required—TOEFL (minimum score 550 paper-based; 79 iBT); Recommended—IELTS (minimum score 6.5). *Application deadline:* For fall admission, 2/1 priority date for domestic and international students. Applications are processed on a rolling basis. Application fee: $60 ($80 for international students). Electronic applications accepted. *Expenses:* Tuition, state resident: full-time $8450; part-time $360.59 per credit hour. Tuition, nonresident: full-time $23,140; part-time $969.09 per credit hour. *Required fees:* $110. One-time fee: $55 full-time. Part-time tuition and fees vary according to course load, degree level, campus/location and reciprocity agreements. *Financial support:* In 2018–19, 6 research assistantships (averaging $10,050 per year), 6 teaching assistantships with full tuition reimbursements (averaging $8,401 per year) were awarded; career-related internships or fieldwork, Federal Work-Study, institutionally sponsored loans, and unspecified assistantships also available. Financial award application deadline: 2/1; financial award applicants required to submit FAFSA. *Faculty research:* HIV/AIDS in college population, substance abuse in youth and college students, ADHD and conduct disorders in youth, assessment and identification of early childhood disabilities, assessment and vocational transition of the disabled. *Unit head:* Dr. Daniel Gadke, Professor and Interim Head, 662-325-3426, Fax: 662-325-3263, E-mail: dgadke@colled.msstate.edu. *Application contact:* Ryan King, Admissions and Enrollment Assistant, 662-325-8951, E-mail: rjk101@grad.msstate.edu.
Website: http://www.cep.msstate.edu/

Mississippi State University, College of Education, Educational Leadership Program, Mississippi State, MS 39762. Offers community college education (MAT); community college leadership (PhD); higher education leadership (PhD); P-12 school leadership (PhD); school administration (MS, Ed S); student affairs and higher education (MS); workforce education leadership (MS). MS in workforce education leadership held jointly with Alcorn State University. *Faculty:* 12 full-time (9 women). *Students:* 74 full-time (43 women), 145 part-time (89 women); includes 86 minority (75 Black or African American, non-Hispanic/Latino; 1 American Indian or Alaska Native, non-Hispanic/Latino; 6 Hispanic/Latino; 4 Two or more races, non-Hispanic/Latino). Average age 35. 83 applicants, 82% accepted, 55 enrolled. In 2018, 48 master's, 12 doctorates, 13 other advanced degrees awarded. *Degree requirements:* For master's and Ed S, comprehensive exam, thesis; for doctorate, comprehensive exam, thesis/dissertation. *Entrance requirements:* For master's, GRE, minimum GPA of 2.75 in junior and senior courses; for doctorate, GRE, minimum GPA of 3.4 on previous graduate work; for Ed S, GRE, minimum GPA of 3.2, master's degree. Additional exam requirements/recommendations for international students: Required—TOEFL (minimum score 550 paper-based; 79 iBT); Recommended—IELTS (minimum score 6.5). *Application deadline:* For fall admission, 7/1 for domestic students, 5/1 for international students; for spring admission, 11/1 for domestic students, 9/1 for international students. Application fee: $60 ($80 for international students). Electronic applications accepted. *Expenses:* Tuition, state resident: full-time $8450; part-time $360.59 per credit hour. Tuition, nonresident: full-time $23,140; part-time $969.09 per credit hour. *Required fees:* $110. One-time fee: $55 full-time. Part-time tuition and fees vary according to course load, degree level, campus/location and reciprocity agreements. *Financial support:* In 2018–19, 1 research assistantship with full tuition reimbursement (averaging $11,861 per year) was awarded; Federal Work-Study, institutionally sponsored loans, and unspecified assistantships also available. Financial award application deadline: 4/1; financial award applicants required to submit FAFSA. *Unit head:* Dr. Eric Moyen, Associate Professor and Head, 662-325-0969, Fax: 662-325-0975, E-mail: em1621@msstate.edu. *Application contact:* Nathan Drake, Admissions and Enrollment Assistant, 662-325-3804, E-mail: ndrake@grad.msstate.edu.
Website: http://www.educationalleadership.msstate.edu/

Missouri State University, Graduate College, College of Education, Department of Counseling, Leadership, and Special Education, Program in Student Affairs in Higher Education, Springfield, MO 65897. Offers MS. *Program availability:* Part-time. *Faculty:* 6 full-time (4 women). *Students:* 20 full-time (11 women), 3 part-time (2 women); includes 5 minority (1 Black or African American, non-Hispanic/Latino; 1 Asian, non-Hispanic/Latino; 1 Hispanic/Latino; 2 Two or more races, non-Hispanic/Latino). Average age 24. 17 applicants, 76% accepted. In 2018, 21 master's awarded. *Degree requirements:* For master's, comprehensive exam, thesis or alternative. *Entrance requirements:* For master's, GRE, statement of purpose; three references. Additional exam requirements/recommendations for international students: Required—TOEFL (minimum score 550 paper-based; 79 iBT), IELTS (minimum score 6). *Application deadline:* For fall admission, 2/1 priority date for domestic students, 2/1 for international students. Applications are processed on a rolling basis. Application fee: $55 ($60 for international students). Electronic applications accepted. Tuition and fees vary according to class time, course level, course load, degree level, campus/location, program and student level. *Financial support:* Federal Work-Study, institutionally sponsored loans, scholarships/grants, and unspecified assistantships available. Financial award application deadline: 1/31; financial award applicants required to submit FAFSA. *Unit head:* Dr. James Satterfield, Department Head, 417-836-5392, E-mail: clse@missouristate.edu. *Application contact:* Lakan Drinker, Director, Graduate Enrollment Management, 417-836-5330, Fax: 417-836-6200, E-mail: lakandrinker@missouristate.edu.
Website: http://education.missouristate.edu/edadmin/MSEDSA.htm

Monmouth University, Graduate Studies, School of Education, West Long Branch, NJ 07764-1898. Offers applied behavior analysis (Certificate); autism (Certificate); director of school counseling services (Post-Master's Certificate); early childhood (M Ed); educational leadership (Ed D); elementary education (MAT), including elementary level, secondary level; English as a second language (M Ed); learning disabilities teacher-consultant (Post-Master's Certificate); literacy (MS Ed); school counseling (MS Ed); special education (MS Ed), including autism, learning disabilities teacher-consultant, teacher of students with disabilities, teaching in inclusive settings; speech-language pathology (MS Ed); student affairs and college counseling (MS Ed); supervisor (Post-Master's Certificate); teaching English to speakers of other languages (Certificate). *Accreditation:* NCATE. *Program availability:* Part-time, evening/weekend, 100% online, blended/hybrid learning. *Faculty:* 29 full-time (23 women), 32 part-time/adjunct (24 women). *Students:* 214 full-time (187 women), 148 part-time (127 women); includes 60 minority (13 Black or African American, non-Hispanic/Latino; 2 Asian, non-Hispanic/Latino; 40 Hispanic/Latino; 5 Two or more races, non-Hispanic/Latino). Average age 27. In 2018, 108 master's, 9 other advanced degrees awarded. *Entrance requirements:* For master's, GRE taken within last 5 years (for MS Ed in speech-language pathology); SAT (minimum combined score of 1660 in 3 sections), ACT (23), GRE (minimum score of 4.0 on analytical writing section and minimum combined score of 310 on quantitative and verbal sections), or passing scores on 3 parts of Core Academic Skills Educators, minimum GPA of 3.0 in major; 2 letters of recommendation (for some programs); resume, personal statement or essay (depending on program). Additional exam requirements/recommendations for international students: Required—TOEFL (minimum score 550 paper-based; 79 iBT), IELTS (minimum score 6), Michigan English Language Assessment Battery (minimum score 77) or Certificate of Advanced English (minimum score 160). *Application deadline:* For fall admission, 7/15 priority date for domestic students, 7/1 for international students; for spring admission, 12/1 priority date for domestic students, 11/1 for international students; for summer admission, 5/1 for domestic students. Applications are processed on a rolling basis. Application fee: $50. Electronic applications accepted. *Expenses: Tuition:* Part-time $1233 per credit. *Required fees:* $178 per term. *Financial support:* In 2018–19, 290 students received support. Institutionally sponsored loans, scholarships/grants, and unspecified

assistantships available. Support available to part-time students. Financial award applicants required to submit FAFSA. *Faculty research:* Multicultural literacy, science and mathematics teaching strategies, teacher as reflective practitioner, children with disabilities. *Unit head:* Dr. John E. Henning, Dean, 732-263-5513, Fax: 732-263-5277, E-mail: kodonnel@monmouth.edu. *Application contact:* Kirsten Sneeringer, Graduate Admission Counselor, 732-571-3452, Fax: 732-263-5123, E-mail: gradadm@monmouth.edu.
Website: http://www.monmouth.edu/academics/schools/education/default.asp

Morgan State University, School of Graduate Studies, School of Education and Urban Studies, Department of Advanced Studies, Leadership and Policy, Program in Higher Education Administration, Baltimore, MD 21251. Offers higher education (PhD); higher education and student affairs administration (MA). *Degree requirements:* For doctorate, comprehensive exam, thesis/dissertation. *Entrance requirements:* For doctorate, GRE General Test or MAT, minimum GPA of 3.0.

New York University, Steinhardt School of Culture, Education, and Human Development, Department of Administration, Leadership, and Technology, Program in Higher Education, New York, NY 10012. Offers higher and postsecondary education (PhD); higher education administration (Ed D); higher education and student affairs (MA). *Accreditation:* TEAC. *Program availability:* Part-time. *Entrance requirements:* For master's, interview, 2 letters of recommendation; for doctorate, GRE General Test, interview. Additional exam requirements/recommendations for international students: Required—TOEFL (minimum score 100 iBT). Electronic applications accepted. *Faculty research:* Organizational theory and culture, systemic change, leadership development, access, equity and diversity.

Northern Arizona University, College of Education, Department of Educational Psychology, Flagstaff, AZ 86011. Offers clinical mental health counseling (MA); combined counseling/school psychology (PhD), including counseling psychology; counseling (M Ed), including school counseling, student affairs; human relations (M Ed); psychology of human development and learning (Graduate Certificate); school psychology (Ed S). *Program availability:* Part-time, 100% online, blended/hybrid learning. Terminal master's awarded for partial completion of doctoral program. *Degree requirements:* For master's, variable foreign language requirement, comprehensive exam (for some programs), thesis (for some programs); for doctorate, variable foreign language requirement, comprehensive exam (for some programs), thesis/dissertation (for some programs); for other advanced degree, comprehensive exam (for some programs). *Entrance requirements:* Additional exam requirements/recommendations for international students: Required—TOEFL (minimum score 80 iBT), IELTS (minimum score 6.5). Electronic applications accepted.

Northwestern State University of Louisiana, Graduate Studies and Research, College of Education and Human Development, Program in Student Affairs in Higher Education, Natchitoches, LA 71497. Offers MA. *Accreditation:* NCATE. *Degree requirements:* For master's, comprehensive exam, thesis or alternative. *Entrance requirements:* For master's, GRE General Test, GRE Subject Test, minimum undergraduate GPA of 2.5. Additional exam requirements/recommendations for international students: Required—TOEFL. Electronic applications accepted.

Nova Southeastern University, College of Arts, Humanities, and Social Sciences, Fort Lauderdale, FL 33314-7796. Offers advanced conflict resolution practice (Graduate Certificate); child protection (MHS); college student affairs (MS); conflict analysis and resolution (MS, PhD); criminal justice (MS, PhD); cross-disciplinary studies (MA); developmental disabilities (MS); family studies (Graduate Certificate); family systems health care (Graduate Certificate); family therapy (MS, PhD); marriage and family therapy (DMFT); peace studies (Graduate Certificate); qualitative research (Graduate Certificate); solution focused coaching (Graduate Certificate). *Accreditation:* AAMFT/COAMFTE (one or more programs are accredited). *Program availability:* Part-time, evening/weekend, 100% online, blended/hybrid learning. *Degree requirements:* For master's, thesis optional, comprehensive exams, portfolios (for some programs), table-top exams (for some programs); for doctorate, comprehensive exam, thesis/dissertation, qualifying exams, portfolios (for some programs). *Entrance requirements:* For master's, interview, minimum GPA of 3.0, writing sample; for doctorate, interview, minimum GPA of 3.5, master's degree in related field, writing sample; for Graduate Certificate, minimum GPA of 3.0. Additional exam requirements/recommendations for international students: Required—TOEFL. Electronic applications accepted. *Expenses:* Contact institution. *Faculty research:* Conflict resolution, family therapy, peace research, international conflict, multi-disciplinary studies, college student affairs, national security affairs, health care conflict resolution, family systems health care, advanced family systems, qualitative research, solution-focused coaching.

Ohio University, Graduate College, Gladys W. and David H. Patton College of Education and Human Services, Department of Counseling and Higher Education, Athens, OH 45701-2979. Offers college student personnel (M Ed); community/agency counseling (M Ed); counselor education (PhD); higher education (PhD); rehabilitation counseling (M Ed); school counseling (M Ed). *Accreditation:* ACA; CORE. *Program availability:* Part-time, evening/weekend. *Degree requirements:* For master's, comprehensive exam (for some programs), thesis or alternative; for doctorate, comprehensive exam, thesis/dissertation. *Entrance requirements:* For master's, GRE General Test or MAT (if GPA less than 2.9), 3 letters of reference; for doctorate, GRE General Test, work experience, minimum GPA of 3.4. Additional exam requirements/recommendations for international students: Required—TOEFL (minimum score 550 paper-based; 80 iBT) or IELTS (minimum score 6.5). Electronic applications accepted. *Faculty research:* Youth violence, gender studies, student affairs, chemical dependency, disabilities issues.

Oregon State University, College of Liberal Arts, Program in College Student Services Administration, Corvallis, OR 97331. Offers Ed M, MS. *Entrance requirements:* For master's, minimum GPA of 3.0 in last 90 hours of course work. Additional exam requirements/recommendations for international students: Required—TOEFL (minimum score 80 iBT), IELTS (minimum score 6.5).

Providence University College & Theological Seminary, Theological Seminary, Otterburne, MB R0A 1G0, Canada. Offers children's ministry (Certificate); Christian studies (MA, Certificate); counseling (MA); cross-cultural discipleship (Certificate); divinity (M Div); educational studies (MA), including counseling psychology, educational ministries, student development, teaching English to speakers of other languages, training teachers of English to speakers of other languages; global studies (MA); lay counseling (Diploma); ministry (D Min); teaching English to speakers of other languages (Certificate); theological studies (MA); training teacher of English to speakers of other languages (Certificate); youth ministry (Certificate). *Accreditation:* ATS. *Program availability:* Part-time. *Degree requirements:* For master's, variable foreign language requirement, thesis (for some programs); for doctorate, thesis/dissertation. *Entrance requirements:* Additional exam requirements/recommendations for international students: Recommended—TOEFL (minimum score 550 paper-based). *Faculty research:* Studies in Isaiah, theology of sin.

Purdue University Global, School of Higher Education Studies, Davenport, IA 52807. Offers college administration and leadership (MS); college teaching and learning (MS); student services (MS). *Program availability:* Part-time, evening/weekend, online learning. *Entrance requirements:* Additional exam requirements/recommendations for international students: Required—TOEFL (minimum score 550 paper-based; 80 iBT).

Quincy University, Master of Science in Education Counseling Program, Quincy, IL 62301-2699. Offers clinical mental health counseling (MS Ed); college student personnel (MS Ed); school counseling (MS Ed). *Program availability:* Part-time, evening/weekend. *Degree requirements:* For master's, comprehensive exam, practicum, internship. *Entrance requirements:* For master's, MAT or GRE. Additional exam requirements/recommendations for international students: Required—TOEFL (minimum score 550 paper-based; 79 iBT). Electronic applications accepted.

Regent University, Graduate School, School of Education, Virginia Beach, VA 23464-9800. Offers education (M Ed, Ed D, PhD), including adult education (Ed D, PhD, Ed S), advanced educational leadership (Ed D, PhD, Ed S), character education (Ed D, PhD, Ed S), Christian education leadership (Ed D, PhD, Ed S), Christian school administration (M Ed), curriculum and instruction (Ed D, PhD, Ed S), curriculum and instruction - adult education (M Ed), curriculum and instruction - Christian school (M Ed), curriculum and instruction - gifted and talented (M Ed), curriculum and instruction - STEM education (M Ed), curriculum and instruction - teacher leader (M Ed), discipleship for ministry (M Ed), educational leadership (M Ed), educational psychology (Ed D, PhD, Ed S), educational technology and online learning (Ed D, PhD, Ed S), elementary education (M Ed), exceptional education executive leadership (Ed D, PhD, Ed S), higher education (Ed D, PhD, Ed S), higher education leadership and management (Ed D, PhD, Ed S), instructional design and technology (M Ed), K-12 school leadership (Ed D, PhD, Ed S), K-12 special education (M Ed), leadership in mathematics education (M Ed), reading specialist (M Ed), special education (Ed D, PhD, Ed S), student affairs (M Ed), TESOL - adult education (M Ed), TESOL - K-12 (M Ed); educational specialist (Ed S), including adult education (Ed D, PhD, Ed S), advanced educational leadership (Ed D, PhD, Ed S), character education (Ed D, PhD, Ed S), Christian education leadership (Ed D, PhD, Ed S), curriculum and instruction (Ed D, PhD, Ed S), educational psychology (Ed D, PhD, Ed S), educational technology and online learning (Ed D, PhD, Ed S), exceptional education executive leadership (Ed D, PhD, Ed S), higher education (Ed D, PhD, Ed S), higher education leadership and management (Ed D, PhD, Ed S), K-12 school leadership (Ed D, PhD, Ed S), special education (Ed D, PhD, Ed S). *Accreditation:* TEAC. *Program availability:* Part-time, evening/weekend, 100% online, blended/hybrid learning. *Degree requirements:* For master's, thesis or alternative; for doctorate, comprehensive exam, thesis/dissertation. *Entrance requirements:* For master's, Virginia Communication and Literacy Assessment (VCLA), PRAXIS, college transcripts, writing sample, interview; for doctorate, GRE, writing sample, resume, transcripts, interview. Additional exam requirements/recommendations for international students: Required—TOEFL (minimum score 577 paper-based). Electronic applications accepted. *Expenses:* Contact institution. *Faculty research:* Christian school administration, curriculum and instruction, educational technology and online learning, higher education, special education.

Rutgers University–New Brunswick, Graduate School of Education, Department of Educational Psychology, Program in College Student Affairs, Piscataway, NJ 08854-8097. Offers Ed M. *Accreditation:* ACA. *Degree requirements:* For master's, comprehensive exam. *Entrance requirements:* For master's, GRE General Test, 3 letters of recommendation, resume. Additional exam requirements/recommendations for international students: Required—TOEFL (minimum score 550 paper-based; 83 iBT). Electronic applications accepted. *Faculty research:* Higher education equality, Latino college student experience.

St. Cloud State University, School of Graduate Studies, School of Education, Department of Educational Leadership and Higher Education, Program in College Counseling and Student Development, St. Cloud, MN 56301-4498. Offers MS. *Degree requirements:* For master's, comprehensive exam, thesis or alternative. *Entrance requirements:* For master's, GRE General Test, minimum GPA of 2.75. Additional exam requirements/recommendations for international students: Required—Michigan English Language Assessment Battery; Recommended—TOEFL (minimum score 550 paper-based), IELTS (minimum score 6.5). Electronic applications accepted.

St. Edward's University, School of Education, Master of Arts in College Student Development Program, Austin, TX 78704. Offers MA. *Program availability:* Part-time-only, evening/weekend. *Entrance requirements:* Additional exam requirements/recommendations for international students: Required—TOEFL, IELTS. Electronic applications accepted.

Saint Louis University, Graduate Programs, School of Education, Department of Educational Leadership and Higher Education, St. Louis, MO 63103. Offers Catholic school leadership (MA); educational administration (MA, Ed D, PhD, Ed S); higher education (MA, Ed D, PhD); student personnel administration (MA). *Accreditation:* NCATE. *Program availability:* Part-time. *Degree requirements:* For master's, comprehensive written and oral exam; for doctorate, comprehensive exam, thesis/dissertation, preliminary oral and written exams. *Entrance requirements:* For master's, GRE General Test, MAT, LSAT, GMAT or MCAT, letters of recommendation, resume; for doctorate and Ed S, GRE General Test, LSAT, GMAT or MCAT, letters of recommendation, resumé, goal statement, transcripts. Additional exam requirements/recommendations for international students: Required—TOEFL (minimum score 525 paper-based). Electronic applications accepted. *Faculty research:* Superintendent of schools, school finance, school facilities, student personal administration, building leadership.

San Jose State University, Program in Counselor Education, San Jose, CA 95192-0001. Offers MA. *Accreditation:* NCATE. *Program availability:* Evening/weekend. *Degree requirements:* For master's, thesis or alternative. Electronic applications accepted.

Seton Hall University, College of Education and Human Services, Department of Education Leadership, Management and Policy, Program in College Student Personnel Administration, South Orange, NJ 07079-2697. Offers MA. *Program availability:* Part-time, evening/weekend. *Entrance requirements:* For master's, GRE or MAT (within past 5 years), minimum GPA of 3.0. Additional exam requirements/recommendations for international students: Required—TOEFL.

Shippensburg University of Pennsylvania, School of Graduate Studies, College of Education and Human Services, Department of Counseling, Shippensburg, PA 17257-2299. Offers college counseling (MS); college student personnel (MS); counselor education and supervision (Ed D); mental health counseling (MS); school counseling (M Ed). *Accreditation:* ACA (one or more programs are accredited); NCATE. *Program availability:* Part-time, evening/weekend, online only, blended/hybrid learning. *Faculty:* 6 full-time (2 women), 6 part-time/adjunct (all women). *Students:* 79 full-time (70 women), 37 part-time (28 women); includes 27 minority (16 Black or African American, non-Hispanic/Latino; 3 Asian, non-Hispanic/Latino; 7 Hispanic/Latino; 1 Two or more races, non-Hispanic/Latino), 3 international. Average age 29. 103 applicants, 40% accepted, 28 enrolled. In 2018, 45 master's awarded. *Degree requirements:* For master's, fieldwork, research project, internship, candidacy; for doctorate, thesis/dissertation, practicum, internship. *Entrance requirements:* For master's, GRE or MAT (for MS if GPA is less than 2.75), minimum GPA of 2.75 (3.0 for M Ed), resume, 3 letter of recommendation forms, one year of relevant work experience, on-campus interview,

autobiographical statement; for doctorate, master's degree in counseling or related discipline; resume; three recommendation letters (1 each from employer, clinical supervisor, and prior graduate school faculty member); personal essay; interview with department chair. Additional exam requirements/recommendations for international students: Required—TOEFL (minimum score 550 paper-based; 68 iBT), IELTS (minimum score 6), TOEFL (minimum score 550 paper-based, 68 iBT) or IELTS (minimum score 6). *Application deadline:* Applications are processed on a rolling basis. Application fee: $45. Electronic applications accepted. *Expenses:* Tuition, state resident: part-time $516 per credit. Tuition, nonresident: part-time $750 per credit. *Required fees:* $149 per credit. *Financial support:* In 2018–19, 50 students received support. Career-related internships or fieldwork, scholarships/grants, unspecified assistantships, and resident hall director and student payroll positions available. Support available to part-time students. Financial award application deadline: 3/1; financial award applicants required to submit FAFSA. *Unit head:* Dr. Kurt L. Kraus, Departmental Chair and Program Coordinator, 717-477-1603, Fax: 717-477-4056, E-mail: klkrau@ship.edu. *Application contact:* Maya T. Mapp, Director of Admissions, 717-477-1231, Fax: 717-477-4016, E-mail: mtmapp@ship.edu.
Website: http://www.ship.edu/counsel

Slippery Rock University of Pennsylvania, Graduate Studies (Recruitment), College of Education, Department of Counseling and Development, Slippery Rock, PA 16057-1383. Offers clinical mental health (MA); school counseling (M Ed); student affairs in higher education (MA); student affairs in higher education with college counseling (MA). *Accreditation:* ACA (one or more programs are accredited); NCATE. *Program availability:* Part-time, evening/weekend. *Faculty:* 8 full-time (5 women), 1 (woman) part-time/adjunct. *Students:* 86 full-time (68 women), 23 part-time (16 women); includes 13 minority (7 Black or African American, non-Hispanic/Latino; 1 Asian, non-Hispanic/Latino; 5 Hispanic/Latino), 1 international. Average age 26. 126 applicants, 58% accepted, 44 enrolled. In 2018, 36 master's awarded. *Degree requirements:* For master's, comprehensive exam, thesis (for some programs). *Entrance requirements:* For master's, GRE General Test or MAT, official transcripts, personal statement, three letters of recommendation, interview. Additional exam requirements/recommendations for international students: Required—TOEFL (minimum score 550 paper-based; 80 iBT). *Application deadline:* For fall admission, 1/15 priority date for domestic and international students. Applications are processed on a rolling basis. Application fee: $25 ($30 for international students). Electronic applications accepted. *Expenses:* Contact institution. *Financial support:* In 2018–19, 55 students received support. Career-related internships or fieldwork, Federal Work-Study, institutionally sponsored loans, scholarships/grants, tuition waivers (partial), and unspecified assistantships available. Support available to part-time students. Financial award application deadline: 5/1; financial award applicants required to submit FAFSA. *Unit head:* Dr. Stacy Jacob, Graduate Coordinator, 724-738-2758, Fax: 724-738-4859, E-mail: stacy.jacob@sru.edu. *Application contact:* Brandi Weber-Mortimer, Director of Graduate Admissions, 724-738-2051, Fax: 724-738-2146, E-mail: graduate.admissions@sru.edu.
Website: http://www.sru.edu/academics/colleges-and-departments/coe/departments/counseling-and-development

Southern Arkansas University–Magnolia, School of Graduate Studies, Magnolia, AR 71753. Offers agriculture (MS); business administration (MBA), including agribusiness, social entrepreneurship, supply chain management; clinical and mental health counseling (MS); computer and information sciences (MS), including cyber security and privacy, data science, information technology; gifted and talented (M Ed), including curriculum and instruction, educational administration and supervision, gifted and talented P-8/7-12, instructional specialist P-4; higher, adult and lifelong education (M Ed); kinesiology (M Ed), including coaching; library media and information specialist (M Ed); public administration (MPA); school counseling K-12 (M Ed); student affairs and college counseling (M Ed); teaching (MAT). *Accreditation:* NCATE. *Program availability:* Part-time, 100% online, blended/hybrid learning. *Faculty:* 36 full-time (21 women), 32 part-time/adjunct (15 women). *Students:* 164 full-time (77 women), 762 part-time (510 women); includes 192 minority (163 Black or African American, non-Hispanic/Latino; 7 American Indian or Alaska Native, non-Hispanic/Latino; 13 Asian, non-Hispanic/Latino; 1 Hispanic/Latino; 8 Two or more races, non-Hispanic/Latino), 213 international. Average age 28. 363 applicants, 100% accepted, 237 enrolled. In 2018, 716 master's awarded. *Degree requirements:* For master's, comprehensive exam (for some programs), thesis optional. *Entrance requirements:* For master's, GRE, MAT or GMAT, minimum GPA of 2.5. Additional exam requirements/recommendations for international students: Required—TOEFL (minimum score 550 paper-based), IELTS (minimum score 6). *Application deadline:* For fall admission, 8/1 for domestic and international students; for spring admission, 12/1 for domestic students, 11/15 for international students; for summer admission, 4/1 for domestic students, 5/10 for international students. Applications are processed on a rolling basis. Application fee: $25 ($90 for international students). Electronic applications accepted. *Expenses: Tuition, area resident:* Full-time $5130; part-time $3420 per year. Tuition, state resident: full-time $5130; part-time $3420 per year. Tuition, nonresident: full-time $7866; part-time $5244 per year. *International tuition:* $7866 full-time. *Required fees:* $1052; $710 per unit. Tuition and fees vary according to course load. *Financial support:* Career-related internships or fieldwork, Federal Work-Study, scholarships/grants, tuition waivers (full), and unspecified assistantships available. Financial award applicants required to submit FAFSA. *Faculty research:* Alternative certification for teachers, supervision of instruction, instructional leadership, counseling. *Unit head:* Dr. Kim Bloss, Dean, School of Graduate Studies, 870-235-4150, Fax: 870-235-5227, E-mail: kkbloss@saumag.edu. *Application contact:* Talia Jett, Admissions Coordinator, 870-2355450, Fax: 870-235-5227, E-mail: taliajett@saumag.edu.
Website: http://www.saumag.edu/graduate

Southern Illinois University Edwardsville, Graduate School, School of Education, Health, and Human Behavior, Department of Educational Leadership, Program in College Student Personnel Administration, Edwardsville, IL 62026. Offers MS Ed. *Program availability:* Part-time, evening/weekend. *Degree requirements:* For master's, thesis or alternative, research project. *Entrance requirements:* Additional exam requirements/recommendations for international students: Required—TOEFL (minimum score 550 paper-based; 79 iBT), IELTS (minimum score 6.5). Electronic applications accepted.

Springfield College, Graduate Programs, Programs in Psychology, Springfield, MA 01109-3797. Offers athletic counseling (MS, CAGS); clinical mental health counseling (M Ed, CAGS); counseling psychology (Psy D); general counseling (M Ed); industrial/organizational psychology (M Ed, CAGS); school counseling (M Ed, CAGS); student personnel administration in higher education (M Ed, CAGS). *Accreditation:* APA. *Program availability:* Part-time. *Degree requirements:* For master's, research project, portfolio; for doctorate, dissertation project, 1500 hours of counseling psychology practicum, full-year internship. *Entrance requirements:* For doctorate, GRE. Additional exam requirements/recommendations for international students: Required—TOEFL (minimum score 550 paper-based); Recommended—IELTS (minimum score 7). Electronic applications accepted.

State University of New York at Plattsburgh, School of Education, Health, and Human Services, Department of Counselor Education, Plattsburgh, NY 12901-2681.

Offers clinical mental health counseling (MS, Advanced Certificate); school counselor (MS Ed, CAS); student affairs counseling (MS). *Accreditation:* ACA (one or more programs are accredited); TEAC. *Program availability:* Part-time. *Entrance requirements:* For master's, GRE General Test or MAT, minimum GPA of 2.8. Additional exam requirements/recommendations for international students: Required—TOEFL. *Faculty research:* Campus violence, program accreditation, substance abuse, vocational assessment, group counseling, divorce.

Syracuse University, School of Education, MS Program in Student Affairs Counseling, Syracuse, NY 13244. Offers MS. *Program availability:* Part-time. *Students:* Average age 28. *Entrance requirements:* For master's, GRE or MAT, baccalaureate degree from regionally-accredited college/university, three letters of recommendation, personal statement, transcripts, interview. Additional exam requirements/recommendations for international students: Required—TOEFL (minimum score 100 iBT). *Application deadline:* For fall admission, 6/15 priority date for domestic and international students; for spring admission, 10/15 priority date for domestic and international students; for summer admission, 1/15 priority date for domestic and international students. Applications are processed on a rolling basis. Application fee: $75. Electronic applications accepted. *Financial support:* Fellowships with full tuition reimbursements, research assistantships, teaching assistantships, career-related internships or fieldwork, and scholarships/grants available. Financial award application deadline: 1/15. *Faculty research:* Group work in counseling, theories of counseling and psychotherapy, social and cultural dimensions of counseling, life-span human development, assessment in counseling. *Unit head:* Dr. Derek Seward, Professor/Chair of the Department of Counseling and Human Service, 315-443-2266, E-mail: dxseward@syr.edu. *Application contact:* Speranza Migliore, Graduate Admissions Recruiter, 315-443-2505, E-mail: gradrcrt@syr.edu.
Website: http://soe.syr.edu/academic/counseling_and_human_services/graduate/masters/student_affairs_counseling/default.aspx

Texas State University, The Graduate College, College of Education, Program in Student Affairs in Higher Education, San Marcos, TX 78666. Offers M Ed. *Accreditation:* ACA. *Program availability:* Part-time, evening/weekend. *Faculty:* 3 full-time (all women), 7 part-time/adjunct (4 women). *Students:* 36 full-time (24 women), 1 part-time (0 women); includes 24 minority (5 Black or African American, non-Hispanic/Latino; 1 Asian, non-Hispanic/Latino; 13 Hispanic/Latino; 5 Two or more races, non-Hispanic/Latino). Average age 24. 46 applicants, 70% accepted, 19 enrolled. In 2018, 19 master's awarded. *Degree requirements:* For master's, comprehensive exam. *Entrance requirements:* For master's, baccalaureate degree from regionally-accredited institution, competitive GPA in last 60 hours of undergraduate course work, resume, statement of purpose, 3 letters of recommendation. Additional exam requirements/recommendations for international students: Required—TOEFL (minimum score 550 paper-based; 78 iBT), IELTS (minimum score 6.5). *Application deadline:* For fall admission, 1/15 for domestic and international students. Applications are processed on a rolling basis. Application fee: $55 ($90 for international students). Electronic applications accepted. *Expenses:* Tuition, state resident: full-time $8102; part-time $4051 per semester. Tuition, nonresident: full-time $18,229; part-time $9115 per semester. *International tuition:* $18,229 full-time. *Required fees:* $2116; $120 per credit hour. Tuition and fees vary according to course load. *Financial support:* In 2018–19, 37 students received support, including 37 teaching assistantships (averaging $11,742 per year); research assistantships, career-related internships or fieldwork, Federal Work-Study, institutionally sponsored loans, scholarships/grants, and unspecified assistantships also available. Support available to part-time students. Financial award application deadline: 1/15; financial award applicants required to submit FAFSA. *Unit head:* Dr. Paige Haber-Curran, Graduate Advisor, 512-245-7628, Fax: 512-245-8872, E-mail: sahe@txstate.edu. *Application contact:* Dr. Andrea Golato, Dean of Graduate School, 512-245-2581, Fax: 512-245-8365, E-mail: gradcollege@txstate.edu.
Website: http://www.gradcollege.txstate.edu/programs/sahe.html

University of Arkansas at Little Rock, Graduate School, College of Education and Health Professions, Department of Educational Leadership, Program in Higher Education, Little Rock, AR 72204-1099. Offers administration (MA); college student affairs (MA); health professions teaching and learning (MA); higher education (Ed D); two-year college teaching (MA). *Degree requirements:* For doctorate, comprehensive exam, oral defense of dissertation, residency. *Entrance requirements:* For master's, GRE General Test or MAT, interview, minimum graduate GPA of 3.0; for doctorate, GRE General Test, interview, minimum graduate GPA of 3.5, teaching certificate, three years of work experience.

University of Bridgeport, School of Arts and Sciences, Department of Counseling, Bridgeport, CT 06604. Offers clinical mental health counseling (MS); college student personnel (MS); community counseling (MS); human resource development (MS); human service (MS). *Program availability:* Part-time, evening/weekend. *Degree requirements:* For master's, thesis, project. *Entrance requirements:* Additional exam requirements/recommendations for international students: Recommended—TOEFL (minimum score 550 paper-based; 80 iBT), IELTS (minimum score 6.5). Electronic applications accepted. *Expenses:* Contact institution.

University of Central Arkansas, Graduate School, College of Education, Department of Leadership Studies, Program in College Student Personnel, Conway, AR 72035-0001. Offers MS. *Degree requirements:* For master's, comprehensive exam, thesis. *Entrance requirements:* For master's, GRE General Test, minimum GPA of 2.7. Additional exam requirements/recommendations for international students: Required—TOEFL (minimum score 550 paper-based). Electronic applications accepted. *Expenses:* Contact institution.

University of Central Florida, College of Community Innovation and Education, Department of Educational Leadership and Higher Education, Orlando, FL 32816. Offers career and technical education (MA); educational leadership (M Ed, MA, Ed S); higher education/college teaching and leadership (MA); higher education/student personnel (MA). *Program availability:* Part-time, evening/weekend. *Degree requirements:* For master's, thesis or alternative; for Ed S, thesis or alternative, final exam. *Entrance requirements:* For master's, GRE General Test; for Ed S, GRE General Test, minimum GPA of 3.0, resume, letters of recommendation. Additional exam requirements/recommendations for international students: Required—TOEFL. Electronic applications accepted.

University of Central Missouri, The Graduate School, Warrensburg, MO 64093. Offers accountancy (MA); accounting (MBA); applied mathematics (MS); aviation safety (MA); biology (MS); business administration (MBA); career and technical education leadership (MS); college student personnel administration (MS); communication (MA); computer science (MS); counseling (MS); criminal justice (MS); educational leadership (Ed D); educational technology (MS); elementary and early childhood education (MSE); English (MA); environmental studies (MA); finance (MBA); history (MA); human services/educational technology (Ed S); human services/learning resources (Ed S); human services/professional counseling (Ed S); industrial hygiene (MS); industrial management (MS); information systems (MBA); information technology (MS); kinesiology (MS); library science and information services (MS); literacy education (MSE); marketing (MBA); mathematics (MS); music (MA); occupational safety management (MS); psychology (MS); rural family nursing (MS); school administration (MSE); social gerontology (MS);

sociology (MA); special education (MSE); speech language pathology (MS); superintendency (Ed S); teaching (MAT); teaching English as a second language (MA); technology (MS); technology management (PhD); theatre (MA). *Accreditation:* ASHA. *Program availability:* Part-time, 100% online, blended/hybrid learning. *Degree requirements:* For master's and Ed S, comprehensive exam (for some programs), thesis (for some programs). *Entrance requirements:* Additional exam requirements/ recommendations for international students: Required—TOEFL (minimum score 550 paper-based; 79 iBT). Electronic applications accepted.

University of Central Oklahoma, The Jackson College of Graduate Studies, College of Education and Professional Studies, Department of Adult Education and Safety Science, Edmond, OK 73034-5209. Offers adult and higher education (M Ed), including interdisciplinary studies, student personnel, training. *Program availability:* Part-time. *Degree requirements:* For master's, comprehensive exam (for some programs), thesis (for some programs). *Entrance requirements:* Additional exam requirements/ recommendations for international students: Required—TOEFL (minimum score 550 paper-based; 79 iBT), IELTS (minimum score 6.5). Electronic applications accepted.

University of Dayton, Department of Counselor Education and Human Services, Dayton, OH 45469. Offers clinical mental health counseling (MS Ed); college student personnel (MS Ed); higher education administration (MS Ed); human services (MS Ed); school counseling (MS Ed); school psychology (MS Ed, Ed S). *Accreditation:* ACA; NCATE. *Program availability:* Part-time. *Degree requirements:* For master's, thesis (for some programs); for Ed S, thesis (for some programs), professional portfolio. *Entrance requirements:* For master's, MAT or GRE (if GPA less than 2.75), essays (for some programs). Additional exam requirements/recommendations for international students: Required—TOEFL (minimum score 550 paper-based; 80 iBT). Electronic applications accepted. *Expenses:* Contact institution. *Faculty research:* Student school bonding, traumatic brain injuries, wellness and counseling, creativity in education.

University of Florida, Graduate School, College of Education, School of Human Development and Organizational Studies in Education, Gainesville, FL 32611. Offers counseling and counselor education (Ed D, PhD), including counseling and counselor education, marriage and family counseling, mental health counseling, school counseling and guidance; educational leadership (M Ed, MAE, Ed D, PhD, Ed S), including educational leadership (Ed D, PhD), educational policy (Ed D, PhD); higher education administration (Ed D, PhD), including education policy (Ed D), educational policy, higher education administration; marriage and family counseling (M Ed, MAE, Ed D, PhD, Ed S); mental health counseling (M Ed, MAE, Ed D, PhD, Ed S); research and evaluation methodology (M Ed, MAE, Ed D, PhD); school counseling and guidance (M Ed, MAE, Ed D, PhD, Ed S); student personnel in higher education (M Ed, MAE). *Accreditation:* ACA (one or more programs are accredited); NCATE. *Program availability:* Part-time, online learning. Terminal master's awarded for partial completion of doctoral program. *Degree requirements:* For master's, thesis optional; for doctorate, comprehensive exam, thesis/dissertation. *Entrance requirements:* For master's and doctorate, GRE General Test, minimum GPA of 3.0 (undergraduate), 3.5 (graduate); for Ed S, GRE General Test. Additional exam requirements/recommendations for international students: Required—TOEFL (minimum score 550 paper-based; 80 iBT), IELTS (minimum score 6). Electronic applications accepted.

University of Georgia, College of Education, Department of Counseling and Human Development Services, Athens, GA 30602. Offers college student affairs administration (M Ed, PhD); professional school counseling (Ed S). *Accreditation:* ACA (one or more programs are accredited); APA (one or more programs are accredited); NCATE. *Degree requirements:* For master's, thesis (MA); for doctorate, variable foreign language requirement, thesis/dissertation. *Entrance requirements:* For master's, GRE General Test or MAT; for doctorate, GRE General Test. Electronic applications accepted.

The University of Iowa, Graduate College, College of Education, Department of Educational Policy and Leadership Studies, Program in Higher Education and Student Affairs, Iowa City, IA 52242-1316. Offers MA, PhD. *Degree requirements:* For master's, exam; for doctorate, comprehensive exam, thesis/dissertation. *Entrance requirements:* For master's and doctorate, GRE General Test, minimum GPA of 3.0. Additional exam requirements/recommendations for international students: Required—TOEFL (minimum score 550 paper-based; 81 iBT). Electronic applications accepted.

University of La Verne, LaFetra College of Education, Program in Social Justice Higher Education Administration, La Verne, CA 91750-4443. Offers MA. *Program availability:* Part-time. *Entrance requirements:* Additional exam requirements/recommendations for international students: Required—TOEFL (minimum score 550 paper-based; 80 iBT), IELTS (minimum score 6.5). Electronic applications accepted.

University of Louisville, Graduate School, College of Education and Human Development, Department of Counseling and Human Development, Louisville, KY 40292-0001. Offers counseling and personnel services (M Ed, PhD), including art therapy (M Ed), college student personnel, counseling psychology, counselor education and supervision (PhD), educational psychology, measurement, and evaluation (PhD), mental health counseling (M Ed), school counseling (M Ed). *Accreditation:* APA; NCATE. *Program availability:* Part-time, evening/weekend, 100% online, blended/hybrid learning. *Students:* 136 full-time (109 women), 53 part-time (38 women); includes 40 minority (26 Black or African American, non-Hispanic/Latino; 1 American Indian or Alaska Native, non-Hispanic/Latino; 1 Asian, non-Hispanic/Latino; 8 Hispanic/Latino; 4 Two or more races, non-Hispanic/Latino), 4 international. Average age 29. 180 applicants, 47% accepted, 54 enrolled. In 2018, 39 master's awarded. Terminal master's awarded for partial completion of doctoral program. *Degree requirements:* For master's, comprehensive exam (for some programs), thesis optional; for doctorate, comprehensive exam (for some programs), thesis/dissertation. *Entrance requirements:* For master's, GRE (for most programs), PRAXIS (for educator preparation programs), professional statement, recommendation letters, resume, transcripts; for doctorate, GRE, professional statement, recommendation letters, resume, transcripts. Additional exam requirements/recommendations for international students: Required—TOEFL (minimum score 550 paper-based; 79 iBT); Recommended—IELTS (minimum score 6.5). *Application deadline:* For fall admission, 6/1 priority date for domestic students, 5/1 priority date for international students; for spring admission, 10/1 priority date for domestic students, 11/1 priority date for international students; for summer admission, 3/1 priority date for domestic students, 4/1 priority date for international students. Application fee: $65. *Expenses: Tuition, area resident:* Full-time $6500; part-time $723 per credit hour. Tuition, state resident: full-time $6500. Tuition, nonresident: full-time $13,557; part-time $1507 per credit hour. Tuition and fees vary according to course load and program. *Financial support:* In 2018–19, 95 students received support, including 5 fellowships with full tuition reimbursements available (averaging $21,024 per year), 32 research assistantships with full tuition reimbursements available (averaging $21,024 per year), 18 teaching assistantships with full tuition reimbursements available (averaging $21,024 per year); Federal Work-Study, scholarships/grants, health care benefits, and unspecified assistantships also available. Financial award application deadline: 3/1; financial award applicants required to submit FAFSA. *Faculty research:* Mental health services and under-served populations; health disparities and outcomes; well-being identity development; measurement and evaluation; college student personnel. *Unit head:* Dr. Mark M. Leach, Chair and Professor, 502-852-6884, E-mail: ecpy@louisville.edu. *Application contact:* Dr. Margaret Pentecost, Assistant Dean for Graduate Student Success, 502-852-2628, Fax: 502-852-1417, E-mail: gedadm@louisville.edu.
Website: http://www.louisville.edu/education/departments/ecpy

University of Maryland, College Park, Academic Affairs, College of Education, Department of Counseling, Higher Education and Special Education, College Park, MD 20742. Offers college student personnel (M Ed, MA); college student personnel administration (PhD); community counseling (CAGS); community/career counseling (M Ed, MA); counseling and personnel services (M Ed, MA, PhD), including art therapy (M Ed), college student personnel (M Ed), counseling and personnel services (PhD), counseling psychology (M Ed), mental health counseling (M Ed), school counseling (M Ed); counseling psychology (PhD); counselor education (PhD); rehabilitation counseling (M Ed, MA, AGSC); school counseling (M Ed, MA); school psychology (M Ed, MA, PhD). *Accreditation:* APA (one or more programs are accredited); NCATE. *Program availability:* Part-time, evening/weekend, online learning. *Degree requirements:* For master's, thesis (for some programs); for doctorate, thesis/dissertation. *Entrance requirements:* For master's, GRE General Test or MAT, minimum GPA of 3.0, 3 letters of recommendation; for doctorate, GRE General Test or MAT, minimum GPA of 3.5, 3 letters of recommendation. Additional exam requirements/recommendations for international students: Required—TOEFL. Electronic applications accepted. *Faculty research:* Educational psychology, counseling, health.

University of Minnesota, Twin Cities Campus, Graduate School, College of Education and Human Development, Department of Educational Psychology, Program in Counseling and Student Personnel Psychology, Minneapolis, MN 55455-0213. Offers MA. *Students:* 63 full-time (46 women), 3 part-time (all women); includes 8 minority (3 Asian, non-Hispanic/Latino; 2 Hispanic/Latino; 3 Two or more races, non-Hispanic/Latino), 9 international. Average age 26. 64 applicants, 67% accepted, 29 enrolled. In 2018, 34 master's awarded. Application fee: $75 ($95 for international students). *Unit head:* Dr. Kristen McMaster, Chair, 612-624-6083, Fax: 612-624-8241, E-mail: mcmas004@umn.edu. *Application contact:* Dr. Panayiota Kendeou, Director of Graduate Studies, 612-626-7814, E-mail: kend0040@umn.edu.
Website: http://www.cehd.umn.edu/EdPsych/Programs/CSPP/default.html

University of Nebraska at Kearney, College of Education, Department of Counseling and School Psychology, Kearney, NE 68849-0001. Offers clinical mental health counseling (MS Ed); school counseling (MS Ed), including elementary, secondary; school psychology (Ed S); student affairs (MS Ed). *Accreditation:* ACA; NCATE. *Program availability:* Part-time, evening/weekend, 100% online. *Degree requirements:* For master's, comprehensive exam, thesis optional; for Ed S, thesis. *Entrance requirements:* For master's and Ed S, personal statement, recommendations, resume, interview. Additional exam requirements/recommendations for international students: Recommended—TOEFL (minimum score 550 paper-based; 79 iBT), IELTS (minimum score 6.5). Electronic applications accepted. *Faculty research:* Multicultural counseling and diversity issues, team decision-making, adult development, women's issues, brief therapy.

University of Northern Colorado, Graduate School, College of Education and Behavioral Sciences, Department of Leadership, Policy and Development: Higher Education and P-12 Education, Program in Higher Education and Student Affairs Leadership, Greeley, CO 80639. Offers MA, PhD. *Program availability:* Part-time. *Entrance requirements:* For doctorate, GRE General Test, transcripts, 3 letters of recommendation. Electronic applications accepted.

University of Northern Iowa, Graduate College, College of Education, Department of Educational Leadership and Postsecondary Education, MA Program in Postsecondary Education: Student Affairs, Cedar Falls, IA 50614. Offers MA. *Degree requirements:* For master's, comprehensive exam, thesis or alternative. *Entrance requirements:* For master's, minimum GPA of 3.0. Additional exam requirements/recommendations for international students: Required—TOEFL (minimum score 500 paper-based; 61 iBT). Electronic applications accepted.

University of Rhode Island, Graduate School, College of Health Sciences, Department of Human Development and Family Studies, Kingston, RI 02881. Offers college student personnel (MS); human development and family studies (MS); marriage and family therapy (MS). *Accreditation:* AAMFT/COAMFTE. *Program availability:* Part-time. *Faculty:* 16 full-time (11 women). *Students:* 50 full-time (39 women), 9 part-time (8 women); includes 17 minority (3 Black or African American, non-Hispanic/Latino; 1 American Indian or Alaska Native, non-Hispanic/Latino; 5 Asian, non-Hispanic/Latino; 5 Hispanic/Latino; 3 Two or more races, non-Hispanic/Latino), 2 international. 100 applicants, 41% accepted, 28 enrolled. In 2018, 22 master's awarded. *Entrance requirements:* Additional exam requirements/recommendations for international students: Required—TOEFL. *Application deadline:* For fall admission, 1/15 for domestic and international students. Application fee: $65. Electronic applications accepted. *Expenses: Tuition, area resident:* Full-time $13,226; part-time $735 per credit. Tuition, state resident: full-time $13,226; part-time $735 per credit. Tuition, nonresident: full-time $25,854; part-time $1436 per credit. *International tuition:* $25,854 full-time. *Required fees:* $1698; $50 per credit. $35 per semester. One-time fee: $165. *Financial support:* In 2018–19, 2 research assistantships with tuition reimbursements (averaging $5,064 per year), 5 teaching assistantships with tuition reimbursements (averaging $11,078 per year) were awarded. Financial award application deadline: 1/15; financial award applicants required to submit FAFSA. *Unit head:* Dr. Sue Adam, Chair, 401-874-5958, E-mail: suekadams@uri.edu. *Application contact:* Dr. Sue Adam, Chair, 401-874-5958, E-mail: suekadams@uri.edu.
Website: http://www.uri.edu/hss/hdf/

University of Rochester, Margaret Warner Graduate School of Education and Human Development, Master's Program in Higher Education, Rochester, NY 14627. Offers higher education (MS); higher education student affairs (MS). *Expenses: Tuition:* Full-time $52,974; part-time $1654 per credit hour. *Required fees:* $612. One-time fee: $30 part-time. Tuition and fees vary according to campus/location and program.

University of St. Thomas, College of Education, Leadership and Counseling, Department of Leadership, Policy and Administration, St. Paul, MN 55105-1096. Offers education leadership and administration (MA); educational leadership and learning (Ed D); executive coaching (Certificate); K-12 administration (Ed S); leadership in student affairs (MA). *Program availability:* Part-time, evening/weekend. Terminal master's awarded for partial completion of doctoral program. *Degree requirements:* For master's, thesis (for some programs); for doctorate, thesis/dissertation; for other advanced degree, thesis or alternative. *Entrance requirements:* For master's, minimum GPA of 3.0 or MAT; for doctorate, MAT, minimum graduate GPA of 3.5; for other advanced degree, minimum graduate GPA of 3.25 or MAT. Additional exam requirements/recommendations for international students: Required—TOEFL (minimum score 550 paper-based). Electronic applications accepted. *Expenses:* Contact institution.

University of South Carolina, The Graduate School, College of Education, Department of Educational Leadership and Policies, Program in Higher Education and Student Affairs, Columbia, SC 29208. Offers M Ed. *Accreditation:* NCATE. *Program availability:* Part-time. *Degree requirements:* For master's, comprehensive exam, thesis (for some programs). *Entrance requirements:* For master's, GRE General Test or MAT, letters of

reference. Electronic applications accepted. *Faculty research:* Minorities in higher education, community college transfer problem, federal role in educational research.

University of Southern California, Graduate School, Rossier School of Education, Master's Programs in Education, Los Angeles, CA 90089-4038. Offers educational counseling (ME); marriage, family and child counseling (MMFT); postsecondary administration and student affairs [PASA] (ME); school counseling (ME); teaching (online) (MAT); teaching and teaching credential (MAT); teaching English to speakers of other languages (MAT). *Program availability:* Part-time, evening/weekend, online learning. *Degree requirements:* For master's, thesis optional. *Entrance requirements:* For master's, GRE (for all programs except MAT). Additional exam requirements/ recommendations for international students: Required—TOEFL (minimum score 100 iBT). Electronic applications accepted. *Faculty research:* College access and equity, preparing teachers for culturally diverse populations, sociocultural basis of learning as mediated by instruction with focus on reading and literacy in English learners, social and political aspects of teaching and learning English, school counselor development and training.

University of Southern Mississippi, College of Education and Human Sciences, Department of Educational Research and Administration, Hattiesburg, MS 39406-0001. Offers educational administration (M Ed, Ed D, PhD, Ed S); educational administration and supervision (M Ed); educational studies and research (MS); higher education (Ed D); higher education administration (PhD); higher education: student affairs (M Ed); research, evaluation, statistics, assessment (PhD). *Degree requirements:* For master's and Ed S, comprehensive exam, thesis (for some programs); for doctorate, comprehensive exam, thesis/dissertation. *Entrance requirements:* For master's and doctorate, GRE General Test, minimum GPA of 2.75. Additional exam requirements/ recommendations for international students: Required—TOEFL.

University of South Florida, College of Education, Department of Educational and Psychological Studies, Tampa, FL 33620-9951. Offers college student affairs (M Ed); counselor education (MA, PhD, Ed S); interdisciplinary education (PhD, Ed S); school psychology (PhD, Ed S). *Faculty:* 27 full-time (14 women). *Students:* 133 full-time (92 women), 113 part-time (81 women); includes 64 minority (23 Black or African American, non-Hispanic/Latino; 6 Asian, non-Hispanic/Latino; 27 Hispanic/Latino; 1 Native Hawaiian or other Pacific Islander, non-Hispanic/Latino; 7 Two or more races, non-Hispanic/Latino), 29 international. Average age 32. 205 applicants, 57% accepted, 85 enrolled. In 2018, 49 master's, 11 doctorates awarded. *Degree requirements:* For master's, comprehensive exam, thesis (for some programs); for doctorate, comprehensive exam, thesis/dissertation (for some programs). *Entrance requirements:* For master's, GRE may be required, Letters of recommendation, personal statement, interview, resume; CLAST/GKT may be required; for doctorate, GRE may be required, 3.5 master's GPA; letter of intent; resume; letters of reference. Additional exam requirements/recommendations for international students: Required—TOEFL. Application fee: $30. *Expenses:* Tuition, state resident: full-time $6350. Tuition, nonresident: full-time $19,048. *International tuition:* $19,048 full-time. *Required fees:* $2079. *Financial support:* In 2018–19, 1 student received support. *Faculty research:* College student affairs, counselor education, educational psychology, school psychology, social foundations. *Total annual research expenditures:* $10.8 million. *Unit head:* Dr. Barabara Shircliff, Chair, 813-974-4001, E-mail: shirclif@usf.edu. *Application contact:* Dr. Barbara Shircliff, Chair, 813-974-4001, E-mail: shirclif@usf.edu.

The University of Tennessee, Graduate School, College of Education, Health and Human Sciences, Department of Educational Psychology and Counseling, Program in College Student Personnel, Knoxville, TN 37996. Offers MS. *Accreditation:* NCATE. *Program availability:* Part-time. *Degree requirements:* For master's, thesis optional. *Entrance requirements:* For master's, GRE General Test, minimum GPA of 2.7. Additional exam requirements/recommendations for international students: Required—TOEFL. Electronic applications accepted.

The University of Tennessee at Martin, Graduate Programs, College of Education, Health and Behavioral Sciences, Program in Counseling, Martin, TN 38238. Offers addictions counseling (MS Ed); community counseling (MS Ed); school counseling (MS Ed); student affairs and college counseling (MS Ed). *Accreditation:* NCATE. *Program availability:* Part-time, online only, 100% online. *Students:* 18 full-time (16 women), 56 part-time (53 women); includes 12 minority (11 Black or African American, non-Hispanic/Latino; 1 Hispanic/Latino). Average age 34. 56 applicants, 36% accepted, 18 enrolled. In 2018, 16 master's awarded. *Degree requirements:* For master's, comprehensive exam. *Entrance requirements:* For master's, GRE General Test, minimum GPA of 2.5, resume, letters of reference. Additional exam requirements/ recommendations for international students: Required—TOEFL (minimum score 525 paper-based; 71 iBT). *Application deadline:* For fall admission, 7/27 priority date for domestic and international students; for spring admission, 12/17 priority date for domestic and international students; for summer admission, 5/10 priority date for domestic and international students. Applications are processed on a rolling basis. Application fee: $30 ($130 for international students). Electronic applications accepted. *Expenses: Tuition, area resident:* Full-time $8918; part-time $495 per credit hour. Tuition, state resident: full-time $8918; part-time $485 per credit hour. Tuition, nonresident: full-time $14,958; part-time $831 per credit hour. *International tuition:* $22,862 full-time. *Required fees:* $1446; $81 per credit hour. Part-time tuition and fees vary according to course load. *Financial support:* In 2018–19, 13 students received support, including 1 teaching assistantship with full tuition reimbursement available (averaging $6,283 per year); research assistantships with full tuition reimbursements available, scholarships/grants, and tuition waivers (full and partial) also available. Financial award application deadline: 2/1; financial award applicants required to submit FAFSA. *Unit head:* Cynthia West, Dean, 731-881-7125, Fax: 731-881-7975, E-mail: cwest@utm.edu. *Application contact:* Jolene L. Cunningham, Student Services Specialist, 731-881-7012, Fax: 731-881-7499, E-mail: jcunningham@utm.edu.

University of the Cumberlands, Graduate Programs in Education, Williamsburg, KY 40769-1372. Offers all grades (P-12) (M Ed); business and marketing (MA Ed, MAT); counselor education and supervision (Ed D); director of pupil personnel (Certificate); director of special education (Certificate); educational administration and supervision (Ed S); educational leadership (Ed D); elementary education (MA Ed, MAT); instructional leadership - principalship (MA Ed); instructional leadership - school principal (Certificate); middle school education (MA Ed, MAT); reading and writing (MA Ed); school counseling (MA Ed); school superintendent (Certificate); secondary education (MA Ed, MAT); special education (MAT); supervisor of instruction (Certificate); teacher leader (MA Ed). *Program availability:* Part-time, evening/weekend, online learning. *Degree requirements:* For master's, comprehensive exam. Electronic applications accepted.

University of Utah, Graduate School, College of Education, Department of Educational Leadership and Policy, Salt Lake City, UT 84084. Offers educational leadership and policy (Ed D, PhD), including higher education administration (Ed D), K-12 (Ed D); K-12 school administration (M Ed); k-12 teacher leadership (M Ed); student affairs (M Ed); MPA/PhD. *Program availability:* Part-time, evening/weekend. *Faculty:* 10 full-time (8 women), 2 part-time/adjunct (both women). *Students:* 51 full-time (35 women), 184 part-time (127 women); includes 65 minority (14 Black or African American, non-Hispanic/ Latino; 3 American Indian or Alaska Native, non-Hispanic/Latino; 10 Asian, non-Hispanic/Latino; 31 Hispanic/Latino; 3 Native Hawaiian or other Pacific Islander, non-Hispanic/Latino; 4 Two or more races, non-Hispanic/Latino), 1 international. Average age 35. 181 applicants, 69% accepted, 90 enrolled. In 2018, 68 master's, 5 doctorates awarded. *Degree requirements:* For master's, comprehensive exam (for some programs), internship, capstone; for doctorate, thesis/dissertation, qualifying exam. *Entrance requirements:* For master's, minimum undergraduate GPA of 3.0, valid bachelor's degree, 3 years' teaching or leadership experience, Level 1 or 2 UT educator's license (for K-12 programs only); for doctorate, GRE General Test (taken with five years of applying), minimum undergraduate GPA of 3.0, valid master's degree. Additional exam requirements/recommendations for international students: Required—TOEFL (minimum score 550 paper-based). *Application deadline:* For fall admission, 1/ 15 priority date for domestic and international students; for winter admission, 2/1 for domestic and international students; for spring admission, 11/1 priority date for domestic and international students; for summer admission, 3/1 priority date for domestic and international students. Applications are processed on a rolling basis. Application fee: $55 ($65 for international students). Electronic applications accepted. *Expenses: Tuition, area resident:* Full-time $7190.66; part-time $2112.48 per year. Tuition, state resident: full-time $7190.66. Tuition, nonresident: full-time $25,195. *Required fees:* $558; $555.04 per unit. Tuition and fees vary according to course level, course load, degree level, program and student level. *Financial support:* In 2018–19, 12 students received support, including 2 fellowships with full tuition reimbursements available (averaging $15,900 per year), 4 research assistantships with full tuition reimbursements available (averaging $15,900 per year), 3 teaching assistantships with full tuition reimbursements available (averaging $15,900 per year); career-related internships or fieldwork, scholarships/grants, health care benefits, and unspecified assistantships also available. Support available to part-time students. Financial award application deadline: 3/1; financial award applicants required to submit FAFSA. *Faculty research:* Education accountability, college student diversity, K-12 educational administration and school leadership, student affairs, higher education. *Unit head:* Dr. Yongmei Ni, Chair, 801-587-9298, Fax: 801-585-6756, E-mail: yongmei.ni@utah.edu. *Application contact:* Marilynn S. Howard, Administrative Officer, 801-581-6714, Fax: 801-585-6756, E-mail: marilynn.howard@utah.edu.
Website: http://elp.utah.edu/

University of Virginia, Curry School of Education, Department of Leadership, Foundations and Policy, Program in Higher Education, Charlottesville, VA 22903. Offers higher education (Ed S); student affairs practice (M Ed). *Entrance requirements:* For master's, doctorate, and Ed S, GRE General Test, 2 letters of recommendation. Additional exam requirements/recommendations for international students: Required—TOEFL (minimum score 600 paper-based; 90 iBT), IELTS (minimum score 7). Electronic applications accepted.

The University of West Alabama, School of Graduate Studies, College of Education, Program in Student Affairs in Higher Education, Livingston, AL 35470. Offers M Ed. *Program availability:* Part-time, evening/weekend, 100% online. *Faculty:* 1 (woman) full-time, 3 part-time/adjunct (2 women). *Students:* 104 full-time (80 women), 3 part-time (2 women); includes 62 minority (58 Black or African American, non-Hispanic/Latino; 2 Hispanic/Latino; 2 Two or more races, non-Hispanic/Latino), 2 international. Average age 32. 34 applicants, 97% accepted, 32 enrolled. In 2018, 16 master's awarded. *Degree requirements:* For master's, comprehensive exam. *Entrance requirements:* For master's, GRE, minimum GPA of 2.75, criminal background check. Additional exam requirements/recommendations for international students: Required—TOEFL (minimum score 500 paper-based; 61 iBT). *Application deadline:* Applications are processed on a rolling basis. Application fee: $40. Electronic applications accepted. *Expenses: Tuition, area resident:* Full-time $9100. Tuition, state resident: full-time $9100. Tuition, nonresident: full-time $19,200. *Required fees:* $1890; $130. *Financial support:* Teaching assistantships, Federal Work-Study, scholarships/grants, and unspecified assistantships available. Support available to part-time students. Financial award application deadline: 3/1; financial award applicants required to submit FAFSA. *Unit head:* Dr. Jodie Winship, Chair of College of Education, 205-652-5415, E-mail: jwinship@uwa.edu. *Application contact:* Dr. B. J. Kimbrough, Dean of Graduate Studies, 205-652-3647, Fax: 205-652-3670, E-mail: bkimbrough@uwa.edu.

University of West Florida, College of Education and Professional Studies, Department of Research and Advanced Studies, Program in College Student Affairs Administration, Pensacola, FL 32514-5750. Offers M Ed. *Program availability:* Part-time, evening/weekend. *Degree requirements:* For master's, internship. *Entrance requirements:* For master's, GRE General Test, minimum GPA of 3.0. Additional exam requirements/recommendations for international students: Required—TOEFL (minimum score 550 paper-based).

University of Wisconsin–La Crosse, College of Liberal Studies, Department of Student Affairs Administration, La Crosse, WI 54601-3742. Offers MS Ed, Ed D. *Program availability:* Part-time, evening/weekend, 100% online, blended/hybrid learning. *Degree requirements:* For master's, comprehensive exam (for some programs), thesis optional, electronic portfolio, applied research project. *Entrance requirements:* For master's, bachelor's degree from accredited institution, minimum GPA of 2.85, resume, essay, 2 references. Additional exam requirements/recommendations for international students: Required—TOEFL (minimum score 550 paper-based; 79 iBT). Electronic applications accepted. *Faculty research:* Persistence; developing positive social justice behaviors in heterosexual white college men; equity; diversity; inclusion in higher education at both interpersonal and institutional levels; expanding student affairs administration research and practice beyond the traditional, majority, or dominant student experience; underrepresented students at historically white institutions; college men and masculinities; Latina/o college student leadership; ethnic cultural centers at HWIs.

University of Wyoming, College of Education, Programs in Counselor Education, Laramie, WY 82071. Offers community mental health (MS); counselor education and supervision (PhD); school counseling (MS); student affairs (MS). *Accreditation:* ACA (one or more programs are accredited). *Degree requirements:* For master's, comprehensive exam (for some programs), thesis optional; for doctorate, thesis/ dissertation, video demonstration. *Entrance requirements:* For master's, interview, background check; for doctorate, video tape session, interview, writing sample, master's degree, background check. Additional exam requirements/recommendations for international students: Required—TOEFL. *Expenses: Tuition, area resident:* Full-time $6504; part-time $271 per credit hour. Tuition, state resident: full-time $6504; part-time $271 per credit hour. Tuition, nonresident: full-time $19,464; part-time $811 per credit hour. *International tuition:* $19,464 full-time. *Required fees:* $1410.94; $343.82 per semester. $343.82 per semester. Tuition and fees vary according to course load, program and reciprocity agreements. *Faculty research:* Wyoming SAGE photovoice project; accountable school counseling programs; GLBT issues; addictions; play therapy-early childhood mental health.

Virginia Commonwealth University, Graduate School, School of Education, Program in Counselor Education, Richmond, VA 23284-9005. Offers college student development and counseling (M Ed); school counseling (M Ed). *Accreditation:* ACA; NCATE. *Entrance requirements:* For master's, GRE General Test or MAT. Additional

exam requirements/recommendations for international students: Required—TOEFL (minimum score 600 paper-based; 100 iBT). Electronic applications accepted.

Walsh University, Graduate Programs, Program in Counseling and Human Development, North Canton, OH 44720-3396. Offers clinical mental health counseling (MA); school counseling (MA); student affairs in higher education (MA). *Accreditation:* ACA. *Program availability:* Part-time, evening/weekend. *Degree requirements:* For master's, comprehensive exam, internship, practicum. *Entrance requirements:* For master's, GRE (minimum score of 145 verbal and 146 quantitative) or MAT (minimum score of 397), interview, minimum GPA of 3.0, writing sample, reference forms, notarized affidavit of good moral conduct. Additional exam requirements/recommendations for international students: Required—TOEFL (minimum score 500 paper-based; 61 iBT). Electronic applications accepted. Application fee is waived when completed online. *Expenses:* Contact institution. *Faculty research:* Supervision of clinical mental health, clinical mental health practice/issues, clinical mental health skills development, advocacy, teaching and professional development, career development, refugee development in US, supervision in student affairs, offender treatment, domestic violence issues, alcohol and drug treatment issues, Professional identity and advocacy in school counseling, Efficacy in counseling clinic.

West Chester University of Pennsylvania, College of Education and Social Work, Department of Counselor Education, West Chester, PA 19383. Offers clinical mental health counseling (MS); counseling (Certificate); higher education counseling (Post Master's Certificate); higher education counseling/student affairs (MS, Certificate); school counseling (M Ed). *Accreditation:* ACA; NCATE. *Program availability:* Part-time, evening/weekend. *Degree requirements:* For master's, comprehensive exam. *Entrance requirements:* For master's, minimum GPA of 3.0, three letters of reference. Additional exam requirements/recommendations for international students: Required—TOEFL or IELTS. Electronic applications accepted. *Faculty research:* Bullying in the schools, adolescent cognitive development, counseling pedagogy, motivational interviewing.

West Chester University of Pennsylvania, College of Education and Social Work, Department of Educational Foundations and Policy Studies, West Chester, PA 19383. Offers education for sustainability (Certificate); educational technology (Certificate); higher education policy and student affairs (MS); transformative education and social change (MS). *Program availability:* Part-time. *Degree requirements:* For master's, comprehensive exam (for some programs), thesis, 36 credits (42 credits for MS in higher education policy and student affairs). *Entrance requirements:* For master's, teaching certification (strongly recommended); for Certificate, minimum GPA of 3.0. Additional exam requirements/recommendations for international students: Required—TOEFL or IELTS. Electronic applications accepted. *Faculty research:* Technology integration: preparing our teachers for the twenty-first century, critical pedagogy, education for sustainability.

Western Illinois University, School of Graduate Studies, College of Education and Human Services, Department of Educational Studies, Program in College Student Personnel, Macomb, IL 61455-1390. Offers college student personnel (MS), including higher education leadership, student affairs. *Accreditation:* NCATE. *Program availability:* Part-time. *Students:* 54 full-time (37 women), 12 part-time (8 women); includes 21 minority (5 Black or African American, non-Hispanic/Latino; 11 Hispanic/Latino; 5 Two or more races, non-Hispanic/Latino), 2 international. Average age 25. 56 applicants, 77% accepted, 22 enrolled. In 2018, 46 master's awarded. *Entrance requirements:* For master's, interview. Additional exam requirements/recommendations for international students: Required—TOEFL (minimum score 550 paper-based; 80 iBT). *Application deadline:* For fall admission, 1/5 priority date for domestic students. Application fee: $30. Electronic applications accepted. *Financial support:* Unspecified assistantships available. Financial award applicants required to submit FAFSA. *Unit head:* Dr. Tracy Davis, Coordinator, 309-298-1183. *Application contact:* Dr. Mark Mossman, Associate Provost and Director of Graduate Studies, 309-298-1806, Fax: 309-298-2345, E-mail: grad-office@wiu.edu.
Website: http://wiu.edu/csp/

Western Kentucky University, Graduate School, College of Education and Behavioral Sciences, Department of Counseling and Student Affairs, Bowling Green, KY 42101. Offers counseling (MA Ed), including marriage and family therapy, mental health counseling; school counseling (P-12) (MA Ed); student affairs in higher education (MA Ed). *Accreditation:* ACA; NCATE. *Program availability:* Part-time, evening/weekend. *Degree requirements:* For master's, comprehensive exam, thesis optional. *Entrance requirements:* For master's, GRE General Test. Additional exam requirements/recommendations for international students: Required—TOEFL (minimum score 555 paper-based; 79 iBT). *Faculty research:* Counselor education, research for residential workers.

William James College, Graduate Programs, Newton, MA 02459. Offers applied psychology in higher education student personnel administration (MA); clinical psychology (Psy D); counseling psychology (MA); counseling psychology and community mental health (MA); counseling psychology and global mental health (MA); executive coaching (Graduate Certificate); forensic and counseling psychology (MA); leadership psychology (Psy D); organizational psychology (MA); primary care psychology (MA); respecialization in clinical psychology (Certificate); school psychology (Psy D); MA/CAGS. *Accreditation:* APA. *Degree requirements:* For master's, comprehensive exam (for some programs); for doctorate, thesis/dissertation (for some programs). Electronic applications accepted. *Expenses: Tuition:* Full-time $33,000. *Required fees:* $960.

Section 24
Instructional Levels

This section contains a directory of institutions offering graduate work in instructional levels. Additional information about programs listed in the directory may be obtained by writing directly to the dean of a graduate school or chair of a department at the address given in the directory.

For programs offering related work, see also in this book *Administration, Instruction, and Theory; Education; Leisure Studies and Recreation; Physical Education and Kinesiology; Special Focus;* and *Subject Areas.* In other guides in this series:

Graduate Programs in the Humanities, Arts & Social Sciences
See *Psychology and Counseling (School Psychology)*
Graduate Programs in the Biological/Biomedical Sciences and Health-Related Medical Professions
See *Health-Related Professions*

CONTENTS

Program Directories

Adult Education

Alverno College, School of Professional Studies - Education Division, Milwaukee, WI 53234-3922. Offers adaptive education (MA); administrative leadership (MA); adult education and organizational development (MA); adult educational and instructional design (MA); adult educational and instructional technology (MA); global connections in the humanities (MA); instructional leadership (MA); instructional technology for K-12 settings (MA); professional development (MA); reading education (MA); reading education with adaptive education (MA); science education (MA); special education (MA); teaching in alternative schools (MA). *Accreditation:* NCATE. *Program availability:* Part-time, evening/weekend. *Degree requirements:* For master's, presentation/defense of proposal, conference presentation of inquiry projects. *Entrance requirements:* For master's, bachelor's degree in related field, communication samples from work setting, 3 letters of recommendation. Additional exam requirements/recommendations for international students: Required—TOEFL. Electronic applications accepted. *Expenses:* Contact institution. *Faculty research:* Student self-assessment, self-reflection, integration of curriculum, identifying needs of students in strategic situations and designing appropriate classroom strategies.

Antioch University Seattle, Program in Education, Seattle, WA 98121. Offers adult education (MA); drama therapy (MA); individualized studies (MA); leadership in edible education (MA); teaching (MAT); urban environmental education (MA). *Program availability:* Part-time, evening/weekend. *Degree requirements:* For master's, comprehensive exam (for some programs), thesis. *Entrance requirements:* For master's, WEST-B, WEST-E, current resume, transcripts of undergraduate degree and coursework (or for highest degree completed), two letters of recommendation, proof of fingerprinting and background check, moral character with fitness statement of understanding, documentation of 40 hours' experience in school classroom(s). *Expenses:* Contact institution. *Faculty research:* Visual thinking and science education, K-8 equity and engaged pedagogy in science education, K-12 inquiry-based mathematics education, education in prisons and other institutions of confinement.

Argosy University, Chicago, College of Education, Chicago, IL 60601. Offers adult education and training (MA Ed); community college executive leadership (Ed D); educational leadership (MA Ed, Ed D, Ed S), including district leadership (Ed D), higher education administration (Ed D), K-12 education (Ed D); instructional leadership (Ed D, Ed S), including higher education (Ed D), K-12 education (Ed D). *Program availability:* Online learning.

Argosy University, Hawai`i, College of Education, Honolulu, HI 96813. Offers adult education and training (MAEd); educational leadership (Ed D), including higher education administration, K-12 education; instructional leadership (Ed D), including higher education, K-12 education; school psychology (MA).

Argosy University, Phoenix, College of Education, Phoenix, AZ 85021. Offers adult education and training (MA Ed); advanced educational administration (Ed D, Ed S); community college executive leadership (Ed D); educational administration (MA Ed); educational leadership (MA Ed, Ed D, Ed S), including education technology (Ed D), higher education administration (Ed D), K-12 education (Ed D); higher and postsecondary education (MA Ed); initial educational administration (Ed D, Ed S); school psychology (MA); teaching and learning (MA Ed, Ed D, Ed S), including education technology (Ed D), higher education (Ed D), K-12 education (Ed D).

Argosy University, Seattle, College of Education, Seattle, WA 98121. Offers adult education and training (MA Ed); community college executive leadership (Ed D); educational leadership (MA Ed, Ed D), including higher education administration (Ed D), K-12 education (Ed D); higher and postsecondary education (MA Ed); instructional leadership (MA Ed, Ed D), including education technology (Ed D), higher education (Ed D), K-12 education (Ed D).

Athabasca University, Centre for Interdisciplinary Studies, Athabasca, AB T9S 3A3, Canada. Offers adult education (MA); community studies (MA); cultural studies (MA); educational studies (MA); global change (MA); heritage resource management (Postbaccalaureate Certificate); legislative drafting (Postbaccalaureate Certificate); work, organization, and leadership (MA). *Program availability:* Part-time, evening/weekend, online learning. *Degree requirements:* For master's, project. *Entrance requirements:* Additional exam requirements/recommendations for international students: Required—TOEFL (minimum score 560 paper-based). Electronic applications accepted. *Faculty research:* Women's history, literature and culture studies, sustainable development, labor and education.

Auburn University, Graduate School, College of Education, Department of Educational Foundations, Leadership, and Technology, Auburn University, AL 36849. Offers adult education (PhD, Ed S); curriculum supervision (M Ed, PhD); higher education administration (PhD); library media (Ed S); school administration (M Ed, PhD). *Accreditation:* NCATE. *Program availability:* Part-time. *Degree requirements:* For master's, thesis (for some programs); for doctorate, thesis/dissertation; for Ed S, field project. *Entrance requirements:* For master's, doctorate, and Ed S, GRE General Test. Electronic applications accepted. *Expenses:* Tuition, state resident: full-time $11,282; part-time $535 per credit hour. Tuition, nonresident: full-time $30,542; part-time $1605 per credit hour. *Required fees:* $826 per semester. Tuition and fees vary according to degree level and program.

Aurora University, School of Education and Human Performance, Aurora, IL 60506-4892. Offers applied behavioral analysis (MS); bilingual-ESL education (MA); educational leadership with principal endorsement (MA); educational technology (MA); leadership in adult learning higher education (Ed D); leadership in curriculum and instruction (Ed D); leadership in educational administration (Ed D); reading instruction (MA); special education (MA). *Accreditation:* NCATE. *Program availability:* Part-time, evening/weekend, 100% online. *Faculty:* 14 full-time (6 women), 32 part-time/adjunct (17 women). *Students:* 28 full-time (25 women), 537 part-time (359 women); includes 101 minority (25 Black or African American, non-Hispanic/Latino; 8 Asian, non-Hispanic/Latino; 58 Hispanic/Latino; 2 Native Hawaiian or other Pacific Islander, non-Hispanic/Latino; 8 Two or more races, non-Hispanic/Latino), 2 international. Average age 38. 191 applicants, 98% accepted, 133 enrolled. In 2018, 213 master's, 16 doctorates awarded. *Degree requirements:* For master's, student teaching, research seminar, and practicum; for doctorate, comprehensive exam, thesis/dissertation. *Entrance requirements:* For master's, 2 years of teaching experience, valid teaching certificate, resume; for doctorate, appropriate master's degree, two references, curriculum vitae, personal statement, professional project, reflective essay. Additional exam requirements/recommendations for international students: Required—TOEFL (minimum score 550 paper-based; 79 iBT). *Application deadline:* For fall admission, 6/1 for international students; for spring admission, 10/1 for international students. Applications are processed on a rolling basis. Application fee: $0. Electronic applications accepted. *Expenses:* The reported tuition amount is for the program with the greatest enrollment, MA in Educational Leadership with Principal Endorsement. Other programs may require

more semester hours, and thus have a greater total cost. The Education doctoral programs are roughly double the amount of the master's programs. *Financial support:* In 2018–19, 31 students received support. Federal Work-Study, scholarships/grants, and unspecified assistantships available. Financial award applicants required to submit FAFSA. *Unit head:* Dr. Jen Buckley, Dean, School of Education and Human Performance, 630-844-1542, Fax: 630-844-6155, E-mail: jbuckley@aurora.edu. *Application contact:* Center for Graduate Studies, 630-947-8955, E-mail: AUadmission@aurora.edu.
Website: http://aurora.edu/education

Ball State University, Graduate School, Teachers College, Department of Educational Studies, Program in Adult Education, Muncie, IN 47306. Offers adult and community education (MA); adult, higher and community education (Ed D). *Accreditation:* NCATE. *Program availability:* Part-time, 100% online, blended/hybrid learning. *Degree requirements:* For doctorate, thesis/dissertation. *Entrance requirements:* For master's, minimum baccalaureate GPA of 2.75 or 3.0 in latter half of baccalaureate; for doctorate, GRE General Test, minimum graduate GPA of 3.2. Additional exam requirements/recommendations for international students: Required—TOEFL (minimum score 550 paper-based; 79 iBT), IELTS (minimum score 6.5). Electronic applications accepted. *Faculty research:* Community education, executive development for public services.

Buffalo State College, State University of New York, The Graduate School, School of Education, Department of Adult Education, Buffalo, NY 14222-1095. Offers adult education (MS, Certificate); human resource development (Certificate). *Program availability:* Part-time, evening/weekend, online learning. *Degree requirements:* For master's, comprehensive exam. *Entrance requirements:* Additional exam requirements/recommendations for international students: Required—TOEFL (minimum score 550 paper-based).

California Baptist University, Program in Education, Riverside, CA 92504-3206. Offers educational leadership (MS); educational leadership for faith-based institutions (MS); educational leadership for public institutions (MS); educational technology (MS); instructional computer applications (MS); international education (MS); leadership and adult learning (MS); leadership and organizational studies (MS); online teaching and learning (MS); reading (MS); science education (MA); special education in mild/moderate disabilities (MS); special education in moderate/severe disabilities (MS); teacher leadership (MS); teaching (MS); teaching and learning (MS). *Program availability:* Part-time, evening/weekend, 100% online, blended/hybrid learning. *Faculty:* 26 full-time (13 women), 28 part-time/adjunct (21 women). *Students:* 201 full-time (164 women), 265 part-time (209 women); includes 226 minority (23 Black or African American, non-Hispanic/Latino; 4 American Indian or Alaska Native, non-Hispanic/Latino; 7 Asian, non-Hispanic/Latino; 169 Hispanic/Latino; 6 Native Hawaiian or other Pacific Islander, non-Hispanic/Latino; 17 Two or more races, non-Hispanic/Latino), 2 international. Average age 39. 145 applicants, 97% accepted, 141 enrolled. In 2018, 253 master's awarded. *Degree requirements:* For master's, comprehensive exam, project, or thesis. *Entrance requirements:* For master's, minimum undergraduate GPA of 2.75; 500-word essay; three letters of recommendation; two prerequisite courses completed with minimum C grade. Additional exam requirements/recommendations for international students: Required—TOEFL (minimum score 80 iBT). *Application deadline:* For fall admission, 8/1 priority date for domestic students, 7/1 for international students; for spring admission, 12/1 priority date for domestic students, 11/1 for international students. Applications are processed on a rolling basis. Application fee: $45. Electronic applications accepted. *Expenses:* $634 per unit. *Financial support:* In 2018–19, 312 students received support. Federal Work-Study and scholarships/grants available. Financial award applicants required to submit CSS PROFILE or FAFSA. *Faculty research:* Leadership development, complexity theory, faith and learning, special education, social and philosophical contexts of education. *Unit head:* Dr. Robin Duncan, Dean, School of Education, 951-552-8948, E-mail: rduncan@calbaptist.edu. *Application contact:* Dr. Shari Farris, Program Director, Online MS in Education, 951-343-2455, E-mail: sfarris@calbaptist.edu.
Website: http://www.calbaptist.edu/mastersined/

Capella University, School of Education, Doctoral Programs in Education, Minneapolis, MN 55402. Offers curriculum and instruction (PhD); educational leadership and management (Ed D); instructional design for online learning (PhD); K-12 studies in education (PhD); leadership for higher education (PhD); leadership in educational administration (PhD); postsecondary and adult education (PhD); professional studies in education (PhD); reading and literacy (Ed D); special education leadership (PhD); training and performance improvement (PhD).

Capella University, School of Education, Master's Programs in Education, Minneapolis, MN 55402. Offers adult education (MS); curriculum and instruction (MS); early childhood education (MS); enrollment management (MS); higher education leadership and management (MS); instructional design for online learning (MS); integrative studies (MS); K-12 studies in education (MS); leadership in educational administration (MS); reading and literacy (MS); special education teaching (MS).

Carroll University, Graduate Programs in Education, Waukesha, WI 53186-5593. Offers adult and continuing education (M Ed); educational leadership (MS); PK-12 (M Ed). *Program availability:* Part-time, evening/weekend. *Degree requirements:* For master's, thesis. *Entrance requirements:* For master's, minimum undergraduate GPA of 2.5 in related field. Additional exam requirements/recommendations for international students: Required—TOEFL. Electronic applications accepted. *Faculty research:* Qualitative research methods, whole language approaches to teaching, the writing process, multicultural education, gifted/talented learners.

Chicago State University, School of Graduate and Professional Studies, College of Education, Department of Educational Leadership, Curriculum and Foundations, Program in Curriculum and Instruction, Chicago, IL 60628. Offers instructional foundations (MS Ed), including adult education, elementary education, secondary education. *Degree requirements:* For master's, comprehensive exam, thesis optional. *Entrance requirements:* For master's, minimum GPA of 2.75.

Cleveland State University, College of Graduate Studies, College of Education and Human Services, Department of Counseling, Administration, Supervision and Adult Learning (CASAL), Cleveland, OH 44115. Offers adult learning and development (M Ed); counselor education (PhD); early childhood mental health counseling (Certificate); educational administration and supervision (M Ed). *Accreditation:* ACA (one or more programs are accredited). *Program availability:* Part-time, evening/weekend. *Faculty:* 15 full-time (8 women), 19 part-time/adjunct (10 women). *Students:* 134 full-time (118 women), 259 part-time (195 women); includes 131 minority (93 Black or African American, non-Hispanic/Latino; 2 American Indian or Alaska Native, non-Hispanic/Latino; 4 Asian, non-Hispanic/Latino; 23 Hispanic/Latino; 9 Two or more races, non-Hispanic/Latino), 11 international. Average age 33. 57 applicants, 93% accepted,

51 enrolled. In 2018, 119 master's, 1 other advanced degree awarded. *Degree requirements:* For master's, comprehensive exam (for some programs), thesis optional, internship. *Entrance requirements:* For master's, GRE General Test or MAT, letter of recommendation and minimum GPA of 2.75 (for counseling); 2 letters of recommendation and interviews (for organizational leadership). Additional exam requirements/recommendations for international students: Required—TOEFL (minimum score 550 paper-based; 78 iBT), IELTS (minimum score 6). *Application deadline:* For fall admission, 6/21 for domestic students, 5/15 for international students; for spring admission, 8/31 for domestic students, 11/1 for international students. Application fee: $40. Electronic applications accepted. *Expenses:* Tuition, state resident: full-time $7232.55; part-time $6676 per credit hour. Tuition, nonresident: full-time $12,375. *International tuition:* $18,914 full-time. *Required fees:* $80; $80 $40. Tuition and fees vary according to program. *Financial support:* In 2018–19, 19 students received support, including 10 research assistantships with tuition reimbursements available (averaging $11,882 per year), 5 teaching assistantships with tuition reimbursements available (averaging $11,882 per year); scholarships/grants and unspecified assistantships also available. Support available to part-time students. *Faculty research:* Education law, career development, bullying, psychopharmacology, counseling and spirituality. *Total annual research expenditures:* $225,821. *Unit head:* Dr. R. Elliott Ingersoll, Chair/Professor, 216-687-4582, Fax: 216-687-5378, E-mail: r.ingersoll@csuohio.edu. *Application contact:* Deborah L. Brown, Interim Assistant Director, Graduate Admissions, 216-523-7572, Fax: 216-687-5400, E-mail: d.l.brown@csuohio.edu.
Website: http://www.csuohio.edu/cehs/departments/CASAL/casal_dept.html

Cleveland State University, College of Graduate Studies, College of Education and Human Services, Program in Urban Education, Specialization in Adult, Continuing, and Higher Education, Cleveland, OH 44115. Offers PhD. *Program availability:* Part-time. *Faculty:* 4 full-time (3 women). *Students:* 3 full-time (2 women), 7 part-time (6 women); includes 3 minority (all Black or African American, non-Hispanic/Latino). Average age 41. In 2018, 1 doctorate awarded. *Entrance requirements:* For doctorate, GRE General Test (minimum score of 297 for combined Verbal and Quantitative exams, 4.0 preferred for Analytical Writing), minimum graduate GPA of 3.25, curriculum vitae or resume, personal statement, 2 letters of recommendation. Additional exam requirements/recommendations for international students: Required—TOEFL (minimum score 550 paper-based; 78 iBT), IELTS (minimum score 6). Application fee: $40. Electronic applications accepted. *Expenses:* Tuition, state resident: full-time $7232.55; part-time $6676 per credit hour. Tuition, nonresident: full-time $12,375. *International tuition:* $18,914 full-time. *Required fees:* $80; $80 $40. Tuition and fees vary according to program. *Financial support:* In 2018–19, 2 students received support. Research assistantships, teaching assistantships, and tuition waivers (full) available. Support available to part-time students. Financial award application deadline: 4/1; financial award applicants required to submit FAFSA. *Faculty research:* Adult education research, practice in diverse contexts. *Unit head:* Dr. Graham Stead, Director, Doctoral Studies, 216-875-9869, E-mail: g.b.stead@csuohio.edu. *Application contact:* Rita M. Grabowski, Administrative Coordinator, 216-687-4697, Fax: 216-875-9697, E-mail: r.grabowski@csuohio.edu.
Website: http://www.csuohio.edu/cehs/departments/DOC/lll_doc.html

Colorado State University, College of Health and Human Sciences, School of Education, Fort Collins, CO 80523-1588. Offers adult education and training (M Ed); counseling and career development (MA); education and human resources (M Ed); education, equity, and transformation (PhD); higher education leadership (PhD); organizational learning, performance, and change (M Ed, PhD); student affairs in higher education (MS). *Accreditation:* ACA; TEAC. *Program availability:* Part-time, online only, 100% online, blended/hybrid learning. *Degree requirements:* For master's, thesis optional, professional portfolio or capstone project; for doctorate, comprehensive exam, thesis/dissertation. *Entrance requirements:* For master's, bachelor's degree; minimum GPA of 3.0 in last degree earned; for doctorate, GRE; GRE or GMAT (for organizational learning, performance and change only), master's degree; minimum GPA of 3.0 in last degree earned. Additional exam requirements/recommendations for international students: Required—TOEFL (minimum score 550 paper-based; 80 iBT), IELTS (minimum score 6.5), PTE (minimum score 58). Electronic applications accepted. *Expenses:* Contact institution. *Faculty research:* Diversity, equity, and inclusion; STEM education; higher education; occupational learning, performance, and change; teacher education.

Concordia University, School of Graduate Studies, Faculty of Arts and Science, Department of Education, Program in Adult Education, Montréal, QC H3G 1M8, Canada. Offers Certificate, Diploma. *Degree requirements:* For other advanced degree, internship. *Entrance requirements:* For degree, interview. *Faculty research:* Staff development, human relations training, adult learning, professional development, learning in the workplace.

Concordia University, School of Graduate Studies, Faculty of Arts and Science, Department of Education, Program in Educational Studies, Montréal, QC H3G 1M8, Canada. Offers MA. *Degree requirements:* For master's, one foreign language, thesis optional. *Faculty research:* Social aspects of microtechnology, gender and education, minorities and immigrants in Canadian education, professional development, political education.

Coppin State University, School of Graduate Studies, School of Education, Department of Instruction Leadership and Professional Development, Program in Adult and Continuing Education, Baltimore, MD 21216-3698. Offers MS. *Program availability:* Part-time, evening/weekend. *Degree requirements:* For master's, thesis optional, research paper, internship. *Entrance requirements:* For master's, GRE or PRAXIS, minimum GPA of 2.5, interview, resume, references.

Cornell University, Graduate School, Graduate Fields of Agriculture and Life Sciences, Field of Education, Ithaca, NY 14853. Offers adult and extension education (MPS, MS, PhD); learning, teaching, and social policy (MPS, MS, PhD); mathematics 7-12 (MS). Terminal master's awarded for partial completion of doctoral program. *Degree requirements:* For master's, thesis (MS); for doctorate, comprehensive exam, thesis/dissertation. *Entrance requirements:* For master's and doctorate, GRE General Test, sample of written work (recommended), 2 letters of recommendation. Additional exam requirements/recommendations for international students: Required—TOEFL (minimum score 550 paper-based; 77 iBT). Electronic applications accepted. *Faculty research:* Moral development and professional ethics, public issues education and community development, socio/political issues in public education, teacher education and curriculum in agricultural science and mathematics, extension research.

Dallas Theological Seminary, Graduate Programs, Dallas, TX 75204-6499. Offers adult education (Th M); apologetics (Th M); Bible backgrounds (Th M); Bible translation (Th M); Biblical and theological studies (Certificate); biblical counseling (MA); biblical exegesis and linguistics (MA); biblical exposition (PhD); biblical studies (MA); Biblical theology (Th M); children's education (Th M); Christian education (MA, D Min); Christian leadership (MA); cross-cultural ministries (MA); educational administration (Th M); educational leadership (Th M); evangelism and discipleship (Th M); exposition of Biblical books (Th M); family life education (Th M); general studies (Th M); Hebrew and cognate studies (Th M); hermeneutics (Th M); historical theology (Th M); homiletics (Th M); intercultural ministries (Th M); Jesus studies (Th M); leadership studies (Th M); media and communication (MA); media arts (Th M); ministry (D Min); ministry with women (Th M); New Testament studies (Th M, PhD); Old Testament studies (Th M, PhD); parachurch ministries (Th M); pastoral care and counseling (Th M); pastoral theology and practice (Th M); philosophy (Th M); sacred theology (STM); spiritual formation (Th M); systematic theology (Th M); teaching in Christian institutions (Th M); theological studies (PhD); urban ministries (Th M); worship studies (Th M); youth education (Th M). *Program availability:* Part-time, online learning. *Degree requirements:* For master's, variable foreign language requirement, thesis (for some programs); for doctorate, 2 foreign languages, thesis/dissertation. *Entrance requirements:* For master's, GRE or MAT (if minimum undergraduate cumulative GPA is below 2.5 or undergraduate degree is unaccredited). Additional exam requirements/recommendations for international students: Required—TOEFL (minimum score 575 paper-based; 85 iBT), TWE. Electronic applications accepted.

Delaware State University, Graduate Programs, College of Education, Health and Public Policy, Program in Adult Literacy and Basic Education, Dover, DE 19901-2277. Offers MA. *Entrance requirements:* Additional exam requirements/recommendations for international students: Required—TOEFL (minimum score 550 paper-based). Electronic applications accepted.

DePaul University, School for New Learning, Chicago, IL 60604. Offers applied professional studies (MA); applied technology (MS); educating adults (MA). *Program availability:* Part-time, evening/weekend. *Degree requirements:* For master's, thesis or alternative. *Entrance requirements:* For master's, resume, interview, official transcript. Electronic applications accepted.

East Carolina University, Graduate School, College of Education, Department of Interdisciplinary Professions, Greenville, NC 27858-4353. Offers adult education (MA Ed); business and marketing education (MA Ed); community college instruction (Certificate); counselor education (MS); education in the healthcare professions (Certificate); library science (MLS); student affairs in higher education (Certificate); vocational education (MS). *Accreditation:* ACA; ALA; NCATE. *Program availability:* Part-time, evening/weekend. *Application deadline:* For fall admission, 5/15 priority date for domestic students. *Expenses: Tuition, area resident:* Full-time $4749. Tuition, state resident: full-time $4749. Tuition, nonresident: full-time $17,898. *International tuition:* $17,898 full-time. *Required fees:* $2787. Part-time tuition and fees vary according to course load and program. *Financial support:* Application deadline: 6/1. *Unit head:* Dr. Scott Glass, Professor, 252-328-5670, E-mail: glassj@ecu.edu. *Application contact:* Graduate School Admissions, 252-328-6012, Fax: 252-328-6071, E-mail: gradschool@ecu.edu.
Website: http://www.ecu.edu/cs-educ/idp/index.cfm

Eastern Washington University, Graduate Studies, College of Arts, Letters and Education, Department of Education, Program in Adult Education, Cheney, WA 99004-2431. Offers M Ed. *Degree requirements:* For master's, comprehensive exam, thesis or alternative. *Entrance requirements:* For master's, minimum GPA of 3.0. Additional exam requirements/recommendations for international students: Required—PTE (minimum score 63), TOEFL (minimum score 580 paper-based, 92 iBT) or IELTS (7). *Expenses:* Contact institution.

Florida Agricultural and Mechanical University, Division of Graduate Studies, Research, and Continuing Education, College of Education, Department of Educational Leadership and Human Services, Tallahassee, FL 32307-3200. Offers administration and supervision (M Ed, MS, PhD); adult education (M Ed, MS); educational leadership (PhD); guidance and counseling (M Ed, MS). *Accreditation:* NCATE. *Degree requirements:* For master's, thesis (for some programs); for doctorate, thesis/dissertation. *Entrance requirements:* For master's, GRE General Test, minimum GPA of 3.0. Additional exam requirements/recommendations for international students: Required—TOEFL.

Florida Atlantic University, College of Education, Department of Educational Leadership and Research Methodology, Boca Raton, FL 33431-0991. Offers adult and community education (M Ed, PhD, Ed S); educational leadership (M Ed, PhD, Ed S); higher education (M Ed, PhD); K-12 school leadership (M Ed, PhD, Ed S). *Accreditation:* NCATE. *Program availability:* Part-time, evening/weekend, online learning. *Faculty:* 22 full-time (12 women), 22 part-time/adjunct (11 women). *Students:* 91 full-time (56 women), 260 part-time (177 women); includes 172 minority (107 Black or African American, non-Hispanic/Latino; 5 Asian, non-Hispanic/Latino; 53 Hispanic/Latino; 7 Two or more races, non-Hispanic/Latino), 8 international. Average age 37. 226 applicants, 68% accepted, 131 enrolled. In 2018, 96 master's, 19 doctorates, 2 other advanced degrees awarded. *Degree requirements:* For doctorate, comprehensive exam, thesis/dissertation, departmental qualifying exam; for Ed S, departmental qualifying exam. *Entrance requirements:* For master's, GRE General Test, minimum GPA of 3.0 during previous 2 years; for doctorate, GRE General Test, minimum GPA of 3.5; for Ed S, GRE General Test. Additional exam requirements/recommendations for international students: Required—TOEFL (minimum score 500 paper-based; 61 iBT), IELTS (minimum score 6). *Application deadline:* For fall admission, 7/1 for domestic students, 2/15 for international students; for spring admission, 9/15 for domestic students, 7/15 for international students. Applications are processed on a rolling basis. Application fee: $30. Electronic applications accepted. *Expenses: Tuition, area resident:* Full-time $7400; part-time $369.82 per credit. Tuition, state resident: full-time $7400; part-time $369.82 per credit. Tuition, nonresident: full-time $20,496; part-time $1024.81 per credit. *Financial support:* Fellowships, research assistantships, teaching assistantships, career-related internships or fieldwork, and tuition waivers (partial) available. *Faculty research:* Self-directed learning, school reform issues, legal issues, mentoring, school leadership. *Unit head:* Dr. Robert E. Shockley, Chair, 561-297-3551, Fax: 561-297-3618, E-mail: shockley@fau.edu. *Application contact:* Kathy DuBois, Senior Secretary, 561-297-6551, Fax: 561-297-3618, E-mail: edleadership@fau.edu.
Website: http://www.coe.fau.edu/academicdepartments/el/

Florida International University, College of Arts, Sciences, and Education, Department of Leadership and Professional Studies, Miami, FL 33199. Offers adult education and human resource development (MS, Ed D); counseling (MS), including rehabilitation counseling, school counseling; counselor education (MS), including clinical mental health counseling; educational administration and supervision (Ed D); educational leadership (MS, Certificate, Ed S); higher education (Ed D); higher education administration (MS); international and comparative education (MS); recreation and sport management (MS), including recreation and sport management, recreational therapy; school psychology (Ed S); urban education (MS), including instruction in urban settings, learning technologies, multicultural/bilingual, multicultural/TESOL, urban education. *Program availability:* Part-time, evening/weekend. *Faculty:* 64 full-time (43 women), 104 part-time/adjunct (76 women). *Students:* 258 full-time (196 women), 217 part-time (155 women); includes 387 minority (118 Black or African American, non-Hispanic/Latino; 8 Asian, non-Hispanic/Latino; 249 Hispanic/Latino; 12 Two or more races, non-Hispanic/Latino), 11 international. Average age 31. 345 applicants, 57% accepted, 126 enrolled. In 2018, 172 master's, 11 doctorates awarded. *Entrance requirements:* For master's, minimum GPA of 3.0; for doctorate and other advanced degree, GRE General Test. Additional exam requirements/recommendations for international students: Required—TOEFL (minimum score 550 paper-based; 80 iBT),

IELTS (minimum score 6.3). *Application deadline:* For fall admission, 6/1 priority date for domestic students, 4/1 for international students; for winter admission, 10/1 priority date for domestic students, 9/1 for international students; for spring admission, 3/1 priority date for domestic students, 2/1 for international students. Applications are processed on a rolling basis. Application fee: $30. Electronic applications accepted. *Financial support:* Fellowships, research assistantships, teaching assistantships, Federal Work-Study, and tuition waivers (full and partial) available. Support available to part-time students. Financial award applicants required to submit FAFSA. *Unit head:* Dr. Benjamin Baez, Chair, 305-348-3214, Fax: 305-348-1515, E-mail: benjamin.baez@fiu.edu. *Application contact:* Nanett Rojas, Manager, Admissions Operations, 305-348-7464, Fax: 305-348-7441, E-mail: gradadm@fiu.edu.
Website: http://education.fiu.edu

The George Washington University, Graduate School of Education and Human Development, Department of Human and Organizational Learning, Program in Design and Assessment of Adult Learning, Washington, DC 20052. Offers Graduate Certificate. *Entrance requirements:* For degree, two letters of recommendation, resume, statement of purpose. Electronic applications accepted. *Unit head:* Michael Feuer, Dean, 202-994-6161, E-mail: mjfeuer@gwu.edu. *Application contact:* Sarah Lang, Director of Graduate Admissions, 202-994-1447, Fax: 202-994-7207, E-mail: slang@gwu.edu.
Website: http://gsehd.gwu.edu/

Grand Valley State University, College of Education, Programs in General Education, Allendale, MI 49401-9403. Offers adult and higher education (M Ed); early childhood education (M Ed); educational differentiation (M Ed); educational leadership (M Ed); educational technology integration (M Ed); elementary education (M Ed); middle level education (M Ed); school library media services (M Ed); secondary level education (M Ed); teaching English to speakers of other languages (M Ed). *Program availability:* Part-time, evening/weekend, 100% online, blended/hybrid learning. *Students:* 20 part-time (10 women); includes 1 minority (Black or African American, non-Hispanic/Latino). Average age 44. In 2018, 1 master's awarded. *Entrance requirements:* For master's, GRE General Test or minimum GPA of 3.0, last 60 credits from regionally-accredited college/university, 3 letters of recommendation. Additional exam requirements/recommendations for international students: Required—TOEFL (minimum iBT score of 80), IELTS (6.5), or Michigan English Language Assessment Battery (77). *Application deadline:* Applications are processed on a rolling basis. Application fee: $30. Electronic applications accepted. *Expenses:* $677 per credit hour, 33 credits. *Financial support:* In 2018–19, 1 student received support, including 1 fellowship; career-related internships or fieldwork, Federal Work-Study, scholarships/grants, and unspecified assistantships also available. *Faculty research:* Effectiveness of technology in education, parental involvement, effective teaching, effective schools research. *Unit head:* Dr. David Bair, Department Director, 616-331-6489, Fax: 616-331-6489, E-mail: baird@gvsu.edu. *Application contact:* Annukka Thelen, Director, Student Information and Services Center, 616-331-6205, Fax: 616-331-6217, E-mail: thelenan@gvsu.edu.
Website: http://www.gvsu.edu/coe/

Indiana University of Pennsylvania, School of Graduate Studies and Research, College of Education and Communications, Department of Adult and Community Education, Program in Adult and Community Education, Indiana, PA 15705. Offers MA. *Program availability:* Part-time, online learning. *Faculty:* 2 full-time (both women). *Students:* 1 (woman) full-time, 13 part-time (10 women); includes 6 minority (5 Black or African American, non-Hispanic/Latino; 1 Hispanic/Latino). Average age 34. 6 applicants, 67% accepted, 4 enrolled. In 2018, 3 master's awarded. *Degree requirements:* For master's, thesis optional. *Entrance requirements:* For master's, goal statement, letters of recommendation, official transcripts. Additional exam requirements/recommendations for international students: Required—TOEFL (minimum score 540 paper-based; 76 iBT). *Application deadline:* Applications are processed on a rolling basis. Application fee: $50. Electronic applications accepted. *Expenses:* Tuition, state resident: full-time $12,384; part-time $516 per credit hour. Tuition, nonresident: full-time $18,576; part-time $774 per credit hour. *Required fees:* $4454; $186 per credit hour. $65 per semester. Tuition and fees vary according to program and reciprocity agreements. *Financial support:* In 2018–19, 4 research assistantships with tuition reimbursements (averaging $2,250 per year) were awarded; career-related internships or fieldwork, Federal Work-Study, scholarships/grants, and unspecified assistantships also available. Support available to part-time students. Financial award application deadline: 4/15; financial award applicants required to submit FAFSA. *Unit head:* Prof. Jacqueline McGinty, Coordinator, 724-357-2470, E-mail: jacqueline.mcginty@iup.edu. *Application contact:* Prof. Jacqueline McGinty, Coordinator, 724-357-2470, E-mail: jacqueline.mcginty@iup.edu.
Website: http://www.iup.edu/grad/ace/default.aspx

Indiana University of Pennsylvania, School of Graduate Studies and Research, College of Education and Communications, Department of Adult and Community Education, Program in Adult and Community Education/Communications Technology, Indiana, PA 15705. Offers MA. *Program availability:* Part-time, evening/weekend. *Faculty:* 2 full-time (both women). *Students:* 1 (woman) full-time. Average age 38. 16 applicants, 81% accepted, 7 enrolled. In 2018, 15 master's awarded. *Degree requirements:* For master's, thesis optional. *Entrance requirements:* For master's, 2 letters of recommendation, resume. Additional exam requirements/recommendations for international students: Required—TOEFL (minimum score 540 paper-based; 76 iBT). *Application deadline:* Applications are processed on a rolling basis. Application fee: $50. Electronic applications accepted. *Expenses:* Tuition, state resident: full-time $12,384; part-time $516 per credit hour. Tuition, nonresident: full-time $18,576; part-time $774 per credit hour. *Required fees:* $4454; $186 per credit hour. $65 per semester. Tuition and fees vary according to program and reciprocity agreements. *Financial support:* Fellowships, research assistantships with tuition reimbursements, teaching assistantships, career-related internships or fieldwork, Federal Work-Study, scholarships/grants, and unspecified assistantships available. Support available to part-time students. Financial award application deadline: 4/15; financial award applicants required to submit FAFSA. *Unit head:* Prof. Jacqueline McGinty, Coordinator, 724-357-2470, E-mail: jacqueline.mcginty@iup.edu. *Application contact:* Prof. Jacqueline McGinty, Coordinator, 724-357-2470, E-mail: jacqueline.mcginty@iup.edu.
Website: http://www.iup.edu/aec

Instituto Tecnologico de Santo Domingo, Graduate School, Area of Humanities and Social Sciences, Santo Domingo, Dominican Republic. Offers accounting (Certificate); adult education (Certificate); applied linguistics (MA); economics (MA); education (M Ed); educational psychology (MA, Certificate); gender and development (MA, Certificate); humanistic studies (MA); international marketing management (Certificate); international relations in the Caribbean basin (Certificate); intervention systems in family therapy (MA); linguistic and literary communication (Certificate); pedagogical support (MA); social science education (M Ed); sustainable human development (MA); terminal illness and death psychology (Certificate); youth and adult education (M Ed).

Kansas State University, Graduate School, College of Education, Department of Educational Leadership, Manhattan, KS 66506. Offers adult learning (Certificate); educational leadership (MS, Ed D, PhD); leadership dynamics for adult learners (Certificate); qualitative research (Certificate); social justice education (Certificate); teaching English as a second language for adult learners (Certificate). *Accreditation:* NCATE. *Program availability:* Online learning. *Degree requirements:* For master's, comprehensive exam; for doctorate, comprehensive exam, thesis/dissertation. *Entrance requirements:* For master's, minimum undergraduate GPA of 3.0; for doctorate, MAT (for educational administration); GRE General Test (for adult education), minimum GPA of 3.0 in last 60 hours. Additional exam requirements/recommendations for international students: Required—TOEFL. Electronic applications accepted. *Faculty research:* Educational law, school finance, school facilities, organizational leadership, adult learning, distance learning/education.

Lesley University, Graduate School of Education, Cambridge, MA 02138-2790. Offers arts, community, and education (M Ed); autism studies (Certificate); curriculum and instruction (M Ed, CAGS); early childhood education (M Ed); ecological teaching and learning (MS); educational studies (PhD), including adult learning, educational leadership, individually designed; elementary education (M Ed); emergent technologies for educators (Certificate); ESLArts: language learning through the arts (M Ed); high school education (M Ed); individually designed (M Ed); integrated teaching through the arts (M Ed); literacy for K-8 classroom teachers (M Ed); mathematics education (M Ed); middle school education (M Ed); moderate disabilities (M Ed); online learning (Certificate); reading (CAGS); science in education (M Ed); severe disabilities (M Ed); special needs (CAGS); specialist teacher of reading (M Ed); teacher of visual art (M Ed); technology in education (M Ed, CAGS). *Accreditation:* TEAC. *Program availability:* Part-time, evening/weekend, online learning. *Degree requirements:* For master's, practicum; for doctorate, thesis/dissertation. *Entrance requirements:* For master's, Massachusetts Tests for Educator Licensure (MTEL), transcripts, statement of purpose, recommendations; interview (for special education); for doctorate, GRE General Test, transcripts, statement of purpose, recommendations, interview, master's degree, resume; for other advanced degree, interview, master's degree. Additional exam requirements/recommendations for international students: Required—TOEFL (minimum score 550 paper-based; 80 iBT). Electronic applications accepted. *Faculty research:* Assessment in literacy, mathematics and science; autism spectrum disorders; instructional technology and online learning; multicultural education and English language learners.

Marshall University, Academic Affairs Division, College of Education and Professional Development, Program in Adult and Continuing Education, Huntington, WV 25755. Offers MS. *Accreditation:* NCATE. *Program availability:* Evening/weekend. *Degree requirements:* For master's, thesis optional, comprehensive assessment.

Memorial University of Newfoundland, School of Graduate Studies, Faculty of Education, St. John's, NL A1C 5S7, Canada. Offers counseling psychology (M Ed); curriculum, teaching, and learning studies (M Ed); education (PhD); educational leadership studies (M Ed, Graduate Diploma); information technology (M Ed); post-secondary studies (M Ed, Diploma), including health professional education (Diploma). *Program availability:* Part-time. *Degree requirements:* For master's, thesis optional, internship, paper folio, project; for doctorate, comprehensive exam, thesis/dissertation, thesis seminar, oral defense of thesis. *Entrance requirements:* For master's, undergraduate degree with at least 2nd class standing, 1-2 years of work experience; for doctorate, minimum A average in graduate course work, MA in education, 2 years of professional experience; for other advanced degree, 2nd class degree, 2 years of work experience with adult learners, appropriate academic qualifications and work experience in a health-related field. Electronic applications accepted. *Faculty research:* Critical thinking, literacy, cognitive studies and counseling, educational change, technology in instruction.

Michigan State University, The Graduate School, College of Education, Department of Educational Administration, East Lansing, MI 48824. Offers higher, adult and lifelong education (MA, PhD); K–12 educational administration (MA, PhD, Ed S); student affairs administration (MA). *Program availability:* Part-time. *Entrance requirements:* Additional exam requirements/recommendations for international students: Required—TOEFL. Electronic applications accepted.

Montana State University, The Graduate School, College of Education, Health, and Human Development, Department of Education, Bozeman, MT 59717. Offers adult and higher education (Ed D); curriculum and instruction (M Ed, Ed D), including professional educator (M Ed), technology education (M Ed); education (M Ed), including adult and higher education, educational leadership, school counseling; educational leadership (Ed D, Ed S). *Accreditation:* TEAC. *Program availability:* Part-time, online learning. *Degree requirements:* For master's, comprehensive exam; for doctorate, comprehensive exam, thesis/dissertation. *Entrance requirements:* For master's, GRE, 3 letters of reference, essays, BA transcripts; for doctorate, GRE, MAT, 3 letters of reference, essay, BA and M Ed transcripts; for Ed S, PRAXIS. Additional exam requirements/recommendations for international students: Required—TOEFL (minimum score 550 paper-based). Electronic applications accepted. *Faculty research:* Critical literacy; standards-based education; school Improvement, organizational change, leadership in rural education, leadership in Indian education; student Learning; multicultural/culturally responsive education for social justice Native American indigenous education, community-centered education teacher preparation.

Morehead State University, Graduate School, College of Education, Department of Foundational and Graduate Studies in Education, Morehead, KY 40351. Offers adult and higher education (MA, Ed S); certified professional counselor (Ed S); counseling P-12 (MA); curriculum and instruction (Ed S); educational technology (MA Ed); instructional leadership (Ed S); school administration (MA); school counseling (Ed S); teacher leader business and marketing content (MA Ed); teacher leader business and marketing technology (MA Ed); teacher leader educational technology (MA Ed); teacher leader English (MA Ed); teacher leader gifted education (MA Ed); teacher leader IECE certification (MA Ed); teacher leader interdisciplinary education P-5 (MA Ed); teacher leader middle grades (MA Ed); teacher leader non IECE certification (MA Ed); teacher leader reading/writing - non-certification (MA Ed); teacher leader reading/writing certification (MA Ed); teacher leader school communication - certification (MA Ed); teacher leader school communication - non-certification (MA Ed); teacher leader social studies (MA Ed); teacher leader special education (MA Ed). *Accreditation:* NCATE. *Program availability:* Part-time, evening/weekend. *Degree requirements:* For master's, thesis optional, oral and/or written comprehensive exams; for Ed S, thesis, oral exam. *Entrance requirements:* For master's, GRE General Test, minimum overall undergraduate GPA of 2.5; for Ed S, GRE General Test, interview, master's degree, minimum GPA of 3.5, work experience. Additional exam requirements/recommendations for international students: Required—TOEFL (minimum score 500 paper-based). Electronic applications accepted. *Faculty research:* Character education, school accountability, computer applications for school administrators.

Mount Saint Vincent University, Graduate Programs, Faculty of Education, Program in Lifelong Learning, Halifax, NS B3M 2J6, Canada. Offers M Ed, MA Ed, MA-R. *Program availability:* Part-time, evening/weekend, online learning. *Degree requirements:* For master's, thesis (for some programs), practicum. *Entrance requirements:* For master's, bachelor's degree in related field, minimum B average. Electronic applications accepted.

National Louis University, College of Arts and Sciences, Chicago, IL 60603. Offers adult education (Ed D); counseling and human services (MS); language and academic

development (M Ed, Certificate); psychology (MA, PhD, Certificate); public policy (MA); written communication (MS, Certificate). *Program availability:* Part-time, evening/weekend, online learning. *Degree requirements:* For master's and Certificate, comprehensive exam (for some programs), thesis (for some programs); for doctorate, thesis/dissertation. *Entrance requirements:* For master's, MAT or GRE, 3 professional or academic references, interview, minimum GPA of 3.0; for doctorate, GRE General Test, MAT, or Watson-Glaser Critical Thinking Appraisal, three professional or academic references, statement of academic and professional goals, 3 years of experience in field, interview, master's degree, resume, writing sample; for Certificate, GRE, MAT, or Watson-Glaser Critical Thinking Appraisal, three professional or academic references, statement of academic and professional goals, interview, minimum GPA of 3.0. Additional exam requirements/recommendations for international students: Required—Department of Language Studies Assessment or TOEFL (minimum score 550 paper-based; 79 iBT). Electronic applications accepted.

North Carolina Agricultural and Technical State University, The Graduate College, College of Education, Department of Leadership Studies and Adult Education, Greensboro, NC 27411. Offers adult education (MS); interdisciplinary leadership studies (PhD). *Accreditation:* NCATE. *Program availability:* Part-time, evening/weekend. *Degree requirements:* For master's, comprehensive exam, comprehensive portfolio. *Entrance requirements:* For master's, GRE General Test, minimum GPA of 3.0.

North Carolina State University, Graduate School, College of Education, Department of Educational Leadership, Policy, and Human Development, Program in Adult and Community College Education, Raleigh, NC 27695. Offers M Ed, MS, Ed D. *Degree requirements:* For master's, thesis (for some programs); for doctorate, thesis/dissertation. *Entrance requirements:* For master's and doctorate, GRE or MAT. Electronic applications accepted.

Northern Illinois University, Graduate School, College of Education, Department of Counseling, Adult and Higher Education, De Kalb, IL 60115-2854. Offers adult and higher education (MS Ed, Ed D); counseling (MS Ed, Ed D). *Accreditation:* ACA. *Program availability:* Part-time, evening/weekend. *Faculty:* 19 full-time (11 women), 2 part-time/adjunct (1 woman). *Students:* 129 full-time (94 women), 225 part-time (158 women); includes 150 minority (68 Black or African American, non-Hispanic/Latino; 8 American Indian or Alaska Native, non-Hispanic/Latino; 12 Asian, non-Hispanic/Latino; 50 Hispanic/Latino; 12 Two or more races, non-Hispanic/Latino), 7 international. Average age 36. 158 applicants, 61% accepted, 67 enrolled. In 2018, 58 master's, 19 doctorates awarded. Terminal master's awarded for partial completion of doctoral program. *Degree requirements:* For master's, comprehensive exam, thesis optional; for doctorate, thesis/dissertation, candidacy exam, dissertation defense. *Entrance requirements:* For master's, GRE General Test or MAT, minimum undergraduate GPA of 2.75, interview (for counseling); for doctorate, GRE General Test, minimum undergraduate GPA of 2.75, 3.2 graduate; interview (for counseling). Additional exam requirements/recommendations for international students: Required—TOEFL (minimum score 550 paper-based). *Application deadline:* For fall admission, 6/1 for domestic students, 5/1 for international students; for spring admission, 11/1 for domestic students, 10/1 for international students. Applications are processed on a rolling basis. Application fee: $40. Electronic applications accepted. *Financial support:* In 2018–19, 15 research assistantships with full tuition reimbursements, 7 teaching assistantships with full tuition reimbursements were awarded; fellowships with full tuition reimbursements, career-related internships or fieldwork, Federal Work-Study, scholarships/grants, tuition waivers (full), and staff assistantships also available. Support available to part-time students. Financial award applicants required to submit FAFSA. *Unit head:* Dr. Suzanne Degges-White, Interim Chair, 815-753-1448, E-mail: cahe@niu.edu. *Application contact:* Graduate School Office, 815-753-0395, E-mail: gradsch@niu.edu. Website: http://www.cedu.niu.edu/cahe/index.html

Northwestern Oklahoma State University, School of Professional Studies, Program in Adult Education Management and Administration, Alva, OK 73717-2799. Offers M Ed. *Program availability:* Part-time. *Degree requirements:* For master's, thesis optional, portfolio. *Entrance requirements:* For master's, GRE or MAT, minimum GPA of 2.75.

Northwestern State University of Louisiana, Graduate Studies and Research, College of Education and Human Development, Program in Adult and Continuing Education, Natchitoches, LA 71497. Offers MA. *Degree requirements:* For master's, comprehensive exam, thesis or alternative. *Entrance requirements:* For master's, GRE General Test, minimum undergraduate GPA of 2.5. Additional exam requirements/recommendations for international students: Required—TOEFL. Electronic applications accepted.

Oregon State University, College of Education, Program in Adult and Higher Education, Corvallis, OR 97331. Offers Ed M, Ed D, PhD. *Accreditation:* NCATE. *Program availability:* Part-time, blended/hybrid learning. *Entrance requirements:* For master's, minimum GPA of 3.0 in last 90 hours. Additional exam requirements/recommendations for international students: Required—TOEFL (minimum score 575 paper-based).

Penn State Harrisburg, Graduate School, School of Behavioral Sciences and Education, Middletown, PA 17057. Offers adult education in the health and medical professions (Certificate); applied behavior analysis (MA); applied clinical psychology (MA); applied psychological research (MA); community psychology and social change (MA); English as a second language (ESL) program specialist and leadership (Certificate); health education (M Ed); lifelong learning and adult education (M Ed, D Ed); literacy education (M Ed); literacy leadership (Certificate); psychology: applications in clinical psychology (Certificate); psychology: health psychology (Certificate); teaching and curriculum (M Ed); training and development (M Ed, Certificate). *Program availability:* Part-time, evening/weekend.

Penn State University Park, Graduate School, College of Education, Department of Learning and Performance Systems, University Park, PA 16802. Offers learning, design, and technology (M Ed, MS, PhD, Certificate); lifelong learning and adult education (M Ed, D Ed, PhD, Certificate); workforce education and development (M Ed, MS, PhD).

Plymouth State University, College of Graduate Studies, Graduate Studies in Education, Program in Learning, Leadership and Community, Plymouth, NH 03264-1595. Offers Ed D.

Point Park University, School of Arts and Sciences, Department of Education, Pittsburgh, PA 15222-1984. Offers adult learning and training (MA); athletic coaching (M Ed); curriculum and instruction (MA); educational administration (MA); leadership and administration (Ed D); secondary education (M Ed); special education grades 7-12 (M Ed); special education PreK-grade 8 (M Ed). *Program availability:* Part-time, evening/weekend, 100% online, blended/hybrid learning. *Degree requirements:* For master's, comprehensive exam (for some programs), thesis or alternative. *Entrance requirements:* For master's, minimum GPA of 3.0, resume, 2 letters of recommendation. Additional exam requirements/recommendations for international students: Required—TOEFL. Electronic applications accepted.

Regent University, Graduate School, School of Education, Virginia Beach, VA 23464-9800. Offers education (M Ed, Ed D, PhD), including adult education (Ed D, PhD, Ed S), advanced educational leadership (Ed D, PhD, Ed S), character education (Ed D, PhD, Ed S), Christian education leadership (Ed D, PhD, Ed S), Christian school administration (M Ed), curriculum and instruction (Ed D, PhD, Ed S), curriculum and instruction - adult education (M Ed), curriculum and instruction - Christian school (M Ed), curriculum and instruction - gifted and talented (M Ed), curriculum and instruction - STEM education (M Ed), curriculum and instruction - teacher leader (M Ed), discipleship for ministry (M Ed), educational leadership (M Ed), educational psychology (Ed D, PhD, Ed S), educational technology and online learning (Ed D, PhD, Ed S), elementary education (M Ed), exceptional education executive leadership (Ed D, PhD, Ed S), higher education (Ed D, PhD, Ed S), higher education leadership and management (Ed D, PhD, Ed S), instructional design and technology (M Ed), K-12 school leadership (Ed D, PhD, Ed S), K-12 special education (M Ed), leadership in mathematics education (M Ed), reading specialist (M Ed), special education (Ed D, PhD, Ed S), student affairs (M Ed), TESOL - adult education (M Ed), TESOL - K-12 (M Ed); educational specialist (Ed S), including adult education (Ed D, PhD, Ed S), advanced educational leadership (Ed D, PhD, Ed S), character education (Ed D, PhD, Ed S), Christian education leadership (Ed D, PhD, Ed S), curriculum and instruction (Ed D, PhD, Ed S), educational psychology (Ed D, PhD, Ed S), educational technology and online learning (Ed D, PhD, Ed S), exceptional education executive leadership (Ed D, PhD, Ed S), higher education (Ed D, PhD, Ed S), higher education leadership and management (Ed D, PhD, Ed S), K-12 school leadership (Ed D, PhD, Ed S), special education (Ed D, PhD, Ed S). *Accreditation:* TEAC. *Program availability:* Part-time, evening/weekend, 100% online, blended/hybrid learning. *Degree requirements:* For master's, thesis or alternative; for doctorate, comprehensive exam, thesis/dissertation. *Entrance requirements:* For master's, Virginia Communication and Literacy Assessment (VCLA), PRAXIS, college transcripts, writing sample, interview; for doctorate, GRE, writing sample, resume, transcripts, interview. Additional exam requirements/recommendations for international students: Required—TOEFL (minimum score 577 paper-based). Electronic applications accepted. *Expenses:* Contact institution. *Faculty research:* Christian school administration, curriculum and instruction, educational technology and online learning, higher education, special education.

St. Francis Xavier University, Graduate Studies, Department of Adult Education, Antigonish, NS B2G 2W5, Canada. Offers adult education (M Ad Ed); community development (M Ad Ed). *Program availability:* Part-time, online learning. *Degree requirements:* For master's, thesis. *Entrance requirements:* For master's, minimum undergraduate B average, 2 years of work experience in field. Additional exam requirements/recommendations for international students: Required—TOEFL (minimum score 580 paper-based). *Expenses: Tuition, area resident:* Full-time $7547 Canadian dollars. Tuition, state resident: full-time $7547 Canadian dollars; part-time $804.19 Canadian dollars per course. Tuition, nonresident: full-time $8839 Canadian dollars; part-time $932.49 Canadian dollars per course. *International tuition:* $932.49 Canadian dollars full-time. *Required fees:* $90.20 Canadian dollars; $90.20 Canadian dollars per course. One-time fee: $6 Canadian dollars. Tuition and fees vary according to course load, degree level and program. *Faculty research:* Adult learning and development, religious education, women's issues, literacy, action research.

Saint Joseph's College of Maine, Master of Science in Education Program, Standish, ME 04084. Offers adult education and training (MS Ed); Catholic school leadership (MS Ed); health care educator (MS Ed); school educator (MS Ed). Program available by correspondence. *Program availability:* Part-time, online learning. Electronic applications accepted.

San Francisco State University, Division of Graduate Studies, College of Education, Department of Equity, Leadership Studies, and Instructional Technologies, Program in Adult Education, San Francisco, CA 94132-1722. Offers MA. *Accreditation:* NCATE. *Unit head:* Dr. Doris Flowers', Chair, 415-338-2614, Fax: 415-338-0568, E-mail: dflowers@sfsu.edu. *Application contact:* Dr. Ming Yeh Lee, Graduate Coordinator, 415-338-1061, Fax: 415-338-0568, E-mail: mylee@sfsu.edu. Website: http://elsit.sfsu.edu/

Seattle University, College of Education, Program in Adult Education and Training, Seattle, WA 98122-1090. Offers M Ed, MA, Certificate. *Accreditation:* NCATE. *Program availability:* Part-time, evening/weekend. *Faculty:* 1 (woman) full-time, 2 part-time/adjunct (1 woman). *Students:* 2 full-time (both women), 14 part-time (10 women); includes 7 minority (2 Black or African American, non-Hispanic/Latino; 1 Asian, non-Hispanic/Latino; 2 Hispanic/Latino; 2 Two or more races, non-Hispanic/Latino). Average age 34. 9 applicants, 67% accepted, 5 enrolled. In 2018, 11 master's awarded. *Degree requirements:* For master's, comprehensive exam. *Entrance requirements:* For master's, GRE, MAT, or minimum GPA of 3.0; 1 year of related experience. Additional exam requirements/recommendations for international students: Required—TOEFL. *Application deadline:* For fall admission, 8/20 priority date for domestic students; for winter admission, 11/20 for domestic students; for spring admission, 2/20 for domestic students. Applications are processed on a rolling basis. Application fee: $55. *Financial support:* In 2018–19, 2 students received support. Career-related internships or fieldwork and Federal Work-Study available. Support available to part-time students. Financial award applicants required to submit FAFSA. *Unit head:* Dr. Carol Weaver, Director, 206-296-5908, E-mail: cweaver@seattleu.edu. *Application contact:* Janet Shandley, Associate Dean of Graduate Admissions, 206-296-5900, Fax: 206-298-5656, E-mail: grad_admissions@seattleu.edu. Website: https://www.seattleu.edu/education/adulted/

Southern Arkansas University–Magnolia, School of Graduate Studies, Magnolia, AR 71753. Offers agriculture (MS); business administration (MBA), including agribusiness, social entrepreneurship, supply chain management; clinical and mental health counseling (MS); computer and information sciences (MS), including cyber security and privacy, data science, information technology; gifted and talented (M Ed), including curriculum and instruction, educational administration and supervision, gifted and talented P-8/7-12, instructional specialist P-4; higher, adult and lifelong education (M Ed); kinesiology (M Ed), including coaching; library media and information specialist (M Ed); public administration (MPA); school counseling K-12 (M Ed); student affairs and college counseling (M Ed); teaching (MAT). *Accreditation:* NCATE. *Program availability:* Part-time, 100% online, blended/hybrid learning. *Faculty:* 36 full-time (21 women), 32 part-time/adjunct (15 women). *Students:* 164 full-time (77 women), 762 part-time (510 women); includes 192 minority (163 Black or African American, non-Hispanic/Latino; 7 American Indian or Alaska Native, non-Hispanic/Latino; 13 Asian, non-Hispanic/Latino; 1 Hispanic/Latino; 8 Two or more races, non-Hispanic/Latino), 213 international. Average age 28. 363 applicants, 100% accepted, 237 enrolled. In 2018, 716 master's awarded. *Degree requirements:* For master's, comprehensive exam (for some programs), thesis optional. *Entrance requirements:* For master's, GRE, MAT or GMAT, minimum GPA of 2.5. Additional exam requirements/recommendations for international students: Required—TOEFL (minimum score 550 paper-based), IELTS (minimum score 6). *Application deadline:* For fall admission, 8/1 for domestic and international students; for spring admission, 12/1 for domestic students, 11/15 for international students; for summer admission, 4/1 for domestic students, 5/10 for international students. Applications are processed on a rolling basis. Application fee: $25 ($90 for international students). Electronic applications accepted. *Expenses: Tuition, area resident:* Full-time $5130; part-time $3420 per year. Tuition, state resident: full-time $5130; part-time $3420 per year. Tuition, nonresident: full-time $7866; part-time $5244 per year.

International tuition: $7866 full-time. *Required fees:* $1052; $710 per unit. Tuition and fees vary according to course load. *Financial support:* Career-related internships or fieldwork, Federal Work-Study, scholarships/grants, tuition waivers (full), and unspecified assistantships available. Financial award applicants required to submit FAFSA. *Faculty research:* Alternative certification for teachers, supervision of instruction, instructional leadership, counseling. *Unit head:* Dr. Kim Bloss, Dean, School of Graduate Studies, 870-235-4150, Fax: 870-235-5227, E-mail: kkbloss@saumag.edu. *Application contact:* Talia Jett, Admissions Coordinator, 870-2355450, Fax: 870-235-5227, E-mail: taliajett@saumag.edu.
Website: http://www.saumag.edu/graduate

State University of New York Empire State College, School for Graduate Studies, Programs in Education, Saratoga Springs, NY 12866-4391. Offers adult learning (MA); learning and emerging technologies (MA); teaching (MAT); teaching and learning (M Ed). *Program availability:* Online learning.

Teachers College, Columbia University, Department of Organization and Leadership, New York, NY 10027-6696. Offers adult education guided intensive study (Ed D); adult learning and leadership (Ed M, MA, Ed D); educational leadership (Ed D); higher and postsecondary education (MA, Ed D); leadership, policy and politics (Ed D); nurse executive (MA, Ed D), including administration studies (MA), professorial studies (MA); private school leadership (Ed M, MA); public school building leadership (Ed M, MA); social and organizational psychology (MA); urban education leaders (Ed D); MA/MBA. *Program availability:* Part-time, evening/weekend. *Students:* 249 full-time (165 women), 427 part-time (299 women); includes 275 minority (99 Black or African American, non-Hispanic/Latino; 75 Asian, non-Hispanic/Latino; 82 Hispanic/Latino; 1 Native Hawaiian or other Pacific Islander, non-Hispanic/Latino; 18 Two or more races, non-Hispanic/Latino), 84 international. Average age 34. 770 applicants, 59% accepted, 267 enrolled. *Unit head:* Prof. Bill Baldwin, Chair, 212-678-3043, E-mail: wjb12@tc.columbia.edu. *Application contact:* Kelly Sutton-Skinner, Director of Admission & New Student Enrollment, E-mail: kms2237@tc.columbia.edu.

Texas A&M University–Kingsville, College of Graduate Studies, College of Education and Human Performance, Department of Educational Leadership and Counseling, Program in Adult Education, Kingsville, TX 78363. Offers M Ed. Program offered jointly with Texas A&M University. *Program availability:* Part-time, evening/weekend. *Degree requirements:* For master's, variable foreign language requirement, comprehensive exam, thesis (for some programs). *Entrance requirements:* For master's, GRE, MAT, GMAT. Additional exam requirements/recommendations for international students: Required—TOEFL (minimum score 550 paper-based; 79 iBT). Electronic applications accepted. *Faculty research:* Continuing education efforts in south Texas, adult education methodologies.

Texas A&M University–Texarkana, Graduate Studies and Research, College of Education and Liberal Arts, Texarkana, TX 75503. Offers adult education (MS); curriculum and instruction (M Ed); education (MS); educational administration (M Ed); English (MA); instructional technology (MS); interdisciplinary studies (MA, MS); special education (MS). *Program availability:* Part-time, evening/weekend. *Degree requirements:* For master's, comprehensive exam (for some programs), thesis optional. *Entrance requirements:* For master's, minimum GPA of 2.5 on last 60 hours of bachelor's degree. Additional exam requirements/recommendations for international students: Required—TOEFL. Electronic applications accepted.

Texas State University, The Graduate College, College of Education, Program in Adult Education, San Marcos, TX 78666. Offers MA. *Program availability:* Part-time. *Faculty:* 7 full-time (4 women). *Students:* 3 full-time (1 woman), 13 part-time (10 women); includes 9 minority (2 Black or African American, non-Hispanic/Latino; 3 Asian, non-Hispanic/Latino; 4 Hispanic/Latino). Average age 39. 10 applicants, 60% accepted, 5 enrolled. In 2018, 8 master's awarded. *Degree requirements:* For master's, comprehensive exam, thesis optional, internship practicum. *Entrance requirements:* For master's, baccalaureate degree from regionally-accredited university; minimum GPA of 2.75 on last 60 undergraduate semester hours of letter-grade work earned at four-year college or university before receipt of bachelor's degree (plus any previously completed graduate work); 3 letters of recommendation; writing sample addressing current adult education issue. Additional exam requirements/recommendations for international students: Required—TOEFL (minimum score 78 iBT), IELTS (minimum score 6.5). *Application deadline:* For fall admission, 2/1 priority date for domestic and international students; for spring admission, 10/15 for domestic students, 10/1 for international students; for summer admission, 4/15 for domestic and international students. Applications are processed on a rolling basis. Application fee: $55 ($90 for international students). Electronic applications accepted. *Expenses:* Tuition, state resident: full-time $8102; part-time $4051 per semester. Tuition, nonresident: full-time $18,229; part-time $9115 per semester. *International tuition:* $18,229 full-time. *Required fees:* $2116; $120 per credit hour. Tuition and fees vary according to course load. *Financial support:* In 2018–19, 5 students received support. Research assistantships, teaching assistantships, scholarships/grants, and unspecified assistantships available. Financial award application deadline: 1/15; financial award applicants required to submit FAFSA. *Faculty research:* Adult learning in study abroad; Immigrants to the US and adult education services; Disabilities and adult and lifelong education; a multicultural perspective on informed consent; Partnering with industry: a community college model for corporate training;. *Total annual research expenditures:* $15,723. *Unit head:* Dr. Clarena Larrotta, Graduate Advisor, 512-245-2531, E-mail: cl24@txstate.edu. *Application contact:* Dr. Andrea Golato, Dean of Graduate School, 512-245-2581, Fax: 512-245-8365, E-mail: gradcollege@txstate.edu.
Website: http://www.gradcollege.txstate.edu/programs/adult-ed.html

Texas State University, The Graduate College, College of Education, Program in Adult, Professional and Community Education, San Marcos, TX 78666. Offers PhD. *Program availability:* Part-time. *Faculty:* 7 full-time (4 women). *Students:* 17 full-time (14 women), 39 part-time (25 women); includes 31 minority (9 Black or African American, non-Hispanic/Latino; 1 Asian, non-Hispanic/Latino; 20 Hispanic/Latino; 1 Two or more races, non-Hispanic/Latino), 3 international. Average age 40. 38 applicants, 37% accepted, 9 enrolled. In 2018, 15 doctorates awarded. *Degree requirements:* For doctorate, comprehensive exam, thesis/dissertation. *Entrance requirements:* For doctorate, baccalaureate and master's degrees from regionally-accredited institution with minimum GPA of 3.5 in all related graduate course work; 3 complete recommendation forms addressing professional and academic background; statement of purpose including rationale for doctoral degree; interview with program faculty. Additional exam requirements/recommendations for international students: Required—TOEFL (minimum score 550 paper-based; 78 iBT), IELTS (minimum score 6.5). *Application deadline:* For fall admission, 2/1 for domestic and international students. Applications are processed on a rolling basis. Application fee: $55 ($90 for international students). Electronic applications accepted. *Expenses:* Tuition, state resident: full-time $8102; part-time $4051 per semester. Tuition, nonresident: full-time $18,229; part-time $9115 per semester. *International tuition:* $18,229 full-time. *Required fees:* $2116; $120 per credit hour. Tuition and fees vary according to course load. *Financial support:* In 2018–19, 29 students received support, including 8 research assistantships (averaging $26,081 per year); teaching assistantships, career-related internships or fieldwork, Federal Work-Study, institutionally sponsored loans, and scholarships/grants also available. Support available to part-time students. Financial award application deadline: 1/15; financial award applicants required to submit FAFSA. *Faculty research:* Adult learning in study abroad; Immigrants to the US and adult education services; Disabilities and adult and lifelong education; a multicultural perspective on informed consent; Partnering with industry: a community college model for corporate training. *Total annual research expenditures:* $15,723. *Unit head:* Dr. Joellen Coryell, PhD Program Director, 512-245-2531, Fax: 512-245-8872, E-mail: jc59@txstate.edu. *Application contact:* Dr. Andrea Golato, Dean of Graduate School, 512-245-2531, Fax: 512-245-8365, E-mail: gradcollege@txstate.edu.
Website: http://www.gradcollege.txstate.edu/programs/apce-phd.html

Trident University International, College of Education, Program in Education, Cypress, CA 90630. Offers adult education (MA Ed); aviation education (MA Ed); children's literacy development (MA Ed); e-learning (MA Ed); early childhood education (MA Ed); enrollment management (MA Ed); higher education (MA Ed); teaching and instruction (MA Ed); training and development (MA Ed). *Program availability:* Part-time, evening/weekend, online learning. *Degree requirements:* For master's, capstone project with integrative paper. *Entrance requirements:* For master's, minimum GPA of 2.5 (students with GPA 3.0 or greater may transfer up to 30% of graduate level credits). Additional exam requirements/recommendations for international students: Required—TOEFL (minimum score 525 paper-based). Electronic applications accepted.

Troy University, Graduate School, College of Education, Program in Adult Education, Troy, AL 36082. Offers MS. *Program availability:* Part-time, evening/weekend. *Faculty:* 5 full-time (2 women), 3 part-time/adjunct (0 women). *Students:* 15 full-time (7 women), 73 part-time (56 women); includes 35 minority (32 Black or African American, non-Hispanic/Latino; 1 American Indian or Alaska Native, non-Hispanic/Latino; 1 Asian, non-Hispanic/Latino; 1 Two or more races, non-Hispanic/Latino). Average age 40. 62 applicants, 94% accepted, 37 enrolled. In 2018, 31 master's awarded. *Degree requirements:* For master's, comprehensive exam, capstone course or thesis. *Entrance requirements:* For master's, GRE (minimum score of 850 on old exam or 290 on new exam), GMAT (minimum score of 380), or MAT (minimum score of 385), bachelor's degree; minimum undergraduate GPA of 2.5 or 3.0 on last 30 semester hours, letter of recommendation. Additional exam requirements/recommendations for international students: Required—TOEFL (minimum score 523 paper-based; 70 iBT), IELTS (minimum score 6). *Application deadline:* Applications are processed on a rolling basis. Application fee: $50. Electronic applications accepted. *Expenses: Tuition, area resident:* Full-time $425; part-time $425 per credit hour. Tuition, state resident: full-time $425; part-time $425 per credit hour. Tuition, nonresident: full-time $850; part-time $850 per credit hour. *International tuition:* $850 full-time. *Required fees:* $50 per semester. Tuition and fees vary according to campus/location and program. *Financial support:* Fellowships, career-related internships or fieldwork, and scholarships/grants available. Support available to part-time students. Financial award applicants required to submit FAFSA. *Unit head:* Dr. Trellys Riley, Assoc. Professor, Assistant Dean Chair, Adult Education, 334-241-9575, E-mail: tariley@troy.edu. *Application contact:* Jessica A. Kimbro, Assistant Director of Graduate Programs, 334-670-3189, E-mail: jacord@troy.edu.
Website: https://www.troy.edu/academics/academic-programs/college-education-programs.php

Troy University, Graduate School, College of Education, Program in Postsecondary Education, Troy, AL 36082. Offers MS Ed. *Accreditation:* NCATE. *Program availability:* Part-time, evening/weekend. *Faculty:* 1 (woman) full-time. *Students:* Average age 36. 7 applicants, 86% accepted, 3 enrolled. In 2018, 2 master's awarded. *Degree requirements:* For master's, comprehensive exam (for some programs), thesis (for some programs), thesis or comprehensive exam. *Entrance requirements:* For master's, GRE (minimum score of 850 on old exam or 290 on new exam), GMAT (minimum score of 380), or MAT (minimum score of 385), bachelor's degree; minimum undergraduate GPA of 2.5 or 3.0 on last 30 semester hours, letter of recommendation. Additional exam requirements/recommendations for international students: Required—TOEFL (minimum score 523 paper-based; 70 iBT), IELTS (minimum score 6). *Application deadline:* Applications are processed on a rolling basis. Application fee: $50. Electronic applications accepted. *Expenses: Tuition, area resident:* Full-time $425; part-time $425 per credit hour. Tuition, state resident: full-time $425; part-time $425 per credit hour. Tuition, nonresident: full-time $850; part-time $850 per credit hour. *International tuition:* $850 full-time. *Required fees:* $50 per semester. Tuition and fees vary according to campus/location and program. *Financial support:* Fellowships, career-related internships or fieldwork, and scholarships/grants available. Support available to part-time students. Financial award applicants required to submit FAFSA. *Unit head:* Dr. Fred Figliano, Assistant Professor, Chair, Teacher Education, 334-808-6509, E-mail: ffigliano@troy.edu. *Application contact:* Jessica A. Kimbro, Assistant Director of Graduate Programs, 334-670-3189, E-mail: jacord@troy.edu.

Universidad del Este, Graduate School, Carolina, PR 00984. Offers accounting (MBA); adult education (M Ed); agribusiness (MBA); criminal justice and criminology (MA); curriculum and instruction - early education (M Ed); curriculum and instruction - elementary (M Ed); curriculum and instruction - English (M Ed); curriculum and instruction - Spanish (M Ed); human resources (MBA); information security management (MBA); information technology and Web business development (MBA); management (MBA); public policy (MPA); social work (MA), including clinical social work; special education (M Ed); strategic leadership (MBA).

Universidad Metropolitana, School of Education, Program in Teaching of Physical Education, San Juan, PR 00928-1150. Offers teaching of adult physical education (M Ed); teaching of elementary physical education (M Ed); teaching of secondary physical education (M Ed). *Degree requirements:* For master's, thesis or alternative. *Entrance requirements:* For master's, EXADEP, interview. Electronic applications accepted.

University of Alberta, Faculty of Graduate Studies and Research, Department of Educational Policy Studies, Edmonton, AB T6G 2E1, Canada. Offers adult education (M Ed, Ed D, PhD); educational administration and leadership (M Ed, Ed D, PhD, Postgraduate Diploma); First Nations education (M Ed, Ed D, PhD); theoretical, cultural and international studies in education (M Ed, Ed D, PhD). *Degree requirements:* For master's, thesis (for some programs); for doctorate, thesis/dissertation. *Entrance requirements:* For master's, minimum GPA of 6.5 on a 9.0 scale; for doctorate, minimum GPA of 7.5 on a 9.0 scale. Additional exam requirements/recommendations for international students: Required—TOEFL (minimum score 580 paper-based). Electronic applications accepted.

University of Arkansas, Graduate School, College of Education and Health Professions, Department of Rehabilitation, Human Resources and Communication Disorders, Adult and Lifelong Learning Program, Fayetteville, AR 72701. Offers M Ed, Ed D. *Program availability:* Part-time, evening/weekend, online learning. In 2018, 3 master's, 4 doctorates awarded. *Application deadline:* For fall admission, 8/1 for domestic students, 4/1 for international students; for spring admission, 12/1 for domestic students, 10/1 for international students; for summer admission, 4/15 for domestic students, 3/1 for international students. Applications are processed on a rolling basis. Application fee: $60. Electronic applications accepted. *Financial support:* Fellowships, research assistantships, teaching assistantships, career-related internships or fieldwork, and Federal Work-Study available. Support available to part-time students. Financial

award application deadline: 4/1; financial award applicants required to submit FAFSA. *Unit head:* Dr. Michael Hevel, Department Chair, 479-575-4924, Fax: 479-575-3119, E-mail: hevel@uark.edu. *Application contact:* Kenda Grover, Assistant Prof. of Adult and Lifelong Learning, 479-575-2675, E-mail: kgrover@uark.edu.
Website: http://adll.uark.edu

University of Arkansas at Little Rock, Graduate School, College of Education and Health Professions, Department of Counseling, Adult and Rehabilitation Education, Program in Adult Education, Little Rock, AR 72204-1099. Offers M Ed. *Accreditation:* NCATE. *Program availability:* Part-time, online learning. *Degree requirements:* For master's, comprehensive exam. *Entrance requirements:* For master's, minimum GPA of 2.75. *Faculty research:* Adult literacy, volunteer training, in-services education.

The University of British Columbia, Faculty of Education, Department of Educational Studies, Vancouver, BC V6T 1Z1, Canada. Offers adult learning and education (M Ed); adult learning and global change (M Ed); curriculum and leadership (M Ed); educational administration and leadership (M Ed); educational leadership and policy (Ed D); educational studies (M Ed, MA, PhD); higher education (M Ed); society, culture and politics in education (M Ed). *Program availability:* Part-time, evening/weekend. Terminal master's awarded for partial completion of doctoral program. *Degree requirements:* For master's, thesis; for doctorate, comprehensive exam, thesis/dissertation. *Entrance requirements:* For master's, minimum B+ average, 4-year undergraduate degree, field-related experience; for doctorate, minimum B+ average, 4-year undergraduate degree, master's degree, field-related experience. Additional exam requirements/recommendations for international students: Required—TOEFL (minimum score 600 paper-based; 100 iBT) or IELTS (minimum score 6.5). Electronic applications accepted. *Expenses:* Contact institution. *Faculty research:* Educational leadership educational administration adult education politics in education, global change and adult learning.

University of Calgary, Faculty of Graduate Studies, Werklund School of Education, Program in Educational Research, Calgary, AB T2N 1N4, Canada. Offers adult learning (M Ed, MA, Ed D, PhD); curriculum and learning (M Ed, MA, Ed D, PhD); educational leadership (M Ed, MA, Ed D, PhD); languages and diversity (M Ed, MA, Ed D, PhD); learning sciences (M Ed, MA, Ed D, PhD). Ed D in educational leadership offered via distance delivery. *Program availability:* Part-time, evening/weekend, online learning. *Degree requirements:* For master's, thesis (for some programs); for doctorate, thesis/dissertation, candidacy exam. *Entrance requirements:* For master's, minimum GPA of 3.0, 3 letters of reference; for doctorate, minimum GPA of 3.5, 3 letters of reference. Additional exam requirements/recommendations for international students: Required—TOEFL, IELTS. Electronic applications accepted. *Faculty research:* Curriculum, leadership, technology, contexts, gifted, second language teaching, work place and adult learning.

University of Central Arkansas, Graduate School, College of Education, Department of Leadership Studies, Conway, AR 72035-0001. Offers college student personnel (MS); district-level administration (PMC); educational leadership - district level (Ed S); instructional technology (MS); library media and information technology (MS); school counseling (MS); school leadership (MS); school-based leadership adult education program administration (PMC); school-based leadership building administration (PMC); school-based leadership curriculum administration (PMC); school-based leadership gifted and talented program administration (PMC); school-based leadership special education program administration (PMC). *Accreditation:* NCATE. *Program availability:* Part-time, evening/weekend, online learning. *Degree requirements:* For master's and other advanced degree, comprehensive exam. *Entrance requirements:* For master's, GRE. Additional exam requirements/recommendations for international students: Required—TOEFL (minimum score 80 iBT). Electronic applications accepted. *Expenses:* Contact institution.

University of Central Oklahoma, The Jackson College of Graduate Studies, College of Education and Professional Studies, Department of Adult Education and Safety Science, Edmond, OK 73034-5209. Offers adult and higher education (M Ed), including interdisciplinary studies, student personnel, training. *Program availability:* Part-time. *Degree requirements:* For master's, comprehensive exam (for some programs), thesis (for some programs). *Entrance requirements:* Additional exam requirements/recommendations for international students: Required—TOEFL (minimum score 550 paper-based; 79 iBT), IELTS (minimum score 6.5). Electronic applications accepted.

University of Colorado Denver, School of Education and Human Development, Information and Learning Technologies Program, Denver, CO 80217. Offers e-learning design and implementation (MA); instructional design and adult learning (MA); K-12 teaching (MA). *Program availability:* Part-time, evening/weekend, online learning. *Degree requirements:* For master's, comprehensive exam (for some programs), comprehensive exam or online portfolio; 30 credit hours. *Entrance requirements:* For master's, GRE or MAT (if GPA is below 2.75), resume, statement of intent, three letters of recommendation, transcripts from all colleges/universities previously attended. Additional exam requirements/recommendations for international students: Required—TOEFL (minimum score 537 paper-based; 75 iBT); Recommended—IELTS (minimum score 6.5). Electronic applications accepted. *Expenses:* Contact institution. *Faculty research:* Technology for educational management, instructional design foundations, e-learning, educational design.

University of Connecticut, Graduate School, Neag School of Education, Department of Educational Leadership, Field of Adult Learning, Storrs, CT 06269. Offers MA, Certificate. *Accreditation:* NCATE. Terminal master's awarded for partial completion of doctoral program. *Degree requirements:* For master's, comprehensive exam, thesis or alternative. *Entrance requirements:* For master's, GRE General Test. Additional exam requirements/recommendations for international students: Required—TOEFL (minimum score 550 paper-based). Electronic applications accepted.

University of Georgia, College of Education, Department of Lifelong Education, Administration and Policy, Athens, GA 30602. Offers adult education (Ed D, Ed S); lifelong education, administration and policy (PhD). *Accreditation:* NCATE. *Entrance requirements:* For doctorate, GRE General Test; for Ed S, GRE General Test or MAT. Electronic applications accepted.

University of Houston–Victoria, School of Education, Health Professions and Human Development, Victoria, TX 77901-4450. Offers administration and supervision (M Ed); adult and higher education (M Ed); counselor education (M Ed); curriculum and instruction (M Ed); dyslexia education (Certificate); educational technology (M Ed); special education (M Ed). *Program availability:* Part-time, evening/weekend, online learning. *Degree requirements:* For master's, comprehensive exam, project or thesis. *Entrance requirements:* For master's, GRE General Test. Additional exam requirements/recommendations for international students: Required—TOEFL. Electronic applications accepted. *Expenses: Tuition, area resident:* Full-time $6154; part-time $3077 per semester. Tuition, state resident: full-time $6154; part-time $3077 per semester. Tuition, nonresident: full-time $13,624; part-time $6812 per semester. *International tuition:* $13,624 full-time. *Required fees:* $1405; $847 per semester. $423 per semester. Tuition and fees vary according to program. *Faculty research:* Reading and language arts education, evaluation and diagnosis of special children's abilities.

University of Manitoba, Faculty of Graduate Studies, Faculty of Education, Department of Educational Administration, Foundations and Psychology, Winnipeg, MB R3T 2N2, Canada. Offers adult and post-secondary education (M Ed); educational administration (M Ed); guidance and counseling (M Ed); inclusive special education (M Ed); social foundations of education (M Ed). *Degree requirements:* For master's, thesis or alternative.

University of Memphis, Graduate School, College of Education, Department of Leadership, Memphis, TN 38152. Offers adult education (Ed D); community college teaching and leadership (Graduate Certificate); community education (Ed D); educational leadership (Ed D); higher education (Ed D); leadership (MS); policy studies (Ed D); school administration and supervision (MS); student personnel (MS). *Accreditation:* NCATE. *Program availability:* Part-time, evening/weekend, online learning. *Students:* 19 full-time (12 women), 137 part-time (90 women); includes 87 minority (80 Black or African American, non-Hispanic/Latino; 2 Asian, non-Hispanic/Latino; 4 Hispanic/Latino; 1 Two or more races, non-Hispanic/Latino), 1 international. Average age 41. 44 applicants, 98% accepted, 37 enrolled. In 2018, 11 master's, 17 doctorates, 2 other advanced degrees awarded. *Degree requirements:* For master's, comprehensive exam, thesis optional; for doctorate, comprehensive exam, thesis/dissertation. *Entrance requirements:* For master's, GRE, resume, letters of reference, statement of professional goals, current teacher certification, sample work, interview; for doctorate, GRE, resume, letters of reference, statement of professional goals, interview. Additional exam requirements/recommendations for international students: Required—TOEFL (minimum score 550 paper-based; 79 iBT). *Application deadline:* For fall admission, 6/15 for domestic students; for spring admission, 9/15 for domestic students; for summer admission, 2/15 for domestic students. Application fee: $35 ($60 for international students). Electronic applications accepted. *Expenses: Tuition, area resident:* Full-time $10,240; part-time $503 per credit hour. Tuition, state resident: full-time $10,464. Tuition, nonresident: full-time $20,224; part-time $991 per credit hour. *Required fees:* $850; $106 per credit hour. *Financial support:* Research assistantships with full tuition reimbursements, teaching assistantships, Federal Work-Study, scholarships/grants, and unspecified assistantships available. Financial award application deadline: 2/1; financial award applicants required to submit FAFSA. *Faculty research:* School improvement, social justice, online learning, adult learning, diversity. *Unit head:* Dr. R Eric Platt, Interim Chair, 901-678-4229, E-mail: replatt@memphis.edu. *Application contact:* Dr. R Eric Platt, Interim Chair, 901-678-4229, E-mail: replatt@memphis.edu.
Website: http://www.memphis.edu/lead

University of Minnesota, Twin Cities Campus, Graduate School, College of Education and Human Development, Department of Organizational Leadership, Policy and Development, Minneapolis, MN 55455-0213. Offers adult literacy (Certificate); comparative and international development education (MA, PhD); disability policy and services (Certificate); education policy and leadership (M Ed, MA, Ed D, PhD), including educational policy and leadership (MA, Ed D, PhD), leadership in education (M Ed); evaluation studies (MA, PhD); higher education (MA, Ed D, PhD), including higher education (MA, PhD), multicultural college teaching and learning (MA); human resource development (M Ed, MA, Ed D, PhD, Certificate); PK-12 administrative licensure (Certificate); private college leadership (Certificate); professional development (Certificate); program evaluation (Certificate); technical education (Certificate); undergraduate multicultural teaching and learning (Certificate). *Faculty:* 33 full-time (16 women). *Students:* 332 full-time (220 women), 194 part-time (139 women); includes 130 minority (46 Black or African American, non-Hispanic/Latino; 5 American Indian or Alaska Native, non-Hispanic/Latino; 37 Asian, non-Hispanic/Latino; 22 Hispanic/Latino; 20 Two or more races, non-Hispanic/Latino), 75 international. Average age 36. 379 applicants, 68% accepted, 187 enrolled. In 2018, 67 master's, 39 doctorates, 64 other advanced degrees awarded. Application fee: $75 ($95 for international students). *Financial support:* In 2018–19, 6 fellowships, 34 research assistantships with full tuition reimbursements (averaging $10,071 per year), 17 teaching assistantships with full tuition reimbursements (averaging $9,608 per year) were awarded; scholarships/grants also available. *Faculty research:* Organizational issues in schools, universities, and other organizations; international education and development; program evaluation and research on applied evaluation methods; international human resource development and change; gender and race/ethnicity in relation to learning and leadership. *Total annual research expenditures:* $732,047. *Unit head:* Dr. Kenneth Bartlett, Chair, 612-625-1006, Fax: 612-624-3377, E-mail: bartlett@umn.edu. *Application contact:* Dr. Jeremy J. Hernandez, Coordinator of Graduate Studies, 612-626-9377, E-mail: olpd@umn.edu.
Website: http://www.cehd.umn.edu/olpd/

University of Missouri, Office of Research and Graduate Studies, College of Education, Department of Educational Leadership and Policy Analysis, Columbia, MO 65211. Offers education administration (M Ed, MA, Ed D, PhD, Ed S); higher and adult education (M Ed, MA, Ed D, PhD, Ed S). *Program availability:* Part-time. *Entrance requirements:* For master's, doctorate, and Ed S, minimum GPA of 3.0.

University of Missouri–St. Louis, College of Education, Department of Education Sciences and Professional Programs, St. Louis, MO 63121. Offers adult and higher education (M Ed); educational psychology (M Ed), including character and citizenship education, research and program evaluation; program evaluation (Certificate); school psychology (Ed S). *Degree requirements:* For other advanced degree, comprehensive exam, thesis or alternative, internship. *Entrance requirements:* For degree, GRE General Test, 2-4 letters of recommendation, personal interview. Additional exam requirements/recommendations for international students: Required—IELTS (minimum score 6.5); Recommended—TOEFL (minimum score 550 paper-based; 79 iBT). Electronic applications accepted. *Faculty research:* Child/adolescent psychology, quantitative and qualitative methodology, evaluation processes, measurement and assessment.

University of Nebraska–Lincoln, Graduate College, College of Education and Human Sciences, Department of Teaching, Learning and Teacher Education, Lincoln, NE 68588. Offers adult and continuing education (MA); educational studies (Ed D, PhD), including special education (Ed D); teaching, learning and teacher education (M Ed, MA, MST, Ed D, PhD); vocational and adult education (M Ed, MA). *Accreditation:* NCATE. *Degree requirements:* For master's, thesis optional. *Entrance requirements:* Additional exam requirements/recommendations for international students: Required—TOEFL (minimum score 550 paper-based). Electronic applications accepted. *Faculty research:* Teacher education, instructional leadership, literacy education, technology, improvement of school curriculum.

The University of North Carolina at Greensboro, Graduate School, School of Education, Department of Teacher Education and Higher Education, Greensboro, NC 27412-5001. Offers college teaching and adult learning (Certificate); curriculum and instruction (M Ed), including chemistry education, elementary education, English as a second language, French education, instructional technology, mathematics education, middle grades education, reading education, science education, social studies education, Spanish education; curriculum and teaching (PhD), including higher education, teacher education and development; English as a second language (Certificate); higher education (M Ed); supervision (M Ed). *Accreditation:* NCATE. *Program availability:* Part-time. *Degree requirements:* For doctorate, thesis/dissertation. *Entrance requirements:* For master's and doctorate, GRE General Test. Additional exam

requirements/recommendations for international students: Required—TOEFL. Electronic applications accepted. *Faculty research:* Community college literacy program, middle school mathematics/computer mathematics.

University of North Florida, College of Education and Human Services, Department of Foundations and Secondary Education, Jacksonville, FL 32224. Offers adult learning (M Ed); professional education (M Ed). *Accreditation:* NCATE. *Program availability:* Part-time, evening/weekend. *Faculty:* 13 full-time (6 women). *Students:* 4 part-time (3 women); includes 3 minority (1 Asian, non-Hispanic/Latino; 2 Two or more races, non-Hispanic/Latino). Average age 30. 1 applicant, 100% accepted, 1 enrolled. In 2018, 6 master's awarded. *Entrance requirements:* For master's, GRE General Test, minimum GPA of 3.0 in last 60 hours, interview, 3 letters of recommendation. Additional exam requirements/recommendations for international students: Required—TOEFL (minimum score 500 paper-based; 61 iBT). *Application deadline:* For fall admission, 5/1 for international students; for spring admission, 10/1 for international students. Application fee: $30. Electronic applications accepted. *Expenses: Tuition, area resident:* Part-time $408.10 per credit hour. Tuition, state resident: part-time $408.10 per credit hour. Tuition, nonresident: part-time $932.61 per credit hour. *Required fees:* $111.81 per credit hour. Tuition and fees vary according to course load, campus/location and program. *Financial support:* Research assistantships, teaching assistantships, career-related internships or fieldwork, Federal Work-Study, and tuition waivers (partial) available. Support available to part-time students. Financial award application deadline: 4/1; financial award applicants required to submit FAFSA. *Faculty research:* Using children's literature to enhance metalinguistic awareness, education, oral language diagnosis of middle-schoolers, science inquiry teaching and learning. *Total annual research expenditures:* $173,438. *Unit head:* Dr. Jeffery Cornett, Chair, 904-620-2610, Fax: 904-620-1821, E-mail: jcornett@unf.edu. *Application contact:* Dr. Amanda Pascale, Director, The Graduate School, 904-620-1360, Fax: 904-620-1362, E-mail: graduateschool@unf.edu.
Website: http://www.unf.edu/coehs/fse/

University of Oklahoma, Jeannine Rainbolt College of Education, Department of Educational Leadership and Policy Studies, Norman, OK 73019. Offers adult and higher education (M Ed, PhD), including adult and higher education; educational administration, curriculum and supervision (M Ed, Ed D, PhD); educational studies (M Ed, PhD). *Accreditation:* NCATE. *Program availability:* Part-time, evening/weekend, blended/hybrid learning. Terminal master's awarded for partial completion of doctoral program. *Degree requirements:* For master's, comprehensive exam, thesis (for some programs); for doctorate, comprehensive exam, thesis/dissertation. *Entrance requirements:* Additional exam requirements/recommendations for international students: Required—TOEFL (minimum score 79 iBT) or IELTS (minimum score 6.5). Electronic applications accepted. *Expenses:* Tuition, state resident: full-time $5683.20; part-time $236.80 per credit hour. Tuition, nonresident: full-time $20,342; part-time $847.60 per credit hour. *International tuition:* $20,342.40 full-time. *Required fees:* $2894.20; $110.05 per credit hour. $126.50 per semester. Tuition and fees vary according to course load and program. *Faculty research:* Improvement science, leadership and ethics, education and social policy, gender and equity, collegiate athletics.

University of Phoenix–Bay Area Campus, College of Education, San Jose, CA 95134-1805. Offers administration and supervision (MA Ed); adult education and training (MA Ed); early childhood education (MA Ed); education (Ed S); educational leadership (Ed D); elementary teacher education (MA Ed); higher education administration (PhD); secondary teacher education (MA Ed); special education (MA Ed); teacher leadership (MA Ed). *Program availability:* Evening/weekend, online learning. *Degree requirements:* For master's, thesis (for some programs). *Entrance requirements:* For master's, minimum undergraduate GPA of 2.5, 3 years of work experience. Additional exam requirements/recommendations for international students: Required—TOEFL (minimum score 550 paper-based; 79 iBT). Electronic applications accepted.

University of Phoenix–Online Campus, College of Education, Phoenix, AZ 85034-7209. Offers administration and supervision (MAEd, Certificate); adult education and training (MAEd); curriculum and instruction (MAEd), including computer education, curriculum and instruction, English as a second language, language arts, mathematics, reading; early childhood education (MAEd); educational studies (MAEd); elementary teacher education (MAEd), including early childhood, elementary teacher education, high school middle level, middle level; principal licensure (Certificate); secondary teacher education (MAEd); special education (MAEd, Certificate); teacher education (MAEd), including middle level generalist; teacher education middle level mathematics (MAEd), including middle level mathematics; teacher education middle level science (MAEd), including middle level science; teacher education secondary mathematics (MAEd); teacher education secondary science (MAEd); teacher leadership (MAEd); teachers of English learners (Certificate); transition to teaching (Certificate), including elementary education, secondary education. *Program availability:* Evening/weekend, online learning. *Entrance requirements:* Additional exam requirements/recommendations for international students: Required—TOEFL, TOEIC (Test of English as an International Communication), Berlitz Online English Proficiency Exam, PTE, or IELTS. Electronic applications accepted. *Expenses:* Contact institution.

University of Phoenix–Phoenix Campus, College of Education, Tempe, AZ 85282-2371. Offers administration and supervision (MA Ed); adult education and training (MA Ed); curriculum and instruction reading (MA Ed); early childhood education (MA Ed); education studies (MA Ed); elementary teacher education (MA Ed); secondary teacher education (MA Ed); special education (MA Ed); teacher leadership (MA Ed). *Program availability:* Evening/weekend, online learning. *Entrance requirements:* Additional exam requirements/recommendations for international students: Required—TOEFL, TOEIC (Test of English as an International Communication), Berlitz Online English Proficiency Exam, PTE, or IELTS. Electronic applications accepted. *Expenses:* Contact institution.

University of Phoenix–Sacramento Valley Campus, College of Education, Sacramento, CA 95833-4334. Offers adult education (MA Ed); curriculum instruction (MA Ed); elementary teacher education (MA Ed); secondary teacher education (MA Ed); teacher education (Certificate). *Program availability:* Evening/weekend. *Degree requirements:* For master's, thesis (for some programs). *Entrance requirements:* For master's, 3 years of work experience, minimum undergraduate GPA of 2.5. Additional exam requirements/recommendations for international students: Required—TOEFL (minimum score 550 paper-based; 79 iBT). Electronic applications accepted.

University of Regina, Faculty of Graduate Studies and Research, Faculty of Education, Department of Adult Education, Regina, SK S4S 0A2, Canada. Offers MA Ed. *Program availability:* Part-time. *Faculty:* 3 full-time (2 women). *Students:* 3 full-time (all women), 12 part-time (9 women). Average age 30. 4 applicants, 75% accepted. In 2018, 10 master's awarded. *Degree requirements:* For master's, thesis (for some programs), practicum, project, or thesis. *Entrance requirements:* For master's, bachelor's degree in education, 2 years of teaching or other relevant professional experience. Additional exam requirements/recommendations for international students: Required—TOEFL (minimum score 580 paper-based; 80 iBT), IELTS (minimum score 6.5), PTE (minimum score 59), options are CAEL, MELAB, Cantest and U of R ESL. *Application deadline:* For fall admission, 2/15 for domestic and international students; for winter admission, 10/15 for domestic and international students; for spring admission, 2/15 for domestic students. Application fee: $100. Electronic applications accepted. Tuition and fees vary according to course level, course load, degree level and program. *Financial support:* Fellowships, research assistantships, teaching assistantships, career-related internships or fieldwork, Federal Work-Study, scholarships/grants, unspecified assistantships, and travel award and Graduate Scholarship Base funds available. Support available to part-time students. Financial award application deadline: 9/30. *Unit head:* Dr. Twyla Salm, Associate Dean, Research and Graduate Programs in Education, 306-585-4604, Fax: 306-585-4006, E-mail: Twyla.Salm@uregina.ca. *Application contact:* Linda Jiang, Graduate Program Coordinator, 306-585-4506, Fax: 306-585-5387, E-mail: edgrad@uregina.ca.
Website: http://www.uregina.ca/education/

University of South Africa, College of Human Sciences, Pretoria, South Africa. Offers adult education (M Ed); African languages (MA, PhD); African politics (MA, PhD); Afrikaans (MA, PhD); ancient history (MA, PhD); ancient Near Eastern studies (MA, PhD); anthropology (MA, PhD); applied linguistics (MA); Arabic (MA, PhD); archaeology (MA); art history (MA); Biblical archaeology (MA); Biblical studies (M Th, D Th, PhD); Christian spirituality (M Th, D Th); church history (M Th, D Th); classical studies (MA, PhD); clinical psychology (MA); communication (MA, PhD); comparative education (M Ed, Ed D); consulting psychology (D Admin, D Com, PhD); curriculum studies (M Ed, Ed D); development studies (M Admin, MA, D Admin, PhD); didactics (M Ed, Ed D); education (M Tech); education management (M Ed, Ed D); educational psychology (M Ed); English (MA); environmental education (M Ed); French (MA, PhD); German (MA, PhD); Greek (MA); guidance and counseling (M Ed); health studies (MA, PhD), including health sciences education (MA), health services management (MA), medical and surgical nursing science (critical care general) (MA), midwifery and neonatal nursing science (MA), trauma and emergency care (MA); history (MA, PhD); history of education (Ed D); inclusive education (M Ed, Ed D); information and communications technology policy and regulation (MA); information science (MA, MIS, PhD); international politics (MA, PhD); Islamic studies (MA, PhD); Italian (MA, PhD); Judaica (MA, PhD); linguistics (MA, PhD); mathematical education (M Ed); mathematics education (MA); missiology (M Th, D Th); modern Hebrew (MA, PhD); musicology (MA, MMus, D Mus, PhD); natural science education (M Ed); New Testament (M Th, D Th); Old Testament (D Th); pastoral therapy (M Th, D Th); philosophy (MA); philosophy of education (M Ed, Ed D); politics (MA, PhD); Portuguese (MA, PhD); practical theology (M Th, D Th); psychology (MA, MS, PhD); psychology of education (M Ed, Ed D); public health (MA); religious studies (MA, D Th, PhD); Romance languages (MA); Russian (MA, PhD); Semitic languages (MA, PhD); social behavior studies in HIV/AIDS (MA); social science (mental health) (MA); social science in development studies (MA); social science in psychology (MA); social science in social work (MA); social science in sociology (MA); social work (MSW, DSW, PhD); socio-education (M Ed, Ed D); sociolinguistics (MA); sociology (MA, PhD); Spanish (MA, PhD); systematic theology (M Th, D Th); TESOL (teaching English to speakers of other languages) (MA); theological ethics (M Th, D Th); theory of literature (MA, PhD); urban ministries (D Th); urban ministry (M Th).

University of South Dakota, Graduate School, School of Education, Division of Educational Leadership, Vermillion, SD 57069. Offers educational administration (MA, Ed D, Ed S), including adult and higher education (MA, Ed D), curriculum director, director of special education (Ed D, Ed S), preK-12 principal, school district superintendent (Ed D, Ed S). *Accreditation:* NCATE. *Program availability:* Part-time, evening/weekend, 100% online, blended/hybrid learning. *Degree requirements:* For master's and Ed S, comprehensive exam, thesis or alternative; for doctorate, comprehensive exam, thesis/dissertation. *Entrance requirements:* For master's, GRE General Test, MAT, minimum GPA of 2.7; for doctorate, minimum GPA of 2.7. Additional exam requirements/recommendations for international students: Required—TOEFL (minimum score 550 paper-based; 79 iBT). Electronic applications accepted.

University of Southern Maine, College of Management and Human Service, School of Education and Human Development, Program in Adult Education, Portland, ME 04103. Offers adult and higher education (MS); adult learning (CAS). *Accreditation:* TEAC. *Program availability:* Part-time, evening/weekend, online learning. *Degree requirements:* For master's and CAS, thesis or alternative. *Entrance requirements:* For master's, interview; for CAS, master's degree. Additional exam requirements/recommendations for international students: Required—TOEFL (minimum score 550 paper-based; 79 iBT). Electronic applications accepted. *Faculty research:* Older learners, lifelong learning institutes, teaching and learning in later age.

University of South Florida, College of Education, Department of Leadership, Counseling, Adult, Career and Higher Education, Tampa, FL 33620-9951. Offers adult education (MA, Ed D, PhD, Ed S); career and technical education (MA); career and workforce education (PhD); higher education/community college teaching (MA, Ed D, PhD); vocational education (Ed S). *Faculty:* 19 full-time (11 women). *Students:* 107 full-time (81 women), 275 part-time (185 women); includes 143 minority (67 Black or African American, non-Hispanic/Latino; 2 American Indian or Alaska Native, non-Hispanic/Latino; 10 Asian, non-Hispanic/Latino; 56 Hispanic/Latino; 8 Two or more races, non-Hispanic/Latino), 14 international. Average age 36. 188 applicants, 54% accepted, 73 enrolled. In 2018, 51 master's, 8 doctorates, 3 other advanced degrees awarded. *Entrance requirements:* For master's, GRE may be required, goals statement; letters of recommendation; proof of educational or professional experience; prerequisites, if needed; for doctorate, GRE may be required, letters of recommendation; masters degree in appropriate field; optional interview; evidence of professional experience; personal statement. Additional exam requirements/recommendations for international students: Required—TOEFL. Application fee: $30. *Expenses:* Tuition, state resident: full-time $6350. Tuition, nonresident: full-time $19,048. *International tuition:* $19,048 full-time. *Required fees:* $2079. *Financial support:* In 2018–19, 19 students received support. *Total annual research expenditures:* $40,520. *Unit head:* Dr. Judith Ponticell, Chair, 813-974-4897, Fax: 813-974-5423, E-mail: jponticell@usf.edu. *Application contact:* Dr. Judith Ponticell, Chair, 813-974-4897, Fax: 813-974-5423, E-mail: jponticell@usf.edu.
Website: http://www.coedu.usf.edu/main/departments/ache/ache.html

University of South Florida, Innovative Education, Tampa, FL 33620-9951. Offers adult, career and higher education (Graduate Certificate), including college teaching, leadership in developing human resources, leadership in higher education; Africana studies (Graduate Certificate), including diasporas and health disparities, genocide and human rights; aging studies (Graduate Certificate), including gerontology; art research (Graduate Certificate), including museum studies; business foundations (Graduate Certificate); chemical and biomedical engineering (Graduate Certificate), including materials science and engineering, water, health and sustainability; child and family studies (Graduate Certificate), including positive behavior support; civil and industrial engineering (Graduate Certificate), including transportation systems analysis; community and family health (Graduate Certificate), including maternal and child health, social marketing and public health, violence and injury: prevention and intervention, women's health; criminology (Graduate Certificate), including criminal justice administration; data science for public administration (Graduate Certificate); digital humanities (Graduate Certificate); educational measurement and research (Graduate Certificate), including evaluation; English (Graduate Certificate), including comparative

literary studies, creative writing, professional and technical communication; entrepreneurship (Graduate Certificate); environmental health (Graduate Certificate), including safety management; epidemiology and biostatistics (Graduate Certificate), including applied biostatistics, biostatistics, concepts and tools of epidemiology, epidemiology, epidemiology of infectious diseases; geography, environment and planning (Graduate Certificate), including community development, environmental policy and management, geographical information systems; geology (Graduate Certificate), including hydrogeology; global health (Graduate Certificate), including disaster management, global health and Latin American and Caribbean studies, global health practice, humanitarian assistance, infection control; government and international affairs (Graduate Certificate), including Cuban studies, globalization studies; health policy and management (Graduate Certificate), including health management and leadership, public health policy and programs; hearing specialist: early intervention (Graduate Certificate); industrial and management systems engineering (Graduate Certificate), including systems engineering, technology management; information studies (Graduate Certificate), including school library media specialist; information systems/decision sciences (Graduate Certificate), including analytics and business intelligence; instructional technology (Graduate Certificate), including distance education, Florida digital/virtual educator, instructional design, multimedia design, Web design; internal medicine, bioethics and medical humanities (Graduate Certificate), including biomedical ethics; Latin American and Caribbean studies (Graduate Certificate); leadership for coastal resiliency planning (Graduate Certificate); mass communications (Graduate Certificate), including multimedia journalism; mathematics and statistics (Graduate Certificate), including mathematics; medicine (Graduate Certificate), including aging and neuroscience, bioinformatics, biotechnology, brain fitness and memory management, clinical investigation, hand and upper limb rehabilitation, health informatics, health sciences, integrative weight management, intellectual property, medicine and gender, metabolic and nutritional medicine, metabolic cardiology, pharmacy sciences; national and competitive intelligence (Graduate Certificate); nursing (Graduate Certificate), including simulation based academic fellowship in advanced pain management; psychological and social foundations (Graduate Certificate), including career counseling, college teaching, diversity in education, mental health counseling, school counseling; public affairs (Graduate Certificate), including nonprofit management, public management, research administration; public health (Graduate Certificate), including assessing chemical toxicity and public health risks, health equity, pharmacoepidemiology, public health generalist, toxicology, translational research in adolescent behavioral health; public health practices (Graduate Certificate), including planning for healthy communities; rehabilitation and mental health counseling (Graduate Certificate), including integrative mental health care, marriage and family therapy, rehabilitation technology; secondary education (Graduate Certificate), including ESOL, foreign language education: culture and content, foreign language education: professional; social work (Graduate Certificate), including geriatric social work/clinical gerontology; special education (Graduate Certificate), including autism spectrum disorder, disabilities education: severe/profound; world languages (Graduate Certificate), including teaching English as a second language (TESL) or foreign language. *Expenses:* Tuition, state resident: full-time $6350. Tuition, nonresident: full-time $19,048. *International tuition:* $19,048 full-time. *Required fees:* $2079. *Unit head:* Dr. Cynthia DeLuca, Associate Vice President and Assistant Vice Provost, 813-974-3077, Fax: 813-974-7061, E-mail: deluca@usf.edu. *Application contact:* Owen Hooper, Director, Summer and Alternative Calendar Programs, 813-974-6917, E-mail: hooper@usf.edu.
Website: http://www.usf.edu/innovative-education/

The University of Tennessee, Graduate School, College of Education, Health and Human Sciences, Department of Educational Psychology and Counseling, Knoxville, TN 37996. Offers adult education (MS); applied educational psychology (MS); collaborative learning (Ed D); college student personnel (MS); mental health counseling (MS); rehabilitation counseling (MS); school counseling (MS). *Accreditation:* ACA (one or more programs are accredited); CORE (one or more programs are accredited); NCATE. *Program availability:* Part-time, evening/weekend. *Degree requirements:* For master's, thesis optional. *Entrance requirements:* For master's, GRE General Test, minimum GPA of 2.7. Additional exam requirements/recommendations for international students: Required—TOEFL. Electronic applications accepted.

University of the District of Columbia, College of Arts and Sciences, Program in Adult Education, Washington, DC 20008-1175. Offers Graduate Certificate.

The University of West Alabama, School of Graduate Studies, College of Education, Program in Continuing Education, Livingston, AL 35470. Offers counseling and psychology (MSCE); general (MSCE); library media (MSCE). *Accreditation:* NCATE. *Program availability:* Part-time, evening/weekend, 100% online. *Faculty:* 10 full-time (8 women), 53 part-time/adjunct (35 women). *Students:* 157 full-time (133 women), 2 part-time (both women); includes 105 minority (102 Black or African American, non-Hispanic/Latino; 1 Hispanic/Latino; 2 Two or more races, non-Hispanic/Latino), 2 international. Average age 35. 44 applicants, 98% accepted, 35 enrolled. In 2018, 57 master's awarded. *Degree requirements:* For master's, comprehensive exam, thesis optional. *Entrance requirements:* For master's, GRE, minimum GPA of 2.75. Additional exam requirements/recommendations for international students: Required—TOEFL (minimum score 500 paper-based; 61 iBT). *Application deadline:* Applications are processed on a rolling basis. Application fee: $40. Electronic applications accepted. *Expenses: Tuition, area resident:* Full-time $9100. Tuition, state resident: full-time $9100. Tuition, nonresident: full-time $19,200. *Required fees:* $1890; $130. *Financial support:* Teaching assistantships, Federal Work-Study, scholarships/grants, and unspecified assistantships available. Support available to part-time students. Financial award application deadline: 3/1; financial award applicants required to submit FAFSA. *Unit head:* Dr. Jodie Winship, Chair of College of Education, 205-652-5415, E-mail: jwinship@uwa.edu. *Application contact:* Dr. B. J. Kimbrough, Dean of Graduate Studies, 205-652-3647, Fax: 205-652-3670, E-mail: bkimbrough@uwa.edu.

University of Wisconsin–Milwaukee, Graduate School, College of Letters and Science, Department of Linguistics, Milwaukee, WI 53201-0413. Offers linguistics (MA, PhD), including teaching English to speakers of other languages (MA); teaching English to speakers of other languages, adult- and university-level (Graduate Certificate). *Students:* 21 full-time (10 women), 12 part-time (8 women); includes 2 minority (both Two or more races, non-Hispanic/Latino), 18 international. Average age 34. 56 applicants, 25% accepted, 7 enrolled. In 2018, 1 master's, 4 doctorates, 1 other advanced degree awarded. Electronic applications accepted. *Unit head:* Hamid Ouali, Department Chair, 414-229-1113, E-mail: ouali@uwm.edu. *Application contact:* General Information Contact, 414-229-4982, Fax: 414-229-6967, E-mail: gradschool@uwm.edu.
Website: http://www4.uwm.edu/letsci/linguistics/

University of Wisconsin–Milwaukee, Graduate School, School of Education, Department of Administrative Leadership, Milwaukee, WI 53201-0413. Offers administrative leadership (MS), including adult and continuing education leadership, educational administration and supervision, higher education administration; support services for online students in higher education (Graduate Certificate); teaching and learning in higher education (Graduate Certificate). *Program availability:* Part-time. *Students:* 12 full-time (10 women), 163 part-time (124 women); includes 51 minority (19 Black or African American, non-Hispanic/Latino; 5 American Indian or Alaska Native, non-Hispanic/Latino; 4 Asian, non-Hispanic/Latino; 3 Hispanic/Latino; 20 Two or more races, non-Hispanic/Latino). Average age 35. 98 applicants, 70% accepted, 43 enrolled. In 2018, 43 master's, 3 other advanced degrees awarded. *Degree requirements:* For master's, comprehensive exam, thesis or alternative. *Entrance requirements:* For master's, GRE General Test. Additional exam requirements/recommendations for international students: Required—TOEFL (minimum score 550 paper-based; 79 iBT), IELTS (minimum score 6.5). *Application deadline:* For fall admission, 1/1 priority date for domestic students; for spring admission, 9/1 for domestic students. Application fee: $56 ($96 for international students). Electronic applications accepted. *Financial support:* In 2018–19, 2 fellowships were awarded; research assistantships, teaching assistantships, career-related internships or fieldwork, health care benefits, unspecified assistantships, and project assistantships also available. Support available to part-time students. Financial award application deadline: 4/15; financial award applicants required to submit FAFSA. *Unit head:* Alan Shoho, Dean, 414-229-4181, E-mail: shoho@uwm.edu. *Application contact:* General Information Contact, 414-229-4721, E-mail: soeinfo@uwm.edu.
Website: http://uwm.edu/education/academics/administrative-leadership-department/

University of Wisconsin–Milwaukee, Graduate School, School of Education, Department of Exceptional Education, Milwaukee, WI 53201-0413. Offers autism spectrum disorders (Graduate Certificate); exceptional education (MS); transition for students with disabilities (Graduate Certificate); urban education (PhD), including adult, continuing and higher education leadership, art education, curriculum and instruction, exceptional education, mathematics education, multicultural studies, social foundations of education. *Program availability:* Part-time. *Students:* 38 full-time (29 women), 67 part-time (50 women); includes 39 minority (23 Black or African American, non-Hispanic/Latino; 1 American Indian or Alaska Native, non-Hispanic/Latino; 6 Asian, non-Hispanic/Latino; 1 Hispanic/Latino; 8 Two or more races, non-Hispanic/Latino), 2 international. Average age 40. 47 applicants, 40% accepted, 11 enrolled. In 2018, 13 master's, 14 doctorates, 4 other advanced degrees awarded. *Entrance requirements:* Additional exam requirements/recommendations for international students: Required—TOEFL (minimum score 550 paper-based; 79 iBT), IELTS (minimum score 6.5). *Application deadline:* For fall admission, 1/1 priority date for domestic students; for spring admission, 9/1 for domestic students. Application fee: $56 ($96 for international students). Electronic applications accepted. *Financial support:* Fellowships, research assistantships, teaching assistantships, career-related internships or fieldwork, health care benefits, and unspecified assistantships available. Support available to part-time students. Financial award application deadline: 4/15; financial award applicants required to submit FAFSA. *Faculty research:* Emotional disturbance, hearing impairment, learning disabilities, mental retardation. *Application contact:* General Information Contact, 414-229-4721, E-mail: soeinfo@uwm.edu.
Website: http://uwm.edu/education/academics/exceptional-edu-department/

University of Wisconsin–Platteville, School of Graduate Studies, College of Liberal Arts and Education, School of Education, Platteville, WI 53818-3099. Offers adult education (MSE). *Accreditation:* NCATE. *Program availability:* Part-time, evening/weekend. *Degree requirements:* For master's, thesis or alternative. *Entrance requirements:* Additional exam requirements/recommendations for international students: Required—TOEFL (minimum score 550 paper-based; 79 iBT), IELTS (minimum score 6.5). Electronic applications accepted.

Virginia Commonwealth University, Graduate School, School of Education, Program in Adult Learning, Richmond, VA 23284-9005. Offers adult literacy (M Ed); human resource development (M Ed); teaching and learning with technology (M Ed). *Accreditation:* NCATE. *Program availability:* Part-time. *Entrance requirements:* For master's, GRE General Test or MAT. Additional exam requirements/recommendations for international students: Required—TOEFL (minimum score 600 paper-based; 100 iBT). Electronic applications accepted. *Faculty research:* Adult development and learning, program planning and evaluation.

Walden University, Graduate Programs, Richard W. Riley College of Education and Leadership, Minneapolis, MN 55401. Offers adult education (Post-Master's Certificate); adult learning (Graduate Certificate); college teaching and learning (Graduate Certificate); community college leadership (Ed D); curriculum, instruction and assessment (Ed D, Ed S, Graduate Certificate); developmental education (Graduate Certificate); early childhood administration, management, and leadership (Graduate Certificate); early childhood education (Ed D, Ed S); early childhood public policy and advocacy (Graduate Certificate); early childhood studies (MS), including administration, management and leadership, early childhood public policy and advocacy, teaching adults in the early childhood field, teaching and diversity in early childhood education; education (MS, PhD), including adolescent literacy and learning (MS), curriculum, instruction, and assessment (grades K-12) (MS), curriculum, instruction, assessment, and evaluation (PhD), early childhood leadership and advocacy (PhD), early childhood special education (PhD), educational leadership (MS), educational leadership and administration (principal preparation) (MS), educational technology and design (PhD), elementary reading and literacy (PreK-6) (MS), elementary reading and mathematics (grades K-6) (MS), global and comparative education (PhD), higher education leadership management and policy (PhD), integrating technology in the classroom (grades K-12) (MS), learning, instruction and innovation (PhD), mathematics (grades 5-8) (MS), mathematics (grades K-6) (MS), mathematics and science (grades K-8) (MS), organizational research, assessment, and evaluation (PhD), reading and literacy with a reading K-12 endorsement (MS), reading literacy assessment and evaluation (PhD), science (grades K-8) (MS), special education (non-licensure) (grades K-12) (MS), teacher leadership (grades K-12) (MS), teaching English language learners (grades K-12) (MS); educational administration and leadership (Ed D); educational leadership and administration (principal preparation) (Ed S); educational technology (Ed D, Ed S, Post Master's Certificate); elementary reading and literacy (Graduate Certificate); engaging culturally diverse learners (Graduate Certificate); enrollment management and institutional marketing (Graduate Certificate); higher education (MS), including adult learning, college teaching and learning, enrollment management and institutional marketing, global higher education, leadership for student success, online and distance learning; higher education and adult learning (Ed D); higher education leadership and management (Ed D); higher education leadership for student success (Graduate Certificate); instructional design and technology (MS, Postbaccalaureate Certificate), including general program (MS), online learning (MS), training and performance improvement (MS); integrating technology in the classroom (Graduate Certificate); mathematics 5-8 (Graduate Certificate); mathematics K-6 (Graduate Certificate); online teaching for adult educators (Graduate Certificate); reading, literacy, and assessment (Ed D, Ed S); science K-8 (Graduate Certificate); special education (Ed D, Ed S, Graduate Certificate); special education (K-age 21) (MAT); teacher leadership (Graduate Certificate); teaching adults English as a second language (Graduate Certificate); teaching adults in the early childhood field (Graduate Certificate); teaching and diversity in early childhood education (Graduate Certificate); teaching English language learners (grades K-12) (Graduate Certificate); teaching K-12 students online (Graduate Certificate). *Accreditation:* NCATE. *Program availability:* Part-time, evening/weekend, online only, 100% online. *Degree requirements:* For doctorate, thesis/dissertation (for some programs), residency; for other advanced degree, residency (for

some programs). *Entrance requirements:* For master's, bachelor's degree or higher; minimum GPA of 2.5; official transcripts; goal statement (for some programs); access to computer and Internet; for doctorate, master's degree or higher; three years of related professional or academic experience (preferred); minimum GPA of 3.0; goal statement and current resume (for select programs); official transcripts; access to computer and Internet; for other advanced degree, relevant work experience; access to computer and Internet. Additional exam requirements/recommendations for international students: Required—TOEFL (minimum score 550 paper-based, 79 iBT), IELTS (minimum score 6.5), Michigan English Language Assessment Battery (minimum score 82), or PTE (minimum score 53). Electronic applications accepted.

Western Kentucky University, Graduate School, College of Education and Behavioral Sciences, Department of Educational Administration, Leadership, and Research, Bowling Green, KY 42101. Offers adult education (MAE); educational leadership (Ed D); school administration (Ed S); school principal (MAE). *Accreditation:* NCATE. *Program availability:* Part-time, evening/weekend. *Degree requirements:* For master's, comprehensive exam, thesis or applied project and oral defense; for Ed S, thesis. *Entrance requirements:* For master's, GRE General Test, minimum GPA of 2.75. Additional exam requirements/recommendations for international students: Required—TOEFL (minimum score 555 paper-based; 79 iBT). *Faculty research:* Principal internship, superintendent assessment, administrative leadership, group training for residential workers.

Western Washington University, Graduate School, Woodring College of Education, Department of Educational Leadership, Program in Continuing and College Education, Bellingham, WA 98225-5996. Offers M Ed. *Program availability:* Part-time, evening/weekend, online learning. *Degree requirements:* For master's, comprehensive exam, thesis optional. *Entrance requirements:* For master's, GRE General Test or MAT, minimum GPA of 3.0 in last 60 semester hours or last 90 quarter hours. Additional exam requirements/recommendations for international students: Required—TOEFL (minimum score 567 paper-based). Electronic applications accepted. *Faculty research:* Transfer of learning, postsecondary faculty development, action research as professional development, literacy education in community colleges, adult education in the Middle East, distance learning tools for graduate students.

Widener University, School of Human Service Professions, Center for Education, Chester, PA 19013-5792. Offers adult education (M Ed); counseling in higher education (M Ed); counselor education (M Ed); early childhood education (M Ed); educational foundations (M Ed); educational leadership (M Ed); educational psychology (M Ed); elementary education (M Ed); English and language arts (M Ed); health education (M Ed); higher education leadership (Ed D); home and school visitor (M Ed); human sexuality (M Ed, PhD); mathematics education (M Ed); middle school education (M Ed); principalship (M Ed); reading and language arts (Ed D); reading education (M Ed); school administration (Ed D); science education (M Ed); social studies education (M Ed); special education (M Ed); technology education (M Ed). *Accreditation:* NCATE. *Program availability:* Part-time, evening/weekend. Terminal master's awarded for partial completion of doctoral program. *Degree requirements:* For doctorate, thesis/dissertation. *Entrance requirements:* For master's, minimum GPA of 2.5; for doctorate, GRE or MAT, minimum GPA of 2.0 (undergraduate), 3.5 (graduate). Electronic applications accepted. *Expenses:* Contact institution. *Faculty research:* Reading and cognition, adult education, technology education, educational leadership, special education.

Community College Education

Argosy University, Chicago, College of Education, Chicago, IL 60601. Offers adult education and training (MA Ed); community college executive leadership (Ed D); educational leadership (MA Ed, Ed D, Ed S), including district leadership (Ed D), higher education administration (Ed D), K-12 education (Ed D); instructional leadership (Ed D, Ed S), including higher education (Ed D), K-12 education (Ed D). *Program availability:* Online learning.

Argosy University, Los Angeles, College of Education, Los Angeles, CA 90045. Offers community college executive leadership (Ed D); educational leadership (MA Ed, Ed D), including higher education administration (Ed D), K-12 education (Ed D); instructional leadership (MA Ed, Ed D), including higher education (Ed D), K-12 education (Ed D), multiple subject teacher preparation (MA Ed), single subject teacher preparation (MA Ed).

Argosy University, Northern Virginia, College of Education, Arlington, VA 22209. Offers community college executive leadership (Ed D); educational leadership (MA Ed, Ed D, Ed S), including higher education administration (Ed D), K-12 education (Ed D); instructional leadership (MA Ed, Ed D, Ed S), including higher education (Ed D), K-12 education (Ed D).

Argosy University, Orange County, College of Education, Orange, CA 92868. Offers community college executive leadership (Ed D); educational leadership (MA Ed, Ed D), including higher education administration (Ed D), K-12 education (Ed D); instructional leadership (MA Ed, Ed D), including education technology (Ed D), higher education (Ed D), K-12 education (Ed D), multiple subject teacher preparation (MA Ed), single subject teacher preparation (MA Ed).

Argosy University, Phoenix, College of Education, Phoenix, AZ 85021. Offers adult education and training (MA Ed); advanced educational administration (Ed D, Ed S); community college executive leadership (Ed D); educational administration (MA Ed); educational leadership (MA Ed, Ed D, Ed S), including education technology (Ed D), higher education administration (Ed D), K-12 education (Ed D); higher and postsecondary education (MA Ed); initial educational administration (Ed D, Ed S); school psychology (MA); teaching and learning (MA Ed, Ed D, Ed S), including education technology (Ed D), higher education (Ed D), K-12 education (Ed D).

Argosy University, Seattle, College of Education, Seattle, WA 98121. Offers adult education and training (MA Ed); community college executive leadership (Ed D); educational leadership (MA Ed, Ed D), including higher education administration (Ed D), K-12 education (Ed D); higher and postsecondary education (MA Ed); instructional leadership (MA Ed, Ed D), including education technology (Ed D), higher education (Ed D), K-12 education (Ed D).

Argosy University, Tampa, College of Education, Tampa, FL 33607. Offers community college executive leadership (Ed D); educational leadership (MA Ed, Ed D, Ed S), including higher education administration (Ed D), K-12 education (Ed D); school counseling (MA); teaching and learning (MA Ed, Ed D, Ed S), including higher education (Ed D), K-12 education (Ed D).

Arkansas State University, Graduate School, College of Education and Behavioral Science, School of Teacher Education and Leadership, State University, AR 72467. Offers community college administration (SCCT); curriculum and instruction (MSE); early childhood education (MSE); early childhood services (MS); educational leadership (MSE, Ed D, Ed S); educational theory and practice (MSE); middle level education (MAT, MSE); reading (MSE, Ed S); special education - gifted, talented, and creative (MSE); special education - instructional specialist grades 4-12 (MSE); special education - instructional specialist grades P-4 (MSE); special education, K-12 (MSE). *Accreditation:* NCATE. *Program availability:* Part-time, online learning. *Degree requirements:* For master's, comprehensive exam, thesis or alternative; for doctorate, comprehensive exam, thesis/dissertation; for other advanced degree, comprehensive exam. *Entrance requirements:* For master's, GRE General Test or MAT, appropriate bachelor's degree, official transcripts, immunization records, letters of reference, interview; for doctorate, GRE General Test or MAT, interview, master's degree, letters of reference, official transcript, personal statement, writing sample, immunization records; for other advanced degree, GRE General Test or MAT, interview, master's degree, official transcript, immunization records, letters of reference, 3 years of teaching experience, teaching license. Additional exam requirements/recommendations for international students: Required—TOEFL (minimum score 550 paper-based; 79 iBT), IELTS (minimum score 6), PTE (minimum score 56). Electronic applications accepted.

California State University, San Bernardino, Graduate Studies, College of Education, Program in Educational Leadership: Community College Specialization, San Bernardino, CA 92407. Offers MA. *Program availability:* Part-time, evening/weekend. *Students:* 12 full-time (8 women), 21 part-time (11 women); includes 21 minority (3 Black or African American, non-Hispanic/Latino; 3 Asian, non-Hispanic/Latino; 14 Hispanic/Latino; 1 Two or more races, non-Hispanic/Latino), 2 international. Average age 43. 24 applicants, 67% accepted, 11 enrolled. *Degree requirements:* For master's, thesis optional. *Entrance requirements:* Additional exam requirements/recommendations for international students: Required—TOEFL. *Application deadline:* For fall admission, 7/17 for domestic students. Application fee: $55. *Unit head:* Dr. Lynne Diaz- Rico, Co-Director, 909-537-5651, E-mail: diazrico@csusb.edu. *Application contact:* Dr. Dorota Huizinga, Dean of Graduate Studies, 909-537-3064, E-mail: dorota.huizinga@csusb.edu.

California State University, Stanislaus, College of Education, Kinesiology and Social Work, Doctor of Education in Educational Leadership Programs, Turlock, CA 95382. Offers community college leadership (Ed D); P-12 leadership (Ed D). *Program availability:* Part-time, evening/weekend. *Degree requirements:* For doctorate, thesis/dissertation. *Entrance requirements:* For doctorate, GRE, minimum GPA of 3.0, 3 letters of reference, interview, personal statement. Additional exam requirements/recommendations for international students: Required—TOEFL (minimum score 550 paper-based). Electronic applications accepted.

Central Michigan University, Central Michigan University Global Campus, Program in Education, Mount Pleasant, MI 48859. Offers college teaching (Graduate Certificate); community college (MA); curriculum and instruction (MA); educational technology (MA, DET); reading and literacy K-12 (MA); school principalship (MA), including charter school leadership; training and development (MA). *Accreditation:* TEAC. *Program availability:* Part-time, evening/weekend. *Entrance requirements:* For master's, minimum GPA of 2.7 in major. Additional exam requirements/recommendations for international students: Required—TOEFL. Electronic applications accepted.

Drew University, Caspersen School of Graduate Studies, Madison, NJ 07940-1493. Offers conflict resolution and leadership (Certificate), including community leadership, moderation, peace building; education (M Ed); finance (MA); history and culture (MA, PhD), including American history, book history, British history, European history, intellectual history, Irish history, print culture, public history; K-12 education (MAT), including art, biology, chemistry, elementary education, English, French, Italian, math, secondary education, special education, teacher of students with disabilities; liberal studies (M Litt, D Litt), including history, Irish/Irish-American studies, literature (M Litt, MMH, D Litt, DMH, CMH), religion, spirituality, teaching in the two-year college, writing; medical humanities (MMH, DMH, CMH), including arts, health, healthcare, literature (M Litt, MMH, D Litt, DMH, CMH), scientific research; poetry (MFA). *Program availability:* Part-time, evening/weekend. *Faculty:* 3 full-time (2 women), 27 part-time/adjunct (13 women). *Students:* 66 full-time (38 women), 179 part-time (117 women); includes 37 minority (15 Black or African American, non-Hispanic/Latino; 2 Asian, non-Hispanic/Latino; 15 Hispanic/Latino; 5 Two or more races, non-Hispanic/Latino), 14 international. Average age 42. 157 applicants, 82% accepted, 57 enrolled. In 2018, 34 master's, 24 doctorates, 17 other advanced degrees awarded. Terminal master's awarded for partial completion of doctoral program. *Degree requirements:* For master's and other advanced degree, thesis (for some programs); for doctorate, one foreign language, comprehensive exam (for some programs), thesis/dissertation. *Entrance requirements:* For master's, PRAXIS Core and Subject Area tests (for MAT), GRE/GMAT (for MFin MS in Data Analytics), resume, transcripts, writing sample, personal statement, letters of recommendation; for doctorate, GRE (PhD in history and culture), resume, transcripts, writing sample, personal statement, letters of recommendation; for other advanced degree, resume, transcripts, personal statement. Additional exam requirements/recommendations for international students: Required—TOEFL (minimum score 587 paper-based; 80 iBT), IELTS (minimum score 6), TWE (minimum score 4). *Application deadline:* For fall admission, 8/1 for domestic students, 6/1 for international students; for spring admission, 12/1 for domestic students, 10/1 for international students. Applications are processed on a rolling basis. Application fee: $35. Electronic applications accepted. *Financial support:* Fellowships, research assistantships, teaching assistantships, career-related internships or fieldwork, Federal Work-Study, scholarships/grants, and unspecified assistantships available. Support available to part-time students. Financial award applicants required to submit FAFSA. *Unit head:* Dr. Debra Liebowitz, Provost and Dean of the College of Liberal Arts & Caspersen School of Graduate Studies, 973-4083139, E-mail: dliebowi@drew.edu. *Application contact:* Amo-Augustus Kubeyinje, Associate Vice President for Graduate Enrollment, 973-408-3111, E-mail: akubeyinje@drew.edu.
Website: http://www.drew.edu/caspersen

East Carolina University, Graduate School, Thomas Harriot College of Arts and Sciences, Department of English, Greenville, NC 27858-4353. Offers creative writing (MA); English studies (MA); linguistics (MA); literature (MA); multicultural and transnational literatures (MA, Certificate); professional communication (Certificate);

rhetoric and composition (MA); rhetoric, writing, and professional communication (PhD); teaching English in the two-year college (Certificate); teaching English to speakers of other languages (MA, Certificate); technical and professional communication (MA). *Program availability:* Part-time, evening/weekend, online learning. *Application deadline:* For fall admission, 7/31 priority date for domestic students, 2/1 priority date for international students; for spring admission, 11/30 priority date for domestic students, 10/1 priority date for international students. *Expenses: Tuition, area resident:* Full-time $4749. Tuition, state resident: full-time $4749. Tuition, nonresident: full-time $17,898. *International tuition:* $17,898 full-time. *Required fees:* $2787. Part-time tuition and fees vary according to course load and program. *Financial support:* Application deadline: 3/1. *Unit head:* Dr. Marianne Montgomery, Chair, 252-328-6041, E-mail: montgomerym@ecu.edu. *Application contact:* Graduate School Admissions, 252-328-6012, Fax: 252-328-6071, E-mail: gradschool@ecu.edu.
Website: http://www.ecu.edu/cs-cas/engl/

East Carolina University, Graduate School, Thomas Harriot College of Arts and Sciences, Department of Mathematics, Greenville, NC 27858-4353. Offers mathematics (MA), including mathematics in the community college, statistics. *Program availability:* Part-time, evening/weekend. *Application deadline:* For fall admission, 6/1 priority date for domestic students, 2/1 priority date for international students; for spring admission, 10/15 priority date for domestic students, 10/1 priority date for international students. *Expenses: Tuition, area resident:* Full-time $4749. Tuition, state resident: full-time $4749. Tuition, nonresident: full-time $17,898. *International tuition:* $17,898 full-time. *Required fees:* $2787. Part-time tuition and fees vary according to course load and program. *Financial support:* Application deadline: 3/1. *Unit head:* Dr. Johannes H. Hattingh, Chair, 252-328-6461, E-mail: hattinghj@ecu.edu. *Application contact:* Graduate School Admissions, 252-328-6012, Fax: 252-328-6071, E-mail: gradschool@ecu.edu.
Website: http://www.ecu.edu/cs-cas/math/

Eastern Michigan University, Graduate School, College of Education, Department of Leadership and Counseling, Programs in Educational Leadership, Ypsilanti, MI 48197. Offers community college leadership (Graduate Certificate); educational leadership (MA, Ed D, SPA); higher education/general administration (MA); higher education/student affairs (MA); K-12 administration (MA); K-12 basic administration (Post Master's Certificate). *Program availability:* Part-time, evening/weekend, online learning. *Students:* 39 full-time (29 women), 283 part-time (195 women); includes 92 minority (67 Black or African American, non-Hispanic/Latino; 2 Asian, non-Hispanic/Latino; 12 Hispanic/Latino; 11 Two or more races, non-Hispanic/Latino), 2 international. Average age 36. 192 applicants, 74% accepted, 80 enrolled. In 2018, 98 master's, 18 doctorates, 22 other advanced degrees awarded. *Entrance requirements:* For doctorate, GRE. Additional exam requirements/recommendations for international students: Required—TOEFL. *Application deadline:* For winter admission, 2/1 for domestic and international students. Applications are processed on a rolling basis. Application fee: $45. *Financial support:* Fellowships, research assistantships with full tuition reimbursements, teaching assistantships with full tuition reimbursements, career-related internships or fieldwork, Federal Work-Study, institutionally sponsored loans, scholarships/grants, tuition waivers (partial), and unspecified assistantships available. Support available to part-time students. *Application contact:* Dr. Jaclynn Tracy, Coordinator of Advising, Programs in Educational Leadership, 734-487-0255, Fax: 734-487-4608, E-mail: jtracy@emich.edu.

Elizabeth City State University, Department of Mathematics and Computer Science, Master of Science in Mathematics Program, Elizabeth City, NC 27909-7806. Offers applied mathematics (MS); community college teaching (MS); mathematics education (MS); remote sensing (MS). *Program availability:* Part-time, evening/weekend. *Degree requirements:* For master's, thesis. *Entrance requirements:* For master's, MAT and/or GRE, minimum GPA of 3.0, 3 letters of recommendation, two official transcripts from all undergraduate/graduate schools attended, typewritten one-page request for entry into program that includes description of student's educational preparation. Additional exam requirements/recommendations for international students: Required—TOEFL (minimum score 550 paper-based, 80 iBT) or IELTS (minimum score 6.5). Electronic applications accepted. *Faculty research:* Oceanic temperature effects, mathematics strategies in elementary schools, multimedia, Antarctic temperature mapping, computer networks, water quality, remote sensing, polar ice, satellite imagery.

Ferris State University, Extended and International Operations, Big Rapids, MI 49307. Offers community college leadership (Ed D). *Program availability:* Evening/weekend, blended/hybrid learning. *Faculty:* 27 part-time/adjunct (18 women). *Students:* 119 full-time (79 women), 2 part-time (1 woman); includes 46 minority (31 Black or African American, non-Hispanic/Latino; 1 American Indian or Alaska Native, non-Hispanic/Latino; 1 Asian, non-Hispanic/Latino; 12 Hispanic/Latino; 1 Two or more races, non-Hispanic/Latino). Average age 45. 40 applicants, 75% accepted, 26 enrolled. In 2018, 17 doctorates awarded. *Degree requirements:* For doctorate, thesis/dissertation, course work completed (minimum GPA of 2.7), e-portfolio demonstration of program & additional comprehensive requirements, successful dissertation. *Entrance requirements:* For doctorate, master's degree with minimum GPA of 3.25, fierce commitment to the mission of community colleges, essay, writing samples. *Application deadline:* For spring admission, 10/31 for domestic and international students; for summer admission, 4/15 for domestic and international students. Applications are processed on a rolling basis. Application fee: $0. Electronic applications accepted. *Expenses:* $690 per credit hour with no additional fees. Total is $42,090. *Financial support:* In 2018–19, 15 students received support, including 6 teaching assistantships (averaging $690 per year). Financial award applicants required to submit FAFSA. *Faculty research:* Community college leadership. *Unit head:* Dr. Roberta Teahen, Director, 231-591-3805, E-mail: robertateahen@ferris.edu. *Application contact:* Megan Biller, Coordinator, 231-591-2710, Fax: 231-591-3539, E-mail: meganbiller@ferris.edu.

Lenoir-Rhyne University, Graduate Programs, School of Education, Program in Community College Administration, Hickory, NC 28601. Offers MA. *Program availability:* Online learning. *Entrance requirements:* For master's, GRE or MAT, official transcripts, essay, resume. Electronic applications accepted. *Expenses:* Contact institution.

Marymount University, School of Design, Arts, and Humanities, Program in English and Humanities, Arlington, VA 22207-4299. Offers English and humanities (MA); teaching English at the community college (Certificate). *Program availability:* Part-time, evening/weekend. *Faculty:* 2 full-time (both women), 1 (woman) part-time/adjunct. *Students:* 4 full-time (2 women), 10 part-time (6 women); includes 6 minority (2 Black or African American, non-Hispanic/Latino; 1 Asian, non-Hispanic/Latino; 2 Hispanic/Latino; 1 Two or more races, non-Hispanic/Latino), 1 international. Average age 32. 9 applicants, 100% accepted, 3 enrolled. In 2018, 3 master's awarded. *Degree requirements:* For master's, thesis, capstone. *Entrance requirements:* For master's, 2 letters of recommendation, resume, bachelor's degree in English or other humanities discipline, writing sample of 8-10 pages, personal statement. Additional exam requirements/recommendations for international students: Required—TOEFL (minimum score 600 paper-based; 96 iBT), IELTS (minimum score 6.5), PTE (minimum score 58). *Application deadline:* For fall admission, 7/16 priority date for domestic and international students; for spring admission, 11/16 priority date for domestic and international students; for summer admission, 4/16 priority date for domestic and international students. Applications are processed on a rolling basis. Application fee: $40. Electronic applications accepted. *Expenses: Tuition:* Full-time $18,900; part-time $1050 per credit. *Required fees:* $396; $22 per credit hour. One-time fee: $270. Tuition and fees vary according to program. *Financial support:* In 2018–19, 2 students received support. Research assistantships, teaching assistantships, career-related internships or fieldwork, scholarships/grants, and unspecified assistantships available. Support available to part-time students. Financial award application deadline: 3/1; financial award applicants required to submit FAFSA. *Unit head:* Dr. Tonya-Marie Howe, Chair, Literature and Languages, 703-284-5762, E-mail: thowe@marymount.edu. *Application contact:* Rebecca Esposito, Senior Associate Director, Graduate Admissions, 703-284-5901, Fax: 703-527-3815, E-mail: grad.admissions@marymount.edu.
Website: https://www.marymount.edu/English-Humanities

Mississippi State University, College of Education, Educational Leadership Program, Mississippi State, MS 39762. Offers community college education (MAT); community college leadership (PhD); higher education leadership (PhD); P-12 school leadership (PhD); school administration (MS, Ed S); student affairs and higher education (MS); workforce education leadership (MS). MS in workforce education leadership held jointly with Alcorn State University. *Faculty:* 12 full-time (9 women). *Students:* 74 full-time (43 women), 145 part-time (89 women); includes 86 minority (75 Black or African American, non-Hispanic/Latino; 1 American Indian or Alaska Native, non-Hispanic/Latino; 6 Hispanic/Latino; 4 Two or more races, non-Hispanic/Latino). Average age 35. 83 applicants, 82% accepted, 55 enrolled. In 2018, 48 master's, 12 doctorates, 13 other advanced degrees awarded. *Degree requirements:* For master's and Ed S, comprehensive exam, thesis; for doctorate, comprehensive exam, thesis/dissertation. *Entrance requirements:* For master's, GRE, minimum GPA of 2.75 in junior and senior courses; for doctorate, GRE, minimum GPA of 3.4 on previous graduate work; for Ed S, GRE, minimum GPA of 3.2, master's degree. Additional exam requirements/recommendations for international students: Required—TOEFL (minimum score 550 paper-based; 79 iBT); Recommended—IELTS (minimum score 6.5). *Application deadline:* For fall admission, 7/1 for domestic students, 5/1 for international students; for spring admission, 11/1 for domestic students, 9/1 for international students. Application fee: $60 ($80 for international students). Electronic applications accepted. *Expenses:* Tuition, state resident: full-time $8450; part-time $360.59 per credit hour. Tuition, nonresident: full-time $23,140; part-time $969.09 per credit hour. *Required fees:* $110. One-time fee: $55 full-time. Part-time tuition and fees vary according to course load, degree level, campus/location and reciprocity agreements. *Financial support:* In 2018–19, 1 research assistantship with full tuition reimbursement (averaging $11,861 per year) was awarded; Federal Work-Study, institutionally sponsored loans, and unspecified assistantships also available. Financial award application deadline: 4/1; financial award applicants required to submit FAFSA. *Unit head:* Dr. Eric Moyen, Associate Professor and Head, 662-325-0969, Fax: 662-325-0975, E-mail: em1621@msstate.edu. *Application contact:* Nathan Drake, Admissions and Enrollment Assistant, 662-325-3804, E-mail: ndrake@grad.msstate.edu.
Website: http://www.educationalleadership.msstate.edu/

Morgan State University, School of Graduate Studies, School of Education and Urban Studies, Department of Advanced Studies, Leadership and Policy, Program in Community College Leadership, Baltimore, MD 21251. Offers Ed D. *Accreditation:* NCATE. *Program availability:* Part-time, evening/weekend. *Degree requirements:* For doctorate, comprehensive exam, thesis/dissertation. *Entrance requirements:* For doctorate, GRE General Test or MAT. Additional exam requirements/recommendations for international students: Required—TOEFL (minimum score 550 paper-based). *Faculty research:* Multicultural education, cooperative learning, psychology of cognition.

National American University, Roueche Graduate Center, Austin, TX 78731. Offers accounting (MBA); aviation management (MBA, MM); care coordination (MSN); community college leadership (Ed D); criminal justice (MM); e-marketing (MBA, MM); health care administration (MBA, MM); higher education (MM); human resources management (MBA, MM); information technology management (MBA, MM); international business (MBA); leadership (EMBA); management (MBA); nursing administration (MSN); nursing education (MSN); nursing informatics (MSN); operations and configuration management (MBA, MM); project and process management (MBA, MM). Master's programs offered online through the Harold D. Buckingham Graduate School. *Program availability:* Part-time, evening/weekend, online learning. *Entrance requirements:* For master's, minimum undergraduate GPA of 2.75. Additional exam requirements/recommendations for international students: Required—TOEFL, TWE. Electronic applications accepted. *Faculty research:* Tourism, finance, marketing.

North Carolina State University, Graduate School, College of Education, Department of Educational Leadership, Policy, and Human Development, Program in Adult and Community College Education, Raleigh, NC 27695. Offers M Ed, MS, Ed D. *Degree requirements:* For master's, thesis (for some programs); for doctorate, thesis/dissertation. *Entrance requirements:* For master's and doctorate, GRE or MAT. Electronic applications accepted.

Northern Arizona University, College of Education, Department of Educational Leadership, Flagstaff, AZ 86011. Offers community college teaching and learning (Graduate Certificate); educational leadership (M Ed, Ed D), including community college/higher education (M Ed), educational foundations (M Ed), instructional leadership K-12 school leadership (M Ed), principal certification K-12 (M Ed); principal (Graduate Certificate); superintendent (Graduate Certificate). *Program availability:* Part-time. *Degree requirements:* For master's, comprehensive exam, thesis (for some programs); for doctorate, comprehensive exam, thesis/dissertation; for Graduate Certificate, comprehensive exam (for some programs). *Entrance requirements:* Additional exam requirements/recommendations for international students: Required—TOEFL (minimum score 80 iBT), IELTS (minimum score 6.5). Electronic applications accepted.

Old Dominion University, Darden College of Education, Doctoral Program in Community College Leadership, Norfolk, VA 23529. Offers PhD. *Program availability:* Evening/weekend, online only, 100% online, blended/hybrid learning. *Degree requirements:* For doctorate, comprehensive exam, thesis/dissertation, internship. *Entrance requirements:* For doctorate, GRE, master's degree, writing sample, 3 letters of reference, resume, essay, interview with faculty. Additional exam requirements/recommendations for international students: Required—TOEFL (minimum score 600 paper-based). Electronic applications accepted. *Faculty research:* Rural community colleges, inter-institutional collaboration in higher education.

Old Dominion University, Darden College of Education, Programs in STEM Education and Professional Studies, Norfolk, VA 23529. Offers community college teaching (MS); human resources training (PhD); technology education (PhD). *Accreditation:* NCATE (one or more programs are accredited). *Program availability:* Part-time, evening/weekend, mix of synchronous and asynchronous study. Terminal master's awarded for partial completion of doctoral program. *Degree requirements:* For master's, comprehensive exam, thesis optional, writing exam, candidacy exam; for doctorate, comprehensive exam, thesis/dissertation, writing exam, candidacy exam. *Entrance requirements:* For master's, GRE General Test or MAT, minimum GPA of 2.8, 2 letters of reference; for doctorate, GRE, minimum GPA of 3.0, 3 letters of reference. Additional exam requirements/recommendations for international students: Required—TOEFL.

Electronic applications accepted. *Faculty research:* Training and development, STEM education, visualization, leadership, technology literacy.

University of Arkansas at Little Rock, Graduate School, College of Education and Health Professions, Department of Educational Leadership, Program in Higher Education, Little Rock, AR 72204-1099. Offers administration (MA); college student affairs (MA); health professions teaching and learning (MA); higher education (Ed D); two-year college teaching (MA). *Degree requirements:* For doctorate, comprehensive exam, oral defense of dissertation, residency. *Entrance requirements:* For master's, GRE General Test or MAT, interview, minimum graduate GPA of 3.0; for doctorate, GRE General Test, interview, minimum graduate GPA of 3.5, teaching certificate, three years of work experience.

University of Central Florida, College of Community Innovation and Education, Department of Educational Leadership and Higher Education, Orlando, FL 32816. Offers career and technical education (MA); educational leadership (M Ed, MA, Ed S); higher education/college teaching and leadership (MA); higher education/student personnel (MA). *Program availability:* Part-time, evening/weekend. *Degree requirements:* For master's, thesis or alternative; for Ed S, thesis or alternative, final exam. *Entrance requirements:* For master's, GRE General Test; for Ed S, GRE General Test, minimum GPA of 3.0, resume, letters of recommendation. Additional exam requirements/recommendations for international students: Required—TOEFL. Electronic applications accepted.

University of Memphis, Graduate School, College of Education, Department of Leadership, Memphis, TN 38152. Offers adult education (Ed D); community college teaching and leadership (Graduate Certificate); community education (Ed D); educational leadership (Ed D); higher education (Ed D); leadership (MS); policy studies (Ed D); school administration and supervision (MS); student personnel (MS). *Accreditation:* NCATE. *Program availability:* Part-time, evening/weekend, online learning. *Students:* 19 full-time (12 women), 137 part-time (90 women); includes 87 minority (80 Black or African American, non-Hispanic/Latino; 2 Asian, non-Hispanic/Latino; 4 Hispanic/Latino; 1 Two or more races, non-Hispanic/Latino), 1 international. Average age 41. 44 applicants, 98% accepted, 37 enrolled. In 2018, 11 master's, 17 doctorates, 2 other advanced degrees awarded. *Degree requirements:* For master's, comprehensive exam, thesis optional; for doctorate, comprehensive exam, thesis/dissertation. *Entrance requirements:* For master's, GRE, resume, letters of reference, statement of professional goals, current teacher certification, sample work, interview; for doctorate, GRE, resume, letters of reference, statement of professional goals, interview. Additional exam requirements/recommendations for international students: Required—TOEFL (minimum score 550 paper-based; 79 iBT). *Application deadline:* For fall admission, 6/15 for domestic students; for spring admission, 9/15 for domestic students; for summer admission, 2/15 for domestic students. Application fee: $35 ($60 for international students). Electronic applications accepted. *Expenses: Tuition, area resident:* Full-time $10,240; part-time $503 per credit hour. Tuition, state resident: full-time $10,464. Tuition, nonresident: full-time $20,224; part-time $991 per credit hour. *Required fees:* $850; $106 per credit hour. *Financial support:* Research assistantships with full tuition reimbursements, teaching assistantships, Federal Work-Study, scholarships/grants, and unspecified assistantships available. Financial award application deadline: 2/1; financial award applicants required to submit FAFSA. *Faculty research:* School improvement, social justice, online learning, adult learning, diversity. *Unit head:* Dr. R Eric Platt, Interim Chair, 901-678-4229, E-mail: replatt@memphis.edu. *Application contact:* Dr. R Eric Platt, Interim Chair, 901-678-4229, E-mail: replatt@memphis.edu.
Website: http://www.memphis.edu/lead

University of Northern Iowa, Graduate College, College of Humanities, Arts and Sciences, Department of Mathematics, MA Program in Mathematics, Cedar Falls, IA 50614. Offers community college teaching (MA); mathematics (MA); secondary teaching (MA).

University of South Florida, College of Education, Department of Leadership, Counseling, Adult, Career and Higher Education, Tampa, FL 33620-9951. Offers adult education (MA, Ed D, PhD, Ed S); career and technical education (MA); career and workforce education (PhD); higher education/community college teaching (MA, Ed D, PhD); vocational education (Ed S). *Faculty:* 19 full-time (11 women). *Students:* 107 full-time (81 women), 275 part-time (185 women); includes 143 minority (67 Black or African American, non-Hispanic/Latino; 2 American Indian or Alaska Native, non-Hispanic/Latino; 10 Asian, non-Hispanic/Latino; 56 Hispanic/Latino; 8 Two or more races, non-Hispanic/Latino), 14 international. Average age 36. 188 applicants, 54% accepted, 73 enrolled. In 2018, 51 master's, 8 doctorates, 3 other advanced degrees awarded. *Entrance requirements:* For master's, GRE may be required, goals statement; letters of recommendation; proof of educational or professional experience; prerequisites, if needed; for doctorate, GRE may be required, letters of recommendation; masters degree in appropriate field; optional interview; evidence of professional experience; personal statement. Additional exam requirements/recommendations for international students: Required—TOEFL. Application fee: $30. *Expenses:* Tuition, state resident: full-time $6350. Tuition, nonresident: full-time $19,048. *International tuition:* $19,048 full-time. *Required fees:* $2079. *Financial support:* In 2018–19, 19 students received support. *Total annual research expenditures:* $40,520. *Unit head:* Dr. Judith Ponticell, Chair, 813-974-4897, Fax: 813-974-5423, E-mail: jponticell@usf.edu. *Application contact:* Dr. Judith Ponticell, Chair, 813-974-4897, Fax: 813-974-5423, E-mail: jponticell@usf.edu.
Website: http://www.coedu.usf.edu/main/departments/ache/ache.html

Wingate University, Thayer School of Education, Wingate, NC 28174. Offers community college executive leadership (Ed D); educational leadership (MA Ed, Ed S); elementary education (MA Ed, MAT). *Accreditation:* NCATE. *Program availability:* Part-time, evening/weekend. *Degree requirements:* For master's, portfolio. *Entrance requirements:* For master's, GRE General Test or MAT, teaching certificate (MA Ed).

Early Childhood Education

Alabama Agricultural and Mechanical University, School of Graduate Studies, College of Education, Humanities, and Behavioral Sciences, Department of Reading, Elementary, Early Childhood and Special Education, Huntsville, AL 35811. Offers early childhood education (MS Ed, Ed S); elementary education (MS Ed, Ed S); reading/literacy (PhD); special education collaborative teacher training (MS Ed, Ed S). *Accreditation:* NCATE. *Program availability:* Evening/weekend. *Degree requirements:* For master's, comprehensive exam; for Ed S, thesis. *Entrance requirements:* For master's, GRE General Test. Additional exam requirements/recommendations for international students: Required—TOEFL (minimum score 500 paper-based; 61 iBT). Electronic applications accepted. *Faculty research:* Multicultural education, learning styles, diagnostic-prescriptive instruction.

Alabama State University, College of Education, Department of Curriculum and Instruction, Montgomery, AL 36101-0271. Offers early childhood education (Ed S); secondary education (M Ed), including biology education, English language arts education, history education, math education, music education, reading education, social science education. *Program availability:* Part-time, evening/weekend, online only, 100% online. *Faculty:* 7 full-time (4 women), 7 part-time/adjunct (4 women). *Students:* 22 full-time (19 women), 58 part-time (49 women); includes 235 minority (234 Black or African American, non-Hispanic/Latino; 1 Hispanic/Latino), 5 international. Average age 36. 45 applicants, 33% accepted, 6 enrolled. In 2018, 34 master's awarded. *Degree requirements:* For master's, comprehensive exam, thesis optional; for Ed S, comprehensive exam, thesis. *Entrance requirements:* For master's, GRE General Test, MAT, writing competency test; for Ed S, writing competency test, GRE, MAT. Additional exam requirements/recommendations for international students: Required—TOEFL (minimum score 500 paper-based). *Application deadline:* For fall admission, 4/15 for domestic and international students; for spring admission, 11/15 for domestic and international students; for summer admission, 3/15 for domestic and international students. Applications are processed on a rolling basis. Application fee: $25. Electronic applications accepted. *Expenses:* Contact institution. *Financial support:* Fellowships, teaching assistantships, career-related internships or fieldwork, scholarships/grants, tuition waivers (partial), and unspecified assistantships available. Financial award application deadline: 6/30; financial award applicants required to submit FAFSA. *Unit head:* Dr. Joyce Johnson, Acting Chairperson, 334-229-4485, Fax: 334-229-5603, E-mail: jjohnson@alasu.edu. *Application contact:* Dr. Ed Brown, Dean of Graduate Studies, 334-229-4274, Fax: 334-229-4928, E-mail: ebrown@alasu.edu.
Website: http://www.alasu.edu/academics/colleges—departments/college-of-education/curriculum—instruction/index.aspx

Albany State University, College of Education, Albany, GA 31705-2717. Offers early childhood education (M Ed); educational leadership (Ed S); health and physical education (M Ed); middle grades education (M Ed); school counseling (M Ed); special education (M Ed). *Accreditation:* NCATE. *Program availability:* Part-time, evening/weekend, online learning. *Degree requirements:* For master's, comprehensive exam, internship, GACE Content Exam. *Entrance requirements:* For master's, GRE or MAT. Electronic applications accepted. *Faculty research:* GACE preparation, STEM (science, technology, engineering, and mathematics), technology education, special education, professional teacher development, health implications liberation philosophy, NET-Q, learning community, disabled or at-risk students.

Albright College, Graduate Division, Reading, PA 19612-5234. Offers early childhood education (MS); elementary education (MS); English as a second language (MA); general education (MA); special education (MS). *Program availability:* Part-time, evening/weekend. *Degree requirements:* For master's, thesis. *Entrance requirements:* For master's, GRE General Test or MAT, minimum undergraduate GPA of 3.0, 2 letters of recommendation, interview. Additional exam requirements/recommendations for international students: Recommended—TOEFL (minimum score 525 paper-based). Electronic applications accepted.

American International College, School of Education, Springfield, MA 01109-3189. Offers early childhood education (M Ed, CAGS); education (MA, Ed D), including counseling psychology (MA), educational leadership and supervision (Ed D), professional counseling and supervision (Ed D), teaching and learning (Ed D); elementary education (M Ed, CAGS); middle education/secondary education (M Ed, CAGS); moderate disabilities (M Ed, CAGS); reading specialist (M Ed, CAGS); school adjustment counseling (MAEP, CAGS); school guidance counseling (MAEP, CAGS); school leadership (M Ed, CAGS). *Program availability:* Evening/weekend. *Degree requirements:* For master's and CAGS, practicum/culminating experience. *Entrance requirements:* For master's, Communication and Literacy portion of the Massachusetts Tests for Education Licensure, graduate of accredited four-year college with minimum B-average in undergraduate course work; for CAGS, M Ed or master's degree in field related to licensure from accredited institution. Electronic applications accepted. *Expenses:* Contact institution.

Anna Maria College, Graduate Division, Program in Education, Paxton, MA 01612. Offers early childhood education (M Ed); education (CAGS); elementary education (M Ed); English language arts (M Ed); visual arts (M Ed). *Program availability:* Part-time, evening/weekend. *Entrance requirements:* For master's, bachelor's degree in liberal arts or sciences, minimum GPA of 3.0. Additional exam requirements/recommendations for international students: Required—TOEFL (minimum score 500 paper-based). Electronic applications accepted.

Antioch University New England, Graduate School, Department of Education, Integrated Learning Program, Keene, NH 03431-3552. Offers early childhood education (M Ed); elementary education (M Ed), including arts and humanities, science and environmental education; special education (M Ed). *Degree requirements:* For master's, internship. *Entrance requirements:* For master's, previous course work or work experience in education. Additional exam requirements/recommendations for international students: Required—TOEFL (minimum score 550 paper-based). Electronic applications accepted. *Expenses:* Contact institution. *Faculty research:* Problem-based learning, place-based education, mathematics education, democratic classrooms, art education.

Arcadia University, School of Education, Glenside, PA 19038-3295. Offers art education (M Ed); computer education (CAS); curriculum (CAS); curriculum studies (M Ed); early childhood education (M Ed), including individualized, master teacher, research in child development; educational leadership (M Ed, Ed D, CAS); elementary education (M Ed); English education (MA Ed); environmental education (MA Ed); instructional technology (M Ed); language arts (M Ed); library science (M Ed); mathematics education (M Ed, MA Ed); music education (MA Ed); psychology (MA Ed); reading (M Ed, CAS); science education (M Ed, CAS); secondary education (M Ed, CAS); special education (M Ed, Ed D, CAS); theater arts (MA Ed); written communication (MA Ed). *Accreditation:* NASAD. *Program availability:* Part-time, evening/weekend, online learning. *Faculty:* 14 full-time (10 women). *Students:* 35 full-time (24 women), 299 part-time (243 women); includes 72 minority (49 Black or African American, non-Hispanic/Latino; 1 American Indian or Alaska Native, non-Hispanic/Latino; 12 Asian, non-Hispanic/Latino; 8 Hispanic/Latino; 2 Two or more races, non-Hispanic/Latino), 5 international. In 2018, 152 master's, 8 doctorates awarded. *Entrance*

requirements: Additional exam requirements/recommendations for international students: Required—Official results from the TOEFL or IELTS are required. *Application deadline:* Applications are processed on a rolling basis. Application fee: $25. Electronic applications accepted. *Expenses:* Contact institution. *Financial support:* Career-related internships or fieldwork, tuition waivers (partial), and unspecified assistantships available. *Unit head:* Kimberly Dean, Chair, 215-572-8629. *Application contact:* 215-572-2925, Fax: 215-572-2126, E-mail: grad@arcadia.edu.

Arkansas State University, Graduate School, College of Education and Behavioral Science, School of Teacher Education and Leadership, State University, AR 72467. Offers community college administration (SCCT); curriculum and instruction (MSE); early childhood education (MSE); early childhood services (MS); educational leadership (MSE, Ed D, Ed S); educational theory and practice (MSE); middle level education (MAT, MSE); reading (MSE, Ed S); special education - gifted, talented, and creative (MSE); special education - instructional specialist grades 4-12 (MSE); special education - instructional specialist grades P-4 (MSE); special education, K-12 (MSE). *Accreditation:* NCATE. *Program availability:* Part-time, online learning. *Degree requirements:* For master's, comprehensive exam, thesis or alternative; for doctorate, comprehensive exam, thesis/dissertation; for other advanced degree, comprehensive exam. *Entrance requirements:* For master's, GRE General Test or MAT, appropriate bachelor's degree, official transcripts, immunization records, letters of reference, interview; for doctorate, GRE General Test or MAT, interview, master's degree, letters of reference, official transcript, personal statement, writing sample, immunization records; for other advanced degree, GRE General Test or MAT, interview, master's degree, official transcript, immunization records, letters of reference, 3 years of teaching experience, teaching license. Additional exam requirements/recommendations for international students: Required—TOEFL (minimum score 550 paper-based; 79 iBT), IELTS (minimum score 6), PTE (minimum score 56). Electronic applications accepted.

Auburn University at Montgomery, College of Education, Department of Counselor, Leadership, and Special Education, Montgomery, AL 36124-4023. Offers counselor education (M Ed, Ed S), including clinical mental health counseling, school counseling; early childhood special education (M Ed); instructional leadership (M Ed, Ed S); special education/collaborative teacher (M Ed, Ed S). *Accreditation:* ACA; NCATE. *Program availability:* Part-time, evening/weekend. *Students:* Average age 34. 76 applicants, 72% accepted, 26 enrolled. In 2018, 37 master's awarded. *Entrance requirements:* For master's, GRE General Test or MAT, certification, BS in teaching; for Ed S, GRE General Test or MAT, certification. Additional exam requirements/recommendations for international students: Recommended—TOEFL (minimum score 500 paper-based; 61 iBT), IELTS (minimum score 5.5), TSE (minimum score 44). *Application deadline:* For fall admission, 7/15 for international students; for spring admission, 11/15 for international students; for summer admission, 4/15 for international students. Applications are processed on a rolling basis. Electronic applications accepted. *Expenses: Tuition, area resident:* Full-time $7146; part-time $4764 per credit hour. Tuition, state resident: full-time $7146; part-time $4764 per credit hour. Tuition, nonresident: full-time $16,056; part-time $10,704 per credit hour. *International tuition:* $16,056 full-time. *Required fees:* $766. One-time fee: $25 full-time. *Financial support:* Career-related internships or fieldwork and scholarships/grants available. Support available to part-time students. Financial award application deadline: 3/1; financial award applicants required to submit FAFSA. *Unit head:* Dr. Samuel Flynt, Head, 334-244-3835, Fax: 334-244-3101, E-mail: sflynt@aum.edu. *Application contact:* Dr. Rhonda Morton, Associate Dean/Graduate Coordinator, 334-244-3287, Fax: 334-244-3978, E-mail: rmorton@aum.edu.
Website: http://education.aum.edu/academic-departments/counselor-leadership-and-special-education

Avila University, School of Education, Kansas City, MO 64145-1698. Offers advanced classroom management (MA); elementary education (Teaching Certificate); English language learners (Advanced Certificate); middle school (Teaching Certificate); physical education K-12 (Teaching Certificate); secondary education (Teaching Certificate). *Program availability:* Part-time, evening/weekend, online learning. *Faculty:* 6 full-time (5 women), 9 part-time/adjunct (8 women). *Students:* 83 full-time (71 women), 84 part-time (69 women); includes 13 minority (6 Black or African American, non-Hispanic/Latino; 2 Asian, non-Hispanic/Latino; 4 Hispanic/Latino; 1 Two or more races, non-Hispanic/Latino), 2 international. Average age 40. 92 applicants, 62% accepted, 40 enrolled. In 2018, 21 master's awarded. *Entrance requirements:* For master's, minimum GPA of 3.0, writing sample, recommendation, interview; for other advanced degree, foreign language. Additional exam requirements/recommendations for international students: Required—TOEFL (minimum score 580 paper-based; 92 iBT). *Application deadline:* Applications are processed on a rolling basis. Electronic applications accepted. *Expenses:* Contact institution. *Financial support:* In 2018–19, 12 students received support. Unspecified assistantships available. Financial award applicants required to submit FAFSA. *Unit head:* Dr. Stacy Keith, Director of Graduate Education, 816-501-2446, Fax: 816-501-2915, E-mail: stacy.keith@avila.edu. *Application contact:* Cory Roup, Graduate Education Enrollment and Academic Advisor, 816-501-2464, E-mail: cory.roup@avila.edu.
Website: https://www.avila.edu/academics/graduate-studies/grad-education

Bank Street College of Education, Graduate School, Program in Early Childhood Education, New York, NY 10025. Offers MS Ed. *Degree requirements:* For master's, thesis. *Entrance requirements:* For master's, interview, essays. Additional exam requirements/recommendations for international students: Required—TOEFL (minimum score 600 paper-based; 100 iBT), IELTS (minimum score 7). Electronic applications accepted. *Faculty research:* Play in early childhood settings, early childhood learning environments, family-teacher interaction, child-centered education, developmental interaction.

Bank Street College of Education, Graduate School, Program in Infant and Family Development and Early Intervention, New York, NY 10025. Offers infant and family development (MS Ed); infant and family early childhood special and general education (MS Ed); infant and family/early childhood special education (Ed M). *Degree requirements:* For master's, thesis. *Entrance requirements:* For master's, interview, essays. Additional exam requirements/recommendations for international students: Required—TOEFL (minimum score 600 paper-based; 100 iBT), IELTS (minimum score 7). Electronic applications accepted. *Faculty research:* Early intervention, early attachment practice in infant and toddler childcare, parenting skills in adolescents.

Bank Street College of Education, Graduate School, Program in Reading and Literacy, New York, NY 10025. Offers advanced literacy specialization (Ed M); reading and literacy (MS Ed); teaching literacy (MS Ed); teaching literacy and childhood general education (MS Ed). *Degree requirements:* For master's, thesis. *Entrance requirements:* For master's, interview, essays. Additional exam requirements/recommendations for international students: Required—TOEFL (minimum score 600 paper-based; 100 iBT), IELTS (minimum score 7). Electronic applications accepted. *Faculty research:* Language development, children's literature, whole language, the reading and writing processes, reading difficulties in multicultural classrooms.

Bank Street College of Education, Graduate School, Programs in Educational Leadership, New York, NY 10025. Offers early childhood leadership (MS Ed); educational leadership (MS Ed); leadership for educational change (Ed M, MS Ed); leadership in community-based learning (MS Ed); leadership in mathematics education (MS Ed); leadership in museum education (MS Ed); leadership in the arts: creative writing (MS Ed); leadership in the arts: visual arts (MS Ed). *Degree requirements:* For master's, thesis. *Entrance requirements:* For master's, interview, essays, minimum of 2 years experience as a classroom teacher. Additional exam requirements/recommendations for international students: Required—TOEFL (minimum score 600 paper-based; 100 iBT), IELTS (minimum score 7). Electronic applications accepted. *Faculty research:* Leadership in urban schools, leadership in small schools, mathematics in elementary schools, professional development in early childhood, leadership in arts education, leadership in special education, museum leadership, community-based leadership.

Barry University, School of Education, Program in Curriculum and Instruction, Miami Shores, FL 33161-6695. Offers accomplished teacher (Ed S); culture, language and literacy (TESOL) (PhD); curriculum evaluation and research (PhD); early childhood (Ed S); early childhood education (PhD); elementary (Ed S); elementary education (PhD); ESOL (Ed S); gifted (Ed S); Montessori (Ed S); PKP/elementary (Ed S); reading (Ed S); reading, language and cognition (PhD). *Entrance requirements:* For doctorate, GRE, minimum GPA of 3.25.

Barry University, School of Education, Program in Montessori Education, Miami Shores, FL 33161-6695. Offers MS, Ed S. *Program availability:* Part-time, evening/weekend. *Degree requirements:* For master's, comprehensive exam, practicum; for Ed S, practicum. *Entrance requirements:* For master's, GRE General Test or MAT, minimum GPA of 3.0; for Ed S, GRE General Test, minimum GPA of 3.0. Electronic applications accepted.

Barry University, School of Education, Program in Pre-Kindergarten and Primary Education, Miami Shores, FL 33161-6695. Offers pre-k/primary (MS); pre-k/primary/ESOL (MS). *Program availability:* Part-time, evening/weekend. *Degree requirements:* For master's, comprehensive exam, practicum. *Entrance requirements:* For master's, GRE General Test or MAT, minimum GPA of 3.0. Electronic applications accepted.

Bayamón Central University, Graduate Programs, Program in Education, Bayamón, PR 00960-1725. Offers administration and supervision (MA Ed); commercial education (MA Ed); elementary education (K–3) (MA Ed); family counseling (Graduate Certificate); guidance and counseling (MA Ed); pre-elementary teacher (MA Ed); rehabilitation counseling (MA Ed); special education (MA Ed), including attention deficit disorder, education of the autistic, learning disabilities. *Program availability:* Part-time, evening/weekend. *Degree requirements:* For master's, comprehensive exam. *Entrance requirements:* For master's, EXADEP, bachelor's degree in education or related field.

Binghamton University, State University of New York, Graduate School, College of Community and Public Affairs, Department of Teaching, Learning and Educational Leadership, Program in Childhood and Early Childhood Education, Binghamton, NY 13902-6000. Offers MS Ed. *Accreditation:* TEAC. *Program availability:* Part-time, evening/weekend. *Entrance requirements:* For master's, GRE General Test. Additional exam requirements/recommendations for international students: Required—TOEFL (minimum score 550 paper-based; 80 iBT). Electronic applications accepted.

Biola University, School of Education, La Mirada, CA 90639-0001. Offers curriculum and instruction (Certificate); early childhood (MA Ed, MAT); multiple subject (MAT); single subject (MAT); special education (MA Ed, MAT, Certificate). *Program availability:* Part-time, evening/weekend, online learning. *Entrance requirements:* For master's, CBEST, CSET, GRE (waived if cumulative GPA is 3.5 or above or if CBEST and all CSET subtests are passed). Additional exam requirements/recommendations for international students: Required—TOEFL (minimum score 100 iBT). Electronic applications accepted. *Faculty research:* Early childhood education, elementary education, special education, curriculum development, teacher preparation.

Bloomsburg University of Pennsylvania, School of Graduate Studies, College of Education, Department of Teaching and Learning, Program in Early Childhood Education, Bloomsburg, PA 17815-1301. Offers M Ed. *Accreditation:* NCATE. *Degree requirements:* For master's, thesis, practicum, student teaching. *Entrance requirements:* For master's, MAT, GRE, minimum QPA of 3.0, valid teaching certificate, U.S. citizenship. Additional exam requirements/recommendations for international students: Required—TOEFL, IELTS. Electronic applications accepted.

Boise State University, College of Education, Department of Early and Special Education, Boise, ID 83725-0399. Offers early and special education (M Ed). *Accreditation:* NCATE. *Program availability:* Part-time. *Degree requirements:* For master's, thesis optional. *Entrance requirements:* For master's, minimum GPA of 3.0. Additional exam requirements/recommendations for international students: Required—TOEFL (minimum score 587 paper-based; 95 iBT), IELTS (minimum score 6.5). Electronic applications accepted.

Boston College, Lynch School of Education and Human Development, Department of Counseling, Developmental, and Educational Psychology, Chestnut Hill, MA 02467-3800. Offers applied developmental and education psychology (MA, PhD); counseling psychology (PhD); mental health counseling (MA); school counseling (MA); theology and ministry and counseling (MA/MA); MA/MA. *Accreditation:* APA (one or more programs are accredited). *Program availability:* Part-time, evening/weekend. *Faculty:* 27 full-time (20 women). *Students:* 219 full-time (167 women), 23 part-time (19 women); includes 70 minority (17 Black or African American, non-Hispanic/Latino; 1 American Indian or Alaska Native, non-Hispanic/Latino; 18 Asian, non-Hispanic/Latino; 25 Hispanic/Latino; 9 Two or more races, non-Hispanic/Latino), 41 international. Average age 26. In 2018, 71 master's, 10 doctorates awarded. Terminal master's awarded for partial completion of doctoral program. *Degree requirements:* For master's, comprehensive exam; for doctorate, comprehensive exam, thesis/dissertation. Application fee: $75. Electronic applications accepted. *Financial support:* Fellowships with full and partial tuition reimbursements, research assistantships with full and partial tuition reimbursements, teaching assistantships with full and partial tuition reimbursements, career-related internships or fieldwork, Federal Work-Study, scholarships/grants, traineeships, health care benefits, tuition waivers (full and partial), and unspecified assistantships available. Support available to part-time students. Financial award applicants required to submit FAFSA. *Faculty research:* Gender, racial and social class differences; psychopathological disorders; impact of violence, community well-being and social justice, psychology of working; child development within impoverished and dangerous contexts. *Unit head:* Dr. Rebekah Levine Coley, Chairperson, 617-552-4214, Fax: 617-552-0812. *Application contact:* Jessica Rivers, Assistant Dean, Graduate Admissions and Financial Aid, 617-552-4214, Fax: 617-552-0398, E-mail: riversja@bc.edu.
Website: http://www.bc.edu/education

Boston College, Lynch School of Education and Human Development, Department of Teacher Education, Special Education and Curriculum and Instruction, Chestnut Hill, MA 02467-3800. Offers curriculum and instruction (M Ed, PhD, CAES); early childhood education (M Ed); elementary education (M Ed); law and curriculum and instruction (JD/M Ed); reading specialist (M Ed, CAES); religious education (M Ed, CAES); secondary education (M Ed, MAT, MST), including biology (MST), chemistry (MST), English (MAT), French (MAT), geology (MST), history (MAT), Latin and classical humanities (MAT), mathematics (MST), physics (MST), secondary teaching (M Ed), Spanish (MAT); special

needs: moderate disabilities (M Ed, CAES); special needs: severe disabilities (M Ed); JD/M Ed. *Program availability:* Part-time, evening/weekend, 100% online. *Faculty:* 19 full-time (11 women). *Students:* 186 full-time (140 women), 92 part-time (74 women); includes 58 minority (20 Black or African American, non-Hispanic/Latino; 4 Asian, non-Hispanic/Latino; 29 Hispanic/Latino; 5 Two or more races, non-Hispanic/Latino), 33 international. Average age 28. In 2018, 132 master's, 13 doctorates awarded. Terminal master's awarded for partial completion of doctoral program. *Degree requirements:* For master's, comprehensive exam; for doctorate, comprehensive exam, thesis/dissertation. *Entrance requirements:* Additional exam requirements/recommendations for international students: Required—TOEFL. Application fee: $75. Electronic applications accepted. *Financial support:* Fellowships with full and partial tuition reimbursements, research assistantships with full and partial tuition reimbursements, teaching assistantships with full and partial tuition reimbursements, career-related internships or fieldwork, Federal Work-Study, institutionally sponsored loans, scholarships/grants, traineeships, health care benefits, tuition waivers (full and partial), and unspecified assistantships available. Support available to part-time students. Financial award applicants required to submit FAFSA. *Faculty research:* Teacher education, education research and policy, bilingual education, science education, disabilities, urban education. *Unit head:* Dr. Susan Bruce, Chairperson, 617-552-4214, Fax: 617-552-0812. *Application contact:* Jessica Rivers, Assistant Dean of Graduate Admission and Financial Aid, 617-552-4214, Fax: 617-552-0398, E-mail: riversja@bc.edu.
Website: http://www.bc.edu/education

Brandman University, School of Education, Irvine, CA 92618. Offers curriculum and instruction (MAE); educational administration (MAE); educational leadership (MAE); educational leadership and administration (MA); elementary education (MAT); instructional technology: teaching the 21st century learner (MAE); leadership in early childhood education (MAE); organizational leadership (Ed D); school counseling (MA); secondary education (MAT); special education (MA); teaching and learning (MAE).

Brenau University, Sydney O. Smith Graduate School, College of Education, Gainesville, GA 30501. Offers early childhood (Ed S); early childhood education (M Ed, MAT); middle grades (Ed S); middle grades education (M Ed, MAT); secondary education (MAT); special education (M Ed, MAT). *Accreditation:* NCATE. *Program availability:* Part-time, evening/weekend, online learning. *Degree requirements:* For master's, thesis optional, comprehensive exam or applied research project, effective portfolio; for Ed S, thesis, applied research project. *Entrance requirements:* For master's, GRE, MAT, interview, minimum GPA of 3.0, 3 references, writing samples; for Ed S, GRE, MAT, master's degree, minimum GPA of 3.0, writing sample, letters of reference. Additional exam requirements/recommendations for international students: Required—TOEFL (minimum score 500 paper-based; 61 iBT); Recommended—IELTS (minimum score 5). Electronic applications accepted. *Expenses:* Contact institution.

Bridgewater State University, College of Graduate Studies, College of Education and Allied Studies, Department of Elementary and Early Childhood Education, Program in Early Childhood Education, Bridgewater, MA 02325. Offers M Ed. *Accreditation:* NCATE. *Program availability:* Part-time, evening/weekend. *Entrance requirements:* For master's, GRE General Test or Massachusetts Test for Educator Licensure.

Brooklyn College of the City University of New York, School of Education, Program in Early Childhood Education, Brooklyn, NY 11210-2889. Offers art teacher (K-12) (MA); birth-grade 2 (MS Ed). *Program availability:* Part-time, evening/weekend. *Entrance requirements:* For master's, LAST, bachelor's degree in early childhood education, resume, 2 letters of recommendation, essay. Additional exam requirements/recommendations for international students: Required—TOEFL (minimum score 500 paper-based; 61 iBT). Electronic applications accepted. *Faculty research:* Children's narrations, language acquisition, culture and education.

Brooklyn College of the City University of New York, School of Education, Program in Special Education, Brooklyn, NY 11210-2889. Offers autism spectrum disorders (AC); teacher of students with disabilities (MS Ed), including adolescence education, childhood education, early childhood education. *Program availability:* Part-time. *Entrance requirements:* For master's, LAST, interview; previous course work in education and psychology; minimum GPA of 3.0 in education, 2.8 overall; resume, 2 letters of recommendation; essay. Additional exam requirements/recommendations for international students: Required—TOEFL (minimum score 500 paper-based; 61 iBT). Electronic applications accepted. *Faculty research:* School reform, conflict resolution, curriculum for inclusive settings, urban issues in special education.

Buffalo State College, State University of New York, The Graduate School, School of Education, Department of Elementary Education, Literacy, and Educational Leadership, Program in Childhood Education, Buffalo, NY 14222-1095. Offers childhood education (grades 1-6) (MS Ed); early childhood and childhood curriculum and instruction (MS Ed); early childhood education (birth-grade 2) (MS Ed). *Accreditation:* NCATE. *Program availability:* Part-time. *Degree requirements:* For master's, thesis or project. *Entrance requirements:* For master's, minimum GPA of 2.5 in last 60 hours, New York teaching certificate. Additional exam requirements/recommendations for international students: Required—TOEFL (minimum score 550 paper-based).

Cabrini University, Academic Affairs, Radnor, PA 19087. Offers accounting (M Acc); autism spectrum disorder (M Ed); biological sciences (MS), including civic leadership; criminology and criminal justice (MA); curriculum, instruction, and assessment (M Ed); educational leadership (M Ed, Ed D), including curriculum and instructional leadership (Ed D), preK-12 leadership (Ed D); English as a second language (M Ed); organizational leadership (DBA, PhD); preK to 4 (M Ed); reading specialist (M Ed); secondary education (M Ed), including biology, chemistry, English, English/communication, mathematics, social studies; special education grades 7-12 (M Ed); special education preK-8 (M Ed); teaching and learning (M Ed). *Program availability:* Part-time, evening/weekend. *Degree requirements:* For master's, comprehensive exam (for some programs), thesis (for some programs); for doctorate, comprehensive exam (for some programs), thesis/dissertation. *Entrance requirements:* For master's, professional resume, personal statement, two recommendations, official transcripts; for doctorate, official transcripts, minimum master's GPA of 3.0, two recommendations, interview with admissions committee. Additional exam requirements/recommendations for international students: Required—TOEFL (minimum score 80 iBT). Electronic applications accepted. Application fee is waived when completed online. *Expenses:* Contact institution.

California State University, Dominguez Hills, College of Education, Division of Teacher Education, Program in Special Education, Carson, CA 90747-0001. Offers early childhood special education (MA). *Program availability:* Part-time, evening/weekend. *Degree requirements:* For master's, comprehensive exam, thesis or alternative. *Entrance requirements:* For master's, minimum GPA of 2.75 in last 60 units, 3 letters of recommendation. Additional exam requirements/recommendations for international students: Required—TOEFL.

California State University, East Bay, Office of Graduate Studies, College of Education and Allied Studies, Department of Teacher Education, Hayward, CA 94542-3000. Offers education (MS), including curriculum, early childhood education, educational technology and leadership, reading instruction. *Program availability:* Online learning. *Degree requirements:* For master's, project or thesis. *Entrance requirements:* For master's, minimum GPA of 3.0 in field, 2.5 overall; teaching experience; baccalaureate degree; 3 letters of recommendation. Additional exam requirements/recommendations for international students: Required—TOEFL (minimum score 550 paper-based), IELTS. Electronic applications accepted. *Faculty research:* Online, pedagogy, writing, learning, teaching.

California State University, Fresno, Division of Research and Graduate Studies, Kremen School of Education and Human Development, Department of Literacy, Early, Bilingual, and Special Education, Fresno, CA 93740-8027. Offers education (MA), including early childhood education, reading/language arts; special education (MA). *Accreditation:* NCATE. *Program availability:* Part-time, evening/weekend. *Degree requirements:* For master's, thesis or alternative. *Entrance requirements:* For master's, GRE General Test, MAT, minimum GPA of 2.75. Additional exam requirements/recommendations for international students: Required—TOEFL. Electronic applications accepted. *Faculty research:* Reading recovery, monitoring/tutoring programs, character and academics, professional ethics, low-performing partnership schools.

California State University, Northridge, Graduate Studies, Michael D. Eisner College of Education, Department of Educational Psychology and Counseling, Northridge, CA 91330. Offers counseling (MS), including career counseling, college counseling and student services, marriage and family therapy, school counseling, school psychology; educational psychology (MA Ed), including development, learning, and instruction, early childhood education. *Accreditation:* ACA (one or more programs are accredited); NCATE. *Program availability:* Part-time, evening/weekend. *Entrance requirements:* For master's, GRE General Test or minimum GPA of 3.0. Additional exam requirements/recommendations for international students: Required—TOEFL.

California State University, Sacramento, College of Education, Graduate and Professional Studies in Education, Sacramento, CA 95819. Offers behavioral science and gender equity (MA); child development (MA); counseling (MS); curriculum and instruction (MA); education (Ed D), including K-12 and community college; education leadership and policy studies (MA), including higher education, PreK-12; education specialist (Ed S), including school psychology; educational technology (MA); language and literacy (MA); multicultural education (MA); school psychology (MA); special education (MA); workforce development advocacy (MA). *Program availability:* Part-time, evening/weekend, blended/hybrid learning. *Degree requirements:* For master's, thesis or project; writing proficiency exam; for doctorate, thesis/dissertation. *Entrance requirements:* For master's and doctorate, GRE. Additional exam requirements/recommendations for international students: Required—TOEFL (minimum score 550 paper-based; 80 iBT); Recommended—IELTS (minimum score 7), TSE. Electronic applications accepted. *Expenses:* Contact institution.

California University of Pennsylvania, School of Graduate Studies and Research, College of Education and Human Services, Department of Childhood Education, California, PA 15419-1394. Offers early childhood education (M Ed); elementary education (M Ed); STEM education (M Ed). *Accreditation:* NCATE. *Program availability:* Part-time, evening/weekend. *Degree requirements:* For master's, comprehensive exam, thesis optional. *Entrance requirements:* For master's, MAT, PRAXIS, minimum GPA of 3.0, state police clearances. Additional exam requirements/recommendations for international students: Required—TOEFL (minimum score 550 paper-based; 80 iBT). Electronic applications accepted. *Faculty research:* English as a second language, adult literacy, emerging literacy, diagnosis and remediation, phonemic awareness.

Cambridge College, School of Education, Boston, MA 02129. Offers autism specialist (M Ed); autism/behavior analyst (M Ed); behavior analyst (Post-Master's Certificate); curriculum and instruction (CAGS); early childhood teacher (M Ed); educational leadership (M Ed, Ed D); elementary teacher (M Ed); English as a second language (M Ed, Certificate); general science (M Ed); health education (Post-Master's Certificate); interdisciplinary studies (M Ed); library teacher (M Ed); mathematics education (M Ed); mathematics specialist (Certificate); school administration (M Ed, CAGS); school nurse education (M Ed); teacher of students with moderate disabilities (M Ed); teaching skills and methodologies (M Ed). *Program availability:* Part-time, evening/weekend, online learning. *Degree requirements:* For master's, thesis, internship/practicum (licensure program only); for doctorate, thesis/dissertation; for other advanced degree, thesis. *Entrance requirements:* For master's, interview, resume, documentation of licensure, 2 professional references; for doctorate, official transcripts, interview, resume, written personal statement/essay, portfolio of scholarly and professional work, 2 professional references, health insurance, immunizations form; for other advanced degree, official transcripts, interview, resume, written personal statement/essay, 2 professional references, health insurance, immunizations form. Additional exam requirements/recommendations for international students: Required—TOEFL (minimum score 550 paper-based; 79 iBT), Michigan English Language Assessment Battery (minimum score 85); Recommended—IELTS (minimum score 6). *Application deadline:* Applications are processed on a rolling basis. Application fee: $30. Electronic applications accepted. *Expenses:* Contact institution. *Financial support:* Career-related internships or fieldwork, Federal Work-Study, and scholarships/grants available. Financial award applicants required to submit FAFSA. *Faculty research:* Adult education, accelerated learning, mathematics education, brain compatible learning, special education and law. *Unit head:* Dr. Mary Garrity, Interim Dean, 617-873-0168, E-mail: mary.garrity@cambridgecollege.edu. *Application contact:* Salvadore Liberto, Interim Assistant Vice President of Enrollment, 800-877-4723, E-mail: admissions@cambridgecollege.edu.
Website: https://www.cambridgecollege.edu/school/school-education

Canisius College, Graduate Division, School of Education and Human Services, Department of Teacher Education, Buffalo, NY 14208-1098. Offers adolescence education (MS Ed); childhood education (MS Ed); general education (MS Ed); special education (MS), including adolescence special education, advanced special education, childhood education grade 1-6, childhood special education. *Program availability:* Part-time, evening/weekend, 100% online, blended/hybrid learning. *Faculty:* 10 full-time (all women), 16 part-time/adjunct (14 women). *Students:* 69 full-time (50 women), 23 part-time (16 women); includes 10 minority (4 Black or African American, non-Hispanic/Latino; 1 Asian, non-Hispanic/Latino; 4 Hispanic/Latino; 1 Two or more races, non-Hispanic/Latino), 3 international. Average age 26. 85 applicants, 75% accepted, 54 enrolled. In 2018, 32 master's awarded. *Degree requirements:* For master's, research project or thesis, project internship. *Entrance requirements:* For master's, GRE (if cumulative GPA less than 2.7), official transcripts, letters of recommendation. Additional exam requirements/recommendations for international students: Required—TOEFL (minimum score 550 paper-based, 79 iBT), IELTS (minimum score 6.5), or CAEL (minimum score 70). *Application deadline:* Applications are processed on a rolling basis. Application fee: $0. Electronic applications accepted. *Expenses: Tuition:* Part-time $820 per credit hour. *Required fees:* $25 per semester. One-time fee: $65 part-time. Tuition and fees vary according to program. *Financial support:* In 2018–19, 90 students received support. Career-related internships or fieldwork, Federal Work-Study, scholarships/grants, tuition waivers (partial), and unspecified assistantships available. Support available to part-time students. Financial award application deadline: 4/30; financial award applicants required to submit FAFSA. *Unit head:* Dr. Barbara A. Burns, CHAIR/PROFESSOR OF TEACHER EDUCATION, 716-888-3291, Fax: 716-888-2766, E-mail: burns1@canisius.edu. *Application contact:* Dr. Barbara A. Burns, CHAIR/PROFESSOR OF TEACHER EDUCATION, 716-888-3291, Fax: 716-888-2766, E-mail: burns1@canisius.edu.
Website: http://www.canisius.edu/academics/graduate/

Capella University, School of Education, Master's Programs in Education, Minneapolis, MN 55402. Offers adult education (MS); curriculum and instruction (MS); early childhood education (MS); enrollment management (MS); higher education leadership and management (MS); instructional design for online learning (MS); integrative studies (MS); K-12 studies in education (MS); leadership in educational administration (MS); reading and literacy (MS); special education teaching (MS).

Caribbean University, Graduate School, Bayamón, PR 00960-0493. Offers administration and supervision (MA Ed); criminal justice (MA); curriculum and instruction (MA Ed, PhD), including elementary education (MA Ed), English education (MA Ed), history education (MA Ed), mathematics education (MA Ed), primary education (MA Ed), science education (MA Ed), Spanish education (MA Ed); educational technology in instructional systems (MA Ed); gerontology (MSN); human resources (MBA); museology, archiving and art history (MA Ed); neonatal pediatrics (MSN); physical education (MA Ed); special education (MA Ed). *Entrance requirements:* For master's, interview, minimum GPA of 2.5.

Carlow University, College of Learning and Innovation, Program in Education, Pittsburgh, PA 15213-3165. Offers early childhood education (M Ed); education (M Ed); online instructional design and technology (Certificate); special education (M Ed), including early childhood. *Program availability:* Part-time, evening/weekend, 100% online, blended/hybrid learning. *Students:* 41 full-time (33 women), 9 part-time (all women); includes 12 minority (10 Black or African American, non-Hispanic/Latino; 1 Asian, non-Hispanic/Latino; 1 Two or more races, non-Hispanic/Latino). Average age 32. 32 applicants, 100% accepted, 22 enrolled. In 2018, 24 master's, 5 Certificates awarded. *Entrance requirements:* For master's, personal essay; resume or curriculum vitae; two recommendations; official transcripts; interview; minimum undergraduate GPA of 3.0. Additional exam requirements/recommendations for international students: Required—TOEFL (minimum score 550 paper-based). *Application deadline:* Applications are processed on a rolling basis. Electronic applications accepted. *Expenses: Tuition:* Full-time $13,090; part-time $5100 per semester. *Required fees:* $215; $84. Tuition and fees vary according to course load, degree level and program. *Financial support:* Application deadline: 4/1; applicants required to submit FAFSA. *Unit head:* Dr. Keeley Baronak, Chair, Department of Education, 412-578-6135, Fax: 412-578-8816, E-mail: kobaronak@carlow.edu. *Application contact:* Dr. Keeley Baronak, Chair, Department of Education, 412-578-6135, Fax: 412-578-8816, E-mail: kobaronak@carlow.edu.
Website: http://www.carlow.edu/education.aspx

Carroll University, Graduate Programs in Education, Waukesha, WI 53186-5593. Offers adult and continuing education (M Ed); educational leadership (MS); PK-12 (M Ed). *Program availability:* Part-time, evening/weekend. *Degree requirements:* For master's, thesis. *Entrance requirements:* For master's, minimum undergraduate GPA of 2.5 in related field. Additional exam requirements/recommendations for international students: Required—TOEFL. Electronic applications accepted. *Faculty research:* Qualitative research methods, whole language approaches to teaching, the writing process, multicultural education, gifted/talented learners.

The Catholic University of America, School of Arts and Sciences, Department of Education, Washington, DC 20064. Offers Catholic school leadership (MA); education (Certificate); secondary education (MA); special education (MA), including early childhood, non-categorical. *Accreditation:* NCATE. *Program availability:* Part-time. *Faculty:* 7 full-time (6 women), 7 part-time/adjunct (5 women). *Students:* 12 full-time (11 women), 15 part-time (6 women); includes 3 minority (2 Hispanic/Latino; 1 Two or more races, non-Hispanic/Latino), 2 international. Average age 37. 12 applicants, 75% accepted, 8 enrolled. In 2018, 14 master's awarded. *Degree requirements:* For master's, comprehensive exam, thesis or alternative; for Certificate, action research project. *Entrance requirements:* For master's, GRE General Test or MAT, statement of purpose, official copies of academic transcripts, three letters of recommendation, interview; for Certificate, PRAXIS I, statement of purpose, official copies of academic transcripts, three letters of recommendation, interview. Additional exam requirements/recommendations for international students: Required—TOEFL (minimum score 550 paper-based; 80 iBT). *Application deadline:* For fall admission, 7/15 priority date for domestic students, 7/1 for international students; for spring admission, 11/15 priority date for domestic students, 11/1 for international students. Applications are processed on a rolling basis. Application fee: $55. Electronic applications accepted. *Expenses:* Contact institution. *Financial support:* Fellowships, research assistantships, teaching assistantships, Federal Work-Study, scholarships/grants, tuition waivers (full and partial), and unspecified assistantships available. Financial award application deadline: 2/1; financial award applicants required to submit FAFSA. *Faculty research:* Special education, early childhood education, educational psychology, Catholic school administration, leadership and policy studies, counseling, curriculum and instruction. *Unit head:* Dr. Agnes Cave, Chair, 202-319-5805, Fax: 202-319-5815, E-mail: cave@cua.edu. *Application contact:* Dr. Steven Brown, Director of Graduate Admissions, 202-319-5057, Fax: 202-319-6533, E-mail: cua-admissions@cua.edu.
Website: http://education.cua.edu/

Central Connecticut State University, School of Graduate Studies, School of Education and Professional Studies, Department of Literacy, Elementary, and Early Childhood Education, New Britain, CT 06050-4010. Offers MS, AC, Sixth Year Certificate. *Program availability:* Part-time, evening/weekend. *Faculty:* 5 full-time (4 women), 5 part-time/adjunct (all women). *Students:* 9 full-time (8 women), 100 part-time (97 women); includes 7 minority (6 Hispanic/Latino; 1 Two or more races, non-Hispanic/Latino). Average age 30. 62 applicants, 77% accepted, 32 enrolled. In 2018, 29 master's, 9 other advanced degrees awarded. *Degree requirements:* For master's, comprehensive exam, thesis or alternative; for other advanced degree, qualifying exam. *Entrance requirements:* For master's, minimum undergraduate GPA of 2.7, teacher certification, interview, essay, letters of recommendation; for other advanced degree, master's degree, essay, teacher certification, interview, letters of recommendation. Additional exam requirements/recommendations for international students: Required—TOEFL (minimum score 550 paper-based; 79 iBT); Recommended—IELTS (minimum score 6.5). *Application deadline:* For fall admission, 6/1 for domestic students, 5/1 for international students; for spring admission, 11/1 for domestic and international students. Applications are processed on a rolling basis. Application fee: $50. Electronic applications accepted. *Expenses: Tuition, area resident:* Full-time $7027; part-time $388 per credit. Tuition, state resident: full-time $9750; part-time $388 per credit. Tuition, nonresident: full-time $18,102; part-time $388 per credit. *International tuition:* $18,102 full-time. *Required fees:* $266 per semester. *Financial support:* In 2018–19, 6 students received support. Career-related internships or fieldwork, Federal Work-Study, scholarships/grants, and unspecified assistantships available. Support available to part-time students. Financial award application deadline: 3/1. *Faculty research:* Developmental, clinical, and administrative aspects of reading and language arts instruction. *Unit head:* Dr. Helen Abadiano, Chair, 860-832-2175, E-mail: abadiano@ccsu.edu. *Application contact:* Patricia Gardner, Associate Director of Graduate Studies, 860-832-2350, Fax: 860-832-2362.
Website: http://www.ccsu.edu/leece/index.html

Central Michigan University, College of Graduate Studies, College of Education and Human Services, Department of Teacher Education and Professional Development, Mount Pleasant, MI 48859. Offers educational technology (MA, Graduate Certificate); elementary education (MA), including classroom teaching, early childhood; reading and literacy K-12 (MA); secondary education (MA). *Program availability:* Part-time, evening/weekend. *Degree requirements:* For master's, thesis or alternative. Electronic applications accepted. *Faculty research:* Integrating literacy across the curriculum, science teaching and aesthetic learning in science, diversity education, educational technology, educational psychology and child development.

Chaminade University of Honolulu, Graduate, Program in Education, Honolulu, HI 96816-1578. Offers child development (M Ed); early childhood education (Montessori) (MAT); early childhood education (PK-3) (MAT); educational leadership (M Ed); elementary education (MAT); instructional leadership (M Ed); Montessori (M Ed); secondary education (MAT); special education (MAT); teacher leader (M Ed). *Program availability:* Part-time, evening/weekend, 100% online, blended/hybrid learning. *Faculty:* 8 full-time (3 women), 11 part-time/adjunct (8 women). *Students:* 80 full-time (57 women), 100 part-time (77 women); includes 113 minority (6 Black or African American, non-Hispanic/Latino; 4 American Indian or Alaska Native, non-Hispanic/Latino; 45 Asian, non-Hispanic/Latino; 6 Hispanic/Latino; 50 Native Hawaiian or other Pacific Islander, non-Hispanic/Latino; 2 Two or more races, non-Hispanic/Latino), 2 international. Average age 35. 53 applicants, 92% accepted, 40 enrolled. In 2018, 92 master's awarded. *Degree requirements:* For master's, thesis or alternative. *Entrance requirements:* For master's, PRAXIS (for MAT), official transcripts, writing sample (for MAT). Additional exam requirements/recommendations for international students: Required—TOEFL (minimum score 550 paper-based; 79 iBT). *Application deadline:* Applications are processed on a rolling basis. Application fee: $40. Electronic applications accepted. *Expenses:* $780 per credit; $93 fee per online course. *Financial support:* Applicants required to submit FAFSA. *Unit head:* Dr. Dale Fryxell, Dean, 808-739-4652, Fax: 808-739-4607, E-mail: edu-office@chaminade.edu. *Application contact:* 808-739-7478, E-mail: gradserv@chaminade.edu.
Website: https://chaminade.edu/academics/education-behavioral-sciences/

Champlain College, Graduate Studies, Burlington, VT 05402-0670. Offers business (MBA); digital forensic science (MS); early childhood education (M Ed); emergent media (MFA, MS); executive leadership (MS); health care administration (MS); information security operations (MS); law (MS); mediation and applied conflict studies (MS). MS in emergent media program held in Shanghai. *Program availability:* Part-time, online learning. *Degree requirements:* For master's, capstone project. *Entrance requirements:* Additional exam requirements/recommendations for international students: Required—TOEFL (minimum score 550 paper-based; 80 iBT). Electronic applications accepted.

Chatham University, Program in Education, Pittsburgh, PA 15232-2826. Offers early childhood education (MAT); elementary education (MAT); environmental education (K-12) (MAT); secondary art (MAT); secondary biology education (MAT); secondary chemistry education (MAT); secondary English education (MAT); secondary math education (MAT); secondary physics education (MAT); secondary social studies education (MAT); special education (MAT). *Degree requirements:* For master's, thesis, teaching experience. *Entrance requirements:* For master's, minimum GPA of 3.0, sample of written work, recommendation letters. Additional exam requirements/recommendations for international students: Required—TOEFL (minimum score 600 paper-based; 100 iBT), IELTS (minimum score 7), TWE. Electronic applications accepted. Application fee is waived when completed online. *Faculty research:* Gifted education, environmental education, technology in education, writing as learning, class size and achievement.

Chestnut Hill College, School of Graduate Studies, Department of Education, Program in Early Education, Philadelphia, PA 19118-2693. Offers early education (M Ed), including Montessori certificate preparation, preK-4 education, preK-4 education and special education preK-8. *Program availability:* Part-time, evening/weekend. *Degree requirements:* For master's, thesis optional. *Entrance requirements:* For master's, PRAXIS I or proof of teaching certification, writing sample, letters of recommendation, 6 graduate credits with minimum B grade or minimum undergraduate GPA of 3.0. Additional exam requirements/recommendations for international students: Required—TOEFL (minimum score 500 paper-based), IELTS (minimum score 6.0), or TWE (minimum score 22). Electronic applications accepted. *Expenses:* Contact institution. *Faculty research:* Gender issues, early childhood education standardized testing.

Chestnut Hill College, School of Graduate Studies, Department of Education, Program in Reading, Philadelphia, PA 19118-2693. Offers reading specialist (M Ed), including K-12, special education 7-12, special education PreK-8. *Program availability:* Part-time, evening/weekend. *Degree requirements:* For master's, thesis optional. *Entrance requirements:* Additional exam requirements/recommendations for international students: Required—TOEFL (minimum score 500 paper-based) or IELTS (minimum score 6). Electronic applications accepted. *Expenses:* Contact institution. *Faculty research:* Inclusive education, cultural issues in education.

Chicago State University, School of Graduate and Professional Studies, College of Education, Department of Special Education, Early Childhood Education and Bilingual Education, Program in Early Childhood Education, Chicago, IL 60628. Offers MAT, MS Ed. *Accreditation:* NCATE. *Entrance requirements:* For master's, minimum GPA of 2.75.

The Citadel, The Military College of South Carolina, Citadel Graduate College, Zucker Family School of Education, Charleston, SC 29409. Offers elementary/secondary school administration and supervision (M Ed); elementary/secondary school counseling (M Ed); interdisciplinary STEM education (M Ed); literacy education (M Ed, Graduate Certificate); middle grades (MAT), including English, mathematics, science, social studies; physical education (grades K-12) (MAT); school superintendency (Ed S); secondary education (MAT), including biology, English, mathematics, social studies; student affairs (Graduate Certificate); student affairs and college counseling (M Ed). *Accreditation:* NCATE. *Program availability:* Part-time, evening/weekend, 100% online, blended/hybrid learning. *Degree requirements:* For master's, comprehensive exam (for some programs). *Entrance requirements:* For master's, GRE (minimum combined verbal and quantitative score of 290) or MAT (minimum score 396). Additional exam requirements/recommendations for international students: Required—TOEFL (minimum score 550 paper-based; 79 iBT). Electronic applications accepted. *Expenses:* Tuition, state resident: part-time $595 per credit hour. Tuition, nonresident: part-time $1020 per credit hour. *Required fees:* $90 per term.

City College of the City University of New York, Graduate School, School of Education, Department of Teaching, Learning and Culture, New York, NY 10031-9198. Offers bilingual education (MS); childhood education (MS); early childhood education (MS); educational theatre (MS); literacy (MS); TESOL (MS). *Accreditation:* NCATE. *Degree requirements:* For master's, thesis. *Entrance requirements:* For master's, Liberal Arts and Sciences Test (LAST), Content Specialty Test (CST). Additional exam requirements/recommendations for international students: Required—TOEFL.

Clarion University of Pennsylvania, College of Arts, Education and Sciences, Master of Education Program, Clarion, PA 16214. Offers curriculum and instruction (M Ed); early childhood (M Ed); math education (M Ed); reading (M Ed); science education (M Ed); special education (M Ed); technology (M Ed). *Accreditation:* NCATE. *Program availability:* Part-time, evening/weekend, 100% online, blended/hybrid learning. *Faculty:*

6 full-time (3 women). *Students:* 5 full-time (all women), 85 part-time (73 women); includes 3 minority (2 Black or African American, non-Hispanic/Latino; 1 Two or more races, non-Hispanic/Latino). Average age 30. 57 applicants, 61% accepted, 26 enrolled. In 2018, 51 master's awarded. *Degree requirements:* For master's, comprehensive exam (for some programs), thesis or alternative. *Entrance requirements:* For master's, minimum QPA of 3.0. Additional exam requirements/recommendations for international students: Required—TOEFL (minimum score 550 paper-based; 80 iBT), Or IELTS. Satisfactory completion of a bachelor's degree from an accredited US college or university is also acceptable evidence of English language. *Application deadline:* For fall admission, 8/1 priority date for domestic students, 7/15 priority date for international students; for winter admission, 11/1 priority date for domestic students; for spring admission, 12/1 priority date for domestic students, 11/15 priority date for international students; for summer admission, 4/1 priority date for domestic students. Applications are processed on a rolling basis. Application fee: $40. Electronic applications accepted. *Expenses: Tuition, area resident:* Part-time $516 per credit hour. Tuition, state resident: part-time $516 per credit hour. Tuition, nonresident: part-time $774 per credit hour. *Required fees:* $159 per credit hour. One-time fee: $50 part-time. Tuition and fees vary according to degree level, campus/location and program. *Financial support:* Federal Work-Study, institutionally sponsored loans, and scholarships/grants available. Financial award application deadline: 3/1; financial award applicants required to submit FAFSA. *Unit head:* Dr. John McCullough, Chair, Department of Education, 814-393-2404, Fax: 814-393-2446, E-mail: gradstudies@clarion.edu. *Application contact:* Susan Staub, Graduate Admissions Counselor, 814-393-2337, Fax: 814-393-2722, E-mail: gradstudies@clarion.edu.

Clemson University, Graduate School, College of Education, Department of Educational and Organizational Leadership Development, Clemson, SC 29634. Offers administration and supervision (M Ed, Ed S); athletic leadership (MS, Certificate); education systems improvement science (Ed D); educational leadership (PhD), including higher education, P-12; human resource development (MHRD), including human resource development; leadership (Certificate); student affairs (M Ed). *Program availability:* Part-time, evening/weekend, 100% online. *Faculty:* 17 full-time (11 women). *Students:* 105 full-time (64 women), 265 part-time (170 women); includes 76 minority (61 Black or African American, non-Hispanic/Latino; 1 American Indian or Alaska Native, non-Hispanic/Latino; 3 Asian, non-Hispanic/Latino; 5 Hispanic/Latino; 6 Two or more races, non-Hispanic/Latino). Average age 32. 204 applicants, 83% accepted, 123 enrolled. In 2018, 93 master's, 17 doctorates, 28 other advanced degrees awarded. *Degree requirements:* For master's, thesis (for some programs); for doctorate, comprehensive exam, thesis/dissertation. *Entrance requirements:* For master's, doctorate, and other advanced degree, GRE General Test, unofficial transcripts, letters of recommendation. Additional exam requirements/recommendations for international students: Required—TOEFL (minimum score 80 paper-based; 80 iBT); Recommended—IELTS (minimum score 6.5), TSE (minimum score 54). *Application deadline:* For fall admission, 4/15 priority date for international students; for spring admission, 10/15 priority date for international students. Applications are processed on a rolling basis. Application fee: $80 ($90 for international students). Electronic applications accepted. *Expenses:* $5198 per semester full-time resident, $10123 per semester full-time non-resident, $556 per credit hour part-time resident, $1109 per credit hour part-time non-resident, online $770 per credit hour, $4938 doctoral programs resident, $10405 doctoral programs non-resident, $1144 full-time graduate assistant, other fees may apply per session. *Financial support:* In 2018–19, 30 students received support, including 8 fellowships with full and partial tuition reimbursements available (averaging $4,525 per year), 3 research assistantships with full and partial tuition reimbursements available (averaging $7,500 per year); career-related internships or fieldwork and unspecified assistantships also available. *Faculty research:* Leadership, ethics, policy development, performance improvement. *Total annual research expenditures:* $79,638. *Unit head:* Dr. Roy Jones, Interim Department Chair, 864-656-7915, E-mail: royj@clemson.edu. *Application contact:* Alison Search, Student Services Program Coordinator, 864-250-8880, E-mail: alisonp@clemson.edu.
Website: http://www.clemson.edu/education/departments/educational-organizational-leadership-development/index.html

Cleveland State University, College of Graduate Studies, College of Education and Human Services, Department of Teacher Education, Cleveland, OH 44115. Offers art education (M Ed); early childhood education (M Ed); foreign language education (M Ed); middle childhood mathematics and science education (M Ed); special education (M Ed), including mild/moderate disabilities, moderate/intensive disabilities; teaching English to speakers of other languages (M Ed). *Program availability:* Part-time, evening/weekend. *Faculty:* 19 full-time (14 women), 32 part-time/adjunct (27 women). *Students:* 56 full-time (40 women), 344 part-time (278 women); includes 104 minority (74 Black or African American, non-Hispanic/Latino; 1 American Indian or Alaska Native, non-Hispanic/Latino; 5 Asian, non-Hispanic/Latino; 9 Hispanic/Latino; 15 Two or more races, non-Hispanic/Latino), 14 international. Average age 34. 177 applicants, 55% accepted, 68 enrolled. In 2018, 117 master's awarded. *Degree requirements:* For master's, comprehensive exam (for some programs), thesis or alternative. *Entrance requirements:* For master's, GRE General Test or MAT, minimum GPA of 2.75. Additional exam requirements/recommendations for international students: Required—TOEFL (minimum score 550 paper-based; 78 iBT), IELTS (minimum score 6). *Application deadline:* For fall admission, 7/1 priority date for domestic students, 5/15 for international students; for spring admission, 11/15 for domestic students, 11/1 for international students; for summer admission, 4/1 for domestic students, 3/15 for international students. Applications are processed on a rolling basis. Application fee: $30. *Expenses:* Tuition, state resident: full-time $7232.55; part-time $6676 per credit hour. Tuition, nonresident: full-time $12,375. *International tuition:* $18,914 full-time. *Required fees:* $80; $80 $40. Tuition and fees vary according to program. *Financial support:* In 2018–19, 13 research assistantships with full tuition reimbursements (averaging $15,845 per year) were awarded; tuition waivers (partial) and unspecified assistantships also available. Financial award application deadline: 2/15; financial award applicants required to submit FAFSA. *Faculty research:* Early childhood education, literacy education, special education: mild/moderate, moderate/intensive, early childhood intervention specialist), teaching English to speakers of other languages (TESOL). *Total annual research expenditures:* $275,907. *Unit head:* Dr. Tachelle Banks, Department Chairperson, 216-687-4600, Fax: 216-687-5379, E-mail: t.i.banks@csuohio.edu. *Application contact:* Rosalyn Adams, Administrative Coordinator, 216-523-7139, Fax: 216-687-5491, E-mail: r.m.adams@csuohio.edu.
Website: http://www.csuohio.edu/cehs/te/te

The College at Brockport, State University of New York, School of Education, Health, and Human Services, Department of Education and Human Development, Brockport, NY 14420-2997. Offers adolescence education (MS Ed), including adolescence biology education, adolescence chemistry education, adolescence English, adolescence mathematics, adolescence physics, adolescence physics education, adolescence social studies education; bilingual education (MS Ed, AGC); childhood curriculum specialist (MS Ed); inclusive generalist education (MS Ed, AGC, Advanced Certificate), including biology (MS Ed, AGC), chemistry (MS Ed), English (MS Ed, Advanced Certificate), mathematics (MS Ed, Advanced Certificate), science (MS Ed, Advanced Certificate), social studies (MS Ed, Advanced Certificate); literacy education B-12 (MS Ed). *Accreditation:* NCATE. *Faculty:* 12 full-time (7 women), 10 part-time/adjunct (6 women). *Students:* 60 full-time (39 women), 227 part-time (157 women); includes 9 minority (1 Asian, non-Hispanic/Latino; 8 Hispanic/Latino). 135 applicants, 71% accepted, 59 enrolled. In 2018, 107 master's, 13 AGCs awarded. *Degree requirements:* For master's, thesis or alternative. *Entrance requirements:* For master's, minimum GPA of 3.0, letters of recommendation, interview (for some programs); statement of objectives, current resume. Additional exam requirements/recommendations for international students: Required—TOEFL (minimum score 550 paper-based; 79 iBT), IELTS (minimum score 6.5). *Application deadline:* For fall admission, 3/15 priority date for domestic and international students; for spring admission, 10/15 priority date for domestic and international students; for summer admission, 3/15 priority date for domestic and international students. Application fee: $80. Electronic applications accepted. *Expenses:* Tuition, state resident: part-time $471 per credit. Tuition, nonresident: part-time $963 per credit. *Financial support:* In 2018–19, 1 fellowship with full tuition reimbursement (averaging $7,500 per year), 1 teaching assistantship with full tuition reimbursement (averaging $6,000 per year) were awarded; Federal Work-Study, scholarships/grants, and unspecified assistantships also available. Support available to part-time students. Financial award application deadline: 3/15; financial award applicants required to submit FAFSA. *Faculty research:* Educational assessment, literacy education, inclusive education, teacher preparation, qualitative methodology. *Unit head:* Dr. Janka Szilagyi, Chairperson, 585-395-5945, Fax: 585-395-2172, E-mail: jszilagy@brockport.edu. *Application contact:* Buffie Edick, Graduate Program Director, 585-395-2326, Fax: 585-395-2172, E-mail: bedick@brockport.edu.
Website: https://www.brockport.edu/academics/education_human_development/department.html

College of Charleston, Graduate School, School of Education, Health, and Human Performance, Department of Elementary and Early Childhood Education, Program in Early Childhood Education, Charleston, SC 29424-0001. Offers MAT. *Accreditation:* NCATE. *Program availability:* Part-time, evening/weekend. *Degree requirements:* For master's, thesis or alternative, written qualifying exam, student teaching experience (MAT). *Entrance requirements:* For master's, GRE, minimum GPA of 2.5, 2 letters of recommendation. Additional exam requirements/recommendations for international students: Required—TOEFL (minimum score 81 iBT). Electronic applications accepted. *Faculty research:* Teacher education and creative arts, integrated curriculum, multicultural awareness, teaching models, cooperative learning.

The College of New Jersey, Office of Graduate and Advancing Education, School of Education, Department of Elementary and Early Childhood Education, Program in Early Childhood Education, Ewing, NJ 08628. Offers M Ed, MAT. *Program availability:* Part-time. *Entrance requirements:* For master's, GRE, minimum GPA of 3.0 in field or 2.75 overall. Additional exam requirements/recommendations for international students: Required—TOEFL. Electronic applications accepted.

The College of New Rochelle, Graduate School, Division of Education, Program in Childhood Education/Early Childhood Education, New Rochelle, NY 10805-2308. Offers childhood education (MS Ed); early childhood education (MS Ed). *Program availability:* Part-time. *Degree requirements:* For master's, comprehensive exam (for some programs), thesis (for some programs), practicum. *Entrance requirements:* For master's, interview, minimum GPA of 3.0 in field, 2.7 overall.

College of Saint Elizabeth, Program in Education, Morristown, NJ 07960-6989. Offers assistive technology (Certificate); education (MA); ESL (Certificate); Holocaust/genocide education (Certificate); middle school science (Certificate); online teaching in the 21st century (Certificate); teaching (Certificate), including K-12, K-6, teacher of students with disabilities. *Program availability:* Part-time. *Degree requirements:* For master's and Certificate, thesis. *Entrance requirements:* For master's, certification. Additional exam requirements/recommendations for international students: Required—TOEFL (minimum score 550 paper-based; 79 iBT), IELTS (minimum score 6.5). Electronic applications accepted. Application fee is waived when completed online.

The College of Saint Rose, Graduate Studies, Thelma P. Lally School of Education, Programs in Special Education, Albany, NY 12203-1419. Offers adolescence education/special education (MS Ed); childhood education/special education (MS Ed); childhood special education (MS Ed); early childhood special education (MS Ed); special education (Certificate); special education professional (MS Ed). *Accreditation:* NCATE. *Students:* 8 full-time (5 women), 7 part-time (4 women). Average age 28. 15 applicants, 47% accepted, 5 enrolled. In 2018, 11 master's awarded. *Degree requirements:* For master's, comprehensive exam (for some programs), thesis or alternative, research project. *Entrance requirements:* For master's, minimum undergraduate GPA of 3.0. Additional exam requirements/recommendations for international students: Required—TOEFL (minimum score 550 paper-based; 80 iBT), IELTS (minimum score 6), PTE (minimum score 56). *Application deadline:* For fall admission, 4/1 priority date for domestic and international students; for spring admission, 10/15 priority date for domestic and international students; for summer admission, 3/15 priority date for domestic and international students. Applications are processed on a rolling basis. Application fee: $40. Electronic applications accepted. *Expenses: Tuition:* Full-time $14,382; part-time $799 per credit hour. *Required fees:* $924; $408 per credit. $286. *Financial support:* Career-related internships or fieldwork, scholarships/grants, tuition waivers (partial), and unspecified assistantships available. Support available to part-time students. Financial award application deadline: 4/15. *Unit head:* Franics Ihle, Chair, 518-337-4885, E-mail: ihlef@strose.edu. *Application contact:* Daniel Gallagher, Assistant Vice President for Graduate Recruitment and Enrollment, 518-485-3390, E-mail: grad@strose.edu.
Website: https://www.strose.edu/special-education/

The College of Saint Rose, Graduate Studies, Thelma P. Lally School of Education, Teacher Education Programs, Albany, NY 12203-1419. Offers adolescence education (MS Ed, Advanced Certificate); adolescence education/special education (Advanced Certificate); childhood education (MS Ed); curriculum and instruction (MS Ed); early childhood education (MS Ed). *Students:* 49 full-time (39 women), 21 part-time (17 women); includes 3 minority (2 Black or African American, non-Hispanic/Latino; 1 Hispanic/Latino). Average age 27. 41 applicants, 66% accepted, 21 enrolled. In 2018, 48 master's, 1 Advanced Certificate awarded. *Entrance requirements:* For master's, minimum undergraduate GPA of 3.0. Additional exam requirements/recommendations for international students: Required—TOEFL (minimum score 550 paper-based; 80 iBT), IELTS (minimum score 6), PTE (minimum score 56). *Application deadline:* For fall admission, 4/1 priority date for domestic and international students; for spring admission, 10/15 priority date for domestic and international students; for summer admission, 3/15 priority date for domestic and international students. Applications are processed on a rolling basis. Application fee: $40. Electronic applications accepted. *Expenses: Tuition:* Full-time $14,382; part-time $799 per credit hour. *Required fees:* $924; $408 per credit. $286. *Financial support:* Career-related internships or fieldwork, scholarships/grants, tuition waivers (partial), and unspecified assistantships available. Support available to part-time students. Financial award application deadline: 4/15. *Unit head:* Dr. Drey Martone, Chair, 518-454-5262, E-mail: martoned@strose.edu. *Application contact:* Daniel Gallagher, Assistant Vice President for Graduate Recruitment and Enrollment, 518-485-3390, Fax: 518-458-5479, E-mail: grad@strose.edu.
Website: https://www.strose.edu/academics/schools/school-of-education/

College of Staten Island of the City University of New York, Graduate Programs, School of Education, Program in Special Education, Staten Island, NY 10314-6600. Offers special education (MS Ed), including adolescence generalist: grades 7-12, grades 1-6. *Program availability:* Part-time, evening/weekend. *Students:* 130. 58 applicants, 71% accepted, 32 enrolled. In 2018, 42 master's awarded. *Degree requirements:* For master's, comprehensive exam, fieldwork; ten three-credit required courses and one elective for a total of 11 courses (33 credits) or 14 three-credit required courses and a three- to six-credit, field-based requirement for a total of 45-48 credits; research project. *Entrance requirements:* For master's, GRE General Test or an approved equivalent examination, BA/BS or 36 approved credits with a 3.0 GPA, 2 letters of recommendations, 1-2 page statement of experience; must have completed courses for NYS initial certificate in childhood education/early childhood education (Sequence 1); 6 credits each in English, history, math, and science, and 1 year of foreign language (Sequence 2). Additional exam requirements/recommendations for international students: Required—TOEFL (minimum score 550 paper-based; 79 iBT), IELTS (minimum score 6.5). *Application deadline:* For fall admission, 4/25 for domestic and international students; for spring admission, 11/25 for domestic and international students. Applications are processed on a rolling basis. Application fee: $75. Electronic applications accepted. *Expenses: Tuition, area resident:* Full-time $10,770; part-time $455 per credit. Tuition, state resident: full-time $10,770; part-time $455 per credit. Tuition, nonresident: full-time $19,920; part-time $830 per credit. *International tuition:* $19,920 full-time. *Required fees:* $559.20; $181.10 per semester. Tuition and fees vary according to program. *Faculty research:* Disabilities studies, social justice, arts-based research on disabilities, assessment of students with disabilities, technological pedagogical and content knowledge (TPACK) in special education teachers, juvenile justice. *Unit head:* Diane Brescia, 718-982-3877, E-mail: diane.brescia@csi.cuny.edu. *Application contact:* Sasha Spence, Associate Director for Graduate Admissions, 718-982-2019, Fax: 718-982-2500, E-mail: sasha.spence@csi.cuny.edu. Website: https://www.csi.cuny.edu/sites/default/files/pdf/admissions/grad/pdf/Education%20Fact%20Sheet.pdf

Colorado Christian University, Program in Curriculum and Instruction, Lakewood, CO 80226. Offers corporate education (MACI); early childhood educator (MACI); elementary educator (MACI); instructional technology (MACI); master educator (MACI); online course developer (MACI); online teaching and learning (MACI); special education generalist (MACI). *Program availability:* Part-time, evening/weekend. *Degree requirements:* For master's, thesis optional, practicum. *Entrance requirements:* For master's, interviews, letters of recommendation. Additional exam requirements/recommendations for international students: Required—TOEFL. Electronic applications accepted. *Expenses:* Contact institution.

Columbia International University, Columbia Graduate School, Columbia, SC 29203. Offers Bible teaching (MABT); counseling (MACN); early childhood and elementary education (MAT); educational administration (M Ed); educational leadership (PhD); instruction and learning (M Ed); teaching English as a foreign language (Certificate); teaching English as a foreign language and intercultural studies (MATF). *Program availability:* Part-time, evening/weekend, online learning. *Degree requirements:* For master's, internships, professional project. *Entrance requirements:* For master's, MAT, GRE (for some programs), minimum GPA of 2.7. Additional exam requirements/recommendations for international students: Required—TOEFL. Electronic applications accepted.

Columbus State University, Graduate Studies, College of Education and Health Professions, Department of Teacher Education, Columbus, GA 31907-5645. Offers curriculum and instruction in accomplished teaching (M Ed); early childhood education (M Ed, MAT, Ed S); middle grades education (M Ed, MAT, Ed S); secondary education (M Ed, MAT, Ed S), including biology (MAT), chemistry (MAT), earth and space science (MAT), English/language arts, general science (M Ed), history (MAT), mathematics, science (Ed S), social science (M Ed, Ed S); special education (M Ed, MAT, Ed S), including general curriculum (M Ed, MAT); teacher leadership (M Ed). *Accreditation:* NCATE. *Program availability:* Part-time, evening/weekend, 100% online, blended/hybrid learning. *Faculty:* 20 full-time (12 women), 20 part-time/adjunct (15 women). *Students:* 110 full-time (84 women), 143 part-time (115 women); includes 105 minority (96 Black or African American, non-Hispanic/Latino; 4 Hispanic/Latino; 5 Two or more races, non-Hispanic/Latino). Average age 33. 147 applicants, 56% accepted, 62 enrolled. In 2018, 112 master's, 11 other advanced degrees awarded. *Degree requirements:* For Ed S, thesis or alternative. *Entrance requirements:* For master's, GRE General Test, minimum undergraduate GPA of 2.75; for Ed S, GRE General Test, minimum undergraduate GPA of 2.75, graduate 3.0. Additional exam requirements/recommendations for international students: Required—TOEFL (minimum score 550 paper-based; 79 iBT). *Application deadline:* For fall admission, 6/30 for domestic students, 5/1 for international students; for spring admission, 11/1 for domestic and international students; for summer admission, 3/1 for domestic and international students. Applications are processed on a rolling basis. Application fee: $50. Electronic applications accepted. *Expenses: Tuition, area resident:* Full-time $4924; part-time $618 per credit hour. Tuition, state resident: full-time $4924; part-time $618 per credit hour. Tuition, nonresident: full-time $19,218; part-time $2403 per credit hour. *International tuition:* $19,218 full-time. *Required fees:* $1870; $802. Tuition and fees vary according to course load, degree level and program. *Financial support:* In 2018–19, 29 students received support, including 7 research assistantships with partial tuition reimbursements available (averaging $3,000 per year); career-related internships or fieldwork, Federal Work-Study, institutionally sponsored loans, scholarships/grants, tuition waivers (partial), and unspecified assistantships also available. Support available to part-time students. Financial award application deadline: 5/1; financial award applicants required to submit FAFSA. *Unit head:* Dr. Jan Burcham, Department Chair, 706-507-8519, Fax: 706-568-3134, E-mail: burcham_jan@columbusstate.edu. *Application contact:* Catrina Smith-Edmond, Assistant Director for Graduate and Global Admission, 706-507-8824, Fax: 706-568-5091, E-mail: smithedmond_catrina@columbusstate.edu.
Website: http://te.columbusstate.edu/

Concordia University, College of Education, Portland, OR 97211-6099. Offers administrative leadership (Ed D); career and technical education (M Ed); curriculum and instruction (M Ed), including adolescent literacy, early childhood education, educational technology leadership, English for speakers of other languages, environmental education, health and physical education, mathematics, methods and curriculum, reading interventionist, science, social studies, STEAM education, teacher leadership, the inclusive classroom, trauma and resilience in educational settings; educational administration (M Ed); educational leadership (M Ed); elementary education (MAT); higher education (Ed D); instructional leadership (Ed D); professional leadership, inquiry, and transformation (Ed D); secondary education (MAT); transformational leadership (Ed D). *Program availability:* Part-time, online learning. *Degree requirements:* For master's, comprehensive exam, work samples/portfolio. *Entrance requirements:* For master's, California Basic Educational Skills Test or PRAXIS I, minimum undergraduate GPA of 2.8, graduate 3.0; 2 letters of recommendation. Additional exam requirements/recommendations for international students: Required—TOEFL (minimum score 525 paper-based). Electronic applications accepted. *Faculty research:* Learner-centered classroom, brain-based learning, future of online learning.

Concordia University Chicago, College of Graduate Studies, Program in Early Childhood Education, River Forest, IL 60305-1499. Offers MA. *Program availability:* Part-time, evening/weekend, online learning. *Degree requirements:* For master's, comprehensive exam, thesis. *Entrance requirements:* For master's, minimum GPA of 2.9. Additional exam requirements/recommendations for international students: Required—TOEFL (minimum score 550 paper-based). Electronic applications accepted. *Faculty research:* Child care training project, "Children in Worship" project, ethical development of children.

Concordia University, Nebraska, Graduate Programs in Education, Program in Early Childhood Education, Seward, NE 68434. Offers M Ed. *Accreditation:* NCATE. *Program availability:* Part-time. *Degree requirements:* For master's, comprehensive exam, thesis or alternative. *Entrance requirements:* For master's, GRE, MAT, or NTE, minimum GPA of 3.0, BS in education or equivalent. Additional exam requirements/recommendations for international students: Required—TOEFL.

Concordia University, St. Paul, College of Education, St. Paul, MN 55104-5494. Offers classroom instruction (MA Ed), including K-12 reading; differentiated instruction (MA Ed); early childhood education (MA Ed); education (Ed D); educational leadership (MA Ed); educational technology (MA Ed, Certificate); K-12 principal licensure (Ed S); special education (MA Ed), including autism spectrum disorder, emotional and behavioral disorders, learning disabilities; superintendent (Ed S); teaching (MAT). *Accreditation:* NCATE. *Program availability:* Part-time, evening/weekend, 100% online, blended/hybrid learning. *Faculty:* 13 full-time (9 women), 82 part-time/adjunct (51 women). *Students:* 979 full-time (748 women), 40 part-time (28 women); includes 124 minority (49 Black or African American, non-Hispanic/Latino; 6 American Indian or Alaska Native, non-Hispanic/Latino; 34 Asian, non-Hispanic/Latino; 22 Hispanic/Latino; 1 Native Hawaiian or other Pacific Islander, non-Hispanic/Latino; 12 Two or more races, non-Hispanic/Latino), 11 international. Average age 34. 423 applicants, 99% accepted, 335 enrolled. In 2018, 358 master's, 3 doctorates, 119 other advanced degrees awarded. *Degree requirements:* For master's, thesis (for some programs); for doctorate, thesis/dissertation, capstone projects; for other advanced degree, e-folio review of competencies. *Entrance requirements:* For master's, official transcripts from regionally-accredited institution stating the conferral of a bachelor's degree with minimum cumulative GPA of 3.0; personal statement; professional resume; practitioner in field through work or volunteerism; resume; for doctorate, minimum master's or specialist degree GPA of 3.25; transcript; writing sample; three letters of recommendation; current resume; on-campus interview; for other advanced degree, minimum master's or specialist degree GPA of 3.25; transcript; statement covering employment history and long-term academic and professional goals; two letters of recommendation; interview with program director. Additional exam requirements/recommendations for international students: Recommended—TOEFL (minimum score 547 paper-based; 78 iBT), IELTS (minimum score 6). *Application deadline:* For fall admission, 8/1 for domestic and international students; for spring admission, 12/1 for domestic and international students; for summer admission, 5/1 for domestic and international students. Applications are processed on a rolling basis. Application fee: $0. Electronic applications accepted. *Expenses:* $395 per credit for 30 credits (for MA programs), $440 per credit for 42 credits (for MAT), $415 per credit for 30 credits (for EdS), $615 per credit for 64 credits (for EdD). *Financial support:* In 2018–19, 163 students received support. Federal Work-Study, scholarships/grants, and unspecified assistantships available. Financial award applicants required to submit FAFSA. *Faculty research:* School design for innovative learning practices, equine-assisted instruction, best practices for leadership in early childhood education, mental health needs in K-12 focusing on children of incarcerated parents, competency-based education. *Unit head:* Lonn Maly, Dean, 651-641-8203, E-mail: maly@csp.edu. *Application contact:* Amber Faletti, Director of Enrollment Management, 651-641-8838, Fax: 651-603-6320, E-mail: faletti@csp.edu.

Concordia University Wisconsin, Graduate Programs, School of Education, Program in Early Childhood, Mequon, WI 53097-2402. Offers MS Ed. *Degree requirements:* For master's, comprehensive exam, thesis or alternative. *Entrance requirements:* For master's, minimum GPA of 3.0, teaching license. Additional exam requirements/recommendations for international students: Required—TOEFL.

Daemen College, Education Programs, Amherst, NY 14226-3592. Offers adolescence education (MS); childhood education (MS); childhood special education (MS); childhood special-alternative certification (MS); early childhood special-alternative certification (MS). *Accreditation:* TEAC. *Program availability:* Part-time. *Faculty:* 16 full-time (12 women), 19 part-time/adjunct (14 women). *Students:* 233 full-time (210 women), 21 part-time (18 women); includes 4 minority (1 Black or African American, non-Hispanic/Latino; 3 Hispanic/Latino), 1 international. Average age 22. 76 applicants, 93% accepted, 68 enrolled. In 2018, 204 master's awarded. *Degree requirements:* For master's, comprehensive exam, A minimum grade of B earned in all courses, thereby resulting in a minimum cumulative grade point average of 3.00. *Entrance requirements:* For master's, Submit scores from taking the Graduate Record Exam (GRE) by no later than December 16 for fall applicants, no later than May 1 for spring applicants, bachelor's degree, GPA of 3.0 or above, resume, letter of intent, 2 letters of recommendation, interview with department chair. Additional exam requirements/recommendations for international students: Required—TOEFL (minimum score 77 paper-based), IELTS (minimum score 6.5). *Application deadline:* Applications are processed on a rolling basis. Application fee: $25. Electronic applications accepted. Application fee is waived when completed online. *Expenses: Tuition:* Part-time $977 per credit hour. *Required fees:* $125; $14 per credit hour. *Financial support:* Scholarships/grants and unspecified assistantships available. Support available to part-time students. Financial award applicants required to submit FAFSA. *Unit head:* Dr. Elizabeth Heilman, Department Chair, 716-839-8553, E-mail: eheilman@daemen.edu. *Application contact:* Megan Beardi, Senior Assistant Director of Graduate Admissions, 716-566-7861, Fax: 716-839-8229, E-mail: mbeardi@daemen.edu.
Website: https://www.daemen.edu/academics/areas-study/education

Dallas Baptist University, Dorothy M. Bush College of Education, Program in Educational Leadership, Dallas, TX 75211-9299. Offers charter school administration (M Ed); educational leadership (M Ed); educational leadership K-12 (Ed D). *Program availability:* Part-time, evening/weekend, online learning. *Application deadline:* Applications are processed on a rolling basis. Application fee: $25. Electronic applications accepted. Application fee is waived when completed online. *Expenses: Tuition:* Full-time $17,262; part-time $959 per credit hour. *Required fees:* $1000; $500 per semester. Tuition and fees vary according to course load and degree level. *Unit head:* Dr. Neil Dugger, Dean, 214-333-5202, E-mail: neil@dbu.edu. *Application contact:* Dr. Carolyn Spain, Program Director, 214-333-5217, E-mail: carolyns@dbu.edu.
Website: http://www3.dbu.edu/graduate/education.asp

Dallas Baptist University, Dorothy M. Bush College of Education, Teaching Program, Dallas, TX 75211-9299. Offers distance learning (MAT); early childhood through grade 6 certification (MAT); early childhood-12 (MAT); elementary (MAT); English as a second language (MAT); Montessori (MAT); multisensory (MAT); secondary (MAT). *Program availability:* Part-time, evening/weekend, 100% online, blended/hybrid learning. *Application deadline:* Applications are processed on a rolling basis. Application fee: $25. Electronic applications accepted. Application fee is waived when completed online.

Expenses: Tuition: Full-time $17,262; part-time $959 per credit hour. *Required fees:* $1000; $500 per semester. Tuition and fees vary according to course load and degree level. *Unit head:* Dr. Neil Dugger, Dean, 214-333-5202, E-mail: neil@dbu.edu. *Application contact:* Dr. DeAnna Jenkins, Program Director, 214-333-5402, E-mail: deannaj@dbu.edu.
Website: https://www.dbu.edu/graduate/degree-programs/ma-teaching

DePaul University, College of Education, Chicago, IL 60614. Offers bilingual-bicultural education (M Ed, MA); counseling (M Ed, MA), including clinical mental health counseling, college student development, school counseling; curriculum studies (M Ed, MA, Ed D); early childhood education (M Ed, MA, Ed D); educational leadership (M Ed, MA, Ed D), including Catholic leadership (M Ed, MA), general (M Ed, MA), higher education (M Ed, MA), physical education (M Ed, MA), principal preparation (M Ed), teacher preparation (M Ed); elementary education (M Ed, MA); middle grades education (M Ed); middle school mathematics education (MS); reading specialist (M Ed, MA); secondary education (M Ed, MA); social and cultural foundations in education (M Ed, MA); special education (M Ed); sport, fitness and recreation leadership (MS); value-creating education for global citizenship (M Ed); world languages education (M Ed, MA). *Program availability:* Part-time, evening/weekend, online learning. *Degree requirements:* For doctorate, thesis/dissertation. Electronic applications accepted.

Dickinson State University, Department of Teacher Education, Dickinson, ND 58601-4896. Offers master of arts in teaching (MAT); master of entrepreneurship (ME); middle school education (MAT); reading (MAT). *Program availability:* Part-time, blended/hybrid learning. *Faculty:* 2 full-time (both women). *Students:* 2 full-time (1 woman), 15 part-time (9 women); includes 1 minority (Hispanic/Latino). Average age 36. 8 applicants, 100% accepted, 8 enrolled. *Degree requirements:* For master's, comprehensive exam (for some programs). *Entrance requirements:* For master's, additional admission requirements for the Master of Entrepreneurship Program: complete the SoBE ME Peregrine Entrance Examination, personal statement; transcripts; additional admission requirements for the Master of Entrepreneurship Program: 2 letters of reference in support of their admission to the program. Reference letters should be from prior academic advisors, faculty, professional colleagues, or supervisors. Additional exam requirements/recommendations for international students: Required—TOEFL (minimum score 71 iBT). *Application deadline:* For fall admission, 8/1 for domestic students, 7/1 for international students; for spring admission, 12/1 for domestic students, 11/15 for international students. Applications are processed on a rolling basis. Application fee: $35. Electronic applications accepted. *Expenses: Tuition, area resident:* Full-time $3735; part-time $311 per credit hour. Tuition, state resident: full-time $3735; part-time $311 per credit hour. Tuition, nonresident: full-time $3735; part-time $311 per credit hour. *Required fees:* $138; $138 per credit hour. *Financial support:* Application deadline: 12/1; applicants required to submit FAFSA. *Unit head:* Dr. Deborah Secord, Chair, Department of Teacher Education, 701-483-2178, E-mail: Deborah.Secord@dickinsonstate.edu. *Application contact:* Pamela Krueger, Graduate Studies Coordinator, 701-483-5631, E-mail: Pamela.j.krueger@dickinsonstate.edu.
Website: https://dickinsonstate.edu/academics/fields-of-study/graduate-studies/

Dominican University, School of Education, River Forest, IL 60305-1099. Offers child life studies (MS); early childhood education (MS); education (MAT); elementary education (MA Ed); English as a second language (MA Ed); reading (MA Ed); secondary education (MAT); special education (MS). *Accreditation:* NCATE. *Program availability:* Part-time, evening/weekend, 100% online, blended/hybrid learning. *Entrance requirements:* For master's, Illinois Test of Basic Skills. Additional exam requirements/recommendations for international students: Required—TOEFL (minimum score 550 paper-based; 79 iBT). *Expenses:* Contact institution. *Faculty research:* Governance of private education institutions, reading and language arts, inclusion, organizational planning, leadership and vision.

Duquesne University, School of Education, Department of Instruction and Leadership, Program in Early Level (PreK-4) Education, Pittsburgh, PA 15282-0001. Offers MS Ed. *Program availability:* Part-time, evening/weekend. *Faculty:* 3 full-time (2 women). *Students:* 23 full-time (all women), 4 part-time (all women); includes 3 minority (1 Black or African American, non-Hispanic/Latino; 1 Asian, non-Hispanic/Latino; 1 Two or more races, non-Hispanic/Latino), 1 international. Average age 29. 26 applicants, 92% accepted, 9 enrolled. In 2018, 9 master's awarded. *Entrance requirements:* For master's, bachelor's degree; minimum GPA of 3.0 overall or on most recent 48 credits. Additional exam requirements/recommendations for international students: Required—TOEFL (minimum score 550 paper-based), IELTS (minimum score 7). *Application deadline:* For fall admission, 9/1 for domestic students; for spring admission, 1/2 for domestic students. Applications are processed on a rolling basis. Application fee: $0. Electronic applications accepted. *Expenses: Tuition:* Full-time $23,112; part-time $1284 per credit. Tuition and fees vary according to program. *Financial support:* In 2018–19, 1 student received support, including 1 research assistantship with full tuition reimbursement available (averaging $6,468 per year). Financial award applicants required to submit FAFSA. *Faculty research:* How young students perceive moral learning; using storytelling for moral learning; faith and character development in young students; early literacy development; engaging parents and families. *Unit head:* Dr. Julia Williams, Assistant Professor, 412-396-6098, Fax: 412-396-5388, E-mail: williamsj@duq.edu. *Application contact:* Kelly McGinley, Graduate Admissions Assistant, 412-396-1559, Fax: 412-396-5585, E-mail: mcginleyk@duq.edu.
Website: http://www.duq.edu/academics/schools/education/graduate-programs/ms-early-level-prek-4

East Carolina University, Graduate School, College of Health and Human Performance, Department of Human Development and Family Science, Greenville, NC 27858-4353. Offers birth through kindergarten education (MA Ed); human development and family science (MS); marriage and family therapy (MS); medical family therapy (PhD). *Accreditation:* AAMFT/COAMFTE. *Program availability:* Part-time. *Application deadline:* For fall admission, 1/15 for domestic students; for spring admission, 10/15 for domestic students. *Expenses: Tuition, area resident:* Full-time $4749. Tuition, state resident: full-time $4749. Tuition, nonresident: full-time $17,898. *International tuition:* $17,898 full-time. *Required fees:* $2787. Part-time tuition and fees vary according to course load and program. *Financial support:* Application deadline: 6/1. *Unit head:* Dr. Sharon Ballard, Chair, 252-328-4220, E-mail: ballards@ecu.edu. *Application contact:* Graduate School Admissions, 252-328-6012, Fax: 252-328-6071, E-mail: gradschool@ecu.edu.
Website: https://hhp.ecu.edu/hdfs/

Eastern Connecticut State University, School of Education and Professional Studies/Graduate Division, Program in Early Childhood Education, Willimantic, CT 06226-2295. Offers MS. *Accreditation:* NCATE. *Program availability:* Part-time, evening/weekend. *Degree requirements:* For master's, thesis optional. *Entrance requirements:* For master's, PRAXIS I, GRE, SAT, ACT, or PAA and PRAXIS II, minimum GPA of 3.0, bachelor's degree from accredited institution. Additional exam requirements/recommendations for international students: Required—TOEFL (minimum score 550 paper-based; 79 iBT); Recommended—IELTS (minimum score 6). Electronic applications accepted.

Eastern Illinois University, Graduate School, College of Education, Department of Teaching, Learning, and Foundations, Charleston, IL 61920. Offers curriculum and instruction (MS Ed). *Accreditation:* NCATE. *Program availability:* Part-time, evening/weekend. *Degree requirements:* For master's, comprehensive exam (for some programs), thesis (for some programs). *Entrance requirements:* For master's, GMAT or GRE. Additional exam requirements/recommendations for international students: Required—TOEFL (minimum score 500 paper-based; 61 iBT), IELTS (minimum score 6). *Application deadline:* For fall admission, 5/15 for domestic and international students; for spring admission, 10/15 for domestic and international students. Applications are processed on a rolling basis. Application fee: $30. Electronic applications accepted. *Expenses:* Tuition, state resident: part-time $299 per credit hour. Tuition, nonresident: part-time $718 per credit hour. *Required fees:* $214.50 per credit hour. *Financial support:* Research assistantships with full tuition reimbursements, teaching assistantships with full tuition reimbursements, career-related internships or fieldwork, Federal Work-Study, scholarships/grants, and unspecified assistantships available. Support available to part-time students. Financial award application deadline: 3/1; financial award applicants required to submit FAFSA. *Unit head:* Jeanne E. Okrasinski, Ph.D., Chair, 217-581-5728, Fax: 217-581-6300, E-mail: jeokrasinski@eiu.edu. *Application contact:* Jeanne E. Okrasinski, Ph.D., Chair, 217-581-5728, Fax: 217-581-6300, E-mail: jeokrasinski@eiu.edu.
Website: http://www.eiu.edu/elegrad/

Eastern Michigan University, Graduate School, College of Education, Department of Teacher Education, Program in Early Childhood Education, Ypsilanti, MI 48197. Offers MA. *Accreditation:* NCATE. *Program availability:* Part-time, evening/weekend. *Students:* 1 (woman) full-time, 35 part-time (33 women); includes 8 minority (4 Black or African American, non-Hispanic/Latino; 2 Hispanic/Latino; 2 Two or more races, non-Hispanic/Latino). Average age 35. 17 applicants, 88% accepted, 10 enrolled. In 2018, 10 master's awarded. *Entrance requirements:* For master's, GRE. Additional exam requirements/recommendations for international students: Required—TOEFL. *Application deadline:* Applications are processed on a rolling basis. Application fee: $45. *Financial support:* Fellowships and teaching assistantships available. Support available to part-time students. Financial award applicants required to submit FAFSA. *Application contact:* Dr. Brigid Beaubien, Coordinator, 734-487-3260, Fax: 734-487-2101, E-mail: brigid.beaubien@emich.edu.

Eastern Nazarene College, Adult and Graduate Studies, Division of Teacher Education, Quincy, MA 02170. Offers administration (M Ed); early childhood education (M Ed, Certificate); elementary education (M Ed, Certificate); English as a second language (Certificate); instructional enrichment and development (Certificate); middle school education (M Ed, Certificate); moderate special needs education (Certificate); principal (Certificate); program development and supervision (Certificate); secondary education (M Ed, Certificate); special education administrator (Certificate); special needs (M Ed); supervisor (Certificate); teacher of reading (M Ed, Certificate). M Ed also available through weekend program for administration, special needs, and teacher of reading only. *Program availability:* Part-time, evening/weekend. *Entrance requirements:* Additional exam requirements/recommendations for international students: Required—TOEFL (minimum score 550 paper-based).

Eastern New Mexico University, Graduate School, College of Education and Technology, Department of Educational Studies, Program in Special Education, Portales, NM 88130. Offers early childhood special education (M Sp Ed); general special education (M Sp Ed); gifted education pedagogy (M Ed); special education pedagogy (M Ed). *Program availability:* Part-time. *Degree requirements:* For master's, comprehensive exam, thesis optional. *Entrance requirements:* For master's, writing assessment, minimum GPA of 3.0, letter of recommendation, photocopy of teaching license or confirmation of entrance into alternative licensure program, special education license or minimum 30 hours of undergraduate course work. Additional exam requirements/recommendations for international students: Required—TOEFL (minimum score 550 paper-based; 79 iBT), IELTS (minimum score 6). Electronic applications accepted. *Expenses: Tuition, area resident:* Full-time $6776. Tuition, state resident: full-time $6776; part-time $282 per credit hour. Tuition, nonresident: full-time $8986; part-time $374 per credit hour. *Required fees:* $60 per semester. One-time fee: $25.

Eastern University, Graduate Education Programs, St. Davids, PA 19087-3696. Offers ESL program specialist (K-12) (Certificate); general supervisor (PreK-12) (Certificate); health and physical education (K-12) (Certificate); middle level (4-8) (Certificate); multicultural education (M Ed); music (K-12) (Certificate); Pre K-4 (Certificate); Pre K-4 with special education (Certificate); reading (M Ed); reading specialist (K-12) (Certificate); reading supervisor (K-12) (Certificate); school counseling (MA, CAGS); school principalship (preK-12) (Certificate); school psychology (MS, CAGS); secondary biology education (7-12) (Certificate); secondary chemistry education (7-12) (Certificate); secondary communication education (7-12) (Certificate); secondary English education (7-12) (Certificate); secondary math education (7-12) (Certificate); secondary social studies education (7-12) (Certificate); special education (M Ed); special education (7-12) (Certificate); special education (Pre K-8) (Certificate); special education supervisor (K-12) (Certificate); TESOL (M Ed); world language (Certificate), including Spanish. *Program availability:* Part-time, evening/weekend, online learning. *Entrance requirements:* Additional exam requirements/recommendations for international students: Required—TOEFL. Electronic applications accepted. Application fee is waived when completed online. *Expenses:* Contact institution.

Eastern Washington University, Graduate Studies, College of Arts, Letters and Education, Department of Education, Program in Early Childhood Education, Cheney, WA 99004-2431. Offers M Ed. *Degree requirements:* For master's, comprehensive exam, thesis (for some programs). *Entrance requirements:* For master's, GRE, minimum GPA of 3.0. Additional exam requirements/recommendations for international students: Required—TOEFL (minimum score 580 paper-based; 92 iBT), IELTS (minimum score 7), PTE (minimum score 63). Electronic applications accepted.

East Stroudsburg University of Pennsylvania, Graduate and Extended Studies, College of Education, Department of Early Childhood and Elementary Education, East Stroudsburg, PA 18301-2999. Offers M Ed. *Program availability:* Part-time, evening/weekend, online learning. *Faculty:* 2 full-time (0 women). *Students:* 11 part-time (all women). Average age 36. 5 applicants, 80% accepted, 3 enrolled. In 2018, 5 master's awarded. *Degree requirements:* For master's, comprehensive exam, professional portfolio, curriculum project or action research. *Entrance requirements:* For master's, PRAXIS/teacher certification, letter of recommendation, Pennsylvania Department of Education requirements. Additional exam requirements/recommendations for international students: Recommended—TOEFL (minimum score 560 paper-based; 83 iBT), IELTS. *Application deadline:* For fall admission, 7/31 priority date for domestic students, 6/30 priority date for international students; for spring admission, 11/30 for domestic students, 10/31 for international students. Applications are processed on a rolling basis. Application fee: $50. Electronic applications accepted. *Expenses: Tuition, area resident:* Full-time $9288; part-time $516 per credit. Tuition, state resident: full-time $9288. Tuition, nonresident: full-time $13,932; part-time $774 per credit. *International tuition:* $13,932 full-time. *Required fees:* $2059; $114 per credit. Tuition and fees vary according to course load and degree level. *Financial support:* Research assistantships with tuition reimbursements, Federal Work-Study, and unspecified assistantships available. Support available to part-time students. Financial award application deadline: 3/1; financial award applicants required to submit FAFSA. *Unit*

head: Andrew Whitehead, Chair, 570-422-3356, Fax: 570-422-3942, E-mail: awhitehead@esu.edu. *Application contact:* Kevin Quintero, Associate Director, Graduate and Extended Studies, 570-422-3890, Fax: 570-422-2711, E-mail: kquintero@esu.edu.
Website: https://www.esu.edu/early_childhood_elementary_education/ undergraduate_programs/eced.cfm

East Tennessee State University, School of Graduate Studies, College of Education, Department of Early Childhood Education, Johnson City, TN 37614. Offers early childhood education (MA, PhD); early childhood education emergent inquiry (Postbaccalaureate Certificate). *Degree requirements:* For master's, thesis optional, practicum; for doctorate, comprehensive exam, thesis/dissertation, research apprenticeship and at least one of the additional apprenticeship options, oral exam. *Entrance requirements:* For master's, GRE, PRAXIS, ACT, SAT, minimum undergraduate GPA of 3.0; for doctorate, GRE, resume, 4 letters of recommendation, personal essay that includes written statement of career and educational goals, master's degree in early childhood or related field, interview; for Postbaccalaureate Certificate, bachelor or master's degree in early childhood or related field, 2 letters of recommendation. Additional exam requirements/recommendations for international students: Required—TOEFL (minimum score 550 paper-based; 79 iBT). Electronic applications accepted.

East Tennessee State University, School of Graduate Studies, College of Education, Department of Educational Foundations and Special Education, Johnson City, TN 37614. Offers community leadership (Post-Master's Certificate), including early childhood special education (M Ed, Post-Master's Certificate), high incidence disabilities (M Ed, Post-Master's Certificate), low incidence disabilities (M Ed, Post-Master's Certificate); special education (M Ed, Post-Master's Certificate), including advanced studies in special education (M Ed), early childhood special education, high incidence disabilities, low incidence disabilities. *Program availability:* Part-time. *Degree requirements:* For master's, thesis (for some programs), practicum, residency, or thesis. *Entrance requirements:* For master's, PRAXIS I or Tennessee teaching license (for special education only), minimum GPA of 3.0 (or complete probationary period with no grade lower than B for first 9 graduate hours for early childhood education), 2-page essay outlining past experience with individuals with disabilities and goals for acquiring an advanced degree in special education; for Post-Master's Certificate, bachelor's or master's degree in early childhood or related field; two years of experience working with young children (preferred). Additional exam requirements/recommendations for international students: Required—TOEFL (minimum score 550 paper-based; 79 iBT). *Faculty research:* Teaching students with significant disabilities, problem-solving in toddlers, children and their development and learning, connecting classroom environment to student engagement in PreK-3, bilingual education in Ecuador, positive discipline/behavior support programs, early childhood relationships, international and comparative special education.

Edinboro University of Pennsylvania, Department of Early Childhood and Reading, Edinboro, PA 16444. Offers arts infusion (Graduate Certificate); early childhood education (M Ed); reading (M Ed); reading specialist (Graduate Certificate). *Program availability:* Part-time, evening/weekend. *Degree requirements:* For master's, thesis or alternative, competency exam; for Graduate Certificate, thesis or alternative. *Entrance requirements:* For master's and Graduate Certificate, GRE or MAT, minimum QPA of 2.5. Electronic applications accepted.

Elms College, Division of Education, Chicopee, MA 01013-2839. Offers early childhood education (MAT); education (M Ed, CAGS); elementary education (MAT); English as a second language (MAT); reading (MAT); secondary education (MAT), including biology education, English education, Spanish education; special education (MAT). *Program availability:* Part-time, evening/weekend. *Faculty:* 5 full-time (all women), 6 part-time/adjunct (5 women). *Students:* 3 full-time (all women), 117 part-time (94 women); includes 12 minority (1 Black or African American, non-Hispanic/Latino; 2 Asian, non-Hispanic/Latino; 9 Hispanic/Latino). Average age 34. 27 applicants, 96% accepted, 23 enrolled. In 2018, 34 master's, 3 other advanced degrees awarded. *Degree requirements:* For master's, thesis (for some programs). *Entrance requirements:* For master's, Massachusetts Educators Certification Test, minimum GPA of 3.0; for CAGS, master's degree in education. Additional exam requirements/recommendations for international students: Required—TOEFL. *Application deadline:* For fall admission, 7/1 priority date for domestic students; for spring admission, 11/1 priority date for domestic students. Applications are processed on a rolling basis. Application fee: $30. *Expenses: Tuition:* Full-time $14,328; part-time $796 per credit. *Required fees:* $200. Tuition and fees vary according to degree level and program. *Financial support:* In 2018–19, 2 teaching assistantships with partial tuition reimbursements were awarded. Financial award applicants required to submit FAFSA. *Unit head:* Dr. Mary Janeczek, Chair, Division of Education, 413-594-2761, Fax: 413-592-4871, E-mail: janeczeke@elms.edu. *Application contact:* Nancy Davis, Director, Office of Graduate and Continuing Education Admissions, 413-265-2239, E-mail: davisn@elms.edu.

Emporia State University, Program in Early Childhood Education, Emporia, KS 66801-5415. Offers MS. *Accreditation:* NCATE. *Program availability:* Part-time, online learning. *Degree requirements:* For master's, comprehensive exam or thesis, practicum. *Entrance requirements:* For master's, GRE General Test or MAT, essay exam, appropriate bachelor's degree, letters of recommendation. Additional exam requirements/ recommendations for international students: Required—TOEFL (minimum score 520 paper-based; 68 iBT). Electronic applications accepted.

Endicott College, Van Loan School of Graduate and Professional Studies, Program in Early Childhood and Elementary Education, Beverly, MA 01915-2096. Offers early childhood and elementary education (M Ed); early childhood education (M Ed); elementary education (M Ed). *Program availability:* Part-time, evening/weekend, 100% online, blended/hybrid learning. *Degree requirements:* For master's, comprehensive exam, thesis, practicum. *Entrance requirements:* For master's, MAT or GRE, Massachusetts Tests for Educator Licensure (MTEL), Massachusetts teaching certificate, 2 professional letters of recommendation, personal statement. Additional exam requirements/recommendations for international students: Required—TOEFL. Electronic applications accepted. *Expenses:* Contact institution.

Endicott College, Van Loan School of Graduate and Professional Studies, Program in Integrative Education, Beverly, MA 01915-2096. Offers M Ed. Program offered in conjunction with The Institute for Educational Studies (TIES). *Program availability:* Part-time, online only, 100% online. *Degree requirements:* For master's, thesis. *Entrance requirements:* For master's, undergraduate transcript. Additional exam requirements/ recommendations for international students: Required—TOEFL. Electronic applications accepted. *Expenses:* Contact institution. *Faculty research:* Neurophenomenology, autopoiesis, systems view.

Erikson Institute, Erikson Institute, Chicago, IL 60654. Offers child development (MS); early childhood education (M Ed, MS, PhD). PhD offered through the Graduate School. *Accreditation:* NCA. *Degree requirements:* For master's, comprehensive exam, internship; for doctorate, one foreign language, comprehensive exam, thesis/ dissertation. *Entrance requirements:* For master's, experience working with young children, interview; for doctorate, GRE General Test, interview. *Faculty research:* Early

childhood development, cognitive development, sociocultural contexts, early childhood education, family and culture, early literacy.

Erikson Institute, Academic Programs, Program in Early Childhood Education, Chicago, IL 60654. Offers MS. *Degree requirements:* For master's, comprehensive exam. *Entrance requirements:* For master's, 3 letters of recommendation, minimum GPA of 2.75. Additional exam requirements/recommendations for international students: Required—TOEFL.

Fairleigh Dickinson University, Florham Campus, University College: Arts, Sciences, and Professional Studies, Peter Sammartino School of Education, Program in Education for Certified Teachers, Madison, NJ 07940-1099. Offers PreK - 3 certification (MA).

Fairleigh Dickinson University, Florham Campus, University College: Arts, Sciences, and Professional Studies, Peter Sammartino School of Education, Program in Teaching, Madison, NJ 07940-1099. Offers PreK - 3 certification (MAT).

Fairleigh Dickinson University, Metropolitan Campus, University College: Arts, Sciences, and Professional Studies, Peter Sammartino School of Education, Program in Education for Certified Teachers, Teaneck, NJ 07666-1914. Offers PreK - 3 certification (MA).

Fairleigh Dickinson University, Metropolitan Campus, University College: Arts, Sciences, and Professional Studies, Peter Sammartino School of Education, Program in Teaching, Teaneck, NJ 07666-1914. Offers PreK - 3 certification (MAT).

Fielding Graduate University, Graduate Programs, School of Leadership Studies, Programs in Infant and Early Childhood Development, Santa Barbara, CA 93105-3814. Offers infant and early childhood development (MA, PhD, Graduate Certificate), including early childhood development: education, mental health, and disruptive behaviors (MA), infant mental health and neurodevelopment (MA), reflective practice and supervision (Graduate Certificate). *Program availability:* Part-time, evening/ weekend. *Faculty:* 1 (woman) full-time, 18 part-time/adjunct (14 women). *Students:* 97 full-time (90 women), 3 part-time (all women); includes 37 minority (14 Black or African American, non-Hispanic/Latino; 4 American Indian or Alaska Native, non-Hispanic/ Latino; 3 Asian, non-Hispanic/Latino; 12 Hispanic/Latino; 4 Two or more races, non-Hispanic/Latino), 1 international. Average age 43. 22 applicants, 77% accepted, 11 enrolled. In 2018, 6 doctorates awarded. *Degree requirements:* For doctorate, comprehensive exam, thesis/dissertation. *Entrance requirements:* For master's and Graduate Certificate, bachelor's degree from regionally-accredited U.S. institution or equivalent; for doctorate, bachelor's or master's degree from regionally-accredited U.S. institution or equivalent, curriculum vitae, statement of purpose, critical thinking writing sample, 2 letters of recommendation, official transcripts. *Application deadline:* For fall admission, 7/16 for domestic and international students; for spring admission, 11/21 for domestic and international students; for summer admission, 2/18 for domestic and international students. Application fee: $75. Electronic applications accepted. *Expenses:* Https://www.fielding.edu/how-to-apply/tuition-financial-aid/tuition-fees/. *Financial support:* In 2018–19, 30 students received support. Research assistantships, teaching assistantships, scholarships/grants, and tuition waivers available. Support available to part-time students. Financial award applicants required to submit FAFSA. *Faculty research:* Infant, childhood, development. *Unit head:* Dr. Jenene Craig, Program Director, E-mail: jcraig@fielding.edu. *Application contact:* Enrollment Coordinator, 800-340-1099 Ext. 4098, Fax: 805-687-9793, E-mail: hodadmission@fielding.edu. Website: http://www.fielding.edu/our-programs/school-of-leadership-studies/phd-infant-early-childhood-development/

Fitchburg State University, Division of Graduate and Continuing Education, Program in Early Childhood Education, Fitchburg, MA 01420-2697. Offers M Ed. *Accreditation:* NCATE. *Program availability:* Part-time, evening/weekend. *Entrance requirements:* Additional exam requirements/recommendations for international students: Required— TOEFL (minimum score 550 paper-based; 79 iBT). Electronic applications accepted. *Expenses:* Contact institution.

Five Towns College, Graduate Programs, Dix Hills, NY 11746-6055. Offers childhood education (MS Ed); composition and arranging (DMA); jazz/commercial music (MM); music education (MM, DMA); music history and literature (DMA); music performance (DMA). *Program availability:* Part-time. *Degree requirements:* For master's, thesis, exams, major composition or capstone project, recital; for doctorate, comprehensive exam, thesis/dissertation, final oral exam. *Entrance requirements:* For master's, audition (for MM); New York state teaching certification (for MS Ed); personal statement, two letters of recommendation; for doctorate, 3 letters of recommendation, audition, essay. Additional exam requirements/recommendations for international students: Required— TOEFL (minimum score 520 paper-based; 85 iBT); Recommended—IELTS (minimum score 7). Electronic applications accepted. *Faculty research:* Teaching methods, teaching strategies and techniques, analysis of modern music, jazz.

Florida Atlantic University, College of Education, Department of Curriculum, Culture, and Educational Inquiry, Boca Raton, FL 33431-0991. Offers curriculum and instruction (M Ed, PhD, Ed S); early childhood education (M Ed); multicultural education (M Ed); TESOL and bilingual education (MA). *Program availability:* Part-time, evening/weekend. *Faculty:* 10 full-time (8 women), 2 part-time/adjunct (both women). *Students:* 15 full-time (11 women), 60 part-time (46 women); includes 24 minority (12 Black or African American, non-Hispanic/Latino; 2 Asian, non-Hispanic/Latino; 8 Hispanic/Latino; 2 Two or more races, non-Hispanic/Latino), 2 international. Average age 36. 45 applicants, 62% accepted, 21 enrolled. In 2018, 21 master's, 14 doctorates, 1 other advanced degree awarded. *Entrance requirements:* Additional exam requirements/ recommendations for international students: Required—TOEFL (minimum score 500 paper-based; 61 iBT), IELTS (minimum score 6). *Application deadline:* For fall admission, 7/1 for domestic students, 2/15 for international students; for spring admission, 11/1 for domestic students, 7/15 for international students. Application fee: $30. *Expenses: Tuition,* area resident: Full-time $7400; part-time $369.82 per credit. Tuition, state resident: full-time $7400; part-time $369.82 per credit. Tuition, nonresident: full-time $20,496; part-time $1024.81 per credit. *Faculty research:* Multicultural education, early intervention strategies, family literacy, religious diversity in schools, early childhood curriculum. *Unit head:* Dr. Hanizah Zainuddin, Chair, 561-297-6594, E-mail: zainuddi@fau.edu. *Application contact:* Dr. Deborah Shepherd, Associate Dean, 561-297-3570, E-mail: dshep@fau.edu.
Website: http://www.coe.fau.edu/academicdepartments/ccei/

Florida International University, College of Arts, Sciences, and Education, Department of Teaching and Learning, Miami, FL 33199. Offers art education (MA, MS); curriculum and instruction (MS, Ed D, PhD, Ed S), including curriculum development (MS), elementary education (MS), English education (MS), learning technologies (MS), mathematics education (MS), modern language education (MS), physical education (MS), science education (MS), social studies education (MS), special education (MS); early childhood education (MS); exceptional student education (Ed D); foreign language education (MS), including foreign language education, teaching English to speakers of other languages (TESOL); language, literacy and culture (PhD); mathematics, science, and learning technologies (PhD); physical education (MS), including sport and fitness; reading education (MS). *Program availability:* Part-time, evening/weekend. *Faculty:* 64 full-time (43 women), 104 part-time/adjunct (76 women). *Students:* 169 full-time (144 women), 155 part-time (130 women); includes 260 minority (53 Black or African

American, non-Hispanic/Latino; 7 Asian, non-Hispanic/Latino; 193 Hispanic/Latino; 7 Two or more races, non-Hispanic/Latino), 13 international. Average age 33. 184 applicants, 62% accepted, 87 enrolled. In 2018, 153 master's, 10 doctorates awarded. *Degree requirements:* For doctorate, comprehensive exam, thesis/dissertation. *Entrance requirements:* For master's, GRE General Test, Florida General Knowledge Test or Florida College Level Academic Skills Test; for doctorate and Ed S, GRE General Test. Additional exam requirements/recommendations for international students: Required—TOEFL (minimum score 550 paper-based; 80 iBT), IELTS (minimum score 6.3). *Application deadline:* For fall admission, 6/1 priority date for domestic students, 4/1 for international students; for winter admission, 10/1 priority date for domestic students, 9/1 for international students; for spring admission, 3/1 priority date for domestic students, 2/1 for international students. Applications are processed on a rolling basis. Application fee: $30. Electronic applications accepted. *Financial support:* Research assistantships and teaching assistantships available. *Unit head:* Dr. Maria Fernandez, Chair, 305-348-0193, Fax: 305-348-2086, E-mail: Maria.Fernandez9@fiu.edu. *Application contact:* Nanett Rojas, Manager, Admissions Operations, 305-348-7464, Fax: 305-348-7441, E-mail: gradadm@fiu.edu.
Website: https://tl.fiu.edu/

Fontbonne University, Graduate Programs, St. Louis, MO 63105-3098. Offers accounting (MBA, MS); art (MA); art (K-12) (MAT); business (MBA); computer science (MS); deaf education (MA); early intervention in deaf education (MA); education (MA), including autism spectrum disorders, curriculum and instruction, diverse learners, early childhood education, reading, special education; elementary education (MAT); family and consumer sciences (MA), including multidisciplinary health communication studies; fine arts (MFA); instructional design and technology (MS); management and leadership (MM); middle school education (MAT); secondary education (MAT); special education (MAT); speech-language pathology (MS); supply chain management (MS); theatre (MA). *Accreditation:* ASHA. *Program availability:* Part-time, evening/weekend, online learning. *Degree requirements:* For master's, comprehensive exam (for some programs), thesis (for some programs). *Entrance requirements:* Additional exam requirements/recommendations for international students: Required—TOEFL (minimum score 500 paper-based; 65 iBT). Electronic applications accepted.

Fordham University, Graduate School of Education, Division of Curriculum and Teaching, New York, NY 10023. Offers curriculum and teaching (MSE); early childhood education (MSE); elementary education (MST); special education (MSE, Adv C); teaching English as a second language (MSE). *Accreditation:* NCATE. *Program availability:* Part-time, evening/weekend. *Degree requirements:* For Adv C, thesis. *Entrance requirements:* Additional exam requirements/recommendations for international students: Required—TOEFL (minimum score 577 paper-based; 90 iBT), IELTS (minimum score 7). Electronic applications accepted.

Framingham State University, Graduate Studies, Program in Early Childhood Education, Framingham, MA 01701-9101. Offers M Ed.

Furman University, Graduate Division, Department of Education, Greenville, SC 29613. Offers curriculum and instruction (MA); early childhood education (MA); educational leadership (Ed S); English as a second language (MA); literacy (MA); school leadership (MA); special education (MA). *Accreditation:* NCATE. *Program availability:* Part-time, online learning. *Degree requirements:* For master's, comprehensive exam (for some programs), thesis or alternative. *Entrance requirements:* For master's, PRAXIS II. *Expenses: Tuition:* Full-time $27,500; part-time $7290 per credit. Tuition and fees vary according to program. *Faculty research:* Literacy, pedagogy and practice, social justice, advanced leadership, achievement in high poverty schools.

Gallaudet University, The Graduate School, Washington, DC 20002-3625. Offers American Sign Language/English bilingual early childhood deaf education: birth to 5 (Certificate); audiology (Au D); clinical psychology (PhD); deaf and hard of hearing infants, toddlers, and their families (Certificate); deaf education (MA, Ed S); deaf history (Certificate); deaf studies (Certificate); educating deaf students with disabilities (Certificate); education: teacher preparation (MA), including deaf education, early childhood education and deaf education, elementary education and deaf education, secondary education and deaf education; educational neuroscience (PhD); hearing, speech and language sciences (MS, PhD); international development (MA); interpretation (MA, PhD), including combined interpreting practice and research (MA), interpreting research (MA); linguistics (MA, PhD); mental health counseling (MA); peer mentoring (Certificate); public administration (MPA); school counseling (MA); school psychology (Psy S); sign language teaching (MA); social work (MSW); speech-language pathology (MS). *Program availability:* Part-time. Terminal master's awarded for partial completion of doctoral program. *Degree requirements:* For master's, comprehensive exam (for some programs), thesis optional; for doctorate, comprehensive exam, thesis/dissertation. *Entrance requirements:* For master's and doctorate, GRE General Test or MAT, letters of recommendation, interviews, goals statement, American Sign Language proficiency interview, written English competency. Additional exam requirements/recommendations for international students: Required—TOEFL. Electronic applications accepted. *Faculty research:* Signing math dictionaries, telecommunications access, cancer genetics, linguistics, visual language and visual learning, integrated quantum materials, deaf legal discourse, advance recruitment and retention in geosciences.

Gateway Seminary, Graduate and Professional Programs, Ontario, CA 91761-8642. Offers divinity (M Div); early childhood education (Certificate); education leadership (MAEL, Diploma); ministry (D Min); theological studies (MTS); theology (Th M); youth ministry (Certificate). *Accreditation:* ACIPE; ATS. *Program availability:* Part-time, evening/weekend. *Degree requirements:* For master's, thesis (for some programs); for doctorate, 2 foreign languages, thesis/dissertation. *Entrance requirements:* For doctorate, MAT. Additional exam requirements/recommendations for international students: Required—TOEFL (minimum score 550 paper-based). Electronic applications accepted.

George Mason University, College of Education and Human Development, Programs in Curriculum and Instruction, Fairfax, VA 22030. Offers assistive technology (M Ed); designing digital learning in schools (M Ed); early childhood education (M Ed); early childhood education for diverse learners (M Ed); elementary education (M Ed); English as a second language (M Ed); gifted child education (M Ed); literacy (M Ed), including PK-12 classroom teachers, reading specialist; literacy leadership for diverse schools (M Ed), including K-12 reading; physical education (M Ed); science K-12 (M Ed); secondary education (M Ed), including biology, chemistry, earth science, English, history/social science, math, physics; special education (M Ed); teacher leadership (M Ed); transformative teaching (M Ed). *Program availability:* Part-time, evening/weekend, 100% online, blended/hybrid learning. *Faculty:* 48 full-time (40 women), 28 part-time/adjunct (20 women). *Students:* 165 full-time (147 women), 697 part-time (579 women); includes 243 minority (47 Black or African American, non-Hispanic/Latino; 3 American Indian or Alaska Native, non-Hispanic/Latino; 88 Asian, non-Hispanic/Latino; 85 Hispanic/Latino; 4 Native Hawaiian or other Pacific Islander, non-Hispanic/Latino; 16 Two or more races, non-Hispanic/Latino), 26 international. Average age 34. 450 applicants, 93% accepted, 315 enrolled. In 2018, 421 master's awarded. *Entrance requirements:* For master's, PRAXIS Core (for some programs), 2 letters of recommendation, interview, program goals statement; 9 hours of complete licensure endorsement requirements (for elementary education); minimum GPA of 3.0 in applicant's last 60 hours of undergraduate coursework (for secondary education); at least 1 year of teaching experience (for literacy). Additional exam requirements/recommendations for international students: Required—TOEFL (minimum score 575 paper-based; 88 iBT), IELTS (minimum score 6.5), PTE (minimum score 59). *Application deadline:* For fall admission, 4/2 priority date for domestic and international students; for spring admission, 11/1 for domestic and international students. Application fee: $75 ($80 for international students). Electronic applications accepted. *Financial support:* In 2018–19, 4 students received support, including 1 fellowship, 3 teaching assistantships (averaging $3,745 per year); career-related internships or fieldwork, Federal Work-Study, scholarships/grants, unspecified assistantships, and health care benefits (for full-time research or teaching assistantship recipients) also available. Support available to part-time students. Financial award application deadline: 3/1; financial award applicants required to submit FAFSA. *Faculty research:* Teacher preparation and professional development; adaptive teaching; wonder in science teacher preparation; literacy (digital, adolescent); site based course instruction. *Unit head:* Rebecca Fox, Professor and Academic Program Coordinator, 703-993-4123, E-mail: rfox@gmu.edu. *Application contact:* Rebecca Fox, Professor and Academic Program Coordinator, 703-993-4123, E-mail: rfox@gmu.edu.
Website: http://gse.gmu.edu/programs/gsemasters

The George Washington University, Graduate School of Education and Human Development, Department of Special Education and Disability Studies, Program in Early Childhood Special Education, Washington, DC 20052. Offers infant special education (MA Ed/HD). *Accreditation:* NCATE. *Students:* 13 full-time (all women), 4 part-time (all women); includes 4 minority (2 Black or African American, non-Hispanic/Latino; 1 Asian, non-Hispanic/Latino; 1 Two or more races, non-Hispanic/Latino), 10 international. Average age 29. 31 applicants, 77% accepted, 7 enrolled. In 2018, 10 master's awarded. *Entrance requirements:* For master's, GRE General Test or MAT, minimum GPA of 2.75. *Application deadline:* For fall admission, 1/15 priority date for domestic students; for spring admission, 10/1 for domestic students. Applications are processed on a rolling basis. Application fee: $75. *Financial support:* In 2018–19, 19 students received support. Fellowships, career-related internships or fieldwork, Federal Work-Study, and tuition waivers (full) available. Financial award application deadline: 1/15; financial award applicants required to submit FAFSA. *Faculty research:* Computer-assisted instruction and learning, disabled learner assessment of preschool, handicapped children. *Unit head:* Dr. Marian H. Jarrett, Faculty Coordinator, 202-994-1509, E-mail: mjarrett@gwu.edu. *Application contact:* Sarah Lang, Director of Graduate Admissions, 202-994-1447, Fax: 202-994-7207, E-mail: slang@gwu.edu.

Georgia College & State University, Graduate School, The John H. Lounsbury College of Education, Program in Early Childhood Education, Milledgeville, GA 31061. Offers M Ed. *Accreditation:* NCATE. *Program availability:* Part-time, evening/weekend. *Degree requirements:* For master's, minimum GPA of 3.0, complete program within 6 years. *Entrance requirements:* For master's, 2 professional recommendations, transcript, T-4 certificate, verification of immunization; minimum GPA of 2.75 or 3 successful years' teaching experience. Electronic applications accepted. *Expenses:* Contact institution.

Georgia Southwestern State University, School of Education, Americus, GA 31709-4693. Offers early childhood education (M Ed, Ed S); middle grades education (Ed S); middle grades language arts (M Ed); middle grades mathematics (M Ed); special education (M Ed). *Accreditation:* NCATE. *Degree requirements:* For master's, minimum cumulative GPA of 3.0; maximum of 6 credit hours with C grade; no courses with D grade; degree completed within 7 calendar years; for Ed S, minimum GPA of 3.25 in all courses with no grade less than a B; degree must be completed within 7 calendar years from date of initial enrollment in graduate work. *Entrance requirements:* For master's, undergraduate degree from accredited institution; professional Georgia Teaching Certificate or eligibility; minimum undergraduate GPA of 2.75 as reported on official final transcripts from all accredited institutions attended; 2 confidential Administrative Recommendation Forms; for Ed S, master's degree from accredited college or university; professional Georgia Teaching Certificate or eligibility; minimum graduate GPA of 3.0 as reported on official final graduate transcripts from all accredited institutions attended; 2 confidential Administrative Recommendation Forms. Electronic applications accepted. *Expenses:* Contact institution.

Georgia State University, College of Education and Human Development, Department of Early Childhood Education, Atlanta, GA 30302-3083. Offers early childhood and elementary education (PhD); early childhood education (M Ed, Ed S); mathematics education (M Ed); urban education (M Ed). *Accreditation:* NCATE. *Program availability:* Part-time, evening/weekend. *Faculty:* 20 full-time (17 women), 1 (woman) part-time/adjunct. *Students:* 82 full-time (74 women), 30 part-time (27 women); includes 69 minority (48 Black or African American, non-Hispanic/Latino; 3 Asian, non-Hispanic/Latino; 11 Hispanic/Latino; 7 Two or more races, non-Hispanic/Latino), 3 international. Average age 31. 116 applicants, 70% accepted, 77 enrolled. In 2018, 36 master's, 6 doctorates awarded. *Entrance requirements:* For master's, GRE, undergraduate diploma; for doctorate and Ed S, GRE, master's degree. *Application deadline:* Applications are processed on a rolling basis. Application fee: $50. Electronic applications accepted. *Expenses: Tuition, area resident:* Full-time $9360; part-time $390 per credit hour. Tuition, state resident: full-time $9360; part-time $390 per credit hour. Tuition, nonresident: full-time $30,024; part-time $1251 per credit hour. *International tuition:* $30,024 full-time. *Required fees:* $2128. *Financial support:* In 2018–19, fellowships with full tuition reimbursements (averaging $24,000 per year), research assistantships with tuition reimbursements (averaging $4,000 per year), teaching assistantships with full tuition reimbursements (averaging $2,000 per year) were awarded; career-related internships or fieldwork, Federal Work-Study, institutionally sponsored loans, scholarships/grants, traineeships, health care benefits, tuition waivers (partial), and unspecified assistantships also available. Support available to part-time students. Financial award applicants required to submit FAFSA. *Faculty research:* Teacher development; language arts/literacy education; mathematics education; intersection of science, urban, and multicultural education; diversity in education.
Website: http://ecee.education.gsu.edu/

Georgia State University, College of Education and Human Development, Department of Learning Sciences, Program in Education of Students with Exceptionalities, Atlanta, GA 30302-3083. Offers autism spectrum disorders (PhD); behavior disorders (PhD); communication disorders (PhD); early childhood special education (PhD); learning disabilities (PhD); mental retardation (PhD); orthopedic impairments (PhD); sensory impairments (PhD). *Accreditation:* NCATE. *Program availability:* Part-time, evening/weekend. Application fee: $50. Electronic applications accepted. *Expenses: Tuition, area resident:* Full-time $9360; part-time $390 per credit hour. Tuition, state resident: full-time $9360; part-time $390 per credit hour. Tuition, nonresident: full-time $30,024; part-time $1251 per credit hour. *International tuition:* $30,024 full-time. *Required fees:* $2128. *Financial support:* Fellowships, research assistantships, scholarships/grants, health care benefits, and unspecified assistantships available. *Faculty research:* Academic and behavioral supports for students with emotional/behavior disorders; academic interventions for learning disabilities; cultural, socioeconomic, and linguistic diversity; language and literacy development, disorders, and instruction. *Unit head:* Dr. Brendan Calandra, Chair, 404-413-8420, Fax: 404-413-8420, E-mail: bcalandra@

gsu.edu. *Application contact:* Sandy Vaughn, Senior Administrative Coordinator, 404-413-8318, Fax: 404-413-8043, E-mail: svaughn@gsu.edu. Website: https://education.gsu.edu/program/phd-education-students-exceptionalities/

Gordon College, Graduate Education Program, Wenham, MA 01984-1899. Offers early childhood (M Ed); educational leadership (M Ed, Ed S); elementary education (M Ed); English as a second language (M Ed, Ed S); math specialist (M Ed); mathematics specialist (Ed S); middle school education (M Ed); moderate disabilities (M Ed); Montessori education (M Ed); reading (M Ed, Ed S); secondary education (M Ed). *Program availability:* Part-time, evening/weekend. *Degree requirements:* For master's, action research or clinical experience (for most programs); for Ed S, action research or clinical experience (for some programs). *Entrance requirements:* For master's, minimum undergraduate GPA of 3.0; 2 official undergraduate transcripts; professional resume; 3 recommendation letters (one professional reference, one academic reference, one personal reference); 500-700 word statement of purpose; for Ed S, minimum master's GPA of 3.3; 2 official transcripts from undergraduate and graduate schools; professional resume; 3 recommendation letters (one professional reference, one academic reference, one personal reference); 500-700 word statement of purpose. Additional exam requirements/recommendations for international students: Required—TOEFL (minimum score 550 paper-based, 80 iBT) or IELTS (minimum score 6.5). *Expenses:* Contact institution. *Faculty research:* Reading, early childhood development, English language learners, universal design for learning.

Governors State University, College of Education, Program in Early Childhood Education, University Park, IL 60484. Offers MA. *Accreditation:* NCATE. *Program availability:* Part-time. *Faculty:* 19 full-time (12 women), 20 part-time/adjunct (13 women). In 2018, 1 master's awarded. *Application deadline:* For fall admission, 4/1 for domestic students. Applications are processed on a rolling basis. Application fee: $50. Electronic applications accepted. *Financial support:* Application deadline: 5/1; applicants required to submit FAFSA. *Unit head:* Timothy Harrington, Chair, Division of Education, 708-534-5000 Ext. 4361, E-mail: tharrington2@govst.edu. *Application contact:* Timothy Harrington, Chair, Division of Education, 708-534-5000 Ext. 4361, E-mail: tharrington2@govst.edu.

Grand Canyon University, College of Education, Phoenix, AZ 85017-1097. Offers autism spectrum disorders (MA); curriculum and instruction (MA); early childhood education (M Ed); educational administration (M Ed); educational leadership (M Ed); elementary education (M Ed); gifted education (MA); instructional technology (MS); K-12 leadership (Ed S); reading (MA); secondary education (M Ed); secondary humanities education (M Ed); secondary STEM education (M Ed); special education (M Ed); teaching and learning (Ed D); teaching English to speakers of other languages (MA). *Program availability:* Part-time, evening/weekend, online learning. *Degree requirements:* For master's, publishable research paper (M Ed), e-portfolio. *Entrance requirements:* For master's, undergraduate degree from accredited, GCU-approved college, university, or program with minimum GPA 2.8. Additional exam requirements/recommendations for international students: Required—TOEFL (minimum score 550 paper-based; 79 iBT), IELTS (minimum score 6). Electronic applications accepted.

Grand Valley State University, College of Education, Program in Special Education, Allendale, MI 49401-9403. Offers cognitive impairment (M Ed); early childhood developmental delay (M Ed); emotional impairment (M Ed); learning disabilities (M Ed); special education (M Ed). *Accreditation:* NCATE. *Program availability:* Part-time, evening/weekend. *Students:* 4 full-time (3 women), 66 part-time (55 women); includes 4 minority (3 Hispanic/Latino; 1 Two or more races, non-Hispanic/Latino), 2 international. Average age 33. 16 applicants, 88% accepted, 9 enrolled. In 2018, 23 master's awarded. *Entrance requirements:* For master's, GRE General Test or minimum GPA of 3.0, last 60 credits from regionally-accredited college/university, 3 letters of recommendation. Additional exam requirements/recommendations for international students: Required—TOEFL (minimum iBT score of 80), IELTS (6.5), or Michigan English Language Assessment Battery (77). *Application deadline:* Applications are processed on a rolling basis. Application fee: $30. Electronic applications accepted. *Expenses:* $677 per credit hour, 33 credit hours. *Financial support:* In 2018–19, 11 students received support, including 11 fellowships; career-related internships or fieldwork, Federal Work-Study, scholarships/grants, and unspecified assistantships also available. *Faculty research:* Evaluation of special education program effects, adaptive behavior assessment, language development, writing disorders, comparative effects of presentation methods. *Unit head:* Dr. Amy Schelling, Director of Special Education, 616-331-6243, Fax: 616-331-6294, E-mail: schellia@gvsu.edu. *Application contact:* Annukka Thelen, Director, Student Information and Services Center, 616-331-6205, Fax: 616-331-6217, E-mail: thelenan@gvsu.edu.

Grand Valley State University, College of Education, Programs in General Education, Allendale, MI 49401-9403. Offers adult and higher education (M Ed); early childhood education (M Ed); educational differentiation (M Ed); educational leadership (M Ed); educational technology integration (M Ed); elementary education (M Ed); middle level education (M Ed); school library media services (M Ed); secondary level education (M Ed); teaching English to speakers of other languages (M Ed). *Program availability:* Part-time, evening/weekend, 100% online, blended/hybrid learning. *Students:* 20 part-time (10 women); includes 1 minority (Black or African American, non-Hispanic/Latino). Average age 44. In 2018, 1 master's awarded. *Entrance requirements:* For master's, GRE General Test or minimum GPA of 3.0, last 60 credits from regionally-accredited college/university, 3 letters of recommendation. Additional exam requirements/recommendations for international students: Required—TOEFL (minimum iBT score of 80), IELTS (6.5), or Michigan English Language Assessment Battery (77). *Application deadline:* Applications are processed on a rolling basis. Application fee: $30. Electronic applications accepted. *Expenses:* $677 per credit hour, 33 credits. *Financial support:* In 2018–19, 1 student received support, including 1 fellowship; career-related internships or fieldwork, Federal Work-Study, scholarships/grants, and unspecified assistantships also available. *Faculty research:* Effectiveness of technology in education, parental involvement, effective teaching, effective schools research. *Unit head:* Dr. David Bair, Department Director, 616-331-6489, Fax: 616-331-6489, E-mail: baird@gvsu.edu. *Application contact:* Annukka Thelen, Director, Student Information and Services Center, 616-331-6205, Fax: 616-331-6217, E-mail: thelenan@gvsu.edu. Website: http://www.gvsu.edu/coe/

Harding University, Cannon-Clary College of Education, Searcy, AR 72149-0001. Offers advanced studies in teaching and learning (M Ed); art (MSE); behavioral science (MSE); counseling (MS, Ed S); early childhood special education (M Ed, MSE); education (MSE); educational leadership (M Ed, Ed S); elementary education (M Ed); English (MSE); French (MSE); history/social science (MSE); kinesiology (MSE); math (MSE); reading (M Ed); secondary education (M Ed); Spanish (MSE); teaching (MAT); teaching English as a second language (MSE). *Accreditation:* NCATE. *Program availability:* Part-time, evening/weekend. *Degree requirements:* For master's, comprehensive exam (for some programs), thesis optional, portfolio(s); for Ed S, comprehensive exam, portfolio, project. *Entrance requirements:* For master's, GRE, MAT, PRAXIS; for Ed S, MAT or GRE. Additional exam requirements/recommendations for international students: Required—TOEFL (minimum score 550 paper-based; 79 iBT). *Faculty research:* Reading, comprehension, school violence, educational technology, behavior, college choice, differentiated instruction, brain-based teaching.

Hebrew College, Shoolman Graduate School of Jewish Education, Newton Centre, MA 02459. Offers early childhood Jewish education (Certificate); Jewish day school education (Certificate); Jewish education (MJ Ed); Jewish family education (Certificate); Jewish special education (Certificate); Jewish youth education, informal education and camping (Certificate). *Program availability:* Part-time, evening/weekend, online learning. *Degree requirements:* For master's, one foreign language. *Entrance requirements:* For master's, GRE, interview. Additional exam requirements/recommendations for international students: Required—TOEFL.

Henderson State University, Graduate Studies, Teachers College, Department of Advanced Instructional Studies, Arkadelphia, AR 71999-0001. Offers developmental therapy (MSE); dyslexia therapy (Graduate Certificate); education (MAT); educational technology leadership (Graduate Certificate); English as a second language (MSE, Graduate Certificate); instructional facilitator (MSE, Graduate Certificate); middle level education (MAT); special education (K-12) (MAT, MSE); special education/early childhood (MAT). *Accreditation:* NCATE. *Program availability:* Part-time. *Entrance requirements:* For master's, GRE General Test or MAT, minimum GPA of 2.7, teacher certification. Additional exam requirements/recommendations for international students: Required—TOEFL (minimum score 600 paper-based); Recommended—IELTS (minimum score 6.5).

Hofstra University, School of Education, Programs in Teacher Education, Hempstead, NY 11549. Offers bilingual education (MA); bilingual extension (Advanced Certificate); business education (MS Ed); curriculum studies (MS Ed); early childhood and childhood education (MS Ed); early childhood education (MA, MS Ed); educational technology (Advanced Certificate); elementary education (MA, MS Ed); English education (MS Ed); family and consumer science (MS Ed); fine arts and music education (Advanced Certificate); fine arts education (MS Ed); foreign language and TESOL (MS Ed); foreign language education (MA, MS Ed); languages other than English and teaching English as a second language (MA); learning and teaching (Ed D); mathematics education (MA, MS Ed); middle childhood extension (Advanced Certificate); music education (MA, MS Ed); science education (MA); secondary education (Advanced Certificate); social studies education (MA, MS Ed); teaching languages other than English and TESOL (MS Ed); technology for learning (MA); TESOL (MS Ed, Advanced Certificate); TESOL with specialization in STEM (MA); work based learning extension (Advanced Certificate). *Program availability:* Part-time, evening/weekend, blended/hybrid learning. *Students:* 138 full-time (94 women), 109 part-time (78 women); includes 66 minority (16 Black or African American, non-Hispanic/Latino; 17 Asian, non-Hispanic/Latino; 31 Hispanic/Latino; 2 Native Hawaiian or other Pacific Islander, non-Hispanic/Latino), 6 international. Average age 29. 217 applicants, 86% accepted, 113 enrolled. In 2018, 105 master's, 11 doctorates, 25 other advanced degrees awarded. *Degree requirements:* For master's, comprehensive exam, thesis (for some programs), exit project, student teaching, fieldwork, electronic portfolio, curriculum project, minimum GPA of 3.0; for doctorate, dissertation; for Advanced Certificate, 3 foreign languages, comprehensive exam (for some programs), thesis project. *Entrance requirements:* For master's, GRE, 2 letters of recommendation, portfolio, teacher certification (MA), interview, essay; for doctorate, GMAT, GRE, LSAT, or MAT; for Advanced Certificate, 2 letters of recommendation, essay, interview and/or portfolio, teaching certificate. Additional exam requirements/recommendations for international students: Required—TOEFL (minimum score 550 paper-based; 80 iBT). *Application deadline:* Applications are processed on a rolling basis. Application fee: $75. Electronic applications accepted. *Financial support:* In 2018–19, 86 students received support, including 51 fellowships with full and partial tuition reimbursements available (averaging $5,080 per year), 2 research assistantships with full and partial tuition reimbursements available (averaging $3,470 per year); career-related internships or fieldwork, Federal Work-Study, institutionally sponsored loans, scholarships/grants, traineeships, tuition waivers (full and partial), unspecified assistantships, and scholarships and endowed scholarships also available. Support available to part-time students. Financial award applicants required to submit FAFSA. *Faculty research:* Impact of memory on learning; brain function, cognitive-development, learning, and achievement; student activism and civic education; using children's literature to promote diversity; 2nd language acquisition. *Unit head:* Dr. Alan Singer, Chairperson, 516-463-5853, Fax: 516-463-6275, E-mail: alan.j.singer@hofstra.edu. *Application contact:* Sunil Samuel, Assistant Vice President of Admissions, 516-463-4723, Fax: 516-463-4664, E-mail: graduateadmission@hofstra.edu. Website: http://www.hofstra.edu/education/

Hofstra University, School of Education, Specialized Programs in Education, Hempstead, NY 11549. Offers applied behavior analysis (Advanced Certificate); childhood special education (MS Ed); early childhood special education (MS Ed, Advanced Certificate); educational and policy leadership (Ed D); educational leadership (Advanced Certificate); educational leadership and policy studies (MS Ed), including K-12; elementary special education (MS Ed); gifted education (Advanced Certificate); health education (MS); health professions pedagogy and leadership (MS); higher education leadership and policy studies (MS Ed); inclusive early childhood special education (MS Ed); inclusive elementary special education (MS Ed); inclusive secondary special education (MS Ed); literacy studies (MA, MS Ed, Ed D, Advanced Certificate); pedagogy for health professions (Advanced Certificate); physical education (MS); school district business leader (Advanced Certificate); secondary education generalist - students with disabilities 7-12 (MS Ed); secondary special education generalist - secondary education (MS Ed); special education (MS Ed, Advanced Certificate); special education assessment and diagnosis (Advanced Certificate); special education early childhood intervention (MS Ed); special education: international perspectives (MS Ed); teaching students with severe or multiple disabilities (Advanced Certificate). *Program availability:* Part-time, evening/weekend, blended/hybrid learning. *Students:* 126 full-time (91 women), 230 part-time (175 women); includes 90 minority (40 Black or African American, non-Hispanic/Latino; 4 American Indian or Alaska Native, non-Hispanic/Latino; 11 Asian, non-Hispanic/Latino; 32 Hispanic/Latino; 3 Two or more races, non-Hispanic/Latino), 4 international. Average age 32. 215 applicants, 90% accepted, 117 enrolled. In 2018, 130 master's, 9 doctorates, 23 other advanced degrees awarded. *Degree requirements:* For master's, one foreign language, comprehensive exam (for some programs), thesis (for some programs), electronic portfolio, capstone course, internship, practicum, student teaching, seminars, minimum GPA of 3.0; for doctorate, one foreign language, comprehensive exam, thesis/dissertation, qualifying hearing. *Entrance requirements:* For master's, GRE, interview, letters of recommendation, portfolio, essay, certification; for doctorate, GRE or MAT, interview, resume, essay, master's degree, 3 letters of recommendation, writing sample; for Advanced Certificate, GRE, interview, letters of recommendation, essay, professional experience, resume, master's degree. Additional exam requirements/recommendations for international students: Required—TOEFL (minimum score 550 paper-based; 80 iBT). *Application deadline:* Applications are processed on a rolling basis. Application fee: $75. Electronic applications accepted. *Financial support:* In 2018–19, 208 students received support, including 105 fellowships with full and partial tuition reimbursements available (averaging $3,948 per year), 12 research assistantships with full and partial tuition reimbursements available (averaging $6,573 per year); career-related internships or fieldwork, Federal Work-Study, institutionally sponsored loans, scholarships/grants, traineeships, tuition waivers (full and partial), unspecified assistantships, and scholarships and endowed scholarships also available. Support available to part-time

students. Financial award applicants required to submit FAFSA. *Faculty research:* Water quality and income inequality; girls and stem; new media literacies; applied behavior analysis; k-12 leadership development. *Unit head:* Dr. Alan Flurkey, Chairperson, 516-463-5237, E-mail: alan.d.flurkey@hofstra.edu. *Application contact:* Sunil Samuel, Assistant Vice President of Admissions, 516-463-4723, Fax: 516-463-4664, E-mail: graduateadmission@hofstra.edu.
Website: http://www.hofstra.edu/education/

Holy Family University, Graduate and Professional Programs, School of Education, Master of Education Programs, Philadelphia, PA 19114. Offers early elementary education (PreK-Grade 4) (M Ed); education leadership (M Ed); general education (M Ed); reading specialist (M Ed); special education (M Ed); TESOL and literacy (M Ed). *Program availability:* Part-time. *Degree requirements:* For master's, thesis optional. Electronic applications accepted.

Hunter College of the City University of New York, Graduate School, School of Education, Department of Curriculum and Teaching, New York, NY 10065-5085. Offers bilingual education (MS); early childhood education (MS); educational supervision and administration (Ed D, AC), including administration and supervision (AC), instructional leadership (Ed D); teaching English as a second language (MA). *Degree requirements:* For master's, thesis; for AC, portfolio review. *Entrance requirements:* For degree, minimum B average in graduate course work, teaching certificate, minimum 3 years of full-time teaching experience, interview, 2 letters of support. Additional exam requirements/recommendations for international students: Required—TOEFL, TWE. *Faculty research:* Teacher opportunity corps (mentor program for first-year teachers), adult literacy, student literacy corporation.

Indiana University–Purdue University Indianapolis, School of Education, Indianapolis, IN 46202-5155. Offers curriculum and instruction (MS); early childhood (MS); educational leadership (MS, Certificate); English as a second language (Certificate); kindergarten (Certificate); language education (MS); reading (Certificate); school counseling (MS); special education (MS, Certificate). *Program availability:* Part-time, evening/weekend. Terminal master's awarded for partial completion of doctoral program. *Degree requirements:* For master's, thesis optional. *Entrance requirements:* For master's, GRE General Test, minimum GPA of 2.5; for Certificate, official transcripts. Additional exam requirements/recommendations for international students: Required—TOEFL (minimum score 60 iBT), IELTS (minimum score 5.5). Electronic applications accepted. *Expenses:* Contact institution. *Faculty research:* Educational policies and school leaders' responses to these; issues of intersectionality in the experiences of African American lesbian, gay, and bisexual students attending historically black colleges and universities and those who belong to black Greek-letter organizations; students' experiential knowledge and their evolving disciplinary-specific literacy and understanding; innovative program development; urban ESL teacher preparation; target-based instructional coaching.

Inter American University of Puerto Rico, Guayama Campus, Department of Education and Social Sciences, Guayama, PR 00785. Offers early childhood education (0-4 years) (M Ed); elementary education (M Ed). *Program availability:* Part-time. *Entrance requirements:* For master's, GRE, MAT, EXADEP, letters of recommendation, minimum GPA of 2.5. Electronic applications accepted.

Iona College, School of Arts and Science, Department of Education, New Rochelle, NY 10801-1890. Offers adolescence education: biology (MS Ed, MST); adolescence education: English (MS Ed); adolescence education: mathematics (MST); adolescence education: social studies (MS Ed, MST); adolescence education: Spanish (MS Ed); adolescence special education 5-12 (MST); childhood and special education (MST); early childhood and childhood (MST); educational leadership (MS Ed). *Accreditation:* NCATE. *Program availability:* Part-time, evening/weekend. *Faculty:* 7 full-time (5 women), 9 part-time/adjunct (5 women). *Students:* 33 full-time (30 women), 26 part-time (20 women); includes 21 minority (6 Black or African American, non-Hispanic/Latino; 1 Asian, non-Hispanic/Latino; 13 Hispanic/Latino; 1 Two or more races, non-Hispanic/Latino). Average age 25. 39 applicants, 87% accepted, 14 enrolled. In 2018, 20 master's awarded. *Degree requirements:* For master's, thesis or alternative. *Entrance requirements:* For master's, minimum GPA of 3.0, NY State teaching certificate and bachelor's degree (for MS Ed). Additional exam requirements/recommendations for international students: Required—TOEFL (minimum score 550 paper-based; 80 iBT), IELTS (minimum score 6.5). *Application deadline:* For fall admission, 8/1 priority date for domestic students, 5/1 priority date for international students; for spring admission, 1/1 priority date for domestic students, 9/1 priority date for international students. Applications are processed on a rolling basis. Electronic applications accepted. *Expenses:* Tuition: Full-time $14,064; part-time $7032 per credit. *Required fees:* $245 per semester. One-time fee: $250. Tuition and fees vary according to program. *Financial support:* In 2018-19, 2 students received support. Unspecified assistantships available. Support available to part-time students. Financial award application deadline: 4/15; financial award applicants required to submit FAFSA. *Faculty research:* Engaging teacher educators in scientific process, cross-national comparisons of mathematics teaching, questioning strategies in the classroom, research methods, literacy development. *Unit head:* Malissa Scheuring Leipold, EdD, Chair, 914-633-2210, Fax: 914-633-2281, E-mail: mleipold@iona.edu. *Application contact:* Christopher Kash, Assistant Director of Graduate Admissions, 914-633-2403, E-mail: ckash@iona.edu. Website: http://www.iona.edu/Academics/School-of-Arts-Science/Departments/Education/Graduate-Programs.aspx

Jackson State University, Graduate School, College of Education and Human Development, Department of Elementary and Early Childhood Education, Jackson, MS 39217. Offers early childhood education (MS Ed, Ed D); elementary education (MS Ed, Ed S); reading education (MS Ed). *Accreditation:* NCATE. *Program availability:* Part-time, evening/weekend, 100% online, blended/hybrid learning. Terminal master's awarded for partial completion of doctoral program. *Degree requirements:* For master's, comprehensive exam, thesis or alternative; for doctorate, comprehensive exam, thesis/dissertation. *Entrance requirements:* For master's, GRE General Test; for doctorate, MAT, teaching experience. Additional exam requirements/recommendations for international students: Required—TOEFL (minimum score 520 paper-based; 67 iBT). Electronic applications accepted. *Expenses:* Contact institution.

Jacksonville State University, Graduate Studies, School of Education, Program in Early Childhood Education, Jacksonville, AL 36265-1602. Offers MS Ed. *Accreditation:* NCATE. *Program availability:* Part-time, evening/weekend. *Degree requirements:* For master's, comprehensive exam, thesis (for some programs). *Entrance requirements:* For master's, GRE General Test or MAT. Additional exam requirements/recommendations for international students: Required—TOEFL (minimum score 500 paper-based; 61 iBT). Electronic applications accepted.

James Madison University, The Graduate School, College of Education, Program in Early Childhood Education, Harrisonburg, VA 22807. Offers MAT. *Accreditation:* NCATE. *Program availability:* Part-time. *Students:* Average age 27. *Entrance requirements:* For master's, GRE General Test or MAT, PRAXIS I and II, 2-3 page written statement, faculty interview, minimum undergraduate GPA of 2.75. Additional exam requirements/recommendations for international students: Required—TOEFL. *Application deadline:* For fall admission, 5/1 priority date for domestic students; for

spring admission, 9/1 priority date for domestic students. Applications are processed on a rolling basis. Electronic applications accepted. *Expenses:* Tuition, state resident: full-time $10,848. Tuition, nonresident: full-time $27,888. *Required fees:* $1128. *Financial support:* Career-related internships or fieldwork and unspecified assistantships available. Financial award application deadline: 3/1; financial award applicants required to submit FAFSA. *Unit head:* Dr. Martha Ross, Academic Unit Head, 540-568-6255. *Application contact:* Lynette M. Bible, Director of Graduate Admissions, 540-568-6395, Fax: 540-568-7860, E-mail: biblelm@jmu.edu.

James Madison University, The Graduate School, College of Education, Program in Education, Harrisonburg, VA 22807. Offers early childhood education (preK-3) (MAT); educational leadership (M Ed); educational technology (M Ed); elementary education (MAT); equity and cultural diversity (M Ed); inclusive early childhood education (MAT); K-8 mathematics specialist (M Ed); middle education (MAT); reading education (M Ed); secondary education (MAT); Spanish language and culture for educators (M Ed); TESOL (MAT). *Accreditation:* NCATE. *Program availability:* Part-time, evening/weekend. *Students:* 255 full-time (224 women), 200 part-time (140 women); includes 56 minority (13 Black or African American, non-Hispanic/Latino; 8 Asian, non-Hispanic/Latino; 21 Hispanic/Latino; 14 Two or more races, non-Hispanic/Latino), 1 international. Average age 30. In 2018, 295 master's awarded. Application fee: $60. Electronic applications accepted. *Expenses:* Tuition, state resident: full-time $10,848. Tuition, nonresident: full-time $27,888. *Required fees:* $1128. *Financial support:* In 2018–19, 22 students received support. Teaching assistantships, career-related internships or fieldwork, Federal Work-Study, and assistantships (averaging $7911) available. Financial award application deadline: 3/1; financial award applicants required to submit FAFSA. *Unit head:* Dr. Phillip M. Wishon, Dean, 540-568-6572, E-mail: wishonpm@jmu.edu. *Application contact:* Lynette D. Michael, Director of Graduate Admissions, 540-568-6131 Ext. 6395, Fax: 540-568-7860, E-mail: michaeld@jmu.edu. Website: http://www.jmu.edu/coe/index.shtml

Jose Maria Vargas University, Program in Preschool Education, Pembroke Pines, FL 33026. Offers MS.

Kansas State University, Graduate School, College of Human Ecology, School of Family Studies and Human Services, Manhattan, KS 66506-1403. Offers applied family sciences (MS); communication sciences and disorders (MS); conflict resolution (Graduate Certificate); couple and family therapy (MS); early childhood education (MS); family and community service (MS); life-span human development (MS); personal financial planning (MS, PhD, Graduate Certificate); youth development (MS, Graduate Certificate). *Accreditation:* AAMFT/COAMFTE; ASHA. *Program availability:* Part-time, online learning. *Degree requirements:* For master's, comprehensive exam (for some programs), thesis optional. *Entrance requirements:* For master's, GRE, minimum GPA of 3.0 in last 2 years (60 semester hours) of undergraduate study; for doctorate, GRE. Additional exam requirements/recommendations for international students: Required—TOEFL (minimum score 600 paper-based). Electronic applications accepted. *Faculty research:* Health and security of military families, training in and evaluation of professional human services (marriage and couple therapy, family life education, treatment of speech and swallowing disorders, financial therapy), disorders of communication and swallowing, family and relationship development and health, financial decision-making.

Kean University, College of Education, Program in Early Childhood Education, Union, NJ 07083. Offers MA. *Accreditation:* NCATE. *Program availability:* Part-time. *Faculty:* 14 full-time (8 women). *Students:* 6 full-time (all women), 9 part-time (6 women); includes 8 minority (2 Black or African American, non-Hispanic/Latino; 2 Asian, non-Hispanic/Latino; 4 Hispanic/Latino). Average age 29. 7 applicants, 100% accepted, 6 enrolled. In 2018, 5 master's awarded. *Entrance requirements:* For master's, GRE General Test, PRAXIS Early Childhood Content Knowledge (for some programs), minimum GPA of 3.0, 2 letters of recommendation, teacher certification (for some programs), personal statement, official transcripts, resume. Additional exam requirements/recommendations for international students: Required—TOEFL (minimum score 550 paper-based; 79 iBT), IELTS (minimum score 6.5). *Application deadline:* For fall admission, 6/30 for domestic and international students; for spring admission, 12/1 for domestic and international students. Applications are processed on a rolling basis. Application fee: $75. Electronic applications accepted. *Expenses:* Tuition, state resident: full-time $15,025; part-time $733.50 per credit. Tuition, nonresident: full-time $19,890; part-time $884.50 per credit. *Required fees:* $2107.50; $89.50 per credit. Tuition and fees vary according to course level, course load, degree level and program. *Financial support:* Scholarships/grants and unspecified assistantships available. Financial award applicants required to submit FAFSA. *Unit head:* Robert Messano, Program Coordinator, 908-737-0301, E-mail: rmessano@kean.edu. *Application contact:* Brittany Gerstenhaber, Admissions Counselor, 908-737-7100, E-mail: gradadmissions@kean.edu.

Kennesaw State University, Bagwell College of Education, Program in Early Childhood Education, Kennesaw, GA 30144. Offers M Ed. *Program availability:* Evening/weekend, online only, 100% online. *Students:* 78 full-time (all women), 5 part-time (3 women); includes 18 minority (9 Black or African American, non-Hispanic/Latino; 2 Asian, non-Hispanic/Latino; 5 Hispanic/Latino; 2 Two or more races, non-Hispanic/Latino). Average age 29. 2 applicants, 100% accepted, 1 enrolled. In 2018, 71 master's awarded. *Degree requirements:* For master's, Capstone. *Entrance requirements:* Additional exam requirements/recommendations for international students: Required—TOEFL (minimum score 80 iBT), IELTS (minimum score 6.5). *Application deadline:* For summer admission, 4/1 for domestic and international students. Application fee: $60. Electronic applications accepted. *Expenses:* Tuition, area resident: Full-time $6960; part-time $290 per credit hour. Tuition, state resident: full-time $6960; part-time $290 per credit hour. Tuition, nonresident: full-time $25,080; part-time $1045 per credit hour. *International tuition:* $25,080 full-time. *Required fees:* $2006; $1706 per semester. $853 per semester. *Application contact:* Admission Counselor, 470-578-4377, Fax: 470-578-9172, E-mail: ksugrad@kennesaw.edu.

Kent State University, College of Education, Health and Human Services, School of Lifespan Development and Educational Sciences, Program in Special Education, Kent, OH 44242-0001. Offers deaf education (M Ed); early childhood education (M Ed); educational interpreter K-12 (M Ed); general special education (M Ed); mild/moderate intervention (M Ed); special education (PhD, Ed S); transition to work (M Ed). *Accreditation:* NCATE. *Faculty:* 12 full-time (8 women), 11 part-time/adjunct (all women). *Students:* 56 full-time (46 women), 45 part-time (42 women); includes 11 minority (8 Black or African American, non-Hispanic/Latino; 1 Asian, non-Hispanic/Latino; 2 Native Hawaiian or other Pacific Islander, non-Hispanic/Latino), 3 international. 81 applicants, 26% accepted. In 2018, 35 master's, 4 doctorates awarded. *Degree requirements:* For doctorate, comprehensive exam, thesis/dissertation. *Entrance requirements:* For master's, minimum undergraduate GPA of 2.75, moral character form, 2 letters of reference, goals statement; for doctorate and Ed S, GRE General Test, goals statement, 2 letters of reference, interview, resume. Additional exam requirements/recommendations for international students: Required—TOEFL (minimum score 550 paper-based; 80 iBT). *Application deadline:* Applications are processed on a rolling basis. Application fee: $45 ($60 for international students). Electronic applications accepted. *Expenses:* Tuition, state resident: full-time $11,766; part-time $536 per credit. Tuition, nonresident: full-time $21,952; part-time $999 per credit. *International tuition:*

$21,952 full-time. Tuition and fees vary according to course load. *Financial support:* In 2018–19, 6 research assistantships with full tuition reimbursements (averaging $9,667 per year) were awarded; teaching assistantships with full tuition reimbursements, career-related internships or fieldwork, Federal Work-Study, institutionally sponsored loans, scholarships/grants, health care benefits, unspecified assistantships, and 1 administrative assistantship (averaging $8,500 per year) also available. Support available to part-time students. Financial award application deadline: 4/1; financial award applicants required to submit FAFSA. *Faculty research:* Social/emotional needs of gifted, inclusion transition services, early intervention/ecobehavioral assessments, applied behavioral analysis. *Unit head:* Sonya Wisdom, Coordinator, 330-672-0452, E-mail: swisdom@kent.edu. *Application contact:* Cheryl Slusarczyk, Academic Program Director, Office of Graduate Student Services, 330-672-2576, Fax: 330-672-9162, E-mail: ogs@kent.edu.
Website: http://www.kent.edu/ehhs/ldes/sped

Kent State University, College of Education, Health and Human Services, School of Teaching, Learning and Curriculum Studies, Program in Early Childhood Education, Kent, OH 44242-0001. Offers M Ed, MA, MAT. *Accreditation:* NCATE. *Faculty:* 5 full-time (all women), 1 (woman) part-time/adjunct. *Students:* 23 full-time (22 women), 5 part-time (all women); includes 2 minority (1 Black or African American, non-Hispanic/Latino; 1 Asian, non-Hispanic/Latino), 1 international. 41 applicants, 37% accepted. In 2018, 15 master's awarded. *Degree requirements:* For master's, thesis (for some programs). *Entrance requirements:* For master's, GRE General Test (for licensure), 2 letters of reference, goals statement. Additional exam requirements/recommendations for international students: Required—TOEFL (minimum score 550 paper-based; 80 iBT). *Application deadline:* For summer admission, 3/1 for domestic students. Applications are processed on a rolling basis. Application fee: $45 ($60 for international students). Electronic applications accepted. *Expenses:* Tuition, state resident: full-time $11,766; part-time $536 per credit. Tuition, nonresident: full-time $21,952; part-time $999 per credit. *International tuition:* $21,952 full-time. Tuition and fees vary according to course load. *Financial support:* In 2018–19, 1 research assistantship with full tuition reimbursement (averaging $9,000 per year) was awarded; teaching assistantships, Federal Work-Study, scholarships/grants, and unspecified assistantships also available. Financial award application deadline: 4/1; financial award applicants required to submit FAFSA. *Faculty research:* Parent-child relationships, professional preparation, curriculum and assessment. *Unit head:* Janice Kroeger, Coordinator, 330-672-0617, E-mail: jkroege1@kent.edu. *Application contact:* Cheryl Slusarczyk, Academic Program Director, Office of Graduate Student Services, 330-672-2576, Fax: 330-672-9162, E-mail: ogs@kent.edu.

Keuka College, Program in Childhood Education/Literacy, Keuka Park, NY 14478. Offers literacy 5-12 (MS); literacy B-6 (MS). *Degree requirements:* For master's, thesis, capstone project/student-led research project. *Entrance requirements:* For master's, GRE, minimum GPA of 3.0; 3 letters of recommendation (2 academic and one from cooperating teacher from student teaching or other professional). Additional exam requirements/recommendations for international students: Required—TOEFL (minimum score 550 paper-based). Electronic applications accepted. *Expenses:* Contact institution. *Faculty research:* Marginalized populations, international literacy, teacher assessment.

Keystone College, Master's in Early Childhood Education Leadership, La Plume, PA 18440. Offers M Ed. *Program availability:* Part-time, blended/hybrid learning. *Faculty:* 1 (woman) full-time, 4 part-time/adjunct (all women). *Students:* 48. 22 applicants, 100% accepted, 18 enrolled. In 2018, 20 master's awarded. *Degree requirements:* For master's, thesis or alternative. *Entrance requirements:* For master's, GRE, college transcripts, resume or curriculum vitae, current clearances. Additional exam requirements/recommendations for international students: Required—TOEFL (minimum score 80 iBT), IELTS (minimum score 6.5), TOEFL (minimum score 80 iBT) or IELTS (minimum score 6.5). *Application deadline:* For fall admission, 8/1 for domestic students; for spring admission, 1/1 for domestic students; for summer admission, 5/1 for domestic students. Applications are processed on a rolling basis. Application fee: $0. Electronic applications accepted. *Expenses:* Contact institution. *Financial support:* Unspecified assistantships available. Financial award application deadline: 5/1; financial award applicants required to submit FAFSA. *Unit head:* Heather Shanks-McElroy, PhD, Professor, 570-945-8475, E-mail: heather.mcelroy@keystone.edu. *Application contact:* Jennifer Sekol, Director of Admissions, 570-945-8117, Fax: 570-945-7916, E-mail: jennifer.sekol@keystone.edu.

Lander University, Graduate Studies, Greenwood, SC 29649-2099. Offers clinical nurse leader (MSN); emergency management (MS); Montessori education (M Ed); teaching and learning (M Ed). *Accreditation:* NCATE. *Program availability:* Part-time, online learning. *Degree requirements:* For master's, comprehensive exam, thesis or alternative. *Entrance requirements:* For master's, GRE General Test. Additional exam requirements/recommendations for international students: Required—TOEFL (minimum score 550 paper-based). Electronic applications accepted.

La Salle University, School of Arts and Sciences, Program in Education, Philadelphia, PA 19141-1199. Offers autism spectrum disorders (MA, Certificate); bilingual/bicultural studies (MA); classroom management (MA); dual early childhood and special education (MA); dual middle-level science and math and special education (MA); education (MA); English (MA); English as a second language (Certificate); history (MA); instructional coach (Certificate); instructional leadership (MA); reading specialist (MA, Certificate); secondary education (MA); special education (MA, Certificate). *Program availability:* Part-time, evening/weekend. *Degree requirements:* For master's, comprehensive exam. *Entrance requirements:* For master's, MAT or GRE, 2 letters of recommendation; for Certificate, GMAT or GRE, 2 letters of recommendation. Additional exam requirements/recommendations for international students: Required—TOEFL. Electronic applications accepted. Application fee is waived when completed online. *Expenses:* Contact institution.

Lee University, Program in Education, Cleveland, TN 37320-3450. Offers art (MAT); curriculum and instruction (M Ed, Ed S); early childhood (MAT); educational leadership (M Ed, Ed S); elementary education (MAT); English and math (MAT); English and science (MAT); English and social studies (MAT); higher education administration (MS); history (MAT); history and economics (MAT); math and science (MAT); math and social studies (MAT); middle grades (MAT); science and social studies (MASW); secondary education (MAT); Spanish (MAT); special education (M Ed, MAT); TESOL (MAT). *Accreditation:* NCATE. *Program availability:* Part-time. *Faculty:* 13 full-time (5 women), 13 part-time/adjunct (7 women). *Students:* 32 full-time (26 women), 73 part-time (49 women); includes 13 minority (10 Black or African American, non-Hispanic/Latino; 3 Two or more races, non-Hispanic/Latino), 3 international. Average age 30. 56 applicants, 73% accepted, 34 enrolled. In 2018, 60 master's, 3 other advanced degrees awarded. *Degree requirements:* For master's, variable foreign language requirement, thesis optional, internship. *Entrance requirements:* For master's, MAT or GRE General Test, minimum undergraduate GPA of 2.75, 3 letters of recommendation, interview, writing sample, official transcripts, background check; for Ed S, minimum undergraduate and master's GPA of 2.75, official transcripts for undergraduate and master's degrees. Additional exam requirements/recommendations for international students: Required—TOEFL (minimum score 61 iBT). *Application deadline:* For fall admission, 6/1 priority date for domestic and international students; for spring admission, 11/1 priority date for domestic and international students; for summer admission, 4/1 priority date for domestic and international students. Applications are processed on a rolling basis. Application fee: $25. Electronic applications accepted. *Financial support:* In 2018–19, 43 students received support. Career-related internships or fieldwork, Federal Work-Study, institutionally sponsored loans, scholarships/grants, and unspecified assistantships available. Financial award application deadline: 3/1; financial award applicants required to submit FAFSA. *Unit head:* Dr. William Kamm, Director, 423-614-8544, E-mail: wkamm@leeuniversity.edu. *Application contact:* Jeffery McGirt, Director of Graduate Enrollment, 423-614-8691, Fax: 423-614-8317, E-mail: jmcgirt@leeuniversity.edu.
Website: http://www.leeuniversity.edu/academics/graduate/education

Lehigh University, College of Education, Program in Educational Leadership, Bethlehem, PA 18015. Offers curriculum and instruction (Certificate); educational leadership (M Ed, Ed D); K-12 principal (Certificate); superintendent letter (Certificate). *Program availability:* Part-time, evening/weekend, online only, blended/hybrid learning. *Faculty:* 4 full-time (1 woman), 7 part-time/adjunct (2 women). *Students:* 11 full-time (7 women), 104 part-time (62 women); includes 24 minority (7 Black or African American, non-Hispanic/Latino; 2 Asian, non-Hispanic/Latino; 14 Hispanic/Latino; 1 Two or more races, non-Hispanic/Latino), 7 international. Average age 34. 42 applicants, 62% accepted, 14 enrolled. In 2018, 40 master's, 2 doctorates awarded. *Degree requirements:* For master's, thesis (for some programs); for doctorate, comprehensive exam, thesis/dissertation. *Entrance requirements:* For master's, minimum undergraduate GPA of 3.0, essay, transcripts, 2 letters of recommendation; for doctorate, GRE General Test or MAT, minimum graduate GPA of 3.6, 2 letters of recommendation, essay, transcript; for Certificate, minimum undergraduate GPA of 3.0. Additional exam requirements/recommendations for international students: Required—TOEFL (minimum score 600 paper-based; 93 iBT), IELTS (minimum score 6.5), Either TOEFL or IELTS is required. *Application deadline:* For fall admission, 1/15 for domestic and international students; for spring admission, 12/1 for domestic and international students; for summer admission, 5/8 for domestic and international students. Applications are processed on a rolling basis. Application fee: $65. Electronic applications accepted. *Expenses:* MBA/Educational Leadership $825 per credit. COE (per 3 credits) intern courses require a special supervision fee which varies from $225 to $350. *Financial support:* In 2018–19, 18 students received support, including 4 research assistantships (averaging $8,600 per year); fellowships, scholarships/grants, and unspecified assistantships also available. Financial award application deadline: 1/31; financial award applicants required to submit FAFSA. *Faculty research:* Supervision of instruction, middle-level education, organizational change, leadership preparation and development, international school leadership, urban school leadership, comparative education, social justice, education and human services, social network, principal leadership, policy implementation, teacher evaluation, teaching quality. *Total annual research expenditures:* $16,829. *Unit head:* Dr. Floyd D. Beachum, Director, 610-758-5955, Fax: 610-758-3227, E-mail: fdb209@lehigh.edu. *Application contact:* Lynn Spina, Coordinator, 610-758-3250, Fax: 610-758-6223, E-mail: lys218@lehigh.edu.
Website: https://ed.lehigh.edu/academics/programs/educational-leadership

Lehman College of the City University of New York, School of Education, Department of Early Childhood and Childhood Education, Program in Early Childhood Education, Bronx, NY 10468-1589. Offers MS Ed. *Accreditation:* NCATE. *Program availability:* Part-time, evening/weekend. *Entrance requirements:* For master's, minimum GPA of 2.7. *Faculty research:* TV programming, literacy, children's trauma conceptualization.

Le Moyne College, Department of Education, Syracuse, NY 13214. Offers adolescent education (MS Ed, MST); adolescent education/special education (MS Ed, MST); adolescent English (MST), including grades 7-12; adolescent English/special education (MST), including grades 7-12; adolescent foreign language (MST), including grades 7-12; adolescent history (MST), including grades 7-12; childhood education (MS Ed); childhood education/special education (MS Ed); elementary education (MS Ed); general education (MS Ed); inclusive childhood education (MST); literacy education (MS Ed), including birth to grade 6, grades 5-12; school building leader (MS Ed); school building leadership (CAS); school district business leader (MS Ed, CAS); school district leader (MS Ed); school district leadership (CAS); secondary education (MS Ed); special education (MS Ed); teaching English to speakers of other languages (MS Ed); urban studies (MS Ed). *Accreditation:* TEAC. *Program availability:* Part-time, evening/weekend. *Faculty:* 7 full-time (5 women), 16 part-time/adjunct (11 women). *Students:* 35 full-time (28 women), 119 part-time (84 women); includes 14 minority (5 Black or African American, non-Hispanic/Latino; 1 Asian, non-Hispanic/Latino; 7 Hispanic/Latino; 1 Two or more races, non-Hispanic/Latino), 1 international. Average age 30. 123 applicants, 89% accepted, 96 enrolled. In 2018, 66 master's, 48 CASs awarded. Terminal master's awarded for partial completion of doctoral program. *Degree requirements:* For master's, thesis. *Entrance requirements:* For master's, bachelor's degree with minimum undergraduate GPA of 3.0, 2 letters of recommendation, transcripts. Additional exam requirements/recommendations for international students: Required—TOEFL (minimum score 79 iBT); Recommended—IELTS (minimum score 6.5). *Application deadline:* For fall admission, 4/1 priority date for domestic and international students; for spring admission, 10/1 priority date for domestic and international students; for summer admission, 3/1 priority date for domestic and international students. Applications are processed on a rolling basis. Electronic applications accepted. *Expenses:* $734 per credit hour; wellness fee $70 per semester for full-time graduate students taking 9+ credit hours; technology fee $75 per semester for full-time graduate students taking 9+ credit hours, $25 per semester for part-time students; $1,470 per credit hour (for ED.D.). *Financial support:* In 2018–19, 44 students received support. Career-related internships or fieldwork, scholarships/grants, and health care benefits available. Support available to part-time students. Financial award applicants required to submit FAFSA. *Faculty research:* Minority teachers, special education, multiculturalism, literacy, technology, media literacy learning, autism, school district organization, service-learning, higher level problem solving, teacher leadership. *Unit head:* Dr. Stephen C. Fleury, Chair, Department of Education, 315-445-4376, Fax: 315-445-4744, E-mail: fleurysc@lemoyne.edu. *Application contact:* Jody F Manning, Assistant Director for Graduate Admission, 315-445-5444, Fax: 315-445-6092, E-mail: manninjf@lemoyne.edu.
Website: http://www.lemoyne.edu/education

Lesley University, Graduate School of Education, Cambridge, MA 02138-2790. Offers arts, community, and education (M Ed); autism studies (Certificate); curriculum and instruction (M Ed, CAGS); early childhood education (M Ed); ecological teaching and learning (MS); educational studies (PhD), including adult learning, educational leadership, individually designed; elementary education (M Ed); emergent technologies for educators (Certificate); ESLArts: language learning through the arts (M Ed); high school education (M Ed); individually designed (M Ed); integrated teaching through the arts (M Ed); literacy for K-8 classroom teachers (M Ed); mathematics education (M Ed); middle school education (M Ed); moderate disabilities (M Ed); online learning (Certificate); reading (CAGS); science in education (M Ed); severe disabilities (M Ed); special needs (CAGS); specialist teacher of reading (M Ed); teacher of visual art (M Ed); technology in education (M Ed, CAGS). *Accreditation:* TEAC. *Program availability:* Part-time, evening/weekend, online learning. *Degree requirements:* For master's, practicum;

for doctorate, thesis/dissertation. *Entrance requirements:* For master's, Massachusetts Tests for Educator Licensure (MTEL), transcripts, statement of purpose, recommendations; interview (for special education); for doctorate, GRE General Test, transcripts, statement of purpose, recommendations, interview, master's degree, resume; for other advanced degree, interview, master's degree. Additional exam requirements/recommendations for international students: Required—TOEFL (minimum score 550 paper-based; 80 iBT). Electronic applications accepted. *Faculty research:* Assessment in literacy, mathematics and science; autism spectrum disorders; instructional technology and online learning; multicultural education and English language learners.

Lewis University, College of Education, Program in Early Childhood Special Education, Romeoville, IL 60446. Offers MA. *Program availability:* Part-time. *Students:* 14 full-time (all women), 8 part-time (7 women); includes 8 minority (all Hispanic/Latino). Average age 33. *Degree requirements:* For master's, comprehensive exam. *Entrance requirements:* For master's, writing exam, Test of Academic Proficiency/Basic Skills Test/ACT/SAT, bachelor's degree, minimum undergraduate GPA of 2.75, two letters of recommendation, professional educator license, interview. Additional exam requirements/recommendations for international students: Required—TOEFL (minimum score 550 paper-based; 79 iBT), IELTS (minimum score 6). *Application deadline:* For fall admission, 5/1 priority date for international students; for spring admission, 11/1 priority date for international students. Application fee: $40. Electronic applications accepted. *Financial support:* Federal Work-Study and unspecified assistantships available. Financial award application deadline: 5/1; financial award applicants required to submit FAFSA. *Unit head:* Dr. Rebecca Pruitt, Program Director. *Application contact:* Kathy Lisak, Graduate Admission Counselor, 815-836-5610, E-mail: grad@lewisu.edu. Website: http://www.lewisu.edu/academics/grad-education/earlychildhood/index.htm

Lincoln University, The School of Adult & Continuing Education, Philadelphia, PA 19104. Offers counseling (MSC); early childhood education (M Ed), including PreK-4; early childhood education and special education (M Ed); educational leadership (M Ed), including principal certification; finance (MBA); human resources management (MBA); human services delivery (MAHS). *Program availability:* Part-time, evening/weekend. *Faculty:* 8 full-time (3 women), 22 part-time/adjunct (12 women). *Students:* 192 full-time (154 women), 62 part-time (40 women); includes 230 minority (218 Black or African American, non-Hispanic/Latino; 9 Hispanic/Latino; 3 Two or more races, non-Hispanic/Latino), 3 international. Average age 33. 278 applicants, 58% accepted, 94 enrolled. In 2018, 105 master's awarded. *Degree requirements:* For master's, comprehensive exam, thesis or alternative, capstone, grant proposal. *Entrance requirements:* For master's, GRE/GMAT (Optional), Official academic transcript(s), letters of recommendation, personal statement, resume, supervisor's evaluation form, Application fee. Additional exam requirements/recommendations for international students: Required—TOEFL (minimum score 500 paper-based; 71 iBT); Recommended—IELTS (minimum score 6.5). *Application deadline:* For fall admission, 8/19 for domestic and international students; for spring admission, 12/30 for domestic and international students. Applications are processed on a rolling basis. Application fee: $50. Electronic applications accepted. *Financial support:* Scholarships/grants available. Financial award application deadline: 4/1; financial award applicants required to submit FAFSA. *Unit head:* Dr. Patricia Joseph, Dean of Faculty, 484-365-7659, E-mail: joseph@lincoln.edu. *Application contact:* Jernice Lea, Director, Student Services and Admissions, 215-590-8231, Fax: 215-387-3859, E-mail: jlea@lincoln.edu. Website: http://www.lincoln.edu/admissions/graduate-admissions

London Metropolitan University, Graduate Programs, London, United Kingdom. Offers applied psychology (M Sc); architecture (MA); biomedical science (M Sc); blood science (M Sc); cancer pharmacology (M Sc); computer networking and cyber security (M Sc); computing and information systems (M Sc); conference interpreting (MA); counter-terrorism studies (M Sc); creative, digital and professional writing (MA); crime, violence and prevention (M Sc); criminology (M Sc); curating contemporary art (MA); data analytics (M Sc); digital media (MA); early childhood studies (MA); education (MA, Ed D); financial services law, regulation and compliance (LL M); food science (M Sc); forensic psychology (M Sc); health and social care management and policy (M Sc); human nutrition (M Sc); human resource management (MA); human rights and international conflict (MA); information technology (M Sc); intelligence and security studies (M Sc); international oil, gas and energy law (LL M); international relations (MA); interpreting (MA); learning and teaching in higher education (MA); legal practice (LL M); media and entertainment law (LL M); organizational and consumer psychology (M Sc); psychological therapy (M Sc); psychology of mental health (M Sc); public health (M Sc); public policy and management (MPA); security studies (M Sc); social work (M Sc); spatial planning and urban design (MA); sports therapy (M Sc); supporting older children and young people with dyslexia (MA); teaching languages (MA), including Arabic, English; translation (MA); woman and child abuse (MA).

Long Island University–Brentwood Campus, Graduate Programs, Brentwood, NY 11717. Offers childhood education (MS), including grades 1-6; childhood education/literacy B-6 (MS); childhood education/special education (grades 1-6) (MS); clinical mental health counseling (MS, Advanced Certificate); criminal justice (MS); early childhood education (MS); educational leadership (MS Ed); family nurse practitioner (MS, Advanced Certificate); health administration (MPA); library and information science (MS); literacy (B-6) (MS Ed); school counselor (MS, Advanced Certificate); social work (MSW); special education (MS Ed); students with disabilities generalist (grades 7-12) (Advanced Certificate). *Program availability:* Part-time. *Entrance requirements:* For master's and Advanced Certificate, GRE. Additional exam requirements/recommendations for international students: Required—TOEFL or IELTS. Electronic applications accepted.

Long Island University–Hudson, Graduate School, Purchase, NY 10577. Offers autism (Advanced Certificate); bilingual education (Advanced Certificate); childhood education (MS Ed); crisis management (Advanced Certificate); early childhood education (MS Ed); educational leadership (MS Ed); health administration (MPA); literacy (MS Ed); marriage and family therapy (MS); mental health counseling (MS, Advanced Certificate), including credentialed alcoholism and substance abuse counselor (MS); middle childhood and adolescence education (MS Ed); pharmaceutics (MS), including cosmetic science, industrial pharmacy; public administration (MPA); school counseling (MS Ed, Advanced Certificate); school psychology (MS Ed); special education (MS Ed); TESOL (MS Ed); TESOL (all grades) (Advanced Certificate). *Program availability:* Part-time, evening/weekend. *Entrance requirements:* Additional exam requirements/recommendations for international students: Required—TOEFL. Electronic applications accepted. *Expenses:* Contact institution.

Long Island University–LIU Brooklyn, School of Education, Brooklyn, NY 11201-8423. Offers adolescence urban education (MS Ed); applied behavior analysis (Advanced Certificate); bilingual education (Advanced Certificate); bilingual education in urban setting (MS Ed); bilingual school counselor (MS Ed, Advanced Certificate); childhood urban education (MS Ed); childhood/early childhood education (MS Ed); childhood/early childhood urban education (MS Ed); early childhood urban education (MS Ed, Advanced Certificate); educational leadership (Advanced Certificate); marriage and family therapy (MS, Advanced Certificate); mental health counseling (MS, Advanced Certificate); school building district leader (Advanced Certificate); school counselor (MS Ed, Advanced Certificate); school psychologist (MS Ed); teaching students with disabilities (MS Ed); teaching urban children with disabilities (MS Ed); TESOL (MS Ed, Advanced Certificate). *Accreditation:* TEAC. *Program availability:* Part-time, evening/weekend, 100% online. *Entrance requirements:* For master's, GRE. Additional exam requirements/recommendations for international students: Required—TOEFL (minimum score 527 paper-based, 75 iBT), IELTS, or PTE. Electronic applications accepted. *Faculty research:* Diversity issues in education and mental health care, inclusion - disability studies, sustainability, teacher professional development.

Long Island University–LIU Post, College of Education, Information and Technology, Brookville, NY 11548-1300. Offers adolescence education (MS); adolescence education 7-12 (MS); archives and records management (AC); art education (MS); childhood education (MS); childhood education/literacy B-6 (MS); childhood education/special education (MS); clinical mental health counseling (MS, AC); early childhood education (MS); early childhood education/childhood education (MS); educational leadership (AC); educational technology (MS); information studies (PhD); interdisciplinary educational studies (Ed D); middle childhood education (MS); music education (MS); public library administration (AC); school counselor (MS); special education (MS Ed); speech-language pathology (MA); students with disabilities, 7-12 generalist (AC); TESOL (MA). *Accreditation:* ASHA; TEAC. *Program availability:* Part-time, 100% online, blended/hybrid learning. Terminal master's awarded for partial completion of doctoral program. *Degree requirements:* For master's, variable foreign language requirement, comprehensive exam (for some programs), thesis optional; for doctorate, comprehensive exam, thesis/dissertation. *Entrance requirements:* For master's and AC, GRE (for some programs). Additional exam requirements/recommendations for international students: Required—TOEFL (minimum score 550 paper-based, 75 iBT), IELTS, or PTE. Electronic applications accepted. *Faculty research:* Sleep; use of technology to develop executive function by students with disabilities; early childhood literacy development through play; social justice through education; using a structured protocol to discuss Bad News.

Long Island University–Riverhead, Graduate Programs, Riverhead, NY 11901. Offers applied behavior analysis (Advanced Certificate); childhood education (MS), including grades 1-6; cybersecurity policy (Advanced Certificate); homeland security management (MS, Advanced Certificate); literacy education (MS); literacy education B-6 (MS); teaching students with disabilities (MS), including grades 1-6; TESOL (Advanced Certificate). *Accreditation:* TEAC. *Program availability:* Part-time. *Entrance requirements:* Additional exam requirements/recommendations for international students: Required—TOEFL or IELTS. Electronic applications accepted. *Expenses:* Contact institution.

Louisiana Tech University, Graduate School, College of Education, Ruston, LA 71272. Offers counseling and guidance (MA), including clinical mental health counseling, human services, orientation and mobility; counseling psychology (PhD); curriculum and instruction (M Ed); cyber education (Graduate Certificate); dynamics of domestic and family violence (Graduate Certificate); early childhood education - PreK-3 (MAT); educational leadership (M Ed, Ed D); elementary education and special education mild/moderate grades 1-5 (MAT); higher education administration (Graduate Certificate); industrial/organizational psychology (MA, PhD); kinesiology (MS); middle school education (MAT), including mathematics; orientation and mobility (Graduate Certificate); rehabilitation teaching for the blind (Graduate Certificate); secondary education (MAT), including agriculture, biology, business, chemistry, English; special education: visually impaired (MAT); teacher leader education (Graduate Certificate); visual impairments - blind education (Graduate Certificate). *Accreditation:* NCATE. *Program availability:* Part-time. *Degree requirements:* For master's, thesis; for doctorate, thesis/dissertation. *Entrance requirements:* For master's and doctorate, GRE General Test. Additional exam requirements/recommendations for international students: Required—TOEFL (minimum score 550 paper-based; 80 iBT), IELTS (minimum score 6.5). Electronic applications accepted. *Faculty research:* Blindness and the best methods for increasing independence for individuals who are blind or visually impaired; educating and investigating factors contributing to improvements in human performance across the lifespan and a reduction in injury rates during training.

Loyola University Maryland, Graduate Programs, School of Education, Program in Montessori Education, Baltimore, MD 21210-2699. Offers elementary education (M Ed); Montessori education (CAS). *Accreditation:* NCATE. *Degree requirements:* For master's, thesis. *Entrance requirements:* For master's, essay, transcripts. Additional exam requirements/recommendations for international students: Required—TOEFL (minimum score 550 paper-based), IELTS (minimum score 7). *Expenses:* Contact institution.

Lynn University, Donald E. and Helen L. Ross College of Education, Boca Raton, FL 33431-5598. Offers educational leadership (M Ed, Ed D), including K-12 (Ed D, school administration K-12 (M Ed); exceptional student education (M Ed), including school administration K-12. *Program availability:* Part-time, evening/weekend, online learning. *Faculty:* 6 full-time (4 women), 8 part-time/adjunct (7 women). *Students:* 38 full-time (30 women), 85 part-time (63 women); includes 50 minority (33 Black or African American, non-Hispanic/Latino; 1 Asian, non-Hispanic/Latino; 15 Hispanic/Latino; 1 Two or more races, non-Hispanic/Latino), 5 international. Average age 38. 78 applicants, 65% accepted, 41 enrolled. In 2018, 13 master's, 14 doctorates awarded. *Degree requirements:* For master's, comprehensive exam, thesis (for some programs), completion of degree in maximum of four calendar years; minimum cumulative GPA of 3.0 and B grade or higher in each course; orientation seminar (one credit); minimum of 40 credits; FTCE ESE K-12 Exam; for doctorate, thesis/dissertation, mid-program review; minimum cumulative GPA of 3.25 and B grade or higher in each course. *Entrance requirements:* For master's, bachelor's degree from accredited institution, minimum undergraduate GPA of 3.0, official undergraduate and graduate transcripts of all academic coursework attempted, current resume, statement of professional goals, writing sample, 2 recent letters of recommendation; for doctorate, professional practice statement that identifies applicant's goals and explains how Lynn's program will help attain them, official transcript showing conferral of master's degree, 2 letters of recommendation from previous professors or employers, current resume, interview. Additional exam requirements/recommendations for international students: Required—TOEFL (minimum score 550 paper-based; 80 iBT), IELTS (minimum score 6.5). *Application deadline:* For fall admission, 8/18 for domestic students, 8/4 for international students; for spring admission, 12/15 for domestic students, 12/1 for international students; for summer admission, 4/17 for domestic students, 4/3 for international students. Applications are processed on a rolling basis. Application fee: $45. Electronic applications accepted. *Expenses:* 850 per credit hour. *Financial support:* In 2018–19, 85 students received support. Career-related internships or fieldwork, Federal Work-Study, scholarships/grants, tuition waivers (partial), and unspecified assistantships available. Support available to part-time students. Financial award application deadline: 3/1; financial award applicants required to submit FAFSA. *Faculty research:* Student achievement, students with learning differences, teacher and student retention, student motivation and cognition, neuroscience leadership and learning. *Unit head:* Dr. Kathleen Weigel, Dean, College of Education, 561-237-7441, E-mail: kweigel@lynn.edu. *Application contact:* Steven Pruitt, Director of Graduate and Undergraduate Evening Admission, 561-237-7834, Fax: 561-237-7100, E-mail: spruitt@lynn.edu. Website: http://www.lynn.edu/academics/colleges/education

Manhattan College, Graduate Programs, School of Education and Health, Program in Special Education, Riverdale, NY 10471. Offers adolescence education students with disabilities generalist extension in English or math or social studies - grades 7-12 (MS Ed); bilingual education (Advanced Certificate); dual childhood/students with disabilities - grades 1-6 (MS Ed); students with disabilities - grades 1-6 (MS Ed). *Program availability:* Part-time, evening/weekend. *Degree requirements:* For master's, thesis, internship (if not certified). *Entrance requirements:* For master's, GRE, minimum GPA of 3.0. Additional exam requirements/recommendations for international students: Required—TOEFL (minimum score 550 paper-based; 80 iBT), IELTS (minimum score 6). Electronic applications accepted. Application fee is waived when completed online. *Expenses:* Contact institution.

Manhattanville College, School of Education, Jump Start Program, Purchase, NY 10577-2132. Offers childhood education and special education (grades 1-6) (MPS); early childhood education (birth-grade 2) (MAT); education (Advanced Certificate); English and special education (grades 5-12) (MPS); mathematics and special education (grades 5-12) (MPS); science and special education (grades 5-12) (MPS); social studies and special education (grades 5-12) (MPS); Spanish (grades 7-12) (MAT); tesol - teaching English as a second language (all grades) (MPS). *Program availability:* Part-time, evening/weekend. *Faculty:* 11 full-time (7 women), 78 part-time/adjunct (50 women). *Students:* 3 full-time (2 women), 16 part-time (11 women); includes 5 minority (1 Black or African American, non-Hispanic/Latino; 3 Hispanic/Latino; 1 Native Hawaiian or other Pacific Islander, non-Hispanic/Latino). Average age 31. 48 applicants, 54% accepted, 22 enrolled. In 2018, 23 master's, 1 other advanced degree awarded. *Degree requirements:* For master's, comprehensive exam (for some programs), thesis (for some programs), student teaching, research seminars, portfolios, internships, writing assessment; for Advanced Certificate, comprehensive exam (for some programs). *Entrance requirements:* For master's, for programs leading to certification, candidates must submit scores from GRE or MAT(miller analogies test), minimum undergraduate GPA of 3.0, all transcripts from all colleges and universities attended, 2 letters of recommendation, interview, essay (2-3 page personal statement that describes reasons for choosing education as profession and personal philosophy of education), proof of immunization (for those born after 1957). Additional exam requirements/ recommendations for international students: Required—TOEFL (minimum score 600 paper-based; 110 iBT); Recommended—IELTS (minimum score 8). *Application deadline:* Applications are processed on a rolling basis. Application fee: $75. Electronic applications accepted. *Expenses:* 935 per credit. *Financial support:* Teaching assistantships, career-related internships or fieldwork, Federal Work-Study, institutionally sponsored loans, scholarships/grants, and unspecified assistantships available. Financial award application deadline: 3/15; financial award applicants required to submit FAFSA. *Faculty research:* Early childhood and technology, professional development schools and community schools, students with emotional difficulties, literacy and adolescents, mindfulness, changing suburbs institute, and community schools, studying the effects of the environment on special populations, the most difficult cases, students who are presented with multiple challenges: learning, behavioral and ACE experiences who see criminal behavior as a way to cope; working on giving them the tools they need to succeed. *Unit head:* Dr. Shelley Wepner, Dean, 914-323-3153, E-mail: Shelly.Wepner@mville.edu. *Application contact:* Alissa Wilson, Director, SOE Graduate Enrollment Management, 914-323-3150, Fax: 914-694-1732, E-mail: edschool@mville.edu.
Website: http://www.mville.edu/programs/jump-start

Manhattanville College, School of Education, Program in Childhood Education, Purchase, NY 10577-2132. Offers childhood education (grades 1-6) (MAT); childhood education (grades 1-6) and special education: childhood (grades 1-6) (MPS); early childhood (birth-grade 2) & childhood ed (grades 1-6) (MAT); special ed early childhood and childhood (birth-grade 6) (MPS); special education childhood (grades 1-6) (MPS); special education: childhood (grades 1-6) (Certificate); special education: early childhood (birth-grade 2) and childhood (grades 1-6) (Certificate). *Program availability:* Part-time, evening/weekend. *Faculty:* 5 full-time (4 women), 3 part-time/adjunct (all women). *Students:* 4 full-time (3 women), 27 part-time (25 women); includes 6 minority (1 Black or African American, non-Hispanic/Latino; 1 Asian, non-Hispanic/Latino; 4 Hispanic/Latino). Average age 25. 18 applicants, 56% accepted, 8 enrolled. In 2018, 15 master's awarded. *Degree requirements:* For master's, comprehensive exam (for some programs), thesis (for some programs), student teaching, research seminars, portfolios, internships, writing assessment; for Certificate, comprehensive exam (for some programs). *Entrance requirements:* For master's, for programs leading to certification, candidates must submit scores from GRE or MAT(Miller Analogies Test), minimum undergraduate GPA of 3.0, all transcripts from all colleges and universities attended, 2 letters of recommendation, interview, essay (2-3 page personal statement that describes reasons for choosing education as profession and personal philosophy of education), proof of immunization (for those born after 1957). Additional exam requirements/ recommendations for international students: Required—TOEFL (minimum score 600 paper-based; 110 iBT); Recommended—IELTS (minimum score 8). *Application deadline:* Applications are processed on a rolling basis. Application fee: $75. Electronic applications accepted. *Expenses:* 935 per credit. *Financial support:* Teaching assistantships, career-related internships or fieldwork, Federal Work-Study, institutionally sponsored loans, scholarships/grants, and unspecified assistantships available. Financial award application deadline: 3/15; financial award applicants required to submit FAFSA. *Faculty research:* Early childhood and technology, professional development schools and community schools. *Unit head:* Dr. Shelley Wepner, Dean, 914-323-3153, Fax: 914-323-5493, E-mail: Shelley.Wepner@mville.edu. *Application contact:* Alissa Wilson, Director, SOE Graduate Enrollment Management, 914-323-3150, Fax: 914-694-1732, E-mail: edschool@mville.edu.
Website: http://www.mville.edu/programs/childhood-education

Manhattanville College, School of Education, Program in Early Childhood Education, Purchase, NY 10577-2132. Offers early childhood (birth-grade 2) & childhood ed (grades 1-6) (MAT); early childhood (birth-grade 2) and special education: early childhood (birth-grade 2) (MPS); early childhood education (birth-grade 2) (MAT); special ed early childhood and childhood (birth-grade 6) (MPS); special education: early childhood (birth-grade 2) (MPS, Certificate); special education: early childhood (birth-grade 2) and childhood (grades 1-6) (Certificate). *Program availability:* Part-time, evening/weekend. *Faculty:* 1 (woman) full-time, 5 part-time/adjunct (all women). *Students:* 6 full-time (all women), 18 part-time (17 women); includes 2 minority (1 Black or African American, non-Hispanic/Latino; 1 Hispanic/Latino). Average age 29. 13 applicants, 69% accepted, 5 enrolled. In 2018, 13 master's awarded. *Degree requirements:* For master's, comprehensive exam (for some programs), thesis (for some programs), student teaching, research seminars, portfolios, internships, writing assessment; for Certificate, comprehensive exam (for some programs). *Entrance requirements:* For master's, for programs leading to certification, candidates must submit scores from GRE or MAT(Miller Analogies Test), minimum undergraduate GPA of 3.0, all transcripts from all colleges and universities attended, 2 letters of recommendation, interview, essay (2-3 page personal statement that describes reasons for choosing education as profession and personal philosophy of education), proof of immunization (for those born after 1957). Additional exam requirements/ recommendations for international students: Required—TOEFL (minimum score 600 paper-based; 110 iBT); Recommended—IELTS (minimum score 8). *Application deadline:* Applications are processed on a rolling basis. Application fee: $75. Electronic applications accepted. *Expenses:* 935 per credit. *Financial support:* Teaching assistantships, career-related internships or fieldwork, Federal Work-Study, institutionally sponsored loans, scholarships/grants, and unspecified assistantships available. Financial award application deadline: 3/15; financial award applicants required to submit FAFSA. *Faculty research:* Early childhood and technology. *Unit head:* Dr. Shelley Wepner, Dean, 914-323-3153, Fax: 914-323-5493, E-mail: Shelley.Wepner@mville.edu. *Application contact:* Alissa Wilson, Director, SOE Graduate Enrollment Management, 914-323-3150, Fax: 914-694-1732, E-mail: edschool@mville.edu.
Website: http://www.mville.edu/programs/early-childhood-education

Manhattanville College, School of Education, Program in Literacy Education, Purchase, NY 10577-2132. Offers literacy (birth-grade 6) and special education childhood (grades 1-6) (MPS); literacy 5-12; special education generalist 7-12; special ed specialist 7-12 (MPS); literacy specialist (birth-grade 6) (MPS); literacy specialist (grades 5-12) (MPS); science of reading: multisensory instruction – the rose institute for learning and literacy (Advanced Certificate). *Program availability:* Part-time, evening/ weekend. *Faculty:* 3 full-time (all women), 15 part-time/adjunct (14 women). *Students:* 2 full-time (both women), 8 part-time (all women). Average age 26. 6 applicants, 50% accepted, 1 enrolled. In 2018, 8 master's, 11 Advanced Certificates awarded. *Degree requirements:* For master's, comprehensive exam (for some programs), thesis (for some programs), student teaching, research seminars, portfolios, internships, writing assessment; for Advanced Certificate, comprehensive exam (for some programs). *Entrance requirements:* For master's, for programs leading to certification, candidates must submit scores from GRE or MAT(Miller Analogies Test), minimum undergraduate GPA of 3.0, all transcripts from all colleges and universities attended, 2 letters of recommendation, interview, essay (2-3 page personal statement that describes reasons for choosing education as profession and personal philosophy of education), proof of immunization (for those born after 1957). Additional exam requirements/ recommendations for international students: Required—TOEFL (minimum score 600 paper-based; 110 iBT); Recommended—IELTS (minimum score 8). *Application deadline:* Applications are processed on a rolling basis. Application fee: $75. Electronic applications accepted. *Expenses:* 935 per credit. *Financial support:* Teaching assistantships, career-related internships or fieldwork, Federal Work-Study, institutionally sponsored loans, scholarships/grants, and unspecified assistantships available. Financial award application deadline: 3/15; financial award applicants required to submit FAFSA. *Faculty research:* Power of story for literacy development, English learners. *Total annual research expenditures:* $800. *Unit head:* Dr. Shelley Wepner, Dean, 914-323-3153, Fax: 914-323-5493, E-mail: Shelley.Wepner@mville.edu. *Application contact:* Alissa Wilson, Director, SOE Graduate Enrollment Management, 914-323-3150, Fax: 914-694-1732, E-mail: edschool@mville.edu.
Website: http://www.mville.edu/programs/literacy-education

Manhattanville College, School of Education, Program in Special Education, Purchase, NY 10577-2132. Offers childhood education (grades 1-6) and special education: childhood (grades 1-6) (MPS); early childhood (birth-grade 2) and special education: early childhood (birth-grade 2) (MPS); English (5-9 and 7-12); special ed generalist (7-12); se English (7-12) (MPS); literacy (birth-grade 6) and special education childhood (grades 1-6) (MPS); literacy 5-12; special education generalist 7-12; special ed specialist 7-12 (MPS); math (5-9 and 7-12); special ed generalist (7-12); se math (7-12) (MPS); science: biology or chemistry (5-9 and 7-12); special ed generalist (7-12); se science (7-12) (MPS); social studies (5-9 and 7-12); special ed generalist (7-12); se soc.st. (7-12) (MPS); special ed early childhood and childhood (birth-grade 6) (MPS); special education childhood (grades 1-6) (MPS); special education: childhood (grades 1-6) (Certificate); special education: early childhood (birth-grade 2) (MPS, Certificate); special education: early childhood (birth-grade 2) and childhood (grades 1-6) (Certificate); special education: grades 7-12 generalist (MPS, Certificate). *Program availability:* Part-time, evening/weekend. *Faculty:* 5 full-time (3 women), 35 part-time/ adjunct (23 women). *Students:* 45 full-time (36 women), 179 part-time (152 women); includes 31 minority (6 Black or African American, non-Hispanic/Latino; 4 Asian, non-Hispanic/Latino; 19 Hispanic/Latino; 2 Native Hawaiian or other Pacific Islander, non-Hispanic/Latino), 1 international. Average age 28. 76 applicants, 68% accepted, 40 enrolled. In 2018, 99 master's, 2 Certificates awarded. *Degree requirements:* For master's, comprehensive exam (for some programs), thesis (for some programs), student teaching, research seminars, portfolios, internships, writing assessment; for Certificate, comprehensive exam (for some programs). *Entrance requirements:* For master's, for programs leading to certification, candidates must submit scores from GRE or MAT(Miller Analogies Test), minimum undergraduate GPA of 3.0, all transcripts from all colleges and universities attended, 2 letters of recommendation, interview, essay (2-3 page personal statement that describes reasons for choosing education as profession and personal philosophy of education), proof of immunization (for those born after 1957). Additional exam requirements/recommendations for international students: Required—TOEFL (minimum score 600 paper-based; 110 iBT); Recommended—IELTS (minimum score 8). *Application deadline:* Applications are processed on a rolling basis. Application fee: $75. Electronic applications accepted. *Expenses:* 935 per credit. *Financial support:* Teaching assistantships, career-related internships or fieldwork, Federal Work-Study, institutionally sponsored loans, scholarships/grants, and unspecified assistantships available. Financial award application deadline: 3/15; financial award applicants required to submit FAFSA. *Faculty research:* Students with emotional difficulties, literacy and adolescents, mindfulness, studying the effects of the environment on special populations, the most difficult cases, students who are presented with multiple challenges: learning, behavioral and ACE experiences who see criminal behavior as a way to cope; working on giving them the tools they need to succeed emotionally and cognitively despite the odds stacked against them. *Unit head:* Dr. Shelley Wepner, Dean, 914-323-3153, Fax: 914-323-5493, E-mail: Shelley.Wepner@mville.edu. *Application contact:* Alissa Wilson, Director, SOE Graduate Enrollment Management, 914-323-3150, Fax: 914-694-1732, E-mail: edschool@mville.edu.
Website: http://www.mville.edu/programs/special-education

Martin Luther College, Graduate Studies, New Ulm, MN 56073. Offers early childhood director (MS Ed Admin); educational technology (MS Ed); instruction (MS Ed); leadership (MS Ed); principal (MS Ed Admin); special education (MS Ed). *Program availability:* Part-time, evening/weekend, online only, 100% online. *Faculty:* 13 full-time (2 women), 31 part-time/adjunct (10 women). *Students:* 1 full-time (0 women), 86 part-time (26 women); includes 1 minority (Two or more races, non-Hispanic/Latino), 1 international. Average age 38. 35 applicants, 100% accepted, 35 enrolled. In 2018, 26 master's awarded. *Degree requirements:* For master's, capstone project or comprehensive exam. *Entrance requirements:* For master's, undergraduate degree in education from an accredited college or university, minimum undergraduate GPA of 3.0. Additional exam requirements/recommendations for international students: Required—TOEFL (minimum score 550 paper-based; 80 iBT); Recommended—IELTS (minimum score 6.5). *Application deadline:* Applications are processed on a rolling basis. Application fee: $35. Electronic applications accepted. *Financial support:* In 2018–19, 1 student received support. Scholarships/grants available. Financial award application deadline: 9/1. *Faculty research:* Principal effectiveness, principal support, cognitive load

in math instruction, reading strategies in multigrade classrooms, mentor provided professional development for new teachers. *Unit head:* John E. Meyer, Director of Graduate Studies, 507-354-8221 Ext. 398, E-mail: meyerjd@mlc-wels.edu. *Application contact:* John E. Meyer, Director of Graduate Studies, 507-354-8221 Ext. 398, E-mail: meyerjd@mlc-wels.edu.
Website: https://mlc-wels.edu/graduate-studies/

Marygrove College, Graduate Studies, Detroit, MI 48221-2599. Offers autism spectrum disorders (M Ed, Certificate); curriculum instruction and assessment (MAT); educational leadership (MA); educational technology (M Ed); effective teaching in the 21st century-classroom focus (MAT); effective teaching in the 21st century-technology focus (MAT); human resource management (MA, Certificate); mathematics 6-8 (MAT); mathematics K-5 (MAT); reading and literacy K-6 (MAT); reading specialist (M Ed); school administrator (Certificate); social justice (MA); special education (MAT); special education - learning disabilities (M Ed); teaching - pre-elementary education (M Ed); teaching - pre-secondary education (M Ed). *Program availability:* Part-time, evening/weekend, 100% online, blended/hybrid learning. *Entrance requirements:* For master's, all official bachelor's transcripts. Additional exam requirements/recommendations for international students: Required—TOEFL (minimum score 550 paper-based; 80 iBT). Electronic applications accepted.

Maryville University of Saint Louis, School of Education, St. Louis, MO 63141-7299. Offers early childhood education (MA Ed); educational leadership (Ed D); educational leadership w/principal certification (MA Ed); elementary education (MA Ed); gifted (MA Ed); higher education leadership (Ed D); middle grades education (MA Ed); reading/literacy specialist (MA Ed); teacher as leader (Ed D). *Accreditation:* NCATE. *Program availability:* Part-time, 100% online, blended/hybrid learning. *Faculty:* 16 full-time (8 women), 18 part-time/adjunct (11 women). *Students:* 12 full-time (all women), 311 part-time (234 women); includes 99 minority (84 Black or African American, non-Hispanic/Latino; 2 Asian, non-Hispanic/Latino; 9 Hispanic/Latino; 4 Two or more races, non-Hispanic/Latino), 2 international. Average age 38. In 2018, 25 master's, 100 doctorates awarded. *Degree requirements:* For master's, thesis, project. *Entrance requirements:* For master's, minimum cumulative GPA of 3.0, 3 professional recommendations, essays, interview with program faculty; for doctorate, minimum GPA of 3.0, 3 professional recommendations, essay, interview, on-site writing sample. Additional exam requirements/recommendations for international students: Required—TOEFL (minimum score 550 paper-based; 79 iBT). *Application deadline:* Applications are processed on a rolling basis. Electronic applications accepted. *Expenses:* $449 per credit hour for master's programs; $897 per credit hour for doctoral programs. *Financial support:* Career-related internships or fieldwork, Federal Work-Study, tuition waivers (partial), and professional educator discounts available. Financial award application deadline: 4/1; financial award applicants required to submit FAFSA. *Faculty research:* Collaboration with public schools, pre-service program development, mathematics, diversity, literacy. *Unit head:* Dr. Maschael Schappe, Dean, 314-529-9670, Fax: 314-529-9921, E-mail: mschappe@maryville.edu. *Application contact:* Stacey Ruffin, Director of Clinical Experiences & Partnerships, 314-529-9542, Fax: 314-529-9921, E-mail: sruffin@maryville.edu.
Website: http://www.maryville.edu/ed/graduate-programs/

Marywood University, Academic Affairs, Reap College of Education and Human Development, Department of Education, Program in Early Childhood Intervention, Scranton, PA 18509-1598. Offers MS. *Accreditation:* NCATE. *Program availability:* Part-time. Electronic applications accepted. *Faculty research:* Montessori education, developmentally-appropriate practice, child care environment.

McNeese State University, Doré School of Graduate Studies, Burton College of Education, Department of Education Professions, Program in Early Childhood Education Grades PK-3, Lake Charles, LA 70609. Offers Postbaccalaureate Certificate. *Entrance requirements:* For degree, PRAXIS, 2 letters of recommendation, autobiography.

Mercer University, Graduate Studies, Cecil B. Day Campus, Tift College of Education (Atlanta), Atlanta, GA 30341. Offers curriculum and instruction (PhD); early childhood education (M Ed, MAT, Ed S); educational leadership (PhD), including higher education leadership, P-12 school leadership; educational leadership P-12 (M Ed, Ed S); higher education leadership (M Ed); independent and charter school leadership (M Ed); middle grades education (M Ed, MAT); secondary education (M Ed, MAT); teacher leadership (Ed S). *Accreditation:* NCATE. *Program availability:* Part-time, evening/weekend. *Degree requirements:* For master's and Ed S, research project; for doctorate, comprehensive exam, thesis/dissertation. *Entrance requirements:* For master's, GRE or MAT, minimum undergraduate GPA of 2.75; for doctorate, GRE; for Ed S, GRE or MAT, minimum GPA of 3.25; 3 years of certified teaching experience (for educational leadership and teacher leadership). Additional exam requirements/recommendations for international students: Required—TOEFL (minimum score 80 iBT). Electronic applications accepted. *Expenses:* Contact institution. *Faculty research:* Educational technology, multicultural and minority issues in education, educational leadership (P-12 and higher education), school discipline and school bullying, standards-based mathematics education.

Mercer University, Graduate Studies, Macon Campus, Tift College of Education (Macon), Macon, GA 31207. Offers curriculum and instruction (PhD); early childhood education (M Ed, Ed S); educational leadership (M Ed, PhD, Ed S), including higher education (PhD), P-12; higher education leadership (M Ed); independent and charter school leadership (M Ed); secondary education (MAT), including STEM; teacher leadership (Ed S). *Accreditation:* NCATE. *Program availability:* Part-time, evening/weekend, 100% online, blended/hybrid learning. *Degree requirements:* For master's, research project report; for doctorate, comprehensive exam, thesis/dissertation. *Entrance requirements:* For master's, GRE or MAT, minimum GPA of 2.75; for doctorate, GRE, minimum GPA of 3.5; interview; writing sample; 3 recommendations; for Ed S, GRE or MAT, minimum GPA of 3.5 (for teacher leadership), 3.0 (for educational leadership). Additional exam requirements/recommendations for international students: Required—TOEFL (minimum score 80 iBT). Electronic applications accepted. *Expenses:* Contact institution. *Faculty research:* Teacher effectiveness, specific learning disabilities, inclusion.

Mercy College, School of Education, Program in Early Childhood Education, Dobbs Ferry, NY 10522-1189. Offers MS. *Program availability:* Part-time, evening/weekend, blended/hybrid learning. *Students:* 73 full-time (69 women), 121 part-time (117 women); includes 107 minority (30 Black or African American, non-Hispanic/Latino; 7 Asian, non-Hispanic/Latino; 66 Hispanic/Latino; 4 Two or more races, non-Hispanic/Latino). Average age 31. 134 applicants, 47% accepted, 45 enrolled. In 2018, 84 master's awarded. *Degree requirements:* For master's, Capstone project; clinical practice; for initial New York State certification, passing scores in the following are required: Educating All Students, Content Specialty Test, edTPA. *Entrance requirements:* For master's, GRE or PRAXIS, transcript(s); resume. Additional exam requirements/recommendations for international students: Required—TOEFL (minimum score 600 paper-based; 71 iBT), IELTS (minimum score 8). *Application deadline:* Applications are processed on a rolling basis. Application fee: $40. Electronic applications accepted. *Expenses: Tuition:* Full-time $15,696; part-time $872 per credit. *Required fees:* $642; $161 per term. Tuition and fees vary according to course load, degree level and program. *Financial support:* Career-related internships or fieldwork, Federal Work-Study, scholarships/grants, and unspecified assistantships available. Support available to part-time students. Financial award applicants required to submit FAFSA. *Unit head:* Dr. Eric Martone, Interim Dean, School of Education, 914-674-7618, Fax: 914-674-7352, E-mail: emartone@mercy.edu. *Application contact:* Allison Gurdineer, Executive Director of Admissions, 877-637-2946, Fax: 914-674-7382, E-mail: admissions@mercy.edu.
Website: https://www.mercy.edu/degrees-programs/ms-early-childhood-education-birth-grade-2

Middle Tennessee State University, College of Graduate Studies, College of Education, Department of Elementary and Special Education, Major in Curriculum and Instruction, Murfreesboro, TN 37132. Offers early childhood education (M Ed); elementary education (M Ed, Ed S); middle school education (M Ed). *Accreditation:* NCATE. *Program availability:* Part-time, evening/weekend, online learning. *Degree requirements:* For master's, comprehensive exam; for Ed S, comprehensive exam, thesis or alternative. *Entrance requirements:* For master's and Ed S, GRE, MAT or PRAXIS. Additional exam requirements/recommendations for international students: Required—TOEFL (minimum score 525 paper-based; 71 iBT) or IELTS (minimum score 6). Electronic applications accepted.

Millersville University of Pennsylvania, College of Graduate Studies and Adult Learning, College of Education and Human Services, Department of Early, Middle, and Exceptional Education, Millersville, PA 17551-0302. Offers early childhood education (M Ed); gifted education (M Ed); language and literacy (M Ed); language and literacy education (M Ed); special education (M Ed); special education: 7-12 (M Ed); special education: PreK-8 (M Ed). *Accreditation:* NCATE. *Program availability:* Part-time, evening/weekend, 100% online, blended/hybrid learning. *Faculty:* 10 full-time (6 women), 13 part-time/adjunct (9 women). *Students:* 9 full-time (6 women), 113 part-time (102 women); includes 11 minority (2 Black or African American, non-Hispanic/Latino; 3 Asian, non-Hispanic/Latino; 5 Hispanic/Latino; 1 Two or more races, non-Hispanic/Latino). Average age 32. 40 applicants, 98% accepted, 28 enrolled. In 2018, 25 master's awarded. *Entrance requirements:* For master's, GRE or MAT, required only if cumulative GPA is lower than 3.0, Teaching Certificate; Interview. Additional exam requirements/recommendations for international students: Required—TOEFL, IELTS (minimum score 6), PTE (minimum score 60). *Application deadline:* Applications are processed on a rolling basis. Application fee: $40. Electronic applications accepted. *Expenses: Tuition, area resident:* Full-time $9288; part-time $516 per credit. Tuition, state resident: full-time $9288; part-time $516 per credit. Tuition, nonresident: full-time $13,932; part-time $774 per credit. *International tuition:* $13,932 full-time. *Required fees:* $2623.50; $145.75 per credit. Tuition and fees vary according to course load, degree level and program. *Financial support:* In 2018–19, 5 students received support. Unspecified assistantships available. Financial award application deadline: 3/15; financial award applicants required to submit FAFSA. *Faculty research:* Co-teaching, needs of new teachers, use of popular culture in education. *Unit head:* Dr. Rich Mehrenberg, Department Chair, 717-871-7343, E-mail: richard.mehrenberg@millersville.edu. *Application contact:* Dr. James A. Delle, Acting Dean of College of Graduate Studies and Adult Learning/Associate Provost, Academic Administration, 717-871-7462, E-mail: James.Delle@millersville.edu.
Website: http://www.millersville.edu/eled/

Milligan College, Area of Education, Milligan College, TN 37682. Offers combined preK-3/K-5 education (M Ed); educational leadership (Ed D); educational specialist (Ed S); K-5 education (M Ed); middle grades education (M Ed); preK-3 education (M Ed); preK-3 special education (M Ed); secondary education (M Ed). *Accreditation:* NCATE. *Program availability:* Part-time, 100% online, blended/hybrid learning. *Faculty:* 5 full-time (3 women), 6 part-time/adjunct (3 women). *Students:* 38 full-time (31 women), 8 part-time (4 women); includes 2 minority (1 Hispanic/Latino; 1 Two or more races, non-Hispanic/Latino), 1 international. Average age 35. 36 applicants, 97% accepted, 32 enrolled. In 2018, 18 master's awarded. *Degree requirements:* For master's, thesis, portfolio, research project; for doctorate, thesis/dissertation, portfolio, research project. *Entrance requirements:* For master's, MAT, GRE General Test, ACT, SAT, or PRAXIS, undergraduate degree and supporting transcripts, professional recommendations, interview; for doctorate, MAT or GRE, master's degree and supporting transcripts, demonstrated scholastic ability, recognized leadership role within education, professional recommendations, essay/personal statement, portfolio (professional development plan, evidence of ability, knowledge and qualities), interview. Additional exam requirements/recommendations for international students: Required—TOEFL (minimum score 550 paper-based, 79 iBT) or IELTS (6.5). *Application deadline:* For fall admission, 8/1 priority date for domestic students, 6/1 for international students; for spring admission, 11/15 priority date for domestic students, 12/1 for international students; for summer admission, 4/1 for domestic students. Applications are processed on a rolling basis. Application fee: $30. Electronic applications accepted. *Expenses:* $365 per hour (for masters); $485 per hour (for doctoral); $375 fees per semester; $75 one-time records fee. *Financial support:* Scholarships/grants available. Financial award application deadline: 12/1; financial award applicants required to submit FAFSA. *Faculty research:* Assessment; school mental health; literacy; technology; educator preparation. *Unit head:* Dr. Angela Hilton-Prillhart, Area Chair of Education, 423-461-8769, Fax: 423-461-3103, E-mail: anhilton-prillhart@milligan.edu. *Application contact:* Melissa Dillow, Graduate Admissions Recruiter, Education, 423-461-8306, Fax: 423-461-8982, E-mail: msdillow@milligan.edu.
Website: http://www.Milligan.edu/GPS

Mills College, Graduate Studies, Program in Infant Mental Health, Oakland, CA 94613-1000. Offers MA. *Program availability:* Part-time. *Entrance requirements:* For master's, bachelor's degree, preferably in psychology, and the following prerequisite courses: fundamentals of psychology, developmental psychology, psychopathology, analytical methods/statistics, and research methods; three letters of recommendation; statement of purpose essay. Additional exam requirements/recommendations for international students: Required—TOEFL (minimum score 550 paper-based; 80 iBT) or IELTS (minimum score 6). Electronic applications accepted. *Faculty research:* Development and sequelae of attachment in children and adults in normative and clinical/risk populations, identifying the mental health needs of young children who have experienced extraordinary traumatic situations during critical points in their early development, examining the effects of early childhood trauma, work on helping professionals' psychological well-being.

Mississippi State University, College of Education, Department of Curriculum, Instruction and Special Education, Mississippi State, MS 39762. Offers early childhood education (PhD); elementary education (MS, PhD, Ed S), including early childhood education (MS), general elementary education (MS), middle level education (MS); general curriculum and instruction (PhD); reading education (PhD); secondary education (MAT, MS, PhD, Ed S); special education (MAT, MS, PhD, Ed S). *Accreditation:* NCATE. *Program availability:* Part-time, evening/weekend. *Faculty:* 20 full-time (14 women), 1 (woman) part-time/adjunct. *Students:* 24 full-time (16 women), 151 part-time (109 women); includes 44 minority (38 Black or African American, non-Hispanic/Latino; 3 American Indian or Alaska Native, non-Hispanic/Latino; 1 Hispanic/Latino; 2 Two or more races, non-Hispanic/Latino), 3 international. Average age 32. 65 applicants, 65% accepted, 38 enrolled. In 2018, 57 master's, 3 doctorates, 1 other advanced degree

awarded. *Degree requirements:* For master's, comprehensive exam; for doctorate, thesis/dissertation; for Ed S, comprehensive exam, thesis or alternative. *Entrance requirements:* For master's, GRE, minimum GPA of 2.75 in junior and senior year, eligibility for initial teacher certification; for doctorate, GRE, minimum GPA of 3.4 on previous graduate work; for Ed S, GRE, minimum GPA of 3.2 on master's degree. Additional exam requirements/recommendations for international students: Required—TOEFL (minimum score 550 paper-based; 79 iBT); Recommended—IELTS (minimum score 6.5). *Application deadline:* For fall admission, 3/1 priority date for domestic students, 5/1 for international students; for spring admission, 9/1 priority date for domestic students, 9/1 for international students. Applications are processed on a rolling basis. Application fee: $60 ($80 for international students). Electronic applications accepted. *Expenses:* Tuition, state resident: full-time $8450; part-time $360.59 per credit hour. Tuition, nonresident: full-time $23,140; part-time $969.09 per credit hour. *Required fees:* $110. One-time fee: $55 full-time. Part-time tuition and fees vary according to course load, degree level, campus/location and reciprocity agreements. *Financial support:* In 2018–19, 5 research assistantships with partial tuition reimbursements (averaging $11,453 per year), 1 teaching assistantship (averaging $11,700 per year) were awarded; Federal Work-Study, institutionally sponsored loans, scholarships/grants, and unspecified assistantships also available. Financial award application deadline: 4/1; financial award applicants required to submit FAFSA. *Faculty research:* Early childhood education, reading, rural schools, multicultural education, use of technology in instruction. *Unit head:* Dr. Linda Cornelious, Professor and Head, 662-325-3747, Fax: 662-325-7857, E-mail: lcornelious@colled.msstate.edu. *Application contact:* Robbie Salters, Admissions and Enrollment Assistant, 662-325-7400, E-mail: rsalters@grad.msstate.edu.
Website: http://www.cise.msstate.edu/

Mississippi State University, College of Education, Educational Leadership Program, Mississippi State, MS 39762. Offers community college education (MAT); community college leadership (PhD); higher education leadership (PhD); P-12 school leadership (PhD); school administration (MS, Ed S); student affairs and higher education (MS); workforce education leadership (MS). MS in workforce education leadership held jointly with Alcorn State University. *Faculty:* 12 full-time (9 women). *Students:* 74 full-time (43 women), 145 part-time (89 women); includes 86 minority (75 Black or African American, non-Hispanic/Latino; 1 American Indian or Alaska Native, non-Hispanic/Latino; 6 Hispanic/Latino; 4 Two or more races, non-Hispanic/Latino). Average age 35. 83 applicants, 82% accepted, 55 enrolled. In 2018, 48 master's, 12 doctorates, 13 other advanced degrees awarded. *Degree requirements:* For master's and Ed S, comprehensive exam, thesis; for doctorate, comprehensive exam, thesis/dissertation. *Entrance requirements:* For master's, GRE, minimum GPA of 2.75 in junior and senior courses; for doctorate, GRE, minimum GPA of 3.4 on previous graduate work; for Ed S, GRE, minimum GPA of 3.2, master's degree. Additional exam requirements/recommendations for international students: Required—TOEFL (minimum score 550 paper-based; 79 iBT); Recommended—IELTS (minimum score 6.5). *Application deadline:* For fall admission, 7/1 for domestic students, 5/1 for international students; for spring admission, 11/1 for domestic students, 9/1 for international students. Application fee: $60 ($80 for international students). Electronic applications accepted. *Expenses:* Tuition, state resident: full-time $8450; part-time $360.59 per credit hour. Tuition, nonresident: full-time $23,140; part-time $969.09 per credit hour. *Required fees:* $110. One-time fee: $55 full-time. Part-time tuition and fees vary according to course load, degree level, campus/location and reciprocity agreements. *Financial support:* In 2018–19, 1 research assistantship with full tuition reimbursement (averaging $11,861 per year) was awarded; Federal Work-Study, institutionally sponsored loans, and unspecified assistantships also available. Financial award application deadline: 4/1; financial award applicants required to submit FAFSA. *Unit head:* Dr. Eric Moyen, Associate Professor and Head, 662-325-0969, Fax: 662-325-0975, E-mail: em1621@msstate.edu. *Application contact:* Nathan Drake, Admissions and Enrollment Assistant, 662-325-3804, E-mail: ndrake@grad.msstate.edu.
Website: http://www.educationalleadership.msstate.edu/

Missouri Southern State University, Program in Early Childhood Education, Joplin, MO 64801-1595. Offers MS Ed. Program offered jointly with Northwest Missouri State University. *Accreditation:* NCATE. *Entrance requirements:* For master's, GRE, minimum cumulative undergraduate GPA of 2.5.

Missouri State University, Graduate College, College of Education, Department of Childhood Education and Family Studies, Springfield, MO 65897. Offers early childhood and family development (MS); elementary education (MS Ed). *Program availability:* Part-time. *Faculty:* 11 full-time (8 women), 2 part-time/adjunct (both women). *Students:* 25 full-time (24 women), 99 part-time (90 women); includes 11 minority (3 Black or African American, non-Hispanic/Latino; 1 Asian, non-Hispanic/Latino; 4 Hispanic/Latino; 3 Two or more races, non-Hispanic/Latino), 5 international. Average age 23. 73 applicants, 58% accepted. In 2018, 30 master's awarded. *Degree requirements:* For master's, comprehensive exam. *Entrance requirements:* For master's, GRE, minimum GPA of 3.0. Additional exam requirements/recommendations for international students: Required—TOEFL (minimum score 550 paper-based; 79 iBT), IELTS (minimum score 6). *Application deadline:* For fall admission, 7/20 priority date for domestic students, 5/1 for international students; for spring admission, 12/20 priority date for domestic students, 9/1 for international students; for summer admission, 5/20 priority date for domestic students. Applications are processed on a rolling basis. Application fee: $55 ($60 for international students). Electronic applications accepted. Tuition and fees vary according to class time, course level, course load, degree level, campus/location, program and student level. *Financial support:* Federal Work-Study, institutionally sponsored loans, scholarships/grants, and unspecified assistantships available. Financial award application deadline: 1/31; financial award applicants required to submit FAFSA. *Faculty research:* Infant development, play advocacy, building mathematical concepts. *Unit head:* Dr. Denise Cunningham, Department Head, 417-836-8915, Fax: 417-836-8900, E-mail: cefs@missouristate.edu. *Application contact:* Lakan Drinker, Director, Graduate Enrollment Management, 417-836-5330, Fax: 417-836-6200, E-mail: lakandrinker@missouristate.edu.
Website: http://education.missouristate.edu/cefs/

Missouri Western State University, Program in Assessment, St. Joseph, MO 64507-2294. Offers K-12 cross-categorical special education (MAS); TESOL (Graduate Certificate). *Program availability:* Part-time. *Students:* 1 (woman) full-time, 33 part-time (32 women); includes 3 minority (2 American Indian or Alaska Native, non-Hispanic/Latino; 1 Asian, non-Hispanic/Latino). Average age 40. 16 applicants, 100% accepted, 8 enrolled. In 2018, 12 master's, 4 other advanced degrees awarded. *Entrance requirements:* For master's, minimum GPA of 2.75. Additional exam requirements/recommendations for international students: Recommended—TOEFL (minimum score 79 iBT), IELTS (minimum score 6). *Application deadline:* For fall admission, 7/15 for domestic and international students; for spring admission, 11/1 for domestic and international students; for summer admission, 4/29 for domestic and international students. Applications are processed on a rolling basis. Application fee: $45 ($50 for international students). Electronic applications accepted. *Expenses: Tuition, area resident:* Part-time $359.39 per credit hour. Tuition, state resident: part-time $359.39 per credit hour. Tuition, nonresident: part-time $643.39 per credit hour. Tuition and fees vary according to program. *Financial support:* Scholarships/grants and unspecified

assistantships available. Support available to part-time students. *Unit head:* Dr. Susan Bashinski, Dean of Graduate Programs, 816-271-4394, E-mail: graduate@missouriwestern.edu. *Application contact:* Dr. Susan Bashinski, Dean of Graduate Programs, 816-271-4394, Fax: 816-271-4525, E-mail: graduate@missouriwestern.edu.
Website: https://www.missouriwestern.edu/graduate/

Molloy College, Graduate Education Program, Rockville Centre, NY 11571-5002. Offers adolescent education in biology (MS); adolescent special education (Advanced Certificate); bilingual extension (Advanced Certificate); childhood education (MS); childhood special education (Advanced Certificate); early childhood education (MS); educational technology (MS); English (MS); mathematics (MS); social studies (MS); Spanish (MS); special education on both childhood and adolescent levels (MS); teaching English to speakers of other languages (TESOL) in grades pre-K to 12 (MS); TESOL (Advanced Certificate). *Accreditation:* NCATE. *Program availability:* Part-time, evening/weekend. *Faculty:* 24 full-time (22 women), 26 part-time/adjunct (19 women). *Students:* 106 full-time (78 women), 203 part-time (154 women); includes 65 minority (14 Black or African American, non-Hispanic/Latino; 5 Asian, non-Hispanic/Latino; 41 Hispanic/Latino; 5 Two or more races, non-Hispanic/Latino). Average age 41. 147 applicants, 63% accepted, 79 enrolled. In 2018, 120 master's, 1 other advanced degree awarded. *Entrance requirements:* Additional exam requirements/recommendations for international students: Required—TOEFL (minimum score 550 paper-based; 79 iBT). *Application deadline:* Applications are processed on a rolling basis. Application fee: $60. Electronic applications accepted. *Expenses: Tuition:* Full-time $20,790; part-time $1155 per credit. *Required fees:* $1060; $900. Tuition and fees vary according to course load and degree level. *Financial support:* Application deadline: 3/1; applicants required to submit FAFSA. *Faculty research:* English Language Learners; social emotional needs of students; gifted education; cultural diversity; collaborative teaching methods. *Unit head:* Joanne O'Brien, Dean, 516-323-3116, E-mail: jobrien@molloy.edu. *Application contact:* Faye Hood, Assistant Director for Admissions, 516-323-4009, E-mail: fhood@molloy.edu.

Monmouth University, Graduate Studies, School of Education, West Long Branch, NJ 07764-1898. Offers applied behavior analysis (Certificate); autism (Certificate); director of school counseling services (Post-Master's Certificate); early childhood (M Ed); educational leadership (Ed D); elementary education (MAT), including elementary level, secondary level; English as a second language (M Ed); learning disabilities teacher-consultant (Post-Master's Certificate); literacy (MS Ed); school counseling (MS Ed); special education (MS Ed), including autism, learning disabilities teacher-consultant, teacher of students with disabilities, teaching in inclusive settings; speech-language pathology (MS Ed); student affairs and college counseling (MS Ed); supervisor (Post-Master's Certificate); teaching English to speakers of other languages (Certificate). *Accreditation:* NCATE. *Program availability:* Part-time, evening/weekend, 100% online, blended/hybrid learning. *Faculty:* 29 full-time (23 women), 32 part-time/adjunct (24 women). *Students:* 214 full-time (187 women), 148 part-time (127 women); includes 60 minority (13 Black or African American, non-Hispanic/Latino; 2 Asian, non-Hispanic/Latino; 40 Hispanic/Latino; 5 Two or more races, non-Hispanic/Latino). Average age 27. In 2018, 108 master's, 9 other advanced degrees awarded. *Entrance requirements:* For master's, GRE taken within last 5 years (for MS Ed in speech-language pathology); SAT (minimum combined score of 1660 in 3 sections), ACT (23), GRE (minimum score of 4.0 on analytical writing section and minimum combined score of 310 on quantitative and verbal sections), or passing scores on 3 parts of Core Academic Skills Educators, minimum GPA of 3.0 in major; 2 letters of recommendation (for some programs); resume, personal statement or essay (depending on program). Additional exam requirements/recommendations for international students: Required—TOEFL (minimum score 550 paper-based; 79 iBT), IELTS (minimum score 6), Michigan English Language Assessment Battery (minimum score 77) or Certificate of Advanced English (minimum score 160). *Application deadline:* For fall admission, 7/15 priority date for domestic students, 7/1 for international students; for spring admission, 12/1 priority date for domestic students, 11/1 for international students; for summer admission, 5/1 for domestic students. Applications are processed on a rolling basis. Application fee: $50. Electronic applications accepted. *Expenses: Tuition:* Part-time $1233 per credit. *Required fees:* $178 per term. *Financial support:* In 2018–19, 290 students received support. Institutionally sponsored loans, scholarships/grants, and unspecified assistantships available. Support available to part-time students. Financial award applicants required to submit FAFSA. *Faculty research:* Multicultural literacy, science and mathematics teaching strategies, teacher as reflective practitioner, children with disabilities. *Unit head:* Dr. John E. Henning, Dean, 732-263-5513, Fax: 732-263-5277, E-mail: kodonnel@monmouth.edu. *Application contact:* Kirsten Sneeringer, Graduate Admission Counselor, 732-571-3452, Fax: 732-263-5123, E-mail: gradadm@monmouth.edu.
Website: http://www.monmouth.edu/academics/schools/education/default.asp

Mount St. Joseph University, Graduate Education Program, Cincinnati, OH 45233-1670. Offers adolescent to young adult education (MA); dyslexia (Certificate); inclusive early childhood education (MA); middle childhood education (MA); multicultural special education (MA); reading science (MA). *Accreditation:* TEAC. *Program availability:* Part-time, evening/weekend, 100% online, blended/hybrid learning. *Degree requirements:* For master's, comprehensive exam, thesis, research project, student teaching, clinical and field-based experiences. *Entrance requirements:* For master's, GRE (if GPA is below 3.0), letter of intent, 2 referrals, background check, interview, resume, minimum undergraduate GPA of 3.0. Additional exam requirements/recommendations for international students: Required—TOEFL (minimum score 560 paper-based; 83 iBT). Electronic applications accepted. *Expenses:* Contact institution. *Faculty research:* Foreign and second language learning problems/reading disabilities, multicultural/bilingual special education, science education, pedagogical content knowledge, early childhood, response to intervention.

Murray State University, College of Education and Human Services, Department of Early Childhood and Elementary Education, Murray, KY 42071. Offers elementary teacher leader (MA Ed); interdisciplinary early childhood education (MA Ed), including elementary education (MA Ed, Ed S); reading and writing; teacher education and professional development (Ed S), including elementary education (MA Ed, Ed S). *Accreditation:* NCATE. *Program availability:* Part-time. *Entrance requirements:* For master's and Ed S, GRE or GMAT, minimum university GPA of 2.75. Additional exam requirements/recommendations for international students: Required—TOEFL (minimum score 527 paper-based; 71 iBT). Electronic applications accepted.

National Louis University, National College of Education, Chicago, IL 60603. Offers administration and supervision (M Ed, Ed D, CAS, Ed S); curriculum and instruction (M Ed, MS Ed, CAS); early childhood administration (M Ed, CAS); early childhood education (M Ed, MAT, MS Ed, CAS); education (Ed D); educational psychology/human learning and development (M Ed, MS Ed, CAS, Ed S); elementary education (MAT); interdisciplinary curriculum and instruction (M Ed); mathematics education (M Ed, MS Ed, CAS); middle grades education (MAT); reading and language (M Ed, MS Ed, CAS); school psychology (M Ed, Ed S); science education (M Ed, MS Ed, CAS); secondary education (MAT); special education (M Ed, MAT, CAS); technology in education (M Ed, CAS). *Accreditation:* NCATE. *Program availability:* Part-time, evening/weekend. *Degree requirements:* For doctorate, comprehensive exam, thesis/

dissertation. *Entrance requirements:* For master's, MAT or GRE, minimum GPA of 3.0; for doctorate, GRE General Test, minimum GPA of 3.25, interview, resume, writing sample, 4 recommendations. Additional exam requirements/recommendations for international students: Required—TOEFL (minimum score 550 paper-based; 79 iBT).

Nazareth College of Rochester, Graduate Studies, Department of Education, Program in Inclusive Early Childhood Education, Rochester, NY 14618. Offers MS Ed. *Accreditation:* TEAC. *Program availability:* Part-time, evening/weekend. *Entrance requirements:* For master's, minimum GPA of 3.0. Additional exam requirements/ recommendations for international students: Required—TOEFL or IELTS.

New Jersey City University, Debra Cannon Partridge Wolfe College of Education, Department of Early Childhood Education, Jersey City, NJ 07305-1597. Offers MAT. *Accreditation:* TEAC. *Program availability:* Part-time, evening/weekend. *Entrance requirements:* Additional exam requirements/recommendations for international students: Required—TOEFL (minimum score 79 iBT).

New Mexico State University, College of Education, Department of Curriculum and Instruction, Las Cruces, NM 88003-8001. Offers bilingual education (MA); curriculum and instruction (Ed D, PhD); early childhood education (MA); educational diagnostics (Ed S); language, literacy and culture (MA); learning design and technologies (MA); teaching (MAT); teaching English to speakers of other languages (MA). *Accreditation:* NCATE. *Program availability:* Part-time, evening/weekend, 100% online. *Faculty:* 22 full-time (17 women), 7 part-time/adjunct (5 women). *Students:* 82 full-time (49 women), 186 part-time (134 women); includes 153 minority (13 Black or African American, non-Hispanic/Latino; 2 American Indian or Alaska Native, non-Hispanic/Latino; 3 Asian, non-Hispanic/Latino; 129 Hispanic/Latino; 6 Two or more races, non-Hispanic/Latino), 33 international. Average age 37. 110 applicants, 79% accepted, 60 enrolled. In 2018, 75 master's, 13 doctorates, 16 other advanced degrees awarded. *Degree requirements:* For master's, comprehensive exam, thesis; for doctorate, comprehensive exam, thesis/ dissertation. *Entrance requirements:* For master's, minimum cumulative GPA of 3.0; for doctorate, portfolio, minimum cumulative GPA of 3.0. Additional exam requirements/ recommendations for international students: Required—TOEFL (minimum score 550 paper-based; 79 iBT), IELTS (minimum score 6.5). *Application deadline:* For fall admission, 12/15 priority date for domestic and international students. Applications are processed on a rolling basis. Application fee: $40 ($50 for international students). Electronic applications accepted. *Expenses: Tuition, area resident:* Full-time $4216.70; part-time $252.70 per credit hour. Tuition, state resident: full-time $4216.70; part-time $252.70 per credit hour. Tuition, nonresident: full-time $12,769; part-time $881.10 per credit hour. *International tuition:* $12,769.30 full-time. *Required fees:* $878.40; $48.80 per credit hour. Full-time tuition and fees vary according to course load and reciprocity agreements. *Financial support:* In 2018–19, 111 students received support, including 2 fellowships (averaging $4,548 per year), 11 research assistantships (averaging $11,673 per year), 10 teaching assistantships (averaging $10,582 per year); career-related internships or fieldwork, Federal Work-Study, scholarships/grants, traineeships, health care benefits, and unspecified assistantships also available. Support available to part-time students. Financial award application deadline: 3/1. *Faculty research:* STEM education, bilingual and English as a second language education, critical pedagogy/ multicultural education, learning design and technology, early childhood education. *Total annual research expenditures:* $10,685. *Unit head:* Dr. David Rutledge, Department Head, 575-646-5411, Fax: 575-646-5436, E-mail: rutledge@nmsu.edu. *Application contact:* Dr. David Rutledge, Associate Department Head for Graduate Programs, 575-646-5411, Fax: 575-646-5436, E-mail: rutledge@nmsu.edu.
Website: http://ci.education.nmsu.edu

New Mexico State University, College of Education, Department of Educational Leadership and Administration, Las Cruces, NM 88003-8001. Offers educational administration (MA), including community college and university administration, PK-12 public school administration; educational leadership (Ed D, PhD). *Accreditation:* NCATE. *Program availability:* Part-time-only, evening/weekend, blended/hybrid learning. *Faculty:* 7 full-time (6 women), 1 (woman) part-time/adjunct. *Students:* 10 full-time (9 women), 111 part-time (76 women); includes 75 minority (2 Black or African American, non-Hispanic/Latino; 8 American Indian or Alaska Native, non-Hispanic/ Latino; 3 Asian, non-Hispanic/Latino; 61 Hispanic/Latino; 1 Native Hawaiian or other Pacific Islander, non-Hispanic/Latino), 2 international. Average age 41. 23 applicants, 26% accepted, 4 enrolled. In 2018, 35 master's, 5 doctorates awarded. *Degree requirements:* For master's, comprehensive exam, internship; for doctorate, comprehensive exam, thesis/dissertation, internship. *Entrance requirements:* For master's, PK-12 educational administration: minimum GPA 3.0, current U.S. teaching license, minimum 3 years of teaching in PK-12 sector; higher education administration: minimum bachelor's degree GPA 3.0; for doctorate, minimum GPA of 3.0, master's degree. Additional exam requirements/recommendations for international students: Required—TOEFL (minimum score 550 paper-based; 79 iBT), IELTS (minimum score 6.5). *Application deadline:* For spring admission, 11/15 for domestic and international students. Application fee: $40 ($50 for international students). Electronic applications accepted. *Expenses: Tuition, area resident:* Full-time $4216.70; part-time $252.70 per credit hour. Tuition, state resident: full-time $4216.70; part-time $252.70 per credit hour. Tuition, nonresident: full-time $12,769; part-time $881.10 per credit hour. *International tuition:* $12,769.30 full-time. *Required fees:* $878.40; $48.80 per credit hour. Full-time tuition and fees vary according to course load and reciprocity agreements. *Financial support:* In 2018–19, 27 students received support, including 1 fellowship (averaging $4,548 per year), 7 research assistantships (averaging $9,896 per year), 5 teaching assistantships (averaging $12,558 per year); career-related internships or fieldwork, Federal Work-Study, scholarships/grants, traineeships, health care benefits, and unspecified assistantships also available. Support available to part-time students. Financial award application deadline: 3/1. *Faculty research:* Leadership in pk-12 and postsecondary education, community college administration, distance education administration, leadership for social justice, educational change. *Total annual research expenditures:* $514,604. *Unit head:* Dr. Azadeh Osanloo, Department Head, 575-646-5976, Fax: 575-646-4767, E-mail: azadeh@nmsu.edu. *Application contact:* Denise Rodriguez-Strawn, Program Coordinator, 575-646-3825, Fax: 575-646-4767, E-mail: edmandev@nmsu.edu.
Website: http://ela.education.nmsu.edu

New York Institute of Technology, School of Interdisciplinary Studies and Education, Department of Teacher Education, Old Westbury, NY 11568-8000. Offers adolescence education (MS), including math (MAT, MS), science; adolescent education (MAT), including biology, chemistry, English, math (MAT, MS), social studies; childhood education (MS); early childhood (MS). *Program availability:* Part-time, evening/weekend, 100% online, blended/hybrid learning. *Faculty:* 2 full-time (both women), 8 part-time/ adjunct (5 women). *Students:* 47 full-time (45 women), 56 part-time (47 women); includes 36 minority (13 Black or African American, non-Hispanic/Latino; 1 American Indian or Alaska Native, non-Hispanic/Latino; 7 Asian, non-Hispanic/Latino; 12 Hispanic/ Latino; 1 Native Hawaiian or other Pacific Islander, non-Hispanic/Latino; 2 Two or more races, non-Hispanic/Latino), 3 international. Average age 31. 81 applicants, 53% accepted, 27 enrolled. In 2018, 27 master's awarded. *Entrance requirements:* For master's, GRE or MAT, BS or equivalent; minimum cumulative undergraduate GPA of 3.0; NY state initial certification; BS with major (or minimum 30 credits in a concentration) in biology, chemistry, English, math, physics, or social studies (for MS in childhood, early childhood education, and MAT); interview; personal statement. Additional exam requirements/recommendations for international students: Required—TOEFL (minimum score 79 iBT), IELTS (minimum score 6), PTE (minimum score 53). *Application deadline:* Applications are processed on a rolling basis. Application fee: $50. Electronic applications accepted. *Expenses:* $1285 per credit plus $215 fees per year (full-time) or $175 fees per year (part-time); $1395 per 3-credit education UFT or off-site graduate course. *Financial support:* Career-related internships or fieldwork, Federal Work-Study, scholarships/grants, tuition waivers (full and partial), and unspecified assistantships available. Support available to part-time students. Financial award application deadline: 2/15; financial award applicants required to submit FAFSA. *Faculty research:* Evolving definition of new literacies and its impact on teaching and learning (twenty-first century skills), new literacies practices in teacher education, teachers' professional development, English language and literacy learning through mobile learning, teaching reading to culturally and linguistically diverse children. *Application contact:* Alice Dolitsky, Director, Graduate Admissions, 516-686-7520, Fax: 516-686-1116, E-mail: admissions@nyit.edu.
Website: http://www.nyit.edu/departments/teacher_education

New York University, Steinhardt School of Culture, Education, and Human Development, Department of Teaching and Learning, Program in Early Childhood and Childhood Education, New York, NY 10012. Offers childhood education (MA); early childhood education (MA); early childhood education/early childhood special education (MA). *Accreditation:* TEAC. *Program availability:* Part-time. *Degree requirements:* For master's, thesis (for some programs). *Entrance requirements:* Additional exam requirements/recommendations for international students: Required—TOEFL (minimum score 100 iBT). Electronic applications accepted. *Faculty research:* Teacher evaluation and beliefs about teaching, early literacy development, language arts, child development and education, cultural differences.

New York University, Steinhardt School of Culture, Education, and Human Development, Department of Teaching and Learning, Program in Special Education, New York, NY 10012-1019. Offers childhood (MA); early childhood (MA). *Accreditation:* TEAC. *Program availability:* Part-time. *Entrance requirements:* Additional exam requirements/recommendations for international students: Required—TOEFL (minimum score 100 iBT). Electronic applications accepted. *Faculty research:* Special education referrals, attention deficit disorders in children, mainstreaming, curriculum-based assessment and program implementation, special education policy.

Niagara University, Graduate Division of Education, Concentration in Teacher Education, Niagara University, NY 14109. Offers early childhood and childhood education (MS Ed, Certificate); early childhood special education (MS); middle and adolescence education (MS Ed); special education (MS Ed), including 1-6, 7-12; special education (grades 1-12) (Certificate); teaching English to speakers of other languages (MS Ed, Certificate). *Accreditation:* NCATE. *Students:* 106 full-time (75 women), 105 part-time (90 women); includes 15 minority (5 Black or African American, non-Hispanic/ Latino; 2 American Indian or Alaska Native, non-Hispanic/Latino; 2 Asian, non-Hispanic/ Latino; 2 Hispanic/Latino; 4 Two or more races, non-Hispanic/Latino), 40 international. Average age 28. In 2018, 81 master's, 21 other advanced degrees awarded. *Entrance requirements:* For master's, GRE General Test or Academic Literacy Skills Test (ALST). Additional exam requirements/recommendations for international students: Required—TOEFL (minimum score 550 paper-based; 79 iBT), IELTS (minimum score 6). *Application deadline:* For fall admission, 8/1 for domestic students. Applications are processed on a rolling basis. Electronic applications accepted. *Expenses:* Contact institution. *Financial support:* Research assistantships with tuition reimbursements, teaching assistantships with tuition reimbursements, career-related internships or fieldwork, Federal Work-Study, scholarships/grants, and unspecified assistantships available. Support available to part-time students. Financial award application deadline: 4/15; financial award applicants required to submit FAFSA. *Unit head:* Dr. Chandra Foote, Dean, College of Education, 716-286-8549, E-mail: cjf@niagara.edu. *Application contact:* Evan Pierce, Associate Director, Graduate Studies, 716-286-8327, E-mail: epierce@niagara.edu.
Website: http://www.niagara.edu/teacher-education

Norfolk State University, School of Graduate Studies, School of Education, Department of Early Childhood and Elementary Education, Norfolk, VA 23504. Offers early childhood education (MAT); pre-elementary education (MA). *Accreditation:* NCATE. *Program availability:* Part-time. *Degree requirements:* For master's, comprehensive exam, thesis or alternative. *Entrance requirements:* For master's, PRAXIS I and II, minimum GPA of 2.5, letters of recommendation, interview. *Faculty research:* Parent involvement in education.

North Carolina Agricultural and Technical State University, The Graduate College, College of Agriculture and Environmental Sciences, Department of Family and Consumer Sciences, Greensboro, NC 27411. Offers child development, early education and family studies (MAT); family and consumer sciences education (MAT); food and nutritional sciences (MS). *Program availability:* Part-time, evening/weekend. *Degree requirements:* For master's, comprehensive exam, thesis or alternative, qualifying exam. *Entrance requirements:* For master's, GRE General Test, minimum GPA of 2.6.

Northeastern Illinois University, College of Graduate Studies and Research, Daniel L. Goodwin College of Education, Program in Early Childhood Education, Chicago, IL 60625. Offers MAT. *Entrance requirements:* For master's, bachelor's degree from accredited college or university; minimum undergraduate GPA of 3.0; three professional references. Electronic applications accepted.

Northeastern State University, College of Education, Department of Curriculum and Instruction, Program in Early Childhood Education, Tahlequah, OK 74464-2399. Offers M Ed. *Program availability:* Part-time, evening/weekend. *Faculty:* 15 full-time (11 women), 2 part-time/adjunct (0 women). *Students:* 4 full-time (all women), 16 part-time (all women); includes 5 minority (3 American Indian or Alaska Native, non-Hispanic/ Latino; 2 Two or more races, non-Hispanic/Latino), 1 international. Average age 34. In 2018, 5 master's awarded. *Degree requirements:* For master's, thesis. *Entrance requirements:* For master's, GRE or MAT, minimum GPA of 2.5. Additional exam requirements/recommendations for international students: Required—TOEFL. *Application deadline:* For fall admission, 6/1 priority date for domestic students. Applications are processed on a rolling basis. Application fee: $25. Electronic applications accepted. *Expenses: Tuition, area resident:* Full-time $4500; part-time $250 per credit hour. Tuition, state resident: full-time $4500; part-time $250 per credit hour. Tuition, nonresident: full-time $9999; part-time $555.50 per credit hour. *International tuition:* $9999 full-time. *Required fees:* $601.20; $33.40 per credit hour. *Financial support:* Teaching assistantships and Federal Work-Study available. Financial award application deadline: 3/1. *Unit head:* Dr. Anita Ede, Program Chair, 918-449-6523, E-mail: edear@nsuok.edu. *Application contact:* Josh McCollum, Graduate Coordinator, 918-444-2093, E-mail: mccolluj@nsuok.edu.
Website: https://academics.nsuok.edu/education/EducationHome/COEDepartments/ CurriculumInstruction.aspx

Northern Arizona University, College of Education, Department of Educational Specialties, Flagstaff, AZ 86011. Offers autism spectrum disorders (Certificate);

bilingual/multicultural education (M Ed), including bilingual, ESL; career and technical education (M Ed, Certificate); educational technology (M Ed, Certificate); English as a second language (Certificate); positive behavior support (Certificate); special education (M Ed), including early childhood special education, mild/moderate disabilities. *Program availability:* Part-time, 100% online, blended/hybrid learning. *Degree requirements:* For master's, variable foreign language requirement, comprehensive exam (for some programs), thesis (for some programs); for Certificate, comprehensive exam (for some programs). *Entrance requirements:* Additional exam requirements/recommendations for international students: Required—TOEFL (minimum score 80 iBT), IELTS (minimum score 6.5). Electronic applications accepted.

Northern Arizona University, College of Education, Department of Teaching and Learning, Flagstaff, AZ 86011. Offers curriculum and instruction (Ed D); early childhood education (M Ed); elementary education (M Ed); secondary education (M Ed). *Program availability:* Part-time, 100% online, blended/hybrid learning. *Degree requirements:* For master's, variable foreign language requirement, comprehensive exam (for some programs), thesis (for some programs); for doctorate, variable foreign language requirement, comprehensive exam (for some programs), thesis/dissertation (for some programs). *Entrance requirements:* Additional exam requirements/recommendations for international students: Required—TOEFL (minimum score 80 iBT), IELTS (minimum score 6.5). Electronic applications accepted.

Northern Illinois University, Graduate School, College of Education, Department of Special and Early Education, De Kalb, IL 60115-2854. Offers curriculum and instruction (MS Ed); early childhood education (MS Ed); elementary education (MS Ed); special education (MS Ed). *Program availability:* Part-time, evening/weekend. *Faculty:* 22 full-time (14 women), 2 part-time/adjunct (both women). *Students:* 43 full-time (33 women), 87 part-time (70 women); includes 22 minority (5 Black or African American, non-Hispanic/Latino; 1 Asian, non-Hispanic/Latino; 12 Hispanic/Latino; 4 Two or more races, non-Hispanic/Latino), 3 international. Average age 32. 75 applicants, 77% accepted, 37 enrolled. In 2018, 41 master's awarded. *Degree requirements:* For master's, comprehensive exam, thesis optional. *Entrance requirements:* For master's, GRE General Test or MAT, minimum undergraduate GPA of 2.75. Additional exam requirements/recommendations for international students: Required—TOEFL (minimum score 550 paper-based). *Application deadline:* For fall admission, 6/1 for domestic students, 5/1 for international students; for spring admission, 11/1 for domestic students, 10/1 for international students. Applications are processed on a rolling basis. Application fee: $40. Electronic applications accepted. *Financial support:* In 2018–19, 17 research assistantships with full tuition reimbursements were awarded; fellowships with full tuition reimbursements, teaching assistantships with full tuition reimbursements, career-related internships or fieldwork, Federal Work-Study, scholarships/grants, tuition waivers (full), and unspecified assistantships also available. Support available to part-time students. Financial award applicants required to submit FAFSA. *Faculty research:* Teacher certification, stress reduction during student teaching, teaching history, portfolios in student teaching. *Unit head:* Gregory Conderman, Chair, 815-753-1619, E-mail: seed@niu.edu. *Application contact:* Gail Myers, Clerk, Graduate Advising, 815-753-0381, E-mail: gmyers@niu.edu.
Website: http://www.cedu.niu.edu/seed/

Northwestern College, Program in Education, Orange City, IA 51041-1996. Offers early childhood (M Ed); master teacher (M Ed); teacher leadership (M Ed, Graduate Certificate). *Program availability:* Online learning.

Northwestern State University of Louisiana, Graduate Studies and Research, College of Education and Human Development, Program in Early Childhood Education, Natchitoches, LA 71497. Offers early childhood education and teaching (M Ed, MAT). *Degree requirements:* For master's, comprehensive exam, thesis or alternative. *Entrance requirements:* For master's, GRE General Test. Additional exam requirements/recommendations for international students: Required—TOEFL. Electronic applications accepted.

Northwest Missouri State University, Graduate School, School of Education, Maryville, MO 64468-6001. Offers early childhood education (MS Ed); education leadership (MS Ed), including elementary, K-12, secondary; educational leadership (Ed S), including elementary school principalship, secondary school principalship, superintendency; educational leadership and policy analysis (Ed D); elementary education (MS Ed); elementary mathematics (MS Ed); higher education leadership (MS); middle school education (MS Ed); reading (MS Ed); special education (MS Ed); teacher leadership (MS Ed); teaching English language learners (MS Ed). *Accreditation:* NCATE. *Program availability:* Part-time. *Faculty:* 26 full-time (16 women). *Students:* 109 full-time (87 women), 385 part-time (270 women); includes 30 minority (10 Black or African American, non-Hispanic/Latino; 2 American Indian or Alaska Native, non-Hispanic/Latino; 3 Asian, non-Hispanic/Latino; 12 Hispanic/Latino; 1 Native Hawaiian or other Pacific Islander, non-Hispanic/Latino; 2 Two or more races, non-Hispanic/Latino), 1 international. Average age 33. 210 applicants, 72% accepted, 142 enrolled. In 2018, 71 master's, 11 other advanced degrees awarded. *Degree requirements:* For master's, comprehensive exam; for Ed S, comprehensive exam, thesis. *Entrance requirements:* For master's, GRE General Test, writing sample; for Ed S, minimum graduate GPA of 3.25. Additional exam requirements/recommendations for international students: Required—TOEFL (minimum score 550 paper-based). *Application deadline:* For fall admission, 7/1 for domestic and international students; for spring admission, 11/15 for domestic and international students. Applications are processed on a rolling basis. Application fee: $0 ($75 for international students). Electronic applications accepted. *Expenses:* $389.11 in-state and $653.92 out-of-state per credit hour. *Financial support:* Research assistantships with full tuition reimbursements, teaching assistantships with full tuition reimbursements, and unspecified assistantships available. Financial award application deadline: 4/1; financial award applicants required to submit FAFSA. *Unit head:* Dr. Tim Wall, Director, 660-562-1179, E-mail: timwall@nwmissouri.edu. *Application contact:* Dr. Tim Wall, Director, 660-562-1179, E-mail: timwall@nwmissouri.edu.
Website: https://www.nwmissouri.edu/education/index.htm

Oakland University, Graduate Study and Lifelong Learning, School of Education and Human Services, Department of Human Development and Child Studies, Program in Early Childhood Education, Rochester, MI 48309-4401. Offers early childhood education (M Ed, PhD); early education and intervention (Ed S). *Accreditation:* TEAC. *Degree requirements:* For doctorate, thesis/dissertation. *Entrance requirements:* For master's, minimum GPA of 3.0; for doctorate, GRE General Test, minimum GPA of 3.0. Additional exam requirements/recommendations for international students: Required—TOEFL (minimum score 550 paper-based).

Oklahoma City University, Petree College of Arts and Sciences, Oklahoma City, OK 73106-1402. Offers applied behavioral studies (M Ed); applied sociology: nonprofit leadership (MA); creative writing (MFA); criminology (MS); early childhood education (M Ed); elementary education (M Ed); general studies (MLA); leadership/management (MLA); moving image arts (MFA); professional counseling (M Ed); teaching (MA); teaching English to speakers of other languages (MA). *Program availability:* Part-time, evening/weekend. *Degree requirements:* For master's, capstone/practicum. *Entrance requirements:* For master's, bachelor's degree from accredited institution with minimum GPA of 3.0, essay, recommendation letters. Additional exam requirements/recommendations for international students: Required—TOEFL (minimum score 550 paper-based; 80 iBT). Electronic applications accepted. *Expenses:* Contact institution.

Old Dominion University, Darden College of Education, Program in Early Childhood Education, Norfolk, VA 23529. Offers MS Ed, PhD. *Accreditation:* NCATE. *Program availability:* Part-time, evening/weekend. *Degree requirements:* For master's, comprehensive exam, written exams; for doctorate, comprehensive exam, thesis/dissertation. *Entrance requirements:* For master's, GRE General Test, PRAXIS I, minimum undergraduate GPA of 2.8; for doctorate, GRE General Test. Additional exam requirements/recommendations for international students: Required—TOEFL. *Faculty research:* Creativity, informal learning environment, children's thinking, early childhood teacher professional development, integrated curriculum.

Old Dominion University, Darden College of Education, Program in Special Education, Norfolk, VA 23529. Offers adapted curriculum K-12 (MS Ed); early childhood special education (MS Ed); general curriculum K-12 (MS Ed); special education (PhD). *Accreditation:* NCATE. *Program availability:* Part-time, evening/weekend, 100% online, blended/hybrid learning. *Degree requirements:* For master's, comprehensive exam, thesis or alternative, VCLA; for doctorate, comprehensive exam, thesis/dissertation. *Entrance requirements:* For master's, GRE General Test or MAT, PRAXIS Core Academic Skills for Educator Tests, minimum GPA of 2.8; for doctorate, GRE General Test or MAT. Additional exam requirements/recommendations for international students: Recommended—TOEFL (minimum score 550 paper-based). Electronic applications accepted. Application fee is waived when completed online. *Expenses:* Contact institution. *Faculty research:* Inclusion, autism spectrum disorder, functional behavioral assessment, infant, preschool, and school-age children and youth with disabilities, distance learning.

Ottawa University, Graduate Studies-Arizona, Program in Education, Ottawa, KS 66067-3399. Offers community college counseling (MA); curriculum and instruction (MA); early childhood (MA); education intervention (MA); education leadership (MA); education technology (MA); Montessori early childhood education (MA); Montessori elementary education (MA); professional development (MA); school guidance counseling (MA); special education - cross categorical (MA). Programs offered in Mesa, Phoenix, Tempe and West Valley, AZ. *Accreditation:* NCATE. *Program availability:* Part-time. *Degree requirements:* For master's, thesis or alternative. *Entrance requirements:* For master's, minimum undergraduate GPA of 3.0, copy of current state certification or teaching license. Additional exam requirements/recommendations for international students: Required—TOEFL (minimum score 550 paper-based). Electronic applications accepted. *Expenses:* Contact institution.

Pace University, School of Education, New York, NY 10038. Offers adolescent education (MST), including biology, chemistry, earth science, English, foreign languages, mathematics, physics, social studies; childhood education (MST); early childhood development, learning and intervention (MST); educational technology studies (MS); inclusive adolescent education (MST), including biology, chemistry, earth science, English, foreign languages, mathematics, physics, social studies; integrated instruction for educational technology (Certificate); integrated instruction for literacy and technology (Certificate); literacy (MS Ed); special education (MS Ed). *Accreditation:* NCATE. *Program availability:* Part-time, evening/weekend, 100% online, blended/hybrid learning. *Faculty:* 19 full-time (13 women), 86 part-time/adjunct (49 women). *Students:* 98 full-time (82 women), 542 part-time (391 women); includes 256 minority (116 Black or African American, non-Hispanic/Latino; 2 American Indian or Alaska Native, non-Hispanic/Latino; 45 Asian, non-Hispanic/Latino; 83 Hispanic/Latino; 10 Two or more races, non-Hispanic/Latino), 4 international. Average age 30. 223 applicants, 89% accepted, 130 enrolled. In 2018, 269 master's, 12 other advanced degrees awarded. *Degree requirements:* For master's and Certificate, certification exams. *Entrance requirements:* For master's, GRE (for initial certification programs only), teaching certificate (for MS Ed in literacy and special education programs only). Additional exam requirements/recommendations for international students: Required—TOEFL (minimum score 88 iBT), IELTS or PTE. *Application deadline:* For fall admission, 8/1 priority date for domestic students, 6/1 for international students; for spring admission, 12/1 priority date for domestic students, 10/1 for international students. Applications are processed on a rolling basis. Application fee: $70. Electronic applications accepted. *Expenses:* Contact institution. *Financial support:* In 2018–19, 17 students received support, including 17 research assistantships with partial tuition reimbursements available (averaging $6,020 per year); career-related internships or fieldwork, Federal Work-Study, scholarships/grants, and unspecified assistantships also available. Financial award application deadline: 9/1; financial award applicants required to submit FAFSA. *Faculty research:* STEM education, TESOL, teacher education, special education, language and literary development. *Total annual research expenditures:* $1.4 million. *Unit head:* Dr. Harriet Feldman, Dean, School of Education, 914-773-3829, E-mail: hfeldman@pace.edu. *Application contact:* Susan Ford-Goldschein, Director of Graduate Admissions, 212-346-1531, Fax: 212-346-1585, E-mail: graduateadmission@pace.edu.
Website: http://www.pace.edu/school-of-education

Pacific Oaks College, Graduate School, Program in Early Childhood Education, Pasadena, CA 91103. Offers MA. *Program availability:* Part-time, online learning.

Pacific University, College of Education, Forest Grove, OR 97116-1797. Offers early childhood education (MAT); education (MAE); elementary education (MAT); ESOL (MAT); high school education (MAT); middle school education (MAT); special education (MAT); speech-language pathology (MS); STEM education (MAT); talented and gifted (M Ed); visual function in learning (M Ed). *Accreditation:* ASHA; NCATE. *Program availability:* Part-time, evening/weekend. *Degree requirements:* For master's, research project. *Entrance requirements:* For master's, California Basic Educational Skills Test, PRAXIS II, minimum undergraduate GPA of 2.75, 3.0 graduate. Additional exam requirements/recommendations for international students: Required—TOEFL. Electronic applications accepted. *Expenses:* Contact institution. *Faculty research:* Defining a culturally competent classroom, technology in the K-12 classroom, Socratic seminars, social studies education.

Piedmont College, School of Education, Demorest, GA 30535. Offers art education (MAT); curriculum and instruction (Ed D, Ed S); early childhood education (MA, MAT); middle grades education (MA, MAT); music education (MAT); secondary education (MA, MAT); special education (MA, MAT). *Program availability:* Part-time, evening/weekend. *Students:* 496 full-time (416 women), 650 part-time (560 women); includes 185 minority (137 Black or African American, non-Hispanic/Latino; 2 American Indian or Alaska Native, non-Hispanic/Latino; 13 Asian, non-Hispanic/Latino; 31 Hispanic/Latino; 1 Native Hawaiian or other Pacific Islander, non-Hispanic/Latino; 1 Two or more races, non-Hispanic/Latino). Average age 37. 483 applicants, 89% accepted, 372 enrolled. In 2018, 275 master's, 10 doctorates, 229 other advanced degrees awarded. *Degree requirements:* For master's, thesis, field experience in the classroom teaching; for doctorate, thesis/dissertation. *Entrance requirements:* For master's, GRE General Test, MAT; for Ed S, minimum graduate GPA of 3.5, valid teaching certificate. Additional exam requirements/recommendations for international students: Required—TOEFL (minimum score 550 paper-based). *Application deadline:* For fall admission, 7/15 for domestic students; for spring admission, 12/1 for domestic students. Applications are processed on a rolling basis. Electronic applications accepted. *Expenses: Tuition:* Full-time $9738; part-time $541 per credit. *Required fees:* $200 per semester. *Financial*

support: Career-related internships or fieldwork, Federal Work-Study, and unspecified assistantships available. Support available to part-time students. Financial award applicants required to submit FAFSA. *Unit head:* Dr. R.D. Nordgren, Dean, 706-778-3000 Ext. 1201, Fax: 706-776-9608, E-mail: rdnordgren@piedmont.edu. *Application contact:* Kathleen Carter, Director of Graduate Enrollment Management, 706-778-8500 Ext. 1181, Fax: 706-778-0150, E-mail: kanderson@piedmont.edu.

Pontificia Universidad Catolica Madre y Maestra, Graduate School, Faculty of Sciences and Humanities, Santiago, Dominican Republic. Offers architecture (M Arch), including architecture of interiors, architecture of tourist lodgings, landscaping; early childhood education (M Ed).

Prescott College, Graduate Programs, Program in Education, Prescott, AZ 86301. Offers early childhood education (MA); early childhood special education (MA); education (MA); elementary education (MA); environmental education leadership and administration (MA); equine-assisted learning (MA); school guidance counseling (MA); secondary education (MA); special education: learning disabilities (MA); special education: mental retardation (MA); special education: serious emotional disabilities (MA); student-directed independent study (MA); sustainability education (PhD). *Program availability:* Part-time, online learning. *Degree requirements:* For master's, thesis, fieldwork or internship, practicum; for doctorate, thesis/dissertation. *Entrance requirements:* For master's, 2 letters of recommendation, resume; for doctorate, 3 letters of recommendation, resume, official transcripts, personal statement, program proposal. Additional exam requirements/recommendations for international students: Required—TOEFL (minimum score 500 paper-based). Electronic applications accepted.

Queens College of the City University of New York, Division of Education, Department of Educational and Community Programs, Queens, NY 11367-1597. Offers bilingual pupil personnel (AC); counselor education (MS Ed); mental health counseling (MS); school building leader (AC); school district leader (AC); school psychologist (MS Ed); special education-childhood education (AC); special education-early childhood (MS Ed); teacher of special education 1-6 (MS Ed); teacher of special education birth-2 (MS Ed); teaching students with disabilities, grades 7-12 (MS Ed, AC). *Program availability:* Part-time. *Faculty:* 19 full-time (13 women), 53 part-time/adjunct (31 women). *Students:* 90 full-time (83 women), 380 part-time (316 women); includes 217 minority (42 Black or African American, non-Hispanic/Latino; 1 American Indian or Alaska Native, non-Hispanic/Latino; 53 Asian, non-Hispanic/Latino; 114 Hispanic/Latino; 7 Two or more races, non-Hispanic/Latino), 6 international. Average age 29. 470 applicants, 65% accepted, 236 enrolled. In 2018, 164 master's, 59 other advanced degrees awarded. *Degree requirements:* For master's, Research project; for AC, internship, research project. *Entrance requirements:* For master's, minimum GPA of 3.0. Additional exam requirements/recommendations for international students: Required—TOEFL, IELTS. *Application deadline:* For fall admission, 3/1 for domestic students. Applications are processed on a rolling basis. Application fee: $125. Electronic applications accepted. *Financial support:* Fellowships available. Financial award application deadline: 4/1; financial award applicants required to submit FAFSA. *Unit head:* Dr. Emilia Lopez, Chair, 718-997-5250, E-mail: emilia.lopez@qc.cuny.edu. *Application contact:* Elizabeth D'Amico-Ramirez, Assistant Director of Graduate Admissions, 718-997-5203, E-mail: elizabeth.damicoramirez@qc.cuny.edu.

Queens College of the City University of New York, Division of Education, Department of Elementary and Early Childhood Education, Queens, NY 11367-1597. Offers bilingual education (MAT, MS Ed, AC); childhood education (MAT, MS Ed); early childhood education birth-2 (MAT, MS Ed, AC); literacy education birth-grade 6 (MS Ed, AC). *Program availability:* Part-time, evening/weekend. *Faculty:* 19 full-time (13 women), 35 part-time/adjunct (32 women). *Students:* 117 full-time (102 women), 376 part-time (344 women); includes 264 minority (27 Black or African American, non-Hispanic/Latino; 75 Asian, non-Hispanic/Latino; 154 Hispanic/Latino; 1 Native Hawaiian or other Pacific Islander, non-Hispanic/Latino; 7 Two or more races, non-Hispanic/Latino), 15 international. Average age 30. 351 applicants, 75% accepted, 204 enrolled. In 2018, 156 master's, 48 other advanced degrees awarded. *Degree requirements:* For master's, Research project; for AC, Field-based research project. *Entrance requirements:* For master's, GRE General Test, minimum undergraduate cumulative GPA of 3.00; for AC, GRE General Test (required for all MAT and other graduate programs leading to NYS initial teacher certification), NYS initial teacher certification in the appropriate certification area is required for admission into MSEd programs. Additional exam requirements/recommendations for international students: Required—TOEFL (minimum score 575 paper-based; 90 iBT). *Application deadline:* For fall admission, 4/1 for domestic students. Applications are processed on a rolling basis. Application fee: $125. Electronic applications accepted. *Financial support:* Career-related internships or fieldwork and Federal Work-Study available. Financial award application deadline: 4/1; financial award applicants required to submit FAFSA. *Faculty research:* Biliteracy, computational thinking, social justice education, technology in early childhood education, children from immigrant families. *Unit head:* Daisuke Akiba, Chair, 718-997-5300, E-mail: daisuke.akiba@qc.cuny.edu. *Application contact:* Elizabeth D'Amico-Ramirez, Assistant Director of Graduate Admissions, 718-997-5203, E-mail: elizabeth.damicoramirez@qc.cuny.edu.

Radford University, College of Graduate Studies and Research, Program in Education, Radford, VA 24142. Offers early childhood education (MS); mathematics education (MS). *Accreditation:* NCATE. *Program availability:* Part-time, evening/weekend. *Faculty:* 28 full-time (21 women), 8 part-time/adjunct (6 women). *Students:* 39 full-time (28 women), 65 part-time (48 women); includes 10 minority (6 Black or African American, non-Hispanic/Latino; 1 Asian, non-Hispanic/Latino; 1 Hispanic/Latino; 2 Two or more races, non-Hispanic/Latino). Average age 31. 40 applicants, 93% accepted, 29 enrolled. In 2018, 42 master's awarded. *Degree requirements:* For master's, comprehensive exam. *Entrance requirements:* For master's, GRE (waived for any applicant with advanced degree), minimum GPA of 3.0, 2 letters of professional reference, personal statement, resume, official transcripts. Additional exam requirements/recommendations for international students: Required—TOEFL (minimum score 550 paper-based; 79 iBT), IELTS (minimum score 6.5). *Application deadline:* For fall admission, 2/15 priority date for domestic students, 12/1 for international students; for spring admission, 7/1 for international students. Applications are processed on a rolling basis. Application fee: $50. Electronic applications accepted. *Expenses: Tuition, area resident:* Full-time $8915; part-time $371 per credit hour. Tuition, state resident: full-time $8915; part-time $371 per credit hour. Tuition, nonresident: full-time $17,441. *Required fees:* $3288; $138 per credit hour. *Financial support:* In 2018–19, 5 students received support. Research assistantships, career-related internships or fieldwork, scholarships/grants, and unspecified assistantships available. Support available to part-time students. Financial award application deadline: 3/1; financial award applicants required to submit FAFSA. *Unit head:* Dr. Wendy Eckenrod-Green, Coordinator, 540-831-5302, E-mail: stel@radford.edu. *Application contact:* Dr. Wendy Eckenrod-Green, Coordinator, 540-831-5302, E-mail: stel@radford.edu.
Website: http://www.radford.edu/content/cehd/home/teacher-ed/programs/education-master.html

Regent University, Graduate School, School of Education, Virginia Beach, VA 23464-9800. Offers education (M Ed, Ed D, PhD), including adult education (Ed D, PhD, Ed S), advanced educational leadership (Ed D, PhD, Ed S), character education (Ed D, PhD, Ed S), Christian education leadership (Ed D, PhD, Ed S), Christian school administration (M Ed), curriculum and instruction (Ed D, PhD, Ed S), curriculum and instruction - adult education (M Ed), curriculum and instruction - Christian school (M Ed), curriculum and instruction - gifted and talented (M Ed), curriculum and instruction - STEM education (M Ed), curriculum and instruction - teacher leader (M Ed), discipleship for ministry (M Ed), educational leadership (M Ed), educational psychology (Ed D, PhD, Ed S), educational technology and online learning (Ed D, PhD, Ed S), elementary education (M Ed), exceptional education executive leadership (Ed D, PhD, Ed S), higher education (Ed D, PhD, Ed S), higher education leadership and management (Ed D, PhD, Ed S), instructional design and technology (M Ed), K-12 school leadership (Ed D, PhD, Ed S), K-12 special education (M Ed), leadership in mathematics education (M Ed), reading specialist (M Ed), special education (Ed D, PhD, Ed S), student affairs (M Ed), TESOL - adult education (M Ed), TESOL - K-12 (M Ed); educational specialist (Ed S), including adult education (Ed D, PhD, Ed S), advanced educational leadership (Ed D, PhD, Ed S), character education (Ed D, PhD, Ed S), Christian education leadership (Ed D, PhD, Ed S), curriculum and instruction (Ed D, PhD, Ed S), educational psychology (Ed D, PhD, Ed S), educational technology and online learning (Ed D, PhD, Ed S), exceptional education executive leadership (Ed D, PhD, Ed S), higher education (Ed D, PhD, Ed S), higher education leadership and management (Ed D, PhD, Ed S), K-12 school leadership (Ed D, PhD, Ed S), special education (Ed D, PhD, Ed S). *Accreditation:* TEAC. *Program availability:* Part-time, evening/weekend, 100% online, blended/hybrid learning. *Degree requirements:* For master's, thesis or alternative; for doctorate, comprehensive exam, thesis/dissertation. *Entrance requirements:* For master's, Virginia Communication and Literacy Assessment (VCLA), PRAXIS, college transcripts, writing sample, interview; for doctorate, GRE, writing sample, resume, transcripts, interview. Additional exam requirements/recommendations for international students: Required—TOEFL (minimum score 577 paper-based). Electronic applications accepted. *Expenses:* Contact institution. *Faculty research:* Christian school administration, curriculum and instruction, educational technology and online learning, higher education, special education.

Reinhardt University, Price School of Education, Waleska, GA 30183-2981. Offers M Ed, MAT. *Program availability:* Part-time. *Faculty:* 2 full-time (both women), 3 part-time/adjunct (all women). *Students:* 17 full-time (14 women); includes 4 minority (3 Black or African American, non-Hispanic/Latino; 1 Hispanic/Latino). Average age 33. In 2018, 54 master's awarded. *Entrance requirements:* For master's, GACE. Additional exam requirements/recommendations for international students: Required—TOEFL (minimum score 500 paper-based). *Application deadline:* Applications are processed on a rolling basis. Application fee: $50. Electronic applications accepted. Application fee is waived when completed online. *Expenses: Tuition:* Full-time $8732; part-time $495 per credit. *Required fees:* $200. Tuition and fees vary according to course load and program. *Financial support:* Application deadline: 7/1; applicants required to submit FAFSA. *Unit head:* Dr. Nancy Marsh, Dean, 770-720-5657, Fax: 770-720-9173, E-mail: njm@reinhardt.edu. *Application contact:* Graduate Admissions, 770-720-5760, E-mail: gradadmissions@reinhardt.edu.

Rhode Island College, School of Graduate Studies, Feinstein School of Education and Human Development, Department of Elementary Education, Providence, RI 02908-1991. Offers early childhood education (M Ed); elementary education (M Ed, MAT); reading (M Ed). *Accreditation:* NCATE. *Program availability:* Part-time, evening/weekend. *Faculty:* 7 full-time (all women), 4 part-time/adjunct (2 women). *Students:* 18 full-time (17 women), 20 part-time (17 women); includes 1 minority (Black or African American, non-Hispanic/Latino). Average age 31. In 2018, 21 master's awarded. *Degree requirements:* For master's, comprehensive exam (for some programs), comprehensive assessment. *Entrance requirements:* For master's, GRE General Test or MAT, PRAXIS II (elementary content knowledge), undergraduate transcripts; minimum undergraduate GPA of 3.0; 3 letters of recommendation. Additional exam requirements/recommendations for international students: Required—TOEFL (minimum score 550 paper-based; 80 iBT). *Application deadline:* For fall admission, 3/1 for domestic students; for spring admission, 11/1 for domestic students. Applications are processed on a rolling basis. Application fee: $50. Electronic applications accepted. *Expenses: Tuition, area resident:* Part-time $407 per credit. Tuition, nonresident: part-time $792 per credit. *Required fees:* $29 per credit. $100 per semester. *Financial support:* Teaching assistantships with full tuition reimbursements, Federal Work-Study, scholarships/grants, and health care benefits available. Support available to part-time students. Financial award application deadline: 5/15; financial award applicants required to submit FAFSA. *Unit head:* Dr. Carolyn Obel-Omia, Chair, 401-456-8016. *Application contact:* Dr. Carolyn Obel-Omia, Chair, 401-456-8016.
Website: http://www.ric.edu/elementaryeducation/Pages/Graduate-Programs.aspx

Rider University, College of Education and Human Services, Program in Teaching, Lawrenceville, NJ 08648-3001. Offers bilingual education (MAT); early childhood education (MAT); elementary education (MAT); English as a second language (MAT); secondary education (MAT); world language (MAT). *Students:* 35 full-time (26 women), 88 part-time (67 women); includes 12 minority (1 Black or African American, non-Hispanic/Latino; 1 American Indian or Alaska Native, non-Hispanic/Latino; 2 Asian, non-Hispanic/Latino; 8 Hispanic/Latino). Average age 34. 104 applicants, 67% accepted, 54 enrolled. In 2018, 70 master's awarded. *Entrance requirements:* For master's, Praxis exams, resume,application fee, statement of aims and objectives, official prior college transcripts, interview. Additional exam requirements/recommendations for international students: Required—TOEFL (minimum score 540 paper-based; 79 iBT). *Application deadline:* For fall admission, 5/1 priority date for domestic students, 6/1 priority date for international students; for spring admission, 12/1 priority date for domestic students, 11/1 priority date for international students. Applications are processed on a rolling basis. Application fee: $50. Electronic applications accepted. *Expenses: Tuition:* Full-time $850; part-time $850 per credit hour. *Required fees:* $50; $50 per course. Tuition and fees vary according to program. *Financial support:* Applicants required to submit FAFSA. *Unit head:* Kathleen Pierce, Professor, 609-895-5478, E-mail: kpierce@rider.edu. *Application contact:* Jamie L Mitchell, Director of Graduate Admissions, 609-896-5036, Fax: 609-895-5680, E-mail: jmitchell@rider.edu.

Rivier University, School of Graduate Studies, Department of Education, Nashua, NH 03060. Offers curriculum and instruction (M Ed); early childhood education (M Ed); educational administration (M Ed); educational studies (M Ed); elementary education (M Ed); elementary education and general special education (M Ed); emotional and behavioral disorders (M Ed); general social education (M Ed); leadership and learning (Ed D, CAGS); learning disabilities (M Ed); learning disabilities and reading (M Ed); mental health counseling (MA); reading (M Ed); school counseling (M Ed). *Program availability:* Part-time, evening/weekend. *Degree requirements:* For master's, comprehensive exam (for some programs), internships. *Entrance requirements:* For master's, GRE General Test or MAT.

Roberts Wesleyan College, Graduate Teacher Education Programs, Rochester, NY 14624-1997. Offers adolescence and special education (M Ed); childhood and special education (M Ed); literacy education (M Ed); special education (M Ed). *Program availability:* Part-time, evening/weekend. *Degree requirements:* For master's, thesis. Electronic applications accepted.

Rockford University, Graduate Studies, Department of Education, Program in Early Childhood Education, Rockford, IL 61108-2393. Offers MAT. *Program availability:* Part-time, evening/weekend. *Degree requirements:* For master's, thesis optional. *Entrance requirements:* For master's, GRE General Test, basic skills test (for students seeking certification), 3 letters of recommendation. Additional exam requirements/recommendations for international students: Required—TOEFL. Electronic applications accepted.

Roosevelt University, Graduate Division, College of Education, Program in Teaching and Learning, Chicago, IL 60605. Offers early childhood education (MA). *Program availability:* Part-time, evening/weekend. Electronic applications accepted.

Rutgers University–New Brunswick, Graduate School of Education, Department of Learning and Teaching, Program in Early Childhood/Elementary Education, Piscataway, NJ 08854-8097. Offers Ed M, Ed D. *Program availability:* Part-time. Terminal master's awarded for partial completion of doctoral program. *Degree requirements:* For master's, comprehensive exam (for some programs); for doctorate, thesis/dissertation, qualifying exam. *Entrance requirements:* For master's, GRE General Test, minimum GPA of 3.0; for doctorate, GRE General Test, minimum GPA of 3.5. Additional exam requirements/recommendations for international students: Required—TOEFL. Electronic applications accepted.

Saginaw Valley State University, College of Education, Program in Early Childhood Education, University Center, MI 48710. Offers MAT. *Accreditation:* NCATE. *Program availability:* Part-time, evening/weekend. *Students:* 4 full-time (all women), 45 part-time (all women); includes 2 minority (both Two or more races, non-Hispanic/Latino). Average age 36. 8 applicants, 100% accepted, 6 enrolled. In 2018, 17 master's awarded. *Degree requirements:* For master's, capstone course. *Entrance requirements:* For master's, minimum GPA of 3.0, teaching certificate. Additional exam requirements/recommendations for international students: Required—TOEFL (minimum score 550 paper-based; 79 iBT). *Application deadline:* For fall admission, 7/15 for international students; for winter admission, 11/15 for international students; for spring admission, 4/15 for international students. Applications are processed on a rolling basis. Application fee: $30 ($90 for international students). Electronic applications accepted. *Expenses:* Tuition, area resident: Full-time $6225; part-time $623 per credit hour. Tuition, state resident: full-time $6225; part-time $623 per credit hour. Tuition, nonresident: full-time $14,215; part-time $1185 per credit hour. *International tuition:* $14,215 full-time. *Required fees:* $263; $14.60 per credit hour. Tuition and fees vary according to degree level. *Financial support:* Federal Work-Study and scholarships/grants available. Support available to part-time students. Financial award applicants required to submit FAFSA. *Unit head:* Dr. Mary Harmon, Dean, 989-964-4057, Fax: 989-964-4563, E-mail: coeconnect@svsu.edu. *Application contact:* Jenna Briggs, Director, Graduate and International Admissions, 989-964-6096, Fax: 989-964-2788, E-mail: gradadm@svsu.edu.

St. Ambrose University, School of Education, Davenport, IA 52803-2898. Offers early childhood education (M Ed); educational administration (M Ed). *Accreditation:* TEAC. *Program availability:* Part-time, evening/weekend, online learning. *Degree requirements:* For master's, comprehensive exam. *Entrance requirements:* For master's, GRE General Test or MAT, minimum GPA of 2.75. Additional exam requirements/recommendations for international students: Required—TOEFL. Electronic applications accepted. *Faculty research:* Disabilities and postsecondary career avenues, self-determination.

St. Bonaventure University, School of Graduate School, School of Education, Literacy Programs, St. Bonaventure, NY 14778-2284. Offers adolescent literacy 5-12 (MS Ed); childhood literacy B-6 (MS Ed). *Accreditation:* NCATE. *Program availability:* Part-time, evening/weekend. *Faculty:* 1 (woman) full-time, 1 part-time/adjunct. *Students:* 9 full-time (all women), 2 part-time (1 woman); all minorities (all Black or African American, non-Hispanic/Latino). Average age 22. 10 applicants, 100% accepted. In 2018, 12 master's awarded. *Degree requirements:* For master's, comprehensive exam, thesis optional, minimum cumulative GPA of 3.0, clinical practicum, literacy coaching internship, electronic portfolio. *Entrance requirements:* For master's, GRE or MAT, teaching certificate in matching area in-hand or pending, transcripts from all previous colleges, minimum GPA of 3.0, 2 references, interview, writing sample. Additional exam requirements/recommendations for international students: Required—TOEFL (minimum score 550 paper-based; 80 iBT). *Application deadline:* For fall admission, 3/15 priority date for domestic students, 2/1 for international students; for spring admission, 10/15 priority date for domestic students, 7/1 for international students. Applications are processed on a rolling basis. Application fee: $0. Electronic applications accepted. *Financial support:* Scholarships/grants, health care benefits, and unspecified assistantships available. Financial award application deadline: 4/15; financial award applicants required to submit FAFSA. *Unit head:* Dr. Sheri Voss, Director, 716-375-2368, Fax: 716-375-2360, E-mail: svoss@sbu.edu. *Application contact:* Matthew Retchless, Director of Graduate Admissions, 716-375-2021, Fax: 716-375-4015, E-mail: gradsch@sbu.edu. Website: http://www.sbu.edu/academics/schools/education/graduate-degrees-certificates/msed-in-childhood-literacy

St. Catherine University, Graduate Programs, Program in Education - Montessori Education, St. Paul, MN 55105. Offers MA. *Program availability:* Part-time, evening/weekend, online learning.

St. John's University, The School of Education, Department of Curriculum and Instruction, PhD in Curriculum and Instruction Program, Queens, NY 11439. Offers early childhood (PhD); global education (PhD); STEM education (PhD); teaching, learning, and knowing (PhD). *Program availability:* Part-time-only. *Degree requirements:* For doctorate, comprehensive exam, thesis/dissertation. *Entrance requirements:* For doctorate, teacher certification (or equivalent), at least three years' teaching experience or the equivalent in informal learning environments, master's degree. Additional exam requirements/recommendations for international students: Required—TOEFL. Electronic applications accepted. *Faculty research:* Literacies, early childhood, STEM, school culture, global education.

St. John's University, The School of Education, Department of Curriculum and Instruction, Program in Early Childhood Education, Queens, NY 11439. Offers MS Ed. *Program availability:* Part-time, evening/weekend, online learning. *Degree requirements:* For master's, thesis. *Entrance requirements:* For master's, GRE, MAT, or PRAXIS, statement of goals (personal essay), official undergraduate transcripts, initial teaching certification. Additional exam requirements/recommendations for international students: Required—TOEFL, IELTS. Electronic applications accepted. *Faculty research:* Improving children's learning in math, science and technology; health and nutrition education to prevent obesity; oral language and literacy development in diverse populations; multicultural and international education; special needs and inclusive education.

St. John's University, The School of Education, Department of Education Specialties, Program in Teaching English to Speakers of Other Languages and Bilingual Education, Queens, NY 11439. Offers bilingual education (Adv C); childhood education and teaching English to speakers of other languages (MS Ed); teaching English to speakers of other languages (MS Ed, Adv C). *Degree requirements:* For Adv C, one foreign language. *Entrance requirements:* For master's, GRE, MAT, or PRAXIS, statement of goals (personal essay), official undergraduate transcripts, initial teaching certification; for Adv C, initial teaching certification, first master's transcripts, statement of purpose. Additional exam requirements/recommendations for international students: Required—TOEFL, IELTS. Electronic applications accepted. *Faculty research:* Second language learning and academic achievement, heritage language education, assessing the progress of English language learners toward English acquisition, dual language acquisition, study of English Creoles and dialects of other English's, literacy development for ESL learners; investigating Caribbean and Creole language and culture, education law.

Saint Joseph's University, College of Arts and Sciences, Graduate Programs in Education, Philadelphia, PA 19131-1395. Offers curriculum supervisor (Certificate); educational leadership (MS, Ed D); elementary education (MS, Certificate); elementary/middle school education (Certificate); organizational development and leadership (MS); principal (Certificate); professional education (MS); reading specialist (MS, Certificate); reading supervisor (Certificate); secondary education (MS, Certificate); special education (MS); special education 7-12 (Certificate); special education PK-8 (Certificate); superintendent's letter of eligibility (Certificate); supervisor of special education (Certificate); teacher of the deaf and hard of hearing (Certificate). *Program availability:* Part-time, evening/weekend, blended/hybrid learning. *Degree requirements:* For master's, thesis or alternative; for doctorate, comprehensive exam, thesis/dissertation. *Entrance requirements:* For master's, 2 letters of recommendation, minimum GPA of 3.0, official transcripts, personal statement; for doctorate, GRE, master's degree from accredited institution, minimum graduate GPA of 3.5, computer competence, interview with program director. Additional exam requirements/recommendations for international students: Required—TOEFL (minimum score 550 paper-based; 80 iBT), IELTS (minimum score 6.5), PTE (minimum score 60). Electronic applications accepted. *Expenses:* Contact institution. *Faculty research:* Factors predicting early mathematics skills for low income children, early child care and development, preschool quality, parent communication and home-school collaboration issues, education of terminally ill children, preparing literacy teachers for urban schools.

Saint Mary's College of California, Kalmanovitz School of Education, Program in Early Childhood Education, Moraga, CA 94575. Offers supervision and leadership (MA). *Program availability:* Part-time, evening/weekend. *Degree requirements:* For master's, thesis or alternative. *Entrance requirements:* For master's, interview, minimum GPA of 3.0.

Saint Mary's College of California, Kalmanovitz School of Education, Program in Montessori Education, Moraga, CA 94575. Offers MA. *Degree requirements:* For master's, thesis or project. *Entrance requirements:* For master's, writing proficiency exam.

Saint Xavier University, Graduate Studies, School of Education, Chicago, IL 60655-3105. Offers counseling (MA); curriculum and instruction (MA); early childhood education (MA); educational administration (MA); elementary education (MA); individualized studies (MA), including educational technology, English as a second language (ESL), ISTEM (integrative science, technology, engineering, and math); science education; music education (MA); reading (MA); secondary education (MA); Spanish education (MA); special education (MA); teaching and leadership (MA). *Accreditation:* NCATE. *Program availability:* Part-time, evening/weekend. *Degree requirements:* For master's, thesis or project. *Entrance requirements:* For master's, minimum GPA of 3.0. *Expenses:* Contact institution.

Salem State University, School of Graduate Studies, Program in Early Childhood Education, Salem, MA 01970-5353. Offers M Ed. *Accreditation:* NCATE. *Program availability:* Part-time, evening/weekend. *Entrance requirements:* For master's, GRE or MAT. Additional exam requirements/recommendations for international students: Required—TOEFL (minimum score 550 paper-based; 80 iBT) or IELTS (minimum score 5.5).

San Francisco State University, Division of Graduate Studies, College of Education, Department of Elementary Education, Program in Early Childhood Education, San Francisco, CA 94132-1722. Offers MA. *Accreditation:* NCATE. *Unit head:* Dr. Stephanie Sisk-Hilton, Chair, 415-338-1562, Fax: 415-338-0567, E-mail: stephhsh@sfsu.edu. *Application contact:* Dr. Daniel Meier, MA Program Coordinator, 415-338-3417, Fax: 415-338-0567, E-mail: dmeier@sfsu.edu. Website: https://eed.sfsu.edu/

San Francisco State University, Division of Graduate Studies, College of Education, Department of Special Education, San Francisco, CA 94132-1722. Offers augmentative and alternative communication (AC); autism spectrum (AC); early childhood practices (AC); education specialist (Credential); orientation and mobility (Credential); special education (MA, PhD). PhD offered jointly with University of California, Berkeley. *Accreditation:* NCATE. *Unit head:* Dr. Yvonne Bui, Chair, 415-338-2503, Fax: 415-338-0566, E-mail: ybui@sfsu.edu. *Application contact:* Jeanne Oh, Academic Office Coordinator, 415-338-2501, Fax: 415-338-0566, E-mail: joh2@sfsu.edu. Website: http://sped.sfsu.edu/home

San Ignacio University, Graduate Programs, Doral, FL 33178. Offers business administration (MBA), including human resources management, international business, marketing management; education (M Ed), including early childhood education, educational leadership, special education; hospitality management (MA), including gastronomy and restaurant management, tourism management.

Shenandoah University, School of Education and Leadership, Winchester, VA 22601. Offers early childhood literacy (MS); reading licensure (MS); writing (MS). *Accreditation:* TEAC. *Program availability:* Part-time, evening/weekend. *Faculty:* 8 full-time (6 women), 26 part-time/adjunct (19 women). *Students:* 11 full-time (8 women), 211 part-time (163 women); includes 27 minority (14 Black or African American, non-Hispanic/Latino; 1 American Indian or Alaska Native, non-Hispanic/Latino; 4 Asian, non-Hispanic/Latino; 3 Hispanic/Latino; 1 Native Hawaiian or other Pacific Islander, non-Hispanic/Latino; 4 Two or more races, non-Hispanic/Latino), 2 international. Average age 38. 82 applicants, 96% accepted, 54 enrolled. In 2018, 62 master's, 11 doctorates, 34 other advanced degrees awarded. *Degree requirements:* For master's, comprehensive exam (for some programs), thesis (for some programs); for doctorate, comprehensive exam, thesis/dissertation. *Entrance requirements:* For degree, PRAXIS Academic Core, SAT/ACT, PRAXIS Academic Core Math, or VCLA, 3 letters of recommendation, writing sample, undergraduate degree, https://www.su.edu/admissions/graduate-students/education-application-information/. Additional exam requirements/recommendations for international students: Required—TOEFL (minimum score 550 paper-based; 79 iBT), IELTS (minimum score 6.5), TOEFL (minimum score 550 paper-based, 79 iBT) OR IELTS (6.5). *Application deadline:* For fall admission, 3/15 for domestic students, 3/17 for international students. Applications are processed on a rolling basis. Application fee: $30. Electronic applications accepted. *Expenses:* $525 per credit hour, $160 student services fee, $170 technology fee. *Financial support:* In 2018–19, 3 students received support. Scholarships/grants and unspecified assistantships available. Financial award application deadline: 1/15; financial award applicants required to submit FAFSA. *Faculty research:* Mentoring, behavior support for students, teacher change agency, educational technology in pedagogy, literacy education, leadership and pedagogy. *Total annual research expenditures:* $70,000. *Unit head:* Jill Lindsey, PhD, Director, School of

Education and Leadership, 540-545-7324, Fax: 540-665-4726, E-mail: jlindsey@su.edu. *Application contact:* Andrew Woodall, Assistant Vice President for Admissions & Recruitment, 540-665-4581, Fax: 540-665-4627, E-mail: admit@su.edu.
Website: http://www.su.edu/education/

Shippensburg University of Pennsylvania, School of Graduate Studies, College of Education and Human Services, Department of Teacher Education, Shippensburg, PA 17257-2299. Offers curriculum and instruction (M Ed), including biology, early childhood education, elementary education, geography/earth science, history, mathematics, middle school education, modern languages; reading (M Ed). *Accreditation:* NCATE. *Program availability:* Part-time, evening/weekend, 100% online, blended/hybrid learning. *Faculty:* 12 full-time (9 women), 2 part-time/adjunct (0 women). *Students:* 10 full-time (8 women), 68 part-time (64 women); includes 7 minority (2 Black or African American, non-Hispanic/Latino; 4 Hispanic/Latino; 1 Two or more races, non-Hispanic/Latino). Average age 31. 41 applicants, 73% accepted, 19 enrolled. In 2018, 34 master's awarded. *Degree requirements:* For master's, comprehensive exam (for some programs), thesis optional, practicum or internship; capstone seminar (for some programs). *Entrance requirements:* For master's, MAT or GRE (if GPA less than 2.75), interview, 3 letters of reference, questionnaire of teaching background and future goals, resume. Additional exam requirements/recommendations for international students: Required—TOEFL (minimum score 550 paper-based; 68 iBT), IELTS (minimum score 6), TOEFL (minimum score 550 paper-based, 68 iBT) or IELTS (minimum score 6). *Application deadline:* For fall admission, 4/1 priority date for domestic students, 4/30 for international students; for spring admission, 9/1 priority date for domestic students, 9/30 for international students; for summer admission, 2/1 priority date for domestic students. Applications are processed on a rolling basis. Application fee: $45. Electronic applications accepted. *Expenses:* Tuition, state resident: part-time $516 per credit. Tuition, nonresident: part-time $750 per credit. *Required fees:* $149 per credit. *Financial support:* In 2018–19, 5 students received support. Career-related internships or fieldwork, scholarships/grants, unspecified assistantships, and resident hall director and student payroll positions available. Support available to part-time students. Financial award application deadline: 3/1; financial award applicants required to submit FAFSA. *Unit head:* Dr. Christine A. Royce, Chairperson, 717-477-1688, Fax: 717-477-4046, E-mail: caroyc@ship.edu. *Application contact:* Maya T. Mapp, Director of Admissions, 717-477-1231, Fax: 717-477-4016, E-mail: mtmapp@ship.edu.
Website: http://www.ship.edu/teacher/

Siena Heights University, Graduate College, Adrian, MI 49221-1796. Offers clinical mental health counseling (MA); educational leadership (Specialist); leadership (MA), including health care leadership, organizational leadership; teacher education (MA), including early childhood education, early childhood education: Montessori, education leadership: principal, elementary education: reading K-12, leadership: higher education, secondary education: reading K-12, special education: cognitive impairment, special education: learning disabilities. *Program availability:* Part-time, evening/weekend. *Faculty:* 10 full-time (6 women), 16 part-time/adjunct (6 women). *Students:* 34 full-time (20 women), 183 part-time (126 women); includes 64 minority (38 Black or African American, non-Hispanic/Latino; 2 American Indian or Alaska Native, non-Hispanic/Latino; 4 Asian, non-Hispanic/Latino; 14 Hispanic/Latino; 6 Two or more races, non-Hispanic/Latino). Average age 36. 97 applicants, 41% accepted, 30 enrolled. In 2018, 72 master's awarded. *Degree requirements:* For master's, thesis, Presentation. *Entrance requirements:* For master's, Minimum GPA of 3.0, current resume, essay, all post-secondary transcripts, 3 letters of reference, conviction disclosure form; copy of teaching certificate (for some education programs); for Specialist, Master's degree, minimum GPA of 3.0, current resume, essay, all post-secondary transcripts, 3 letters of reference, conviction disclosure form; copy of teaching certificate (for some education programs). Additional exam requirements/recommendations for international students: Recommended—TOEFL, IELTS, TWE, TSE. *Application deadline:* Applications are processed on a rolling basis. Application fee: $50. Electronic applications accepted. *Expenses: Tuition:* Full-time $11,340; part-time $7560 per year. *Required fees:* $454; $454 per unit. $227 per semester. One-time fee: $100. Tuition and fees vary according to program. *Financial support:* In 2018–19, 55 students received support. Scholarships/grants, tuition waivers (full and partial), unspecified assistantships, and State of Michigan Scholarships/Grants available. Support available to part-time students. Financial award application deadline: 9/1; financial award applicants required to submit FAFSA. *Unit head:* Dr. Cheryl Betz, Dean, College for Professional Studies and Graduate College, 517-264-7234, Fax: 517-264-7714, E-mail: cbetz@sienaheights.edu. *Application contact:* Elizabeth Brooks, Assistant Director, 517-264-7165, Fax: 517-264-7714, E-mail: ebrooks@sienaheights.edu.
Website: http://www.sienaheights.edu

Sonoma State University, School of Education, Rohnert Park, CA 94928-3609. Offers administrative services (Credential); curriculum, teaching, and learning (MA); early childhood education (MA); education specialist (Credential); educational leadership (MA); multiple subject (Credential); reading and literacy (MA, Credential); single subject (Credential); special education (MA). *Accreditation:* NCATE. *Program availability:* Part-time, evening/weekend. *Entrance requirements:* For master's, minimum GPA of 2.5. Additional exam requirements/recommendations for international students: Required—TOEFL (minimum score 500 paper-based).

South Carolina State University, College of Graduate and Professional Studies, Department of Education, Orangeburg, SC 29117-0001. Offers early childhood education (MAT); education (M Ed); elementary education (M Ed, MAT); English (MAT); general science/biology (MAT); mathematics (MAT); secondary education (M Ed), including biology education, business education, counselor education, English education, home economics education, industrial education, mathematics education, science education, social studies education; special education (M Ed), including emotionally handicapped, learning disabilities, mentally handicapped. *Accreditation:* NCATE. *Program availability:* Part-time, evening/weekend. *Faculty:* 17 full-time (6 women), 12 part-time/adjunct (5 women). *Students:* 42 full-time (32 women), 93 part-time (64 women); includes 121 minority (119 Black or African American, non-Hispanic/Latino; 2 Asian, non-Hispanic/Latino), 2 international. Average age 40. 50 applicants, 98% accepted, 39 enrolled. In 2018, 9 master's awarded. *Degree requirements:* For master's, thesis optional, departmental qualifying exam. *Entrance requirements:* For master's, GRE General Test, NTE, interview, teaching certificate. *Application deadline:* For fall admission, 6/15 priority date for domestic students, 6/15 for international students; for spring admission, 11/1 for domestic and international students. Application fee: $25. Electronic applications accepted. *Expenses: Tuition, area resident:* Full-time $9928; part-time $552 per credit hour. Tuition, state resident: full-time $9928. Tuition, nonresident: full-time $21,038; part-time $1169 per credit hour. *Required fees:* $1532; $85 per credit hour. *Financial support:* Fellowships, career-related internships or fieldwork, Federal Work-Study, and scholarships/grants available. Financial award application deadline: 6/1. *Unit head:* Dr. Charlie Spell, Chair, Department of Education, 803-536-8963, Fax: 803-516-4568, E-mail: cspell@scsu.edu. *Application contact:* Curtis Foskey, Coordinator of Graduate Studies, 803-536-8419, Fax: 803-536-8812, E-mail: cfoskey@scsu.edu.

Southern New Hampshire University, School of Education, Manchester, NH 03106-1045. Offers curriculum and instruction (M Ed), including dyslexia studies and language-based learning disabilities, educational leadership, reading, special education, technology integration; dyslexia studies and language-based learning disabilities (Certificate); early childhood and special education (M Ed); educational leadership (M Ed, Ed D); educational studies (M Ed); elementary and special education (M Ed); field based education (M Ed); higher education administration (MS); teaching English as a foreign language (MS). *Program availability:* Part-time, evening/weekend, online learning. *Degree requirements:* For master's, comprehensive exam (for some programs), thesis or alternative. *Entrance requirements:* For master's, PRAXIS I, minimum GPA of 2.75. Additional exam requirements/recommendations for international students: Required—TOEFL (minimum score 550 paper-based). Electronic applications accepted. *Expenses:* Contact institution.

Southern Oregon University, Graduate Studies, School of Education, Ashland, OR 97520. Offers elementary education (MA Ed, MS Ed), including classroom teacher, early childhood, handicapped learner, reading, supervision; secondary education (MA Ed, MS Ed), including classroom teacher, handicapped learner, reading, supervision; teaching (MAT). *Program availability:* Online learning. *Degree requirements:* For master's, thesis optional. *Entrance requirements:* For master's, GRE General Test, minimum cumulative GPA of 3.0 in the last 90 quarter credits (60 semester credits) of undergraduate coursework. Additional exam requirements/recommendations for international students: Required—TOEFL (minimum score 540 paper-based; 76 iBT), IELTS (minimum score 6), ELPT (minimum score 964) or ELS (minimum score 112). Electronic applications accepted.

Southwestern College, Education Programs, Winfield, KS 67156-2499. Offers curriculum and instruction (M Ed); early childhood education (M Ed); educational leadership (Ed D), including higher education leadership, PK-12 education leadership; special education (M Ed), including high-incidence disabilities, low-incidence disabilities; teaching (MA). *Accreditation:* NCATE. *Program availability:* Part-time, evening/weekend, 100% online, blended/hybrid learning. *Faculty:* 7 full-time (5 women), 14 part-time/adjunct (12 women). *Students:* 6 full-time (5 women), 79 part-time (54 women); includes 11 minority (4 Black or African American, non-Hispanic/Latino; 2 American Indian or Alaska Native, non-Hispanic/Latino; 1 Asian, non-Hispanic/Latino; 3 Hispanic/Latino; 1 Two or more races, non-Hispanic/Latino), 4 international. Average age 38. 31 applicants, 74% accepted, 18 enrolled. In 2018, 24 master's, 8 doctorates awarded. *Degree requirements:* For master's, practicum, portfolio; for doctorate, thesis/dissertation, professional portfolio. *Entrance requirements:* For master's, baccalaureate degree, minimum GPA of 3.0, valid teaching certificate (for special education); for doctorate, GRE if no master's degree, baccalaureate degree with minimum GPA of 3.25 and current teaching experience, or master's degree with minimum GPA of 3.5. Additional exam requirements/recommendations for international students: Required—TOEFL (minimum score 60 paper-based; 70 iBT), IELTS (minimum score 5.5). *Application deadline:* Applications are processed on a rolling basis. Application fee: $40. Electronic applications accepted. *Expenses:* Masters programs are $606 per credit hour, $535 per online credit hour; doctorate program is $639 per credit hour. *Financial support:* In 2018–19, 13 students received support. Unspecified assistantships and employee tuition waivers available. Financial award applicants required to submit FAFSA. *Unit head:* J.K. Campbell, Education Division Chair, 620-229-6115, E-mail: JK.Campbell@sckans.edu. *Application contact:* Jen Caughron, Director of Enrollment Services & Marketing, 888-684-5335 Ext. 3312, Fax: 888-684-5218, E-mail: jennifer.caughron@sckans.edu.
Website: http://www.sckans.edu/graduate/education-med/

Southwestern Oklahoma State University, College of Professional and Graduate Studies, School of Behavioral Sciences and Education, Specialization in Early Childhood Education, Weatherford, OK 73096-3098. Offers M Ed. *Accreditation:* NCATE. *Program availability:* Part-time, evening/weekend. *Degree requirements:* For master's, exam. *Entrance requirements:* For master's, GRE General Test or minimum undergraduate GPA of 3.0. Additional exam requirements/recommendations for international students: Required—TOEFL (minimum score 550 paper-based), IELTS (minimum score 6.5).

Southwest Minnesota State University, Department of Education, Marshall, MN 56258. Offers ESL (MS); math (MS); reading (MS); special education (MS), including developmental disabilities, early childhood education, emotional behavioral disorders, learning disabilities; teaching, learning and leadership (MS). *Program availability:* Part-time, evening/weekend, online learning. *Entrance requirements:* Additional exam requirements/recommendations for international students: Required—TOEFL or IELTS; Recommended—TOEFL (minimum score 550 paper-based; 80 iBT), IELTS.

Springfield College, Graduate Programs, Programs in Education, Springfield, MA 01109-3797. Offers early childhood education (M Ed); educational studies (M Ed); elementary education (M Ed); secondary education (M Ed); special education (M Ed, CAGS). *Program availability:* Part-time, evening/weekend. *Entrance requirements:* For master's, Massachusetts Tests for Educator Licensure (MTEL). Additional exam requirements/recommendations for international students: Required—TOEFL (minimum score 550 paper-based); Recommended—IELTS (minimum score 7). Electronic applications accepted. *Expenses:* Contact institution.

Spring Hill College, Graduate Programs, Program in Education, Mobile, AL 36608-1791. Offers early childhood education (MAT, MS Ed); educational theory (MS Ed); elementary education (MAT, MS Ed); secondary education (MAT, MS Ed). *Program availability:* Part-time. *Faculty:* 3 full-time (all women). *Students:* 1 full-time (0 women), 8 part-time (5 women); includes 2 minority (1 Hispanic/Latino; 1 Two or more races, non-Hispanic/Latino), 1 international. Average age 32. In 2018, 6 master's awarded. *Degree requirements:* For master's, comprehensive exam, completion of program within 6 calendar years of entrance into graduate studies at Spring Hill; documentation of course field assignments (MS) or completion of internship (MAT). *Entrance requirements:* For master's, GRE, MAT, or PRAXIS (varies by program), bachelor's degree with minimum undergraduate GPA of 3.0; class B certificate (for MS); minimum number of hours in specific fields (for MAT). Additional exam requirements/recommendations for international students: Required—TOEFL (minimum score 550 paper-based; 80 iBT), IELTS (minimum score 6.5), CPE or CAE (minimum score C), Michigan English Language Assessment Battery (minimum score 90). *Application deadline:* For fall admission, 8/1 priority date for domestic and international students; for spring admission, 12/1 priority date for domestic and international students. Applications are processed on a rolling basis. Application fee: $25 ($35 for international students). Electronic applications accepted. *Expenses:* Contact institution. *Financial support:* Fellowships, research assistantships, teaching assistantships, and tuition waivers available. Financial award applicants required to submit FAFSA. *Unit head:* Dr. Lori P. Aultman, Chair of Education, 251-380-3473, Fax: 251-460-2184, E-mail: laultman@shc.edu. *Application contact:* Gary Bracken, Vice President of Enrollment Management, 251-380-3038, Fax: 251-460-2186, E-mail: gbracken@shc.edu.
Website: http://ug.shc.edu/graduate-degrees/master-science-education/

State University of New York at Fredonia, College of Education, Fredonia, NY 14063-1136. Offers curriculum and instruction (MS Ed); literacy education (MS Ed), including birth-grade 12, grades 5-12; music education (M Mus), including k-12; TESOL (MS Ed). *Accreditation:* NCATE. *Program availability:* Part-time. *Faculty:* 16 full-time (14 women), 13 part-time/adjunct (11 women). *Students:* 39 full-time (33 women), 44 part-time (36

women); includes 5 minority (1 Asian, non-Hispanic/Latino; 3 Hispanic/Latino; 1 Two or more races, non-Hispanic/Latino), 4 international. Average age 27. 44 applicants, 89% accepted, 34 enrolled. In 2018, 25 master's awarded. *Degree requirements:* For master's, thesis. *Entrance requirements:* For master's, GRE, minimum undergraduate GPA of 3.0. Additional exam requirements/recommendations for international students: Required—TOEFL (minimum score 79 iBT), IELTS (minimum score 6.5). *Application deadline:* For fall admission, 4/1 priority date for domestic and international students; for spring admission, 11/1 priority date for domestic students, 11/1 for international students. Applications are processed on a rolling basis. Application fee: $75. Electronic applications accepted. *Expenses:* Tuition, state resident: full-time $6870; part-time $462 per credit hour. Tuition, nonresident: full-time $16,650; part-time $944 per credit hour. *International tuition:* $16,650 full-time. *Required fees:* $25; $2 per credit hour. $1 per semester. *Financial support:* In 2018–19, 13 students received support. Unspecified assistantships available. Financial award application deadline: 3/15; financial award applicants required to submit FAFSA. *Faculty research:* Positive behavioral intervention and support (PBIS), place-based science education, peer support for education, primary source material for social studies education, policies and practices in learning English language. *Unit head:* Dr. Christine Givner, Dean, 716-673-3311, E-mail: christine.givner@fredonia.edu. *Application contact:* Wendy S. Dunst, Interim Graduate Recruitment and Admissions Associate, 716-673-3808, Fax: 716-673-3712, E-mail: wendy.dunst@fredonia.edu.
Website: http://www.fredonia.edu/coe/

State University of New York at New Paltz, Graduate and Extended Learning School, School of Education, Program in Early Childhood and Childhood Education, New Paltz, NY 12561. Offers childhood education (MS Ed), including early childhood; childhood education 1-6 (MST), including childhood education 1-6. *Accreditation:* NCATE. *Program availability:* Part-time, evening/weekend. *Faculty:* 9 full-time (7 women), 6 part-time/adjunct (all women). *Students:* 32 full-time (29 women), 14 part-time (13 women); includes 8 minority (1 Black or African American, non-Hispanic/Latino; 6 Hispanic/Latino; 1 Two or more races, non-Hispanic/Latino). 20 applicants, 75% accepted, 14 enrolled. In 2018, 29 master's awarded. *Degree requirements:* For master's, comprehensive exam (for some programs), portfolio. *Entrance requirements:* For master's, GRE or MAT (for MST), minimum GPA of 3.0 (3.2 for literacy and special education), New York state teaching certificate (for MS Ed). Additional exam requirements/recommendations for international students: Required—TOEFL (minimum score 550 paper-based; 80 iBT), IELTS (minimum score 6.5). *Application deadline:* For fall admission, 4/1 for domestic and international students; for spring admission, 11/1 priority date for domestic and international students; for summer admission, 4/15 priority date for domestic and international students. Applications are processed on a rolling basis. Application fee: $50. Electronic applications accepted. *Financial support:* Application deadline: 8/1. *Faculty research:* Multi-sensory teaching methods, volunteer tutoring programs for struggling readers, school readiness and transition, math/science/technology, university-school partnerships. *Unit head:* Dr. Aaron Isabelle, Chair, 845-257-2837, E-mail: isabella@newpaltz.edu. *Application contact:* Vika Shock, Assistant Director of Graduate Admissions, 845-257-3285, Fax: 845-257-3284, E-mail: gradstudies@newpaltz.edu.
Website: http://www.newpaltz.edu/elementaryed/

State University of New York at New Paltz, Graduate and Extended Learning School, School of Education, Program of Educational Administration, Program in Special Education, New Paltz, NY 12561. Offers adolescence special education (7-12) (MS Ed); adolescence special education and literacy (MS Ed); childhood special education (1-6) (MS Ed); childhood special education and literacy (MS Ed); early childhood special education (B-2) (MS Ed). *Accreditation:* NCATE. *Program availability:* Part-time, evening/weekend. *Faculty:* 4 full-time (3 women), 1 (woman) part-time/adjunct. *Students:* 14 full-time (11 women), 34 part-time (26 women); includes 4 minority (all Hispanic/Latino). 26 applicants, 85% accepted, 21 enrolled. In 2018, 15 master's awarded. *Entrance requirements:* For master's, minimum GPA of 3.0 (3.2 for special education and literacy programs), New York state teaching certificate. Additional exam requirements/recommendations for international students: Required—TOEFL (minimum score 550 paper-based; 80 iBT), IELTS (minimum score 6.5). *Application deadline:* For fall admission, 3/15 priority date for domestic students, 3/15 for international students; for spring admission, 11/1 for domestic and international students. Application fee: $50. Electronic applications accepted. *Financial support:* Application deadline: 8/1. *Unit head:* Dr. Jane Sileo, Coordinator, 845-257-2835, E-mail: sileoj@newpaltz.edu. *Application contact:* Vika Shock, Director of Graduate Admissions, 845-257-3286, E-mail: gradstudies@newpaltz.edu.
Website: http://www.newpaltz.edu/schoolofed/department-of-teaching—learning/special_ed.html

State University of New York at Oswego, Graduate Studies, School of Education, Department of Curriculum and Instruction, Oswego, NY 13126. Offers adolescence education (MST); art education (MAT); childhood education (MST); curriculum and instruction (MS Ed); literacy education (MS Ed); special education (MS Ed). *Program availability:* Part-time, evening/weekend. *Degree requirements:* For master's, comprehensive exam (for some programs), thesis optional. *Entrance requirements:* For master's, GRE General Test, minimum GPA of 2.7, provisional teaching certificate. Additional exam requirements/recommendations for international students: Required—TOEFL (minimum score 560 paper-based). *Faculty research:* Classroom applications for microcomputers; classroom questioning, wait-time, and achievement; values clarification and academic achievement.

State University of New York at Plattsburgh, School of Education, Health, and Human Services, Program in Early Childhood Education, Plattsburgh, NY 12901-2681. Offers early childhood birth-grade 6 (Advanced Certificate).

State University of New York College at Cortland, Graduate Studies, School of Education, Program in Childhood Education, Cortland, NY 13045. Offers MST. *Accreditation:* NCATE.

State University of New York College at Potsdam, School of Education and Professional Studies, Program in Special Education, Potsdam, NY 13676. Offers adolescence (grades 7-12) (MS Ed); childhood (grades 1-6) (MS Ed); early childhood (birth-grade 2) (MS Ed). *Accreditation:* NCATE. *Program availability:* Part-time. *Degree requirements:* For master's, culminating experience. *Entrance requirements:* For master's, minimum GPA of 3.0 in last 60 hours of course work. Additional exam requirements/recommendations for international students: Required—TOEFL (minimum score 550 paper-based; 80 iBT), IELTS (minimum score 6). Electronic applications accepted.

Stephen F. Austin State University, Graduate School, James I. Perkins College of Education, Department of Elementary Education, Program in Early Childhood Education, Nacogdoches, TX 75962. Offers M Ed. *Accreditation:* NCATE. *Degree requirements:* For master's, comprehensive exam. *Entrance requirements:* For master's, GRE General Test. Additional exam requirements/recommendations for international students: Required—TOEFL (minimum score 550 paper-based).

Syracuse University, School of Education, MS Program in Early Childhood Special Education, Syracuse, NY 13244. Offers MS. *Program availability:* Part-time. *Entrance requirements:* For master's, GRE, baccalaureate degree from regionally-accredited college/university, strong teacher and/or employer recommendations, personal statement, experience working with children. Additional exam requirements/recommendations for international students: Required—TOEFL (minimum score 100 iBT). *Application deadline:* For fall admission, 1/15 priority date for domestic and international students; for spring admission, 10/15 priority date for domestic and international students; for summer admission, 1/15 priority date for domestic and international students. Applications are processed on a rolling basis. Application fee: $75. Electronic applications accepted. *Financial support:* Fellowships with full tuition reimbursements, research assistantships, teaching assistantships, career-related internships or fieldwork, and scholarships/grants available. Financial award application deadline: 1/15; financial award applicants required to submit FAFSA. *Faculty research:* Teaching children with diverse backgrounds and abilities, home-based itinerant teaching, early childhood special education, general preschool teaching, teacher consulting. *Unit head:* Dr. Benjamin Dotger, Department Chair, 315-443-2685, E-mail: bdotger@syr.edu. *Application contact:* Speranza Migliore, Graduate Admissions Recruiter, 315-443-2505, E-mail: gradrcrt@syr.edu.
Website: http://soe.syr.edu/academic/teaching_and_leadership/graduate/masters/early_childhood_special_education/default.aspx

Teachers College, Columbia University, Department of Curriculum and Teaching, New York, NY 10027-6696. Offers curriculum and teaching (Ed M, MA, Ed D); curriculum and teaching: elementary education (MA); curriculum and teaching: secondary education (MA); early childhood education (MA, Ed D); early childhood education: special education (MA); elementary education-gifted extension (MA); elementary inclusive education (MA); gifted education (MA); literacy specialist (MA); secondary inclusive education (MA); special inclusive elementary education (MA). *Program availability:* Part-time, evening/weekend. *Students:* 88 full-time (77 women), 264 part-time (239 women); includes 129 minority (45 Black or African American, non-Hispanic/Latino; 1 American Indian or Alaska Native, non-Hispanic/Latino; 41 Asian, non-Hispanic/Latino; 28 Hispanic/Latino; 14 Two or more races, non-Hispanic/Latino), 48 international. Average age 30. 460 applicants, 73% accepted, 149 enrolled. Terminal master's awarded for partial completion of doctoral program. *Unit head:* Prof. Daniel Friedrich, Chair, 212-678-3263, E-mail: friedrich@exchange.tc.columbia.edu. *Application contact:* Kelly Sutton-Skinner, Director of Admission & New Student Enrollment, E-mail: kms2237@tc.columbia.edu.

Teachers College of San Joaquin, Master's Program in Education, Stockton, CA 95206. Offers early education (M Ed); educational inquiry (M Ed); educational leadership and school development (M Ed); science, technology, engineering, and mathematics (M Ed); special education (M Ed). *Expenses: Tuition:* Full-time $5520. Tuition and fees vary according to course load and program.

Tennessee Technological University, College of Graduate Studies, College of Education, Department of Curriculum and Instruction, Program in Early Childhood Education, Cookeville, TN 38505. Offers MA, Ed S. *Accreditation:* NCATE. *Program availability:* Part-time, evening/weekend. *Faculty:* 2 full-time (both women). *Students:* 2 full-time (both women), 12 part-time (all women); includes 2 minority (1 Black or African American, non-Hispanic/Latino; 1 Hispanic/Latino), 2 international. 6 applicants, 50% accepted, 2 enrolled. *Degree requirements:* For master's and Ed S, comprehensive exam, thesis or alternative. *Entrance requirements:* For master's and Ed S, MAT or GRE. Additional exam requirements/recommendations for international students: Required—TOEFL (minimum score 527 paper-based; 71 iBT), IELTS (minimum score 5.5), PTE (minimum score 48), or TOEIC (Test of English as an International Communication). *Application deadline:* For fall admission, 8/1 priority date for domestic students, 5/1 for international students; for spring admission, 12/1 for domestic students, 10/1 for international students; for summer admission, 5/1 for domestic students, 2/1 for international students. Application fee: $35 ($40 for international students). Electronic applications accepted. *Financial support:* Fellowships, research assistantships, teaching assistantships, and career-related internships or fieldwork available. Financial award application deadline: 4/1. *Unit head:* Dr. Jeremy Wendt, Chairperson, 931-372-3181, Fax: 931-372-6270, E-mail: jwendt@tntech.edu. *Application contact:* Shelia K. Kendrick, Coordinator of Graduate Studies, 931-372-3808, Fax: 931-372-3497, E-mail: skendrick@tntech.edu.

Texas A&M University–Commerce, College of Education and Human Services, Commerce, TX 75429. Offers counseling (M Ed, MS, PhD); early childhood education (M Ed, MS); educational administration (M Ed, MS, Ed D); educational psychology (PhD); educational technology leadership (M Ed, MS); educational technology library science (M Ed, MS); elementary education (M Ed); health, kinesiology and sports studies (MS); higher education (MS, Ed D); psychology (MS); reading (M Ed, MS); school psychology (SSP); secondary education (M Ed, MS); social work (MSW); special education (M Ed, MS); supervision, curriculum and instruction-elementary education (Ed D); training and development (MS). *Program availability:* Part-time, evening/weekend, 100% online, blended/hybrid learning. *Faculty:* 95 full-time (59 women), 29 part-time/adjunct (22 women). *Students:* 356 full-time (295 women), 1,262 part-time (992 women); includes 683 minority (349 Black or African American, non-Hispanic/Latino; 9 American Indian or Alaska Native, non-Hispanic/Latino; 30 Asian, non-Hispanic/Latino; 238 Hispanic/Latino; 57 Two or more races, non-Hispanic/Latino), 9 international. Average age 37. 951 applicants, 42% accepted, 304 enrolled. In 2018, 532 master's, 51 doctorates awarded. *Degree requirements:* For master's, comprehensive exam, thesis optional, departmental qualifying exams (for some programs); for doctorate, comprehensive exam, thesis/dissertation, departmental qualifying exam; for SSP, comprehensive exam. *Entrance requirements:* For master's, GRE General Test, official transcripts, letters of recommendation, resume, statement of goals; for doctorate, GRE General Test, letters of recommendation, statement of goals, writing samples, writing sessions, resumes. Additional exam requirements/recommendations for international students: Required—TOEFL (minimum score 550 paper-based; 79 iBT), IELTS (minimum score 6), PTE (minimum score 53). *Application deadline:* For fall admission, 6/1 priority date for international students; for spring admission, 10/15 priority date for international students; for summer admission, 3/15 priority date for international students. Applications are processed on a rolling basis. Application fee: $50 ($75 for international students). Electronic applications accepted. *Expenses: Tuition, area resident:* Full-time $3630. Tuition, state resident: full-time $3630. Tuition, nonresident: full-time $11,100. *International tuition:* $11,100 full-time. *Required fees:* $2794. Tuition and fees vary according to course load, degree level and program. *Financial support:* In 2018–19, 116 students received support, including 94 research assistantships with partial tuition reimbursements available (averaging $3,863 per year), 38 teaching assistantships with partial tuition reimbursements available (averaging $4,728 per year); career-related internships or fieldwork, Federal Work-Study, institutionally sponsored loans, scholarships/grants, health care benefits, and unspecified assistantships also available. Financial award application deadline: 5/1; financial award applicants required to submit FAFSA. *Faculty research:* Cognitive and bilingual education, positive behavioral intervention, literacy, math readiness. *Total annual research expenditures:* $1.1 million. *Unit head:* Dr. Madeline Justice, Interim Dean, 903-886-5181, Fax: 903-886-5905, E-mail: madeline.justice@tamuc.edu. *Application contact:* Vicky Turner, Doctoral Degree and Special Programs Coordinator, 903-886-5167, E-mail: vicky.turner@tamuc.edu.
Website: http://www.tamuc.edu/academics/graduateSchool/programs/education/default.aspx

Early Childhood Education

Texas A&M University–Commerce, College of Humanities, Social Sciences and Arts, Commerce, TX 75429. Offers applied criminology (MS); applied linguistics (MA, MS); art (MA, MFA); computational linguistics (Graduate Certificate); creative writing (Graduate Certificate); criminal justice management (Graduate Certificate); criminal justice studies (Graduate Certificate); English (MA, MS, PhD); film studies (Graduate Certificate); history (MA, MS); history of Christianity (Graduate Certificate); Holocaust studies (Graduate Certificate); homeland security (Graduate Certificate); music (MM); music performance (MM); political science (MA, MS); public history (Graduate Certificate); sociology (MS); Spanish (MA); studies in children's and adolescent literature and culture (Graduate Certificate); teaching English to speakers of other languages (Graduate Certificate); theater (MA, MS); world history (Graduate Certificate). *Program availability:* Part-time. *Faculty:* 50 full-time (26 women), 11 part-time/adjunct (2 women). *Students:* 125 full-time (83 women), 393 part-time (278 women); includes 197 minority (75 Black or African American, non-Hispanic/Latino; 2 American Indian or Alaska Native, non-Hispanic/Latino; 13 Asian, non-Hispanic/Latino; 92 Hispanic/Latino; 1 Native Hawaiian or other Pacific Islander, non-Hispanic/Latino; 14 Two or more races, non-Hispanic/Latino), 16 international. Average age 37. 261 applicants, 46% accepted, 106 enrolled. In 2018, 124 master's, 8 doctorates awarded. *Degree requirements:* For master's, one foreign language, comprehensive exam, thesis (for some programs); for doctorate, one foreign language, comprehensive exam, thesis/dissertation, departmental qualifying exam. *Entrance requirements:* For master's, GRE General Test, official transcripts, letters of recommendation, resume, statement of goals; for doctorate, GRE General Test, official transcripts, letters of recommendation, statement of goals, writing samples, writing sessions, resumes. Additional exam requirements/recommendations for international students: Required—TOEFL (minimum score 550 paper-based; 79 iBT), IELTS (minimum score 6), PTE (minimum score 53). *Application deadline:* For fall admission, 6/1 priority date for international students; for spring admission, 10/15 priority date for international students; for summer admission, 3/15 priority date for international students. Applications are processed on a rolling basis. Application fee: $50 ($75 for international students). Electronic applications accepted. *Expenses: Tuition, area resident:* Full-time $3630. Tuition, state resident: full-time $3630. Tuition, nonresident: full-time $11,100. *International tuition:* $11,100 full-time. *Required fees:* $2794. Tuition and fees vary according to course load, degree level and program. *Financial support:* In 2018–19, 39 students received support, including 18 research assistantships with partial tuition reimbursements available (averaging $3,231 per year), 136 teaching assistantships with partial tuition reimbursements available (averaging $4,053 per year); Federal Work-Study, institutionally sponsored loans, scholarships/grants, health care benefits, and unspecified assistantships also available. Financial award application deadline: 5/1; financial award applicants required to submit FAFSA. *Unit head:* Dr. William F. Kuracina, Interim Dean, 903-886-5166, Fax: 903-886-5774, E-mail: william.kuracina@tamuc.edu. *Application contact:* Vicky Turner, Doctoral Degree and Special Programs Coordinator, 903-886-5167, E-mail: vicky.turner@tamuc.edu.
Website: http://www.tamuc.edu/academics/colleges/humanitiesSocialSciencesArts/

Texas A&M University–Corpus Christi, College of Graduate Studies, College of Education and Human Development, Corpus Christi, TX 78412. Offers counseling (MS), including counseling; counselor education (PhD); curriculum and instruction (MS, PhD); early childhood education (MS); educational administration (MS); educational leadership (Ed D); elementary education (MS); instructional design and educational technology (MS); kinesiology (MS); reading (MS); secondary education (MS); special education (MS). *Program availability:* Part-time, evening/weekend, blended/hybrid learning. *Degree requirements:* For master's, comprehensive exam, capstone; for doctorate, thesis/dissertation. *Entrance requirements:* For master's, GRE General Test, essay (300 words); for doctorate, GRE, essay, resume, 3-4 reference forms. Electronic applications accepted.

Texas A&M University–Kingsville, College of Graduate Studies, College of Education and Human Performance, Department of Teacher and Bilingual Education, Program in Early Childhood Education, Kingsville, TX 78363. Offers M Ed. *Program availability:* Part-time, evening/weekend. *Degree requirements:* For master's, variable foreign language requirement, comprehensive exam, thesis (for some programs). *Entrance requirements:* For master's, GRE, MAT, GMAT. Additional exam requirements/recommendations for international students: Required—TOEFL (minimum score 550 paper-based; 79 iBT). Electronic applications accepted.

Texas A&M University–San Antonio, Department of Educator and Leadership Preparation, San Antonio, TX 78224. Offers bilingual education (MS); early childhood education (M Ed); educational administration (MA); reading specialization (MS); special education (M Ed), including educational diagnostician. *Program availability:* Part-time, evening/weekend, online learning. *Degree requirements:* For master's, comprehensive exam, thesis or alternative. *Entrance requirements:* For master's, GRE (Quantitative and Verbal) or MAT. Additional exam requirements/recommendations for international students: Required—TOEFL (minimum score 550 paper-based; 79 iBT), IELTS (minimum score 6). Electronic applications accepted. *Faculty research:* Equity in education, biliteracy practices among Latina and immigrants, academic achievement of low socio-economic students, equity practices in instruction and educational leadership in diverse settings, racial identity development and multicultural education.

Texas State University, The Graduate College, College of Education, Program in Reading Education, San Marcos, TX 78666. Offers early childhood-12 reading specialist (M Ed). *Program availability:* Part-time, evening/weekend. *Faculty:* 12 full-time (11 women), 1 (woman) part-time/adjunct. *Students:* 1 (woman) full-time, 9 part-time (8 women); includes 5 minority (1 Black or African American, non-Hispanic/Latino; 4 Hispanic/Latino). Average age 36. 5 applicants, 80% accepted, 4 enrolled. In 2018, 9 master's awarded. *Degree requirements:* For master's, comprehensive exam. *Entrance requirements:* For master's, baccalaureate degree from regionally-accredited institution with minimum GPA of 3.0 in last 60 hours of course work, statement of purpose, official teaching certificate. Additional exam requirements/recommendations for international students: Required—TOEFL, IELTS, TOEFL (minimum iBT scores: 22 listening, 22 reading, 24 speaking, 21 writing). *Application deadline:* For fall admission, 2/1 priority date for domestic and international students; for spring admission, 10/15 priority date for domestic students, 10/1 for international students; for summer admission, 4/15 for domestic students, 3/15 for international students. Applications are processed on a rolling basis. Application fee: $55 ($90 for international students). Electronic applications accepted. *Expenses:* Tuition, state resident: full-time $8102; part-time $4051 per semester. Tuition, nonresident: full-time $18,229; part-time $9115 per semester. *International tuition:* $18,229 full-time. *Required fees:* $2116; $120 per credit hour. Tuition and fees vary according to course load. *Financial support:* In 2018–19, 5 students received support. Research assistantships, teaching assistantships, career-related internships or fieldwork, Federal Work-Study, institutionally sponsored loans, scholarships/grants, and unspecified assistantships available. Support available to part-time students. Financial award application deadline: 1/15; financial award applicants required to submit FAFSA. *Faculty research:* Reciprocal Teaching; Instructional design for "long-term English learners; Bilingual students' linguistic experiences and literacy instruction; motivation to read; teacher perceptions of teaching literacy; Oral History methodology; literacies of linguistically and culturally diverse children, families, and communities; developing reading through mentoring. *Total annual research expenditures:* $91,671. *Unit head:* Dr. Jesse Gainer, Graduate Advisor, 512-245-3534, Fax: 512-245-8365, E-mail: jg51@txstate.edu. *Application contact:* Dr. Andrea Golato, Dean of Graduate School, 512-245-2581, Fax: 512-245-8365, E-mail: gradcollege@txstate.edu.
Website: http://www.education.txstate.edu/ci/degrees-certifications/graduate/reading.html

Texas Woman's University, Graduate School, College of Professional Education, Department of Family Sciences, Denton, TX 76204. Offers child development (MS); child life (MS); counseling and development (MS); early childhood development and education (PhD); early childhood education (M Ed); family studies (MS, PhD); family therapy (MS, PhD). *Accreditation:* ACA (one or more programs are accredited). *Program availability:* Part-time, evening/weekend, 100% online, blended/hybrid learning. *Faculty:* 25 full-time (18 women), 19 part-time/adjunct (16 women). *Students:* 180 full-time (172 women), 247 part-time (229 women); includes 176 minority (86 Black or African American, non-Hispanic/Latino; 11 Asian, non-Hispanic/Latino; 68 Hispanic/Latino; 11 Two or more races, non-Hispanic/Latino), 9 international. Average age 32. 203 applicants, 69% accepted, 100 enrolled. In 2018, 101 master's, 18 doctorates awarded. *Degree requirements:* For master's, comprehensive exam (for some programs), thesis (for some programs), thesis, professional paper, portfolio, or coursework; practicums (for some programs); for doctorate, comprehensive exam, thesis/dissertation, seminars, qualifying exam, dissertation. *Entrance requirements:* For master's, minimum GPA of 3.0 (3.25 for family therapy), letter of intent, curriculum vitae/resume, interview, writing sample, letter of recommendation,; for doctorate, minimum GPA of 3.5 (3.35 for family studies) on all prior graduate work, curriculum vitae/resume, letter of intent. Additional exam requirements/recommendations for international students: Required—TOEFL (minimum score 550 paper-based; 79 iBT); Recommended—IELTS (minimum score 6.5), TSE (minimum score 53). *Application deadline:* For fall admission, 3/15 for domestic students, 3/1 priority date for international students; for spring admission, 9/15 for domestic students, 7/1 priority date for international students. Application fee: $50 ($75 for international students). Electronic applications accepted. *Expenses: Tuition, area resident:* Full-time $4852; part-time $270 per semester hour. Tuition, state resident: full-time $4852; part-time $270 per semester hour. Tuition, nonresident: full-time $12,322; part-time $685 per semester hour. *International tuition:* $12,322 full-time. *Required fees:* $2714; $113 per semester hour. $296 per semester. Tuition and fees vary according to course level, course load, degree level, campus/location and program. *Financial support:* In 2018–19, 106 students received support, including 1 research assistantship, 17 teaching assistantships (averaging $10,232 per year); career-related internships or fieldwork, Federal Work-Study, institutionally sponsored loans, scholarships/grants, traineeships, health care benefits, and unspecified assistantships also available. Support available to part-time students. Financial award application deadline: 3/1; financial award applicants required to submit FAFSA. *Faculty research:* Parenting/parent education, play therapy, healthy relationships, child development, technology integration. *Unit head:* Ron Hovis, Interim Chair, 940-898-2685, Fax: 940-898-2676, E-mail: famsci@twu.edu. *Application contact:* Korie Hawkins, Associate Director of Admissions, Graduate Recruitment, 940-898-3188, Fax: 940-898-3081, E-mail: admissions@twu.edu.
Website: http://www.twu.edu/family-sciences/

Theological University of the Caribbean, Graduate Programs, Saint Just, PR 00978-0901. Offers childhood and adolescent education (MA); counseling and pastoral care (MA); ministry (D Min); missions (MA).

Towson University, College of Education, Program in Early Childhood Education, Towson, MD 21252-0001. Offers M Ed, CAS. *Accreditation:* NCATE. *Program availability:* Part-time, evening/weekend. *Degree requirements:* For master's, thesis optional. *Entrance requirements:* For master's, bachelor's degree with minimum GPA of 3.0, resume, teacher certification, work experience or course work in early childhood education; for CAS, master's degree in early childhood education or related field from nationally-accredited institution; minimum overall GPA of 3.75 for graduate work; resume; 3 letters of recommendation. Electronic applications accepted. *Expenses: Tuition, area resident:* Full-time $9196; part-time $418 per unit. Tuition, state resident: full-time $9196; part-time $418 per unit. Tuition, nonresident: full-time $19,030; part-time $865 per unit. *International tuition:* $19,030 full-time. *Required fees:* $3102; $141 per year. $423 per term. Tuition and fees vary according to campus/location and program.

Towson University, College of Education, Program in Teaching, Towson, MD 21252-0001. Offers early childhood education (MAT); elementary education (MAT); secondary education (MAT); special education (MAT). *Entrance requirements:* For master's, ACT, GRE, PRAXIS I or SAT, 2 letters of reference, resume, minimum GPA of 3.0, essay. Electronic applications accepted. *Expenses: Tuition, area resident:* Full-time $9196; part-time $418 per unit. Tuition, state resident: full-time $9196; part-time $418 per unit. Tuition, nonresident: full-time $19,030; part-time $865 per unit. *International tuition:* $19,030 full-time. *Required fees:* $3102; $141 per year. $423 per term. Tuition and fees vary according to campus/location and program.

Trident University International, College of Education, Program in Education, Cypress, CA 90630. Offers adult education (MA Ed); aviation education (MA Ed); children's literacy development (MA Ed); e-learning (MA Ed); early childhood education (MA Ed); enrollment management (MA Ed); higher education (MA Ed); teaching and instruction (MA Ed); training and development (MA Ed). *Program availability:* Part-time, evening/weekend, online learning. *Degree requirements:* For master's, capstone project with integrative paper. *Entrance requirements:* For master's, minimum GPA of 2.5 (students with GPA 3.0 or greater may transfer up to 30% of graduate level credits). Additional exam requirements/recommendations for international students: Required—TOEFL (minimum score 525 paper-based). Electronic applications accepted.

Trinity Washington University, School of Education, Washington, DC 20017-1094. Offers clinical mental health counseling (MA); early childhood education (MAT); educating for change (M Ed); educational administration (MSA); elementary education (MAT); reading (M Ed); school counseling (MA); secondary education (MAT), including English, social studies; special education (MAT). *Accreditation:* NCATE. *Program availability:* Part-time, evening/weekend. *Degree requirements:* For master's, thesis (for some programs), capstone project(s). *Entrance requirements:* For master's, PRAXIS I, minimum GPA of 2.8. Additional exam requirements/recommendations for international students: Required—TOEFL (minimum score 550 paper-based). *Faculty research:* Technology, literacy, special education, organizations, inclusion models.

Troy University, Graduate School, College of Education, Program in Early Childhood Education, Troy, AL 36082. Offers MS, Ed S. *Program availability:* Part-time, evening/weekend, 100% online, blended/hybrid learning. *Faculty:* 2 full-time (both women), 1 (woman) part-time/adjunct. *Students:* 2 full-time (both women), 4 part-time (all women); includes 1 minority (Black or African American, non-Hispanic/Latino). Average age 28. 5 applicants, 40% accepted, 1 enrolled. In 2018, 28 master's, 4 other advanced degrees awarded. *Entrance requirements:* For master's, GRE (minimum score of 850 on old exam or 290 on new exam), GMAT (minimum score of 380), or MAT (minimum score of 385), bachelor's degree; minimum undergraduate GPA of 2.5 or 3.0 on last 30 semester hours, letter of recommendation. Additional exam requirements/recommendations for international students: Required—TOEFL (minimum score 523 paper-based; 70 iBT), IELTS (minimum score 6). *Application deadline:* Applications are processed on a rolling

basis. Application fee: $50. Electronic applications accepted. *Expenses: Tuition, area resident:* Full-time $425; part-time $425 per credit hour. Tuition, state resident: full-time $425; part-time $425 per credit hour. Tuition, nonresident: full-time $850; part-time $850 per credit hour. *International tuition:* $850 full-time. *Required fees:* $50 per semester. Tuition and fees vary according to campus/location and program. *Financial support:* Fellowships, career-related internships or fieldwork, and scholarships/grants available. Support available to part-time students. Financial award applicants required to submit FAFSA. *Unit head:* Dr. Fred Figliano, Chair, Early Childhood Education, 334-808-6509, E-mail: ffigliano@troy.edu. *Application contact:* Jessica A. Kimbro, Assistant Director of Graduate Programs, 334-670-3189, E-mail: jacord@troy.edu.

Universidad del Turabo, Graduate Programs, Programs in Education, Program in Teaching at Primary Level, Gurabo, PR 00778-3030. Offers M Ed. *Entrance requirements:* For master's, GRE, EXADEP, GMAT, interview, official transcript, essay, recommendation letters. Electronic applications accepted.

University at Buffalo, the State University of New York, Graduate School, Graduate School of Education, Department of Learning and Instruction, Buffalo, NY 14260. Offers biology education (Ed M, Certificate); chemistry education (Ed M, Certificate); childhood education (Ed M); childhood education with bilingual extension (Ed M); college teaching (Advanced Certificate); curriculum, instruction and the science of learning (PhD); early childhood education (Ed M); early childhood education with bilingual extension (Ed M); earth science education (Ed M, Certificate); education and technology (Ed M); education studies (Ed M); educational technology and new literacies (Certificate); educational technology and new literacies (Advanced Certificate); elementary education (Ed D); English education (Ed M, Certificate); English education studies (Ed M); English for speakers of other languages (Ed M); foreign and second language education (PhD); French education (Ed M, Certificate); German education (Ed M, Certificate); gifted education (Certificate); Latin education (Ed M, Certificate); literacy education studies (Ed M); literacy specialist (Ed M); literacy teaching and learning (Certificate); mathematics education (Ed M, Certificate); music education (Ed M, Certificate); music education studies (Ed M); music learning theory (Advanced Certificate); online education (Advanced Certificate); physics education (Ed M, Certificate); science and the public (Ed M); social studies education (Ed M, Certificate); Spanish education (Ed M, Certificate); special education (PhD); teaching English to speakers of other languages (Ed M). *Program availability:* Part-time, evening/weekend, 100% online. *Faculty:* 31 full-time (22 women), 41 part-time/adjunct (27 women). *Students:* 161 full-time (107 women), 369 part-time (260 women); includes 76 minority (26 Black or African American, non-Hispanic/Latino; 3 American Indian or Alaska Native, non-Hispanic/Latino; 30 Asian, non-Hispanic/Latino; 14 Hispanic/Latino; 3 Two or more races, non-Hispanic/Latino), 41 international. Average age 34. 368 applicants, 70% accepted, 179 enrolled. In 2018, 100 master's, 26 doctorates, 19 other advanced degrees awarded. *Degree requirements:* For master's, comprehensive exam; for doctorate, thesis/dissertation, research analysis exam, research experience. *Entrance requirements:* For master's, letters of reference; for doctorate, GRE General Test or MAT, interview, writing sample, letters of recommendation. Additional exam requirements/recommendations for international students: Required—TOEFL (minimum score 600 paper-based; 96 iBT), IELTS (minimum score 6.5), PTE (minimum score 55). *Application deadline:* For fall admission, 2/1 priority date for domestic and international students; for spring admission, 11/15 priority date for domestic students, 10/1 for international students. Applications are processed on a rolling basis. Application fee: $50. Electronic applications accepted. *Financial support:* In 2018–19, 42 fellowships (averaging $5,181 per year), 44 research assistantships with tuition reimbursements (averaging $10,908 per year) were awarded; teaching assistantships, career-related internships or fieldwork, Federal Work-Study, institutionally sponsored loans, scholarships/grants, tuition waivers (full and partial), and unspecified assistantships also available. Financial award application deadline: 2/28; financial award applicants required to submit FAFSA. *Faculty research:* Science assessment, foreign language teaching and learning, early learning, new literacies, gender and education. *Total annual research expenditures:* $413,233. *Unit head:* Dr. Julie Gorlewski, Department Chair, 716-645-2455, Fax: 716-645-3161, E-mail: jgorlews@buffalo.edu. *Application contact:* Renad Aref, Assistant Director of Admission Recruitment, 716-645-2110, Fax: 716-645-7937, E-mail: gseinfo@buffalo.edu.
Website: http://ed.buffalo.edu/teaching.html

The University of Alabama at Birmingham, School of Education, Program in Early Childhood Education, Birmingham, AL 35294. Offers MA Ed, PhD. *Accreditation:* NCATE. *Degree requirements:* For master's, comprehensive exam, thesis optional; for doctorate, thesis/dissertation. *Entrance requirements:* For master's, GRE General Test or MAT; for doctorate, GRE General Test, MAT, minimum GPA of 3.25, at least 3 years' teaching experience, essay, recommendations, interview. Electronic applications accepted. *Expenses: Tuition, area resident:* Full-time $8100; part-time $8100 per year. Tuition, state resident: full-time $8100. Tuition, nonresident: full-time $19,188; part-time $19,188 per year. Tuition and fees vary according to program.

University of Alaska Anchorage, School of Education, Program in Special Education, Anchorage, AK 99508. Offers early childhood special education (M Ed); special education (M Ed, Certificate). *Program availability:* Part-time. *Degree requirements:* For master's, comprehensive exam (for some programs), thesis or alternative. *Entrance requirements:* For master's, GRE or MAT, interview, minimum GPA of 2.75. Additional exam requirements/recommendations for international students: Required—TOEFL (minimum score 550 paper-based). *Faculty research:* Mild disabilities, substance abuse issues for educators, partnerships to improve at-risk youth, analysis of planning models for teachers in special education.

University of Arkansas, Graduate School, College of Education and Health Professions, Department of Curriculum and Instruction, Program in Childhood Education, Fayetteville, AR 72701. Offers MAT. *Accreditation:* NCATE. In 2018, 1 master's awarded. *Application deadline:* For fall admission, 8/1 for domestic students, 4/1 for international students; for spring admission, 12/1 for domestic students, 10/1 for international students; for summer admission, 4/15 for domestic students, 3/1 for international students. Applications are processed on a rolling basis. Application fee: $60. Electronic applications accepted. *Financial support:* Fellowships, research assistantships, and teaching assistantships available. *Unit head:* Dr. Cheryl Murphy, Department Head, 479-575-5111, Fax: 479-575-2492, E-mail: cmurphy@uark.edu. *Application contact:* Jason Endacott, CIED Graduate Program Coordinator, 479-575-2657, Fax: 479-575-6676, E-mail: jendacot@uark.edu.
Website: http://cied.uark.edu/

University of Bridgeport, School of Education, Department of Education, Bridgeport, CT 06604. Offers education (MS); educational management (Ed D, Diploma), including intermediate administrator or supervisor (Diploma), leadership (Ed D); elementary education (MS, Diploma), including early childhood education, elementary education; middle school education (MS); music education (MS); remedial reading and language arts (Diploma); secondary education (MS, Diploma), including computer specialist (Diploma), international education (Diploma), reading specialist, secondary education. *Program availability:* Part-time, evening/weekend. *Degree requirements:* For master's, final exam, final project, or thesis; for doctorate, comprehensive exam, thesis/dissertation; for Diploma, thesis or alternative, final project. *Entrance requirements:* For master's, minimum undergraduate QPA of 2.67; for doctorate, GRE, MAT; for Diploma, GRE General Test or MAT, minimum graduate QPA of 3.0. Additional exam requirements/recommendations for international students: Recommended—TOEFL (minimum score 550 paper-based; 80 iBT), IELTS (minimum score 6.5). Electronic applications accepted. *Expenses:* Contact institution.

University of Central Missouri, The Graduate School, Warrensburg, MO 64093. Offers accountancy (MA); accounting (MBA); applied mathematics (MS); aviation safety (MA); biology (MS); business administration (MBA); career and technical education leadership (MS); college student personnel administration (MS); communication (MA); computer science (MS); counseling (MS); criminal justice (MS); educational leadership (Ed D); educational technology (MS); elementary and early childhood education (MSE); English (MA); environmental studies (MA); finance (MBA); history (MA); human services/educational technology (Ed S); human services/learning resources (Ed S); human services/professional counseling (Ed S); industrial hygiene (MS); industrial management (MS); information systems (MBA); information technology (MS); kinesiology (MS); library science and information services (MS); literacy education (MSE); marketing (MBA); mathematics (MS); music (MA); occupational safety management (MS); psychology (MS); rural family nursing (MS); school administration (MSE); social gerontology (MS); sociology (MA); special education (MSE); speech language pathology (MS); superintendency (Ed S); teaching (MAT); teaching English as a second language (MA); technology (MS); technology management (PhD); theatre (MA). *Accreditation:* ASHA. *Program availability:* Part-time, 100% online, blended/hybrid learning. *Degree requirements:* For master's and Ed S, comprehensive exam (for some programs), thesis (for some programs). *Entrance requirements:* Additional exam requirements/recommendations for international students: Required—TOEFL (minimum score 550 paper-based; 79 iBT). Electronic applications accepted.

University of Central Oklahoma, The Jackson College of Graduate Studies, College of Education and Professional Studies, Department of Curriculum and Instruction, Edmond, OK 73034-5209. Offers bilingual education/teaching English as a second language (M Ed); early childhood education (M Ed); elementary education (M Ed). *Program availability:* Part-time. *Degree requirements:* For master's, comprehensive exam (for some programs), thesis optional. *Entrance requirements:* Additional exam requirements/recommendations for international students: Required—TOEFL (minimum score 550 paper-based; 79 iBT), IELTS (minimum score 6.5). Electronic applications accepted.

University of Colorado Denver, School of Education and Human Development, Early Childhood Education Program, Denver, CO 80217. Offers early childhood education (MA); special education (MA). *Accreditation:* NCATE. *Program availability:* Part-time, evening/weekend, online learning. *Degree requirements:* For master's, comprehensive exam, fieldwork, practica, 40 credit hours. *Entrance requirements:* For master's, GRE or MAT (if GPA is below 2.75), minimum GPA of 2.75, resume, three letters of recommendation, documented experience with young children, transcripts from all previous colleges/universities attended. Additional exam requirements/recommendations for international students: Required—TOEFL (minimum score 537 paper-based; 75 iBT); Recommended—IELTS (minimum score 6.5). Electronic applications accepted. *Expenses:* Tuition, state resident: full-time $6786; part-time $337 per credit hour. Tuition, nonresident: full-time $22,590; part-time $1255 per credit hour. *Required fees:* $1231; $137 per credit hour. Tuition and fees vary according to program and reciprocity agreements. *Faculty research:* Early childhood growth and development, faculty development, adult learning, gender and equity issues, research methodology.

University of Colorado Denver, School of Education and Human Development, Program in Educational Leadership and Innovation, Denver, CO 80217. Offers educational studies and research (PhD), including administrative leadership and policy, early childhood special education, math education, research, assessment and evaluation, science education, urban ecologies. *Program availability:* Part-time, evening/weekend. *Degree requirements:* For doctorate, comprehensive exam, thesis/dissertation, 75 credit hours (for PhD). *Entrance requirements:* For doctorate, GRE or equivalent, resume or curriculum vitae, letters of recommendation, master's degree or equivalent, completion of basic or advanced statistics course with minimum B grade. Additional exam requirements/recommendations for international students: Required—TOEFL (minimum score 537 paper-based; 75 iBT); Recommended—IELTS (minimum score 6.5). Electronic applications accepted. *Expenses:* Tuition, state resident: full-time $6786; part-time $337 per credit hour. Tuition, nonresident: full-time $22,590; part-time $1255 per credit hour. *Required fees:* $1231; $137 per credit hour. Tuition and fees vary according to program and reciprocity agreements. *Faculty research:* Administrative leadership and policy studies, early childhood education, research in diversity, paraprofessionals in education, urban schools lab.

University of Colorado Denver, School of Education and Human Development, Program in Education and Human Development, Denver, CO 80217. Offers administrative leadership and policy (PhD); assessment (MA); early childhood special education/early childhood education (PhD); family science and human development (PhD); human development and family relations (MA); learning (MA); mathematics education (PhD); research and evaluation methods (MA); research, assessment and evaluation (PhD); science education (PhD); urban ecologies (PhD). MA program also offered in partnership with Boulder Journey School, Friends School and Stanley British Primary School. *Program availability:* Part-time, evening/weekend. *Degree requirements:* For master's, comprehensive exam, 9 hours of core courses embedded within a minimum of 36 to 38 hours of relevant coursework, including an educational psychology practicum, independent study project or thesis (recommended). *Entrance requirements:* For master's, GRE if undergraduate GPA below 2.75, resume, three letters of recommendation, transcripts. Additional exam requirements/recommendations for international students: Required—TOEFL (minimum score 537 paper-based; 75 iBT); Recommended—IELTS (minimum score 6.5). Electronic applications accepted. *Expenses:* Contact institution. *Faculty research:* Crisis response and intervention, school violence prevention, immigrant experience, educational environments for English language learners, culturally competent assessment and intervention, child and youth suicide.

University of Dayton, Department of Teacher Education, Dayton, OH 45469. Offers adolescence to young adult education (MS Ed); early childhood leadership and advocacy (MS Ed); interdisciplinary education (MS Ed), including visual arts; interdisciplinary education studies (MS Ed); leadership in educational systems (MS Ed); literacy (MS Ed); mathematics education (MS Ed); middle childhood education (MS Ed); multi-age education (MS Ed), including world languages; music education (MS Ed); teacher as leader (MS Ed); teacher education (MS Ed); technology-enhanced learning (MS Ed); trans-disciplinary early childhood education (MS Ed). *Program availability:* Part-time, 100% online. *Degree requirements:* For master's, variable foreign language requirement, thesis or alternative, internship (for teaching licensure or endorsement). *Entrance requirements:* For master's, GRE (minimum score of 149 verbal, 4 on writing) or MAT (minimum score of 396) if undergraduate GPA was under 2.75, minimum GPA of 2.75, 3 letters of recommendation, personal statement or resume, official transcripts. Additional exam requirements/recommendations for international students: Required—TOEFL (minimum score 550 paper-based; 80 iBT); Recommended—IELTS (minimum score 6.5). Electronic applications accepted. *Expenses:* Contact institution. *Faculty research:* Social emotional learning, culturally responsive teaching, urban teaching, literacy, instructional strategies, pre-service teacher education preparation.

Early Childhood Education

University of Denver, Morgridge College of Education, Denver, CO 80208. Offers child, family and school psychology (MA, PhD, Ed S); counseling psychology (MA, PhD); curriculum and instruction (MA, Ed D, PhD); curriculum instruction and teaching (Certificate); early childhood special education (MA, Certificate); educational leadership and policy studies (MA, Ed D, PhD, Certificate); higher education (Ed D, PhD); library and information science (MLIS); research methods and statistics (MA, PhD). *Accreditation:* ALA; APA (one or more programs are accredited). *Program availability:* Part-time, evening/weekend, online learning. *Faculty:* 49 full-time (35 women), 33 part-time/adjunct (20 women). *Students:* 509 full-time (400 women), 365 part-time (277 women); includes 236 minority (53 Black or African American, non-Hispanic/Latino; 6 American Indian or Alaska Native, non-Hispanic/Latino; 28 Asian, non-Hispanic/Latino; 116 Hispanic/Latino; 33 Two or more races, non-Hispanic/Latino), 56 international. Average age 31. 1,372 applicants, 57% accepted, 382 enrolled. In 2018, 258 master's, 41 doctorates, 162 other advanced degrees awarded. Terminal master's awarded for partial completion of doctoral program. *Degree requirements:* For master's, comprehensive exam (for some programs); for doctorate, comprehensive exam (for some programs), thesis/dissertation. *Entrance requirements:* For master's, GRE General Test or GMAT, bachelors degree; transcripts; two letters of recommendation; personal statement; resume; for doctorate, GRE General Test or GMAT, Masters degree; transcripts; two letters of recommendation; personal statement(s); resume. Additional exam requirements/recommendations for international students: Required—TOEFL (minimum score 550 paper-based; 80 iBT). *Application deadline:* Applications are processed on a rolling basis. Application fee: $65. Electronic applications accepted. *Expenses:* $33,183 per year full-time. *Financial support:* In 2018–19, 690 students received support, including 29 research assistantships with tuition reimbursements available (averaging $11,465 per year), 9 teaching assistantships with tuition reimbursements available (averaging $2,527 per year); career-related internships or fieldwork, Federal Work-Study, institutionally sponsored loans, scholarships/grants, and unspecified assistantships also available. Support available to part-time students. Financial award application deadline: 2/15; financial award applicants required to submit FAFSA. *Faculty research:* Early childhood education, educational leadership, access and opportunity to postsecondary education, marriage and family therapy, data management and archival research. *Total annual research expenditures:* $2.3 million. *Unit head:* Dr. Karen Riley, Dean, 303-871-3665, E-mail: karen.riley@du.edu. *Application contact:* Jodi Dye, Director of Admissions, 303-871-2510, E-mail: jodi.dye@du.edu.
Website: http://morgridge.du.edu

University of Florida, Graduate School, College of Education, School of Special Education, School Psychology and Early Childhood Studies, Gainesville, FL 32611. Offers early childhood education (M Ed, MAE); school psychology (M Ed, MAE, Ed D, PhD, Ed S); special education (M Ed, MAE, Ed D, PhD, Ed S). *Accreditation:* NCATE. *Program availability:* Part-time, evening/weekend, online learning. *Degree requirements:* For master's, comprehensive exam (for some programs), thesis (MAE); for doctorate, comprehensive exam, thesis/dissertation. *Entrance requirements:* For master's and doctorate, GRE General Test, minimum GPA of 3.0; for Ed S, GRE General Test. Additional exam requirements/recommendations for international students: Required—TOEFL (minimum score 550 paper-based; 80 iBT), IELTS (minimum score 6). Electronic applications accepted. *Faculty research:* Teacher quality/teacher education, early childhood, autism, academic and behavioral assessment and interventions.

University of Hartford, College of Education, Nursing, and Health Professions, Program in Early Childhood Education, West Hartford, CT 06117-1599. Offers M Ed. *Accreditation:* NCATE. *Program availability:* Part-time, evening/weekend. *Degree requirements:* For master's, comprehensive exam. *Entrance requirements:* For master's, PRAXIS I or waiver, interview, 2 letters of recommendation. Additional exam requirements/recommendations for international students: Required—TOEFL (minimum score 550 paper-based). Electronic applications accepted.

University of Hawaii at Manoa, Office of Graduate Education, College of Education, Department of Curriculum Studies, Program in Early Childhood Education, Honolulu, HI 96822. Offers M Ed. *Accreditation:* NCATE. *Program availability:* Part-time. *Degree requirements:* For master's, thesis optional. *Entrance requirements:* Additional exam requirements/recommendations for international students: Required—TOEFL (minimum score 580 paper-based; 92 iBT), IELTS (minimum score 5).

University of Houston–Clear Lake, School of Education, Program in Curriculum and Instruction, Houston, TX 77058-1002. Offers curriculum and instruction (MS); early childhood education (MS); reading (MS); school library and information science (MS). *Program availability:* Part-time, evening/weekend. *Degree requirements:* For master's, thesis (for some programs). *Entrance requirements:* For master's, GRE or minimum GPA of 3.0 in last 60 hours. Additional exam requirements/recommendations for international students: Required—TOEFL (minimum score 550 paper-based). Electronic applications accepted.

University of Illinois at Chicago, College of Education, Department of Educational Psychology, Chicago, IL 60607-7128. Offers early childhood education (M Ed); educational psychology (PhD); measurement, evaluation, statistics, and assessment (M Ed); youth development (M Ed). *Program availability:* Part-time, online learning. *Faculty research:* Children's construction of morality, development of resilience in the face of enduring economical difficulties, cognition and cognitive development, test fairness.

The University of Kansas, Graduate Studies, School of Education, Department of Special Education, Lawrence, KS 66045. Offers autism spectrum disorder (Certificate); early childhood unified (MS Ed); special and inclusive education leadership (Certificate); special education (PhD). *Accreditation:* NCATE. *Program availability:* Part-time, online learning. *Students:* 60 full-time (50 women), 295 part-time (257 women); includes 51 minority (17 Black or African American, non-Hispanic/Latino; 12 Asian, non-Hispanic/Latino; 12 Hispanic/Latino; 1 Native Hawaiian or other Pacific Islander, non-Hispanic/Latino; 9 Two or more races, non-Hispanic/Latino), 19 international. Average age 34. 189 applicants, 77% accepted, 123 enrolled. In 2018, 136 master's, 7 doctorates, 34 other advanced degrees awarded. *Entrance requirements:* For master's, minimum GPA of 3.0, official transcripts, 3 letters of reference, professional resume; for doctorate, GRE General Test, official transcripts, 3 letters of reference, professional resume, professional writing sample. Additional exam requirements/recommendations for international students: Required—TOEFL, IELTS. *Application deadline:* For fall admission, 8/1 for domestic students; for spring admission, 12/13 for domestic students. Application fee: $65 ($85 for international students). Electronic applications accepted. *Financial support:* Fellowships, research assistantships, teaching assistantships, Federal Work-Study, scholarships/grants, and unspecified assistantships available. Support available to part-time students. Financial award application deadline: 2/21; financial award applicants required to submit FAFSA. *Faculty research:* Autism spectrum disorders, learning disabilities research, leadership development, qualitative research and evaluation. *Unit head:* Michael L. Wehmeyer, Chair, 785-864-0723, E-mail: wehmeyer@ku.edu. *Application contact:* Shaunna Price, Graduate Admission Contact, 785-864-4342, E-mail: shaunna.price@ku.edu.
Website: http://specialedu.ku.edu/

University of Kentucky, Graduate School, College of Education, Program in Special Education, Lexington, KY 40506-0032. Offers early childhood (MS Ed); rehabilitation counseling (MRC, PhD); special education (MS Ed, PhD). *Accreditation:* CORE; NCATE. Terminal master's awarded for partial completion of doctoral program. *Degree requirements:* For master's, comprehensive exam, thesis optional; for doctorate, comprehensive exam, thesis/dissertation. *Entrance requirements:* For master's, GRE General Test, minimum undergraduate GPA of 2.75; for doctorate, GRE General Test, minimum graduate GPA of 3.0. Additional exam requirements/recommendations for international students: Required—TOEFL (minimum score 550 paper-based). Electronic applications accepted. *Faculty research:* Applied behavior analysis applications in special education, single subject research design in classroom settings, transition research across life span, rural special education personnel.

University of Louisiana at Lafayette, College of Education, Department of Educational Curriculum and Instruction, Program in Curriculum and Instruction, Lafayette, LA 70504. Offers instructional specialist (M Ed); K-8 mathematics education (M Ed); non-public school administration (M Ed); special education diagnostics (M Ed); teacher researcher (M Ed). *Accreditation:* NCATE. *Entrance requirements:* For master's, GRE General Test, teaching certificate. Additional exam requirements/recommendations for international students: Required—TOEFL (minimum score 550 paper-based). Electronic applications accepted.

University of Louisville, Graduate School, College of Education and Human Development, Departments of Early Childhood and Elementary Education, Middle and Secondary Education, and Special Education, Louisville, KY 40292-0001. Offers art education (MAT); autism and applied behavior analysis (Certificate); curriculum and instruction (PhD); early elementary education (MAT); exercise physiology (MS); health and physical education (MAT); health professions education (Certificate); higher education (MA); human resources and organization development (MS); instructional technology (M Ed); interdisciplinary early childhood education (MAT); middle school education (MAT); music education (MAT); secondary education (MAT); special education (MAT); sport administration (MS); teacher leadership (M Ed). *Program availability:* Part-time, evening/weekend, 100% online, blended/hybrid learning. *Faculty:* 97 full-time (64 women), 131 part-time/adjunct (86 women). *Students:* 109 full-time (72 women), 139 part-time (87 women); includes 43 minority (18 Black or African American, non-Hispanic/Latino; 6 Asian, non-Hispanic/Latino; 10 Hispanic/Latino; 9 Two or more races, non-Hispanic/Latino), 9 international. Average age 29. 108 applicants, 75% accepted, 59 enrolled. In 2018, 64 master's awarded. Terminal master's awarded for partial completion of doctoral program. *Degree requirements:* For master's, comprehensive exam (for some programs), thesis optional; for doctorate, comprehensive exam (for some programs), thesis/dissertation. *Entrance requirements:* For master's, GRE (for most programs), PRAXIS (for educator preparation programs), professional statement, recommendation letters, resume, transcripts; for doctorate and Certificate, GRE, professional statement, recommendation letters, resume, transcripts. Additional exam requirements/recommendations for international students: Required—TOEFL (minimum score 550 paper-based; 79 iBT); Recommended—IELTS (minimum score 6.5). *Application deadline:* For fall admission, 6/1 priority date for domestic students, 5/1 priority date for international students; for spring admission, 10/1 for domestic students, 11/1 priority date for international students; for summer admission, 3/1 priority date for domestic students, 4/1 priority date for international students. Application fee: $65. *Expenses: Tuition, area resident:* Full-time $6500; part-time $723 per credit hour. Tuition, state resident: full-time $6500. Tuition, nonresident: full-time $13,557; part-time $1507 per credit hour. Tuition and fees vary according to course load and program. *Financial support:* In 2018–19, 144 students received support, including fellowships with full tuition reimbursements available (averaging $21,024 per year), research assistantships with full tuition reimbursements available (averaging $21,024 per year), teaching assistantships with full tuition reimbursements available (averaging $21,024 per year); Federal Work-Study, scholarships/grants, health care benefits, tuition waivers (full), and unspecified assistantships also available. Financial award application deadline: 3/1; financial award applicants required to submit FAFSA. *Faculty research:* Children's early reading and writing development, crelevance of basic facts in elementary mathematics instruction, clinical model of teacher education, cultural and linguistic context of diverse learners, and STEM-integrated curriculum design and development. STEM teaching and learning, content literacy for English language learners, social justice in teacher education, adolescent literacy, mathematics teacher development. Classroom and behavior management; moderate/severe disabilities, autism. *Unit head:* Dr. Amy Lingo, Interim Dean, 502-852-3235, Fax: 502-852-1464, E-mail: cehdinfo@louisville.edu. *Application contact:* Dr. Margaret Pentecost, Assistant Dean for Graduate Student Success, 502-852-6437, Fax: 502-852-1417, E-mail: gedadm@louisville.edu.
Website: http://louisville.edu/delphi

University of Maine, Graduate School, College of Education and Human Development, School of Learning and Teaching, Orono, ME 04469. Offers counselor education (M Ed, MA, MS, CAS); early childhood teacher (CGS); education (PhD), including counselor education, literacy education, prevention and intervention studies; elementary education (M Ed, CAS); individualized education (M Ed); literacy education (CAS); response to intervention for behavior (CGS); secondary education (M Ed, CAS); social studies education (M Ed); special education (M Ed, CAS). *Program availability:* Part-time. *Faculty:* 21 full-time (12 women), 37 part-time/adjunct (29 women). *Students:* 113 full-time (96 women), 224 part-time (191 women); includes 11 minority (3 Black or African American, non-Hispanic/Latino; 4 American Indian or Alaska Native, non-Hispanic/Latino; 1 Asian, non-Hispanic/Latino; 2 Hispanic/Latino; 1 Two or more races, non-Hispanic/Latino), 3 international. Average age 37. 195 applicants, 99% accepted, 147 enrolled. In 2018, 82 master's, 2 doctorates, 49 other advanced degrees awarded. *Degree requirements:* For master's, thesis (for some programs); for doctorate, comprehensive exam, thesis/dissertation. *Entrance requirements:* For master's, GRE General Test, MAT. Additional exam requirements/recommendations for international students: Required—TOEFL (minimum score 550 paper-based; 80 iBT), IELTS (minimum score 6.5). *Application deadline:* For fall admission, 2/1 priority date for domestic students. Applications are processed on a rolling basis. Application fee: $65. Electronic applications accepted. *Financial support:* In 2018–19, 22 students received support, including 8 teaching assistantships with full tuition reimbursements available (averaging $1,600 per year); Federal Work-Study, scholarships/grants, and unspecified assistantships also available. Financial award application deadline: 3/1. *Faculty research:* Gender and leadership, virtual reality, using writing to improve performance in athletics, digital citizenship, professional development for special and general education. *Total annual research expenditures:* $2.1 million. *Unit head:* Dr. Jim Artesani, Associate Dean of Accreditation and Graduate Affairs, 207-581-4061. *Application contact:* Scott G. Delcourt, Assistant Vice President for Graduate Studies and Senior Associate Dean, 207-581-3291, Fax: 207-581-3232, E-mail: graduate@maine.edu.
Website: http://umaine.edu/edhd/

University of Maine at Farmington, Graduate Programs in Education, Farmington, ME 04938. Offers early childhood education (MS Ed); educational leadership (MS Ed); instructional technology (M Ed). M Ed offered in collaboration with University of Maine and University of Southern Maine. *Accreditation:* NCATE. *Program availability:* Part-time-only, evening/weekend, 100% online, blended/hybrid learning. *Degree*

requirements: For master's, thesis, capstone research project. *Entrance requirements:* For master's, baccalaureate degree from accredited institution, valid teaching certificate or professional experience in education. Additional exam requirements/recommendations for international students: Required—TOEFL. Electronic applications accepted. *Expenses:* Contact institution. *Faculty research:* Teacher leadership, school improvement strategies, technology integration.

University of Maryland, Baltimore County, The Graduate School, College of Arts, Humanities and Social Sciences, Department of Education, Program in Teaching, Baltimore, MD 21250. Offers early childhood education (MAT); elementary education (MAT); teaching (MAT), including art, biology, chemistry, choral music, classical foreign language, dance, earth/space science, English, instrumental music, mathematics, modern foreign language, physical science, physics, social studies, theatre. *Program availability:* Part-time, evening/weekend. *Degree requirements:* For master's, comprehensive exam (for some programs), thesis (for some programs). *Entrance requirements:* For master's, PRAXIS Core Examination or GRE (minimum score of 1000), minimum GPA of 3.0. Additional exam requirements/recommendations for international students: Required—TOEFL. Electronic applications accepted. *Faculty research:* STEM teacher education, culturally sensitive pedagogy, ESOL/bilingual education, early childhood education, language, literacy and culture.

University of Massachusetts Amherst, Graduate School, College of Education, Program in Education, Amherst, MA 01003. Offers bilingual, English as a second language, and multicultural education (M Ed, Ed S); child study and early education (M Ed); children, families and schools (Ed D, Ed S); early childhood and elementary teacher education (M Ed); educational leadership (M Ed); educational policy and leadership (Ed D); higher education (M Ed); international education (M Ed); language, literacy and culture (Ed D); learning, media and technology (M Ed, Ed S); mathematics, science, and learning technologies (Ed D); reading and writing (M Ed); research, educational measurement and psychometrics (Ed D); school counselor education (M Ed, Ed S); school psychology (Ed S); science education (Ed S); secondary teacher education (M Ed); social justice education (M Ed, Ed D, Ed S); special education (M Ed, Ed D, Ed S); teacher education and school improvement (Ed D, Ed S). *Accreditation:* NCATE. *Program availability:* Part-time, online learning. Terminal master's awarded for partial completion of doctoral program. *Degree requirements:* For doctorate, comprehensive exam, thesis/dissertation. *Entrance requirements:* Additional exam requirements/recommendations for international students: Required—TOEFL (minimum score 550 paper-based; 80 iBT), IELTS (minimum score 6.5). Electronic applications accepted.

University of Massachusetts Boston, College of Education and Human Development, Program in Early Childhood Education and Care, Boston, MA 02125-3393. Offers PhD. *Students:* 12 full-time (11 women), 2 part-time (both women); includes 1 minority (Hispanic/Latino), 6 international. Average age 34. 7 applicants, 71% accepted, 5 enrolled. *Application deadline:* For fall admission, 1/15 for domestic students. Application fee: $60 ($100 for international students). Electronic applications accepted. *Expenses: Tuition, area resident:* Full-time $17,896. Tuition, state resident: full-time $17,896. Tuition, nonresident: full-time $34,932. *International tuition:* $34,932 full-time. *Required fees:* $355. *Unit head:* Dr. Lianna Pizzo, Assistant Professor, 617-287.4517, E-mail: lianna.pizzo@umb.edu. *Application contact:* Graduate Admissions Coordinator, 617-287-6400, Fax: 617-287-6236, E-mail: graduate.admissions@umb.edu.

University of Memphis, Graduate School, College of Education, Department of Instruction and Curriculum Leadership, Memphis, TN 38152. Offers advanced studies in teaching and learning (M Ed); applied behavior analysis (Graduate Certificate); autism studies (Graduate Certificate); early childhood education (MAT, MS, Ed D); elementary education (MAT); instruction and curriculum (MS, Ed D); instruction design and technology (MS, Ed D); instructional design and technology (Graduate Certificate); literacy, leadership, and coaching (Graduate Certificate); reading (MS, Ed D); school library information specialist (Graduate Certificate); secondary education (MAT); special education (MAT, MS, Ed D); STEM teacher leadership (Graduate Certificate); urban education (Graduate Certificate). *Accreditation:* NCATE (one or more programs are accredited). *Program availability:* Part-time. *Students:* 62 full-time (45 women), 412 part-time (326 women); includes 209 minority (179 Black or African American, non-Hispanic/Latino; 1 American Indian or Alaska Native, non-Hispanic/Latino; 5 Asian, non-Hispanic/Latino; 17 Hispanic/Latino; 7 Two or more races, non-Hispanic/Latino), 4 international. Average age 35. 195 applicants, 91% accepted, 143 enrolled. In 2018, 122 master's, 13 doctorates, 29 other advanced degrees awarded. Terminal master's awarded for partial completion of doctoral program. *Degree requirements:* For master's, comprehensive exam, thesis or alternative; for doctorate, comprehensive exam, thesis/dissertation. *Entrance requirements:* For master's, GRE General Test, PRAXIS, minimum GPA of 2.5, letters of reference; for doctorate, GRE General Test, GRE Subject Test, 2 years of teaching experience, letters of reference, statement of purpose, interview. Additional exam requirements/recommendations for international students: Required—TOEFL (minimum score 550 paper-based; 79 iBT). *Application deadline:* For fall admission, 4/1 priority date for domestic students; for spring admission, 10/1 priority date for domestic students; for summer admission, 2/1 priority date for domestic students. Applications are processed on a rolling basis. Application fee: $35 ($60 for international students). Electronic applications accepted. *Expenses: Tuition, area resident:* Full-time $10,240; part-time $503 per credit hour. Tuition, state resident: full-time $10,464. Tuition, nonresident: full-time $20,224; part-time $991 per credit hour. *Required fees:* $850; $106 per credit hour. *Financial support:* Research assistantships with full tuition reimbursements, teaching assistantships with full tuition reimbursements, career-related internships or fieldwork, Federal Work-Study, institutionally sponsored loans, scholarships/grants, traineeships, and unspecified assistantships available. Support available to part-time students. Financial award application deadline: 2/1; financial award applicants required to submit FAFSA. *Faculty research:* Effective urban teachers, preparation and retention of urban teachers, technology utilization in schools, field-based teacher preparation programs, effective use of online instruction. *Unit head:* Dr. Christian Mueller, Chair, 901-678-2365, E-mail: cemuellr@memphis.edu. *Application contact:* Dr. Lee Allen, Director of Graduate Programs, 901-678-4073, E-mail: allenlee@memphis.edu.
Website: http://www.memphis.edu/icl/

University of Miami, Graduate School, School of Education and Human Development, Department of Teaching and Learning, Program in Early Childhood Special Education, Coral Gables, FL 33124. Offers MS Ed, Ed S. *Program availability:* Part-time, evening/weekend. *Faculty:* 4 full-time (3 women), 6 part-time/adjunct (all women). *Students:* 13 part-time (12 women); includes 10 minority (2 Black or African American, non-Hispanic/Latino; 8 Hispanic/Latino). Average age 35. In 2018, 13 master's awarded. *Degree requirements:* For master's, electronic portfolio. *Entrance requirements:* For master's, GRE General Test. Additional exam requirements/recommendations for international students: Required—TOEFL (minimum score 550 paper-based; 80 iBT); Recommended—IELTS (minimum score 6.5). *Application deadline:* Applications are processed on a rolling basis. Application fee: $75. Electronic applications accepted. *Financial support:* Scholarships/grants available. Financial award application deadline: 3/1; financial award applicants required to submit FAFSA. *Unit head:* Dr. Elizabeth Harry, Professor, 305-284-4961, Fax: 305-284-6998, E-mail: bharry@miami.edu. *Application contact:* Lois Heffernan, Graduate Admissions Coordinator, 305-284-2167, E-mail: lheffernan@miami.edu.
Website: http://www.education.miami.edu

University of Michigan–Dearborn, College of Education, Health, and Human Services, Master of Arts Program in Early Childhood Education, Dearborn, MI 48126. Offers MA. *Program availability:* Part-time, evening/weekend. *Faculty:* 2 full-time (both women), 2 part-time/adjunct (both women). *Students:* 26 part-time (all women); includes 8 minority (4 Black or African American, non-Hispanic/Latino; 3 Hispanic/Latino; 1 Two or more races, non-Hispanic/Latino). Average age 37. 7 applicants, 86% accepted, 5 enrolled. In 2018, 8 master's awarded. *Entrance requirements:* Additional exam requirements/recommendations for international students: Required—TOEFL (minimum score 560 paper-based; 84 iBT), IELTS (minimum score 6.5). *Application deadline:* For fall admission, 8/1 priority date for domestic students, 5/1 for international students; for winter admission, 12/1 priority date for domestic students, 9/1 for international students; for spring admission, 4/1 priority date for domestic students, 1/1 for international students. Applications are processed on a rolling basis. Application fee: $60. Electronic applications accepted. *Expenses:* $12,140 per academic year (typical full-time in-state); $20,708 per academic year (typical full-time out-of-state). *Financial support:* In 2018–19, 2 students received support. Career-related internships or fieldwork and scholarships/grants available. Financial award application deadline: 3/1; financial award applicants required to submit FAFSA. *Faculty research:* Place based education, curriculum development, early childhood learning and development, literacy, multicultural education. *Unit head:* Dr. Paul Fossum, Director, Master's Programs, 313-593-0982, E-mail: pfossum@umich.edu. *Application contact:* Office of Graduate Studies, 313-583-6321, E-mail: umd-graduatestudies@umich.edu.
Website: http://umdearborn.edu/cehhs/cehhs_maeced/

University of Michigan–Flint, School of Education and Human Services, Department of Education, Flint, MI 48502-1950. Offers curriculum and instruction (Ed S); early childhood education (MA); education (Ed D); educational leadership (Ed S); educational technology (MA), including curriculum and instruction, developer; literacy education (MA); secondary education with certification (MA). *Program availability:* Part-time, evening/weekend, online only, 100% online, mixed mode format (for some programs). *Faculty:* 16 full-time (10 women), 28 part-time/adjunct (14 women). *Students:* 31 full-time (23 women), 179 part-time (135 women); includes 54 minority (42 Black or African American, non-Hispanic/Latino; 3 Asian, non-Hispanic/Latino; 4 Hispanic/Latino; 1 Native Hawaiian or other Pacific Islander, non-Hispanic/Latino; 4 Two or more races, non-Hispanic/Latino), 1 international. Average age 39. 133 applicants, 72% accepted, 61 enrolled. In 2018, 60 master's awarded. *Degree requirements:* For master's, thesis optional; for doctorate, thesis/dissertation. *Entrance requirements:* For master's, bachelor's degree from regionally-accredited institution, minimum overall undergraduate GPA of 3.0 on 4.0 scale; for doctorate, completion of Eds minimum overall graduate GPA of 3.3 (6.0 on a 9.0 scale) or equivalent; at least 3 years of work experience in a P-16 educational institution or in an education-related position; for Ed S, MA or MS in education-related field from accredited institution; minimum overall graduate GPA of 3.0 (6.0 on a 9.0 scale) or equivalent; at least 3 years of work experience in an educational setting. Additional exam requirements/recommendations for international students: Required—TOEFL (minimum score 84 iBT), IELTS (minimum score 6.5). *Application deadline:* For fall admission, 8/1 for domestic students, 5/1 for international students; for winter admission, 11/15 for domestic students, 9/15 for international students; for spring admission, 3/15 for domestic students, 1/15 for international students; for summer admission, 5/15 for domestic students. Applications are processed on a rolling basis. Application fee: $55. Electronic applications accepted. *Expenses:* Contact institution. *Financial support:* Federal Work-Study, scholarships/grants, and unspecified assistantships available. Financial award application deadline: 3/1; financial award applicants required to submit FAFSA. *Unit head:* Dr. Mary Jo Finney, Department Chair/Associate Professor, 810-766-6617, E-mail: mjfinney@umflint.edu. *Application contact:* Matt Bohlen, Director of Graduate Admissions, 810-762-3171, Fax: 810-766-6789, E-mail: mbohlen@umflint.edu.
Website: https://www.umflint.edu/education/graduate-programs

University of Minnesota, Twin Cities Campus, Graduate School, College of Education and Human Development, Department of Educational Psychology, Minneapolis, MN 55455-0213. Offers autism spectrum disorder (Certificate); counseling and student personnel psychology (MA); early childhood special education (M Ed); psychological foundations of education (MA, PhD); quantitative methods in education (MA, PhD); school psychology (MA, PhD, Ed S); special education (M Ed, MA, PhD); talent development and gifted education (Certificate). *Accreditation:* APA (one or more programs are accredited). *Faculty:* 29 full-time (13 women). *Students:* 243 full-time (181 women), 38 part-time (31 women); includes 45 minority (6 Black or African American, non-Hispanic/Latino; 17 Asian, non-Hispanic/Latino; 12 Hispanic/Latino; 10 Two or more races, non-Hispanic/Latino), 42 international. Average age 29. 278 applicants, 46% accepted, 95 enrolled. In 2018, 100 master's, 21 doctorates, 16 other advanced degrees awarded. Application fee: $75 ($95 for international students). *Financial support:* In 2018–19, 16 fellowships, 65 research assistantships (averaging $13,491 per year), 37 teaching assistantships (averaging $11,583 per year) were awarded. *Faculty research:* Achievement gap; autism; behavioral and social-emotional development; improving skills in mathematics, reading, and comprehension; measuring and analyzing student change. *Total annual research expenditures:* $6.9 million. *Unit head:* Dr. Kristen McMaster, Chair, 612-624-6083, Fax: 612-624-8241, E-mail: mcmas004@umn.edu. *Application contact:* Dr. Panayiota Kendeou, Director of Graduate Studies, 612-626-7814, E-mail: kend0040@umn.edu.
Website: http://www.cehd.umn.edu/EdPsych

University of Minnesota, Twin Cities Campus, Graduate School, College of Education and Human Development, Institute of Child Development, Minneapolis, MN 55455-0213. Offers applied child and adolescent development (MA); developmental psychology (PhD); early childhood education (M Ed). *Program availability:* Online learning. *Faculty:* 15 full-time (8 women). *Students:* 83 full-time (77 women), 11 part-time (all women); includes 18 minority (5 Black or African American, non-Hispanic/Latino; 2 Asian, non-Hispanic/Latino; 7 Hispanic/Latino; 4 Two or more races, non-Hispanic/Latino), 4 international. Average age 28. 181 applicants, 36% accepted, 59 enrolled. In 2018, 23 master's, 3 doctorates awarded. Application fee: $75 ($95 for international students). *Financial support:* In 2018–19, 20 fellowships, 19 research assistantships with full tuition reimbursements (averaging $18,356 per year), 17 teaching assistantships with full tuition reimbursements (averaging $15,438 per year) were awarded. *Faculty research:* Developmental affective and cognitive neuroscience; developmental psychopathology; intervention and prevention science; social and emotional development; cognitive, language, and perceptual development. *Total annual research expenditures:* $7.5 million. *Unit head:* Dr. Megan Gunnar, Director, 612-624-2713, E-mail: gunnar@umn.edu. *Application contact:* Dr. Kathleen Thomas, Director of Graduate Studies, 612-625-3389, E-mail: thoma114@umn.edu.
Website: http://www.cehd.umn.edu/ICD

University of Mississippi, Graduate School, School of Education, University, MS 38677. Offers counselor education (M Ed, PhD); counselor education - play therapy (Ed S); early childhood (M Ed); educational leadership K-12 (M Ed, Ed D, PhD, Ed S);

elementary education (M Ed, Ed D, Ed S); higher education/student personnel (Ed D, PhD); literacy education (M Ed); math education (Ed D); secondary education (M Ed, PhD, Ed S); special education (M Ed, PhD, Ed S); teacher corporations (MA); teacher education (MA). *Accreditation:* NCATE. *Faculty:* 59 full-time (35 women), 34 part-time/adjunct (26 women). *Students:* 169 full-time (137 women), 461 part-time (329 women); includes 199 minority (185 Black or African American, non-Hispanic/Latino; 3 Asian, non-Hispanic/Latino; 7 Hispanic/Latino; 4 Two or more races, non-Hispanic/Latino), 5 international. Average age 33. In 2018, 180 master's, 57 doctorates, 37 other advanced degrees awarded. *Entrance requirements:* For master's, GRE General Test, minimum GPA of 3.0; for doctorate, GRE General Test. Additional exam requirements/recommendations for international students: Required—TOEFL. *Application deadline:* Applications are processed on a rolling basis. Application fee: $50. Electronic applications accepted. *Financial support:* Scholarships/grants available. Financial award application deadline: 3/1; financial award applicants required to submit FAFSA. *Unit head:* Dr. David Rock, Dean, 662-915-7063, Fax: 662-915-7249, E-mail: soe@olemiss.edu. *Application contact:* Temeka Smith, Graduate Activities Specialist for Admissions, 662-915-7474, Fax: 662-915-7577, E-mail: gschool@olemiss.edu.

University of Missouri, Office of Research and Graduate Studies, College of Education, Department of Learning, Teaching and Curriculum, Columbia, MO 65211. Offers agricultural education (M Ed, PhD, Ed S); art education (M Ed, PhD, Ed S); business and office education (M Ed, PhD, Ed S); early childhood education (M Ed, PhD, Ed S); elementary education (M Ed, PhD, Ed S); English education (M Ed, PhD, Ed S); foreign language education (M Ed, PhD, Ed S); health education and promotion (M Ed, PhD); learning and instruction (M Ed); marketing education (M Ed, PhD, Ed S); mathematics education (M Ed, PhD, Ed S); music education (M Ed, PhD, Ed S); reading education (M Ed, PhD, Ed S); science education (M Ed, PhD, Ed S); social studies education (M Ed, PhD, Ed S); vocational education (M Ed, PhD, Ed S). *Program availability:* Part-time. Terminal master's awarded for partial completion of doctoral program. *Entrance requirements:* For master's and Ed S, GRE General Test or MAT, minimum GPA of 3.0; for doctorate, GRE General Test, minimum GPA of 3.0. Additional exam requirements/recommendations for international students: Required—TOEFL.

University of Missouri–St. Louis, College of Education, Department of Educator Preparation, Innovation and Research, St. Louis, MO 63121. Offers elementary education (M Ed), including early childhood, general, reading; secondary education (M Ed), including curriculum and instruction, general, middle level education, reading, teaching English to speakers of other languages (TESOL); special education (M Ed), including autism and developmental disabilities, early childhood special education. *Program availability:* Part-time, evening/weekend. *Degree requirements:* For master's, comprehensive exam. *Entrance requirements:* Additional exam requirements/recommendations for international students: Recommended—TOEFL (minimum score 550 paper-based; 79 iBT), IELTS (minimum score 6.5). Electronic applications accepted.

University of Montana, Graduate School, Phyllis J. Washington College of Education and Human Sciences, Department of Teaching and Learning, Missoula, MT 59812. Offers curriculum and instruction (M Ed, Ed D); early childhood education (M Ed); education (MA); teaching and learning (PhD). *Program availability:* Part-time. *Degree requirements:* For doctorate, thesis/dissertation. *Entrance requirements:* For master's, GRE General Test. Additional exam requirements/recommendations for international students: Required—TOEFL.

University of Nebraska at Kearney, College of Education, Department of Teacher Education, Kearney, NE 68849-0001. Offers curriculum and instruction (MA Ed), including early childhood education, elementary education, English as a second language, instructional effectiveness, reading/special education, secondary education; instructional technology (MS Ed), including information technology, instructional technology, school librarian; reading PK-12 (MA Ed); special education (MA Ed), including advanced practitioner: assistive technology specialist, advanced practitioner: behavioral interventionist, advanced practitioner: inclusive collaboration specialist, gifted, teacher education. *Program availability:* Part-time, evening/weekend, online only, 100% online. *Degree requirements:* For master's, comprehensive exam, thesis optional. *Entrance requirements:* For master's, portfolio or GRE. Additional exam requirements/recommendations for international students: Recommended—TOEFL (minimum score 550 paper-based; 79 iBT), IELTS (minimum score 6.5). Electronic applications accepted. *Expenses:* Contact institution.

University of Nebraska–Lincoln, Graduate College, College of Education and Human Sciences, Department of Child, Youth and Family Studies, Lincoln, NE 68588. Offers child development/early childhood education (MS, PhD); child, youth and family studies (MS); family and consumer sciences education (MS, PhD); family financial planning (MS); family science (MS, PhD); gerontology (PhD); human sciences (PhD), including child, youth and family studies, gerontology, medical family therapy; marriage and family therapy (MS); medical family therapy (PhD); youth development (MS). *Accreditation:* AAMFT/COAMFTE (one or more programs are accredited). *Program availability:* Online learning. *Degree requirements:* For master's, thesis optional. *Entrance requirements:* For master's, GRE. Additional exam requirements/recommendations for international students: Required—TOEFL (minimum score 550 paper-based). Electronic applications accepted. *Faculty research:* Marriage and family therapy, child development/early childhood education, family financial management.

University of Nevada, Las Vegas, Graduate College, College of Education, Department of Educational and Clinical Studies, Las Vegas, NV 89154-3066. Offers addiction studies (Advanced Certificate); counselor education (M Ed, MS), including clinical mental health (MS), school counseling (M Ed); early childhood education (M Ed); early childhood special education (Certificate), including infancy, preschool; English language learning (M Ed); mental health counseling (Advanced Certificate); special education (M Ed, PhD); PhD/JD. *Program availability:* Part-time. *Degree requirements:* For master's, comprehensive exam (for some programs); for doctorate, comprehensive exam, thesis/dissertation; for other advanced degree, final project. *Entrance requirements:* For master's, bachelor's degree; letter of recommendation; statement of purpose; for doctorate, GRE General Test, statement of purpose; writing sample; 3 letters of recommendation. Additional exam requirements/recommendations for international students: Required—TOEFL (minimum score 550 paper-based; 80 iBT), IELTS (minimum score 7). Electronic applications accepted. *Expenses:* Contact institution. *Faculty research:* Multicultural issues in counseling, academic interventions for students with disabilities, establishment of pro-social skills in young children with severe disabilities, inclusive strategies for students with disabilities, language and literacy for English language learners.

University of New England, College of Graduate and Professional Studies, Portland, ME 04005-9526. Offers advanced educational leadership (CAGS); applied nutrition (MS); career and technical education (MS Ed); curriculum and instruction (MS Ed); education (CAGS, Post-Master's Certificate); educational leadership (MS Ed, Ed D); generalist (MS Ed); health informatics (MS, Graduate Certificate); inclusion education (MS Ed); literacy K-12 (MS Ed); medical education leadership (MMEL); public health (MPH, Graduate Certificate); reading specialist (MS Ed); social work (MSW). *Program availability:* Part-time, evening/weekend, online only, 100% online. *Faculty:* 109 part-time/adjunct (78 women). *Students:* 1,207 full-time (972 women), 561 part-time (450 women); includes 411 minority (280 Black or African American, non-Hispanic/Latino; 17 American Indian or Alaska Native, non-Hispanic/Latino; 74 Asian, non-Hispanic/Latino; 25 Hispanic/Latino; 9 Native Hawaiian or other Pacific Islander, non-Hispanic/Latino; 6 Two or more races, non-Hispanic/Latino). Average age 36. 740 applicants, 92% accepted, 494 enrolled. In 2018, 586 master's, 44 doctorates, 85 other advanced degrees awarded. *Application deadline:* Applications are processed on a rolling basis. Electronic applications accepted. *Financial support:* Application deadline: 5/1; applicants required to submit FAFSA. *Unit head:* Dr. Martha Wilson, Dean of the College of Graduate and Professional Studies, 207-221-4985, E-mail: mwilson13@une.edu. *Application contact:* Nicole Lindsay, Director of Online Admissions, 207-221-4966, E-mail: nlindsay1@une.edu.
Website: http://online.une.edu

University of New Hampshire, Graduate School, College of Liberal Arts, Department of Education, Program in Early Childhood Education, Durham, NH 03824. Offers early childhood education (M Ed); early childhood education: special needs (M Ed). *Program availability:* Part-time. *Entrance requirements:* For master's, PRAXIS, Department of Education background check. Additional exam requirements/recommendations for international students: Required—TOEFL (minimum score 550 paper-based; 80 iBT). Electronic applications accepted.

University of New Mexico, Graduate Studies, College of Education, Program in Multicultural Teacher and Childhood Education, Albuquerque, NM 87131-2039. Offers Ed D, PhD. *Accreditation:* NCATE. *Program availability:* Part-time. *Students:* Average age 47. 5 applicants, 20% accepted. In 2018, 1 doctorate awarded. *Degree requirements:* For doctorate, comprehensive exam, thesis/dissertation. *Entrance requirements:* For doctorate, GRE, master's degree, minimum GPA of 3.0, 3 years of teaching experience, 3-5 letters of reference, letter of intent, professional writing sample. Additional exam requirements/recommendations for international students: Required—TOEFL (minimum score 550 paper-based). *Application deadline:* For fall admission, 1/15 priority date for domestic students, 1/15 for international students; for spring admission, 10/30 for domestic and international students. Application fee: $50. Electronic applications accepted. *Financial support:* Fellowships, research assistantships, teaching assistantships with partial tuition reimbursements, scholarships/grants, and unspecified assistantships available. Financial award application deadline: 3/1; financial award applicants required to submit FAFSA. *Faculty research:* Teacher education, clinical preparation, reflective practice, science education, mathematics education, social justice, technology education, media literacy. *Unit head:* Dr. Cheryl Torrez, Department Chair, 505-277-9611, Fax: 505-277-0455, E-mail: ted@unm.edu. *Application contact:* Robert Romero, Program Coordinator, 505-277-0513, Fax: 505-277-0455, E-mail: ted@unm.edu.
Website: https://coe.unm.edu/departments-programs/ifce/ecme/

The University of North Carolina at Chapel Hill, Graduate School, School of Education, Master of Education Program for Experienced Teachers: Early Childhood Intervention and Family Support, Chapel Hill, NC 27599. Offers M Ed. *Accreditation:* NCATE. *Program availability:* Part-time. *Degree requirements:* For master's, comprehensive exam. *Entrance requirements:* For master's, minimum GPA of 3.0 during last 2 years of undergraduate course work. Electronic applications accepted.

The University of North Carolina at Chapel Hill, Graduate School, School of Education, Program in Education, Chapel Hill, NC 27599. Offers culture, curriculum and change (MA, PhD); early childhood, intervention and literacy (MA, PhD); educational psychology, measurement and evaluation (MA, PhD). *Accreditation:* NCATE. *Degree requirements:* For master's, thesis; for doctorate, comprehensive exam, thesis/dissertation. *Entrance requirements:* For master's, GRE General Test, minimum GPA of 3.0 during last 2 years of undergraduates course work; for doctorate, GRE General Test, minimum GPA of 3.0 during last 2 years of undergraduate course work. Additional exam requirements/recommendations for international students: Required—TOEFL (minimum score 550 paper-based). Electronic applications accepted.

The University of North Carolina at Charlotte, Cato College of Education, Interdisciplinary Education Programs, Charlotte, NC 28223-0001. Offers art education (Graduate Certificate); child and family development: early childhood education (MAT); curriculum and instruction (PhD); elementary education (MAT); foreign language education (MAT); middle grades education (MAT); secondary education (MAT); special education (MAT); teaching (Graduate Certificate); teaching English as a second language (MAT); theatre education (Graduate Certificate). *Program availability:* Part-time, 100% online, blended/hybrid learning. *Students:* 70 full-time (55 women), 511 part-time (414 women); includes 228 minority (160 Black or African American, non-Hispanic/Latino; 1 American Indian or Alaska Native, non-Hispanic/Latino; 11 Asian, non-Hispanic/Latino; 38 Hispanic/Latino; 18 Two or more races, non-Hispanic/Latino), 8 international. Average age 34. 343 applicants, 92% accepted, 219 enrolled. In 2018, 69 master's, 13 doctorates, 161 other advanced degrees awarded. *Entrance requirements:* For master's, GRE or MAT, bachelor's degree, or its U.S. equivalent, from regionally-accredited college or university; minimum overall GPA of 3.0 on all previous work beyond high school; statement of purpose (essay); at least three recommendation forms; for doctorate, GRE or MAT, bachelor's degree (or its U.S. equivalent) from regionally-accredited college or university; minimum overall GPA of 3.5 in master's degree program; for Graduate Certificate, bachelor's degree from regionally-accredited university; minimum GPA of 2.75 on all post-secondary work attempted; transcripts; personal statement outlining why the applicant seeks admission to the program. Additional exam requirements/recommendations for international students: Required—TOEFL (minimum score 523 paper-based; 70 iBT), IELTS (minimum score 6), TOEFL (minimum score 523 paper-based, 70 iBT) or IELTS (6). *Application deadline:* Applications are processed on a rolling basis. Application fee: $75. Electronic applications accepted. Tuition and fees vary according to course load and program. *Financial support:* Career-related internships or fieldwork, institutionally sponsored loans, scholarships/grants, and unspecified assistantships available. Support available to part-time students. Financial award application deadline: 3/1; financial award applicants required to submit FAFSA. *Unit head:* Dr. Ellen McIntyre, Dean, 704-687-8722, E-mail: ellen.mcintyre@uncc.edu. *Application contact:* Kathy B. Giddings, Director of Graduate Admissions, 704-687-5503, Fax: 704-687-1668, E-mail: gradadm@uncc.edu.
Website: http://education.uncc.edu/academic-programs

The University of North Carolina at Greensboro, Graduate School, School of Education, Department of Specialized Education Services, Greensboro, NC 27412-5001. Offers cross-categorical special education (M Ed); interdisciplinary studies in special education (M Ed); leadership early care and education (Certificate); special education (M Ed, PhD). *Degree requirements:* For master's, thesis or alternative. *Entrance requirements:* For master's, GRE General Test. Additional exam requirements/recommendations for international students: Required—TOEFL. Electronic applications accepted.

The University of North Carolina Wilmington, Watson College of Education, Department of Early Childhood, Elementary, Middle, Literacy and Special Education, Wilmington, NC 28403-3297. Offers educational leadership, policy, and advocacy (M Ed); elementary education (M Ed, MAT); language and literacy (M Ed); middle grades education (MAT). *Accreditation:* NCATE. *Program availability:* Part-time,

blended/hybrid learning. *Degree requirements:* For master's, thesis or alternative, exit portfolio, oral presentation, internship, research project (depending on specialization). *Entrance requirements:* For master's, 3 letters of recommendations, NC Class A teacher license in related field, education statement of interest essay. Additional exam requirements/recommendations for international students: Required—TOEFL (minimum score 550 paper-based; 79 iBT), IELTS (minimum score 6.5). Electronic applications accepted.

University of North Dakota, Graduate School, College of Education and Human Development, Program in Early Childhood Education, Grand Forks, ND 58202. Offers MS. *Accreditation:* NCATE. *Program availability:* Part-time. *Degree requirements:* For master's, comprehensive exam, thesis or alternative. *Entrance requirements:* For master's, minimum GPA of 3.0. Additional exam requirements/recommendations for international students: Required—TOEFL (minimum score 550 paper-based; 79 iBT), IELTS (minimum score 6.5). Electronic applications accepted.

University of Northern Iowa, Graduate College, College of Education, Department of Curriculum and Instruction, MAE Program in Early Childhood Education, Cedar Falls, IA 50614. Offers MAE. *Degree requirements:* For master's, comprehensive exam, thesis or alternative. *Entrance requirements:* For master's, minimum GPA of 3.0. Additional exam requirements/recommendations for international students: Required—TOEFL (minimum score 500 paper-based; 61 iBT). Electronic applications accepted.

University of North Georgia, Program in Early Childhood Education, Dahlonega, GA 30597. Offers M Ed. *Program availability:* Part-time, blended/hybrid learning. *Degree requirements:* For master's, content field capstone. *Entrance requirements:* For master's, GRE or MAT (exempt with GPA 3.0 or higher), renewable teaching certificate. Additional exam requirements/recommendations for international students: Required—TOEFL (minimum score 550 paper-based; 79 iBT), IELTS (minimum score 6.5). Electronic applications accepted.

University of North Texas, Toulouse Graduate School, Denton, TX 76203-5459. Offers accounting (MS); applied anthropology (MA, MS); applied behavior analysis (Certificate); applied geography (MA); applied technology and performance improvement (M Ed, MS); art education (MA); art history (MA); arts leadership (Certificate); audiology (Au D); behavior analysis (MS); behavioral science (PhD); biochemistry and molecular biology (MS); biology (MA, MS); biomedical engineering (MS); business analysis (MS); chemistry (MS); clinical health psychology (PhD); communication studies (MA, MS); computer engineering (MS); computer science (MS); counseling (M Ed, MS), including clinical mental health counseling (MS), college and university counseling, elementary school counseling, secondary school counseling; creative writing (MA); criminal justice (MS); curriculum and instruction (M Ed); decision sciences (MBA); design (MA, MFA), including fashion design (MFA), innovation studies, interior design (MFA); early childhood studies (MS); economics (MS); educational leadership (M Ed, Ed D); educational psychology (MS, PhD), including family studies (MS), gifted and talented (MS), human development (MS), learning and cognition (MS), research, measurement and evaluation (MS); electrical engineering (MS); emergency management (MPA); engineering technology (MS); English (MA); English as a second language (MA); environmental science (MS); finance (MBA, MS); financial management (MPA); French (MA); health services management (MBA); higher education (M Ed, Ed D); history (MA, MS); hospitality management (MS); human resources management (MPA); information science (MS); information systems (PhD); information technologies (MBA); interdisciplinary studies (MA, MS); international studies (MA); international sustainable tourism (MS); jazz studies (MM); journalism (MA, MJ, Graduate Certificate), including interactive and virtual digital communication (Graduate Certificate), narrative journalism (Graduate Certificate), public relations (Graduate Certificate); kinesiology (MS); linguistics (MA); local government management (MPA); logistics (PhD); logistics and supply chain management (MBA); long-term care, senior housing, and aging services (MA); management (PhD); marketing (MBA); mathematics (MA, MS); mechanical and energy engineering (MS, PhD); music (MA), including ethnomusicology, music theory, musicology, performance; music composition (PhD); music education (MM Ed, PhD); nonprofit management (MPA); operations and supply chain management (MBA); performance (MM, DMA); philosophy (MA); political science (MA); professional and technical communication (MA); radio, television and film (MA, MFA); rehabilitation counseling (Certificate); sociology (MA); Spanish (MA); special education (M Ed); speech-language pathology (MA); strategic management (MBA); studio art (MFA); teaching (M Ed); MBA/MS. *Program availability:* Part-time, evening/weekend, online learning. Terminal master's awarded for partial completion of doctoral program. *Degree requirements:* For master's, variable foreign language requirement, comprehensive exam (for some programs), thesis (for some programs); for doctorate, variable foreign language requirement, comprehensive exam (for some programs), thesis/dissertation; for other advanced degree, variable foreign language requirement, comprehensive exam (for some programs). *Entrance requirements:* For master's and doctorate, GRE, GMAT. Additional exam requirements/recommendations for international students: Required—TOEFL (minimum score 550 paper-based; 79 iBT). Electronic applications accepted.

University of Oklahoma, Jeannine Rainbolt College of Education, Department of Instructional Leadership and Academic Curriculum, Norman, OK 73072. Offers instructional leadership and academic curriculum (M Ed, PhD), including biomedical education (PhD), early childhood education, elementary education, English education, instructional leadership, mathematics education, reading education, science education, social studies education, world languages education (M Ed); reading specialist (M Ed). *Accreditation:* NCATE. *Program availability:* Part-time. *Faculty:* 26 full-time (12 women), 1 part-time/adjunct (0 women). *Students:* 42 full-time (32 women), 113 part-time (85 women); includes 33 minority (9 Black or African American, non-Hispanic/Latino; 5 American Indian or Alaska Native, non-Hispanic/Latino; 6 Asian, non-Hispanic/Latino; 4 Hispanic/Latino; 1 Native Hawaiian or other Pacific Islander, non-Hispanic/Latino; 8 Two or more races, non-Hispanic/Latino), 9 international. Average age 35. 42 applicants, 79% accepted, 21 enrolled. In 2018, 30 master's, 17 doctorates awarded. Terminal master's awarded for partial completion of doctoral program. *Degree requirements:* For master's, comprehensive exam (for some programs), thesis (for some programs); for doctorate, comprehensive exam (for some programs), thesis/dissertation. *Entrance requirements:* For doctorate, GRE. Additional exam requirements/recommendations for international students: Required—TOEFL (minimum score 79 iBT) or IELTS (minimum score 6.5). Application fee: $50 ($100 for international students). Electronic applications accepted. *Expenses:* Tuition, state resident: full-time $5683.20; part-time $236.80 per credit hour. Tuition, nonresident: full-time $20,342; part-time $847.60 per credit hour. *International tuition:* $20,342.40 full-time. *Required fees:* $2894.20; $110.05 per credit hour. $126.50 per semester. Tuition and fees vary according to course load and program. *Financial support:* Fellowships, research assistantships, teaching assistantships, scholarships/grants, and unspecified assistantships available. Financial award application deadline: 6/1; financial award applicants required to submit FAFSA. *Faculty research:* Teacher preparation; instruction; curriculum; learning; constructivist theory. *Unit head:* Dr. Stacy Reeder, Chair, 405-325-1498, Fax: 405-325-4061, E-mail: reeder@ou.edu. *Application contact:* Anna Steele, Graduate Programs Officer, 405-325-4525, E-mail: anna.steele@ou.edu.
Website: http://www.ou.edu/education/ilac

University of Phoenix–Bay Area Campus, College of Education, San Jose, CA 95134-1805. Offers administration and supervision (MA Ed); adult education and training (MA Ed); early childhood education (MA Ed); education (Ed S); educational leadership (Ed D); elementary teacher education (MA Ed); higher education administration (PhD); secondary teacher education (MA Ed); special education (MA Ed); teacher leadership (MA Ed). *Program availability:* Evening/weekend, online learning. *Degree requirements:* For master's, thesis (for some programs). *Entrance requirements:* For master's, minimum undergraduate GPA of 2.5, 3 years of work experience. Additional exam requirements/recommendations for international students: Required—TOEFL (minimum score 550 paper-based; 79 iBT). Electronic applications accepted.

University of Phoenix–Online Campus, College of Education, Phoenix, AZ 85034-7209. Offers administration and supervision (MAEd, Certificate); adult education and training (MAEd); curriculum and instruction (MAEd), including computer education, curriculum and instruction, English as a second language, language arts, mathematics, reading; early childhood education (MAEd); educational studies (MAEd); elementary teacher education (MAEd), including early childhood, elementary teacher education, high school middle level, middle level; principal licensure (Certificate); secondary teacher education (MAEd); special education (MAEd, Certificate); teacher education (MAEd), including middle level generalist; teacher education middle level mathematics (MAEd), including middle level mathematics; teacher education middle level science (MAEd), including middle level science; teacher education secondary mathematics (MAEd); teacher education secondary science (MAEd); teacher leadership (MAEd); teachers of English learners (Certificate); transition to teaching (Certificate), including elementary education, secondary education. *Program availability:* Evening/weekend, online learning. *Entrance requirements:* Additional exam requirements/recommendations for international students: Required—TOEFL, TOEIC (Test of English as an International Communication), Berlitz Online English Proficiency Exam, PTE, or IELTS. Electronic applications accepted. *Expenses:* Contact institution.

University of Phoenix–Phoenix Campus, College of Education, Tempe, AZ 85282-2371. Offers administration and supervision (MA Ed); adult education and training (MA Ed); curriculum and instruction reading (MA Ed); early childhood education (MA Ed); education studies (MA Ed); elementary teacher education (MA Ed); secondary teacher education (MA Ed); special education (MA Ed); teacher leadership (MA Ed). *Program availability:* Evening/weekend, online learning. *Entrance requirements:* Additional exam requirements/recommendations for international students: Required—TOEFL, TOEIC (Test of English as an International Communication), Berlitz Online English Proficiency Exam, PTE, or IELTS. Electronic applications accepted. *Expenses:* Contact institution.

University of Pittsburgh, School of Education, Department of Instruction and Learning, Program in Early Childhood Education, Pittsburgh, PA 15260. Offers M Ed. *Program availability:* Part-time, evening/weekend. *Degree requirements:* For master's, thesis. *Entrance requirements:* For master's, PRAXIS I. Additional exam requirements/recommendations for international students: Required—TOEFL. Electronic applications accepted.

University of Puerto Rico–Río Piedras, College of Education, Program in Early Child Education, San Juan, PR 00931-3300. Offers M Ed. *Program availability:* Part-time. *Degree requirements:* For master's, thesis. *Entrance requirements:* For master's, EXADEP, GRE General Test or PAEG, interview, minimum GPA of 3.0, letter of recommendation.

University of South Alabama, College of Education and Professional Studies, Department of Leadership and Teacher Education, Mobile, AL 36688. Offers art education (M Ed); early childhood education (M Ed); educational leadership (M Ed, Ed D); elementary education (M Ed); reading education (M Ed); science education (M Ed); secondary education (M Ed); special education (M Ed). *Accreditation:* NCATE. *Program availability:* Part-time. *Degree requirements:* For master's, comprehensive exam, thesis (for some programs); for doctorate, comprehensive exam, thesis/dissertation. *Entrance requirements:* For master's, GRE General Test or MAT, minimum GPA of 3.0; for doctorate, GRE, minimum graduate GPA of 3.25, 3 years of experience in field, 3 letters of recommendation, interview, official transcripts. Additional exam requirements/recommendations for international students: Required—TOEFL. Electronic applications accepted.

University of South Carolina, The Graduate School, College of Education, Department of Instruction and Teacher Education, Program in Early Childhood Education, Columbia, SC 29208. Offers M Ed, Ed D, PhD. *Accreditation:* NCATE. *Degree requirements:* For master's, comprehensive exam; for doctorate, one foreign language, comprehensive exam, thesis/dissertation. *Entrance requirements:* For master's, GRE General Test, MAT, interview; for doctorate, GRE General Test, MAT, interview, teaching experience. *Faculty research:* Parent involvement, play, multicultural education, global education.

University of South Carolina Upstate, Graduate Programs, Spartanburg, SC 29303-4999. Offers early childhood education (M Ed); elementary education (M Ed); informatics (MS); special education: visual impairment (M Ed). *Accreditation:* NCATE. *Program availability:* Part-time, evening/weekend. *Degree requirements:* For master's, professional portfolio. *Entrance requirements:* For master's, GRE General Test or MAT, interview, minimum undergraduate GPA of 2.5, teaching certificate, 2 letters of recommendation. *Faculty research:* Promoting university diversity awareness, rough and tumble play, social justice education, American Indian literatures and cultures, diversity and multicultural education, science teaching strategy.

University of South Dakota, Graduate School, School of Education, Division of Curriculum and Instruction, Program in Elementary Education, Vermillion, SD 57069. Offers elementary education (MA), including early childhood education, English language learning, reading specialist/literacy coach, science, technology and math (STEM). *Accreditation:* NCATE. *Program availability:* Part-time, 100% online, blended/hybrid learning. *Degree requirements:* For master's, comprehensive exam, thesis or alternative. *Entrance requirements:* For master's, GRE General Test, MAT, minimum GPA of 2.7. Additional exam requirements/recommendations for international students: Required—TOEFL (minimum score 550 paper-based; 79 iBT). Electronic applications accepted.

University of South Dakota, Graduate School, School of Education, Division of Curriculum and Instruction, Program in Special Education, Vermillion, SD 57069. Offers special education (MA), including advanced specialist in disabilities, early childhood special education, multicategorical special education K-12. *Accreditation:* NCATE. *Program availability:* Part-time, online learning. *Degree requirements:* For master's, comprehensive exam, thesis or alternative. *Entrance requirements:* For master's, GRE General Test, MAT, minimum GPA of 2.7. Additional exam requirements/recommendations for international students: Required—TOEFL (minimum score 550 paper-based; 79 iBT). Electronic applications accepted.

University of South Dakota, Graduate School, School of Education, Division of Educational Leadership, Vermillion, SD 57069. Offers educational administration (MA, Ed D, Ed S), including adult and higher education (MA, Ed D), curriculum director, director of special education (Ed D, Ed S), preK-12 principal, school district superintendent (Ed D, Ed S). *Accreditation:* NCATE. *Program availability:* Part-time, evening/weekend, 100% online, blended/hybrid learning. *Degree requirements:* For

master's and Ed S, comprehensive exam, thesis or alternative; for doctorate, comprehensive exam, thesis/dissertation. *Entrance requirements:* For master's, GRE General Test, MAT, minimum GPA of 2.7; for doctorate, minimum GPA of 2.7. Additional exam requirements/recommendations for international students: Required—TOEFL (minimum score 550 paper-based; 79 iBT). Electronic applications accepted.

University of South Florida, College of Education, Department of Teaching and Learning, Tampa, FL 33620-9951. Offers early childhood education (M Ed, MA, PhD); elementary education (MA, MAT, PhD); reading/language arts (MA, PhD, Ed S). *Accreditation:* NCATE. *Faculty:* 36 full-time (27 women). *Students:* 244 full-time (193 women), 283 part-time (204 women); includes 140 minority (62 Black or African American, non-Hispanic/Latino; 2 American Indian or Alaska Native, non-Hispanic/Latino; 10 Asian, non-Hispanic/Latino; 61 Hispanic/Latino; 5 Two or more races, non-Hispanic/Latino), 70 international. Average age 36. 204 applicants, 84% accepted, 131 enrolled. In 2018, 67 master's, 3 doctorates awarded. *Degree requirements:* For master's, comprehensive exam, thesis (for some programs); for doctorate, comprehensive exam, thesis/dissertation (for some programs). *Entrance requirements:* For master's, GRE may be required (varies by major), statement of purpose; letters of recommendation; be eligible for professional certification (if applicable to major); passing GKT (if applicable to major); for doctorate, GRE may be required (varies by major), Master's degree with 3.5 GPA; CV; statement of purpose; letters of recommendation; faculty interview; language proficiency (if applicable). Additional exam requirements/recommendations for international students: Required—TOEFL. Application fee: $30. *Expenses:* Tuition, state resident: full-time $6350. Tuition, nonresident: full-time $19,048. *International tuition:* $19,048 full-time. *Required fees:* $2079. *Total annual research expenditures:* $2.7 million. *Unit head:* Dr. Denisse Thompson, Chair, 813-974-4110. *Application contact:* Dr. Denisse Thompson, Chair, 813-974-4110.
Website: http://www.coedu.usf.edu/main/departments/ce/ce.html

The University of Tennessee, Graduate School, College of Education, Health and Human Sciences, Department of Child and Family Studies, Knoxville, TN 37996. Offers child and family studies (MS); early childhood education (MS). *Program availability:* Part-time. *Degree requirements:* For master's, thesis or alternative. *Entrance requirements:* For master's, GRE General Test, minimum GPA of 2.7. Additional exam requirements/recommendations for international students: Required—TOEFL. Electronic applications accepted.

The University of Tennessee, Graduate School, College of Education, Health and Human Sciences, Program in Education, Knoxville, TN 37996. Offers art education (MS); counseling education (PhD); cultural studies in education (PhD); curriculum (MS, Ed S); curriculum, educational research and evaluation (Ed D, PhD); early childhood education (PhD); early childhood special education (MS); education of deaf and hard of hearing (MS); educational administration and policy studies (Ed D, PhD); educational administration and supervision (Ed S); educational psychology (Ed D, PhD); elementary education (MS, Ed S); elementary teaching (MS); English education (MS, Ed S); exercise science (PhD); foreign language/ESL education (MS, Ed S); instructional technology (MS, Ed D, PhD, Ed S); literacy, language and ESL education (PhD); literacy, language education, and ESL education (Ed D); mathematics education (MS, Ed S); modified and comprehensive special education (MS); reading education (MS, Ed S); school counseling (Ed S); school psychology (PhD, Ed S); science education (MS, Ed S); secondary teaching (MS); social foundations (MS); social science education (MS, Ed S); socio-cultural foundations of sports and education (PhD); special education (Ed S); teacher education (Ed D, PhD). *Accreditation:* NCATE. *Program availability:* Part-time, evening/weekend. *Degree requirements:* For master's and Ed S, thesis optional; for doctorate, variable foreign language requirement, thesis/dissertation. *Entrance requirements:* For master's, minimum GPA of 2.7; for doctorate and Ed S, GRE General Test, minimum GPA of 2.7. Additional exam requirements/recommendations for international students: Required—TOEFL. Electronic applications accepted.

The University of Texas at Austin, Graduate School, College of Education, Department of Curriculum and Instruction, Austin, TX 78712-1111. Offers bilingual/bicultural education (M Ed, MA, PhD); cultural studies in education (M Ed, MA, PhD); early childhood education (M Ed, MA, PhD); language and literacy studies (M Ed, PhD); learning technologies (M Ed, MA, PhD); physical education (M Ed, MA, PhD). Terminal master's awarded for partial completion of doctoral program. *Degree requirements:* For doctorate, thesis/dissertation. *Entrance requirements:* For master's and doctorate, GRE General Test. Electronic applications accepted.

The University of Texas at Austin, Graduate School, College of Education, Department of Special Education, Austin, TX 78712-1111. Offers autism and developmental disabilities (Ed D, PhD); autism and developmental disability (M Ed, MA); early childhood special education (M Ed, MA, Ed D, PhD); learning disabilities (Ed D, PhD); learning disabilities/behavior disorders (M Ed, MA); multicultural special education (M Ed, MA, Ed D, PhD); rehabilitation counselor (M Ed); rehabilitation counselor education (Ed D, PhD); special education administration (Ed D, PhD). *Accreditation:* CORE. *Program availability:* Part-time, evening/weekend, online learning. *Degree requirements:* For master's, thesis or alternative; for doctorate, thesis/dissertation. *Entrance requirements:* For master's and doctorate, GRE General Test. *Faculty research:* Anchored instruction, reading disabilities, multicultural/bilingual.

The University of Texas at San Antonio, College of Education and Human Development, Department of Interdisciplinary Learning and Teaching, San Antonio, TX 78249-0617. Offers education (MA), including curriculum and instruction, early childhood and elementary education, instructional technology, reading and literacy, special education; interdisciplinary learning and teaching (PhD). *Program availability:* Part-time, evening/weekend. *Degree requirements:* For master's, comprehensive exam, thesis optional, 36 hours of course work without thesis (33 with thesis); for doctorate, comprehensive exam, thesis/dissertation, minimum of 60 semester credit hours. *Entrance requirements:* For master's, bachelor's degree with minimum GPA of 3.0 in last 60 hours of coursework; 18 hours of undergraduate coursework in education or related field; for doctorate, GRE, transcripts from all colleges and universities attended, professional vitae demonstrating experience in work environment where education was primary professional emphasis, 3 letters of recommendation, statement of purpose, minimum GPA of 3.5. Additional exam requirements/recommendations for international students: Required—TOEFL (minimum score 550 paper-based; 79 iBT), IELTS (minimum score 6.5). Electronic applications accepted. *Faculty research:* Explorations of science, learning and teaching, family involvement in early childhood, culturally-responsive literacy instruction in diverse settings, STEM education, autism spectrum disorder.

The University of Texas at Tyler, College of Education and Psychology, School of Education, Tyler, TX 75799-0001. Offers early childhood education (M Ed, MA); reading (M Ed, MA); special education (M Ed, MA). *Program availability:* Part-time, evening/weekend. *Students:* 4 full-time (3 women), 30 part-time (all women); includes 4 minority (3 Black or African American, non-Hispanic/Latino; 1 Hispanic/Latino), 2 international. Average age 37. 13 applicants, 100% accepted, 6 enrolled. In 2018, 14 master's awarded. *Degree requirements:* For master's, comprehensive exam, thesis (for some programs), research project. *Entrance requirements:* For master's, GRE General Test. Additional exam requirements/recommendations for international students: Required—TOEFL. *Application deadline:* For fall admission, 8/17 priority date for domestic students, 7/1 priority date for international students; for spring admission, 12/21 priority date for domestic students, 11/1 priority date for international students. Applications are processed on a rolling basis. Application fee: $25 ($50 for international students). Electronic applications accepted. *Financial support:* In 2018–19, 2 research assistantships (averaging $12,000 per year) were awarded; scholarships/grants also available. Financial award application deadline: 7/1. *Faculty research:* Improving quality in childcare settings, play and creativity, teacher interactions, effects of modeling on early childhood teachers, biofeedback, literacy instruction. *Unit head:* Dr. Wes Hickey, Dean, 903-565-5669, E-mail: whickey@uttyler.edu. *Application contact:* Dr. Wes Hickey, Dean, 903-565-5669, E-mail: whickey@uttyler.edu.
Website: http://www.uttyler.edu/education/

The University of Texas of the Permian Basin, Office of Graduate Studies, School of Education, Program in Early Childhood Education, Odessa, TX 79762-0001. Offers MA. *Degree requirements:* For master's, comprehensive exam (for some programs), thesis (for some programs). *Entrance requirements:* For master's, GRE General Test. Additional exam requirements/recommendations for international students: Required—TOEFL (minimum score 550 paper-based).

The University of Texas Rio Grande Valley, College of Education and P-16 Integration, Department of Human Development and School Services, Edinburg, TX 78539. Offers early childhood education (M Ed); early childhood special education (M Ed); school psychology (MA); special education (M Ed). *Program availability:* Part-time, evening/weekend. *Degree requirements:* For master's, comprehensive exam (for some programs). *Entrance requirements:* For master's, minimum GPA of 3.0. Additional exam requirements/recommendations for international students: Required—TOEFL (minimum score 550 paper-based; 79 iBT), IELTS (minimum score 6.5). Electronic applications accepted. *Expenses: Tuition, area resident:* Full-time $6888. Tuition, state resident: full-time $6888. Tuition, nonresident: full-time $14,484. *International tuition:* $14,484 full-time. *Required fees:* $1468. *Faculty research:* Special education, assessment practice, behavior interventions, mental retardation, early childhood.

University of the District of Columbia, College of Arts and Sciences, Program in Early Childhood Education, Washington, DC 20008-1175. Offers MA. *Accreditation:* NCATE. *Program availability:* Part-time. *Degree requirements:* For master's, comprehensive exam, research paper. *Entrance requirements:* For master's, GRE General Test, writing proficiency exam, minimum GPA of 3.0.

University of the Sacred Heart, Graduate Programs, Department of Education, San Juan, PR 00914-0383. Offers early childhood education (M Ed); information technology and multimedia (Certificate); instruction systems and education technology (M Ed), including English, information technology and multimedia, instructional design, mathematics, Spanish. *Program availability:* Part-time, evening/weekend. *Degree requirements:* For master's, thesis. *Entrance requirements:* For master's, EXADEP, minimum undergraduate GPA of 2.75, interview.

University of the Southwest, Graduate Programs, Hobbs, NM 88240-9129. Offers business administration (MBA); curriculum and instruction (MSE); curriculum and instruction: bilingual (MSE); curriculum and instruction: TESOL (MSE); early childhood education (MSE); educational administration (MSE); mental health counseling (MSE); school counseling (MSE); special education (MSE); sports management (MBA). *Program availability:* Part-time, evening/weekend, online learning. *Degree requirements:* For master's, comprehensive exam, thesis (for some programs). *Entrance requirements:* Additional exam requirements/recommendations for international students: Recommended—TOEFL. Electronic applications accepted.

The University of Toledo, College of Graduate Studies, Judith Herb College of Education, Department of Curriculum and Instruction, Toledo, OH 43606-3390. Offers art education (ME); career and technical education (ME, Ed S); curriculum and instruction (ME, PhD, Ed S); early childhood education (Ed S); education and anthropology (MAE); education and biology (MES); education and chemistry (MES); education and classics (MAE); education and economics (MAE); education and English (MAE); education and French (MAE); education and geology (MES); education and German (MAE); education and history (MAE); education and mathematics (MAE, MES); education and physics (MES); education and political science (MAE); education and sociology (MAE); education and Spanish (MAE); educational media (PhD); educational technology (ME); educational technology: virtual educator (Certificate); elementary education (PhD); English as a second language (MAE); gifted and talented education (PhD); middle childhood education (ME); secondary education (ME, PhD); special education (PhD). *Accreditation:* NCATE. *Program availability:* Part-time, evening/weekend. *Degree requirements:* For master's, comprehensive exam, thesis or alternative; for doctorate, comprehensive exam, thesis/dissertation; for other advanced degree, thesis optional. *Entrance requirements:* For master's, doctorate, and other advanced degree, minimum cumulative GPA of 2.7 for all previous academic work, letters of recommendation. Additional exam requirements/recommendations for international students: Required—TOEFL (minimum score 550 paper-based; 80 iBT). Electronic applications accepted.

The University of Toledo, College of Graduate Studies, Judith Herb College of Education, Department of Early Childhood, Physical and Special Education, Toledo, OH 43606-3390. Offers early childhood education (ME); physical education (ME); special education (ME). *Program availability:* Part-time. *Degree requirements:* For master's, thesis. *Entrance requirements:* For master's, minimum cumulative GPA of 2.7 for all previous academic work, letters of recommendation. Additional exam requirements/recommendations for international students: Required—TOEFL (minimum score 550 paper-based; 80 iBT). Electronic applications accepted.

University of Utah, Graduate School, College of Education, Department of Special Education, Salt Lake City, UT 84112. Offers board certified behavior analyst (M Ed, MS, PhD); deaf and hard of hearing (M Ed); deafblind (M Ed, MS); early childhood deaf and hard of hearing (MS); early childhood special education (M Ed, MS, PhD); early childhood visual impairments (M Ed); mild/moderate disabilities (M Ed, MS, PhD); severe disabilities (M Ed, MS, PhD); visual impairments (M Ed, MS). *Program availability:* Part-time, 100% online, blended/hybrid learning, Interactive Video Conferencing. *Faculty:* 17 full-time (13 women), 31 part-time/adjunct (25 women). *Students:* 62 full-time (53 women), 8 part-time (all women); includes 10 minority (4 Asian, non-Hispanic/Latino; 5 Hispanic/Latino; 1 Two or more races, non-Hispanic/Latino). Average age 31. 53 applicants, 83% accepted, 36 enrolled. In 2018, 13 master's, 1 doctorate awarded. Terminal master's awarded for partial completion of doctoral program. *Degree requirements:* For master's, comprehensive exam, thesis (for some programs), qualifying exam; for doctorate, thesis/dissertation, qualifying exam. *Entrance requirements:* For master's, minimum GPA of 3.0; for doctorate, GRE General Test, minimum GPA of 3.5, Master's Degree. Additional exam requirements/recommendations for international students: Required—TOEFL (minimum score 600 paper-based; 100 iBT); Recommended—IELTS (minimum score 7). *Application deadline:* For fall admission, 3/1 for domestic and international students; for spring admission, 10/1 for domestic and international students; for summer admission, 5/16 for domestic and international students. Application fee: $55 ($65 for international students). Electronic applications accepted. *Expenses:* $12,000 per year. *Financial*

support: In 2018–19, 8 students received support, including 35 fellowships with full and partial tuition reimbursements available (averaging $18,200 per year), 42 research assistantships with partial tuition reimbursements available (averaging $14,500 per year), 2 teaching assistantships with full tuition reimbursements available (averaging $15,500 per year); scholarships/grants, traineeships, health care benefits, and unspecified assistantships also available. Financial award application deadline: 3/1; financial award applicants required to submit FAFSA. *Faculty research:* Inclusion, positive behavior supports, embedded instruction, functional communication, literacy intervention. *Total annual research expenditures:* $142,545. *Unit head:* Dr. Susan Johnston, PhD, Chair, 801-581-5187, Fax: 801-585-6476, E-mail: susan.johnston@utah.edu. *Application contact:* Kaitlin Lindsey, Academic Advisor/Student Recruiting Contact, 801-581-4764, Fax: 801-585-6476, E-mail: k.lindsey@utah.edu. Website: http://special-ed.utah.edu/

University of Vermont, Graduate College, College of Education and Social Services, Program in Early Childhood Special Education, Burlington, VT 05405. Offers M Ed. *Program availability:* Part-time, evening/weekend. *Entrance requirements:* Additional exam requirements/recommendations for international students: Required—TOEFL (minimum iBT score of 90) or IELTS (6.5). Electronic applications accepted.

University of Vermont, Graduate College, College of Education and Social Services, Program in Special Education, Grades K-12, Burlington, VT 05405. Offers M Ed. *Accreditation:* NCATE. *Degree requirements:* For master's, thesis or alternative. *Entrance requirements:* For master's, license (or eligible for licensure). Additional exam requirements/recommendations for international students: Required—TOEFL (minimum score 550 paper-based, 90 iBT) or IELTS (6.5). Electronic applications accepted.

University of Victoria, Faculty of Graduate Studies, Faculty of Education, Department of Curriculum and Instruction, Victoria, BC V8W 2Y2, Canada. Offers art education (M Ed, PhD); curriculum studies (M Ed, MA, PhD); early childhood education (M Ed, PhD); educational studies (PhD); language and literacy (M Ed, MA, PhD); mathematics (M Ed, MA, PhD); music education (M Ed, MA, PhD); science (M Ed, MA, PhD); social studies (M Ed, MA); social, cultural and foundational studies (MA, PhD); technology and environmental education (PhD). *Program availability:* Part-time. *Degree requirements:* For master's, thesis, project (M Ed); for doctorate, comprehensive exam, thesis/dissertation. *Entrance requirements:* For master's, minimum B average. Additional exam requirements/recommendations for international students: Required—TOEFL (minimum score 575 paper-based), IELTS (minimum score 7). Electronic applications accepted. *Faculty research:* Elementary and secondary English, language arts, curriculum theory and practice, educational media and technology, educational administration and leadership, history and philosophy of education.

University of Virginia, Curry School of Education, Program in Education, Charlottesville, VA 22903. Offers administration and supervision (PhD); applied developmental science (PhD); counselor education (PhD); curriculum and instruction (PhD); early childhood special education (MT); education evaluation (PhD); educational psychology (PhD); educational research (PhD); elementary education (MT); English education (MT, PhD); foreign language education (MT); higher education (PhD); instructional technology (PhD); kinesiology (MT, PhD); math education (PhD); reading education (PhD); research, statistics and evaluation (PhD); school psychology (PhD); science education (PhD); social studies education (MT, PhD); special education (PhD); world languages education (MT). *Degree requirements:* For master's, comprehensive exam (for some programs), field project; for doctorate, comprehensive exam, thesis/dissertation. *Entrance requirements:* For doctorate, GRE General Test. Additional exam requirements/recommendations for international students: Required—TOEFL (minimum score 600 paper-based; 90 iBT), IELTS (minimum score 7). Electronic applications accepted.

The University of West Alabama, School of Graduate Studies, College of Education, Program in Early Childhood Education, Livingston, AL 35470. Offers early childhood development (M Ed); early childhood education P-3 (M Ed, Ed S). *Accreditation:* NCATE. *Program availability:* Part-time, evening/weekend, 100% online. *Faculty:* 4 full-time (all women), 27 part-time/adjunct (18 women). *Students:* 148 full-time (143 women), 8 part-time (all women); includes 69 minority (67 Black or African American, non-Hispanic/Latino; 1 Asian, non-Hispanic/Latino; 1 Two or more races, non-Hispanic/Latino). Average age 33. 42 applicants, 95% accepted, 35 enrolled. In 2018, 29 master's, 6 Ed Ss awarded. *Degree requirements:* For master's, comprehensive exam, thesis optional; for Ed S, comprehensive exam. *Entrance requirements:* For master's, GRE, minimum GPA of 2.75, verification of background clearance/fingerprints, valid bachelor's-level Professional Educator Certificate in same teaching field. Additional exam requirements/recommendations for international students: Required—TOEFL (minimum score 500 paper-based; 61 iBT). *Application deadline:* Applications are processed on a rolling basis. Application fee: $40. Electronic applications accepted. *Expenses: Tuition, area resident:* Full-time $9100. *Tuition, state resident:* full-time $9100. *Tuition, nonresident:* full-time $19,200. *Required fees:* $1890; $130. *Financial support:* Teaching assistantships, Federal Work-Study, scholarships/grants, and unspecified assistantships available. Support available to part-time students. Financial award application deadline: 3/1; financial award applicants required to submit FAFSA. *Unit head:* Dr. Jodie Winship, Chair of College of Education, 205-652-5415, Fax: 205-652-3706, E-mail: jwinship@uwa.edu. *Application contact:* Dr. B. J. Kimbrough, Dean of Graduate Studies, 205-652-3647, Fax: 205-652-3670, E-mail: bkimbrough@uwa.edu.

University of West Georgia, College of Education, Carrollton, GA 30118. Offers business education (M Ed); early childhood education (M Ed, Ed S); educational leadership (M Ed, Ed S); media (M Ed, Ed S); professional counseling (M Ed, Ed S); professional counseling and supervision (Ed D); reading instruction (M Ed); school improvement (Ed D); secondary education (M Ed); special education (M Ed, Ed S), including teaching (M Ed); speech language pathology (M Ed); teaching (MAT). *Accreditation:* NCATE. *Program availability:* Part-time, evening/weekend, 100% online, blended/hybrid learning. *Faculty:* 39 full-time (23 women). *Students:* 368 full-time (316 women), 1,140 part-time (960 women); includes 460 minority (376 Black or African American, non-Hispanic/Latino; 1 American Indian or Alaska Native, non-Hispanic/Latino; 11 Asian, non-Hispanic/Latino; 44 Hispanic/Latino; 28 Two or more races, non-Hispanic/Latino), 6 international. Average age 35. 625 applicants, 77% accepted, 401 enrolled. In 2018, 399 master's, 25 doctorates, 273 other advanced degrees awarded. *Entrance requirements:* Additional exam requirements/recommendations for international students: Required—TOEFL (minimum score 523 paper-based; 69 iBT), Recommended—IELTS (minimum score 6.5). *Application deadline:* For fall admission, 7/21 for domestic students, 6/1 for international students; for spring admission, 11/30 for domestic students, 10/15 for international students; for summer admission, 4/15 for domestic students, 3/30 for international students. Applications are processed on a rolling basis. Application fee: $40. Electronic applications accepted. Tuition and fees vary according to course load, degree level, campus/location and program. *Financial support:* Fellowships, research assistantships, teaching assistantships, career-related internships or fieldwork, Federal Work-Study, institutionally sponsored loans, scholarships/grants, and unspecified assistantships available. Support available to part-time students. Financial award application deadline: 4/1; financial award applicants required to submit FAFSA. *Unit head:* Dr. Diane Hoff, Dean, College of Education, 678-839-6570, Fax: 678-839-6098, E-mail: dhoff@westga.edu. *Application contact:* Dr. Toby

Ziglar, Assistant Dean of the Graduate School, 678-839-1394, Fax: 678-839-1395, E-mail: graduate@westga.edu. Website: http://www.westga.edu/education/

University of Wisconsin–Milwaukee, Graduate School, School of Education, Department of Curriculum and Instruction, Milwaukee, WI 53201-0413. Offers curriculum and instruction (MS), including cross-curricular focus, early childhood education, English education, mathematics education, middle childhood/early adolescence education, reading education, science education, urban social studies education. *Program availability:* Part-time. *Students:* 19 full-time (15 women), 56 part-time (49 women); includes 15 minority (3 Black or African American, non-Hispanic/Latino; 1 American Indian or Alaska Native, non-Hispanic/Latino; 3 Asian, non-Hispanic/Latino; 1 Hispanic/Latino; 7 Two or more races, non-Hispanic/Latino), 2 international. Average age 33. 27 applicants, 44% accepted, 11 enrolled. In 2018, 20 master's awarded. *Entrance requirements:* Additional exam requirements/recommendations for international students: Required—TOEFL (minimum score 550 paper-based; 79 iBT), IELTS (minimum score 6.5). *Application deadline:* For fall admission, 1/1 priority date for domestic students; for spring admission, 9/1 for domestic students. Application fee: $56 ($96 for international students). Electronic applications accepted. *Financial support:* Fellowships, research assistantships, teaching assistantships, career-related internships or fieldwork, health care benefits, unspecified assistantships, and project assistantships available. Support available to part-time students. Financial award application deadline: 4/15; financial award applicants required to submit FAFSA. *Application contact:* General Information Contact, 414-229-4721, E-mail: soeinfo@uwm.edu. Website: http://uwm.edu/education/academics/curriculum-instruction-department/

University of Wisconsin–Oshkosh, Graduate Studies, College of Education and Human Services, Department of Special Education, Oshkosh, WI 54901. Offers cross-categorical (MSE); early childhood: exceptional education needs (MSE); non-licensure (MSE). *Program availability:* Part-time, evening/weekend. *Degree requirements:* For master's, comprehensive exam (for some programs), thesis or alternative, field report. *Entrance requirements:* For master's, interview, minimum GPA of 3.0, teaching license, letters of recommendation. Additional exam requirements/recommendations for international students: Required—TOEFL (minimum score 550 paper-based; 79 iBT). Electronic applications accepted. *Faculty research:* Private agency contributions to the disabled, graduation requirements for exceptional education needs students, direct instruction in spelling for learning disabled, effects of behavioral parent training, secondary education programming issues.

Upper Iowa University, Master of Education Program, Fayette, IA 52142-1857. Offers early childhood (M Ed); English as a second language (M Ed); higher education (M Ed); instructional strategist (M Ed); reading (M Ed); teacher leadership (M Ed).

Virginia Commonwealth University, Graduate School, School of Education, Program in Special Education, Richmond, VA 23284-9005. Offers early childhood (M Ed); general education (M Ed); severe disabilities (M Ed). *Accreditation:* NCATE. *Degree requirements:* For master's, comprehensive exam. *Entrance requirements:* For master's, GRE General Test or MAT. Additional exam requirements/recommendations for international students: Required—TOEFL (minimum score 600 paper-based; 100 iBT). Electronic applications accepted.

Virginia Commonwealth University, Graduate School, School of Education, Program in Teaching and Learning, Richmond, VA 23284-9005. Offers early and elementary education (MT). *Accreditation:* NCATE. *Program availability:* Part-time. *Entrance requirements:* For master's, GRE General Test or MAT. Additional exam requirements/recommendations for international students: Required—TOEFL (minimum score 600 paper-based; 100 iBT). Electronic applications accepted.

Viterbo University, Graduate Programs in Education, La Crosse, WI 54601-4797. Offers cross-categorical special education (Certificate); director of instruction (Certificate); director of special education and pupil services (Certificate); early childhood (Certificate); education (MAE); literacy coaching (Certificate); PreK-12 principal/supervisor of special education (Certificate); principal (Certificate); reading specialist endorsement (Certificate); reading teacher (Certificate); reading teacher 5-12 endorsement (Certificate); reading teacher K-8 endorsement (Certificate); superintendent (Certificate); talented and gifted endorsement (Certificate); Wisconsin school business administrator (Certificate). Weekend courses available in summer. *Accreditation:* NCATE. *Program availability:* Part-time, evening/weekend. *Degree requirements:* For master's, comprehensive exam, thesis, 30 credits of course work. *Entrance requirements:* For master's, BS, transcripts, teaching license, written narrative. Electronic applications accepted. *Expenses:* Contact institution.

Wagner College, Division of Graduate Studies, Education Department, Program in Early Childhood Education/Students with Disabilities (Birth-Grade 2), Staten Island, NY 10301-4495. Offers MS Ed. *Program availability:* Part-time, evening/weekend. *Degree requirements:* For master's, thesis. *Entrance requirements:* For master's, minimum GPA of 3.0, valid initial NY State Certificate or equivalent, interview, recommendations. Additional exam requirements/recommendations for international students: Recommended—TOEFL (minimum score 550 paper-based; 79 iBT), IELTS (minimum score 6.5). Electronic applications accepted. *Expenses:* Contact institution.

Walden University, Graduate Programs, Richard W. Riley College of Education and Leadership, Minneapolis, MN 55401. Offers adult education (Post-Master's Certificate); adult learning (Graduate Certificate); college teaching and learning (Graduate Certificate); community college leadership (Ed D); curriculum, instruction and assessment (Ed D, Ed S, Graduate Certificate); developmental education (Graduate Certificate); early childhood administration, management, and leadership (Graduate Certificate); early childhood education (Ed D, Ed S); early childhood public policy and advocacy (Graduate Certificate); early childhood studies (MS), including administration, management and leadership, early childhood public policy and advocacy, teaching adults in the early childhood field, teaching and diversity in early childhood education; education (MS, PhD), including adolescent literacy and learning (MS), curriculum, instruction, and assessment (grades K-12) (MS), curriculum, instruction, assessment, and evaluation (PhD), early childhood leadership and advocacy (PhD), early childhood special education (PhD), educational leadership (MS), educational leadership and administration (principal preparation) (MS), educational technology and design (PhD), elementary reading and literacy (PreK-6) (MS), elementary reading and mathematics (grades K-6) (MS), global and comparative education (PhD), higher education leadership management and policy (PhD), integrating technology in the classroom (grades K-12) (MS), learning, instruction and innovation (PhD), mathematics (grades 5-8) (MS), mathematics (grades K-6) (MS), mathematics and science (grades K-8) (MS), organizational research, assessment, and evaluation (PhD), reading and literacy with a reading K-12 endorsement (MS), reading literacy assessment and evaluation (PhD), science (grades K-8) (MS), special education (non-licensure) (grades K-12) (MS), teacher leadership (grades K-12) (MS), teaching English language learners (grades K-12) (MS); educational administration and leadership (Ed D); educational leadership and administration (principal preparation) (Ed S); educational technology (Ed D, Ed S, Post Master's Certificate); elementary reading and literacy (Graduate Certificate); engaging culturally diverse learners (Graduate Certificate); enrollment management and

institutional marketing (Graduate Certificate); higher education (MS), including adult learning, college teaching and learning, enrollment management and institutional marketing, global higher education, leadership for student success, online and distance learning; higher education and adult learning (Ed D); higher education leadership and management (Ed D); higher education leadership for student success (Graduate Certificate); instructional design and technology (MS, Postbaccalaureate Certificate), including general program (MS), online learning (MS), training and performance improvement (MS); integrating technology in the classroom (Graduate Certificate); mathematics 5-8 (Graduate Certificate); mathematics K-6 (Graduate Certificate); online teaching for adult educators (Graduate Certificate); reading, literacy, and assessment (Ed D, Ed S); science K-8 (Graduate Certificate); special education (Ed D, Ed S, Graduate Certificate); special education (K-age 21) (MAT); teacher leadership (Graduate Certificate); teaching adults English as a second language (Graduate Certificate); teaching adults in the early childhood field (Graduate Certificate); teaching and diversity in early childhood education (Graduate Certificate); teaching English language learners (grades K-12) (Graduate Certificate); teaching K-12 students online (Graduate Certificate). *Accreditation:* NCATE. *Program availability:* Part-time, evening/weekend, online only, 100% online. *Degree requirements:* For doctorate, thesis/dissertation (for some programs), residency; for other advanced degree, residency (for some programs). *Entrance requirements:* For master's, bachelor's degree or higher; minimum GPA of 2.5; official transcripts; goal statement (for some programs); access to computer and Internet; for doctorate, master's degree or higher; three years of related professional or academic experience (preferred); minimum GPA of 3.0; goal statement and current resume (for select programs); official transcripts; access to computer and Internet; for other advanced degree, relevant work experience; access to computer and Internet. Additional exam requirements/recommendations for international students: Required—TOEFL (minimum score 550 paper-based, 79 iBT), IELTS (minimum score 6.5), Michigan English Language Assessment Battery (minimum score 82), or PTE (minimum score 53). Electronic applications accepted.

Wayne State College, School of Education and Counseling, Department of Educational Foundations and Leadership, Program in Curriculum and Instruction, Wayne, NE 68787. Offers alternative education (MSE); business and information technology education (MSE); communication arts education (MSE); early childhood education (MSE); elementary education (MSE); English as a second language (MSE); English education (MSE); family and consumer sciences education (MSE); industrial technology and vocational education (MSE); learning communities (MSE); mathematics education (MSE); music education (MSE); science education (MSE); social science education (MSE). *Accreditation:* NCATE. *Program availability:* Part-time, evening/weekend. *Degree requirements:* For master's, comprehensive exam, thesis optional. *Entrance requirements:* For master's, GRE General Test. Additional exam requirements/recommendations for international students: Required—TOEFL (minimum score 550 paper-based).

Wayne State University, College of Education, Division of Teacher Education, Detroit, MI 48202. Offers art education (M Ed); bilingual/bicultural education (Certificate); curriculum and instruction (Ed D, PhD, Ed S), including English as a second language (MAT, Ed D, Ed S), K-12 curriculum (PhD); elementary education (MAT), including bilingual/bicultural education (M Ed, MAT), early childhood education (M Ed, MAT), English as a second language (MAT, Ed D, Ed S), foreign language education, science education (M Ed, MAT), special education (M Ed, MAT); elementary mathematics specialist (Certificate); English as a second language (Certificate); reading (M Ed, Ed S); reading, language and literature (Ed D); secondary education (MAT), including bilingual/bicultural education (M Ed, MAT), early childhood education (M Ed, MAT), English as a second language (MAT, Ed D, Ed S), English education, foreign language education, mathematics education (M Ed, MAT), science education (M Ed, MAT), social studies education (M Ed, MAT); special education (MAT), including career and technical education; teaching and learning (M Ed), including bilingual/bicultural education (M Ed, MAT), early childhood education (M Ed, MAT), elementary education, foreign language, mathematics education (M Ed, MAT), science education (M Ed, MAT), social studies education (M Ed, MAT), special education (M Ed, MAT). *Program availability:* Part-time, evening/weekend. *Faculty:* 20. *Students:* 121 full-time (94 women), 251 part-time (209 women); includes 116 minority (83 Black or African American, non-Hispanic/Latino; 3 American Indian or Alaska Native, non-Hispanic/Latino; 3 Asian, non-Hispanic/Latino; 14 Hispanic/Latino; 13 Two or more races, non-Hispanic/Latino), 11 international. Average age 37. 171 applicants, 23% accepted, 32 enrolled. In 2018, 112 master's, 8 doctorates, 11 other advanced degrees awarded. *Degree requirements:* For master's, thesis (for some programs), essay or project (for some M Ed programs), professional field experience (for MAT programs); for doctorate, comprehensive exam, thesis/dissertation. *Entrance requirements:* For master's, undergraduate degree, verification of participation in group work with children, Michigan State Police criminal background check, negative tb test, personal statement (for MAT programs); for all other master's programs: undergraduate degree, personal statement; for doctorate, minimum undergraduate GPA of 3.0, graduate 3.5; interview; curriculum vitae; references; writing sample; letter of application; master's degree (for most programs); for other advanced degree, education specialist certificate: undergraduate with GPA of 2.5 or better and master's degree with GPA of 2.75 or better; personal statement. Additional exam requirements/recommendations for international students: Required—TOEFL (minimum score 550 paper-based; 79 iBT); Recommended—IELTS (minimum score 6.5), TWE (minimum score 5.5), TSE (minimum score 58). *Application deadline:* Applications are processed on a rolling basis. Application fee: $50. Electronic applications accepted. *Financial support:* In 2018–19, 85 students received support, including 3 fellowships (averaging $14,275 per year); research assistantships with tuition reimbursements available, Federal Work-Study, scholarships/grants, and unspecified assistantships also available. Support available to part-time students. Financial award applicants required to submit FAFSA. *Faculty research:* Improving students' skill achievement in mathematics, improving elementary children's understanding of informational text, teachers' use of their pedagogical and mathematical knowledge in the interactive work of teaching, the intersection of identity construction in teaching and learning, identifying effective methods of literacy instruction and assessments for bilingual students in elementary language arts classrooms. *Unit head:* Dr. Roland Coloma, Assistant Dean for Teacher Education, 313-577-0902, E-mail: rscoloma@wayne.edu. *Application contact:* Dr. Mary L. Waker, Graduate Admissions Officer, 313-577-1601, Fax: 313-577-7904, E-mail: m.waker@wayne.edu.
Website: http://coe.wayne.edu/ted/index.php

Webster University, School of Education, Department of Multidisciplinary Studies, St. Louis, MO 63119-3194. Offers applied educational psychology (MA, Ed S); communication arts (MA); early childhood education (MA, MAT); education and innovation (MA); educational technology (MET); elementary education (MAT); mathematics for educators (MA); middle school education (MAT); multidisciplinary studies (MAT); multimodal literacy for global impact (MA); reading (MA); secondary school education (MAT); special education (MA, MAT); teaching English as a second language (MA); transformative learning in the global community (Ed S). *Program availability:* Part-time. *Entrance requirements:* For master's, minimum GPA of 2.5. Additional exam requirements/recommendations for international students: Required—TOEFL. *Expenses: Tuition:* Full-time $22,500; part-time $750 per credit hour. Tuition and fees vary according to degree level, campus/location and program.

Wesleyan College, Department of Education, Program in Early Childhood Education, Macon, GA 31210-4462. Offers MA. *Program availability:* Part-time. *Entrance requirements:* For master's, two letters of professional reference, official transcript from the institution in which a Bachelor's degree was earned with an undergraduate GPA of 3.0, a copy of a valid professional teaching certificate or evidence of having been the teacher of record in a classroom for at least two years. Additional exam requirements/recommendations for international students: Required—TOEFL (minimum score 550 paper-based). *Application deadline:* Applications are processed on a rolling basis. Electronic applications accepted. *Expenses:* Contact institution. *Unit head:* Dr. Virginia Wilcox, Associate Professor of Education, 478-7575279, E-mail: vwilcox@wesleyancollege.edu. *Application contact:* Mariana Furlin, Assessment Coordinator for Education Department, Program Assistant to the EMBA, 478-7572801, E-mail: mfurlin@wesleyancollege.edu.

West Chester University of Pennsylvania, College of Education and Social Work, Department of Early and Middle Grades Education, West Chester, PA 19383. Offers applied studies in teaching and learning (M Ed); early childhood education (M Ed), including accomplished teacher, program administrator; grades 4-8 (Teaching Certificate); grades preK-4 (Teaching Certificate). *Accreditation:* NCATE. *Program availability:* Part-time, 100% online. *Degree requirements:* For master's, teacher research project, portfolio. *Entrance requirements:* For master's, certification (for applied studies in teaching and learning track); one year of full time teaching; minimum GPA of 3.0; for Teaching Certificate, math, social studies, or science concentration exams (for middle grades preparation), minimum GPA of 3.0. Additional exam requirements/recommendations for international students: Required—TOEFL or IELTS. Electronic applications accepted. *Faculty research:* Cooperative learning, creative expression and critical thinking, teacher research, learning styles, middle school education.

Western Kentucky University, Graduate School, College of Education and Behavioral Sciences, School of Teacher Education, Bowling Green, KY 42101. Offers elementary education (MAE, Ed S); exceptional education: learning and behavioral disorders (MAE); instructional design (MS); interdisciplinary early childhood education (MAE); library media education (MS); literacy education (MAE); middle grades education (MAE); secondary education (MAE, Ed S); special education: moderate and severe disabilities (MAE). *Program availability:* Part-time, evening/weekend, online learning. *Degree requirements:* For master's, comprehensive exam. *Entrance requirements:* For master's, GRE General Test. Additional exam requirements/recommendations for international students: Required—TOEFL (minimum score 555 paper-based; 79 iBT). *Faculty research:* Teacher preparation in moderate/severe disabilities.

Western Oregon University, Graduate Programs, College of Education, Division of Special Education, Program in Early Childhood Special Education, Monmouth, OR 97361. Offers MS Ed. *Accreditation:* NCATE. *Program availability:* Part-time, evening/weekend. *Degree requirements:* For master's, thesis optional, written exam, portfolio. *Entrance requirements:* For master's, CBEST, PRAXIS or GRE General Test, minimum GPA of 3.0, teaching license. Additional exam requirements/recommendations for international students: Required—TOEFL (minimum score 550 paper-based; 79 iBT), IELTS (minimum score 6.5). *Faculty research:* High school through university articulation, career development for early childhood educators professional collaboration/cooperation.

Westfield State University, College of Graduate and Continuing Education, Department of Education, Program in Early Childhood Education, Westfield, MA 01086. Offers M Ed. *Accreditation:* NCATE. *Program availability:* Part-time, evening/weekend. *Degree requirements:* For master's, comprehensive exam, practicum. *Entrance requirements:* For master's, GRE General Test or MAT, minimum undergraduate GPA of 2.8. Additional exam requirements/recommendations for international students: Recommended—TOEFL (minimum score 550 paper-based; 79 iBT).

Westminster College, Graduate School, Program in Educational Administration, New Wilmington, PA 16172-0001. Offers school principal K-12 (M Ed); school superintendent (M Ed).

West Virginia University, College of Education and Human Services, Morgantown, WV 26506. Offers audiology (Au D); autism spectrum disorder (MA); clinical rehabilitation and mental health counseling (MS); communication science and disorders (PhD); counseling (MA); counseling psychology (PhD); curriculum and instruction (Ed D); early childhood education (MA); early intervention/ early childhood special education (MA); education (PhD); educational leadership (MA); educational leadership/ public school administration (Ed D); educational leadership/public school administration (MA); educational psychology (MA, Ed D); elementary education (MA); gifted education (MA); higher education administration (MA, Ed D); higher education curriculum and teaching (MA); institutional design and technology (MA); instructional design and technology (Ed D); literacy education (MA); secondary education (MA); secondary education/English (MA); special education (Ed D); speech pathology (MS). *Accreditation:* ASHA; NCATE. *Program availability:* Part-time, evening/weekend, online learning. *Students:* 392 full-time (325 women), 337 part-time (285 women); includes 44 minority (16 Black or African American, non-Hispanic/Latino; 16 Hispanic/Latino; 12 Two or more races, non-Hispanic/Latino), 11 international. In 2018, 303 master's, 6 doctorates awarded. *Degree requirements:* For master's, content exams; for doctorate, comprehensive exam, thesis/dissertation. *Entrance requirements:* Additional exam requirements/recommendations for international students: Required—TOEFL (minimum score 500 paper-based; 61 iBT). *Application deadline:* For fall admission, 8/1 for domestic students; for spring admission, 1/1 for domestic students; for summer admission, 5/1 for domestic students. Application fee: $60. Electronic applications accepted. *Financial support:* Fellowships, research assistantships, teaching assistantships, career-related internships or fieldwork, Federal Work-Study, institutionally sponsored loans, health care benefits, tuition waivers (full and partial), and administrative assistantships available. Financial award applicants required to submit FAFSA. *Faculty research:* Internet training and integration for teachers, rural education, teacher preparation, organization of schools, evaluation of personnel. *Unit head:* Dr. Tracy L. Morris, Interim Dean, 304-293-0816, Fax: 304-293-7565, E-mail: Tracy.Morris@mail.wvu.edu. *Application contact:* Dr. Melissa Luna, Associate Dean for Research, 304-293-2174, Fax: 304-293-3802, E-mail: Melissa.Luna@mail.wvu.edu.
Website: http://cehs.wvu.edu/

Wichita State University, Graduate School, College of Applied Studies, School of Education, Wichita, KS 67260. Offers learning and instructional design (M Ed); special education (M Ed), including early childhood (M Ed, MAT), gifted, high incidence, low incidence; teaching (MAT), including early childhood (M Ed, MAT), middle level/secondary, transition to teaching. *Accreditation:* NCATE. *Program availability:* Part-time, evening/weekend, 100% online, blended/hybrid learning. *Entrance requirements:* For master's, MAT, minimum GPA of 2.75. *Unit head:* Dr. Edward Robeck, Department Head, 316-978-3322, E-mail: edward.robeck@wichita.edu. *Application contact:* Jordan Oleson, Admission Coordinator, 316-978-3095, Fax: 316-978-3253, E-mail: jordan.oleson@wichita.edu.

Widener University, School of Human Service Professions, Center for Education, Chester, PA 19013-5792. Offers adult education (M Ed); counseling in higher education (M Ed); counselor education (M Ed); early childhood education (M Ed); educational foundations (M Ed); educational leadership (M Ed); educational psychology (M Ed); elementary education (M Ed); English and language arts (M Ed); health education (M Ed); higher education leadership (Ed D); home and school visitor (M Ed); human sexuality (M Ed, PhD); mathematics education (M Ed); middle school education (M Ed); principalship (M Ed); reading and language arts (Ed D); reading education (M Ed); school administration (Ed D); science education (M Ed); social studies education (M Ed); special education (M Ed); technology education (M Ed). *Accreditation:* NCATE. *Program availability:* Part-time, evening/weekend. Terminal master's awarded for partial completion of doctoral program. *Degree requirements:* For doctorate, thesis/dissertation. *Entrance requirements:* For master's, minimum GPA of 2.5; for doctorate, GRE or MAT, minimum GPA of 2.0 (undergraduate), 3.5 (graduate). Electronic applications accepted. *Expenses:* Contact institution. *Faculty research:* Reading and cognition, adult education, technology education, educational leadership, special education.

William Paterson University of New Jersey, College of Education, Wayne, NJ 07470-8420. Offers curriculum and learning (M Ed); early childhood education (Certificate); educational leadership (M Ed); educational media specialist (Certificate); elementary education (MAT, Certificate); elementary education subject area (Certificate); higher education administration (MA); learning disabilities consultant (Certificate); literacy (M Ed); middle level education (M Ed); middle school education subject area (Certificate); professional counseling (M Ed); reading specialist (Certificate); school library media specialist (Certificate); school principal (Certificate); school supervisor (Certificate); secondary education (MAT); special education (M Ed); teacher of students with disabilities (Certificate). *Accreditation:* NCATE. *Program availability:* Part-time, evening/weekend. *Students:* Average age 35. 347 applicants, 87% accepted, 226 enrolled. In 2018, 136 master's awarded. *Degree requirements:* For master's, comprehensive exam, thesis (for some programs), exit interview (for some programs); practicum/internship; minimum GPA of 3.0 (for some programs); exit portfolio (for some programs). *Entrance requirements:* For master's, GRE/MAT, minimum GPA of 2.75; teaching certificate; essay; interview; 2 letters of recommendation; personal statement. Additional exam requirements/recommendations for international students: Required—TOEFL (minimum score 550 paper-based; 79 iBT), IELTS (minimum score 6). *Application deadline:* For fall admission, 6/1 for domestic students, 3/1 for international students; for spring admission, 11/1 for domestic students, 10/1 for international students. Applications are processed on a rolling basis. Application fee: $50. Electronic applications accepted. *Expenses: Tuition, area resident:* Full-time $14,714; part-time $727 per credit. Tuition, state resident: full-time $14,714; part-time $727 per credit. Tuition, nonresident: full-time $22,952; part-time $727 per credit. *International tuition:* $22,952 full-time. *Required fees:* $4 per semester. Tuition and fees vary according to course load, degree level and program. *Financial support:* In 2018–19, 8,416 students received support. Career-related internships or fieldwork, Federal Work-Study, scholarships/grants, and unspecified assistantships available. Support available to part-time students. Financial award application deadline: 3/15; financial award applicants

required to submit FAFSA. *Faculty research:* Code switching and creative writing, language instruction, teacher evaluation, preschools, history of educational theories. *Total annual research expenditures:* $311,226. *Unit head:* Dr. Dorothy Feola, Dean, 973-720-2138, Fax: 973-720-3647, E-mail: feolad@wpunj.edu. *Application contact:* Liana Fornarotto, Director of Education Enrollment and Certification, 973-720-2206, Fax: 973-720-2989, E-mail: fornarottol@wpunj.edu.
Website: http://www.wpunj.edu/coe

Worcester State University, Graduate School, Department of Education, Program in Early Childhood Education, Worcester, MA 01602-2597. Offers M Ed, Postbaccalaureate Certificate. *Faculty:* 4 full-time (all women), 14 part-time/adjunct (8 women). *Students:* 1 full-time (0 women), 13 part-time (all women). Average age 34. 5 applicants, 100% accepted, 3 enrolled. In 2018, 13 master's awarded. *Degree requirements:* For master's, comprehensive exam (for some programs), thesis, research project. For a detail list of degree completion requirements please see the graduate catalog at catalog.worcester.edu. *Entrance requirements:* For master's, GRE General Test or MAT, initial license or its equivalent in early childhood education. For a detail list of entrance requirements please see the graduate catalog at catalog.worcester.edu. Additional exam requirements/recommendations for international students: Required—TOEFL (minimum score 550 paper-based; 79 iBT), IELTS (minimum score 6). *Application deadline:* For fall admission, 3/1 for domestic and international students; for spring admission, 11/1 for domestic and international students; for summer admission, 3/1 for domestic and international students. Applications are processed on a rolling basis. Application fee: $50. Electronic applications accepted. *Expenses: Tuition, area resident:* Full-time $3042; part-time $169 per credit hour. Tuition, state resident: full-time $3042; part-time $169 per credit hour. Tuition, nonresident: full-time $3042; part-time $169 per credit hour. *International tuition:* $3042 full-time. *Required fees:* $2754; $153 per credit hour. *Financial support:* Scholarships/grants and unspecified assistantships available. Support available to part-time students. Financial award application deadline: 3/1; financial award applicants required to submit FAFSA. *Unit head:* Dr. Carol Donnelly, Early Childhood Graduate Coordinator, 508-929-8667, Fax: 508-929-8164, E-mail: cdonnelly@worcester.edu. *Application contact:* Sara Grady, Associate Dean of Graduate Studies and Professional Development, 508-929-8130, Fax: 508-929-8100, E-mail: sara.grady@worcester.edu.

Xavier University, College of Professional Sciences, School of Education, Department of Childhood Education and Literacy, Cincinnati, OH 45207. Offers children's multicultural literature (M Ed); elementary education (M Ed); Montessori education (M Ed); reading (M Ed). *Program availability:* Part-time. *Degree requirements:* For master's, comprehensive exam, thesis, 30 semester hours. *Entrance requirements:* For master's, GRE, MAT, official transcript; 3 letters of recommendation (for Montessori education); resume; statement of purpose. Additional exam requirements/recommendations for international students: Required—TOEFL (minimum score 550 paper-based; 79 iBT). Electronic applications accepted. Application fee is waived when completed online. *Expenses:* Contact institution. *Faculty research:* Multicultural literacy/fluency, early literacy development, writing/creative and across curriculum, assessment of reading abilities.

Elementary Education

Acacia University, American Graduate School of Education, Tempe, AZ 85284. Offers educational administration (M Ed); elementary education (MA); English as a second language (M Ed); secondary education (MA); special education (M Ed).

Adelphi University, College of Education & Health Sciences, College of Education and Health Services, Garden City, NY 11530-0701. Offers MA. *Program availability:* Part-time, evening/weekend. *Students:* 42 full-time (40 women), 14 part-time (11 women); includes 15 minority (2 Black or African American, non-Hispanic/Latino; 1 Asian, non-Hispanic/Latino; 12 Hispanic/Latino). Average age 24. 39 applicants, 44% accepted, 12 enrolled. In 2018, 11 master's awarded. *Entrance requirements:* For master's, official transcripts, bachelor's degree, 500 work essay, letters of recommendation, resume. Additional exam requirements/recommendations for international students: Required—TOEFL (minimum score 550 paper-based; 80 iBT), IELTS (minimum score 6.5). *Application deadline:* For fall admission, 3/1 for international students; for spring admission, 11/1 for international students. Application fee: $50. Electronic applications accepted. *Expenses:* Contact institution. *Financial support:* Research assistantships, teaching assistantships, career-related internships or fieldwork, institutionally sponsored loans, scholarships/grants, traineeships, and unspecified assistantships available. Support available to part-time students. Financial award application deadline: 1/1; financial award applicants required to submit FAFSA. *Faculty research:* Diversity; parental involvement; teacher education; psychoanalytic understanding of racial formation; relationships between ideology, language, culture and individual subject formation. *Unit head:* Dr. Shilpi Sinha, Director, 516-877-4144, E-mail: sinha@adelphi.edu. *Application contact:* Dr. Shilpi Sinha, Director, 516-877-4144, E-mail: sinha@adelphi.edu.

Alabama Agricultural and Mechanical University, School of Graduate Studies, College of Education, Humanities, and Behavioral Sciences, Department of Reading, Elementary, Early Childhood and Special Education, Huntsville, AL 35811. Offers early childhood education (MS Ed, Ed S); elementary education (MS Ed, Ed S); reading/literacy (PhD); special education collaborative teacher training (MS Ed, Ed S). *Accreditation:* NCATE. *Program availability:* Evening/weekend. *Degree requirements:* For master's, comprehensive exam; for Ed S, thesis. *Entrance requirements:* For master's, GRE General Test. Additional exam requirements/recommendations for international students: Required—TOEFL (minimum score 500 paper-based; 61 iBT). Electronic applications accepted. *Faculty research:* Multicultural education, learning styles, diagnostic-prescriptive instruction.

Alaska Pacific University, Graduate Programs, Education Department, Program in Teaching, Anchorage, AK 99508-4672. Offers teaching (K-8) (MAT). *Degree requirements:* For master's, research project. *Entrance requirements:* For master's, GRE or MAT, PRAXIS, minimum GPA of 3.0.

Albright College, Graduate Division, Reading, PA 19612-5234. Offers early childhood education (MS); elementary education (MS); English as a second language (MA); general education (MA); special education (MS). *Program availability:* Part-time, evening/weekend. *Degree requirements:* For master's, thesis. *Entrance requirements:* For master's, GRE General Test or MAT, minimum undergraduate GPA of 3.0, 2 letters of recommendation, interview. Additional exam requirements/recommendations for international students: Recommended—TOEFL (minimum score 525 paper-based). Electronic applications accepted.

Alcorn State University, School of Graduate Studies, School of Education and Psychology, Lorman, MS 39096-7500. Offers agricultural education (MS Ed); elementary education (MAT, MS Ed, Ed S); guidance and counseling (MS Ed); industrial education (MS Ed); secondary education (MAT, MS Ed), including health and physical education (MS Ed), NCAA compliance and academic progress reporting (MS Ed); special education (MS Ed). *Accreditation:* NCATE. *Degree requirements:* For master's, thesis optional.

American International College, School of Education, Springfield, MA 01109-3189. Offers early childhood education (M Ed, CAGS); education (MA, Ed D), including counseling psychology (MA), educational leadership and supervision (Ed D), professional counseling and supervision (Ed D), teaching and learning (Ed D); elementary education (M Ed, CAGS); middle education/secondary education (M Ed, CAGS); moderate disabilities (M Ed, CAGS); reading specialist (M Ed, CAGS); school adjustment counseling (MAEP, CAGS); school guidance counseling (MAEP, CAGS); school leadership (M Ed, CAGS). *Program availability:* Evening/weekend. *Degree requirements:* For master's and CAGS, practicum/culminating experience. *Entrance requirements:* For master's, Communication and Literacy portion of the Massachusetts Tests for Education Licensure, graduate of accredited four-year college with minimum B-average in undergraduate course work; for CAGS, M Ed or master's degree in field related to licensure from accredited institution. Electronic applications accepted. *Expenses:* Contact institution.

American University of Beirut, Graduate Programs, Faculty of Arts and Sciences, Beirut 1107 2020, Lebanon. Offers anthropology (MA); Arab and Middle Eastern history (PhD); Arabic language and literature (MA, PhD); archaeology (MA); art history and curating (MA); biology (MS); cell and molecular biology (PhD); chemistry (MS); clinical psychology (MA); computational sciences (MS); computer science (MS); economics (MA); education (MA), including administration and policy studies, elementary education, mathematics education, psychology school guidance, psychology test and measurements, science education, teaching English as a foreign language; English language (MA); English literature (MA); environmental policy planning (MS); financial economics (MAFE); general psychology (MA); geology (MS); history (MA); Islamic studies (MA); mathematics (MS); media studies (MA); Middle East studies (MA); philosophy (MA); physics (MS); political studies (MA); public administration (MA); public policy and international affairs (MA); sociology (MA); theoretical physics (PhD). *Program availability:* Part-time. *Faculty:* 187 full-time (64 women), 27 part-time/adjunct (15 women). *Students:* 292 full-time (215 women), 216 part-time (148 women). Average age 27. 422 applicants, 64% accepted, 124 enrolled. In 2018, 90 master's, 3 doctorates awarded. *Degree requirements:* For master's, comprehensive exam, thesis (for some programs), project; for doctorate, comprehensive exam, thesis/dissertation (for some programs). *Entrance requirements:* For master's, GRE General Test (for archaeology, clinical psychology, general psychology, economics, financial economics and biology); for doctorate, GRE General Test for all PhD programs, GRE Subject Test for theoretical physics. Additional exam requirements/recommendations for international students: Required—TOEFL (minimum score 583 paper-based; 97 iBT), IELTS (minimum score 7). *Application deadline:* For fall admission, 3/18 for domestic students; for spring admission, 11/5 for domestic students. Application fee: $50. Electronic applications accepted. *Expenses:* MA/MS: Humanities and social sciences=$912/credit. Sciences=$943/credit. Financial economics=$986/credit. Thesis: Humanities/social

sciences=$6565 and sciences=$6865. *Financial support:* In 2018–19, 227 fellowships with full tuition reimbursements, 17 research assistantships with full tuition reimbursements, 83 teaching assistantships with full tuition reimbursements were awarded; scholarships/grants, tuition waivers (full and partial), and unspecified assistantships also available. Financial award application deadline: 3/18. *Faculty research:* Sciences: Physics: High energy, Particle, Polymer and Soft Matter, Thermal, Plasma; String Theory, Mathematical physics, Astrophysics (stellar evolution, planet and galaxy formation and evolution, astrophysical dynamics), Solid State physics/thin films, Spintronics, Magnetic properties of materials, Mineralogy, Petrology, and Geochemistry of Hard Rocks, Geophysics and Petrophysics, Hydrogeology, Micropaleontology, Sedimentology, and Stratigraphy, Structural Geology and Geotectonics, Renewable en. *Total annual research expenditures:* $4.3 million. *Unit head:* Dr. Nadia Maria El Cheikh, Dean, Faculty of Arts and Sciences, 961-1-350000 Ext. 3800, Fax: 961-1-744461, E-mail: nmcheikh@aub.edu.lb. *Application contact:* Adriana Michelle Zanaty, Curriculum and Graduate Studies Officer, 961-1-350000 Ext. 3833, Fax: 961-1-744461, E-mail: az48@aub.edu.lb.
Website: https://www.aub.edu.lb/fas/Pages/default.aspx

American University of Puerto Rico, Program in Education, Bayamon, PR 00960-2037. Offers art education (M Ed); elementary education 4-6 (M Ed); elementary education K-3 (M Ed); general science education (M Ed); physical education (M Ed); special education (M Ed). *Program availability:* Part-time, evening/weekend. *Entrance requirements:* For master's, EXADEP, GRE, or MAT, 2 letters of recommendation, minimum GPA of 2.5.

Anderson University, College of Education, Anderson, SC 29621-4035. Offers administration and supervision (M Ed); education (M Ed); elementary education (MAT). *Accreditation:* NCATE. *Program availability:* 100% online. *Expenses: Tuition:* Full-time $400; part-time $400 per credit. *Required fees:* $200; $200 per semester. Tuition and fees vary according to course load. *Financial support:* Scholarships/grants and tuition waivers available. Financial award application deadline: 3/1; financial award applicants required to submit FAFSA. *Unit head:* Dr. Mark Butler, Dean, 864-231-2042. *Application contact:* Dr. Mark Butler, Dean, 864-231-2042.
Website: https://www.andersonuniversity.edu/education

Andrews University, School of Graduate Studies, School of Education, Department of Teaching, Learning, and Curriculum, Berrien Springs, MI 49104. Offers curriculum and instruction (MA, Ed D, PhD, Ed S); elementary education (MAT); secondary education (MAT), including biology, education, English, English as a second language, French, history, physics; teacher education (MAT). *Entrance requirements:* For master's, GRE Subject Test. Additional exam requirements/recommendations for international students: Required—TOEFL (minimum score 550 paper-based).

Anna Maria College, Graduate Division, Program in Education, Paxton, MA 01612. Offers early childhood education (M Ed); education (CAGS); elementary education (M Ed); English language arts (M Ed); visual arts (M Ed). *Program availability:* Part-time, evening/weekend. *Entrance requirements:* For master's, bachelor's degree in liberal arts or sciences, minimum GPA of 3.0. Additional exam requirements/recommendations for international students: Required—TOEFL (minimum score 500 paper-based). Electronic applications accepted.

Antioch University New England, Graduate School, Department of Education, Integrated Learning Program, Keene, NH 03431-3552. Offers early childhood education (M Ed); elementary education (M Ed), including arts and humanities, science and environmental education; special education (M Ed). *Degree requirements:* For master's, internship. *Entrance requirements:* For master's, previous course work or work experience in education. Additional exam requirements/recommendations for international students: Required—TOEFL (minimum score 550 paper-based). Electronic applications accepted. *Expenses:* Contact institution. *Faculty research:* Problem-based learning, place-based education, mathematics education, democratic classrooms, art education.

Antioch University New England, Graduate School, Department of Education, Waldorf Teacher Training Program, Keene, NH 03431-3552. Offers elementary education (M Ed, Certificate). *Degree requirements:* For master's, thesis (for some programs), internship. *Entrance requirements:* For master's, foundation studies in anthroposophy or equivalent. Additional exam requirements/recommendations for international students: Required—TOEFL (minimum score 550 paper-based). Electronic applications accepted. *Expenses:* Contact institution. *Faculty research:* Teacher renewal, early childhood education, collaborative leadership.

Appalachian State University, Cratis D. Williams School of Graduate Studies, Department of Curriculum and Instruction, Boone, NC 28608. Offers curriculum specialist (MA); educational media (MA); elementary education (MA); middle grades education (MA), including language arts, mathematics, science, social studies. *Accreditation:* NCATE. *Program availability:* Part-time, evening/weekend, online learning. *Degree requirements:* For master's, comprehensive exam, thesis or alternative. *Entrance requirements:* For master's, GRE General Test or MAT, 3 letters of recommendation. Additional exam requirements/recommendations for international students: Required—TOEFL (minimum score 570 paper-based; 79 iBT), IELTS (minimum score 6.5). Electronic applications accepted. *Expenses: Tuition, area resident:* Full-time $4839; part-time $237 per credit hour. Tuition, state resident: full-time $4839; part-time $237 per credit hour. Tuition, nonresident: full-time $18,271; part-time $895.50 per credit hour. *Faculty research:* Media literacy, elementary teaching, curriculum development, online learning environments.

Aquinas College, School of Education, Nashville, TN 37205-2005. Offers elementary education (MAT); secondary education (MAT); teaching and learning (M Ed).

Arcadia University, School of Education, Glenside, PA 19038-3295. Offers art education (M Ed); computer education (CAS); curriculum (CAS); curriculum studies (M Ed); early childhood education (M Ed), including individualized, master teacher, research in child development; educational leadership (M Ed, Ed D, CAS); elementary education (M Ed); English education (MA Ed); environmental education (MA Ed); instructional technology (M Ed); language arts (M Ed); library science (M Ed); mathematics education (M Ed, MA Ed); music education (MA Ed); psychology (MA Ed); reading (M Ed, CAS); science education (M Ed, CAS); secondary education (M Ed, CAS); special education (M Ed, Ed D, CAS); theater arts (MA Ed); written communication (MA Ed). *Accreditation:* NASAD. *Program availability:* Part-time, evening/weekend, online learning. *Faculty:* 14 full-time (10 women). *Students:* 35 full-time (24 women), 299 part-time (243 women); includes 72 minority (49 Black or African American, non-Hispanic/Latino; 1 American Indian or Alaska Native, non-Hispanic/Latino; 12 Asian, non-Hispanic/Latino; 8 Hispanic/Latino; 2 Two or more races, non-Hispanic/Latino), 5 international. In 2018, 152 master's, 8 doctorates awarded. *Entrance requirements:* Additional exam requirements/recommendations for international students: Required—Official results from the TOEFL or IELTS are required. *Application deadline:* Applications are processed on a rolling basis. Application fee: $25. Electronic applications accepted. *Expenses:* Contact institution. *Financial support:* Career-related internships or fieldwork, tuition waivers (partial), and unspecified assistantships available. *Unit head:* Kimberly Dean, Chair, 215-572-8629. *Application contact:* 215-572-2925, Fax: 215-572-2126, E-mail: grad@arcadia.edu.

Argosy University, Atlanta, College of Education, Atlanta, GA 30328. Offers educational leadership (MAEd, Ed D, Ed S), including higher education administration (Ed D), K-12 education (Ed D); teaching and learning (MAEd, Ed D, Ed S), including education technology (Ed D), higher education (Ed D), K-12 education (Ed D).

Argosy University, Chicago, College of Education, Chicago, IL 60601. Offers adult education and training (MA Ed); community college executive leadership (Ed D); educational leadership (MA Ed, Ed D, Ed S), including district leadership (Ed D), higher education administration (Ed D), K-12 education (Ed D); instructional leadership (Ed D, Ed S), including higher education (Ed D), K-12 education (Ed D). *Program availability:* Online learning.

Argosy University, Hawai`i, College of Education, Honolulu, HI 96813. Offers adult education and training (MAEd); educational leadership (Ed D), including higher education administration, K-12 education; instructional leadership (Ed D), including higher education, K-12 education; school psychology (MA).

Argosy University, Los Angeles, College of Education, Los Angeles, CA 90045. Offers community college executive leadership (Ed D); educational leadership (MA Ed, Ed D), including higher education administration (Ed D), K-12 education (Ed D); instructional leadership (MA Ed, Ed D), including higher education (Ed D), K-12 education (Ed D), multiple subject teacher preparation (MA Ed), single subject teacher preparation (MA Ed).

Argosy University, Northern Virginia, College of Education, Arlington, VA 22209. Offers community college executive leadership (Ed D); educational leadership (MA Ed, Ed D, Ed S), including higher education administration (Ed D), K-12 education (Ed D); instructional leadership (MA Ed, Ed D, Ed S), including higher education (Ed D), K-12 education (Ed D).

Argosy University, Orange County, College of Education, Orange, CA 92868. Offers community college executive leadership (Ed D); educational leadership (MA Ed, Ed D), including higher education administration (Ed D), K-12 education (Ed D); instructional leadership (MA Ed, Ed D), including education technology (Ed D), higher education (Ed D), K-12 education (Ed D), multiple subject teacher preparation (MA Ed), single subject teacher preparation (MA Ed).

Argosy University, Phoenix, College of Education, Phoenix, AZ 85021. Offers adult education and training (MA Ed); advanced educational administration (Ed D, Ed S); community college executive leadership (Ed D); educational administration (MA Ed); educational leadership (MA Ed, Ed D, Ed S), including education technology (Ed D), higher education administration (Ed D), K-12 education (Ed D); higher and postsecondary education (MA Ed); initial educational administration (Ed D, Ed S); school psychology (MA); teaching and learning (MA Ed, Ed D, Ed S), including education technology (Ed D), higher education (Ed D), K-12 education (Ed D).

Argosy University, Seattle, College of Education, Seattle, WA 98121. Offers adult education and training (MA Ed); community college executive leadership (Ed D); educational leadership (MA Ed, Ed D), including higher education administration (Ed D), K-12 education (Ed D); higher and postsecondary education (MA Ed); instructional leadership (MA Ed, Ed D), including education technology (Ed D), higher education (Ed D), K-12 education (Ed D).

Argosy University, Tampa, College of Education, Tampa, FL 33607. Offers community college executive leadership (Ed D); educational leadership (MA Ed, Ed D, Ed S), including higher education administration (Ed D), K-12 education (Ed D); school counseling (MA); teaching and learning (MA Ed, Ed D, Ed S), including higher education (Ed D), K-12 education (Ed D).

Argosy University, Twin Cities, College of Education, Eagan, MN 55121. Offers advanced educational administration (Ed D, Ed S); educational leadership (MA Ed, Ed D, Ed S), including higher education administration (Ed D), K-12 education (Ed D); higher and postsecondary education (MA Ed); initial educational administration (Ed D, Ed S); instructional leadership (MA Ed, Ed D, Ed S), including education technology (Ed D), higher education (Ed D), K-12 education (Ed D).

Arizona State University at the Tempe campus, Mary Lou Fulton Teachers College, Program in Curriculum and Instruction, Phoenix, AZ 85069. Offers curriculum and instruction (M Ed, MA); elementary education (M Ed); physical education (MPE); secondary education (M Ed). *Program availability:* Part-time, evening/weekend, online learning. Terminal master's awarded for partial completion of doctoral program. *Degree requirements:* For master's, thesis or alternative, applied project, interactive Program of Study (iPOS) submitted before completing 50 percent of required credit hours. *Entrance requirements:* For master's, GRE or GMAT (for some programs), minimum GPA of 3.0 or equivalent in last 2 years of work leading to bachelor's degree, 3 letters of recommendation, personal statement describing research and career goals, curriculum vitae or resume, IVP fingerprint clearance card (for those seeking Arizona certification). Additional exam requirements/recommendations for international students: Required—TOEFL, IELTS, or PTE. Electronic applications accepted. *Expenses:* Contact institution. *Faculty research:* Early childhood, media and computers, elementary education, secondary education, English education, bilingual education, language and literacy, science education, engineering education, exercise and wellness education.

Arkansas State University, Graduate School, College of Education and Behavioral Science, School of Teacher Education and Leadership, State University, AR 72467. Offers community college administration (SCCT); curriculum and instruction (MSE); early childhood education (MSE); early childhood services (MS); educational leadership (MSE, Ed D, Ed S); educational theory and practice (MSE); middle level education (MAT, MSE); reading (MSE, Ed S); special education - gifted, talented, and creative (MSE); special education - instructional specialist grades 4-12 (MSE); special education - instructional specialist grades P-4 (MSE); special education, K-12 (MSE). *Accreditation:* NCATE. *Program availability:* Part-time, online learning. *Degree requirements:* For master's, comprehensive exam, thesis or alternative; for doctorate, comprehensive exam, thesis/dissertation; for other advanced degree, comprehensive exam. *Entrance requirements:* For master's, GRE General Test or MAT, appropriate bachelor's degree, official transcripts, immunization records, letters of reference, interview; for doctorate, GRE General Test or MAT, interview, master's degree, letters of reference, official transcript, personal statement, writing sample, immunization records; for other advanced degree, GRE General Test or MAT, interview, master's degree, official transcript, immunization records, letters of reference, 3 years of teaching experience, teaching license. Additional exam requirements/recommendations for international students: Required—TOEFL (minimum score 550 paper-based; 79 iBT), IELTS (minimum score 6), PTE (minimum score 56). Electronic applications accepted.

Arkansas Tech University, College of Education, Russellville, AR 72801. Offers college student personnel (MS); educational leadership (M Ed, Ed S); instructional technology (M Ed); school counseling and leadership (M Ed); school leadership (Ed D); special education K-12 (M Ed); strength and conditioning studies (MS); teaching (MAT); teaching, learning, and leadership (M Ed). *Accreditation:* NCATE. *Program availability:* Part-time, evening/weekend, 100% online, blended/hybrid learning. *Students:* 90 full-time (52 women), 450 part-time (359 women); includes 100 minority (63 Black or African American, non-Hispanic/Latino; 6 American Indian or Alaska Native, non-Hispanic/Latino; 1 Asian, non-Hispanic/Latino; 15 Hispanic/Latino; 15 Two or more races, non-

Hispanic/Latino), 4 international. Average age 34. In 2018, 130 master's, 14 doctorates, 1 other advanced degree awarded. *Degree requirements:* For master's, comprehensive exam, thesis optional, action research project; for doctorate, thesis/dissertation. *Entrance requirements:* Additional exam requirements/recommendations for international students: Required—TOEFL (minimum score 550 paper-based; 79 iBT), IELTS (minimum score 6.5), PTE (minimum score 58). *Application deadline:* For fall admission, 3/1 priority date for domestic students, 5/1 priority date for international students; for spring admission, 10/1 priority date for domestic and international students. Applications are processed on a rolling basis. Application fee: $40 ($90 for international students). Electronic applications accepted. *Expenses: Tuition, area resident:* Full-time $6816; part-time $284 per credit hour. Tuition, state resident: full-time $6816; part-time $284 per credit hour. Tuition, nonresident: full-time $13,632; part-time $568 per credit hour. *International tuition:* $13,632 full-time. *Required fees:* $457.50 per semester. Tuition and fees vary according to course load and degree level. *Financial support:* In 2018–19, research assistantships with full and partial tuition reimbursements (averaging $4,800 per year), teaching assistantships with full and partial tuition reimbursements (averaging $4,800 per year) were awarded; career-related internships or fieldwork, Federal Work-Study, scholarships/grants, health care benefits, and unspecified assistantships also available. Support available to part-time students. Financial award application deadline: 4/15; financial award applicants required to submit FAFSA. *Unit head:* Dr. Linda Bean, Dean, 479-964-3217, E-mail: lbean@atu.edu. *Application contact:* Dr. Jeff Robertson, Interim Dean of Graduate College, 479-968-0398, Fax: 479-964-0542, E-mail: gradcollege@atu.edu.
Website: http://www.atu.edu/education/

Auburn University at Montgomery, College of Education, Department of Curriculum, Instruction, and Technology, Montgomery, AL 36124-4023. Offers elementary education (M Ed, Ed S); instructional technology (Ed S); secondary education (M Ed). *Faculty:* 12 full-time (8 women), 8 part-time/adjunct (all women). *Students:* 43 full-time (34 women), 81 part-time (65 women); includes 39 minority (38 Black or African American, non-Hispanic/Latino; 1 Hispanic/Latino), 2 international. Average age 33. 99 applicants, 70% accepted, 37 enrolled. In 2018, 47 master's awarded. *Degree requirements:* For master's, comprehensive exam, thesis (for some programs). *Entrance requirements:* For master's, GRE or MAT. Additional exam requirements/recommendations for international students: Recommended—TOEFL (minimum score 500 paper-based; 61 iBT), IELTS (minimum score 5.5), TSE (minimum score 44). *Application deadline:* For fall admission, 7/15 for international students; for spring admission, 11/15 for international students; for summer admission, 4/15 for international students. Applications are processed on a rolling basis. Application fee: $25. Electronic applications accepted. *Expenses: Tuition, area resident:* Full-time $7146; part-time $4764 per credit hour. Tuition, state resident: full-time $7146; part-time $4764 per credit hour. Tuition, nonresident: full-time $16,056; part-time $10,704 per credit hour. *International tuition:* $16,056 full-time. *Required fees:* $766. One-time fee: $25 full-time. *Financial support:* Application deadline: 3/1; applicants required to submit FAFSA. *Unit head:* Dr. Kellie Shumack, Head, 334-244-3737, Fax: 334-244-3835, E-mail: kshumack@aum.edu. *Application contact:* Dr. Rhonda Morton, Associate Dean/Graduate Coordinator, 334-224-3287, Fax: 334-244-3978, E-mail: rmorton@aum.edu. Website: http://education.aum.edu/academic-departments/curriculum-instruction-technology

Augusta University, College of Education, Program in Curriculum and Instruction, Augusta, GA 30912. Offers curriculum and instruction (Ed S); elementary education (MAT); foreign language education (MAT); instruction (M Ed); middle grades education (MAT); music education (MAT); secondary education (MAT); special education (MAT). *Degree requirements:* For master's, thesis, portfolio. *Entrance requirements:* For master's, GRE, MAT, minimum GPA of 2.5.

Avila University, School of Education, Kansas City, MO 64145-1698. Offers advanced classroom management (MA); elementary education (Teaching Certificate); English language learners (Advanced Certificate); middle school (Teaching Certificate); physical education K-12 (Teaching Certificate); secondary education (Teaching Certificate). *Program availability:* Part-time, evening/weekend, online learning. *Faculty:* 6 full-time (5 women), 9 part-time/adjunct (8 women). *Students:* 83 full-time (71 women), 84 part-time (69 women); includes 13 minority (6 Black or African American, non-Hispanic/Latino; 2 Asian, non-Hispanic/Latino; 4 Hispanic/Latino; 1 Two or more races, non-Hispanic/Latino), 2 international. Average age 40. 92 applicants, 62% accepted, 40 enrolled. In 2018, 21 master's awarded. *Entrance requirements:* For master's, minimum GPA of 3.0, writing sample, recommendation, interview; for other advanced degree, foreign language. Additional exam requirements/recommendations for international students: Required—TOEFL (minimum score 580 paper-based; 92 iBT). *Application deadline:* Applications are processed on a rolling basis. Electronic applications accepted. *Expenses:* Contact institution. *Financial support:* In 2018–19, 12 students received support. Unspecified assistantships available. Financial award applicants required to submit FAFSA. *Unit head:* Dr. Stacy Keith, Director of Graduate Education, 816-501-2446, Fax: 816-501-2915, E-mail: stacy.keith@avila.edu. *Application contact:* Cory Roup, Graduate Education Enrollment and Academic Advisor, 816-501-2464, E-mail: cory.roup@avila.edu.
Website: https://www.avila.edu/academics/graduate-studies/grad-education

Ball State University, Graduate School, College of Sciences and Humanities, Department of Mathematical Sciences, Muncie, IN 47306. Offers actuarial science (MA); elementary mathematics teacher leadership (Certificate); mathematics (MA, MS), including mathematics; mathematics education (MA), including mathematics education; middle school mathematics education (Certificate); post-secondary foundational mathematics teaching (MA, Certificate); statistical modeling (Certificate); statistics (MA, MS), including statistics. *Program availability:* Part-time, 100% online, blended/hybrid learning. *Entrance requirements:* For master's, minimum baccalaureate GPA of 2.75 or 3.0 in latter half of baccalaureate. Additional exam requirements/recommendations for international students: Required—TOEFL (minimum score 550 paper-based; 79 iBT), IELTS (minimum score 6.5). Electronic applications accepted. *Faculty research:* Differential equations.

Ball State University, Graduate School, Teachers College, Department of Elementary Education, Muncie, IN 47306. Offers early childhood administration (Certificate); elementary education (MAE, Ed D, PhD); enhanced teaching practices for elementary teachers (Certificate); literacy instruction (Certificate). *Accreditation:* NCATE. *Program availability:* Part-time, 100% online. *Entrance requirements:* For master's, minimum baccalaureate GPA of 2.75 or 3.0 in latter half of baccalaureate; for doctorate, GRE General Test, minimum graduate GPA of 3.2. Additional exam requirements/recommendations for international students: Required—TOEFL (minimum score 550 paper-based; 79 iBT), IELTS (minimum score 6.5). Electronic applications accepted.

Bank Street College of Education, Graduate School, Program in Elementary/Childhood Education, New York, NY 10025. Offers early childhood and elementary/childhood education (MS Ed); elementary/childhood education (MS Ed). *Degree requirements:* For master's, thesis. *Entrance requirements:* For master's, interview, essays. Additional exam requirements/recommendations for international students: Required—TOEFL (minimum score 600 paper-based; 100 iBT), IELTS (minimum score

7). Electronic applications accepted. *Faculty research:* Social studies in the elementary grades, urban education, experiential learning, child-centered classrooms.

Barry University, School of Education, Program in Curriculum and Instruction, Miami Shores, FL 33161-6695. Offers accomplished teacher (Ed S); culture, language and literacy (TESOL) (PhD); curriculum evaluation and research (PhD); early childhood (Ed S); early childhood education (PhD); elementary (Ed S); elementary education (PhD); ESOL (Ed S); gifted (Ed S); Montessori (Ed S); PKP/elementary (Ed S); reading (Ed S); reading, language and cognition (PhD). *Entrance requirements:* For doctorate, GRE, minimum GPA of 3.25.

Barry University, School of Education, Program in Elementary Education, Miami Shores, FL 33161-6695. Offers elementary education (MS); elementary education/ESOL (MS). *Program availability:* Part-time, evening/weekend. *Degree requirements:* For master's, comprehensive exam, practicum. *Entrance requirements:* For master's, GRE General Test or MAT, minimum GPA of 3.0. Electronic applications accepted.

Barton College, Program in Elementary Education, Wilson, NC 27893-7000. Offers M Ed. *Entrance requirements:* For master's, MAT or GRE taken within last five years, bachelor's degree from accredited college or university, minimum GPA of 3.0 for undergraduate work (recommended), official transcript, one year of teaching experience, copy of recognized teaching license in elementary education, personal statement, recommendation form from current employer or administrator, interview. Additional exam requirements/recommendations for international students: Required—TOEFL (minimum score 550 paper-based). Electronic applications accepted. Tuition and fees vary according to program.

Bayamón Central University, Graduate Programs, Program in Education, Bayamón, PR 00960-1725. Offers administration and supervision (MA Ed); commercial education (MA Ed); elementary education (K–3) (MA Ed); family counseling (Graduate Certificate); guidance and counseling (MA Ed); pre-elementary teacher (MA Ed); rehabilitation counseling (MA Ed); special education (MA Ed), including attention deficit disorder, education of the autistic, learning disabilities. *Program availability:* Part-time, evening/weekend. *Degree requirements:* For master's, comprehensive exam. *Entrance requirements:* For master's, EXADEP, bachelor's degree in education or related field.

Bellarmine University, Annsley Frazier Thornton School of Education, Louisville, KY 40205. Offers education and district leadership (Ed D); education and social change (PhD); elementary education (MA Ed, MAT); leadership in higher education (PhD); middle school education (MA Ed, MAT); principalship (Ed S); reading and writing (MA Ed); secondary education (MAT); teacher leadership (MA Ed). *Accreditation:* NCATE. *Program availability:* Part-time, evening/weekend. *Faculty:* 14 full-time (7 women), 17 part-time/adjunct (11 women). *Students:* 27 full-time (19 women), 205 part-time (156 women); includes 74 minority (53 Black or African American, non-Hispanic/Latino; 6 Asian, non-Hispanic/Latino; 7 Hispanic/Latino; 8 Two or more races, non-Hispanic/Latino). Average age 34. 155 applicants, 71% accepted, 95 enrolled. In 2018, 69 master's, 10 doctorates, 30 other advanced degrees awarded. *Degree requirements:* For master's, comprehensive exam (for some programs), thesis (for some programs); for doctorate, comprehensive exam (for some programs), thesis/dissertation; for Ed S, comprehensive exam (for some programs). *Entrance requirements:* For master's, GRE, baccalaureate degree from accredited institution; minimum cumulative GPA of 2.75; recommendations from employers, supervisors, or professors attesting to applicant's potential as graduate student; statement of intent to pursue graduate degree; for doctorate, GRE, minimum GPA of 3.5 in all graduate coursework; baccalaureate and master's degrees in education or fields directly relevant to education; three letters of recommendation; two essays (no more than 1,000 words each); resume or curriculum vitae; interview; for Ed S, master's degree in education; valid teaching certificate; three years of experience in teaching; three recommendations; minimum GPA of 3.0 in all graduate work; interview; essays; personal goal statement. Additional exam requirements/recommendations for international students: Required—TOEFL (minimum score 80 iBT), IELTS (minimum score 6), TOEFL (minimum score 550 paper-based, 68 iBT), IELTS (minimum score 6), or Michigan English Language Assessment Battery. *Application deadline:* For fall admission, 8/1 priority date for domestic and international students; for spring admission, 12/1 priority date for domestic and international students; for summer admission, 4/10 priority date for domestic and international students. Applications are processed on a rolling basis. Application fee: $40. Electronic applications accepted. *Expenses:* Doctor of Education: $855 per credit hour; Educational Specialist: $410 per credit hour; Master of Arts in Education: $410 per credit hour; Master of Arts in Teaching: $665 per credit hour; Master of Arts in Teaching, undergraduate content courses: $410 per credit hour; Master of Education in Higher Education Leadership and Social Justice: $665 per credit hour; Ph.D., Social Change: $855 per credit hour; Ph.D., Leadership in Higher Education: $855 per credit hour; Rank I Programs: $410 per credit hour. *Financial support:* Scholarships/grants available. Financial award applicants required to submit FAFSA. *Faculty research:* Literacy, service-learning, dispositions, educational technology, special education. *Unit head:* Dr. Elizabeth Dinkins, Dean, 502-272-7958, Fax: 502-272-8189, E-mail: edinkins@bellarmine.edu. *Application contact:* Sarah Schuble, Assistant Director of Graduate Student Enrollment, 502-272-8271, Fax: 502-272-8002, E-mail: sschuble@bellarmine.edu.
Website: http://www.bellarmine.edu/education/graduate

Bethel University, Graduate School, St. Paul, MN 55112-6999. Offers business administration (MBA); classroom management (Certificate); counseling (MA); K-12 education (MA); leadership (Ed D); leadership foundations (Certificate); nurse educator (MS, Certificate); nurse-midwifery (MS); physician assistant (MS); special education (MA); strategic leadership (MA); teaching (MA); teaching and learning (Certificate). *Program availability:* Part-time, evening/weekend, 100% online, blended/hybrid learning. *Faculty:* 23 full-time (17 women), 73 part-time/adjunct (45 women). *Students:* 586 full-time (426 women), 372 part-time (244 women); includes 141 minority (49 Black or African American, non-Hispanic/Latino; 6 American Indian or Alaska Native, non-Hispanic/Latino; 19 Asian, non-Hispanic/Latino; 40 Hispanic/Latino; 2 Native Hawaiian or other Pacific Islander, non-Hispanic/Latino; 25 Two or more races, non-Hispanic/Latino), 25 international. Average age 35. 642 applicants, 39% accepted, 194 enrolled. In 2018, 312 master's, 28 doctorates, 134 other advanced degrees awarded. *Degree requirements:* For master's, comprehensive exam (for some programs), thesis (for some programs); for doctorate, comprehensive exam, thesis/dissertation. *Entrance requirements:* Additional exam requirements/recommendations for international students: Required—TOEFL (minimum score 550 paper-based; 80 iBT), TOEFL (minimum score 550 paper-based, 80 iBT) or IELTS. *Application deadline:* Applications are processed on a rolling basis. Application fee: $0. Electronic applications accepted. *Expenses:* Contact institution. *Financial support:* Teaching assistantships, career-related internships or fieldwork, and scholarships/grants available. Support available to part-time students. Financial award applicants required to submit FAFSA. *Unit head:* Dr. Randy Bergen, Associate Provost, 651-635-8000, Fax: 651-635-8004, E-mail: r-bergen@bethel.edu. *Application contact:* Director of Admissions, 651-635-8000, Fax: 651-635-8004, E-mail: gs@bethel.edu.
Website: https://www.bethel.edu/graduate/

Blue Mountain College, Program in Elementary Education, Blue Mountain, MS 38610. Offers M Ed. *Program availability:* Part-time, evening/weekend. *Degree requirements:*

Elementary Education

For master's, comprehensive exam. *Entrance requirements:* For master's, PRAXIS, GRE or MAT, official transcripts; bachelor's degree in a field of education from accredited university or college; teaching certificate; three recommendations. Additional exam requirements/recommendations for international students: Required—TOEFL (minimum score 550 paper-based). Electronic applications accepted.

Bob Jones University, Graduate Programs, Greenville, SC 29614. Offers accountancy (MS); Bible (MA); Bible translation (MA); Biblical studies (Certificate); business administration (MBA); church history (MA, PhD); church ministries (MA); church music (MM); cinema and video production (MA); counseling (MS); curriculum and instruction (Ed D); divinity (M Div); dramatic production (MA); educational leadership (MS, Ed D, Ed S); elementary education (M Ed, MAT); English (M Ed, MA, MAT); fine arts (MA); graphic design (MA); history (M Ed, MA); illustration (MA); interpretative speech (MA); mathematics (M Ed, MAT); medical missions (Certificate); ministry (MM, D Min); multicategorical special education (M Ed, MAT); music (M Ed); New Testament interpretation (PhD); Old Testament interpretation (PhD); orchestral instrument performance (MM); organ performance (MM); pastoral studies (MA); personnel services (MS, Ed S); piano pedagogy (MM); piano performance (MM); platform arts (MA); rhetoric and public address (MA); secondary education (M Ed); studio art (MA); teaching Bible (MA); theology (MA, PhD); voice performance (MM); youth ministries (MA); M Div/MM.

Boston College, Lynch School of Education and Human Development, Department of Teacher Education, Special Education and Curriculum and Instruction, Chestnut Hill, MA 02467-3800. Offers curriculum and instruction (M Ed, PhD, CAES); early childhood education (M Ed); elementary education (M Ed); law and curriculum and instruction (JD/M Ed); reading specialist (M Ed, CAES); religious education (M Ed, CAES); secondary education (M Ed, MAT, MST), including biology (MST), chemistry (MST), English (MAT), French (MAT), geology (MST), history (MAT), Latin and classical humanities (MAT), mathematics (MST), physics (MST), secondary teaching (M Ed), Spanish (MAT); special needs: moderate disabilities (M Ed, CAES); special needs: severe disabilities (M Ed); JD/M Ed. *Program availability:* Part-time, evening/weekend, 100% online. *Faculty:* 19 full-time (11 women). *Students:* 186 full-time (140 women), 92 part-time (74 women); includes 58 minority (20 Black or African American, non-Hispanic/Latino; 4 Asian, non-Hispanic/Latino; 29 Hispanic/Latino; 5 Two or more races, non-Hispanic/Latino), 33 international. Average age 28. In 2018, 132 master's, 13 doctorates awarded. Terminal master's awarded for partial completion of doctoral program. *Degree requirements:* For master's, comprehensive exam; for doctorate, comprehensive exam, thesis/dissertation. *Entrance requirements:* Additional exam requirements/recommendations for international students: Required—TOEFL. Application fee: $75. Electronic applications accepted. *Financial support:* Fellowships with full and partial tuition reimbursements, research assistantships with full and partial tuition reimbursements, teaching assistantships with full and partial tuition reimbursements, career-related internships or fieldwork, Federal Work-Study, institutionally sponsored loans, scholarships/grants, traineeships, health care benefits, tuition waivers (full and partial), and unspecified assistantships available. Support available to part-time students. Financial award applicants required to submit FAFSA. *Faculty research:* Teacher education, education research and policy, bilingual education, science education, disabilities, urban education. *Unit head:* Dr. Susan Bruce, Chairperson, 617-552-4214, Fax: 617-552-0812. *Application contact:* Jessica Rivers, Assistant Dean of Graduate Admission and Financial Aid, 617-552-4214, Fax: 617-552-0398, E-mail: riversja@bc.edu.
Website: http://www.bc.edu/education

Bowie State University, Graduate Programs, Program in Elementary Education, Bowie, MD 20715-9465. Offers M Ed. *Accreditation:* NCATE. *Program availability:* Part-time, evening/weekend. *Degree requirements:* For master's, comprehensive exam, thesis optional, research paper. *Entrance requirements:* For master's, minimum GPA of 2.5, teaching certificate, teaching experience. Electronic applications accepted.

Brandeis University, Graduate School of Arts and Sciences, Department of Education, Waltham, MA 02454-9110. Offers Jewish day schools (MAT); public elementary education (MAT); secondary education (MAT), including Bible, biology, chemistry, Chinese, English, history, Jewish day schools, math, physics; teacher leadership (Ed M, AGC). *Faculty:* 5 full-time (3 women), 9 part-time/adjunct (all women). *Students:* 17 full-time (13 women), 36 part-time (33 women); includes 9 minority (1 Black or African American, non-Hispanic/Latino; 6 Asian, non-Hispanic/Latino; 1 Hispanic/Latino; 1 Two or more races, non-Hispanic/Latino). Average age 36. 90 applicants, 79% accepted, 50 enrolled. In 2018, 44 master's, 18 other advanced degrees awarded. *Degree requirements:* For master's, thesis or alternative, internship, research project, capstone. *Entrance requirements:* For master's, GRE or MAT, transcripts, letters of recommendation, resume, statement of purpose; for AGC, transcripts, letters of recommendation, resume, statement of purpose, interview. Additional exam requirements/recommendations for international students: Required—TOEFL, IELTS, PTE. *Application deadline:* For fall admission, 3/15 priority date for domestic students. Applications are processed on a rolling basis. Application fee: $75. Electronic applications accepted. *Financial support:* Scholarships/grants available. *Faculty research:* Teacher education, education, teaching, elementary education, secondary education, Jewish education, English, history, biology, chemistry, physics, math, Chinese, Bible/Tanakh. *Unit head:* Danielle Igra, Director of Graduate Study, 781-736-8519, E-mail: digra@brandeis.edu. *Application contact:* Manuel Tuan, Administrator, 781-736-2002, E-mail: tuan@brandeis.edu.
Website: http://www.brandeis.edu/gsas/programs/education.html

Brandman University, School of Education, Irvine, CA 92618. Offers curriculum and instruction (MAE); educational administration (MAE); educational leadership (MAE); educational leadership and administration (MA); elementary education (MAT); instructional technology: teaching the 21st century learner (MAE); leadership in early childhood education (MAE); organizational leadership (Ed D); school counseling (MA); secondary education (MAT); special education (MA); teaching and learning (MAE).

Bridgewater State University, College of Graduate Studies, College of Education and Allied Studies, Department of Elementary and Early Childhood Education, Program in Elementary Education, Bridgewater, MA 02325. Offers M Ed. *Accreditation:* NCATE. *Program availability:* Part-time, evening/weekend. *Entrance requirements:* For master's, GRE General Test or Massachusetts Test for Educator Licensure.

Brooklyn College of the City University of New York, School of Education, Program in Childhood Education, Brooklyn, NY 11210-2889. Offers bilingual education (MS Ed); liberal arts (MS Ed); mathematics (MS Ed); science and environmental education (MS Ed). *Program availability:* Part-time, evening/weekend. *Entrance requirements:* For master's, LAST, interview, previous course work in education, writing sample, resume, 2 letters of recommendation. Additional exam requirements/recommendations for international students: Required—TOEFL (minimum score 500 paper-based; 61 iBT). Electronic applications accepted. *Faculty research:* Emotional intelligence, multiculturalism, arts immersion, the Holocaust.

Brooklyn College of the City University of New York, School of Education, Program in Special Education, Brooklyn, NY 11210-2889. Offers autism spectrum disorders (AC); teacher of students with disabilities (MS Ed), including adolescence education, childhood education, early childhood education. *Program availability:* Part-time. *Entrance requirements:* For master's, LAST, interview; previous course work in education and psychology; minimum GPA of 3.0 in education, 2.8 overall; resume, 2 letters of recommendation; essay. Additional exam requirements/recommendations for international students: Required—TOEFL (minimum score 500 paper-based; 61 iBT). Electronic applications accepted. *Faculty research:* School reform, conflict resolution, curriculum for inclusive settings, urban issues in special education.

Brown University, Graduate School, Department of Education, Providence, RI 02912. Offers teaching (MAT), including elementary education, English, history/social studies, science, secondary education; urban education policy (AM). *Degree requirements:* For master's, student teaching, portfolio. *Entrance requirements:* For master's, GRE General Test, letters of recommendation, interview. Additional exam requirements/recommendations for international students: Recommended—TOEFL.

Cabrini University, Academic Affairs, Radnor, PA 19087. Offers accounting (M Acc); autism spectrum disorder (M Ed); biological sciences (MS), including civic leadership; criminology and criminal justice (MA); curriculum, instruction, and assessment (M Ed); educational leadership (M Ed, Ed D), including curriculum and instructional leadership (Ed D), preK-12 leadership (Ed D); English as a second language (M-Ed); organizational leadership (DBA, PhD); preK to 4 (M Ed); reading specialist (M Ed); secondary education (M Ed), including biology, chemistry, English, English/communication, mathematics, social studies; special education grades 7-12 (M Ed); special education preK-8 (M Ed); teaching and learning (M Ed). *Program availability:* Part-time, evening/weekend. *Degree requirements:* For master's, comprehensive exam (for some programs), thesis (for some programs); for doctorate, comprehensive exam (for some programs), thesis/dissertation. *Entrance requirements:* For master's, professional resume, personal statement, two recommendations, official transcripts; for doctorate, official transcripts, minimum master's GPA of 3.0, two recommendations, interview with admissions committee. Additional exam requirements/recommendations for international students: Required—TOEFL (minimum score 80 iBT). Electronic applications accepted. Application fee is waived when completed online. *Expenses:* Contact institution.

California Lutheran University, Graduate Studies, Graduate School of Education, Thousand Oaks, CA 91360-2787. Offers counseling and guidance (MS), including college student personnel, counseling and guidance; educational leadership (MA, Ed D), including educational leadership (K-12) (Ed D), higher education leadership (Ed D); special education (MS); teacher leadership (M Ed); teaching (M Ed). *Accreditation:* NCATE. *Program availability:* Part-time, evening/weekend. *Degree requirements:* For master's, comprehensive exam or thesis; for doctorate, thesis/dissertation. *Entrance requirements:* For master's, GRE General Test, interview, minimum GPA of 3.0. Electronic applications accepted.

California State University, Fullerton, Graduate Studies, College of Education, Department of Elementary and Bilingual Education, Fullerton, CA 92831-3599. Offers bilingual/bicultural education (MS); educational technology (MS); elementary curriculum and instruction (MS). *Accreditation:* NCATE. *Program availability:* Part-time. *Degree requirements:* For master's, comprehensive exam, project or thesis. *Entrance requirements:* For master's, minimum GPA of 2.5, teaching certificate. *Faculty research:* Teacher training and tracking, model for improvement of teaching.

California State University, Long Beach, Graduate Studies, College of Education, Department of Teacher Education, Long Beach, CA 90840. Offers elementary education (MA); secondary education (MA). *Program availability:* Part-time, evening/weekend. *Degree requirements:* For master's, comprehensive exam or thesis. *Entrance requirements:* For master's, GRE General Test, minimum GPA of 2.75. *Application deadline:* For fall admission, 7/1 for domestic students; for spring admission, 12/1 for domestic students. Applications are processed on a rolling basis. Application fee: $55. Electronic applications accepted. *Expenses: Required fees:* $2628 per term. Tuition and fees vary according to class time, course level, course load, degree level, campus/location and program. *Financial support:* Federal Work-Study, institutionally sponsored loans, and scholarships/grants available. Financial award application deadline: 3/2; financial award applicants required to submit FAFSA. *Faculty research:* Teacher stress and burnout, new teacher induction. *Unit head:* Huong Tran Nguyen, Chair, 562-985-4506. *Application contact:* Lisa Isbell, Director Preparation Advising Center, 562-985-1105, Fax: 562-985-1106, E-mail: ced-tpac@csulb.edu.
Website: http://www.csulb.edu/college-of-education/teacher-preparation-advising-center-tpac

California State University, Los Angeles, Graduate Studies, Charter College of Education, Division of Curriculum and Instruction, Los Angeles, CA 90032-8530. Offers elementary teaching (MA). *Program availability:* Part-time, evening/weekend. *Entrance requirements:* For master's, minimum GPA of 2.75 in last 90 units of course work, teaching certificate. Additional exam requirements/recommendations for international students: Required—TOEFL (minimum score 500 paper-based). Electronic applications accepted. *Faculty research:* Media, language arts, mathematics, computers, drug-free schools.

California State University, Northridge, Graduate Studies, Michael D. Eisner College of Education, Department of Elementary Education, Northridge, CA 91330. Offers curriculum and instruction (MA); language and literacy (MA); multilingual/multicultural education (MA). *Accreditation:* NCATE. *Program availability:* Part-time, evening/weekend. *Degree requirements:* For master's, comprehensive exam. *Entrance requirements:* For master's, GRE General Test or minimum GPA of 3.0. Additional exam requirements/recommendations for international students: Required—TOEFL.

California State University, Sacramento, College of Education, Graduate and Professional Studies in Education, Sacramento, CA 95819. Offers behavioral science and gender equity (MA); child development (MA); counseling (MS); curriculum and instruction (MA); education (Ed D), including K-12 and community college; education leadership and policy studies (MA), including higher education, PreK-12; education specialist (Ed S), including school psychology; educational technology (MA); language and literacy (MA); multicultural education (MA); school psychology (MA); special education (MA); workforce development advocacy (MA). *Program availability:* Part-time, evening/weekend, blended/hybrid learning. *Degree requirements:* For master's, thesis or project; writing proficiency exam; for doctorate, thesis/dissertation. *Entrance requirements:* For master's and doctorate, GRE. Additional exam requirements/recommendations for international students: Required—TOEFL (minimum score 550 paper-based; 80 iBT); Recommended—IELTS (minimum score 7), TSE. Electronic applications accepted. *Expenses:* Contact institution.

California State University, Stanislaus, College of Education, Kinesiology and Social Work, MA Program in Education, Turlock, CA 95382. Offers curriculum and instruction (MA), including education technology, elementary education, multilingual education, physical education, reading, secondary education, special education; school administration (MA); school counseling (MA). *Program availability:* Part-time, evening/weekend. *Degree requirements:* For master's, comprehensive exam (for some programs), thesis (for some programs). *Entrance requirements:* For master's, MAT, GRE, or CBEST (varies by concentration), 3 letters of recommendation, personal statement. Additional exam requirements/recommendations for international students: Required—TOEFL (minimum score 550 paper-based). Electronic applications accepted. *Faculty research:* Children's perspectives on historical events, method elementary schools dual language education, K-12 reading programs.

California University of Pennsylvania, School of Graduate Studies and Research, College of Education and Human Services, Department of Childhood Education, California, PA 15419-1394. Offers early childhood education (M Ed); elementary education (M Ed); STEM education (M Ed). *Accreditation:* NCATE. *Program availability:* Part-time, evening/weekend. *Degree requirements:* For master's, comprehensive exam, thesis optional. *Entrance requirements:* For master's, MAT, PRAXIS, minimum GPA of 3.0, state police clearances. Additional exam requirements/recommendations for international students: Required—TOEFL (minimum score 550 paper-based; 80 iBT). Electronic applications accepted. *Faculty research:* English as a second language, adult literacy, emerging literacy, diagnosis and remediation, phonemic awareness.

Calvary University, Graduate School and Seminary, Kansas City, MO 64147. Offers Bible and theology (MS); Biblical counseling (MA); education (MS), including administration and leadership, Christian education, curriculum and instruction, elementary education; organizational development (MS); pastoral studies (M Div); worship arts (MS). *Program availability:* Part-time, evening/weekend. *Degree requirements:* For master's, variable foreign language requirement, comprehensive exam, thesis or alternative. *Entrance requirements:* For master's, minimum GPA of 2.5, BA or BS, doctrine agreement. Additional exam requirements/recommendations for international students: Required—TOEFL (minimum score 550 paper-based). Electronic applications accepted. *Expenses:* Contact institution.

Cambridge College, School of Education, Boston, MA 02129. Offers autism specialist (M Ed); autism/behavior analyst (M Ed); behavior analyst (Post-Master's Certificate); curriculum and instruction (CAGS); early childhood teacher (M Ed); educational leadership (M Ed, Ed D); elementary teacher (M Ed); English as a second language (M Ed, Certificate); general science (M Ed); health education (Post-Master's Certificate); interdisciplinary studies (M Ed); library teacher (M Ed); mathematics education (M Ed); mathematics specialist (Certificate); school administration (M Ed, CAGS); school nurse education (M Ed); teacher of students with moderate disabilities (M Ed); teaching skills and methodologies (M Ed). *Program availability:* Part-time, evening/weekend, online learning. *Degree requirements:* For master's, thesis, internship/practicum (licensure program only); for doctorate, thesis/dissertation; for other advanced degree, thesis. *Entrance requirements:* For master's, interview, resume, documentation of licensure, 2 professional references; for doctorate, official transcripts, interview, resume, written personal statement/essay, portfolio of scholarly and professional work, 2 professional references, health insurance, immunizations form; for other advanced degree, official transcripts, interview, resume, written personal statement/essay, 2 professional references, health insurance, immunizations form. Additional exam requirements/recommendations for international students: Required—TOEFL (minimum score 550 paper-based; 79 iBT), Michigan English Language Assessment Battery (minimum score 85); Recommended—IELTS (minimum score 6). *Application deadline:* Applications are processed on a rolling basis. Application fee: $30. Electronic applications accepted. *Expenses:* Contact institution. *Financial support:* Career-related internships or fieldwork, Federal Work-Study, and scholarships/grants available. Financial award applicants required to submit FAFSA. *Faculty research:* Adult education, accelerated learning, mathematics education, brain compatible learning, special education and law. *Unit head:* Dr. Mary Garrity, Interim Dean, 617-873-0168, E-mail: mary.garrity@cambridgecollege.edu. *Application contact:* Salvadore Liberto, Interim Assistant Vice President of Enrollment, 800-877-4723, E-mail: admissions@cambridgecollege.edu. Website: https://www.cambridgecollege.edu/school/school-education

Campbell University, Graduate and Professional Programs, School of Education, Buies Creek, NC 27506. Offers elementary education (M Ed); interdisciplinary studies (M Ed); middle grades education (M Ed); physical education (M Ed); school administration (MSA); school counseling (M Ed); secondary education (M Ed). *Accreditation:* NCATE. *Program availability:* Part-time, evening/weekend. *Degree requirements:* For master's, comprehensive exam. *Entrance requirements:* For master's, GRE General Test, minimum GPA of 2.7. *Faculty research:* Spiritual values and wellness issues in counseling, stress and professional burnout among counselors, thinking strategies, leadership, adaptive technology.

Canisius College, Graduate Division, School of Education and Human Services, Department of Graduate Education and Leadership, Buffalo, NY 14208-1098. Offers business and marketing education (MS Ed); college student personnel (MS Ed); deaf education (MS Ed); deaf/adolescent education, grades 7-12 (MS Ed); deaf/childhood education, grades 1-6 (MS Ed); differentiated instruction (MS Ed); education administration (MS); educational administration (MS Ed); educational technologies (Certificate); gifted education extension (Certificate); literacy (MS Ed); reading (Certificate); school building leadership (MS Ed, Certificate); school district leadership (Certificate); teacher leader (Certificate); TESOL (MS Ed). *Accreditation:* NCATE. *Program availability:* Part-time, evening/weekend, 100% online, blended/hybrid learning. *Faculty:* 5 full-time (all women), 21 part-time/adjunct (16 women). *Students:* 79 full-time (66 women), 135 part-time (106 women); includes 45 minority (27 Black or African American, non-Hispanic/Latino; 1 American Indian or Alaska Native, non-Hispanic/Latino; 3 Asian, non-Hispanic/Latino; 9 Hispanic/Latino; 5 Two or more races, non-Hispanic/Latino), 1 international. Average age 32. 83 applicants, 96% accepted, 74 enrolled. In 2018, 94 master's, 47 other advanced degrees awarded. *Entrance requirements:* For master's, GRE (if cumulative GPA less than 2.7), transcripts, two letters of recommendation. Additional exam requirements/recommendations for international students: Required—TOEFL (minimum score 550 paper-based, 79 iBT), IELTS (minimum score 6.5), or CAEL (minimum score 70). *Application deadline:* Applications are processed on a rolling basis. Application fee: $0. Electronic applications accepted. *Expenses: Tuition:* Part-time $820 per credit hour. *Required fees:* $25 per semester. One-time fee: $65 part-time. Tuition and fees vary according to program. *Financial support:* In 2018–19, 206 students received support. Career-related internships or fieldwork, Federal Work-Study, scholarships/grants, tuition waivers (partial), and unspecified assistantships available. Support available to part-time students. Financial award application deadline: 4/30; financial award applicants required to submit FAFSA. *Faculty research:* Asperger's disease, autism, private higher education, reading strategies. *Unit head:* Dr. Anne Marie Tryjankowski, Chair/Associate Professor of Graduate Education and Leadership, 716-888-3715, Fax: 716-888-3142, E-mail: tryjanka@canisius.edu. *Application contact:* Dr. Anne Marie Tryjankowski, Chair/Associate Professor of Graduate Education and Leadership, 716-888-3715, Fax: 716-888-3142, E-mail: tryjanka@canisius.edu.

Capella University, School of Education, Doctoral Programs in Education, Minneapolis, MN 55402. Offers curriculum and instruction (PhD); educational leadership and management (Ed D); instructional design for online learning (PhD); K-12 studies in education (PhD); leadership for higher education (PhD); leadership in educational administration (PhD); postsecondary and adult education (PhD); professional studies in education (PhD); reading and literacy (Ed D); special education leadership (PhD); training and performance improvement (PhD).

Capella University, School of Education, Master's Programs in Education, Minneapolis, MN 55402. Offers adult education (MS); curriculum and instruction (MS); early childhood education (MS); enrollment management (MS); higher education leadership and management (MS); instructional design for online learning (MS); integrative studies

(MS); K-12 studies in education (MS); leadership in educational administration (MS); reading and literacy (MS); special education teaching (MS).

Caribbean University, Graduate School, Bayamón, PR 00960-0493. Offers administration and supervision (MA Ed); criminal justice (MA); curriculum and instruction (MA Ed, PhD), including elementary education (MA Ed), English education (MA Ed), history education (MA Ed), mathematics education (MA Ed), primary education (MA Ed), science education (MA Ed), Spanish education (MA Ed); educational technology in instructional systems (MA Ed); gerontology (MSN); human resources (MBA); museology, archiving and art history (MA Ed); neonatal pediatrics (MSN); physical education (MA Ed); special education (MA Ed). *Entrance requirements:* For master's, interview, minimum GPA of 2.5.

Carroll University, Graduate Programs in Education, Waukesha, WI 53186-5593. Offers adult and continuing education (M Ed); educational leadership (MS); PK-12 (M Ed). *Program availability:* Part-time, evening/weekend. *Degree requirements:* For master's, thesis. *Entrance requirements:* For master's, minimum undergraduate GPA of 2.5 in related field. Additional exam requirements/recommendations for international students: Required—TOEFL. Electronic applications accepted. *Faculty research:* Qualitative research methods, whole language approaches to teaching, the writing process, multicultural education, gifted/talented learners.

Carson-Newman University, Graduate Program in Education, Jefferson City, TN 37760. Offers curriculum and instruction (M Ed); educational leadership (M Ed); elementary education (MAT); school counseling (MS); secondary education (MAT); teaching English as a second language (MATESL). *Accreditation:* NCATE. *Program availability:* Part-time, evening/weekend, 100% online, blended/hybrid learning. *Faculty:* 20 full-time (11 women), 16 part-time/adjunct (13 women). *Students:* 14 full-time (8 women), 401 part-time (294 women); includes 45 minority (34 Black or African American, non-Hispanic/Latino; 1 American Indian or Alaska Native, non-Hispanic/Latino; 4 Hispanic/Latino; 1 Native Hawaiian or other Pacific Islander, non-Hispanic/Latino; 5 Two or more races, non-Hispanic/Latino). Average age 36. 223 applicants, 100% accepted, 199 enrolled. In 2018, 211 master's awarded. *Degree requirements:* For master's, thesis or alternative. *Entrance requirements:* For master's, PRAXIS II or GRE with minimum score of 290 on the verbal and quantitative components (for MAT), minimum GPA of 3.0 in major, 2.5 overall. Additional exam requirements/recommendations for international students: Recommended—TOEFL (minimum score 79 iBT), IELTS (minimum score 6.5), TSE (minimum score 53). *Application deadline:* For fall admission, 7/15 priority date for domestic students. Applications are processed on a rolling basis. Application fee: $50. *Expenses: Tuition:* Full-time $9036; part-time $502 per credit hour. *Required fees:* $900; $25 per credit hour. $300 per semester. One-time fee: $150. *Financial support:* Federal Work-Study and unspecified assistantships available. Financial award applicants required to submit FAFSA. *Unit head:* Dr. Kim Hawkins, Chair, 865-471-3314, E-mail: khawkins@cn.edu. *Application contact:* Nilma Stewart, Graduate Admissions and Services Adviser, 865-471-3230, Fax: 865-471-3875, E-mail: adults@cn.edu.
Website: http://www.cn.edu/adult-graduate-studies

Catawba College, Department of Teacher Education, Salisbury, NC 28144-2488. Offers STEM education (M Ed). *Accreditation:* NCATE. *Program availability:* Part-time-only. *Degree requirements:* For master's, portfolio. *Entrance requirements:* For master's, NTE, PRAXIS II, minimum undergraduate GPA of 3.0, valid teaching license, official transcripts, 3 references, essay, interview, practicing teacher. Electronic applications accepted. *Expenses:* Contact institution.

Centenary College of Louisiana, Graduate Programs, Department of Education, Shreveport, LA 71104. Offers elementary education (MAT); secondary education (MAT). *Program availability:* Part-time, evening/weekend. *Degree requirements:* For master's, comprehensive exam. *Entrance requirements:* For master's, PRAXIS I and II (for MAT), undergraduate degree, minimum GPA of 2.5. *Expenses:* Contact institution. *Faculty research:* Teachers as advocates for teachers, portfolio assessment, disabled readers.

Central Connecticut State University, School of Graduate Studies, School of Education and Professional Studies, Department of Literacy, Elementary, and Early Childhood Education, New Britain, CT 06050-4010. Offers MS, AC, Sixth Year Certificate. *Program availability:* Part-time, evening/weekend. *Faculty:* 5 full-time (4 women), 5 part-time/adjunct (all women). *Students:* 9 full-time (8 women), 100 part-time (97 women); includes 7 minority (6 Hispanic/Latino; 1 Two or more races, non-Hispanic/Latino). Average age 30. 62 applicants, 77% accepted, 32 enrolled. In 2018, 29 master's, 9 other advanced degrees awarded. *Degree requirements:* For master's, comprehensive exam, thesis or alternative; for other advanced degree, qualifying exam. *Entrance requirements:* For master's, minimum undergraduate GPA of 2.7, teacher certification, interview, essay, letters of recommendation; for other advanced degree, master's degree, essay, teacher certification, interview, letters of recommendation. Additional exam requirements/recommendations for international students: Required—TOEFL (minimum score 550 paper-based; 79 iBT); Recommended—IELTS (minimum score 6.5). *Application deadline:* For fall admission, 6/1 for domestic students, 5/1 for international students; for spring admission, 11/1 for domestic and international students. Applications are processed on a rolling basis. Application fee: $50. Electronic applications accepted. *Expenses: Tuition, area resident:* Full-time $7027; part-time $388 per credit. Tuition, state resident: full-time $9750; part-time $388 per credit. Tuition, nonresident: full-time $18,102; part-time $388 per credit. *International tuition:* $18,102 full-time. *Required fees:* $266 per semester. *Financial support:* In 2018–19, 6 students received support. Career-related internships or fieldwork, Federal Work-Study, scholarships/grants, and unspecified assistantships available. Support available to part-time students. Financial award application deadline: 3/1. *Faculty research:* Developmental, clinical, and administrative aspects of reading and language arts instruction. *Unit head:* Dr. Helen Abadiano, Chair, 860-832-2175, E-mail: abadiano@ccsu.edu. *Application contact:* Patricia Gardner, Associate Director of Graduate Studies, 860-832-2350, Fax: 860-832-2362.
Website: http://www.ccsu.edu/leece/index.html

Central Michigan University, Central Michigan University Global Campus, Program in Educational Leadership, Mount Pleasant, MI 48859. Offers K-12 leadership (Ed D). *Program availability:* Part-time, evening/weekend. *Entrance requirements:* Additional exam requirements/recommendations for international students: Required—TOEFL. Electronic applications accepted.

Central Michigan University, College of Graduate Studies, College of Education and Human Services, Department of Teacher Education and Professional Development, Mount Pleasant, MI 48859. Offers educational technology (MA, Graduate Certificate); elementary education (MA), including classroom teaching, early childhood; reading and literacy K-12 (MA); secondary education (MA). *Program availability:* Part-time, evening/weekend. *Degree requirements:* For master's, thesis or alternative. Electronic applications accepted. *Faculty research:* Integrating literacy across the curriculum, science teaching and aesthetic learning in science, diversity education, educational technology, educational psychology and child development.

Chadron State College, School of Professional and Graduate Studies, Department of Education, Chadron, NE 69337. Offers business (MA Ed); community counseling (MA Ed); educational administration (MS Ed, Sp Ed); elementary education (MS Ed);

history (MA Ed); language and literature (MA Ed); secondary administration (MS Ed); secondary education (MS Ed). *Accreditation:* NCATE. *Program availability:* Part-time, evening/weekend, online learning. *Degree requirements:* For master's, thesis optional. *Entrance requirements:* For master's, GRE General Test, GRE Writing Test, minimum GPA of 2.75 or 12 graduate hours at CSC with minimum GPA of 3.25. Additional exam requirements/recommendations for international students: Required—TOEFL. Electronic applications accepted. *Faculty research:* Rural education, technology, mental health.

Chaminade University of Honolulu, Graduate, Program in Education, Honolulu, HI 96816-1578. Offers child development (M Ed); early childhood education (Montessori) (MAT); early childhood education (PK-3) (MAT); educational leadership (M Ed); elementary education (MAT); instructional leadership (M Ed); Montessori (M Ed); secondary education (MAT); special education (MAT); teacher leader (M Ed). *Program availability:* Part-time, evening/weekend, 100% online, blended/hybrid learning. *Faculty:* 8 full-time (3 women), 11 part-time/adjunct (8 women). *Students:* 80 full-time (57 women), 100 part-time (77 women); includes 113 minority (6 Black or African American, non-Hispanic/Latino; 4 American Indian or Alaska Native, non-Hispanic/Latino; 45 Asian, non-Hispanic/Latino; 6 Hispanic/Latino; 50 Native Hawaiian or other Pacific Islander, non-Hispanic/Latino; 2 Two or more races, non-Hispanic/Latino), 2 international. Average age 35. 53 applicants, 92% accepted, 40 enrolled. In 2018, 92 master's awarded. *Degree requirements:* For master's, thesis or alternative. *Entrance requirements:* For master's, PRAXIS (for MAT), official transcripts, writing sample (for MAT). Additional exam requirements/recommendations for international students: Required—TOEFL (minimum score 550 paper-based; 79 iBT). *Application deadline:* Applications are processed on a rolling basis. Application fee: $40. Electronic applications accepted. *Expenses:* $780 per credit; $93 fee per online course. *Financial support:* Applicants required to submit FAFSA. *Unit head:* Dr. Dale Fryxell, Dean, 808-739-4652, Fax: 808-739-4607, E-mail: edu-office@chaminade.edu. *Application contact:* 808-739-7478, E-mail: gradserv@chaminade.edu.
Website: https://chaminade.edu/academics/education-behavioral-sciences/

Chapman University, Donna Ford Attallah College of Educational Studies, Orange, CA 92866. Offers counseling (MA), including school counseling (MA, Credential); curriculum and instruction (MA), including elementary education, secondary education; education (PhD), including cultural and curricular studies, disability studies, leadership studies, school psychology (PhD, Credential); educational psychology (MA); leadership development (MA); multiple subjects (Credential), including Spanish/English bilingual; pupil personnel services (Credential), including school counseling (MA, Credential), school psychology (PhD, Credential); school psychology (Ed S); single subject (Credential); special education (MA, Credential), including mild/moderate (Credential), moderate/severe (Credential); teaching (MA), including elementary education, secondary education, secondary music education. *Accreditation:* TEAC. *Program availability:* Part-time, evening/weekend. Electronic applications accepted. *Expenses:* Contact institution.

Charleston Southern University, College of Education, Charleston, SC 29423-8087. Offers elementary administration and supervision (M Ed); elementary education (M Ed); secondary administration and supervision (M Ed). *Accreditation:* NCATE. *Program availability:* Part-time, evening/weekend. *Degree requirements:* For master's, thesis optional. *Entrance requirements:* For master's, GRE or MAT. Additional exam requirements/recommendations for international students: Required—TOEFL (minimum score 550 paper-based; 79 iBT). Electronic applications accepted. *Expenses:* Contact institution.

Chatham University, Program in Education, Pittsburgh, PA 15232-2826. Offers early childhood education (MAT); elementary education (MAT); environmental education (K-12) (MAT); secondary art (MAT); secondary biology education (MAT); secondary chemistry education (MAT); secondary English education (MAT); secondary math education (MAT); secondary physics education (MAT); secondary social studies education (MAT); special education (MAT). *Degree requirements:* For master's, thesis, teaching experience. *Entrance requirements:* For master's, minimum GPA of 3.0, sample of written work, recommendation letters. Additional exam requirements/recommendations for international students: Required—TOEFL (minimum score 600 paper-based; 100 iBT), IELTS (minimum score 7), TWE. Electronic applications accepted. Application fee is waived when completed online. *Faculty research:* Gifted education, environmental education, technology in education, writing as learning, class size and achievement.

Chestnut Hill College, School of Graduate Studies, Department of Education, Program in Elementary/Middle Education, Philadelphia, PA 19118-2693. Offers M Ed. *Program availability:* Part-time, evening/weekend. *Degree requirements:* For master's, thesis optional. *Entrance requirements:* For master's, PRAXIS I or proof of teaching certification, letters of recommendation, writing sample, 6 graduate credits with minimum B grade if undergraduate GPA less than 3.0. Additional exam requirements/recommendations for international students: Required—TOEFL (minimum score 500 paper-based), IELTS (minimum score 6.0), or TWE (minimum score 22). Electronic applications accepted. *Expenses:* Contact institution. *Faculty research:* Inclusive education, cultural issues in education.

Cheyney University of Pennsylvania, Graduate Programs, Program in Elementary Education, Cheyney, PA 19319. Offers M Ed. *Program availability:* Part-time, evening/weekend. *Degree requirements:* For master's, thesis. *Entrance requirements:* For master's, GRE General Test, MAT, minimum GPA of 2.75. Electronic applications accepted.

Chicago State University, School of Graduate and Professional Studies, College of Education, Department of Educational Leadership, Curriculum and Foundations, Program in Curriculum and Instruction, Chicago, IL 60628. Offers instructional foundations (MS Ed), including adult education, elementary education, secondary education. *Degree requirements:* For master's, comprehensive exam, thesis optional. *Entrance requirements:* For master's, minimum GPA of 2.75.

Chicago State University, School of Graduate and Professional Studies, College of Education, Department of Reading, Elementary Education, Library Information and Media Studies, Program in Elementary Education, Chicago, IL 60628. Offers MAT. *Accreditation:* NCATE. *Degree requirements:* For master's, comprehensive exam, thesis optional. *Entrance requirements:* For master's, minimum GPA of 3.0 in last 60 hours.

City University of Seattle, Graduate Division, Albright School of Education, Seattle, WA 98121. Offers administrator certification (Certificate); curriculum and instruction (M Ed); elementary education (MIT); guidance and counseling (M Ed); leadership (M Ed); reading and literacy (M Ed); school counseling (M Ed); special education (MIT); superintendent certification (Certificate). *Program availability:* Part-time, evening/weekend, online learning. *Degree requirements:* For master's, comprehensive exam (for some programs), thesis (for some programs). *Entrance requirements:* For master's, baccalaureate degree or equivalent from an accredited or otherwise recognized institution. Additional exam requirements/recommendations for international students: Required—TOEFL (minimum score 567 paper-based; 87 iBT); Recommended—IELTS. Electronic applications accepted. *Expenses:* Contact institution.

Clemson University, Graduate School, College of Education, Department of Educational and Organizational Leadership Development, Clemson, SC 29634. Offers administration and supervision (M Ed, Ed S); athletic leadership (MS, Certificate); education systems improvement science (Ed D); educational leadership (PhD), including higher education, P-12; human resource development (MHRD), including human resource development; leadership (Certificate); student affairs (M Ed). *Program availability:* Part-time, evening/weekend, 100% online. *Faculty:* 17 full-time (11 women). *Students:* 105 full-time (64 women), 265 part-time (170 women); includes 76 minority (61 Black or African American, non-Hispanic/Latino; 1 American Indian or Alaska Native, non-Hispanic/Latino; 3 Asian, non-Hispanic/Latino; 5 Hispanic/Latino; 6 Two or more races, non-Hispanic/Latino). Average age 32. 204 applicants, 83% accepted, 123 enrolled. In 2018, 93 master's, 17 doctorates, 28 other advanced degrees awarded. *Degree requirements:* For master's, thesis (for some programs); for doctorate, comprehensive exam, thesis/dissertation. *Entrance requirements:* For master's, doctorate, and other advanced degree, GRE General Test, unofficial transcripts, letters of recommendation. Additional exam requirements/recommendations for international students: Required—TOEFL (minimum score 80 paper-based; 80 iBT); Recommended—IELTS (minimum score 6.5), TSE (minimum score 54). *Application deadline:* For fall admission, 4/15 priority date for international students; for spring admission, 10/15 priority date for international students. Applications are processed on a rolling basis. Application fee: $80 ($90 for international students). Electronic applications accepted. *Expenses:* $5198 per semester full-time resident, $10123 per semester full-time non-resident, $556 per credit hour part-time resident, $1109 per credit hour part-time non-resident, online $770 per credit hour, $4938 doctoral programs resident, $10405 doctoral programs non-resident, $1144 full-time graduate assistant, other fees may apply per session. *Financial support:* In 2018–19, 30 students received support, including 8 fellowships with full and partial tuition reimbursements available (averaging $4,525 per year), 3 research assistantships with full and partial tuition reimbursements available (averaging $7,500 per year); career-related internships or fieldwork and unspecified assistantships also available. *Faculty research:* Leadership, ethics, policy development, performance improvement. *Total annual research expenditures:* $79,638. *Unit head:* Dr. Roy Jones, Interim Department Chair, 864-656-7915, E-mail: royj@clemson.edu. *Application contact:* Alison Search, Student Services Program Coordinator, 864-250-8880, E-mail: alisonp@clemson.edu.
Website: http://www.clemson.edu/education/departments/educational-organizational-leadership-development/index.html

College of Charleston, Graduate School, School of Education, Health, and Human Performance, Department of Elementary and Early Childhood Education, Program in Elementary Education, Charleston, SC 29424-0001. Offers MAT. *Accreditation:* NCATE. *Program availability:* Part-time, evening/weekend. *Degree requirements:* For master's, thesis or alternative, written qualifying exam, student teaching experience. *Entrance requirements:* For master's, GRE, 2 letters of recommendation. Additional exam requirements/recommendations for international students: Required—TOEFL (minimum score 81 iBT). Electronic applications accepted.

The College of New Jersey, Office of Graduate and Advancing Education, School of Education, Department of Elementary and Early Childhood Education, Program in Elementary Education, Ewing, NJ 08628. Offers M Ed, MAT. *Accreditation:* NCATE. *Program availability:* Part-time. *Degree requirements:* For master's, comprehensive exam. *Entrance requirements:* For master's, GRE General Test, minimum GPA of 3.0 in field or 2.75 overall. Additional exam requirements/recommendations for international students: Required—TOEFL. Electronic applications accepted.

The College of New Rochelle, Graduate School, Division of Education, Program in Childhood Education/Early Childhood Education, New Rochelle, NY 10805-2308. Offers childhood education (MS Ed); early childhood education (MS Ed). *Program availability:* Part-time. *Degree requirements:* For master's, comprehensive exam (for some programs), thesis (for some programs), practicum. *Entrance requirements:* For master's, interview, minimum GPA of 3.0 in field, 2.7 overall.

College of Saint Elizabeth, Program in Education, Morristown, NJ 07960-6989. Offers assistive technology (Certificate); education (MA); ESL (Certificate); Holocaust/genocide education (Certificate); middle school science (Certificate); online teaching in the 21st century (Certificate); teaching (Certificate), including K-12, K-6, teacher of students with disabilities. *Program availability:* Part-time. *Degree requirements:* For master's and Certificate, thesis. *Entrance requirements:* For master's, certification. Additional exam requirements/recommendations for international students: Required—TOEFL (minimum score 550 paper-based; 79 iBT), IELTS (minimum score 6.5). Electronic applications accepted. Application fee is waived when completed online.

College of St. Joseph, Graduate Programs, Division of Education, Program in Elementary Education, Rutland, VT 05701-3899. Offers M Ed. *Program availability:* Part-time, evening/weekend. *Degree requirements:* For master's, comprehensive exam. *Entrance requirements:* For master's, PRAXIS I (for initial licensure), official college transcripts; 2 letters of reference; minimum GPA of 3.0 (initial licensure) or 2.7 (nonlicensure); interview. Additional exam requirements/recommendations for international students: Required—TOEFL (minimum score 550 paper-based). Electronic applications accepted.

College of Staten Island of the City University of New York, Graduate Programs, School of Education, Program in Childhood Education, Staten Island, NY 10314-6600. Offers childhood (MS Ed). *Program availability:* Part-time, evening/weekend. *Students:* 60. 23 applicants, 61% accepted, 13 enrolled. In 2018, 20 master's awarded. *Degree requirements:* For master's, educational research project; Sequence 1 consists of ten courses and a minimum of 32-38 graduate credits in five required areas of study. Sequence 2 consists of a minimum of 45-49 graduate credits. Students complete six required core courses before selecting from an array of advanced graduate courses. *Entrance requirements:* For master's, GRE General Test or approved equivalent examination, relevant bachelor's degree, letters of recommendation, one- or two-page personal statement. For Sequence 1, candidates must have completed the coursework leading to a New York State initial certificate in childhood education or early childhood education. Overall GPA over 3.0. Additional exam requirements/recommendations for international students: Required—TOEFL (minimum score 550 paper-based; 79 iBT), IELTS (minimum score 6.5). *Application deadline:* For fall admission, 4/25 for domestic and international students; for spring admission, 11/25 for domestic and international students. Applications are processed on a rolling basis. Application fee: $75. Electronic applications accepted. *Expenses: Tuition, area resident:* Full-time $10,770; part-time $455 per credit. Tuition, state resident: full-time $10,770; part-time $455 per credit. Tuition, nonresident: full-time $19,920; part-time $830 per credit. *International tuition:* $19,920 full-time. *Required fees:* $559.20; $181.10 per semester. Tuition and fees vary according to program. *Faculty research:* Preservice teacher preparation, music education and integration, literacy, emergent bilingual. *Unit head:* Diane Brescia, 718-982-3877, E-mail: diane.brescia@csi.cuny.edu. *Application contact:* Sasha Spence, Associate Director for Graduate Admissions, 718-982-2019, Fax: 718-982-2500, E-mail: sasha.spence@csi.cuny.edu.
Website: https://www.csi.cuny.edu/sites/default/files/pdf/admissions/grad/pdf/Education%20Fact%20Sheet.pdf

College of Staten Island of the City University of New York, Graduate Programs, School of Education, Program in Special Education, Staten Island, NY 10314-6600. Offers special education (MS Ed), including adolescence generalist: grades 7-12, grades 1-6. *Program availability:* Part-time, evening/weekend. *Students:* 130. 58 applicants, 71% accepted, 32 enrolled. In 2018, 42 master's awarded. *Degree requirements:* For master's, comprehensive exam, fieldwork; ten three-credit required courses and one elective for a total of 11 courses (33 credits) or 14 three-credit required courses and a three- to six-credit, field-based requirement for a total of 45-48 credits; research project. *Entrance requirements:* For master's, GRE General Test or an approved equivalent examination, BA/BS or 36 approved credits with a 3.0 GPA, 2 letters of recommendations, 1-2 page statement of experience; must have completed courses for NYS initial certificate in childhood education/early childhood education (Sequence 1); 6 credits each in English, history, math, and science, and 1 year of foreign language (Sequence 2). Additional exam requirements/recommendations for international students: Required—TOEFL (minimum score 550 paper-based; 79 iBT), IELTS (minimum score 6.5). *Application deadline:* For fall admission, 4/25 for domestic and international students; for spring admission, 11/25 for domestic and international students. Applications are processed on a rolling basis. Application fee: $75. Electronic applications accepted. *Expenses: Tuition, area resident:* Full-time $10,770; part-time $455 per credit. Tuition, state resident: full-time $10,770; part-time $455 per credit. Tuition, nonresident: full-time $19,920; part-time $830 per credit. *International tuition:* $19,920 full-time. *Required fees:* $559.20; $181.10 per semester. Tuition and fees vary according to program. *Faculty research:* Disabilities studies, social justice, arts-based research on disabilities, assessment of students with disabilities, technological pedagogical and content knowledge (TPACK) in special education teachers, juvenile justice. *Unit head:* Diane Brescia, 718-982-3877, E-mail: diane.brescia@csi.cuny.edu. *Application contact:* Sasha Spence, Associate Director for Graduate Admissions, 718-982-2019, Fax: 718-982-2500, E-mail: sasha.spence@csi.cuny.edu.
Website: https://www.csi.cuny.edu/sites/default/files/pdf/admissions/grad/pdf/Education%20Fact%20Sheet.pdf

Colorado Christian University, Program in Curriculum and Instruction, Lakewood, CO 80226. Offers corporate education (MACI); early childhood educator (MACI); elementary educator (MACI); instructional technology (MACI); master educator (MACI); online course developer (MACI); online teaching and learning (MACI); special education generalist (MACI). *Program availability:* Part-time, evening/weekend. *Degree requirements:* For master's, thesis optional, practicum. *Entrance requirements:* For master's, interviews, letters of recommendation. Additional exam requirements/recommendations for international students: Required—TOEFL. Electronic applications accepted. *Expenses:* Contact institution.

The Colorado College, Education Department, Program in Elementary Education, Colorado Springs, CO 80903-3294. Offers elementary school teaching (MAT). *Degree requirements:* For master's, thesis, internship. Electronic applications accepted.

Columbia College, Graduate Programs, Education Division, Columbia, SC 29203-5998. Offers divergent learning (M Ed); higher education administration (M Ed). *Accreditation:* NCATE. *Program availability:* Part-time, evening/weekend, online learning. *Degree requirements:* For master's, thesis. *Entrance requirements:* For master's, GRE General Test, MAT, 2 recommendations, current South Carolina teaching certificate, minimum GPA of 3.2. Electronic applications accepted. *Expenses:* Contact institution.

Columbia International University, Columbia Graduate School, Columbia, SC 29203. Offers Bible teaching (MABT); counseling (MACN); early childhood and elementary education (MAT); educational administration (M Ed); educational leadership (PhD); instruction and learning (M Ed); teaching English as a foreign language (Certificate); teaching English as a foreign language and intercultural studies (MATF). *Program availability:* Part-time, evening/weekend, online learning. *Degree requirements:* For master's, internships, professional project. *Entrance requirements:* For master's, MAT; GRE (for some programs), minimum GPA of 2.7. Additional exam requirements/recommendations for international students: Required—TOEFL. Electronic applications accepted.

Concordia University, College of Education, Portland, OR 97211-6099. Offers administrative leadership (Ed D); career and technical education (M Ed); curriculum and instruction (M Ed), including adolescent literacy, early childhood education, educational technology leadership, English for speakers of other languages, environmental education, health and physical education, mathematics, methods and curriculum, reading interventionist, science, social studies, STEAM education, teacher leadership, the inclusive classroom, trauma and resilience in educational settings; educational administration (M Ed); educational leadership (M Ed); elementary education (MAT); higher education (Ed D); instructional leadership (Ed D); professional leadership, inquiry, and transformation (Ed D); secondary education (MAT); transformational leadership (Ed D). *Program availability:* Part-time, online learning. *Degree requirements:* For master's, comprehensive exam, work samples/portfolio. *Entrance requirements:* For master's, California Basic Educational Skills Test or PRAXIS I, minimum undergraduate GPA of 2.8, graduate 3.0; 2 letters of recommendation. Additional exam requirements/recommendations for international students: Required—TOEFL (minimum score 525 paper-based). Electronic applications accepted. *Faculty research:* Learner-centered classroom, brain-based learning, future of online learning.

Concordia University Chicago, College of Graduate Studies, Program in Teaching, River Forest, IL 60305-1499. Offers elementary education (MAT); secondary education (MAT). *Degree requirements:* For master's, thesis or alternative. *Entrance requirements:* For master's, minimum GPA of 2.9. Additional exam requirements/recommendations for international students: Required—TOEFL (minimum score 550 paper-based). Electronic applications accepted.

Concordia University, Nebraska, Graduate Programs in Education, Program in Educational Administration, Seward, NE 68434. Offers elementary and secondary education (M Ed); elementary education (M Ed); secondary education (M Ed). *Accreditation:* NCATE. *Program availability:* Part-time. *Degree requirements:* For master's, thesis or alternative. *Entrance requirements:* For master's, GRE, MAT, or NTE, BS in education or equivalent, minimum GPA of 3.0.

Converse College, Program in Elementary Education, Spartanburg, SC 29302. Offers M Ed, MAT. *Program availability:* Part-time. *Degree requirements:* For master's, capstone paper. *Entrance requirements:* For master's, NTE or PRAXIS II (M Ed), minimum GPA of 2.75, 2 recommendations. Electronic applications accepted.

Creighton University, Graduate School, College of Arts and Sciences, Department of Education, Program in Teaching, Omaha, NE 68178-0001. Offers elementary teaching (M Ed); secondary teaching (M Ed). *Program availability:* Part-time. *Faculty:* 10 full-time (5 women). *Students:* 3 full-time (2 women), 26 part-time (17 women); includes 2 minority (1 Asian, non-Hispanic/Latino; 1 Two or more races, non-Hispanic/Latino), 1 international. Average age 26. In 2018, 12 master's awarded. *Degree requirements:* For master's, portfolio. *Entrance requirements:* For master's, 3 letters of recommendation, 2 writing samples. Additional exam requirements/recommendations for international students: Required—TOEFL (minimum score 90 iBT). *Application deadline:* For fall admission, 7/1 priority date for domestic students, 3/1 priority date for international students; for winter admission, 12/1 priority date for domestic students, 6/1 priority date for international students; for spring admission, 3/1 priority date for domestic and international students; for summer admission, 3/1 for domestic and international students. Application fee: $50. Electronic applications accepted. *Financial support:* Scholarships/grants and tuition waivers (partial) available. Support available to part-time students. Financial award applicants required to submit FAFSA. *Unit head:* Dr. Max Engel, Director, 402-280-3162, E-mail: MaxEngel@creighton.edu. *Application contact:* Lindsay Johnson, Director of Graduate and Adult Recruitment, 402-280-2703, Fax: 402-280-2423, E-mail: gradschool@creighton.edu.

Curry College, Graduate Studies, Program in Education, Milton, MA 02186-9984. Offers elementary education (M Ed); foundations (non-license) (M Ed); reading (M Ed, Certificate); special education (M Ed). *Program availability:* Part-time, evening/weekend. *Degree requirements:* For master's, project or thesis. *Entrance requirements:* For master's, interview, recommendations, resume, written statement. Additional exam requirements/recommendations for international students: Required—TOEFL (minimum score 550 paper-based; 80 iBT). *Expenses:* Contact institution. *Faculty research:* Classroom trauma, therapeutic writing, inclusionary practices.

Dallas Baptist University, Dorothy M. Bush College of Education, Teaching Program, Dallas, TX 75211-9299. Offers distance learning (MAT); early childhood through grade 6 certification (MAT); early childhood-12 (MAT); elementary (MAT); English as a second language (MAT); Montessori (MAT); multisensory (MAT); secondary (MAT). *Program availability:* Part-time, evening/weekend, 100% online, blended/hybrid learning. *Application deadline:* Applications are processed on a rolling basis. Application fee: $25. Electronic applications accepted. Application fee is waived when completed online. *Expenses: Tuition:* Full-time $17,262; part-time $959 per credit hour. *Required fees:* $1000; $500 per semester. Tuition and fees vary according to course load and degree level. *Unit head:* Dr. Neil Dugger, Dean, 214-333-5202, E-mail: neil@dbu.edu. *Application contact:* Dr. DeAnna Jenkins, Program Director, 214-333-5402, E-mail: deannaj@dbu.edu.
Website: https://www.dbu.edu/graduate/degree-programs/ma-teaching

Delta State University, Graduate Programs, College of Education, Division of Teacher Education, Leadership, and Research, Program in Professional Studies, Cleveland, MS 38733-0001. Offers counselor education (Ed D); elementary education (Ed D); higher education (Ed D). *Program availability:* Part-time, evening/weekend. *Degree requirements:* For doctorate, thesis/dissertation. *Entrance requirements:* For doctorate, GRE General Test. *Expenses: Tuition, area resident:* Full-time $7076; part-time $393 per credit hour. Tuition, state resident: full-time $7076; part-time $393 per credit hour. Tuition, nonresident: full-time $7076; part-time $393 per credit hour. *International tuition:* $7076 full-time. *Required fees:* $170; $18.90 per credit hour. $9.45 per semester. Part-time tuition and fees vary according to program.

Delta State University, Graduate Programs, College of Education, Division of Teacher Education, Leadership, and Research, Programs in Elementary Education, Cleveland, MS 38733-0001. Offers M Ed, MAT, Ed S. *Accreditation:* NCATE. *Program availability:* Part-time, evening/weekend. *Degree requirements:* For master's, thesis optional. *Entrance requirements:* For master's, GRE General Test; for Ed S, master's degree, teaching certificate. *Expenses: Tuition, area resident:* Full-time $7076; part-time $393 per credit hour. Tuition, state resident: full-time $7076; part-time $393 per credit hour. Tuition, nonresident: full-time $7076; part-time $393 per credit hour. *International tuition:* $7076 full-time. *Required fees:* $170; $18.90 per credit hour. $9.45 per semester. Part-time tuition and fees vary according to program.

DePaul University, College of Education, Chicago, IL 60614. Offers bilingual-bicultural education (M Ed, MA); counseling (M Ed, MA), including clinical mental health counseling, college student development, school counseling; curriculum studies (M Ed, MA, Ed D); early childhood education (M Ed, MA, Ed D); educational leadership (M Ed, MA, Ed D), including Catholic leadership (M Ed, MA), general (M Ed, MA), higher education (M Ed, MA), physical education (M Ed, MA), principal preparation (M Ed), teacher preparation (M Ed); elementary education (M Ed, MA); middle grades education (M Ed); middle school mathematics education (MS); reading specialist (M Ed, MA); secondary education (M Ed, MA); social and cultural foundations in education (M Ed, MA); special education (M Ed); sport, fitness and recreation leadership (MS); value-creating education for global citizenship (M Ed); world languages education (M Ed, MA). *Program availability:* Part-time, evening/weekend, online learning. *Degree requirements:* For doctorate, thesis/dissertation. Electronic applications accepted.

Dominican College, Division of Teacher Education, Orangeburg, NY 10962-1210. Offers education/teaching of individuals with multiple disabilities (MS Ed). *Program availability:* Part-time, evening/weekend, online learning. *Faculty:* 5 part-time/adjunct (all women). *Students:* 4 full-time (all women), 52 part-time (40 women); includes 11 minority (1 Black or African American, non-Hispanic/Latino; 2 Asian, non-Hispanic/Latino; 8 Hispanic/Latino). Average age 33. In 2018, 24 master's awarded. *Degree requirements:* For master's, comprehensive exam (for some programs), thesis. *Entrance requirements:* For master's, 3 letters of recommendation (atleast 1 from a former professor), current resume, Official transcripts (not student copies) of all undergraduate and graduate records, results from GRE/MAT/SAT or ACT scores, interview, State issued teaching certificate & State Certification Exam Scores are Required for TVI program. Additional exam requirements/recommendations for international students: Required—TOEFL (minimum score 90 iBT). *Application deadline:* For fall admission, 8/1 for domestic students, 6/1 for international students. Applications are processed on a rolling basis. Application fee: $50. Electronic applications accepted. *Expenses: Tuition:* Part-time $965 per credit. *Required fees:* $200 per semester. One-time fee: $200. Tuition and fees vary according to course load, degree level and program. *Financial support:* Application deadline: 2/1; applicants required to submit FAFSA. *Unit head:* Dr. Mike Kelly, Director, 845-848-4090, Fax: 845-359-7802, E-mail: mike.kelly@dc.edu. *Application contact:* Heather Karsenty, Assistant Director of Graduate Admissions, 845-848-7908 Ext. 15, Fax: 845-365-3150, E-mail: admissions@dc.edu.

Dominican University, School of Education, River Forest, IL 60305-1099. Offers child life studies (MS); early childhood education (MS); education (MAT); elementary education (MA Ed); English as a second language (MA Ed); reading (MA Ed); secondary education (MAT); special education (MS). *Accreditation:* NCATE. *Program availability:* Part-time, evening/weekend, 100% online, blended/hybrid learning. *Entrance requirements:* For master's, Illinois Test of Basic Skills. Additional exam requirements/recommendations for international students: Required—TOEFL (minimum score 550 paper-based; 79 iBT). *Expenses:* Contact institution. *Faculty research:* Governance of private education institutions, reading and language arts, inclusion, organizational planning, leadership and vision.

Drew University, Caspersen School of Graduate Studies, Madison, NJ 07940-1493. Offers conflict resolution and leadership (Certificate), including community leadership, moderation, peace building; education (M Ed); finance (MA); history and culture (MA, PhD), including American history, book history, British history, European history, intellectual history, Irish history, print culture, public history; K-12 education (MAT), including art, biology, chemistry, elementary education, English, French, Italian, math, secondary education, special education, teacher of students with disabilities; liberal studies (M Litt, D Litt), including history, Irish/Irish-American studies, literature (M Litt,

MMH, D Litt, DMH, CMH), religion, spirituality, teaching in the two-year college, writing; medical humanities (MMH, DMH, CMH), including arts, health, healthcare, literature (M Litt, MMH, D Litt, DMH, CMH), scientific research; poetry (MFA). *Program availability:* Part-time, evening/weekend. *Faculty:* 3 full-time (2 women), 27 part-time/adjunct (13 women). *Students:* 66 full-time (38 women), 179 part-time (117 women); includes 37 minority (15 Black or African American, non-Hispanic/Latino; 2 Asian, non-Hispanic/Latino; 15 Hispanic/Latino; 5 Two or more races, non-Hispanic/Latino), 14 international. Average age 42. 157 applicants, 82% accepted, 57 enrolled. In 2018, 34 master's, 24 doctorates, 17 other advanced degrees awarded. Terminal master's awarded for partial completion of doctoral program. *Degree requirements:* For master's and other advanced degree, thesis (for some programs); for doctorate, one foreign language, comprehensive exam (for some programs), thesis/dissertation. *Entrance requirements:* For master's, PRAXIS Core and Subject Area tests (for MAT), GRE/GMAT (for MFin MS in Data Analytics), resume, transcripts, writing sample, personal statement, letters of recommendation; for doctorate, GRE (PhD in history and culture), resume, transcripts, writing sample, personal statement, letters of recommendation; for other advanced degree, resume, transcripts, personal statement. Additional exam requirements/ recommendations for international students: Required—TOEFL (minimum score 587 paper-based; 80 iBT), IELTS (minimum score 6), TWE (minimum score 4). *Application deadline:* For fall admission, 8/1 for domestic students, 6/1 for international students; for spring admission, 12/1 for domestic students, 10/1 for international students. Applications are processed on a rolling basis. Application fee: $35. Electronic applications accepted. *Financial support:* Fellowships, research assistantships, teaching assistantships, career-related internships or fieldwork, Federal Work-Study, scholarships/grants, and unspecified assistantships available. Support available to part-time students. Financial award applicants required to submit FAFSA. *Unit head:* Dr. Debra Liebowitz, Provost and Dean of the College of Liberal Arts & Caspersen School of Graduate Studies, 973-4083139, E-mail: dliebowi@drew.edu. *Application contact:* Amo-Augustus Kubeyinje, Associate Vice President for Graduate Enrollment, 973-408-3111, E-mail: akubeyinje@drew.edu.
Website: http://www.drew.edu/caspersen

Drury University, Master in Education Program, Springfield, MO 65802. Offers curriculum and instruction (M Ed), including elementary education, middle school education, secondary education; instructional leadership (M Ed); instructional technology (M Ed); integrated learning (M Ed); special education (M Ed); special reading (M Ed). *Accreditation:* NCATE. *Program availability:* Part-time, evening/weekend, 100% online, blended/hybrid learning. *Faculty:* 10 full-time (6 women), 8 part-time/adjunct (6 women). *Students:* 167 full-time (133 women). Average age 32. 92 applicants, 92% accepted, 69 enrolled. In 2018, 44 master's awarded. *Entrance requirements:* For master's, bachelor's degree with minimum GPA of 2.75. Additional exam requirements/ recommendations for international students: Recommended—TOEFL (minimum score 80 iBT), IELTS (minimum score 6.5). *Application deadline:* For fall admission, 8/4 priority date for domestic and international students; for spring admission, 1/5 priority date for domestic and international students; for summer admission, 5/26 priority date for domestic and international students. Applications are processed on a rolling basis. Application fee: $25. Electronic applications accepted. *Expenses:* Tuition is $366 per credit hour. Fees are $7 per credit hour. Most M.Ed. degrees are 33 credit hours. *Financial support:* In 2018–19, 5 students received support. Career-related internships or fieldwork, scholarships/grants, and unspecified assistantships available. Financial award application deadline: 6/30; financial award applicants required to submit FAFSA. *Faculty research:* Instructional technology, autism, diversity, and social justice. *Unit head:* Dr. Asikaa Cosgrove, Director, Master in Education Program, 417-873-7806, E-mail: acosgrov@drury.edu. *Application contact:* Dr. Asikaa Cosgrove, Director, Master in Education Program, 417-873-7806, E-mail: acosgrov@drury.edu.
Website: http://www.drury.edu/education-masters

Duquesne University, School of Education, Department of Instruction and Leadership, Program in Secondary Education, Pittsburgh, PA 15282-0001. Offers biology (MS Ed); chemistry (MS Ed); English (MS Ed); K-12 education (MS Ed), including Latin; mathematics (MS Ed); physics (MS Ed); social studies (MS Ed). *Program availability:* Part-time, evening/weekend. *Faculty:* 5 full-time (4 women). *Students:* 20 full-time (12 women); includes 3 minority (1 Black or African American, non-Hispanic/Latino; 1 Hispanic/Latino; 1 Two or more races, non-Hispanic/Latino). Average age 24. 20 applicants, 85% accepted, 13 enrolled. In 2018, 14 master's awarded. *Entrance requirements:* For master's, two letters of recommendation, letter of intent, interview, bachelor's degree. Additional exam requirements/recommendations for international students: Required—TOEFL (minimum score 550 paper-based), IELTS (minimum score 7). *Application deadline:* For fall admission, 9/1 for domestic students; for spring admission, 1/2 for domestic students. Applications are processed on a rolling basis. Application fee: $0. Electronic applications accepted. *Expenses: Tuition:* Full-time $23,112; part-time $1284 per credit. Tuition and fees vary according to program. *Financial support:* In 2018–19, 1 student received support, including 1 teaching assistantship with full tuition reimbursement available; Federal Work-Study also available. Support available to part-time students. Financial award applicants required to submit FAFSA. *Faculty research:* Factors that create highly effective teachers; how to best support teachers to support students in reform-oriented environments; urban education; models of teacher leadership; improving instruction in mathematics/science/ social studies/English. *Total annual research expenditures:* $120,139. *Unit head:* Dr. Melissa Boston, Associate Dean for Teacher Education/Professor, 412-396.6109, Fax: 412-396-5585, E-mail: bostonm@duq.edu. *Application contact:* Kelly McGinley, Graduate Admissions Assistant, 412-396-1559, Fax: 412-396-5585, E-mail: mcginleyk@duq.edu.
Website: http://www.duq.edu/academics/schools/education/graduate-programs-education/ms-ed-secondary-education

D'Youville College, Department of Education, Buffalo, NY 14201-1084. Offers educational leadership (Ed D); elementary education (MS Ed); secondary education (MS Ed); special education (MS Ed). *Program availability:* Part-time, evening/weekend. *Degree requirements:* For master's, one foreign language, comprehensive exam, project or thesis. *Entrance requirements:* For master's, GRE (if GPA less than 2.75), minimum GPA of 3.0. Additional exam requirements/recommendations for international students: Required—TOEFL (minimum score 500 paper-based). Electronic applications accepted. *Faculty research:* Developmental disabilities, multiculturalism, early childhood education.

East Carolina University, Graduate School, College of Education, Department of Elementary and Middle Grades Education, Greenville, NC 27858-4353. Offers elementary education (MA Ed, MAT); middle grades education (MA Ed, MAT). *Accreditation:* NCATE. *Program availability:* Part-time, evening/weekend, online learning. *Application deadline:* For fall admission, 6/1 priority date for domestic students. *Expenses: Tuition, area resident:* Full-time $4749. Tuition, state resident: full-time $4749. Tuition, nonresident: full-time $17,898. *International tuition:* $17,898 full-time. *Required fees:* $2787. Part-time tuition and fees vary according to course load and program. *Financial support:* Application deadline: 3/1. *Unit head:* Dr. Patricia Jean Anderson, Interim Chair, 252-328-4123, E-mail: andersonp@ecu.edu. *Application contact:* Graduate School Admissions, 252-328-6012, Fax: 252-328-6071, E-mail: gradschool@ecu.edu.
Website: http://www.ecu.edu/cs-educ/elmid/index.cfm

East Carolina University, Graduate School, College of Education, Department of Mathematics, Science, and Instructional Technology Education, Greenville, NC 27858-4353. Offers distance learning and administration (Certificate); elementary mathematics education (Certificate); instructional technology (MA Ed, MS); mathematics education (MA Ed, MAT); science education (MA Ed, MAT); special endorsement in computer education (Certificate). *Program availability:* Part-time, evening/weekend. *Application deadline:* For fall admission, 6/1 priority date for domestic students. *Expenses: Tuition, area resident:* Full-time $4749. Tuition, state resident: full-time $4749. Tuition, nonresident: full-time $17,898. *International tuition:* $17,898 full-time. *Required fees:* $2787. Part-time tuition and fees vary according to course load and program. *Financial support:* Application deadline: 6/1. *Unit head:* Dr. Ron Preston, Director of Students, 252-737-9355, E-mail: prestonr@ecu.edu. *Application contact:* Graduate School Admissions, 252-328-6012, Fax: 252-328-6071, E-mail: gradschool@ecu.edu.
Website: http://www.ecu.edu/cs-educ/msite/

Eastern Connecticut State University, School of Education and Professional Studies/ Graduate Division, Program in Elementary Education, Willimantic, CT 06226-2295. Offers MS. *Accreditation:* NCATE. *Program availability:* Part-time, evening/weekend. *Degree requirements:* For master's, comprehensive exam or thesis. *Entrance requirements:* For master's, PRAXIS I, PRAXIS II, GRE, minimum GPA of 3.0, bachelor's degree from accredited institution. Additional exam requirements/ recommendations for international students: Required—TOEFL (minimum score 550 paper-based; 79 iBT); Recommended—IELTS (minimum score 6). Electronic applications accepted.

Eastern Illinois University, Graduate School, College of Education, Department of Teaching, Learning, and Foundations, Charleston, IL 61920. Offers curriculum and instruction (MS Ed). *Accreditation:* NCATE. *Program availability:* Part-time, evening/ weekend. *Degree requirements:* For master's, comprehensive exam (for some programs), thesis (for some programs). *Entrance requirements:* For master's, GMAT or GRE. Additional exam requirements/recommendations for international students: Required—TOEFL (minimum score 500 paper-based; 61 iBT), IELTS (minimum score 6). *Application deadline:* For fall admission, 5/15 for domestic and international students; for spring admission, 10/15 for domestic and international students. Applications are processed on a rolling basis. Application fee: $30. Electronic applications accepted. *Expenses:* Tuition, state resident: part-time $299 per credit hour. Tuition, nonresident: part-time $718 per credit hour. *Required fees:* $214.50 per credit hour. *Financial support:* Research assistantships with full tuition reimbursements, teaching assistantships with full tuition reimbursements, career-related internships or fieldwork, Federal Work-Study, scholarships/grants, and unspecified assistantships available. Support available to part-time students. Financial award application deadline: 3/1; financial award applicants required to submit FAFSA. *Unit head:* Jeanne E. Okrasinski, Ph.D., Chair, 217-581-5728, Fax: 217-581-6300, E-mail: jeokrasinski@eiu.edu. *Application contact:* Jeanne E. Okrasinski, Ph.D., Chair, 217-581-5728, Fax: 217-581-6300, E-mail: jeokrasinski@eiu.edu.
Website: http://www.eiu.edu/elegrad/

Eastern Illinois University, Graduate School, College of Liberal Arts and Sciences, Department of Mathematics and Computer Science, Charleston, IL 61920. Offers elementary/middle school mathematics education (MA); mathematics (MA); secondary mathematics education (MA). *Program availability:* Part-time, evening/weekend. *Degree requirements:* For master's, comprehensive exam (for some programs), thesis (for some programs). *Entrance requirements:* For master's, GMAT or GRE. Additional exam requirements/recommendations for international students: Required—TOEFL (minimum score 500 paper-based; 61 iBT), IELTS (minimum score 6). Electronic applications accepted. *Expenses:* Tuition, state resident: part-time $299 per credit hour. Tuition, nonresident: part-time $718 per credit hour. *Required fees:* $214.50 per credit hour.

Eastern Kentucky University, The Graduate School, College of Education, Department of Curriculum and Instruction, Richmond, KY 40475-3102. Offers elementary education (MA Ed), including early elementary education, reading; library science (MA Ed); music education (MA Ed); secondary and higher education (MA Ed), including secondary education; teaching (MAT). *Accreditation:* NCATE. *Program availability:* Part-time. *Degree requirements:* For master's, portfolio is part of exam. *Entrance requirements:* For master's, GRE General Test, PRAXIS II (KY), minimum GPA of 2.5. *Faculty research:* Technology in education, reading instruction, e-portfolios, induction to teacher education, dispositions of teachers.

Eastern Nazarene College, Adult and Graduate Studies, Division of Teacher Education, Quincy, MA 02170. Offers administration (M Ed); early childhood education (M Ed, Certificate); elementary education (M Ed, Certificate); English as a second language (Certificate); instructional enrichment and development (Certificate); middle school education (M Ed, Certificate); moderate special needs education (Certificate); principal (Certificate); program development and supervision (Certificate); secondary education (M Ed, Certificate); special education administrator (Certificate); special needs (M Ed); supervisor (Certificate); teacher of reading (M Ed, Certificate). M Ed also available through weekend program for administration, special needs, and teacher of reading only. *Program availability:* Part-time, evening/weekend. *Entrance requirements:* Additional exam requirements/recommendations for international students: Required—TOEFL (minimum score 550 paper-based).

Eastern New Mexico University, Graduate School, College of Education and Technology, Department of Curriculum and Instruction, Portales, NM 88130. Offers alternative licensure in elementary education (M Ed); bilingual education (M Ed); career and technical education (M Ed); educational technology (M Ed); elementary education (M Ed); English as a second language (M Ed); pedagogy and learning (M Ed); reading/ literacy (M Ed). *Program availability:* Part-time, online learning. *Degree requirements:* For master's, comprehensive exam, thesis optional. *Entrance requirements:* For master's, writing assessment, minimum GPA of 3.0, photocopy of teaching license, letter of recommendation. Additional exam requirements/recommendations for international students: Required—TOEFL (minimum score 550 paper-based; 79 iBT), IELTS (minimum score 6). Electronic applications accepted. *Expenses: Tuition, area resident:* Full-time $6776. Tuition, state resident: full-time $6776; part-time $282 per credit hour. Tuition, nonresident: full-time $8986; part-time $374 per credit hour. *Required fees:* $60 per semester. One-time fee: $25.

Eastern Oregon University, Master of Arts in Teaching Program, La Grande, OR 97850-2899. Offers elementary education (MAT); secondary education (MAT). *Faculty:* 10 full-time (6 women), 5 part-time/adjunct (2 women). *Students:* 48 full-time (26 women), 3 part-time (all women); includes 4 minority (1 Asian, non-Hispanic/Latino; 2 Hispanic/Latino; 1 Two or more races, non-Hispanic/Latino). Average age 32. In 2018, 47 master's awarded. *Degree requirements:* For master's, thesis. *Entrance requirements:* For master's, NTE. Secondary candidates will be required to pass the state approved subject-specific test(s), prior to entry into the program (ORELA/NES or Praxis II, depending upon which is required of your subject). Elementary-Multiple Subjects candidates will be required to pass the state approved Elementary Education, subtest II (ORELA/NES). Additional exam requirements/recommendations for

international students: Required—TOEFL (minimum score 550 paper-based; 79 iBT), IELTS (minimum score 6), Can also be satisfied by successful completion of the American Classroom Readiness course. *Application deadline:* For fall admission, 3/1 for domestic students. Applications are processed on a rolling basis. Electronic applications accepted. *Expenses:* $466.50/credit hour. *Financial support:* In 2018–19, 23 students received support. Federal Work-Study, scholarships/grants, and tuition waivers (full and partial) available. Support available to part-time students. *Unit head:* Dr. Matt Seimears, Dean of College of Business and Education, 541-962-3399, Fax: 541-962-3701, E-mail: mseimears@eou.edu. *Application contact:* Janet Frye, Administrative Support, MAT/MS Graduate Admission, 541-962-3772, Fax: 541-962-3701, E-mail: jfrye@eou.edu.
Website: https://www.eou.edu/cobe/ed/mat/

Eastern University, Graduate Education Programs, St. Davids, PA 19087-3696. Offers ESL program specialist (K-12) (Certificate); general supervisor (PreK-12) (Certificate); health and physical education (K-12) (Certificate); middle level (4-8) (Certificate); multicultural education (M Ed); music (K-12) (Certificate); Pre K-4 (Certificate); Pre K-4 with special education (Certificate); reading (M Ed); reading specialist (K-12) (Certificate); reading supervisor (K-12) (Certificate); school counseling (MA, CAGS); school principalship (preK-12) (Certificate); school psychology (MS, CAGS); secondary biology education (7-12) (Certificate); secondary chemistry education (7-12) (Certificate); secondary communication education (7-12) (Certificate); secondary English education (7-12) (Certificate); secondary math education (7-12) (Certificate); secondary social studies education (7-12) (Certificate); special education (M Ed); special education (7-12) (Certificate); special education (Pre K-8) (Certificate); special education supervisor (K-12) (Certificate); TESOL (M Ed); world language (Certificate), including Spanish. *Program availability:* Part-time, evening/weekend, online learning. *Entrance requirements:* Additional exam requirements/recommendations for international students: Required—TOEFL. Electronic applications accepted. Application fee is waived when completed online. *Expenses:* Contact institution.

Eastern Washington University, Graduate Studies, College of Arts, Letters and Education, Department of Education, Cheney, WA 99004-2431. Offers adult education (M Ed); curriculum development (M Ed); early childhood education (M Ed); educational foundations (M Ed); educational leadership (M Ed); literacy (M Ed); teaching K-8 (M Ed). *Program availability:* Part-time. *Degree requirements:* For master's, comprehensive exam. *Entrance requirements:* For master's, minimum GPA of 3.0. Additional exam requirements/recommendations for international students: Required—TOEFL (minimum score 580 paper-based; 92 iBT), IELTS (minimum score 7), PTE (minimum score 63). Electronic applications accepted.

East Stroudsburg University of Pennsylvania, Graduate and Extended Studies, College of Education, Department of Early Childhood and Elementary Education, East Stroudsburg, PA 18301-2999. Offers M Ed. *Program availability:* Part-time, evening/weekend, online learning. *Faculty:* 2 full-time (0 women). *Students:* 11 part-time (all women). Average age 36. 5 applicants, 80% accepted, 3 enrolled. In 2018, 5 master's awarded. *Degree requirements:* For master's, comprehensive exam, professional portfolio, curriculum project or action research. *Entrance requirements:* For master's, PRAXIS/teacher certification, letter of recommendation, Pennsylvania Department of Education requirements. Additional exam requirements/recommendations for international students: Recommended—TOEFL (minimum score 560 paper-based; 83 iBT), IELTS. *Application deadline:* For fall admission, 7/31 priority date for domestic students, 6/30 priority date for international students; for spring admission, 11/30 for domestic students, 10/31 for international students. Applications are processed on a rolling basis. Application fee: $50. Electronic applications accepted. *Expenses: Tuition, area resident:* Full-time $9288; part-time $516 per credit. Tuition, state resident: full-time $9288. Tuition, nonresident: full-time $13,932; part-time $774 per credit. *International tuition:* $13,932 full-time. *Required fees:* $2059; $114 per credit. Tuition and fees vary according to course load and degree level. *Financial support:* Research assistantships with tuition reimbursements, Federal Work-Study, and unspecified assistantships available. Support available to part-time students. Financial award application deadline: 3/1; financial award applicants required to submit FAFSA. *Unit head:* Andrew Whitehead, Chair, 570-422-3356, Fax: 570-422-3942, E-mail: awhitehead@esu.edu. *Application contact:* Kevin Quintero, Associate Director, Graduate and Extended Studies, 570-422-3890, Fax: 570-422-2711, E-mail: kquintero@esu.edu.
Website: https://www.esu.edu/early_childhood_elementary_education/undergraduate_programs/eced.cfm

East Tennessee State University, School of Graduate Studies, College of Education, Department of Curriculum and Instruction, Johnson City, TN 37614. Offers advanced studies in teaching and learning (M Ed), including childhood literacy; educational technology (M Ed), including educational communications and technology, school library media; elementary education (M Ed); reading (M Ed, MA), including reading education (MA), storytelling (MA); response to intervention (Post-Master's Certificate); school library professional (Post-Master's Certificate); secondary education (M Ed); STEAM K-12 education (Postbaccalaureate Certificate); storytelling (Postbaccalaureate Certificate); teacher education (MAT), including elementary education K-5, middle grades education 4-8, middle grades education 6-8, secondary education 6-12 and preK-12, secondary education K-12. *Accreditation:* NCATE. *Program availability:* Part-time, evening/weekend, online learning. *Degree requirements:* For master's, comprehensive exam, thesis optional, student teaching, practicum; for other advanced degree, field work (school library); culminating experience (storytelling). *Entrance requirements:* For master's, GRE, SAT, ACT, PRAXIS, minimum GPA of 3.0, interview, 3 letters of recommendation, background check; for other advanced degree, master's degree, TN teaching license. Additional exam requirements/recommendations for international students: Required—TOEFL (minimum score 550 paper-based; 79 iBT). Electronic applications accepted. *Faculty research:* Critical thinking; curriculum development in reading, math, and science education; cultural diversity; cognitive processes; effective teaching strategies.

Elizabeth City State University, Department of Education, Psychology and Health, Master of Education in Elementary Education Program, Elizabeth City, NC 27909-7806. Offers M Ed. *Accreditation:* NCATE. *Program availability:* Part-time, evening/weekend. *Degree requirements:* For master's, comprehensive exam (for some programs), thesis or alternative, electronic transformational teaching project. *Entrance requirements:* For master's, GRE and/or MAT, minimum GPA of 2.5, 3 letters of recommendation, 2 official transcripts from all undergraduate/graduate schools attended, teacher license, typewritten 2-page essay specifying educational philosophy. Additional exam requirements/recommendations for international students: Required—TOEFL (minimum score 550 paper-based, 80 iBT) or IELTS (minimum score 6.5). Electronic applications accepted. Application fee is waived when completed online. *Faculty research:* Diverse learners, disproportionality, inclusionary classrooms, international curriculum development.

Elms College, Division of Education, Chicopee, MA 01013-2839. Offers early childhood education (MAT); education (M Ed, CAGS); elementary education (MAT); English as a second language (MAT); reading (MAT); secondary education (MAT), including biology education, English education, Spanish education; special education (MAT). *Program availability:* Part-time, evening/weekend. *Faculty:* 5 full-time (all women), 6 part-time/adjunct (5 women). *Students:* 3 full-time (all women), 117 part-time (94 women); includes 12 minority (1 Black or African American, non-Hispanic/Latino; 2 Asian, non-Hispanic/Latino; 9 Hispanic/Latino). Average age 34. 27 applicants, 96% accepted, 23 enrolled. In 2018, 34 master's, 3 other advanced degrees awarded. *Degree requirements:* For master's, thesis (for some programs). *Entrance requirements:* For master's, Massachusetts Educators Certification Test, minimum GPA of 3.0; for CAGS, master's degree in education. Additional exam requirements/recommendations for international students: Required—TOEFL. *Application deadline:* For fall admission, 7/1 priority date for domestic students; for spring admission, 11/1 priority date for domestic students. Applications are processed on a rolling basis. Application fee: $30. *Expenses: Tuition:* Full-time $14,328; part-time $796 per credit. *Required fees:* $200. Tuition and fees vary according to degree level and program. *Financial support:* In 2018–19, 2 teaching assistantships with partial tuition reimbursements were awarded. Financial award applicants required to submit FAFSA. *Unit head:* Dr. Mary Janeczek, Chair, Division of Education, 413-594-2761, Fax: 413-592-4871, E-mail: janeczeke@elms.edu. *Application contact:* Nancy Davis, Director, Office of Graduate and Continuing Education Admissions, 413-265-2239, E-mail: davisn@elms.edu.

Elon University, Program in Education, Elon, NC 27244-2010. Offers elementary education (M Ed). *Accreditation:* NCATE. *Program availability:* Part-time. *Faculty:* 7 full-time (4 women), 4 part-time/adjunct (all women). *Students:* 49 part-time (43 women); includes 20 minority (6 Black or African American, non-Hispanic/Latino; 2 Asian, non-Hispanic/Latino; 10 Hispanic/Latino; 2 Two or more races, non-Hispanic/Latino), 1 international. Average age 34. 51 applicants, 90% accepted, 37 enrolled. In 2018, 10 master's awarded. *Entrance requirements:* For master's, GRE, MAT. Additional exam requirements/recommendations for international students: Required—TOEFL (minimum score 550 paper-based; 79 iBT). *Application deadline:* For fall admission, 5/1 for domestic students. Applications are processed on a rolling basis. Application fee: $50. Electronic applications accepted. *Financial support:* Federal Work-Study and scholarships/grants available. Support available to part-time students. Financial award application deadline: 6/1; financial award applicants required to submit FAFSA. *Faculty research:* Teaching reading to low-achieving second and third graders, pre- and post-student teaching attitudes, children's writing, whole language methodology, critical creative thinking. *Unit head:* Dr. Ann Bullock, Dean of the School of Education/Professor, 336-278-5900, E-mail: abullock9@elon.edu. *Application contact:* Art Fadde, Director of Graduate Admissions, 800-334-8448 Ext. 3, Fax: 336-278-7699, E-mail: afadde@elon.edu.
Website: http://www.elon.edu/med

Emporia State University, Program in Instructional Specialist, Emporia, KS 66801-5415. Offers elementary subject matter (MS); reading (MS). *Accreditation:* NCATE. *Program availability:* Part-time. *Degree requirements:* For master's, comprehensive exam or thesis, practicum. *Entrance requirements:* For master's, GRE General Test or MAT, essay exam, appropriate bachelor's degree, letters of recommendation. Additional exam requirements/recommendations for international students: Required—TOEFL (minimum score 520 paper-based; 68 iBT). Electronic applications accepted.

Endicott College, Van Loan School of Graduate and Professional Studies, Program in Early Childhood and Elementary Education, Beverly, MA 01915-2096. Offers early childhood and elementary education (M Ed); early childhood education (M Ed); elementary education (M Ed). *Program availability:* Part-time, evening/weekend, 100% online, blended/hybrid learning. *Degree requirements:* For master's, comprehensive exam, thesis, practicum. *Entrance requirements:* For master's, MAT or GRE, Massachusetts Tests for Educator Licensure (MTEL), Massachusetts teaching certificate, 2 professional letters of recommendation, personal statement. Additional exam requirements/recommendations for international students: Required—TOEFL. Electronic applications accepted. *Expenses:* Contact institution.

Fairfield University, Graduate School of Education and Allied Professions, Fairfield, CT 06824. Offers applied behavior analysis (ATC); applied psychology (MA); clinical mental health counseling (MA, CAS); educational technology (MA); elementary education (MA, CAS); family studies (MA); integration of spirituality and religion in counseling (ATC); marriage and family therapy (MA); reading and language development (Sixth Year Certificate); school counseling (MA, CAS); school psychology (MA, CAS); school-based marriage and family therapy (ATC); secondary education (MA); special education (MA, CAS); substance abuse counseling (ATC); teaching (Certificate); teaching and foundations (MA, CAS); TESOL, world languages, and bilingual education (MA, CAS). *Accreditation:* NCATE. *Program availability:* Part-time, evening/weekend. *Degree requirements:* For master's, comprehensive exam. *Entrance requirements:* For master's, minimum GPA of 3.0, 2 recommendations, resume. Additional exam requirements/recommendations for international students: Required—TOEFL (minimum score 550 paper-based; 84 iBT) or IELTS (minimum score 7.5). Electronic applications accepted. *Expenses:* Contact institution. *Faculty research:* Reading and literacy, writing, social justice and inequality in education, addictions and mental health issues, therapeutic relationships and clinical supervision.

Faulkner University, College of Education, Montgomery, AL 36109-3398. Offers counseling (MS); curriculum and instruction (M Ed); elementary education (M Ed); school counseling (M Ed). *Program availability:* Part-time, evening/weekend, 100% online, blended/hybrid learning. *Degree requirements:* For master's, 5+ hours in clinical training (for MS, M Ed in school counseling). *Entrance requirements:* For master's, MAT (minimum score of 370) or GRE (minimum score of 280) taken within last five years, bachelor's degree from regionally-accredited college or university; official transcripts from all colleges and universities attended; 3 letters of recommendation; goal statement (approximately 600 words); minimum cumulative GPA of 2.75 in undergraduate courses, 3.0 in graduate courses. Additional exam requirements/recommendations for international students: Required—TOEFL (minimum score 500 paper-based). Electronic applications accepted. *Expenses:* Contact institution.

Fayetteville State University, Graduate School, Programs in Middle Grades, Secondary, Special and Elementary Education, Fayetteville, NC 28301-4298. Offers middle grades (MA Ed); sociology (MA Ed); special education (MA Ed), including behavioral-emotional handicaps, mentally handicapped, specific training disability. *Accreditation:* NCATE. *Program availability:* Part-time, evening/weekend. *Faculty:* 10 full-time (6 women), 1 (woman) part-time/adjunct. *Students:* 24 full-time (20 women), 31 part-time (29 women); includes 38 minority (35 Black or African American, non-Hispanic/Latino; 2 Hispanic/Latino; 1 Two or more races, non-Hispanic/Latino), 1 international. Average age 35. 8 applicants, 88% accepted, 3 enrolled. In 2018, 7 master's awarded. *Degree requirements:* For master's, comprehensive exam, internship. *Entrance requirements:* Additional exam requirements/recommendations for international students: Required—TOEFL. *Application deadline:* For fall admission, 4/15 for domestic students; for spring admission, 10/15 for domestic students. Applications are processed on a rolling basis. Application fee: $40. Electronic applications accepted. *Financial support:* Application deadline: 3/1; applicants required to submit FAFSA. *Faculty research:* Reading assessment; reading remediation; learning disabilities; parenting; and adolescents with autism spectrum disorders social-communication development. *Unit head:* Dr. Cynthia Shamberger, Chair of Middle Grades, Secondary and Specialized Subjects, 910-672-2464, Fax: 910-672-1941, E-mail: cshamber@uncfsu.edu. *Application contact:* Dr. Cynthia Shamberger, Chair of Middle Grades, Secondary and Specialized Subjects, 910-672-2464, Fax: 910-672-1941, E-mail: cshamber@uncfsu.edu.

Elementary Education

Fitchburg State University, Division of Graduate and Continuing Education, Program in Elementary Education, Fitchburg, MA 01420-2697. Offers M Ed. *Accreditation:* NCATE. *Program availability:* Part-time, evening/weekend. *Entrance requirements:* Additional exam requirements/recommendations for international students: Required—TOEFL (minimum score 550 paper-based; 79 iBT). Electronic applications accepted. *Expenses:* Contact institution.

Florida Agricultural and Mechanical University, Division of Graduate Studies, Research, and Continuing Education, College of Education, Department of Elementary Education, Tallahassee, FL 32307-3200. Offers M Ed, MS. *Accreditation:* NCATE. *Degree requirements:* For master's, thesis (for some programs). *Entrance requirements:* For master's, GRE General Test, minimum GPA of 3.0. Additional exam requirements/recommendations for international students: Required—TOEFL.

Florida Atlantic University, College of Education, Department of Teaching and Learning, Boca Raton, FL 33431-0991. Offers elementary education (M Ed); environmental education (M Ed); instructional technology (M Ed); reading education (M Ed); secondary education (M Ed). *Accreditation:* NCATE. *Program availability:* Part-time, evening/weekend. *Faculty:* 16 full-time (12 women), 1 part-time/adjunct (0 women). *Students:* 30 full-time (21 women), 45 part-time (36 women); includes 27 minority (14 Black or African American, non-Hispanic/Latino; 3 Asian, non-Hispanic/Latino; 8 Hispanic/Latino; 2 Two or more races, non-Hispanic/Latino), 6 international. Average age 30. 71 applicants, 58% accepted, 28 enrolled. In 2018, 23 master's awarded. *Entrance requirements:* For master's, GRE General Test, minimum GPA of 3.0 in last 2 years of undergraduate course work. Additional exam requirements/recommendations for international students: Required—TOEFL (minimum score 500 paper-based; 61 iBT), IELTS (minimum score 6). *Application deadline:* For fall admission, 7/1 for domestic students, 2/15 for international students; for spring admission, 11/1 for domestic students, 7/15 for international students. Applications are processed on a rolling basis. Application fee: $30. *Expenses: Tuition, area resident:* Full-time $7400; part-time $369.82 per credit. Tuition, state resident: full-time $7400; part-time $369.82 per credit. Tuition, nonresident: full-time $20,496; part-time $1024.81 per credit. *Financial support:* Fellowships with partial tuition reimbursements, research assistantships with partial tuition reimbursements, teaching assistantships with partial tuition reimbursements, career-related internships or fieldwork, scholarships/grants, and unspecified assistantships available. *Faculty research:* Technology, teaching English to speakers of other languages, math teaching, electronic portfolio assessment, global perspectives through social studies. *Unit head:* Dr. Barbara Ridener, Chairperson, 561-297-3588, E-mail: bridener@fau.edu. *Application contact:* Dr. Debora Shepherd, Associate Dean, 561-296-3570, E-mail: dshep@fau.edu.
Website: http://www.coe.fau.edu/academicdepartments/tl/

Florida Gulf Coast University, College of Education, Program in Curriculum and Instruction, Fort Myers, FL 33965-6565. Offers elementary education (M Ed); English education (M Ed); English speakers of other languages endorsement (M Ed); gifted education (M Ed); mathematics education (M Ed); middle school education (M Ed); reading education (M Ed); science education (M Ed); social science education (M Ed); special education (M Ed). *Program availability:* Part-time, evening/weekend, online learning. *Degree requirements:* For master's, final project or portfolio. *Entrance requirements:* For master's, GRE General Test, MAT, minimum undergraduate GPA of 3.0 in last 2 years. Additional exam requirements/recommendations for international students: Required—TOEFL (minimum score 550 paper-based). Electronic applications accepted. *Faculty research:* Internet in schools, technology in pre-service and in-service teacher training.

Florida International University, College of Arts, Sciences, and Education, Department of Teaching and Learning, Miami, FL 33199. Offers art education (MA, MS); curriculum and instruction (MS, Ed D, PhD, Ed S), including curriculum development (MS), elementary education (MS), English education (MS), learning technologies (MS), mathematics education (MS), modern language education (MS), physical education (MS), science education (MS), social studies education (MS), special education (MS); early childhood education (MS); exceptional student education (Ed D); foreign language education (MS), including foreign language education, teaching English to speakers of other languages (TESOL); language, literacy and culture (PhD); mathematics, science, and learning technologies (PhD); physical education (MS), including sport and fitness; reading education (MS). *Program availability:* Part-time, evening/weekend. *Faculty:* 64 full-time (43 women), 104 part-time/adjunct (76 women). *Students:* 169 full-time (144 women), 155 part-time (130 women); includes 260 minority (53 Black or African American, non-Hispanic/Latino; 7 Asian, non-Hispanic/Latino; 193 Hispanic/Latino; 7 Two or more races, non-Hispanic/Latino), 13 international. Average age 33. 184 applicants, 62% accepted, 87 enrolled. In 2018, 153 master's, 10 doctorates awarded. *Degree requirements:* For doctorate, comprehensive exam, thesis/dissertation. *Entrance requirements:* For master's, GRE General Test, Florida General Knowledge Test or Florida College Level Academic Skills Test; for doctorate and Ed S, GRE General Test. Additional exam requirements/recommendations for international students: Required—TOEFL (minimum score 550 paper-based; 80 iBT), IELTS (minimum score 6.3). *Application deadline:* For fall admission, 6/1 priority date for domestic students, 4/1 for international students; for winter admission, 10/1 priority date for domestic students, 9/1 for international students; for spring admission, 3/1 priority date for domestic students, 2/1 for international students. Applications are processed on a rolling basis. Application fee: $30. Electronic applications accepted. *Financial support:* Research assistantships and teaching assistantships available. *Unit head:* Dr. Maria Fernandez, Chair, 305-348-0193, Fax: 305-348-2086, E-mail: Maria.Fernandez9@fiu.edu. *Application contact:* Nanett Rojas, Manager, Admissions Operations, 305-348-7464, Fax: 305-348-7441, E-mail: gradadm@fiu.edu.
Website: https://tl.fiu.edu/

Florida Memorial University, School of Education, Miami-Dade, FL 33054. Offers elementary education (MS); exceptional student education (MS); reading (MS). *Degree requirements:* For master's, comprehensive exam or thesis, field and clinical experiences, exit exam. *Entrance requirements:* For master's, GRE, CLAST, PRAXIS I, baccalaureate or graduate degree with minimum GPA of 3.0 in last 60 hours, 3 recommendations. Additional exam requirements/recommendations for international students: Recommended—TOEFL.

Fontbonne University, Graduate Programs, St. Louis, MO 63105-3098. Offers accounting (MBA, MS); art (MA); art (K-12) (MAT); business (MBA); computer science (MS); deaf education (MA); early intervention in deaf education (MA); education (MA), including autism spectrum disorders, curriculum and instruction, diverse learners, early childhood education, reading, special education; elementary education (MAT); family and consumer sciences (MA), including multidisciplinary health communication studies; fine arts (MFA); instructional design and technology (MS); management and leadership (MM); middle school education (MAT); secondary education (MAT); special education (MAT); speech-language pathology (MS); supply chain management (MS); theatre (MA). *Accreditation:* ASHA. *Program availability:* Part-time, evening/weekend, online learning. *Degree requirements:* For master's, comprehensive exam (for some programs), thesis (for some programs). *Entrance requirements:* Additional exam requirements/recommendations for international students: Required—TOEFL (minimum score 500 paper-based; 65 iBT). Electronic applications accepted.

Fordham University, Graduate School of Education, Division of Curriculum and Teaching, New York, NY 10023. Offers curriculum and teaching (MSE); early childhood education (MSE); elementary education (MST); special education (MSE, Adv C); teaching English as a second language (MSE). *Accreditation:* NCATE. *Program availability:* Part-time, evening/weekend. *Degree requirements:* For Adv C, thesis. *Entrance requirements:* Additional exam requirements/recommendations for international students: Required—TOEFL (minimum score 577 paper-based; 90 iBT), IELTS (minimum score 7). Electronic applications accepted.

Framingham State University, Graduate Studies, Program in Elementary Education, Framingham, MA 01701-9101. Offers M Ed.

Franklin Pierce University, Graduate and Professional Studies, Rindge, NH 03461-0060. Offers curriculum and instruction (M Ed); elementary education (MS Ed); emerging network technologies (Graduate Certificate); energy and sustainability studies (MBA, Graduate Certificate); health administration (MBA, Graduate Certificate); human resource management (MBA, Graduate Certificate); information technology (MBA); leadership (MBA); nursing education (MS); nursing leadership (MS); physical therapy (DPT); physician assistant studies (MPAS); special education (M Ed); sports management (MBA). *Accreditation:* APTA. *Program availability:* Part-time, 100% online, blended/hybrid learning. *Degree requirements:* For master's, concentrated original research projects; student teaching; fieldwork and/or internship; leadership project; PRAXIS I and II (for M Ed); for doctorate, concentrated original research projects, clinical fieldwork and/or internship, leadership project. *Entrance requirements:* For master's, minimum GPA of 2.5, 3 letters of recommendation; competencies in accounting, economics, statistics, and computer skills through life experience or undergraduate coursework (for MBA); certification/e-portfolio, minimum C grade in all education courses (for M Ed); license to practice as RN (for MS); for doctorate, GRE, 80 hours of observation/work in PT settings; completion of anatomy, chemistry, physics, and statistics; minimum GPA of 3.0. Additional exam requirements/recommendations for international students: Required—TOEFL (minimum score 550 paper-based; 61 iBT). Electronic applications accepted. *Faculty research:* Evidence-based practice in sports physical therapy, human resource management in economic crisis, leadership in nursing, innovation in sports facility management, differentiated learning and understanding by design.

Frostburg State University, College of Education, Department of Educational Professions, Program in Curriculum and Instruction, Frostburg, MD 21532-1099. Offers curriculum and instruction (Ed D); educational technology (M Ed); elementary education (M Ed); secondary education (M Ed). *Program availability:* Part-time, evening/weekend. *Degree requirements:* For master's, thesis or alternative. *Entrance requirements:* For master's, teaching certificate. Additional exam requirements/recommendations for international students: Required—TOEFL. Electronic applications accepted.

Frostburg State University, College of Education, Department of Educational Professions, Program in Elementary Teaching, Frostburg, MD 21532-1099. Offers MAT. *Accreditation:* NCATE. *Degree requirements:* For master's, thesis or alternative, PRAXIS II. *Entrance requirements:* For master's, PRAXIS I, entry portfolio. Additional exam requirements/recommendations for international students: Required—TOEFL. Electronic applications accepted.

Gallaudet University, The Graduate School, Washington, DC 20002-3625. Offers American Sign Language/English bilingual early childhood deaf education: birth to 5 (Certificate); audiology (Au D); clinical psychology (PhD); deaf and hard of hearing infants, toddlers, and their families (Certificate); deaf education (MA, Ed S); deaf history (Certificate); deaf studies (Certificate); educating deaf students with disabilities (Certificate); education: teacher preparation (MA), including deaf education, early childhood education and deaf education, elementary education and deaf education, secondary education and deaf education; educational neuroscience (PhD); hearing, speech and language sciences (MS, PhD); international development (MA); interpretation (MA, PhD), including combined interpreting practice and research (MA), interpreting research (MA); linguistics (MA, PhD); mental health counseling (MA); peer mentoring (Certificate); public administration (MPA); school counseling (MA); school psychology (Psy S); sign language teaching (MA); social work (MSW); speech-language pathology (MS). *Program availability:* Part-time. Terminal master's awarded for partial completion of doctoral program. *Degree requirements:* For master's, comprehensive exam (for some programs), thesis optional; for doctorate, comprehensive exam, thesis/dissertation. *Entrance requirements:* For master's and doctorate, GRE General Test or MAT, letters of recommendation, interviews, goals statement, American Sign Language proficiency interview, written English competency. Additional exam requirements/recommendations for international students: Required—TOEFL. Electronic applications accepted. *Faculty research:* Signing math dictionaries, telecommunications access, cancer genetics, linguistics, visual language and visual learning, integrated quantum materials, deaf legal discourse, advance recruitment and retention in geosciences.

George Mason University, College of Education and Human Development, Programs in Curriculum and Instruction, Fairfax, VA 22030. Offers assistive technology (M Ed); designing digital learning in schools (M Ed); early childhood education (M Ed); early childhood education for diverse learners (M Ed); elementary education (M Ed); English as a second language (M Ed); gifted child education (M Ed); literacy (M Ed), including PK-12 classroom teachers, reading specialist; literacy leadership for diverse schools (M Ed), including K-12 reading; physical education (M Ed); science K-12 (M Ed); secondary education (M Ed), including biology, chemistry, earth science, English, history/social science, math, physics; special education (M Ed); teacher leadership (M Ed); transformative teaching (M Ed). *Program availability:* Part-time, evening/weekend, 100% online, blended/hybrid learning. *Faculty:* 48 full-time (40 women), 28 part-time/adjunct (20 women). *Students:* 165 full-time (147 women), 697 part-time (579 women); includes 243 minority (47 Black or African American, non-Hispanic/Latino; 3 American Indian or Alaska Native, non-Hispanic/Latino; 88 Asian, non-Hispanic/Latino; 85 Hispanic/Latino; 4 Native Hawaiian or other Pacific Islander, non-Hispanic/Latino; 16 Two or more races, non-Hispanic/Latino), 26 international. Average age 34. 450 applicants, 93% accepted, 315 enrolled. In 2018, 421 master's awarded. *Entrance requirements:* For master's, PRAXIS Core (for some programs), 2 letters of recommendation, interview, program goals statement; 9 hours of complete licensure endorsement requirements (for elementary education); minimum GPA of 3.0 in applicant's last 60 hours of undergraduate coursework (for secondary education); at least 1 year of teaching experience (for literacy). Additional exam requirements/recommendations for international students: Required—TOEFL (minimum score 575 paper-based; 88 iBT), IELTS (minimum score 6.5), PTE (minimum score 59). *Application deadline:* For fall admission, 4/2 priority date for domestic and international students; for spring admission, 11/1 for domestic and international students. Application fee: $75 ($80 for international students). Electronic applications accepted. *Financial support:* In 2018–19, 4 students received support, including 1 fellowship, 3 teaching assistantships (averaging $3,745 per year); career-related internships or fieldwork, Federal Work-Study, scholarships/grants, unspecified assistantships, and health care benefits (for full-time research or teaching assistantship recipients) also available. Support available to part-time students. Financial award application deadline: 3/1; financial award applicants required to submit FAFSA. *Faculty research:* Teacher preparation and professional development; adaptive teaching; wonder in science

teacher preparation; literacy (digital, adolescent); site based course instruction. *Unit head:* Rebecca Fox, Professor and Academic Program Coordinator, 703-993-4123, E-mail: rfox@gmu.edu. *Application contact:* Rebecca Fox, Professor and Academic Program Coordinator, 703-993-4123, E-mail: rfox@gmu.edu. Website: http://gse.gmu.edu/programs/gsemasters

The George Washington University, Graduate School of Education and Human Development, Department of Curriculum and Pedagogy, Program in Elementary Education, Washington, DC 20052. Offers MA Ed/HD. *Accreditation:* NCATE. *Program availability:* Part-time. *Students:* 21 full-time (19 women), 5 part-time (4 women); includes 7 minority (4 Black or African American, non-Hispanic/Latino; 2 Asian, non-Hispanic/Latino; 1 Hispanic/Latino), 3 international. Average age 28. 46 applicants, 87% accepted, 23 enrolled. In 2018, 17 master's awarded. *Entrance requirements:* For master's, GRE General Test or MAT, minimum GPA of 2.75. *Application deadline:* For fall admission, 1/15 priority date for domestic students; for spring admission, 10/1 for domestic students. Applications are processed on a rolling basis. Application fee: $75. *Financial support:* In 2018–19, 20 students received support. Fellowships, career-related internships or fieldwork, Federal Work-Study, and tuition waivers (partial) available. Financial award application deadline: 1/15; financial award applicants required to submit FAFSA. *Faculty research:* Issues in teacher training. *Unit head:* Dr. Sylvan S. Beck, Director, 202-994-3365, E-mail: sbeck@gwu.edu. *Application contact:* Sarah Lang, Director of Graduate Admissions, 202-994-1447, Fax: 202-994-7207, E-mail: slang@gwu.edu.

Georgia Southern University, Jack N. Averitt College of Graduate Studies, College of Education, Department of Elementary and Special Education, Program in Elementary Education, Statesboro, GA 30460. Offers M Ed, MAT, Ed S. *Accreditation:* NCATE. *Program availability:* Part-time, evening/weekend, online only, 100% online. *Degree requirements:* For master's, portfolio, transition point assessments, exit assessment; for Ed S, field based research projects, assessments. *Entrance requirements:* For master's, minimum cumulative GPA of 2.5. Additional exam requirements/recommendations for international students: Required—TOEFL (minimum score 550 paper-based; 80 iBT), IELTS (minimum score 6). Electronic applications accepted. *Expenses: Tuition, area resident:* Part-time $3324 per semester. Tuition, state resident: full-time $5814; part-time $3324 per semester. Tuition, nonresident: full-time $23,204; part-time $13,260 per semester. *Required fees:* $2092; $2092. Tuition and fees vary according to course load, degree level, campus/location and program. *Faculty research:* Technology, effective instructional strategies, multiculturalism, children's literature, school violence.

Georgia State University, College of Education and Human Development, Department of Early Childhood Education, Atlanta, GA 30302-3083. Offers early childhood and elementary education (PhD); early childhood education (M Ed, Ed S); mathematics education (M Ed); urban education (M Ed). *Accreditation:* NCATE. *Program availability:* Part-time, evening/weekend. *Faculty:* 20 full-time (17 women), 1 (woman) part-time/adjunct. *Students:* 82 full-time (74 women), 30 part-time (27 women); includes 69 minority (48 Black or African American, non-Hispanic/Latino; 3 Asian, non-Hispanic/Latino; 11 Hispanic/Latino; 7 Two or more races, non-Hispanic/Latino), 3 international. Average age 31. 116 applicants, 70% accepted, 77 enrolled. In 2018, 36 master's, 6 doctorates awarded. *Entrance requirements:* For master's, GRE, undergraduate diploma; for doctorate and Ed S, GRE, master's degree. *Application deadline:* Applications are processed on a rolling basis. Application fee: $50. Electronic applications accepted. *Expenses: Tuition, area resident:* Full-time $9360; part-time $390 per credit hour. Tuition, state resident: full-time $9360; part-time $390 per credit hour. Tuition, nonresident: full-time $30,024; part-time $1251 per credit hour. *International tuition:* $30,024 full-time. *Required fees:* $2128. *Financial support:* In 2018–19, fellowships with full tuition reimbursements (averaging $24,000 per year), research assistantships with tuition reimbursements (averaging $4,000 per year), teaching assistantships with full tuition reimbursements (averaging $2,000 per year) were awarded; career-related internships or fieldwork, Federal Work-Study, institutionally sponsored loans, scholarships/grants, traineeships, health care benefits, tuition waivers (partial), and unspecified assistantships also available. Support available to part-time students. Financial award applicants required to submit FAFSA. *Faculty research:* Teacher development; language arts/literacy education; mathematics education; intersection of science, urban, and multicultural education; diversity in education. Website: http://ecee.education.gsu.edu/

Gonzaga University, School of Education, Spokane, WA 99258. Offers clinical mental health counseling (MA); educational leadership (M Ed, Ed D); elementary education (MIT); marriage and family counseling (MA); school counseling (MA); secondary education (MIT); special education (M Ed, MIT); sport and athletic administration (MA). *Accreditation:* NCATE. *Program availability:* Part-time, evening/weekend, 100% online, blended/hybrid learning. *Degree requirements:* For master's, comprehensive exam. *Entrance requirements:* For master's, GRE, MAT, and/or Washington Educator Skills Test-Basic (WEST-B), Washington Educator Skills Test-Endorsements (WEST-E), official transcripts from all colleges or universities attended, interview, two letters of recommendation, resume, essay, minimum GPA of 3.0. Additional exam requirements/recommendations for international students: Required—TOEFL (minimum score 580 paper-based, 88 iBT) or IELTS (minimum score 6.5). Electronic applications accepted. *Expenses:* Contact institution.

Gordon College, Graduate Education Program, Wenham, MA 01984-1899. Offers early childhood (M Ed); educational leadership (M Ed, Ed S); elementary education (M Ed); English as a second language (M Ed, Ed S); math specialist (M Ed); mathematics specialist (Ed S); middle school education (M Ed); moderate disabilities (M Ed); Montessori education (M Ed); reading (M Ed, Ed S); secondary education (M Ed). *Program availability:* Part-time, evening/weekend. *Degree requirements:* For master's, action research or clinical experience (for most programs); for Ed S, action research or clinical experience (for some programs). *Entrance requirements:* For master's, minimum undergraduate GPA of 3.0; 2 official undergraduate transcripts; professional resume; 3 recommendation letters (one professional reference, one academic reference, one personal reference); 500-700 word statement of purpose; for Ed S, minimum master's GPA of 3.3; 2 official transcripts from undergraduate and graduate schools; professional resume; 3 recommendation letters (one professional reference, one academic reference, one personal reference); 500-700 word statement of purpose. Additional exam requirements/recommendations for international students: Required—TOEFL (minimum score 550 paper-based, 80 iBT) or IELTS (minimum score 6.5). *Expenses:* Contact institution. *Faculty research:* Reading, early childhood development, English language learners, universal design for learning.

Goucher College, Graduate Programs in Education, Baltimore, MD 21204-2794. Offers at-risk and diverse learners (M Ed, Certificate); athletic program leadership and administration (M Ed, Certificate); elementary education (MAT); literacy strategies for content learning (M Ed); middle school (M Ed, Certificate); Montessori studies (M Ed); reading instruction (M Ed, Certificate); reducing student, classroom, and school disruption (M Ed); school improvement leadership (M Ed); secondary education (MAT); special education (MAT), including elementary education; special education for certified elementary and secondary teachers (M Ed); teacher as leader in technology (M Ed). *Program availability:* Part-time, evening/weekend. *Degree requirements:* For master's, thesis (M Ed), final presentation (MAT). *Entrance requirements:* For master's, minimum

GPA of 3.0. Additional exam requirements/recommendations for international students: Required—TOEFL (minimum score 550 paper-based; 80 iBT), IELTS (minimum score 7). Electronic applications accepted. *Expenses:* Contact institution. *Faculty research:* Urban education, middle school, school improvement, teacher education, at-risk student achievement.

Grand Canyon University, College of Education, Phoenix, AZ 85017-1097. Offers autism spectrum disorders (MA); curriculum and instruction (MA); early childhood education (M Ed); educational administration (M Ed); educational leadership (M Ed); elementary education (M Ed); gifted education (MA); instructional technology (MS); K-12 leadership (Ed S); reading (MA); secondary education (M Ed); secondary humanities education (M Ed); secondary STEM education (M Ed); special education (M Ed); teaching and learning (Ed D); teaching English to speakers of other languages (MA). *Program availability:* Part-time, evening/weekend, online learning. *Degree requirements:* For master's, publishable research paper (M Ed), e-portfolio. *Entrance requirements:* For master's, undergraduate degree from accredited, GCU-approved college, university, or program with minimum GPA 2.8. Additional exam requirements/recommendations for international students: Required—TOEFL (minimum score 550 paper-based; 79 iBT), IELTS (minimum score 6). Electronic applications accepted.

Grand Valley State University, College of Education, Programs in General Education, Allendale, MI 49401-9403. Offers adult and higher education (M Ed); early childhood education (M Ed); educational differentiation (M Ed); educational leadership (M Ed); educational technology integration (M Ed); elementary education (M Ed); middle level education (M Ed); school library media services (M Ed); secondary level education (M Ed); teaching English to speakers of other languages (M Ed). *Program availability:* Part-time, evening/weekend, 100% online, blended/hybrid learning. *Students:* 20 part-time (10 women); includes 1 minority (Black or African American, non-Hispanic/Latino). Average age 44. In 2018, 1 master's awarded. *Entrance requirements:* For master's, GRE General Test or minimum GPA of 3.0, last 60 credits from regionally-accredited college/university, 3 letters of recommendation. Additional exam requirements/recommendations for international students: Required—TOEFL (minimum iBT score of 80), IELTS (6.5), or Michigan English Language Assessment Battery (77). *Application deadline:* Applications are processed on a rolling basis. Application fee: $30. Electronic applications accepted. *Expenses:* $677 per credit hour, 33 credits. *Financial support:* In 2018–19, 1 student received support, including 1 fellowship; career-related internships or fieldwork, Federal Work-Study, scholarships/grants, and unspecified assistantships also available. *Faculty research:* Effectiveness of technology in education, parental involvement, effective teaching, effective schools research. *Unit head:* Dr. David Bair, Department Director, 616-331-6489, Fax: 616-331-6489, E-mail: baird@gvsu.edu. *Application contact:* Annukka Thelen, Director, Student Information and Services Center, 616-331-6205, Fax: 616-331-6217, E-mail: thelenan@gvsu.edu. Website: http://www.gvsu.edu/coe/

Greensboro College, Program in Education, Greensboro, NC 27401-1875. Offers elementary education (M Ed); special education (M Ed). *Program availability:* Part-time, evening/weekend. *Degree requirements:* For master's, thesis. *Entrance requirements:* For master's, GRE, teacher license, 2 years of teaching experience, 2 letters of recommendation. Additional exam requirements/recommendations for international students: Required—TOEFL (minimum score 550 paper-based). Electronic applications accepted.

Greenville University, Program in Education, Greenville, IL 62246-0159. Offers education (MAT); elementary education (MAE); secondary education (MAE). *Degree requirements:* For master's, thesis (for some programs). *Entrance requirements:* For master's, GRE, Illinois Basic Skills Test, teacher certification. Electronic applications accepted.

Harding University, Cannon-Clary College of Education, Searcy, AR 72149-0001. Offers advanced studies in teaching and learning (M Ed); art (MSE); behavioral science (MSE); counseling (MS, Ed S); early childhood special education (M Ed, MSE); education (MSE); educational leadership (M Ed, Ed S); elementary education (M Ed); English (MSE); French (MSE); history/social science (MSE); kinesiology (MSE); math (MSE); reading (M Ed); secondary education (M Ed); Spanish (MSE); teaching (MAT); teaching English as a second language (MSE). *Accreditation:* NCATE. *Program availability:* Part-time, evening/weekend. *Degree requirements:* For master's, comprehensive exam (for some programs), thesis optional, portfolio(s); for Ed S, comprehensive exam, portfolio, project. *Entrance requirements:* For master's, GRE, MAT, PRAXIS; for Ed S, MAT or GRE. Additional exam requirements/recommendations for international students: Required—TOEFL (minimum score 550 paper-based; 79 iBT). *Faculty research:* Reading, comprehension, school violence, educational technology, behavior, college choice, differentiated instruction, brain-based teaching.

Hawai'i Pacific University, College of Professional Studies, Program in Elementary Education, Honolulu, HI 96813. Offers M Ed. *Accreditation:* TEAC. *Program availability:* Part-time, evening/weekend. *Entrance requirements:* For master's, minimum undergraduate GPA of 3.0, background check, interview. Additional exam requirements/recommendations for international students: Recommended—TOEFL (minimum score 550 paper-based; 80 iBT), IELTS (minimum score 6), TWE (minimum score 5). Electronic applications accepted.

High Point University, Norcross Graduate School, High Point, NC 27268. Offers athletic training (MSAT); business administration (MBA); educational leadership (M Ed, Ed D); elementary education (M Ed, MAT); pharmacy (Pharm D); physical therapy (DPT); physician assistant studies (MPAS); secondary mathematics (M Ed, MAT); special education (M Ed); strategic communication (MA). *Accreditation:* NCATE. *Program availability:* Part-time, evening/weekend. *Degree requirements:* For master's, comprehensive exam (for some programs), thesis (for some programs). *Entrance requirements:* For master's, GMAT (MBA), GRE, MAT, minimum GPA of 3.0. Additional exam requirements/recommendations for international students: Required—TOEFL (minimum score 550 paper-based). Electronic applications accepted.

Hofstra University, School of Education, Programs in Teacher Education, Hempstead, NY 11549. Offers bilingual education (MA); bilingual extension (Advanced Certificate); business education (MS Ed); curriculum studies (MS Ed); early childhood and childhood education (MS Ed); early childhood education (MA, MS Ed); educational technology (Advanced Certificate); elementary education (MA, MS Ed); English education (MS Ed); family and consumer science (MS Ed); fine arts and music education (Advanced Certificate); fine arts education (MS Ed); foreign language and TESOL (MS Ed); foreign language education (MA, MS Ed); languages other than English and teaching English as a second language (MA); learning and teaching (Ed D); mathematics education (MA, MS Ed); middle childhood extension (Advanced Certificate); music education (MA, MS Ed); science education (MA); secondary education (Advanced Certificate); social studies education (MA, MS Ed); teaching languages other than English and TESOL (MS Ed); technology for learning (MA); TESOL (MS Ed, Advanced Certificate); TESOL with specialization in STEM (MA); work based learning extension (Advanced Certificate). *Program availability:* Part-time, evening/weekend, blended/hybrid learning. *Students:* 138 full-time (94 women), 109 part-time (78 women); includes 66 minority (16 Black or African American, non-Hispanic/Latino; 17 Asian, non-Hispanic/Latino; 31 Hispanic/Latino; 2 Native Hawaiian or other Pacific Islander, non-Hispanic/Latino), 6

international. Average age 29. 217 applicants, 86% accepted, 113 enrolled. In 2018, 105 master's, 11 doctorates, 25 other advanced degrees awarded. *Degree requirements:* For master's, comprehensive exam, thesis (for some programs), exit project, student teaching, fieldwork, electronic portfolio, curriculum project, minimum GPA of 3.0; for doctorate, dissertation; for Advanced Certificate, 3 foreign languages, comprehensive exam (for some programs), thesis project. *Entrance requirements:* For master's, GRE, 2 letters of recommendation, portfolio, teacher certification (MA), interview, essay; for doctorate, GMAT, GRE, LSAT, or MAT; for Advanced Certificate, 2 letters of recommendation, essay, interview and/or portfolio, teaching certificate. Additional exam requirements/recommendations for international students: Required—TOEFL (minimum score 550 paper-based; 80 iBT). *Application deadline:* Applications are processed on a rolling basis. Application fee: $75. Electronic applications accepted. *Financial support:* In 2018–19, 86 students received support, including 51 fellowships with full and partial tuition reimbursements available (averaging $5,080 per year), 2 research assistantships with full and partial tuition reimbursements available (averaging $3,470 per year); career-related internships or fieldwork, Federal Work-Study, institutionally sponsored loans, scholarships/grants, traineeships, tuition waivers (full and partial), unspecified assistantships, and scholarships and endowed scholarships also available. Support available to part-time students. Financial award applicants required to submit FAFSA. *Faculty research:* Impact of memory on learning; brain function, cognitive-development, learning, and achievement; student activism and civic education; using children's literature to promote diversity; 2nd language acquisition. *Unit head:* Dr. Alan Singer, Chairperson, 516-463-5853, Fax: 516-463-6275, E-mail: alan.j.singer@hofstra.edu. *Application contact:* Sunil Samuel, Assistant Vice President of Admissions, 516-463-4723, Fax: 516-463-4664, E-mail: graduateadmission@hofstra.edu.
Website: http://www.hofstra.edu/education/

Hofstra University, School of Education, Specialized Programs in Education, Hempstead, NY 11549. Offers applied behavior analysis (Advanced Certificate); childhood special education (MS Ed); early childhood special education (MS Ed, Advanced Certificate); educational and policy leadership (Ed D); educational leadership (Advanced Certificate); educational leadership and policy studies (MS Ed), including K-12; elementary special education (MS Ed); gifted education (Advanced Certificate); health education (MS); health professions pedagogy and leadership (MS); higher education leadership and policy studies (MS Ed); inclusive early childhood special education (MS Ed); inclusive elementary special education (MS Ed); inclusive secondary special education (MS Ed); literacy studies (MA, MS Ed, Ed D, Advanced Certificate); pedagogy for health professions (Advanced Certificate); physical education (MS); school district business leader (Advanced Certificate); secondary education generalist - students with disabilities 7-12 (MS Ed); secondary special education generalist - secondary education (MS Ed); special education (MS Ed, Advanced Certificate); special education assessment and diagnosis (Advanced Certificate); special education early childhood intervention (MS Ed); special education: international perspectives (MS Ed); teaching students with severe or multiple disabilities (Advanced Certificate). *Program availability:* Part-time, evening/weekend, blended/hybrid learning. *Students:* 126 full-time (91 women), 230 part-time (175 women); includes 90 minority (40 Black or African American, non-Hispanic/Latino; 4 American Indian or Alaska Native, non-Hispanic/Latino; 11 Asian, non-Hispanic/Latino; 32 Hispanic/Latino; 3 Two or more races, non-Hispanic/Latino), 4 international. Average age 32. 215 applicants, 90% accepted, 117 enrolled. In 2018, 130 master's, 9 doctorates, 23 other advanced degrees awarded. *Degree requirements:* For master's, one foreign language, comprehensive exam (for some programs), thesis (for some programs), electronic portfolio, capstone course, internship, practicum, student teaching, seminars, minimum GPA of 3.0; for doctorate, one foreign language, comprehensive exam, thesis/dissertation, qualifying hearing. *Entrance requirements:* For master's, GRE, interview, letters of recommendation, portfolio, essay, certification; for doctorate, GRE or MAT, interview, resume, essay, master's degree, 3 letters of recommendation, writing sample; for Advanced Certificate, GRE, interview, letters of recommendation, essay, professional experience, resume, master's degree. Additional exam requirements/recommendations for international students: Required—TOEFL (minimum score 550 paper-based; 80 iBT). *Application deadline:* Applications are processed on a rolling basis. Application fee: $75. Electronic applications accepted. *Financial support:* In 2018–19, 208 students received support, including 105 fellowships with full and partial tuition reimbursements available (averaging $3,948 per year), 12 research assistantships with full and partial tuition reimbursements available (averaging $6,573 per year); career-related internships or fieldwork, Federal Work-Study, institutionally sponsored loans, scholarships/grants, traineeships, tuition waivers (full and partial), unspecified assistantships, and scholarships and endowed scholarships also available. Support available to part-time students. Financial award applicants required to submit FAFSA. *Faculty research:* Water quality and income inequality; girls and stem; new media literacies; applied behavior analysis; k-12 leadership development. *Unit head:* Dr. Alan Flurkey, Chairperson, 516-463-5237, E-mail: alan.d.flurkey@hofstra.edu. *Application contact:* Sunil Samuel, Assistant Vice President of Admissions, 516-463-4723, Fax: 516-463-4664, E-mail: graduateadmission@hofstra.edu.
Website: http://www.hofstra.edu/education/

Holy Family University, Graduate and Professional Programs, School of Education, Master of Education Programs, Philadelphia, PA 19114. Offers early elementary education (PreK-Grade 4) (M Ed); education leadership (M Ed); general education (M Ed); reading specialist (M Ed); special education (M Ed); TESOL and literacy (M Ed). *Program availability:* Part-time. *Degree requirements:* For master's, thesis optional. Electronic applications accepted.

Hood College, Graduate School, Department of Education, Frederick, MD 21701-8575. Offers curriculum and instruction (MS), including elementary education, elementary science and mathematics education, secondary education, special education; education, multidisciplinary studies (MS); educational leadership (MS, Certificate); reading specialization (MS); STEM education (Certificate). *Accreditation:* NCATE. *Program availability:* Part-time-only, evening/weekend. *Faculty:* 5 full-time (3 women), 32 part-time/adjunct (24 women). *Students:* 3 full-time (all women), 306 part-time (253 women); includes 65 minority (22 Black or African American, non-Hispanic/Latino; 9 Asian, non-Hispanic/Latino; 17 Hispanic/Latino; 17 Two or more races, non-Hispanic/Latino), 3 international. Average age 33. 80 applicants, 99% accepted, 45 enrolled. In 2018, 59 master's, 47 other advanced degrees awarded. *Degree requirements:* For master's, action research project, portfolio (for reading specialization); for Certificate, STEM capstone activity. *Entrance requirements:* For master's, minimum GPA of 2.75, teaching certification, writing sample during interview, letter of recommendation from principal (for educational leadership program only). Additional exam requirements/recommendations for international students: Required—TOEFL (minimum score 575 paper-based; 89 iBT), IELTS (minimum score 6.5). *Application deadline:* For fall admission, 8/15 priority date for domestic students, 8/5 for international students; for spring admission, 12/1 priority date for domestic students, 12/1 for international students; for summer admission, 5/1 priority date for domestic students, 4/15 for international students. Applications are processed on a rolling basis. Application fee: $50 ($100 for international students). Electronic applications accepted. *Expenses: Tuition:* Full-time $17,640; part-time $4410 per semester. *Required fees:* $125 per semester. Tuition and fees vary according to degree level and program. *Financial support:* Tuition waivers (partial) and unspecified assistantships available. Financial award applicants required to submit FAFSA. *Faculty research:* Leadership, action research, brain research, learning styles. *Unit head:* Dr. April M. Boulton, Dean of the Graduate School, 301-696-3612, E-mail: gofurther@hood.edu. *Application contact:* Tanith Fowler Corsi, Assistant Director of Graduate Admissions, 301-696-3603, E-mail: gofurther@hood.edu.
Website: https://www.hood.edu/academics/departments/department-education/programs-offered

Hope International University, School of Graduate and Professional Studies, Program in Education, Fullerton, CA 92831-3138. Offers education administration (MA); elementary education (ME); secondary education (ME). *Program availability:* Part-time, evening/weekend. *Degree requirements:* For master's, comprehensive exam (for some programs), thesis. *Entrance requirements:* For master's, minimum GPA of 3.0, 2 references. Additional exam requirements/recommendations for international students: Required—TOEFL (minimum score 550 paper-based; 86 iBT); Recommended—IELTS (minimum score 6.5). Electronic applications accepted. *Expenses:* Contact institution. *Faculty research:* Distance education.

Houston Baptist University, School of Humanities, Program in Liberal Arts, Houston, TX 77074-3298. Offers education (EC-12 art, music, physical education, or Spanish) (MLA); education (EC-6 generalist) (MLA); general liberal arts (MLA); specialization in education (4-8 or 7-12) (MLA). *Program availability:* Part-time, evening/weekend. *Entrance requirements:* For master's, minimum GPA of 2.5, essay/personal statement, resume, bachelor's degree transcript. Additional exam requirements/recommendations for international students: Required—TOEFL (minimum score 80 iBT), IELTS (minimum score 6.5). Electronic applications accepted. Application fee is waived when completed online. *Expenses:* Contact institution.

Howard University, School of Education, Department of Curriculum and Instruction, Program in Elementary Education, Washington, DC 20059-0002. Offers M Ed. *Accreditation:* NCATE. *Degree requirements:* For master's, comprehensive exam, expository writing exam, internships, seminar paper. *Entrance requirements:* For master's, PRAXIS I, GRE, minimum GPA of 2.7. Additional exam requirements/recommendations for international students: Required—TOEFL (minimum score 550 paper-based; 79 iBT). Electronic applications accepted.

Huntington University, Graduate School, Huntington, IN 46750-1299. Offers adolescent and young adult education (M Ed); business administration (MBA); counseling (MA), including licensed mental health counselor; early adolescent education (M Ed); elementary education (M Ed); global youth ministry (MA); occupational therapy (OTD); organizational leadership (MA); pastoral leadership (MA); TESOL education (M Ed). *Accreditation:* AOTA. *Program availability:* Part-time, online learning. *Degree requirements:* For master's, comprehensive exam (for some programs), thesis (for some programs). *Entrance requirements:* For master's, GRE (for counseling and education students only); for doctorate, GRE (for occupational therapy students). Additional exam requirements/recommendations for international students: Required—TOEFL (minimum score 85 iBT), IELTS (minimum score 6.5). Electronic applications accepted. *Expenses:* Contact institution. *Faculty research:* Leadership, educational technology trends, evangelism, youth ministry, mental health.

Idaho State University, Graduate School, College of Education, Department of Teaching and Educational Studies, Pocatello, ID 83209-8059. Offers deaf education (M Ed); elementary education (M Ed); human exceptionality (M Ed); literacy (M Ed); music education (M Ed); secondary education (M Ed). *Program availability:* Part-time. *Degree requirements:* For master's, comprehensive exam, thesis (for some programs), oral thesis defense or written comprehensive exam and oral exam. *Entrance requirements:* For master's, GRE or MAT, minimum undergraduate GPA of 3.0, bachelor's degree, professional experience in an educational context. Additional exam requirements/recommendations for international students: Required—TOEFL (minimum score 550 paper-based; 80 iBT). Electronic applications accepted. *Faculty research:* Literacy, school psychology, special education.

Indiana University Bloomington, School of Education, Department of Curriculum and Instruction, Bloomington, IN 47405-7000. Offers art education (MS, Ed D, PhD); curriculum studies (Ed D, PhD); elementary education (MS, Ed D, PhD, Ed S); mathematics education (MS, Ed D, PhD); science education (MS, Ed D, PhD); secondary education (MS, Ed D, PhD); social studies education (MS, PhD); special education (PhD, Ed S). *Accreditation:* NCATE. *Program availability:* Part-time, evening/weekend. Terminal master's awarded for partial completion of doctoral program. *Degree requirements:* For doctorate, thesis/dissertation; for Ed S, comprehensive exam or project. *Entrance requirements:* For master's, doctorate, and Ed S, GRE General Test. Electronic applications accepted.

Indiana University Northwest, School of Education, Gary, IN 46408. Offers educational leadership (MS Ed); elementary education (MS Ed); K-12 online teaching (Graduate Certificate); secondary education (MS Ed). *Accreditation:* NCATE. *Program availability:* Part-time, evening/weekend. *Entrance requirements:* For master's, GRE General Test or MAT, minimum GPA of 3.0. Electronic applications accepted. *Expenses:* Contact institution.

Indiana University South Bend, School of Education, South Bend, IN 46615. Offers addiction counseling (MS Ed); alcohol and drug counseling (Graduate Certificate); clinical mental health counseling (MS Ed); educational leadership (MS Ed); elementary education (MS Ed); marriage, couple, and family counseling (MS Ed); school counseling (MS Ed); secondary education (MS Ed); special education (MAT, MS Ed), including intense intervention (MS Ed), mild intervention (MS Ed). *Accreditation:* NCATE. *Program availability:* Part-time, evening/weekend. *Degree requirements:* For master's, thesis or alternative, exit project. *Entrance requirements:* For master's, letters of recommendation, GRE or minimum GPA of 3.0. Additional exam requirements/recommendations for international students: Required—TOEFL. Electronic applications accepted. *Expenses:* Contact institution. *Faculty research:* Professional dispositions, early childhood literacy, online learning, program assessments, problem-based learning.

Indiana University Southeast, School of Education, New Albany, IN 47150. Offers counselor education (MS Ed); elementary education (MS Ed); secondary education (MS Ed). *Accreditation:* NCATE. *Program availability:* Part-time, evening/weekend. *Entrance requirements:* For master's, minimum undergraduate GPA of 2.5, graduate 3.0. Electronic applications accepted. *Faculty research:* Learning styles, technology, constructivism, group process, innovative math strategies.

Inter American University of Puerto Rico, Aguadilla Campus, Graduate School, Aguadilla, PR 00605. Offers accounting (MBA); counseling psychology specializing in family (MS); criminal justice (MA); educative management and leadership (MA); elementary education (M Ed); finance (MBA); human resources (MBA); industrial management (MBA); management information systems (MBA); marketing (MBA). *Program availability:* Part-time, evening/weekend. *Degree requirements:* For master's, comprehensive exam. *Entrance requirements:* For master's, EXADEP, 2 letters of recommendation, minimum GPA of 2.5. Electronic applications accepted.

Inter American University of Puerto Rico, Arecibo Campus, Programs in Education, Arecibo, PR 00614-4050. Offers administration and educational supervision (MA Ed);

counseling and guidance (MA Ed); curriculum and teaching (MA Ed), including biology education, English as a second language, history education, math education, Spanish; elementary education (MA Ed). *Accreditation:* TEAC. *Degree requirements:* For master's, comprehensive exam, thesis optional. *Entrance requirements:* For master's, GRE, EXADEP, bachelor's degree in education or teaching license (administration and supervision) or courses in education and psychology (counseling and guidance), minimum GPA of 2.5 in last 60 credits.

Inter American University of Puerto Rico, Barranquitas Campus, Program in Education, Barranquitas, PR 00794. Offers curriculum and teaching (M Ed), including biology, English as a second language, history, Spanish; educational leadership and management (MA); elementary education (M Ed); information and library service technology (M Ed); special education (MA). *Accreditation:* TEAC. *Program availability:* Part-time, evening/weekend. *Degree requirements:* For master's, 2 foreign languages, comprehensive exam, thesis (for some programs). *Entrance requirements:* For master's, GRE or EXADEP, bachelor's degree or its equivalent from accredited institution, official academic transcript from institution that conferred bachelor's degree, minimum GPA of 2.5, two recommendation letters, interview (for some programs), essay (for some programs). Electronic applications accepted. *Expenses:* Contact institution.

Inter American University of Puerto Rico, Guayama Campus, Department of Education and Social Sciences, Guayama, PR 00785. Offers early childhood education (0-4 years) (M Ed); elementary education (M Ed). *Program availability:* Part-time. *Entrance requirements:* For master's, GRE, MAT, EXADEP, letters of recommendation, minimum GPA of 2.5. Electronic applications accepted.

Inter American University of Puerto Rico, Metropolitan Campus, Graduate Programs, Program in Elementary Education, San Juan, PR 00919-1293. Offers MA. *Degree requirements:* For master's, comprehensive exam. *Entrance requirements:* For master's, GRE or EXADEP, interview. Electronic applications accepted.

Inter American University of Puerto Rico, Ponce Campus, Graduate School, Mercedita, PR 00715-1602. Offers accounting (MBA); biology (M Ed); chemistry (M Ed); criminal justice (MA); elementary education (M Ed); English as a Second Language (M Ed); finance (MBA); history (M Ed); human resources (MBA); marketing (MBA); mathematics (M Ed); Spanish (M Ed). *Entrance requirements:* For master's, minimum GPA of 2.5.

Inter American University of Puerto Rico, San Germán Campus, Graduate Studies Center, Program in Elementary Education, San Germán, PR 00683-5008. Offers MA. *Program availability:* Part-time, evening/weekend. *Degree requirements:* For master's, comprehensive exam. *Entrance requirements:* For master's, GRE General Test or EXADEP, minimum GPA of 3.0. *Expenses: Tuition:* Full-time $212; part-time $212 per credit. *Required fees:* $366 per semester. One-time fee: $31. Tuition and fees vary according to degree level and program.

Iowa State University of Science and Technology, Department of Education, Ames, IA 50011. Offers curriculum and instructional technology (M Ed, MS, PhD); elementary education (M Ed, MS); historical, philosophical, and comparative studies in education (M Ed, MS); special education (M Ed, MS, PhD). *Degree requirements:* For master's, thesis or alternative; for doctorate, thesis/dissertation. *Entrance requirements:* For master's and doctorate, GRE General Test. Additional exam requirements/recommendations for international students: Required—TOEFL (minimum score 560 paper-based; 83 iBT), IELTS (minimum score 6.5). Electronic applications accepted.

Ithaca College, School of Humanities and Sciences, Program in Childhood Education, Ithaca, NY 14850. Offers MS. *Faculty:* 14 full-time (7 women). *Students:* 9 full-time (7 women); includes 1 minority (Asian, non-Hispanic/Latino). Average age 31. 13 applicants, 85% accepted, 8 enrolled. In 2018, 4 master's awarded. *Degree requirements:* For master's, one foreign language, student teaching, portfolio, teacher inquiry project. *Entrance requirements:* Additional exam requirements/recommendations for international students: Required—TOEFL (minimum score 550 paper-based; 80 iBT). *Application deadline:* For fall admission, 3/19 for domestic and international students. Applications are processed on a rolling basis. Application fee: $40. Electronic applications accepted. *Expenses:* Contact institution. *Financial support:* In 2018–19, 8 students received support, including 8 research assistantships (averaging $11,355 per year); career-related internships or fieldwork, Federal Work-Study, and scholarships/grants also available. Support available to part-time students. Financial award application deadline: 3/1; financial award applicants required to submit FAFSA. *Unit head:* Dr. Peter Martin, Chair, 607-274-1076, Fax: 607-274-1263, E-mail: pmartin@ithaca.edu. *Application contact:* Nicole Eversley Bradwell, Director, Office of Admission, 800-429-4274, Fax: 607-274-1263, E-mail: admission@ithaca.edu.
Website: http://www.ithaca.edu/gradprograms/education/programs/childhooded/

Jackson State University, Graduate School, College of Education and Human Development, Department of Elementary and Early Childhood Education, Jackson, MS 39217. Offers early childhood education (MS Ed, Ed D); elementary education (MS Ed, Ed S); reading education (MS Ed). *Accreditation:* NCATE. *Program availability:* Part-time, evening/weekend, 100% online, blended/hybrid learning. Terminal master's awarded for partial completion of doctoral program. *Degree requirements:* For master's, comprehensive exam, thesis or alternative; for doctorate, comprehensive exam, thesis/dissertation. *Entrance requirements:* For master's, GRE General Test; for doctorate, MAT, teaching experience. Additional exam requirements/recommendations for international students: Required—TOEFL (minimum score 520 paper-based; 67 iBT). Electronic applications accepted. *Expenses:* Contact institution.

Jacksonville State University, Graduate Studies, School of Education, Program in Elementary Education, Jacksonville, AL 36265-1602. Offers MS Ed. *Accreditation:* NCATE. *Program availability:* Part-time, evening/weekend. *Degree requirements:* For master's, comprehensive exam, thesis (for some programs). *Entrance requirements:* For master's, GRE General Test or MAT. Additional exam requirements/recommendations for international students: Required—TOEFL (minimum score 500 paper-based; 61 iBT). Electronic applications accepted.

James Madison University, The Graduate School, College of Education, Program in Education, Harrisonburg, VA 22807. Offers early childhood education (preK-3) (MAT); educational leadership (M Ed); educational technology (M Ed); elementary education (MAT); equity and cultural diversity (M Ed); inclusive early childhood education (MAT); K-8 mathematics specialist (M Ed); middle education (MAT); reading education (M Ed); secondary education (MAT); Spanish language and culture for educators (M Ed); TESOL (MAT). *Accreditation:* NCATE. *Program availability:* Part-time, evening/weekend. *Students:* 255 full-time (224 women), 200 part-time (140 women); includes 56 minority (13 Black or African American, non-Hispanic/Latino; 8 Asian, non-Hispanic/Latino; 21 Hispanic/Latino; 14 Two or more races, non-Hispanic/Latino), 1 international. Average age 30. In 2018, 295 master's awarded. Application fee: $60. Electronic applications accepted. *Expenses:* Tuition, state resident: full-time $10,848. Tuition, nonresident: full-time $27,888. *Required fees:* $1128. *Financial support:* In 2018–19, 22 students received support. Teaching assistantships, career-related internships or fieldwork, Federal Work-Study, and assistantships (averaging $7911) available. Financial award application deadline: 3/1; financial award applicants required to submit FAFSA. *Unit head:* Dr. Phillip M. Wishon, Dean, 540-568-6572, E-mail: wishonpm@jmu.edu. *Application contact:* Lynette D. Michael, Director of Graduate Admissions, 540-568-6131 Ext. 6395, Fax: 540-568-7860, E-mail: michaeld@jmu.edu.
Website: http://www.jmu.edu/coe/index.shtml

James Madison University, The Graduate School, College of Education, Program in Elementary Education, Harrisonburg, VA 22807. Offers MAT. *Students:* Average age 27. *Entrance requirements:* For master's, GRE General Test, PRAXIS II, minimum undergraduate GPA of 2.75, 2-page essay, interview. Additional exam requirements/recommendations for international students: Required—TOEFL. *Application deadline:* For fall admission, 5/1 for domestic students; for spring admission, 9/1 for domestic students. Applications are processed on a rolling basis. Electronic applications accepted. *Expenses:* Tuition, state resident: full-time $10,848. Tuition, nonresident: full-time $27,888. *Required fees:* $1128. *Unit head:* Dr. Martha Ross, Academic Unit Head, 540-568-6255. *Application contact:* Lynette M. Bible, Director of Graduate Admissions, 540-568-6395, Fax: 540-568-7860, E-mail: biblelm@jmu.edu.

Johnson & Wales University, Graduate Studies, MAT Program in Teacher Education, Providence, RI 02903-3703. Offers business education and secondary special education (MAT); culinary arts education (MAT); elementary education and elementary special education (MAT). *Program availability:* Part-time, evening/weekend. *Entrance requirements:* For master's, MAT, minimum GPA of 2.75. Additional exam requirements/recommendations for international students: Required—TOEFL (minimum score 550 paper-based) or IELTS (recommended). *Faculty research:* Secondary education, student teaching, educational reform, evaluation procedures.

Kansas State University, Graduate School, College of Education, Department of Curriculum and Instruction, Manhattan, KS 66506. Offers curriculum and instruction (Ed D, PhD); digital teaching and learning (MS); educational computing, design and online learning (MS); elementary/middle level curriculum and instruction (MS); online learning (Certificate); reading specialist endorsement (MS); reading/language arts (MS); teacher leader/school improvement (MS); teaching and learning (Certificate). *Accreditation:* NCATE. *Program availability:* Part-time, online learning. *Degree requirements:* For master's, comprehensive exam, portfolio, project, report or thesis; for doctorate, comprehensive exam, thesis/dissertation, preliminary exam; for Certificate, comprehensive exam, portfolio. *Entrance requirements:* For master's, minimum GPA of 3.0, 3 letters of recommendation; for doctorate, GRE, minimum GPA of 3.0, 3 letters of recommendation, evidence of scholarly writing; for Certificate, minimum GPA of 3.0, letters of recommendation. Additional exam requirements/recommendations for international students: Required—TOEFL (minimum score 550 paper-based; 80 iBT) or IELTS. Electronic applications accepted. *Faculty research:* Literacy and technology, critical race theory and diversity, achievement gaps, school improvement, teacher education.

Keuka College, Program in Childhood Education/Literacy, Keuka Park, NY 14478. Offers literacy 5-12 (MS); literacy B-6 (MS). *Degree requirements:* For master's, thesis, capstone project/student-led research project. *Entrance requirements:* For master's, GRE, minimum GPA of 3.0; 3 letters of recommendation (2 academic and one from cooperating teacher from student teaching or other professional). Additional exam requirements/recommendations for international students: Required—TOEFL (minimum score 550 paper-based). Electronic applications accepted. *Expenses:* Contact institution. *Faculty research:* Marginalized populations, international literacy, teacher assessment.

Kutztown University of Pennsylvania, College of Education, Program in Elementary Education, Kutztown, PA 19530-0730. Offers M Ed. *Accreditation:* NCATE. *Program availability:* Part-time, evening/weekend. *Faculty:* 9 full-time (8 women). *Students:* 5 full-time (4 women), 57 part-time (47 women); includes 6 minority (2 Black or African American, non-Hispanic/Latino; 1 Asian, non-Hispanic/Latino; 3 Hispanic/Latino), 1 international. Average age 31. 79 applicants, 70% accepted, 32 enrolled. In 2018, 24 master's awarded. *Degree requirements:* For master's, comprehensive exam, thesis optional, comprehensive project. *Entrance requirements:* For master's, GRE General Test, PA teaching certificate in elementary education, 3 letters of recommendation. Additional exam requirements/recommendations for international students: Required—TOEFL (minimum score 550 paper-based, 79 iBT), IELTS (minimum score 6.5), or PTE (minimum score 53). *Application deadline:* For fall admission, 8/1 for domestic and international students; for spring admission, 12/1 for domestic and international students. Application fee: $35. Electronic applications accepted. *Expenses:* Tuition, state resident: part-time $516 per credit. Tuition, nonresident: part-time $774 per credit. *Required fees:* $119 per credit. One-time fee: $50 part-time. Tuition and fees vary according to degree level. *Financial support:* Career-related internships or fieldwork, Federal Work-Study, and unspecified assistantships available. Financial award application deadline: 3/1; financial award applicants required to submit FAFSA. *Faculty research:* Whole language, middle schools, cooperative learning discussion techniques, oral reading techniques, hemisphericity. *Unit head:* Dr. Tracy Keyes, Department Chair, 610-683-4286, Fax: 610-683-1327, E-mail: keyes@kutztown.edu. *Application contact:* Dr. Tracy Keyes, Department Chair, 610-683-4286, Fax: 610-683-1327, E-mail: keyes@kutztown.edu.
Website: https://www.kutztown.edu/academics/graduate-programs/elementary-education.htm

Lake Forest College, Master of Arts in Teaching Program, Lake Forest, IL 60045. Offers elementary education (MAT); K-12 French (MAT); K-12 music (MAT); K-12 Spanish (MAT); K-12 visual art (MAT); secondary biology (MAT); secondary chemistry (MAT); secondary English (MAT); secondary history (MAT); secondary mathematics (MAT). *Degree requirements:* For master's, comprehensive exam, portfolio. *Entrance requirements:* For master's, GRE.

Lancaster Bible College, Graduate School, Lancaster, PA 17601-5036. Offers adult ministries (MA); Bible (MA); children and family ministry (MA); church planting (MA); consulting resource teacher (M Ed); elementary school counseling (M Ed); leadership (PhD); leadership studies (MA); marriage and family counseling (MA); mental health counseling (MA); pastoral studies (MA); secondary school counseling (M Ed); sports ministry (MA); student ministry (MA); town and country ministry (MA). *Program availability:* Part-time, evening/weekend. *Faculty:* 8 full-time (1 woman), 5 part-time/adjunct (1 woman). *Students:* 94 full-time (47 women), 89 part-time (45 women); includes 21 minority (15 Black or African American, non-Hispanic/Latino; 5 Asian, non-Hispanic/Latino; 1 Hispanic/Latino). Average age 36. *Degree requirements:* For master's, comprehensive exam (for some programs), thesis (for some programs). *Entrance requirements:* For master's, bachelor's degree with a minimum of 30 credits of course work in Bible, minimum undergraduate GPA of 3.0, interview. Additional exam requirements/recommendations for international students: Required—TOEFL. *Application deadline:* Applications are processed on a rolling basis. Application fee: $25. *Financial support:* In 2018–19, 31 students received support. Teaching assistantships, scholarships/grants, and unspecified assistantships available. Support available to part-time students. Financial award application deadline: 6/1; financial award applicants required to submit FAFSA. *Unit head:* Dr. Gary Bredfeldt, Associate Vice President/Dean of iLead Center, 717-560-8297, Fax: 717-560-8236. *Application contact:* Mark Wilson, Admissions Counselor, 717-560-8229, E-mail: mwilson@lbc.edu.

Langston University, School of Education and Behavioral Sciences, Langston, OK 73050. Offers bilingual/multicultural (M Ed); elementary education (M Ed); English as a

second language (M Ed); rehabilitation counseling (M Sc); urban education (M Ed). *Accreditation:* CORE; NCATE (one or more programs are accredited). *Program availability:* Part-time. *Degree requirements:* For master's, comprehensive exam, thesis optional. *Entrance requirements:* For master's, GRE, writing skills test, minimum GPA of 2.5, 3 letters of recommendation. Additional exam requirements/recommendations for international students: Required—TOEFL, TWE. *Faculty research:* Bilingual/multicultural education, financing post-secondary education.

Lasell College, Graduate and Professional Studies in Education, Newton, MA 02466-2709. Offers curriculum, leadership, and inclusion (M Ed); elementary education (M Ed); special education (M Ed), including moderate disabilities; teaching bilingual/English learners with disabilities (Graduate Certificate). *Program availability:* Part-time-only, evening/weekend, blended/hybrid learning. *Faculty:* 1 (woman) full-time, 5 part-time/adjunct (4 women). *Students:* 4 full-time (3 women), 45 part-time (37 women); includes 4 minority (3 Asian, non-Hispanic/Latino; 1 Hispanic/Latino). Average age 28. 23 applicants, 70% accepted, 10 enrolled. In 2018, 22 master's awarded. *Degree requirements:* For master's, minimum GPA of 3.0; practicum. *Entrance requirements:* For master's, Massachusetts Tests for Educator Licensure (MTEL) Curriculum and Literacy foundations of reading and writing subtest, one-page personal statement, 2 letters of recommendation, resume, bachelor's degree transcript. Additional exam requirements/recommendations for international students: Required—TOEFL (minimum score 550 paper-based, 79 iBT) or IELTS (minimum score 6). *Application deadline:* For fall admission, 8/31 priority date for domestic students, 6/30 priority date for international students; for spring admission, 12/31 priority date for domestic students, 10/31 priority date for international students. Applications are processed on a rolling basis. Electronic applications accepted. *Expenses: Tuition:* Part-time $600 per credit. *Required fees:* $40 per course. *Financial support:* Federal Work-Study, scholarships/grants, and tuition discounts available. Support available to part-time students. Financial award application deadline: 8/31; financial award applicants required to submit FAFSA. *Faculty research:* Inclusion, English language learners, literacy, and urban education; teacher inquiry; universal design for learning, deaf-blindness, and visual impairments; social and emotional learning; educational law, applied behavior analysis, and classroom management. *Unit head:* Eric Turner, Vice President of Graduate and Professional Studies, 617-243-2071, Fax: 617-243-2450, E-mail: gradinfo@lasell.edu. *Application contact:* Adrienne Franciosi, Director of Graduate Enrollment, 617-243-2214, Fax: 617-243-2450, E-mail: gradinfo@lasell.edu.
Website: http://www.lasell.edu/academics/graduate-and-professional-studies/programs-of-study/master-of-education.html

Lee University, Program in Education, Cleveland, TN 37320-3450. Offers art (MAT); curriculum and instruction (M Ed, Ed S); early childhood (MAT); educational leadership (M Ed, Ed S); elementary education (MAT); English and math (MAT); English and science (MAT); English and social studies (MAT); higher education administration (MS); history (MAT); history and economics (MAT); math and science (MAT); math and social studies (MAT); middle grades (MAT); science and social studies (MASW); secondary education (MAT); Spanish (MAT); special education (M Ed, MAT); TESOL (MAT). *Accreditation:* NCATE. *Program availability:* Part-time. *Faculty:* 13 full-time (5 women), 13 part-time/adjunct (7 women). *Students:* 32 full-time (26 women), 73 part-time (49 women); includes 13 minority (10 Black or African American, non-Hispanic/Latino; 3 Two or more races, non-Hispanic/Latino), 3 international. Average age 30. 56 applicants, 73% accepted, 34 enrolled. In 2018, 60 master's, 3 other advanced degrees awarded. *Degree requirements:* For master's, variable foreign language requirement, thesis optional, internship. *Entrance requirements:* For master's, MAT or GRE General Test, minimum undergraduate GPA of 2.75, 3 letters of recommendation, interview, writing sample, official transcripts, background check; for Ed S, minimum undergraduate and master's GPA of 2.75, official transcripts for undergraduate and master's degrees. Additional exam requirements/recommendations for international students: Required—TOEFL (minimum score 61 iBT). *Application deadline:* For fall admission, 6/1 priority date for domestic and international students; for spring admission, 11/1 priority date for domestic and international students; for summer admission, 4/1 priority date for domestic and international students. Applications are processed on a rolling basis. Application fee: $25. Electronic applications accepted. *Financial support:* In 2018–19, 43 students received support. Career-related internships or fieldwork, Federal Work-Study, institutionally sponsored loans, scholarships/grants, and unspecified assistantships available. Financial award application deadline: 3/1; financial award applicants required to submit FAFSA. *Unit head:* Dr. William Kamm, Director, 423-614-8544, E-mail: wkamm@leeuniversity.edu. *Application contact:* Jeffery McGirt, Director of Graduate Enrollment, 423-614-8691, Fax: 423-614-8317, E-mail: jmcgirt@leeuniversity.edu.
Website: http://www.leeuniversity.edu/academics/graduate/education

Lehigh University, College of Education, Program in Teaching, Learning and Technology, Bethlehem, PA 18015. Offers elementary education (M Ed); instructional technology (MS); teaching, learning and technology (PhD); M Ed/MA. *Program availability:* Part-time. *Faculty:* 6 full-time (4 women), 8 part-time/adjunct (5 women). *Students:* 18 full-time (12 women), 55 part-time (32 women); includes 9 minority (1 Asian, non-Hispanic/Latino; 7 Hispanic/Latino; 1 Native Hawaiian or other Pacific Islander, non-Hispanic/Latino), 6 international. Average age 32. 50 applicants, 70% accepted, 9 enrolled. In 2018, 28 master's, 4 doctorates awarded. Terminal master's awarded for partial completion of doctoral program. *Degree requirements:* For doctorate, comprehensive exam, thesis/dissertation, qualifying exam. *Entrance requirements:* For master's, minimum GPA of 3.0, 2 letters of recommendation, essay, transcript; for doctorate, GRE General Test, minimum graduate GPA of 3.0, writing sample, 2 letters of recommendation, essay, transcript. Additional exam requirements/recommendations for international students: Required—TOEFL (minimum score 93 iBT), IELTS (minimum score 6.5), TOEFL or IELTS is required. *Application deadline:* For fall admission, 7/15 for domestic and international students; for spring admission, 12/15 for domestic and international students; for summer admission, 4/15 for domestic and international students. Application fee: $65. Electronic applications accepted. *Expenses:* $565 per credit. *Financial support:* In 2018–19, 11 students received support, including 3 research assistantships with full and partial tuition reimbursements available (averaging $15,778 per year); fellowships, scholarships/grants, and unspecified assistantships also available. Financial award application deadline: 1/31. *Faculty research:* Teaching and learning, K-16 curriculum development, web-based learning, teaching and technology, language and literacy, teaching, learning with spatial technologies, visual instructional technologies, environmental science curriculum, multicultural issues, English language education, educational access and equity, elLs with disabilities, integrated curriculum, augmented. *Total annual research expenditures:* $786,227. *Unit head:* Dr. Lynn Columba, Director, 610-758-3237, Fax: 610-758-3243, E-mail: hlc0@lehigh.edu. *Application contact:* Donna Toothman, Coordinator, 610-758-3230, Fax: 610-758-3243, E-mail: djt2@lehigh.edu.
Website: https://ed.lehigh.edu/academics/programs/teacher-education

Lehman College of the City University of New York, School of Education, Department of Early Childhood and Childhood Education, Program in Childhood Education, Bronx, NY 10468-1589. Offers MS Ed. *Accreditation:* NCATE. *Program availability:* Part-time, evening/weekend. *Degree requirements:* For master's, thesis. *Entrance requirements:* For master's, minimum GPA of 3.0. *Faculty research:* POS network, emotional and intellectual learning, realistic picture books.

Le Moyne College, Department of Education, Syracuse, NY 13214. Offers adolescent education (MS Ed, MST); adolescent education/special education (MS Ed, MST); adolescent English (MST), including grades 7-12; adolescent English/special education (MST), including grades 7-12; adolescent foreign language (MST), including grades 7-12; adolescent history (MST), including grades 7-12; childhood education (MS Ed); childhood education/special education (MS Ed); elementary education (MS Ed); general education (MS Ed); inclusive childhood education (MST); literacy education (MS Ed), including birth to grade 6, grades 5-12; school building leader (MS Ed); school building leadership (CAS); school district business leader (MS Ed, CAS); school district leader (MS Ed); school district leadership (CAS); secondary education (MS Ed); special education (MS Ed); teaching English to speakers of other languages (MS Ed); urban studies (MS Ed). *Accreditation:* TEAC. *Program availability:* Part-time, evening/weekend. *Faculty:* 7 full-time (5 women), 16 part-time/adjunct (11 women). *Students:* 35 full-time (28 women), 119 part-time (84 women); includes 14 minority (5 Black or African American, non-Hispanic/Latino; 1 Asian, non-Hispanic/Latino; 7 Hispanic/Latino; 1 Two or more races, non-Hispanic/Latino), 1 international. Average age 30. 123 applicants, 89% accepted, 96 enrolled. In 2018, 66 master's, 48 CASs awarded. Terminal master's awarded for partial completion of doctoral program. *Degree requirements:* For master's, thesis. *Entrance requirements:* For master's, bachelor's degree with minimum undergraduate GPA of 3.0, 2 letters of recommendation, transcripts. Additional exam requirements/recommendations for international students: Required—TOEFL (minimum score 79 iBT); Recommended—IELTS (minimum score 6.5). *Application deadline:* For fall admission, 4/1 priority date for domestic and international students; for spring admission, 10/1 priority date for domestic and international students; for summer admission, 3/1 priority date for domestic and international students. Applications are processed on a rolling basis. Electronic applications accepted. *Expenses:* $734 per credit hour; wellness fee $70 per semester for full-time graduate students taking 9+ credit hours; technology fee $75 per semester for full-time graduate students taking 9+ credit hours, $25 per semester for part-time students; $1,470 per credit hour (for ED.D.). *Financial support:* In 2018–19, 44 students received support. Career-related internships or fieldwork, scholarships/grants, and health care benefits available. Support available to part-time students. Financial award applicants required to submit FAFSA. *Faculty research:* Minority teachers, special education, multiculturalism, literacy, technology, media literacy learning, autism, school district organization, service-learning, higher level problem solving, teacher leadership. *Unit head:* Dr. Stephen C. Fleury, Chair, Department of Education, 315-445-4376, Fax: 315-445-4744, E-mail: fleurysc@lemoyne.edu. *Application contact:* Jody F Manning, Assistant Director for Graduate Admission, 315-445-5444, Fax: 315-445-6092, E-mail: manninjf@lemoyne.edu.
Website: http://www.lemoyne.edu/education

Lesley University, Graduate School of Education, Cambridge, MA 02138-2790. Offers arts, community, and education (M Ed); autism studies (Certificate); curriculum and instruction (M Ed, CAGS); early childhood education (M Ed); ecological teaching and learning (MS); educational studies (PhD), including adult learning, educational leadership, individually designed; elementary education (M Ed); emergent technologies for educators (Certificate); ESLArts: language learning through the arts (M Ed); high school education (M Ed); individually designed (M Ed); integrated teaching through the arts (M Ed); literacy for K-8 classroom teachers (M Ed); mathematics education (M Ed); middle school education (M Ed); moderate disabilities (M Ed); online learning (Certificate); reading (CAGS); science in education (M Ed); severe disabilities (M Ed); special needs (CAGS); specialist teacher of reading (M Ed); teacher of visual art (M Ed); technology in education (M Ed, CAGS). *Accreditation:* TEAC. *Program availability:* Part-time, evening/weekend, online learning. *Degree requirements:* For master's, practicum; for doctorate, thesis/dissertation. *Entrance requirements:* For master's, Massachusetts Tests for Educator Licensure (MTEL), transcripts, statement of purpose, recommendations; interview (for special education); for doctorate, GRE General Test, transcripts, statement of purpose, recommendations, interview, master's degree, resume; for other advanced degree, interview, master's degree. Additional exam requirements/recommendations for international students: Required—TOEFL (minimum score 550 paper-based; 80 iBT). Electronic applications accepted. *Faculty research:* Assessment in literacy, mathematics and science; autism spectrum disorders; instructional technology and online learning; multicultural education and English language learners.

Lewis & Clark College, Graduate School of Education and Counseling, Department of Teacher Education, Program in Elementary Education, Portland, OR 97219-7899. Offers MAT. *Accreditation:* NCATE. *Entrance requirements:* For master's, minimum undergraduate GPA of 2.75; history of work, either volunteer or paid, with children in grades K-6. Additional exam requirements/recommendations for international students: Required—TOEFL (minimum score 575 paper-based). Electronic applications accepted. *Faculty research:* Classroom ethnography, assessing student learning, reading, moral development, language arts.

Lewis University, College of Education, Program in Elementary Education, Romeoville, IL 60446. Offers MA. *Program availability:* Part-time. *Students:* 21 full-time (18 women), 14 part-time (10 women); includes 12 minority (3 Black or African American, non-Hispanic/Latino; 2 Asian, non-Hispanic/Latino; 7 Hispanic/Latino). Average age 32. *Degree requirements:* For master's, comprehensive exam, departmental qualifying exam. *Entrance requirements:* For master's, writing exam, Test of Academic Proficiency/Basic Skills Test/ACT/SAT, bachelor's degree, minimum undergraduate GPA of 2.75, two letter of recommendation. Additional exam requirements/recommendations for international students: Required—TOEFL (minimum score 550 paper-based; 80 iBT), IELTS (minimum score 6). *Application deadline:* For fall admission, 5/1 priority date for international students; for spring admission, 11/15 priority date for international students. Applications are processed on a rolling basis. Application fee: $40. Electronic applications accepted. *Financial support:* Federal Work-Study, scholarships/grants, and unspecified assistantships available. Financial award application deadline: 5/1; financial award applicants required to submit FAFSA. *Unit head:* Dr. Ann O'Brien, Program Director. *Application contact:* Kathy Lisak, Graduate Admission Counselor, 815-838-5610, E-mail: grad@lewisu.edu.

Lincoln University, Graduate Studies, Jefferson City, MO 65101. Offers business administration (MBA); counseling (M Ed); environmental science (MS); higher education (MA); history (MA); natural sciences (MS); school teaching middle school with certification (M Ed); school teaching-elementary (M Ed); school teaching-secondary (M Ed); sociology (MA); sociology/criminal justice (MS); sustainable agriculture (MS). *Program availability:* Part-time, evening/weekend, 100% online, blended/hybrid learning. *Students:* 37 full-time (23 women), 52 part-time (25 women); includes 26 minority (24 Black or African American, non-Hispanic/Latino; 1 Asian, non-Hispanic/Latino; 1 Two or more races, non-Hispanic/Latino), 11 international. Average age 34. 67 applicants, 52% accepted, 29 enrolled. In 2018, 48 master's awarded. *Degree requirements:* For master's, comprehensive exam, thesis optional. *Entrance requirements:* For master's, GRE, MAT, or GMAT, minimum GPA of 2.75 overall, 3.0 in courses related to specialization; 3 letters of recommendation; minimum C average in English composition; personal statement of purpose. Additional exam requirements/recommendations for

international students: Required—TOEFL (minimum score 500 paper-based; 61 iBT), IELTS (minimum score 5.5), Michigan English Language Assessment Battery (minimum score 80). *Application deadline:* For fall admission, 7/1 priority date for domestic students, 5/1 priority date for international students; for spring admission, 11/1 priority date for domestic students, 10/1 priority date for international students; for summer admission, 6/1 priority date for domestic students. Applications are processed on a rolling basis. Application fee: $30. Electronic applications accepted. *Expenses: Tuition, area resident:* Full-time $6984; part-time $291 per credit. Tuition, state resident: full-time $6984; part-time $291 per credit. Tuition, nonresident: full-time $12,996; part-time $541.50 per credit. *International tuition:* $12,996 full-time. *Required fees:* $1242.20. *Financial support:* In 2018–19, 9 research assistantships with tuition reimbursements (averaging $4,050 per year) were awarded; fellowships with tuition reimbursements, Federal Work-Study, scholarships/grants, and unspecified assistantships also available. Support available to part-time students. Financial award application deadline: 3/1; financial award applicants required to submit FAFSA. *Unit head:* Dr. Benjamin Arnold, Assistant Vice President of Academic Affairs, 573-681-5247, Fax: 573-681-5106, E-mail: gradschool@lincolnu.edu. *Application contact:* Sarah Robinett, Administrative Assistant, 573-681-5247, Fax: 573-681-5106, E-mail: gradschool@lincolnu.edu. Website: http://www.lincolnu.edu/web/graduate-studies/graduate-studies

Lock Haven University of Pennsylvania, College of Liberal Arts and Education, Lock Haven, PA 17745-2390. Offers alternative education (M Ed); educational leadership (M Ed); teaching and learning (M Ed). *Accreditation:* NCATE. *Program availability:* Part-time, evening/weekend, online learning. *Degree requirements:* For master's, thesis. *Entrance requirements:* For master's, minimum undergraduate GPA of 3.0. Additional exam requirements/recommendations for international students: Required—TOEFL. Electronic applications accepted.

Long Island University–Brentwood Campus, Graduate Programs, Brentwood, NY 11717. Offers childhood education (MS), including grades 1-6; childhood education/literacy B-6 (MS); childhood education/special education (grades 1-6) (MS); clinical mental health counseling (MS, Advanced Certificate); criminal justice (MS); early childhood education (MS); educational leadership (MS Ed); family nurse practitioner (MS, Advanced Certificate); health administration (MPA); library and information science (MS); literacy (B-6) (MS Ed); school counselor (MS, Advanced Certificate); social work (MSW); special education (MS Ed); students with disabilities generalist (grades 7-12) (Advanced Certificate). *Program availability:* Part-time. *Entrance requirements:* For master's and Advanced Certificate, GRE. Additional exam requirements/recommendations for international students: Required—TOEFL or IELTS. Electronic applications accepted.

Long Island University–Hudson, Graduate School, Purchase, NY 10577. Offers autism (Advanced Certificate); bilingual education (Advanced Certificate); childhood education (MS Ed); crisis management (Advanced Certificate); early childhood education (MS Ed); educational leadership (MS Ed); health administration (MPA); literacy (MS Ed); marriage and family therapy (MS); mental health counseling (MS, Advanced Certificate), including credentialed alcoholism and substance abuse counselor (MS); middle childhood and adolescence education (MS Ed); pharmaceutics (MS), including cosmetic science, industrial pharmacy; public administration (MPA); school counseling (MS Ed, Advanced Certificate); school psychology (MS Ed); special education (MS Ed); TESOL (MS Ed); TESOL (all grades) (Advanced Certificate). *Program availability:* Part-time, evening/weekend. *Entrance requirements:* Additional exam requirements/recommendations for international students: Required—TOEFL. Electronic applications accepted. *Expenses:* Contact institution.

Long Island University–Riverhead, Graduate Programs, Riverhead, NY 11901. Offers applied behavior analysis (Advanced Certificate); childhood education (MS), including grades 1-6; cybersecurity policy (Advanced Certificate); homeland security management (MS, Advanced Certificate); literacy education (MS); literacy education B-6 (MS); teaching students with disabilities (MS), including grades 1-6; TESOL (Advanced Certificate). *Accreditation:* TEAC. *Program availability:* Part-time. *Entrance requirements:* Additional exam requirements/recommendations for international students: Required—TOEFL or IELTS. Electronic applications accepted. *Expenses:* Contact institution.

Longwood University, College of Graduate and Professional Studies, College of Education and Human Services, Farmville, VA 23909. Offers education (MS), including algebra and middle school mathematics, counselor education, elementary and middle school mathematics, elementary education, elementary education initial licensure, health and physical education, special education general curriculum, special education initial licensure; reading, literacy and learning (M Ed); school librarianship (M Ed); social work and communication sciences and disorders (MS), including communication sciences and disorders. *Accreditation:* NCATE. *Program availability:* Part-time, evening/weekend. *Degree requirements:* For master's, comprehensive exam (for some programs), thesis optional, professional portfolio, internship, clinical experience, or practicum. *Entrance requirements:* For master's, PRAXIS I (for initial teaching licensure programs); GRE (for some programs), bachelor's degree from regionally-accredited institution, 2 recommendations (3 for some programs), minimum 500-word personal essay, official transcripts, minimum GPA of 2.75, valid teaching license (for some programs). Additional exam requirements/recommendations for international students: Required—TOEFL (minimum score 570 paper-based), IELTS (minimum score 6.5). Electronic applications accepted. *Expenses:* Contact institution.

Louisiana State University and Agricultural & Mechanical College, Graduate School, College of Human Sciences and Education, Department of Educational Theory, Policy and Practice, Baton Rouge, LA 70803. Offers counseling (M Ed, MA, Ed S); educational administration (M Ed, MA, PhD, Ed S); educational technology (MA); elementary education (M Ed, MAT); higher education (PhD); research methodology (PhD); secondary education (M Ed, MAT). *Accreditation:* ACA (one or more programs are accredited); NCATE.

Louisiana Tech University, Graduate School, College of Education, Ruston, LA 71272. Offers counseling and guidance (MA), including clinical mental health counseling, human services, orientation and mobility; counseling psychology (PhD); curriculum and instruction (M Ed); cyber education (Graduate Certificate); dynamics of domestic and family violence (Graduate Certificate); early childhood education - PreK-3 (MAT); educational leadership (M Ed, Ed D); elementary education and special education mild/moderate grades 1-5 (MAT); higher education administration (Graduate Certificate); industrial/organizational psychology (MA, PhD); kinesiology (MS); middle school education (MAT), including mathematics; orientation and mobility (Graduate Certificate); rehabilitation teaching for the blind (Graduate Certificate); secondary education (MAT), including agriculture, biology, business, chemistry, English; special education: visually impaired (MAT); teacher leader education (Graduate Certificate); visual impairments - blind education (Graduate Certificate). *Accreditation:* NCATE. *Program availability:* Part-time. *Degree requirements:* For master's, thesis; for doctorate, thesis/dissertation. *Entrance requirements:* For master's and doctorate, GRE General Test. Additional exam requirements/recommendations for international students: Required—TOEFL (minimum score 550 paper-based; 80 iBT), IELTS (minimum score 6.5). Electronic applications accepted. *Faculty research:* Blindness and the best methods for increasing independence for individuals who are blind or visually impaired; educating and

investigating factors contributing to improvements in human performance across the lifespan and a reduction in injury rates during training.

Loyola Marymount University, School of Education, Program in Elementary Education, Los Angeles, CA 90045. Offers MA. *Unit head:* Dr. Liza Mastrippolito, Assistant Director, Department of Elementary and Secondary Education, 310-568-6697, E-mail: liza.mastrippolito@lmu.edu. *Application contact:* Ammar Dalal, Assistant Vice Provost for Graduate Enrollment, 310-338-2721, Fax: 310-338-6086, E-mail: graduateinfo@lmu.edu. Website: http://soe.lmu.edu/academics/elementaryeducation

Loyola University Chicago, School of Education, Program in Teaching and Learning, Chicago, IL 60660. Offers elementary education (M Ed); English language teaching and learning (M Ed); secondary education (M Ed); special education (M Ed). *Accreditation:* NCATE. *Faculty:* 18 full-time (12 women), 33 part-time/adjunct (29 women). *Students:* 5 full-time (all women), 30 part-time (21 women); includes 11 minority (2 Asian, non-Hispanic/Latino; 9 Hispanic/Latino). Average age 28. 28 applicants, 61% accepted, 12 enrolled. In 2018, 20 master's awarded. *Entrance requirements:* For master's, Illinois Basic Skills Test, 3 letters of recommendation, minimum GPA of 3.0, resume. Additional exam requirements/recommendations for international students: Required—TOEFL (minimum score 550 paper-based; 79 iBT). *Application deadline:* For summer admission, 3/1 priority date for domestic and international students. Application fee: $50. Electronic applications accepted. Application fee is waived when completed online. *Expenses:* Contact institution. *Financial support:* In 2018–19, 12 fellowships with partial tuition reimbursements were awarded; institutionally sponsored loans, scholarships/grants, and unspecified assistantships also available. Support available to part-time students. Financial award application deadline: 2/1; financial award applicants required to submit FAFSA. *Faculty research:* Positive behavior support, school reform, school improvement. *Unit head:* Dr. Hank Bohanon, Program Chair, 312-915-7009, E-mail: hbohano@luc.edu. *Application contact:* Dr. Hank Bohanon, Program Chair, 312-915-7009, E-mail: hbohano@luc.edu.

Loyola University Maryland, Graduate Programs, School of Education, Master of Arts in Teaching Program, Baltimore, MD 21210-2699. Offers elementary education (MAT); secondary education (MAT). *Program availability:* Part-time. *Entrance requirements:* For master's, essay, 2 letters of recommendation, resume, transcript. Additional exam requirements/recommendations for international students: Required—TOEFL (minimum score 550 paper-based), IELTS (minimum score 7). Electronic applications accepted. *Expenses:* Contact institution.

Loyola University Maryland, Graduate Programs, School of Education, Program in Montessori Education, Baltimore, MD 21210-2699. Offers elementary education (M Ed); Montessori education (CAS). *Accreditation:* NCATE. *Degree requirements:* For master's, thesis. *Entrance requirements:* For master's, essay, transcripts. Additional exam requirements/recommendations for international students: Required—TOEFL (minimum score 550 paper-based), IELTS (minimum score 7). *Expenses:* Contact institution.

Manhattan College, Graduate Programs, School of Education and Health, Program in Special Education, Riverdale, NY 10471. Offers adolescence education students with disabilities generalist extension in English or math or social studies - grades 7-12 (MS Ed); bilingual education (Advanced Certificate); dual childhood/students with disabilities - grades 1-6 (MS Ed); students with disabilities - grades 1-6 (MS Ed). *Program availability:* Part-time, evening/weekend. *Degree requirements:* For master's, thesis, internship (if not certified). *Entrance requirements:* For master's, GRE, minimum GPA of 3.0. Additional exam requirements/recommendations for international students: Required—TOEFL (minimum score 550 paper-based; 80 iBT), IELTS (minimum score 6). Electronic applications accepted. Application fee is waived when completed online. *Expenses:* Contact institution.

Manhattanville College, School of Education, Jump Start Program, Purchase, NY 10577-2132. Offers childhood education and special education (grades 1-6) (MPS); early childhood education (birth-grade 2) (MAT); education (Advanced Certificate); English and special education (grades 5-12) (MPS); mathematics and special education (grades 5-12) (MPS); science and special education (grades 5-12) (MPS); social studies and special education (grades 5-12) (MPS); Spanish (grades 7-12) (MAT); tesol - teaching English as a second language (all grades) (MPS). *Program availability:* Part-time, evening/weekend. *Faculty:* 11 full-time (7 women), 78 part-time/adjunct (50 women). *Students:* 3 full-time (2 women), 16 part-time (11 women); includes 5 minority (1 Black or African American, non-Hispanic/Latino; 3 Hispanic/Latino; 1 Native Hawaiian or other Pacific Islander, non-Hispanic/Latino). Average age 31. 48 applicants, 54% accepted, 22 enrolled. In 2018, 23 master's, 1 other advanced degree awarded. *Degree requirements:* For master's, comprehensive exam (for some programs), thesis (for some programs), student teaching, research seminars, portfolios, internships, writing assessment; for Advanced Certificate, comprehensive exam (for some programs). *Entrance requirements:* For master's, for programs leading to certification, candidates must submit scores from GRE or MAT(miller analogies test), minimum undergraduate GPA of 3.0, all transcripts from all colleges and universities attended, 2 letters of recommendation, interview, essay (2-3 page personal statement that describes reasons for choosing education as profession and personal philosophy of education), proof of immunization (for those born after 1957). Additional exam requirements/recommendations for international students: Required—TOEFL (minimum score 600 paper-based; 110 iBT); Recommended—IELTS (minimum score 8). *Application deadline:* Applications are processed on a rolling basis. Application fee: $75. Electronic applications accepted. *Expenses:* 935 per credit. *Financial support:* Teaching assistantships, career-related internships or fieldwork, Federal Work-Study, institutionally sponsored loans, scholarships/grants, and unspecified assistantships available. Financial award application deadline: 3/15; financial award applicants required to submit FAFSA. *Faculty research:* Early childhood and technology, professional development schools and community schools, students with emotional difficulties, literacy and adolescents, mindfulness, changing suburbs institute, and community schools, studying the effects of the environment on special populations, the most difficult cases, students who are presented with multiple challenges: learning, behavioral and ACE experiences who see criminal behavior as a way to cope; working on giving them the tools they need to succeed. *Unit head:* Dr. Shelley Wepner, Dean, 914-323-3153, E-mail: Shelly.Wepner@mville.edu. *Application contact:* Alissa Wilson, Director, SOE Graduate Enrollment Management, 914-323-3150, Fax: 914-694-1732, E-mail: edschool@mville.edu.
Website: http://www.mville.edu/programs/jump-start

Manhattanville College, School of Education, Program in Childhood Education, Purchase, NY 10577-2132. Offers childhood education (grades 1-6) (MAT); childhood education (grades 1-6) and special education: childhood (grades 1-6) (MPS); early childhood (birth-grade 2) & childhood ed (grades 1-6) (MAT); special ed early childhood and childhood (birth-grade 6) (MPS); special education childhood (grades 1-6) (MPS); special education: childhood (grades 1-6) (Certificate); special education: early childhood (birth-grade 2) and childhood (grades 1-6) (Certificate). *Program availability:* Part-time, evening/weekend. *Faculty:* 5 full-time (4 women), 3 part-time/adjunct (all women). *Students:* 4 full-time (3 women), 27 part-time (25 women); includes 6 minority (1 Black or African American, non-Hispanic/Latino; 1 Asian, non-Hispanic/Latino; 4

Hispanic/Latino). Average age 25. 18 applicants, 56% accepted, 8 enrolled. In 2018, 15 master's awarded. *Degree requirements:* For master's, comprehensive exam (for some programs), thesis (for some programs), student teaching, research seminars, portfolios, internships, writing assessment; for Certificate, comprehensive exam (for some programs). *Entrance requirements:* For master's, for programs leading to certification, candidates must submit scores from GRE or MAT(Miller Analogies Test), minimum undergraduate GPA of 3.0, all transcripts from all colleges and universities attended, 2 letters of recommendation, interview, essay (2-3 page personal statement that describes reasons for choosing education as profession and personal philosophy of education), proof of immunization (for those born after 1957). Additional exam requirements/recommendations for international students: Required—TOEFL (minimum score 600 paper-based; 110 iBT); Recommended—IELTS (minimum score 8). *Application deadline:* Applications are processed on a rolling basis. Application fee: $75. Electronic applications accepted. *Expenses:* 935 per credit. *Financial support:* Teaching assistantships, career-related internships or fieldwork, Federal Work-Study, institutionally sponsored loans, scholarships/grants, and unspecified assistantships available. Financial award application deadline: 3/15; financial award applicants required to submit FAFSA. *Faculty research:* Early childhood and technology, professional development schools and community schools. *Unit head:* Dr. Shelley Wepner, Dean, 914-323-3153, Fax: 914-323-5493, E-mail: Shelley.Wepner@mville.edu. *Application contact:* Alissa Wilson, Director, SOE Graduate Enrollment Management, 914-323-3150, Fax: 914-694-1732, E-mail: edschool@mville.edu.
Website: http://www.mville.edu/programs/childhood-education

Manhattanville College, School of Education, Program in Literacy Education, Purchase, NY 10577-2132. Offers literacy (birth-grade 6) and special education childhood (grades 1-6) (MPS); literacy 5-12; special education generalist 7-12; special ed specialist 7-12 (MPS); literacy specialist (birth-grade 6) (MPS); literacy specialist (grades 5-12) (MPS); science of reading: multisensory instruction – the rose institute for learning and literacy (Advanced Certificate). *Program availability:* Part-time, evening/weekend. *Faculty:* 3 full-time (all women), 15 part-time/adjunct (14 women). *Students:* 2 full-time (both women), 8 part-time (all women). Average age 26. 6 applicants, 50% accepted, 1 enrolled. In 2018, 8 master's, 11 Advanced Certificates awarded. *Degree requirements:* For master's, comprehensive exam (for some programs), thesis (for some programs), student teaching, research seminars, portfolios, internships, writing assessment; for Advanced Certificate, comprehensive exam (for some programs). *Entrance requirements:* For master's, for programs leading to certification, candidates must submit scores from GRE or MAT(Miller Analogies Test), minimum undergraduate GPA of 3.0, all transcripts from all colleges and universities attended, 2 letters of recommendation, interview, essay (2-3 page personal statement that describes reasons for choosing education as profession and personal philosophy of education), proof of immunization (for those born after 1957). Additional exam requirements/recommendations for international students: Required—TOEFL (minimum score 600 paper-based; 110 iBT); Recommended—IELTS (minimum score 8). *Application deadline:* Applications are processed on a rolling basis. Application fee: $75. Electronic applications accepted. *Expenses:* 935 per credit. *Financial support:* Teaching assistantships, career-related internships or fieldwork, Federal Work-Study, institutionally sponsored loans, scholarships/grants, and unspecified assistantships available. Financial award application deadline: 3/15; financial award applicants required to submit FAFSA. *Faculty research:* Power of story for literacy development, English learners. *Total annual research expenditures:* $800. *Unit head:* Dr. Shelley Wepner, Dean, 914-323-3153, Fax: 914-323-5493, E-mail: Shelley.Wepner@mville.edu. *Application contact:* Alissa Wilson, Director, SOE Graduate Enrollment Management, 914-323-3150, Fax: 914-694-1732, E-mail: edschool@mville.edu.
Website: http://www.mville.edu/programs/literacy-education

Manhattanville College, School of Education, Program in Special Education, Purchase, NY 10577-2132. Offers childhood education (grades 1-6) and special education: childhood (grades 1-6) (MPS); early childhood (birth-grade 2) and special education: early childhood (birth-grade 2) (MPS); English (5-9 and 7-12); special ed generalist (7-12); se English (7-12) (MPS); literacy (birth-grade 6) and special education childhood (grades 1-6) (MPS); literacy 5-12; special education generalist 7-12; special ed specialist 7-12 (MPS); math (5-9 and 7-12); special ed generalist (7-12); se math (7-12) (MPS); science: biology or chemistry (5-9 and 7-12); special ed generalist (7-12); se science (7-12) (MPS); social studies (5-9 and 7-12); special ed generalist (7-12); se soc.st. (7-12) (MPS); special ed early childhood and childhood (birth-grade 6) (MPS); special education childhood (grades 1-6) (MPS); special education: childhood (grades 1-6) (Certificate); special education: early childhood (birth-grade 2) (MPS, Certificate); special education: early childhood (birth-grade 2) and childhood (grades 1-6) (Certificate); special education: grades 7-12 generalist (MPS, Certificate). *Program availability:* Part-time, evening/weekend. *Faculty:* 5 full-time (3 women), 35 part-time/adjunct (23 women). *Students:* 45 full-time (36 women), 179 part-time (152 women); includes 31 minority (6 Black or African American, non-Hispanic/Latino; 4 Asian, non-Hispanic/Latino; 19 Hispanic/Latino; 2 Native Hawaiian or other Pacific Islander, non-Hispanic/Latino), 1 international. Average age 28. 76 applicants, 68% accepted, 40 enrolled. In 2018, 99 master's, 2 Certificates awarded. *Degree requirements:* For master's, comprehensive exam (for some programs), thesis (for some programs), student teaching, research seminars, portfolios, internships, writing assessment; for Certificate, comprehensive exam (for some programs). *Entrance requirements:* For master's, for programs leading to certification, candidates must submit scores from GRE or MAT(Miller Analogies Test), minimum undergraduate GPA of 3.0, all transcripts from all colleges and universities attended, 2 letters of recommendation, interview, essay (2-3 page personal statement that describes reasons for choosing education as profession and personal philosophy of education), proof of immunization (for those born after 1957). Additional exam requirements/recommendations for international students: Required—TOEFL (minimum score 600 paper-based; 110 iBT); Recommended—IELTS (minimum score 8). *Application deadline:* Applications are processed on a rolling basis. Application fee: $75. Electronic applications accepted. *Expenses:* 935 per credit. *Financial support:* Teaching assistantships, career-related internships or fieldwork, Federal Work-Study, institutionally sponsored loans, scholarships/grants, and unspecified assistantships available. Financial award application deadline: 3/15; financial award applicants required to submit FAFSA. *Faculty research:* Students with emotional difficulties, literacy and adolescents, mindfulness, studying the effects of the environment on special populations, the most difficult cases, students who are presented with multiple challenges: learning, behavioral and ACE experiences who see criminal behavior as a way to cope; working on giving them the tools they need to succeed emotionally and cognitively despite the odds stacked against them. *Unit head:* Dr. Shelley Wepner, Dean, 914-323-3153, Fax: 914-323-5493, E-mail: Shelley.Wepner@mville.edu. *Application contact:* Alissa Wilson, Director, SOE Graduate Enrollment Management, 914-323-3150, Fax: 914-694-1732, E-mail: edschool@mville.edu.
Website: http://www.mville.edu/programs/special-education

Mansfield University of Pennsylvania, Graduate Studies, Department of Education and Special Education, Mansfield, PA 16933. Offers elementary education (M Ed); secondary education (MS); special education (M Ed). *Accreditation:* NCATE (one or more programs are accredited). *Program availability:* Part-time, evening/weekend, online learning. *Degree requirements:* For master's, comprehensive exam, thesis optional. *Entrance requirements:* For master's, minimum GPA of 3.0. Additional exam requirements/recommendations for international students: Required—TOEFL (minimum score 550 paper-based). Electronic applications accepted.

Marquette University, Graduate School, College of Education, Department of Educational Policy and Leadership, Milwaukee, WI 53201-1881. Offers college student personnel administration (M Ed); curriculum and instruction (MA); education (MA); educational administration (M Ed); educational policy and foundations (MA); elementary education (Certificate); literacy (MA); principal (Certificate); reading specialist (Certificate); reading teacher (Certificate); secondary education (Certificate); superintendent (Certificate). *Program availability:* Part-time, evening/weekend. Terminal master's awarded for partial completion of doctoral program. *Degree requirements:* For master's, comprehensive exam, thesis (for some programs); for doctorate, thesis/dissertation, qualifying exam. *Entrance requirements:* For master's, GRE General Test or MAT, official transcripts from all current and previous colleges/universities except Marquette, three letters of recommendation, statement of purpose; for doctorate, GRE General Test, MAT, sample of written work, official transcripts from all current and previous colleges/universities except Marquette, three letters of recommendation, statement of purpose, resume/curriculum vitae; for Certificate, GRE General Test or MAT, master's degree. Additional exam requirements/recommendations for international students: Required—TOEFL (minimum score 530 paper-based). *Expenses:* Contact institution. *Faculty research:* Leadership; social justice in education; development of lifelong learners; race, class, and schooling in historical perspective; urban teacher education.

Mars Hill University, Adult and Graduate Studies, Mars Hill, NC 28754. Offers elementary education (K-6) (M Ed). *Degree requirements:* For master's, project.

Mary Baldwin University, Graduate Studies, Programs in Education, Staunton, VA 24401-3610. Offers applied behavior analysis (MS); autism spectrum disorders (M Ed); elementary education (M Ed, MAT); English as a second language (M Ed); environment-based learning (M Ed); gifted education (M Ed); higher education (MS); leadership (M Ed); middle grades education (MAT); reading education (M Ed); special education (M Ed). *Accreditation:* TEAC.

Marygrove College, Graduate Studies, Detroit, MI 48221-2599. Offers autism spectrum disorders (M Ed, Certificate); curriculum instruction and assessment (MAT); educational leadership (MA); educational technology (M Ed); effective teaching in the 21st century-classroom focus (MAT); effective teaching in the 21st century-technology focus (MAT); human resource management (MA, Certificate); mathematics 6-8 (MAT); mathematics K-5 (MAT); reading and literacy K-6 (MAT); reading specialist (M Ed); school administrator (Certificate); social justice (MA); special education (MAT); special education - learning disabilities (M Ed); teaching - pre-elementary education (M Ed); teaching - pre-secondary education (M Ed). *Program availability:* Part-time, evening/weekend, 100% online, blended/hybrid learning. *Entrance requirements:* For master's, all official bachelor's transcripts. Additional exam requirements/recommendations for international students: Required—TOEFL (minimum score 550 paper-based; 80 iBT). Electronic applications accepted.

Marymount University, School of Sciences, Mathematics, and Education, Program in Education, Arlington, VA 22207-4299. Offers curriculum and instruction (M Ed); elementary education (M Ed); professional studies (M Ed); secondary education (M Ed); special education: general curriculum (M Ed). *Accreditation:* NCATE. *Program availability:* Part-time, evening/weekend. *Faculty:* 7 full-time (all women), 8 part-time/adjunct (6 women). *Students:* 42 full-time (29 women), 103 part-time (80 women); includes 31 minority (8 Black or African American, non-Hispanic/Latino; 11 Asian, non-Hispanic/Latino; 10 Hispanic/Latino; 1 Native Hawaiian or other Pacific Islander, non-Hispanic/Latino; 1 Two or more races, non-Hispanic/Latino), 12 international. Average age 36. 44 applicants, 100% accepted, 30 enrolled. In 2018, 61 master's awarded. *Degree requirements:* For master's, thesis or alternative, capstone/internship. *Entrance requirements:* For master's, PRAXIS MATH or SAT/ACT, and Virginia Communication and Literacy Assessment (VCLA), 2 letters of recommendation, resume, interview, minimum undergraduate GPA of 2.75 or 3.25 in the last 60 hours. Additional exam requirements/recommendations for international students: Required—TOEFL (minimum score 600 paper-based; 96 iBT), IELTS (minimum score 6.5), PTE (minimum score 58). *Application deadline:* For fall admission, 7/16 priority date for domestic and international students; for spring admission, 11/16 priority date for domestic and international students. Applications are processed on a rolling basis. Application fee: $40. Electronic applications accepted. *Expenses:* $770 per credit. *Financial support:* In 2018–19, 3 students received support. Research assistantships, teaching assistantships, career-related internships or fieldwork, scholarships/grants, and unspecified assistantships available. Support available to part-time students. Financial award application deadline: 3/1; financial award applicants required to submit FAFSA. *Unit head:* Dr. Lisa Turissini, Chair, Education, 703-526-1668, E-mail: lisa.turissini@marymount.edu. *Application contact:* Rebecca Esposito, Senior Associate Director, Graduate Admissions, 703-284-5901, Fax: 703-527-3815, E-mail: grad.admissions@marymount.edu.
Website: https://www.marymount.edu/Academics/School-of-Sciences-Mathematics-and-Education/Graduate-Programs/Education-(M-Ed-)

Maryville University of Saint Louis, School of Education, St. Louis, MO 63141-7299. Offers early childhood education (MA Ed); educational leadership (Ed D); educational leadership w/principal certification (MA Ed); elementary education (MA Ed); gifted (MA Ed); higher education leadership (Ed D); middle grades education (MA Ed); reading/literacy specialist (MA Ed); teacher as leader (Ed D). *Accreditation:* NCATE. *Program availability:* Part-time, 100% online, blended/hybrid learning. *Faculty:* 16 full-time (8 women), 18 part-time/adjunct (11 women). *Students:* 12 full-time (all women), 311 part-time (234 women); includes 99 minority (84 Black or African American, non-Hispanic/Latino; 2 Asian, non-Hispanic/Latino; 9 Hispanic/Latino; 4 Two or more races, non-Hispanic/Latino), 2 international. Average age 38. In 2018, 25 master's, 100 doctorates awarded. *Degree requirements:* For master's, thesis, project. *Entrance requirements:* For master's, minimum cumulative GPA of 3.0, 3 professional recommendations, essays, interview with program faculty; for doctorate, minimum GPA of 3.0, 3 professional recommendations, essay, interview, on-site writing sample. Additional exam requirements/recommendations for international students: Required—TOEFL (minimum score 550 paper-based; 79 iBT). *Application deadline:* Applications are processed on a rolling basis. Electronic applications accepted. *Expenses:* $449 per credit hour for master's programs; $897 per credit hour for doctoral programs. *Financial support:* Career-related internships or fieldwork, Federal Work-Study, tuition waivers (partial), and professional educator discounts available. Financial award application deadline: 4/1; financial award applicants required to submit FAFSA. *Faculty research:* Collaboration with public schools, pre-service program development, mathematics, diversity, literacy. *Unit head:* Dr. Maschael Schappe, Dean, 314-529-9670, Fax: 314-529-9921, E-mail: mschappe@maryville.edu. *Application contact:* Stacey Ruffin, Director of Clinical Experiences & Partnerships, 314-529-9542, Fax: 314-529-9921, E-mail: sruffin@maryville.edu.
Website: http://www.maryville.edu/ed/graduate-programs/

Marywood University, Academic Affairs, Reap College of Education and Human Development, Department of Education, Program in PK-4 Education, Scranton, PA 18509-1598. Offers MAT. *Accreditation:* NCATE. *Program availability:* Part-time. Electronic applications accepted.

McDaniel College, Graduate and Professional Studies, Program in Elementary and Secondary Education, Westminster, MD 21157-4390. Offers elementary education (MS); elementary STEM instructional leader (Postbaccalaureate Certificate); equity and excellence in education (Postbaccalaureate Certificate); learning technology specialist (Postbaccalaureate Certificate); secondary education (MS). *Accreditation:* NCATE. *Program availability:* Part-time, evening/weekend. *Degree requirements:* For master's, comprehensive exam (for some programs), thesis optional. *Entrance requirements:* For master's, PRAXIS, 2 references. Additional exam requirements/recommendations for international students: Required—TOEFL (minimum score 79 iBT), IELTS (minimum score 6). Electronic applications accepted.

McNeese State University, Doré School of Graduate Studies, Burton College of Education, Department of Education Professions, Program in Curriculum and Instruction, Lake Charles, LA 70609. Offers academically gifted education (M Ed); elementary education (M Ed); reading (M Ed); secondary education (M Ed); special education (M Ed). *Program availability:* Evening/weekend. *Entrance requirements:* For master's, GRE, teaching certificate.

McNeese State University, Doré School of Graduate Studies, Burton College of Education, Department of Education Professions, Program in Elementary Education, Lake Charles, LA 70609. Offers MAT. *Program availability:* Evening/weekend. *Degree requirements:* For master's, comprehensive exam, field experiences. *Entrance requirements:* For master's, GRE General Test, PRAXIS I and II, autobiography, two letters of recommendation.

McNeese State University, Doré School of Graduate Studies, Burton College of Education, Department of Education Professions, Program in Elementary Education Grades 1-5, Lake Charles, LA 70609. Offers Postbaccalaureate Certificate. *Entrance requirements:* For degree, PRAXIS, 2 letters of recommendation, autobiography.

Medaille College, Program in Education, Buffalo, NY 14214-2695. Offers adolescent education (MS Ed); curriculum and instruction (MS Ed); education preparation (MS Ed); literacy (MS Ed); special education (MS). *Accreditation:* TEAC. *Program availability:* Part-time, evening/weekend. *Degree requirements:* For master's, comprehensive exam (for some programs), thesis or alternative. *Entrance requirements:* For master's, minimum undergraduate GPA of 2.7. Additional exam requirements/recommendations for international students: Required—TOEFL (minimum score 550 paper-based). Electronic applications accepted. *Faculty research:* Curriculum planning, truancy, tracking minority students, curriculum design, mentoring students.

Mercy College, School of Education, Program in Childhood Education, Dobbs Ferry, NY 10522-1189. Offers MS. *Program availability:* Part-time, evening/weekend, blended/hybrid learning. *Students:* 22 full-time (20 women), 35 part-time (30 women); includes 27 minority (9 Black or African American, non-Hispanic/Latino; 2 Asian, non-Hispanic/Latino; 16 Hispanic/Latino). Average age 32. 82 applicants, 41% accepted, 19 enrolled. In 2018, 19 master's awarded. *Degree requirements:* For master's, Capstone project; clinical practice; for initial New York State certification, passing scores in the following are required: Educating All Students, Content Specialty Test, edTPA. *Entrance requirements:* For master's, GRE or PRAXIS, transcript(s); resume. Additional exam requirements/recommendations for international students: Required—TOEFL (minimum score 600 paper-based; 71 iBT), IELTS (minimum score 8). *Application deadline:* Applications are processed on a rolling basis. Application fee: $40. Electronic applications accepted. *Expenses:* Tuition: Full-time $15,696; part-time $872 per credit. *Required fees:* $642; $161 per term. Tuition and fees vary according to course load, degree level and program. *Financial support:* Career-related internships or fieldwork, Federal Work-Study, scholarships/grants, and unspecified assistantships available. Financial award applicants required to submit FAFSA. *Unit head:* Dr. Eric Martone, Interim Dean, School of Education, 914-674-7618, Fax: 914-674-7352, E-mail: emartone@mercy.edu. *Application contact:* Allison Gurdineer, Executive Director of Admissions, 877-637-2946, Fax: 914-674-7382, E-mail: admissions@mercy.edu. Website: https://www.mercy.edu/degrees-programs/ms-childhood-education-grade-1-6

Meredith College, School of Education, Health and Human Sciences, Raleigh, NC 27607-5298. Offers academically and intellectually gifted (M Ed); elementary education (M Ed, MAT); English as a second language (M Ed, MAT); health and physical education (MAT); nutrition, health and human performance (MS, Postbaccalaureate Certificate), including dietetic internship (Postbaccalaureate Certificate), nutrition (MS); psychology (MA), including industrial/organizational psychology; reading (M Ed); special education (MAT); special education (general curriculum) (M Ed). *Accreditation:* NCATE. *Program availability:* Part-time, evening/weekend. *Students:* 97 full-time (89 women), 76 part-time (73 women); includes 39 minority (17 Black or African American, non-Hispanic/Latino; 1 American Indian or Alaska Native, non-Hispanic/Latino; 9 Asian, non-Hispanic/Latino; 10 Hispanic/Latino; 2 Two or more races, non-Hispanic/Latino). Average age 28. In 2018, 56 master's, 36 other advanced degrees awarded. *Degree requirements:* For master's, thesis optional. *Entrance requirements:* For master's, GRE General Test or MAT, minimum GPA of 2.5, teaching license, recommendations. Additional exam requirements/recommendations for international students: Required—TOEFL. *Application deadline:* For fall admission, 7/1 priority date for domestic students; for spring admission, 11/1 priority date for domestic students. Applications are processed on a rolling basis. Application fee: $50. Electronic applications accepted. *Expenses:* $575 per credit hour for masters degree in education, $725 (for MS. PSY.IO degree), $20,295 (for pre-health post-baccalaureate certificate), $13,600 (for dietetic internship). *Financial support:* Career-related internships or fieldwork, institutionally sponsored loans, and tuition waivers (partial) available. Support available to part-time students. Financial award application deadline: 2/15; financial award applicants required to submit FAFSA. *Unit head:* Dr. Monica McKinney, Graduate Program Manager, 919-760-8056, Fax: 919-760-2303, E-mail: mckinneym@meredith.edu. *Application contact:* Dr. Monica McKinney, Graduate Program Manager, 919-760-8056, Fax: 919-760-2303, E-mail: mckinneym@meredith.edu. Website: https://www.meredith.edu/school-of-education-health-and-human-sciences

Metropolitan College of New York, Program in Childhood/Special Education, New York, NY 10006. Offers dual childhood 1-6 special education (MS). *Accreditation:* NCATE. *Entrance requirements:* For master's, GRE or MAT, minimum GPA of 3.0, 2 letters of reference, interview, resume. Additional exam requirements/recommendations for international students: Required—TOEFL (minimum score 550 paper-based; 80 iBT), IELTS (minimum score 6.5). Electronic applications accepted. *Expenses:* Contact institution. *Faculty research:* Classroom management, learner autonomy, teacher research, math and gender, intelligence.

Metropolitan State University of Denver, School of Education, Denver, CO 80204. Offers elementary education (MAT); special education (MAT). *Expenses:* Contact institution.

Middle Tennessee State University, College of Graduate Studies, College of Education, Department of Elementary and Special Education, Major in Curriculum and Instruction, Murfreesboro, TN 37132. Offers early childhood education (M Ed); elementary education (M Ed, Ed S); middle school education (M Ed). *Accreditation:* NCATE. *Program availability:* Part-time, evening/weekend, online learning. *Degree requirements:* For master's, comprehensive exam; for Ed S, comprehensive exam, thesis or alternative. *Entrance requirements:* For master's and Ed S, GRE, MAT or

PRAXIS. Additional exam requirements/recommendations for international students: Required—TOEFL (minimum score 525 paper-based; 71 iBT) or IELTS (minimum score 6). Electronic applications accepted.

Milligan College, Area of Education, Milligan College, TN 37682. Offers combined preK-3/K-5 education (M Ed); educational leadership (Ed D); educational specialist (Ed S); K-5 education (M Ed); middle grades education (M Ed); preK-3 education (M Ed); preK-3 special education (M Ed); secondary education (M Ed). *Accreditation:* NCATE. *Program availability:* Part-time, 100% online, blended/hybrid learning. *Faculty:* 5 full-time (3 women), 6 part-time/adjunct (3 women). *Students:* 38 full-time (31 women), 8 part-time (4 women); includes 2 minority (1 Hispanic/Latino; 1 Two or more races, non-Hispanic/Latino), 1 international. Average age 35. 36 applicants, 97% accepted, 32 enrolled. In 2018, 18 master's awarded. *Degree requirements:* For master's, thesis, portfolio, research project; for doctorate, thesis/dissertation, portfolio, research project. *Entrance requirements:* For master's, MAT, GRE General Test, ACT, SAT, or PRAXIS, undergraduate degree and supporting transcripts, professional recommendations, interview; for doctorate, MAT or GRE, master's degree and supporting transcripts, demonstrated scholastic ability, recognized leadership role within education, professional recommendations, essay/personal statement, portfolio (professional development plan, evidence of ability, knowledge and qualities), interview. Additional exam requirements/recommendations for international students: Required—TOEFL (minimum score 550 paper-based, 79 iBT) or IELTS (6.5). *Application deadline:* For fall admission, 8/1 priority date for domestic students, 6/1 for international students; for spring admission, 11/15 priority date for domestic students, 12/1 for international students; for summer admission, 4/1 for domestic students. Applications are processed on a rolling basis. Application fee: $30. Electronic applications accepted. *Expenses:* $365 per hour (for masters); $485 per hour (for doctoral); $375 fees per semester; $75 one-time records fee. *Financial support:* Scholarships/grants available. Financial award application deadline: 12/1; financial award applicants required to submit FAFSA. *Faculty research:* Assessment; school mental health; literacy; technology; educator preparation. *Unit head:* Dr. Angela Hilton-Prillhart, Area Chair of Education, 423-461-8769, Fax: 423-461-3103, E-mail: anhilton-prillhart@milligan.edu. *Application contact:* Melissa Dillow, Graduate Admissions Recruiter, Education, 423-461-8306, Fax: 423-461-8982, E-mail: msdillow@milligan.edu.
Website: http://www.Milligan.edu/GPS

Minot State University, Graduate School, Teacher Education and Human Performance Department, Minot, ND 58707-0002. Offers elementary education (M Ed). *Accreditation:* NCATE. *Degree requirements:* For master's, thesis. *Entrance requirements:* For master's, 2 years of teaching experience, bachelor's degree in education, minimum GPA of 2.75. Additional exam requirements/recommendations for international students: Required—TOEFL (minimum score 79 iBT), IELTS (minimum score 6).

Mississippi College, Graduate School, School of Education, Department of Teacher Education and Leadership, Clinton, MS 39058. Offers art (M Ed); biological science (M Ed); business education (M Ed); computer science (M Ed); dyslexia therapy (M Ed); educational leadership (M Ed, Ed D, Ed S); elementary education (M Ed, Ed S); English (M Ed); higher education administration (MS); mathematics (M Ed); secondary education (M Ed); social studies (history) (M Ed); teaching arts (M Ed). *Program availability:* Part-time, online learning. *Degree requirements:* For master's, comprehensive exam, thesis optional. *Entrance requirements:* For master's, NTE. Additional exam requirements/recommendations for international students: Recommended—TOEFL, IELTS. Electronic applications accepted.

Mississippi State University, College of Education, Department of Curriculum, Instruction and Special Education, Mississippi State, MS 39762. Offers early childhood education (PhD); elementary education (MS, PhD, Ed S), including early childhood education (MS), general elementary education (MS), middle level education (MS); general curriculum and instruction (PhD); reading education (PhD); secondary education (MAT, MS, PhD, Ed S); special education (MAT, MS, PhD, Ed S). *Accreditation:* NCATE. *Program availability:* Part-time, evening/weekend. *Faculty:* 20 full-time (14 women), 1 (woman) part-time/adjunct. *Students:* 24 full-time (16 women), 151 part-time (109 women); includes 44 minority (38 Black or African American, non-Hispanic/Latino; 3 American Indian or Alaska Native, non-Hispanic/Latino; 1 Hispanic/Latino; 2 Two or more races, non-Hispanic/Latino), 3 international. Average age 32. 65 applicants, 65% accepted, 38 enrolled. In 2018, 57 master's, 3 doctorates, 1 other advanced degree awarded. *Degree requirements:* For master's, comprehensive exam; for doctorate, thesis/dissertation; for Ed S, comprehensive exam, thesis or alternative. *Entrance requirements:* For master's, GRE, minimum GPA of 2.75 in junior and senior year, eligibility for initial teacher certification; for doctorate, GRE, minimum GPA of 3.4 on previous graduate work; for Ed S, GRE, minimum GPA of 3.2 on master's degree. Additional exam requirements/recommendations for international students: Required—TOEFL (minimum score 550 paper-based; 79 iBT); Recommended—IELTS (minimum score 6.5). *Application deadline:* For fall admission, 3/1 priority date for domestic students, 5/1 for international students; for spring admission, 9/1 priority date for domestic students, 9/1 for international students. Applications are processed on a rolling basis. Application fee: $60 ($80 for international students). Electronic applications accepted. *Expenses:* Tuition, state resident: full-time $8450; part-time $360.59 per credit hour. Tuition, nonresident: full-time $23,140; part-time $969.09 per credit hour. *Required fees:* $110. One-time fee: $55 full-time. Part-time tuition and fees vary according to course load, degree level, campus/location and reciprocity agreements. *Financial support:* In 2018–19, 5 research assistantships with partial tuition reimbursements (averaging $11,453 per year), 1 teaching assistantship (averaging $11,700 per year) were awarded; Federal Work-Study, institutionally sponsored loans, scholarships/grants, and unspecified assistantships also available. Financial award application deadline: 4/1; financial award applicants required to submit FAFSA. *Faculty research:* Early childhood education, reading, rural schools, multicultural education, use of technology in instruction. *Unit head:* Dr. Linda Cornelious, Professor and Head, 662-325-3747, Fax: 662-325-7857, E-mail: lcornelious@colled.msstate.edu. *Application contact:* Robbie Salters, Admissions and Enrollment Assistant, 662-325-7400, E-mail: rsalters@grad.msstate.edu.
Website: http://www.cise.msstate.edu/

Missouri State University, Graduate College, College of Education, Department of Childhood Education and Family Studies, Program in Elementary Education, Springfield, MO 65897. Offers MS Ed. *Program availability:* Part-time, evening/weekend, 100% online, blended/hybrid learning. *Faculty:* 22 full-time (1 woman), 11 part-time/adjunct (6 women). *Students:* 6 full-time (all women), 43 part-time (36 women); includes 3 minority (2 Black or African American, non-Hispanic/Latino; 1 Asian, non-Hispanic/Latino), 1 international. Average age 24. 17 applicants, 65% accepted. In 2018, 18 master's awarded. *Degree requirements:* For master's, comprehensive exam, thesis or alternative. *Entrance requirements:* For master's, GRE (if GPA less than 3.0), minimum GPA of 2.75, teaching certificate. Additional exam requirements/recommendations for international students: Required—TOEFL (minimum score 550 paper-based; 79 iBT), IELTS (minimum score 6). *Application deadline:* For fall admission, 7/20 priority date for domestic students, 5/1 for international students; for spring admission, 12/20 priority date for domestic students, 9/1 for international students; for summer admission, 5/20 priority date for domestic students. Applications are processed on a rolling basis.

Elementary Education

Application fee: $55 ($60 for international students). Electronic applications accepted. Tuition and fees vary according to class time, course level, course load, degree level, campus/location, program and student level. *Financial support:* Federal Work-Study, institutionally sponsored loans, and scholarships/grants available. Financial award application deadline: 1/31; financial award applicants required to submit FAFSA. *Unit head:* Dr. Denise Cunningham, Department Head, 417-836-8915, E-mail: cefs@missouristate.edu. *Application contact:* Lakan Drinker, Director, Graduate Enrollment Management, 417-836-5300, Fax: 417-836-6200, E-mail: lakandrinker@missouristate.edu.
Website: http://education.missouristate.edu/ele/

Missouri State University, Graduate College, College of Education, Department of Counseling, Leadership, and Special Education, Program in Educational Administration, Springfield, MO 65897. Offers elementary principal (MS Ed, Ed S); secondary principal (MS Ed, Ed S); superintendent (Ed S). *Program availability:* Part-time, evening/weekend. *Faculty:* 5 full-time (2 women), 1 part-time/adjunct (0 women). *Students:* 6 full-time (all women), 84 part-time (56 women); includes 9 minority (1 Black or African American, non-Hispanic/Latino; 1 American Indian or Alaska Native, non-Hispanic/Latino; 4 Hispanic/Latino; 3 Two or more races, non-Hispanic/Latino). Average age 26. 46 applicants, 98% accepted. In 2018, 10 master's, 3 Ed Ss awarded. *Degree requirements:* For master's and Ed S, comprehensive exam, thesis or alternative. *Entrance requirements:* For master's, minimum GPA of 2.75; for Ed S, GRE General Test, MAT, minimum GPA of 2.75. Additional exam requirements/recommendations for international students: Required—TOEFL (minimum score 550 paper-based; 79 iBT), IELTS (minimum score 6). *Application deadline:* For fall admission, 7/20 priority date for domestic students, 5/1 for international students; for spring admission, 12/20 priority date for domestic students, 9/1 for international students; for summer admission, 5/20 priority date for domestic students. Applications are processed on a rolling basis. Application fee: $55 ($60 for international students). Electronic applications accepted. Tuition and fees vary according to class time, course level, course load, degree level, campus/location, program and student level. *Financial support:* Career-related internships or fieldwork, Federal Work-Study, institutionally sponsored loans, scholarships/grants, and unspecified assistantships available. Financial award application deadline: 1/31; financial award applicants required to submit FAFSA. *Unit head:* Dr. James Satterfield, Department Head, 417-836-5392, Fax: 417-836-4918, E-mail: clse@missouristate.edu. *Application contact:* Lakan Drinker, Director, Graduate Enrollment Management, 417-836-5330, Fax: 417-836-6200, E-mail: lakandrinker@missouristate.edu.
Website: http://education.missouristate.edu/edadmin/

Monmouth University, Graduate Studies, School of Education, West Long Branch, NJ 07764-1898. Offers applied behavior analysis (Certificate); autism (Certificate); director of school counseling services (Post-Master's Certificate); early childhood (M Ed); educational leadership (Ed D); elementary education (MAT), including elementary level, secondary level; English as a second language (M Ed); learning disabilities teacher-consultant (Post-Master's Certificate); literacy (MS Ed); school counseling (MS Ed); special education (MS Ed), including autism, learning disabilities teacher-consultant, teacher of students with disabilities, teaching in inclusive settings; speech-language pathology (MS Ed); student affairs and college counseling (MS Ed); supervisor (Post-Master's Certificate); teaching English to speakers of other languages (Certificate). *Accreditation:* NCATE. *Program availability:* Part-time, evening/weekend, 100% online, blended/hybrid learning. *Faculty:* 29 full-time (23 women), 32 part-time/adjunct (24 women). *Students:* 214 full-time (187 women), 148 part-time (127 women); includes 60 minority (13 Black or African American, non-Hispanic/Latino; 2 Asian, non-Hispanic/Latino; 40 Hispanic/Latino; 5 Two or more races, non-Hispanic/Latino). Average age 27. In 2018, 108 master's, 9 other advanced degrees awarded. *Entrance requirements:* For master's, GRE taken within last 5 years (for MS Ed in speech-language pathology); SAT (minimum combined score of 1660 in 3 sections), ACT (23), GRE (minimum score of 4.0 on analytical writing section and minimum combined score of 310 on quantitative and verbal sections), or passing scores on 3 parts of Core Academic Skills Educators, minimum GPA of 3.0 in major; 2 letters of recommendation (for some programs); resume, personal statement or essay (depending on program). Additional exam requirements/recommendations for international students: Required—TOEFL (minimum score 550 paper-based; 79 iBT), IELTS (minimum score 6), Michigan English Language Assessment Battery (minimum score 77) or Certificate of Advanced English (minimum score 160). *Application deadline:* For fall admission, 7/15 priority date for domestic students, 7/1 for international students; for spring admission, 12/1 priority date for domestic students, 11/1 for international students; for summer admission, 5/1 for domestic students. Applications are processed on a rolling basis. Application fee: $50. Electronic applications accepted. *Expenses: Tuition:* Part-time $1233 per credit. *Required fees:* $178 per term. *Financial support:* In 2018–19, 290 students received support. Institutionally sponsored loans, scholarships/grants, and unspecified assistantships available. Support available to part-time students. Financial award applicants required to submit FAFSA. *Faculty research:* Multicultural literacy, science and mathematics teaching strategies, teacher as reflective practitioner, children with disabilities. *Unit head:* Dr. John E. Henning, Dean, 732-263-5513, Fax: 732-263-5277, E-mail: kodonnel@monmouth.edu. *Application contact:* Kirsten Sneeringer, Graduate Admission Counselor, 732-571-3452, Fax: 732-263-5123, E-mail: gradadm@monmouth.edu.
Website: http://www.monmouth.edu/academics/schools/education/default.asp

Montana State University Billings, College of Education, Department of Educational Theory and Practice, Option in Curriculum and Instruction, Billings, MT 59101. Offers K-8 elementary education (M Ed); secondary education (M Ed). *Accreditation:* NCATE. *Program availability:* Part-time. *Degree requirements:* For master's, thesis or professional paper and/or field experience. *Entrance requirements:* For master's, GRE General Test or MAT, minimum GPA of 3.0. Additional exam requirements/recommendations for international students: Required—TOEFL (minimum score 79 iBT), IELTS (minimum score 6.5). Electronic applications accepted. *Faculty research:* Social studies education, science education.

Morehead State University, Graduate School, College of Education, Department of Foundational and Graduate Studies in Education, Morehead, KY 40351. Offers adult and higher education (MA, Ed S); certified professional counselor (Ed S); counseling P-12 (MA); curriculum and instruction (Ed S); educational technology (MA Ed); instructional leadership (Ed S); school administration (MA); school counseling (Ed S); teacher leader business and marketing content (MA Ed); teacher leader business and marketing technology (MA Ed); teacher leader educational technology (MA Ed); teacher leader English (MA Ed); teacher leader gifted education (MA Ed); teacher leader IECE certification (MA Ed); teacher leader interdisciplinary education P-5 (MA Ed); teacher leader middle grades (MA Ed); teacher leader non IECE certification (MA Ed); teacher leader reading/writing - non-certification (MA Ed); teacher leader reading/writing certification (MA Ed); teacher leader school communication - certification (MA Ed); teacher leader school communication - non-certification (MA Ed); teacher leader social studies (MA Ed); teacher leader special education (MA Ed). *Accreditation:* NCATE. *Program availability:* Part-time, evening/weekend. *Degree requirements:* For master's, thesis optional, oral and/or written comprehensive exams; for Ed S, thesis, oral exam. *Entrance requirements:* For master's, GRE General Test, minimum overall undergraduate GPA of 2.5; for Ed S, GRE General Test, interview, master's degree, minimum GPA of 3.5, work experience. Additional exam requirements/recommendations for international students: Required—TOEFL (minimum score 500 paper-based). Electronic applications accepted. *Faculty research:* Character education, school accountability, computer applications for school administrators.

Morgan State University, School of Graduate Studies, School of Education and Urban Studies, MAT Program, Baltimore, MD 21251. Offers elementary education (MAT). *Program availability:* Part-time. *Entrance requirements:* For master's, GRE General Test or MAT. *Faculty research:* Multicultural education, cooperative learning, psychology of cognition.

Mount Saint Vincent University, Graduate Programs, Faculty of Education, Program in Elementary and Middle School Education, Halifax, NS B3M 2J6, Canada. Offers M Ed, MA Ed, MA-R. *Program availability:* Part-time, evening/weekend, online learning. *Degree requirements:* For master's, thesis (for some programs). *Entrance requirements:* For master's, bachelor's degree in education, 1 year of teaching experience. Electronic applications accepted. *Faculty research:* Curriculum theory, mathematics education, philosophy in teacher education, science education, literacy education.

Murray State University, College of Education and Human Services, Department of Early Childhood and Elementary Education, Murray, KY 42071. Offers elementary teacher leader (MA Ed); interdisciplinary early childhood education (MA Ed), including elementary education (MA Ed, Ed S), reading and writing; teacher education and professional development (Ed S), including elementary education (MA Ed, Ed S). *Accreditation:* NCATE. *Program availability:* Part-time. *Entrance requirements:* For master's and Ed S, GRE or GMAT, minimum university GPA of 2.75. Additional exam requirements/recommendations for international students: Required—TOEFL (minimum score 527 paper-based; 71 iBT). Electronic applications accepted.

National Louis University, National College of Education, Chicago, IL 60603. Offers administration and supervision (M Ed, Ed D, CAS, Ed S); curriculum and instruction (M Ed, MS Ed, CAS); early childhood administration (M Ed, CAS); early childhood education (M Ed, MAT, MS Ed, CAS); education (Ed D); educational psychology/human learning and development (M Ed, MS Ed, CAS, Ed S); elementary education (MAT); interdisciplinary curriculum and instruction (M Ed); mathematics education (M Ed, MS Ed, CAS); middle grades education (MAT); reading and language (M Ed, MS Ed, CAS); school psychology (M Ed, Ed S); science education (M Ed, MS Ed, CAS); secondary education (MAT); special education (M Ed, MAT, CAS); technology in education (M Ed, CAS). *Accreditation:* NCATE. *Program availability:* Part-time, evening/weekend. *Degree requirements:* For doctorate, comprehensive exam, thesis/dissertation. *Entrance requirements:* For master's, MAT or GRE, minimum GPA of 3.0; for doctorate, GRE General Test, minimum GPA of 3.25, interview, resume, writing sample, 4 recommendations. Additional exam requirements/recommendations for international students: Required—TOEFL (minimum score 550 paper-based; 79 iBT).

Nazareth College of Rochester, Graduate Studies, Department of Education, Program in Inclusive Childhood Education, Rochester, NY 14618. Offers MS Ed. *Accreditation:* TEAC. *Program availability:* Part-time, evening/weekend. *Entrance requirements:* For master's, minimum GPA of 3.0. Additional exam requirements/recommendations for international students: Required—TOEFL or IELTS.

Nebraska Christian College of Hope International University, Graduate Programs, Papillion, NE 68046. Offers biblical studies (M Div); business as mission/social entrepreneurship (MBA); children, youth, and family (M Div); church planting (M Div); counseling psychology (MS); educational administration (MA); elementary education (M Ed); general management (MBA); gifted and talented education (M Ed); intercultural studies (M Div); international development (MBA); marketing management (MBA); ministry (MA); ministry and leadership (M Div); music education (M Ed); non-profit management (MBA); pastoral care (M Div); secondary education (M Ed); spiritual formation (M Div); worship ministry (M Div).

Neumann University, Graduate Program in Education, Aston, PA 19014-1298. Offers education (MS), including administrative certification (school principal PK-12), autism, early elementary education, secondary education, special education. *Program availability:* Part-time, evening/weekend, 100% online, blended/hybrid learning. *Entrance requirements:* For master's, official transcripts from all institutions attended, letter of intent, three professional references, copy of any teaching certifications. Additional exam requirements/recommendations for international students: Required—TOEFL (minimum score 70 iBT). Electronic applications accepted. *Expenses:* Contact institution.

New Jersey City University, Debra Cannon Partridge Wolfe College of Education, Department of Elementary and Secondary Education, Jersey City, NJ 07305-1597. Offers elementary education (MAT); secondary education (MAT). *Program availability:* Part-time, evening/weekend. *Entrance requirements:* Additional exam requirements/recommendations for international students: Required—TOEFL (minimum score 79 iBT).

New York Institute of Technology, School of Interdisciplinary Studies and Education, Department of Teacher Education, Old Westbury, NY 11568-8000. Offers adolescence education (MS), including math (MAT, MS), science; adolescent education (MAT), including biology, chemistry, English, math (MAT, MS), social studies; childhood education (MS); early childhood (MS). *Program availability:* Part-time, evening/weekend, 100% online, blended/hybrid learning. *Faculty:* 2 full-time (both women), 8 part-time/adjunct (5 women). *Students:* 47 full-time (45 women), 56 part-time (47 women); includes 36 minority (13 Black or African American, non-Hispanic/Latino; 1 American Indian or Alaska Native, non-Hispanic/Latino; 7 Asian, non-Hispanic/Latino; 12 Hispanic/Latino; 1 Native Hawaiian or other Pacific Islander, non-Hispanic/Latino; 2 Two or more races, non-Hispanic/Latino), 3 international. Average age 31. 81 applicants, 53% accepted, 27 enrolled. In 2018, 27 master's awarded. *Entrance requirements:* For master's, GRE or MAT, BS or equivalent; minimum cumulative undergraduate GPA of 3.0; NY state initial certification; BS with major (or minimum 30 credits in a concentration) in biology, chemistry, English, math, physics, or social studies (for MS in childhood, early childhood education, and MAT); interview; personal statement. Additional exam requirements/recommendations for international students: Required—TOEFL (minimum score 79 iBT), IELTS (minimum score 6), PTE (minimum score 53). *Application deadline:* Applications are processed on a rolling basis. Application fee: $50. Electronic applications accepted. *Expenses:* $1285 per credit plus $215 fees per year (full-time) or $175 fees per year (part-time); $1395 per 3-credit education UFT or off-site graduate course. *Financial support:* Career-related internships or fieldwork, Federal Work-Study, scholarships/grants, tuition waivers (full and partial), and unspecified assistantships available. Support available to part-time students. Financial award application deadline: 2/15; financial award applicants required to submit FAFSA. *Faculty research:* Evolving definition of new literacies and its impact on teaching and learning (twenty-first century skills), new literacies practices in teacher education, teachers' professional development, English language and literacy learning through mobile learning, teaching reading to culturally and linguistically diverse children. *Application contact:* Alice Dolitsky, Director, Graduate Admissions, 516-686-7520, Fax: 516-686-1116, E-mail: admissions@nyit.edu.
Website: http://www.nyit.edu/departments/teacher_education

New York University, Steinhardt School of Culture, Education, and Human Development, Department of Teaching and Learning, Program in Early Childhood and Childhood Education, New York, NY 10012. Offers childhood education (MA); early childhood education (MA); early childhood education/early childhood special education (MA). *Accreditation:* TEAC. *Program availability:* Part-time. *Degree requirements:* For master's, thesis (for some programs). *Entrance requirements:* Additional exam requirements/recommendations for international students: Required—TOEFL (minimum score 100 iBT). Electronic applications accepted. *Faculty research:* Teacher evaluation and beliefs about teaching, early literacy development, language arts, child development and education, cultural differences.

Niagara University, Graduate Division of Education, Concentration in Teacher Education, Niagara University, NY 14109. Offers early childhood and childhood education (MS Ed, Certificate); early childhood special education (MS); middle and adolescence education (MS Ed); special education (MS Ed), including 1-6, 7-12; special education (grades 1-12) (Certificate); teaching English to speakers of other languages (MS Ed, Certificate). *Accreditation:* NCATE. *Students:* 106 full-time (75 women), 105 part-time (90 women); includes 15 minority (5 Black or African American, non-Hispanic/Latino; 2 American Indian or Alaska Native, non-Hispanic/Latino; 2 Asian, non-Hispanic/Latino; 2 Hispanic/Latino; 4 Two or more races, non-Hispanic/Latino), 40 international. Average age 28. In 2018, 81 master's, 21 other advanced degrees awarded. *Entrance requirements:* For master's, GRE General Test or Academic Literacy Skills Test (ALST). Additional exam requirements/recommendations for international students: Required—TOEFL (minimum score 550 paper-based; 79 iBT), IELTS (minimum score 6). *Application deadline:* For fall admission, 8/1 for domestic students. Applications are processed on a rolling basis. Electronic applications accepted. *Expenses:* Contact institution. *Financial support:* Research assistantships with tuition reimbursements, teaching assistantships with tuition reimbursements, career-related internships or fieldwork, Federal Work-Study, scholarships/grants, and unspecified assistantships available. Support available to part-time students. Financial award application deadline: 4/15; financial award applicants required to submit FAFSA. *Unit head:* Dr. Chandra Foote, Dean, College of Education, 716-286-8549, E-mail: cjf@niagara.edu. *Application contact:* Evan Pierce, Associate Director, Graduate Studies, 716-286-8327, E-mail: epierce@niagara.edu.
Website: http://www.niagara.edu/teacher-education

Nicholls State University, Graduate Studies, College of Education, Department of Teacher Education, Thibodaux, LA 70310. Offers curriculum and instruction (M Ed); educational leadership (M Ed); elementary education (MAT); human performance education (MAT); middle school education (MAT); secondary education (MAT). *Accreditation:* NCATE. *Program availability:* Part-time, evening/weekend, online learning. *Degree requirements:* For master's, comprehensive exam, portfolio. *Entrance requirements:* For master's, GRE General Test, teaching license. Electronic applications accepted.

North Carolina Agricultural and Technical State University, The Graduate College, College of Education, Department of Educator Preparation, Greensboro, NC 27411. Offers elementary education (MA Ed). *Accreditation:* NCATE. *Program availability:* Part-time, evening/weekend. *Degree requirements:* For master's, comprehensive exam, research project or comprehensive portfolio. *Entrance requirements:* For master's, GRE General Test, minimum GPA of 3.0.

North Carolina State University, Graduate School, College of Education, Department of Teacher Education and Learning Sciences, Program in Elementary Education, Raleigh, NC 27695. Offers M Ed. *Entrance requirements:* For master's, MAT or GRE, 3 letters of reference.

Northeastern Illinois University, College of Graduate Studies and Research, Daniel L. Goodwin College of Education, MAT Program in Elementary Education, Chicago, IL 60625. Offers MAT.

Northeastern University, College of Professional Studies, Boston, MA 02115-5096. Offers applied nutrition (MS); college athletics administration (MSL); commerce and economic development (MS); corporate and organizational communication (MS); criminal justice (MS); digital media (MPS); elearning and instructional design (M Ed); elementary education (MAT); geographic information technology (MPS); global studies and international relations (MS); higher education administration (M Ed); homeland security (MA); human services (MS); informatics (MPS); leadership (MS); learning analytics (M Ed); learning and instruction (M Ed); nonprofit management (MS); professional sports administration (MSL); project management (MS); regulatory affairs for drugs, biologics, and medical devices (MS); respiratory care leadership (MS); special education (M Ed); technical communication (MS). *Program availability:* Part-time, evening/weekend, 100% online, blended/hybrid learning. Electronic applications accepted. *Expenses:* Contact institution.

Northern Arizona University, College of Education, Department of Teaching and Learning, Flagstaff, AZ 86011. Offers curriculum and instruction (Ed D); early childhood education (M Ed); elementary education (M Ed); secondary education (M Ed). *Program availability:* Part-time, 100% online, blended/hybrid learning. *Degree requirements:* For master's, variable foreign language requirement, comprehensive exam (for some programs), thesis (for some programs); for doctorate, variable foreign language requirement, comprehensive exam (for some programs), thesis/dissertation (for some programs). *Entrance requirements:* Additional exam requirements/recommendations for international students: Required—TOEFL (minimum score 80 iBT), IELTS (minimum score 6.5). Electronic applications accepted.

Northern Illinois University, Graduate School, College of Education, Department of Special and Early Education, De Kalb, IL 60115-2854. Offers curriculum and instruction (MS Ed); early childhood education (MS Ed); elementary education (MS Ed); special education (MS Ed). *Program availability:* Part-time, evening/weekend. *Faculty:* 22 full-time (14 women), 2 part-time/adjunct (both women). *Students:* 43 full-time (33 women), 87 part-time (70 women); includes 22 minority (5 Black or African American, non-Hispanic/Latino; 1 Asian, non-Hispanic/Latino; 12 Hispanic/Latino; 4 Two or more races, non-Hispanic/Latino), 3 international. Average age 32. 75 applicants, 77% accepted, 37 enrolled. In 2018, 41 master's awarded. *Degree requirements:* For master's, comprehensive exam, thesis optional. *Entrance requirements:* For master's, GRE General Test or MAT, minimum undergraduate GPA of 2.75. Additional exam requirements/recommendations for international students: Required—TOEFL (minimum score 550 paper-based). *Application deadline:* For fall admission, 6/1 for domestic students, 5/1 for international students; for spring admission, 11/1 for domestic students, 10/1 for international students. Applications are processed on a rolling basis. Application fee: $40. Electronic applications accepted. *Financial support:* In 2018–19, 17 research assistantships with full tuition reimbursements were awarded; fellowships with full tuition reimbursements, teaching assistantships with full tuition reimbursements, career-related internships or fieldwork, Federal Work-Study, scholarships/grants, tuition waivers (full), and unspecified assistantships also available. Support available to part-time students. Financial award applicants required to submit FAFSA. *Faculty research:* Teacher certification, stress reduction during student teaching, teaching history, portfolios in student teaching. *Unit head:* Gregory Conderman, Chair, 815-753-1619, E-mail: seed@niu.edu. *Application contact:* Gail Myers, Clerk, Graduate Advising, 815-753-0381, E-mail: gmyers@niu.edu.
Website: http://www.cedu.niu.edu/seed/

Northwest Christian University, School of Education and Counseling, Eugene, OR 97401-3745. Offers clinical mental health counseling (MA); elementary teaching (MAT); English for speakers of other languages (MAT); physical education (MAT); school counseling (MA); secondary teaching (MAT); special education (MAT). *Program availability:* Part-time, evening/weekend, online learning. *Degree requirements:* For master's, thesis (for some programs). *Entrance requirements:* For master's, GRE or MAT, minimum undergraduate GPA of 3.0, interview, 2-3 page statement of purpose, two letters of recommendation, resume, background check. Additional exam requirements/recommendations for international students: Required—TOEFL (minimum score 550 paper-based; 80 iBT). Electronic applications accepted. *Expenses:* Contact institution.

Northwestern Oklahoma State University, School of Professional Studies, Program in Elementary Education, Alva, OK 73717-2799. Offers M Ed. *Accreditation:* NCATE. *Program availability:* Part-time. *Degree requirements:* For master's, thesis optional, portfolio. *Entrance requirements:* For master's, GRE General Test or MAT, minimum GPA of 2.75.

Northwestern State University of Louisiana, Graduate Studies and Research, College of Education and Human Development, Program in Elementary Education, Natchitoches, LA 71497. Offers MAT. *Degree requirements:* For master's, comprehensive exam, thesis or alternative. *Entrance requirements:* For master's, GRE General Test, minimum undergraduate GPA of 2.5. Additional exam requirements/recommendations for international students: Required—TOEFL. Electronic applications accepted.

Northwestern State University of Louisiana, Graduate Studies and Research, College of Education and Human Development, Programs in Educational Leadership and Instruction, Natchitoches, LA 71497. Offers counseling (Ed S); educational leadership (M Ed, Ed S); educational technology (Ed S); elementary teaching (Ed S); reading (Ed S); secondary teaching (Ed S); special education (Ed S). *Accreditation:* NASAD. *Degree requirements:* For master's, comprehensive exam, thesis (for some programs). *Entrance requirements:* For master's and Ed S, GRE General Test. Additional exam requirements/recommendations for international students: Required—TOEFL. Electronic applications accepted.

Northwestern University, The Graduate School, School of Education and Social Policy, Education and Social Policy Program, Evanston, IL 60035. Offers elementary teaching (MS); secondary teaching (MS); teacher leadership (MS). *Program availability:* Part-time, evening/weekend. *Degree requirements:* For master's, research project. *Entrance requirements:* For master's, GRE General Test, Illinois State Board of Education Basic Skills Exam (secondary and elementary), bachelor's degree. Additional exam requirements/recommendations for international students: Recommended—TOEFL. Electronic applications accepted. *Faculty research:* Cultural context and literacy, philosophy of education and interpretive discussion, productivity, enhancing research and teaching, motivation, new and junior faculty issues, professional development for K-12 teachers to improve math and science teaching, female/underrepresented students/faculty in STEM disciplines.

Northwest Missouri State University, Graduate School, School of Education, Maryville, MO 64468-6001. Offers early childhood education (MS Ed); education leadership (MS Ed), including elementary, K-12, secondary; educational leadership (Ed S), including elementary school principalship, secondary school principalship, superintendency; educational leadership and policy analysis (Ed D); elementary education (MS Ed); elementary mathematics (MS Ed); higher education leadership (MS); middle school education (MS Ed); reading (MS Ed); special education (MS Ed); teacher leadership (MS Ed); teaching English language learners (MS Ed). *Accreditation:* NCATE. *Program availability:* Part-time. *Faculty:* 26 full-time (16 women). *Students:* 109 full-time (87 women), 385 part-time (270 women); includes 30 minority (10 Black or African American, non-Hispanic/Latino; 2 American Indian or Alaska Native, non-Hispanic/Latino; 3 Asian, non-Hispanic/Latino; 12 Hispanic/Latino; 1 Native Hawaiian or other Pacific Islander, non-Hispanic/Latino; 2 Two or more races, non-Hispanic/Latino), 1 international. Average age 33. 210 applicants, 72% accepted, 142 enrolled. In 2018, 71 master's, 11 other advanced degrees awarded. *Degree requirements:* For master's, comprehensive exam; for Ed S, comprehensive exam, thesis. *Entrance requirements:* For master's, GRE General Test, writing sample; for Ed S, minimum graduate GPA of 3.25. Additional exam requirements/recommendations for international students: Required—TOEFL (minimum score 550 paper-based). *Application deadline:* For fall admission, 7/1 for domestic and international students; for spring admission, 11/15 for domestic and international students. Applications are processed on a rolling basis. Application fee: $0 ($75 for international students). Electronic applications accepted. *Expenses:* $389.11 in-state and $653.92 out-of-state per credit hour. *Financial support:* Research assistantships with full tuition reimbursements, teaching assistantships with full tuition reimbursements, and unspecified assistantships available. Financial award application deadline: 4/1; financial award applicants required to submit FAFSA. *Unit head:* Dr. Tim Wall, Director, 660-562-1179, E-mail: timwall@nwmissouri.edu. *Application contact:* Dr. Tim Wall, Director, 660-562-1179, E-mail: timwall@nwmissouri.edu.
Website: https://www.nwmissouri.edu/education/index.htm

Nyack College, School of Education, Nyack, NY 10960. Offers childhood education (MS); childhood special education (MS); TESOL (MAT, MS). *Program availability:* Part-time, evening/weekend, 100% online, blended/hybrid learning. *Students:* 28 full-time (24 women), 22 part-time (19 women); includes 21 minority (10 Black or African American, non-Hispanic/Latino; 1 American Indian or Alaska Native, non-Hispanic/Latino; 3 Asian, non-Hispanic/Latino; 6 Hispanic/Latino; 1 Two or more races, non-Hispanic/Latino), 4 international. Average age 32. In 2018, 17 master's awarded. *Degree requirements:* For master's, comprehensive exam, clinical experience. *Entrance requirements:* For master's, GRE, transcripts, autobiography and statement on reasons for pursuing graduate study in education, recommendations, 6 credits of language, evidence of computer literacy, introductory course in psychology. Additional exam requirements/recommendations for international students: Required—TOEFL (minimum score 550 paper-based; 80 iBT), GRE. *Application deadline:* Applications are processed on a rolling basis. Application fee: $30. Electronic applications accepted. *Expenses:* $725/credit. *Financial support:* Scholarships/grants available. Financial award applicants required to submit FAFSA. *Unit head:* Dr. JoAnn Looney, Dean, 845-675-4538. *Application contact:* Dr. JoAnn Looney, Dean, 845-675-4538.
Website: http://www.nyack.edu/edu

Oakland City University, School of Education, Oakland City, IN 47660-1099. Offers building level administration (MS Ed); curriculum and instruction (MS Ed, Ed D); education (MS Ed); elementary education (MAT); organizational management (Ed D); secondary education (MAT); superintendency (Ed D). *Accreditation:* NCATE. Terminal master's awarded for partial completion of doctoral program. *Degree requirements:* For master's, thesis; for doctorate, comprehensive exam, thesis/dissertation. *Entrance requirements:* For master's, MAT, minimum GPA of 3.0, interview, resume, letters of recommendation; for doctorate, MAT, GRE, minimum GPA of 3.2, interview, resume,

letters of recommendation. *Expenses:* Contact institution. *Faculty research:* Assessment, cultural diversity, teacher education, education leadership.

Oakland University, Graduate Study and Lifelong Learning, School of Education and Human Services, Department of Teacher Development and Educational Studies, Rochester, MI 48309-4401. Offers educational studies (M Ed); elementary education (MAT); secondary education (MAT); teaching and learning (Graduate Certificate). *Entrance requirements:* For master's, minimum GPA of 3.0. Electronic applications accepted.

Oklahoma City University, Petree College of Arts and Sciences, Oklahoma City, OK 73106-1402. Offers applied behavioral studies (M Ed); applied sociology: nonprofit leadership (MA); creative writing (MFA); criminology (MS); early childhood education (M Ed); elementary education (M Ed); general studies (MLA); leadership/management (MLA); moving image arts (MFA); professional counseling (M Ed); teaching (MA); teaching English to speakers of other languages (MA). *Program availability:* Part-time, evening/weekend. *Degree requirements:* For master's, capstone/practicum. *Entrance requirements:* For master's, bachelor's degree from accredited institution with minimum GPA of 3.0, essay, recommendation letters. Additional exam requirements/recommendations for international students: Required—TOEFL (minimum score 550 paper-based; 80 iBT). Electronic applications accepted. *Expenses:* Contact institution.

Old Dominion University, Darden College of Education, Program in Elementary/Middle Education, Norfolk, VA 23529. Offers elementary education (Postbaccalaureate Certificate); instructional technology (MS Ed); library science (MS Ed). *Accreditation:* NCATE. *Program availability:* Part-time, evening/weekend, 100% online, blended/hybrid learning. *Degree requirements:* For master's, comprehensive exam. *Entrance requirements:* For master's, GRE General Test or MAT; PRAXIS I, SAT or ACT, minimum GPA of 2.8. Additional exam requirements/recommendations for international students: Required—TOEFL (minimum score 600 paper-based). Electronic applications accepted. *Expenses:* Contact institution. *Faculty research:* Education pre-K to 6, school librarianship, reading, TESOL, literacy.

Olivet Nazarene University, Graduate School, Division of Education, Program in Elementary Education, Bourbonnais, IL 60914. Offers MAT. *Accreditation:* NCATE. *Program availability:* Evening/weekend. *Degree requirements:* For master's, thesis or alternative.

Oregon State University, College of Education, Program in Teaching, Corvallis, OR 97331. Offers clinically based elementary education (MAT); elementary education (MAT); language arts (MAT); mathematics (MAT); music education (MAT); science (MAT); social studies (MAT). *Program availability:* Part-time, blended/hybrid learning. *Entrance requirements:* For master's, CBEST. Additional exam requirements/recommendations for international students: Required—TOEFL (minimum score 575 paper-based). *Expenses:* Contact institution.

Ottawa University, Graduate Studies-Arizona, Program in Education, Ottawa, KS 66067-3399. Offers community college counseling (MA); curriculum and instruction (MA); early childhood (MA); education intervention (MA); education leadership (MA); education technology (MA); Montessori early childhood education (MA); Montessori elementary education (MA); professional development (MA); school guidance counseling (MA); special education - cross categorical (MA). Programs offered in Mesa, Phoenix, Tempe and West Valley, AZ. *Accreditation:* NCATE. *Program availability:* Part-time. *Degree requirements:* For master's, thesis or alternative. *Entrance requirements:* For master's, minimum undergraduate GPA of 3.0, copy of current state certification or teaching license. Additional exam requirements/recommendations for international students: Required—TOEFL (minimum score 550 paper-based). Electronic applications accepted. *Expenses:* Contact institution.

Pace University, School of Education, New York, NY 10038. Offers adolescent education (MST), including biology, chemistry, earth science, English, foreign languages, mathematics, physics, social studies; childhood education (MST); early childhood development, learning and intervention (MST); educational technology studies (MS); inclusive adolescent education (MST), including biology, chemistry, earth science, English, foreign languages, mathematics, physics, social studies; integrated instruction for educational technology (Certificate); integrated instruction for literacy and technology (Certificate); literacy (MS Ed); special education (MS Ed). *Accreditation:* NCATE. *Program availability:* Part-time, evening/weekend, 100% online, blended/hybrid learning. *Faculty:* 19 full-time (13 women), 86 part-time/adjunct (49 women). *Students:* 98 full-time (82 women), 542 part-time (391 women); includes 256 minority (116 Black or African American, non-Hispanic/Latino; 2 American Indian or Alaska Native, non-Hispanic/Latino; 45 Asian, non-Hispanic/Latino; 83 Hispanic/Latino; 10 Two or more races, non-Hispanic/Latino), 4 international. Average age 30. 223 applicants, 89% accepted, 130 enrolled. In 2018, 269 master's, 12 other advanced degrees awarded. *Degree requirements:* For master's and Certificate, certification exams. *Entrance requirements:* For master's, GRE (for initial certification programs only), teaching certificate (for MS Ed in literacy and special education programs only). Additional exam requirements/recommendations for international students: Required—TOEFL (minimum score 88 iBT), IELTS or PTE. *Application deadline:* For fall admission, 8/1 priority date for domestic students, 6/1 for international students; for spring admission, 12/1 priority date for domestic students, 10/1 for international students. Applications are processed on a rolling basis. Application fee: $70. Electronic applications accepted. *Expenses:* Contact institution. *Financial support:* In 2018–19, 17 students received support, including 17 research assistantships with partial tuition reimbursements available (averaging $6,020 per year); career-related internships or fieldwork, Federal Work-Study, scholarships/grants, and unspecified assistantships also available. Financial award application deadline: 9/1; financial award applicants required to submit FAFSA. *Faculty research:* STEM education, TESOL, teacher education, special education, language and literary development. *Total annual research expenditures:* $1.4 million. *Unit head:* Dr. Harriet Feldman, Dean, School of Education, 914-773-3829, E-mail: hfeldman@pace.edu. *Application contact:* Susan Ford-Goldschein, Director of Graduate Admissions, 212-346-1531, Fax: 212-346-1585, E-mail: graduateadmission@pace.edu. Website: http://www.pace.edu/school-of-education

Pacific Union College, Education Department, Angwin, CA 94508-9707. Offers education (M Ed); elementary teaching (MAT); secondary teaching (MAT). *Program availability:* Part-time. *Faculty:* 3 full-time (1 woman), 1 (woman) part-time/adjunct. *Students:* 3 full-time (2 women). Average age 20. 4 applicants, 100% accepted, 4 enrolled. In 2018, 1 master's awarded. *Degree requirements:* For master's, thesis, action research project, field experiences. *Entrance requirements:* For master's, GRE General Test, two interviews, teaching credential, letters of recommendation, essay. *Application deadline:* For fall admission, 8/30 for domestic and international students; for summer admission, 6/1 for domestic and international students. Applications are processed on a rolling basis. Application fee: $0. *Expenses:* Contact institution. *Financial support:* Scholarships/grants available. Support available to part-time students. Financial award application deadline: 9/25. *Unit head:* Dr. Jean Buller, Department Chair, 707-965-7266, Fax: 707-965-6645, E-mail: jbuller@puc.edu. *Application contact:* Sarah Gitter, Credential Analyst, 707-965-6643, Fax: 707-965-6645, E-mail: teachingcredentials@puc.edu. Website: http://www.puc.edu/academics/departments/education/

Pacific University, College of Education, Forest Grove, OR 97116-1797. Offers early childhood education (MAT); education (MAE); elementary education (MAT); ESOL (MAT); high school education (MAT); middle school education (MAT); special education (MAT); speech-language pathology (MS); STEM education (MAT); talented and gifted (M Ed); visual function in learning (M Ed). *Accreditation:* ASHA; NCATE. *Program availability:* Part-time, evening/weekend. *Degree requirements:* For master's, research project. *Entrance requirements:* For master's, California Basic Educational Skills Test, PRAXIS II, minimum undergraduate GPA of 2.75, 3.0 graduate. Additional exam requirements/recommendations for international students: Required—TOEFL. Electronic applications accepted. *Expenses:* Contact institution. *Faculty research:* Defining a culturally competent classroom, technology in the K-12 classroom, Socratic seminars, social studies education.

Pfeiffer University, Program in Elementary Education, Misenheimer, NC 28109-0960. Offers MAT, MS. *Accreditation:* NCATE. *Entrance requirements:* For master's, GRE, MAT, minimum GPA of 2.75.

Point Park University, School of Arts and Sciences, Department of Education, Pittsburgh, PA 15222-1984. Offers adult learning and training (MA); athletic coaching (M Ed); curriculum and instruction (MA); educational administration (MA); leadership and administration (Ed D); secondary education (M Ed); special education grades 7-12 (M Ed); special education PreK-grade 8 (M Ed). *Program availability:* Part-time, evening/weekend, 100% online, blended/hybrid learning. *Degree requirements:* For master's, comprehensive exam (for some programs), thesis or alternative. *Entrance requirements:* For master's, minimum GPA of 3.0, resume, 2 letters of recommendation. Additional exam requirements/recommendations for international students: Required—TOEFL. Electronic applications accepted.

Prescott College, Graduate Programs, Program in Education, Prescott, AZ 86301. Offers early childhood education (MA); early childhood special education (MA); education (MA); elementary education (MA); environmental education leadership and administration (MA); equine-assisted learning (MA); school guidance counseling (MA); secondary education (MA); special education: learning disabilities (MA); special education: mental retardation (MA); special education: serious emotional disabilities (MA); student-directed independent study (MA); sustainability education (PhD). *Program availability:* Part-time, online learning. *Degree requirements:* For master's, thesis, fieldwork or internship, practicum; for doctorate, thesis/dissertation. *Entrance requirements:* For master's, 2 letters of recommendation, resume; for doctorate, 3 letters of recommendation, resume, official transcripts, personal statement, program proposal. Additional exam requirements/recommendations for international students: Required—TOEFL (minimum score 500 paper-based). Electronic applications accepted.

Providence College, Program in Special Education, Providence, RI 02918. Offers special education (M Ed), including elementary teaching, secondary teaching. *Program availability:* Part-time, evening/weekend. *Degree requirements:* For master's, comprehensive exam, portfolio. *Entrance requirements:* Additional exam requirements/recommendations for international students: Required—TOEFL (minimum score 577 paper-based; 90 iBT).

Providence College, Programs in Administration, Providence, RI 02918. Offers elementary administration (M Ed); secondary administration (M Ed). *Program availability:* Part-time, evening/weekend. *Degree requirements:* For master's, comprehensive exam, portfolio. *Entrance requirements:* Additional exam requirements/recommendations for international students: Required—TOEFL (minimum score 577 paper-based; 90 iBT).

Purdue University, Graduate School, College of Education, Department of Curriculum and Instruction, West Lafayette, IN 47907. Offers agricultural and extension education (MS, MS Ed, PhD, Ed S); art education (PhD); career and technical education (MS Ed, PhD, Ed S); curriculum studies (MS Ed, PhD, Ed S); educational technology (MS Ed, PhD, Ed S); elementary education (MS Ed); family and consumer sciences education (MS Ed, PhD, Ed S); foreign language education (MS Ed, PhD, Ed S); industrial technology (PhD, Ed S); language arts (MS Ed, PhD, Ed S); literacy (MS Ed, PhD, Ed S); mathematics education (MS, MS Ed, PhD, Ed S); science education (MS, MS Ed, PhD, Ed S); social studies education (MS Ed, PhD, Ed S). *Accreditation:* NCATE. *Program availability:* Part-time, evening/weekend, online learning. *Faculty:* 34 full-time (24 women), 3 part-time/adjunct (1 woman). *Students:* 75 full-time (52 women), 357 part-time (271 women); includes 83 minority (29 Black or African American, non-Hispanic/Latino; 1 American Indian or Alaska Native, non-Hispanic/Latino; 14 Asian, non-Hispanic/Latino; 29 Hispanic/Latino; 1 Native Hawaiian or other Pacific Islander, non-Hispanic/Latino; 9 Two or more races, non-Hispanic/Latino), 43 international. Average age 36. 169 applicants, 83% accepted, 102 enrolled. In 2018, 141 master's, 15 doctorates awarded. *Degree requirements:* For master's, thesis optional; for doctorate, thesis/dissertation, oral and written exams; for Ed S, oral presentation, project. *Entrance requirements:* For master's, GRE General Test (if undergraduate GPA is below 3.0), minimum undergraduate GPA of 3.0 or equivalent; for doctorate, GRE General Test (minimum combined verbal and quantitative score of 1000, 300 for new scoring), minimum undergraduate GPA of 3.0 or equivalent; master's degree with minimum GPA of 3.0 or equivalent; for Ed S, GRE General Test (minimum combined verbal and quantitative score of 1000, 300 for new scoring), minimum undergraduate GPA of 3.0 or equivalent; master's degree. Additional exam requirements/recommendations for international students: Required—TOEFL (minimum score 550 paper-based; 77 iBT). *Application deadline:* For fall admission, 12/15 for domestic students, 3/1 for international students; for spring admission, 9/15 for domestic students, 8/1 for international students. Application fee: $60 ($75 for international students). Electronic applications accepted. *Financial support:* Fellowships with full tuition reimbursements, research assistantships with full tuition reimbursements, teaching assistantships with full tuition reimbursements, career-related internships or fieldwork, and tuition waivers (full) available. Support available to part-time students. Financial award application deadline: 3/1; financial award applicants required to submit FAFSA. *Faculty research:* Literacy acquisition and development, teacher beliefs and knowledge, recruitment and retention of underrepresented students, economic education, literacy discourse. *Unit head:* Janet M. Alsup, Head, 765-494-9667, E-mail: alsupj@purdue.edu. *Application contact:* Heather Brinkman, Graduate Contact, 765-494-2345, E-mail: hbrinkma@purdue.edu. Website: http://www.edci.purdue.edu/

Purdue University Fort Wayne, College of Professional Studies, School of Education, Fort Wayne, IN 46805-1499. Offers couple and family counseling (MS Ed); educational leadership (MS Ed); elementary education (MS Ed); school counseling (MS Ed); secondary education (MS Ed); special education (MS Ed, Certificate). *Accreditation:* NCATE. *Program availability:* Part-time. *Entrance requirements:* For master's, minimum GPA of 2.5, three professional letters of recommendation. Additional exam requirements/recommendations for international students: Required—TOEFL (minimum score 550 paper-based; 79 iBT). *Faculty research:* International faculty, gender in Burmese refugee narratives, planning effective instruction.

Queens College of the City University of New York, Division of Education, Department of Elementary and Early Childhood Education, Queens, NY 11367-1597. Offers bilingual education (MAT, MS Ed, AC); childhood education (MAT, MS Ed); early childhood education birth-2 (MAT, MS Ed, AC); literacy education birth-grade 6 (MS Ed,

AC). *Program availability:* Part-time, evening/weekend. *Faculty:* 19 full-time (13 women), 35 part-time/adjunct (32 women). *Students:* 117 full-time (102 women), 376 part-time (344 women); includes 264 minority (27 Black or African American, non-Hispanic/Latino; 75 Asian, non-Hispanic/Latino; 154 Hispanic/Latino; 1 Native Hawaiian or other Pacific Islander, non-Hispanic/Latino; 7 Two or more races, non-Hispanic/Latino), 15 international. Average age 30. 351 applicants, 75% accepted, 204 enrolled. In 2018, 156 master's, 48 other advanced degrees awarded. *Degree requirements:* For master's, Research project; for AC, Field-based research project. *Entrance requirements:* For master's, GRE General Test, minimum undergraduate cumulative GPA of 3.00; for AC, GRE General Test (required for all MAT and other graduate programs leading to NYS initial teacher certification), NYS initial teacher certification in the appropriate certification area is required for admission into MSEd programs. Additional exam requirements/recommendations for international students: Required—TOEFL (minimum score 575 paper-based; 90 iBT). *Application deadline:* For fall admission, 4/1 for domestic students. Applications are processed on a rolling basis. Application fee: $125. Electronic applications accepted. *Financial support:* Career-related internships or fieldwork and Federal Work-Study available. Financial award application deadline: 4/1; financial award applicants required to submit FAFSA. *Faculty research:* Biliteracy, computational thinking, social justice education, technology in early childhood education, children from immigrant families. *Unit head:* Daisuke Akiba, Chair, 718-997-5300, E-mail: daisuke.akiba@qc.cuny.edu. *Application contact:* Elizabeth D'Amico-Ramirez, Assistant Director of Graduate Admissions, 718-997-5203, E-mail: elizabeth.damicoramirez@qc.cuny.edu.

Queens University of Charlotte, Wayland H. Cato, Jr. School of Education, Charlotte, NC 28274-0002. Offers educational leadership (MA); K-6 (MAT); literacy K-12 (M Ed). *Accreditation:* NCATE. *Program availability:* Part-time, evening/weekend, online learning. *Degree requirements:* For master's, comprehensive exam. *Entrance requirements:* For master's, GRE General Test. *Expenses:* Contact institution.

Quinnipiac University, School of Education, Program in Elementary Education, Hamden, CT 06518-1940. Offers MAT. *Accreditation:* NCATE. *Entrance requirements:* For master's, PRAXIS I or PRAXIS Core Academic Skills Exam, minimum GPA of 3.0, interview. Electronic applications accepted. *Faculty research:* Multicultural and urban education/leadership, challenges of teaching diverse learners, scholarship of teaching and learning, technology and teaching, humor and education.

Regent University, Graduate School, School of Education, Virginia Beach, VA 23464-9800. Offers education (M Ed, Ed D, PhD), including adult education (Ed D, PhD, Ed S), advanced educational leadership (Ed D, PhD, Ed S), character education (Ed D, PhD, Ed S), Christian education leadership (Ed D, PhD, Ed S), Christian school administration (M Ed), curriculum and instruction (Ed D, PhD, Ed S), curriculum and instruction - adult education (M Ed), curriculum and instruction - Christian school (M Ed), curriculum and instruction - gifted and talented (M Ed), curriculum and instruction - STEM education (M Ed), curriculum and instruction - teacher leader (M Ed), discipleship for ministry (M Ed), educational leadership (M Ed), educational psychology (Ed D, PhD, Ed S), educational technology and online learning (Ed D, PhD, Ed S), elementary education (M Ed), exceptional education executive leadership (Ed D, PhD, Ed S), higher education (Ed D, PhD, Ed S), higher education leadership and management (Ed D, PhD, Ed S), instructional design and technology (M Ed), K-12 school leadership (Ed D, PhD, Ed S), K-12 special education (M Ed), leadership in mathematics education (M Ed), reading specialist (M Ed), special education (Ed D, PhD, Ed S), student affairs (M Ed), TESOL - adult education (M Ed), TESOL - K-12 (M Ed); educational specialist (Ed S), including adult education (Ed D, PhD, Ed S), advanced educational leadership (Ed D, PhD, Ed S), character education (Ed D, PhD, Ed S), Christian education leadership (Ed D, PhD, Ed S), curriculum and instruction (Ed D, PhD, Ed S), educational psychology (Ed D, PhD, Ed S), educational technology and online learning (Ed D, PhD, Ed S), exceptional education executive leadership (Ed D, PhD, Ed S), higher education (Ed D, PhD, Ed S), higher education leadership and management (Ed D, PhD, Ed S), K-12 school leadership (Ed D, PhD, Ed S), special education (Ed D, PhD, Ed S). *Accreditation:* TEAC. *Program availability:* Part-time, evening/weekend, 100% online, blended/hybrid learning. *Degree requirements:* For master's, thesis or alternative; for doctorate, comprehensive exam, thesis/dissertation. *Entrance requirements:* For master's, Virginia Communication and Literacy Assessment (VCLA), PRAXIS, college transcripts, writing sample, interview; for doctorate, GRE, writing sample, resume, transcripts, interview. Additional exam requirements/recommendations for international students: Required—TOEFL (minimum score 577 paper-based). Electronic applications accepted. *Expenses:* Contact institution. *Faculty research:* Christian school administration, curriculum and instruction, educational technology and online learning, higher education, special education.

Regis College, Department of Education, Weston, MA 02493. Offers elementary teacher (M Ed); higher education leadership (Ed D); special education (M Ed). *Program availability:* Part-time, evening/weekend. *Degree requirements:* For doctorate, thesis/dissertation, capstone project. *Entrance requirements:* For master's, GRE or MAT, personal statement, recommendations, resume/curriculum vitae, official transcripts, interview; for doctorate, personal statement, recommendations, resume/curriculum vitae, official transcripts, presentation/interview. Additional exam requirements/recommendations for international students: Required—TOEFL (minimum score 560 paper-based; 79 iBT); Recommended—IELTS (minimum score 6.5). *Application deadline:* Applications are processed on a rolling basis. Application fee: $65. Electronic applications accepted. *Financial support:* Federal Work-Study, scholarships/grants, and unspecified assistantships available. Financial award applicants required to submit FAFSA. *Unit head:* Dr. Priscilla Boerger, Department Chair/Graduate Program Director, 781-768-7422, E-mail: priscilla.boerger@regiscollege.edu. *Application contact:* Dr. Priscilla Boerger, Department Chair/Graduate Program Director, 781-768-7422, E-mail: priscilla.boerger@regiscollege.edu.

Regis University, College of Contemporary Liberal Studies, Denver, CO 80221-1099. Offers creative writing (MFA); criminology (M Sc); curriculum, instruction and assessment (M Ed); education - teacher leadership (M Ed); educational leadership (M Ed); elementary education (M Ed); literacy (Certificate); reading (M Ed); secondary education (M Ed); special education (M Ed); teacher academic leadership (Certificate); teacher leadership (MA); teacher/educational leadership (M Ed); teaching the linguistically diverse (M Ed). *Program availability:* Part-time, evening/weekend, 100% online, blended/hybrid learning. *Degree requirements:* For master's, thesis (for some programs). *Entrance requirements:* For master's, official transcript reflecting baccalaureate degree awarded from regionally-accredited college or university, work experience, resume, letters of recommendation. Additional exam requirements/recommendations for international students: Required—TOEFL (minimum score 550 paper-based; 82 iBT). Electronic applications accepted. *Expenses:* Contact institution.

Rhode Island College, School of Graduate Studies, Feinstein School of Education and Human Development, Department of Elementary Education, Providence, RI 02908-1991. Offers early childhood education (M Ed); elementary education (M Ed, MAT); reading (M Ed). *Accreditation:* NCATE. *Program availability:* Part-time, evening/weekend. *Faculty:* 7 full-time (all women), 4 part-time/adjunct (2 women). *Students:* 18 full-time (17 women), 20 part-time (17 women); includes 1 minority (Black or African American, non-Hispanic/Latino). Average age 31. In 2018, 21 master's awarded. *Degree requirements:* For master's, comprehensive exam (for some programs), comprehensive assessment. *Entrance requirements:* For master's, GRE General Test or MAT, PRAXIS II (elementary content knowledge), undergraduate transcripts; minimum undergraduate GPA of 3.0; 3 letters of recommendation. Additional exam requirements/recommendations for international students: Required—TOEFL (minimum score 550 paper-based; 80 iBT). *Application deadline:* For fall admission, 3/1 for domestic students; for spring admission, 11/1 for domestic students. Applications are processed on a rolling basis. Application fee: $50. Electronic applications accepted. *Expenses: Tuition, area resident:* Part-time $407 per credit. Tuition, nonresident: part-time $792 per credit. *Required fees:* $29 per credit. $100 per semester. *Financial support:* Teaching assistantships with full tuition reimbursements, Federal Work-Study, scholarships/grants, and health care benefits available. Support available to part-time students. Financial award application deadline: 5/15; financial award applicants required to submit FAFSA. *Unit head:* Dr. Carolyn Obel-Omia, Chair, 401-456-8016. *Application contact:* Dr. Carolyn Obel-Omia, Chair, 401-456-8016.
Website: http://www.ric.edu/elementaryeducation/Pages/Graduate-Programs.aspx

Rider University, College of Education and Human Services, Program in Teaching, Lawrenceville, NJ 08648-3001. Offers bilingual education (MAT); early childhood education (MAT); elementary education (MAT); English as a second language (MAT); secondary education (MAT); world language (MAT). *Students:* 35 full-time (26 women), 88 part-time (67 women); includes 12 minority (1 Black or African American, non-Hispanic/Latino; 1 American Indian or Alaska Native, non-Hispanic/Latino; 2 Asian, non-Hispanic/Latino; 8 Hispanic/Latino). Average age 34. 104 applicants, 67% accepted, 54 enrolled. In 2018, 70 master's awarded. *Entrance requirements:* For master's, Praxis exams, resume,application fee, statement of aims and objectives, official prior college transcripts, interview. Additional exam requirements/recommendations for international students: Required—TOEFL (minimum score 540 paper-based; 79 iBT). *Application deadline:* For fall admission, 5/1 priority date for domestic students, 6/1 priority date for international students; for spring admission, 12/1 priority date for domestic students, 11/1 priority date for international students. Applications are processed on a rolling basis. Application fee: $50. Electronic applications accepted. *Expenses: Tuition:* Full-time $850; part-time $850 per credit hour. *Required fees:* $50; $50 per course. Tuition and fees vary according to program. *Financial support:* Applicants required to submit FAFSA. *Unit head:* Kathleen Pierce, Professor, 609-895-5478, E-mail: kpierce@rider.edu. *Application contact:* Jamie L Mitchell, Director of Graduate Admissions, 609-896-5036, Fax: 609-895-5680, E-mail: jmitchell@rider.edu.

Rivier University, School of Graduate Studies, Department of Education, Nashua, NH 03060. Offers curriculum and instruction (M Ed); early childhood education (M Ed); educational administration (M Ed); educational studies (M Ed); elementary education (M Ed); elementary education and general special education (M Ed); emotional and behavioral disorders (M Ed); general social education (M Ed); leadership and learning (Ed D, CAGS); learning disabilities (M Ed); learning disabilities and reading (M Ed); mental health counseling (MA); reading (M Ed); school counseling (M Ed). *Program availability:* Part-time, evening/weekend. *Degree requirements:* For master's, comprehensive exam (for some programs), internships. *Entrance requirements:* For master's, GRE General Test or MAT.

Rockford University, Graduate Studies, Department of Education, Program in Elementary Education, Rockford, IL 61108-2393. Offers MAT. *Program availability:* Part-time, evening/weekend. *Degree requirements:* For master's, thesis optional. *Entrance requirements:* For master's, GRE General Test, basic skills test (for students seeking certification), 3 letters of recommendation. Additional exam requirements/recommendations for international students: Required—TOEFL (minimum score 550 paper-based; 79 iBT). Electronic applications accepted.

Rollins College, Hamilton Holt School, Graduate Education Programs, Winter Park, FL 32789-4499. Offers elementary education (M Ed, MAT). *Program availability:* Part-time, evening/weekend. *Degree requirements:* For master's, comprehensive exam, Professional Education Test (PED) and Subject Area Examination (SAE) of the Florida Teacher Certification Examinations (FTCE), successful review of the Expanded Teacher Education Portfolio (ETEP). *Entrance requirements:* For master's, General Knowledge Test of the Florida Teacher Certification Examination (FTCE), official transcripts, letter(s) of recommendation, essay. Additional exam requirements/recommendations for international students: Required—TOEFL (minimum score 550 paper-based; 80 iBT). *Expenses:* Contact institution.

Roosevelt University, Graduate Division, College of Education, Program in Elementary Education, Chicago, IL 60605. Offers MA. Electronic applications accepted.

Rosemont College, Schools of Graduate and Professional Studies, Graduate Education PreK-4 Program, Rosemont, PA 19010-1699. Offers elementary certification (MA); PreK-4 (MA). *Program availability:* Part-time, evening/weekend. *Degree requirements:* For master's, thesis optional. *Entrance requirements:* For master's, minimum college GPA of 3.0, 3 letters of recommendation. Additional exam requirements/recommendations for international students: Required—TOEFL. Electronic applications accepted. Application fee is waived when completed online.

Rutgers University–New Brunswick, Graduate School of Education, Department of Learning and Teaching, Program in Early Childhood/Elementary Education, Piscataway, NJ 08854-8097. Offers Ed M, Ed D. *Program availability:* Part-time. Terminal master's awarded for partial completion of doctoral program. *Degree requirements:* For master's, comprehensive exam (for some programs); for doctorate, thesis/dissertation, qualifying exam. *Entrance requirements:* For master's, GRE General Test, minimum GPA of 3.0; for doctorate, GRE General Test, minimum GPA of 3.5. Additional exam requirements/recommendations for international students: Required—TOEFL. Electronic applications accepted.

Sage Graduate School, Esteves School of Education, Program in Childhood Education/Literacy, Troy, NY 12180-4115. Offers MS. *Program availability:* Part-time, evening/weekend. *Faculty:* 2 full-time (both women), 9 part-time/adjunct (5 women). *Students:* 13 full-time (12 women), 2 part-time (both women); includes 2 minority (both Black or African American, non-Hispanic/Latino). Average age 30. 20 applicants, 50% accepted, 6 enrolled. In 2018, 6 master's awarded. *Degree requirements:* For master's, thesis optional. *Entrance requirements:* For master's, GRE (minimum scores: Verbal Reasoning 145, Quantitative Reasoning 145, Analytical Writing 3.5) or MAT (minimum score: 350), bachelor's degree in a liberal arts or science area, minimum cumulative GPA of 3.0. Additional exam requirements/recommendations for international students: Required—TOEFL (minimum score 550 paper-based). *Application deadline:* Applications are processed on a rolling basis. Application fee: $30. Electronic applications accepted. *Financial support:* Fellowships, research assistantships, scholarships/grants, and unspecified assistantships available. Financial award application deadline: 3/1; financial award applicants required to submit FAFSA. *Unit head:* Dr. John Pelizza, Dean, Esteves School of Education, 518-244-2051, Fax: 518-244-2334, E-mail: pelizj@sage.edu. *Application contact:* Dr. Kathleen Gormley, Chair and Professor of Education, 518-244-2403, Fax: 518-244-2334, E-mail: gormlk@sage.edu.

Sage Graduate School, Esteves School of Education, Program in Childhood Special Education, Troy, NY 12180-4115. Offers MS Ed. *Accreditation:* NCATE. *Program*

availability: Part-time, evening/weekend. *Faculty:* 2 full-time (both women), 9 part-time/adjunct (5 women). *Students:* 5 full-time (4 women), 3 part-time (2 women); includes 1 minority (Asian, non-Hispanic/Latino). Average age 24. 16 applicants, 56% accepted, 3 enrolled. In 2018, 2 master's awarded. *Degree requirements:* For master's, thesis optional. *Entrance requirements:* For master's, bachelor's degree in a liberal arts or sciences area or the equivalent. Additional exam requirements/recommendations for international students: Required—TOEFL (minimum score 550 paper-based). *Application deadline:* Applications are processed on a rolling basis. Application fee: $30. Electronic applications accepted. *Financial support:* Fellowships, research assistantships, scholarships/grants, and unspecified assistantships available. Financial award application deadline: 3/1; financial award applicants required to submit FAFSA. *Faculty research:* Effective behavioral strategies for classroom instruction. *Unit head:* Dr. John Pelizza, Dean, Esteves School of Education, 518-244-2051, Fax: 518-244-2334, E-mail: pelizj@sage.edu. *Application contact:* Kathleen Gormley, Chair & Professor of Education, 518-244-2403, Fax: 518-244-2334, E-mail: gormlk@sage.edu.

St. John Fisher College, Ralph C. Wilson Jr. School of Education, Program in Childhood Education/Special Education, Rochester, NY 14618-3597. Offers childhood education (MS); childhood education/special education (Certificate). *Program availability:* Part-time, evening/weekend. *Faculty:* 8 full-time (6 women), 2 part-time/adjunct (both women). *Students:* 14 full-time (11 women), 4 part-time (2 women); includes 1 minority (Hispanic/Latino). Average age 28. 27 applicants, 48% accepted, 6 enrolled. In 2018, 14 master's awarded. *Degree requirements:* For master's, field experience, student teaching. *Entrance requirements:* For master's, LAST, 2 letters of recommendation, personal statement, current resume. Additional exam requirements/recommendations for international students: Required—TOEFL (minimum score 575 paper-based; 80 iBT). *Application deadline:* Applications are processed on a rolling basis. Application fee: $30. Electronic applications accepted. *Expenses:* Contact institution. *Financial support:* Scholarships/grants available. Financial award applicants required to submit FAFSA. *Faculty research:* Professional development, science assessment, multi-cultural, educational technology. *Unit head:* Dr. Susan Hildenbrand, Program Director, 585-385-7297, E-mail: shildenbrand@sjfc.edu. *Application contact:* Michelle Gosier, Associate Director of Transfer and Graduate Admissions, 585-385-8064, E-mail: mgosier@sjfc.edu.
Website: https://www.sjfc.edu/graduate-programs/ms-in-childhood-special-education/

St. John's University, The School of Education, Department of Curriculum and Instruction, Program in Childhood Education, Queens, NY 11439. Offers MS Ed. *Program availability:* Part-time, evening/weekend. *Degree requirements:* For master's, thesis. *Entrance requirements:* For master's, GRE, MAT, or PRAXIS, statement of goals (personal essay), official undergraduate transcripts, initial teaching certification. Additional exam requirements/recommendations for international students: Required—TOEFL, IELTS. Electronic applications accepted. *Faculty research:* Self-determination in the special education setting; parent, teacher, and student views on testing in elementary school; children's play; children's acquisition of STEM related subjects; the politics of preschool.

Saint Joseph's University, College of Arts and Sciences, Graduate Programs in Education, Philadelphia, PA 19131-1395. Offers curriculum supervisor (Certificate); educational leadership (MS, Ed D); elementary education (MS, Certificate); elementary/middle school education (Certificate); organizational development and leadership (MS); principal (Certificate); professional education (MS); reading specialist (MS, Certificate); reading supervisor (Certificate); secondary education (MS, Certificate); special education (MS); special education 7-12 (Certificate); special education PK-8 (Certificate); superintendent's letter of eligibility (Certificate); supervisor of special education (Certificate); teacher of the deaf and hard of hearing (Certificate). *Program availability:* Part-time, evening/weekend, blended/hybrid learning. *Degree requirements:* For master's, thesis or alternative; for doctorate, comprehensive exam, thesis/dissertation. *Entrance requirements:* For master's, 2 letters of recommendation, minimum GPA of 3.0, official transcripts, personal statement; for doctorate, GRE, master's degree from accredited institution, minimum graduate GPA of 3.5, computer competence, interview with program director. Additional exam requirements/recommendations for international students: Required—TOEFL (minimum score 550 paper-based; 80 iBT), IELTS (minimum score 6.5), PTE (minimum score 60). Electronic applications accepted. *Expenses:* Contact institution. *Faculty research:* Factors predicting early mathematics skills for low income children, early child care and development, preschool quality, parent communication and home-school collaboration issues, education of terminally ill children, preparing literacy teachers for urban schools.

Saint Mary's University of Minnesota, Schools of Graduate and Professional Programs, Graduate School of Education, Teaching Program, Winona, MN 55987-1399. Offers MA. *Unit head:* Delores Roethke, Director, 612-238-4511, E-mail: droethke@smumn.edu. *Application contact:* Laurie Roy, Director of Admission of Schools of Graduate and Professional Programs, 507-457-8606, Fax: 612-728-5121, E-mail: lroy@smumn.edu.
Website: http://www.smumn.edu/graduate-home/areas-of-study/graduate-school-of-education/ma-in-instruction

Saint Peter's University, Graduate Programs in Education, Program in Teaching, Jersey City, NJ 07306-5997. Offers 6-8 middle school education (MA Ed, Certificate); K-12 secondary education (MA Ed, Certificate); K-5 elementary education (MA Ed, Certificate). *Program availability:* Part-time, evening/weekend. *Degree requirements:* For master's, comprehensive exam. *Entrance requirements:* For master's, GRE or MAT. Additional exam requirements/recommendations for international students: Required—TOEFL. Electronic applications accepted.

St. Thomas Aquinas College, Division of Teacher Education, Sparkill, NY 10976. Offers adolescence education (MST); childhood and special education (MST); childhood education (MST); educational leadership (MS Ed); reading (MS Ed, PMC); special education (MS Ed, PMC); teaching (MS Ed), including elementary education, middle school education, secondary education. *Accreditation:* NCATE. *Program availability:* Part-time, evening/weekend. *Degree requirements:* For master's, comprehensive exam, comprehensive professional portfolio; for PMC, action research project. *Entrance requirements:* For master's, New York State Qualifying Exam, GRE General Test or minimum GPA of 3.0, teaching certificate; for PMC, GRE General Test or minimum GPA of 3.0. Electronic applications accepted. *Faculty research:* Computer applications in education, adolescent special education students, literacy development, inclusive practices for special education students.

St. Thomas University, School of Leadership Studies, Institute for Education, Miami Gardens, FL 33054-6459. Offers earth/space science (Certificate); educational administration (MS, Certificate); educational leadership (Ed D); elementary education (MS); ESOL (Certificate); gifted education (Certificate); instructional technology (MS, Certificate); professional/studies (Certificate); reading (MS, Certificate); special education (MS). *Program availability:* Part-time, evening/weekend. *Degree requirements:* For master's, comprehensive exam; for doctorate, comprehensive exam, thesis/dissertation. *Entrance requirements:* For master's, interview, minimum GPA of 3.0 or GRE; for doctorate, GRE or MAT. Additional exam requirements/recommendations for international students: Required—TOEFL (minimum score 550 paper-based; 79 iBT). Electronic applications accepted.

Saint Xavier University, Graduate Studies, School of Education, Chicago, IL 60655-3105. Offers counseling (MA); curriculum and instruction (MA); early childhood education (MA); educational administration (MA); elementary education (MA); individualized studies (MA), including educational technology, English as a second language (ESL), ISTEM (integrative science, technology, engineering, and math), science education; music education (MA); reading (MA); secondary education (MA); Spanish education (MA); special education (MA); teaching and leadership (MA). *Accreditation:* NCATE. *Program availability:* Part-time, evening/weekend. *Degree requirements:* For master's, thesis or project. *Entrance requirements:* For master's, minimum GPA of 3.0. *Expenses:* Contact institution.

Salem College, Graduate Studies, Winston-Salem, NC 27101. Offers art education (MAT); elementary education (M Ed, MAT); language and literacy (M Ed); middle school education (MAT); organ (MM); piano (MM); school counseling (M Ed); second language studies (MAT); secondary education (MAT); special education (M Ed, MAT). *Accreditation:* NCATE. *Program availability:* Part-time, evening/weekend, online learning. *Degree requirements:* For master's, practicum (MAT), action research project (M Ed). *Entrance requirements:* For master's, minimum GPA of 3.0, two academic/professional recommendations, acceptable criminal background check. Additional exam requirements/recommendations for international students: Recommended—TOEFL. Electronic applications accepted. *Faculty research:* Teacher professional development, adolescent literacy, instructional technology.

Salem State University, School of Graduate Studies, Program in Elementary Education, Salem, MA 01970-5353. Offers M Ed. *Accreditation:* NCATE. *Program availability:* Part-time, evening/weekend. *Entrance requirements:* For master's, GRE or MAT. Additional exam requirements/recommendations for international students: Required—TOEFL (minimum score 550 paper-based; 80 iBT) or IELTS (minimum score 5.5).

Salem State University, School of Graduate Studies, Program in Spanish, Salem, MA 01970-5353. Offers MAT. *Program availability:* Part-time, evening/weekend. *Entrance requirements:* For master's, GRE or MAT. Additional exam requirements/recommendations for international students: Required—TOEFL (minimum score 550 paper-based; 80 iBT) or IELTS (minimum score 5.5).

Samford University, Orlean Beeson School of Education, Birmingham, AL 35229. Offers educational leadership (MSE, Ed D); elementary education (MS Ed, MSE); gifted (MSE); instructional design and technology (MSE); instructional leadership (MSE, Ed S); secondary education (MSE); special education (MSE). *Accreditation:* NCATE. *Program availability:* Part-time, evening/weekend, 100% online, blended/hybrid learning. *Faculty:* 12 full-time (10 women), 16 part-time/adjunct (11 women). *Students:* 156 full-time (111 women), 101 part-time (73 women); includes 106 minority (100 Black or African American, non-Hispanic/Latino; 1 American Indian or Alaska Native, non-Hispanic/Latino; 5 Two or more races, non-Hispanic/Latino), 1 international. Average age 37. 107 applicants, 94% accepted, 65 enrolled. In 2018, 94 master's, 40 doctorates, 11 other advanced degrees awarded. *Degree requirements:* For master's and Ed S, comprehensive exam; for doctorate, comprehensive exam, thesis/dissertation. *Entrance requirements:* For master's, GRE, MAT, PRAXIS II, interview, transcripts, essay, recommendations, teaching certification; for doctorate, resume, transcripts, interview, essay, recommendations; for Ed S, teaching certification, transcripts, essay, interview, recommendations. Additional exam requirements/recommendations for international students: Required—TOEFL (minimum score 90 iBT); Recommended—IELTS (minimum score 6.5). *Application deadline:* For fall admission, 7/15 for domestic and international students; for winter admission, 11/15 for domestic and international students; for spring admission, 11/15 for domestic and international students; for summer admission, 4/15 for domestic and international students. Applications are processed on a rolling basis. Application fee: $35. Electronic applications accepted. *Expenses:* $862 Per Hour $100 School of Education $175 Technology Fee $100 Per Fully Online Class. *Financial support:* In 2018–19, 173 students received support. Scholarships/grants available. Financial award application deadline: 2/15; financial award applicants required to submit FAFSA. *Faculty research:* Principal leadership's and teacher organizational commitment mentoring, professional development, and middle grades leadership coaching and administrator effectiveness character development programs in schools teacher efficacy related STEM and professional growth. *Unit head:* Dr. Howard Finch, Interim Dean, 205-726-2745, E-mail: hfinch@samford.edu. *Application contact:* Brooke Karr, Graduate Admissions Office Coordinator, 205-729-2783, E-mail: kbgilrea@samford.edu.
Website: http://www.samford.edu/education

San Diego State University, Graduate and Research Affairs, College of Education, School of Teacher Education, Program in Elementary Curriculum and Instruction, San Diego, CA 92182. Offers MA. *Accreditation:* NCATE. *Program availability:* Evening/weekend. *Entrance requirements:* For master's, GRE General Test, letters of reference. Additional exam requirements/recommendations for international students: Required—TOEFL. Electronic applications accepted.

San Francisco State University, Division of Graduate Studies, College of Education, Department of Elementary Education, Program in Elementary Education, San Francisco, CA 94132-1722. Offers MA. *Accreditation:* NCATE. *Unit head:* Dr. Stephanie Sisk-Hilton, Chair, 415-338-1562, Fax: 415-338-0567, E-mail: stephsh@sfsu.edu. *Application contact:* Dr. Stephanie Sisk-Hilton, Chair, 415-338-1562, Fax: 415-338-0567, E-mail: stephsh@sfsu.edu.
Website: https://eed.sfsu.edu/

San Jose State University, Program in Elementary Education, San Jose, CA 95192-0001. Offers curriculum and instruction (MA); reading (Certificate). *Accreditation:* NCATE. *Degree requirements:* For master's, thesis or alternative. Electronic applications accepted.

Seton Hill University, Master of Arts Program in Elementary/Middle Level Education, Greensburg, PA 15601. Offers MA. *Program availability:* Part-time, evening/weekend, blended/hybrid learning. *Entrance requirements:* For master's, teacher's certification, 3 letters of recommendation, personal statement, transcripts, resume. Additional exam requirements/recommendations for international students: Required—TOEFL (minimum score 600 paper-based; 100 iBT), IELTS (minimum score 6.5). *Application deadline:* Applications are processed on a rolling basis. Application fee: $0. Electronic applications accepted. *Financial support:* Federal Work-Study, scholarships/grants, and tuition discounts available. Financial award application deadline: 8/15; financial award applicants required to submit FAFSA.
Website: https://www.setonhill.edu/academics/graduate-programs/elementary-middle-level-education-ma/

Shippensburg University of Pennsylvania, School of Graduate Studies, College of Education and Human Services, Department of Teacher Education, Shippensburg, PA 17257-2299. Offers curriculum and instruction (M Ed), including biology, early childhood education, elementary education, geography/earth science, history, mathematics, middle school education, modern languages; reading (M Ed). *Accreditation:* NCATE. *Program availability:* Part-time, evening/weekend, 100% online, blended/hybrid learning. *Faculty:* 12 full-time (9 women), 2 part-time/adjunct (0 women). *Students:* 10 full-time (8 women), 68 part-time (64 women); includes 7 minority (2 Black or African American,

non-Hispanic/Latino; 4 Hispanic/Latino; 1 Two or more races, non-Hispanic/Latino). Average age 31. 41 applicants, 73% accepted, 19 enrolled. In 2018, 34 master's awarded. *Degree requirements:* For master's, comprehensive exam (for some programs), thesis optional, practicum or internship; capstone seminar (for some programs). *Entrance requirements:* For master's, MAT or GRE (if GPA less than 2.75), interview, 3 letters of reference, questionnaire of teaching background and future goals, resume. Additional exam requirements/recommendations for international students: Required—TOEFL (minimum score 550 paper-based; 68 iBT), IELTS (minimum score 6), TOEFL (minimum score 550 paper-based, 68 iBT) or IELTS (minimum score 6). *Application deadline:* For fall admission, 4/1 priority date for domestic students, 4/30 for international students; for spring admission, 9/1 priority date for domestic students, 9/30 for international students; for summer admission, 2/1 priority date for domestic students. Applications are processed on a rolling basis. Application fee: $45. Electronic applications accepted. *Expenses:* Tuition, state resident: part-time $516 per credit. Tuition, nonresident: part-time $750 per credit. *Required fees:* $149 per credit. *Financial support:* In 2018–19, 5 students received support. Career-related internships or fieldwork, scholarships/grants, unspecified assistantships, and resident hall director and student payroll positions available. Support available to part-time students. Financial award application deadline: 3/1; financial award applicants required to submit FAFSA. *Unit head:* Dr. Christine A. Royce, Chairperson, 717-477-1688, Fax: 717-477-4046, E-mail: caroyc@ship.edu. *Application contact:* Maya T. Mapp, Director of Admissions, 717-477-1231, Fax: 717-477-4016, E-mail: mtmapp@ship.edu.
Website: http://www.ship.edu/teacher/

Siena Heights University, Graduate College, Adrian, MI 49221-1796. Offers clinical mental health counseling (MA); educational leadership (Specialist); leadership (MA), including health care leadership, organizational leadership; teacher education (MA), including early childhood education, early childhood education: Montessori, education leadership: principal, elementary education: reading K-12, leadership: higher education, secondary education: reading K-12, special education: cognitive impairment, special education: learning disabilities. *Program availability:* Part-time, evening/weekend. *Faculty:* 10 full-time (6 women), 16 part-time/adjunct (6 women). *Students:* 34 full-time (20 women), 183 part-time (126 women); includes 64 minority (38 Black or African American, non-Hispanic/Latino; 2 American Indian or Alaska Native, non-Hispanic/Latino; 4 Asian, non-Hispanic/Latino; 14 Hispanic/Latino; 6 Two or more races, non-Hispanic/Latino). Average age 36. 97 applicants, 41% accepted, 30 enrolled. In 2018, 72 master's awarded. *Degree requirements:* For master's, thesis, Presentation. *Entrance requirements:* For master's, Minimum GPA of 3.0, current resume, essay, all post-secondary transcripts, 3 letters of reference, conviction disclosure form; copy of teaching certificate (for some education programs); for Specialist, Master's degree, minimum GPA of 3.0, current resume, essay, all post-secondary transcripts, 3 letters of reference, conviction disclosure form; copy of teaching certificate (for some education programs). Additional exam requirements/recommendations for international students: Recommended—TOEFL, IELTS, TWE, TSE. *Application deadline:* Applications are processed on a rolling basis. Application fee: $50. Electronic applications accepted. *Expenses: Tuition:* Full-time $11,340; part-time $7560 per year. *Required fees:* $454; $454 per unit. $227 per semester. One-time fee: $100. Tuition and fees vary according to program. *Financial support:* In 2018–19, 55 students received support. Scholarships/grants, tuition waivers (full and partial), unspecified assistantships, and State of Michigan Scholarships/Grants available. Support available to part-time students. Financial award application deadline: 9/1; financial award applicants required to submit FAFSA. *Unit head:* Dr. Cheryl Betz, Dean, College for Professional Studies and Graduate College, 517-264-7234, Fax: 517-264-7714, E-mail: cbetz@sienaheights.edu. *Application contact:* Elizabeth Brooks, Assistant Director, 517-264-7165, Fax: 517-264-7714, E-mail: ebrooks@sienaheights.edu.
Website: http://www.sienaheights.edu

Sierra Nevada College, Teacher Education Program, Incline Village, NV 89451. Offers advanced teaching and leadership (M Ed); elementary education (MAT); secondary education (MAT). *Program availability:* Part-time, evening/weekend, online learning. *Degree requirements:* For master's, comprehensive exam, thesis, PRAXIS I and II. *Entrance requirements:* For master's, 2 letters of recommendation, minimum GPA of 3.0. Electronic applications accepted.

Simmons University, Gwen Ifill College of Media, Arts, and Humanities, Boston, MA 02115. Offers behavior analysis (MS, PhD, Ed S); children's literature (MA); dietetics (Certificate); elementary education (MAT); English (MA); gender/cultural studies (MA); history (MA); nutrition and health promotion (MS); physical therapy (DPT); public health (MPH); public policy (MPP); special education: moderate and severe disabilities (MS Ed); sports nutrition (Certificate); writing for children (MFA). *Program availability:* Part-time. *Faculty:* 16 full-time (13 women), 4 part-time/adjunct (3 women). *Students:* 5 full-time (all women), 70 part-time (61 women); includes 12 minority (2 Black or African American, non-Hispanic/Latino; 4 Asian, non-Hispanic/Latino; 4 Hispanic/Latino; 2 Two or more races, non-Hispanic/Latino). Average age 29. 84 applicants, 79% accepted, 32 enrolled. In 2018, 24 master's awarded. *Degree requirements:* For master's, thesis optional. *Entrance requirements:* For master's, GRE, bachelor's degree from accredited college or university; minimum B average (preferred). Additional exam requirements/recommendations for international students: Required—TOEFL (minimum score 600 paper-based; 100 iBT). *Application deadline:* For fall admission, 8/1 for domestic and international students; for spring admission, 12/15 for domestic and international students; for summer admission, 5/1 for domestic and international students. Applications are processed on a rolling basis. Application fee: $35. Electronic applications accepted. *Expenses:* $1,085 per credit hour plus fees. *Financial support:* In 2018–19, 14 students received support, including 1 fellowship (averaging $15,360 per year), 13 teaching assistantships (averaging $2,000 per year); scholarships/grants also available. Financial award applicants required to submit FAFSA. *Faculty research:* Film and media studies, postcolonial literature, critical theory, arts and culture. *Unit head:* Dr. Brian Norman, Dean, 617-521-2472, E-mail: brian.norman@simmons.edu. *Application contact:* Patricia Flaherty, Director, Graduate Studies Admission, 617-521-3902, Fax: 617-521-3058, E-mail: gsa@simmons.edu.
Website: https://www.simmons.edu/academics/colleges-schools-departments/ifill

Sinte Gleska University, Graduate Education Program, Mission, SD 57555. Offers elementary education (M Ed). *Program availability:* Part-time, evening/weekend. *Degree requirements:* For master's, thesis. *Entrance requirements:* For master's, 2 years of experience in elementary education, minimum GPA of 2.5, South Dakota elementary education certification. *Faculty research:* American Indian graduate education, teaching of Native American students.

Slippery Rock University of Pennsylvania, Graduate Studies (Recruitment), College of Education, Department of Elementary Education and Early Childhood, Slippery Rock, PA 16057-1383. Offers instructional coach (M Ed); K-12 reading (M Ed); K-12 science and math (M Ed); reading specialist (M Ed). *Accreditation:* NCATE. *Program availability:* Part-time, evening/weekend, online only, 100% online. *Faculty:* 5 full-time (all women). *Students:* 6 full-time (all women), 115 part-time (107 women); includes 3 minority (1 Asian, non-Hispanic/Latino; 2 Hispanic/Latino). Average age 29. 106 applicants, 83% accepted, 45 enrolled. In 2018, 73 master's awarded. *Degree requirements:* For master's, comprehensive exam (for some programs), thesis optional. *Entrance requirements:* For master's, minimum GPA of 3.0, resume, teaching certification, transcripts, letters of recommendation (depending on program). Additional exam requirements/recommendations for international students: Required—TOEFL (minimum score 550 paper-based; 80 iBT). *Application deadline:* For fall admission, 3/1 priority date for domestic students, 5/1 priority date for international students; for spring admission, 10/1 priority date for domestic students, 9/1 priority date for international students. Applications are processed on a rolling basis. Application fee: $25 ($30 for international students). Electronic applications accepted. *Expenses:* Contact institution. *Financial support:* Career-related internships or fieldwork, Federal Work-Study, institutionally sponsored loans, scholarships/grants, tuition waivers (partial), and unspecified assistantships available. Support available to part-time students. Financial award application deadline: 5/1; financial award applicants required to submit FAFSA. *Unit head:* Dr. Suzanne Rose, Graduate Coordinator, 724-738-2042, Fax: 724-738-2779, E-mail: suzanne.rose@sru.edu. *Application contact:* Brandi Weber-Mortimer, Director of Graduate Admissions, 724-738-2051, Fax: 724-738-2146, E-mail: graduate.admissions@sru.edu.
Website: http://www.sru.edu/academics/colleges-and-departments/coe/departments/elementary-education-/-early-childhood/graduate-programs

Smith College, Graduate and Special Programs, Department of Education and Child Study, Program in Elementary Education, Northampton, MA 01063. Offers elementary education (MAT); middle school education (MAT). *Program availability:* Part-time. *Students:* 9 full-time (6 women), 7 part-time (6 women); includes 5 minority (2 Black or African American, non-Hispanic/Latino; 2 Asian, non-Hispanic/Latino; 1 Hispanic/Latino), 2 international. Average age 25. 19 applicants, 89% accepted, 13 enrolled. In 2018, 11 master's awarded. *Entrance requirements:* Additional exam requirements/recommendations for international students: Required—TOEFL (minimum score 595 paper-based; 97 iBT), IELTS (minimum score 7.5). *Application deadline:* For fall admission, 4/15 for domestic students, 1/15 priority date for international students; for spring admission, 12/1 for domestic students. Applications are processed on a rolling basis. Application fee: $60. *Expenses:* The total tuition cost to each M.A.T. student (the full program fee, after 'built-in' scholarship award) is $18,500. *Financial support:* In 2018–19, 15 students received support, including 4 fellowships with full tuition reimbursements available; scholarships/grants and human resources employee benefit also available. Support available to part-time students. Financial award application deadline: 4/15; financial award applicants required to submit CSS PROFILE or FAFSA. *Unit head:* Alan Rudnitsky, Graduate Student Adviser, 413-585-3261, E-mail: arudnits@smith.edu. *Application contact:* Ruth Morgan, Program Coordinator, 413-585-3050, Fax: 413-585-3054, E-mail: gradstdy@smith.edu.
Website: http://www.smith.edu/educ/

South Carolina State University, College of Graduate and Professional Studies, Department of Education, Orangeburg, SC 29117-0001. Offers early childhood education (MAT); education (M Ed); elementary education (M Ed, MAT); English (MAT); general science/biology (MAT); mathematics (MAT); secondary education (M Ed), including biology education, business education, counselor education, English education, home economics education, industrial education, mathematics education, science education, social studies education; special education (M Ed), including emotionally handicapped, learning disabilities, mentally handicapped. *Accreditation:* NCATE. *Program availability:* Part-time, evening/weekend. *Faculty:* 17 full-time (6 women), 12 part-time/adjunct (5 women). *Students:* 42 full-time (32 women), 93 part-time (64 women); includes 121 minority (119 Black or African American, non-Hispanic/Latino; 2 Asian, non-Hispanic/Latino), 2 international. Average age 40. 50 applicants, 98% accepted, 39 enrolled. In 2018, 9 master's awarded. *Degree requirements:* For master's, thesis optional, departmental qualifying exam. *Entrance requirements:* For master's, GRE General Test, NTE, interview, teaching certificate. *Application deadline:* For fall admission, 6/15 priority date for domestic students, 6/15 for international students; for spring admission, 11/1 for domestic and international students. Application fee: $25. Electronic applications accepted. *Expenses: Tuition, area resident:* Full-time $9928; part-time $552 per credit hour. Tuition, state resident: full-time $9928. Tuition, nonresident: full-time $21,038; part-time $1169 per credit hour. *Required fees:* $1532; $85 per credit hour. *Financial support:* Fellowships, career-related internships or fieldwork, Federal Work-Study, and scholarships/grants available. Financial award application deadline: 6/1. *Unit head:* Dr. Charlie Spell, Chair, Department of Education, 803-536-8963, Fax: 803-516-4568, E-mail: cspell@scsu.edu. *Application contact:* Curtis Foskey, Coordinator of Graduate Studies, 803-536-8419, Fax: 803-536-8812, E-mail: cfoskey@scsu.edu.

Southeastern Louisiana University, College of Education, Department of Teaching and Learning, Hammond, LA 70402. Offers curriculum and instruction (M Ed); elementary education (MAT); special education (M Ed); special education: early interventionist (MAT). *Accreditation:* NCATE. *Program availability:* Part-time. *Faculty:* 10 full-time (9 women). *Students:* 23 full-time (18 women), 118 part-time (102 women); includes 20 minority (14 Black or African American, non-Hispanic/Latino; 3 Hispanic/Latino; 3 Two or more races, non-Hispanic/Latino), 1 international. Average age 37. 78 applicants, 71% accepted, 40 enrolled. In 2018, 12 master's awarded. *Degree requirements:* For master's, comprehensive exam (for some programs), thesis (for some programs), action research project, oral defense of research project, portfolio, teaching certificate, minimum cumulative GPA of 3.0. *Entrance requirements:* For master's, GRE (verbal and quantitative), PRAXIS (for MAT), Prospective Education Candidate (PEC) self-assessment survey; competency on a technology performance assessment in education or three-hour graduate-level technology course; orientation seminar. Additional exam requirements/recommendations for international students: Required—TOEFL (minimum score 500 paper-based; 61 iBT). *Application deadline:* For fall admission, 7/15 priority date for domestic students, 6/1 priority date for international students; for spring admission, 12/1 priority date for domestic students, 10/1 priority date for international students. Applications are processed on a rolling basis. Application fee: $20 ($30 for international students). Electronic applications accepted. *Expenses: Tuition, area resident:* Full-time $6684. Tuition, state resident: full-time $6684. Tuition, nonresident: full-time $19,162. *Required fees:* $2097. *Financial support:* In 2018–19, 7 students received support, including 1 fellowship with tuition reimbursement available (averaging $3,500 per year); career-related internships or fieldwork, Federal Work-Study, institutionally sponsored loans, scholarships/grants, and unspecified assistantships also available. Support available to part-time students. Financial award application deadline: 5/1; financial award applicants required to submit FAFSA. *Faculty research:* Early childhood education, STEM education, literacy, special education early intervention, math education. *Total annual research expenditures:* $404,225. *Unit head:* Dr. Colleen Klein-Ezell, Department Head, 985-549-2221, Fax: 985-549-5009, E-mail: colleen.klein-ezell@southeastern.edu. *Application contact:* Dr. Colleen Klein-Ezell, Department Head, 985-549-2221, Fax: 985-549-5009, E-mail: colleen.klein-ezell@southeastern.edu.
Website: http://www.southeastern.edu/acad_research/depts/teach_lrn/index.html

Southeastern University, College of Education, Lakeland, FL 33801-6099. Offers curriculum and instruction (Ed D); educational leadership (M Ed); elementary education (M Ed); exceptional student education (M Ed); exceptional student education/educational therapy (M Ed); kinesiology (M Ed); organizational leadership (Ed D); reading education (M Ed); teaching English to speakers of other languages (M Ed). Electronic applications accepted.

Elementary Education

Southeast Missouri State University, School of Graduate Studies, Department of Elementary, Early and Special Education, Program in Elementary Education, Cape Girardeau, MO 63701-4799. Offers MA. *Accreditation:* NCATE. *Program availability:* Part-time, evening/weekend, online only, 100% online. *Faculty:* 11 full-time (9 women), 1 (woman) part-time/adjunct. *Students:* 1 (woman) full-time, 51 part-time (all women); includes 2 minority (both Black or African American, non-Hispanic/Latino). Average age 31. 21 applicants, 100% accepted, 21 enrolled. In 2018, 24 master's awarded. *Degree requirements:* For master's, comprehensive exam, action research project and presentation. *Entrance requirements:* For master's, state licensure exam or GRE, minimum GPA of 2.75; teaching certificate. Additional exam requirements/recommendations for international students: Required—TOEFL (minimum score 95 iBT), IELTS (minimum score 7), PTE. *Application deadline:* For fall admission, 8/1 for domestic students, 6/1 for international students; for spring admission, 11/21 for domestic students, 10/1 for international students; for summer admission, 5/15 for domestic students. Applications are processed on a rolling basis. Application fee: $30 ($40 for international students). Electronic applications accepted. *Expenses:* Contact institution. *Financial support:* In 2018–19, 2 students received support. Career-related internships or fieldwork, Federal Work-Study, scholarships/grants, traineeships, tuition waivers (full), and unspecified assistantships available. Financial award application deadline: 6/30; financial award applicants required to submit FAFSA. *Faculty research:* Instructional technology, field and clinical experiences, teacher candidate professional dispositions, family engagement in P-12 schools, learning communities. *Unit head:* Dr. Julie Ray, Department of Elementary, Early, and Special Education Chair/Professor, 573-651-2444, E-mail: jaray@semo.edu. *Application contact:* Dr. Min Zou, Assistant Professor, 573-651-2122, E-mail: mzou@semo.edu.
Website: http://www.semo.edu/eese/

Southeast Missouri State University, School of Graduate Studies, Leadership, Middle and Secondary Education, Cape Girardeau, MO 63701-4799. Offers counseling (MA, Ed S), including career counseling (MA), counseling education (Ed S), mental health counseling (MA), school counseling (MA); educational administration (MA, Ed D, Ed S), including educational administration (Ed S), educational leadership (Ed D), elementary administration (MA), higher education administration (MA), secondary administration (MA), teacher leadership (MA, Ed S). *Accreditation:* NCATE. *Program availability:* Part-time, evening/weekend, online only, 100% online, blended/hybrid learning. *Faculty:* 11 full-time (7 women), 6 part-time/adjunct (3 women). *Students:* 45 full-time (28 women), 210 part-time (135 women); includes 22 minority (16 Black or African American, non-Hispanic/Latino; 2 American Indian or Alaska Native, non-Hispanic/Latino; 1 Asian, non-Hispanic/Latino; 3 Two or more races, non-Hispanic/Latino), 13 international. Average age 32. 111 applicants, 100% accepted, 111 enrolled. In 2018, 102 master's, 29 other advanced degrees awarded. *Degree requirements:* For master's and Ed S, comprehensive exam, thesis or alternative, paper; for doctorate, comprehensive exam, thesis/dissertation. *Entrance requirements:* For master's, minimum GPA of 3.5; for doctorate, minimum GPA of 3.7. Additional exam requirements/recommendations for international students: Required—TOEFL (minimum score 550 paper-based; 79 iBT), IELTS (minimum score 6), PTE (minimum score 53). *Application deadline:* For fall admission, 8/1 for domestic students, 6/1 for international students; for spring admission, 11/21 for domestic students, 10/1 for international students; for summer admission, 5/15 for domestic students. Applications are processed on a rolling basis. Application fee: $30 ($40 for international students). Electronic applications accepted. *Expenses:* Contact institution. *Financial support:* In 2018–19, 22 students received support. Career-related internships or fieldwork, Federal Work-Study, scholarships/grants, traineeships, tuition waivers (full), and unspecified assistantships available. Financial award application deadline: 6/30; financial award applicants required to submit FAFSA. *Faculty research:* Mental health counseling; technology in the classroom; administration and student success; school counseling; social justice in leadership and higher education; career counseling; leadership, equity, and social justice in P-12 schools and higher education; gender identity and queer youth; building level and district level leadership; school culture and climate; higher education; equity and social justice; organizational analysis and program planning; global leadership. *Unit head:* Dr. C. P. Gause, Professor/Department Chair, 573-651-2137, Fax: 573-986-6512, E-mail: cgause@semo.edu. *Application contact:* Dr. C. P. Gause, Professor/Department Chair, 573-651-2137, Fax: 573-986-6512, E-mail: cgause@semo.edu.
Website: http://www.semo.edu/eduleadcounsel/

Southern Connecticut State University, School of Graduate Studies, School of Education, Department of Elementary Education, New Haven, CT 06515-1355. Offers classroom teacher specialist (Diploma); educational coach (Diploma); elementary education (MS). *Accreditation:* NCATE. *Program availability:* Part-time, evening/weekend. *Degree requirements:* For master's, thesis or alternative. *Entrance requirements:* For master's, interview, minimum QPA of 2.5; for Diploma, master's degree. Electronic applications accepted.

Southern New Hampshire University, School of Education, Manchester, NH 03106-1045. Offers curriculum and instruction (M Ed), including dyslexia studies and language-based learning disabilities, educational leadership, reading, special education, technology integration; dyslexia studies and language-based learning disabilities (Certificate); early childhood and special education (M Ed); educational leadership (M Ed, Ed D); educational studies (M Ed); elementary and special education (M Ed); field based education (M Ed); higher education administration (MS); teaching English as a foreign language (MS). *Program availability:* Part-time, evening/weekend, online learning. *Degree requirements:* For master's, comprehensive exam (for some programs), thesis or alternative. *Entrance requirements:* For master's, PRAXIS I, minimum GPA of 2.75. Additional exam requirements/recommendations for international students: Required—TOEFL (minimum score 550 paper-based). Electronic applications accepted. *Expenses:* Contact institution.

Southern Oregon University, Graduate Studies, School of Education, Ashland, OR 97520. Offers elementary education (MA Ed, MS Ed), including classroom teacher, early childhood, handicapped learner, reading, supervision; secondary education (MA Ed, MS Ed), including classroom teacher, handicapped learner, reading, supervision; teaching (MAT). *Program availability:* Online learning. *Degree requirements:* For master's, thesis optional. *Entrance requirements:* For master's, GRE General Test, minimum cumulative GPA of 3.0 in the last 90 quarter credits (60 semester credits) of undergraduate coursework. Additional exam requirements/recommendations for international students: Required—TOEFL (minimum score 540 paper-based; 76 iBT), IELTS (minimum score 6), ELPT (minimum score 964) or ELS (minimum score 112). Electronic applications accepted.

Southern University and Agricultural and Mechanical College, Graduate School, College of Humanities and Interdisciplinary Studies, School of Education, Department of Curriculum and Instruction, Baton Rouge, LA 70813. Offers elementary education (M Ed); media (M Ed); secondary education (M Ed). *Degree requirements:* For master's, comprehensive exam, thesis optional. *Entrance requirements:* For master's, GMAT or GRE General Test. Additional exam requirements/recommendations for international students: Required—TOEFL (minimum score 525 paper-based).

Southwestern College, Education Programs, Winfield, KS 67156-2499. Offers curriculum and instruction (M Ed); early childhood education (M Ed); educational leadership (Ed D), including higher education leadership, PK-12 education leadership; special education (M Ed), including high-incidence disabilities, low-incidence disabilities; teaching (MA). *Accreditation:* NCATE. *Program availability:* Part-time, evening/weekend, 100% online, blended/hybrid learning. *Faculty:* 7 full-time (5 women), 14 part-time/adjunct (12 women). *Students:* 6 full-time (5 women), 79 part-time (54 women); includes 11 minority (4 Black or African American, non-Hispanic/Latino; 2 American Indian or Alaska Native, non-Hispanic/Latino; 1 Asian, non-Hispanic/Latino; 3 Hispanic/Latino; 1 Two or more races, non-Hispanic/Latino), 4 international. Average age 38. 31 applicants, 74% accepted, 18 enrolled. In 2018, 24 master's, 8 doctorates awarded. *Degree requirements:* For master's, practicum, portfolio; for doctorate, thesis/dissertation, professional portfolio. *Entrance requirements:* For master's, baccalaureate degree, minimum GPA of 3.0, valid teaching certificate (for special education); for doctorate, GRE if no master's degree, baccalaureate degree with minimum GPA of 3.25 and current teaching experience, or master's degree with minimum GPA of 3.5. Additional exam requirements/recommendations for international students: Required—TOEFL (minimum score 60 paper-based; 70 iBT), IELTS (minimum score 5.5). *Application deadline:* Applications are processed on a rolling basis. Application fee: $40. Electronic applications accepted. *Expenses:* Masters programs are $606 per credit hour, $535 per online credit hour; doctorate program is $639 per credit hour. *Financial support:* In 2018–19, 13 students received support. Unspecified assistantships and employee tuition waivers available. Financial award applicants required to submit FAFSA. *Unit head:* J.K. Campbell, Education Division Chair, 620-229-6115, E-mail: JK.Campbell@sckans.edu. *Application contact:* Jen Caughron, Director of Enrollment Services & Marketing, 888-684-5335 Ext. 3312, Fax: 888-684-5218, E-mail: jennifer.caughron@sckans.edu.
Website: http://www.sckans.edu/graduate/education-med/

Southwestern Oklahoma State University, College of Professional and Graduate Studies, School of Behavioral Sciences and Education, Specialization in Elementary Education, Weatherford, OK 73096-3098. Offers M Ed. *Accreditation:* NCATE. *Program availability:* Part-time, evening/weekend. *Degree requirements:* For master's, exam. *Entrance requirements:* For master's, GRE General Test or minimum undergraduate GPA of 3.0. Additional exam requirements/recommendations for international students: Required—TOEFL (minimum score 550 paper-based), IELTS (minimum score 6.5).

Spalding University, Graduate Studies, College of Education, Programs in Education, Louisville, KY 40203-2188. Offers art teacher education (MAT); business teacher education (MAT); elementary school education (MAT); foreign language (MAT); high school education (MAT); middle school education (MAT); secondary education (MAT); special education (learning and behavioral disorders) (MAT); student guidance counselor (MA); teacher leader (M Ed). *Accreditation:* NCATE. *Program availability:* Part-time, evening/weekend. *Entrance requirements:* For master's, GRE General Test or MAT, interview, letters of recommendation, resume. Additional exam requirements/recommendations for international students: Required—TOEFL (minimum score 535 paper-based). Electronic applications accepted. *Faculty research:* Instructional technology, achievement gap, classroom management, assessment.

Springfield College, Graduate Programs, Programs in Education, Springfield, MA 01109-3797. Offers early childhood education (M Ed); educational studies (M Ed); elementary education (M Ed); secondary education (M Ed); special education (M Ed, CAGS). *Program availability:* Part-time, evening/weekend. *Entrance requirements:* For master's, Massachusetts Tests for Educator Licensure (MTEL). Additional exam requirements/recommendations for international students: Required—TOEFL (minimum score 550 paper-based); Recommended—IELTS (minimum score 7). Electronic applications accepted. *Expenses:* Contact institution.

Spring Hill College, Graduate Programs, Program in Education, Mobile, AL 36608-1791. Offers early childhood education (MAT, MS Ed); educational theory (MS Ed); elementary education (MAT, MS Ed); secondary education (MAT, MS Ed). *Program availability:* Part-time. *Faculty:* 3 full-time (all women). *Students:* 1 full-time (0 women), 8 part-time (5 women); includes 2 minority (1 Hispanic/Latino; 1 Two or more races, non-Hispanic/Latino), 1 international. Average age 32. In 2018, 6 master's awarded. *Degree requirements:* For master's, comprehensive exam, completion of program within 6 calendar years of entrance into graduate studies at Spring Hill; documentation of course field assignments (MS) or completion of internship (MAT). *Entrance requirements:* For master's, GRE, MAT, or PRAXIS (varies by program), bachelor's degree with minimum undergraduate GPA of 3.0; class B certificate (for MS); minimum number of hours in specific fields (for MAT). Additional exam requirements/recommendations for international students: Required—TOEFL (minimum score 550 paper-based; 80 iBT), IELTS (minimum score 6.5), CPE or CAE (minimum score C), Michigan English Language Assessment Battery (minimum score 90). *Application deadline:* For fall admission, 8/1 priority date for domestic and international students; for spring admission, 12/1 priority date for domestic and international students. Applications are processed on a rolling basis. Application fee: $25 ($35 for international students). Electronic applications accepted. *Expenses:* Contact institution. *Financial support:* Fellowships, research assistantships, teaching assistantships, and tuition waivers available. Financial award applicants required to submit FAFSA. *Unit head:* Dr. Lori P. Aultman, Chair of Education, 251-380-3473, Fax: 251-460-2184, E-mail: laultman@shc.edu. *Application contact:* Gary Bracken, Vice President of Enrollment Management, 251-380-3038, Fax: 251-460-2186, E-mail: gbracken@shc.edu.
Website: http://ug.shc.edu/graduate-degrees/master-science-education/

Stanford University, Graduate School of Education, Teacher Education Program, Stanford, CA 94305-2004. Offers elementary education (MAE); secondary education (MAE). *Expenses: Tuition:* Full-time $50,703; part-time $32,970 per year. *Required fees:* $651.

State University of New York at New Paltz, Graduate and Extended Learning School, School of Education, Program in Early Childhood and Childhood Education, New Paltz, NY 12561. Offers childhood education (MS Ed), including early childhood; childhood education 1-6 (MST), including childhood education 1-6. *Accreditation:* NCATE. *Program availability:* Part-time, evening/weekend. *Faculty:* 9 full-time (7 women), 6 part-time/adjunct (all women). *Students:* 32 full-time (29 women), 14 part-time (13 women); includes 8 minority (1 Black or African American, non-Hispanic/Latino; 6 Hispanic/Latino; 1 Two or more races, non-Hispanic/Latino). 20 applicants, 75% accepted, 14 enrolled. In 2018, 29 master's awarded. *Degree requirements:* For master's, comprehensive exam (for some programs), portfolio. *Entrance requirements:* For master's, GRE or MAT (for MST), minimum GPA of 3.0 (3.2 for literacy and special education), New York state teaching certificate (for MS Ed). Additional exam requirements/recommendations for international students: Required—TOEFL (minimum score 550 paper-based; 80 iBT), IELTS (minimum score 6.5). *Application deadline:* For fall admission, 4/1 for domestic and international students; for spring admission, 11/1 priority date for domestic and international students; for summer admission, 4/15 priority date for domestic and international students. Applications are processed on a rolling basis. Application fee: $50. Electronic applications accepted. *Financial support:* Application deadline: 8/1. *Faculty research:* Multi-sensory teaching methods, volunteer tutoring programs for struggling readers, school readiness and transition, math/science/technology, university-school partnerships. *Unit head:* Dr. Aaron Isabelle, Chair, 845-257-2837, E-mail: isabella@newpaltz.edu. *Application contact:* Vika Shock, Assistant

Director of Graduate Admissions, 845-257-3285, Fax: 845-257-3284, E-mail: gradstudies@newpaltz.edu.
Website: http://www.newpaltz.edu/elementaryed/

State University of New York at Oswego, Graduate Studies, School of Education, Department of Curriculum and Instruction, Oswego, NY 13126. Offers adolescence education (MST); art education (MAT); childhood education (MST); curriculum and instruction (MS Ed); literacy education (MS Ed); special education (MS Ed). *Program availability:* Part-time, evening/weekend. *Degree requirements:* For master's, comprehensive exam (for some programs), thesis optional. *Entrance requirements:* For master's, GRE General Test, minimum GPA of 2.7, provisional teaching certificate. Additional exam requirements/recommendations for international students: Required—TOEFL (minimum score 560 paper-based). *Faculty research:* Classroom applications for microcomputers; classroom questioning, wait-time, and achievement; values clarification and academic achievement.

State University of New York at Plattsburgh, School of Education, Health, and Human Services, Program in Early Childhood Education, Plattsburgh, NY 12901-2681. Offers early childhood birth-grade 6 (Advanced Certificate).

State University of New York at Plattsburgh, School of Education, Health, and Human Services, Program in Teacher Education: Adolescence Education, Plattsburgh, NY 12901-2681. Offers adolescence education (MST); biology 7-12 (MST); chemistry 7-12 (MST); earth science 7-12 (MST); English 7-12 (MST); French 7-12 (MST); mathematics 7-12 (MST); physics 7-12 (MST); social studies 7-12 (MST); Spanish 7-12 (MST). *Accreditation:* TEAC. *Program availability:* Part-time, evening/weekend. *Entrance requirements:* For master's, minimum GPA of 2.75. Additional exam requirements/recommendations for international students: Required—TOEFL.

State University of New York at Plattsburgh, School of Education, Health, and Human Services, Program in Teacher Education: Childhood Education, Plattsburgh, NY 12901-2681. Offers childhood education (grades 1-6) (MST). *Accreditation:* TEAC. *Program availability:* Part-time, evening/weekend. *Entrance requirements:* For master's, minimum GPA of 2.75. Additional exam requirements/recommendations for international students: Required—TOEFL.

State University of New York College at Oneonta, Graduate Programs, Division of Education, Department of Elementary Education and Reading, Oneonta, NY 13820-4015. Offers childhood education (MS Ed); literacy education (MS Ed). *Accreditation:* NCATE. *Program availability:* Part-time, evening/weekend. *Entrance requirements:* For master's, GRE General Test.

State University of New York College at Potsdam, School of Education and Professional Studies, Program in Curriculum and Instruction, Potsdam, NY 13676. Offers childhood education (MST); curriculum and instruction (MS Ed). *Accreditation:* NCATE. *Program availability:* Online learning. *Degree requirements:* For master's, thesis (for some programs). *Entrance requirements:* For master's, minimum GPA of 2.75 in last 60 credit hours of undergraduate study. Additional exam requirements/recommendations for international students: Required—TOEFL (minimum score 550 paper-based; 80 iBT), IELTS (minimum score 6). Electronic applications accepted.

State University of New York College at Potsdam, School of Education and Professional Studies, Program in Special Education, Potsdam, NY 13676. Offers adolescence (grades 7-12) (MS Ed); childhood (grades 1-6) (MS Ed); early childhood (birth-grade 2) (MS Ed). *Accreditation:* NCATE. *Program availability:* Part-time. *Degree requirements:* For master's, culminating experience. *Entrance requirements:* For master's, minimum GPA of 3.0 in last 60 hours of course work. Additional exam requirements/recommendations for international students: Required—TOEFL (minimum score 550 paper-based; 80 iBT), IELTS (minimum score 6). Electronic applications accepted.

Stephen F. Austin State University, Graduate School, James I. Perkins College of Education, Department of Elementary Education, Program in Elementary Education, Nacogdoches, TX 75962. Offers M Ed. *Accreditation:* NCATE. *Degree requirements:* For master's, comprehensive exam. *Entrance requirements:* For master's, GRE General Test. Additional exam requirements/recommendations for international students: Required—TOEFL.

Sul Ross State University, Rio Grande College of Sul Ross State University, Alpine, TX 79832. Offers business administration (MBA); teacher education (M Ed), including bilingual education, counseling, educational diagnostics, elementary education, general education, reading, school administration, secondary education. *Program availability:* Part-time, evening/weekend, online learning. *Degree requirements:* For master's, comprehensive exam, thesis optional, minimum GPA of 3.0. *Entrance requirements:* For master's, GMAT or GRE General Test, minimum GPA of 2.5 in last 60 hours of undergraduate work. Additional exam requirements/recommendations for international students: Required—TOEFL.

Tarleton State University, College of Graduate Studies, College of Education, Department of Curriculum and Instruction, Stephenville, TX 76402. Offers curriculum and instruction (M Ed); educational diagnostician (M Ed); elementary education (M Ed); instructional design and technology (M Ed); instructional leadership (M Ed); secondary education (M Ed); special education (M Ed); technology applications (M Ed); technology director (M Ed). *Program availability:* Part-time, evening/weekend. *Faculty:* 11 full-time (10 women), 4 part-time/adjunct (1 woman). *Students:* 16 full-time (14 women), 158 part-time (143 women). Average age 40. 54 applicants, 87% accepted, 41 enrolled. In 2018, 46 master's awarded. *Degree requirements:* For master's, comprehensive exam, thesis (for some programs). *Entrance requirements:* For master's, GRE General Test, minimum GPA of 3.0. Additional exam requirements/recommendations for international students: Required—TOEFL (minimum score 520 paper-based; 69 iBT); Recommended—IELTS (minimum score 6), TSE (minimum score 50). *Application deadline:* For fall admission, 8/15 priority date for domestic students; for spring admission, 1/7 for domestic students. Applications are processed on a rolling basis. Application fee: $50 ($130 for international students). Electronic applications accepted. *Expenses:* Contact institution. *Financial support:* Research assistantships, teaching assistantships, career-related internships or fieldwork, Federal Work-Study, and institutionally sponsored loans available. Support available to part-time students. Financial award application deadline: 5/1; financial award applicants required to submit FAFSA. *Unit head:* Dr. Amber Lynn Diaz, Department Head, 254-968-0730, E-mail: adiaz@tarleton.edu. *Application contact:* Information Contact, 254-968-9104, Fax: 254-968-9670, E-mail: gradoffice@tarleton.edu.
Website: http://www.tarleton.edu/cimasters/

Teachers College, Columbia University, Department of Curriculum and Teaching, New York, NY 10027-6696. Offers curriculum and teaching (Ed M, MA, Ed D); curriculum and teaching: elementary education (MA); curriculum and teaching: secondary education (MA); early childhood education (MA, Ed D); early childhood education: special education (MA); elementary education-gifted extension (MA); elementary inclusive education (MA); gifted education (MA); literacy specialist (MA); secondary inclusive education (MA); special inclusive elementary education (MA). *Program availability:* Part-time, evening/weekend. *Students:* 88 full-time (77 women), 264 part-time (239 women); includes 129 minority (45 Black or African American, non-

Hispanic/Latino; 1 American Indian or Alaska Native, non-Hispanic/Latino; 41 Asian, non-Hispanic/Latino; 28 Hispanic/Latino; 14 Two or more races, non-Hispanic/Latino); 48 international. Average age 30. 460 applicants, 73% accepted, 149 enrolled. Terminal master's awarded for partial completion of doctoral program. *Unit head:* Prof. Daniel Friedrich, Chair, 212-678-3263, E-mail: friedrich@exchange.tc.columbia.edu. *Application contact:* Kelly Sutton-Skinner, Director of Admission & New Student Enrollment, E-mail: kms2237@tc.columbia.edu.

Tennessee State University, The School of Graduate Studies and Research, College of Education, Department of Teaching and Learning, Nashville, TN 37209-1561. Offers curriculum and instruction (M Ed, Ed D); elementary education (M Ed); special education (M Ed). *Accreditation:* NCATE. *Degree requirements:* For doctorate, thesis/dissertation. *Entrance requirements:* For master's, GRE General Test, GRE Subject Test, or MAT, minimum GPA of 2.5; for doctorate, GRE General Test, GRE Subject Test, or MAT, minimum GPA of 3.25. Electronic applications accepted. *Faculty research:* Multicultural education, teacher education reform, whole language, interactive video teaching, English as a second language.

Tennessee Technological University, College of Graduate Studies, College of Education, Department of Curriculum and Instruction, Program in Elementary Education, Cookeville, TN 38505. Offers MA, Ed S. *Accreditation:* NCATE. *Program availability:* Part-time, evening/weekend. *Faculty:* 8 full-time (2 women). *Students:* 6 full-time (5 women), 19 part-time (18 women); includes 1 minority (Black or African American, non-Hispanic/Latino). 5 applicants, 100% accepted, 5 enrolled. *Degree requirements:* For master's and Ed S, comprehensive exam, thesis or alternative. *Entrance requirements:* For master's and Ed S, MAT or GRE. Additional exam requirements/recommendations for international students: Required—TOEFL (minimum score 527 paper-based; 71 iBT), IELTS (minimum score 5.5), PTE (minimum score 48), or TOEIC (Test of English as an International Communication). *Application deadline:* For fall admission, 8/1 for domestic students, 5/1 for international students; for spring admission, 12/1 for domestic students, 10/1 for international students; for summer admission, 5/1 for domestic students, 2/1 for international students. Applications are processed on a rolling basis. Application fee: $35 ($40 for international students). Electronic applications accepted. *Financial support:* Fellowships, research assistantships, teaching assistantships, and career-related internships or fieldwork available. Financial award application deadline: 4/1. *Faculty research:* Educational television art program. *Unit head:* Dr. Jeremy Wendt, Chairperson, 931-372-3181, Fax: 931-372-6270, E-mail: jwendt@tntech.edu. *Application contact:* Shelia K. Kendrick, Coordinator of Graduate Studies, 931-372-3808, Fax: 931-372-3497, E-mail: skendrick@tntech.edu.

Tennessee Technological University, College of Graduate Studies, College of Education, Department of Exercise Science, Physical Education and Wellness, Cookeville, TN 38505. Offers adapted physical education (MA); elementary/middle school physical education (MA); lifetime wellness (MA); sport management (MA). *Accreditation:* NCATE. *Program availability:* Part-time, online learning. *Faculty:* 7 full-time (0 women). *Students:* 12 full-time (10 women), 45 part-time (22 women); includes 8 minority (3 Black or African American, non-Hispanic/Latino; 1 Asian, non-Hispanic/Latino; 2 Hispanic/Latino; 2 Two or more races, non-Hispanic/Latino), 1 international. 43 applicants, 67% accepted, 22 enrolled. In 2018, 17 master's awarded. *Degree requirements:* For master's, comprehensive exam, thesis or alternative. *Entrance requirements:* For master's, MAT or GRE. Additional exam requirements/recommendations for international students: Required—TOEFL (minimum score 527 paper-based; 71 iBT), IELTS (minimum score 5.5), PTE (minimum score 48), or TOEIC (Test of English as an International Communication). *Application deadline:* For fall admission, 8/1 for domestic students, 5/1 for international students; for spring admission, 12/1 for domestic students, 10/1 for international students; for summer admission, 5/1 for domestic students, 2/1 for international students. Applications are processed on a rolling basis. Application fee: $35 ($40 for international students). Electronic applications accepted. *Financial support:* Fellowships, research assistantships, teaching assistantships, and career-related internships or fieldwork available. Financial award application deadline: 4/1. *Unit head:* Dr. Christy Killman, Chairperson, 931-372-3467, Fax: 931-372-6319, E-mail: ckillman@tntech.edu. *Application contact:* Shelia K. Kendrick, Coordinator of Graduate Studies, 931-372-3808, Fax: 931-372-3497, E-mail: skendrick@tntech.edu.

Texas A&M University–Commerce, College of Education and Human Services, Commerce, TX 75429. Offers counseling (M Ed, MS, PhD); early childhood education (M Ed, MS); educational administration (M Ed, MS, Ed D); educational psychology (PhD); educational technology leadership (M Ed, MS); educational technology library science (M Ed, MS); elementary education (M Ed); health, kinesiology and sports studies (MS); higher education (MS, Ed D); psychology (MS); reading (M Ed, MS); school psychology (SSP); secondary education (M Ed, MS); social work (MSW); special education (M Ed, MS); supervision, curriculum and instruction-elementary education (Ed D); training and development (MS). *Program availability:* Part-time, evening/weekend, 100% online, blended/hybrid learning. *Faculty:* 95 full-time (59 women), 29 part-time/adjunct (22 women). *Students:* 356 full-time (295 women), 1,262 part-time (992 women); includes 683 minority (349 Black or African American, non-Hispanic/Latino; 9 American Indian or Alaska Native, non-Hispanic/Latino; 30 Asian, non-Hispanic/Latino; 238 Hispanic/Latino; 57 Two or more races, non-Hispanic/Latino), 9 international. Average age 37. 951 applicants, 42% accepted, 304 enrolled. In 2018, 532 master's, 51 doctorates awarded. *Degree requirements:* For master's, comprehensive exam, thesis optional, departmental qualifying exams (for some programs); for doctorate, comprehensive exam, thesis/dissertation, departmental qualifying exam; for SSP, comprehensive exam. *Entrance requirements:* For master's, GRE General Test, official transcripts, letters of recommendation, resume, statement of goals; for doctorate, GRE General Test, letters of recommendation, statement of goals, writing samples, writing sessions, resumes. Additional exam requirements/recommendations for international students: Required—TOEFL (minimum score 550 paper-based; 79 iBT), IELTS (minimum score 6), PTE (minimum score 53). *Application deadline:* For fall admission, 6/1 priority date for international students; for spring admission, 10/15 priority date for international students; for summer admission, 3/15 priority date for international students. Applications are processed on a rolling basis. Application fee: $50 ($75 for international students). Electronic applications accepted. *Expenses: Tuition, area resident:* Full-time $3630. Tuition, state resident: full-time $3630. Tuition, nonresident: full-time $11,100. *International tuition:* $11,100 full-time. *Required fees:* $2794. Tuition and fees vary according to course load, degree level and program. *Financial support:* In 2018–19, 116 students received support, including 94 research assistantships with partial tuition reimbursements available (averaging $3,863 per year), 38 teaching assistantships with partial tuition reimbursements available (averaging $4,728 per year); career-related internships or fieldwork, Federal Work-Study, institutionally sponsored loans, scholarships/grants, health care benefits, and unspecified assistantships also available. Financial award application deadline: 5/1; financial award applicants required to submit FAFSA. *Faculty research:* Cognitive and bilingual education, positive behavioral intervention, literacy, math readiness. *Total annual research expenditures:* $1.1 million. *Unit head:* Dr. Madeline Justice, Interim Dean, 903-886-5181, Fax: 903-886-5905, E-mail: madeline.justice@tamuc.edu. *Application contact:* Vicky Turner, Doctoral Degree and Special Programs Coordinator, 903-886-5167, E-mail: vicky.turner@tamuc.edu.
Website: http://www.tamuc.edu/academics/graduateSchool/programs/education/default.aspx

Elementary Education

Texas A&M University–Commerce, College of Humanities, Social Sciences and Arts, Commerce, TX 75429. Offers applied criminology (MS); applied linguistics (MA, MS); art (MA, MFA); computational linguistics (Graduate Certificate); creative writing (Graduate Certificate); criminal justice management (Graduate Certificate); criminal justice studies (Graduate Certificate); English (MA, MS, PhD); film studies (Graduate Certificate); history (MA, MS); history of Christianity (Graduate Certificate); Holocaust studies (Graduate Certificate); homeland security (Graduate Certificate); music (MM); music performance (MM); political science (MA, MS); public history (Graduate Certificate); sociology (MS); Spanish (MA); studies in children's and adolescent literature and culture (Graduate Certificate); teaching English to speakers of other languages (Graduate Certificate); theater (MA, MS); world history (Graduate Certificate). *Program availability:* Part-time. *Faculty:* 50 full-time (26 women), 11 part-time/adjunct (2 women). *Students:* 125 full-time (83 women), 393 part-time (278 women); includes 197 minority (75 Black or African American, non-Hispanic/Latino; 2 American Indian or Alaska Native, non-Hispanic/Latino; 13 Asian, non-Hispanic/Latino; 92 Hispanic/Latino; 1 Native Hawaiian or other Pacific Islander, non-Hispanic/Latino; 14 Two or more races, non-Hispanic/Latino), 16 international. Average age 37. 261 applicants, 46% accepted, 106 enrolled. In 2018, 124 master's, 8 doctorates awarded. *Degree requirements:* For master's, one foreign language, comprehensive exam, thesis (for some programs); for doctorate, one foreign language, comprehensive exam, thesis/dissertation, departmental qualifying exam. *Entrance requirements:* For master's, GRE General Test, official transcripts, letters of recommendation, resume, statement of goals; for doctorate, GRE General Test, official transcripts, letters of recommendation, statement of goals, writing samples, writing sessions, resumes. Additional exam requirements/recommendations for international students: Required—TOEFL (minimum score 550 paper-based; 79 iBT), IELTS (minimum score 6), PTE (minimum score 53). *Application deadline:* For fall admission, 6/1 priority date for international students; for spring admission, 10/15 priority date for international students; for summer admission, 3/15 priority date for international students. Applications are processed on a rolling basis. Application fee: $50 ($75 for international students). Electronic applications accepted. *Expenses: Tuition, area resident:* Full-time $3630. Tuition, state resident: full-time $3630. Tuition, nonresident: full-time $11,100. *International tuition:* $11,100 full-time. *Required fees:* $2794. Tuition and fees vary according to course load, degree level and program. *Financial support:* In 2018–19, 39 students received support, including 18 research assistantships with partial tuition reimbursements available (averaging $3,231 per year), 136 teaching assistantships with partial tuition reimbursements available (averaging $4,053 per year); Federal Work-Study, institutionally sponsored loans, scholarships/grants, health care benefits, and unspecified assistantships also available. Financial award application deadline: 5/1; financial award applicants required to submit FAFSA. *Unit head:* Dr. William F. Kuracina, Interim Dean, 903-886-5166, Fax: 903-886-5774, E-mail: william.kuracina@tamuc.edu. *Application contact:* Vicky Turner, Doctoral Degree and Special Programs Coordinator, 903-886-5167, E-mail: vicky.turner@tamuc.edu.
Website: http://www.tamuc.edu/academics/colleges/humanitiesSocialSciencesArts/

Texas A&M University–Corpus Christi, College of Graduate Studies, College of Education and Human Development, Program in Elementary Education, Corpus Christi, TX 78412. Offers MS. *Program availability:* Part-time, evening/weekend, online learning. *Degree requirements:* For master's, comprehensive exam, capstone experience. *Entrance requirements:* For master's, minimum GPA of 3.0 in last 60 hours. Additional exam requirements/recommendations for international students: Required—TOEFL (minimum score 550 paper-based; 79 iBT), IELTS (minimum score 6.5). Electronic applications accepted.

Texas State University, The Graduate College, College of Education, Program in Elementary Education, San Marcos, TX 78666. Offers M Ed, MA. *Program availability:* Part-time, evening/weekend. *Faculty:* 13 full-time (11 women), 2 part-time/adjunct (1 woman). *Students:* 59 full-time (53 women), 76 part-time (69 women); includes 54 minority (8 Black or African American, non-Hispanic/Latino; 6 Asian, non-Hispanic/Latino; 39 Hispanic/Latino; 1 Two or more races, non-Hispanic/Latino), 6 international. Average age 30. 78 applicants, 67% accepted, 38 enrolled. In 2018, 49 master's awarded. *Degree requirements:* For master's, comprehensive exam, thesis (for some programs). *Entrance requirements:* For master's, baccalaureate degree from regionally-accredited institution with minimum GPA of 2.75 in last 60 hours of course work; a statement of purpose; 3 letters of recommendation. Additional exam requirements/recommendations for international students: Required—TOEFL (minimum score 550 paper-based; 78 iBT), IELTS (minimum score 6.5), TOEFL (minimum iBT scores: 22 listening, 22 reading, 24 speaking, 21 writing). *Application deadline:* For fall admission, 2/1 priority date for domestic and international students; for spring admission, 10/15 for domestic students, 10/1 for international students; for summer admission, 4/15 for domestic students, 3/15 for international students. Applications are processed on a rolling basis. Application fee: $55 ($90 for international students). Electronic applications accepted. *Expenses:* Tuition, state resident: full-time $8102; part-time $4051 per semester. Tuition, nonresident: full-time $18,229; part-time $9115 per semester. *International tuition:* $18,229 full-time. *Required fees:* $2116; $120 per credit hour. Tuition and fees vary according to course load. *Financial support:* In 2018–19, 39 students received support, including 18 teaching assistantships (averaging $13,500 per year); research assistantships, career-related internships or fieldwork, Federal Work-Study, institutionally sponsored loans, scholarships/grants, and unspecified assistantships also available. Support available to part-time students. Financial award application deadline: 1/15; financial award applicants required to submit FAFSA. *Faculty research:* Multi-cultural teaching; Improving Teaching for English Learners; the use of literature in science instruction; leadership and mentoring; aesthetics; Cultivating change through participatory action research; Advocacy and effective professional development; Classroom Instruction and Implementation;. *Unit head:* Dr. Cheryll Dennis, Graduate Advisor, 512-716-4533, Fax: 512-245-7911, E-mail: elemedgrad@txstate.edu. *Application contact:* Dr. Andrea Golato, Dean of Graduate School, 512-245-2581, Fax: 512-245-8365, E-mail: gradcollege@txstate.edu.
Website: http://www.education.txstate.edu/ci/degrees-programs/graduate/elementary-education.html

Texas State University, The Graduate College, College of Education, Program in Elementary Education - Bilingual/Bicultural, San Marcos, TX 78666. Offers M Ed, MA. *Program availability:* Part-time. *Faculty:* 5 full-time (4 women), 1 (woman) part-time/adjunct. *Students:* 5 part-time (all women); all minorities (all Hispanic/Latino). Average age 36. 2 applicants, 50% accepted, 1 enrolled. In 2018, 3 master's awarded. *Degree requirements:* For master's, comprehensive exam, thesis (for some programs). *Entrance requirements:* For master's, baccalaureate degree from regionally-accredited institution with minimum GPA of 2.75 in last 60 hours of course work; meeting with bilingual coordinator to ensure proficiency in written and spoken Spanish; statement of purpose; three letters of recommendation. Additional exam requirements/recommendations for international students: Required—TOEFL (minimum score 550 paper-based; 78 iBT), IELTS (minimum score 6.5). *Application deadline:* For fall admission, 2/1 priority date for domestic and international students; for spring admission, 10/15 for domestic students, 10/1 for international students; for summer admission, 4/15 for domestic students, 3/15 for international students. Applications are processed on a rolling basis. Application fee: $55 ($90 for international students). Electronic applications accepted. *Expenses:* Tuition, state resident: full-time $8102; part-time $4051 per semester. Tuition, nonresident: full-time $18,229; part-time $9115 per semester. *International tuition:* $18,229 full-time. *Required fees:* $2116; $120 per credit hour. Tuition and fees vary according to course load. *Financial support:* Research assistantships, teaching assistantships, career-related internships or fieldwork, Federal Work-Study, institutionally sponsored loans, scholarships/grants, and unspecified assistantships available. Support available to part-time students. Financial award application deadline: 1/15; financial award applicants required to submit FAFSA. *Faculty research:* Examining five problem solving process skills in subtraction in limited English proficient students; Expanding research approaches in underserved communities; Transformative Learning In Living and Working Abroad. *Unit head:* Dr. Charise Pimentel, Graduate Advisor, 512-245-3678, Fax: 512-245-7911, E-mail: cp26@txstate.edu. *Application contact:* Dr. Andrea Golato, Dean of Graduate School, 512-245-2581, Fax: 512-245-8365, E-mail: gradcollege@txstate.edu.
Website: http://www.gradcollege.txstate.edu/programs/bilingual-bicultural.html

Texas State University, The Graduate College, College of Education, Program in Reading Education, San Marcos, TX 78666. Offers early childhood-12 reading specialist (M Ed). *Program availability:* Part-time, evening/weekend. *Faculty:* 12 full-time (11 women), 1 (woman) part-time/adjunct. *Students:* 1 (woman) full-time, 9 part-time (8 women); includes 5 minority (1 Black or African American, non-Hispanic/Latino; 4 Hispanic/Latino). Average age 36. 5 applicants, 80% accepted, 4 enrolled. In 2018, 9 master's awarded. *Degree requirements:* For master's, comprehensive exam. *Entrance requirements:* For master's, baccalaureate degree from regionally-accredited institution with minimum GPA of 3.0 in last 60 hours of course work, statement of purpose, official teaching certificate. Additional exam requirements/recommendations for international students: Required—TOEFL, IELTS, TOEFL (minimum iBT scores: 22 listening, 22 reading, 24 speaking, 21 writing). *Application deadline:* For fall admission, 2/1 priority date for domestic and international students; for spring admission, 10/15 priority date for domestic students, 10/1 for international students; for summer admission, 4/15 for domestic students, 3/15 for international students. Applications are processed on a rolling basis. Application fee: $55 ($90 for international students). Electronic applications accepted. *Expenses:* Tuition, state resident: full-time $8102; part-time $4051 per semester. Tuition, nonresident: full-time $18,229; part-time $9115 per semester. *International tuition:* $18,229 full-time. *Required fees:* $2116; $120 per credit hour. Tuition and fees vary according to course load. *Financial support:* In 2018–19, 5 students received support. Research assistantships, teaching assistantships, career-related internships or fieldwork, Federal Work-Study, institutionally sponsored loans, scholarships/grants, and unspecified assistantships available. Support available to part-time students. Financial award application deadline: 1/15; financial award applicants required to submit FAFSA. *Faculty research:* Reciprocal Teaching; Instructional design for "long-term English learners; Bilingual students' linguistic experiences and literacy instruction; motivation to read; teacher perceptions of teaching literacy; Oral History methodology; literacies of linguistically and culturally diverse children, families, and communities; developing reading through mentoring. *Total annual research expenditures:* $91,671. *Unit head:* Dr. Jesse Gainer, Graduate Advisor, 512-245-3534, Fax: 512-245-8365, E-mail: jg51@txstate.edu. *Application contact:* Dr. Andrea Golato, Dean of Graduate School, 512-245-2581, Fax: 512-245-8365, E-mail: gradcollege@txstate.edu.
Website: http://www.education.txstate.edu/ci/degrees-certifications/graduate/reading.html

Texas Tech University, Graduate School, College of Education, Department of Curriculum and Instruction, Lubbock, TX 79409-1071. Offers bilingual education (M Ed); curriculum and instruction (M Ed, PhD); elementary education (M Ed); language/literacy education (M Ed); multidisciplinary science (MS); secondary education (M Ed). *Accreditation:* NCATE. *Program availability:* Part-time, evening/weekend, online learning. *Faculty:* 17 full-time (11 women), 1 (woman) part-time/adjunct. *Students:* 48 full-time (41 women), 265 part-time (220 women); includes 103 minority (25 Black or African American, non-Hispanic/Latino; 9 Asian, non-Hispanic/Latino; 64 Hispanic/Latino; 5 Two or more races, non-Hispanic/Latino), 27 international. Average age 40. 101 applicants, 65% accepted, 51 enrolled. In 2018, 26 master's, 21 doctorates awarded. Terminal master's awarded for partial completion of doctoral program. *Degree requirements:* For master's, comprehensive exam (for some programs), thesis optional; for doctorate, comprehensive exam, thesis/dissertation. *Entrance requirements:* For master's, bachelor's degree; resume; letter of intent; academic writing sample; 2 letters of recommendation; for doctorate, GRE, master's degree; resume; letter of intent; academic writing sample; 3 letters of recommendation. Additional exam requirements/recommendations for international students: Required—TOEFL (minimum score 550 paper-based; 79 iBT). *Application deadline:* For fall admission, 6/1 priority date for domestic students, 1/15 priority date for international students; for spring admission, 9/1 priority date for domestic students, 6/15 priority date for international students. Applications are processed on a rolling basis. Application fee: $65. Electronic applications accepted. *Expenses:* Contact institution. *Financial support:* In 2018–19, 142 students received support, including 136 fellowships (averaging $2,895 per year), 28 research assistantships (averaging $12,296 per year), 7 teaching assistantships (averaging $14,175 per year); Federal Work-Study, institutionally sponsored loans, scholarships/grants, health care benefits, and unspecified assistantships also available. Support available to part-time students. Financial award application deadline: 2/1; financial award applicants required to submit FAFSA. *Faculty research:* Teacher education, curriculum studies, bilingual education, science and math education, language and literacy education. *Total annual research expenditures:* $79,025. *Unit head:* Dr. Jerry Dwyer, Professor, Interim Department Chair, 806-834-7399, Fax: 806-742-2179, E-mail: jerry.dwyer@ttu.edu. *Application contact:* Brandi Stephens, Graduate Academic Advisor, 806-834-4554, Fax: 806-742-2179, E-mail: brandi.stephens@ttu.edu.
Website: www.educ.ttu.edu

Towson University, College of Education, Program in Elementary Education, Towson, MD 21252-0001. Offers M Ed. *Accreditation:* NCATE. *Program availability:* Part-time, evening/weekend. *Entrance requirements:* For master's, minimum GPA of 3.0, bachelor's degree in education, teaching certification or eligibility for certification. Electronic applications accepted. *Expenses: Tuition, area resident:* Full-time $9196; part-time $418 per unit. Tuition, state resident: full-time $9196; part-time $418 per unit. Tuition, nonresident: full-time $19,030; part-time $865 per unit. *International tuition:* $19,030 full-time. *Required fees:* $3102; $141 per year. $423 per term. Tuition and fees vary according to campus/location and program.

Towson University, College of Education, Program in Teaching, Towson, MD 21252-0001. Offers early childhood education (MAT); elementary education (MAT); secondary education (MAT); special education (MAT). *Entrance requirements:* For master's, ACT, GRE, PRAXIS I or SAT, 2 letters of reference, resume, minimum GPA of 3.0, essay. Electronic applications accepted. *Expenses: Tuition, area resident:* Full-time $9196; part-time $418 per unit. Tuition, state resident: full-time $9196; part-time $418 per unit. Tuition, nonresident: full-time $19,030; part-time $865 per unit. *International tuition:* $19,030 full-time. *Required fees:* $3102; $141 per year. $423 per term. Tuition and fees vary according to campus/location and program.

Trevecca Nazarene University, Graduate Education Program, Nashville, TN 37210-2877. Offers accountability and instructional leadership (Ed S); curriculum and instruction for Christian school educators (M Ed); curriculum and instruction K-12 (M Ed); educational leadership (M Ed); English second language (M Ed); library and information science (MLI Sc); special education: visual impairments (M Ed); teaching (MAT), including teaching 6-12, teaching K-5. *Accreditation:* NCATE. *Program availability:* Part-time, evening/weekend, online learning. *Degree requirements:* For master's, comprehensive exam, exit assessment/e-portfolio. *Entrance requirements:* For master's, GRE or MAT; PRAXIS (for MAT), minimum GPA of 3.0, official transcript from regionally-accredited institution, references, interview, writing sample, at least 3 years' successful teaching experience (for M Ed in educational leadership); for Ed S, GRE or MAT, master's degree with minimum GPA of 3.0, official transcript from regionally accredited institution, at least 3 years' successful teaching experience, interview, writing sample, background and fingerprinting check, recommendations. Additional exam requirements/recommendations for international students: Required—TOEFL (minimum score 550 paper-based). Electronic applications accepted. *Expenses:* Contact institution.

Trinity Washington University, School of Education, Washington, DC 20017-1094. Offers clinical mental health counseling (MA); early childhood education (MAT); educating for change (M Ed); educational administration (MSA); elementary education (MAT); reading (M Ed); school counseling (MA); secondary education (MAT), including English, social studies; special education (MAT). *Accreditation:* NCATE. *Program availability:* Part-time, evening/weekend. *Degree requirements:* For master's, thesis (for some programs), capstone project(s). *Entrance requirements:* For master's, PRAXIS I, minimum GPA of 2.8. Additional exam requirements/recommendations for international students: Required—TOEFL (minimum score 550 paper-based). *Faculty research:* Technology, literacy, special education, organizations, inclusion models.

Troy University, Graduate School, College of Education, Program in K–6 Elementary and Collaborative Education, Troy, AL 36082. Offers MS, Ed S. *Accreditation:* NCATE. *Program availability:* Part-time, evening/weekend. *Faculty:* 5 full-time (3 women), 6 part-time/adjunct (5 women). *Students:* 38 full-time (35 women), 45 part-time (40 women); includes 24 minority (23 Black or African American, non-Hispanic/Latino; 1 Hispanic/Latino). Average age 34. 79 applicants, 76% accepted, 43 enrolled. In 2018, 2 master's awarded. *Degree requirements:* For master's, comprehensive exam, thesis. *Entrance requirements:* For master's, GRE (minimum score of 850 on old exam or 290 on new exam), GMAT (minimum score of 380), or MAT (minimum score of 385), bachelor's degree; minimum undergraduate GPA of 2.5 or 3.0 on last 30 semester hours, letter of recommendation; for Ed S, GRE (minimum score of 850 on old exam or 286 on new exam) or GMAT (minimum score of 380), Alabama Class A certificate or equivalent, master's degree, minimum graduate GPA of 3.0. Additional exam requirements/recommendations for international students: Required—TOEFL (minimum score 523 paper-based; 70 iBT), IELTS (minimum score 5.5). *Application deadline:* Applications are processed on a rolling basis. Application fee: $50. Electronic applications accepted. *Expenses: Tuition, area resident:* Full-time $425; part-time $425 per credit hour. Tuition, state resident: full-time $425; part-time $425 per credit hour. Tuition, nonresident: full-time $850; part-time $850 per credit hour. *International tuition:* $850 full-time. *Required fees:* $50 per semester. Tuition and fees vary according to campus/location and program. *Financial support:* Fellowships, career-related internships or fieldwork, and scholarships/grants available. Support available to part-time students. Financial award applicants required to submit FAFSA. *Unit head:* Dr. Fred Figliano, Assistant Professor, Chair, Teacher Education, 334-808-6509, E-mail: ffigliano@troy.edu. *Application contact:* Jessica A. Kimbro, Assistant Director of Graduate Programs, 334-670-3189, E-mail: jacord@troy.edu.

Tufts University, Graduate School of Arts and Sciences, Department of Education, Program in Education, Medford, MA 02155. Offers educational studies (MA); elementary education (MAT); middle and secondary education (MAT); museum education (MA); secondary education (MA); STEM education (MS, PhD). *Program availability:* Part-time. *Degree requirements:* For master's, thesis optional. *Entrance requirements:* For master's, GRE General Test, portfolio (for art education only); for doctorate, GRE General Test, writing sample. Additional exam requirements/recommendations for international students: Required—TOEFL (minimum score 550 paper-based; 80 iBT), IELTS (minimum score 6.5). Electronic applications accepted. *Expenses:* Contact institution.

Union College, Graduate Programs, Department of Education, Program in Elementary Education, Barbourville, KY 40906-1499. Offers MA. *Degree requirements:* For master's, thesis optional. *Entrance requirements:* For master's, GRE General Test, NTE.

Universidad del Este, Graduate School, Carolina, PR 00984. Offers accounting (MBA); adult education (M Ed); agribusiness (MBA); criminal justice and criminology (MA); curriculum and instruction - early education (M Ed); curriculum and instruction - elementary (M Ed); curriculum and instruction - English (M Ed); curriculum and instruction - Spanish (M Ed); human resources (MBA); information security management (MBA); information technology and Web business development (MBA); management (MBA); public policy (MPA); social work (MA), including clinical social work; special education (M Ed); strategic leadership (MBA).

Universidad Metropolitana, School of Education, Program in Teaching of Physical Education, San Juan, PR 00928-1150. Offers teaching of adult physical education (M Ed); teaching of elementary physical education (M Ed); teaching of secondary physical education (M Ed). *Degree requirements:* For master's, thesis or alternative. *Entrance requirements:* For master's, EXADEP, interview. Electronic applications accepted.

Université de Sherbrooke, Faculty of Education, Program in Elementary Education, Sherbrooke, QC J1K 2R1, Canada. Offers M Ed, Diploma. *Program availability:* Part-time, evening/weekend. *Degree requirements:* For master's, thesis.

University at Buffalo, the State University of New York, Graduate School, Graduate School of Education, Department of Learning and Instruction, Buffalo, NY 14260. Offers biology education (Ed M, Certificate); chemistry education (Ed M, Certificate); childhood education (Ed M); childhood education with bilingual extension (Ed M); college teaching (Advanced Certificate); curriculum, instruction and the science of learning (PhD); early childhood education (Ed M); early childhood education with bilingual extension (Ed M); earth science education (Ed M, Certificate); education and technology (Ed M); education studies (Ed M); educational technology and new literacies (Certificate); educational technology and new literacies (Advanced Certificate); elementary education (Ed D); English education (Ed M, Certificate); English education studies (Ed M); English for speakers of other languages (Ed M); foreign and second language education (PhD); French education (Ed M, Certificate); German education (Ed M, Certificate); gifted education (Certificate); Latin education (Ed M, Certificate); literacy education studies (Ed M); literacy specialist (Ed M); literacy teaching and learning (Certificate); mathematics education (Ed M, Certificate); music education (Ed M, Certificate); music education studies (Ed M); music learning theory (Advanced Certificate); online education (Advanced Certificate); physics education (Ed M, Certificate); science and the public (Ed M); social studies education (Ed M, Certificate); Spanish education (Ed M, Certificate); special education (PhD); teaching English to speakers of other languages (Ed M). *Program availability:* Part-time, evening/weekend, 100% online. *Faculty:* 31 full-time (22 women), 41 part-time/adjunct (27 women). *Students:* 161 full-time (107 women), 369 part-time (260 women); includes 76 minority (26 Black or African American, non-Hispanic/Latino; 3 American Indian or Alaska Native, non-Hispanic/Latino; 30 Asian, non-Hispanic/Latino; 14 Hispanic/Latino; 3 Two or more races, non-Hispanic/Latino), 41 international. Average age 34. 368 applicants, 70% accepted, 179 enrolled. In 2018, 100 master's, 26 doctorates, 19 other advanced degrees awarded. *Degree requirements:* For master's, comprehensive exam; for doctorate, thesis/dissertation, research analysis exam, research experience. *Entrance requirements:* For master's, letters of reference; for doctorate, GRE General Test or MAT, interview, writing sample, letters of recommendation. Additional exam requirements/recommendations for international students: Required—TOEFL (minimum score 600 paper-based; 96 iBT), IELTS (minimum score 6.5), PTE (minimum score 55). *Application deadline:* For fall admission, 2/1 priority date for domestic and international students; for spring admission, 11/15 priority date for domestic students, 10/1 for international students. Applications are processed on a rolling basis. Application fee: $50. Electronic applications accepted. *Financial support:* In 2018–19, 42 fellowships (averaging $5,181 per year), 44 research assistantships with tuition reimbursements (averaging $10,908 per year) were awarded; teaching assistantships, career-related internships or fieldwork, Federal Work-Study, institutionally sponsored loans, scholarships/grants, tuition waivers (full and partial), and unspecified assistantships also available. Financial award application deadline: 2/28; financial award applicants required to submit FAFSA. *Faculty research:* Science assessment, foreign language teaching and learning, early learning, new literacies, gender and education. *Total annual research expenditures:* $413,233. *Unit head:* Dr. Julie Gorlewski, Department Chair, 716-645-2455, Fax: 716-645-3161, E-mail: jgorlews@buffalo.edu. *Application contact:* Renad Aref, Assistant Director of Admission Recruitment, 716-645-2110, Fax: 716-645-7937, E-mail: gseinfo@buffalo.edu.
Website: http://ed.buffalo.edu/teaching.html

The University of Akron, Graduate School, College of Education, Department of Curricular and Instructional Studies, Program in Elementary Education - Literacy Option, Akron, OH 44325. Offers MA. *Accreditation:* NCATE. *Degree requirements:* For master's, comprehensive exam, thesis optional. *Entrance requirements:* For master's, valid teaching license. Additional exam requirements/recommendations for international students: Required—TOEFL (minimum score 79 iBT), IELTS (minimum score 6.5). Electronic applications accepted.

The University of Alabama, Graduate School, College of Education, Department of Curriculum and Instruction, Tuscaloosa, AL 35487. Offers elementary education (MA, Ed D, PhD, Ed S); secondary education (MA, Ed D, PhD, Ed S). *Program availability:* Part-time, evening/weekend, 100% online, blended/hybrid learning. *Degree requirements:* For master's, comprehensive exam, thesis (for some programs); for doctorate, comprehensive exam, thesis/dissertation; for Ed S, comprehensive exam, thesis. *Entrance requirements:* For master's and Ed S, MAT and/or GRE; for doctorate, GRE. Additional exam requirements/recommendations for international students: Recommended—TOEFL (minimum score 550 paper-based), IELTS (minimum score 6.5). Electronic applications accepted. *Faculty research:* Teacher education, diversity, integration of curriculum, technology, pedagogical content knowledge.

The University of Alabama at Birmingham, School of Education, Program in Elementary Education, Birmingham, AL 35294. Offers MA Ed. *Accreditation:* NCATE. *Program availability:* Part-time, online learning. *Degree requirements:* For master's, thesis optional. *Entrance requirements:* For master's, GRE General Test or MAT. Electronic applications accepted. *Expenses: Tuition, area resident:* Full-time $8100; part-time $8100 per year. Tuition, state resident: full-time $8100. Tuition, nonresident: full-time $19,188; part-time $19,188 per year. Tuition and fees vary according to program.

University of Alaska Southeast, Graduate Programs, Program in Education, Juneau, AK 99801. Offers educational leadership (M Ed); elementary education (MAT); learning design and technology (M Ed); mathematics education (M Ed); reading specialist (M Ed); secondary education (MAT); special education (M Ed, MAT). *Accreditation:* NCATE. *Program availability:* Part-time, evening/weekend, online learning. *Degree requirements:* For master's, comprehensive exam or project, portfolio. *Entrance requirements:* For master's, PRAXIS, minimum GPA of 3.0, writing sample, letters of recommendation. Electronic applications accepted. *Faculty research:* Applied classroom research, culturally responsive practices, action research, teaching effectiveness.

University of Alberta, Faculty of Graduate Studies and Research, Department of Elementary Education, Edmonton, AB T6G 2E1, Canada. Offers M Ed, Ed D, PhD. *Program availability:* Part-time, evening/weekend, online learning. *Degree requirements:* For master's, thesis (for some programs); for doctorate, thesis/dissertation. *Entrance requirements:* For master's and doctorate, 1 year of teaching experience, minimum GPA of 6.5 on a 9.0 scale. *Faculty research:* Literacy education, early childhood education, teacher education, curriculum studies, instructional studies.

The University of Arizona, College of Education, Department of Teaching, Learning and Sociocultural Studies, Program in Teaching and Teacher Education, Tucson, AZ 85721. Offers M Ed, MA, PhD. *Program availability:* Part-time, evening/weekend. *Degree requirements:* For master's, thesis optional; for doctorate, comprehensive exam, thesis/dissertation. *Entrance requirements:* For master's, writing sample, 1 year of teaching experience, 3 letters of recommendation; for doctorate, GRE General Test (minimum score 1000), minimum GPA of 3.5, 2 years of teaching experience, 3 letters of recommendation, writing sample. Additional exam requirements/recommendations for international students: Required—TOEFL (minimum score 550 paper-based; 79 iBT). Electronic applications accepted. *Faculty research:* Staff development, science education, environmental education, math education.

University of Arkansas at Pine Bluff, School of Education, Pine Bluff, AR 71601-2799. Offers elementary education (M Ed); secondary education (M Ed), including English education, mathematics education, science education, social studies education; teaching (MAT). *Accreditation:* NCATE. *Program availability:* Part-time, evening/weekend. *Degree requirements:* For master's, comprehensive exam. *Entrance requirements:* For master's, GRE, minimum GPA of 2.75, NTE or Standard Arkansas Teaching Certificate. *Faculty research:* Teacher certification, accreditation, assessment, standards, portfolio development, rehabilitation, technology.

University of Bridgeport, School of Education, Department of Education, Bridgeport, CT 06604. Offers education (MS); educational management (Ed D, Diploma), including intermediate administrator or supervisor (Diploma), leadership (Ed D); elementary education (MS, Diploma), including early childhood education, elementary education; middle school education (MS); music education (MS); remedial reading and language arts (Diploma); secondary education (MS, Diploma), including computer specialist (Diploma), international education (Diploma), reading specialist, secondary education. *Program availability:* Part-time, evening/weekend. *Degree requirements:* For master's, final exam, final project, or thesis; for doctorate, comprehensive exam, thesis/dissertation; for Diploma, thesis or alternative, final project. *Entrance requirements:* For master's, minimum undergraduate QPA of 2.67; for doctorate, GRE, MAT; for Diploma,

Elementary Education

GRE General Test or MAT, minimum graduate QPA of 3.0. Additional exam requirements/recommendations for international students: Recommended—TOEFL (minimum score 550 paper-based; 80 iBT), IELTS (minimum score 6.5). Electronic applications accepted. *Expenses:* Contact institution.

University of California, Irvine, School of Education, Irvine, CA 92697. Offers educational administration (Ed D); educational administration and leadership (Ed D); elementary and secondary education (MAT). *Program availability:* Part-time, evening/weekend. *Students:* 213 full-time (155 women), 3 part-time (2 women); includes 107 minority (1 Black or African American, non-Hispanic/Latino; 51 Asian, non-Hispanic/Latino; 40 Hispanic/Latino; 15 Two or more races, non-Hispanic/Latino), 23 international. Average age 28. 482 applicants, 47% accepted, 148 enrolled. In 2018, 141 master's, 8 doctorates awarded. *Entrance requirements:* For master's, GRE, minimum GPA of 3.0; for doctorate, GRE General Test, minimum GPA of 3.0. Additional exam requirements/recommendations for international students: Required—TOEFL (minimum score 550 paper-based). *Application deadline:* For fall admission, 1/2 priority date for domestic students, 1/2 for international students. Application fee: $105 ($125 for international students). Electronic applications accepted. *Financial support:* Fellowships, research assistantships with full tuition reimbursements, institutionally sponsored loans, traineeships, health care benefits, and unspecified assistantships available. Financial award application deadline: 3/1; financial award applicants required to submit FAFSA. *Faculty research:* Education technology, learning theory, social theory, cultural diversity, postmodernism. *Unit head:* Richard Arum, Dean, 949-824-2534, E-mail: richard.arum@uci.edu. *Application contact:* Denise Earley, Assistant Director of Student Affairs, 949-824-4022, E-mail: denise.earley@uci.edu.
Website: http://education.uci.edu/

University of Central Florida, College of Community Innovation and Education, School of Teacher Education, Program in Elementary Education, Orlando, FL 32816. Offers M Ed, MA. *Accreditation:* NCATE. *Students:* 20 full-time (19 women), 27 part-time (26 women); includes 8 minority (2 Black or African American, non-Hispanic/Latino; 6 Hispanic/Latino). Average age 27. 31 applicants, 45% accepted, 12 enrolled. In 2018, 20 master's awarded. *Entrance requirements:* For master's, Florida Professional Teaching Certificate in subject area or professional teaching certificate. Additional exam requirements/recommendations for international students: Required—TOEFL. *Application deadline:* For fall admission, 7/15 for domestic students; for spring admission, 12/1 for domestic students; for summer admission, 4/15 for domestic students. Application fee: $30. Electronic applications accepted. *Financial support:* In 2018–19, 1 student received support, including 1 teaching assistantship with partial tuition reimbursement available (averaging $1,286 per year); career-related internships or fieldwork, Federal Work-Study, institutionally sponsored loans, tuition waivers (partial), and unspecified assistantships also available. Financial award application deadline: 3/1; financial award applicants required to submit FAFSA. *Unit head:* Dr. Robert Everett, Program Coordinator, 407-823-5788, E-mail: robert.everett@ucf.edu. *Application contact:* Associate Director, Graduate Admissions, 321-823-2766, Fax: 407-823-6442, E-mail: gradadmissions@ucf.edu.
Website: https://edcollege.ucf.edu/academic-programs/graduate/elementary-education/#ma

University of Central Missouri, The Graduate School, Warrensburg, MO 64093. Offers accountancy (MA); accounting (MBA); applied mathematics (MS); aviation safety (MA); biology (MS); business administration (MBA); career and technical education leadership (MS); college student personnel administration (MS); communication (MA); computer science (MS); counseling (MS); criminal justice (MS); educational leadership (Ed D); educational technology (MS); elementary and early childhood education (MSE); English (MA); environmental studies (MA); finance (MBA); history (MA); human services/educational technology (Ed S); human services/learning resources (Ed S); human services/professional counseling (Ed S); industrial hygiene (MS); industrial management (MS); information systems (MBA); information technology (MS); kinesiology (MS); library science and information services (MS); literacy education (MSE); marketing (MBA); mathematics (MS); music (MA); occupational safety management (MS); psychology (MS); rural family nursing (MS); school administration (MSE); social gerontology (MS); sociology (MA); special education (MSE); speech language pathology (MS); superintendency (Ed S); teaching (MAT); teaching English as a second language (MA); technology (MS); technology management (PhD); theatre (MA). *Accreditation:* ASHA. *Program availability:* Part-time, 100% online, blended/hybrid learning. *Degree requirements:* For master's and Ed S, comprehensive exam (for some programs), thesis (for some programs). *Entrance requirements:* Additional exam requirements/recommendations for international students: Required—TOEFL (minimum score 550 paper-based; 79 iBT). Electronic applications accepted.

University of Central Oklahoma, The Jackson College of Graduate Studies, College of Education and Professional Studies, Department of Curriculum and Instruction, Edmond, OK 73034-5209. Offers bilingual education/teaching English as a second language (M Ed); early childhood education (M Ed); elementary education (M Ed). *Program availability:* Part-time. *Degree requirements:* For master's, comprehensive exam (for some programs), thesis optional. *Entrance requirements:* Additional exam requirements/recommendations for international students: Required—TOEFL (minimum score 550 paper-based; 79 iBT), IELTS (minimum score 6.5). Electronic applications accepted.

University of Colorado Denver, School of Education and Human Development, Information and Learning Technologies Program, Denver, CO 80217. Offers e-learning design and implementation (MA); instructional design and adult learning (MA); K-12 teaching (MA). *Program availability:* Part-time, evening/weekend, online learning. *Degree requirements:* For master's, comprehensive exam (for some programs), comprehensive exam or online portfolio; 30 credit hours. *Entrance requirements:* For master's, GRE or MAT (if GPA is below 2.75), resume, statement of intent, three letters of recommendation, transcripts from all colleges/universities previously attended. Additional exam requirements/recommendations for international students: Required—TOEFL (minimum score 537 paper-based; 75 iBT); Recommended—IELTS (minimum score 6.5). Electronic applications accepted. *Expenses:* Contact institution. *Faculty research:* Technology for educational management, instructional design foundations, e-learning, educational design.

University of Colorado Denver, School of Education and Human Development, Teacher Education Programs, Denver, CO 80217. Offers elementary linguistically diverse education (MA); elementary math and science education (MA); elementary math education (MA); elementary reading and writing (MA); elementary science education (MA); secondary English education (MA); secondary linguistically diverse education (MA); secondary math education (MA); secondary reading and writing (MA); secondary science education (MA); special education (MA). *Accreditation:* NCATE. *Program availability:* Part-time, evening/weekend. *Degree requirements:* For master's, comprehensive exam. *Entrance requirements:* For master's, GRE or MAT (for those with GPA below 2.75), transcripts, resume, letters of recommendation. Additional exam requirements/recommendations for international students: Required—TOEFL (minimum score 537 paper-based; 75 iBT); Recommended—IELTS (minimum score 6.5). Electronic applications accepted. *Expenses:* Tuition, state resident: full-time $6786; part-time $337 per credit hour. Tuition, nonresident: full-time $22,590; part-time $1255 per credit hour. *Required fees:* $1231; $137 per credit hour. Tuition and fees vary according to program and reciprocity agreements. *Faculty research:* Linguistically diverse education/ESL, elementary reading and writing, elementary teacher education, secondary teacher education, special education.

University of Connecticut, Graduate School, Neag School of Education, Department of Curriculum and Instruction, Program in Elementary Education, Storrs, CT 06269. Offers MA, PhD. *Accreditation:* NCATE. Terminal master's awarded for partial completion of doctoral program. *Degree requirements:* For master's, comprehensive exam, thesis or alternative; for doctorate, thesis/dissertation. *Entrance requirements:* For doctorate, GRE General Test. Additional exam requirements/recommendations for international students: Required—TOEFL (minimum score 550 paper-based). Electronic applications accepted.

University of Dayton, Department of Teacher Education, Dayton, OH 45469. Offers adolescence to young adult education (MS Ed); early childhood leadership and advocacy (MS Ed); interdisciplinary education (MS Ed), including visual arts; interdisciplinary education studies (MS Ed); leadership in educational systems (MS Ed); literacy (MS Ed); mathematics education (MS Ed); middle childhood education (MS Ed); multi-age education (MS Ed), including world languages; music education (MS Ed); teacher as leader (MS Ed); teacher education (MS Ed); technology-enhanced learning (MS Ed); trans-disciplinary early childhood education (MS Ed). *Program availability:* Part-time, 100% online. *Degree requirements:* For master's, variable foreign language requirement, thesis or alternative, internship (for teaching licensure or endorsement). *Entrance requirements:* For master's, GRE (minimum score of 149 verbal, 4 on writing) or MAT (minimum score of 396) if undergraduate GPA was under 2.75, minimum GPA of 2.75, 3 letters of recommendation, personal statement or resume, official transcripts. Additional exam requirements/recommendations for international students: Required—TOEFL (minimum score 550 paper-based; 80 iBT); Recommended—IELTS (minimum score 6.5). Electronic applications accepted. *Expenses:* Contact institution. *Faculty research:* Social emotional learning, culturally responsive teaching, urban teaching, literacy, instructional strategies, pre-service teacher education preparation.

University of Florida, Graduate School, College of Education, School of Teaching and Learning, Gainesville, FL 32611. Offers curriculum and instruction (M Ed, MAE, Ed D, PhD, Ed S); elementary education (M Ed, MAE); English education (M Ed, MAE); mathematics education (M Ed, MAE); reading education (M Ed, MAE); science education (M Ed, MAE); social studies education (M Ed, MAE). *Accreditation:* NCATE. *Program availability:* Part-time, evening/weekend, online learning. Terminal master's awarded for partial completion of doctoral program. *Degree requirements:* For master's, comprehensive exam (for some programs), thesis (for some programs); for doctorate, comprehensive exam (for some programs), thesis/dissertation (for some programs). *Entrance requirements:* For master's and doctorate, GRE General Test, minimum GPA of 3.0; for Ed S, GRE General Test. Additional exam requirements/recommendations for international students: Required—TOEFL (minimum score 550 paper-based; 80 iBT), IELTS (minimum score 6). Electronic applications accepted. *Faculty research:* STEM education; curriculum; teaching and teacher education; languages and literacy; schools, culture, and society; theories and processes of learning.

University of Hartford, College of Education, Nursing, and Health Professions, Program in Elementary and Special Education, West Hartford, CT 06117-1599. Offers elementary education (M Ed). *Accreditation:* NCATE. *Program availability:* Part-time, evening/weekend. *Degree requirements:* For master's, comprehensive exam. *Entrance requirements:* For master's, PRAXIS I or waiver, interview, 2 letters of recommendation. Additional exam requirements/recommendations for international students: Required—TOEFL (minimum score 550 paper-based). Electronic applications accepted.

University of Illinois at Chicago, College of Education, Department of Curriculum and Instruction, Chicago, IL 60607-7128. Offers curriculum studies (PhD); elementary education (M Ed); secondary education (M Ed). *Program availability:* Part-time, evening/weekend. *Degree requirements:* For doctorate, thesis/dissertation. *Entrance requirements:* For master's, minimum GPA of 2.75; for doctorate, GRE General Test, minimum GPA of 2.75. Additional exam requirements/recommendations for international students: Required—TOEFL. Electronic applications accepted. *Faculty research:* Curriculum theory, curriculum development, research on teaching, curriculum and context, reading/literacy.

University of Indianapolis, Graduate Programs, School of Education, Indianapolis, IN 46227-3697. Offers art education (MAT); biology (MAT); chemistry (MAT); curriculum and instruction (MA); earth sciences (MAT); education (MA, MAT); educational leadership (MA); elementary education (MA); English (MAT); French (MAT); math (MAT); physical education (MAT); physics (MAT); secondary education (MA), including art education, education, English education, social studies education; social studies (MAT); Spanish (MAT). *Accreditation:* NCATE. *Program availability:* Part-time, evening/weekend. *Entrance requirements:* For master's, GRE Subject Test, PRAXIS I, minimum GPA of 2.5, 3 letters of recommendation, interview. Additional exam requirements/recommendations for international students: Required—TOEFL (minimum score 550 paper-based). *Faculty research:* Assessment of teacher education, perceptions of prospective teachers by parents.

The University of Iowa, Graduate College, College of Education, Department of Teaching and Learning, Program in Education, Iowa City, IA 52242-1316. Offers art education (MA); developmental reading (MA); elementary education (MA); English education (MA, MAT); foreign and second language education (MAT); foreign language education (MA); foreign language/ESL education (PhD); language, literacy and culture (PhD); mathematics education (MA, MAT, PhD); music education (MM, PhD); science education (MA); secondary education (MA); social studies (MA, PhD). *Degree requirements:* For master's, thesis optional, exam; for doctorate, comprehensive exam, thesis/dissertation. *Entrance requirements:* For master's and doctorate, GRE General Test, minimum GPA of 3.0. Additional exam requirements/recommendations for international students: Required—TOEFL (minimum score 550 paper-based; 81 iBT). Electronic applications accepted.

University of Kentucky, Graduate School, College of Education, Program in Curriculum and Instruction, Lexington, KY 40506-0032. Offers curriculum and instruction (Ed D, PhD); elementary education (MA Ed); instructional system design (MS Ed); literacy (MA Ed); middle school education (MA Ed, MS Ed); secondary education (MA Ed, MS Ed). *Accreditation:* NCATE. *Degree requirements:* For master's, comprehensive exam, thesis optional; for doctorate, comprehensive exam, thesis/dissertation. *Entrance requirements:* For master's, GRE General Test, minimum undergraduate GPA of 2.75; for doctorate, GRE General Test, minimum graduate GPA of 3.0. Additional exam requirements/recommendations for international students: Required—TOEFL (minimum score 550 paper-based). Electronic applications accepted. *Faculty research:* Educational reform, multicultural education, classroom instructional practices, performance based assessment, primary school programs.

University of La Verne, Regional and Online Campuses, Graduate Programs, High Desert Campus, Victorville, CA 92392. Offers business administration for experienced professionals (MBA); educational (special emphasis) (M Ed); educational counseling (MS); leadership and management (MS); multiple subject (elementary) (Credential); preliminary administrative services (Credential); pupil personnel services (Credential); single subject (secondary) (Credential). *Expenses:* Contact institution.

University of La Verne, Regional and Online Campuses, Graduate Programs, Kern County Campus, Bakersfield, CA 93301. Offers business administration for experienced professionals (MBA-EP); education (special emphasis) (M Ed); educational counseling (MS); educational leadership (M Ed); health administration (MHA); leadership and management (MS); mild/moderate education specialist (Credential); multiple subject (elementary) (Credential); organizational leadership (Ed D); preliminary administrative services (Credential); single subject (secondary) (Credential); special education studies (MS). *Program availability:* Part-time, evening/weekend. *Expenses:* Contact institution.

University of La Verne, Regional and Online Campuses, Graduate Programs, Ventura County/Point Mugu Naval Air Station Campuses, Oxnard, CA 93036. Offers business administration for experienced professionals (MS); educational counseling (MS); educational leadership (M Ed); leadership and management (MS); multiple subject (elementary) (Credential); pupil personnel services (Credential); single subject (secondary) (Credential). *Program availability:* Part-time, evening/weekend. *Expenses:* Contact institution.

University of Louisiana at Monroe, Graduate School, College of Arts, Education, and Sciences, School of Education, Program in Elementary Education, Monroe, LA 71209-0001. Offers MAT. *Accreditation:* NCATE. *Program availability:* Part-time, evening/weekend. *Faculty:* 11 full-time (7 women). *Students:* 5 full-time (all women), 12 part-time (11 women); includes 5 minority (2 Black or African American, non-Hispanic/Latino; 1 Hispanic/Latino; 2 Two or more races, non-Hispanic/Latino). Average age 28. 9 applicants, 56% accepted, 5 enrolled. In 2018, 16 master's awarded. *Degree requirements:* For master's, thesis optional. *Entrance requirements:* For master's, GRE General Test, minimum GPA of 2.5. Additional exam requirements/recommendations for international students: Required—TOEFL (minimum score 500 paper-based; 61 iBT). *Application deadline:* For fall admission, 8/24 for domestic students, 7/1 for international students; for winter admission, 12/14 priority date for domestic students; for spring admission, 1/19 for domestic students, 11/1 for international students. Applications are processed on a rolling basis. Application fee: $20 ($30 for international students). Electronic applications accepted. *Financial support:* Career-related internships or fieldwork, Federal Work-Study, and unspecified assistantships available. Financial award application deadline: 4/1; financial award applicants required to submit FAFSA. *Faculty research:* Student attitudes.

University of Louisville, Graduate School, College of Education and Human Development, Departments of Early Childhood and Elementary Education, Middle and Secondary Education, and Special Education, Louisville, KY 40292-0001. Offers art education (MAT); autism and applied behavior analysis (Certificate); curriculum and instruction (PhD); early elementary education (MAT); exercise physiology (MS); health and physical education (MAT); health professions education (Certificate); higher education (MA); human resources and organization development (MS); instructional technology (M Ed); interdisciplinary early childhood education (MAT); middle school education (MAT); music education (MAT); secondary education (MAT); special education (MAT); sport administration (MS); teacher leadership (M Ed). *Program availability:* Part-time, evening/weekend, 100% online, blended/hybrid learning. *Faculty:* 97 full-time (64 women), 131 part-time/adjunct (86 women). *Students:* 109 full-time (72 women), 139 part-time (87 women); includes 43 minority (18 Black or African American, non-Hispanic/Latino; 6 Asian, non-Hispanic/Latino; 10 Hispanic/Latino; 9 Two or more races, non-Hispanic/Latino), 9 international. Average age 29. 108 applicants, 75% accepted, 59 enrolled. In 2018, 64 master's awarded. Terminal master's awarded for partial completion of doctoral program. *Degree requirements:* For master's, comprehensive exam (for some programs), thesis optional; for doctorate, comprehensive exam (for some programs), thesis/dissertation. *Entrance requirements:* For master's, GRE (for most programs), PRAXIS (for educator preparation programs), professional statement, recommendation letters, resume, transcripts; for doctorate and Certificate, GRE, professional statement, recommendation letters, resume, transcripts. Additional exam requirements/recommendations for international students: Required—TOEFL (minimum score 550 paper-based; 79 iBT); Recommended—IELTS (minimum score 6.5). *Application deadline:* For fall admission, 6/1 priority date for domestic students, 5/1 priority date for international students; for spring admission, 10/1 for domestic students, 11/1 priority date for international students; for summer admission, 3/1 priority date for domestic students, 4/1 priority date for international students. Application fee: $65. *Expenses: Tuition, area resident:* Full-time $6500; part-time $723 per credit hour. Tuition, state resident: full-time $6500. Tuition, nonresident: full-time $13,557; part-time $1507 per credit hour. Tuition and fees vary according to course load and program. *Financial support:* In 2018–19, 144 students received support, including fellowships with full tuition reimbursements available (averaging $21,024 per year), research assistantships with full tuition reimbursements available (averaging $21,024 per year), teaching assistantships with full tuition reimbursements available (averaging $21,024 per year); Federal Work-Study, scholarships/grants, health care benefits, tuition waivers (full), and unspecified assistantships also available. Financial award application deadline: 3/1; financial award applicants required to submit FAFSA. *Faculty research:* Children's early reading and writing development, crelevance of basic facts in elementary mathematics instruction, clinical model of teacher education, cultural and linguistic context of diverse learners, and STEM-integrated curriculum design and development. STEM teaching and learning, content literacy for English language learners, social justice in teacher education, adolescent literacy, mathematics teacher development. Classroom and behavior management; moderate/severe disabilities, autism. *Unit head:* Dr. Amy Lingo, Interim Dean, 502-852-3235, Fax: 502-852-1464, E-mail: cehdinfo@louisville.edu. *Application contact:* Dr. Margaret Pentecost, Assistant Dean for Graduate Student Success, 502-852-6437, Fax: 502-852-1417, E-mail: gedadm@louisville.edu.
Website: http://louisville.edu/delphi

University of Mary Hardin-Baylor, Graduate Studies in Education, Belton, TX 76513. Offers curriculum and instruction (M Ed); educational administration (M Ed, Ed D), including higher education (Ed D), leadership in nursing education (Ed D), P-12 (Ed D). *Program availability:* Part-time, evening/weekend. *Degree requirements:* For master's, comprehensive exam; for doctorate, thesis/dissertation. *Entrance requirements:* For master's, minimum GPA of 3.0, interview; for doctorate, minimum GPA of 3.5, interview, essay, resume, employment verification, 3 letters of recommendation. Additional exam requirements/recommendations for international students: Required—TOEFL (minimum score 60 iBT), IELTS (minimum score 4.5). Electronic applications accepted. *Expenses:* Contact institution. *Faculty research:* Motivational orientation of preservice teachers.

University of Maryland, Baltimore County, The Graduate School, College of Arts, Humanities and Social Sciences, Department of Education, Program in Teaching, Baltimore, MD 21250. Offers early childhood education (MAT); elementary education (MAT); teaching (MAT), including art, biology, chemistry, choral music, classical foreign language, dance, earth/space science, English, instrumental music, mathematics, modern foreign language, physical science, physics, social studies, theatre. *Program availability:* Part-time, evening/weekend. *Degree requirements:* For master's, comprehensive exam (for some programs), thesis (for some programs). *Entrance requirements:* For master's, PRAXIS Core Examination or GRE (minimum score of 1000), minimum GPA of 3.0. Additional exam requirements/recommendations for international students: Required—TOEFL. Electronic applications accepted. *Faculty research:* STEM teacher education, culturally sensitive pedagogy, ESOL/bilingual education, early childhood education, language, literacy and culture.

University of Mary Washington, College of Education, Fredericksburg, VA 22401. Offers education (M Ed); elementary education (MS). *Program availability:* Part-time, evening/weekend. *Degree requirements:* For master's, one foreign language, comprehensive exam (for some programs). *Entrance requirements:* For master's, PRAXIS Core Academic Skills for Educators (Reading; Writing; Math or Virginia Department of Education accepted equivalent). Additional exam requirements/recommendations for international students: Required—TOEFL (minimum score 570 paper-based; 88 iBT), IELTS (minimum score 6.5). Electronic applications accepted. Application fee is waived when completed online. *Expenses:* Contact institution.

University of Massachusetts Amherst, Graduate School, College of Education, Program in Education, Amherst, MA 01003. Offers bilingual, English as a second language, and multicultural education (M Ed, Ed S); child study and early education (M Ed); children, families and schools (Ed D, Ed S); early childhood and elementary teacher education (M Ed); educational leadership (M Ed); educational policy and leadership (Ed D); higher education (M Ed); international education (M Ed); language, literacy and culture (Ed D); learning, media and technology (M Ed, Ed S); mathematics, science, and learning technologies (Ed D); reading and writing (M Ed); research, educational measurement and psychometrics (Ed D); school counselor education (M Ed, Ed S); school psychology (Ed S); science education (Ed S); secondary teacher education (M Ed); social justice education (M Ed, Ed D, Ed S); special education (M Ed, Ed D, Ed S); teacher education and school improvement (Ed D, Ed S). *Accreditation:* NCATE. *Program availability:* Part-time, online learning. Terminal master's awarded for partial completion of doctoral program. *Degree requirements:* For doctorate, comprehensive exam, thesis/dissertation. *Entrance requirements:* Additional exam requirements/recommendations for international students: Required—TOEFL (minimum score 550 paper-based; 80 iBT), IELTS (minimum score 6.5). Electronic applications accepted.

University of Memphis, Graduate School, College of Education, Department of Instruction and Curriculum Leadership, Memphis, TN 38152. Offers advanced studies in teaching and learning (M Ed); applied behavior analysis (Graduate Certificate); autism studies (Graduate Certificate); early childhood education (MAT, MS, Ed D); elementary education (MAT); instruction and curriculum (MS, Ed D); instruction design and technology (MS, Ed D); instructional design and technology (Graduate Certificate); literacy, leadership, and coaching (Graduate Certificate); reading (MS, Ed D); school library information specialist (Graduate Certificate); secondary education (MAT); special education (MAT, MS, Ed D); STEM teacher leadership (Graduate Certificate); urban education (Graduate Certificate). *Accreditation:* NCATE (one or more programs are accredited). *Program availability:* Part-time. *Students:* 62 full-time (45 women), 412 part-time (326 women); includes 209 minority (179 Black or African American, non-Hispanic/Latino; 1 American Indian or Alaska Native, non-Hispanic/Latino; 5 Asian, non-Hispanic/Latino; 17 Hispanic/Latino; 7 Two or more races, non-Hispanic/Latino), 4 international. Average age 35. 195 applicants, 91% accepted, 143 enrolled. In 2018, 122 master's, 13 doctorates, 29 other advanced degrees awarded. Terminal master's awarded for partial completion of doctoral program. *Degree requirements:* For master's, comprehensive exam, thesis or alternative; for doctorate, comprehensive exam, thesis/dissertation. *Entrance requirements:* For master's, GRE General Test, PRAXIS, minimum GPA of 2.5, letters of reference; for doctorate, GRE General Test, GRE Subject Test, 2 years of teaching experience, letters of reference, statement of purpose, interview. Additional exam requirements/recommendations for international students: Required—TOEFL (minimum score 550 paper-based; 79 iBT). *Application deadline:* For fall admission, 4/1 priority date for domestic students; for spring admission, 10/1 priority date for domestic students; for summer admission, 2/1 priority date for domestic students. Applications are processed on a rolling basis. Application fee: $35 ($60 for international students). Electronic applications accepted. *Expenses: Tuition, area resident:* Full-time $10,240; part-time $503 per credit hour. Tuition, state resident: full-time $10,464. Tuition, nonresident: full-time $20,224; part-time $991 per credit hour. *Required fees:* $850; $106 per credit hour. *Financial support:* Research assistantships with full tuition reimbursements, teaching assistantships with full tuition reimbursements, career-related internships or fieldwork, Federal Work-Study, institutionally sponsored loans, scholarships/grants, traineeships, and unspecified assistantships available. Support available to part-time students. Financial award application deadline: 2/1; financial award applicants required to submit FAFSA. *Faculty research:* Effective urban teachers, preparation and retention of urban teachers, technology utilization in schools, field-based teacher preparation programs, effective use of online instruction. *Unit head:* Dr. Christian Mueller, Chair, 901-678-2365, E-mail: cemuellr@memphis.edu. *Application contact:* Dr. Lee Allen, Director of Graduate Programs, 901-678-4073, E-mail: allenlee@memphis.edu.
Website: http://www.memphis.edu/icl/

University of Minnesota, Twin Cities Campus, Graduate School, College of Education and Human Development, Department of Curriculum and Instruction, Program in Teaching, Minneapolis, MN 55455-0213. Offers teaching (M Ed), including arts in education, elementary education, English education, mathematics, science, second language education, social studies. *Students:* 249 full-time (182 women), 101 part-time (59 women); includes 57 minority (5 Black or African American, non-Hispanic/Latino; 16 Asian, non-Hispanic/Latino; 25 Hispanic/Latino; 11 Two or more races, non-Hispanic/Latino), 12 international. Average age 28. 383 applicants, 79% accepted, 261 enrolled. In 2018, 292 master's awarded. Application fee: $75 ($95 for international students). *Unit head:* Dr. Mark Vagle, Chair, 612-625-4006, Fax: 612-624-8277, E-mail: mvagle@umn.edu. *Application contact:* Dr. Mark Vagle, Chair, 612-625-4006, Fax: 612-624-8277, E-mail: mvagle@umn.edu.
Website: http://www.cehd.umn.edu/ci/

University of Mississippi, Graduate School, School of Education, University, MS 38677. Offers counselor education (M Ed, PhD); counselor education - play therapy (Ed S); early childhood (M Ed); educational leadership K-12 (M Ed, Ed D, PhD, Ed S); elementary education (M Ed, Ed D, Ed S); higher education/student personnel (Ed D, PhD); literacy education (M Ed); math education (Ed D); secondary education (M Ed, PhD, Ed S); special education (M Ed, PhD, Ed S); teacher corporations (MA); teacher education (MA). *Accreditation:* NCATE. *Faculty:* 59 full-time (35 women), 34 part-time/adjunct (26 women). *Students:* 169 full-time (137 women), 461 part-time (329 women); includes 199 minority (185 Black or African American, non-Hispanic/Latino; 3 Asian, non-Hispanic/Latino; 7 Hispanic/Latino; 4 Two or more races, non-Hispanic/Latino), 5 international. Average age 33. In 2018, 180 master's, 57 doctorates, 37 other advanced degrees awarded. *Entrance requirements:* For master's, GRE General Test, minimum GPA of 3.0; for doctorate, GRE General Test. Additional exam requirements/recommendations for international students: Required—TOEFL. *Application deadline:* Applications are processed on a rolling basis. Application fee: $50. Electronic applications accepted. *Financial support:* Scholarships/grants available. Financial award application deadline: 3/1; financial award applicants required to submit FAFSA. *Unit head:* Dr. David Rock, Dean, 662-915-7063, Fax: 662-915-7249, E-mail: soe@olemiss.edu. *Application contact:* Temeka Smith, Graduate Activities Specialist for Admissions, 662-915-7474, Fax: 662-915-7577, E-mail: gschool@olemiss.edu.

Elementary Education

University of Missouri, Office of Research and Graduate Studies, College of Education, Department of Learning, Teaching and Curriculum, Columbia, MO 65211. Offers agricultural education (M Ed, PhD, Ed S); art education (M Ed, PhD, Ed S); business and office education (M Ed, PhD, Ed S); early childhood education (M Ed, PhD, Ed S); elementary education (M Ed, PhD, Ed S); English education (M Ed, PhD, Ed S); foreign language education (M Ed, PhD, Ed S); health education and promotion (M Ed, PhD); learning and instruction (M Ed); marketing education (M Ed, PhD, Ed S); mathematics education (M Ed, PhD, Ed S); music education (M Ed, PhD, Ed S); reading education (M Ed, PhD, Ed S); science education (M Ed, PhD, Ed S); social studies education (M Ed, PhD, Ed S); vocational education (M Ed, PhD, Ed S). *Program availability:* Part-time. Terminal master's awarded for partial completion of doctoral program. *Entrance requirements:* For master's and Ed S, GRE General Test or MAT, minimum GPA of 3.0; for doctorate, GRE General Test, minimum GPA of 3.0. Additional exam requirements/recommendations for international students: Required—TOEFL.

University of Missouri–St. Louis, College of Education, Department of Educator Preparation, Innovation and Research, St. Louis, MO 63121. Offers elementary education (M Ed), including early childhood, general, reading; secondary education (M Ed), including curriculum and instruction, general, middle level education, reading, teaching English to speakers of other languages (TESOL); special education (M Ed), including autism and developmental disabilities, early childhood special education. *Program availability:* Part-time, evening/weekend. *Degree requirements:* For master's, comprehensive exam. *Entrance requirements:* Additional exam requirements/recommendations for international students: Recommended—TOEFL (minimum score 550 paper-based; 79 iBT), IELTS (minimum score 6.5). Electronic applications accepted.

University of Montevallo, College of Education, Program in Elementary Education, Montevallo, AL 35115. Offers M Ed. *Accreditation:* NCATE. *Program availability:* Part-time. *Students:* 10 full-time (8 women), 16 part-time (all women); includes 4 minority (2 Black or African American, non-Hispanic/Latino; 1 Hispanic/Latino; 1 Two or more races, non-Hispanic/Latino). In 2018, 11 master's awarded. *Entrance requirements:* For master's, GRE General Test, MAT, minimum undergraduate GPA of 2.5. Additional exam requirements/recommendations for international students: Required—TOEFL (minimum score 550 paper-based). *Application deadline:* For fall admission, 7/15 for domestic students; for spring admission, 11/15 for domestic students. Application fee: $30. *Expenses: Tuition, area resident:* Full-time $10,512. Tuition, state resident: full-time $10,512. Tuition, nonresident: full-time $22,464. *International tuition:* $22,464 full-time. *Financial support:* Federal Work-Study, scholarships/grants, and unspecified assistantships available. *Unit head:* Dr. Charlotte Daughhetee, Interim Dean, 205-665-6360, E-mail: daughc@montevallo.edu. *Application contact:* Colleen Kennedy, Graduate Program Assistant, 205-665-6350, E-mail: ckennedy@montevallo.edu. Website: https://www.montevallo.edu/academics/colleges/college-of-education/

University of Nebraska at Kearney, College of Education, Department of Teacher Education, Kearney, NE 68849-0001. Offers curriculum and instruction (MA Ed), including early childhood education, elementary education, English as a second language, instructional effectiveness, reading/special education, secondary education; instructional technology (MS Ed), including information technology, instructional technology, school librarian; reading PK-12 (MA Ed); special education (MA Ed), including advanced practitioner: assistive technology specialist, advanced practitioner: behavioral interventionist, advanced practitioner: inclusive collaboration specialist, gifted, teacher education. *Program availability:* Part-time, evening/weekend, online only, 100% online. *Degree requirements:* For master's, comprehensive exam, thesis optional. *Entrance requirements:* For master's, portfolio or GRE. Additional exam requirements/recommendations for international students: Recommended—TOEFL (minimum score 550 paper-based; 79 iBT), IELTS (minimum score 6.5). Electronic applications accepted. *Expenses:* Contact institution.

University of Nebraska at Omaha, Graduate Studies, College of Education, Department of Teacher Education, Program in Elementary Education, Omaha, NE 68182. Offers MS. *Accreditation:* NCATE. *Program availability:* Part-time, evening/weekend. *Degree requirements:* For master's, comprehensive exam (for some programs), thesis (for some programs). *Entrance requirements:* For master's, minimum GPA of 3.0, transcripts. Additional exam requirements/recommendations for international students: Required—TOEFL, IELTS, PTE. Electronic applications accepted.

University of Nevada, Las Vegas, Graduate College, College of Education, Department of Teaching and Learning, Las Vegas, NV 89154-3005. Offers curriculum and instruction (M Ed, MS, Ed D, PhD, Ed S), including teacher education (PhD); elementary teaching (Certificate); online teaching and training (Certificate); secondary teaching (Certificate); social justice studies (Certificate); teaching and learning (PhD). *Program availability:* Part-time, evening/weekend. *Faculty:* 25 full-time (12 women), 11 part-time/adjunct (8 women). *Students:* 304 full-time (212 women), 271 part-time (181 women); includes 255 minority (56 Black or African American, non-Hispanic/Latino; 1 American Indian or Alaska Native, non-Hispanic/Latino; 38 Asian, non-Hispanic/Latino; 124 Hispanic/Latino; 1 Native Hawaiian or other Pacific Islander, non-Hispanic/Latino; 35 Two or more races, non-Hispanic/Latino), 16 international. Average age 34. 228 applicants, 86% accepted, 164 enrolled. In 2018, 135 master's, 12 doctorates, 10 other advanced degrees awarded. *Degree requirements:* For master's, comprehensive exam (for some programs), thesis (for some programs); for doctorate, comprehensive exam, thesis/dissertation, defense of dissertation; for other advanced degree, comprehensive exam (for some programs), oral presentation of special project or professional paper. *Entrance requirements:* For master's, bachelor's degree with minimum GPA 2.75; for doctorate, GRE General Test, master's degree with minimum GPA of 3.0; statement of purpose; demonstration of oral communication skills; 3 letters of recommendation; for other advanced degree, PRAXIS Core (for some programs); PRAXIS II (for some programs), bachelor's degree (for some programs). Additional exam requirements/recommendations for international students: Required—TOEFL (minimum score 550 paper-based; 80 iBT), IELTS (minimum score 7). *Application deadline:* For fall admission, 6/1 for domestic students, 5/1 for international students; for spring admission, 11/1 for domestic students, 10/1 for international students; for summer admission, 3/15 for domestic students. Application fee: $60 ($95 for international students). Electronic applications accepted. *Financial support:* In 2018–19, 31 students received support, including 7 research assistantships with full tuition reimbursements available (averaging $18,286 per year), 24 teaching assistantships with full tuition reimbursements available (averaging $19,271 per year); institutionally sponsored loans, scholarships/grants, health care benefits, and unspecified assistantships also available. Financial award application deadline: 3/15; financial award applicants required to submit FAFSA. *Faculty research:* Content area and critical literacy, education in content areas, teacher education, science, technology, engineering and mathematics education, immersive environments/simulations/games. *Total annual research expenditures:* $1.1 million. *Unit head:* Dr. P.G. Schrader, Chair/Professor, 702-895-3331, Fax: 702-895-4898, E-mail: tl.chair@unlv.edu. *Application contact:* Dr. Micah Stohlmann, Graduate Coordinator, 702-895-0836, Fax: 702-895-4898, E-mail: tl.gradcoord@unlv.edu. Website: http://tl.unlv.edu/

University of Nevada, Reno, Graduate School, College of Education, Department of Curriculum, Teaching and Learning, Program in Elementary Education, Reno, NV 89557. Offers M Ed, MA, MS. *Degree requirements:* For master's, thesis optional. *Entrance requirements:* For master's, GRE General Test, minimum GPA of 2.75. Additional exam requirements/recommendations for international students: Required—TOEFL (minimum score 500 paper-based; 61 iBT), IELTS (minimum score 6). Electronic applications accepted. *Faculty research:* Child development, educational trends.

University of New Hampshire, Graduate School, College of Liberal Arts, Department of Education, Program in Elementary Education, Durham, NH 03824. Offers M Ed. *Program availability:* Part-time. *Entrance requirements:* For master's, PRAXIS. Additional exam requirements/recommendations for international students: Required—TOEFL (minimum score 550 paper-based; 80 iBT). Electronic applications accepted.

University of New Hampshire, Graduate School Manchester Campus, Manchester, NH 03101. Offers business administration (MBA); cybersecurity policy and risk management (MS); educational administration and supervision (Ed S); educational studies (M Ed); elementary education (M Ed); information technology (MS); public administration (MPA); public health (MPH, Certificate); secondary education (M Ed, MAT); social work (MSW); substance use disorders (Certificate). *Program availability:* Part-time, evening/weekend. *Entrance requirements:* Additional exam requirements/recommendations for international students: Required—TOEFL (minimum score 550 paper-based; 80 iBT). Electronic applications accepted.

University of New Mexico, Graduate Studies, College of Education, Program in Elementary Education, Albuquerque, NM 87131-2039. Offers math, science, and educational technology (MA). *Program availability:* Part-time. *Students:* Average age 33. 39 applicants, 79% accepted, 26 enrolled. In 2018, 71 master's awarded. *Degree requirements:* For master's, comprehensive exam, thesis optional. *Entrance requirements:* For master's, minimum overall GPA of 3.0, some experience working with students, NMTA or teacher's license, 3 letters of reference, letter of intent. Additional exam requirements/recommendations for international students: Required—TOEFL (minimum score 550 paper-based). *Application deadline:* For fall admission, 2/15 for domestic students; for spring admission, 10/1 for domestic students. Application fee: $50. Electronic applications accepted. *Financial support:* Fellowships, career-related internships or fieldwork, scholarships/grants, and unspecified assistantships available. Financial award application deadline: 4/15; financial award applicants required to submit FAFSA. *Faculty research:* Elementary education, science education, technology education, reflective practice, teacher education. *Unit head:* Dr. Cheryl Torrez, Chair, 505-277-0911, Fax: 505-277-0455, E-mail: ted@unm.edu. *Application contact:* Lea Briggs, Administrative Assistant, 505-277-9439, Fax: 505-277-0455, E-mail: ted@unm.edu. Website: http://coe.unm.edu/departments-programs/teelp/elementary-education/index.html

University of North Alabama, College of Education, Department of Elementary Education, Program in Elementary Education, Florence, AL 35632-0001. Offers MA Ed, Ed S. *Accreditation:* NCATE. *Program availability:* Part-time, 100% online. *Degree requirements:* For master's, comprehensive exam. *Entrance requirements:* For master's, GRE, MAT, or NTE, minimum GPA of 2.5, Alabama Class B Certificate or equivalent, teaching experience. Additional exam requirements/recommendations for international students: Required—TOEFL (minimum score 79 iBT), IELTS (minimum score 6), PTE (minimum score 54). Electronic applications accepted.

The University of North Carolina at Charlotte, Cato College of Education, Department of Reading and Elementary Education, Charlotte, NC 28223-0001. Offers elementary education (M Ed, Graduate Certificate); elementary mathematics education (Graduate Certificate); reading education (M Ed). *Program availability:* Part-time, evening/weekend, 100% online, blended/hybrid learning. *Students:* 58 part-time (all women); includes 15 minority (12 Black or African American, non-Hispanic/Latino; 1 American Indian or Alaska Native, non-Hispanic/Latino; 2 Two or more races, non-Hispanic/Latino). Average age 31. 39 applicants, 95% accepted, 35 enrolled. In 2018, 29 master's, 23 other advanced degrees awarded. *Entrance requirements:* For master's, GRE or MAT, three letters of recommendation, official transcripts, academic and professional goals statement, valid teacher's license, bachelor's degree in elementary education; NC A-level license or its equivalent in another state (for reading education). Additional exam requirements/recommendations for international students: Required—TOEFL (minimum score 523 paper-based; 70 iBT), IELTS (minimum score 6), TOEFL (minimum score 523 paper-based, 70 iBT) or IELTS (6). *Application deadline:* Applications are processed on a rolling basis. Application fee: $75. Electronic applications accepted. Tuition and fees vary according to course load and program. *Financial support:* Research assistantships, career-related internships or fieldwork, institutionally sponsored loans, scholarships/grants, and unspecified assistantships available. Support available to part-time students. Financial award application deadline: 3/1; financial award applicants required to submit FAFSA. *Total annual research expenditures:* $146,699. *Unit head:* Dr. Mike Putman, Chair, 704-687-8019, E-mail: michael.putman@uncc.edu. *Application contact:* Kathy B. Giddings, Director of Graduate Admissions, 704-687-5503, Fax: 704-687-1668, E-mail: gradadm@uncc.edu. Website: http://reel.uncc.edu/

The University of North Carolina at Greensboro, Graduate School, School of Education, Department of Teacher Education and Higher Education, Program in Curriculum and Teaching, Greensboro, NC 27412-5001. Offers higher education (PhD); teacher education and development (PhD). *Accreditation:* NCATE. *Degree requirements:* For doctorate, comprehensive exam, thesis/dissertation. *Entrance requirements:* For doctorate, GRE General Test. Additional exam requirements/recommendations for international students: Required—TOEFL. Electronic applications accepted.

The University of North Carolina at Pembroke, The Graduate School, School of Education, Program in Elementary Education, Pembroke, NC 28372-1510. Offers MA Ed, MAT. *Accreditation:* NCATE. *Program availability:* Part-time, evening/weekend, online learning. *Degree requirements:* For master's, comprehensive exam, thesis optional. *Entrance requirements:* For master's, GRE General Test or MAT, minimum GPA of 3.0 in major, 2.5 overall; teaching license; two years of full-time teaching experience (recommended). Additional exam requirements/recommendations for international students: Required—TOEFL.

The University of North Carolina Wilmington, Watson College of Education, Department of Early Childhood, Elementary, Middle, Literacy and Special Education, Wilmington, NC 28403-3297. Offers educational leadership, policy, and advocacy (M Ed); elementary education (M Ed, MAT); language and literacy (M Ed); middle grades education (MAT). *Accreditation:* NCATE. *Program availability:* Part-time, blended/hybrid learning. *Degree requirements:* For master's, thesis or alternative, exit portfolio, oral presentation, internship, research project (depending on specialization). *Entrance requirements:* For master's, 3 letters of recommendations, NC Class A teacher license in related field, education statement of interest essay. Additional exam requirements/recommendations for international students: Required—TOEFL (minimum score 550 paper-based; 79 iBT), IELTS (minimum score 6.5). Electronic applications accepted.

University of North Dakota, Graduate School, College of Education and Human Development, Program in Elementary Education, Grand Forks, ND 58202. Offers M Ed, MS. *Accreditation:* NCATE. *Program availability:* Part-time, online learning. *Degree requirements:* For master's, comprehensive exam, thesis or alternative. *Entrance requirements:* For master's, minimum GPA of 3.0. Additional exam requirements/recommendations for international students: Required—TOEFL (minimum score 550 paper-based; 79 iBT), IELTS (minimum score 6.5). Electronic applications accepted. *Faculty research:* Whole language, multicultural education, child-focused learning, experiential science, cooperative learning.

University of Northern Colorado, Graduate School, College of Education and Behavioral Sciences, School of Teacher Education, Program in Elementary Education, Greeley, CO 80639. Offers MAT. *Accreditation:* NCATE. *Program availability:* Part-time, evening/weekend. *Degree requirements:* For master's, comprehensive exam, thesis or alternative. *Entrance requirements:* For master's, GRE General Test. Electronic applications accepted.

University of Northern Iowa, Graduate College, College of Education, Department of Curriculum and Instruction, MAE Program in Elementary Education, Cedar Falls, IA 50614. Offers MAE. *Program availability:* Part-time, evening/weekend. *Degree requirements:* For master's, comprehensive exam, thesis or alternative. *Entrance requirements:* For master's, minimum GPA of 3.0. Additional exam requirements/recommendations for international students: Required—TOEFL (minimum score 500 paper-based; 61 iBT).

University of North Florida, College of Education and Human Services, Department of Childhood Education, Literacy, and TESOL, Jacksonville, FL 32224. Offers literacy (M Ed); professional education (M Ed); TESOL (M Ed). *Accreditation:* NCATE. *Program availability:* Part-time, evening/weekend. *Faculty:* 9 full-time (6 women), 3 part-time/adjunct (2 women). *Students:* 12 full-time (all women), 23 part-time (20 women); includes 15 minority (10 Black or African American, non-Hispanic/Latino; 4 Hispanic/Latino; 1 Two or more races, non-Hispanic/Latino), 2 international. Average age 32. 18 applicants, 67% accepted, 8 enrolled. In 2018, 14 master's awarded. *Entrance requirements:* For master's, GRE General Test, minimum GPA of 3.0 in last 60 hours, 3 letters of recommendation, interview. Additional exam requirements/recommendations for international students: Required—TOEFL (minimum score 500 paper-based). *Application deadline:* For fall admission, 8/1 priority date for domestic students, 5/1 for international students; for spring admission, 12/1 priority date for domestic students, 10/1 for international students; for summer admission, 3/15 priority date for domestic students, 2/1 for international students. Application fee: $30. Electronic applications accepted. *Expenses: Tuition, area resident:* Part-time $408.10 per credit hour. Tuition, state resident: part-time $408.10 per credit hour. Tuition, nonresident: part-time $932.61 per credit hour. *Required fees:* $111.81 per credit hour. Tuition and fees vary according to course load, campus/location and program. *Financial support:* In 2018–19, 2 students received support. Federal Work-Study, tuition waivers (partial), and unspecified assistantships available. Support available to part-time students. Financial award application deadline: 4/1; financial award applicants required to submit FAFSA. *Faculty research:* Social context of and processes in learning, inter-disciplinary instruction, cross-cultural conflict resolution, the Vygotskian perspective on literacy diagnosis and instruction, performance poetry and teaching the language arts through drama. *Total annual research expenditures:* $630. *Unit head:* Dr. Paul Parkison, Chair, 904-620-5352, Fax: 904-620-1025, E-mail: n01230143@unf.edu. *Application contact:* Dr. Amanda Pascale, Director, The Graduate School, 904-620-1360, Fax: 904-620-1362, E-mail: graduateschool@unf.edu.
Website: http://www.unf.edu/coehs/celt/

University of Oklahoma, Jeannine Rainbolt College of Education, Department of Instructional Leadership and Academic Curriculum, Norman, OK 73072. Offers instructional leadership and academic curriculum (M Ed, PhD), including biomedical education (PhD), early childhood education, elementary education, English education, instructional leadership, mathematics education, reading education, science education, social studies education, world languages education (M Ed); reading specialist (M Ed). *Accreditation:* NCATE. *Program availability:* Part-time. *Faculty:* 26 full-time (12 women), 1 part-time/adjunct (0 women). *Students:* 42 full-time (32 women), 113 part-time (85 women); includes 33 minority (9 Black or African American, non-Hispanic/Latino; 5 American Indian or Alaska Native, non-Hispanic/Latino; 6 Asian, non-Hispanic/Latino; 4 Hispanic/Latino; 1 Native Hawaiian or other Pacific Islander, non-Hispanic/Latino; 8 Two or more races, non-Hispanic/Latino), 9 international. Average age 35. 42 applicants, 79% accepted, 21 enrolled. In 2018, 30 master's, 17 doctorates awarded. Terminal master's awarded for partial completion of doctoral program. *Degree requirements:* For master's, comprehensive exam (for some programs), thesis (for some programs); for doctorate, comprehensive exam (for some programs), thesis/dissertation. *Entrance requirements:* For doctorate, GRE. Additional exam requirements/recommendations for international students: Required—TOEFL (minimum score 79 iBT) or IELTS (minimum score 6.5). Application fee: $50 ($100 for international students). Electronic applications accepted. *Expenses:* Tuition, state resident: full-time $5683.20; part-time $236.80 per credit hour. Tuition, nonresident: full-time $20,342; part-time $847.60 per credit hour. *International tuition:* $20,342.40 full-time. *Required fees:* $2894.20; $110.05 per credit hour. $126.50 per semester. Tuition and fees vary according to course load and program. *Financial support:* Fellowships, research assistantships, teaching assistantships, scholarships/grants, and unspecified assistantships available. Financial award application deadline: 6/1; financial award applicants required to submit FAFSA. *Faculty research:* Teacher preparation; instruction; curriculum; learning; constructivist theory. *Unit head:* Dr. Stacy Reeder, Chair, 405-325-1498, Fax: 405-325-4061, E-mail: reeder@ou.edu. *Application contact:* Anna Steele, Graduate Programs Officer, 405-325-4525, E-mail: anna.steele@ou.edu.
Website: http://www.ou.edu/education/ilac

University of Pennsylvania, Graduate School of Education, Division of Teaching, Learning, and Leadership, Teacher Education Program, Philadelphia, PA 19104. Offers elementary education (MS Ed); secondary education (MS Ed). *Students:* 49 full-time (37 women), 2 part-time (both women); includes 13 minority (2 Black or African American, non-Hispanic/Latino; 6 Asian, non-Hispanic/Latino; 2 Hispanic/Latino; 3 Two or more races, non-Hispanic/Latino), 1 international. Average age 25. 140 applicants, 86% accepted, 59 enrolled. In 2018, 36 master's awarded. *Degree requirements:* For master's, thesis or alternative, student teaching, portfolio. *Entrance requirements:* For master's, GRE, bachelor's degree. Additional exam requirements/recommendations for international students: Required—TOEFL, IELTS. *Application deadline:* For summer admission, 6/1 priority date for domestic students, 6/1 for international students. Applications are processed on a rolling basis. Application fee: $80. Electronic applications accepted. *Financial support:* In 2018–19, 53 students received support. Federal Work-Study and scholarships/grants available. Financial award applicants required to submit FAFSA. *Faculty research:* Teacher competencies, social justice teaching, teacher practitioner inquiry. *Unit head:* Maureen Cotterill, Program Manager, 215-898-7364. *Application contact:* Maureen Cotterill, Program Manager, 215-898-7364.
Website: http://www2.gse.upenn.edu/tep/

University of Phoenix–Bay Area Campus, College of Education, San Jose, CA 95134-1805. Offers administration and supervision (MA Ed); adult education and training (MA Ed); early childhood education (MA Ed); education (Ed S); educational leadership (Ed D); elementary teacher education (MA Ed); higher education administration (PhD); secondary teacher education (MA Ed); special education (MA Ed); teacher leadership (MA Ed). *Program availability:* Evening/weekend, online learning. *Degree requirements:* For master's, thesis (for some programs). *Entrance requirements:* For master's, minimum undergraduate GPA of 2.5, 3 years of work experience. Additional exam requirements/recommendations for international students: Required—TOEFL (minimum score 550 paper-based; 79 iBT). Electronic applications accepted.

University of Phoenix–Central Valley Campus, College of Education, Fresno, CA 93720-1552. Offers curriculum and instruction (MA Ed); curriculum and instruction-computer education (MA Ed); elementary teacher education (MA Ed); secondary teacher education (MA Ed).

University of Phoenix–Hawaii Campus, College of Education, Honolulu, HI 96813-3800. Offers administration and supervision (MA Ed); curriculum and instruction (MA Ed); elementary education (MA Ed); secondary education (MA Ed); special education (MA Ed); teacher education for elementary licensure (MA Ed). *Program availability:* Evening/weekend. *Degree requirements:* For master's, thesis (for some programs). *Entrance requirements:* For master's, minimum undergraduate GPA of 2.5, 3 years of work experience. Additional exam requirements/recommendations for international students: Required—TOEFL (minimum score 550 paper-based; 79 iBT). Electronic applications accepted.

University of Phoenix–Las Vegas Campus, College of Education, Las Vegas, NV 89135. Offers administration and supervision (MA Ed); curriculum and instruction (MA Ed); school counseling (MSC); teacher education-elementary licensure (MA Ed). *Program availability:* Evening/weekend. *Degree requirements:* For master's, thesis (for some programs). *Entrance requirements:* For master's, minimum undergraduate GPA of 2.5, 3 years of work experience. Additional exam requirements/recommendations for international students: Required—TOEFL (minimum score 550 paper-based; 79 iBT). Electronic applications accepted.

University of Phoenix–Online Campus, College of Education, Phoenix, AZ 85034-7209. Offers administration and supervision (MAEd, Certificate); adult education and training (MAEd); curriculum and instruction (MAEd), including computer education, curriculum and instruction, English as a second language, language arts, mathematics, reading; early childhood education (MAEd); educational studies (MAEd); elementary teacher education (MAEd), including early childhood, elementary teacher education, high school middle level, middle level; principal licensure (Certificate); secondary teacher education (MAEd); special education (MAEd, Certificate); teacher education (MAEd), including middle level generalist; teacher education middle level mathematics (MAEd), including middle level mathematics; teacher education middle level science (MAEd), including middle level science; teacher education secondary mathematics (MAEd); teacher education secondary science (MAEd); teacher leadership (MAEd); teachers of English learners (Certificate); transition to teaching (Certificate), including elementary education, secondary education. *Program availability:* Evening/weekend, online learning. *Entrance requirements:* Additional exam requirements/recommendations for international students: Required—TOEFL, TOEIC (Test of English as an International Communication), Berlitz Online English Proficiency Exam, PTE, or IELTS. Electronic applications accepted. *Expenses:* Contact institution.

University of Phoenix–Phoenix Campus, College of Education, Tempe, AZ 85282-2371. Offers administration and supervision (MA Ed); adult education and training (MA Ed); curriculum and instruction reading (MA Ed); early childhood education (MA Ed); education studies (MA Ed); elementary teacher education (MA Ed); secondary teacher education (MA Ed); special education (MA Ed); teacher leadership (MA Ed). *Program availability:* Evening/weekend, online learning. *Entrance requirements:* Additional exam requirements/recommendations for international students: Required—TOEFL, TOEIC (Test of English as an International Communication), Berlitz Online English Proficiency Exam, PTE, or IELTS. Electronic applications accepted. *Expenses:* Contact institution.

University of Phoenix–Sacramento Valley Campus, College of Education, Sacramento, CA 95833-4334. Offers adult education (MA Ed); curriculum instruction (MA Ed); elementary teacher education (MA Ed); secondary teacher education (MA Ed); teacher education (Certificate). *Program availability:* Evening/weekend. *Degree requirements:* For master's, thesis (for some programs). *Entrance requirements:* For master's, 3 years of work experience, minimum undergraduate GPA of 2.5. Additional exam requirements/recommendations for international students: Required—TOEFL (minimum score 550 paper-based; 79 iBT). Electronic applications accepted.

University of Phoenix–San Diego Campus, College of Education, San Diego, CA 92123. Offers curriculum and instruction (MA Ed), including computer education, curriculum and instruction, English as a second language; elementary teacher education (MA Ed); secondary teacher education (MA Ed). *Program availability:* Evening/weekend. *Degree requirements:* For master's, thesis (for some programs). *Entrance requirements:* For master's, 3 years of work experience, minimum undergraduate GPA of 3.0. Additional exam requirements/recommendations for international students: Required—TOEFL (minimum score 550 paper-based; 79 iBT). Electronic applications accepted.

University of Pittsburgh, School of Education, Department of Instruction and Learning, Program in Elementary Education, Pittsburgh, PA 15260. Offers M Ed, MAT. *Degree requirements:* For master's, thesis. *Entrance requirements:* For master's, PRAXIS I. Additional exam requirements/recommendations for international students: Required—TOEFL. Electronic applications accepted.

University of Puget Sound, School of Education, Program in Teaching, Tacoma, WA 98416. Offers elementary education (MAT); secondary education (MAT). *Accreditation:* NASM. *Degree requirements:* For master's, project. *Entrance requirements:* For master's, WEST-E or NES, WEST-B or ACT/SAT, two education foundation prerequisite courses; minor in content area (for secondary education). Additional exam requirements/recommendations for international students: Required—TOEFL (minimum score 550 paper-based; 90 iBT). Electronic applications accepted. *Expenses:* Contact institution. *Faculty research:* Pre-service teacher learning, public school partnerships and professional development, creating equitable classrooms, literacy development, teaching social studies.

University of St. Francis, College of Education, Joliet, IL 60435-6169. Offers educational leadership (MS, Ed D); elementary education (M Ed); reading (MS); secondary education (M Ed), including English education, math education, science education, social studies education, visual arts education; special education (M Ed); teaching and learning (MS); TESOL (Certificate). *Accreditation:* NCATE. *Program availability:* Part-time, evening/weekend, 100% online, blended/hybrid learning. *Faculty:* 11 full-time (8 women), 58 part-time/adjunct (38 women). *Students:* 43 full-time (35 women), 453 part-time (354 women); includes 110 minority (48 Black or African American, non-Hispanic/Latino; 7 Asian, non-Hispanic/Latino; 52 Hispanic/Latino; 3 Two or more races, non-Hispanic/Latino), 3 international. Average age 37. 300 applicants, 66% accepted, 164 enrolled. In 2018, 151 master's, 42 doctorates, 4 other advanced degrees awarded. *Degree requirements:* For master's, comprehensive exam; for doctorate, thesis/dissertation. *Entrance requirements:* Additional exam requirements/recommendations for international students: Required—TOEFL (minimum score 550

paper-based; 79 iBT), IELTS (minimum score 6). *Application deadline:* Applications are processed on a rolling basis. Electronic applications accepted. Application fee is waived when completed online. *Expenses:* Contact institution. *Financial support:* In 2018–19, 33 students received support. Scholarships/grants and tuition waivers (partial) available. Support available to part-time students. Financial award applicants required to submit FAFSA. *Unit head:* Dr. John Gambro, Dean, 815-740-3456, E-mail: jgambro@stfrancis.edu. *Application contact:* Sandee Sloka, Director Adult & Graduate Admissions, 800-735-7500, E-mail: ssloka@stfrancis.edu.
Website: https://www.stfrancis.edu/education/

University of Saint Joseph, Department of Education, West Hartford, CT 06117-2700. Offers curriculum and instruction (MA); elementary education (MAT); instructional technology (MA); literacy (MA); secondary education (MAT); TESOL (MA). *Program availability:* Part-time, evening/weekend. *Degree requirements:* For master's, comprehensive exam, thesis or alternative. *Entrance requirements:* For master's, 2 letters of recommendation. Electronic applications accepted. Application fee is waived when completed online.

University of Saint Mary, Graduate Programs, Program in Elementary Education, Leavenworth, KS 66048-5082. Offers MA. *Program availability:* Part-time, evening/weekend. *Students:* 22 full-time (20 women), 1 (woman) part-time; includes 2 minority (both Hispanic/Latino). Average age 32. *Entrance requirements:* For master's, PPST or CBase, minimum GPA of 2.75, interview, essay, two letters of reference. *Application deadline:* Applications are processed on a rolling basis. Application fee: $25. Electronic applications accepted. *Expenses:* Contact institution. *Financial support:* Applicants required to submit FAFSA. *Unit head:* Dr. Cheryl Reding, Unit Head of Education, 913-758-6159, E-mail: cheryl.reding@stmary.edu. *Application contact:* Dr. Cheryl Reding, Unit Head of Education, 913-758-6159, E-mail: cheryl.reding@stmary.edu.
Website: http://www.stmary.edu/success/Grad-Program/Master-of-Arts-Elementary-Education.aspx

University of St. Thomas, School of Education and Human Services, Houston, TX 77006-4696. Offers all level education (M Ed); bilingual/dual language (M Ed); Catholic school teaching (M Ed); Catholic/private school leadership (M Ed); counselor education (M Ed); curriculum and instruction (M Ed); education (Ed D); educational leadership (M Ed); elementary teaching (M Ed); English as a second language (M Ed); exceptionality/educational diagnostician (M Ed); exceptionality/special education (M Ed); generalist (M Ed); reading (M Ed); secondary teaching (M Ed); teaching (MAT). *Accreditation:* TEAC. *Program availability:* Part-time, evening/weekend, online learning. *Degree requirements:* For master's, thesis, field experience. *Entrance requirements:* For master's, GRE or MAT if GPA is below 3.0, bachelor's degree; minimum GPA of 2.75 in bachelor's degree or last 60 credit hours; official transcripts from all institutions; goal statement of 250-300 words; 1 reference. Additional exam requirements/recommendations for international students: Required—TOEFL (minimum score 94 iBT), IELTS (minimum score 7), PTE (minimum score 53). Electronic applications accepted. *Expenses:* Contact institution. *Faculty research:* Leadership, diversity, personality traits, second language acquisition.

University of South Alabama, College of Education and Professional Studies, Department of Leadership and Teacher Education, Mobile, AL 36688. Offers art education (M Ed); early childhood education (M Ed); educational leadership (M Ed, Ed D); elementary education (M Ed); reading education (M Ed); science education (M Ed); secondary education (M Ed); special education (M Ed). *Accreditation:* NCATE. *Program availability:* Part-time. *Degree requirements:* For master's, comprehensive exam, thesis (for some programs); for doctorate, comprehensive exam, thesis/dissertation. *Entrance requirements:* For master's, GRE General Test or MAT, minimum GPA of 3.0; for doctorate, GRE, minimum graduate GPA of 3.25, 3 years of experience in field, 3 letters of recommendation, interview, official transcripts. Additional exam requirements/recommendations for international students: Required—TOEFL. Electronic applications accepted.

University of South Carolina, The Graduate School, College of Education, Department of Instruction and Teacher Education, Program in Elementary Education, Columbia, SC 29208. Offers MAT, Ed D, PhD. *Accreditation:* NCATE. *Degree requirements:* For master's, comprehensive exam; for doctorate, one foreign language, comprehensive exam, thesis/dissertation. *Entrance requirements:* For master's, GRE General Test, MAT, interview, letters of reference, resume; for doctorate, GRE General Test, MAT, interview, letters of reference, letters of intent, resum&e, transcript. *Faculty research:* Children's conception of science, whole language, middle school curriculum.

University of South Carolina Upstate, Graduate Programs, Spartanburg, SC 29303-4999. Offers early childhood education (M Ed); elementary education (M Ed); informatics (MS); special education: visual impairment (M Ed). *Accreditation:* NCATE. *Program availability:* Part-time, evening/weekend. *Degree requirements:* For master's, professional portfolio. *Entrance requirements:* For master's, GRE General Test or MAT, interview, minimum undergraduate GPA of 2.5, teaching certificate, 2 letters of recommendation. *Faculty research:* Promoting university diversity awareness, rough and tumble play, social justice education, American Indian literatures and cultures, diversity and multicultural education, science teaching strategy.

University of South Dakota, Graduate School, School of Education, Division of Curriculum and Instruction, Program in Elementary Education, Vermillion, SD 57069. Offers elementary education (MA), including early childhood education, English language learning, reading specialist/literacy coach, science, technology and math (STEM). *Accreditation:* NCATE. *Program availability:* Part-time, 100% online, blended/hybrid learning. *Degree requirements:* For master's, comprehensive exam, thesis or alternative. *Entrance requirements:* For master's, GRE General Test, MAT, minimum GPA of 2.7. Additional exam requirements/recommendations for international students: Required—TOEFL (minimum score 550 paper-based; 79 iBT). Electronic applications accepted.

University of Southern Indiana, Graduate Studies, Pott College of Science, Engineering, and Education, Department of Teacher Education, Program in Elementary Education, Evansville, IN 47712-3590. Offers MSE. *Accreditation:* NCATE. *Program availability:* Part-time, evening/weekend. *Entrance requirements:* For master's, PRAXIS II, bachelor's degree with minimum cumulative GPA of 2.75 from college or university accredited by NCATE or comparable association; minimum GPA of 3.0 in all courses taken at graduate level at all schools attended; teaching license. Additional exam requirements/recommendations for international students: Required—TOEFL (minimum score 550 paper-based; 79 iBT), IELTS (minimum score 6). Electronic applications accepted.

University of Southern Mississippi, College of Education and Human Sciences, Department of Curriculum, Instruction and Special Education, Hattiesburg, MS 39406-0001. Offers elementary education (M Ed, PhD); instructional technology (MS); instructional technology and design (PhD); secondary education (MAT); special education (M Ed, PhD). *Program availability:* Part-time, online learning. *Degree requirements:* For master's, comprehensive exam, thesis (for some programs); for doctorate, comprehensive exam, thesis/dissertation. *Entrance requirements:* For master's, GRE General Test, MAT, minimum GPA of 3.0; for doctorate, GRE General Test, minimum GPA of 3.5. Additional exam requirements/recommendations for international students: Required—TOEFL, IELTS. *Faculty research:* Mathematical problem solving, integrative curriculum, writing process, teacher education models.

University of South Florida, College of Education, Department of Teaching and Learning, Tampa, FL 33620-9951. Offers early childhood education (M Ed, MA, PhD); elementary education (MA, MAT, PhD); reading/language arts (MA, PhD, Ed S). *Accreditation:* NCATE. *Faculty:* 36 full-time (27 women). *Students:* 244 full-time (193 women), 283 part-time (204 women); includes 140 minority (62 Black or African American, non-Hispanic/Latino; 2 American Indian or Alaska Native, non-Hispanic/Latino; 10 Asian, non-Hispanic/Latino; 61 Hispanic/Latino; 5 Two or more races, non-Hispanic/Latino), 70 international. Average age 36. 204 applicants, 84% accepted, 131 enrolled. In 2018, 67 master's, 3 doctorates awarded. *Degree requirements:* For master's, comprehensive exam, thesis (for some programs); for doctorate, comprehensive exam, thesis/dissertation (for some programs). *Entrance requirements:* For master's, GRE may be required (varies by major), statement of purpose; letters of recommendation; be eligible for professional certification (if applicable to major); passing GKT (if applicable to major); for doctorate, GRE may be required (varies by major), Master's degree with 3.5 GPA; CV; statement of purpose; letters of recommendation; faculty interview; language proficiency (if applicable). Additional exam requirements/recommendations for international students: Required—TOEFL. Application fee: $30. *Expenses:* Tuition, state resident: full-time $6350. Tuition, nonresident: full-time $19,048. *International tuition:* $19,048 full-time. *Required fees:* $2079. *Total annual research expenditures:* $2.7 million. *Unit head:* Dr. Denisse Thompson, Chair, 813-974-4110. *Application contact:* Dr. Denisse Thompson, Chair, 813-974-4110.
Website: http://www.coedu.usf.edu/main/departments/ce/ce.html

University of South Florida, St. Petersburg, College of Education, St. Petersburg, FL 33701. Offers educational leadership development (M Ed); elementary education (MA), including math/science; English education (MA); middle grades STEM education (MS); reading education (MA). *Program availability:* Part-time. *Degree requirements:* For master's, comprehensive exam, practicum, internship, comprehensive portfolio. *Entrance requirements:* For master's, State of Florida General Knowledge Test (GKT), Florida Teaching Certificate (for non-initial certification programs), letters of recommendation. Additional exam requirements/recommendations for international students: Required—TOEFL (minimum score 550 paper-based; 79 iBT); Recommended—IELTS. Electronic applications accepted.

University of South Florida Sarasota-Manatee, College of Liberal Arts and Social Sciences, Sarasota, FL 34243. Offers criminal justice (MA); education (MA); educational leadership (M Ed), including curriculum leadership, K-12 public school leadership, non-public/charter school leadership; elementary education (MAT); English education (MA); social work (MSW). *Program availability:* Part-time, 100% online, blended/hybrid learning. *Faculty:* 14 full-time (9 women), 6 part-time/adjunct (5 women). *Students:* 10 full-time (8 women), 46 part-time (40 women); includes 17 minority (6 Black or African American, non-Hispanic/Latino; 7 Hispanic/Latino; 4 Two or more races, non-Hispanic/Latino). Average age 33. 57 applicants, 46% accepted, 24 enrolled. In 2018, 12 master's awarded. *Degree requirements:* For master's, comprehensive exam (for some programs). *Entrance requirements:* For master's, GRE. Additional exam requirements/recommendations for international students: Required—TOEFL (minimum score 550 paper-based; 79 iBT), IELTS (minimum score 6.5). *Application deadline:* For fall admission, 3/1 priority date for domestic students, 3/1 for international students; for spring admission, 10/1 priority date for domestic students, 10/1 for international students. Applications are processed on a rolling basis. Application fee: $30. Electronic applications accepted. *Expenses: Tuition, area resident:* Full-time $8350; part-time $348 per credit hour. Tuition, state resident: full-time $8350; part-time $348 per credit hour. Tuition, nonresident: full-time $19,048; part-time $794 per credit hour. *Required fees:* $1689; $70 per credit hour. $5 per semester. Tuition and fees vary according to program. *Financial support:* Career-related internships or fieldwork, institutionally sponsored loans, scholarships/grants, health care benefits, and unspecified assistantships available. Support available to part-time students. Financial award application deadline: 6/30; financial award applicants required to submit FAFSA. *Faculty research:* Educational leadership, secondary education, elementary education, and criminal justice. *Total annual research expenditures:* $97,764. *Unit head:* Dr. Jane Rose, Dean, 941-359-4469, Fax: 941-359-4778, E-mail: jane.rose@sar.usf.edu. *Application contact:* Brandon Avery, Assistant Director, Admissions, 941-359-4331, E-mail: bavery@sar.usf.edu.

The University of Tennessee, Graduate School, College of Education, Health and Human Sciences, Program in Education, Knoxville, TN 37996. Offers art education (MS); counseling education (PhD); cultural studies in education (PhD); curriculum (MS, Ed S); curriculum, educational research and evaluation (Ed D, PhD); early childhood education (PhD); early childhood special education (MS); education of deaf and hard of hearing (MS); educational administration and policy studies (Ed D, PhD); educational administration and supervision (Ed S); educational psychology (Ed D, PhD); elementary education (MS, Ed S); elementary teaching (MS); English education (MS, Ed S); exercise science (PhD); foreign language/ESL education (MS, Ed S); instructional technology (MS, Ed D, PhD, Ed S); literacy, language and ESL education (PhD); literacy, language education, and ESL education (Ed D); mathematics education (MS, Ed S); modified and comprehensive special education (MS); reading education (MS, Ed S); school counseling (Ed S); school psychology (PhD, Ed S); science education (MS, Ed S); secondary teaching (MS); social foundations (MS); social science education (MS, Ed S); socio-cultural foundations of sports and education (PhD); special education (Ed S); teacher education (Ed D, PhD). *Accreditation:* NCATE. *Program availability:* Part-time, evening/weekend. *Degree requirements:* For master's and Ed S, thesis optional; for doctorate, variable foreign language requirement, thesis/dissertation. *Entrance requirements:* For master's, minimum GPA of 2.7; for doctorate and Ed S, GRE General Test, minimum GPA of 2.7. Additional exam requirements/recommendations for international students: Required—TOEFL. Electronic applications accepted.

The University of Tennessee at Chattanooga, School of Education, Chattanooga, TN 37403. Offers counseling (M Ed), including community counseling, school counseling; education (M Ed, Post-Master's Certificate), including elementary education (M Ed), school leadership (Post-Master's Certificate); elementary education (M Ed); learning and leadership (Ed D), including educational leadership; school leadership (Post-Master's Certificate); school leadership: principal licensure (Ed S); secondary education (M Ed); special education (M Ed). *Accreditation:* ACA; NCATE. *Program availability:* Part-time. *Degree requirements:* For master's, comprehensive exam, thesis optional, culminating experience; for other advanced degree, internship. *Entrance requirements:* For master's, GRE General Test, PPST 1, teaching certificate; for other advanced degree, two letters of recommendation, graduate degree in education, teaching certificate with three years of experience. Additional exam requirements/recommendations for international students: Required—TOEFL (minimum score 550 paper-based; 79 iBT), IELTS (minimum score 6). Electronic applications accepted. *Expenses:* Contact institution. *Faculty research:* School counseling, community counseling, elementary and secondary education, school leadership and administration.

The University of Tennessee at Martin, Graduate Programs, College of Education, Health and Behavioral Sciences, Program in Teaching, Martin, TN 38238. Offers

curriculum and instruction (MS Ed), including 7-12, K-6; initial licensure (MS Ed), including elementary education, secondary education; initial licensure k-8 (MS Ed), including library service, special education; interdisciplinary (MS Ed). *Program availability:* Part-time, online only, 100% online. *Students:* 24 full-time (20 women), 126 part-time (90 women); includes 19 minority (11 Black or African American, non-Hispanic/Latino; 3 Hispanic/Latino; 5 Two or more races, non-Hispanic/Latino). Average age 34. 69 applicants, 58% accepted, 21 enrolled. In 2018, 28 master's awarded. *Degree requirements:* For master's, comprehensive exam. *Entrance requirements:* For master's, GRE General Test, minimum GPA of 2.5, teaching license. Additional exam requirements/recommendations for international students: Required—TOEFL (minimum score 525 paper-based; 71 iBT). *Application deadline:* For fall admission, 7/27 for domestic and international students; for spring admission, 12/17 for domestic and international students; for summer admission, 5/10 for domestic and international students. Applications are processed on a rolling basis. Application fee: $30 ($130 for international students). Electronic applications accepted. *Expenses: Tuition, area resident:* Full-time $8918; part-time $495 per credit hour. Tuition, state resident: full-time $8918; part-time $485 per credit hour. Tuition, nonresident: full-time $14,958; part-time $831 per credit hour. *International tuition:* $22,862 full-time. *Required fees:* $1446; $81 per credit hour. Part-time tuition and fees vary according to course load. *Financial support:* In 2018–19, 26 students received support, including 1 research assistantship with full tuition reimbursement available (averaging $6,283 per year), 5 teaching assistantships with full tuition reimbursements available (averaging $7,464 per year); scholarships/grants and tuition waivers also available. Financial award application deadline: 2/1; financial award applicants required to submit FAFSA. *Faculty research:* Special education, science/math/technology, school reform, reading. *Unit head:* Cynthia West, Dean, 731-881-7125, Fax: 731-881-7975, E-mail: cwest@utm.edu. *Application contact:* Jolene L. Cunningham, Student Services Specialist, 731-881-7012, Fax: 731-881-7499, E-mail: jcunningham@utm.edu.

The University of Texas Rio Grande Valley, College of Education and P-16 Integration, Department of Teaching and Learning, Edinburg, TX 78539. Offers curriculum and instruction (M Ed, Ed D); educational technology (M Ed). *Program availability:* Part-time, evening/weekend. *Degree requirements:* For master's, comprehensive exam, thesis optional; for doctorate, comprehensive exam, thesis/dissertation. *Entrance requirements:* For master's, minimum GPA of 3.0. Additional exam requirements/recommendations for international students: Required—TOEFL (minimum score 550 paper-based; 79 iBT), IELTS (minimum score 6.5). Electronic applications accepted. *Expenses: Tuition, area resident:* Full-time $6888. Tuition, state resident: full-time $6888. Tuition, nonresident: full-time $14,484. *International tuition:* $14,484 full-time. *Required fees:* $1468. *Faculty research:* Teacher education, mathematics education, science education, educational technology, pedagogy.

University of the Cumberlands, Graduate Programs in Education, Williamsburg, KY 40769-1372. Offers all grades (P-12) (M Ed); business and marketing (MA Ed, MAT); counselor education and supervision (Ed D); director of pupil personnel (Certificate); director of special education (Certificate); educational administration and supervision (Ed S); educational leadership (Ed D); elementary education (MA Ed, MAT); instructional leadership - principalship (MA Ed); instructional leadership - school principal (Certificate); middle school education (MA Ed, MAT); reading and writing (MA Ed); school counseling (MA Ed); school superintendent (Certificate); secondary education (MA Ed, MAT); special education (MAT); supervisor of instruction (Certificate); teacher leader (MA Ed). *Program availability:* Part-time, evening/weekend, online learning. *Degree requirements:* For master's, comprehensive exam. Electronic applications accepted.

University of the District of Columbia, College of Arts and Sciences, Program in Teaching, Washington, DC 20008-1175. Offers elementary education (MAT); middle school mathematics (MAT); secondary English language arts (MAT); secondary social studies (MAT).

The University of Toledo, College of Graduate Studies, Judith Herb College of Education, Department of Curriculum and Instruction, Toledo, OH 43606-3390. Offers art education (ME); career and technical education (ME, Ed S); curriculum and instruction (ME, PhD, Ed S); early childhood education (Ed S); education and anthropology (MAE); education and biology (MES); education and chemistry (MES); education and classics (MAE); education and economics (MAE); education and English (MAE); education and French (MAE); education and geology (MES); education and German (MAE); education and history (MAE); education and mathematics (MAE, MES); education and physics (MES); education and political science (MAE); education and sociology (MAE); education and Spanish (MAE); educational media (PhD); educational technology (ME); educational technology: virtual educator (Certificate); elementary education (PhD); English as a second language (MAE); gifted and talented education (PhD); middle childhood education (ME); secondary education (ME, PhD); special education (PhD). *Accreditation:* NCATE. *Program availability:* Part-time, evening/weekend. *Degree requirements:* For master's, comprehensive exam, thesis or alternative; for doctorate, comprehensive exam, thesis/dissertation; for other advanced degree, thesis optional. *Entrance requirements:* For master's, doctorate, and other advanced degree, minimum cumulative GPA of 2.7 for all previous academic work, letters of recommendation. Additional exam requirements/recommendations for international students: Required—TOEFL (minimum score 550 paper-based; 80 iBT). Electronic applications accepted.

University of Utah, Graduate School, College of Education, Department of Educational Psychology, Salt Lake City, UT 84112. Offers clinical mental health counseling (M Ed); counseling psychology (PhD); elementary education (M Ed); instructional design and educational technology (M Ed); instructional design and technology (MS); learning and cognition (MS, PhD); reading and literacy (M Ed, PhD); school counseling (M Ed); school psychology (M Ed, PhD, Ed S); statistics (M Stat). *Accreditation:* APA (one or more programs are accredited). *Faculty:* 20 full-time (12 women), 50 part-time/adjunct (34 women). *Students:* 127 full-time (93 women), 92 part-time (63 women); includes 33 minority (1 Black or African American, non-Hispanic/Latino; 7 Asian, non-Hispanic/Latino; 18 Hispanic/Latino; 1 Native Hawaiian or other Pacific Islander, non-Hispanic/Latino; 6 Two or more races, non-Hispanic/Latino), 5 international. Average age 32. 296 applicants, 27% accepted, 73 enrolled. In 2018, 68 master's, 10 doctorates, 3 other advanced degrees awarded. Terminal master's awarded for partial completion of doctoral program. *Degree requirements:* For master's, thesis (for some programs); for doctorate, thesis/dissertation. *Entrance requirements:* For master's and doctorate, GRE General Test, minimum GPA of 3.0. Additional exam requirements/recommendations for international students: Required—TOEFL (minimum score 80 iBT). *Application deadline:* For fall admission, 12/15 for domestic and international students; for winter admission, 11/1 for domestic and international students; for spring admission, 3/15 for domestic and international students. Application fee: $55 ($65 for international students). Electronic applications accepted. *Expenses:* Contact institution. *Financial support:* In 2018–19, 72 students received support, including 6 fellowships with full and partial tuition reimbursements available (averaging $17,000 per year), 14 research assistantships with full and partial tuition reimbursements available (averaging $15,750 per year), 27 teaching assistantships with full and partial tuition reimbursements available (averaging $15,500 per year); career-related internships or fieldwork, scholarships/grants,

traineeships, health care benefits, and unspecified assistantships also available. Financial award application deadline: 4/1; financial award applicants required to submit FAFSA. *Faculty research:* Autism, computer technology and instruction, cognitive behavior, aging, group counseling. *Total annual research expenditures:* $620,935. *Unit head:* Dr. Anne E. Cook, Chair, 801-581-7148, Fax: 801-581-5566, E-mail: anne.cook@utah.edu. *Application contact:* JoLynn N. Yates, Academic Coordinator, 801-581-7148, Fax: 801-581-5566, E-mail: jo.yates@utah.edu. Website: http://www.ed.utah.edu/edps/

University of Vermont, Graduate College, College of Education and Social Services, Program in Special Education, Grades K-12, Burlington, VT 05405. Offers M Ed. *Accreditation:* NCATE. *Degree requirements:* For master's, thesis or alternative. *Entrance requirements:* For master's, license (or eligible for licensure). Additional exam requirements/recommendations for international students: Required—TOEFL (minimum score 550 paper-based, 90 iBT) or IELTS (6.5). Electronic applications accepted.

University of Virginia, Curry School of Education, Department of Curriculum, Instruction, and Special Education, Program in Curriculum and Instruction, Charlottesville, VA 22903. Offers curriculum and instruction (M Ed, Ed S); elementary education (M Ed, Ed D); English education (M Ed, Ed D); foreign language education (M Ed); mathematics education (M Ed, Ed D); science education (Ed D); social studies education (M Ed); MBA/M Ed. *Program availability:* 100% online. *Degree requirements:* For master's, comprehensive exam (for some programs); for doctorate, comprehensive exam, thesis/dissertation; for Ed S, comprehensive exam. *Entrance requirements:* For master's, doctorate, and Ed S, GRE General Test, 2 letters of recommendation. Additional exam requirements/recommendations for international students: Required—TOEFL (minimum score 600 paper-based; 90 iBT), IELTS (minimum score 7). Electronic applications accepted.

University of Virginia, Curry School of Education, Program in Education, Charlottesville, VA 22903. Offers administration and supervision (PhD); applied developmental science (PhD); counselor education (PhD); curriculum and instruction (PhD); early childhood special education (MT); education evaluation (PhD); educational psychology (PhD); educational research (PhD); elementary education (MT); English education (MT, PhD); foreign language education (MT); higher education (PhD); instructional technology (PhD); kinesiology (MT, PhD); math education (PhD); reading education (PhD); research, statistics and evaluation (PhD); school psychology (PhD); science education (PhD); social studies education (MT, PhD); special education (PhD); world languages education (MT). *Degree requirements:* For master's, comprehensive exam (for some programs), field project; for doctorate, comprehensive exam, thesis/dissertation. *Entrance requirements:* For doctorate, GRE General Test. Additional exam requirements/recommendations for international students: Required—TOEFL (minimum score 600 paper-based; 90 iBT), IELTS (minimum score 7). Electronic applications accepted.

University of Washington, Tacoma, Graduate Programs, Program in Education, Tacoma, WA 98402-3100. Offers education (M Ed); educational administration (principal or program administrator certification) (M Ed); elementary education teacher certification (M Ed); elementary education/special education teacher certification (M Ed); secondary science or math teacher certification (M Ed). *Program availability:* Part-time, evening/weekend. *Degree requirements:* For master's, culminating project. *Entrance requirements:* For master's, WEST-B, WEST-E (teacher certification programs only), official sealed transcript from every college/university attended, personal goal statement, letters of recommendation, copy of valid teaching certificate. Additional exam requirements/recommendations for international students: Required—TOEFL (minimum score 580 paper-based; 92 iBT). Electronic applications accepted. *Faculty research:* Global learning communities for English/Chinese languages, evaluation of mathematics and reading intervention programs, response to intervention, school-wide behavioral and emotional support, mathematics education and culturally responsive mathematics education.

The University of West Alabama, School of Graduate Studies, College of Education, Program in Elementary Education, Livingston, AL 35470. Offers elementary education (Ed S); elementary education K-6 (M Ed). *Accreditation:* NCATE. *Program availability:* Part-time, evening/weekend, 100% online. *Faculty:* 5 full-time (all women), 35 part-time/adjunct (26 women). *Students:* 451 full-time (431 women), 16 part-time (15 women); includes 137 minority (128 Black or African American, non-Hispanic/Latino; 2 American Indian or Alaska Native, non-Hispanic/Latino; 5 Hispanic/Latino; 2 Two or more races, non-Hispanic/Latino). Average age 32. 133 applicants, 97% accepted, 106 enrolled. In 2018, 117 master's, 23 Ed Ss awarded. *Degree requirements:* For master's, comprehensive exam, thesis optional; for Ed S, comprehensive exam. *Entrance requirements:* For master's, GRE, minimum GPA of 2.75, verification of background clearance/fingerprints, valid bachelor's-level Professional Educator Certificate in same teaching field. Additional exam requirements/recommendations for international students: Required—TOEFL (minimum score 500 paper-based; 61 iBT). *Application deadline:* Applications are processed on a rolling basis. Application fee: $40. Electronic applications accepted. *Expenses: Tuition, area resident:* Full-time $9100. Tuition, state resident: full-time $9100. Tuition, nonresident: full-time $19,200. *Required fees:* $1890; $130. *Financial support:* Teaching assistantships, Federal Work-Study, and unspecified assistantships available. Support available to part-time students. Financial award application deadline: 3/1; financial award applicants required to submit FAFSA. *Unit head:* Dr. Jodie Winship, Chair of College of Education, 205-652-5415, Fax: 205-652-3706, E-mail: jwinship@uwa.edu. *Application contact:* Dr. B. J. Kimbrough, Dean of Graduate Studies, 205-652-3647, Fax: 205-652-3670, E-mail: bkimbrough@uwa.edu. Website: http://www.uwa.edu/elementaryeducationk6.aspx

University of West Florida, College of Education and Professional Studies, Department of Teacher Education and Educational Leadership, Program in Curriculum and Instruction, Pensacola, FL 32514-5750. Offers elementary education (M Ed); middle level education (M Ed); secondary education (M Ed). *Program availability:* Part-time, evening/weekend. *Entrance requirements:* For master's, GRE (minimum score 450 verbal) or MAT (minimum score 396) if bachelor's GPA less than 3.0, state teaching certification; letter of intent; two professional references. Additional exam requirements/recommendations for international students: Required—TOEFL (minimum score 550 paper-based).

University of Wisconsin–Milwaukee, Graduate School, School of Education, Department of Curriculum and Instruction, Milwaukee, WI 53201-0413. Offers curriculum and instruction (MS), including cross-curricular focus, early childhood education, English education, mathematics education, middle childhood/early adolescence education, reading education, science education, urban social studies education. *Program availability:* Part-time. *Students:* 19 full-time (15 women), 56 part-time (49 women); includes 15 minority (3 Black or African American, non-Hispanic/Latino; 1 American Indian or Alaska Native, non-Hispanic/Latino; 3 Asian, non-Hispanic/Latino; 1 Hispanic/Latino; 7 Two or more races, non-Hispanic/Latino), 2 international. Average age 33. 27 applicants, 44% accepted, 11 enrolled. In 2018, 20 master's awarded. *Entrance requirements:* Additional exam requirements/recommendations for international students: Required—TOEFL (minimum score 550 paper-based; 79 iBT), IELTS (minimum score 6.5). *Application deadline:* For fall admission, 1/1 priority date for domestic students; for spring admission, 9/1 for domestic students. Application fee: $56

($96 for international students). Electronic applications accepted. *Financial support:* Fellowships, research assistantships, teaching assistantships, career-related internships or fieldwork, health care benefits, unspecified assistantships, and project assistantships available. Support available to part-time students. Financial award application deadline: 4/15; financial award applicants required to submit FAFSA. *Application contact:* General Information Contact, 414-229-4721, E-mail: soeinfo@uwm.edu.
Website: http://uwm.edu/education/academics/curriculum-instruction-department/

University of Wisconsin–River Falls, Outreach and Graduate Studies, College of Education and Professional Studies, Department of Teacher Education, River Falls, WI 54022. Offers elementary education (MSE); professional development shared inquiry communities (MSE); reading (MSE). *Program availability:* Part-time. *Degree requirements:* For master's, comprehensive exam, thesis or alternative. *Entrance requirements:* For master's, minimum GPA of 2.75. Additional exam requirements/recommendations for international students: Required—TOEFL (minimum score 500 paper-based; 65 iBT), IELTS (minimum score 5.5). Electronic applications accepted.

University of Wisconsin–Stevens Point, College of Fine Arts and Communication, Department of Music, Stevens Point, WI 54481-3897. Offers elementary/secondary music education (MM Ed); studio pedagogy (MM Ed); Suzuki talent education (MM Ed). *Accreditation:* NASM. *Program availability:* Part-time. *Degree requirements:* For master's, thesis or alternative. *Entrance requirements:* For master's, teaching certificate. *Faculty research:* Music education, music composition, music performance.

University of Wisconsin–Stevens Point, College of Professional Studies, School of Education, Program in Elementary Education, Stevens Point, WI 54481-3897. Offers MSE. *Program availability:* Part-time. *Degree requirements:* For master's, comprehensive exam, thesis or alternative. *Entrance requirements:* For master's, teacher certification, minimum undergraduate GPA of 3.0. Additional exam requirements/recommendations for international students: Required—TOEFL (minimum score 523 paper-based). *Faculty research:* Gifted education, early childhood special education, curriculum and instruction, standards-based education.

Utah State University, School of Graduate Studies, Emma Eccles Jones College of Education and Human Services, Program in Elementary Education, Logan, UT 84322. Offers M Ed, MA, MS. *Program availability:* Part-time, online learning. *Degree requirements:* For master's, comprehensive exam (for some programs), thesis (for some programs). *Entrance requirements:* For master's, GRE General Test or MAT, minimum GPA of 3.0, teaching certificate, 3 recommendations, 1 year teaching department record. Additional exam requirements/recommendations for international students: Required—TOEFL. *Faculty research:* Teacher education, supervision, gifted and talented education, language arts/writing, early childhood education.

Utah Valley University, Program in Education, Orem, UT 84058-5999. Offers educational technology (M Ed); elementary mathematics (M Ed); elementary STEM (M Ed); English as a second language (M Ed); reading (M Ed); teachers as leaders (M Ed). *Accreditation:* TEAC. *Program availability:* Part-time. *Degree requirements:* For master's, project. *Entrance requirements:* For master's, GRE, 3 letters of recommendation, interview, essay. Additional exam requirements/recommendations for international students: Required—TOEFL (minimum score 83 iBT). Electronic applications accepted. *Expenses:* Contact institution.

Valdosta State University, Department of Elementary Education, Valdosta, GA 31698. Offers M Ed. *Accreditation:* ASHA; NCATE. *Program availability:* Part-time, evening/weekend, blended/hybrid learning. *Degree requirements:* For master's, thesis (for some programs), comprehensive written and/or oral exams. *Entrance requirements:* For master's, GRE General Test or MAT, minimum GPA of 2.75. Additional exam requirements/recommendations for international students: Required—TOEFL (minimum score 523 paper-based); Recommended—IELTS. Electronic applications accepted. *Expenses:* Contact institution.

Valley City State University, Online Graduate Programs, Valley City, ND 58072. Offers elementary education (M Ed); English education (M Ed); library and information technologies (M Ed); teaching (MAT); teaching and technology (M Ed); teaching English language learners (M Ed); technology education (M Ed). *Accreditation:* NCATE. *Program availability:* Part-time, evening/weekend, online only, 100% online. *Faculty:* 20 full-time (11 women), 13 part-time/adjunct (8 women). *Students:* 5 full-time (2 women), 133 part-time (100 women); includes 8 minority (1 Black or African American, non-Hispanic/Latino; 3 American Indian or Alaska Native, non-Hispanic/Latino; 2 Asian, non-Hispanic/Latino; 2 Hispanic/Latino). Average age 36. 23 applicants, 74% accepted, 12 enrolled. In 2018, 47 master's awarded. *Degree requirements:* For master's, action research report, comprehensive portfolio. *Entrance requirements:* For master's, GRE, MAT, PRAXIS II or National Teaching Board for Professional Standards (if GPA is less than 3.0). Additional exam requirements/recommendations for international students: Required—TOEFL (minimum score 525 paper-based; 71 iBT); Recommended—IELTS (minimum score 5.5). *Application deadline:* For fall admission, 7/26 for domestic and international students; for spring admission, 12/13 for domestic and international students; for summer admission, 5/18 for domestic and international students. Applications are processed on a rolling basis. Application fee: $35. Electronic applications accepted. *Expenses:* $396.39 per credit for all students regardless of residency. *Financial support:* In 2018–19, 16 students received support. Scholarships/grants, tuition waivers (full and partial), and unspecified assistantships available. Financial award applicants required to submit FAFSA. *Faculty research:* Universal accessibility, instructional design and technology, gender communication, STEM education in K-12, English language learners. *Unit head:* Dr. Sheri Okland, Dean, 701-845-7184, E-mail: sheri.l.okland@vcsu.edu. *Application contact:* Misty Lindgren, Graduate Studies, 701-845-7303, Fax: 701-845-7190, E-mail: misty.lindgren@vcsu.edu.
Website: http://www.vcsu.edu/graduate

Valparaiso University, Graduate School and Continuing Education, Programs in Education, Valparaiso, IN 46383. Offers initial licensure (M Ed), including Chinese teaching, elementary education, secondary education; instructional leadership (M Ed); school psychology (Ed S); secondary education (M Ed); M Ed/Ed S. *Accreditation:* NCATE. *Program availability:* Part-time, evening/weekend, online learning. *Entrance requirements:* For master's, GRE General Test, minimum GPA of 3.0. Additional exam requirements/recommendations for international students: Required—TOEFL (minimum score 550 paper-based; 80 iBT), IELTS (minimum score 6). Electronic applications accepted.

Vanderbilt University, Peabody College, Department of Teaching and Learning, Nashville, TN 37240-1001. Offers elementary education (M Ed); English language learners (M Ed); reading education (M Ed); secondary education (M Ed). *Accreditation:* NCATE. *Program availability:* Part-time. *Faculty:* 47 full-time (34 women), 19 part-time/adjunct (16 women). *Students:* 122 full-time (99 women), 37 part-time (27 women); includes 34 minority (22 Black or African American, non-Hispanic/Latino; 2 American Indian or Alaska Native, non-Hispanic/Latino; 4 Asian, non-Hispanic/Latino; 4 Hispanic/Latino; 2 Two or more races, non-Hispanic/Latino), 41 international. Average age 26. 359 applicants, 74% accepted, 106 enrolled. In 2018, 113 master's awarded. *Degree requirements:* For master's, comprehensive exam, thesis optional. *Entrance requirements:* For master's, GRE General Test, MAT. Additional exam requirements/recommendations for international students: Required—TOEFL (minimum score 550 paper-based; 80 iBT). *Application deadline:* For fall admission, 12/31 priority date for domestic and international students; for spring admission, 11/1 priority date for domestic and international students. Applications are processed on a rolling basis. Application fee: $0. Electronic applications accepted. *Expenses: Tuition:* Full-time $47,208; part-time $2026 per credit hour. *Required fees:* $478. *Financial support:* Fellowships with partial tuition reimbursements, research assistantships with partial tuition reimbursements, teaching assistantships with partial tuition reimbursements, Federal Work-Study, institutionally sponsored loans, scholarships/grants, tuition waivers (partial), and unspecified assistantships available. Support available to part-time students. Financial award application deadline: 1/15; financial award applicants required to submit FAFSA. *Faculty research:* Literacy education; science education; math education; learning sciences; diversity studies. *Unit head:* Dr. Deborah Rowe, Chair, 615-322-8100, Fax: 615-322-8999, E-mail: deborah.w.rowe@vanderbilt.edu. *Application contact:* Angela Saylor, Educational Coordinator, 615-322-8092, Fax: 615-322-8999, E-mail: angela.saylor@vanderbilt.edu.

Virginia Commonwealth University, Graduate School, School of Education, Program in Teaching and Learning, Richmond, VA 23284-9005. Offers early and elementary education (MT). *Accreditation:* NCATE. *Program availability:* Part-time. *Entrance requirements:* For master's, GRE General Test or MAT. Additional exam requirements/recommendations for international students: Required—TOEFL (minimum score 600 paper-based; 100 iBT). Electronic applications accepted.

Wagner College, Division of Graduate Studies, Education Department, Program in Childhood Education/Students with Disabilities, Staten Island, NY 10301-4495. Offers childhood education (MS Ed). *Program availability:* Part-time, evening/weekend. *Degree requirements:* For master's, thesis (for some programs), passage of New York State certification exams before student teaching. *Entrance requirements:* For master's, GRE, minimum GPA of 3.0, interview, recommendations. Additional exam requirements/recommendations for international students: Required—TOEFL (minimum score 550 paper-based; 79 iBT), IELTS (minimum score 6.5). Electronic applications accepted. *Expenses:* Contact institution.

Walden University, Graduate Programs, Richard W. Riley College of Education and Leadership, Minneapolis, MN 55401. Offers adult education (Post-Master's Certificate); adult learning (Graduate Certificate); college teaching and learning (Graduate Certificate); community college leadership (Ed D); curriculum, instruction and assessment (Ed D, Ed S, Graduate Certificate); developmental education (Graduate Certificate); early childhood administration, management, and leadership (Graduate Certificate); early childhood education (Ed D, Ed S); early childhood public policy and advocacy (Graduate Certificate); early childhood studies (MS), including administration, management and leadership, early childhood public policy and advocacy, teaching adults in the early childhood field, teaching and diversity in early childhood education; education (MS, PhD), including adolescent literacy and learning (MS), curriculum, instruction, and assessment (grades K-12) (MS), curriculum, instruction, assessment, and evaluation (PhD), early childhood leadership and advocacy (PhD), early childhood special education (PhD), educational leadership (MS), educational leadership and administration (principal preparation) (MS), educational technology and design (PhD), elementary reading and literacy (PreK-6) (MS), elementary reading and mathematics (grades K-6) (MS), global and comparative education (PhD), higher education leadership management and policy (PhD), integrating technology in the classroom (grades K-12) (MS), learning, instruction and innovation (PhD), mathematics (grades 5-8) (MS), mathematics (grades K-6) (MS), mathematics and science (grades K-8) (MS), organizational research, assessment, and evaluation (PhD), reading and literacy with a reading K-12 endorsement (MS), reading literacy assessment and evaluation (PhD), science (grades K-8) (MS), special education (non-licensure) (grades K-12) (MS), teacher leadership (grades K-12) (MS), teaching English language learners (grades K-12) (MS); educational administration and leadership (Ed D); educational leadership and administration (principal preparation) (Ed S); educational technology (Ed D, Ed S, Post Master's Certificate); elementary reading and literacy (Graduate Certificate); engaging culturally diverse learners (Graduate Certificate); enrollment management and institutional marketing (Graduate Certificate); higher education (MS), including adult learning, college teaching and learning, enrollment management and institutional marketing, global higher education, leadership for student success, online and distance learning; higher education and adult learning (Ed D); higher education leadership and management (Ed D); higher education leadership for student success (Graduate Certificate); instructional design and technology (MS, Postbaccalaureate Certificate), including general program (MS), online learning (MS), training and performance improvement (MS); integrating technology in the classroom (Graduate Certificate); mathematics 5-8 (Graduate Certificate); mathematics K-6 (Graduate Certificate); online teaching for adult educators (Graduate Certificate); reading, literacy, and assessment (Ed D, Ed S); science K-8 (Graduate Certificate); special education (Ed D, Ed S, Graduate Certificate); special education (K-age 21) (MAT); teacher leadership (Graduate Certificate); teaching adults English as a second language (Graduate Certificate); teaching adults in the early childhood field (Graduate Certificate); teaching and diversity in early childhood education (Graduate Certificate); teaching English language learners (grades K-12) (Graduate Certificate); teaching K-12 students online (Graduate Certificate). *Accreditation:* NCATE. *Program availability:* Part-time, evening/weekend, online only, 100% online. *Degree requirements:* For doctorate, thesis/dissertation (for some programs), residency; for other advanced degree, residency (for some programs). *Entrance requirements:* For master's, bachelor's degree or higher; minimum GPA of 2.5; official transcripts; goal statement (for some programs); access to computer and Internet; for doctorate, master's degree or higher; three years of related professional or academic experience (preferred); minimum GPA of 3.0; goal statement and current resume (for select programs); official transcripts; access to computer and Internet; for other advanced degree, relevant work experience; access to computer and Internet. Additional exam requirements/recommendations for international students: Required—TOEFL (minimum score 550 paper-based, 79 iBT), IELTS (minimum score 6.5), Michigan English Language Assessment Battery (minimum score 82), or PTE (minimum score 53). Electronic applications accepted.

Warner University, School of Education, Lake Wales, FL 33859. Offers curriculum and instruction (MAEd); elementary education (MAEd); science, technology, engineering, and mathematics (STEM) (MAEd). *Program availability:* Part-time, evening/weekend, online learning. *Degree requirements:* For master's, thesis, accomplished practices portfolio. *Entrance requirements:* For master's, minimum GPA of 3.0 in last 60 hours of undergraduate coursework; 2 letters of recommendation. Additional exam requirements/recommendations for international students: Required—TOEFL (minimum score 550 paper-based). Electronic applications accepted.

Washington State University, College of Education, Department of Teaching and Learning, Pullman, WA 99164-2132. Offers cultural studies and social thought in education (PhD); curriculum and instruction (Ed M, MA); English language learners (Ed M, MA); language, literacy and technology (PhD); literacy education (Ed M, MA); mathematics education (PhD); special education (Ed M, MA, PhD); teacher leadership (Ed D); teaching (MIT), including elementary education, secondary education. Programs offered at the Pullman, Spokane, Tri-cities, Vancouver and Global (online) campuses.

Program availability: Part-time, online learning. *Degree requirements:* For master's, comprehensive exam, thesis, oral or written exam; for doctorate, comprehensive exam, thesis/dissertation, oral and written exam. *Entrance requirements:* For master's, GRE General Test, minimum GPA of 3.0, 3 letters of recommendation, letter of intent, transcripts, resume/curriculum vitae; for doctorate, GRE General Test, minimum GPA of 3.0, 3 letters of recommendation, letter of intent, transcripts, writing sample, resume/ curriculum vitae. Additional exam requirements/recommendations for international students: Required—TOEFL (minimum score 550 paper-based; 80 iBT). Electronic applications accepted. *Faculty research:* Intersection of gender, youth cultures and schooling; examination of ideology of power in children's literature; early childhood special education; analyzing pre-service and in-service teacher development; second language acquisition.

Washington University in St. Louis, The Graduate School, Department of Education, Program in Elementary Education, St. Louis, MO 63130-4899. Offers MA Ed. *Degree requirements:* For master's, thesis or alternative. *Entrance requirements:* For master's, GRE General Test or MAT. Additional exam requirements/recommendations for international students: Required—TOEFL. Electronic applications accepted.

Wayland Baptist University, Graduate Programs, Program in Education, Plainview, TX 79072-6998. Offers education administration (M Ed); education diagnostics (M Ed); education literacy (M Ed); elementary certification (M Ed); English (M Ed); English as a second language (M Ed); higher education administration (M Ed); human resources (M Ed); instructional leadership (M Ed); instructional technology (M Ed); leadership training and development (M Ed); science education (M Ed); secondary certification (M Ed); social studies (M Ed); special education (M Ed); sports administration and management (M Ed). *Program availability:* Part-time, evening/weekend, 100% online. *Degree requirements:* For master's, comprehensive exam, capstone course. *Entrance requirements:* For master's, GRE, GMAT or MAT. Additional exam requirements/ recommendations for international students: Required—TOEFL (minimum score 500 paper-based; 61 iBT). Electronic applications accepted.

Wayne State College, School of Education and Counseling, Department of Educational Foundations and Leadership, Program in Curriculum and Instruction, Wayne, NE 68787. Offers alternative education (MSE); business and information technology education (MSE); communication arts education (MSE); early childhood education (MSE); elementary education (MSE); English as a second language (MSE); English education (MSE); family and consumer sciences education (MSE); industrial technology and vocational education (MSE); learning communities (MSE); mathematics education (MSE); music education (MSE); science education (MSE); social science education (MSE). *Accreditation:* NCATE. *Program availability:* Part-time, evening/weekend. *Degree requirements:* For master's, comprehensive exam, thesis optional. *Entrance requirements:* For master's, GRE General Test. Additional exam requirements/ recommendations for international students: Required—TOEFL (minimum score 550 paper-based).

Wayne State University, College of Education, Division of Teacher Education, Detroit, MI 48202. Offers art education (M Ed); bilingual/bicultural education (Certificate); curriculum and instruction (Ed D, PhD, Ed S), including English as a second language (MAT, Ed D, Ed S), K-12 curriculum (PhD); elementary education (MAT), including bilingual/bicultural education (M Ed, MAT), early childhood education (M Ed, MAT), English as a second language (MAT, Ed D, Ed S), foreign language education, science education (M Ed, MAT), special education (M Ed, MAT); elementary mathematics specialist (Certificate); English as a second language (Certificate); reading (M Ed, Ed S); reading, language and literature (Ed D); secondary education (MAT), including bilingual/ bicultural education (M Ed, MAT), early childhood education (M Ed, MAT), English as a second language (MAT, Ed D, Ed S), English education, foreign language education, mathematics education (M Ed, MAT), science education (M Ed, MAT), social studies education (M Ed, MAT); special education (MAT), including career and technical education; teaching and learning (M Ed), including bilingual/bicultural education (M Ed, MAT), early childhood education (M Ed, MAT), elementary education, foreign language, mathematics education (M Ed, MAT), science education (M Ed, MAT), social studies education (M Ed, MAT), special education (M Ed, MAT). *Program availability:* Part-time, evening/weekend. *Faculty:* 20. *Students:* 121 full-time (94 women), 251 part-time (209 women); includes 116 minority (83 Black or African American, non-Hispanic/Latino; 3 American Indian or Alaska Native, non-Hispanic/Latino; 3 Asian, non-Hispanic/Latino; 14 Hispanic/Latino; 13 Two or more races, non-Hispanic/Latino), 11 international. Average age 37. 171 applicants, 23% accepted, 32 enrolled. In 2018, 112 master's, 8 doctorates, 11 other advanced degrees awarded. *Degree requirements:* For master's, thesis (for some programs), essay or project (for some M Ed programs), professional field experience (for MAT programs); for doctorate, comprehensive exam, thesis/ dissertation. *Entrance requirements:* For master's, undergraduate degree, verification of participation in group work with children, Michigan State Police criminal background check, negative tb test, personal statement (for MAT programs); for all other master's programs: undergraduate degree, personal statement; for doctorate, minimum undergraduate GPA of 3.0, graduate 3.5; interview; curriculum vitae; references; writing sample; letter of application; master's degree (for most programs); for other advanced degree, education specialist certificate: undergraduate with GPA of 2.5 or better and master's degree with GPA of 2.75 or better; personal statement. Additional exam requirements/recommendations for international students: Required—TOEFL (minimum score 550 paper-based; 79 iBT); Recommended—IELTS (minimum score 6.5), TWE (minimum score 5.5), TSE (minimum score 58). *Application deadline:* Applications are processed on a rolling basis. Application fee: $50. Electronic applications accepted. *Financial support:* In 2018–19, 85 students received support, including 3 fellowships (averaging $14,275 per year); research assistantships with tuition reimbursements available, Federal Work-Study, scholarships/grants, and unspecified assistantships also available. Support available to part-time students. Financial award applicants required to submit FAFSA. *Faculty research:* Improving students' skill achievement in mathematics, improving elementary children's understanding of informational text, teachers' use of their pedagogical and mathematical knowledge in the interactive work of teaching, the intersection of identity construction in teaching and learning, identifying effective methods of literacy instruction and assessments for bilingual students in elementary language arts classrooms. *Unit head:* Dr. Roland Coloma, Assistant Dean for Teacher Education, 313-577-0902, E-mail: rscoloma@wayne.edu. *Application contact:* Dr. Mary L. Waker, Graduate Admissions Officer, 313-577-1601, Fax: 313-577-7904, E-mail: m.waker@wayne.edu.
Website: http://coe.wayne.edu/ted/index.php

Webster University, School of Education, Department of Multidisciplinary Studies, St. Louis, MO 63119-3194. Offers applied educational psychology (MA, Ed S); communication arts (MA); early childhood education (MA, MAT); education and innovation (MA); educational technology (MET); elementary education (MAT); mathematics for educators (MA); middle school education (MAT); multidisciplinary studies (MAT); multimodal literacy for global impact (MA); reading (MA); secondary school education (MAT); special education (MA, MAT); teaching English as a second language (MA); transformative learning in the global community (Ed S). *Program availability:* Part-time. *Entrance requirements:* For master's, minimum GPA of 2.5. Additional exam requirements/recommendations for international students: Required—TOEFL. *Expenses: Tuition:* Full-time $22,500; part-time $750 per credit hour. Tuition and fees vary according to degree level, campus/location and program.

Western Governors University, Teachers College, Salt Lake City, UT 84107. Offers curriculum and instruction (MS); educational leadership (MS); elementary education (MAT, Postbaccalaureate Certificate); English education (5-12) (MAT); English language learning (PreK-12) (MA); instructional design (M Ed); learning and technology (M Ed); mathematics (5-12) (MAT); mathematics (5-9) (MAT); mathematics education (5-12) (MA); mathematics education (5-9) (MA); mathematics education (K-6) (MA); science (5-12) (MAT); science education (5-12) (MA), including biology, chemistry, earth science, physics; science education (5-9) (MA); special education (MS). *Accreditation:* NCATE. *Program availability:* Evening/weekend, online learning. *Degree requirements:* For master's, capstone project. *Entrance requirements:* For master's and Postbaccalaureate Certificate, transcripts. Additional exam requirements/ recommendations for international students: Required—TOEFL (minimum score 450 paper-based; 80 iBT). Electronic applications accepted. Application fee is waived when completed online. *Expenses:* Contact institution.

Western Kentucky University, Graduate School, College of Education and Behavioral Sciences, School of Teacher Education, Bowling Green, KY 42101. Offers elementary education (MAE, Ed S); exceptional education: learning and behavioral disorders (MAE); instructional design (MS); interdisciplinary early childhood education (MAE); library media education (MS); literacy education (MAE); middle grades education (MAE); secondary education (MAE, Ed S); special education: moderate and severe disabilities (MAE). *Program availability:* Part-time, evening/weekend, online learning. *Degree requirements:* For master's, comprehensive exam. *Entrance requirements:* For master's, GRE General Test. Additional exam requirements/recommendations for international students: Required—TOEFL (minimum score 555 paper-based; 79 iBT). *Faculty research:* Teacher preparation in moderate/severe disabilities.

Western New Mexico University, Graduate Division, School of Education, Silver City, NM 88062-0680. Offers bilingual education (MAT); educational leadership (MA); elementary education (MAT); reading (MAT); secondary education (MAT); special education (MAT); TESOL (teaching English to speakers of other languages) (MAT). *Accreditation:* NCATE. *Program availability:* Part-time, online learning. *Degree requirements:* For master's, comprehensive exam. *Entrance requirements:* For master's, minimum GPA of 3.0 in last 64 hours of undergraduate study. Additional exam requirements/recommendations for international students: Required—TOEFL (minimum score 550 paper-based; 79 iBT). Electronic applications accepted. *Faculty research:* International education, electronic reading assessment, developing STEM teachers.

Western Washington University, Graduate School, Woodring College of Education, Department of Elementary Education, Bellingham, WA 98225-5996. Offers M Ed. *Accreditation:* NCATE. *Program availability:* Part-time. *Degree requirements:* For master's, comprehensive exam, thesis optional. *Entrance requirements:* For master's, GRE General Test or MAT, minimum GPA of 3.0 in last 60 semester hours or last 90 quarter hours, elementary teaching certificate. Additional exam requirements/ recommendations for international students: Required—TOEFL (minimum score 567 paper-based). Electronic applications accepted. *Faculty research:* Teacher learning through National Board certification.

Westfield State University, College of Graduate and Continuing Education, Department of Education, Program in Elementary Education, Westfield, MA 01086. Offers M Ed. *Accreditation:* NCATE. *Program availability:* Part-time, evening/weekend. *Degree requirements:* For master's, comprehensive exam, practicum. *Entrance requirements:* For master's, GRE General Test or MAT, minimum undergraduate GPA of 2.8. Additional exam requirements/recommendations for international students: Recommended—TOEFL (minimum score 550 paper-based; 79 iBT).

West Virginia University, College of Education and Human Services, Morgantown, WV 26506. Offers audiology (Au D); autism spectrum disorder (MA); clinical rehabilitation and mental health counseling (MS); communication science and disorders (PhD); counseling (MA); counseling psychology (PhD); curriculum and instruction (Ed D); early childhood education (MA); early intervention/ early childhood special education (MA); education (PhD); educational leadership (MA); educational leadership/ public school administration (Ed D); educational leadership/public school administration (MA); educational psychology (MA, Ed D); elementary education (MA); gifted education (MA); higher education administration (MA, Ed D); higher education curriculum and teaching (MA); institutional design and technology (MA); instructional design and technology (Ed D); literacy education (MA); secondary education (MA); secondary education/ English (MA); special education (Ed D); speech pathology (MS). *Accreditation:* ASHA; NCATE. *Program availability:* Part-time, evening/weekend, online learning. *Students:* 392 full-time (325 women), 337 part-time (285 women); includes 44 minority (16 Black or African American, non-Hispanic/Latino; 16 Hispanic/Latino; 12 Two or more races, non-Hispanic/Latino), 11 international. In 2018, 303 master's, 6 doctorates awarded. *Degree requirements:* For master's, content exams; for doctorate, comprehensive exam, thesis/ dissertation. *Entrance requirements:* Additional exam requirements/recommendations for international students: Required—TOEFL (minimum score 500 paper-based; 61 iBT). *Application deadline:* For fall admission, 8/1 for domestic students; for spring admission, 1/1 for domestic students; for summer admission, 5/1 for domestic students. Application fee: $60. Electronic applications accepted. *Financial support:* Fellowships, research assistantships, teaching assistantships, career-related internships or fieldwork, Federal Work-Study, institutionally sponsored loans, health care benefits, tuition waivers (full and partial), and administrative assistantships available. Financial award applicants required to submit FAFSA. *Faculty research:* Internet training and integration for teachers, rural education, teacher preparation, organization of schools, evaluation of personnel. *Unit head:* Dr. Tracy L. Morris, Interim Dean, 304-293-0816, Fax: 304-293-7565, E-mail: Tracy.Morris@mail.wvu.edu. *Application contact:* Dr. Melissa Luna, Associate Dean for Research, 304-293-2174, Fax: 304-293-3802, E-mail: Melissa.Luna@mail.wvu.edu.
Website: http://cehs.wvu.edu/

Wheaton College, Graduate School, Department of Education, Wheaton, IL 60187-5593. Offers elementary education (MAT); secondary education (MAT). *Accreditation:* NCATE. *Faculty:* 1 full-time (0 women), 1 part-time/adjunct (0 women). *Students:* 18 full-time (13 women), 22 part-time (10 women); includes 7 minority (3 Asian, non-Hispanic/ Latino; 3 Hispanic/Latino; 1 Two or more races, non-Hispanic/Latino), 1 international. Average age 24. 21 applicants, 86% accepted, 13 enrolled. In 2018, 14 master's awarded. *Degree requirements:* For master's, thesis or alternative. *Entrance requirements:* For master's, GRE General Test or MAT. Additional exam requirements/ recommendations for international students: Required—TOEFL (minimum score 550 paper-based; 80 iBT), IELTS (minimum score 6.5). *Application deadline:* For fall admission, 5/1 for domestic students, 1/1 for international students; for spring admission, 11/1 for domestic students. Applications are processed on a rolling basis. Application fee: $30. Electronic applications accepted. *Expenses: Tuition:* Full-time $20,400; part-time $850 per credit hour. Tuition and fees vary according to degree level and program. *Financial support:* Career-related internships or fieldwork and Federal Work-Study available. Financial award application deadline: 3/1; financial award applicants required to submit FAFSA. *Unit head:* Dr. Paul Egeland, Chair, 630-752-5041, E-mail: education.dept@wheaton.edu. *Application contact:* Terrance Campbell,

Director of Graduate Admissions, 630-752-5195, Fax: 630-752-7047, E-mail: graduate.admissions@wheaton.edu.
Website: https://www.wheaton.edu/graduate-school/degrees/ma-in-teaching/

Whittier College, Graduate Programs, Department of Education and Child Development, Program in Elementary Education, Whittier, CA 90608-0634. Offers MA Ed. *Program availability:* Part-time, evening/weekend. *Degree requirements:* For master's, thesis. *Entrance requirements:* For master's, GRE General Test, MAT.

Whitworth University, School of Education, Graduate Studies in Education, Spokane, WA 99251-0001. Offers administration (M Ed); counseling (M Ed), including school counselors, social agency/church setting; elementary education (M Ed); gifted and talented (MAT); secondary education (M Ed); special education (MAT); teaching (MIT). *Accreditation:* NCATE. *Program availability:* Part-time, evening/weekend. *Degree requirements:* For master's, comprehensive exam, thesis (for some programs). *Entrance requirements:* For master's, GRE General Test, MAT. Additional exam requirements/recommendations for international students: Required—TOEFL. *Faculty research:* Rural program development, mainstreaming, special needs learners.

Widener University, School of Human Service Professions, Center for Education, Chester, PA 19013-5792. Offers adult education (M Ed); counseling in higher education (M Ed); counselor education (M Ed); early childhood education (M Ed); educational foundations (M Ed); educational leadership (M Ed); educational psychology (M Ed); elementary education (M Ed); English and language arts (M Ed); health education (M Ed); higher education leadership (Ed D); home and school visitor (M Ed); human sexuality (M Ed, PhD); mathematics education (M Ed); middle school education (M Ed); principalship (M Ed); reading and language arts (Ed D); reading education (M Ed); school administration (Ed D); science education (M Ed); social studies education (M Ed); special education (M Ed); technology education (M Ed). *Accreditation:* NCATE. *Program availability:* Part-time, evening/weekend. Terminal master's awarded for partial completion of doctoral program. *Degree requirements:* For doctorate, thesis/dissertation. *Entrance requirements:* For master's, minimum GPA of 2.5; for doctorate, GRE or MAT, minimum GPA of 2.0 (undergraduate), 3.5 (graduate). Electronic applications accepted. *Expenses:* Contact institution. *Faculty research:* Reading and cognition, adult education, technology education, educational leadership, special education.

William Carey University, School of Education, Hattiesburg, MS 39401. Offers art education (M Ed); art of teaching (M Ed); elementary education (M Ed, Ed S); English education (M Ed); gifted education (M Ed); history and social science (M Ed); mild/moderate disabilities (M Ed); secondary education (M Ed). *Accreditation:* NCATE. *Program availability:* Part-time. *Degree requirements:* For master's, comprehensive exam. *Entrance requirements:* For master's, GRE, MAT, minimum GPA of 2.5, Class A teacher's license. Additional exam requirements/recommendations for international students: Required—TOEFL (minimum score 550 paper-based).

William Paterson University of New Jersey, College of Education, Wayne, NJ 07470-8420. Offers curriculum and learning (M Ed); early childhood education (Certificate); educational leadership (M Ed); educational media specialist (Certificate); elementary education (MAT, Certificate); elementary education subject area (Certificate); higher education administration (MA); learning disabilities consultant (Certificate); literacy (M Ed); middle level education (M Ed); middle school education subject area (Certificate); professional counseling (M Ed); reading specialist (Certificate); school library media specialist (Certificate); school principal (Certificate); school supervisor (Certificate); secondary education (MAT); special education (M Ed); teacher of students with disabilities (Certificate). *Accreditation:* NCATE. *Program availability:* Part-time, evening/weekend. *Students:* Average age 35. 347 applicants, 87% accepted, 226 enrolled. In 2018, 136 master's awarded. *Degree requirements:* For master's, comprehensive exam, thesis (for some programs), exit interview (for some programs); practicum/internship; minimum GPA of 3.0 (for some programs); exit portfolio (for some programs). *Entrance requirements:* For master's, GRE/MAT, minimum GPA of 2.75; teaching certificate; essay; interview; 2 letters of recommendation; personal statement. Additional exam requirements/recommendations for international students: Required—TOEFL (minimum score 550 paper-based; 79 iBT), IELTS (minimum score 6). *Application deadline:* For fall admission, 6/1 for domestic students, 3/1 for international students; for spring admission, 11/1 for domestic students, 10/1 for international students. Applications are processed on a rolling basis. Application fee: $50. Electronic applications accepted. *Expenses: Tuition, area resident:* Full-time $14,714; part-time $727 per credit. Tuition, state resident: full-time $14,714; part-time $727 per credit. Tuition, nonresident: full-time $22,952; part-time $727 per credit. *International tuition:* $22,952 full-time. *Required fees:* $4 per semester. Tuition and fees vary according to course load, degree level and program. *Financial support:* In 2018–19, 8,416 students received support. Career-related internships or fieldwork, Federal Work-Study, scholarships/grants, and unspecified assistantships available. Support available to part-time students. Financial award application deadline: 3/15; financial award applicants required to submit FAFSA. *Faculty research:* Code switching and creative writing, language instruction, teacher evaluation, preschools, history of educational theories. *Total annual research expenditures:* $311,226. *Unit head:* Dr. Dorothy Feola, Dean, 973-720-2138, Fax: 973-720-3647, E-mail: feolad@wpunj.edu. *Application contact:* Liana Fornarotto, Director of Education Enrollment and Certification, 973-720-2206, Fax: 973-720-2989, E-mail: fornarottol@wpunj.edu.
Website: http://www.wpunj.edu/coe

Wilmington University, College of Education, New Castle, DE 19720-6491. Offers applied technology in education (M Ed); career and technical education (M Ed); educational leadership (Ed D); elementary and secondary school counseling (M Ed); elementary studies (M Ed); ESOL literacy (M Ed); higher education leadership (Ed D); instruction: gifted and talented (M Ed); instruction: teacher of reading (M Ed); instruction: teaching and learning (M Ed); organizational leadership (Ed D); school leadership (M Ed); secondary education (MAT); special education (M Ed). *Accreditation:* NCATE. *Program availability:* Part-time, evening/weekend. *Entrance requirements:* For master's, 2 letters of recommendation, interview. Additional exam requirements/recommendations for international students: Required—TOEFL (minimum score 500 paper-based). Electronic applications accepted.

Wilson College, Graduate Programs, Chambersburg, PA 17201-1285. Offers accounting (M Acc); choreography and visual art (MFA); education (M Ed); educational technology (MET); healthcare administration (MHA); humanities (MA), including art and culture, critical/cultural theory, English language and literature, women's studies; management (MSM); nursing (MSN), including nursing education, nursing leadership and management; special education (MSE). *Program availability:* Evening/weekend. *Degree requirements:* For master's, project. *Entrance requirements:* For master's, PRAXIS, minimum undergraduate cumulative GPA of 3.0, 2 letters of recommendation, current certification for eligibility to teach in grades K-12, resume, personal interview. Electronic applications accepted.

Wingate University, Thayer School of Education, Wingate, NC 28174. Offers community college executive leadership (Ed D); educational leadership (MA Ed, Ed S); elementary education (MA Ed, MAT). *Accreditation:* NCATE. *Program availability:* Part-time, evening/weekend. *Degree requirements:* For master's, portfolio. *Entrance requirements:* For master's, GRE General Test or MAT, teaching certificate (MA Ed).

Worcester State University, Graduate School, Department of Education, Worcester, MA 01602-2597. Offers adult English as a esl (Postbaccalaureate Certificate); curriculum and instruction (Ed S); early childhood education (M Ed); education (M Ed); elementary education (M Ed); English as a second language (M Ed, Postbaccalaureate Certificate); middle school education (M Ed); middle/secondary school education (Postbaccalaureate Certificate); moderate disabilities (M Ed, Postbaccalaureate Certificate); reading (M Ed, Postbaccalaureate Certificate); reading specialist (Postbaccalaureate Certificate); school leadership and education administration (M Ed); school psychology (M Ed, Ed S); secondary education (M Ed, Ed S, Postbaccalaureate Certificate). *Faculty:* 10 full-time (9 women), 23 part-time/adjunct (11 women). *Students:* 38 full-time (33 women), 281 part-time (212 women); includes 30 minority (4 Black or African American, non-Hispanic/Latino; 3 American Indian or Alaska Native, non-Hispanic/Latino; 2 Asian, non-Hispanic/Latino; 16 Hispanic/Latino; 5 Two or more races, non-Hispanic/Latino), 2 international. Average age 41. 102 applicants, 98% accepted, 88 enrolled. In 2018, 132 master's, 52 Ed Ss awarded. *Degree requirements:* For master's, comprehensive exam (for some programs), thesis (for some programs), For a detail list of degree completion requirements please see the graduate catalog at catalog.worcester.edu. *Entrance requirements:* For master's, GRE General Test, MAT or GMAT, teaching certificate. For a detail list of entrance requirements please see the graduate catalog at catalog.worcester.edu. Additional exam requirements/recommendations for international students: Required—TOEFL (minimum score 550 paper-based; 79 iBT), PTE. *Application deadline:* For fall admission, 3/1 for domestic and international students; for spring admission, 11/1 for domestic and international students; for summer admission, 3/1 for domestic and international students. Applications are processed on a rolling basis. Application fee: $50. Electronic applications accepted. *Expenses: Tuition, area resident:* Full-time $3042; part-time $169 per credit hour. Tuition, state resident: full-time $3042; part-time $169 per credit hour. Tuition, nonresident: full-time $3042; part-time $169 per credit hour. *International tuition:* $3042 full-time. *Required fees:* $2754; $153 per credit hour. *Financial support:* Career-related internships or fieldwork, scholarships/grants, and unspecified assistantships available. Support available to part-time students. Financial award application deadline: 3/1; financial award applicants required to submit FAFSA. *Unit head:* Dr. Sara Young, Graduate Program Coordinator, 508-929-8246, Fax: 508-929-8164, E-mail: syoung3@worcester.edu. *Application contact:* Sara Grady, Associate Dean of Graduate and Continuing Education, 508-929-8130, Fax: 508-929-8100, E-mail: sara.grady@worcester.edu.

Wright State University, Graduate School, College of Education and Human Services, Department of Teacher Education, Programs in Classroom Teacher Education, Dayton, OH 45435. Offers M Ed, MA. *Accreditation:* NCATE. *Degree requirements:* For master's, thesis (for some programs). *Entrance requirements:* For master's, GRE General Test, MAT, PRAXIS II. Additional exam requirements/recommendations for international students: Required—TOEFL.

Xavier University, College of Professional Sciences, School of Education, Department of Childhood Education and Literacy, Cincinnati, OH 45207. Offers children's multicultural literature (M Ed); elementary education (M Ed); Montessori education (M Ed); reading (M Ed). *Program availability:* Part-time. *Degree requirements:* For master's, comprehensive exam, thesis, 30 semester hours. *Entrance requirements:* For master's, GRE, MAT, official transcript; 3 letters of recommendation (for Montessori education); resume; statement of purpose. Additional exam requirements/recommendations for international students: Required—TOEFL (minimum score 550 paper-based; 79 iBT). Electronic applications accepted. Application fee is waived when completed online. *Expenses:* Contact institution. *Faculty research:* Multicultural literacy/fluency, early literacy development, writing/creative and across curriculum, assessment of reading abilities.

Higher Education

Abilene Christian University, College of Graduate and Professional Studies, Program in Higher Education, Addison, TX 79699. Offers conflict management (M Ed); enrollment management (M Ed). *Program availability:* Part-time, online only. *Faculty:* 2 full-time (0 women), 1 part-time/adjunct (0 women). *Students:* 28 full-time (22 women), 16 part-time (10 women); includes 24 minority (11 Black or African American, non-Hispanic/Latino; 1 American Indian or Alaska Native, non-Hispanic/Latino; 8 Hispanic/Latino; 4 Two or more races, non-Hispanic/Latino), 1 international. 19 applicants, 95% accepted, 10 enrolled. In 2018, 22 master's awarded. *Degree requirements:* For master's, internship, capstone. *Entrance requirements:* Additional exam requirements/recommendations for international students: Required—TOEFL (minimum score 80 iBT), IELTS (minimum score 6), PTE. *Application deadline:* For fall admission, 10/7 for domestic students; for winter admission, 12/20 for domestic students; for spring admission, 2/24 for domestic students; for summer admission, 4/20 for domestic students. Applications are processed on a rolling basis. Application fee: $50. Electronic applications accepted. *Expenses:* $726 per hour. *Financial support:* In 2018–19, 7 students received support. Scholarships/grants available. Financial award application deadline: 7/1; financial award applicants required to submit FAFSA. *Unit head:* Dr. Jason Morris, Graduate Director, 325-674-2830, Fax: 325-674-2123, E-mail: morrisj@acu.edu. *Application contact:* Graduate Advisor, 855-219-7300, E-mail: onlineadmissions@acu.edu.
Website: http://www.acu.edu/online/academics/higher-education.html

Alliant International University–San Diego, Shirley M. Hufstedler School of Education, Educational Leadership Programs, San Diego, CA 92131. Offers educational administration (MA); educational leadership and management (K-12) (Ed D); higher education (Ed D, Certificate); preliminary administrative services (Credential). *Program availability:* Part-time. *Degree requirements:* For doctorate, comprehensive exam, thesis/dissertation. *Entrance requirements:* For master's, minimum GPA of 2.5, letters of recommendation; for doctorate, minimum GPA of 3.0, letters of recommendation.

Additional exam requirements/recommendations for international students: Required—TOEFL (minimum score 550 paper-based; 80 iBT), TWE (minimum score 5). Electronic applications accepted. *Faculty research:* Global education, women and international educational opportunities.

Alliant International University–San Francisco, Shirley M. Hufstedler School of Education, Educational Leadership Programs, San Francisco, CA 94133. Offers community college administration (Ed D); educational administration (MA); educational leadership and management (K-12) (Ed D); higher education (Ed D); preliminary administrative services (Credential). *Program availability:* Part-time. *Degree requirements:* For doctorate, comprehensive exam, thesis/dissertation. *Entrance requirements:* For master's and doctorate, minimum GPA of 3.0, letters of recommendation. Additional exam requirements/recommendations for international students: Required—TOEFL (minimum score 550 paper-based; 80 iBT), TWE (minimum score 5). Electronic applications accepted. *Faculty research:* Leadership in higher education, community colleges.

Andrews University, School of Graduate Studies, School of Education, Department of Leadership and Educational Administration, Berrien Springs, MI 49104. Offers educational administration and leadership (MA, Ed D, PhD, Ed S); higher education administration (MA, Ed D, PhD, Ed S); leadership (MA, Ed D, PhD, Ed S). *Degree requirements:* For doctorate, thesis/dissertation. *Entrance requirements:* For master's, GRE. Additional exam requirements/recommendations for international students: Required—TOEFL (minimum score 550 paper-based).

Angelo State University, College of Graduate Studies and Research, College of Education, Department of Curriculum and Instruction, San Angelo, TX 76909. Offers curriculum and instruction (MA); educational administration (M Ed); guidance and counseling (M Ed); student development and leadership in higher education (M Ed). *Program availability:* Part-time, evening/weekend, online learning. *Students:* 360 full-time (307 women), 456 part-time (364 women); includes 312 minority (93 Black or African American, non-Hispanic/Latino; 3 American Indian or Alaska Native, non-Hispanic/Latino; 7 Asian, non-Hispanic/Latino; 193 Hispanic/Latino; 1 Native Hawaiian or other Pacific Islander, non-Hispanic/Latino; 15 Two or more races, non-Hispanic/Latino). Average age 35. *Application deadline:* For fall admission, 7/15 priority date for domestic students, 6/10 for international students; for spring admission, 12/1 priority date for domestic students, 11/1 for international students. Application fee: $40 ($50 for international students). *Expenses: Tuition, area resident:* Full-time $3964; part-time $220 per credit hour. Tuition, state resident: full-time $3964; part-time $220 per credit hour. Tuition, nonresident: full-time $11,434; part-time $635 per credit hour. *International tuition:* $11,434 full-time. *Unit head:* Dr. Kim Livengood, Chair, 325-942-2647, Fax: 325-942-2039, E-mail: kim.livengood@angelo.edu. *Application contact:* Dr. Kim Livengood, Chair, 325-942-2647, Fax: 325-942-2039, E-mail: kim.livengood@angelo.edu.
Website: http://www.angelo.edu/dept/ci/

Appalachian State University, Cratis D. Williams School of Graduate Studies, Department of Leadership and Educational Studies, Boone, NC 28608. Offers educational administration (Ed S); educational media (MA); higher education (MA, Ed S); library science (MLS); school administration (MSA). *Program availability:* Part-time, evening/weekend, online learning. *Degree requirements:* For master's and Ed S, comprehensive exam, thesis optional. *Entrance requirements:* For master's and Ed S, GRE or MAT, 3 letters of recommendation. Additional exam requirements/recommendations for international students: Required—TOEFL (minimum score 570 paper-based; 79 iBT), IELTS (minimum score 6.5). Electronic applications accepted. *Expenses: Tuition, area resident:* Full-time $4839; part-time $237 per credit hour. Tuition, state resident: full-time $4839; part-time $237 per credit hour. Tuition, nonresident: full-time $18,271; part-time $895.50 per credit hour. *Faculty research:* Brain, learning and meditation; leadership of teaching and learning.

Argosy University, Atlanta, College of Education, Atlanta, GA 30328. Offers educational leadership (MAEd, Ed D, Ed S), including higher education administration (Ed D), K-12 education (Ed D); teaching and learning (MAEd, Ed D, Ed S), including education technology (Ed D), higher education (Ed D), K-12 education (Ed D).

Argosy University, Chicago, College of Education, Chicago, IL 60601. Offers adult education and training (MA Ed); community college executive leadership (Ed D); educational leadership (MA Ed, Ed D, Ed S), including district leadership (Ed D), higher education administration (Ed D), K-12 education (Ed D); instructional leadership (Ed D, Ed S), including higher education (Ed D), K-12 education (Ed D). *Program availability:* Online learning.

Argosy University, Hawai`i, College of Education, Honolulu, HI 96813. Offers adult education and training (MAEd); educational leadership (Ed D), including higher education administration, K-12 education; instructional leadership (Ed D), including higher education, K-12 education; school psychology (MA).

Argosy University, Los Angeles, College of Education, Los Angeles, CA 90045. Offers community college executive leadership (Ed D); educational leadership (MA Ed, Ed D), including higher education administration (Ed D), K-12 education (Ed D); instructional leadership (MA Ed, Ed D), including higher education (Ed D), K-12 education (Ed D), multiple subject teacher preparation (MA Ed), single subject teacher preparation (MA Ed).

Argosy University, Northern Virginia, College of Education, Arlington, VA 22209. Offers community college executive leadership (Ed D); educational leadership (MA Ed, Ed D, Ed S), including higher education administration (Ed D), K-12 education (Ed D); instructional leadership (MA Ed, Ed D, Ed S), including higher education (Ed D), K-12 education (Ed D).

Argosy University, Orange County, College of Education, Orange, CA 92868. Offers community college executive leadership (Ed D); educational leadership (MA Ed, Ed D), including higher education administration (Ed D), K-12 education (Ed D); instructional leadership (MA Ed, Ed D), including education technology (Ed D), higher education (Ed D), K-12 education (Ed D), multiple subject teacher preparation (MA Ed), single subject teacher preparation (MA Ed).

Argosy University, Phoenix, College of Education, Phoenix, AZ 85021. Offers adult education and training (MA Ed); advanced educational administration (Ed D, Ed S); community college executive leadership (Ed D); educational administration (MA Ed); educational leadership (MA Ed, Ed D, Ed S), including education technology (Ed D), higher education administration (Ed D), K-12 education (Ed D); higher and postsecondary education (MA Ed); initial educational administration (Ed D, Ed S); school psychology (MA); teaching and learning (MA Ed, Ed D, Ed S), including education technology (Ed D), higher education (Ed D), K-12 education (Ed D).

Argosy University, Seattle, College of Education, Seattle, WA 98121. Offers adult education and training (MA Ed); community college executive leadership (Ed D); educational leadership (MA Ed, Ed D), including higher education administration (Ed D), K-12 education (Ed D); higher and postsecondary education (MA Ed); instructional leadership (MA Ed, Ed D), including education technology (Ed D), higher education (Ed D), K-12 education (Ed D).

Argosy University, Tampa, College of Education, Tampa, FL 33607. Offers community college executive leadership (Ed D); educational leadership (MA Ed, Ed D, Ed S), including higher education administration (Ed D), K-12 education (Ed D); school counseling (MA); teaching and learning (MA Ed, Ed D, Ed S), including higher education (Ed D), K-12 education (Ed D).

Argosy University, Twin Cities, College of Education, Eagan, MN 55121. Offers advanced educational administration (Ed D, Ed S); educational leadership (MA Ed, Ed D, Ed S), including higher education administration (Ed D), K-12 education (Ed D); higher and postsecondary education (MA Ed); initial educational administration (Ed D, Ed S); instructional leadership (MA Ed, Ed D, Ed S), including education technology (Ed D), higher education (Ed D), K-12 education (Ed D).

Arizona State University at the Tempe campus, Mary Lou Fulton Teachers College, Program in Higher and Post-Secondary Education, Phoenix, AZ 85069. Offers M Ed. *Program availability:* Part-time, evening/weekend. *Degree requirements:* For master's, thesis or alternative, applied project, interactive Program of Study (iPOS) submitted before completing 50 percent of required credit hours. *Entrance requirements:* For master's, minimum GPA of 3.0 or equivalent in last 2 years of work leading to bachelor's degree, 3 letters of recommendation, personal statement describing research and career goals, curriculum vitae or resume. Additional exam requirements/recommendations for international students: Required—TOEFL, IELTS, or PTE. Electronic applications accepted.

Auburn University, Graduate School, College of Education, Department of Educational Foundations, Leadership, and Technology, Auburn University, AL 36849. Offers adult education (PhD, Ed S); curriculum supervision (M Ed, PhD); higher education administration (PhD); library media (Ed S); school administration (M Ed, PhD). *Accreditation:* NCATE. *Program availability:* Part-time. *Degree requirements:* For master's, thesis (for some programs); for doctorate, thesis/dissertation; for Ed S, field project. *Entrance requirements:* For master's, doctorate, and Ed S, GRE General Test. Electronic applications accepted. *Expenses:* Tuition, state resident: full-time $11,282; part-time $535 per credit hour. Tuition, nonresident: full-time $30,542; part-time $1605 per credit hour. *Required fees:* $826 per semester. Tuition and fees vary according to degree level and program.

Azusa Pacific University, School of Behavioral and Applied Sciences, Department of Higher Education, Azusa, CA 91702-7000. Offers college counseling and student development (MS); higher education (PhD); higher education leadership (Ed D).

Ball State University, Graduate School, Teachers College, Department of Educational Studies, Program in Adult Education, Muncie, IN 47306. Offers adult and community education (MA); adult, higher and community education (Ed D). *Accreditation:* NCATE. *Program availability:* Part-time, 100% online, blended/hybrid learning. *Degree requirements:* For doctorate, thesis/dissertation. *Entrance requirements:* For master's, minimum baccalaureate GPA of 2.75 or 3.0 in latter half of baccalaureate; for doctorate, GRE General Test, minimum graduate GPA of 3.2. Additional exam requirements/recommendations for international students: Required—TOEFL (minimum score 550 paper-based; 79 iBT), IELTS (minimum score 6.5). Electronic applications accepted. *Faculty research:* Community education, executive development for public services.

Ball State University, Graduate School, Teachers College, Department of Educational Studies, Program in Student Affairs Administration in Higher Education, Muncie, IN 47306. Offers MA. *Accreditation:* NCATE. *Entrance requirements:* For master's, GRE General Test, minimum baccalaureate GPA of 2.75 or 3.0 in latter half of baccalaureate, resume, three professional references. Additional exam requirements/recommendations for international students: Required—TOEFL (minimum score 550 paper-based; 79 iBT), IELTS (minimum score 6.5). Electronic applications accepted.

Barry University, School of Education, Program in Higher Education Administration, Miami Shores, FL 33161-6695. Offers MS. *Program availability:* Part-time, evening/weekend. *Degree requirements:* For master's, comprehensive exam. *Entrance requirements:* For master's, GRE General Test or MAT, minimum GPA of 3.0. Electronic applications accepted.

Barry University, School of Education, Program in Leadership and Education, Miami Shores, FL 33161-6695. Offers educational technology (PhD); exceptional student education (PhD); higher education administration (PhD); human resource development (PhD); leadership (PhD). *Program availability:* Part-time, evening/weekend. *Degree requirements:* For doctorate, thesis/dissertation. *Entrance requirements:* For doctorate, GRE General Test, minimum GPA of 3.25. Electronic applications accepted.

Baruch College of the City University of New York, Austin W. Marxe School of Public and International Affairs, Program in Higher Education Administration, New York, NY 10010-5585. Offers MS Ed. *Program availability:* Part-time, evening/weekend. *Entrance requirements:* For master's, GRE General Test. Additional exam requirements/recommendations for international students: Required—TOEFL. Electronic applications accepted. *Expenses:* Contact institution.

Bay Path University, Program in Higher Education Administration, Longmeadow, MA 01106-2292. Offers enrollment management (MS); general administration (MS); institutional advancement (MS); online teaching and program administration (MS). *Program availability:* Part-time, online only, 100% online. *Students:* 2 full-time (both women), 34 part-time (25 women); includes 11 minority (6 Black or African American, non-Hispanic/Latino; 1 Asian, non-Hispanic/Latino; 3 Hispanic/Latino; 1 Two or more races, non-Hispanic/Latino). Average age 34. *Entrance requirements:* For master's, completed application; official undergraduate and graduate transcripts (a GPA of 3.0 or higher is preferred); original essay of at least 250 words on the topic: "Why the MS in Higher Education Administration is important to my personal and professional goals"; current resume; 2 recommendations. *Application deadline:* Applications are processed on a rolling basis. Electronic applications accepted. Application fee is waived when completed online. *Expenses:* Contact institution. *Financial support:* Unspecified assistantships available. Financial award applicants required to submit FAFSA. *Unit head:* Dr. Lauren Way, Program Director, 413-565-1193, E-mail: lway@baypath.edu. *Application contact:* Jennifer Palma, Director of Graduate Admissions, 413-565-1181, Fax: 413-565-1250, E-mail: jpalma@baypath.edu.
Website: https://www.baypath.edu/academics/graduate-programs/higher-education-administration-ms/

Bay Path University, Program in Strategic Fundraising and Philanthropy, Longmeadow, MA 01106-2292. Offers higher education fundraising (MS); nonprofit fundraising (MS). *Program availability:* Part-time, 100% online. *Students:* 10 part-time (9 women); includes 1 minority (Black or African American, non-Hispanic/Latino). Average age 41. In 2018, 4 master's awarded. *Entrance requirements:* For master's, completed application; official undergraduate and graduate transcripts (a GPA of 3.0 higher is preferred); original essay of at least 250 words on the topic: "Why the MS in Strategic Fundraising & Philanthropy is important to my personal and professional goals?"; current resume; 2 recommendations. *Application deadline:* Applications are processed on a rolling basis. Electronic applications accepted. Application fee is waived when completed online. *Expenses:* Contact institution. *Financial support:* Unspecified assistantships available. Financial award applicants required to submit FAFSA. *Unit head:* Silvia de Haas-Phillips, Program Director, E-mail: sdphillips@

baypath.edu. *Application contact:* Jennifer Palma, Director of Graduate Admissions, 413-565-1181, Fax: 413-565-1250, E-mail: jpalma@baypath.edu.
Website: https://www.baypath.edu/academics/graduate-programs/strategic-fundraising-philanthropy-ms/

Bellarmine University, Annsley Frazier Thornton School of Education, Louisville, KY 40205. Offers education and district leadership (Ed D); education and social change (PhD); elementary education (MA Ed, MAT); leadership in higher education (PhD); middle school education (MA Ed, MAT); principalship (Ed S); reading and writing (MA Ed); secondary education (MAT); teacher leadership (MA Ed). *Accreditation:* NCATE. *Program availability:* Part-time, evening/weekend. *Faculty:* 14 full-time (7 women), 17 part-time/adjunct (11 women). *Students:* 27 full-time (19 women), 205 part-time (156 women); includes 74 minority (53 Black or African American, non-Hispanic/Latino; 6 Asian, non-Hispanic/Latino; 7 Hispanic/Latino; 8 Two or more races, non-Hispanic/Latino). Average age 34. 155 applicants, 71% accepted, 95 enrolled. In 2018, 69 master's, 10 doctorates, 30 other advanced degrees awarded. *Degree requirements:* For master's, comprehensive exam (for some programs), thesis (for some programs); for doctorate, comprehensive exam (for some programs), thesis/dissertation; for Ed S, comprehensive exam (for some programs). *Entrance requirements:* For master's, GRE, baccalaureate degree from accredited institution; minimum cumulative GPA of 2.75; recommendations from employers, supervisors, or professors attesting to applicant's potential as graduate student; statement of intent to pursue graduate degree; for doctorate, GRE, minimum GPA of 3.5 in all graduate coursework; baccalaureate and master's degrees in education or fields directly relevant to education; three letters of recommendation; two essays (no more than 1,000 words each); resume or curriculum vitae; interview; for Ed S, master's degree in education; valid teaching certificate; three years of experience in teaching; three recommendations; minimum GPA of 3.0 in all graduate work; interview; essays; personal goal statement. Additional exam requirements/recommendations for international students: Required—TOEFL (minimum score 80 iBT), IELTS (minimum score 6), TOEFL (minimum score 550 paper-based, 68 iBT), IELTS (minimum score 6), or Michigan English Language Assessment Battery. *Application deadline:* For fall admission, 8/1 priority date for domestic and international students; for spring admission, 12/1 priority date for domestic and international students; for summer admission, 4/10 priority date for domestic and international students. Applications are processed on a rolling basis. Application fee: $40. Electronic applications accepted. *Expenses:* Doctor of Education: $855 per credit hour; Educational Specialist: $410 per credit hour; Master of Arts in Education: $410 per credit hour; Master of Arts in Teaching: $665 per credit hour; Master of Arts in Teaching, undergraduate content courses: $410 per credit hour; Master of Education in Higher Education Leadership and Social Justice: $665 per credit hour; Ph.D., Social Change: $855 per credit hour; Ph.D., Leadership in Higher Education: $855 per credit hour; Rank I Programs: $410 per credit hour. *Financial support:* Scholarships/grants available. Financial award applicants required to submit FAFSA. *Faculty research:* Literacy, service-learning, dispositions, educational technology, special education. *Unit head:* Dr. Elizabeth Dinkins, Dean, 502-272-7958, Fax: 502-272-8189, E-mail: edinkins@bellarmine.edu. *Application contact:* Sarah Schuble, Assistant Director of Graduate Student Enrollment, 502-272-8271, Fax: 502-272-8002, E-mail: sschuble@bellarmine.edu.
Website: http://www.bellarmine.edu/education/graduate

Bowling Green State University, Graduate College, College of Education and Human Development, Department of Higher Education and Student Affairs, Program in Higher Education Administration, Bowling Green, OH 43403. Offers PhD. *Accreditation:* NCATE. *Program availability:* Part-time. *Degree requirements:* For doctorate, comprehensive exam, thesis/dissertation. *Entrance requirements:* For doctorate, GRE General Test. Additional exam requirements/recommendations for international students: Required—TOEFL. Electronic applications accepted. *Faculty research:* Adult learners, legal issues, intellectual development.

California Baptist University, Program in Higher Education Leadership and Student Development, Riverside, CA 92504-3206. Offers MS. *Program availability:* Part-time. *Faculty:* 8 full-time (3 women), 3 part-time/adjunct (1 woman). *Students:* 11 full-time (10 women), 5 part-time (all women); includes 8 minority (3 Black or African American, non-Hispanic/Latino; 5 Hispanic/Latino). Average age 31. 18 applicants, 100% accepted, 18 enrolled. In 2018, 14 master's awarded. *Entrance requirements:* For master's, minimum cumulative GPA of 2.75, three letters of recommendation, current resume, 500-word comprehensive essay. Additional exam requirements/recommendations for international students: Required—TOEFL (minimum score 80 iBT). *Application deadline:* For fall admission, 8/1 priority date for domestic students; 7/1 for international students; for spring admission, 12/1 priority date for domestic students, 11/1 for international students. Applications are processed on a rolling basis. Application fee: $45. Electronic applications accepted. *Expenses:* $607 per unit. *Financial support:* In 2018–19, 11 students received support. Federal Work-Study and scholarships/grants available. Financial award applicants required to submit CSS PROFILE or FAFSA. *Faculty research:* Sociology of education, student retention, women in academic leadership, curriculum and instruction, global education. *Unit head:* Dr. Robin Duncan, Dean, School of Education, 951-552-8948, E-mail: rduncan@calbaptist.edu. *Application contact:* Dr. Robin Duncan, Dean, School of Education, 951-552-8948, E-mail: rduncan@calbaptist.edu.
Website: http://www.calbaptist.edu/academics/schools-colleges/school-education/programs/graduate/master-science-higher-education-leadership-and-student-develop

California Lutheran University, Graduate Studies, Graduate School of Education, Thousand Oaks, CA 91360-2787. Offers counseling and guidance (MS), including college student personnel, counseling and guidance; educational leadership (MA, Ed D), including educational leadership (K-12) (Ed D), higher education leadership (Ed D); special education (MS); teacher leadership (M Ed); teaching (M Ed). *Accreditation:* NCATE. *Program availability:* Part-time, evening/weekend. *Degree requirements:* For master's, comprehensive exam or thesis; for doctorate, thesis/dissertation. *Entrance requirements:* For master's, GRE General Test, interview, minimum GPA of 3.0. Electronic applications accepted.

California State University, Long Beach, Graduate Studies, College of Education, Department of Advanced Studies in Education and Counseling, Long Beach, CA 90840. Offers counseling (MS), including marriage and family therapy, school counseling, student development in higher education; education (MA, Ed D); educational administration (MA, Ed D); educational psychology (MA); special education (MS). *Program availability:* Part-time, evening/weekend. *Entrance requirements:* For master's, GRE General Test, minimum GPA of 2.75. *Application deadline:* For fall admission, 3/1 for domestic students. Applications are processed on a rolling basis. Application fee: $55. Electronic applications accepted. *Expenses: Required fees:* $2628 per term. Tuition and fees vary according to class time, course level, course load, degree level, campus/location and program. *Financial support:* Federal Work-Study, institutionally sponsored loans, and scholarships/grants available. Financial award application deadline: 3/2; financial award applicants required to submit FAFSA. *Unit head:* Dr. Hiromi Masunaga, Chair, 562-985-4517, E-mail: asec@csulb.edu. *Application contact:* Dr. Hiromi Masunaga, Chair, 562-985-4517, E-mail: asec@csulb.edu.

Website: http://www.csulb.edu/college-of-education/advanced-studies-education-and-counseling

California State University, Sacramento, College of Education, Graduate and Professional Studies in Education, Sacramento, CA 95819. Offers behavioral science and gender equity (MA); child development (MA); counseling (MS); curriculum and instruction (MA); education (Ed D), including K-12 and community college; education leadership and policy studies (MA), including higher education, PreK-12; education specialist (Ed S), including school psychology; educational technology (MA); language and literacy (MA); multicultural education (MA); school psychology (MA); special education (MA); workforce development advocacy (MA). *Program availability:* Part-time, evening/weekend, blended/hybrid learning. *Degree requirements:* For master's, thesis or project; writing proficiency exam; for doctorate, thesis/dissertation. *Entrance requirements:* For master's and doctorate, GRE. Additional exam requirements/recommendations for international students: Required—TOEFL (minimum score 550 paper-based; 80 iBT); Recommended—IELTS (minimum score 7), TSE. Electronic applications accepted. *Expenses:* Contact institution.

Capella University, School of Education, Doctoral Programs in Education, Minneapolis, MN 55402. Offers curriculum and instruction (PhD); educational leadership and management (Ed D); instructional design for online learning (PhD); K-12 studies in education (PhD); leadership for higher education (PhD); leadership in educational administration (PhD); postsecondary and adult education (PhD); professional studies in education (PhD); reading and literacy (Ed D); special education leadership (PhD); training and performance improvement (PhD).

Capella University, School of Education, Master's Programs in Education, Minneapolis, MN 55402. Offers adult education (MS); curriculum and instruction (MS); early childhood education (MS); enrollment management (MS); higher education leadership and management (MS); instructional design for online learning (MS); integrative studies (MS); K-12 studies in education (MS); leadership in educational administration (MS); reading and literacy (MS); special education teaching (MS).

Cardinal Stritch University, College of Education and Leadership, Department of Education, Milwaukee, WI 53217-3985. Offers educational leadership (MS); higher education student affairs leadership (MS); leadership for the advancement of learning and service (Ed D, PhD); leadership for the advancement of learning and service in higher education (Ed D, PhD); teaching (MAT); urban education (MA). *Accreditation:* NCATE. *Program availability:* Part-time, evening/weekend, 100% online, blended/hybrid learning. *Degree requirements:* For master's, comprehensive exam, thesis (for some programs), research project, faculty recommendation; for doctorate, thesis/dissertation, practica, field experience. *Entrance requirements:* For master's, 2 letters of recommendation, minimum GPA of 3.0; for doctorate, minimum GPA of 3.5 in master's coursework, 3 letters of recommendation. Additional exam requirements/recommendations for international students: Required—TOEFL (minimum score 550 paper-based; 79 iBT), IELTS (minimum score 6.5). Electronic applications accepted. *Expenses:* Contact institution.

Central Michigan University, Central Michigan University Global Campus, Program in Education, Mount Pleasant, MI 48859. Offers college teaching (Graduate Certificate); community college (MA); curriculum and instruction (MA); educational technology (MA, DET); reading and literacy K-12 (MA); school principalship (MA), including charter school leadership; training and development (MA). *Accreditation:* TEAC. *Program availability:* Part-time, evening/weekend. *Entrance requirements:* For master's, minimum GPA of 2.7 in major. Additional exam requirements/recommendations for international students: Required—TOEFL. Electronic applications accepted.

Central Michigan University, College of Graduate Studies, College of Education and Human Services, Department of Educational Leadership, Mount Pleasant, MI 48859. Offers educational leadership (Ed D), including educational technology (Ed D, Ed S), higher education leadership, K-12 curriculum, K-12 leadership; general educational administration (Ed S), including administrative leadership K-12, educational technology (Ed D, Ed S), higher education administration, instructional leadership K-12; school principalship (MA), including charter school leadership, site-based leadership; student affairs administration (MA); teacher leadership (MA). *Program availability:* Part-time, evening/weekend. *Degree requirements:* For master's and Ed S, thesis or alternative; for doctorate, thesis/dissertation. *Entrance requirements:* For doctorate, GRE or MAT, master's degree, minimum GPA of 3.5, 3 years of professional education experience. Electronic applications accepted. *Faculty research:* Elementary administration, secondary administration, student achievement, in-service training, internships in administration.

Central Washington University, School of Graduate Studies and Research, College of Education and Professional Studies, Department of Curriculum, Supervision, and Educational Leadership, Ellensburg, WA 98926. Offers higher education (M Ed); master teacher (M Ed). *Program availability:* Part-time. *Degree requirements:* For master's, comprehensive exam (for some programs), thesis or alternative. *Entrance requirements:* For master's, 1 year of contracted teaching experience. Additional exam requirements/recommendations for international students: Required—TOEFL (minimum score 550 paper-based; 79 iBT), IELTS (minimum score 6.5). Electronic applications accepted.

Chicago State University, School of Graduate and Professional Studies, College of Education, Department of Educational Leadership, Curriculum and Foundations, Program in Educational Leadership, Chicago, IL 60628. Offers educational leadership (Ed D); higher education administration (MA); principal preparation (MA). *Accreditation:* NCATE. *Degree requirements:* For master's, comprehensive exam, thesis optional. *Entrance requirements:* For master's, minimum GPA of 2.75.

Claremont Graduate University, Graduate Programs, School of Educational Studies, Claremont, CA 91711-6160. Offers Africana education (Certificate); education and policy (MA, PhD); higher education/student affairs (MA, PhD); human development (MA, PhD); public school administration (MA, PhD); quantitative evaluation (MA, PhD); special education (MA, PhD); teacher education (MA); teaching and learning (MA, PhD); urban leadership (PhD); MBA/PhD. PhD program offered jointly with San Diego State University. *Program availability:* Part-time. Terminal master's awarded for partial completion of doctoral program. *Entrance requirements:* For master's and doctorate, GRE General Test. Additional exam requirements/recommendations for international students: Required—TOEFL (minimum score 75 iBT). Electronic applications accepted. *Faculty research:* Education administration, K-12 and higher education, multicultural education, education policy, diversity in higher education, faculty issues.

Clemson University, Graduate School, College of Education, Department of Educational and Organizational Leadership Development, Clemson, SC 29634. Offers administration and supervision (M Ed, Ed S); athletic leadership (MS, Certificate); education systems improvement science (Ed D); educational leadership (PhD), including higher education, P-12; human resource development (MHRD), including human resource development; leadership (Certificate); student affairs (M Ed). *Program availability:* Part-time, evening/weekend, 100% online. *Faculty:* 17 full-time (11 women). *Students:* 105 full-time (64 women), 265 part-time (170 women); includes 76 minority (61 Black or African American, non-Hispanic/Latino; 1 American Indian or Alaska Native, non-Hispanic/Latino; 3 Asian, non-Hispanic/Latino; 5 Hispanic/Latino; 6 Two or more races, non-Hispanic/Latino). Average age 32. 204 applicants, 83% accepted, 123

enrolled. In 2018, 93 master's, 17 doctorates, 28 other advanced degrees awarded. *Degree requirements:* For master's, thesis (for some programs); for doctorate, comprehensive exam, thesis/dissertation. *Entrance requirements:* For master's, doctorate, and other advanced degree, GRE General Test, unofficial transcripts, letters of recommendation. Additional exam requirements/recommendations for international students: Required—TOEFL (minimum score 80 paper-based; 80 iBT); Recommended—IELTS (minimum score 6.5), TSE (minimum score 54). *Application deadline:* For fall admission, 4/15 priority date for international students; for spring admission, 10/15 priority date for international students. Applications are processed on a rolling basis. Application fee: $80 ($90 for international students). Electronic applications accepted. *Expenses:* $5198 per semester full-time resident, $10123 per semester full-time non-resident, $556 per credit hour part-time resident, $1109 per credit hour part-time non-resident, online $770 per credit hour, $4938 doctoral programs resident, $10405 doctoral programs non-resident, $1144 full-time graduate assistant, other fees may apply per session. *Financial support:* In 2018–19, 30 students received support, including 8 fellowships with full and partial tuition reimbursements available (averaging $4,525 per year), 3 research assistantships with full and partial tuition reimbursements available (averaging $7,500 per year); career-related internships or fieldwork and unspecified assistantships also available. *Faculty research:* Leadership, ethics, policy development, performance improvement. *Total annual research expenditures:* $79,638. *Unit head:* Dr. Roy Jones, Interim Department Chair, 864-656-7915, E-mail: royj@clemson.edu. *Application contact:* Alison Search, Student Services Program Coordinator, 864-250-8880, E-mail: alisonp@clemson.edu.
Website: http://www.clemson.edu/education/departments/educational-organizational-leadership-development/index.html

Cleveland State University, College of Graduate Studies, College of Education and Human Services, Program in Urban Education, Specialization in Adult, Continuing, and Higher Education, Cleveland, OH 44115. Offers PhD. *Program availability:* Part-time. *Faculty:* 4 full-time (3 women). *Students:* 3 full-time (2 women), 7 part-time (6 women); includes 3 minority (all Black or African American, non-Hispanic/Latino). Average age 41. In 2018, 1 doctorate awarded. *Entrance requirements:* For doctorate, GRE General Test (minimum score of 297 for combined Verbal and Quantitative exams, 4.0 preferred for Analytical Writing), minimum graduate GPA of 3.25, curriculum vitae or resume, personal statement, 2 letters of recommendation. Additional exam requirements/recommendations for international students: Required—TOEFL (minimum score 550 paper-based; 78 iBT), IELTS (minimum score 6). Application fee: $40. Electronic applications accepted. *Expenses:* Tuition, state resident: full-time $7232.55; part-time $6676 per credit hour. Tuition, nonresident: full-time $12,375. *International tuition:* $18,914 full-time. *Required fees:* $80; $80 $40. Tuition and fees vary according to program. *Financial support:* In 2018–19, 2 students received support. Research assistantships, teaching assistantships, and tuition waivers (full) available. Support available to part-time students. Financial award application deadline: 4/1; financial award applicants required to submit FAFSA. *Faculty research:* Adult education research, practice in diverse contexts. *Unit head:* Dr. Graham Stead, Director, Doctoral Studies, 216-875-9869, E-mail: g.b.stead@csuohio.edu. *Application contact:* Rita M. Grabowski, Administrative Coordinator, 216-687-4697, Fax: 216-875-9697, E-mail: r.grabowski@csuohio.edu.
Website: http://www.csuohio.edu/cehs/departments/DOC/lll_doc.html

College of Saint Elizabeth, Department of Educational Leadership, Morristown, NJ 07960-6989. Offers educational leadership (MA, Ed D), including higher education (Ed D), Pre-K to 12th grade (Ed D); supervisor (Certificate). *Program availability:* Part-time. *Degree requirements:* For master's, thesis or alternative; for doctorate, thesis/dissertation. *Entrance requirements:* For master's, baccalaureate degree with minimum GPA of 2.75, standard teaching certificate, three years of exemplary certified teaching experience, writing sample, two letters of recommendation from school(s) of employment, personal interview (for educational leadership); for doctorate, MA in educational leadership or related field; leadership experience including certification as principal and/or supervisor; letter of recommendation from college/university professor attesting to candidate's ability to perform a high level of academic work in the program; for Certificate, MA in education; certification; baccalaureate degree with minimum GPA of 2.75; personal written statement; two letters of recommendation; official transcripts from all colleges attended. Additional exam requirements/recommendations for international students: Required—TOEFL (minimum score 550 paper-based; 79 iBT), IELTS (minimum score 6.5). Electronic applications accepted. Application fee is waived when completed online. *Expenses:* Contact institution.

The College of Saint Rose, Graduate Studies, Thelma P. Lally School of Education, Programs in Higher Education Leadership and Administration, Albany, NY 12203-1419. Offers MS Ed, Advanced Certificate. *Program availability:* Part-time, evening/weekend. *Students:* 3 full-time (1 woman), 10 part-time (5 women); includes 2 minority (1 Hispanic/Latino; 1 Two or more races, non-Hispanic/Latino), 2 international. Average age 30. 6 applicants, 67% accepted, 2 enrolled. In 2018, 6 master's awarded. *Degree requirements:* For master's, capstone seminar. *Entrance requirements:* For master's, resume, letter of recommendation. Additional exam requirements/recommendations for international students: Required—TOEFL (minimum score 550 paper-based; 80 iBT), IELTS (minimum score 6), PTE (minimum score 56). *Application deadline:* For fall admission, 4/1 priority date for domestic and international students; for spring admission, 10/15 priority date for domestic and international students; for summer admission, 3/15 priority date for domestic and international students. Applications are processed on a rolling basis. Application fee: $40. Electronic applications accepted. *Expenses: Tuition:* Full-time $14,382; part-time $799 per credit hour. *Required fees:* $924; $408 per credit. $286. *Financial support:* Scholarships/grants, tuition waivers (partial), and unspecified assistantships available. Support available to part-time students. Financial award application deadline: 4/15. *Unit head:* Dr. Margaret McLane, Institutional Strategist, 518-485-3334, E-mail: mclanem@strose.edu. *Application contact:* Daniel Gallagher, Assistant Vice President for Graduate Recruitment and Enrollment, 518-454-5136, Fax: 518-458-5479, E-mail: grad@strose.edu.
Website: https://www.strose.edu/higher-education-leadership-and-administration/

Colorado State University, College of Health and Human Sciences, School of Education, Fort Collins, CO 80523-1588. Offers adult education and training (M Ed); counseling and career development (MA); education and human resources (M Ed); education, equity, and transformation (PhD); higher education leadership (PhD); organizational learning, performance, and change (M Ed, PhD); student affairs in higher education (MS). *Accreditation:* ACA; TEAC. *Program availability:* Part-time, online only, 100% online, blended/hybrid learning. *Degree requirements:* For master's, thesis optional, professional portfolio or capstone project; for doctorate, comprehensive exam, thesis/dissertation. *Entrance requirements:* For master's, bachelor's degree; minimum GPA of 3.0 in last degree earned; for doctorate, GRE; GRE or GMAT (for organizational learning, performance and change only), master's degree; minimum GPA of 3.0 in last degree earned. Additional exam requirements/recommendations for international students: Required—TOEFL (minimum score 550 paper-based; 80 iBT), IELTS (minimum score 6.5), PTE (minimum score 58). Electronic applications accepted. *Expenses:* Contact institution. *Faculty research:* Diversity, equity, and inclusion; STEM education; higher education; occupational learning, performance, and change; teacher education.

Columbia College, Graduate Programs, Education Division, Columbia, SC 29203-5998. Offers divergent learning (M Ed); higher education administration (M Ed). *Accreditation:* NCATE. *Program availability:* Part-time, evening/weekend, online learning. *Degree requirements:* For master's, thesis. *Entrance requirements:* For master's, GRE General Test, MAT, 2 recommendations, current South Carolina teaching certificate, minimum GPA of 3.2. Electronic applications accepted. *Expenses:* Contact institution.

Columbus State University, Graduate Studies, College of Education and Health Professions, Department of Counseling, Foundations, and Leadership, Columbus, GA 31907-5645. Offers clinical mental health counseling (MS); curriculum and leadership (Ed D), including curriculum, educational leadership, higher education (M Ed, Ed D); educational leadership (M Ed, Ed S), including higher education (M Ed, Ed D); school counseling (M Ed, Ed S). *Accreditation:* ACA; NCATE. *Program availability:* Part-time, evening/weekend, 100% online, blended/hybrid learning. *Faculty:* 13 full-time (5 women), 17 part-time/adjunct (8 women). *Students:* 66 full-time (50 women), 209 part-time (158 women); includes 145 minority (124 Black or African American, non-Hispanic/Latino; 5 Asian, non-Hispanic/Latino; 10 Hispanic/Latino; 6 Two or more races, non-Hispanic/Latino), 1 international. Average age 39. 168 applicants, 48% accepted, 54 enrolled. In 2018, 44 master's, 25 doctorates, 129 other advanced degrees awarded. *Degree requirements:* For master's, thesis, exit exam; for doctorate, comprehensive exam, thesis/dissertation; for Ed S, thesis or alternative. *Entrance requirements:* For master's, GRE General Test, minimum undergraduate GPA of 2.75; for doctorate, GRE General Test, minimum graduate GPA of 3.5, four years of professional service; for Ed S, GRE General Test, minimum undergraduate GPA of 2.75, graduate 3.0. Additional exam requirements/recommendations for international students: Required—TOEFL (minimum score 550 paper-based; 79 iBT). *Application deadline:* For fall admission, 6/30 for domestic and international students; for spring admission, 11/1 for domestic and international students; for summer admission, 3/1 for domestic and international students. Applications are processed on a rolling basis. Application fee: $50. Electronic applications accepted. *Expenses: Tuition, area resident:* Full-time $4924; part-time $618 per credit hour. Tuition, state resident: full-time $4924; part-time $618 per credit hour. Tuition, nonresident: full-time $19,218; part-time $2403 per credit hour. *International tuition:* $19,218 full-time. *Required fees:* $1870; $802. Tuition and fees vary according to course load, degree level and program. *Financial support:* In 2018–19, 30 students received support, including 6 research assistantships with partial tuition reimbursements available (averaging $3,000 per year); career-related internships or fieldwork, Federal Work-Study, institutionally sponsored loans, scholarships/grants, tuition waivers (partial), and unspecified assistantships also available. Support available to part-time students. Financial award application deadline: 5/1; financial award applicants required to submit FAFSA. *Unit head:* Dr. Tom Hackett, Department Chair, 706-507-8968, Fax: 706-569-3134, E-mail: hackett_paul@columbusstate.edu. *Application contact:* Catrina Smith-Edmond, Assistant Director for Graduate and Global Admission, 706-507-8824, Fax: 706-568-5091, E-mail: smithedmond_catrina@columbusstate.edu.
Website: http://cfl.columbusstate.edu/

Concordia University, College of Education, Portland, OR 97211-6099. Offers administrative leadership (Ed D); career and technical education (M Ed); curriculum and instruction (M Ed), including adolescent literacy, early childhood education, educational technology leadership, English for speakers of other languages, environmental education, health and physical education, mathematics, methods and curriculum, reading interventionist, science, social studies, STEAM education, teacher leadership, the inclusive classroom, trauma and resilience in educational settings; educational administration (M Ed); educational leadership (M Ed); elementary education (MAT); higher education (Ed D); instructional leadership (Ed D); professional leadership, inquiry, and transformation (Ed D); secondary education (MAT); transformational leadership (Ed D). *Program availability:* Part-time, online learning. *Degree requirements:* For master's, comprehensive exam, work samples/portfolio. *Entrance requirements:* For master's, California Basic Educational Skills Test or PRAXIS I, minimum undergraduate GPA of 2.8, graduate 3.0; 2 letters of recommendation. Additional exam requirements/recommendations for international students: Required—TOEFL (minimum score 525 paper-based). Electronic applications accepted. *Faculty research:* Learner-centered classroom, brain-based learning, future of online learning.

Dallas Baptist University, Gary Cook School of Leadership, Program in Educational Leadership, Dallas, TX 75211-9299. Offers higher education leadership (Ed D), including educational ministry leadership, general leadership, higher education leadership. *Program availability:* Part-time. *Degree requirements:* For doctorate, thesis/dissertation. *Application deadline:* Applications are processed on a rolling basis. Application fee: $25. Electronic applications accepted. Application fee is waived when completed online. *Expenses: Tuition:* Full-time $17,262; part-time $959 per credit hour. *Required fees:* $1000; $500 per semester. Tuition and fees vary according to course load and degree level. *Unit head:* Dr. Jack Goodyear, Dean, 214-333-5595, E-mail: jackg@dbu.edu. *Application contact:* Dr. Ozzie Ingram, Program Director, 214-333-6875, E-mail: ozzie@dbu.edu.
Website: http://www4.dbu.edu/leadership/education-leadership-ed-d

Dallas Baptist University, Gary Cook School of Leadership, Program in Higher Education, Dallas, TX 75211-9299. Offers leadership studies (M Ed); student affairs leadership (M Ed), including community college leadership, distance learning, interdisciplinary studies, student affairs leadership. *Program availability:* Part-time, evening/weekend, online learning. *Application deadline:* Applications are processed on a rolling basis. Application fee: $25. Electronic applications accepted. Application fee is waived when completed online. *Expenses: Tuition:* Full-time $17,262; part-time $959 per credit hour. *Required fees:* $1000; $500 per semester. Tuition and fees vary according to course load and degree level. *Unit head:* Dr. Jack Goodyear, Dean, 214-333-5595, Fax: 214-333-6809, E-mail: jackg@dbu.edu. *Application contact:* Dr. Jack Goodyear, Dean, 214-333-5595, Fax: 214-333-6809, E-mail: jackg@dbu.edu.
Website: https://www.dbu.edu/graduate/degree-programs/med-higher-education/

Dallas Baptist University, Professional Development Program, Dallas, TX 75211-9299. Offers accounting (MA); church leadership (MA); communication (MA); counseling (MA); criminal justice (MA); English as a second language (MA); finance (MA); higher education (MA); leadership studies (MA); management (MA). *Program availability:* Part-time, evening/weekend, online learning. *Application deadline:* Applications are processed on a rolling basis. Application fee: $25. Electronic applications accepted. Application fee is waived when completed online. *Expenses: Tuition:* Full-time $17,262; part-time $959 per credit hour. *Required fees:* $1000; $500 per semester. Tuition and fees vary according to course load and degree level. *Unit head:* Jared Ingram, Program Director, 214-333-5584, E-mail: jaredi@dbu.edu. *Application contact:* Jared Ingram, Program Director, 214-333-5584, E-mail: jaredi@dbu.edu.
Website: https://www.dbu.edu/graduate/degree-programs/ma-professional-development

Delta State University, Graduate Programs, College of Education, Division of Teacher Education, Leadership, and Research, Program in Professional Studies, Cleveland, MS 38733-0001. Offers counselor education (Ed D); elementary education (Ed D); higher education (Ed D). *Program availability:* Part-time, evening/weekend. *Degree*

requirements: For doctorate, thesis/dissertation. *Entrance requirements:* For doctorate, GRE General Test. *Expenses: Tuition, area resident:* Full-time $7076; part-time $393 per credit hour. Tuition, state resident: full-time $7076; part-time $393 per credit hour. Tuition, nonresident: full-time $7076; part-time $393 per credit hour. *International tuition:* $7076 full-time. *Required fees:* $170; $18.90 per credit hour. $9.45 per semester. Part-time tuition and fees vary according to program.

DePaul University, College of Education, Chicago, IL 60614. Offers bilingual-bicultural education (M Ed, MA); counseling (M Ed, MA), including clinical mental health counseling, college student development, school counseling; curriculum studies (M Ed, MA, Ed D); early childhood education (M Ed, MA, Ed D); educational leadership (M Ed, MA, Ed D), including Catholic leadership (M Ed, MA), general (M Ed, MA), higher education (M Ed, MA), physical education (M Ed, MA), principal preparation (M Ed), teacher preparation (M Ed); elementary education (M Ed, MA); middle grades education (M Ed); middle school mathematics education (MS); reading specialist (M Ed, MA); secondary education (M Ed, MA); social and cultural foundations in education (M Ed, MA); special education (M Ed); sport, fitness and recreation leadership (MS); value-creating education for global citizenship (M Ed); world languages education (M Ed, MA). *Program availability:* Part-time, evening/weekend, online learning. *Degree requirements:* For doctorate, thesis/dissertation. Electronic applications accepted.

DeVry University–Folsom Campus, Graduate Programs, Folsom, CA 95630. Offers accounting (M Acc); accounting and financial management (MAFM); business administration (MBA); curriculum leadership (M Ed); educational leadership (M Ed); educational technology (M Ed); higher education leadership (M Ed); human resource management (MHRM); information systems management (MISM); network and communications management (MNCM); project management (MPM); public administration (MPA).

Drexel University, Goodwin College of Professional Studies, School of Education, Philadelphia, PA 19104-2875. Offers applied behavior analysis (MS); creativity and innovation (MS); education improvement and transformation (MS); educational administration (MS); educational leadership and management (Ed D); educational leadership development and learning technologies (PhD); global and international education (MS); higher education (MS); human resources development (MS); learning technologies (MS); mathematics, learning and teaching (MS); special education (MS); teaching, learning and curriculum (MS). *Program availability:* Part-time, evening/weekend, online learning. *Degree requirements:* For doctorate, thesis/dissertation. *Entrance requirements:* For doctorate, GRE or GMAT. Additional exam requirements/recommendations for international students: Required—TOEFL, IELTS. Electronic applications accepted. Application fee is waived when completed online. *Expenses:* Contact institution. *Faculty research:* Leadership development, mathematics education, literacy, autism, educational technology.

East Carolina University, Graduate School, College of Education, Department of Interdisciplinary Professions, Greenville, NC 27858-4353. Offers adult education (MA Ed); business and marketing education (MA Ed); community college instruction (Certificate); counselor education (MS); education in the healthcare professions (Certificate); library science (MLS); student affairs in higher education (Certificate); vocational education (MS). *Accreditation:* ACA; ALA; NCATE. *Program availability:* Part-time, evening/weekend. *Application deadline:* For fall admission, 5/15 priority date for domestic students. *Expenses: Tuition, area resident:* Full-time $4749. Tuition, state resident: full-time $4749. Tuition, nonresident: full-time $17,898. *International tuition:* $17,898 full-time. *Required fees:* $2787. Part-time tuition and fees vary according to course load and program. *Financial support:* Application deadline: 6/1. *Unit head:* Dr. Scott Glass, Professor, 252-328-5670, E-mail: glassj@ecu.edu. *Application contact:* Graduate School Admissions, 252-328-6012, Fax: 252-328-6071, E-mail: gradschool@ecu.edu.
Website: http://www.ecu.edu/cs-educ/idp/index.cfm

Eastern Kentucky University, The Graduate School, College of Education, Department of Curriculum and Instruction, Program in Secondary and Higher Education, Richmond, KY 40475-3102. Offers secondary education (MA Ed), including agricultural education, art education, biological sciences education, business education, English education, geography education, history education, home economics education, industrial education, mathematical sciences education, physical education, school health education. *Accreditation:* NCATE. *Program availability:* Part-time. *Entrance requirements:* For master's, GRE General Test, minimum GPA of 2.5.

Eastern Michigan University, Graduate School, College of Education, Department of Leadership and Counseling, Programs in Educational Leadership, Ypsilanti, MI 48197. Offers community college leadership (Graduate Certificate); educational leadership (MA, Ed D, SPA); higher education/general administration (MA); higher education/student affairs (MA); K-12 administration (MA); K-12 basic administration (Post Master's Certificate). *Program availability:* Part-time, evening/weekend, online learning. *Students:* 39 full-time (29 women), 283 part-time (195 women); includes 92 minority (67 Black or African American, non-Hispanic/Latino; 2 Asian, non-Hispanic/Latino; 12 Hispanic/Latino; 11 Two or more races, non-Hispanic/Latino), 2 international. Average age 36. 192 applicants, 74% accepted, 80 enrolled. In 2018, 98 master's, 18 doctorates, 22 other advanced degrees awarded. *Entrance requirements:* For doctorate, GRE. Additional exam requirements/recommendations for international students: Required—TOEFL. *Application deadline:* For winter admission, 2/1 for domestic and international students. Applications are processed on a rolling basis. Application fee: $45. *Financial support:* Fellowships, research assistantships with full tuition reimbursements, teaching assistantships with full tuition reimbursements, career-related internships or fieldwork, Federal Work-Study, institutionally sponsored loans, scholarships/grants, tuition waivers (partial), and unspecified assistantships available. Support available to part-time students. *Application contact:* Dr. Jaclynn Tracy, Coordinator of Advising, Programs in Educational Leadership, 734-487-0255, Fax: 734-487-4608, E-mail: jtracy@emich.edu.

Fitchburg State University, Division of Graduate and Continuing Education, Program in Educational Leadership and Management, Fitchburg, MA 01420-2697. Offers education technology (Certificate); educational leadership and management (M Ed, CAGS); higher education administration (CAGS); school principal (M Ed, CAGS); supervisor/director (M Ed, CAGS). *Accreditation:* NCATE. *Program availability:* Part-time, evening/weekend. *Entrance requirements:* Additional exam requirements/recommendations for international students: Required—TOEFL (minimum score 550 paper-based; 79 iBT). Electronic applications accepted. *Expenses:* Contact institution.

Florida Atlantic University, College of Education, Department of Educational Leadership and Research Methodology, Boca Raton, FL 33431-0991. Offers adult and community education (M Ed, PhD, Ed S); educational leadership (M Ed, PhD, Ed S); higher education (M Ed, PhD); K-12 school leadership (M Ed, PhD, Ed S). *Accreditation:* NCATE. *Program availability:* Part-time, evening/weekend, online learning. *Faculty:* 22 full-time (12 women), 22 part-time/adjunct (11 women). *Students:* 91 full-time (56 women), 260 part-time (177 women); includes 172 minority (107 Black or African American, non-Hispanic/Latino; 5 Asian, non-Hispanic/Latino; 53 Hispanic/Latino; 7 Two or more races, non-Hispanic/Latino), 8 international. Average age 37. 226 applicants, 68% accepted, 131 enrolled. In 2018, 96 master's, 19 doctorates, 2 other advanced degrees awarded. *Degree requirements:* For doctorate, comprehensive exam, thesis/

dissertation, departmental qualifying exam; for Ed S, departmental qualifying exam. *Entrance requirements:* For master's, GRE General Test, minimum GPA of 3.0 during previous 2 years; for doctorate, GRE General Test, minimum GPA of 3.5; for Ed S, GRE General Test. Additional exam requirements/recommendations for international students: Required—TOEFL (minimum score 500 paper-based; 61 iBT), IELTS (minimum score 6). *Application deadline:* For fall admission, 7/1 for domestic students, 2/15 for international students; for spring admission, 9/15 for domestic students, 7/15 for international students. Applications are processed on a rolling basis. Application fee: $30. Electronic applications accepted. *Expenses: Tuition, area resident:* Full-time $7400; part-time $369.82 per credit. Tuition, state resident: full-time $7400; part-time $369.82 per credit. Tuition, nonresident: full-time $20,496; part-time $1024.81 per credit. *Financial support:* Fellowships, research assistantships, teaching assistantships, career-related internships or fieldwork, and tuition waivers (partial) available. *Faculty research:* Self-directed learning, school reform issues, legal issues, mentoring, school leadership. *Unit head:* Dr. Robert E. Shockley, Chair, 561-297-3551, Fax: 561-297-3618, E-mail: shockley@fau.edu. *Application contact:* Kathy DuBois, Senior Secretary, 561-297-6551, Fax: 561-297-3618, E-mail: edleadership@fau.edu.
Website: http://www.coe.fau.edu/academicdepartments/el/

Florida International University, College of Arts, Sciences, and Education, Department of Leadership and Professional Studies, Miami, FL 33199. Offers adult education and human resource development (MS, Ed D); counseling (MS), including rehabilitation counseling, school counseling; counselor education (MS), including clinical mental health counseling; educational administration and supervision (Ed D); educational leadership (MS, Certificate, Ed S); higher education (Ed D); higher education administration (MS); international and comparative education (MS); recreation and sport management (MS), including recreation and sport management, recreational therapy; school psychology (Ed S); urban education (MS), including instruction in urban settings, learning technologies, multicultural/bilingual, multicultural/TESOL, urban education. *Program availability:* Part-time, evening/weekend. *Faculty:* 64 full-time (43 women), 104 part-time/adjunct (76 women). *Students:* 258 full-time (196 women), 217 part-time (155 women); includes 387 minority (118 Black or African American, non-Hispanic/Latino; 8 Asian, non-Hispanic/Latino; 249 Hispanic/Latino; 12 Two or more races, non-Hispanic/Latino), 11 international. Average age 31. 345 applicants, 57% accepted, 126 enrolled. In 2018, 172 master's, 11 doctorates awarded. *Entrance requirements:* For master's, minimum GPA of 3.0; for doctorate and other advanced degree, GRE General Test. Additional exam requirements/recommendations for international students: Required—TOEFL (minimum score 550 paper-based; 80 iBT), IELTS (minimum score 6.3). *Application deadline:* For fall admission, 6/1 priority date for domestic students, 4/1 for international students; for winter admission, 10/1 priority date for domestic students, 9/1 for international students; for spring admission, 3/1 priority date for domestic students, 2/1 for international students. Applications are processed on a rolling basis. Application fee: $30. Electronic applications accepted. *Financial support:* Fellowships, research assistantships, teaching assistantships, Federal Work-Study, and tuition waivers (full and partial) available. Support available to part-time students. Financial award applicants required to submit FAFSA. *Unit head:* Dr. Benjamin Baez, Chair, 305-348-3214, Fax: 305-348-1515, E-mail: benjamin.baez@fiu.edu. *Application contact:* Nanett Rojas, Manager, Admissions Operations, 305-348-7464, Fax: 305-348-7441, E-mail: gradadm@fiu.edu.
Website: http://education.fiu.edu

Florida State University, The Graduate School, College of Education, Department of Educational Leadership and Policy Studies, Tallahassee, FL 32306. Offers educational leadership and administration (Certificate); educational leadership and policy (MS, Ed D, PhD, Ed S), including education policy and evaluation (MS, Ed D, PhD), educational leadership and administration, foundations of education (MS, PhD), including history and philosophy of education, international and multicultural education; higher education (MS, PhD); institutional research (Certificate); program evaluation (Certificate). *Program availability:* Part-time, evening/weekend, 100% online, blended/hybrid learning, asynchronous, minimal on-campus study. *Degree requirements:* For master's, comprehensive exam, thesis optional; for doctorate, comprehensive exam, thesis/dissertation, diagnostic exam, preliminary exam, prospectus defense, dissertation defense. *Entrance requirements:* For master's, doctorate, and other advanced degree, GRE General Test, minimum GPA of 3.0. Additional exam requirements/recommendations for international students: Required—TOEFL (minimum score 550 paper-based, 80 iBT), IELTS (minimum score 6.5), Michigan English Language Assessment Battery (minimum score 77), or PTE (minimum score 55). Electronic applications accepted. *Expenses: Tuition, area resident:* Part-time $479.32 per credit hour. Tuition and fees vary according to campus/location and program. *Faculty research:* Post-secondary success; leadership education; education policy; international education; multicultural education.

Geneva College, Master of Arts in Higher Education Program, Beaver Falls, PA 15010-3599. Offers campus ministry (MA); college teaching (MA); educational leadership (MA); student affairs administration (MA). *Program availability:* Part-time, evening/weekend, blended/hybrid learning. *Degree requirements:* For master's, 36 hours (27 in core courses) including a capstone research project. *Entrance requirements:* For master's, minimum GPA of 3.0, writing sample, 3 letters of recommendation, essay on motivation for participation in the program. Additional exam requirements/recommendations for international students: Required—TOEFL. Electronic applications accepted. *Expenses:* Contact institution. *Faculty research:* Learning theories, church-related higher education, organizational culture, sexual assault and transgender students at Christian colleges, emerging technology in higher education.

George Mason University, College of Education and Human Development, Program in Education, Fairfax, VA 22030. Offers higher education (PhD). *Faculty:* 63 full-time (44 women). *Students:* 80 full-time (58 women), 215 part-time (159 women); includes 75 minority (29 Black or African American, non-Hispanic/Latino; 18 Asian, non-Hispanic/Latino; 22 Hispanic/Latino; 6 Two or more races, non-Hispanic/Latino), 33 international. Average age 39. 103 applicants, 51% accepted, 33 enrolled. In 2018, 46 doctorates awarded. *Degree requirements:* For doctorate, thesis/dissertation, portfolio review. *Entrance requirements:* For doctorate, GRE (no more than 5 years old); resume; official transcripts from graduate and undergraduate institutions; 3 letters of recommendation; goal statement of 750-1000 words. Additional exam requirements/recommendations for international students: Required—TOEFL (minimum score 575 paper-based; 88 iBT), IELTS, PTE (minimum score 59). *Application deadline:* For fall admission, 1/15 for domestic and international students; for spring admission, 10/1 for domestic and international students. Application fee: $75 ($80 for international students). Electronic applications accepted. *Financial support:* In 2018–19, 79 students received support, including 1 fellowship, 60 research assistantships with tuition reimbursements available (averaging $14,242 per year), 28 teaching assistantships with tuition reimbursements available (averaging $5,854 per year); career-related internships or fieldwork, Federal Work-Study, unspecified assistantships, and health care benefits (for full-time research or teaching assistantship recipients) also available. Support available to part-time students. Financial award application deadline: 3/1; financial award applicants required to submit FAFSA. *Unit head:* Anastasia Kitsantis, Director, 703-993-2688, E-mail: akitsant@gmu.edu. *Application contact:* Nicole Mariam, Graduate Admissions Coordinator, 703-993-3832, Fax: 703-993-2020, E-mail: nwhite5@gmu.edu.

George Mason University, College of Humanities and Social Sciences, Department of English, Fairfax, VA 22030. Offers college teaching (Certificate), including higher education pedagogy; creative writing (MFA), including fiction, nonfiction writing, poetry; English (MA), including cultural studies, linguistics, literature, professional writing and rhetoric, teaching of writing and literature; English pedagogy (Certificate); folklore studies (Certificate); linguistics (PhD); writing and rhetoric (PhD). *Program availability:* Part-time. *Faculty:* 86 full-time (47 women), 38 part-time/adjunct (26 women). *Students:* 116 full-time (81 women), 112 part-time (83 women); includes 37 minority (7 Black or African American, non-Hispanic/Latino; 1 American Indian or Alaska Native, non-Hispanic/Latino; 6 Asian, non-Hispanic/Latino; 12 Hispanic/Latino; 1 Native Hawaiian or other Pacific Islander, non-Hispanic/Latino; 10 Two or more races, non-Hispanic/Latino), 18 international. Average age 33. 152 applicants, 79% accepted, 57 enrolled. In 2018, 67 master's, 1 doctorate, 16 other advanced degrees awarded. *Degree requirements:* For master's, thesis (for some programs), proficiency in a foreign language by course work or translation test; for doctorate, comprehensive exam, thesis/dissertation, 2 papers. *Entrance requirements:* For master's, official transcripts; expanded goals statement; writing sample; portfolio; 2 letters of recommendation; resume; for doctorate, GRE (for linguistics), expanded goals statement; 2 letters of recommendation (writing and rhetoric); 3 letters of recommendation (linguistics); writing sample; introductory course in linguistics; official transcripts; master's degree in relevant field; for Certificate, official transcripts; expanded goals statement; 2 letters of recommendation; writing sample; resume. Additional exam requirements/recommendations for international students: Required—TOEFL (minimum score 575 paper-based; 88 iBT), IELTS (minimum score 6.5), PTE (minimum score 59). *Application deadline:* For fall admission, 3/15 for domestic and international students; for spring admission, 10/15 for domestic and international students. Application fee: $75 ($80 for international students). Electronic applications accepted. *Financial support:* In 2018–19, 81 students received support, including 8 research assistantships with tuition reimbursements available (averaging $20,666 per year), 74 teaching assistantships with tuition reimbursements available (averaging $14,714 per year); career-related internships or fieldwork, Federal Work-Study, scholarships/grants, unspecified assistantships, and health care benefits (for full-time research or teaching assistantship recipients) also available. Support available to part-time students. Financial award application deadline: 3/1; financial award applicants required to submit FAFSA. *Faculty research:* Literature, professional writing and editing, writing of fiction or poetry. *Total annual research expenditures:* $68,592. *Unit head:* Debra Lattanzi-Shutika, Chair, 703-993-1170, Fax: 703-993-1161, E-mail: dshutika@gmu.edu. *Application contact:* Alex Walsh, Graduate Admissions Coordinator, 703-993-1185, Fax: 703-993-1161, E-mail: awalsh7@gmu.edu.
Website: http://english.gmu.edu

George Mason University, College of Humanities and Social Sciences, Higher Education Program, Fairfax, VA 22030. Offers MA, Certificate. *Faculty:* 3 full-time (all women). *Students:* 7 part-time (6 women); includes 3 minority (2 Black or African American, non-Hispanic/Latino; 1 Hispanic/Latino). Average age 37. 5 applicants, 100% accepted, 2 enrolled. In 2018, 4 other advanced degrees awarded. *Degree requirements:* For master's, thesis optional, practicum; for Certificate, practicum. *Entrance requirements:* For master's and Certificate, transcript, resume, writing sample, goals statement, 3 letters of recommendation. Additional exam requirements/recommendations for international students: Required—TOEFL (minimum score 575 paper-based; 88 iBT), IELTS (minimum score 6.5), PTE (minimum score 59). *Application deadline:* For fall admission, 3/1 for domestic and international students; for spring admission, 10/15 for domestic and international students. Application fee: $75 ($80 for international students). Electronic applications accepted. *Financial support:* Career-related internships or fieldwork, Federal Work-Study, and scholarships/grants available. Support available to part-time students. Financial award application deadline: 3/1; financial award applicants required to submit FAFSA. *Faculty research:* Multicultural issues, leadership, assessment, scholarship of teaching and learning, learning analytics. *Total annual research expenditures:* $24,019. *Unit head:* Jan Arminio, Director, 703-993-2064, Fax: 703-993-2307, E-mail: jarminio@gmu.edu. *Application contact:* Katie Richards, Administrative Coordinator, 703-993-2310, Fax: 703-993-2307, E-mail: kricha22@gmu.edu.
Website: http://highered.gmu.edu/

George Mason University, College of Humanities and Social Sciences, Interdisciplinary Studies Program, Fairfax, VA 22030. Offers computational social science (MAIS); energy and sustainability (MAIS); folklore studies (MAIS); higher education (MAIS); individualized studies (MAIS); religion, culture, and values (MAIS); social entrepreneurship (MAIS); social justice and human rights (MAIS); war and the military in society (MAIS); women and gender studies (MAIS). *Faculty:* 9 full-time (4 women), 3 part-time/adjunct (2 women). *Students:* 32 full-time (18 women), 67 part-time (45 women); includes 37 minority (14 Black or African American, non-Hispanic/Latino; 6 Asian, non-Hispanic/Latino; 11 Hispanic/Latino; 6 Two or more races, non-Hispanic/Latino), 4 international. Average age 32. 49 applicants, 86% accepted, 20 enrolled. In 2018, 29 master's awarded. *Degree requirements:* For master's, thesis or alternative, experiential learning (for some programs). *Entrance requirements:* Additional exam requirements/recommendations for international students: Required—TOEFL (minimum score 575 paper-based; 88 iBT), IELTS (minimum score 6.5), PTE (minimum score 59). *Application deadline:* For fall admission, 3/1 for domestic and international students; for spring admission, 10/15 for domestic and international students. Application fee: $75 ($80 for international students). Electronic applications accepted. *Financial support:* In 2018–19, 9 students received support, including 2 research assistantships with tuition reimbursements available, 9 teaching assistantships with tuition reimbursements available (averaging $10,628 per year); career-related internships or fieldwork, Federal Work-Study, scholarships/grants, unspecified assistantships, and health care benefits (for full-time research or teaching assistantship recipients) also available. Support available to part-time students. Financial award application deadline: 3/1; financial award applicants required to submit FAFSA. *Faculty research:* Combined English and folklore, religious and cultural studies (Christianity and Muslim society). *Unit head:* Meredith H. Lair, Director, 703-993-2159, Fax: 703-993-1251, E-mail: mlair@gmu.edu. *Application contact:* Morgan Fisher, Graduate Coordinator, 703-993-8762, E-mail: mfisherb@gmu.edu.
Website: http://mais.gmu.edu

The George Washington University, Graduate School of Education and Human Development, Department of Educational Leadership, Program in Higher Education Administration, Washington, DC 20052. Offers college teaching and academic leadership (MA Ed/HD, Ed S); general administration (MA Ed/HD, Ed S); higher education administration (Ed D); higher education finance (MA Ed/HD, Ed S); international education (MA Ed/HD, Ed S); policy (MA Ed/HD, Ed S); student affairs administration (MA Ed/HD, Ed S). *Accreditation:* NCATE. *Students:* 27 full-time (19 women), 55 part-time (41 women); includes 37 minority (21 Black or African American, non-Hispanic/Latino; 5 Asian, non-Hispanic/Latino; 8 Hispanic/Latino; 3 Two or more races, non-Hispanic/Latino), 4 international. Average age 32. 131 applicants, 85% accepted, 37 enrolled. In 2018, 15 master's, 4 doctorates, 1 other advanced degree awarded. *Degree requirements:* For master's and Ed S, comprehensive exam; for doctorate, comprehensive exam, thesis/dissertation. *Entrance requirements:* For master's, GRE General Test or MAT, minimum GPA of 2.75; for doctorate, GRE General

Test or MAT, interview, minimum GPA of 3.3; for Ed S, GRE General Test or MAT, minimum GPA of 3.3. *Application deadline:* For fall admission, 1/15 priority date for domestic students; for spring admission, 10/1 for domestic students. Applications are processed on a rolling basis. Application fee: $75. *Financial support:* In 2018–19, 17 students received support. Fellowships, research assistantships, career-related internships or fieldwork, Federal Work-Study, and tuition waivers (partial) available. Financial award application deadline: 1/15; financial award applicants required to submit FAFSA. *Faculty research:* Technology in higher education administration. *Unit head:* Michael Feuer, Dean, 202-994-6161, E-mail: mjfeuer@gwu.edu. *Application contact:* Sarah Lang, Director of Graduate Admissions, 202-994-1447, Fax: 202-994-7207, E-mail: slang@gwu.edu.

Georgia Southern University, Jack N. Averitt College of Graduate Studies, College of Education, Department of Leadership, Technology, and Human Development, Program in Higher Education, Statesboro, GA 30460. Offers educational leadership (Ed D); higher education administration (M Ed). *Accreditation:* NCATE. *Program availability:* Part-time, evening/weekend. *Degree requirements:* For master's, portfolio, practicum, transition point assessments; for doctorate, comprehensive exam, thesis/dissertation. *Entrance requirements:* For master's, minimum GPA of 2.5. Additional exam requirements/recommendations for international students: Required—TOEFL (minimum score 550 paper-based; 80 iBT), IELTS (minimum score 6). Electronic applications accepted. *Expenses: Tuition, area resident:* Part-time $3324 per semester. Tuition, state resident: full-time $5814; part-time $3324 per semester. Tuition, nonresident: full-time $23,204; part-time $13,260 per semester. *Required fees:* $2092; $2092. Tuition and fees vary according to course load, degree level, campus/location and program. *Faculty research:* Global issues in higher education, leadership and identity development in higher education, student affairs.

Georgia Southern University, Jack N. Averitt College of Graduate Studies, College of Education, Department of Leadership, Technology, and Human Development, Program in Higher Education Administration, Statesboro, GA 30458. Offers M Ed. *Program availability:* Part-time, evening/weekend. *Entrance requirements:* For master's, GRE, minimum GPA of 2.5. Additional exam requirements/recommendations for international students: Required—TOEFL (minimum score 550 paper-based; 80 iBT), IELTS (minimum score 6). Electronic applications accepted. *Expenses: Tuition, area resident:* Part-time $3324 per semester. Tuition, state resident: full-time $5814; part-time $3324 per semester. Tuition, nonresident: full-time $23,204; part-time $13,260 per semester. *Required fees:* $2092; $2092. Tuition and fees vary according to course load, degree level, campus/location and program. *Faculty research:* Higher education administration, student affairs.

Grambling State University, School of Graduate Studies and Research, College of Education, Department of Educational Leadership, Grambling, LA 71245. Offers developmental education (MS, Ed D, PMC), including curriculum and instructional design (Ed D), English (MS), guidance and counseling (MS), higher education administration and management (Ed D), mathematics (MS), reading (MS), science (MS), student development and personnel services (Ed D); educational leadership (M Ed). *Program availability:* Part-time, evening/weekend. *Degree requirements:* For master's, comprehensive exam, thesis (for some programs); for doctorate, comprehensive exam, thesis/dissertation. *Entrance requirements:* For master's, GRE, minimum GPA of 2.5 on last degree; for doctorate, GRE (minimum score 1000, 500 on Verbal), master's degree, minimum GPA of 3.0 on last degree. Additional exam requirements/recommendations for international students: Required—TOEFL (minimum score 500 paper-based; 62 iBT). Electronic applications accepted.

Grand Valley State University, College of Education, Program in College Student Affairs Leadership, Allendale, MI 49401-9403. Offers M Ed. *Students:* 64 full-time (41 women), 3 part-time (all women); includes 11 minority (5 Black or African American, non-Hispanic/Latino; 1 American Indian or Alaska Native, non-Hispanic/Latino; 4 Hispanic/Latino; 1 Two or more races, non-Hispanic/Latino), 2 international. Average age 25. In 2018, 33 master's awarded. *Degree requirements:* For master's, project or thesis. *Entrance requirements:* For master's, GRE General Test or minimum GPA of 3.0, last 60 credits from regionally-accredited college/university, 3 letters of recommendation. Additional exam requirements/recommendations for international students: Required—TOEFL (minimum iBT score of 80), IELTS (6.5), or Michigan English Language Assessment Battery (77). *Application deadline:* Applications are processed on a rolling basis. Application fee: $30. Electronic applications accepted. *Expenses:* $677 per credit hour, 36 credit hours. *Financial support:* In 2018–19, 61 students received support, including 12 fellowships, 50 research assistantships with full and partial tuition reimbursements available (averaging $9,000 per year); unspecified assistantships also available. *Faculty research:* Adult learners, diversity and multiculturalism. *Unit head:* Dr. John Shinsky, Department Director, 616-331-6682, Fax: 616-331-6515, E-mail: shinskjo@gvsu.edu. *Application contact:* Dr. Karyn Rabourn, Graduate Program Director, 616-331-6250, Fax: 616-331-6422, E-mail: rabournk@gvsu.edu.

Grand Valley State University, College of Education, Program in Higher Education, Allendale, MI 49401-9403. Offers M Ed. *Program availability:* Part-time. *Students:* 4 full-time (1 woman), 38 part-time (31 women); includes 9 minority (6 Black or African American, non-Hispanic/Latino; 3 Hispanic/Latino). Average age 33. 102 applicants, 88% accepted, 2 enrolled. In 2018, 16 master's awarded. *Degree requirements:* For master's, project or thesis. *Entrance requirements:* For master's, minimum undergraduate GPA of 3.0 or GRE General Test, last 60 credits from regionally-accredited college/university, 3 letters of recommendation. Additional exam requirements/recommendations for international students: Required—TOEFL (minimum iBT score of 80), IELTS (6.5), or Michigan English Language Assessment Battery (77). *Application deadline:* Applications are processed on a rolling basis. Application fee: $30. Electronic applications accepted. *Expenses:* $677 per credit hour, 36 credit hours. *Financial support:* In 2018–19, 3 students received support, including 2 fellowships, 1 research assistantship; unspecified assistantships also available. *Unit head:* Dr. John Shinsky, Director, Educational Leadership and Counseling, 616-331-6682, Fax: 616-331-515, E-mail: shinskjo@gvsu.edu. *Application contact:* Annukka Thelen, Director, Student Information and Services Center, 616-331-6205, Fax: 616-331-6217, E-mail: thelenan@gvsu.edu.
Website: http://www.gvsu.edu/grad/highered/

Grand Valley State University, College of Education, Programs in General Education, Allendale, MI 49401-9403. Offers adult and higher education (M Ed); early childhood education (M Ed); educational differentiation (M Ed); educational leadership (M Ed); educational technology integration (M Ed); elementary education (M Ed); middle level education (M Ed); school library media services (M Ed); secondary level education (M Ed); teaching English to speakers of other languages (M Ed). *Program availability:* Part-time, evening/weekend, 100% online, blended/hybrid learning. *Students:* 20 part-time (10 women); includes 1 minority (Black or African American, non-Hispanic/Latino). Average age 44. In 2018, 1 master's awarded. *Entrance requirements:* For master's, GRE General Test or minimum GPA of 3.0, last 60 credits from regionally-accredited college/university, 3 letters of recommendation. Additional exam requirements/recommendations for international students: Required—TOEFL (minimum iBT score of 80), IELTS (6.5), or Michigan English Language Assessment Battery (77). *Application*

deadline: Applications are processed on a rolling basis. Application fee: $30. Electronic applications accepted. *Expenses:* $677 per credit hour, 33 credits. *Financial support:* In 2018–19, 1 student received support, including 1 fellowship; career-related internships or fieldwork, Federal Work-Study, scholarships/grants, and unspecified assistantships also available. *Faculty research:* Effectiveness of technology in education, parental involvement, effective teaching, effective schools research. *Unit head:* Dr. David Bair, Department Director, 616-331-6489, Fax: 616-331-6489, E-mail: baird@gvsu.edu. *Application contact:* Annukka Thelen, Director, Student Information and Services Center, 616-331-6205, Fax: 616-331-6217, E-mail: thelenan@gvsu.edu.
Website: http://www.gvsu.edu/coe/

Hardin-Simmons University, Graduate School, College of Human Sciences and Educational Studies, Program in Education Leadership, Abilene, TX 79698-0001. Offers educational leadership in superintendency (Ed D); higher education leadership (Ed D). *Program availability:* Part-time. *Students:* 32 part-time (26 women); includes 3 minority (all Hispanic/Latino). Average age 41. 10 applicants, 70% accepted, 6 enrolled. In 2018, 5 doctorates awarded. *Entrance requirements:* For doctorate, minimum master's GPA of 3.5; resume or curriculum vitae; three recommendations from doctoral degree holder, employer/supervisor, and professional colleague. Additional exam requirements/recommendations for international students: Required—TOEFL (minimum score 550 paper-based; 79 iBT), TWE (minimum score 5). *Application deadline:* For fall admission, 7/15 priority date for domestic students, 4/1 for international students; for spring admission, 1/5 priority date for domestic students, 8/1 for international students. Applications are processed on a rolling basis. Application fee: $50. Electronic applications accepted. *Expenses: Tuition:* Full-time $750; part-time $750 per credit hour. *Required fees:* $1300; $880 per credit. Tuition and fees vary according to degree level and program. *Financial support:* Fellowships and scholarships/grants available. Support available to part-time students. Financial award application deadline: 6/30; financial award applicants required to submit FAFSA. *Unit head:* Dr. Mary Christopher, Program Director, 325-670-1510, Fax: 325-670-5859, E-mail: leadership@hsutx.edu. *Application contact:* Dr. Nancy Kucinski, Dean of Graduate Studies, 325-670-1298, Fax: 325-670-1564, E-mail: gradoff@hsutx.edu.
Website: http://www.hsutx.edu/doctorateinleadership

Hofstra University, School of Education, Specialized Programs in Education, Hempstead, NY 11549. Offers applied behavior analysis (Advanced Certificate); childhood special education (MS Ed); early childhood special education (MS Ed, Advanced Certificate); educational and policy leadership (Ed D); educational leadership (Advanced Certificate); educational leadership and policy studies (MS Ed), including K-12; elementary special education (MS Ed); gifted education (Advanced Certificate); health education (MS); health professions pedagogy and leadership (MS); higher education leadership and policy studies (MS Ed); inclusive early childhood special education (MS Ed); inclusive elementary special education (MS Ed); inclusive secondary special education (MS Ed); literacy studies (MA, MS Ed, Ed D, Advanced Certificate); pedagogy for health professions (Advanced Certificate); physical education (MS); school district business leader (Advanced Certificate); secondary education generalist - students with disabilities 7-12 (MS Ed); secondary special education generalist - secondary education (MS Ed); special education (MS Ed, Advanced Certificate); special education assessment and diagnosis (Advanced Certificate); special education early childhood intervention (MS Ed); special education: international perspectives (MS Ed); teaching students with severe or multiple disabilities (Advanced Certificate). *Program availability:* Part-time, evening/weekend, blended/hybrid learning. *Students:* 126 full-time (91 women), 230 part-time (175 women); includes 90 minority (40 Black or African American, non-Hispanic/Latino; 4 American Indian or Alaska Native, non-Hispanic/Latino; 11 Asian, non-Hispanic/Latino; 32 Hispanic/Latino; 3 Two or more races, non-Hispanic/Latino), 4 international. Average age 32. 215 applicants, 90% accepted, 117 enrolled. In 2018, 130 master's, 9 doctorates, 23 other advanced degrees awarded. *Degree requirements:* For master's, one foreign language, comprehensive exam (for some programs), thesis (for some programs), electronic portfolio, capstone course, internship, practicum, student teaching, seminars, minimum GPA of 3.0; for doctorate, one foreign language, comprehensive exam, thesis/dissertation, qualifying hearing. *Entrance requirements:* For master's, GRE, interview, letters of recommendation, portfolio, essay, certification; for doctorate, GRE or MAT, interview, resume, essay, master's degree, 3 letters of recommendation, writing sample; for Advanced Certificate, GRE, interview, letters of recommendation, essay, professional experience, resume, master's degree. Additional exam requirements/recommendations for international students: Required—TOEFL (minimum score 550 paper-based; 80 iBT). *Application deadline:* Applications are processed on a rolling basis. Application fee: $75. Electronic applications accepted. *Financial support:* In 2018–19, 208 students received support, including 105 fellowships with full and partial tuition reimbursements available (averaging $3,948 per year), 12 research assistantships with full and partial tuition reimbursements available (averaging $6,573 per year); career-related internships or fieldwork, Federal Work-Study, institutionally sponsored loans, scholarships/grants, traineeships, tuition waivers (full and partial), unspecified assistantships, and scholarships and endowed scholarships also available. Support available to part-time students. Financial award applicants required to submit FAFSA. *Faculty research:* Water quality and income inequality; girls and stem; new media literacies; applied behavior analysis; k-12 leadership development. *Unit head:* Dr. Alan Flurkey, Chairperson, 516-463-5237, E-mail: alan.d.flurkey@hofstra.edu. *Application contact:* Sunil Samuel, Assistant Vice President of Admissions, 516-463-4723, Fax: 516-463-4664, E-mail: graduateadmission@hofstra.edu.
Website: http://www.hofstra.edu/education/

Houston Baptist University, College of Education and Behavioral Sciences, Programs in Education, Houston, TX 77074-3298. Offers bilingual education (M Ed); counselor education (M Ed); curriculum and instruction (M Ed); curriculum and instruction (EC-6 bilingual) (M Ed); curriculum and instruction in all-level art, Spanish, music, or physical education (M Ed); curriculum and instruction in EC-6 and special education (EC-12) (M Ed); curriculum and instruction in instructional technology (M Ed); curriculum and instruction in mathematics, science, or social studies (4-8) (M Ed); curriculum and instruction with EC-6 generalist (M Ed); curriculum and instruction with English language arts and reading (4-8) (M Ed); educational administration (M Ed); educational diagnostician (M Ed); executive educational leadership (Ed D); higher education in business management (M Ed); higher education in Christian studies (M Ed); higher education in counseling (M Ed); higher education in educational technology (M Ed); reading (M Ed); special educational leadership (Ed D). *Program availability:* Part-time, evening/weekend, 100% online, blended/hybrid learning. *Degree requirements:* For master's, comprehensive exam; for doctorate, thesis/dissertation. *Entrance requirements:* For master's, minimum GPA of 2.75, two recommendations, resume, bachelor's degree conferred transcript; interview (for non-certified teachers); for doctorate, GRE, 5 letters of recommendation. Additional exam requirements/recommendations for international students: Required—TOEFL (minimum score 80 iBT), IELTS (minimum score 6.5). Electronic applications accepted. Application fee is waived when completed online. *Expenses:* Contact institution. *Faculty research:* Autism and inclusion, integrating technology into instruction, school change and leadership trust.

Illinois State University, Graduate School, College of Education, Department of Curriculum and Instruction, Normal, IL 61790. Offers curriculum and instruction (MS, MS Ed, Ed D); educational policies (Ed D); postsecondary education (Ed D); reading (MS Ed); supervision (Ed D). *Accreditation:* NCATE. *Faculty:* 49 full-time (31 women), 80 part-time/adjunct (64 women). *Students:* 7 full-time (2 women), 21 part-time (18 women); includes 4 minority (2 Black or African American, non-Hispanic/Latino; 2 Hispanic/Latino), 5 international. Average age 33. 43 applicants, 93% accepted, 28 enrolled. In 2018, 51 master's, 7 doctorates awarded. *Degree requirements:* For master's, variable foreign language requirement, thesis or alternative; for doctorate, variable foreign language requirement, thesis/dissertation, 2 terms of residency, internship. *Entrance requirements:* For master's, GRE General Test, minimum GPA of 3.0 in last 60 hours of course work; for doctorate, GRE General Test. *Application deadline:* Applications are processed on a rolling basis. Application fee: $40. *Expenses: Tuition, area resident:* Full-time $7264.62. Tuition, state resident: full-time $9466. Tuition, nonresident: full-time $17,290. *International tuition:* $15,089.40 full-time. *Required fees:* $1481.04. *Financial support:* In 2018–19, 18 research assistantships were awarded; tuition waivers (full) and unspecified assistantships also available. Financial award application deadline: 4/1. *Faculty research:* In-service and pre-service teacher education for teachers of English language learners; teachers for all children: developing a model for alternative, bilingual elementary certification for paraprofessionals in Illinois; Illinois Geographic Alliance, Connections Project. *Unit head:* Dr. Alan Bates, Interim Director, 309-438-5425, E-mail: abates@ilstu.edu. *Application contact:* Dr. Ryan Brown, Graduate Coordinator, 309-438-3964, E-mail: rbrown@ilstu.edu.
Website: http://ci.illinoisstate.edu/

Indiana State University, College of Graduate and Professional Studies, Bayh College of Education, Department of Educational Leadership, Terre Haute, IN 47809. Offers educational administration (PhD); higher education leadership (PhD); K-12 district leadership (PhD); school administration (Ed S); school administration and supervision (M Ed); student affairs and higher education (MS). *Accreditation:* NCATE. *Program availability:* Part-time, evening/weekend. Terminal master's awarded for partial completion of doctoral program. *Degree requirements:* For master's, thesis; for doctorate, thesis/dissertation. *Entrance requirements:* For master's, GRE General Test, minimum undergraduate GPA of 2.5; for doctorate, GRE General Test, minimum undergraduate GPA of 3.5; for Ed S, GRE General Test, minimum graduate GPA of 3.25. Electronic applications accepted.

Indiana University Bloomington, School of Education, Department of Educational Leadership and Policy Studies, Bloomington, IN 47405. Offers educational leadership (MS, Ed D, Ed S); higher education (Ed D, PhD); higher education and student affairs (MS); history and philosophy of education (MS); history, philosophy, and policy in education (PhD), including education policy studies, history of education, philosophy of education; international and comparative education (MS). *Accreditation:* NCATE. *Degree requirements:* For master's, thesis optional; for doctorate, comprehensive exam, thesis/dissertation; for Ed S, comprehensive exam or project. *Entrance requirements:* For master's, doctorate, and Ed S, GRE General Test. Additional exam requirements/recommendations for international students: Required—TOEFL (minimum score 79 iBT). Electronic applications accepted. *Faculty research:* Culturally engaging campus environments, school choice policy analysis, democracy and education in the national and international context, and principal leadership.

Indiana University of Pennsylvania, School of Graduate Studies and Research, College of Education and Communications, Department of Student Affairs in Higher Education, Indiana, PA 15705. Offers MA. *Accreditation:* NCATE. *Program availability:* Part-time. *Faculty:* 3 full-time (1 woman), 1 (woman) part-time/adjunct. *Students:* 47 full-time (24 women), 1 part-time (0 women); includes 11 minority (5 Black or African American, non-Hispanic/Latino; 2 Asian, non-Hispanic/Latino; 4 Hispanic/Latino), 1 international. Average age 23. 76 applicants, 84% accepted, 28 enrolled. In 2018, 25 master's awarded. *Degree requirements:* For master's, comprehensive exam, thesis optional. *Entrance requirements:* For master's, resume, interview, 2 letters of recommendation, writing sample, minimum GPA of 2.8. Additional exam requirements/recommendations for international students: Required—TOEFL (minimum score 540 paper-based). *Application deadline:* For fall admission, 1/15 priority date for domestic students. Application fee: $50. Electronic applications accepted. *Expenses:* Contact institution. *Financial support:* In 2018–19, 21 research assistantships with tuition reimbursements (averaging $5,129 per year) were awarded; fellowships, career-related internships or fieldwork, Federal Work-Study, scholarships/grants, and unspecified assistantships also available. Support available to part-time students. Financial award application deadline: 4/15; financial award applicants required to submit FAFSA. *Unit head:* Dr. John Wesley Lowery, Chairperson, 724-357-4545, Fax: 724-357-7821, E-mail: jlowery@iup.edu. *Application contact:* Dr. John Wesley Lowery, Chairperson, 724-357-4545, Fax: 724-357-7821, E-mail: jlowery@iup.edu.
Website: http://www.iup.edu/sahe

Indiana Wesleyan University, Graduate School, College of Arts and Sciences, Marion, IN 46953. Offers addictions counseling (MS); clinical mental health counseling (MS); community counseling (MS); marriage and family therapy (MS); school counseling (MS); student development counseling and administration (MS). *Accreditation:* ACA. *Program availability:* Part-time. *Degree requirements:* For master's, thesis or alternative. *Entrance requirements:* For master's, GRE General Test. Additional exam requirements/recommendations for international students: Required—TOEFL. Electronic applications accepted. *Expenses:* Contact institution. *Faculty research:* Community counseling, multicultural counseling, addictions.

Inter American University of Puerto Rico, Metropolitan Campus, Graduate Programs, Program in Higher Education Administration, San Juan, PR 00919-1293. Offers MA. *Degree requirements:* For master's, comprehensive exam. *Entrance requirements:* For master's, GRE or EXADEP, interview. Electronic applications accepted.

Iowa State University of Science and Technology, Department of Educational Leadership and Policy Studies, Ames, IA 50011. Offers counselor education (M Ed, MS); educational administration (M Ed, MS); educational leadership (PhD); higher education (M Ed, MS); organizational learning and human resource development (M Ed, MS); research and evaluation (MS); student affairs (MS). *Degree requirements:* For master's, thesis or alternative; for doctorate, thesis/dissertation. *Entrance requirements:* For master's and doctorate, GRE General Test. Additional exam requirements/recommendations for international students: Required—TOEFL (minimum score 560 paper-based; 83 iBT), IELTS (minimum score 6.5). Electronic applications accepted.

Jackson State University, Graduate School, College of Education and Human Development, Department of Educational Leadership, Jackson, MS 39217. Offers education administration and supervision (Ed S); educational administration and supervision (MS Ed, PhD); higher education (Ed S). *Accreditation:* NCATE. *Program availability:* Part-time, evening/weekend, online only, 100% online, blended/hybrid learning. *Degree requirements:* For master's and Ed S, comprehensive exam, thesis; for doctorate, comprehensive exam, thesis/dissertation. *Entrance requirements:* For master's, GRE General Test; for doctorate, MAT, GRE, teaching experience. Additional exam requirements/recommendations for international students: Required—TOEFL (minimum score 520 paper-based; 67 iBT). Electronic applications accepted. *Expenses:* Contact institution.

James Madison University, The Graduate School, College of Education, Program in Adult Education and Human Resource Development, Harrisonburg, VA 22807. Offers higher education (MS Ed); human resource management (MS Ed); individualized (MS Ed); instructional design (MS Ed); leadership and facilitation (MS Ed); program evaluation and measurement (MS Ed). *Accreditation:* NCATE. *Program availability:* Part-time, evening/weekend. *Students:* 10 full-time (7 women), 11 part-time (8 women); includes 8 minority (5 Black or African American, non-Hispanic/Latino; 1 American Indian or Alaska Native, non-Hispanic/Latino; 1 Hispanic/Latino; 1 Two or more races, non-Hispanic/Latino), 1 international. Average age 30. In 2018, 10 master's awarded. Application fee: $60. Electronic applications accepted. *Expenses:* Tuition, state resident: full-time $10,848. Tuition, nonresident: full-time $27,888. *Required fees:* $1128. *Financial support:* In 2018–19, 8 students received support. Teaching assistantships, Federal Work-Study, and assistantships (averaging $7911) available. Financial award application deadline: 3/1; financial award applicants required to submit FAFSA. *Unit head:* Dr. Jane B. Thall, Department Head, 540-568-5531, E-mail: thalljb@jmu.edu. *Application contact:* Lynette D. Michael, Director of Graduate Admissions, 540-568-6131 Ext. 6395, Fax: 540-568-7860, E-mail: michaeld@jmu.edu.

Johnson University, Graduate and Professional Programs, Knoxville, TN 37998-1001. Offers biblical interpretation (Graduate Certificate); business administration (MBA); Christian ministries (Graduate Certificate); clinical mental health counseling (MA); educational technology (MA); intercultural studies (MA); leadership (MBA); leadership studies (PhD); New Testament (MA); nonprofit management (MBA); school counseling (MA); spiritual formation and leadership (Graduate Certificate); strategic ministry (MA); teacher education (MA). *Program availability:* Part-time, evening/weekend, 100% online, blended/hybrid learning. *Degree requirements:* For master's, variable foreign language requirement, comprehensive exam, thesis (for some programs), internships; for doctorate, variable foreign language requirement, comprehensive exam, thesis/dissertation, internships. *Entrance requirements:* For master's, PRAXIS (for MA in teacher education); MAT (for counseling); GRE or GMAT (for MBA), interview, 3 references, transcripts, essay, minimum GPA of 2.5 or 3.0 (depending on program); for doctorate, GRE or MAT (taken not less than 5 years prior), interview, 3 references, transcripts, essay, minimum GPA of 3.0; for Graduate Certificate, interview, 3 references, transcripts, essay, minimum GPA of 3.0. Additional exam requirements/recommendations for international students: Required—TOEFL (minimum score 527 paper-based; 71 iBT). Electronic applications accepted. *Expenses:* Contact institution.

Kent State University, College of Education, Health and Human Services, School of Foundations, Leadership and Administration, Program in Higher Education, Kent, OH 44242-0001. Offers PhD, Ed S. *Accreditation:* NCATE. *Program availability:* Part-time, evening/weekend. *Faculty:* 5 full-time (3 women), 2 part-time/adjunct (1 woman). *Students:* 31 full-time (19 women), 32 part-time (21 women); includes 6 minority (3 Black or African American, non-Hispanic/Latino; 1 Asian, non-Hispanic/Latino; 1 Hispanic/Latino; 1 Native Hawaiian or other Pacific Islander, non-Hispanic/Latino), 2 international. 40 applicants, 33% accepted. In 2018, 2 doctorates awarded. *Degree requirements:* For doctorate, comprehensive exam, thesis/dissertation. *Entrance requirements:* For doctorate, GRE General Test, 2 letters of reference, resume, interview, goals statement. Additional exam requirements/recommendations for international students: Required—TOEFL (minimum score 550 paper-based; 80 iBT). *Application deadline:* For fall admission, 2/1 priority date for domestic and international students. Applications are processed on a rolling basis. Application fee: $45 ($60 for international students). Electronic applications accepted. *Expenses:* Tuition, state resident: full-time $11,766; part-time $536 per credit. Tuition, nonresident: full-time $21,952; part-time $999 per credit. *International tuition:* $21,952 full-time. Tuition and fees vary according to course load. *Financial support:* In 2018–19, 3 research assistantships with full tuition reimbursements (averaging $12,000 per year), 3 teaching assistantships with full tuition reimbursements (averaging $12,000 per year) were awarded; career-related internships or fieldwork, Federal Work-Study, institutionally sponsored loans, scholarships/grants, health care benefits, unspecified assistantships, and 2 administrative assistantships (averaging $12,000 per year) also available. Support available to part-time students. Financial award application deadline: 4/1; financial award applicants required to submit FAFSA. *Faculty research:* Leadership. *Unit head:* Dr. Stephen Thomas, Coordinator, 330-672-0654, E-mail: sbthomas@kent.edu. *Application contact:* Cheryl Slusarczyk, Academic Program Director, Office of Graduate Student Services, 330-672-2576, Fax: 330-672-9162, E-mail: ogs@kent.edu.

Kent State University, College of Education, Health and Human Services, School of Foundations, Leadership and Administration, Program in Higher Education Administration and Student Affairs, Kent, OH 44242-0001. Offers M Ed. *Accreditation:* NCATE. *Program availability:* Part-time, evening/weekend. *Faculty:* 5 full-time (3 women), 2 part-time/adjunct (1 woman). *Students:* 75 full-time (49 women), 24 part-time (20 women); includes 21 minority (13 Black or African American, non-Hispanic/Latino; 1 American Indian or Alaska Native, non-Hispanic/Latino; 1 Asian, non-Hispanic/Latino; 6 Native Hawaiian or other Pacific Islander, non-Hispanic/Latino), 3 international. 164 applicants, 30% accepted. In 2018, 56 master's awarded. *Degree requirements:* For master's, thesis. *Entrance requirements:* For master's, GRE if undergraduate GPA is below 3.0, resume, interview, 2 letters of recommendation, goals statement. Additional exam requirements/recommendations for international students: Required—TOEFL (minimum score 550 paper-based; 80 iBT). *Application deadline:* For fall admission, 1/5 priority date for domestic and international students. Applications are processed on a rolling basis. Application fee: $45 ($60 for international students). Electronic applications accepted. *Expenses:* Tuition, state resident: full-time $11,766; part-time $536 per credit. Tuition, nonresident: full-time $21,952; part-time $999 per credit. *International tuition:* $21,952 full-time. Tuition and fees vary according to course load. *Financial support:* In 2018–19, 4 research assistantships with full tuition reimbursements (averaging $8,500 per year) were awarded; teaching assistantships with full tuition reimbursements, Federal Work-Study, scholarships/grants, unspecified assistantships, and 8 administrative assistantships (averaging $8,500 per year) also available. Financial award application deadline: 4/1; financial award applicants required to submit FAFSA. *Faculty research:* History/sociology of higher education, organization and administration in higher education. *Unit head:* Dr. Mark Kretovics, Coordinator, 330-672-0642, E-mail: mkretov1@kent.edu. *Application contact:* Cheryl Slusarczyk, Academic Program Director, Office of Graduate Student Services, 330-672-2576, Fax: 330-672-9162, E-mail: ogs@kent.edu.

Lee University, Program in Education, Cleveland, TN 37320-3450. Offers art (MAT); curriculum and instruction (M Ed, Ed S); early childhood (MAT); educational leadership (M Ed, Ed S); elementary education (MAT); English and math (MAT); English and science (MAT); English and social studies (MAT); higher education administration (MS); history (MAT); history and economics (MAT); math and science (MAT); math and social studies (MAT); middle grades (MAT); science and social studies (MASW); secondary education (MAT); Spanish (MAT); special education (M Ed, MAT); TESOL (MAT). *Accreditation:* NCATE. *Program availability:* Part-time. *Faculty:* 13 full-time (5 women), 13 part-time/adjunct (7 women). *Students:* 32 full-time (26 women), 73 part-time (49 women); includes 13 minority (10 Black or African American, non-Hispanic/Latino; 3 Two or more races, non-Hispanic/Latino), 3 international. Average age 30. 56 applicants, 73% accepted, 34 enrolled. In 2018, 60 master's, 3 other advanced degrees awarded. *Degree requirements:* For master's, variable foreign language requirement, thesis optional, internship. *Entrance requirements:* For master's, MAT or GRE General Test, minimum undergraduate GPA of 2.75, 3 letters of recommendation, interview, writing sample, official transcripts, background check; for Ed S, minimum undergraduate and master's GPA of 2.75, official transcripts for undergraduate and master's degrees. Additional exam requirements/recommendations for international students: Required—TOEFL (minimum score 61 iBT). *Application deadline:* For fall admission, 6/1 priority date for domestic and international students; for spring admission, 11/1 priority date for domestic and international students; for summer admission, 4/1 priority date for domestic and international students. Applications are processed on a rolling basis. Application fee: $25. Electronic applications accepted. *Financial support:* In 2018–19, 43 students received support. Career-related internships or fieldwork, Federal Work-Study, institutionally sponsored loans, scholarships/grants, and unspecified assistantships available. Financial award application deadline: 3/1; financial award applicants required to submit FAFSA. *Unit head:* Dr. William Kamm, Director, 423-614-8544, E-mail: wkamm@leeuniversity.edu. *Application contact:* Jeffery McGirt, Director of Graduate Enrollment, 423-614-8691, Fax: 423-614-8317, E-mail: jmcgirt@leeuniversity.edu.
Website: http://www.leeuniversity.edu/academics/graduate/education

Lewis University, College of Arts and Sciences, Program in Organizational Leadership, Romeoville, IL 60446. Offers higher education/student services (MA); organizational and leadership coaching (MA); training and development (MA). *Program availability:* Part-time, evening/weekend, 100% online, blended/hybrid learning. *Students:* 13 full-time (9 women), 150 part-time (115 women); includes 45 minority (28 Black or African American, non-Hispanic/Latino; 3 Asian, non-Hispanic/Latino; 10 Hispanic/Latino; 4 Two or more races, non-Hispanic/Latino), 2 international. Average age 38. *Entrance requirements:* For master's, bachelor's degree, personal statement, minimum GPA of 3.0, letters of recommendation. Additional exam requirements/recommendations for international students: Required—TOEFL (minimum score 550 paper-based; 79 iBT), IELTS (minimum score 6). *Application deadline:* For fall admission, 5/1 priority date for international students; for spring admission, 11/15 priority date for international students. Applications are processed on a rolling basis. Application fee: $40. Electronic applications accepted. *Financial support:* Federal Work-Study, tuition waivers, and unspecified assistantships available. Financial award application deadline: 5/1; financial award applicants required to submit FAFSA. *Unit head:* Dr. Lesley Page, Chair, Organizational Leadership. *Application contact:* Kathy Lisak, Graduate Admission Counselor, 815-836-5610, E-mail: grad@lewisu.edu.

Lincoln Memorial University, Carter and Moyers School of Education, Harrogate, TN 37752-1901. Offers administration and supervision (M Ed, Ed S); counseling and guidance (M Ed); curriculum and instruction (M Ed, Ed D, Ed S); English (M Ed); executive leadership (Ed D); higher education administration (Ed D); human resource development (Ed D); leadership and administration (Ed D). *Program availability:* Part-time, evening/weekend, online learning. *Degree requirements:* For master's, comprehensive exam, thesis optional; for Ed S, comprehensive exam. *Entrance requirements:* For master's, PRAXIS, NTE, GRE, MAT, letters of recommendation; for Ed S, graduate transcripts. Additional exam requirements/recommendations for international students: Recommended—TOEFL. *Faculty research:* Brain compatible teaching and learning; poverty in Appalachia; leadership for change; ethics, moral responsibility and social justice; human and organizational learning.

Lincoln University, Graduate Studies, Jefferson City, MO 65101. Offers business administration (MBA); counseling (M Ed); environmental science (MS); higher education (MA); history (MA); natural sciences (MS); school teaching middle school with certification (M Ed); school teaching-elementary (M Ed); school teaching-secondary (M Ed); sociology (MA); sociology/criminal justice (MA); sustainable agriculture (MS). *Program availability:* Part-time, evening/weekend, 100% online, blended/hybrid learning. *Students:* 37 full-time (23 women), 52 part-time (25 women); includes 26 minority (24 Black or African American, non-Hispanic/Latino; 1 Asian, non-Hispanic/Latino; 1 Two or more races, non-Hispanic/Latino), 11 international. Average age 34. 67 applicants, 52% accepted, 29 enrolled. In 2018, 48 master's awarded. *Degree requirements:* For master's, comprehensive exam, thesis optional. *Entrance requirements:* For master's, GRE, MAT, or GMAT, minimum GPA of 2.75 overall, 3.0 in courses related to specialization; 3 letters of recommendation; minimum C average in English composition; personal statement of purpose. Additional exam requirements/recommendations for international students: Required—TOEFL (minimum score 500 paper-based; 61 iBT), IELTS (minimum score 5.5), Michigan English Language Assessment Battery (minimum score 80). *Application deadline:* For fall admission, 7/1 priority date for domestic students, 5/1 priority date for international students; for spring admission, 11/1 priority date for domestic students, 10/1 priority date for international students; for summer admission, 6/1 priority date for domestic students. Applications are processed on a rolling basis. Application fee: $30. Electronic applications accepted. *Expenses: Tuition, area resident:* Full-time $6984; part-time $291 per credit. Tuition, state resident: full-time $6984; part-time $291 per credit. Tuition, nonresident: full-time $12,996; part-time $541.50 per credit. *International tuition:* $12,996 full-time. *Required fees:* $1242.20. *Financial support:* In 2018–19, 9 research assistantships with tuition reimbursements (averaging $4,050 per year) were awarded; fellowships with tuition reimbursements, Federal Work-Study, scholarships/grants, and unspecified assistantships also available. Support available to part-time students. Financial award application deadline: 3/1; financial award applicants required to submit FAFSA. *Unit head:* Dr. Benjamin Arnold, Assistant Vice President of Academic Affairs, 573-681-5247, Fax: 573-681-5106, E-mail: gradschool@lincolnu.edu. *Application contact:* Sarah Robinett, Administrative Assistant, 573-681-5247, Fax: 573-681-5106, E-mail: gradschool@lincolnu.edu.
Website: http://www.lincolnu.edu/web/graduate-studies/graduate-studies

London Metropolitan University, Graduate Programs, London, United Kingdom. Offers applied psychology (M Sc); architecture (MA); biomedical science (M Sc); blood science (M Sc); cancer pharmacology (M Sc); computer networking and cyber security (M Sc); computing and information systems (M Sc); conference interpreting (MA); counter-terrorism studies (M Sc); creative, digital and professional writing (MA); crime, violence and prevention (M Sc); criminology (M Sc); curating contemporary art (MA); data analytics (M Sc); digital media (MA); early childhood studies (MA); education (MA, Ed D); financial services law, regulation and compliance (LL M); food science (M Sc); forensic psychology (M Sc); health and social care management and policy (M Sc); human nutrition (M Sc); human resource management (MA); human rights and international conflict (MA); information technology (M Sc); intelligence and security studies (M Sc); international oil, gas and energy law (LL M); international relations (MA); interpreting (MA); learning and teaching in higher education (MA); legal practice (LL M); media and entertainment law (LL M); organizational and consumer psychology (M Sc); psychological therapy (M Sc); psychology of mental health (M Sc); public health (M Sc); public policy and management (MPA); security studies (M Sc); social work (M Sc); spatial planning and urban design (MA); sports therapy (M Sc); supporting older children and young people with dyslexia (MA); teaching languages (MA), including Arabic, English; translation (MA); woman and child abuse (MA).

Louisiana State University and Agricultural & Mechanical College, Graduate School, College of Human Sciences and Education, Department of Educational Theory, Policy and Practice, Baton Rouge, LA 70803. Offers counseling (M Ed, MA, Ed S);

educational administration (M Ed, MA, PhD, Ed S); educational technology (MA); elementary education (M Ed, MAT); higher education (PhD); research methodology (PhD); secondary education (M Ed, MAT). *Accreditation:* ACA (one or more programs are accredited); NCATE.

Louisiana Tech University, Graduate School, College of Education, Ruston, LA 71272. Offers counseling and guidance (MA), including clinical mental health counseling, human services, orientation and mobility; counseling psychology (PhD); curriculum and instruction (M Ed); cyber education (Graduate Certificate); dynamics of domestic and family violence (Graduate Certificate); early childhood education - PreK-3 (MAT); educational leadership (M Ed, Ed D); elementary education and special education mild/moderate grades 1-5 (MAT); higher education administration (Graduate Certificate); industrial/organizational psychology (MA, PhD); kinesiology (MS); middle school education (MAT), including mathematics; orientation and mobility (Graduate Certificate); rehabilitation teaching for the blind (Graduate Certificate); secondary education (MAT), including agriculture, biology, business, chemistry, English; special education: visually impaired (MAT); teacher leader education (Graduate Certificate); visual impairments - blind education (Graduate Certificate). *Accreditation:* NCATE. *Program availability:* Part-time. *Degree requirements:* For master's, thesis; for doctorate, thesis/dissertation. *Entrance requirements:* For master's and doctorate, GRE General Test. Additional exam requirements/recommendations for international students: Required—TOEFL (minimum score 550 paper-based; 80 iBT), IELTS (minimum score 6.5). Electronic applications accepted. *Faculty research:* Blindness and the best methods for increasing independence for individuals who are blind or visually impaired; educating and investigating factors contributing to improvements in human performance across the lifespan and a reduction in injury rates during training.

Loyola Marymount University, School of Education, Program in Higher Education Administration, Los Angeles, CA 90045. Offers MA. *Unit head:* Dr. Elizabeth Stoddard, Director, Higher Education, 310-258-8803, E-mail: elizabeth.stoddard@lmu.edu. *Application contact:* Ammar Dalal, Assistant Vice Provost for Graduate Enrollment, 310-338-2721, Fax: 310-338-6086, E-mail: graduateinfo@lmu.edu.
Website: http://soe.lmu.edu/academics/highereducationadministration

Loyola University Chicago, School of Education, Program in Higher Education, Chicago, IL 60660. Offers higher education (M Ed, PhD); international higher education (M Ed). PhD offered through the Graduate School. *Accreditation:* NCATE. *Program availability:* Part-time, blended/hybrid learning. *Faculty:* 4 full-time (2 women), 10 part-time/adjunct (9 women). *Students:* 49 full-time (30 women), 63 part-time (50 women); includes 51 minority (17 Black or African American, non-Hispanic/Latino; 8 Asian, non-Hispanic/Latino; 21 Hispanic/Latino; 5 Two or more races, non-Hispanic/Latino). Average age 30. 172 applicants, 83% accepted, 39 enrolled. In 2018, 70 master's, 5 doctorates awarded. *Degree requirements:* For master's, comprehensive exam; for doctorate, comprehensive exam, thesis/dissertation. *Entrance requirements:* For master's, letters of recommendation, minimum GPA of 3.0, resume, transcripts; for doctorate, GMAT, GRE General Test, or MAT, 5 years of higher education work experience, interview. Additional exam requirements/recommendations for international students: Required—TOEFL (minimum score 550 paper-based; 79 iBT). *Application deadline:* For fall admission, 12/1 for domestic and international students. Applications are processed on a rolling basis. Application fee: $50. Electronic applications accepted. Application fee is waived when completed online. *Expenses:* Contact institution. *Financial support:* In 2018–19, 37 fellowships with partial tuition reimbursements, 42 research assistantships with full tuition reimbursements (averaging $14,000 per year), 23 teaching assistantships with full tuition reimbursements (averaging $4,000 per year) were awarded; career-related internships or fieldwork, institutionally sponsored loans, scholarships/grants, traineeships, health care benefits, and unspecified assistantships also available. Support available to part-time students. Financial award application deadline: 2/1; financial award applicants required to submit FAFSA. *Faculty research:* Church-affiliated higher education, enrollment management, academic programs, program evaluation/quality. *Unit head:* Dr. Bridget Kelly, Director, 312-915-6855, Fax: 312-915-6660, E-mail: bkelly4@luc.edu. *Application contact:* Dr. Bridget Kelly, Director, 312-915-6855, Fax: 312-915-6660, E-mail: bkelly4@luc.edu.

Mary Baldwin University, Graduate Studies, Programs in Education, Staunton, VA 24401-3610. Offers applied behavior analysis (MS); autism spectrum disorders (M Ed); elementary education (M Ed, MAT); English as a second language (M Ed); environment-based learning (M Ed); gifted education (M Ed); higher education (MS); leadership (M Ed); middle grades education (MAT); reading education (M Ed); special education (M Ed). *Accreditation:* TEAC.

Maryville University of Saint Louis, School of Education, St. Louis, MO 63141-7299. Offers early childhood education (MA Ed); educational leadership (Ed D); educational leadership w/principal certification (MA Ed); elementary education (MA Ed); gifted (MA Ed); higher education leadership (Ed D); middle grades education (MA Ed); reading/literacy specialist (MA Ed); teacher as leader (Ed D). *Accreditation:* NCATE. *Program availability:* Part-time, 100% online, blended/hybrid learning. *Faculty:* 16 full-time (8 women), 18 part-time/adjunct (11 women). *Students:* 12 full-time (all women), 311 part-time (234 women); includes 99 minority (84 Black or African American, non-Hispanic/Latino; 2 Asian, non-Hispanic/Latino; 9 Hispanic/Latino; 4 Two or more races, non-Hispanic/Latino), 2 international. Average age 38. In 2018, 25 master's, 100 doctorates awarded. *Degree requirements:* For master's, thesis, project. *Entrance requirements:* For master's, minimum cumulative GPA of 3.0, 3 professional recommendations, essays, interview with program faculty; for doctorate, minimum GPA of 3.0, 3 professional recommendations, essay, interview, on-site writing sample. Additional exam requirements/recommendations for international students: Required—TOEFL (minimum score 550 paper-based; 79 iBT). *Application deadline:* Applications are processed on a rolling basis. Electronic applications accepted. *Expenses:* $449 per credit hour for master's programs; $897 per credit hour for doctoral programs. *Financial support:* Career-related internships or fieldwork, Federal Work-Study, tuition waivers (partial), and professional educator discounts available. Financial award application deadline: 4/1; financial award applicants required to submit FAFSA. *Faculty research:* Collaboration with public schools, pre-service program development, mathematics, diversity, literacy. *Unit head:* Dr. Maschael Schappe, Dean, 314-529-9670, Fax: 314-529-9921, E-mail: mschappe@maryville.edu. *Application contact:* Stacey Ruffin, Director of Clinical Experiences & Partnerships, 314-529-9542, Fax: 314-529-9921, E-mail: sruffin@maryville.edu.
Website: http://www.maryville.edu/ed/graduate-programs/

Marywood University, Academic Affairs, Center for Interdisciplinary Studies, Scranton, PA 18509-1598. Offers human development (PhD), including educational administration, health promotion, higher education administration, instructional leadership, social work. *Program availability:* Part-time. Electronic applications accepted. *Expenses:* Contact institution.

Marywood University, Academic Affairs, Reap College of Education and Human Development, Department of Education, Program in Higher Education Administration, Scranton, PA 18509-1598. Offers MS. *Program availability:* Part-time, evening/weekend. Electronic applications accepted. *Faculty research:* Integrated thematic instruction.

McKendree University, Graduate Programs, Programs in Education, Lebanon, IL 62254-1299. Offers curriculum design and instruction (Ed D, Ed S); educational administration and leadership (MA Ed); educational studies (MA Ed); higher education administrative services (MA Ed); music education (MA Ed); reading (MA Ed); special education (MA Ed); teacher leadership (MA Ed); teaching certification (MA Ed). *Accreditation:* NCATE. *Program availability:* Part-time, evening/weekend, online learning. *Entrance requirements:* For master's, official transcripts from all institutions previously attended, minimum GPA of 3.0, resume, references; for doctorate, GRE (within the past 5 years), master's degree in education and Ed S, or the equivalent, from regionally-accredited institution; official transcripts from all institutions previously attended; curriculum vitae/resume; essay/personal statement; two years of teaching/professional experience; for Ed S, GRE (within the past 5 years), master's degree in education from regionally-accredited institution of higher education; official transcripts from all institutions previously attended; curriculum vitae/resume; essay/personal statement; two years of teaching/professional experience. Additional exam requirements/recommendations for international students: Required—TOEFL. Electronic applications accepted.

Mercer University, Graduate Studies, Cecil B. Day Campus, Tift College of Education (Atlanta), Atlanta, GA 30341. Offers curriculum and instruction (PhD); early childhood education (M Ed, MAT, Ed S); educational leadership (PhD), including higher education leadership, P-12 school leadership; educational leadership P-12 (M Ed, Ed S); higher education leadership (M Ed); independent and charter school leadership (M Ed); middle grades education (M Ed, MAT); secondary education (M Ed, MAT); teacher leadership (Ed S). *Accreditation:* NCATE. *Program availability:* Part-time, evening/weekend. *Degree requirements:* For master's and Ed S, research project; for doctorate, comprehensive exam, thesis/dissertation. *Entrance requirements:* For master's, GRE or MAT, minimum undergraduate GPA of 2.75; for doctorate, GRE; for Ed S, GRE or MAT, minimum GPA of 3.25; 3 years of certified teaching experience (for educational leadership and teacher leadership). Additional exam requirements/recommendations for international students: Required—TOEFL (minimum score 80 iBT). Electronic applications accepted. *Expenses:* Contact institution. *Faculty research:* Educational technology, multicultural and minority issues in education, educational leadership (P-12 and higher education), school discipline and school bullying, standards-based mathematics education.

Mercer University, Graduate Studies, Macon Campus, Tift College of Education (Macon), Macon, GA 31207. Offers curriculum and instruction (PhD); early childhood education (M Ed, Ed S); educational leadership (M Ed, PhD, Ed S), including higher education (PhD), P-12; higher education leadership (M Ed); independent and charter school leadership (M Ed); secondary education (MAT), including STEM; teacher leadership (Ed S). *Accreditation:* NCATE. *Program availability:* Part-time, evening/weekend, 100% online, blended/hybrid learning. *Degree requirements:* For master's, research project report; for doctorate, comprehensive exam, thesis/dissertation. *Entrance requirements:* For master's, GRE or MAT, minimum GPA of 2.75; for doctorate, GRE, minimum GPA of 3.5; interview; writing sample; 3 recommendations; for Ed S, GRE or MAT, minimum GPA of 3.5 (for teacher leadership), 3.0 (for educational leadership). Additional exam requirements/recommendations for international students: Required—TOEFL (minimum score 80 iBT). Electronic applications accepted. *Expenses:* Contact institution. *Faculty research:* Teacher effectiveness, specific learning disabilities, inclusion.

Mercyhurst University, Graduate Studies, Program in Organizational Leadership, Erie, PA 16546. Offers accounting (MS); higher education administration (MS); human resources (MS); organizational leadership (MS, Certificate); sports leadership (MS); strategy and innovation (MS). *Program availability:* Part-time, evening/weekend. *Degree requirements:* For master's, thesis. *Entrance requirements:* For master's, GRE General Test or MAT, interview, resume, essay, three professional references, transcripts. Additional exam requirements/recommendations for international students: Required—TOEFL (minimum score 80 iBT), IELTS (minimum score 6.5). Electronic applications accepted. *Faculty research:* Leadership training, organizational communication, leadership pedagogy.

Messiah College, Program in Higher Education, Mechanicsburg, PA 17055. Offers college athletics management (MA); self-designed concentration (MA); student affairs (MA). *Program availability:* Part-time. Electronic applications accepted. *Faculty research:* College athletics management, assessment and student learning outcomes, the life and legacy of Ernest L. Boyer, common learning, student affairs practice.

Michigan State University, The Graduate School, College of Education, Department of Educational Administration, East Lansing, MI 48824. Offers higher, adult and lifelong education (MA, PhD); K–12 educational administration (MA, PhD, Ed S); student affairs administration (MA). *Program availability:* Part-time. *Entrance requirements:* Additional exam requirements/recommendations for international students: Required—TOEFL. Electronic applications accepted.

Minnesota State University Mankato, College of Graduate Studies and Research, College of Social and Behavioral Sciences, Department of Sociology and Corrections, Mankato, MN 56001. Offers sociology (MA); sociology: college teaching (MA); sociology: corrections (MS); sociology: human services planning and administration (MS). *Program availability:* Part-time. *Degree requirements:* For master's, comprehensive exam, thesis or alternative. *Entrance requirements:* For master's, minimum GPA of 3.0 during previous 2 years, 3 letters of reference, resume. Additional exam requirements/recommendations for international students: Required—TOEFL. Electronic applications accepted.

Mississippi College, Graduate School, School of Education, Department of Teacher Education and Leadership, Clinton, MS 39058. Offers art (M Ed); biological science (M Ed); business education (M Ed); computer science (M Ed); dyslexia therapy (M Ed); educational leadership (M Ed, Ed D, Ed S); elementary education (M Ed, Ed S); English (M Ed); higher education administration (MS); mathematics (M Ed); secondary education (M Ed); social studies (history) (M Ed); teaching arts (M Ed). *Program availability:* Part-time, online learning. *Degree requirements:* For master's, comprehensive exam, thesis optional. *Entrance requirements:* For master's, NTE. Additional exam requirements/recommendations for international students: Recommended—TOEFL, IELTS. Electronic applications accepted.

Mississippi College, Graduate School, School of Education, Program in Higher Education Administration, Clinton, MS 39058. Offers MS. *Program availability:* Part-time, online learning. *Degree requirements:* For master's, comprehensive exam, thesis optional. *Entrance requirements:* For master's, GRE or GMAT, minimum GPA of 3.0. Additional exam requirements/recommendations for international students: Recommended—TOEFL, IELTS.

Mississippi State University, College of Education, Educational Leadership Program, Mississippi State, MS 39762. Offers community college education (MAT); community college leadership (PhD); higher education leadership (PhD); P-12 school leadership (PhD); school administration (MS, Ed S); student affairs and higher education (MS); workforce education leadership (MS). MS in workforce education leadership held jointly with Alcorn State University. *Faculty:* 12 full-time (9 women). *Students:* 74 full-time (43 women), 145 part-time (89 women); includes 86 minority (75 Black or African American,

non-Hispanic/Latino; 1 American Indian or Alaska Native, non-Hispanic/Latino; 6 Hispanic/Latino; 4 Two or more races, non-Hispanic/Latino). Average age 35. 83 applicants, 82% accepted, 55 enrolled. In 2018, 48 master's, 12 doctorates, 13 other advanced degrees awarded. *Degree requirements:* For master's and Ed S, comprehensive exam, thesis; for doctorate, comprehensive exam, thesis/dissertation. *Entrance requirements:* For master's, GRE, minimum GPA of 2.75 in junior and senior courses; for doctorate, GRE, minimum GPA of 3.4 on previous graduate work; for Ed S, GRE, minimum GPA of 3.2, master's degree. Additional exam requirements/recommendations for international students: Required—TOEFL (minimum score 550 paper-based; 79 iBT); Recommended—IELTS (minimum score 6.5). *Application deadline:* For fall admission, 7/1 for domestic students, 5/1 for international students; for spring admission, 11/1 for domestic students, 9/1 for international students. Application fee: $60 ($80 for international students). Electronic applications accepted. *Expenses:* Tuition, state resident: full-time $8450; part-time $360.59 per credit hour. Tuition, nonresident: full-time $23,140; part-time $969.09 per credit hour. *Required fees:* $110. One-time fee: $55 full-time. Part-time tuition and fees vary according to course load, degree level, campus/location and reciprocity agreements. *Financial support:* In 2018–19, 1 research assistantship with full tuition reimbursement (averaging $11,861 per year) was awarded; Federal Work-Study, institutionally sponsored loans, and unspecified assistantships also available. Financial award application deadline: 4/1; financial award applicants required to submit FAFSA. *Unit head:* Dr. Eric Moyen, Associate Professor and Head, 662-325-0969, Fax: 662-325-0975, E-mail: em1621@msstate.edu. *Application contact:* Nathan Drake, Admissions and Enrollment Assistant, 662-325-3804, E-mail: ndrake@grad.msstate.edu.
Website: http://www.educationalleadership.msstate.edu/

Missouri State University, Graduate College, College of Education, Department of Counseling, Leadership, and Special Education, Program in Student Affairs in Higher Education, Springfield, MO 65897. Offers MS. *Program availability:* Part-time. *Faculty:* 6 full-time (4 women). *Students:* 20 full-time (11 women), 3 part-time (2 women); includes 5 minority (1 Black or African American, non-Hispanic/Latino; 1 Asian, non-Hispanic/Latino; 1 Hispanic/Latino; 2 Two or more races, non-Hispanic/Latino). Average age 24. 17 applicants, 76% accepted. In 2018, 21 master's awarded. *Degree requirements:* For master's, comprehensive exam, thesis or alternative. *Entrance requirements:* For master's, GRE, statement of purpose; three references. Additional exam requirements/recommendations for international students: Required—TOEFL (minimum score 550 paper-based; 79 iBT), IELTS (minimum score 6). *Application deadline:* For fall admission, 2/1 priority date for domestic students, 2/1 for international students. Applications are processed on a rolling basis. Application fee: $55 ($60 for international students). Electronic applications accepted. Tuition and fees vary according to class time, course level, course load, degree level, campus/location, program and student level. *Financial support:* Federal Work-Study, institutionally sponsored loans, scholarships/grants, and unspecified assistantships available. Financial award application deadline: 1/31; financial award applicants required to submit FAFSA. *Unit head:* Dr. James Satterfield, Department Head, 417-836-5392, E-mail: clse@missouristate.edu. *Application contact:* Lakan Drinker, Director, Graduate Enrollment Management, 417-836-5330, Fax: 417-836-6200, E-mail: lakandrinker@missouristate.edu.
Website: http://education.missouristate.edu/edadmin/MSEDSA.htm

Montana State University, The Graduate School, College of Education, Health, and Human Development, Department of Education, Bozeman, MT 59717. Offers adult and higher education (Ed D); curriculum and instruction (M Ed, Ed D), including professional educator (M Ed), technology education (M Ed); education (M Ed), including adult and higher education, educational leadership, school counseling; educational leadership (Ed D, Ed S). *Accreditation:* TEAC. *Program availability:* Part-time, online learning. *Degree requirements:* For master's, comprehensive exam; for doctorate, comprehensive exam, thesis/dissertation. *Entrance requirements:* For master's, GRE, 3 letters of reference, essays, BA transcripts; for doctorate, GRE, MAT, 3 letters of reference, essay, BA and M Ed transcripts; for Ed S, PRAXIS. Additional exam requirements/recommendations for international students: Required—TOEFL (minimum score 550 paper-based). Electronic applications accepted. *Faculty research:* Critical literacy; standards-based education; school Improvement, organizational change, leadership in rural education, leadership in Indian education; student Learning; multicultural/culturally responsive education for social justice Native American indigenous education, community-centered education teacher preparation.

Morehead State University, Graduate School, College of Education, Department of Foundational and Graduate Studies in Education, Morehead, KY 40351. Offers adult and higher education (MA, Ed S); certified professional counselor (Ed S); counseling P-12 (MA); curriculum and instruction (Ed S); educational technology (MA Ed); instructional leadership (Ed S); school administration (MA); school counseling (Ed S); teacher leader business and marketing content (MA Ed); teacher leader business and marketing technology (MA Ed); teacher leader educational technology (MA Ed); teacher leader English (MA Ed); teacher leader gifted education (MA Ed); teacher leader IECE certification (MA Ed); teacher leader interdisciplinary education P-5 (MA Ed); teacher leader middle grades (MA Ed); teacher leader non IECE certification (MA Ed); teacher leader reading/writing - non-certification (MA Ed); teacher leader reading/writing certification (MA Ed); teacher leader school communication - certification (MA Ed); teacher leader school communication - non-certification (MA Ed); teacher leader social studies (MA Ed); teacher leader special education (MA Ed). *Accreditation:* NCATE. *Program availability:* Part-time, evening/weekend. *Degree requirements:* For master's, thesis optional, oral and/or written comprehensive exams; for Ed S, thesis, oral exam. *Entrance requirements:* For master's, GRE General Test, minimum overall undergraduate GPA of 2.5; for Ed S, GRE General Test, interview, master's degree, minimum GPA of 3.5, work experience. Additional exam requirements/recommendations for international students: Required—TOEFL (minimum score 500 paper-based). Electronic applications accepted. *Faculty research:* Character education, school accountability, computer applications for school administrators.

Morgan State University, School of Graduate Studies, School of Education and Urban Studies, Department of Advanced Studies, Leadership and Policy, Program in Higher Education Administration, Baltimore, MD 21251. Offers higher education (PhD); higher education and student affairs administration (MA). *Degree requirements:* For doctorate, comprehensive exam, thesis/dissertation, *Entrance requirements:* For doctorate, GRE General Test or MAT, minimum GPA of 3.0.

National American University, Roueche Graduate Center, Austin, TX 78731. Offers accounting (MBA); aviation management (MBA, MM); care coordination (MSN); community college leadership (Ed D); criminal justice (MM); e-marketing (MBA, MM); health care administration (MBA, MM); higher education (MM); human resources management (MBA, MM); information technology management (MBA, MM); international business (MBA); leadership (EMBA); management (MBA); nursing administration (MSN); nursing education (MSN); nursing informatics (MSN); operations and configuration management (MBA, MM); project and process management (MBA, MM). Master's programs offered online through the Harold D. Buckingham Graduate School. *Program availability:* Part-time, evening/weekend, online learning. *Entrance requirements:* For master's, minimum undergraduate GPA of 2.75. Additional exam

requirements/recommendations for international students: Required—TOEFL, TWE. Electronic applications accepted. *Faculty research:* Tourism, finance, marketing.

National University, Sanford College of Education, La Jolla, CA 92037-1011. Offers advanced teaching practices (MS); applied behavior analysis (MS); applied school leadership (MS); e-teaching and learning (Certificate); education (MA); educational administration (MS); educational and instructional technology (MS); educational counseling (MS); higher education administration (MS); inspired teaching and learning (M Ed); school psychology (MS); special education (MA, MS). *Program availability:* Part-time, evening/weekend, 100% online, blended/hybrid learning. *Degree requirements:* For master's, thesis (for some programs). *Entrance requirements:* For master's, interview, minimum GPA of 2.5. Additional exam requirements/recommendations for international students: Required—TOEFL (minimum score 550 paper-based; 79 iBT), IELTS (minimum score 6). Electronic applications accepted. *Expenses: Tuition:* Full-time $10,320; part-time $430 per unit. Tuition and fees vary according to degree level. *Faculty research:* Teacher education, special education, educational effectiveness, teaching abroad, school counseling.

New England College, Program in Education, Henniker, NH 03242-3293. Offers higher education administration (MS, Ed D); K-12 leadership (Ed D); literacy and language arts (M Ed); meeting the needs of all learners/special education (M Ed); teacher leadership/school reform (M Ed). *Program availability:* Part-time, evening/weekend.

New Mexico State University, College of Education, Department of Educational Leadership and Administration, Las Cruces, NM 88003-8001. Offers educational administration (MA), including community college and university administration, PK-12 public school administration; educational leadership (Ed D, PhD). *Accreditation:* NCATE. *Program availability:* Part-time-only, evening/weekend, blended/hybrid learning. *Faculty:* 7 full-time (6 women), 1 (woman) part-time/adjunct. *Students:* 10 full-time (9 women), 111 part-time (76 women); includes 75 minority (2 Black or African American, non-Hispanic/Latino; 8 American Indian or Alaska Native, non-Hispanic/Latino; 3 Asian, non-Hispanic/Latino; 61 Hispanic/Latino; 1 Native Hawaiian or other Pacific Islander, non-Hispanic/Latino), 2 international. Average age 41. 23 applicants, 26% accepted, 4 enrolled. In 2018, 35 master's, 5 doctorates awarded. *Degree requirements:* For master's, comprehensive exam, internship; for doctorate, comprehensive exam, thesis/dissertation, internship. *Entrance requirements:* For master's, PK-12 educational administration: minimum GPA 3.0, current U.S. teaching license, minimum 3 years of teaching in PK-12 sector; higher education administration: minimum bachelor's degree GPA 3.0; for doctorate, minimum GPA of 3.0, master's degree. Additional exam requirements/recommendations for international students: Required—TOEFL (minimum score 550 paper-based; 79 iBT), IELTS (minimum score 6.5). *Application deadline:* For spring admission, 11/15 for domestic and international students. Application fee: $40 ($50 for international students). Electronic applications accepted. *Expenses: Tuition,* area resident: Full-time $4216.70; part-time $252.70 per credit hour. Tuition, state resident: full-time $4216.70; part-time $252.70 per credit hour. Tuition, nonresident: full-time $12,769; part-time $881.10 per credit hour. *International tuition:* $12,769.30 full-time. *Required fees:* $878.40; $48.80 per credit hour. Full-time tuition and fees vary according to course load and reciprocity agreements. *Financial support:* In 2018–19, 27 students received support, including 1 fellowship (averaging $4,548 per year), 7 research assistantships (averaging $9,896 per year), 5 teaching assistantships (averaging $12,558 per year); career-related internships or fieldwork, Federal Work-Study, scholarships/grants, traineeships, health care benefits, and unspecified assistantships also available. Support available to part-time students. Financial award application deadline: 3/1. *Faculty research:* Leadership in pk-12 and postsecondary education, community college administration, distance education administration, leadership for social justice, educational change. *Total annual research expenditures:* $514,604. *Unit head:* Dr. Azadeh Osanloo, Department Head, 575-646-5976, Fax: 575-646-4767, E-mail: azadeh@nmsu.edu. *Application contact:* Denise Rodriguez-Strawn, Program Coordinator, 575-646-3825, Fax: 575-646-4767, E-mail: edmandev@nmsu.edu.
Website: http://ela.education.nmsu.edu

New York University, Steinhardt School of Culture, Education, and Human Development, Department of Administration, Leadership, and Technology, Program in Higher Education, New York, NY 10012. Offers higher and postsecondary education (PhD); higher education administration (Ed D); higher education and student affairs (MA). *Accreditation:* TEAC. *Program availability:* Part-time. *Entrance requirements:* For master's, interview, 2 letters of recommendation; for doctorate, GRE General Test, interview. Additional exam requirements/recommendations for international students: Required—TOEFL (minimum score 100 iBT). Electronic applications accepted. *Faculty research:* Organizational theory and culture, systemic change, leadership development, access, equity and diversity.

New York University, Steinhardt School of Culture, Education, and Human Development, Department of Music and Performing Arts Professions, Program in Educational Theatre, New York, NY 10012. Offers educational theatre and English 7-12 (MA); educational theatre and social studies 7-12 (MA); educational theatre in colleges and communities (MA, Ed D, PhD); educational theatre, all grades (MA). *Program availability:* Part-time. *Entrance requirements:* For master's, audition; for doctorate, GRE General Test, interview. Additional exam requirements/recommendations for international students: Required—TOEFL (minimum score 100 iBT). Electronic applications accepted. *Faculty research:* Theatre for young audiences, drama in education, applied theatre, arts education assessment, reflective praxis.

North Dakota State University, College of Graduate and Interdisciplinary Studies, Program in College Teaching, Fargo, ND 58102. Offers Certificate. *Entrance requirements:* For degree, minimum cumulative GPA of 3.0. Electronic applications accepted.

Northeastern University, College of Professional Studies, Boston, MA 02115-5096. Offers applied nutrition (MS); college athletics administration (MSL); commerce and economic development (MS); corporate and organizational communication (MS); criminal justice (MS); digital media (MPS); elearning and instructional design (M Ed); elementary education (MAT); geographic information technology (MPS); global studies and international relations (MS); higher education administration (M Ed); homeland security (MA); human services (MS); informatics (MPS); leadership (MS); learning analytics (M Ed); learning and instruction (M Ed); nonprofit management (MS); professional sports administration (MSL); project management (MS); regulatory affairs for drugs, biologics, and medical devices (MS); respiratory care leadership (MS); special education (M Ed); technical communication (MS). *Program availability:* Part-time, evening/weekend, 100% online, blended/hybrid learning. Electronic applications accepted. *Expenses:* Contact institution.

Northern Arizona University, College of Education, Department of Educational Leadership, Flagstaff, AZ 86011. Offers community college teaching and learning (Graduate Certificate); educational leadership (M Ed, Ed D), including community college/higher education (M Ed), educational foundations (M Ed), instructional leadership K-12 school leadership (M Ed), principal certification K-12 (M Ed); principal (Graduate Certificate); superintendent (Graduate Certificate). *Program availability:* Part-time. *Degree requirements:* For master's, comprehensive exam, thesis (for some

programs); for doctorate, comprehensive exam, thesis/dissertation; for Graduate Certificate, comprehensive exam (for some programs). *Entrance requirements:* Additional exam requirements/recommendations for international students: Required—TOEFL (minimum score 80 iBT), IELTS (minimum score 6.5). Electronic applications accepted.

Northern Illinois University, Graduate School, College of Education, Department of Counseling, Adult and Higher Education, De Kalb, IL 60115-2854. Offers adult and higher education (MS Ed, Ed D); counseling (MS Ed, Ed D). *Accreditation:* ACA. *Program availability:* Part-time, evening/weekend. *Faculty:* 19 full-time (11 women), 2 part-time/adjunct (1 woman). *Students:* 129 full-time (94 women), 225 part-time (158 women); includes 150 minority (68 Black or African American, non-Hispanic/Latino; 8 American Indian or Alaska Native, non-Hispanic/Latino; 12 Asian, non-Hispanic/Latino; 50 Hispanic/Latino; 12 Two or more races, non-Hispanic/Latino), 7 international. Average age 36. 158 applicants, 61% accepted, 67 enrolled. In 2018, 58 master's, 19 doctorates awarded. Terminal master's awarded for partial completion of doctoral program. *Degree requirements:* For master's, comprehensive exam, thesis optional; for doctorate, thesis/dissertation, candidacy exam, dissertation defense. *Entrance requirements:* For master's, GRE General Test or MAT, minimum undergraduate GPA of 2.75, interview (for counseling); for doctorate, GRE General Test, minimum undergraduate GPA of 2.75, 3.2 graduate; interview (for counseling). Additional exam requirements/recommendations for international students: Required—TOEFL (minimum score 550 paper-based). *Application deadline:* For fall admission, 6/1 for domestic students, 5/1 for international students; for spring admission, 11/1 for domestic students, 10/1 for international students. Applications are processed on a rolling basis. Application fee: $40. Electronic applications accepted. *Financial support:* In 2018–19, 15 research assistantships with full tuition reimbursements, 7 teaching assistantships with full tuition reimbursements were awarded; fellowships with full tuition reimbursements, career-related internships or fieldwork, Federal Work-Study, scholarships/grants, tuition waivers (full), and staff assistantships also available. Support available to part-time students. Financial award applicants required to submit FAFSA. *Unit head:* Dr. Suzanne Degges-White, Interim Chair, 815-753-1448, E-mail: cahe@niu.edu. *Application contact:* Graduate School Office, 815-753-0395, E-mail: gradsch@niu.edu.
Website: http://www.cedu.niu.edu/cahe/index.html

Northwest Missouri State University, Graduate School, School of Education, Maryville, MO 64468-6001. Offers early childhood education (MS Ed); education leadership (MS Ed), including elementary, K-12, secondary; educational leadership (Ed S), including elementary school principalship, secondary school principalship, superintendency; educational leadership and policy analysis (Ed D); elementary education (MS Ed); elementary mathematics (MS Ed); higher education leadership (MS); middle school education (MS Ed); reading (MS Ed); special education (MS Ed); teacher leadership (MS Ed); teaching English language learners (MS Ed). *Accreditation:* NCATE. *Program availability:* Part-time. *Faculty:* 26 full-time (16 women). *Students:* 109 full-time (87 women), 385 part-time (270 women); includes 30 minority (10 Black or African American, non-Hispanic/Latino; 2 American Indian or Alaska Native, non-Hispanic/Latino; 3 Asian, non-Hispanic/Latino; 12 Hispanic/Latino; 1 Native Hawaiian or other Pacific Islander, non-Hispanic/Latino; 2 Two or more races, non-Hispanic/Latino), 1 international. Average age 33. 210 applicants, 72% accepted, 142 enrolled. In 2018, 71 master's, 11 other advanced degrees awarded. *Degree requirements:* For master's, comprehensive exam; for Ed S, comprehensive exam, thesis. *Entrance requirements:* For master's, GRE General Test, writing sample; for Ed S, minimum graduate GPA of 3.25. Additional exam requirements/recommendations for international students: Required—TOEFL (minimum score 550 paper-based). *Application deadline:* For fall admission, 7/1 for domestic and international students; for spring admission, 11/15 for domestic and international students. Applications are processed on a rolling basis. Application fee: $0 ($75 for international students). Electronic applications accepted. *Expenses:* $389.11 in-state and $653.92 out-of-state per credit hour. *Financial support:* Research assistantships with full tuition reimbursements, teaching assistantships with full tuition reimbursements, and unspecified assistantships available. Financial award application deadline: 4/1; financial award applicants required to submit FAFSA. *Unit head:* Dr. Tim Wall, Director, 660-562-1179, E-mail: timwall@nwmissouri.edu. *Application contact:* Dr. Tim Wall, Director, 660-562-1179, E-mail: timwall@nwmissouri.edu.
Website: https://www.nwmissouri.edu/education/index.htm

Oakland University, Graduate Study and Lifelong Learning, School of Education and Human Services, Department of Organizational Leadership, Rochester, MI 48309-4401. Offers educational leadership (M Ed, PhD); higher education (Certificate); school administration (Ed S). *Entrance requirements:* Additional exam requirements/recommendations for international students: Required—TOEFL (minimum score 550 paper-based).

Ohio University, Graduate College, Gladys W. and David H. Patton College of Education and Human Services, Department of Counseling and Higher Education, Athens, OH 45701-2979. Offers college student personnel (M Ed); community/agency counseling (M Ed); counselor education (PhD); higher education (PhD); rehabilitation counseling (M Ed); school counseling (M Ed). *Accreditation:* ACA; CORE. *Program availability:* Part-time, evening/weekend. *Degree requirements:* For master's, comprehensive exam (for some programs), thesis or alternative; for doctorate, comprehensive exam, thesis/dissertation. *Entrance requirements:* For master's, GRE General Test or MAT (if GPA less than 2.9), 3 letters of reference; for doctorate, GRE General Test, work experience, minimum GPA of 3.4. Additional exam requirements/recommendations for international students: Required—TOEFL (minimum score 550 paper-based; 80 iBT) or IELTS (minimum score 6.5). Electronic applications accepted. *Faculty research:* Youth violence, gender studies, student affairs, chemical dependency, disabilities issues.

Oklahoma State University, College of Education, Health and Aviation, School of Educational Studies, Stillwater, OK 74078. Offers higher education (Ed D). *Program availability:* Part-time. *Entrance requirements:* For master's and doctorate, GRE or GMAT. Additional exam requirements/recommendations for international students: Required—TOEFL (minimum score 550 paper-based; 79 iBT). Electronic applications accepted. *Expenses: Tuition, area resident:* Full-time $4148. Tuition, state resident: full-time $4148. Tuition, nonresident: full-time $10,517. *International tuition:* $10,517 full-time. *Required fees:* $4394; $2929 per credit hour. Tuition and fees vary according to course load and program.

Old Dominion University, Darden College of Education, Doctoral Program in Higher Education, Norfolk, VA 23529. Offers PhD. *Program availability:* Part-time, online learning. *Degree requirements:* For doctorate, comprehensive exam, thesis/dissertation. *Entrance requirements:* For doctorate, GRE, master's degree, minimum graduate GPA of 3.5. Additional exam requirements/recommendations for international students: Required—TOEFL. Electronic applications accepted. *Faculty research:* Law leadership, student development, research administration, international higher education administration, academic integrity, leadership.

Old Dominion University, Darden College of Education, Programs in Higher Education, Norfolk, VA 23529. Offers MS Ed, Ed S. *Program availability:* Part-time. *Degree requirements:* For master's, comprehensive exam. *Entrance requirements:* For master's, GRE; for Ed S, GRE, 2 letters of reference, minimum GPA of 3.5, master's degree. Additional exam requirements/recommendations for international students: Required—TOEFL. Electronic applications accepted. *Faculty research:* Law leadership, student development, research administration, international higher education administration.

Oral Roberts University, School of Education, Tulsa, OK 74171. Offers Christian school administration (K-12) (MA Ed, Ed D); college and higher education administration (Ed D); curriculum and instruction (MA Ed); initial teaching with alternative licensure (MAT); initial teaching with licensure (MAT); public school administration (K-12) (MA Ed, Ed D). *Accreditation:* NCATE. *Program availability:* Part-time, online learning. *Degree requirements:* For master's, comprehensive exam, thesis optional; for doctorate, comprehensive exam, thesis/dissertation. *Entrance requirements:* For master's, GRE General Test or MAT (minimum score in 80th percentile or higher); Oklahoma general education or subject area test (for MAT), minimum GPA of 3.0, bachelor's degree from regionally-accredited institution; for doctorate, minimum GPA of 3.0, master's degree from regionally-accredited institution. Electronic applications accepted. Application fee is waived when completed online. *Expenses:* Contact institution. *Faculty research:* Teacher effectiveness, college success in high achieving African-Americans, professional development practices.

Oregon State University, College of Education, Program in Adult and Higher Education, Corvallis, OR 97331. Offers Ed M, Ed D, PhD. *Accreditation:* NCATE. *Program availability:* Part-time, blended/hybrid learning. *Entrance requirements:* For master's, minimum GPA of 3.0 in last 90 hours. Additional exam requirements/recommendations for international students: Required—TOEFL (minimum score 575 paper-based).

Penn State University Park, Graduate School, College of Education, Department of Education Policy Studies, University Park, PA 16802. Offers educational leadership (M Ed, D Ed, PhD, Certificate); educational theory and policy (MA, PhD); higher education (M Ed, D Ed, PhD). *Accreditation:* NCATE. *Program availability:* Online learning.

Phillips Theological Seminary, Programs in Theology, Tulsa, OK 74116. Offers administration of church agencies (M Div); campus ministry (M Div); church-related social work (M Div); college and seminary teaching (M Div); global mission work (M Div); institutional chaplaincy (M Div); ministerial vocations in Christian education (M Div); ministry (D Min), including parish ministry, pastoral counseling, practices of ministry; ministry and culture (MAMC), including Christian education, congregational leadership, history and practice of Christian spirituality, theology, ethics, and culture; ministry of music (M Div); pastoral care and counseling (M Div); pastoral ministry (M Div); theological studies (MTS). *Accreditation:* ATS. *Program availability:* Part-time, online learning. *Degree requirements:* For master's, thesis (for some programs); for doctorate, thesis/dissertation. *Entrance requirements:* For master's, minimum GPA of 2.5; for doctorate, M Div, minimum GPA of 3.0. *Faculty research:* Biblical studies, historical studies, theology and culture, practical theology, theology and film.

Plymouth State University, College of Graduate Studies, Graduate Studies in Education, Certificate of Advanced Graduate Studies Programs, Plymouth, NH 03264-1595. Offers clinical mental health counseling (CAGS); educational leadership (CAGS); higher education (CAGS); school psychology (CAGS). *Program availability:* Part-time, evening/weekend.

Plymouth State University, College of Graduate Studies, Graduate Studies in Education, Program in Higher Education, Plymouth, NH 03264-1595. Offers administrative leadership (Ed D); curriculum and instruction (Ed D).

Purdue University, Graduate School, College of Education, Department of Educational Studies, West Lafayette, IN 47907. Offers administration (MS Ed, Ed S); foundations of education (MS Ed); higher education administration (PhD). *Accreditation:* ACA (one or more programs are accredited); NCATE (one or more programs are accredited). *Program availability:* Part-time, evening/weekend. *Faculty:* 30 full-time (21 women), 2 part-time/adjunct (0 women). *Students:* 72 full-time (55 women), 240 part-time (186 women); includes 46 minority (13 Black or African American, non-Hispanic/Latino; 12 Asian, non-Hispanic/Latino; 14 Hispanic/Latino; 7 Two or more races, non-Hispanic/Latino), 47 international. Average age 32. 218 applicants, 51% accepted, 83 enrolled. In 2018, 86 master's, 15 doctorates awarded. *Degree requirements:* For master's, thesis optional; for doctorate, thesis/dissertation, oral and written exams; for Ed S, oral presentation, project. *Entrance requirements:* For master's, GRE General Test (except for special education if undergraduate GPA is higher than a 3.0), minimum undergraduate GPA of 3.0; for doctorate and Ed S, GRE General Test (minimum combined score of 1000, 300 for new scoring), minimum undergraduate GPA of 3.0. Additional exam requirements/recommendations for international students: Required—TOEFL (minimum score 550 paper-based; 77 iBT), TWE (minimum score 5). *Application deadline:* Applications are processed on a rolling basis. Application fee: $60 ($75 for international students). Electronic applications accepted. *Financial support:* Fellowships with full tuition reimbursements, research assistantships with full tuition reimbursements, teaching assistantships with full tuition reimbursements, career-related internships or fieldwork, and tuition waivers (full) available. Support available to part-time students. Financial award application deadline: 3/1; financial award applicants required to submit FAFSA. *Faculty research:* Motivation, learning disabilities, school learning, group processes, cognitive development. *Unit head:* F. Richard Olenchak, Head, 765-494-9170, E-mail: olenchak@purdue.edu. *Application contact:* Heather Brinkman, Graduate Contact, 765-494-2345, Fax: 765-494-5832, E-mail: hbrinkma@purdue.edu.
Website: http://www.edst.purdue.edu/

Purdue University Global, School of Higher Education Studies, Davenport, IA 52807. Offers college administration and leadership (MS); college teaching and learning (MS); student services (MS). *Program availability:* Part-time, evening/weekend, online learning. *Entrance requirements:* Additional exam requirements/recommendations for international students: Required—TOEFL (minimum score 550 paper-based; 80 iBT).

Regent University, Graduate School, School of Education, Virginia Beach, VA 23464-9800. Offers education (M Ed, Ed D, PhD), including adult education (Ed D, PhD, Ed S), advanced educational leadership (Ed D, PhD, Ed S), character education (Ed D, PhD, Ed S), Christian education leadership (Ed D, PhD, Ed S), Christian school administration (M Ed), curriculum and instruction (Ed D, PhD, Ed S), curriculum and instruction - adult education (M Ed), curriculum and instruction - Christian school (M Ed), curriculum and instruction - gifted and talented (M Ed), curriculum and instruction - STEM education (M Ed), curriculum and instruction - teacher leader (M Ed), discipleship for ministry (M Ed), educational leadership (M Ed), educational psychology (Ed D, PhD, Ed S), educational technology and online learning (Ed D, PhD, Ed S), elementary education (M Ed), exceptional education executive leadership (Ed D, PhD, Ed S), higher education (Ed D, PhD, Ed S), higher education leadership and management (Ed D, PhD, Ed S), instructional design and technology (M Ed), K-12 school leadership (Ed D, PhD, Ed S), K-12 special education (M Ed), leadership in mathematics education (M Ed), reading specialist (M Ed), special education (Ed D, PhD, Ed S), student affairs (M Ed), TESOL - adult education (M Ed), TESOL - K-12 (M Ed); educational specialist (Ed S), including adult education (Ed D, PhD, Ed S), advanced educational leadership (Ed D, PhD, Ed S), character education (Ed D, PhD, Ed S), Christian education leadership (Ed D, PhD,

Ed S), curriculum and instruction (Ed D, PhD, Ed S), educational psychology (Ed D, PhD, Ed S), educational technology and online learning (Ed D, PhD, Ed S), exceptional education executive leadership (Ed D, PhD, Ed S), higher education (Ed D, PhD, Ed S), higher education leadership and management (Ed D, PhD, Ed S), K-12 school leadership (Ed D, PhD, Ed S), special education (Ed D, PhD, Ed S). *Accreditation:* TEAC. *Program availability:* Part-time, evening/weekend, 100% online, blended/hybrid learning. *Degree requirements:* For master's, thesis or alternative; for doctorate, comprehensive exam, thesis/dissertation. *Entrance requirements:* For master's, Virginia Communication and Literacy Assessment (VCLA), PRAXIS, college transcripts, writing sample, interview; for doctorate, GRE, writing sample, resume, transcripts, interview. Additional exam requirements/recommendations for international students: Required—TOEFL (minimum score 577 paper-based). Electronic applications accepted. *Expenses:* Contact institution. *Faculty research:* Christian school administration, curriculum and instruction, educational technology and online learning, higher education, special education.

Regis College, Department of Education, Weston, MA 02493. Offers elementary teacher (M Ed); higher education leadership (Ed D); special education (M Ed). *Program availability:* Part-time, evening/weekend. *Degree requirements:* For doctorate, thesis/dissertation, capstone project. *Entrance requirements:* For master's, GRE or MAT, personal statement, recommendations, resume/curriculum vitae, official transcripts, interview; for doctorate, personal statement, recommendations, resume/curriculum vitae, official transcripts, presentation/interview. Additional exam requirements/recommendations for international students: Required—TOEFL (minimum score 560 paper-based; 79 iBT); Recommended—IELTS (minimum score 6.5). *Application deadline:* Applications are processed on a rolling basis. Application fee: $65. Electronic applications accepted. *Financial support:* Federal Work-Study, scholarships/grants, and unspecified assistantships available. Financial award applicants required to submit FAFSA. *Unit head:* Dr. Priscilla Boerger, Department Chair/Graduate Program Director, 781-768-7422, E-mail: priscilla.boerger@regiscollege.edu. *Application contact:* Dr. Priscilla Boerger, Department Chair/Graduate Program Director, 781-768-7422, E-mail: priscilla.boerger@regiscollege.edu.

Robert Morris University Illinois, Morris Graduate School of Management, Chicago, IL 60605. Offers accounting (MBA); accounting/finance (MBA); business analytics (MIS); health care administration (MM); higher education administration (MM); human performance (MS); human resource management (MBA); information security (MIS); information systems management (MIS); law enforcement administration (MM); management (MBA); management/finance (MBA); management/human resource management (MBA); sports administration (MM). *Program availability:* Part-time, evening/weekend. *Entrance requirements:* For master's, official transcripts and letters of recommendation (for some programs); written personal statement. Additional exam requirements/recommendations for international students: Required—TOEFL (minimum score 550 paper-based). Electronic applications accepted.

Rowan University, Graduate School, College of Education, Department of Educational Services and Leadership, Program in Higher Education Administration, Glassboro, NJ 08028-1701. Offers MA. *Accreditation:* NCATE. *Program availability:* Part-time, evening/weekend. *Degree requirements:* For master's, comprehensive exam, thesis. *Entrance requirements:* For master's, GRE General Test, minimum GPA of 2.8, 2 years of teaching experience. Additional exam requirements/recommendations for international students: Required—TOEFL. Electronic applications accepted.

St. Cloud State University, School of Graduate Studies, School of Education, Department of Educational Leadership and Higher Education, Program in Higher Education Administration, St. Cloud, MN 56301-4498. Offers Ed D.

Saint Louis University, Graduate Programs, School of Education, Department of Educational Leadership and Higher Education, St. Louis, MO 63103. Offers Catholic school leadership (MA); educational administration (MA, Ed D, PhD, Ed S); higher education (MA, Ed D, PhD); student personnel administration (MA). *Accreditation:* NCATE. *Program availability:* Part-time. *Degree requirements:* For master's, comprehensive written and oral exam; for doctorate, comprehensive exam, thesis/dissertation, preliminary oral and written exams. *Entrance requirements:* For master's, GRE General Test, MAT, LSAT, GMAT or MCAT, letters of recommendation, resume; for doctorate and Ed S, GRE General Test, LSAT, GMAT or MCAT, letters of recommendation, resumé, goal statement, transcripts. Additional exam requirements/recommendations for international students: Required—TOEFL (minimum score 525 paper-based). Electronic applications accepted. *Faculty research:* Superintendent of schools, school finance, school facilities, student personal administration, building leadership.

Saint Peter's University, Graduate Programs in Education, Program in Higher Education, Jersey City, NJ 07306-5997. Offers educational leadership (Ed D); general administration (MHE). *Degree requirements:* For doctorate, comprehensive exam, thesis/dissertation, qualifying examination, internship. *Entrance requirements:* For doctorate, GRE or MAT (taken within the last 5 years), official transcripts from all previously attended postsecondary institutions; bachelor's degree; master's degree; three letters of recommendation; essay; current resume; personal interview.

Salem State University, School of Graduate Studies, Program in Higher Education in Student Affairs, Salem, MA 01970-5353. Offers M Ed. *Program availability:* Part-time, evening/weekend. *Entrance requirements:* For master's, GRE or MAT. Additional exam requirements/recommendations for international students: Required—TOEFL (minimum score 550 paper-based; 80 iBT) or IELTS (minimum score 5.5).

Sam Houston State University, College of Education, Department of Educational Leadership, Huntsville, TX 77341. Offers administration (M Ed); developmental education administration (Ed D); educational leadership (Ed D); higher education administration (MA); higher education leadership (Ed D); instructional leadership (M Ed, MA). *Program availability:* Part-time, evening/weekend, online learning. *Degree requirements:* For master's, comprehensive exam (for some programs), thesis (for some programs); for doctorate, comprehensive exam, thesis/dissertation. *Entrance requirements:* For master's, GRE General Test, references, personal essay, resume, professional statement; for doctorate, GRE General Test, master's degree, references, personal essay, resume. Additional exam requirements/recommendations for international students: Required—TOEFL (minimum score 550 paper-based; 79 iBT), IELTS (minimum score 6.5). Electronic applications accepted.

San Diego State University, Graduate and Research Affairs, College of Education, Department of Administration, Rehabilitation and Post-Secondary Education, San Diego, CA 92182. Offers educational leadership in post-secondary education (MA); rehabilitation counseling (MS), including deafness. *Program availability:* Evening/weekend, online learning. *Degree requirements:* For master's, comprehensive exam (for some programs), thesis (for some programs). *Entrance requirements:* For master's, GRE General Test, letters of reference. Additional exam requirements/recommendations for international students: Required—TOEFL. Electronic applications accepted. *Faculty research:* Rehabilitation in cultural diversity, distance learning technology.

San Jose State University, Program in Educational Leadership, San Jose, CA 95192-0001. Offers educational administration (K-12) (MA); educational leadership (Ed D); higher education administration (MA). *Accreditation:* NCATE. *Degree requirements:* For master's, thesis or alternative. Electronic applications accepted.

Seton Hall University, College of Education and Human Services, Department of Education Leadership, Management and Policy, Program in Higher Education Administration, South Orange, NJ 07079-2697. Offers Ed D, PhD. *Accreditation:* NCATE. *Program availability:* Part-time, evening/weekend. *Degree requirements:* For doctorate, comprehensive exam, thesis/dissertation, internship. *Entrance requirements:* For doctorate, GRE or MAT, interview, minimum GPA of 3.5. Additional exam requirements/recommendations for international students: Required—TOEFL.

Siena Heights University, Graduate College, Adrian, MI 49221-1796. Offers clinical mental health counseling (MA); educational leadership (Specialist); leadership (MA), including health care leadership, organizational leadership; teacher education (MA), including early childhood education, early childhood education: Montessori, education leadership: principal, elementary education: reading K-12, leadership: higher education, secondary education: reading K-12, special education: cognitive impairment, special education: learning disabilities. *Program availability:* Part-time, evening/weekend. *Faculty:* 10 full-time (6 women), 16 part-time/adjunct (6 women). *Students:* 34 full-time (20 women), 183 part-time (126 women); includes 64 minority (38 Black or African American, non-Hispanic/Latino; 2 American Indian or Alaska Native, non-Hispanic/Latino; 4 Asian, non-Hispanic/Latino; 14 Hispanic/Latino; 6 Two or more races, non-Hispanic/Latino). Average age 36. 97 applicants, 41% accepted, 30 enrolled. In 2018, 72 master's awarded. *Degree requirements:* For master's, thesis, Presentation. *Entrance requirements:* For master's, Minimum GPA of 3.0, current resume, essay, all post-secondary transcripts, 3 letters of reference, conviction disclosure form; copy of teaching certificate (for some education programs); for Specialist, Master's degree, minimum GPA of 3.0, current resume, essay, all post-secondary transcripts, 3 letters of reference, conviction disclosure form; copy of teaching certificate (for some education programs). Additional exam requirements/recommendations for international students: Recommended—TOEFL, IELTS, TWE, TSE. *Application deadline:* Applications are processed on a rolling basis. Application fee: $50. Electronic applications accepted. *Expenses: Tuition:* Full-time $11,340; part-time $7560 per year. *Required fees:* $454; $454 per unit. $227 per semester. One-time fee: $100. Tuition and fees vary according to program. *Financial support:* In 2018–19, 55 students received support. Scholarships/grants, tuition waivers (full and partial), unspecified assistantships, and State of Michigan Scholarships/Grants available. Support available to part-time students. Financial award application deadline: 9/1; financial award applicants required to submit FAFSA. *Unit head:* Dr. Cheryl Betz, Dean, College for Professional Studies and Graduate College, 517-264-7234, Fax: 517-264-7714, E-mail: cbetz@sienaheights.edu. *Application contact:* Elizabeth Brooks, Assistant Director, 517-264-7165, Fax: 517-264-7714, E-mail: ebrooks@sienaheights.edu.
Website: http://www.sienaheights.edu

Southeast Missouri State University, School of Graduate Studies, Leadership, Middle and Secondary Education, Program in Educational Administration, Cape Girardeau, MO 63701-4799. Offers educational leadership (Ed D); higher education administration (MA); secondary administration (MA); teacher leadership (MA, Ed S). *Accreditation:* NCATE. *Program availability:* Part-time, evening/weekend, online only, 100% online, blended/hybrid learning. *Faculty:* 7 full-time (4 women), 4 part-time/adjunct (1 woman). *Students:* 45 full-time (28 women), 210 part-time (135 women); includes 22 minority (16 Black or African American, non-Hispanic/Latino; 2 American Indian or Alaska Native, non-Hispanic/Latino; 1 Asian, non-Hispanic/Latino; 3 Two or more races, non-Hispanic/Latino), 13 international. Average age 32. 111 applicants, 100% accepted, 111 enrolled. In 2018, 63 master's, 26 other advanced degrees awarded. *Degree requirements:* For master's and Ed S, comprehensive exam, thesis or alternative, paper; for doctorate, comprehensive exam, thesis/dissertation. *Entrance requirements:* For master's, minimum GPA of 3.5; for doctorate, GRE, interview; for Ed S, minimum GPA of 3.7. Additional exam requirements/recommendations for international students: Required—TOEFL (minimum score 550 paper-based; 79 iBT), IELTS (minimum score 6), PTE (minimum score 53). *Application deadline:* For fall admission, 8/1 for domestic students, 6/1 for international students; for spring admission, 11/21 for domestic students, 10/1 for international students; for summer admission, 5/15 for domestic students. Applications are processed on a rolling basis. Application fee: $30 ($40 for international students). Electronic applications accepted. *Expenses:* Contact institution. *Financial support:* In 2018–19, 22 students received support. Career-related internships or fieldwork, Federal Work-Study, scholarships/grants, traineeships, tuition waivers (full), and unspecified assistantships available. Financial award application deadline: 6/30; financial award applicants required to submit FAFSA. *Faculty research:* Learning and technology; leadership, equity and social justice in P-12 schools and higher education; school culture; leadership and academic achievement; school leadership and student success. *Unit head:* Dr. C. P. Gause, Professor/Chair, 573-651-2137, Fax: 573-986-6512, E-mail: cgause@semo.edu. *Application contact:* Dr. Lisa Bertrand, Professor/Coordinator, 573-651-5080, Fax: 573-986-6512, E-mail: lbertrand@semo.edu.
Website: http://www.semo.edu/eduleadcounsel/

Southern Arkansas University–Magnolia, School of Graduate Studies, Magnolia, AR 71753. Offers agriculture (MS); business administration (MBA), including agribusiness, social entrepreneurship, supply chain management; clinical and mental health counseling (MS); computer and information sciences (MS), including cyber security and privacy, data science, information technology; gifted and talented (M Ed), including curriculum and instruction, educational administration and supervision, gifted and talented P-8/7-12, instructional specialist P-4; higher, adult and lifelong education (M Ed); kinesiology (M Ed), including coaching; library media and information specialist (M Ed); public administration (MPA); school counseling K-12 (M Ed); student affairs and college counseling (M Ed); teaching (MAT). *Accreditation:* NCATE. *Program availability:* Part-time, 100% online, blended/hybrid learning. *Faculty:* 36 full-time (21 women), 32 part-time/adjunct (15 women). *Students:* 164 full-time (77 women), 762 part-time (510 women); includes 192 minority (163 Black or African American, non-Hispanic/Latino; 7 American Indian or Alaska Native, non-Hispanic/Latino; 13 Asian, non-Hispanic/Latino; 1 Hispanic/Latino; 8 Two or more races, non-Hispanic/Latino), 213 international. Average age 28. 363 applicants, 100% accepted, 237 enrolled. In 2018, 716 master's awarded. *Degree requirements:* For master's, comprehensive exam (for some programs), thesis optional. *Entrance requirements:* For master's, GRE, MAT or GMAT, minimum GPA of 2.5. Additional exam requirements/recommendations for international students: Required—TOEFL (minimum score 550 paper-based), IELTS (minimum score 6). *Application deadline:* For fall admission, 8/1 for domestic and international students; for spring admission, 12/1 for domestic students, 11/15 for international students; for summer admission, 4/1 for domestic students, 5/10 for international students. Applications are processed on a rolling basis. Application fee: $25 ($90 for international students). Electronic applications accepted. *Expenses: Tuition, area resident:* Full-time $5130; part-time $3420 per year. Tuition, state resident: full-time $5130; part-time $3420 per year. Tuition, nonresident: full-time $7866; part-time $5244 per year. *International tuition:* $7866 full-time. *Required fees:* $1052; $710 per unit. Tuition and fees vary according to course load. *Financial support:* Career-related internships or fieldwork, Federal Work-Study, scholarships/grants, tuition waivers (full), and unspecified assistantships available. Financial award applicants required to submit FAFSA. *Faculty research:* Alternative certification for teachers, supervision of

instruction, instructional leadership, counseling. *Unit head:* Dr. Kim Bloss, Dean, School of Graduate Studies, 870-235-4150, Fax: 870-235-5227, E-mail: kkbloss@saumag.edu. *Application contact:* Talia Jett, Admissions Coordinator, 870-2355450, Fax: 870-235-5227, E-mail: taliajett@saumag.edu.
Website: http://www.saumag.edu/graduate

Southern Illinois University Carbondale, Graduate School, College of Education and Human Services, Department of Educational Administration and Higher Education, Program in Higher Education, Carbondale, IL 62901-4701. Offers education (MS Ed). *Accreditation:* NCATE. *Program availability:* Part-time. *Degree requirements:* For master's, thesis. *Entrance requirements:* For master's, GRE General Test or MAT, minimum GPA of 2.7. Additional exam requirements/recommendations for international students: Required—TOEFL. *Faculty research:* Student affairs administration, international education, community college teaching.

Southern Illinois University Edwardsville, Graduate School, College of Arts and Sciences, Department of Mathematics and Statistics, Program in Postsecondary Mathematics Education, Edwardsville, IL 62026. Offers MS. *Program availability:* Part-time. *Degree requirements:* For master's, thesis (for some programs), special project. *Entrance requirements:* Additional exam requirements/recommendations for international students: Required—TOEFL (minimum score 550 paper-based, 79 iBT), IELTS (minimum score 6.5), Michigan Test of English Language Proficiency or PTE. Electronic applications accepted.

Southern Methodist University, Simmons School of Education and Human Development, Department of Education Policy and Leadership, Dallas, TX 75275. Offers higher education (M Ed, Ed D); PK-12 school leadership (M Ed, Ed D).

Southern New Hampshire University, School of Education, Manchester, NH 03106-1045. Offers curriculum and instruction (M Ed), including dyslexia studies and language-based learning disabilities, educational leadership, reading, special education, technology integration; dyslexia studies and language-based learning disabilities (Certificate); early childhood and special education (M Ed); educational leadership (M Ed, Ed D); educational studies (M Ed); elementary and special education (M Ed); field based education (M Ed); higher education administration (MS); teaching English as a foreign language (MS). *Program availability:* Part-time, evening/weekend, online learning. *Degree requirements:* For master's, comprehensive exam (for some programs), thesis or alternative. *Entrance requirements:* For master's, PRAXIS I, minimum GPA of 2.75. Additional exam requirements/recommendations for international students: Required—TOEFL (minimum score 550 paper-based). Electronic applications accepted. *Expenses:* Contact institution.

Southwestern College, Education Programs, Winfield, KS 67156-2499. Offers curriculum and instruction (M Ed); early childhood education (M Ed); educational leadership (Ed D), including higher education leadership, PK-12 education leadership; special education (M Ed), including high-incidence disabilities, low-incidence disabilities; teaching (MA). *Accreditation:* NCATE. *Program availability:* Part-time, evening/weekend, 100% online, blended/hybrid learning. *Faculty:* 7 full-time (5 women), 14 part-time/adjunct (12 women). *Students:* 6 full-time (5 women), 79 part-time (54 women); includes 11 minority (4 Black or African American, non-Hispanic/Latino; 2 American Indian or Alaska Native, non-Hispanic/Latino; 1 Asian, non-Hispanic/Latino; 3 Hispanic/Latino; 1 Two or more races, non-Hispanic/Latino), 4 international. Average age 38. 31 applicants, 74% accepted, 18 enrolled. In 2018, 24 master's, 8 doctorates awarded. *Degree requirements:* For master's, practicum, portfolio; for doctorate, thesis/dissertation, professional portfolio. *Entrance requirements:* For master's, baccalaureate degree, minimum GPA of 3.0, valid teaching certificate (for special education); for doctorate, GRE if no master's degree, baccalaureate degree with minimum GPA of 3.25 and current teaching experience, or master's degree with minimum GPA of 3.5. Additional exam requirements/recommendations for international students: Required—TOEFL (minimum score 60 paper-based; 70 iBT), IELTS (minimum score 5.5). *Application deadline:* Applications are processed on a rolling basis. Application fee: $40. Electronic applications accepted. *Expenses:* Masters programs are $606 per credit hour, $535 per online credit hour; doctorate program is $639 per credit hour. *Financial support:* In 2018–19, 13 students received support. Unspecified assistantships and employee tuition waivers available. Financial award applicants required to submit FAFSA. *Unit head:* J.K. Campbell, Education Division Chair, 620-229-6115, E-mail: JK.Campbell@sckans.edu. *Application contact:* Jen Caughron, Director of Enrollment Services & Marketing, 888-684-5335 Ext. 3312, Fax: 888-684-5218, E-mail: jennifer.caughron@sckans.edu.
Website: http://www.sckans.edu/graduate/education-med/

Springfield College, Graduate Programs, Programs in Psychology, Springfield, MA 01109-3797. Offers athletic counseling (MS, CAGS); clinical mental health counseling (M Ed, CAGS); counseling psychology (Psy D); general counseling (M Ed); industrial/organizational psychology (M Ed, CAGS); school counseling (M Ed, CAGS); student personnel administration in higher education (M Ed, CAGS). *Accreditation:* APA. *Program availability:* Part-time. *Degree requirements:* For master's, research project, portfolio; for doctorate, dissertation project, 1500 hours of counseling psychology practicum, full-year internship. *Entrance requirements:* For doctorate, GRE. Additional exam requirements/recommendations for international students: Required—TOEFL (minimum score 550 paper-based); Recommended—IELTS (minimum score 7). Electronic applications accepted.

Stony Brook University, State University of New York, School of Professional Development, Stony Brook, NY 11794. Offers coaching (Graduate Certificate); environmental management (MPS); German (MAT); higher education administration (MA, Certificate); human resource management (MS, Graduate Certificate); Italian (MAT); liberal studies (MA); mathematics (MAT); school district business leadership (Advanced Certificate); social studies (MAT); Spanish (MAT). *Program availability:* Part-time, evening/weekend, online learning. *Faculty:* 3 full-time (2 women), 94 part-time/adjunct (40 women). *Students:* 214 full-time (138 women), 1,100 part-time (813 women); includes 313 minority (117 Black or African American, non-Hispanic/Latino; 2 American Indian or Alaska Native, non-Hispanic/Latino; 32 Asian, non-Hispanic/Latino; 140 Hispanic/Latino; 3 Native Hawaiian or other Pacific Islander, non-Hispanic/Latino; 19 Two or more races, non-Hispanic/Latino), 7 international. Average age 33. 483 applicants, 89% accepted, 337 enrolled. In 2018, 315 master's, 178 other advanced degrees awarded. *Entrance requirements:* Additional exam requirements/recommendations for international students: Required—TOEFL (minimum score 85 iBT). *Application deadline:* For fall admission, 1/15 for domestic students, 6/1 for international students; for spring admission, 10/1 for domestic and international students. Applications are processed on a rolling basis. Application fee: $100. *Expenses:* Contact institution. *Financial support:* Fellowships, research assistantships, teaching assistantships, and career-related internships or fieldwork available. Support available to part-time students. *Unit head:* Patricia Malone, Associate Vice President for Professional Education and Assistant Provost for Engaged Learning, 631-632-7512, Fax: 631-632-9046, E-mail: patricia.malone@stonybrook.edu. *Application contact:* Melissa Jordan, Assistant Dean, 631-632-7751, E-mail: melissa.jordan@stonybrook.edu.
Website: http://www.stonybrook.edu/spd/

Syracuse University, College of Arts and Sciences, Program in College Science Teaching, Syracuse, NY 13244. Offers PhD. *Program availability:* Part-time. *Entrance requirements:* For doctorate, GRE General Test, three letters of recommendation, personal statement, transcripts, scholarly writing sample. Additional exam requirements/recommendations for international students: Required—TOEFL (minimum score 100 iBT). *Application deadline:* For fall admission, 2/1 priority date for domestic and international students. Applications are processed on a rolling basis. Application fee: $75. Electronic applications accepted. *Financial support:* Fellowships with full tuition reimbursements, research assistantships, teaching assistantships, and scholarships/grants available. Financial award application deadline: 1/15; financial award applicants required to submit FAFSA. *Faculty research:* Philosophy of science, methods of teaching science in higher education, research focused on the problems of college teaching, curriculum development. *Unit head:* Dr. John W. Tillotson, Department Chairperson, 315-443-9137, E-mail: jwtillot@syr.edu. *Application contact:* Heather Thompson, Administrative Assistant, Earth Sciences and Science Teaching, 315-443-2672, E-mail: hethomps@syr.edu.
Website: http://sciteach.syr.edu/academics/program-science-teaching-phd.html

Syracuse University, School of Education, Programs in Higher Education, Syracuse, NY 13244. Offers MS, PhD. *Program availability:* Part-time. *Students:* Average age 30. *Degree requirements:* For master's, thesis or alternative; for doctorate, comprehensive exam, thesis/dissertation. *Entrance requirements:* For master's, baccalaureate degree from regionally-accredited college/university, experience in student affairs or higher education, personal statement, resume, transcripts, three letters of recommendation; for doctorate, GRE, master's degree in higher education, student affairs, or related area; three years of work experience in higher education, student affairs, related area, or college teaching; strong writing skills; transcripts; three letters of recommendation. Additional exam requirements/recommendations for international students: Required—TOEFL (minimum score 100 iBT). *Application deadline:* For fall admission, 2/1 priority date for domestic and international students; for spring admission, 10/15 priority date for domestic and international students. Applications are processed on a rolling basis. Application fee: $75. Electronic applications accepted. *Financial support:* Fellowships with full tuition reimbursements, research assistantships, teaching assistantships, career-related internships or fieldwork, and scholarships/grants available. Financial award application deadline: 1/15. *Faculty research:* Student culture, college student personnel development, programming advising, policy-making, faculty roles on behalf of students from diverse groups. *Unit head:* Dr. Dawn Johnson, Associate Professor/Chair, 315-443-3130, E-mail: drjohn02@syr.edu. *Application contact:* Speranza Migliore, Graduate Admissions Recruiter, 315-443-2505, E-mail: gradrcrt@syr.edu.
Website: http://soe.syr.edu/academic/higher_education/

Taylor University, Master of Arts in Higher Education Program, Upland, IN 46989-1001. Offers MA. *Accreditation:* NCATE. *Program availability:* Part-time. *Degree requirements:* For master's, thesis. *Entrance requirements:* For master's, resume, official transcripts, three references, interview. *Expenses:* Contact institution.

Teachers College, Columbia University, Department of Organization and Leadership, New York, NY 10027-6696. Offers adult education guided intensive study (Ed D); adult learning and leadership (Ed M, MA, Ed D); educational leadership (Ed D); higher and postsecondary education (MA, Ed D); leadership, policy and politics (Ed D); nurse executive (MA, Ed D), including administration studies (MA), professional studies (MA); private school leadership (Ed M, MA); public school building leadership (Ed M, MA); social and organizational psychology (MA); urban education leaders (Ed D); MA/MBA. *Program availability:* Part-time, evening/weekend. *Students:* 249 full-time (165 women), 427 part-time (299 women); includes 275 minority (99 Black or African American, non-Hispanic/Latino; 75 Asian, non-Hispanic/Latino; 82 Hispanic/Latino; 1 Native Hawaiian or other Pacific Islander, non-Hispanic/Latino; 18 Two or more races, non-Hispanic/Latino), 84 international. Average age 34. 770 applicants, 59% accepted, 267 enrolled. *Unit head:* Prof. Bill Baldwin, Chair, 212-678-3043, E-mail: wjb12@tc.columbia.edu. *Application contact:* Kelly Sutton-Skinner, Director of Admission & New Student Enrollment, E-mail: kms2237@tc.columbia.edu.

Texas A&M University–Commerce, College of Education and Human Services, Commerce, TX 75429. Offers counseling (M Ed, MS, PhD); early childhood education (M Ed, MS); educational administration (M Ed, MS, Ed D); educational psychology (PhD); educational technology leadership (M Ed, MS); educational technology library science (M Ed, MS); elementary education (M Ed); health, kinesiology and sports studies (MS); higher education (MS, Ed D); psychology (MS); reading (M Ed, MS); school psychology (SSP); secondary education (M Ed, MS); social work (MSW); special education (M Ed, MS); supervision, curriculum and instruction-elementary education (Ed D); training and development (MS). *Program availability:* Part-time, evening/weekend, 100% online, blended/hybrid learning. *Faculty:* 95 full-time (59 women), 29 part-time/adjunct (22 women). *Students:* 356 full-time (295 women), 1,262 part-time (992 women); includes 683 minority (349 Black or African American, non-Hispanic/Latino; 9 American Indian or Alaska Native, non-Hispanic/Latino; 30 Asian, non-Hispanic/Latino; 238 Hispanic/Latino; 57 Two or more races, non-Hispanic/Latino), 9 international. Average age 37. 951 applicants, 42% accepted, 304 enrolled. In 2018, 532 master's, 51 doctorates awarded. *Degree requirements:* For master's, comprehensive exam, thesis optional, departmental qualifying exams (for some programs); for doctorate, comprehensive exam, thesis/dissertation, departmental qualifying exam; for SSP, comprehensive exam. *Entrance requirements:* For master's, GRE General Test, official transcripts, letters of recommendation, resume, statement of goals; for doctorate, GRE General Test, letters of recommendation, statement of goals, writing samples, writing sessions, resumes. Additional exam requirements/recommendations for international students: Required—TOEFL (minimum score 550 paper-based; 79 iBT), IELTS (minimum score 6), PTE (minimum score 53). *Application deadline:* For fall admission, 6/1 priority date for international students; for spring admission, 10/15 priority date for international students; for summer admission, 3/15 priority date for international students. Applications are processed on a rolling basis. Application fee: $50 ($75 for international students). Electronic applications accepted. *Expenses: Tuition, area resident:* Full-time $3630. Tuition, state resident: full-time $3630. Tuition, nonresident: full-time $11,100. *International tuition:* $11,100 full-time. *Required fees:* $2794. Tuition and fees vary according to course load, degree level and program. *Financial support:* In 2018–19, 116 students received support, including 94 research assistantships with partial tuition reimbursements available (averaging $3,863 per year), 38 teaching assistantships with partial tuition reimbursements available (averaging $4,728 per year); career-related internships or fieldwork, Federal Work-Study, institutionally sponsored loans, scholarships/grants, health care benefits, and unspecified assistantships also available. Financial award application deadline: 5/1; financial award applicants required to submit FAFSA. *Faculty research:* Cognitive and bilingual education, positive behavioral intervention, literacy, math readiness. *Total annual research expenditures:* $1.1 million. *Unit head:* Dr. Madeline Justice, Interim Dean, 903-886-5181, Fax: 903-886-5905, E-mail: madeline.justice@tamuc.edu. *Application contact:* Vicky Turner, Doctoral Degree and Special Programs Coordinator, 903-886-5167, E-mail: vicky.turner@tamuc.edu.
Website: http://www.tamuc.edu/academics/graduateSchool/programs/education/default.aspx

Texas Southern University, College of Education, Department of Educational Administration and Foundation, Houston, TX 77004-4584. Offers educational administration (M Ed, Ed D). *Program availability:* Part-time, evening/weekend. *Degree requirements:* For master's, comprehensive exam; for doctorate, comprehensive exam, thesis/dissertation. *Entrance requirements:* For master's, GRE General Test, minimum GPA of 2.5; for doctorate, GRE General Test or MAT, master's degree, minimum B+ average. Additional exam requirements/recommendations for international students: Required—TOEFL. Electronic applications accepted.

Texas State University, The Graduate College, College of Education, Program in Student Affairs in Higher Education, San Marcos, TX 78666. Offers M Ed. *Accreditation:* ACA. *Program availability:* Part-time, evening/weekend. *Faculty:* 3 full-time (all women), 7 part-time/adjunct (4 women). *Students:* 36 full-time (24 women), 1 part-time (0 women); includes 24 minority (5 Black or African American, non-Hispanic/Latino; 1 Asian, non-Hispanic/Latino; 13 Hispanic/Latino; 5 Two or more races, non-Hispanic/Latino). Average age 24. 46 applicants, 70% accepted, 19 enrolled. In 2018, 19 master's awarded. *Degree requirements:* For master's, comprehensive exam. *Entrance requirements:* For master's, baccalaureate degree from regionally-accredited institution, competitive GPA in last 60 hours of undergraduate course work, resume, statement of purpose, 3 letters of recommendation. Additional exam requirements/recommendations for international students: Required—TOEFL (minimum score 550 paper-based; 78 iBT), IELTS (minimum score 6.5). *Application deadline:* For fall admission, 1/15 for domestic and international students. Applications are processed on a rolling basis. Application fee: $55 ($90 for international students). Electronic applications accepted. *Expenses:* Tuition, state resident: full-time $8102; part-time $4051 per semester. Tuition, nonresident: full-time $18,229; part-time $9115 per semester. *International tuition:* $18,229 full-time. *Required fees:* $2116; $120 per credit hour. Tuition and fees vary according to course load. *Financial support:* In 2018–19, 37 students received support, including 37 teaching assistantships (averaging $11,742 per year); research assistantships, career-related internships or fieldwork, Federal Work-Study, institutionally sponsored loans, scholarships/grants, and unspecified assistantships also available. Support available to part-time students. Financial award application deadline: 1/15; financial award applicants required to submit FAFSA. *Unit head:* Dr. Paige Haber-Curran, Graduate Advisor, 512-245-7628, Fax: 512-245-8872, E-mail: sahe@txstate.edu. *Application contact:* Dr. Andrea Golato, Dean of Graduate School, 512-245-2581, Fax: 512-245-8365, E-mail: gradcollege@txstate.edu.
Website: http://www.gradcollege.txstate.edu/programs/sahe.html

Texas Tech University, Graduate School, College of Education, Department of Educational Psychology and Leadership, Lubbock, TX 79409-1071. Offers counselor education (M Ed, PhD); educational leadership (M Ed, Ed D, PhD); educational psychology (M Ed, PhD); higher education administration (M Ed, Ed D); higher education research (PhD); instructional technology (M Ed, Ed D); special education (M Ed, Ed D, PhD). *Accreditation:* ACA; NCATE. *Program availability:* Part-time, evening/weekend, 100% online, blended/hybrid learning. *Faculty:* 65 full-time (29 women), 3 part-time/adjunct (all women). *Students:* 261 full-time (184 women), 624 part-time (482 women); includes 325 minority (88 Black or African American, non-Hispanic/Latino; 3 American Indian or Alaska Native, non-Hispanic/Latino; 12 Asian, non-Hispanic/Latino; 192 Hispanic/Latino; 1 Native Hawaiian or other Pacific Islander, non-Hispanic/Latino; 29 Two or more races, non-Hispanic/Latino), 39 international. Average age 36. 437 applicants, 73% accepted, 252 enrolled. In 2018, 278 master's, 40 doctorates awarded. Terminal master's awarded for partial completion of doctoral program. *Degree requirements:* For master's, comprehensive exam, thesis optional; for doctorate, comprehensive exam, thesis/dissertation. *Entrance requirements:* For master's, GRE (for some programs); for doctorate, GRE. Additional exam requirements/recommendations for international students: Required—TOEFL (minimum score 550 paper-based; 79 iBT). *Application deadline:* For fall admission, 6/1 priority date for domestic students, 1/15 priority date for international students; for spring admission, 9/1 priority date for domestic students, 6/15 priority date for international students. Applications are processed on a rolling basis. Application fee: $65. Electronic applications accepted. *Expenses:* Contact institution. *Financial support:* In 2018–19, 493 students received support, including 489 fellowships (averaging $3,305 per year), 61 research assistantships (averaging $12,558 per year), 5 teaching assistantships (averaging $13,161 per year); scholarships/grants and unspecified assistantships also available. Support available to part-time students. Financial award application deadline: 1/3; financial award applicants required to submit FAFSA. *Faculty research:* Cognitive, motivational, and developmental processes in learning; counseling education; instructional technology; generic special education and sensory impairment; community college administration; K-12 school administration. *Total annual research expenditures:* $204,930. *Unit head:* Dr. Hansel Burley, Professor, Department Chair, 806-834-5135, Fax: 806-742-2179, E-mail: hansel.burley@ttu.edu. *Application contact:* Pam Smith, Admissions Advisor, 806-834-2969, Fax: 806-742-2179, E-mail: pam.smith@ttu.edu.
Website: www.educ.ttu.edu/

Tiffin University, Program in Education, Tiffin, OH 44883-2161. Offers educational technology management (M Ed); higher education administration (M Ed). *Program availability:* Part-time, evening/weekend, online only, 100% online, blended/hybrid learning. *Entrance requirements:* Additional exam requirements/recommendations for international students: Required—TOEFL. Electronic applications accepted. *Expenses:* Contact institution.

Trident University International, College of Education, Program in Education, Cypress, CA 90630. Offers adult education (MA Ed); aviation education (MA Ed); children's literacy development (MA Ed); e-learning (MA Ed); early childhood education (MA Ed); enrollment management (MA Ed); higher education (MA Ed); teaching and instruction (MA Ed); training and development (MA Ed). *Program availability:* Part-time, evening/weekend, online learning. *Degree requirements:* For master's, capstone project with integrative paper. *Entrance requirements:* For master's, minimum GPA of 2.5 (students with GPA 3.0 or greater may transfer up to 30% of graduate level credits). Additional exam requirements/recommendations for international students: Required—TOEFL (minimum score 525 paper-based). Electronic applications accepted.

Trident University International, College of Education, Program in Educational Leadership, Cypress, CA 90630. Offers e-learning leadership (MA Ed, PhD); educational leadership (MA Ed); higher education leadership (PhD); K-12 leadership (PhD). *Program availability:* Part-time, evening/weekend, online learning. *Degree requirements:* For doctorate, comprehensive exam, thesis/dissertation, defense of dissertation. *Entrance requirements:* For master's, minimum GPA of 2.5 (students with GPA 3.0 or greater may transfer up to 30% of graduate level credits); for doctorate, minimum GPA of 3.4, course work in research methods or statistics. Additional exam requirements/recommendations for international students: Required—TOEFL. Electronic applications accepted.

Union University, School of Education, Jackson, TN 38305-3697. Offers education (M Ed, MA Ed); education administration generalist (Ed S); educational leadership (Ed D); educational supervision (Ed S); higher education (Ed D). M Ed also available at Germantown campus. *Accreditation:* NCATE. *Program availability:* Part-time, evening/weekend, online learning. *Degree requirements:* For master's, thesis (for some programs), capstone research course (for MA Ed); performance exhibition (for M Ed); for doctorate, comprehensive exam, thesis/dissertation; for Ed S, thesis or alternative. *Entrance requirements:* For master's, MAT, PRAXIS II or GRE, minimum GPA of 3.0, teaching license (for M Ed only), writing sample; for doctorate, GRE, minimum graduate GPA of 3.2, writing sample; for Ed S, PRAXIS II, minimum graduate GPA of 3.2, writing sample. Additional exam requirements/recommendations for international students: Required—TOEFL (minimum score 560 paper-based; 80 iBT). Electronic applications accepted. *Expenses:* Contact institution. *Faculty research:* Mathematics education, brain compatible learning, transformational teaching, cognitive strategy development, instructional technology.

Universidad Central del Este, Graduate School, San Pedro de Macoris, Dominican Republic. Offers environmental engineering (ME); financial management (M Ad); higher education (M Ed), including higher education management, higher education pedagogy; human resources (M Ad). *Entrance requirements:* For master's, letters of recommendation.

Université de Sherbrooke, Faculty of Education, Program in Postsecondary Education Training, Sherbrooke, QC J1K 2R1, Canada. Offers M Ed, Diploma. *Degree requirements:* For master's, thesis.

University at Albany, State University of New York, School of Education, Department of Educational Policy and Leadership, Albany, NY 12222-0001. Offers educational policy and leadership (MS, PhD); higher education (MS); international education management (CAS). *Program availability:* Evening/weekend. *Faculty:* 12 full-time (5 women), 3 part-time/adjunct (2 women). *Students:* 42 full-time (31 women), 132 part-time (84 women); includes 47 minority (21 Black or African American, non-Hispanic/Latino; 4 Asian, non-Hispanic/Latino; 20 Hispanic/Latino; 2 Two or more races, non-Hispanic/Latino), 23 international. Average age 32. 72 applicants, 71% accepted, 48 enrolled. In 2018, 11 master's, 7 doctorates, 12 other advanced degrees awarded. *Degree requirements:* For doctorate, one foreign language, thesis/dissertation. *Entrance requirements:* For doctorate, GRE General Test, GRE Subject Test. Additional exam requirements/recommendations for international students: Required—TOEFL (minimum score 550 paper-based). *Application deadline:* For fall admission, 2/1 for domestic students, 5/1 for international students; for spring admission, 9/1 for domestic students, 11/1 for international students. Applications are processed on a rolling basis. Application fee: $75. Electronic applications accepted. *Financial support:* Fellowships and career-related internships or fieldwork available. Financial award application deadline: 3/15. *Unit head:* Jason Lane, Chair, 518-442-5092, E-mail: jlane@albany.edu. *Application contact:* Jason Lane, Chair, 518-442-5092, E-mail: jlane@albany.edu.
Website: http://www.albany.edu/epl/

University at Buffalo, the State University of New York, Graduate School, Graduate School of Education, Department of Educational Leadership and Policy, Buffalo, NY 14260. Offers economics and education policy analysis (MA); education studies (Ed M); educational administration (Ed M, Ed D, PhD); educational culture, policy and society (PhD); higher education administration (Ed M, PhD); school building leadership (Certificate); school business and human resource administration (Certificate); school district business leadership (Certificate); school district leadership (Certificate). *Program availability:* Part-time, evening/weekend. *Faculty:* 16 full-time (10 women), 11 part-time/adjunct (4 women). *Students:* 73 full-time (50 women), 128 part-time (82 women); includes 40 minority (21 Black or African American, non-Hispanic/Latino; 7 Asian, non-Hispanic/Latino; 11 Hispanic/Latino; 1 Two or more races, non-Hispanic/Latino), 19 international. Average age 34. 136 applicants, 69% accepted, 53 enrolled. In 2018, 39 master's, 20 doctorates, 25 other advanced degrees awarded. *Degree requirements:* For master's, comprehensive exam (for some programs), thesis optional; for doctorate, comprehensive exam, thesis/dissertation. *Entrance requirements:* For master's, interview, letters of reference; for doctorate, GRE General Test or MAT, writing sample, letters of reference. Additional exam requirements/recommendations for international students: Required—TOEFL (minimum score 600 paper-based; 79 iBT), IELTS (minimum score 6.5), PTE (minimum score 55). *Application deadline:* For fall admission, 2/1 priority date for domestic students, 2/1 for international students; for spring admission, 11/15 priority date for domestic students, 10/1 for international students. Applications are processed on a rolling basis. Application fee: $50. Electronic applications accepted. *Financial support:* In 2018–19, 18 fellowships (averaging $5,673 per year), 34 research assistantships with tuition reimbursements (averaging $12,055 per year) were awarded; career-related internships or fieldwork, Federal Work-Study, institutionally sponsored loans, scholarships/grants, health care benefits, tuition waivers (full and partial), and unspecified assistantships also available. Financial award application deadline: 3/15; financial award applicants required to submit FAFSA. *Faculty research:* College access and choice, school leadership preparation and practice, public policy, curriculum and pedagogy, comparative and international education. *Total annual research expenditures:* $637,951. *Unit head:* Dr. Nathan Daun-Barnett, Department Chair, 716-645-1096, Fax: 716-645-2481, E-mail: nbarnett@buffalo.edu. *Application contact:* Renad Aref, Assistant Director of Admission Recruitment, 716-645-2110, Fax: 716-645-7937, E-mail: gseinfo@buffalo.edu.
Website: http://gse.buffalo.edu/elp

The University of Alabama, Graduate School, College of Education, Department of Educational Leadership, Policy, and Technology Studies, Higher Education Administration Program, Tuscaloosa, AL 35487. Offers MA, Ed D, PhD. *Program availability:* Evening/weekend, 100% online. Terminal master's awarded for partial completion of doctoral program. *Degree requirements:* For master's, capstone seminar; for doctorate, comprehensive exam, thesis/dissertation. *Entrance requirements:* For master's, GRE or MAT, minimum GPA of 3.0; for doctorate, GRE (for PhD), GRE or MAT (for Ed D), master's degree, minimum GPA of 3.0. Additional exam requirements/recommendations for international students: Required—TOEFL. Electronic applications accepted. *Faculty research:* College teaching and learning, faculty-administration relations, community colleges, organizational change, student affairs.

The University of Arizona, College of Education, Department of Educational Policy Studies and Practice, Program in Higher Education, Tucson, AZ 85721. Offers MA, PhD. *Program availability:* Part-time. Terminal master's awarded for partial completion of doctoral program. *Degree requirements:* For master's, comprehensive exam, thesis; for doctorate, comprehensive exam, thesis/dissertation. *Entrance requirements:* For master's, GRE General Test or MAT, minimum undergraduate GPA of 3.0; for doctorate, GRE General Test or MAT, minimum undergraduate GPA of 3.0, graduate 3.5. Additional exam requirements/recommendations for international students: Required—TOEFL (minimum score 550 paper-based; 79 iBT). Electronic applications accepted. *Faculty research:* Technology transfer, higher education policy, finance, curricular change.

University of Arkansas, Graduate School, College of Education and Health Professions, Department of Rehabilitation, Human Resources and Communication Disorders, Program in Higher Education, Fayetteville, AR 72701. Offers M Ed, Ed D, Ed S. *Accreditation:* NCATE. *Program availability:* Part-time, evening/weekend. In 2018, 17 master's, 9 doctorates awarded. *Entrance requirements:* For master's, GRE General Test, MAT or minimum GPA of 3.0; for doctorate, GRE General Test or MAT. *Application deadline:* For fall admission, 8/1 for domestic students, 4/1 for international students; for spring admission, 12/1 for domestic students, 10/1 for international students; for summer admission, 4/15 for domestic students, 3/1 for international

students. Applications are processed on a rolling basis. Application fee: $60. Electronic applications accepted. *Financial support:* In 2018–19, 30 research assistantships, 1 teaching assistantship were awarded; fellowships with tuition reimbursements, career-related internships or fieldwork, and Federal Work-Study also available. Support available to part-time students. Financial award application deadline: 4/1; financial award applicants required to submit FAFSA. *Unit head:* Dr. Michael Hevel, Department Head, 479-575-4924, Fax: 479-575-3119, E-mail: hevel@uark.edu. *Application contact:* Dr. Michael Hevel, Department Head, 479-575-4924, Fax: 479-575-3119, E-mail: hevel@uark.edu.
Website: http://hied.uark.edu

University of Arkansas at Little Rock, Graduate School, College of Education and Health Professions, Department of Educational Leadership, Program in Higher Education, Little Rock, AR 72204-1099. Offers administration (MA); college student affairs (MA); health professions teaching and learning (MA); higher education (Ed D); two-year college teaching (MA). *Degree requirements:* For doctorate, comprehensive exam, oral defense of dissertation, residency. *Entrance requirements:* For master's, GRE General Test or MAT, interview, minimum graduate GPA of 3.0; for doctorate, GRE General Test, interview, minimum graduate GPA of 3.5, teaching certificate, three years of work experience.

The University of British Columbia, Faculty of Education, Department of Educational Studies, Vancouver, BC V6T 1Z1, Canada. Offers adult learning and education (M Ed); adult learning and global change (M Ed); curriculum and leadership (M Ed); educational administration and leadership (M Ed); educational leadership and policy (Ed D); educational studies (M Ed, MA, PhD); higher education (M Ed); society, culture and politics in education (M Ed). *Program availability:* Part-time, evening/weekend. Terminal master's awarded for partial completion of doctoral program. *Degree requirements:* For master's, thesis; for doctorate, comprehensive exam, thesis/dissertation. *Entrance requirements:* For master's, minimum B+ average, 4-year undergraduate degree, field-related experience; for doctorate, minimum B+ average, 4-year undergraduate degree, master's degree, field-related experience. Additional exam requirements/recommendations for international students: Required—TOEFL (minimum score 600 paper-based; 100 iBT) or IELTS (minimum score 6.5). Electronic applications accepted. *Expenses:* Contact institution. *Faculty research:* Educational leadership educational administration adult education politics in education, global change and adult learning.

University of California, Riverside, Graduate Division, Graduate School of Education, Riverside, CA 92521. Offers applied behavior analysis (M Ed); diversity and equity (M Ed); education policy analysis and leadership (PhD); education specialist (Credential); education, society, and culture (MA, PhD); educational psychology (MA, PhD); general education (M Ed); higher education administration and policy (M Ed, PhD); multiple subject (Credential); research, evaluation, measurement and statistics (MA); school psychology (PhD); single subject (Credential); special education (M Ed, PhD); special education and autism (MA); TESOL (M Ed). Terminal master's awarded for partial completion of doctoral program. *Degree requirements:* For master's, comprehensive exams or thesis (MA), case study or analytical report (M Ed); for doctorate, comprehensive exam, thesis/dissertation, written and oral qualifying exams, college teaching practicum. *Entrance requirements:* For master's, GRE General Test (for MA); CBEST and CSET (for M Ed in general education only), UCR Extension TESOL certificate (for M Ed with TESOL emphasis only); for doctorate, GRE General Test, writing sample; for Credential, CBEST, CSET. Additional exam requirements/recommendations for international students: Required—TOEFL (minimum score 550 paper-based; 80 iBT), IELTS (minimum score 7). Electronic applications accepted. *Faculty research:* Responsiveness to intervention, faculty core, response to intervention of English language learners, advanced modeling techniques, study on social capital, trust, and motivation.

University of Central Florida, College of Community Innovation and Education, Department of Educational Leadership and Higher Education, Orlando, FL 32816. Offers career and technical education (MA); educational leadership (M Ed, MA, Ed S); higher education/college teaching and leadership (MA); higher education/student personnel (MA). *Program availability:* Part-time, evening/weekend. *Degree requirements:* For master's, thesis or alternative; for Ed S, thesis or alternative, final exam. *Entrance requirements:* For master's, GRE General Test; for Ed S, GRE General Test, minimum GPA of 3.0, resume, letters of recommendation. Additional exam requirements/recommendations for international students: Required—TOEFL. Electronic applications accepted.

University of Connecticut, Graduate School, Neag School of Education, Department of Educational Leadership, Field of Higher Education and Student Affairs, Storrs, CT 06269. Offers MA. *Accreditation:* NCATE. *Degree requirements:* For master's, comprehensive exam, thesis or alternative. *Entrance requirements:* Additional exam requirements/recommendations for international students: Required—TOEFL (minimum score 550 paper-based). Electronic applications accepted.

University of Delaware, College of Education and Human Development, School of Education, Newark, DE 19716. Offers education (PhD); educational leadership (Ed D); higher education (M Ed); instruction (MI); reading (M Ed); school leadership (M Ed); school psychology (MA, Ed S); teaching English as a second language (TESL) (MA). *Accreditation:* NCATE. *Program availability:* Part-time, evening/weekend. Terminal master's awarded for partial completion of doctoral program. *Degree requirements:* For master's, comprehensive exam (for some programs), thesis (for some programs); for doctorate, comprehensive exam (for some programs), thesis/dissertation. *Entrance requirements:* For master's and doctorate, GRE, 3 letters of recommendation. Additional exam requirements/recommendations for international students: Required—TOEFL (minimum score 600 paper-based). Electronic applications accepted. *Faculty research:* Teacher education; curriculum theory and development; community based education models, educational leadership.

University of Denver, Morgridge College of Education, Denver, CO 80208. Offers child, family and school psychology (MA, PhD, Ed S); counseling psychology (MA, PhD); curriculum and instruction (MA, Ed D, PhD); curriculum instruction and teaching (Certificate); early childhood special education (MA, Certificate); educational leadership and policy studies (MA, Ed D, PhD, Certificate); higher education (Ed D, PhD); library and information science (MLIS); research methods and statistics (MA, PhD). *Accreditation:* ALA; APA (one or more programs are accredited). *Program availability:* Part-time, evening/weekend, online learning. *Faculty:* 49 full-time (35 women), 33 part-time/adjunct (20 women). *Students:* 509 full-time (400 women), 365 part-time (277 women); includes 236 minority (53 Black or African American, non-Hispanic/Latino; 6 American Indian or Alaska Native, non-Hispanic/Latino; 28 Asian, non-Hispanic/Latino; 116 Hispanic/Latino; 33 Two or more races, non-Hispanic/Latino), 56 international. Average age 31. 1,372 applicants, 57% accepted, 382 enrolled. In 2018, 258 master's, 41 doctorates, 162 other advanced degrees awarded. Terminal master's awarded for partial completion of doctoral program. *Degree requirements:* For master's, comprehensive exam (for some programs); for doctorate, comprehensive exam (for some programs), thesis/dissertation. *Entrance requirements:* For master's, GRE General Test or GMAT, bachelors degree; transcripts; two letters of recommendation; personal statement; resume; for doctorate, GRE General Test or GMAT, Masters degree; transcripts; two letters of recommendation; personal statement(s); resume. Additional exam requirements/recommendations for international students: Required—TOEFL (minimum score 550 paper-based; 80 iBT). *Application deadline:* Applications are processed on a rolling basis. Application fee: $65. Electronic applications accepted. *Expenses:* $33,183 per year full-time. *Financial support:* In 2018–19, 690 students received support, including 29 research assistantships with tuition reimbursements available (averaging $11,465 per year), 9 teaching assistantships with tuition reimbursements available (averaging $2,527 per year); career-related internships or fieldwork, Federal Work-Study, institutionally sponsored loans, scholarships/grants, and unspecified assistantships also available. Support available to part-time students. Financial award application deadline: 2/15; financial award applicants required to submit FAFSA. *Faculty research:* Early childhood education, educational leadership, access and opportunity to postsecondary education, marriage and family therapy, data management and archival research. *Total annual research expenditures:* $2.3 million. *Unit head:* Dr. Karen Riley, Dean, 303-871-3665, E-mail: karen.riley@du.edu. *Application contact:* Jodi Dye, Director of Admissions, 303-871-2510, E-mail: jodi.dye@du.edu.
Website: http://morgridge.du.edu

University of Florida, Graduate School, College of Education, School of Human Development and Organizational Studies in Education, Gainesville, FL 32611. Offers counseling and counselor education (Ed D, PhD), including counseling and counselor education, marriage and family counseling, mental health counseling, school counseling and guidance; educational leadership (M Ed, MAE, Ed D, PhD, Ed S), including educational leadership (Ed D, PhD), educational policy (Ed D, PhD); higher education administration (Ed D, PhD), including education policy (Ed D), educational policy, higher education administration; marriage and family counseling (M Ed, MAE, Ed D, PhD, Ed S); mental health counseling (M Ed, MAE, Ed D, PhD, Ed S); research and evaluation methodology (M Ed, MAE, Ed D, PhD); school counseling and guidance (M Ed, MAE, Ed D, PhD, Ed S); student personnel in higher education (M Ed, MAE). *Accreditation:* ACA (one or more programs are accredited); NCATE. *Program availability:* Part-time, online learning. Terminal master's awarded for partial completion of doctoral program. *Degree requirements:* For master's, thesis optional; for doctorate, comprehensive exam, thesis/dissertation. *Entrance requirements:* For master's and doctorate, GRE General Test, minimum GPA of 3.0 (undergraduate), 3.5 (graduate); for Ed S, GRE General Test. Additional exam requirements/recommendations for international students: Required—TOEFL (minimum score 550 paper-based; 80 iBT), IELTS (minimum score 6). Electronic applications accepted.

University of Georgia, College of Education, Program in Higher Education, Athens, GA 30602. Offers M Ed, Ed D, PhD. *Accreditation:* NCATE. *Degree requirements:* For doctorate, thesis/dissertation. *Entrance requirements:* For doctorate, GRE General Test. Electronic applications accepted.

University of Houston, College of Education, Department of Educational Leadership and Policy Studies, Houston, TX 77204. Offers administration and supervision (M Ed, Ed D); higher education (M Ed); historical, social, and cultural foundations of education (M Ed). None. *Accreditation:* NCATE. *Program availability:* Part-time, evening/weekend, 100% online, blended/hybrid learning. *Faculty:* 20 full-time (12 women), 2 part-time/adjunct (both women). *Students:* 99 full-time (76 women), 226 part-time (159 women); includes 207 minority (103 Black or African American, non-Hispanic/Latino; 2 American Indian or Alaska Native, non-Hispanic/Latino; 10 Asian, non-Hispanic/Latino; 84 Hispanic/Latino; 8 Two or more races, non-Hispanic/Latino), 5 international. Average age 37. 213 applicants, 78% accepted, 87 enrolled. In 2018, 78 master's, 18 doctorates awarded. Terminal master's awarded for partial completion of doctoral program. *Degree requirements:* For master's, comprehensive exam or thesis; for doctorate, comprehensive exam, thesis/dissertation. *Entrance requirements:* For master's, GRE General Test, minimum cumulative GPA of 2.6, 3 letters of recommendation, resume/vitae, goal statement; for doctorate, GRE General Test, minimum cumulative GPA of 2.6, 3 letters of recommendation, resume/vitae, goal statement, writing sample, interview. Additional exam requirements/recommendations for international students: Required—TOEFL (minimum score 550 paper-based; 79 iBT). *Application deadline:* For fall admission, 3/1 for domestic students; for spring admission, 10/1 for domestic students. Applications are processed on a rolling basis. Application fee: $80 ($75 for international students). Electronic applications accepted. Application fee is waived when completed online. *Financial support:* In 2018–19, 10 students received support, including 13 research assistantships with full tuition reimbursements available (averaging $18,000 per year); career-related internships or fieldwork, Federal Work-Study, institutionally sponsored loans, scholarships/grants, health care benefits, and unspecified assistantships also available. Support available to part-time students. Financial award application deadline: 2/1; financial award applicants required to submit FAFSA. *Faculty research:* Change, supervision, multiculturalism, evaluation, policy. *Total annual research expenditures:* $220,018. *Unit head:* Dr. Catherine Horn, Dean, 713-743-5032, Fax: 713-743-8650, E-mail: clhorn2@uh.edu. *Application contact:* Bridgette Jones, Director of Student Affairs, 713-743-2978, E-mail: bajones5@uh.edu.
Website: http://www.uh.edu/education/departments/elps/

University of Houston, College of Education, Department of Psychological, Health and Learning Sciences, Houston, TX 77204. Offers administration and supervision - higher education (M Ed); counseling (M Ed); counseling psychology (PhD); educational psychology (M Ed); school psychology (PhD); school psychology and individual differences (PhD); special education (M Ed). None. *Accreditation:* NCATE. *Program availability:* Part-time, evening/weekend, 100% online, blended/hybrid learning. *Faculty:* 31 full-time (23 women), 3 part-time/adjunct (1 woman). *Students:* 163 full-time (135 women), 51 part-time (43 women); includes 106 minority (35 Black or African American, non-Hispanic/Latino; 1 American Indian or Alaska Native, non-Hispanic/Latino; 18 Asian, non-Hispanic/Latino; 46 Hispanic/Latino; 6 Two or more races, non-Hispanic/Latino), 17 international. Average age 29. 216 applicants, 58% accepted, 60 enrolled. In 2018, 39 master's, 18 doctorates awarded. Terminal master's awarded for partial completion of doctoral program. *Degree requirements:* For master's, comprehensive exam or thesis; for doctorate, comprehensive exam, thesis/dissertation. *Entrance requirements:* For master's, GRE, transcripts, 3 letters of recommendation, curriculum vita, goal statement; for doctorate, GRE, transcripts, 3 letters of recommendation, curriculum vita, goal statement, writing sample, interview. Additional exam requirements/recommendations for international students: Required—TOEFL (minimum score 550 paper-based; 79 iBT). *Application deadline:* For fall admission, 1/15 for domestic and international students; for spring admission, 9/15 for domestic and international students. Applications are processed on a rolling basis. Application fee: $80 ($75 for international students). Electronic applications accepted. Application fee is waived when completed online. *Financial support:* In 2018–19, 10 students received support, including 5 fellowships with full tuition reimbursements available (averaging $2,000 per year), 8 research assistantships with full tuition reimbursements available (averaging $8,664 per year), 56 teaching assistantships with full tuition reimbursements available (averaging $8,760 per year); career-related internships or fieldwork, Federal Work-Study, institutionally sponsored loans, scholarships/grants, health care benefits, and unspecified assistantships also available. Support available to part-time students. Financial award application deadline: 2/1. *Faculty research:* Evidence-based assessment and intervention, multicultural issues in psychology, social and cultural context of learning, systemic barriers to college, motivational aspects of self-regulated

learning. *Total annual research expenditures:* $1.9 million. *Unit head:* Dr. Nathan Grant Smith, Interim Department Chair, 713-743-7648, Fax: 713-743-4996, E-mail: ngsmith@uh.edu. *Application contact:* Bridgette Jones, Director of Student Affairs, 713-743-2978, E-mail: bajones5@uh.edu.
Website: http://www.uh.edu/education/departments/phls/

University of Houston–Victoria, School of Education, Health Professions and Human Development, Victoria, TX 77901-4450. Offers administration and supervision (M Ed); adult and higher education (M Ed); counselor education (M Ed); curriculum and instruction (M Ed); dyslexia education (Certificate); educational technology (M Ed); special education (M Ed). *Program availability:* Part-time, evening/weekend, online learning. *Degree requirements:* For master's, comprehensive exam, project or thesis. *Entrance requirements:* For master's, GRE General Test. Additional exam requirements/recommendations for international students: Required—TOEFL. Electronic applications accepted. *Expenses: Tuition, area resident:* Full-time $6154; part-time $3077 per semester. Tuition, state resident: full-time $6154; part-time $3077 per semester. Tuition, nonresident: full-time $13,624; part-time $6812 per semester. *International tuition:* $13,624 full-time. *Required fees:* $1405; $847 per semester. $423 per semester. Tuition and fees vary according to program. *Faculty research:* Reading and language arts education, evaluation and diagnosis of special children's abilities.

The University of Iowa, Graduate College, College of Education, Department of Educational Policy and Leadership Studies, Program in Higher Education and Student Affairs, Iowa City, IA 52242-1316. Offers MA, PhD. *Degree requirements:* For master's, exam; for doctorate, comprehensive exam, thesis/dissertation. *Entrance requirements:* For master's and doctorate, GRE General Test, minimum GPA of 3.0. Additional exam requirements/recommendations for international students: Required—TOEFL (minimum score 550 paper-based; 81 iBT). Electronic applications accepted.

The University of Kansas, Graduate Studies, School of Education, Department of Educational Leadership and Policy Studies, Program in Higher Education Administration, Lawrence, KS 66045-3101. Offers MS Ed, Ed D, PhD. *Program availability:* Part-time, evening/weekend. *Students:* 49 full-time (40 women), 16 part-time (12 women); includes 25 minority (9 Black or African American, non-Hispanic/Latino; 1 American Indian or Alaska Native, non-Hispanic/Latino; 2 Asian, non-Hispanic/Latino; 9 Hispanic/Latino; 4 Two or more races, non-Hispanic/Latino). Average age 26. 68 applicants, 94% accepted, 28 enrolled. In 2018, 25 master's awarded. *Entrance requirements:* For master's, minimum GPA of 3.0, resume, statement of purpose, official transcript, three letters of recommendation; for doctorate, GRE General Test, minimum graduate GPA of 3.5, resume, statement of purpose, official transcripts, three letters of recommendation, writing sample; minimum of three years of professional experience in higher education or related organization and master's degree (preferred for Ed D). Additional exam requirements/recommendations for international students: Required—TOEFL, IELTS. *Application deadline:* For fall admission, 7/1 for domestic and international students; for spring admission, 11/1 for domestic and international students; for summer admission, 3/1 for domestic and international students. Application fee: $65 ($85 for international students). Electronic applications accepted. *Financial support:* Fellowships, career-related internships or fieldwork, scholarships/grants, and unspecified assistantships available. Financial award application deadline: 1/3; financial award applicants required to submit FAFSA. *Faculty research:* Higher education policy, faculty issues, research on college students, financial aid, access to higher education. *Unit head:* Dr. Susan B. Twombly, Chair, 785-864-9721, Fax: 785-864-4697, E-mail: stwombly@ku.edu. *Application contact:* Denise Brubaker, Admissions Coordinator, 785-864-7973, Fax: 785-864-4697, E-mail: brubaker@ku.edu.

University of Kentucky, Graduate School, College of Education, Program in Educational Policy Studies and Evaluation, Lexington, KY 40506-0032. Offers educational policy studies and evaluation (Ed D); higher education (MS Ed, PhD); social and philosophical studies (MS Ed). *Accreditation:* NCATE. Terminal master's awarded for partial completion of doctoral program. *Degree requirements:* For master's, comprehensive exam, thesis optional; for doctorate, comprehensive exam, thesis/dissertation. *Entrance requirements:* For master's, GRE General Test, minimum undergraduate GPA of 2.75; for doctorate, GRE General Test, minimum graduate GPA of 3.0. Additional exam requirements/recommendations for international students: Required—TOEFL (minimum score 550 paper-based). Electronic applications accepted. *Faculty research:* Studies in higher education; comparative and international education; evaluation of educational programs, policies, and reform; student, teacher, and faculty cultures; gender and education.

University of La Verne, LaFetra College of Education, Program in Social Justice Higher Education Administration, La Verne, CA 91750-4443. Offers MA. *Program availability:* Part-time. *Entrance requirements:* Additional exam requirements/recommendations for international students: Required—TOEFL (minimum score 550 paper-based; 80 iBT), IELTS (minimum score 6.5). Electronic applications accepted.

University of Louisville, Graduate School, College of Education and Human Development, Department of Educational Leadership, Evaluation and Organizational Development, Louisville, KY 40292-0001. Offers educational leadership and organizational development (Ed D, PhD), including evaluation (PhD), human resource development (PhD), P-12 administration (PhD), post-secondary administration (PhD), sport administration (MA, PhD); health professions education (Certificate); higher education administration (MA), including sport administration (MA, PhD); human resources and organization development (MS), including health professions education, human resource leadership, workplace learning and performance; P-12 educational administration (Ed S), including principalship, supervisor of instruction. *Accreditation:* NCATE. *Program availability:* Part-time, evening/weekend, 100% online, blended/hybrid learning. *Students:* 200 full-time (82 women), 474 part-time (262 women); includes 218 minority (127 Black or African American, non-Hispanic/Latino; 1 American Indian or Alaska Native, non-Hispanic/Latino; 18 Asian, non-Hispanic/Latino; 46 Hispanic/Latino; 2 Native Hawaiian or other Pacific Islander, non-Hispanic/Latino; 24 Two or more races, non-Hispanic/Latino), 5 international. Average age 36. 257 applicants, 77% accepted, 170 enrolled. In 2018, 111 master's, 10 doctorates, 22 other advanced degrees awarded. Terminal master's awarded for partial completion of doctoral program. *Degree requirements:* For master's, comprehensive exam (for some programs), thesis (for some programs); for doctorate, comprehensive exam (for some programs), thesis/dissertation. *Entrance requirements:* For master's, GRE (for most programs), PRAXIS (for educator preparation programs), professional statement, recommendation letters, resume, transcripts; for doctorate and other advanced degree, GRE, professional statement, recommendation letters, resume, transcripts. Additional exam requirements/recommendations for international students: Required—TOEFL (minimum score 550 paper-based; 79 iBT); Recommended—IELTS (minimum score 6.5). *Application deadline:* For fall admission, 6/1 priority date for domestic students, 5/1 priority date for international students; for spring admission, 10/1 priority date for domestic students, 11/1 priority date for international students; for summer admission, 3/1 for domestic students, 4/1 priority date for international students. Application fee: $65. *Expenses: Tuition, area resident:* Full-time $6500; part-time $723 per credit hour. Tuition, state resident: full-time $6500. Tuition, nonresident: full-time $13,557; part-time $1507 per credit hour. Tuition and fees vary according to course load and program. *Financial support:* In 2018–19, 144 students received support, including fellowships (averaging $21,024 per year), research assistantships with full tuition reimbursements available (averaging $21,024 per year), teaching assistantships with full tuition reimbursements available (averaging $21,024 per year); Federal Work-Study, scholarships/grants, health care benefits, tuition waivers (full), and unspecified assistantships also available. Financial award application deadline: 3/1; financial award applicants required to submit FAFSA. *Faculty research:* Human resources and organizational development; career, technical, health professions, and economic education; health professions education; community and military partnerships; higher education. *Unit head:* Dr. Sharron Kerrick, Chair, 502-852-6475, E-mail: lead@louisville.edu. *Application contact:* Dr. Margaret Pentecost, Assistant Dean for Graduate Student Success, 502-852-6437, Fax: 502-852-1417, E-mail: gedadm@louisville.edu.
Website: http://louisville.edu/education/departments/eleod

University of Louisville, Graduate School, College of Education and Human Development, Departments of Early Childhood and Elementary Education, Middle and Secondary Education, and Special Education, Louisville, KY 40292-0001. Offers art education (MAT); autism and applied behavior analysis (Certificate); curriculum and instruction (PhD); early elementary education (MAT); exercise physiology (MS); health and physical education (MAT); health professions education (Certificate); higher education (MA); human resources and organization development (MS); instructional technology (M Ed); interdisciplinary early childhood education (MAT); middle school education (MAT); music education (MAT); secondary education (MAT); special education (MAT); sport administration (MS); teacher leadership (M Ed). *Program availability:* Part-time, evening/weekend, 100% online, blended/hybrid learning. *Faculty:* 97 full-time (64 women), 131 part-time/adjunct (86 women). *Students:* 109 full-time (72 women), 139 part-time (87 women); includes 43 minority (18 Black or African American, non-Hispanic/Latino; 6 Asian, non-Hispanic/Latino; 10 Hispanic/Latino; 9 Two or more races, non-Hispanic/Latino), 9 international. Average age 29. 108 applicants, 75% accepted, 59 enrolled. In 2018, 64 master's awarded. Terminal master's awarded for partial completion of doctoral program. *Degree requirements:* For master's, comprehensive exam (for some programs), thesis optional; for doctorate, comprehensive exam (for some programs), thesis/dissertation. *Entrance requirements:* For master's, GRE (for most programs), PRAXIS (for educator preparation programs), professional statement, recommendation letters, resume, transcripts; for doctorate and Certificate, GRE, professional statement, recommendation letters, resume, transcripts. Additional exam requirements/recommendations for international students: Required—TOEFL (minimum score 550 paper-based; 79 iBT); Recommended—IELTS (minimum score 6.5). *Application deadline:* For fall admission, 6/1 priority date for domestic students, 5/1 priority date for international students; for spring admission, 10/1 priority date for domestic students, 11/1 priority date for international students; for summer admission, 3/1 priority date for domestic students, 4/1 priority date for international students. Application fee: $65. *Expenses: Tuition, area resident:* Full-time $6500; part-time $723 per credit hour. Tuition, state resident: full-time $6500. Tuition, nonresident: full-time $13,557; part-time $1507 per credit hour. Tuition and fees vary according to course load and program. *Financial support:* In 2018–19, 144 students received support, including fellowships with full tuition reimbursements available (averaging $21,024 per year), research assistantships with full tuition reimbursements available (averaging $21,024 per year), teaching assistantships with full tuition reimbursements available (averaging $21,024 per year); Federal Work-Study, scholarships/grants, health care benefits, tuition waivers (full), and unspecified assistantships also available. Financial award application deadline: 3/1; financial award applicants required to submit FAFSA. *Faculty research:* Children's early reading and writing development, crelevance of basic facts in elementary mathematics instruction, clinical model of teacher education, cultural and linguistic context of diverse learners, and STEM-integrated curriculum design and development. STEM teaching and learning, content literacy for English language learners, social justice in teacher education, adolescent literacy, mathematics teacher development. Classroom and behavior management; moderate/severe disabilities, autism. *Unit head:* Dr. Amy Lingo, Interim Dean, 502-852-3235, Fax: 502-852-1464, E-mail: cehdinfo@louisville.edu. *Application contact:* Dr. Margaret Pentecost, Assistant Dean for Graduate Student Success, 502-852-6437, Fax: 502-852-1417, E-mail: gedadm@louisville.edu.
Website: http://louisville.edu/delphi

University of Lynchburg, Graduate Studies, M Ed Program in Educational Leadership, Lynchburg, VA 24501-3199. Offers higher education (M Ed); PK-12 administrative and supervisory (M Ed). *Program availability:* Part-time, evening/weekend. *Degree requirements:* For master's, comprehensive exam (for some programs), internship; SLLC exam or comprehensive exam. *Entrance requirements:* For master's, GRE, minimum GPA of 3.0 (preferred), official transcripts (bachelor's, others as relevant), three letters of recommendation, career goals statement. Additional exam requirements/recommendations for international students: Required—TOEFL (minimum score 550 paper-based; 80 iBT), IELTS (minimum score 6). Electronic applications accepted. Application fee is waived when completed online. *Expenses:* Contact institution.

University of Maine, Graduate School, College of Education and Human Development, School of Educational Leadership, Higher Education, and Human Development, Orono, ME 04469. Offers educational leadership (M Ed, CAS); higher education (CAS); human development (MS). *Program availability:* Part-time. *Faculty:* 11 full-time (7 women), 10 part-time/adjunct (5 women). *Students:* 72 full-time (53 women), 64 part-time (44 women); includes 11 minority (3 Black or African American, non-Hispanic/Latino; 4 Asian, non-Hispanic/Latino; 4 Hispanic/Latino), 1 international. Average age 37. 101 applicants, 85% accepted, 49 enrolled. In 2018, 18 master's, 4 doctorates, 10 other advanced degrees awarded. *Degree requirements:* For master's, thesis (for some programs); for doctorate, comprehensive exam, thesis/dissertation. *Entrance requirements:* For master's, GRE General Test, MAT; for doctorate, GRE. Additional exam requirements/recommendations for international students: Required—TOEFL (minimum score 550 paper-based; 80 iBT), IELTS (minimum score 6.5). *Application deadline:* For fall admission, 2/1 priority date for domestic students. Applications are processed on a rolling basis. Application fee: $65. Electronic applications accepted. *Financial support:* In 2018–19, 39 students received support, including 3 teaching assistantships with full tuition reimbursements available (averaging $15,600 per year); career-related internships or fieldwork, Federal Work-Study, institutionally sponsored loans, tuition waivers (full and partial), and unspecified assistantships also available. Financial award application deadline: 3/1. *Faculty research:* Student hazing and hazing prevention, sexuality education, cross cultural perspectives on family, early childhood development, fatherhood/parenting, campus climate, social justice, rural higher education, gender in higher education, discourse, rural sociology, school-community relationships, instructional supervision, rural educational leadership. *Unit head:* Dr. Jim Artesani, Associate Dean of Accreditation and Graduate Affairs, 207-581-4061, Fax: 207-581-3120. *Application contact:* Scott G. Delcourt, Senior Associate Dean of the Graduate School, 207-581-3291, Fax: 207-581-3232, E-mail: graduate@maine.edu.
Website: http://www.umaine.edu/edhd/

University of Manitoba, Faculty of Graduate Studies, Faculty of Education, Department of Educational Administration, Foundations and Psychology, Winnipeg, MB R3T 2N2, Canada. Offers adult and post-secondary education (M Ed); educational administration (M Ed); guidance and counseling (M Ed); inclusive special education (M Ed); social foundations of education (M Ed). *Degree requirements:* For master's, thesis or alternative.

Higher Education

University of Mary Hardin-Baylor, Graduate Studies in Education, Belton, TX 76513. Offers curriculum and instruction (M Ed); educational administration (M Ed, Ed D), including higher education (Ed D), leadership in nursing education (Ed D), P-12 (Ed D). *Program availability:* Part-time, evening/weekend. *Degree requirements:* For master's, comprehensive exam; for doctorate, thesis/dissertation. *Entrance requirements:* For master's, minimum GPA of 3.0, interview; for doctorate, minimum GPA of 3.5, interview, essay, resume, employment verification, 3 letters of recommendation. Additional exam requirements/recommendations for international students: Required—TOEFL (minimum score 60 iBT), IELTS (minimum score 4.5). Electronic applications accepted. *Expenses:* Contact institution. *Faculty research:* Motivational orientation of preservice teachers.

University of Massachusetts Amherst, Graduate School, College of Education, Program in Education, Amherst, MA 01003. Offers bilingual, English as a second language, and multicultural education (M Ed, Ed S); child study and early education (M Ed); children, families and schools (Ed D, Ed S); early childhood and elementary teacher education (M Ed); educational leadership (M Ed); educational policy and leadership (Ed D); higher education (M Ed); international education (M Ed); language, literacy and culture (Ed D); learning, media and technology (M Ed, Ed S); mathematics, science, and learning technologies (Ed D); reading and writing (M Ed); research, educational measurement and psychometrics (Ed D); school counselor education (M Ed, Ed S); school psychology (Ed S); science education (Ed S); secondary teacher education (M Ed); social justice education (M Ed, Ed D, Ed S); special education (M Ed, Ed D, Ed S); teacher education and school improvement (Ed D, Ed S). *Accreditation:* NCATE. *Program availability:* Part-time, online learning. Terminal master's awarded for partial completion of doctoral program. *Degree requirements:* For doctorate, comprehensive exam, thesis/dissertation. *Entrance requirements:* Additional exam requirements/recommendations for international students: Required—TOEFL (minimum score 550 paper-based; 80 iBT), IELTS (minimum score 6.5). Electronic applications accepted.

University of Massachusetts Amherst, Graduate School, Interdisciplinary Programs, Dual Degree Program in Education and Public Policy and Administration, Amherst, MA 01003. Offers MPPA/M Ed. *Entrance requirements:* Additional exam requirements/recommendations for international students: Required—TOEFL (minimum score 550 paper-based; 80 iBT), IELTS (minimum score 6.5). Electronic applications accepted.

University of Massachusetts Boston, College of Education and Human Development, Program in Higher Education, Boston, MA 02125-3393. Offers Ed D, PhD. *Students:* 6 full-time (3 women), 67 part-time (46 women); includes 38 minority (15 Black or African American, non-Hispanic/Latino; 9 Asian, non-Hispanic/Latino; 14 Hispanic/Latino). Average age 41. 24 applicants, 58% accepted, 12 enrolled. In 2018, 6 doctorates awarded. *Application deadline:* For summer admission, 2/1 for domestic students. Application fee: $60 ($100 for international students). Electronic applications accepted. *Expenses: Tuition, area resident:* Full-time $17,896. Tuition, state resident: full-time $17,896. Tuition, nonresident: full-time $34,932. *International tuition:* $34,932 full-time. *Required fees:* $355. *Unit head:* Dr. Katalin Szelényi, Graduate Program Director, 617-287.7765, E-mail: Katalin.Szelenyi@umb.edu. *Application contact:* Graduate Admissions Coordinator, 617-287-6400, Fax: 617-287-6236, E-mail: graduate.admissions@umb.edu.

University of Memphis, Graduate School, College of Education, Department of Leadership, Memphis, TN 38152. Offers adult education (Ed D); community college teaching and leadership (Graduate Certificate); community education (Ed D); educational leadership (Ed D); higher education (Ed D); leadership (MS); policy studies (Ed D); school administration and supervision (MS); student personnel (MS). *Accreditation:* NCATE. *Program availability:* Part-time, evening/weekend, online learning. *Students:* 19 full-time (12 women), 137 part-time (90 women); includes 87 minority (80 Black or African American, non-Hispanic/Latino; 2 Asian, non-Hispanic/Latino; 4 Hispanic/Latino; 1 Two or more races, non-Hispanic/Latino), 1 international. Average age 41. 44 applicants, 98% accepted, 37 enrolled. In 2018, 11 master's, 17 doctorates, 2 other advanced degrees awarded. *Degree requirements:* For master's, comprehensive exam, thesis optional; for doctorate, comprehensive exam, thesis/dissertation. *Entrance requirements:* For master's, GRE, resume, letters of reference, statement of professional goals, current teacher certification, sample work, interview; for doctorate, GRE, resume, letters of reference, statement of professional goals, interview. Additional exam requirements/recommendations for international students: Required—TOEFL (minimum score 550 paper-based; 79 iBT). *Application deadline:* For fall admission, 6/15 for domestic students; for spring admission, 9/15 for domestic students; for summer admission, 2/15 for domestic students. Application fee: $35 ($60 for international students). Electronic applications accepted. *Expenses: Tuition, area resident:* Full-time $10,240; part-time $503 per credit hour. Tuition, state resident: full-time $10,464. Tuition, nonresident: full-time $20,224; part-time $991 per credit hour. *Required fees:* $850; $106 per credit hour. *Financial support:* Research assistantships with full tuition reimbursements, teaching assistantships, Federal Work-Study, scholarships/grants, and unspecified assistantships available. Financial award application deadline: 2/1; financial award applicants required to submit FAFSA. *Faculty research:* School improvement, social justice, online learning, adult learning, diversity. *Unit head:* Dr. R Eric Platt, Interim Chair, 901-678-4229, E-mail: replatt@memphis.edu. *Application contact:* Dr. R Eric Platt, Interim Chair, 901-678-4229, E-mail: replatt@memphis.edu.
Website: http://www.memphis.edu/lead

University of Miami, Graduate School, School of Education and Human Development, Department of Educational and Psychological Studies, Program in Higher Education Administration, Coral Gables, FL 33124. Offers enrollment management (MS Ed, Certificate); higher education leadership (Ed D); student life and development (MS Ed, Certificate). *Program availability:* Part-time, evening/weekend. *Faculty:* 2 full-time (1 woman), 9 part-time/adjunct (3 women). *Students:* 36 full-time (25 women), 13 part-time (10 women); includes 30 minority (10 Black or African American, non-Hispanic/Latino; 2 Asian, non-Hispanic/Latino; 17 Hispanic/Latino; 1 Two or more races, non-Hispanic/Latino), 3 international. Average age 32. 39 applicants, 85% accepted, 21 enrolled. In 2018, 26 master's, 12 doctorates, 2 Certificates awarded. Terminal master's awarded for partial completion of doctoral program. *Degree requirements:* For master's, comprehensive exam; for doctorate, thesis/dissertation, qualifying exam. *Entrance requirements:* For master's and doctorate, GRE General Test. Additional exam requirements/recommendations for international students: Required—TOEFL (minimum score 550 paper-based; 80 iBT); Recommended—IELTS (minimum score 6.5). *Application deadline:* Applications are processed on a rolling basis. Application fee: $75. Electronic applications accepted. *Financial support:* Institutionally sponsored loans, scholarships/grants, health care benefits, and tuition waivers (full and partial) available. Support available to part-time students. Financial award application deadline: 3/1; financial award applicants required to submit FAFSA. *Unit head:* Dr. Carol Anne Phekoo, Associate Professor of Professional Practice/Program Director, 305-284-5013, E-mail: cphekoo@miami.edu. *Application contact:* Lois Heffernan, Graduate Admissions Coordinator, 305-284-2167, Fax: 305-284-9395, E-mail: lheffernan@miami.edu.
Website: http://www.education.miami.edu

University of Minnesota, Twin Cities Campus, Graduate School, College of Education and Human Development, Department of Organizational Leadership, Policy and Development, Program in Higher Education, Minneapolis, MN 55455-0213. Offers higher education (MA, PhD); multicultural college teaching and learning (MA). *Students:* 63 full-time (38 women), 48 part-time (33 women); includes 40 minority (15 Black or African American, non-Hispanic/Latino; 2 American Indian or Alaska Native, non-Hispanic/Latino; 10 Asian, non-Hispanic/Latino; 8 Hispanic/Latino; 5 Two or more races, non-Hispanic/Latino), 4 international. Average age 36. 59 applicants, 58% accepted, 28 enrolled. In 2018, 10 master's, 13 doctorates awarded. Application fee: $75 ($95 for international students). *Unit head:* Dr. Kenneth Bartlett, Chair, 612-624-1006, E-mail: bartlett@umn.edu. *Application contact:* Dr. Jeremy J. Hernandez, Director of Graduate Studies, 612-626-9377, E-mail: olpd@umn.edu.
Website: http://www.cehd.umn.edu/olpd/grad-programs/HiEd/

University of Mississippi, Graduate School, School of Education, University, MS 38677. Offers counselor education (M Ed, PhD); counselor education - play therapy (Ed S); early childhood (M Ed); educational leadership K-12 (M Ed, Ed D, PhD, Ed S); elementary education (M Ed, Ed D, Ed S); higher education/student personnel (Ed D, PhD); literacy education (M Ed); math education (Ed D); secondary education (M Ed, PhD, Ed S); special education (M Ed, PhD, Ed S); teacher corporations (MA); teacher education (MA). *Accreditation:* NCATE. *Faculty:* 59 full-time (35 women), 34 part-time/adjunct (26 women). *Students:* 169 full-time (137 women), 461 part-time (329 women); includes 199 minority (185 Black or African American, non-Hispanic/Latino; 3 Asian, non-Hispanic/Latino; 7 Hispanic/Latino; 4 Two or more races, non-Hispanic/Latino), 5 international. Average age 33. In 2018, 180 master's, 57 doctorates, 37 other advanced degrees awarded. *Entrance requirements:* For master's, GRE General Test, minimum GPA of 3.0; for doctorate, GRE General Test. Additional exam requirements/recommendations for international students: Required—TOEFL. *Application deadline:* Applications are processed on a rolling basis. Application fee: $50. Electronic applications accepted. *Financial support:* Scholarships/grants available. Financial award application deadline: 3/1; financial award applicants required to submit FAFSA. *Unit head:* Dr. David Rock, Dean, 662-915-7063, Fax: 662-915-7249, E-mail: soe@olemiss.edu. *Application contact:* Temeka Smith, Graduate Activities Specialist for Admissions, 662-915-7474, Fax: 662-915-7577, E-mail: gschool@olemiss.edu.

University of Missouri, Office of Research and Graduate Studies, College of Education, Department of Educational Leadership and Policy Analysis, Columbia, MO 65211. Offers education administration (M Ed, MA, Ed D, PhD, Ed S); higher and adult education (M Ed, MA, Ed D, PhD, Ed S). *Program availability:* Part-time. *Entrance requirements:* For master's, doctorate, and Ed S, minimum GPA of 3.0.

University of Missouri–Kansas City, School of Education, Kansas City, MO 64110-2499. Offers administration (Ed D); counseling and guidance (MA, Ed S), including mental health counseling (Ed S), school counseling (Ed S); counseling psychology (PhD); curriculum and instruction (MA, Ed S), including language and literacy (Ed S); education (PhD), including higher education administration, PK-12 education administration; educational administration (MA, Ed S), including advanced principal (Ed S), beginning principal (Ed S), district-level administration (Ed S); reading education (MA); special education (MA). PhD in education offered through the School of Graduate Studies. *Accreditation:* NCATE. *Program availability:* Part-time, evening/weekend. *Degree requirements:* For doctorate, thesis/dissertation, internship, practicum. *Entrance requirements:* For master's, GRE, minimum GPA of 2.75, 2 letters of reference, written statement of purpose; for doctorate, GRE, minimum GPA of 3.0; for Ed S, minimum GPA of 3.0. Additional exam requirements/recommendations for international students: Required—TOEFL (minimum score 550 paper-based; 80 iBT). *Faculty research:* Urban education, inquiry-based field study, theories of counseling and psychotherapy, school literacy, educational technology.

University of Missouri–St. Louis, College of Education, Department of Education Sciences and Professional Programs, St. Louis, MO 63121. Offers adult and higher education (M Ed); educational psychology (M Ed), including character and citizenship education, research and program evaluation; program evaluation (Certificate); school psychology (Ed S). *Degree requirements:* For other advanced degree, comprehensive exam, thesis or alternative, internship. *Entrance requirements:* For degree, GRE General Test, 2-4 letters of recommendation, personal interview. Additional exam requirements/recommendations for international students: Required—IELTS (minimum score 6.5); Recommended—TOEFL (minimum score 550 paper-based; 79 iBT). Electronic applications accepted. *Faculty research:* Child/adolescent psychology, quantitative and qualitative methodology, evaluation processes, measurement and assessment.

University of Nevada, Las Vegas, Graduate College, College of Education, Department of Educational Psychology and Higher Education, Las Vegas, NV 89154-3002. Offers chief diversity officer in higher education (Certificate); college sport leadership (Certificate); educational policy and leadership (M Ed); educational psychology (MS, PhD, Ed S); educational psychology/law (PhD/JD); higher education (M Ed, PhD, Certificate); psychology/learning and technology (PhD), including learning and technology; workforce development/educational leadership (PhD); PhD/JD. *Program availability:* Part-time, evening/weekend, 100% online, blended/hybrid learning. *Faculty:* 20 full-time (12 women), 6 part-time/adjunct (5 women). *Students:* 74 full-time (50 women), 95 part-time (61 women); includes 64 minority (20 Black or African American, non-Hispanic/Latino; 9 Asian, non-Hispanic/Latino; 26 Hispanic/Latino; 9 Two or more races, non-Hispanic/Latino), 10 international. Average age 36. 106 applicants, 49% accepted, 40 enrolled. In 2018, 57 master's, 4 doctorates, 12 other advanced degrees awarded. *Degree requirements:* For master's, comprehensive exam (for some programs), thesis (for some programs); for doctorate, comprehensive exam, thesis/dissertation. *Entrance requirements:* For master's, GRE General Test or GMAT (for some programs), letters of recommendation; writing sample; bachelor's degree; for doctorate, GMAT or GRE General Test, writing exam; for other advanced degree, GRE General Test (for some programs). Additional exam requirements/recommendations for international students: Required—TOEFL (minimum score 550 paper-based; 80 iBT), IELTS (minimum score 7). Application fee: $60 ($95 for international students). Electronic applications accepted. *Financial support:* In 2018–19, 43 students received support, including 28 research assistantships with full tuition reimbursements available (averaging $14,674 per year), 15 teaching assistantships with full tuition reimbursements available (averaging $18,733 per year); institutionally sponsored loans, scholarships/grants, health care benefits, and unspecified assistantships also available. Financial award application deadline: 3/15; financial award applicants required to submit FAFSA. *Faculty research:* Innovation and change in educational settings; educational policy, finance, and marketing; psycho-educational assessment; student retention, persistence, development, language, and culture; statistical modeling, program evaluation, qualitative and quantitative research methods. *Total annual research expenditures:* $426,511. *Unit head:* Dr. Alice Corkill, Chair/Professor, 702-895-4164, E-mail: ephe.chair@unlv.edu. *Application contact:* Dr. Nancy Lough, Graduate Coordinator, 702-895-5392, E-mail: highered.gradcoord@unlv.edu.
Website: http://education.unlv.edu/ephe/

University of New Hampshire, Graduate School, Interdisciplinary Programs, Program in College Teaching, Durham, NH 03824. Offers Postbaccalaureate Certificate. *Program availability:* Part-time. *Entrance requirements:* Additional exam requirements/recommendations for international students: Required—TOEFL (minimum score 550 paper-based; 80 iBT). Electronic applications accepted.

University of New Mexico, School of Medicine, Program in University Science Teaching, Albuquerque, NM 87131-2039. Offers Certificate.

University of New Orleans, Graduate School, College of Liberal Arts, Education and Human Development, Department of Educational Leadership, Counseling, and Foundations, Program in Educational Leadership, New Orleans, LA 70148. Offers educational administration (PhD); educational leadership (M Ed); higher education (M Ed). *Accreditation:* NCATE. *Program availability:* Evening/weekend. Terminal master's awarded for partial completion of doctoral program. *Degree requirements:* For doctorate, variable foreign language requirement, thesis/dissertation. *Entrance requirements:* For master's and doctorate, GRE General Test. Additional exam requirements/recommendations for international students: Required—TOEFL (minimum score 550 paper-based; 79 iBT). Electronic applications accepted.

University of North Alabama, College of Arts and Sciences, Department of Interdisciplinary and Professional Studies, Florence, AL 35632-0001. Offers professional studies (MPS), including community development, higher education administration, information technology, security and safety leadership. *Program availability:* Part-time, 100% online. *Degree requirements:* For master's, thesis optional. *Entrance requirements:* For master's, ETS PPI, personal statement; three letters of recommendation. Additional exam requirements/recommendations for international students: Required—TOEFL (minimum score 79 iBT), IELTS (minimum score 6), PTE (minimum score 54). Electronic applications accepted.

The University of North Carolina at Greensboro, Graduate School, School of Education, Department of Teacher Education and Higher Education, Program in Curriculum and Teaching, Greensboro, NC 27412-5001. Offers higher education (PhD); teacher education and development (PhD). *Accreditation:* NCATE. *Degree requirements:* For doctorate, comprehensive exam, thesis/dissertation. *Entrance requirements:* For doctorate, GRE General Test. Additional exam requirements/recommendations for international students: Required—TOEFL. Electronic applications accepted.

The University of North Carolina Wilmington, Watson College of Education, Department of Educational Leadership, Wilmington, NC 28403-3297. Offers curriculum, instruction and supervision (M Ed); educational leadership and administration (Ed D), including curriculum and instruction; higher education (M Ed); school administration (MSA), including school administration. *Program availability:* Part-time, 100% online. *Degree requirements:* For master's, thesis or culminating project, e-Portfolio (for school administration); for doctorate, comprehensive exam, thesis/dissertation. *Entrance requirements:* For master's, GRE General Test, MAT, minimum B average in undergraduate work, 3 letters of recommendation, education statement of interest essay, autobiographical statement, NC Class A teacher licensure in related field, minimum of 3 years' teaching experience; for doctorate, education statement of interest essay, master's degree in education field, 3 years of leadership experience. Additional exam requirements/recommendations for international students: Required—TOEFL (minimum score 550 paper-based; 79 iBT), IELTS (minimum score 6.5). Electronic applications accepted.

University of Northern Colorado, Graduate School, College of Education and Behavioral Sciences, Department of Leadership, Policy and Development: Higher Education and P-12 Education, Program in Higher Education and Student Affairs Leadership, Greeley, CO 80639. Offers MA, PhD. *Program availability:* Part-time. *Entrance requirements:* For doctorate, GRE General Test, transcripts, 3 letters of recommendation. Electronic applications accepted.

University of Northern Iowa, Graduate College, College of Education, Department of Educational Leadership and Postsecondary Education, MA Program in Postsecondary Education: Student Affairs, Cedar Falls, IA 50614. Offers MA. *Degree requirements:* For master's, comprehensive exam, thesis or alternative. *Entrance requirements:* For master's, minimum GPA of 3.0. Additional exam requirements/recommendations for international students: Required—TOEFL (minimum score 500 paper-based; 61 iBT). Electronic applications accepted.

University of North Georgia, Doctor of Education Program in Higher Education Leadership and Practice, Dahlonega, GA 30597. Offers Ed D. *Program availability:* Part-time, evening/weekend, online only, 100% online. *Degree requirements:* For doctorate, thesis/dissertation. *Entrance requirements:* Additional exam requirements/recommendations for international students: Required—TOEFL (minimum score 550 paper-based; 79 iBT), IELTS (minimum score 6.5). Electronic applications accepted. *Expenses:* Contact institution.

University of North Texas, Toulouse Graduate School, Denton, TX 76203-5459. Offers accounting (MS); applied anthropology (MA, MS); applied behavior analysis (Certificate); applied geography (MA); applied technology and performance improvement (M Ed, MS); art education (MA); art history (MA); arts leadership (Certificate); audiology (Au D); behavior analysis (MS); behavioral science (PhD); biochemistry and molecular biology (MS); biology (MA, MS); biomedical engineering (MS); business analysis (MS); chemistry (MS); clinical health psychology (PhD); communication studies (MA, MS); computer engineering (MS); computer science (MS); counseling (M Ed, MS), including clinical mental health counseling (MS), college and university counseling, elementary school counseling, secondary school counseling; creative writing (MA); criminal justice (MS); curriculum and instruction (M Ed); decision sciences (MBA); design (MA, MFA), including fashion design (MFA), innovation studies, interior design (MFA); early childhood studies (MS); economics (MS); educational leadership (M Ed, Ed D); educational psychology (MS, PhD), including family studies (MS), gifted and talented (MS), human development (MS), learning and cognition (MS), research, measurement and evaluation (MS); electrical engineering (MS); emergency management (MPA); engineering technology (MS); English (MA); English as a second language (MA); environmental science (MS); finance (MBA, MS); financial management (MPA); French (MA); health services management (MBA); higher education (M Ed, Ed D); history (MA, MS); hospitality management (MS); human resources management (MPA); information science (MS); information systems (PhD); information technologies (MBA); interdisciplinary studies (MA, MS); international studies (MA); international sustainable tourism (MS); jazz studies (MM); journalism (MA, MJ, Graduate Certificate), including interactive and virtual digital communication (Graduate Certificate), narrative journalism (Graduate Certificate), public relations (Graduate Certificate); kinesiology (MS); linguistics (MA); local government management (MPA); logistics (PhD); logistics and supply chain management (MBA); long-term care, senior housing, and aging services (MA); management (PhD); marketing (MBA); mathematics (MA, MS); mechanical and energy engineering (MS, PhD); music (MA), including ethnomusicology, music theory, musicology, performance; music composition (PhD); music education (MM Ed, PhD); nonprofit management (MPA); operations and supply chain management (MBA); performance (MM, DMA); philosophy (MA); political science (MA); professional and technical communication (MA); radio, television and film (MA, MFA); rehabilitation counseling (Certificate); sociology (MA); Spanish (MA); special education (M Ed); speech-language pathology (MA); strategic management (MBA); studio art (MFA); teaching (M Ed); MBA/MS. *Program availability:* Part-time, evening/weekend, online learning. Terminal master's awarded for partial completion of doctoral program. *Degree requirements:* For master's, variable foreign language requirement,

comprehensive exam (for some programs), thesis (for some programs); for doctorate, variable foreign language requirement, comprehensive exam (for some programs), thesis/dissertation; for other advanced degree, variable foreign language requirement, comprehensive exam (for some programs). *Entrance requirements:* For master's and doctorate, GRE, GMAT. Additional exam requirements/recommendations for international students: Required—TOEFL (minimum score 550 paper-based; 79 iBT). Electronic applications accepted.

University of Oklahoma, Jeannine Rainbolt College of Education, Department of Educational Leadership and Policy Studies, Norman, OK 73019. Offers adult and higher education (M Ed, PhD), including adult and higher education; educational administration, curriculum and supervision (M Ed, Ed D, PhD); educational studies (M Ed, PhD). *Accreditation:* NCATE. *Program availability:* Part-time, evening/weekend, blended/hybrid learning. Terminal master's awarded for partial completion of doctoral program. *Degree requirements:* For master's, comprehensive exam, thesis (for some programs); for doctorate, comprehensive exam, thesis/dissertation. *Entrance requirements:* Additional exam requirements/recommendations for international students: Required—TOEFL (minimum score 79 iBT) or IELTS (minimum score 6.5). Electronic applications accepted. *Expenses:* Tuition, state resident: full-time $5683.20; part-time $236.80 per credit hour. Tuition, nonresident: full-time $20,342; part-time $847.60 per credit hour. *International tuition:* $20,342.40 full-time. *Required fees:* $2894.20; $110.05 per credit hour. $126.50 per semester. Tuition and fees vary according to course load and program. *Faculty research:* Improvement science, leadership and ethics, education and social policy, gender and equity, collegiate athletics.

University of Pennsylvania, Graduate School of Education, Division of Higher Education, Executive Doctorate Program in Higher Education Management, Philadelphia, PA 19104. Offers Ed D. *Program availability:* Evening/weekend. *Students:* 52 full-time (25 women); includes 19 minority (8 Black or African American, non-Hispanic/Latino; 6 Asian, non-Hispanic/Latino; 5 Hispanic/Latino). Average age 44. 75 applicants, 36% accepted, 25 enrolled. In 2018, 21 doctorates awarded. *Entrance requirements:* For doctorate, bachelor's degree. Additional exam requirements/recommendations for international students: Required—TOEFL, IELTS. *Application deadline:* For summer admission, 3/1 priority date for domestic and international students. Application fee: $80. Electronic applications accepted. *Faculty research:* Access, choice, and equity in higher education, college finance and affordability, academic governance and leadership. *Unit head:* Eric Kaplan, Director, 215-573-9404. *Application contact:* Jessica Lundeen, Program Coordinator, 215-573-0588, E-mail: mlundeen@upenn.edu.
Website: http://www2.gse.upenn.edu/execdoc/

University of Pennsylvania, Graduate School of Education, Division of Higher Education, Program in Higher Education, Philadelphia, PA 19104. Offers MS Ed, Ed D, PhD. *Program availability:* Part-time. *Students:* 54 full-time (32 women), 44 part-time (31 women); includes 48 minority (24 Black or African American, non-Hispanic/Latino; 9 Asian, non-Hispanic/Latino; 10 Hispanic/Latino; 5 Two or more races, non-Hispanic/Latino), 4 international. Average age 30. 259 applicants, 61% accepted, 71 enrolled. In 2018, 53 master's, 12 doctorates awarded. Application fee: $80.

University of Phoenix–Bay Area Campus, College of Education, San Jose, CA 95134-1805. Offers administration and supervision (MA Ed); adult education and training (MA Ed); early childhood education (MA Ed); education (Ed S); educational leadership (Ed D); elementary teacher education (MA Ed); higher education administration (PhD); secondary teacher education (MA Ed); special education (MA Ed); teacher leadership (MA Ed). *Program availability:* Evening/weekend, online learning. *Degree requirements:* For master's, thesis (for some programs). *Entrance requirements:* For master's, minimum undergraduate GPA of 2.5, 3 years of work experience. Additional exam requirements/recommendations for international students: Required—TOEFL (minimum score 550 paper-based; 79 iBT). Electronic applications accepted.

University of Phoenix–Online Campus, School of Advanced Studies, Phoenix, AZ 85034-7209. Offers business administration (DBA); education (Ed S); educational leadership (Ed D), including curriculum and instruction, education technology, educational leadership; health administration (DHA); higher education administration (PhD); industrial/organizational psychology (PhD); nursing (PhD); organizational leadership (DM), including information systems and technology, organizational leadership. *Program availability:* Evening/weekend, online learning. *Degree requirements:* For doctorate, thesis/dissertation. *Entrance requirements:* Additional exam requirements/recommendations for international students: Required—TOEFL, TOEIC (Test of English as an International Communication), Berlitz Online English Proficiency Exam, PTE, or IELTS. Electronic applications accepted. *Expenses:* Contact institution.

University of Pittsburgh, School of Education, Department of Administrative and Policy Studies, Program in Higher Education Management, Pittsburgh, PA 15260. Offers M Ed, Ed D, PhD. *Program availability:* Part-time, evening/weekend. *Degree requirements:* For master's, thesis; for doctorate, thesis/dissertation. *Entrance requirements:* For doctorate, GRE General Test. Additional exam requirements/recommendations for international students: Required—TOEFL (minimum score 80 iBT). Electronic applications accepted.

University of Puerto Rico–Mayagüez, Graduate Studies, College of Arts and Sciences, Department of Mathematical Sciences, Mayagüez, PR 00681-9000. Offers applied mathematics (MS); pre-college math education (MS); pure mathematics (MS); scientific computing (MS); statistics (MS). *Program availability:* Part-time. *Degree requirements:* For master's, one foreign language, comprehensive exam, thesis. *Entrance requirements:* For master's, undergraduate degree in mathematics or its equivalent. Electronic applications accepted. *Faculty research:* Automata theory, linear algebra, logic.

University of Rochester, Margaret Warner Graduate School of Education and Human Development, Doctoral Programs in Education, Rochester, NY 14627. Offers counseling (Ed D); educational administration (Ed D); educational policy and theory (PhD); higher education (PhD); human development in educational context (PhD); teaching, curriculum, and change (PhD). *Expenses: Tuition:* Full-time $52,974; part-time $1654 per credit hour. *Required fees:* $612. One-time fee: $30 part-time. Tuition and fees vary according to campus/location and program.

University of Rochester, Margaret Warner Graduate School of Education and Human Development, Master's Program in Higher Education, Rochester, NY 14627. Offers higher education (MS); higher education student affairs (MS). *Expenses: Tuition:* Full-time $52,974; part-time $1654 per credit hour. *Required fees:* $612. One-time fee: $30 part-time. Tuition and fees vary according to campus/location and program.

University of San Diego, School of Leadership and Education Sciences, Department of Leadership Studies, San Diego, CA 92110-2492. Offers higher education leadership (MA); leadership studies (MA, PhD, Certificate); nonprofit leadership and management (MA). *Program availability:* Part-time, evening/weekend. *Faculty:* 8 full-time (3 women), 24 part-time/adjunct (11 women). *Students:* 46 full-time (28 women), 225 part-time (147 women); includes 124 minority (19 Black or African American, non-Hispanic/Latino; 25 Asian, non-Hispanic/Latino; 66 Hispanic/Latino; 14 Two or more races, non-Hispanic/

Latino), 17 international. Average age 34. 299 applicants, 67% accepted, 105 enrolled. In 2018, 93 master's, 17 doctorates awarded. *Degree requirements:* For master's, thesis (for some programs), international experience; for doctorate, comprehensive exam, thesis/dissertation, international experience. *Entrance requirements:* For master's, GRE (recommended with GPA less than 3.25); for doctorate, GRE (less than 5 years old) strongly encouraged, master's degree, minimum GPA of 3.5 (graduate coursework), resume. Additional exam requirements/recommendations for international students: Required—TOEFL (minimum score 580 paper-based; 83 iBT), TWE. Application fee: $45. Electronic applications accepted. *Financial support:* In 2018–19, 190 students received support. Career-related internships or fieldwork, Federal Work-Study, institutionally sponsored loans, unspecified assistantships, and stipends available. Support available to part-time students. Financial award application deadline: 4/1; financial award applicants required to submit FAFSA. *Faculty research:* Higher education administration policy and relations, organizational leadership, nonprofits and philanthropy, student affairs leadership. *Unit head:* Dr. Lea Hubbard, Graduate Program Director, 619-260-7818, E-mail: lhubbard@sandiego.edu. *Application contact:* Erika Garwood, Associate Director of Graduate Admissions, 619-260-4524, Fax: 619-260-4158, E-mail: grads@sandiego.edu.
Website: https://www.sandiego.edu/soles/leadership-studies/

University of South Carolina, The Graduate School, College of Education, Department of Educational Leadership and Policies, Program in Higher Education and Student Affairs, Columbia, SC 29208. Offers M Ed. *Accreditation:* NCATE. *Program availability:* Part-time. *Degree requirements:* For master's, comprehensive exam, thesis (for some programs). *Entrance requirements:* For master's, GRE General Test or MAT, letters of reference. Electronic applications accepted. *Faculty research:* Minorities in higher education, community college transfer problem, federal role in educational research.

University of South Dakota, Graduate School, School of Education, Division of Educational Leadership, Vermillion, SD 57069. Offers educational administration (MA, Ed D, Ed S), including adult and higher education (MA, Ed D), curriculum director, director of special education (Ed D, Ed S), preK-12 principal, school district superintendent (Ed D, Ed S). *Accreditation:* NCATE. *Program availability:* Part-time, evening/weekend, 100% online, blended/hybrid learning. *Degree requirements:* For master's and Ed S, comprehensive exam, thesis or alternative; for doctorate, comprehensive exam, thesis/dissertation. *Entrance requirements:* For master's, GRE General Test, MAT, minimum GPA of 2.7; for doctorate, minimum GPA of 2.7. Additional exam requirements/recommendations for international students: Required—TOEFL (minimum score 550 paper-based; 79 iBT). Electronic applications accepted.

University of Southern California, Graduate School, Rossier School of Education, Doctor of Education Programs, Los Angeles, CA 90089. Offers educational psychology (Ed D); higher education administration (Ed D); K-12 leadership in urban school settings (Ed D); teacher education in multicultural societies (Ed D). *Program availability:* Part-time, evening/weekend. *Degree requirements:* For doctorate, thesis/dissertation. *Entrance requirements:* For doctorate, GRE. Additional exam requirements/recommendations for international students: Required—TOEFL (minimum score 100 iBT). Electronic applications accepted. *Faculty research:* Data-driven decision-making in K-12 schools and districts; examination of college and university leadership and management in U. S. and Asia; studies in facilitating student learning; organizational change and the role of leaders; leadership, diversity, learning and accountability.

University of Southern California, Graduate School, Rossier School of Education, Doctor of Philosophy in Education Programs, Los Angeles, CA 90089. Offers educational psychology (PhD); higher education administration and policy (PhD); K-12 policy and practice (PhD). *Degree requirements:* For doctorate, thesis/dissertation, 63 units; qualifying exam; dissertation proposal and defense. *Entrance requirements:* For doctorate, GRE. Additional exam requirements/recommendations for international students: Required—TOEFL (minimum score 100 iBT). Electronic applications accepted. *Faculty research:* Diversity in higher education, organizational change, educational psychology, policy and politics of educational reform, economics of education and education policy.

University of Southern Maine, College of Management and Human Service, School of Education and Human Development, Program in Adult Education, Portland, ME 04103. Offers adult and higher education (MS); adult learning (CAS). *Accreditation:* TEAC. *Program availability:* Part-time, evening/weekend, online learning. *Degree requirements:* For master's and CAS, thesis or alternative. *Entrance requirements:* For master's, interview; for CAS, master's degree. Additional exam requirements/recommendations for international students: Required—TOEFL (minimum score 550 paper-based; 79 iBT). Electronic applications accepted. *Faculty research:* Older learners, lifelong learning institutes, teaching and learning in later age.

University of Southern Mississippi, College of Education and Human Sciences, Department of Educational Research and Administration, Hattiesburg, MS 39406-0001. Offers educational administration (M Ed, Ed D, PhD, Ed S); educational administration and supervision (M Ed); educational studies and research (MS); higher education (Ed D); higher education administration (PhD); higher education: student affairs (M Ed); research, evaluation, statistics, assessment (PhD). *Degree requirements:* For master's and Ed S, comprehensive exam, thesis (for some programs); for doctorate, comprehensive exam, thesis/dissertation. *Entrance requirements:* For master's and doctorate, GRE General Test, minimum GPA of 2.75. Additional exam requirements/ recommendations for international students: Required—TOEFL.

University of South Florida, College of Education, Department of Leadership, Counseling, Adult, Career and Higher Education, Tampa, FL 33620-9951. Offers adult education (MA, Ed D, PhD, Ed S); career and technical education (MA); career and workforce education (PhD); higher education/community college teaching (MA, Ed D, PhD); vocational education (Ed S). *Faculty:* 19 full-time (11 women). *Students:* 107 full-time (81 women), 275 part-time (185 women); includes 143 minority (67 Black or African American, non-Hispanic/Latino; 2 American Indian or Alaska Native, non-Hispanic/Latino; 10 Asian, non-Hispanic/Latino; 56 Hispanic/Latino; 8 Two or more races, non-Hispanic/Latino), 14 international. Average age 36. 188 applicants, 54% accepted, 73 enrolled. In 2018, 51 master's, 8 doctorates, 3 other advanced degrees awarded. *Entrance requirements:* For master's, GRE may be required, goals statement; letters of recommendation; proof of educational or professional experience; prerequisites, if needed; for doctorate, GRE may be required, letters of recommendation; masters degree in appropriate field; optional interview; evidence of professional experience; personal statement. Additional exam requirements/recommendations for international students: Required—TOEFL. Application fee: $30. *Expenses:* Tuition, state resident: full-time $6350. Tuition, nonresident: full-time $19,048. International tuition: $19,048 full-time. *Required fees:* $2079. *Financial support:* In 2018–19, 19 students received support. *Total annual research expenditures:* $40,520. *Unit head:* Dr. Judith Ponticell, Chair, 813-974-4897, Fax: 813-974-5423, E-mail: jponticell@usf.edu. *Application contact:* Dr. Judith Ponticell, Chair, 813-974-4897, Fax: 813-974-5423, E-mail: jponticell@usf.edu.
Website: http://www.coedu.usf.edu/main/departments/ache/ache.html

University of South Florida, Innovative Education, Tampa, FL 33620-9951. Offers adult, career and higher education (Graduate Certificate), including college teaching,

leadership in developing human resources, leadership in higher education; Africana studies (Graduate Certificate), including diasporas and health disparities, genocide and human rights; aging studies (Graduate Certificate), including gerontology; art research (Graduate Certificate), including museum studies; business foundations (Graduate Certificate); chemical and biomedical engineering (Graduate Certificate), including materials science and engineering, water, health and sustainability; child and family studies (Graduate Certificate), including positive behavior support; civil and industrial engineering (Graduate Certificate), including transportation systems analysis; community and family health (Graduate Certificate), including maternal and child health, social marketing and public health, violence and injury: prevention and intervention, women's health; criminology (Graduate Certificate), including criminal justice administration; data science for public administration (Graduate Certificate); digital humanities (Graduate Certificate); educational measurement and research (Graduate Certificate), including evaluation; English (Graduate Certificate), including comparative literary studies, creative writing, professional and technical communication; entrepreneurship (Graduate Certificate); environmental health (Graduate Certificate), including safety management; epidemiology and biostatistics (Graduate Certificate), including applied biostatistics, biostatistics, concepts and tools of epidemiology, epidemiology, epidemiology of infectious diseases; geography, environment and planning (Graduate Certificate), including community development, environmental policy and management, geographical information systems; geology (Graduate Certificate), including hydrogeology; global health (Graduate Certificate), including disaster management, global health and Latin American and Caribbean studies, global health practice, humanitarian assistance, infection control; government and international affairs (Graduate Certificate), including Cuban studies, globalization studies; health policy and management (Graduate Certificate), including health management and leadership, public health policy and programs; hearing specialist: early intervention (Graduate Certificate); industrial and management systems engineering (Graduate Certificate), including systems engineering, technology management; information studies (Graduate Certificate), including school library media specialist; information systems/decision sciences (Graduate Certificate), including analytics and business intelligence; instructional technology (Graduate Certificate), including distance education, Florida digital/virtual educator, instructional design, multimedia design, Web design; internal medicine, bioethics and medical humanities (Graduate Certificate), including biomedical ethics; Latin American and Caribbean studies (Graduate Certificate); leadership for coastal resiliency planning (Graduate Certificate); mass communications (Graduate Certificate), including multimedia journalism; mathematics and statistics (Graduate Certificate), including mathematics; medicine (Graduate Certificate), including aging and neuroscience, bioinformatics, biotechnology, brain fitness and memory management, clinical investigation, hand and upper limb rehabilitation, health informatics, health sciences, integrative weight management, intellectual property, medicine and gender, metabolic and nutritional medicine, metabolic cardiology, pharmacy sciences; national and competitive intelligence (Graduate Certificate); nursing (Graduate Certificate), including simulation based academic fellowship in advanced pain management; psychological and social foundations (Graduate Certificate), including career counseling, college teaching, diversity in education, mental health counseling, school counseling; public affairs (Graduate Certificate), including nonprofit management, public management, research administration; public health (Graduate Certificate), including assessing chemical toxicity and public health risks, health equity, pharmacoepidemiology, public health generalist, toxicology, translational research in adolescent behavioral health; public health practices (Graduate Certificate), including planning for healthy communities; rehabilitation and mental health counseling (Graduate Certificate), including integrative mental health care, marriage and family therapy, rehabilitation technology; secondary education (Graduate Certificate), including ESOL, foreign language education: culture and content, foreign language education: professional; social work (Graduate Certificate), including geriatric social work/clinical gerontology; special education (Graduate Certificate), including autism spectrum disorder, disabilities education: severe/profound; world languages (Graduate Certificate), including teaching English as a second language (TESL) or foreign language. *Expenses:* Tuition, state resident: full-time $6350. Tuition, nonresident: full-time $19,048. International tuition: $19,048 full-time. *Required fees:* $2079. *Unit head:* Dr. Cynthia DeLuca, Associate Vice President and Assistant Vice Provost, 813-974-3077, Fax: 813-974-7061, E-mail: deluca@usf.edu. *Application contact:* Owen Hooper, Director, Summer and Alternative Calendar Programs, 813-974-6917, E-mail: hooper@usf.edu.
Website: http://www.usf.edu/innovative-education/

The University of Texas at Arlington, Graduate School, College of Education, Department of Educational Leadership and Policy Studies, Arlington, TX 76019. Offers educational leadership (PhD); higher education (M Ed); principal certification (M Ed). *Program availability:* Part-time, evening/weekend, online learning. *Degree requirements:* For master's, 2 field-based practica; for doctorate, comprehensive exam, thesis/dissertation, 2 research-based practica. *Entrance requirements:* For master's, GRE, 3 references, minimum undergraduate GPA of 3.0 in last 60 hours of course work; for doctorate, GRE, resume, statement of intent, 3 reference forms, applicable master's degree. *Faculty research:* Lived realities of students of color in K-16 contexts, K-16 faculty, K-16 policy and law, K-16 student access, K-16 student success.

The University of Texas at San Antonio, College of Education and Human Development, Department of Educational Leadership and Policy Studies, San Antonio, TX 78249-0617. Offers educational leadership (Ed D); educational leadership and policy studies (M Ed), including educational leadership, higher education administration. *Program availability:* Part-time. *Degree requirements:* For master's, comprehensive exam, thesis or alternative; for doctorate, comprehensive exam, thesis/dissertation. *Entrance requirements:* For master's, transcripts, statement of purpose, resume or curriculum vitae; for doctorate, GRE General Test, minimum GPA of 3.5 in a master's program, resume, three letters of recommendation, statement of purpose. Additional exam requirements/recommendations for international students: Required—TOEFL (minimum score 550 paper-based; 79 iBT), IELTS (minimum score 6.5). Electronic applications accepted. *Faculty research:* Urban and international school leadership, student success, college access, higher education policy, multiculturalism, minority student achievement.

The University of Toledo, College of Graduate Studies, College of Social Justice and Human Service, Department of School Psychology, Higher Education and Counselor Education, Toledo, OH 43606-3390. Offers counselor education (MA, PhD); higher education (ME, PhD, Certificate); school psychology (MA, Ed S). *Program availability:* Part-time. *Degree requirements:* For master's, comprehensive exam, thesis or alternative; for doctorate, comprehensive exam, thesis/dissertation; for other advanced degree, thesis optional. *Entrance requirements:* For master's, doctorate, and other advanced degree, minimum cumulative GPA of 2.7 for all previous academic work, letters of recommendation. Additional exam requirements/recommendations for international students: Required—TOEFL (minimum score 550 paper-based; 80 iBT). Electronic applications accepted.

University of Utah, Graduate School, College of Education, Department of Educational Leadership and Policy, Salt Lake City, UT 84084. Offers educational leadership and policy (Ed D, PhD), including higher education administration (Ed D), K-12 (Ed D); K-12

school administration (M Ed); k-12 teacher leadership (M Ed); student affairs (M Ed); MPA/PhD. *Program availability:* Part-time, evening/weekend. *Faculty:* 10 full-time (8 women), 2 part-time/adjunct (both women). *Students:* 51 full-time (35 women), 184 part-time (127 women); includes 65 minority (14 Black or African American, non-Hispanic/Latino; 3 American Indian or Alaska Native, non-Hispanic/Latino; 10 Asian, non-Hispanic/Latino; 31 Hispanic/Latino; 3 Native Hawaiian or other Pacific Islander, non-Hispanic/Latino; 4 Two or more races, non-Hispanic/Latino), 1 international. Average age 35. 181 applicants, 69% accepted, 90 enrolled. In 2018, 68 master's, 5 doctorates awarded. *Degree requirements:* For master's, comprehensive exam (for some programs), internship, capstone; for doctorate, thesis/dissertation, qualifying exam. *Entrance requirements:* For master's, minimum undergraduate GPA of 3.0, valid bachelor's degree, 3 years' teaching or leadership experience, Level 1 or 2 UT educator's license (for K-12 programs only); for doctorate, GRE General Test (taken with five years of applying), minimum undergraduate GPA of 3.0, valid master's degree. Additional exam requirements/recommendations for international students: Required—TOEFL (minimum score 550 paper-based). *Application deadline:* For fall admission, 1/15 priority date for domestic and international students; for winter admission, 2/1 for domestic and international students; for spring admission, 11/1 priority date for domestic and international students; for summer admission, 3/1 priority date for domestic and international students. Applications are processed on a rolling basis. Application fee: $55 ($65 for international students). Electronic applications accepted. *Expenses: Tuition, area resident:* Full-time $7190.66; part-time $2112.48 per year. Tuition, state resident: full-time $7190.66. Tuition, nonresident: full-time $25,195. *Required fees:* $558; $555.04 per unit. Tuition and fees vary according to course level, course load, degree level, program and student level. *Financial support:* In 2018–19, 12 students received support, including 2 fellowships with full tuition reimbursements available (averaging $15,900 per year), 4 research assistantships with full tuition reimbursements available (averaging $15,900 per year), 3 teaching assistantships with full tuition reimbursements available (averaging $15,900 per year); career-related internships or fieldwork, scholarships/grants, health care benefits, and unspecified assistantships also available. Support available to part-time students. Financial award application deadline: 3/1; financial award applicants required to submit FAFSA. *Faculty research:* Education accountability, college student diversity, K-12 educational administration and school leadership, student affairs, higher education. *Unit head:* Dr. Yongmei Ni, Chair, 801-587-9298, Fax: 801-585-6756, E-mail: yongmei.ni@utah.edu. *Application contact:* Marilynn S. Howard, Administrative Officer, 801-581-6714, Fax: 801-585-6756, E-mail: marilynn.howard@utah.edu.
Website: http://elp.utah.edu/

University of Vermont, Graduate College, College of Education and Social Services, Program in Special Education, Grades K-12, Burlington, VT 05405. Offers M Ed. *Accreditation:* NCATE. *Degree requirements:* For master's, thesis or alternative. *Entrance requirements:* For master's, license (or eligible for licensure). Additional exam requirements/recommendations for international students: Required—TOEFL (minimum score 550 paper-based, 90 iBT) or IELTS (6.5). Electronic applications accepted.

University of Virginia, Curry School of Education, Department of Leadership, Foundations and Policy, Program in Higher Education, Charlottesville, VA 22903. Offers higher education (Ed S); student affairs practice (M Ed). *Entrance requirements:* For master's, doctorate, and Ed S, GRE General Test, 2 letters of recommendation. Additional exam requirements/recommendations for international students: Required—TOEFL (minimum score 600 paper-based; 90 iBT), IELTS (minimum score 7). Electronic applications accepted.

University of Virginia, Curry School of Education, Program in Education, Charlottesville, VA 22903. Offers administration and supervision (PhD); applied developmental science (PhD); counselor education (PhD); curriculum and instruction (PhD); early childhood special education (MT); education evaluation (PhD); educational psychology (PhD); educational research (PhD); elementary education (MT); English education (MT, PhD); foreign language education (MT); higher education (PhD); instructional technology (PhD); kinesiology (MT, PhD); math education (PhD); reading education (PhD); research, statistics and evaluation (PhD); school psychology (PhD); science education (PhD); social studies education (MT, PhD); special education (PhD); world languages education (MT). *Degree requirements:* For master's, comprehensive exam (for some programs), field project; for doctorate, comprehensive exam, thesis/dissertation. *Entrance requirements:* For doctorate, GRE General Test. Additional exam requirements/recommendations for international students: Required—TOEFL (minimum score 600 paper-based; 90 iBT), IELTS (minimum score 7). Electronic applications accepted.

University of Washington, Graduate School, College of Education, Seattle, WA 98195. Offers curriculum and instruction (M Ed, Ed D, PhD), including educational technology, general curriculum (Ed D, PhD), language, literacy, and culture, mathematics education, multicultural education, reading and language arts education (Ed D), science education, social studies education, teaching and curriculum (M Ed); educational leadership and policy studies (M Ed, Ed D, PhD), including administration (Ed D), educational policy, organization, and leadership (M Ed, PhD), higher education, leadership for learning (Ed D), social and cultural foundations of education (M Ed, PhD); educational psychology (M Ed, PhD), including educational psychology (PhD), human development and cognition (M Ed), learning sciences, measurement, statistics and research design (M Ed), school psychology (M Ed); instructional leadership (M Ed); intercollegiate athletic leadership (M Ed); special education (M Ed, Ed D, PhD), including early childhood special education (M Ed), emotional and behavioral disabilities (M Ed), learning disabilities (M Ed), low-incidence disabilities (M Ed), severe disabilities (M Ed), special education (Ed D, PhD); teacher education (MIT). *Accreditation:* APA. *Program availability:* Part-time, evening/weekend. *Degree requirements:* For master's, thesis optional; for doctorate, thesis/dissertation. *Entrance requirements:* For master's and doctorate, GRE General Test, minimum GPA of 3.0. Additional exam requirements/recommendations for international students: Required—TOEFL. Electronic applications accepted. *Faculty research:* School restructuring/effective schools, special education interventions, literacy and writing, technology, school partnerships, teacher preparation.

The University of West Alabama, School of Graduate Studies, College of Education, Program in Student Affairs in Higher Education, Livingston, AL 35470. Offers M Ed. *Program availability:* Part-time, evening/weekend, 100% online. *Faculty:* 1 (woman) full-time, 3 part-time/adjunct (2 women). *Students:* 104 full-time (80 women), 3 part-time (2 women); includes 62 minority (58 Black or African American, non-Hispanic/Latino; 2 Hispanic/Latino; 2 Two or more races, non-Hispanic/Latino), 2 international. Average age 32. 34 applicants, 97% accepted, 32 enrolled. In 2018, 16 master's awarded. *Degree requirements:* For master's, comprehensive exam. *Entrance requirements:* For master's, GRE, minimum GPA of 2.75, criminal background check. Additional exam requirements/recommendations for international students: Required—TOEFL (minimum score 500 paper-based; 61 iBT). *Application deadline:* Applications are processed on a rolling basis. Application fee: $40. Electronic applications accepted. *Expenses: Tuition, area resident:* Full-time $9100. Tuition, state resident: full-time $9100. Tuition, nonresident: full-time $19,200. *Required fees:* $1890; $130. *Financial support:* Teaching assistantships, Federal Work-Study, scholarships/grants, and unspecified assistantships available. Support available to part-time students. Financial award application deadline: 3/1; financial award applicants required to submit FAFSA. *Unit head:* Dr. Jodie Winship, Chair of College of Education, 205-652-5415, E-mail: jwinship@uwa.edu. *Application contact:* Dr. B. J. Kimbrough, Dean of Graduate Studies, 205-652-3647, Fax: 205-652-3670, E-mail: bkimbrough@uwa.edu.

University of Wisconsin–La Crosse, College of Liberal Studies, Department of Student Affairs Administration, La Crosse, WI 54601-3742. Offers MS Ed, Ed D. *Program availability:* Part-time, evening/weekend, 100% online, blended/hybrid learning. *Degree requirements:* For master's, comprehensive exam (for some programs), thesis optional, electronic portfolio, applied research project. *Entrance requirements:* For master's, bachelor's degree from accredited institution, minimum GPA of 2.85, resume, essay, 2 references. Additional exam requirements/recommendations for international students: Required—TOEFL (minimum score 550 paper-based; 79 iBT). Electronic applications accepted. *Faculty research:* Persistence; developing positive social justice behaviors in heterosexual white college men; equity; diversity; inclusion in higher education at both interpersonal and institutional levels; expanding student affairs administration research and practice beyond the traditional, majority, or dominant student experience; underrepresented students at historically white institutions; college men and masculinities; Latina/o college student leadership; ethnic cultural centers at HWIs.

University of Wisconsin–Madison, Graduate School, School of Education, Department of Educational Leadership and Policy Analysis, Madison, WI 53706-1380. Offers administration (Certificate); educational policy (MS, PhD); global higher education (MS). *Degree requirements:* For doctorate, thesis/dissertation. *Entrance requirements:* For master's and doctorate, GRE General Test. Electronic applications accepted.

University of Wisconsin–Milwaukee, Graduate School, School of Education, Department of Administrative Leadership, Milwaukee, WI 53201-0413. Offers administrative leadership (MS), including adult and continuing education leadership, educational administration and supervision, higher education administration; support services for online students in higher education (Graduate Certificate); teaching and learning in higher education (Graduate Certificate). *Program availability:* Part-time. *Students:* 12 full-time (10 women), 163 part-time (124 women); includes 51 minority (19 Black or African American, non-Hispanic/Latino; 5 American Indian or Alaska Native, non-Hispanic/Latino; 4 Asian, non-Hispanic/Latino; 3 Hispanic/Latino; 20 Two or more races, non-Hispanic/Latino). Average age 35. 98 applicants, 70% accepted, 43 enrolled. In 2018, 43 master's, 3 other advanced degrees awarded. *Degree requirements:* For master's, comprehensive exam, thesis or alternative. *Entrance requirements:* For master's, GRE General Test. Additional exam requirements/recommendations for international students: Required—TOEFL (minimum score 550 paper-based; 79 iBT), IELTS (minimum score 6.5). *Application deadline:* For fall admission, 1/1 priority date for domestic students; for spring admission, 9/1 for domestic students. Application fee: $56 ($96 for international students). Electronic applications accepted. *Financial support:* In 2018–19, 2 fellowships were awarded; research assistantships, teaching assistantships, career-related internships or fieldwork, health care benefits, unspecified assistantships, and project assistantships also available. Support available to part-time students. Financial award application deadline: 4/15; financial award applicants required to submit FAFSA. *Unit head:* Alan Shoho, Dean, 414-229-4181, E-mail: shoho@uwm.edu. *Application contact:* General Information Contact, 414-229-4721, E-mail: soeinfo@uwm.edu.
Website: http://uwm.edu/education/academics/administrative-leadership-department/

Upper Iowa University, Master of Education Program, Fayette, IA 52142-1857. Offers early childhood (M Ed); English as a second language (M Ed); higher education (M Ed); instructional strategist (M Ed); reading (M Ed); teacher leadership (M Ed).

Wagner College, Division of Graduate Studies, Education Department, Staten Island, NY 10301-4495. Offers childhood education/students with disabilities (MS Ed), including childhood education; early childhood education/students with disabilities (birth-grade 2) (MS Ed); higher education and learning organizations leadership (MA); secondary education/students with disabilities (MS Ed), including secondary education 7-12. *Accreditation:* NCATE. *Program availability:* Part-time, evening/weekend. *Degree requirements:* For master's, thesis (for some programs). *Entrance requirements:* For master's, GRE, minimum GPA of 3.0. Additional exam requirements/recommendations for international students: Required—TOEFL (minimum score 550 paper-based; 79 iBT), IELTS (minimum score 6.5). Electronic applications accepted. *Faculty research:* School-community partnerships, civic engagement, educational accountability, micro-aggression and bullying, cross-cultural pedagogy with students and families.

Walden University, Graduate Programs, Richard W. Riley College of Education and Leadership, Minneapolis, MN 55401. Offers adult education (Post-Master's Certificate); adult learning (Graduate Certificate); college teaching and learning (Graduate Certificate); community college leadership (Ed D); curriculum, instruction and assessment (Ed D, Ed S, Graduate Certificate); developmental education (Graduate Certificate); early childhood administration, management, and leadership (Graduate Certificate); early childhood education (Ed D, Ed S); early childhood public policy and advocacy (Graduate Certificate); early childhood studies (MS), including administration, management and leadership, early childhood public policy and advocacy, teaching adults in the early childhood field, teaching and diversity in early childhood education; education (MS, PhD), including adolescent literacy and learning (MS), curriculum, instruction, and assessment (grades K-12) (MS), curriculum, instruction, assessment, and evaluation (PhD), early childhood leadership and advocacy (PhD), early childhood special education (PhD), educational leadership (MS), educational leadership and administration (principal preparation) (MS), educational technology and design (PhD), elementary reading and literacy (PreK-6) (MS), elementary reading and mathematics (grades K-6) (MS), global and comparative education (PhD), higher education leadership management and policy (PhD), integrating technology in the classroom (grades K-12) (MS), learning, instruction and innovation (PhD), mathematics (grades 5-8) (MS), mathematics (grades K-6) (MS), mathematics and science (grades K-8) (MS), organizational research, assessment, and evaluation (PhD), reading and literacy with a reading K-12 endorsement (MS), reading literacy assessment and evaluation (PhD), science (grades K-8) (MS), special education (non-licensure) (grades K-12) (MS), teacher leadership (grades K-12) (MS), teaching English language learners (grades K-12) (MS); educational administration and leadership (Ed D); educational leadership and administration (principal preparation) (Ed S); educational technology (Ed D, Ed S, Post Master's Certificate); elementary reading and literacy (Graduate Certificate); engaging culturally diverse learners (Graduate Certificate); enrollment management and institutional marketing (Graduate Certificate); higher education (MS), including adult learning, college teaching and learning, enrollment management and institutional marketing, global higher education, leadership for student success, online and distance learning; higher education and adult learning (Ed D); higher education leadership and management (Ed D); higher education leadership for student success (Graduate Certificate); instructional design and technology (MS, Postbaccalaureate Certificate), including general program (MS), online learning (MS), training and performance improvement (MS); integrating technology in the classroom (Graduate Certificate); mathematics 5-8 (Graduate Certificate); mathematics K-6 (Graduate Certificate); online teaching for adult educators (Graduate Certificate); reading, literacy, and assessment (Ed D, Ed S); science K-8 (Graduate Certificate); special education (Ed D, Ed S,

Graduate Certificate); special education (K-age 21) (MAT); teacher leadership (Graduate Certificate); teaching adults English as a second language (Graduate Certificate); teaching adults in the early childhood field (Graduate Certificate); teaching and diversity in early childhood education (Graduate Certificate); teaching English language learners (grades K-12) (Graduate Certificate); teaching K-12 students online (Graduate Certificate). *Accreditation:* NCATE. *Program availability:* Part-time, evening/weekend, online only, 100% online. *Degree requirements:* For doctorate, thesis/dissertation (for some programs), residency; for other advanced degree, residency (for some programs). *Entrance requirements:* For master's, bachelor's degree or higher; minimum GPA of 2.5; official transcripts; goal statement (for some programs); access to computer and Internet; for doctorate, master's degree or higher; three years of related professional or academic experience (preferred); minimum GPA of 3.0; goal statement and current resume (for select programs); official transcripts; access to computer and Internet; for other advanced degree, relevant work experience; access to computer and Internet. Additional exam requirements/recommendations for international students: Required—TOEFL (minimum score 550 paper-based, 79 iBT), IELTS (minimum score 6.5), Michigan English Language Assessment Battery (minimum score 82), or PTE (minimum score 53). Electronic applications accepted.

Walden University, Graduate Programs, School of Social Work and Human Services, Minneapolis, MN 55401. Offers addictions and social work (DSW); advanced clinical practice (MSW); clinical expertise (DSW); criminal justice (DSW); disaster, crisis, and intervention (DSW); family studies and interventions (DSW); human and social services (PhD), including advanced research, community and social services, community intervention and leadership, conflict management, criminal justice, disaster crisis and intervention, family studies and intervention, gerontology, global social services, higher education, human services and nonprofit administration, mental health facilitation; medical social work (DSW); military social work (MSW); policy practice (DSW); social work (PhD), including addictions and social work, clinical expertise, criminal justice, disaster, crisis and intervention, family studies and interventions, medical social work, policy practice, social work administration; social work administration (DSW); social work in healthcare (MSW); social work with children and families (MSW). *Accreditation:* CSWE. *Program availability:* Part-time, evening/weekend, online only, 100% online. *Degree requirements:* For master's, residency (for some programs); for doctorate, thesis/dissertation, residency. *Entrance requirements:* For master's, bachelor's degree or higher; minimum GPA of 2.5; official transcripts; goal statement (for some programs); access to computer and Internet; for doctorate, master's degree or higher; three years of related professional or academic experience (preferred); minimum GPA of 3.0; goal statement and current resume (for select programs); official transcripts; access to computer and Internet. Additional exam requirements/recommendations for international students: Required—TOEFL (minimum score 550 paper-based, 79 iBT), IELTS (minimum score 6.5), Michigan English Language Assessment Battery (minimum score 82), or PTE (minimum score 53). Electronic applications accepted.

Walsh University, Graduate Programs, Program in Counseling and Human Development, North Canton, OH 44720-3396. Offers clinical mental health counseling (MA); school counseling (MA); student affairs in higher education (MA). *Accreditation:* ACA. *Program availability:* Part-time, evening/weekend. *Degree requirements:* For master's, comprehensive exam, internship, practicum. *Entrance requirements:* For master's, GRE (minimum score of 145 verbal and 146 quantitative) or MAT (minimum score of 397), interview, minimum GPA of 3.0, writing sample, reference forms, notarized affidavit of good moral conduct. Additional exam requirements/recommendations for international students: Required—TOEFL (minimum score 500 paper-based; 61 iBT). Electronic applications accepted. Application fee is waived when completed online. *Expenses:* Contact institution. *Faculty research:* Supervision of clinical mental health, clinical mental health practice/issues, clinical mental health skills development, advocacy, teaching and professional development, career development, refugee development in US, supervision in student affairs, offender treatment, domestic violence issues, alcohol and drug treatment issues, Professional identity and advocacy in school counseling, Efficacy in counseling clinic.

Wayland Baptist University, Graduate Programs, Program in Education, Plainview, TX 79072-6998. Offers education administration (M Ed); education diagnostics (M Ed); education literacy (M Ed); elementary certification (M Ed); English (M Ed); English as a second language (M Ed); higher education administration (M Ed); human resources (M Ed); instructional leadership (M Ed); instructional technology (M Ed); leadership training and development (M Ed); science education (M Ed); secondary certification (M Ed); social studies (M Ed); special education (M Ed); sports administration and management (M Ed). *Program availability:* Part-time, evening/weekend, 100% online. *Degree requirements:* For master's, comprehensive exam, capstone course. *Entrance requirements:* For master's, GRE, GMAT or MAT. Additional exam requirements/recommendations for international students: Required—TOEFL (minimum score 500 paper-based; 61 iBT). Electronic applications accepted.

West Chester University of Pennsylvania, College of Education and Social Work, Department of Counselor Education, West Chester, PA 19383. Offers clinical mental health counseling (MS); counseling (Certificate); higher education counseling (Post Master's Certificate); higher education counseling/student affairs (MS, Certificate); school counseling (M Ed). *Accreditation:* ACA; NCATE. *Program availability:* Part-time, evening/weekend. *Degree requirements:* For master's, comprehensive exam. *Entrance requirements:* For master's, minimum GPA of 3.0, three letters of reference. Additional exam requirements/recommendations for international students: Required—TOEFL or IELTS. Electronic applications accepted. *Faculty research:* Bullying in the schools, adolescent cognitive development, counseling pedagogy, motivational interviewing.

Western Illinois University, School of Graduate Studies, College of Education and Human Services, Department of Educational Studies, Program in College Student Personnel, Macomb, IL 61455-1390. Offers college student personnel (MS), including higher education leadership, student affairs. *Accreditation:* NCATE. *Program availability:* Part-time. *Students:* 54 full-time (37 women), 12 part-time (8 women); includes 21 minority (5 Black or African American, non-Hispanic/Latino; 11 Hispanic/Latino; 5 Two or more races, non-Hispanic/Latino), 2 international. Average age 25. 56 applicants, 77% accepted, 22 enrolled. In 2018, 46 master's awarded. *Entrance requirements:* For master's, interview. Additional exam requirements/recommendations for international students: Required—TOEFL (minimum score 550 paper-based; 80 iBT). *Application deadline:* For fall admission, 1/5 priority date for domestic students. Application fee: $30. Electronic applications accepted. *Financial support:* Unspecified assistantships available. Financial award applicants required to submit FAFSA. *Unit head:* Dr. Tracy Davis, Coordinator, 309-298-1183. *Application contact:* Dr. Mark Mossman, Associate Provost and Director of Graduate Studies, 309-298-1806, Fax: 309-298-2345, E-mail: grad-office@wiu.edu.
Website: http://wiu.edu/csp/

Western Kentucky University, Graduate School, College of Education and Behavioral Sciences, Department of Counseling and Student Affairs, Bowling Green, KY 42101. Offers counseling (MA Ed), including marriage and family therapy, mental health counseling; school counseling (P-12) (MA Ed); student affairs in higher education (MA Ed). *Accreditation:* ACA; NCATE. *Program availability:* Part-time, evening/weekend. *Degree requirements:* For master's, comprehensive exam, thesis optional. *Entrance requirements:* For master's, GRE General Test. Additional exam requirements/recommendations for international students: Required—TOEFL (minimum score 555 paper-based; 79 iBT). *Faculty research:* Counselor education, research for residential workers.

Western Michigan University, Graduate College, College of Arts and Sciences, Department of Mathematics, Kalamazoo, MI 49008. Offers applied and computational mathematics (MS); mathematics education (MA, PhD), including collegiate mathematics education (PhD). *Degree requirements:* For doctorate, one foreign language, thesis/dissertation.

Western Washington University, Graduate School, Woodring College of Education, Department of Educational Leadership, Program in Continuing and College Education, Bellingham, WA 98225-5996. Offers M Ed. *Program availability:* Part-time, evening/weekend, online learning. *Degree requirements:* For master's, comprehensive exam, thesis optional. *Entrance requirements:* For master's, GRE General Test or MAT, minimum GPA of 3.0 in last 60 semester hours or last 90 quarter hours. Additional exam requirements/recommendations for international students: Required—TOEFL (minimum score 567 paper-based). Electronic applications accepted. *Faculty research:* Transfer of learning, postsecondary faculty development, action research as professional development, literacy education in community colleges, adult education in the Middle East, distance learning tools for graduate students.

West Virginia University, College of Education and Human Services, Morgantown, WV 26506. Offers audiology (Au D); autism spectrum disorder (MA); clinical rehabilitation and mental health counseling (MS); communication science and disorders (PhD); counseling (MA); counseling psychology (PhD); curriculum and instruction (Ed D); early childhood education (MA); early intervention/ early childhood special education (MA); education (PhD); educational leadership (MA); educational leadership/ public school administration (Ed D); educational leadership/public school administration (MA); educational psychology (MA, Ed D); elementary education (MA); gifted education (MA); higher education administration (MA, Ed D); higher education curriculum and teaching (MA); institutional design and technology (MA); instructional design and technology (Ed D); literacy education (MA); secondary education (MA); secondary education/English (MA); special education (Ed D); speech pathology (MS). *Accreditation:* ASHA; NCATE. *Program availability:* Part-time, evening/weekend, online learning. *Students:* 392 full-time (325 women), 337 part-time (285 women); includes 44 minority (16 Black or African American, non-Hispanic/Latino; 16 Hispanic/Latino; 12 Two or more races, non-Hispanic/Latino), 11 international. In 2018, 303 master's, 6 doctorates awarded. *Degree requirements:* For master's, content exams; for doctorate, comprehensive exam, thesis/dissertation. *Entrance requirements:* Additional exam requirements/recommendations for international students: Required—TOEFL (minimum score 500 paper-based; 61 iBT). *Application deadline:* For fall admission, 8/1 for domestic students; for spring admission, 1/1 for domestic students; for summer admission, 5/1 for domestic students. Application fee: $60. Electronic applications accepted. *Financial support:* Fellowships, research assistantships, teaching assistantships, career-related internships or fieldwork, Federal Work-Study, institutionally sponsored loans, health care benefits, tuition waivers (full and partial), and administrative assistantships available. Financial award applicants required to submit FAFSA. *Faculty research:* Internet training and integration for teachers, rural education, teacher preparation, organization of schools, evaluation of personnel. *Unit head:* Dr. Tracy L. Morris, Interim Dean, 304-293-0816, Fax: 304-293-7565, E-mail: Tracy.Morris@mail.wvu.edu. *Application contact:* Dr. Melissa Luna, Associate Dean for Research, 304-293-2174, Fax: 304-293-3802, E-mail: Melissa.Luna@mail.wvu.edu.
Website: http://cehs.wvu.edu/

William Paterson University of New Jersey, College of Education, Wayne, NJ 07470-8420. Offers curriculum and learning (M Ed); early childhood education (Certificate); educational leadership (M Ed); educational media specialist (Certificate); elementary education (MAT, Certificate); elementary education subject area (Certificate); higher education administration (MA); learning disabilities consultant (Certificate); literacy (M Ed); middle level education (M Ed); middle school education subject area (Certificate); professional counseling (M Ed); reading specialist (Certificate); school library media specialist (Certificate); school principal (Certificate); school supervisor (Certificate); secondary education (MAT); special education (M Ed); teacher of students with disabilities (Certificate). *Accreditation:* NCATE. *Program availability:* Part-time, evening/weekend. *Students:* Average age 35. 347 applicants, 87% accepted, 226 enrolled. In 2018, 136 master's awarded. *Degree requirements:* For master's, comprehensive exam, thesis (for some programs), exit interview (for some programs); practicum/internship; minimum GPA of 3.0 (for some programs); exit portfolio (for some programs). *Entrance requirements:* For master's, GRE/MAT, minimum GPA of 2.75; teaching certificate; essay; interview; 2 letters of recommendation; personal statement. Additional exam requirements/recommendations for international students: Required—TOEFL (minimum score 550 paper-based; 79 iBT), IELTS (minimum score 6). *Application deadline:* For fall admission, 6/1 for domestic students, 3/1 for international students; for spring admission, 11/1 for domestic students, 10/1 for international students. Applications are processed on a rolling basis. Application fee: $50. Electronic applications accepted. *Expenses: Tuition, area resident:* Full-time $14,714; part-time $727 per credit. Tuition, state resident: full-time $14,714; part-time $727 per credit. Tuition, nonresident: full-time $22,952; part-time $727 per credit. *International tuition:* $22,952 full-time. *Required fees:* $4 per semester. Tuition and fees vary according to course load, degree level and program. *Financial support:* In 2018–19, 8,416 students received support. Career-related internships or fieldwork, Federal Work-Study, scholarships/grants, and unspecified assistantships available. Support available to part-time students. Financial award application deadline: 3/15; financial award applicants required to submit FAFSA. *Faculty research:* Code switching and creative writing, language instruction, teacher evaluation, preschools, history of educational theories. *Total annual research expenditures:* $311,226. *Unit head:* Dr. Dorothy Feola, Dean, 973-720-2138, Fax: 973-720-3647, E-mail: feolad@wpunj.edu. *Application contact:* Liana Fornarotto, Director of Education Enrollment and Certification, 973-720-2206, Fax: 973-720-2989, E-mail: fornarottol@wpunj.edu.
Website: http://www.wpunj.edu/coe

Wilmington University, College of Education, New Castle, DE 19720-6491. Offers applied technology in education (M Ed); career and technical education (M Ed); educational leadership (Ed D); elementary and secondary school counseling (M Ed); elementary studies (M Ed); ESOL literacy (M Ed); higher education leadership (Ed D); instruction: gifted and talented (M Ed); instruction: teacher of reading (M Ed); instruction: teaching and learning (M Ed); organizational leadership (Ed D); school leadership (M Ed); secondary education (MAT); special education (M Ed). *Accreditation:* NCATE. *Program availability:* Part-time, evening/weekend. *Entrance requirements:* For master's, 2 letters of recommendation, interview. Additional exam requirements/recommendations for international students: Required—TOEFL (minimum score 500 paper-based). Electronic applications accepted.

Middle School Education

Alaska Pacific University, Graduate Programs, Education Department, Program in Teaching, Anchorage, AK 99508-4672. Offers teaching (K-8) (MAT). *Degree requirements:* For master's, research project. *Entrance requirements:* For master's, GRE or MAT, PRAXIS, minimum GPA of 3.0.

Albany State University, College of Education, Albany, GA 31705-2717. Offers early childhood education (M Ed); educational leadership (Ed S); health and physical education (M Ed); middle grades education (M Ed); school counseling (M Ed); special education (M Ed). *Accreditation:* NCATE. *Program availability:* Part-time, evening/weekend, online learning. *Degree requirements:* For master's, comprehensive exam, internship, GACE Content Exam. *Entrance requirements:* For master's, GRE or MAT. Electronic applications accepted. *Faculty research:* GACE preparation, STEM (science, technology, engineering, and mathematics), technology education, special education, professional teacher development, health implications liberation philosophy, NET-Q, learning community, disabled or at-risk students.

American International College, School of Education, Springfield, MA 01109-3189. Offers early childhood education (M Ed, CAGS); education (MA, Ed D), including counseling psychology (MA), educational leadership and supervision (Ed D), professional counseling and supervision (Ed D), teaching and learning (Ed D); elementary education (M Ed, CAGS); middle education/secondary education (M Ed, CAGS); moderate disabilities (M Ed, CAGS); reading specialist (M Ed, CAGS); school adjustment counseling (MAEP, CAGS); school guidance counseling (MAEP, CAGS); school leadership (M Ed, CAGS). *Program availability:* Evening/weekend. *Degree requirements:* For master's and CAGS, practicum/culminating experience. *Entrance requirements:* For master's, Communication and Literacy portion of the Massachusetts Tests for Education Licensure, graduate of accredited four-year college with minimum B-average in undergraduate course work; for CAGS, M Ed or master's degree in field related to licensure from accredited institution. Electronic applications accepted. *Expenses:* Contact institution.

Appalachian State University, Cratis D. Williams School of Graduate Studies, Department of Curriculum and Instruction, Boone, NC 28608. Offers curriculum specialist (MA); educational media (MA); elementary education (MA); middle grades education (MA), including language arts, mathematics, science, social studies. *Accreditation:* NCATE. *Program availability:* Part-time, evening/weekend, online learning. *Degree requirements:* For master's, comprehensive exam, thesis or alternative. *Entrance requirements:* For master's, GRE General Test or MAT, 3 letters of recommendation. Additional exam requirements/recommendations for international students: Required—TOEFL (minimum score 570 paper-based; 79 iBT), IELTS (minimum score 6.5). Electronic applications accepted. *Expenses: Tuition, area resident:* Full-time $4839; part-time $237 per credit hour. Tuition, state resident: full-time $4839; part-time $237 per credit hour. Tuition, nonresident: full-time $18,271; part-time $895.50 per credit hour. *Faculty research:* Media literacy, elementary teaching, curriculum development, online learning environments.

Arkansas State University, Graduate School, College of Education and Behavioral Science, School of Teacher Education and Leadership, State University, AR 72467. Offers community college administration (SCCT); curriculum and instruction (MSE); early childhood education (MSE); early childhood services (MS); educational leadership (MSE, Ed D, Ed S); educational theory and practice (MSE); middle level education (MAT, MSE); reading (MSE, Ed S); special education - gifted, talented, and creative (MSE); special education - instructional specialist grades 4-12 (MSE); special education - instructional specialist grades P-4 (MSE); special education, K-12 (MSE). *Accreditation:* NCATE. *Program availability:* Part-time, online learning. *Degree requirements:* For master's, comprehensive exam, thesis or alternative; for doctorate, comprehensive exam, thesis/dissertation; for other advanced degree, comprehensive exam. *Entrance requirements:* For master's, GRE General Test or MAT, appropriate bachelor's degree, official transcripts, immunization records, letters of reference, interview; for doctorate, GRE General Test or MAT, interview, master's degree, letters of reference, official transcript, personal statement, writing sample, immunization records; for other advanced degree, GRE General Test or MAT, interview, master's degree, official transcript, immunization records, letters of reference, 3 years of teaching experience, teaching license. Additional exam requirements/recommendations for international students: Required—TOEFL (minimum score 550 paper-based; 79 iBT), IELTS (minimum score 6), PTE (minimum score 56). Electronic applications accepted.

Augusta University, College of Education, Program in Curriculum and Instruction, Augusta, GA 30912. Offers curriculum and instruction (Ed S); elementary education (MAT); foreign language education (MAT); instruction (M Ed); middle grades education (MAT); music education (MAT); secondary education (MAT); special education (MAT). *Degree requirements:* For master's, thesis, portfolio. *Entrance requirements:* For master's, GRE, MAT, minimum GPA of 2.5.

Avila University, School of Education, Kansas City, MO 64145-1698. Offers advanced classroom management (MA); elementary education (Teaching Certificate); English language learners (Advanced Certificate); middle school (Teaching Certificate); physical education K-12 (Teaching Certificate); secondary education (Teaching Certificate). *Program availability:* Part-time, evening/weekend, online learning. *Faculty:* 6 full-time (5 women), 9 part-time/adjunct (8 women). *Students:* 83 full-time (71 women), 84 part-time (69 women); includes 13 minority (6 Black or African American, non-Hispanic/Latino; 2 Asian, non-Hispanic/Latino; 4 Hispanic/Latino; 1 Two or more races, non-Hispanic/Latino), 2 international. Average age 40. 92 applicants, 62% accepted, 40 enrolled. In 2018, 21 master's awarded. *Entrance requirements:* For master's, minimum GPA of 3.0, writing sample, recommendation, interview; for other advanced degree, foreign language. Additional exam requirements/recommendations for international students: Required—TOEFL (minimum score 580 paper-based; 92 iBT). *Application deadline:* Applications are processed on a rolling basis. Electronic applications accepted. *Expenses:* Contact institution. *Financial support:* In 2018–19, 12 students received support. Unspecified assistantships available. Financial award applicants required to submit FAFSA. *Unit head:* Dr. Stacy Keith, Director of Graduate Education, 816-501-2446, Fax: 816-501-2915, E-mail: stacy.keith@avila.edu. *Application contact:* Cory Roup, Graduate Education Enrollment and Academic Advisor, 816-501-2464, E-mail: cory.roup@avila.edu.
Website: https://www.avila.edu/academics/graduate-studies/grad-education

Ball State University, Graduate School, College of Sciences and Humanities, Department of Mathematical Sciences, Muncie, IN 47306. Offers actuarial science (MA); elementary mathematics teacher leadership (Certificate); mathematics (MA, MS), including mathematics; mathematics education (MA), including mathematics education; middle school mathematics education (Certificate); post-secondary foundational mathematics teaching (MA, Certificate); statistical modeling (Certificate); statistics (MA, MS), including statistics. *Program availability:* Part-time, 100% online, blended/hybrid learning. *Entrance requirements:* For master's, minimum baccalaureate GPA of 2.75 or 3.0 in latter half of baccalaureate. Additional exam requirements/recommendations for international students: Required—TOEFL (minimum score 550 paper-based; 79 iBT), IELTS (minimum score 6.5). Electronic applications accepted. *Faculty research:* Differential equations.

Bellarmine University, Annsley Frazier Thornton School of Education, Louisville, KY 40205. Offers education and district leadership (Ed D); education and social change (PhD); elementary education (MA Ed, MAT); leadership in higher education (PhD); middle school education (MA Ed, MAT); principalship (Ed S); reading and writing (MA Ed); secondary education (MAT); teacher leadership (MA Ed). *Accreditation:* NCATE. *Program availability:* Part-time, evening/weekend. *Faculty:* 14 full-time (7 women), 17 part-time/adjunct (11 women). *Students:* 27 full-time (19 women), 205 part-time (156 women); includes 74 minority (53 Black or African American, non-Hispanic/Latino; 6 Asian, non-Hispanic/Latino; 7 Hispanic/Latino; 8 Two or more races, non-Hispanic/Latino). Average age 34. 155 applicants, 71% accepted, 95 enrolled. In 2018, 69 master's, 10 doctorates, 30 other advanced degrees awarded. *Degree requirements:* For master's, comprehensive exam (for some programs), thesis (for some programs); for doctorate, comprehensive exam (for some programs), thesis/dissertation; for Ed S, comprehensive exam (for some programs). *Entrance requirements:* For master's, GRE, baccalaureate degree from accredited institution; minimum cumulative GPA of 2.75; recommendations from employers, supervisors, or professors attesting to applicant's potential as graduate student; statement of intent to pursue graduate degree; for doctorate, GRE, minimum GPA of 3.5 in all graduate coursework; baccalaureate and master's degrees in education or fields directly relevant to education; three letters of recommendation; two essays (no more than 1,000 words each); resume or curriculum vitae; interview; for Ed S, master's degree in education; valid teaching certificate; three years of experience in teaching; three recommendations; minimum GPA of 3.0 in all graduate work; interview; essays; personal goal statement. Additional exam requirements/recommendations for international students: Required—TOEFL (minimum score 80 iBT), IELTS (minimum score 6), TOEFL (minimum score 550 paper-based, 68 iBT), IELTS (minimum score 6), or Michigan English Language Assessment Battery. *Application deadline:* For fall admission, 8/1 priority date for domestic and international students; for spring admission, 12/1 priority date for domestic and international students; for summer admission, 4/10 priority date for domestic and international students. Applications are processed on a rolling basis. Application fee: $40. Electronic applications accepted. *Expenses:* Doctor of Education: $855 per credit hour; Educational Specialist: $410 per credit hour; Master of Arts in Education: $410 per credit hour; Master of Arts in Teaching: $665 per credit hour; Master of Arts in Teaching, undergraduate content courses: $410 per credit hour; Master of Education in Higher Education Leadership and Social Justice: $665 per credit hour; Ph.D., Social Change: $855 per credit hour; Ph.D., Leadership in Higher Education: $855 per credit hour; Rank I Programs: $410 per credit hour. *Financial support:* Scholarships/grants available. Financial award applicants required to submit FAFSA. *Faculty research:* Literacy, service-learning, dispositions, educational technology, special education. *Unit head:* Dr. Elizabeth Dinkins, Dean, 502-272-7958, Fax: 502-272-8189, E-mail: edinkins@bellarmine.edu. *Application contact:* Sarah Schuble, Assistant Director of Graduate Student Enrollment, 502-272-8271, Fax: 502-272-8002, E-mail: sschuble@bellarmine.edu.
Website: http://www.bellarmine.edu/education/graduate

Berry College, Graduate Programs, Graduate Programs in Education, Program in Middle-Grades Education and Reading, Mount Berry, GA 30149. Offers middle grades education (MAT); middle-grades education (M Ed); reading (M Ed). *Accreditation:* NCATE. *Program availability:* Part-time. *Degree requirements:* For master's, thesis, portfolio, oral exams. *Entrance requirements:* For master's, GRE General Test or MAT, minimum GPA of 2.5. Additional exam requirements/recommendations for international students: Required—TOEFL (minimum score 550 paper-based). *Application deadline:* For fall admission, 7/26 for domestic students, 5/1 for international students; for spring admission, 12/1 for domestic students, 10/1 for international students. Applications are processed on a rolling basis. Application fee: $25 ($30 for international students). Electronic applications accepted. *Expenses:* Contact institution. *Financial support:* Research assistantships with full tuition reimbursements, scholarships/grants, tuition waivers (partial), and unspecified assistantships available. Support available to part-time students. Financial award application deadline: 3/1; financial award applicants required to submit FAFSA. *Unit head:* Dr. Jacqueline McDowell, Dean, 706-236-1717, Fax: 706-238-5827, E-mail: jmcdowell@berry.edu. *Application contact:* Admissions, 706-236-2215, Fax: 706-290-2178, E-mail: admissions@berry.edu.

Bloomsburg University of Pennsylvania, School of Graduate Studies, College of Education, Department of Teaching and Learning, Program in Middle Level Education Grades 4-8, Bloomsburg, PA 17815-1301. Offers language arts (M Ed); math (M Ed); science (M Ed); social studies (M Ed). *Accreditation:* NCATE. *Degree requirements:* For master's, thesis optional, practicum, student teaching. *Entrance requirements:* For master's, MAT, GRE, or PRAXIS, minimum QPA of 3.0, teaching certificate, U.S. citizenship, related undergraduate coursework, professional liability insurance, recent TB test. Additional exam requirements/recommendations for international students: Required—TOEFL (minimum score 550 paper-based), IELTS. Electronic applications accepted.

Brenau University, Sydney O. Smith Graduate School, College of Education, Gainesville, GA 30501. Offers early childhood (Ed S); early childhood education (M Ed, MAT); middle grades (Ed S); middle grades education (M Ed, MAT); secondary education (MAT); special education (M Ed, MAT). *Accreditation:* NCATE. *Program availability:* Part-time, evening/weekend, online learning. *Degree requirements:* For master's, thesis optional, comprehensive exam or applied research project, effective portfolio; for Ed S, thesis, applied research project. *Entrance requirements:* For master's, GRE, MAT, interview, minimum GPA of 3.0, 3 references, writing samples; for Ed S, GRE, MAT, master's degree, minimum GPA of 3.0, writing sample, letters of reference. Additional exam requirements/recommendations for international students: Required—TOEFL (minimum score 500 paper-based; 61 iBT); Recommended—IELTS (minimum score 5). Electronic applications accepted. *Expenses:* Contact institution.

Brooklyn College of the City University of New York, School of Education, Program in Middle Childhood Mathematics Education, Brooklyn, NY 11210-2889. Offers MS Ed. *Entrance requirements:* For master's, LAST, 2 letters of recommendation, essay, resume. Additional exam requirements/recommendations for international students: Required—TOEFL (minimum score 500 paper-based; 61 iBT). Electronic applications accepted.

Brooklyn College of the City University of New York, School of Education, Program in Middle Childhood Science Education, Brooklyn, NY 11210-2889. Offers biology (MA);

chemistry (MA); earth science (MA); general science (MA); physics (MA). *Program availability:* Part-time, evening/weekend. *Entrance requirements:* For master's, LAST, interview, previous course work in education and mathematics, resume, 2 letters of recommendation, essay. Additional exam requirements/recommendations for international students: Required—TOEFL (minimum score 500 paper-based; 61 iBT). Electronic applications accepted. *Faculty research:* Geometric thinking, mastery of basic facts, problem-solving strategies, history of mathematics.

Brooklyn College of the City University of New York, School of Education, Program in Special Education, Brooklyn, NY 11210-2889. Offers autism spectrum disorders (AC); teacher of students with disabilities (MS Ed), including adolescence education, childhood education, early childhood education. *Program availability:* Part-time. *Entrance requirements:* For master's, LAST, interview; previous course work in education and psychology; minimum GPA of 3.0 in education, 2.8 overall; resume, 2 letters of recommendation; essay. Additional exam requirements/recommendations for international students: Required—TOEFL (minimum score 500 paper-based; 61 iBT). Electronic applications accepted. *Faculty research:* School reform, conflict resolution, curriculum for inclusive settings, urban issues in special education.

Cabrini University, Academic Affairs, Radnor, PA 19087. Offers accounting (M Acc); autism spectrum disorder (M Ed); biological sciences (MS), including civic leadership; criminology and criminal justice (MA); curriculum, instruction, and assessment (M Ed); educational leadership (M Ed, Ed D), including curriculum and instructional leadership (Ed D), preK-12 leadership (Ed D); English as a second language (M Ed); organizational leadership (DBA, PhD); preK to 4 (M Ed); reading specialist (M Ed); secondary education (M Ed), including biology, chemistry, English, English/communication, mathematics, social studies; special education grades 7-12 (M Ed); special education preK-8 (M Ed); teaching and learning (M Ed). *Program availability:* Part-time, evening/weekend. *Degree requirements:* For master's, comprehensive exam (for some programs), thesis (for some programs); for doctorate, comprehensive exam (for some programs), thesis/dissertation. *Entrance requirements:* For master's, professional resume, personal statement, two recommendations, official transcripts; for doctorate, official transcripts, minimum master's GPA of 3.0, two recommendations, interview with admissions committee. Additional exam requirements/recommendations for international students: Required—TOEFL (minimum score 80 iBT). Electronic applications accepted. Application fee is waived when completed online. *Expenses:* Contact institution.

California Lutheran University, Graduate Studies, Graduate School of Education, Thousand Oaks, CA 91360-2787. Offers counseling and guidance (MS), including college student personnel, counseling and guidance; educational leadership (MA, Ed D), including educational leadership (K-12) (Ed D), higher education leadership (Ed D); special education (MS); teacher leadership (M Ed); teaching (M Ed). *Accreditation:* NCATE. *Program availability:* Part-time, evening/weekend. *Degree requirements:* For master's, comprehensive exam or thesis; for doctorate, thesis/dissertation. *Entrance requirements:* For master's, GRE General Test, interview, minimum GPA of 3.0. Electronic applications accepted.

Campbell University, Graduate and Professional Programs, School of Education, Buies Creek, NC 27506. Offers elementary education (M Ed); interdisciplinary studies (M Ed); middle grades education (M Ed); physical education (M Ed); school administration (MSA); school counseling (M Ed); secondary education (M Ed). *Accreditation:* NCATE. *Program availability:* Part-time, evening/weekend. *Degree requirements:* For master's, comprehensive exam. *Entrance requirements:* For master's, GRE General Test, minimum GPA of 2.7. *Faculty research:* Spiritual values and wellness issues in counseling, stress and professional burnout among counselors, thinking strategies, leadership, adaptive technology.

Canisius College, Graduate Division, School of Education and Human Services, Department of Teacher Education, Buffalo, NY 14208-1098. Offers adolescence education (MS Ed); childhood education (MS Ed); general education (MS Ed); special education (MS), including adolescence special education, advanced special education, childhood education grade 1-6, childhood special education. *Program availability:* Part-time, evening/weekend, 100% online, blended/hybrid learning. *Faculty:* 10 full-time (all women), 16 part-time/adjunct (14 women). *Students:* 69 full-time (50 women), 23 part-time (16 women); includes 10 minority (4 Black or African American, non-Hispanic/Latino; 1 Asian, non-Hispanic/Latino; 4 Hispanic/Latino; 1 Two or more races, non-Hispanic/Latino), 3 international. Average age 26. 85 applicants, 75% accepted, 54 enrolled. In 2018, 32 master's awarded. *Degree requirements:* For master's, research project or thesis, project internship. *Entrance requirements:* For master's, GRE (if cumulative GPA less than 2.7), official transcripts, letters of recommendation. Additional exam requirements/recommendations for international students: Required—TOEFL (minimum score 550 paper-based, 79 iBT), IELTS (minimum score 6.5), or CAEL (minimum score 70). *Application deadline:* Applications are processed on a rolling basis. Application fee: $0. Electronic applications accepted. *Expenses: Tuition:* Part-time $820 per credit hour. *Required fees:* $25 per semester. One-time fee: $65 part-time. Tuition and fees vary according to program. *Financial support:* In 2018–19, 90 students received support. Career-related internships or fieldwork, Federal Work-Study, scholarships/grants, tuition waivers (partial), and unspecified assistantships available. Support available to part-time students. Financial award application deadline: 4/30; financial award applicants required to submit FAFSA. *Unit head:* Dr. Barbara A. Burns, CHAIR/PROFESSOR OF TEACHER EDUCATION, 716-888-3291, Fax: 716-888-2766, E-mail: burns1@canisius.edu. *Application contact:* Dr. Barbara A. Burns, CHAIR/PROFESSOR OF TEACHER EDUCATION, 716-888-3291, Fax: 716-888-2766, E-mail: burns1@canisius.edu.
Website: http://www.canisius.edu/academics/graduate/

Capella University, School of Education, Doctoral Programs in Education, Minneapolis, MN 55402. Offers curriculum and instruction (PhD); educational leadership and management (Ed D); instructional design for online learning (PhD); K-12 studies in education (PhD); leadership for higher education (PhD); leadership in educational administration (PhD); postsecondary and adult education (PhD); professional studies in education (PhD); reading and literacy (Ed D); special education leadership (PhD); training and performance improvement (PhD).

Capella University, School of Education, Master's Programs in Education, Minneapolis, MN 55402. Offers adult education (MS); curriculum and instruction (MS); early childhood education (MS); enrollment management (MS); higher education leadership and management (MS); instructional design for online learning (MS); integrative studies (MS); K-12 studies in education (MS); leadership in educational administration (MS); reading and literacy (MS); special education teaching (MS).

Chestnut Hill College, School of Graduate Studies, Department of Education, Program in Elementary/Middle Education, Philadelphia, PA 19118-2693. Offers M Ed. *Program availability:* Part-time, evening/weekend. *Degree requirements:* For master's, thesis optional. *Entrance requirements:* For master's, PRAXIS I or proof of teaching certification, letters of recommendation, writing sample, 6 graduate credits with minimum B grade if undergraduate GPA less than 3.0. Additional exam requirements/recommendations for international students: Required—TOEFL (minimum score 500 paper-based), IELTS (minimum score 6.0), or TWE (minimum score 22). Electronic applications accepted. *Expenses:* Contact institution. *Faculty research:* Inclusive education, cultural issues in education.

Chestnut Hill College, School of Graduate Studies, Department of Education, Program in Reading, Philadelphia, PA 19118-2693. Offers reading specialist (M Ed), including K-12, special education 7-12, special education PreK-8. *Program availability:* Part-time, evening/weekend. *Degree requirements:* For master's, thesis optional. *Entrance requirements:* Additional exam requirements/recommendations for international students: Required—TOEFL (minimum score 500 paper-based) or IELTS (minimum score 6). Electronic applications accepted. *Expenses:* Contact institution. *Faculty research:* Inclusive education, cultural issues in education.

Chicago State University, School of Graduate and Professional Studies, College of Education, Department of Reading, Elementary Education, Library Information and Media Studies, Program in Middle School Education, Chicago, IL 60628. Offers MAT.

The Citadel, The Military College of South Carolina, Citadel Graduate College, Zucker Family School of Education, Charleston, SC 29409. Offers elementary/secondary school administration and supervision (M Ed); elementary/secondary school counseling (M Ed); interdisciplinary STEM education (M Ed); literacy education (M Ed, Graduate Certificate); middle grades (MAT), including English, mathematics, science, social studies; physical education (grades K-12) (MAT); school superintendency (Ed S); secondary education (MAT), including biology, English, mathematics, social studies; student affairs (Graduate Certificate); student affairs and college counseling (M Ed). *Accreditation:* NCATE. *Program availability:* Part-time, evening/weekend, 100% online, blended/hybrid learning. *Degree requirements:* For master's, comprehensive exam (for some programs). *Entrance requirements:* For master's, GRE (minimum combined verbal and quantitative score of 290) or MAT (minimum score 396). Additional exam requirements/recommendations for international students: Required—TOEFL (minimum score 550 paper-based; 79 iBT). Electronic applications accepted. *Expenses:* Tuition, state resident: part-time $595 per credit hour. Tuition, nonresident: part-time $1020 per credit hour. *Required fees:* $90 per term.

City College of the City University of New York, Graduate School, School of Education, Department of Secondary Education, New York, NY 10031-9198. Offers adolescent mathematics education (MA, AC); English education (MA); middle school mathematics education (MS); science education (MA); social studies education (AC). *Accreditation:* NCATE. *Entrance requirements:* For master's, Liberal Arts and Sciences Test (LAST), Content Specialty Test (CST). Additional exam requirements/recommendations for international students: Required—TOEFL.

Clemson University, Graduate School, College of Education, Department of Teaching and Learning, Clemson, SC 29634. Offers curriculum and instruction (PhD); middle level education (MAT); secondary math and science (MAT); STEAM education (Certificate); teaching and learning (M Ed). *Program availability:* Part-time, evening/weekend, 100% online. *Faculty:* 16 full-time (13 women). *Students:* 40 full-time (36 women), 198 part-time (171 women); includes 32 minority (10 Black or African American, non-Hispanic/Latino; 1 American Indian or Alaska Native, non-Hispanic/Latino; 3 Asian, non-Hispanic/Latino; 12 Hispanic/Latino; 1 Native Hawaiian or other Pacific Islander, non-Hispanic/Latino; 5 Two or more races, non-Hispanic/Latino), 8 international. Average age 31. 257 applicants, 77% accepted, 163 enrolled. In 2018, 38 master's, 5 doctorates awarded. *Degree requirements:* For master's, comprehensive exam; for doctorate, comprehensive exam, thesis/dissertation. *Entrance requirements:* For master's, doctorate, and Certificate, GRE General Test, unofficial transcripts, letters of recommendation. Additional exam requirements/recommendations for international students: Required—TOEFL (minimum score 80 paper-based; 80 iBT); Recommended—IELTS (minimum score 6.5), TSE (minimum score 54). *Application deadline:* For fall admission, 4/15 for international students; for spring admission, 10/15 for international students. Applications are processed on a rolling basis. Application fee: $80 ($90 for international students). Electronic applications accepted. *Expenses:* $5198 per semester full-time resident, $10123 per semester full-time non-resident, $556 per credit hour part-time resident, $1109 per credit hour part-time non-resident, online $770 per credit hour, $4938 doctoral programs resident, $10405 doctoral programs non-resident, $1144 full-time graduate assistant, other fees may apply per session; MAT Programs: $5898 per semester full-time resident, $11623 per semester full-time non-resident, $724 per credit hour part-time resident, $1451 per credit hour part-time non-resident, online $955 per credit hour, $1144 full-time graduate assistant, other fees may apply per session. *Financial support:* In 2018–19, 8 students received support, including 9 fellowships with full and partial tuition reimbursements available (averaging $3,414 per year), 3 research assistantships with full and partial tuition reimbursements available (averaging $17,500 per year), 28 teaching assistantships with full and partial tuition reimbursements available (averaging $18,020 per year); career-related internships or fieldwork also available. *Faculty research:* STEAM education, inquiry-based instruction, cultural hegemony and mathematics, equity and ethics, teacher effectiveness. *Total annual research expenditures:* $1.3 million. *Unit head:* Dr. Jeff Marshall, Department Chair, 864-656-2059, E-mail: marsha9@clemson.edu. *Application contact:* Julie Jones, Student Services Manager, 864-656-5096, E-mail: jgambre@clemson.edu.
Website: http://www.clemson.edu/education/departments/teaching-learning/index.html

The College at Brockport, State University of New York, School of Education, Health, and Human Services, Department of Education and Human Development, Brockport, NY 14420-2997. Offers adolescence education (MS Ed), including adolescence biology education, adolescence chemistry education, adolescence English, adolescence mathematics, adolescence physics, adolescence physics education, adolescence social studies education; bilingual education (MS Ed, AGC); childhood curriculum specialist (MS Ed); inclusive generalist education (MS Ed, AGC, Advanced Certificate), including biology (MS Ed, AGC), chemistry (MS Ed), English (MS Ed, Advanced Certificate), mathematics (MS Ed, Advanced Certificate), science (MS Ed, Advanced Certificate), social studies (MS Ed, Advanced Certificate); literacy education B-12 (MS Ed). *Accreditation:* NCATE. *Faculty:* 12 full-time (7 women), 10 part-time/adjunct (6 women). *Students:* 60 full-time (39 women), 227 part-time (157 women); includes 9 minority (1 Asian, non-Hispanic/Latino; 8 Hispanic/Latino). 135 applicants, 71% accepted, 59 enrolled. In 2018, 107 master's, 13 AGCs awarded. *Degree requirements:* For master's, thesis or alternative. *Entrance requirements:* For master's, minimum GPA of 3.0, letters of recommendation, interview (for some programs); statement of objectives, current resume. Additional exam requirements/recommendations for international students: Required—TOEFL (minimum score 550 paper-based; 79 iBT), IELTS (minimum score 6.5). *Application deadline:* For fall admission, 3/15 priority date for domestic and international students; for spring admission, 10/15 priority date for domestic and international students; for summer admission, 3/15 priority date for domestic and international students. Application fee: $80. Electronic applications accepted. *Expenses:* Tuition, state resident: part-time $471 per credit. Tuition, nonresident: part-time $963 per credit. *Financial support:* In 2018–19, 1 fellowship with full tuition reimbursement (averaging $7,500 per year), 1 teaching assistantship with full tuition reimbursement (averaging $6,000 per year) were awarded; Federal Work-Study, scholarships/grants, and unspecified assistantships also available. Support available to part-time students. Financial award application deadline: 3/15; financial award applicants required to submit FAFSA. *Faculty research:* Educational assessment, literacy education, inclusive education, teacher preparation, qualitative

methodology. *Unit head:* Dr. Janka Szilagyi, Chairperson, 585-395-5945, Fax: 585-395-2172, E-mail: jszilagy@brockport.edu. *Application contact:* Buffie Edick, Graduate Program Director, 585-395-2326, Fax: 585-395-2172, E-mail: bedick@brockport.edu. Website: https://www.brockport.edu/academics/education_human_development/department.html

College of Mount Saint Vincent, School of Professional and Graduate Studies, Department of Teacher Education, Riverdale, NY 10471-1093. Offers instructional technology and global perspectives (Certificate); middle level education (Certificate); multicultural studies (Certificate); teaching English to speakers of other languages (MS Ed); urban and multicultural education (MS Ed). *Accreditation:* TEAC. *Program availability:* Part-time. *Degree requirements:* For master's, comprehensive exam. *Entrance requirements:* For master's, interview, New York teaching certificate. Additional exam requirements/recommendations for international students: Required—TOEFL.

College of Saint Elizabeth, Program in Education, Morristown, NJ 07960-6989. Offers assistive technology (Certificate); education (MA); ESL (Certificate); Holocaust/genocide education (Certificate); middle school science (Certificate); online teaching in the 21st century (Certificate); teaching (Certificate), including K-12, K-6, teacher of students with disabilities. *Program availability:* Part-time. *Degree requirements:* For master's and Certificate, thesis. *Entrance requirements:* For master's, certification. Additional exam requirements/recommendations for international students: Required—TOEFL (minimum score 550 paper-based; 79 iBT), IELTS (minimum score 6.5). Electronic applications accepted. Application fee is waived when completed online.

The College of Saint Rose, Graduate Studies, Thelma P. Lally School of Education, Teacher Education Programs, Albany, NY 12203-1419. Offers adolescence education (MS Ed, Advanced Certificate); adolescence education/special education (Advanced Certificate); childhood education (MS Ed); curriculum and instruction (MS Ed); early childhood education (MS Ed). *Students:* 49 full-time (39 women), 21 part-time (17 women); includes 3 minority (2 Black or African American, non-Hispanic/Latino; 1 Hispanic/Latino). Average age 27. 41 applicants, 66% accepted, 21 enrolled. In 2018, 48 master's, 1 Advanced Certificate awarded. *Entrance requirements:* For master's, minimum undergraduate GPA of 3.0. Additional exam requirements/recommendations for international students: Required—TOEFL (minimum score 550 paper-based; 80 iBT), IELTS (minimum score 6), PTE (minimum score 56). *Application deadline:* For fall admission, 4/1 priority date for domestic and international students; for spring admission, 10/15 priority date for domestic and international students; for summer admission, 3/15 priority date for domestic and international students. Applications are processed on a rolling basis. Application fee: $40. Electronic applications accepted. *Expenses: Tuition:* Full-time $14,382; part-time $799 per credit hour. *Required fees:* $924; $408 per credit. $286. *Financial support:* Career-related internships or fieldwork, scholarships/grants, tuition waivers (partial), and unspecified assistantships available. Support available to part-time students. Financial award application deadline: 4/15. *Unit head:* Dr. Drey Martone, Chair, 518-454-5262, E-mail: martoned@strose.edu. *Application contact:* Daniel Gallagher, Assistant Vice President for Graduate Recruitment and Enrollment, 518-485-3390, Fax: 518-458-5479, E-mail: grad@strose.edu. Website: https://www.strose.edu/academics/schools/school-of-education/

College of Staten Island of the City University of New York, Graduate Programs, School of Education, Program in Special Education, Staten Island, NY 10314-6600. Offers special education (MS Ed), including adolescence generalist: grades 7-12, grades 1-6. *Program availability:* Part-time, evening/weekend. *Students:* 130. 58 applicants, 71% accepted, 32 enrolled. In 2018, 42 master's awarded. *Degree requirements:* For master's, comprehensive exam, fieldwork; ten three-credit required courses and one elective for a total of 11 courses (33 credits) or 14 three-credit required courses and a three- to six-credit, field-based requirement for a total of 45-48 credits; research project. *Entrance requirements:* For master's, GRE General Test or an approved equivalent examination, BA/BS or 36 approved credits with a 3.0 GPA, 2 letters of recommendations, 1-2 page statement of experience; must have completed courses for NYS initial certificate in childhood education/early childhood education (Sequence 1); 6 credits each in English, history, math, and science, and 1 year of foreign language (Sequence 2). Additional exam requirements/recommendations for international students: Required—TOEFL (minimum score 550 paper-based; 79 iBT), IELTS (minimum score 6.5). *Application deadline:* For fall admission, 4/25 for domestic and international students; for spring admission, 11/25 for domestic and international students. Applications are processed on a rolling basis. Application fee: $75. Electronic applications accepted. *Expenses: Tuition, area resident:* Full-time $10,770; part-time $455 per credit. Tuition, state resident: full-time $10,770; part-time $455 per credit. Tuition, nonresident: full-time $19,920; part-time $830 per credit. *International tuition:* $19,920 full-time. *Required fees:* $559.20; $181.10 per semester. Tuition and fees vary according to program. *Faculty research:* Disabilities studies, social justice, arts-based research on disabilities, assessment of students with disabilities, technological pedagogical and content knowledge (TPACK) in special education teachers, juvenile justice. *Unit head:* Diane Brescia, 718-982-3877, E-mail: diane.brescia@csi.cuny.edu. *Application contact:* Sasha Spence, Associate Director for Graduate Admissions, 718-982-2019, Fax: 718-982-2500, E-mail: sasha.spence@csi.cuny.edu. Website: https://www.csi.cuny.edu/sites/default/files/pdf/admissions/grad/pdf/Education%20Fact%20Sheet.pdf

Columbus State University, Graduate Studies, College of Education and Health Professions, Department of Teacher Education, Columbus, GA 31907-5645. Offers curriculum and instruction in accomplished teaching (M Ed); early childhood education (M Ed, MAT, Ed S); middle grades education (M Ed, MAT, Ed S); secondary education (M Ed, MAT, Ed S), including biology (MAT), chemistry (MAT), earth and space science (MAT), English/language arts, general science (M Ed), history (MAT), mathematics, science (Ed S), social science (M Ed, Ed S); special education (M Ed, MAT, Ed S), including general curriculum (M Ed, MAT); teacher leadership (M Ed). *Accreditation:* NCATE. *Program availability:* Part-time, evening/weekend, 100% online, blended/hybrid learning. *Faculty:* 20 full-time (12 women), 20 part-time/adjunct (15 women). *Students:* 110 full-time (84 women), 143 part-time (115 women); includes 105 minority (96 Black or African American, non-Hispanic/Latino; 4 Hispanic/Latino; 5 Two or more races, non-Hispanic/Latino). Average age 33. 147 applicants, 56% accepted, 62 enrolled. In 2018, 112 master's, 11 other advanced degrees awarded. *Degree requirements:* For Ed S, thesis or alternative. *Entrance requirements:* For master's, GRE General Test, minimum undergraduate GPA of 2.75; for Ed S, GRE General Test, minimum undergraduate GPA of 2.75, graduate 3.0. Additional exam requirements/recommendations for international students: Required—TOEFL (minimum score 550 paper-based; 79 iBT). *Application deadline:* For fall admission, 6/30 for domestic students, 5/1 for international students; for spring admission, 11/1 for domestic and international students; for summer admission, 3/1 for domestic and international students. Applications are processed on a rolling basis. Application fee: $50. Electronic applications accepted. *Expenses: Tuition, area resident:* Full-time $4924; part-time $618 per credit hour. Tuition, state resident: full-time $4924; part-time $618 per credit hour. Tuition, nonresident: full-time $19,218; part-time $2403 per credit hour. *International tuition:* $19,218 full-time. *Required fees:* $1870; $802. Tuition and fees vary according to course load, degree level and program.

Financial support: In 2018–19, 29 students received support, including 7 research assistantships with partial tuition reimbursements available (averaging $3,000 per year); career-related internships or fieldwork, Federal Work-Study, institutionally sponsored loans, scholarships/grants, tuition waivers (partial), and unspecified assistantships also available. Support available to part-time students. Financial award application deadline: 5/1; financial award applicants required to submit FAFSA. *Unit head:* Dr. Jan Burcham, Department Chair, 706-507-8519, Fax: 706-568-3134, E-mail: burcham_jan@columbusstate.edu. *Application contact:* Catrina Smith-Edmond, Assistant Director for Graduate and Global Admission, 706-507-8824, Fax: 706-568-5091, E-mail: smithedmond_catrina@columbusstate.edu. Website: http://te.columbusstate.edu/

Converse College, Program in Middle Level Education, Spartanburg, SC 29302. Offers language arts/English (MAT); mathematics (MAT); middle level education (M Ed); science (MAT); social studies (MAT).

Daemen College, Education Programs, Amherst, NY 14226-3592. Offers adolescence education (MS); childhood education (MS); childhood special education (MS); childhood special-alternative certification (MS); early childhood special-alternative certification (MS). *Accreditation:* TEAC. *Program availability:* Part-time. *Faculty:* 16 full-time (12 women), 19 part-time/adjunct (14 women). *Students:* 233 full-time (210 women), 21 part-time (18 women); includes 4 minority (1 Black or African American, non-Hispanic/Latino; 3 Hispanic/Latino), 1 international. Average age 22. 76 applicants, 93% accepted, 68 enrolled. In 2018, 204 master's awarded. *Degree requirements:* For master's, comprehensive exam, A minimum grade of B earned in all courses, thereby resulting in a minimum cumulative grade point average of 3.00. *Entrance requirements:* For master's, Submit scores from taking the Graduate Record Exam (GRE) by no later than December 16 for fall applicants, no later than May 1 for spring applicants, bachelor's degree, GPA of 3.0 or above, resume, letter of intent, 2 letters of recommendation, interview with department chair. Additional exam requirements/recommendations for international students: Required—TOEFL (minimum score 77 paper-based), IELTS (minimum score 6.5). *Application deadline:* Applications are processed on a rolling basis. Application fee: $25. Electronic applications accepted. Application fee is waived when completed online. *Expenses: Tuition:* Part-time $977 per credit hour. *Required fees:* $125; $14 per credit hour. *Financial support:* Scholarships/grants and unspecified assistantships available. Support available to part-time students. Financial award applicants required to submit FAFSA. *Unit head:* Dr. Elizabeth Heilman, Department Chair, 716-839-8553, E-mail: eheilman@daemen.edu. *Application contact:* Megan Beardi, Senior Assistant Director of Graduate Admissions, 716-566-7861, Fax: 716-839-8229, E-mail: mbeardi@daemen.edu. Website: https://www.daemen.edu/academics/areas-study/education

DePaul University, College of Education, Chicago, IL 60614. Offers bilingual-bicultural education (M Ed, MA); counseling (M Ed, MA), including clinical mental health counseling, college student development, school counseling; curriculum studies (M Ed, MA, Ed D); early childhood education (M Ed, MA, Ed D); educational leadership (M Ed, MA, Ed D), including Catholic leadership (M Ed, MA), general (M Ed, MA), higher education (M Ed, MA), physical education (M Ed, MA), principal preparation (M Ed), teacher preparation (M Ed); elementary education (M Ed, MA); middle grades education (M Ed); middle school mathematics education (MS); reading specialist (M Ed, MA); secondary education (M Ed, MA); social and cultural foundations in education (M Ed, MA); special education (M Ed); sport, fitness and recreation leadership (MS); value-creating education for global citizenship (M Ed); world languages education (M Ed, MA). *Program availability:* Part-time, evening/weekend, online learning. *Degree requirements:* For doctorate, thesis/dissertation. Electronic applications accepted.

Dickinson State University, Department of Teacher Education, Dickinson, ND 58601-4896. Offers master of arts in teaching (MAT); master of entrepreneurship (ME); middle school education (MAT); reading (MAT). *Program availability:* Part-time, blended/hybrid learning. *Faculty:* 2 full-time (both women). *Students:* 2 full-time (1 woman), 15 part-time (9 women); includes 1 minority (Hispanic/Latino). Average age 36. 8 applicants, 100% accepted, 8 enrolled. *Degree requirements:* For master's, comprehensive exam (for some programs). *Entrance requirements:* For master's, additional admission requirements for the Master of Entrepreneurship Program: complete the SoBE ME Peregrine Entrance Examination, personal statement; transcripts; additional admission requirements for the Master of Entrepreneurship Program: 2 letters of reference in support of their admission to the program. Reference letters should be from prior academic advisors, faculty, professional colleagues, or supervisors. Additional exam requirements/recommendations for international students: Required—TOEFL (minimum score 71 iBT). *Application deadline:* For fall admission, 8/1 for domestic students, 7/1 for international students; for spring admission, 12/1 for domestic students, 11/15 for international students. Applications are processed on a rolling basis. Application fee: $35. Electronic applications accepted. *Expenses: Tuition, area resident:* Full-time $3735; part-time $311 per credit hour. Tuition, state resident: full-time $3735; part-time $311 per credit hour. Tuition, nonresident: full-time $3735; part-time $311 per credit hour. *Required fees:* $138; $138 per credit hour. *Financial support:* Application deadline: 12/1; applicants required to submit FAFSA. *Unit head:* Dr. Deborah Secord, Chair, Department of Teacher Education, 701-483-2178, E-mail: Deborah.Secord@dickinsonstate.edu. *Application contact:* Pamela Krueger, Graduate Studies Coordinator, 701-483-5631, E-mail: Pamela.j.krueger@dickinsonstate.edu. Website: https://dickinsonstate.edu/academics/fields-of-study/graduate-studies/

Drury University, Master in Education Program, Springfield, MO 65802. Offers curriculum and instruction (M Ed), including elementary education, middle school education, secondary education; instructional leadership (M Ed); instructional technology (M Ed); integrated learning (M Ed); special education (M Ed); special reading (M Ed). *Accreditation:* NCATE. *Program availability:* Part-time, evening/weekend, 100% online, blended/hybrid learning. *Faculty:* 10 full-time (6 women), 8 part-time/adjunct (6 women). *Students:* 167 full-time (133 women). Average age 32. 92 applicants, 92% accepted, 69 enrolled. In 2018, 44 master's awarded. *Entrance requirements:* For master's, bachelor's degree with minimum GPA of 2.75. Additional exam requirements/recommendations for international students: Recommended—TOEFL (minimum score 80 iBT), IELTS (minimum score 6.5). *Application deadline:* For fall admission, 8/4 priority date for domestic and international students; for spring admission, 1/5 priority date for domestic and international students; for summer admission, 5/26 priority date for domestic and international students. Applications are processed on a rolling basis. Application fee: $25. Electronic applications accepted. *Expenses: Tuition* is $366 per credit hour. Fees are $7 per credit hour. Most M.Ed. degrees are 33 credit hours. *Financial support:* In 2018–19, 5 students received support. Career-related internships or fieldwork, scholarships/grants, and unspecified assistantships available. Financial award application deadline: 6/30; financial award applicants required to submit FAFSA. *Faculty research:* Instructional technology, autism, diversity, and social justice. *Unit head:* Dr. Asikaa Cosgrove, Director, Master in Education Program, 417-873-7806, E-mail: acosgrov@drury.edu. *Application contact:* Dr. Asikaa Cosgrove, Director, Master in Education Program, 417-873-7806, E-mail: acosgrov@drury.edu. Website: http://www.drury.edu/education-masters

Duquesne University, School of Education, Department of Instruction and Leadership, Program in Middle Level (4-8) Education, Pittsburgh, PA 15282-0001. Offers MS Ed.

Middle School Education

Program availability: Part-time, evening/weekend. *Faculty:* 1 (woman) full-time. *Students:* 1 (woman) full-time. Average age 33. In 2018, 1 master's awarded. *Entrance requirements:* For master's, bachelor's degree. Additional exam requirements/recommendations for international students: Required—TOEFL (minimum score 550 paper-based). *Application deadline:* For fall admission, 9/1 for domestic students; for spring admission, 1/1 for domestic students. Applications are processed on a rolling basis. Application fee: $0. Electronic applications accepted. *Expenses: Tuition:* Full-time $23,112; part-time $1284 per credit. Tuition and fees vary according to program. *Financial support:* Research assistantships available. *Faculty research:* Adolescent literacy; family engagement and community partnerships; factors that create highly effective teachers; notions and perceptions of being a well-educated person, models of teacher leadership. *Unit head:* Dr. Carla Meyer, Assistant Professor, 412-396-5838, Fax: 412-396-5388, E-mail: meyerc2@duq.edu. *Application contact:* Kelly McGinley, Graduate Admissions Assistant, 412-396-1559, Fax: 412-396-5585, E-mail: mcginleyk@duq.edu.
Website: http://www.duq.edu/academics/schools/education/graduate-programs-education/ms-middle-level-4-8

East Carolina University, Graduate School, College of Education, Department of Elementary and Middle Grades Education, Greenville, NC 27858-4353. Offers elementary education (MA Ed, MAT); middle grades education (MA Ed, MAT). *Accreditation:* NCATE. *Program availability:* Part-time, evening/weekend, online learning. *Application deadline:* For fall admission, 6/1 priority date for domestic students. *Expenses: Tuition, area resident:* Full-time $4749. Tuition, state resident: full-time $4749. Tuition, nonresident: full-time $17,898. *International tuition:* $17,898 full-time. *Required fees:* $2787. Part-time tuition and fees vary according to course load and program. *Financial support:* Application deadline: 3/1. *Unit head:* Dr. Patricia Jean Anderson, Interim Chair, 252-328-4123, E-mail: andersonp@ecu.edu. *Application contact:* Graduate School Admissions, 252-328-6012, Fax: 252-328-6071, E-mail: gradschool@ecu.edu.
Website: http://www.ecu.edu/cs-educ/elmid/index.cfm

Eastern Illinois University, Graduate School, College of Education, Department of Teaching, Learning, and Foundations, Charleston, IL 61920. Offers curriculum and instruction (MS Ed). *Accreditation:* NCATE. *Program availability:* Part-time, evening/weekend. *Degree requirements:* For master's, comprehensive exam (for some programs), thesis (for some programs). *Entrance requirements:* For master's, GMAT or GRE. Additional exam requirements/recommendations for international students: Required—TOEFL (minimum score 500 paper-based; 61 iBT), IELTS (minimum score 6). *Application deadline:* For fall admission, 5/15 for domestic and international students; for spring admission, 10/15 for domestic and international students. Applications are processed on a rolling basis. Application fee: $30. Electronic applications accepted. *Expenses:* Tuition, state resident: part-time $299 per credit hour. Tuition, nonresident: part-time $718 per credit hour. *Required fees:* $214.50 per credit hour. *Financial support:* Research assistantships with full tuition reimbursements, teaching assistantships with full tuition reimbursements, career-related internships or fieldwork, Federal Work-Study, scholarships/grants, and unspecified assistantships available. Support available to part-time students. Financial award application deadline: 3/1; financial award applicants required to submit FAFSA. *Unit head:* Jeanne E. Okrasinski, Ph.D., Chair, 217-581-5728, Fax: 217-581-6300, E-mail: jeokrasinski@eiu.edu. *Application contact:* Jeanne E. Okrasinski, Ph.D., Chair, 217-581-5728, Fax: 217-581-6300, E-mail: jeokrasinski@eiu.edu.
Website: http://www.eiu.edu/elegrad/

Eastern Illinois University, Graduate School, College of Liberal Arts and Sciences, Department of Mathematics and Computer Science, Charleston, IL 61920. Offers elementary/middle school mathematics education (MA); mathematics (MA); secondary mathematics education (MA). *Program availability:* Part-time, evening/weekend. *Degree requirements:* For master's, comprehensive exam (for some programs), thesis (for some programs). *Entrance requirements:* For master's, GMAT or GRE. Additional exam requirements/recommendations for international students: Required—TOEFL (minimum score 500 paper-based; 61 iBT), IELTS (minimum score 6). Electronic applications accepted. *Expenses:* Tuition, state resident: part-time $299 per credit hour. Tuition, nonresident: part-time $718 per credit hour. *Required fees:* $214.50 per credit hour.

Eastern Michigan University, Graduate School, College of Education, Department of Teacher Education, Programs in K–12 Education, Ypsilanti, MI 48197. Offers middle school education (MA); secondary school education (MA). *Accreditation:* NCATE. *Program availability:* Part-time, evening/weekend, online learning. *Students:* 20 full-time (13 women), 21 part-time (13 women); includes 6 minority (2 Black or African American, non-Hispanic/Latino; 2 Asian, non-Hispanic/Latino; 2 Hispanic/Latino), 6 international. Average age 31. 28 applicants, 54% accepted, 10 enrolled. In 2018, 2 master's awarded. *Entrance requirements:* For master's, GRE. Additional exam requirements/recommendations for international students: Required—TOEFL. *Application deadline:* Applications are processed on a rolling basis. Application fee: $45. *Financial support:* Fellowships, research assistantships with full tuition reimbursements, teaching assistantships with full tuition reimbursements, career-related internships or fieldwork, Federal Work-Study, institutionally sponsored loans, scholarships/grants, tuition waivers (partial), and unspecified assistantships available. Support available to part-time students. Financial award applicants required to submit FAFSA. *Application contact:* Dr. Molly Thornbladh, Advisor, 734-487-1416, Fax: 734-487-2101, E-mail: mthornbl@emich.edu.

Eastern Nazarene College, Adult and Graduate Studies, Division of Teacher Education, Quincy, MA 02170. Offers administration (M Ed); early childhood education (M Ed, Certificate); elementary education (M Ed, Certificate); English as a second language (Certificate); instructional enrichment and development (Certificate); middle school education (M Ed, Certificate); moderate special needs education (Certificate); principal (Certificate); program development and supervision (Certificate); secondary education (M Ed, Certificate); special education administrator (Certificate); special needs (M Ed); supervisor (Certificate); teacher of reading (M Ed, Certificate). M Ed also available through weekend program for administration, special needs, and teacher of reading only. *Program availability:* Part-time, evening/weekend. *Entrance requirements:* Additional exam requirements/recommendations for international students: Required—TOEFL (minimum score 550 paper-based).

Eastern University, Graduate Education Programs, St. Davids, PA 19087-3696. Offers ESL program specialist (K-12) (Certificate); general supervisor (PreK-12) (Certificate); health and physical education (K-12) (Certificate); middle level (4-8) (Certificate); multicultural education (M Ed); music (K-12) (Certificate); Pre K-4 (Certificate); Pre K-4 with special education (Certificate); reading (M Ed); reading specialist (K-12) (Certificate); reading supervisor (K-12) (Certificate); school counseling (MA, CAGS); school principalship (preK-12) (Certificate); school psychology (MS, CAGS); secondary biology education (7-12) (Certificate); secondary chemistry education (7-12) (Certificate); secondary communication education (7-12) (Certificate); secondary English education (7-12) (Certificate); secondary math education (7-12) (Certificate); secondary social studies education (7-12) (Certificate); special education (M Ed); special education (7-12) (Certificate); special education (Pre K-8) (Certificate); special education supervisor (K-12) (Certificate); TESOL (M Ed); world language (Certificate), including Spanish. *Program availability:* Part-time, evening/weekend, online learning. *Entrance requirements:* Additional exam requirements/recommendations for international students: Required—TOEFL. Electronic applications accepted. Application fee is waived when completed online. *Expenses:* Contact institution.

East Tennessee State University, School of Graduate Studies, College of Education, Department of Curriculum and Instruction, Johnson City, TN 37614. Offers advanced studies in teaching and learning (M Ed), including childhood literacy; educational technology (M Ed), including educational communications and technology, school library media; elementary education (M Ed); reading (M Ed, MA), including reading education (MA), storytelling (MA); response to intervention (Post-Master's Certificate); school library professional (Post-Master's Certificate); secondary education (M Ed); STEAM K-12 education (Postbaccalaureate Certificate); storytelling (Postbaccalaureate Certificate); teacher education (MAT), including elementary education K-5, middle grades education 4-8, middle grades education 6-8, secondary education 6-12 and preK-12, secondary education K-12. *Accreditation:* NCATE. *Program availability:* Part-time, evening/weekend, online learning. *Degree requirements:* For master's, comprehensive exam, thesis optional, student teaching, practicum; for other advanced degree, field work (school library); culminating experience (storytelling). *Entrance requirements:* For master's, GRE, SAT, ACT, PRAXIS, minimum GPA of 3.0, interview, 3 letters of recommendation, background check; for other advanced degree, master's degree, TN teaching license. Additional exam requirements/recommendations for international students: Required—TOEFL (minimum score 550 paper-based; 79 iBT). Electronic applications accepted. *Faculty research:* Critical thinking; curriculum development in reading, math, and science education; cultural diversity; cognitive processes; effective teaching strategies.

Edinboro University of Pennsylvania, Department of Middle and Secondary Education and Educational Leadership, Edinboro, PA 16444. Offers educational leadership (M Ed); middle and secondary instruction (M Ed). *Program availability:* Part-time, evening/weekend. *Degree requirements:* For master's, comprehensive exam, thesis or alternative, project. *Entrance requirements:* For master's, GRE or MAT, minimum QPA of 2.5. Electronic applications accepted.

Emory University, Laney Graduate School, Division of Educational Studies, Atlanta, GA 30322-1100. Offers educational studies (MA, PhD); middle grades teaching (MAT); secondary teaching (MAT). *Accreditation:* NCATE. Terminal master's awarded for partial completion of doctoral program. *Degree requirements:* For master's, thesis; for doctorate, comprehensive exam, thesis/dissertation. *Entrance requirements:* For master's and doctorate, GRE General Test, minimum GPA of 3.0. Additional exam requirements/recommendations for international students: Required—TOEFL. Electronic applications accepted. *Faculty research:* Educational policy, educational measurement, urban and multicultural education, mathematics and science education, comparative education.

Fayetteville State University, Graduate School, Programs in Middle Grades, Secondary, Special and Elementary Education, Fayetteville, NC 28301-4298. Offers middle grades (MA Ed); sociology (MA Ed); special education (MA Ed), including behavioral-emotional handicaps, mentally handicapped, specific training disability. *Accreditation:* NCATE. *Program availability:* Part-time, evening/weekend. *Faculty:* 10 full-time (6 women), 1 (woman) part-time/adjunct. *Students:* 24 full-time (20 women), 31 part-time (29 women); includes 38 minority (35 Black or African American, non-Hispanic/Latino; 2 Hispanic/Latino; 1 Two or more races, non-Hispanic/Latino), 1 international. Average age 35. 8 applicants, 88% accepted, 3 enrolled. In 2018, 7 master's awarded. *Degree requirements:* For master's, comprehensive exam, internship. *Entrance requirements:* Additional exam requirements/recommendations for international students: Required—TOEFL. *Application deadline:* For fall admission, 4/15 for domestic students; for spring admission, 10/15 for domestic students. Applications are processed on a rolling basis. Application fee: $40. Electronic applications accepted. *Financial support:* Application deadline: 3/1; applicants required to submit FAFSA. *Faculty research:* Reading assessment; reading remediation; learning disabilities; parenting; and adolescents with autism spectrum disorders social-communication development. *Unit head:* Dr. Cynthia Shamberger, Chair of Middle Grades, Secondary and Specialized Subjects, 910-672-2464, Fax: 910-672-1941, E-mail: cshamber@uncfsu.edu. *Application contact:* Dr. Cynthia Shamberger, Chair of Middle Grades, Secondary and Specialized Subjects, 910-672-2464, Fax: 910-672-1941, E-mail: cshamber@uncfsu.edu.

Fitchburg State University, Division of Graduate and Continuing Education, Program in Middle School Education, Fitchburg, MA 01420-2697. Offers English (M Ed); general science (M Ed); history (M Ed); math (M Ed). *Accreditation:* NCATE. *Program availability:* Part-time, evening/weekend. *Entrance requirements:* Additional exam requirements/recommendations for international students: Required—TOEFL (minimum score 550 paper-based; 79 iBT). Electronic applications accepted. *Expenses:* Contact institution.

Florida Gulf Coast University, College of Education, Program in Curriculum and Instruction, Fort Myers, FL 33965-6565. Offers elementary education (M Ed); English education (M Ed); English speakers of other languages endorsement (M Ed); gifted education (M Ed); mathematics education (M Ed); middle school education (M Ed); reading education (M Ed); science education (M Ed); social science education (M Ed); special education (M Ed). *Program availability:* Part-time, evening/weekend, online learning. *Degree requirements:* For master's, final project or portfolio. *Entrance requirements:* For master's, GRE General Test, MAT, minimum undergraduate GPA of 3.0 in last 2 years. Additional exam requirements/recommendations for international students: Required—TOEFL (minimum score 550 paper-based). Electronic applications accepted. *Faculty research:* Internet in schools, technology in pre-service and in-service teacher training.

Fontbonne University, Graduate Programs, St. Louis, MO 63105-3098. Offers accounting (MBA, MS); art (MA); art (K-12) (MAT); business (MBA); computer science (MS); deaf education (MA); early intervention in deaf education (MA); education (MA), including autism spectrum disorders, curriculum and instruction, diverse learners, early childhood education, reading, special education; elementary education (MAT); family and consumer sciences (MA), including multidisciplinary health communication studies; fine arts (MFA); instructional design and technology (MS); management and leadership (MM); middle school education (MAT); secondary education (MAT); special education (MAT); speech-language pathology (MS); supply chain management (MS); theatre (MA). *Accreditation:* ASHA. *Program availability:* Part-time, evening/weekend, online learning. *Degree requirements:* For master's, comprehensive exam (for some programs), thesis (for some programs). *Entrance requirements:* Additional exam requirements/recommendations for international students: Required—TOEFL (minimum score 500 paper-based; 65 iBT). Electronic applications accepted.

Georgia College & State University, Graduate School, The John H. Lounsbury College of Education, Program in Middle Grades Education, Milledgeville, GA 31061. Offers M Ed, MAT. *Accreditation:* NCATE. *Program availability:* Part-time, evening/weekend. *Degree requirements:* For master's, comprehensive exam, portfolio presentation, complete program within 6 years, minimum GPA of 3.0. *Entrance requirements:* For master's, 2 professional recommendations, transcripts, resume,

verification of immunization, and minimum GPA of 2.75; Georgia T4 certification or evidence of qualification for one (for M Ed). Electronic applications accepted. *Expenses:* Contact institution.

Georgia Southern University, Jack N. Averitt College of Graduate Studies, College of Education, Department of Middle Grades and Secondary Education, Program in Middle Grades Education, Statesboro, GA 30460. Offers M Ed, MAT, Ed S. *Accreditation:* NCATE. *Program availability:* Part-time, evening/weekend, 100% online, blended/hybrid learning. *Degree requirements:* For master's, portfolio, transition point assessments, exit assessment; for Ed S, field-based research projects, assessments. *Entrance requirements:* For master's, GACE Basic Skills and Content Assessments (for MAT), minimum cumulative GPA of 2.5. Additional exam requirements/recommendations for international students: Required—TOEFL (minimum score 550 paper-based; 80 iBT), IELTS (minimum score 6). Electronic applications accepted. *Expenses: Tuition, area resident:* Part-time $3324 per semester. Tuition, state resident: full-time $5814; part-time $3324 per semester. Tuition, nonresident: full-time $23,204; part-time $13,260 per semester. *Required fees:* $2092; $2092. Tuition and fees vary according to course load, degree level, campus/location and program. *Faculty research:* Gender, technology applications, early and young adolescent literature, content subjects and literacy, integrated curriculum, content subject learning.

Georgia Southwestern State University, School of Education, Americus, GA 31709-4693. Offers early childhood education (M Ed, Ed S); middle grades education (Ed S); middle grades language arts (M Ed); middle grades mathematics (M Ed); special education (M Ed). *Accreditation:* NCATE. *Degree requirements:* For master's, minimum cumulative GPA of 3.0; maximum of 6 credit hours with C grade; no courses with D grade; degree completed within 7 calendar years; for Ed S, minimum GPA of 3.25 in all courses with no grade less than a B; degree must be completed within 7 calendar years from date of initial enrollment in graduate work. *Entrance requirements:* For master's, undergraduate degree from accredited institution; professional Georgia Teaching Certificate or eligibility; minimum undergraduate GPA of 2.75 as reported on official final transcripts from all accredited institutions attended; 2 confidential Administrative Recommendation Forms; for Ed S, master's degree from accredited college or university; professional Georgia Teaching Certificate or eligibility; minimum graduate GPA of 3.0 as reported on official final graduate transcripts from all accredited institutions attended; 2 confidential Administrative Recommendation Forms. Electronic applications accepted. *Expenses:* Contact institution.

Georgia State University, College of Education and Human Development, Department of Middle and Secondary Education, Atlanta, GA 30302-3083. Offers curriculum and instruction (Ed D); English education (MAT); mathematics education (M Ed, MAT); middle level education (MAT); reading, language and literacy education (M Ed, MAT), including reading instruction (M Ed); science education (M Ed, MAT), including biology (MAT), broad field science (MAT), chemistry (MAT), earth science (MAT), physics (MAT); social studies education (M Ed, MAT), including economics (MAT), geography (MAT), history (MAT), political science (MAT); teaching and learning (PhD), including language and literacy, mathematics education, music education, science education, social studies education, teaching and teacher education. *Accreditation:* NCATE. *Program availability:* Part-time, evening/weekend, online learning. *Faculty:* 19 full-time (15 women), 9 part-time/adjunct (7 women). *Students:* 217 full-time (136 women), 203 part-time (140 women); includes 229 minority (156 Black or African American, non-Hispanic/Latino; 23 Asian, non-Hispanic/Latino; 31 Hispanic/Latino; 19 Two or more races, non-Hispanic/Latino), 3 international. Average age 34. 149 applicants, 60% accepted, 70 enrolled. In 2018, 112 master's, 23 doctorates awarded. *Entrance requirements:* For master's, GRE; GACE I (for initial teacher preparation programs), baccalaureate degree or equivalent, resume, goals statement, two letters of recommendation, minimum undergraduate GPA of 2.5; proof of initial teacher certification in the content area (for M Ed); for doctorate, GRE, resume, goals statement, writing sample, two letters of recommendation, minimum graduate GPA of 3.3, interview. *Application deadline:* For fall admission, 1/15 priority date for domestic and international students; for spring admission, 10/1 for domestic and international students. Application fee: $50. Electronic applications accepted. *Expenses: Tuition, area resident:* Full-time $9360; part-time $390 per credit hour. Tuition, state resident: full-time $9360; part-time $390 per credit hour. Tuition, nonresident: full-time $30,024; part-time $1251 per credit hour. *International tuition:* $30,024 full-time. *Required fees:* $2128. *Financial support:* In 2018–19, fellowships with full tuition reimbursements (averaging $19,667 per year), research assistantships with full tuition reimbursements (averaging $5,436 per year), teaching assistantships with full tuition reimbursements (averaging $2,779 per year) were awarded; career-related internships or fieldwork, Federal Work-Study, scholarships/grants, health care benefits, tuition waivers (full and partial), and unspecified assistantships also available. Financial award application deadline: 3/15. *Faculty research:* Teacher education in language and literacy, mathematics, science, and social studies in urban middle and secondary school settings; learning technologies in school, community, and corporate settings; multicultural education and education for social justice; urban education; international education. *Unit head:* Dr. Gertrude Marilyn Tinker Sachs, Chair, 404-413-8384, Fax: 404-413-8063, E-mail: gtinkersachs@gsu.edu. *Application contact:* Shaleen Tibbs, Administrative Specialist, 404-413-8385, Fax: 404-413-8063, E-mail: stibbs@gsu.edu.
Website: http://mse.education.gsu.edu/

Gordon College, Graduate Education Program, Wenham, MA 01984-1899. Offers early childhood (M Ed); educational leadership (M Ed, Ed S); elementary education (M Ed); English as a second language (M Ed, Ed S); math specialist (M Ed); mathematics specialist (Ed S); middle school education (M Ed); moderate disabilities (M Ed); Montessori education (M Ed); reading (M Ed, Ed S); secondary education (M Ed). *Program availability:* Part-time, evening/weekend. *Degree requirements:* For master's, action research or clinical experience (for most programs); for Ed S, action research or clinical experience (for some programs). *Entrance requirements:* For master's, minimum undergraduate GPA of 3.0; 2 official undergraduate transcripts; professional resume; 3 recommendation letters (one professional reference, one academic reference, one personal reference); 500-700 word statement of purpose; for Ed S, minimum master's GPA of 3.3; 2 official transcripts from undergraduate and graduate schools; professional resume; 3 recommendation letters (one professional reference, one academic reference, one personal reference); 500-700 word statement of purpose. Additional exam requirements/recommendations for international students: Required—TOEFL (minimum score 550 paper-based, 80 iBT) or IELTS (minimum score 6.5). *Expenses:* Contact institution. *Faculty research:* Reading, early childhood development, English language learners, universal design for learning.

Goucher College, Graduate Programs in Education, Baltimore, MD 21204-2794. Offers at-risk and diverse learners (M Ed, Certificate); athletic program leadership and administration (M Ed, Certificate); elementary education (MAT); literacy strategies for content learning (M Ed); middle school (M Ed, Certificate); Montessori studies (M Ed); reading instruction (M Ed, Certificate); reducing student, classroom, and school disruption (M Ed); school improvement leadership (M Ed); secondary education (MAT); special education (MAT), including elementary education; special education for certified elementary and secondary teachers (M Ed); teacher as leader in technology (M Ed). *Program availability:* Part-time, evening/weekend. *Degree requirements:* For master's,

thesis (M Ed), final presentation (MAT). *Entrance requirements:* For master's, minimum GPA of 3.0. Additional exam requirements/recommendations for international students: Required—TOEFL (minimum score 550 paper-based; 80 iBT), IELTS (minimum score 7). Electronic applications accepted. *Expenses:* Contact institution. *Faculty research:* Urban education, middle school, school improvement, teacher education, at-risk student achievement.

Grand Valley State University, College of Education, Programs in General Education, Allendale, MI 49401-9403. Offers adult and higher education (M Ed); early childhood education (M Ed); educational differentiation (M Ed); educational leadership (M Ed); educational technology integration (M Ed); elementary education (M Ed); middle level education (M Ed); school library media services (M Ed); secondary level education (M Ed); teaching English to speakers of other languages (M Ed). *Program availability:* Part-time, evening/weekend, 100% online, blended/hybrid learning. *Students:* 20 part-time (10 women); includes 1 minority (Black or African American, non-Hispanic/Latino). Average age 44. In 2018, 1 master's awarded. *Entrance requirements:* For master's, GRE General Test or minimum GPA of 3.0, last 60 credits from regionally-accredited college/university, 3 letters of recommendation. Additional exam requirements/recommendations for international students: Required—TOEFL (minimum iBT score of 80), IELTS (6.5), or Michigan English Language Assessment Battery (77). *Application deadline:* Applications are processed on a rolling basis. Application fee: $30. Electronic applications accepted. *Expenses:* $677 per credit hour, 33 credits. *Financial support:* In 2018–19, 1 student received support, including 1 fellowship; career-related internships or fieldwork, Federal Work-Study, scholarships/grants, and unspecified assistantships also available. *Faculty research:* Effectiveness of technology in education, parental involvement, effective teaching, effective schools research. *Unit head:* Dr. David Bair, Department Director, 616-331-6489, Fax: 616-331-6489, E-mail: baird@gvsu.edu. *Application contact:* Annukka Thelen, Director, Student Information and Services Center, 616-331-6205, Fax: 616-331-6217, E-mail: thelenan@gvsu.edu.
Website: http://www.gvsu.edu/coe/

Hampton University, School of Liberal Arts and Education, Program in Teaching, Hampton, VA 23668. Offers English education 6-12 (MT); mathematics education 6-12 (MT). *Program availability:* Part-time. *Students:* 2 full-time (both women); both minorities (both Black or African American, non-Hispanic/Latino). Average age 30. 2 applicants, 50% accepted, 1 enrolled. In 2018, 1 master's awarded. *Entrance requirements:* For master's, GRE General Test. Additional exam requirements/recommendations for international students: Required—TOEFL (minimum score 525 paper-based) or IELTS (6.5). *Application deadline:* For fall admission, 6/1 priority date for domestic students, 4/1 for international students; for spring admission, 11/1 priority date for domestic students, 9/1 for international students; for summer admission, 4/1 priority date for domestic students, 2/1 priority date for international students. Applications are processed on a rolling basis. Application fee: $35. Electronic applications accepted. *Financial support:* Application deadline: 6/30; applicants required to submit FAFSA. *Unit head:* Dr. Martha Jallim-Hall, Program Coordinator, 757-727-5793. *Application contact:* Dr. Martha Jallim-Hall, Program Coordinator, 757-727-5793.

Hebrew College, Shoolman Graduate School of Jewish Education, Newton Centre, MA 02459. Offers early childhood Jewish education (Certificate); Jewish day school education (Certificate); Jewish education (MJ Ed); Jewish family education (Certificate); Jewish special education (Certificate); Jewish youth education, informal education and camping (Certificate). *Program availability:* Part-time, evening/weekend, online learning. *Degree requirements:* For master's, one foreign language. *Entrance requirements:* For master's, GRE, interview. Additional exam requirements/recommendations for international students: Required—TOEFL.

Henderson State University, Graduate Studies, Teachers College, Department of Advanced Instructional Studies, Arkadelphia, AR 71999-0001. Offers developmental therapy (MSE); dyslexia therapy (Graduate Certificate); education (MAT); educational technology leadership (Graduate Certificate); English as a second language (MSE, Graduate Certificate); instructional facilitator (MSE, Graduate Certificate); middle level education (MAT); special education (K-12) (MAT, MSE); special education/early childhood (MAT). *Accreditation:* NCATE. *Program availability:* Part-time. *Entrance requirements:* For master's, GRE General Test or MAT, minimum GPA of 2.7, teacher certification. Additional exam requirements/recommendations for international students: Required—TOEFL (minimum score 600 paper-based); Recommended—IELTS (minimum score 6.5).

Hofstra University, School of Education, Programs in Teacher Education, Hempstead, NY 11549. Offers bilingual education (MA); bilingual extension (Advanced Certificate); business education (MS Ed); curriculum studies (MS Ed); early childhood and childhood education (MS Ed); early childhood education (MA, MS Ed); educational technology (Advanced Certificate); elementary education (MA, MS Ed); English education (MS Ed); family and consumer science (MS Ed); fine arts and music education (Advanced Certificate); fine arts education (MS Ed); foreign language and TESOL (MS Ed); foreign language education (MA, MS Ed); languages other than English and teaching English as a second language (MA); learning and teaching (Ed D); mathematics education (MA, MS Ed); middle childhood extension (Advanced Certificate); music education (MA, MS Ed); science education (MA); secondary education (Advanced Certificate); social studies education (MA, MS Ed); teaching languages other than English and TESOL (MS Ed); technology for learning (MA); TESOL (MS Ed, Advanced Certificate); TESOL with specialization in STEM (MA); work based learning extension (Advanced Certificate). *Program availability:* Part-time, evening/weekend, blended/hybrid learning. *Students:* 138 full-time (94 women), 109 part-time (78 women); includes 66 minority (16 Black or African American, non-Hispanic/Latino; 17 Asian, non-Hispanic/Latino; 31 Hispanic/Latino; 2 Native Hawaiian or other Pacific Islander, non-Hispanic/Latino), 6 international. Average age 29. 217 applicants, 86% accepted, 113 enrolled. In 2018, 105 master's, 11 doctorates, 25 other advanced degrees awarded. *Degree requirements:* For master's, comprehensive exam, thesis (for some programs), exit project, student teaching, fieldwork, electronic portfolio, curriculum project, minimum GPA of 3.0; for doctorate, dissertation; for Advanced Certificate, 3 foreign languages, comprehensive exam (for some programs), thesis project. *Entrance requirements:* For master's, GRE, 2 letters of recommendation, portfolio, teacher certification (MA), interview, essay; for doctorate, GMAT, GRE, LSAT, or MAT; for Advanced Certificate, 2 letters of recommendation, essay, interview and/or portfolio, teaching certificate. Additional exam requirements/recommendations for international students: Required—TOEFL (minimum score 550 paper-based; 80 iBT). *Application deadline:* Applications are processed on a rolling basis. Application fee: $75. Electronic applications accepted. *Financial support:* In 2018–19, 86 students received support, including 51 fellowships with full and partial tuition reimbursements available (averaging $5,080 per year), 2 research assistantships with full and partial tuition reimbursements available (averaging $3,470 per year); career-related internships or fieldwork, Federal Work-Study, institutionally sponsored loans, scholarships/grants, traineeships, tuition waivers (full and partial), unspecified assistantships, and scholarships and endowed scholarships also available. Support available to part-time students. Financial award applicants required to submit FAFSA. *Faculty research:* Impact of memory on learning; brain function, cognitive-development, learning, and achievement; student activism and civic education; using children's literature to promote diversity; 2nd language acquisition. *Unit head:* Dr. Alan Singer,

Chairperson, 516-463-5853, Fax: 516-463-6275, E-mail: alan.j.singer@hofstra.edu. *Application contact:* Sunil Samuel, Assistant Vice President of Admissions, 516-463-4723, Fax: 516-463-4664, E-mail: graduateadmission@hofstra.edu.
Website: http://www.hofstra.edu/education/

Hofstra University, School of Education, Specialized Programs in Education, Hempstead, NY 11549. Offers applied behavior analysis (Advanced Certificate); childhood special education (MS Ed); early childhood special education (MS Ed, Advanced Certificate); educational and policy leadership (Ed D); educational leadership (Advanced Certificate); educational leadership and policy studies (MS Ed), including K-12; elementary special education (MS Ed); gifted education (Advanced Certificate); health education (MS); health professions pedagogy and leadership (MS); higher education leadership and policy studies (MS Ed); inclusive early childhood special education (MS Ed); inclusive elementary special education (MS Ed); inclusive secondary special education (MS Ed); literacy studies (MA, MS Ed, Ed D, Advanced Certificate); pedagogy for health professions (Advanced Certificate); physical education (MS); school district business leader (Advanced Certificate); secondary education generalist - students with disabilities 7-12 (MS Ed); secondary special education generalist - secondary education (MS Ed); special education (MS Ed, Advanced Certificate); special education assessment and diagnosis (Advanced Certificate); special education early childhood intervention (MS Ed); special education: international perspectives (MS Ed); teaching students with severe or multiple disabilities (Advanced Certificate). *Program availability:* Part-time, evening/weekend, blended/hybrid learning. *Students:* 126 full-time (91 women), 230 part-time (175 women); includes 90 minority (40 Black or African American, non-Hispanic/Latino; 4 American Indian or Alaska Native, non-Hispanic/Latino; 11 Asian, non-Hispanic/Latino; 32 Hispanic/Latino; 3 Two or more races, non-Hispanic/Latino), 4 international. Average age 32. 215 applicants, 90% accepted, 117 enrolled. In 2018, 130 master's, 9 doctorates, 23 other advanced degrees awarded. *Degree requirements:* For master's, one foreign language, comprehensive exam (for some programs), thesis (for some programs), electronic portfolio, capstone course, internship, practicum, student teaching, seminars, minimum GPA of 3.0; for doctorate, one foreign language, comprehensive exam, thesis/dissertation, qualifying hearing. *Entrance requirements:* For master's, GRE, interview, letters of recommendation, portfolio, essay, certification; for doctorate, GRE or MAT, interview, resume, essay, master's degree, 3 letters of recommendation, writing sample; for Advanced Certificate, GRE, interview, letters of recommendation, essay, professional experience, resume, master's degree. Additional exam requirements/recommendations for international students: Required—TOEFL (minimum score 550 paper-based; 80 iBT). *Application deadline:* Applications are processed on a rolling basis. Application fee: $75. Electronic applications accepted. *Financial support:* In 2018–19, 208 students received support, including 105 fellowships with full and partial tuition reimbursements available (averaging $3,948 per year), 12 research assistantships with full and partial tuition reimbursements available (averaging $6,573 per year); career-related internships or fieldwork, Federal Work-Study, institutionally sponsored loans, scholarships/grants, traineeships, tuition waivers (full and partial), unspecified assistantships, and scholarships and endowed scholarships also available. Support available to part-time students. Financial award applicants required to submit FAFSA. *Faculty research:* Water quality and income inequality; girls and stem; new media literacies; applied behavior analysis; k-12 leadership development. *Unit head:* Dr. Alan Flurkey, Chairperson, 516-463-5237, E-mail: alan.d.flurkey@hofstra.edu. *Application contact:* Sunil Samuel, Assistant Vice President of Admissions, 516-463-4723, Fax: 516-463-4664, E-mail: graduateadmission@hofstra.edu.
Website: http://www.hofstra.edu/education/

Hood College, Graduate School, Program in Secondary Mathematics Education, Frederick, MD 21701-8575. Offers high school (MS); middle school (MS); secondary mathematics education (Certificate). *Program availability:* Part-time-only, evening/weekend. *Faculty:* 1 (woman) full-time, 2 part-time/adjunct (both women). *Students:* 20 part-time (13 women); includes 3 minority (1 Black or African American, non-Hispanic/Latino; 2 Hispanic/Latino). Average age 33. 6 applicants, 100% accepted, 4 enrolled. In 2018, 3 master's awarded. *Degree requirements:* For master's, exitfolio, capstone/research project. *Entrance requirements:* For master's, minimum GPA of 2.75, initial teacher certification, essay. Additional exam requirements/recommendations for international students: Required—TOEFL (minimum score 575 paper-based; 89 iBT), IELTS (minimum score 6.5). *Application deadline:* For fall admission, 8/15 priority date for domestic students, 8/15 for international students; for spring admission, 12/1 priority date for domestic students, 12/1 for international students; for summer admission, 5/1 priority date for domestic students, 4/15 for international students. Applications are processed on a rolling basis. Application fee: $50 ($100 for international students). Electronic applications accepted. *Expenses: Tuition:* Full-time $17,640; part-time $4410 per semester. *Required fees:* $125 per semester. Tuition and fees vary according to degree level and program. *Financial support:* Tuition waivers (partial) and unspecified assistantships available. Financial award applicants required to submit FAFSA. *Unit head:* Dr. April M. Boulton, Dean of the Graduate School, 301-696-3600, E-mail: gofurther@hood.edu. *Application contact:* Tanith Fowler Corsi, Assistant Director of Graduate Admissions, 301-696-3603, E-mail: gofurther@hood.edu.
Website: http://www.hood.edu/graduate

Houston Baptist University, School of Humanities, Program in Liberal Arts, Houston, TX 77074-3298. Offers education (EC-12 art, music, physical education, or Spanish) (MLA); education (EC-6 generalist) (MLA); general liberal arts (MLA); specialization in education (4-8 or 7-12) (MLA). *Program availability:* Part-time, evening/weekend. *Entrance requirements:* For master's, minimum GPA of 2.5, essay/personal statement, resume, bachelor's degree transcript. Additional exam requirements/recommendations for international students: Required—TOEFL (minimum score 80 iBT), IELTS (minimum score 6.5). Electronic applications accepted. Application fee is waived when completed online. *Expenses:* Contact institution.

Huntington University, Graduate School, Huntington, IN 46750-1299. Offers adolescent and young adult education (M Ed); business administration (MBA); counseling (MA), including licensed mental health counselor; early adolescent education (M Ed); elementary education (M Ed); global youth ministry (MA); occupational therapy (OTD); organizational leadership (MA); pastoral leadership (MA); TESOL education (M Ed). *Accreditation:* AOTA. *Program availability:* Part-time, online learning. *Degree requirements:* For master's, comprehensive exam (for some programs), thesis (for some programs). *Entrance requirements:* For master's, GRE (for counseling and education students only); for doctorate, GRE (for occupational therapy students). Additional exam requirements/recommendations for international students: Required—TOEFL (minimum score 85 iBT), IELTS (minimum score 6.5). Electronic applications accepted. *Expenses:* Contact institution. *Faculty research:* Leadership, educational technology trends, evangelism, youth ministry, mental health.

James Madison University, The Graduate School, College of Education, Program in Education, Harrisonburg, VA 22807. Offers early childhood education (preK-3) (MAT); educational leadership (M Ed); educational technology (M Ed); elementary education (MAT); equity and cultural diversity (M Ed); inclusive early childhood education (MAT); K-8 mathematics specialist (M Ed); middle education (MAT); reading education (M Ed); secondary education (MAT); Spanish language and culture for educators (M Ed); TESOL (MAT). *Accreditation:* NCATE. *Program availability:* Part-time, evening/weekend. *Students:* 255 full-time (224 women), 200 part-time (140 women); includes 56 minority (13 Black or African American, non-Hispanic/Latino; 8 Asian, non-Hispanic/Latino; 21 Hispanic/Latino; 14 Two or more races, non-Hispanic/Latino), 1 international. Average age 30. In 2018, 295 master's awarded. Application fee: $60. Electronic applications accepted. *Expenses:* Tuition, state resident: full-time $10,848. Tuition, nonresident: full-time $27,888. *Required fees:* $1128. *Financial support:* In 2018–19, 22 students received support. Teaching assistantships, career-related internships or fieldwork, Federal Work-Study, and assistantships (averaging $7911) available. Financial award application deadline: 3/1; financial award applicants required to submit FAFSA. *Unit head:* Dr. Phillip M. Wishon, Dean, 540-568-6572, E-mail: wishonpm@jmu.edu. *Application contact:* Lynette D. Michael, Director of Graduate Admissions, 540-568-6131 Ext. 6395, Fax: 540-568-7860, E-mail: michaeld@jmu.edu.
Website: http://www.jmu.edu/coe/index.shtml

James Madison University, The Graduate School, College of Education, Program in Middle Education, Harrisonburg, VA 22807. Offers MAT. *Accreditation:* NCATE. *Program availability:* Part-time, evening/weekend. *Entrance requirements:* For master's, GRE General Test, minimum undergraduate GPA of 2.5. Additional exam requirements/recommendations for international students: Required—TOEFL. *Application deadline:* For fall admission, 5/1 priority date for domestic students; for spring admission, 9/1 priority date for domestic students. Applications are processed on a rolling basis. Electronic applications accepted. *Expenses:* Tuition, state resident: full-time $10,848. Tuition, nonresident: full-time $27,888. *Required fees:* $1128. *Financial support:* Federal Work-Study and unspecified assistantships available. Financial award application deadline: 3/1; financial award applicants required to submit FAFSA. *Unit head:* Dr. Steven L. Purcell, Academic Unit Head, 540-568-6793. *Application contact:* Lynette M. Bible, Director of Graduate Admissions, 540-568-6395, Fax: 540-568-7860, E-mail: biblelm@jmu.edu.

Kansas State University, Graduate School, College of Education, Department of Curriculum and Instruction, Manhattan, KS 66506. Offers curriculum and instruction (Ed D, PhD); digital teaching and learning (MS); educational computing, design and online learning (MS); elementary/middle level curriculum and instruction (MS); online learning (Certificate); reading specialist endorsement (MS); reading/language arts (MS); teacher leader/school improvement (MS); teaching and learning (Certificate). *Accreditation:* NCATE. *Program availability:* Part-time, online learning. *Degree requirements:* For master's, comprehensive exam, portfolio, project, report or thesis; for doctorate, comprehensive exam, thesis/dissertation, preliminary exam; for Certificate, comprehensive exam, portfolio. *Entrance requirements:* For master's, minimum GPA of 3.0, 3 letters of recommendation; for doctorate, GRE, minimum GPA of 3.0, 3 letters of recommendation, evidence of scholarly writing; for Certificate, minimum GPA of 3.0, letters of recommendation. Additional exam requirements/recommendations for international students: Required—TOEFL (minimum score 550 paper-based; 80 iBT) or IELTS. Electronic applications accepted. *Faculty research:* Literacy and technology, critical race theory and diversity, achievement gaps, school improvement, teacher education.

Kennesaw State University, Bagwell College of Education, Program in Middle Grades and Secondary Education, Kennesaw, GA 30144. Offers Ed D, Ed S. *Program availability:* Part-time, evening/weekend, 100% online, blended/hybrid learning. *Students:* 41 full-time (27 women), 148 part-time (105 women); includes 35 minority (25 Black or African American, non-Hispanic/Latino; 2 Asian, non-Hispanic/Latino; 4 Hispanic/Latino; 4 Two or more races, non-Hispanic/Latino), 1 international. Average age 34. 80 applicants, 84% accepted, 59 enrolled. In 2018, 4 doctorates, 25 other advanced degrees awarded. *Entrance requirements:* Additional exam requirements/recommendations for international students: Required—TOEFL (minimum score 80 iBT), IELTS (minimum score 6.5). *Application deadline:* For fall admission, 7/1 for domestic students; for summer admission, 4/1 for domestic students. Applications are processed on a rolling basis. Application fee: $60. Electronic applications accepted. *Expenses: Tuition, area resident:* Full-time $6960; part-time $290 per credit hour. Tuition, state resident: full-time $6960; part-time $290 per credit hour. Tuition, nonresident: full-time $25,080; part-time $1045 per credit hour. *International tuition:* $25,080 full-time. *Required fees:* $2006; $1706 per semester. $853 per semester. *Application contact:* Admission Counselor, 470-578-4377, Fax: 470-578-9172, E-mail: ksugrad@kennesaw.edu.

Kent State University, College of Education, Health and Human Services, School of Teaching, Learning and Curriculum Studies, Kent, OH 44242-0001. Offers career technical teacher education (M Ed); curriculum and instruction (M Ed, PhD, Ed S); early childhood education (M Ed, MA, MAT); junior high/middle school (M Ed, MA); math specialization (M Ed, MA); reading specialization (M Ed, MA); secondary education (MAT). *Program availability:* Part-time, evening/weekend. *Faculty:* 43 full-time (25 women), 7 part-time/adjunct (6 women). *Students:* 116 full-time (88 women), 110 part-time (83 women); includes 23 minority (6 Black or African American, non-Hispanic/Latino; 1 American Indian or Alaska Native, non-Hispanic/Latino; 13 Asian, non-Hispanic/Latino; 1 Hispanic/Latino; 2 Native Hawaiian or other Pacific Islander, non-Hispanic/Latino), 17 international. 202 applicants, 35% accepted. In 2018, 71 master's, 13 doctorates, 2 other advanced degrees awarded. *Degree requirements:* For master's, thesis (for some programs); for doctorate, comprehensive exam, thesis/dissertation. *Entrance requirements:* For doctorate and Ed S, GRE General Test. Additional exam requirements/recommendations for international students: Required—TOEFL (minimum score 550 paper-based; 80 iBT). *Application deadline:* Applications are processed on a rolling basis. Application fee: $45 ($60 for international students). Electronic applications accepted. *Expenses:* Tuition, state resident: full-time $11,766; part-time $536 per credit. Tuition, nonresident: full-time $21,952; part-time $999 per credit. *International tuition:* $21,952 full-time. Tuition and fees vary according to course load. *Financial support:* In 2018–19, 21 research assistantships with full tuition reimbursements (averaging $12,642 per year), 3 teaching assistantships with full tuition reimbursements (averaging $13,500 per year) were awarded; Federal Work-Study, scholarships/grants, unspecified assistantships, and 3 administrative assistantships (averaging $10,500 per year) also available. Financial award application deadline: 4/1. *Unit head:* Dr. Alexa Sandmann, Director, 330-672-0652, E-mail: asandman@kent.edu. *Application contact:* Cheryl Slusarczyk, Academic Program Director, Office of Graduate Student Services, 330-672-2576, Fax: 330-672-9162, E-mail: ogs@kent.edu.
Website: http://www.kent.edu/ehhs/tlcs/

Kutztown University of Pennsylvania, College of Education, Program in Secondary Education, Kutztown, PA 19530-0730. Offers biology (M Ed); curriculum and instruction (M Ed); English (M Ed); mathematics (M Ed); middle level (M Ed); social studies (M Ed); teaching (M Ed); transformational teaching and learning (Ed D). *Accreditation:* NCATE. *Program availability:* Part-time, evening/weekend, 100% online, blended/hybrid learning. *Faculty:* 5 full-time (3 women), 3 part-time/adjunct (0 women). *Students:* 25 full-time (16 women), 80 part-time (51 women); includes 8 minority (1 Black or African American, non-Hispanic/Latino; 5 Hispanic/Latino; 2 Two or more races, non-Hispanic/Latino), 1 international. Average age 32. 86 applicants, 93% accepted, 45 enrolled. In 2018, 3,531 master's awarded. *Degree requirements:* For master's, comprehensive exam, thesis optional; for doctorate, thesis/dissertation. *Entrance requirements:* For master's, GRE

General Test, minimum undergraduate major GPA of 3.0, 3 letters of recommendation, copy of PRAXIS II or valid instructional I or II teaching certificate; for doctorate, master's or specialist degree in education or related field from regionally-accredited institution of higher learning with minimum graduate GPA of 3.25, significant educational experience, employment in an education setting (preferred). Additional exam requirements/ recommendations for international students: Required—TOEFL (minimum score 550 paper-based, 79 iBT), IELTS (minimum score 6.5), or PTE (minimum score 53). *Application deadline:* For fall admission, 8/1 for domestic and international students; for spring admission, 12/1 for domestic and international students. Application fee: $35. Electronic applications accepted. *Expenses:* Tuition, state resident: part-time $516 per credit. Tuition, nonresident: part-time $774 per credit. *Required fees:* $119 per credit. One-time fee: $50 part-time. Tuition and fees vary according to degree level. *Financial support:* Career-related internships or fieldwork, Federal Work-Study, scholarships/ grants, and unspecified assistantships available. Financial award application deadline: 3/1; financial award applicants required to submit FAFSA. *Unit head:* Dr. Georgeos Sirrakos, Department Chair, 610-683-4279, Fax: 610-683-1338, E-mail: sirrakos@kutztown.edu. *Application contact:* Dr. Patricia Walsh Coates, Graduate Coordinator, 610-638-4289, Fax: 610-683-1338, E-mail: coates@kutztown.edu.
Website: https://www.kutztown.edu/academcs/graduate-programs/secondary-education.htm

LaGrange College, Graduate Programs, Department of Education, LaGrange, GA 30240-2999. Offers curriculum and instruction (M Ed, Ed S); middle grades (MAT); secondary education (MAT). *Program availability:* Part-time, evening/weekend. *Degree requirements:* For master's, comprehensive exam. *Entrance requirements:* For master's, GRE, MAT, minimum GPA of 2.5. Additional exam requirements/ recommendations for international students: Required—TOEFL (minimum score 550 paper-based).

La Salle University, School of Arts and Sciences, Program in Education, Philadelphia, PA 19141-1199. Offers autism spectrum disorders (MA, Certificate); bilingual/bicultural studies (MA); classroom management (MA); dual early childhood and special education (MA); dual middle-level science and math and special education (MA); education (MA); English (MA); English as a second language (Certificate); history (MA); instructional coach (Certificate); instructional leadership (MA); reading specialist (MA, Certificate); secondary education (MA); special education (MA, Certificate). *Program availability:* Part-time, evening/weekend. *Degree requirements:* For master's, comprehensive exam. *Entrance requirements:* For master's, MAT or GRE, 2 letters of recommendation; for Certificate, GMAT or GRE, 2 letters of recommendation. Additional exam requirements/ recommendations for international students: Required—TOEFL. Electronic applications accepted. Application fee is waived when completed online. *Expenses:* Contact institution.

Lee University, Program in Education, Cleveland, TN 37320-3450. Offers art (MAT); curriculum and instruction (M Ed, Ed S); early childhood (MAT); educational leadership (M Ed, Ed S); elementary education (MAT); English and math (MAT); English and science (MAT); English and social studies (MAT); higher education administration (MS); history (MAT); history and economics (MAT); math and science (MAT); math and social studies (MAT); middle grades (MAT); science and social studies (MASW); secondary education (MAT); Spanish (MAT); special education (M Ed, MAT); TESOL (MAT). *Accreditation:* NCATE. *Program availability:* Part-time. *Faculty:* 13 full-time (5 women), 13 part-time/adjunct (7 women). *Students:* 32 full-time (26 women), 73 part-time (49 women); includes 13 minority (10 Black or African American, non-Hispanic/Latino; 3 Two or more races, non-Hispanic/Latino), 3 international. Average age 30. 56 applicants, 73% accepted, 34 enrolled. In 2018, 60 master's, 3 other advanced degrees awarded. *Degree requirements:* For master's, variable foreign language requirement, thesis optional, internship. *Entrance requirements:* For master's, MAT or GRE General Test, minimum undergraduate GPA of 2.75, 3 letters of recommendation, interview, writing sample, official transcripts, background check; for Ed S, minimum undergraduate and master's GPA of 2.75, official transcripts for undergraduate and master's degrees. Additional exam requirements/recommendations for international students: Required—TOEFL (minimum score 61 iBT). *Application deadline:* For fall admission, 6/1 priority date for domestic and international students; for spring admission, 11/1 priority date for domestic and international students; for summer admission, 4/1 priority date for domestic and international students. Applications are processed on a rolling basis. Application fee: $25. Electronic applications accepted. *Financial support:* In 2018–19, 43 students received support. Career-related internships or fieldwork, Federal Work-Study, institutionally sponsored loans, scholarships/grants, and unspecified assistantships available. Financial award application deadline: 3/1; financial award applicants required to submit FAFSA. *Unit head:* Dr. William Kamm, Director, 423-614-8544, E-mail: wkamm@leeuniversity.edu. *Application contact:* Jeffery McGirt, Director of Graduate Enrollment, 423-614-8691, Fax: 423-614-8317, E-mail: jmcgirt@leeuniversity.edu.
Website: http://www.leeuniversity.edu/academics/graduate/education

Lehman College of the City University of New York, School of Education, Department of Middle and High School Education, Bronx, NY 10468-1589. Offers English education (MS Ed); mathematics education (MA); science education (MS Ed); social studies education (MA); teaching English to speakers of other languages (MS Ed). *Program availability:* Part-time, evening/weekend.

Le Moyne College, Department of Education, Syracuse, NY 13214. Offers adolescent education (MS Ed, MST); adolescent education/special education (MS Ed, MST); adolescent English (MST), including grades 7-12; adolescent English/special education (MST), including grades 7-12; adolescent foreign language (MST), including grades 7-12; adolescent history (MST), including grades 7-12; childhood education (MS Ed); childhood education/special education (MS Ed); elementary education (MS Ed); general education (MS Ed); inclusive childhood education (MST); literacy education (MS Ed), including birth to grade 6, grades 5-12; school building leader (MS Ed); school building leadership (CAS); school district business leader (MS Ed, CAS); school district leader (MS Ed); school district leadership (CAS); secondary education (MS Ed); special education (MS Ed); teaching English to speakers of other languages (MS Ed); urban studies (MS Ed). *Accreditation:* TEAC. *Program availability:* Part-time, evening/ weekend. *Faculty:* 7 full-time (5 women), 16 part-time/adjunct (11 women). *Students:* 35 full-time (28 women), 119 part-time (84 women); includes 14 minority (5 Black or African American, non-Hispanic/Latino; 1 Asian, non-Hispanic/Latino; 7 Hispanic/Latino; 1 Two or more races, non-Hispanic/Latino), 1 international. Average age 30. 123 applicants, 89% accepted, 96 enrolled. In 2018, 66 master's, 48 CASs awarded. Terminal master's awarded for partial completion of doctoral program. *Degree requirements:* For master's, thesis. *Entrance requirements:* For master's, bachelor's degree with minimum undergraduate GPA of 3.0, 2 letters of recommendation, transcripts. Additional exam requirements/recommendations for international students: Required—TOEFL (minimum score 79 iBT); Recommended—IELTS (minimum score 6.5). *Application deadline:* For fall admission, 4/1 priority date for domestic and international students; for spring admission, 10/1 priority date for domestic and international students; for summer admission, 3/1 priority date for domestic and international students. Applications are processed on a rolling basis. Electronic applications accepted. *Expenses:* $734 per credit hour; wellness fee $70 per semester for full-time graduate students taking 9+ credit hours; technology fee $75 per semester for full-time graduate students taking 9+ credit hours, $25 per semester for part-time students; $1,470 per credit hour (for ED.D.). *Financial support:* In 2018–19, 44 students received support. Career-related internships or fieldwork, scholarships/grants, and health care benefits available. Support available to part-time students. Financial award applicants required to submit FAFSA. *Faculty research:* Minority teachers, special education, multiculturalism, literacy, technology, media literacy learning, autism, school district organization, service-learning, higher level problem solving, teacher leadership. *Unit head:* Dr. Stephen C. Fleury, Chair, Department of Education, 315-445-4376, Fax: 315-445-4744, E-mail: fleurysc@lemoyne.edu. *Application contact:* Jody F Manning, Assistant Director for Graduate Admission, 315-445-5444, Fax: 315-445-6092, E-mail: manninjf@lemoyne.edu.
Website: http://www.lemoyne.edu/education

Lesley University, Graduate School of Education, Cambridge, MA 02138-2790. Offers arts, community, and education (M Ed); autism studies (Certificate); curriculum and instruction (M Ed, CAGS); early childhood education (M Ed); ecological teaching and learning (MS); educational studies (PhD), including adult learning, educational leadership, individually designed; elementary education (M Ed); emergent technologies for educators (Certificate); ESLArts: language learning through the arts (M Ed); high school education (M Ed); individually designed (M Ed); integrated teaching through the arts (M Ed); literacy for K-8 classroom teachers (M Ed); mathematics education (M Ed); middle school education (M Ed); moderate disabilities (M Ed); online learning (Certificate); reading (CAGS); science in education (M Ed); severe disabilities (M Ed); special needs (CAGS); specialist teacher of reading (M Ed); teacher of visual art (M Ed); technology in education (M Ed, CAGS). *Accreditation:* TEAC. *Program availability:* Part-time, evening/weekend, online learning. *Degree requirements:* For master's, practicum; for doctorate, thesis/dissertation. *Entrance requirements:* For master's, Massachusetts Tests for Educator Licensure (MTEL), transcripts, statement of purpose, recommendations; interview (for special education); for doctorate, GRE General Test, transcripts, statement of purpose, recommendations, interview, master's degree, resume; for other advanced degree, interview, master's degree. Additional exam requirements/recommendations for international students: Required—TOEFL (minimum score 550 paper-based; 80 iBT). Electronic applications accepted. *Faculty research:* Assessment in literacy, mathematics and science; autism spectrum disorders; instructional technology and online learning; multicultural education and English language learners.

Lewis University, College of Education, Program in Middle Level Education, Romeoville, IL 60446. Offers MA. *Program availability:* Part-time. *Students:* 6 full-time (all women), 6 part-time (5 women); includes 1 minority (Hispanic/Latino). Average age 34. *Degree requirements:* For master's, comprehensive exam. *Entrance requirements:* For master's, writing exam, Test of Academic Proficiency/Basic Skills Test/ACT/SAT, bachelor's degree, minimum GPA of 2.75, 2 letters of recommendation. Additional exam requirements/recommendations for international students: Required—TOEFL (minimum score 550 paper-based; 79 iBT), IELTS (minimum score 6). *Application deadline:* For fall admission, 5/1 priority date for international students; for spring admission, 11/1 priority date for international students. Application fee: $40. Electronic applications accepted. *Financial support:* Federal Work-Study, scholarships/grants, and unspecified assistantships available. Financial award application deadline: 5/1; financial award applicants required to submit FAFSA. *Unit head:* Dr. Chris Palmi, Program Director. *Application contact:* Kathy Lisak, Graduate Admission Counselor, 815-836-5610, E-mail: grad@lewisu.edu.
Website: http://www.lewisu.edu/academics/mastersmiddleleveleducation/index.htm

Lincoln University, Graduate Studies, Jefferson City, MO 65101. Offers business administration (MBA); counseling (M Ed); environmental science (MS); higher education (MA); history (MA); natural sciences (MS); school teaching middle school with certification (M Ed); school teaching-elementary (M Ed); school teaching-secondary (M Ed); sociology (MA); sociology/criminal justice (MA); sustainable agriculture (MS). *Program availability:* Part-time, evening/weekend, 100% online, blended/hybrid learning. *Students:* 37 full-time (23 women), 52 part-time (25 women); includes 26 minority (24 Black or African American, non-Hispanic/Latino; 1 Asian, non-Hispanic/Latino; 1 Two or more races, non-Hispanic/Latino), 11 international. Average age 34. 67 applicants, 52% accepted, 29 enrolled. In 2018, 48 master's awarded. *Degree requirements:* For master's, comprehensive exam, thesis optional. *Entrance requirements:* For master's, GRE, MAT, or GMAT, minimum GPA of 2.75 overall, 3.0 in courses related to specialization; 3 letters of recommendation; minimum C average in English composition; personal statement of purpose. Additional exam requirements/recommendations for international students: Required—TOEFL (minimum score 500 paper-based; 61 iBT), IELTS (minimum score 5.5), Michigan English Language Assessment Battery (minimum score 80). *Application deadline:* For fall admission, 7/1 priority date for domestic students, 5/1 priority date for international students; for spring admission, 11/1 priority date for domestic students, 10/1 priority date for international students; for summer admission, 6/1 priority date for domestic students. Applications are processed on a rolling basis. Application fee: $30. Electronic applications accepted. *Expenses: Tuition, area resident:* Full-time $6984; part-time $291 per credit. Tuition, state resident: full-time $6984; part-time $291 per credit. Tuition, nonresident: full-time $12,996; part-time $541.50 per credit. *International tuition:* $12,996 full-time. *Required fees:* $1242.20. *Financial support:* In 2018–19, 9 research assistantships with tuition reimbursements (averaging $4,050 per year) were awarded; fellowships with tuition reimbursements, Federal Work-Study, scholarships/grants, and unspecified assistantships also available. Support available to part-time students. Financial award application deadline: 3/1; financial award applicants required to submit FAFSA. *Unit head:* Dr. Benjamin Arnold, Assistant Vice President of Academic Affairs, 573-681-5247, Fax: 573-681-5106, E-mail: gradschool@lincolnu.edu. *Application contact:* Sarah Robinett, Administrative Assistant, 573-681-5247, Fax: 573-681-5106, E-mail: gradschool@lincolnu.edu.
Website: http://www.lincolnu.edu/web/graduate-studies/graduate-studies

Long Island University–Hudson, Graduate School, Purchase, NY 10577. Offers autism (Advanced Certificate); bilingual education (Advanced Certificate); childhood education (MS Ed); crisis management (Advanced Certificate); early childhood education (MS Ed); educational leadership (MS Ed); health administration (MPA); literacy (MS Ed); marriage and family therapy (MS); mental health counseling (MS, Advanced Certificate), including credentialed alcoholism and substance abuse counselor (MS); middle childhood and adolescence education (MS Ed); pharmaceutics (MS), including cosmetic science, industrial pharmacy; public administration (MPA); school counseling (MS Ed, Advanced Certificate); school psychology (MS Ed); special education (MS Ed); TESOL (MS Ed); TESOL (all grades) (Advanced Certificate). *Program availability:* Part-time, evening/weekend. *Entrance requirements:* Additional exam requirements/recommendations for international students: Required—TOEFL. Electronic applications accepted. *Expenses:* Contact institution.

Long Island University–LIU Post, College of Education, Information and Technology, Brookville, NY 11548-1300. Offers adolescence education (MS); adolescence education 7-12 (MS); archives and records management (AC); art education (MS); childhood education (MS); childhood education/literacy B-6 (MS); childhood education/special education (MS); clinical mental health counseling (MS, AC); early childhood education (MS); early childhood education/childhood education (MS); educational leadership (AC);

educational technology (MS); information studies (PhD); interdisciplinary educational studies (Ed D); middle childhood education (MS); music education (MS); public library administration (AC); school counselor (MS); special education (MS Ed); speech-language pathology (MA); students with disabilities, 7-12 generalist (AC); TESOL (MA). *Accreditation:* ASHA; TEAC. *Program availability:* Part-time, 100% online, blended/hybrid learning. Terminal master's awarded for partial completion of doctoral program. *Degree requirements:* For master's, variable foreign language requirement, comprehensive exam (for some programs), thesis optional; for doctorate, comprehensive exam, thesis/dissertation. *Entrance requirements:* For master's and AC, GRE (for some programs). Additional exam requirements/recommendations for international students: Required—TOEFL (minimum score 550 paper-based, 75 iBT), IELTS, or PTE. Electronic applications accepted. *Faculty research:* Sleep; use of technology to develop executive function by students with disabilities; early childhood literacy development through play; social justice through education; using a structured protocol to discuss Bad News.

Longwood University, College of Graduate and Professional Studies, College of Education and Human Services, Farmville, VA 23909. Offers education (MS), including algebra and middle school mathematics, counselor education, elementary and middle school mathematics, elementary education, elementary education initial licensure, health and physical education, special education general curriculum, special education initial licensure; reading, literacy and learning (M Ed); school librarianship (M Ed); social work and communication sciences and disorders (MS), including communication sciences and disorders. *Accreditation:* NCATE. *Program availability:* Part-time, evening/weekend. *Degree requirements:* For master's, comprehensive exam (for some programs), thesis optional, professional portfolio, internship, clinical experience, or practicum. *Entrance requirements:* For master's, PRAXIS I (for initial teaching licensure programs); GRE (for some programs), bachelor's degree from regionally-accredited institution, 2 recommendations (3 for some programs), minimum 500-word personal essay, official transcripts, minimum GPA of 2.75, valid teaching license (for some programs). Additional exam requirements/recommendations for international students: Required—TOEFL (minimum score 570 paper-based), IELTS (minimum score 6.5). Electronic applications accepted. *Expenses:* Contact institution.

Louisiana Tech University, Graduate School, College of Education, Ruston, LA 71272. Offers counseling and guidance (MA), including clinical mental health counseling, human services, orientation and mobility; counseling psychology (PhD); curriculum and instruction (M Ed); cyber education (Graduate Certificate); dynamics of domestic and family violence (Graduate Certificate); early childhood education - PreK-3 (MAT); educational leadership (M Ed, Ed D); elementary education and special education mild/moderate grades 1-5 (MAT); higher education administration (Graduate Certificate); industrial/organizational psychology (MA, PhD); kinesiology (MS); middle school education (MAT), including mathematics; orientation and mobility (Graduate Certificate); rehabilitation teaching for the blind (Graduate Certificate); secondary education (MAT), including agriculture, biology, business, chemistry, English; special education: visually impaired (MAT); teacher leader education (Graduate Certificate); visual impairments - blind education (Graduate Certificate). *Accreditation:* NCATE. *Program availability:* Part-time. *Degree requirements:* For master's, thesis; for doctorate, thesis/dissertation. *Entrance requirements:* For master's and doctorate, GRE General Test. Additional exam requirements/recommendations for international students: Required—TOEFL (minimum score 550 paper-based; 80 iBT), IELTS (minimum score 6.5). Electronic applications accepted. *Faculty research:* Blindness and the best methods for increasing independence for individuals who are blind or visually impaired; educating and investigating factors contributing to improvements in human performance across the lifespan and a reduction in injury rates during training.

Lynn University, Donald E. and Helen L. Ross College of Education, Boca Raton, FL 33431-5598. Offers educational leadership (M Ed, Ed D), including K-12 (Ed D), school administration K-12 (M Ed); exceptional student education (M Ed), including school administration K-12. *Program availability:* Part-time, evening/weekend, online learning. *Faculty:* 6 full-time (4 women), 8 part-time/adjunct (7 women). *Students:* 38 full-time (30 women), 85 part-time (63 women); includes 50 minority (33 Black or African American, non-Hispanic/Latino; 1 Asian, non-Hispanic/Latino; 15 Hispanic/Latino; 1 Two or more races, non-Hispanic/Latino), 5 international. Average age 38. 78 applicants, 65% accepted, 41 enrolled. In 2018, 13 master's, 14 doctorates awarded. *Degree requirements:* For master's, comprehensive exam, thesis (for some programs), completion of degree in maximum of four calendar years; minimum cumulative GPA of 3.0 and B grade or higher in each course; orientation seminar (one credit); minimum of 40 credits; FTCE ESE K-12 Exam; for doctorate, thesis/dissertation, mid-program review; minimum cumulative GPA of 3.25 and B grade or higher in each course. *Entrance requirements:* For master's, bachelor's degree from accredited institution, minimum undergraduate GPA of 3.0, official undergraduate and graduate transcripts of all academic coursework attempted, current resume, statement of professional goals, writing sample, 2 recent letters of recommendation; for doctorate, professional practice statement that identifies applicant's goals and explains how Lynn's program will help attain them, official transcript showing conferral of master's degree, 2 letters of recommendation from previous professors or employers, current resume, interview. Additional exam requirements/recommendations for international students: Required—TOEFL (minimum score 550 paper-based; 80 iBT), IELTS (minimum score 6.5). *Application deadline:* For fall admission, 8/18 for domestic students, 8/4 for international students; for spring admission, 12/15 for domestic students, 12/1 for international students; for summer admission, 4/17 for domestic students, 4/3 for international students. Applications are processed on a rolling basis. Application fee: $45. Electronic applications accepted. *Expenses:* 850 per credit hour. *Financial support:* In 2018–19, 85 students received support. Career-related internships or fieldwork, Federal Work-Study, scholarships/grants, tuition waivers (partial), and unspecified assistantships available. Support available to part-time students. Financial award application deadline: 3/1; financial award applicants required to submit FAFSA. *Faculty research:* Student achievement, students with learning differences, teacher and student retention, student motivation and cognition, neuroscience leadership and learning. *Unit head:* Dr. Kathleen Weigel, Dean, College of Education, 561-237-7441, E-mail: kweigel@lynn.edu. *Application contact:* Steven Pruitt, Director of Graduate and Undergraduate Evening Admission, 561-237-7834, Fax: 561-237-7100, E-mail: spruitt@lynn.edu.
Website: http://www.lynn.edu/academics/colleges/education

Manhattanville College, School of Education, Jump Start Program, Purchase, NY 10577-2132. Offers childhood education and special education (grades 1-6) (MPS); early childhood education (birth-grade 2) (MAT); education (Advanced Certificate); English and special education (grades 5-12) (MPS); mathematics and special education (grades 5-12) (MPS); science and special education (grades 5-12) (MPS); social studies and special education (grades 5-12) (MPS); Spanish (grades 7-12) (MAT); tesol - teaching English as a second language (all grades) (MPS). *Program availability:* Part-time, evening/weekend. *Faculty:* 11 full-time (7 women), 78 part-time/adjunct (50 women). *Students:* 3 full-time (2 women), 16 part-time (11 women); includes 5 minority (1 Black or African American, non-Hispanic/Latino; 3 Hispanic/Latino; 1 Native Hawaiian or other Pacific Islander, non-Hispanic/Latino). Average age 31. 48 applicants, 54% accepted, 22 enrolled. In 2018, 23 master's, 1 other advanced degree awarded. *Degree requirements:* For master's, comprehensive exam (for some programs), thesis (for some programs), student teaching, research seminars, portfolios, internships, writing assessment; for Advanced Certificate, comprehensive exam (for some programs). *Entrance requirements:* For master's, for programs leading to certification, candidates must submit scores from GRE or MAT(miller analogies test), minimum undergraduate GPA of 3.0, all transcripts from all colleges and universities attended, 2 letters of recommendation, interview, essay (2-3 page personal statement that describes reasons for choosing education as profession and personal philosophy of education), proof of immunization (for those born after 1957). Additional exam requirements/recommendations for international students: Required—TOEFL (minimum score 600 paper-based; 110 iBT); Recommended—IELTS (minimum score 8). *Application deadline:* Applications are processed on a rolling basis. Application fee: $75. Electronic applications accepted. *Expenses:* 935 per credit. *Financial support:* Teaching assistantships, career-related internships or fieldwork, Federal Work-Study, institutionally sponsored loans, scholarships/grants, and unspecified assistantships available. Financial award application deadline: 3/15; financial award applicants required to submit FAFSA. *Faculty research:* Early childhood and technology, professional development schools and community schools, students with emotional difficulties, literacy and adolescents, mindfulness, changing suburbs institute, and community schools, studying the effects of the environment on special populations, the most difficult cases, students who are presented with multiple challenges: learning, behavioral and ACE experiences who see criminal behavior as a way to cope; working on giving them the tools they need to succeed. *Unit head:* Dr. Shelley Wepner, Dean, 914-323-3153, E-mail: Shelly.Wepner@mville.edu. *Application contact:* Alissa Wilson, Director, SOE Graduate Enrollment Management, 914-323-3150, Fax: 914-694-1732, E-mail: edschool@mville.edu.
Website: http://www.mville.edu/programs/jump-start

Manhattanville College, School of Education, Program in Literacy Education, Purchase, NY 10577-2132. Offers literacy (birth-grade 6) and special education childhood (grades 1-6) (MPS); literacy 5-12; special education generalist 7-12; special ed specialist 7-12 (MPS); literacy specialist (birth-grade 6) (MPS); literacy specialist (grades 5-12) (MPS); science of reading: multisensory instruction – the rose institute for learning and literacy (Advanced Certificate). *Program availability:* Part-time, evening/weekend. *Faculty:* 3 full-time (all women), 15 part-time/adjunct (14 women). *Students:* 2 full-time (both women), 8 part-time (all women). Average age 26. 6 applicants, 50% accepted, 1 enrolled. In 2018, 8 master's, 11 Advanced Certificates awarded. *Degree requirements:* For master's, comprehensive exam (for some programs), thesis (for some programs), student teaching, research seminars, portfolios, internships, writing assessment; for Advanced Certificate, comprehensive exam (for some programs). *Entrance requirements:* For master's, for programs leading to certification, candidates must submit scores from GRE or MAT(Miller Analogies Test), minimum undergraduate GPA of 3.0, all transcripts from all colleges and universities attended, 2 letters of recommendation, interview, essay (2-3 page personal statement that describes reasons for choosing education as profession and personal philosophy of education), proof of immunization (for those born after 1957). Additional exam requirements/recommendations for international students: Required—TOEFL (minimum score 600 paper-based; 110 iBT); Recommended—IELTS (minimum score 8). *Application deadline:* Applications are processed on a rolling basis. Application fee: $75. Electronic applications accepted. *Expenses:* 935 per credit. *Financial support:* Teaching assistantships, career-related internships or fieldwork, Federal Work-Study, institutionally sponsored loans, scholarships/grants, and unspecified assistantships available. Financial award application deadline: 3/15; financial award applicants required to submit FAFSA. *Faculty research:* Power of story for literacy development, English learners. *Total annual research expenditures:* $800. *Unit head:* Dr. Shelley Wepner, Dean, 914-323-3153, Fax: 914-323-5493, E-mail: Shelley.Wepner@mville.edu. *Application contact:* Alissa Wilson, Director, SOE Graduate Enrollment Management, 914-323-3150, Fax: 914-694-1732, E-mail: edschool@mville.edu.
Website: http://www.mville.edu/programs/literacy-education

Manhattanville College, School of Education, Program in Middle Childhood/Adolescence Education (Grades 5-12), Purchase, NY 10577-2132. Offers biology and special education (MPS); chemistry and special education (MPS); education for sustainability (Advanced Certificate); English and special education (MPS); literacy and special education (MPS); literacy specialist (MPS); math and special education (MPS); mathematics (Advanced Certificate); middle childhood/adolescence ed science (biology or chemistry grades 5-12) or (physics grades 7-12) (MAT); middle childhood/adolescence education (grades 5-12) English (MAT, Advanced Certificate); middle childhood/adolescence education (grades 5-12) mathematics (MAT, Advanced Certificate); middle childhood/adolescence education (grades 5-12) science (biology chemistry, physics, earth science) (Advanced Certificate); middle childhood/adolescence education (grades 5-12) social studies (MAT, Advanced Certificate); physics (MAT, Advanced Certificate); social studies (MAT); social studies and special education (MPS); special education generalist (MPS). *Program availability:* Part-time, evening/weekend. *Faculty:* 3 full-time (2 women), 9 part-time/adjunct (4 women). *Students:* 11 full-time (6 women), 17 part-time (12 women); includes 3 minority (1 Black or African American, non-Hispanic/Latino; 2 Hispanic/Latino). Average age 31. 17 applicants, 71% accepted, 7 enrolled. In 2018, 8 master's, 3 other advanced degrees awarded. *Degree requirements:* For master's, comprehensive exam (for some programs), thesis (for some programs), student teaching, research seminars, portfolios, internships, writing assessment; for Advanced Certificate, comprehensive exam (for some programs). *Entrance requirements:* For master's, for programs leading to certification, candidates must submit scores from GRE or MAT(Miller Analogies Test), minimum undergraduate GPA of 3.0, all transcripts from all colleges and universities attended, 2 letters of recommendation, interview, essay (2-3 page personal statement that describes reasons for choosing education as profession and personal philosophy of education), proof of immunization (for those born after 1957). Additional exam requirements/recommendations for international students: Required—TOEFL (minimum score 600 paper-based; 110 iBT); Recommended—IELTS (minimum score 8). *Application deadline:* Applications are processed on a rolling basis. Application fee: $75. Electronic applications accepted. *Expenses:* 935 per credit. *Financial support:* Teaching assistantships, career-related internships or fieldwork, Federal Work-Study, institutionally sponsored loans, scholarships/grants, and unspecified assistantships available. Financial award application deadline: 3/15; financial award applicants required to submit FAFSA. *Faculty research:* Education for sustainability. *Unit head:* Dr. Shelley Wepner, Dean, 914-323-3153, Fax: 914-323-5493, E-mail: Shelley.Wepner@mville.edu. *Application contact:* Alissa Wilson, Director, Graduate Admissions, 914-323-3150, Fax: 914-694-1732, E-mail: edschool@mville.edu.
Website: http://www.mville.edu/programs#/search/19

Manhattanville College, School of Education, Program in Special Education, Purchase, NY 10577-2132. Offers childhood education (grades 1-6) and special education: childhood (grades 1-6) (MPS); early childhood (birth-grade 2) and special education: early childhood (birth-grade 2) (MPS); English (5-9 and 7-12); special ed generalist (7-12); se English (7-12) (MPS); literacy (birth-grade 6) and special education childhood (grades 1-6) (MPS); literacy 5-12; special education generalist 7-12; special ed specialist 7-12 (MPS); math (5-9 and 7-12); special ed generalist (7-12); se math (7-12) (MPS); science: biology or chemistry (5-9 and 7-12); special ed generalist (7-12); se

science (7-12) (MPS); social studies (5-9 and 7-12); special ed generalist (7-12); se soc.st. (7-12) (MPS); special ed early childhood and childhood (birth-grade 6) (MPS); special education childhood (grades 1-6) (MPS); special education: childhood (grades 1-6) (Certificate); special education: early childhood (birth-grade 2) (MPS, Certificate); special education: early childhood (birth-grade 2) and childhood (grades 1-6) (Certificate); special education: grades 7-12 generalist (MPS, Certificate). *Program availability:* Part-time, evening/weekend. *Faculty:* 5 full-time (3 women), 35 part-time/adjunct (23 women). *Students:* 45 full-time (36 women), 179 part-time (152 women); includes 31 minority (6 Black or African American, non-Hispanic/Latino; 4 Asian, non-Hispanic/Latino; 19 Hispanic/Latino; 2 Native Hawaiian or other Pacific Islander, non-Hispanic/Latino), 1 international. Average age 28. 76 applicants, 68% accepted, 40 enrolled. In 2018, 99 master's, 2 Certificates awarded. *Degree requirements:* For master's, comprehensive exam (for some programs), thesis (for some programs), student teaching, research seminars, portfolios, internships, writing assessment; for Certificate, comprehensive exam (for some programs). *Entrance requirements:* For master's, for programs leading to certification, candidates must submit scores from GRE or MAT(Miller Analogies Test), minimum undergraduate GPA of 3.0, all transcripts from all colleges and universities attended, 2 letters of recommendation, interview, essay (2-3 page personal statement that describes reasons for choosing education as profession and personal philosophy of education), proof of immunization (for those born after 1957). Additional exam requirements/recommendations for international students: Required—TOEFL (minimum score 600 paper-based; 110 iBT); Recommended—IELTS (minimum score 8). *Application deadline:* Applications are processed on a rolling basis. Application fee: $75. Electronic applications accepted. *Expenses:* 935 per credit. *Financial support:* Teaching assistantships, career-related internships or fieldwork, Federal Work-Study, institutionally sponsored loans, scholarships/grants, and unspecified assistantships available. Financial award application deadline: 3/15; financial award applicants required to submit FAFSA. *Faculty research:* Students with emotional difficulties, literacy and adolescents, mindfulness, studying the effects of the environment on special populations, the most difficult cases, students who are presented with multiple challenges: learning, behavioral and ACE experiences who see criminal behavior as a way to cope; working on giving them the tools they need to succeed emotionally and cognitively despite the odds stacked against them. *Unit head:* Dr. Shelley Wepner, Dean, 914-323-3153, Fax: 914-323-5493, E-mail: Shelley.Wepner@mville.edu. *Application contact:* Alissa Wilson, Director, SOE Graduate Enrollment Management, 914-323-3150, Fax: 914-694-1732, E-mail: edschool@mville.edu.
Website: http://www.mville.edu/programs/special-education

Manhattanville College, School of Education, Program in Teaching of Languages Other than English, Purchase, NY 10577-2132. Offers adolescence education (grades 7-12) foreign language(French, Spanish, Italian and Latin) (MAT, Advanced Certificate). *Program availability:* Part-time, evening/weekend. *Faculty:* 2 full-time (1 woman), 1 (woman) part-time/adjunct. *Students:* 2 full-time (both women), 2 part-time (both women). Average age 28. 4 applicants, 75% accepted, 3 enrolled. In 2018, 2 master's awarded. *Degree requirements:* For master's, comprehensive exam (for some programs), thesis (for some programs), student teaching, research seminars, portfolios, internships, writing assessment; for Advanced Certificate, comprehensive exam (for some programs). *Entrance requirements:* For master's, for programs leading to certification, candidates must submit scores from GRE or MAT(Miller Analogies Test), minimum undergraduate GPA of 3.0, all transcripts from all colleges and universities attended, 2 letters of recommendation, interview, essay (2-3 page personal statement that describes reasons for choosing education as profession and personal philosophy of education), proof of immunization (for those born after 1957). Additional exam requirements/recommendations for international students: Required—TOEFL (minimum score 600 paper-based; 110 iBT); Recommended—IELTS (minimum score 8). *Application deadline:* Applications are processed on a rolling basis. Application fee: $75. Electronic applications accepted. *Expenses:* 935 per credit. *Financial support:* Teaching assistantships, career-related internships or fieldwork, Federal Work-Study, institutionally sponsored loans, scholarships/grants, and unspecified assistantships available. Financial award application deadline: 3/15; financial award applicants required to submit FAFSA. *Faculty research:* Changing suburbs institute and community schools. *Unit head:* Dr. Shelley Wepner, Dean, 914-323-3153, Fax: 914-323-5493, E-mail: Shelley.Wepner@mville.edu. *Application contact:* Alissa Wilson, Director, SOE Graduate Enrollment Management, 914-323-3150, Fax: 914-694-1732, E-mail: edschool@mville.edu.
Website: https://www.mville.edu/programs/teaching-languages-other-english

Mary Baldwin University, Graduate Studies, Programs in Education, Staunton, VA 24401-3610. Offers applied behavior analysis (MS); autism spectrum disorders (M Ed); elementary education (M Ed, MAT); English as a second language (M Ed); environment-based learning (M Ed); gifted education (M Ed); higher education (MS); leadership (M Ed); middle grades education (MAT); reading education (M Ed); special education (M Ed). *Accreditation:* TEAC.

Marygrove College, Graduate Studies, Detroit, MI 48221-2599. Offers autism spectrum disorders (M Ed, Certificate); curriculum instruction and assessment (MAT); educational leadership (MA); educational technology (M Ed); effective teaching in the 21st century-classroom focus (MAT); effective teaching in the 21st century-technology focus (MAT); human resource management (MA, Certificate); mathematics 6-8 (MAT); mathematics K-5 (MAT); reading and literacy K-6 (MAT); reading specialist (M Ed); school administrator (Certificate); social justice (MA); special education (MAT); special education - learning disabilities (M Ed); teaching - pre-elementary education (M Ed); teaching - pre-secondary education (M Ed). *Program availability:* Part-time, evening/weekend, 100% online, blended/hybrid learning. *Entrance requirements:* For master's, all official bachelor's transcripts. Additional exam requirements/recommendations for international students: Required—TOEFL (minimum score 550 paper-based; 80 iBT). Electronic applications accepted.

Maryville University of Saint Louis, School of Education, St. Louis, MO 63141-7299. Offers early childhood education (MA Ed); educational leadership (Ed D); educational leadership w/principal certification (MA Ed); elementary education (MA Ed); gifted (MA Ed); higher education leadership (Ed D); middle grades education (MA Ed); reading/literacy specialist (MA Ed); teacher as leader (Ed D). *Accreditation:* NCATE. *Program availability:* Part-time, 100% online, blended/hybrid learning. *Faculty:* 16 full-time (8 women), 18 part-time/adjunct (11 women). *Students:* 12 full-time (all women), 311 part-time (234 women); includes 99 minority (84 Black or African American, non-Hispanic/Latino; 2 Asian, non-Hispanic/Latino; 9 Hispanic/Latino; 4 Two or more races, non-Hispanic/Latino), 2 international. Average age 38. In 2018, 25 master's, 100 doctorates awarded. *Degree requirements:* For master's, thesis, project. *Entrance requirements:* For master's, minimum cumulative GPA of 3.0, 3 professional recommendations, essays, interview with program faculty; for doctorate, minimum GPA of 3.0, 3 professional recommendations, essay, interview, on-site writing sample. Additional exam requirements/recommendations for international students: Required—TOEFL (minimum score 550 paper-based; 79 iBT). *Application deadline:* Applications are processed on a rolling basis. Electronic applications accepted. *Expenses:* $449 per credit hour for master's programs; $897 per credit hour for doctoral programs. *Financial support:* Career-related internships or fieldwork, Federal Work-Study, tuition waivers (partial), and professional educator discounts available. Financial award application deadline: 4/1; financial award applicants required to submit FAFSA. *Faculty research:* Collaboration with public schools, pre-service program development, mathematics, diversity, literacy. *Unit head:* Dr. Maschael Schappe, Dean, 314-529-9670, Fax: 314-529-9921, E-mail: mschappe@maryville.edu. *Application contact:* Stacey Ruffin, Director of Clinical Experiences & Partnerships, 314-529-9542, Fax: 314-529-9921, E-mail: sruffin@maryville.edu.
Website: http://www.maryville.edu/ed/graduate-programs/

McNeese State University, Doré School of Graduate Studies, Burton College of Education, Department of Education Professions, Program in Middle School Education Grades 4-8, Lake Charles, LA 70609. Offers middle school education grades 4-8 (Postbaccalaureate Certificate), including mathematics, science. *Entrance requirements:* For degree, PRAXIS, 2 letters of recommendation, autobiography.

Mercer University, Graduate Studies, Cecil B. Day Campus, Tift College of Education (Atlanta), Atlanta, GA 30341. Offers curriculum and instruction (PhD); early childhood education (M Ed, MAT, Ed S); educational leadership (PhD), including higher education leadership, P-12 school leadership; educational leadership P-12 (M Ed, Ed S); higher education leadership (M Ed); independent and charter school leadership (M Ed); middle grades education (M Ed, MAT); secondary education (M Ed, MAT); teacher leadership (Ed S). *Accreditation:* NCATE. *Program availability:* Part-time, evening/weekend. *Degree requirements:* For master's and Ed S, research project; for doctorate, comprehensive exam, thesis/dissertation. *Entrance requirements:* For master's, GRE or MAT, minimum undergraduate GPA of 2.75; for doctorate, GRE; for Ed S, GRE or MAT, minimum GPA of 3.25; 3 years of certified teaching experience (for educational leadership and teacher leadership). Additional exam requirements/recommendations for international students: Required—TOEFL (minimum score 80 iBT). Electronic applications accepted. *Expenses:* Contact institution. *Faculty research:* Educational technology, multicultural and minority issues in education, educational leadership (P-12 and higher education), school discipline and school bullying, standards-based mathematics education.

Mercy College, School of Education, Program in Teaching Literacy, Dobbs Ferry, NY 10522-1189. Offers teaching literacy (Advanced Certificate); teaching literacy, birth-6 (MS); teaching literacy, grades 5-12 (MS). *Program availability:* Part-time, evening/weekend. *Students:* 7 full-time (all women), 27 part-time (24 women); includes 9 minority (2 Black or African American, non-Hispanic/Latino; 7 Hispanic/Latino). Average age 35. 33 applicants, 64% accepted, 17 enrolled. In 2018, 2 master's, 10 other advanced degrees awarded. *Degree requirements:* For master's and Advanced Certificate, Capstone project; clinical practice; for initial New York State certification, passing scores in the following are required: Educating All Students, Content Specialty Test, edTPA. *Entrance requirements:* For master's and Advanced Certificate, GRE or PRAXIS, transcript(s); resume. Additional exam requirements/recommendations for international students: Required—TOEFL (minimum score 600 paper-based; 71 iBT), IELTS (minimum score 8). *Application deadline:* Applications are processed on a rolling basis. Application fee: $40. Electronic applications accepted. *Expenses: Tuition:* Full-time $15,696; part-time $872 per credit. *Required fees:* $642; $161 per term. Tuition and fees vary according to course load, degree level and program. *Financial support:* Career-related internships or fieldwork, Federal Work-Study, scholarships/grants, and unspecified assistantships available. Support available to part-time students. Financial award applicants required to submit FAFSA. *Unit head:* Dr. Eric Martone, Interim Dean, School of Education, 914-674-7618, Fax: 914-674-7352, E-mail: emartone@mercy.edu. *Application contact:* Allison Gurdineer, Executive Director of Admissions, 877-637-2946, Fax: 914-674-7382, E-mail: admissions@mercy.edu.
Website: https://www.mercy.edu/education/literacy-and-multilingual-studies

Middle Tennessee State University, College of Graduate Studies, College of Education, Department of Elementary and Special Education, Major in Curriculum and Instruction, Murfreesboro, TN 37132. Offers early childhood education (M Ed); elementary education (M Ed, Ed S); middle school education (M Ed). *Accreditation:* NCATE. *Program availability:* Part-time, evening/weekend, online learning. *Degree requirements:* For master's, comprehensive exam; for Ed S, comprehensive exam, thesis or alternative. *Entrance requirements:* For master's and Ed S, GRE, MAT or PRAXIS. Additional exam requirements/recommendations for international students: Required—TOEFL (minimum score 525 paper-based; 71 iBT) or IELTS (minimum score 6). Electronic applications accepted.

Milligan College, Area of Education, Milligan College, TN 37682. Offers combined preK-3/K-5 education (M Ed); educational leadership (Ed D); educational specialist (Ed S); K-5 education (M Ed); middle grades education (M Ed); preK-3 education (M Ed); preK-3 special education (M Ed); secondary education (M Ed). *Accreditation:* NCATE. *Program availability:* Part-time, 100% online, blended/hybrid learning. *Faculty:* 5 full-time (3 women), 6 part-time/adjunct (3 women). *Students:* 38 full-time (31 women), 8 part-time (4 women); includes 2 minority (1 Hispanic/Latino; 1 Two or more races, non-Hispanic/Latino), 1 international. Average age 35. 36 applicants, 97% accepted, 32 enrolled. In 2018, 18 master's awarded. *Degree requirements:* For master's, thesis, portfolio, research project; for doctorate, thesis/dissertation, portfolio, research project. *Entrance requirements:* For master's, MAT, GRE General Test, ACT, SAT, or PRAXIS, undergraduate degree and supporting transcripts, professional recommendations, interview; for doctorate, MAT or GRE, master's degree and supporting transcripts, demonstrated scholastic ability, recognized leadership role within education, professional recommendations, essay/personal statement, portfolio (professional development plan, evidence of ability, knowledge and qualities), interview. Additional exam requirements/recommendations for international students: Required—TOEFL (minimum score 550 paper-based, 79 iBT) or IELTS (6.5). *Application deadline:* For fall admission, 8/1 priority date for domestic students, 6/1 for international students; for spring admission, 11/15 priority date for domestic students, 12/1 for international students; for summer admission, 4/1 for domestic students. Applications are processed on a rolling basis. Application fee: $30. Electronic applications accepted. *Expenses:* $365 per hour (for masters); $485 per hour (for doctoral); $375 fees per semester; $75 one-time records fee. *Financial support:* Scholarships/grants available. Financial award application deadline: 12/1; financial award applicants required to submit FAFSA. *Faculty research:* Assessment; school mental health; literacy; technology; educator preparation. *Unit head:* Dr. Angela Hilton-Prillhart, Area Chair of Education, 423-461-8769, Fax: 423-461-3103, E-mail: anhilton-prillhart@milligan.edu. *Application contact:* Melissa Dillow, Graduate Admissions Recruiter, Education, 423-461-8306, Fax: 423-461-8982, E-mail: msdillow@milligan.edu.
Website: http://www.Milligan.edu/GPS

Minot State University, Graduate School, Teacher Education and Human Performance Department, Minot, ND 58707-0002. Offers elementary education (M Ed). *Accreditation:* NCATE. *Degree requirements:* For master's, thesis. *Entrance requirements:* For master's, 2 years of teaching experience, bachelor's degree in education, minimum GPA of 2.75. Additional exam requirements/recommendations for international students: Required—TOEFL (minimum score 79 iBT), IELTS (minimum score 6).

Mississippi State University, College of Education, Department of Curriculum, Instruction and Special Education, Mississippi State, MS 39762. Offers early childhood education (PhD); elementary education (MS, PhD, Ed S), including early childhood

education (MS), general elementary education (MS), middle level education (MS); general curriculum and instruction (PhD); reading education (PhD); secondary education (MAT, MS, PhD, Ed S); special education (MAT, MS, PhD, Ed S). *Accreditation:* NCATE. *Program availability:* Part-time, evening/weekend. *Faculty:* 20 full-time (14 women), 1 (woman) part-time/adjunct. *Students:* 24 full-time (16 women), 151 part-time (109 women); includes 44 minority (38 Black or African American, non-Hispanic/Latino; 3 American Indian or Alaska Native, non-Hispanic/Latino; 1 Hispanic/Latino; 2 Two or more races, non-Hispanic/Latino), 3 international. Average age 32. 65 applicants, 65% accepted, 38 enrolled. In 2018, 57 master's, 3 doctorates, 1 other advanced degree awarded. *Degree requirements:* For master's, comprehensive exam; for doctorate, thesis/dissertation; for Ed S, comprehensive exam, thesis or alternative. *Entrance requirements:* For master's, GRE, minimum GPA of 2.75 in junior and senior year, eligibility for initial teacher certification; for doctorate, GRE, minimum GPA of 3.4 on previous graduate work; for Ed S, GRE, minimum GPA of 3.2 on master's degree. Additional exam requirements/recommendations for international students: Required—TOEFL (minimum score 550 paper-based; 79 iBT); Recommended—IELTS (minimum score 6.5). *Application deadline:* For fall admission, 3/1 priority date for domestic students, 5/1 for international students; for spring admission, 9/1 priority date for domestic students, 9/1 for international students. Applications are processed on a rolling basis. Application fee: $60 ($80 for international students). Electronic applications accepted. *Expenses:* Tuition, state resident: full-time $8450; part-time $360.59 per credit hour. Tuition, nonresident: full-time $23,140; part-time $969.09 per credit hour. *Required fees:* $110. One-time fee: $55 full-time. Part-time tuition and fees vary according to course load, degree level, campus/location and reciprocity agreements. *Financial support:* In 2018–19, 5 research assistantships with partial tuition reimbursements (averaging $11,453 per year), 1 teaching assistantship (averaging $11,700 per year) were awarded; Federal Work-Study, institutionally sponsored loans, scholarships/grants, and unspecified assistantships also available. Financial award application deadline: 4/1; financial award applicants required to submit FAFSA. *Faculty research:* Early childhood education, reading, rural schools, multicultural education, use of technology in instruction. *Unit head:* Dr. Linda Cornelious, Professor and Head, 662-325-3747, Fax: 662-325-7857, E-mail: lcornelious@colled.msstate.edu. *Application contact:* Robbie Salters, Admissions and Enrollment Assistant, 662-325-7400, E-mail: rsalters@grad.msstate.edu.
Website: http://www.cise.msstate.edu/

Morehead State University, Graduate School, College of Education, Department of Foundational and Graduate Studies in Education, Morehead, KY 40351. Offers adult and higher education (MA, Ed S); certified professional counselor (Ed S); counseling P-12 (MA); curriculum and instruction (Ed S); educational technology (MA Ed); instructional leadership (Ed S); school administration (MA); school counseling (Ed S); teacher leader business and marketing content (MA Ed); teacher leader business and marketing technology (MA Ed); teacher leader educational technology (MA Ed); teacher leader English (MA Ed); teacher leader gifted education (MA Ed); teacher leader IECE certification (MA Ed); teacher leader interdisciplinary education P-5 (MA Ed); teacher leader middle grades (MA Ed); teacher leader non IECE certification (MA Ed); teacher leader reading/writing - non-certification (MA Ed); teacher leader reading/writing certification (MA Ed); teacher leader school communication - certification (MA Ed); teacher leader school communication - non-certification (MA Ed); teacher leader social studies (MA Ed); teacher leader special education (MA Ed). *Accreditation:* NCATE. *Program availability:* Part-time, evening/weekend. *Degree requirements:* For master's, thesis optional, oral and/or written comprehensive exams; for Ed S, thesis, oral exam. *Entrance requirements:* For master's, GRE General Test, minimum overall undergraduate GPA of 2.5; for Ed S, GRE General Test, interview, master's degree, minimum GPA of 3.5, work experience. Additional exam requirements/recommendations for international students: Required—TOEFL (minimum score 500 paper-based). Electronic applications accepted. *Faculty research:* Character education, school accountability, computer applications for school administrators.

Morehead State University, Graduate School, College of Education, Department of Middle Grades and Secondary Education, Morehead, KY 40351. Offers business and marketing education (MAT); English/language arts 5-9 (MAT); French (MAT); health P-12 (MAT); mathematics 5-9 (MAT); physical education P-12 (MAT); science 5-9 (MAT); secondary biology (MAT); secondary chemistry (MAT); secondary earth science (MAT); secondary English (MAT); secondary math (MAT); secondary physics (MAT); secondary social studies (MAT); social studies 5-9 (MAT); Spanish (MAT). *Program availability:* Part-time, evening/weekend. *Degree requirements:* For master's, portfolio. *Entrance requirements:* For master's, GRE or PRAXIS II content exam, minimum overall undergraduate GPA of 2.5. Additional exam requirements/recommendations for international students: Required—TOEFL (minimum score 500 paper-based). Electronic applications accepted.

Mount St. Joseph University, Graduate Education Program, Cincinnati, OH 45233-1670. Offers adolescent to young adult education (MA); dyslexia (Certificate); inclusive early childhood education (MA); middle childhood education (MA); multicultural special education (MA); reading science (MA). *Accreditation:* TEAC. *Program availability:* Part-time, evening/weekend, 100% online, blended/hybrid learning. *Degree requirements:* For master's, comprehensive exam, thesis, research project, student teaching, clinical and field-based experiences. *Entrance requirements:* For master's, GRE (if GPA is below 3.0), letter of intent, 2 referrals, background check, interview, resume, minimum undergraduate GPA of 3.0. Additional exam requirements/recommendations for international students: Required—TOEFL (minimum score 560 paper-based; 83 iBT). Electronic applications accepted. *Expenses:* Contact institution. *Faculty research:* Foreign and second language learning problems/reading disabilities, multicultural/bilingual special education, science education, pedagogical content knowledge, early childhood, response to intervention.

Mount Saint Mary College, Division of Education, Newburgh, NY 12550-3494. Offers adolescence and special education (MS Ed); childhood education (MS Ed); literacy education (MS Ed); middle school (7-9) (MS Ed). *Accreditation:* NCATE. *Program availability:* Part-time, evening/weekend. *Faculty:* 7 full-time (6 women), 7 part-time/adjunct (all women). *Students:* 19 full-time (14 women), 78 part-time (64 women); includes 7 minority (5 Hispanic/Latino; 1 Native Hawaiian or other Pacific Islander, non-Hispanic/Latino; 1 Two or more races, non-Hispanic/Latino). Average age 28. 31 applicants, 61% accepted, 17 enrolled. In 2018, 28 master's awarded. *Entrance requirements:* Additional exam requirements/recommendations for international students: Required—TOEFL (minimum score 80 iBT). *Application deadline:* Applications are processed on a rolling basis. Application fee: $45. Electronic applications accepted. Application fee is waived when completed online. *Expenses: Tuition:* Full-time $14,454; part-time $803 per credit. *Required fees:* $172; $86 per semester. *Financial support:* In 2018–19, 17 students received support. Institutionally sponsored loans, scholarships/grants, and unspecified assistantships available. Financial award application deadline: 4/15; financial award applicants required to submit FAFSA. *Faculty research:* Learning and teaching styles, computers in special education, language development. *Unit head:* Dr. Vicki Caruana, Graduate Coordinator, 845-569-3530, Fax: 845-569-3551, E-mail: Victoria.caruana@msmc.edu. *Application contact:* Eileen Bardney, Director of Admissions, 845-569-3254, Fax: 845-569-3438, E-mail: Eileen.Bardney@msmc.edu.
Website: http://www.msmc.edu/Academics/Graduate_Programs/Master_of_Science_in_Education

Mount Saint Vincent University, Graduate Programs, Faculty of Education, Program in Elementary and Middle School Education, Halifax, NS B3M 2J6, Canada. Offers M Ed, MA Ed, MA-R. *Program availability:* Part-time, evening/weekend, online learning. *Degree requirements:* For master's, thesis (for some programs). *Entrance requirements:* For master's, bachelor's degree in education, 1 year of teaching experience. Electronic applications accepted. *Faculty research:* Curriculum theory, mathematics education, philosophy in teacher education, science education, literacy education.

Murray State University, College of Education and Human Services, Department of Adolescent, Career, and Special Education, Murray, KY 42071. Offers career and technical education (MS); middle school teacher leader (MA Ed); secondary teacher leader (MA Ed); special education (MA Ed), including mild learning and behavior disorders, moderate to severe disabilities (P-12), teacher leader in special education learning and behavior disorders; teacher education and professional development (Ed S). *Accreditation:* NCATE. *Program availability:* Part-time. *Entrance requirements:* For master's and Ed S, GRE or GMAT, minimum university GPA of 2.75. Additional exam requirements/recommendations for international students: Required—TOEFL (minimum score 527 paper-based; 71 iBT). Electronic applications accepted.

Murray State University, College of Education and Human Services, Department of Educational Studies, Leadership and Counseling, Murray, KY 42071. Offers college advising (Certificate); education administration (MA Ed); human development and leadership (MS, Certificate); library media (MA Ed); middle school teacher leader (MA Ed); P-20 and community leadership (Ed D); postsecondary education administration (MA Ed); school counseling (MA Ed); school guidance and counseling (Ed S); secondary teacher leader (MA Ed). *Program availability:* Part-time, evening/weekend, 100% online, blended/hybrid learning. *Entrance requirements:* For master's and other advanced degree, GRE or GMAT, minimum university GPA of 2.75. Additional exam requirements/recommendations for international students: Required—TOEFL (minimum score 527 paper-based; 71 iBT). Electronic applications accepted.

National Louis University, National College of Education, Chicago, IL 60603. Offers administration and supervision (M Ed, Ed D, CAS, Ed S); curriculum and instruction (M Ed, MS Ed, CAS); early childhood administration (M Ed, CAS); early childhood education (M Ed, MAT, MS Ed, CAS); education (Ed D); educational psychology/human learning and development (M Ed, MS Ed, CAS, Ed S); elementary education (MAT); interdisciplinary curriculum and instruction (M Ed); mathematics education (M Ed, MS Ed, CAS); middle grades education (MAT); reading and language (M Ed, MS Ed, CAS); school psychology (M Ed, Ed S); science education (M Ed, MS Ed, CAS); secondary education (MAT); special education (M Ed, MAT, CAS); technology in education (M Ed, CAS). *Accreditation:* NCATE. *Program availability:* Part-time, evening/weekend. *Degree requirements:* For doctorate, comprehensive exam, thesis/dissertation. *Entrance requirements:* For master's, MAT or GRE, minimum GPA of 3.0; for doctorate, GRE General Test, minimum GPA of 3.25, interview, resume, writing sample, 4 recommendations. Additional exam requirements/recommendations for international students: Required—TOEFL (minimum score 550 paper-based; 79 iBT).

Nazareth College of Rochester, Graduate Studies, Department of Education, Program in Inclusive Adolescence Education, Rochester, NY 14618. Offers MS Ed. *Accreditation:* TEAC. *Entrance requirements:* For master's, minimum GPA of 3.0. Additional exam requirements/recommendations for international students: Required—TOEFL or IELTS.

New York Institute of Technology, School of Interdisciplinary Studies and Education, Department of Teacher Education, Old Westbury, NY 11568-8000. Offers adolescence education (MS), including math (MAT, MS), science; adolescent education (MAT), including biology, chemistry, English, math (MAT, MS), social studies; childhood education (MS); early childhood (MS). *Program availability:* Part-time, evening/weekend, 100% online, blended/hybrid learning. *Faculty:* 2 full-time (both women), 8 part-time/adjunct (5 women). *Students:* 47 full-time (45 women), 56 part-time (47 women); includes 36 minority (13 Black or African American, non-Hispanic/Latino; 1 American Indian or Alaska Native, non-Hispanic/Latino; 7 Asian, non-Hispanic/Latino; 12 Hispanic/Latino; 1 Native Hawaiian or other Pacific Islander, non-Hispanic/Latino; 2 Two or more races, non-Hispanic/Latino), 3 international. Average age 31. 81 applicants, 53% accepted, 27 enrolled. In 2018, 27 master's awarded. *Entrance requirements:* For master's, GRE or MAT, BS or equivalent; minimum cumulative undergraduate GPA of 3.0; NY state initial certification; BS with major (or minimum 30 credits in a concentration) in biology, chemistry, English, math, physics, or social studies (for MS in childhood, early childhood education, and MAT); interview; personal statement. Additional exam requirements/recommendations for international students: Required—TOEFL (minimum score 79 iBT), IELTS (minimum score 6), PTE (minimum score 53). *Application deadline:* Applications are processed on a rolling basis. Application fee: $50. Electronic applications accepted. *Expenses:* $1285 per credit plus $215 fees per year (full-time) or $175 fees per year (part-time); $1395 per 3-credit education UFT or off-site graduate course. *Financial support:* Career-related internships or fieldwork, Federal Work-Study, scholarships/grants, tuition waivers (full and partial), and unspecified assistantships available. Support available to part-time students. Financial award application deadline: 2/15; financial award applicants required to submit FAFSA. *Faculty research:* Evolving definition of new literacies and its impact on teaching and learning (twenty-first century skills), new literacies practices in teacher education, teachers' professional development, English language and literacy learning through mobile learning, teaching reading to culturally and linguistically diverse children. *Application contact:* Alice Dolitsky, Director, Graduate Admissions, 516-686-7520, Fax: 516-686-1116, E-mail: admissions@nyit.edu.
Website: http://www.nyit.edu/departments/teacher_education

Niagara University, Graduate Division of Education, Concentration in Teacher Education, Niagara University, NY 14109. Offers early childhood and childhood education (MS Ed, Certificate); early childhood special education (MS); middle and adolescence education (MS Ed); special education (MS Ed), including 1-6, 7-12; special education (grades 1-12) (Certificate); teaching English to speakers of other languages (MS Ed, Certificate). *Accreditation:* NCATE. *Students:* 106 full-time (75 women), 105 part-time (90 women); includes 15 minority (5 Black or African American, non-Hispanic/Latino; 2 American Indian or Alaska Native, non-Hispanic/Latino; 2 Asian, non-Hispanic/Latino; 2 Hispanic/Latino; 4 Two or more races, non-Hispanic/Latino), 40 international. Average age 28. In 2018, 81 master's, 21 other advanced degrees awarded. *Entrance requirements:* For master's, GRE General Test or Academic Literacy Skills Test (ALST). Additional exam requirements/recommendations for international students: Required—TOEFL (minimum score 550 paper-based; 79 iBT), IELTS (minimum score 6). *Application deadline:* For fall admission, 8/1 for domestic students. Applications are processed on a rolling basis. Electronic applications accepted. *Expenses:* Contact institution. *Financial support:* Research assistantships with tuition reimbursements, teaching assistantships with tuition reimbursements, career-related internships or fieldwork, Federal Work-Study, scholarships/grants, and unspecified assistantships available. Support available to part-time students. Financial award application deadline: 4/15; financial award applicants required to submit FAFSA. *Unit head:* Dr. Chandra Foote, Dean, College of Education, 716-286-8549, E-mail: cjf@niagara.edu. *Application contact:* Evan Pierce, Associate Director, Graduate Studies, 716-286-8327, E-mail: epierce@niagara.edu.
Website: http://www.niagara.edu/teacher-education

Nicholls State University, Graduate Studies, College of Education, Department of Teacher Education, Thibodaux, LA 70310. Offers curriculum and instruction (M Ed); educational leadership (M Ed); elementary education (MAT); human performance education (MAT); middle school education (MAT); secondary education (MAT). *Accreditation:* NCATE. *Program availability:* Part-time, evening/weekend, online learning. *Degree requirements:* For master's, comprehensive exam, portfolio. *Entrance requirements:* For master's, GRE General Test, teaching license. Electronic applications accepted.

North Carolina State University, Graduate School, College of Education, Department of Teacher Education and Learning Sciences, Program in Middle Grades Education, Raleigh, NC 27695. Offers M Ed, MS. *Accreditation:* NCATE. *Degree requirements:* For master's, thesis optional. *Entrance requirements:* For master's, GRE General Test or MAT, minimum GPA of 3.0 in major.

Northeastern Illinois University, College of Graduate Studies and Research, Daniel L. Goodwin College of Education, Program in Middle Level Education, Chicago, IL 60625-4699. Offers MAT.

Northwestern State University of Louisiana, Graduate Studies and Research, College of Education and Human Development, Program in Middle School Education, Natchitoches, LA 71497. Offers MAT. *Degree requirements:* For master's, comprehensive exam, thesis or alternative. *Entrance requirements:* For master's, GRE General Test, minimum undergraduate GPA of 2.5. Additional exam requirements/recommendations for international students: Required—TOEFL. Electronic applications accepted.

Northwest Missouri State University, Graduate School, School of Education, Maryville, MO 64468-6001. Offers early childhood education (MS Ed); education leadership (MS Ed), including elementary, K-12, secondary; educational leadership (Ed S), including elementary school principalship, secondary school principalship, superintendency; educational leadership and policy analysis (Ed D); elementary education (MS Ed); elementary mathematics (MS Ed); higher education leadership (MS); middle school education (MS Ed); reading (MS Ed); special education (MS Ed); teacher leadership (MS Ed); teaching English language learners (MS Ed). *Accreditation:* NCATE. *Program availability:* Part-time. *Faculty:* 26 full-time (16 women). *Students:* 109 full-time (87 women), 385 part-time (270 women); includes 30 minority (10 Black or African American, non-Hispanic/Latino; 2 American Indian or Alaska Native, non-Hispanic/Latino; 3 Asian, non-Hispanic/Latino; 12 Hispanic/Latino; 1 Native Hawaiian or other Pacific Islander, non-Hispanic/Latino; 2 Two or more races, non-Hispanic/Latino), 1 international. Average age 33. 210 applicants, 72% accepted, 142 enrolled. In 2018, 71 master's, 11 other advanced degrees awarded. *Degree requirements:* For master's, comprehensive exam; for Ed S, comprehensive exam, thesis. *Entrance requirements:* For master's, GRE General Test, writing sample; for Ed S, minimum graduate GPA of 3.25. Additional exam requirements/recommendations for international students: Required—TOEFL (minimum score 550 paper-based). *Application deadline:* For fall admission, 7/1 for domestic and international students; for spring admission, 11/15 for domestic and international students. Applications are processed on a rolling basis. Application fee: $0 ($75 for international students). Electronic applications accepted. *Expenses:* $389.11 in-state and $653.92 out-of-state per credit hour. *Financial support:* Research assistantships with full tuition reimbursements, teaching assistantships with full tuition reimbursements, and unspecified assistantships available. Financial award application deadline: 4/1; financial award applicants required to submit FAFSA. *Unit head:* Dr. Tim Wall, Director, 660-562-1179, E-mail: timwall@nwmissouri.edu. *Application contact:* Dr. Tim Wall, Director, 660-562-1179, E-mail: timwall@nwmissouri.edu.
Website: https://www.nwmissouri.edu/education/index.htm

Ohio University, Graduate College, Gladys W. and David H. Patton College of Education and Human Services, Department of Teacher Education, Athens, OH 45701-2979. Offers adolescent to young adult education (M Ed); curriculum and instruction (M Ed, PhD); early childhood/special education (M Ed); intervention specialist/mild-moderate needs (M Ed); intervention specialist/moderate-intensive needs (M Ed); middle childhood education (M Ed); reading education (M Ed). *Program availability:* Part-time, evening/weekend. *Degree requirements:* For master's, thesis or alternative; for doctorate, comprehensive exam, thesis/dissertation. *Entrance requirements:* For master's, GRE General Test or MAT (if GPA is below 2.9); for doctorate, GRE General Test, minimum GPA of 3.4, work experience. Additional exam requirements/recommendations for international students: Required—TOEFL (minimum score 550 paper-based; 80 iBT) or IELTS (minimum score 6.5). Electronic applications accepted. *Faculty research:* Cognition literacy, character education, teacher's education reform, disabilities.

Old Dominion University, Darden College of Education, Program in Elementary/Middle Education, Norfolk, VA 23529. Offers elementary education (Postbaccalaureate Certificate); instructional technology (MS Ed); library science (MS Ed). *Accreditation:* NCATE. *Program availability:* Part-time, evening/weekend, 100% online, blended/hybrid learning. *Degree requirements:* For master's, comprehensive exam. *Entrance requirements:* For master's, GRE General Test or MAT; PRAXIS I, SAT or ACT, minimum GPA of 2.8. Additional exam requirements/recommendations for international students: Required—TOEFL (minimum score 600 paper-based). Electronic applications accepted. *Expenses:* Contact institution. *Faculty research:* Education pre-K to 6, school librarianship, reading, TESOL, literacy.

Pacific University, College of Education, Forest Grove, OR 97116-1797. Offers early childhood education (MAT); education (MAE); elementary education (MAT); ESOL (MAT); high school education (MAT); middle school education (MAT); special education (MAT); speech-language pathology (MS); STEM education (MAT); talented and gifted (M Ed); visual function in learning (M Ed). *Accreditation:* ASHA; NCATE. *Program availability:* Part-time, evening/weekend. *Degree requirements:* For master's, research project. *Entrance requirements:* For master's, California Basic Educational Skills Test, PRAXIS II, minimum undergraduate GPA of 2.75, 3.0 graduate. Additional exam requirements/recommendations for international students: Required—TOEFL. Electronic applications accepted. *Expenses:* Contact institution. *Faculty research:* Defining a culturally competent classroom, technology in the K-12 classroom, Socratic seminars, social studies education.

Piedmont College, School of Education, Demorest, GA 30535. Offers art education (MAT); curriculum and instruction (Ed D, Ed S); early childhood education (MA, MAT); middle grades education (MA, MAT); music education (MAT); secondary education (MA, MAT); special education (MA, MAT). *Program availability:* Part-time, evening/weekend. *Students:* 496 full-time (416 women), 650 part-time (560 women); includes 185 minority (137 Black or African American, non-Hispanic/Latino; 2 American Indian or Alaska Native, non-Hispanic/Latino; 13 Asian, non-Hispanic/Latino; 31 Hispanic/Latino; 1 Native Hawaiian or other Pacific Islander, non-Hispanic/Latino; 1 Two or more races, non-Hispanic/Latino). Average age 37. 483 applicants, 89% accepted, 372 enrolled. In 2018, 275 master's, 10 doctorates, 229 other advanced degrees awarded. *Degree requirements:* For master's, thesis, field experience in the classroom teaching; for doctorate, thesis/dissertation. *Entrance requirements:* For master's, GRE General Test, MAT; for Ed S, minimum graduate GPA of 3.5, valid teaching certificate. Additional exam requirements/recommendations for international students: Required—TOEFL (minimum score 550 paper-based). *Application deadline:* For fall admission, 7/15 for domestic students; for spring admission, 12/1 for domestic students. Applications are processed on a rolling basis. Electronic applications accepted. *Expenses: Tuition:* Full-time $9738; part-time $541 per credit. *Required fees:* $200 per semester. *Financial support:* Career-related internships or fieldwork, Federal Work-Study, and unspecified assistantships available. Support available to part-time students. Financial award applicants required to submit FAFSA. *Unit head:* Dr. R.D. Nordgren, Dean, 706-778-3000 Ext. 1201, Fax: 706-776-9608, E-mail: rdnordgren@piedmont.edu. *Application contact:* Kathleen Carter, Director of Graduate Enrollment Management, 706-778-8500 Ext. 1181, Fax: 706-778-0150, E-mail: kanderson@piedmont.edu.

Point Park University, School of Arts and Sciences, Department of Education, Pittsburgh, PA 15222-1984. Offers adult learning and training (MA); athletic coaching (M Ed); curriculum and instruction (MA); educational administration (MA); leadership and administration (Ed D); secondary education (M Ed); special education grades 7-12 (M Ed); special education PreK-grade 8 (M Ed). *Program availability:* Part-time, evening/weekend, 100% online, blended/hybrid learning. *Degree requirements:* For master's, comprehensive exam (for some programs), thesis or alternative. *Entrance requirements:* For master's, minimum GPA of 3.0, resume, 2 letters of recommendation. Additional exam requirements/recommendations for international students: Required—TOEFL. Electronic applications accepted.

Portland State University, Graduate Studies, College of Liberal Arts and Sciences, Fariborz Maseeh Department of Mathematics and Statistics, Portland, OR 97207-0751. Offers applied statistics (Certificate); mathematical sciences (PhD); mathematics education (PhD); mathematics for middle school (Certificate); mathematics for teachers (MS); statistics (MS); MA/MS. *Degree requirements:* For master's, comprehensive exam, thesis or alternative, 2 written examinations; for doctorate, thesis/dissertation, preliminary and comprehensive examinations. *Entrance requirements:* For master's, GRE General Test, GRE Subject Test, minimum GPA of 3.0 in upper-division course work or 2.75 cumulative undergraduate; for doctorate, GRE General Test. Additional exam requirements/recommendations for international students: Required—TOEFL (minimum score 550 paper-based; 80 iBT). *Faculty research:* Algebra, topology, statistical distribution theory, control theory, statistical robustness.

Queens College of the City University of New York, Division of Education, Department of Educational and Community Programs, Queens, NY 11367-1597. Offers bilingual pupil personnel (AC); counselor education (MS Ed); mental health counseling (MS); school building leader (AC); school district leader (AC); school psychologist (MS Ed); special education-childhood education (AC); special education-early childhood (MS Ed); teacher of special education 1-6 (MS Ed); teacher of special education birth-2 (MS Ed); teaching students with disabilities, grades 7-12 (MS Ed, AC). *Program availability:* Part-time. *Faculty:* 19 full-time (13 women), 53 part-time/adjunct (31 women). *Students:* 90 full-time (83 women), 380 part-time (316 women); includes 217 minority (42 Black or African American, non-Hispanic/Latino; 1 American Indian or Alaska Native, non-Hispanic/Latino; 53 Asian, non-Hispanic/Latino; 114 Hispanic/Latino; 7 Two or more races, non-Hispanic/Latino), 6 international. Average age 29. 470 applicants, 65% accepted, 236 enrolled. In 2018, 164 master's, 59 other advanced degrees awarded. *Degree requirements:* For master's, Research project; for AC, internship, research project. *Entrance requirements:* For master's, minimum GPA of 3.0. Additional exam requirements/recommendations for international students: Required—TOEFL, IELTS. *Application deadline:* For fall admission, 3/1 for domestic students. Applications are processed on a rolling basis. Application fee: $125. Electronic applications accepted. *Financial support:* Fellowships available. Financial award application deadline: 4/1; financial award applicants required to submit FAFSA. *Unit head:* Dr. Emilia Lopez, Chair, 718-997-5250, E-mail: emilia.lopez@qc.cuny.edu. *Application contact:* Elizabeth D'Amico-Ramirez, Assistant Director of Graduate Admissions, 718-997-5203, E-mail: elizabeth.damicoramirez@qc.cuny.edu.

Queens College of the City University of New York, Division of Education, Department of Elementary and Early Childhood Education, Queens, NY 11367-1597. Offers bilingual education (MAT, MS Ed, AC); childhood education (MAT, MS Ed); early childhood education birth-2 (MAT, MS Ed, AC); literacy education birth-grade 6 (MS Ed, AC). *Program availability:* Part-time, evening/weekend. *Faculty:* 19 full-time (13 women), 35 part-time/adjunct (32 women). *Students:* 117 full-time (102 women), 376 part-time (344 women); includes 264 minority (27 Black or African American, non-Hispanic/Latino; 75 Asian, non-Hispanic/Latino; 154 Hispanic/Latino; 1 Native Hawaiian or other Pacific Islander, non-Hispanic/Latino; 7 Two or more races, non-Hispanic/Latino), 15 international. Average age 30. 351 applicants, 75% accepted, 204 enrolled. In 2018, 156 master's, 48 other advanced degrees awarded. *Degree requirements:* For master's, Research project; for AC, Field-based research project. *Entrance requirements:* For master's, GRE General Test, minimum undergraduate cumulative GPA of 3.00; for AC, GRE General Test (required for all MAT and other graduate programs leading to NYS initial teacher certification), NYS initial teacher certification in the appropriate certification area is required for admission into MSEd programs. Additional exam requirements/recommendations for international students: Required—TOEFL (minimum score 575 paper-based; 90 iBT). *Application deadline:* For fall admission, 4/1 for domestic students. Applications are processed on a rolling basis. Application fee: $125. Electronic applications accepted. *Financial support:* Career-related internships or fieldwork and Federal Work-Study available. Financial award application deadline: 4/1; financial award applicants required to submit FAFSA. *Faculty research:* Biliteracy, computational thinking, social justice education, technology in early childhood education, children from immigrant families. *Unit head:* Daisuke Akiba, Chair, 718-997-5300, E-mail: daisuke.akiba@qc.cuny.edu. *Application contact:* Elizabeth D'Amico-Ramirez, Assistant Director of Graduate Admissions, 718-997-5203, E-mail: elizabeth.damicoramirez@qc.cuny.edu.

Roberts Wesleyan College, Graduate Teacher Education Programs, Rochester, NY 14624-1997. Offers adolescence and special education (M Ed); childhood and special education (M Ed); literacy education (M Ed); special education (M Ed). *Program availability:* Part-time, evening/weekend. *Degree requirements:* For master's, thesis. Electronic applications accepted.

Roger Williams University, Feinstein School of Humanities, Arts and Education, Bristol, RI 02809. Offers literacy education (MA); middle school certification (Certificate). *Program availability:* Part-time-only, evening/weekend. *Faculty:* 5 full-time (4 women), 5 part-time/adjunct (2 women). *Students:* 7 part-time (all women). Average age 36. 1 applicant, 100% accepted, 1 enrolled. In 2018, 6 master's awarded. *Entrance requirements:* For master's, resume, 2 letters of recommendation, college transcript, letter of intent, verification of active teaching license. Additional exam requirements/recommendations for international students: Required—TOEFL (minimum score 85 iBT), IELTS (minimum score 6.5). *Application deadline:* Applications are processed on a rolling basis. Application fee: $50. Electronic applications accepted. *Expenses:* $593 per credit hour for academic year 2018-2019 (for Master of Arts in Literacy, Middle School Endorsement Certificate), $267 graduation fee for all programs for academic year 2018-2019. *Financial support:* Application deadline: 3/15; applicants required to submit FAFSA. *Unit head:* Dr. Cynthia Scheinberg, Dean, 401-254-3828, E-mail: cscheinberg@rwu.edu. *Application contact:* Marcus Hanscom, Director of Graduate Admissions, 401-

254-3345, Fax: 401-254-3557, E-mail: gradadmit@rwu.edu.
Website: http://www.rwu.edu/academics/schools-and-colleges/fshae

Rowan University, Graduate School, College of Science and Mathematics, Department of Mathematics, Program in Middle Grades Math Education, Glassboro, NJ 08028-1701. Offers CGS. Electronic applications accepted.

St. Bonaventure University, School of Graduate School, School of Education, Adolescence Education Program, St. Bonaventure, NY 14778-2284. Offers MS Ed. *Program availability:* Part-time, evening/weekend. *Faculty:* 2 full-time (both women), 5 part-time/adjunct (4 women). *Students:* 5 full-time (2 women), 4 part-time (2 women); includes 1 minority (Hispanic/Latino). Average age 26. 5 applicants, 100% accepted. In 2018, 5 master's awarded. *Degree requirements:* For master's, comprehensive exam, minimum cumulative GPA of 3.0, electronic portfolio, student teaching. *Entrance requirements:* For master's, New York State Teacher Certification Exams, CST in subject area; SAT, ACT, GRE or MAT, bachelor's degree or thirty semester hours in an arts or sciences major in the subject area of teaching certification from an accredited college or university; official transcripts showing proof of degree and all college and university courses taken; at least six semester hours of university-level credit; letters of recommendation. Additional exam requirements/recommendations for international students: Required—TOEFL (minimum score 550 paper-based; 79 iBT). *Application deadline:* For fall admission, 3/15 priority date for domestic students, 2/1 priority date for international students; for spring admission, 10/1 for domestic students, 7/1 for international students. Applications are processed on a rolling basis. Application fee: $0. Electronic applications accepted. *Expenses:* $755.00 per credit hour; $100 one time fee. *Financial support:* Scholarships/grants, health care benefits, and unspecified assistantships available. Financial award application deadline: 4/15; financial award applicants required to submit FAFSA. *Faculty research:* Critical, multicultural, and transformative pedagogy and its effect on pre-service teachers, disproportionality in special education. *Unit head:* Dr. Lisa Buenaventura, Director, 716-375-2394, Fax: 716-375-2360, E-mail: lbuenave@sbu.edu. *Application contact:* Matthew Retchless, Director of Graduate Admissions, 716-375-2021, Fax: 716-375-4015, E-mail: gradsch@sbu.edu.
Website: http://www.sbu.edu/academics/schools/education/graduate-degrees-certificates/msed-in-adolescence-education

St. Bonaventure University, School of Graduate School, School of Education, Literacy Programs, St. Bonaventure, NY 14778-2284. Offers adolescent literacy 5-12 (MS Ed); childhood literacy B-6 (MS Ed). *Accreditation:* NCATE. *Program availability:* Part-time, evening/weekend. *Faculty:* 1 (woman) full-time, 1 part-time/adjunct. *Students:* 9 full-time (all women), 2 part-time (1 woman); all minorities (all Black or African American, non-Hispanic/Latino). Average age 22. 10 applicants, 100% accepted. In 2018, 12 master's awarded. *Degree requirements:* For master's, comprehensive exam, thesis optional, minimum cumulative GPA of 3.0, clinical practicum, literacy coaching internship, electronic portfolio. *Entrance requirements:* For master's, GRE or MAT, teaching certificate in matching area in-hand or pending, transcripts from all previous colleges, minimum GPA of 3.0, 2 references, interview, writing sample. Additional exam requirements/recommendations for international students: Required—TOEFL (minimum score 550 paper-based; 80 iBT). *Application deadline:* For fall admission, 3/15 priority date for domestic students, 2/1 for international students; for spring admission, 10/15 priority date for domestic students, 7/1 for international students. Applications are processed on a rolling basis. Application fee: $0. Electronic applications accepted. *Financial support:* Scholarships/grants, health care benefits, and unspecified assistantships available. Financial award application deadline: 4/15; financial award applicants required to submit FAFSA. *Unit head:* Dr. Sheri Voss, Director, 716-375-2368, Fax: 716-375-2360, E-mail: svoss@sbu.edu. *Application contact:* Matthew Retchless, Director of Graduate Admissions, 716-375-2021, Fax: 716-375-4015, E-mail: gradsch@sbu.edu.
Website: http://www.sbu.edu/academics/schools/education/graduate-degrees-certificates/msed-in-childhood-literacy

St. John Fisher College, Ralph C. Wilson Jr. School of Education, Program in Adolescence Education and Special Education, Rochester, NY 14618-3597. Offers adolescence education: biology with special education (MS Ed); adolescence education: chemistry with special education (MS Ed); adolescence education: English with special education (MS Ed); adolescence education: French with special education (MS Ed); adolescence education: math with special education (MS Ed); adolescence education: physics with special education (MS Ed); adolescence education: social studies with special education (MS Ed); adolescence education: Spanish with special education (MS Ed). *Program availability:* Part-time, evening/weekend. *Faculty:* 8 full-time (6 women), 2 part-time/adjunct (both women). *Students:* 13 full-time (4 women), 2 part-time (1 woman); includes 2 minority (1 Black or African American, non-Hispanic/Latino; 1 Two or more races, non-Hispanic/Latino). Average age 27. 24 applicants, 58% accepted, 4 enrolled. In 2018, 9 master's awarded. *Degree requirements:* For master's, field experiences, student teaching. *Entrance requirements:* For master's, LAST, 2 letters of recommendation, personal statement, current resume. Additional exam requirements/recommendations for international students: Required—TOEFL (minimum score 575 paper-based; 80 iBT). *Application deadline:* Applications are processed on a rolling basis. Application fee: $30. Electronic applications accepted. *Expenses:* Contact institution. *Financial support:* Scholarships/grants available. Financial award applicants required to submit FAFSA. *Faculty research:* Arts and humanities, urban schools, constructivist learning, at-risk students, mentoring. *Unit head:* Dr. Susan Hildenbrand, Program Director, 585-385-7297, E-mail: shildenbrand@sjfc.edu. *Application contact:* Michelle Gosier, Director of Transfer and Graduate Admissions, 585-385-8064, E-mail: mgosier@sjfc.edu.

Saint Joseph's University, College of Arts and Sciences, Graduate Programs in Education, Philadelphia, PA 19131-1395. Offers curriculum supervisor (Certificate); educational leadership (MS, Ed D); elementary education (MS, Certificate); elementary/middle school education (Certificate); organizational development and leadership (MS); principal (Certificate); professional education (MS); reading specialist (MS, Certificate); reading supervisor (Certificate); secondary education (MS, Certificate); special education (MS); special education 7-12 (Certificate); special education PK-8 (Certificate); superintendent's letter of eligibility (Certificate); supervisor of special education (Certificate); teacher of the deaf and hard of hearing (Certificate). *Program availability:* Part-time, evening/weekend, blended/hybrid learning. *Degree requirements:* For master's, thesis or alternative; for doctorate, comprehensive exam, thesis/dissertation. *Entrance requirements:* For master's, 2 letters of recommendation, minimum GPA of 3.0, official transcripts, personal statement; for doctorate, GRE, master's degree from accredited institution, minimum graduate GPA of 3.5, computer competence, interview with program director. Additional exam requirements/recommendations for international students: Required—TOEFL (minimum score 550 paper-based; 80 iBT), IELTS (minimum score 6.5), PTE (minimum score 60). Electronic applications accepted. *Expenses:* Contact institution. *Faculty research:* Factors predicting early mathematics skills for low income children, early child care and development, preschool quality, parent communication and home-school collaboration issues, education of terminally ill children, preparing literacy teachers for urban schools.

Saint Peter's University, Graduate Programs in Education, Program in Teaching, Jersey City, NJ 07306-5997. Offers 6-8 middle school education (MA Ed, Certificate); K-12 secondary education (MA Ed, Certificate); K-5 elementary education (MA Ed, Certificate). *Program availability:* Part-time, evening/weekend. *Degree requirements:* For master's, comprehensive exam. *Entrance requirements:* For master's, GRE or MAT. Additional exam requirements/recommendations for international students: Required—TOEFL. Electronic applications accepted.

St. Thomas Aquinas College, Division of Teacher Education, Sparkill, NY 10976. Offers adolescence education (MST); childhood and special education (MST); childhood education (MST); educational leadership (MS Ed); reading (MS Ed, PMC); special education (MS Ed, PMC); teaching (MS Ed), including elementary education, middle school education, secondary education. *Accreditation:* NCATE. *Program availability:* Part-time, evening/weekend. *Degree requirements:* For master's, comprehensive exam, comprehensive professional portfolio; for PMC, action research project. *Entrance requirements:* For master's, New York State Qualifying Exam, GRE General Test or minimum GPA of 3.0, teaching certificate; for PMC, GRE General Test or minimum GPA of 3.0. Electronic applications accepted. *Faculty research:* Computer applications in education, adolescent special education students, literacy development, inclusive practices for special education students.

Salem College, Graduate Studies, Winston-Salem, NC 27101. Offers art education (MAT); elementary education (M Ed, MAT); language and literacy (M Ed); middle school education (MAT); organ (MM); piano (MM); school counseling (M Ed); second language studies (MAT); secondary education (MAT); special education (M Ed, MAT). *Accreditation:* NCATE. *Program availability:* Part-time, evening/weekend, online learning. *Degree requirements:* For master's, practicum (MAT), action research project (M Ed). *Entrance requirements:* For master's, minimum GPA of 3.0, two academic/professional recommendations, acceptable criminal background check. Additional exam requirements/recommendations for international students: Recommended—TOEFL. Electronic applications accepted. *Faculty research:* Teacher professional development, adolescent literacy, instructional technology.

Salem State University, School of Graduate Studies, Program in Middle School Education, Salem, MA 01970-5353. Offers humanities (M Ed); math/science (MAT). *Program availability:* Part-time, evening/weekend. *Entrance requirements:* For master's, GRE or MAT. Additional exam requirements/recommendations for international students: Required—TOEFL (minimum score 550 paper-based; 80 iBT) or IELTS (minimum score 5.5).

Salem State University, School of Graduate Studies, Program in Middle School General Science, Salem, MA 01970-5353. Offers MAT. *Program availability:* Part-time, evening/weekend. *Entrance requirements:* For master's, GRE or MAT. Additional exam requirements/recommendations for international students: Required—TOEFL (minimum score 550 paper-based; 80 iBT) or IELTS (minimum score 5.5).

Salem State University, School of Graduate Studies, Program in Middle School Math, Salem, MA 01970-5353. Offers MAT. *Program availability:* Part-time, evening/weekend. *Entrance requirements:* For master's, GRE or MAT. Additional exam requirements/recommendations for international students: Required—TOEFL (minimum score 550 paper-based; 80 iBT) or IELTS (minimum score 5.5).

Salisbury University, Program in Mathematics Education, Salisbury, MD 21801-6837. Offers mathematics (MSME), including high school, middle school. *Program availability:* Part-time. *Faculty:* 2 full-time (1 woman). *Students:* 1 (woman) full-time, 11 part-time (10 women). Average age 26. 7 applicants, 100% accepted, 6 enrolled. In 2018, 1 master's awarded. *Degree requirements:* For master's, capstone experience. *Entrance requirements:* For master's, transcripts from colleges and universities attended; personal statement; two letters of recommendation. Additional exam requirements/recommendations for international students: Required—TOEFL (minimum score 550 paper-based; 79 iBT), IELTS (minimum score 6.5). *Application deadline:* For fall admission, 8/15 priority date for domestic and international students; for spring admission, 10/1 priority date for domestic and international students. Applications are processed on a rolling basis. Application fee: $65. Electronic applications accepted. *Expenses:* Resident - $412 per credit hour; Non-resident - $746 per credit hour; Fees - $108. *Financial support:* In 2018–19, 1 teaching assistantship with full tuition reimbursement (averaging $8,000 per year) was awarded; career-related internships or fieldwork and scholarships/grants also available. Support available to part-time students. Financial award application deadline: 3/1; financial award applicants required to submit FAFSA. *Faculty research:* Multiplicative reasoning of children; the mathematics of games; probabilistic reasoning of middle grade children; fractional reasoning of children; pre-service teacher education. *Unit head:* Dr. Jennifer Bergner, Graduate Program Director, 410-677-5429, E-mail: jabergner@salisbury.edu. *Application contact:* Dr. Jennifer Bergner, Graduate Program Director, 410-677-5429, E-mail: jabergner@salisbury.edu.
Website: https://www.salisbury.edu/explore-academics/programs/graduate-degree-programs/mathematics-education-masters/

Seton Hill University, Master of Arts Program in Elementary/Middle Level Education, Greensburg, PA 15601. Offers MA. *Program availability:* Part-time, evening/weekend, blended/hybrid learning. *Entrance requirements:* For master's, teacher's certification, 3 letters of recommendation, personal statement, transcripts, resume. Additional exam requirements/recommendations for international students: Required—TOEFL (minimum score 600 paper-based; 100 iBT), IELTS (minimum score 6.5). *Application deadline:* Applications are processed on a rolling basis. Application fee: $0. Electronic applications accepted. *Financial support:* Federal Work-Study, scholarships/grants, and tuition discounts available. Financial award application deadline: 8/15; financial award applicants required to submit FAFSA.
Website: https://www.setonhill.edu/academics/graduate-programs/elementary-middle-level-education-ma/

Shippensburg University of Pennsylvania, School of Graduate Studies, College of Education and Human Services, Department of Teacher Education, Shippensburg, PA 17257-2299. Offers curriculum and instruction (M Ed), including biology, early childhood education, elementary education, geography/earth science, history, mathematics, middle school education, modern languages; reading (M Ed). *Accreditation:* NCATE. *Program availability:* Part-time, evening/weekend, 100% online, blended/hybrid learning. *Faculty:* 12 full-time (9 women), 2 part-time/adjunct (0 women). *Students:* 10 full-time (8 women), 68 part-time (64 women); includes 7 minority (2 Black or African American, non-Hispanic/Latino; 4 Hispanic/Latino; 1 Two or more races, non-Hispanic/Latino). Average age 31. 41 applicants, 73% accepted, 19 enrolled. In 2018, 34 master's awarded. *Degree requirements:* For master's, comprehensive exam (for some programs), thesis optional, practicum or internship; capstone seminar (for some programs). *Entrance requirements:* For master's, MAT or GRE (if GPA less than 2.75), interview, 3 letters of reference, questionnaire of teaching background and future goals, resume. Additional exam requirements/recommendations for international students: Required—TOEFL (minimum score 550 paper-based; 68 iBT), IELTS (minimum score 6), TOEFL (minimum score 550 paper-based, 68 iBT) or IELTS (minimum score 6). *Application deadline:* For fall admission, 4/1 priority date for domestic students, 4/30 for international students; for spring admission, 9/1 priority date for domestic students, 9/30 for international students; for summer admission, 2/1 priority date for domestic students. Applications are processed on a rolling basis. Application fee: $45. Electronic

applications accepted. *Expenses:* Tuition, state resident: part-time $516 per credit. Tuition, nonresident: part-time $750 per credit. *Required fees:* $149 per credit. *Financial support:* In 2018–19, 5 students received support. Career-related internships or fieldwork, scholarships/grants, unspecified assistantships, and resident hall director and student payroll positions available. Support available to part-time students. Financial award application deadline: 3/1; financial award applicants required to submit FAFSA. *Unit head:* Dr. Christine A. Royce, Chairperson, 717-477-1688, Fax: 717-477-4046, E-mail: caroyc@ship.edu. *Application contact:* Maya T. Mapp, Director of Admissions, 717-477-1231, Fax: 717-477-4016, E-mail: mtmapp@ship.edu.
Website: http://www.ship.edu/teacher/

Smith College, Graduate and Special Programs, Department of Education and Child Study, Program in Elementary Education, Northampton, MA 01063. Offers elementary education (MAT); middle school education (MAT). *Program availability:* Part-time. *Students:* 9 full-time (6 women), 7 part-time (6 women); includes 5 minority (2 Black or African American, non-Hispanic/Latino; 2 Asian, non-Hispanic/Latino; 1 Hispanic/ Latino), 2 international. Average age 25. 19 applicants, 89% accepted, 13 enrolled. In 2018, 11 master's awarded. *Entrance requirements:* Additional exam requirements/ recommendations for international students: Required—TOEFL (minimum score 595 paper-based; 97 iBT), IELTS (minimum score 7.5). *Application deadline:* For fall admission, 4/15 for domestic students, 1/15 priority date for international students; for spring admission, 12/1 for domestic students. Applications are processed on a rolling basis. Application fee: $60. *Expenses:* The total tuition cost to each M.A.T. student (the full program fee, after 'built-in' scholarship award) is $18,500. *Financial support:* In 2018–19, 15 students received support, including 4 fellowships with full tuition reimbursements available; scholarships/grants and human resources employee benefit also available. Support available to part-time students. Financial award application deadline: 4/15; financial award applicants required to submit CSS PROFILE or FAFSA. *Unit head:* Alan Rudnitsky, Graduate Student Adviser, 413-585-3261, E-mail: arudnits@ smith.edu. *Application contact:* Ruth Morgan, Program Coordinator, 413-585-3050, Fax: 413-585-3054, E-mail: gradstdy@smith.edu.
Website: http://www.smith.edu/educ/

Southeast Missouri State University, School of Graduate Studies, Leadership, Middle and Secondary, Cape Girardeau, MO 63701-4799. Offers MA. *Accreditation:* NCATE. *Program availability:* Part-time, online only, 100% online. *Faculty:* 5 full-time (3 women), 1 (woman) part-time/adjunct. *Students:* 7 full-time (6 women), 80 part-time (39 women); includes 5 minority (4 Black or African American, non-Hispanic/Latino; 1 American Indian or Alaska Native, non-Hispanic/Latino). Average age 31. 37 applicants, 100% accepted, 37 enrolled. In 2018, 50 master's awarded. *Degree requirements:* For master's, comprehensive exam, research paper. *Entrance requirements:* For master's, minimum undergraduate GPA of 2.75. Additional exam requirements/recommendations for international students: Required—TOEFL (minimum score 550 paper-based; 79 iBT), IELTS (minimum score 6), PTE (minimum score 53). *Application deadline:* For fall admission, 8/1 for domestic students, 6/1 for international students; for spring admission, 11/21 for domestic students, 10/1 for international students; for summer admission, 5/15 for domestic students. Applications are processed on a rolling basis. Application fee: $30 ($40 for international students). Electronic applications accepted. *Expenses:* Contact institution. *Financial support:* In 2018–19, 3 students received support. Career-related internships or fieldwork, Federal Work-Study, scholarships/ grants, tuition waivers (full), and unspecified assistantships available. Financial award application deadline: 6/30; financial award applicants required to submit FAFSA. *Faculty research:* Assessment, technology, diversity. *Unit head:* Dr. C.P. Gause, Professor and Department Chair, 573-651-5965, E-mail: scwick@semo.edu. *Application contact:* Alisa Aleen McFerron, Assistant Director of Admissions for Operations, 573-651-5937, E-mail: amcferron@semo.edu.
Website: http://www.semo.edu/midsecondaryed/

Spalding University, Graduate Studies, College of Education, Programs in Education, Louisville, KY 40203-2188. Offers art teacher education (MAT); business teacher education (MAT); elementary school education (MAT); foreign language (MAT); high school education (MAT); middle school education (MAT); secondary education (MAT); special education (learning and behavioral disorders) (MAT); student guidance counselor (MA); teacher leader (M Ed). *Accreditation:* NCATE. *Program availability:* Part-time, evening/weekend. *Entrance requirements:* For master's, GRE General Test or MAT, interview, letters of recommendation, resume. Additional exam requirements/ recommendations for international students: Required—TOEFL (minimum score 535 paper-based). Electronic applications accepted. *Faculty research:* Instructional technology, achievement gap, classroom management, assessment.

State University of New York at Fredonia, College of Education, Fredonia, NY 14063-1136. Offers curriculum and instruction (MS Ed); literacy education (MS Ed), including birth-grade 12, grades 5-12; music education (M Mus), including k-12; TESOL (MS Ed). *Accreditation:* NCATE. *Program availability:* Part-time. *Faculty:* 16 full-time (14 women), 13 part-time/adjunct (11 women). *Students:* 39 full-time (33 women), 44 part-time (36 women); includes 5 minority (1 Asian, non-Hispanic/Latino; 3 Hispanic/Latino; 1 Two or more races, non-Hispanic/Latino), 4 international. Average age 27. 44 applicants, 89% accepted, 34 enrolled. In 2018, 25 master's awarded. *Degree requirements:* For master's, thesis. *Entrance requirements:* For master's, GRE, minimum undergraduate GPA of 3.0. Additional exam requirements/recommendations for international students: Required—TOEFL (minimum score 79 iBT), IELTS (minimum score 6.5). *Application deadline:* For fall admission, 4/1 priority date for domestic and international students; for spring admission, 11/1 priority date for domestic students, 11/1 for international students. Applications are processed on a rolling basis. Application fee: $75. Electronic applications accepted. *Expenses:* Tuition, state resident: full-time $6870; part-time $462 per credit hour. Tuition, nonresident: full-time $16,650; part-time $944 per credit hour. *International tuition:* $16,650 full-time. *Required fees:* $25; $2 per credit hour. $1 per semester. *Financial support:* In 2018–19, 13 students received support. Unspecified assistantships available. Financial award application deadline: 3/15; financial award applicants required to submit FAFSA. *Faculty research:* Positive behavioral intervention and support (PBIS), place-based science education, peer support for education, primary source material for social studies education, policies and practices in learning English language. *Unit head:* Dr. Christine Givner, Dean, 716-673-3311, E-mail: christine.givner@fredonia.edu. *Application contact:* Wendy S. Dunst, Interim Graduate Recruitment and Admissions Associate, 716-673-3808, Fax: 716-673-3712, E-mail: wendy.dunst@fredonia.edu.
Website: http://www.fredonia.edu/coe/

State University of New York at Fredonia, College of Liberal Arts and Sciences, Fredonia, NY 14063-1136. Offers biology (MS); English (MA); English education 7-12 (MA); interdisciplinary studies (MA, MS); math education (MS Ed); professional writing (CAS); speech pathology (MS); MA/MS. *Program availability:* Part-time, evening/ weekend. *Faculty:* 23 full-time (12 women), 3 part-time/adjunct (1 woman). *Students:* 67 full-time (60 women), 6 part-time (5 women); includes 9 minority (2 Black or African American, non-Hispanic/Latino; 5 Asian, non-Hispanic/Latino; 1 Hispanic/Latino; 1 Two or more races, non-Hispanic/Latino), 9 international. Average age 23. 131 applicants, 77% accepted, 36 enrolled. In 2018, 37 master's, 1 other advanced degree awarded. *Degree requirements:* For master's, comprehensive exam (for some programs), thesis (for some programs). *Entrance requirements:* For master's, GRE. Additional exam requirements/recommendations for international students: Required—TOEFL (minimum score 79 iBT), IELTS (minimum score 6.5). *Application deadline:* For fall admission, 4/1 for domestic and international students; for spring admission, 11/1 for domestic and international students. Applications are processed on a rolling basis. Application fee: $75. Electronic applications accepted. *Expenses:* Tuition, state resident: full-time $6870; part-time $462 per credit hour. Tuition, nonresident: full-time $16,650; part-time $944 per credit hour. *International tuition:* $16,650 full-time. *Required fees:* $25; $2 per credit hour. $1 per semester. *Financial support:* In 2018–19, 17 students received support, including 14 teaching assistantships with full and partial tuition reimbursements available (averaging $5,957 per year); tuition waivers (full and partial) and unspecified assistantships also available. *Faculty research:* Immunology/microbiology, applied human physiology, ecology and evolution, invertebrate biology, molecular biology, biochemistry, physiology, animal behavior, science education, vertebrate physiology, cell biology, plant biology, developmental biology, aquatic ecology, bilingual language acquisition, bilingual language acquisition and disorders, augmentative and alternate communication with ALS, World War I, Zweig, environmental literature, editing, adolescent literature, pedagogy. *Unit head:* Dr. Andy Karafa, Dean, 716-673-3173, Fax: 716-673-3338, E-mail: andy.karafa@gmail.com. *Application contact:* Wendy S. Dunst, Interim Graduate Recruitment and Admissions Associate, 716-673-3808, Fax: 716-673-3712, E-mail: wendy.dunst@fredonia.edu.
Website: http://www.fredonia.edu/clas/

State University of New York at Oswego, Graduate Studies, School of Education, Department of Curriculum and Instruction, Oswego, NY 13126. Offers adolescence education (MST); art education (MAT); childhood education (MST); curriculum and instruction (MS Ed); literacy education (MS Ed); special education (MS Ed). *Program availability:* Part-time, evening/weekend. *Degree requirements:* For master's, comprehensive exam (for some programs), thesis optional. *Entrance requirements:* For master's, GRE General Test, minimum GPA of 2.7, provisional teaching certificate. Additional exam requirements/recommendations for international students: Required—TOEFL (minimum score 560 paper-based). *Faculty research:* Classroom applications for microcomputers; classroom questioning, wait-time, and achievement; values clarification and academic achievement.

State University of New York College at Potsdam, School of Education and Professional Studies, Program in Special Education, Potsdam, NY 13676. Offers adolescence (grades 7-12) (MS Ed); childhood (grades 1-6) (MS Ed); early childhood (birth-grade 2) (MS Ed). *Accreditation:* NCATE. *Program availability:* Part-time. *Degree requirements:* For master's, culminating experience. *Entrance requirements:* For master's, minimum GPA of 3.0 in last 60 hours of course work. Additional exam requirements/recommendations for international students: Required—TOEFL (minimum score 550 paper-based; 80 iBT), IELTS (minimum score 6). Electronic applications accepted.

Temple University, College of Education, Department of Teaching and Learning, Philadelphia, PA 19122-6096. Offers career and technical education (Ed M), including business, computing, and information technology, industrial education, marketing education; middle grades education (Ed M), including math and language arts, math and science, science and language arts; secondary education (Ed M), including English, math, social studies; teaching English to speakers of other languages (MS Ed); urban education (Ed M). *Program availability:* Part-time, evening/weekend. *Faculty:* 27 full-time (19 women), 71 part-time/adjunct (51 women). *Students:* 181 full-time (126 women), 128 part-time (78 women); includes 71 minority (25 Black or African American, non-Hispanic/Latino; 1 American Indian or Alaska Native, non-Hispanic/Latino; 20 Asian, non-Hispanic/Latino; 19 Hispanic/Latino; 1 Native Hawaiian or other Pacific Islander, non-Hispanic/Latino; 5 Two or more races, non-Hispanic/Latino), 12 international. 234 applicants, 67% accepted, 103 enrolled. In 2018, 148 master's awarded. *Degree requirements:* For master's, thesis (for some programs). *Entrance requirements:* For master's, statement of goals, 2 letters of recommendation. Additional exam requirements/recommendations for international students: Required—TOEFL (minimum score 79 iBT), IELTS, PTE, one of three is required. Application fee: $60. Electronic applications accepted. *Financial support:* Fellowships, research assistantships, teaching assistantships, career-related internships or fieldwork, Federal Work-Study, scholarships/grants, health care benefits, and unspecified assistantships available. Financial award applicants required to submit FAFSA. *Faculty research:* Career & technical education, early childhood education, middle grades education, secondary education, special education. *Unit head:* Matthew Tincani, Prof. of Applied Behavior Analysis and Dept. Chairperson, 215-204-8073, E-mail: matthew.tincani@ temple.edu. *Application contact:* Stacey Sanginette, Academic Coordinator, 215-204-6143, E-mail: stacey.sangtinette@temple.edu.
Website: http://education.temple.edu/tl

Tennessee Technological University, College of Graduate Studies, College of Education, Department of Exercise Science, Physical Education and Wellness, Cookeville, TN 38505. Offers adapted physical education (MA); elementary/middle school physical education (MA); lifetime wellness (MA); sport management (MA). *Accreditation:* NCATE. *Program availability:* Part-time, online learning. *Faculty:* 7 full-time (0 women). *Students:* 12 full-time (10 women), 45 part-time (22 women); includes 8 minority (3 Black or African American, non-Hispanic/Latino; 1 Asian, non-Hispanic/ Latino; 2 Hispanic/Latino; 2 Two or more races, non-Hispanic/Latino), 1 international. 43 applicants, 67% accepted, 22 enrolled. In 2018, 17 master's awarded. *Degree requirements:* For master's, comprehensive exam, thesis or alternative. *Entrance requirements:* For master's, MAT or GRE. Additional exam requirements/ recommendations for international students: Required—TOEFL (minimum score 527 paper-based; 71 iBT), IELTS (minimum score 5.5), PTE (minimum score 48), or TOEIC (Test of English as an International Communication). *Application deadline:* For fall admission, 8/1 for domestic students, 5/1 for international students; for spring admission, 12/1 for domestic students, 10/1 for international students; for summer admission, 5/1 for domestic students, 2/1 for international students. Applications are processed on a rolling basis. Application fee: $35 ($40 for international students). Electronic applications accepted. *Financial support:* Fellowships, research assistantships, teaching assistantships, and career-related internships or fieldwork available. Financial award application deadline: 4/1. *Unit head:* Dr. Christy Killman, Chairperson, 931-372-3467, Fax: 931-372-6319, E-mail: ckillman@tntech.edu. *Application contact:* Shelia K. Kendrick, Coordinator of Graduate Studies, 931-372-3808, Fax: 931-372-3497, E-mail: skendrick@tntech.edu.

Theological University of the Caribbean, Graduate Programs, Saint Just, PR 00978-0901. Offers childhood and adolescent education (MA); counseling and pastoral care (MA); ministry (D Min); missions (MA).

Tufts University, Graduate School of Arts and Sciences, Department of Education, Program in Education, Medford, MA 02155. Offers educational studies (MA); elementary education (MAT); middle and secondary education (MAT); museum education (MA); secondary education (MA); STEM education (MS, PhD). *Program availability:* Part-time. *Degree requirements:* For master's, thesis optional. *Entrance requirements:* For master's, GRE General Test, portfolio (for art education only); for doctorate, GRE General Test, writing sample. Additional exam requirements/recommendations for

international students: Required—TOEFL (minimum score 550 paper-based; 80 iBT), IELTS (minimum score 6.5). Electronic applications accepted. *Expenses:* Contact institution.

Union College, Graduate Programs, Department of Education, Program in Middle Grades, Barbourville, KY 40906-1499. Offers MA. *Degree requirements:* For master's, thesis optional. *Entrance requirements:* For master's, GRE General Test, NTE.

University of Arkansas, Graduate School, College of Education and Health Professions, Department of Curriculum and Instruction, Fayetteville, AR 72701. Offers childhood education (MAT); curriculum and instruction (M Ed, PhD, Ed S); educational leadership (M Ed, Ed D, Ed S); educational technology (M Ed); middle-level education (MAT); secondary education (M Ed, MAT, Ed S); special education (M Ed, MAT). *Accreditation:* NCATE. In 2018, 75 master's, 14 doctorates, 10 other advanced degrees awarded. *Entrance requirements:* For doctorate, GRE General Test or MAT. *Application deadline:* For fall admission, 8/1 for domestic students, 4/1 for international students; for spring admission, 12/1 for domestic students, 10/1 for international students; for summer admission, 4/15 for domestic students, 3/1 for international students. Applications are processed on a rolling basis. Application fee: $60. Electronic applications accepted. *Financial support:* In 2018–19, 41 research assistantships, 2 teaching assistantships were awarded; fellowships with tuition reimbursements, career-related internships or fieldwork, and Federal Work-Study also available. Support available to part-time students. Financial award application deadline: 4/1; financial award applicants required to submit FAFSA. *Unit head:* Dr. Cheryl A. Murphy, Interim Department Head, 479-575-5111, Fax: 479-575-5119, E-mail: cmurphy@uark.edu. *Application contact:* Dr. Derrick Mears, Graduate Coordinator, 479-575-6195, Fax: 479-575-6676, E-mail: dmears@uark.edu.
Website: http://cied.uark.edu/

University of Arkansas at Little Rock, Graduate School, College of Education and Health Professions, Department of Teacher Education, Program in Middle Childhood Education, Little Rock, AR 72204-1099. Offers M Ed. *Degree requirements:* For master's, electronic portfolio. *Entrance requirements:* For master's, PRAXIS, minimum undergraduate GPA of 2.75 overall or 3.0 in the last 60 hours of undergraduate work; interview.

University of Bridgeport, School of Education, Department of Education, Bridgeport, CT 06604. Offers education (MS); educational management (Ed D, Diploma), including intermediate administrator or supervisor (Diploma), leadership (Ed D); elementary education (MS, Diploma), including early childhood education, elementary education; middle school education (MS); music education (MS); remedial reading and language arts (Diploma); secondary education (MS, Diploma), including computer specialist (Diploma), international education (Diploma), reading specialist, secondary education. *Program availability:* Part-time, evening/weekend. *Degree requirements:* For master's, final exam, final project, or thesis; for doctorate, comprehensive exam, thesis/dissertation; for Diploma, thesis or alternative, final project. *Entrance requirements:* For master's, minimum undergraduate QPA of 2.67; for doctorate, GRE, MAT; for Diploma, GRE General Test or MAT, minimum graduate QPA of 3.0. Additional exam requirements/recommendations for international students: Recommended—TOEFL (minimum score 550 paper-based; 80 iBT), IELTS (minimum score 6.5). Electronic applications accepted. *Expenses:* Contact institution.

University of Central Florida, College of Community Innovation and Education, School of Teacher Education, Orlando, FL 32816. Offers applied learning and instruction (MA); curriculum and instruction (M Ed); elementary education (M Ed, MA); exceptional student education (M Ed, MA, Certificate), including autism spectrum disorders (Certificate), exceptional student education (M Ed), exceptional student education K-12 (MA), intervention specialist (Certificate), pre-kindergarten disabilities (Certificate), severe or profound disabilities (Certificate), special education (Certificate); K-8 mathematics and science education (M Ed, Certificate); reading education (M Ed, Certificate); teacher education (MAT), including art education, English language, mathematics education, middle school mathematics, middle school science, science education, social science education; world languages education - English for speakers of other languages (ESOL) (Certificate); world languages education - languages other than English (LOTE) (Certificate). *Program availability:* Part-time, evening/weekend. *Degree requirements:* For Certificate, thesis or alternative. *Entrance requirements:* For degree, GRE General Test, minimum GPA of 3.0. Additional exam requirements/recommendations for international students: Required—TOEFL. Electronic applications accepted.

University of Dayton, Department of Teacher Education, Dayton, OH 45469. Offers adolescence to young adult education (MS Ed); early childhood leadership and advocacy (MS Ed); interdisciplinary education (MS Ed), including visual arts; interdisciplinary education studies (MS Ed); leadership in educational systems (MS Ed); literacy (MS Ed); mathematics education (MS Ed); middle childhood education (MS Ed); multi-age education (MS Ed), including world languages; music education (MS Ed); teacher as leader (MS Ed); teacher education (MS Ed); technology-enhanced learning (MS Ed); trans-disciplinary early childhood education (MS Ed). *Program availability:* Part-time, 100% online. *Degree requirements:* For master's, variable foreign language requirement, thesis or alternative, internship (for teaching licensure or endorsement). *Entrance requirements:* For master's, GRE (minimum score of 149 verbal, 4 on writing) or MAT (minimum score of 396) if undergraduate GPA was under 2.75, minimum GPA of 2.75, 3 letters of recommendation, personal statement or resume, official transcripts. Additional exam requirements/recommendations for international students: Required—TOEFL (minimum score 550 paper-based; 80 iBT); Recommended—IELTS (minimum score 6.5). Electronic applications accepted. *Expenses:* Contact institution. *Faculty research:* Social emotional learning, culturally responsive teaching, urban teaching, literacy, instructional strategies, pre-service teacher education preparation.

University of Kentucky, Graduate School, College of Education, Program in Curriculum and Instruction, Lexington, KY 40506-0032. Offers curriculum and instruction (Ed D, PhD); elementary education (MA Ed); instructional system design (MS Ed); literacy (MA Ed); middle school education (MA Ed, MS Ed); secondary education (MA Ed, MS Ed). *Accreditation:* NCATE. *Degree requirements:* For master's, comprehensive exam, thesis optional; for doctorate, comprehensive exam, thesis/dissertation. *Entrance requirements:* For master's, GRE General Test, minimum undergraduate GPA of 2.75; for doctorate, GRE General Test, minimum graduate GPA of 3.0. Additional exam requirements/recommendations for international students: Required—TOEFL (minimum score 550 paper-based). Electronic applications accepted. *Faculty research:* Educational reform, multicultural education, classroom instructional practices, performance based assessment, primary school programs.

University of Louisville, Graduate School, College of Education and Human Development, Departments of Early Childhood and Elementary Education, Middle and Secondary Education, and Special Education, Louisville, KY 40292-0001. Offers art education (MAT); autism and applied behavior analysis (Certificate); curriculum and instruction (PhD); early elementary education (MAT); exercise physiology (MS); health and physical education (MAT); health professions education (Certificate); higher education (MA); human resources and organization development (MS); instructional technology (M Ed); interdisciplinary early childhood education (MAT); middle school education (MAT); music education (MAT); secondary education (MAT); special education (MAT); sport administration (MS); teacher leadership (M Ed). *Program availability:* Part-time, evening/weekend, 100% online, blended/hybrid learning. *Faculty:* 97 full-time (64 women), 131 part-time/adjunct (86 women). *Students:* 109 full-time (72 women), 139 part-time (87 women); includes 43 minority (18 Black or African American, non-Hispanic/Latino; 6 Asian, non-Hispanic/Latino; 10 Hispanic/Latino; 9 Two or more races, non-Hispanic/Latino), 9 international. Average age 29. 108 applicants, 75% accepted, 59 enrolled. In 2018, 64 master's awarded. Terminal master's awarded for partial completion of doctoral program. *Degree requirements:* For master's, comprehensive exam (for some programs), thesis optional; for doctorate, comprehensive exam (for some programs), thesis/dissertation. *Entrance requirements:* For master's, GRE (for most programs), PRAXIS (for educator preparation programs), professional statement, recommendation letters, resume, transcripts; for doctorate and Certificate, GRE, professional statement, recommendation letters, resume, transcripts. Additional exam requirements/recommendations for international students: Required—TOEFL (minimum score 550 paper-based; 79 iBT); Recommended—IELTS (minimum score 6.5). *Application deadline:* For fall admission, 6/1 priority date for domestic students, 5/1 priority date for international students; for spring admission, 10/1 for domestic students, 11/1 priority date for international students; for summer admission, 3/1 priority date for domestic students, 4/1 priority date for international students. Application fee: $65. *Expenses: Tuition, area resident:* Full-time $6500; part-time $723 per credit hour. Tuition, state resident: full-time $6500. Tuition, nonresident: full-time $13,557; part-time $1507 per credit hour. Tuition and fees vary according to course load and program. *Financial support:* In 2018–19, 144 students received support, including fellowships with full tuition reimbursements available (averaging $21,024 per year), research assistantships with full tuition reimbursements available (averaging $21,024 per year), teaching assistantships with full tuition reimbursements available (averaging $21,024 per year); Federal Work-Study, scholarships/grants, health care benefits, tuition waivers (full), and unspecified assistantships also available. Financial award application deadline: 3/1; financial award applicants required to submit FAFSA. *Faculty research:* Children's early reading and writing development, crelevance of basic facts in elementary mathematics instruction, clinical model of teacher education, cultural and linguistic context of diverse learners, and STEM-integrated curriculum design and development. STEM teaching and learning, content literacy for English language learners, social justice in teacher education, adolescent literacy, mathematics teacher development. Classroom and behavior management; moderate/severe disabilities, autism. *Unit head:* Dr. Amy Lingo, Interim Dean, 502-852-3235, Fax: 502-852-1464, E-mail: cehdinfo@louisville.edu. *Application contact:* Dr. Margaret Pentecost, Assistant Dean for Graduate Student Success, 502-852-6437, Fax: 502-852-1417, E-mail: gedadm@louisville.edu.
Website: http://louisville.edu/delphi

University of Massachusetts Dartmouth, Graduate School, College of Arts and Sciences, School of Education, Department of STEM Education and Teacher Development, North Dartmouth, MA 02747-2300. Offers English as a second language (Postbaccalaureate Certificate); mathematics education (PhD); middle school education (MAT); secondary school education (MAT). *Program availability:* Part-time. *Faculty:* 9 full-time (6 women), 3 part-time/adjunct (2 women). *Students:* 21 full-time (18 women), 100 part-time (53 women); includes 20 minority (3 Black or African American, non-Hispanic/Latino; 2 Asian, non-Hispanic/Latino; 11 Hispanic/Latino; 4 Two or more races, non-Hispanic/Latino), 3 international. Average age 34. 63 applicants, 90% accepted, 45 enrolled. In 2018, 68 master's, 1 doctorate, 1 other advanced degree awarded. *Degree requirements:* For doctorate, thesis/dissertation. *Entrance requirements:* For master's, Statement of Purpose, Resume, Official Transcripts, copy of MA MTELs, 2 letters of recommendation, Proof of License (for Professional Licensure Program); for doctorate, GRE Score, Statement of Purpose, Resume, Official transcripts, 3 letters of recommendation; for Postbaccalaureate Certificate, Statement of Purpose, Resume, Official Transcripts, 2 letters of recommendation, MTEL Score Report. Additional exam requirements/recommendations for international students: Required—TOEFL (minimum score 550 paper-based; 79 iBT), IELTS (minimum score 6.5). *Application deadline:* For fall admission, 1/15 priority date for domestic students, 12/15 priority date for international students; for spring admission, 12/15 priority date for domestic students, 11/15 priority date for international students. Application fee: $60. Electronic applications accepted. *Financial support:* In 2018–19, 1 fellowship (averaging $18,000 per year), 3 research assistantships (averaging $10,897 per year), 6 teaching assistantships (averaging $8,017 per year) were awarded; tuition waivers (full) and doctoral support also available. Financial award application deadline: 3/1; financial award applicants required to submit FAFSA. *Faculty research:* Mindfulness in education, literacies, assessment of teacher knowledge, curriculum tools for supporting mathematics learning. *Total annual research expenditures:* $1.8 million. *Unit head:* Traci Almeida, Coordinator of Graduate Admissions and Licensure, 508-999-8098, Fax: 508-910-8183, E-mail: talmeida@umassd.edu. *Application contact:* Scott Webster, Director of Graduate Studies and Admissions, 508-999-8604, Fax: 508-999-8183, E-mail: graduate@umassd.edu.
Website: http://www.umassd.edu/cas/schoolofeducation/departments/stemeducationandteacherdevelopment/

University of Missouri–St. Louis, College of Education, Department of Educator Preparation, Innovation and Research, St. Louis, MO 63121. Offers elementary education (M Ed), including early childhood, general, reading; secondary education (M Ed), including curriculum and instruction, general, middle level education, reading, teaching English to speakers of other languages (TESOL); special education (M Ed), including autism and developmental disabilities, early childhood special education. *Program availability:* Part-time, evening/weekend. *Degree requirements:* For master's, comprehensive exam. *Entrance requirements:* Additional exam requirements/recommendations for international students: Recommended—TOEFL (minimum score 550 paper-based; 79 iBT), IELTS (minimum score 6.5). Electronic applications accepted.

The University of North Carolina at Charlotte, Cato College of Education, Department of Middle, Secondary and K-12 Education, Charlotte, NC 28223-0001. Offers middle grades and secondary education (M Ed); teaching English as a second language (M Ed, Graduate Certificate). *Program availability:* Part-time. *Students:* 3 full-time (all women), 88 part-time (77 women); includes 21 minority (19 Black or African American, non-Hispanic/Latino; 1 Asian, non-Hispanic/Latino; 1 Hispanic/Latino), 3 international. Average age 34. 36 applicants, 94% accepted, 30 enrolled. In 2018, 25 master's awarded. *Entrance requirements:* For master's, GRE or MAT, bachelor's degree from accredited college or university; minimum GPA of 3.0 in undergraduate work; North Carolina Class A teaching license in appropriate middle grades or secondary education field; minimum of two years' teaching experience; written narrative providing statement of purpose for master's degree study; letters of recommendation; for Graduate Certificate, bachelor's degree from accredited institution; minimum undergraduate GPA of 2.5 overall or 3.0 in senior year, or 15 hours taken in the last 5 years; satisfactory recommendations from three persons knowledgeable of applicant's interactions with children or adolescents; statement of purpose. Additional exam requirements/recommendations for international students: Required—TOEFL (minimum score 523 paper-based; 70 iBT), IELTS (minimum score 6), TOEFL (minimum score 523 paper-

based, 70 iBT) or IELTS (6). *Application deadline:* Applications are processed on a rolling basis. Application fee: $75. Electronic applications accepted. Tuition and fees vary according to course load and program. *Financial support:* Research assistantships, teaching assistantships, career-related internships or fieldwork, institutionally sponsored loans, scholarships/grants, and unspecified assistantships available. Support available to part-time students. Financial award application deadline: 3/1; financial award applicants required to submit FAFSA. *Total annual research expenditures:* $309,255. *Unit head:* Scott Kissau, Chair, 704-687-8875, E-mail: spkissau@uncc.edu. *Application contact:* Kathy B. Giddings, Director of Graduate Admissions, 704-687-5503, Fax: 704-687-1668, E-mail: gradadm@uncc.edu.
Website: http://mdsk.uncc.edu/

The University of North Carolina at Charlotte, Cato College of Education, Interdisciplinary Education Programs, Charlotte, NC 28223-0001. Offers art education (Graduate Certificate); child and family development: early childhood education (MAT); curriculum and instruction (PhD); elementary education (MAT); foreign language education (MAT); middle grades education (MAT); secondary education (MAT); special education (MAT); teaching (Graduate Certificate); teaching English as a second language (MAT); theatre education (Graduate Certificate). *Program availability:* Part-time, 100% online, blended/hybrid learning. *Students:* 70 full-time (55 women), 511 part-time (414 women); includes 228 minority (160 Black or African American, non-Hispanic/Latino; 1 American Indian or Alaska Native, non-Hispanic/Latino; 11 Asian, non-Hispanic/Latino; 38 Hispanic/Latino; 18 Two or more races, non-Hispanic/Latino), 8 international. Average age 34. 343 applicants, 92% accepted, 219 enrolled. In 2018, 69 master's, 13 doctorates, 161 other advanced degrees awarded. *Entrance requirements:* For master's, GRE or MAT, bachelor's degree, or its U.S. equivalent, from regionally-accredited college or university; minimum overall GPA of 3.0 on all previous work beyond high school; statement of purpose (essay); at least three recommendation forms; for doctorate, GRE or MAT, bachelor's degree (or its U.S. equivalent) from regionally-accredited college or university; minimum overall GPA of 3.5 in master's degree program; for Graduate Certificate, bachelor's degree from regionally-accredited university; minimum GPA of 2.75 on all post-secondary work attempted; transcripts; personal statement outlining why the applicant seeks admission to the program. Additional exam requirements/recommendations for international students: Required—TOEFL (minimum score 523 paper-based; 70 iBT), IELTS (minimum score 6), TOEFL (minimum score 523 paper-based, 70 iBT) or IELTS (6). *Application deadline:* Applications are processed on a rolling basis. Application fee: $75. Electronic applications accepted. Tuition and fees vary according to course load and program. *Financial support:* Career-related internships or fieldwork, institutionally sponsored loans, scholarships/grants, and unspecified assistantships available. Support available to part-time students. Financial award application deadline: 3/1; financial award applicants required to submit FAFSA. *Unit head:* Dr. Ellen McIntyre, Dean, 704-687-8722, E-mail: ellen.mcintyre@uncc.edu. *Application contact:* Kathy B. Giddings, Director of Graduate Admissions, 704-687-5503, Fax: 704-687-1668, E-mail: gradadm@uncc.edu.
Website: http://education.uncc.edu/academic-programs

The University of North Carolina at Greensboro, Graduate School, School of Education, Department of Teacher Education and Higher Education, Greensboro, NC 27412-5001. Offers college teaching and adult learning (Certificate); curriculum and instruction (M Ed), including chemistry education, elementary education, English as a second language, French education, instructional technology, mathematics education, middle grades education, reading education, science education, social studies education, Spanish education; curriculum and teaching (PhD), including higher education, teacher education and development; English as a second language (Certificate); higher education (M Ed); supervision (M Ed). *Accreditation:* NCATE. *Program availability:* Part-time. *Degree requirements:* For doctorate, thesis/dissertation. *Entrance requirements:* For master's and doctorate, GRE General Test. Additional exam requirements/recommendations for international students: Required—TOEFL. Electronic applications accepted. *Faculty research:* Community college literacy program, middle school mathematics/computer mathematics.

The University of North Carolina Wilmington, Watson College of Education, Department of Early Childhood, Elementary, Middle, Literacy and Special Education, Wilmington, NC 28403-3297. Offers educational leadership, policy, and advocacy (M Ed); elementary education (M Ed, MAT); language and literacy (M Ed); middle grades education (MAT). *Accreditation:* NCATE. *Program availability:* Part-time, blended/hybrid learning. *Degree requirements:* For master's, thesis or alternative, exit portfolio, oral presentation, internship, research project (depending on specialization). *Entrance requirements:* For master's, 3 letters of recommendations, NC Class A teacher license in related field, education statement of interest essay. Additional exam requirements/recommendations for international students: Required—TOEFL (minimum score 550 paper-based; 79 iBT), IELTS (minimum score 6.5). Electronic applications accepted.

University of Northern Iowa, Graduate College, College of Humanities, Arts and Sciences, Department of Mathematics, MA Program in Mathematics for the Middle Grades, Cedar Falls, IA 50614. Offers MA.

University of North Georgia, Master of Arts in Teaching Program, Dahlonega, GA 30597. Offers physical education (MAT); secondary education - English (MAT); secondary education - history (MAT); secondary education - mathematics (MAT); secondary education - middle grades (MAT). *Degree requirements:* For master's, internship, capstone. *Entrance requirements:* For master's, GRE or MAT, GACE I and II, GA pre-service application, lawful presence verification, official transcripts, GA Educator Ethics Program entry assessment. Additional exam requirements/recommendations for international students: Required—TOEFL (minimum score 550 paper-based; 79 iBT), IELTS (minimum score 6.5). Electronic applications accepted. *Expenses:* Contact institution.

University of North Georgia, Program in Middle Grades Math and Science, Dahlonega, GA 30597. Offers M Ed. *Program availability:* Part-time, evening/weekend, online only, 100% online. *Degree requirements:* For master's, teaching practicum. *Entrance requirements:* For master's, baccalaureate degree from regionally-accredited, four-year institution with minimum cumulative GPA of 2.75; employment as teacher in middle grades classroom working with students at least 20 hours per week; clear/renewable teaching certificate in middle grades math or science in the state of Georgia or equivalent. Additional exam requirements/recommendations for international students: Required—TOEFL (minimum score 550 paper-based; 79 iBT), IELTS (minimum score 6.5). Electronic applications accepted. *Expenses:* Contact institution.

University of Phoenix–Online Campus, College of Education, Phoenix, AZ 85034-7209. Offers administration and supervision (MAEd, Certificate); adult education and training (MAEd); curriculum and instruction (MAEd), including computer education, curriculum and instruction, English as a second language, language arts, mathematics, reading; early childhood education (MAEd); educational studies (MAEd); elementary teacher education (MAEd), including early childhood, elementary teacher education, high school middle level, middle level; principal licensure (Certificate); secondary teacher education (MAEd); special education (MAEd, Certificate); teacher education (MAEd), including middle level generalist; teacher education middle level mathematics

(MAEd), including middle level mathematics; teacher education middle level science (MAEd), including middle level science; teacher education secondary mathematics (MAEd); teacher education secondary science (MAEd); teacher leadership (MAEd); teachers of English learners (Certificate); transition to teaching (Certificate), including elementary education, secondary education. *Program availability:* Evening/weekend, online learning. *Entrance requirements:* Additional exam requirements/recommendations for international students: Required—TOEFL, TOEIC (Test of English as an International Communication), Berlitz Online English Proficiency Exam, PTE, or IELTS. Electronic applications accepted. *Expenses:* Contact institution.

University of South Florida, St. Petersburg, College of Education, St. Petersburg, FL 33701. Offers educational leadership development (M Ed); elementary education (MA), including math/science; English education (MA); middle grades STEM education (MS); reading education (MA). *Program availability:* Part-time. *Degree requirements:* For master's, comprehensive exam, practicum, internship, comprehensive portfolio. *Entrance requirements:* For master's, State of Florida General Knowledge Test (GKT), Florida Teaching Certificate (for non-initial certification programs), letters of recommendation. Additional exam requirements/recommendations for international students: Required—TOEFL (minimum score 550 paper-based; 79 iBT); Recommended—IELTS. Electronic applications accepted.

University of the Cumberlands, Graduate Programs in Education, Williamsburg, KY 40769-1372. Offers all grades (P-12) (M Ed); business and marketing (MA Ed, MAT); counselor education and supervision (Ed D); director of pupil personnel (Certificate); director of special education (Certificate); educational administration and supervision (Ed S); educational leadership (Ed D); elementary education (MA Ed, MAT); instructional leadership - principalship (MA Ed); instructional leadership - school principal (Certificate); middle school education (MA Ed, MAT); reading and writing (MA Ed); school counseling (MA Ed); school superintendent (Certificate); secondary education (MA Ed, MAT); special education (MAT); supervisor of instruction (Certificate); teacher leader (MA Ed). *Program availability:* Part-time, evening/weekend, online learning. *Degree requirements:* For master's, comprehensive exam. Electronic applications accepted.

University of the District of Columbia, College of Arts and Sciences, Program in Teaching, Washington, DC 20008-1175. Offers elementary education (MAT); middle school mathematics (MAT); secondary English language arts (MAT); secondary social studies (MAT).

The University of Toledo, College of Graduate Studies, Judith Herb College of Education, Department of Curriculum and Instruction, Toledo, OH 43606-3390. Offers art education (ME); career and technical education (ME, Ed S); curriculum and instruction (ME, PhD, Ed S); early childhood education (Ed S); education and anthropology (MAE); education and biology (MES); education and chemistry (MES); education and classics (MAE); education and economics (MAE); education and English (MAE); education and French (MAE); education and geology (MES); education and German (MAE); education and history (MAE); education and mathematics (MAE, MES); education and physics (MES); education and political science (MAE); education and sociology (MAE); education and Spanish (MAE); educational media (PhD); educational technology (ME); educational technology: virtual educator (Certificate); elementary education (PhD); English as a second language (MAE); gifted and talented education (PhD); middle childhood education (ME); secondary education (ME, PhD); special education (PhD). *Accreditation:* NCATE. *Program availability:* Part-time, evening/weekend. *Degree requirements:* For master's, comprehensive exam, thesis or alternative; for doctorate, comprehensive exam, thesis/dissertation; for other advanced degree, thesis optional. *Entrance requirements:* For master's, doctorate, and other advanced degree, minimum cumulative GPA of 2.7 for all previous academic work, letters of recommendation. Additional exam requirements/recommendations for international students: Required—TOEFL (minimum score 550 paper-based; 80 iBT). Electronic applications accepted.

University of Vermont, Graduate College, College of Education and Social Services, Program in Middle Level Education, Burlington, VT 05405. Offers curriculum and instruction (MAT), including middle level education. *Program availability:* Part-time. *Entrance requirements:* For master's, resume, writing sample. Additional exam requirements/recommendations for international students: Required—TOEFL (minimum iBT score of 90) or IELTS (6.5). Electronic applications accepted.

University of Vermont, Graduate College, College of Education and Social Services, Program in Special Education, Grades K-12, Burlington, VT 05405. Offers M Ed. *Accreditation:* NCATE. *Degree requirements:* For master's, thesis or alternative. *Entrance requirements:* For master's, license (or eligible for licensure). Additional exam requirements/recommendations for international students: Required—TOEFL (minimum score 550 paper-based, 90 iBT) or IELTS (6.5). Electronic applications accepted.

University of Washington, Bothell, Program in Education, Bothell, WA 98011. Offers education (M Ed); leadership development for educators (M Ed); secondary/middle level endorsement (M Ed). *Program availability:* Part-time, evening/weekend. *Degree requirements:* For master's, thesis. *Entrance requirements:* Additional exam requirements/recommendations for international students: Required—TOEFL. Electronic applications accepted. *Faculty research:* Multicultural education in citizenship education, intercultural education, knowledge and practice in the principalship, educational public policy, national board certification for teachers, teacher learning in literacy, technology and its impact on teaching and learning of mathematics, reading assessments, professional development in literacy education and mobility, digital media, education and class.

University of West Florida, College of Education and Professional Studies, Department of Teacher Education and Educational Leadership, Program in Curriculum and Instruction, Pensacola, FL 32514-5750. Offers elementary education (M Ed); middle level education (M Ed); secondary education (M Ed). *Program availability:* Part-time, evening/weekend. *Entrance requirements:* For master's, GRE (minimum score 450 verbal) or MAT (minimum score 396) if bachelor's GPA less than 3.0, state teaching certification; letter of intent; two professional references. Additional exam requirements/recommendations for international students: Required—TOEFL (minimum score 550 paper-based).

University of Wisconsin–Milwaukee, Graduate School, School of Education, Department of Curriculum and Instruction, Milwaukee, WI 53201-0413. Offers curriculum and instruction (MS), including cross-curricular focus, early childhood education, English education, mathematics education, middle childhood/early adolescence education, reading education, science education, urban social studies education. *Program availability:* Part-time. *Students:* 19 full-time (15 women), 56 part-time (49 women); includes 15 minority (3 Black or African American, non-Hispanic/Latino; 1 American Indian or Alaska Native, non-Hispanic/Latino; 3 Asian, non-Hispanic/Latino; 1 Hispanic/Latino; 7 Two or more races, non-Hispanic/Latino), 2 international. Average age 33. 27 applicants, 44% accepted, 11 enrolled. In 2018, 20 master's awarded. *Entrance requirements:* Additional exam requirements/recommendations for international students: Required—TOEFL (minimum score 550 paper-based; 79 iBT), IELTS (minimum score 6.5). *Application deadline:* For fall admission, 1/1 priority date for domestic students; for spring admission, 9/1 for domestic students. Application fee: $56

($96 for international students). Electronic applications accepted. *Financial support:* Fellowships, research assistantships, teaching assistantships, career-related internships or fieldwork, health care benefits, unspecified assistantships, and project assistantships available. Support available to part-time students. Financial award application deadline: 4/15; financial award applicants required to submit FAFSA. *Application contact:* General Information Contact, 414-229-4721, E-mail: soeinfo@uwm.edu.
Website: http://uwm.edu/education/academics/curriculum-instruction-department/

Wagner College, Division of Graduate Studies, Education Department, Program in Secondary Education/Students with Disabilities, Staten Island, NY 10301-4495. Offers secondary education 7-12 (MS Ed), including language arts, languages other than English, mathematics and technology, science and technology, social studies. *Program availability:* Evening/weekend. *Degree requirements:* For master's, thesis (for some programs), completion of state certification exams before student teaching. *Entrance requirements:* For master's, GRE, minimum GPA of 3.0, interview, recommendations. Additional exam requirements/recommendations for international students: Required—TOEFL (minimum score 550 paper-based; 79 iBT), IELTS (minimum score 6.5). Electronic applications accepted. *Expenses:* Contact institution.

Webster University, School of Education, Department of Multidisciplinary Studies, St. Louis, MO 63119-3194. Offers applied educational psychology (MA, Ed S); communication arts (MA); early childhood education (MA, MAT); education and innovation (MA); educational technology (MET); elementary education (MAT); mathematics for educators (MA); middle school education (MAT); multidisciplinary studies (MAT); multimodal literacy for global impact (MA); reading (MA); secondary school education (MAT); special education (MA, MAT); teaching English as a second language (MA); transformative learning in the global community (Ed S). *Program availability:* Part-time. *Entrance requirements:* For master's, minimum GPA of 2.5. Additional exam requirements/recommendations for international students: Required—TOEFL. *Expenses: Tuition:* Full-time $22,500; part-time $750 per credit hour. Tuition and fees vary according to degree level, campus/location and program.

Western Kentucky University, Graduate School, College of Education and Behavioral Sciences, School of Teacher Education, Bowling Green, KY 42101. Offers elementary education (MAE, Ed S); exceptional education: learning and behavioral disorders (MAE); instructional design (MS); interdisciplinary early childhood education (MAE); library media education (MS); literacy education (MAE); middle grades education (MAE); secondary education (MAE, Ed S); special education: moderate and severe disabilities (MAE). *Program availability:* Part-time, evening/weekend, online learning. *Degree requirements:* For master's, comprehensive exam. *Entrance requirements:* For master's, GRE General Test. Additional exam requirements/recommendations for international students: Required—TOEFL (minimum score 555 paper-based; 79 iBT). *Faculty research:* Teacher preparation in moderate/severe disabilities.

Wichita State University, Graduate School, College of Applied Studies, School of Education, Wichita, KS 67260. Offers learning and instructional design (M Ed); special education (M Ed), including early childhood (M Ed, MAT), gifted, high incidence, low incidence; teaching (MAT), including early childhood (M Ed, MAT), middle level/secondary, transition to teaching. *Accreditation:* NCATE. *Program availability:* Part-time, evening/weekend, 100% online, blended/hybrid learning. *Entrance requirements:* For master's, MAT, minimum GPA of 2.75. *Unit head:* Dr. Edward Robeck, Department Head, 316-978-3322, E-mail: edward.robeck@wichita.edu. *Application contact:* Jordan Oleson, Admission Coordinator, 316-978-3095, Fax: 316-978-3253, E-mail: jordan.oleson@wichita.edu.

Widener University, School of Human Service Professions, Center for Education, Chester, PA 19013-5792. Offers adult education (M Ed); counseling in higher education (M Ed); counselor education (M Ed); early childhood education (M Ed); educational foundations (M Ed); educational leadership (M Ed); educational psychology (M Ed); elementary education (M Ed); English and language arts (M Ed); health education (M Ed); higher education leadership (Ed D); home and school visitor (M Ed); human sexuality (M Ed, PhD); mathematics education (M Ed); middle school education (M Ed); principalship (M Ed); reading and language arts (Ed D); reading education (M Ed); school administration (Ed D); science education (M Ed); social studies education (M Ed); special education (M Ed); technology education (M Ed). *Accreditation:* NCATE. *Program availability:* Part-time, evening/weekend. Terminal master's awarded for partial completion of doctoral program. *Degree requirements:* For doctorate, thesis/dissertation. *Entrance requirements:* For master's, minimum GPA of 2.5; for doctorate, GRE or MAT, minimum GPA of 2.0 (undergraduate), 3.5 (graduate). Electronic applications accepted. *Expenses:* Contact institution. *Faculty research:* Reading and cognition, adult education, technology education, educational leadership, special education.

Wilkes University, College of Graduate and Professional Studies, School of Education, Wilkes-Barre, PA 18766-0002. Offers educational development and strategies (MS Ed); educational leadership (MS Ed, Ed D); effective teaching (MS Ed); instructional media (MS Ed); instructional technology (MS Ed); international school leadership (MS Ed); international teaching and learning (MS Ed); literacy (MS Ed); middle level education (MS Ed); online teaching (MS Ed); school business leadership (MS Ed); special education (MS Ed); teaching English to speakers of other languages (MS Ed). *Program availability:* Part-time, evening/weekend, 100% online, blended/hybrid learning. *Students:* 87 full-time (67 women), 1,418 part-time (1,078 women); includes 87 minority (13 Black or African American, non-Hispanic/Latino; 1 American Indian or Alaska Native, non-Hispanic/Latino; 11 Asian, non-Hispanic/Latino; 40 Hispanic/Latino; 22 Two or more races, non-Hispanic/Latino). Average age 35. In 2018, 611 master's, 9 doctorates awarded. *Entrance requirements:* Additional exam requirements/recommendations for international students: Required—TOEFL (minimum score 550 paper-based; 79 iBT). *Application deadline:* Applications are processed on a rolling basis. Application fee: $45 ($65 for international students). Electronic applications accepted. *Expenses:* Contact institution. *Financial support:* Unspecified assistantships available. Financial award application deadline: 3/1; financial award applicants required to submit FAFSA. *Unit head:* Dr. Rhonda Rabbitt, Dean, 570-408-4680, Fax: 570-408-7872, E-mail: rhonda.rabbitt@wilkes.edu. *Application contact:* Stephanie Wasmanski, Associate Director of Graduate Admissions, 570-408-5535, Fax: 570-408-7846, E-mail: stephanie.wasmanski@wilkes.edu.
Website: http://www.wilkes.edu/academics/graduate-programs/masters-programs/graduate-education/index.aspx

William Paterson University of New Jersey, College of Education, Wayne, NJ 07470-8420. Offers curriculum and learning (M Ed); early childhood education (Certificate); educational leadership (M Ed); educational media specialist (Certificate); elementary education (MAT, Certificate); elementary education subject area (Certificate); higher education administration (MA); learning disabilities consultant (Certificate); literacy (M Ed); middle level education (M Ed); middle school education subject area (Certificate); professional counseling (M Ed); reading specialist (Certificate); school library media specialist (Certificate); school principal (Certificate); school supervisor (Certificate); secondary education (MAT); special education (M Ed); teacher of students with disabilities (Certificate). *Accreditation:* NCATE. *Program availability:* Part-time, evening/weekend. *Students:* Average age 35. 347 applicants, 87% accepted, 226 enrolled. In 2018, 136 master's awarded. *Degree requirements:* For master's, comprehensive exam, thesis (for some programs), exit interview (for some programs); practicum/internship; minimum GPA of 3.0 (for some programs); exit portfolio (for some programs). *Entrance requirements:* For master's, GRE/MAT, minimum GPA of 2.75; teaching certificate; essay; interview; 2 letters of recommendation; personal statement. Additional exam requirements/recommendations for international students: Required—TOEFL (minimum score 550 paper-based; 79 iBT), IELTS (minimum score 6). *Application deadline:* For fall admission, 6/1 for domestic students, 3/1 for international students; for spring admission, 11/1 for domestic students, 10/1 for international students. Applications are processed on a rolling basis. Application fee: $50. Electronic applications accepted. *Expenses: Tuition, area resident:* Full-time $14,714; part-time $727 per credit. Tuition, state resident: full-time $14,714; part-time $727 per credit. Tuition, nonresident: full-time $22,952; part-time $727 per credit. *International tuition:* $22,952 full-time. *Required fees:* $4 per semester. Tuition and fees vary according to course load, degree level and program. *Financial support:* In 2018–19, 8,416 students received support. Career-related internships or fieldwork, Federal Work-Study, scholarships/grants, and unspecified assistantships available. Support available to part-time students. Financial award application deadline: 3/15; financial award applicants required to submit FAFSA. *Faculty research:* Code switching and creative writing, language instruction, teacher evaluation, preschools, history of educational theories. *Total annual research expenditures:* $311,226. *Unit head:* Dr. Dorothy Feola, Dean, 973-720-2138, Fax: 973-720-3647, E-mail: feolad@wpunj.edu. *Application contact:* Liana Fornarotto, Director of Education Enrollment and Certification, 973-720-2206, Fax: 973-720-2989, E-mail: fornarottol@wpunj.edu.
Website: http://www.wpunj.edu/coe

Winston-Salem State University, MAT Program, Winston-Salem, NC 27110-0003. Offers middle grades education (MAT); special education (MAT). *Accreditation:* NCATE. *Program availability:* Part-time, evening/weekend, online learning. *Entrance requirements:* For master's, GRE, MAT, NC teacher licensure. Electronic applications accepted. *Faculty research:* Action research on issues in elementary classroom.

Worcester State University, Graduate School, Department of Education, Worcester, MA 01602-2597. Offers adult English as a esl (Postbaccalaureate Certificate); curriculum and instruction (Ed S); early childhood education (M Ed); education (M Ed); elementary education (M Ed); English as a second language (M Ed, Postbaccalaureate Certificate); middle school education (M Ed); middle/secondary school education (Postbaccalaureate Certificate); moderate disabilities (M Ed, Postbaccalaureate Certificate); reading (M Ed, Postbaccalaureate Certificate); reading specialist (Postbaccalaureate Certificate); school leadership and education administration (M Ed); school psychology (M Ed, Ed S); secondary education (M Ed, Ed S, Postbaccalaureate Certificate). *Faculty:* 10 full-time (9 women), 23 part-time/adjunct (11 women). *Students:* 38 full-time (33 women), 281 part-time (212 women); includes 30 minority (4 Black or African American, non-Hispanic/Latino; 3 American Indian or Alaska Native, non-Hispanic/Latino; 2 Asian, non-Hispanic/Latino; 16 Hispanic/Latino; 5 Two or more races, non-Hispanic/Latino), 2 international. Average age 41. 102 applicants, 98% accepted, 88 enrolled. In 2018, 132 master's, 52 Ed Ss awarded. *Degree requirements:* For master's, comprehensive exam (for some programs), thesis (for some programs), For a detail list of degree completion requirements please see the graduate catalog at catalog.worcester.edu. *Entrance requirements:* For master's, GRE General Test, MAT or GMAT, teaching certificate. For a detail list of entrance requirements please see the graduate catalog at catalog.worcester.edu. Additional exam requirements/recommendations for international students: Required—TOEFL (minimum score 550 paper-based; 79 iBT), PTE. *Application deadline:* For fall admission, 3/1 for domestic and international students; for spring admission, 11/1 for domestic and international students; for summer admission, 3/1 for domestic and international students. Applications are processed on a rolling basis. Application fee: $50. Electronic applications accepted. *Expenses: Tuition, area resident:* Full-time $3042; part-time $169 per credit hour. Tuition, state resident: full-time $3042; part-time $169 per credit hour. Tuition, nonresident: full-time $3042; part-time $169 per credit hour. *International tuition:* $3042 full-time. *Required fees:* $2754; $153 per credit hour. *Financial support:* Career-related internships or fieldwork, scholarships/grants, and unspecified assistantships available. Support available to part-time students. Financial award application deadline: 3/1; financial award applicants required to submit FAFSA. *Unit head:* Dr. Sara Young, Graduate Program Coordinator, 508-929-8246, Fax: 508-929-8164, E-mail: syoung3@worcester.edu. *Application contact:* Sara Grady, Associate Dean of Graduate and Continuing Education, 508-929-8130, Fax: 508-929-8100, E-mail: sara.grady@worcester.edu.

Secondary Education

Acacia University, American Graduate School of Education, Tempe, AZ 85284. Offers educational administration (M Ed); elementary education (MA); English as a second language (M Ed); secondary education (MA); special education (M Ed).

Adelphi University, College of Education & Health Sciences, College of Education and Health Services, Garden City, NY 11530-0701. Offers MA. *Program availability:* Part-time, evening/weekend. *Students:* 28 full-time (20 women), 2 part-time (1 woman); includes 6 minority (1 Asian, non-Hispanic/Latino; 5 Hispanic/Latino). Average age 22. 66 applicants, 62% accepted, 17 enrolled. In 2018, 11 master's awarded. *Entrance requirements:* For master's, official transcripts, bachelor's degree, 500 word essay, letters of recommendation, resume. Additional exam requirements/recommendations for international students: Required—TOEFL (minimum score 550 paper-based; 80 iBT), IELTS (minimum score 6.5). *Application deadline:* For fall admission, 3/1 for international students; for spring admission, 11/1 for international students. Applications are processed on a rolling basis. Application fee: $50. Electronic applications accepted. *Expenses:* Contact institution. *Financial support:* Research assistantships, teaching

assistantships, career-related internships or fieldwork, institutionally sponsored loans, scholarships/grants, traineeships, and unspecified assistantships available. Support available to part-time students. Financial award application deadline: 1/1; financial award applicants required to submit FAFSA. *Faculty research:* Methods to enhance the development of teaching dispositions, ethical and moral issues in education. *Unit head:* Dr. Robert Linne, Director, 516-877-4411, E-mail: linne@adelphi.edu. *Application contact:* Michael Myers, Director of Graduate Admissions, 516-877-3010, Fax: 516-877-3039, E-mail: graduateadmissions@adelphi.edu.

Alabama Agricultural and Mechanical University, School of Graduate Studies, College of Education, Humanities, and Behavioral Sciences, Department of Educational Leadership and Secondary Education, Huntsville, AL 35811. Offers biology (M Ed); business/marketing education (M Ed, Ed S); chemistry (M Ed); collaborative teacher secondary education (M Ed, Ed S); education (M Ed, Ed S); English language arts (M Ed); family/consumer science education (M Ed, Ed S); general science (M Ed); general social science (M Ed); mathematics (M Ed, Ed S); physics (M Ed, Ed S); technology education (M Ed). *Accreditation:* NCATE. *Program availability:* Evening/weekend. *Degree requirements:* For master's, comprehensive exam; for Ed S, thesis. *Entrance requirements:* For master's, GRE General Test. Additional exam requirements/recommendations for international students: Required—TOEFL (minimum score 500 paper-based; 61 iBT). Electronic applications accepted. *Faculty research:* World peace through education, computer-assisted instruction.

Alabama State University, College of Education, Department of Curriculum and Instruction, Montgomery, AL 36101-0271. Offers early childhood education (Ed S); secondary education (M Ed), including biology education, English language arts education, history education, math education, music education, reading education, social science education. *Program availability:* Part-time, evening/weekend, online only, 100% online. *Faculty:* 7 full-time (4 women), 7 part-time/adjunct (4 women). *Students:* 22 full-time (19 women), 58 part-time (49 women); includes 235 minority (234 Black or African American, non-Hispanic/Latino; 1 Hispanic/Latino), 5 international. Average age 36. 45 applicants, 33% accepted, 6 enrolled. In 2018, 34 master's awarded. *Degree requirements:* For master's, comprehensive exam, thesis optional; for Ed S, comprehensive exam, thesis. *Entrance requirements:* For master's, GRE General Test, MAT, writing competency test; for Ed S, writing competency test, GRE, MAT. Additional exam requirements/recommendations for international students: Required—TOEFL (minimum score 500 paper-based). *Application deadline:* For fall admission, 4/15 for domestic and international students; for spring admission, 11/15 for domestic and international students; for summer admission, 3/15 for domestic and international students. Applications are processed on a rolling basis. Application fee: $25. Electronic applications accepted. *Expenses:* Contact institution. *Financial support:* Fellowships, teaching assistantships, career-related internships or fieldwork, scholarships/grants, tuition waivers (partial), and unspecified assistantships available. Financial award application deadline: 6/30; financial award applicants required to submit FAFSA. *Unit head:* Dr. Joyce Johnson, Acting Chairperson, 334-229-4485, Fax: 334-229-5603, E-mail: jjohnson@alasu.edu. *Application contact:* Dr. Ed Brown, Dean of Graduate Studies, 334-229-4274, Fax: 334-229-4928, E-mail: ebrown@alasu.edu.
Website: http://www.alasu.edu/academics/colleges—departments/college-of-education/curriculum—instruction/index.aspx

Alcorn State University, School of Graduate Studies, School of Education and Psychology, Lorman, MS 39096-7500. Offers agricultural education (MS Ed); elementary education (MAT, MS Ed, Ed S); guidance and counseling (MS Ed); industrial education (MS Ed); secondary education (MAT, MS Ed), including health and physical education (MS Ed), NCAA compliance and academic progress reporting (MS Ed); special education (MS Ed). *Accreditation:* NCATE. *Degree requirements:* For master's, thesis optional.

American International College, School of Education, Springfield, MA 01109-3189. Offers early childhood education (M Ed, CAGS); education (MA, Ed D), including counseling psychology (MA), educational leadership and supervision (Ed D), professional counseling and supervision (Ed D), teaching and learning (Ed D); elementary education (M Ed, CAGS); middle education/secondary education (M Ed, CAGS); moderate disabilities (M Ed, CAGS); reading specialist (M Ed, CAGS); school adjustment counseling (MAEP, CAGS); school guidance counseling (MAEP, CAGS); school leadership (M Ed, CAGS). *Program availability:* Evening/weekend. *Degree requirements:* For master's and CAGS, practicum/culminating experience. *Entrance requirements:* For master's, Communication and Literacy portion of the Massachusetts Tests for Education Licensure, graduate of accredited four-year college with minimum B-average in undergraduate course work; for CAGS, M Ed or master's degree in field related to licensure from accredited institution. Electronic applications accepted. *Expenses:* Contact institution.

American Public University System, AMU/APU Graduate Programs, Charles Town, WV 25414. Offers accounting (MS); applied business analytics (MS); business administration (MBA); criminal justice (MA); cybersecurity studies (MS); educational leadership (M Ed); environmental policy and management (MS); global security (DGS); health information management (MS); history (MA), including American military history, American Revolution, civil war, war since 1945, World War II; information technology (MS); international relations and conflict resolution (MA), including American politics and government, comparative government and development, general, international relations, public policy; national security studies (MA); nursing (MSN); political science (MA); public policy (MPP); reverse logistics management (MA), including comparative and security issues, conflict resolution, international and transnational security issues, peacekeeping; space studies (MS); sports management (MS); strategic intelligence (DSI); teaching (M Ed), including secondary social studies; transportation and logistics management (MA). *Program availability:* Part-time, evening/weekend, online only, 100% online. *Students:* 406 full-time (180 women), 7,826 part-time (3,329 women); includes 2,781 minority (1,438 Black or African American, non-Hispanic/Latino; 44 American Indian or Alaska Native, non-Hispanic/Latino; 193 Asian, non-Hispanic/Latino; 747 Hispanic/Latino; 53 Native Hawaiian or other Pacific Islander, non-Hispanic/Latino; 306 Two or more races, non-Hispanic/Latino), 121 international. Average age 38. In 2018, 2,717 master's awarded. *Degree requirements:* For master's, comprehensive exam or practicum; for doctorate, practicum. *Entrance requirements:* For master's, official transcript showing earned bachelor's degree from institution accredited by recognized accrediting body. Additional exam requirements/recommendations for international students: Required—TOEFL (minimum score 550 paper-based), IELTS (minimum score 6.5). *Application deadline:* Applications are processed on a rolling basis. Application fee: $0. Electronic applications accepted. *Financial support:* Scholarships/grants available. Financial award applicants required to submit FAFSA. *Unit head:* Dr. Wallace Boston, President, 877-468-6268, Fax: 304-728-2348, E-mail: president@apus.edu. *Application contact:* Yoci Deal, Associate Vice President, Graduate and International Admissions, 877-468-6268, Fax: 304-724-3764, E-mail: info@apus.edu.
Website: http://www.apus.edu

Andrews University, School of Graduate Studies, School of Education, Department of Teaching, Learning, and Curriculum, Berrien Springs, MI 49104. Offers curriculum and instruction (MA, Ed D, PhD, Ed S); elementary education (MAT); secondary education (MAT), including biology, education, English, English as a second language, French, history, physics; teacher education (MAT). *Entrance requirements:* For master's, GRE Subject Test. Additional exam requirements/recommendations for international students: Required—TOEFL (minimum score 550 paper-based).

Aquinas College, School of Education, Nashville, TN 37205-2005. Offers elementary education (MAT); secondary education (MAT); teaching and learning (M Ed).

Arcadia University, School of Education, Glenside, PA 19038-3295. Offers art education (M Ed); computer education (CAS); curriculum (CAS); curriculum studies (M Ed); early childhood education (M Ed), including individualized, master teacher, research in child development; educational leadership (M Ed, Ed D, CAS); elementary education (M Ed); English education (MA Ed); environmental education (MA Ed); instructional technology (M Ed); language arts (M Ed); library science (M Ed); mathematics education (M Ed, MA Ed); music education (MA Ed); psychology (MA Ed); reading (M Ed, CAS); science education (M Ed, CAS); secondary education (M Ed, CAS); special education (M Ed, Ed D, CAS); theater arts (MA Ed); written communication (MA Ed). *Accreditation:* NASAD. *Program availability:* Part-time, evening/weekend, online learning. *Faculty:* 14 full-time (10 women). *Students:* 35 full-time (24 women), 299 part-time (243 women); includes 72 minority (49 Black or African American, non-Hispanic/Latino; 1 American Indian or Alaska Native, non-Hispanic/Latino; 12 Asian, non-Hispanic/Latino; 8 Hispanic/Latino; 2 Two or more races, non-Hispanic/Latino), 5 international. In 2018, 152 master's, 8 doctorates awarded. *Entrance requirements:* Additional exam requirements/recommendations for international students: Required—Official results from the TOEFL or IELTS are required. *Application deadline:* Applications are processed on a rolling basis. Application fee: $25. Electronic applications accepted. *Expenses:* Contact institution. *Financial support:* Career-related internships or fieldwork, tuition waivers (partial), and unspecified assistantships available. *Unit head:* Kimberly Dean, Chair, 215-572-8629. *Application contact:* 215-572-2925, Fax: 215-572-2126, E-mail: grad@arcadia.edu.

Argosy University, Atlanta, College of Education, Atlanta, GA 30328. Offers educational leadership (MAEd, Ed D, Ed S), including higher education administration (Ed D), K-12 education (Ed D); teaching and learning (MAEd, Ed D, Ed S), including education technology (Ed D), higher education (Ed D), K-12 education (Ed D).

Argosy University, Chicago, College of Education, Chicago, IL 60601. Offers adult education and training (MA Ed); community college executive leadership (Ed D); educational leadership (MA Ed, Ed D, Ed S), including district leadership (Ed D), higher education administration (Ed D), K-12 education (Ed D); instructional leadership (Ed D, Ed S), including higher education (Ed D), K-12 education (Ed D). *Program availability:* Online learning.

Argosy University, Hawai`i, College of Education, Honolulu, HI 96813. Offers adult education and training (MAEd); educational leadership (Ed D), including higher education administration, K-12 education; instructional leadership (Ed D), including higher education, K-12 education; school psychology (MA).

Argosy University, Los Angeles, College of Education, Los Angeles, CA 90045. Offers community college executive leadership (Ed D); educational leadership (MA Ed, Ed D), including higher education administration (Ed D), K-12 education (Ed D); instructional leadership (MA Ed, Ed D), including higher education (Ed D), K-12 education (Ed D), multiple subject teacher preparation (MA Ed), single subject teacher preparation (MA Ed).

Argosy University, Northern Virginia, College of Education, Arlington, VA 22209. Offers community college executive leadership (Ed D); educational leadership (MA Ed, Ed D, Ed S), including higher education administration (Ed D), K-12 education (Ed D); instructional leadership (MA Ed, Ed D, Ed S), including higher education (Ed D), K-12 education (Ed D).

Argosy University, Orange County, College of Education, Orange, CA 92868. Offers community college executive leadership (Ed D); educational leadership (MA Ed, Ed D), including higher education administration (Ed D), K-12 education (Ed D); instructional leadership (MA Ed, Ed D), including education technology (Ed D), higher education (Ed D), K-12 education (Ed D), multiple subject teacher preparation (MA Ed), single subject teacher preparation (MA Ed).

Argosy University, Phoenix, College of Education, Phoenix, AZ 85021. Offers adult education and training (MA Ed); advanced educational administration (Ed D, Ed S); community college executive leadership (Ed D); educational administration (MA Ed); educational leadership (MA Ed, Ed D, Ed S), including education technology (Ed D), higher education administration (Ed D), K-12 education (Ed D); higher and postsecondary education (MA Ed); initial educational administration (Ed D, Ed S); school psychology (MA); teaching and learning (MA Ed, Ed D, Ed S), including education technology (Ed D), higher education (Ed D), K-12 education (Ed D).

Argosy University, Seattle, College of Education, Seattle, WA 98121. Offers adult education and training (MA Ed); community college executive leadership (Ed D); educational leadership (MA Ed, Ed D), including higher education administration (Ed D), K-12 education (Ed D); higher and postsecondary education (MA Ed); instructional leadership (MA Ed, Ed D), including education technology (Ed D), higher education (Ed D), K-12 education (Ed D).

Argosy University, Tampa, College of Education, Tampa, FL 33607. Offers community college executive leadership (Ed D); educational leadership (MA Ed, Ed D, Ed S), including higher education administration (Ed D), K-12 education (Ed D); school counseling (MA); teaching and learning (MA Ed, Ed D, Ed S), including higher education (Ed D), K-12 education (Ed D).

Argosy University, Twin Cities, College of Education, Eagan, MN 55121. Offers advanced educational administration (Ed D, Ed S); educational leadership (MA Ed, Ed D, Ed S), including higher education administration (Ed D), K-12 education (Ed D); higher and postsecondary education (MA Ed); initial educational administration (Ed D, Ed S); instructional leadership (MA Ed, Ed D, Ed S), including education technology (Ed D), higher education (Ed D), K-12 education (Ed D).

Arizona State University at the Tempe campus, Mary Lou Fulton Teachers College, Program in Curriculum and Instruction, Phoenix, AZ 85069. Offers curriculum and instruction (M Ed, MA); elementary education (M Ed); physical education (MPE); secondary education (M Ed). *Program availability:* Part-time, evening/weekend, online learning. Terminal master's awarded for partial completion of doctoral program. *Degree requirements:* For master's, thesis or alternative, applied project, interactive Program of Study (iPOS) submitted before completing 50 percent of required credit hours. *Entrance requirements:* For master's, GRE or GMAT (for some programs), minimum GPA of 3.0 or equivalent in last 2 years of work leading to bachelor's degree, 3 letters of recommendation, personal statement describing research and career goals, curriculum vitae or resume, IVP fingerprint clearance card (for those seeking Arizona certification). Additional exam requirements/recommendations for international students: Required—TOEFL, IELTS, or PTE. Electronic applications accepted. *Expenses:* Contact institution. *Faculty research:* Early childhood, media and computers, elementary education, secondary education, English education, bilingual education, language and literacy, science education, engineering education, exercise and wellness education.

Secondary Education

Auburn University at Montgomery, College of Education, Department of Curriculum, Instruction, and Technology, Montgomery, AL 36124-4023. Offers elementary education (M Ed, Ed S); instructional technology (Ed S); secondary education (M Ed). *Faculty:* 12 full-time (8 women), 8 part-time/adjunct (all women). *Students:* 43 full-time (34 women), 81 part-time (65 women); includes 39 minority (38 Black or African American, non-Hispanic/Latino; 1 Hispanic/Latino), 2 international. Average age 33. 99 applicants, 70% accepted, 37 enrolled. In 2018, 47 master's awarded. *Degree requirements:* For master's, comprehensive exam, thesis (for some programs). *Entrance requirements:* For master's, GRE or MAT. Additional exam requirements/recommendations for international students: Recommended—TOEFL (minimum score 500 paper-based; 61 iBT), IELTS (minimum score 5.5), TSE (minimum score 44). *Application deadline:* For fall admission, 7/15 for international students; for spring admission, 11/15 for international students; for summer admission, 4/15 for international students. Applications are processed on a rolling basis. Application fee: $25. Electronic applications accepted. *Expenses:* Tuition, area resident: Full-time $7146; part-time $4764 per credit hour. Tuition, state resident: full-time $7146; part-time $4764 per credit hour. Tuition, nonresident: full-time $16,056; part-time $10,704 per credit hour. *International tuition:* $16,056 full-time. *Required fees:* $766. One-time fee: $25 full-time. *Financial support:* Application deadline: 3/1; applicants required to submit FAFSA. *Unit head:* Dr. Kellie Shumack, Head, 334-244-3737, Fax: 334-244-3835, E-mail: kshumack@aum.edu. *Application contact:* Dr. Rhonda Morton, Associate Dean/Graduate Coordinator, 334-224-3287, Fax: 334-244-3978, E-mail: rmorton@aum.edu. Website: http://education.aum.edu/academic-departments/curriculum-instruction-technology

Augusta University, College of Education, Program in Curriculum and Instruction, Augusta, GA 30912. Offers curriculum and instruction (Ed S); elementary education (MAT); foreign language education (MAT); instruction (M Ed); middle grades education (MAT); music education (MAT); secondary education (MAT); special education (MAT). *Degree requirements:* For master's, thesis, portfolio. *Entrance requirements:* For master's, GRE, MAT, minimum GPA of 2.5.

Avila University, School of Education, Kansas City, MO 64145-1698. Offers advanced classroom management (MA); elementary education (Teaching Certificate); English language learners (Advanced Certificate); middle school (Teaching Certificate); physical education K-12 (Teaching Certificate); secondary education (Teaching Certificate). *Program availability:* Part-time, evening/weekend, online learning. *Faculty:* 6 full-time (5 women), 9 part-time/adjunct (8 women). *Students:* 83 full-time (71 women), 84 part-time (69 women); includes 13 minority (6 Black or African American, non-Hispanic/Latino; 2 Asian, non-Hispanic/Latino; 4 Hispanic/Latino; 1 Two or more races, non-Hispanic/Latino), 2 international. Average age 40. 92 applicants, 62% accepted, 40 enrolled. In 2018, 21 master's awarded. *Entrance requirements:* For master's, minimum GPA of 3.0, writing sample, recommendation, interview; for other advanced degree, foreign language. Additional exam requirements/recommendations for international students: Required—TOEFL (minimum score 580 paper-based; 92 iBT). *Application deadline:* Applications are processed on a rolling basis. Electronic applications accepted. *Expenses:* Contact institution. *Financial support:* In 2018–19, 12 students received support. Unspecified assistantships available. Financial award applicants required to submit FAFSA. *Unit head:* Dr. Stacy Keith, Director of Graduate Education, 816-501-2446, Fax: 816-501-2915, E-mail: stacy.keith@avila.edu. *Application contact:* Cory Roup, Graduate Education Enrollment and Academic Advisor, 816-501-2464, E-mail: cory.roup@avila.edu. Website: https://www.avila.edu/academics/graduate-studies/grad-education

Ball State University, Graduate School, Teachers College, Department of Educational Studies, Program in Secondary Education, Muncie, IN 47306. Offers MA. *Accreditation:* NCATE. *Program availability:* Part-time, online only, 100% online. *Entrance requirements:* For master's, minimum baccalaureate GPA of 2.75 or 3.0 in latter half of baccalaureate. Additional exam requirements/recommendations for international students: Required—TOEFL (minimum score 550 paper-based; 79 iBT), IELTS (minimum score 6.5). Electronic applications accepted.

Bard College, Master of Arts in Teaching Program, Annandale-on-Hudson, NY 12504. Offers secondary education (MAT), including biology, history, literature, mathematics, Spanish; MS/MAT. *Program availability:* Part-time. *Degree requirements:* For master's, year-long teaching residencies in area middle and high schools. *Entrance requirements:* For master's, GRE General Test, resume, 3 letters of recommendation, personal statement, official transcripts. Additional exam requirements/recommendations for international students: Required—TOEFL. Electronic applications accepted. Application fee is waived when completed online.

Bellarmine University, Annsley Frazier Thornton School of Education, Louisville, KY 40205. Offers education and district leadership (Ed D); education and social change (PhD); elementary education (MA Ed, MAT); leadership in higher education (PhD); middle school education (MA Ed, MAT); principalship (Ed S); reading and writing (MA Ed); secondary education (MAT); teacher leadership (MA Ed). *Accreditation:* NCATE. *Program availability:* Part-time, evening/weekend. *Faculty:* 14 full-time (7 women), 17 part-time/adjunct (11 women). *Students:* 27 full-time (19 women), 205 part-time (156 women); includes 74 minority (53 Black or African American, non-Hispanic/Latino; 6 Asian, non-Hispanic/Latino; 7 Hispanic/Latino; 8 Two or more races, non-Hispanic/Latino). Average age 34. 155 applicants, 71% accepted, 95 enrolled. In 2018, 69 master's, 10 doctorates, 30 other advanced degrees awarded. *Degree requirements:* For master's, comprehensive exam (for some programs), thesis (for some programs); for doctorate, comprehensive exam (for some programs), thesis/dissertation; for Ed S, comprehensive exam (for some programs). *Entrance requirements:* For master's, GRE, baccalaureate degree from accredited institution; minimum cumulative GPA of 2.75; recommendations from employers, supervisors, or professors attesting to applicant's potential as graduate student; statement of intent to pursue graduate degree; for doctorate, GRE, minimum GPA of 3.5 in all graduate coursework; baccalaureate and master's degrees in education or fields directly relevant to education; three letters of recommendation; two essays (no more than 1,000 words each); resume or curriculum vitae; interview; for Ed S, master's degree in education; valid teaching certificate; three years of experience in teaching; three recommendations; minimum GPA of 3.0 in all graduate work; interview; essays; personal goal statement. Additional exam requirements/recommendations for international students: Required—TOEFL (minimum score 80 iBT), IELTS (minimum score 6), TOEFL (minimum score 550 paper-based, 68 iBT), IELTS (minimum score 6), or Michigan English Language Assessment Battery. *Application deadline:* For fall admission, 8/1 priority date for domestic and international students; for spring admission, 12/1 priority date for domestic and international students; for summer admission, 4/10 priority date for domestic and international students. Applications are processed on a rolling basis. Application fee: $40. Electronic applications accepted. *Expenses:* Doctor of Education: $855 per credit hour; Educational Specialist: $410 per credit hour; Master of Arts in Education: $410 per credit hour; Master of Arts in Teaching: $665 per credit hour; Master of Arts in Teaching, undergraduate content courses: $410 per credit hour; Master of Education in Higher Education Leadership and Social Justice: $665 per credit hour; Ph.D., Social Change: $855 per credit hour; Ph.D., Leadership in Higher Education: $855 per credit hour; Rank I Programs: $410 per credit hour. *Financial support:* Scholarships/grants available.

Financial award applicants required to submit FAFSA. *Faculty research:* Literacy, service-learning, dispositions, educational technology, special education. *Unit head:* Dr. Elizabeth Dinkins, Dean, 502-272-7958, Fax: 502-272-8189, E-mail: edinkins@bellarmine.edu. *Application contact:* Sarah Schuble, Assistant Director of Graduate Student Enrollment, 502-272-8271, Fax: 502-272-8002, E-mail: sschuble@bellarmine.edu. Website: http://www.bellarmine.edu/education/graduate

Berry College, Graduate Programs, Graduate Programs in Education, Program in Secondary Education, Mount Berry, GA 30149. Offers MAT. *Degree requirements:* For master's, thesis, portfolio, oral exams. *Entrance requirements:* For master's, GRE General Test or MAT, minimum GPA of 2.5. Additional exam requirements/recommendations for international students: Required—TOEFL (minimum score 550 paper-based). *Application deadline:* For fall admission, 7/26 for domestic students, 5/1 for international students; for spring admission, 12/1 for domestic students, 10/1 for international students. Applications are processed on a rolling basis. Application fee: $25 ($30 for international students). Electronic applications accepted. *Expenses:* Contact institution. *Financial support:* Research assistantships with full tuition reimbursements, scholarships/grants, tuition waivers (partial), and unspecified assistantships available. Support available to part-time students. Financial award application deadline: 3/1; financial award applicants required to submit FAFSA. *Unit head:* Dr. Jacqueline McDowell, Dean, Charter School of Education and Human Sciences, 706-236-1717, Fax: 706-238-5827, E-mail: jmcdowell@berry.edu. *Application contact:* Admissions, 706-236-2215, Fax: 706-290-2178, E-mail: admissions@berry.edu. Website: http://www.berry.edu/academics/education/graduate/

Bethel University, Graduate School, St. Paul, MN 55112-6999. Offers business administration (MBA); classroom management (Certificate); counseling (MA); K-12 education (MA); leadership (Ed D); leadership foundations (Certificate); nurse educator (MS, Certificate); nurse-midwifery (MS); physician assistant (MS); special education (MA); strategic leadership (MA); teaching (MA); teaching and learning (Certificate). *Program availability:* Part-time, evening/weekend, 100% online, blended/hybrid learning. *Faculty:* 23 full-time (17 women), 73 part-time/adjunct (45 women). *Students:* 586 full-time (426 women), 372 part-time (244 women); includes 141 minority (49 Black or African American, non-Hispanic/Latino; 6 American Indian or Alaska Native, non-Hispanic/Latino; 19 Asian, non-Hispanic/Latino; 40 Hispanic/Latino; 2 Native Hawaiian or other Pacific Islander, non-Hispanic/Latino; 25 Two or more races, non-Hispanic/Latino), 25 international. Average age 35. 642 applicants, 39% accepted, 194 enrolled. In 2018, 312 master's, 28 doctorates, 134 other advanced degrees awarded. *Degree requirements:* For master's, comprehensive exam (for some programs), thesis (for some programs); for doctorate, comprehensive exam, thesis/dissertation. *Entrance requirements:* Additional exam requirements/recommendations for international students: Required—TOEFL (minimum score 550 paper-based; 80 iBT), TOEFL (minimum score 550 paper-based, 80 iBT) or IELTS. *Application deadline:* Applications are processed on a rolling basis. Application fee: $0. Electronic applications accepted. *Expenses:* Contact institution. *Financial support:* Teaching assistantships, career-related internships or fieldwork, and scholarships/grants available. Support available to part-time students. Financial award applicants required to submit FAFSA. *Unit head:* Dr. Randy Bergen, Associate Provost, 651-635-8000, Fax: 651-635-8004, E-mail: r-bergen@bethel.edu. *Application contact:* Director of Admissions, 651-635-8000, Fax: 651-635-8004, E-mail: gs@bethel.edu. Website: https://www.bethel.edu/graduate/

Binghamton University, State University of New York, Graduate School, College of Community and Public Affairs, Department of Teaching, Learning and Educational Leadership, Program in Adolescence Education, Binghamton, NY 13902-6000. Offers biology education (MAT, MS Ed); chemistry education (MAT, MS Ed); earth science education (MAT, MS Ed); English education (MAT, MS Ed); French education (MAT, MS Ed); mathematical sciences education (MAT, MS Ed); physics (MAT, MS Ed); social studies (MAT, MS Ed); Spanish education (MAT, MS Ed). *Accreditation:* TEAC. *Program availability:* Part-time, evening/weekend. *Degree requirements:* For master's, portfolio. *Entrance requirements:* For master's, GRE General Test, teaching certification. Additional exam requirements/recommendations for international students: Required—TOEFL (minimum score 550 paper-based; 80 iBT). Electronic applications accepted.

Blue Mountain College, Program in Secondary Education - Biology, Blue Mountain, MS 38610. Offers M Ed. *Program availability:* Part-time, evening/weekend. *Degree requirements:* For master's, comprehensive exam. *Entrance requirements:* For master's, PRAXIS, GRE, or MAT, official transcripts; bachelor's degree in a field of education from an accredited college or university; teaching certificate; three recommendations. Additional exam requirements/recommendations for international students: Required—TOEFL (minimum score 550 paper-based). Electronic applications accepted.

Bob Jones University, Graduate Programs, Greenville, SC 29614. Offers accountancy (MS); Bible (MA); Bible translation (MA); Biblical studies (Certificate); business administration (MBA); church history (MA, PhD); church ministries (MA); church music (MM); cinema and video production (MA); counseling (MS); curriculum and instruction (Ed D); divinity (M Div); dramatic production (MA); educational leadership (MS, Ed D, Ed S); elementary education (M Ed, MAT); English (M Ed, MA, MAT); fine arts (MA); graphic design (MA); history (M Ed, MA); illustration (MA); interpretative speech (MA); mathematics (M Ed, MAT); medical missions (Certificate); ministry (MM, D Min); multi-categorical special education (M Ed, MAT); music (M Ed); New Testament interpretation (PhD); Old Testament interpretation (PhD); orchestral instrument performance (MM); organ performance (MM); pastoral studies (MA); personnel services (MS, Ed S); piano pedagogy (MM); piano performance (MM); platform arts (MA); rhetoric and public address (MA); secondary education (M Ed); studio art (MA); teaching Bible (MA); theology (MA, PhD); voice performance (MM); youth ministries (MA); M Div/MM.

Boston College, Lynch School of Education and Human Development, Department of Teacher Education, Special Education and Curriculum and Instruction, Chestnut Hill, MA 02467-3800. Offers curriculum and instruction (M Ed, PhD, CAES); early childhood education (M Ed); elementary education (M Ed); law and curriculum and instruction (JD/M Ed); reading specialist (M Ed, CAES); religious education (M Ed, CAES); secondary education (M Ed, MAT, MST), including biology (MST), chemistry (MST), English (MAT), French (MAT), geology (MST), history (MAT), Latin and classical humanities (MAT), mathematics (MST), physics (MST), secondary teaching (M Ed), Spanish (MAT); special needs: moderate disabilities (M Ed, CAES); special needs: severe disabilities (M Ed); JD/M Ed. *Program availability:* Part-time, evening/weekend, 100% online. *Faculty:* 19 full-time (11 women). *Students:* 186 full-time (140 women), 92 part-time (74 women); includes 58 minority (20 Black or African American, non-Hispanic/Latino; 4 Asian, non-Hispanic/Latino; 29 Hispanic/Latino; 5 Two or more races, non-Hispanic/Latino), 33 international. Average age 28. In 2018, 132 master's, 13 doctorates awarded. Terminal master's awarded for partial completion of doctoral program. *Degree requirements:* For master's, comprehensive exam; for doctorate, comprehensive exam, thesis/dissertation. *Entrance requirements:* Additional exam requirements/recommendations for international students: Required—TOEFL. Application fee: $75. Electronic applications accepted. *Financial support:* Fellowships with full and partial tuition reimbursements,

research assistantships with full and partial tuition reimbursements, teaching assistantships with full and partial tuition reimbursements, career-related internships or fieldwork, Federal Work-Study, institutionally sponsored loans, scholarships/grants, traineeships, health care benefits, tuition waivers (full and partial), and unspecified assistantships available. Support available to part-time students. Financial award applicants required to submit FAFSA. *Faculty research:* Teacher education, education research and policy, bilingual education, science education, disabilities, urban education. *Unit head:* Dr. Susan Bruce, Chairperson, 617-552-4214, Fax: 617-552-0812. *Application contact:* Jessica Rivers, Assistant Dean of Graduate Admission and Financial Aid, 617-552-4214, Fax: 617-552-0398, E-mail: riversja@bc.edu.
Website: http://www.bc.edu/education

Bowie State University, Graduate Programs, Program in Secondary Education, Bowie, MD 20715-9465. Offers M Ed. *Accreditation:* NCATE. *Program availability:* Part-time, evening/weekend. *Degree requirements:* For master's, comprehensive exam, thesis optional, research paper. *Entrance requirements:* For master's, minimum undergraduate GPA of 3.0, bachelor's degree in education, teaching certificate, teaching experience. Electronic applications accepted.

Brandeis University, Graduate School of Arts and Sciences, Department of Education, Waltham, MA 02454-9110. Offers Jewish day schools (MAT); public elementary education (MAT); secondary education (MAT), including Bible, biology, chemistry, Chinese, English, history, Jewish day schools, math, physics; teacher leadership (Ed M, AGC). *Faculty:* 5 full-time (3 women), 9 part-time/adjunct (all women). *Students:* 17 full-time (13 women), 36 part-time (33 women); includes 9 minority (1 Black or African American, non-Hispanic/Latino; 6 Asian, non-Hispanic/Latino; 1 Hispanic/Latino; 1 Two or more races, non-Hispanic/Latino). Average age 36. 90 applicants, 79% accepted, 50 enrolled. In 2018, 44 master's, 18 other advanced degrees awarded. *Degree requirements:* For master's, thesis or alternative, internship, research project, capstone. *Entrance requirements:* For master's, GRE or MAT, transcripts, letters of recommendation, resume, statement of purpose; for AGC, transcripts, letters of recommendation, resume, statement of purpose, interview. Additional exam requirements/recommendations for international students: Required—TOEFL, IELTS, PTE. *Application deadline:* For fall admission, 3/15 priority date for domestic students. Applications are processed on a rolling basis. Application fee: $75. Electronic applications accepted. *Financial support:* Scholarships/grants available. *Faculty research:* Teacher education, education, teaching, elementary education, secondary education, Jewish education, English, history, biology, chemistry, physics, math, Chinese, Bible/Tanakh. *Unit head:* Danielle Igra, Director of Graduate Study, 781-736-8519, E-mail: digra@brandeis.edu. *Application contact:* Manuel Tuan, Administrator, 781-736-2002, E-mail: tuan@brandeis.edu.
Website: http://www.brandeis.edu/gsas/programs/education.html

Brandman University, School of Education, Irvine, CA 92618. Offers curriculum and instruction (MAE); educational administration (MAE); educational leadership (MAE); educational leadership and administration (MA); elementary education (MAT); instructional technology: teaching the 21st century learner (MAE); leadership in early childhood education (MAE); organizational leadership (Ed D); school counseling (MA); secondary education (MAT); special education (MA); teaching and learning (MAE).

Brenau University, Sydney O. Smith Graduate School, College of Education, Gainesville, GA 30501. Offers early childhood (Ed S); early childhood education (M Ed, MAT); middle grades (Ed S); middle grades education (M Ed, MAT); secondary education (MAT); special education (M Ed, MAT). *Accreditation:* NCATE. *Program availability:* Part-time, evening/weekend, online learning. *Degree requirements:* For master's, thesis optional, comprehensive exam or applied research project, effective portfolio; for Ed S, thesis, applied research project. *Entrance requirements:* For master's, GRE, MAT, interview, minimum GPA of 3.0, 3 references, writing samples; for Ed S, GRE, MAT, master's degree, minimum GPA of 3.0, writing sample, letters of reference. Additional exam requirements/recommendations for international students: Required—TOEFL (minimum score 500 paper-based; 61 iBT); Recommended—IELTS (minimum score 5). Electronic applications accepted. *Expenses:* Contact institution.

Bridgewater State University, College of Graduate Studies, College of Education and Allied Studies, Department of Secondary Education and Professional Programs, Program in Secondary Education, Bridgewater, MA 02325. Offers MAT. *Accreditation:* NCATE. *Program availability:* Part-time, evening/weekend. *Entrance requirements:* For master's, GRE General Test.

Brooklyn College of the City University of New York, School of Education, Program in Adolescence Science Education and Special Subjects, Brooklyn, NY 11210-2889. Offers adolescence science education (MAT); biology teacher (7-12) (MA); chemistry teacher (7-12) (MA); earth science teacher (7-12) (MAT); English teacher (7-12) (MA); French teacher (7-12) (MA); mathematics teacher (7-12) (MA); music teacher (MA); physics teacher (7-12) (MA); social studies teacher (7-12) (MA); Spanish teacher (7-12) (MA). *Program availability:* Part-time, evening/weekend. *Degree requirements:* For master's, comprehensive exam (for some programs), thesis (for some programs). *Entrance requirements:* For master's, LAST, previous course work in education, resume, 2 letters of recommendation, essay. Additional exam requirements/recommendations for international students: Required—TOEFL (minimum score 500 paper-based; 61 iBT). Electronic applications accepted. *Faculty research:* Interdisciplinary education, semiotics, discourse analysis, autobiography, teacher identity.

Brown University, Graduate School, Department of Education, Program in Teaching, Providence, RI 02912. Offers elementary education (MAT); English (MAT); history/social studies (MAT); science (MAT); secondary education (MAT). *Degree requirements:* For master's, student teaching, portfolio. *Entrance requirements:* For master's, GRE General Test, transcript, personal statement, 3 letters of recommendation, interview, writing sample (English applicants only). Additional exam requirements/recommendations for international students: Required—TOEFL (minimum score 577 paper-based). Electronic applications accepted. *Faculty research:* Literacy, English language learners, diversity, special education, biodiversity.

Cabrini University, Academic Affairs, Radnor, PA 19087. Offers accounting (M Acc); autism spectrum disorder (M Ed); biological sciences (MS), including civic leadership; criminology and criminal justice (MA); curriculum, instruction, and assessment (M Ed); educational leadership (M Ed, Ed D), including curriculum and instructional leadership (Ed D), preK-12 leadership (Ed D); English as a second language (M Ed); organizational leadership (DBA, PhD); preK to 4 (M Ed); reading specialist (M Ed); secondary education (M Ed), including biology, chemistry, English, English/communication, mathematics, social studies; special education grades 7-12 (M Ed); special education preK-8 (M Ed); teaching and learning (M Ed). *Program availability:* Part-time, evening/weekend. *Degree requirements:* For master's, comprehensive exam (for some programs), thesis (for some programs); for doctorate, comprehensive exam (for some programs), thesis/dissertation. *Entrance requirements:* For master's, professional resume, personal statement, two recommendations, official transcripts; for doctorate, official transcripts, minimum master's GPA of 3.0, two recommendations, interview with admissions committee. Additional exam requirements/recommendations for international students: Required—TOEFL (minimum score 80 iBT). Electronic applications accepted. Application fee is waived when completed online. *Expenses:* Contact institution.

California State University, Fullerton, Graduate Studies, College of Education, Department of Secondary Education, Fullerton, CA 92831-3599. Offers teacher instruction (MS); teaching foundational mathematics (MS). *Program availability:* Part-time.

California State University, Long Beach, Graduate Studies, College of Education, Department of Teacher Education, Long Beach, CA 90840. Offers elementary education (MA); secondary education (MA). *Program availability:* Part-time, evening/weekend. *Degree requirements:* For master's, comprehensive exam or thesis. *Entrance requirements:* For master's, GRE General Test, minimum GPA of 2.75. *Application deadline:* For fall admission, 7/1 for domestic students; for spring admission, 12/1 for domestic students. Applications are processed on a rolling basis. Application fee: $55. Electronic applications accepted. *Expenses: Required fees:* $2628 per term. Tuition and fees vary according to class time, course level, course load, degree level, campus/location and program. *Financial support:* Federal Work-Study, institutionally sponsored loans, and scholarships/grants available. Financial award application deadline: 3/2; financial award applicants required to submit FAFSA. *Faculty research:* Teacher stress and burnout, new teacher induction. *Unit head:* Huong Tran Nguyen, Chair, 562-985-4506. *Application contact:* Lisa Isbell, Director Preparation Advising Center, 562-985-1105, Fax: 562-985-1106, E-mail: ced-tpac@csulb.edu.
Website: http://www.csulb.edu/college-of-education/teacher-preparation-advising-center-tpac

California State University, Long Beach, Graduate Studies, College of Natural Sciences and Mathematics, Department of Mathematics and Statistics, Long Beach, CA 90840. Offers mathematics (MS), including applied mathematics, applied statistics, mathematics education for secondary school teachers. *Program availability:* Part-time. *Degree requirements:* For master's, comprehensive exam or thesis. *Application deadline:* For fall admission, 6/1 for domestic students; for spring admission, 11/1 for domestic students. Applications are processed on a rolling basis. Application fee: $55. Electronic applications accepted. *Expenses: Required fees:* $2628 per term. Tuition and fees vary according to class time, course level, course load, degree level, campus/location and program. *Financial support:* Teaching assistantships, Federal Work-Study, institutionally sponsored loans, scholarships/grants, and traineeships available. Financial award application deadline: 3/2; financial award applicants required to submit FAFSA. *Faculty research:* Algebra, functional analysis, partial differential equations, operator theory, numerical analysis. *Unit head:* Dr. Tangan Gao, Chair, 562-985-4721, Fax: 562-985-8227, E-mail: tangan.gao@csulb.edu. *Application contact:* Dr. Tangan Gao, Chair, 562-985-4721, Fax: 562-985-8227, E-mail: tangan.gao@csulb.edu.

California State University, Northridge, Graduate Studies, Michael D. Eisner College of Education, Department of Secondary Education, Northridge, CA 91330. Offers educational technology (MA); English education (MA); mathematics education (MA); secondary science education (MA); teaching and learning (MA). *Accreditation:* NCATE. *Program availability:* Part-time. *Degree requirements:* For master's, thesis optional. *Entrance requirements:* For master's, GRE General Test or minimum GPA of 3.0. Additional exam requirements/recommendations for international students: Required—TOEFL.

California State University, Stanislaus, College of Education, Kinesiology and Social Work, MA Program in Education, Turlock, CA 95382. Offers curriculum and instruction (MA), including education technology, elementary education, multilingual education, physical education, reading, secondary education, special education; school administration (MA); school counseling (MA). *Program availability:* Part-time, evening/weekend. *Degree requirements:* For master's, comprehensive exam (for some programs), thesis (for some programs). *Entrance requirements:* For master's, MAT, GRE, or CBEST (varies by concentration), 3 letters of recommendation, personal statement. Additional exam requirements/recommendations for international students: Required—TOEFL (minimum score 550 paper-based). Electronic applications accepted. *Faculty research:* Children's perspectives on historical events, method elementary schools dual language education, K-12 reading programs.

California University of Pennsylvania, School of Graduate Studies and Research, College of Education and Human Services, Program in Secondary Education, California, PA 15419-1394. Offers advanced studies in secondary education and teacher leadership (M Ed); secondary education (MAT). *Program availability:* Part-time, evening/weekend, online learning. *Degree requirements:* For master's, comprehensive exam, thesis. *Entrance requirements:* For master's, PRAXIS, minimum GPA of 3.0. Additional exam requirements/recommendations for international students: Required—TOEFL (minimum score 550 paper-based; 80 iBT). Electronic applications accepted. *Faculty research:* The effectiveness of online instruction, student-centered instruction strategies in secondary education, computer technology in education, environmental education, multi-media in education.

Campbell University, Graduate and Professional Programs, School of Education, Buies Creek, NC 27506. Offers elementary education (M Ed); interdisciplinary studies (M Ed); middle grades education (M Ed); physical education (M Ed); school administration (MSA); school counseling (M Ed); secondary education (M Ed). *Accreditation:* NCATE. *Program availability:* Part-time, evening/weekend. *Degree requirements:* For master's, comprehensive exam. *Entrance requirements:* For master's, GRE General Test, minimum GPA of 2.7. *Faculty research:* Spiritual values and wellness issues in counseling, stress and professional burnout among counselors, thinking strategies, leadership, adaptive technology.

Canisius College, Graduate Division, School of Education and Human Services, Department of Graduate Education and Leadership, Buffalo, NY 14208-1098. Offers business and marketing education (MS Ed); college student personnel (MS Ed); deaf education (MS Ed); deaf/adolescent education, grades 7-12 (MS Ed); deaf/childhood education, grades 1-6 (MS Ed); differentiated instruction (MS Ed); education administration (MS); educational administration (MS Ed); educational technologies (Certificate); gifted education extension (Certificate); literacy (MS Ed); reading (Certificate); school building leadership (MS Ed, Certificate); school district leadership (Certificate); teacher leader (Certificate); TESOL (MS Ed). *Accreditation:* NCATE. *Program availability:* Part-time, evening/weekend, 100% online, blended/hybrid learning. *Faculty:* 5 full-time (all women), 21 part-time/adjunct (16 women). *Students:* 79 full-time (66 women), 135 part-time (106 women); includes 45 minority (27 Black or African American, non-Hispanic/Latino; 1 American Indian or Alaska Native, non-Hispanic/Latino; 3 Asian, non-Hispanic/Latino; 9 Hispanic/Latino; 5 Two or more races, non-Hispanic/Latino), 1 international. Average age 32. 83 applicants, 96% accepted, 74 enrolled. In 2018, 94 master's, 47 other advanced degrees awarded. *Entrance requirements:* For master's, GRE (if cumulative GPA less than 2.7), transcripts, two letters of recommendation. Additional exam requirements/recommendations for international students: Required—TOEFL (minimum score 550 paper-based, 79 iBT), IELTS (minimum score 6.5), or CAEL (minimum score 70). *Application deadline:* Applications are processed on a rolling basis. Application fee: $0. Electronic applications accepted. *Expenses: Tuition:* Part-time $820 per credit hour. *Required fees:* $25 per semester. One-time fee: $65 part-time. Tuition and fees vary according to program.

Financial support: In 2018–19, 206 students received support. Career-related internships or fieldwork, Federal Work-Study, scholarships/grants, tuition waivers (partial), and unspecified assistantships available. Support available to part-time students. Financial award application deadline: 4/30; financial award applicants required to submit FAFSA. *Faculty research:* Asperger's disease, autism, private higher education, reading strategies. *Unit head:* Dr. Anne Marie Tryjankowski, Chair/Associate Professor of Graduate Education and Leadership, 716-888-3715, Fax: 716-888-3142, E-mail: tryjanka@canisius.edu. *Application contact:* Dr. Anne Marie Tryjankowski, Chair/Associate Professor of Graduate Education and Leadership, 716-888-3715, Fax: 716-888-3142, E-mail: tryjanka@canisius.edu.

Carroll University, Graduate Programs in Education, Waukesha, WI 53186-5593. Offers adult and continuing education (M Ed); educational leadership (MS); PK-12 (M Ed). *Program availability:* Part-time, evening/weekend. *Degree requirements:* For master's, thesis. *Entrance requirements:* For master's, minimum undergraduate GPA of 2.5 in related field. Additional exam requirements/recommendations for international students: Required—TOEFL. Electronic applications accepted. *Faculty research:* Qualitative research methods, whole language approaches to teaching, the writing process, multicultural education, gifted/talented learners.

Carson-Newman University, Graduate Program in Education, Jefferson City, TN 37760. Offers curriculum and instruction (M Ed); educational leadership (M Ed); elementary education (MAT); school counseling (MS); secondary education (MAT); teaching English as a second language (MATESL). *Accreditation:* NCATE. *Program availability:* Part-time, evening/weekend, 100% online, blended/hybrid learning. *Faculty:* 20 full-time (11 women), 16 part-time/adjunct (13 women). *Students:* 14 full-time (8 women), 401 part-time (294 women); includes 45 minority (34 Black or African American, non-Hispanic/Latino; 1 American Indian or Alaska Native, non-Hispanic/Latino; 4 Hispanic/Latino; 1 Native Hawaiian or other Pacific Islander, non-Hispanic/Latino; 5 Two or more races, non-Hispanic/Latino). Average age 36. 223 applicants, 100% accepted, 199 enrolled. In 2018, 211 master's awarded. *Degree requirements:* For master's, thesis or alternative. *Entrance requirements:* For master's, PRAXIS II or GRE with minimum score of 290 on the verbal and quantitative components (for MAT), minimum GPA of 3.0 in major, 2.5 overall. Additional exam requirements/recommendations for international students: Recommended—TOEFL (minimum score 79 iBT), IELTS (minimum score 6.5), TSE (minimum score 53). *Application deadline:* For fall admission, 7/15 priority date for domestic students. Applications are processed on a rolling basis. Application fee: $50. *Expenses: Tuition:* Full-time $9036; part-time $502 per credit hour. *Required fees:* $900; $25 per credit hour. $300 per semester. One-time fee: $150. *Financial support:* Federal Work-Study and unspecified assistantships available. Financial award applicants required to submit FAFSA. *Unit head:* Dr. Kim Hawkins, Chair, 865-471-3314, E-mail: khawkins@cn.edu. *Application contact:* Nilma Stewart, Graduate Admissions and Services Adviser, 865-471-3230, Fax: 865-471-3875, E-mail: adults@cn.edu.
Website: http://www.cn.edu/adult-graduate-studies

The Catholic University of America, School of Arts and Sciences, Department of Education, Washington, DC 20064. Offers Catholic school leadership (MA); education (Certificate); secondary education (MA); special education (MA), including early childhood, non-categorical. *Accreditation:* NCATE. *Program availability:* Part-time. *Faculty:* 7 full-time (6 women), 7 part-time/adjunct (5 women). *Students:* 12 full-time (11 women), 15 part-time (6 women); includes 3 minority (2 Hispanic/Latino; 1 Two or more races, non-Hispanic/Latino), 2 international. Average age 37. 12 applicants, 75% accepted, 8 enrolled. In 2018, 14 master's awarded. *Degree requirements:* For master's, comprehensive exam, thesis or alternative; for Certificate, action research project. *Entrance requirements:* For master's, GRE General Test or MAT, statement of purpose, official copies of academic transcripts, three letters of recommendation, interview; for Certificate, PRAXIS I, statement of purpose, official copies of academic transcripts, three letters of recommendation, interview. Additional exam requirements/recommendations for international students: Required—TOEFL (minimum score 550 paper-based; 80 iBT). *Application deadline:* For fall admission, 7/15 priority date for domestic students, 7/1 for international students; for spring admission, 11/15 priority date for domestic students, 11/1 for international students. Applications are processed on a rolling basis. Application fee: $55. Electronic applications accepted. *Expenses:* Contact institution. *Financial support:* Fellowships, research assistantships, teaching assistantships, Federal Work-Study, scholarships/grants, tuition waivers (full and partial), and unspecified assistantships available. Financial award application deadline: 2/1; financial award applicants required to submit FAFSA. *Faculty research:* Special education, early childhood education, educational psychology, Catholic school administration, leadership and policy studies, counseling, curriculum and instruction. *Unit head:* Dr. Agnes Cave, Chair, 202-319-5805, Fax: 202-319-5815, E-mail: cave@cua.edu. *Application contact:* Dr. Steven Brown, Director of Graduate Admissions, 202-319-5057, Fax: 202-319-6533, E-mail: cua-admissions@cua.edu.
Website: http://education.cua.edu/

Centenary College of Louisiana, Graduate Programs, Department of Education, Shreveport, LA 71104. Offers elementary education (MAT); secondary education (MAT). *Program availability:* Part-time, evening/weekend. *Degree requirements:* For master's, comprehensive exam. *Entrance requirements:* For master's, PRAXIS I and II (for MAT), undergraduate degree, minimum GPA of 2.5. *Expenses:* Contact institution. *Faculty research:* Teachers as advocates for teachers, portfolio assessment, disabled readers.

Central Connecticut State University, School of Graduate Studies, School of Engineering, Science and Technology, Department of Mathematical Sciences, New Britain, CT 06050-4010. Offers data mining (MS, Certificate); mathematics (MA, MS), including actuarial science (MA), computer science (MA), statistics (MA); mathematics education leadership (Sixth Year Certificate); mathematics for secondary education (Certificate). *Program availability:* Part-time, evening/weekend, 100% online. *Faculty:* 13 full-time (4 women). *Students:* 14 full-time (9 women), 70 part-time (39 women); includes 21 minority (8 Black or African American, non-Hispanic/Latino; 9 Asian, non-Hispanic/Latino; 3 Hispanic/Latino; 1 Two or more races, non-Hispanic/Latino), 2 international. Average age 33. 57 applicants, 70% accepted, 20 enrolled. In 2018, 20 master's, 3 other advanced degrees awarded. *Degree requirements:* For master's, comprehensive exam, thesis or alternative, special project; for other advanced degree, qualifying exam. *Entrance requirements:* For master's, minimum undergraduate GPA of 2.7; for other advanced degree, minimum undergraduate GPA of 3.0, essay, letters of recommendation. Additional exam requirements/recommendations for international students: Required—TOEFL (minimum score 550 paper-based; 79 iBT); Recommended—IELTS (minimum score 6.5). *Application deadline:* For fall admission, 6/1 for domestic students, 5/1 for international students; for spring admission, 11/1 for domestic and international students. Applications are processed on a rolling basis. Application fee: $50. Electronic applications accepted. *Expenses: Tuition, area resident:* Full-time $7027; part-time $388 per credit. Tuition, state resident: full-time $9750; part-time $388 per credit. Tuition, nonresident: full-time $18,102; part-time $388 per credit. *International tuition:* $18,102 full-time. *Required fees:* $266 per semester. *Financial support:* In 2018–19, 22 students received support. Career-related internships or fieldwork, Federal Work-Study, scholarships/grants, and unspecified assistantships available. Support available to part-time students. Financial award application deadline: 3/1; financial award applicants required to submit FAFSA. *Faculty research:* Statistics, actuarial mathematics, computer systems and engineering, computer programming techniques, operations research. *Unit head:* Dr. Robin Kalder, Chair, 860-832-2835, E-mail: kalderr@ccsu.edu. *Application contact:* Patricia Gardner, Associate Director of Graduate Studies, 860-832-2350, Fax: 860-832-2362.
Website: http://www.ccsu.edu/mathematics/

Central Michigan University, Central Michigan University Global Campus, Program in Educational Leadership, Mount Pleasant, MI 48859. Offers K-12 leadership (Ed D). *Program availability:* Part-time, evening/weekend. *Entrance requirements:* Additional exam requirements/recommendations for international students: Required—TOEFL. Electronic applications accepted.

Central Michigan University, College of Graduate Studies, College of Education and Human Services, Department of Teacher Education and Professional Development, Mount Pleasant, MI 48859. Offers educational technology (MA, Graduate Certificate); elementary education (MA), including classroom teaching, early childhood; reading and literacy K-12 (MA); secondary education (MA). *Program availability:* Part-time, evening/weekend. *Degree requirements:* For master's, thesis or alternative. Electronic applications accepted. *Faculty research:* Integrating literacy across the curriculum, science teaching and aesthetic learning in science, diversity education, educational technology, educational psychology and child development.

Central Michigan University, College of Graduate Studies, College of Science and Engineering, Department of Chemistry, Mount Pleasant, MI 48859. Offers chemistry (MS); teaching chemistry (MA), including teaching college chemistry, teaching high school chemistry. *Program availability:* Part-time. *Degree requirements:* For master's, comprehensive exam, thesis or alternative. *Entrance requirements:* For master's, GRE. Electronic applications accepted. *Faculty research:* Analytical and organic-inorganic chemistry, biochemistry, catalysis, dendrimer and polymer studies, nanotechnology.

Chadron State College, School of Professional and Graduate Studies, Department of Education, Chadron, NE 69337. Offers business (MA Ed); community counseling (MA Ed); educational administration (MS Ed, Sp Ed); elementary education (MS Ed); history (MA Ed); language and literature (MA Ed); secondary administration (MS Ed); secondary education (MS Ed). *Accreditation:* NCATE. *Program availability:* Part-time, evening/weekend, online learning. *Degree requirements:* For master's, thesis optional. *Entrance requirements:* For master's, GRE General Test, GRE Writing Test, minimum GPA of 2.75 or 12 graduate hours at CSC with minimum GPA of 3.25. Additional exam requirements/recommendations for international students: Required—TOEFL. Electronic applications accepted. *Faculty research:* Rural education, technology, mental health.

Chaminade University of Honolulu, Graduate, Program in Education, Honolulu, HI 96816-1578. Offers child development (M Ed); early childhood education (Montessori) (MAT); early childhood education (PK-3) (MAT); educational leadership (M Ed); elementary education (MAT); instructional leadership (M Ed); Montessori (M Ed); secondary education (MAT); special education (MAT); teacher leader (M Ed). *Program availability:* Part-time, evening/weekend, 100% online, blended/hybrid learning. *Faculty:* 8 full-time (3 women), 11 part-time/adjunct (8 women). *Students:* 80 full-time (57 women), 100 part-time (77 women); includes 113 minority (6 Black or African American, non-Hispanic/Latino; 4 American Indian or Alaska Native, non-Hispanic/Latino; 45 Asian, non-Hispanic/Latino; 6 Hispanic/Latino; 50 Native Hawaiian or other Pacific Islander, non-Hispanic/Latino; 2 Two or more races, non-Hispanic/Latino), 2 international. Average age 35. 53 applicants, 92% accepted, 40 enrolled. In 2018, 92 master's awarded. *Degree requirements:* For master's, thesis or alternative. *Entrance requirements:* For master's, PRAXIS (for MAT), official transcripts, writing sample (for MAT). Additional exam requirements/recommendations for international students: Required—TOEFL (minimum score 550 paper-based; 79 iBT). *Application deadline:* Applications are processed on a rolling basis. Application fee: $40. Electronic applications accepted. *Expenses:* $780 per credit; $93 fee per online course. *Financial support:* Applicants required to submit FAFSA. *Unit head:* Dr. Dale Fryxell, Dean, 808-739-4652, Fax: 808-739-4607, E-mail: edu-office@chaminade.edu. *Application contact:* 808-739-7478, E-mail: gradserv@chaminade.edu.
Website: https://chaminade.edu/academics/education-behavioral-sciences/

Chapman University, Donna Ford Attallah College of Educational Studies, Orange, CA 92866. Offers counseling (MA), including school counseling (MA, Credential); curriculum and instruction (MA), including elementary education, secondary education; education (PhD), including cultural and curricular studies, disability studies, leadership studies, school psychology (PhD, Credential); educational psychology (MA); leadership development (MA); multiple subjects (Credential), including Spanish/English bilingual; pupil personnel services (Credential), including school counseling (MA, Credential), school psychology (PhD, Credential); school psychology (Ed S); single subject (Credential); special education (MA, Credential), including mild/moderate (Credential), moderate/severe (Credential); teaching (MA), including elementary education, secondary education, secondary music education. *Accreditation:* TEAC. *Program availability:* Part-time, evening/weekend. Electronic applications accepted. *Expenses:* Contact institution.

Chatham University, Program in Education, Pittsburgh, PA 15232-2826. Offers early childhood education (MAT); elementary education (MAT); environmental education (K-12) (MAT); secondary art (MAT); secondary biology education (MAT); secondary chemistry education (MAT); secondary English education (MAT); secondary math education (MAT); secondary physics education (MAT); secondary social studies education (MAT); special education (MAT). *Degree requirements:* For master's, thesis, teaching experience. *Entrance requirements:* For master's, minimum GPA of 3.0, sample of written work, recommendation letters. Additional exam requirements/recommendations for international students: Required—TOEFL (minimum score 600 paper-based; 100 iBT), IELTS (minimum score 7), TWE. Electronic applications accepted. Application fee is waived when completed online. *Faculty research:* Gifted education, environmental education, technology in education, writing as learning, class size and achievement.

Chestnut Hill College, School of Graduate Studies, Department of Education, Program in Secondary Education, Philadelphia, PA 19118-2693. Offers M Ed. *Program availability:* Part-time, evening/weekend. *Degree requirements:* For master's, thesis optional. *Entrance requirements:* For master's, PRAXIS I or proof of teaching certification, letters of recommendation; writing sample; 6 graduate credits with minimum B grade if undergraduate GPA less than 3.0. Additional exam requirements/recommendations for international students: Required—TOEFL (minimum score 500 paper-based), IELTS (minimum score 6.0), or TWE (minimum score 22). Electronic applications accepted. *Expenses:* Contact institution. *Faculty research:* Science teaching.

Chicago State University, School of Graduate and Professional Studies, College of Education, Department of Educational Leadership, Curriculum and Foundations, Program in Curriculum and Instruction, Chicago, IL 60628. Offers instructional foundations (MS Ed), including adult education, elementary education, secondary education. *Degree requirements:* For master's, comprehensive exam, thesis optional. *Entrance requirements:* For master's, minimum GPA of 2.75.

The Citadel, The Military College of South Carolina, Citadel Graduate College, Zucker Family School of Education, Charleston, SC 29409. Offers elementary/ secondary school administration and supervision (M Ed); elementary/secondary school counseling (M Ed); interdisciplinary STEM education (M Ed); literacy education (M Ed, Graduate Certificate); middle grades (MAT), including English, mathematics, science, social studies; physical education (grades K-12) (MAT); school superintendency (Ed S); secondary education (MAT), including biology, English, mathematics, social studies; student affairs (Graduate Certificate); student affairs and college counseling (M Ed). *Accreditation:* NCATE. *Program availability:* Part-time, evening/weekend, 100% online, blended/hybrid learning. *Degree requirements:* For master's, comprehensive exam (for some programs). *Entrance requirements:* For master's, GRE (minimum combined verbal and quantitative score of 290) or MAT (minimum score 396). Additional exam requirements/recommendations for international students: Required—TOEFL (minimum score 550 paper-based; 79 iBT). Electronic applications accepted. *Expenses:* Tuition, state resident: part-time $595 per credit hour. Tuition, nonresident: part-time $1020 per credit hour. *Required fees:* $90 per term.

City College of the City University of New York, Graduate School, School of Education, Department of Secondary Education, New York, NY 10031-9198. Offers adolescent mathematics education (MA, AC); English education (MA); middle school mathematics education (MS); science education (MA); social studies education (AC). *Accreditation:* NCATE. *Entrance requirements:* For master's, Liberal Arts and Sciences Test (LAST), Content Specialty Test (CST). Additional exam requirements/ recommendations for international students: Required—TOEFL.

Clemson University, Graduate School, College of Education, Department of Teaching and Learning, Clemson, SC 29634. Offers curriculum and instruction (PhD); middle level education (MAT); secondary math and science (MAT); STEAM education (Certificate); teaching and learning (M Ed). *Program availability:* Part-time, evening/weekend, 100% online. *Faculty:* 16 full-time (13 women). *Students:* 40 full-time (36 women), 198 part-time (171 women); includes 32 minority (10 Black or African American, non-Hispanic/ Latino; 1 American Indian or Alaska Native, non-Hispanic/Latino; 3 Asian, non-Hispanic/ Latino; 12 Hispanic/Latino; 1 Native Hawaiian or other Pacific Islander, non-Hispanic/ Latino; 5 Two or more races, non-Hispanic/Latino), 8 international. Average age 31. 257 applicants, 77% accepted, 163 enrolled. In 2018, 38 master's, 5 doctorates awarded. *Degree requirements:* For master's, comprehensive exam; for doctorate, comprehensive exam, thesis/dissertation. *Entrance requirements:* For master's, doctorate, and Certificate, GRE General Test, unofficial transcripts, letters of recommendation. Additional exam requirements/recommendations for international students: Required—TOEFL (minimum score 80 paper-based; 80 iBT); Recommended—IELTS (minimum score 6.5), TSE (minimum score 54). *Application deadline:* For fall admission, 4/15 for international students; for spring admission, 10/15 for international students. Applications are processed on a rolling basis. Application fee: $80 ($90 for international students). Electronic applications accepted. *Expenses:* $5198 per semester full-time resident, $10123 per semester full-time non-resident, $556 per credit hour part-time resident, $1109 per credit hour part-time non-resident, online $770 per credit hour, $4938 doctoral programs resident, $10405 doctoral programs non-resident, $1144 full-time graduate assistant, other fees may apply per session; MAT Programs: $5898 per semester full-time resident, $11623 per semester full-time non-resident, $724 per credit hour part-time resident, $1451 per credit hour part-time non-resident, online $955 per credit hour, $1144 full-time graduate assistant, other fees may apply per session. *Financial support:* In 2018–19, 8 students received support, including 9 fellowships with full and partial tuition reimbursements available (averaging $3,414 per year), 3 research assistantships with full and partial tuition reimbursements available (averaging $17,500 per year), 28 teaching assistantships with full and partial tuition reimbursements available (averaging $18,020 per year); career-related internships or fieldwork also available. *Faculty research:* STEAM education, inquiry-based instruction, cultural hegemony and mathematics, equity and ethics, teacher effectiveness. *Total annual research expenditures:* $1.3 million. *Unit head:* Dr. Jeff Marshall, Department Chair, 864-656-2059, E-mail: marsha9@clemson.edu. *Application contact:* Julie Jones, Student Services Manager, 864-656-5096, E-mail: jgambre@clemson.edu. Website: http://www.clemson.edu/education/departments/teaching-learning/index.html

Colgate University, Master of Arts in Teaching Program, Hamilton, NY 13346-1386. Offers MAT. *Accreditation:* TEAC. *Degree requirements:* For master's, special project or thesis. *Entrance requirements:* For master's, GRE General Test, interview. *Faculty research:* Culturally-responsive teaching, comparative education, moral development in education, politics in education, educational psychology.

The College of New Jersey, Office of Graduate and Advancing Education, School of Education, Department of Educational Administration and Secondary Education, Program in Secondary Education, Ewing, NJ 08628. Offers MAT. *Degree requirements:* For master's, comprehensive exam. *Entrance requirements:* For master's, GRE, minimum GPA of 3.0 in field or 2.75 overall. Additional exam requirements/ recommendations for international students: Required—TOEFL. Electronic applications accepted.

College of St. Joseph, Graduate Programs, Division of Education, Program in Secondary Education, Rutland, VT 05701-3899. Offers English (M Ed); social studies (M Ed). *Program availability:* Part-time, evening/weekend. *Degree requirements:* For master's, comprehensive exam. *Entrance requirements:* For master's, PRAXIS I, official college transcripts; 2 letters of reference; minimum GPA of 3.0 (initial licensure) or 2.7 (nonlicensure); interview. Additional exam requirements/recommendations for international students: Required—TOEFL (minimum score 550 paper-based). Electronic applications accepted.

The College of Saint Rose, Graduate Studies, Thelma P. Lally School of Education, Programs in Special Education, Albany, NY 12203-1419. Offers adolescence education/ special education (MS Ed); childhood education/special education (MS Ed); childhood special education (MS Ed); early childhood special education (MS Ed); special education (Certificate); special education professional (MS Ed). *Accreditation:* NCATE. *Students:* 8 full-time (5 women), 7 part-time (4 women). Average age 28. 15 applicants, 47% accepted, 5 enrolled. In 2018, 11 master's awarded. *Degree requirements:* For master's, comprehensive exam (for some programs), thesis or alternative, research project. *Entrance requirements:* For master's, minimum undergraduate GPA of 3.0. Additional exam requirements/recommendations for international students: Required—TOEFL (minimum score 550 paper-based; 80 iBT), IELTS (minimum score 6), PTE (minimum score 56). *Application deadline:* For fall admission, 4/1 priority date for domestic and international students; for spring admission, 10/15 priority date for domestic and international students; for summer admission, 3/15 priority date for domestic and international students. Applications are processed on a rolling basis. Application fee: $40. Electronic applications accepted. *Expenses: Tuition:* Full-time $14,382; part-time $799 per credit hour. *Required fees:* $924; $408 per credit. $286. *Financial support:* Career-related internships or fieldwork, scholarships/grants, tuition waivers (partial), and unspecified assistantships available. Support available to part-time students. Financial award application deadline: 4/15. *Unit head:* Franics Ihle, Chair, 518-337-4885, E-mail: ihlef@ strose.edu. *Application contact:* Daniel Gallagher, Assistant Vice President for Graduate Recruitment and Enrollment, 518-485-3390, E-mail: grad@strose.edu. Website: https://www.strose.edu/special-education/

The College of Saint Rose, Graduate Studies, Thelma P. Lally School of Education, Teacher Education Programs, Albany, NY 12203-1419. Offers adolescence education (MS Ed, Advanced Certificate); adolescence education/special education (Advanced Certificate); childhood education (MS Ed); curriculum and instruction (MS Ed); early childhood education (MS Ed). *Students:* 49 full-time (39 women), 21 part-time (17 women); includes 3 minority (2 Black or African American, non-Hispanic/Latino; 1 Hispanic/Latino). Average age 27. 41 applicants, 66% accepted, 21 enrolled. In 2018, 48 master's, 1 Advanced Certificate awarded. *Entrance requirements:* For master's, minimum undergraduate GPA of 3.0. Additional exam requirements/recommendations for international students: Required—TOEFL (minimum score 550 paper-based; 80 iBT), IELTS (minimum score 6), PTE (minimum score 56). *Application deadline:* For fall admission, 4/1 priority date for domestic and international students; for spring admission, 10/15 priority date for domestic and international students; for summer admission, 3/15 priority date for domestic and international students. Applications are processed on a rolling basis. Application fee: $40. Electronic applications accepted. *Expenses: Tuition:* Full-time $14,382; part-time $799 per credit hour. *Required fees:* $924; $408 per credit. $286. *Financial support:* Career-related internships or fieldwork, scholarships/grants, tuition waivers (partial), and unspecified assistantships available. Support available to part-time students. Financial award application deadline: 4/15. *Unit head:* Dr. Drey Martone, Chair, 518-454-5262, E-mail: martoned@strose.edu. *Application contact:* Daniel Gallagher, Assistant Vice President for Graduate Recruitment and Enrollment, 518-485-3390, Fax: 518-458-5479, E-mail: grad@strose.edu. Website: https://www.strose.edu/academics/schools/school-of-education/

College of Staten Island of the City University of New York, Graduate Programs, School of Education, Program in Adolescence Education, Staten Island, NY 10314-6600. Offers adolescence education (MS Ed), including biology, English, mathematics, social studies. *Program availability:* Part-time, evening/weekend. *Students:* 76. 34 applicants, 59% accepted, 14 enrolled. In 2018, 28 master's awarded. *Degree requirements:* For master's, thesis, educational research project supervised by faculty; Sequence 1 consists of a minimum of 33-38 graduate credits among 11 courses. Sequence 2 consists of a minimum of 46-53 graduate credits. *Entrance requirements:* For master's, The candidate must also take the General Test of the Graduate Record Examination (GRE) or an approved equivalent examination and request the submission of official scores to the College. The CSI Code is 2778. Applicants should apply directly to the Educational Testing Service (ETS) to take the examination., relevant bachelor's degree, minimum overall GPA of 3.0, two letters of recommendation, one- or two-page personal statement. Additional exam requirements/recommendations for international students: Required—TOEFL (minimum score 550 paper-based; 79 iBT), IELTS (minimum score 6.5). *Application deadline:* For fall admission, 4/25 for domestic and international students; for spring admission, 11/25 for domestic and international students. Applications are processed on a rolling basis. Application fee: $75. Electronic applications accepted. *Expenses: Tuition, area resident:* Full-time $10,770; part-time $455 per credit. Tuition, state resident: full-time $10,770; part-time $455 per credit. Tuition, nonresident: full-time $19,920; part-time $830 per credit. *International tuition:* $19,920 full-time. *Required fees:* $559.20; $181.10 per semester. Tuition and fees vary according to program. *Faculty research:* Social Studies curriculum and Pedagogy; Civics Education; Teacher effectiveness and student achievement; Teacher knowledge, Knowledge transfer from college to classroom. *Unit head:* Diane Brescia, 718-982-3877, E-mail: diane.brescia@csi.cuny.edu. *Application contact:* Sasha Spence, Associate Director for Graduate Admissions, 718-982-2019, Fax: 718-982-2500, E-mail: sasha.spence@csi.cuny.edu. Website: https://www.csi.cuny.edu/academics-and-research/divisions-and-schools/school-education/programs-and-courses/adolescence-graduate

College of Staten Island of the City University of New York, Graduate Programs, School of Education, Program in Special Education, Staten Island, NY 10314-6600. Offers special education (MS Ed), including adolescence generalist: grades 7-12, grades 1-6. *Program availability:* Part-time, evening/weekend. *Students:* 130. 58 applicants, 71% accepted, 32 enrolled. In 2018, 42 master's awarded. *Degree requirements:* For master's, comprehensive exam, fieldwork; ten three-credit required courses and one elective for a total of 11 courses (33 credits) or 14 three-credit required courses and a three- to six-credit, field-based requirement for a total of 45-48 credits; research project. *Entrance requirements:* For master's, GRE General Test or an approved equivalent examination, BA/BS or 36 approved credits with a 3.0 GPA, 2 letters of recommendations, 1-2 page statement of experience; must have completed courses for NYS initial certificate in childhood education/early childhood education (Sequence 1); 6 credits each in English, history, math, and science, and 1 year of foreign language (Sequence 2). Additional exam requirements/recommendations for international students: Required—TOEFL (minimum score 550 paper-based; 79 iBT), IELTS (minimum score 6.5). *Application deadline:* For fall admission, 4/25 for domestic and international students; for spring admission, 11/25 for domestic and international students. Applications are processed on a rolling basis. Application fee: $75. Electronic applications accepted. *Expenses: Tuition, area resident:* Full-time $10,770; part-time $455 per credit. Tuition, state resident: full-time $10,770; part-time $455 per credit. Tuition, nonresident: full-time $19,920; part-time $830 per credit. *International tuition:* $19,920 full-time. *Required fees:* $559.20; $181.10 per semester. Tuition and fees vary according to program. *Faculty research:* Disabilities studies, social justice, arts-based research on disabilities, assessment of students with disabilities, technological pedagogical and content knowledge (TPACK) in special education teachers, juvenile justice. *Unit head:* Diane Brescia, 718-982-3877, E-mail: diane.brescia@csi.cuny.edu. *Application contact:* Sasha Spence, Associate Director for Graduate Admissions, 718-982-2019, Fax: 718-982-2500, E-mail: sasha.spence@csi.cuny.edu. Website: https://www.csi.cuny.edu/sites/default/files/pdf/admissions/grad/pdf/Education%20Fact%20Sheet.pdf

The Colorado College, Education Department, Program in Secondary Education, Colorado Springs, CO 80903-3294. Offers art teaching (K-12) (MAT); English teaching (MAT); foreign language teaching (MAT); mathematics teaching (MAT); music teaching (MAT); science teaching (MAT); social studies teaching (MAT). *Degree requirements:* For master's, thesis, internship. Electronic applications accepted.

Columbus State University, Graduate Studies, College of Education and Health Professions, Department of Teacher Education, Columbus, GA 31907-5645. Offers curriculum and instruction in accomplished teaching (M Ed); early childhood education (M Ed, MAT, Ed S); middle grades education (M Ed, MAT, Ed S); secondary education (M Ed, MAT, Ed S), including biology (MAT), chemistry (MAT), earth and space science (MAT), English/language arts, general science (M Ed), history (MAT), mathematics, science (Ed S), social science (M Ed, Ed S); special education (M Ed, MAT, Ed S), including general curriculum (M Ed, MAT); teacher leadership (M Ed). *Accreditation:* NCATE. *Program availability:* Part-time, evening/weekend, 100% online, blended/hybrid learning. *Faculty:* 20 full-time (12 women), 20 part-time/adjunct (15 women). *Students:* 110 full-time (84 women), 143 part-time (115 women); includes 105 minority (96 Black or African American, non-Hispanic/Latino; 4 Hispanic/Latino; 5 Two or more races, non-Hispanic/Latino). Average age 33. 147 applicants, 56% accepted, 62 enrolled. In 2018, 112 master's, 11 other advanced degrees awarded. *Degree requirements:* For Ed S, thesis or alternative. *Entrance requirements:* For master's, GRE General Test, minimum

undergraduate GPA of 2.75; for Ed S, GRE General Test, minimum undergraduate GPA of 2.75, graduate 3.0. Additional exam requirements/recommendations for international students: Required—TOEFL (minimum score 550 paper-based; 79 iBT). *Application deadline:* For fall admission, 6/30 for domestic students, 5/1 for international students; for spring admission, 11/1 for domestic and international students; for summer admission, 3/1 for domestic and international students. Applications are processed on a rolling basis. Application fee: $50. Electronic applications accepted. *Expenses: Tuition, area resident:* Full-time $4924; part-time $618 per credit hour. Tuition, state resident: full-time $4924; part-time $618 per credit hour. Tuition, nonresident: full-time $19,218; part-time $2403 per credit hour. *International tuition:* $19,218 full-time. *Required fees:* $1870; $802. Tuition and fees vary according to course load, degree level and program. *Financial support:* In 2018–19, 29 students received support, including 7 research assistantships with partial tuition reimbursements available (averaging $3,000 per year); career-related internships or fieldwork, Federal Work-Study, institutionally sponsored loans, scholarships/grants, tuition waivers (partial), and unspecified assistantships also available. Support available to part-time students. Financial award application deadline: 5/1; financial award applicants required to submit FAFSA. *Unit head:* Dr. Jan Burcham, Department Chair, 706-507-8519, Fax: 706-568-3134, E-mail: burcham_jan@columbusstate.edu. *Application contact:* Catrina Smith-Edmond, Assistant Director for Graduate and Global Admission, 706-507-8824, Fax: 706-568-5091, E-mail: smithedmond_catrina@columbusstate.edu.
Website: http://te.columbusstate.edu/

Concordia University, College of Education, Portland, OR 97211-6099. Offers administrative leadership (Ed D); career and technical education (M Ed); curriculum and instruction (M Ed), including adolescent literacy, early childhood education, educational technology leadership, English for speakers of other languages, environmental education, health and physical education, mathematics, methods and curriculum, reading interventionist, science, social studies, STEAM education, teacher leadership, the inclusive classroom, trauma and resilience in educational settings; educational administration (M Ed); educational leadership (M Ed); elementary education (MAT); higher education (Ed D); instructional leadership (Ed D); professional leadership, inquiry, and transformation (Ed D); secondary education (MAT); transformational leadership (Ed D). *Program availability:* Part-time, online learning. *Degree requirements:* For master's, comprehensive exam, work samples/portfolio. *Entrance requirements:* For master's, California Basic Educational Skills Test or PRAXIS I, minimum undergraduate GPA of 2.8, graduate 3.0; 2 letters of recommendation. Additional exam requirements/recommendations for international students: Required—TOEFL (minimum score 525 paper-based). Electronic applications accepted. *Faculty research:* Learner-centered classroom, brain-based learning, future of online learning.

Concordia University Chicago, College of Graduate Studies, Program in Teaching, River Forest, IL 60305-1499. Offers elementary education (MAT); secondary education (MAT). *Degree requirements:* For master's, thesis or alternative. *Entrance requirements:* For master's, minimum GPA of 2.9. Additional exam requirements/recommendations for international students: Required—TOEFL (minimum score 550 paper-based). Electronic applications accepted.

Concordia University, Nebraska, Graduate Programs in Education, Program in Educational Administration, Seward, NE 68434. Offers elementary and secondary education (M Ed); elementary education (M Ed); secondary education (M Ed). *Accreditation:* NCATE. *Program availability:* Part-time. *Degree requirements:* For master's, thesis or alternative. *Entrance requirements:* For master's, GRE, MAT, or NTE, BS in education or equivalent, minimum GPA of 3.0.

Converse College, Program in Secondary Education, Spartanburg, SC 29302. Offers biology (MAT); chemistry (MAT); English (M Ed, MAT); mathematics (M Ed, MAT); natural sciences (M Ed); social sciences (M Ed, MAT). *Program availability:* Part-time. *Degree requirements:* For master's, capstone paper. *Entrance requirements:* For master's, NTE or PRAXIS II (M Ed), minimum GPA of 2.75, 2 recommendations. Electronic applications accepted.

Cornell University, Graduate School, Graduate Fields of Agriculture and Life Sciences, Field of Education, Ithaca, NY 14853. Offers adult and extension education (MPS, MS, PhD); learning, teaching, and social policy (MPS, MS, PhD); mathematics 7-12 (MS). Terminal master's awarded for partial completion of doctoral program. *Degree requirements:* For master's, thesis (MS); for doctorate, comprehensive exam, thesis/dissertation. *Entrance requirements:* For master's and doctorate, GRE General Test, sample of written work (recommended), 2 letters of recommendation. Additional exam requirements/recommendations for international students: Required—TOEFL (minimum score 550 paper-based; 77 iBT). Electronic applications accepted. *Faculty research:* Moral development and professional ethics, public issues education and community development, socio/political issues in public education, teacher education and curriculum in agricultural science and mathematics, extension research.

Creighton University, Graduate School, College of Arts and Sciences, Department of Education, Program in Teaching, Omaha, NE 68178-0001. Offers elementary teaching (M Ed); secondary teaching (M Ed). *Program availability:* Part-time. *Faculty:* 10 full-time (5 women). *Students:* 3 full-time (2 women), 26 part-time (17 women); includes 2 minority (1 Asian, non-Hispanic/Latino; 1 Two or more races, non-Hispanic/Latino), 1 international. Average age 26. In 2018, 12 master's awarded. *Degree requirements:* For master's, portfolio. *Entrance requirements:* For master's, 3 letters of recommendation, 2 writing samples. Additional exam requirements/recommendations for international students: Required—TOEFL (minimum score 90 iBT). *Application deadline:* For fall admission, 7/1 priority date for domestic students, 3/1 priority date for international students; for winter admission, 12/1 priority date for domestic students, 6/1 priority date for international students; for spring admission, 3/1 priority date for domestic and international students; for summer admission, 3/1 for domestic and international students. Application fee: $50. Electronic applications accepted. *Financial support:* Scholarships/grants and tuition waivers (partial) available. Support available to part-time students. Financial award applicants required to submit FAFSA. *Unit head:* Dr. Max Engel, Director, 402-280-3162, E-mail: MaxEngel@creighton.edu. *Application contact:* Lindsay Johnson, Director of Graduate and Adult Recruitment, 402-280-2703, Fax: 402-280-2423, E-mail: gradschool@creighton.edu.

Dakota Wesleyan University, Program in Education, Mitchell, SD 57301. Offers curriculum and instruction (MA Ed); educational policy and administration (MA Ed); preK-12 principal certification (MA Ed); secondary certification (MA Ed). *Program availability:* Part-time, evening/weekend, online only, 100% online. *Faculty:* 5 part-time/adjunct (2 women). *Students:* 20 full-time (6 women), 4 part-time (1 woman); includes 8 minority (4 Black or African American, non-Hispanic/Latino; 3 Hispanic/Latino; 1 Two or more races, non-Hispanic/Latino). Average age 26. 12 applicants, 83% accepted, 8 enrolled. In 2018, 13 master's awarded. *Degree requirements:* For master's, comprehensive exam, thesis optional, electronic portfolio. *Entrance requirements:* For master's, minimum GPA of 2.7, elementary statistics course, statement of purpose, official transcripts, resume, three letters of recommendation. Additional exam requirements/recommendations for international students: Required—TOEFL (minimum score 500 paper-based), IELTS (minimum score 6.5). *Application deadline:* For fall admission, 8/1 priority date for domestic and international students; for winter admission, 12/1 priority date for domestic students; for spring admission, 4/1 priority date for domestic students, 12/1 priority date for international students. Applications are processed on a rolling basis. Application fee: $0. Electronic applications accepted. Application fee is waived when completed online. *Expenses:* Contact institution. *Financial support:* Applicants required to submit FAFSA. *Faculty research:* Technology in the classroom, current educational trends, higher education. *Unit head:* Dr. Melissa Weber, Director of Graduate Studies, 605-995-2630, Fax: 605-995-2609, E-mail: melissa.weber@dwu.edu. *Application contact:* Stacy Mock, Coordinator of Adult and Online Admissions, 605-995-2650, Fax: 605-995-2699, E-mail: admissions@dwu.edu.
Website: www.dwu.edu

Dallas Baptist University, Dorothy M. Bush College of Education, Teaching Program, Dallas, TX 75211-9299. Offers distance learning (MAT); early childhood through grade 6 certification (MAT); early childhood-12 (MAT); elementary (MAT); English as a second language (MAT); Montessori (MAT); multisensory (MAT); secondary (MAT). *Program availability:* Part-time, evening/weekend, 100% online, blended/hybrid learning. *Application deadline:* Applications are processed on a rolling basis. Application fee: $25. Electronic applications accepted. Application fee is waived when completed online. *Expenses: Tuition:* Full-time $17,262; part-time $959 per credit hour. *Required fees:* $1000; $500 per semester. Tuition and fees vary according to course load and degree level. *Unit head:* Dr. Neil Dugger, Dean, 214-333-5202, E-mail: neil@dbu.edu. *Application contact:* Dr. DeAnna Jenkins, Program Director, 214-333-5402, E-mail: deannaj@dbu.edu.
Website: https://www.dbu.edu/graduate/degree-programs/ma-teaching

Delta State University, Graduate Programs, College of Arts and Sciences, Division of Languages and Literature, Cleveland, MS 38733-0001. Offers secondary education (M Ed), including English. *Program availability:* Part-time. *Degree requirements:* For master's, thesis or alternative. *Expenses: Tuition, area resident:* Full-time $7076; part-time $393 per credit hour. Tuition, state resident: full-time $7076; part-time $393 per credit hour. Tuition, nonresident: full-time $7076; part-time $393 per credit hour. *International tuition:* $7076 full-time. *Required fees:* $170; $18.90 per credit hour. $9.45 per semester. Part-time tuition and fees vary according to program.

Delta State University, Graduate Programs, College of Arts and Sciences, Division of Social Sciences and History, Cleveland, MS 38733-0001. Offers community development (MS); social justice and criminology (MSJC); social science secondary education (M Ed), including history, social sciences. *Program availability:* Part-time, online learning. *Degree requirements:* For master's, thesis or alternative. *Expenses: Tuition, area resident:* Full-time $7076; part-time $393 per credit hour. Tuition, state resident: full-time $7076; part-time $393 per credit hour. Tuition, nonresident: full-time $7076; part-time $393 per credit hour. *International tuition:* $7076 full-time. *Required fees:* $170; $18.90 per credit hour. $9.45 per semester. Part-time tuition and fees vary according to program.

Delta State University, Graduate Programs, College of Education, Division of Teacher Education, Leadership, and Research, Cleveland, MS 38733-0001. Offers educational administration and supervision (M Ed, Ed S); elementary education (M Ed, MAT, Ed S); professional studies (Ed D), including counselor education, elementary education, higher education; secondary education (MAT); special education (M Ed). *Accreditation:* NCATE. *Program availability:* Part-time, evening/weekend. *Degree requirements:* For master's, thesis optional. *Entrance requirements:* For master's, GRE General Test; for Ed S, master's degree, teaching certificate. Electronic applications accepted. *Expenses: Tuition, area resident:* Full-time $7076; part-time $393 per credit hour. Tuition, state resident: full-time $7076; part-time $393 per credit hour. Tuition, nonresident: full-time $7076; part-time $393 per credit hour. *International tuition:* $7076 full-time. *Required fees:* $170; $18.90 per credit hour. $9.45 per semester. Part-time tuition and fees vary according to program. *Faculty research:* Thinking skills, writing across the curriculum, mathematics/science education.

DePaul University, College of Education, Chicago, IL 60614. Offers bilingual-bicultural education (M Ed, MA); counseling (M Ed, MA), including clinical mental health counseling, college student development, school counseling; curriculum studies (M Ed, MA, Ed D); early childhood education (M Ed, MA, Ed D); educational leadership (M Ed, MA, Ed D), including Catholic leadership (M Ed, MA), general (M Ed, MA), higher education (M Ed, MA), physical education (M Ed, MA), principal preparation (M Ed), teacher preparation (M Ed); elementary education (M Ed, MA); middle grades education (M Ed); middle school mathematics education (MS); reading specialist (M Ed, MA); secondary education (M Ed, MA); social and cultural foundations in education (M Ed, MA); special education (M Ed); sport, fitness and recreation leadership (MS); value-creating education for global citizenship (M Ed); world languages education (M Ed, MA). *Program availability:* Part-time, evening/weekend, online learning. *Degree requirements:* For doctorate, thesis/dissertation. Electronic applications accepted.

DeSales University, Division of Liberal Arts and Social Sciences, Center Valley, PA 18034-9568. Offers criminal justice (MCJ); digital forensics (MCJ, Postbaccalaureate Certificate); education (M Ed), including instructional technology, secondary education, special education, teaching English to speakers of other languages; investigative forensics (MCJ, Postbaccalaureate Certificate). *Program availability:* Part-time, 100% online, blended/hybrid learning. *Entrance requirements:* For master's, bachelor's degree from accredited institution, minimum undergraduate GPA of 3.0, personal statement showing potential of graduate work, three letters of recommendation, professional goal statement. Additional exam requirements/recommendations for international students: Required—TOEFL. Electronic applications accepted.

Dominican University, School of Education, River Forest, IL 60305-1099. Offers child life studies (MS); early childhood education (MS); education (MAT); elementary education (MA Ed); English as a second language (MA Ed); reading (MA Ed); secondary education (MAT); special education (MS). *Accreditation:* NCATE. *Program availability:* Part-time, evening/weekend, 100% online, blended/hybrid learning. *Entrance requirements:* For master's, Illinois Test of Basic Skills. Additional exam requirements/recommendations for international students: Required—TOEFL (minimum score 550 paper-based; 79 iBT). *Expenses:* Contact institution. *Faculty research:* Governance of private education institutions, reading and language arts, inclusion, organizational planning, leadership and vision.

Drew University, Caspersen School of Graduate Studies, Madison, NJ 07940-1493. Offers conflict resolution and leadership (Certificate), including community leadership, moderation, peace building; education (M Ed); finance (MA); history and culture (MA, PhD), including American history, book history, British history, European history, intellectual history, Irish history, print culture, public history; K-12 education (MAT), including art, biology, chemistry, elementary education, English, French, Italian, math, secondary education, special education, teacher of students with disabilities; liberal studies (M Litt, D Litt), including history, Irish/Irish-American studies, literature (M Litt, MMH, D Litt, DMH, CMH), religion, spirituality, teaching in the two-year college, writing; medical humanities (MMH, DMH, CMH), including arts, health, healthcare, literature (M Litt, MMH, D Litt, DMH, CMH), scientific research; poetry (MFA). *Program availability:* Part-time, evening/weekend. *Faculty:* 3 full-time (2 women), 27 part-time/adjunct (13 women). *Students:* 66 full-time (38 women), 179 part-time (117 women); includes 37 minority (15 Black or African American, non-Hispanic/Latino; 2 Asian, non-Hispanic/Latino; 15 Hispanic/Latino; 5 Two or more races, non-Hispanic/Latino), 14 international.

Average age 42. 157 applicants, 82% accepted, 57 enrolled. In 2018, 34 master's, 24 doctorates, 17 other advanced degrees awarded. Terminal master's awarded for partial completion of doctoral program. *Degree requirements:* For master's and other advanced degree, thesis (for some programs); for doctorate, one foreign language, comprehensive exam (for some programs), thesis/dissertation. *Entrance requirements:* For master's, PRAXIS Core and Subject Area tests (for MAT), GRE/GMAT (for MFin MS in Data Analytics), resume, transcripts, writing sample, personal statement, letters of recommendation; for doctorate, GRE (PhD in history and culture), resume, transcripts, writing sample, personal statement, letters of recommendation; for other advanced degree, resume, transcripts, personal statement. Additional exam requirements/recommendations for international students: Required—TOEFL (minimum score 587 paper-based; 80 iBT), IELTS (minimum score 6), TWE (minimum score 4). *Application deadline:* For fall admission, 8/1 for domestic students, 6/1 for international students; for spring admission, 12/1 for domestic students, 10/1 for international students. Applications are processed on a rolling basis. Application fee: $35. Electronic applications accepted. *Financial support:* Fellowships, research assistantships, teaching assistantships, career-related internships or fieldwork, Federal Work-Study, scholarships/grants, and unspecified assistantships available. Support available to part-time students. Financial award applicants required to submit FAFSA. *Unit head:* Dr. Debra Liebowitz, Provost and Dean of the College of Liberal Arts & Caspersen School of Graduate Studies, 973-4083139, E-mail: dliebowi@drew.edu. *Application contact:* Amo-Augustus Kubeyinje, Associate Vice President for Graduate Enrollment, 973-408-3111, E-mail: akubeyinje@drew.edu.
Website: http://www.drew.edu/caspersen

Drury University, Master in Education Program, Springfield, MO 65802. Offers curriculum and instruction (M Ed), including elementary education, middle school education, secondary education; instructional leadership (M Ed); instructional technology (M Ed); integrated learning (M Ed); special education (M Ed); special reading (M Ed). *Accreditation:* NCATE. *Program availability:* Part-time, evening/weekend, 100% online, blended/hybrid learning. *Faculty:* 10 full-time (6 women), 8 part-time/adjunct (6 women). *Students:* 167 full-time (133 women). Average age 32. 92 applicants, 92% accepted, 69 enrolled. In 2018, 44 master's awarded. *Entrance requirements:* For master's, bachelor's degree with minimum GPA of 2.75. Additional exam requirements/recommendations for international students: Recommended—TOEFL (minimum score 80 iBT), IELTS (minimum score 6.5). *Application deadline:* For fall admission, 8/4 priority date for domestic and international students; for spring admission, 1/5 priority date for domestic and international students; for summer admission, 5/26 priority date for domestic and international students. Applications are processed on a rolling basis. Application fee: $25. Electronic applications accepted. *Expenses:* Tuition is $366 per credit hour. Fees are $7 per credit hour. Most M.Ed. degrees are 33 credit hours. *Financial support:* In 2018–19, 5 students received support. Career-related internships or fieldwork, scholarships/grants, and unspecified assistantships available. Financial award application deadline: 6/30; financial award applicants required to submit FAFSA. *Faculty research:* Instructional technology, autism, diversity, and social justice. *Unit head:* Dr. Asikaa Cosgrove, Director, Master in Education Program, 417-873-7806, E-mail: acosgrov@drury.edu. *Application contact:* Dr. Asikaa Cosgrove, Director, Master in Education Program, 417-873-7806, E-mail: acosgrov@drury.edu.
Website: http://www.drury.edu/education-masters

Duquesne University, School of Education, Department of Instruction and Leadership, Program in Secondary Education, Pittsburgh, PA 15282-0001. Offers biology (MS Ed); chemistry (MS Ed); English (MS Ed); K-12 education (MS Ed), including Latin; mathematics (MS Ed); physics (MS Ed); social studies (MS Ed). *Program availability:* Part-time, evening/weekend. *Faculty:* 5 full-time (4 women). *Students:* 20 full-time (12 women); includes 3 minority (1 Black or African American, non-Hispanic/Latino; 1 Hispanic/Latino; 1 Two or more races, non-Hispanic/Latino). Average age 24. 20 applicants, 85% accepted, 13 enrolled. In 2018, 14 master's awarded. *Entrance requirements:* For master's, two letters of recommendation, letter of intent, interview, bachelor's degree. Additional exam requirements/recommendations for international students: Required—TOEFL (minimum score 550 paper-based), IELTS (minimum score 7). *Application deadline:* For fall admission, 9/1 for domestic students; for spring admission, 1/2 for domestic students. Applications are processed on a rolling basis. Application fee: $0. Electronic applications accepted. *Expenses: Tuition:* Full-time $23,112; part-time $1284 per credit. Tuition and fees vary according to program. *Financial support:* In 2018–19, 1 student received support, including 1 teaching assistantship with full tuition reimbursement available; Federal Work-Study also available. Support available to part-time students. Financial award applicants required to submit FAFSA. *Faculty research:* Factors that create highly effective teachers; how to best support teachers to support students in reform-oriented environments; urban education; models of teacher leadership; improving instruction in mathematics/science/social studies/English. *Total annual research expenditures:* $120,139. *Unit head:* Dr. Melissa Boston, Associate Dean for Teacher Education/Professor, 412-396.6109, Fax: 412-396-5585, E-mail: bostonm@duq.edu. *Application contact:* Kelly McGinley, Graduate Admissions Assistant, 412-396-1559, Fax: 412-396-5585, E-mail: mcginleyk@duq.edu.
Website: http://www.duq.edu/academics/schools/education/graduate-programs-education/ms-ed-secondary-education

D'Youville College, Department of Education, Buffalo, NY 14201-1084. Offers educational leadership (Ed D); elementary education (MS Ed); secondary education (MS Ed); special education (MS Ed). *Program availability:* Part-time, evening/weekend. *Degree requirements:* For master's, one foreign language, comprehensive exam, project or thesis. *Entrance requirements:* For master's, GRE (if GPA less than 2.75), minimum GPA of 3.0. Additional exam requirements/recommendations for international students: Required—TOEFL (minimum score 500 paper-based). Electronic applications accepted. *Faculty research:* Developmental disabilities, multiculturalism, early childhood education.

Eastern Connecticut State University, School of Education and Professional Studies/Graduate Division, Program in Secondary Education, Willimantic, CT 06226-2295. Offers MS. *Accreditation:* NCATE. *Program availability:* Part-time, evening/weekend. *Degree requirements:* For master's, thesis optional. *Entrance requirements:* For master's, PRAXIS I, PRAXIS II, minimum GPA of 3.0, bachelor's degree from accredited institution. Additional exam requirements/recommendations for international students: Required—TOEFL (minimum score 550 paper-based; 79 iBT); Recommended—IELTS (minimum score 6). Electronic applications accepted.

Eastern Illinois University, Graduate School, College of Liberal Arts and Sciences, Department of Mathematics and Computer Science, Charleston, IL 61920. Offers elementary/middle school mathematics education (MA); mathematics (MA); secondary mathematics education (MA). *Program availability:* Part-time, evening/weekend. *Degree requirements:* For master's, comprehensive exam (for some programs), thesis (for some programs). *Entrance requirements:* For master's, GMAT or GRE. Additional exam requirements/recommendations for international students: Required—TOEFL (minimum score 500 paper-based; 61 iBT), IELTS (minimum score 6). Electronic applications accepted. *Expenses:* Tuition, state resident: part-time $299 per credit hour. Tuition, nonresident: part-time $718 per credit hour. *Required fees:* $214.50 per credit hour.

Eastern Kentucky University, The Graduate School, College of Education, Department of Curriculum and Instruction, Program in Secondary and Higher Education, Richmond, KY 40475-3102. Offers secondary education (MA Ed), including agricultural education, art education, biological sciences education, business education, English education, geography education, history education, home economics education, industrial education, mathematical sciences education, physical education, school health education. *Accreditation:* NCATE. *Program availability:* Part-time. *Entrance requirements:* For master's, GRE General Test, minimum GPA of 2.5.

Eastern Michigan University, Graduate School, College of Education, Department of Teacher Education, Programs in K–12 Education, Ypsilanti, MI 48197. Offers middle school education (MA); secondary school education (MA). *Accreditation:* NCATE. *Program availability:* Part-time, evening/weekend, online learning. *Students:* 20 full-time (13 women), 21 part-time (13 women); includes 6 minority (2 Black or African American, non-Hispanic/Latino; 2 Asian, non-Hispanic/Latino; 2 Hispanic/Latino), 6 international. Average age 31. 28 applicants, 54% accepted, 10 enrolled. In 2018, 2 master's awarded. *Entrance requirements:* For master's, GRE. Additional exam requirements/recommendations for international students: Required—TOEFL. *Application deadline:* Applications are processed on a rolling basis. Application fee: $45. *Financial support:* Fellowships, research assistantships with full tuition reimbursements, teaching assistantships with full tuition reimbursements, career-related internships or fieldwork, Federal Work-Study, institutionally sponsored loans, scholarships/grants, tuition waivers (partial), and unspecified assistantships available. Support available to part-time students. Financial award applicants required to submit FAFSA. *Application contact:* Dr. Molly Thornbladh, Advisor, 734-487-1416, Fax: 734-487-2101, E-mail: mthornbl@emich.edu.

Eastern Nazarene College, Adult and Graduate Studies, Division of Teacher Education, Quincy, MA 02170. Offers administration (M Ed); early childhood education (M Ed, Certificate); elementary education (M Ed, Certificate); English as a second language (Certificate); instructional enrichment and development (Certificate); middle school education (M Ed, Certificate); moderate special needs education (Certificate); principal (Certificate); program development and supervision (Certificate); secondary education (M Ed, Certificate); special education administrator (Certificate); special needs (M Ed); supervisor (Certificate); teacher of reading (M Ed, Certificate). M Ed also available through weekend program for administration, special needs, and teacher of reading only. *Program availability:* Part-time, evening/weekend. *Entrance requirements:* Additional exam requirements/recommendations for international students: Required—TOEFL (minimum score 550 paper-based).

Eastern New Mexico University, Graduate School, College of Education and Technology, Department of Educational Studies, Portales, NM 88130. Offers counseling (MA); education (M Ed), including educational administration, secondary education; school counseling (M Ed); special education (M Ed, M Sp Ed), including early childhood special education (M Sp Ed), general special education (M Sp Ed), gifted education pedagogy (M Ed), special education pedagogy (M Ed). *Accreditation:* NCATE. *Program availability:* Part-time, evening/weekend, online learning. *Degree requirements:* For master's, comprehensive exam, thesis optional. *Entrance requirements:* For master's, writing assessment, minimum GPA of 3.0, letter of recommendation, photocopy of teaching license; Level II teaching license (for M Ed in educational administration). Additional exam requirements/recommendations for international students: Required—TOEFL (minimum score 550 paper-based; 79 iBT), IELTS (minimum score 6). Electronic applications accepted. *Expenses: Tuition, area resident:* Full-time $6776. Tuition, state resident: full-time $6776; part-time $282 per credit hour. Tuition, nonresident: full-time $8986; part-time $374 per credit hour. *Required fees:* $60 per semester. One-time fee: $25.

Eastern Oregon University, Master of Arts in Teaching Program, La Grande, OR 97850-2899. Offers elementary education (MAT); secondary education (MAT). *Faculty:* 10 full-time (6 women), 5 part-time/adjunct (2 women). *Students:* 48 full-time (26 women), 3 part-time (all women); includes 4 minority (1 Asian, non-Hispanic/Latino; 2 Hispanic/Latino; 1 Two or more races, non-Hispanic/Latino). Average age 32. In 2018, 47 master's awarded. *Degree requirements:* For master's, thesis. *Entrance requirements:* For master's, NTE. Secondary candidates will be required to pass the state approved subject-specific test(s), prior to entry into the program (ORELA/NES or Praxis II, depending upon which is required of your subject). Elementary-Multiple Subjects candidates will be required to pass the state approved Elementary Education, subtest II (ORELA/NES). Additional exam requirements/recommendations for international students: Required—TOEFL (minimum score 550 paper-based; 79 iBT), IELTS (minimum score 6), Can also be satisfied by successful completion of the American Classroom Readiness course. *Application deadline:* For fall admission, 3/1 for domestic students. Applications are processed on a rolling basis. Electronic applications accepted. *Expenses:* $466.50/credit hour. *Financial support:* In 2018–19, 23 students received support. Federal Work-Study, scholarships/grants, and tuition waivers (full and partial) available. Support available to part-time students. *Unit head:* Dr. Matt Seimears, Dean of College of Business and Education, 541-962-3399, Fax: 541-962-3701, E-mail: mseimears@eou.edu. *Application contact:* Janet Frye, Administrative Support, MAT/MS Graduate Admission, 541-962-3772, Fax: 541-962-3701, E-mail: jfrye@eou.edu.
Website: https://www.eou.edu/cobe/ed/mat/

Eastern University, Graduate Education Programs, St. Davids, PA 19087-3696. Offers ESL program specialist (K-12) (Certificate); general supervisor (PreK-12) (Certificate); health and physical education (K-12) (Certificate); middle level (4-8) (Certificate); multicultural education (M Ed); music (K-12) (Certificate); Pre K-4 (Certificate); Pre K-4 with special education (Certificate); reading (M Ed); reading specialist (K-12) (Certificate); reading supervisor (K-12) (Certificate); school counseling (MA, CAGS); school principalship (preK-12) (Certificate); school psychology (MS, CAGS); secondary biology education (7-12) (Certificate); secondary chemistry education (7-12) (Certificate); secondary communication education (7-12) (Certificate); secondary English education (7-12) (Certificate); secondary math education (7-12) (Certificate); secondary social studies education (7-12) (Certificate); special education (M Ed); special education (7-12) (Certificate); special education (Pre K-8) (Certificate); special education supervisor (K-12) (Certificate); TESOL (M Ed); world language (Certificate), including Spanish. *Program availability:* Part-time, evening/weekend, online learning. *Entrance requirements:* Additional exam requirements/recommendations for international students: Required—TOEFL. Electronic applications accepted. Application fee is waived when completed online. *Expenses:* Contact institution.

East Stroudsburg University of Pennsylvania, Graduate and Extended Studies, College of Education, Department of Professional and Secondary Education, East Stroudsburg, PA 18301-2999. Offers professional and secondary education (Ed D); secondary education (M Ed). *Accreditation:* NCATE. *Program availability:* Part-time, evening/weekend, online learning. *Faculty:* 7 full-time (5 women), 5 part-time/adjunct (2 women). *Students:* 28 full-time (18 women), 129 part-time (84 women); includes 33 minority (11 Black or African American, non-Hispanic/Latino; 3 Asian, non-Hispanic/Latino; 15 Hispanic/Latino; 4 Two or more races, non-Hispanic/Latino), 1 international. Average age 39. 67 applicants, 79% accepted, 47 enrolled. In 2018, 8 master's, 5 doctorates awarded. *Degree requirements:* For master's, independent research problem or comprehensive assessment portfolio. *Entrance requirements:* For master's, PRAXIS/

teacher certification, letter of recommendation, Pennsylvania Department of Education requirements; for doctorate, Two letters of recommendation, resume, professional goals statement. Additional exam requirements/recommendations for international students: Recommended—TOEFL (minimum score 560 paper-based; 83 iBT), IELTS. *Application deadline:* For fall admission, 7/31 priority date for domestic students, 5/30 priority date for international students; for spring admission, 11/30 for domestic students, 10/31 for international students. Applications are processed on a rolling basis. Application fee: $50. Electronic applications accepted. *Expenses: Tuition, area resident:* Full-time $9288; part-time $516 per credit. Tuition, state resident: full-time $9288. Tuition, nonresident: full-time $13,932; part-time $774 per credit. *International tuition:* $13,932 full-time. *Required fees:* $2059; $114 per credit. Tuition and fees vary according to course load and degree level. *Financial support:* Research assistantships with tuition reimbursements, career-related internships or fieldwork, Federal Work-Study, and unspecified assistantships available. Support available to part-time students. Financial award application deadline: 3/1; financial award applicants required to submit FAFSA. *Unit head:* Dr. Beth Sockman, Co-Department Chair, 570-422-3621, Fax: 570-422-3942, E-mail: bsockman@esu.edu. *Application contact:* Kevin Quintero, Associate Director, Graduate and Extended Studies, 570-422-3890, Fax: 570-422-2711, E-mail: kquintero@esu.edu.
Website: https://www.esu.edu/college_education/graduate-programs.cfm

East Tennessee State University, School of Graduate Studies, College of Education, Department of Curriculum and Instruction, Johnson City, TN 37614. Offers advanced studies in teaching and learning (M Ed), including childhood literacy; educational technology (M Ed), including educational communications and technology, school library media; elementary education (M Ed); reading (M Ed, MA), including reading education (MA), storytelling (MA); response to intervention (Post-Master's Certificate); school library professional (Post-Master's Certificate); secondary education (M Ed); STEAM K-12 education (Postbaccalaureate Certificate); storytelling (Postbaccalaureate Certificate); teacher education (MAT), including elementary education K-5, middle grades education 4-8, middle grades education 6-8, secondary education 6-12 and preK-12, secondary education K-12. *Accreditation:* NCATE. *Program availability:* Part-time, evening/weekend, online learning. *Degree requirements:* For master's, comprehensive exam, thesis optional, student teaching, practicum; for other advanced degree, field work (school library); culminating experience (storytelling). *Entrance requirements:* For master's, GRE, SAT, ACT, PRAXIS, minimum GPA of 3.0, interview, 3 letters of recommendation, background check; for other advanced degree, master's degree, TN teaching license. Additional exam requirements/recommendations for international students: Required—TOEFL (minimum score 550 paper-based; 79 iBT). Electronic applications accepted. *Faculty research:* Critical thinking; curriculum development in reading, math, and science education; cultural diversity; cognitive processes; effective teaching strategies.

Edinboro University of Pennsylvania, Department of Middle and Secondary Education and Educational Leadership, Edinboro, PA 16444. Offers educational leadership (M Ed); middle and secondary instruction (M Ed). *Program availability:* Part-time, evening/weekend. *Degree requirements:* For master's, comprehensive exam, thesis or alternative, project. *Entrance requirements:* For master's, GRE or MAT, minimum QPA of 2.5. Electronic applications accepted.

Elms College, Division of Education, Chicopee, MA 01013-2839. Offers early childhood education (MAT); education (M Ed, CAGS); elementary education (MAT); English as a second language (MAT); reading (MAT); secondary education (MAT), including biology education, English education, Spanish education; special education (MAT). *Program availability:* Part-time, evening/weekend. *Faculty:* 5 full-time (all women), 6 part-time/adjunct (5 women). *Students:* 3 full-time (all women), 117 part-time (94 women); includes 12 minority (1 Black or African American, non-Hispanic/Latino; 2 Asian, non-Hispanic/Latino; 9 Hispanic/Latino). Average age 34. 27 applicants, 96% accepted, 23 enrolled. In 2018, 34 master's, 3 other advanced degrees awarded. *Degree requirements:* For master's, thesis (for some programs). *Entrance requirements:* For master's, Massachusetts Educators Certification Test, minimum GPA of 3.0; for CAGS, master's degree in education. Additional exam requirements/recommendations for international students: Required—TOEFL. *Application deadline:* For fall admission, 7/1 priority date for domestic students; for spring admission, 11/1 priority date for domestic students. Applications are processed on a rolling basis. Application fee: $30. *Expenses: Tuition:* Full-time $14,328; part-time $796 per credit. *Required fees:* $200. Tuition and fees vary according to degree level and program. *Financial support:* In 2018–19, 2 teaching assistantships with partial tuition reimbursements were awarded. Financial award applicants required to submit FAFSA. *Unit head:* Dr. Mary Janeczek, Chair, Division of Education, 413-594-2761, Fax: 413-592-4871, E-mail: janeczeke@elms.edu. *Application contact:* Nancy Davis, Director, Office of Graduate and Continuing Education Admissions, 413-265-2239, E-mail: davisn@elms.edu.

Emory University, Laney Graduate School, Division of Educational Studies, Atlanta, GA 30322-1100. Offers educational studies (MA, PhD); middle grades teaching (MAT); secondary teaching (MAT). *Accreditation:* NCATE. Terminal master's awarded for partial completion of doctoral program. *Degree requirements:* For master's, thesis; for doctorate, comprehensive exam, thesis/dissertation. *Entrance requirements:* For master's and doctorate, GRE General Test, minimum GPA of 3.0. Additional exam requirements/recommendations for international students: Required—TOEFL. Electronic applications accepted. *Faculty research:* Educational policy, educational measurement, urban and multicultural education, mathematics and science education, comparative education.

Endicott College, Van Loan School of Graduate and Professional Studies, Program in Secondary Education, Beverly, MA 01915-2096. Offers M Ed. *Program availability:* Part-time, evening/weekend, 100% online, blended/hybrid learning. *Degree requirements:* For master's, thesis, practicum, seminar. *Entrance requirements:* For master's, Massachusetts Tests for Educator Licensure (MTEL) Communication and Literacy Test and Subject Matter Test, MAT or GRE, bachelor's degree from accredited college, transcript, two recommendations, essay. Additional exam requirements/recommendations for international students: Required—TOEFL. Electronic applications accepted. *Expenses:* Contact institution.

Evangel University, Department of Education, Springfield, MO 65802. Offers curriculum and instruction (M Ed); educational leadership (M Ed); literacy (M Ed); secondary teaching (M Ed). *Accreditation:* NCATE. *Program availability:* Part-time, evening/weekend, 100% online, blended/hybrid learning. *Entrance requirements:* For master's, PRAXIS II (preferred) or GRE, minimum undergraduate GPA of 3.0. Additional exam requirements/recommendations for international students: Required—TOEFL (minimum score 550 paper-based). Electronic applications accepted. Application fee is waived when completed online.

Fairfield University, Graduate School of Education and Allied Professions, Fairfield, CT 06824. Offers applied behavior analysis (ATC); applied psychology (MA); clinical mental health counseling (MA, CAS); educational technology (MA); elementary education (MA, CAS); family studies (MA); integration of spirituality and religion in counseling (ATC); marriage and family therapy (MA); reading and language development (Sixth Year Certificate); school counseling (MA, CAS); school psychology (MA, CAS); school-based marriage and family therapy (ATC); secondary education (MA); special education (MA,

CAS); substance abuse counseling (ATC); teaching (Certificate); teaching and foundations (MA, CAS); TESOL, world languages, and bilingual education (MA, CAS). *Accreditation:* NCATE. *Program availability:* Part-time, evening/weekend. *Degree requirements:* For master's, comprehensive exam. *Entrance requirements:* For master's, minimum GPA of 3.0, 2 recommendations, resume. Additional exam requirements/recommendations for international students: Required—TOEFL (minimum score 550 paper-based; 84 iBT) or IELTS (minimum score 7.5). Electronic applications accepted. *Expenses:* Contact institution. *Faculty research:* Reading and literacy, writing, social justice and inequality in education, addictions and mental health issues, therapeutic relationships and clinical supervision.

Fayetteville State University, Graduate School, Programs in Middle Grades, Secondary, Special and Elementary Education, Fayetteville, NC 28301-4298. Offers middle grades (MA Ed); sociology (MA Ed); special education (MA Ed), including behavioral-emotional handicaps, mentally handicapped, specific training disability. *Accreditation:* NCATE. *Program availability:* Part-time, evening/weekend. *Faculty:* 10 full-time (6 women), 1 (woman) part-time/adjunct. *Students:* 24 full-time (20 women), 31 part-time (29 women); includes 38 minority (35 Black or African American, non-Hispanic/Latino; 2 Hispanic/Latino; 1 Two or more races, non-Hispanic/Latino), 1 international. Average age 35. 8 applicants, 88% accepted, 3 enrolled. In 2018, 7 master's awarded. *Degree requirements:* For master's, comprehensive exam, internship. *Entrance requirements:* Additional exam requirements/recommendations for international students: Required—TOEFL. *Application deadline:* For fall admission, 4/15 for domestic students; for spring admission, 10/15 for domestic students. Applications are processed on a rolling basis. Application fee: $40. Electronic applications accepted. *Financial support:* Application deadline: 3/1; applicants required to submit FAFSA. *Faculty research:* Reading assessment; reading remediation; learning disabilities; parenting; and adolescents with autism spectrum disorders social-communication development. *Unit head:* Dr. Cynthia Shamberger, Chair of Middle Grades, Secondary and Specialized Subjects, 910-672-2464, Fax: 910-672-1941, E-mail: cshamber@uncfsu.edu. *Application contact:* Dr. Cynthia Shamberger, Chair of Middle Grades, Secondary and Specialized Subjects, 910-672-2464, Fax: 910-672-1941, E-mail: cshamber@uncfsu.edu.

Florida Agricultural and Mechanical University, Division of Graduate Studies, Research, and Continuing Education, College of Education, Program in Secondary Education and Foundation, Tallahassee, FL 32307-3200. Offers biology (M Ed); chemistry (MS Ed); English (MS Ed); history (MS Ed); math (MS Ed); physics (MS Ed). *Accreditation:* NCATE. *Degree requirements:* For master's, thesis (for some programs). *Entrance requirements:* For master's, GRE General Test, minimum GPA of 3.0. Additional exam requirements/recommendations for international students: Required—TOEFL.

Florida Atlantic University, College of Education, Department of Teaching and Learning, Boca Raton, FL 33431-0991. Offers elementary education (M Ed); environmental education (M Ed); instructional technology (M Ed); reading education (M Ed); secondary education (M Ed). *Accreditation:* NCATE. *Program availability:* Part-time, evening/weekend. *Faculty:* 16 full-time (12 women), 1 part-time/adjunct (0 women). *Students:* 30 full-time (21 women), 45 part-time (36 women); includes 27 minority (14 Black or African American, non-Hispanic/Latino; 3 Asian, non-Hispanic/Latino; 8 Hispanic/Latino; 2 Two or more races, non-Hispanic/Latino), 6 international. Average age 30. 71 applicants, 58% accepted, 28 enrolled. In 2018, 23 master's awarded. *Entrance requirements:* For master's, GRE General Test, minimum GPA of 3.0 in last 2 years of undergraduate course work. Additional exam requirements/recommendations for international students: Required—TOEFL (minimum score 500 paper-based; 61 iBT), IELTS (minimum score 6). *Application deadline:* For fall admission, 7/1 for domestic students, 2/15 for international students; for spring admission, 11/1 for domestic students, 7/15 for international students. Applications are processed on a rolling basis. Application fee: $30. *Expenses: Tuition, area resident:* Full-time $7400; part-time $369.82 per credit. Tuition, state resident: full-time $7400; part-time $369.82 per credit. Tuition, nonresident: full-time $20,496; part-time $1024.81 per credit. *Financial support:* Fellowships with partial tuition reimbursements, research assistantships with partial tuition reimbursements, teaching assistantships with partial tuition reimbursements, career-related internships or fieldwork, scholarships/grants, and unspecified assistantships available. *Faculty research:* Technology, teaching English to speakers of other languages, math teaching, electronic portfolio assessment, global perspectives through social studies. *Unit head:* Dr. Barbara Ridener, Chairperson, 561-297-3588, E-mail: bridener@fau.edu. *Application contact:* Dr. Debora Shepherd, Associate Dean, 561-296-3570, E-mail: dshep@fau.edu.
Website: http://www.coe.fau.edu/academicdepartments/tl/

Fontbonne University, Graduate Programs, St. Louis, MO 63105-3098. Offers accounting (MBA, MS); art (MA); art (K-12) (MAT); business (MBA); computer science (MS); deaf education (MA); early intervention in deaf education (MA); education (MA), including autism spectrum disorders, curriculum and instruction, diverse learners, early childhood education, reading, special education; elementary education (MAT); family and consumer sciences (MA), including multidisciplinary health communication studies; fine arts (MFA); instructional design and technology (MS); management and leadership (MM); middle school education (MAT); secondary education (MAT); special education (MAT); speech-language pathology (MS); supply chain management (MS); theatre (MA). *Accreditation:* ASHA. *Program availability:* Part-time, evening/weekend, online learning. *Degree requirements:* For master's, comprehensive exam (for some programs), thesis (for some programs). *Entrance requirements:* Additional exam requirements/recommendations for international students: Required—TOEFL (minimum score 500 paper-based; 65 iBT). Electronic applications accepted.

Frostburg State University, College of Education, Department of Educational Professions, Program in Curriculum and Instruction, Frostburg, MD 21532-1099. Offers curriculum and instruction (Ed D); educational technology (M Ed); elementary education (M Ed); secondary education (M Ed). *Program availability:* Part-time, evening/weekend. *Degree requirements:* For master's, thesis or alternative. *Entrance requirements:* For master's, teaching certificate. Additional exam requirements/recommendations for international students: Required—TOEFL. Electronic applications accepted.

Frostburg State University, College of Education, Department of Educational Professions, Program in Secondary Teaching, Frostburg, MD 21532-1099. Offers MAT. *Entrance requirements:* For master's, PRAXIS I, entry portfolio. Additional exam requirements/recommendations for international students: Required—TOEFL.

Gallaudet University, The Graduate School, Washington, DC 20002-3625. Offers American Sign Language/English bilingual early childhood deaf education: birth to 5 (Certificate); audiology (Au D); clinical psychology (PhD); deaf and hard of hearing infants, toddlers, and their families (Certificate); deaf education (MA, Ed S); deaf history (Certificate); deaf studies (Certificate); educating deaf students with disabilities (Certificate); education: teacher preparation (MA), including deaf education, early childhood education and deaf education, elementary education and deaf education, secondary education and deaf education; educational neuroscience (PhD); hearing, speech and language sciences (MS, PhD); international development (MA); interpretation (MA, PhD), including combined interpreting practice and research (MA), interpreting research (MA); linguistics (MA, PhD); mental health counseling (MA); peer

mentoring (Certificate); public administration (MPA); school counseling (MA); school psychology (Psy S); sign language teaching (MA); social work (MSW); speech-language pathology (MS). *Program availability:* Part-time. Terminal master's awarded for partial completion of doctoral program. *Degree requirements:* For master's, comprehensive exam (for some programs), thesis optional; for doctorate, comprehensive exam, thesis/dissertation. *Entrance requirements:* For master's and doctorate, GRE General Test or MAT, letters of recommendation, interviews, goals statement, American Sign Language proficiency interview, written English competency. Additional exam requirements/recommendations for international students: Required—TOEFL. Electronic applications accepted. *Faculty research:* Signing math dictionaries, telecommunications access, cancer genetics, linguistics, visual language and visual learning, integrated quantum materials, deaf legal discourse, advance recruitment and retention in geosciences.

George Mason University, College of Education and Human Development, Programs in Curriculum and Instruction, Fairfax, VA 22030. Offers assistive technology (M Ed); designing digital learning in schools (M Ed); early childhood education (M Ed); early childhood education for diverse learners (M Ed); elementary education (M Ed); English as a second language (M Ed); gifted child education (M Ed); literacy (M Ed), including PK-12 classroom teachers, reading specialist; literacy leadership for diverse schools (M Ed), including K-12 reading; physical education (M Ed); science K-12 (M Ed); secondary education (M Ed), including biology, chemistry, earth science, English, history/social science, math, physics; special education (M Ed); teacher leadership (M Ed); transformative teaching (M Ed). *Program availability:* Part-time, evening/weekend, 100% online, blended/hybrid learning. *Faculty:* 48 full-time (40 women), 28 part-time/adjunct (20 women). *Students:* 165 full-time (147 women), 697 part-time (579 women); includes 243 minority (47 Black or African American, non-Hispanic/Latino; 3 American Indian or Alaska Native, non-Hispanic/Latino; 88 Asian, non-Hispanic/Latino; 85 Hispanic/Latino; 4 Native Hawaiian or other Pacific Islander, non-Hispanic/Latino; 16 Two or more races, non-Hispanic/Latino), 26 international. Average age 34. 450 applicants, 93% accepted, 315 enrolled. In 2018, 421 master's awarded. *Entrance requirements:* For master's, PRAXIS Core (for some programs), 2 letters of recommendation, interview, program goals statement; 9 hours of complete licensure endorsement requirements (for elementary education); minimum GPA of 3.0 in applicant's last 60 hours of undergraduate coursework (for secondary education); at least 1 year of teaching experience (for literacy). Additional exam requirements/recommendations for international students: Required—TOEFL (minimum score 575 paper-based; 88 iBT), IELTS (minimum score 6.5), PTE (minimum score 59). *Application deadline:* For fall admission, 4/2 priority date for domestic and international students; for spring admission, 11/1 for domestic and international students. Application fee: $75 ($80 for international students). Electronic applications accepted. *Financial support:* In 2018–19, 4 students received support, including 1 fellowship, 3 teaching assistantships (averaging $3,745 per year); career-related internships or fieldwork, Federal Work-Study, scholarships/grants, unspecified assistantships, and health care benefits (for full-time research or teaching assistantship recipients) also available. Support available to part-time students. Financial award application deadline: 3/1; financial award applicants required to submit FAFSA. *Faculty research:* Teacher preparation and professional development; adaptive teaching; wonder in science teacher preparation; literacy (digital, adolescent); site based course instruction. *Unit head:* Rebecca Fox, Professor and Academic Program Coordinator, 703-993-4123, E-mail: rfox@gmu.edu. *Application contact:* Rebecca Fox, Professor and Academic Program Coordinator, 703-993-4123, E-mail: rfox@gmu.edu. Website: http://gse.gmu.edu/programs/gsemasters

The George Washington University, Graduate School of Education and Human Development, Department of Curriculum and Pedagogy, Program in Secondary Education, Washington, DC 20052. Offers Arabic (M Ed); Italian (M Ed); math (M Ed); physics (M Ed); Russian (M Ed). Programs also offered in Arlington and Ashburn, VA. *Accreditation:* NCATE. *Students:* 7 full-time (3 women), 23 part-time (13 women); includes 10 minority (5 Black or African American, non-Hispanic/Latino; 2 American Indian or Alaska Native, non-Hispanic/Latino; 1 Hispanic/Latino; 1 Native Hawaiian or other Pacific Islander, non-Hispanic/Latino; 1 Two or more races, non-Hispanic/Latino). Average age 33. 55 applicants, 69% accepted, 16 enrolled. In 2018, 17 master's awarded. *Entrance requirements:* For master's, GRE General Test or MAT, interview, minimum GPA of 2.75. *Application deadline:* For fall admission, 1/15 priority date for domestic students; for spring admission, 10/1 for domestic students. Applications are processed on a rolling basis. Application fee: $75. *Financial support:* Fellowships, career-related internships or fieldwork, Federal Work-Study, tuition waivers (full and partial), and stipends available. Financial award application deadline: 1/15; financial award applicants required to submit FAFSA. *Unit head:* Prof. Curtis Pyke, Chair, 202-994-4516, E-mail: cpyke@gwu.edu. *Application contact:* Sarah Lang, Director of Graduate Admissions, 202-994-1447, Fax: 202-994-7207, E-mail: slang@gwu.edu.

Georgia College & State University, Graduate School, The John H. Lounsbury College of Education, Program in Secondary Education, Milledgeville, GA 31061. Offers MAT. *Program availability:* Part-time, evening/weekend, online learning. *Degree requirements:* For master's, comprehensive exam, minimum GPA of 3.0, complete program within 6 years. *Entrance requirements:* For master's, GACE, 2 recommendations, transcripts, proof of immunization, resume, minimum GPA of 2.75. Electronic applications accepted. *Expenses:* Contact institution.

Georgia Southern University, Jack N. Averitt College of Graduate Studies, College of Education, Department of Middle Grades and Secondary Education, Program in Secondary Education, Statesboro, GA 30460. Offers M Ed, MAT, Ed S. *Program availability:* Part-time, evening/weekend, 100% online, blended/hybrid learning. *Degree requirements:* For master's, portfolio, transition point assessments, exit assessment; for Ed S, field based research project, assessments. *Entrance requirements:* For master's, GACE (for MAT), minimum cumulative GPA of 2.5. Additional exam requirements/recommendations for international students: Required—TOEFL (minimum score 550 paper-based; 80 iBT), IELTS (minimum score 6). Electronic applications accepted. *Expenses: Tuition, area resident:* Part-time $3324 per semester. Tuition, state resident: full-time $5814; part-time $3324 per semester. Tuition, nonresident: full-time $23,204; part-time $13,260 per semester. *Required fees:* $2092; $2092. Tuition and fees vary according to course load, degree level, campus/location and program. *Faculty research:* Social studies education, mathematics education, science education, language arts education, dispositions.

Georgia State University, College of Education and Human Development, Department of Middle and Secondary Education, Atlanta, GA 30302-3083. Offers curriculum and instruction (Ed D); English education (MAT); mathematics education (M Ed, MAT); middle level education (MAT); reading, language and literacy education (M Ed, MAT), including reading instruction (M Ed); science education (M Ed, MAT), including biology (MAT), broad field science (MAT), chemistry (MAT), earth science (MAT), physics (MAT); social studies education (M Ed, MAT), including economics (MAT), geography (MAT), history (MAT), political science (MAT); teaching and learning (PhD), including language and literacy, mathematics education, music education, science education, social studies education, teaching and teacher education. *Accreditation:* NCATE. *Program availability:* Part-time, evening/weekend, online learning. *Faculty:* 19 full-time (15 women), 9 part-time/adjunct (7 women). *Students:* 217 full-time (136 women), 203 part-time (140 women); includes 229 minority (156 Black or African American, non-Hispanic/Latino; 23 Asian, non-Hispanic/Latino; 31 Hispanic/Latino; 19 Two or more races, non-Hispanic/Latino), 3 international. Average age 34. 149 applicants, 60% accepted, 70 enrolled. In 2018, 112 master's, 23 doctorates awarded. *Entrance requirements:* For master's, GRE; GACE I (for initial teacher preparation programs), baccalaureate degree or equivalent, resume, goals statement, two letters of recommendation, minimum undergraduate GPA of 2.5; proof of initial teacher certification in the content area (for M Ed); for doctorate, GRE, resume, goals statement, writing sample, two letters of recommendation, minimum graduate GPA of 3.3, interview. *Application deadline:* For fall admission, 1/15 priority date for domestic and international students; for spring admission, 10/1 for domestic and international students. Application fee: $50. Electronic applications accepted. *Expenses: Tuition, area resident:* Full-time $9360; part-time $390 per credit hour. Tuition, state resident: full-time $9360; part-time $390 per credit hour. Tuition, nonresident: full-time $30,024; part-time $1251 per credit hour. *International tuition:* $30,024 full-time. *Required fees:* $2128. *Financial support:* In 2018–19, fellowships with full tuition reimbursements (averaging $19,667 per year), research assistantships with full tuition reimbursements (averaging $5,436 per year), teaching assistantships with full tuition reimbursements (averaging $2,779 per year) were awarded; career-related internships or fieldwork, Federal Work-Study, scholarships/grants, health care benefits, tuition waivers (full and partial), and unspecified assistantships also available. Financial award application deadline: 3/15. *Faculty research:* Teacher education in language and literacy, mathematics, science, and social studies in urban middle and secondary school settings; learning technologies in school, community, and corporate settings; multicultural education and education for social justice; urban education; international education. *Unit head:* Dr. Gertrude Marilyn Tinker Sachs, Chair, 404-413-8384, Fax: 404-413-8063, E-mail: gtinkersachs@gsu.edu. *Application contact:* Shaleen Tibbs, Administrative Specialist, 404-413-8385, Fax: 404-413-8063, E-mail: stibbs@gsu.edu. Website: http://mse.education.gsu.edu/

Gonzaga University, School of Education, Spokane, WA 99258. Offers clinical mental health counseling (MA); educational leadership (M Ed, Ed D); elementary education (MIT); marriage and family counseling (MA); school counseling (MA); secondary education (MIT); special education (M Ed, MIT); sport and athletic administration (MA). *Accreditation:* NCATE. *Program availability:* Part-time, evening/weekend, 100% online, blended/hybrid learning. *Degree requirements:* For master's, comprehensive exam. *Entrance requirements:* For master's, GRE, MAT, and/or Washington Educator Skills Test-Basic (WEST-B), Washington Educator Skills Test-Endorsements (WEST-E), official transcripts from all colleges or universities attended, interview, two letters of recommendation, resume, essay, minimum GPA of 3.0. Additional exam requirements/recommendations for international students: Required—TOEFL (minimum score 580 paper-based, 88 iBT) or IELTS (minimum score 6.5). Electronic applications accepted. *Expenses:* Contact institution.

Gordon College, Graduate Education Program, Wenham, MA 01984-1899. Offers early childhood (M Ed); educational leadership (M Ed, Ed S); elementary education (M Ed); English as a second language (M Ed, Ed S); math specialist (M Ed); mathematics specialist (Ed S); middle school education (M Ed); moderate disabilities (M Ed); Montessori education (M Ed); reading (M Ed, Ed S); secondary education (M Ed). *Program availability:* Part-time, evening/weekend. *Degree requirements:* For master's, action research or clinical experience (for most programs); for Ed S, action research or clinical experience (for some programs). *Entrance requirements:* For master's, minimum undergraduate GPA of 3.0; 2 official undergraduate transcripts; professional resume; 3 recommendation letters (one professional reference, one academic reference, one personal reference); 500-700 word statement of purpose; for Ed S, minimum master's GPA of 3.3; 2 official transcripts from undergraduate and graduate schools; professional resume; 3 recommendation letters (one professional reference, one academic reference, one personal reference); 500-700 word statement of purpose. Additional exam requirements/recommendations for international students: Required—TOEFL (minimum score 550 paper-based, 80 iBT) or IELTS (minimum score 6.5). *Expenses:* Contact institution. *Faculty research:* Reading, early childhood development, English language learners, universal design for learning.

Goucher College, Graduate Programs in Education, Baltimore, MD 21204-2794. Offers at-risk and diverse learners (M Ed, Certificate); athletic program leadership and administration (M Ed, Certificate); elementary education (MAT); literacy strategies for content learning (M Ed); middle school (M Ed, Certificate); Montessori studies (M Ed); reading instruction (M Ed, Certificate); reducing student, classroom, and school disruption (M Ed); school improvement leadership (M Ed); secondary education (MAT); special education (MAT), including elementary education; special education for certified elementary and secondary teachers (M Ed); teacher as leader in technology (M Ed). *Program availability:* Part-time, evening/weekend. *Degree requirements:* For master's, thesis (M Ed), final presentation (MAT). *Entrance requirements:* For master's, minimum GPA of 3.0. Additional exam requirements/recommendations for international students: Required—TOEFL (minimum score 550 paper-based; 80 iBT), IELTS (minimum score 7). Electronic applications accepted. *Expenses:* Contact institution. *Faculty research:* Urban education, middle school, school improvement, teacher education, at-risk student achievement.

Grand Canyon University, College of Education, Phoenix, AZ 85017-1097. Offers autism spectrum disorders (MA); curriculum and instruction (MA); early childhood education (M Ed); educational administration (M Ed); educational leadership (M Ed); elementary education (M Ed); gifted education (MA); instructional technology (MS); K-12 leadership (Ed S); reading (MA); secondary education (M Ed); secondary humanities education (M Ed); secondary STEM education (M Ed); special education (M Ed); teaching and learning (Ed D); teaching English to speakers of other languages (MA). *Program availability:* Part-time, evening/weekend, online learning. *Degree requirements:* For master's, publishable research paper (M Ed), e-portfolio. *Entrance requirements:* For master's, undergraduate degree from accredited, GCU-approved college, university, or program with minimum GPA 2.8. Additional exam requirements/recommendations for international students: Required—TOEFL (minimum score 550 paper-based; 79 iBT), IELTS (minimum score 6). Electronic applications accepted.

Grand Valley State University, College of Education, Programs in General Education, Allendale, MI 49401-9403. Offers adult and higher education (M Ed); early childhood education (M Ed); educational differentiation (M Ed); educational leadership (M Ed); educational technology integration (M Ed); elementary education (M Ed); middle level education (M Ed); school library media services (M Ed); secondary level education (M Ed); teaching English to speakers of other languages (M Ed). *Program availability:* Part-time, evening/weekend, 100% online, blended/hybrid learning. *Students:* 20 part-time (10 women); includes 1 minority (Black or African American, non-Hispanic/Latino). Average age 44. In 2018, 1 master's awarded. *Entrance requirements:* For master's, GRE General Test or minimum GPA of 3.0, last 60 credits from regionally-accredited college/university, 3 letters of recommendation. Additional exam requirements/recommendations for international students: Required—TOEFL (minimum iBT score of 80), IELTS (6.5), or Michigan English Language Assessment Battery (77). *Application deadline:* Applications are processed on a rolling basis. Application fee: $30. Electronic applications accepted. *Expenses:* $677 per credit hour, 33 credits. *Financial support:* In

2018–19, 1 student received support, including 1 fellowship; career-related internships or fieldwork, Federal Work-Study, scholarships/grants, and unspecified assistantships also available. *Faculty research:* Effectiveness of technology in education, parental involvement, effective teaching, effective schools research. *Unit head:* Dr. David Bair, Department Director, 616-331-6489, Fax: 616-331-6489, E-mail: baird@gvsu.edu. *Application contact:* Annukka Thelen, Director, Student Information and Services Center, 616-331-6205, Fax: 616-331-6217, E-mail: thelenan@gvsu.edu.
Website: http://www.gvsu.edu/coe/

Greenville University, Program in Education, Greenville, IL 62246-0159. Offers education (MAT); elementary education (MAE); secondary education (MAE). *Degree requirements:* For master's, thesis (for some programs). *Entrance requirements:* For master's, GRE, Illinois Basic Skills Test, teacher certification. Electronic applications accepted.

Harding University, Cannon-Clary College of Education, Searcy, AR 72149-0001. Offers advanced studies in teaching and learning (M Ed); art (MSE); behavioral science (MSE); counseling (MS, Ed S); early childhood special education (M Ed, MSE); education (MSE); educational leadership (M Ed, Ed S); elementary education (M Ed); English (MSE); French (MSE); history/social science (MSE); kinesiology (MSE); math (MSE); reading (M Ed); secondary education (M Ed); Spanish (MSE); teaching (MAT); teaching English as a second language (MSE). *Accreditation:* NCATE. *Program availability:* Part-time, evening/weekend. *Degree requirements:* For master's, comprehensive exam (for some programs), thesis optional, portfolio(s); for Ed S, comprehensive exam, portfolio, project. *Entrance requirements:* For master's, GRE, MAT, PRAXIS; for Ed S, MAT or GRE. Additional exam requirements/recommendations for international students: Required—TOEFL (minimum score 550 paper-based; 79 iBT). *Faculty research:* Reading, comprehension, school violence, educational technology, behavior, college choice, differentiated instruction, brain-based teaching.

Hawai`i Pacific University, College of Professional Studies, Program in Secondary Education, Honolulu, HI 96813. Offers M Ed. *Accreditation:* TEAC. *Program availability:* Part-time, evening/weekend. *Entrance requirements:* For master's, minimum undergraduate GPA of 3.0, background check. Additional exam requirements/recommendations for international students: Recommended—TOEFL (minimum score 550 paper-based; 80 iBT), IELTS (minimum score 6), TWE (minimum score 5). Electronic applications accepted.

High Point University, Norcross Graduate School, High Point, NC 27268. Offers athletic training (MSAT); business administration (MBA); educational leadership (M Ed, Ed D); elementary education (M Ed, MAT); pharmacy (Pharm D); physical therapy (DPT); physician assistant studies (MPAS); secondary mathematics (M Ed, MAT); special education (M Ed); strategic communication (MA). *Accreditation:* NCATE. *Program availability:* Part-time, evening/weekend. *Degree requirements:* For master's, comprehensive exam (for some programs), thesis (for some programs). *Entrance requirements:* For master's, GMAT (MBA), GRE, MAT, minimum GPA of 3.0. Additional exam requirements/recommendations for international students: Required—TOEFL (minimum score 550 paper-based). Electronic applications accepted.

Hofstra University, School of Education, Programs in Teacher Education, Hempstead, NY 11549. Offers bilingual education (MA); bilingual extension (Advanced Certificate); business education (MS Ed); curriculum studies (MS Ed); early childhood and childhood education (MS Ed); early childhood education (MA, MS Ed); educational technology (Advanced Certificate); elementary education (MA, MS Ed); English education (MS Ed); family and consumer science (MS Ed); fine arts and music education (Advanced Certificate); fine arts education (MS Ed); foreign language and TESOL (MS Ed); foreign language education (MA, MS Ed); languages other than English and teaching English as a second language (MA); learning and teaching (Ed D); mathematics education (MA, MS Ed); middle childhood extension (Advanced Certificate); music education (MA, MS Ed); science education (MA); secondary education (Advanced Certificate); social studies education (MA, MS Ed); teaching languages other than English and TESOL (MS Ed); technology for learning (MA); TESOL (MS Ed, Advanced Certificate); TESOL with specialization in STEM (MA); work based learning extension (Advanced Certificate). *Program availability:* Part-time, evening/weekend, blended/hybrid learning. *Students:* 138 full-time (94 women), 109 part-time (78 women); includes 66 minority (16 Black or African American, non-Hispanic/Latino; 17 Asian, non-Hispanic/Latino; 31 Hispanic/Latino; 2 Native Hawaiian or other Pacific Islander, non-Hispanic/Latino), 6 international. Average age 29. 217 applicants, 86% accepted, 113 enrolled. In 2018, 105 master's, 11 doctorates, 25 other advanced degrees awarded. *Degree requirements:* For master's, comprehensive exam, thesis (for some programs), exit project, student teaching, fieldwork, electronic portfolio, curriculum project, minimum GPA of 3.0; for doctorate, dissertation; for Advanced Certificate, 3 foreign languages, comprehensive exam (for some programs), thesis project. *Entrance requirements:* For master's, GRE, 2 letters of recommendation, portfolio, teacher certification (MA), interview, essay; for doctorate, GMAT, GRE, LSAT, or MAT; for Advanced Certificate, 2 letters of recommendation, essay, interview and/or portfolio, teaching certificate. Additional exam requirements/recommendations for international students: Required—TOEFL (minimum score 550 paper-based; 80 iBT). *Application deadline:* Applications are processed on a rolling basis. Application fee: $75. Electronic applications accepted. *Financial support:* In 2018–19, 86 students received support, including 51 fellowships with full and partial tuition reimbursements available (averaging $5,080 per year), 2 research assistantships with full and partial tuition reimbursements available (averaging $3,470 per year); career-related internships or fieldwork, Federal Work-Study, institutionally sponsored loans, scholarships/grants, traineeships, tuition waivers (full and partial), unspecified assistantships, and scholarships and endowed scholarships also available. Support available to part-time students. Financial award applicants required to submit FAFSA. *Faculty research:* Impact of memory on learning; brain function, cognitive-development, learning, and achievement; student activism and civic education; using children's literature to promote diversity; 2nd language acquisition. *Unit head:* Dr. Alan Singer, Chairperson, 516-463-5853, Fax: 516-463-6275, E-mail: alan.j.singer@hofstra.edu. *Application contact:* Sunil Samuel, Assistant Vice President of Admissions, 516-463-4723, Fax: 516-463-4664, E-mail: graduateadmission@hofstra.edu.
Website: http://www.hofstra.edu/education/

Hofstra University, School of Education, Specialized Programs in Education, Hempstead, NY 11549. Offers applied behavior analysis (Advanced Certificate); childhood special education (MS Ed); early childhood special education (MS Ed, Advanced Certificate); educational and policy leadership (Ed D); educational leadership (Advanced Certificate); educational leadership and policy studies (MS Ed), including K-12; elementary special education (MS Ed); gifted education (Advanced Certificate); health education (MS); health professions pedagogy and leadership (MS); higher education leadership and policy studies (MS Ed); inclusive early childhood special education (MS Ed); inclusive elementary special education (MS Ed); inclusive secondary special education (MS Ed); literacy studies (MA, MS Ed, Ed D, Advanced Certificate); pedagogy for health professions (Advanced Certificate); physical education (MS); school district business leader (Advanced Certificate); secondary education generalist - students with disabilities 7-12 (MS Ed); secondary special education generalist - secondary education (MS Ed); special education (MS Ed, Advanced Certificate); special education assessment and diagnosis (Advanced Certificate); special education early childhood intervention (MS Ed); special education: international perspectives (MS Ed); teaching students with severe or multiple disabilities (Advanced Certificate). *Program availability:* Part-time, evening/weekend, blended/hybrid learning. *Students:* 126 full-time (91 women), 230 part-time (175 women); includes 90 minority (40 Black or African American, non-Hispanic/Latino; 4 American Indian or Alaska Native, non-Hispanic/Latino; 11 Asian, non-Hispanic/Latino; 32 Hispanic/Latino; 3 Two or more races, non-Hispanic/Latino), 4 international. Average age 32. 215 applicants, 90% accepted, 117 enrolled. In 2018, 130 master's, 9 doctorates, 23 other advanced degrees awarded. *Degree requirements:* For master's, one foreign language, comprehensive exam (for some programs), thesis (for some programs), electronic portfolio, capstone course, internship, practicum, student teaching, seminars, minimum GPA of 3.0; for doctorate, one foreign language, comprehensive exam, thesis/dissertation, qualifying hearing. *Entrance requirements:* For master's, GRE, interview, letters of recommendation, portfolio, essay, certification; for doctorate, GRE or MAT, interview, resume, essay, master's degree, 3 letters of recommendation, writing sample; for Advanced Certificate, GRE, interview, letters of recommendation, essay, professional experience, resume, master's degree. Additional exam requirements/recommendations for international students: Required—TOEFL (minimum score 550 paper-based; 80 iBT). *Application deadline:* Applications are processed on a rolling basis. Application fee: $75. Electronic applications accepted. *Financial support:* In 2018–19, 208 students received support, including 105 fellowships with full and partial tuition reimbursements available (averaging $3,948 per year), 12 research assistantships with full and partial tuition reimbursements available (averaging $6,573 per year); career-related internships or fieldwork, Federal Work-Study, institutionally sponsored loans, scholarships/grants, traineeships, tuition waivers (full and partial), unspecified assistantships, and scholarships and endowed scholarships also available. Support available to part-time students. Financial award applicants required to submit FAFSA. *Faculty research:* Water quality and income inequality; girls and stem; new media literacies; applied behavior analysis; k-12 leadership development. *Unit head:* Dr. Alan Flurkey, Chairperson, 516-463-5237, E-mail: alan.d.flurkey@hofstra.edu. *Application contact:* Sunil Samuel, Assistant Vice President of Admissions, 516-463-4723, Fax: 516-463-4664, E-mail: graduateadmission@hofstra.edu.
Website: http://www.hofstra.edu/education/

Hood College, Graduate School, Department of Education, Frederick, MD 21701-8575. Offers curriculum and instruction (MS), including elementary education, elementary science and mathematics education, secondary education, special education; education, multidisciplinary studies (MS); educational leadership (MS, Certificate); reading specialization (MS); STEM education (Certificate). *Accreditation:* NCATE. *Program availability:* Part-time-only, evening/weekend. *Faculty:* 5 full-time (3 women), 32 part-time/adjunct (24 women). *Students:* 3 full-time (all women), 306 part-time (253 women); includes 65 minority (22 Black or African American, non-Hispanic/Latino; 9 Asian, non-Hispanic/Latino; 17 Hispanic/Latino; 17 Two or more races, non-Hispanic/Latino), 3 international. Average age 33. 80 applicants, 99% accepted, 45 enrolled. In 2018, 59 master's, 47 other advanced degrees awarded. *Degree requirements:* For master's, action research project, portfolio (for reading specialization); for Certificate, STEM capstone activity. *Entrance requirements:* For master's, minimum GPA of 2.75, teaching certification, writing sample during interview, letter of recommendation from principal (for educational leadership program only). Additional exam requirements/recommendations for international students: Required—TOEFL (minimum score 575 paper-based; 89 iBT), IELTS (minimum score 6.5). *Application deadline:* For fall admission, 8/15 priority date for domestic students, 8/5 for international students; for spring admission, 12/1 priority date for domestic students, 12/1 for international students; for summer admission, 5/1 priority date for domestic students, 4/15 for international students. Applications are processed on a rolling basis. Application fee: $50 ($100 for international students). Electronic applications accepted. *Expenses: Tuition:* Full-time $17,640; part-time $4410 per semester. *Required fees:* $125 per semester. Tuition and fees vary according to degree level and program. *Financial support:* Tuition waivers (partial) and unspecified assistantships available. Financial award applicants required to submit FAFSA. *Faculty research:* Leadership, action research, brain research, learning styles. *Unit head:* Dr. April M. Boulton, Dean of the Graduate School, 301-696-3612, E-mail: gofurther@hood.edu. *Application contact:* Tanith Fowler Corsi, Assistant Director of Graduate Admissions, 301-696-3603, E-mail: gofurther@hood.edu.
Website: https://www.hood.edu/academics/departments/department-education/programs-offered

Hood College, Graduate School, Program in Secondary Mathematics Education, Frederick, MD 21701-8575. Offers high school (MS); middle school (MS); secondary mathematics education (Certificate). *Program availability:* Part-time-only, evening/weekend. *Faculty:* 1 (woman) full-time, 2 part-time/adjunct (both women). *Students:* 20 part-time (13 women); includes 3 minority (1 Black or African American, non-Hispanic/Latino; 2 Hispanic/Latino). Average age 33. 6 applicants, 100% accepted, 4 enrolled. In 2018, 3 master's awarded. *Degree requirements:* For master's, exitfolio, capstone/research project. *Entrance requirements:* For master's, minimum GPA of 2.75, initial teacher certification, essay. Additional exam requirements/recommendations for international students: Required—TOEFL (minimum score 575 paper-based; 89 iBT), IELTS (minimum score 6.5). *Application deadline:* For fall admission, 8/15 priority date for domestic students, 8/15 for international students; for spring admission, 12/1 priority date for domestic students, 12/1 for international students; for summer admission, 5/1 priority date for domestic students, 4/15 for international students. Applications are processed on a rolling basis. Application fee: $50 ($100 for international students). Electronic applications accepted. *Expenses: Tuition:* Full-time $17,640; part-time $4410 per semester. *Required fees:* $125 per semester. Tuition and fees vary according to degree level and program. *Financial support:* Tuition waivers (partial) and unspecified assistantships available. Financial award applicants required to submit FAFSA. *Unit head:* Dr. April M. Boulton, Dean of the Graduate School, 301-696-3600, E-mail: gofurther@hood.edu. *Application contact:* Tanith Fowler Corsi, Assistant Director of Graduate Admissions, 301-696-3603, E-mail: gofurther@hood.edu.
Website: http://www.hood.edu/graduate

Hope International University, School of Graduate and Professional Studies, Program in Education, Fullerton, CA 92831-3138. Offers education administration (MA); elementary education (ME); secondary education (ME). *Program availability:* Part-time, evening/weekend. *Degree requirements:* For master's, comprehensive exam (for some programs), thesis. *Entrance requirements:* For master's, minimum GPA of 3.0, 2 references. Additional exam requirements/recommendations for international students: Required—TOEFL (minimum score 550 paper-based; 86 iBT); Recommended—IELTS (minimum score 6.5). Electronic applications accepted. *Expenses:* Contact institution. *Faculty research:* Distance education.

Howard University, School of Education, Department of Curriculum and Instruction, Program in Secondary Education, Washington, DC 20059-0002. Offers M Ed. *Accreditation:* NCATE. *Degree requirements:* For master's, comprehensive exam, thesis (for some programs), expository writing exam, internships, practicum. *Entrance requirements:* For master's, PRAXIS I, GRE, minimum GPA of 2.7. Additional exam requirements/recommendations for international students: Required—TOEFL (minimum score 550 paper-based; 79 iBT). Electronic applications accepted.

Hunter College of the City University of New York, Graduate School, School of Arts and Sciences, Department of Mathematics and Statistics, New York, NY 10065-5085. Offers adolescent mathematics education (MA); applied mathematics (MA); bioinformatics (MA); pure mathematics (MA); statistics (MA). *Program availability:* Part-time, evening/weekend. *Degree requirements:* For master's, one foreign language, comprehensive exam, thesis (for some programs). *Entrance requirements:* For master's, GRE General Test, 24 credits in mathematics. Additional exam requirements/recommendations for international students: Required—TOEFL. *Faculty research:* Data analysis, dynamical systems, computer graphics, topology, statistical decision theory.

Hunter College of the City University of New York, Graduate School, School of Education, Programs in Secondary Education, New York, NY 10065-5085. Offers biology education (MA); chemistry education (MA); earth science (MA); English education (MA); French education (MA); Italian education (MA); mathematics education (MA); physics education (MA); social studies education (MA); Spanish education (MA). *Accreditation:* NCATE. *Degree requirements:* For master's, thesis. *Entrance requirements:* Additional exam requirements/recommendations for international students: Required—TOEFL.

Idaho State University, Graduate School, College of Education, Department of Teaching and Educational Studies, Pocatello, ID 83209-8059. Offers deaf education (M Ed); elementary education (M Ed); human exceptionality (M Ed); literacy (M Ed); music education (M Ed); secondary education (M Ed). *Program availability:* Part-time. *Degree requirements:* For master's, comprehensive exam, thesis (for some programs), oral thesis defense or written comprehensive exam and oral exam. *Entrance requirements:* For master's, GRE or MAT, minimum undergraduate GPA of 3.0, bachelor's degree, professional experience in an educational context. Additional exam requirements/recommendations for international students: Required—TOEFL (minimum score 550 paper-based; 80 iBT). Electronic applications accepted. *Faculty research:* Literacy, school psychology, special education.

Immaculata University, College of Graduate Studies, Program in Educational Leadership, Immaculata, PA 19345. Offers educational leadership (MA, Ed D); principal (Certificate); secondary education (Certificate); supervisor of special education (Certificate). *Program availability:* Part-time, evening/weekend. *Degree requirements:* For master's, comprehensive exam, thesis optional; for doctorate, comprehensive exam, thesis/dissertation. *Entrance requirements:* For master's, GRE or MAT, minimum GPA of 3.0; for doctorate, GRE General Test or MAT, minimum GPA of 3.5. Additional exam requirements/recommendations for international students: Required—TOEFL. Electronic applications accepted. *Faculty research:* Cooperative learning, school-based management, whole language, performance assessment.

Indiana University Bloomington, School of Education, Department of Curriculum and Instruction, Bloomington, IN 47405-7000. Offers art education (MS, Ed D, PhD); curriculum studies (Ed D, PhD); elementary education (MS, Ed D, PhD, Ed S); mathematics education (MS, Ed D, PhD); science education (MS, Ed D, PhD); secondary education (MS, Ed D, PhD); social studies education (MS, PhD); special education (PhD, Ed S). *Accreditation:* NCATE. *Program availability:* Part-time, evening/weekend. Terminal master's awarded for partial completion of doctoral program. *Degree requirements:* For doctorate, thesis/dissertation; for Ed S, comprehensive exam or project. *Entrance requirements:* For master's, doctorate, and Ed S, GRE General Test. Electronic applications accepted.

Indiana University Northwest, School of Education, Gary, IN 46408. Offers educational leadership (MS Ed); elementary education (MS Ed); K-12 online teaching (Graduate Certificate); secondary education (MS Ed). *Accreditation:* NCATE. *Program availability:* Part-time, evening/weekend. *Entrance requirements:* For master's, GRE General Test or MAT, minimum GPA of 3.0. Electronic applications accepted. *Expenses:* Contact institution.

Indiana University South Bend, School of Education, South Bend, IN 46615. Offers addiction counseling (MS Ed); alcohol and drug counseling (Graduate Certificate); clinical mental health counseling (MS Ed); educational leadership (MS Ed); elementary education (MS Ed); marriage, couple, and family counseling (MS Ed); school counseling (MS Ed); secondary education (MS Ed); special education (MAT, MS Ed), including intense intervention (MS Ed), mild intervention (MS Ed). *Accreditation:* NCATE. *Program availability:* Part-time, evening/weekend. *Degree requirements:* For master's, thesis or alternative, exit project. *Entrance requirements:* For master's, letters of recommendation, GRE or minimum GPA of 3.0. Additional exam requirements/recommendations for international students: Required—TOEFL. Electronic applications accepted. *Expenses:* Contact institution. *Faculty research:* Professional dispositions, early childhood literacy, online learning, program assessments, problem-based learning.

Indiana University Southeast, School of Education, New Albany, IN 47150. Offers counselor education (MS Ed); elementary education (MS Ed); secondary education (MS Ed). *Accreditation:* NCATE. *Program availability:* Part-time, evening/weekend. *Entrance requirements:* For master's, minimum undergraduate GPA of 2.5, graduate 3.0. Electronic applications accepted. *Faculty research:* Learning styles, technology, constructivism, group process, innovative math strategies.

Instituto Tecnologico de Santo Domingo, Graduate School, Area of Humanities and Social Sciences, Santo Domingo, Dominican Republic. Offers accounting (Certificate); adult education (Certificate); applied linguistics (MA); economics (MA); education (M Ed); educational psychology (MA, Certificate); gender and development (MA, Certificate); humanistic studies (MA); international marketing management (Certificate); international relations in the Caribbean basin (Certificate); intervention systems in family therapy (MA); linguistic and literary communication (Certificate); pedagogical support (MA); social science education (M Ed); sustainable human development (MA); terminal illness and death psychology (Certificate); youth and adult education (M Ed).

Ithaca College, School of Humanities and Sciences, Program in Adolescence Education, Ithaca, NY 14850. Offers English (MAT). *Faculty:* 14 full-time (7 women). *Students:* 6 full-time (2 women); includes 1 minority (Hispanic/Latino). Average age 30. 12 applicants, 83% accepted, 6 enrolled. In 2018, 7 master's awarded. *Degree requirements:* For master's, one foreign language, student teaching, portfolio, teacher inquiry project. *Entrance requirements:* Additional exam requirements/recommendations for international students: Required—TOEFL (minimum score 550 paper-based; 80 iBT). *Application deadline:* For fall admission, 3/19 for domestic and international students. Applications are processed on a rolling basis. Application fee: $40. Electronic applications accepted. *Expenses:* Contact institution. *Financial support:* In 2018–19, 6 students received support, including 6 research assistantships (averaging $12,112 per year); career-related internships or fieldwork, Federal Work-Study, and scholarships/grants also available. Support available to part-time students. Financial award application deadline: 3/1; financial award applicants required to submit FAFSA. *Unit head:* Dr. Peter Martin, Chair, 607-274-1076, E-mail: pmartin@ithaca.edu. *Application contact:* Nicole Eversley Bradwell, Director, Office of Admission, 800-429-4274, Fax: 607-274-1263, E-mail: admission@ithaca.edu.
Website: http://www.ithaca.edu/gradprograms/education/programs/aded

Jacksonville State University, Graduate Studies, School of Education, Program in Secondary Education, Jacksonville, AL 36265-1602. Offers MS Ed. *Accreditation:* NCATE. *Program availability:* Part-time, evening/weekend. *Degree requirements:* For master's, comprehensive exam, thesis (for some programs). *Entrance requirements:* For master's, GRE General Test or MAT. Additional exam requirements/recommendations for international students: Required—TOEFL (minimum score 500 paper-based; 61 iBT). Electronic applications accepted.

James Madison University, The Graduate School, College of Education, Program in Education, Harrisonburg, VA 22807. Offers early childhood education (preK-3) (MAT); educational leadership (M Ed); educational technology (M Ed); elementary education (MAT); equity and cultural diversity (M Ed); inclusive early childhood education (MAT); K-8 mathematics specialist (M Ed); middle education (MAT); reading education (M Ed); secondary education (MAT); Spanish language and culture for educators (M Ed); TESOL (MAT). *Accreditation:* NCATE. *Program availability:* Part-time, evening/weekend. *Students:* 255 full-time (224 women), 200 part-time (140 women); includes 56 minority (13 Black or African American, non-Hispanic/Latino; 8 Asian, non-Hispanic/Latino; 21 Hispanic/Latino; 14 Two or more races, non-Hispanic/Latino), 1 international. Average age 30. In 2018, 295 master's awarded. Application fee: $60. Electronic applications accepted. *Expenses:* Tuition, state resident: full-time $10,848. Tuition, nonresident: full-time $27,888. *Required fees:* $1128. *Financial support:* In 2018–19, 22 students received support. Teaching assistantships, career-related internships or fieldwork, Federal Work-Study, and assistantships (averaging $7911) available. Financial award application deadline: 3/1; financial award applicants required to submit FAFSA. *Unit head:* Dr. Phillip M. Wishon, Dean, 540-568-6572, E-mail: wishonpm@jmu.edu. *Application contact:* Lynette D. Michael, Director of Graduate Admissions, 540-568-6131 Ext. 6395, Fax: 540-568-7860, E-mail: michaeld@jmu.edu.
Website: http://www.jmu.edu/coe/index.shtml

James Madison University, The Graduate School, College of Education, Program in Secondary Education, Harrisonburg, VA 22807. Offers MAT. *Accreditation:* NCATE. *Program availability:* Part-time, evening/weekend. *Entrance requirements:* For master's, GRE General Test. Additional exam requirements/recommendations for international students: Required—TOEFL. *Application deadline:* For fall admission, 5/1 priority date for domestic students; for spring admission, 9/1 priority date for domestic students. Applications are processed on a rolling basis. Electronic applications accepted. *Expenses:* Tuition, state resident: full-time $10,848. Tuition, nonresident: full-time $27,888. *Required fees:* $1128. *Financial support:* Application deadline: 3/1; applicants required to submit FAFSA. *Unit head:* Dr. Steven L. Purcell, Academic Unit Head, 540-568-6793. *Application contact:* Lynette M. Bible, Director of Graduate Admissions, 540-568-6395, Fax: 540-568-7860, E-mail: biblelm@jmu.edu.

John Brown University, Graduate Education Programs, Siloam Springs, AR 72761-2121. Offers curriculum and instruction (M Ed); secondary education (MAT). *Program availability:* Part-time, evening/weekend. *Entrance requirements:* For master's, GRE (minimum score of 300). Additional exam requirements/recommendations for international students: Required—TOEFL (minimum score 550 paper-based; 79 iBT). Electronic applications accepted.

Johnson & Wales University, Graduate Studies, MAT Program in Teacher Education, Providence, RI 02903-3703. Offers business education and secondary special education (MAT); culinary arts education (MAT); elementary education and elementary special education (MAT). *Program availability:* Part-time, evening/weekend. *Entrance requirements:* For master's, MAT, minimum GPA of 2.75. Additional exam requirements/recommendations for international students: Required—TOEFL (minimum score 550 paper-based) or IELTS (recommended). *Faculty research:* Secondary education, student teaching, educational reform, evaluation procedures.

Kennesaw State University, Bagwell College of Education, MAT Program, Kennesaw, GA 30144. Offers art education (MAT); secondary English (MAT); secondary mathematics (MAT); secondary science (MAT); special education (MAT); teaching English to speakers of other languages (MAT). *Program availability:* Part-time, evening/weekend. *Students:* 44 full-time (36 women), 10 part-time (6 women); includes 15 minority (10 Black or African American, non-Hispanic/Latino; 4 Hispanic/Latino; 1 Two or more races, non-Hispanic/Latino). Average age 32. 3 applicants. In 2018, 32 master's awarded. *Entrance requirements:* For master's, GRE, GACE I (state certificate exam), minimum GPA of 2.75, 2 recommendations, resume. Additional exam requirements/recommendations for international students: Required—TOEFL (minimum score 550 paper-based; 80 iBT), IELTS (minimum score 6.5). *Application deadline:* For fall admission, 6/1 for domestic and international students; for spring admission, 3/1 for domestic and international students; for summer admission, 4/15 for domestic and international students. Applications are processed on a rolling basis. Application fee: $60. Electronic applications accepted. *Expenses: Tuition, area resident:* Full-time $6960; part-time $290 per credit hour. Tuition, state resident: full-time $6960; part-time $290 per credit hour. Tuition, nonresident: full-time $25,080; part-time $1045 per credit hour. *International tuition:* $25,080 full-time. *Required fees:* $2006; $1706 per semester. $853 per semester. *Financial support:* Research assistantships with tuition reimbursements and unspecified assistantships available. Financial award application deadline: 4/1; financial award applicants required to submit FAFSA. *Unit head:* Director, 470-578-3093. *Application contact:* Admissions Counselor, 470-578-4377, Fax: 470-578-9172, E-mail: ksugrad@kennesaw.edu.

Kennesaw State University, Bagwell College of Education, Program in Middle Grades and Secondary Education, Kennesaw, GA 30144. Offers Ed D, Ed S. *Program availability:* Part-time, evening/weekend, 100% online, blended/hybrid learning. *Students:* 41 full-time (27 women), 148 part-time (105 women); includes 35 minority (25 Black or African American, non-Hispanic/Latino; 2 Asian, non-Hispanic/Latino; 4 Hispanic/Latino; 4 Two or more races, non-Hispanic/Latino), 1 international. Average age 34. 80 applicants, 84% accepted, 59 enrolled. In 2018, 4 doctorates, 25 other advanced degrees awarded. *Entrance requirements:* Additional exam requirements/recommendations for international students: Required—TOEFL (minimum score 80 iBT), IELTS (minimum score 6.5). *Application deadline:* For fall admission, 7/1 for domestic students; for summer admission, 4/1 for domestic students. Applications are processed on a rolling basis. Application fee: $60. Electronic applications accepted. *Expenses: Tuition, area resident:* Full-time $6960; part-time $290 per credit hour. Tuition, state resident: full-time $6960; part-time $290 per credit hour. Tuition, nonresident: full-time $25,080; part-time $1045 per credit hour. *International tuition:* $25,080 full-time. *Required fees:* $2006; $1706 per semester. $853 per semester. *Application contact:* Admission Counselor, 470-578-4377, Fax: 470-578-9172, E-mail: ksugrad@kennesaw.edu.

Kent State University, College of Arts and Sciences, Department of Mathematical Sciences, Kent, OH 44242-0001. Offers applied mathematics (MA, MS, PhD); mathematics for secondary teachers (MA); pure mathematics (MA, MS, PhD). *Program availability:* Part-time. *Faculty:* 23 full-time (7 women). *Students:* 84 full-time (33 women), 39 part-time (17 women); includes 7 minority (2 Black or African American, non-Hispanic/Latino; 4 Asian, non-Hispanic/Latino; 1 Hispanic/Latino), 43 international. Average age 31. 66 applicants, 79% accepted, 12 enrolled. In 2018, 16 master's, 10 doctorates awarded. *Degree requirements:* For master's, comprehensive exam (for some programs), thesis (for some programs); for doctorate, comprehensive exam, thesis/dissertation. *Entrance requirements:* For master's, bachelor's degree with proficiency in numerical analysis and statistics, goal statement, resume or vita, 3 letters of recommendation; for doctorate, official transcript(s), goal statement, three letters of

recommendation, resume or vita, passage of the departmental qualifying examination at the master's level. Additional exam requirements/recommendations for international students: Required—TOEFL (minimum score 525 paper-based, 71 iBT), Michigan English Language Assessment Battery (minimum score 74), IELTS (minimum score 6.0) or PTE (minimum score 50). *Application deadline:* For fall admission, 5/1 for domestic and international students; for spring admission, 10/1 for domestic and international students; for summer admission, 2/1 for domestic and international students. Applications are processed on a rolling basis. Application fee: $45 ($70 for international students). Electronic applications accepted. *Expenses:* Tuition, state resident: full-time $11,766; part-time $536 per credit. Tuition, nonresident: full-time $21,952; part-time $999 per credit. *International tuition:* $21,952 full-time. Tuition and fees vary according to course load. *Financial support:* Fellowships with full tuition reimbursements, research assistantships with full tuition reimbursements, teaching assistantships with full tuition reimbursements, scholarships/grants, and unspecified assistantships available. Financial award application deadline: 1/31. *Unit head:* Dr. Andrew Tonge, Professor and Chair, 330-672-9046, E-mail: atonge@kent.edu. *Application contact:* Artem Zvavitch, Professor and Graduate Coordinator, 330-672-3316, E-mail: zvavitch@math.kent.edu.
Website: http://www.kent.edu/math/

Kent State University, College of Education, Health and Human Services, School of Teaching, Learning and Curriculum Studies, Program in Secondary Education, Kent, OH 44242-0001. Offers MAT. *Accreditation:* NCATE. *Faculty:* 4 full-time (3 women), 1 part-time/adjunct (0 women). *Students:* 17 full-time (9 women); includes 3 minority (1 American Indian or Alaska Native, non-Hispanic/Latino; 1 Asian, non-Hispanic/Latino; 1 Native Hawaiian or other Pacific Islander, non-Hispanic/Latino). 57 applicants, 37% accepted. In 2018, 15 master's awarded. *Entrance requirements:* For master's, GRE General Test, 2 letters of reference, moral character form. Additional exam requirements/recommendations for international students: Required—TOEFL (minimum score 550 paper-based; 80 iBT). *Application deadline:* For summer admission, 1/15 for domestic and international students. Application fee: $45 ($60 for international students). Electronic applications accepted. *Expenses:* Tuition, state resident: full-time $11,766; part-time $536 per credit. Tuition, nonresident: full-time $21,952; part-time $999 per credit. *International tuition:* $21,952 full-time. Tuition and fees vary according to course load. *Financial support:* Research assistantships with full tuition reimbursements, career-related internships or fieldwork, Federal Work-Study, institutionally sponsored loans, scholarships/grants, health care benefits, and unspecified assistantships available. Support available to part-time students. Financial award application deadline: 4/1; financial award applicants required to submit FAFSA. *Faculty research:* Creativity in science, women in science, teaching of writing, curriculum theory, mathematical reasoning. *Unit head:* Dr. Lisa Testa, Coordinator, 330-672-0647, E-mail: etesta@kent.edu. *Application contact:* Cheryl Slusarczyk, Academic Program Director, Office of Graduate Student Services, 330-672-2576, Fax: 330-672-9162, E-mail: ogs@kent.edu.
Website: http://www.kent.edu/ehhs/aded/

Keuka College, Program in Childhood Education/Literacy, Keuka Park, NY 14478. Offers literacy 5-12 (MS); literacy B-6 (MS). *Degree requirements:* For master's, thesis, capstone project/student-led research project. *Entrance requirements:* For master's, GRE, minimum GPA of 3.0; 3 letters of recommendation (2 academic and one from cooperating teacher from student teaching or other professional). Additional exam requirements/recommendations for international students: Required—TOEFL (minimum score 550 paper-based). Electronic applications accepted. *Expenses:* Contact institution. *Faculty research:* Marginalized populations, international literacy, teacher assessment.

Kutztown University of Pennsylvania, College of Education, Program in Secondary Education, Kutztown, PA 19530-0730. Offers biology (M Ed); curriculum and instruction (M Ed); English (M Ed); mathematics (M Ed); middle level (M Ed); social studies (M Ed); teaching (M Ed); transformational teaching and learning (Ed D). *Accreditation:* NCATE. *Program availability:* Part-time, evening/weekend, 100% online, blended/hybrid learning. *Faculty:* 5 full-time (3 women), 3 part-time/adjunct (0 women). *Students:* 25 full-time (16 women), 80 part-time (51 women); includes 8 minority (1 Black or African American, non-Hispanic/Latino; 5 Hispanic/Latino; 2 Two or more races, non-Hispanic/Latino), 1 international. Average age 32. 86 applicants, 93% accepted, 45 enrolled. In 2018, 3,531 master's awarded. *Degree requirements:* For master's, comprehensive exam, thesis optional; for doctorate, thesis/dissertation. *Entrance requirements:* For master's, GRE General Test, minimum undergraduate major GPA of 3.0, 3 letters of recommendation, copy of PRAXIS II or valid instructional I or II teaching certificate; for doctorate, master's or specialist degree in education or related field from regionally-accredited institution of higher learning with minimum graduate GPA of 3.25, significant educational experience, employment in an education setting (preferred). Additional exam requirements/recommendations for international students: Required—TOEFL (minimum score 550 paper-based, 79 iBT), IELTS (minimum score 6.5), or PTE (minimum score 53). *Application deadline:* For fall admission, 8/1 for domestic and international students; for spring admission, 12/1 for domestic and international students. Application fee: $35. Electronic applications accepted. *Expenses:* Tuition, state resident: part-time $516 per credit. Tuition, nonresident: part-time $774 per credit. *Required fees:* $119 per credit. One-time fee: $50 part-time. Tuition and fees vary according to degree level. *Financial support:* Career-related internships or fieldwork, Federal Work-Study, scholarships/grants, and unspecified assistantships available. Financial award application deadline: 3/1; financial award applicants required to submit FAFSA. *Unit head:* Dr. Georgeos Sirrakos, Department Chair, 610-683-4279, Fax: 610-683-1338, E-mail: sirrakos@kutztown.edu. *Application contact:* Dr. Patricia Walsh Coates, Graduate Coordinator, 610-638-4289, Fax: 610-683-1338, E-mail: coates@kutztown.edu.
Website: https://www.kutztown.edu/academcs/graduate-programs/secondary-education.htm

LaGrange College, Graduate Programs, Department of Education, LaGrange, GA 30240-2999. Offers curriculum and instruction (M Ed, Ed S); middle grades (MAT); secondary education (MAT). *Program availability:* Part-time, evening/weekend. *Degree requirements:* For master's, comprehensive exam. *Entrance requirements:* For master's, GRE, MAT, minimum GPA of 2.5. Additional exam requirements/recommendations for international students: Required—TOEFL (minimum score 550 paper-based).

Lake Forest College, Master of Arts in Teaching Program, Lake Forest, IL 60045. Offers elementary education (MAT); K-12 French (MAT); K-12 music (MAT); K-12 Spanish (MAT); K-12 visual art (MAT); secondary biology (MAT); secondary chemistry (MAT); secondary English (MAT); secondary history (MAT); secondary mathematics (MAT). *Degree requirements:* For master's, comprehensive exam, portfolio. *Entrance requirements:* For master's, GRE.

Lancaster Bible College, Graduate School, Lancaster, PA 17601-5036. Offers adult ministries (MA); Bible (MA); children and family ministry (MA); church planting (MA); consulting resource teacher (M Ed); elementary school counseling (M Ed); leadership (PhD); leadership studies (MA); marriage and family counseling (MA); mental health counseling (MA); pastoral studies (MA); secondary school counseling (M Ed); sports ministry (MA); student ministry (MA); town and country ministry (MA). *Program availability:* Part-time, evening/weekend. *Faculty:* 8 full-time (1 woman), 5 part-time/adjunct (1 woman). *Students:* 94 full-time (47 women), 89 part-time (45 women); includes 21 minority (15 Black or African American, non-Hispanic/Latino; 5 Asian, non-Hispanic/Latino; 1 Hispanic/Latino). Average age 36. *Degree requirements:* For master's, comprehensive exam (for some programs), thesis (for some programs). *Entrance requirements:* For master's, bachelor's degree with a minimum of 30 credits of course work in Bible, minimum undergraduate GPA of 3.0, interview. Additional exam requirements/recommendations for international students: Required—TOEFL. *Application deadline:* Applications are processed on a rolling basis. Application fee: $25. *Financial support:* In 2018–19, 31 students received support. Teaching assistantships, scholarships/grants, and unspecified assistantships available. Support available to part-time students. Financial award application deadline: 6/1; financial award applicants required to submit FAFSA. *Unit head:* Dr. Gary Bredfeldt, Associate Vice President/Dean of iLead Center, 717-560-8297, Fax: 717-560-8236. *Application contact:* Mark Wilson, Admissions Counselor, 717-560-8229, E-mail: mwilson@lbc.edu.

La Salle University, School of Arts and Sciences, Program in Education, Philadelphia, PA 19141-1199. Offers autism spectrum disorders (MA, Certificate); bilingual/bicultural studies (MA); classroom management (MA); dual early childhood and special education (MA); dual middle-level science and math and special education (MA); education (MA); English (MA); English as a second language (Certificate); history (MA); instructional coach (Certificate); instructional leadership (MA); reading specialist (MA, Certificate); secondary education (MA); special education (MA, Certificate). *Program availability:* Part-time, evening/weekend. *Degree requirements:* For master's, comprehensive exam. *Entrance requirements:* For master's, MAT or GRE, 2 letters of recommendation; for Certificate, GMAT or GRE, 2 letters of recommendation. Additional exam requirements/recommendations for international students: Required—TOEFL. Electronic applications accepted. Application fee is waived when completed online. *Expenses:* Contact institution.

Lee University, Program in Education, Cleveland, TN 37320-3450. Offers art (MAT); curriculum and instruction (M Ed, Ed S); early childhood (MAT); educational leadership (M Ed, Ed S); elementary education (MAT); English and math (MAT); English and science (MAT); English and social studies (MAT); higher education administration (MS); history (MAT); history and economics (MAT); math and science (MAT); math and social studies (MAT); middle grades (MAT); science and social studies (MASW); secondary education (MAT); Spanish (MAT); special education (M Ed, MAT); TESOL (MAT). *Accreditation:* NCATE. *Program availability:* Part-time. *Faculty:* 13 full-time (5 women), 13 part-time/adjunct (7 women). *Students:* 32 full-time (26 women), 73 part-time (49 women); includes 13 minority (10 Black or African American, non-Hispanic/Latino; 3 Two or more races, non-Hispanic/Latino), 3 international. Average age 30. 56 applicants, 73% accepted, 34 enrolled. In 2018, 60 master's, 3 other advanced degrees awarded. *Degree requirements:* For master's, variable foreign language requirement, thesis optional, internship. *Entrance requirements:* For master's, MAT or GRE General Test, minimum undergraduate GPA of 2.75, 3 letters of recommendation, interview, writing sample, official transcripts, background check; for Ed S, minimum undergraduate and master's GPA of 2.75, official transcripts for undergraduate and master's degrees. Additional exam requirements/recommendations for international students: Required—TOEFL (minimum score 61 iBT). *Application deadline:* For fall admission, 6/1 priority date for domestic and international students; for spring admission, 11/1 priority date for domestic and international students; for summer admission, 4/1 priority date for domestic and international students. Applications are processed on a rolling basis. Application fee: $25. Electronic applications accepted. *Financial support:* In 2018–19, 43 students received support. Career-related internships or fieldwork, Federal Work-Study, institutionally sponsored loans, scholarships/grants, and unspecified assistantships available. Financial award application deadline: 3/1; financial award applicants required to submit FAFSA. *Unit head:* Dr. William Kamm, Director, 423-614-8544, E-mail: wkamm@leeuniversity.edu. *Application contact:* Jeffery McGirt, Director of Graduate Enrollment, 423-614-8691, Fax: 423-614-8317, E-mail: jmcgirt@leeuniversity.edu.
Website: http://www.leeuniversity.edu/academics/graduate/education

Lehman College of the City University of New York, School of Education, Department of Middle and High School Education, Bronx, NY 10468-1589. Offers English education (MS Ed); mathematics education (MA); science education (MS Ed); social studies education (MA); teaching English to speakers of other languages (MS Ed). *Program availability:* Part-time, evening/weekend.

Le Moyne College, Department of Education, Syracuse, NY 13214. Offers adolescent education (MS Ed, MST); adolescent education/special education (MS Ed, MST); adolescent English (MST), including grades 7-12; adolescent English/special education (MST), including grades 7-12; adolescent foreign language (MST), including grades 7-12; adolescent history (MST), including grades 7-12; childhood education (MS Ed); childhood education/special education (MS Ed); elementary education (MS Ed); general education (MS Ed); inclusive childhood education (MST); literacy education (MS Ed), including birth to grade 6, grades 5-12; school building leader (MS Ed); school building leadership (CAS); school district business leader (MS Ed, CAS); school district leader (MS Ed); school district leadership (CAS); secondary education (MS Ed); special education (MS Ed); teaching English to speakers of other languages (MS Ed); urban studies (MS Ed). *Accreditation:* TEAC. *Program availability:* Part-time, evening/weekend. *Faculty:* 7 full-time (5 women), 16 part-time/adjunct (11 women). *Students:* 35 full-time (28 women), 119 part-time (84 women); includes 14 minority (5 Black or African American, non-Hispanic/Latino; 1 Asian, non-Hispanic/Latino; 7 Hispanic/Latino; 1 Two or more races, non-Hispanic/Latino), 1 international. Average age 30. 123 applicants, 89% accepted, 96 enrolled. In 2018, 66 master's, 48 CASs awarded. Terminal master's awarded for partial completion of doctoral program. *Degree requirements:* For master's, thesis. *Entrance requirements:* For master's, bachelor's degree with minimum undergraduate GPA of 3.0, 2 letters of recommendation, transcripts. Additional exam requirements/recommendations for international students: Required—TOEFL (minimum score 79 iBT); Recommended—IELTS (minimum score 6.5). *Application deadline:* For fall admission, 4/1 priority date for domestic and international students; for spring admission, 10/1 priority date for domestic and international students; for summer admission, 3/1 priority date for domestic and international students. Applications are processed on a rolling basis. Electronic applications accepted. *Expenses:* $734 per credit hour; wellness fee $70 per semester for full-time graduate students taking 9+ credit hours; technology fee $75 per semester for full-time graduate students taking 9+ credit hours, $25 per semester for part-time students; $1,470 per credit hour (for ED.D.). *Financial support:* In 2018–19, 44 students received support. Career-related internships or fieldwork, scholarships/grants, and health care benefits available. Support available to part-time students. Financial award applicants required to submit FAFSA. *Faculty research:* Minority teachers, special education, multiculturalism, literacy, technology, media literacy learning, autism, school district organization, service-learning, higher level problem solving, teacher leadership. *Unit head:* Dr. Stephen C. Fleury, Chair, Department of Education, 315-445-4376, Fax: 315-445-4744, E-mail: fleurysc@lemoyne.edu. *Application contact:* Jody F Manning, Assistant Director for Graduate Admission, 315-445-5444, Fax: 315-445-6092, E-mail: manninjf@lemoyne.edu.
Website: http://www.lemoyne.edu/education

Lenoir-Rhyne University, Graduate Programs, School of Education, Master of Arts in Teaching Secondary Education Program, Hickory, NC 28601. Offers MAT. *Entrance requirements:* For master's, GRE (minimum score of 147 on each of the verbal and quantitative sections and 3.5 on the analytical) or MAT (minimum score of 390); or PRAXIS I (minimum scores of Reading 176, Writing 173, and Math 173), official transcripts from all undergraduate and graduate institutions attended, resume, essay, criminal background check. *Expenses:* Contact institution.

Lesley University, Graduate School of Education, Cambridge, MA 02138-2790. Offers arts, community, and education (M Ed); autism studies (Certificate); curriculum and instruction (M Ed, CAGS); early childhood education (M Ed); ecological teaching and learning (MS); educational studies (PhD), including adult learning, educational leadership, individually designed; elementary education (M Ed); emergent technologies for educators (Certificate); ESLArts: language learning through the arts (M Ed); high school education (M Ed); individually designed (M Ed); integrated teaching through the arts (M Ed); literacy for K-8 classroom teachers (M Ed); mathematics education (M Ed); middle school education (M Ed); moderate disabilities (M Ed); online learning (Certificate); reading (CAGS); science in education (M Ed); severe disabilities (M Ed); special needs (CAGS); specialist teacher of reading (M Ed); teacher of visual art (M Ed); technology in education (M Ed, CAGS). *Accreditation:* TEAC. *Program availability:* Part-time, evening/weekend, online learning. *Degree requirements:* For master's, practicum; for doctorate, thesis/dissertation. *Entrance requirements:* For master's, Massachusetts Tests for Educator Licensure (MTEL), transcripts, statement of purpose, recommendations; interview (for special education); for doctorate, GRE General Test, transcripts, statement of purpose, recommendations, interview, master's degree, resume; for other advanced degree, interview, master's degree. Additional exam requirements/recommendations for international students: Required—TOEFL (minimum score 550 paper-based; 80 iBT). Electronic applications accepted. *Faculty research:* Assessment in literacy, mathematics and science; autism spectrum disorders; instructional technology and online learning; multicultural education and English language learners.

Lewis & Clark College, Graduate School of Education and Counseling, Department of Teacher Education, Program in Secondary Education, Portland, OR 97219-7899. Offers MAT. *Accreditation:* NCATE. *Entrance requirements:* For master's, prior experience working with children and/or youth; minimum undergraduate GPA of 2.75. Additional exam requirements/recommendations for international students: Required—TOEFL (minimum score 575 paper-based). Electronic applications accepted. *Faculty research:* Classroom management, classroom assessment, science education, classroom ethnography, moral development.

Lewis University, College of Education, Program in Secondary Education, Romeoville, IL 60446. Offers chemistry (MA); English (MA); history (MA); physics (MA); psychology and social science (MA). *Program availability:* Part-time. *Students:* 24 full-time (9 women), 28 part-time (17 women); includes 16 minority (2 Black or African American, non-Hispanic/Latino; 2 Asian, non-Hispanic/Latino; 10 Hispanic/Latino; 2 Two or more races, non-Hispanic/Latino). Average age 27. *Degree requirements:* For master's, comprehensive exam, departmental qualifying exam. *Entrance requirements:* For master's, writing exam, Test of Academic Proficiency/Basic Skills Test/ACT/SAT, bachelor's degree, minimum GPA of 2.75, 2 letters of recommendation. Additional exam requirements/recommendations for international students: Required—TOEFL (minimum score 550 paper-based; 79 iBT), IELTS (minimum score 6). *Application deadline:* For fall admission, 5/1 priority date for international students; for spring admission, 11/15 priority date for international students. Applications are processed on a rolling basis. Application fee: $40. Electronic applications accepted. *Financial support:* Federal Work-Study, scholarships/grants, and unspecified assistantships available. Financial award application deadline: 5/1; financial award applicants required to submit FAFSA. *Unit head:* Dr. Chris Palmi, Program Director. *Application contact:* Kathy Lisak, Graduate Admission Counselor, 815-836-5610, E-mail: grad@lewisu.edu.

Lincoln University, Graduate Studies, Jefferson City, MO 65101. Offers business administration (MBA); counseling (M Ed); environmental science (MS); higher education (MA); history (MA); natural sciences (MS); school teaching middle school with certification (M Ed); school teaching-elementary (M Ed); school teaching-secondary (M Ed); sociology (MA); sociology/criminal justice (MA); sustainable agriculture (MS). *Program availability:* Part-time, evening/weekend, 100% online, blended/hybrid learning. *Students:* 37 full-time (23 women), 52 part-time (25 women); includes 26 minority (24 Black or African American, non-Hispanic/Latino; 1 Asian, non-Hispanic/Latino; 1 Two or more races, non-Hispanic/Latino), 11 international. Average age 34. 67 applicants, 52% accepted, 29 enrolled. In 2018, 48 master's awarded. *Degree requirements:* For master's, comprehensive exam, thesis optional. *Entrance requirements:* For master's, GRE, MAT, or GMAT, minimum GPA of 2.75 overall, 3.0 in courses related to specialization; 3 letters of recommendation; minimum C average in English composition; personal statement of purpose. Additional exam requirements/recommendations for international students: Required—TOEFL (minimum score 500 paper-based; 61 iBT), IELTS (minimum score 5.5), Michigan English Language Assessment Battery (minimum score 80). *Application deadline:* For fall admission, 7/1 priority date for domestic students, 5/1 priority date for international students; for spring admission, 11/1 priority date for domestic students, 10/1 priority date for international students; for summer admission, 6/1 priority date for domestic students. Applications are processed on a rolling basis. Application fee: $30. Electronic applications accepted. *Expenses: Tuition, area resident:* Full-time $6984; part-time $291 per credit. Tuition, state resident: full-time $6984; part-time $291 per credit. Tuition, nonresident: full-time $12,996; part-time $541.50 per credit. *International tuition:* $12,996 full-time. *Required fees:* $1242.20. *Financial support:* In 2018–19, 9 research assistantships with tuition reimbursements (averaging $4,050 per year) were awarded; fellowships with tuition reimbursements, Federal Work-Study, scholarships/grants, and unspecified assistantships also available. Support available to part-time students. Financial award application deadline: 3/1; financial award applicants required to submit FAFSA. *Unit head:* Dr. Benjamin Arnold, Assistant Vice President of Academic Affairs, 573-681-5247, Fax: 573-681-5106, E-mail: gradschool@lincolnu.edu. *Application contact:* Sarah Robinett, Administrative Assistant, 573-681-5247, Fax: 573-681-5106, E-mail: gradschool@lincolnu.edu.
Website: http://www.lincolnu.edu/web/graduate-studies/graduate-studies

Long Island University–LIU Post, College of Education, Information and Technology, Brookville, NY 11548-1300. Offers adolescence education (MS); adolescence education 7-12 (MS); archives and records management (AC); art education (MS); childhood education (MS); childhood education/literacy B-6 (MS); childhood education/special education (MS); clinical mental health counseling (MS, AC); early childhood education (MS); early childhood education/childhood education (MS); educational leadership (AC); educational technology (MS); information studies (PhD); interdisciplinary educational studies (Ed D); middle childhood education (MS); music education (MS); public library administration (AC); school counselor (MS); special education (MS Ed); speech-language pathology (MA); students with disabilities, 7-12 generalist (AC); TESOL (MA). *Accreditation:* ASHA; TEAC. *Program availability:* Part-time, 100% online, blended/hybrid learning. Terminal master's awarded for partial completion of doctoral program. *Degree requirements:* For master's, variable foreign language requirement, comprehensive exam (for some programs), thesis optional; for doctorate, comprehensive exam, thesis/dissertation. *Entrance requirements:* For master's and AC, GRE (for some programs). Additional exam requirements/recommendations for international students: Required—TOEFL (minimum score 550 paper-based, 75 iBT), IELTS, or PTE. Electronic applications accepted. *Faculty research:* Sleep; use of technology to develop executive function by students with disabilities; early childhood literacy development through play; social justice through education; using a structured protocol to discuss Bad News.

Louisiana State University and Agricultural & Mechanical College, Graduate School, College of Human Sciences and Education, Department of Educational Theory, Policy and Practice, Baton Rouge, LA 70803. Offers counseling (M Ed, MA, Ed S); educational administration (M Ed, MA, PhD, Ed S); educational technology (MA); elementary education (M Ed, MAT); higher education (PhD); research methodology (PhD); secondary education (M Ed, MAT). *Accreditation:* ACA (one or more programs are accredited); NCATE.

Louisiana Tech University, Graduate School, College of Education, Ruston, LA 71272. Offers counseling and guidance (MA), including clinical mental health counseling, human services, orientation and mobility; counseling psychology (PhD); curriculum and instruction (M Ed); cyber education (Graduate Certificate); dynamics of domestic and family violence (Graduate Certificate); early childhood education - PreK-3 (MAT); educational leadership (M Ed, Ed D); elementary education and special education mild/moderate grades 1-5 (MAT); higher education administration (Graduate Certificate); industrial/organizational psychology (MA, PhD); kinesiology (MS); middle school education (MAT), including mathematics; orientation and mobility (Graduate Certificate); rehabilitation teaching for the blind (Graduate Certificate); secondary education (MAT), including agriculture, biology, business, chemistry, English; special education: visually impaired (MAT); teacher leader education (Graduate Certificate); visual impairments - blind education (Graduate Certificate). *Accreditation:* NCATE. *Program availability:* Part-time. *Degree requirements:* For master's, thesis; for doctorate, thesis/dissertation. *Entrance requirements:* For master's and doctorate, GRE General Test. Additional exam requirements/recommendations for international students: Required—TOEFL (minimum score 550 paper-based; 80 iBT), IELTS (minimum score 6.5). Electronic applications accepted. *Faculty research:* Blindness and the best methods for increasing independence for individuals who are blind or visually impaired; educating and investigating factors contributing to improvements in human performance across the lifespan and a reduction in injury rates during training.

Loyola Marymount University, School of Education, Program in Secondary Education, Los Angeles, CA 90045. Offers MA. *Unit head:* Dr. Liza Mastrippolito, Assistant Director, Department of Elementary and Secondary Education, 310-568-6697, E-mail: liza.mastrippolito@lmu.edu. *Application contact:* Ammar Dalal, Assistant Vice Provost for Graduate Enrollment, 310-338-2721, Fax: 310-338-6086, E-mail: graduateinfo@lmu.edu.
Website: http://soe.lmu.edu/academics/secondaryeducation

Loyola University Chicago, School of Education, Program in Teaching and Learning, Chicago, IL 60660. Offers elementary education (M Ed); English language teaching and learning (M Ed); secondary education (M Ed); special education (M Ed). *Accreditation:* NCATE. *Faculty:* 18 full-time (12 women), 33 part-time/adjunct (29 women). *Students:* 5 full-time (all women), 30 part-time (21 women); includes 11 minority (2 Asian, non-Hispanic/Latino; 9 Hispanic/Latino). Average age 28. 28 applicants, 61% accepted, 12 enrolled. In 2018, 20 master's awarded. *Entrance requirements:* For master's, Illinois Basic Skills Test, 3 letters of recommendation, minimum GPA of 3.0, resume. Additional exam requirements/recommendations for international students: Required—TOEFL (minimum score 550 paper-based; 79 iBT). *Application deadline:* For summer admission, 3/1 priority date for domestic and international students. Application fee: $50. Electronic applications accepted. Application fee is waived when completed online. *Expenses:* Contact institution. *Financial support:* In 2018–19, 12 fellowships with partial tuition reimbursements were awarded; institutionally sponsored loans, scholarships/grants, and unspecified assistantships also available. Support available to part-time students. Financial award application deadline: 2/1; financial award applicants required to submit FAFSA. *Faculty research:* Positive behavior support, school reform, school improvement. *Unit head:* Dr. Hank Bohanon, Program Chair, 312-915-7009, E-mail: hbohano@luc.edu. *Application contact:* Dr. Hank Bohanon, Program Chair, 312-915-7009, E-mail: hbohano@luc.edu.

Loyola University Maryland, Graduate Programs, School of Education, Master of Arts in Teaching Program, Baltimore, MD 21210-2699. Offers elementary education (MAT); secondary education (MAT). *Program availability:* Part-time. *Entrance requirements:* For master's, essay, 2 letters of recommendation, resume, transcript. Additional exam requirements/recommendations for international students: Required—TOEFL (minimum score 550 paper-based), IELTS (minimum score 7). Electronic applications accepted. *Expenses:* Contact institution.

Loyola University New Orleans, College of Arts and Sciences, Master of Arts in Teaching Program, New Orleans, LA 70118-6195. Offers MAT. *Program availability:* Part-time. *Faculty:* 2 full-time (both women). *Students:* 21 part-time (15 women); includes 9 minority (8 Black or African American, non-Hispanic/Latino; 1 American Indian or Alaska Native, non-Hispanic/Latino). Average age 31. 17 applicants, 100% accepted, 13 enrolled. In 2018, 1 master's awarded. *Degree requirements:* For master's, comprehensive exam, Praxis II content-specific exam and Teaching (PLT). *Entrance requirements:* For master's, GRE; Praxis I (or have an ACT composite score of 22 or higher, an SAT combined verbal and math score of 1030, or a graduate degree), 3 professional references, a non-education baccalaureate degree from a regionally accredited institution with a 3.0 or higher GPA. *Application deadline:* Applications are processed on a rolling basis. Electronic applications accepted. *Expenses:* $409 per credit hour tuition, $733 per semester full-time fees, $376.50 per semester part-time fees. *Financial support:* Application deadline: 5/1; applicants required to submit FAFSA. *Unit head:* Dr. Glenda Hembree, Office of Teacher Education, 504-865-3081, E-mail: gghembre@loyno.edu. *Application contact:* Dr. Glenda Hembree, Office of Teacher Education, 504-865-3081, E-mail: gghembre@loyno.edu.
Website: http://cas.loyno.edu/teacher-education/mat

Manhattanville College, School of Education, Program in Middle Childhood/Adolescence Education (Grades 5-12), Purchase, NY 10577-2132. Offers biology and special education (MPS); chemistry and special education (MPS); education for sustainability (Advanced Certificate); English and special education (MPS); literacy and special education (MPS); literacy specialist (MPS); math and special education (MPS); mathematics (Advanced Certificate); middle childhood/adolescence ed science (biology or chemistry grades 5-12) or (physics grades 7-12) (MAT); middle childhood/adolescence education (grades 5-12) English (MAT, Advanced Certificate); middle childhood/adolescence education (grades 5-12) mathematics (MAT, Advanced Certificate); middle childhood/adolescence education (grades 5-12) science (biology chemistry, physics, earth science) (Advanced Certificate); middle childhood/adolescence education (grades 5-12) social studies (MAT, Advanced Certificate); physics (MAT, Advanced Certificate); social studies (MAT); social studies and special education (MPS); special education generalist (MPS). *Program availability:* Part-time, evening/weekend. *Faculty:* 3 full-time (2 women), 9 part-time/adjunct (4 women). *Students:* 11 full-time (6 women), 17 part-time (12 women); includes 3 minority (1 Black

or African American, non-Hispanic/Latino; 2 Hispanic/Latino). Average age 31. 17 applicants, 71% accepted, 7 enrolled. In 2018, 8 master's, 3 other advanced degrees awarded. *Degree requirements:* For master's, comprehensive exam (for some programs), thesis (for some programs), student teaching, research seminars, portfolios, internships, writing assessment; for Advanced Certificate, comprehensive exam (for some programs). *Entrance requirements:* For master's, for programs leading to certification, candidates must submit scores from GRE or MAT(Miller Analogies Test), minimum undergraduate GPA of 3.0, all transcripts from all colleges and universities attended, 2 letters of recommendation, interview, essay (2-3 page personal statement that describes reasons for choosing education as profession and personal philosophy of education), proof of immunization (for those born after 1957). Additional exam requirements/recommendations for international students: Required—TOEFL (minimum score 600 paper-based; 110 iBT); Recommended—IELTS (minimum score 8). *Application deadline:* Applications are processed on a rolling basis. Application fee: $75. Electronic applications accepted. *Expenses:* 935 per credit. *Financial support:* Teaching assistantships, career-related internships or fieldwork, Federal Work-Study, institutionally sponsored loans, scholarships/grants, and unspecified assistantships available. Financial award application deadline: 3/15; financial award applicants required to submit FAFSA. *Faculty research:* Education for sustainability. *Unit head:* Dr. Shelley Wepner, Dean, 914-323-3153, Fax: 914-323-5493, E-mail: Shelley.Wepner@mville.edu. *Application contact:* Alissa Wilson, Director, Graduate Admissions, 914-323-3150, Fax: 914-694-1732, E-mail: edschool@mville.edu.
Website: http://www.mville.edu/programs#/search/19

Manhattanville College, School of Education, Program in Special Education, Purchase, NY 10577-2132. Offers childhood education (grades 1-6) and special education: childhood (grades 1-6) (MPS); early childhood (birth-grade 2) and special education: early childhood (birth-grade 2) (MPS); English (5-9 and 7-12); special ed generalist (7-12); se English (7-12) (MPS); literacy (birth-grade 6) and special education childhood (grades 1-6) (MPS); literacy 5-12; special education generalist 7-12; special ed specialist 7-12 (MPS); math (5-9 and 7-12); special ed generalist (7-12); se math (7-12) (MPS); science: biology or chemistry (5-9 and 7-12); special ed generalist (7-12); se science (7-12) (MPS); social studies (5-9 and 7-12); special ed generalist (7-12); se soc.st. (7-12) (MPS); special ed early childhood and childhood (birth-grade 6) (MPS); special education childhood (grades 1-6) (MPS); special education: childhood (grades 1-6) (Certificate); special education: early childhood (birth-grade 2) (MPS, Certificate); special education: early childhood (birth-grade 2) and childhood (grades 1-6) (Certificate); special education: grades 7-12 generalist (MPS, Certificate). *Program availability:* Part-time, evening/weekend. *Faculty:* 5 full-time (3 women), 35 part-time/adjunct (23 women). *Students:* 45 full-time (36 women), 179 part-time (152 women); includes 31 minority (6 Black or African American, non-Hispanic/Latino; 4 Asian, non-Hispanic/Latino; 19 Hispanic/Latino; 2 Native Hawaiian or other Pacific Islander, non-Hispanic/Latino), 1 international. Average age 28. 76 applicants, 68% accepted, 40 enrolled. In 2018, 99 master's, 2 Certificates awarded. *Degree requirements:* For master's, comprehensive exam (for some programs), thesis (for some programs), student teaching, research seminars, portfolios, internships, writing assessment; for Certificate, comprehensive exam (for some programs). *Entrance requirements:* For master's, for programs leading to certification, candidates must submit scores from GRE or MAT(Miller Analogies Test), minimum undergraduate GPA of 3.0, all transcripts from all colleges and universities attended, 2 letters of recommendation, interview, essay (2-3 page personal statement that describes reasons for choosing education as profession and personal philosophy of education), proof of immunization (for those born after 1957). Additional exam requirements/recommendations for international students: Required—TOEFL (minimum score 600 paper-based; 110 iBT); Recommended—IELTS (minimum score 8). *Application deadline:* Applications are processed on a rolling basis. Application fee: $75. Electronic applications accepted. *Expenses:* 935 per credit. *Financial support:* Teaching assistantships, career-related internships or fieldwork, Federal Work-Study, institutionally sponsored loans, scholarships/grants, and unspecified assistantships available. Financial award application deadline: 3/15; financial award applicants required to submit FAFSA. *Faculty research:* Students with emotional difficulties, literacy and adolescents, mindfulness, studying the effects of the environment on special populations, the most difficult cases, students who are presented with multiple challenges: learning, behavioral and ACE experiences who see criminal behavior as a way to cope; working on giving them the tools they need to succeed emotionally and cognitively despite the odds stacked against them. *Unit head:* Dr. Shelley Wepner, Dean, 914-323-3153, Fax: 914-323-5493, E-mail: Shelley.Wepner@mville.edu. *Application contact:* Alissa Wilson, Director, SOE Graduate Enrollment Management, 914-323-3150, Fax: 914-694-1732, E-mail: edschool@mville.edu.
Website: http://www.mville.edu/programs/special-education

Mansfield University of Pennsylvania, Graduate Studies, Department of Education and Special Education, Mansfield, PA 16933. Offers elementary education (M Ed); secondary education (MS); special education (M Ed). *Accreditation:* NCATE (one or more programs are accredited). *Program availability:* Part-time, evening/weekend, online learning. *Degree requirements:* For master's, comprehensive exam, thesis optional. *Entrance requirements:* For master's, minimum GPA of 3.0. Additional exam requirements/recommendations for international students: Required—TOEFL (minimum score 550 paper-based). Electronic applications accepted.

Marquette University, Graduate School, College of Education, Department of Educational Policy and Leadership, Milwaukee, WI 53201-1881. Offers college student personnel administration (M Ed); curriculum and instruction (MA); education (MA); educational administration (M Ed); educational policy and foundations (MA); elementary education (Certificate); literacy (MA); principal (Certificate); reading specialist (Certificate); reading teacher (Certificate); secondary education (Certificate); superintendent (Certificate). *Program availability:* Part-time, evening/weekend. Terminal master's awarded for partial completion of doctoral program. *Degree requirements:* For master's, comprehensive exam, thesis (for some programs); for doctorate, thesis/dissertation, qualifying exam. *Entrance requirements:* For master's, GRE General Test or MAT, official transcripts from all current and previous colleges/universities except Marquette, three letters of recommendation, statement of purpose; for doctorate, GRE General Test, MAT, sample of written work, official transcripts from all current and previous colleges/universities except Marquette, three letters of recommendation, statement of purpose, resume/curriculum vitae; for Certificate, GRE General Test or MAT, master's degree. Additional exam requirements/recommendations for international students: Required—TOEFL (minimum score 530 paper-based). *Expenses:* Contact institution. *Faculty research:* Leadership; social justice in education; development of lifelong learners; race, class, and schooling in historical perspective; urban teacher education.

Marymount University, School of Sciences, Mathematics, and Education, Program in Education, Arlington, VA 22207-4299. Offers curriculum and instruction (M Ed); elementary education (M Ed); professional studies (M Ed); secondary education (M Ed); special education: general curriculum (M Ed). *Accreditation:* NCATE. *Program availability:* Part-time, evening/weekend. *Faculty:* 7 full-time (all women), 8 part-time/adjunct (6 women). *Students:* 42 full-time (29 women), 103 part-time (80 women); includes 31 minority (8 Black or African American, non-Hispanic/Latino; 11 Asian, non-

Hispanic/Latino; 10 Hispanic/Latino; 1 Native Hawaiian or other Pacific Islander, non-Hispanic/Latino; 1 Two or more races, non-Hispanic/Latino), 12 international. Average age 36. 44 applicants, 100% accepted, 30 enrolled. In 2018, 61 master's awarded. *Degree requirements:* For master's, thesis or alternative, capstone/internship. *Entrance requirements:* For master's, PRAXIS MATH or SAT/ACT, and Virginia Communication and Literacy Assessment (VCLA), 2 letters of recommendation, resume, interview, minimum undergraduate GPA of 2.75 or 3.25 in the last 60 hours. Additional exam requirements/recommendations for international students: Required—TOEFL (minimum score 600 paper-based; 96 iBT), IELTS (minimum score 6.5), PTE (minimum score 58). *Application deadline:* For fall admission, 7/16 priority date for domestic and international students; for spring admission, 11/16 priority date for domestic and international students. Applications are processed on a rolling basis. Application fee: $40. Electronic applications accepted. *Expenses:* $770 per credit. *Financial support:* In 2018–19, 3 students received support. Research assistantships, teaching assistantships, career-related internships or fieldwork, scholarships/grants, and unspecified assistantships available. Support available to part-time students. Financial award application deadline: 3/1; financial award applicants required to submit FAFSA. *Unit head:* Dr. Lisa Turissini, Chair, Education, 703-526-1668, E-mail: lisa.turissini@marymount.edu. *Application contact:* Rebecca Esposito, Senior Associate Director, Graduate Admissions, 703-284-5901, Fax: 703-527-3815, E-mail: grad.admissions@marymount.edu.
Website: https://www.marymount.edu/Academics/School-of-Sciences-Mathematics-and-Education/Graduate-Programs/Education-(M-Ed-)

Maryville University of Saint Louis, School of Education, St. Louis, MO 63141-7299. Offers early childhood education (MA Ed); educational leadership (Ed D); educational leadership w/principal certification (MA Ed); elementary education (MA Ed); gifted (MA Ed); higher education leadership (Ed D); middle grades education (MA Ed); reading/literacy specialist (MA Ed); teacher as leader (Ed D). *Accreditation:* NCATE. *Program availability:* Part-time, 100% online, blended/hybrid learning. *Faculty:* 16 full-time (8 women), 18 part-time/adjunct (11 women). *Students:* 12 full-time (all women), 311 part-time (234 women); includes 99 minority (84 Black or African American, non-Hispanic/Latino; 2 Asian, non-Hispanic/Latino; 9 Hispanic/Latino; 4 Two or more races, non-Hispanic/Latino), 2 international. Average age 38. In 2018, 25 master's, 100 doctorates awarded. *Degree requirements:* For master's, thesis, project. *Entrance requirements:* For master's, minimum cumulative GPA of 3.0, 3 professional recommendations, essays, interview with program faculty; for doctorate, minimum GPA of 3.0, 3 professional recommendations, essay, interview, on-site writing sample. Additional exam requirements/recommendations for international students: Required—TOEFL (minimum score 550 paper-based; 79 iBT). *Application deadline:* Applications are processed on a rolling basis. Electronic applications accepted. *Expenses:* $449 per credit hour for master's programs; $897 per credit hour for doctoral programs. *Financial support:* Career-related internships or fieldwork, Federal Work-Study, tuition waivers (partial), and professional educator discounts available. Financial award application deadline: 4/1; financial award applicants required to submit FAFSA. *Faculty research:* Collaboration with public schools, pre-service program development, mathematics, diversity, literacy. *Unit head:* Dr. Maschael Schappe, Dean, 314-529-9670, Fax: 314-529-9921, E-mail: mschappe@maryville.edu. *Application contact:* Stacey Ruffin, Director of Clinical Experiences & Partnerships, 314-529-9542, Fax: 314-529-9921, E-mail: sruffin@maryville.edu.
Website: http://www.maryville.edu/ed/graduate-programs/

Marywood University, Academic Affairs, Reap College of Education and Human Development, Department of Education, Program in Secondary/K-12 Education, Scranton, PA 18509-1598. Offers MAT. *Program availability:* Part-time. Electronic applications accepted.

McDaniel College, Graduate and Professional Studies, Program in Elementary and Secondary Education, Westminster, MD 21157-4390. Offers elementary education (MS); elementary STEM instructional leader (Postbaccalaureate Certificate); equity and excellence in education (Postbaccalaureate Certificate); learning technology specialist (Postbaccalaureate Certificate); secondary education (MS). *Accreditation:* NCATE. *Program availability:* Part-time, evening/weekend. *Degree requirements:* For master's, comprehensive exam (for some programs), thesis optional. *Entrance requirements:* For master's, PRAXIS, 2 references. Additional exam requirements/recommendations for international students: Required—TOEFL (minimum score 79 iBT), IELTS (minimum score 6). Electronic applications accepted.

McNeese State University, Doré School of Graduate Studies, Burton College of Education, Department of Education Professions, Program in Curriculum and Instruction, Lake Charles, LA 70609. Offers academically gifted education (M Ed); elementary education (M Ed); reading (M Ed); secondary education (M Ed); special education (M Ed). *Program availability:* Evening/weekend. *Entrance requirements:* For master's, GRE, teaching certificate.

McNeese State University, Doré School of Graduate Studies, Burton College of Education, Department of Education Professions, Program in Secondary Education, Lake Charles, LA 70609. Offers MAT. *Program availability:* Evening/weekend. *Degree requirements:* For master's, comprehensive exam, field experiences. *Entrance requirements:* For master's, GRE General Test, PRAXIS I and II, autobiography, two letters of recommendation.

McNeese State University, Doré School of Graduate Studies, Burton College of Education, Department of Education Professions, Program in Secondary Education Grades 6-12, Lake Charles, LA 70609. Offers Postbaccalaureate Certificate. *Entrance requirements:* For degree, PRAXIS, 2 letters of recommendation, autobiography.

Medaille College, Program in Education, Buffalo, NY 14214-2695. Offers adolescent education (MS Ed); curriculum and instruction (MS Ed); education preparation (MS Ed); literacy (MS Ed); special education (MS). *Accreditation:* TEAC. *Program availability:* Part-time, evening/weekend. *Degree requirements:* For master's, comprehensive exam (for some programs), thesis or alternative. *Entrance requirements:* For master's, minimum undergraduate GPA of 2.7. Additional exam requirements/recommendations for international students: Required—TOEFL (minimum score 550 paper-based). Electronic applications accepted. *Faculty research:* Curriculum planning, truancy, tracking minority students, curriculum design, mentoring students.

Mercer University, Graduate Studies, Cecil B. Day Campus, Tift College of Education (Atlanta), Atlanta, GA 30341. Offers curriculum and instruction (PhD); early childhood education (M Ed, MAT, Ed S); educational leadership (PhD), including higher education leadership, P-12 school leadership; educational leadership P-12 (M Ed, Ed S); higher education leadership (M Ed); independent and charter school leadership (M Ed); middle grades education (M Ed, MAT); secondary education (M Ed, MAT); teacher leadership (Ed S). *Accreditation:* NCATE. *Program availability:* Part-time, evening/weekend. *Degree requirements:* For master's and Ed S, research project; for doctorate, comprehensive exam, thesis/dissertation. *Entrance requirements:* For master's, GRE or MAT, minimum undergraduate GPA of 2.75; for doctorate, GRE; for Ed S, GRE or MAT, minimum GPA of 3.25; 3 years of certified teaching experience (for educational leadership and teacher leadership). Additional exam requirements/recommendations for international students: Required—TOEFL (minimum score 80 iBT). Electronic applications accepted. *Expenses:* Contact institution. *Faculty research:* Educational

technology, multicultural and minority issues in education, educational leadership (P-12 and higher education), school discipline and school bullying, standards-based mathematics education.

Mercer University, Graduate Studies, Macon Campus, Tift College of Education (Macon), Macon, GA 31207. Offers curriculum and instruction (PhD); early childhood education (M Ed, Ed S); educational leadership (M Ed, PhD, Ed S), including higher education (PhD), P-12; higher education leadership (M Ed); independent and charter school leadership (M Ed); secondary education (MAT), including STEM; teacher leadership (Ed S). *Accreditation:* NCATE. *Program availability:* Part-time, evening/weekend, 100% online, blended/hybrid learning. *Degree requirements:* For master's, research project report; for doctorate, comprehensive exam, thesis/dissertation. *Entrance requirements:* For master's, GRE or MAT, minimum GPA of 2.75; for doctorate, GRE, minimum GPA of 3.5; interview; writing sample; 3 recommendations; for Ed S, GRE or MAT, minimum GPA of 3.5 (for teacher leadership), 3.0 (for educational leadership). Additional exam requirements/recommendations for international students: Required—TOEFL (minimum score 80 iBT). Electronic applications accepted. *Expenses:* Contact institution. *Faculty research:* Teacher effectiveness, specific learning disabilities, inclusion.

Mercy College, School of Education, Program in Adolescence Education, Dobbs Ferry, NY 10522-1189. Offers MS. *Program availability:* Part-time, evening/weekend, blended/hybrid learning. *Students:* 44 full-time (20 women), 31 part-time (19 women); includes 36 minority (9 Black or African American, non-Hispanic/Latino; 7 Asian, non-Hispanic/Latino; 19 Hispanic/Latino; 1 Two or more races, non-Hispanic/Latino). Average age 31. 68 applicants, 50% accepted, 28 enrolled. In 2018, 30 master's awarded. *Degree requirements:* For master's, Capstone project; clinical practice; for initial New York State certification, passing scores in the following are required: Educating All Students, Content Specialty Test, edTPA. *Entrance requirements:* For master's, GRE or PRAXIS, transcript(s); resume. Additional exam requirements/recommendations for international students: Required—TOEFL (minimum score 600 paper-based; 71 iBT), IELTS (minimum score 8). *Application deadline:* Applications are processed on a rolling basis. Application fee: $40. Electronic applications accepted. *Expenses: Tuition:* Full-time $15,696; part-time $872 per credit. *Required fees:* $642; $161 per term. Tuition and fees vary according to course load, degree level and program. *Financial support:* Career-related internships or fieldwork, Federal Work-Study, scholarships/grants, and unspecified assistantships available. Support available to part-time students. Financial award applicants required to submit FAFSA. *Unit head:* Dr. Eric Martone, Interim Dean, School of Education, 914-674-7618, Fax: 914-674-7352, E-mail: emartone@mercy.edu. *Application contact:* Allison Gurdineer, Executive Director of Admissions, 877-637-2946, Fax: 914-674-7382, E-mail: admissions@mercy.edu.
Website: https://www.mercy.edu/education/secondary-education

Mercy College, School of Education, Program in Teaching Literacy, Dobbs Ferry, NY 10522-1189. Offers teaching literacy (Advanced Certificate); teaching literacy, birth-6 (MS); teaching literacy, grades 5-12 (MS). *Program availability:* Part-time, evening/weekend. *Students:* 7 full-time (all women), 27 part-time (24 women); includes 9 minority (2 Black or African American, non-Hispanic/Latino; 7 Hispanic/Latino). Average age 35. 33 applicants, 64% accepted, 17 enrolled. In 2018, 2 master's, 10 other advanced degrees awarded. *Degree requirements:* For master's and Advanced Certificate, Capstone project; clinical practice; for initial New York State certification, passing scores in the following are required: Educating All Students, Content Specialty Test, edTPA. *Entrance requirements:* For master's and Advanced Certificate, GRE or PRAXIS, transcript(s); resume. Additional exam requirements/recommendations for international students: Required—TOEFL (minimum score 600 paper-based; 71 iBT), IELTS (minimum score 8). *Application deadline:* Applications are processed on a rolling basis. Application fee: $40. Electronic applications accepted. *Expenses: Tuition:* Full-time $15,696; part-time $872 per credit. *Required fees:* $642; $161 per term. Tuition and fees vary according to course load, degree level and program. *Financial support:* Career-related internships or fieldwork, Federal Work-Study, scholarships/grants, and unspecified assistantships available. Support available to part-time students. Financial award applicants required to submit FAFSA. *Unit head:* Dr. Eric Martone, Interim Dean, School of Education, 914-674-7618, Fax: 914-674-7352, E-mail: emartone@mercy.edu. *Application contact:* Allison Gurdineer, Executive Director of Admissions, 877-637-2946, Fax: 914-674-7382, E-mail: admissions@mercy.edu.
Website: https://www.mercy.edu/education/literacy-and-multilingual-studies

Mercyhurst University, Graduate Studies, Program in Secondary Education: Pedagogy and Practice, Erie, PA 16546. Offers MS. *Program availability:* Part-time, evening/weekend. *Entrance requirements:* For master's, GRE or PRAXIS I, resume, essay, three professional references, transcripts. Additional exam requirements/recommendations for international students: Required—TOEFL.

Metropolitan State University, School of Urban Education, St. Paul, MN 55106-5000. Offers curriculum, pedagogy and schooling (MS); English as a second language (MS); secondary education (MS), including English teaching, life sciences teaching, mathematics teaching, social studies teaching; special education (MS).

Middle Tennessee State University, College of Graduate Studies, College of Education, Department of Educational Leadership, Program in Curriculum and Instruction, Murfreesboro, TN 37132. Offers curriculum and instruction (M Ed, Ed S); English as a second language (M Ed, Ed S); secondary education (M Ed); technology and curriculum design (Ed S). *Accreditation:* NCATE. *Program availability:* Part-time, evening/weekend, online learning. *Degree requirements:* For master's, comprehensive exam; for Ed S, comprehensive exam, thesis or alternative. *Entrance requirements:* For master's and Ed S, GRE, MAT or PRAXIS. Additional exam requirements/recommendations for international students: Required—TOEFL (minimum score 525 paper-based; 71 iBT) or IELTS (minimum score 6). Electronic applications accepted.

Milligan College, Area of Education, Milligan College, TN 37682. Offers combined preK-3/K-5 education (M Ed); educational leadership (Ed D); educational specialist (Ed S); K-5 education (M Ed); middle grades education (M Ed); preK-3 education (M Ed); preK-3 special education (M Ed); secondary education (M Ed). *Accreditation:* NCATE. *Program availability:* Part-time, 100% online, blended/hybrid learning. *Faculty:* 5 full-time (3 women), 6 part-time/adjunct (3 women). *Students:* 38 full-time (31 women), 8 part-time (4 women); includes 2 minority (1 Hispanic/Latino; 1 Two or more races, non-Hispanic/Latino), 1 international. Average age 35. 36 applicants, 97% accepted, 32 enrolled. In 2018, 18 master's awarded. *Degree requirements:* For master's, thesis, portfolio, research project; for doctorate, thesis/dissertation, portfolio, research project. *Entrance requirements:* For master's, MAT, GRE General Test, ACT, SAT, or PRAXIS, undergraduate degree and supporting transcripts, professional recommendations, interview; for doctorate, MAT or GRE, master's degree and supporting transcripts, demonstrated scholastic ability, recognized leadership role within education, professional recommendations, essay/personal statement, portfolio (professional development plan, evidence of ability, knowledge and qualities), interview. Additional exam requirements/recommendations for international students: Required—TOEFL (minimum score 550 paper-based, 79 iBT) or IELTS (6.5). *Application deadline:* For fall admission, 8/1 priority date for domestic students, 6/1 for international students; for spring admission, 11/15 priority date for domestic students, 12/1 for international students; for summer admission, 4/1 for domestic students. Applications are processed

on a rolling basis. Application fee: $30. Electronic applications accepted. *Expenses:* $365 per hour (for masters); $485 per hour (for doctoral); $375 fees per semester; $75 one-time records fee. *Financial support:* Scholarships/grants available. Financial award application deadline: 12/1; financial award applicants required to submit FAFSA. *Faculty research:* Assessment; school mental health; literacy; technology; educator preparation. *Unit head:* Dr. Angela Hilton-Prillhart, Area Chair of Education, 423-461-8769, Fax: 423-461-3103, E-mail: anhilton-prillhart@milligan.edu. *Application contact:* Melissa Dillow, Graduate Admissions Recruiter, Education, 423-461-8306, Fax: 423-461-8982, E-mail: msdillow@milligan.edu.
Website: http://www.Milligan.edu/GPS

Mississippi College, Graduate School, School of Education, Department of Teacher Education and Leadership, Clinton, MS 39058. Offers art (M Ed); biological science (M Ed); business education (M Ed); computer science (M Ed); dyslexia therapy (M Ed); educational leadership (M Ed, Ed D, Ed S); elementary education (M Ed, Ed S); English (M Ed); higher education administration (MS); mathematics (M Ed); secondary education (M Ed); social studies (history) (M Ed); teaching arts (M Ed). *Program availability:* Part-time, online learning. *Degree requirements:* For master's, comprehensive exam, thesis optional. *Entrance requirements:* For master's, NTE. Additional exam requirements/recommendations for international students: Recommended—TOEFL, IELTS. Electronic applications accepted.

Mississippi State University, College of Education, Department of Curriculum, Instruction and Special Education, Mississippi State, MS 39762. Offers early childhood education (PhD); elementary education (MS, PhD, Ed S), including early childhood education (MS), general elementary education (MS), middle level education (MS); general curriculum and instruction (PhD); reading education (PhD); secondary education (MAT, MS, PhD, Ed S); special education (MAT, MS, PhD, Ed S). *Accreditation:* NCATE. *Program availability:* Part-time, evening/weekend. *Faculty:* 20 full-time (14 women), 1 (woman) part-time/adjunct. *Students:* 24 full-time (16 women), 151 part-time (109 women); includes 44 minority (38 Black or African American, non-Hispanic/Latino; 3 American Indian or Alaska Native, non-Hispanic/Latino; 1 Hispanic/Latino; 2 Two or more races, non-Hispanic/Latino), 3 international. Average age 32. 65 applicants, 65% accepted, 38 enrolled. In 2018, 57 master's, 3 doctorates, 1 other advanced degree awarded. *Degree requirements:* For master's, comprehensive exam; for doctorate, thesis/dissertation; for Ed S, comprehensive exam, thesis or alternative. *Entrance requirements:* For master's, GRE, minimum GPA of 2.75 in junior and senior year, eligibility for initial teacher certification; for doctorate, GRE, minimum GPA of 3.4 on previous graduate work; for Ed S, GRE, minimum GPA of 3.2 on master's degree. Additional exam requirements/recommendations for international students: Required—TOEFL (minimum score 550 paper-based; 79 iBT); Recommended—IELTS (minimum score 6.5). *Application deadline:* For fall admission, 3/1 priority date for domestic students, 5/1 for international students; for spring admission, 9/1 priority date for domestic students, 9/1 for international students. Applications are processed on a rolling basis. Application fee: $60 ($80 for international students). Electronic applications accepted. *Expenses:* Tuition, state resident: full-time $8450; part-time $360.59 per credit hour. Tuition, nonresident: full-time $23,140; part-time $969.09 per credit hour. *Required fees:* $110. One-time fee: $55 full-time. Part-time tuition and fees vary according to course load, degree level, campus/location and reciprocity agreements. *Financial support:* In 2018–19, 5 research assistantships with partial tuition reimbursements (averaging $11,453 per year), 1 teaching assistantship (averaging $11,700 per year) were awarded; Federal Work-Study, institutionally sponsored loans, scholarships/grants, and unspecified assistantships also available. Financial award application deadline: 4/1; financial award applicants required to submit FAFSA. *Faculty research:* Early childhood education, reading, rural schools, multicultural education, use of technology in instruction. *Unit head:* Dr. Linda Cornelious, Professor and Head, 662-325-3747, Fax: 662-325-7857, E-mail: lcornelious@colled.msstate.edu. *Application contact:* Robbie Salters, Admissions and Enrollment Assistant, 662-325-7400, E-mail: rsalters@grad.msstate.edu.
Website: http://www.cise.msstate.edu/

Missouri State University, Graduate College, College of Education, Department of Counseling, Leadership, and Special Education, Program in Educational Administration, Springfield, MO 65897. Offers elementary principal (MS Ed, Ed S); secondary principal (MS Ed, Ed S); superintendent (Ed S). *Program availability:* Part-time, evening/weekend. *Faculty:* 5 full-time (2 women), 1 part-time/adjunct (0 women). *Students:* 6 full-time (all women), 84 part-time (56 women); includes 9 minority (1 Black or African American, non-Hispanic/Latino; 1 American Indian or Alaska Native, non-Hispanic/Latino; 4 Hispanic/Latino; 3 Two or more races, non-Hispanic/Latino). Average age 26. 46 applicants, 98% accepted. In 2018, 10 master's, 3 Ed Ss awarded. *Degree requirements:* For master's and Ed S, comprehensive exam, thesis or alternative. *Entrance requirements:* For master's, minimum GPA of 2.75; for Ed S, GRE General Test, MAT, minimum GPA of 2.75. Additional exam requirements/recommendations for international students: Required—TOEFL (minimum score 550 paper-based; 79 iBT), IELTS (minimum score 6). *Application deadline:* For fall admission, 7/20 priority date for domestic students, 5/1 for international students; for spring admission, 12/20 priority date for domestic students, 9/1 for international students; for summer admission, 5/20 priority date for domestic students. Applications are processed on a rolling basis. Application fee: $55 ($60 for international students). Electronic applications accepted. Tuition and fees vary according to class time, course level, course load, degree level, campus/location, program and student level. *Financial support:* Career-related internships or fieldwork, Federal Work-Study, institutionally sponsored loans, scholarships/grants, and unspecified assistantships available. Financial award application deadline: 1/31; financial award applicants required to submit FAFSA. *Unit head:* Dr. James Satterfield, Department Head, 417-836-5392, Fax: 417-836-4918, E-mail: clse@missouristate.edu. *Application contact:* Lakan Drinker, Director, Graduate Enrollment Management, 417-836-5330, Fax: 417-836-6200, E-mail: lakandrinker@missouristate.edu.
Website: http://education.missouristate.edu/edadmin/

Missouri State University, Graduate College, College of Education, Department of Reading, Foundations, and Technology, Master of Arts in Teaching Program, Springfield, MO 65897. Offers MAT. *Program availability:* Part-time. *Faculty:* 17 full-time (11 women), 14 part-time/adjunct (13 women). *Students:* 13 full-time (8 women), 49 part-time (34 women); includes 6 minority (4 Hispanic/Latino; 2 Two or more races, non-Hispanic/Latino). Average age 28. 32 applicants, 91% accepted. In 2018, 30 master's awarded. *Degree requirements:* For master's, comprehensive exam, project. *Entrance requirements:* For master's, PRAXIS II. Additional exam requirements/recommendations for international students: Required—TOEFL (minimum score 550 paper-based; 79 iBT), IELTS (minimum score 6). *Application deadline:* For fall admission, 2/15 priority date for domestic and international students; for summer admission, 2/15 priority date for domestic students. Application fee: $55 ($60 for international students). Electronic applications accepted. Tuition and fees vary according to class time, course level, course load, degree level, campus/location, program and student level. *Financial support:* Federal Work-Study, institutionally sponsored loans, scholarships/grants, tuition waivers (full), and unspecified assistantships available. Financial award application deadline: 1/31; financial award applicants required to submit FAFSA. *Unit head:* Dr. Emmett Sawyer, Interim Department Head, 417-836-6769, E-mail: rft@

missouristate.edu. *Application contact:* Lakan Drinker, Coordinator of Graduate Admissions, 417-836-5330, Fax: 417-836-6200, E-mail: lakandrinker@missouristate.edu.

Missouri State University, Graduate College, College of Health and Human Services, Department of Kinesiology, Springfield, MO 65897. Offers health promotion and wellness management (MS); secondary education (MS Ed), including physical education. *Program availability:* Part-time. *Faculty:* 14 full-time (6 women). *Students:* 14 full-time (5 women), 16 part-time (10 women); includes 2 minority (both Black or African American, non-Hispanic/Latino), 2 international. Average age 23. 23 applicants, 48% accepted. In 2018, 16 master's awarded. *Degree requirements:* For master's, comprehensive exam, thesis or alternative. *Entrance requirements:* For master's, GRE (for MS), minimum GPA of 2.8 (MS); 9-12 teaching certification (MS Ed). Additional exam requirements/recommendations for international students: Required—TOEFL (minimum score 550 paper-based; 79 iBT), IELTS (minimum score 6). *Application deadline:* For fall admission, 7/20 priority date for domestic students, 5/1 for international students; for spring admission, 12/20 priority date for domestic students, 9/1 for international students. Applications are processed on a rolling basis. Application fee: $55 ($60 for international students). Electronic applications accepted. Tuition and fees vary according to class time, course level, course load, degree level, campus/location, program and student level. *Financial support:* In 2018–19, 7 teaching assistantships with partial tuition reimbursements (averaging $8,772 per year) were awarded; Federal Work-Study, institutionally sponsored loans, scholarships/grants, and unspecified assistantships also available. Financial award application deadline: 1/31; financial award applicants required to submit FAFSA. *Unit head:* Dr. Sarah McCallister, Department Head, 417-836-6582, Fax: 417-836-5371, E-mail: sarahmccallister@missouristate.edu. *Application contact:* Lakan Drinker, Director, Graduate Enrollment Management, 417-836-5330, Fax: 417-836-6200, E-mail: lakandrinker@missouristate.edu.
Website: http://www.missouristate.edu/kinesiology/

Missouri State University, Graduate College, College of Natural and Applied Sciences, Department of Biology, Springfield, MO 65897. Offers biology (MS); natural and applied science (MNAS), including biology (MNAS, MS Ed); secondary education (MS Ed), including biology (MNAS, MS Ed). *Faculty:* 18 full-time (3 women), 7 part-time/adjunct (2 women). *Students:* 23 full-time (12 women), 21 part-time (13 women); includes 2 minority (1 Black or African American, non-Hispanic/Latino; 1 Two or more races, non-Hispanic/Latino), 8 international. Average age 24. 28 applicants, 46% accepted. In 2018, 17 master's awarded. *Degree requirements:* For master's, comprehensive exam, thesis or alternative. *Entrance requirements:* For master's, GRE (MS, MNAS), 24 hours of course work in biology (MS); minimum GPA of 3.0 (MS, MNAS); 9-12 teacher certification (MS Ed). Additional exam requirements/recommendations for international students: Required—TOEFL (minimum score 550 paper-based; 79 iBT), IELTS (minimum score 6). *Application deadline:* For fall admission, 7/20 priority date for domestic students, 5/1 for international students; for spring admission, 12/20 priority date for domestic students, 9/1 for international students; for summer admission, 5/20 priority date for domestic students. Applications are processed on a rolling basis. Application fee: $55 ($60 for international students). Electronic applications accepted. Tuition and fees vary according to class time, course level, course load, degree level, campus/location, program and student level. *Financial support:* In 2018–19, 2 research assistantships with full tuition reimbursements (averaging $10,672 per year), 26 teaching assistantships with full tuition reimbursements (averaging $9,746 per year) were awarded; Federal Work-Study, institutionally sponsored loans, scholarships/grants, and unspecified assistantships also available. Financial award application deadline: 1/31; financial award applicants required to submit FAFSA. *Faculty research:* Hibernation physiology of bats, behavioral ecology of salamanders, mussel conservation, plant evolution and systematics, cellular/molecular mechanisms involved in migraine pathology. *Unit head:* Dr. S. Alicia Mathis, Department Head, 417-836-5126, Fax: 417-836-6934, E-mail: biology@missouristate.edu. *Application contact:* Lakan Drinker, Director, Graduate Enrollment Management, 417-836-5330, Fax: 417-836-6200, E-mail: lakandrinker@missouristate.edu.
Website: http://biology.missouristate.edu/

Missouri State University, Graduate College, College of Natural and Applied Sciences, Department of Chemistry, Springfield, MO 65897. Offers chemistry (MS); natural and applied science (MNAS), including chemistry (MNAS, MS Ed); secondary education (MS Ed), including chemistry (MNAS, MS Ed). *Program availability:* Part-time. *Faculty:* 15 full-time (2 women). *Students:* 12 full-time (5 women), 9 part-time (4 women); includes 2 minority (1 Hispanic/Latino; 1 Two or more races, non-Hispanic/Latino), 5 international. Average age 23. 11 applicants, 45% accepted. In 2018, 8 master's awarded. *Degree requirements:* For master's, comprehensive exam, thesis. *Entrance requirements:* For master's, GRE General Test (MS, MNAS), minimum undergraduate GPA of 3.0 (MS and MNAS), 9-12 teacher certification (MS Ed). Additional exam requirements/recommendations for international students: Required—TOEFL (minimum score 550 paper-based; 79 iBT), IELTS (minimum score 6). *Application deadline:* For fall admission, 7/20 priority date for domestic students, 5/1 for international students; for spring admission, 12/20 priority date for domestic students, 9/1 for international students; for summer admission, 5/20 priority date for domestic students. Applications are processed on a rolling basis. Application fee: $55 ($60 for international students). Electronic applications accepted. Tuition and fees vary according to class time, course level, course load, degree level, campus/location, program and student level. *Financial support:* In 2018–19, 17 teaching assistantships with full tuition reimbursements (averaging $8,772 per year) were awarded; Federal Work-Study, institutionally sponsored loans, scholarships/grants, and unspecified assistantships also available. Financial award application deadline: 1/31; financial award applicants required to submit FAFSA. *Faculty research:* Polyethylene glycol derivatives, electrochemiluminescence of environmental systems, enzymology, environmental organic pollutants, DNA repair via nuclear magnetic resonance (NMR). *Unit head:* Dr. Bryan Breyfogle, Department Head, 417-836-5601, Fax: 417-836-5507, E-mail: chemistry@missouristate.edu. *Application contact:* Lakan Drinker, Director, Graduate Enrollment Management, 417-836-5330, Fax: 417-836-6200, E-mail: lakandrinker@missouristate.edu.
Website: http://chemistry.missouristate.edu/

Missouri State University, Graduate College, College of Natural and Applied Sciences, Department of Geography, Geology, and Planning, Springfield, MO 65897. Offers geography, geology, and planning (Certificate); natural and applied science (MNAS), including geography, geology and planning; secondary education (MS Ed), including earth science, physical geography. *Program availability:* Part-time, evening/weekend. *Faculty:* 18 full-time (4 women), 1 part-time/adjunct (0 women). *Students:* 24 full-time (10 women), 10 part-time (5 women); includes 2 minority (1 Hispanic/Latino; 1 Two or more races, non-Hispanic/Latino), 5 international. Average age 25. 26 applicants, 50% accepted. In 2018, 8 master's awarded. *Degree requirements:* For master's, comprehensive exam, thesis (for some programs). *Entrance requirements:* For master's, GRE General Test (MS, MNAS), minimum undergraduate GPA of 3.0 (MS, MNAS), 9-12 teacher certification (MS Ed). Additional exam requirements/recommendations for international students: Required—TOEFL (minimum score 550 paper-based; 79 iBT), IELTS (minimum score 6). *Application deadline:* For fall admission, 7/20 priority date for domestic students, 5/1 for international students; for spring admission, 12/20 priority date for domestic students, 9/1 for international students. Applications are processed on a rolling basis. Application fee: $55 ($60 for international students). Electronic applications accepted. Tuition and fees vary according to class time, course level, course load, degree level, campus/location, program and student level. *Financial support:* In 2018–19, 3 research assistantships with full tuition reimbursements (averaging $11,574 per year), 15 teaching assistantships with full tuition reimbursements (averaging $9,365 per year) were awarded; career-related internships or fieldwork, Federal Work-Study, institutionally sponsored loans, scholarships/grants, and unspecified assistantships also available. Financial award application deadline: 1/31; financial award applicants required to submit FAFSA. *Faculty research:* Stratigraphy and ancient meteorite impacts, environmental geochemistry of karst, hyperspectral image processing, water quality, small town planning. *Unit head:* Dr. Toby Dogwiler, Department Head, 417-836-5800, Fax: 417-836-6934, E-mail: tobydogwiler@missouristate.edu. *Application contact:* Lakan Drinker, Director, Graduate Enrollment Management, 417-836-5330, Fax: 417-836-6200, E-mail: lakandrinker@missouristate.edu.
Website: http://geosciences.missouristate.edu/

Missouri State University, Graduate College, College of Natural and Applied Sciences, Department of Mathematics, Springfield, MO 65897. Offers mathematics (MS); natural and applied science (MNAS), including mathematics (MNAS, MS Ed); secondary education (MS Ed), including mathematics (MNAS, MS Ed). *Program availability:* Part-time. *Faculty:* 21 full-time (4 women). *Students:* 13 full-time (4 women), 15 part-time (10 women); includes 2 minority (1 American Indian or Alaska Native, non-Hispanic/Latino; 1 Hispanic/Latino), 6 international. Average age 24. 18 applicants, 56% accepted. In 2018, 11 master's awarded. *Degree requirements:* For master's, comprehensive exam, thesis or alternative. *Entrance requirements:* For master's, GRE (MS, MNAS), minimum undergraduate GPA of 3.0 (MS, MNAS), 9-12 teacher certification (MS Ed). Additional exam requirements/recommendations for international students: Required—TOEFL (minimum score 550 paper-based; 79 iBT), IELTS (minimum score 6). *Application deadline:* For fall admission, 7/20 priority date for domestic students, 5/1 for international students; for spring admission, 12/20 priority date for domestic students, 9/1 for international students. Applications are processed on a rolling basis. Application fee: $55 ($60 for international students). Electronic applications accepted. Tuition and fees vary according to class time, course level, course load, degree level, campus/location, program and student level. *Financial support:* In 2018–19, 11 teaching assistantships with full tuition reimbursements (averaging $10,672 per year) were awarded; Federal Work-Study, institutionally sponsored loans, scholarships/grants, and unspecified assistantships also available. Financial award application deadline: 1/31; financial award applicants required to submit FAFSA. *Faculty research:* Harmonic analysis, commutative algebra, number theory, K-theory, probability. *Unit head:* Dr. William Bray, Department Head, 417-836-5112, Fax: 417-836-6966, E-mail: mathematics@missouristate.edu. *Application contact:* Lakan Drinker, Director, Graduate Enrollment Management, 417-836-5330, Fax: 417-836-6200, E-mail: lakandrinker@missouristate.edu.
Website: http://math.missouristate.edu/

Missouri State University, Graduate College, College of Natural and Applied Sciences, Department of Physics, Astronomy, and Materials Science, Springfield, MO 65897. Offers materials science (MS); natural and applied science (MNAS), including physics (MNAS, MS Ed); secondary education (MS Ed), including physics (MNAS, MS Ed). *Program availability:* Part-time. *Faculty:* 9 full-time (0 women). *Students:* 11 full-time (1 woman), 4 part-time (1 woman); includes 1 minority (Hispanic/Latino), 13 international. Average age 26. 12 applicants, 92% accepted. In 2018, 9 master's awarded. *Degree requirements:* For master's, comprehensive exam, thesis. *Entrance requirements:* For master's, GRE (MS, MNAS), minimum undergraduate GPA of 3.0 (MS and MNAS), 9-12 teaching certification (MS Ed). Additional exam requirements/recommendations for international students: Required—TOEFL (minimum score 550 paper-based; 79 iBT), IELTS (minimum score 6). *Application deadline:* For fall admission, 7/20 priority date for domestic students, 5/1 for international students; for spring admission, 12/20 priority date for domestic students, 9/1 for international students. Applications are processed on a rolling basis. Application fee: $55 ($60 for international students). Electronic applications accepted. Tuition and fees vary according to class time, course level, course load, degree level, campus/location, program and student level. *Financial support:* In 2018–19, 6 research assistantships with full tuition reimbursements (averaging $10,672 per year), 11 teaching assistantships with full tuition reimbursements (averaging $10,672 per year) were awarded; Federal Work-Study, institutionally sponsored loans, scholarships/grants, and unspecified assistantships also available. Financial award application deadline: 1/31; financial award applicants required to submit FAFSA. *Faculty research:* Nanocomposites, ferroelectricity, infrared focal plane array sensors, biosensors, pulsating stars. *Unit head:* Dr. Robert Mayanovic, Department Head, 417-836-5131, Fax: 417-836-6226, E-mail: physics@missouristate.edu. *Application contact:* Lakan Drinker, Director, Graduate Enrollment Management, 417-836-5330, Fax: 417-836-6200, E-mail: lakandrinker@missouristate.edu.
Website: http://physics.missouristate.edu/

Missouri State University, Graduate College, Darr College of Agriculture, Springfield, MO 65897. Offers plant science (MS); secondary education (MS Ed), including agriculture. *Program availability:* Part-time. *Faculty:* 16 full-time (5 women), 1 part-time/adjunct (0 women). *Students:* 22 full-time (9 women), 32 part-time (17 women); includes 3 minority (1 American Indian or Alaska Native, non-Hispanic/Latino; 2 Two or more races, non-Hispanic/Latino). Average age 23. 24 applicants, 42% accepted. In 2018, 21 master's awarded. *Degree requirements:* For master's, comprehensive exam, thesis or alternative. *Entrance requirements:* For master's, GRE (MS in plant science, MNAS), 9-12 teacher certification (MS Ed), minimum GPA of 3.0 (MS plant science, MNAS). Additional exam requirements/recommendations for international students: Required—TOEFL (minimum score 550 paper-based; 79 iBT), IELTS (minimum score 6). *Application deadline:* For fall admission, 7/20 priority date for domestic students, 5/1 for international students; for spring admission, 12/20 priority date for domestic students, 9/1 for international students; for summer admission, 5/20 priority date for domestic students. Applications are processed on a rolling basis. Application fee: $55 ($60 for international students). Electronic applications accepted. Tuition and fees vary according to class time, course level, course load, degree level, campus/location, program and student level. *Financial support:* In 2018–19, 7 research assistantships with full tuition reimbursements (averaging $9,365 per year), 6 teaching assistantships with full tuition reimbursements (averaging $8,450 per year) were awarded; Federal Work-Study, institutionally sponsored loans, scholarships/grants, and unspecified assistantships also available. Financial award application deadline: 1/31; financial award applicants required to submit FAFSA. *Faculty research:* Grapevine biotechnology, agricultural marketing, Asian elephant reproduction, poultry science, integrated pest management. *Unit head:* Dr. Ronald Del Vecchio, Dean, 417-836-5050, E-mail: darr@missouristate.edu. *Application contact:* Lakan Drinker, Director, Graduate Enrollment Management, 417-836-5330, Fax: 417-836-6200, E-mail: lakandrinker@missouristate.edu.
Website: http://ag.missouristate.edu/

Monmouth University, Graduate Studies, School of Education, West Long Branch, NJ 07764-1898. Offers applied behavior analysis (Certificate); autism (Certificate); director

of school counseling services (Post-Master's Certificate); early childhood (M Ed); educational leadership (Ed D); elementary education (MAT), including elementary level, secondary level; English as a second language (M Ed); learning disabilities teacher-consultant (Post-Master's Certificate); literacy (MS Ed); school counseling (MS Ed); special education (MS Ed), including autism, learning disabilities teacher-consultant, teacher of students with disabilities, teaching in inclusive settings; speech-language pathology (MS Ed); student affairs and college counseling (MS Ed); supervisor (Post-Master's Certificate); teaching English to speakers of other languages (Certificate). *Accreditation:* NCATE. *Program availability:* Part-time, evening/weekend, 100% online, blended/hybrid learning. *Faculty:* 29 full-time (23 women), 32 part-time/adjunct (24 women). *Students:* 214 full-time (187 women), 148 part-time (127 women); includes 60 minority (13 Black or African American, non-Hispanic/Latino; 2 Asian, non-Hispanic/Latino; 40 Hispanic/Latino; 5 Two or more races, non-Hispanic/Latino). Average age 27. In 2018, 108 master's, 9 other advanced degrees awarded. *Entrance requirements:* For master's, GRE taken within last 5 years (for MS Ed in speech-language pathology), SAT (minimum combined score of 1660 in 3 sections), ACT (23), GRE (minimum score of 4.0 on analytical writing section and minimum combined score of 310 on quantitative and verbal sections), or passing scores on 3 parts of Core Academic Skills Educators, minimum GPA of 3.0 in major; 2 letters of recommendation (for some programs); resume, personal statement or essay (depending on program). Additional exam requirements/recommendations for international students: Required—TOEFL (minimum score 550 paper-based; 79 iBT), IELTS (minimum score 6), Michigan English Language Assessment Battery (minimum score 77) or Certificate of Advanced English (minimum score 160). *Application deadline:* For fall admission, 7/15 priority date for domestic students, 7/1 for international students; for spring admission, 12/1 priority date for domestic students, 11/1 for international students; for summer admission, 5/1 for domestic students. Applications are processed on a rolling basis. Application fee: $50. Electronic applications accepted. *Expenses: Tuition:* Part-time $1233 per credit. *Required fees:* $178 per term. *Financial support:* In 2018–19, 290 students received support. Institutionally sponsored loans, scholarships/grants, and unspecified assistantships available. Support available to part-time students. Financial award applicants required to submit FAFSA. *Faculty research:* Multicultural literacy, science and mathematics teaching strategies, teacher as reflective practitioner, children with disabilities. *Unit head:* Dr. John E. Henning, Dean, 732-263-5513, Fax: 732-263-5277, E-mail: kodonnel@monmouth.edu. *Application contact:* Kirsten Sneeringer, Graduate Admission Counselor, 732-571-3452, Fax: 732-263-5123, E-mail: gradadm@monmouth.edu.
Website: http://www.monmouth.edu/academics/schools/education/default.asp

Montana State University Billings, College of Education, Department of Educational Theory and Practice, Option in Curriculum and Instruction, Billings, MT 59101. Offers K-8 elementary education (M Ed); secondary education (M Ed). *Accreditation:* NCATE. *Program availability:* Part-time. *Degree requirements:* For master's, thesis or professional paper and/or field experience. *Entrance requirements:* For master's, GRE General Test or MAT, minimum GPA of 3.0. Additional exam requirements/recommendations for international students: Required—TOEFL (minimum score 79 iBT), IELTS (minimum score 6.5). Electronic applications accepted. *Faculty research:* Social studies education, science education.

Morehead State University, Graduate School, College of Education, Department of Middle Grades and Secondary Education, Morehead, KY 40351. Offers business and marketing education (MAT); English/language arts 5-9 (MAT); French (MAT); health P-12 (MAT); mathematics 5-9 (MAT); physical education P-12 (MAT); science 5-9 (MAT); secondary biology (MAT); secondary chemistry (MAT); secondary earth science (MAT); secondary English (MAT); secondary math (MAT); secondary physics (MAT); secondary social studies (MAT); social studies 5-9 (MAT); Spanish (MAT). *Program availability:* Part-time, evening/weekend. *Degree requirements:* For master's, portfolio. *Entrance requirements:* For master's, GRE or PRAXIS II content exam, minimum overall undergraduate GPA of 2.5. Additional exam requirements/recommendations for international students: Required—TOEFL (minimum score 500 paper-based). Electronic applications accepted.

Mount St. Joseph University, Graduate Education Program, Cincinnati, OH 45233-1670. Offers adolescent to young adult education (MA); dyslexia (Certificate); inclusive early childhood education (MA); middle childhood education (MA); multicultural special education (MA); reading science (MA). *Accreditation:* TEAC. *Program availability:* Part-time, evening/weekend, 100% online, blended/hybrid learning. *Degree requirements:* For master's, comprehensive exam, thesis, research project, student teaching, clinical and field-based experiences. *Entrance requirements:* For master's, GRE (if GPA is below 3.0), letter of intent, 2 referrals, background check, interview, resume, minimum undergraduate GPA of 3.0. Additional exam requirements/recommendations for international students: Required—TOEFL (minimum score 560 paper-based; 83 iBT). Electronic applications accepted. *Expenses:* Contact institution. *Faculty research:* Foreign and second language learning problems/reading disabilities, multicultural/bilingual special education, science education, pedagogical content knowledge, early childhood, response to intervention.

Murray State University, College of Education and Human Services, Department of Adolescent, Career, and Special Education, Murray, KY 42071. Offers career and technical education (MS); middle school teacher leader (MA Ed); secondary teacher leader (MA Ed); special education (MA Ed), including mild learning and behavior disorders, moderate to severe disabilities (P-12), teacher leader in special education learning and behavior disorders; teacher education and professional development (Ed S). *Accreditation:* NCATE. *Program availability:* Part-time. *Entrance requirements:* For master's and Ed S, GRE or GMAT, minimum university GPA of 2.75. Additional exam requirements/recommendations for international students: Required—TOEFL (minimum score 527 paper-based; 71 iBT). Electronic applications accepted.

Murray State University, College of Education and Human Services, Department of Educational Studies, Leadership and Counseling, Murray, KY 42071. Offers college advising (Certificate); education administration (MA Ed); human development and leadership (MS, Certificate); library media (MA Ed); middle school teacher leader (MA Ed); P-20 and community leadership (Ed D); postsecondary education administration (MA Ed); school counseling (MA Ed); school guidance and counseling (Ed S); secondary teacher leader (MA Ed). *Program availability:* Part-time, evening/weekend, 100% online, blended/hybrid learning. *Entrance requirements:* For master's and other advanced degree, GRE or GMAT, minimum university GPA of 2.75. Additional exam requirements/recommendations for international students: Required—TOEFL (minimum score 527 paper-based; 71 iBT). Electronic applications accepted.

National Louis University, National College of Education, Chicago, IL 60603. Offers administration and supervision (M Ed, Ed D, CAS, Ed S); curriculum and instruction (M Ed, MS Ed, CAS); early childhood administration (M Ed, CAS); early childhood education (M Ed, MAT, MS Ed, CAS); education (Ed D); educational psychology/human learning and development (M Ed, MS Ed, CAS, Ed S); elementary education (MAT); interdisciplinary curriculum and instruction (M Ed); mathematics education (M Ed, MS Ed, CAS); middle grades education (MAT); reading and language (M Ed, MS Ed, CAS); school psychology (M Ed, Ed S); science education (M Ed, MS Ed, CAS); secondary education (MAT); special education (M Ed, MAT, CAS); technology in

education (M Ed, CAS). *Accreditation:* NCATE. *Program availability:* Part-time, evening/weekend. *Degree requirements:* For doctorate, comprehensive exam, thesis/dissertation. *Entrance requirements:* For master's, MAT or GRE, minimum GPA of 3.0; for doctorate, GRE General Test, minimum GPA of 3.25, interview, resume, writing sample, 4 recommendations. Additional exam requirements/recommendations for international students: Required—TOEFL (minimum score 550 paper-based; 79 iBT).

Nebraska Christian College of Hope International University, Graduate Programs, Papillion, NE 68046. Offers biblical studies (M Div); business as mission/social entrepreneurship (MBA); children, youth, and family (M Div); church planting (M Div); counseling psychology (MS); educational administration (MA); elementary education (M Ed); general management (MBA); gifted and talented education (M Ed); intercultural studies (M Div); international development (MBA); marketing management (MBA); ministry (MA); ministry and leadership (M Div); music education (M Ed); non-profit management (MBA); pastoral care (M Div); secondary education (M Ed); spiritual formation (M Div); worship ministry (M Div).

Neumann University, Graduate Program in Education, Aston, PA 19014-1298. Offers education (MS), including administrative certification (school principal PK-12), autism, early elementary education, secondary education, special education. *Program availability:* Part-time, evening/weekend, 100% online, blended/hybrid learning. *Entrance requirements:* For master's, official transcripts from all institutions attended, letter of intent, three professional references, copy of any teaching certifications. Additional exam requirements/recommendations for international students: Required—TOEFL (minimum score 70 iBT). Electronic applications accepted. *Expenses:* Contact institution.

New Jersey City University, Debra Cannon Partridge Wolfe College of Education, Department of Elementary and Secondary Education, Jersey City, NJ 07305-1597. Offers elementary education (MAT); secondary education (MAT). *Program availability:* Part-time, evening/weekend. *Entrance requirements:* Additional exam requirements/recommendations for international students: Required—TOEFL (minimum score 79 iBT).

New York Institute of Technology, School of Interdisciplinary Studies and Education, Department of Teacher Education, Old Westbury, NY 11568-8000. Offers adolescence education (MS), including math (MAT, MS), science; adolescent education (MAT), including biology, chemistry, English, math (MAT, MS), social studies; childhood education (MS); early childhood (MS). *Program availability:* Part-time, evening/weekend, 100% online, blended/hybrid learning. *Faculty:* 2 full-time (both women), 8 part-time/adjunct (5 women). *Students:* 47 full-time (45 women), 56 part-time (47 women); includes 36 minority (13 Black or African American, non-Hispanic/Latino; 1 American Indian or Alaska Native, non-Hispanic/Latino; 7 Asian, non-Hispanic/Latino; 12 Hispanic/Latino; 1 Native Hawaiian or other Pacific Islander, non-Hispanic/Latino; 2 Two or more races, non-Hispanic/Latino), 3 international. Average age 31. 81 applicants, 53% accepted, 27 enrolled. In 2018, 27 master's awarded. *Entrance requirements:* For master's, GRE or MAT, BS or equivalent; minimum cumulative undergraduate GPA of 3.0; NY state initial certification; BS with major (or minimum 30 credits in a concentration) in biology, chemistry, English, math, physics, or social studies (for MS in childhood, early childhood education, and MAT); interview; personal statement. Additional exam requirements/recommendations for international students: Required—TOEFL (minimum score 79 iBT), IELTS (minimum score 6), PTE (minimum score 53). *Application deadline:* Applications are processed on a rolling basis. Application fee: $50. Electronic applications accepted. *Expenses:* $1285 per credit plus $215 fees per year (full-time) or $175 fees per year (part-time); $1395 per 3-credit education UFT or off-site graduate course. *Financial support:* Career-related internships or fieldwork, Federal Work-Study, scholarships/grants, tuition waivers (full and partial), and unspecified assistantships available. Support available to part-time students. Financial award application deadline: 2/15; financial award applicants required to submit FAFSA. *Faculty research:* Evolving definition of new literacies and its impact on teaching and learning (twenty-first century skills), new literacies practices in teacher education, teachers' professional development, English language and literacy learning through mobile learning, teaching reading to culturally and linguistically diverse children. *Application contact:* Alice Dolitsky, Director, Graduate Admissions, 516-686-7520, Fax: 516-686-1116, E-mail: admissions@nyit.edu.
Website: http://www.nyit.edu/departments/teacher_education

New York University, Steinhardt School of Culture, Education, and Human Development, Department of Art and Art Professions, Program in Art Education, New York, NY 10003-5799. Offers art, education, and community practice (MA); teachers of art, all grades (MA); teaching art/social studies 7-12 (MA), including 5-6 extension. *Accreditation:* TEAC. *Program availability:* Part-time. *Entrance requirements:* For master's, portfolio. Additional exam requirements/recommendations for international students: Required—TOEFL (minimum score 100 iBT). Electronic applications accepted. *Faculty research:* Multicultural aesthetic inquiry, urban art education, feminism, equity and social justice.

New York University, Steinhardt School of Culture, Education, and Human Development, Department of Music and Performing Arts Professions, Program in Educational Theatre, New York, NY 10012. Offers educational theatre and English 7-12 (MA); educational theatre and social studies 7-12 (MA); educational theatre in colleges and communities (MA, Ed D, PhD); educational theatre, all grades (MA). *Program availability:* Part-time. *Entrance requirements:* For master's, audition; for doctorate, GRE General Test, interview. Additional exam requirements/recommendations for international students: Required—TOEFL (minimum score 100 iBT). Electronic applications accepted. *Faculty research:* Theatre for young audiences, drama in education, applied theatre, arts education assessment, reflective praxis.

New York University, Steinhardt School of Culture, Education, and Human Development, Department of Teaching and Learning, Program in English Education, New York, NY 10012-1019. Offers clinically-based English education, grades 7-12 (MA); English education (PhD, Advanced Certificate); English education, grades 7-12 (MA). *Accreditation:* TEAC. *Program availability:* Part-time. *Entrance requirements:* For doctorate, GRE General Test, interview; for Advanced Certificate, master's degree. Additional exam requirements/recommendations for international students: Required—TOEFL (minimum score 100 iBT). Electronic applications accepted. *Faculty research:* Making meaning of literature, teaching of literature, urban adolescent literacy and equity, literacy development and globalization, digital media and literacy.

New York University, Steinhardt School of Culture, Education, and Human Development, Department of Teaching and Learning, Program in Multilingual/Multicultural Studies, New York, NY 10012. Offers bilingual education (MA, PhD, Advanced Certificate); foreign language education (MA); teaching English to speakers of other languages (MA, PhD); teaching foreign languages, 7-12 (MA), including Chinese, French, Italian, Japanese, Spanish; teaching French as a foreign language (MA), including teaching English to speakers of other languages; teaching Spanish as a foreign language (MA), including teaching English to speakers of other languages. MA in teaching English to speakers of other languages also offered in collaboration with NYU Shanghai. *Accreditation:* TEAC. *Program availability:* Part-time, evening/weekend. *Entrance requirements:* For doctorate, GRE General Test, interview; for Advanced

Certificate, master's degree. Additional exam requirements/recommendations for international students: Required—TOEFL (minimum score 100 iBT). Electronic applications accepted. *Faculty research:* Second language acquisition, cross-cultural communication, technology-enhanced language learning, language variation, action learning.

New York University, Steinhardt School of Culture, Education, and Human Development, Department of Teaching and Learning, Program in Social Studies Education, New York, NY 10012. Offers teaching art/social studies 7-12 (MA), including 5-6 extension; teaching social studies 7-12 (MA). *Accreditation:* TEAC. *Program availability:* Part-time, evening/weekend. *Entrance requirements:* Additional exam requirements/recommendations for international students: Required—TOEFL (minimum score 100 iBT). Electronic applications accepted. *Faculty research:* Social studies education reform, ethnography and oral history, civic education, labor history and social studies curriculum, material culture.

Niagara University, Graduate Division of Education, Concentration in Teacher Education, Niagara University, NY 14109. Offers early childhood and childhood education (MS Ed, Certificate); early childhood special education (MS); middle and adolescence education (MS Ed); special education (MS Ed), including 1-6, 7-12; special education (grades 1-12) (Certificate); teaching English to speakers of other languages (MS Ed, Certificate). *Accreditation:* NCATE. *Students:* 106 full-time (75 women), 105 part-time (90 women); includes 15 minority (5 Black or African American, non-Hispanic/Latino; 2 American Indian or Alaska Native, non-Hispanic/Latino; 2 Asian, non-Hispanic/Latino; 2 Hispanic/Latino; 4 Two or more races, non-Hispanic/Latino), 40 international. Average age 28. In 2018, 81 master's, 21 other advanced degrees awarded. *Entrance requirements:* For master's, GRE General Test or Academic Literacy Skills Test (ALST). Additional exam requirements/recommendations for international students: Required—TOEFL (minimum score 550 paper-based; 79 iBT), IELTS (minimum score 6). *Application deadline:* For fall admission, 8/1 for domestic students. Applications are processed on a rolling basis. Electronic applications accepted. *Expenses:* Contact institution. *Financial support:* Research assistantships with tuition reimbursements, teaching assistantships with tuition reimbursements, career-related internships or fieldwork, Federal Work-Study, scholarships/grants, and unspecified assistantships available. Support available to part-time students. Financial award application deadline: 4/15; financial award applicants required to submit FAFSA. *Unit head:* Dr. Chandra Foote, Dean, College of Education, 716-286-8549, E-mail: cjf@niagara.edu. *Application contact:* Evan Pierce, Associate Director, Graduate Studies, 716-286-8327, E-mail: epierce@niagara.edu.
Website: http://www.niagara.edu/teacher-education

Nicholls State University, Graduate Studies, College of Education, Department of Teacher Education, Thibodaux, LA 70310. Offers curriculum and instruction (M Ed); educational leadership (M Ed); elementary education (MAT); human performance education (MAT); middle school education (MAT); secondary education (MAT). *Accreditation:* NCATE. *Program availability:* Part-time, evening/weekend, online learning. *Degree requirements:* For master's, comprehensive exam, portfolio. *Entrance requirements:* For master's, GRE General Test, teaching license. Electronic applications accepted.

Norfolk State University, School of Graduate Studies, School of Education, Department of Secondary Education and School Leadership, Norfolk, VA 23504. Offers principal preparation (MA); secondary education (MAT); urban education/administration (MA), including teaching. *Accreditation:* NCATE. *Program availability:* Part-time. *Entrance requirements:* For master's, GRE General Test, PRAXIS I, minimum GPA of 3.0 in major, 2.5 overall. Additional exam requirements/recommendations for international students: Required—TOEFL (minimum score 500 paper-based).

North Carolina Agricultural and Technical State University, The Graduate College, College of Science and Technology, Department of Mathematics, Greensboro, NC 27411. Offers applied mathematics (MS), including secondary education; mathematics (MAT). *Accreditation:* NCATE (one or more programs are accredited). *Program availability:* Part-time, evening/weekend. *Degree requirements:* For master's, comprehensive exam, thesis or alternative, qualifying exam. *Entrance requirements:* For master's, GRE General Test, minimum GPA of 3.0.

Northeastern Illinois University, College of Graduate Studies and Research, Daniel L. Goodwin College of Education, MAT Program in Secondary Education, Chicago, IL 60625. Offers English language arts (MAT); mathematics (MAT); science (MAT); social science (MAT).

Northeastern Illinois University, College of Graduate Studies and Research, Daniel L. Goodwin College of Education, MSI Program in Language Arts - Secondary Education, Chicago, IL 60625-4699. Offers MSI.

Northern Arizona University, College of Arts and Letters, Department of English, Flagstaff, AZ 86011. Offers applied linguistics (PhD); creative writing (MFA), including creative writing; English (MA), including literature, professional writing, rhetoric, writing, and digital media studies, secondary education; professional writing (Graduate Certificate); rhetoric, writing and digital media studies (Graduate Certificate); teaching English as a second language (MA, Graduate Certificate). *Program availability:* Part-time, 100% online, blended/hybrid learning. *Degree requirements:* For master's, variable foreign language requirement, comprehensive exam (for some programs), thesis (for some programs); for doctorate, variable foreign language requirement, comprehensive exam (for some programs), thesis/dissertation (for some programs); for Graduate Certificate, comprehensive exam (for some programs). *Entrance requirements:* Additional exam requirements/recommendations for international students: Required—TOEFL (minimum score 80 iBT), IELTS (minimum score 6.5). Electronic applications accepted.

Northern Arizona University, College of Education, Department of Teaching and Learning, Flagstaff, AZ 86011. Offers curriculum and instruction (Ed D); early childhood education (M Ed); elementary education (M Ed); secondary education (M Ed). *Program availability:* Part-time, 100% online, blended/hybrid learning. *Degree requirements:* For master's, variable foreign language requirement, comprehensive exam (for some programs), thesis (for some programs); for doctorate, variable foreign language requirement, comprehensive exam (for some programs), thesis/dissertation (for some programs). *Entrance requirements:* Additional exam requirements/recommendations for international students: Required—TOEFL (minimum score 80 iBT), IELTS (minimum score 6.5). Electronic applications accepted.

Northwest Christian University, School of Education and Counseling, Eugene, OR 97401-3745. Offers clinical mental health counseling (MA); elementary teaching (MAT); English for speakers of other languages (MAT); physical education (MAT); school counseling (MA); secondary teaching (MAT); special education (MAT). *Program availability:* Part-time, evening/weekend, online learning. *Degree requirements:* For master's, thesis (for some programs). *Entrance requirements:* For master's, GRE or MAT, minimum undergraduate GPA of 3.0, interview, 2-3 page statement of purpose, two letters of recommendation, resume, background check. Additional exam requirements/recommendations for international students: Required—TOEFL (minimum score 550 paper-based; 80 iBT). Electronic applications accepted. *Expenses:* Contact institution.

Northwestern Oklahoma State University, School of Professional Studies, Program in Secondary Education, Alva, OK 73717-2799. Offers M Ed. *Accreditation:* NCATE. *Program availability:* Part-time. *Degree requirements:* For master's, thesis optional, portfolio. *Entrance requirements:* For master's, GRE General Test or MAT, minimum GPA of 2.75. *Faculty research:* Teacher education, professional school models of pedagogy, competency exams for teachers, teacher accreditation/certification.

Northwestern State University of Louisiana, Graduate Studies and Research, College of Education and Human Development, Program in Secondary Education, Natchitoches, LA 71497. Offers MAT. *Degree requirements:* For master's, comprehensive exam, thesis or alternative. *Entrance requirements:* For master's, GRE General Test, minimum undergraduate GPA of 2.5. Additional exam requirements/recommendations for international students: Required—TOEFL. Electronic applications accepted.

Northwestern State University of Louisiana, Graduate Studies and Research, College of Education and Human Development, Programs in Educational Leadership and Instruction, Natchitoches, LA 71497. Offers counseling (Ed S); educational leadership (M Ed, Ed S); educational technology (Ed S); elementary teaching (Ed S); reading (Ed S); secondary teaching (Ed S); special education (Ed S). *Accreditation:* NASAD. *Degree requirements:* For master's, comprehensive exam, thesis (for some programs). *Entrance requirements:* For master's and Ed S, GRE General Test. Additional exam requirements/recommendations for international students: Required—TOEFL. Electronic applications accepted.

Northwestern University, The Graduate School, School of Education and Social Policy, Education and Social Policy Program, Evanston, IL 60035. Offers elementary teaching (MS); secondary teaching (MS); teacher leadership (MS). *Program availability:* Part-time, evening/weekend. *Degree requirements:* For master's, research project. *Entrance requirements:* For master's, GRE General Test, Illinois State Board of Education Basic Skills Exam (secondary and elementary), bachelor's degree. Additional exam requirements/recommendations for international students: Recommended—TOEFL. Electronic applications accepted. *Faculty research:* Cultural context and literacy, philosophy of education and interpretive discussion, productivity, enhancing research and teaching, motivation, new and junior faculty issues, professional development for K-12 teachers to improve math and science teaching, female/underrepresented students/faculty in STEM disciplines.

Oakland City University, School of Education, Oakland City, IN 47660-1099. Offers building level administration (MS Ed); curriculum and instruction (MS Ed, Ed D); education (MS Ed); elementary education (MAT); organizational management (Ed D); secondary education (MAT); superintendency (Ed D). *Accreditation:* NCATE. Terminal master's awarded for partial completion of doctoral program. *Degree requirements:* For master's, thesis; for doctorate, comprehensive exam, thesis/dissertation. *Entrance requirements:* For master's, MAT, minimum GPA of 3.0, interview, resume, letters of recommendation; for doctorate, MAT, GRE, minimum GPA of 3.2, interview, resume, letters of recommendation. *Expenses:* Contact institution. *Faculty research:* Assessment, cultural diversity, teacher education, education leadership.

Oakland University, Graduate Study and Lifelong Learning, School of Education and Human Services, Department of Teacher Development and Educational Studies, Rochester, MI 48309-4401. Offers educational studies (M Ed); elementary education (MAT); secondary education (MAT); teaching and learning (Graduate Certificate). *Entrance requirements:* For master's, minimum GPA of 3.0. Electronic applications accepted.

Ohio University, Graduate College, Gladys W. and David H. Patton College of Education and Human Services, Department of Teacher Education, Athens, OH 45701-2979. Offers adolescent to young adult education (M Ed); curriculum and instruction (M Ed, PhD); early childhood/special education (M Ed); intervention specialist/mild-moderate needs (M Ed); intervention specialist/moderate-intensive needs (M Ed); middle childhood education (M Ed); reading education (M Ed). *Program availability:* Part-time, evening/weekend. *Degree requirements:* For master's, thesis or alternative; for doctorate, comprehensive exam, thesis/dissertation. *Entrance requirements:* For master's, GRE General Test or MAT (if GPA is below 2.9); for doctorate, GRE General Test, minimum GPA of 3.4, work experience. Additional exam requirements/recommendations for international students: Required—TOEFL (minimum score 550 paper-based; 80 iBT) or IELTS (minimum score 6.5). Electronic applications accepted. *Faculty research:* Cognition literacy, character education, teacher's education reform, disabilities.

Old Dominion University, Darden College of Education, Programs in Secondary Education, Norfolk, VA 23529. Offers chemistry (MS Ed); English (MS Ed); secondary education (MS Ed). *Accreditation:* NCATE. *Program availability:* Part-time, evening/weekend, online learning. *Degree requirements:* For master's, comprehensive exam, thesis. *Entrance requirements:* For master's, GRE General Test or MAT, PRAXIS I (for licensure), minimum GPA of 2.8, teaching certificate. Additional exam requirements/recommendations for international students: Required—TOEFL. Electronic applications accepted. *Faculty research:* Use of technology, writing project for teachers, geography teaching, reading.

Olivet Nazarene University, Graduate School, Division of Education, Program in Secondary Education, Bourbonnais, IL 60914. Offers MAT. *Accreditation:* NCATE. *Program availability:* Evening/weekend. *Degree requirements:* For master's, thesis or alternative.

Pacific Union College, Education Department, Angwin, CA 94508-9707. Offers education (M Ed); elementary teaching (MAT); secondary teaching (MAT). *Program availability:* Part-time. *Faculty:* 3 full-time (1 woman), 1 (woman) part-time/adjunct. *Students:* 3 full-time (2 women). Average age 20. 4 applicants, 100% accepted, 4 enrolled. In 2018, 1 master's awarded. *Degree requirements:* For master's, thesis, action research project, field experiences. *Entrance requirements:* For master's, GRE General Test, two interviews, teaching credential, letters of recommendation, essay. *Application deadline:* For fall admission, 8/30 for domestic and international students; for summer admission, 6/1 for domestic and international students. Applications are processed on a rolling basis. Application fee: $0. *Expenses:* Contact institution. *Financial support:* Scholarships/grants available. Support available to part-time students. Financial award application deadline: 9/25. *Unit head:* Dr. Jean Buller, Department Chair, 707-965-7266, Fax: 707-965-6645, E-mail: jbuller@puc.edu. *Application contact:* Sarah Gitter, Credential Analyst, 707-965-6643, Fax: 707-965-6645, E-mail: teachingcredentials@puc.edu.
Website: http://www.puc.edu/academics/departments/education/

Pacific University, College of Education, Forest Grove, OR 97116-1797. Offers early childhood education (MAT); education (MAE); elementary education (MAT); ESOL (MAT); high school education (MAT); middle school education (MAT); special education (MAT); speech-language pathology (MS); STEM education (MAT); talented and gifted (M Ed); visual function in learning (M Ed). *Accreditation:* ASHA; NCATE. *Program availability:* Part-time, evening/weekend. *Degree requirements:* For master's, research project. *Entrance requirements:* For master's, California Basic Educational Skills Test, PRAXIS II, minimum undergraduate GPA of 2.75, 3.0 graduate. Additional exam requirements/recommendations for international students: Required—TOEFL.

Electronic applications accepted. *Expenses:* Contact institution. *Faculty research:* Defining a culturally competent classroom, technology in the K-12 classroom, Socratic seminars, social studies education.

Piedmont College, School of Education, Demorest, GA 30535. Offers art education (MAT); curriculum and instruction (Ed D, Ed S); early childhood education (MA, MAT); middle grades education (MA, MAT); music education (MAT); secondary education (MA, MAT); special education (MA, MAT). *Program availability:* Part-time, evening/weekend. *Students:* 496 full-time (416 women), 650 part-time (560 women); includes 185 minority (137 Black or African American, non-Hispanic/Latino; 2 American Indian or Alaska Native, non-Hispanic/Latino; 13 Asian, non-Hispanic/Latino; 31 Hispanic/Latino; 1 Native Hawaiian or other Pacific Islander, non-Hispanic/Latino; 1 Two or more races, non-Hispanic/Latino). Average age 37. 483 applicants, 89% accepted, 372 enrolled. In 2018, 275 master's, 10 doctorates, 229 other advanced degrees awarded. *Degree requirements:* For master's, thesis, field experience in the classroom teaching; for doctorate, thesis/dissertation. *Entrance requirements:* For master's, GRE General Test, MAT; for Ed S, minimum graduate GPA of 3.5, valid teaching certificate. Additional exam requirements/recommendations for international students: Required—TOEFL (minimum score 550 paper-based). *Application deadline:* For fall admission, 7/15 for domestic students; for spring admission, 12/1 for domestic students. Applications are processed on a rolling basis. Electronic applications accepted. *Expenses: Tuition:* Full-time $9738; part-time $541 per credit. *Required fees:* $200 per semester. *Financial support:* Career-related internships or fieldwork, Federal Work-Study, and unspecified assistantships available. Support available to part-time students. Financial award applicants required to submit FAFSA. *Unit head:* Dr. R.D. Nordgren, Dean, 706-778-3000 Ext. 1201, Fax: 706-776-9608, E-mail: rdnordgren@piedmont.edu. *Application contact:* Kathleen Carter, Director of Graduate Enrollment Management, 706-778-8500 Ext. 1181, Fax: 706-778-0150, E-mail: kanderson@piedmont.edu.

Pittsburg State University, Graduate School, College of Education, Department of Teaching and Leadership, Pittsburg, KS 66762. Offers autism spectrum disorder (Certificate); district level (Certificate); education (MS), including school health; educational leadership (MS); educational technology (MS); general school administration (Ed S), including advanced studies in leadership; secondary education (MAT); special education (MAT, MS), including special education teaching (MS); teaching (MS); TESOL (Certificate). *Program availability:* Part-time, online only, 100% online, blended/hybrid learning. Terminal master's awarded for partial completion of doctoral program. *Degree requirements:* For master's and other advanced degree, thesis or alternative. *Entrance requirements:* For master's, PPST. Additional exam requirements/recommendations for international students: Required—TOEFL (minimum score 520 paper-based; 68 iBT), IELTS (minimum score 6), PTE (minimum score 47). Electronic applications accepted. *Expenses:* Contact institution. *Faculty research:* Special education, autism spectrum disorder, reading, educational technology, leadership.

Point Park University, School of Arts and Sciences, Department of Education, Pittsburgh, PA 15222-1984. Offers adult learning and training (MA); athletic coaching (M Ed); curriculum and instruction (MA); educational administration (MA); leadership and administration (Ed D); secondary education (M Ed); special education grades 7-12 (M Ed); special education PreK-grade 8 (M Ed). *Program availability:* Part-time, evening/weekend, 100% online, blended/hybrid learning. *Degree requirements:* For master's, comprehensive exam (for some programs), thesis or alternative. *Entrance requirements:* For master's, minimum GPA of 3.0, resume, 2 letters of recommendation. Additional exam requirements/recommendations for international students: Required—TOEFL. Electronic applications accepted.

Prescott College, Graduate Programs, Program in Education, Prescott, AZ 86301. Offers early childhood education (MA); early childhood special education (MA); education (MA); elementary education (MA); environmental education leadership and administration (MA); equine-assisted learning (MA); school guidance counseling (MA); secondary education (MA); special education: learning disabilities (MA); special education: mental retardation (MA); special education: serious emotional disabilities (MA); student-directed independent study (MA); sustainability education (PhD). *Program availability:* Part-time, online learning. *Degree requirements:* For master's, thesis, fieldwork or internship, practicum; for doctorate, thesis/dissertation. *Entrance requirements:* For master's, 2 letters of recommendation, resume; for doctorate, 3 letters of recommendation, resume, official transcripts, personal statement, program proposal. Additional exam requirements/recommendations for international students: Required—TOEFL (minimum score 500 paper-based). Electronic applications accepted.

Providence College, Program in Special Education, Providence, RI 02918. Offers special education (M Ed), including elementary teaching, secondary teaching. *Program availability:* Part-time, evening/weekend. *Degree requirements:* For master's, comprehensive exam, portfolio. *Entrance requirements:* Additional exam requirements/recommendations for international students: Required—TOEFL (minimum score 577 paper-based; 90 iBT).

Providence College, Programs in Administration, Providence, RI 02918. Offers elementary administration (M Ed); secondary administration (M Ed). *Program availability:* Part-time, evening/weekend. *Degree requirements:* For master's, comprehensive exam, portfolio. *Entrance requirements:* Additional exam requirements/recommendations for international students: Required—TOEFL (minimum score 577 paper-based; 90 iBT).

Providence College, Providence Alliance for Catholic Teachers (PACT) Program, Providence, RI 02918. Offers secondary education (M Ed). *Entrance requirements:* For master's, GRE/MAT/PRAXIS. Additional exam requirements/recommendations for international students: Required—TOEFL (minimum score 550 paper-based; 90 iBT).

Purdue University Fort Wayne, College of Professional Studies, School of Education, Fort Wayne, IN 46805-1499. Offers couple and family counseling (MS Ed); educational leadership (MS Ed); elementary education (MS Ed); school counseling (MS Ed); secondary education (MS Ed); special education (MS Ed, Certificate). *Accreditation:* NCATE. *Program availability:* Part-time. *Entrance requirements:* For master's, minimum GPA of 2.5, three professional letters of recommendation. Additional exam requirements/recommendations for international students: Required—TOEFL (minimum score 550 paper-based; 79 iBT). *Faculty research:* International faculty, gender in Burmese refugee narratives, planning effective instruction.

Purdue University Global, School of Teacher Education, Davenport, IA 52807. Offers education (M Ed); secondary education (M Ed); teaching and learning (MA); teaching literacy and language: grades 6-12 (MA); teaching literacy and language: grades K-6 (MA); teaching mathematics: grades 6-8 (MA); teaching mathematics: grades 9-12 (MA); teaching mathematics: grades K-5 (MA); teaching science: grades 6-12 (MA); teaching science: grades K-6 (MA); teaching students with special needs (MA); teaching with technology (MA). *Program availability:* Part-time, evening/weekend, online learning. *Entrance requirements:* Additional exam requirements/recommendations for international students: Required—TOEFL (minimum score 550 paper-based; 80 iBT).

Queens College of the City University of New York, Division of Education, Department of Secondary Education and Youth Services, Queens, NY 11367-1597. Offers adolescent biology (MAT); art (MS Ed); biology (MS Ed, AC); chemistry (MS Ed, AC); earth sciences (MS Ed, AC); English (MS Ed, AC); French (MS Ed); Italian (MS Ed, AC); literacy education (MS Ed); mathematics (MS Ed, AC); music (MS Ed, AC); physics (MS Ed, AC); social studies (MS Ed, AC); Spanish (MS Ed, AC). *Program availability:* Part-time, evening/weekend. *Faculty:* 22 full-time (14 women), 35 part-time/adjunct (24 women). *Students:* 33 full-time (19 women), 358 part-time (228 women); includes 182 minority (15 Black or African American, non-Hispanic/Latino; 62 Asian, non-Hispanic/Latino; 91 Hispanic/Latino; 4 Native Hawaiian or other Pacific Islander, non-Hispanic/Latino; 10 Two or more races, non-Hispanic/Latino), 13 international. Average age 29. 216 applicants, 74% accepted, 109 enrolled. In 2018, 108 master's, 35 other advanced degrees awarded. *Degree requirements:* For master's, research project. *Entrance requirements:* For master's, GRE, minimum GPA of 3.0. Additional exam requirements/recommendations for international students: Required—TOEFL, IELTS. *Application deadline:* For fall admission, 4/1 for domestic students; for spring admission, 11/1 for domestic students. Applications are processed on a rolling basis. Application fee: $125. Electronic applications accepted. *Financial support:* Career-related internships or fieldwork available. Financial award application deadline: 4/1; financial award applicants required to submit FAFSA. *Faculty research:* Self regulated learning, teacher learning, assessment and teaching, language diversity, teaching and learning history. *Unit head:* Dr. Eleanor Armour-Thomas, Chairperson, 718-997-5150, E-mail: eleanor.armour-thomas@qc.cuny.edu. *Application contact:* Elizabeth D'Amico-Ramirez, Assistant Director of Graduate Admissions, 718-997-5203, E-mail: elizabeth.damicoramirez@qc.cuny.edu.

Quinnipiac University, School of Education, Program in Secondary Education, Hamden, CT 06518-1940. Offers biology (MAT); English (MAT); history (MAT); mathematics (MAT); Spanish (MAT). *Accreditation:* NCATE. *Entrance requirements:* For master's, PRAXIS I or PRAXIS Core Academic Skills Exam, minimum GPA of 3.0, interview. Electronic applications accepted. *Faculty research:* Multicultural and urban education/leadership, challenges of teaching diverse learners, scholarship of teaching and learning, technology and teaching, humor and education.

Regis University, College of Contemporary Liberal Studies, Denver, CO 80221-1099. Offers creative writing (MFA); criminology (M Sc); curriculum, instruction and assessment (M Ed); education - teacher leadership (M Ed); educational leadership (M Ed); elementary education (M Ed); literacy (Certificate); reading (M Ed); secondary education (M Ed); special education (M Ed); teacher academic leadership (Certificate); teacher leadership (MA); teacher/educational leadership (M Ed); teaching the linguistically diverse (M Ed). *Program availability:* Part-time, evening/weekend, 100% online, blended/hybrid learning. *Degree requirements:* For master's, thesis (for some programs). *Entrance requirements:* For master's, official transcript reflecting baccalaureate degree awarded from regionally-accredited college or university, work experience, resume, letters of recommendation. Additional exam requirements/recommendations for international students: Required—TOEFL (minimum score 550 paper-based; 82 iBT). Electronic applications accepted. *Expenses:* Contact institution.

Rhode Island College, School of Graduate Studies, Feinstein School of Education and Human Development, Department of Educational Studies, Providence, RI 02908-1991. Offers advanced studies in teaching and learning (M Ed); English (MAT); French (MAT); history (MAT); math (MAT); secondary education (MAT); Spanish (MAT); teaching English as a second language (M Ed). *Accreditation:* NCATE. *Program availability:* Part-time, evening/weekend. *Faculty:* 12 full-time (9 women), 7 part-time/adjunct (6 women). *Students:* 12 full-time (10 women), 31 part-time (28 women); includes 5 minority (1 Black or African American, non-Hispanic/Latino; 1 Asian, non-Hispanic/Latino; 3 Hispanic/Latino). Average age 33. In 2018, 24 master's awarded. *Degree requirements:* For master's, capstone or comprehensive assessment. *Entrance requirements:* For master's, GRE or MAT (for most programs), minimum undergraduate GPA of 3.0; baccalaureate degree in English, French, history, math or Spanish; 3 letters of recommendation; interview. Additional exam requirements/recommendations for international students: Required—TOEFL (minimum score 550 paper-based; 80 iBT). *Application deadline:* For fall admission, 3/1 for domestic students; for spring admission, 11/1 for domestic students. Applications are processed on a rolling basis. Application fee: $50. Electronic applications accepted. *Expenses: Tuition, area resident:* Part-time $407 per credit. Tuition, nonresident: part-time $792 per credit. *Required fees:* $29 per credit. $100 per semester. *Financial support:* Teaching assistantships, career-related internships or fieldwork, Federal Work-Study, scholarships/grants, health care benefits, and unspecified assistantships available. Support available to part-time students. Financial award application deadline: 5/15; financial award applicants required to submit FAFSA. *Unit head:* Dr. Leslie Bogad, Chair, 401-456-8170. *Application contact:* Dr. Leslie Bogad, Chair, 401-456-8170.
Website: http://www.ric.edu/educationalStudies/Pages/default.aspx

Rider University, College of Education and Human Services, Program in Teaching, Lawrenceville, NJ 08648-3001. Offers bilingual education (MAT); early childhood education (MAT); elementary education (MAT); English as a second language (MAT); secondary education (MAT); world language (MAT). *Students:* 35 full-time (26 women), 88 part-time (67 women); includes 12 minority (1 Black or African American, non-Hispanic/Latino; 1 American Indian or Alaska Native, non-Hispanic/Latino; 2 Asian, non-Hispanic/Latino; 8 Hispanic/Latino). Average age 34. 104 applicants, 67% accepted, 54 enrolled. In 2018, 70 master's awarded. *Entrance requirements:* For master's, Praxis exams, resume, application fee, statement of aims and objectives, official prior college transcripts, interview. Additional exam requirements/recommendations for international students: Required—TOEFL (minimum score 540 paper-based; 79 iBT). *Application deadline:* For fall admission, 5/1 priority date for domestic students, 6/1 priority date for international students; for spring admission, 12/1 priority date for domestic students, 11/1 priority date for international students. Applications are processed on a rolling basis. Application fee: $50. Electronic applications accepted. *Expenses: Tuition:* Full-time $850; part-time $850 per credit hour. *Required fees:* $50; $50 per course. Tuition and fees vary according to program. *Financial support:* Applicants required to submit FAFSA. *Unit head:* Kathleen Pierce, Professor, 609-895-5478, E-mail: kpierce@rider.edu. *Application contact:* Jamie L Mitchell, Director of Graduate Admissions, 609-896-5036, Fax: 609-895-5680, E-mail: jmitchell@rider.edu.

Roberts Wesleyan College, Graduate Teacher Education Programs, Rochester, NY 14624-1997. Offers adolescence and special education (M Ed); childhood and special education (M Ed); literacy education (M Ed); special education (M Ed). *Program availability:* Part-time, evening/weekend. *Degree requirements:* For master's, thesis. Electronic applications accepted.

Rochester Institute of Technology, Graduate Enrollment Services, National Technical Institute for the Deaf, Research and Teacher Education Department, MS Program in Secondary Education for the Deaf and Hard of Hearing, Rochester, NY 14623-5603. Offers MS. *Program availability:* Part-time, evening/weekend, blended/hybrid learning. *Students:* 17 full-time (12 women); includes 2 minority (1 Asian, non-Hispanic/Latino; 1 Hispanic/Latino), 5 international. Average age 27. 13 applicants, 54% accepted, 7 enrolled. In 2018, 11 master's awarded. *Degree requirements:* For master's, Student Teaching and Professional Portfolio. *Entrance requirements:* For master's, GRE required for students with a GPA below 3.25, minimum cumulative GPA of 2.8, expository essay, interview, two letters of recommendation, Sign Language Self-Assessment. *Application deadline:* For fall admission, 6/1 priority date for domestic and

international students. Applications are processed on a rolling basis. Application fee: $65. Electronic applications accepted. *Financial support:* Fellowships with partial tuition reimbursements, research assistantships with partial tuition reimbursements, teaching assistantships with partial tuition reimbursements, career-related internships or fieldwork, scholarships/grants, and unspecified assistantships available. Support available to part-time students. Financial award applicants required to submit FAFSA. *Faculty research:* Effective use of technology and online learning in teaching deaf students; strategies for inclusive instruction/deaf students with other disabilities; effective literacy instruction strategies for DHH readers; single case experimental design methods; STEM language, literacy and learning; deaf studies; international deaf education; stereotype threat effects on mathematical performance. *Unit head:* Dr. Gerald C. Bateman, Director, 585-475-6480, E-mail: gcbnmp@rit.edu. *Application contact:* Diane Ellison, Senior Associate Vice President, Graduate Enrollment Services, 585-475-2229, Fax: 585-475-7164, E-mail: gradinfo@rit.edu.
Website: https://www.rit.edu/study/secondary-education-students-who-are-deaf-or-hard-hearing-ms

Rockford University, Graduate Studies, Department of Education, Program in Secondary Education, Rockford, IL 61108-2393. Offers MAT. *Program availability:* Part-time, evening/weekend. *Degree requirements:* For master's, thesis optional. *Entrance requirements:* For master's, GRE General Test, basic skills test (for students seeking certification), 3 letters of recommendation. Additional exam requirements/recommendations for international students: Required—TOEFL (minimum score 550 paper-based; 79 iBT). Electronic applications accepted.

Roosevelt University, Graduate Division, College of Education, Program in Secondary Education, Chicago, IL 60605. Offers MA. Electronic applications accepted.

St. Bonaventure University, School of Graduate School, School of Education, Literacy Programs, St. Bonaventure, NY 14778-2284. Offers adolescent literacy 5-12 (MS Ed); childhood literacy B-6 (MS Ed). *Accreditation:* NCATE. *Program availability:* Part-time, evening/weekend. *Faculty:* 1 (woman) full-time, 1 part-time/adjunct. *Students:* 9 full-time (all women), 2 part-time (1 woman); all minorities (all Black or African American, non-Hispanic/Latino). Average age 22. 10 applicants, 100% accepted. In 2018, 12 master's awarded. *Degree requirements:* For master's, comprehensive exam, thesis optional, minimum cumulative GPA of 3.0, clinical practicum, literacy coaching internship, electronic portfolio. *Entrance requirements:* For master's, GRE or MAT, teaching certificate in matching area in-hand or pending, transcripts from all previous colleges, minimum GPA of 3.0, 2 references, interview, writing sample. Additional exam requirements/recommendations for international students: Required—TOEFL (minimum score 550 paper-based; 80 iBT). *Application deadline:* For fall admission, 3/15 priority date for domestic students, 2/1 for international students; for spring admission, 10/15 priority date for domestic students, 7/1 for international students. Applications are processed on a rolling basis. Application fee: $0. Electronic applications accepted. *Financial support:* Scholarships/grants, health care benefits, and unspecified assistantships available. Financial award application deadline: 4/15; financial award applicants required to submit FAFSA. *Unit head:* Dr. Sheri Voss, Director, 716-375-2368, Fax: 716-375-2360, E-mail: svoss@sbu.edu. *Application contact:* Matthew Retchless, Director of Graduate Admissions, 716-375-2021, Fax: 716-375-4015, E-mail: gradsch@sbu.edu.
Website: http://www.sbu.edu/academics/schools/education/graduate-degrees-certificates/msed-in-childhood-literacy

St. John's University, The School of Education, Department of Curriculum and Instruction, Program in Adolescent Education, Queens, NY 11439. Offers MS Ed. *Program availability:* Part-time, online learning. *Degree requirements:* For master's, thesis. *Entrance requirements:* For master's, GRE, MAT, or PRAXIS, statement of goals (personal essay), official undergraduate transcripts, initial teaching certification. Additional exam requirements/recommendations for international students: Required—TOEFL, IELTS. Electronic applications accepted. *Faculty research:* Digital and nondigital literacies; youth participatory action research; young adolescents' learning; self-efficacy in literacy learning; using problem solving as an approach for math learning.

Saint Joseph's University, College of Arts and Sciences, Graduate Programs in Education, Philadelphia, PA 19131-1395. Offers curriculum supervisor (Certificate); educational leadership (MS, Ed D); elementary education (MS, Certificate); elementary/middle school education (Certificate); organizational development and leadership (MS); principal (Certificate); professional education (MS); reading specialist (MS, Certificate); reading supervisor (Certificate); secondary education (MS, Certificate); special education (MS); special education 7-12 (Certificate); special education PK-8 (Certificate); superintendent's letter of eligibility (Certificate); supervisor of special education (Certificate); teacher of the deaf and hard of hearing (Certificate). *Program availability:* Part-time, evening/weekend, blended/hybrid learning. *Degree requirements:* For master's, thesis or alternative; for doctorate, comprehensive exam, thesis/dissertation. *Entrance requirements:* For master's, 2 letters of recommendation, minimum GPA of 3.0, official transcripts, personal statement; for doctorate, GRE, master's degree from accredited institution, minimum graduate GPA of 3.5, computer competence, interview with program director. Additional exam requirements/recommendations for international students: Required—TOEFL (minimum score 550 paper-based; 80 iBT), IELTS (minimum score 6.5), PTE (minimum score 60). Electronic applications accepted. *Expenses:* Contact institution. *Faculty research:* Factors predicting early mathematics skills for low income children, early child care and development, preschool quality, parent communication and home-school collaboration issues, education of terminally ill children, preparing literacy teachers for urban schools.

Saint Mary's University of Minnesota, Schools of Graduate and Professional Programs, Graduate School of Education, Teaching Program, Winona, MN 55987-1399. Offers MA. *Unit head:* Delores Roethke, Director, 612-238-4511, E-mail: droethke@smumn.edu. *Application contact:* Laurie Roy, Director of Admission of Schools of Graduate and Professional Programs, 507-457-8606, Fax: 612-728-5121, E-mail: lroy@smumn.edu.
Website: http://www.smumn.edu/graduate-home/areas-of-study/graduate-school-of-education/ma-in-instruction

Saint Peter's University, Graduate Programs in Education, Program in Teaching, Jersey City, NJ 07306-5997. Offers 6-8 middle school education (MA Ed, Certificate); K-12 secondary education (MA Ed, Certificate); K-5 elementary education (MA Ed, Certificate). *Program availability:* Part-time, evening/weekend. *Degree requirements:* For master's, comprehensive exam. *Entrance requirements:* For master's, GRE or MAT. Additional exam requirements/recommendations for international students: Required—TOEFL. Electronic applications accepted.

St. Thomas Aquinas College, Division of Teacher Education, Sparkill, NY 10976. Offers adolescence education (MST); childhood and special education (MST); childhood education (MST); educational leadership (MS Ed); reading (MS Ed, PMC); special education (MS Ed, PMC); teaching (MS Ed), including elementary education, middle school education, secondary education. *Accreditation:* NCATE. *Program availability:* Part-time, evening/weekend. *Degree requirements:* For master's, comprehensive exam, comprehensive professional portfolio; for PMC, action research project. *Entrance requirements:* For master's, New York State Qualifying Exam, GRE General Test or minimum GPA of 3.0, teaching certificate; for PMC, GRE General Test or minimum GPA of 3.0. Electronic applications accepted. *Faculty research:* Computer applications in education, adolescent special education students, literacy development, inclusive practices for special education students.

Saint Xavier University, Graduate Studies, School of Education, Chicago, IL 60655-3105. Offers counseling (MA); curriculum and instruction (MA); early childhood education (MA); educational administration (MA); elementary education (MA); individualized studies (MA), including educational technology, English as a second language (ESL), ISTEM (integrative science, technology, engineering, and math), science education; music education (MA); reading (MA); secondary education (MA); Spanish education (MA); special education (MA); teaching and leadership (MA). *Accreditation:* NCATE. *Program availability:* Part-time, evening/weekend. *Degree requirements:* For master's, thesis or project. *Entrance requirements:* For master's, minimum GPA of 3.0. *Expenses:* Contact institution.

Salem College, Graduate Studies, Winston-Salem, NC 27101. Offers art education (MAT); elementary education (M Ed, MAT); language and literacy (M Ed); middle school education (MAT); organ (MM); piano (MM); school counseling (M Ed); second language studies (MAT); secondary education (MAT); special education (M Ed, MAT). *Accreditation:* NCATE. *Program availability:* Part-time, evening/weekend, online learning. *Degree requirements:* For master's, practicum (MAT), action research project (M Ed). *Entrance requirements:* For master's, minimum GPA of 3.0, two academic/professional recommendations, acceptable criminal background check. Additional exam requirements/recommendations for international students: Recommended—TOEFL. Electronic applications accepted. *Faculty research:* Teacher professional development, adolescent literacy, instructional technology.

Salem State University, School of Graduate Studies, Program in Secondary Education, Salem, MA 01970-5353. Offers M Ed. *Program availability:* Part-time, evening/weekend. *Entrance requirements:* For master's, GRE or MAT. Additional exam requirements/recommendations for international students: Required—TOEFL (minimum score 550 paper-based; 80 iBT) or IELTS (minimum score 5.5).

Salem State University, School of Graduate Studies, Program in Spanish, Salem, MA 01970-5353. Offers MAT. *Program availability:* Part-time, evening/weekend. *Entrance requirements:* For master's, GRE or MAT. Additional exam requirements/recommendations for international students: Required—TOEFL (minimum score 550 paper-based; 80 iBT) or IELTS (minimum score 5.5).

Salisbury University, Program in Mathematics Education, Salisbury, MD 21801-6837. Offers mathematics (MSME), including high school, middle school. *Program availability:* Part-time. *Faculty:* 2 full-time (1 woman). *Students:* 1 (woman) full-time, 11 part-time (10 women). Average age 26. 7 applicants, 100% accepted, 6 enrolled. In 2018, 1 master's awarded. *Degree requirements:* For master's, capstone experience. *Entrance requirements:* For master's, transcripts from colleges and universities attended; personal statement; two letters of recommendation. Additional exam requirements/recommendations for international students: Required—TOEFL (minimum score 550 paper-based; 79 iBT), IELTS (minimum score 6.5). *Application deadline:* For fall admission, 8/15 priority date for domestic and international students; for spring admission, 10/1 priority date for domestic and international students. Applications are processed on a rolling basis. Application fee: $65. Electronic applications accepted. *Expenses:* Resident - $412 per credit hour; Non-resident - $746 per credit hour; Fees - $108. *Financial support:* In 2018–19, 1 teaching assistantship with full tuition reimbursement (averaging $8,000 per year) was awarded; career-related internships or fieldwork and scholarships/grants also available. Support available to part-time students. Financial award application deadline: 3/1; financial award applicants required to submit FAFSA. *Faculty research:* Multiplicative reasoning of children; the mathematics of games; probabilistic reasoning of middle grade children; fractional reasoning of children; pre-service teacher education. *Unit head:* Dr. Jennifer Bergner, Graduate Program Director, 410-677-5429, E-mail: jabergner@salisbury.edu. *Application contact:* Dr. Jennifer Bergner, Graduate Program Director, 410-677-5429, E-mail: jabergner@salisbury.edu.
Website: https://www.salisbury.edu/explore-academics/programs/graduate-degree-programs/mathematics-education-masters/

Salisbury University, Program in Teaching, Salisbury, MD 21801-6837. Offers secondary education (MAT). *Program availability:* Part-time, evening/weekend. *Faculty:* 5 full-time (3 women). *Students:* 5 full-time (4 women), 3 part-time (all women). Average age 30. 2 applicants, 100% accepted, 2 enrolled. In 2018, 5 master's awarded. *Degree requirements:* For master's, comprehensive exam. *Entrance requirements:* For master's, PRAXIS or SAT/GRE/ACT, transcripts from all institutions attended; undergraduate degree in specified area; minimum cumulative GPA of 3.0; three letters of recommendation; structured interview. Additional exam requirements/recommendations for international students: Required—TOEFL (minimum score 550 paper-based; 79 iBT), IELTS (minimum score 6.5). *Application deadline:* For winter admission, 10/1 priority date for domestic and international students. Application fee: $65. Electronic applications accepted. *Expenses:* Residents - $412 per credit hour; Non-Residents - $746 per credit hour; Fees - $108. *Financial support:* In 2018–19, 4 students received support, including 2 teaching assistantships with full tuition reimbursements available (averaging $8,000 per year); career-related internships or fieldwork and scholarships/grants also available. Support available to part-time students. Financial award application deadline: 3/1; financial award applicants required to submit FAFSA. *Faculty research:* Social studies education; science education; mathematics education; classroom management; inclusive education. *Unit head:* Dr. Alexander Pope, IV, Graduate Program Director, 410-543-6391, E-mail: axpope@salisbury.edu. *Application contact:* Claire Williams, Program Management Specialist, 410-677-0001, E-mail: clwilliams@salisbury.edu.
Website: https://www.salisbury.edu/explore-academics/programs/graduate-degree-programs/teaching-masters/

Samford University, Orlean Beeson School of Education, Birmingham, AL 35229. Offers educational leadership (MSE, Ed D); elementary education (MS Ed, MSE); gifted (MSE); instructional design and technology (MSE); instructional leadership (MSE, Ed S); secondary education (MSE); special education (MSE). *Accreditation:* NCATE. *Program availability:* Part-time, evening/weekend, 100% online, blended/hybrid learning. *Faculty:* 12 full-time (10 women), 16 part-time/adjunct (11 women). *Students:* 156 full-time (111 women), 101 part-time (73 women); includes 106 minority (100 Black or African American, non-Hispanic/Latino; 1 American Indian or Alaska Native, non-Hispanic/Latino; 5 Two or more races, non-Hispanic/Latino), 1 international. Average age 37. 107 applicants, 94% accepted, 65 enrolled. In 2018, 94 master's, 40 doctorates, 11 other advanced degrees awarded. *Degree requirements:* For master's and Ed S, comprehensive exam; for doctorate, comprehensive exam, thesis/dissertation. *Entrance requirements:* For master's, GRE, MAT, PRAXIS II, interview, transcripts, essay, recommendations, teaching certificate; for doctorate, resume, transcripts, interview, essay, recommendations; for Ed S, teaching certification, transcripts, essay, interview, recommendations. Additional exam requirements/recommendations for international students: Required—TOEFL (minimum score 90 iBT); Recommended—IELTS (minimum score 6.5). *Application deadline:* For fall admission, 7/15 for domestic and international students; for winter admission, 11/15 for domestic and international

students; for spring admission, 11/15 for domestic and international students; for summer admission, 4/15 for domestic and international students. Applications are processed on a rolling basis. Application fee: $35. Electronic applications accepted. *Expenses:* $862 Per Hour $100 School of Education $175 Technology Fee $100 Per Fully Online Class. *Financial support:* In 2018–19, 173 students received support. Scholarships/grants available. Financial award application deadline: 2/15; financial award applicants required to submit FAFSA. *Faculty research:* Principal leadership's and teacher organizational commitment mentoring, professional development, and middle grades leadership coaching and administrator effectiveness character development programs in schools teacher efficacy related STEM and professional growth. *Unit head:* Dr. Howard Finch, Interim Dean, 205-726-2745, E-mail: hfinch@samford.edu. *Application contact:* Brooke Karr, Graduate Admissions Office Coordinator, 205-729-2783, E-mail: kbgilrea@samford.edu.
Website: http://www.samford.edu/education

San Diego State University, Graduate and Research Affairs, College of Education, School of Teacher Education, Program in Secondary Curriculum and Instruction, San Diego, CA 92182. Offers MA. *Accreditation:* NCATE. *Entrance requirements:* For master's, GRE General Test, letters of reference. Additional exam requirements/recommendations for international students: Required—TOEFL. Electronic applications accepted.

San Francisco State University, Division of Graduate Studies, College of Education, Department of Secondary Education, San Francisco, CA 94132-1722. Offers mathematics education (MA); secondary education (MA, Credential). *Accreditation:* NCATE. *Unit head:* Dr. Maika Watanabe, Chair, 415-338-1622, Fax: 415-338-0914, E-mail: watanabe@sfsu.edu. *Application contact:* Marisol Del Rio, Administrative Office Coordinator, 415-338-7649, Fax: 415-338-0914, E-mail: seced@sfsu.edu.
Website: http://secondaryed.sfsu.edu/

Seattle Pacific University, Master of Arts in Teaching Program, Seattle, WA 98119-1997. Offers MAT. *Accreditation:* NCATE. *Program availability:* Part-time, evening/weekend. *Students:* 56 full-time (35 women), 59 part-time (43 women); includes 20 minority (1 American Indian or Alaska Native, non-Hispanic/Latino; 9 Asian, non-Hispanic/Latino; 6 Hispanic/Latino; 4 Two or more races, non-Hispanic/Latino). Average age 33. 54 applicants, 74% accepted, 28 enrolled. In 2018, 78 master's awarded. *Degree requirements:* For master's, field experience, internship. *Entrance requirements:* For master's, GRE or MAT, WEST-B, WEST-E, official transcript(s) from each college/university attended, resume, personal statement (one to two pages), two to four letters of recommendation, endorsement verification form, moral character and personal fitness policy form. *Application deadline:* For fall admission, 3/15 for domestic students. Application fee: $50. Electronic applications accepted. *Expenses:* Contact institution. *Financial support:* Scholarships/grants available. Financial award applicants required to submit FAFSA. *Application contact:* Graduate Admission, 206-281-2091.
Website: https://spu.edu/academics/school-of-education/graduate-programs/masters-programs/masters-of-arts-in-teaching

Siena Heights University, Graduate College, Adrian, MI 49221-1796. Offers clinical mental health counseling (MA); educational leadership (Specialist); leadership (MA), including health care leadership, organizational leadership; teacher education (MA), including early childhood education, early childhood education: Montessori, education leadership: principal, elementary education: reading K-12, leadership: higher education, secondary education: reading K-12, special education: cognitive impairment, special education: learning disabilities. *Program availability:* Part-time, evening/weekend. *Faculty:* 10 full-time (6 women), 16 part-time/adjunct (6 women). *Students:* 34 full-time (20 women), 183 part-time (126 women); includes 64 minority (38 Black or African American, non-Hispanic/Latino; 2 American Indian or Alaska Native, non-Hispanic/Latino; 4 Asian, non-Hispanic/Latino; 14 Hispanic/Latino; 6 Two or more races, non-Hispanic/Latino). Average age 36. 97 applicants, 41% accepted, 30 enrolled. In 2018, 72 master's awarded. *Degree requirements:* For master's, thesis, Presentation. *Entrance requirements:* For master's, Minimum GPA of 3.0, current resume, essay, all post-secondary transcripts, 3 letters of reference, conviction disclosure form; copy of teaching certificate (for some education programs); for Specialist, Master's degree, minimum GPA of 3.0, current resume, essay, all post-secondary transcripts, 3 letters of reference, conviction disclosure form; copy of teaching certificate (for some education programs). Additional exam requirements/recommendations for international students: Recommended—TOEFL, IELTS, TWE, TSE. *Application deadline:* Applications are processed on a rolling basis. Application fee: $50. Electronic applications accepted. *Expenses:* Tuition: Full-time $11,340; part-time $7560 per year. *Required fees:* $454; $454 per unit. $227 per semester. One-time fee: $100. Tuition and fees vary according to program. *Financial support:* In 2018–19, 55 students received support. Scholarships/grants, tuition waivers (full and partial), unspecified assistantships, and State of Michigan Scholarships/Grants available. Support available to part-time students. Financial award application deadline: 9/1; financial award applicants required to submit FAFSA. *Unit head:* Dr. Cheryl Betz, Dean, College for Professional Studies and Graduate College, 517-264-7234, Fax: 517-264-7714, E-mail: cbetz@sienaheights.edu. *Application contact:* Elizabeth Brooks, Assistant Director, 517-264-7165, Fax: 517-264-7714, E-mail: ebrooks@sienaheights.edu.
Website: http://www.sienaheights.edu

Sierra Nevada College, Teacher Education Program, Incline Village, NV 89451. Offers advanced teaching and leadership (M Ed); elementary education (MAT); secondary education (MAT). *Program availability:* Part-time, evening/weekend, online learning. *Degree requirements:* For master's, comprehensive exam, thesis, PRAXIS I and II. *Entrance requirements:* For master's, 2 letters of recommendation, minimum GPA of 3.0. Electronic applications accepted.

Simpson College, Department of Education, Indianola, IA 50125-1297. Offers secondary education (MAT). *Degree requirements:* For master's, PRAXIS II, electronic portfolio. *Entrance requirements:* For master's, bachelor's degree; minimum cumulative GPA of 2.75, 3.0 in major; 3 letters of recommendation.

Slippery Rock University of Pennsylvania, Graduate Studies (Recruitment), College of Education, Department of Secondary Education/Foundations of Education, Slippery Rock, PA 16057-1383. Offers secondary education (M Ed), including English, math/science, social studies. *Accreditation:* NCATE. *Program availability:* Part-time, evening/weekend, 100% online. *Faculty:* 9 full-time (4 women), 1 part-time/adjunct (0 women). *Students:* 45 full-time (36 women), 232 part-time (191 women); includes 2 minority (both Black or African American, non-Hispanic/Latino). Average age 28. 58 applicants, 76% accepted, 28 enrolled. In 2018, 34 master's awarded. *Degree requirements:* For master's, comprehensive exam, thesis (for some programs). *Entrance requirements:* For master's, copy of teaching certification and two letters of recommendation (for some programs). Additional exam requirements/recommendations for international students: Required—TOEFL (minimum score 550 paper-based; 80 iBT). *Application deadline:* For fall admission, 3/1 priority date for domestic students, 5/1 priority date for international students; for spring admission, 10/1 priority date for domestic students, 9/1 priority date for international students. Applications are processed on a rolling basis. Application fee: $25 ($30 for international students). Electronic applications accepted. *Expenses:* Contact institution. *Financial support:* In 2018–19, 9 students received support. Career-related internships or fieldwork, Federal Work-Study, institutionally sponsored loans,

scholarships/grants, tuition waivers (partial), and unspecified assistantships available. Support available to part-time students. Financial award application deadline: 5/1; financial award applicants required to submit FAFSA. *Unit head:* Dr. Jeffrey Lehman, Graduate Coordinator, 724-738-2311, Fax: 724-738-4987, E-mail: jeffrey.lehman@sru.edu. *Application contact:* Brandi Weber-Mortimer, Director of Graduate Studies, 724-738-2051, Fax: 724-738-2146, E-mail: graduate.admissions@sru.edu.
Website: http://www.sru.edu/academics/colleges-and-departments/coe/departments/secondary-education-/-foundations-of-education

Smith College, Graduate and Special Programs, Department of Chemistry, Northampton, MA 01063. Offers secondary education (MAT), including chemistry. *Program availability:* Part-time. *Students:* 2 full-time (both women); includes 1 minority (Asian, non-Hispanic/Latino). Average age 22. 2 applicants, 100% accepted, 2 enrolled. In 2018, 2 master's awarded. *Entrance requirements:* Additional exam requirements/recommendations for international students: Required—TOEFL (minimum score 595 paper-based; 97 iBT), IELTS (minimum score 7.5). *Application deadline:* For fall admission, 4/15 for domestic students, 1/15 for international students; for spring admission, 12/1 for domestic students. Applications are processed on a rolling basis. Application fee: $60. *Expenses:* The total tuition cost to each M.A.T. student (the full program fee, after 'built-in' scholarship award) is $18,500. *Financial support:* In 2018–19, 2 students received support, including 2 fellowships with full tuition reimbursements available; scholarships/grants also available. Support available to part-time students. Financial award application deadline: 4/15; financial award applicants required to submit CSS PROFILE or FAFSA. *Unit head:* Kate Queeney, Department Chair, 413-585-3835, E-mail: kqueeney@smith.edu. *Application contact:* Ruth Morgan, Program Coordinator, 413-585-3050, Fax: 413-585-3054, E-mail: gradstdy@smith.edu.
Website: http://www.science.smith.edu/departments/chem/

Smith College, Graduate and Special Programs, Department of Education and Child Study, Program in Secondary Education, Northampton, MA 01063. Offers secondary education (MAT), including biological sciences education, chemistry education, English education, geology education, government education, history education, mathematics education, physics education. *Program availability:* Part-time. *Students:* 8 full-time (all women), 2 part-time (0 women); includes 2 minority (1 Black or African American, non-Hispanic/Latino; 1 Asian, non-Hispanic/Latino), 2 international. Average age 27. 25 applicants, 84% accepted, 10 enrolled. In 2018, 8 master's awarded. *Entrance requirements:* Additional exam requirements/recommendations for international students: Required—TOEFL (minimum score 595 paper-based; 97 iBT), IELTS (minimum score 7.5). *Application deadline:* For fall admission, 4/15 for domestic students, 1/15 priority date for international students; for spring admission, 12/1 for domestic students. Applications are processed on a rolling basis. Application fee: $60. *Expenses:* The total tuition cost to each M.A.T. student (the full program fee, after 'built-in' scholarship award) is $18,500. *Financial support:* In 2018–19, 9 students received support, including 2 fellowships with full tuition reimbursements available; scholarships/grants and human resources employee benefit also available. Support available to part-time students. Financial award application deadline: 4/15; financial award applicants required to submit CSS PROFILE or FAFSA. *Unit head:* Rosetta Cohen, Graduate Student Advisor, 413-585-3266, E-mail: rcohen@smith.edu. *Application contact:* Ruth Morgan, Program Coordinator, 413-585-3050, Fax: 413-585-3054, E-mail: gradstdy@smith.edu.
Website: http://www.smith.edu/educ/

Smith College, Graduate and Special Programs, Department of English Language and Literature, Northampton, MA 01063. Offers secondary education (MAT), including English education. *Program availability:* Part-time. *Students:* 3 full-time (all women). Average age 29. 11 applicants, 82% accepted, 3 enrolled. In 2018, 3 master's awarded. *Entrance requirements:* Additional exam requirements/recommendations for international students: Required—TOEFL (minimum score 595 paper-based; 97 iBT), IELTS (minimum score 7.5). *Application deadline:* For fall admission, 4/15 for domestic students, 1/15 for international students; for spring admission, 12/1 for domestic students. Applications are processed on a rolling basis. Application fee: $60. *Expenses:* The total tuition cost to each M.A.T. student (the full program fee, after 'built-in' scholarship award) is $18,500. *Financial support:* In 2018–19, 3 students received support. Fellowships and scholarships/grants available. Support available to part-time students. Financial award application deadline: 4/15; financial award applicants required to submit CSS PROFILE or FAFSA. *Unit head:* Craig Davis, Graduate Adviser, 413-585-3327, E-mail: crdavis@smith.edu. *Application contact:* Ruth Morgan, Program Coordinator, 413-585-3050, Fax: 413-585-3054, E-mail: gradstdy@smith.edu.
Website: http://www.smith.edu/english/

Smith College, Graduate and Special Programs, Department of Government, Northampton, MA 01063. Offers secondary education (MAT), including government education. *Program availability:* Part-time. *Students:* 1 (woman) full-time, all international. Average age 30. 2 applicants, 100% accepted, 1 enrolled. *Entrance requirements:* Additional exam requirements/recommendations for international students: Required—TOEFL (minimum score 595 paper-based; 97 iBT), IELTS. *Application deadline:* For fall admission, 4/15 for domestic students, 1/15 for international students; for spring admission, 12/1 for domestic students. Applications are processed on a rolling basis. Application fee: $60. *Expenses:* The total tuition cost to each M.A.T. student (the full program fee, after 'built-in' scholarship award) is $18,500. *Financial support:* In 2018–19, 1 student received support. Fellowships and scholarships/grants available. Support available to part-time students. Financial award application deadline: 4/15; financial award applicants required to submit CSS PROFILE or FAFSA. *Unit head:* Don Baumer, Department Chair / Graduate Adviser, 413-585-3534, E-mail: dbaumer@smith.edu. *Application contact:* Ruth Morgan, Program Coordinator, 413-585-3050, Fax: 413-585-3054, E-mail: gradstdy@smith.edu.
Website: http://www.smith.edu/gov/

Smith College, Graduate and Special Programs, Department of History, Northampton, MA 01063. Offers secondary education (MAT), including history education. *Program availability:* Part-time. *Students:* 1 (woman) full-time, 1 part-time (0 women); includes 1 minority (Black or African American, non-Hispanic/Latino). Average age 26. 3 applicants, 67% accepted, 2 enrolled. In 2018, 1 master's awarded. *Entrance requirements:* Additional exam requirements/recommendations for international students: Required—TOEFL (minimum score 595 paper-based; 97 iBT), IELTS. *Application deadline:* For fall admission, 4/15 for domestic students, 1/15 for international students; for spring admission, 12/1 for domestic students. Applications are processed on a rolling basis. Application fee: $60. *Expenses:* The total tuition cost to each M.A.T. student (the full program fee, after 'built-in' scholarship award) is $18,500. *Financial support:* In 2018–19, 2 students received support. Fellowships and scholarships/grants available. Support available to part-time students. Financial award application deadline: 4/15; financial award applicants required to submit CSS PROFILE or FAFSA. *Unit head:* Joshua Birk, Graduate Student Adviser, 413-585-3740, E-mail: jbirk@smith.edu. *Application contact:* Ruth Morgan, Program Coordinator, 413-585-3050, Fax: 413-585-3054, E-mail: gradstdy@smith.edu.
Website: http://www.smith.edu/history/

Smith College, Graduate and Special Programs, Department of Mathematics, Northampton, MA 01063. Offers secondary education (MAT), including mathematics

education. *Program availability:* Part-time. *Students:* 3 applicants, 67% accepted. *Entrance requirements:* Additional exam requirements/recommendations for international students: Required—TOEFL (minimum score 595 paper-based; 97 iBT), IELTS (minimum score 7.5). *Application deadline:* For fall admission, 11/1 for domestic students, 1/15 for international students; for spring admission, 4/15 for domestic students. Applications are processed on a rolling basis. Application fee: $60. *Expenses:* The total tuition cost to each M.A.T. student (the full program fee, after automatic scholarship award) is $18,500. *Financial support:* Fellowships and scholarships/grants available. Support available to part-time students. Financial award application deadline: 4/15; financial award applicants required to submit CSS PROFILE or FAFSA. *Unit head:* Julianna Tymoczko, Program Director, 413-585-3775, E-mail: jtymoczko@smith.edu. *Application contact:* Ruth Morgan, Program Coordinator, 413-585-3050, Fax: 413-585-3054, E-mail: gradstdy@smith.edu.
Website: http://www.math.smith.edu/

Smith College, Graduate and Special Programs, Department of Physics, Northampton, MA 01063. Offers secondary education (MAT), including physics education. *Program availability:* Part-time. *Students:* 1 part-time (0 women). Average age 38. In 2018, 1 master's awarded. *Entrance requirements:* Additional exam requirements/recommendations for international students: Required—TOEFL (minimum score 595 paper-based; 97 iBT), IELTS. *Application deadline:* For fall admission, 4/15 for domestic students, 1/15 for international students; for spring admission, 12/1 for domestic students. Applications are processed on a rolling basis. Application fee: $60. *Expenses:* The total tuition cost to each M.A.T. student (the full program fee, after 'built-in' scholarship award) is $18,500. *Financial support:* In 2018–19, 1 student received support. Fellowships and scholarships/grants available. Support available to part-time students. Financial award application deadline: 4/15; financial award applicants required to submit CSS PROFILE or FAFSA. *Unit head:* Gary Felder, Graduate Adviser, 413-585-4489, E-mail: gfelder@smith.edu. *Application contact:* Ruth Morgan, Program Coordinator, 413-585-3050, Fax: 413-585-3054, E-mail: gradstdy@smith.edu.

South Carolina State University, College of Graduate and Professional Studies, Department of Education, Orangeburg, SC 29117-0001. Offers early childhood education (MAT); education (M Ed); elementary education (M Ed, MAT); English (MAT); general science/biology (MAT); mathematics (MAT); secondary education (M Ed), including biology education, business education, counselor education, English education, home economics education, industrial education, mathematics education, science education, social studies education; special education (M Ed), including emotionally handicapped, learning disabilities, mentally handicapped. *Accreditation:* NCATE. *Program availability:* Part-time, evening/weekend. *Faculty:* 17 full-time (6 women), 12 part-time/adjunct (5 women). *Students:* 42 full-time (32 women), 93 part-time (64 women); includes 121 minority (119 Black or African American, non-Hispanic/Latino; 2 Asian, non-Hispanic/Latino), 2 international. Average age 40. 50 applicants, 98% accepted, 39 enrolled. In 2018, 9 master's awarded. *Degree requirements:* For master's, thesis optional, departmental qualifying exam. *Entrance requirements:* For master's, GRE General Test, NTE, interview, teaching certificate. *Application deadline:* For fall admission, 6/15 priority date for domestic students, 6/15 for international students; for spring admission, 11/1 for domestic and international students. Application fee: $25. Electronic applications accepted. *Expenses: Tuition, area resident:* Full-time $9928; part-time $552 per credit hour. Tuition, state resident: full-time $9928. Tuition, nonresident: full-time $21,038; part-time $1169 per credit hour. *Required fees:* $1532; $85 per credit hour. *Financial support:* Fellowships, career-related internships or fieldwork, Federal Work-Study, and scholarships/grants available. Financial award application deadline: 6/1. *Unit head:* Dr. Charlie Spell, Chair, Department of Education, 803-536-8963, Fax: 803-516-4568, E-mail: cspell@scsu.edu. *Application contact:* Curtis Foskey, Coordinator of Graduate Studies, 803-536-8419, Fax: 803-536-8812, E-mail: cfoskey@scsu.edu.

Southeast Missouri State University, School of Graduate Studies, Leadership, Middle and Secondary, Cape Girardeau, MO 63701-4799. Offers MA. *Accreditation:* NCATE. *Program availability:* Part-time, online only, 100% online. *Faculty:* 5 full-time (3 women), 1 (woman) part-time/adjunct. *Students:* 7 full-time (6 women), 80 part-time (39 women); includes 5 minority (4 Black or African American, non-Hispanic/Latino; 1 American Indian or Alaska Native, non-Hispanic/Latino). Average age 31. 37 applicants, 100% accepted, 37 enrolled. In 2018, 50 master's awarded. *Degree requirements:* For master's, comprehensive exam, research paper. *Entrance requirements:* For master's, minimum undergraduate GPA of 2.75. Additional exam requirements/recommendations for international students: Required—TOEFL (minimum score 550 paper-based; 79 iBT), IELTS (minimum score 6), PTE (minimum score 53). *Application deadline:* For fall admission, 8/1 for domestic students, 6/1 for international students; for spring admission, 11/21 for domestic students, 10/1 for international students; for summer admission, 5/15 for domestic students. Applications are processed on a rolling basis. Application fee: $30 ($40 for international students). Electronic applications accepted. *Expenses:* Contact institution. *Financial support:* In 2018–19, 3 students received support. Career-related internships or fieldwork, Federal Work-Study, scholarships/grants, tuition waivers (full), and unspecified assistantships available. Financial award application deadline: 6/30; financial award applicants required to submit FAFSA. *Faculty research:* Assessment, technology, diversity. *Unit head:* Dr. C.P. Gause, Professor and Department Chair, 573-651-5965, E-mail: scwick@semo.edu. *Application contact:* Alisa Aleen McFerron, Assistant Director of Admissions for Operations, 573-651-5937, E-mail: amcferron@semo.edu.
Website: http://www.semo.edu/midsecondaryed/

Southeast Missouri State University, School of Graduate Studies, Leadership, Middle and Secondary Education, Program in Educational Administration, Cape Girardeau, MO 63701-4799. Offers educational leadership (Ed D); higher education administration (MA); secondary administration (MA); teacher leadership (MA, Ed S). *Accreditation:* NCATE. *Program availability:* Part-time, evening/weekend, online only, 100% online, blended/hybrid learning. *Faculty:* 7 full-time (4 women), 4 part-time/adjunct (1 woman). *Students:* 45 full-time (28 women), 210 part-time (135 women); includes 22 minority (16 Black or African American, non-Hispanic/Latino; 2 American Indian or Alaska Native, non-Hispanic/Latino; 1 Asian, non-Hispanic/Latino; 3 Two or more races, non-Hispanic/Latino), 13 international. Average age 32. 111 applicants, 100% accepted, 111 enrolled. In 2018, 63 master's, 26 other advanced degrees awarded. *Degree requirements:* For master's and Ed S, comprehensive exam, thesis or alternative, paper; for doctorate, comprehensive exam, thesis/dissertation. *Entrance requirements:* For master's, minimum GPA of 3.5; for doctorate, GRE, interview; for Ed S, minimum GPA of 3.7. Additional exam requirements/recommendations for international students: Required—TOEFL (minimum score 550 paper-based; 79 iBT), IELTS (minimum score 6), PTE (minimum score 53). *Application deadline:* For fall admission, 8/1 for domestic students, 6/1 for international students; for spring admission, 11/21 for domestic students, 10/1 for international students; for summer admission, 5/15 for domestic students. Applications are processed on a rolling basis. Application fee: $30 ($40 for international students). Electronic applications accepted. *Expenses:* Contact institution. *Financial support:* In 2018–19, 22 students received support. Career-related internships or fieldwork, Federal Work-Study, scholarships/grants, traineeships, tuition waivers (full), and unspecified assistantships available. Financial award application deadline: 6/30; financial award applicants required to submit FAFSA. *Faculty research:* Learning and technology; leadership, equity and social justice in P-12 schools and higher education; school culture; leadership and academic achievement; school leadership and student success. *Unit head:* Dr. C. P. Gause, Professor/Chair, 573-651-2137, Fax: 573-986-6512, E-mail: cgause@semo.edu. *Application contact:* Dr. Lisa Bertrand, Professor/Coordinator, 573-651-5080, Fax: 573-986-6512, E-mail: lbertrand@semo.edu.
Website: http://www.semo.edu/eduleadcounsel/

Southern Oregon University, Graduate Studies, School of Education, Ashland, OR 97520. Offers elementary education (MA Ed, MS Ed), including classroom teacher, early childhood, handicapped learner, reading, supervision; secondary education (MA Ed, MS Ed), including classroom teacher, handicapped learner, reading, supervision; teaching (MAT). *Program availability:* Online learning. *Degree requirements:* For master's, thesis optional. *Entrance requirements:* For master's, GRE General Test, minimum cumulative GPA of 3.0 in the last 90 quarter credits (60 semester credits) of undergraduate coursework. Additional exam requirements/recommendations for international students: Required—TOEFL (minimum score 540 paper-based; 76 iBT), IELTS (minimum score 6), ELPT (minimum score 964) or ELS (minimum score 112). Electronic applications accepted.

Southern University and Agricultural and Mechanical College, Graduate School, College of Humanities and Interdisciplinary Studies, School of Education, Department of Curriculum and Instruction, Baton Rouge, LA 70813. Offers elementary education (M Ed); media (M Ed); secondary education (M Ed). *Degree requirements:* For master's, comprehensive exam, thesis optional. *Entrance requirements:* For master's, GMAT or GRE General Test. Additional exam requirements/recommendations for international students: Required—TOEFL (minimum score 525 paper-based).

Southwestern Assemblies of God University, Thomas F. Harrison School of Graduate Studies, Program in Education, Waxahachie, TX 75165-5735. Offers Christian school administration (MS); curriculum development (MS); early education administration (M Ed); middle and secondary education (M Ed). *Degree requirements:* For master's, comprehensive written and oral exams. *Entrance requirements:* For master's, GRE General Test, minimum GPA of 2.5. Electronic applications accepted.

Spalding University, Graduate Studies, College of Education, Programs in Education, Louisville, KY 40203-2188. Offers art teacher education (MAT); business teacher education (MAT); elementary school education (MAT); foreign language (MAT); high school education (MAT); middle school education (MAT); secondary education (MAT); special education (learning and behavioral disorders) (MAT); student guidance counselor (MA); teacher leader (M Ed). *Accreditation:* NCATE. *Program availability:* Part-time, evening/weekend. *Entrance requirements:* For master's, GRE General Test or MAT, interview, letters of recommendation, resume. Additional exam requirements/recommendations for international students: Required—TOEFL (minimum score 535 paper-based). Electronic applications accepted. *Faculty research:* Instructional technology, achievement gap, classroom management, assessment.

Springfield College, Graduate Programs, Programs in Education, Springfield, MA 01109-3797. Offers early childhood education (M Ed); educational studies (M Ed); elementary education (M Ed); secondary education (M Ed); special education (M Ed, CAGS). *Program availability:* Part-time, evening/weekend. *Entrance requirements:* For master's, Massachusetts Tests for Educator Licensure (MTEL). Additional exam requirements/recommendations for international students: Required—TOEFL (minimum score 550 paper-based); Recommended—IELTS (minimum score 7). Electronic applications accepted. *Expenses:* Contact institution.

Spring Hill College, Graduate Programs, Program in Education, Mobile, AL 36608-1791. Offers early childhood education (MAT, MS Ed); educational theory (MS Ed); elementary education (MAT, MS Ed); secondary education (MAT, MS Ed). *Program availability:* Part-time. *Faculty:* 3 full-time (all women). *Students:* 1 full-time (0 women), 8 part-time (5 women); includes 2 minority (1 Hispanic/Latino; 1 Two or more races, non-Hispanic/Latino), 1 international. Average age 32. In 2018, 6 master's awarded. *Degree requirements:* For master's, comprehensive exam, completion of program within 6 calendar years of entrance into graduate studies at Spring Hill; documentation of course field assignments (MS) or completion of internship (MAT). *Entrance requirements:* For master's, GRE, MAT, or PRAXIS (varies by program), bachelor's degree with minimum undergraduate GPA of 3.0; class B certificate (for MS); minimum number of hours in specific fields (for MAT). Additional exam requirements/recommendations for international students: Required—TOEFL (minimum score 550 paper-based; 80 iBT), IELTS (minimum score 6.5), CPE or CAE (minimum score C), Michigan English Language Assessment Battery (minimum score 90). *Application deadline:* For fall admission, 8/1 priority date for domestic and international students; for spring admission, 12/1 priority date for domestic and international students. Applications are processed on a rolling basis. Application fee: $25 ($35 for international students). Electronic applications accepted. *Expenses:* Contact institution. *Financial support:* Fellowships, research assistantships, teaching assistantships, and tuition waivers available. Financial award applicants required to submit FAFSA. *Unit head:* Dr. Lori P. Aultman, Chair of Education, 251-380-3473, Fax: 251-460-2184, E-mail: laultman@shc.edu. *Application contact:* Gary Bracken, Vice President of Enrollment Management, 251-380-3038, Fax: 251-460-2186, E-mail: gbracken@shc.edu.
Website: http://ug.shc.edu/graduate-degrees/master-science-education/

Stanford University, Graduate School of Education, Teacher Education Program, Stanford, CA 94305-2004. Offers elementary education (MAE); secondary education (MAE). *Expenses: Tuition:* Full-time $50,703; part-time $32,970 per year. *Required fees:* $651.

State University of New York at Fredonia, College of Education, Fredonia, NY 14063-1136. Offers curriculum and instruction (MS Ed); literacy education (MS Ed), including birth-grade 12, grades 5-12; music education (M Mus), including k-12; TESOL (MS Ed). *Accreditation:* NCATE. *Program availability:* Part-time. *Faculty:* 16 full-time (14 women), 13 part-time/adjunct (11 women). *Students:* 39 full-time (33 women), 44 part-time (36 women); includes 5 minority (1 Asian, non-Hispanic/Latino; 3 Hispanic/Latino; 1 Two or more races, non-Hispanic/Latino), 4 international. Average age 27. 44 applicants, 89% accepted, 34 enrolled. In 2018, 25 master's awarded. *Degree requirements:* For master's, thesis. *Entrance requirements:* For master's, GRE, minimum undergraduate GPA of 3.0. Additional exam requirements/recommendations for international students: Required—TOEFL (minimum score 79 iBT), IELTS (minimum score 6.5). *Application deadline:* For fall admission, 4/1 priority date for domestic and international students; for spring admission, 11/1 priority date for domestic students, 11/1 for international students. Applications are processed on a rolling basis. Application fee: $75. Electronic applications accepted. *Expenses:* Tuition, state resident: full-time $6870; part-time $462 per credit hour. Tuition, nonresident: full-time $16,650; part-time $944 per credit hour. *International tuition:* $16,650 full-time. *Required fees:* $25; $2 per credit hour. $1 per semester. *Financial support:* In 2018–19, 13 students received support. Unspecified assistantships available. Financial award application deadline: 3/15; financial award applicants required to submit FAFSA. *Faculty research:* Positive behavioral intervention and support (PBIS), place-based science education, peer support for education, primary source material for social studies education, policies and practices in learning English language. *Unit head:* Dr. Christine Givner, Dean, 716-673-3311, E-mail: christine.givner@fredonia.edu. *Application contact:* Wendy S. Dunst, Interim Graduate

Recruitment and Admissions Associate, 716-673-3808, Fax: 716-673-3712, E-mail: wendy.dunst@fredonia.edu.
Website: http://www.fredonia.edu/coe/

State University of New York at New Paltz, Graduate and Extended Learning School, School of Education, Program of Educational Administration, Program in Special Education, New Paltz, NY 12561. Offers adolescence special education (7-12) (MS Ed); adolescence special education and literacy (MS Ed); childhood special education (1-6) (MS Ed); childhood special education and literacy (MS Ed); early childhood special education (B-2) (MS Ed). *Accreditation:* NCATE. *Program availability:* Part-time, evening/weekend. *Faculty:* 4 full-time (3 women), 1 (woman) part-time/adjunct. *Students:* 14 full-time (11 women), 34 part-time (26 women); includes 4 minority (all Hispanic/Latino). 26 applicants, 85% accepted, 21 enrolled. In 2018, 15 master's awarded. *Entrance requirements:* For master's, minimum GPA of 3.0 (3.2 for special education and literacy programs), New York state teaching certificate. Additional exam requirements/recommendations for international students: Required—TOEFL (minimum score 550 paper-based; 80 iBT), IELTS (minimum score 6.5). *Application deadline:* For fall admission, 3/15 priority date for domestic students, 3/15 for international students; for spring admission, 11/1 for domestic and international students. Application fee: $50. Electronic applications accepted. *Financial support:* Application deadline: 8/1. *Unit head:* Dr. Jane Sileo, Coordinator, 845-257-2835, E-mail: sileoj@newpaltz.edu. *Application contact:* Vika Shock, Director of Graduate Admissions, 845-257-3286, E-mail: gradstudies@newpaltz.edu.
Website: http://www.newpaltz.edu/schoolofed/department-of-teaching—learning/special_ed.html

State University of New York at Oswego, Graduate Studies, School of Education, Department of Curriculum and Instruction, Oswego, NY 13126. Offers adolescence education (MST); art education (MAT); childhood education (MST); curriculum and instruction (MS Ed); literacy education (MS Ed); special education (MS Ed). *Program availability:* Part-time, evening/weekend. *Degree requirements:* For master's, comprehensive exam (for some programs), thesis optional. *Entrance requirements:* For master's, GRE General Test, minimum GPA of 2.7, provisional teaching certificate. Additional exam requirements/recommendations for international students: Required—TOEFL (minimum score 560 paper-based). *Faculty research:* Classroom applications for microcomputers; classroom questioning, wait-time, and achievement; values clarification and academic achievement.

State University of New York at Plattsburgh, School of Education, Health, and Human Services, Program in Teacher Education: Adolescence Education, Plattsburgh, NY 12901-2681. Offers adolescence education (MST); biology 7-12 (MST); chemistry 7-12 (MST); earth science 7-12 (MST); English 7-12 (MST); French 7-12 (MST); mathematics 7-12 (MST); physics 7-12 (MST); social studies 7-12 (MST); Spanish 7-12 (MST). *Accreditation:* TEAC. *Program availability:* Part-time, evening/weekend. *Entrance requirements:* For master's, minimum GPA of 2.75. Additional exam requirements/recommendations for international students: Required—TOEFL.

State University of New York College at Cortland, Graduate Studies, School of Arts and Sciences, Programs in Adolescence Education, Cortland, NY 13045. Offers biology (MAT); chemistry (MAT); English (MAT, MS Ed); mathematics (MAT); mathematics and physics (MS Ed); physics (MAT, MS Ed). *Accreditation:* NCATE. *Program availability:* Part-time, evening/weekend. *Degree requirements:* For master's, one foreign language, comprehensive exam (for some programs), thesis (for some programs). *Entrance requirements:* For master's, GRE General Test.

State University of New York College at Geneseo, Graduate Studies, School of Education, Program in Adolescence Education, Geneseo, NY 14454-1401. Offers English 7-12 (MS Ed); French 7-12 (MS Ed); social studies 7-12 (MS Ed); Spanish 7-12 (MS Ed). *Program availability:* Part-time, evening/weekend. *Degree requirements:* For master's, 2 foreign languages, comprehensive examination, thesis or research project. *Entrance requirements:* For master's, GRE, MAT, EAS, edTPA, PRAXIS, or another substantially equivalent test, proof of New York State initial certification or equivalent certification from another state. Additional exam requirements/recommendations for international students: Required—TOEFL (minimum score 525 paper-based; 71 iBT), IELTS (minimum score 6.5), PTE, iTEP. Electronic applications accepted. *Expenses:* Contact institution.

State University of New York College at Potsdam, School of Education and Professional Studies, Program in Secondary Education, Potsdam, NY 13676. Offers English education (MST); mathematics education (MST); science education (MST), including biology, chemistry, earth science, physics; social studies education (MST). *Accreditation:* NCATE. *Degree requirements:* For master's, culminating experience. *Entrance requirements:* For master's, minimum GPA of 2.75 in last 60 hours of course work (3.0 for English program). Additional exam requirements/recommendations for international students: Required—TOEFL (minimum score 550 paper-based; 80 iBT), IELTS (minimum score 6). Electronic applications accepted.

Stephen F. Austin State University, Graduate School, James I. Perkins College of Education, Department of Secondary Education and Educational Leadership, Nacogdoches, TX 75962. Offers educational leadership (Ed D); secondary education (M Ed); secondary education leadership (MAT). *Accreditation:* NCATE. *Degree requirements:* For master's, comprehensive exam; for doctorate, thesis/dissertation. *Entrance requirements:* For master's, GRE General Test; for doctorate, GRE General Test, interview, writing sample. Additional exam requirements/recommendations for international students: Required—TOEFL. Electronic applications accepted.

Sul Ross State University, Rio Grande College of Sul Ross State University, Alpine, TX 79832. Offers business administration (MBA); teacher education (M Ed), including bilingual education, counseling, educational diagnostics, elementary education, general education, reading, school administration, secondary education. *Program availability:* Part-time, evening/weekend, online learning. *Degree requirements:* For master's, comprehensive exam, thesis optional, minimum GPA of 3.0. *Entrance requirements:* For master's, GMAT or GRE General Test, minimum GPA of 2.5 in last 60 hours of undergraduate work. Additional exam requirements/recommendations for international students: Required—TOEFL.

Tarleton State University, College of Graduate Studies, College of Education, Department of Curriculum and Instruction, Stephenville, TX 76402. Offers curriculum and instruction (M Ed); educational diagnostician (M Ed); elementary education (M Ed); instructional design and technology (M Ed); instructional leadership (M Ed); secondary education (M Ed); special education (M Ed); technology applications (M Ed); technology director (M Ed). *Program availability:* Part-time, evening/weekend. *Faculty:* 11 full-time (10 women), 4 part-time/adjunct (1 woman). *Students:* 16 full-time (14 women), 158 part-time (143 women). Average age 40. 54 applicants, 87% accepted, 41 enrolled. In 2018, 46 master's awarded. *Degree requirements:* For master's, comprehensive exam, thesis (for some programs). *Entrance requirements:* For master's, GRE General Test, minimum GPA of 3.0. Additional exam requirements/recommendations for international students: Required—TOEFL (minimum score 520 paper-based; 69 iBT); Recommended—IELTS (minimum score 6), TSE (minimum score 50). *Application deadline:* For fall admission, 8/15 priority date for domestic students; for spring admission, 1/7 for domestic students. Applications are processed on a rolling basis. Application fee: $50 ($130 for international students). Electronic applications accepted. *Expenses:* Contact institution. *Financial support:* Research assistantships, teaching assistantships, career-related internships or fieldwork, Federal Work-Study, and institutionally sponsored loans available. Support available to part-time students. Financial award application deadline: 5/1; financial award applicants required to submit FAFSA. *Unit head:* Dr. Amber Lynn Diaz, Department Head, 254-968-0730, E-mail: adiaz@tarleton.edu. *Application contact:* Information Contact, 254-968-9104, Fax: 254-968-9670, E-mail: gradoffice@tarleton.edu.
Website: http://www.tarleton.edu/cimasters/

Teachers College, Columbia University, Department of Curriculum and Teaching, New York, NY 10027-6696. Offers curriculum and teaching (Ed M, MA, Ed D); curriculum and teaching: elementary education (MA); curriculum and teaching: secondary education (MA); early childhood education (MA, Ed D); early childhood education: special education (MA); elementary education-gifted extension (MA); elementary inclusive education (MA); gifted education (MA); literacy specialist (MA); secondary inclusive education (MA); special inclusive elementary education (MA). *Program availability:* Part-time, evening/weekend. *Students:* 88 full-time (77 women), 264 part-time (239 women); includes 129 minority (45 Black or African American, non-Hispanic/Latino; 1 American Indian or Alaska Native, non-Hispanic/Latino; 41 Asian, non-Hispanic/Latino; 28 Hispanic/Latino; 14 Two or more races, non-Hispanic/Latino), 48 international. Average age 30. 460 applicants, 73% accepted, 149 enrolled. Terminal master's awarded for partial completion of doctoral program. *Unit head:* Prof. Daniel Friedrich, Chair, 212-678-3263, E-mail: friedrich@exchange.tc.columbia.edu. *Application contact:* Kelly Sutton-Skinner, Director of Admission & New Student Enrollment, E-mail: kms2237@tc.columbia.edu.

Temple University, College of Education, Department of Teaching and Learning, Philadelphia, PA 19122-6096. Offers career and technical education (Ed M), including business, computing, and information technology, industrial education, marketing education; middle grades education (Ed M), including math and language arts, math and science, science and language arts; secondary education (Ed M), including English, math, social studies; teaching English to speakers of other languages (MS Ed); urban education (Ed M). *Program availability:* Part-time, evening/weekend. *Faculty:* 27 full-time (19 women), 71 part-time/adjunct (51 women). *Students:* 181 full-time (126 women), 128 part-time (78 women); includes 71 minority (25 Black or African American, non-Hispanic/Latino; 1 American Indian or Alaska Native, non-Hispanic/Latino; 20 Asian, non-Hispanic/Latino; 19 Hispanic/Latino; 1 Native Hawaiian or other Pacific Islander, non-Hispanic/Latino; 5 Two or more races, non-Hispanic/Latino), 12 international. 234 applicants, 67% accepted, 103 enrolled. In 2018, 148 master's awarded. *Degree requirements:* For master's, thesis (for some programs). *Entrance requirements:* For master's, statement of goals, 2 letters of recommendation. Additional exam requirements/recommendations for international students: Required—TOEFL (minimum score 79 iBT), IELTS, PTE, one of three is required. Application fee: $60. Electronic applications accepted. *Financial support:* Fellowships, research assistantships, teaching assistantships, career-related internships or fieldwork, Federal Work-Study, scholarships/grants, health care benefits, and unspecified assistantships available. Financial award applicants required to submit FAFSA. *Faculty research:* Career & technical education, early childhood education, middle grades education, secondary education, special education. *Unit head:* Matthew Tincani, Prof. of Applied Behavior Analysis and Dept. Chairperson, 215-204-8073, E-mail: matthew.tincani@temple.edu. *Application contact:* Stacey Sanginette, Academic Coordinator, 215-204-6143, E-mail: stacey.sangtinette@temple.edu.
Website: http://education.temple.edu/tl

Tennessee Technological University, College of Graduate Studies, College of Education, Department of Curriculum and Instruction, Program in Secondary Education, Cookeville, TN 38505. Offers MA, Ed S. *Accreditation:* NCATE. *Program availability:* Part-time, evening/weekend. *Faculty:* 7 full-time (0 women). *Students:* 17 full-time (9 women), 30 part-time (14 women); includes 2 minority (1 Black or African American, non-Hispanic/Latino; 1 Two or more races, non-Hispanic/Latino). 34 applicants, 85% accepted, 21 enrolled. *Degree requirements:* For master's and Ed S, comprehensive exam, thesis or alternative. *Entrance requirements:* For master's and Ed S, MAT or GRE. Additional exam requirements/recommendations for international students: Required—TOEFL (minimum score 527 paper-based; 71 iBT), IELTS (minimum score 5.5), PTE (minimum score 48), or TOEIC (Test of English as an International Communication). *Application deadline:* For fall admission, 8/1 for domestic students, 5/1 for international students; for spring admission, 12/1 for domestic students, 10/1 for international students; for summer admission, 5/1 for domestic students, 2/1 for international students. Applications are processed on a rolling basis. Application fee: $35 ($40 for international students). Electronic applications accepted. *Financial support:* Fellowships, research assistantships, teaching assistantships, and career-related internships or fieldwork available. Financial award application deadline: 4/1. *Unit head:* Dr. Jeremy Wendt, Chairperson, 931-372-3181, Fax: 931-372-6270, E-mail: jwendt@tntech.edu. *Application contact:* Shelia K. Kendrick, Coordinator of Graduate Studies, 931-372-3808, Fax: 931-372-3497, E-mail: skendrick@tntech.edu.

Texas A&M University–Commerce, College of Education and Human Services, Commerce, TX 75429. Offers counseling (M Ed, MS, PhD); early childhood education (M Ed, MS); educational administration (M Ed, MS, Ed D); educational psychology (PhD); educational technology leadership (M Ed, MS); educational technology library science (M Ed, MS); elementary education (M Ed); health, kinesiology and sports studies (MS); higher education (MS, Ed D); psychology (MS); reading (M Ed, MS); school psychology (SSP); secondary education (M Ed, MS); social work (MSW); special education (M Ed, MS); supervision, curriculum and instruction-elementary education (Ed D); training and development (MS). *Program availability:* Part-time, evening/weekend, 100% online, blended/hybrid learning. *Faculty:* 95 full-time (59 women), 29 part-time/adjunct (22 women). *Students:* 356 full-time (295 women), 1,262 part-time (992 women); includes 683 minority (349 Black or African American, non-Hispanic/Latino; 9 American Indian or Alaska Native, non-Hispanic/Latino; 30 Asian, non-Hispanic/Latino; 238 Hispanic/Latino; 57 Two or more races, non-Hispanic/Latino), 9 international. Average age 37. 951 applicants, 42% accepted, 304 enrolled. In 2018, 532 master's, 51 doctorates awarded. *Degree requirements:* For master's, comprehensive exam, thesis optional, departmental qualifying exams (for some programs); for doctorate, comprehensive exam, thesis/dissertation, departmental qualifying exam; for SSP, comprehensive exam. *Entrance requirements:* For master's, GRE General Test, official transcripts, letters of recommendation, resume, statement of goals; for doctorate, GRE General Test, letters of recommendation, statement of goals, writing samples, writing sessions, resumes. Additional exam requirements/recommendations for international students: Required—TOEFL (minimum score 550 paper-based; 79 iBT), IELTS (minimum score 6), PTE (minimum score 53). *Application deadline:* For fall admission, 6/1 priority date for international students; for spring admission, 10/15 priority date for international students; for summer admission, 3/15 priority date for international students. Applications are processed on a rolling basis. Application fee: $50 ($75 for international students). Electronic applications accepted. *Expenses: Tuition, area resident:* Full-time $3630. Tuition, state resident: full-time $3630. Tuition, nonresident: full-time $11,100. *International tuition:* $11,100 full-time. *Required fees:* $2794. Tuition and fees vary according to course load, degree level and program. *Financial support:* In

2018–19, 116 students received support, including 94 research assistantships with partial tuition reimbursements available (averaging $3,863 per year), 38 teaching assistantships with partial tuition reimbursements available (averaging $4,728 per year); career-related internships or fieldwork, Federal Work-Study, institutionally sponsored loans, scholarships/grants, health care benefits, and unspecified assistantships also available. Financial award application deadline: 5/1; financial award applicants required to submit FAFSA. *Faculty research:* Cognitive and bilingual education, positive behavioral intervention, literacy, math readiness. *Total annual research expenditures:* $1.1 million. *Unit head:* Dr. Madeline Justice, Interim Dean, 903-886-5181, Fax: 903-886-5905, E-mail: madeline.justice@tamuc.edu. *Application contact:* Vicky Turner, Doctoral Degree and Special Programs Coordinator, 903-886-5167, E-mail: vicky.turner@tamuc.edu.
Website: http://www.tamuc.edu/academics/graduateSchool/programs/education/default.aspx

Texas A&M University–Corpus Christi, College of Graduate Studies, College of Education and Human Development, Program in Secondary Education, Corpus Christi, TX 78412. Offers MS. *Program availability:* Part-time, evening/weekend, online learning. *Degree requirements:* For master's, comprehensive exam, capstone experience. *Entrance requirements:* For master's, minimum GPA of 3.0 in last 60 hours. Additional exam requirements/recommendations for international students: Required—TOEFL (minimum score 550 paper-based; 79 iBT), IELTS (minimum score 6.5). Electronic applications accepted.

Texas Southern University, College of Education, Area of Curriculum and Instruction, Houston, TX 77004-4584. Offers bilingual education (M Ed); curriculum and instruction (Ed D); secondary education (M Ed). *Program availability:* Part-time, evening/weekend. *Degree requirements:* For master's, comprehensive exam; for doctorate, comprehensive exam, thesis/dissertation. *Entrance requirements:* For master's, GRE General Test, minimum GPA of 2.5; for doctorate, GRE General Test or MAT, master's degree, minimum B+ average. Additional exam requirements/recommendations for international students: Required—TOEFL. Electronic applications accepted.

Texas State University, The Graduate College, College of Education, Program in Secondary Education, San Marcos, TX 78666. Offers M Ed, MA. *Program availability:* Part-time, evening/weekend. *Faculty:* 12 full-time (8 women), 2 part-time/adjunct (both women). *Students:* 31 full-time (24 women), 34 part-time (25 women); includes 27 minority (2 Black or African American, non-Hispanic/Latino; 2 Asian, non-Hispanic/Latino; 21 Hispanic/Latino; 2 Two or more races, non-Hispanic/Latino), 1 international. Average age 31. 56 applicants, 77% accepted, 19 enrolled. In 2018, 31 master's awarded. *Degree requirements:* For master's, comprehensive exam, thesis (for some programs). *Entrance requirements:* For master's, baccalaureate degree from regionally-accredited institution with minimum GPA of 2.75 in last 60 hour of undergrad work for M. Ed and a 3.4 (for MA); statement of purpose identifying research interest (for MA). Additional exam requirements/recommendations for international students: Required—TOEFL (minimum iBT scores: 22 listening, 22 reading, 24 speaking, 21 writing). *Application deadline:* For fall admission, 2/1 priority date for domestic and international students; for spring admission, 10/15 for domestic students, 10/1 for international students; for summer admission, 4/15 for domestic students, 3/15 for international students. Applications are processed on a rolling basis. Application fee: $55 ($90 for international students). Electronic applications accepted. *Expenses:* Tuition, state resident: full-time $8102; part-time $4051 per semester. Tuition, nonresident: full-time $18,229; part-time $9115 per semester. *International tuition:* $18,229 full-time. *Required fees:* $2116; $120 per credit hour. Tuition and fees vary according to course load. *Financial support:* In 2018–19, 30 students received support, including 6 teaching assistantships (averaging $13,058 per year); research assistantships, career-related internships or fieldwork, Federal Work-Study, institutionally sponsored loans, scholarships/grants, and unspecified assistantships also available. Support available to part-time students. Financial award application deadline: 1/15; financial award applicants required to submit FAFSA. *Faculty research:* Psychosocial, motivational, and self-regulatory factors; Developing a Mentoring Framework Through the Examination of Mentoring Paradigms; needs assessment for learning centers; Facilitating School-Based Teacher Learning Through a District/University Partnership. *Total annual research expenditures:* $3.5 million. *Unit head:* Dr. Nathan Bond, Graduate Advisor, 512-245-3098, Fax: 512-245-7911, E-mail: jb50@txstate.edu. *Application contact:* Dr. Andrea Golato, Dean of Graduate School, 512-245-2581, Fax: 512-245-8365, E-mail: gradcollege@txstate.edu.
Website: http://www.education.txstate.edu/ci/degrees-programs/graduate/secondary-education.html

Texas Tech University, Graduate School, College of Education, Department of Curriculum and Instruction, Lubbock, TX 79409-1071. Offers bilingual education (M Ed); curriculum and instruction (M Ed, PhD); elementary education (M Ed); language/literacy education (M Ed); multidisciplinary science (MS); secondary education (M Ed). *Accreditation:* NCATE. *Program availability:* Part-time, evening/weekend, online learning. *Faculty:* 17 full-time (11 women), 1 (woman) part-time/adjunct. *Students:* 48 full-time (41 women), 265 part-time (220 women); includes 103 minority (25 Black or African American, non-Hispanic/Latino; 9 Asian, non-Hispanic/Latino; 64 Hispanic/Latino; 5 Two or more races, non-Hispanic/Latino), 27 international. Average age 40. 101 applicants, 65% accepted, 51 enrolled. In 2018, 26 master's, 21 doctorates awarded. Terminal master's awarded for partial completion of doctoral program. *Degree requirements:* For master's, comprehensive exam (for some programs), thesis optional; for doctorate, comprehensive exam, thesis/dissertation. *Entrance requirements:* For master's, bachelor's degree; resume; letter of intent; academic writing sample; 2 letters of recommendation; for doctorate, GRE, master's degree; resume; letter of intent; academic writing sample; 3 letters of recommendation. Additional exam requirements/recommendations for international students: Required—TOEFL (minimum score 550 paper-based; 79 iBT). *Application deadline:* For fall admission, 6/1 priority date for domestic students, 1/15 priority date for international students; for spring admission, 9/1 priority date for domestic students, 6/15 priority date for international students. Applications are processed on a rolling basis. Application fee: $65. Electronic applications accepted. *Expenses:* Contact institution. *Financial support:* In 2018–19, 142 students received support, including 136 fellowships (averaging $2,895 per year), 28 research assistantships (averaging $12,296 per year), 7 teaching assistantships (averaging $14,175 per year); Federal Work-Study, institutionally sponsored loans, scholarships/grants, health care benefits, and unspecified assistantships also available. Support available to part-time students. Financial award application deadline: 2/1; financial award applicants required to submit FAFSA. *Faculty research:* Teacher education, curriculum studies, bilingual education, science and math education, language and literacy education. *Total annual research expenditures:* $79,025. *Unit head:* Dr. Jerry Dwyer, Professor, Interim Department Chair, 806-834-7399, Fax: 806-742-2179, E-mail: jerry.dwyer@ttu.edu. *Application contact:* Brandi Stephens, Graduate Academic Advisor, 806-834-4554, Fax: 806-742-2179, E-mail: brandi.stephens@ttu.edu.
Website: www.educ.ttu.edu

Towson University, College of Education, Program in Secondary Education, Towson, MD 21252-0001. Offers M Ed. *Accreditation:* NCATE. *Program availability:* Part-time, evening/weekend. *Degree requirements:* For master's, thesis optional. *Entrance requirements:* For master's, Maryland teaching certification or permission of program director, minimum GPA of 3.0. Electronic applications accepted. *Expenses: Tuition, area resident:* Full-time $9196; part-time $418 per unit. Tuition, state resident: full-time $9196; part-time $418 per unit. Tuition, nonresident: full-time $19,030; part-time $865 per unit. *International tuition:* $19,030 full-time. *Required fees:* $3102; $141 per year. $423 per term. Tuition and fees vary according to campus/location and program.

Towson University, College of Education, Program in Teaching, Towson, MD 21252-0001. Offers early childhood education (MAT); elementary education (MAT); secondary education (MAT); special education (MAT). *Entrance requirements:* For master's, ACT, GRE, PRAXIS I or SAT, 2 letters of reference, resume, minimum GPA of 3.0, essay. Electronic applications accepted. *Expenses: Tuition, area resident:* Full-time $9196; part-time $418 per unit. Tuition, state resident: full-time $9196; part-time $418 per unit. Tuition, nonresident: full-time $19,030; part-time $865 per unit. *International tuition:* $19,030 full-time. *Required fees:* $3102; $141 per year. $423 per term. Tuition and fees vary according to campus/location and program.

Trevecca Nazarene University, Graduate Education Program, Nashville, TN 37210-2877. Offers accountability and instructional leadership (Ed S); curriculum and instruction for Christian school educators (M Ed); curriculum and instruction K-12 (M Ed); educational leadership (M Ed); English second language (M Ed); library and information science (MLI Sc); special education: visual impairments (M Ed); teaching (MAT), including teaching 6-12, teaching K-5. *Accreditation:* NCATE. *Program availability:* Part-time, evening/weekend, online learning. *Degree requirements:* For master's, comprehensive exam, exit assessment/e-portfolio. *Entrance requirements:* For master's, GRE or MAT; PRAXIS (for MAT), minimum GPA of 3.0, official transcript from regionally-accredited institution, references, interview, writing sample, at least 3 years' successful teaching experience (for M Ed in educational leadership); for Ed S, GRE or MAT, master's degree with minimum GPA of 3.0, official transcript from regionally accredited institution, at least 3 years' successful teaching experience, interview, writing sample, background and fingerprinting check, recommendations. Additional exam requirements/recommendations for international students: Required—TOEFL (minimum score 550 paper-based). Electronic applications accepted. *Expenses:* Contact institution.

Trinity Washington University, School of Education, Washington, DC 20017-1094. Offers clinical mental health counseling (MA); early childhood education (MAT); educating for change (M Ed); educational administration (MSA); elementary education (MAT); reading (M Ed); school counseling (MA); secondary education (MAT), including English, social studies; special education (MAT). *Accreditation:* NCATE. *Program availability:* Part-time, evening/weekend. *Degree requirements:* For master's, thesis (for some programs), capstone project(s). *Entrance requirements:* For master's, PRAXIS I, minimum GPA of 2.8. Additional exam requirements/recommendations for international students: Required—TOEFL (minimum score 550 paper-based). *Faculty research:* Technology, literacy, special education, organizations, inclusion models.

Troy University, Graduate School, College of Education, Program in Secondary Education, Troy, AL 36082. Offers MS. *Accreditation:* NCATE. *Program availability:* Part-time, evening/weekend. *Faculty:* 3 full-time (2 women). *Students:* 6 full-time (all women), 5 part-time (4 women); includes 1 minority (Black or African American, non-Hispanic/Latino). Average age 27. 6 applicants, 67% accepted, 3 enrolled. *Degree requirements:* For master's, comprehensive exam, thesis. *Entrance requirements:* For master's, GRE (minimum score of 850 on old exam or 290 on new exam), GMAT (minimum score of 380), or MAT (minimum score of 385), bachelor's degree; minimum undergraduate GPA of 2.5 or 3.0 on last 30 semester hours, letter of recommendation. Additional exam requirements/recommendations for international students: Required—TOEFL (minimum score 523 paper-based; 70 iBT), IELTS (minimum score 6). *Application deadline:* Applications are processed on a rolling basis. Application fee: $50. Electronic applications accepted. *Expenses: Tuition, area resident:* Full-time $425; part-time $425 per credit hour. Tuition, state resident: full-time $425; part-time $425 per credit hour. Tuition, nonresident: full-time $850; part-time $850 per credit hour. *International tuition:* $850 full-time. *Required fees:* $50 per semester. Tuition and fees vary according to campus/location and program. *Financial support:* Fellowships, career-related internships or fieldwork, and scholarships/grants available. Support available to part-time students. Financial award applicants required to submit FAFSA. *Unit head:* Dr. Fred Figliano, Assistant Professor, Chair, Teacher Education, 334-808-6509, E-mail: ffigliano@troy.edu. *Application contact:* Jessica A. Kimbro, Assistant Director of Graduate Programs, 334-670-3189, E-mail: jacord@troy.edu.
Website: https://www.troy.edu/academics/academic-programs/college-education-programs.php

Tufts University, Graduate School of Arts and Sciences, Department of Education, Program in Education, Medford, MA 02155. Offers educational studies (MA); elementary education (MAT); middle and secondary education (MAT); museum education (MA); secondary education (MA); STEM education (MS, PhD). *Program availability:* Part-time. *Degree requirements:* For master's, thesis optional. *Entrance requirements:* For master's, GRE General Test, portfolio (for art education only); for doctorate, GRE General Test, writing sample. Additional exam requirements/recommendations for international students: Required—TOEFL (minimum score 550 paper-based; 80 iBT), IELTS (minimum score 6.5). Electronic applications accepted. *Expenses:* Contact institution.

Union College, Graduate Programs, Department of Education, Program in Secondary Education, Barbourville, KY 40906-1499. Offers MA. *Degree requirements:* For master's, thesis optional. *Entrance requirements:* For master's, GRE General Test, NTE.

Universidad Metropolitana, School of Education, Program in Teaching of Physical Education, San Juan, PR 00928-1150. Offers teaching of adult physical education (M Ed); teaching of elementary physical education (M Ed); teaching of secondary physical education (M Ed). *Degree requirements:* For master's, thesis or alternative. *Entrance requirements:* For master's, EXADEP, interview. Electronic applications accepted.

The University of Akron, Graduate School, College of Education, Department of Curricular and Instructional Studies, Program in Adolescent to Young Adult Education, Akron, OH 44325. Offers chemistry (MS); chemistry and physics (MS); earth science (MS); earth science and chemistry (MS); earth science and physics (MS); integrated language arts (MS); integrated mathematics (MS); integrated social studies (MS); life science (MS); life science and chemistry (MS); life science and earth science (MS); life science and physics (MS); physics (MS). *Accreditation:* NCATE. *Degree requirements:* For master's, comprehensive exam. *Entrance requirements:* For master's, minimum GPA of 3.0. Additional exam requirements/recommendations for international students: Required—TOEFL (minimum score 79 iBT), IELTS (minimum score 6.5). Electronic applications accepted.

The University of Alabama, Graduate School, College of Education, Department of Curriculum and Instruction, Tuscaloosa, AL 35487. Offers elementary education (MA, Ed D, PhD, Ed S); secondary education (MA, Ed D, PhD, Ed S). *Program availability:* Part-time, evening/weekend, 100% online, blended/hybrid learning. *Degree*

requirements: For master's, comprehensive exam, thesis (for some programs); for doctorate, comprehensive exam, thesis/dissertation; for Ed S, comprehensive exam, thesis. *Entrance requirements:* For master's and Ed S, MAT and/or GRE; for doctorate, GRE. Additional exam requirements/recommendations for international students: Recommended—TOEFL (minimum score 550 paper-based), IELTS (minimum score 6.5). Electronic applications accepted. *Faculty research:* Teacher education, diversity, integration of curriculum, technology, pedagogical content knowledge.

The University of Alabama at Birmingham, School of Education, Program in High School Education, Birmingham, AL 35294. Offers MA Ed. *Accreditation:* NCATE. *Degree requirements:* For master's, thesis optional. *Entrance requirements:* For master's, GRE General Test, MAT, or NTE, minimum GPA of 3.0. Electronic applications accepted. *Expenses: Tuition, area resident:* Full-time $8100; part-time $8100 per year. Tuition, state resident: full-time $8100. Tuition, nonresident: full-time $19,188; part-time $19,188 per year. Tuition and fees vary according to program.

The University of Alabama in Huntsville, School of Graduate Studies, College of Education, Huntsville, AL 35899. Offers autism spectrum disorders (M Ed, Graduate Certificate); biology (MAT); chemistry (MAT); differentiated instruction in elementary education (M Ed); English language arts (MAT); English speakers of other languages (M Ed, MAT); history (MAT); mathematics (MAT); physics (MAT); reading education (M Ed); secondary education (M Ed). *Program availability:* Part-time. *Faculty:* 13 full-time (10 women). *Students:* 38 full-time (30 women), 39 part-time (37 women); includes 17 minority (10 Black or African American, non-Hispanic/Latino; 3 American Indian or Alaska Native, non-Hispanic/Latino; 2 Asian, non-Hispanic/Latino; 2 Two or more races, non-Hispanic/Latino). Average age 33. 47 applicants, 83% accepted, 29 enrolled. In 2018, 31 master's awarded. *Degree requirements:* For master's, comprehensive exam, thesis or alternative, oral and written. *Entrance requirements:* For master's, GRE General Test, minimum GPA of 3.0. Additional exam requirements/recommendations for international students: Required—TOEFL (minimum score 500 paper-based; 80 iBT), IELTS (minimum score 6.5). *Application deadline:* For fall admission, 7/15 priority date for domestic students, 4/1 priority date for international students; for spring admission, 11/30 priority date for domestic students, 9/1 priority date for international students. Applications are processed on a rolling basis. Application fee: $50. Electronic applications accepted. *Expenses: Tuition, area resident:* Full-time $10,632; part-time $412 per credit hour. Tuition, state resident: full-time $10,632. Tuition, nonresident: full-time $23,604; part-time $412 per credit hour. *Required fees:* $582; $582. Tuition and fees vary according to course load and program. *Financial support:* In 2018–19, 2 students received support, including 1 teaching assistantship with full tuition reimbursement available (averaging $4,500 per year); career-related internships or fieldwork, Federal Work-Study, institutionally sponsored loans, scholarships/grants, health care benefits, tuition waivers (full and partial), and unspecified assistantships also available. Support available to part-time students. Financial award application deadline: 4/1; financial award applicants required to submit FAFSA. *Unit head:* Dr. Beth Nason Quick, Dean, 256-824-2325, E-mail: beth.quick@uah.edu. *Application contact:* Kim Gray, Graduate Studies Admissions Coordinator, 256-824-6002, Fax: 256-824-6405, E-mail: deangrad@uah.edu.
Website: http://www.uah.edu/education/

University of Alaska Southeast, Graduate Programs, Program in Education, Juneau, AK 99801. Offers educational leadership (M Ed); elementary education (MAT); learning design and technology (M Ed); mathematics education (M Ed); reading specialist (M Ed); secondary education (MAT); special education (M Ed, MAT). *Accreditation:* NCATE. *Program availability:* Part-time, evening/weekend, online learning. *Degree requirements:* For master's, comprehensive exam or project, portfolio. *Entrance requirements:* For master's, PRAXIS, minimum GPA of 3.0, writing sample, letters of recommendation. Electronic applications accepted. *Faculty research:* Applied classroom research, culturally responsive practices, action research, teaching effectiveness.

University of Alberta, Faculty of Graduate Studies and Research, Department of Secondary Education, Edmonton, AB T6G 2E1, Canada. Offers M Ed, Ed D, PhD. *Program availability:* Part-time. *Degree requirements:* For master's, thesis or alternative, 1 year of residency; for doctorate, thesis/dissertation, 2 years of residency (PhD), 1 year of residency (Ed D). *Entrance requirements:* For master's, teaching certificate, 2 years of teaching experience; for doctorate, master's degree. *Faculty research:* Curriculum studies, teacher education, subject area specializations.

The University of Arizona, College of Education, Department of Teaching, Learning and Sociocultural Studies, Program in Teaching and Teacher Education, Tucson, AZ 85721. Offers M Ed, MA, PhD. *Program availability:* Part-time, evening/weekend. *Degree requirements:* For master's, thesis optional; for doctorate, comprehensive exam, thesis/dissertation. *Entrance requirements:* For master's, writing sample, 1 year of teaching experience, 3 letters of recommendation; for doctorate, GRE General Test (minimum score 1000), minimum GPA of 3.5, 2 years of teaching experience, 3 letters of recommendation, writing sample. Additional exam requirements/recommendations for international students: Required—TOEFL (minimum score 550 paper-based; 79 iBT). Electronic applications accepted. *Faculty research:* Staff development, science education, environmental education, math education.

The University of Arizona, College of Science, Department of Mathematics, Program in Secondary Mathematics Education, Tucson, AZ 85721. Offers MA. *Program availability:* Part-time. *Degree requirements:* For master's, thesis, internships, colloquium, business courses. *Entrance requirements:* For master's, GRE, minimum GPA of 3.0, statement of purpose. Additional exam requirements/recommendations for international students: Required—TOEFL (minimum score 550 paper-based). *Faculty research:* Algebra, coding theory, graph theory, combinatorics, probability.

University of Arkansas, Graduate School, College of Education and Health Professions, Department of Curriculum and Instruction, Program in Secondary Education, Fayetteville, AR 72701. Offers M Ed, MAT, Ed S. *Accreditation:* NCATE. In 2018, 30 master's awarded. *Application deadline:* For fall admission, 8/1 for domestic students, 4/1 for international students; for spring admission, 12/1 for domestic students, 10/1 for international students; for summer admission, 4/15 for domestic students, 3/1 for international students. Applications are processed on a rolling basis. Application fee: $60. Electronic applications accepted. *Financial support:* Fellowships with tuition reimbursements, research assistantships, teaching assistantships, career-related internships or fieldwork, and Federal Work-Study available. Support available to part-time students. Financial award application deadline: 4/1; financial award applicants required to submit FAFSA. *Faculty research:* Mathematics. *Unit head:* Dr. Cheryl Murphy, Department Head, 479-575-5111, Fax: 479-575-2492, E-mail: cmurphy@uark.edu. *Application contact:* Jason Endacott, CIED Graduate Program Coordinator, 479-575-2657, Fax: 479-575-6676, E-mail: jendacot@uark.edu.
Website: https://seed.uark.edu

University of Arkansas at Little Rock, Graduate School, College of Education and Health Professions, Department of Teacher Education, Program in Secondary Education, Little Rock, AR 72204-1099. Offers M Ed. *Accreditation:* NCATE. *Program availability:* Part-time. *Degree requirements:* For master's, comprehensive exam. *Entrance requirements:* For master's, interview, minimum GPA of 2.75, GRE General Test or teaching certificate.

University of Arkansas at Pine Bluff, School of Education, Pine Bluff, AR 71601-2799. Offers elementary education (M Ed); secondary education (M Ed), including English education, mathematics education, science education, social studies education; teaching (MAT). *Accreditation:* NCATE. *Program availability:* Part-time, evening/weekend. *Degree requirements:* For master's, comprehensive exam. *Entrance requirements:* For master's, GRE, minimum GPA of 2.75, NTE or Standard Arkansas Teaching Certificate. *Faculty research:* Teacher certification, accreditation, assessment, standards, portfolio development, rehabilitation, technology.

University of Bridgeport, School of Education, Department of Education, Bridgeport, CT 06604. Offers education (MS); educational management (Ed D, Diploma), including intermediate administrator or supervisor (Diploma), leadership (Ed D); elementary education (MS, Diploma), including early childhood education, elementary education; middle school education (MS); music education (MS); remedial reading and language arts (Diploma); secondary education (MS, Diploma), including computer specialist (Diploma), international education (Diploma), reading specialist, secondary education. *Program availability:* Part-time, evening/weekend. *Degree requirements:* For master's, final exam, final project, or thesis; for doctorate, comprehensive exam, thesis/dissertation; for Diploma, thesis or alternative, final project. *Entrance requirements:* For master's, minimum undergraduate QPA of 2.67; for doctorate, GRE, MAT; for Diploma, GRE General Test or MAT, minimum graduate QPA of 3.0. Additional exam requirements/recommendations for international students: Recommended—TOEFL (minimum score 550 paper-based; 80 iBT), IELTS (minimum score 6.5). Electronic applications accepted. *Expenses:* Contact institution.

University of California, Irvine, School of Education, Irvine, CA 92697. Offers educational administration (Ed D); educational administration and leadership (Ed D); elementary and secondary education (MAT). *Program availability:* Part-time, evening/weekend. *Students:* 213 full-time (155 women), 3 part-time (2 women); includes 107 minority (1 Black or African American, non-Hispanic/Latino; 51 Asian, non-Hispanic/Latino; 40 Hispanic/Latino; 15 Two or more races, non-Hispanic/Latino), 23 international. Average age 28. 482 applicants, 47% accepted, 148 enrolled. In 2018, 141 master's, 8 doctorates awarded. *Entrance requirements:* For master's, GRE, minimum GPA of 3.0; for doctorate, GRE General Test, minimum GPA of 3.0. Additional exam requirements/recommendations for international students: Required—TOEFL (minimum score 550 paper-based). *Application deadline:* For fall admission, 1/2 priority date for domestic students, 1/2 for international students. Application fee: $105 ($125 for international students). Electronic applications accepted. *Financial support:* Fellowships, research assistantships with full tuition reimbursements, institutionally sponsored loans, traineeships, health care benefits, and unspecified assistantships available. Financial award application deadline: 3/1; financial award applicants required to submit FAFSA. *Faculty research:* Education technology, learning theory, social theory, cultural diversity, postmodernism. *Unit head:* Richard Arum, Dean, 949-824-2534, E-mail: richard.arum@uci.edu. *Application contact:* Denise Earley, Assistant Director of Student Affairs, 949-824-4022, E-mail: denise.earley@uci.edu.
Website: http://education.uci.edu/

University of Central Oklahoma, The Jackson College of Graduate Studies, College of Education and Professional Studies, Department of Educational Sciences, Foundations and Research, Edmond, OK 73034-5209. Offers secondary education (M Ed). *Program availability:* Part-time. *Degree requirements:* For master's, comprehensive exam (for some programs). *Entrance requirements:* Additional exam requirements/recommendations for international students: Required—TOEFL (minimum score 550 paper-based; 79 iBT), IELTS (minimum score 6.5). Electronic applications accepted.

University of Colorado Denver, School of Education and Human Development, Information and Learning Technologies Program, Denver, CO 80217. Offers e-learning design and implementation (MA); instructional design and adult learning (MA); K-12 teaching (MA). *Program availability:* Part-time, evening/weekend, online learning. *Degree requirements:* For master's, comprehensive exam (for some programs), comprehensive exam or online portfolio; 30 credit hours. *Entrance requirements:* For master's, GRE or MAT (if GPA is below 2.75), resume, statement of intent, three letters of recommendation, transcripts from all colleges/universities previously attended. Additional exam requirements/recommendations for international students: Required—TOEFL (minimum score 537 paper-based; 75 iBT); Recommended—IELTS (minimum score 6.5). Electronic applications accepted. *Expenses:* Contact institution. *Faculty research:* Technology for educational management, instructional design foundations, e-learning, educational design.

University of Colorado Denver, School of Education and Human Development, Teacher Education Programs, Denver, CO 80217. Offers elementary linguistically diverse education (MA); elementary math and science education (MA); elementary math education (MA); elementary reading and writing (MA); elementary science education (MA); secondary English education (MA); secondary linguistically diverse education (MA); secondary math education (MA); secondary reading and writing (MA); secondary science education (MA); special education (MA). *Accreditation:* NCATE. *Program availability:* Part-time, evening/weekend. *Degree requirements:* For master's, comprehensive exam. *Entrance requirements:* For master's, GRE or MAT (for those with GPA below 2.75), transcripts, resume, letters of recommendation. Additional exam requirements/recommendations for international students: Required—TOEFL (minimum score 537 paper-based; 75 iBT); Recommended—IELTS (minimum score 6.5). Electronic applications accepted. *Expenses:* Tuition, state resident: full-time $6786; part-time $337 per credit hour. Tuition, nonresident: full-time $22,590; part-time $1255 per credit hour. *Required fees:* $1231; $137 per credit hour. Tuition and fees vary according to program and reciprocity agreements. *Faculty research:* Linguistically diverse education/ESL, elementary reading and writing, elementary teacher education, secondary teacher education, special education.

University of Connecticut, Graduate School, Neag School of Education, Department of Curriculum and Instruction, Program in Secondary Education, Storrs, CT 06269. Offers MA, PhD. *Accreditation:* NCATE. Terminal master's awarded for partial completion of doctoral program. *Degree requirements:* For master's, comprehensive exam, thesis or alternative; for doctorate, thesis/dissertation. *Entrance requirements:* For doctorate, GRE General Test. Additional exam requirements/recommendations for international students: Required—TOEFL (minimum score 550 paper-based). Electronic applications accepted.

University of Dayton, Department of Teacher Education, Dayton, OH 45469. Offers adolescence to young adult education (MS Ed); early childhood leadership and advocacy (MS Ed); interdisciplinary education (MS Ed), including visual arts; interdisciplinary education studies (MS Ed); leadership in educational systems (MS Ed); literacy (MS Ed); mathematics education (MS Ed); middle childhood education (MS Ed); multi-age education (MS Ed), including world languages; music education (MS Ed); teacher as leader (MS Ed); teacher education (MS Ed); technology-enhanced learning (MS Ed); trans-disciplinary early childhood education (MS Ed). *Program availability:* Part-time, 100% online. *Degree requirements:* For master's, variable foreign language requirement, thesis or alternative, internship (for teaching licensure or endorsement). *Entrance requirements:* For master's, GRE (minimum score of 149 verbal, 4 on writing) or MAT (minimum score of 396) if undergraduate GPA was under 2.75, minimum GPA of 2.75, 3 letters of recommendation, personal statement or resume, official transcripts.

Additional exam requirements/recommendations for international students: Required—TOEFL (minimum score 550 paper-based; 80 iBT); Recommended—IELTS (minimum score 6.5). Electronic applications accepted. *Expenses:* Contact institution. *Faculty research:* Social emotional learning, culturally responsive teaching, urban teaching, literacy, instructional strategies, pre-service teacher education preparation.

University of Guam, Office of Graduate Studies, School of Education, Program in Secondary Education, Mangilao, GU 96923. Offers M Ed. *Degree requirements:* For master's, thesis, comprehensive oral and written exams. *Entrance requirements:* For master's, GRE General Test. Additional exam requirements/recommendations for international students: Required—TOEFL.

University of Illinois at Chicago, College of Education, Department of Curriculum and Instruction, Chicago, IL 60607-7128. Offers curriculum studies (PhD); elementary education (M Ed); secondary education (M Ed). *Program availability:* Part-time, evening/weekend. *Degree requirements:* For doctorate, thesis/dissertation. *Entrance requirements:* For master's, minimum GPA of 2.75; for doctorate, GRE General Test, minimum GPA of 2.75. Additional exam requirements/recommendations for international students: Required—TOEFL. Electronic applications accepted. *Faculty research:* Curriculum theory, curriculum development, research on teaching, curriculum and context, reading/literacy.

University of Indianapolis, Graduate Programs, School of Education, Indianapolis, IN 46227-3697. Offers art education (MAT); biology (MAT); chemistry (MAT); curriculum and instruction (MA); earth sciences (MAT); education (MA, MAT); educational leadership (MA); elementary education (MA); English (MAT); French (MAT); math (MAT); physical education (MAT); physics (MAT); secondary education (MA), including art education, education, English education, social studies education; social studies (MAT); Spanish (MAT). *Accreditation:* NCATE. *Program availability:* Part-time, evening/weekend. *Entrance requirements:* For master's, GRE Subject Test, PRAXIS I, minimum GPA of 2.5, 3 letters of recommendation, interview. Additional exam requirements/recommendations for international students: Required—TOEFL (minimum score 550 paper-based). *Faculty research:* Assessment of teacher education, perceptions of prospective teachers by parents.

The University of Iowa, Graduate College, College of Education, Department of Teaching and Learning, Program in Education, Iowa City, IA 52242-1316. Offers art education (MA); developmental reading (MA); elementary education (MA); English education (MA, MAT); foreign and second language education (MAT); foreign language education (MA); foreign language/ESL education (PhD); language, literacy and culture (PhD); mathematics education (MA, MAT, PhD); music education (MM, PhD); science education (MA); secondary education (MA); social studies (MA, PhD). *Degree requirements:* For master's, thesis optional, exam; for doctorate, comprehensive exam, thesis/dissertation. *Entrance requirements:* For master's and doctorate, GRE General Test, minimum GPA of 3.0. Additional exam requirements/recommendations for international students: Required—TOEFL (minimum score 550 paper-based; 81 iBT). Electronic applications accepted.

University of Kentucky, Graduate School, College of Education, Program in Curriculum and Instruction, Lexington, KY 40506-0032. Offers curriculum and instruction (Ed D, PhD); elementary education (MA Ed); instructional system design (MS Ed); literacy (MA Ed); middle school education (MA Ed, MS Ed); secondary education (MA Ed, MS Ed). *Accreditation:* NCATE. *Degree requirements:* For master's, comprehensive exam, thesis optional; for doctorate, comprehensive exam, thesis/dissertation. *Entrance requirements:* For master's, GRE General Test, minimum undergraduate GPA of 2.75; for doctorate, GRE General Test, minimum graduate GPA of 3.0. Additional exam requirements/recommendations for international students: Required—TOEFL (minimum score 550 paper-based). Electronic applications accepted. *Faculty research:* Educational reform, multicultural education, classroom instructional practices, performance based assessment, primary school programs.

University of La Verne, Regional and Online Campuses, Graduate Programs, High Desert Campus, Victorville, CA 92392. Offers business administration for experienced professionals (MBA); educational (special emphasis) (M Ed); educational counseling (MS); leadership and management (MS); multiple subject (elementary) (Credential); preliminary administrative services (Credential); pupil personnel services (Credential); single subject (secondary) (Credential). *Expenses:* Contact institution.

University of La Verne, Regional and Online Campuses, Graduate Programs, Kern County Campus, Bakersfield, CA 93301. Offers business administration for experienced professionals (MBA-EP); education (special emphasis) (M Ed); educational counseling (MS); educational leadership (M Ed); health administration (MHA); leadership and management (MS); mild/moderate education specialist (Credential); multiple subject (elementary) (Credential); organizational leadership (Ed D); preliminary administrative services (Credential); single subject (secondary) (Credential); special education studies (MS). *Program availability:* Part-time, evening/weekend. *Expenses:* Contact institution.

University of La Verne, Regional and Online Campuses, Graduate Programs, Ventura County/Point Mugu Naval Air Station Campuses, Oxnard, CA 93036. Offers business administration for experienced professionals (MS); educational counseling (MS); educational leadership (M Ed); leadership and management (MS); multiple subject (elementary) (Credential); pupil personnel services (Credential); single subject (secondary) (Credential). *Program availability:* Part-time, evening/weekend. *Expenses:* Contact institution.

University of Louisiana at Monroe, Graduate School, College of Arts, Education, and Sciences, School of Education, Program in Secondary Education, Monroe, LA 71209-0001. Offers MAT. *Accreditation:* NCATE. *Program availability:* Part-time, evening/weekend. *Faculty:* 11 full-time (7 women). *Students:* 1 (woman) full-time, 9 part-time (5 women); includes 1 minority (Black or African American, non-Hispanic/Latino). Average age 30. 6 applicants, 83% accepted, 3 enrolled. In 2018, 7 master's awarded. *Entrance requirements:* For master's, GRE General Test, PRAXIS, minimum GPA of 2.5. Additional exam requirements/recommendations for international students: Required—TOEFL (minimum score 500 paper-based; 61 iBT). *Application deadline:* For fall admission, 8/24 priority date for domestic students, 7/1 for international students; for winter admission, 12/14 priority date for domestic students; for spring admission, 1/19 for domestic students, 11/1 for international students. Applications are processed on a rolling basis. Application fee: $20 ($30 for international students). Electronic applications accepted. *Financial support:* Career-related internships or fieldwork, Federal Work-Study, and unspecified assistantships available. Financial award application deadline: 4/1; financial award applicants required to submit FAFSA.

University of Louisville, Graduate School, College of Education and Human Development, Departments of Early Childhood and Elementary Education, Middle and Secondary Education, and Special Education, Louisville, KY 40292-0001. Offers art education (MAT); autism and applied behavior analysis (Certificate); curriculum and instruction (PhD); early elementary education (MAT); exercise physiology (MS); health and physical education (MAT); health professions education (Certificate); higher education (MA); human resources and organization development (MS); instructional technology (M Ed); interdisciplinary early childhood education (MAT); middle school education (MAT); music education (MAT); secondary education (MAT); special education (MAT); sport administration (MS); teacher leadership (M Ed). *Program*

availability: Part-time, evening/weekend, 100% online, blended/hybrid learning. *Faculty:* 97 full-time (64 women), 131 part-time/adjunct (86 women). *Students:* 109 full-time (72 women), 139 part-time (87 women); includes 43 minority (18 Black or African American, non-Hispanic/Latino; 6 Asian, non-Hispanic/Latino; 10 Hispanic/Latino; 9 Two or more races, non-Hispanic/Latino), 9 international. Average age 29. 108 applicants, 75% accepted, 59 enrolled. In 2018, 64 master's awarded. Terminal master's awarded for partial completion of doctoral program. *Degree requirements:* For master's, comprehensive exam (for some programs), thesis optional; for doctorate, comprehensive exam (for some programs), thesis/dissertation. *Entrance requirements:* For master's, GRE (for most programs), PRAXIS (for educator preparation programs), professional statement, recommendation letters, resume, transcripts; for doctorate and Certificate, GRE, professional statement, recommendation letters, resume, transcripts. Additional exam requirements/recommendations for international students: Required—TOEFL (minimum score 550 paper-based; 79 iBT); Recommended—IELTS (minimum score 6.5). *Application deadline:* For fall admission, 6/1 priority date for domestic students, 5/1 priority date for international students; for spring admission, 10/1 for domestic students, 11/1 priority date for international students; for summer admission, 3/1 priority date for domestic students, 4/1 priority date for international students. Application fee: $65. *Expenses: Tuition, area resident:* Full-time $6500; part-time $723 per credit hour. Tuition, state resident: full-time $6500. Tuition, nonresident: full-time $13,557; part-time $1507 per credit hour. Tuition and fees vary according to course load and program. *Financial support:* In 2018–19, 144 students received support, including fellowships with full tuition reimbursements available (averaging $21,024 per year), research assistantships with full tuition reimbursements available (averaging $21,024 per year), teaching assistantships with full tuition reimbursements available (averaging $21,024 per year); Federal Work-Study, scholarships/grants, health care benefits, tuition waivers (full), and unspecified assistantships also available. Financial award application deadline: 3/1; financial award applicants required to submit FAFSA. *Faculty research:* Children's early reading and writing development, crelevance of basic facts in elementary mathematics instruction, clinical model of teacher education, cultural and linguistic context of diverse learners, and STEM-integrated curriculum design and development. STEM teaching and learning, content literacy for English language learners, social justice in teacher education, adolescent literacy, mathematics teacher development. Classroom and behavior management; moderate/severe disabilities, autism. *Unit head:* Dr. Amy Lingo, Interim Dean, 502-852-3235, Fax: 502-852-1464, E-mail: cehdinfo@louisville.edu. *Application contact:* Dr. Margaret Pentecost, Assistant Dean for Graduate Student Success, 502-852-6437, Fax: 502-852-1417, E-mail: gedadm@louisville.edu.
Website: http://louisville.edu/delphi

University of Mary Hardin-Baylor, Graduate Studies in Education, Belton, TX 76513. Offers curriculum and instruction (M Ed); educational administration (M Ed, Ed D), including higher education (Ed D), leadership in nursing education (Ed D), P-12 (Ed D). *Program availability:* Part-time, evening/weekend. *Degree requirements:* For master's, comprehensive exam; for doctorate, thesis/dissertation. *Entrance requirements:* For master's, minimum GPA of 3.0, interview; for doctorate, minimum GPA of 3.5, interview, essay, resume, employment verification, 3 letters of recommendation. Additional exam requirements/recommendations for international students: Required—TOEFL (minimum score 60 iBT), IELTS (minimum score 4.5). Electronic applications accepted. *Expenses:* Contact institution. *Faculty research:* Motivational orientation of preservice teachers.

University of Maryland, College Park, Academic Affairs, College of Education, Department of Teaching, Learning, Policy and Leadership, College Park, MD 20742. Offers reading (M Ed, MA, PhD, CAGS); secondary education (M Ed, MA, Ed D, PhD, CAGS); teaching English to speakers of other languages (M Ed). *Accreditation:* NCATE. *Program availability:* Part-time, evening/weekend, online learning. *Degree requirements:* For master's, comprehensive exam, seminar paper; for doctorate, comprehensive exam, thesis/dissertation, published paper, oral exam. *Entrance requirements:* For master's, GRE General Test or MAT, minimum GPA of 3.0, 3 letters of recommendation; for doctorate, GRE General Test or MAT, minimum undergraduate GPA of 3.0, graduate 3.5; 3 letters of recommendation. Electronic applications accepted. *Faculty research:* Teacher preparation, curriculum study, in-service education.

University of Massachusetts Amherst, Graduate School, College of Education, Program in Education, Amherst, MA 01003. Offers bilingual, English as a second language, and multicultural education (M Ed, Ed S); child study and early education (M Ed); children, families and schools (Ed D, Ed S); early childhood and elementary teacher education (M Ed); educational leadership (M Ed); educational policy and leadership (Ed D); higher education (M Ed); international education (M Ed); language, literacy and culture (Ed D); learning, media and technology (M Ed, Ed S); mathematics, science, and learning technologies (Ed D); reading and writing (M Ed); research, educational measurement and psychometrics (Ed D); school counselor education (M Ed, Ed S); school psychology (Ed S); science education (Ed S); secondary teacher education (M Ed); social justice education (M Ed, Ed D, Ed S); special education (M Ed, Ed D, Ed S); teacher education and school improvement (Ed D, Ed S). *Accreditation:* NCATE. *Program availability:* Part-time, online learning. Terminal master's awarded for partial completion of doctoral program. *Degree requirements:* For doctorate, comprehensive exam, thesis/dissertation. *Entrance requirements:* Additional exam requirements/recommendations for international students: Required—TOEFL (minimum score 550 paper-based; 80 iBT), IELTS (minimum score 6.5). Electronic applications accepted.

University of Massachusetts Dartmouth, Graduate School, College of Arts and Sciences, School of Education, Department of STEM Education and Teacher Development, North Dartmouth, MA 02747-2300. Offers English as a second language (Postbaccalaureate Certificate); mathematics education (PhD); middle school education (MAT); secondary school education (MAT). *Program availability:* Part-time. *Faculty:* 9 full-time (6 women), 3 part-time/adjunct (2 women). *Students:* 21 full-time (18 women), 100 part-time (53 women); includes 20 minority (3 Black or African American, non-Hispanic/Latino; 2 Asian, non-Hispanic/Latino; 11 Hispanic/Latino; 4 Two or more races, non-Hispanic/Latino), 3 international. Average age 34. 63 applicants, 90% accepted, 45 enrolled. In 2018, 68 master's, 1 doctorate, 1 other advanced degree awarded. *Degree requirements:* For doctorate, thesis/dissertation. *Entrance requirements:* For master's, Statement of Purpose, Resume, Official Transcripts, copy of MA MTELs, 2 letters of recommendation, Proof of License (for Professional Licensure Program); for doctorate, GRE Score, Statement of Purpose, Resume, Official transcripts, 3 letters of recommendation; for Postbaccalaureate Certificate, Statement of Purpose, Resume, Official Transcripts, 2 letters of recommendation, MTEL Score Report. Additional exam requirements/recommendations for international students: Required—TOEFL (minimum score 550 paper-based; 79 iBT), IELTS (minimum score 6.5). *Application deadline:* For fall admission, 1/15 priority date for domestic students, 12/15 priority date for international students; for spring admission, 12/15 priority date for domestic students, 11/15 priority date for international students. Application fee: $60. Electronic applications accepted. *Financial support:* In 2018–19, 1 fellowship (averaging $18,000 per year), 3 research assistantships (averaging $10,897 per year), 6 teaching assistantships (averaging $8,017 per year) were awarded; tuition waivers (full) and doctoral support also available. Financial award application deadline: 3/1; financial award applicants required to submit FAFSA. *Faculty research:* Mindfulness in education, literacies,

assessment of teacher knowledge, curriculum tools for supporting mathematics learning. *Total annual research expenditures:* $1.8 million. *Unit head:* Traci Almeida, Coordinator of Graduate Admissions and Licensure, 508-999-8098, Fax: 508-910-8183, E-mail: talmeida@umassd.edu. *Application contact:* Scott Webster, Director of Graduate Studies and Admissions, 508-999-8604, Fax: 508-999-8183, E-mail: graduate@umassd.edu.
Website: http://www.umassd.edu/cas/schoolofeducation/departments/stemeducationandteacherdevelopment/

University of Memphis, Graduate School, College of Education, Department of Instruction and Curriculum Leadership, Memphis, TN 38152. Offers advanced studies in teaching and learning (M Ed); applied behavior analysis (Graduate Certificate); autism studies (Graduate Certificate); early childhood education (MAT, MS, Ed D); elementary education (MAT); instruction and curriculum (MS, Ed D); instruction design and technology (MS, Ed D); instructional design and technology (Graduate Certificate); literacy, leadership, and coaching (Graduate Certificate); reading (MS, Ed D); school library information specialist (Graduate Certificate); secondary education (MAT); special education (MAT, MS, Ed D); STEM teacher leadership (Graduate Certificate); urban education (Graduate Certificate). *Accreditation:* NCATE (one or more programs are accredited). *Program availability:* Part-time. *Students:* 62 full-time (45 women), 412 part-time (326 women); includes 209 minority (179 Black or African American, non-Hispanic/Latino; 1 American Indian or Alaska Native, non-Hispanic/Latino; 5 Asian, non-Hispanic/Latino; 17 Hispanic/Latino; 7 Two or more races, non-Hispanic/Latino), 4 international. Average age 35. 195 applicants, 91% accepted, 143 enrolled. In 2018, 122 master's, 13 doctorates, 29 other advanced degrees awarded. Terminal master's awarded for partial completion of doctoral program. *Degree requirements:* For master's, comprehensive exam, thesis or alternative; for doctorate, comprehensive exam, thesis/dissertation. *Entrance requirements:* For master's, GRE General Test, PRAXIS, minimum GPA of 2.5, letters of reference; for doctorate, GRE General Test, GRE Subject Test, 2 years of teaching experience, letters of reference, statement of purpose, interview. Additional exam requirements/recommendations for international students: Required—TOEFL (minimum score 550 paper-based; 79 iBT). *Application deadline:* For fall admission, 4/1 priority date for domestic students; for spring admission, 10/1 priority date for domestic students; for summer admission, 2/1 priority date for domestic students. Applications are processed on a rolling basis. Application fee: $35 ($60 for international students). Electronic applications accepted. *Expenses: Tuition, area resident:* Full-time $10,240; part-time $503 per credit hour. Tuition, state resident: full-time $10,464. Tuition, nonresident: full-time $20,224; part-time $991 per credit hour. *Required fees:* $850; $106 per credit hour. *Financial support:* Research assistantships with full tuition reimbursements, teaching assistantships with full tuition reimbursements, career-related internships or fieldwork, Federal Work-Study, institutionally sponsored loans, scholarships/grants, traineeships, and unspecified assistantships available. Support available to part-time students. Financial award application deadline: 2/1; financial award applicants required to submit FAFSA. *Faculty research:* Effective urban teachers, preparation and retention of urban teachers, technology utilization in schools, field-based teacher preparation programs, effective use of online instruction. *Unit head:* Dr. Christian Mueller, Chair, 901-678-2365, E-mail: cemuellr@memphis.edu. *Application contact:* Dr. Lee Allen, Director of Graduate Programs, 901-678-4073, E-mail: allenlee@memphis.edu.
Website: http://www.memphis.edu/icl/

University of Michigan–Flint, School of Education and Human Services, Department of Education, Flint, MI 48502-1950. Offers curriculum and instruction (Ed S); early childhood education (MA); education (Ed D); educational leadership (Ed S); educational technology (MA), including curriculum and instruction, developer; literacy education (MA); secondary education with certification (MA). *Program availability:* Part-time, evening/weekend, online only, 100% online, mixed mode format (for some programs). *Faculty:* 16 full-time (10 women), 28 part-time/adjunct (14 women). *Students:* 31 full-time (23 women), 179 part-time (135 women); includes 54 minority (42 Black or African American, non-Hispanic/Latino; 3 Asian, non-Hispanic/Latino; 4 Hispanic/Latino; 1 Native Hawaiian or other Pacific Islander, non-Hispanic/Latino; 4 Two or more races, non-Hispanic/Latino), 1 international. Average age 39. 133 applicants, 72% accepted, 61 enrolled. In 2018, 60 master's awarded. *Degree requirements:* For master's, thesis optional; for doctorate, thesis/dissertation. *Entrance requirements:* For master's, bachelor's degree from regionally-accredited institution, minimum overall undergraduate GPA of 3.0 on 4.0 scale; for doctorate, completion of Eds minimum overall graduate GPA of 3.3 (6.0 on a 9.0 scale) or equivalent; at least 3 years of work experience in a P-16 educational institution or in an education-related position; for Ed S, MA or MS in education-related field from accredited institution; minimum overall graduate GPA of 3.0 (6.0 on a 9.0 scale) or equivalent; at least 3 years of work experience in an educational setting. Additional exam requirements/recommendations for international students: Required—TOEFL (minimum score 84 iBT), IELTS (minimum score 6.5). *Application deadline:* For fall admission, 8/1 for domestic students, 5/1 for international students; for winter admission, 11/15 for domestic students, 9/15 for international students; for spring admission, 3/15 for domestic students, 1/15 for international students; for summer admission, 5/15 for domestic students. Applications are processed on a rolling basis. Application fee: $55. Electronic applications accepted. *Expenses:* Contact institution. *Financial support:* Federal Work-Study, scholarships/grants, and unspecified assistantships available. Financial award application deadline: 3/1; financial award applicants required to submit FAFSA. *Unit head:* Dr. Mary Jo Finney, Department Chair/Associate Professor, 810-766-6617, E-mail: mjfinney@umflint.edu. *Application contact:* Matt Bohlen, Director of Graduate Admissions, 810-762-3171, Fax: 810-766-6789, E-mail: mbohlen@umflint.edu.
Website: https://www.umflint.edu/education/graduate-programs

University of Mississippi, Graduate School, School of Education, University, MS 38677. Offers counselor education (M Ed, PhD); counselor education - play therapy (Ed S); early childhood (M Ed); educational leadership K-12 (M Ed, Ed D, PhD, Ed S); elementary education (M Ed, Ed D, Ed S); higher education/student personnel (Ed D, PhD); literacy education (M Ed); math education (Ed D); secondary education (M Ed, PhD, Ed S); special education (M Ed, PhD, Ed S); teacher corporations (MA); teacher education (MA). *Accreditation:* NCATE. *Faculty:* 59 full-time (35 women), 34 part-time/adjunct (26 women). *Students:* 169 full-time (137 women), 461 part-time (329 women); includes 199 minority (185 Black or African American, non-Hispanic/Latino; 3 Asian, non-Hispanic/Latino; 7 Hispanic/Latino; 4 Two or more races, non-Hispanic/Latino), 5 international. Average age 33. In 2018, 180 master's, 57 doctorates, 37 other advanced degrees awarded. *Entrance requirements:* For master's, GRE General Test, minimum GPA of 3.0; for doctorate, GRE General Test. Additional exam requirements/recommendations for international students: Required—TOEFL. *Application deadline:* Applications are processed on a rolling basis. Application fee: $50. Electronic applications accepted. *Financial support:* Scholarships/grants available. Financial award application deadline: 3/1; financial award applicants required to submit FAFSA. *Unit head:* Dr. David Rock, Dean, 662-915-7063, Fax: 662-915-7249, E-mail: soe@olemiss.edu. *Application contact:* Temeka Smith, Graduate Activities Specialist for Admissions, 662-915-7474, Fax: 662-915-7577, E-mail: gschool@olemiss.edu.

University of Missouri–St. Louis, College of Education, Department of Educator Preparation, Innovation and Research, St. Louis, MO 63121. Offers elementary education (M Ed), including early childhood, general, reading; secondary education (M Ed), including curriculum and instruction, general, middle level education, reading, teaching English to speakers of other languages (TESOL); special education (M Ed), including autism and developmental disabilities, early childhood special education. *Program availability:* Part-time, evening/weekend. *Degree requirements:* For master's, comprehensive exam. *Entrance requirements:* Additional exam requirements/recommendations for international students: Recommended—TOEFL (minimum score 550 paper-based; 79 iBT), IELTS (minimum score 6.5). Electronic applications accepted.

University of Montevallo, College of Education, Program in Secondary/High School Education, Montevallo, AL 35115. Offers M Ed. *Accreditation:* NCATE. *Students:* 16 full-time (12 women), 50 part-time (33 women); includes 17 minority (16 Black or African American, non-Hispanic/Latino; 1 Two or more races, non-Hispanic/Latino), 1 international. In 2018, 36 master's awarded. *Entrance requirements:* For master's, GRE General Test, MAT, minimum undergraduate GPA of 2.5. Additional exam requirements/recommendations for international students: Required—TOEFL (minimum score 550 paper-based). *Application deadline:* For fall admission, 7/15 for domestic students; for spring admission, 11/15 for domestic students. Application fee: $30. *Expenses: Tuition, area resident:* Full-time $10,512. Tuition, state resident: full-time $10,512. Tuition, nonresident: full-time $22,464. *International tuition:* $22,464 full-time. *Financial support:* Federal Work-Study, scholarships/grants, and unspecified assistantships available. *Unit head:* Dr. Charlotte Daughhetee, Interim Dean, 205-665-6360, E-mail: daughc@montevallo.edu. *Application contact:* Colleen Kennedy, Graduate Program Assistant, 205-665-6350, E-mail: ckennedy@montevallo.edu.

University of Nebraska at Kearney, College of Education, Department of Teacher Education, Kearney, NE 68849-0001. Offers curriculum and instruction (MA Ed), including early childhood education, elementary education, English as a second language, instructional effectiveness, reading/special education, secondary education; instructional technology (MS Ed), including information technology, instructional technology, school librarian; reading PK-12 (MA Ed); special education (MA Ed), including advanced practitioner: assistive technology specialist, advanced practitioner: behavioral interventionist, advanced practitioner: inclusive collaboration specialist, gifted, teacher education. *Program availability:* Part-time, evening/weekend, online only, 100% online. *Degree requirements:* For master's, comprehensive exam, thesis optional. *Entrance requirements:* For master's, portfolio or GRE. Additional exam requirements/recommendations for international students: Recommended—TOEFL (minimum score 550 paper-based; 79 iBT), IELTS (minimum score 6.5). Electronic applications accepted. *Expenses:* Contact institution.

University of Nebraska at Omaha, Graduate Studies, College of Education, Department of Teacher Education, Program in Secondary Education, Omaha, NE 68182. Offers instruction in urban schools (Certificate); secondary education (MS). *Accreditation:* NCATE. *Program availability:* Part-time, evening/weekend. *Degree requirements:* For master's, comprehensive exam, thesis (for some programs). *Entrance requirements:* For master's, minimum GPA of 3.0, transcripts. Additional exam requirements/recommendations for international students: Required—TOEFL, IELTS, PTE. Electronic applications accepted.

University of Nevada, Las Vegas, Graduate College, College of Education, Department of Teaching and Learning, Las Vegas, NV 89154-3005. Offers curriculum and instruction (M Ed, MS, Ed D, PhD, Ed S), including teacher education (PhD); elementary teaching (Certificate); online teaching and training (Certificate); secondary teaching (Certificate); social justice studies (Certificate); teaching and learning (PhD). *Program availability:* Part-time, evening/weekend. *Faculty:* 25 full-time (12 women), 11 part-time/adjunct (8 women). *Students:* 304 full-time (212 women), 271 part-time (181 women); includes 255 minority (56 Black or African American, non-Hispanic/Latino; 1 American Indian or Alaska Native, non-Hispanic/Latino; 38 Asian, non-Hispanic/Latino; 124 Hispanic/Latino; 1 Native Hawaiian or other Pacific Islander, non-Hispanic/Latino; 35 Two or more races, non-Hispanic/Latino), 16 international. Average age 34. 228 applicants, 86% accepted, 164 enrolled. In 2018, 135 master's, 12 doctorates, 10 other advanced degrees awarded. *Degree requirements:* For master's, comprehensive exam (for some programs), thesis (for some programs); for doctorate, comprehensive exam, thesis/dissertation, defense of dissertation; for other advanced degree, comprehensive exam (for some programs), oral presentation of special project or professional paper. *Entrance requirements:* For master's, bachelor's degree with minimum GPA 2.75; for doctorate, GRE General Test, master's degree with minimum GPA of 3.0; statement of purpose; demonstration of oral communication skills; 3 letters of recommendation; for other advanced degree, PRAXIS Core (for some programs); PRAXIS II (for some programs), bachelor's degree (for some programs). Additional exam requirements/recommendations for international students: Required—TOEFL (minimum score 550 paper-based; 80 iBT), IELTS (minimum score 7). *Application deadline:* For fall admission, 6/1 for domestic students, 5/1 for international students; for spring admission, 11/1 for domestic students, 10/1 for international students; for summer admission, 3/15 for domestic students. Application fee: $60 ($95 for international students). Electronic applications accepted. *Financial support:* In 2018–19, 31 students received support, including 7 research assistantships with full tuition reimbursements available (averaging $18,286 per year), 24 teaching assistantships with full tuition reimbursements available (averaging $19,271 per year); institutionally sponsored loans, scholarships/grants, health care benefits, and unspecified assistantships also available. Financial award application deadline: 3/15; financial award applicants required to submit FAFSA. *Faculty research:* Content area and critical literacy, education in content areas, teacher education, science, technology, engineering and mathematics education, immersive environments/simulations/games. *Total annual research expenditures:* $1.1 million. *Unit head:* Dr. P.G. Schrader, Chair/Professor, 702-895-3331, Fax: 702-895-4898, E-mail: tl.chair@unlv.edu. *Application contact:* Dr. Micah Stohlmann, Graduate Coordinator, 702-895-0836, Fax: 702-895-4898, E-mail: tl.gradcoord@unlv.edu.
Website: http://tl.unlv.edu/

University of Nevada, Reno, Graduate School, College of Education, Department of Curriculum, Teaching and Learning, Program in Secondary Education, Reno, NV 89557. Offers M Ed, MA, MS. *Degree requirements:* For master's, thesis optional. *Entrance requirements:* For master's, GRE General Test, minimum GPA of 2.75. Additional exam requirements/recommendations for international students: Required—TOEFL (minimum score 500 paper-based; 61 iBT), IELTS (minimum score 6). Electronic applications accepted. *Faculty research:* Educational trends, pedagogy.

University of New Hampshire, Graduate School, College of Liberal Arts, Department of Education, Program in Secondary Education, Durham, NH 03824. Offers M Ed, MAT. *Program availability:* Part-time. *Entrance requirements:* For master's, PRAXIS, Department of Education background check. Additional exam requirements/recommendations for international students: Required—TOEFL (minimum score 550 paper-based; 80 iBT). Electronic applications accepted.

University of New Hampshire, Graduate School Manchester Campus, Manchester, NH 03101. Offers business administration (MBA); cybersecurity policy and risk management (MS); educational administration and supervision (Ed S); educational studies (M Ed); elementary education (M Ed); information technology (MS); public administration (MPA); public health (MPH, Certificate); secondary education (M Ed,

MAT); social work (MSW); substance use disorders (Certificate). *Program availability:* Part-time, evening/weekend. *Entrance requirements:* Additional exam requirements/ recommendations for international students: Required—TOEFL (minimum score 550 paper-based; 80 iBT). Electronic applications accepted.

University of New Mexico, Graduate Studies, College of Education, Program in Secondary Education, Albuquerque, NM 87131-2039. Offers math, science, and educational technology (MA). *Program availability:* Part-time. *Students:* Average age 33. 35 applicants, 80% accepted, 22 enrolled. In 2018, 42 master's awarded. *Degree requirements:* For master's, comprehensive exam, thesis optional. *Entrance requirements:* For master's, minimum overall GPA of 3.0, some experience working with students, NMTA or teacher's licensure, 3 letters of reference, letter of intent. Additional exam requirements/recommendations for international students: Required—TOEFL (minimum score 550 paper-based). *Application deadline:* For fall admission, 2/1 for domestic students; for spring admission, 10/1 for domestic students. Application fee: $50. Electronic applications accepted. *Financial support:* Teaching assistantships with partial tuition reimbursements, career-related internships or fieldwork, scholarships/ grants, and unspecified assistantships available. Financial award application deadline: 4/15. *Faculty research:* Secondary education, teacher education, reflective practice, teacher leadership, student learning. *Unit head:* Dr. Cheryl Torrez, Chair, 505-277-0911, Fax: 505-277-0455, E-mail: ted@unm.edu. *Application contact:* Robert Romero, Administrative Assistant, 505-277-0513, Fax: 505-277-0455, E-mail: ted@unm.edu.
Website: http://coe.unm.edu/departments-programs/teelp/secondary-education/index.html

University of North Alabama, College of Education, Department of Secondary Education, Program in Secondary Education, Florence, AL 35632-0001. Offers secondary education (MA Ed); special education (MA Ed). *Accreditation:* NCATE. *Program availability:* Part-time, 100% online, blended/hybrid learning. *Degree requirements:* For master's, comprehensive exam. *Entrance requirements:* For master's, GRE, MAT, or NTE, minimum GPA of 2.5, Alabama Class B Certificate or equivalent, teaching experience. Additional exam requirements/recommendations for international students: Required—TOEFL (minimum score 79 iBT), IELTS (minimum score 6), PTE (minimum score 54). Electronic applications accepted.

The University of North Carolina at Chapel Hill, Graduate School, School of Education, Program in Secondary Education, Chapel Hill, NC 27599. Offers English (Grades 9-12) (MAT); English as a second language (MAT); French (Grades K-12) (MAT); German (Grades K-12) (MAT); Japanese (Grades K-12) (MAT); Latin (Grades 9-12) (MAT); mathematics (Grades 9-12) (MAT); music (Grades K-12) (MAT); science (Grades 9-12) (MAT); social studies (Grades 9-12) (MAT); Spanish (Grades K-12) (MAT). *Accreditation:* NCATE. *Degree requirements:* For master's, comprehensive exam. *Entrance requirements:* For master's, GRE General Test, minimum GPA of 3.0 during last 2 years of undergraduate course work. Additional exam requirements/ recommendations for international students: Required—TOEFL (minimum score 550 paper-based). Electronic applications accepted.

The University of North Carolina at Charlotte, Cato College of Education, Department of Middle, Secondary and K-12 Education, Charlotte, NC 28223-0001. Offers middle grades and secondary education (M Ed); teaching English as a second language (M Ed, Graduate Certificate). *Program availability:* Part-time. *Students:* 3 full-time (all women), 88 part-time (77 women); includes 21 minority (19 Black or African American, non-Hispanic/Latino; 1 Asian, non-Hispanic/Latino; 1 Hispanic/Latino), 3 international. Average age 34. 36 applicants, 94% accepted, 30 enrolled. In 2018, 25 master's awarded. *Entrance requirements:* For master's, GRE or MAT, bachelor's degree from accredited college or university; minimum GPA of 3.0 in undergraduate work; North Carolina Class A teaching license in appropriate middle grades or secondary education field; minimum of two years' teaching experience; written narrative providing statement of purpose for master's degree study; letters of recommendation; for Graduate Certificate, bachelor's degree from accredited institution; minimum undergraduate GPA of 2.5 overall or 3.0 in senior year, or 15 hours taken in the last 5 years; satisfactory recommendations from three persons knowledgeable of applicant's interactions with children or adolescents; statement of purpose. Additional exam requirements/ recommendations for international students: Required—TOEFL (minimum score 523 paper-based; 70 iBT), IELTS (minimum score 6), TOEFL (minimum score 523 paper-based, 70 iBT) or IELTS (6). *Application deadline:* Applications are processed on a rolling basis. Application fee: $75. Electronic applications accepted. Tuition and fees vary according to course load and program. *Financial support:* Research assistantships, teaching assistantships, career-related internships or fieldwork, institutionally sponsored loans, scholarships/grants, and unspecified assistantships available. Support available to part-time students. Financial award application deadline: 3/1; financial award applicants required to submit FAFSA. *Total annual research expenditures:* $309,255. *Unit head:* Scott Kissau, Chair, 704-687-8875, E-mail: spkissau@uncc.edu. *Application contact:* Kathy B. Giddings, Director of Graduate Admissions, 704-687-5503, Fax: 704-687-1668, E-mail: gradadm@uncc.edu.
Website: http://mdsk.uncc.edu/

The University of North Carolina at Charlotte, Cato College of Education, Interdisciplinary Education Programs, Charlotte, NC 28223-0001. Offers art education (Graduate Certificate); child and family development: early childhood education (MAT); curriculum and instruction (PhD); elementary education (MAT); foreign language education (MAT); middle grades education (MAT); secondary education (MAT); special education (MAT); teaching (Graduate Certificate); teaching English as a second language (MAT); theatre education (Graduate Certificate). *Program availability:* Part-time, 100% online, blended/hybrid learning. *Students:* 70 full-time (55 women), 511 part-time (414 women); includes 228 minority (160 Black or African American, non-Hispanic/ Latino; 1 American Indian or Alaska Native, non-Hispanic/Latino; 11 Asian, non-Hispanic/Latino; 38 Hispanic/Latino; 18 Two or more races, non-Hispanic/Latino), 8 international. Average age 34. 343 applicants, 92% accepted, 219 enrolled. In 2018, 69 master's, 13 doctorates, 161 other advanced degrees awarded. *Entrance requirements:* For master's, GRE or MAT, bachelor's degree, or its U.S. equivalent, from regionally-accredited college or university; minimum overall GPA of 3.0 on all previous work beyond high school; statement of purpose (essay); at least three recommendation forms; for doctorate, GRE or MAT, bachelor's degree (or its U.S. equivalent) from regionally-accredited college or university; minimum overall GPA of 3.5 in master's degree program; for Graduate Certificate, bachelor's degree from regionally-accredited university; minimum GPA of 2.75 on all post-secondary work attempted; transcripts; personal statement outlining why the applicant seeks admission to the program. Additional exam requirements/recommendations for international students: Required—TOEFL (minimum score 523 paper-based; 70 iBT), IELTS (minimum score 6), TOEFL (minimum score 523 paper-based, 70 iBT) or IELTS (6). *Application deadline:* Applications are processed on a rolling basis. Application fee: $75. Electronic applications accepted. Tuition and fees vary according to course load and program. *Financial support:* Career-related internships or fieldwork, institutionally sponsored loans, scholarships/grants, and unspecified assistantships available. Support available to part-time students. Financial award application deadline: 3/1; financial award applicants required to submit FAFSA. *Unit head:* Dr. Ellen McIntyre, Dean, 704-687-8722, E-mail: ellen.mcintyre@uncc.edu. *Application contact:* Kathy B. Giddings, Director of Graduate Admissions, 704-687-5503, Fax: 704-687-1668, E-mail: gradadm@uncc.edu.
Website: http://education.uncc.edu/academic-programs

The University of North Carolina Wilmington, Watson College of Education, Department of Instructional Technology, Foundations and Secondary Education, Wilmington, NC 28403-3297. Offers English as a second language (M Ed, MAT); instructional technology (MS); secondary education (M Ed, MAT). *Program availability:* Part-time, blended/hybrid learning. *Degree requirements:* For master's, thesis or research project/portfolio. *Entrance requirements:* For master's, GRE or MAT, education statement of interest essay, 3 letters of recommendation. Additional exam requirements/ recommendations for international students: Required—TOEFL (minimum score 550 paper-based; 79 iBT), IELTS (minimum score 6.5). Electronic applications accepted.

University of Northern Iowa, Graduate College, College of Humanities, Arts and Sciences, Department of Languages and Literatures, MA Program in Teaching English in Secondary Schools, Cedar Falls, IA 50614. Offers MA.

University of Northern Iowa, Graduate College, College of Humanities, Arts and Sciences, Department of Mathematics, MA Program in Mathematics, Cedar Falls, IA 50614. Offers community college teaching (MA); mathematics (MA); secondary teaching (MA).

University of North Florida, College of Education and Human Services, Department of Foundations and Secondary Education, Jacksonville, FL 32224. Offers adult learning (M Ed); professional education (M Ed). *Accreditation:* NCATE. *Program availability:* Part-time, evening/weekend. *Faculty:* 13 full-time (6 women). *Students:* 4 part-time (3 women); includes 3 minority (1 Asian, non-Hispanic/Latino; 2 Two or more races, non-Hispanic/Latino). Average age 30. 1 applicant, 100% accepted, 1 enrolled. In 2018, 6 master's awarded. *Entrance requirements:* For master's, GRE General Test, minimum GPA of 3.0 in last 60 hours, interview, 3 letters of recommendation. Additional exam requirements/recommendations for international students: Required—TOEFL (minimum score 500 paper-based; 61 iBT). *Application deadline:* For fall admission, 5/1 for international students; for spring admission, 10/1 for international students. Application fee: $30. Electronic applications accepted. *Expenses: Tuition, area resident:* Part-time $408.10 per credit hour. Tuition, state resident: part-time $408.10 per credit hour. Tuition, nonresident: part-time $932.61 per credit hour. *Required fees:* $111.81 per credit hour. Tuition and fees vary according to course load, campus/location and program. *Financial support:* Research assistantships, teaching assistantships, career-related internships or fieldwork, Federal Work-Study, and tuition waivers (partial) available. Support available to part-time students. Financial award application deadline: 4/1; financial award applicants required to submit FAFSA. *Faculty research:* Using children's literature to enhance metalinguistic awareness, education, oral language diagnosis of middle-schoolers, science inquiry teaching and learning. *Total annual research expenditures:* $173,438. *Unit head:* Dr. Jeffery Cornett, Chair, 904-620-2610, Fax: 904-620-1821, E-mail: jcornett@unf.edu. *Application contact:* Dr. Amanda Pascale, Director, The Graduate School, 904-620-1360, Fax: 904-620-1362, E-mail: graduateschool@unf.edu.
Website: http://www.unf.edu/coehs/fse/

University of North Georgia, Master of Arts in Teaching Program, Dahlonega, GA 30597. Offers physical education (MAT); secondary education - English (MAT); secondary education - history (MAT); secondary education - mathematics (MAT); secondary education - middle grades (MAT). *Degree requirements:* For master's, internship, capstone. *Entrance requirements:* For master's, GRE or MAT, GACE I and II, GA pre-service application, lawful presence verification, official transcripts, GA Educator Ethics Program entry assessment. Additional exam requirements/recommendations for international students: Required—TOEFL (minimum score 550 paper-based; 79 iBT), IELTS (minimum score 6.5). Electronic applications accepted. *Expenses:* Contact institution.

University of Pennsylvania, Graduate School of Education, Division of Teaching, Learning, and Leadership, Teacher Education Program, Philadelphia, PA 19104. Offers elementary education (MS Ed); secondary education (MS Ed). *Students:* 49 full-time (37 women), 2 part-time (both women); includes 13 minority (2 Black or African American, non-Hispanic/Latino; 6 Asian, non-Hispanic/Latino; 2 Hispanic/Latino; 3 Two or more races, non-Hispanic/Latino), 1 international. Average age 25. 140 applicants, 86% accepted, 59 enrolled. In 2018, 36 master's awarded. *Degree requirements:* For master's, thesis or alternative, student teaching, portfolio. *Entrance requirements:* For master's, GRE, bachelor's degree. Additional exam requirements/recommendations for international students: Required—TOEFL, IELTS. *Application deadline:* For summer admission, 6/1 priority date for domestic students, 6/1 for international students. Applications are processed on a rolling basis. Application fee: $80. Electronic applications accepted. *Financial support:* In 2018–19, 53 students received support. Federal Work-Study and scholarships/grants available. Financial award applicants required to submit FAFSA. *Faculty research:* Teacher competencies, social justice teaching, teacher practitioner inquiry. *Unit head:* Maureen Cotterill, Program Manager, 215-898-7364. *Application contact:* Maureen Cotterill, Program Manager, 215-898-7364.
Website: http://www2.gse.upenn.edu/tep/

University of Phoenix–Bay Area Campus, College of Education, San Jose, CA 95134-1805. Offers administration and supervision (MA Ed); adult education and training (MA Ed); early childhood education (MA Ed); education (Ed S); educational leadership (Ed D); elementary teacher education (MA Ed); higher education administration (PhD); secondary teacher education (MA Ed); special education (MA Ed); teacher leadership (MA Ed). *Program availability:* Evening/weekend, online learning. *Degree requirements:* For master's, thesis (for some programs). *Entrance requirements:* For master's, minimum undergraduate GPA of 2.5, 3 years of work experience. Additional exam requirements/recommendations for international students: Required—TOEFL (minimum score 550 paper-based; 79 iBT). Electronic applications accepted.

University of Phoenix–Central Valley Campus, College of Education, Fresno, CA 93720-1552. Offers curriculum and instruction (MA Ed); curriculum and instruction-computer education (MA Ed); elementary teacher education (MA Ed); secondary teacher education (MA Ed).

University of Phoenix–Hawaii Campus, College of Education, Honolulu, HI 96813-3800. Offers administration and supervision (MA Ed); curriculum and instruction (MA Ed); elementary education (MA Ed); secondary education (MA Ed); special education (MA Ed); teacher education for elementary licensure (MA Ed). *Program availability:* Evening/weekend. *Degree requirements:* For master's, thesis (for some programs). *Entrance requirements:* For master's, minimum undergraduate GPA of 2.5, 3 years of work experience. Additional exam requirements/recommendations for international students: Required—TOEFL (minimum score 550 paper-based; 79 iBT). Electronic applications accepted.

University of Phoenix–Online Campus, College of Education, Phoenix, AZ 85034-7209. Offers administration and supervision (MAEd, Certificate); adult education and training (MAEd); curriculum and instruction (MAEd), including computer education, curriculum and instruction, English as a second language, language arts, mathematics, reading; early childhood education (MAEd); educational studies (MAEd); elementary teacher education (MAEd), including early childhood, elementary teacher education,

high school middle level, middle level; principal licensure (Certificate); secondary teacher education (MAEd); special education (MAEd, Certificate); teacher education (MAEd), including middle level generalist; teacher education middle level mathematics (MAEd), including middle level mathematics; teacher education middle level science (MAEd), including middle level science; teacher education secondary mathematics (MAEd); teacher education secondary science (MAEd); teacher leadership (MAEd); teachers of English learners (Certificate); transition to teaching (Certificate), including elementary education, secondary education. *Program availability:* Evening/weekend, online learning. *Entrance requirements:* Additional exam requirements/recommendations for international students: Required—TOEFL, TOEIC (Test of English as an International Communication), Berlitz Online English Proficiency Exam, PTE, or IELTS. Electronic applications accepted. *Expenses:* Contact institution.

University of Phoenix–Phoenix Campus, College of Education, Tempe, AZ 85282-2371. Offers administration and supervision (MA Ed); adult education and training (MA Ed); curriculum and instruction reading (MA Ed); early childhood education (MA Ed); education studies (MA Ed); elementary teacher education (MA Ed); secondary teacher education (MA Ed); special education (MA Ed); teacher leadership (MA Ed). *Program availability:* Evening/weekend, online learning. *Entrance requirements:* Additional exam requirements/recommendations for international students: Required—TOEFL, TOEIC (Test of English as an International Communication), Berlitz Online English Proficiency Exam, PTE, or IELTS. Electronic applications accepted. *Expenses:* Contact institution.

University of Phoenix–Sacramento Valley Campus, College of Education, Sacramento, CA 95833-4334. Offers adult education (MA Ed); curriculum instruction (MA Ed); elementary teacher education (MA Ed); secondary teacher education (MA Ed); teacher education (Certificate). *Program availability:* Evening/weekend. *Degree requirements:* For master's, thesis (for some programs). *Entrance requirements:* For master's, 3 years of work experience, minimum undergraduate GPA of 2.5. Additional exam requirements/recommendations for international students: Required—TOEFL (minimum score 550 paper-based; 79 iBT). Electronic applications accepted.

University of Phoenix–San Diego Campus, College of Education, San Diego, CA 92123. Offers curriculum and instruction (MA Ed), including computer education, curriculum and instruction, English as a second language; elementary teacher education (MA Ed); secondary teacher education (MA Ed). *Program availability:* Evening/weekend. *Degree requirements:* For master's, thesis (for some programs). *Entrance requirements:* For master's, 3 years of work experience, minimum undergraduate GPA of 3.0. Additional exam requirements/recommendations for international students: Required—TOEFL (minimum score 550 paper-based; 79 iBT). Electronic applications accepted.

University of Pittsburgh, School of Education, Department of Instruction and Learning, Program in Secondary Education, Pittsburgh, PA 15260. Offers English and communications education (M Ed, MAT); foreign language education (M Ed, MAT); language, literacy and culture education (Ed D, PhD); mathematics education (M Ed, MAT, Ed D, PhD); science education (M Ed, MAT, Ed D, PhD); secondary education (PhD); social studies education (M Ed, MAT); STEM education (Ed D). *Program availability:* Part-time, evening/weekend. *Degree requirements:* For master's, thesis; for doctorate, thesis/dissertation. *Entrance requirements:* For master's, PRAXIS I; for doctorate, GRE General Test. Additional exam requirements/recommendations for international students: Required—TOEFL. Electronic applications accepted.

University of Puget Sound, School of Education, Program in Teaching, Tacoma, WA 98416. Offers elementary education (MAT); secondary education (MAT). *Accreditation:* NASM. *Degree requirements:* For master's, project. *Entrance requirements:* For master's, WEST-E or NES, WEST-B or ACT/SAT, two education foundation prerequisite courses; minor in content area (for secondary education). Additional exam requirements/recommendations for international students: Required—TOEFL (minimum score 550 paper-based; 90 iBT). Electronic applications accepted. *Expenses:* Contact institution. *Faculty research:* Pre-service teacher learning, public school partnerships and professional development, creating equitable classrooms, literacy development, teaching social studies.

University of St. Francis, College of Education, Joliet, IL 60435-6169. Offers educational leadership (MS, Ed D); elementary education (M Ed); reading (MS); secondary education (M Ed), including English education, math education, science education, social studies education, visual arts education; special education (M Ed); teaching and learning (MS); TESOL (Certificate). *Accreditation:* NCATE. *Program availability:* Part-time, evening/weekend, 100% online, blended/hybrid learning. *Faculty:* 11 full-time (8 women), 58 part-time/adjunct (38 women). *Students:* 43 full-time (35 women), 453 part-time (354 women); includes 110 minority (48 Black or African American, non-Hispanic/Latino; 7 Asian, non-Hispanic/Latino; 52 Hispanic/Latino; 3 Two or more races, non-Hispanic/Latino), 3 international. Average age 37. 300 applicants, 66% accepted, 164 enrolled. In 2018, 151 master's, 42 doctorates, 4 other advanced degrees awarded. *Degree requirements:* For master's, comprehensive exam; for doctorate, thesis/dissertation. *Entrance requirements:* Additional exam requirements/recommendations for international students: Required—TOEFL (minimum score 550 paper-based; 79 iBT), IELTS (minimum score 6). *Application deadline:* Applications are processed on a rolling basis. Electronic applications accepted. Application fee is waived when completed online. *Expenses:* Contact institution. *Financial support:* In 2018–19, 33 students received support. Scholarships/grants and tuition waivers (partial) available. Support available to part-time students. Financial award applicants required to submit FAFSA. *Unit head:* Dr. John Gambro, Dean, 815-740-3456, E-mail: jgambro@stfrancis.edu. *Application contact:* Sandee Sloka, Director Adult & Graduate Admissions, 800-735-7500, E-mail: ssloka@stfrancis.edu.
Website: https://www.stfrancis.edu/education/

University of Saint Francis, Graduate School, Department of Education, Fort Wayne, IN 46808-3994. Offers secondary education (MAT); special education (MS Ed), including intense intervention, mild intervention. *Accreditation:* NCATE. *Program availability:* Part-time, evening/weekend, online only, 100% online. *Faculty:* 2 full-time (1 woman), 3 part-time/adjunct (all women). *Students:* 3 full-time (2 women), 27 part-time (18 women); includes 3 minority (1 Black or African American, non-Hispanic/Latino; 1 Hispanic/Latino; 1 Two or more races, non-Hispanic/Latino). Average age 33. 19 applicants, 95% accepted, 18 enrolled. In 2018, 12 master's awarded. *Expenses: Tuition:* Full-time $22,440; part-time $935 per credit hour. *Required fees:* $330 per semester. Tuition and fees vary according to degree level, campus/location and program. *Unit head:* Mary Riepenhoff, Chair of the Department of Education, 260-399-7700 Ext. 8409, E-mail: mriepenhoff@sf.edu. *Application contact:* Kyle Richardson, Associate Director of Enrollment Services for Adult Learning, 260-399-7700 Ext. 6310, Fax: 260-399-8152, E-mail: krichardson@sf.edu.
Website: https://admissions.sf.edu/graduate/

University of Saint Joseph, Department of Education, West Hartford, CT 06117-2700. Offers curriculum and instruction (MA); elementary education (MAT); instructional technology (MA); literacy (MA); secondary education (MAT); TESOL (MA). *Program availability:* Part-time, evening/weekend. *Degree requirements:* For master's, comprehensive exam, thesis or alternative. *Entrance requirements:* For master's, 2 letters of recommendation. Electronic applications accepted. Application fee is waived when completed online.

University of St. Thomas, School of Education and Human Services, Houston, TX 77006-4696. Offers all level education (M Ed); bilingual/dual language (M Ed); Catholic school teaching (M Ed); Catholic/private school leadership (M Ed); counselor education (M Ed); curriculum and instruction (M Ed); education (Ed D); educational leadership (M Ed); elementary teaching (M Ed); English as a second language (M Ed); exceptionality/educational diagnostician (M Ed); exceptionality/special education (M Ed); generalist (M Ed); reading (M Ed); secondary teaching (M Ed); teaching (MAT). *Accreditation:* TEAC. *Program availability:* Part-time, evening/weekend, online learning. *Degree requirements:* For master's, thesis, field experience. *Entrance requirements:* For master's, GRE or MAT if GPA is below 3.0, bachelor's degree; minimum GPA of 2.75 in bachelor's degree or last 60 credit hours; official transcripts from all institutions; goal statement of 250-300 words; 1 reference. Additional exam requirements/recommendations for international students: Required—TOEFL (minimum score 94 iBT), IELTS (minimum score 7), PTE (minimum score 53). Electronic applications accepted. *Expenses:* Contact institution. *Faculty research:* Leadership, diversity, personality traits, second language acquisition.

The University of Scranton, Panuska College of Professional Studies, Department of Education, Program in Secondary Education, Scranton, PA 18510. Offers MS. *Accreditation:* NCATE. *Program availability:* Part-time, evening/weekend. *Degree requirements:* For master's, comprehensive exam (for some programs), thesis (for some programs), capstone experience. *Entrance requirements:* For master's, minimum GPA of 3.0, three letters of reference. Additional exam requirements/recommendations for international students: Required—TOEFL (minimum score 500 paper-based; 80 iBT), IELTS (minimum score 6.5). Electronic applications accepted.

University of South Alabama, College of Education and Professional Studies, Department of Leadership and Teacher Education, Mobile, AL 36688. Offers art education (M Ed); early childhood education (M Ed); educational leadership (M Ed, Ed D); elementary education (M Ed); reading education (M Ed); science education (M Ed); secondary education (M Ed); special education (M Ed). *Accreditation:* NCATE. *Program availability:* Part-time. *Degree requirements:* For master's, comprehensive exam, thesis (for some programs); for doctorate, comprehensive exam, thesis/dissertation. *Entrance requirements:* For master's, GRE General Test or MAT, minimum GPA of 3.0; for doctorate, GRE, minimum graduate GPA of 3.25, 3 years of experience in field, 3 letters of recommendation, interview, official transcripts. Additional exam requirements/recommendations for international students: Required—TOEFL. Electronic applications accepted.

University of South Carolina, The Graduate School, College of Education, Department of Instruction and Teacher Education, Program in Secondary Education, Columbia, SC 29208. Offers art education (IMA, MAT); business education (IMA, MAT); English (MAT); foreign language (MAT); health education (MAT); mathematics (MAT); science (IMA, MAT); secondary (Ed D); secondary education (MT, PhD); social studies (MAT); theatre and speech (MAT). IMA and MT offered jointly with the subject areas. *Accreditation:* NCATE. *Degree requirements:* For master's, comprehensive exam, thesis (for some programs), foreign language (MA); for doctorate, one foreign language, comprehensive exam, thesis/dissertation. *Entrance requirements:* For master's, GRE General Test or MAT, teaching certificate (IMA, M Ed), interview; for doctorate, GRE General Test or MAT, interview. *Faculty research:* Middle school programs, professional development, school collaboration.

University of South Dakota, Graduate School, School of Education, Division of Curriculum and Instruction, Program in Secondary Education, Vermillion, SD 57069. Offers secondary education (MA), including English language learning, science, technology and math (STEM), secondary education plus certification. *Accreditation:* NCATE. *Program availability:* Part-time, online learning. *Degree requirements:* For master's, comprehensive exam, thesis or alternative. *Entrance requirements:* For master's, GRE General Test, MAT, minimum GPA of 2.7. Additional exam requirements/recommendations for international students: Required—TOEFL (minimum score 550 paper-based; 79 iBT). Electronic applications accepted.

University of Southern Indiana, Graduate Studies, Pott College of Science, Engineering, and Education, Department of Teacher Education, Program in Secondary Education, Evansville, IN 47712-3590. Offers secondary education (MSE), including mathematics teaching. *Accreditation:* NCATE. *Program availability:* Part-time, evening/weekend. *Entrance requirements:* For master's, PRAXIS II, bachelor's degree with minimum cumulative GPA of 2.75 from college or university accredited by NCATE or comparable association; minimum GPA of 3.0 in all courses taken at graduate level at all schools attended; teaching license. Additional exam requirements/recommendations for international students: Required—TOEFL (minimum score 550 paper-based; 79 iBT), IELTS (minimum score 6). Electronic applications accepted.

University of Southern Mississippi, College of Education and Human Sciences, Department of Curriculum, Instruction and Special Education, Hattiesburg, MS 39406-0001. Offers elementary education (M Ed, PhD); instructional technology (MS); instructional technology and design (PhD); secondary education (MAT); special education (M Ed, PhD). *Program availability:* Part-time, online learning. *Degree requirements:* For master's, comprehensive exam, thesis (for some programs); for doctorate, comprehensive exam, thesis/dissertation. *Entrance requirements:* For master's, GRE General Test, MAT, minimum GPA of 3.0; for doctorate, GRE General Test, minimum GPA of 3.5. Additional exam requirements/recommendations for international students: Required—TOEFL, IELTS. *Faculty research:* Mathematical problem solving, integrative curriculum, writing process, teacher education models.

University of South Florida, Innovative Education, Tampa, FL 33620-9951. Offers adult, career and higher education (Graduate Certificate), including college teaching, leadership in developing human resources, leadership in higher education; Africana studies (Graduate Certificate), including diasporas and health disparities, genocide and human rights; aging studies (Graduate Certificate), including gerontology; art research (Graduate Certificate), including museum studies; business foundations (Graduate Certificate); chemical and biomedical engineering (Graduate Certificate), including materials science and engineering, water, health and sustainability; child and family studies (Graduate Certificate), including positive behavior support; civil and industrial engineering (Graduate Certificate), including transportation systems analysis; community and family health (Graduate Certificate), including maternal and child health, social marketing and public health, violence and injury: prevention and intervention, women's health; criminology (Graduate Certificate), including criminal justice administration; data science for public administration (Graduate Certificate); digital humanities (Graduate Certificate); educational measurement and research (Graduate Certificate), including evaluation; English (Graduate Certificate), including comparative literary studies, creative writing, professional and technical communication; entrepreneurship (Graduate Certificate); environmental health (Graduate Certificate), including safety management; epidemiology and biostatistics (Graduate Certificate), including applied biostatistics, biostatistics, concepts and tools of epidemiology, epidemiology, epidemiology of infectious diseases; geography, environment and planning (Graduate Certificate), including community development, environmental policy

and management, geographical information systems; geology (Graduate Certificate), including hydrogeology; global health (Graduate Certificate), including disaster management, global health and Latin American and Caribbean studies, global health practice, humanitarian assistance, infection control; government and international affairs (Graduate Certificate), including Cuban studies, globalization studies; health policy and management (Graduate Certificate), including health management and leadership, public health policy and programs; hearing specialist: early intervention (Graduate Certificate); industrial and management systems engineering (Graduate Certificate), including systems engineering, technology management; information studies (Graduate Certificate), including school library media specialist; information systems/decision sciences (Graduate Certificate), including analytics and business intelligence; instructional technology (Graduate Certificate), including distance education, Florida digital/virtual educator, instructional design, multimedia design, Web design; internal medicine, bioethics and medical humanities (Graduate Certificate), including biomedical ethics; Latin American and Caribbean studies (Graduate Certificate); leadership for coastal resiliency planning (Graduate Certificate); mass communications (Graduate Certificate), including multimedia journalism; mathematics and statistics (Graduate Certificate), including mathematics; medicine (Graduate Certificate), including aging and neuroscience, bioinformatics, biotechnology, brain fitness and memory management, clinical investigation, hand and upper limb rehabilitation, health informatics, health sciences, integrative weight management, intellectual property, medicine and gender, metabolic and nutritional medicine, metabolic cardiology, pharmacy sciences; national and competitive intelligence (Graduate Certificate); nursing (Graduate Certificate), including simulation based academic fellowship in advanced pain management; psychological and social foundations (Graduate Certificate), including career counseling, college teaching, diversity in education, mental health counseling, school counseling; public affairs (Graduate Certificate), including nonprofit management, public management, research administration; public health (Graduate Certificate), including assessing chemical toxicity and public health risks, health equity, pharmacoepidemiology, public health generalist, toxicology, translational research in adolescent behavioral health; public health practices (Graduate Certificate), including planning for healthy communities; rehabilitation and mental health counseling (Graduate Certificate), including integrative mental health care, marriage and family therapy, rehabilitation technology; secondary education (Graduate Certificate), including ESOL, foreign language education: culture and content, foreign language education: professional; social work (Graduate Certificate), including geriatric social work/clinical gerontology; special education (Graduate Certificate), including autism spectrum disorder, disabilities education: severe/profound; world languages (Graduate Certificate), including teaching English as a second language (TESL) or foreign language. *Expenses:* Tuition, state resident: full-time $6350. Tuition, nonresident: full-time $19,048. *International tuition:* $19,048 full-time. *Required fees:* $2079. *Unit head:* Dr. Cynthia DeLuca, Associate Vice President and Assistant Vice Provost, 813-974-3077, Fax: 813-974-7061, E-mail: deluca@usf.edu. *Application contact:* Owen Hooper, Director, Summer and Alternative Calendar Programs, 813-974-6917, E-mail: hooper@usf.edu.
Website: http://www.usf.edu/innovative-education/

The University of Tennessee, Graduate School, College of Education, Health and Human Sciences, Program in Education, Knoxville, TN 37996. Offers art education (MS); counseling education (PhD); cultural studies in education (PhD); curriculum (MS, Ed S); curriculum, educational research and evaluation (Ed D, PhD); early childhood education (PhD); early childhood special education (MS); education of deaf and hard of hearing (MS); educational administration and policy studies (Ed D, PhD); educational administration and supervision (Ed S); educational psychology (Ed D, PhD); elementary education (MS, Ed S); elementary teaching (MS); English education (MS, Ed S); exercise science (PhD); foreign language/ESL education (MS, Ed S); instructional technology (MS, Ed D, PhD, Ed S); literacy, language and ESL education (PhD); literacy, language education, and ESL education (Ed D); mathematics education (MS, Ed S); modified and comprehensive special education (MS); reading education (MS, Ed S); school counseling (Ed S); school psychology (PhD, Ed S); science education (MS, Ed S); secondary teaching (MS); social foundations (MS); social science education (MS, Ed S); socio-cultural foundations of sports and education (PhD); special education (Ed S); teacher education (Ed D, PhD). *Accreditation:* NCATE. *Program availability:* Part-time, evening/weekend. *Degree requirements:* For master's and Ed S, thesis optional; for doctorate, variable foreign language requirement, thesis/dissertation. *Entrance requirements:* For master's, minimum GPA of 2.7; for doctorate and Ed S, GRE General Test, minimum GPA of 2.7. Additional exam requirements/recommendations for international students: Required—TOEFL. Electronic applications accepted.

The University of Tennessee at Chattanooga, School of Education, Chattanooga, TN 37403. Offers counseling (M Ed), including community counseling, school counseling; education (M Ed, Post-Master's Certificate), including elementary education (M Ed), school leadership (Post-Master's Certificate); elementary education (M Ed); learning and leadership (Ed D), including educational leadership; school leadership (Post-Master's Certificate); school leadership: principal licensure (Ed S); secondary education (M Ed); special education (M Ed). *Accreditation:* ACA; NCATE. *Program availability:* Part-time. *Degree requirements:* For master's, comprehensive exam, thesis optional, culminating experience; for other advanced degree, internship. *Entrance requirements:* For master's, GRE General Test, PPST 1, teaching certificate; for other advanced degree, two letters of recommendation, graduate degree in education, teaching certificate with three years of experience. Additional exam requirements/recommendations for international students: Required—TOEFL (minimum score 550 paper-based; 79 iBT), IELTS (minimum score 6). Electronic applications accepted. *Expenses:* Contact institution. *Faculty research:* School counseling, community counseling, elementary and secondary education, school leadership and administration.

The University of Tennessee at Martin, Graduate Programs, College of Education, Health and Behavioral Sciences, Program in Teaching, Martin, TN 38238. Offers curriculum and instruction (MS Ed), including 7-12, K-6; initial licensure (MS Ed), including elementary education, secondary education; initial licensure k-8 (MS Ed), including library service, special education; interdisciplinary (MS Ed). *Program availability:* Part-time, online only, 100% online. *Students:* 24 full-time (20 women), 126 part-time (90 women); includes 19 minority (11 Black or African American, non-Hispanic/Latino; 3 Hispanic/Latino; 5 Two or more races, non-Hispanic/Latino). Average age 34. 69 applicants, 58% accepted, 21 enrolled. In 2018, 28 master's awarded. *Degree requirements:* For master's, comprehensive exam. *Entrance requirements:* For master's, GRE General Test, minimum GPA of 2.5, teaching license. Additional exam requirements/recommendations for international students: Required—TOEFL (minimum score 525 paper-based; 71 iBT). *Application deadline:* For fall admission, 7/27 for domestic and international students; for spring admission, 12/17 for domestic and international students; for summer admission, 5/10 for domestic and international students. Applications are processed on a rolling basis. Application fee: $30 ($130 for international students). Electronic applications accepted. *Expenses: Tuition, area resident:* Full-time $8918; part-time $495 per credit hour. Tuition, state resident: full-time $8918; part-time $485 per credit hour. Tuition, nonresident: full-time $14,958; part-time $831 per credit hour. *International tuition:* $22,862 full-time. *Required fees:* $1446; $81 per credit hour. Part-time tuition and fees vary according to course load. *Financial support:* In 2018–19, 26 students received support, including 1 research assistantship with full tuition reimbursement available (averaging $6,283 per year), 5 teaching assistantships with full tuition reimbursements available (averaging $7,464 per year); scholarships/grants and tuition waivers also available. Financial award application deadline: 2/1; financial award applicants required to submit FAFSA. *Faculty research:* Special education, science/math/technology, school reform, reading. *Unit head:* Cynthia West, Dean, 731-881-7125, Fax: 731-881-7975, E-mail: cwest@utm.edu. *Application contact:* Jolene L. Cunningham, Student Services Specialist, 731-881-7012, Fax: 731-881-7499, E-mail: jcunningham@utm.edu.

The University of Texas Rio Grande Valley, College of Education and P-16 Integration, Department of Teaching and Learning, Edinburg, TX 78539. Offers curriculum and instruction (M Ed, Ed D); educational technology (M Ed). *Program availability:* Part-time, evening/weekend. *Degree requirements:* For master's, comprehensive exam, thesis optional; for doctorate, comprehensive exam, thesis/dissertation. *Entrance requirements:* For master's, minimum GPA of 3.0. Additional exam requirements/recommendations for international students: Required—TOEFL (minimum score 550 paper-based; 79 iBT), IELTS (minimum score 6.5). Electronic applications accepted. *Expenses: Tuition, area resident:* Full-time $6888. Tuition, state resident: full-time $6888. Tuition, nonresident: full-time $14,484. *International tuition:* $14,484 full-time. *Required fees:* $1468. *Faculty research:* Teacher education, mathematics education, science education, educational technology, pedagogy.

University of the Cumberlands, Graduate Programs in Education, Williamsburg, KY 40769-1372. Offers all grades (P-12) (M Ed); business and marketing (MA Ed, MAT); counselor education and supervision (Ed D); director of pupil personnel (Certificate); director of special education (Certificate); educational administration and supervision (Ed S); educational leadership (Ed D); elementary education (MA Ed, MAT); instructional leadership - principalship (MA Ed); instructional leadership - school principal (Certificate); middle school education (MA Ed, MAT); reading and writing (MA Ed); school counseling (MA Ed); school superintendent (Certificate); secondary education (MA Ed, MAT); special education (MAT); supervisor of instruction (Certificate); teacher leader (MA Ed). *Program availability:* Part-time, evening/weekend, online learning. *Degree requirements:* For master's, comprehensive exam. Electronic applications accepted.

University of the District of Columbia, College of Arts and Sciences, Program in Teaching, Washington, DC 20008-1175. Offers elementary education (MAT); middle school mathematics (MAT); secondary English language arts (MAT); secondary social studies (MAT).

University of the Virgin Islands, College of Science and Mathematics, St. Thomas, VI 00802. Offers marine and environmental science (MS); mathematics for secondary teachers (MA). *Faculty:* 5 full-time (4 women), 7 part-time/adjunct (2 women). *Students:* 16 full-time (13 women), 19 part-time (13 women); includes 10 minority (4 Black or African American, non-Hispanic/Latino; 1 American Indian or Alaska Native, non-Hispanic/Latino; 2 Hispanic/Latino; 1 Native Hawaiian or other Pacific Islander, non-Hispanic/Latino; 2 Two or more races, non-Hispanic/Latino), 1 international. Average age 27. In 2018, 8 master's awarded. *Degree requirements:* For master's, comprehensive exam, thesis. *Entrance requirements:* For master's, GRE, minimum GPA of 2.5. Additional exam requirements/recommendations for international students: Required—TOEFL (minimum score 550 paper-based). *Application deadline:* For fall admission, 4/30 for domestic and international students; for spring admission, 10/30 for domestic and international students. Application fee: $30. Electronic applications accepted. *Expenses:* Tuition, state resident: full-time $6948; part-time $386 per credit. Tuition, nonresident: full-time $13,230; part-time $735 per credit. *International tuition:* $13,230 full-time. *Required fees:* $508. *Financial support:* Fellowships, research assistantships, teaching assistantships, career-related internships or fieldwork, and scholarships/grants available. Financial award application deadline: 4/15; financial award applicants required to submit FAFSA. *Unit head:* Dr. Sandra Romano, Dean, 340-693-1230, Fax: 340-693-1245, E-mail: sromano@uvi.edu. *Application contact:* Charmaine Smith, Director of Admissions, 340-690-4070, E-mail: csmith@uvi.edu.

The University of Toledo, College of Graduate Studies, Judith Herb College of Education, Department of Curriculum and Instruction, Toledo, OH 43606-3390. Offers art education (ME); career and technical education (ME, Ed S); curriculum and instruction (ME, PhD, Ed S); early childhood education (Ed S); education and anthropology (MAE); education and biology (MES); education and chemistry (MES); education and classics (MAE); education and economics (MAE); education and English (MAE); education and French (MAE); education and geology (MES); education and German (MAE); education and history (MAE); education and mathematics (MAE, MES); education and physics (MES); education and political science (MAE); education and sociology (MAE); education and Spanish (MAE); educational media (PhD); educational technology (ME); educational technology: virtual educator (Certificate); elementary education (PhD); English as a second language (MAE); gifted and talented education (PhD); middle childhood education (ME); secondary education (ME, PhD); special education (PhD). *Accreditation:* NCATE. *Program availability:* Part-time, evening/weekend. *Degree requirements:* For master's, comprehensive exam, thesis or alternative; for doctorate, comprehensive exam, thesis/dissertation; for other advanced degree, thesis optional. *Entrance requirements:* For master's, doctorate, and other advanced degree, minimum cumulative GPA of 2.7 for all previous academic work, letters of recommendation. Additional exam requirements/recommendations for international students: Required—TOEFL (minimum score 550 paper-based; 80 iBT). Electronic applications accepted.

University of Vermont, Graduate College, College of Education and Social Services, Program in Secondary Education, Burlington, VT 05405. Offers curriculum and instruction (MAT), including secondary education. *Entrance requirements:* For master's, major or its equivalent in a state-approved licensing area. Additional exam requirements/recommendations for international students: Required—TOEFL (minimum iBT score of 90) or IELTS (6.5). Electronic applications accepted.

University of Washington, Bothell, Program in Education, Bothell, WA 98011. Offers education (M Ed); leadership development for educators (M Ed); secondary/middle level endorsement (M Ed). *Program availability:* Part-time, evening/weekend. *Degree requirements:* For master's, thesis. *Entrance requirements:* Additional exam requirements/recommendations for international students: Required—TOEFL. Electronic applications accepted. *Faculty research:* Multicultural education in citizenship education, intercultural education, knowledge and practice in the principalship, educational public policy, national board certification for teachers, teacher learning in literacy, technology and its impact on teaching and learning of mathematics, reading assessments, professional development in literacy education and mobility, digital media, education and class.

The University of West Alabama, School of Graduate Studies, College of Education, Program in Secondary Education, Livingston, AL 35470. Offers biology (MAT); English language arts (MAT); high school 6-12 (M Ed); history (MAT); mathematics (MAT); science (MAT); social science (MAT). *Program availability:* Part-time, evening/weekend, 100% online. *Faculty:* 18 full-time (6 women), 8 part-time/adjunct (2 women). *Students:*

232 full-time (165 women), 34 part-time (24 women); includes 53 minority (44 Black or African American, non-Hispanic/Latino; 3 American Indian or Alaska Native, non-Hispanic/Latino; 2 Hispanic/Latino; 4 Two or more races, non-Hispanic/Latino), 3 international. Average age 31. 84 applicants, 93% accepted, 67 enrolled. In 2018, 100 master's awarded. *Degree requirements:* For master's, comprehensive exam, thesis optional. *Entrance requirements:* For master's, GRE, minimum GPA of 2.75, verification of background clearance/fingerprints, valid bachelor's-level Professional Educator Certificate in same teaching field. Additional exam requirements/recommendations for international students: Required—TOEFL (minimum score 500 paper-based; 61 iBT). *Application deadline:* Applications are processed on a rolling basis. Application fee: $40. Electronic applications accepted. *Expenses: Tuition, area resident:* Full-time $9100. Tuition, state resident: full-time $9100. Tuition, nonresident: full-time $19,200. *Required fees:* $1890; $130. *Financial support:* Teaching assistantships, Federal Work-Study, scholarships/grants, and unspecified assistantships available. Support available to part-time students. Financial award application deadline: 3/1; financial award applicants required to submit FAFSA. *Unit head:* Dr. Jodie Winship, Chair of College of Education, 205-652-5415, Fax: 205-652-3706, E-mail: jwinship@uwa.edu. *Application contact:* Dr. B. J. Kimbrough, Dean of Graduate Studies, 205-652-3647, Fax: 205-652-3670, E-mail: bkimbrough@uwa.edu.

University of West Florida, College of Education and Professional Studies, Department of Teacher Education and Educational Leadership, Program in Curriculum and Instruction, Pensacola, FL 32514-5750. Offers elementary education (M Ed); middle level education (M Ed); secondary education (M Ed). *Program availability:* Part-time, evening/weekend. *Entrance requirements:* For master's, GRE (minimum score 450 verbal) or MAT (minimum score 396) if bachelor's GPA less than 3.0, state teaching certification; letter of intent; two professional references. Additional exam requirements/recommendations for international students: Required—TOEFL (minimum score 550 paper-based).

University of West Georgia, College of Education, Carrollton, GA 30118. Offers business education (M Ed); early childhood education (M Ed, Ed S); educational leadership (M Ed, Ed S); media (M Ed, Ed S); professional counseling (M Ed, Ed S); professional counseling and supervision (Ed D); reading instruction (M Ed); school improvement (Ed D); secondary education (M Ed); special education (M Ed, Ed S); including teaching (M Ed); speech language pathology (M Ed); teaching (MAT). *Accreditation:* NCATE. *Program availability:* Part-time, evening/weekend, 100% online, blended/hybrid learning. *Faculty:* 39 full-time (23 women). *Students:* 368 full-time (316 women), 1,140 part-time (960 women); includes 460 minority (376 Black or African American, non-Hispanic/Latino; 1 American Indian or Alaska Native, non-Hispanic/Latino; 11 Asian, non-Hispanic/Latino; 44 Hispanic/Latino; 28 Two or more races, non-Hispanic/Latino), 6 international. Average age 35. 625 applicants, 77% accepted, 401 enrolled. In 2018, 399 master's, 25 doctorates, 273 other advanced degrees awarded. *Entrance requirements:* Additional exam requirements/recommendations for international students: Required—TOEFL (minimum score 523 paper-based; 69 iBT); Recommended—IELTS (minimum score 6.5). *Application deadline:* For fall admission, 7/21 for domestic students, 6/1 for international students; for spring admission, 11/30 for domestic students, 10/15 for international students; for summer admission, 4/15 for domestic students, 3/30 for international students. Applications are processed on a rolling basis. Application fee: $40. Electronic applications accepted. Tuition and fees vary according to course load, degree level, campus/location and program. *Financial support:* Fellowships, research assistantships, teaching assistantships, career-related internships or fieldwork, Federal Work-Study, institutionally sponsored loans, scholarships/grants, and unspecified assistantships available. Support available to part-time students. Financial award application deadline: 4/1; financial award applicants required to submit FAFSA. *Unit head:* Dr. Diane Hoff, Dean, College of Education, 678-839-6570, Fax: 678-839-6098, E-mail: dhoff@westga.edu. *Application contact:* Dr. Toby Ziglar, Assistant Dean of the Graduate School, 678-839-1394, Fax: 678-839-1395, E-mail: graduate@westga.edu.
Website: http://www.westga.edu/education/

University of Wisconsin–Eau Claire, College of Education and Human Sciences, Program in Secondary Education, Eau Claire, WI 54702-4004. Offers professional development (ME-PD), including library science, professional development. *Program availability:* Part-time, online learning. *Degree requirements:* For master's, comprehensive exam, thesis, research paper, portfolio or written exam; oral exam. *Entrance requirements:* For master's, certification to teach, minimum GPA of 2.75. Additional exam requirements/recommendations for international students: Required—TOEFL (minimum score 79 iBT).

University of Wisconsin–Milwaukee, Graduate School, College of Letters and Science, Department of English, Milwaukee, WI 53201-0413. Offers English (MA, PhD), including creative writing, English language and linguistics, English secondary education, literary and critical studies, literature and cultural theory (PhD), literature and language studies, literature, culture, and media, media, cinema and digital studies, professional and technical communication (MA), professional and technical writing, professional writing (PhD), rhetoric and composition (PhD), rhetoric and writing. *Students:* 82 full-time (46 women), 44 part-time (21 women); includes 9 minority (2 American Indian or Alaska Native, non-Hispanic/Latino; 3 Asian, non-Hispanic/Latino; 1 Hispanic/Latino; 3 Two or more races, non-Hispanic/Latino), 11 international. Average age 34. 161 applicants, 27% accepted, 32 enrolled. In 2018, 13 master's, 9 doctorates awarded. *Degree requirements:* For master's, thesis or alternative; for doctorate, one foreign language, thesis/dissertation. *Entrance requirements:* For master's, GRE General Test, GRE Subject Test; for doctorate, GRE. Additional exam requirements/recommendations for international students: Required—TOEFL (minimum score 550 paper-based; 79 iBT), IELTS (minimum score 6.5). *Application deadline:* For fall admission, 1/1 priority date for domestic students; for spring admission, 9/1 for domestic students. Application fee: $56 ($96 for international students). Electronic applications accepted. *Financial support:* Fellowships, research assistantships, teaching assistantships, career-related internships or fieldwork, unspecified assistantships, and project assistantships available. Support available to part-time students. Financial award application deadline: 4/15; financial award applicants required to submit FAFSA. *Unit head:* Mark Netzloff, Department Chair, 414-229-4511, E-mail: netzloff@uwm.edu. *Application contact:* General Information Contact, 414-229-4982, Fax: 414-229-6967, E-mail: gradschool@uwm.edu.
Website: https://uwm.edu/english/

University of Wisconsin–Stevens Point, College of Fine Arts and Communication, Department of Music, Stevens Point, WI 54481-3897. Offers elementary/secondary music education (MM Ed); studio pedagogy (MM Ed); Suzuki talent education (MM Ed). *Accreditation:* NASM. *Program availability:* Part-time. *Degree requirements:* For master's, thesis or alternative. *Entrance requirements:* For master's, teaching certificate. *Faculty research:* Music education, music composition, music performance.

Utah State University, School of Graduate Studies, Emma Eccles Jones College of Education and Human Services, Program in Secondary Education, Logan, UT 84322. Offers M Ed, MA, MS. *Program availability:* Part-time, evening/weekend. *Degree requirements:* For master's, thesis (for some programs). *Entrance requirements:* For master's, GRE General Test or MAT, minimum GPA of 3.0, 1 year teaching, teaching

license, letters of recommendation. Additional exam requirements/recommendations for international students: Required—TOEFL. Electronic applications accepted. *Faculty research:* Character education, science education, reading/writing skills, mathematics education, pre-service teacher education.

Valparaiso University, Graduate School and Continuing Education, Programs in Education, Valparaiso, IN 46383. Offers initial licensure (M Ed), including Chinese teaching, elementary education, secondary education; instructional leadership (M Ed); school psychology (Ed S); secondary education (M Ed); M Ed/Ed S. *Accreditation:* NCATE. *Program availability:* Part-time, evening/weekend, online learning. *Entrance requirements:* For master's, GRE General Test, minimum GPA of 3.0. Additional exam requirements/recommendations for international students: Required—TOEFL (minimum score 550 paper-based; 80 iBT), IELTS (minimum score 6). Electronic applications accepted.

Vanderbilt University, Peabody College, Department of Teaching and Learning, Nashville, TN 37240-1001. Offers elementary education (M Ed); English language learners (M Ed); reading education (M Ed); secondary education (M Ed). *Accreditation:* NCATE. *Program availability:* Part-time. *Faculty:* 47 full-time (34 women), 19 part-time/adjunct (16 women). *Students:* 122 full-time (99 women), 37 part-time (27 women); includes 34 minority (22 Black or African American, non-Hispanic/Latino; 2 American Indian or Alaska Native, non-Hispanic/Latino; 4 Asian, non-Hispanic/Latino; 4 Hispanic/Latino; 2 Two or more races, non-Hispanic/Latino), 41 international. Average age 26. 359 applicants, 74% accepted, 106 enrolled. In 2018, 113 master's awarded. *Degree requirements:* For master's, comprehensive exam, thesis optional. *Entrance requirements:* For master's, GRE General Test, MAT. Additional exam requirements/recommendations for international students: Required—TOEFL (minimum score 550 paper-based; 80 iBT). *Application deadline:* For fall admission, 12/31 priority date for domestic and international students; for spring admission, 11/1 priority date for domestic and international students. Applications are processed on a rolling basis. Application fee: $0. Electronic applications accepted. *Expenses: Tuition:* Full-time $47,208; part-time $2026 per credit hour. *Required fees:* $478. *Financial support:* Fellowships with partial tuition reimbursements, research assistantships with partial tuition reimbursements, teaching assistantships with partial tuition reimbursements, Federal Work-Study, institutionally sponsored loans, scholarships/grants, tuition waivers (partial), and unspecified assistantships available. Support available to part-time students. Financial award application deadline: 1/15; financial award applicants required to submit FAFSA. *Faculty research:* Literacy education; science education; math education; learning sciences; diversity studies. *Unit head:* Dr. Deborah Rowe, Chair, 615-322-8100, Fax: 615-322-8999, E-mail: deborah.w.rowe@vanderbilt.edu. *Application contact:* Angela Saylor, Educational Coordinator, 615-322-8092, Fax: 615-322-8999, E-mail: angela.saylor@vanderbilt.edu.

Virginia Wesleyan University, Graduate Studies, Virginia Beach, VA 23455. Offers business administration (MBA); secondary and PreK-12 education (MA Ed). *Program availability:* Online learning.

Wagner College, Division of Graduate Studies, Education Department, Program in Secondary Education/Students with Disabilities, Staten Island, NY 10301-4495. Offers secondary education 7-12 (MS Ed), including language arts, languages other than English, mathematics and technology, science and technology, social studies. *Program availability:* Evening/weekend. *Degree requirements:* For master's, thesis (for some programs), completion of state certification exams before student teaching. *Entrance requirements:* For master's, GRE, minimum GPA of 3.0, interview, recommendations. Additional exam requirements/recommendations for international students: Required—TOEFL (minimum score 550 paper-based; 79 iBT), IELTS (minimum score 6.5). Electronic applications accepted. *Expenses:* Contact institution.

Wake Forest University, Graduate School of Arts and Sciences, Department of Education, Winston-Salem, NC 27109. Offers secondary education (MA Ed). *Accreditation:* ACA; NCATE. *Faculty:* 7 full-time (4 women). *Students:* 13 full-time (8 women); includes 1 minority (Black or African American, non-Hispanic/Latino). Average age 24. 20 applicants, 65% accepted, 11 enrolled. In 2018, 11 master's awarded. *Degree requirements:* For master's, thesis optional. *Entrance requirements:* For master's, GRE General Test. Additional exam requirements/recommendations for international students: Required—TOEFL (minimum score 550 paper-based). *Application deadline:* For fall admission, 1/15 for domestic students, 1/15 priority date for international students. Application fee: $75. Electronic applications accepted. *Expenses:* Contact institution. *Financial support:* In 2018–19, 11 students received support, including 11 fellowships with full tuition reimbursements available (averaging $49,000 per year), 3 teaching assistantships with full tuition reimbursements available (averaging $49,000 per year); scholarships/grants and tuition waivers (full and partial) also available. Financial award application deadline: 2/15. *Faculty research:* Teaching and learning. *Unit head:* Dr. Adam Friedman, Chair, 336-758-5507, Fax: 336-758-4591, E-mail: amfriedman@wfu.edu. *Application contact:* Dr. Leah McCoy, Program Director, 336-758-5498, Fax: 336-758-4591, E-mail: mccoy@wfu.edu.
Website: https://education.wfu.edu/graduate-program/overview-of-graduate-programs/

Washington State University, College of Education, Department of Teaching and Learning, Pullman, WA 99164-2132. Offers cultural studies and social thought in education (PhD); curriculum and instruction (Ed M, MA); English language learners (Ed M, MA); language, literacy and technology (PhD); literacy education (Ed M, MA); mathematics education (PhD); special education (Ed M, MA, PhD); teacher leadership (Ed D); teaching (MIT), including elementary education, secondary education. Programs offered at the Pullman, Spokane, Tri-cities, Vancouver and Global (online) campuses. *Program availability:* Part-time, online learning. *Degree requirements:* For master's, comprehensive exam, thesis, oral or written exam; for doctorate, comprehensive exam, thesis/dissertation, oral and written exam. *Entrance requirements:* For master's, GRE General Test, minimum GPA of 3.0, 3 letters of recommendation, letter of intent, transcripts, resume/curriculum vitae; for doctorate, GRE General Test, minimum GPA of 3.0, 3 letters of recommendation, letter of intent, transcripts, writing sample, resume/curriculum vitae. Additional exam requirements/recommendations for international students: Required—TOEFL (minimum score 550 paper-based; 80 iBT). Electronic applications accepted. *Faculty research:* Intersection of gender, youth cultures and schooling; examination of ideology of power in children's literature; early childhood special education; analyzing pre-service and in-service teacher development; second language acquisition.

Washington University in St. Louis, The Graduate School, Department of Education, Program in Secondary Education, St. Louis, MO 63130-4899. Offers MAT. *Degree requirements:* For master's, thesis or alternative. *Entrance requirements:* For master's, GRE General Test or MAT. Additional exam requirements/recommendations for international students: Required—TOEFL. Electronic applications accepted.

Wayland Baptist University, Graduate Programs, Program in Education, Plainview, TX 79072-6998. Offers education administration (M Ed); education diagnostics (M Ed); education literacy (M Ed); elementary certification (M Ed); English (M Ed); English as a second language (M Ed); higher education administration (M Ed); human resources (M Ed); instructional leadership (M Ed); instructional technology (M Ed); leadership training and development (M Ed); science education (M Ed); secondary certification

(M Ed); social studies (M Ed); special education (M Ed); sports administration and management (M Ed). *Program availability:* Part-time, evening/weekend, 100% online. *Degree requirements:* For master's, comprehensive exam, capstone course. *Entrance requirements:* For master's, GRE, GMAT or MAT. Additional exam requirements/recommendations for international students: Required—TOEFL (minimum score 500 paper-based; 61 iBT). Electronic applications accepted.

Wayne State University, College of Education, Division of Teacher Education, Detroit, MI 48202. Offers art education (M Ed); bilingual/bicultural education (Certificate); curriculum and instruction (Ed D, PhD, Ed S), including English as a second language (MAT, Ed D, Ed S), K-12 curriculum (PhD); elementary education (MAT), including bilingual/bicultural education (M Ed, MAT), early childhood education (M Ed, MAT), English as a second language (MAT, Ed D, Ed S), foreign language education, science education (M Ed, MAT), special education (M Ed, MAT); elementary mathematics specialist (Certificate); English as a second language (Certificate); reading (M Ed, Ed S); reading, language and literature (Ed D); secondary education (MAT), including bilingual/bicultural education (M Ed, MAT), early childhood education (M Ed, MAT), English as a second language (MAT, Ed D, Ed S), English education, foreign language education, mathematics education (M Ed, MAT), science education (M Ed, MAT), social studies education (M Ed, MAT); special education (MAT), including career and technical education; teaching and learning (M Ed), including bilingual/bicultural education (M Ed, MAT), early childhood education (M Ed, MAT), elementary education, foreign language, mathematics education (M Ed, MAT), science education (M Ed, MAT), social studies education (M Ed, MAT), special education (M Ed, MAT). *Program availability:* Part-time, evening/weekend. *Faculty:* 20. *Students:* 121 full-time (94 women), 251 part-time (209 women); includes 116 minority (83 Black or African American, non-Hispanic/Latino; 3 American Indian or Alaska Native, non-Hispanic/Latino; 3 Asian, non-Hispanic/Latino; 14 Hispanic/Latino; 13 Two or more races, non-Hispanic/Latino), 11 international. Average age 37. 171 applicants, 23% accepted, 32 enrolled. In 2018, 112 master's, 8 doctorates, 11 other advanced degrees awarded. *Degree requirements:* For master's, thesis (for some programs), essay or project (for some M Ed programs), professional field experience (for MAT programs); for doctorate, comprehensive exam, thesis/dissertation. *Entrance requirements:* For master's, undergraduate degree, verification of participation in group work with children, Michigan State Police criminal background check, negative tb test, personal statement (for MAT programs); for all other master's programs: undergraduate degree, personal statement; for doctorate, minimum undergraduate GPA of 3.0, graduate 3.5; interview; curriculum vitae; references; writing sample; letter of application; master's degree (for most programs); for other advanced degree, education specialist certificate: undergraduate with GPA of 2.5 or better and master's degree with GPA of 2.75 or better; personal statement. Additional exam requirements/recommendations for international students: Required—TOEFL (minimum score 550 paper-based; 79 iBT); Recommended—IELTS (minimum score 6.5), TWE (minimum score 5.5), TSE (minimum score 58). *Application deadline:* Applications are processed on a rolling basis. Application fee: $50. Electronic applications accepted. *Financial support:* In 2018–19, 85 students received support, including 3 fellowships (averaging $14,275 per year); research assistantships with tuition reimbursements available, Federal Work-Study, scholarships/grants, and unspecified assistantships also available. Support available to part-time students. Financial award applicants required to submit FAFSA. *Faculty research:* Improving students' skill achievement in mathematics, improving elementary children's understanding of informational text, teachers' use of their pedagogical and mathematical knowledge in the interactive work of teaching, the intersection of identity construction in teaching and learning, identifying effective methods of literacy instruction and assessments for bilingual students in elementary language arts classrooms. *Unit head:* Dr. Roland Coloma, Assistant Dean for Teacher Education, 313-577-0902, E-mail: rscoloma@wayne.edu. *Application contact:* Dr. Mary L. Waker, Graduate Admissions Officer, 313-577-1601, Fax: 313-577-7904, E-mail: m.waker@wayne.edu.
Website: http://coe.wayne.edu/ted/index.php

Webster University, School of Education, Department of Multidisciplinary Studies, St. Louis, MO 63119-3194. Offers applied educational psychology (MA, Ed S); communication arts (MA); early childhood education (MA, MAT); education and innovation (MA); educational technology (MET); elementary education (MAT); mathematics for educators (MA); middle school education (MAT); multidisciplinary studies (MAT); multimodal literacy for global impact (MA); reading (MA); secondary school education (MAT); special education (MA, MAT); teaching English as a second language (MA); transformative learning in the global community (Ed S). *Program availability:* Part-time. *Entrance requirements:* For master's, minimum GPA of 2.5. Additional exam requirements/recommendations for international students: Required—TOEFL. *Expenses: Tuition:* Full-time $22,500; part-time $750 per credit hour. Tuition and fees vary according to degree level, campus/location and program.

Western Kentucky University, Graduate School, College of Education and Behavioral Sciences, School of Teacher Education, Bowling Green, KY 42101. Offers elementary education (MAE, Ed S); exceptional education: learning and behavioral disorders (MAE); instructional design (MS); interdisciplinary early childhood education (MAE); library media education (MS); literacy education (MAE); middle grades education (MAE); secondary education (MAE, Ed S); special education: moderate and severe disabilities (MAE). *Program availability:* Part-time, evening/weekend, online learning. *Degree requirements:* For master's, comprehensive exam. *Entrance requirements:* For master's, GRE General Test. Additional exam requirements/recommendations for international students: Required—TOEFL (minimum score 555 paper-based; 79 iBT). *Faculty research:* Teacher preparation in moderate/severe disabilities.

Western New Mexico University, Graduate Division, School of Education, Silver City, NM 88062-0680. Offers bilingual education (MAT); educational leadership (MA); elementary education (MAT); reading (MAT); secondary education (MAT); special education (MAT); TESOL (teaching English to speakers of other languages) (MAT). *Accreditation:* NCATE. *Program availability:* Part-time, online learning. *Degree requirements:* For master's, comprehensive exam. *Entrance requirements:* For master's, minimum GPA of 3.0 in last 64 hours of undergraduate study. Additional exam requirements/recommendations for international students: Required—TOEFL (minimum score 550 paper-based; 79 iBT). Electronic applications accepted. *Faculty research:* International education, electronic reading assessment, developing STEM teachers.

Western Oregon University, Graduate Programs, College of Education, Division of Teacher Education, Program in Secondary Education, Monmouth, OR 97361. Offers bilingual education (MS Ed); health (MS Ed); humanities (MAT, MS Ed); initial licensure (MAT); mathematics (MAT, MS Ed); science (MAT, MS Ed); social science (MAT, MS Ed). *Accreditation:* NCATE. *Program availability:* Part-time, evening/weekend. *Degree requirements:* For master's, thesis optional, written exam. *Entrance requirements:* For master's, minimum GPA of 3.0, teaching license. Additional exam requirements/recommendations for international students: Required—TOEFL (minimum score 550 paper-based; 79 iBT), IELTS (minimum score 6.5). *Faculty research:* Literacy, science in primary grades, geography education, retention, teacher burnout.

Western Washington University, Graduate School, Woodring College of Education, Department of Secondary Education, Bellingham, WA 98225-5996. Offers MIT. *Accreditation:* NCATE. *Program availability:* Part-time. *Degree requirements:* For master's, comprehensive exam, thesis optional. *Entrance requirements:* For master's, GRE General Test or MAT, minimum GPA of 3.0 in last 60 semester hours or last 90 quarter hours, secondary teaching certification. Additional exam requirements/recommendations for international students: Required—TOEFL (minimum score 567 paper-based). Electronic applications accepted. *Faculty research:* Service learning, controversial issues in classroom, trauma-sensitive teaching-learning, measuring a teacher's "withitness".

Westfield State University, College of Graduate and Continuing Education, Department of Education, Programs in Secondary Education, Westfield, MA 01086. Offers biology teacher education (M Ed), including secondary education-biology; history teacher education (M Ed), including secondary education-history; mathematics teacher education (M Ed), including secondary education-mathematics; physical education teacher education (M Ed), including secondary education-physical education. *Accreditation:* NCATE. *Program availability:* Part-time, evening/weekend. *Degree requirements:* For master's, comprehensive exam, practicum. *Entrance requirements:* For master's, GRE General Test or MAT, minimum undergraduate GPA of 2.8. Additional exam requirements/recommendations for international students: Recommended—TOEFL (minimum score 550 paper-based; 79 iBT).

West Virginia University, College of Education and Human Services, Morgantown, WV 26506. Offers audiology (Au D); autism spectrum disorder (MA); clinical rehabilitation and mental health counseling (MS); communication science and disorders (PhD); counseling (MA); counseling psychology (PhD); curriculum and instruction (Ed D); early childhood education (MA); early intervention/ early childhood special education (MA); education (PhD); educational leadership (MA); educational leadership/ public school administration (Ed D); educational leadership/public school administration (MA); educational psychology (MA, Ed D); elementary education (MA); gifted education (MA); higher education administration (MA, Ed D); higher education curriculum and teaching (MA); institutional design and technology (MA); instructional design and technology (Ed D); literacy education (MA); secondary education (MA); secondary education/ English (MA); special education (Ed D); speech pathology (MS). *Accreditation:* ASHA; NCATE. *Program availability:* Part-time, evening/weekend, online learning. *Students:* 392 full-time (325 women), 337 part-time (285 women); includes 44 minority (16 Black or African American, non-Hispanic/Latino; 16 Hispanic/Latino; 12 Two or more races, non-Hispanic/Latino), 11 international. In 2018, 303 master's, 6 doctorates awarded. *Degree requirements:* For master's, content exams; for doctorate, comprehensive exam, thesis/dissertation. *Entrance requirements:* Additional exam requirements/recommendations for international students: Required—TOEFL (minimum score 500 paper-based; 61 iBT). *Application deadline:* For fall admission, 8/1 for domestic students; for spring admission, 1/1 for domestic students; for summer admission, 5/1 for domestic students. Application fee: $60. Electronic applications accepted. *Financial support:* Fellowships, research assistantships, teaching assistantships, career-related internships or fieldwork, Federal Work-Study, institutionally sponsored loans, health care benefits, tuition waivers (full and partial), and administrative assistantships available. Financial award applicants required to submit FAFSA. *Faculty research:* Internet training and integration for teachers, rural education, teacher preparation, organization of schools, evaluation of personnel. *Unit head:* Dr. Tracy L. Morris, Interim Dean, 304-293-0816, Fax: 304-293-7565, E-mail: Tracy.Morris@mail.wvu.edu. *Application contact:* Dr. Melissa Luna, Associate Dean for Research, 304-293-2174, Fax: 304-293-3802, E-mail: Melissa.Luna@mail.wvu.edu.
Website: http://cehs.wvu.edu/

Wheaton College, Graduate School, Department of Education, Wheaton, IL 60187-5593. Offers elementary education (MAT); secondary education (MAT). *Accreditation:* NCATE. *Faculty:* 1 full-time (0 women), 1 part-time/adjunct (0 women). *Students:* 18 full-time (13 women), 22 part-time (10 women); includes 7 minority (3 Asian, non-Hispanic/Latino; 3 Hispanic/Latino; 1 Two or more races, non-Hispanic/Latino), 1 international. Average age 24. 21 applicants, 86% accepted, 13 enrolled. In 2018, 14 master's awarded. *Degree requirements:* For master's, thesis or alternative. *Entrance requirements:* For master's, GRE General Test or MAT. Additional exam requirements/recommendations for international students: Required—TOEFL (minimum score 550 paper-based; 80 iBT), IELTS (minimum score 6.5). *Application deadline:* For fall admission, 5/1 for domestic students, 1/1 for international students; for spring admission, 11/1 for domestic students. Applications are processed on a rolling basis. Application fee: $30. Electronic applications accepted. *Expenses: Tuition:* Full-time $20,400; part-time $850 per credit hour. Tuition and fees vary according to degree level and program. *Financial support:* Career-related internships or fieldwork and Federal Work-Study available. Financial award application deadline: 3/1; financial award applicants required to submit FAFSA. *Unit head:* Dr. Paul Egeland, Chair, 630-752-5041, E-mail: education.dept@wheaton.edu. *Application contact:* Terrance Campbell, Director of Graduate Admissions, 630-752-5195, Fax: 630-752-7047, E-mail: graduate.admissions@wheaton.edu.
Website: https://www.wheaton.edu/graduate-school/degrees/ma-in-teaching/

Whittier College, Graduate Programs, Department of Education and Child Development, Program in Secondary Education, Whittier, CA 90608-0634. Offers MA Ed. *Program availability:* Part-time, evening/weekend. *Degree requirements:* For master's, thesis. *Entrance requirements:* For master's, GRE General Test, MAT.

Whitworth University, School of Education, Graduate Studies in Education, Spokane, WA 99251-0001. Offers administration (M Ed); counseling (M Ed), including school counselors, social agency/church setting; elementary education (M Ed); gifted and talented (MAT); secondary education (M Ed); special education (MAT); teaching (MIT). *Accreditation:* NCATE. *Program availability:* Part-time, evening/weekend. *Degree requirements:* For master's, comprehensive exam, thesis (for some programs). *Entrance requirements:* For master's, GRE General Test, MAT. Additional exam requirements/recommendations for international students: Required—TOEFL. *Faculty research:* Rural program development, mainstreaming, special needs learners.

Wichita State University, Graduate School, College of Applied Studies, School of Education, Wichita, KS 67260. Offers learning and instructional design (M Ed); special education (M Ed), including early childhood (M Ed, MAT), gifted, high incidence, low incidence; teaching (MAT), including early childhood (M Ed, MAT), middle level/secondary, transition to teaching. *Accreditation:* NCATE. *Program availability:* Part-time, evening/weekend, 100% online, blended/hybrid learning. *Entrance requirements:* For master's, MAT, minimum GPA of 2.75. *Unit head:* Dr. Edward Robeck, Department Head, 316-978-3322, E-mail: edward.robeck@wichita.edu. *Application contact:* Jordan Oleson, Admission Coordinator, 316-978-3095, Fax: 316-978-3253, E-mail: jordan.oleson@wichita.edu.

William Carey University, School of Education, Hattiesburg, MS 39401. Offers art education (M Ed); art of teaching (M Ed); elementary education (M Ed, Ed S); English education (M Ed); gifted education (M Ed); history and social science (M Ed); mild/moderate disabilities (M Ed); secondary education (M Ed). *Accreditation:* NCATE. *Program availability:* Part-time. *Degree requirements:* For master's, comprehensive exam. *Entrance requirements:* For master's, GRE, MAT, minimum GPA of 2.5, Class A teacher's license. Additional exam requirements/recommendations for international students: Required—TOEFL (minimum score 550 paper-based).

William Paterson University of New Jersey, College of Education, Wayne, NJ 07470-8420. Offers curriculum and learning (M Ed); early childhood education (Certificate); educational leadership (M Ed); educational media specialist (Certificate); elementary education (MAT, Certificate); elementary education subject area (Certificate); higher education administration (MA); learning disabilities consultant (Certificate); literacy (M Ed); middle level education (M Ed); middle school education subject area (Certificate); professional counseling (M Ed); reading specialist (Certificate); school library media specialist (Certificate); school principal (Certificate); school supervisor (Certificate); secondary education (MAT); special education (M Ed); teacher of students with disabilities (Certificate). *Accreditation:* NCATE. *Program availability:* Part-time, evening/weekend. *Students:* Average age 35. 347 applicants, 87% accepted, 226 enrolled. In 2018, 136 master's awarded. *Degree requirements:* For master's, comprehensive exam, thesis (for some programs), exit interview (for some programs); practicum/internship; minimum GPA of 3.0 (for some programs); exit portfolio (for some programs). *Entrance requirements:* For master's, GRE/MAT, minimum GPA of 2.75; teaching certificate; essay; interview; 2 letters of recommendation; personal statement. Additional exam requirements/recommendations for international students: Required—TOEFL (minimum score 550 paper-based; 79 iBT), IELTS (minimum score 6). *Application deadline:* For fall admission, 6/1 for domestic students, 3/1 for international students; for spring admission, 11/1 for domestic students, 10/1 for international students. Applications are processed on a rolling basis. Application fee: $50. Electronic applications accepted. *Expenses: Tuition, area resident:* Full-time $14,714; part-time $727 per credit. Tuition, state resident: full-time $14,714; part-time $727 per credit. Tuition, nonresident: full-time $22,952; part-time $727 per credit. *International tuition:* $22,952 full-time. *Required fees:* $4 per semester. Tuition and fees vary according to course load, degree level and program. *Financial support:* In 2018–19, 8,416 students received support. Career-related internships or fieldwork, Federal Work-Study, scholarships/grants, and unspecified assistantships available. Support available to part-time students. Financial award application deadline: 3/15; financial award applicants required to submit FAFSA. *Faculty research:* Code switching and creative writing, language instruction, teacher evaluation, preschools, history of educational theories. *Total annual research expenditures:* $311,226. *Unit head:* Dr. Dorothy Feola, Dean, 973-720-2138, Fax: 973-720-3647, E-mail: feolad@wpunj.edu. *Application contact:* Liana Fornarotto, Director of Education Enrollment and Certification, 973-720-2206, Fax: 973-720-2989, E-mail: fornarottol@wpunj.edu.
Website: http://www.wpunj.edu/coe

Wilmington University, College of Education, New Castle, DE 19720-6491. Offers applied technology in education (M Ed); career and technical education (M Ed); educational leadership (Ed D); elementary and secondary school counseling (M Ed); elementary studies (M Ed); ESOL literacy (M Ed); higher education leadership (Ed D); instruction: gifted and talented (M Ed); instruction: teacher of reading (M Ed); instruction: teaching and learning (M Ed); organizational leadership (Ed D); school leadership (M Ed); secondary education (MAT); special education (M Ed). *Accreditation:* NCATE. *Program availability:* Part-time, evening/weekend. *Entrance requirements:* For master's, 2 letters of recommendation, interview. Additional exam requirements/recommendations for international students: Required—TOEFL (minimum score 500 paper-based). Electronic applications accepted.

Wilson College, Graduate Programs, Chambersburg, PA 17201-1285. Offers accounting (M Acc); choreography and visual art (MFA); education (M Ed); educational technology (MET); healthcare administration (MHA); humanities (MA), including art and culture, critical/cultural theory, English language and literature, women's studies; management (MSM); nursing (MSN), including nursing education, nursing leadership and management; special education (MSE). *Program availability:* Evening/weekend. *Degree requirements:* For master's, project. *Entrance requirements:* For master's, PRAXIS, minimum undergraduate cumulative GPA of 3.0, 2 letters of recommendation, current certification for eligibility to teach in grades K-12, resume, personal interview. Electronic applications accepted.

Winthrop University, College of Education, Program in Secondary Education, Rock Hill, SC 29733. Offers M Ed. *Accreditation:* NCATE. *Program availability:* Part-time. *Students:* 22 full-time (17 women), 25 part-time (15 women); includes 14 minority (10 Black or African American, non-Hispanic/Latino; 1 Hispanic/Latino; 3 Two or more races, non-Hispanic/Latino), 1 international. Average age 26. In 2018, 24 master's awarded. *Entrance requirements:* For master's, PRAXIS, minimum GPA of 3.0, South Carolina Class III Teaching Certificate. Additional exam requirements/recommendations for international students: Required—TOEFL (minimum score 550 paper-based; 79 iBT), IELTS (minimum score 6). *Application deadline:* For fall admission, 7/15 priority date for domestic students; for spring admission, 12/1 for domestic students. Applications are processed on a rolling basis. Application fee: $50. Electronic applications accepted. *Expenses:* Tuition, state resident: full-time $15,166; part-time $635 per credit hour. Tuition, nonresident: full-time $29,214. *Required fees:* $500; $180 per semester. *Financial support:* Career-related internships or fieldwork, Federal Work-Study, scholarships/grants, and unspecified assistantships available. Support available to part-time students. Financial award application deadline: 2/1; financial award applicants required to submit FAFSA. *Unit head:* Marshall Jones, Graduate Program Advisor, 803-323-4937, E-mail: jonesmg@winthrop.edu. *Application contact:* 800-411-7041, Fax: 803-323-2292, E-mail: gradschool@winthrop.edu.
Website: http://www.winthrop.edu/graduateschool

Worcester State University, Graduate School, Department of Education, Worcester, MA 01602-2597. Offers adult English as a esl (Postbaccalaureate Certificate); curriculum and instruction (Ed S); early childhood education (M Ed); education (M Ed); elementary education (M Ed); English as a second language (M Ed, Postbaccalaureate Certificate); middle school education (M Ed); middle/secondary school education (Postbaccalaureate Certificate); moderate disabilities (M Ed, Postbaccalaureate Certificate); reading (M Ed, Postbaccalaureate Certificate); reading specialist (Postbaccalaureate Certificate); school leadership and education administration (M Ed); school psychology (M Ed, Ed S); secondary education (M Ed, Ed S, Postbaccalaureate Certificate). *Faculty:* 10 full-time (9 women), 23 part-time/adjunct (11 women). *Students:* 38 full-time (33 women), 281 part-time (212 women); includes 30 minority (4 Black or African American, non-Hispanic/Latino; 3 American Indian or Alaska Native, non-Hispanic/Latino; 2 Asian, non-Hispanic/Latino; 16 Hispanic/Latino; 5 Two or more races, non-Hispanic/Latino), 2 international. Average age 41. 102 applicants, 98% accepted, 88 enrolled. In 2018, 132 master's, 52 Ed Ss awarded. *Degree requirements:* For master's, comprehensive exam (for some programs), thesis (for some programs), For a detail list of degree completion requirements please see the graduate catalog at catalog.worcester.edu. *Entrance requirements:* For master's, GRE General Test, MAT or GMAT, teaching certificate. For a detail list of entrance requirements please see the graduate catalog at catalog.worcester.edu. Additional exam requirements/recommendations for international students: Required—TOEFL (minimum score 550 paper-based; 79 iBT), PTE. *Application deadline:* For fall admission, 3/1 for domestic and international students; for spring admission, 11/1 for domestic and international students; for summer admission, 3/1 for domestic and international students. Applications are processed on a rolling basis. Application fee: $50. Electronic applications accepted. *Expenses: Tuition, area resident:* Full-time $3042; part-time $169 per credit hour. Tuition, state resident: full-time $3042; part-time $169 per credit hour. Tuition, nonresident: full-time $3042; part-time $169 per credit hour. *International tuition:* $3042 full-time. *Required fees:* $2754; $153 per credit hour. *Financial support:* Career-related internships or fieldwork, scholarships/grants, and unspecified assistantships available. Support available to part-time students. Financial award application deadline: 3/1; financial award applicants required to submit FAFSA. *Unit head:* Dr. Sara Young, Graduate Program Coordinator, 508-929-8246, Fax: 508-929-8164, E-mail: syoung3@worcester.edu. *Application contact:* Sara Grady, Associate Dean of Graduate and Continuing Education, 508-929-8130, Fax: 508-929-8100, E-mail: sara.grady@worcester.edu.

Wright State University, Graduate School, College of Education and Human Services, Department of Teacher Education, Programs in Classroom Teacher Education, Dayton, OH 45435. Offers M Ed, MA. *Accreditation:* NCATE. *Degree requirements:* For master's, thesis (for some programs). *Entrance requirements:* For master's, GRE General Test, MAT, PRAXIS II. Additional exam requirements/recommendations for international students: Required—TOEFL.

Xavier University, College of Professional Sciences, School of Education, Department of Secondary and Special Education, Cincinnati, OH 45207. Offers secondary education (M Ed); special education (M Ed). *Entrance requirements:* Additional exam requirements/recommendations for international students: Required—TOEFL (minimum score 550 paper-based; 79 iBT). Application fee is waived when completed online. *Expenses:* Contact institution.

Section 25
Special Focus

This section contains a directory of institutions offering graduate work in special focus. Additional information about programs listed in the directory may be obtained by writing directly to the dean of a graduate school or chair of a department at the address given in the directory.

For programs offering related work, see also in this book *Administration, Instruction, and Theory; Education; Instructional Levels; Leisure Studies and Recreation; Physical Education and Kinesiology;* and *Subject Areas.* In other guides in this series:

Graduate Programs in the Humanities, Arts & Social Sciences
See *Psychology and Counseling (School Psychology)* and *Public, Regional, and Industrial Affairs (Urban Studies)*

Graduate Programs in the Biological/Biomedical Sciences and Health-Related Medical Professions
See *Health-Related Professions*

CONTENTS

Program Directories

Education of Students with Severe/Multiple Disabilities

California Baptist University, Program in Education, Riverside, CA 92504-3206. Offers educational leadership (MS); educational leadership for faith-based institutions (MS); educational leadership for public institutions (MS); educational technology (MS); instructional computer applications (MS); international education (MS); leadership and adult learning (MS); leadership and organizational studies (MS); online teaching and learning (MS); reading (MS); science education (MA); special education in mild/moderate disabilities (MS); special education in moderate/severe disabilities (MS); teacher leadership (MS); teaching (MS); teaching and learning (MS). *Program availability:* Part-time, evening/weekend, 100% online, blended/hybrid learning. *Faculty:* 26 full-time (13 women), 28 part-time/adjunct (21 women). *Students:* 201 full-time (164 women), 265 part-time (209 women); includes 226 minority (23 Black or African American, non-Hispanic/Latino; 4 American Indian or Alaska Native, non-Hispanic/Latino; 7 Asian, non-Hispanic/Latino; 169 Hispanic/Latino; 6 Native Hawaiian or other Pacific Islander, non-Hispanic/Latino; 17 Two or more races, non-Hispanic/Latino), 2 international. Average age 39. 145 applicants, 97% accepted, 141 enrolled. In 2018, 253 master's awarded. *Degree requirements:* For master's, comprehensive exam, project, or thesis. *Entrance requirements:* For master's, minimum undergraduate GPA of 2.75; 500-word essay; three letters of recommendation; two prerequisite courses completed with minimum C grade. Additional exam requirements/recommendations for international students: Required—TOEFL (minimum score 80 iBT). *Application deadline:* For fall admission, 8/1 priority date for domestic students, 7/1 for international students; for spring admission, 12/1 priority date for domestic students, 11/1 for international students. Applications are processed on a rolling basis. Application fee: $45. Electronic applications accepted. *Expenses:* $634 per unit. *Financial support:* In 2018–19, 312 students received support. Federal Work-Study and scholarships/grants available. Financial award applicants required to submit CSS PROFILE or FAFSA. *Faculty research:* Leadership development, complexity theory, faith and learning, special education, social and philosophical contexts of education. *Unit head:* Dr. Robin Duncan, Dean, School of Education, 951-552-8948, E-mail: rduncan@calbaptist.edu. *Application contact:* Dr. Shari Farris, Program Director, Online MS in Education, 951-343-2455, E-mail: sfarris@calbaptist.edu.
Website: http://www.calbaptist.edu/mastersined/

California State University, East Bay, Office of Graduate Studies, College of Education and Allied Studies, Department of Educational Psychology, Special Education Program, Hayward, CA 94542-3000. Offers mild-moderate disabilities (MS); moderate-severe disabilities (MS). *Accreditation:* NCATE. *Degree requirements:* For master's, project or thesis. *Entrance requirements:* For master's, GRE or MAT, interview, minimum GPA of 2.5 during previous 2 years of course work. Additional exam requirements/recommendations for international students: Required—TOEFL (minimum score 550 paper-based). Electronic applications accepted.

California State University, Northridge, Graduate Studies, Michael D. Eisner College of Education, Department of Special Education, Northridge, CA 91330. Offers early childhood special education (MA); education of the deaf and hard of hearing (MA); educational therapy (MA); mild/moderate disabilities (MA); moderate/severe disabilities (MA). *Accreditation:* NCATE. *Entrance requirements:* For master's, GRE General Test (if cumulative undergraduate GPA less than 3.0). Additional exam requirements/recommendations for international students: Required—TOEFL. *Faculty research:* Teacher training, classroom aide training.

Chapman University, Donna Ford Attallah College of Educational Studies, Orange, CA 92866. Offers counseling (MA), including school counseling (MA, Credential); curriculum and instruction (MA), including elementary education, secondary education; education (PhD), including cultural and curricular studies, disability studies, leadership studies, school psychology (PhD, Credential); educational psychology (MA); leadership development (MA); multiple subjects (Credential), including Spanish/English bilingual; pupil personnel services (Credential), including school counseling (MA, Credential), school psychology (PhD, Credential); school psychology (Ed S); single subject (Credential); special education (MA, Credential), including mild/moderate (Credential), moderate/severe (Credential); teaching (MA), including elementary education, secondary education, secondary music education. *Accreditation:* TEAC. *Program availability:* Part-time, evening/weekend. Electronic applications accepted. *Expenses:* Contact institution.

Cleveland State University, College of Graduate Studies, College of Education and Human Services, Department of Teacher Education, Cleveland, OH 44115. Offers art education (M Ed); early childhood education (M Ed); foreign language education (M Ed); middle childhood mathematics and science education (M Ed); special education (M Ed), including mild/moderate disabilities, moderate/intensive disabilities; teaching English to speakers of other languages (M Ed). *Program availability:* Part-time, evening/weekend. *Faculty:* 19 full-time (14 women), 32 part-time/adjunct (27 women). *Students:* 56 full-time (40 women), 344 part-time (278 women); includes 104 minority (74 Black or African American, non-Hispanic/Latino; 1 American Indian or Alaska Native, non-Hispanic/Latino; 5 Asian, non-Hispanic/Latino; 9 Hispanic/Latino; 15 Two or more races, non-Hispanic/Latino), 14 international. Average age 34. 177 applicants, 55% accepted, 68 enrolled. In 2018, 117 master's awarded. *Degree requirements:* For master's, comprehensive exam (for some programs), thesis or alternative. *Entrance requirements:* For master's, GRE General Test or MAT, minimum GPA of 2.75. Additional exam requirements/recommendations for international students: Required—TOEFL (minimum score 550 paper-based; 78 iBT), IELTS (minimum score 6). *Application deadline:* For fall admission, 7/1 priority date for domestic students, 5/15 for international students; for spring admission, 11/15 for domestic students, 11/1 for international students; for summer admission, 4/1 for domestic students, 3/15 for international students. Applications are processed on a rolling basis. Application fee: $30. *Expenses:* Tuition, state resident: full-time $7232.55; part-time $6676 per credit hour. Tuition, nonresident: full-time $12,375. *International tuition:* $18,914 full-time. *Required fees:* $80; $80 $40. Tuition and fees vary according to program. *Financial support:* In 2018–19, 13 research assistantships with full tuition reimbursements (averaging $15,845 per year) were awarded; tuition waivers (partial) and unspecified assistantships also available. Financial award application deadline: 2/15; financial award applicants required to submit FAFSA. *Faculty research:* Early childhood education, literacy education, special education: mild/moderate, moderate/intensive, early childhood intervention specialist), teaching English to speakers of other languages (TESOL). *Total annual research expenditures:* $275,907. *Unit head:* Dr. Tachelle Banks, Department Chairperson, 216-687-4600, Fax: 216-687-5379, E-mail: t.i.banks@csuohio.edu. *Application contact:* Rosalyn Adams, Administrative Coordinator, 216-523-7139, Fax: 216-687-5491, E-mail: r.m.adams@csuohio.edu.
Website: http://www.csuohio.edu/cehs/te/te

Georgia State University, College of Education and Human Development, Department of Learning Sciences, Atlanta, GA 30302-3083. Offers behavior and learning disabilities (M Ed); communication disorders (M Ed); education of students with exceptionalities (PhD), including autism spectrum disorders, behavior disorders, communication disorders, early childhood special education (M Ed, PhD), learning disabilities, mental retardation, orthopedic impairments, sensory impairments; educational psychology (MS, PhD); multiple and severe disabilities (M Ed), including early childhood special education (M Ed, PhD), special education adapted curriculum (intellectual disabilities), special education deaf education, special education general and adapted curriculum (autism spectrum disorders), special education physical and health disabilities (orthopedic impairments). *Accreditation:* NCATE. *Program availability:* Part-time, evening/weekend. *Faculty:* 7 full-time (all women). *Students:* 155 full-time (127 women), 122 part-time (100 women); includes 178 minority (135 Black or African American, non-Hispanic/Latino; 13 Asian, non-Hispanic/Latino; 15 Hispanic/Latino; 15 Two or more races, non-Hispanic/Latino), 6 international. Average age 35. 206 applicants, 61% accepted, 88 enrolled. In 2018, 60 master's, 8 doctorates awarded. *Entrance requirements:* For master's, GRE (minimum scores at or above the 50th percentile), GACE Basics Skills Assessment, two official transcripts, minimum GPA of 3.0, certificate in special education/T4 certificate, written statement of goals, resume, two letters of recommendation. *Application deadline:* For fall admission, 6/1 for domestic and international students; for winter admission, 11/1 for domestic and international students; for spring admission, 5/1 for domestic and international students. Application fee: $50. Electronic applications accepted. *Expenses: Tuition, area resident:* Full-time $9360; part-time $390 per credit hour. Tuition, state resident: full-time $9360; part-time $390 per credit hour. Tuition, nonresident: full-time $30,024; part-time $1251 per credit hour. *International tuition:* $30,024 full-time. *Required fees:* $2128. *Financial support:* In 2018–19, fellowships with full tuition reimbursements (averaging $30,000 per year), research assistantships with full tuition reimbursements (averaging $2,000 per year) were awarded; teaching assistantships with full tuition reimbursements, scholarships/grants, and unspecified assistantships also available. *Faculty research:* Academic and behavioral supports for students with emotional/behavior disorders; academic interventions for learning disabilities; communication disorders; language and literacy development, disorders, and instruction; educational psychology. *Application contact:* Sandy Vaughn, Administrative Specialist, 404-413-8318, Fax: 404-413-8043, E-mail: svaughn@gsu.edu.

Hofstra University, School of Education, Specialized Programs in Education, Hempstead, NY 11549. Offers applied behavior analysis (Advanced Certificate); childhood special education (MS Ed); early childhood special education (MS Ed, Advanced Certificate); educational and policy leadership (Ed D); educational leadership (Advanced Certificate); educational leadership and policy studies (MS Ed), including K-12; elementary special education (MS Ed); gifted education (Advanced Certificate); health education (MS); health professions pedagogy and leadership (MS); higher education leadership and policy studies (MS Ed); inclusive early childhood special education (MS Ed); inclusive elementary special education (MS Ed); inclusive secondary special education (MS Ed); literacy studies (MA, MS Ed, Ed D, Advanced Certificate); pedagogy for health professions (Advanced Certificate); physical education (MS); school district business leader (Advanced Certificate); secondary education generalist - students with disabilities 7-12 (MS Ed); secondary special education generalist - secondary education (MS Ed); special education (MS Ed, Advanced Certificate); special education assessment and diagnosis (Advanced Certificate); special education early childhood intervention (MS Ed); special education: international perspectives (MS Ed); teaching students with severe or multiple disabilities (Advanced Certificate). *Program availability:* Part-time, evening/weekend, blended/hybrid learning. *Students:* 126 full-time (91 women), 230 part-time (175 women); includes 90 minority (40 Black or African American, non-Hispanic/Latino; 4 American Indian or Alaska Native, non-Hispanic/Latino; 11 Asian, non-Hispanic/Latino; 32 Hispanic/Latino; 3 Two or more races, non-Hispanic/Latino), 4 international. Average age 32. 215 applicants, 90% accepted, 117 enrolled. In 2018, 130 master's, 9 doctorates, 23 other advanced degrees awarded. *Degree requirements:* For master's, one foreign language, comprehensive exam (for some programs), thesis (for some programs), electronic portfolio, capstone course, internship, practicum, student teaching, seminars, minimum GPA of 3.0; for doctorate, one foreign language, comprehensive exam, thesis/dissertation, qualifying hearing. *Entrance requirements:* For master's, GRE, interview, letters of recommendation, portfolio, essay, certification; for doctorate, GRE or MAT, interview, resume, essay, master's degree, 3 letters of recommendation, writing sample; for Advanced Certificate, GRE, interview, letters of recommendation, essay, professional experience, resume, master's degree. Additional exam requirements/recommendations for international students: Required—TOEFL (minimum score 550 paper-based; 80 iBT). *Application deadline:* Applications are processed on a rolling basis. Application fee: $75. Electronic applications accepted. *Financial support:* In 2018–19, 208 students received support, including 105 fellowships with full and partial tuition reimbursements available (averaging $3,948 per year), 12 research assistantships with full and partial tuition reimbursements available (averaging $6,573 per year); career-related internships or fieldwork, Federal Work-Study, institutionally sponsored loans, scholarships/grants, traineeships, tuition waivers (full and partial), unspecified assistantships, and scholarships and endowed scholarships also available. Support available to part-time students. Financial award applicants required to submit FAFSA. *Faculty research:* Water quality and income inequality; girls and stem; new media literacies; applied behavior analysis; k-12 leadership development. *Unit head:* Dr. Alan Flurkey, Chairperson, 516-463-5237, E-mail: alan.d.flurkey@hofstra.edu. *Application contact:* Sunil Samuel, Assistant Vice President of Admissions, 516-463-4723, Fax: 516-463-4664, E-mail: graduateadmission@hofstra.edu.
Website: http://www.hofstra.edu/education/

Hunter College of the City University of New York, Graduate School, School of Education, Department of Special Education, New York, NY 10065-5085. Offers blind and visually impaired (MS Ed); severe/multiple disabilities (MS Ed). *Accreditation:* NCATE. *Degree requirements:* For master's, comprehensive exam, thesis, student teaching practica, clinical teaching lab courses, New York State Teacher Certification Exams. *Entrance requirements:* For master's, minimum GPA of 2.8. Additional exam requirements/recommendations for international students: Required—TOEFL, TWE. *Faculty research:* Mathematics learning disabilities; street behavior; assessment; bilingual special education; families, diversity, and disabilities.

Lesley University, Graduate School of Education, Cambridge, MA 02138-2790. Offers arts, community, and education (M Ed); autism studies (Certificate); curriculum and instruction (M Ed, CAGS); early childhood education (M Ed); ecological teaching and learning (MS); educational studies (PhD), including adult learning, educational leadership, individually designed; elementary education (M Ed); emergent technologies for educators (Certificate); ESLArts: language learning through the arts (M Ed); high school education (M Ed); individually designed (M Ed); integrated teaching through the arts (M Ed); literacy for K-8 classroom teachers (M Ed); mathematics education (M Ed); middle school education (M Ed); moderate disabilities (M Ed); online learning (Certificate); reading (CAGS); science in education (M Ed); severe disabilities (M Ed); special needs (CAGS); specialist teacher of reading (M Ed); teacher of visual art (M Ed); technology in education (M Ed, CAGS). *Accreditation:* TEAC. *Program availability:* Part-time, evening/weekend, online learning. *Degree requirements:* For master's, practicum; for doctorate, thesis/dissertation. *Entrance requirements:* For master's, Massachusetts Tests for Educator Licensure (MTEL), transcripts, statement of purpose, recommendations; interview (for special education); for doctorate, GRE General Test, transcripts, statement of purpose, recommendations, interview, master's degree, resume; for other advanced degree, interview, master's degree. Additional exam requirements/recommendations for international students: Required—TOEFL (minimum score 550 paper-based; 80 iBT). Electronic applications accepted. *Faculty research:* Assessment in literacy, mathematics and science; autism spectrum disorders; instructional technology and online learning; multicultural education and English language learners.

Murray State University, College of Education and Human Services, Department of Adolescent, Career, and Special Education, Murray, KY 42071. Offers career and technical education (MS); middle school teacher leader (MA Ed); secondary teacher leader (MA Ed); special education (MA Ed), including mild learning and behavior disorders, moderate to severe disabilities (P-12), teacher leader in special education learning and behavior disorders; teacher education and professional development (Ed S). *Accreditation:* NCATE. *Program availability:* Part-time. *Entrance requirements:* For master's and Ed S, GRE or GMAT, minimum university GPA of 2.75. Additional exam requirements/recommendations for international students: Required—TOEFL (minimum score 527 paper-based; 71 iBT). Electronic applications accepted.

Norfolk State University, School of Graduate Studies, School of Education, Department of Special Education, Program in Severe Disabilities, Norfolk, VA 23504. Offers MA. *Accreditation:* NCATE. *Program availability:* Part-time. *Degree requirements:* For master's, thesis or alternative. *Entrance requirements:* For master's, GRE, minimum GPA of 3.0 in major, 2.5 overall.

Rhode Island College, School of Graduate Studies, Feinstein School of Education and Human Development, Department of Special Education, Providence, RI 02908-1991. Offers autism education (CGS); severe intellectual disabilities (CGS); special education (M Ed). *Accreditation:* NCATE. *Program availability:* Part-time, evening/weekend. *Faculty:* 5 full-time (4 women), 6 part-time/adjunct (all women). *Students:* 10 full-time (all women), 52 part-time (51 women); includes 5 minority (1 Black or African American, non-Hispanic/Latino; 2 Hispanic/Latino; 2 Two or more races, non-Hispanic/Latino). Average age 32. In 2018, 34 master's awarded. *Degree requirements:* For master's, comprehensive assessment/assignment. *Entrance requirements:* For master's, GRE General Test or MAT, undergraduate transcripts; minimum undergraduate GPA of 3.0; 3 letters of recommendation; for CGS, GRE or MAT, master's degree or equivalent, teaching certificate, 3 letters of recommendation, interview. Additional exam requirements/recommendations for international students: Required—TOEFL (minimum score 550 paper-based; 80 iBT). *Application deadline:* For fall admission, 3/1 for domestic students; for spring admission, 11/1 for domestic students. Applications are processed on a rolling basis. Application fee: $50. Electronic applications accepted. *Expenses: Tuition, area resident:* Part-time $407 per credit. Tuition, nonresident: part-time $792 per credit. *Required fees:* $29 per credit. $100 per semester. *Financial support:* Teaching assistantships with full tuition reimbursements, career-related internships or fieldwork, Federal Work-Study, scholarships/grants, health care benefits, and unspecified assistantships available. Support available to part-time students. Financial award application deadline: 5/15; financial award applicants required to submit FAFSA. *Unit head:* Dr. Ying Hui-Michael, Chair, 401-456-8024, E-mail: yhui@ric.edu. *Application contact:* Dr. Ying Hui-Michael, Chair, 401-456-8024, E-mail: yhui@ric.edu.
Website: http://www.ric.edu/specialeducation/Pages/default.aspx

Simmons University, Gwen Ifill College of Media, Arts, and Humanities, Boston, MA 02115. Offers behavior analysis (MS, PhD, Ed S); children's literature (MA); dietetics (Certificate); elementary education (MAT); English (MA); gender/cultural studies (MA); history (MA); nutrition and health promotion (MS); physical therapy (DPT); public health (MPH); public policy (MPP); special education: moderate and severe disabilities (MS Ed); sports nutrition (Certificate); writing for children (MFA). *Program availability:* Part-time. *Faculty:* 16 full-time (13 women), 4 part-time/adjunct (3 women). *Students:* 5 full-time (all women), 70 part-time (61 women); includes 12 minority (2 Black or African American, non-Hispanic/Latino; 4 Asian, non-Hispanic/Latino; 4 Hispanic/Latino; 2 Two or more races, non-Hispanic/Latino). Average age 29. 84 applicants, 79% accepted, 32 enrolled. In 2018, 24 master's awarded. *Degree requirements:* For master's, thesis optional. *Entrance requirements:* For master's, GRE, bachelor's degree from accredited college or university; minimum B average (preferred). Additional exam requirements/recommendations for international students: Required—TOEFL (minimum score 600 paper-based; 100 iBT). *Application deadline:* For fall admission, 8/1 for domestic and international students; for spring admission, 12/15 for domestic and international students; for summer admission, 5/1 for domestic and international students. Applications are processed on a rolling basis. Application fee: $35. Electronic applications accepted. *Expenses:* $1,085 per credit hour plus fees. *Financial support:* In 2018–19, 14 students received support, including 1 fellowship (averaging $15,360 per year), 13 teaching assistantships (averaging $2,000 per year); scholarships/grants also available. Financial award applicants required to submit FAFSA. *Faculty research:* Film and media studies, postcolonial literature, critical theory, arts and culture. *Unit head:* Dr. Brian Norman, Dean, 617-521-2472, E-mail: brian.norman@simmons.edu. *Application contact:* Patricia Flaherty, Director, Graduate Studies Admission, 617-521-3902, Fax: 617-521-3058, E-mail: gsa@simmons.edu.
Website: https://www.simmons.edu/academics/colleges-schools-departments/ifill

Syracuse University, School of Education, MS Program in Inclusive Special Education: Severe/Multiple Disabilities, Syracuse, NY 13244. Offers MS. *Program availability:* Part-time. *Students:* Average age 27. *Entrance requirements:* For master's, GRE, baccalaureate degree from regionally-accredited college/university, New York State initial certification in students with disabilities, strong professor and/or employer recommendations, personal statement, interview. Additional exam requirements/recommendations for international students: Required—TOEFL (minimum score 100 iBT). *Application deadline:* For fall admission, 1/15 priority date for domestic and international students; for spring admission, 10/15 priority date for domestic and international students. Applications are processed on a rolling basis. Application fee: $75. Electronic applications accepted. *Financial support:* Fellowships with full tuition reimbursements, research assistantships, teaching assistantships, career-related internships or fieldwork, and scholarships/grants available. Financial award application deadline: 1/15. *Faculty research:* Teaching children and adolescents with autism, augmentation of communication in the inclusive classroom, families of students with disabilities, positive approaches to challenging behaviors, creating safe and peaceful schools. *Unit head:* Dr. Gail Ensher, Program Coordinator, 315-443-9650, E-mail: glensher@syr.edu. *Application contact:* Speranza Migliore, Graduate Admissions Recruiter, 315-443-2505, E-mail: gradrcrt@syr.edu.
Website: http://soe.syr.edu/academic/teaching_and_leadership/graduate/masters/inclusive_special_education_grades_1_6/admissions.aspx

Teachers College, Columbia University, Department of Health and Behavior Studies, New York, NY 10027-6696. Offers applied behavior analysis (MA, PhD); applied educational psychology: school psychology (Ed M, PhD); behavioral nutrition (PhD), including nutrition (Ed D, PhD); community health education (MS); community nutrition education (Ed M), including community nutrition education; education of deaf and hard of hearing (MA, PhD); health education (MA, Ed D); hearing impairment (Ed D); intellectual disability/autism (MA, Ed D, PhD); nursing education (Ed D, Advanced Certificate); nutrition and education (MS); nutrition and exercise physiology (MS); nutrition and public health (MS); nutrition education (Ed D), including nutrition (Ed D, PhD); physical disabilities (Ed D); reading specialist (MA); severe or multiple disabilities (MA); special education (Ed M, MA, Ed D); teaching of sign language (MA). *Program availability:* Part-time, evening/weekend. *Students:* 157 full-time (145 women), 344 part-time (310 women); includes 169 minority (46 Black or African American, non-Hispanic/Latino; 2 American Indian or Alaska Native, non-Hispanic/Latino; 55 Asian, non-Hispanic/Latino; 57 Hispanic/Latino; 9 Two or more races, non-Hispanic/Latino), 64 international. Average age 31. 495 applicants, 64% accepted, 171 enrolled. Terminal master's awarded for partial completion of doctoral program. *Unit head:* Prof. Dolores Perin, Chair, 212-678-3091, E-mail: dp111@tc.columbia.edu. *Application contact:* Kelly Sutton-Skinner, Director of Admission & New Student Enrollment, E-mail: kms2237@tc.columbia.edu.
Website: http://www.tc.columbia.edu/health-and-behavior-studies/

The University of Arizona, College of Education, Department of Disability and Psychoeducational Studies, Tucson, AZ 85721. Offers counseling and mental health (MA), including rehabilitation counseling, school counseling; family studies and human development (M Ed); rehabilitation counseling (PhD); school counseling (MA); school psychology (PhD, Ed S); special education (MA, PhD), including cross-categorical special education (MA), deaf and hard of hearing (MA), learning disabilities (MA), severe and multiple disabilities (MA), special education (PhD), visual impairment (MA). *Accreditation:* CORE. *Program availability:* Part-time. Terminal master's awarded for partial completion of doctoral program. *Degree requirements:* For master's, comprehensive exam, thesis optional; for doctorate, comprehensive exam, thesis/dissertation. *Entrance requirements:* For master's, statement of purpose; for doctorate, GRE General Test (minimum score 1100) or MAT, 3 letters of recommendation. Additional exam requirements/recommendations for international students: Required—TOEFL (minimum score 550 paper-based; 79 iBT).

University of Central Oklahoma, The Jackson College of Graduate Studies, College of Education and Professional Studies, Donna Nigh Department of Advanced Professional and Special Services, Edmond, OK 73034-5209. Offers educational leadership (M Ed); library media education (M Ed); reading (M Ed); school counseling (M Ed); special education (M Ed), including mild/moderate disabilities, severe-profound/multiple disabilities; speech-language pathology (MS). *Accreditation:* ASHA. *Program availability:* Part-time. *Degree requirements:* For master's, comprehensive exam (for some programs), thesis (for some programs). *Entrance requirements:* Additional exam requirements/recommendations for international students: Required—TOEFL (minimum score 550 paper-based; 79 iBT), IELTS (minimum score 6.5). Electronic applications accepted.

University of Illinois at Urbana–Champaign, Graduate College, College of Education, Department of Special Education, Champaign, IL 61820. Offers Ed M, MS, Ed D, PhD, CAS. *Program availability:* Part-time, online learning.

University of New Mexico, Graduate Studies, College of Education, Program in Special Education, Albuquerque, NM 87131-2039. Offers intellectual disability and severe disabilities (MA); learning and behavioral exceptionalities (MA); special education (Ed D, PhD, Ed S). *Accreditation:* NCATE. *Program availability:* Part-time, evening/weekend. *Students:* Average age 37. 24 applicants, 50% accepted, 12 enrolled. In 2018, 37 master's, 6 doctorates, 4 other advanced degrees awarded. *Degree requirements:* For master's, comprehensive exam, thesis optional; for doctorate, comprehensive exam, thesis/dissertation, screening, proposal hearing. *Entrance requirements:* For master's, minimum GPA of 3.2; for doctorate, minimum GPA of 3.2, 2 years of relevant experience; for Ed S, special education degree, 2 years of teaching experience with people with disabilities, writing sample, minimum GPA of 3.2. *Application deadline:* For fall admission, 3/31 priority date for domestic students; for spring admission, 9/30 priority date for domestic students. Applications are processed on a rolling basis. Application fee: $50. Electronic applications accepted. *Financial support:* Fellowships, research assistantships, teaching assistantships, career-related internships or fieldwork, Federal Work-Study, scholarships/grants, traineeships, health care benefits, unspecified assistantships, and stipends available. Support available to part-time students. Financial award application deadline: 3/1; financial award applicants required to submit FAFSA. *Faculty research:* Mathematics instruction, bilingual special education, inclusive education, autism, reading instruction for students with cognitive disabilities, alternative assessment, human rights and disability, applied behavior analysis, bilingualism, language and literacy, mathematics, science instruction, special education. *Unit head:* Prof. Ruth Luckasson, Chair, 505-277-6510, Fax: 505-277-6929, E-mail: luckasson@unm.edu. *Application contact:* Della Gallegos, Information Contact, 505-277-5018, Fax: 505-277-8679, E-mail: dgalle06@unm.edu.
Website: http://coe.unm.edu/departments-programs/es/special-education-program/index.html

University of South Florida, Innovative Education, Tampa, FL 33620-9951. Offers adult, career and higher education (Graduate Certificate), including college teaching, leadership in developing human resources, leadership in higher education; Africana studies (Graduate Certificate), including diasporas and health disparities, genocide and human rights; aging studies (Graduate Certificate), including gerontology; art research (Graduate Certificate), including museum studies; business foundations (Graduate Certificate); chemical and biomedical engineering (Graduate Certificate), including materials science and engineering, water, health and sustainability; child and family studies (Graduate Certificate), including positive behavior support; civil and industrial engineering (Graduate Certificate), including transportation systems analysis; community and family health (Graduate Certificate), including maternal and child health, social marketing and public health, violence and injury: prevention and intervention, women's health; criminology (Graduate Certificate), including criminal justice administration; data science for public administration (Graduate Certificate); digital humanities (Graduate Certificate); educational measurement and research (Graduate Certificate), including evaluation; English (Graduate Certificate), including comparative literary studies, creative writing, professional and technical communication; entrepreneurship (Graduate Certificate); environmental health (Graduate Certificate), including safety management; epidemiology and biostatistics (Graduate Certificate),

including applied biostatistics, biostatistics, concepts and tools of epidemiology, epidemiology, epidemiology of infectious diseases; geography, environment and planning (Graduate Certificate), including community development, environmental policy and management, geographical information systems; geology (Graduate Certificate), including hydrogeology; global health (Graduate Certificate), including disaster management, global health and Latin American and Caribbean studies, global health practice, humanitarian assistance, infection control; government and international affairs (Graduate Certificate), including Cuban studies, globalization studies; health policy and management (Graduate Certificate), including health management and leadership, public health policy and programs; hearing specialist: early intervention (Graduate Certificate); industrial and management systems engineering (Graduate Certificate), including systems engineering, technology management; information studies (Graduate Certificate), including school library media specialist; information systems/decision sciences (Graduate Certificate), including analytics and business intelligence; instructional technology (Graduate Certificate), including distance education, Florida digital/virtual educator, instructional design, multimedia design, Web design; internal medicine, bioethics and medical humanities (Graduate Certificate), including biomedical ethics; Latin American and Caribbean studies (Graduate Certificate); leadership for coastal resiliency planning (Graduate Certificate); mass communications (Graduate Certificate), including multimedia journalism; mathematics and statistics (Graduate Certificate), including mathematics; medicine (Graduate Certificate), including aging and neuroscience, bioinformatics, biotechnology, brain fitness and memory management, clinical investigation, hand and upper limb rehabilitation, health informatics, health sciences, integrative weight management, intellectual property, medicine and gender, metabolic and nutritional medicine, metabolic cardiology, pharmacy sciences; national and competitive intelligence (Graduate Certificate); nursing (Graduate Certificate), including simulation based academic fellowship in advanced pain management; psychological and social foundations (Graduate Certificate), including career counseling, college teaching, diversity in education, mental health counseling, school counseling; public affairs (Graduate Certificate), including nonprofit management, public management, research administration; public health (Graduate Certificate), including assessing chemical toxicity and public health risks, health equity, pharmacoepidemiology, public health generalist, toxicology, translational research in adolescent behavioral health; public health practices (Graduate Certificate), including planning for healthy communities; rehabilitation and mental health counseling (Graduate Certificate), including integrative mental health care, marriage and family therapy, rehabilitation technology; secondary education (Graduate Certificate), including ESOL, foreign language education: culture and content, foreign language education: professional; social work (Graduate Certificate), including geriatric social work/clinical gerontology; special education (Graduate Certificate), including autism spectrum disorder, disabilities education: severe/profound; world languages (Graduate Certificate), including teaching English as a second language (TESL) or foreign language. *Expenses:* Tuition, state resident: full-time $6350. Tuition, nonresident: full-time $19,048. *International tuition:* $19,048 full-time. *Required fees:* $2079. *Unit head:* Dr. Cynthia DeLuca, Associate Vice President and Assistant Vice Provost, 813-974-3077, Fax: 813-974-7061, E-mail: deluca@usf.edu. *Application contact:* Owen Hooper, Director, Summer and Alternative Calendar Programs, 813-974-6917, E-mail: hooper@usf.edu.
Website: http://www.usf.edu/innovative-education/

University of Utah, Graduate School, College of Education, Department of Special Education, Salt Lake City, UT 84112. Offers board certified behavior analyst (M Ed, MS, PhD); deaf and hard of hearing (M Ed); deafblind (M Ed, MS); early childhood deaf and hard of hearing (MS); early childhood special education (M Ed, MS, PhD); early childhood visual impairments (M Ed); mild/moderate disabilities (M Ed, MS, PhD); severe disabilities (M Ed, MS, PhD); visual impairments (M Ed, MS). *Program availability:* Part-time, 100% online, blended/hybrid learning, Interactive Video Conferencing. *Faculty:* 17 full-time (13 women), 31 part-time/adjunct (25 women). *Students:* 62 full-time (53 women), 8 part-time (all women); includes 10 minority (4 Asian, non-Hispanic/Latino; 5 Hispanic/Latino; 1 Two or more races, non-Hispanic/Latino). Average age 31. 53 applicants, 83% accepted, 36 enrolled. In 2018, 13 master's, 1 doctorate awarded. Terminal master's awarded for partial completion of doctoral program. *Degree requirements:* For master's, comprehensive exam, thesis (for some programs), qualifying exam; for doctorate, thesis/dissertation, qualifying exam. *Entrance requirements:* For master's, minimum GPA of 3.0; for doctorate, GRE General Test, minimum GPA of 3.5, Master's Degree. Additional exam requirements/recommendations for international students: Required—TOEFL (minimum score 600 paper-based; 100 iBT); Recommended—IELTS (minimum score 7). *Application deadline:* For fall admission, 3/1 for domestic and international students; for spring admission, 10/1 for domestic and international students; for summer admission, 5/16 for domestic and international students. Application fee: $55 ($65 for international students). Electronic applications accepted. *Expenses:* $12,000 per year. *Financial support:* In 2018–19, 8 students received support, including 35 fellowships with full and partial tuition reimbursements available (averaging $18,200 per year), 42 research assistantships with partial tuition reimbursements available (averaging $14,500 per year), 2 teaching assistantships with full tuition reimbursements available (averaging $15,500 per year); scholarships/grants, traineeships, health care benefits, and unspecified assistantships also available. Financial award application deadline: 3/1; financial award applicants required to submit FAFSA. *Faculty research:* Inclusion, positive behavior supports, embedded instruction, functional communication, literacy intervention. *Total annual research expenditures:* $142,545. *Unit head:* Dr. Susan Johnston, PhD, Chair, 801-581-5187, Fax: 801-585-6476, E-mail: susan.johnston@utah.edu. *Application contact:* Kaitlin Lindsey, Academic Advisor/Student Recruiting Contact, 801-581-4764, Fax: 801-585-6476, E-mail: k.lindsey@utah.edu.
Website: http://special-ed.utah.edu/

University of Washington, Graduate School, College of Education, Seattle, WA 98195. Offers curriculum and instruction (M Ed, Ed D, PhD), including educational technology, general curriculum (Ed D, PhD), language, literacy, and culture, mathematics education, multicultural education, reading and language arts education (Ed D), science education, social studies education, teaching and curriculum (M Ed); educational leadership and policy studies (M Ed, Ed D, PhD), including administration (Ed D), educational policy, organization, and leadership (M Ed, PhD), higher education, leadership for learning (Ed D), social and cultural foundations of education (M Ed, PhD); educational psychology (M Ed, PhD), including educational psychology (PhD), human development and cognition (M Ed), learning sciences, measurement, statistics and research design (M Ed), school psychology (M Ed); instructional leadership (M Ed); intercollegiate athletic leadership (M Ed); special education (M Ed, Ed D, PhD), including early childhood special education (M Ed), emotional and behavioral disabilities (M Ed), learning disabilities (M Ed), low-incidence disabilities (M Ed), severe disabilities (M Ed), special education (Ed D, PhD); teacher education (MIT). *Accreditation:* APA. *Program availability:* Part-time, evening/weekend. *Degree requirements:* For master's, thesis optional; for doctorate, thesis/dissertation. *Entrance requirements:* For master's and doctorate, GRE General Test, minimum GPA of 3.0. Additional exam requirements/recommendations for international students: Required—TOEFL. Electronic applications accepted. *Faculty research:* School restructuring/effective schools, special education interventions, literacy and writing, technology, school partnerships, teacher preparation.

Western Kentucky University, Graduate School, College of Education and Behavioral Sciences, School of Teacher Education, Bowling Green, KY 42101. Offers elementary education (MAE, Ed S); exceptional education: learning and behavioral disorders (MAE); instructional design (MS); interdisciplinary early childhood education (MAE); library media education (MS); literacy education (MAE); middle grades education (MAE); secondary education (MAE, Ed S); special education: moderate and severe disabilities (MAE). *Program availability:* Part-time, evening/weekend, online learning. *Degree requirements:* For master's, comprehensive exam. *Entrance requirements:* For master's, GRE General Test. Additional exam requirements/recommendations for international students: Required—TOEFL (minimum score 555 paper-based; 79 iBT). *Faculty research:* Teacher preparation in moderate/severe disabilities.

West Liberty University, College of Education and Human Performance, West Liberty, WV 26074. Offers community education research and leadership (MA Ed); innovative instruction (MA Ed); leadership in disability services (MA Ed); leadership studies (MA Ed); multi-categorical special education (MA Ed); reading specialist (MA Ed); sports leadership and coaching (MA Ed). *Accreditation:* NCATE. *Program availability:* Part-time, evening/weekend. *Degree requirements:* For master's, capstone experience. *Entrance requirements:* For master's, minimum GPA of 2.5 or 3.0 (depending on track). Additional exam requirements/recommendations for international students: Required—TOEFL. Electronic applications accepted.

Education of the Gifted

Albizu University, Miami Campus, Graduate Programs, Miami, FL 33172-2209. Offers clinical psychology (PhD, Psy D); entrepreneurship (MBA); exceptional student education (MS); human services (PhD); industrial/organizational psychology (MS); marriage and family therapy (MS); mental health counseling (MS); nonprofit management (MBA); organizational management (MBA); school counseling (MS); speech and language pathology (MS); teaching English for speakers of other languages (MS). *Accreditation:* APA. *Program availability:* Part-time, evening/weekend, 100% online, blended/hybrid learning. *Faculty:* 32 full-time (24 women), 27 part-time/adjunct (15 women). *Students:* 479 full-time (410 women), 146 part-time (126 women); includes 539 minority (42 Black or African American, non-Hispanic/Latino; 2 Asian, non-Hispanic/Latino; 490 Hispanic/Latino; 5 Two or more races, non-Hispanic/Latino), 22 international. Average age 33. 314 applicants, 45% accepted, 92 enrolled. In 2018, 101 master's, 64 doctorates awarded. Terminal master's awarded for partial completion of doctoral program. *Degree requirements:* For master's, comprehensive exam (for some programs), integrative project (for MBA); research project (for exceptional student education, teaching English as a second language); for doctorate, comprehensive exam, thesis/dissertation, comprehensive examinations, internship, project/dissertation. *Entrance requirements:* For master's, GRE/EXADEP, bachelor's degree from accredited institution, minimum GPA of 3.0, 3 letters of recommendation, interview, resume, statement of purpose, official transcripts; for doctorate, GRE (for Psy D), 3 letters of recommendation, resume, interview, statement of purpose, official transcripts; bachelor's degree and minimum GPA of 3.25 (for Psy D); master's degree and minimum GPA of 3.0 (for PhD). Additional exam requirements/recommendations for international students: Required—Michigan Test of English Language Proficiency. *Application deadline:* For fall admission, 4/1 priority date for domestic students, 5/1 priority date for international students; for spring admission, 11/1 priority date for domestic students, 9/1 priority date for international students. Applications are processed on a rolling basis. Application fee: $50. Electronic applications accepted. Application fee is waived when completed online. *Expenses:* Contact institution. *Financial support:* In 2018–19, 141 students received support. Federal Work-Study, scholarships/grants, unspecified assistantships, and tuition discounts available. Financial award application deadline: 6/1; financial award applicants required to submit FAFSA. *Faculty research:* Psychotherapy, forensic psychology, neuropsychology, special education, speech-language pathology, criminal justice, human services. *Unit head:* Dr. Jose Pons-Madera, PhD, President, 305-593-1223 Ext. 3120, Fax: 305-477-8983, E-mail: jpons@albizu.edu. *Application contact:* Nancy Alvarez, Director of Enrollment Management, 305-593-1223 Ext. 3136, Fax: 305-593-1854, E-mail: nalvarez@albizu.edu.

Arkansas State University, Graduate School, College of Education and Behavioral Science, School of Teacher Education and Leadership, State University, AR 72467. Offers community college administration (SCCT); curriculum and instruction (MSE); early childhood education (MSE); early childhood services (MS); educational leadership (MSE, Ed D, Ed S); educational theory and practice (MSE); middle level education (MAT, MSE); reading (MSE, Ed S); special education - gifted, talented, and creative (MSE); special education - instructional specialist grades 4-12 (MSE); special education - instructional specialist grades P-4 (MSE); special education, K-12 (MSE). *Accreditation:* NCATE. *Program availability:* Part-time, online learning. *Degree requirements:* For master's, comprehensive exam, thesis or alternative; for doctorate, comprehensive exam, thesis/dissertation; for other advanced degree, comprehensive exam. *Entrance requirements:* For master's, GRE General Test or MAT, appropriate bachelor's degree, official transcripts, immunization records, letters of reference, interview; for doctorate, GRE General Test or MAT, interview, master's degree, letters of reference, official transcript, personal statement, writing sample, immunization records; for other advanced degree, GRE General Test or MAT, interview, master's degree, official transcript, immunization records, letters of reference, 3 years of teaching experience, teaching license. Additional exam requirements/recommendations for international students: Required—TOEFL (minimum score 550 paper-based; 79 iBT), IELTS (minimum score 6), PTE (minimum score 56). Electronic applications accepted.

Ball State University, Graduate School, Teachers College, Department of Educational Psychology, Muncie, IN 47306. Offers educational psychology (MA, MS), including educational psychology (MA, MS, PhD); educational psychology (PhD), including educational psychology (MA, MS, PhD); gifted and talented education (Certificate); human development and learning (Certificate); instructional design and assessment

(Certificate); neuropsychology (Certificate); quantitative psychology (MS); response to intervention (Certificate); school psychology (MA, PhD), including school psychology (MA, PhD, Ed S); school psychology (Ed S), including school psychology (MA, PhD, Ed S). *Program availability:* 100% online. *Degree requirements:* For doctorate, thesis/dissertation; for other advanced degree, thesis. *Entrance requirements:* For master's, GRE General Test, minimum baccalaureate GPA of 2.75 or 3.0 in latter half of baccalaureate, professional goals and self-assessment; for doctorate, GRE General Test, minimum graduate GPA of 3.2; for other advanced degree, GRE General Test. Additional exam requirements/recommendations for international students: Required—TOEFL (minimum score 550 paper-based; 79 iBT), IELTS (minimum score 6.5). Electronic applications accepted.

Barry University, School of Education, Program in Curriculum and Instruction, Miami Shores, FL 33161-6695. Offers accomplished teacher (Ed S); culture, language and literacy (TESOL) (PhD); curriculum evaluation and research (PhD); early childhood (Ed S); early childhood education (PhD); elementary (Ed S); elementary education (PhD); ESOL (Ed S); gifted (Ed S); Montessori (Ed S); PKP/elementary (Ed S); reading (Ed S); reading, language and cognition (PhD). *Entrance requirements:* For doctorate, GRE, minimum GPA of 3.25.

Barry University, School of Education, Program in Exceptional Student Education, Miami Shores, FL 33161-6695. Offers MS, Ed S. *Program availability:* Part-time, evening/weekend. *Degree requirements:* For master's, comprehensive exam; for Ed S, practicum. *Entrance requirements:* For master's, GRE General Test or MAT, minimum GPA of 3.0; for Ed S, GRE General Test, minimum GPA of 3.0. Electronic applications accepted.

Barry University, School of Education, Program in Leadership and Education, Miami Shores, FL 33161-6695. Offers educational technology (PhD); exceptional student education (PhD); higher education administration (PhD); human resource development (PhD); leadership (PhD). *Program availability:* Part-time, evening/weekend. *Degree requirements:* For doctorate, thesis/dissertation. *Entrance requirements:* For doctorate, GRE General Test, minimum GPA of 3.25. Electronic applications accepted.

Canisius College, Graduate Division, School of Education and Human Services, Department of Graduate Education and Leadership, Buffalo, NY 14208-1098. Offers business and marketing education (MS Ed); college student personnel (MS Ed); deaf education (MS Ed); deaf/adolescent education, grades 7-12 (MS Ed); deaf/childhood education, grades 1-6 (MS Ed); differentiated instruction (MS Ed); education administration (MS); educational administration (MS Ed); educational technologies (Certificate); gifted education extension (Certificate); literacy (MS Ed); reading (Certificate); school building leadership (MS Ed, Certificate); school district leadership (Certificate); teacher leader (Certificate); TESOL (MS Ed). *Accreditation:* NCATE. *Program availability:* Part-time, evening/weekend, 100% online, blended/hybrid learning. *Faculty:* 5 full-time (all women), 21 part-time/adjunct (16 women). *Students:* 79 full-time (66 women), 135 part-time (106 women); includes 45 minority (27 Black or African American, non-Hispanic/Latino; 1 American Indian or Alaska Native, non-Hispanic/Latino; 3 Asian, non-Hispanic/Latino; 9 Hispanic/Latino; 5 Two or more races, non-Hispanic/Latino), 1 international. Average age 32. 83 applicants, 96% accepted, 74 enrolled. In 2018, 94 master's, 47 other advanced degrees awarded. *Entrance requirements:* For master's, GRE (if cumulative GPA less than 2.7), transcripts, two letters of recommendation. Additional exam requirements/recommendations for international students: Required—TOEFL (minimum score 550 paper-based, 79 iBT), IELTS (minimum score 6.5), or CAEL (minimum score 70). *Application deadline:* Applications are processed on a rolling basis. Application fee: $0. Electronic applications accepted. *Expenses: Tuition:* Part-time $820 per credit hour. *Required fees:* $25 per semester. One-time fee: $65 part-time. Tuition and fees vary according to program. *Financial support:* In 2018–19, 206 students received support. Career-related internships or fieldwork, Federal Work-Study, scholarships/grants, tuition waivers (partial), and unspecified assistantships available. Support available to part-time students. Financial award application deadline: 4/30; financial award applicants required to submit FAFSA. *Faculty research:* Asperger's disease, autism, private higher education, reading strategies. *Unit head:* Dr. Anne Marie Tryjankowski, Chair/Associate Professor of Graduate Education and Leadership, 716-888-3715, Fax: 716-888-3142, E-mail: tryjanka@canisius.edu. *Application contact:* Dr. Anne Marie Tryjankowski, Chair/Associate Professor of Graduate Education and Leadership, 716-888-3715, Fax: 716-888-3142, E-mail: tryjanka@canisius.edu.

Carthage College, Division of Teacher Education, Kenosha, WI 53140. Offers classroom guidance and counseling (M Ed); creative arts (M Ed); gifted and talented children (M Ed); language arts (M Ed); modern language (M Ed); natural sciences (M Ed); reading (M Ed, Certificate); social sciences (M Ed); teacher leadership (M Ed). *Program availability:* Part-time, evening/weekend. *Degree requirements:* For master's, thesis optional. *Entrance requirements:* For master's, MAT, minimum B average, letters of reference.

The College of New Rochelle, Graduate School, Division of Education, Program in Gifted Education, New Rochelle, NY 10805-2308. Offers Certificate. *Program availability:* Part-time. *Degree requirements:* For Certificate, practicum.

Colorado Mesa University, Center for Teacher Education, Grand Junction, CO 81501-3122. Offers educational leadership (MAEd); English for speakers of other languages (MAEd); exceptional learner/special education (MAEd); teacher education (Graduate Certificate); teacher leader (MAEd). *Accreditation:* NCATE. *Program availability:* Part-time. *Degree requirements:* For master's, comprehensive exam (for some programs), capstone presentation. *Entrance requirements:* For master's, 3 professional letters of recommendation, Colorado teaching license, minimum baccalaureate GPA of 3.0; for Graduate Certificate, minimum baccalaureate GPA of 3.0. Additional exam requirements/recommendations for international students: Required—TOEFL (minimum score 550 paper-based). Electronic applications accepted. *Expenses:* Contact institution. *Faculty research:* K-8 STEM instruction, special education inclusion, elementary math literacy, secondary literacy, elementary/early childhood education literacy.

Converse College, Program in Gifted Education, Spartanburg, SC 29302. Offers M Ed. *Program availability:* Part-time. *Degree requirements:* For master's, capstone paper. *Entrance requirements:* For master's, NTE or PRAXIS II, minimum GPA of 2.75, teaching certificate, 2 recommendations. Electronic applications accepted. *Faculty research:* Identification of gifted minorities, arts in gifted education.

Eastern New Mexico University, Graduate School, College of Education and Technology, Department of Educational Studies, Program in Special Education, Portales, NM 88130. Offers early childhood special education (M Sp Ed); general special education (M Sp Ed); gifted education pedagogy (M Ed); special education pedagogy (M Ed). *Program availability:* Part-time. *Degree requirements:* For master's, comprehensive exam, thesis optional. *Entrance requirements:* For master's, writing assessment, minimum GPA of 3.0, letter of recommendation, photocopy of teaching license or confirmation of entrance into alternative licensure program, special education license or minimum 30 hours of undergraduate course work. Additional exam requirements/recommendations for international students: Required—TOEFL (minimum score 550 paper-based; 79 iBT), IELTS (minimum score 6). Electronic applications

accepted. *Expenses: Tuition, area resident:* Full-time $6776. Tuition, state resident: full-time $6776; part-time $282 per credit hour. Tuition, nonresident: full-time $8986; part-time $374 per credit hour. *Required fees:* $60 per semester. One-time fee: $25.

Emporia State University, Program in Special Education, Emporia, KS 66801-5415. Offers behavior disorders (MS); gifted, talented, and creative (MS); interrelated special education (MS). *Accreditation:* NCATE. *Program availability:* Part-time. *Degree requirements:* For master's, comprehensive exam or thesis, practicum. *Entrance requirements:* For master's, GRE General Test or MAT, essay exam, appropriate bachelor's degree, teacher certification, letters of recommendation. Additional exam requirements/recommendations for international students: Required—TOEFL (minimum score 520 paper-based; 68 iBT). Electronic applications accepted.

Florida Gulf Coast University, College of Education, Program in Curriculum and Instruction, Fort Myers, FL 33965-6565. Offers elementary education (M Ed); English education (M Ed); English speakers of other languages endorsement (M Ed); gifted education (M Ed); mathematics education (M Ed); middle school education (M Ed); reading education (M Ed); science education (M Ed); social science education (M Ed); special education (M Ed). *Program availability:* Part-time, evening/weekend, online learning. *Degree requirements:* For master's, final project or portfolio. *Entrance requirements:* For master's, GRE General Test, MAT, minimum undergraduate GPA of 3.0 in last 2 years. Additional exam requirements/recommendations for international students: Required—TOEFL (minimum score 550 paper-based). Electronic applications accepted. *Faculty research:* Internet in schools, technology in pre-service and in-service teacher training.

George Mason University, College of Education and Human Development, Programs in Curriculum and Instruction, Fairfax, VA 22030. Offers assistive technology (M Ed); designing digital learning in schools (M Ed); early childhood education (M Ed); early childhood education for diverse learners (M Ed); elementary education (M Ed); English as a second language (M Ed); gifted child education (M Ed); literacy (M Ed), including PK-12 classroom teachers, reading specialist; literacy leadership for diverse schools (M Ed), including K-12 reading; physical education (M Ed); science K-12 (M Ed); secondary education (M Ed), including biology, chemistry, earth science, English, history/social science, math, physics; special education (M Ed); teacher leadership (M Ed); transformative teaching (M Ed). *Program availability:* Part-time, evening/weekend, 100% online, blended/hybrid learning. *Faculty:* 48 full-time (40 women), 28 part-time/adjunct (20 women). *Students:* 165 full-time (147 women), 697 part-time (579 women); includes 243 minority (47 Black or African American, non-Hispanic/Latino; 3 American Indian or Alaska Native, non-Hispanic/Latino; 88 Asian, non-Hispanic/Latino; 85 Hispanic/Latino; 4 Native Hawaiian or other Pacific Islander, non-Hispanic/Latino; 16 Two or more races, non-Hispanic/Latino), 26 international. Average age 34. 450 applicants, 93% accepted, 315 enrolled. In 2018, 421 master's awarded. *Entrance requirements:* For master's, PRAXIS Core (for some programs), 2 letters of recommendation, interview, program goals statement; 9 hours of complete licensure endorsement requirements (for elementary education); minimum GPA of 3.0 in applicant's last 60 hours of undergraduate coursework (for secondary education); at least 1 year of teaching experience (for literacy). Additional exam requirements/recommendations for international students: Required—TOEFL (minimum score 575 paper-based; 88 iBT), IELTS (minimum score 6.5), PTE (minimum score 59). *Application deadline:* For fall admission, 4/2 priority date for domestic and international students; for spring admission, 11/1 for domestic and international students. Application fee: $75 ($80 for international students). Electronic applications accepted. *Financial support:* In 2018–19, 4 students received support, including 1 fellowship, 3 teaching assistantships (averaging $3,745 per year); career-related internships or fieldwork, Federal Work-Study, scholarships/grants, unspecified assistantships, and health care benefits (for full-time research or teaching assistantship recipients) also available. Support available to part-time students. Financial award application deadline: 3/1; financial award applicants required to submit FAFSA. *Faculty research:* Teacher preparation and professional development; adaptive teaching; wonder in science teacher preparation; literacy (digital, adolescent); site based course instruction. *Unit head:* Rebecca Fox, Professor and Academic Program Coordinator, 703-993-4123, E-mail: rfox@gmu.edu. *Application contact:* Rebecca Fox, Professor and Academic Program Coordinator, 703-993-4123, E-mail: rfox@gmu.edu. Website: http://gse.gmu.edu/programs/gsemasters

Grand Canyon University, College of Education, Phoenix, AZ 85017-1097. Offers autism spectrum disorders (MA); curriculum and instruction (MA); early childhood education (M Ed); educational administration (M Ed); educational leadership (M Ed); elementary education (M Ed); gifted education (MA); instructional technology (MS); K-12 leadership (Ed S); reading (MA); secondary education (M Ed); secondary humanities education (M Ed); secondary STEM education (M Ed); special education (M Ed); teaching and learning (Ed D); teaching English to speakers of other languages (MA). *Program availability:* Part-time, evening/weekend, online learning. *Degree requirements:* For master's, publishable research paper (M Ed), e-portfolio. *Entrance requirements:* For master's, undergraduate degree from accredited, GCU-approved college, university, or program with minimum GPA 2.8. Additional exam requirements/recommendations for international students: Required—TOEFL (minimum score 550 paper-based; 79 iBT), IELTS (minimum score 6). Electronic applications accepted.

Hardin-Simmons University, Graduate School, College of Human Sciences and Educational Studies, Department of Educational Studies, Program in Gifted Education, Abilene, TX 79698-0001. Offers M Ed. *Program availability:* Part-time. *Students:* 1 (woman) full-time, 30 part-time (all women); includes 8 minority (2 Black or African American, non-Hispanic/Latino; 5 Hispanic/Latino; 1 Two or more races, non-Hispanic/Latino). Average age 36. 11 applicants, 100% accepted, 11 enrolled. In 2018, 6 master's awarded. *Degree requirements:* For master's, comprehensive exam. *Entrance requirements:* For master's, minimum undergraduate GPA of 3.0 in major, 2.7 overall. Additional exam requirements/recommendations for international students: Required—TOEFL (minimum score 550 paper-based; 79 iBT). *Application deadline:* For fall admission, 8/15 priority date for domestic students, 4/1 for international students; for spring admission, 1/5 priority date for domestic students, 9/1 for international students. Applications are processed on a rolling basis. Application fee: $50. Electronic applications accepted. *Expenses: Tuition:* Full-time $750; part-time $750 per credit hour. *Required fees:* $1300; $880 per credit. Tuition and fees vary according to degree level and program. *Financial support:* In 2018–19, 8 students received support. Fellowships and scholarships/grants available. Support available to part-time students. Financial award application deadline: 6/30; financial award applicants required to submit FAFSA. *Faculty research:* Experiences of gifted learners in college, use of authentic assessment, brain research and how it works in learning, theories of multiple intelligence beyond Howard Gardner. *Unit head:* Dr. Mary Christopher, Program Director, 325-670-1510, Fax: 325-670-1397, E-mail: mchris@hsutx.edu. *Application contact:* Dr. Nancy Kucinski, Dean of Graduate Studies, 325-670-1298, Fax: 325-670-1564, E-mail: gradoff@hsutx.edu.

Hofstra University, School of Education, Specialized Programs in Education, Hempstead, NY 11549. Offers applied behavior analysis (Advanced Certificate); childhood special education (MS Ed); early childhood special education (MS Ed, Advanced Certificate); educational and policy leadership (Ed D); educational leadership

(Advanced Certificate); educational leadership and policy studies (MS Ed), including K-12; elementary special education (MS Ed); gifted education (Advanced Certificate); health education (MS); health professions pedagogy and leadership (MS); higher education leadership and policy studies (MS Ed); inclusive early childhood special education (MS Ed); inclusive elementary special education (MS Ed); inclusive secondary special education (MS Ed); literacy studies (MA, MS Ed, Ed D, Advanced Certificate); pedagogy for health professions (Advanced Certificate); physical education (MS); school district business leader (Advanced Certificate); secondary education generalist - students with disabilities 7-12 (MS Ed); secondary special education generalist - secondary education (MS Ed); special education (MS Ed, Advanced Certificate); special education assessment and diagnosis (Advanced Certificate); special education early childhood intervention (MS Ed); special education: international perspectives (MS Ed); teaching students with severe or multiple disabilities (Advanced Certificate). *Program availability:* Part-time, evening/weekend, blended/hybrid learning. *Students:* 126 full-time (91 women), 230 part-time (175 women); includes 90 minority (40 Black or African American, non-Hispanic/Latino; 4 American Indian or Alaska Native, non-Hispanic/Latino; 11 Asian, non-Hispanic/Latino; 32 Hispanic/Latino; 3 Two or more races, non-Hispanic/Latino), 4 international. Average age 32. 215 applicants, 90% accepted, 117 enrolled. In 2018, 130 master's, 9 doctorates, 23 other advanced degrees awarded. *Degree requirements:* For master's, one foreign language, comprehensive exam (for some programs), thesis (for some programs), electronic portfolio, capstone course, internship, practicum, student teaching, seminars, minimum GPA of 3.0; for doctorate, one foreign language, comprehensive exam, thesis/dissertation, qualifying hearing. *Entrance requirements:* For master's, GRE, interview, letters of recommendation, portfolio, essay, certification; for doctorate, GRE or MAT, interview, resume, essay, master's degree, 3 letters of recommendation, writing sample; for Advanced Certificate, GRE, interview, letters of recommendation, essay, professional experience, resume, master's degree. Additional exam requirements/recommendations for international students: Required—TOEFL (minimum score 550 paper-based; 80 iBT). *Application deadline:* Applications are processed on a rolling basis. Application fee: $75. Electronic applications accepted. *Financial support:* In 2018–19, 208 students received support, including 105 fellowships with full and partial tuition reimbursements available (averaging $3,948 per year), 12 research assistantships with full and partial tuition reimbursements available (averaging $6,573 per year); career-related internships or fieldwork, Federal Work-Study, institutionally sponsored loans, scholarships/grants, traineeships, tuition waivers (full and partial), unspecified assistantships, and scholarships and endowed scholarships also available. Support available to part-time students. Financial award applicants required to submit FAFSA. *Faculty research:* Water quality and income inequality; girls and stem; new media literacies; applied behavior analysis; k-12 leadership development. *Unit head:* Dr. Alan Flurkey, Chairperson, 516-463-5237, E-mail: alan.d.flurkey@hofstra.edu. *Application contact:* Sunil Samuel, Assistant Vice President of Admissions, 516-463-4723, Fax: 516-463-4664, E-mail: graduateadmission@hofstra.edu.
Website: http://www.hofstra.edu/education/

James Madison University, The Graduate School, College of Education, Program in Special Education, Harrisonburg, VA 22807. Offers adapted curriculum (MAT); autism (M Ed); behavior specialist (M Ed); early childhood special education (MAT); general curriculum K-12 special education (MAT); gifted education (M Ed); inclusive early childhood special education (MAT); instructional specialist (M Ed); K-12 special education (MAT); visual impairments (MAT). *Accreditation:* NCATE. *Program availability:* Part-time. *Students:* 28 full-time (23 women), 9 part-time (5 women); includes 7 minority (3 Black or African American, non-Hispanic/Latino; 2 Hispanic/Latino; 2 Two or more races, non-Hispanic/Latino). Average age 30. In 2018, 25 master's awarded. Application fee: $60. Electronic applications accepted. *Expenses:* Tuition, state resident: full-time $10,848. Tuition, nonresident: full-time $27,888. *Required fees:* $1128. *Financial support:* In 2018–19, 6 students received support. Fellowships, Federal Work-Study, and assistantships (averaging $7911) available. Financial award application deadline: 3/1; financial award applicants required to submit FAFSA. *Unit head:* Dr. David A. Slykhuis, Interim Department Head, 540-568-4314, E-mail: slykhuda@jmu.edu. *Application contact:* Lynette D. Michael, Director of Graduate Admissions, 540-568-6131 Ext. 6395, Fax: 540-568-7860, E-mail: michaeld@jmu.edu.
Website: http://www.jmu.edu/coe/efex/index.shtml

Kent State University, College of Education, Health and Human Services, School of Lifespan Development and Educational Sciences, Kent, OH 44242-0001. Offers clinical mental health counseling (M Ed); counseling (Ed S); counseling and human development services (PhD); educational psychology (M Ed, MA); human development and family studies (MA); instructional technology (M Ed, PhD), including computer technology (M Ed), educational psychology (PhD), general instructional technology (M Ed); rehabilitation counseling (M Ed); school counseling (M Ed); school psychology (PhD, Ed S); special education (M Ed, PhD, Ed S), including deaf education (M Ed), early childhood education (M Ed), educational interpreter K-12 (M Ed), general special education (M Ed), gifted education (M Ed), mild/moderate intervention (M Ed), moderate/intensive intervention (M Ed), special education (PhD, Ed S), transition to work (M Ed). *Program availability:* Part-time, evening/weekend. *Faculty:* 71 full-time (37 women), 80 part-time/adjunct (61 women). *Students:* 341 full-time (272 women), 238 part-time (193 women); includes 66 minority (40 Black or African American, non-Hispanic/Latino; 5 American Indian or Alaska Native, non-Hispanic/Latino; 5 Asian, non-Hispanic/Latino; 8 Hispanic/Latino; 7 Native Hawaiian or other Pacific Islander, non-Hispanic/Latino; 1 Two or more races, non-Hispanic/Latino), 16 international. 461 applicants, 35% accepted. In 2018, 162 master's, 21 doctorates, 14 other advanced degrees awarded. *Degree requirements:* For master's, thesis optional; for doctorate, comprehensive exam, thesis/dissertation. *Entrance requirements:* For master's, doctorate, and Ed S, GRE General Test. Additional exam requirements/recommendations for international students: Required—TOEFL (minimum score 550 paper-based; 80 iBT). *Application deadline:* Applications are processed on a rolling basis. Application fee: $45 ($60 for international students). Electronic applications accepted. *Expenses:* Tuition, state resident: full-time $11,766; part-time $536 per credit. Tuition, nonresident: full-time $21,952; part-time $999 per credit. *International tuition:* $21,952 full-time. Tuition and fees vary according to course load. *Financial support:* In 2018–19, 35 research assistantships with full tuition reimbursements (averaging $10,000 per year), 8 teaching assistantships with full tuition reimbursements (averaging $12,000 per year) were awarded; Federal Work-Study, scholarships/grants, unspecified assistantships, and 16 administrative assistantships (averaging $9,594 per year) also available. Financial award application deadline: 4/1. *Unit head:* Dr. Mary Dellmann-Jenkins, Director, 330-672-6958, E-mail: mdellman@kent.edu. *Application contact:* Cheryl Slusarczyk, Academic Program Director, Office of Graduate Student Services, 330-672-2576, Fax: 330-672-9162, E-mail: ogs@kent.edu.
Website: http://www.kent.edu/ehhs/ldes/

Lindenwood University, Graduate Programs, School of Education, St. Charles, MO 63301-1695. Offers behavioral analysis (MA); education (MA), including autism spectrum disorders, character education, early intervention in autism and sensory impairment, gifted, technology; educational administration (MA, Ed D, Ed S); English to speakers of other languages (MA); instructional leadership (Ed D, Ed S); library media (MA); professional counseling (MA); school administration (MA, Ed S); school counseling (MA); teaching (MA). *Program availability:* Part-time, evening/weekend, 100% online, blended/hybrid learning. *Faculty:* 38 full-time (28 women), 111 part-time/adjunct (66 women). *Students:* 456 full-time (341 women), 1,107 part-time (851 women); includes 374 minority (296 Black or African American, non-Hispanic/Latino; 7 American Indian or Alaska Native, non-Hispanic/Latino; 8 Asian, non-Hispanic/Latino; 38 Hispanic/Latino; 1 Native Hawaiian or other Pacific Islander, non-Hispanic/Latino; 24 Two or more races, non-Hispanic/Latino), 17 international. Average age 36. 496 applicants, 72% accepted, 275 enrolled. In 2018, 454 master's, 64 doctorates, 66 other advanced degrees awarded. *Degree requirements:* For master's, thesis (for some programs), minimum GPA of 3.0; for doctorate, thesis/dissertation, minimum GPA of 3.0; for Ed S, comprehensive exam, project, minimum GPA of 3.0. *Entrance requirements:* For master's, interview, minimum undergraduate cumulative GPA of 3.0, writing sample, letter of recommendation; for doctorate, minimum graduate GPA of 3.4, resume, interview, writing sample, 4 letters of recommendation; for Ed S, master's degree in education, relevant work experience. Additional exam requirements/recommendations for international students: Required—TOEFL (minimum score 553 paper-based; 81 iBT); Recommended—IELTS (minimum score 6.5). *Application deadline:* For fall admission, 8/9 priority date for domestic students, 6/1 priority date for international students; for spring admission, 12/20 priority date for domestic students, 11/1 priority date for international students; for summer admission, 5/15 priority date for domestic students, 3/27 priority date for international students. Applications are processed on a rolling basis. Application fee: $0 ($100 for international students). Electronic applications accepted. *Expenses: Tuition:* Full-time $16,900; part-time $480 per credit hour. *Required fees:* $700; $350 per unit. Tuition and fees vary according to degree level. *Financial support:* In 2018–19, 316 students received support. Career-related internships or fieldwork, Federal Work-Study, institutionally sponsored loans, scholarships/grants, tuition waivers (partial), and unspecified assistantships available. Financial award application deadline: 6/30; financial award applicants required to submit FAFSA. *Unit head:* Dr. Anthony Scheffler, Dean, School of Education, 636-949-4618, Fax: 636-949-4197, E-mail: ascheffler@lindenwood.edu. *Application contact:* Kara Schilli, Assistant Vice President, University Admissions, 636-949-4349, Fax: 636-949-4109, E-mail: adultadmissions@lindenwood.edu.
Website: https://www.lindenwood.edu/academics/academic-schools/school-of-education/

Lynn University, Donald E. and Helen L. Ross College of Education, Boca Raton, FL 33431-5598. Offers educational leadership (M Ed, Ed D), including K-12 (Ed D), school administration K-12 (M Ed); exceptional student education (M Ed), including school administration K-12. *Program availability:* Part-time, evening/weekend, online learning. *Faculty:* 6 full-time (4 women), 8 part-time/adjunct (7 women). *Students:* 38 full-time (30 women), 85 part-time (63 women); includes 50 minority (33 Black or African American, non-Hispanic/Latino; 1 Asian, non-Hispanic/Latino; 15 Hispanic/Latino; 1 Two or more races, non-Hispanic/Latino), 5 international. Average age 38. 78 applicants, 65% accepted, 41 enrolled. In 2018, 13 master's, 14 doctorates awarded. *Degree requirements:* For master's, comprehensive exam, thesis (for some programs), completion of degree in maximum of four calendar years; minimum cumulative GPA of 3.0 and B grade or higher in each course; orientation seminar (one credit); minimum of 40 credits; FTCE ESE K-12 Exam; for doctorate, thesis/dissertation, mid-program review; minimum cumulative GPA of 3.25 and B grade or higher in each course. *Entrance requirements:* For master's, bachelor's degree from accredited institution, minimum undergraduate GPA of 3.0, official undergraduate and graduate transcripts of all academic coursework attempted, current resume, statement of professional goals, writing sample, 2 recent letters of recommendation; for doctorate, professional practice statement that identifies applicant's goals and explains how Lynn's program will help attain them, official transcript showing conferral of master's degree, 2 letters of recommendation from previous professors or employers, current resume, interview. Additional exam requirements/recommendations for international students: Required—TOEFL (minimum score 550 paper-based; 80 iBT), IELTS (minimum score 6.5). *Application deadline:* For fall admission, 8/18 for domestic students, 8/4 for international students; for spring admission, 12/15 for domestic students, 12/1 for international students; for summer admission, 4/17 for domestic students, 4/3 for international students. Applications are processed on a rolling basis. Application fee: $45. Electronic applications accepted. *Expenses:* 850 per credit hour. *Financial support:* In 2018–19, 85 students received support. Career-related internships or fieldwork, Federal Work-Study, scholarships/grants, tuition waivers (partial), and unspecified assistantships available. Support available to part-time students. Financial award application deadline: 3/1; financial award applicants required to submit FAFSA. *Faculty research:* Student achievement, students with learning differences, teacher and student retention, student motivation and cognition, neuroscience leadership and learning. *Unit head:* Dr. Kathleen Weigel, Dean, College of Education, 561-237-7441, E-mail: kweigel@lynn.edu. *Application contact:* Steven Pruitt, Director of Graduate and Undergraduate Evening Admission, 561-237-7834, Fax: 561-237-7100, E-mail: spruitt@lynn.edu.
Website: http://www.lynn.edu/academics/colleges/education

Mary Baldwin University, Graduate Studies, Programs in Education, Staunton, VA 24401-3610. Offers applied behavior analysis (MS); autism spectrum disorders (M Ed); elementary education (M Ed, MAT); English as a second language (M Ed); environment-based learning (M Ed); gifted education (M Ed); higher education (MS); leadership (M Ed); middle grades education (MAT); reading education (M Ed); special education (M Ed). *Accreditation:* TEAC.

McNeese State University, Doré School of Graduate Studies, Burton College of Education, Department of Education Professions, Program in Curriculum and Instruction, Lake Charles, LA 70609. Offers academically gifted education (M Ed); elementary education (M Ed); reading (M Ed); secondary education (M Ed); special education (M Ed). *Program availability:* Evening/weekend. *Entrance requirements:* For master's, GRE, teaching certificate.

Meredith College, School of Education, Health and Human Sciences, Raleigh, NC 27607-5298. Offers academically and intellectually gifted (M Ed); elementary education (M Ed, MAT); English as a second language (M Ed, MAT); health and physical education (MAT); nutrition, health and human performance (MS, Postbaccalaureate Certificate), including dietetic internship (Postbaccalaureate Certificate), nutrition (MS); psychology (MA), including industrial/organizational psychology; reading (M Ed); special education (MAT); special education (general curriculum) (M Ed). *Accreditation:* NCATE. *Program availability:* Part-time, evening/weekend. *Students:* 97 full-time (89 women), 76 part-time (73 women); includes 39 minority (17 Black or African American, non-Hispanic/Latino; 1 American Indian or Alaska Native, non-Hispanic/Latino; 9 Asian, non-Hispanic/Latino; 10 Hispanic/Latino; 2 Two or more races, non-Hispanic/Latino). Average age 28. In 2018, 56 master's, 36 other advanced degrees awarded. *Degree requirements:* For master's, thesis optional. *Entrance requirements:* For master's, GRE General Test or MAT, minimum GPA of 2.5, teaching license, recommendations. Additional exam requirements/recommendations for international students: Required—TOEFL. *Application deadline:* For fall admission, 7/1 priority date for domestic students; for spring admission, 11/1 priority date for domestic students. Applications are processed on a rolling basis. Application fee: $50. Electronic applications accepted. *Expenses:* $575 per credit hour for masters degree in education, $725 (for MS. PSY.IO degree),

$20,295 (for pre-health post-baccalaureate certificate), $13,600 (for dietetic internship). *Financial support:* Career-related internships or fieldwork, institutionally sponsored loans, and tuition waivers (partial) available. Support available to part-time students. Financial award application deadline: 2/15; financial award applicants required to submit FAFSA. *Unit head:* Dr. Monica McKinney, Graduate Program Manager, 919-760-8056, Fax: 919-760-2303, E-mail: mckinneym@meredith.edu. *Application contact:* Dr. Monica McKinney, Graduate Program Manager, 919-760-8056, Fax: 919-760-2303, E-mail: mckinneym@meredith.edu.
Website: https://www.meredith.edu/school-of-education-health-and-human-sciences

Midwest University, Graduate Programs, Wentzville, MO 63385. Offers asset management/investment/real estate (MBA); Christian counseling (D Min); Christian education (D Min); counseling (MA), including marriage and family counseling, school counseling; divinity (M Div); education (MA), including brain and gifted education, Christian education; global business management (MBA); global leadership (MBA); leadership (PhD), including brain and gifted educational leadership, entrepreneurial leadership, international aviation leadership, organizational leadership, political leadership; mission studies (D Min); music (MM, DMA); pastoral theology (D Min); public policy/administration (MBA); teaching English to speakers of other languages (MA). *Program availability:* Part-time, online learning. *Degree requirements:* For master's, thesis (for some programs); for doctorate, thesis/dissertation. *Entrance requirements:* Additional exam requirements/recommendations for international students: Recommended—TOEFL (minimum score 550 paper-based).

Millersville University of Pennsylvania, College of Graduate Studies and Adult Learning, College of Education and Human Services, Department of Early, Middle, and Exceptional Education, Millersville, PA 17551-0302. Offers early childhood education (M Ed); gifted education (M Ed); language and literacy (M Ed); language and literacy education (M Ed); special education (M Ed); special education: 7-12 (M Ed); special education: PreK-8 (M Ed). *Accreditation:* NCATE. *Program availability:* Part-time, evening/weekend, 100% online, blended/hybrid learning. *Faculty:* 10 full-time (6 women), 13 part-time/adjunct (9 women). *Students:* 9 full-time (6 women), 113 part-time (102 women); includes 11 minority (2 Black or African American, non-Hispanic/Latino; 3 Asian, non-Hispanic/Latino; 5 Hispanic/Latino; 1 Two or more races, non-Hispanic/Latino). Average age 32. 40 applicants, 98% accepted, 28 enrolled. In 2018, 25 master's awarded. *Entrance requirements:* For master's, GRE or MAT, required only if cumulative GPA is lower than 3.0, Teaching Certificate; Interview. Additional exam requirements/recommendations for international students: Required—TOEFL, IELTS (minimum score 6), PTE (minimum score 60). *Application deadline:* Applications are processed on a rolling basis. Application fee: $40. Electronic applications accepted. *Expenses: Tuition, area resident:* Full-time $9288; part-time $516 per credit. Tuition, state resident: full-time $9288; part-time $516 per credit. Tuition, nonresident: full-time $13,932; part-time $774 per credit. *International tuition:* $13,932 full-time. *Required fees:* $2623.50; $145.75 per credit. Tuition and fees vary according to course load, degree level and program. *Financial support:* In 2018–19, 5 students received support. Unspecified assistantships available. Financial award application deadline: 3/15; financial award applicants required to submit FAFSA. *Faculty research:* Co-teaching, needs of new teachers, use of popular culture in education. *Unit head:* Dr. Rich Mehrenberg, Department Chair, 717-871-7343, E-mail: richard.mehrenberg@millersville.edu. *Application contact:* Dr. James A. Delle, Acting Dean of College of Graduate Studies and Adult Learning/Associate Provost, Academic Administration, 717-871-7462, E-mail: James.Delle@millersville.edu.
Website: http://www.millersville.edu/eled/

Mississippi University for Women, Graduate School, College of Education and Human Sciences, Columbus, MS 39701-9998. Offers differentiated instruction (M Ed); educational leadership (M Ed); gifted studies (M Ed); reading/literacy (M Ed); teaching (MAT). *Accreditation:* ASHA; NCATE. *Program availability:* Part-time. *Degree requirements:* For master's, comprehensive exam, thesis optional. *Entrance requirements:* For master's, GRE General Test or NTE (M Ed in gifted education or MS in speech/language pathology), MAT (M Ed in instructional management), minimum QPA of 3.0.

Morehead State University, Graduate School, College of Education, Department of Foundational and Graduate Studies in Education, Morehead, KY 40351. Offers adult and higher education (MA, Ed S); certified professional counselor (Ed S); counseling P-12 (MA); curriculum and instruction (Ed S); educational technology (MA Ed); instructional leadership (Ed S); school administration (MA); school counseling (Ed S); teacher leader business and marketing content (MA Ed); teacher leader business and marketing technology (MA Ed); teacher leader educational technology (MA Ed); teacher leader English (MA Ed); teacher leader gifted education (MA Ed); teacher leader IECE certification (MA Ed); teacher leader interdisciplinary education P-5 (MA Ed); teacher leader middle grades (MA Ed); teacher leader non IECE certification (MA Ed); teacher leader reading/writing - non-certification (MA Ed); teacher leader reading/writing certification (MA Ed); teacher leader school communication - certification (MA Ed); teacher leader school communication - non-certification (MA Ed); teacher leader social studies (MA Ed); teacher leader special education (MA Ed). *Accreditation:* NCATE. *Program availability:* Part-time, evening/weekend. *Degree requirements:* For master's, thesis optional, oral and/or written comprehensive exams; for Ed S, thesis, oral exam. *Entrance requirements:* For master's, GRE General Test, minimum overall undergraduate GPA of 2.5; for Ed S, GRE General Test, interview, master's degree, minimum GPA of 3.5, work experience. Additional exam requirements/recommendations for international students: Required—TOEFL (minimum score 500 paper-based). Electronic applications accepted. *Faculty research:* Character education, school accountability, computer applications for school administrators.

Nebraska Christian College of Hope International University, Graduate Programs, Papillion, NE 68046. Offers biblical studies (M Div); business as mission/social entrepreneurship (MBA); children, youth, and family (M Div); church planting (M Div); counseling psychology (MS); educational administration (MA); elementary education (M Ed); general management (MBA); gifted and talented education (M Ed); intercultural studies (M Div); international development (MBA); marketing management (MBA); ministry (MA); ministry and leadership (M Div); music education (M Ed); non-profit management (MBA); pastoral care (M Div); secondary education (M Ed); spiritual formation (M Div); worship ministry (M Div).

Northeastern Illinois University, College of Graduate Studies and Research, Daniel L. Goodwin College of Education, Program in Gifted Education, Chicago, IL 60625. Offers MA. *Program availability:* Part-time, evening/weekend. *Degree requirements:* For master's, comprehensive exam, thesis or alternative. *Entrance requirements:* For master's, teaching certificate or previous course work in history or philosophy of education, minimum GPA of 2.75. Additional exam requirements/recommendations for international students: Required—TOEFL (minimum score 550 paper-based; 79 iBT). Electronic applications accepted. *Faculty research:* Effect of inclusion in public school gifted programs, social and emotional needs of gifted children, problem-based learning strategies.

Pacific University, College of Education, Forest Grove, OR 97116-1797. Offers early childhood education (MAT); education (MAE); elementary education (MAT); ESOL (MAT); high school education (MAT); middle school education (MAT); special education

(MAT); speech-language pathology (MS); STEM education (MAT); talented and gifted (M Ed); visual function in learning (M Ed). *Accreditation:* ASHA; NCATE. *Program availability:* Part-time, evening/weekend. *Degree requirements:* For master's, research project. *Entrance requirements:* For master's, California Basic Educational Skills Test, PRAXIS II, minimum undergraduate GPA of 2.75, 3.0 graduate. Additional exam requirements/recommendations for international students: Required—TOEFL. Electronic applications accepted. *Expenses:* Contact institution. *Faculty research:* Defining a culturally competent classroom, technology in the K-12 classroom, Socratic seminars, social studies education.

Regent University, Graduate School, School of Education, Virginia Beach, VA 23464-9800. Offers education (M Ed, Ed D, PhD), including adult education (Ed D, PhD, Ed S), advanced educational leadership (Ed D, PhD, Ed S), character education (Ed D, PhD, Ed S), Christian education leadership (Ed D, PhD, Ed S), Christian school administration (M Ed), curriculum and instruction (Ed D, PhD, Ed S), curriculum and instruction - adult education (M Ed), curriculum and instruction - Christian school (M Ed), curriculum and instruction - gifted and talented (M Ed), curriculum and instruction - STEM education (M Ed), curriculum and instruction - teacher leader (M Ed), discipleship for ministry (M Ed), educational leadership (M Ed), educational psychology (Ed D, PhD, Ed S), educational technology and online learning (Ed D, PhD, Ed S), elementary education (M Ed), exceptional education executive leadership (Ed D, PhD, Ed S), higher education (Ed D, PhD, Ed S), higher education leadership and management (Ed D, PhD, Ed S), instructional design and technology (M Ed), K-12 school leadership (Ed D, PhD, Ed S), K-12 special education (M Ed), leadership in mathematics education (M Ed), reading specialist (M Ed), special education (Ed D, PhD, Ed S), student affairs (M Ed), TESOL - adult education (M Ed), TESOL - K-12 (M Ed); educational specialist (Ed S), including adult education (Ed D, PhD, Ed S), advanced educational leadership (Ed D, PhD, Ed S), character education (Ed D, PhD, Ed S), Christian education leadership (Ed D, PhD, Ed S), curriculum and instruction (Ed D, PhD, Ed S), educational psychology (Ed D, PhD, Ed S), educational technology and online learning (Ed D, PhD, Ed S), exceptional education executive leadership (Ed D, PhD, Ed S), higher education (Ed D, PhD, Ed S), higher education leadership and management (Ed D, PhD, Ed S), K-12 school leadership (Ed D, PhD, Ed S), special education (Ed D, PhD, Ed S). *Accreditation:* TEAC. *Program availability:* Part-time, evening/weekend, 100% online, blended/hybrid learning. *Degree requirements:* For master's, thesis or alternative; for doctorate, comprehensive exam, thesis/dissertation. *Entrance requirements:* For master's, Virginia Communication and Literacy Assessment (VCLA), PRAXIS, college transcripts, writing sample, interview; for doctorate, GRE, writing sample, resume, transcripts, interview. Additional exam requirements/recommendations for international students: Required—TOEFL (minimum score 577 paper-based). Electronic applications accepted. *Expenses:* Contact institution. *Faculty research:* Christian school administration, curriculum and instruction, educational technology and online learning, higher education, special education.

St. Bonaventure University, School of Graduate School, School of Education, Inclusive Special Education, St. Bonaventure, NY 14778-2284. Offers gifted education (MS Ed, Adv C); gifted education and students with disabilities (MS Ed). *Program availability:* Part-time, evening/weekend. *Faculty:* 2 full-time (both women), 3 part-time/adjunct (1 woman). *Students:* 2 full-time (1 woman), 12 part-time (9 women); includes 2 minority (1 Hispanic/Latino; 1 Two or more races, non-Hispanic/Latino). Average age 26. 6 applicants, 100% accepted, 3 enrolled. In 2018, 10 master's awarded. *Degree requirements:* For master's, comprehensive exam, internship, portfolio; for Adv C, practicum, portfolio. *Entrance requirements:* For master's, GRE or MAT, disabilities or special education teaching certification (or letter of eligibility); interview; transcripts from all colleges previously attended; 2 letters of recommendation; writing sample; for Adv C, teaching certification (or letter of eligibility); interview; transcripts from all colleges previously attended; 2 references; master's degree; writing sample. Additional exam requirements/recommendations for international students: Required—TOEFL (minimum score 550 paper-based; 79 iBT). *Application deadline:* For fall admission, 3/15 priority date for domestic students, 2/1 priority date for international students; for spring admission, 10/15 priority date for domestic students, 7/1 priority date for international students. Applications are processed on a rolling basis. Application fee: $0. Electronic applications accepted. *Expenses:* $755.00 per credit hour; $100 one time fee. *Financial support:* Scholarships/grants, health care benefits, and unspecified assistantships available. Financial award application deadline: 4/15; financial award applicants required to submit FAFSA. *Faculty research:* Differentiated instruction, Teacher education and curriculum, specializing in authentic and responsive pedagogy for diverse learners, history of education. *Unit head:* Dr. Rene' Hauser, Director, 716-375-4078, Fax: 716-375-2360, E-mail: rhauser@sbu.edu. *Application contact:* Matthew Retchless, Director of Graduate Admissions, 716-375-2021, Fax: 716-375-4015, E-mail: gradsch@sbu.edu.
Website: http://www.sbu.edu/academics/post-master's-in-differentiated-instruction

St. John's University, The School of Education, Department of Administrative and Instructional Leadership, Program in Instructional Leadership, Queens, NY 11439. Offers gifted education (Adv C); instructional leadership (Ed D, Adv C). *Program availability:* Part-time, blended/hybrid learning. *Degree requirements:* For doctorate, comprehensive exam, thesis/dissertation. *Entrance requirements:* For doctorate, GRE, official master's transcript, statement of purpose; for Adv C, statement of purpose, official master's transcripts, teaching certification. Additional exam requirements/recommendations for international students: Required—TOEFL, IELTS. Electronic applications accepted. *Faculty research:* Mathematics learning disabilities and difficulties with students identified as learning disabled or students who are English language learners, identification of mathematical giftedness in students who are English language learners, effects of parental participation and parenting behaviors on the science and mathematics academic achievement of school-age students, analysis of major theoretical perspectives in curriculum design and implementation.

St. Thomas University, School of Leadership Studies, Institute for Education, Miami Gardens, FL 33054-6459. Offers earth/space science (Certificate); educational administration (MS, Certificate); educational leadership (Ed D); elementary education (MS); ESOL (Certificate); gifted education (Certificate); instructional technology (MS, Certificate); professional/studies (Certificate); reading (MS, Certificate); special education (MS). *Program availability:* Part-time, evening/weekend. *Degree requirements:* For master's, comprehensive exam; for doctorate, comprehensive exam, thesis/dissertation. *Entrance requirements:* For master's, interview, minimum GPA of 3.0 or GRE; for doctorate, GRE or MAT. Additional exam requirements/recommendations for international students: Required—TOEFL (minimum score 550 paper-based; 79 iBT). Electronic applications accepted.

Samford University, Orlean Beeson School of Education, Birmingham, AL 35229. Offers educational leadership (MSE, Ed D); elementary education (MS Ed, MSE); gifted (MSE); instructional design and technology (MSE); instructional leadership (MSE, Ed S); secondary education (MSE); special education (MSE). *Accreditation:* NCATE. *Program availability:* Part-time, evening/weekend, 100% online, blended/hybrid learning. *Faculty:* 12 full-time (10 women), 16 part-time/adjunct (11 women). *Students:* 156 full-time (111 women), 101 part-time (73 women); includes 106 minority (100 Black or African American, non-Hispanic/Latino; 1 American Indian or Alaska Native, non-Hispanic/Latino; 5 Two or more races, non-Hispanic/Latino), 1 international. Average age 37. 107

applicants, 94% accepted, 65 enrolled. In 2018, 94 master's, 40 doctorates, 11 other advanced degrees awarded. *Degree requirements:* For master's and Ed S, comprehensive exam; for doctorate, comprehensive exam, thesis/dissertation. *Entrance requirements:* For master's, GRE, MAT, PRAXIS II, interview, transcripts, essay, recommendations, teaching certification; for doctorate, resume, transcripts, interview, essay, recommendations; for Ed S, teaching certification, transcripts, essay, interview, recommendations. Additional exam requirements/recommendations for international students: Required—TOEFL (minimum score 90 iBT); Recommended—IELTS (minimum score 6.5). *Application deadline:* For fall admission, 7/15 for domestic and international students; for winter admission, 11/15 for domestic and international students; for spring admission, 11/15 for domestic and international students; for summer admission, 4/15 for domestic and international students. Applications are processed on a rolling basis. Application fee: $35. Electronic applications accepted. *Expenses:* $862 Per Hour $100 School of Education $175 Technology Fee $100 Per Fully Online Class. *Financial support:* In 2018–19, 173 students received support. Scholarships/grants available. Financial award application deadline: 2/15; financial award applicants required to submit FAFSA. *Faculty research:* Principal leadership's and teacher organizational commitment mentoring, professional development, and middle grades leadership coaching and administrator effectiveness character development programs in schools teacher efficacy related STEM and professional growth. *Unit head:* Dr. Howard Finch, Interim Dean, 205-726-2745, E-mail: hfinch@samford.edu. *Application contact:* Brooke Karr, Graduate Admissions Office Coordinator, 205-729-2783, E-mail: kbgilrea@samford.edu. Website: http://www.samford.edu/education

Southeastern University, College of Education, Lakeland, FL 33801-6099. Offers curriculum and instruction (Ed D); educational leadership (M Ed); elementary education (M Ed); exceptional student education (M Ed); exceptional student education/educational therapy (M Ed); kinesiology (M Ed); organizational leadership (Ed D); reading education (M Ed); teaching English to speakers of other languages (M Ed). Electronic applications accepted.

Southern Arkansas University–Magnolia, School of Graduate Studies, Magnolia, AR 71753. Offers agriculture (MS); business administration (MBA), including agribusiness, social entrepreneurship, supply chain management; clinical and mental health counseling (MS); computer and information sciences (MS), including cyber security and privacy, data science, information technology; gifted and talented (M Ed), including curriculum and instruction, educational administration and supervision, gifted and talented P-8/7-12, instructional specialist P-4; higher, adult and lifelong education (M Ed); kinesiology (M Ed), including coaching; library media and information specialist (M Ed); public administration (MPA); school counseling K-12 (M Ed); student affairs and college counseling (M Ed); teaching (MAT). *Accreditation:* NCATE. *Program availability:* Part-time, 100% online, blended/hybrid learning. *Faculty:* 36 full-time (21 women), 32 part-time/adjunct (15 women). *Students:* 164 full-time (77 women), 762 part-time (510 women); includes 192 minority (163 Black or African American, non-Hispanic/Latino; 7 American Indian or Alaska Native, non-Hispanic/Latino; 13 Asian, non-Hispanic/Latino; 1 Hispanic/Latino; 8 Two or more races, non-Hispanic/Latino), 213 international. Average age 28. 363 applicants, 100% accepted, 237 enrolled. In 2018, 716 master's awarded. *Degree requirements:* For master's, comprehensive exam (for some programs), thesis optional. *Entrance requirements:* For master's, GRE, MAT or GMAT, minimum GPA of 2.5. Additional exam requirements/recommendations for international students: Required—TOEFL (minimum score 550 paper-based), IELTS (minimum score 6). *Application deadline:* For fall admission, 8/1 for domestic and international students; for spring admission, 12/1 for domestic students, 11/15 for international students; for summer admission, 4/1 for domestic students, 5/10 for international students. Applications are processed on a rolling basis. Application fee: $25 ($90 for international students). Electronic applications accepted. *Expenses:* Tuition, area resident: Full-time $5130; part-time $3420 per year. Tuition, state resident: full-time $5130; part-time $3420 per year. Tuition, nonresident: full-time $7866; part-time $5244 per year. International tuition: $7866 full-time. *Required fees:* $1052; $710 per unit. Tuition and fees vary according to course load. *Financial support:* Career-related internships or fieldwork, Federal Work-Study, scholarships/grants, tuition waivers (full), and unspecified assistantships available. Financial award applicants required to submit FAFSA. *Faculty research:* Alternative certification for teachers, supervision of instruction, instructional leadership, counseling. *Unit head:* Dr. Kim Bloss, Dean, School of Graduate Studies, 870-235-4150, Fax: 870-235-5227, E-mail: kkbloss@saumag.edu. *Application contact:* Talia Jett, Admissions Coordinator, 870-2355450, Fax: 870-235-5227, E-mail: taliajett@saumag.edu. Website: http://www.saumag.edu/graduate

Southern Methodist University, Simmons School of Education and Human Development, Department of Teaching and Learning, Dallas, TX 75275. Offers bilingual education (MBE); education (M Ed, PhD); English as a second language (M Ed); gifted and talented (M Ed); literacy studies (M Ed); special education (M Ed). *Program availability:* Part-time, evening/weekend. Terminal master's awarded for partial completion of doctoral program. *Degree requirements:* For master's, comprehensive exam, minimum GPA of 3.0; for doctorate, thesis/dissertation, qualifying exams, major area paper, evidence of teaching competency, dissemination of research (e.g., conference presentation), professional portfolio. *Entrance requirements:* For master's, minimum GPA of 3.0 or GRE, 3 letters of recommendation; for doctorate, GRE, minimum GPA of 3.3, 3 years of full-time teaching, 3 letters of recommendation, interview. Additional exam requirements/recommendations for international students: Required—TOEFL. Electronic applications accepted. *Faculty research:* Reading intervention, mathematics intervention, bilingual education, new literacies.

Teachers College, Columbia University, Department of Curriculum and Teaching, New York, NY 10027-6696. Offers curriculum and teaching (Ed M, MA, Ed D); curriculum and teaching: elementary education (MA); curriculum and teaching: secondary education (MA); early childhood education (MA, Ed D); early childhood education: special education (MA); elementary education-gifted extension (MA); elementary inclusive education (MA); gifted education (MA); literacy specialist (MA); secondary inclusive education (MA); special inclusive elementary education (MA). *Program availability:* Part-time, evening/weekend. *Students:* 88 full-time (77 women), 264 part-time (239 women); includes 129 minority (45 Black or African American, non-Hispanic/Latino; 1 American Indian or Alaska Native, non-Hispanic/Latino; 41 Asian, non-Hispanic/Latino; 28 Hispanic/Latino; 14 Two or more races, non-Hispanic/Latino), 48 international. Average age 30. 460 applicants, 73% accepted, 149 enrolled. Terminal master's awarded for partial completion of doctoral program. *Unit head:* Prof. Daniel Friedrich, Chair, 212-678-3263, E-mail: friedrich@exchange.tc.columbia.edu. *Application contact:* Kelly Sutton-Skinner, Director of Admission & New Student Enrollment, E-mail: kms2237@tc.columbia.edu.

Tennessee Technological University, College of Graduate Studies, College of Education, Department of Curriculum and Instruction, Program in Exceptional Learning, Cookeville, TN 38505. Offers applied behavior analysis (PhD); literacy (PhD); program planning and evaluation (PhD); STEM education (PhD). *Program availability:* Part-time, evening/weekend. *Students:* 14 full-time (8 women), 20 part-time (12 women); includes 2 minority (1 Black or African American, non-Hispanic/Latino; 1 Two or more races, non-

Hispanic/Latino), 3 international. 16 applicants, 56% accepted, 2 enrolled. In 2018, 8 doctorates awarded. *Degree requirements:* For doctorate, comprehensive exam, thesis/dissertation. *Entrance requirements:* For doctorate, GRE, minimum GPA of 3.0. Additional exam requirements/recommendations for international students: Required—TOEFL (minimum score 550 paper-based; 79 iBT), IELTS (minimum score 5.5), PTE (minimum score 53), or TOEIC (Test of English as an International Communication). *Application deadline:* For fall admission, 8/1 for domestic students, 5/1 for international students; for spring admission, 12/1 for domestic students, 10/1 for international students; for summer admission, 5/1 for domestic students, 2/1 for international students. Applications are processed on a rolling basis. Application fee: $35 ($40 for international students). Electronic applications accepted. *Financial support:* Fellowships, research assistantships, and teaching assistantships available. Financial award application deadline: 4/1. *Unit head:* Dr. Lisa Zagumny, Dean, College of Education, 931-372-3078, Fax: 931-372-3517, E-mail: lzagumny@tntech.edu. *Application contact:* Shelia K. Kendrick, Coordinator of Graduate Studies, 931-372-3808, Fax: 931-372-3497, E-mail: skendrick@tntech.edu. Website: https://www.tntech.edu/education/elphd

University at Buffalo, the State University of New York, Graduate School, Graduate School of Education, Department of Learning and Instruction, Buffalo, NY 14260. Offers biology education (Ed M, Certificate); chemistry education (Ed M, Certificate); childhood education (Ed M); childhood education with bilingual extension (Ed M); college teaching (Advanced Certificate); curriculum, instruction and the science of learning (PhD); early childhood education (Ed M); early childhood education with bilingual extension (Ed M); earth science education (Ed M, Certificate); education and technology (Ed M); education studies (Ed M); educational technology and new literacies (Certificate); educational technology and new literacies (Advanced Certificate); elementary education (Ed D); English education (Ed M, Certificate); English education studies (Ed M); English for speakers of other languages (Ed M); foreign and second language education (PhD); French education (Ed M, Certificate); German education (Ed M, Certificate); gifted education (Certificate); Latin education (Ed M, Certificate); literacy education studies (Ed M); literacy specialist (Ed M); literacy teaching and learning (Certificate); mathematics education (Ed M, Certificate); music education (Ed M, Certificate); music education studies (Ed M); music learning theory (Advanced Certificate); online education (Advanced Certificate); physics education (Ed M, Certificate); science and the public (Ed M); social studies education (Ed M, Certificate); Spanish education (Ed M, Certificate); special education (PhD); teaching English to speakers of other languages (Ed M). *Program availability:* Part-time, evening/weekend, 100% online. *Faculty:* 31 full-time (22 women), 41 part-time/adjunct (27 women). *Students:* 161 full-time (107 women), 369 part-time (260 women); includes 76 minority (26 Black or African American, non-Hispanic/Latino; 3 American Indian or Alaska Native, non-Hispanic/Latino; 30 Asian, non-Hispanic/Latino; 14 Hispanic/Latino; 3 Two or more races, non-Hispanic/Latino), 41 international. Average age 34. 368 applicants, 70% accepted, 179 enrolled. In 2018, 100 master's, 26 doctorates, 19 other advanced degrees awarded. *Degree requirements:* For master's, comprehensive exam; for doctorate, thesis/dissertation, research analysis exam, research experience. *Entrance requirements:* For master's, letters of reference; for doctorate, GRE General Test or MAT, interview, writing sample, letters of recommendation. Additional exam requirements/recommendations for international students: Required—TOEFL (minimum score 600 paper-based; 96 iBT), IELTS (minimum score 6.5), PTE (minimum score 55). *Application deadline:* For fall admission, 2/1 priority date for domestic and international students; for spring admission, 11/15 priority date for domestic students, 10/1 for international students. Applications are processed on a rolling basis. Application fee: $50. Electronic applications accepted. *Financial support:* In 2018–19, 42 fellowships (averaging $5,181 per year), 44 research assistantships with tuition reimbursements (averaging $10,908 per year) were awarded; teaching assistantships, career-related internships or fieldwork, Federal Work-Study, institutionally sponsored loans, scholarships/grants, tuition waivers (full and partial), and unspecified assistantships also available. Financial award application deadline: 2/28; financial award applicants required to submit FAFSA. *Faculty research:* Science assessment, foreign language teaching and learning, early learning, new literacies, gender and education. *Total annual research expenditures:* $413,233. *Unit head:* Dr. Julie Gorlewski, Department Chair, 716-645-2455, Fax: 716-645-3161, E-mail: jgorlews@buffalo.edu. *Application contact:* Renad Aref, Assistant Director of Admission Recruitment, 716-645-2110, Fax: 716-645-7937, E-mail: gseinfo@buffalo.edu. Website: http://ed.buffalo.edu/teaching.html

The University of Alabama, Graduate School, College of Education, Department of Special Education and Multiple Abilities, Tuscaloosa, AL 35487. Offers collaborative special education (M Ed, Ed S); early intervention (M Ed, Ed S); gifted and talented education (M Ed, Ed S); multiple abilities (M Ed); special education (Ed D, PhD). *Program availability:* Part-time, evening/weekend. Terminal master's awarded for partial completion of doctoral program. *Degree requirements:* For master's, comprehensive exam, thesis optional; for doctorate, one foreign language, comprehensive exam, thesis/dissertation. *Entrance requirements:* For master's, GRE, minimum undergraduate GPA of 3.0, teaching certificate, 3 letters of recommendation; for doctorate, GRE, 3 years of teaching experience, minimum undergraduate GPA of 3.25. Additional exam requirements/recommendations for international students: Required—TOEFL. Electronic applications accepted. *Faculty research:* Gifted education, mild disabilities, early intervention, severe disabilities, behavior disorders.

University of Arkansas at Little Rock, Graduate School, College of Education and Health Professions, Department of Educational Leadership, Program in Gifted and Talented Education, Little Rock, AR 72204-1099. Offers M Ed, Graduate Certificate. *Degree requirements:* For Graduate Certificate, comprehensive exam. *Entrance requirements:* For degree, teacher license.

University of Central Arkansas, Graduate School, College of Education, Department of Early Childhood and Special Education, Conway, AR 72035-0001. Offers gifted and talented education (Graduate Certificate); instructional facilitator (Graduate Certificate); reading education (MSE); special education (MSE, Graduate Certificate), including collaborative instructional specialist (ages 0-8) (MSE), collaborative instructional specialist (grades 4-12) (MSE), special education instructional specialist grades 4-12 (Graduate Certificate), special education instructional specialist P-4 (Graduate Certificate). *Program availability:* Part-time, evening/weekend, online learning. *Degree requirements:* For master's, comprehensive exam, thesis optional. *Entrance requirements:* For master's, GRE General Test, minimum GPA of 2.7. Additional exam requirements/recommendations for international students: Required—TOEFL (minimum score 550 paper-based; 80 iBT). Electronic applications accepted.

University of Central Arkansas, Graduate School, College of Education, Department of Leadership Studies, Conway, AR 72035-0001. Offers college student personnel (MS); district-level administration (PMC); educational leadership - district level (Ed S); instructional technology (MS); library media and information technology (MS); school counseling (MS); school leadership (MS); school-based leadership adult education program administration (PMC); school-based leadership building administration (PMC); school-based leadership curriculum administration (PMC); school-based leadership gifted and talented program administration (PMC); school-based leadership special

education program administration (PMC). *Accreditation:* NCATE. *Program availability:* Part-time, evening/weekend, online learning. *Degree requirements:* For master's and other advanced degree, comprehensive exam. *Entrance requirements:* For master's, GRE. Additional exam requirements/recommendations for international students: Required—TOEFL (minimum score 80 iBT). Electronic applications accepted. *Expenses:* Contact institution.

University of Connecticut, Graduate School, Neag School of Education, Department of Educational Psychology, Program in Gifted and Talented Education, Storrs, CT 06269. Offers Graduate Certificate. *Accreditation:* NCATE. Terminal master's awarded for partial completion of doctoral program. *Entrance requirements:* Additional exam requirements/recommendations for international students: Required—TOEFL (minimum score 550 paper-based). Electronic applications accepted.

University of Louisiana at Lafayette, College of Education, Department of Educational Curriculum and Instruction, Program in Education of the Gifted, Lafayette, LA 70504. Offers M Ed. *Accreditation:* NCATE. *Entrance requirements:* For master's, GRE General Test, teaching certificate. Additional exam requirements/recommendations for international students: Required—TOEFL (minimum score 550 paper-based). Electronic applications accepted.

University of Minnesota, Twin Cities Campus, Graduate School, College of Education and Human Development, Department of Educational Psychology, Minneapolis, MN 55455-0213. Offers autism spectrum disorder (Certificate); counseling and student personnel psychology (MA); early childhood special education (M Ed); psychological foundations of education (MA, PhD); quantitative methods in education (MA, PhD); school psychology (MA, PhD, Ed S); special education (M Ed, MA, PhD); talent development and gifted education (Certificate). *Accreditation:* APA (one or more programs are accredited). *Faculty:* 29 full-time (13 women). *Students:* 243 full-time (181 women), 38 part-time (31 women); includes 45 minority (6 Black or African American, non-Hispanic/Latino; 17 Asian, non-Hispanic/Latino; 12 Hispanic/Latino; 10 Two or more races, non-Hispanic/Latino), 42 international. Average age 29. 278 applicants, 46% accepted, 95 enrolled. In 2018, 100 master's, 21 doctorates, 16 other advanced degrees awarded. Application fee: $75 ($95 for international students). *Financial support:* In 2018–19, 16 fellowships, 65 research assistantships (averaging $13,491 per year), 37 teaching assistantships (averaging $11,583 per year) were awarded. *Faculty research:* Achievement gap; autism; behavioral and social-emotional development; improving skills in mathematics, reading, and comprehension; measuring and analyzing student change. *Total annual research expenditures:* $6.9 million. *Unit head:* Dr. Kristen McMaster, Chair, 612-624-6083, Fax: 612-624-8241, E-mail: mcmas004@umn.edu. *Application contact:* Dr. Panayiota Kendeou, Director of Graduate Studies, 612-626-7814, E-mail: kend0040@umn.edu. Website: http://www.cehd.umn.edu/EdPsych

University of Nebraska at Kearney, College of Education, Department of Teacher Education, Kearney, NE 68849-0001. Offers curriculum and instruction (MA Ed), including early childhood education, elementary education, English as a second language, instructional effectiveness, reading/special education, secondary education; instructional technology (MS Ed), including information technology, instructional technology, school librarian; reading PK-12 (MA Ed); special education (MA Ed), including advanced practitioner: assistive technology specialist, advanced practitioner: behavioral interventionist, advanced practitioner: inclusive collaboration specialist, gifted, teacher education. *Program availability:* Part-time, evening/weekend, online only, 100% online. *Degree requirements:* For master's, comprehensive exam, thesis optional. *Entrance requirements:* For master's, portfolio or GRE. Additional exam requirements/recommendations for international students: Recommended—TOEFL (minimum score 550 paper-based; 79 iBT), IELTS (minimum score 6.5). Electronic applications accepted. *Expenses:* Contact institution.

The University of North Carolina at Charlotte, Cato College of Education, Department of Special Education and Child Development, Charlotte, NC 28223-0001. Offers academically or intellectually gifted (Graduate Certificate); autism spectrum disorders (Graduate Certificate); child and family development: birth through kindergarten (Graduate Certificate); child and family studies: early education (M Ed); special education (M Ed, PhD, Graduate Certificate), including academically or intellectually gifted (M Ed). *Program availability:* Part-time, 100% online, blended/hybrid learning. *Students:* 16 full-time (11 women), 64 part-time (61 women); includes 16 minority (13 Black or African American, non-Hispanic/Latino; 1 Hispanic/Latino; 2 Two or more races, non-Hispanic/Latino), 3 international. Average age 32. 65 applicants, 78% accepted, 32 enrolled. In 2018, 16 master's, 6 doctorates, 33 other advanced degrees awarded. *Entrance requirements:* For master's, GRE or MAT, personal statement, letters of recommendation; for doctorate, GRE or MAT, 2 official transcripts of all academic work attempted since high school indicating minimum GPA of 3.5 in graduate degree program; at least 3 references of someone who knows applicant's current work and/or academic achievements in previous degree work; two-page essay; current resume or curriculum vitae; writing sample; documentation of teaching; for Graduate Certificate, undergraduate degree from regionally-accredited four-year institution; minimum cumulative undergraduate GPA of 3.0; three recommendations from persons knowledgeable of applicant's interaction with children and families; statement of purpose; clear criminal background check. Additional exam requirements/recommendations for international students: Required—TOEFL (minimum score 523 paper-based; 70 iBT), IELTS (minimum score 6), TOEFL (minimum score 523 paper-based, 70 iBT) or IELTS (6). *Application deadline:* Applications are processed on a rolling basis. Application fee: $75. Electronic applications accepted. Tuition and fees vary according to course load and program. *Financial support:* Research assistantships, teaching assistantships, career-related internships or fieldwork, institutionally sponsored loans, scholarships/grants, and unspecified assistantships available. Support available to part-time students. Financial award application deadline: 3/1; financial award applicants required to submit FAFSA. *Total annual research expenditures:* $3.9 million. *Unit head:* Dr. Belva Collins, Chair, 704-687-8828, E-mail: belva.collins@uncc.edu. *Application contact:* Kathy B. Giddings, Director of Graduate Admissions, 704-687-5503, Fax: 704-687-1668, E-mail: gradadm@uncc.edu. Website: http://spcd.uncc.edu/

University of Northern Colorado, Graduate School, College of Education and Behavioral Sciences, School of Special Education, Greeley, CO 80639. Offers deaf/hard of hearing (MA); early childhood special education (MA); gifted and talented (MA); special education (MA, PhD); visual impairment (MA). *Program availability:* Part-time, evening/weekend, online learning. *Degree requirements:* For master's, comprehensive exam, thesis or alternative; for doctorate, comprehensive exam, thesis/dissertation. *Entrance requirements:* For master's, letters of recommendation, interview; for doctorate, GRE General Test, resume. Electronic applications accepted.

University of North Texas, Toulouse Graduate School, Denton, TX 76203-5459. Offers accounting (MS); applied anthropology (MA, MS); applied behavior analysis (Certificate); applied geography (MA); applied technology and performance improvement (M Ed, MS); art education (MA); art history (MA); arts leadership (Certificate); audiology (Au D); behavior analysis (MS); behavioral science (PhD); biochemistry and molecular biology (MS); biology (MA, MS); biomedical engineering (MS); business analysis (MS); chemistry (MS); clinical health psychology (PhD);

communication studies (MA, MS); computer engineering (MS); computer science (MS); counseling (M Ed, MS), including clinical mental health counseling (MS), college and university counseling, elementary school counseling, secondary school counseling; creative writing (MA); criminal justice (MS); curriculum and instruction (M Ed); decision sciences (MBA); design (MA, MFA), including fashion design (MFA), innovation studies, interior design (MFA); early childhood studies (MS); economics (MS); educational leadership (M Ed, Ed D); educational psychology (MS, PhD), including family studies (MS), gifted and talented (MS), human development (MS), learning and cognition (MS), research, measurement and evaluation (MS); electrical engineering (MS); emergency management (MPA); engineering technology (MS); English (MA); English as a second language (MA); environmental science (MS); finance (MBA, MS); financial management (MPA); French (MA); health services management (MBA); higher education (M Ed, Ed D); history (MA, MS); hospitality management (MS); human resources management (MPA); information science (MS); information systems (PhD); information technologies (MBA); interdisciplinary studies (MA, MS); international studies (MA); international sustainable tourism (MS); jazz studies (MM); journalism (MA, MJ, Graduate Certificate), including interactive and virtual digital communication (Graduate Certificate), narrative journalism (Graduate Certificate), public relations (Graduate Certificate); kinesiology (MS); linguistics (MA); local government management (MPA); logistics (PhD); logistics and supply chain management (MBA); long-term care, senior housing, and aging services (MA); management (PhD); marketing (MBA); mathematics (MA, MS); mechanical and energy engineering (MS, PhD); music (MA), including ethnomusicology, music theory, musicology, performance; music composition (PhD); music education (MM Ed, PhD); nonprofit management (MPA); operations and supply chain management (MBA); performance (MM, DMA); philosophy (MA); political science (MA); professional and technical communication (MA); radio, television and film (MA, MFA); rehabilitation counseling (Certificate); sociology (MA); Spanish (MA); special education (M Ed); speech-language pathology (MA); strategic management (MBA); studio art (MFA); teaching (M Ed); MBA/MS. *Program availability:* Part-time, evening/weekend, online learning. Terminal master's awarded for partial completion of doctoral program. *Degree requirements:* For master's, variable foreign language requirement, comprehensive exam (for some programs), thesis (for some programs); for doctorate, variable foreign language requirement, comprehensive exam (for some programs), thesis/dissertation; for other advanced degree, variable foreign language requirement, comprehensive exam (for some programs). *Entrance requirements:* For master's and doctorate, GRE, GMAT. Additional exam requirements/recommendations for international students: Required—TOEFL (minimum score 550 paper-based; 79 iBT). Electronic applications accepted.

University of Southern Maine, College of Management and Human Service, School of Education and Human Development, Program in Special Education, Portland, ME 04103. Offers gifted and talented education (CGS); special education (MS); teaching all students (CGS). *Accreditation:* TEAC. *Program availability:* Part-time, evening/weekend. *Degree requirements:* For master's, thesis or alternative, portfolio. *Entrance requirements:* For master's, proof of teacher certification. Additional exam requirements/recommendations for international students: Required—TOEFL (minimum score 550 paper-based; 79 iBT). Electronic applications accepted. *Faculty research:* Special education, gifted and talented education, diversity education, positive behavioral interventions and supports.

The University of Toledo, College of Graduate Studies, Judith Herb College of Education, Department of Curriculum and Instruction, Toledo, OH 43606-3390. Offers art education (ME); career and technical education (ME, Ed S); curriculum and instruction (ME, PhD, Ed S); early childhood education (Ed S); education and anthropology (MAE); education and biology (MES); education and chemistry (MES); education and classics (MAE); education and economics (MAE); education and English (MAE); education and French (MAE); education and geology (MES); education and German (MAE); education and history (MAE); education and mathematics (MAE, MES); education and physics (MES); education and political science (MAE); education and sociology (MAE); education and Spanish (MAE); educational media (PhD); educational technology (ME); educational technology: virtual educator (Certificate); elementary education (PhD); English as a second language (MAE); gifted and talented education (PhD); middle childhood education (ME); secondary education (ME, PhD); special education (PhD). *Accreditation:* NCATE. *Program availability:* Part-time, evening/weekend. *Degree requirements:* For master's, comprehensive exam, thesis or alternative; for doctorate, comprehensive exam, thesis/dissertation; for other advanced degree, thesis optional. *Entrance requirements:* For master's, doctorate, and other advanced degree, minimum cumulative GPA of 2.7 for all previous academic work, letters of recommendation. Additional exam requirements/recommendations for international students: Required—TOEFL (minimum score 550 paper-based; 80 iBT). Electronic applications accepted.

University of Virginia, Curry School of Education, Department of Leadership, Foundations and Policy, Program in Educational Psychology, Charlottesville, VA 22903. Offers applied developmental science (M Ed); educational evaluation (M Ed); educational psychology (M Ed, Ed D, Ed S); educational research (Ed D); gifted education (M Ed); instructional technology (M Ed, Ed S); research statistics and evaluation (Ed D); school psychology (Ed D). *Degree requirements:* For master's, comprehensive exam. *Entrance requirements:* For master's and doctorate, GRE General Test, 2 letters of recommendation. Additional exam requirements/recommendations for international students: Required—TOEFL (minimum score 600 paper-based; 90 iBT), IELTS (minimum score 7). Electronic applications accepted.

Viterbo University, Graduate Programs in Education, La Crosse, WI 54601-4797. Offers cross-categorical special education (Certificate); director of instruction (Certificate); director of special education and pupil services (Certificate); early childhood (Certificate); education (MAE); literacy coaching (Certificate); PreK-12 principal/supervisor of special education (Certificate); principal (Certificate); reading specialist endorsement (Certificate); reading teacher (Certificate); reading teacher 5-12 endorsement (Certificate); reading teacher K-8 endorsement (Certificate); superintendent (Certificate); talented and gifted endorsement (Certificate); Wisconsin school business administrator (Certificate). Weekend courses available in summer. *Accreditation:* NCATE. *Program availability:* Part-time, evening/weekend. *Degree requirements:* For master's, comprehensive exam, thesis, 30 credits of course work. *Entrance requirements:* For master's, BS, transcripts, teaching license, written narrative. Electronic applications accepted. *Expenses:* Contact institution.

Western Washington University, Graduate School, Woodring College of Education, Department of Special Education, Bellingham, WA 98225-5996. Offers M Ed. *Accreditation:* NCATE. *Program availability:* Part-time. *Degree requirements:* For master's, comprehensive exam, thesis optional. *Entrance requirements:* For master's, GRE General Test or MAT, minimum GPA of 3.0 in last 60 semester hours or last 90 quarter hours. Additional exam requirements/recommendations for international students: Required—TOEFL (minimum score 567 paper-based). Electronic applications accepted. *Faculty research:* Applied behavioral analysis, controversial practices, infant/toddler social-emotional interventions, reflective practices in teacher education.

West Virginia University, College of Education and Human Services, Morgantown, WV 26506. Offers audiology (Au D); autism spectrum disorder (MA); clinical rehabilitation

and mental health counseling (MS); communication science and disorders (PhD); counseling (MA); counseling psychology (PhD); curriculum and instruction (Ed D); early childhood education (MA); early intervention/ early childhood special education (MA); education (PhD); educational leadership (MA); educational leadership/ public school administration (Ed D); educational leadership/public school administration (MA); educational psychology (MA, Ed D); elementary education (MA); gifted education (MA); higher education administration (MA, Ed D); higher education curriculum and teaching (MA); institutional design and technology (MA); instructional design and technology (Ed D); literacy education (MA); secondary education (MA); secondary education/ English (MA); special education (Ed D); speech pathology (MS). *Accreditation:* ASHA; NCATE. *Program availability:* Part-time, evening/weekend, online learning. *Students:* 392 full-time (325 women), 337 part-time (285 women); includes 44 minority (16 Black or African American, non-Hispanic/Latino; 16 Hispanic/Latino; 12 Two or more races, non-Hispanic/Latino), 11 international. In 2018, 303 master's, 6 doctorates awarded. *Degree requirements:* For master's, content exams; for doctorate, comprehensive exam, thesis/dissertation. *Entrance requirements:* Additional exam requirements/recommendations for international students: Required—TOEFL (minimum score 500 paper-based; 61 iBT). *Application deadline:* For fall admission, 8/1 for domestic students; for spring admission, 1/1 for domestic students; for summer admission, 5/1 for domestic students. Application fee: $60. Electronic applications accepted. *Financial support:* Fellowships, research assistantships, teaching assistantships, career-related internships or fieldwork, Federal Work-Study, institutionally sponsored loans, health care benefits, tuition waivers (full and partial), and administrative assistantships available. Financial award applicants required to submit FAFSA. *Faculty research:* Internet training and integration for teachers, rural education, teacher preparation, organization of schools, evaluation of personnel. *Unit head:* Dr. Tracy L. Morris, Interim Dean, 304-293-0816, Fax: 304-293-7565, E-mail: Tracy.Morris@mail.wvu.edu. *Application contact:* Dr. Melissa Luna, Associate Dean for Research, 304-293-2174, Fax: 304-293-3802, E-mail: Melissa.Luna@mail.wvu.edu.
Website: http://cehs.wvu.edu/

Whitworth University, School of Education, Graduate Studies in Education, Program in Gifted and Talented, Spokane, WA 99251-0001. Offers MAT. *Accreditation:* NCATE. *Program availability:* Part-time, evening/weekend. *Degree requirements:* For master's, comprehensive exam, thesis (for some programs). *Entrance requirements:* For master's, GRE General Test, MAT.

Wichita State University, Graduate School, College of Applied Studies, School of Education, Wichita, KS 67260. Offers learning and instructional design (M Ed); special education (M Ed), including early childhood (M Ed, MAT), gifted, high incidence, low incidence; teaching (MAT), including early childhood (M Ed, MAT), middle level/secondary, transition to teaching. *Accreditation:* NCATE. *Program availability:* Part-time, evening/weekend, 100% online, blended/hybrid learning. *Entrance requirements:* For master's, MAT, minimum GPA of 2.75. *Unit head:* Dr. Edward Robeck, Department Head, 316-978-3322, E-mail: edward.robeck@wichita.edu. *Application contact:* Jordan Oleson, Admission Coordinator, 316-978-3095, Fax: 316-978-3253, E-mail: jordan.oleson@wichita.edu.

William Carey University, School of Education, Hattiesburg, MS 39401. Offers art education (M Ed); art of teaching (M Ed); elementary education (M Ed, Ed S); English education (M Ed); gifted education (M Ed); history and social science (M Ed); mild/moderate disabilities (M Ed); secondary education (M Ed). *Accreditation:* NCATE. *Program availability:* Part-time. *Degree requirements:* For master's, comprehensive exam. *Entrance requirements:* For master's, GRE, MAT, minimum GPA of 2.5, Class A teacher's license. Additional exam requirements/recommendations for international students: Required—TOEFL (minimum score 550 paper-based).

Wilmington University, College of Education, New Castle, DE 19720-6491. Offers applied technology in education (M Ed); career and technical education (M Ed); educational leadership (Ed D); elementary and secondary school counseling (M Ed); elementary studies (M Ed); ESOL literacy (M Ed); higher education leadership (Ed D); instruction: gifted and talented (M Ed); instruction: teacher of reading (M Ed); instruction: teaching and learning (M Ed); organizational leadership (Ed D); school leadership (M Ed); secondary education (MAT); special education (M Ed). *Accreditation:* NCATE. *Program availability:* Part-time, evening/weekend. *Entrance requirements:* For master's, 2 letters of recommendation, interview. Additional exam requirements/recommendations for international students: Required—TOEFL (minimum score 500 paper-based). Electronic applications accepted.

English as a Second Language

Acacia University, American Graduate School of Education, Tempe, AZ 85284. Offers educational administration (M Ed); elementary education (MA); English as a second language (M Ed); secondary education (MA); special education (M Ed).

Adelphi University, College of Education & Health Sciences, College of Education and Health Sciences, Garden City, NY 11530-0701. Offers p - 12 (MA). *Program availability:* Part-time, evening/weekend. *Students:* 20 full-time (16 women), 26 part-time (24 women); includes 23 minority (4 Black or African American, non-Hispanic/Latino; 3 Asian, non-Hispanic/Latino; 16 Hispanic/Latino), 4 international. Average age 30. 42 applicants, 62% accepted, 12 enrolled. In 2018, 36 master's, 11 other advanced degrees awarded. *Entrance requirements:* For master's, 2 letters of recommendation, resume, bachelor's degree with 3.0 min average, personal essay. Additional exam requirements/recommendations for international students: Required—TOEFL (minimum score 550 paper-based; 80 iBT), IELTS (minimum score 6.5). *Application deadline:* For fall admission, 5/1 for international students; for spring admission, 11/1 for international students; for summer admission, 3/1 for international students. Applications are processed on a rolling basis. Application fee: $50. Electronic applications accepted. *Expenses:* Contact institution. *Financial support:* Research assistantships, teaching assistantships, career-related internships or fieldwork, institutionally sponsored loans, scholarships/grants, traineeships, and unspecified assistantships available. Support available to part-time students. Financial award application deadline: 1/1; financial award applicants required to submit FAFSA. *Faculty research:* Theories of language acquisition, English as a second language in the content areas, apprenticeship in English as a second language instruction. *Unit head:* Eva Roca, Director, 516-877-4072, E-mail: roca2@adelphi.edu. *Application contact:* Eva Roca, Director, 516-877-4072, E-mail: roca2@adelphi.edu.

Albizu University, Miami Campus, Graduate Programs, Miami, FL 33172-2209. Offers clinical psychology (PhD, Psy D); entrepreneurship (MBA); exceptional student education (MS); human services (PhD); industrial/organizational psychology (MS); marriage and family therapy (MS); mental health counseling (MS); nonprofit management (MBA); organizational management (MBA); school counseling (MS); speech and language pathology (MS); teaching English for speakers of other languages (MS). *Accreditation:* APA. *Program availability:* Part-time, evening/weekend, 100% online, blended/hybrid learning. *Faculty:* 32 full-time (24 women), 27 part-time/adjunct (15 women). *Students:* 479 full-time (410 women), 146 part-time (126 women); includes 539 minority (42 Black or African American, non-Hispanic/Latino; 2 Asian, non-Hispanic/Latino; 490 Hispanic/Latino; 5 Two or more races, non-Hispanic/Latino), 22 international. Average age 33. 314 applicants, 45% accepted, 92 enrolled. In 2018, 101 master's, 64 doctorates awarded. Terminal master's awarded for partial completion of doctoral program. *Degree requirements:* For master's, comprehensive exam (for some programs), integrative project (for MBA); research project (for exceptional student education, teaching English as a second language); for doctorate, comprehensive exam, thesis/dissertation, comprehensive examinations, internship, project/dissertation. *Entrance requirements:* For master's, GRE/EXADEP, bachelor's degree from accredited institution, minimum GPA of 3.0, 3 letters of recommendation, interview, resume, statement of purpose, official transcripts; for doctorate, GRE (for Psy D), 3 letters of recommendation, resume, interview, statement of purpose, official transcripts; bachelor's degree and minimum GPA of 3.25 (for Psy D); master's degree and minimum GPA of 3.0 (for PhD). Additional exam requirements/recommendations for international students: Required—Michigan Test of English Language Proficiency. *Application deadline:* For fall admission, 4/1 priority date for domestic students, 5/1 priority date for international students; for spring admission, 11/1 priority date for domestic students, 9/1 priority date for international students. Applications are processed on a rolling basis. Application fee: $50. Electronic applications accepted. Application fee is waived when completed online. *Expenses:* Contact institution. *Financial support:* In 2018–19, 141 students received support. Federal Work-Study, scholarships/grants, unspecified assistantships, and tuition discounts available. Financial award application deadline: 6/1; financial award applicants required to submit FAFSA. *Faculty research:* Psychotherapy, forensic psychology, neuropsychology, special education, speech-language pathology, criminal justice, human services. *Unit head:* Dr. Jose Pons-Madera, PhD, President, 305-593-1223 Ext. 3120, Fax: 305-477-8983, E-mail: jpons@albizu.edu. *Application contact:* Nancy Alvarez, Director of Enrollment Management, 305-593-1223 Ext. 3136, Fax: 305-593-1854, E-mail: nalvarez@albizu.edu.

Albright College, Graduate Division, Reading, PA 19612-5234. Offers early childhood education (MS); elementary education (MS); English as a second language (MA); general education (MA); special education (MS). *Program availability:* Part-time, evening/weekend. *Degree requirements:* For master's, thesis. *Entrance requirements:* For master's, GRE General Test or MAT, minimum undergraduate GPA of 3.0, 2 letters of recommendation, interview. Additional exam requirements/recommendations for international students: Recommended—TOEFL (minimum score 525 paper-based). Electronic applications accepted.

Alliant International University–San Diego, Shirley M. Hufstedler School of Education, Program in Teaching English to Speakers of Other Languages, San Diego, CA 92131. Offers MA, Ed D, Certificate. *Program availability:* Part-time. *Degree requirements:* For doctorate, thesis/dissertation. *Entrance requirements:* For master's, minimum GPA of 2.5, letters of recommendation; for doctorate, minimum GPA of 3.0, letters of recommendation. Additional exam requirements/recommendations for international students: Required—TOEFL (minimum score 575 paper-based; 83 iBT), TWE (minimum score 5). Electronic applications accepted. *Faculty research:* Global education, psycho-linguistics, bilingualism and education, curriculum and instruction.

Alliant International University–San Francisco, Shirley M. Hufstedler School of Education, Teacher Education Programs, San Francisco, CA 94133. Offers auditory oral education (Certificate); CLAD (Certificate); education specialist: mild/moderate disabilities (Credential); preliminary multiple subject (Credential); preliminary single subject (Credential); professional clear multiple subject (Credential); professional clear single subject (Credential); special education (MA); teaching (MA); TESOL (Certificate). *Program availability:* Part-time, evening/weekend. *Degree requirements:* For master's, thesis. *Entrance requirements:* For degree, California Basic Educational Skills Test, minimum GPA of 2.5. Additional exam requirements/recommendations for international students: Required—TOEFL (minimum score 550 paper-based), TWE (minimum score 5). Electronic applications accepted. *Faculty research:* Curriculum development, first year teachers, cross-cultural issues in teaching, biliteracy.

American College of Education, Graduate Programs, Indianapolis, IN 46204. Offers curriculum and instruction (M Ed), including bilingual, ESL; educational leadership (M Ed); educational technology (M Ed).

American University, College of Arts and Sciences, Department of World Languages and Cultures, Washington, DC 20016-8045. Offers Spanish: Latin American studies (MA); teaching English as a foreign language (MA); teaching English to speakers of other languages (MA, Certificate); translation: French (Certificate); translation: Russian (Certificate); translation: Spanish (Certificate). *Program availability:* Part-time, evening/weekend. *Faculty:* 41 full-time (31 women), 26 part-time/adjunct (21 women). *Students:* 15 full-time (14 women), 20 part-time (15 women); includes 9 minority (3 Black or African American, non-Hispanic/Latino; 1 Asian, non-Hispanic/Latino; 4 Hispanic/Latino; 1 Two or more races, non-Hispanic/Latino), 10 international. Average age 33. 51 applicants, 88% accepted, 13 enrolled. In 2018, 11 master's, 6 other advanced degrees awarded. *Degree requirements:* For master's, one foreign language, comprehensive exam, thesis or alternative. *Entrance requirements:* For master's, GRE; Please see website:https://www.american.edu/cas/wlc/, writing sample, statement of purpose, transcripts, 2 letters of recommendation, resume; for Certificate, bachelor's degree, statement of purpose, transcripts, resume. Additional exam requirements/recommendations for international students: Required—TOEFL (minimum score 600 paper-based; 100 iBT). Application fee: $55. *Expenses:* Contact institution. *Financial support:* Institutionally sponsored loans, scholarships/grants, and unspecified assistantships available. Financial award applicants required to submit FAFSA. *Unit head:* Dr. Brenda Werth, Chair, World Languages and Cultures, 202-885-2381, E-mail: wlc@american.edu. *Application contact:* Jonathan Harper, Director of Graduate Recruitment, 202-885-3620, E-mail: casgrad@american.edu.
Website: http://www.american.edu/cas/wlc/

The American University in Cairo, School of Humanities and Social Sciences, Cairo, Egypt. Offers Arab and Islamic civilizations (Graduate Diploma); Arabic studies (MA);

comparative literary studies (Graduate Diploma); Egyptology and Coptology (MA); English and comparative literature (MA); humanities and social sciences (Graduate Diploma); philosophy (MA); psychology (MA); sociology and anthropology (MA); teaching Arabic as a foreign language (MA); teaching English to speakers of other languages (MA). *Program availability:* Part-time, evening/weekend. *Degree requirements:* For master's, comprehensive exam (for some programs), thesis (for some programs). *Entrance requirements:* Additional exam requirements/recommendations for international students: Required—TOEFL (minimum score 450 paper-based; 45 iBT), IELTS (minimum score 5). Electronic applications accepted. *Faculty research:* English literature, political science, psychology, sociology, anthropology and Egyptology, philosophy, Arabic studies, history, teaching Arabic as a foreign language, teaching English to speakers of other languages.

American University of Armenia, Graduate Programs, Yerevan, Armenia. Offers business administration (MBA); computer and information science (MS), including business management, design and manufacturing, energy (ME, MS), industrial engineering and systems management; economics (MS); industrial engineering and systems management (ME), including business, computer aided design/manufacturing, energy (ME, MS), information technology; law (LL M); political science and international affairs (MPSIA); public health (MPH); teaching English as a foreign language (MA). *Program availability:* Part-time, evening/weekend. *Degree requirements:* For master's, thesis (for some programs), capstone/project. *Entrance requirements:* For master's, GRE, GMAT, or LSAT. Additional exam requirements/recommendations for international students: Recommended—TOEFL (minimum score 79 iBT), IELTS (minimum score 6.5). *Faculty research:* Microfinance, finance (rural/development, international, corporate), firm life cycle theory, TESOL, language proficiency testing, public policy, administrative law, economic development, cryptography, artificial intelligence, energy efficiency/renewable energy, computer-aided design/manufacturing, health financing, tuberculosis control, mother/child health, preventive ophthalmology, post-earthquake psychopathological investigations, tobacco control, environmental health risk assessments.

American University of Beirut, Graduate Programs, Faculty of Arts and Sciences, Beirut 1107 2020, Lebanon. Offers anthropology (MA); Arab and Middle Eastern history (PhD); Arabic language and literature (MA, PhD); archaeology (MA); art history and curating (MA); biology (MS); cell and molecular biology (PhD); chemistry (MS); clinical psychology (MA); computational sciences (MS); computer science (MS); economics (MA); education (MA), including administration and policy studies, elementary education, mathematics education, psychology school guidance, psychology test and measurements, science education, teaching English as a foreign language; English language (MA); English literature (MA); environmental policy planning (MS); financial economics (MAFE); general psychology (MA); geology (MS); history (MA); Islamic studies (MA); mathematics (MS); media studies (MA); Middle East studies (MA); philosophy (MA); physics (MS); political studies (MA); public administration (MA); public policy and international affairs (MA); sociology (MA); theoretical physics (PhD). *Program availability:* Part-time. *Faculty:* 187 full-time (64 women), 27 part-time/adjunct (15 women). *Students:* 292 full-time (215 women), 216 part-time (148 women). Average age 27. 422 applicants, 64% accepted, 124 enrolled. In 2018, 90 master's, 3 doctorates awarded. *Degree requirements:* For master's, comprehensive exam, thesis (for some programs), project; for doctorate, comprehensive exam, thesis/dissertation (for some programs). *Entrance requirements:* For master's, GRE General Test (for archaeology, clinical psychology, general psychology, economics, financial economics and biology); for doctorate, GRE General Test for all PhD programs, GRE Subject Test for theoretical physics. Additional exam requirements/recommendations for international students: Required—TOEFL (minimum score 583 paper-based; 97 iBT), IELTS (minimum score 7). *Application deadline:* For fall admission, 3/18 for domestic students; for spring admission, 11/5 for domestic students. Application fee: $50. Electronic applications accepted. *Expenses:* MA/MS: Humanities and social sciences=$912/credit. Sciences=$943/credit. Financial economics=$986/credit. Thesis: Humanities/social sciences=$6565 and sciences=$6865. *Financial support:* In 2018–19, 227 fellowships with full tuition reimbursements, 17 research assistantships with full tuition reimbursements, 83 teaching assistantships with full tuition reimbursements were awarded; scholarships/grants, tuition waivers (full and partial), and unspecified assistantships also available. Financial award application deadline: 3/18. *Faculty research:* Sciences: Physics: High energy, Particle, Polymer and Soft Matter, Thermal, Plasma; String Theory, Mathematical physics, Astrophysics (stellar evolution, planet and galaxy formation and evolution, astrophysical dynamics), Solid State physics/thin films, Spintronics, Magnetic properties of materials, Mineralogy, Petrology, and Geochemistry of Hard Rocks, Geophysics and Petrophysics, Hydrogeology, Micropaleontology, Sedimentology, and Stratigraphy, Structural Geology and Geotectonics, Renewable en. *Total annual research expenditures:* $4.3 million. *Unit head:* Dr. Nadia Maria El Cheikh, Dean, Faculty of Arts and Sciences, 961-1-350000 Ext. 3800, Fax: 961-1-744461, E-mail: nmcheikh@aub.edu.lb. *Application contact:* Adriana Michelle Zanaty, Curriculum and Graduate Studies Officer, 961-1-350000 Ext. 3833, Fax: 961-1-744461, E-mail: az48@aub.edu.lb.
Website: https://www.aub.edu.lb/fas/Pages/default.aspx

American University of Sharjah, Graduate Programs, Sharjah, United Arab Emirates. Offers accounting (MS); biomedical engineering (MSBME); business administration (MBA); chemical engineering (MS Ch E); civil engineering (MSCE); computer engineering (MS); electrical engineering (MSEE); engineering systems management (MS, PhD); mathematics (MS); mechanical engineering (MSME); mechatronics engineering (MS); teaching English to speakers of other languages (MA); translation and interpreting (MA); urban planning (MUP). *Program availability:* Part-time, evening/weekend. *Degree requirements:* For master's, thesis (for some programs). *Entrance requirements:* For master's, GMAT (for MBA). Additional exam requirements/recommendations for international students: Required—TOEFL (minimum score 550 paper-based; 80 iBT), TWE (minimum score 5); Recommended—IELTS (minimum score 6.5). Electronic applications accepted. *Faculty research:* Water pollution, management and waste water treatment, energy and sustainability, air pollution, Islamic finance, family business and small and medium enterprises.

Anaheim University, Program in Teaching English to Speakers of Other Languages, Anaheim, CA 92806-5150. Offers MA, Ed D, Certificate, Diploma. *Program availability:* Part-time, evening/weekend, online only, 100% online. In 2018, 1 master's, 1 doctorate awarded. *Application deadline:* Applications are processed on a rolling basis. Electronic applications accepted. *Unit head:* Dr. Hayo Reinders, Director, Doctor of Education in TESOL Program, 714-772-3330, Fax: 714-772-3331, E-mail: admissions@anaheim.edu. *Application contact:* Dr. Hayo Reinders, Director, Doctor of Education in TESOL Program, 714-772-3330, Fax: 714-772-3331, E-mail: admissions@anaheim.edu.

Andrews University, School of Graduate Studies, School of Education, Department of Teaching, Learning, and Curriculum, Berrien Springs, MI 49104. Offers curriculum and instruction (MA, Ed D, PhD, Ed S); elementary education (MAT); secondary education (MAT), including biology, education, English, English as a second language, French, history, physics; teacher education (MAT). *Entrance requirements:* For master's, GRE Subject Test. Additional exam requirements/recommendations for international students: Required—TOEFL (minimum score 550 paper-based).

Angelo State University, College of Graduate Studies and Research, College of Arts and Humanities, Department of English and Modern Languages, San Angelo, TX 76909. Offers English (MA); TESOL (MA). *Program availability:* Part-time, evening/weekend. *Students:* 8 full-time (7 women), 12 part-time (10 women); includes 4 minority (1 Asian, non-Hispanic/Latino; 3 Hispanic/Latino), 2 international. Average age 32. *Entrance requirements:* For master's, essay. Additional exam requirements/recommendations for international students: Required—TOEFL or IELTS. *Application deadline:* For fall admission, 7/15 priority date for domestic students, 6/10 for international students; for spring admission, 12/1 priority date for domestic students, 11/1 for international students. Applications are processed on a rolling basis. Application fee: $40 ($50 for international students). Electronic applications accepted. *Expenses: Tuition, area resident:* Full-time $3964; part-time $220 per credit hour. Tuition, state resident: full-time $3964; part-time $220 per credit hour. Tuition, nonresident: full-time $11,434; part-time $635 per credit hour. *International tuition:* $11,434 full-time. *Financial support:* Teaching assistantships, Federal Work-Study, scholarships/grants, and unspecified assistantships available. Support available to part-time students. Financial award application deadline: 3/1; financial award applicants required to submit FAFSA. *Unit head:* Dr. Erin Ashworth-King, Chair, 325-943-2273, Fax: 325-942-2208, E-mail: erin.ashworth-king@angelo.edu. *Application contact:* Dr. Erin Ashworth-King, Chair, 325-943-2273, Fax: 325-942-2208, E-mail: erin.ashworth-king@angelo.edu.
Website: http://www.angelo.edu/dept/english_modern_languages/

Arizona State University at the Tempe campus, College of Liberal Arts and Sciences, Department of English, Tempe, AZ 85287-0302. Offers applied linguistics (PhD); creative writing (MFA); English (MA, PhD), including comparative literature (MA), linguistics (MA), literature, rhetoric and composition (MA), rhetoric, composition, and linguistics (PhD); film and media studies (MAS), including American media and popular culture; linguistics (Graduate Certificate); teaching English to speakers of other languages (MTESOL); translation studies (Graduate Certificate). Terminal master's awarded for partial completion of doctoral program. *Degree requirements:* For master's, variable foreign language requirement, comprehensive exam (for some programs), thesis (for some programs), interactive Program of Study (iPOS) submitted before completing 50 percent of required credit hours; for doctorate, variable foreign language requirement, comprehensive exam, thesis/dissertation, interactive Program of Study (iPOS) submitted before completing 50 percent of required credit hours. *Entrance requirements:* For master's and doctorate, GRE, minimum GPA of 3.0 or equivalent in last 2 years of work leading to bachelor's degree. Additional exam requirements/recommendations for international students: Required—TOEFL, IELTS, or PTE. Electronic applications accepted.

Arkansas Tech University, College of Arts and Humanities, Russellville, AR 72801. Offers applied sociology (MS); English (M Ed, MA); history (MA); liberal arts (MLA); multi-media journalism (MA); psychology (MS); teaching English as a second language (MA). *Program availability:* Part-time, 100% online, blended/hybrid learning. *Students:* 34 full-time (21 women), 150 part-time (108 women); includes 38 minority (10 Black or African American, non-Hispanic/Latino; 4 Asian, non-Hispanic/Latino; 20 Hispanic/Latino; 4 Two or more races, non-Hispanic/Latino), 11 international. Average age 34. In 2018, 75 master's awarded. *Degree requirements:* For master's, comprehensive exam (for some programs), thesis (for some programs), project. *Entrance requirements:* Additional exam requirements/recommendations for international students: Required—TOEFL (minimum score 550 paper-based; 79 iBT), IELTS (minimum score 6.5), PTE (minimum score 58). *Application deadline:* For fall admission, 3/1 priority date for domestic students, 5/1 priority date for international students; for spring admission, 10/1 priority date for domestic and international students. Applications are processed on a rolling basis. Application fee: $40 ($90 for international students). Electronic applications accepted. *Expenses: Tuition, area resident:* Full-time $6816; part-time $284 per credit hour. Tuition, state resident: full-time $6816; part-time $284 per credit hour. Tuition, nonresident: full-time $13,632; part-time $568 per credit hour. *International tuition:* $13,632 full-time. *Required fees:* $457.50 per semester. Tuition and fees vary according to course load and degree level. *Financial support:* In 2018–19, research assistantships with full and partial tuition reimbursements (averaging $4,800 per year), teaching assistantships with full and partial tuition reimbursements (averaging $4,800 per year) were awarded; career-related internships or fieldwork, Federal Work-Study, scholarships/grants, health care benefits, and unspecified assistantships also available. Support available to part-time students. Financial award application deadline: 4/15; financial award applicants required to submit FAFSA. *Unit head:* Dr. Wayne Powell, Dean, 479-968-0274, Fax: 479-964-0812, E-mail: wpowell4@atu.edu. *Application contact:* Dr. Jeff Robertson, Interim Dean of Graduate College, 479-968-0398, Fax: 479-964-0542, E-mail: gradcollege@atu.edu.
Website: http://www.atu.edu/humanities/

Asbury University, School of Graduate and Professional Studies, Wilmore, KY 40390-1198. Offers biology: alternative certificate (MA Ed); chemistry: alternative certificate (MA Ed); English (MA Ed); English as a second language (MA Ed); ESL (MA Ed); French (MA Ed); Latin: alternative certificate (MA Ed); mathematics: alternative certificate (MA Ed); reading/writing endorsement (MA Ed); social studies (MA Ed); social work (MSW), including child and family services; Spanish (MA Ed); special education (MA Ed); special education: alternative certificate (MA Ed); teacher as leader endorsement (MA Ed). *Accreditation:* NCATE. *Program availability:* Part-time. *Degree requirements:* For master's, action research project, portfolio. *Entrance requirements:* For master's, PRAXIS/NTE, minimum GPA of 2.75, letters of recommendation. Additional exam requirements/recommendations for international students: Required—TOEFL (minimum score 550 paper-based). Electronic applications accepted.

Aurora University, School of Education and Human Performance, Aurora, IL 60506-4892. Offers applied behavioral analysis (MS); bilingual-ESL education (MA); educational leadership with principal endorsement (MA); educational technology (MA); leadership in adult learning higher education (Ed D); leadership in curriculum and instruction (Ed D); leadership in educational administration (Ed D); reading instruction (MA); special education (MA). *Accreditation:* NCATE. *Program availability:* Part-time, evening/weekend, 100% online. *Faculty:* 14 full-time (6 women), 32 part-time/adjunct (17 women). *Students:* 28 full-time (25 women), 537 part-time (359 women); includes 101 minority (25 Black or African American, non-Hispanic/Latino; 8 Asian, non-Hispanic/Latino; 58 Hispanic/Latino; 2 Native Hawaiian or other Pacific Islander, non-Hispanic/Latino; 8 Two or more races, non-Hispanic/Latino), 2 international. Average age 38. 191 applicants, 98% accepted, 133 enrolled. In 2018, 213 master's, 16 doctorates awarded. *Degree requirements:* For master's, student teaching, research seminar, and practicum; for doctorate, comprehensive exam, thesis/dissertation. *Entrance requirements:* For master's, 2 years of teaching experience, valid teaching certificate, resume; for doctorate, appropriate master's degree, two references, curriculum vitae, personal statement, professional project, reflective essay. Additional exam requirements/recommendations for international students: Required—TOEFL (minimum score 550 paper-based; 79 iBT). *Application deadline:* For fall admission, 6/1 for international students; for spring admission, 10/1 for international students. Applications are processed on a rolling basis. Application fee: $0. Electronic applications accepted. *Expenses:* The reported tuition amount is for the program with the greatest enrollment, MA in Educational Leadership with Principal Endorsement. Other programs may require more semester hours, and thus have a greater total cost. The Education doctoral

programs are roughly double the amount of the master's programs. *Financial support:* In 2018–19, 31 students received support. Federal Work-Study, scholarships/grants, and unspecified assistantships available. Financial award applicants required to submit FAFSA. *Unit head:* Dr. Jen Buckley, Dean, School of Education and Human Performance, 630-844-1542, Fax: 630-844-6155, E-mail: jbuckley@aurora.edu. *Application contact:* Center for Graduate Studies, 630-947-8955, E-mail: AUadmission@aurora.edu.
Website: http://aurora.edu/education

Avila University, School of Education, Kansas City, MO 64145-1698. Offers advanced classroom management (MA); elementary education (Teaching Certificate); English language learners (Advanced Certificate); middle school (Teaching Certificate); physical education K-12 (Teaching Certificate); secondary education (Teaching Certificate). *Program availability:* Part-time, evening/weekend, online learning. *Faculty:* 6 full-time (5 women), 9 part-time/adjunct (8 women). *Students:* 83 full-time (71 women), 84 part-time (69 women); includes 13 minority (6 Black or African American, non-Hispanic/Latino; 2 Asian, non-Hispanic/Latino; 4 Hispanic/Latino; 1 Two or more races, non-Hispanic/Latino), 2 international. Average age 40. 92 applicants, 62% accepted, 40 enrolled. In 2018, 21 master's awarded. *Entrance requirements:* For master's, minimum GPA of 3.0, writing sample, recommendation, interview; for other advanced degree, foreign language. Additional exam requirements/recommendations for international students: Required—TOEFL (minimum score 580 paper-based; 92 iBT). *Application deadline:* Applications are processed on a rolling basis. Electronic applications accepted. *Expenses:* Contact institution. *Financial support:* In 2018–19, 12 students received support. Unspecified assistantships available. Financial award applicants required to submit FAFSA. *Unit head:* Dr. Stacy Keith, Director of Graduate Education, 816-501-2446, Fax: 816-501-2915, E-mail: stacy.keith@avila.edu. *Application contact:* Cory Roup, Graduate Education Enrollment and Academic Advisor, 816-501-2464, E-mail: cory.roup@avila.edu.
Website: https://www.avila.edu/academics/graduate-studies/grad-education

Azusa Pacific University, College of Liberal Arts and Sciences, Program in Teaching English to Speakers of Other Languages, Azusa, CA 91702-7000. Offers MA. *Program availability:* 100% online.

Ball State University, Graduate School, College of Sciences and Humanities, Department of English, Program in Linguistics, Muncie, IN 47306. Offers linguistics (MA); teaching English to speakers of other languages (TESOL) and linguistics (MA). *Program availability:* Part-time. *Entrance requirements:* For master's, GRE General Test, minimum baccalaureate GPA of 2.75 or 3.0 in latter half of baccalaureate, statement of purpose, writing sample, three letters of recommendation. Additional exam requirements/recommendations for international students: Required—TOEFL (minimum score 550 paper-based; 79 iBT), IELTS (minimum score 6.5). Electronic applications accepted. *Faculty research:* Descriptive and theoretical linguistics.

Barry University, School of Education, Program in Curriculum and Instruction, Miami Shores, FL 33161-6695. Offers accomplished teacher (Ed S); culture, language and literacy (TESOL) (PhD); curriculum evaluation and research (PhD); early childhood (Ed S); early childhood education (PhD); elementary (Ed S); elementary education (PhD); ESOL (Ed S); gifted (Ed S); Montessori (Ed S); PKP/elementary (Ed S); reading (Ed S); reading, language and cognition (PhD). *Entrance requirements:* For doctorate, GRE, minimum GPA of 3.25.

Barry University, School of Education, Program in Technology and TESOL, Miami Shores, FL 33161-6695. Offers MS, Ed S.

Barry University, School of Education, Program in TESOL, Miami Shores, FL 33161-6695. Offers TESOL (MS); TESOL international (MS). *Entrance requirements:* For master's, GRE or MAT.

Binghamton University, State University of New York, Graduate School, College of Community and Public Affairs, Department of Teaching, Learning and Educational Leadership, Program in TESOL Education, Binghamton, NY 13902-6000. Offers MA, MS Ed. *Degree requirements:* For master's, capstone project or thesis, practicum.

Biola University, Cook School of Intercultural Studies, La Mirada, CA 90639-0001. Offers anthropology (MA); applied linguistics (MA); intercultural education (PhD); intercultural studies (MA, PhD); linguistics (Certificate); linguistics and Biblical languages (MA); missiology (D Miss); missions (MA); teaching English to speakers of other languages (MA, Certificate). *Program availability:* Part-time, 100% online. *Entrance requirements:* For master's, minimum undergraduate GPA of 3.0; for doctorate, master's degree or equivalent, 3 years of cross-cultural experience, minimum graduate GPA of 3.3. Additional exam requirements/recommendations for international students: Required—TOEFL. Electronic applications accepted. *Faculty research:* Linguistics, anthropology, intercultural studies, teaching English to speakers of other languages, missions, missiology.

Bishop's University, School of Education, Sherbrooke, QC J1M 1Z7, Canada. Offers advanced studies in education (Diploma); education (M Ed, MA); teaching English as a second language (Certificate). *Program availability:* Part-time, online learning. *Degree requirements:* For master's, thesis (for some programs). *Entrance requirements:* For master's, teaching license, 2 years of teaching experience. *Faculty research:* Integration of special needs students, multigrade classes/small schools, leadership in organizational development, second language acquisition.

Boise State University, College of Arts and Sciences, Department of English, Boise, ID 83725-0399. Offers English literature (MA); English, rhetoric and composition (MA); teaching English language (MA); technical communication (MA). *Program availability:* Part-time. *Degree requirements:* For master's, thesis (for some programs). *Entrance requirements:* For master's, GRE General Test, minimum GPA of 3.0. Additional exam requirements/recommendations for international students: Required—TOEFL (minimum score 550 paper-based; 80 iBT), IELTS (minimum score 6). Electronic applications accepted.

Boise State University, College of Education, Department of Literacy, Language and Culture, Boise, ID 83725-0399. Offers bilingual education (M Ed); English as a new language (M Ed); literacy (MA). *Accreditation:* NCATE. *Program availability:* Part-time, evening/weekend. *Degree requirements:* For master's, thesis optional. *Entrance requirements:* For master's, minimum GPA of 3.0. Additional exam requirements/recommendations for international students: Required—TOEFL (minimum score 550 paper-based; 80 iBT), IELTS (minimum score 6). Electronic applications accepted.

Boricua College, Program in TESOL Education (K-12), New York, NY 10032-1560. Offers MS. Program offered in Brooklyn Campus and Bronx Campus. *Program availability:* Evening/weekend. *Faculty:* 2 full-time (0 women), 2 part-time/adjunct (both women). *Students:* 59 full-time (52 women); includes 55 minority (9 Black or African American, non-Hispanic/Latino; 46 Hispanic/Latino). Average age 34. 92 applicants, 76% accepted, 59 enrolled. In 2018, 53 master's awarded. *Degree requirements:* For master's, thesis. *Entrance requirements:* For master's, interview by the faculty. *Application deadline:* Applications are processed on a rolling basis. Application fee: $100 ($500 for international students). *Expenses:* *Tuition:* Full-time $15,000. One-time fee: $100 full-time. *Financial support:* Career-related internships or fieldwork and Federal Work-Study available. Financial award applicants required to submit FAFSA. *Unit head:* Dr. Joseph H. Gaines, Co-Chairperson, 347-964-8600 Ext. 451, E-mail: jgaines@boricuacollege.edu. *Application contact:* Dr. Shivaji Sengupta, Vice President, 212-694-1000 Ext. 650, Fax: 212-694-1015, E-mail: ssengupta@boricuacollege.edu.

Brigham Young University, Graduate Studies, College of Humanities, Department of Linguistics, Provo, UT 84602. Offers linguistics (MA); teaching English as a second language (MA). *Program availability:* Part-time. *Faculty:* 23 full-time (3 women). *Students:* 40 full-time (29 women), 17 part-time (10 women), 11 international. Average age 31. 33 applicants, 91% accepted, 23 enrolled. In 2018, 19 master's awarded. *Degree requirements:* For master's, 2 foreign languages, thesis. *Entrance requirements:* For master's, GRE General Test, minimum GPA of 3.0 in last 60 hours of course work. Additional exam requirements/recommendations for international students: Required—TOEFL (minimum score 580 paper-based; 90 iBT), TWE. *Application deadline:* 1/15 for domestic and international students. Application fee: $50. Electronic applications accepted. *Financial support:* In 2018–19, 57 students received support, including 7 research assistantships (averaging $7,200 per year), 11 teaching assistantships (averaging $2,067 per year); fellowships with partial tuition reimbursements available, career-related internships or fieldwork, scholarships/grants, unspecified assistantships, and travel to conference presentations also available. Financial award application deadline: 7/1. *Faculty research:* Teaching English to speakers of other languages, second language acquisition, computational linguistics, semiotics and semantics, computer-assisted language instruction, forensic linguistics, endangered language documentation. *Unit head:* Dr. Norman Evans, Chair, 801-422-8472, E-mail: norm_evans@byu.edu. *Application contact:* Mary Beth Wald, Graduate Program Manager, 801-422-9010, E-mail: marybeth_wald@byu.edu.
Website: http://linguistics.byu.edu/

Brock University, Faculty of Graduate Studies, Faculty of Humanities, Program in Applied Linguistics, St. Catharines, ON L2S 3A1, Canada. Offers MA. *Program availability:* Part-time. *Degree requirements:* For master's, thesis optional. *Entrance requirements:* For master's, honours degree with a background in English, English linguistics, teaching English as a second language, or a comparable field. Additional exam requirements/recommendations for international students: Required—TOEFL (minimum score 630 paper-based; 109 iBT), IELTS (minimum score 8), TWE (minimum score 5.5). Electronic applications accepted. *Expenses:* Contact institution. *Faculty research:* Metalinguistic ability in subsequent language learning, language teaching methodology, forensic linguistics, philosophy of education, culturally appropriate pedagogy.

Brown University, Graduate School, Department of Portuguese and Brazilian Studies, Providence, RI 02912. Offers Brazilian studies (AM); English as a second language and cross-cultural studies (AM); Portuguese and Brazilian studies (AM, PhD); Portuguese bilingual education and cross-cultural studies (AM). *Degree requirements:* For doctorate, thesis/dissertation.

Buena Vista University, School of Education, Storm Lake, IA 50588. Offers curriculum and instruction (M Ed), including effective teaching, TESL; school guidance and counseling (MS Ed). Program offered in summer only. *Program availability:* Part-time, evening/weekend, online learning. *Degree requirements:* For master's, thesis, fieldwork/practicum, capstone portfolio. *Entrance requirements:* For master's, Analytical Writing Assessment (in-house), minimum undergraduate GPA of 2.75. Electronic applications accepted. *Faculty research:* Reading, curriculum, educational psychology, special education.

Cabrini University, Academic Affairs, Radnor, PA 19087. Offers accounting (M Acc); autism spectrum disorder (M Ed); biological sciences (MS), including civic leadership; criminology and criminal justice (MA); curriculum, instruction, and assessment (M Ed); educational leadership (M Ed, Ed D), including curriculum and instructional leadership (Ed D), preK-12 leadership (Ed D); English as a second language (M Ed); organizational leadership (DBA, PhD); preK to 4 (M Ed); reading specialist (M Ed); secondary education (M Ed), including biology, chemistry, English, English/communication, mathematics, social studies; special education grades 7-12 (M Ed); special education preK-8 (M Ed); teaching and learning (M Ed). *Program availability:* Part-time, evening/weekend. *Degree requirements:* For master's, comprehensive exam (for some programs), thesis (for some programs); for doctorate, comprehensive exam (for some programs), thesis/dissertation. *Entrance requirements:* For master's, professional resume, personal statement, two recommendations, official transcripts; for doctorate, official transcripts, minimum master's GPA of 3.0, two recommendations, interview with admissions committee. Additional exam requirements/recommendations for international students: Required—TOEFL (minimum score 80 iBT). Electronic applications accepted. Application fee is waived when completed online. *Expenses:* Contact institution.

California Baptist University, Program in English, Riverside, CA 92504-3206. Offers English pedagogy (MA); literature (MA); teaching English to speakers of other languages (TESOL) (MA). *Program availability:* Part-time. *Faculty:* 17 full-time (11 women). *Students:* 1 (woman) full-time, 19 part-time (12 women); includes 14 minority (8 Black or African American, non-Hispanic/Latino; 6 Hispanic/Latino). Average age 33. 2 applicants, 100% accepted, 2 enrolled. In 2018, 6 master's awarded. *Degree requirements:* For master's, comprehensive exam, project, or thesis. *Entrance requirements:* For master's, GRE (for applicants with a GPA below 2.75) or CSET, minimum undergraduate GPA of 2.75; 18 semester hours of course work in English beyond freshman level; three recommendations; essay; demonstration of writing; interview. Additional exam requirements/recommendations for international students: Required—TOEFL (minimum score 80 iBT). *Application deadline:* For fall admission, 8/1 priority date for domestic students, 7/1 for international students; for spring admission, 12/1 priority date for domestic students, 11/1 for international students. Applications are processed on a rolling basis. Application fee: $45. Electronic applications accepted. *Expenses:* $607 per unit. *Financial support:* In 2018–19, 9 students received support. Federal Work-Study and scholarships/grants available. Financial award applicants required to submit CSS PROFILE or FAFSA. *Faculty research:* Classical mythology and folklore, multicultural literature, genre studies, science fiction and fantasy literature, intercultural rhetoric. *Unit head:* Dr. Lisa Hernandez, Dean, College of Arts and Sciences, 951-343-4767, E-mail: lihernandez@calbaptist.edu. *Application contact:* Dr. Laura Veltman, Director, MA in English, 951-343-4649, E-mail: lveltman@calbaptist.edu.
Website: http://www.calbaptist.edu/maenglish/

California State University, Dominguez Hills, College of Arts and Humanities, Department of English, Carson, CA 90747-0001. Offers English literature (MA); rhetoric and composition (Certificate); teaching English as a second language (MA, Certificate). *Program availability:* Part-time, evening/weekend. *Degree requirements:* For master's, comprehensive exam (for some programs), thesis or alternative. *Entrance requirements:* For master's, minimum GPA of 3.0 in last 60 units. Additional exam requirements/recommendations for international students: Required—TOEFL (minimum score 550 paper-based). Electronic applications accepted. *Faculty research:* Gender studies, transnationalism, discourse analysis, visual culture, Shakespeare.

California State University, East Bay, Office of Graduate Studies, College of Letters, Arts, and Social Sciences, Department of English, Hayward, CA 94542-3000. Offers

English (MA); teaching English to speaker of other languages (MA). *Program availability:* Part-time. *Degree requirements:* For master's, one foreign language, comprehensive exam, thesis optional. *Entrance requirements:* For master's, minimum GPA of 3.0 in field; 2 letters of recommendation; academic or professional writing sample; teaching experience and some degree of bilingualism (preferred for TESOL). Additional exam requirements/recommendations for international students: Required—TOEFL (minimum score 550 paper-based); Recommended—IELTS (minimum score 6.5). Electronic applications accepted.

California State University, Fresno, Division of Research and Graduate Studies, College of Arts and Humanities, Department of Linguistics, Fresno, CA 93740-8027. Offers linguistics (MA), including teaching English as a second language. *Program availability:* Part-time, evening/weekend. *Degree requirements:* For master's, comprehensive exam. *Entrance requirements:* For master's, GRE General Test, minimum GPA of 3.0. Additional exam requirements/recommendations for international students: Required—TOEFL. Electronic applications accepted. *Faculty research:* Communication systems, bilingual education, animal communication, conflict resolution, literacy programs.

California State University, Long Beach, Graduate Studies, College of Liberal Arts, Department of Linguistics, Long Beach, CA 90840. Offers general linguistics (MA); language and culture (MA); special concentration (MA); teaching English to speakers of other languages (MA, Graduate Certificate). *Program availability:* Part-time, evening/ weekend. *Degree requirements:* For master's, one foreign language, comprehensive exam, thesis optional. *Application deadline:* For fall admission, 4/15 for domestic students; for spring admission, 11/1 for domestic students. Applications are processed on a rolling basis. Application fee: $55. Electronic applications accepted. *Expenses: Required fees:* $2628 per term. Tuition and fees vary according to class time, course level, course load, degree level, campus/location and program. *Financial support:* Teaching assistantships, career-related internships or fieldwork, Federal Work-Study, institutionally sponsored loans, and scholarships/grants available. Financial award application deadline: 3/2; financial award applicants required to submit FAFSA. *Faculty research:* Pedagogy of language instruction, role of language in society, Khmer language instruction. *Unit head:* Nancy Hall, Chair, 562-985-5792, Fax: 562-985-2593, E-mail: Nancy.Hall@csulb.edu. *Application contact:* Dr. Rebekha Abbuhl, Graduate Advisor, 562-985-1393, E-mail: Rebekha.Abbuhl@csulb.edu.
Website: http://www.csulb.edu/colleges/cla/departments/linguistics/

California State University, Sacramento, College of Arts and Letters, Department of English, Sacramento, CA 95819. Offers composition (MA); creative writing (MA); literature (MA); teaching English to speakers of other languages (MA). *Program availability:* Part-time. *Degree requirements:* For master's, thesis, project, or comprehensive exam; TESOL exam; writing proficiency exam. *Entrance requirements:* For master's, portfolio (creative writing); minimum GPA of 3.0 in English and overall during previous 2 years. Additional exam requirements/recommendations for international students: Required—TOEFL (minimum score 600 paper-based; 100 iBT). Electronic applications accepted. *Expenses:* Contact institution. *Faculty research:* Teaching composition, remedial writing.

California State University, Stanislaus, College of the Arts, Humanities and Social Sciences, MA Program in English, Turlock, CA 95382. Offers literature (Certificate); rhetoric and teaching writing (MA); teaching English to speakers of other languages (MA). *Program availability:* Part-time. *Degree requirements:* For master's, comprehensive exam, thesis or alternative. *Entrance requirements:* For master's, GRE, minimum GPA of 3.0, 2 letters of reference, personal statement. Additional exam requirements/recommendations for international students: Required—TOEFL (minimum score 575 paper-based), TWE (minimum score 4). Electronic applications accepted. *Faculty research:* Transnational literacies, Renaissance and medieval literature, abolition writings and slave narratives, qualitative writing.

Cambridge College, School of Education, Boston, MA 02129. Offers autism specialist (M Ed); autism/behavior analyst (M Ed); behavior analyst (Post-Master's Certificate); curriculum and instruction (CAGS); early childhood teacher (M Ed); educational leadership (M Ed, Ed D); elementary teacher (M Ed); English as a second language (M Ed, Certificate); general science (M Ed); health education (Post-Master's Certificate); interdisciplinary studies (M Ed); library teacher (M Ed); mathematics education (M Ed); mathematics specialist (Certificate); school administration (M Ed, CAGS); school nurse education (M Ed); teacher of students with moderate disabilities (M Ed); teaching skills and methodologies (M Ed). *Program availability:* Part-time, evening/weekend, online learning. *Degree requirements:* For master's, thesis, internship/practicum (licensure program only); for doctorate, thesis/dissertation; for other advanced degree, thesis. *Entrance requirements:* For master's, interview, resume, documentation of licensure, 2 professional references; for doctorate, official transcripts, interview, resume, written personal statement/essay, portfolio of scholarly and professional work, 2 professional references, health insurance, immunizations form; for other advanced degree, official transcripts, interview, resume, written personal statement/essay, 2 professional references, health insurance, immunizations form. Additional exam requirements/ recommendations for international students: Required—TOEFL (minimum score 550 paper-based; 79 iBT), Michigan English Language Assessment Battery (minimum score 85); Recommended—IELTS (minimum score 6). *Application deadline:* Applications are processed on a rolling basis. Application fee: $30. Electronic applications accepted. *Expenses:* Contact institution. *Financial support:* Career-related internships or fieldwork, Federal Work-Study, and scholarships/grants available. Financial award applicants required to submit FAFSA. *Faculty research:* Adult education, accelerated learning, mathematics education, brain compatible learning, special education and law. *Unit head:* Dr. Mary Garrity, Interim Dean, 617-873-0168, E-mail: mary.garrity@cambridgecollege.edu. *Application contact:* Salvadore Liberto, Interim Assistant Vice President of Enrollment, 800-877-4723, E-mail: admissions@cambridgecollege.edu.
Website: https://www.cambridgecollege.edu/school/school-education

Canisius College, Graduate Division, School of Education and Human Services, Department of Graduate Education and Leadership, Buffalo, NY 14208-1098. Offers business and marketing education (MS Ed); college student personnel (MS Ed); deaf education (MS Ed); deaf/adolescent education, grades 7-12 (MS Ed); deaf/childhood education, grades 1-6 (MS Ed); differentiated instruction (MS Ed); education administration (MS); educational administration (MS Ed); educational technologies (Certificate); gifted education extension (Certificate); literacy (MS Ed); reading (Certificate); school building leadership (MS Ed, Certificate); school district leadership (Certificate); teacher leader (Certificate); TESOL (MS Ed). *Accreditation:* NCATE. *Program availability:* Part-time, evening/weekend, 100% online, blended/hybrid learning. *Faculty:* 5 full-time (all women), 21 part-time/adjunct (16 women). *Students:* 79 full-time (66 women), 135 part-time (106 women); includes 45 minority (27 Black or African American, non-Hispanic/Latino; 1 American Indian or Alaska Native, non-Hispanic/ Latino; 3 Asian, non-Hispanic/Latino; 9 Hispanic/Latino; 5 Two or more races, non-Hispanic/Latino), 1 international. Average age 32. 83 applicants, 96% accepted, 74 enrolled. In 2018, 94 master's, 47 other advanced degrees awarded. *Entrance requirements:* For master's, GRE (if cumulative GPA less than 2.7), transcripts, two letters of recommendation. Additional exam requirements/recommendations for international students: Required—TOEFL (minimum score 550 paper-based, 79 iBT),

IELTS (minimum score 6.5), or CAEL (minimum score 70). *Application deadline:* Applications are processed on a rolling basis. Application fee: $0. Electronic applications accepted. *Expenses: Tuition:* Part-time $820 per credit hour. *Required fees:* $25 per semester. One-time fee: $65 part-time. Tuition and fees vary according to program. *Financial support:* In 2018–19, 206 students received support. Career-related internships or fieldwork, Federal Work-Study, scholarships/grants, tuition waivers (partial), and unspecified assistantships available. Support available to part-time students. Financial award application deadline: 4/30; financial award applicants required to submit FAFSA. *Faculty research:* Asperger's disease, autism, private higher education, reading strategies. *Unit head:* Dr. Anne Marie Tryjankowski, Chair/Associate Professor of Graduate Education and Leadership, 716-888-3715, Fax: 716-888-3142, E-mail: tryjanka@canisius.edu. *Application contact:* Dr. Anne Marie Tryjankowski, Chair/ Associate Professor of Graduate Education and Leadership, 716-888-3715, Fax: 716-888-3142, E-mail: tryjanka@canisius.edu.

Carson-Newman University, Graduate Program in Education, Jefferson City, TN 37760. Offers curriculum and instruction (M Ed); educational leadership (M Ed); elementary education (MAT); school counseling (MS); secondary education (MAT); teaching English as a second language (MATESL). *Accreditation:* NCATE. *Program availability:* Part-time, evening/weekend, 100% online, blended/hybrid learning. *Faculty:* 20 full-time (11 women), 16 part-time/adjunct (13 women). *Students:* 14 full-time (8 women), 401 part-time (294 women); includes 45 minority (34 Black or African American, non-Hispanic/Latino; 1 American Indian or Alaska Native, non-Hispanic/ Latino; 4 Hispanic/Latino; 1 Native Hawaiian or other Pacific Islander, non-Hispanic/ Latino; 5 Two or more races, non-Hispanic/Latino). Average age 36. 223 applicants, 100% accepted, 199 enrolled. In 2018, 211 master's awarded. *Degree requirements:* For master's, thesis or alternative. *Entrance requirements:* For master's, PRAXIS II or GRE with minimum score of 290 on the verbal and quantitative components (for MAT), minimum GPA of 3.0 in major, 2.5 overall. Additional exam requirements/ recommendations for international students: Recommended—TOEFL (minimum score 79 iBT), IELTS (minimum score 6.5), TSE (minimum score 53). *Application deadline:* For fall admission, 7/15 priority date for domestic students. Applications are processed on a rolling basis. Application fee: $50. *Expenses: Tuition:* Full-time $9036; part-time $502 per credit hour. *Required fees:* $900; $25 per credit hour. $300 per semester. One-time fee: $150. *Financial support:* Federal Work-Study and unspecified assistantships available. Financial award applicants required to submit FAFSA. *Unit head:* Dr. Kim Hawkins, Chair, 865-471-3314, E-mail: khawkins@cn.edu. *Application contact:* Nilma Stewart, Graduate Admissions and Services Adviser, 865-471-3230, Fax: 865-471-3875, E-mail: adults@cn.edu.
Website: http://www.cn.edu/adult-graduate-studies

Central Michigan University, College of Graduate Studies, College of Liberal Arts and Social Sciences, Department of English Language and Literature, Mount Pleasant, MI 48859. Offers English composition and communication (MA); English language and literature (MA), including children's and young adult literature, creative writing, English language and literature; TESOL: teaching English to speakers of other languages (MA). *Program availability:* Part-time, evening/weekend. *Degree requirements:* For master's, thesis or alternative. Electronic applications accepted. *Faculty research:* Composition theory, science fiction history and bibliography, children's and young adult literature, nineteenth century American literature, applied linguistics.

Central Washington University, School of Graduate Studies and Research, College of Arts and Humanities, Department of English, Ellensburg, WA 98926. Offers literature (MA); professional and creative writing (MA); teaching English to speakers of other languages (MA). *Program availability:* Part-time. *Entrance requirements:* For master's, GRE General Test, minimum GPA of 3.0, writing sample. Additional exam requirements/ recommendations for international students: Required—TOEFL (minimum score 550 paper-based; 79 iBT) or IELTS (minimum score 6.5). Electronic applications accepted.

City College of the City University of New York, Graduate School, School of Education, Department of Teaching, Learning and Culture, New York, NY 10031-9198. Offers bilingual education (MS); childhood education (MS); early childhood education (MS); educational theatre (MS); literacy (MS); TESOL (MS). *Accreditation:* NCATE. *Degree requirements:* For master's, thesis. *Entrance requirements:* For master's, Liberal Arts and Sciences Test (LAST), Content Specialty Test (CST). Additional exam requirements/recommendations for international students: Required—TOEFL.

Cleveland State University, College of Graduate Studies, College of Education and Human Services, Department of Teacher Education, Cleveland, OH 44115. Offers art education (M Ed); early childhood education (M Ed); foreign language education (M Ed); middle childhood mathematics and science education (M Ed); special education (M Ed), including mild/moderate disabilities, moderate/intensive disabilities; teaching English to speakers of other languages (M Ed). *Program availability:* Part-time, evening/weekend. *Faculty:* 19 full-time (14 women), 32 part-time/adjunct (27 women). *Students:* 56 full-time (40 women), 344 part-time (278 women); includes 104 minority (74 Black or African American, non-Hispanic/Latino; 1 American Indian or Alaska Native, non-Hispanic/ Latino; 5 Asian, non-Hispanic/Latino; 9 Hispanic/Latino; 15 Two or more races, non-Hispanic/Latino), 14 international. Average age 34. 177 applicants, 55% accepted, 68 enrolled. In 2018, 117 master's awarded. *Degree requirements:* For master's, comprehensive exam (for some programs), thesis or alternative. *Entrance requirements:* For master's, GRE General Test or MAT, minimum GPA of 2.75. Additional exam requirements/recommendations for international students: Required—TOEFL (minimum score 550 paper-based; 78 iBT), IELTS (minimum score 6). *Application deadline:* For fall admission, 7/1 priority date for domestic students, 5/15 for international students; for spring admission, 11/15 for domestic students, 11/1 for international students; for summer admission, 4/1 for domestic students, 3/15 for international students. Applications are processed on a rolling basis. Application fee: $30. *Expenses:* Tuition, state resident: full-time $7232.55; part-time $6676 per credit hour. Tuition, nonresident: full-time $12,375. *International tuition:* $18,914 full-time. *Required fees:* $80; $80 $40. Tuition and fees vary according to program. *Financial support:* In 2018–19, 13 research assistantships with full tuition reimbursements (averaging $15,845 per year) were awarded; tuition waivers (partial) and unspecified assistantships also available. Financial award application deadline: 2/15; financial award applicants required to submit FAFSA. *Faculty research:* Early childhood education, literacy education, special education: mild/moderate, moderate/intensive, early childhood intervention specialist; teaching English to speakers of other languages (TESOL). *Total annual research expenditures:* $275,907. *Unit head:* Dr. Tachelle Banks, Department Chairperson, 216-687-4600, Fax: 216-687-5379, E-mail: t.i.banks@csuohio.edu. *Application contact:* Rosalyn Adams, Administrative Coordinator, 216-523-7139, Fax: 216-687-5491, E-mail: r.m.adams@csuohio.edu.
Website: http://www.csuohio.edu/cehs/te/te

Coastal Carolina University, Spadoni College of Education, Conway, SC 29528-6054. Offers education (MAT); educational leadership (M Ed, Ed S); English for speakers of other languages (Certificate); instructional technology (M Ed, Ed S); language, literacy and culture (M Ed); learning and teaching (M Ed); online teaching and training (Certificate); special education (M Ed). *Accreditation:* NCATE. *Program availability:* Part-time, evening/weekend, 100% online, blended/hybrid learning. *Degree requirements:* For master's and other advanced degree, comprehensive exam. *Entrance requirements:*

For master's, GRE, GMAT, 2 letters of recommendation, evidence of teacher certification, official transcripts; for other advanced degree, official transcripts, 3 letters of reference, master's degree in related field with minimum overall cumulative GPA of 3.0. Additional exam requirements/recommendations for international students: Required—TOEFL (minimum score 550 paper-based; 79 iBT), IELTS (minimum score 6.5). Electronic applications accepted.

College of Charleston, Graduate School, School of Education, Health, and Human Performance, Program in English to Speakers of Other Languages, Charleston, SC 29424-0001. Offers Certificate. *Program availability:* Part-time, online learning. *Entrance requirements:* Additional exam requirements/recommendations for international students: Required—TOEFL (minimum score 81 iBT). Electronic applications accepted.

College of Mount Saint Vincent, School of Professional and Graduate Studies, Department of Teacher Education, Riverdale, NY 10471-1093. Offers instructional technology and global perspectives (Certificate); middle level education (Certificate); multicultural studies (Certificate); teaching English to speakers of other languages (MS Ed); urban and multicultural education (MS Ed). *Accreditation:* TEAC. *Program availability:* Part-time. *Degree requirements:* For master's, comprehensive exam. *Entrance requirements:* For master's, interview, New York teaching certificate. Additional exam requirements/recommendations for international students: Required—TOEFL.

The College of New Jersey, Office of Graduate and Advancing Education, School of Education, Department of Special Education, Language and Literacy, Program in Teaching English as a Second Language, Ewing, NJ 08628. Offers English as a second language (M Ed); teaching English as a second language (Certificate). *Accreditation:* NCATE. *Program availability:* Part-time. *Degree requirements:* For master's, comprehensive exam. *Entrance requirements:* For master's, GRE General Test, minimum GPA of 3.0 in field or 2.75 overall. Additional exam requirements/recommendations for international students: Required—TOEFL. Electronic applications accepted.

The College of New Rochelle, Graduate School, Division of Education, Program in Multilingual/Multicultural Education, New Rochelle, NY 10805-2308. Offers bilingual education (Certificate); multilingual/multicultural education (Certificate); teaching English to speakers of other languages (MS Ed, Certificate). *Program availability:* Part-time, evening/weekend. *Degree requirements:* For master's, student teaching or practicum. *Entrance requirements:* For master's, interview, minimum GPA of 3.0 in field, 2.7 overall.

College of Saint Elizabeth, Program in Education, Morristown, NJ 07960-6989. Offers assistive technology (Certificate); education (MA); ESL (Certificate); Holocaust/genocide education (Certificate); middle school science (Certificate); online teaching in the 21st century (Certificate); teaching (Certificate), including K-12, K-6, teacher of students with disabilities. *Program availability:* Part-time. *Degree requirements:* For master's and Certificate, thesis. *Entrance requirements:* For master's, certification. Additional exam requirements/recommendations for international students: Required—TOEFL (minimum score 550 paper-based; 79 iBT), IELTS (minimum score 6.5). Electronic applications accepted. Application fee is waived when completed online.

College of Saint Mary, Program in Education, Omaha, NE 68106. Offers assessment leadership (MSE); English as a second language (MSE). *Program availability:* Part-time. *Entrance requirements:* For master's, technology competency test or equivalent, minimum cumulative GPA of 3.0, teaching certificate, 2 letters of reference, resume.

College of Staten Island of the City University of New York, Graduate Programs, School of Education, Program in Teaching of English to Speakers of Other Languages, Staten Island, NY 10314-6600. Offers MS Ed, Advanced Certificate. *Program availability:* Part-time, evening/weekend. *Faculty:* 4. *Students:* 75. 32 applicants, 78% accepted, 23 enrolled. In 2018, 20 master's, 5 Advanced Certificates awarded. *Degree requirements:* For master's, comprehensive exam, fieldwork; twelve three-credit courses (36 credits); research project under faculty supervision; for Advanced Certificate, seven three-credit courses (21 credits). *Entrance requirements:* For master's, baccalaureate degree in liberal arts and sciences major or 36 approved credits in liberal arts and sciences, one year of college level foreign language, overall GPA at or above 3.0, two letters of recommendation, one- or two- page personal statement. International students must have full command of academic English at the graduate level.; for Advanced Certificate, courses required for New York State initial certificate in early childhood, childhood or adolescence education or its equivalent from another state; baccalaureate degree in a liberal arts and sciences major, or 36 credits in a liberal arts and sciences concentration, with minimum overall GPA of 3.0. Additional exam requirements/recommendations for international students: Required—TOEFL (minimum score 550 paper-based; 79 iBT), IELTS (minimum score 6.5). *Application deadline:* For fall admission, 4/25 for domestic and international students; for spring admission, 11/25 for domestic and international students. Applications are processed on a rolling basis. Application fee: $75. Electronic applications accepted. *Expenses: Tuition, area resident:* Full-time $10,770; part-time $455 per credit. Tuition, state resident: full-time $10,770; part-time $455 per credit. Tuition, nonresident: full-time $19,920; part-time $830 per credit. *International tuition:* $19,920 full-time. *Required fees:* $559.20; $181.10 per semester. Tuition and fees vary according to program. *Faculty research:* Application of critical pedagogies focusing on intersections of race, class, culture, and gender in first and second language literacies; urban education; second language acquisition in secondary education; cross-linguistic predictors in reading comprehension; students with interrupted or inconsistent formal education (SIFE). *Unit head:* Dr. Rachel Grant, Graduate Faculty Advisor, 718-982-3740, E-mail: rachel.grant@csi.cuny.edu. *Application contact:* Sasha Spence, Associate Director for Graduate Admissions, 718-982-2019, Fax: 718-982-2500, E-mail: sasha.spence@csi.cuny.edu.
Website: https://www.csi.cuny.edu/sites/default/files/pdf/admissions/grad/pdf/TESOL%20Advanced%20Certificate%20Fact%20Sheet.pdf

Colorado Mesa University, Center for Teacher Education, Grand Junction, CO 81501-3122. Offers educational leadership (MAEd); English for speakers of other languages (MAEd); exceptional learner/special education (MAEd); teacher education (Graduate Certificate); teacher leader (MAEd). *Accreditation:* NCATE. *Program availability:* Part-time. *Degree requirements:* For master's, comprehensive exam (for some programs), capstone presentation. *Entrance requirements:* For master's, 3 professional letters of recommendation, Colorado teaching license, minimum baccalaureate GPA of 3.0; for Graduate Certificate, minimum baccalaureate GPA of 3.0. Additional exam requirements/recommendations for international students: Required—TOEFL (minimum score 550 paper-based). Electronic applications accepted. *Expenses:* Contact institution. *Faculty research:* K-8 STEM instruction, special education inclusion, elementary math literacy, secondary literacy, elementary/early childhood education literacy.

Columbia International University, Columbia Graduate School, Columbia, SC 29203. Offers Bible teaching (MABT); counseling (MACN); early childhood and elementary education (MAT); educational administration (M Ed); educational leadership (PhD); instruction and learning (M Ed); teaching English as a foreign language (Certificate); teaching English as a foreign language and intercultural studies (MATF). *Program availability:* Part-time, evening/weekend, online learning. *Degree requirements:* For master's, internships, professional project. *Entrance requirements:* For master's, MAT; GRE (for some programs), minimum GPA of 2.7. Additional exam requirements/recommendations for international students: Required—TOEFL. Electronic applications accepted.

Columbus State University, Graduate Studies, College of Letters and Sciences, Program in Teaching English to Speakers of Other Languages, Columbus, GA 31907-5645. Offers teaching English to speakers of other languages (Certificate). *Program availability:* Part-time, evening/weekend, blended/hybrid learning. *Faculty:* 3 full-time (0 women). *Students:* 1 applicant, 100% accepted. In 2018, 2 Certificates awarded. *Entrance requirements:* Additional exam requirements/recommendations for international students: Required—TOEFL (minimum score 550 paper-based; 79 iBT). *Application deadline:* For fall admission, 6/30 for domestic and international students; for spring admission, 11/1 for domestic and international students; for summer admission, 5/1 for domestic and international students. Applications are processed on a rolling basis. Application fee: $50. Electronic applications accepted. *Expenses: Tuition, area resident:* Full-time $4924; part-time $618 per credit hour. Tuition, state resident: full-time $4924; part-time $618 per credit hour. Tuition, nonresident: full-time $19,218; part-time $2403 per credit hour. *International tuition:* $19,218 full-time. *Required fees:* $1870; $802. Tuition and fees vary according to course load, degree level and program. *Financial support:* Application deadline: 5/1; applicants required to submit FAFSA. *Unit head:* Dr. Dennis Rome, Dean, 706-568-2056, E-mail: rome_dennis@columbusstate.edu. *Application contact:* Catrina Smith-Edmond, Assistant Director for Graduate and Global Admission, 706-507-8824, Fax: 706-568-5091, E-mail: smithedmond_catrina@columbusstate.edu.

Concordia University, College of Arts and Sciences, Portland, OR 97211-6099. Offers community psychology (MA); teaching English to speakers of other languages (MA).

Concordia University, College of Education, Portland, OR 97211-6099. Offers administrative leadership (Ed D); career and technical education (M Ed); curriculum and instruction (M Ed), including adolescent literacy, early childhood education, educational technology leadership, English for speakers of other languages, environmental education, health and physical education, mathematics, methods and curriculum, reading interventionist, science, social studies, STEAM education, teacher leadership, the inclusive classroom, trauma and resilience in educational settings; educational administration (M Ed); educational leadership (M Ed); elementary education (MAT); higher education (Ed D); instructional leadership (Ed D); professional leadership, inquiry, and transformation (Ed D); secondary education (MAT); transformational leadership (Ed D). *Program availability:* Part-time, online learning. *Degree requirements:* For master's, comprehensive exam, work samples/portfolio. *Entrance requirements:* For master's, California Basic Educational Skills Test or PRAXIS I, minimum undergraduate GPA of 2.8, graduate 3.0; 2 letters of recommendation. Additional exam requirements/recommendations for international students: Required—TOEFL (minimum score 525 paper-based). Electronic applications accepted. *Faculty research:* Learner-centered classroom, brain-based learning, future of online learning.

Concordia University, School of Graduate Studies, Faculty of Arts and Science, Department of Education, Program in Applied Linguistics, Montréal, QC H3G 1M8, Canada. Offers applied linguistics (MA); teaching English as a second language (Certificate).

Cornerstone University, Graduate Programs, Grand Rapids, MI 49525-5897. Offers business administration (MBA); education (MA Ed); management (MSM); teaching English to speakers of other languages (MA, Graduate Certificate). Programs also offered at Holland, Kalamazoo, and Troy, MI campuses. *Program availability:* Part-time, online learning. *Degree requirements:* For master's, comprehensive exam (for some programs), thesis (for some programs). *Entrance requirements:* For master's, minimum GPA of 2.5, 2 letters of reference. Additional exam requirements/recommendations for international students: Required—TOEFL (minimum score 575 paper-based). Electronic applications accepted.

Dallas Baptist University, Dorothy M. Bush College of Education, Program in Bilingual Education, Dallas, TX 75211-9299. Offers bilingual education (M Ed), including dual language, English as a second language/multilingual. *Program availability:* Part-time, evening/weekend. *Application deadline:* Applications are processed on a rolling basis. Application fee: $25. Electronic applications accepted. Application fee is waived when completed online. *Expenses: Tuition:* Full-time $17,262; part-time $959 per credit hour. *Required fees:* $1000; $500 per semester. Tuition and fees vary according to course load and degree level. *Unit head:* Dr. Neil Dugger, Dean, 214-333-5202, E-mail: neil@dbu.edu. *Application contact:* Dr. Adelita Baker, Program Director, 214-333-5515, E-mail: adelita@dbu.edu.
Website: https://www.dbu.edu/graduate/degree-programs/med-bilingual-education

Dallas Baptist University, Dorothy M. Bush College of Education, Program in Curriculum and Instruction, Dallas, TX 75211-9299. Offers Christian school administration (M Ed); distance learning (M Ed); English as a second language (M Ed); instructional technology (M Ed); professional life coaching (M Ed); special education (M Ed); supervision (M Ed). *Program availability:* Part-time, evening/weekend, online learning. *Application deadline:* Applications are processed on a rolling basis. Application fee: $25. Electronic applications accepted. Application fee is waived when completed online. *Expenses: Tuition:* Full-time $17,262; part-time $959 per credit hour. *Required fees:* $1000; $500 per semester. Tuition and fees vary according to course load and degree level. *Unit head:* Dr. Neil Dugger, Dean, 214-333-5202, E-mail: neil@dbu.edu. *Application contact:* Karla Hagan, Program Director, 214-333-5831, E-mail: karla@dbu.edu.
Website: http://www3.dbu.edu/graduate/curriculum_instruction.asp

Dallas Baptist University, Dorothy M. Bush College of Education, Program in Reading and English as a Second Language, Dallas, TX 75211-9299. Offers bilingual education (M Ed); reading and English as a second language (M Ed). *Program availability:* Part-time, evening/weekend. *Application deadline:* Applications are processed on a rolling basis. Application fee: $25. Electronic applications accepted. Application fee is waived when completed online. *Expenses: Tuition:* Full-time $17,262; part-time $959 per credit hour. *Required fees:* $1000; $500 per semester. Tuition and fees vary according to course load and degree level. *Unit head:* Dr. Neil Dugger, Dean, 214-333-5202, E-mail: neil@dbu.edu. *Application contact:* Dr. Adelita Baker, Program Director, 214-333-5515, E-mail: adelita@dbu.edu.
Website: https://www.dbu.edu/graduate/degree-programs/med-reading-esl

Dallas Baptist University, Dorothy M. Bush College of Education, Teaching Program, Dallas, TX 75211-9299. Offers distance learning (MAT); early childhood through grade 6 certification (MAT); early childhood-12 (MAT); elementary (MAT); English as a second language (MAT); Montessori (MAT); multisensory (MAT); secondary (MAT). *Program availability:* Part-time, evening/weekend, 100% online, blended/hybrid learning. *Application deadline:* Applications are processed on a rolling basis. Application fee: $25. Electronic applications accepted. Application fee is waived when completed online. *Expenses: Tuition:* Full-time $17,262; part-time $959 per credit hour. *Required fees:* $1000; $500 per semester. Tuition and fees vary according to course load and degree level. *Unit head:* Dr. Neil Dugger, Dean, 214-333-5202, E-mail: neil@dbu.edu. *Application contact:* Dr. DeAnna Jenkins, Program Director, 214-333-5402, E-mail: deannaj@dbu.edu.
Website: https://www.dbu.edu/graduate/degree-programs/ma-teaching

Dallas Baptist University, Graduate School of Ministry, Program in Global Leadership, Dallas, TX 75211-9299. Offers church planting (MA); East Asian Studies (MA); English as a second language (MA); general studies (MA); global communication (MA); global studies (MA); international business (MA); leading the nonprofit organization (MA); missions (MA); small group ministry (MA); urban ministry (MA). *Program availability:* Part-time, evening/weekend, online learning. *Application deadline:* Applications are processed on a rolling basis. Application fee: $25. Electronic applications accepted. Application fee is waived when completed online. *Expenses: Tuition:* Full-time $17,262; part-time $959 per credit hour. *Required fees:* $1000; $500 per semester. Tuition and fees vary according to course load and degree level. *Unit head:* Dr. Robert R. Brooks, Dean, 214-333-5494, Fax: 214-333-5673, E-mail: bobb@dbu.edu. *Application contact:* Dr. Brent Thomason, Program Director, 214-333-5236, E-mail: brentt@dbu.edu. Website: http://www.dbu.edu/ministry/degree-programs/m-a-in-global-leadership

Dallas Baptist University, Liberal Arts Program, Dallas, TX 75211-9299. Offers art (MLA); Christian studies (MLA); commercial art (MLA); East Asian studies (MLA); English (MLA); English as a second language (MLA); history (MLA); missions (MLA); political science (MLA). *Program availability:* Part-time, evening/weekend, online learning. *Application deadline:* Applications are processed on a rolling basis. Application fee: $25. Electronic applications accepted. Application fee is waived when completed online. *Expenses: Tuition:* Full-time $17,262; part-time $959 per credit hour. *Required fees:* $1000; $500 per semester. Tuition and fees vary according to course load and degree level. *Unit head:* Jared Ingram, Director, 214-333-5584, E-mail: jaredi@dbu.edu. *Application contact:* Jared Ingram, Director, 214-333-5584, E-mail: jaredi@dbu.edu. Website: https://www.dbu.edu/graduate/degree-programs/mla

Dallas Baptist University, Professional Development Program, Dallas, TX 75211-9299. Offers accounting (MA); church leadership (MA); communication (MA); counseling (MA); criminal justice (MA); English as a second language (MA); finance (MA); higher education (MA); leadership studies (MA); management (MA). *Program availability:* Part-time, evening/weekend, online learning. *Application deadline:* Applications are processed on a rolling basis. Application fee: $25. Electronic applications accepted. Application fee is waived when completed online. *Expenses: Tuition:* Full-time $17,262; part-time $959 per credit hour. *Required fees:* $1000; $500 per semester. Tuition and fees vary according to course load and degree level. *Unit head:* Jared Ingram, Program Director, 214-333-5584, E-mail: jaredi@dbu.edu. *Application contact:* Jared Ingram, Program Director, 214-333-5584, E-mail: jaredi@dbu.edu. Website: https://www.dbu.edu/graduate/degree-programs/ma-professional-development

DeSales University, Division of Liberal Arts and Social Sciences, Center Valley, PA 18034-9568. Offers criminal justice (MCJ); digital forensics (MCJ, Postbaccalaureate Certificate); education (M Ed), including instructional technology, secondary education, special education, teaching English to speakers of other languages; investigative forensics (MCJ, Postbaccalaureate Certificate). *Program availability:* Part-time, 100% online, blended/hybrid learning. *Entrance requirements:* For master's, bachelor's degree from accredited institution, minimum undergraduate GPA of 3.0, personal statement showing potential of graduate work, three letters of recommendation, professional goal statement. Additional exam requirements/recommendations for international students: Required—TOEFL. Electronic applications accepted.

Dominican University, School of Education, River Forest, IL 60305-1099. Offers child life studies (MS); early childhood education (MS); education (MAT); elementary education (MA Ed); English as a second language (MA Ed); reading (MA Ed); secondary education (MAT); special education (MS). *Accreditation:* NCATE. *Program availability:* Part-time, evening/weekend, 100% online, blended/hybrid learning. *Entrance requirements:* For master's, Illinois Test of Basic Skills. Additional exam requirements/recommendations for international students: Required—TOEFL (minimum score 550 paper-based; 79 iBT). *Expenses:* Contact institution. *Faculty research:* Governance of private education institutions, reading and language arts, inclusion, organizational planning, leadership and vision.

Duquesne University, School of Education, Department of Instruction and Leadership, Program in English as a Second Language, Pittsburgh, PA 15282-0001. Offers MS Ed. *Program availability:* Part-time, evening/weekend. *Faculty:* 4 full-time (2 women). *Students:* 18 full-time (14 women); includes 6 minority (2 Black or African American, non-Hispanic/Latino; 1 Asian, non-Hispanic/Latino; 2 Hispanic/Latino; 1 Two or more races, non-Hispanic/Latino), 8 international. Average age 29. 32 applicants, 97% accepted, 6 enrolled. In 2018, 6 master's awarded. *Entrance requirements:* For master's, bachelor's degree. Additional exam requirements/recommendations for international students: Required—TOEFL (minimum score 550 paper-based), IELTS (minimum score 7). *Application deadline:* For fall admission, 9/1 for domestic students; for spring admission, 1/1 for domestic students. Applications are processed on a rolling basis. Application fee: $0. Electronic applications accepted. *Expenses: Tuition:* Full-time $23,112; part-time $1284 per credit. Tuition and fees vary according to program. *Financial support:* In 2018–19, 1 student received support, including 1 teaching assistantship with partial tuition reimbursement available (averaging $3,693 per year). Financial award applicants required to submit FAFSA. *Faculty research:* Bilingual language acquisition; social factors that affect language acquisition; teaching and interaction with English language learners in electronic classrooms; identity and motivation in second language acquisition; second-language teacher education with focus on teacher identity, beliefs, and dispositions. *Total annual research expenditures:* $1,103. *Unit head:* Dr. Laura Mahalingappa, Associate Professor and Director, 412-396-6111, Fax: 412-396-1997, E-mail: mahalingappa1@duq.edu. *Application contact:* Kelly McGinley, Graduate Admissions Assistant, 412-396-1559, Fax: 412-396-5585, E-mail: mcginleyk@duq.edu. Website: http://wwwtest.duq.edu/academics/schools/education/graduate-programs-education/english-second-language

East Carolina University, Graduate School, Thomas Harriot College of Arts and Sciences, Department of English, Greenville, NC 27858-4353. Offers creative writing (MA); English studies (MA); linguistics (MA); literature (MA); multicultural and transnational literatures (MA, Certificate); professional communication (Certificate); rhetoric and composition (MA); rhetoric, writing, and professional communication (PhD); teaching English in the two-year college (Certificate); teaching English to speakers of other languages (MA, Certificate); technical and professional communication (MA). *Program availability:* Part-time, evening/weekend, online learning. *Application deadline:* For fall admission, 7/31 priority date for domestic students, 2/1 priority date for international students; for spring admission, 11/30 priority date for domestic students, 10/1 priority date for international students. *Expenses: Tuition, area resident:* Full-time $4749. Tuition, state resident: full-time $4749. Tuition, nonresident: full-time $17,898. *International tuition:* $17,898 full-time. *Required fees:* $2787. Part-time tuition and fees vary according to course load and program. *Financial support:* Application deadline: 3/1. *Unit head:* Dr. Marianne Montgomery, Chair, 252-328-6041, E-mail: montgomerym@ecu.edu. *Application contact:* Graduate School Admissions, 252-328-6012, Fax: 252-328-6071, E-mail: gradschool@ecu.edu. Website: http://www.ecu.edu/cs-cas/engl/

Eastern Michigan University, Graduate School, College of Arts and Sciences, Department of World Languages, Program in Teaching English to Speakers of Other Languages, Ypsilanti, MI 48197. Offers MA, Graduate Certificate. *Program availability:* Part-time, evening/weekend, online learning. *Students:* 5 full-time (all women), 66 part-time (56 women); includes 15 minority (3 Black or African American, non-Hispanic/Latino; 3 Asian, non-Hispanic/Latino; 6 Hispanic/Latino; 3 Two or more races, non-Hispanic/Latino), 9 international. Average age 36. 26 applicants, 85% accepted, 9 enrolled. In 2018, 15 master's, 3 other advanced degrees awarded. *Entrance requirements:* Additional exam requirements/recommendations for international students: Required—TOEFL. *Application deadline:* Applications are processed on a rolling basis. Application fee: $45. *Financial support:* Fellowships, research assistantships with full tuition reimbursements, teaching assistantships with full tuition reimbursements, career-related internships or fieldwork, Federal Work-Study, institutionally sponsored loans, scholarships/grants, tuition waivers (partial), and unspecified assistantships available. Support available to part-time students. Financial award applicants required to submit FAFSA. *Application contact:* Dr. Ildiko Porter-Szucs, Program Advisor, 734-487-6487, Fax: 734-487-3411, E-mail: jporters@emich.edu.

Eastern Nazarene College, Adult and Graduate Studies, Division of Teacher Education, Quincy, MA 02170. Offers administration (M Ed); early childhood education (M Ed, Certificate); elementary education (M Ed, Certificate); English as a second language (Certificate); instructional enrichment and development (Certificate); middle school education (M Ed, Certificate); moderate special needs education (Certificate); principal (Certificate); program development and supervision (Certificate); secondary education (M Ed, Certificate); special education administrator (Certificate); special needs (M Ed); supervisor (Certificate); teacher of reading (M Ed, Certificate). M Ed also available through weekend program for administration, special needs, and teacher of reading only. *Program availability:* Part-time, evening/weekend. *Entrance requirements:* Additional exam requirements/recommendations for international students: Required—TOEFL (minimum score 550 paper-based).

Eastern New Mexico University, Graduate School, College of Education and Technology, Department of Curriculum and Instruction, Portales, NM 88130. Offers alternative licensure in elementary education (M Ed); bilingual education (M Ed); career and technical education (M Ed); educational technology (M Ed); elementary education (M Ed); English as a second language (M Ed); pedagogy and learning (M Ed); reading/literacy (M Ed). *Program availability:* Part-time, online learning. *Degree requirements:* For master's, comprehensive exam, thesis optional. *Entrance requirements:* For master's, writing assessment, minimum GPA of 3.0, photocopy of teaching license, letter of recommendation. Additional exam requirements/recommendations for international students: Required—TOEFL (minimum score 550 paper-based; 79 iBT), IELTS (minimum score 6). Electronic applications accepted. *Expenses: Tuition, area resident:* Full-time $6776. Tuition, state resident: full-time $6776; part-time $282 per credit hour. Tuition, nonresident: full-time $8986; part-time $374 per credit hour. *Required fees:* $60 per semester. One-time fee: $25.

Eastern University, Graduate Education Programs, St. Davids, PA 19087-3696. Offers ESL program specialist (K-12) (Certificate); general supervisor (PreK-12) (Certificate); health and physical education (K-12) (Certificate); middle level (4-8) (Certificate); multicultural education (M Ed); music (K-12) (Certificate); Pre K-4 (Certificate); Pre K-4 with special education (Certificate); reading (M Ed); reading specialist (K-12) (Certificate); reading supervisor (K-12) (Certificate); school counseling (MA, CAGS); school principalship (preK-12) (Certificate); school psychology (MS, CAGS); secondary biology education (7-12) (Certificate); secondary chemistry education (7-12) (Certificate); secondary communication education (7-12) (Certificate); secondary English education (7-12) (Certificate); secondary math education (7-12) (Certificate); secondary social studies education (7-12) (Certificate); special education (M Ed); special education (7-12) (Certificate); special education (Pre K-8) (Certificate); special education supervisor (K-12) (Certificate); TESOL (M Ed); world language (Certificate), including Spanish. *Program availability:* Part-time, evening/weekend, online learning. *Entrance requirements:* Additional exam requirements/recommendations for international students: Required—TOEFL. Electronic applications accepted. Application fee is waived when completed online. *Expenses:* Contact institution.

Eastern Washington University, Graduate Studies, College of Arts, Letters and Education, Department of English, Cheney, WA 99004-2431. Offers literature (MA); rhetoric, composition, and technical communication (MA); teaching English as a second language (MA). *Degree requirements:* For master's, comprehensive exam, thesis or alternative. *Entrance requirements:* For master's, GRE General Test, minimum GPA of 3.0. Additional exam requirements/recommendations for international students: Required—TOEFL (minimum score 580 paper-based; 92 iBT), IELTS (minimum score 7), PTE (minimum score 6).

East Tennessee State University, School of Graduate Studies, College of Arts and Sciences, Department of Literature and Language, Johnson City, TN 37614. Offers healthcare translation and interpreting (Postbaccalaureate Certificate); literature (MA); teaching English to speakers of other languages (Postbaccalaureate Certificate). *Program availability:* Part-time, evening/weekend. *Degree requirements:* For master's, comprehensive exam, thesis optional; for Postbaccalaureate Certificate, one foreign language. *Entrance requirements:* For master's, GRE General Test, minimum undergraduate GPA of 3.0 in English, writing sample, three letters of recommendation; for Postbaccalaureate Certificate, GRE General Test, speaking and listening assessment, resume, three letters of recommendation, two years of coursework or basic proficiency in a foreign language. Additional exam requirements/recommendations for international students: Required—TOEFL (minimum score 550 paper-based; 79 iBT). Electronic applications accepted. *Faculty research:* Linguistics and dialectology, English education, critical literary theory, literary biography, environmental literature, modern and ancient languages.

Elms College, Division of Education, Chicopee, MA 01013-2839. Offers early childhood education (MAT); education (M Ed, CAGS); elementary education (MAT); English as a second language (MAT); reading (MAT); secondary education (MAT), including biology education, English education, Spanish education; special education (MAT). *Program availability:* Part-time, evening/weekend. *Faculty:* 5 full-time (all women), 6 part-time/adjunct (5 women). *Students:* 3 full-time (all women), 117 part-time (94 women); includes 12 minority (1 Black or African American, non-Hispanic/Latino; 2 Asian, non-Hispanic/Latino; 9 Hispanic/Latino). Average age 34. 27 applicants, 96% accepted, 23 enrolled. In 2018, 34 master's, 3 other advanced degrees awarded. *Degree requirements:* For master's, thesis (for some programs). *Entrance requirements:* For master's, Massachusetts Educators Certification Test, minimum GPA of 3.0; for CAGS, master's degree in education. Additional exam requirements/recommendations for international students: Required—TOEFL. *Application deadline:* For fall admission, 7/1 priority date for domestic students; for spring admission, 11/1 priority date for domestic students. Applications are processed on a rolling basis. Application fee: $30. *Expenses: Tuition:* Full-time $14,328; part-time $796 per credit. *Required fees:* $200. Tuition and fees vary according to degree level and program. *Financial support:* In 2018–19, 2 teaching assistantships with partial tuition reimbursements were awarded. Financial award applicants required to submit FAFSA. *Unit head:* Dr. Mary Janeczek, Chair, Division of Education, 413-594-2761, Fax: 413-592-4871, E-mail: janeczeke@elms.edu. *Application contact:* Nancy Davis, Director, Office of Graduate and Continuing Education Admissions, 413-265-2239, E-mail: davisn@elms.edu.

English as a Second Language

Emporia State University, Program in Teaching English to Speakers of Other Languages, Emporia, KS 66801-5415. Offers TESOL (Certificate). *Program availability:* Part-time. *Degree requirements:* For master's, comprehensive exam, thesis optional. *Entrance requirements:* For master's, minimum undergraduate GPA of 2.75 over last 60 hours. Additional exam requirements/recommendations for international students: Required—TOEFL (minimum score 520 paper-based; 68 iBT). Electronic applications accepted.

Erikson Institute, Academic Programs, Chicago, IL 60654. Offers administration (Certificate); bilingual/ESL (Certificate); child development (MS); early childhood education (MS); infant mental health (Certificate); infant studies (Certificate); social work (MSW); MS/MSW. MS/MSW offered jointly with Loyola University Chicago. *Program availability:* Part-time, evening/weekend. *Degree requirements:* For master's, comprehensive exam, internship; for Certificate, internship. *Entrance requirements:* For master's and Certificate, minimum GPA of 2.75. Additional exam requirements/recommendations for international students: Required—TOEFL. *Faculty research:* Assessment strategies from early childhood through elementary years; language, literacy, and the arts in children's development; inclusive special education; parent-child relationships; cognitive development.

Fairfield University, Graduate School of Education and Allied Professions, Fairfield, CT 06824. Offers applied behavior analysis (ATC); applied psychology (MA); clinical mental health counseling (MA, CAS); educational technology (MA); elementary education (MA, CAS); family studies (MA); integration of spirituality and religion in counseling (ATC); marriage and family therapy (MA); reading and language development (Sixth Year Certificate); school counseling (MA, CAS); school psychology (MA, CAS); school-based marriage and family therapy (ATC); secondary education (MA); special education (MA, CAS); substance abuse counseling (ATC); teaching (Certificate); teaching and foundations (MA, CAS); TESOL, world languages, and bilingual education (MA, CAS). *Accreditation:* NCATE. *Program availability:* Part-time, evening/weekend. *Degree requirements:* For master's, comprehensive exam. *Entrance requirements:* For master's, minimum GPA of 3.0, 2 recommendations, resume. Additional exam requirements/recommendations for international students: Required—TOEFL (minimum score 550 paper-based; 84 iBT) or IELTS (minimum score 7.5). Electronic applications accepted. *Expenses:* Contact institution. *Faculty research:* Reading and literacy, writing, social justice and inequality in education, addictions and mental health issues, therapeutic relationships and clinical supervision.

Florida Atlantic University, College of Education, Department of Curriculum, Culture, and Educational Inquiry, Boca Raton, FL 33431-0991. Offers curriculum and instruction (M Ed, PhD, Ed S); early childhood education (M Ed); multicultural education (M Ed); TESOL and bilingual education (MA). *Program availability:* Part-time, evening/weekend. *Faculty:* 10 full-time (8 women), 2 part-time/adjunct (both women). *Students:* 15 full-time (11 women), 60 part-time (46 women); includes 24 minority (12 Black or African American, non-Hispanic/Latino; 2 Asian, non-Hispanic/Latino; 8 Hispanic/Latino; 2 Two or more races, non-Hispanic/Latino), 2 international. Average age 36. 45 applicants, 62% accepted, 21 enrolled. In 2018, 21 master's, 14 doctorates, 1 other advanced degree awarded. *Entrance requirements:* Additional exam requirements/recommendations for international students: Required—TOEFL (minimum score 500 paper-based; 61 iBT), IELTS (minimum score 6). *Application deadline:* For fall admission, 7/1 for domestic students, 2/15 for international students; for spring admission, 11/1 for domestic students, 7/15 for international students. Application fee: $30. *Expenses: Tuition, area resident:* Full-time $7400; part-time $369.82 per credit. Tuition, state resident: full-time $7400; part-time $369.82 per credit. Tuition, nonresident: full-time $20,496; part-time $1024.81 per credit. *Faculty research:* Multicultural education, early intervention strategies, family literacy, religious diversity in schools, early childhood curriculum. *Unit head:* Dr. Hanizah Zainuddin, Chair, 561-297-6594, E-mail: zainuddi@fau.edu. *Application contact:* Dr. Deborah Shepherd, Associate Dean, 561-297-3570, E-mail: dshep@fau.edu.
Website: http://www.coe.fau.edu/academicdepartments/ccei/

Florida Gulf Coast University, College of Education, Program in Curriculum and Instruction, Fort Myers, FL 33965-6565. Offers elementary education (M Ed); English education (M Ed); English speakers of other languages endorsement (M Ed); gifted education (M Ed); mathematics education (M Ed); middle school education (M Ed); reading education (M Ed); science education (M Ed); social science education (M Ed); special education (M Ed). *Program availability:* Part-time, evening/weekend, online learning. *Degree requirements:* For master's, final project or portfolio. *Entrance requirements:* For master's, GRE General Test, MAT, minimum undergraduate GPA of 3.0 in last 2 years. Additional exam requirements/recommendations for international students: Required—TOEFL (minimum score 550 paper-based). Electronic applications accepted. *Faculty research:* Internet in schools, technology in pre-service and in-service teacher training.

Florida International University, College of Arts, Sciences, and Education, Department of Leadership and Professional Studies, Miami, FL 33199. Offers adult education and human resource development (MS, Ed D); counseling (MS), including rehabilitation counseling, school counseling; counselor education (MS), including clinical mental health counseling; educational administration and supervision (Ed D); educational leadership (MS, Certificate, Ed S); higher education (Ed D); higher education administration (MS); international and comparative education (MS); recreation and sport management (MS), including recreation and sport management, recreational therapy; school psychology (Ed S); urban education (MS), including instruction in urban settings, learning technologies, multicultural/bilingual, multicultural/TESOL, urban education. *Program availability:* Part-time, evening/weekend. *Faculty:* 64 full-time (43 women), 104 part-time/adjunct (76 women). *Students:* 258 full-time (196 women), 217 part-time (155 women); includes 387 minority (118 Black or African American, non-Hispanic/Latino; 8 Asian, non-Hispanic/Latino; 249 Hispanic/Latino; 12 Two or more races, non-Hispanic/Latino), 11 international. Average age 31. 345 applicants, 57% accepted, 126 enrolled. In 2018, 172 master's, 11 doctorates awarded. *Entrance requirements:* For master's, minimum GPA of 3.0; for doctorate and other advanced degree, GRE General Test. Additional exam requirements/recommendations for international students: Required—TOEFL (minimum score 550 paper-based; 80 iBT), IELTS (minimum score 6.3). *Application deadline:* For fall admission, 6/1 priority date for domestic students, 4/1 for international students; for winter admission, 10/1 priority date for domestic students, 9/1 for international students; for spring admission, 3/1 priority date for domestic students, 2/1 for international students. Applications are processed on a rolling basis. Application fee: $30. Electronic applications accepted. *Financial support:* Fellowships, research assistantships, teaching assistantships, Federal Work-Study, and tuition waivers (full and partial) available. Support available to part-time students. Financial award applicants required to submit FAFSA. *Unit head:* Dr. Benjamin Baez, Chair, 305-348-3214, Fax: 305-348-1515, E-mail: benjamin.baez@fiu.edu. *Application contact:* Nanett Rojas, Manager, Admissions Operations, 305-348-7464, Fax: 305-348-7441, E-mail: gradadm@fiu.edu.
Website: http://education.fiu.edu

Florida International University, College of Arts, Sciences, and Education, Department of Teaching and Learning, Miami, FL 33199. Offers art education (MA, MS); curriculum and instruction (MS, Ed D, PhD, Ed S), including curriculum development

(MS), elementary education (MS), English education (MS), learning technologies (MS), mathematics education (MS), modern language education (MS), physical education (MS), science education (MS), social studies education (MS), special education (MS); early childhood education (MS); exceptional student education (Ed D); foreign language education (MS), including foreign language education, teaching English to speakers of other languages (TESOL); language, literacy and culture (PhD); mathematics, science, and learning technologies (PhD); physical education (MS), including sport and fitness; reading education (MS). *Program availability:* Part-time, evening/weekend. *Faculty:* 64 full-time (43 women), 104 part-time/adjunct (76 women). *Students:* 169 full-time (144 women), 155 part-time (130 women); includes 260 minority (53 Black or African American, non-Hispanic/Latino; 7 Asian, non-Hispanic/Latino; 193 Hispanic/Latino; 7 Two or more races, non-Hispanic/Latino), 13 international. Average age 33. 184 applicants, 62% accepted, 87 enrolled. In 2018, 153 master's, 10 doctorates awarded. *Degree requirements:* For doctorate, comprehensive exam, thesis/dissertation. *Entrance requirements:* For master's, GRE General Test, Florida General Knowledge Test or Florida College Level Academic Skills Test; for doctorate and Ed S, GRE General Test. Additional exam requirements/recommendations for international students: Required—TOEFL (minimum score 550 paper-based; 80 iBT), IELTS (minimum score 6.3). *Application deadline:* For fall admission, 6/1 priority date for domestic students, 4/1 for international students; for winter admission, 10/1 priority date for domestic students, 9/1 for international students; for spring admission, 3/1 priority date for domestic students, 2/1 for international students. Applications are processed on a rolling basis. Application fee: $30. Electronic applications accepted. *Financial support:* Research assistantships and teaching assistantships available. *Unit head:* Dr. Maria Fernandez, Chair, 305-348-0193, Fax: 305-348-2086, E-mail: Maria.Fernandez9@fiu.edu. *Application contact:* Nanett Rojas, Manager, Admissions Operations, 305-348-7464, Fax: 305-348-7441, E-mail: gradadm@fiu.edu.
Website: https://tl.fiu.edu/

Florida State University, The Graduate School, College of Education, School of Teacher Education, Tallahassee, FL 32306. Offers curriculum and instruction (MS, PhD, Ed S), including reading and language arts (Ed S); teaching English to speakers of other languages (Certificate). *Program availability:* Part-time, evening/weekend, 100% online, blended/hybrid learning, asynchronous, minimal on-campus study. *Faculty:* 30 full-time (23 women), 8 part-time/adjunct (7 women). *Students:* 90 full-time (66 women), 66 part-time (51 women); includes 56 minority (12 Black or African American, non-Hispanic/Latino; 19 Asian, non-Hispanic/Latino; 15 Hispanic/Latino; 10 Two or more races, non-Hispanic/Latino), 32 international. Average age 32. 146 applicants, 56% accepted, 52 enrolled. In 2018, 50 master's, 15 doctorates, 2 other advanced degrees awarded. Terminal master's awarded for partial completion of doctoral program. *Degree requirements:* For master's and other advanced degree, comprehensive exam, thesis optional; for doctorate, comprehensive exam, thesis/dissertation, diagnostic exam, preliminary exam, prospectus defense, dissertation defense. *Entrance requirements:* For master's, doctorate, and other advanced degree, GRE General Test, minimum upper-division GPA of 3.0. Additional exam requirements/recommendations for international students: Required—TOEFL (minimum score 550 paper-based, 80 iBT), Michigan English Language Assessment Battery (minimum score 77), IELTS (minimum score 6.5) or PTE (minimum score 55). *Application deadline:* For fall admission, 6/17 for domestic students; for spring admission, 10/18 for domestic students; for summer admission, 2/11 for domestic students. Application fee: $30. Electronic applications accepted. *Expenses: Tuition, area resident:* Part-time $479.32 per credit hour. Tuition and fees vary according to campus/location and program. *Financial support:* Fellowships, research assistantships, teaching assistantships, scholarships/grants, tuition waivers (full and partial), and unspecified assistantships available. Financial award application deadline: 1/15; financial award applicants required to submit FAFSA. *Faculty research:* Identifying effective intervention strategies to improve reading skills; improving literacy teaching and learning through technology; understanding of student sense making, problem solving, the history and structure of STEM disciplines, and teacher education to support the development of ambitious instruction that supports the STEM learning of all students; examining practices of international education; identifying ways to support the professional development of teachers. *Unit head:* Dr. Sherry Southerland, Professor/Department Chair, 850-644-6885, Fax: 850-644-2725, E-mail: ssoutherland@admin.fsu.edu. *Application contact:* Britni DeZerga, Academic Program Specialist, 850-644-2122, Fax: 850-644-7736, E-mail: bpurvis@fsu.edu.
Website: http://education.fsu.edu

Fordham University, Graduate School of Education, Division of Curriculum and Teaching, New York, NY 10023. Offers curriculum and teaching (MSE); early childhood education (MSE); elementary education (MST); special education (MSE, Adv C); teaching English as a second language (MSE). *Accreditation:* NCATE. *Program availability:* Part-time, evening/weekend. *Degree requirements:* For Adv C, thesis. *Entrance requirements:* Additional exam requirements/recommendations for international students: Required—TOEFL (minimum score 577 paper-based; 90 iBT), IELTS (minimum score 7). Electronic applications accepted.

Framingham State University, Graduate Studies, Program in the Teaching of English as a Second Language, Framingham, MA 01701-9101. Offers M Ed, Graduate Certificate.

Fresno Pacific University, Graduate Programs, School of Education, Program in Reading and Language Arts, Fresno, CA 93702-4709. Offers reading (Certificate); reading/English as a second language (MA Ed); reading/language arts (MA Ed). *Program availability:* Part-time, evening/weekend. *Degree requirements:* For master's, thesis or alternative. *Entrance requirements:* For master's, three references. Additional exam requirements/recommendations for international students: Required—TOEFL (minimum score 550 paper-based). Electronic applications accepted. *Expenses:* Contact institution.

Furman University, Graduate Division, Department of Education, Greenville, SC 29613. Offers curriculum and instruction (MA); early childhood education (MA); educational leadership (Ed S); English as a second language (MA); literacy (MA); school leadership (MA); special education (MA). *Accreditation:* NCATE. *Program availability:* Part-time, online learning. *Degree requirements:* For master's, comprehensive exam (for some programs), thesis or alternative. *Entrance requirements:* For master's, PRAXIS II. *Expenses: Tuition:* Full-time $27,500; part-time $7290 per credit. Tuition and fees vary according to program. *Faculty research:* Literacy, pedagogy and practice, social justice, advanced leadership, achievement in high poverty schools.

Gannon University, School of Graduate Studies, College of Humanities, Education, and Social Sciences, School of Education, Program in English as a Second Language, Erie, PA 16541-0001. Offers Certificate. *Program availability:* Part-time, evening/weekend, 100% online. *Degree requirements:* For Certificate, comprehensive exam, practicum. *Entrance requirements:* For degree, 3 letters of recommendation, bachelor's degree from regionally-accredited college or university with minimum GPA of 3.0, valid Pennsylvania Instructional I or II teaching certificate. Additional exam requirements/recommendations for international students: Required—TOEFL (minimum score 79 iBT). Electronic applications accepted. Application fee is waived when completed online. *Expenses:* Contact institution.

George Fox University, College of Education, Graduate Teaching and Leading Program, Newberg, OR 97132-2697. Offers administrative leadership (Ed S); continuing administrator license (Certificate); educational leadership (M Ed); educational technology (M Ed); English for speakers of other languages (M Ed); ESOL (Certificate); initial administrator license (Certificate); reading (M Ed, Certificate); special education (M Ed); teaching (MAT). *Accreditation:* NCATE. *Program availability:* Part-time, evening/weekend, online learning. *Degree requirements:* For master's, thesis (for some programs). *Entrance requirements:* For master's, minimum undergraduate GPA of 3.0 during previous 2 years of course work, resume, 3 professional recommendations on university forms, official transcripts. Additional exam requirements/recommendations for international students: Required—TOEFL (minimum score 577 paper-based; 90 iBT). Electronic applications accepted. *Expenses:* Contact institution.

George Mason University, College of Education and Human Development, Programs in Curriculum and Instruction, Fairfax, VA 22030. Offers assistive technology (M Ed); designing digital learning in schools (M Ed); early childhood education (M Ed); early childhood education for diverse learners (M Ed); elementary education (M Ed); English as a second language (M Ed); gifted child education (M Ed); literacy (M Ed), including PK-12 classroom teachers, reading specialist; literacy leadership for diverse schools (M Ed), including K-12 reading; physical education (M Ed); science K-12 (M Ed); secondary education (M Ed), including biology, chemistry, earth science, English, history/social science, math, physics; special education (M Ed); teacher leadership (M Ed); transformative teaching (M Ed). *Program availability:* Part-time, evening/weekend, 100% online, blended/hybrid learning. *Faculty:* 48 full-time (40 women), 28 part-time/adjunct (20 women). *Students:* 165 full-time (147 women), 697 part-time (579 women); includes 243 minority (47 Black or African American, non-Hispanic/Latino; 3 American Indian or Alaska Native, non-Hispanic/Latino; 88 Asian, non-Hispanic/Latino; 85 Hispanic/Latino; 4 Native Hawaiian or other Pacific Islander, non-Hispanic/Latino; 16 Two or more races, non-Hispanic/Latino), 26 international. Average age 34. 450 applicants, 93% accepted, 315 enrolled. In 2018, 421 master's awarded. *Entrance requirements:* For master's, PRAXIS Core (for some programs), 2 letters of recommendation, interview, program goals statement; 9 hours of complete licensure endorsement requirements (for elementary education); minimum GPA of 3.0 in applicant's last 60 hours of undergraduate coursework (for secondary education); at least 1 year of teaching experience (for literacy). Additional exam requirements/recommendations for international students: Required—TOEFL (minimum score 575 paper-based; 88 iBT), IELTS (minimum score 6.5), PTE (minimum score 59). *Application deadline:* For fall admission, 4/2 priority date for domestic and international students; for spring admission, 11/1 for domestic and international students. Application fee: $75 ($80 for international students). Electronic applications accepted. *Financial support:* In 2018–19, 4 students received support, including 1 fellowship, 3 teaching assistantships (averaging $3,745 per year); career-related internships or fieldwork, Federal Work-Study, scholarships/grants, unspecified assistantships, and health care benefits (for full-time research or teaching assistantship recipients) also available. Support available to part-time students. Financial award application deadline: 3/1; financial award applicants required to submit FAFSA. *Faculty research:* Teacher preparation and professional development; adaptive teaching; wonder in science teacher preparation; literacy (digital, adolescent); site based course instruction. *Unit head:* Rebecca Fox, Professor and Academic Program Coordinator, 703-993-4123, E-mail: rfox@gmu.edu. *Application contact:* Rebecca Fox, Professor and Academic Program Coordinator, 703-993-4123, E-mail: rfox@gmu.edu.
Website: http://gse.gmu.edu/programs/gsemasters

Gonzaga University, English Language Center, Spokane, WA 99258. Offers teaching English as a second language (MA). *Program availability:* Part-time. *Degree requirements:* For master's, research thesis or research project. *Entrance requirements:* For master's, two letters of recommendation, written statement of purpose, two official transcripts from each college or university attended. Additional exam requirements/recommendations for international students: Required—TOEFL (minimum score of 580 paper-based, 88 iBT) or IELTS (minimum score of 6.5). Electronic applications accepted. *Expenses:* Contact institution.

Gordon College, Graduate Education Program, Wenham, MA 01984-1899. Offers early childhood (M Ed); educational leadership (M Ed, Ed S); elementary education (M Ed); English as a second language (M Ed, Ed S); math specialist (M Ed); mathematics specialist (Ed S); middle school education (M Ed); moderate disabilities (M Ed); Montessori education (M Ed); reading (M Ed, Ed S); secondary education (M Ed). *Program availability:* Part-time, evening/weekend. *Degree requirements:* For master's, action research or clinical experience (for most programs); for Ed S, action research or clinical experience (for some programs). *Entrance requirements:* For master's, minimum undergraduate GPA of 3.0; 2 official undergraduate transcripts; professional resume; 3 recommendation letters (one professional reference, one academic reference, one personal reference); 500-700 word statement of purpose; for Ed S, minimum master's GPA of 3.3; 2 official transcripts from undergraduate and graduate schools; professional resume; 3 recommendation letters (one professional reference, one academic reference, one personal reference); 500-700 word statement of purpose. Additional exam requirements/recommendations for international students: Required—TOEFL (minimum score 550 paper-based, 80 iBT) or IELTS (minimum score 6.5). *Expenses:* Contact institution. *Faculty research:* Reading, early childhood development, English language learners, universal design for learning.

Grand Canyon University, College of Education, Phoenix, AZ 85017-1097. Offers autism spectrum disorders (MA); curriculum and instruction (MA); early childhood education (M Ed); educational administration (M Ed); educational leadership (M Ed); elementary education (M Ed); gifted education (MA); instructional technology (MS); K-12 leadership (Ed S); reading (MA); secondary education (M Ed); secondary humanities education (M Ed); secondary STEM education (M Ed); special education (M Ed); teaching and learning (Ed D); teaching English to speakers of other languages (MA). *Program availability:* Part-time, evening/weekend, online learning. *Degree requirements:* For master's, publishable research paper (M Ed), e-portfolio. *Entrance requirements:* For master's, undergraduate degree from accredited, GCU-approved college, university, or program with minimum GPA 2.8. Additional exam requirements/recommendations for international students: Required—TOEFL (minimum score 550 paper-based; 79 iBT), IELTS (minimum score 6). Electronic applications accepted.

Grand Valley State University, College of Education, Programs in General Education, Allendale, MI 49401-9403. Offers adult and higher education (M Ed); early childhood education (M Ed); educational differentiation (M Ed); educational leadership (M Ed); educational technology integration (M Ed); elementary education (M Ed); middle level education (M Ed); school library media services (M Ed); secondary level education (M Ed); teaching English to speakers of other languages (M Ed). *Program availability:* Part-time, evening/weekend, 100% online, blended/hybrid learning. *Students:* 20 part-time (10 women); includes 1 minority (Black or African American, non-Hispanic/Latino). Average age 44. In 2018, 1 master's awarded. *Entrance requirements:* For master's, GRE General Test or minimum GPA of 3.0, last 60 credits from regionally-accredited college/university, 3 letters of recommendation. Additional exam requirements/recommendations for international students: Required—TOEFL (minimum iBT score of 80), IELTS (6.5), or Michigan English Language Assessment Battery (77). *Application deadline:* Applications are processed on a rolling basis. Application fee: $30. Electronic applications accepted. *Expenses:* $677 per credit hour, 33 credits. *Financial support:* In 2018–19, 1 student received support, including 1 fellowship; career-related internships or fieldwork, Federal Work-Study, scholarships/grants, and unspecified assistantships also available. *Faculty research:* Effectiveness of technology in education, parental involvement, effective teaching, effective schools research. *Unit head:* Dr. David Bair, Department Director, 616-331-6489, Fax: 616-331-6489, E-mail: baird@gvsu.edu. *Application contact:* Annukka Thelen, Director, Student Information and Services Center, 616-331-6205, Fax: 616-331-6217, E-mail: thelenan@gvsu.edu.
Website: http://www.gvsu.edu/coe/

Greensboro College, Program in Teaching English to Speakers of Other Languages, Greensboro, NC 27401-1875. Offers MA. *Accreditation:* NCATE. *Program availability:* Part-time, evening/weekend. *Degree requirements:* For master's, thesis, portfolio, project. *Entrance requirements:* For master's, GRE or MAT, 2 letters of recommendation, writing sample. Additional exam requirements/recommendations for international students: Required—TOEFL (minimum score 550 paper-based). Electronic applications accepted.

Hamline University, School of Education, St. Paul, MN 55104-1284. Offers education (MA Ed, Ed D); English as a second language (MA); literacy education (MA); natural science and environmental education (MA Ed); teaching (MAT); teaching English to speakers of other languages (MA). *Accreditation:* NCATE (one or more programs are accredited). *Program availability:* Part-time, evening/weekend, 100% online, blended/hybrid learning. *Degree requirements:* For master's, thesis (for some programs), thesis or capstone project; for doctorate, comprehensive exam, thesis/dissertation. *Entrance requirements:* For master's, official transcripts, essay, letters of recommendation, minimum GPA of 3.0 from bachelor's work; resume and/or writing samples (for some programs); for doctorate, personal statement, master's degree with minimum GPA of 3.0, letters of recommendation, writing sample. Additional exam requirements/recommendations for international students: Required—TOEFL (minimum score 550 paper-based; 80 iBT), IELTS (minimum score 6.5). Electronic applications accepted. *Expenses:* Contact institution. *Faculty research:* Adult basic education, service-learning, teacher dispositions, diversity, technology.

Harding University, Cannon-Clary College of Education, Searcy, AR 72149-0001. Offers advanced studies in teaching and learning (M Ed); art (MSE); behavioral science (MSE); counseling (MS, Ed S); early childhood special education (M Ed, MSE); education (MSE); educational leadership (M Ed, Ed S); elementary education (M Ed); English (MSE); French (MSE); history/social science (MSE); kinesiology (MSE); math (MSE); reading (M Ed); secondary education (M Ed); Spanish (MSE); teaching (MAT); teaching English as a second language (MSE). *Accreditation:* NCATE. *Program availability:* Part-time, evening/weekend. *Degree requirements:* For master's, comprehensive exam (for some programs), thesis optional, portfolio(s); for Ed S, comprehensive exam, portfolio, project. *Entrance requirements:* For master's, GRE, MAT, PRAXIS; for Ed S, MAT or GRE. Additional exam requirements/recommendations for international students: Required—TOEFL (minimum score 550 paper-based; 79 iBT). *Faculty research:* Reading, comprehension, school violence, educational technology, behavior, college choice, differentiated instruction, brain-based teaching.

Hawai`i Pacific University, College of Liberal Arts, Program in Teaching English to Speakers of Other Languages, Honolulu, HI 96813. Offers MA. *Program availability:* Part-time. *Entrance requirements:* For master's, two letters of recommendation, statement of purpose, transcripts, second language requirement. Additional exam requirements/recommendations for international students: Required—TOEFL (minimum score 550 paper-based; 80 iBT), IELTS (minimum score 6), TWE (minimum score 5). Electronic applications accepted.

Henderson State University, Graduate Studies, Teachers College, Department of Advanced Instructional Studies, Arkadelphia, AR 71999-0001. Offers developmental therapy (MSE); dyslexia therapy (Graduate Certificate); education (MAT); educational technology leadership (Graduate Certificate); English as a second language (MSE, Graduate Certificate); instructional facilitator (MSE, Graduate Certificate); middle level education (MAT); special education (K-12) (MAT, MSE); special education/early childhood (MAT). *Accreditation:* NCATE. *Program availability:* Part-time. *Entrance requirements:* For master's, GRE General Test or MAT, minimum GPA of 2.7, teacher certification. Additional exam requirements/recommendations for international students: Required—TOEFL (minimum score 600 paper-based); Recommended—IELTS (minimum score 6.5).

Heritage University, Graduate Programs in Education, Program in Professional Studies, Toppenish, WA 98948-9599. Offers bilingual education/ESL (M Ed); biology (M Ed); English and literature (M Ed); reading/literacy (M Ed); special education (M Ed). *Program availability:* Part-time, evening/weekend. *Degree requirements:* For master's, comprehensive exam (for some programs), thesis (for some programs).

Hofstra University, College of Liberal Arts and Sciences, Programs in Forensic Linguistics and Applied Linguistics, Hempstead, NY 11549. Offers applied linguistics (TESOL) (MA); linguistics (MA), including forensic linguistics. *Program availability:* Part-time, blended/hybrid learning. *Students:* 43 full-time (34 women), 2 part-time (1 woman); includes 18 minority (4 Black or African American, non-Hispanic/Latino; 4 Asian, non-Hispanic/Latino; 10 Hispanic/Latino), 1 international. Average age 27. 42 applicants, 86% accepted, 22 enrolled. In 2018, 10 master's awarded. *Degree requirements:* For master's, thesis, 36 credits, capstone, minimum GPA of 3.0. *Entrance requirements:* For master's, bachelor's degree in related area, interview, 2 letters of recommendation. Additional exam requirements/recommendations for international students: Required—TOEFL (minimum score 550 paper-based; 80 iBT). *Application deadline:* Applications are processed on a rolling basis. Application fee: $75. Electronic applications accepted. *Financial support:* In 2018–19, 32 students received support, including 12 fellowships with full and partial tuition reimbursements available (averaging $3,669 per year); research assistantships with full and partial tuition reimbursements available, career-related internships or fieldwork, Federal Work-Study, institutionally sponsored loans, scholarships/grants, tuition waivers (full and partial), unspecified assistantships, and scholarships and endowed scholarships also available. Support available to part-time students. Financial award applicants required to submit FAFSA. *Faculty research:* Threatening language; using corpus tools for legal interpretation; cross-examination strategies in assault trials; non-native speakers of English in the justice system; investigating deception, misrepresentation, and disinformation in civil, criminal, and intelligence cases. *Unit head:* Dr. Patricia Welch, Chairperson, 516-463-6453, E-mail: patricia.m.welch@hofstra.edu. *Application contact:* Sunil Samuel, Assistant Vice President of Admissions, 516-463-4723, Fax: 516-463-4664, E-mail: graduateadmission@hofstra.edu.
Website: http://www.hofstra.edu/hclas

Hofstra University, School of Education, Programs in Teacher Education, Hempstead, NY 11549. Offers bilingual education (MA); bilingual extension (Advanced Certificate); business education (MS Ed); curriculum studies (MS Ed); early childhood and childhood education (MS Ed); early childhood education (MA, MS Ed); educational technology (Advanced Certificate); elementary education (MA, MS Ed); English education (MS Ed); family and consumer science (MS Ed); fine arts and music education (Advanced

Certificate); fine arts education (MS Ed); foreign language and TESOL (MS Ed); foreign language education (MA, MS Ed); languages other than English and teaching English as a second language (MA); learning and teaching (Ed D); mathematics education (MA, MS Ed); middle childhood extension (Advanced Certificate); music education (MA, MS Ed); science education (MA); secondary education (Advanced Certificate); social studies education (MA, MS Ed); teaching languages other than English and TESOL (MS Ed); technology for learning (MA); TESOL (MS Ed, Advanced Certificate); TESOL with specialization in STEM (MA); work based learning extension (Advanced Certificate). *Program availability:* Part-time, evening/weekend, blended/hybrid learning. *Students:* 138 full-time (94 women), 109 part-time (78 women); includes 66 minority (16 Black or African American, non-Hispanic/Latino; 17 Asian, non-Hispanic/Latino; 31 Hispanic/Latino; 2 Native Hawaiian or other Pacific Islander, non-Hispanic/Latino), 6 international. Average age 29. 217 applicants, 86% accepted, 113 enrolled. In 2018, 105 master's, 11 doctorates, 25 other advanced degrees awarded. *Degree requirements:* For master's, comprehensive exam, thesis (for some programs), exit project, student teaching, fieldwork, electronic portfolio, curriculum project, minimum GPA of 3.0; for doctorate, dissertation; for Advanced Certificate, 3 foreign languages, comprehensive exam (for some programs), thesis project. *Entrance requirements:* For master's, GRE, 2 letters of recommendation, portfolio, teacher certification (MA), interview, essay; for doctorate, GMAT, GRE, LSAT, or MAT; for Advanced Certificate, 2 letters of recommendation, essay, interview and/or portfolio, teaching certificate. Additional exam requirements/recommendations for international students: Required—TOEFL (minimum score 550 paper-based; 80 iBT). *Application deadline:* Applications are processed on a rolling basis. Application fee: $75. Electronic applications accepted. *Financial support:* In 2018–19, 86 students received support, including 51 fellowships with full and partial tuition reimbursements available (averaging $5,080 per year), 2 research assistantships with full and partial tuition reimbursements available (averaging $3,470 per year); career-related internships or fieldwork, Federal Work-Study, institutionally sponsored loans, scholarships/grants, traineeships, tuition waivers (full and partial), unspecified assistantships, and scholarships and endowed scholarships also available. Support available to part-time students. Financial award applicants required to submit FAFSA. *Faculty research:* Impact of memory on learning; brain function, cognitive-development, learning, and achievement; student activism and civic education; using children's literature to promote diversity; 2nd language acquisition. *Unit head:* Dr. Alan Singer, Chairperson, 516-463-5853, Fax: 516-463-6275, E-mail: alan.j.singer@hofstra.edu. *Application contact:* Sunil Samuel, Assistant Vice President of Admissions, 516-463-4723, Fax: 516-463-4664, E-mail: graduateadmission@hofstra.edu.
Website: http://www.hofstra.edu/education/

Holy Family University, Graduate and Professional Programs, School of Education, Master of Education Programs, Philadelphia, PA 19114. Offers early elementary education (PreK-Grade 4) (M Ed); education leadership (M Ed); general education (M Ed); reading specialist (M Ed); special education (M Ed); TESOL and literacy (M Ed). *Program availability:* Part-time. *Degree requirements:* For master's, thesis optional. Electronic applications accepted.

Houston Baptist University, College of Education and Behavioral Sciences, Programs in Education, Houston, TX 77074-3298. Offers bilingual education (M Ed); counselor education (M Ed); curriculum and instruction (M Ed); curriculum and instruction (EC-6 bilingual) (M Ed); curriculum and instruction in all-level art, Spanish, music, or physical education (M Ed); curriculum and instruction in EC-6 and special education (EC-12) (M Ed); curriculum and instruction in instructional technology (M Ed); curriculum and instruction in mathematics, science, or social studies (4-8) (M Ed); curriculum and instruction with EC-6 generalist (M Ed); curriculum and instruction with English language arts and reading (4-8) (M Ed); educational administration (M Ed); educational diagnostician (M Ed); executive educational leadership (Ed D); higher education in business management (M Ed); higher education in Christian studies (M Ed); higher education in counseling (M Ed); higher education in educational technology (M Ed); reading (M Ed); special educational leadership (Ed D). *Program availability:* Part-time, evening/weekend, 100% online, blended/hybrid learning. *Degree requirements:* For master's, comprehensive exam; for doctorate, thesis/dissertation. *Entrance requirements:* For master's, minimum GPA of 2.75, two recommendations, resume, bachelor's degree conferred transcript; interview (for non-certified teachers); for doctorate, GRE, 5 letters of recommendation. Additional exam requirements/recommendations for international students: Required—TOEFL (minimum score 80 iBT), IELTS (minimum score 6.5). Electronic applications accepted. Application fee is waived when completed online. *Expenses:* Contact institution. *Faculty research:* Autism and inclusion, integrating technology into instruction, school change and leadership trust.

Humboldt State University, Academic Programs, College of Arts, Humanities, and Social Sciences, Department of English, Arcata, CA 95521-8299. Offers English (MA), including composition studies and pedagogy, literary and cultural studies, teaching English as a second language. *Faculty:* 9 full-time (8 women), 15 part-time/adjunct (all women). *Students:* 8 full-time (6 women), 9 part-time (4 women); includes 4 minority (all Hispanic/Latino). Average age 27. 16 applicants, 75% accepted, 8 enrolled. In 2018, 4 master's awarded. *Degree requirements:* For master's, variable foreign language requirement, thesis or alternative, qualifying exam. *Entrance requirements:* For master's, GRE, minimum GPA of 3.0, 3 letters of recommendation, sample of writing. Additional exam requirements/recommendations for international students: Required—TOEFL (minimum score 500 paper-based). *Application deadline:* For fall admission, 3/1 for domestic students; for spring admission, 11/1 for domestic students. Applications are processed on a rolling basis. Application fee: $55. *Expenses: Tuition:* Part-time $4649 per semester. *Required fees:* $2121; $1673. Tuition and fees vary according to program. *Financial support:* Teaching assistantships, career-related internships or fieldwork, Federal Work-Study, and institutionally sponsored loans available. Financial award application deadline: 3/1; financial award applicants required to submit FAFSA. *Faculty research:* Teaching of writing, literature. *Unit head:* Dr. Janet Winston, English Graduate Program Coordinator, 707-826-3913, E-mail: winston@humboldt.edu. *Application contact:* Dr. Janet Winston, English Graduate Program Coordinator, 707-826-3913, E-mail: winston@humboldt.edu.
Website: http://www.humboldt.edu/english/

Hunter College of the City University of New York, Graduate School, School of Education, Department of Curriculum and Teaching, Program in Teaching English as a Second Language, New York, NY 10065-5085. Offers MA. *Accreditation:* NCATE. *Degree requirements:* For master's, one foreign language, thesis, comprehensive exam or essay, New York state teacher certification exams. *Entrance requirements:* For master's, minimum GPA of 2.8, 2 letters of recommendation, interview. Additional exam requirements/recommendations for international students: Required—TOEFL (minimum score 600 paper-based), TWE (minimum score 5).

Huntington University, Graduate School, Huntington, IN 46750-1299. Offers adolescent and young adult education (M Ed); business administration (MBA); counseling (MA), including licensed mental health counselor; early adolescent education (M Ed); elementary education (M Ed); global youth ministry (MA); occupational therapy (OTD); organizational leadership (MA); pastoral leadership (MA); TESOL education (M Ed). *Accreditation:* AOTA. *Program availability:* Part-time, online learning. *Degree requirements:* For master's, comprehensive exam (for some programs), thesis (for some programs). *Entrance requirements:* For master's, GRE (for counseling and education students only); for doctorate, GRE (for occupational therapy students). Additional exam requirements/recommendations for international students: Required—TOEFL (minimum score 85 iBT), IELTS (minimum score 6.5). Electronic applications accepted. *Expenses:* Contact institution. *Faculty research:* Leadership, educational technology trends, evangelism, youth ministry, mental health.

Idaho State University, Graduate School, College of Arts and Letters, Department of English and Philosophy, Pocatello, ID 83209-8056. Offers English (MA); English and the teaching of English (PhD); TESOL (Post-Master's Certificate). *Program availability:* Part-time. *Degree requirements:* For master's, one foreign language, comprehensive exam, thesis optional; for doctorate, one foreign language, comprehensive exam, thesis/dissertation, 2 papers, 2 teaching internships; for Post-Master's Certificate, 6 credits of elective linguistics, practicum. *Entrance requirements:* For master's, GRE General Test (minimum 50th percentile verbal), general literature exam, minimum GPA of 3.0, 3 letters of recommendation, 5-page writing sample; for doctorate, GRE General Test, GRE Subject Test, minimum GPA of 3.5, writing examples, 3 letters of recommendation, master's degree in English; for Post-Master's Certificate, GRE (minimum 35th percentile on verbal section), bachelor's degree, minimum undergraduate GPA of 3.0 in last 2 years, 3 letters of recommendation, knowledge of second language. Additional exam requirements/recommendations for international students: Required—TOEFL (minimum score 550 paper-based; 80 iBT). Electronic applications accepted. *Faculty research:* American literature, Renaissance literature, composition and rhetoric, Intermountain West studies, ethics.

Immaculata University, College of Graduate Studies, Program in Cultural and Linguistic Diversity, Immaculata, PA 19345. Offers bilingual studies (MA); TESOL (MA). *Program availability:* Part-time, evening/weekend. *Degree requirements:* For master's, one foreign language, comprehensive exam, thesis optional, professional experience. *Entrance requirements:* For master's, GRE or MAT, proficiency in Spanish or Asian language, minimum GPA of 3.0. Additional exam requirements/recommendations for international students: Required—TOEFL, IELTS. Electronic applications accepted. *Faculty research:* Cognitive learning, Caribbean literature and culture, English as a second language, teaching English to speakers of other languages.

Indiana State University, College of Graduate and Professional Studies, College of Arts and Sciences, Department of Languages, Literatures, and Linguistics, Terre Haute, IN 47809. Offers applied linguistics/teaching English as a second language (MA); language education (PhD); Spanish/teaching English as a second language (MA); TESL/TEFL (CAS). *Degree requirements:* For master's, comprehensive exam. Electronic applications accepted.

Indiana University Bloomington, University Graduate School, College of Arts and Sciences, Department of Second Language Studies, Bloomington, IN 47405-7000. Offers second language studies (MA, PhD); TESOL and applied linguistics (MA). *Entrance requirements:* Additional exam requirements/recommendations for international students: Required—TOEFL (minimum score 100 iBT). Electronic applications accepted.

Indiana University of Pennsylvania, School of Graduate Studies and Research, College of Humanities and Social Sciences, Department of English, PhD Program in Composition and Teaching English to Speakers of Other Languages, Indiana, PA 15705. Offers PhD. *Program availability:* Part-time. *Faculty:* 22 full-time (9 women). *Students:* 15 full-time (11 women), 81 part-time (50 women); includes 10 minority (2 Black or African American, non-Hispanic/Latino; 6 Asian, non-Hispanic/Latino; 2 Hispanic/Latino), 39 international. Average age 37. 2 applicants, 100% accepted, 1 enrolled. In 2018, 17 doctorates awarded. *Degree requirements:* For doctorate, one foreign language, comprehensive exam, thesis/dissertation. *Entrance requirements:* For doctorate, 2 letters of recommendation. Additional exam requirements/recommendations for international students: Required—TOEFL (minimum score 600 paper-based). *Application deadline:* For fall admission, 2/1 priority date for domestic students; for summer admission, 11/1 priority date for domestic students. Applications are processed on a rolling basis. Application fee: $50. Electronic applications accepted. *Expenses:* Contact institution. *Financial support:* In 2018–19, 7 fellowships with full tuition reimbursements (averaging $1,093 per year), 8 research assistantships with tuition reimbursements (averaging $6,916 per year), 6 teaching assistantships with partial tuition reimbursements (averaging $22,389 per year) were awarded; career-related internships or fieldwork, Federal Work-Study, scholarships/grants, and unspecified assistantships also available. Support available to part-time students. Financial award application deadline: 4/15; financial award applicants required to submit FAFSA. *Unit head:* Dr. Gloria Park, Graduate Coordinator, 724-357-3095, E-mail: gloria.park@iup.edu. *Application contact:* Dr. Gloria Park, Graduate Coordinator, 724-357-3095, E-mail: gloria.park@iup.edu.
Website: http://www.iup.edu/english/grad/composition-tesol-phd/default.aspx

Indiana University of Pennsylvania, School of Graduate Studies and Research, College of Humanities and Social Sciences, Department of English, Program in English: TESOL, Indiana, PA 15705. Offers MA. *Program availability:* Part-time. *Faculty:* 22 full-time (9 women). *Students:* 11 full-time (5 women), 2 part-time (0 women); includes 1 minority (Hispanic/Latino), 6 international. Average age 29. 22 applicants, 86% accepted, 7 enrolled. In 2018, 12 master's awarded. *Degree requirements:* For master's, thesis optional. *Entrance requirements:* For master's, two letters of recommendation. Additional exam requirements/recommendations for international students: Required—TOEFL (minimum score 580 paper-based). *Application deadline:* Applications are processed on a rolling basis. Application fee: $50. Electronic applications accepted. *Expenses:* Contact institution. *Financial support:* In 2018–19, 4 research assistantships with tuition reimbursements (averaging $4,200 per year) were awarded; fellowships with full tuition reimbursements, Federal Work-Study, scholarships/grants, and unspecified assistantships also available. Financial award application deadline: 4/15; financial award applicants required to submit FAFSA. *Unit head:* Dr. Gloria Park, Director, 724-357-3095, E-mail: gloria.park@iup.edu. *Application contact:* Dr. Gloria Park, Director, 724-357-3095, E-mail: gloria.park@iup.edu.
Website: http://www.iup.edu/english/grad/tesol-ma/default.aspx

Indiana University–Purdue University Indianapolis, School of Education, Indianapolis, IN 46202-5155. Offers curriculum and instruction (MS); early childhood (MS); educational leadership (MS, Certificate); English as a second language (Certificate); kindergarten (Certificate); language education (MS); reading (Certificate); school counseling (MS); special education (MS, Certificate). *Program availability:* Part-time, evening/weekend. Terminal master's awarded for partial completion of doctoral program. *Degree requirements:* For master's, thesis optional. *Entrance requirements:* For master's, GRE General Test, minimum GPA of 2.5; for Certificate, official transcripts. Additional exam requirements/recommendations for international students: Required—TOEFL (minimum score 60 iBT), IELTS (minimum score 5.5). Electronic applications accepted. *Expenses:* Contact institution. *Faculty research:* Educational policies and school leaders' responses to these; issues of intersectionality in the experiences of African American lesbian, gay, and bisexual students attending historically black colleges and universities and those who belong to black Greek-letter organizations; students' experiential knowledge and their evolving disciplinary-specific literacy and understanding; innovative program development; urban ESL teacher preparation; target-based instructional coaching.

Indiana University–Purdue University Indianapolis, School of Liberal Arts, Department of English, Indianapolis, IN 46202. Offers English (MA); teaching English to speakers of other languages (TESOL) (MA, Certificate); teaching literature (Certificate); teaching writing (Certificate). *Entrance requirements:* For master's, GRE. Additional exam requirements/recommendations for international students: Required—TOEFL.

Inter American University of Puerto Rico, Arecibo Campus, Programs in Education, Arecibo, PR 00614-4050. Offers administration and educational supervision (MA Ed); counseling and guidance (MA Ed); curriculum and teaching (MA Ed), including biology education, English as a second language, history education, math education, Spanish; elementary education (MA Ed). *Accreditation:* TEAC. *Degree requirements:* For master's, comprehensive exam, thesis optional. *Entrance requirements:* For master's, GRE, EXADEP, bachelor's degree in education or teaching license (administration and supervision) or courses in education and psychology (counseling and guidance), minimum GPA of 2.5 in last 60 credits.

Inter American University of Puerto Rico, Barranquitas Campus, Program in Education, Barranquitas, PR 00794. Offers curriculum and teaching (M Ed), including biology, English as a second language, history, Spanish; educational leadership and management (MA); elementary education (M Ed); information and library service technology (M Ed); special education (MA). *Accreditation:* TEAC. *Program availability:* Part-time, evening/weekend. *Degree requirements:* For master's, 2 foreign languages, comprehensive exam, thesis (for some programs). *Entrance requirements:* For master's, GRE or EXADEP, bachelor's degree or its equivalent from accredited institution, official academic transcript from institution that conferred bachelor's degree, minimum GPA of 2.5, two recommendation letters, interview (for some programs), essay (for some programs). Electronic applications accepted. *Expenses:* Contact institution.

Inter American University of Puerto Rico, Metropolitan Campus, Graduate Programs, Program in Teaching English as a Second Language, San Juan, PR 00919-1293. Offers MA. *Program availability:* Part-time, evening/weekend. *Degree requirements:* For master's, comprehensive exam, thesis or alternative. *Entrance requirements:* For master's, GRE General Test or EXADEP, interview, minimum GPA of 2.5. Electronic applications accepted.

Inter American University of Puerto Rico, Ponce Campus, Graduate School, Mercedita, PR 00715-1602. Offers accounting (MBA); biology (M Ed); chemistry (M Ed); criminal justice (MA); elementary education (M Ed); English as a Second Language (M Ed); finance (MBA); history (M Ed); human resources (MBA); marketing (MBA); mathematics (M Ed); Spanish (M Ed). *Entrance requirements:* For master's, minimum GPA of 2.5.

Inter American University of Puerto Rico, San Germán Campus, Graduate Studies Center, Program in Teaching English as a Second Language, San Germán, PR 00683-5008. Offers MA. *Accreditation:* TEAC. *Program availability:* Part-time, evening/weekend. *Degree requirements:* For master's, comprehensive exam. *Entrance requirements:* For master's, GRE General Test or EXADEP, minimum GPA of 3.0. *Expenses: Tuition:* Full-time $212; part-time $212 per credit. *Required fees:* $366 per semester. One-time fee: $31. Tuition and fees vary according to degree level and program.

Iowa State University of Science and Technology, Program in Teaching English as a Second Language/Applied Linguistics, Ames, IA 50011. Offers MA. *Entrance requirements:* For master's, GRE, official academic transcripts, resume, three letters of recommendation, statement of personal goals, writing sample. Additional exam requirements/recommendations for international students: Required—TOEFL (minimum score 600 paper-based; 100 iBT), IELTS (minimum score 7). Electronic applications accepted.

James Madison University, The Graduate School, College of Education, Program in Education, Harrisonburg, VA 22807. Offers early childhood education (preK-3) (MAT); educational leadership (M Ed); educational technology (M Ed); elementary education (MAT); equity and cultural diversity (M Ed); inclusive early childhood education (MAT); K-8 mathematics specialist (M Ed); middle education (MAT); reading education (M Ed); secondary education (MAT); Spanish language and culture for educators (MAT); TESOL (MAT). *Accreditation:* NCATE. *Program availability:* Part-time, evening/weekend. *Students:* 255 full-time (224 women), 200 part-time (140 women); includes 56 minority (13 Black or African American, non-Hispanic/Latino; 8 Asian, non-Hispanic/Latino; 21 Hispanic/Latino; 14 Two or more races, non-Hispanic/Latino), 1 international. Average age 30. In 2018, 295 master's awarded. Application fee: $60. Electronic applications accepted. *Expenses:* Tuition, state resident: full-time $10,848. Tuition, nonresident: full-time $27,888. *Required fees:* $1128. *Financial support:* In 2018–19, 22 students received support. Teaching assistantships, career-related internships or fieldwork, Federal Work-Study, and assistantships (averaging $7911) available. Financial award application deadline: 3/1; financial award applicants required to submit FAFSA. *Unit head:* Dr. Phillip M. Wishon, Dean, 540-568-6572, E-mail: wishonpm@jmu.edu. *Application contact:* Lynette D. Michael, Director of Graduate Admissions, 540-568-6131 Ext. 6395, Fax: 540-568-7860, E-mail: michaeld@jmu.edu.
Website: http://www.jmu.edu/coe/index.shtml

Kansas State University, Graduate School, College of Arts and Sciences, Department of Modern Languages, Manhattan, KS 66506. Offers literature (MA), including French, German, Spanish; second language acquisition (MA), including French, German, Spanish, teaching English as a foreign language. *Program availability:* Part-time, evening/weekend, blended/hybrid learning. *Degree requirements:* For master's, thesis optional. *Entrance requirements:* For master's, teaching certificate. Additional exam requirements/recommendations for international students: Required—TOEFL (minimum score 550 paper-based; 83 iBT), TOEFL (minimum speaking-portion score of 26). Electronic applications accepted. *Faculty research:* Second language acquisitions; U.S. Latino literature; Francophone literature; German, French, Spanish, and Spanish-American literature from the Middle Ages to the modern era; teaching English as a foreign language; linguistics.

Kansas State University, Graduate School, College of Education, Department of Educational Leadership, Manhattan, KS 66506. Offers adult learning (Certificate); educational leadership (MS, Ed D, PhD); leadership dynamics for adult learners (Certificate); qualitative research (Certificate); social justice education (Certificate); teaching English as a second language for adult learners (Certificate). *Accreditation:* NCATE. *Program availability:* Online learning. *Degree requirements:* For master's, comprehensive exam; for doctorate, comprehensive exam, thesis/dissertation. *Entrance requirements:* For master's, minimum undergraduate GPA of 3.0; for doctorate, MAT (for educational administration); GRE General Test (for adult education), minimum GPA of 3.0 in last 60 hours. Additional exam requirements/recommendations for international students: Required—TOEFL. Electronic applications accepted. *Faculty research:* Educational law, school finance, school facilities, organizational leadership, adult learning, distance learning/education.

Kean University, College of Education, Program in Instruction and Curriculum, Union, NJ 07083. Offers bilingual/bicultural education (MA); teaching English as a second language (MA). *Accreditation:* NCATE. *Program availability:* Part-time. *Faculty:* 14 full-time (8 women). *Students:* 1 (woman) full-time, 14 part-time (11 women); includes 9 minority (all Hispanic/Latino), 1 international. Average age 33. 5 applicants, 100% accepted, 5 enrolled. In 2018, 19 master's awarded. *Degree requirements:* For master's, comprehensive exam (for some programs), thesis optional, two-semester advanced seminar. *Entrance requirements:* For master's, GRE General Test or MAT; PRAXIS (for some programs), minimum GPA of 3.0, personal statement, professional resume/curriculum vitae, commitment to working with children, certification (for some programs), two letters of recommendation. Additional exam requirements/recommendations for international students: Required—TOEFL (minimum score 550 paper-based; 79 iBT), IELTS (minimum score 6.5). *Application deadline:* For fall admission, 6/30 for domestic and international students; for spring admission, 12/1 for domestic and international students. Applications are processed on a rolling basis. Application fee: $75. Electronic applications accepted. *Expenses:* Tuition, state resident: full-time $15,025; part-time $733.50 per credit. Tuition, nonresident: full-time $19,890; part-time $884.50 per credit. *Required fees:* $2107.50; $89.50 per credit. Tuition and fees vary according to course level, course load, degree level and program. *Financial support:* Scholarships/grants and unspecified assistantships available. Financial award applicants required to submit FAFSA. *Unit head:* Dr. Gail Verdi, Program Coordinator, 908-737-3908, E-mail: gverdi@kean.edu. *Application contact:* Brittany Gerstenhaber, Admissions Counselor, 908-737-7100, E-mail: grad-adm@kean.edu.
Website: http://grad.kean.edu/masters-programs/bilingualbicultural-education-instruction-and-curriculum

Kennesaw State University, Bagwell College of Education, MAT Program, Kennesaw, GA 30144. Offers art education (MAT); secondary English (MAT); secondary mathematics (MAT); secondary science (MAT); special education (MAT); teaching English to speakers of other languages (MAT). *Program availability:* Part-time, evening/weekend. *Students:* 44 full-time (36 women), 10 part-time (6 women); includes 15 minority (10 Black or African American, non-Hispanic/Latino; 4 Hispanic/Latino; 1 Two or more races, non-Hispanic/Latino). Average age 32. 3 applicants. In 2018, 32 master's awarded. *Entrance requirements:* For master's, GRE, GACE I (state certificate exam), minimum GPA of 2.75, 2 recommendations, resume. Additional exam requirements/recommendations for international students: Required—TOEFL (minimum score 550 paper-based; 80 iBT), IELTS (minimum score 6.5). *Application deadline:* For fall admission, 6/1 for domestic and international students; for spring admission, 3/1 for domestic and international students; for summer admission, 4/15 for domestic and international students. Applications are processed on a rolling basis. Application fee: $60. Electronic applications accepted. *Expenses: Tuition, area resident:* Full-time $6960; part-time $290 per credit hour. Tuition, state resident: full-time $6960; part-time $290 per credit hour. Tuition, nonresident: full-time $25,080; part-time $1045 per credit hour. *International tuition:* $25,080 full-time. *Required fees:* $2006; $1706 per semester. $853 per semester. *Financial support:* Research assistantships with tuition reimbursements and unspecified assistantships available. Financial award application deadline: 4/1; financial award applicants required to submit FAFSA. *Unit head:* Director, 470-578-3093. *Application contact:* Admissions Counselor, 470-578-4377, Fax: 470-578-9172, E-mail: ksugrad@kennesaw.edu.

Kennesaw State University, Bagwell College of Education, Program in Teaching English to Speakers of Other Languages, Kennesaw, GA 30144. Offers M Ed. *Program availability:* Part-time, evening/weekend, 100% online. *Students:* 9 full-time (all women), 9 part-time (8 women); includes 1 minority (Asian, non-Hispanic/Latino). Average age 37. 10 applicants, 90% accepted, 8 enrolled. In 2018, 8 master's awarded. *Entrance requirements:* For master's, interview, teaching certification. Additional exam requirements/recommendations for international students: Required—TOEFL (minimum score 80 iBT), IELTS (minimum score 6.5). *Application deadline:* For fall admission, 7/1 for domestic students. Applications are processed on a rolling basis. Application fee: $60. Electronic applications accepted. *Expenses: Tuition, area resident:* Full-time $6960; part-time $290 per credit hour. Tuition, state resident: full-time $6960; part-time $290 per credit hour. Tuition, nonresident: full-time $25,080; part-time $1045 per credit hour. *International tuition:* $25,080 full-time. *Required fees:* $2006; $1706 per semester. $853 per semester. *Application contact:* Admission Counselor, 470-578-4377, Fax: 470-578-9172, E-mail: ksugrad@kennesaw.edu.
Website: http://bagwell.kennesaw.edu/departments/ined/programs/tesol-med/me/index.php

Kent State University, College of Arts and Sciences, Department of English, Kent, OH 44242-0001. Offers creative writing (MFA); English (MA, PhD); English for teachers (MA); literature and writing (MA); rhetoric and composition (PhD); teaching English as a second language (MA). MFA program offered jointly with Cleveland State University, The University of Akron, and Youngstown State University as a consortium. Students must also apply through NEOMFA. *Program availability:* Part-time. *Faculty:* 21 full-time (9 women). *Students:* 98 full-time (62 women), 20 part-time (11 women); includes 9 minority (3 Black or African American, non-Hispanic/Latino; 1 Asian, non-Hispanic/Latino; 2 Hispanic/Latino; 3 Two or more races, non-Hispanic/Latino), 21 international. Average age 35. 75 applicants, 28% accepted, 21 enrolled. In 2018, 18 master's, 7 doctorates awarded. *Degree requirements:* For master's, one foreign language, thesis (for some programs), final portfolio, final exam, or thesis (for MA in teaching English as a second language); for doctorate, one foreign language, comprehensive exam, thesis/dissertation. *Entrance requirements:* For master's, GRE General Test, goal statement, 3 letters of recommendation, 8-15 page writing sample relevant to the field of study (waived for MA in English for teachers concentration), transcripts; for doctorate, GRE General Test, statement of purpose, 3 letters of recommendation, 8-15 page writing sample relevant to field of study, transcripts. Additional exam requirements/recommendations for international students: Required—TOEFL (minimum score 587 paper-based, 94 iBT), Michigan English Language Assessment Battery (minimum score 82), IELTS (minimum score 7.0) or PTE (minimum score 65). *Application deadline:* For fall admission, 1/15 for domestic and international students. Applications are processed on a rolling basis. Application fee: $45 ($70 for international students). Electronic applications accepted. *Expenses:* Tuition, state resident: full-time $11,766; part-time $536 per credit. Tuition, nonresident: full-time $21,952; part-time $999 per credit. *International tuition:* $21,952 full-time. Tuition and fees vary according to course load. *Financial support:* Fellowships with full tuition reimbursements, teaching assistantships with full tuition reimbursements, and unspecified assistantships available. Financial award application deadline: 1/15. *Unit head:* Dr. Robert Trogdon, Chair, 330-672-2676, E-mail: rtrogdon@kent.edu. *Application contact:* Wesley Raabe, Graduate Studies Coordinator, 330-672-1723, E-mail: wraabe@kent.edu.
Website: http://www.kent.edu/english/

Langston University, School of Education and Behavioral Sciences, Langston, OK 73050. Offers bilingual/multicultural (M Ed); elementary education (M Ed); English as a second language (M Ed); rehabilitation counseling (M Sc); urban education (M Ed). *Accreditation:* CORE; NCATE (one or more programs are accredited). *Program availability:* Part-time. *Degree requirements:* For master's, comprehensive exam, thesis optional. *Entrance requirements:* For master's, GRE, writing skills test, minimum GPA of 2.5, 3 letters of recommendation. Additional exam requirements/recommendations for international students: Required—TOEFL, TWE. *Faculty research:* Bilingual/multicultural education, financing post-secondary education.

La Salle University, School of Arts and Sciences, Hispanic Institute, Philadelphia, PA 19141-1199. Offers bilingual/bicultural studies (MA); ESL program specialist

(Certificate); interpretation: English/Spanish-Spanish/English (Certificate); teaching English to speakers of other languages (MA); translation and interpretation (MA); translation: English/Spanish-Spanish/English (Certificate). *Program availability:* Part-time, evening/weekend. *Degree requirements:* For master's, one foreign language, project or thesis. *Entrance requirements:* For master's, GRE, MAT, or GMAT, professional resume; two letters of recommendation; for Certificate, GRE, MAT, or GMAT, professional resume; two letters of recommendation; evidence of an advanced level in Spanish. Additional exam requirements/recommendations for international students: Required—TOEFL. Electronic applications accepted. Application fee is waived when completed online. *Expenses:* Contact institution. *Faculty research:* Puerto Rican literature, cross-cultural communication, English as a second language methodology, Spanish language.

La Salle University, School of Arts and Sciences, Program in Education, Philadelphia, PA 19141-1199. Offers autism spectrum disorders (MA, Certificate); bilingual/bicultural studies (MA); classroom management (MA); dual early childhood and special education (MA); dual middle-level science and math and special education (MA); education (MA); English (MA); English as a second language (Certificate); history (MA); instructional coach (Certificate); instructional leadership (MA); reading specialist (MA, Certificate); secondary education (MA); special education (MA, Certificate). *Program availability:* Part-time, evening/weekend. *Degree requirements:* For master's, comprehensive exam. *Entrance requirements:* For master's, MAT or GRE, 2 letters of recommendation; for Certificate, GMAT or GRE, 2 letters of recommendation. Additional exam requirements/recommendations for international students: Required—TOEFL. Electronic applications accepted. Application fee is waived when completed online. *Expenses:* Contact institution.

Lasell College, Graduate and Professional Studies in Education, Newton, MA 02466-2709. Offers curriculum, leadership, and inclusion (M Ed); elementary education (M Ed); special education (M Ed), including moderate disabilities; teaching bilingual/English learners with disabilities (Graduate Certificate). *Program availability:* Part-time-only, evening/weekend, blended/hybrid learning. *Faculty:* 1 (woman) full-time, 5 part-time/adjunct (4 women). *Students:* 4 full-time (3 women), 45 part-time (37 women); includes 4 minority (3 Asian, non-Hispanic/Latino; 1 Hispanic/Latino). Average age 28. 23 applicants, 70% accepted, 10 enrolled. In 2018, 22 master's awarded. *Degree requirements:* For master's, minimum GPA of 3.0; practicum. *Entrance requirements:* For master's, Massachusetts Tests for Educator Licensure (MTEL) Curriculum and Literacy foundations of reading and writing subtest, one-page personal statement, 2 letters of recommendation, resume, bachelor's degree transcript. Additional exam requirements/recommendations for international students: Required—TOEFL (minimum score 550 paper-based, 79 iBT) or IELTS (minimum score 6). *Application deadline:* For fall admission, 8/31 priority date for domestic students, 6/30 priority date for international students; for spring admission, 12/31 priority date for domestic students, 10/31 priority date for international students. Applications are processed on a rolling basis. Electronic applications accepted. *Expenses: Tuition:* Part-time $600 per credit. *Required fees:* $40 per course. *Financial support:* Federal Work-Study, scholarships/grants, and tuition discounts available. Support available to part-time students. Financial award application deadline: 8/31; financial award applicants required to submit FAFSA. *Faculty research:* Inclusion, English language learners, literacy, and urban education; teacher inquiry; universal design for learning, deaf-blindness, and visual impairments; social and emotional learning; educational law, applied behavior analysis, and classroom management. *Unit head:* Eric Turner, Vice President of Graduate and Professional Studies, 617-243-2071, Fax: 617-243-2450, E-mail: gradinfo@lasell.edu. *Application contact:* Adrienne Franciosi, Director of Graduate Enrollment, 617-243-2214, Fax: 617-243-2450, E-mail: gradinfo@lasell.edu.
Website: http://www.lasell.edu/academics/graduate-and-professional-studies/programs-of-study/master-of-education.html

Lee University, Program in Education, Cleveland, TN 37320-3450. Offers art (MAT); curriculum and instruction (M Ed, Ed S); early childhood (MAT); educational leadership (M Ed, Ed S); elementary education (MAT); English and math (MAT); English and science (MAT); English and social studies (MAT); higher education administration (MS); history (MAT); history and economics (MAT); math and science (MAT); math and social studies (MAT); middle grades (MAT); science and social studies (MASW); secondary education (MAT); Spanish (MAT); special education (M Ed, MAT); TESOL (MAT). *Accreditation:* NCATE. *Program availability:* Part-time. *Faculty:* 13 full-time (5 women), 13 part-time/adjunct (7 women). *Students:* 32 full-time (26 women), 73 part-time (49 women); includes 13 minority (10 Black or African American, non-Hispanic/Latino; 3 Two or more races, non-Hispanic/Latino), 3 international. Average age 30. 56 applicants, 73% accepted, 34 enrolled. In 2018, 60 master's, 3 other advanced degrees awarded. *Degree requirements:* For master's, variable foreign language requirement, thesis optional, internship. *Entrance requirements:* For master's, MAT or GRE General Test, minimum undergraduate GPA of 2.75, 3 letters of recommendation, interview, writing sample, official transcripts, background check; for Ed S, minimum undergraduate and master's GPA of 2.75, official transcripts for undergraduate and master's degrees. Additional exam requirements/recommendations for international students: Required—TOEFL (minimum score 61 iBT). *Application deadline:* For fall admission, 6/1 priority date for domestic and international students; for spring admission, 11/1 priority date for domestic and international students; for summer admission, 4/1 priority date for domestic and international students. Applications are processed on a rolling basis. Application fee: $25. Electronic applications accepted. *Financial support:* In 2018–19, 43 students received support. Career-related internships or fieldwork, Federal Work-Study, institutionally sponsored loans, scholarships/grants, and unspecified assistantships available. Financial award application deadline: 3/1; financial award applicants required to submit FAFSA. *Unit head:* Dr. William Kamm, Director, 423-614-8544, E-mail: wkamm@leeuniversity.edu. *Application contact:* Jeffery McGirt, Director of Graduate Enrollment, 423-614-8691, Fax: 423-614-8317, E-mail: jmcgirt@leeuniversity.edu.
Website: http://www.leeuniversity.edu/academics/graduate/education

Lehman College of the City University of New York, School of Education, Department of Middle and High School Education, Program in Teaching English to Speakers of Other Languages, Bronx, NY 10468-1589. Offers MS Ed. *Accreditation:* NCATE. *Degree requirements:* For master's, thesis. *Entrance requirements:* For master's, minimum GPA of 3.0.

Le Moyne College, Department of Education, Syracuse, NY 13214. Offers adolescent education (MS Ed, MST); adolescent education/special education (MS Ed, MST); adolescent English (MST), including grades 7-12; adolescent English/special education (MST), including grades 7-12; adolescent foreign language (MST), including grades 7-12; adolescent history (MST), including grades 7-12; childhood education (MS Ed); childhood education/special education (MS Ed); elementary education (MS Ed); general education (MS Ed); inclusive childhood education (MST); literacy education (MS Ed), including birth to grade 6, grades 5-12; school building leader (MS Ed); school building leadership (CAS); school district business leader (MS Ed, CAS); school district leader (MS Ed); school district leadership (CAS); secondary education (MS Ed); special education (MS Ed); teaching English to speakers of other languages (MS Ed); urban studies (MS Ed). *Accreditation:* TEAC. *Program availability:* Part-time, evening/weekend. *Faculty:* 7 full-time (5 women), 16 part-time/adjunct (11 women). *Students:* 35 full-time (28 women), 119 part-time (84 women); includes 14 minority (5 Black or African American, non-Hispanic/Latino; 1 Asian, non-Hispanic/Latino; 7 Hispanic/Latino; 1 Two or more races, non-Hispanic/Latino), 1 international. Average age 30. 123 applicants, 89% accepted, 96 enrolled. In 2018, 66 master's, 48 CASs awarded. Terminal master's awarded for partial completion of doctoral program. *Degree requirements:* For master's, thesis. *Entrance requirements:* For master's, bachelor's degree with minimum undergraduate GPA of 3.0, 2 letters of recommendation, transcripts. Additional exam requirements/recommendations for international students: Required—TOEFL (minimum score 79 iBT); Recommended—IELTS (minimum score 6.5). *Application deadline:* For fall admission, 4/1 priority date for domestic and international students; for spring admission, 10/1 priority date for domestic and international students; for summer admission, 3/1 priority date for domestic and international students. Applications are processed on a rolling basis. Electronic applications accepted. *Expenses:* $734 per credit hour; wellness fee $70 per semester for full-time graduate students taking 9+ credit hours; technology fee $75 per semester for full-time graduate students taking 9+ credit hours, $25 per semester for part-time students; $1,470 per credit hour (for ED.D.). *Financial support:* In 2018–19, 44 students received support. Career-related internships or fieldwork, scholarships/grants, and health care benefits available. Support available to part-time students. Financial award applicants required to submit FAFSA. *Faculty research:* Minority teachers, special education, multiculturalism, literacy, technology, media literacy learning, autism, school district organization, service-learning, higher level problem solving, teacher leadership. *Unit head:* Dr. Stephen C. Fleury, Chair, Department of Education, 315-445-4376, Fax: 315-445-4744, E-mail: fleurysc@lemoyne.edu. *Application contact:* Jody F Manning, Assistant Director for Graduate Admission, 315-445-5444, Fax: 315-445-6092, E-mail: manninjf@lemoyne.edu.
Website: http://www.lemoyne.edu/education

Lesley University, Graduate School of Education, Cambridge, MA 02138-2790. Offers arts, community, and education (M Ed); autism studies (Certificate); curriculum and instruction (M Ed, CAGS); early childhood education (M Ed); ecological teaching and learning (MS); educational studies (PhD), including adult learning, educational leadership, individually designed; elementary education (M Ed); emergent technologies for educators (Certificate); ESLArts: language learning through the arts (M Ed); high school education (M Ed); individually designed (M Ed); integrated teaching through the arts (M Ed); literacy for K-8 classroom teachers (M Ed); mathematics education (M Ed); middle school education (M Ed); moderate disabilities (M Ed); online learning (Certificate); reading (CAGS); science in education (M Ed); severe disabilities (M Ed); special needs (CAGS); specialist teacher of reading (M Ed); teacher of visual art (M Ed); technology in education (M Ed, CAGS). *Accreditation:* TEAC. *Program availability:* Part-time, evening/weekend, online learning. *Degree requirements:* For master's, practicum; for doctorate, thesis/dissertation. *Entrance requirements:* For master's, Massachusetts Tests for Educator Licensure (MTEL), transcripts, statement of purpose, recommendations; interview (for special education); for doctorate, GRE General Test, transcripts, statement of purpose, recommendations, interview, master's degree, resume; for other advanced degree, interview, master's degree. Additional exam requirements/recommendations for international students: Required—TOEFL (minimum score 550 paper-based; 80 iBT). Electronic applications accepted. *Faculty research:* Assessment in literacy, mathematics and science; autism spectrum disorders; instructional technology and online learning; multicultural education and English language learners.

Lewis University, College of Education, Program in Curriculum and Instruction: Literacy and English Language Learning, Romeoville, IL 60446. Offers M Ed. *Program availability:* Part-time. *Students:* 1 (woman) full-time, 1 part-time (0 women). Average age 31. *Degree requirements:* For master's, comprehensive exam. *Entrance requirements:* For master's, Test of Academic Proficiency/Basic Skills Test/ACT/SAT, bachelor's degree, minimum undergraduate GPA of 2.75, state licensure with teaching endorsement. Additional exam requirements/recommendations for international students: Required—TOEFL (minimum score 550 paper-based; 79 iBT), IELTS (minimum score 6). *Application deadline:* For fall admission, 5/1 priority date for international students; for spring admission, 11/1 for international students. Application fee: $40. Electronic applications accepted. *Financial support:* Federal Work-Study and unspecified assistantships available. Financial award application deadline: 5/1; financial award applicants required to submit FAFSA. *Unit head:* Dr. Christopher Kline, Foundations, Leadership & Literacy Department Chair. *Application contact:* Kathy Lisak, Graduate Admission Counselor, 815-836-5610, E-mail: grad@lewisu.edu.
Website: http://www.lewisu.edu/academics/literacy-ELL/index.htm

Lewis University, College of Education, Program in English as a Second Language, Romeoville, IL 60446. Offers M Ed. *Program availability:* Part-time, evening/weekend. *Students:* 1 (woman) full-time, 5 part-time (4 women); includes 1 minority (Hispanic/Latino), 2 international. Average age 30. *Degree requirements:* For master's, comprehensive exam, departmental qualifying exam. *Entrance requirements:* For master's, writing exam, Test of Academic Proficiency/Basic Skills Test/ACT/SAT, bachelor's degree, minimum GPA of 2.75, 2 letters of recommendation, writing sample, professional educator license. Additional exam requirements/recommendations for international students: Required—TOEFL (minimum score 550 paper-based; 79 iBT), IELTS (minimum score 6). *Application deadline:* For fall admission, 5/1 priority date for international students; for spring admission, 11/15 priority date for international students. Application fee: $40. Electronic applications accepted. *Financial support:* Federal Work-Study, scholarships/grants, and unspecified assistantships available. Financial award application deadline: 5/1; financial award applicants required to submit FAFSA. *Unit head:* Dr. Jung Kim, Program Director. *Application contact:* Kathy Lisak, Graduate Admission Counselor, 815-836-5610, E-mail: grad@lewisu.edu.

Lindenwood University, Graduate Programs, School of Education, St. Charles, MO 63301-1695. Offers behavioral analysis (MA); education (MA), including autism spectrum disorders, character education, early intervention in autism and sensory impairment, gifted, technology; educational administration (MA, Ed D, Ed S); English to speakers of other languages (MA); instructional leadership (Ed D, Ed S); library media (MA); professional counseling (MA); school administration (MA, Ed S); school counseling (MA); teaching (MA). *Program availability:* Part-time, evening/weekend, 100% online, blended/hybrid learning. *Faculty:* 38 full-time (28 women), 111 part-time/adjunct (66 women). *Students:* 456 full-time (341 women), 1,107 part-time (851 women); includes 374 minority (296 Black or African American, non-Hispanic/Latino; 7 American Indian or Alaska Native, non-Hispanic/Latino; 8 Asian, non-Hispanic/Latino; 38 Hispanic/Latino; 1 Native Hawaiian or other Pacific Islander, non-Hispanic/Latino; 24 Two or more races, non-Hispanic/Latino), 17 international. Average age 36. 496 applicants, 72% accepted, 275 enrolled. In 2018, 454 master's, 64 doctorates, 66 other advanced degrees awarded. *Degree requirements:* For master's, thesis (for some programs), minimum GPA of 3.0; for doctorate, thesis/dissertation, minimum GPA of 3.0; for Ed S, comprehensive exam, project, minimum GPA of 3.0. *Entrance requirements:* For master's, interview, minimum undergraduate cumulative GPA of 3.0, writing sample, letter of recommendation; for doctorate, minimum graduate GPA of 3.4, resume, interview, writing sample, 4 letters of recommendation; for Ed S, master's degree in education, relevant work experience. Additional exam requirements/recommendations for international students: Required—TOEFL (minimum score 553 paper-based; 81 iBT);

Recommended—IELTS (minimum score 6.5). *Application deadline:* For fall admission, 8/9 priority date for domestic students, 6/1 priority date for international students; for spring admission, 12/20 priority date for domestic students, 11/1 priority date for international students; for summer admission, 5/15 priority date for domestic students, 3/27 priority date for international students. Applications are processed on a rolling basis. Application fee: $0 ($100 for international students). Electronic applications accepted. *Expenses: Tuition:* Full-time $16,900; part-time $480 per credit hour. *Required fees:* $700; $350 per unit. Tuition and fees vary according to degree level. *Financial support:* In 2018–19, 316 students received support. Career-related internships or fieldwork, Federal Work-Study, institutionally sponsored loans, scholarships/grants, tuition waivers (partial), and unspecified assistantships available. Financial award application deadline: 6/30; financial award applicants required to submit FAFSA. *Unit head:* Dr. Anthony Scheffler, Dean, School of Education, 636-949-4618, Fax: 636-949-4197, E-mail: ascheffler@lindenwood.edu. *Application contact:* Kara Schilli, Assistant Vice President, University Admissions, 636-949-4349, Fax: 636-949-4109, E-mail: adultadmissions@lindenwood.edu.
Website: https://www.lindenwood.edu/academics/academic-schools/school-of-education/

Long Island University–Hudson, Graduate School, Purchase, NY 10577. Offers autism (Advanced Certificate); bilingual education (Advanced Certificate); childhood education (MS Ed); crisis management (Advanced Certificate); early childhood education (MS Ed); educational leadership (MS Ed); health administration (MPA); literacy (MS Ed); marriage and family therapy (MS); mental health counseling (MS, Advanced Certificate), including credentialed alcoholism and substance abuse counselor (MS); middle childhood and adolescence education (MS Ed); pharmaceutics (MS), including cosmetic science, industrial pharmacy; public administration (MPA); school counseling (MS Ed, Advanced Certificate); school psychology (MS Ed); special education (MS Ed); TESOL (MS Ed); TESOL (all grades) (Advanced Certificate). *Program availability:* Part-time, evening/weekend. *Entrance requirements:* Additional exam requirements/recommendations for international students: Required—TOEFL. Electronic applications accepted. *Expenses:* Contact institution.

Long Island University–LIU Brooklyn, School of Education, Brooklyn, NY 11201-8423. Offers adolescence urban education (MS Ed); applied behavior analysis (Advanced Certificate); bilingual education (Advanced Certificate); bilingual education in urban setting (MS Ed); bilingual school counselor (MS Ed, Advanced Certificate); childhood urban education (MS Ed); childhood/early childhood education (MS Ed); childhood/early childhood urban education (MS Ed); early childhood urban education (MS Ed, Advanced Certificate); educational leadership (Advanced Certificate); marriage and family therapy (MS, Advanced Certificate); mental health counseling (MS, Advanced Certificate); school building district leader (Advanced Certificate); school counselor (MS Ed, Advanced Certificate); school psychologist (MS Ed); teaching students with disabilities (MS Ed); teaching urban children with disabilities (MS Ed); TESOL (MS Ed, Advanced Certificate). *Accreditation:* TEAC. *Program availability:* Part-time, evening/weekend, 100% online. *Entrance requirements:* For master's, GRE. Additional exam requirements/recommendations for international students: Required—TOEFL (minimum score 527 paper-based, 75 iBT), IELTS, or PTE. Electronic applications accepted. *Faculty research:* Diversity issues in education and mental health care, inclusion - disability studies, sustainability, teacher professional development.

Long Island University–LIU Post, College of Education, Information and Technology, Brookville, NY 11548-1300. Offers adolescence education (MS); adolescence education 7-12 (MS); archives and records management (AC); art education (MS); childhood education (MS); childhood education/literacy B-6 (MS); childhood education/special education (MS); clinical mental health counseling (MS, AC); early childhood education (MS); early childhood education/childhood education (MS); educational leadership (AC); educational technology (MS); information studies (PhD); interdisciplinary educational studies (Ed D); middle childhood education (MS); music education (MS); public library administration (AC); school counselor (MS); special education (MS Ed); speech-language pathology (MA); students with disabilities, 7-12 generalist (AC); TESOL (MA). *Accreditation:* ASHA; TEAC. *Program availability:* Part-time, 100% online, blended/hybrid learning. Terminal master's awarded for partial completion of doctoral program. *Degree requirements:* For master's, variable foreign language requirement, comprehensive exam (for some programs), thesis optional; for doctorate, comprehensive exam, thesis/dissertation. *Entrance requirements:* For master's and AC, GRE (for some programs). Additional exam requirements/recommendations for international students: Required—TOEFL (minimum score 550 paper-based, 75 iBT), IELTS, or PTE. Electronic applications accepted. *Faculty research:* Sleep; use of technology to develop executive function by students with disabilities; early childhood literacy development through play; social justice through education; using a structured protocol to discuss Bad News.

Long Island University–Riverhead, Graduate Programs, Riverhead, NY 11901. Offers applied behavior analysis (Advanced Certificate); childhood education (MS), including grades 1-6; cybersecurity policy (Advanced Certificate); homeland security management (MS, Advanced Certificate); literacy education (MS); literacy education B-6 (MS); teaching students with disabilities (MS), including grades 1-6; TESOL (Advanced Certificate). *Accreditation:* TEAC. *Program availability:* Part-time. *Entrance requirements:* Additional exam requirements/recommendations for international students: Required—TOEFL or IELTS. Electronic applications accepted. *Expenses:* Contact institution.

Madonna University, Program in Teaching English to Speakers of Other Languages, Livonia, MI 48150-1173. Offers MATESOL. *Program availability:* Part-time, evening/weekend. *Degree requirements:* For master's, one foreign language, thesis or alternative. Electronic applications accepted. *Expenses: Tuition:* Full-time $15,030; part-time $835 per credit hour. Tuition and fees vary according to degree level and program.

Manhattanville College, School of Education, Jump Start Program, Purchase, NY 10577-2132. Offers childhood education and special education (grades 1-6) (MPS); early childhood education (birth-grade 2) (MAT); education (Advanced Certificate); English and special education (grades 5-12) (MPS); mathematics and special education (grades 5-12) (MPS); science and special education (grades 5-12) (MPS); social studies and special education (grades 5-12) (MPS); Spanish (grades 7-12) (MAT); tesol - teaching English as a second language (all grades) (MPS). *Program availability:* Part-time, evening/weekend. *Faculty:* 11 full-time (7 women), 78 part-time/adjunct (50 women). *Students:* 3 full-time (2 women), 16 part-time (11 women); includes 5 minority (1 Black or African American, non-Hispanic/Latino; 3 Hispanic/Latino; 1 Native Hawaiian or other Pacific Islander, non-Hispanic/Latino). Average age 31. 48 applicants, 54% accepted, 22 enrolled. In 2018, 23 master's, 1 other advanced degree awarded. *Degree requirements:* For master's, comprehensive exam (for some programs), thesis (for some programs), student teaching, research seminars, portfolios, internships, writing assessment; for Advanced Certificate, comprehensive exam (for some programs). *Entrance requirements:* For master's, for programs leading to certification, candidates must submit scores from GRE or MAT(miller analogies test), minimum undergraduate GPA of 3.0, all transcripts from all colleges and universities attended, 2 letters of recommendation, interview, essay (2-3 page personal statement that describes reasons for choosing education as profession and personal philosophy of education), proof of immunization (for those born after 1957). Additional exam requirements/recommendations for international students: Required—TOEFL (minimum score 600 paper-based; 110 iBT); Recommended—IELTS (minimum score 8). *Application deadline:* Applications are processed on a rolling basis. Application fee: $75. Electronic applications accepted. *Expenses:* 935 per credit. *Financial support:* Teaching assistantships, career-related internships or fieldwork, Federal Work-Study, institutionally sponsored loans, scholarships/grants, and unspecified assistantships available. Financial award application deadline: 3/15; financial award applicants required to submit FAFSA. *Faculty research:* Early childhood and technology, professional development schools and community schools, students with emotional difficulties, literacy and adolescents, mindfulness, changing suburbs institute, and community schools, studying the effects of the environment on special populations, the most difficult cases, students who are presented with multiple challenges: learning, behavioral and ACE experiences who see criminal behavior as a way to cope; working on giving them the tools they need to succeed. *Unit head:* Dr. Shelley Wepner, Dean, 914-323-3153, E-mail: Shelly.Wepner@mville.edu. *Application contact:* Alissa Wilson, Director, SOE Graduate Enrollment Management, 914-323-3150, Fax: 914-694-1732, E-mail: edschool@mville.edu.
Website: http://www.mville.edu/programs/jump-start

Manhattanville College, School of Education, Program in Teaching English to Speakers of Other Languages, Purchase, NY 10577-2132. Offers adult and international settings (MPS); bilingual education (childhood/Spanish) (Advanced Certificate); teaching English as a second language (all grades) (MPS, Certificate). *Program availability:* Part-time, evening/weekend. *Faculty:* 2 full-time (1 woman), 13 part-time/adjunct (8 women). *Students:* 4 full-time (3 women), 16 part-time (11 women); includes 2 minority (both Hispanic/Latino). Average age 27. 9 applicants, 67% accepted, 3 enrolled. In 2018, 13 master's, 5 Advanced Certificates awarded. *Degree requirements:* For master's, comprehensive exam (for some programs), thesis (for some programs), student teaching, research seminars, portfolios, internships, writing assessment; for other advanced degree, comprehensive exam (for some programs). *Entrance requirements:* For master's, for programs leading to certification, candidates must submit scores from GRE or MAT(Miller Analogies Test), minimum undergraduate GPA of 3.0, all transcripts from all colleges and universities attended, 2 letters of recommendation, interview, essay (2-3 page personal statement that describes reasons for choosing education as profession and personal philosophy of education), proof of immunization (for those born after 1957). Additional exam requirements/recommendations for international students: Required—TOEFL (minimum score 600 paper-based; 110 iBT); Recommended—IELTS (minimum score 8). *Application deadline:* Applications are processed on a rolling basis. Application fee: $75. Electronic applications accepted. *Expenses:* 935 per credit. *Financial support:* Teaching assistantships, career-related internships or fieldwork, Federal Work-Study, institutionally sponsored loans, scholarships/grants, and unspecified assistantships available. Financial award application deadline: 3/15; financial award applicants required to submit FAFSA. *Faculty research:* Changing suburbs institute and community schools. *Unit head:* Dr. Shelly Wepner, Dean, 914-323-3153, Fax: 914-323-5493, E-mail: Shelly.Wepner@mville.edu. *Application contact:* Alissa Wilson, Director, SOE Graduate Enrollment Management, 914-323-3150, Fax: 914-694-1732, E-mail: edschool@mville.edu.
Website: http://www.mville.edu/programs/tesol-teaching-english-speakers-other-languages

Marlboro College, Graduate and Professional Studies, Program in Teaching English to Speakers of Other Languages, Marlboro, VT 05344. Offers MAT. *Degree requirements:* For master's, 36 credits, final learning portfolio. *Entrance requirements:* For master's, 2 letters of recommendation, letter of intent, transcripts, interview. Additional exam requirements/recommendations for international students: Required—TOEFL (minimum score of 577 paper-based, 90 iBT) or IELTS (minimum score of 7). Electronic applications accepted. *Expenses:* Contact institution.

Mary Baldwin University, Graduate Studies, Programs in Education, Staunton, VA 24401-3610. Offers applied behavior analysis (MS); autism spectrum disorders (M Ed); elementary education (M Ed, MAT); English as a second language (M Ed); environment-based learning (M Ed); gifted education (M Ed); higher education (MS); leadership (M Ed); middle grades education (MAT); reading education (M Ed); special education (M Ed). *Accreditation:* TEAC.

McDaniel College, Graduate and Professional Studies, Program in TESOL, Westminster, MD 21157-4390. Offers MS. *Program availability:* Part-time, evening/weekend, online only, 100% online. *Degree requirements:* For master's, thesis optional, portfolio. *Entrance requirements:* For master's, PRAXIS I, bachelor's degree from accredited institution with minimum cumulative GPA of 2.75; statement of intent; three references. Additional exam requirements/recommendations for international students: Required—TOEFL (minimum score 79 iBT), IELTS (minimum score 6). Electronic applications accepted.

Mercy College, School of Education, Program in Teaching English to Speakers of Other Languages (TESOL), Dobbs Ferry, NY 10522-1189. Offers MS, Advanced Certificate. *Program availability:* Part-time, evening/weekend, blended/hybrid learning. *Students:* 10 full-time (all women), 37 part-time (34 women); includes 24 minority (4 Black or African American, non-Hispanic/Latino; 18 Hispanic/Latino; 2 Two or more races, non-Hispanic/Latino). Average age 33. 40 applicants, 65% accepted, 15 enrolled. In 2018, 16 master's, 9 other advanced degrees awarded. *Degree requirements:* For master's, Capstone project; clinical practice; for initial New York State certification, passing scores in the following are required: Educating All Students, Content Specialty Test, edTPA. *Entrance requirements:* For master's, GRE or PRAXIS, transcript(s); resume. Additional exam requirements/recommendations for international students: Required—TOEFL (minimum score 600 paper-based; 71 iBT), IELTS (minimum score 8). *Application deadline:* Applications are processed on a rolling basis. Application fee: $40. Electronic applications accepted. *Expenses: Tuition:* Full-time $15,696; part-time $872 per credit. *Required fees:* $642; $161 per term. Tuition and fees vary according to course load, degree level and program. *Financial support:* Career-related internships or fieldwork, Federal Work-Study, scholarships/grants, and unspecified assistantships available. Support available to part-time students. Financial award applicants required to submit FAFSA. *Unit head:* Dr. Eric Martone, Interim Dean, School of Education, 914-674-7618, Fax: 914-674-7352, E-mail: emartone@mercy.edu. *Application contact:* Allison Gurdineer, Executive Director of Admissions, 877-637-2946, Fax: 914-674-7382, E-mail: admissions@mercy.edu.
Website: https://www.mercy.edu/degrees-programs/ms-teaching-english-speakers-other-languages-tesol

Meredith College, School of Education, Health and Human Sciences, Raleigh, NC 27607-5298. Offers academically and intellectually gifted (M Ed); elementary education (M Ed, MAT); English as a second language (M Ed, MAT); health and physical education (MAT); nutrition, health and human performance (MS, Postbaccalaureate Certificate), including dietetic internship (Postbaccalaureate Certificate), nutrition (MS); psychology (MA), including industrial/organizational psychology; reading (M Ed); special education (MAT); special education (general curriculum) (M Ed). *Accreditation:* NCATE. *Program availability:* Part-time, evening/weekend. *Students:* 97 full-time (89 women), 76 part-time (73 women); includes 39 minority (17 Black or African American, non-Hispanic/

Latino; 1 American Indian or Alaska Native, non-Hispanic/Latino; 9 Asian, non-Hispanic/Latino; 10 Hispanic/Latino; 2 Two or more races, non-Hispanic/Latino). Average age 28. In 2018, 56 master's, 36 other advanced degrees awarded. *Degree requirements:* For master's, thesis optional. *Entrance requirements:* For master's, GRE General Test or MAT, minimum GPA of 2.5, teaching license, recommendations. Additional exam requirements/recommendations for international students: Required—TOEFL. *Application deadline:* For fall admission, 7/1 priority date for domestic students; for spring admission, 11/1 priority date for domestic students. Applications are processed on a rolling basis. Application fee: $50. Electronic applications accepted. *Expenses:* $575 per credit hour for masters degree in education, $725 (for MS. PSY.IO degree), $20,295 (for pre-health post-baccalaureate certificate), $13,600 (for dietetic internship). *Financial support:* Career-related internships or fieldwork, institutionally sponsored loans, and tuition waivers (partial) available. Support available to part-time students. Financial award application deadline: 2/15; financial award applicants required to submit FAFSA. *Unit head:* Dr. Monica McKinney, Graduate Program Manager, 919-760-8056, Fax: 919-760-2303, E-mail: mckinneym@meredith.edu. *Application contact:* Dr. Monica McKinney, Graduate Program Manager, 919-760-8056, Fax: 919-760-2303, E-mail: mckinneym@meredith.edu.
Website: https://www.meredith.edu/school-of-education-health-and-human-sciences

Messiah College, Program in Education, Mechanicsburg, PA 17055. Offers curriculum and instruction (M Ed); special education (M Ed); teaching English to speakers of other languages (M Ed). *Program availability:* Part-time, online learning. Electronic applications accepted. *Faculty research:* Socio-cultural perspectives on education, TESOL, autism, special education.

Metropolitan State University, School of Urban Education, St. Paul, MN 55106-5000. Offers curriculum, pedagogy and schooling (MS); English as a second language (MS); secondary education (MS), including English teaching, life sciences teaching, mathematics teaching, social studies teaching; special education (MS).

Michigan State University, The Graduate School, College of Arts and Letters, Department of Linguistics and Germanic, Slavic, Asian, and African Languages, East Lansing, MI 48824. Offers German studies (MA, PhD); linguistics (MA, PhD); teaching English to speakers of other languages (MA). *Program availability:* Part-time, evening/weekend. *Entrance requirements:* For master's, GRE General Test, minimum GPA of 3.2 in last 2 undergraduate years, 2 years of college-level foreign language, 3 letters of recommendation, portfolio (German studies); for doctorate, GRE General Test, minimum graduate GPA of 3.5, 3 letters of recommendation, master's degree or sufficient graduate course work in linguistics or language of study, master's thesis or major research paper. Additional exam requirements/recommendations for international students: Required—TOEFL. Electronic applications accepted.

MidAmerica Nazarene University, Professional and Graduate Studies in Education, Olathe, KS 66062-1899. Offers ESOL (M Ed); reading specialist (M Ed); technology enhanced teaching (M Ed). *Accreditation:* NCATE. *Program availability:* Part-time, evening/weekend, online only, 100% online. *Entrance requirements:* For master's, bachelor's degree from an accredited college or university, minimum undergraduate GPA of 3.0, valid teaching license. Additional exam requirements/recommendations for international students: Required—TOEFL (minimum score 81 iBT), IELTS (minimum score 6). Electronic applications accepted. *Expenses:* Contact institution.

Middlebury Institute of International Studies at Monterey, Graduate School of Translation, Interpretation and Language Education, Program in Teaching English to Speakers of Other Languages, Monterey, CA 93940-2691. Offers MATESOL. *Degree requirements:* For master's, portfolio, oral defense. *Entrance requirements:* For master's, minimum GPA of 3.0. Additional exam requirements/recommendations for international students: Required—TOEFL (minimum score 600 paper-based; 100 iBT). Electronic applications accepted.

Middle Tennessee State University, College of Graduate Studies, College of Education, Department of Educational Leadership, Program in Curriculum and Instruction, Murfreesboro, TN 37132. Offers curriculum and instruction (M Ed, Ed S); English as a second language (M Ed, Ed S); secondary education (M Ed); technology and curriculum design (Ed S). *Accreditation:* NCATE. *Program availability:* Part-time, evening/weekend, online learning. *Degree requirements:* For master's, comprehensive exam; for Ed S, comprehensive exam, thesis or alternative. *Entrance requirements:* For master's and Ed S, GRE, MAT or PRAXIS. Additional exam requirements/recommendations for international students: Required—TOEFL (minimum score 525 paper-based; 71 iBT) or IELTS (minimum score 6). Electronic applications accepted.

Midwest University, Graduate Programs, Wentzville, MO 63385. Offers asset management/investment/real estate (MBA); Christian counseling (D Min); Christian education (D Min); counseling (MA), including marriage and family counseling, school counseling; divinity (M Div); education (MA), including brain and gifted education, Christian education; global business management (MBA); global leadership (MBA); leadership (PhD), including brain and gifted educational leadership, entrepreneurial leadership, international aviation leadership, organizational leadership, political leadership; mission studies (D Min); music (MM, DMA); pastoral theology (D Min); public policy/administration (MBA); teaching English to speakers of other languages (MA). *Program availability:* Part-time, online learning. *Degree requirements:* For master's, thesis (for some programs); for doctorate, thesis/dissertation. *Entrance requirements:* Additional exam requirements/recommendations for international students: Recommended—TOEFL (minimum score 550 paper-based).

Minnesota State University Mankato, College of Graduate Studies and Research, College of Arts and Humanities, Department of English, Mankato, MN 56001. Offers communication and composition (MA); creative writing (MFA); English studies (MA); teaching English as a second language (MA, Certificate); technical communication (MA, Certificate). *Program availability:* Part-time. *Degree requirements:* For master's, one foreign language, comprehensive exam, thesis or alternative. *Entrance requirements:* For master's, minimum GPA of 3.0 during previous 2 years, writing sample (MFA). Additional exam requirements/recommendations for international students: Required—TOEFL (minimum score 500 paper-based; 61 iBT). Electronic applications accepted.

Mississippi College, Graduate School, College of Arts and Sciences, School of Humanities and Social Sciences, Department of Modern Languages, Clinton, MS 39058. Offers teaching English to speakers of other languages (MA, MS). *Program availability:* Part-time. *Degree requirements:* For master's, thesis (for some programs). *Entrance requirements:* For master's, GRE or NTE. Additional exam requirements/recommendations for international students: Recommended—TOEFL, IELTS. Electronic applications accepted.

Missouri State University, Graduate College, College of Arts and Letters, Department of English, Springfield, MO 65897. Offers applied second language acquisition (MASLA); English (MA); English education (MS Ed); teaching English to speakers of other languages (Certificate); writing (MA). MASLA offered with the Department of Modern and Classical Languages. *Program availability:* Part-time, evening/weekend. *Faculty:* 25 full-time (18 women), 5 part-time/adjunct (2 women). *Students:* 41 full-time (32 women), 73 part-time (66 women); includes 5 minority (2 Hispanic/Latino; 1 Native Hawaiian or other Pacific Islander, non-Hispanic/Latino; 2 Two or more races, non-Hispanic/Latino), 7 international. Average age 24. 97 applicants, 65% accepted, 56 enrolled. In 2018, 29 master's awarded. *Degree requirements:* For master's, one foreign language, comprehensive exam, thesis or alternative. *Entrance requirements:* For master's, GRE (for MA), 9-12 teacher certification (MS Ed); minimum GPA of 3.0 (MA); personal statement (200- to 250-word description of reasons and goals behind interest in English graduate studies); at least two letters of recommendation from individuals able to speak of the applicant's academic achievements and potential; writing sample. Additional exam requirements/recommendations for international students: Required—TOEFL (minimum score 550 paper-based; 79 iBT), IELTS (minimum score 6). *Application deadline:* For fall admission, 3/1 priority date for domestic students, 3/1 for international students; for spring admission, 10/1 priority date for domestic students, 10/1 for international students. Applications are processed on a rolling basis. Application fee: $55 ($60 for international students). Electronic applications accepted. Tuition and fees vary according to class time, course level, course load, degree level, campus/location, program and student level. *Financial support:* In 2018–19, 23 teaching assistantships with full tuition reimbursements (averaging $8,772 per year) were awarded; Federal Work-Study, institutionally sponsored loans, scholarships/grants, and unspecified assistantships also available. Financial award application deadline: 1/31; financial award applicants required to submit FAFSA. *Faculty research:* History of rhetoric, modern poetry, African-American literature, digital writing, teaching English to speakers of other languages. *Unit head:* Dr. Linda Moser, Interim Department Head, 417-836-6565, Fax: 417-836-6940, E-mail: english@missouristate.edu. *Application contact:* Lakan Drinker, Director, Graduate Enrollment Management, 417-836-5330, Fax: 417-836-6200, E-mail: lakandrinker@missouristate.edu.
Website: https://english.missouristate.edu/

Missouri Western State University, Program in Assessment, St. Joseph, MO 64507-2294. Offers K-12 cross-categorical special education (MAS); TESOL (Graduate Certificate). *Program availability:* Part-time. *Students:* 1 (woman) full-time, 33 part-time (32 women); includes 3 minority (2 American Indian or Alaska Native, non-Hispanic/Latino; 1 Asian, non-Hispanic/Latino). Average age 40. 16 applicants, 100% accepted, 8 enrolled. In 2018, 12 master's, 4 other advanced degrees awarded. *Entrance requirements:* For master's, minimum GPA of 2.75. Additional exam requirements/recommendations for international students: Recommended—TOEFL (minimum score 79 iBT), IELTS (minimum score 6). *Application deadline:* For fall admission, 7/15 for domestic and international students; for spring admission, 11/1 for domestic and international students; for summer admission, 4/29 for domestic and international students. Applications are processed on a rolling basis. Application fee: $45 ($50 for international students). Electronic applications accepted. *Expenses: Tuition, area resident:* Part-time $359.39 per credit hour. Tuition, state resident: part-time $359.39 per credit hour. Tuition, nonresident: part-time $643.39 per credit hour. Tuition and fees vary according to program. *Financial support:* Scholarships/grants and unspecified assistantships available. Support available to part-time students. *Unit head:* Dr. Susan Bashinski, Dean of Graduate Programs, 816-271-4394, E-mail: graduate@missouriwestern.edu. *Application contact:* Dr. Susan Bashinski, Dean of Graduate Programs, 816-271-4394, Fax: 816-271-4525, E-mail: graduate@missouriwestern.edu.
Website: https://www.missouriwestern.edu/graduate/

Molloy College, Graduate Education Program, Rockville Centre, NY 11571-5002. Offers adolescent education in biology (MS); adolescent special education (Advanced Certificate); bilingual extension (Advanced Certificate); childhood education (MS); childhood special education (Advanced Certificate); early childhood education (MS); educational technology (MS); English (MS); mathematics (MS); social studies (MS); Spanish (MS); special education on both childhood and adolescent levels (MS); teaching English to speakers of other languages (TESOL) in grades pre-K to 12 (MS); TESOL (Advanced Certificate). *Accreditation:* NCATE. *Program availability:* Part-time, evening/weekend. *Faculty:* 24 full-time (22 women), 26 part-time/adjunct (19 women). *Students:* 106 full-time (78 women), 203 part-time (154 women); includes 65 minority (14 Black or African American, non-Hispanic/Latino; 5 Asian, non-Hispanic/Latino; 41 Hispanic/Latino; 5 Two or more races, non-Hispanic/Latino). Average age 41. 147 applicants, 63% accepted, 79 enrolled. In 2018, 120 master's, 1 other advanced degree awarded. *Entrance requirements:* Additional exam requirements/recommendations for international students: Required—TOEFL (minimum score 550 paper-based; 79 iBT). *Application deadline:* Applications are processed on a rolling basis. Application fee: $60. Electronic applications accepted. *Expenses: Tuition:* Full-time $20,790; part-time $1155 per credit. *Required fees:* $1060; $900. Tuition and fees vary according to course load and degree level. *Financial support:* Application deadline: 3/1; applicants required to submit FAFSA. *Faculty research:* English Language Learners; social emotional needs of students; gifted education; cultural diversity; collaborative teaching methods. *Unit head:* Joanne O'Brien, Dean, 516-323-3116, E-mail: jobrien@molloy.edu. *Application contact:* Faye Hood, Assistant Director for Admissions, 516-323-4009, E-mail: fhood@molloy.edu.

Monmouth University, Graduate Studies, School of Education, West Long Branch, NJ 07764-1898. Offers applied behavior analysis (Certificate); autism (Certificate); director of school counseling services (Post-Master's Certificate); early childhood (M Ed); educational leadership (Ed D); elementary education (MAT), including elementary level, secondary level; English as a second language (M Ed); learning disabilities teacher-consultant (Post-Master's Certificate); literacy (MS Ed); school counseling (MS Ed); special education (MS Ed), including autism, learning disabilities teacher-consultant, teacher of students with disabilities, teaching in inclusive settings; speech-language pathology (MS Ed); student affairs and college counseling (MS Ed); supervisor (Post-Master's Certificate); teaching English to speakers of other languages (Certificate). *Accreditation:* NCATE. *Program availability:* Part-time, evening/weekend, 100% online, blended/hybrid learning. *Faculty:* 29 full-time (23 women), 32 part-time/adjunct (24 women). *Students:* 214 full-time (187 women), 148 part-time (127 women); includes 60 minority (13 Black or African American, non-Hispanic/Latino; 2 Asian, non-Hispanic/Latino; 40 Hispanic/Latino; 5 Two or more races, non-Hispanic/Latino). Average age 27. In 2018, 108 master's, 9 other advanced degrees awarded. *Entrance requirements:* For master's, GRE taken within last 5 years (for MS Ed in speech-language pathology); SAT (minimum combined score of 1660 in 3 sections), ACT (23), GRE (minimum score of 4.0 on analytical writing section and minimum combined score of 310 on quantitative and verbal sections), or passing scores on 3 parts of Core Academic Skills Educators, minimum GPA of 3.0 in major; 2 letters of recommendation (for some programs); resume, personal statement or essay (depending on program). Additional exam requirements/recommendations for international students: Required—TOEFL (minimum score 550 paper-based; 79 iBT), IELTS (minimum score 6), Michigan English Language Assessment Battery (minimum score 77) or Certificate of Advanced English (minimum score 160). *Application deadline:* For fall admission, 7/15 priority date for domestic students, 7/1 for international students; for spring admission, 12/1 priority date for domestic students, 11/1 for international students; for summer admission, 5/1 for domestic students. Applications are processed on a rolling basis. Application fee: $50. Electronic applications accepted. *Expenses: Tuition:* Part-time $1233 per credit. *Required fees:* $178 per term. *Financial support:* In 2018–19, 290 students received support. Institutionally sponsored loans, scholarships/grants, and unspecified assistantships available. Support available to part-time students. Financial award applicants required to submit FAFSA. *Faculty research:* Multicultural literacy, science and mathematics teaching strategies, teacher as reflective practitioner, children with

disabilities. *Unit head:* Dr. John E. Henning, Dean, 732-263-5513, Fax: 732-263-5277, E-mail: kodonnel@monmouth.edu. *Application contact:* Kirsten Sneeringer, Graduate Admission Counselor, 732-571-3452, Fax: 732-263-5123, E-mail: gradadm@monmouth.edu.
Website: http://www.monmouth.edu/academics/schools/education/default.asp

Montclair State University, The Graduate School, College of Education and Human Services, MAT Program in Teaching, Montclair, NJ 07043-1624. Offers art (MAT); biology (MAT); chemistry (MAT); earth science (MAT); English (MAT); French (MAT); health and physical education (MAT); health education (MAT); mathematics (MAT); music (MAT); physical education (MAT); physical science (MAT); social studies (MAT); Spanish (MAT); teacher of English as a second language (MAT). *Degree requirements:* For master's, comprehensive exam, thesis or alternative. *Entrance requirements:* For master's, interview, 2 letters of recommendation. Additional exam requirements/recommendations for international students: Required—TOEFL (minimum score 83 iBT), IELTS (minimum score 6.5). Electronic applications accepted.

Montclair State University, The Graduate School, College of Humanities and Social Sciences, Teaching English to Speakers of Other Languages Certificate Program, Montclair, NJ 07043-1624. Offers Certificate. *Program availability:* Part-time, evening/weekend. *Degree requirements:* For Certificate, comprehensive exam. *Entrance requirements:* For degree, 2 letters of recommendation, essay. Additional exam requirements/recommendations for international students: Required—TOEFL (minimum score 83 iBT), IELTS (minimum score 6.5). Electronic applications accepted. *Faculty research:* Language learning and technology research, interlanguage, bilingual pragmatics.

Mount Saint Vincent University, Graduate Programs, Faculty of Education, Program in Curriculum Studies, Halifax, NS B3M 2J6, Canada. Offers general curriculum studies (M Ed, MA Ed, MA-R); teaching English to speakers of other languages (M Ed, MA Ed, MA-R). *Program availability:* Part-time, evening/weekend, online learning. *Degree requirements:* For master's, thesis (for some programs). *Entrance requirements:* For master's, bachelor's degree in related field, minimum B average, 1 year of teaching experience. Electronic applications accepted. *Faculty research:* Science education, cultural studies, international education, curriculum development.

Multnomah University, Graduate Programs, Portland, OR 97220-5898. Offers counseling (MA); global development and justice (MA); teaching (MA); TESOL (MA). *Program availability:* Part-time, evening/weekend. *Degree requirements:* For master's, variable foreign language requirement, comprehensive exam (for some programs), thesis (for some programs). *Entrance requirements:* For master's, interview; references; writing sample (for counseling). Additional exam requirements/recommendations for international students: Required—TOEFL (minimum score 550 paper-based). Electronic applications accepted. *Expenses: Tuition:* Full-time $13,440; part-time $6720 per semester hour. *Required fees:* $390; $250 per unit. Tuition and fees vary according to course load.

Murray State University, College of Humanities and Fine Arts, Department of English and Philosophy, Murray, KY 42071. Offers creative writing (MFA); English (MA); English pedagogy and technology (DA); gender studies (Certificate); teaching English to speakers of other languages (TESOL) (MA). *Program availability:* Part-time, 100% online, blended/hybrid learning. *Entrance requirements:* For master's, doctorate, and Certificate, GRE or GMAT, minimum university GPA of 2.75. Additional exam requirements/recommendations for international students: Required—TOEFL (minimum score 527 paper-based; 71 iBT). Electronic applications accepted.

Nazareth College of Rochester, Graduate Studies, Department of Education, Program in Teaching English to Speakers of Other Languages, Rochester, NY 14618. Offers MS Ed. *Accreditation:* TEAC. *Entrance requirements:* For master's, minimum GPA of 3.0. Additional exam requirements/recommendations for international students: Required—TOEFL or IELTS.

New Jersey City University, Debra Cannon Partridge Wolfe College of Education, Department of Multicultural Education, Jersey City, NJ 07305-1597. Offers bilingual/bicultural education (MA); English as a second language (MA). *Program availability:* Part-time, evening/weekend. *Entrance requirements:* For master's, GRE General Test or MAT. Additional exam requirements/recommendations for international students: Required—TOEFL.

Newman University, Master of Science in Education Program, Wichita, KS 67213-2097. Offers building leadership (MS Ed); curriculum and instruction (MS Ed), including English as a second language, reading specialist; organizational leadership (MS Ed). *Accreditation:* NCATE. *Program availability:* Part-time, evening/weekend, online learning. *Degree requirements:* For master's, thesis optional. *Entrance requirements:* For master's, 3 years' full-time teaching experience, minimum GPA of 3.0, writing sample, 2 letters of recommendation, evidence of teaching certification. Additional exam requirements/recommendations for international students: Required—TOEFL (minimum score 600 paper-based; 100 iBT). Electronic applications accepted. *Expenses:* Contact institution. *Faculty research:* Online course design and deliver, staff engagement, classroom action.

New Mexico State University, College of Education, Department of Curriculum and Instruction, Las Cruces, NM 88003-8001. Offers bilingual education (MA); curriculum and instruction (Ed D, PhD); early childhood education (MA); educational diagnostics (Ed S); language, literacy and culture (MA); learning design and technologies (MA); teaching (MAT); teaching English to speakers of other languages (MA). *Accreditation:* NCATE. *Program availability:* Part-time, evening/weekend, 100% online. *Faculty:* 22 full-time (17 women), 7 part-time/adjunct (5 women). *Students:* 82 full-time (49 women), 186 part-time (134 women); includes 153 minority (13 Black or African American, non-Hispanic/Latino; 2 American Indian or Alaska Native, non-Hispanic/Latino; 3 Asian, non-Hispanic/Latino; 129 Hispanic/Latino; 6 Two or more races, non-Hispanic/Latino), 33 international. Average age 37. 110 applicants, 79% accepted, 60 enrolled. In 2018, 75 master's, 13 doctorates, 16 other advanced degrees awarded. *Degree requirements:* For master's, comprehensive exam, thesis; for doctorate, comprehensive exam, thesis/dissertation. *Entrance requirements:* For master's, minimum cumulative GPA of 3.0; for doctorate, portfolio, minimum cumulative GPA of 3.0. Additional exam requirements/recommendations for international students: Required—TOEFL (minimum score 550 paper-based; 79 iBT), IELTS (minimum score 6.5). *Application deadline:* For fall admission, 12/15 priority date for domestic and international students. Applications are processed on a rolling basis. Application fee: $40 ($50 for international students). Electronic applications accepted. *Expenses: Tuition, area resident:* Full-time $4216.70; part-time $252.70 per credit hour. Tuition, state resident: full-time $4216.70; part-time $252.70 per credit hour. Tuition, nonresident: full-time $12,769; part-time $881.10 per credit hour. *International tuition:* $12,769.30 full-time. *Required fees:* $878.40; $48.80 per credit hour. Full-time tuition and fees vary according to course load and reciprocity agreements. *Financial support:* In 2018–19, 111 students received support, including 2 fellowships (averaging $4,548 per year), 11 research assistantships (averaging $11,673 per year), 10 teaching assistantships (averaging $10,582 per year); career-related internships or fieldwork, Federal Work-Study, scholarships/grants, traineeships, health care benefits, and unspecified assistantships also available. Support available to part-time students. Financial award application deadline: 3/1. *Faculty research:* STEM education, bilingual and English as a second language education, critical pedagogy/multicultural education, learning design and technology, early childhood education. *Total annual research expenditures:* $10,685. *Unit head:* Dr. David Rutledge, Department Head, 575-646-5411, Fax: 575-646-5436, E-mail: rutledge@nmsu.edu. *Application contact:* Dr. David Rutledge, Associate Department Head for Graduate Programs, 575-646-5411, Fax: 575-646-5436, E-mail: rutledge@nmsu.edu.
Website: http://ci.education.nmsu.edu

The New School, Schools of Public Engagement, Program in Teaching English to Speakers of Other Languages, New York, NY 10011. Offers teaching English to speakers of other languages (MA). *Program availability:* Part-time, evening/weekend, 100% online. *Degree requirements:* For master's, thesis optional. *Entrance requirements:* For master's, two letters of recommendation, statement of purpose, resume, transcripts, interview. Additional exam requirements/recommendations for international students: Required—TOEFL (minimum score 92 iBT), IELTS (minimum score 7), PTE (minimum score 68). Electronic applications accepted. *Expenses:* Contact institution.

New York University, Steinhardt School of Culture, Education, and Human Development, Department of Teaching and Learning, Program in Multilingual/Multicultural Studies, New York, NY 10012. Offers bilingual education (MA, PhD, Advanced Certificate); foreign language education (MA); teaching English to speakers of other languages (MA, PhD); teaching foreign languages, 7-12 (MA), including Chinese, French, Italian, Japanese, Spanish; teaching French as a foreign language (MA), including teaching English to speakers of other languages; teaching Spanish as a foreign language (MA), including teaching English to speakers of other languages. MA in teaching English to speakers of other languages also offered in collaboration with NYU Shanghai. *Accreditation:* TEAC. *Program availability:* Part-time, evening/weekend. *Entrance requirements:* For doctorate, GRE General Test, interview; for Advanced Certificate, master's degree. Additional exam requirements/recommendations for international students: Required—TOEFL (minimum score 100 iBT). Electronic applications accepted. *Faculty research:* Second language acquisition, cross-cultural communication, technology-enhanced language learning, language variation, action learning.

Niagara University, Graduate Division of Education, Concentration in Teacher Education, Niagara University, NY 14109. Offers early childhood and childhood education (MS Ed, Certificate); early childhood special education (MS); middle and adolescence education (MS Ed); special education (MS Ed), including 1-6, 7-12; special education (grades 1-12) (Certificate); teaching English to speakers of other languages (MS Ed, Certificate). *Accreditation:* NCATE. *Students:* 106 full-time (75 women), 105 part-time (90 women); includes 15 minority (5 Black or African American, non-Hispanic/Latino; 2 American Indian or Alaska Native, non-Hispanic/Latino; 2 Asian, non-Hispanic/Latino; 2 Hispanic/Latino; 4 Two or more races, non-Hispanic/Latino), 40 international. Average age 28. In 2018, 81 master's, 21 other advanced degrees awarded. *Entrance requirements:* For master's, GRE General Test or Academic Literacy Skills Test (ALST). Additional exam requirements/recommendations for international students: Required—TOEFL (minimum score 550 paper-based; 79 iBT), IELTS (minimum score 6). *Application deadline:* For fall admission, 8/1 for domestic students. Applications are processed on a rolling basis. Electronic applications accepted. *Expenses:* Contact institution. *Financial support:* Research assistantships with tuition reimbursements, teaching assistantships with tuition reimbursements, career-related internships or fieldwork, Federal Work-Study, scholarships/grants, and unspecified assistantships available. Support available to part-time students. Financial award application deadline: 4/15; financial award applicants required to submit FAFSA. *Unit head:* Dr. Chandra Foote, Dean, College of Education, 716-286-8549, E-mail: cjf@niagara.edu. *Application contact:* Evan Pierce, Associate Director, Graduate Studies, 716-286-8327, E-mail: epierce@niagara.edu.
Website: http://www.niagara.edu/teacher-education

Northeastern Illinois University, College of Graduate Studies and Research, College of Arts and Sciences, Program in Teaching English to Speakers of Other Languages, Chicago, IL 60625. Offers MA.

Northern Arizona University, College of Arts and Letters, Department of English, Flagstaff, AZ 86011. Offers applied linguistics (PhD); creative writing (MFA), including creative writing; English (MA), including literature, professional writing, rhetoric, writing, and digital media studies, secondary education; professional writing (Graduate Certificate); rhetoric, writing and digital media studies (Graduate Certificate); teaching English as a second language (MA, Graduate Certificate). *Program availability:* Part-time, 100% online, blended/hybrid learning. *Degree requirements:* For master's, variable foreign language requirement, comprehensive exam (for some programs), thesis (for some programs); for doctorate, variable foreign language requirement, comprehensive exam (for some programs), thesis/dissertation (for some programs); for Graduate Certificate, comprehensive exam (for some programs). *Entrance requirements:* Additional exam requirements/recommendations for international students: Required—TOEFL (minimum score 80 iBT), IELTS (minimum score 6.5). Electronic applications accepted.

Northern Arizona University, College of Education, Department of Educational Specialties, Flagstaff, AZ 86011. Offers autism spectrum disorders (Certificate); bilingual/multicultural education (M Ed), including bilingual, ESL; career and technical education (M Ed, Certificate); educational technology (M Ed, Certificate); English as a second language (Certificate); positive behavior support (Certificate); special education (M Ed), including early childhood special education, mild/moderate disabilities. *Program availability:* Part-time, 100% online, blended/hybrid learning. *Degree requirements:* For master's, variable foreign language requirement, comprehensive exam (for some programs), thesis (for some programs); for Certificate, comprehensive exam (for some programs). *Entrance requirements:* Additional exam requirements/recommendations for international students: Required—TOEFL (minimum score 80 iBT), IELTS (minimum score 6.5). Electronic applications accepted.

Northern Michigan University, Office of Graduate Education and Research, College of Arts and Sciences, Department of English, Marquette, MI 49855-5301. Offers creative writing (MFA); literature (MA); pedagogy (MA); teaching English to speakers of other languages (Graduate Certificate); theater (MA); writing (MA). *Program availability:* Part-time, evening/weekend. Terminal master's awarded for partial completion of doctoral program. *Degree requirements:* For master's, capstone project: thesis, practicum or portfolio (for MA); thesis (for MFA); for Graduate Certificate, one foreign language. *Entrance requirements:* For master's, minimum GPA of 3.0; bachelor's degree in English or minimum of 30 credit hours in undergraduate English; statement of purpose; resume; critical essay; 3 letters of recommendation; for Graduate Certificate, bachelor's degree. Additional exam requirements/recommendations for international students: Required—TOEFL (minimum score 550 paper-based; 79 iBT), IELTS (minimum score 6.5). Electronic applications accepted. *Faculty research:* Modern Arabic literature, British literature (medieval to contemporary), postcolonial literature, Native and African-American literature, creative writing, critical theory, pedagogy.

Northwest Christian University, School of Education and Counseling, Eugene, OR 97401-3745. Offers clinical mental health counseling (MA); elementary teaching (MAT);

English for speakers of other languages (MAT); physical education (MAT); school counseling (MA); secondary teaching (MAT); special education (MAT). *Program availability:* Part-time, evening/weekend, online learning. *Degree requirements:* For master's, thesis (for some programs). *Entrance requirements:* For master's, GRE or MAT, minimum undergraduate GPA of 3.0, interview, 2-3 page statement of purpose, two letters of recommendation, resume, background check. Additional exam requirements/recommendations for international students: Required—TOEFL (minimum score 550 paper-based; 80 iBT). Electronic applications accepted. *Expenses:* Contact institution.

Northwest Missouri State University, Graduate School, School of Education, Maryville, MO 64468-6001. Offers early childhood education (MS Ed); education leadership (MS Ed), including elementary, K-12, secondary; educational leadership (Ed S), including elementary school principalship, secondary school principalship, superintendency; educational leadership and policy analysis (Ed D); elementary education (MS Ed); elementary mathematics (MS Ed); higher education leadership (MS); middle school education (MS Ed); reading (MS Ed); special education (MS Ed); teacher leadership (MS Ed); teaching English language learners (MS Ed). *Accreditation:* NCATE. *Program availability:* Part-time. *Faculty:* 26 full-time (16 women). *Students:* 109 full-time (87 women), 385 part-time (270 women); includes 30 minority (10 Black or African American, non-Hispanic/Latino; 2 American Indian or Alaska Native, non-Hispanic/Latino; 3 Asian, non-Hispanic/Latino; 12 Hispanic/Latino; 1 Native Hawaiian or other Pacific Islander, non-Hispanic/Latino; 2 Two or more races, non-Hispanic/Latino), 1 international. Average age 33. 210 applicants, 72% accepted, 142 enrolled. In 2018, 71 master's, 11 other advanced degrees awarded. *Degree requirements:* For master's, comprehensive exam; for Ed S, comprehensive exam, thesis. *Entrance requirements:* For master's, GRE General Test, writing sample; for Ed S, minimum graduate GPA of 3.25. Additional exam requirements/recommendations for international students: Required—TOEFL (minimum score 550 paper-based). *Application deadline:* For fall admission, 7/1 for domestic and international students; for spring admission, 11/15 for domestic and international students. Applications are processed on a rolling basis. Application fee: $0 ($75 for international students). Electronic applications accepted. *Expenses:* $389.11 in-state and $653.92 out-of-state per credit hour. *Financial support:* Research assistantships with full tuition reimbursements, teaching assistantships with full tuition reimbursements, and unspecified assistantships available. Financial award application deadline: 4/1; financial award applicants required to submit FAFSA. *Unit head:* Dr. Tim Wall, Director, 660-562-1179, E-mail: timwall@nwmissouri.edu. *Application contact:* Dr. Tim Wall, Director, 660-562-1179, E-mail: timwall@nwmissouri.edu.
Website: https://www.nwmissouri.edu/education/index.htm

Notre Dame of Maryland University, Graduate Studies, Program in Teaching English to Speakers of Other Languages, Baltimore, MD 21210-2476. Offers MA. *Accreditation:* NCATE. *Program availability:* Part-time, evening/weekend. *Entrance requirements:* Additional exam requirements/recommendations for international students: Required—TOEFL (minimum score 500 paper-based; 61 iBT). Electronic applications accepted.

Nyack College, School of Education, Nyack, NY 10960. Offers childhood education (MS); childhood special education (MS); TESOL (MAT, MS). *Program availability:* Part-time, evening/weekend, 100% online, blended/hybrid learning. *Students:* 28 full-time (24 women), 22 part-time (19 women); includes 21 minority (10 Black or African American, non-Hispanic/Latino; 1 American Indian or Alaska Native, non-Hispanic/Latino; 3 Asian, non-Hispanic/Latino; 6 Hispanic/Latino; 1 Two or more races, non-Hispanic/Latino), 4 international. Average age 32. In 2018, 17 master's awarded. *Degree requirements:* For master's, comprehensive exam, clinical experience. *Entrance requirements:* For master's, GRE, transcripts, autobiography and statement on reasons for pursuing graduate study in education, recommendations, 6 credits of language, evidence of computer literacy, introductory course in psychology. Additional exam requirements/recommendations for international students: Required—TOEFL (minimum score 550 paper-based; 80 iBT), GRE. *Application deadline:* Applications are processed on a rolling basis. Application fee: $30. Electronic applications accepted. *Expenses:* $725/credit. *Financial support:* Scholarships/grants available. Financial award applicants required to submit FAFSA. *Unit head:* Dr. JoAnn Looney, Dean, 845-675-4538. *Application contact:* Dr. JoAnn Looney, Dean, 845-675-4538.
Website: http://www.nyack.edu/edu

Oakland University, Graduate Study and Lifelong Learning, College of Arts and Sciences, Department of Linguistics, Rochester, MI 48309-4401. Offers linguistics (MA); teaching English as a second language (Certificate). *Program availability:* Part-time, evening/weekend. *Entrance requirements:* For master's, minimum GPA of 3.0. Additional exam requirements/recommendations for international students: Required—TOEFL (minimum score 550 paper-based).

Ohio Dominican University, Division of Education, Program in Teaching English to Speakers of Other Languages, Columbus, OH 43219-2099. Offers MA. *Program availability:* Part-time, evening/weekend, 100% online, blended/hybrid learning. *Faculty:* 1 full-time (0 women), 1 (woman) part-time/adjunct. *Students:* 2 full-time (both women), 18 part-time (12 women); includes 3 minority (1 Hispanic/Latino; 2 Two or more races, non-Hispanic/Latino), 6 international. Average age 33. 11 applicants, 64% accepted, 5 enrolled. In 2018, 8 master's awarded. *Degree requirements:* For master's, thesis. *Entrance requirements:* For master's, bachelor's degree with minimum cumulative GPA of 3.0, 3 letters of recommendation. Additional exam requirements/recommendations for international students: Required—TOEFL (minimum score 550 paper-based), IELTS (minimum score 6.5). *Application deadline:* For fall admission, 9/15 for domestic students, 6/10 for international students; for spring admission, 1/4 for domestic students, 11/2 for international students; for summer admission, 5/30 for domestic students. Applications are processed on a rolling basis. Application fee: $25. Electronic applications accepted. *Expenses:* $538/credit hour tuition, $225/semester fees. *Financial support:* Applicants required to submit FAFSA. *Unit head:* Dr. Timothy A. Micek, Director, 614-251-4675, E-mail: micekt@ohiodominican.edu. *Application contact:* John W. Naughton, Vice President for Enrollment and Student Success, 614-251-4721, Fax: 614-251-6654, E-mail: grad@ohiodominican.edu.
Website: http://www.ohiodominican.edu/academics/graduate/ma-tesol

Oklahoma City University, Petree College of Arts and Sciences, Oklahoma City, OK 73106-1402. Offers applied behavioral studies (M Ed); applied sociology: nonprofit leadership (MA); creative writing (MFA); criminology (MS); early childhood education (M Ed); elementary education (M Ed); general studies (MLA); leadership/management (MLA); moving image arts (MFA); professional counseling (M Ed); teaching (MA); teaching English to speakers of other languages (MA). *Program availability:* Part-time, evening/weekend. *Degree requirements:* For master's, capstone/practicum. *Entrance requirements:* For master's, bachelor's degree from accredited institution with minimum GPA of 3.0, essay, recommendation letters. Additional exam requirements/recommendations for international students: Required—TOEFL (minimum score 550 paper-based; 80 iBT). Electronic applications accepted. *Expenses:* Contact institution.

Old Dominion University, College of Arts and Letters, Program in Applied Linguistics, Norfolk, VA 23529. Offers sociolinguistics (MA); TESOL (MA). *Program availability:* Part-time. *Degree requirements:* For master's, one foreign language, comprehensive exam, thesis optional, program portfolio. *Entrance requirements:* For master's, GRE General Test, sample of written work; 12 hours in English, 9 on the upper-level; minimum B average; letters of recommendation; resume; essay. Additional exam requirements/recommendations for international students: Required—TOEFL (minimum score 570 paper-based; 88 iBT). Electronic applications accepted. *Faculty research:* Discourse analysis, phonology, syntax, second language acquisition, gender, sociolinguistics.

Pacific University, College of Education, Forest Grove, OR 97116-1797. Offers early childhood education (MAT); education (MAE); elementary education (MAT); ESOL (MAT); high school education (MAT); middle school education (MAT); special education (MAT); speech-language pathology (MS); STEM education (MAT); talented and gifted (M Ed); visual function in learning (M Ed). *Accreditation:* ASHA; NCATE. *Program availability:* Part-time, evening/weekend. *Degree requirements:* For master's, research project. *Entrance requirements:* For master's, California Basic Educational Skills Test, PRAXIS II, minimum undergraduate GPA of 2.75, 3.0 graduate. Additional exam requirements/recommendations for international students: Required—TOEFL. Electronic applications accepted. *Expenses:* Contact institution. *Faculty research:* Defining a culturally competent classroom, technology in the K-12 classroom, Socratic seminars, social studies education.

Penn State Harrisburg, Graduate School, School of Behavioral Sciences and Education, Middletown, PA 17057. Offers adult education in the health and medical professions (Certificate); applied behavior analysis (MA); applied clinical psychology (MA); applied psychological research (MA); community psychology and social change (MA); English as a second language (ESL) program specialist and leadership (Certificate); health education (M Ed); lifelong learning and adult education (M Ed, D Ed); literacy education (M Ed); literacy leadership (Certificate); psychology: applications in clinical psychology (Certificate); psychology: health psychology (Certificate); teaching and curriculum (M Ed); training and development (M Ed, Certificate). *Program availability:* Part-time, evening/weekend.

Penn State University Park, Graduate School, College of the Liberal Arts, Department of Applied Linguistics, University Park, PA 16802. Offers applied linguistics (PhD); teaching English as a second language (MA).

Penn State York, Graduate School, York, PA 17403. Offers ESL specialist (Certificate); teaching and curriculum (M Ed). *Expenses:* Contact institution.

Pittsburg State University, Graduate School, College of Education, Department of Teaching and Leadership, Pittsburg, KS 66762. Offers autism spectrum disorder (Certificate); district level (Certificate); education (MS), including school health; educational leadership (MS); educational technology (MS); general school administration (Ed S), including advanced studies in leadership; secondary education (MAT); special education (MAT, MS), including special education teaching (MS); teaching (MS); TESOL (Certificate). *Program availability:* Part-time, online only, 100% online, blended/hybrid learning. Terminal master's awarded for partial completion of doctoral program. *Degree requirements:* For master's and other advanced degree, thesis or alternative. *Entrance requirements:* For master's, PPST. Additional exam requirements/recommendations for international students: Required—TOEFL (minimum score 520 paper-based; 68 iBT), IELTS (minimum score 6), PTE (minimum score 47). Electronic applications accepted. *Expenses:* Contact institution. *Faculty research:* Special education, autism spectrum disorder, reading, educational technology, leadership.

Pontifical Catholic University of Puerto Rico, College of Education, Program in English as a Second Language, Ponce, PR 00717-0777. Offers M Ed. *Degree requirements:* For master's, comprehensive exam, thesis (for some programs). *Entrance requirements:* For master's, GRE, 2 letters of recommendation, interview, minimum GPA of 2.75.

Portland State University, Graduate Studies, College of Liberal Arts and Sciences, Department of Applied Linguistics, Portland, OR 97207-0751. Offers teaching English as a second language (Certificate); teaching English to speakers of other languages (MA). *Program availability:* Part-time. *Degree requirements:* For master's, one foreign language, comprehensive exam, thesis, portfolio, culminating experience. *Entrance requirements:* For master's, bachelor's degree with minimum undergraduate GPA of 3.0, 2 letters of recommendation, personal statement, resume. Additional exam requirements/recommendations for international students: Required—TOEFL (minimum score 600 paper-based; 100 iBT), IELTS (minimum score 7). Electronic applications accepted. *Faculty research:* Sociolinguistics, linguistics and cognitive science, language proficiency testing, lexical phrases and language teaching, teaching English as a second language methodology.

Post University, Program in Education, Waterbury, CT 06723-2540. Offers curriculum and instruction (M Ed); education (M Ed); educational technology (M Ed); higher education administration (MS); learning design and technology (M Ed); online teaching (M Ed); teaching English to speakers of other languages (TESOL) (M Ed). *Program availability:* Online learning. *Entrance requirements:* For master's, resume. *Expenses:* *Tuition:* Full-time $8300; part-time $570 per credit. *Required fees:* $140 per term. Tuition and fees vary according to course level, campus/location and program.

Providence University College & Theological Seminary, Theological Seminary, Otterburne, MB R0A 1G0, Canada. Offers children's ministry (Certificate); Christian studies (MA, Certificate); counseling (MA); cross-cultural discipleship (Certificate); divinity (M Div); educational studies (MA), including counseling psychology, educational ministries, student development, teaching English to speakers of other languages, training teachers of English to speakers of other languages; global studies (MA); lay counseling (Diploma); ministry (D Min); teaching English to speakers of other languages (Certificate); theological studies (MA); training teacher of English to speakers of other languages (Certificate); youth ministry (Certificate). *Accreditation:* ATS. *Program availability:* Part-time. *Degree requirements:* For master's, variable foreign language requirement, thesis (for some programs); for doctorate, thesis/dissertation. *Entrance requirements:* Additional exam requirements/recommendations for international students: Recommended—TOEFL (minimum score 550 paper-based). *Faculty research:* Studies in Isaiah, theology of sin.

Purdue University Fort Wayne, College of Arts and Sciences, Department of English and Linguistics, Fort Wayne, IN 46805-1499. Offers English (MA, MAT); TENL (teaching English as a new language) (Certificate). *Program availability:* Part-time. *Degree requirements:* For master's, one foreign language, thesis (for some programs), teaching certificate (for MAT). *Entrance requirements:* For master's, GRE General Test, minimum GPA of 3.0, major or minor in English, 3 letters of recommendation; for Certificate, bachelor's degree with minimum GPA of 2.5. Additional exam requirements/recommendations for international students: Required—TOEFL (minimum score 600 paper-based; 79 iBT). *Faculty research:* Hebrew names and the vernacular Savior in Anglo-Saxon England.

Queens College of the City University of New York, Arts and Humanities Division, Department of Linguistics and Communication Disorders, Queens, NY 11367-1597. Offers applied linguistics (MA); speech-language pathology (MA); TESOL (MS Ed, Post-Master's Certificate); TESOL and bilingual education (Post-Master's Certificate). *Accreditation:* ASHA. *Program availability:* Part-time. *Faculty:* 21 full-time (15 women), 24 part-time/adjunct (18 women). *Students:* 39 full-time (36 women), 108 part-time (98

women); includes 70 minority (8 Black or African American, non-Hispanic/Latino; 26 Asian, non-Hispanic/Latino; 33 Hispanic/Latino; 3 Two or more races, non-Hispanic/ Latino), 5 international. Average age 27. 390 applicants, 25% accepted, 81 enrolled. In 2018, 57 master's, 11 other advanced degrees awarded. *Entrance requirements:* For master's, minimum GPA of 3.0. Additional exam requirements/recommendations for international students: Required—TOEFL, IELTS. *Application deadline:* For fall admission, 4/1 for domestic students; for winter admission, 1/1 for domestic students. Applications are processed on a rolling basis. Application fee: $125. Electronic applications accepted. *Expenses:* Contact institution. *Financial support:* Career-related internships or fieldwork available. Financial award application deadline: 4/1; financial award applicants required to submit FAFSA. *Unit head:* Arlene Kraat, Chair, 718-997-2940, E-mail: arlene.kraat@qc.cuny.edu. *Application contact:* Elizabeth D'Amico-Ramirez, Assistant Director of Graduate Admissions, 718-997-5203, E-mail: elizabeth.damicoramirez@qc.cuny.edu.

Quincy University, Master of Science in Education Programs, Quincy, IL 62301-2699. Offers curriculum and instruction (MS Ed), including bilingual/English as a second language; education studies (MS Ed); leadership (MS Ed); reading education (MS Ed); teacher leader (MS Ed). *Program availability:* Part-time, evening/weekend, online learning. *Degree requirements:* For master's, comprehensive exam (for some programs), thesis optional. *Entrance requirements:* For master's, MAT or GRE, personal resume. Additional exam requirements/recommendations for international students: Required—TOEFL (minimum score 550 paper-based; 79 iBT). Electronic applications accepted. Application fee is waived when completed online.

Regent University, Graduate School, School of Education, Virginia Beach, VA 23464-9800. Offers education (M Ed, Ed D, PhD), including adult education (Ed D, PhD, Ed S), advanced educational leadership (Ed D, PhD, Ed S), character education (Ed D, PhD, Ed S), Christian education leadership (Ed D, PhD, Ed S), Christian school administration (M Ed), curriculum and instruction (Ed D, PhD, Ed S), curriculum and instruction - adult education (M Ed), curriculum and instruction - Christian school (M Ed), curriculum and instruction - gifted and talented (M Ed), curriculum and instruction - STEM education (M Ed), curriculum and instruction - teacher leader (M Ed), discipleship for ministry (M Ed), educational leadership (M Ed), educational psychology (Ed D, PhD, Ed S), educational technology and online learning (Ed D, PhD, Ed S), elementary education (M Ed), exceptional education executive leadership (Ed D, PhD, Ed S), higher education (Ed D, PhD, Ed S), higher education leadership and management (Ed D, PhD, Ed S), instructional design and technology (M Ed), K-12 school leadership (Ed D, PhD, Ed S), K-12 special education (M Ed), leadership in mathematics education (M Ed), reading specialist (M Ed), special education (Ed D, PhD, Ed S), student affairs (M Ed), TESOL - adult education (M Ed), TESOL - K-12 (M Ed); educational specialist (Ed S), including adult education (Ed D, PhD, Ed S), advanced educational leadership (Ed D, PhD, Ed S), character education (Ed D, PhD, Ed S), Christian education leadership (Ed D, PhD, Ed S), curriculum and instruction (Ed D, PhD, Ed S), educational psychology (Ed D, PhD, Ed S), educational technology and online learning (Ed D, PhD, Ed S), exceptional education executive leadership (Ed D, PhD, Ed S), higher education (Ed D, PhD, Ed S), higher education leadership and management (Ed D, PhD, Ed S), K-12 school leadership (Ed D, PhD, Ed S), special education (Ed D, PhD, Ed S). *Accreditation:* TEAC. *Program availability:* Part-time, evening/weekend, 100% online, blended/hybrid learning. *Degree requirements:* For master's, thesis or alternative; for doctorate, comprehensive exam, thesis/dissertation. *Entrance requirements:* For master's, Virginia Communication and Literacy Assessment (VCLA), PRAXIS, college transcripts, writing sample, interview; for doctorate, GRE, writing sample, resume, transcripts, interview. Additional exam requirements/recommendations for international students: Required—TOEFL (minimum score 577 paper-based). Electronic applications accepted. *Expenses:* Contact institution. *Faculty research:* Christian school administration, curriculum and instruction, educational technology and online learning, higher education, special education.

Rhode Island College, School of Graduate Studies, Feinstein School of Education and Human Development, Department of Educational Studies, Providence, RI 02908-1991. Offers advanced studies in teaching and learning (M Ed); English (MAT); French (MAT); history (MAT); math (MAT); secondary education (MAT); Spanish (MAT); teaching English as a second language (M Ed). *Accreditation:* NCATE. *Program availability:* Part-time, evening/weekend. *Faculty:* 12 full-time (9 women), 7 part-time/adjunct (6 women). *Students:* 12 full-time (10 women), 31 part-time (28 women); includes 5 minority (1 Black or African American, non-Hispanic/Latino; 1 Asian, non-Hispanic/Latino; 3 Hispanic/ Latino). Average age 33. In 2018, 24 master's awarded. *Degree requirements:* For master's, capstone or comprehensive assessment. *Entrance requirements:* For master's, GRE or MAT (for most programs), minimum undergraduate GPA of 3.0; baccalaureate degree in English, French, history, math or Spanish; 3 letters of recommendation; interview. Additional exam requirements/recommendations for international students: Required—TOEFL (minimum score 550 paper-based; 80 iBT). *Application deadline:* For fall admission, 3/1 for domestic students; for spring admission, 11/1 for domestic students. Applications are processed on a rolling basis. Application fee: $50. Electronic applications accepted. *Expenses: Tuition, area resident:* Part-time $407 per credit. Tuition, nonresident: part-time $792 per credit. *Required fees:* $29 per credit. $100 per semester. *Financial support:* Teaching assistantships, career-related internships or fieldwork, Federal Work-Study, scholarships/grants, health care benefits, and unspecified assistantships available. Support available to part-time students. Financial award application deadline: 5/15; financial award applicants required to submit FAFSA. *Unit head:* Dr. Leslie Bogad, Chair, 401-456-8170. *Application contact:* Dr. Leslie Bogad, Chair, 401-456-8170.
Website: http://www.ric.edu/educationalStudies/Pages/default.aspx

Rider University, College of Education and Human Services, Program in Teaching, Lawrenceville, NJ 08648-3001. Offers bilingual education (MAT); early childhood education (MAT); elementary education (MAT); English as a second language (MAT); secondary education (MAT); world language (MAT). *Students:* 35 full-time (26 women), 88 part-time (67 women); includes 12 minority (1 Black or African American, non-Hispanic/Latino; 1 American Indian or Alaska Native, non-Hispanic/Latino; 2 Asian, non-Hispanic/Latino; 8 Hispanic/Latino). Average age 34. 104 applicants, 67% accepted, 54 enrolled. In 2018, 70 master's awarded. *Entrance requirements:* For master's, Praxis exams, resume,application fee, statement of aims and objectives, official prior college transcripts, interview. Additional exam requirements/recommendations for international students: Required—TOEFL (minimum score 540 paper-based; 79 iBT). *Application deadline:* For fall admission, 5/1 priority date for domestic students, 6/1 priority date for international students; for spring admission, 12/1 priority date for domestic students, 11/1 priority date for international students. Applications are processed on a rolling basis. Application fee: $50. Electronic applications accepted. *Expenses: Tuition:* Full-time $850; part-time $850 per credit hour. *Required fees:* $50; $50 per course. Tuition and fees vary according to program. *Financial support:* Applicants required to submit FAFSA. *Unit head:* Kathleen Pierce, Professor, 609-895-5478, E-mail: kpierce@rider.edu. *Application contact:* Jamie L Mitchell, Director of Graduate Admissions, 609-896-5036, Fax: 609-895-5680, E-mail: jmitchell@rider.edu.

Rowan University, Graduate School, College of Education, Department of Language, Literacy, and Sociocultural Education, Program in ESL Education, Glassboro, NJ 08028-1701. Offers CGS. Electronic applications accepted.

Rutgers University–New Brunswick, Graduate School of Education, Department of Learning and Teaching, Program in Language Education, Piscataway, NJ 08854-8097. Offers English as a second language education (Ed M); language education (Ed M, Ed D). *Program availability:* Part-time. Terminal master's awarded for partial completion of doctoral program. *Degree requirements:* For master's, comprehensive exam; for doctorate, thesis/dissertation, concept paper, qualifying exam. *Entrance requirements:* For master's, GRE General Test, minimum GPA of 3.0; for doctorate, GRE General Test, minimum GPA of 3.5. Additional exam requirements/recommendations for international students: Required—TOEFL. Electronic applications accepted. *Faculty research:* Linguistics, sociolinguistics, cross-cultural/international communication.

St. John's University, The School of Education, Department of Education Specialties, Program in Teaching English to Speakers of Other Languages and Bilingual Education, Queens, NY 11439. Offers bilingual education (Adv C); childhood education and teaching English to speakers of other languages (MS Ed); teaching English to speakers of other languages (MS Ed, Adv C). *Degree requirements:* For Adv C, one foreign language. *Entrance requirements:* For master's, GRE, MAT, or PRAXIS, statement of goals (personal essay), official undergraduate transcripts, initial teaching certification; for Adv C, initial teaching certification, first master's transcripts, statement of purpose. Additional exam requirements/recommendations for international students: Required—TOEFL, IELTS. Electronic applications accepted. *Faculty research:* Second language learning and academic achievement, heritage language education, assessing the progress of English language learners toward English acquisition, dual language acquisition, study of English Creoles and dialects of other English's, literacy development for ESL learners; investigating Caribbean and Creole language and culture, education law.

Saint Michael's College, Graduate Programs, Program in Teaching English to Speakers of Other Languages, Colchester, VT 05439. Offers MATESOL, Certificate. *Program availability:* Part-time, evening/weekend. *Degree requirements:* For master's, one foreign language, comprehensive exam (for some programs), thesis or alternative, capstone paper or portfolio. *Entrance requirements:* For master's, minimum GPA of 3.0, resume, essay. Additional exam requirements/recommendations for international students: Required—TOEFL (minimum score 550 paper-based; 79 iBT); Recommended—IELTS. *Expenses: Tuition:* Part-time $590 per credit. *Faculty research:* Language teaching methodology, discourse analysis, second language acquisition, language assessment, sociolinguistics, K-12 English as a second language for children.

St. Thomas University, School of Leadership Studies, Institute for Education, Miami Gardens, FL 33054-6459. Offers earth/space science (Certificate); educational administration (MS, Certificate); educational leadership (Ed D); elementary education (MS); ESOL (Certificate); gifted education (Certificate); instructional technology (MS, Certificate); professional/studies (Certificate); reading (MS, Certificate); special education (MS). *Program availability:* Part-time, evening/weekend. *Degree requirements:* For master's, comprehensive exam; for doctorate, comprehensive exam, thesis/dissertation. *Entrance requirements:* For master's, interview, minimum GPA of 3.0 or GRE; for doctorate, GRE or MAT. Additional exam requirements/recommendations for international students: Required—TOEFL (minimum score 550 paper-based; 79 iBT). Electronic applications accepted.

Saint Xavier University, Graduate Studies, School of Education, Chicago, IL 60655-3105. Offers counseling (MA); curriculum and instruction (MA); early childhood education (MA); educational administration (MA); elementary education (MA); individualized studies (MA), including educational technology, English as a second language (ESL), ISTEM (integrative science, technology, engineering, and math), science education; music education (MA); reading (MA); secondary education (MA); Spanish education (MA); special education (MA); teaching and leadership (MA). *Accreditation:* NCATE. *Program availability:* Part-time, evening/weekend. *Degree requirements:* For master's, thesis or project. *Entrance requirements:* For master's, minimum GPA of 3.0. *Expenses:* Contact institution.

Salem College, Graduate Studies, Winston-Salem, NC 27101. Offers art education (MAT); elementary education (M Ed, MAT); language and literacy (M Ed); middle school education (MAT); organ (MM); piano (MM); school counseling (M Ed); second language studies (MAT); secondary education (MAT); special education (M Ed, MAT). *Accreditation:* NCATE. *Program availability:* Part-time, evening/weekend, online learning. *Degree requirements:* For master's, practicum (MAT), action research project (M Ed). *Entrance requirements:* For master's, minimum GPA of 3.0, two academic/ professional recommendations, acceptable criminal background check. Additional exam requirements/recommendations for international students: Recommended—TOEFL. Electronic applications accepted. *Faculty research:* Teacher professional development, adolescent literacy, instructional technology.

Salem State University, School of Graduate Studies, Program in Teaching English as a Second Language, Salem, MA 01970-5353. Offers MAT. *Program availability:* Part-time, evening/weekend. *Entrance requirements:* Additional exam requirements/ recommendations for international students: Required—TOEFL (minimum score 550 paper-based; 80 iBT) or IELTS (minimum score 5.5).

San Diego State University, Graduate and Research Affairs, College of Arts and Letters, Department of Linguistics and Oriental Languages, San Diego, CA 92182. Offers applied linguistics and English as a second language (CAL); computational linguistics (MA); English as a second language/applied linguistics (MA); general linguistics (MA). *Degree requirements:* For master's, one foreign language, comprehensive exam, thesis optional. *Entrance requirements:* For master's, GRE General Test, 2 letters of recommendation. Additional exam requirements/ recommendations for international students: Required—TOEFL (minimum score 570 paper-based). Electronic applications accepted. *Faculty research:* Cross-cultural linguistic studies of semantics.

San Francisco State University, Division of Graduate Studies, College of Liberal and Creative Arts, Department of English Language and Literature, Program in Teaching English to Speakers of Other Languages, San Francisco, CA 94132-1722. Offers MA. *Program availability:* Part-time. *Degree requirements:* For master's, comprehensive exam (for some programs), thesis (for some programs). *Application deadline:* Applications are processed on a rolling basis. Electronic applications accepted. *Unit head:* Dr. Sugie Goen-Salter, Chair, 415-338-7582, Fax: 415-338-6159, E-mail: sgoen@sfsu.edu. *Application contact:* Dr. David Olsher, Coordinator, 415-338-2827, Fax: 415-338-6159, E-mail: olsher@sfsu.edu.
Website: http://english.sfsu.edu/graduate-matesol/

San Jose State University, Program in Linguistics and Language Development, San Jose, CA 95192-0001. Offers computational linguistics (Certificate); linguistics (MA); teaching English to speakers of other languages (MA, Certificate). *Entrance requirements:* Additional exam requirements/recommendations for international students: Required—TOEFL (minimum score 570 paper-based). Electronic applications accepted.

Seattle Pacific University, MA in Teaching English to Speakers of Other Languages Program, Seattle, WA 98119-1997. Offers K-12 (MA). *Program availability:* Part-time. *Students:* 1 full-time (0 women), 1 (woman) part-time. Average age 43. In 2018, 12 master's awarded. *Faculty research:* Second language acquisition. *Unit head:* Dr. Kathryn Bartholomew, Program Director, 206-281-3533, Fax: 206-281-2500, E-mail: kbarthol@spu.edu. *Application contact:* Dr. Kathryn Bartholomew, Program Director, 206-281-3533, Fax: 206-281-2500, E-mail: kbarthol@spu.edu.
Website: http://www.spu.edu/depts/tesol/

Seattle University, College of Education, Program in Teaching English to Speakers of Other Languages, Seattle, WA 98122-1090. Offers M Ed, MA, Certificate. *Accreditation:* NCATE. *Program availability:* Part-time. *Faculty:* 1 full-time (0 women). *Students:* 8 full-time (6 women), 22 part-time (14 women); includes 6 minority (5 Asian, non-Hispanic/Latino; 1 Hispanic/Latino), 3 international. Average age 31. 20 applicants, 80% accepted, 8 enrolled. In 2018, 19 master's, 2 other advanced degrees awarded. *Degree requirements:* For master's, comprehensive exam, thesis, internship. *Entrance requirements:* For master's, GRE, MAT, or minimum GPA of 3.0. Additional exam requirements/recommendations for international students: Required—TOEFL. *Application deadline:* For fall admission, 8/20 priority date for domestic students; for winter admission, 11/20 for domestic students; for spring admission, 2/20 for domestic students. Applications are processed on a rolling basis. Application fee: $55. *Financial support:* In 2018–19, 2 students received support. Career-related internships or fieldwork and Federal Work-Study available. Support available to part-time students. Financial award applicants required to submit FAFSA. *Unit head:* Dr. Jian Yang, Coordinator, 209-296-5908, E-mail: tesol@seattleu.edu. *Application contact:* Janet Shandley, Associate Dean of Graduate Admissions, 206-296-5900, Fax: 206-298-5656, E-mail: grad_admissions@seattleu.edu.
Website: https://www.seattleu.edu/education/tesol/

Simon Fraser University, Office of Graduate Studies and Postdoctoral Fellows, Faculty of Education, Program in Teaching English as a Second/Foreign Language, Burnaby, BC V5A 1S6, Canada. Offers M Ed. *Program availability:* Part-time, evening/weekend. *Degree requirements:* For master's, comprehensive exam. *Entrance requirements:* For master's, minimum GPA of 3.0 (on scale of 4.33) or 3.33 based on last 60 credits of undergraduate courses. Additional exam requirements/recommendations for international students: Recommended—TOEFL (minimum score 580 paper-based; 93 iBT), IELTS (minimum score 7), TWE (minimum score 5). Electronic applications accepted. *Faculty research:* Internationalization of higher education, international student experiences, language practices and language ideology in the globalized political economy, integration of immigrants, minorities and international students in educational settings, critical and psychoanalytical perspectives on second language learning, pedagogy, and curriculum.

SIT Graduate Institute, Graduate Programs, Master's Program in Teaching English as a Second Language, Brattleboro, VT 05302-0676. Offers MAT. *Degree requirements:* For master's, one foreign language, thesis, teaching practice. *Entrance requirements:* For master's, 3 letters of reference. Additional exam requirements/recommendations for international students: Required—TOEFL. *Faculty research:* Teaching English to speakers of other languages (TESOL).

Slippery Rock University of Pennsylvania, Graduate Studies (Recruitment), College of Liberal Arts, Department of Modern Languages and Cultures, Slippery Rock, PA 16057-1383. Offers teaching English to speakers of other languages (MA). *Program availability:* Part-time, evening/weekend, blended/hybrid learning, 1 evening class per week on campus. *Faculty:* 1 (woman) full-time. *Students:* 2 part-time (1 woman). Average age 36. 3 applicants, 67% accepted, 2 enrolled. In 2018, 8 master's awarded. *Degree requirements:* For master's, thesis (for some programs), practicum or end project. *Entrance requirements:* For master's, two letters of recommendation, statement of intent, official transcripts, minimum GPA of 2.75. Additional exam requirements/recommendations for international students: Required—TOEFL (minimum score 550 paper-based; 80 iBT). *Application deadline:* For fall admission, 5/1 priority date for domestic students, 3/1 priority date for international students; for spring admission, 9/1 priority date for domestic students, 10/1 priority date for international students. Applications are processed on a rolling basis. Application fee: $25 ($30 for international students). Electronic applications accepted. *Expenses:* Contact institution. *Financial support:* In 2018–19, 1 student received support. Career-related internships or fieldwork, Federal Work-Study, institutionally sponsored loans, scholarships/grants, tuition waivers (partial), and unspecified assistantships available. Support available to part-time students. Financial award application deadline: 5/1; financial award applicants required to submit FAFSA. *Unit head:* Dr. Marnie Petray-Covey, Graduate Coordinator, 724-738-4577, Fax: 724-738-2263, E-mail: marnie.petray-covey@sru.edu. *Application contact:* Brandi Weber-Mortimer, Director of Graduate Admissions, 724-738-4430, E-mail: graduate.admissions@sru.edu.
Website: http://www.sru.edu/academics/colleges-and-departments/cla/departments/modern-languages-and-cultures

Southeastern University, College of Education, Lakeland, FL 33801-6099. Offers curriculum and instruction (Ed D); educational leadership (M Ed); elementary education (M Ed); exceptional student education (M Ed); exceptional student education/educational therapy (M Ed); kinesiology (M Ed); organizational leadership (Ed D); reading education (M Ed); teaching English to speakers of other languages (M Ed). Electronic applications accepted.

Southeast Missouri State University, School of Graduate Studies, Department of English, Cape Girardeau, MO 63701-4799. Offers teaching English to speakers of other languages (MA). *Program availability:* Part-time, evening/weekend, online learning. *Faculty:* 17 full-time (8 women). *Students:* 34 full-time (24 women), 45 part-time (32 women); includes 9 minority (2 Black or African American, non-Hispanic/Latino; 5 Asian, non-Hispanic/Latino; 1 Hispanic/Latino; 1 Native Hawaiian or other Pacific Islander, non-Hispanic/Latino), 56 international. Average age 31. 43 applicants, 100% accepted, 43 enrolled. In 2018, 30 master's awarded. *Degree requirements:* For master's, comprehensive exam (for some programs), thesis optional. *Entrance requirements:* Additional exam requirements/recommendations for international students: Required—TOEFL (minimum score 550 paper-based; 79 iBT), IELTS (minimum score 6), PTE (minimum score 53). *Application deadline:* For fall admission, 8/1 for domestic students, 6/1 for international students; for spring admission, 11/21 for domestic students, 10/1 for international students; for summer admission, 5/15 for domestic students. Applications are processed on a rolling basis. Application fee: $30 ($40 for international students). Electronic applications accepted. *Expenses:* Contact institution. *Financial support:* In 2018–19, 14 students received support, including 16 teaching assistantships with full tuition reimbursements available; career-related internships or fieldwork, Federal Work-Study, scholarships/grants, traineeships, tuition waivers (full), and unspecified assistantships also available. Financial award application deadline: 6/30; financial award applicants required to submit FAFSA. *Faculty research:* Literature, creative writing, technical writing, secondary English education, teaching English as a second language. *Unit head:* Dr. Susan Kendrick, Department of English Chair, 573-651-2156, Fax: 573-651-5188, E-mail: skendrick@semo.edu. *Application contact:* Dr. Susan Kendrick, Department of English Chair, 573-651-2156, Fax: 573-651-5188, E-mail: skendrick@semo.edu.
Website: http://www.semo.edu/english/

Southern Connecticut State University, School of Graduate Studies, School of Arts and Sciences, Department of World Languages and Literatures, New Haven, CT 06515-1355. Offers multicultural-bilingual education/teaching English to speakers of other languages (MS); romance languages (MA). *Program availability:* Part-time, evening/weekend. *Degree requirements:* For master's, one foreign language, thesis or alternative. *Entrance requirements:* For master's, interview, minimum undergraduate GPA of 2.7. Electronic applications accepted.

Southern Illinois University Carbondale, Graduate School, College of Liberal Arts, Department of Linguistics, Program in Teaching English to Speakers of Other Languages, Carbondale, IL 62901-4701. Offers MA. *Entrance requirements:* Additional exam requirements/recommendations for international students: Required—TOEFL (minimum score 90 iBT).

Southern Illinois University Edwardsville, Graduate School, College of Arts and Sciences, Department of English Language and Literature, Program in Teaching English as a Second Language, Edwardsville, IL 62026. Offers MA, Postbaccalaureate Certificate. *Program availability:* Part-time, evening/weekend. *Degree requirements:* For master's, one foreign language, thesis (for some programs), final exam. *Entrance requirements:* Additional exam requirements/recommendations for international students: Required—TOEFL (minimum score 550 paper-based, 79 iBT), IELTS (minimum score 6.5), Michigan Test of English Language Proficiency or PTE. Electronic applications accepted.

Southern Methodist University, Simmons School of Education and Human Development, Department of Teaching and Learning, Dallas, TX 75275. Offers bilingual education (MBE); education (M Ed, PhD); English as a second language (M Ed); gifted and talented (M Ed); literacy studies (M Ed); special education (M Ed). *Program availability:* Part-time, evening/weekend. Terminal master's awarded for partial completion of doctoral program. *Degree requirements:* For master's, comprehensive exam, minimum GPA of 3.0; for doctorate, thesis/dissertation, qualifying exams, major area paper, evidence of teaching competency, dissemination of research (e.g., conference presentation), professional portfolio. *Entrance requirements:* For master's, minimum GPA of 3.0 or GRE, 3 letters of recommendation; for doctorate, GRE, minimum GPA of 3.3, 3 years of full-time teaching, 3 letters of recommendation, interview. Additional exam requirements/recommendations for international students: Required—TOEFL. Electronic applications accepted. *Faculty research:* Reading intervention, mathematics intervention, bilingual education, new literacies.

Southern New Hampshire University, School of Education, Manchester, NH 03106-1045. Offers curriculum and instruction (M Ed), including dyslexia studies and language-based learning disabilities, educational leadership, reading, special education, technology integration; dyslexia studies and language-based learning disabilities (Certificate); early childhood and special education (M Ed); educational leadership (M Ed, Ed D); educational studies (M Ed); elementary and special education (M Ed); field based education (M Ed); higher education administration (MS); teaching English as a foreign language (MS). *Program availability:* Part-time, evening/weekend, online learning. *Degree requirements:* For master's, comprehensive exam (for some programs), thesis or alternative. *Entrance requirements:* For master's, PRAXIS I, minimum GPA of 2.75. Additional exam requirements/recommendations for international students: Required—TOEFL (minimum score 550 paper-based). Electronic applications accepted. *Expenses:* Contact institution.

Southwest Minnesota State University, Department of Education, Marshall, MN 56258. Offers ESL (MS); math (MS); reading (MS); special education (MS), including developmental disabilities, early childhood education, emotional behavioral disorders, learning disabilities; teaching, learning and leadership (MS). *Program availability:* Part-time, evening/weekend, online learning. *Entrance requirements:* Additional exam requirements/recommendations for international students: Required—TOEFL or IELTS; Recommended—TOEFL (minimum score 550 paper-based; 80 iBT), IELTS.

State University of New York at Fredonia, College of Education, Fredonia, NY 14063-1136. Offers curriculum and instruction (MS Ed); literacy education (MS Ed), including birth-grade 12, grades 5-12; music education (M Mus), including k-12; TESOL (MS Ed). *Accreditation:* NCATE. *Program availability:* Part-time. *Faculty:* 16 full-time (14 women), 13 part-time/adjunct (11 women). *Students:* 39 full-time (33 women), 44 part-time (36 women); includes 5 minority (1 Asian, non-Hispanic/Latino; 3 Hispanic/Latino; 1 Two or more races, non-Hispanic/Latino), 4 international. Average age 27. 44 applicants, 89% accepted, 34 enrolled. In 2018, 25 master's awarded. *Degree requirements:* For master's, thesis. *Entrance requirements:* For master's, GRE, minimum undergraduate GPA of 3.0. Additional exam requirements/recommendations for international students: Required—TOEFL (minimum score 79 iBT), IELTS (minimum score 6.5). *Application deadline:* For fall admission, 4/1 priority date for domestic and international students; for spring admission, 11/1 priority date for domestic students, 11/1 for international students. Applications are processed on a rolling basis. Application fee: $75. Electronic applications accepted. *Expenses:* Tuition, state resident: full-time $6870; part-time $462 per credit hour. Tuition, nonresident: full-time $16,650; part-time $944 per credit hour. *International tuition:* $16,650 full-time. *Required fees:* $25; $2 per credit hour. $1 per semester. *Financial support:* In 2018–19, 13 students received support. Unspecified assistantships available. Financial award application deadline: 3/15; financial award applicants required to submit FAFSA. *Faculty research:* Positive behavioral intervention and support (PBIS), place-based science education, peer support for education, primary source material for social studies education, policies and practices in learning English language. *Unit head:* Dr. Christine Givner, Dean, 716-673-3311, E-mail: christine.givner@fredonia.edu. *Application contact:* Wendy S. Dunst, Interim Graduate Recruitment and Admissions Associate, 716-673-3808, Fax: 716-673-3712, E-mail: wendy.dunst@fredonia.edu.
Website: http://www.fredonia.edu/coe/

State University of New York at New Paltz, Graduate and Extended Learning School, School of Education, Department of Teaching and Learning, New Paltz, NY 12561. Offers adolescence education: biology (MAT, MS Ed); adolescence education: chemistry (MAT, MS Ed); adolescence education: earth science (MAT, MS Ed); adolescence education: English (MAT, MS Ed); adolescence education: French (MAT, MS Ed); adolescence education: social studies (MAT, MS Ed); adolescence education: Spanish (MAT, MS Ed); second language education (MS Ed, AC), including second language education (MS Ed), teaching English language learners (AC). *Accreditation:* NCATE. *Program availability:* Part-time, evening/weekend. *Faculty:* 21 full-time (16 women), 15 part-time/adjunct (12 women). *Students:* 127 full-time (91 women), 171 part-time (149 women); includes 48 minority (5 Black or African American, non-Hispanic/Latino; 2 Asian, non-Hispanic/Latino; 37 Hispanic/Latino; 4 Two or more races, non-Hispanic/Latino). 152 applicants, 84% accepted, 104 enrolled. In 2018, 135 master's, 19 other advanced degrees awarded. *Degree requirements:* For master's, comprehensive exam (for some programs), portfolio. *Entrance requirements:* For master's, minimum GPA of 3.0, New York state teaching certificate (MS Ed). Additional exam requirements/recommendations for international students: Required—TOEFL (minimum score 550 paper-based; 80 iBT), IELTS (minimum score 6.5). *Application deadline:* For fall admission, 3/1 priority date for domestic students, 3/1 for international students; for spring admission, 10/1 priority date for domestic students, 10/1 for international students. Application fee: $50. Electronic applications accepted. *Financial support:*

Application deadline: 8/1. *Unit head:* Dr. Aaron Isabelle, Associate Dean, 845-257-2837, E-mail: isabella@newpaltz.edu. *Application contact:* Vika Shock, Director of Graduate Admissions, 845-257-3285, Fax: 845-257-3284, E-mail: gradstudies@newpaltz.edu.
Website: http://www.newpaltz.edu/secondaryed/

State University of New York College at Cortland, Graduate Studies, School of Arts and Sciences, Department of Modern Languages, Cortland, NY 13045. Offers second language education (MS Ed). *Accreditation:* NCATE.

Stony Brook University, State University of New York, Graduate School, College of Arts and Sciences, Department of Linguistics, Program in Teaching English to Speakers of Other Languages, Stony Brook, NY 11794. Offers MA. *Accreditation:* NCATE. *Students:* 29 full-time (26 women), 20 part-time (19 women); includes 8 minority (1 Black or African American, non-Hispanic/Latino; 1 Asian, non-Hispanic/Latino; 6 Hispanic/Latino). Average age 27. 80 applicants, 45% accepted, 24 enrolled. In 2018, 21 master's awarded. *Entrance requirements:* For master's, GRE, statement of purpose, curriculum vitae, 3 letters of recommendation, official transcripts. Additional exam requirements/recommendations for international students: Required—TOEFL (minimum score 85 iBT). *Application deadline:* For fall admission, 6/20 for domestic students, 4/15 for international students; for spring admission, 10/1 for domestic students. Application fee: $100. Electronic applications accepted. *Expenses:* Contact institution. *Financial support:* In 2018–19, 1 research assistantship was awarded; fellowships and teaching assistantships also available. *Unit head:* Dr. Richard Larson, Chair, 631-632-7776, E-mail: richard.larson@stonybrook.edu. *Application contact:* Michelle Carbone, Coordinator, 631-632-7774, Fax: 631-632-9789, E-mail: michelle.carbone@stonybrook.edu.
Website: https://linguistics.stonybrook.edu/programs/graduate/ma/tesol.html

Syracuse University, College of Arts and Sciences, CAS Program in Language Teaching: TESOL/TLOTE, Syracuse, NY 13244. Offers CAS. *Program availability:* Part-time. In 2018, 12 CASs awarded. *Entrance requirements:* Additional exam requirements/recommendations for international students: Required—TOEFL (minimum score 600 paper-based; 100 iBT), IELTS (minimum score 7). *Application deadline:* For fall admission, 1/10 priority date for domestic and international students. Applications are processed on a rolling basis. Application fee: $75. Electronic applications accepted. *Faculty research:* Linguistic analysis, methods for language teaching, teaching English. *Unit head:* Dr. Amanda Brown, Coordinator, 315-443-2244, E-mail: abrown08@syr.edu. *Application contact:* Dr. Amanda Brown, Coordinator, 315-443-2244, E-mail: abrown08@syr.edu.
Website: http://lll.syr.edu/tesol/certificate.html

Syracuse University, College of Arts and Sciences, MA Program in Linguistic Studies, Syracuse, NY 13244. Offers linguistic studies (MA), including information representation and retrieval, language acquisition, language, culture, and society, linguistic theory, logic and language, teaching language (TESOL/TLOTE). *Program availability:* Part-time. *Students:* Average age 25. *Degree requirements:* For master's, comprehensive exam, thesis or alternative. *Entrance requirements:* For master's, GRE General Test, personal statement detailing interest in field of linguistics and possible concentration areas, transcripts, three recommendation letters. Additional exam requirements/recommendations for international students: Required—TOEFL (minimum score 100 iBT). *Application deadline:* For fall admission, 1/15 priority date for domestic and international students. Application fee: $75. Electronic applications accepted. *Financial support:* Teaching assistantships available. Financial award application deadline: 1/15. *Faculty research:* Information representation and retrieval, language acquisition, linguistic theory, logic and language, teaching languages. *Unit head:* Dr. Gerald R. Greenberg, Director, 315-443-1414, E-mail: ggreenbe@syr.edu. *Application contact:* Jaklin Kornfilt, Professor of Linguistics and Director of the Linguistic Studies Program, 315-443-5375, E-mail: kornfilt@syr.edu.
Website: http://lll.syr.edu/linguistics/graduate.html

Syracuse University, School of Education, MS Program in Teaching English Language Learners (Pre-K-12), Syracuse, NY 13244. Offers MS. *Program availability:* Part-time. *Students:* Average age 22. *Entrance requirements:* For master's, GRE or MAT, baccalaureate degree from regionally-accredited college/university, strong teacher and/or employer recommendations, 12 credits in a language other than English, personal statement. Additional exam requirements/recommendations for international students: Required—TOEFL (minimum score 100 iBT). *Application deadline:* For fall admission, 1/15 priority date for domestic and international students. Application fee: $75. Electronic applications accepted. *Financial support:* Fellowships with full tuition reimbursements, teaching assistantships, career-related internships or fieldwork, scholarships/grants, and tuition waivers available. Financial award application deadline: 1/15; financial award applicants required to submit FAFSA. *Unit head:* Dr. Zaline Roy-Campbell, Program Coordinator, 315-443-8194, E-mail: zmroycam@syr.edu. *Application contact:* Speranza Migliore, Graduate Admissions Recruiter, 315-443-2505, E-mail: gradrcrt@syr.edu.
Website: http://soe.syr.edu/academic/reading_language_arts/graduate/masters/teaching_english_language_learners/default.aspx

Taylor College and Seminary, Graduate and Professional Programs, Edmonton, AB T6J 4T3, Canada. Offers Christian studies (Diploma); intercultural studies (MA, Diploma), including intercultural studies (Diploma), TESOL; theology (M Div, MTS). *Accreditation:* ATS. *Program availability:* Part-time, online learning. *Degree requirements:* For master's, thesis optional. *Entrance requirements:* Additional exam requirements/recommendations for international students: Required—TOEFL (minimum score 550 paper-based; 80 iBT), IELTS (minimum score 6.5). *Faculty research:* Biblical studies, administration and organization, world religions, ethics, missiology.

Teachers College, Columbia University, Department of Arts and Humanities, New York, NY 10027. Offers applied linguistics (MA, Ed D); art and art education (Ed M, MA, Ed D, Ed DCT); arts administration (MA); bilingual and bicultural education (MA); global competence (Certificate); history and education (Ed D, PhD); music and music education (Ed DCT); philosophy and education (MA, Ed D, PhD); social studies education (Ed M, PhD); teaching English to speakers of other languages (Ed M); teaching of English and English education (Ed M, MA, Ed D, PhD), including English education (Ed M, Ed D, PhD), teaching of English (MA); teaching of social studies (MA); TESOL (MA, Ed D). *Program availability:* Part-time, evening/weekend. *Students:* 267 full-time (216 women), 569 part-time (400 women); includes 235 minority (62 Black or African American, non-Hispanic/Latino; 2 American Indian or Alaska Native, non-Hispanic/Latino; 88 Asian, non-Hispanic/Latino; 69 Hispanic/Latino; 14 Two or more races, non-Hispanic/Latino), 229 international. Average age 31. 1,075 applicants, 56% accepted, 342 enrolled. Terminal master's awarded for partial completion of doctoral program. *Financial support:* Fellowships, research assistantships, teaching assistantships, career-related internships or fieldwork, Federal Work-Study, institutionally sponsored loans, tuition waivers (full and partial), and unspecified assistantships available. Support available to part-time students. *Unit head:* Prof. ZhaoHong Han, Department Chair, E-mail: zhh2@tc.columbia.edu. *Application contact:* Kelly Sutton-Skinner, Director of Admissions & New Student Enrollment, E-mail: kms2237@tc.columbia.edu.

Temple University, College of Education, Department of Teaching and Learning, Philadelphia, PA 19122-6096. Offers career and technical education (Ed M), including business, computing, and information technology, industrial education, marketing education; middle grades education (Ed M), including math and language arts, math and science, science and language arts; secondary education (Ed M), including English, math, social studies; teaching English to speakers of other languages (MS Ed); urban education (Ed M). *Program availability:* Part-time, evening/weekend. *Faculty:* 27 full-time (19 women), 71 part-time/adjunct (51 women). *Students:* 181 full-time (126 women), 128 part-time (78 women); includes 71 minority (25 Black or African American, non-Hispanic/Latino; 1 American Indian or Alaska Native, non-Hispanic/Latino; 20 Asian, non-Hispanic/Latino; 19 Hispanic/Latino; 1 Native Hawaiian or other Pacific Islander, non-Hispanic/Latino; 5 Two or more races, non-Hispanic/Latino), 12 international. 234 applicants, 67% accepted, 103 enrolled. In 2018, 148 master's awarded. *Degree requirements:* For master's, thesis (for some programs). *Entrance requirements:* For master's, statement of goals, 2 letters of recommendation. Additional exam requirements/recommendations for international students: Required—TOEFL (minimum score 79 iBT), IELTS, PTE, one of three is required. Application fee: $60. Electronic applications accepted. *Financial support:* Fellowships, research assistantships, teaching assistantships, career-related internships or fieldwork, Federal Work-Study, scholarships/grants, health care benefits, and unspecified assistantships available. Financial award applicants required to submit FAFSA. *Faculty research:* Career & technical education, early childhood education, middle grades education, secondary education, special education. *Unit head:* Matthew Tincani, Prof. of Applied Behavior Analysis and Dept. Chairperson, 215-204-8073, E-mail: matthew.tincani@temple.edu. *Application contact:* Stacey Sanginette, Academic Coordinator, 215-204-6143, E-mail: stacey.sangtinette@temple.edu.
Website: http://education.temple.edu/tl

Tennessee Technological University, College of Graduate Studies, College of Interdisciplinary Studies, School of Professional Studies, Cookeville, TN 38505. Offers health care administration (MPS); human resources leadership (MPS); public safety (MPS); strategic leadership (MPS); teaching English to speakers of other languages (MPS); training and development (MPS). *Program availability:* Part-time, evening/weekend, online learning. *Students:* 23 full-time (8 women), 80 part-time (48 women); includes 20 minority (13 Black or African American, non-Hispanic/Latino; 3 Hispanic/Latino; 4 Two or more races, non-Hispanic/Latino), 1 international. 49 applicants, 73% accepted, 29 enrolled. In 2018, 33 master's awarded. *Degree requirements:* For master's, comprehensive exam, thesis or alternative. *Entrance requirements:* For master's, GRE. Additional exam requirements/recommendations for international students: Required—TOEFL (minimum score 527 paper-based; 71 iBT), IELTS (minimum score 5.5), PTE (minimum score 48), or TOEIC (Test of English as an International Communication). *Application deadline:* For fall admission, 7/1 for domestic students, 5/1 for international students; for spring admission, 11/1 for domestic students, 10/1 for international students; for summer admission, 5/1 for domestic students, 2/1 for international students. Applications are processed on a rolling basis. Application fee: $35 ($40 for international students). Electronic applications accepted. *Financial support:* Application deadline: 4/1. *Unit head:* Dr. Joseph Roberts, Interim Director, School of Professional Studies, 931-372-6223, E-mail: jmroberts@tntech.edu. *Application contact:* Shelia K. Kendrick, Coordinator of Graduate Studies, 931-372-3808, Fax: 931-372-3497, E-mail: skendrick@tntech.edu.
Website: https://www.tntech.edu/is/sps/

Texas A&M University–Commerce, College of Humanities, Social Sciences and Arts, Commerce, TX 75429. Offers applied criminology (MS); applied linguistics (MA, MS); art (MA, MFA); computational linguistics (Graduate Certificate); creative writing (Graduate Certificate); criminal justice management (Graduate Certificate); criminal justice studies (Graduate Certificate); English (MA, MS, PhD); film studies (Graduate Certificate); history (MA, MS); history of Christianity (Graduate Certificate); Holocaust studies (Graduate Certificate); homeland security (Graduate Certificate); music (MM); music performance (MM); political science (MA, MS); public history (Graduate Certificate); sociology (MS); Spanish (MA); studies in children's and adolescent literature and culture (Graduate Certificate); teaching English to speakers of other languages (Graduate Certificate); theater (MA, MS); world history (Graduate Certificate). *Program availability:* Part-time. *Faculty:* 50 full-time (26 women), 11 part-time/adjunct (2 women). *Students:* 125 full-time (83 women), 393 part-time (278 women); includes 197 minority (75 Black or African American, non-Hispanic/Latino; 2 American Indian or Alaska Native, non-Hispanic/Latino; 13 Asian, non-Hispanic/Latino; 92 Hispanic/Latino; 1 Native Hawaiian or other Pacific Islander, non-Hispanic/Latino; 14 Two or more races, non-Hispanic/Latino), 16 international. Average age 37. 261 applicants, 46% accepted, 106 enrolled. In 2018, 124 master's, 8 doctorates awarded. *Degree requirements:* For master's, one foreign language, comprehensive exam, thesis (for some programs); for doctorate, one foreign language, comprehensive exam, thesis/dissertation, departmental qualifying exam. *Entrance requirements:* For master's, GRE General Test, official transcripts, letters of recommendation, resume, statement of goals; for doctorate, GRE General Test, official transcripts, letters of recommendation, statement of goals, writing samples, writing sessions, resumes. Additional exam requirements/recommendations for international students: Required—TOEFL (minimum score 550 paper-based; 79 iBT), IELTS (minimum score 6), PTE (minimum score 53). *Application deadline:* For fall admission, 6/1 priority date for international students; for spring admission, 10/15 priority date for international students; for summer admission, 3/15 priority date for international students. Applications are processed on a rolling basis. Application fee: $50 ($75 for international students). Electronic applications accepted. *Expenses: Tuition, area resident:* Full-time $3630. Tuition, state resident: full-time $3630. Tuition, nonresident: full-time $11,100. *International tuition:* $11,100 full-time. *Required fees:* $2794. Tuition and fees vary according to course load, degree level and program. *Financial support:* In 2018–19, 39 students received support, including 18 research assistantships with partial tuition reimbursements available (averaging $3,231 per year), 136 teaching assistantships with partial tuition reimbursements available (averaging $4,053 per year); Federal Work-Study, institutionally sponsored loans, scholarships/grants, health care benefits, and unspecified assistantships also available. Financial award application deadline: 5/1; financial award applicants required to submit FAFSA. *Unit head:* Dr. William F. Kuracina, Interim Dean, 903-886-5166, Fax: 903-886-5774, E-mail: william.kuracina@tamuc.edu. *Application contact:* Vicky Turner, Doctoral Degree and Special Programs Coordinator, 903-886-5167, E-mail: vicky.turner@tamuc.edu.
Website: http://www.tamuc.edu/academics/colleges/humanitiesSocialSciencesArts/

Texas A&M University–Kingsville, College of Graduate Studies, College of Education and Human Performance, Department of Teacher and Bilingual Education, Program in Bilingual Education, Kingsville, TX 78363. Offers M Ed, Ed D. *Degree requirements:* For master's, comprehensive exam. *Entrance requirements:* For master's, GRE General Test, MAT, minimum GPA of 3.0.

Touro College, Graduate School of Education, New York, NY 10010. Offers education and special education (MS); instructional technology (MS); mathematics education (MS); school leadership (MS); teaching English to speakers of other languages (MS); teaching literacy (MS). *Accreditation:* TEAC. *Program availability:* Part-time, evening/weekend, online learning. *Entrance requirements:* Additional exam requirements/recommendations for international students: Required—TOEFL (minimum score 83 iBT), IELTS (minimum score 6.5). *Faculty research:* Equity assistance, language development, scholarly communications, Latin American studies and cultural sensitivity, behavior management techniques and strategies in special education.

English as a Second Language

Trevecca Nazarene University, Graduate Education Program, Nashville, TN 37210-2877. Offers accountability and instructional leadership (Ed S); curriculum and instruction for Christian school educators (M Ed); curriculum and instruction K-12 (M Ed); educational leadership (M Ed); English second language (M Ed); library and information science (MLI Sc); special education: visual impairments (M Ed); teaching (MAT), including teaching 6-12, teaching K-5. *Accreditation:* NCATE. *Program availability:* Part-time, evening/weekend, online learning. *Degree requirements:* For master's, comprehensive exam, exit assessment/e-portfolio. *Entrance requirements:* For master's, GRE or MAT; PRAXIS (for MAT), minimum GPA of 3.0, official transcript from regionally-accredited institution, references, interview, writing sample, at least 3 years' successful teaching experience (for M Ed in educational leadership); for Ed S, GRE or MAT, master's degree with minimum GPA of 3.0, official transcript from regionally accredited institution, at least 3 years' successful teaching experience, interview, writing sample, background and fingerprinting check, recommendations. Additional exam requirements/recommendations for international students: Required—TOEFL (minimum score 550 paper-based). Electronic applications accepted. *Expenses:* Contact institution.

Trinity Western University, School of Graduate Studies, Program in Teaching English to Speakers of Other Languages (TESOL), Langley, BC V2Y 1Y1, Canada. Offers MA. *Program availability:* Part-time, online learning. *Degree requirements:* For master's, project. *Entrance requirements:* For master's, minimum GPA of 3.0. Additional exam requirements/recommendations for international students: Required—TOEFL (minimum score 600 paper-based). *Faculty research:* ESL methodology, second language acquisition, computer assisted language learning.

Troy University, Graduate School, College of Education, Program in Second Language Instruction, Troy, AL 36082. Offers MS. *Program availability:* Part-time, evening/weekend. *Faculty:* 2 full-time (1 woman), 2 part-time/adjunct (both women). *Students:* 9 full-time (8 women), 1 (woman) part-time; includes 1 minority (Black or African American, non-Hispanic/Latino), 8 international. Average age 26. 8 applicants, 100% accepted, 5 enrolled. In 2018, 15 master's awarded. *Degree requirements:* For master's, thesis or capstone. *Entrance requirements:* For master's, GRE (minimum score of 850 on old exam or 290 on new exam), GMAT (minimum score of 380), or MAT (minimum score of 385), bachelor's degree; minimum undergraduate GPA of 2.5 or 3.0 on last 30 semester hours; letters of recommendation. Additional exam requirements/recommendations for international students: Required—TOEFL (minimum score 523 paper-based; 70 iBT), IELTS (minimum score 6). *Application deadline:* Applications are processed on a rolling basis. Application fee: $50. Electronic applications accepted. *Expenses: Tuition, area resident:* Full-time $425; part-time $425 per credit hour. Tuition, state resident: full-time $425; part-time $425 per credit hour. Tuition, nonresident: full-time $850; part-time $850 per credit hour. *International tuition:* $850 full-time. *Required fees:* $50 per semester. Tuition and fees vary according to campus/location and program. *Financial support:* Fellowships, career-related internships or fieldwork, and scholarships/grants available. Support available to part-time students. Financial award applicants required to submit FAFSA. *Unit head:* Dr. Trellys Riley, Associate Professor, Chair, Leadership Development and Professional Studies, 334-241-9575, E-mail: tariley@troy.edu. *Application contact:* Jessica A. Kimbro, Assistant Director of Graduate Programs, 334-670-3189, E-mail: jacord@troy.edu.
Website: https://www.troy.edu/academics/academic-programs/college-education-programs.php

Universidad del Este, Graduate School, Carolina, PR 00984. Offers accounting (MBA); adult education (M Ed); agribusiness (MBA); criminal justice and criminology (MA); curriculum and instruction - early education (M Ed); curriculum and instruction - elementary (M Ed); curriculum and instruction - English (M Ed); curriculum and instruction - Spanish (M Ed); human resources (MBA); information security management (MBA); information technology and Web business development (MBA); management (MBA); public policy (MPA); social work (MA), including clinical social work; special education (M Ed); strategic leadership (MBA).

Universidad del Turabo, Graduate Programs, Programs in Education, Program in Teaching English as a Second Language, Gurabo, PR 00778-3030. Offers M Ed. *Entrance requirements:* For master's, GRE, EXADEP, GMAT, interview, official transcript, essay, recommendation letters. Electronic applications accepted.

University at Buffalo, the State University of New York, Graduate School, Graduate School of Education, Department of Learning and Instruction, Buffalo, NY 14260. Offers biology education (Ed M, Certificate); chemistry education (Ed M, Certificate); childhood education (Ed M); childhood education with bilingual extension (Ed M); college teaching (Advanced Certificate); curriculum, instruction and the science of learning (PhD); early childhood education (Ed M); early childhood education with bilingual extension (Ed M); earth science education (Ed M, Certificate); education and technology (Ed M); education studies (Ed M); educational technology and new literacies (Certificate); educational technology and new literacies (Advanced Certificate); elementary education (Ed D); English education (Ed M, Certificate); English education studies (Ed M); English for speakers of other languages (Ed M); foreign and second language education (PhD); French education (Ed M, Certificate); German education (Ed M, Certificate); gifted education (Certificate); Latin education (Ed M, Certificate); literacy education studies (Ed M); literacy specialist (Ed M); literacy teaching and learning (Certificate); mathematics education (Ed M, Certificate); music education (Ed M, Certificate); music education studies (Ed M); music learning theory (Advanced Certificate); online education (Advanced Certificate); physics education (Ed M, Certificate); science and the public (Ed M); social studies education (Ed M, Certificate); Spanish education (Ed M, Certificate); special education (PhD); teaching English to speakers of other languages (Ed M). *Program availability:* Part-time, evening/weekend, 100% online. *Faculty:* 31 full-time (22 women), 41 part-time/adjunct (27 women). *Students:* 161 full-time (107 women), 369 part-time (260 women); includes 76 minority (26 Black or African American, non-Hispanic/Latino; 3 American Indian or Alaska Native, non-Hispanic/Latino; 30 Asian, non-Hispanic/Latino; 14 Hispanic/Latino; 3 Two or more races, non-Hispanic/Latino), 41 international. Average age 34. 368 applicants, 70% accepted, 179 enrolled. In 2018, 100 master's, 26 doctorates, 19 other advanced degrees awarded. *Degree requirements:* For master's, comprehensive exam; for doctorate, thesis/dissertation, research analysis exam, research experience. *Entrance requirements:* For master's, letters of reference; for doctorate, GRE General Test or MAT, interview, writing sample, letters of recommendation. Additional exam requirements/recommendations for international students: Required—TOEFL (minimum score 600 paper-based; 96 iBT), IELTS (minimum score 6.5), PTE (minimum score 55). *Application deadline:* For fall admission, 2/1 priority date for domestic and international students; for spring admission, 11/15 priority date for domestic students, 10/1 for international students. Applications are processed on a rolling basis. Application fee: $50. Electronic applications accepted. *Financial support:* In 2018–19, 42 fellowships (averaging $5,181 per year), 44 research assistantships with tuition reimbursements (averaging $10,908 per year) were awarded; teaching assistantships, career-related internships or fieldwork, Federal Work-Study, institutionally sponsored loans, scholarships/grants, tuition waivers (full and partial), and unspecified assistantships also available. Financial award application deadline: 2/28; financial award applicants required to submit FAFSA. *Faculty research:* Science assessment, foreign language teaching and learning, early learning, new literacies, gender and education. *Total annual research expenditures:* $413,233. *Unit head:* Dr. Julie Gorlewski, Department Chair, 716-645-2455, Fax: 716-645-3161, E-mail: jgorlews@buffalo.edu. *Application contact:* Renad Aref, Assistant Director of Admission Recruitment, 716-645-2110, Fax: 716-645-7937, E-mail: gseinfo@buffalo.edu.
Website: http://ed.buffalo.edu/teaching.html

The University of Alabama, Graduate School, College of Arts and Sciences, Department of English, Tuscaloosa, AL 35487. Offers composition and rhetoric (PhD); creative writing (MFA), including fiction, poetry; literature (MA, PhD); rhetoric and composition (MA); teaching English as a second language (MATESOL). *Degree requirements:* For master's, one foreign language, comprehensive exam, thesis; for doctorate, 2 foreign languages, comprehensive exam, thesis/dissertation. *Entrance requirements:* For master's, GRE (minimum score of 300, except for MFA), minimum GPA of 3.0, critical writing sample; for doctorate, GRE (minimum score of 300), minimum GPA of 3.5 on master's or equivalent graduate work, critical writing sample. Additional exam requirements/recommendations for international students: Recommended—TOEFL (minimum score 550 paper-based; 79 iBT). Electronic applications accepted. *Faculty research:* American literature, British literature, composition/rhetoric, applied linguistics, creative writing.

The University of Alabama at Birmingham, School of Education, Program in English as a Second Language, Birmingham, AL 35294-1250. Offers MA Ed, Ed S. *Program availability:* Part-time, evening/weekend. *Degree requirements:* For master's, variable foreign language requirement, comprehensive exam. *Entrance requirements:* For master's, MAT (minimum score of 388 scaled, 35 raw) or GRE (minimum 290 on current test). Additional exam requirements/recommendations for international students: Required—TOEFL, IELTS. Electronic applications accepted. *Expenses:* Contact institution. *Faculty research:* How mainstream teachers learn to implement ESL best practices and how they help their colleagues through collaborative mentoring; language use, identity, and the relationship between school and community empowering K- 12 administrators to become EL advocates; oral English proficiency of non-native English speakers pursuing graduate degrees in education and factors related to their identity and perceptions of self-efficacy as teachers.

The University of Alabama in Huntsville, School of Graduate Studies, College of Arts, Humanities, and Social Sciences, Department of English, Huntsville, AL 35899. Offers education (MA); English (MA); technical writing (Certificate); TESOL (Certificate). *Program availability:* Part-time. *Faculty:* 9 full-time (5 women). *Students:* 13 full-time (7 women), 16 part-time (10 women); includes 7 minority (6 Black or African American, non-Hispanic/Latino; 1 Hispanic/Latino). Average age 34. 8 applicants, 100% accepted, 6 enrolled. In 2018, 11 master's awarded. *Degree requirements:* For master's, one foreign language, comprehensive exam, thesis or alternative, oral and written exams. *Entrance requirements:* For master's and Certificate, GRE General Test, minimum GPA of 3.0. Additional exam requirements/recommendations for international students: Required—TOEFL (minimum score 500 paper-based; 80 iBT), IELTS (minimum score 6.5). *Application deadline:* For fall admission, 7/15 priority date for domestic students, 4/1 priority date for international students; for spring admission, 11/30 priority date for domestic students, 9/1 priority date for international students. Applications are processed on a rolling basis. Application fee: $50. Electronic applications accepted. *Expenses: Tuition, area resident:* Full-time $10,632; part-time $412 per credit hour. Tuition, state resident: full-time $10,632. Tuition, nonresident: full-time $23,604; part-time $412 per credit hour. *Required fees:* $582; $582. Tuition and fees vary according to course load and program. *Financial support:* In 2018–19, 12 students received support, including 10 teaching assistantships with full tuition reimbursements available (averaging $4,500 per year); career-related internships or fieldwork, Federal Work-Study, institutionally sponsored loans, scholarships/grants, health care benefits, tuition waivers (full and partial), and unspecified assistantships also available. Support available to part-time students. Financial award application deadline: 4/1; financial award applicants required to submit FAFSA. *Faculty research:* Fiction and identity, Shakespeare, science fiction, eighteenth-century literature, technical writing. *Unit head:* Dr. Alanna Frost, Chair, 256-824-2373, Fax: 256-824-6949, E-mail: alanna.frost@uah.edu. *Application contact:* Kim Gray, Graduate Studies Admissions Coordinator, 256-824-6002, Fax: 256-824-6405, E-mail: deangrad@uah.edu.
Website: http://www.uah.edu/ahs/departments/english

The University of Alabama in Huntsville, School of Graduate Studies, College of Education, Huntsville, AL 35899. Offers autism spectrum disorders (M Ed, Graduate Certificate); biology (MAT); chemistry (MAT); differentiated instruction in elementary education (M Ed); English language arts (MAT); English speakers of other languages (M Ed, MAT); history (MAT); mathematics (MAT); physics (MAT); reading education (M Ed); secondary education (M Ed). *Program availability:* Part-time. *Faculty:* 13 full-time (10 women). *Students:* 38 full-time (30 women), 39 part-time (37 women); includes 17 minority (10 Black or African American, non-Hispanic/Latino; 3 American Indian or Alaska Native, non-Hispanic/Latino; 2 Asian, non-Hispanic/Latino; 2 Two or more races, non-Hispanic/Latino). Average age 33. 47 applicants, 83% accepted, 29 enrolled. In 2018, 31 master's awarded. *Degree requirements:* For master's, comprehensive exam, thesis or alternative, oral and written. *Entrance requirements:* For master's, GRE General Test, minimum GPA of 3.0. Additional exam requirements/recommendations for international students: Required—TOEFL (minimum score 500 paper-based; 80 iBT), IELTS (minimum score 6.5). *Application deadline:* For fall admission, 7/15 priority date for domestic students, 4/1 priority date for international students; for spring admission, 11/30 priority date for domestic students, 9/1 priority date for international students. Applications are processed on a rolling basis. Application fee: $50. Electronic applications accepted. *Expenses: Tuition, area resident:* Full-time $10,632; part-time $412 per credit hour. Tuition, state resident: full-time $10,632. Tuition, nonresident: full-time $23,604; part-time $412 per credit hour. *Required fees:* $582; $582. Tuition and fees vary according to course load and program. *Financial support:* In 2018–19, 2 students received support, including 1 teaching assistantship with full tuition reimbursement available (averaging $4,500 per year); career-related internships or fieldwork, Federal Work-Study, institutionally sponsored loans, scholarships/grants, health care benefits, tuition waivers (full and partial), and unspecified assistantships also available. Support available to part-time students. Financial award application deadline: 4/1; financial award applicants required to submit FAFSA. *Unit head:* Dr. Beth Nason Quick, Dean, 256-824-2325, E-mail: beth.quick@uah.edu. *Application contact:* Kim Gray, Graduate Studies Admissions Coordinator, 256-824-6002, Fax: 256-824-6405, E-mail: deangrad@uah.edu.
Website: http://www.uah.edu/education/

University of Alberta, Faculty of Graduate Studies and Research, Department of Educational Psychology, Edmonton, AB T6G 2E1, Canada. Offers counseling psychology (M Ed, PhD); educational psychology (M Ed, PhD); instructional technology (M Ed); school counseling (M Ed); school psychology (M Ed, PhD); special education (M Ed, PhD); special education-deafness studies (M Ed); teaching English as a second language (M Ed). *Program availability:* Part-time. *Degree requirements:* For master's, thesis optional; for doctorate, comprehensive exam, thesis/dissertation. *Entrance requirements:* For master's and doctorate, minimum GPA of 3.0. Additional exam requirements/recommendations for international students: Required—TOEFL. *Faculty research:* Human learning, development and assessment.

The University of Arizona, College of Humanities, Department of English, English Language/Linguistics Program, Tucson, AZ 85721. Offers English (MA, PhD); ESL (MA). *Entrance requirements:* Additional exam requirements/recommendations for international students: Required—TOEFL (minimum score 550 paper-based; 79 iBT); Recommended—IELTS (minimum score 7). Electronic applications accepted.

The University of Arizona, Graduate Interdisciplinary Programs, Graduate Interdisciplinary Program in Second Language Acquisition and Teaching, Tucson, AZ 85721. Offers PhD. *Degree requirements:* For doctorate, one foreign language, comprehensive exam, thesis/dissertation. *Entrance requirements:* For doctorate, GRE, 3 letters of recommendation, writing sample. Additional exam requirements/recommendations for international students: Required—TOEFL (minimum score 550 paper-based; 79 iBT); Recommended—TWE. Electronic applications accepted.

University of Arkansas at Little Rock, Graduate School, College of Arts, Letters, and Sciences, Department of International and Second Language Studies, Little Rock, AR 72204-1099. Offers second languages (MA). *Degree requirements:* For master's, comprehensive exam, thesis. *Entrance requirements:* For master's, GRE or MAT, bachelor's degree; 3 letters of reference; personal interview; minimum overall undergraduate GPA of 2.75, 3.0 in last 60 hours.

The University of British Columbia, Faculty of Education, Department of Language and Literacy Education, Vancouver, BC V6T 1Z2, Canada. Offers literacy education (M Ed, MA, PhD); modern languages education (M Ed, MA); teaching English as a second language (M Ed, MA, PhD). *Program availability:* Part-time, evening/weekend. *Degree requirements:* For master's, thesis (MA); for doctorate, thesis/dissertation. *Entrance requirements:* For master's and doctorate, minimum B+ average in last 2 years with minimum 2 courses at A standing. Additional exam requirements/recommendations for international students: Required—TOEFL, TWE. Electronic applications accepted. *Expenses:* Contact institution. *Faculty research:* Language and literacy development, second language acquisition, Asia Pacific language curriculum, children's literature, whole language instruction.

University of California, Berkeley, UC Berkeley Extension, Certificate Programs in Education, Berkeley, CA 94720. Offers college admissions and career planning (Certificate); teaching English as a second language (Certificate).

University of California, Los Angeles, Graduate Division, College of Letters and Science, Department of Applied Linguistics and Teaching English as a Second Language, Los Angeles, CA 90095. Offers applied linguistics (PhD); applied linguistics and teaching English as a second language (MA); teaching English as a second language (Certificate). *Degree requirements:* For master's, one foreign language, thesis; for doctorate, one foreign language, thesis/dissertation, oral and written qualifying exams. *Entrance requirements:* For master's and doctorate, bachelor's degree; minimum undergraduate GPA of 3.0 (or its equivalent if letter grade system not used). Additional exam requirements/recommendations for international students: Required—TOEFL. Electronic applications accepted.

University of California, Riverside, Graduate Division, Graduate School of Education, Riverside, CA 92521. Offers applied behavior analysis (M Ed); diversity and equity (M Ed); education policy analysis and leadership (PhD); education specialist (Credential); education, society, and culture (MA, PhD); educational psychology (MA, PhD); general education (M Ed); higher education administration and policy (M Ed, PhD); multiple subject (Credential); research, evaluation, measurement and statistics (MA); school psychology (PhD); single subject (Credential); special education (M Ed, PhD); special education and autism (MA); TESOL (M Ed). Terminal master's awarded for partial completion of doctoral program. *Degree requirements:* For master's, comprehensive exams or thesis (MA), case study or analytical report (M Ed); for doctorate, comprehensive exam, thesis/dissertation, written and oral qualifying exams, college teaching practicum. *Entrance requirements:* For master's, GRE General Test (for MA); CBEST and CSET (for M Ed in general education only), UCR Extension TESOL certificate (for M Ed with TESOL emphasis only); for doctorate, GRE General Test, writing sample; for Credential, CBEST, CSET. Additional exam requirements/recommendations for international students: Required—TOEFL (minimum score 550 paper-based; 80 iBT), IELTS (minimum score 7). Electronic applications accepted. *Faculty research:* Responsiveness to intervention, faculty core, response to intervention of English language learners, advanced modeling techniques, study on social capital, trust, and motivation.

University of Central Florida, College of Arts and Humanities, Department of Modern Languages and Literatures, Program in Teaching English to Speakers of Other Languages, Orlando, FL 32816. Offers MA, Certificate. *Accreditation:* NCATE. *Program availability:* Part-time, evening/weekend. *Students:* 12 full-time (8 women), 15 part-time (13 women); includes 7 minority (1 Black or African American, non-Hispanic/Latino; 6 Hispanic/Latino), 2 international. Average age 35. 31 applicants, 84% accepted, 14 enrolled. In 2018, 15 master's, 20 other advanced degrees awarded. *Degree requirements:* For master's, comprehensive exam, thesis or alternative. *Entrance requirements:* For master's, GRE General Test, minimum GPA of 3.0 in last 60 hours, letters of recommendation. Additional exam requirements/recommendations for international students: Required—TOEFL. *Application deadline:* For fall admission, 7/1 for domestic students; for spring admission, 12/1 for domestic students; for summer admission, 4/1 for domestic students. Application fee: $30. Electronic applications accepted. *Financial support:* In 2018–19, 6 students received support, including 1 research assistantship with partial tuition reimbursement available (averaging $9,088 per year), 5 teaching assistantships with partial tuition reimbursements available (averaging $9,088 per year); career-related internships or fieldwork, Federal Work-Study, institutionally sponsored loans, health care benefits, tuition waivers (partial), and unspecified assistantships also available. Financial award application deadline: 3/1; financial award applicants required to submit FAFSA. *Unit head:* Dr. Gergana Vitanova, Director, 407-823-2472, E-mail: gergana.vitanova@ucf.edu. *Application contact:* Associate Director, Graduate Admissions, 407-823-2766, Fax: 407-823-6442, E-mail: gradadmissions@ucf.edu.
Website: http://mll.cah.ucf.edu/graduate/index.php#TESOL

University of Central Florida, College of Community Innovation and Education, School of Teacher Education, Orlando, FL 32816. Offers applied learning and instruction (MA); curriculum and instruction (M Ed); elementary education (M Ed, MA); exceptional student education (M Ed, MA, Certificate), including autism spectrum disorders (Certificate), exceptional student education (M Ed), exceptional student education K-12 (MA), intervention specialist (Certificate), pre-kindergarten disabilities (Certificate), severe or profound disabilities (Certificate), special education (Certificate); K-8 mathematics and science education (M Ed, Certificate); reading education (M Ed, Certificate); teacher education (MAT), including art education, English language, mathematics education, middle school mathematics, middle school science, science education, social science education; world languages education - English for speakers of other languages (ESOL) (Certificate); world languages education - languages other than English (LOTE) (Certificate). *Program availability:* Part-time, evening/weekend. *Degree requirements:* For Certificate, thesis or alternative. *Entrance requirements:* For degree, GRE General Test, minimum GPA of 3.0. Additional exam requirements/recommendations for international students: Required—TOEFL. Electronic applications accepted.

University of Central Missouri, The Graduate School, Warrensburg, MO 64093. Offers accountancy (MA); accounting (MBA); applied mathematics (MS); aviation safety (MA); biology (MS); business administration (MBA); career and technical education leadership (MS); college student personnel administration (MS); communication (MA); computer science (MS); counseling (MS); criminal justice (MS); educational leadership (Ed D); educational technology (MS); elementary and early childhood education (MSE); English (MA); environmental studies (MA); finance (MBA); history (MA); human services/educational technology (Ed S); human services/learning resources (Ed S); human services/professional counseling (Ed S); industrial hygiene (MS); industrial management (MS); information systems (MBA); information technology (MS); kinesiology (MS); library science and information services (MS); literacy education (MSE); marketing (MBA); mathematics (MS); music (MA); occupational safety management (MS); psychology (MS); rural family nursing (MS); school administration (MSE); social gerontology (MS); sociology (MA); special education (MSE); speech language pathology (MS); superintendency (Ed S); teaching (MAT); teaching English as a second language (MA); technology (MS); technology management (PhD); theatre (MA). *Accreditation:* ASHA. *Program availability:* Part-time, 100% online, blended/hybrid learning. *Degree requirements:* For master's and Ed S, comprehensive exam (for some programs), thesis (for some programs). *Entrance requirements:* Additional exam requirements/recommendations for international students: Required—TOEFL (minimum score 550 paper-based; 79 iBT). Electronic applications accepted.

University of Central Oklahoma, The Jackson College of Graduate Studies, College of Education and Professional Studies, Department of Curriculum and Instruction, Edmond, OK 73034-5209. Offers bilingual education/teaching English as a second language (M Ed); early childhood education (M Ed); elementary education (M Ed). *Program availability:* Part-time. *Degree requirements:* For master's, comprehensive exam (for some programs), thesis optional. *Entrance requirements:* Additional exam requirements/recommendations for international students: Required—TOEFL (minimum score 550 paper-based; 79 iBT), IELTS (minimum score 6.5). Electronic applications accepted.

University of Central Oklahoma, The Jackson College of Graduate Studies, College of Liberal Arts, Department of English, Edmond, OK 73034-5209. Offers composition and rhetoric (MA); creative writing (MA); literature (MA); teaching English as a second language (MA). *Program availability:* Part-time. *Degree requirements:* For master's, variable foreign language requirement, comprehensive exam (for some programs), thesis (for some programs), portfolio. *Entrance requirements:* For master's, 18-24 hours of course work in English language and literature; writing sample; essay. Additional exam requirements/recommendations for international students: Required—TOEFL (minimum score 550 paper-based; 79 iBT), IELTS (minimum score 6.5). Electronic applications accepted.

University of Cincinnati, Graduate School, College of Education, Criminal Justice, and Human Services, School of Education, Program in Literacy and Second Language Studies, Cincinnati, OH 45221. Offers M Ed, Ed D. *Accreditation:* NCATE. *Program availability:* Part-time. *Degree requirements:* For master's, thesis or alternative; for doctorate, thesis/dissertation. *Entrance requirements:* For master's, GRE General Test. Additional exam requirements/recommendations for international students: Required—TOEFL (minimum score 550 paper-based), TWE (minimum score 4.5), OEPT. Electronic applications accepted.

University of Colorado Colorado Springs, College of Education, Colorado Springs, CO 80918. Offers counseling and human services (MA); curriculum and instruction (MA); educational leadership (MA); educational leadership, research and policy (PhD); special education (MA); teaching English to speakers of other languages (MA). *Accreditation:* ACA; NCATE. *Program availability:* Part-time, evening/weekend, 100% online, blended/hybrid learning. *Faculty:* 31 full-time (22 women), 61 part-time/adjunct (47 women). *Students:* 208 full-time (149 women), 351 part-time (256 women); includes 136 minority (30 Black or African American, non-Hispanic/Latino; 1 American Indian or Alaska Native, non-Hispanic/Latino; 12 Asian, non-Hispanic/Latino; 64 Hispanic/Latino; 29 Two or more races, non-Hispanic/Latino), 8 international. Average age 36. 230 applicants, 80% accepted, 101 enrolled. In 2018, 186 master's, 9 doctorates awarded. *Degree requirements:* For master's, comprehensive exam, thesis or alternative, microcomputer proficiency; for doctorate, comprehensive exam, thesis/dissertation, research lab. *Entrance requirements:* For master's, GRE General Test (recommended but not required), career goal statement, professional references; for doctorate, GRE General Test. Additional exam requirements/recommendations for international students: Recommended—TOEFL (minimum score 90 iBT), IELTS (minimum score 6.5). *Application deadline:* For fall admission, 1/28 priority date for domestic and international students; for spring admission, 11/1 priority date for domestic and international students. Applications are processed on a rolling basis. Application fee: $60 ($100 for international students). Electronic applications accepted. *Expenses:* Tuition and fees vary by program, course load, and residency type. Please visit the University of Colorado Colorado Springs Student Financial Services website to estimate current program costs: https://www.uccs.edu/bursar/index.php/estimate-your-bill. *Financial support:* In 2018–19, 15 students received support. Career-related internships or fieldwork, Federal Work-Study, scholarships/grants, and unspecified assistantships available. Support available to part-time students. Financial award application deadline: 3/1; financial award applicants required to submit FAFSA. *Faculty research:* Linguistically diverse education (LDE), educational policy, evidence-based reading and writing instruction, relational and social aggression, positive behavior supports, inclusive schooling, K-12 education policy. *Total annual research expenditures:* $607,967. *Unit head:* Dr. Valerie Martin Conley, Dean, 719-255-4133, E-mail: vmconley@uccs.edu. *Application contact:* The College of Education Student Resource Office, 719-255-4996, E-mail: education@uccs.edu.
Website: https://www.uccs.edu/coe/

University of Dayton, Department of English, Dayton, OH 45469. Offers literary and cultural studies (MA); teaching English to speakers of other languages (TESOL) (MA); writing and rhetoric (MA). *Program availability:* Part-time. *Degree requirements:* For master's, thesis optional. *Entrance requirements:* For master's, 24 undergraduate-level semester hours in literature and/or writing; minimum GPA of 3.0; transcripts; personal statement; 8-10 page writing sample; three professional letters of recommendation. Additional exam requirements/recommendations for international students: Required—TOEFL (minimum score 550 paper-based, 80 iBT) or IELTS. Electronic applications accepted. *Faculty research:* Gender and Victorian periodicals; literature and human rights; Paul Lawrence Dunbar; the archetype of the Indian princess; Amish country.

University of Delaware, College of Education and Human Development, School of Education, Newark, DE 19716. Offers education (PhD); educational leadership (Ed D); higher education (M Ed); instruction (MI); reading (M Ed); school leadership (M Ed); school psychology (MA, Ed S); teaching English as a second language (TESL) (MA). *Accreditation:* NCATE. *Program availability:* Part-time, evening/weekend. Terminal master's awarded for partial completion of doctoral program. *Degree requirements:* For master's, comprehensive exam (for some programs), thesis (for some programs); for doctorate, comprehensive exam (for some programs), thesis/dissertation. *Entrance*

requirements: For master's and doctorate, GRE, 3 letters of recommendation. Additional exam requirements/recommendations for international students: Required—TOEFL (minimum score 600 paper-based). Electronic applications accepted. *Faculty research:* Teacher education; curriculum theory and development; community based education models, educational leadership.

The University of Findlay, Office of Graduate Admissions, Findlay, OH 45840-3653. Offers applied security and analytics (MSAS); athletic training (MAT); business (MBA), including certified management accountant, certified public accountant, health care management, hospitality management; education (MA Ed, Ed D), including children's literature (MA Ed), curriculum and teaching (MA Ed), education (MA Ed), educational administration (MA Ed), human resource development (MA Ed), mathematics (MA Ed), reading (MA Ed), science education (MA Ed), superintendent (Ed D), teaching (Ed D), technology (MA Ed); environmental, safety, and health management (MSEM); health informatics (MS); occupational therapy (MOT); pharmacy (Pharm D); physical therapy (DPT); physician assistant (MPA); rhetoric and writing (MA); teaching English to speakers of other languages (TESOL) and applied linguistics (MA). *Program availability:* Part-time, evening/weekend, 100% online, blended/hybrid learning. *Degree requirements:* For master's, comprehensive exam (for some programs), thesis (for some programs), cumulative project, capstone project; for doctorate, thesis/dissertation (for some programs). *Entrance requirements:* For master's, GRE/GMAT, bachelor's degree from accredited institution, minimum undergraduate GPA of 2.5 in last 64 hours of course work; for doctorate, GRE, MAT, minimum cumulative GPA of 3.0. Additional exam requirements/recommendations for international students: Required—TOEFL (minimum score 79 iBT), IELTS (minimum score 7), PTE (minimum score 61). Electronic applications accepted.

University of Florida, Graduate School, College of Liberal Arts and Sciences, Department of Linguistics, Gainesville, FL 32611. Offers linguistics (MA, PhD); teaching English as a second language (Certificate). *Program availability:* Part-time. Terminal master's awarded for partial completion of doctoral program. *Degree requirements:* For master's, one foreign language, comprehensive exam, thesis (for some programs); for doctorate, 2 foreign languages, comprehensive exam, thesis/dissertation. *Entrance requirements:* For master's and doctorate, GRE General Test, minimum GPA of 3.0. Additional exam requirements/recommendations for international students: Required—TOEFL (minimum score 550 paper-based; 80 iBT), IELTS (minimum score 6). Electronic applications accepted. *Faculty research:* Language documentation, psycholinguistics and neuro-linguistics, theoretical linguistics, sociolinguistics second language acquisition.

University of Guam, Office of Graduate Studies, School of Education, Program in Teaching English to Speakers of Other Languages, Mangilao, GU 96923. Offers M Ed. *Degree requirements:* For master's, comprehensive oral and written exams, special project or thesis. *Entrance requirements:* For master's, GRE General Test. Additional exam requirements/recommendations for international students: Required—TOEFL.

University of Hawaii at Manoa, Office of Graduate Education, College of Languages, Linguistics and Literature, Department of Second Language Studies, Honolulu, HI 96822. Offers English as a second language (MA, Graduate Certificate); second language acquisition (PhD). *Program availability:* Part-time. *Degree requirements:* For master's, 2 foreign languages, thesis optional; for doctorate, 2 foreign languages, comprehensive exam, thesis/dissertation. *Entrance requirements:* For master's, GRE General Test, minimum GPA of 3.0; for doctorate, GRE General Test, MA, scholarly publications. Additional exam requirements/recommendations for international students: Required—TOEFL (minimum score 600 paper-based; 100 iBT), IELTS (minimum score 7). *Faculty research:* Second language use, second language analysis, second language pedagogy and testing, second language learning, qualitative and quantitative research methods for second languages.

University of Illinois at Chicago, College of Liberal Arts and Sciences, School of Literatures, Cultural Studies and Linguistics, Chicago, IL 60607-7128. Offers French and Francophone studies (MA); Germanic studies (MA); Hispanic and Italian studies (MAT, PhD), including Hispanic linguistics (PhD), Hispanic literary and cultural studies (PhD), teaching of Spanish (MAT); linguistics (MA), including teaching English to speakers of other languages/applied linguistics; Slavic and Baltic languages and literatures (MA), including Slavic studies (MA, PhD); Slavic and Baltic languages and literatures (PhD), including Slavic studies (MA, PhD). *Program availability:* Part-time. Terminal master's awarded for partial completion of doctoral program. *Degree requirements:* For master's, one foreign language, exam. *Entrance requirements:* For master's, minimum GPA of 2.75. Additional exam requirements/recommendations for international students: Required—TOEFL. Electronic applications accepted. *Faculty research:* International studies, religious (Catholic, Jewish) studies, moving image arts.

University of Illinois at Urbana–Champaign, Graduate College, College of Liberal Arts and Sciences, School of Literatures, Cultures and Linguistics, Department of Linguistics, Champaign, IL 61820. Offers linguistics (MA, PhD); teaching of English as a second language (MA).

University of Illinois at Urbana–Champaign, Graduate College, College of Liberal Arts and Sciences, School of Literatures, Cultures and Linguistics, Program in Second Language Acquisition and Teacher Education, Champaign, IL 61820. Offers PhD.

The University of Iowa, Graduate College, College of Education, Department of Teaching and Learning, Program in Education, Iowa City, IA 52242-1316. Offers art education (MA); developmental reading (MA); elementary education (MA); English education (MA, MAT); foreign and second language education (MAT); foreign language education (MA); foreign language/ESL education (PhD); language, literacy and culture (PhD); mathematics education (MA, MAT, PhD); music education (MM, PhD); science education (MA); secondary education (MA); social studies (MA, PhD). *Degree requirements:* For master's, thesis optional, exam; for doctorate, comprehensive exam, thesis/dissertation. *Entrance requirements:* For master's and doctorate, GRE General Test, minimum GPA of 3.0. Additional exam requirements/recommendations for international students: Required—TOEFL (minimum score 550 paper-based; 81 iBT). Electronic applications accepted.

University of Louisiana at Lafayette, College of Liberal Arts, Department of English, Lafayette, LA 70504. Offers American culture (MA, PhD), including history, sociology; American literature and language (PhD); creative writing (MA, PhD), including creative writing (MA), folklore (MA), rhetoric (MA); folklore (MA, PhD); linguistic studies (MA, PhD); professional writing (PhD); rhetoric (MA, PhD); TESOL studies (MA, PhD). *Program availability:* Part-time. Terminal master's awarded for partial completion of doctoral program. *Degree requirements:* For master's, one foreign language, thesis or alternative; for doctorate, 2 foreign languages, comprehensive exam, thesis/dissertation. *Entrance requirements:* For master's, GRE General Test, minimum GPA of 2.75; for doctorate, GRE General Test, minimum GPA of 3.0. Additional exam requirements/recommendations for international students: Required—TOEFL (minimum score 550 paper-based). Electronic applications accepted. *Faculty research:* Composition theory, Southern literature, medieval literature.

University of Manitoba, Faculty of Graduate Studies, Faculty of Education, Department of Curriculum, Teaching and Learning, Winnipeg, MB R3T 2N2, Canada. Offers language and literacy (M Ed); second language education (M Ed); studies in curriculum, teaching and learning (M Ed). *Degree requirements:* For master's, thesis or alternative.

University of Maryland, Baltimore County, The Graduate School, College of Arts, Humanities and Social Sciences, Department of Education, Program in Teaching English to Speakers of Other Languages, Baltimore, MD 21250. Offers MA, Postbaccalaureate Certificate. *Program availability:* Part-time, evening/weekend, 100% online, blended/hybrid learning. *Degree requirements:* For master's, thesis optional; for Postbaccalaureate Certificate, internship. *Entrance requirements:* For master's, GRE (minimum score 500 verbal, 150 on the new version, or 297 composite), 3 letters of reference, statement of purpose. Additional exam requirements/recommendations for international students: Required—TOEFL (minimum score 550 paper-based; 80 iBT). Electronic applications accepted. *Faculty research:* Adult education, bilingual language learning, online instruction, English grammar, cross-culture communication, ESL teacher professional identity.

University of Maryland, College Park, Academic Affairs, College of Education, Department of Teaching, Learning, Policy and Leadership, College Park, MD 20742. Offers reading (M Ed, MA, PhD, CAGS); secondary education (M Ed, MA, Ed D, PhD, CAGS); teaching English to speakers of other languages (M Ed). *Accreditation:* NCATE. *Program availability:* Part-time, evening/weekend, online learning. *Degree requirements:* For master's, comprehensive exam, seminar paper; for doctorate, comprehensive exam, thesis/dissertation, published paper, oral exam. *Entrance requirements:* For master's, GRE General Test or MAT, minimum GPA of 3.0, 3 letters of recommendation; for doctorate, GRE General Test or MAT, minimum undergraduate GPA of 3.0, graduate 3.5; 3 letters of recommendation. Electronic applications accepted. *Faculty research:* Teacher preparation, curriculum study, in-service education.

University of Massachusetts Amherst, Graduate School, College of Education, Program in Education, Amherst, MA 01003. Offers bilingual, English as a second language, and multicultural education (M Ed, Ed S); child study and early education (M Ed); children, families and schools (Ed D, Ed S); early childhood and elementary teacher education (M Ed); educational leadership (M Ed); educational policy and leadership (Ed D); higher education (M Ed); international education (M Ed); language, literacy and culture (Ed D); learning, media and technology (M Ed, Ed S); mathematics, science, and learning technologies (Ed D); reading and writing (M Ed); research, educational measurement and psychometrics (Ed D); school counselor education (M Ed, Ed S); school psychology (Ed S); science education (Ed S); secondary teacher education (M Ed); social justice education (M Ed, Ed D, Ed S); special education (M Ed, Ed D, Ed S); teacher education and school improvement (Ed D, Ed S). *Accreditation:* NCATE. *Program availability:* Part-time, online learning. Terminal master's awarded for partial completion of doctoral program. *Degree requirements:* For doctorate, comprehensive exam, thesis/dissertation. *Entrance requirements:* Additional exam requirements/recommendations for international students: Required—TOEFL (minimum score 550 paper-based; 80 iBT), IELTS (minimum score 6.5). Electronic applications accepted.

University of Massachusetts Dartmouth, Graduate School, College of Arts and Sciences, School of Education, Department of STEM Education and Teacher Development, North Dartmouth, MA 02747-2300. Offers English as a second language (Postbaccalaureate Certificate); mathematics education (PhD); middle school education (MAT); secondary school education (MAT). *Program availability:* Part-time. *Faculty:* 9 full-time (6 women), 3 part-time/adjunct (2 women). *Students:* 21 full-time (18 women), 100 part-time (53 women); includes 20 minority (3 Black or African American, non-Hispanic/Latino; 2 Asian, non-Hispanic/Latino; 11 Hispanic/Latino; 4 Two or more races, non-Hispanic/Latino), 3 international. Average age 34. 63 applicants, 90% accepted, 45 enrolled. In 2018, 68 master's, 1 doctorate, 1 other advanced degree awarded. *Degree requirements:* For doctorate, thesis/dissertation. *Entrance requirements:* For master's, Statement of Purpose, Resume, Official Transcripts, copy of MA MTELs, 2 letters of recommendation, Proof of License (for Professional Licensure Program); for doctorate, GRE Score, Statement of Purpose, Resume, Official transcripts, 3 letters of recommendation; for Postbaccalaureate Certificate, Statement of Purpose, Resume, Official Transcripts, 2 letters of recommendation, MTEL Score Report. Additional exam requirements/recommendations for international students: Required—TOEFL (minimum score 550 paper-based; 79 iBT), IELTS (minimum score 6.5). *Application deadline:* For fall admission, 1/15 priority date for domestic students, 12/15 priority date for international students; for spring admission, 12/15 priority date for domestic students, 11/15 priority date for international students. Application fee: $60. Electronic applications accepted. *Financial support:* In 2018–19, 1 fellowship (averaging $18,000 per year), 3 research assistantships (averaging $10,897 per year), 6 teaching assistantships (averaging $8,017 per year) were awarded; tuition waivers (full) and doctoral support also available. Financial award application deadline: 3/1; financial award applicants required to submit FAFSA. *Faculty research:* Mindfulness in education, literacies, assessment of teacher knowledge, curriculum tools for supporting mathematics learning. *Total annual research expenditures:* $1.8 million. *Unit head:* Traci Almeida, Coordinator of Graduate Admissions and Licensure, 508-999-8098, Fax: 508-910-8183, E-mail: talmeida@umassd.edu. *Application contact:* Scott Webster, Director of Graduate Studies and Admissions, 508-999-8604, Fax: 508-999-8183, E-mail: graduate@umassd.edu.
Website: http://www.umassd.edu/cas/schoolofeducation/departments/stemeducationandteacherdevelopment/

University of Memphis, Graduate School, College of Arts and Sciences, Department of English, Memphis, TN 38152. Offers African-American literature (Graduate Certificate); applied linguistics (PhD); composition studies (PhD); creative writing (MFA); English as a second language (MA); linguistics (MA); literary and cultural studies (PhD), including African-American literature; literature (MA); professional writing (MA, PhD); teaching English as a second/foreign language (Graduate Certificate). *Program availability:* Part-time, evening/weekend, 100% online. *Students:* 72 full-time (42 women), 78 part-time (51 women); includes 41 minority (24 Black or African American, non-Hispanic/Latino; 3 Asian, non-Hispanic/Latino; 11 Hispanic/Latino; 3 Two or more races, non-Hispanic/Latino), 26 international. Average age 35. 49 applicants, 86% accepted, 18 enrolled. In 2018, 19 master's, 15 doctorates, 8 other advanced degrees awarded. Terminal master's awarded for partial completion of doctoral program. *Degree requirements:* For master's, one foreign language, comprehensive exam, thesis optional; for doctorate, 2 foreign languages, comprehensive exam, thesis/dissertation, qualifying exam. *Entrance requirements:* For master's, GRE, minimum undergraduate GPA of 3.0, statement of purpose, two letters of recommendation; for doctorate, GRE, minimum undergraduate and graduate GPA of 3.25, statement of purpose, writing sample, three letters of recommendation. Additional exam requirements/recommendations for international students: Required—TOEFL. *Application deadline:* For fall admission, 1/15 for domestic students; for spring admission, 10/15 for domestic students. Applications are processed on a rolling basis. Application fee: $35 ($60 for international students). Electronic applications accepted. *Expenses: Tuition, area resident:* Full-time $10,240; part-time $503 per credit hour. Tuition, state resident: full-time $10,464. Tuition, nonresident: full-time $20,224; part-time $991 per credit hour. *Required fees:* $850; $106 per credit hour. *Financial support:* Research assistantships with full tuition reimbursements, teaching assistantships with full tuition reimbursements, Federal Work-Study, scholarships/

grants, and unspecified assistantships available. Financial award application deadline: 2/1; financial award applicants required to submit FAFSA. *Faculty research:* Applied linguistics, British and American literature, professional writing, composition studies. *Unit head:* Dr. Joshua Phillips, Chair, 901-678-2651, Fax: 901-678-2226, E-mail: jsphllps@memphis.edu. *Application contact:* Dr. Jeffrey Scraba, Coordinator of Graduate Studies, 901-678-4768, Fax: 901-678-2226, E-mail: jscraba@memphis.edu. Website: http://www.memphis.edu/english

University of Minnesota, Twin Cities Campus, Graduate School, College of Education and Human Development, Department of Curriculum and Instruction, Minneapolis, MN 55455-0213. Offers art education (M Ed, MA, PhD); curriculum and instruction (M Ed, MA, PhD); elementary education (MA, PhD); English education (PhD); language and immersion education (Certificate); learning technologies (MA, PhD); literacy education (MA, PhD); second language education (MA, PhD); social studies education (MA, PhD); STEM education (MA, PhD); teaching (M Ed), including mathematics, science, social studies, teaching; teaching English to speakers of other languages (MA); technology enhanced learning (Certificate). *Faculty:* 33 full-time (18 women). *Students:* 414 full-time (293 women), 247 part-time (170 women); includes 129 minority (16 Black or African American, non-Hispanic/Latino; 3 American Indian or Alaska Native, non-Hispanic/Latino; 38 Asian, non-Hispanic/Latino; 47 Hispanic/Latino; 25 Two or more races, non-Hispanic/Latino), 57 international. Average age 31. 610 applicants, 69% accepted, 349 enrolled. In 2018, 338 master's, 21 doctorates, 41 other advanced degrees awarded. Application fee: $75 ($95 for international students). *Financial support:* In 2018–19, 9 fellowships, 35 research assistantships with full tuition reimbursements (averaging $11,380 per year), 85 teaching assistantships with full tuition reimbursements (averaging $11,180 per year) were awarded. *Faculty research:* Teaching and learning; influence of cultural, linguistic, social, political, and technological factors on teaching, learning and educational research; relationship between educational practice and a democratic and just society; urban education; immigrant education, racial justice and education. *Total annual research expenditures:* $3.9 million. *Unit head:* Dr. Mark Vagle, Chair, 612-625-4006, E-mail: mvagle@umn.edu. *Application contact:* Dr. Mark Vagle, Chair, 612-625-4006, E-mail: mvagle@umn.edu. Website: http://www.cehd.umn.edu/ci

University of Minnesota, Twin Cities Campus, Graduate School, College of Liberal Arts, Institute of Linguistics, English as a Second Language, and Slavic Languages and Literatures (ILES), English as a Second Language Program, Minneapolis, MN 55455-0213. Offers MA. *Degree requirements:* For master's, one foreign language, comprehensive exam, thesis. *Entrance requirements:* For master's, GRE, 3 letters of recommendation. Additional exam requirements/recommendations for international students: Required—TOEFL (minimum score 600 paper-based). Electronic applications accepted. *Faculty research:* Second language acquisitions, communication strategies, English for specific purposes, literacy, speech act, proymatics in general, language assessment, discourse analysis, research methods.

University of Missouri–St. Louis, College of Education, Department of Educator Preparation, Innovation and Research, St. Louis, MO 63121. Offers elementary education (M Ed), including early childhood, general, reading; secondary education (M Ed), including curriculum and instruction, general, middle level education, reading, teaching English to speakers of other languages (TESOL); special education (M Ed), including autism and developmental disabilities, early childhood special education. *Program availability:* Part-time, evening/weekend. *Degree requirements:* For master's, comprehensive exam. *Entrance requirements:* Additional exam requirements/recommendations for international students: Recommended—TOEFL (minimum score 550 paper-based; 79 iBT), IELTS (minimum score 6.5). Electronic applications accepted.

University of Nebraska at Kearney, College of Education, Department of Teacher Education, Kearney, NE 68849-0001. Offers curriculum and instruction (MA Ed), including early childhood education, elementary education, English as a second language, instructional effectiveness, reading/special education, secondary education; instructional technology (MS Ed), including information technology, instructional technology, school librarian; reading PK-12 (MA Ed); special education (MA Ed), including advanced practitioner: assistive technology specialist, advanced practitioner: behavioral interventionist, advanced practitioner: inclusive collaboration specialist, gifted, teacher education. *Program availability:* Part-time, evening/weekend, online only, 100% online. *Degree requirements:* For master's, comprehensive exam, thesis optional. *Entrance requirements:* For master's, portfolio or GRE. Additional exam requirements/recommendations for international students: Recommended—TOEFL (minimum score 550 paper-based; 79 iBT), IELTS (minimum score 6.5). Electronic applications accepted. *Expenses:* Contact institution.

University of Nebraska at Omaha, Graduate Studies, College of Arts and Sciences, Department of English, Omaha, NE 68182. Offers advanced writing (Certificate); English (MA); teaching English to speakers of other languages (Certificate); technical communication (Certificate). *Program availability:* Part-time, evening/weekend. *Degree requirements:* For master's, comprehensive exam, thesis (for some programs). *Entrance requirements:* For master's, GRE or MAT, minimum GPA of 3.0, transcripts, 3 letters of recommendation, statement of purpose, writing sample; for Certificate, minimum GPA of 3.0, transcripts, statement of purpose. Additional exam requirements/recommendations for international students: Required—TOEFL, IELTS, PTE. Electronic applications accepted.

University of Nevada, Las Vegas, Graduate College, College of Education, Department of Educational and Clinical Studies, Las Vegas, NV 89154-3066. Offers addiction studies (Advanced Certificate); counselor education (M Ed, MS), including clinical mental health (MS), school counseling (M Ed); early childhood education (M Ed); early childhood special education (Certificate), including infancy, preschool; English language learning (M Ed); mental health counseling (Advanced Certificate); special education (M Ed, PhD); PhD/JD. *Program availability:* Part-time. *Degree requirements:* For master's, comprehensive exam (for some programs); for doctorate, comprehensive exam, thesis/dissertation; for other advanced degree, final project. *Entrance requirements:* For master's, bachelor's degree; letter of recommendation; statement of purpose; for doctorate, GRE General Test, statement of purpose; writing sample; 3 letters of recommendation. Additional exam requirements/recommendations for international students: Required—TOEFL (minimum score 550 paper-based; 80 iBT), IELTS (minimum score 7). Electronic applications accepted. *Expenses:* Contact institution. *Faculty research:* Multicultural issues in counseling, academic interventions for students with disabilities, establishment of pro-social skills in young children with severe disabilities, inclusive strategies for students with disabilities, language and literacy for English language learners.

University of Nevada, Reno, Graduate School, College of Education, Department of Educational Specialties, Program in Teaching English to Speakers of Other Languages, Reno, NV 89557. Offers MA. Terminal master's awarded for partial completion of doctoral program. *Degree requirements:* For master's, thesis optional. *Entrance requirements:* For master's, minimum GPA of 2.75. Additional exam requirements/recommendations for international students: Required—TOEFL (minimum score 500 paper-based; 61 iBT), IELTS (minimum score 6). Electronic applications accepted. *Faculty research:* Bilingualism, multicultural education.

University of New Mexico, Graduate Studies, College of Education, Program in Language, Literacy and Sociocultural Studies, Albuquerque, NM 87131-2039. Offers American Indian education (MA); bilingual education (MA, PhD); educational linguistics (PhD); educational thought and sociocultural studies (MA, PhD); literacy/language arts (MA, PhD); social studies (MA); TESOL (MA, PhD). *Students:* Average age 40. 61 applicants, 38% accepted, 23 enrolled. In 2018, 36 master's, 4 doctorates awarded. *Degree requirements:* For master's, comprehensive exam, thesis optional; for doctorate, comprehensive exam, thesis/dissertation, research skills. *Entrance requirements:* For master's, letter of intent, 3 letters of recommendation, resume, BA/BS, department demographic form, transcripts; for doctorate, writing sample, letter of intent, 3 letters of recommendation, resume, BA/BS, MA, department demographic form, transcripts. Additional exam requirements/recommendations for international students: Required—TOEFL. *Application deadline:* For fall admission, 12/1 for domestic and international students; for spring admission, 9/15 for domestic and international students. Application fee: $50. Electronic applications accepted. *Financial support:* Fellowships, research assistantships, teaching assistantships, career-related internships or fieldwork, institutionally sponsored loans, scholarships/grants, and unspecified assistantships available. Support available to part-time students. Financial award application deadline: 3/1; financial award applicants required to submit FAFSA. *Faculty research:* School reform, professional development, history of education, Native American education, politics of education, feminism and issues of sexual identity, critical race theory, bilingualism, literacy reading, adolescent literature, second language acquisition, critical theory and schooling, indigenous languages. *Unit head:* Dr. Lois M. Meyer, Chair, 505-277-7244, Fax: 505-277-8362, E-mail: lsmeyer@unm.edu. *Application contact:* Debra Schaffer, Administrative Assistant, 505-277-0437, Fax: 505-277-8362, E-mail: schaffer@unm.edu. Website: http://coe.unm.edu/departments-programs/llss/index.html

The University of North Carolina at Chapel Hill, Graduate School, School of Education, Program in Secondary Education, Chapel Hill, NC 27599. Offers English (Grades 9-12) (MAT); English as a second language (MAT); French (Grades K-12) (MAT); German (Grades K-12) (MAT); Japanese (Grades K-12) (MAT); Latin (Grades 9-12) (MAT); mathematics (Grades 9-12) (MAT); music (Grades K-12) (MAT); science (Grades 9-12) (MAT); social studies (Grades 9-12) (MAT); Spanish (Grades K-12) (MAT). *Accreditation:* NCATE. *Degree requirements:* For master's, comprehensive exam. *Entrance requirements:* For master's, GRE General Test, minimum GPA of 3.0 during last 2 years of undergraduate course work. Additional exam requirements/recommendations for international students: Required—TOEFL (minimum score 550 paper-based). Electronic applications accepted.

The University of North Carolina at Charlotte, Cato College of Education, Department of Middle, Secondary and K-12 Education, Charlotte, NC 28223-0001. Offers middle grades and secondary education (M Ed); teaching English as a second language (M Ed, Graduate Certificate). *Program availability:* Part-time. *Students:* 3 full-time (all women), 88 part-time (77 women); includes 21 minority (19 Black or African American, non-Hispanic/Latino; 1 Asian, non-Hispanic/Latino; 1 Hispanic/Latino), 3 international. Average age 34. 36 applicants, 94% accepted, 30 enrolled. In 2018, 25 master's awarded. *Entrance requirements:* For master's, GRE or MAT, bachelor's degree from accredited college or university; minimum GPA of 3.0 in undergraduate work; North Carolina Class A teaching license in appropriate middle grades or secondary education field; minimum of two years' teaching experience; written narrative providing statement of purpose for master's degree study; letters of recommendation; for Graduate Certificate, bachelor's degree from accredited institution; minimum undergraduate GPA of 2.5 overall or 3.0 in senior year, or 15 hours taken in the last 5 years; satisfactory recommendations from three persons knowledgeable of applicant's interactions with children or adolescents; statement of purpose. Additional exam requirements/recommendations for international students: Required—TOEFL (minimum score 523 paper-based; 70 iBT), IELTS (minimum score 6), TOEFL (minimum score 523 paper-based, 70 iBT) or IELTS (6). *Application deadline:* Applications are processed on a rolling basis. Application fee: $75. Electronic applications accepted. Tuition and fees vary according to course load and program. *Financial support:* Research assistantships, teaching assistantships, career-related internships or fieldwork, institutionally sponsored loans, scholarships/grants, and unspecified assistantships available. Support available to part-time students. Financial award application deadline: 3/1; financial award applicants required to submit FAFSA. *Total annual research expenditures:* $309,255. *Unit head:* Scott Kissau, Chair, 704-687-8875, E-mail: spkissau@uncc.edu. *Application contact:* Kathy B. Giddings, Director of Graduate Admissions, 704-687-5503, Fax: 704-687-1668, E-mail: gradadm@uncc.edu. Website: http://mdsk.uncc.edu/

The University of North Carolina at Charlotte, Cato College of Education, Interdisciplinary Education Programs, Charlotte, NC 28223-0001. Offers art education (Graduate Certificate); child and family development: early childhood education (MAT); curriculum and instruction (PhD); elementary education (MAT); foreign language education (MAT); middle grades education (MAT); secondary education (MAT); special education (MAT); teaching (Graduate Certificate); teaching English as a second language (MAT); theatre education (Graduate Certificate). *Program availability:* Part-time, 100% online, blended/hybrid learning. *Students:* 70 full-time (55 women), 511 part-time (414 women); includes 228 minority (160 Black or African American, non-Hispanic/Latino; 1 American Indian or Alaska Native, non-Hispanic/Latino; 11 Asian, non-Hispanic/Latino; 38 Hispanic/Latino; 18 Two or more races, non-Hispanic/Latino), 8 international. Average age 34. 343 applicants, 92% accepted, 219 enrolled. In 2018, 69 master's, 13 doctorates, 161 other advanced degrees awarded. *Entrance requirements:* For master's, GRE or MAT, bachelor's degree, or its U.S. equivalent, from regionally-accredited college or university; minimum overall GPA of 3.0 on all previous work beyond high school; statement of purpose (essay); at least three recommendation forms; for doctorate, GRE or MAT, bachelor's degree (or its U.S. equivalent) from regionally-accredited college or university; minimum overall GPA of 3.5 in master's degree program; for Graduate Certificate, bachelor's degree from regionally-accredited university; minimum GPA of 2.75 on all post-secondary work attempted; transcripts; personal statement outlining why the applicant seeks admission to the program. Additional exam requirements/recommendations for international students: Required—TOEFL (minimum score 523 paper-based; 70 iBT), IELTS (minimum score 6), TOEFL (minimum score 523 paper-based, 70 iBT) or IELTS (6). *Application deadline:* Applications are processed on a rolling basis. Application fee: $75. Electronic applications accepted. Tuition and fees vary according to course load and program. *Financial support:* Career-related internships or fieldwork, institutionally sponsored loans, scholarships/grants, and unspecified assistantships available. Support available to part-time students. Financial award application deadline: 3/1; financial award applicants required to submit FAFSA. *Unit head:* Dr. Ellen McIntyre, Dean, 704-687-8722, E-mail: ellen.mcintyre@uncc.edu. *Application contact:* Kathy B. Giddings, Director of Graduate Admissions, 704-687-5503, Fax: 704-687-1668, E-mail: gradadm@uncc.edu. Website: http://education.uncc.edu/academic-programs

The University of North Carolina at Greensboro, Graduate School, School of Education, Department of Teacher Education and Higher Education, Greensboro, NC 27412-5001. Offers college teaching and adult learning (Certificate); curriculum and

instruction (M Ed), including chemistry education, elementary education, English as a second language, French education, instructional technology, mathematics education, middle grades education, reading education, science education, social studies education, Spanish education; curriculum and teaching (PhD), including higher education, teacher education and development; English as a second language (Certificate); higher education (M Ed); supervision (M Ed). *Accreditation:* NCATE. *Program availability:* Part-time. *Degree requirements:* For doctorate, thesis/dissertation. *Entrance requirements:* For master's and doctorate, GRE General Test. Additional exam requirements/recommendations for international students: Required—TOEFL. Electronic applications accepted. *Faculty research:* Community college literacy program, middle school mathematics/computer mathematics.

The University of North Carolina Wilmington, Watson College of Education, Department of Instructional Technology, Foundations and Secondary Education, Wilmington, NC 28403-3297. Offers English as a second language (M Ed, MAT); instructional technology (MS); secondary education (M Ed, MAT). *Program availability:* Part-time, blended/hybrid learning. *Degree requirements:* For master's, thesis or research project/portfolio. *Entrance requirements:* For master's, GRE or MAT, education statement of interest essay, 3 letters of recommendation. Additional exam requirements/recommendations for international students: Required—TOEFL (minimum score 550 paper-based; 79 iBT), IELTS (minimum score 6.5). Electronic applications accepted.

University of Northern Colorado, Graduate School, College of Education and Behavioral Sciences, School of Teacher Education, Greeley, CO 80639. Offers curriculum studies (MAT); educational studies (Ed D); elementary education (MAT); English education (MAT); literacy (MA); multilingual education (MA), including TESOL, world languages; teaching diverse learners (MA). *Accreditation:* NCATE. *Program availability:* Part-time, evening/weekend. *Degree requirements:* For master's, comprehensive exam, thesis or alternative; for doctorate, comprehensive exam, thesis/dissertation. *Entrance requirements:* For master's and doctorate, GRE General Test, 3 letters of recommendation. Electronic applications accepted.

University of Northern Iowa, Graduate College, College of Humanities, Arts and Sciences, Department of Languages and Literatures, MA Program in Teaching English to Speakers of Other Languages, Cedar Falls, IA 50614. Offers MA. *Degree requirements:* For master's, comprehensive exam, thesis or research paper.

University of North Florida, College of Education and Human Services, Department of Childhood Education, Literacy, and TESOL, Jacksonville, FL 32224. Offers literacy (M Ed); professional education (M Ed); TESOL (M Ed). *Accreditation:* NCATE. *Program availability:* Part-time, evening/weekend. *Faculty:* 9 full-time (6 women), 3 part-time/adjunct (2 women). *Students:* 12 full-time (all women), 23 part-time (20 women); includes 15 minority (10 Black or African American, non-Hispanic/Latino; 4 Hispanic/Latino; 1 Two or more races, non-Hispanic/Latino), 2 international. Average age 32. 18 applicants, 67% accepted, 8 enrolled. In 2018, 14 master's awarded. *Entrance requirements:* For master's, GRE General Test, minimum GPA of 3.0 in last 60 hours, 3 letters of recommendation, interview. Additional exam requirements/recommendations for international students: Required—TOEFL (minimum score 500 paper-based). *Application deadline:* For fall admission, 8/1 priority date for domestic students, 5/1 for international students; for spring admission, 12/1 priority date for domestic students, 10/1 for international students; for summer admission, 3/15 priority date for domestic students, 2/1 for international students. Application fee: $30. Electronic applications accepted. *Expenses: Tuition, area resident:* Part-time $408.10 per credit hour. Tuition, state resident: part-time $408.10 per credit hour. Tuition, nonresident: part-time $932.61 per credit hour. *Required fees:* $111.81 per credit hour. Tuition and fees vary according to course load, campus/location and program. *Financial support:* In 2018–19, 2 students received support. Federal Work-Study, tuition waivers (partial), and unspecified assistantships available. Support available to part-time students. Financial award application deadline: 4/1; financial award applicants required to submit FAFSA. *Faculty research:* Social context of and processes in learning, inter-disciplinary instruction, cross-cultural conflict resolution, the Vygotskian perspective on literacy diagnosis and instruction, performance poetry and teaching the language arts through drama. *Total annual research expenditures:* $630. *Unit head:* Dr. Paul Parkison, Chair, 904-620-5352, Fax: 904-620-1025, E-mail: n01230143@unf.edu. *Application contact:* Dr. Amanda Pascale, Director, The Graduate School, 904-620-1360, Fax: 904-620-1362, E-mail: graduateschool@unf.edu.
Website: http://www.unf.edu/coehs/celt/

University of North Texas, Toulouse Graduate School, Denton, TX 76203-5459. Offers accounting (MS); applied anthropology (MA, MS); applied behavior analysis (Certificate); applied geography (MA); applied technology and performance improvement (M Ed, MS); art education (MA); art history (MA); arts leadership (Certificate); audiology (Au D); behavior analysis (MS); behavioral science (PhD); biochemistry and molecular biology (MS); biology (MA, MS); biomedical engineering (MS); business analysis (MS); chemistry (MS); clinical health psychology (PhD); communication studies (MA, MS); computer engineering (MS); computer science (MS); counseling (M Ed, MS), including clinical mental health counseling (MS), college and university counseling, elementary school counseling, secondary school counseling; creative writing (MA); criminal justice (MS); curriculum and instruction (M Ed); decision sciences (MBA); design (MA, MFA), including fashion design (MFA), innovation studies, interior design (MFA); early childhood studies (MS); economics (MS); educational leadership (M Ed, Ed D); educational psychology (MS, PhD), including family studies (MS), gifted and talented (MS), human development (MS), learning and cognition (MS), research, measurement and evaluation (MS); electrical engineering (MS); emergency management (MPA); engineering technology (MS); English (MA); English as a second language (MA); environmental science (MS); finance (MBA, MS); financial management (MPA); French (MA); health services management (MBA); higher education (M Ed, Ed D); history (MA, MS); hospitality management (MS); human resources management (MPA); information science (MS); information systems (PhD); information technologies (MBA); interdisciplinary studies (MA, MS); international studies (MA); international sustainable tourism (MS); jazz studies (MM); journalism (MA, MJ, Graduate Certificate), including interactive and virtual digital communication (Graduate Certificate), narrative journalism (Graduate Certificate), public relations (Graduate Certificate); kinesiology (MS); linguistics (MA); local government management (MPA); logistics (PhD); logistics and supply chain management (MBA); long-term care, senior housing, and aging services (MA); management (PhD); marketing (MBA); mathematics (MA, MS); mechanical and energy engineering (MS, PhD); music (MA), including ethnomusicology, music theory, musicology, performance; music composition (PhD); music education (MM Ed, PhD); nonprofit management (MPA); operations and supply chain management (MBA); performance (MM, DMA); philosophy (MA); political science (MA); professional and technical communication (MA); radio, television and film (MA, MFA); rehabilitation counseling (Certificate); sociology (MA); Spanish (MA); special education (M Ed); speech-language pathology (MA); strategic management (MBA); studio art (MFA); teaching (M Ed); MBA/MS. *Program availability:* Part-time, evening/weekend, online learning. Terminal master's awarded for partial completion of doctoral program. *Degree requirements:* For master's, variable foreign language requirement, comprehensive exam (for some programs), thesis (for some programs); for doctorate, variable foreign language requirement, comprehensive exam (for some programs), thesis/dissertation; for other advanced degree, variable foreign language requirement, comprehensive exam (for some programs). *Entrance requirements:* For master's and doctorate, GRE, GMAT. Additional exam requirements/recommendations for international students: Required—TOEFL (minimum score 550 paper-based; 79 iBT). Electronic applications accepted.

University of Pennsylvania, Graduate School of Education, Division of Educational Linguistics, Program in Teaching English to Speakers of Other Languages, Philadelphia, PA 19104. Offers MS Ed. *Program availability:* Part-time, online learning. *Students:* Average age 25. 348 applicants, 39% accepted, 76 enrolled. In 2018, 69 master's awarded.

University of Phoenix–Online Campus, College of Education, Phoenix, AZ 85034-7209. Offers administration and supervision (MAEd, Certificate); adult education and training (MAEd); curriculum and instruction (MAEd), including computer education, curriculum and instruction, English as a second language, language arts, mathematics, reading; early childhood education (MAEd); educational studies (MAEd); elementary teacher education (MAEd), including early childhood, elementary teacher education, high school middle level, middle level; principal licensure (Certificate); secondary teacher education (MAEd); special education (MAEd, Certificate); teacher education (MAEd), including middle level generalist; teacher education middle level mathematics (MAEd), including middle level mathematics; teacher education middle level science (MAEd), including middle level science; teacher education secondary mathematics (MAEd); teacher education secondary science (MAEd); teacher leadership (MAEd); teachers of English learners (Certificate); transition to teaching (Certificate), including elementary education, secondary education. *Program availability:* Evening/weekend, online learning. *Entrance requirements:* Additional exam requirements/recommendations for international students: Required—TOEFL, TOEIC (Test of English as an International Communication), Berlitz Online English Proficiency Exam, PTE, or IELTS. Electronic applications accepted. *Expenses:* Contact institution.

University of Phoenix–San Diego Campus, College of Education, San Diego, CA 92123. Offers curriculum and instruction (MA Ed), including computer education, curriculum and instruction, English as a second language; elementary teacher education (MA Ed); secondary teacher education (MA Ed). *Program availability:* Evening/weekend. *Degree requirements:* For master's, thesis (for some programs). *Entrance requirements:* For master's, 3 years of work experience, minimum undergraduate GPA of 3.0. Additional exam requirements/recommendations for international students: Required—TOEFL (minimum score 550 paper-based; 79 iBT). Electronic applications accepted.

University of Pittsburgh, Kenneth P. Dietrich School of Arts and Sciences, Program in Hispanic Linguistics, Pittsburgh, PA 15260. Offers TESOL (PhD). Terminal master's awarded for partial completion of doctoral program. *Degree requirements:* For doctorate, 2 foreign languages, comprehensive exam, thesis/dissertation. *Entrance requirements:* For doctorate, GRE General Test, proficiency in Spanish. Additional exam requirements/recommendations for international students: Required—TOEFL (minimum score 600 paper-based; 100 iBT). Electronic applications accepted. *Faculty research:* Hispanic linguistics, second language acquisition, phonetics, prosody, language variation and change.

University of Pittsburgh, Kenneth P. Dietrich School of Arts and Sciences, TESOL Certificate Program, Pittsburgh, PA 15260. Offers Certificate. *Program availability:* Part-time. *Entrance requirements:* Additional exam requirements/recommendations for international students: Required—TOEFL (minimum score 600 paper-based; 100 iBT), IELTS (minimum score 7.5). *Faculty research:* Second language acquisition, applied linguistics, sociolinguistics, second language pedagogy, linguistic theory.

University of Portland, School of Education, Portland, OR 97203-5798. Offers education (MA, MAT); educational leadership (M Ed); English for speakers of other languages (M Ed); initial administrator licensure (M Ed); neuroeducation (M Ed, Ed D); organizational leadership and development (Ed D); reading (M Ed); school leadership and development (Ed D); special education (M Ed). *Accreditation:* NCATE. *Program availability:* Part-time, evening/weekend. *Students:* 32 full-time (30 women), 239 part-time (187 women); includes 33 minority (7 Black or African American, non-Hispanic/Latino; 3 American Indian or Alaska Native, non-Hispanic/Latino; 13 Asian, non-Hispanic/Latino; 1 Native Hawaiian or other Pacific Islander, non-Hispanic/Latino; 9 Two or more races, non-Hispanic/Latino). Average age 34. 92 applicants, 60% accepted, 42 enrolled. In 2018, 57 master's, 16 doctorates awarded. *Degree requirements:* For doctorate, thesis/dissertation. *Entrance requirements:* For master's, minimum GPA of 3.0, teaching certificate, letters of recommendation, resume, statement of goals, official transcripts; for doctorate, 2 letters of recommendation, resume, essays, official transcripts. Additional exam requirements/recommendations for international students: Required—TOEFL (minimum score 550 paper-based; 80 iBT), IELTS (minimum score 7). *Application deadline:* For fall admission, 7/15 priority date for domestic and international students; for spring admission, 12/15 priority date for domestic and international students; for summer admission, 4/15 for domestic and international students. Applications are processed on a rolling basis. Electronic applications accepted. *Expenses:* MAT degree - $995/credit hour; EDD and Educational Specialist - $813/credit hour; all other degrees and certificates - $663/credit hour. *Financial support:* Fellowships, Federal Work-Study, and scholarships/grants available. Support available to part-time students. Financial award application deadline: 3/1; financial award applicants required to submit FAFSA. *Faculty research:* Multicultural education, supervision/leadership. *Unit head:* Dr. Bruce Weitzel, Associate Dean, 503-943-7135, E-mail: soed@up.edu. *Application contact:* Caitlin Biddulph, Graduate Programs and Admissions Specialist, 503-943-7107, E-mail: biddulph@up.edu.
Website: http://education.up.edu/default.aspx?cid-4318&pid-5590

University of Puerto Rico–Río Piedras, College of Education, Program in Teaching English as a Second Language, San Juan, PR 00931-3300. Offers M Ed. *Program availability:* Part-time. *Degree requirements:* For master's, thesis. *Entrance requirements:* For master's, PAEG or GRE, minimum GPA of 3.0, letter of recommendation. *Faculty research:* Second language acquisition, bilingual education.

University of St. Francis, College of Education, Joliet, IL 60435-6169. Offers educational leadership (MS, Ed D); elementary education (M Ed); reading (MS); secondary education (M Ed), including English education, math education, science education, social studies education, visual arts education; special education (M Ed); teaching and learning (MS); TESOL (Certificate). *Accreditation:* NCATE. *Program availability:* Part-time, evening/weekend, 100% online, blended/hybrid learning. *Faculty:* 11 full-time (8 women), 58 part-time/adjunct (38 women). *Students:* 43 full-time (35 women), 453 part-time (354 women); includes 110 minority (48 Black or African American, non-Hispanic/Latino; 7 Asian, non-Hispanic/Latino; 52 Hispanic/Latino; 3 Two or more races, non-Hispanic/Latino), 3 international. Average age 37. 300 applicants, 66% accepted, 164 enrolled. In 2018, 151 master's, 42 doctorates, 4 other advanced degrees awarded. *Degree requirements:* For master's, comprehensive exam; for doctorate, thesis/dissertation. *Entrance requirements:* Additional exam requirements/recommendations for international students: Required—TOEFL (minimum score 550 paper-based; 79 iBT), IELTS (minimum score 6). *Application deadline:* Applications are processed on a rolling basis. Electronic applications accepted. Application fee is waived when completed online. *Expenses:* Contact institution. *Financial support:* In 2018–19,

33 students received support. Scholarships/grants and tuition waivers (partial) available. Support available to part-time students. Financial award applicants required to submit FAFSA. *Unit head:* Dr. John Gambro, Dean, 815-740-3456, E-mail: jgambro@stfrancis.edu. *Application contact:* Sandee Sloka, Director Adult & Graduate Admissions, 800-735-7500, E-mail: ssloka@stfrancis.edu.
Website: https://www.stfrancis.edu/education/

University of Saint Joseph, Department of Education, West Hartford, CT 06117-2700. Offers curriculum and instruction (MA); elementary education (MAT); instructional technology (MA); literacy (MA); secondary education (MAT); TESOL (MA). *Program availability:* Part-time, evening/weekend. *Degree requirements:* For master's, comprehensive exam, thesis or alternative. *Entrance requirements:* For master's, 2 letters of recommendation. Electronic applications accepted. Application fee is waived when completed online.

University of St. Thomas, School of Education and Human Services, Houston, TX 77006-4696. Offers all level education (M Ed); bilingual/dual language (M Ed); Catholic school teaching (M Ed); Catholic/private school leadership (M Ed); counselor education (M Ed); curriculum and instruction (M Ed); education (Ed D); educational leadership (M Ed); elementary teaching (M Ed); English as a second language (M Ed); exceptionality/educational diagnostician (M Ed); exceptionality/special education (M Ed); generalist (M Ed); reading (M Ed); secondary teaching (M Ed); teaching (MAT). *Accreditation:* TEAC. *Program availability:* Part-time, evening/weekend, online learning. *Degree requirements:* For master's, thesis, field experience. *Entrance requirements:* For master's, GRE or MAT if GPA is below 3.0, bachelor's degree; minimum GPA of 2.75 in bachelor's degree or last 60 credit hours; official transcripts from all institutions; goal statement of 250-300 words; 1 reference. Additional exam requirements/recommendations for international students: Required—TOEFL (minimum score 94 iBT), IELTS (minimum score 7), PTE (minimum score 53). Electronic applications accepted. *Expenses:* Contact institution. *Faculty research:* Leadership, diversity, personality traits, second language acquisition.

University of San Diego, School of Leadership and Education Sciences, Department of Learning and Teaching, San Diego, CA 92110-2492. Offers curriculum and instruction (M Ed), including inclusive learning, literacy and digital learning, school leadership, steam (science, technology, engineering, arts, and mathematics); inclusive learning (M Ed); literacy and digital learning (M Ed); school leadership (M Ed); special education (M Ed); STEAM (science, technology, engineering, arts, and mathematics) (M Ed); TESOL, literacy and culture (M Ed). *Program availability:* Part-time, evening/weekend. *Faculty:* 9 full-time (7 women), 34 part-time/adjunct (26 women). *Students:* 136 full-time (102 women), 223 part-time (177 women); includes 130 minority (17 Black or African American, non-Hispanic/Latino; 21 Asian, non-Hispanic/Latino; 74 Hispanic/Latino; 3 Native Hawaiian or other Pacific Islander, non-Hispanic/Latino; 15 Two or more races, non-Hispanic/Latino), 10 international. Average age 33. 391 applicants, 85% accepted, 190 enrolled. In 2018, 201 master's awarded. *Degree requirements:* For master's, thesis (for some programs), international experience. *Entrance requirements:* For master's, California Basic Educational Skills Test, California Subject Examination for Teachers. Additional exam requirements/recommendations for international students: Required—TOEFL (minimum score 580 paper-based; 83 iBT), TWE. *Application deadline:* Applications are processed on a rolling basis. Application fee: $45. Electronic applications accepted. *Financial support:* In 2018–19, 127 students received support. Career-related internships or fieldwork, Federal Work-Study, institutionally sponsored loans, scholarships/grants, and stipends available. Financial award application deadline: 4/1; financial award applicants required to submit FAFSA. *Faculty research:* Action research methodology, cultural studies, instructional theories and practices, second language acquisition, school reform. *Unit head:* Dr. Reyes Quezada, Chair, 619-260-7655, E-mail: rquezada@sandiego.edu. *Application contact:* Erika Garwood, Associate Director of Graduate Admissions, 619-260-4524, Fax: 619-260-4158, E-mail: grads@sandiego.edu.
Website: http://www.sandiego.edu/soles/learning-and-teaching/

University of Saskatchewan, College of Graduate and Postdoctoral Studies, College of Arts and Science, Department of Linguistics and Religious Studies, Saskatoon, SK S7N 5A2, Canada. Offers applied linguistics (MA); religion and culture (MA); teaching English to speakers of other languages (MA). *Degree requirements:* For master's, thesis. *Entrance requirements:* Additional exam requirements/recommendations for international students: Required—TOEFL (minimum score 80 iBT); Recommended—IELTS (minimum score 6.5). Electronic applications accepted.

University of South Africa, College of Human Sciences, Pretoria, South Africa. Offers adult education (M Ed); African languages (MA, PhD); African politics (MA, PhD); Afrikaans (MA, PhD); ancient history (MA, PhD); ancient Near Eastern studies (MA, PhD); anthropology (MA, PhD); applied linguistics (MA); Arabic (MA, PhD); archaeology (MA); art history (MA); Biblical archaeology (MA); Biblical studies (M Th, D Th, PhD); Christian spirituality (M Th, D Th); church history (M Th, D Th); classical studies (MA, PhD); clinical psychology (MA); communication (MA, PhD); comparative education (M Ed, Ed D); consulting psychology (D Admin, D Com, PhD); curriculum studies (M Ed, Ed D); development studies (M Admin, MA, D Admin, PhD); didactics (M Ed, Ed D); education (M Tech); education management (M Ed, Ed D); educational psychology (M Ed); English (MA); environmental education (M Ed); French (MA, PhD); German (MA, PhD); Greek (MA); guidance and counseling (M Ed); health studies (MA, PhD), including health sciences education (MA), health services management (MA), medical and surgical nursing science (critical care general) (MA), midwifery and neonatal nursing science (MA), trauma and emergency care (MA); history (MA, PhD); history of education (Ed D); inclusive education (M Ed, Ed D); information and communications technology policy and regulation (MA); information science (MA, MIS, PhD); international politics (MA, PhD); Islamic studies (MA, PhD); Italian (MA, PhD); Judaica (MA, PhD); linguistics (MA, PhD); mathematical education (M Ed); mathematics education (MA); missiology (M Th, D Th); modern Hebrew (MA, PhD); musicology (MA, MMus, D Mus, PhD); natural science education (M Ed); New Testament (M Th, D Th); Old Testament (D Th); pastoral therapy (M Th, D Th); philosophy (MA); philosophy of education (M Ed, Ed D); politics (MA, PhD); Portuguese (MA, PhD); practical theology (M Th, D Th); psychology (MA, MS, PhD); psychology of education (M Ed, Ed D); public health (MA); religious studies (MA, D Th, PhD); Romance languages (MA); Russian (MA, PhD); Semitic languages (MA, PhD); social behavior studies in HIV/AIDS (MA); social science (mental health) (MA); social science in development studies (MA); social science in psychology (MA); social science in social work (MA); social science in sociology (MA); social work (MSW, DSW, PhD); socio-education (M Ed, Ed D); sociolinguistics (MA); sociology (MA, PhD); Spanish (MA, PhD); systematic theology (M Th, D Th); TESOL (teaching English to speakers of other languages) (MA); theological ethics (M Th, D Th); theory of literature (MA, PhD); urban ministries (D Th); urban ministry (M Th).

University of South Carolina, The Graduate School, College of Arts and Sciences, Linguistics Program, Columbia, SC 29208. Offers linguistics (MA, PhD); teaching English to speakers of other languages (Certificate). *Program availability:* Part-time. Terminal master's awarded for partial completion of doctoral program. *Degree requirements:* For master's, one foreign language, comprehensive exam, thesis optional; for doctorate, 3 foreign languages, comprehensive exam, thesis/dissertation. *Entrance requirements:* For master's and Certificate, GRE General Test, minimum GPA of 3.0; for doctorate, GRE General Test, minimum GPA of 3.5. Additional exam requirements/recommendations for international students: Required—TOEFL. Electronic applications accepted. *Faculty research:* Second language acquisition, sociolinguistics, syntax, historical linguistics and phonology.

University of South Dakota, Graduate School, School of Education, Division of Curriculum and Instruction, Program in Elementary Education, Vermillion, SD 57069. Offers elementary education (MA), including early childhood education, English language learning, reading specialist/literacy coach, science, technology and math (STEM). *Accreditation:* NCATE. *Program availability:* Part-time, 100% online, blended/hybrid learning. *Degree requirements:* For master's, comprehensive exam, thesis or alternative. *Entrance requirements:* For master's, GRE General Test, MAT, minimum GPA of 2.7. Additional exam requirements/recommendations for international students: Required—TOEFL (minimum score 550 paper-based; 79 iBT). Electronic applications accepted.

University of South Dakota, Graduate School, School of Education, Division of Curriculum and Instruction, Program in Secondary Education, Vermillion, SD 57069. Offers secondary education (MA), including English language learning, science, technology and math (STEM), secondary education plus certification. *Accreditation:* NCATE. *Program availability:* Part-time, online learning. *Degree requirements:* For master's, comprehensive exam, thesis or alternative. *Entrance requirements:* For master's, GRE General Test, MAT, minimum GPA of 2.7. Additional exam requirements/recommendations for international students: Required—TOEFL (minimum score 550 paper-based; 79 iBT). Electronic applications accepted.

University of Southern California, Graduate School, Rossier School of Education, Master's Programs in Education, Los Angeles, CA 90089-4038. Offers educational counseling (ME); marriage, family and child counseling (MMFT); postsecondary administration and student affairs [PASA] (ME); school counseling (ME); teaching (online) (MAT); teaching and teaching credential (MAT); teaching English to speakers of other languages (MAT). *Program availability:* Part-time, evening/weekend, online learning. *Degree requirements:* For master's, thesis optional. *Entrance requirements:* For master's, GRE (for all programs except MAT). Additional exam requirements/recommendations for international students: Required—TOEFL (minimum score 100 iBT). Electronic applications accepted. *Faculty research:* College access and equity, preparing teachers for culturally diverse populations, sociocultural basis of learning as mediated by instruction with focus on reading and literacy in English learners, social and political aspects of teaching and learning English, school counselor development and training.

University of Southern Indiana, Graduate Studies, College of Liberal Arts, Program in Second Language Acquisition, Policy, and Culture, Evansville, IN 47712-3590. Offers MA. *Program availability:* Part-time. *Entrance requirements:* For master's, minimum GPA of 3.0, letter of intent, 3 letters of recommendation. Additional exam requirements/recommendations for international students: Required—TOEFL (minimum score 550 paper-based; 79 iBT), IELTS (minimum score 6).

University of Southern Maine, College of Management and Human Service, School of Education and Human Development, Program in Literacy Education, Portland, ME 04103. Offers applied literacy (MS Ed); English as a second language (MS Ed, CAS, CGS); literacy education (MS Ed, CAS, CGS). *Accreditation:* TEAC. *Program availability:* Part-time, evening/weekend. *Degree requirements:* For master's, comprehensive exam, thesis or alternative; for other advanced degree, thesis or alternative. *Entrance requirements:* For master's, teacher certification; for other advanced degree, master's degree. Additional exam requirements/recommendations for international students: Required—TOEFL (minimum score 550 paper-based; 79 iBT). Electronic applications accepted. *Faculty research:* Teacher research in literacy, multiliteracies, learning to teach culturally and linguistically diverse students, motivation to read.

University of Southern Mississippi, College of Arts and Sciences, Department of World Languages, Hattiesburg, MS 39406-0001. Offers French (MATL); Spanish (MATL); teaching English to speakers of other languages (MATL). *Program availability:* 100% online. *Degree requirements:* For master's, comprehensive exam. *Entrance requirements:* For master's, GRE General Test, minimum GPA of 3.0 in field of study, 2.75 in last 2 years. Additional exam requirements/recommendations for international students: Required—TOEFL, IELTS. Electronic applications accepted.

University of South Florida, College of Arts and Sciences, Department of World Languages, Tampa, FL 33620-9951. Offers French (MA); linguistics (MA); linguistics and applied linguistics studies (PhD); linguistics: English as a second language (MA); Spanish (MA). *Program availability:* Part-time, evening/weekend. *Faculty:* 15 full-time (11 women). *Students:* 44 full-time (34 women), 8 part-time (all women); includes 17 minority (15 Hispanic/Latino; 2 Two or more races, non-Hispanic/Latino), 20 international. Average age 30. 68 applicants, 56% accepted, 22 enrolled. In 2018, 16 master's, 1 doctorate awarded. *Degree requirements:* For master's, one foreign language, comprehensive exam, thesis optional; for doctorate, one foreign language, comprehensive exam, thesis/dissertation. *Entrance requirements:* For master's, French and Spanish: GRE Not required; Applied Linguistics: GRE required with minimum scores of 149 (40th percentile) V and 4 AW (50th percentile), minimum undergraduate GPA of 3.0; French and Spanish: 3 letters of recommendation, writing sample, oral interview; Applied Linguistics: 3 letters of recommendation, statement of purpose, CV; for doctorate, GRE scores: V: 153 (500, approximately 60% percentile); Q: 144 (500, approximately 20% percentile); AW: 4.00, MA in Applied LInguistics or related field; experience with additional language(s); MA GPA 3.5 or higher; Statement of research interest; CV; writing sample; 3 academic references; interview. Additional exam requirements/recommendations for international students: Required—TOEFL, TOEFL minimum score 600 paper-based; 80 iBT or IELTS minimum score 6.5 (for MA); TOEFL minimum score 550 paper-based; 80 iBT or IELTS minimum score 6.5 (for PhD). *Application deadline:* For fall admission, 1/15 for domestic and international students; for spring admission, 10/15 for domestic students, 9/15 for international students. Application fee: $30. Electronic applications accepted. *Expenses:* Tuition, state resident: full-time $6350. Tuition, nonresident: full-time $19,048. *International tuition:* $19,048 full-time. *Required fees:* $2079. *Financial support:* In 2018–19, 7 students received support, including 43 teaching assistantships with tuition reimbursements available (averaging $10,152 per year); tuition waivers (partial) and unspecified assistantships also available. Financial award application deadline: 6/30. *Faculty research:* Second language acquisition, instructional technology, foreign language education, English for speakers of other languages, distance learning. *Total annual research expenditures:* $1,842. *Unit head:* Dr. Stephan Schindler, Chair and Professor, 813-974-2548, Fax: 813-905-9937, E-mail: skschindler@usf.edu. *Application contact:* Patricia Garcia, Academic Program Specialist, 813-974-2548, Fax: 813-905-9937, E-mail: pgarcia@usf.edu.
Website: http://languages.usf.edu/

University of South Florida, Innovative Education, Tampa, FL 33620-9951. Offers adult, career and higher education (Graduate Certificate), including college teaching, leadership in developing human resources, leadership in higher education; Africana studies (Graduate Certificate), including diasporas and health disparities, genocide and

human rights; aging studies (Graduate Certificate), including gerontology; art research (Graduate Certificate), including museum studies; business foundations (Graduate Certificate); chemical and biomedical engineering (Graduate Certificate), including materials science and engineering, water, health and sustainability; child and family studies (Graduate Certificate), including positive behavior support; civil and industrial engineering (Graduate Certificate), including transportation systems analysis; community and family health (Graduate Certificate), including maternal and child health, social marketing and public health, violence and injury: prevention and intervention, women's health; criminology (Graduate Certificate), including criminal justice administration; data science for public administration (Graduate Certificate); digital humanities (Graduate Certificate); educational measurement and research (Graduate Certificate), including evaluation; English (Graduate Certificate), including comparative literary studies, creative writing, professional and technical communication; entrepreneurship (Graduate Certificate); environmental health (Graduate Certificate), including safety management; epidemiology and biostatistics (Graduate Certificate), including applied biostatistics, biostatistics, concepts and tools of epidemiology, epidemiology, epidemiology of infectious diseases; geography, environment and planning (Graduate Certificate), including community development, environmental policy and management, geographical information systems; geology (Graduate Certificate), including hydrogeology; global health (Graduate Certificate), including disaster management, global health and Latin American and Caribbean studies, global health practice, humanitarian assistance, infection control; government and international affairs (Graduate Certificate), including Cuban studies, globalization studies; health policy and management (Graduate Certificate), including health management and leadership, public health policy and programs; hearing specialist: early intervention (Graduate Certificate); industrial and management systems engineering (Graduate Certificate), including systems engineering, technology management; information studies (Graduate Certificate), including school library media specialist; information systems/decision sciences (Graduate Certificate), including analytics and business intelligence; instructional technology (Graduate Certificate), including distance education, Florida digital/virtual educator, instructional design, multimedia design, Web design; internal medicine, bioethics and medical humanities (Graduate Certificate), including biomedical ethics; Latin American and Caribbean studies (Graduate Certificate); leadership for coastal resiliency planning (Graduate Certificate); mass communications (Graduate Certificate), including multimedia journalism; mathematics and statistics (Graduate Certificate), including mathematics; medicine (Graduate Certificate), including aging and neuroscience, bioinformatics, biotechnology, brain fitness and memory management, clinical investigation, hand and upper limb rehabilitation, health informatics, health sciences, integrative weight management, intellectual property, medicine and gender, metabolic and nutritional medicine, metabolic cardiology, pharmacy sciences; national and competitive intelligence (Graduate Certificate); nursing (Graduate Certificate), including simulation based academic fellowship in advanced pain management; psychological and social foundations (Graduate Certificate), including career counseling, college teaching, diversity in education, mental health counseling, school counseling; public affairs (Graduate Certificate), including nonprofit management, public management, research administration; public health (Graduate Certificate), including assessing chemical toxicity and public health risks, health equity, pharmacoepidemiology, public health generalist, toxicology, translational research in adolescent behavioral health; public health practices (Graduate Certificate), including planning for healthy communities; rehabilitation and mental health counseling (Graduate Certificate), including integrative mental health care, marriage and family therapy, rehabilitation technology; secondary education (Graduate Certificate), including ESOL, foreign language education: culture and content, foreign language education: professional; social work (Graduate Certificate), including geriatric social work/clinical gerontology; special education (Graduate Certificate), including autism spectrum disorder, disabilities education: severe/profound; world languages (Graduate Certificate), including teaching English as a second language (TESL) or foreign language. *Expenses:* Tuition, state resident: full-time $6350. Tuition, nonresident: full-time $19,048. *International tuition:* $19,048 full-time. *Required fees:* $2079. *Unit head:* Dr. Cynthia DeLuca, Associate Vice President and Assistant Vice Provost, 813-974-3077, Fax: 813-974-7061, E-mail: deluca@usf.edu. *Application contact:* Owen Hooper, Director, Summer and Alternative Calendar Programs, 813-974-6917, E-mail: hooper@usf.edu.
Website: http://www.usf.edu/innovative-education/

The University of Tennessee, Graduate School, College of Education, Health and Human Sciences, Program in Education, Knoxville, TN 37996. Offers art education (MS); counseling education (PhD); cultural studies in education (PhD); curriculum (MS, Ed S); curriculum, educational research and evaluation (Ed D, PhD); early childhood education (PhD); early childhood special education (MS); education of deaf and hard of hearing (MS); educational administration and policy studies (Ed D, PhD); educational administration and supervision (Ed S); educational psychology (Ed D, PhD); elementary education (MS, Ed S); elementary teaching (MS); English education (MS, Ed S); exercise science (PhD); foreign language/ESL education (MS, Ed S); instructional technology (MS, Ed D, PhD, Ed S); literacy, language and ESL education (PhD); literacy, language education, and ESL education (Ed D); mathematics education (MS, Ed S); modified and comprehensive special education (MS); reading education (MS, Ed S); school counseling (Ed S); school psychology (PhD, Ed S); science education (MS, Ed S); secondary teaching (MS); social foundations (MS); social science education (MS, Ed S); socio-cultural foundations of sports and education (PhD); special education (Ed S); teacher education (Ed D, PhD). *Accreditation:* NCATE. *Program availability:* Part-time, evening/weekend. *Degree requirements:* For master's and Ed S, thesis optional; for doctorate, variable foreign language requirement, thesis/dissertation. *Entrance requirements:* For master's, minimum GPA of 2.7; for doctorate and Ed S, GRE General Test, minimum GPA of 2.7. Additional exam requirements/recommendations for international students: Required—TOEFL. Electronic applications accepted.

The University of Texas at Arlington, Graduate School, College of Liberal Arts, Department of Linguistics and TESOL, Program in Teaching English to Speakers of Other Languages, Arlington, TX 76019. Offers MA. *Accreditation:* NCATE. *Program availability:* Part-time, evening/weekend. *Degree requirements:* For master's, comprehensive exam (for some programs), thesis optional. *Entrance requirements:* For master's, GRE General Test, minimum undergraduate GPA of 3.0, 6 credits of undergraduate foundation courses, equivalent of 2 years of university-level foreign language study. Additional exam requirements/recommendations for international students: Required—TOEFL (minimum score 550 paper-based). Electronic applications accepted.

The University of Texas at El Paso, Graduate School, College of Liberal Arts, Department of Languages and Linguistics, El Paso, TX 79968-0001. Offers linguistics (MA); Spanish (MA); teaching English to speakers of other languages (Certificate). *Program availability:* Part-time, evening/weekend. *Degree requirements:* For master's, thesis optional. *Entrance requirements:* For master's, GRE General Test, departmental exam, minimum GPA of 3.0, letters of recommendation. Additional exam requirements/recommendations for international students: Required—TOEFL; Recommended—IELTS. Electronic applications accepted.

The University of Texas at San Antonio, College of Education and Human Development, Department of Bicultural and Bilingual Studies, San Antonio, TX 78249-0617. Offers bicultural and bilingual studies (MA), including bicultural and bilingual education, bicultural studies; culture, literacy, and language (PhD); teaching English as a second language (MA). *Program availability:* Part-time, evening/weekend. *Degree requirements:* For master's, one foreign language, comprehensive exam, thesis optional; for doctorate, one foreign language, comprehensive exam, thesis/dissertation. *Entrance requirements:* For master's, bachelor's degree with 18 credit hours in field of study or in another appropriate field of study; for doctorate, GRE General Test, resume or curriculum vitae, 3 letters of recommendation, statement of purpose, master's degree. Additional exam requirements/recommendations for international students: Required—TOEFL (minimum score 550 paper-based; 79 iBT), IELTS (minimum score 6.5). Electronic applications accepted. *Expenses:* Contact institution. *Faculty research:* Bilingual and ESL teacher preparation; transnational communities; applied linguistics; cultural studies; bilingualism, biliteracy and second language acquisition.

The University of Texas at San Antonio, College of Education and Human Development, Department of Educational Psychology, San Antonio, TX 78207. Offers applied behavior analysis (Certificate); educational psychology (MA), including applied educational psychology, behavior assessment and intervention, general educational psychology, program evaluation; language acquisition and bilingual psychoeducational assessment (Certificate); school psychology (MA). *Program availability:* Part-time. *Degree requirements:* For master's, comprehensive exam, thesis (for some programs). *Entrance requirements:* For master's, GRE, bachelor's degree with 18 credit hours in field of study or in another appropriate field of study, two letters of recommendation, statement of purpose; for Certificate, 18 hours in psychology, sociology, education, or anything related (for applied behavioral analysis); minimum GPA of 2.7 in last 30 hours (for language acquisition and bilingual psychoeducational assessment). Additional exam requirements/recommendations for international students: Required—TOEFL (minimum score 550 paper-based; 79 iBT), IELTS (minimum score 6.5). Electronic applications accepted. *Faculty research:* Teacher consultation and culturally responsive school psychology practices, youth mentoring, cross-age peer mentoring, adolescent connectedness, pair counseling.

The University of Texas of the Permian Basin, Office of Graduate Studies, School of Education, Program in Bilingual/English as a Second Language Education, Odessa, TX 79762-0001. Offers MA. *Degree requirements:* For master's, comprehensive exam (for some programs), thesis (for some programs). *Entrance requirements:* For master's, GRE General Test. Additional exam requirements/recommendations for international students: Required—TOEFL (minimum score 550 paper-based).

The University of Texas Rio Grande Valley, College of Education and P-16 Integration, Department of Bilingual and Literacy Studies, Edinburg, TX 78539. Offers bilingual education (M Ed), including dual language, ESL; reading and literacy (M Ed), including adolescent literacy, biliteracy, digital literacy, reading specialist. *Program availability:* Part-time, evening/weekend. *Degree requirements:* For master's, comprehensive exam (for some programs), thesis optional. *Entrance requirements:* For master's, minimum GPA of 3.0 in undergraduate coursework. Additional exam requirements/recommendations for international students: Required—TOEFL (minimum score 550 paper-based; 79 iBT), IELTS (minimum score 6.5). Electronic applications accepted. *Expenses: Tuition, area resident:* Full-time $6888. Tuition, state resident: full-time $6888. Tuition, nonresident: full-time $14,484. *International tuition:* $14,484 full-time. *Required fees:* $1468. *Faculty research:* Bilingual education, reading instruction, multicultural education, English as a second language.

The University of Texas Rio Grande Valley, College of Liberal Arts, Department of Writing and Language Studies, Edinburg, TX 78539. Offers English as a second language (MA). *Program availability:* Part-time. *Degree requirements:* For master's, comprehensive exam, thesis or alternative. *Entrance requirements:* For master's, GRE General Test, minimum GPA of 3.0. Additional exam requirements/recommendations for international students: Required—TOEFL or IELTS. *Expenses: Tuition, area resident:* Full-time $6888. Tuition, state resident: full-time $6888. Tuition, nonresident: full-time $14,484. *International tuition:* $14,484 full-time. *Required fees:* $1468. *Faculty research:* Latin American literature, women's literature, Caribbean literature, Latina/o studies, sociolinguistics, applied linguistics, creative writing.

University of the Southwest, Graduate Programs, Hobbs, NM 88240-9129. Offers business administration (MBA); curriculum and instruction (MSE); curriculum and instruction: bilingual (MSE); curriculum and instruction: TESOL (MSE); early childhood education (MSE); educational administration (MSE); mental health counseling (MSE); school counseling (MSE); special education (MSE); sports management (MBA). *Program availability:* Part-time, evening/weekend, online learning. *Degree requirements:* For master's, comprehensive exam, thesis (for some programs). *Entrance requirements:* Additional exam requirements/recommendations for international students: Recommended—TOEFL. Electronic applications accepted.

The University of Toledo, College of Graduate Studies, College of Languages, Literature and Social Sciences, Department of English Language and Literature, Toledo, OH 43606-3390. Offers English as a second language (MA); teaching of writing (Certificate). *Program availability:* Part-time. *Degree requirements:* For master's, thesis. *Entrance requirements:* For master's, GRE if GPA is less than 3.0, minimum cumulative point-hour ratio of 2.7 for all previous academic work, three letters of recommendation, transcripts from all prior institutions attended, critical essay; for Certificate, statement of purpose, transcripts from all prior institutions attended, 2 letters of recommendation. Additional exam requirements/recommendations for international students: Required—TOEFL (minimum score 550 paper-based; 80 iBT). Electronic applications accepted. *Faculty research:* Literary criticism, linguistics, creative writing, folklore and cultural studies.

The University of Toledo, College of Graduate Studies, Judith Herb College of Education, Department of Curriculum and Instruction, Toledo, OH 43606-3390. Offers art education (ME); career and technical education (ME, Ed S); curriculum and instruction (ME, PhD, Ed S); early childhood education (Ed S); education and anthropology (MAE); education and biology (MES); education and chemistry (MES); education and classics (MAE); education and economics (MAE); education and English (MAE); education and French (MAE); education and geology (MES); education and German (MAE); education and history (MAE); education and mathematics (MAE, MES); education and physics (MES); education and political science (MAE); education and sociology (MAE); education and Spanish (MAE); educational media (PhD); educational technology (ME); educational technology: virtual educator (Certificate); elementary education (PhD); English as a second language (MAE); gifted and talented education (PhD); middle childhood education (ME); secondary education (ME, PhD); special education (PhD). *Accreditation:* NCATE. *Program availability:* Part-time, evening/weekend. *Degree requirements:* For master's, comprehensive exam, thesis or alternative; for doctorate, comprehensive exam, thesis/dissertation; for other advanced degree, thesis optional. *Entrance requirements:* For master's, doctorate, and other advanced degree, minimum cumulative GPA of 2.7 for all previous academic work, letters of recommendation. Additional exam requirements/recommendations for international students: Required—TOEFL (minimum score 550 paper-based; 80 iBT). Electronic applications accepted.

University of Washington, Graduate School, College of Arts and Sciences, Department of English, Seattle, WA 98195. Offers creative writing (MFA); English as a second language (MAT); English literature and language (MA, MAT, PhD). *Program availability:* Part-time. Terminal master's awarded for partial completion of doctoral program. *Degree requirements:* For master's, one foreign language, thesis (for some programs); for doctorate, one foreign language, thesis/dissertation. *Entrance requirements:* For master's, GRE General Test, GRE Subject Test (MA and MAT in English), minimum GPA of 3.0; for doctorate, GRE General Test, GRE Subject Test. Additional exam requirements/recommendations for international students: Required—TOEFL. Electronic applications accepted. *Faculty research:* English and American literature, critical theory, creative writing, language theory.

University of Wisconsin–Madison, Graduate School, School of Education, Department of Curriculum and Instruction, Madison, WI 53706-1380. Offers curriculum and instruction (MS, PhD); English as a second language (MS). *Accreditation:* NASM (one or more programs are accredited). *Degree requirements:* For doctorate, thesis/dissertation.

University of Wisconsin–Milwaukee, Graduate School, College of Letters and Science, Department of Linguistics, Milwaukee, WI 53201-0413. Offers linguistics (MA, PhD), including teaching English to speakers of other languages (MA); teaching English to speakers of other languages, adult- and university-level (Graduate Certificate). *Students:* 21 full-time (10 women), 12 part-time (8 women); includes 2 minority (both Two or more races, non-Hispanic/Latino), 18 international. Average age 34. 56 applicants, 25% accepted, 7 enrolled. In 2018, 1 master's, 4 doctorates, 1 other advanced degree awarded. Electronic applications accepted. *Unit head:* Hamid Ouali, Department Chair, 414-229-1113, E-mail: ouali@uwm.edu. *Application contact:* General Information Contact, 414-229-4982, Fax: 414-229-6967, E-mail: gradschool@uwm.edu. Website: http://www4.uwm.edu/letsci/linguistics/

University of Wisconsin–River Falls, Outreach and Graduate Studies, College of Arts and Science, Program in Teaching English to Speakers of Other Languages, River Falls, WI 54022. Offers MA.

Upper Iowa University, Master of Education Program, Fayette, IA 52142-1857. Offers early childhood (M Ed); English as a second language (M Ed); higher education (M Ed); instructional strategist (M Ed); reading (M Ed); teacher leadership (M Ed).

Utah Valley University, Program in Education, Orem, UT 84058-5999. Offers educational technology (M Ed); elementary mathematics (M Ed); elementary STEM (M Ed); English as a second language (M Ed); reading (M Ed); teachers as leaders (M Ed). *Accreditation:* TEAC. *Program availability:* Part-time. *Degree requirements:* For master's, project. *Entrance requirements:* For master's, GRE, 3 letters of recommendation, interview, essay. Additional exam requirements/recommendations for international students: Required—TOEFL (minimum score 83 iBT). Electronic applications accepted. *Expenses:* Contact institution.

Valley City State University, Online Graduate Programs, Valley City, ND 58072. Offers elementary education (M Ed); English education (M Ed); library and information technologies (M Ed); teaching (MAT); teaching and technology (M Ed); teaching English language learners (M Ed); technology education (M Ed). *Accreditation:* NCATE. *Program availability:* Part-time, evening/weekend, online only, 100% online. *Faculty:* 20 full-time (11 women), 13 part-time/adjunct (8 women). *Students:* 5 full-time (2 women), 133 part-time (100 women); includes 8 minority (1 Black or African American, non-Hispanic/Latino; 3 American Indian or Alaska Native, non-Hispanic/Latino; 2 Asian, non-Hispanic/Latino; 2 Hispanic/Latino). Average age 36. 23 applicants, 74% accepted, 12 enrolled. In 2018, 47 master's awarded. *Degree requirements:* For master's, action research report, comprehensive portfolio. *Entrance requirements:* For master's, GRE, MAT, PRAXIS II or National Teaching Board for Professional Standards (if GPA is less than 3.0). Additional exam requirements/recommendations for international students: Required—TOEFL (minimum score 525 paper-based; 71 iBT); Recommended—IELTS (minimum score 5.5). *Application deadline:* For fall admission, 7/26 for domestic and international students; for spring admission, 12/13 for domestic and international students; for summer admission, 5/18 for domestic and international students. Applications are processed on a rolling basis. Application fee: $35. Electronic applications accepted. *Expenses:* $396.39 per credit for all students regardless of residency. *Financial support:* In 2018–19, 16 students received support. Scholarships/grants, tuition waivers (full and partial), and unspecified assistantships available. Financial award applicants required to submit FAFSA. *Faculty research:* Universal accessibility, instructional design and technology, gender communication, STEM education in K-12, English language learners. *Unit head:* Dr. Sheri Okland, Dean, 701-845-7184, E-mail: sheri.l.okland@vcsu.edu. *Application contact:* Misty Lindgren, Graduate Studies, 701-845-7303, Fax: 701-845-7190, E-mail: misty.lindgren@vcsu.edu. Website: http://www.vcsu.edu/graduate

Valparaiso University, Graduate School and Continuing Education, TESOL Program, Valparaiso, IN 46383. Offers MA, Certificate. *Program availability:* Part-time, evening/weekend. *Entrance requirements:* For master's, minimum GPA of 3.0. Additional exam requirements/recommendations for international students: Required—TOEFL (minimum score 550 paper-based; 80 iBT), IELTS (minimum score 6). Electronic applications accepted.

Virginia International University, School of Education, Fairfax, VA 22030. Offers applied linguistics (MS); education (M Ed); teaching English to speakers of other languages (MA). *Program availability:* Part-time, online learning. *Entrance requirements:* For master's, bachelor's degree. Additional exam requirements/recommendations for international students: Required—TOEFL (minimum score 550 paper-based; 80 iBT), IELTS (minimum score 6). Electronic applications accepted.

Walden University, Graduate Programs, Richard W. Riley College of Education and Leadership, Minneapolis, MN 55401. Offers adult education (Post-Master's Certificate); adult learning (Graduate Certificate); college teaching and learning (Graduate Certificate); community college leadership (Ed D); curriculum, instruction and assessment (Ed D, Ed S, Graduate Certificate); developmental education (Graduate Certificate); early childhood administration, management, and leadership (Graduate Certificate); early childhood education (Ed D, Ed S); early childhood public policy and advocacy (Graduate Certificate); early childhood studies (MS), including administration, management and leadership, early childhood public policy and advocacy, teaching adults in the early childhood field, teaching and diversity in early childhood education; education (MS, PhD), including adolescent literacy and learning (MS), curriculum, instruction, and assessment (grades K-12) (MS), curriculum, instruction, assessment, and evaluation (PhD), early childhood leadership and advocacy (PhD), early childhood special education (PhD), educational leadership (MS), educational leadership and administration (principal preparation) (MS), educational technology and design (PhD), elementary reading and literacy (PreK-6) (MS), elementary reading and mathematics (grades K-6) (MS), global and comparative education (PhD), higher education leadership management and policy (PhD), integrating technology in the classroom (grades K-12) (MS), learning, instruction and innovation (PhD), mathematics (grades 5-8) (MS), mathematics (grades K-6) (MS), mathematics and science (grades K-8) (MS), organizational research, assessment, and evaluation (PhD), reading and literacy with a reading K-12 endorsement (MS), reading literacy assessment and evaluation (PhD), science (grades K-8) (MS), special education (non-licensure) (grades K-12) (MS), teacher leadership (grades K-12) (MS), teaching English language learners (grades K-12) (MS); educational administration and leadership (Ed D); educational leadership and administration (principal preparation) (Ed S); educational technology (Ed D, Ed S, Post Master's Certificate); elementary reading and literacy (Graduate Certificate); engaging culturally diverse learners (Graduate Certificate); enrollment management and institutional marketing (Graduate Certificate); higher education (MS), including adult learning, college teaching and learning, enrollment management and institutional marketing, global higher education, leadership for student success, online and distance learning; higher education and adult learning (Ed D); higher education leadership and management (Ed D); higher education leadership for student success (Graduate Certificate); instructional design and technology (MS, Postbaccalaureate Certificate), including general program (MS), online learning (MS), training and performance improvement (MS); integrating technology in the classroom (Graduate Certificate); mathematics 5-8 (Graduate Certificate); mathematics K-6 (Graduate Certificate); online teaching for adult educators (Graduate Certificate); reading, literacy, and assessment (Ed D, Ed S); science K-8 (Graduate Certificate); special education (Ed D, Ed S, Graduate Certificate); special education (K-age 21) (MAT); teacher leadership (Graduate Certificate); teaching adults English as a second language (Graduate Certificate); teaching adults in the early childhood field (Graduate Certificate); teaching and diversity in early childhood education (Graduate Certificate); teaching English language learners (grades K-12) (Graduate Certificate); teaching K-12 students online (Graduate Certificate). *Accreditation:* NCATE. *Program availability:* Part-time, evening/weekend, online only, 100% online. *Degree requirements:* For doctorate, thesis/dissertation (for some programs), residency; for other advanced degree, residency (for some programs). *Entrance requirements:* For master's, bachelor's degree or higher; minimum GPA of 2.5; official transcripts; goal statement (for some programs); access to computer and Internet; for doctorate, master's degree or higher; three years of related professional or academic experience (preferred); minimum GPA of 3.0; goal statement and current resume (for select programs); official transcripts; access to computer and Internet; for other advanced degree, relevant work experience; access to computer and Internet. Additional exam requirements/recommendations for international students: Required—TOEFL (minimum score 550 paper-based, 79 iBT), IELTS (minimum score 6.5), Michigan English Language Assessment Battery (minimum score 82), or PTE (minimum score 53). Electronic applications accepted.

Washington State University, College of Education, Department of Teaching and Learning, Pullman, WA 99164-2132. Offers cultural studies and social thought in education (PhD); curriculum and instruction (Ed M, MA); English language learners (Ed M, MA); language, literacy and technology (PhD); literacy education (Ed M, MA); mathematics education (PhD); special education (Ed M, MA, PhD); teacher leadership (Ed D); teaching (MIT), including elementary education, secondary education. Programs offered at the Pullman, Spokane, Tri-cities, Vancouver and Global (online) campuses. *Program availability:* Part-time, online learning. *Degree requirements:* For master's, comprehensive exam, thesis, oral or written exam; for doctorate, comprehensive exam, thesis/dissertation, oral and written exam. *Entrance requirements:* For master's, GRE General Test, minimum GPA of 3.0, 3 letters of recommendation, letter of intent, transcripts, resume/curriculum vitae; for doctorate, GRE General Test, minimum GPA of 3.0, 3 letters of recommendation, letter of intent, transcripts, writing sample, resume/curriculum vitae. Additional exam requirements/recommendations for international students: Required—TOEFL (minimum score 550 paper-based; 80 iBT). Electronic applications accepted. *Faculty research:* Intersection of gender, youth cultures and schooling; examination of ideology of power in children's literature; early childhood special education; analyzing pre-service and in-service teacher development; second language acquisition.

Wayland Baptist University, Graduate Programs, Program in Education, Plainview, TX 79072-6998. Offers education administration (M Ed); education diagnostics (M Ed); education literacy (M Ed); elementary certification (M Ed); English (M Ed); English as a second language (M Ed); higher education administration (M Ed); human resources (M Ed); instructional leadership (M Ed); instructional technology (M Ed); leadership training and development (M Ed); science education (M Ed); secondary certification (M Ed); social studies (M Ed); special education (M Ed); sports administration and management (M Ed). *Program availability:* Part-time, evening/weekend, 100% online. *Degree requirements:* For master's, comprehensive exam, capstone course. *Entrance requirements:* For master's, GRE, GMAT or MAT. Additional exam requirements/recommendations for international students: Required—TOEFL (minimum score 500 paper-based; 61 iBT). Electronic applications accepted.

Wayne State College, School of Education and Counseling, Department of Educational Foundations and Leadership, Program in Curriculum and Instruction, Wayne, NE 68787. Offers alternative education (MSE); business and information technology education (MSE); communication arts education (MSE); early childhood education (MSE); elementary education (MSE); English as a second language (MSE); English education (MSE); family and consumer sciences education (MSE); industrial technology and vocational education (MSE); learning communities (MSE); mathematics education (MSE); music education (MSE); science education (MSE); social science education (MSE). *Accreditation:* NCATE. *Program availability:* Part-time, evening/weekend. *Degree requirements:* For master's, comprehensive exam, thesis optional. *Entrance requirements:* For master's, GRE General Test. Additional exam requirements/recommendations for international students: Required—TOEFL (minimum score 550 paper-based).

Wayne State University, College of Education, Division of Teacher Education, Detroit, MI 48202. Offers art education (M Ed); bilingual/bicultural education (Certificate); curriculum and instruction (Ed D, PhD, Ed S), including English as a second language (MAT, Ed D, Ed S), K-12 curriculum (PhD); elementary education (MAT), including bilingual/bicultural education (M Ed, MAT), early childhood education (M Ed, MAT), English as a second language (MAT, Ed D, Ed S), foreign language education, science education (M Ed, MAT), special education (M Ed, MAT); elementary mathematics specialist (Certificate); English as a second language (Certificate); reading (M Ed, Ed S); reading, language and literature (Ed D); secondary education (MAT), including bilingual/bicultural education (M Ed, MAT), early childhood education (M Ed, MAT), English as a second language (MAT, Ed D, Ed S), English education, foreign language education, mathematics education (M Ed, MAT), science education (M Ed, MAT), social studies education (M Ed, MAT); special education (MAT), including career and technical education; teaching and learning (M Ed), including bilingual/bicultural education (M Ed, MAT), early childhood education (M Ed, MAT), elementary education, foreign language, mathematics education (M Ed, MAT), science education (M Ed, MAT), social studies education (M Ed, MAT), special education (M Ed, MAT). *Program availability:* Part-time, evening/weekend. *Faculty:* 20. *Students:* 121 full-time (94 women), 251 part-time (209 women); includes 116 minority (83 Black or African American, non-Hispanic/Latino; 3 American Indian or Alaska Native, non-Hispanic/Latino; 3 Asian, non-Hispanic/Latino; 14 Hispanic/Latino; 13 Two or more races, non-Hispanic/Latino), 11 international. Average age 37. 171 applicants, 23% accepted, 32 enrolled. In 2018, 112 master's, 8 doctorates, 11 other advanced degrees awarded. *Degree requirements:* For master's, thesis (for some programs), essay or project (for some M Ed programs), professional field experience (for MAT programs); for doctorate, comprehensive exam, thesis/dissertation. *Entrance requirements:* For master's, undergraduate degree, verification of participation in group work with children, Michigan State Police criminal background check, negative tb test, personal statement (for MAT

programs); for all other master's programs: undergraduate degree, personal statement; for doctorate, minimum undergraduate GPA of 3.0, graduate 3.5; interview; curriculum vitae; references; writing sample; letter of application; master's degree (for most programs); for other advanced degree, education specialist certificate: undergraduate with GPA of 2.5 or better and master's degree with GPA of 2.75 or better; personal statement. Additional exam requirements/recommendations for international students: Required—TOEFL (minimum score 550 paper-based; 79 iBT); Recommended—IELTS (minimum score 6.5), TWE (minimum score 5.5), TSE (minimum score 58). *Application deadline:* Applications are processed on a rolling basis. Application fee: $50. Electronic applications accepted. *Financial support:* In 2018–19, 85 students received support, including 3 fellowships (averaging $14,275 per year); research assistantships with tuition reimbursements available, Federal Work-Study, scholarships/grants, and unspecified assistantships also available. Support available to part-time students. Financial award applicants required to submit FAFSA. *Faculty research:* Improving students' skill achievement in mathematics, improving elementary children's understanding of informational text, teachers' use of their pedagogical and mathematical knowledge in the interactive work of teaching, the intersection of identity construction in teaching and learning, identifying effective methods of literacy instruction and assessments for bilingual students in elementary language arts classrooms. *Unit head:* Dr. Roland Coloma, Assistant Dean for Teacher Education, 313-577-0902, E-mail: rscoloma@wayne.edu. *Application contact:* Dr. Mary L. Waker, Graduate Admissions Officer, 313-577-1601, Fax: 313-577-7904, E-mail: m.waker@wayne.edu.
Website: http://coe.wayne.edu/ted/index.php

Webster University, School of Education, Department of Multidisciplinary Studies, St. Louis, MO 63119-3194. Offers applied educational psychology (MA, Ed S); communication arts (MA); early childhood education (MA, MAT); education and innovation (MA); educational technology (MET); elementary education (MAT); mathematics for educators (MA); middle school education (MAT); multidisciplinary studies (MAT); multimodal literacy for global impact (MA); reading (MA); secondary school education (MAT); special education (MA, MAT); teaching English as a second language (MA); transformative learning in the global community (Ed S). *Program availability:* Part-time. *Entrance requirements:* For master's, minimum GPA of 2.5. Additional exam requirements/recommendations for international students: Required—TOEFL. *Expenses: Tuition:* Full-time $22,500; part-time $750 per credit hour. Tuition and fees vary according to degree level, campus/location and program.

West Chester University of Pennsylvania, College of Arts and Humanities, Program in Teaching English as a Second Language, West Chester, PA 19383. Offers MA, Certificate. *Program availability:* Part-time, evening/weekend, 100% online. *Degree requirements:* For master's, comprehensive exam, capstone review and teaching philosophy. *Entrance requirements:* For master's, minimum GPA of 2.8, two letters of recommendation, prior introduction to linguistics coursework, goals statement, experience in learning a second language (recommended); for Certificate, prior PA teaching certification. Additional exam requirements/recommendations for international students: Required—TOEFL or IELTS. Electronic applications accepted. *Faculty research:* Second language acquisition, language teaching methods, discourse analysis, computer-assisted language learning, language teacher development.

Westcliff University, College of Education, Irvine, CA 92606. Offers teaching English to speakers of other languages (MA).

Western Carolina University, Graduate School, College of Arts and Sciences, Department of English, Cullowhee, NC 28723. Offers literature (MA); professional writing (MA); rhetoric and composition (MA); teaching English to speakers of other languages (Certificate); technical and professional writing (Certificate). *Program availability:* Part-time, evening/weekend. *Degree requirements:* For master's, one foreign language, comprehensive exam, thesis (for some programs). *Entrance requirements:* For master's, appropriate undergraduate degree, writing sample, 3 letters of recommendation. Additional exam requirements/recommendations for international students: Required—TOEFL (minimum score 550 paper-based, 79 iBT) or IELTS (6.5). Electronic applications accepted. *Expenses:* Contact institution. *Faculty research:* Teaching English to speakers of other languages (TESOL), language assessment, applied linguistics, poetry, folk and fairy tales, post World War II British literature, Appalachian and Southern literature.

Western Illinois University, School of Graduate Studies, College of Education and Human Services, Department of Educational Studies, Educational Studies, Macomb, IL 61455-1390. Offers educational and interdisciplinary studies (MS Ed); teaching English to speakers of other languages (Certificate). *Accreditation:* NCATE. *Program availability:* Part-time. *Students:* 5 full-time (all women), 26 part-time (24 women); includes 3 minority (1 Asian, non-Hispanic/Latino; 1 Hispanic/Latino; 1 Two or more races, non-Hispanic/Latino), 2 international. Average age 35. 9 applicants, 89% accepted, 5 enrolled. In 2018, 7 master's, 1 Certificate awarded. *Entrance requirements:* For master's, minimum GPA of 2.75, interview. Additional exam requirements/recommendations for international students: Required—TOEFL (minimum score 550 paper-based; 80 iBT). *Application deadline:* Applications are processed on a rolling basis. Application fee: $30. Electronic applications accepted. *Financial support:* In 2018–19, 1 research assistantship with full tuition reimbursement (averaging $7,544 per year) was awarded; unspecified assistantships also available. Financial award applicants required to submit FAFSA. *Unit head:* Dr. Eric Sheffield, Chairperson, 309-298-1183. *Application contact:* Dr. Mark Mossman, Associate Provost and Director of Graduate Studies, 309-298-1806, Fax: 309-298-2345, E-mail: grad-office@wiu.edu.
Website: http://www.wiu.edu/coehs/es/programs/eis/eis.php

Western Kentucky University, Graduate School, Potter College of Arts and Letters, Department of English, Bowling Green, KY 42101. Offers education (MA); English (MA Ed); literature (MA), including American literature, British literature, literary theory, women writers, world literature; teaching English as a second language (MA); writing (MA). *Program availability:* Part-time, evening/weekend. *Degree requirements:* For master's, comprehensive exam, thesis optional, final exam. *Entrance requirements:* For master's, GRE General Test, minimum GPA of 2.75. Additional exam requirements/recommendations for international students: Required—TOEFL (minimum score 555 paper-based; 79 iBT). *Faculty research:* Improving writing, linking teacher knowledge and performance, Victorian women writers, Kentucky women writers, Kentucky poets.

Western New Mexico University, Graduate Division, School of Education, Silver City, NM 88062-0680. Offers bilingual education (MAT); educational leadership (MA); elementary education (MAT); reading (MAT); secondary education (MAT); special education (MAT); TESOL (teaching English to speakers of other languages) (MAT). *Accreditation:* NCATE. *Program availability:* Part-time, online learning. *Degree requirements:* For master's, comprehensive exam. *Entrance requirements:* For master's, minimum GPA of 3.0 in last 64 hours of undergraduate study. Additional exam requirements/recommendations for international students: Required—TOEFL (minimum score 550 paper-based; 79 iBT). Electronic applications accepted. *Faculty research:* International education, electronic reading assessment, developing STEM teachers.

Wilkes University, College of Graduate and Professional Studies, School of Education, Wilkes-Barre, PA 18766-0002. Offers educational development and strategies (MS Ed); educational leadership (MS Ed, Ed D); effective teaching (MS Ed); instructional media (MS Ed); instructional technology (MS Ed); international school leadership (MS Ed); international teaching and learning (MS Ed); literacy (MS Ed); middle level education (MS Ed); online teaching (MS Ed); school business leadership (MS Ed); special education (MS Ed); teaching English to speakers of other languages (MS Ed). *Program availability:* Part-time, evening/weekend, 100% online, blended/hybrid learning. *Students:* 87 full-time (67 women), 1,418 part-time (1,078 women); includes 87 minority (13 Black or African American, non-Hispanic/Latino; 1 American Indian or Alaska Native, non-Hispanic/Latino; 11 Asian, non-Hispanic/Latino; 40 Hispanic/Latino; 22 Two or more races, non-Hispanic/Latino). Average age 35. In 2018, 611 master's, 9 doctorates awarded. *Entrance requirements:* Additional exam requirements/recommendations for international students: Required—TOEFL (minimum score 550 paper-based; 79 iBT). *Application deadline:* Applications are processed on a rolling basis. Application fee: $45 ($65 for international students). Electronic applications accepted. *Expenses:* Contact institution. *Financial support:* Unspecified assistantships available. Financial award application deadline: 3/1; financial award applicants required to submit FAFSA. *Unit head:* Dr. Rhonda Rabbitt, Dean, 570-408-4680, Fax: 570-408-7872, E-mail: rhonda.rabbitt@wilkes.edu. *Application contact:* Stephanie Wasmanski, Associate Director of Graduate Admissions, 570-408-5535, Fax: 570-408-7846, E-mail: stephanie.wasmanski@wilkes.edu.
Website: http://www.wilkes.edu/academics/graduate-programs/masters-programs/graduate-education/index.aspx

William Paterson University of New Jersey, College of Humanities and Social Sciences, Wayne, NJ 07470-8420. Offers applied sociology (MA); assessment and evaluation research (Certificate); bilingual education (Certificate); clinical and counseling psychology (MA); clinical psychology (Psy D); creative and professional writing (MFA); English (MA); history (MA); public policy and international affairs (MA); teaching English as a second language (Certificate). *Program availability:* Part-time. *Faculty:* 41 full-time (25 women), 7 part-time/adjunct (5 women). *Students:* 69 full-time (49 women), 65 part-time (42 women); includes 55 minority (6 Black or African American, non-Hispanic/Latino; 2 Asian, non-Hispanic/Latino; 41 Hispanic/Latino; 6 Two or more races, non-Hispanic/Latino), 3 international. Average age 32. 152 applicants, 47% accepted, 44 enrolled. In 2018, 46 master's awarded. *Degree requirements:* For master's, Programs Differ see: https://academiccatalog.wpunj.edu/content.php?catoid=1&navoid=68. *Entrance requirements:* For master's, program details: https://www.wpunj.edu/admissions/graduate/admission-deadlines-and-requirements/. Additional exam requirements/recommendations for international students: Required—TOEFL (minimum score 550 paper-based; 79 iBT), IELTS (minimum score 6). *Application deadline:* For fall admission, 6/1 for domestic students, 3/1 for international students; for spring admission, 11/1 for domestic students, 10/1 for international students. Applications are processed on a rolling basis. Application fee: $50. Electronic applications accepted. *Expenses: Tuition, area resident:* Full-time $14,714; part-time $727 per credit. Tuition, state resident: full-time $14,714; part-time $727 per credit. Tuition, nonresident: full-time $22,952; part-time $727 per credit. *International tuition:* $22,952 full-time. *Required fees:* $4 per semester. Tuition and fees vary according to course load, degree level and program. *Financial support:* In 2018–19, 16 students received support. Career-related internships or fieldwork, Federal Work-Study, scholarships/grants, tuition waivers, and unspecified assistantships available. Support available to part-time students. Financial award application deadline: 3/15; financial award applicants required to submit FAFSA. *Faculty research:* Relationship violence, work-family balance, social development of Japan, theories justifying war, reactions to trauma. *Total annual research expenditures:* $119,089. *Unit head:* Dr. Kara Rabbitt, Dean, 973-720-2180, Fax: 973-720-2955, E-mail: rabbittk@wpunj.edu. *Application contact:* Tinu Adeniran, Associate Director, Graduate Admissions, 973-720-2764, Fax: 973-720-2035, E-mail: adenirant@wpunj.edu.
Website: http://www.wpunj.edu/cohss

Wilmington University, College of Education, New Castle, DE 19720-6491. Offers applied technology in education (M Ed); career and technical education (M Ed); educational leadership (Ed D); elementary and secondary school counseling (M Ed); elementary studies (M Ed); ESOL literacy (M Ed); higher education leadership (Ed D); instruction: gifted and talented (M Ed); instruction: teacher of reading (M Ed); instruction: teaching and learning (M Ed); organizational leadership (Ed D); school leadership (M Ed); secondary education (MAT); special education (M Ed). *Accreditation:* NCATE. *Program availability:* Part-time, evening/weekend. *Entrance requirements:* For master's, 2 letters of recommendation, interview. Additional exam requirements/recommendations for international students: Required—TOEFL (minimum score 500 paper-based). Electronic applications accepted.

Winona State University, College of Liberal Arts, Department of English, Winona, MN 55987. Offers English (MS); literature and language (MA); TESOL (MA). *Program availability:* Part-time. *Degree requirements:* For master's, thesis or alternative.

Worcester State University, Graduate School, Department of Education, Worcester, MA 01602-2597. Offers adult English as a esl (Postbaccalaureate Certificate); curriculum and instruction (Ed S); early childhood education (M Ed); education (M Ed); elementary education (M Ed); English as a second language (M Ed, Postbaccalaureate Certificate); middle school education (M Ed); middle/secondary school education (Postbaccalaureate Certificate); moderate disabilities (M Ed, Postbaccalaureate Certificate); reading (M Ed, Postbaccalaureate Certificate); reading specialist (Postbaccalaureate Certificate); school leadership and education administration (M Ed); school psychology (M Ed, Ed S); secondary education (M Ed, Ed S, Postbaccalaureate Certificate). *Faculty:* 10 full-time (9 women), 23 part-time/adjunct (11 women). *Students:* 38 full-time (33 women), 281 part-time (212 women); includes 30 minority (4 Black or African American, non-Hispanic/Latino; 3 American Indian or Alaska Native, non-Hispanic/Latino; 2 Asian, non-Hispanic/Latino; 16 Hispanic/Latino; 5 Two or more races, non-Hispanic/Latino), 2 international. Average age 41. 102 applicants, 98% accepted, 88 enrolled. In 2018, 132 master's, 52 Ed Ss awarded. *Degree requirements:* For master's, comprehensive exam (for some programs), thesis (for some programs), For a detail list of degree completion requirements please see the graduate catalog at catalog.worcester.edu. *Entrance requirements:* For master's, GRE General Test, MAT or GMAT, teaching certificate. For a detail list of entrance requirements please see the graduate catalog at catalog.worcester.edu. Additional exam requirements/recommendations for international students: Required—TOEFL (minimum score 550 paper-based; 79 iBT), PTE. *Application deadline:* For fall admission, 3/1 for domestic and international students; for spring admission, 11/1 for domestic and international students; for summer admission, 3/1 for domestic and international students. Applications are processed on a rolling basis. Application fee: $50. Electronic applications accepted. *Expenses: Tuition, area resident:* Full-time $3042; part-time $169 per credit hour. Tuition, state resident: full-time $3042; part-time $169 per credit hour. Tuition, nonresident: full-time $3042; part-time $169 per credit hour. *International tuition:* $3042 full-time. *Required fees:* $2754; $153 per credit hour. *Financial support:* Career-related internships or fieldwork, scholarships/grants, and unspecified assistantships available. Support available to part-time students. Financial award application deadline: 3/1; financial award applicants required to submit FAFSA. *Unit head:* Dr. Sara Young, Graduate Program Coordinator, 508-929-8246, Fax: 508-929-8164, E-mail: syoung3@worcester.edu. *Application contact:* Sara Grady, Associate Dean of Graduate and Continuing Education, 508-929-8130, Fax: 508-929-8100, E-mail: sara.grady@worcester.edu.

Multilingual and Multicultural Education

Alliant International University–San Francisco, Shirley M. Hufstedler School of Education, Teacher Education Programs, San Francisco, CA 94133. Offers auditory oral education (Certificate); CLAD (Certificate); education specialist: mild/moderate disabilities (Credential); preliminary multiple subject (Credential); preliminary single subject (Credential); professional clear multiple subject (Credential); professional clear single subject (Credential); special education (MA); teaching (MA); TESOL (Certificate). *Program availability:* Part-time, evening/weekend. *Degree requirements:* For master's, thesis. *Entrance requirements:* For degree, California Basic Educational Skills Test, minimum GPA of 2.5. Additional exam requirements/recommendations for international students: Required—TOEFL (minimum score 550 paper-based), TWE (minimum score 5). Electronic applications accepted. *Faculty research:* Curriculum development, first year teachers, cross-cultural issues in teaching, biliteracy.

American College of Education, Graduate Programs, Indianapolis, IN 46204. Offers curriculum and instruction (M Ed), including bilingual, ESL; educational leadership (M Ed); educational technology (M Ed).

Bank Street College of Education, Graduate School, Program in Bilingual Education, New York, NY 10025. Offers bilingual childhood special education (Ed M); bilingual early childhood general education (MS Ed); bilingual early childhood special and general education (MS Ed); bilingual early childhood special education (Ed M, MS Ed); bilingual elementary/childhood general education (MS Ed); bilingual elementary/childhood special and general education (MS Ed); bilingual elementary/childhood special education (MS Ed). *Degree requirements:* For master's, thesis. *Entrance requirements:* For master's, interview, fluency in Spanish and English, essays. Additional exam requirements/recommendations for international students: Required—TOEFL (minimum score 600 paper-based; 100 iBT), IELTS (minimum score 7). Electronic applications accepted. *Faculty research:* Dual language education, language immersion, bilingual education in the urban classroom, community and school partnerships.

Boise State University, College of Education, Department of Literacy, Language and Culture, Boise, ID 83725-0399. Offers bilingual education (M Ed); English as a new language (M Ed); literacy (MA). *Accreditation:* NCATE. *Program availability:* Part-time, evening/weekend. *Degree requirements:* For master's, thesis optional. *Entrance requirements:* For master's, minimum GPA of 3.0. Additional exam requirements/recommendations for international students: Required—TOEFL (minimum score 550 paper-based; 80 iBT), IELTS (minimum score 6). Electronic applications accepted.

Brooklyn College of the City University of New York, School of Education, Program in Childhood Education, Brooklyn, NY 11210-2889. Offers bilingual education (MS Ed); liberal arts (MS Ed); mathematics (MS Ed); science and environmental education (MS Ed). *Program availability:* Part-time, evening/weekend. *Entrance requirements:* For master's, LAST, interview, previous course work in education, writing sample, resume, 2 letters of recommendation. Additional exam requirements/recommendations for international students: Required—TOEFL (minimum score 500 paper-based; 61 iBT). Electronic applications accepted. *Faculty research:* Emotional intelligence, multiculturalism, arts immersion, the Holocaust.

Brown University, Graduate School, Department of Portuguese and Brazilian Studies, Providence, RI 02912. Offers Brazilian studies (AM); English as a second language and cross-cultural studies (AM); Portuguese and Brazilian studies (AM, PhD); Portuguese bilingual education and cross-cultural studies (AM). *Degree requirements:* For doctorate, thesis/dissertation.

Buffalo State College, State University of New York, The Graduate School, School of Education, Department of Exceptional Education, Program in Teaching Bilingual Exceptional Individuals, Buffalo, NY 14222-1095. Offers Graduate Certificate. *Accreditation:* NCATE. *Program availability:* Part-time, evening/weekend. *Entrance requirements:* Additional exam requirements/recommendations for international students: Required—TOEFL (minimum score 550 paper-based).

California State University, Fullerton, Graduate Studies, College of Education, Department of Elementary and Bilingual Education, Fullerton, CA 92831-3599. Offers bilingual/bicultural education (MS); educational technology (MS); elementary curriculum and instruction (MS). *Accreditation:* NCATE. *Program availability:* Part-time. *Degree requirements:* For master's, comprehensive exam, project or thesis. *Entrance requirements:* For master's, minimum GPA of 2.5, teaching certificate. *Faculty research:* Teacher training and tracking, model for improvement of teaching.

California State University, Northridge, Graduate Studies, Michael D. Eisner College of Education, Department of Elementary Education, Northridge, CA 91330. Offers curriculum and instruction (MA); language and literacy (MA); multilingual/multicultural education (MA). *Accreditation:* NCATE. *Program availability:* Part-time, evening/weekend. *Degree requirements:* For master's, comprehensive exam. *Entrance requirements:* For master's, GRE General Test or minimum GPA of 3.0. Additional exam requirements/recommendations for international students: Required—TOEFL.

California State University, Sacramento, College of Education, Graduate and Professional Studies in Education, Sacramento, CA 95819. Offers behavioral science and gender equity (MA); child development (MA); counseling (MS); curriculum and instruction (MA); education (Ed D), including K-12 and community college; education leadership and policy studies (MA), including higher education, PreK-12; education specialist (Ed S), including school psychology; educational technology (MA); language and literacy (MA); multicultural education (MA); school psychology (MA); special education (MA); workforce development advocacy (MA). *Program availability:* Part-time, evening/weekend, blended/hybrid learning. *Degree requirements:* For master's, thesis or project; writing proficiency exam; for doctorate, thesis/dissertation. *Entrance requirements:* For master's and doctorate, GRE. Additional exam requirements/recommendations for international students: Required—TOEFL (minimum score 550 paper-based; 80 iBT); Recommended—IELTS (minimum score 7), TSE. Electronic applications accepted. *Expenses:* Contact institution.

California State University, Stanislaus, College of Education, Kinesiology and Social Work, MA Program in Education, Turlock, CA 95382. Offers curriculum and instruction (MA), including education technology, elementary education, multilingual education, physical education, reading, secondary education, special education; school administration (MA); school counseling (MA). *Program availability:* Part-time, evening/weekend. *Degree requirements:* For master's, comprehensive exam (for some programs), thesis (for some programs). *Entrance requirements:* For master's, MAT, GRE, or CBEST (varies by concentration), 3 letters of recommendation, personal statement. Additional exam requirements/recommendations for international students: Required—TOEFL (minimum score 550 paper-based). Electronic applications accepted. *Faculty research:* Children's perspectives on historical events, method elementary schools dual language education, K-12 reading programs.

Chicago State University, School of Graduate and Professional Studies, College of Education, Department of Special Education, Early Childhood Education and Bilingual Education, Program in Bilingual Education, Chicago, IL 60628. Offers MS Ed. *Accreditation:* NCATE. *Degree requirements:* For master's, comprehensive exam, thesis optional. *Entrance requirements:* For master's, minimum GPA of 2.75.

City College of the City University of New York, Graduate School, School of Education, Department of Teaching, Learning and Culture, Program in Bilingual Education, New York, NY 10031-9198. Offers MS. *Accreditation:* NCATE. *Program availability:* Part-time. *Degree requirements:* For master's, thesis. *Entrance requirements:* For master's, Liberal Arts and Sciences Test (LAST), Content Specialty Test (CST). Additional exam requirements/recommendations for international students: Required—TOEFL.

The College at Brockport, State University of New York, School of Education, Health, and Human Services, Department of Education and Human Development, Brockport, NY 14420-2997. Offers adolescence education (MS Ed), including adolescence biology education, adolescence chemistry education, adolescence English, adolescence mathematics, adolescence physics, adolescence physics education, adolescence social studies education; bilingual education (MS Ed, AGC); childhood curriculum specialist (MS Ed); inclusive generalist education (MS Ed, AGC, Advanced Certificate), including biology (MS Ed, AGC), chemistry (MS Ed), English (MS Ed, Advanced Certificate), mathematics (MS Ed, Advanced Certificate), science (MS Ed, Advanced Certificate), social studies (MS Ed, Advanced Certificate); literacy education B-12 (MS Ed). *Accreditation:* NCATE. *Faculty:* 12 full-time (7 women), 10 part-time/adjunct (6 women). *Students:* 60 full-time (39 women), 227 part-time (157 women); includes 9 minority (1 Asian, non-Hispanic/Latino; 8 Hispanic/Latino). 135 applicants, 71% accepted, 59 enrolled. In 2018, 107 master's, 13 AGCs awarded. *Degree requirements:* For master's, thesis or alternative. *Entrance requirements:* For master's, minimum GPA of 3.0, letters of recommendation, interview (for some programs); statement of objectives, current resume. Additional exam requirements/recommendations for international students: Required—TOEFL (minimum score 550 paper-based; 79 iBT), IELTS (minimum score 6.5). *Application deadline:* For fall admission, 3/15 priority date for domestic and international students; for spring admission, 10/15 priority date for domestic and international students; for summer admission, 3/15 priority date for domestic and international students. Application fee: $80. Electronic applications accepted. *Expenses:* Tuition, state resident: part-time $471 per credit. Tuition, nonresident: part-time $963 per credit. *Financial support:* In 2018–19, 1 fellowship with full tuition reimbursement (averaging $7,500 per year), 1 teaching assistantship with full tuition reimbursement (averaging $6,000 per year) were awarded; Federal Work-Study, scholarships/grants, and unspecified assistantships also available. Support available to part-time students. Financial award application deadline: 3/15; financial award applicants required to submit FAFSA. *Faculty research:* Educational assessment, literacy education, inclusive education, teacher preparation, qualitative methodology. *Unit head:* Dr. Janka Szilagyi, Chairperson, 585-395-5945, Fax: 585-395-2172, E-mail: jszilagy@brockport.edu. *Application contact:* Buffie Edick, Graduate Program Director, 585-395-2326, Fax: 585-395-2172, E-mail: bedick@brockport.edu.
Website: https://www.brockport.edu/academics/education_human_development/department.html

College of Mount Saint Vincent, School of Professional and Graduate Studies, Department of Teacher Education, Riverdale, NY 10471-1093. Offers instructional technology and global perspectives (Certificate); middle level education (Certificate); multicultural studies (Certificate); teaching English to speakers of other languages (MS Ed); urban and multicultural education (MS Ed). *Accreditation:* TEAC. *Program availability:* Part-time. *Degree requirements:* For master's, comprehensive exam. *Entrance requirements:* For master's, interview, New York teaching certificate. Additional exam requirements/recommendations for international students: Required—TOEFL.

The College of New Rochelle, Graduate School, Division of Education, Program in Multilingual/Multicultural Education, New Rochelle, NY 10805-2308. Offers bilingual education (Certificate); multilingual/multicultural education (Certificate); teaching English to speakers of other languages (MS Ed, Certificate). *Program availability:* Part-time, evening/weekend. *Degree requirements:* For master's, student teaching or practicum. *Entrance requirements:* For master's, interview, minimum GPA of 3.0 in field, 2.7 overall.

College of Staten Island of the City University of New York, Graduate Programs, School of Education, Program in Bilingual Education, Staten Island, NY 10314-6600. Offers Advanced Certificate. *Program availability:* Part-time. *Students:* 1 applicant. *Entrance requirements:* For degree, New York State Initial Teaching Certification (certification in TESOL and World Languages not acceptable); BA with GPA 3.0 or higher; Proficiency in language other than English, Personal Statement, Two academic or professional letters of recommendation, interview. Additional exam requirements/recommendations for international students: Required—TOEFL (minimum score 550 paper-based; 79 iBT), IELTS (minimum score 6.5). *Application deadline:* For fall admission, 4/25 for domestic and international students; for spring admission, 11/25 for domestic and international students. Applications are processed on a rolling basis. Application fee: $75. Electronic applications accepted. *Expenses: Tuition, area resident:* Full-time $10,770; part-time $455 per credit. Tuition, state resident: full-time $10,770; part-time $455 per credit. Tuition, nonresident: full-time $19,920; part-time $830 per credit. *International tuition:* $19,920 full-time. *Required fees:* $559.20; $181.10 per semester. Tuition and fees vary according to program. *Unit head:* Dr. Rachel Grant, Program Coordinator, 719-982-3740, E-mail: rachel.grant@csi.cuny.edu. *Application contact:* Sasha Spence, Associate Director for Graduate Admissions, 718-982-2019, Fax: 718-982-2500, E-mail: sasha.spence@csi.cuny.edu.
Website: https://www.csi.cuny.edu/sites/default/files/pdf/admissions/grad/pdf/Bilingual_Advanced_Certificate.pdf

Columbia International University, Columbia Graduate School, Columbia, SC 29203. Offers Bible teaching (MABT); counseling (MACN); early childhood and elementary education (MAT); educational administration (M Ed); educational leadership (PhD); instruction and learning (M Ed); teaching English as a foreign language (Certificate); teaching English as a foreign language and intercultural studies (MATF). *Program availability:* Part-time, evening/weekend, online learning. *Degree requirements:* For master's, internships, professional project. *Entrance requirements:* For master's, MAT; GRE (for some programs), minimum GPA of 2.7. Additional exam requirements/recommendations for international students: Required—TOEFL. Electronic applications accepted.

Dallas Baptist University, Dorothy M. Bush College of Education, Program in Bilingual Education, Dallas, TX 75211-9299. Offers bilingual education (M Ed), including dual language, English as a second language/multilingual. *Program availability:* Part-time,

evening/weekend. *Application deadline:* Applications are processed on a rolling basis. Application fee: $25. Electronic applications accepted. Application fee is waived when completed online. *Expenses: Tuition:* Full-time $17,262; part-time $959 per credit hour. *Required fees:* $1000; $500 per semester. Tuition and fees vary according to course load and degree level. *Unit head:* Dr. Neil Dugger, Dean, 214-333-5202, E-mail: neil@dbu.edu. *Application contact:* Dr. Adelita Baker, Program Director, 214-333-5515, E-mail: adelita@dbu.edu.
Website: https://www.dbu.edu/graduate/degree-programs/med-bilingual-education

Dallas Baptist University, Dorothy M. Bush College of Education, Program in Reading and English as a Second Language, Dallas, TX 75211-9299. Offers bilingual education (M Ed); reading and English as a second language (M Ed). *Program availability:* Part-time, evening/weekend. *Application deadline:* Applications are processed on a rolling basis. Application fee: $25. Electronic applications accepted. Application fee is waived when completed online. *Expenses: Tuition:* Full-time $17,262; part-time $959 per credit hour. *Required fees:* $1000; $500 per semester. Tuition and fees vary according to course load and degree level. *Unit head:* Dr. Neil Dugger, Dean, 214-333-5202, E-mail: neil@dbu.edu. *Application contact:* Dr. Adelita Baker, Program Director, 214-333-5515, E-mail: adelita@dbu.edu.
Website: https://www.dbu.edu/graduate/degree-programs/med-reading-esl

Dallas International University, Graduate Programs, Dallas, TX 75236. Offers applied linguistics (MA, Certificate); language development (MA). *Program availability:* Part-time. *Degree requirements:* For master's, one foreign language, comprehensive exam (for some programs), thesis (for some programs). *Entrance requirements:* For master's, GRE. Additional exam requirements/recommendations for international students: Required—TOEFL (minimum score 577 paper-based; 90 iBT). Electronic applications accepted. *Faculty research:* Minority languages, endangered languages, language documentation.

DePaul University, College of Education, Chicago, IL 60614. Offers bilingual-bicultural education (M Ed, MA); counseling (M Ed, MA), including clinical mental health counseling, college student development, school counseling; curriculum studies (M Ed, MA, Ed D); early childhood education (M Ed, MA, Ed D); educational leadership (M Ed, MA, Ed D), including Catholic leadership (M Ed, MA), general (M Ed, MA), higher education (M Ed, MA), physical education (M Ed, MA), principal preparation (M Ed); teacher preparation (M Ed); elementary education (M Ed, MA); middle grades education (M Ed); middle school mathematics education (MS); reading specialist (M Ed, MA); secondary education (M Ed, MA); social and cultural foundations in education (M Ed, MA); special education (M Ed); sport, fitness and recreation leadership (MS); value-creating education for global citizenship (M Ed); world languages education (M Ed, MA). *Program availability:* Part-time, evening/weekend, online learning. *Degree requirements:* For doctorate, thesis/dissertation. Electronic applications accepted.

Eastern New Mexico University, Graduate School, College of Education and Technology, Department of Curriculum and Instruction, Portales, NM 88130. Offers alternative licensure in elementary education (M Ed); bilingual education (M Ed); career and technical education (M Ed); educational technology (M Ed); elementary education (M Ed); English as a second language (M Ed); pedagogy and learning (M Ed); reading/literacy (M Ed). *Program availability:* Part-time, online learning. *Degree requirements:* For master's, comprehensive exam, thesis optional. *Entrance requirements:* For master's, writing assessment, minimum GPA of 3.0, photocopy of teaching license, letter of recommendation. Additional exam requirements/recommendations for international students: Required—TOEFL (minimum score 550 paper-based; 79 iBT), IELTS (minimum score 6). Electronic applications accepted. *Expenses: Tuition, area resident:* Full-time $6776. Tuition, state resident: full-time $6776; part-time $282 per credit hour. Tuition, nonresident: full-time $8986; part-time $374 per credit hour. *Required fees:* $60 per semester. One-time fee: $25.

Eastern University, Graduate Education Programs, St. Davids, PA 19087-3696. Offers ESL program specialist (K-12) (Certificate); general supervisor (PreK-12) (Certificate); health and physical education (K-12) (Certificate); middle level (4-8) (Certificate); multicultural education (M Ed); music (K-12) (Certificate); Pre K-4 (Certificate); Pre K-4 with special education (Certificate); reading (M Ed); reading specialist (K-12) (Certificate); reading supervisor (K-12) (Certificate); school counseling (MA, CAGS); school principalship (preK-12) (Certificate); school psychology (MS, CAGS); secondary biology education (7-12) (Certificate); secondary chemistry education (7-12) (Certificate); secondary communication education (7-12) (Certificate); secondary English education (7-12) (Certificate); secondary math education (7-12) (Certificate); secondary social studies education (7-12) (Certificate); special education (M Ed); special education (7-12) (Certificate); special education (Pre K-8) (Certificate); special education supervisor (K-12) (Certificate); TESOL (M Ed); world language (Certificate), including Spanish. *Program availability:* Part-time, evening/weekend, online learning. *Entrance requirements:* Additional exam requirements/recommendations for international students: Required—TOEFL. Electronic applications accepted. Application fee is waived when completed online. *Expenses:* Contact institution.

Fairfield University, Graduate School of Education and Allied Professions, Fairfield, CT 06824. Offers applied behavior analysis (ATC); applied psychology (MA); clinical mental health counseling (MA, CAS); educational technology (MA); elementary education (MA, CAS); family studies (MA); integration of spirituality and religion in counseling (ATC); marriage and family therapy (MA); reading and language development (Sixth Year Certificate); school counseling (MA, CAS); school psychology (MA, CAS); school-based marriage and family therapy (ATC); secondary education (MA); special education (MA, CAS); substance abuse counseling (ATC); teaching (Certificate); teaching and foundations (MA, CAS); TESOL, world languages, and bilingual education (MA, CAS). *Accreditation:* NCATE. *Program availability:* Part-time, evening/weekend. *Degree requirements:* For master's, comprehensive exam. *Entrance requirements:* For master's, minimum GPA of 3.0, 2 recommendations, resume. Additional exam requirements/recommendations for international students: Required—TOEFL (minimum score 550 paper-based; 84 iBT) or IELTS (minimum score 7.5). Electronic applications accepted. *Expenses:* Contact institution. *Faculty research:* Reading and literacy, writing, social justice and inequality in education, addictions and mental health issues, therapeutic relationships and clinical supervision.

Fairleigh Dickinson University, Metropolitan Campus, University College: Arts, Sciences, and Professional Studies, Peter Sammartino School of Education, Program in Multilingual Education, Teaneck, NJ 07666-1914. Offers MA. *Accreditation:* TEAC.

Florida Atlantic University, College of Education, Department of Curriculum, Culture, and Educational Inquiry, Boca Raton, FL 33431-0991. Offers curriculum and instruction (M Ed, PhD, Ed S); early childhood education (M Ed); multicultural education (M Ed); TESOL and bilingual education (MA). *Program availability:* Part-time, evening/weekend. *Faculty:* 10 full-time (8 women), 2 part-time/adjunct (both women). *Students:* 15 full-time (11 women), 60 part-time (46 women); includes 24 minority (12 Black or African American, non-Hispanic/Latino; 2 Asian, non-Hispanic/Latino; 8 Hispanic/Latino; 2 Two or more races, non-Hispanic/Latino), 2 international. Average age 36. 45 applicants, 62% accepted, 21 enrolled. In 2018, 21 master's, 14 doctorates, 1 other advanced degree awarded. *Entrance requirements:* Additional exam requirements/recommendations for international students: Required—TOEFL (minimum score 500

paper-based; 61 iBT), IELTS (minimum score 6). *Application deadline:* For fall admission, 7/1 for domestic students, 2/15 for international students; for spring admission, 11/1 for domestic students, 7/15 for international students. Application fee: $30. *Expenses: Tuition, area resident:* Full-time $7400; part-time $369.82 per credit. Tuition, state resident: full-time $7400; part-time $369.82 per credit. Tuition, nonresident: full-time $20,496; part-time $1024.81 per credit. *Faculty research:* Multicultural education, early intervention strategies, family literacy, religious diversity in schools, early childhood curriculum. *Unit head:* Dr. Hanizah Zainuddin, Chair, 561-297-6594, E-mail: zainuddi@fau.edu. *Application contact:* Dr. Deborah Shepherd, Associate Dean, 561-297-3570, E-mail: dshep@fau.edu.
Website: http://www.coe.fau.edu/academicdepartments/ccei/

Florida International University, College of Arts, Sciences, and Education, Department of Leadership and Professional Studies, Miami, FL 33199. Offers adult education and human resource development (MS, Ed D); counseling (MS), including rehabilitation counseling, school counseling; counselor education (MS), including clinical mental health counseling; educational administration and supervision (Ed D); educational leadership (MS, Certificate, Ed S); higher education (Ed D); higher education administration (MS); international and comparative education (MS); recreation and sport management (MS), including recreation and sport management, recreational therapy; school psychology (Ed S); urban education (MS), including instruction in urban settings, learning technologies, multicultural/bilingual, multicultural/TESOL, urban education. *Program availability:* Part-time, evening/weekend. *Faculty:* 64 full-time (43 women), 104 part-time/adjunct (76 women). *Students:* 258 full-time (196 women), 217 part-time (155 women); includes 387 minority (118 Black or African American, non-Hispanic/Latino; 8 Asian, non-Hispanic/Latino; 249 Hispanic/Latino; 12 Two or more races, non-Hispanic/Latino), 11 international. Average age 31. 345 applicants, 57% accepted, 126 enrolled. In 2018, 172 master's, 11 doctorates awarded. *Entrance requirements:* For master's, minimum GPA of 3.0; for doctorate and other advanced degree, GRE General Test. Additional exam requirements/recommendations for international students: Required—TOEFL (minimum score 550 paper-based; 80 iBT), IELTS (minimum score 6.3). *Application deadline:* For fall admission, 6/1 priority date for domestic students, 4/1 for international students; for winter admission, 10/1 priority date for domestic students, 9/1 for international students; for spring admission, 3/1 priority date for domestic students, 2/1 for international students. Applications are processed on a rolling basis. Application fee: $30. Electronic applications accepted. *Financial support:* Fellowships, research assistantships, teaching assistantships, Federal Work-Study, and tuition waivers (full and partial) available. Support available to part-time students. Financial award applicants required to submit FAFSA. *Unit head:* Dr. Benjamin Baez, Chair, 305-348-3214, Fax: 305-348-1515, E-mail: benjamin.baez@fiu.edu. *Application contact:* Nanett Rojas, Manager, Admissions Operations, 305-348-7464, Fax: 305-348-7441, E-mail: gradadm@fiu.edu.
Website: http://education.fiu.edu

Gallaudet University, The Graduate School, Washington, DC 20002-3625. Offers American Sign Language/English bilingual early childhood deaf education: birth to 5 (Certificate); audiology (Au D); clinical psychology (PhD); deaf and hard of hearing infants, toddlers, and their families (Certificate); deaf education (MA, Ed S); deaf history (Certificate); deaf studies (Certificate); educating deaf students with disabilities (Certificate); education: teacher preparation (MA), including deaf education, early childhood education and deaf education, elementary education and deaf education, secondary education and deaf education; educational neuroscience (PhD); hearing, speech and language sciences (MS, PhD); international development (MA); interpretation (MA, PhD), including combined interpreting practice and research (MA), interpreting research (MA); linguistics (MA, PhD); mental health counseling (MA); peer mentoring (Certificate); public administration (MPA); school counseling (MA); school psychology (Psy S); sign language teaching (MA); social work (MSW); speech-language pathology (MS). *Program availability:* Part-time. Terminal master's awarded for partial completion of doctoral program. *Degree requirements:* For master's, comprehensive exam (for some programs), thesis optional; for doctorate, comprehensive exam, thesis/dissertation. *Entrance requirements:* For master's and doctorate, GRE General Test or MAT, letters of recommendation, interviews, goals statement, American Sign Language proficiency interview, written English competency. Additional exam requirements/recommendations for international students: Required—TOEFL. Electronic applications accepted. *Faculty research:* Signing math dictionaries, telecommunications access, cancer genetics, linguistics, visual language and visual learning, integrated quantum materials, deaf legal discourse, advance recruitment and retention in geosciences.

The George Washington University, Graduate School of Education and Human Development, Department of Counseling and Human Development, Washington, DC 20052. Offers clinical mental health counseling (MA); counseling (PhD, Ed S); counseling culturally and linguistically diverse persons (MA Ed/HD, Certificate); forensic rehabilitation counseling (Graduate Certificate); job development and placement (Graduate Certificate); rehabilitation counseling (MA Ed/HD), including autism spectrum disorder, substance abuse and psychiatric disabilities, traumatic brain injury; school counseling (MA Ed, Graduate Certificate). *Accreditation:* ACA (one or more programs are accredited). *Program availability:* Part-time, evening/weekend. *Faculty:* 14 full-time (9 women). *Students:* 110 full-time (94 women), 80 part-time (63 women); includes 63 minority (21 Black or African American, non-Hispanic/Latino; 2 American Indian or Alaska Native, non-Hispanic/Latino; 16 Asian, non-Hispanic/Latino; 19 Hispanic/Latino; 5 Two or more races, non-Hispanic/Latino), 14 international. Average age 31. 297 applicants, 60% accepted, 66 enrolled. In 2018, 49 master's, 7 doctorates, 2 other advanced degrees awarded. *Degree requirements:* For master's and other advanced degree, comprehensive exam; for doctorate, comprehensive exam, thesis/dissertation. *Entrance requirements:* For master's, GRE General Test or MAT, minimum GPA of 2.75; for doctorate, GRE General Test or MAT, interview, minimum GPA of 3.3; for other advanced degree, GRE General Test or MAT, minimum GPA of 3.3. *Application deadline:* For fall admission, 1/15 priority date for domestic students; for spring admission, 10/1 for domestic students. Applications are processed on a rolling basis. Application fee: $75. *Financial support:* In 2018–19, 58 students received support. Fellowships, research assistantships, teaching assistantships, career-related internships or fieldwork, Federal Work-Study, and tuition waivers (full and partial) available. Financial award application deadline: 1/15. *Faculty research:* Multiculturalism and counseling, models of adult development. *Unit head:* Dr. Kenneth C. Hergenrather, Chair, 202-994-1334, E-mail: hergenkc@gwu.edu. *Application contact:* Sarah Lang, Director of Graduate Admissions, 202-994-1447, Fax: 202-994-7207, E-mail: slang@gwu.edu.

The George Washington University, Graduate School of Education and Human Development, Department of Special Education and Disability Studies, Program in Bilingual Special Education, Washington, DC 20052. Offers MA Ed, Certificate. *Unit head:* Michael Feuer, Dean, 202-994-6161, E-mail: mjfeuer@gwu.edu. *Application contact:* Sarah Lang, Director of Graduate Admissions, 202-994-1447, Fax: 202-994-7207, E-mail: slang@gwu.edu.

The George Washington University, Graduate School of Education and Human Development, Department of Special Education and Disability Studies, Program in Special Education for Culturally and Linguistically Diverse Persons, Washington, DC

20052. Offers MA Ed/HD, Certificate. *Students:* 4 full-time (3 women), 47 part-time (42 women); includes 18 minority (4 Black or African American, non-Hispanic/Latino; 3 Asian, non-Hispanic/Latino; 10 Hispanic/Latino; 1 Two or more races, non-Hispanic/Latino), 1 international. Average age 33. 37 applicants, 81% accepted, 16 enrolled. In 2018, 13 master's, 1 Certificate awarded. *Unit head:* Doran Gresham, Assistant Professor, 202-994-2780, E-mail: dgresham@gwu.edu. *Application contact:* Doran Gresham, Assistant Professor, 202-994-2780, E-mail: dgresham@gwu.edu.

Georgia Southern University, Jack N. Averitt College of Graduate Studies, College of Education, Department of Curriculum, Foundations, and Reading, Program in Curriculum Studies, Statesboro, GA 30460. Offers curriculum studies (Ed D), including cultural curriculum, instructional improvement, multicultural studies, teaching and learning. *Program availability:* Part-time. *Degree requirements:* For doctorate, comprehensive exam, thesis/dissertation, exams; assessments. *Entrance requirements:* For doctorate, GRE or MAT, letters of reference, minimum GPA of 3.5, writing sample. Additional exam requirements/recommendations for international students: Required—TOEFL (minimum score 550 paper-based; 80 iBT), IELTS (minimum score 6). Electronic applications accepted. *Expenses: Tuition, area resident:* Part-time $3324 per semester. Tuition, state resident: full-time $5814; part-time $3324 per semester. Tuition, nonresident: full-time $23,204; part-time $13,260 per semester. *Required fees:* $2092; $2092. Tuition and fees vary according to course load, degree level, campus/location and program. *Faculty research:* Curriculum theory, cultural studies, narrative research, postmodern theory, critical race theory, international education, feminism, media literacy, documentary studies, post human condition, social and cultural foundations of education, democracy and education.

Heritage University, Graduate Programs in Education, Program in Professional Studies, Toppenish, WA 98948-9599. Offers bilingual education/ESL (M Ed); biology (M Ed); English and literature (M Ed); reading/literacy (M Ed); special education (M Ed). *Program availability:* Part-time, evening/weekend. *Degree requirements:* For master's, comprehensive exam (for some programs), thesis (for some programs).

Hofstra University, School of Education, Programs in Teacher Education, Hempstead, NY 11549. Offers bilingual education (MA); bilingual extension (Advanced Certificate); business education (MS Ed); curriculum studies (MS Ed); early childhood and childhood education (MS Ed); early childhood education (MA, MS Ed); educational technology (Advanced Certificate); elementary education (MA, MS Ed); English education (MS Ed); family and consumer science (MS Ed); fine arts and music education (Advanced Certificate); fine arts education (MS Ed); foreign language and TESOL (MS Ed); foreign language education (MA, MS Ed); languages other than English and teaching English as a second language (MA); learning and teaching (Ed D); mathematics education (MA, MS Ed); middle childhood extension (Advanced Certificate); music education (MA, MS Ed); science education (MA); secondary education (Advanced Certificate); social studies education (MA, MS Ed); teaching languages other than English and TESOL (MS Ed); technology for learning (MA); TESOL (MS Ed, Advanced Certificate); TESOL with specialization in STEM (MA); work based learning extension (Advanced Certificate). *Program availability:* Part-time, evening/weekend, blended/hybrid learning. *Students:* 138 full-time (94 women), 109 part-time (78 women); includes 66 minority (16 Black or African American, non-Hispanic/Latino; 17 Asian, non-Hispanic/Latino; 31 Hispanic/Latino; 2 Native Hawaiian or other Pacific Islander, non-Hispanic/Latino), 6 international. Average age 29. 217 applicants, 86% accepted, 113 enrolled. In 2018, 105 master's, 11 doctorates, 25 other advanced degrees awarded. *Degree requirements:* For master's, comprehensive exam, thesis (for some programs), exit project, student teaching, fieldwork, electronic portfolio, curriculum project, minimum GPA of 3.0; for doctorate, dissertation; for Advanced Certificate, 3 foreign languages, comprehensive exam (for some programs), thesis project. *Entrance requirements:* For master's, GRE, 2 letters of recommendation, portfolio, teacher certification (MA), interview, essay; for doctorate, GMAT, GRE, LSAT, or MAT; for Advanced Certificate, 2 letters of recommendation, essay, interview and/or portfolio, teaching certificate. Additional exam requirements/recommendations for international students: Required—TOEFL (minimum score 550 paper-based; 80 iBT). *Application deadline:* Applications are processed on a rolling basis. Application fee: $75. Electronic applications accepted. *Financial support:* In 2018–19, 86 students received support, including 51 fellowships with full and partial tuition reimbursements available (averaging $5,080 per year), 2 research assistantships with full and partial tuition reimbursements available (averaging $3,470 per year); career-related internships or fieldwork, Federal Work-Study, institutionally sponsored loans, scholarships/grants, traineeships, tuition waivers (full and partial), unspecified assistantships, and scholarships and endowed scholarships also available. Support available to part-time students. Financial award applicants required to submit FAFSA. *Faculty research:* Impact of memory on learning; brain function, cognitive-development, learning, and achievement; student activism and civic education; using children's literature to promote diversity; 2nd language acquisition. *Unit head:* Dr. Alan Singer, Chairperson, 516-463-5853, Fax: 516-463-6275, E-mail: alan.j.singer@hofstra.edu. *Application contact:* Sunil Samuel, Assistant Vice President of Admissions, 516-463-4723, Fax: 516-463-4664, E-mail: graduateadmission@hofstra.edu.
Website: http://www.hofstra.edu/education/

Houston Baptist University, College of Education and Behavioral Sciences, Programs in Education, Houston, TX 77074-3298. Offers bilingual education (M Ed); counselor education (M Ed); curriculum and instruction (M Ed); curriculum and instruction (EC-6 bilingual) (M Ed); curriculum and instruction in all-level art, Spanish, music, or physical education (M Ed); curriculum and instruction in EC-6 and special education (EC-12) (M Ed); curriculum and instruction in instructional technology (M Ed); curriculum and instruction in mathematics, science, or social studies (4-8) (M Ed); curriculum and instruction with EC-6 generalist (M Ed); curriculum and instruction with English language arts and reading (4-8) (M Ed); educational administration (M Ed); educational diagnostician (M Ed); executive educational leadership (Ed D); higher education in business management (M Ed); higher education in Christian studies (M Ed); higher education in counseling (M Ed); higher education in educational technology (M Ed); reading (M Ed); special educational leadership (Ed D). *Program availability:* Part-time, evening/weekend, 100% online, blended/hybrid learning. *Degree requirements:* For master's, comprehensive exam; for doctorate, thesis/dissertation. *Entrance requirements:* For master's, minimum GPA of 2.75, two recommendations, resume, bachelor's degree conferred transcript; interview (for non-certified teachers); for doctorate, GRE, 5 letters of recommendation. Additional exam requirements/recommendations for international students: Required—TOEFL (minimum score 80 iBT), IELTS (minimum score 6.5). Electronic applications accepted. Application fee is waived when completed online. *Expenses:* Contact institution. *Faculty research:* Autism and inclusion, integrating technology into instruction, school change and leadership trust.

Howard University, Cathy Hughes School of Communications, Department of Strategic, Legal and Management Communication, Washington, DC 20059-0002. Offers intercultural communication (MA, PhD); organizational communication (MA, PhD). Offered through the Graduate School of Arts and Sciences. *Program availability:* Part-time. Terminal master's awarded for partial completion of doctoral program. *Degree requirements:* For master's, comprehensive exam or thesis; for doctorate, one foreign language, comprehensive exam, thesis/dissertation. *Entrance requirements:* For master's, English proficiency exam, GRE General Test, minimum GPA of 3.0; for doctorate, English proficiency exam, GRE General Test, master's degree in related field, minimum GPA of 3.5. Additional exam requirements/recommendations for international students: Required—TOEFL. *Faculty research:* Media effects, black discourse, development communication, African-American organizations.

Hunter College of the City University of New York, Graduate School, School of Education, Department of Curriculum and Teaching, Program in Bilingual Education, New York, NY 10065-5085. Offers MS. *Accreditation:* NCATE. *Degree requirements:* For master's, one foreign language, thesis, research seminar, student teaching experience or practicum, New York State Teacher Certification Exams. *Entrance requirements:* For master's, interview, minimum GPA of 2.8, writing sample in English and Spanish. Additional exam requirements/recommendations for international students: Required—TOEFL, TWE. *Faculty research:* Teacher effectiveness, language development, Spanish language and linguistics and multicultural education.

Immaculata University, College of Graduate Studies, Program in Cultural and Linguistic Diversity, Immaculata, PA 19345. Offers bilingual studies (MA); TESOL (MA). *Program availability:* Part-time, evening/weekend. *Degree requirements:* For master's, one foreign language, comprehensive exam, thesis optional, professional experience. *Entrance requirements:* For master's, GRE or MAT, proficiency in Spanish or Asian language, minimum GPA of 3.0. Additional exam requirements/recommendations for international students: Required—TOEFL, IELTS. Electronic applications accepted. *Faculty research:* Cognitive learning, Caribbean literature and culture, English as a second language, teaching English to speakers of other languages.

Indiana State University, College of Graduate and Professional Studies, College of Arts and Sciences, Department of Languages, Literatures, and Linguistics, Terre Haute, IN 47809. Offers applied linguistics/teaching English as a second language (MA); language education (PhD); Spanish/teaching English as a second language (MA); TESL/TEFL (CAS). *Degree requirements:* For master's, comprehensive exam. Electronic applications accepted.

Indiana University Bloomington, University Graduate School, College of Arts and Sciences, Department of Second Language Studies, Bloomington, IN 47405-7000. Offers second language studies (MA, PhD); TESOL and applied linguistics (MA). *Entrance requirements:* Additional exam requirements/recommendations for international students: Required—TOEFL (minimum score 100 iBT). Electronic applications accepted.

James Madison University, The Graduate School, College of Education, Program in Education, Harrisonburg, VA 22807. Offers early childhood education (preK-3) (MAT); educational leadership (M Ed); educational technology (M Ed); elementary education (MAT); equity and cultural diversity (M Ed); inclusive early childhood education (MAT); K-8 mathematics specialist (M Ed); middle education (MAT); reading education (M Ed); secondary education (MAT); Spanish language and culture for educators (M Ed); TESOL (MAT). *Accreditation:* NCATE. *Program availability:* Part-time, evening/weekend. *Students:* 255 full-time (224 women), 200 part-time (140 women); includes 56 minority (13 Black or African American, non-Hispanic/Latino; 8 Asian, non-Hispanic/Latino; 21 Hispanic/Latino; 14 Two or more races, non-Hispanic/Latino), 1 international. Average age 30. In 2018, 295 master's awarded. Application fee: $60. Electronic applications accepted. *Expenses:* Tuition, state resident: full-time $10,848. Tuition, nonresident: full-time $27,888. *Required fees:* $1128. *Financial support:* In 2018–19, 22 students received support. Teaching assistantships, career-related internships or fieldwork, Federal Work-Study, and assistantships (averaging $7911) available. Financial award application deadline: 3/1; financial award applicants required to submit FAFSA. *Unit head:* Dr. Phillip M. Wishon, Dean, 540-568-6572, E-mail: wishonpm@jmu.edu. *Application contact:* Lynette D. Michael, Director of Graduate Admissions, 540-568-6131 Ext. 6395, Fax: 540-568-7860, E-mail: michaeld@jmu.edu.
Website: http://www.jmu.edu/coe/index.shtml

Kean University, College of Education, Program in Instruction and Curriculum, Union, NJ 07083. Offers bilingual/bicultural education (MA); teaching English as a second language (MA). *Accreditation:* NCATE. *Program availability:* Part-time. *Faculty:* 14 full-time (8 women). *Students:* 1 (woman) full-time, 14 part-time (11 women); includes 9 minority (all Hispanic/Latino), 1 international. Average age 33. 5 applicants, 100% accepted, 5 enrolled. In 2018, 19 master's awarded. *Degree requirements:* For master's, comprehensive exam (for some programs), thesis optional, two-semester advanced seminar. *Entrance requirements:* For master's, GRE General Test or MAT; PRAXIS (for some programs), minimum GPA of 3.0, personal statement, professional resume/curriculum vitae, commitment to working with children, certification (for some programs), two letters of recommendation. Additional exam requirements/recommendations for international students: Required—TOEFL (minimum score 550 paper-based; 79 iBT), IELTS (minimum score 6.5). *Application deadline:* For fall admission, 6/30 for domestic and international students; for spring admission, 12/1 for domestic and international students. Applications are processed on a rolling basis. Application fee: $75. Electronic applications accepted. *Expenses:* Tuition, state resident: full-time $15,025; part-time $733.50 per credit. Tuition, nonresident: full-time $19,890; part-time $884.50 per credit. *Required fees:* $2107.50; $89.50 per credit. Tuition and fees vary according to course level, course load, degree level and program. *Financial support:* Scholarships/grants and unspecified assistantships available. Financial award applicants required to submit FAFSA. *Unit head:* Dr. Gail Verdi, Program Coordinator, 908-737-3908, E-mail: gverdi@kean.edu. *Application contact:* Brittany Gerstenhaber, Admissions Counselor, 908-737-7100, E-mail: grad-adm@kean.edu.
Website: http://grad.kean.edu/masters-programs/bilingualbicultural-education-instruction-and-curriculum

Langston University, School of Education and Behavioral Sciences, Langston, OK 73050. Offers bilingual/multicultural (M Ed); elementary education (M Ed); English as a second language (M Ed); rehabilitation counseling (M Sc); urban education (M Ed). *Accreditation:* CORE; NCATE (one or more programs are accredited). *Program availability:* Part-time. *Degree requirements:* For master's, comprehensive exam, thesis optional. *Entrance requirements:* For master's, GRE, writing skills test, minimum GPA of 2.5, 3 letters of recommendation. Additional exam requirements/recommendations for international students: Required—TOEFL, TWE. *Faculty research:* Bilingual/multicultural education, financing post-secondary education.

La Salle University, School of Arts and Sciences, Hispanic Institute, Philadelphia, PA 19141-1199. Offers bilingual/bicultural studies (MA); ESL program specialist (Certificate); interpretation: English/Spanish-Spanish/English (Certificate); teaching English to speakers of other languages (MA); translation and interpretation (MA); translation: English/Spanish-Spanish/English (Certificate). *Program availability:* Part-time, evening/weekend. *Degree requirements:* For master's, one foreign language, project or thesis. *Entrance requirements:* For master's, GRE, MAT, or GMAT, professional resume; two letters of recommendation; for Certificate, GRE, MAT, or GMAT, professional resume; two letters of recommendation; evidence of an advanced level in Spanish. Additional exam requirements/recommendations for international students: Required—TOEFL. Electronic applications accepted. Application fee is waived when completed online. *Expenses:* Contact institution. *Faculty research:* Puerto Rican literature, cross-cultural communication, English as a second language methodology, Spanish language.

La Salle University, School of Arts and Sciences, Program in Education, Philadelphia, PA 19141-1199. Offers autism spectrum disorders (MA, Certificate); bilingual/bicultural studies (MA); classroom management (MA); dual early childhood and special education (MA); dual middle-level science and math and special education (MA); education (MA); English (MA); English as a second language (Certificate); history (MA); instructional coach (Certificate); instructional leadership (MA); reading specialist (MA, Certificate); secondary education (MA); special education (MA, Certificate). *Program availability:* Part-time, evening/weekend. *Degree requirements:* For master's, comprehensive exam. *Entrance requirements:* For master's, MAT or GRE, 2 letters of recommendation; for Certificate, GMAT or GRE, 2 letters of recommendation. Additional exam requirements/ recommendations for international students: Required—TOEFL. Electronic applications accepted. Application fee is waived when completed online. *Expenses:* Contact institution.

Lehman College of the City University of New York, School of Education, Department of Counseling, Leadership, Literacy, and Special Education, Bronx, NY 10468-1589. Offers counselor education/school counseling (MS Ed); literacy studies (MS Ed); special education (MS Ed), including bilingual special education, early childhood special education. *Program availability:* Part-time, evening/weekend. *Faculty research:* Battered women, whole language classrooms, parent education, mainstreaming.

Lehman College of the City University of New York, School of Education, Department of Counseling, Leadership, Literacy, and Special Education, Program in Special Education, Option in Bilingual Special Education, Bronx, NY 10468-1589. Offers MS Ed. *Accreditation:* NCATE. *Entrance requirements:* For master's, minimum GPA of 3.0.

Long Island University–Hudson, Graduate School, Purchase, NY 10577. Offers autism (Advanced Certificate); bilingual education (Advanced Certificate); childhood education (MS Ed); crisis management (Advanced Certificate); early childhood education (MS Ed); educational leadership (MS Ed); health administration (MPA); literacy (MS Ed); marriage and family therapy (MS); mental health counseling (MS, Advanced Certificate), including credentialed alcoholism and substance abuse counselor (MS); middle childhood and adolescence education (MS Ed); pharmaceutics (MS), including cosmetic science, industrial pharmacy; public administration (MPA); school counseling (MS Ed, Advanced Certificate); school psychology (MS Ed); special education (MS Ed); TESOL (MS Ed); TESOL (all grades) (Advanced Certificate). *Program availability:* Part-time, evening/weekend. *Entrance requirements:* Additional exam requirements/recommendations for international students: Required—TOEFL. Electronic applications accepted. *Expenses:* Contact institution.

Long Island University–LIU Brooklyn, School of Education, Brooklyn, NY 11201-8423. Offers adolescence urban education (MS Ed); applied behavior analysis (Advanced Certificate); bilingual education (Advanced Certificate); bilingual education in urban setting (MS Ed); bilingual school counselor (MS Ed, Advanced Certificate); childhood urban education (MS Ed); childhood/early childhood education (MS Ed); childhood/early childhood urban education (MS Ed); early childhood urban education (MS Ed, Advanced Certificate); educational leadership (Advanced Certificate); marriage and family therapy (MS, Advanced Certificate); mental health counseling (MS, Advanced Certificate); school building district leader (Advanced Certificate); school counselor (MS Ed, Advanced Certificate); school psychologist (MS Ed); teaching students with disabilities (MS Ed); teaching urban children with disabilities (MS Ed); TESOL (MS Ed, Advanced Certificate). *Accreditation:* TEAC. *Program availability:* Part-time, evening/weekend, 100% online. *Entrance requirements:* For master's, GRE. Additional exam requirements/recommendations for international students: Required—TOEFL (minimum score 527 paper-based, 75 iBT), IELTS, or PTE. Electronic applications accepted. *Faculty research:* Diversity issues in education and mental health care, inclusion - disability studies, sustainability, teacher professional development.

Loyola Marymount University, School of Education, Program in Bilingual Elementary Education, Los Angeles, CA 90045. Offers MA. *Unit head:* Dr. Liza Mastrippolito, Program Director, Bilingual Education, 310-568-6697, E-mail: liza.mastrippolito@lmu.edu. *Application contact:* Ammar Dalal, Assistant Vice Provost for Graduate Enrollment, 310-338-2721, Fax: 310-338-6086, E-mail: graduateinfo@lmu.edu.
Website: http://soe.lmu.edu/academics/bilingualeducation

Loyola Marymount University, School of Education, Program in Bilingual Secondary Education, Los Angeles, CA 90064. Offers MA. *Unit head:* Dr. Liza Mastrippolito, Program Director, Bilingual Education, 310-568-6697, E-mail: liza.mastrippolito@lmu.edu. *Application contact:* Ammar Dalal, Assistant Vice Provost for Graduate Enrollment, 310-338-2721, Fax: 310-388-6086, E-mail: graduateinfo@lmu.edu.
Website: http://soe.lmu.edu/academics/bilingualeducation

Manhattan College, Graduate Programs, School of Education and Health, Program in Special Education, Riverdale, NY 10471. Offers adolescence education students with disabilities generalist extension in English or math or social studies - grades 7-12 (MS Ed); bilingual education (Advanced Certificate); dual childhood/students with disabilities - grades 1-6 (MS Ed); students with disabilities - grades 1-6 (MS Ed). *Program availability:* Part-time, evening/weekend. *Degree requirements:* For master's, thesis, internship (if not certified). *Entrance requirements:* For master's, GRE, minimum GPA of 3.0. Additional exam requirements/recommendations for international students: Required—TOEFL (minimum score 550 paper-based; 80 iBT), IELTS (minimum score 6). Electronic applications accepted. Application fee is waived when completed online. *Expenses:* Contact institution.

Manhattanville College, School of Education, Program in Teaching English to Speakers of Other Languages, Purchase, NY 10577-2132. Offers adult and international settings (MPS); bilingual education (childhood/Spanish) (Advanced Certificate); teaching English as a second language (all grades) (MPS, Certificate). *Program availability:* Part-time, evening/weekend. *Faculty:* 2 full-time (1 woman), 13 part-time/adjunct (8 women). *Students:* 4 full-time (3 women), 16 part-time (11 women); includes 2 minority (both Hispanic/Latino). Average age 27. 9 applicants, 67% accepted, 3 enrolled. In 2018, 13 master's, 5 Advanced Certificates awarded. *Degree requirements:* For master's, comprehensive exam (for some programs), thesis (for some programs), student teaching, research seminars, portfolios, internships, writing assessment; for other advanced degree, comprehensive exam (for some programs). *Entrance requirements:* For master's, for programs leading to certification, candidates must submit scores from GRE or MAT(Miller Analogies Test), minimum undergraduate GPA of 3.0, all transcripts from all colleges and universities attended, 2 letters of recommendation, interview, essay (2-3 page personal statement that describes reasons for choosing education as profession and personal philosophy of education), proof of immunization (for those born after 1957). Additional exam requirements/recommendations for international students: Required—TOEFL (minimum score 600 paper-based; 110 iBT); Recommended—IELTS (minimum score 8). *Application deadline:* Applications are processed on a rolling basis. Application fee: $75. Electronic applications accepted. *Expenses:* 935 per credit. *Financial support:* Teaching assistantships, career-related internships or fieldwork, Federal Work-Study, institutionally sponsored loans, scholarships/grants, and unspecified assistantships available. Financial award application deadline: 3/15; financial award applicants required to submit FAFSA. *Faculty research:* Changing suburbs institute and community schools. *Unit head:* Dr. Shelly Wepner, Dean, 914-323-3153, Fax: 914-323-5493, E-mail: Shelly.Wepner@mville.edu. *Application contact:* Alissa Wilson, Director, SOE Graduate Enrollment Management, 914-323-3150, Fax: 914-694-1732, E-mail: edschool@mville.edu.
Website: http://www.mville.edu/programs/tesol-teaching-english-speakers-other-languages

Molloy College, Graduate Education Program, Rockville Centre, NY 11571-5002. Offers adolescent education in biology (MS); adolescent special education (Advanced Certificate); bilingual extension (Advanced Certificate); childhood education (MS); childhood special education (Advanced Certificate); early childhood education (MS); educational technology (MS); English (MS); mathematics (MS); social studies (MS); Spanish (MS); special education on both childhood and adolescent levels (MS); teaching English to speakers of other languages (TESOL) in grades pre-K to 12 (MS); TESOL (Advanced Certificate). *Accreditation:* NCATE. *Program availability:* Part-time, evening/weekend. *Faculty:* 24 full-time (22 women), 26 part-time/adjunct (19 women). *Students:* 106 full-time (78 women), 203 part-time (154 women); includes 65 minority (14 Black or African American, non-Hispanic/Latino; 5 Asian, non-Hispanic/Latino; 41 Hispanic/Latino; 5 Two or more races, non-Hispanic/Latino). Average age 41. 147 applicants, 63% accepted, 79 enrolled. In 2018, 120 master's, 1 other advanced degree awarded. *Entrance requirements:* Additional exam requirements/recommendations for international students: Required—TOEFL (minimum score 550 paper-based; 79 iBT). *Application deadline:* Applications are processed on a rolling basis. Application fee: $60. Electronic applications accepted. *Expenses: Tuition:* Full-time $20,790; part-time $1155 per credit. *Required fees:* $1060; $900. Tuition and fees vary according to course load and degree level. *Financial support:* Application deadline: 3/1; applicants required to submit FAFSA. *Faculty research:* English Language Learners; social emotional needs of students; gifted education; cultural diversity; collaborative teaching methods. *Unit head:* Joanne O'Brien, Dean, 516-323-3116, E-mail: jobrien@molloy.edu. *Application contact:* Faye Hood, Assistant Director for Admissions, 516-323-4009, E-mail: fhood@molloy.edu.

Mount St. Joseph University, Graduate Education Program, Cincinnati, OH 45233-1670. Offers adolescent to young adult education (MA); dyslexia (Certificate); inclusive early childhood education (MA); middle childhood education (MA); multicultural special education (MA); reading science (MA). *Accreditation:* TEAC. *Program availability:* Part-time, evening/weekend, 100% online, blended/hybrid learning. *Degree requirements:* For master's, comprehensive exam, thesis, research project, student teaching, clinical and field-based experiences. *Entrance requirements:* For master's, GRE (if GPA is below 3.0), letter of intent, 2 referrals, background check, interview, resume, minimum undergraduate GPA of 3.0. Additional exam requirements/recommendations for international students: Required—TOEFL (minimum score 560 paper-based; 83 iBT). Electronic applications accepted. *Expenses:* Contact institution. *Faculty research:* Foreign and second language learning problems/reading disabilities, multicultural/ bilingual special education, science education, pedagogical content knowledge, early childhood, response to intervention.

New Jersey City University, Debra Cannon Partridge Wolfe College of Education, Department of Multicultural Education, Jersey City, NJ 07305-1597. Offers bilingual/ bicultural education (MA); English as a second language (MA). *Program availability:* Part-time, evening/weekend. *Entrance requirements:* For master's, GRE General Test or MAT. Additional exam requirements/recommendations for international students: Required—TOEFL.

New Mexico State University, College of Education, Department of Curriculum and Instruction, Las Cruces, NM 88003-8001. Offers bilingual education (MA); curriculum and instruction (Ed D, PhD); early childhood education (MA); educational diagnostics (Ed S); language, literacy and culture (MA); learning design and technologies (MA); teaching (MAT); teaching English to speakers of other languages (MA). *Accreditation:* NCATE. *Program availability:* Part-time, evening/weekend, 100% online. *Faculty:* 22 full-time (17 women), 7 part-time/adjunct (5 women). *Students:* 82 full-time (49 women), 186 part-time (134 women); includes 153 minority (13 Black or African American, non-Hispanic/Latino; 2 American Indian or Alaska Native, non-Hispanic/Latino; 3 Asian, non-Hispanic/Latino; 129 Hispanic/Latino; 6 Two or more races, non-Hispanic/Latino), 33 international. Average age 37. 110 applicants, 79% accepted, 60 enrolled. In 2018, 75 master's, 13 doctorates, 16 other advanced degrees awarded. *Degree requirements:* For master's, comprehensive exam, thesis; for doctorate, comprehensive exam, thesis/ dissertation. *Entrance requirements:* For master's, minimum cumulative GPA of 3.0; for doctorate, portfolio, minimum cumulative GPA of 3.0. Additional exam requirements/ recommendations for international students: Required—TOEFL (minimum score 550 paper-based; 79 iBT), IELTS (minimum score 6.5). *Application deadline:* For fall admission, 12/15 priority date for domestic and international students. Applications are processed on a rolling basis. Application fee: $40 ($50 for international students). Electronic applications accepted. *Expenses: Tuition, area resident:* Full-time $4216.70; part-time $252.70 per credit hour. Tuition, state resident: full-time $4216.70; part-time $252.70 per credit hour. Tuition, nonresident: full-time $12,769; part-time $881.10 per credit hour. *International tuition:* $12,769.30 full-time. *Required fees:* $878.40; $48.80 per credit hour. Full-time tuition and fees vary according to course load and reciprocity agreements. *Financial support:* In 2018–19, 111 students received support, including 2 fellowships (averaging $4,548 per year), 11 research assistantships (averaging $11,673 per year), 10 teaching assistantships (averaging $10,582 per year); career-related internships or fieldwork, Federal Work-Study, scholarships/grants, traineeships, health care benefits, and unspecified assistantships also available. Support available to part-time students. Financial award application deadline: 3/1. *Faculty research:* STEM education, bilingual and English as a second language education, critical pedagogy/ multicultural education, learning design and technology, early childhood education. *Total annual research expenditures:* $10,685. *Unit head:* Dr. David Rutledge, Department Head, 575-646-5411, Fax: 575-646-5436, E-mail: rutledge@nmsu.edu. *Application contact:* Dr. David Rutledge, Associate Department Head for Graduate Programs, 575-646-5411, Fax: 575-646-5436, E-mail: rutledge@nmsu.edu.
Website: http://ci.education.nmsu.edu

New Mexico State University, College of Education, Department of Special Education and Communication Disorders, Las Cruces, NM 88003-8001. Offers communication disorders (MA); curriculum and instruction (Ed S), including special education (MA, Ed S), special education/deaf-hard of hearing (MA, Ed S); education (MA), including autism spectrum disorders (MA, Ed D, PhD), special education (MA, Ed S), special education/deaf-hard of hearing (MA, Ed S), speech-language pathology; special education (Ed D, PhD), including autism spectrum disorders (MA, Ed D, PhD), bilingual/ multicultural special education. *Accreditation:* ASHA (one or more programs are accredited); NCATE. *Program availability:* Part-time, evening/weekend, online learning. *Faculty:* 13 full-time (10 women), 2 part-time/adjunct (1 woman). *Students:* 49 full-time (46 women), 52 part-time (46 women); includes 514 minority (1 Black or African American, non-Hispanic/Latino; 454 Asian, non-Hispanic/Latino; 55 Hispanic/Latino; 4 Two or more races, non-Hispanic/Latino), 7 international. Average age 32. 150 applicants, 21% accepted, 27 enrolled. In 2018, 25 master's, 3 doctorates, 4 other advanced degrees awarded. *Degree requirements:* For master's, comprehensive exam, thesis optional; for doctorate, comprehensive exam, thesis/dissertation. *Entrance*

requirements: For master's, GRE General Test or MAT. Additional exam requirements/recommendations for international students: Required—TOEFL (minimum score 550 paper-based; 79 iBT), IELTS (minimum score 6.5). *Application deadline:* For fall admission, 2/1 priority date for domestic students. Applications are processed on a rolling basis. Application fee: $40 ($50 for international students). Electronic applications accepted. *Expenses: Tuition, area resident:* Full-time $4216.70; part-time $252.70 per credit hour. Tuition, state resident: full-time $4216.70; part-time $252.70 per credit hour. Tuition, nonresident: full-time $12,769; part-time $881.10 per credit hour. *International tuition:* $12,769.30 full-time. *Required fees:* $878.40; $48.80 per credit hour. Full-time tuition and fees vary according to course load and reciprocity agreements. *Financial support:* In 2018–19, 43 students received support, including 2 fellowships (averaging $4,548 per year), 3 research assistantships (averaging $8,482 per year), 6 teaching assistantships (averaging $8,482 per year); career-related internships or fieldwork, Federal Work-Study, scholarships/grants, traineeships, health care benefits, and unspecified assistantships also available. Support available to part-time students. Financial award application deadline: 3/1. *Faculty research:* Multicultural special education, multicultural communication disorders, mild disability, multicultural assessment, deaf education, early childhood, bilingual special education. *Total annual research expenditures:* $174,534.
Website: spedcd.education.nmsu.edu

New York University, Steinhardt School of Culture, Education, and Human Development, Applied Statistics, Social Science, and Humanities, Program in Sociology of Education, New York, NY 10012. Offers education policy (MA); social and cultural studies of education (MA); sociology of education (PhD). *Program availability:* Part-time. *Entrance requirements:* For master's, letters of recommendation; for doctorate, GRE General Test, interview. Additional exam requirements/recommendations for international students: Required—TOEFL (minimum score 100 iBT). Electronic applications accepted. *Faculty research:* Legal and institutional environments of schools; social inequality; high school reform and achievement; urban schooling, economics and education, educational policy.

New York University, Steinhardt School of Culture, Education, and Human Development, Department of Teaching and Learning, Program in Multilingual/Multicultural Studies, New York, NY 10012. Offers bilingual education (MA, PhD, Advanced Certificate); foreign language education (MA); teaching English to speakers of other languages (MA, PhD); teaching foreign languages, 7-12 (MA), including Chinese, French, Italian, Japanese, Spanish; teaching French as a foreign language (MA), including teaching English to speakers of other languages; teaching Spanish as a foreign language (MA), including teaching English to speakers of other languages. MA in teaching English to speakers of other languages also offered in collaboration with NYU Shanghai. *Accreditation:* TEAC. *Program availability:* Part-time, evening/weekend. *Entrance requirements:* For doctorate, GRE General Test, interview; for Advanced Certificate, master's degree. Additional exam requirements/recommendations for international students: Required—TOEFL (minimum score 100 iBT). Electronic applications accepted. *Faculty research:* Second language acquisition, cross-cultural communication, technology-enhanced language learning, language variation, action learning.

Northern Arizona University, College of Education, Department of Educational Specialties, Flagstaff, AZ 86011. Offers autism spectrum disorders (Certificate); bilingual/multicultural education (M Ed), including bilingual, ESL; career and technical education (M Ed, Certificate); educational technology (M Ed, Certificate); English as a second language (Certificate); positive behavior support (Certificate); special education (M Ed), including early childhood special education, mild/moderate disabilities. *Program availability:* Part-time, 100% online, blended/hybrid learning. *Degree requirements:* For master's, variable foreign language requirement, comprehensive exam (for some programs), thesis (for some programs); for Certificate, comprehensive exam (for some programs). *Entrance requirements:* Additional exam requirements/recommendations for international students: Required—TOEFL (minimum score 80 iBT), IELTS (minimum score 6.5). Electronic applications accepted.

Queens College of the City University of New York, Arts and Humanities Division, Department of Linguistics and Communication Disorders, Queens, NY 11367-1597. Offers applied linguistics (MA); speech-language pathology (MA); TESOL (MS Ed, Post-Master's Certificate); TESOL and bilingual education (Post-Master's Certificate). *Accreditation:* ASHA. *Program availability:* Part-time. *Faculty:* 21 full-time (15 women), 24 part-time/adjunct (18 women). *Students:* 39 full-time (36 women), 108 part-time (98 women); includes 70 minority (8 Black or African American, non-Hispanic/Latino; 26 Asian, non-Hispanic/Latino; 33 Hispanic/Latino; 3 Two or more races, non-Hispanic/Latino), 5 international. Average age 27. 390 applicants, 25% accepted, 81 enrolled. In 2018, 57 master's, 11 other advanced degrees awarded. *Entrance requirements:* For master's, minimum GPA of 3.0. Additional exam requirements/recommendations for international students: Required—TOEFL, IELTS. *Application deadline:* For fall admission, 4/1 for domestic students; for winter admission, 1/1 for domestic students. Applications are processed on a rolling basis. Application fee: $125. Electronic applications accepted. *Expenses:* Contact institution. *Financial support:* Career-related internships or fieldwork available. Financial award application deadline: 4/1; financial award applicants required to submit FAFSA. *Unit head:* Arlene Kraat, Chair, 718-997-2940, E-mail: arlene.kraat@qc.cuny.edu. *Application contact:* Elizabeth D'Amico-Ramirez, Assistant Director of Graduate Admissions, 718-997-5203, E-mail: elizabeth.damicoramirez@qc.cuny.edu.

Queens College of the City University of New York, Division of Education, Department of Elementary and Early Childhood Education, Queens, NY 11367-1597. Offers bilingual education (MAT, MS Ed, AC); childhood education (MAT, MS Ed); early childhood education birth-2 (MAT, MS Ed, AC); literacy education birth-grade 6 (MS Ed, AC). *Program availability:* Part-time, evening/weekend. *Faculty:* 19 full-time (13 women), 35 part-time/adjunct (32 women). *Students:* 117 full-time (102 women), 376 part-time (344 women); includes 264 minority (27 Black or African American, non-Hispanic/Latino; 75 Asian, non-Hispanic/Latino; 154 Hispanic/Latino; 1 Native Hawaiian or other Pacific Islander, non-Hispanic/Latino; 7 Two or more races, non-Hispanic/Latino), 15 international. Average age 30. 351 applicants, 75% accepted, 204 enrolled. In 2018, 156 master's, 48 other advanced degrees awarded. *Degree requirements:* For master's, Research project; for AC, Field-based research project. *Entrance requirements:* For master's, GRE General Test, minimum undergraduate cumulative GPA of 3.00; for AC, GRE General Test (required for all MAT and other graduate programs leading to NYS initial teacher certification), NYS initial teacher certification in the appropriate certification area is required for admission into MSEd programs. Additional exam requirements/recommendations for international students: Required—TOEFL (minimum score 575 paper-based; 90 iBT). *Application deadline:* For fall admission, 4/1 for domestic students. Applications are processed on a rolling basis. Application fee: $125. Electronic applications accepted. *Financial support:* Career-related internships or fieldwork and Federal Work-Study available. Financial award application deadline: 4/1; financial award applicants required to submit FAFSA. *Faculty research:* Biliteracy, computational thinking, social justice education, technology in early childhood education, children from immigrant families. *Unit head:* Daisuke Akiba, Chair, 718-997-5300, E-mail: daisuke.akiba@qc.cuny.edu. *Application contact:* Elizabeth D'Amico-Ramirez, Assistant Director of Graduate Admissions, 718-997-5203, E-mail: elizabeth.damicoramirez@qc.cuny.edu.

Quincy University, Master of Science in Education Programs, Quincy, IL 62301-2699. Offers curriculum and instruction (MS Ed), including bilingual/English as a second language; education studies (MS Ed); leadership (MS Ed); reading education (MS Ed); teacher leader (MS Ed). *Program availability:* Part-time, evening/weekend, online learning. *Degree requirements:* For master's, comprehensive exam (for some programs), thesis optional. *Entrance requirements:* For master's, MAT or GRE, personal resume. Additional exam requirements/recommendations for international students: Required—TOEFL (minimum score 550 paper-based; 79 iBT). Electronic applications accepted. Application fee is waived when completed online.

Rider University, College of Education and Human Services, Program in Teaching, Lawrenceville, NJ 08648-3001. Offers bilingual education (MAT); early childhood education (MAT); elementary education (MAT); English as a second language (MAT); secondary education (MAT); world language (MAT). *Students:* 35 full-time (26 women), 88 part-time (67 women); includes 12 minority (1 Black or African American, non-Hispanic/Latino; 1 American Indian or Alaska Native, non-Hispanic/Latino; 2 Asian, non-Hispanic/Latino; 8 Hispanic/Latino). Average age 34. 104 applicants, 67% accepted, 54 enrolled. In 2018, 70 master's awarded. *Entrance requirements:* For master's, Praxis exams, resume,application fee, statement of aims and objectives, official prior college transcripts, interview. Additional exam requirements/recommendations for international students: Required—TOEFL (minimum score 540 paper-based; 79 iBT). *Application deadline:* For fall admission, 5/1 priority date for domestic students, 6/1 priority date for international students; for spring admission, 12/1 priority date for domestic students, 11/1 priority date for international students. Applications are processed on a rolling basis. Application fee: $50. Electronic applications accepted. *Expenses: Tuition:* Full-time $850; part-time $850 per credit hour. *Required fees:* $50; $50 per course. Tuition and fees vary according to program. *Financial support:* Applicants required to submit FAFSA. *Unit head:* Kathleen Pierce, Professor, 609-895-5478, E-mail: kpierce@rider.edu. *Application contact:* Jamie L Mitchell, Director of Graduate Admissions, 609-896-5036, Fax: 609-895-5680, E-mail: jmitchell@rider.edu.

Rutgers University–New Brunswick, Graduate School-New Brunswick, Program in Spanish, Piscataway, NJ 08854-8097. Offers bilingualism and second language acquisition (MA, PhD); Spanish (MA, MAT, PhD); Spanish literature (MA, PhD); translation (MA). *Program availability:* Part-time. *Degree requirements:* For master's, comprehensive exam (for some programs), thesis (for some programs); for doctorate, 2 foreign languages, comprehensive exam, thesis/dissertation. *Entrance requirements:* For master's and doctorate, GRE General Test. Additional exam requirements/recommendations for international students: Required—TOEFL. Electronic applications accepted. *Faculty research:* Hispanic literature, Luso-Brazilian literature, Spanish linguistics, Spanish translation.

St. John's University, The School of Education, Department of Education Specialties, Program in Teaching English to Speakers of Other Languages and Bilingual Education, Queens, NY 11439. Offers bilingual education (Adv C); childhood education and teaching English to speakers of other languages (MS Ed); teaching English to speakers of other languages (MS Ed, Adv C). *Degree requirements:* For Adv C, one foreign language. *Entrance requirements:* For master's, GRE, MAT, or PRAXIS, statement of goals (personal essay), official undergraduate transcripts, initial teaching certification; for Adv C, initial teaching certification, first master's transcripts, statement of purpose. Additional exam requirements/recommendations for international students: Required—TOEFL, IELTS. Electronic applications accepted. *Faculty research:* Second language learning and academic achievement, heritage language education, assessing the progress of English language learners toward English acquisition, dual language acquisition, study of English Creoles and dialects of other English's, literacy development for ESL learners; investigating Caribbean and Creole language and culture, education law.

San Diego State University, Graduate and Research Affairs, College of Education, Department of Policy Studies in Language and Cross Cultural Education, San Diego, CA 92182. Offers multi-cultural emphasis (PhD); policy studies in language and cross cultural education (MA). *Accreditation:* NCATE. *Entrance requirements:* For master's, GRE General Test, letters of reference; for doctorate, GRE General Test, 3 letters of reference, resumé. Additional exam requirements/recommendations for international students: Required—TOEFL. Electronic applications accepted.

Southern Connecticut State University, School of Graduate Studies, School of Arts and Sciences, Department of World Languages and Literatures, New Haven, CT 06515-1355. Offers multicultural-bilingual education/teaching English to speakers of other languages (MS); romance languages (MA). *Program availability:* Part-time, evening/weekend. *Degree requirements:* For master's, one foreign language, thesis or alternative. *Entrance requirements:* For master's, interview, minimum undergraduate GPA of 2.7. Electronic applications accepted.

Southern Methodist University, Simmons School of Education and Human Development, Department of Teaching and Learning, Dallas, TX 75275. Offers bilingual education (MBE); education (M Ed, PhD); English as a second language (M Ed); gifted and talented (M Ed); literacy studies (M Ed); special education (M Ed). *Program availability:* Part-time, evening/weekend. Terminal master's awarded for partial completion of doctoral program. *Degree requirements:* For master's, comprehensive exam, minimum GPA of 3.0; for doctorate, thesis/dissertation, qualifying exams, major area paper, evidence of teaching competency, dissemination of research (e.g., conference presentation), professional portfolio. *Entrance requirements:* For master's, minimum GPA of 3.0 or GRE, 3 letters of recommendation; for doctorate, GRE, minimum GPA of 3.3, 3 years of full-time teaching, 3 letters of recommendation, interview. Additional exam requirements/recommendations for international students: Required—TOEFL. Electronic applications accepted. *Faculty research:* Reading intervention, mathematics intervention, bilingual education, new literacies.

State University of New York at New Paltz, Graduate and Extended Learning School, School of Education, Program of Educational Administration, Program in Humanistic/Multicultural Education, New Paltz, NY 12561. Offers humanistic/multicultural education (MPS); multicultural education (AC). *Accreditation:* NCATE. *Program availability:* Part-time, evening/weekend. *Faculty:* 4 full-time (3 women), 1 (woman) part-time/adjunct. *Students:* 2 full-time (both women), 32 part-time (25 women); includes 11 minority (4 Black or African American, non-Hispanic/Latino; 7 Hispanic/Latino). 7 applicants, 86% accepted, 5 enrolled. In 2018, 12 master's awarded. *Entrance requirements:* For master's, minimum GPA of 3.0. Additional exam requirements/recommendations for international students: Required—TOEFL (minimum score 550 paper-based; 80 iBT), IELTS (minimum score 6.5). *Application deadline:* For fall admission, 4/15 priority date for domestic students, 4/15 for international students; for spring admission, 10/15 for domestic and international students. Application fee: $50. Electronic applications accepted. *Financial support:* Unspecified assistantships available. Financial award application deadline: 8/1. *Unit head:* Dr. Shannon McManimon, Coordinator, 845-257-2828, E-mail: mcmanims@newpaltz.edu. *Application contact:* Vika Shock, Director of Graduate Admissions, 845-257-3286, E-mail: gradstudies@newpaltz.edu.
Website: http://www.newpaltz.edu/edstudies/humanistic.html

Multilingual and Multicultural Education

State University of New York College at Geneseo, Graduate Studies, School of Education, Program in Childhood Multicultural Education, Geneseo, NY 14454-1401. Offers MS Ed. *Program availability:* Part-time, evening/weekend. *Degree requirements:* For master's, culminating experience: thesis or research project. *Entrance requirements:* For master's, GRE, MAT, EAS, edTPA, PRAXIS, or another substantially equivalent test, proof of New York State initial certification or equivalent certification from another state. Additional exam requirements/recommendations for international students: Required—TOEFL (minimum score 525 paper-based; 71 iBT), IELTS (minimum score 6.5), PTE, iTEP. Electronic applications accepted. *Expenses:* Contact institution.

Sul Ross State University, Rio Grande College of Sul Ross State University, Alpine, TX 79832. Offers business administration (MBA); teacher education (M Ed), including bilingual education, counseling, educational diagnostics, elementary education, general education, reading, school administration, secondary education. *Program availability:* Part-time, evening/weekend, online learning. *Degree requirements:* For master's, comprehensive exam, thesis optional, minimum GPA of 3.0. *Entrance requirements:* For master's, GMAT or GRE General Test, minimum GPA of 2.5 in last 60 hours of undergraduate work. Additional exam requirements/recommendations for international students: Required—TOEFL.

Teachers College, Columbia University, Department of Arts and Humanities, New York, NY 10027. Offers applied linguistics (MA, Ed D); art and art education (Ed M, MA, Ed D, Ed DCT); arts administration (MA); bilingual and bicultural education (MA); global competence (Certificate); history and education (Ed D, PhD); music and music education (Ed DCT); philosophy and education (MA, Ed D, PhD); social studies education (Ed M, PhD); teaching English to speakers of other languages (Ed M); teaching of English and English education (Ed M, MA, Ed D, PhD), including English education (Ed M, Ed D, PhD), teaching of English (MA); teaching of social studies (MA); TESOL (MA, Ed D). *Program availability:* Part-time, evening/weekend. *Students:* 267 full-time (216 women), 569 part-time (400 women); includes 235 minority (62 Black or African American, non-Hispanic/Latino; 2 American Indian or Alaska Native, non-Hispanic/Latino; 88 Asian, non-Hispanic/Latino; 69 Hispanic/Latino; 14 Two or more races, non-Hispanic/Latino), 229 international. Average age 31. 1,075 applicants, 56% accepted, 342 enrolled. Terminal master's awarded for partial completion of doctoral program. *Financial support:* Fellowships, research assistantships, teaching assistantships, career-related internships or fieldwork, Federal Work-Study, institutionally sponsored loans, tuition waivers (full and partial), and unspecified assistantships available. Support available to part-time students. *Unit head:* Prof. ZhaoHong Han, Department Chair, E-mail: zhh2@tc.columbia.edu. *Application contact:* Kelly Sutton-Skinner, Director of Admissions & New Student Enrollment, E-mail: kms2237@tc.columbia.edu.

Texas A&M University, College of Education and Human Development, Department of Educational Psychology, College Station, TX 77843. Offers bilingual education (M Ed, MS); counseling psychology (PhD); educational psychology (M Ed, MS, PhD); educational technology (M Ed); school psychology (PhD); special education (M Ed, MS). *Accreditation:* APA (one or more programs are accredited). *Program availability:* Part-time, evening/weekend, blended/hybrid learning. *Faculty:* 47. *Students:* 146 full-time (118 women), 244 part-time (204 women); includes 146 minority (22 Black or African American, non-Hispanic/Latino; 2 American Indian or Alaska Native, non-Hispanic/Latino; 18 Asian, non-Hispanic/Latino; 92 Hispanic/Latino; 1 Native Hawaiian or other Pacific Islander, non-Hispanic/Latino; 11 Two or more races, non-Hispanic/Latino), 50 international. Average age 33. 142 applicants, 50% accepted, 49 enrolled. In 2018, 152 master's, 23 doctorates awarded. *Degree requirements:* For master's, thesis optional; for doctorate, thesis/dissertation. *Entrance requirements:* For master's and doctorate, GRE General Test. Additional exam requirements/recommendations for international students: Required—TOEFL (minimum score 550 paper-based; 80 iBT), IELTS (minimum score 6), PTE (minimum score 53). *Application deadline:* For fall admission, 12/1 for domestic students; for spring admission, 10/15 for domestic students. Application fee: $50 ($90 for international students). Electronic applications accepted. *Expenses:* Contact institution. *Financial support:* In 2018–19, 125 students received support, including 3 fellowships with tuition reimbursements available (averaging $19,520 per year), 106 research assistantships with tuition reimbursements available (averaging $15,181 per year), 19 teaching assistantships with tuition reimbursements available (averaging $9,322 per year); career-related internships or fieldwork, institutionally sponsored loans, scholarships/grants, traineeships, health care benefits, tuition waivers (full and partial), and unspecified assistantships also available. Support available to part-time students. Financial award application deadline: 3/15; financial award applicants required to submit FAFSA. *Unit head:* Dr. Victor Willson, Department Head, 979-845-1394, E-mail: v-willson@tamu.edu. *Application contact:* Kristie Stramaski, Senior Academic Advisor, 979-845-1833, E-mail: epsyadvisor@tamu.edu.
Website: http://epsy.tamu.edu

Texas A&M University–Kingsville, College of Graduate Studies, College of Education and Human Performance, Department of Teacher and Bilingual Education, Program in Bilingual Education, Kingsville, TX 78363. Offers M Ed, Ed D. *Degree requirements:* For master's, comprehensive exam. *Entrance requirements:* For master's, GRE General Test, MAT, minimum GPA of 3.0.

Texas A&M University–San Antonio, Department of Educator and Leadership Preparation, San Antonio, TX 78224. Offers bilingual education (MS); early childhood education (M Ed); educational administration (MA); reading specialization (MS); special education (M Ed), including educational diagnostician. *Program availability:* Part-time, evening/weekend, online learning. *Degree requirements:* For master's, comprehensive exam, thesis or alternative. *Entrance requirements:* For master's, GRE (Quantitative and Verbal) or MAT. Additional exam requirements/recommendations for international students: Required—TOEFL (minimum score 550 paper-based; 79 iBT), IELTS (minimum score 6). Electronic applications accepted. *Faculty research:* Equity in education, biliteracy practices among Latina and immigrants, academic achievement of low socio-economic students, equity practices in instruction and educational leadership in diverse settings, racial identity development and multicultural education.

Texas Southern University, College of Education, Area of Curriculum and Instruction, Houston, TX 77004-4584. Offers bilingual education (M Ed); curriculum and instruction (Ed D); secondary education (M Ed). *Program availability:* Part-time, evening/weekend. *Degree requirements:* For master's, comprehensive exam; for doctorate, comprehensive exam, thesis/dissertation. *Entrance requirements:* For master's, GRE General Test, minimum GPA of 2.5; for doctorate, GRE General Test or MAT, master's degree, minimum B+ average. Additional exam requirements/recommendations for international students: Required—TOEFL. Electronic applications accepted.

Texas State University, The Graduate College, College of Education, Program in Elementary Education - Bilingual/Bicultural, San Marcos, TX 78666. Offers M Ed, MA. *Program availability:* Part-time. *Faculty:* 5 full-time (4 women), 1 (woman) part-time/adjunct. *Students:* 5 part-time (all women); all minorities (all Hispanic/Latino). Average age 36. 2 applicants, 50% accepted, 1 enrolled. In 2018, 3 master's awarded. *Degree requirements:* For master's, comprehensive exam, thesis (for some programs). *Entrance requirements:* For master's, baccalaureate degree from regionally-accredited institution with minimum GPA of 2.75 in last 60 hours of course work; meeting with bilingual coordinator to ensure proficiency in written and spoken Spanish; statement of purpose; three letters of recommendation. Additional exam requirements/recommendations for international students: Required—TOEFL (minimum score 550 paper-based; 78 iBT), IELTS (minimum score 6.5). *Application deadline:* For fall admission, 2/1 priority date for domestic and international students; for spring admission, 10/15 for domestic students, 10/1 for international students; for summer admission, 4/15 for domestic students, 3/15 for international students. Applications are processed on a rolling basis. Application fee: $55 ($90 for international students). Electronic applications accepted. *Expenses:* Tuition, state resident: full-time $8102; part-time $4051 per semester. Tuition, nonresident: full-time $18,229; part-time $9115 per semester. *International tuition:* $18,229 full-time. *Required fees:* $2116; $120 per credit hour. Tuition and fees vary according to course load. *Financial support:* Research assistantships, teaching assistantships, career-related internships or fieldwork, Federal Work-Study, institutionally sponsored loans, scholarships/grants, and unspecified assistantships available. Support available to part-time students. Financial award application deadline: 1/15; financial award applicants required to submit FAFSA. *Faculty research:* Examining five problem solving process skills in subtraction in limited English proficient students; Expanding research approaches in underserved communities; Transformative Learning In Living and Working Abroad. *Unit head:* Dr. Charise Pimentel, Graduate Advisor, 512-245-3678, Fax: 512-245-7911, E-mail: cp26@txstate.edu. *Application contact:* Dr. Andrea Golato, Dean of Graduate School, 512-245-2581, Fax: 512-245-8365, E-mail: gradcollege@txstate.edu.
Website: http://www.gradcollege.txstate.edu/programs/bilingual-bicultural.html

Texas Tech University, Graduate School, College of Education, Department of Curriculum and Instruction, Lubbock, TX 79409-1071. Offers bilingual education (M Ed); curriculum and instruction (M Ed, PhD); elementary education (M Ed); language/literacy education (M Ed); multidisciplinary science (MS); secondary education (M Ed). *Accreditation:* NCATE. *Program availability:* Part-time, evening/weekend, online learning. *Faculty:* 17 full-time (11 women), 1 (woman) part-time/adjunct. *Students:* 48 full-time (41 women), 265 part-time (220 women); includes 103 minority (25 Black or African American, non-Hispanic/Latino; 9 Asian, non-Hispanic/Latino; 64 Hispanic/Latino; 5 Two or more races, non-Hispanic/Latino), 27 international. Average age 40. 101 applicants, 65% accepted, 51 enrolled. In 2018, 26 master's, 21 doctorates awarded. Terminal master's awarded for partial completion of doctoral program. *Degree requirements:* For master's, comprehensive exam (for some programs), thesis optional; for doctorate, comprehensive exam, thesis/dissertation. *Entrance requirements:* For master's, bachelor's degree; resume; letter of intent; academic writing sample; 2 letters of recommendation; for doctorate, GRE, master's degree; resume; letter of intent; academic writing sample; 3 letters of recommendation. Additional exam requirements/recommendations for international students: Required—TOEFL (minimum score 550 paper-based; 79 iBT). *Application deadline:* For fall admission, 6/1 priority date for domestic students, 1/15 priority date for international students; for spring admission, 9/1 priority date for domestic students, 6/15 priority date for international students. Applications are processed on a rolling basis. Application fee: $65. Electronic applications accepted. *Expenses:* Contact institution. *Financial support:* In 2018–19, 142 students received support, including 136 fellowships (averaging $2,895 per year), 28 research assistantships (averaging $12,296 per year), 7 teaching assistantships (averaging $14,175 per year); Federal Work-Study, institutionally sponsored loans, scholarships/grants, health care benefits, and unspecified assistantships also available. Support available to part-time students. Financial award application deadline: 2/1; financial award applicants required to submit FAFSA. *Faculty research:* Teacher education, curriculum studies, bilingual education, science and math education, language and literacy education. *Total annual research expenditures:* $79,025. *Unit head:* Dr. Jerry Dwyer, Professor, Interim Department Chair, 806-834-7399, Fax: 806-742-2179, E-mail: jerry.dwyer@ttu.edu. *Application contact:* Brandi Stephens, Graduate Academic Advisor, 806-834-4554, Fax: 806-742-2179, E-mail: brandi.stephens@ttu.edu.
Website: www.educ.ttu.edu

University at Buffalo, the State University of New York, Graduate School, Graduate School of Education, Department of Learning and Instruction, Buffalo, NY 14260. Offers biology education (Ed M, Certificate); chemistry education (Ed M, Certificate); childhood education (Ed M); childhood education with bilingual extension (Ed M); college teaching (Advanced Certificate); curriculum, instruction and the science of learning (PhD); early childhood education (Ed M); early childhood education with bilingual extension (Ed M); earth science education (Ed M, Certificate); education and technology (Ed M); education studies (Ed M); educational technology and new literacies (Certificate); educational technology and new literacies (Advanced Certificate); elementary education (Ed D); English education (Ed M, Certificate); English education studies (Ed M); English for speakers of other languages (Ed M); foreign and second language education (PhD); French education (Ed M, Certificate); German education (Ed M, Certificate); gifted education (Certificate); Latin education (Ed M, Certificate); literacy education studies (Ed M); literacy specialist (Ed M); literacy teaching and learning (Certificate); mathematics education (Ed M, Certificate); music education (Ed M, Certificate); music education studies (Ed M); music learning theory (Advanced Certificate); online education (Advanced Certificate); physics education (Ed M, Certificate); science and the public (Ed M); social studies education (Ed M, Certificate); Spanish education (Ed M, Certificate); special education (PhD); teaching English to speakers of other languages (Ed M). *Program availability:* Part-time, evening/weekend, 100% online. *Faculty:* 31 full-time (22 women), 41 part-time/adjunct (27 women). *Students:* 161 full-time (107 women), 369 part-time (260 women); includes 76 minority (26 Black or African American, non-Hispanic/Latino; 3 American Indian or Alaska Native, non-Hispanic/Latino; 30 Asian, non-Hispanic/Latino; 14 Hispanic/Latino; 3 Two or more races, non-Hispanic/Latino), 41 international. Average age 34. 368 applicants, 70% accepted, 179 enrolled. In 2018, 100 master's, 26 doctorates, 19 other advanced degrees awarded. *Degree requirements:* For master's, comprehensive exam; for doctorate, thesis/dissertation, research analysis exam, research experience. *Entrance requirements:* For master's, letters of reference; for doctorate, GRE General Test or MAT, interview, writing sample, letters of recommendation. Additional exam requirements/recommendations for international students: Required—TOEFL (minimum score 600 paper-based; 96 iBT), IELTS (minimum score 6.5), PTE (minimum score 55). *Application deadline:* For fall admission, 2/1 priority date for domestic and international students; for spring admission, 11/15 priority date for domestic students, 10/1 for international students. Applications are processed on a rolling basis. Application fee: $50. Electronic applications accepted. *Financial support:* In 2018–19, 42 fellowships (averaging $5,181 per year), 44 research assistantships with tuition reimbursements (averaging $10,908 per year) were awarded; teaching assistantships, career-related internships or fieldwork, Federal Work-Study, institutionally sponsored loans, scholarships/grants, tuition waivers (full and partial), and unspecified assistantships also available. Financial award application deadline: 2/28; financial award applicants required to submit FAFSA. *Faculty research:* Science assessment, foreign language teaching and learning, early learning, new literacies, gender and education. *Total annual research expenditures:* $413,233. *Unit head:* Dr. Julie Gorlewski, Department Chair, 716-645-2455, Fax: 716-645-3161, E-mail: jgorlews@buffalo.edu. *Application contact:* Renad Aref, Assistant Director of Admission Recruitment, 716-645-2110, Fax: 716-645-7937, E-mail: gseinfo@buffalo.edu.
Website: http://ed.buffalo.edu/teaching.html

University of Alaska Fairbanks, College of Liberal Arts, Center for Cross-Cultural Studies, Fairbanks, AK 99775-6300. Offers MA. *Program availability:* Part-time. *Faculty:* 4 full-time (2 women). *Students:* 2 full-time (both women), 2 part-time (1 woman); includes 2 minority (both American Indian or Alaska Native, non-Hispanic/Latino). Average age 38. 4 applicants, 75% accepted, 2 enrolled. In 2018, 1 master's awarded. *Degree requirements:* For master's, comprehensive exam, project, oral defense of project. *Entrance requirements:* For master's, bachelor's degree from accredited institution with minimum cumulative undergraduate and major GPA of 3.0. Additional exam requirements/recommendations for international students: Required—TOEFL (minimum score 550 paper-based; 79 iBT), IELTS (minimum score 8.5). *Application deadline:* For fall admission, 3/1 for domestic and international students; for spring admission, 9/1 for domestic and international students. Applications are processed on a rolling basis. Application fee: $60. Electronic applications accepted. *Expenses: Tuition, area resident:* Full-time $8802; part-time $5868 per credit hour. Tuition, state resident: full-time $8802; part-time $5868 per credit hour. Tuition, nonresident: full-time $18,504; part-time $12,336 per credit hour. *International tuition:* $18,504 full-time. *Required fees:* $1416; $944 per credit hour. $472 per semester. Tuition and fees vary according to course load and program. *Financial support:* In 2018–19, 1 teaching assistantship with full tuition reimbursement (averaging $5,034 per year) was awarded; fellowships with full tuition reimbursements, research assistantships with full tuition reimbursements, Federal Work-Study, scholarships/grants, health care benefits, and unspecified assistantships also available. Support available to part-time students. Financial award application deadline: 7/1; financial award applicants required to submit FAFSA. *Faculty research:* Alaska native literature, oral traditions, history, law and policy, cultures, art; Native American religion and philosophy. *Unit head:* Michael Koskey, Department Chair, 907-474-1902, E-mail: uaf-cxcs@alaska.edu. *Application contact:* Samara Taber, Director of Admissions, 907-474-7500, E-mail: uaf-admissions@alaska.edu.
Website: http://www.uaf.edu/cxcs

University of Alaska Fairbanks, College of Liberal Arts, Program in Linguistics, Fairbanks, AK 99775-6280. Offers applied linguistics (MA), including language documentation, second language acquisition teacher education. *Program availability:* Part-time, 100% online, blended/hybrid learning. *Faculty:* 2 full-time (both women). *Students:* 5 full-time (2 women), 15 part-time (14 women); includes 5 minority (all American Indian or Alaska Native, non-Hispanic/Latino), 1 international. Average age 35. 10 applicants, 50% accepted, 3 enrolled. In 2018, 1 master's awarded. Terminal master's awarded for partial completion of doctoral program. *Degree requirements:* For master's, one foreign language, comprehensive exam, oral defense of project or thesis. *Entrance requirements:* For master's, bachelor's degree from accredited institution with minimum cumulative undergraduate and major GPA of 3.0. Additional exam requirements/recommendations for international students: Required—TOEFL (minimum score 550 paper-based; 79 iBT), IELTS (minimum score 6.5). *Application deadline:* For fall admission, 6/1 for domestic students, 3/1 for international students; for spring admission, 10/15 for domestic students, 9/1 for international students. Applications are processed on a rolling basis. Application fee: $60. Electronic applications accepted. *Expenses: Tuition, area resident:* Full-time $8802; part-time $5868 per credit hour. Tuition, state resident: full-time $8802; part-time $5868 per credit hour. Tuition, nonresident: full-time $18,504; part-time $12,336 per credit hour. *International tuition:* $18,504 full-time. *Required fees:* $1416; $944 per credit hour. $472 per semester. Tuition and fees vary according to course load and program. *Financial support:* In 2018–19, 5 teaching assistantships with full tuition reimbursements (averaging $5,559 per year) were awarded; fellowships with full tuition reimbursements, research assistantships with full tuition reimbursements, career-related internships or fieldwork, Federal Work-Study, scholarships/grants, health care benefits, and unspecified assistantships also available. Support available to part-time students. Financial award application deadline: 2/15; financial award applicants required to submit FAFSA. *Faculty research:* Second language acquisition/teaching, Alaska Native languages, language documentation, language policy and planning, language maintenance and shift, phonology, morphology, historical linguistics. *Unit head:* Dr. Patrick Marlow, Program Chair, 907-474-7876, E-mail: uaf-ling@alaska.edu. *Application contact:* Samara Taber, Director of Admissions, 907-474-7500, E-mail: uaf-admissions@alaska.edu.
Website: http://www.uaf.edu/linguist/

University of Alberta, Faculty of Graduate Studies and Research, Facultè Saint Jean, Edmonton, AB T6G 2E1, Canada. Offers M Ed. *Program availability:* Part-time, evening/weekend, online learning. *Degree requirements:* For master's, thesis (for some programs). *Entrance requirements:* For master's, proficiency in French, 2 years of teaching experience. *Faculty research:* First and second language acquisition, first and second language learning through subject matter, cultural transmission.

University of Calgary, Faculty of Graduate Studies, Werklund School of Education, Program in Educational Research, Calgary, AB T2N 1N4, Canada. Offers adult learning (M Ed, MA, Ed D, PhD); curriculum and learning (M Ed, MA, Ed D, PhD); educational leadership (M Ed, MA, Ed D, PhD); languages and diversity (M Ed, MA, Ed D, PhD); learning sciences (M Ed, MA, Ed D, PhD). Ed D in educational leadership offered via distance delivery. *Program availability:* Part-time, evening/weekend, online learning. *Degree requirements:* For master's, thesis (for some programs); for doctorate, thesis/dissertation, candidacy exam. *Entrance requirements:* For master's, minimum GPA of 3.0, 3 letters of reference; for doctorate, minimum GPA of 3.5, 3 letters of reference. Additional exam requirements/recommendations for international students: Required—TOEFL, IELTS. Electronic applications accepted. *Faculty research:* Curriculum, leadership, technology, contexts, gifted, second language teaching, work place and adult learning.

University of California, Riverside, Graduate Division, Graduate School of Education, Riverside, CA 92521. Offers applied behavior analysis (M Ed); diversity and equity (M Ed); education policy analysis and leadership (PhD); education specialist (Credential); education, society, and culture (MA, PhD); educational psychology (MA, PhD); general education (M Ed); higher education administration and policy (M Ed, PhD); multiple subject (Credential); research, evaluation, measurement and statistics (MA); school psychology (PhD); single subject (Credential); special education (M Ed, PhD); special education and autism (MA); TESOL (M Ed). Terminal master's awarded for partial completion of doctoral program. *Degree requirements:* For master's, comprehensive exams or thesis (MA), case study or analytical report (M Ed); for doctorate, comprehensive exam, thesis/dissertation, written and oral qualifying exams, college teaching practicum. *Entrance requirements:* For master's, GRE General Test (for MA); CBEST and CSET (for M Ed in general education only), UCR Extension TESOL certificate (for M Ed with TESOL emphasis only); for doctorate, GRE General Test, writing sample; for Credential, CBEST, CSET. Additional exam requirements/recommendations for international students: Required—TOEFL (minimum score 550 paper-based; 80 iBT), IELTS (minimum score 7). Electronic applications accepted. *Faculty research:* Responsiveness to intervention, faculty core, response to intervention of English language learners, advanced modeling techniques, study on social capital, trust, and motivation.

University of California, San Diego, Graduate Division, Program in Education Studies, La Jolla, CA 92093. Offers education (M Ed, PhD); educational leadership (Ed D); teaching and learning (MA, Ed D), including bilingual education (MA), curriculum design (MA). Ed D offered jointly with California State University, San Marcos. *Students:* 100 full-time (78 women), 61 part-time (41 women). 262 applicants, 54% accepted, 81 enrolled. In 2018, 75 master's, 15 doctorates awarded. *Degree requirements:* For master's, thesis (for some programs), student teaching; for doctorate, comprehensive exam, thesis/dissertation. *Entrance requirements:* For master's, GRE General Test; CBEST and appropriate CSET exam (for select tracks), current teaching or educational assignment (for select tracks); for doctorate, GRE General Test, current teaching or educational assignment (for select tracks). Additional exam requirements/recommendations for international students: Required—TOEFL (minimum score 550 paper-based; 80 iBT), IELTS (minimum score 7). *Application deadline:* For fall admission, 12/6 for domestic students. Application fee: $105 ($125 for international students). Electronic applications accepted. *Financial support:* Fellowships, career-related internships or fieldwork, and scholarships/grants available. Financial award applicants required to submit FAFSA. *Faculty research:* Language, culture and literacy development of deaf/hard of hearing children; equity issues in education; educational reform; evaluation, assessment, and research methodologies; distributed learning. *Unit head:* Carolyn Hofstetter, Chair, 858-822-6688, E-mail: ajdaly@ucsd.edu. *Application contact:* Giselle Van Luit, Graduate Coordinator, 858-534-2958, E-mail: edsinfo@ucsd.edu.

University of Colorado Boulder, Graduate School, School of Education, Division of Social Multicultural and Bilingual Foundations, Boulder, CO 80309. Offers educational equity and cultural diversity (PhD); multicultural education (MA). *Accreditation:* NCATE. Terminal master's awarded for partial completion of doctoral program. *Degree requirements:* For master's, comprehensive exam, thesis or alternative; for doctorate, one foreign language, comprehensive exam, thesis/dissertation. *Entrance requirements:* For master's, GRE General Test or MAT, minimum undergraduate GPA of 2.75; for doctorate, GRE General Test. Electronic applications accepted. Application fee is waived when completed online.

University of Colorado Denver, School of Education and Human Development, Teacher Education Programs, Denver, CO 80217. Offers elementary linguistically diverse education (MA); elementary math and science education (MA); elementary math education (MA); elementary reading and writing (MA); elementary science education (MA); secondary English education (MA); secondary linguistically diverse education (MA); secondary math education (MA); secondary reading and writing (MA); secondary science education (MA); special education (MA). *Accreditation:* NCATE. *Program availability:* Part-time, evening/weekend. *Degree requirements:* For master's, comprehensive exam. *Entrance requirements:* For master's, GRE or MAT (for those with GPA below 2.75), transcripts, resume, letters of recommendation. Additional exam requirements/recommendations for international students: Required—TOEFL (minimum score 537 paper-based; 75 iBT); Recommended—IELTS (minimum score 6.5). Electronic applications accepted. *Expenses:* Tuition, state resident: full-time $6786; part-time $337 per credit hour. Tuition, nonresident: full-time $22,590; part-time $1255 per credit hour. *Required fees:* $1231; $137 per credit hour. Tuition and fees vary according to program and reciprocity agreements. *Faculty research:* Linguistically diverse education/ESL, elementary reading and writing, elementary teacher education, secondary teacher education, special education.

University of Connecticut, Graduate School, Neag School of Education, Department of Curriculum and Instruction, Program in Bilingual and Bicultural Education, Storrs, CT 06269. Offers MA, PhD. *Accreditation:* NCATE. Terminal master's awarded for partial completion of doctoral program. *Degree requirements:* For master's, comprehensive exam; for doctorate, thesis/dissertation. *Entrance requirements:* For doctorate, GRE General Test. Additional exam requirements/recommendations for international students: Required—TOEFL (minimum score 550 paper-based). Electronic applications accepted.

University of Delaware, College of Education and Human Development, School of Education, Newark, DE 19716. Offers education (PhD); educational leadership (Ed D); higher education (M Ed); instruction (MI); reading (M Ed); school leadership (M Ed); school psychology (MA, Ed S); teaching English as a second language (TESL) (MA). *Accreditation:* NCATE. *Program availability:* Part-time, evening/weekend. Terminal master's awarded for partial completion of doctoral program. *Degree requirements:* For master's, comprehensive exam (for some programs), thesis (for some programs); for doctorate, comprehensive exam (for some programs), thesis/dissertation. *Entrance requirements:* For master's and doctorate, GRE, 3 letters of recommendation. Additional exam requirements/recommendations for international students: Required—TOEFL (minimum score 600 paper-based). Electronic applications accepted. *Faculty research:* Teacher education; curriculum theory and development; community based education models, educational leadership.

University of Houston–Clear Lake, School of Education, Program in Foundations and Professional Studies, Houston, TX 77058-1002. Offers counseling (MS); instructional technology (MS); multicultural studies (MS). *Program availability:* Part-time, evening/weekend. *Degree requirements:* For master's, thesis optional. *Entrance requirements:* For master's, GRE or minimum GPA of 3.0 in last 60 hours. Additional exam requirements/recommendations for international students: Required—TOEFL (minimum score 550 paper-based). Electronic applications accepted.

University of Maryland, Baltimore County, The Graduate School, College of Arts, Humanities and Social Sciences, Department of Modern Languages, Linguistics and Intercultural Communication, Program in Intercultural Communication, Baltimore, MD 21250. Offers MA. *Program availability:* Part-time, evening/weekend. *Degree requirements:* For master's, one foreign language, comprehensive exam (for some programs), thesis (for some programs). *Entrance requirements:* For master's, GRE General Test, minimum GPA of 3.0, 3 letters of recommendation, self-evaluation and statement of support, resume, writing sample in modern language. Additional exam requirements/recommendations for international students: Required—TOEFL (minimum score 550 paper-based, 80 iBT) or IELTS. Electronic applications accepted. *Expenses:* Contact institution. *Faculty research:* Comparative television research-cross-cultural; cultural studies; social developments in Latin America; intercultural communication; French civilization and cultural studies; language, gender and sexuality; sociolinguistics; African linguistics; immigrants in U.S. and Latin American societies.

University of Maryland, Baltimore County, The Graduate School, College of Arts, Humanities and Social Sciences, Program in Language, Literacy, and Culture, Baltimore, MD 21250. Offers PhD. *Program availability:* Part-time, evening/weekend. *Degree requirements:* For doctorate, comprehensive exam, thesis/dissertation. *Entrance requirements:* For doctorate, research writing sample; resume or curriculum vitae; master's degree; 3 letters of recommendation. Additional exam requirements/recommendations for international students: Required—TOEFL (minimum score 80 iBT). Electronic applications accepted. *Faculty research:* Educational equity, identity, intercultural communication, technology and communication, workplace diversity.

University of Massachusetts Amherst, Graduate School, College of Education, Program in Education, Amherst, MA 01003. Offers bilingual, English as a second language, and multicultural education (M Ed, Ed S); child study and early education (M Ed); children, families and schools (Ed D, Ed S); early childhood and elementary teacher education (M Ed); educational leadership (M Ed); educational policy and

leadership (Ed D); higher education (M Ed); international education (M Ed); language, literacy and culture (Ed D); learning, media and technology (M Ed, Ed S); mathematics, science, and learning technologies (Ed D); reading and writing (M Ed); research, educational measurement and psychometrics (Ed D); school counselor education (M Ed, Ed S); school psychology (Ed S); science education (Ed S); secondary teacher education (M Ed); social justice education (M Ed, Ed D, Ed S); special education (M Ed, Ed D, Ed S); teacher education and school improvement (Ed D, Ed S). *Accreditation:* NCATE. *Program availability:* Part-time, online learning. Terminal master's awarded for partial completion of doctoral program. *Degree requirements:* For doctorate, comprehensive exam, thesis/dissertation. *Entrance requirements:* Additional exam requirements/recommendations for international students: Required—TOEFL (minimum score 550 paper-based; 80 iBT), IELTS (minimum score 6.5). Electronic applications accepted.

University of Miami, Graduate School, School of Education and Human Development, Department of Teaching and Learning, Program in Teaching and Learning, Coral Gables, FL 33124. Offers language and literacy learning in multilingual settings (PhD); science, technology, engineering and mathematics (stem) (PhD); special education (PhD). *Faculty:* 14 full-time (10 women), 9 part-time/adjunct (all women). *Students:* 18 full-time (12 women); includes 8 minority (2 Black or African American, non-Hispanic/Latino; 1 Asian, non-Hispanic/Latino; 4 Hispanic/Latino; 1 Two or more races, non-Hispanic/Latino), 6 international. Average age 36. 15 applicants, 33% accepted, 3 enrolled. In 2018, 4 doctorates awarded. *Degree requirements:* For doctorate, thesis/dissertation, electronic portfolio. *Entrance requirements:* For doctorate, GRE General Test. Additional exam requirements/recommendations for international students: Required—TOEFL (minimum score 550 paper-based; 80 iBT); Recommended—IELTS (minimum score 6.5). *Application deadline:* For fall admission, 6/30 for domestic students, 10/1 for international students. Application fee: $75. Electronic applications accepted. *Financial support:* Fellowships, research assistantships, teaching assistantships, health care benefits, tuition waivers (full and partial), and unspecified assistantships available. Financial award application deadline: 3/1; financial award applicants required to submit FAFSA. *Faculty research:* Teacher education, multicultural education, special education, second language acquisition, math and science education. *Unit head:* Dr. Matthew Deroo, Assistant Professor and Program Director, 305-284-5217, Fax: 305-284-6998, E-mail: deroomat@miami.edu. *Application contact:* Lois Heffernan, Graduate Admission Coordinator, 305-284-2167, Fax: 305-284-9395, E-mail: lheffernan@miami.edu.
Website: http://www.education.miami.edu

University of Minnesota, Twin Cities Campus, Graduate School, College of Education and Human Development, Department of Curriculum and Instruction, Minneapolis, MN 55455-0213. Offers art education (M Ed, MA, PhD); curriculum and instruction (M Ed, MA, PhD); elementary education (MA, PhD); English education (PhD); language and immersion education (Certificate); learning technologies (MA, PhD); literacy education (MA, PhD); second language education (MA, PhD); social studies education (MA, PhD); STEM education (MA, PhD); teaching (M Ed), including mathematics, science, social studies, teaching; teaching English to speakers of other languages (MA); technology enhanced learning (Certificate). *Faculty:* 33 full-time (18 women). *Students:* 414 full-time (293 women), 247 part-time (170 women); includes 129 minority (16 Black or African American, non-Hispanic/Latino; 3 American Indian or Alaska Native, non-Hispanic/Latino; 38 Asian, non-Hispanic/Latino; 47 Hispanic/Latino; 25 Two or more races, non-Hispanic/Latino), 57 international. Average age 31. 610 applicants, 69% accepted, 349 enrolled. In 2018, 338 master's, 21 doctorates, 41 other advanced degrees awarded. Application fee: $75 ($95 for international students). *Financial support:* In 2018–19, 9 fellowships, 35 research assistantships with full tuition reimbursements (averaging $11,380 per year), 85 teaching assistantships with full tuition reimbursements (averaging $11,180 per year) were awarded. *Faculty research:* Teaching and learning; influence of cultural, linguistic, social, political, and technological factors on teaching, learning and educational research; relationship between educational practice and a democratic and just society; urban education; immigrant education, racial justice and education. *Total annual research expenditures:* $3.9 million. *Unit head:* Dr. Mark Vagle, Chair, 612-625-4006, E-mail: mvagle@umn.edu. *Application contact:* Dr. Mark Vagle, Chair, 612-625-4006, E-mail: mvagle@umn.edu.
Website: http://www.cehd.umn.edu/ci

University of New Mexico, Graduate Studies, College of Education, Program in Language, Literacy and Sociocultural Studies, Albuquerque, NM 87131-2039. Offers American Indian education (MA); bilingual education (MA, PhD); educational linguistics (PhD); educational thought and sociocultural studies (MA, PhD); literacy/language arts (MA, PhD); social studies (MA); TESOL (MA, PhD). *Students:* Average age 40. 61 applicants, 38% accepted, 23 enrolled. In 2018, 36 master's, 4 doctorates awarded. *Degree requirements:* For master's, comprehensive exam, thesis optional; for doctorate, comprehensive exam, thesis/dissertation, research skills. *Entrance requirements:* For master's, letter of intent, 3 letters of recommendation, resume, BA/BS, department demographic form, transcripts; for doctorate, writing sample, letter of intent, 3 letters of recommendation, resume, BA/BS, MA, department demographic form, transcripts. Additional exam requirements/recommendations for international students: Required—TOEFL. *Application deadline:* For fall admission, 12/1 for domestic and international students; for spring admission, 9/15 for domestic and international students. Application fee: $50. Electronic applications accepted. *Financial support:* Fellowships, research assistantships, teaching assistantships, career-related internships or fieldwork, institutionally sponsored loans, scholarships/grants, and unspecified assistantships available. Support available to part-time students. Financial award application deadline: 3/1; financial award applicants required to submit FAFSA. *Faculty research:* School reform, professional development, history of education, Native American education, politics of education, feminism and issues of sexual identity, critical race theory, bilingualism, literacy reading, adolescent literature, second language acquisition, critical theory and schooling, indigenous languages. *Unit head:* Dr. Lois M. Meyer, Chair, 505-277-7244, Fax: 505-277-8362, E-mail: lsmeyer@unm.edu. *Application contact:* Debra Schaffer, Administrative Assistant, 505-277-0437, Fax: 505-277-8362, E-mail: schaffer@unm.edu.
Website: http://coe.unm.edu/departments-programs/llss/index.html

University of New Mexico, Graduate Studies, College of Education, Program in Multicultural Teacher and Childhood Education, Albuquerque, NM 87131-2039. Offers Ed D, PhD. *Accreditation:* NCATE. *Program availability:* Part-time. *Students:* Average age 47. 5 applicants, 20% accepted. In 2018, 1 doctorate awarded. *Degree requirements:* For doctorate, comprehensive exam, thesis/dissertation. *Entrance requirements:* For doctorate, GRE, master's degree, minimum GPA of 3.0, 3 years of teaching experience, 3-5 letters of reference, letter of intent, professional writing sample. Additional exam requirements/recommendations for international students: Required—TOEFL (minimum score 550 paper-based). *Application deadline:* For fall admission, 1/15 priority date for domestic students, 1/15 for international students; for spring admission, 10/30 for domestic and international students. Application fee: $50. Electronic applications accepted. *Financial support:* Fellowships, research assistantships, teaching assistantships with partial tuition reimbursements, scholarships/grants, and unspecified assistantships available. Financial award application deadline: 3/1; financial award applicants required to submit FAFSA. *Faculty research:* Teacher education, clinical preparation, reflective practice, science education, mathematics education, social justice, technology education, media literacy. *Unit head:* Dr. Cheryl Torrez, Department Chair, 505-277-9611, Fax: 505-277-0455, E-mail: ted@unm.edu. *Application contact:* Robert Romero, Program Coordinator, 505-277-0513, Fax: 505-277-0455, E-mail: ted@unm.edu.
Website: https://coe.unm.edu/departments-programs/ifce/ecme/

The University of North Carolina at Greensboro, Graduate School, School of Education, Department of Educational Leadership and Cultural Foundations, Greensboro, NC 27412-5001. Offers curriculum and teaching (PhD), including cultural studies; educational leadership (Ed D, Ed S); school administration (MSA). *Accreditation:* NCATE. *Degree requirements:* For doctorate, thesis/dissertation. *Entrance requirements:* For master's, doctorate, and Ed S, GRE General Test. Additional exam requirements/recommendations for international students: Required—TOEFL. Electronic applications accepted.

University of Northern Colorado, Graduate School, College of Education and Behavioral Sciences, School of Teacher Education, Greeley, CO 80639. Offers curriculum studies (MAT); educational studies (Ed D); elementary education (MAT); English education (MAT); literacy (MA); multilingual education (MA), including TESOL, world languages; teaching diverse learners (MA). *Accreditation:* NCATE. *Program availability:* Part-time, evening/weekend. *Degree requirements:* For master's, comprehensive exam, thesis or alternative; for doctorate, comprehensive exam, thesis/dissertation. *Entrance requirements:* For master's and doctorate, GRE General Test, 3 letters of recommendation. Electronic applications accepted.

University of Pennsylvania, Graduate School of Education, Division of Educational Linguistics, Program in Intercultural Communication, Philadelphia, PA 19104. Offers MS Ed. *Program availability:* Part-time. *Students:* 25 full-time (20 women), 3 part-time (all women); includes 7 minority (1 Black or African American, non-Hispanic/Latino; 4 Asian, non-Hispanic/Latino; 1 Hispanic/Latino; 1 Two or more races, non-Hispanic/Latino), 12 international. Average age 27. 98 applicants, 41% accepted, 17 enrolled. In 2018, 14 master's awarded. Application fee: $80.

University of St. Thomas, School of Education and Human Services, Houston, TX 77006-4696. Offers all level education (M Ed); bilingual/dual language (M Ed); Catholic school teaching (M Ed); Catholic/private school leadership (M Ed); counselor education (M Ed); curriculum and instruction (M Ed); education (Ed D); educational leadership (M Ed); elementary teaching (M Ed); English as a second language (M Ed); exceptionality/educational diagnostician (M Ed); exceptionality/special education (M Ed); generalist (M Ed); reading (M Ed); secondary teaching (M Ed); teaching (MAT). *Accreditation:* TEAC. *Program availability:* Part-time, evening/weekend, online learning. *Degree requirements:* For master's, thesis, field experience. *Entrance requirements:* For master's, GRE or MAT if GPA is below 3.0, bachelor's degree; minimum GPA of 2.75 in bachelor's degree or last 60 credit hours; official transcripts from all institutions; goal statement of 250-300 words; 1 reference. Additional exam requirements/recommendations for international students: Required—TOEFL (minimum score 94 iBT), IELTS (minimum score 7), PTE (minimum score 53). Electronic applications accepted. *Expenses:* Contact institution. *Faculty research:* Leadership, diversity, personality traits, second language acquisition.

University of San Francisco, School of Education, Department of International and Multicultural Education, San Francisco, CA 94117. Offers MA, Ed D. *Program availability:* Part-time, evening/weekend. *Students:* 50 full-time (43 women), 34 part-time (27 women); includes 52 minority (9 Black or African American, non-Hispanic/Latino; 11 Asian, non-Hispanic/Latino; 25 Hispanic/Latino; 2 Native Hawaiian or other Pacific Islander, non-Hispanic/Latino; 5 Two or more races, non-Hispanic/Latino), 10 international. Average age 35. 74 applicants, 85% accepted, 21 enrolled. In 2018, 15 master's, 10 doctorates awarded. *Degree requirements:* For doctorate, thesis/dissertation. *Entrance requirements:* Additional exam requirements/recommendations for international students: Required—TOEFL, IELTS, PTE. *Application deadline:* For fall admission, 3/1 priority date for domestic students, 3/1 for international students; for spring admission, 10/15 priority date for domestic and international students. Applications are processed on a rolling basis. Application fee: $55 ($65 for international students). Electronic applications accepted. *Financial support:* Fellowships, research assistantships, and teaching assistantships available. Financial award application deadline: 3/2; financial award applicants required to submit FAFSA. *Unit head:* Dr. Emma Fuentes, Chair, 415-422-6878. *Application contact:* Peter Cole, Admission Coordinator, 415-422-5467, E-mail: schoolofeducation@usfca.edu.

University of Southern California, Graduate School, Rossier School of Education, Doctor of Education Programs, Los Angeles, CA 90089. Offers educational psychology (Ed D); higher education administration (Ed D); K-12 leadership in urban school settings (Ed D); teacher education in multicultural societies (Ed D). *Program availability:* Part-time, evening/weekend. *Degree requirements:* For doctorate, thesis/dissertation. *Entrance requirements:* For doctorate, GRE. Additional exam requirements/recommendations for international students: Required—TOEFL (minimum score 100 iBT). Electronic applications accepted. *Faculty research:* Data-driven decision-making in K-12 schools and districts; examination of college and university leadership and management in U. S. and Asia; studies in facilitating student learning; organizational change and the role of leaders; leadership, diversity, learning and accountability.

The University of Tennessee, Graduate School, College of Education, Health and Human Sciences, Program in Education, Knoxville, TN 37996. Offers art education (MS); counseling education (PhD); cultural studies in education (PhD); curriculum (MS, Ed S); curriculum, educational research and evaluation (Ed D, PhD); early childhood education (PhD); early childhood special education (MS); education of deaf and hard of hearing (MS); educational administration and policy studies (Ed D, PhD); educational administration and supervision (Ed S); educational psychology (Ed D, PhD); elementary education (MS, Ed S); elementary teaching (MS); English education (MS, Ed S); exercise science (PhD); foreign language/ESL education (MS, Ed S); instructional technology (MS, Ed D, PhD, Ed S); literacy, language and ESL education (PhD); literacy, language education, and ESL education (Ed D); mathematics education (MS, Ed S); modified and comprehensive special education (MS); reading education (MS, Ed S); school counseling (Ed S); school psychology (PhD, Ed S); science education (MS, Ed S); secondary teaching (MS); social foundations (MS); social science education (MS, Ed S); socio-cultural foundations of sports and education (PhD); special education (Ed S); teacher education (Ed D, PhD). *Accreditation:* NCATE. *Program availability:* Part-time, evening/weekend. *Degree requirements:* For master's and Ed S, thesis optional; for doctorate, variable foreign language requirement, thesis/dissertation. *Entrance requirements:* For master's, minimum GPA of 2.7; for doctorate and Ed S, GRE General Test, minimum GPA of 2.7. Additional exam requirements/recommendations for international students: Required—TOEFL. Electronic applications accepted.

The University of Texas at Austin, Graduate School, College of Education, Department of Curriculum and Instruction, Austin, TX 78712-1111. Offers bilingual/bicultural education (M Ed, MA, PhD); cultural studies in education (M Ed, MA, PhD); early childhood education (M Ed, MA, PhD); language and literacy studies (M Ed, PhD); learning technologies (M Ed, MA, PhD); physical education (M Ed, MA, PhD). Terminal

master's awarded for partial completion of doctoral program. *Degree requirements:* For doctorate, thesis/dissertation. *Entrance requirements:* For master's and doctorate, GRE General Test. Electronic applications accepted.

The University of Texas at Austin, Graduate School, College of Education, Department of Special Education, Austin, TX 78712-1111. Offers autism and developmental disabilities (Ed D, PhD); autism and developmental disability (M Ed, MA); early childhood special education (M Ed, MA, Ed D, PhD); learning disabilities (Ed D, PhD); learning disabilities/behavior disorders (M Ed, MA); multicultural special education (M Ed, MA, Ed D, PhD); rehabilitation counselor (M Ed); rehabilitation counselor education (Ed D, PhD); special education administration (Ed D, PhD). *Accreditation:* CORE. *Program availability:* Part-time, evening/weekend, online learning. *Degree requirements:* For master's, thesis or alternative; for doctorate, thesis/dissertation. *Entrance requirements:* For master's and doctorate, GRE General Test. *Faculty research:* Anchored instruction, reading disabilities, multicultural/bilingual.

The University of Texas at El Paso, Graduate School, College of Liberal Arts, Department of English, El Paso, TX 79968-0001. Offers bilingual professional writing (Certificate); English and American literature (MA); rhetoric and composition (PhD); rhetoric and writing studies (MA); teaching English (MAT). *Program availability:* Part-time, evening/weekend. *Degree requirements:* For master's, thesis optional. *Entrance requirements:* For master's, GRE General Test, minimum GPA of 3.0. Additional exam requirements/recommendations for international students: Required—TOEFL. Electronic applications accepted. *Faculty research:* Literature, creative writing, literary theory.

The University of Texas at San Antonio, College of Education and Human Development, Department of Bicultural and Bilingual Studies, San Antonio, TX 78249-0617. Offers bicultural and bilingual studies (MA), including bicultural and bilingual education, bicultural studies; culture, literacy, and language (PhD); teaching English as a second language (MA). *Program availability:* Part-time, evening/weekend. *Degree requirements:* For master's, one foreign language, comprehensive exam, thesis optional; for doctorate, one foreign language, comprehensive exam, thesis/dissertation. *Entrance requirements:* For master's, bachelor's degree with 18 credit hours in field of study or in another appropriate field of study; for doctorate, GRE General Test, resume or curriculum vitae, 3 letters of recommendation, statement of purpose, master's degree. Additional exam requirements/recommendations for international students: Required—TOEFL (minimum score 550 paper-based; 79 iBT), IELTS (minimum score 6.5). Electronic applications accepted. *Expenses:* Contact institution. *Faculty research:* Bilingual and ESL teacher preparation; transnational communities; applied linguistics; cultural studies; bilingualism, biliteracy and second language acquisition.

The University of Texas Rio Grande Valley, College of Education and P-16 Integration, Department of Bilingual and Literacy Studies, Edinburg, TX 78539. Offers bilingual education (M Ed), including dual language, ESL; reading and literacy (M Ed), including adolescent literacy, biliteracy, digital literacy, reading specialist. *Program availability:* Part-time, evening/weekend. *Degree requirements:* For master's, comprehensive exam (for some programs), thesis optional. *Entrance requirements:* For master's, minimum GPA of 3.0 in undergraduate coursework. Additional exam requirements/recommendations for international students: Required—TOEFL (minimum score 550 paper-based; 79 iBT), IELTS (minimum score 6.5). Electronic applications accepted. *Expenses: Tuition, area resident:* Full-time $6888. Tuition, state resident: full-time $6888. Tuition, nonresident: full-time $14,484. *International tuition:* $14,484 full-time. *Required fees:* $1468. *Faculty research:* Bilingual education, reading instruction, multicultural education, English as a second language.

University of the Southwest, Graduate Programs, Hobbs, NM 88240-9129. Offers business administration (MBA); curriculum and instruction (MSE); curriculum and instruction: bilingual (MSE); curriculum and instruction: TESOL (MSE); early childhood education (MSE); educational administration (MSE); mental health counseling (MSE); school counseling (MSE); special education (MSE); sports management (MBA). *Program availability:* Part-time, evening/weekend, online learning. *Degree requirements:* For master's, comprehensive exam, thesis (for some programs). *Entrance requirements:* Additional exam requirements/recommendations for international students: Recommended—TOEFL. Electronic applications accepted.

University of Washington, Graduate School, College of Education, Seattle, WA 98195. Offers curriculum and instruction (M Ed, Ed D, PhD), including educational technology, general curriculum (Ed D, PhD), language, literacy, and culture, mathematics education, multicultural education, reading and language arts education (Ed D), science education, social studies education, teaching and curriculum (M Ed); educational leadership and policy studies (M Ed, Ed D, PhD), including administration (Ed D), educational policy, organization, and leadership (M Ed, PhD), higher education, leadership for learning (Ed D), social and cultural foundations of education (M Ed, PhD); educational psychology (M Ed, PhD), including educational psychology (PhD), human development and cognition (M Ed), learning sciences, measurement, statistics and research design (M Ed), school psychology (M Ed); instructional leadership (M Ed); intercollegiate athletic leadership (M Ed); special education (M Ed, Ed D, PhD), including early childhood special education (M Ed), emotional and behavioral disabilities (M Ed), learning disabilities (M Ed), low-incidence disabilities (M Ed), severe disabilities (M Ed), special education (Ed D, PhD); teacher education (MIT). *Accreditation:* APA. *Program availability:* Part-time, evening/weekend. *Degree requirements:* For master's, thesis optional; for doctorate, thesis/dissertation. *Entrance requirements:* For master's and doctorate, GRE General Test, minimum GPA of 3.0. Additional exam requirements/recommendations for international students: Required—TOEFL. Electronic applications accepted. *Faculty research:* School restructuring/effective schools, special education interventions, literacy and writing, technology, school partnerships, teacher preparation.

University of Wisconsin–Milwaukee, Graduate School, School of Education, Department of Exceptional Education, Milwaukee, WI 53201-0413. Offers autism spectrum disorders (Graduate Certificate); exceptional education (MS); transition for students with disabilities (Graduate Certificate); urban education (PhD), including adult, continuing and higher education leadership, art education, curriculum and instruction, exceptional education, mathematics education, multicultural studies, social foundations of education. *Program availability:* Part-time. *Students:* 38 full-time (29 women), 67 part-time (50 women); includes 39 minority (23 Black or African American, non-Hispanic/Latino; 1 American Indian or Alaska Native, non-Hispanic/Latino; 6 Asian, non-Hispanic/Latino; 1 Hispanic/Latino; 8 Two or more races, non-Hispanic/Latino), 2 international. Average age 40. 47 applicants, 40% accepted, 11 enrolled. In 2018, 13 master's, 14 doctorates, 4 other advanced degrees awarded. *Entrance requirements:* Additional exam requirements/recommendations for international students: Required—TOEFL (minimum score 550 paper-based; 79 iBT), IELTS (minimum score 6.5). *Application deadline:* For fall admission, 1/1 priority date for domestic students; for spring admission, 9/1 for domestic students. Application fee: $56 ($96 for international students). Electronic applications accepted. *Financial support:* Fellowships, research assistantships, teaching assistantships, career-related internships or fieldwork, health care benefits, and unspecified assistantships available. Support available to part-time students. Financial award application deadline: 4/15; financial award applicants required to submit FAFSA. *Faculty research:* Emotional disturbance, hearing impairment, learning disabilities, mental retardation. *Application contact:* General Information Contact, 414-229-4721, E-mail: soeinfo@uwm.edu.
Website: http://uwm.edu/education/academics/exceptional-edu-department/

Utah State University, School of Graduate Studies, College of Humanities and Social Sciences, Department of Languages, Philosophy, and Communication Studies, Logan, UT 84322. Offers second language teaching (MSLT). *Entrance requirements:* For master's, GRE General Test or MAT, minimum GPA of 3.0. Additional exam requirements/recommendations for international students: Required—TOEFL.

Vanderbilt University, Program in Learning, Teaching and Diversity, Nashville, TN 37240-1001. Offers PhD. *Faculty:* 19 full-time (10 women), 2 part-time/adjunct (both women). *Students:* 38 full-time (31 women); includes 12 minority (3 Black or African American, non-Hispanic/Latino; 4 Asian, non-Hispanic/Latino; 1 Hispanic/Latino; 4 Two or more races, non-Hispanic/Latino), 3 international. Average age 32. 91 applicants, 12% accepted, 6 enrolled. In 2018, 8 doctorates awarded. *Degree requirements:* For doctorate, comprehensive exam, thesis/dissertation, qualifying examinations. *Entrance requirements:* For doctorate, GRE General Test. Additional exam requirements/recommendations for international students: Required—TOEFL (minimum score 570 paper-based; 88 iBT). *Application deadline:* For fall admission, 12/1 for domestic and international students. Application fee: $0. Electronic applications accepted. *Expenses:* Contact institution. *Financial support:* Fellowships with partial tuition reimbursements, research assistantships with full tuition reimbursements, teaching assistantships with full tuition reimbursements, Federal Work-Study, institutionally sponsored loans, scholarships/grants, traineeships, and health care benefits available. Financial award application deadline: 1/15; financial award applicants required to submit CSS PROFILE or FAFSA. *Faculty research:* New pedagogies for math, science, and language; the support of English language learners; the uses of new technology and media in the classroom; middle school mathematics and the institutional setting of teaching. *Unit head:* Dr. Deborah Rowe, Chair, 615-322-8044, Fax: 615-322-8014, E-mail: deborah.w.rowe@vanderbilt.edu. *Application contact:* Llana Horn, Director of Graduate Studies, 615-322-5884, Fax: 615-322-8014, E-mail: llana.horn@vanderbilt.edu.
Website: http://peabody.vanderbilt.edu/departments/tl/index.php

Walden University, Graduate Programs, Richard W. Riley College of Education and Leadership, Minneapolis, MN 55401. Offers adult education (Post-Master's Certificate); adult learning (Graduate Certificate); college teaching and learning (Graduate Certificate); community college leadership (Ed D); curriculum, instruction and assessment (Ed D, Ed S, Graduate Certificate); developmental education (Graduate Certificate); early childhood administration, management, and leadership (Graduate Certificate); early childhood education (Ed D, Ed S); early childhood public policy and advocacy (Graduate Certificate); early childhood studies (MS), including administration, management and leadership, early childhood public policy and advocacy, teaching adults in the early childhood field, teaching and diversity in early childhood education; education (MS, PhD), including adolescent literacy and learning (MS), curriculum, instruction, and assessment (grades K-12) (MS), curriculum, instruction, assessment, and evaluation (PhD), early childhood leadership and advocacy (PhD), early childhood special education (PhD), educational leadership (MS), educational leadership and administration (principal preparation) (MS), educational technology and design (PhD), elementary reading and literacy (PreK-6) (MS), elementary reading and mathematics (grades K-6) (MS), global and comparative education (PhD), higher education leadership management and policy (PhD), integrating technology in the classroom (grades K-12) (MS), learning, instruction and innovation (PhD), mathematics (grades 5-8) (MS), mathematics (grades K-6) (MS), mathematics and science (grades K-8) (MS), organizational research, assessment, and evaluation (PhD), reading and literacy with a reading K-12 endorsement (MS), reading literacy assessment and evaluation (PhD), science (grades K-8) (MS), special education (non-licensure) (grades K-12) (MS), teacher leadership (grades K-12) (MS), teaching English language learners (grades K-12) (MS); educational administration and leadership (Ed D); educational leadership and administration (principal preparation) (Ed S); educational technology (Ed D, Ed S, Post Master's Certificate); elementary reading and literacy (Graduate Certificate); engaging culturally diverse learners (Graduate Certificate); enrollment management and institutional marketing (Graduate Certificate); higher education (MS), including adult learning, college teaching and learning, enrollment management and institutional marketing, global higher education, leadership for student success, online and distance learning; higher education and adult learning (Ed D); higher education leadership and management (Ed D); higher education leadership for student success (Graduate Certificate); instructional design and technology (MS, Postbaccalaureate Certificate), including general program (MS), online learning (MS), training and performance improvement (MS); integrating technology in the classroom (Graduate Certificate); mathematics 5-8 (Graduate Certificate); mathematics K-6 (Graduate Certificate); online teaching for adult educators (Graduate Certificate); reading, literacy, and assessment (Ed D, Ed S); science K-8 (Graduate Certificate); special education (Ed D, Ed S, Graduate Certificate); special education (K-age 21) (MAT); teacher leadership (Graduate Certificate); teaching adults English as a second language (Graduate Certificate); teaching adults in the early childhood field (Graduate Certificate); teaching and diversity in early childhood education (Graduate Certificate); teaching English language learners (grades K-12) (Graduate Certificate); teaching K-12 students online (Graduate Certificate). *Accreditation:* NCATE. *Program availability:* Part-time, evening/weekend, online only, 100% online. *Degree requirements:* For doctorate, thesis/dissertation (for some programs), residency; for other advanced degree, residency (for some programs). *Entrance requirements:* For master's, bachelor's degree or higher; minimum GPA of 2.5; official transcripts; goal statement (for some programs); access to computer and Internet; for doctorate, master's degree or higher; three years of related professional or academic experience (preferred); minimum GPA of 3.0; goal statement and current resume (for select programs); official transcripts; access to computer and Internet; for other advanced degree, relevant work experience; access to computer and Internet. Additional exam requirements/recommendations for international students: Required—TOEFL (minimum score 550 paper-based, 79 iBT), IELTS (minimum score 6.5), Michigan English Language Assessment Battery (minimum score 82), or PTE (minimum score 53). Electronic applications accepted.

Wayne State University, College of Education, Division of Teacher Education, Detroit, MI 48202. Offers art education (M Ed); bilingual/bicultural education (Certificate); curriculum and instruction (Ed D, PhD, Ed S), including English as a second language (MAT, Ed D, Ed S), K-12 curriculum (PhD); elementary education (MAT), including bilingual/bicultural education (M Ed, MAT), early childhood education (M Ed, MAT), English as a second language (MAT, Ed D, Ed S), foreign language education, science education (M Ed, MAT), special education (M Ed, MAT); elementary mathematics specialist (Certificate); English as a second language (Certificate); reading (M Ed, Ed S); reading, language and literature (Ed D); secondary education (MAT), including bilingual/bicultural education (M Ed, MAT), early childhood education (M Ed, MAT), English as a second language (MAT, Ed D, Ed S), English education, foreign language education, mathematics education (M Ed, MAT), science education (M Ed, MAT), social studies education (M Ed, MAT); special education (MAT), including career and technical education; teaching and learning (M Ed), including bilingual/bicultural education (M Ed, MAT), early childhood education (M Ed, MAT), elementary education, foreign language, mathematics education (M Ed, MAT), science education (M Ed, MAT), social studies education (M Ed, MAT), special education (M Ed, MAT). *Program availability:* Part-time,

evening/weekend. *Faculty:* 20. *Students:* 121 full-time (94 women), 251 part-time (209 women); includes 116 minority (83 Black or African American, non-Hispanic/Latino; 3 American Indian or Alaska Native, non-Hispanic/Latino; 3 Asian, non-Hispanic/Latino; 14 Hispanic/Latino; 13 Two or more races, non-Hispanic/Latino), 11 international. Average age 37. 171 applicants, 23% accepted, 32 enrolled. In 2018, 112 master's, 8 doctorates, 11 other advanced degrees awarded. *Degree requirements:* For master's, thesis (for some programs), essay or project (for some M Ed programs), professional field experience (for MAT programs); for doctorate, comprehensive exam, thesis/dissertation. *Entrance requirements:* For master's, undergraduate degree, verification of participation in group work with children, Michigan State Police criminal background check, negative tb test, personal statement (for MAT programs); for all other master's programs: undergraduate degree, personal statement; for doctorate, minimum undergraduate GPA of 3.0, graduate 3.5; interview; curriculum vitae; references; writing sample; letter of application; master's degree (for most programs); for other advanced degree, education specialist certificate: undergraduate with GPA of 2.5 or better and master's degree with GPA of 2.75 or better; personal statement. Additional exam requirements/recommendations for international students: Required—TOEFL (minimum score 550 paper-based; 79 iBT); Recommended—IELTS (minimum score 6.5), TWE (minimum score 5.5), TSE (minimum score 58). *Application deadline:* Applications are processed on a rolling basis. Application fee: $50. Electronic applications accepted. *Financial support:* In 2018–19, 85 students received support, including 3 fellowships (averaging $14,275 per year); research assistantships with tuition reimbursements available, Federal Work-Study, scholarships/grants, and unspecified assistantships also available. Support available to part-time students. Financial award applicants required to submit FAFSA. *Faculty research:* Improving students' skill achievement in mathematics, improving elementary children's understanding of informational text, teachers' use of their pedagogical and mathematical knowledge in the interactive work of teaching, the intersection of identity construction in teaching and learning, identifying effective methods of literacy instruction and assessments for bilingual students in elementary language arts classrooms. *Unit head:* Dr. Roland Coloma, Assistant Dean for Teacher Education, 313-577-0902, E-mail: rscoloma@wayne.edu. *Application contact:* Dr. Mary L. Waker, Graduate Admissions Officer, 313-577-1601, Fax: 313-577-7904, E-mail: m.waker@wayne.edu.
Website: http://coe.wayne.edu/ted/index.php

Western New Mexico University, Graduate Division, School of Education, Silver City, NM 88062-0680. Offers bilingual education (MAT); educational leadership (MA); elementary education (MAT); reading (MAT); secondary education (MAT); special education (MAT); TESOL (teaching English to speakers of other languages) (MAT). *Accreditation:* NCATE. *Program availability:* Part-time, online learning. *Degree requirements:* For master's, comprehensive exam. *Entrance requirements:* For master's, minimum GPA of 3.0 in last 64 hours of undergraduate study. Additional exam requirements/recommendations for international students: Required—TOEFL (minimum score 550 paper-based; 79 iBT). Electronic applications accepted. *Faculty research:* International education, electronic reading assessment, developing STEM teachers.

Western Oregon University, Graduate Programs, College of Education, Division of Teacher Education, Program in Secondary Education, Monmouth, OR 97361. Offers bilingual education (MS Ed); health (MS Ed); humanities (MAT, MS Ed); initial licensure (MAT); mathematics (MAT, MS Ed); science (MAT, MS Ed); social science (MAT, MS Ed). *Accreditation:* NCATE. *Program availability:* Part-time, evening/weekend. *Degree requirements:* For master's, thesis optional, written exam. *Entrance requirements:* For master's, minimum GPA of 3.0, teaching license. Additional exam requirements/recommendations for international students: Required—TOEFL (minimum score 550 paper-based; 79 iBT), IELTS (minimum score 6.5). *Faculty research:* Literacy, science in primary grades, geography education, retention, teacher burnout.

William Paterson University of New Jersey, College of Humanities and Social Sciences, Wayne, NJ 07470-8420. Offers applied sociology (MA); assessment and evaluation research (Certificate); bilingual education (Certificate); clinical and counseling psychology (MA); clinical psychology (Psy D); creative and professional writing (MFA); English (MA); history (MA); public policy and international affairs (MA); teaching English as a second language (Certificate). *Program availability:* Part-time. *Faculty:* 41 full-time (25 women), 7 part-time/adjunct (5 women). *Students:* 69 full-time (49 women), 65 part-time (42 women); includes 55 minority (6 Black or African American, non-Hispanic/Latino; 2 Asian, non-Hispanic/Latino; 41 Hispanic/Latino; 6 Two or more races, non-Hispanic/Latino), 3 international. Average age 32. 152 applicants, 47% accepted, 44 enrolled. In 2018, 46 master's awarded. *Degree requirements:* For master's, Programs Differ see: https://academiccatalog.wpunj.edu/content.php?catoid=1&navoid=68. *Entrance requirements:* For master's, program details: https://www.wpunj.edu/admissions/graduate/admission-deadlines-and-requirements/. Additional exam requirements/recommendations for international students: Required—TOEFL (minimum score 550 paper-based; 79 iBT), IELTS (minimum score 6). *Application deadline:* For fall admission, 6/1 for domestic students, 3/1 for international students; for spring admission, 11/1 for domestic students, 10/1 for international students. Applications are processed on a rolling basis. Application fee: $50. Electronic applications accepted. *Expenses: Tuition, area resident:* Full-time $14,714; part-time $727 per credit. Tuition, state resident: full-time $14,714; part-time $727 per credit. Tuition, nonresident: full-time $22,952; part-time $727 per credit. *International tuition:* $22,952 full-time. *Required fees:* $4 per semester. Tuition and fees vary according to course load, degree level and program. *Financial support:* In 2018–19, 16 students received support. Career-related internships or fieldwork, Federal Work-Study, scholarships/grants, tuition waivers, and unspecified assistantships available. Support available to part-time students. Financial award application deadline: 3/15; financial award applicants required to submit FAFSA. *Faculty research:* Relationship violence, work-family balance, social development of Japan, theories justifying war, reactions to trauma. *Total annual research expenditures:* $119,089. *Unit head:* Dr. Kara Rabbitt, Dean, 973-720-2180, Fax: 973-720-2955, E-mail: rabbittk@wpunj.edu. *Application contact:* Tinu Adeniran, Associate Director, Graduate Admissions, 973-720-2764, Fax: 973-720-2035, E-mail: adenirant@wpunj.edu.
Website: http://www.wpunj.edu/cohss

Winona State University, College of Education, Department of Education Studies, Winona, MN 55987. Offers multicultural education (Certificate). *Accreditation:* NCATE. *Program availability:* Part-time, evening/weekend.

Xavier University, College of Professional Sciences, School of Education, Department of Childhood Education and Literacy, Cincinnati, OH 45207. Offers children's multicultural literature (M Ed); elementary education (M Ed); Montessori education (M Ed); reading (M Ed). *Program availability:* Part-time. *Degree requirements:* For master's, comprehensive exam, thesis, 30 semester hours. *Entrance requirements:* For master's, GRE, MAT, official transcript; 3 letters of recommendation (for Montessori education); resume; statement of purpose. Additional exam requirements/recommendations for international students: Required—TOEFL (minimum score 550 paper-based; 79 iBT). Electronic applications accepted. Application fee is waived when completed online. *Expenses:* Contact institution. *Faculty research:* Multicultural literacy/fluency, early literacy development, writing/creative and across curriculum, assessment of reading abilities.

Special Education

Acacia University, American Graduate School of Education, Tempe, AZ 85284. Offers educational administration (M Ed); elementary education (MA); English as a second language (M Ed); secondary education (MA); special education (M Ed).

Acadia University, Faculty of Professional Studies, School of Education, Program in Inclusive Education, Wolfville, NS B4P 2R6, Canada. Offers M Ed. *Program availability:* Part-time. *Entrance requirements:* For master's, bachelor's degree in education, minimum B average in undergraduate course work, course work in special education. Additional exam requirements/recommendations for international students: Required—TOEFL (minimum score 580 paper-based; 93 iBT), IELTS (minimum score 6.5). *Faculty research:* Technology and human interaction, inclusive education and community, accommodating diversity, program evaluation.

Adelphi University, College of Education & Health Sciences, College of Education and Health Sciences, Garden City, NY 11530-0701. Offers MS, Certificate. *Program availability:* Part-time, evening/weekend. *Students:* 31 full-time (6 women), 32 part-time (7 women); includes 13 minority (3 Black or African American, non-Hispanic/Latino; 4 Asian, non-Hispanic/Latino; 6 Hispanic/Latino), 1 international. Average age 27. 106 applicants, 57% accepted, 30 enrolled. In 2018, 22 master's, 28 other advanced degrees awarded. *Entrance requirements:* For master's, 2 letters of recommendation, essay, college transcripts, Bachelor's degree with min. 3.0 GPA. Additional exam requirements/recommendations for international students: Required—TOEFL (minimum score 550 paper-based; 80 iBT), IELTS (minimum score 6.5). Application fee: $50. Electronic applications accepted. *Expenses:* Contact institution. *Financial support:* Research assistantships, teaching assistantships, career-related internships or fieldwork, institutionally sponsored loans, scholarships/grants, traineeships, and unspecified assistantships available. Support available to part-time students. Financial award application deadline: 1/1; financial award applicants required to submit FAFSA. *Unit head:* Dori Phalen, Director, 516-877-4025, E-mail: phalen2@adelphi.edu. *Application contact:* Dori Phalen, Director, 516-877-4025, E-mail: phalen2@adelphi.edu.

Alabama Agricultural and Mechanical University, School of Graduate Studies, College of Education, Humanities, and Behavioral Sciences, Department of Reading, Elementary, Early Childhood and Special Education, Huntsville, AL 35811. Offers early childhood education (MS Ed, Ed S); elementary education (MS Ed, Ed S); reading/literacy (PhD); special education collaborative teacher training (MS Ed, Ed S). *Accreditation:* NCATE. *Program availability:* Evening/weekend. *Degree requirements:* For master's, comprehensive exam; for Ed S, thesis. *Entrance requirements:* For master's, GRE General Test. Additional exam requirements/recommendations for international students: Required—TOEFL (minimum score 500 paper-based; 61 iBT). Electronic applications accepted. *Faculty research:* Multicultural education, learning styles, diagnostic-prescriptive instruction.

Albany State University, College of Education, Albany, GA 31705-2717. Offers early childhood education (M Ed); educational leadership (Ed S); health and physical education (M Ed); middle grades education (M Ed); school counseling (M Ed); special education (M Ed). *Accreditation:* NCATE. *Program availability:* Part-time, evening/weekend, online learning. *Degree requirements:* For master's, comprehensive exam, internship, GACE Content Exam. *Entrance requirements:* For master's, GRE or MAT. Electronic applications accepted. *Faculty research:* GACE preparation, STEM (science, technology, engineering, and mathematics), technology education, special education, professional teacher development, health implications liberation philosophy, NET-Q, learning community, disabled or at-risk students.

Albizu University, Miami Campus, Graduate Programs, Miami, FL 33172-2209. Offers clinical psychology (PhD, Psy D); entrepreneurship (MBA); exceptional student education (MS); human services (PhD); industrial/organizational psychology (MS); marriage and family therapy (MS); mental health counseling (MS); nonprofit management (MBA); organizational management (MBA); school counseling (MS); speech and language pathology (MS); teaching English for speakers of other languages (MS). *Accreditation:* APA. *Program availability:* Part-time, evening/weekend, 100% online, blended/hybrid learning. *Faculty:* 32 full-time (24 women), 27 part-time/adjunct (15 women). *Students:* 479 full-time (410 women), 146 part-time (126 women); includes 539 minority (42 Black or African American, non-Hispanic/Latino; 2 Asian, non-Hispanic/Latino; 490 Hispanic/Latino; 5 Two or more races, non-Hispanic/Latino), 22 international. Average age 33. 314 applicants, 45% accepted, 92 enrolled. In 2018, 101 master's, 64 doctorates awarded. Terminal master's awarded for partial completion of doctoral program. *Degree requirements:* For master's, comprehensive exam (for some programs), integrative project (for MBA); research project (for exceptional student education, teaching English as a second language); for doctorate, comprehensive exam, thesis/dissertation, comprehensive examinations, internship, project/dissertation. *Entrance requirements:* For master's, GRE/EXADEP, bachelor's degree from accredited institution, minimum GPA of 3.0, 3 letters of recommendation, interview, resume, statement of purpose, official transcripts; for doctorate, GRE (for Psy D), 3 letters of recommendation, resume, interview, statement of purpose, official transcripts; bachelor's degree and minimum GPA of 3.25 (for Psy D); master's degree and minimum GPA of 3.0 (for PhD). Additional exam requirements/recommendations for international students: Required—Michigan Test of English Language Proficiency. *Application deadline:* For fall admission, 4/1 priority date for domestic students, 5/1 priority date for international students; for spring admission, 11/1 priority date for domestic students, 9/1 priority date for international students. Applications are processed on a rolling basis. Application fee: $50. Electronic applications accepted. Application fee is waived when completed online. *Expenses:* Contact institution. *Financial support:* In 2018–19, 141 students received support. Federal Work-Study, scholarships/grants, unspecified assistantships, and tuition discounts available. Financial award application deadline: 6/1; financial award applicants required to submit FAFSA. *Faculty research:* Psychotherapy, forensic psychology, neuropsychology, special education, speech-language pathology, criminal justice, human services. *Unit head:* Dr. Jose Pons-Madera, PhD, President,

305-593-1223 Ext. 3120, Fax: 305-477-8983, E-mail: jpons@albizu.edu. *Application contact:* Nancy Alvarez, Director of Enrollment Management, 305-593-1223 Ext. 3136, Fax: 305-593-1854, E-mail: nalvarez@albizu.edu.

Albright College, Graduate Division, Reading, PA 19612-5234. Offers early childhood education (MS); elementary education (MS); English as a second language (MA); general education (MA); special education (MS). *Program availability:* Part-time, evening/weekend. *Degree requirements:* For master's, thesis. *Entrance requirements:* For master's, GRE General Test or MAT, minimum undergraduate GPA of 3.0, 2 letters of recommendation, interview. Additional exam requirements/recommendations for international students: Recommended—TOEFL (minimum score 525 paper-based). Electronic applications accepted.

Alcorn State University, School of Graduate Studies, School of Education and Psychology, Lorman, MS 39096-7500. Offers agricultural education (MS Ed); elementary education (MAT, MS Ed, Ed S); guidance and counseling (MS Ed); industrial education (MS Ed); secondary education (MAT, MS Ed), including health and physical education (MS Ed), NCAA compliance and academic progress reporting (MS Ed); special education (MS Ed). *Accreditation:* NCATE. *Degree requirements:* For master's, thesis optional.

Alliant International University–San Francisco, Shirley M. Hufstedler School of Education, Teacher Education Programs, San Francisco, CA 94133. Offers auditory oral education (Certificate); CLAD (Certificate); education specialist: mild/moderate disabilities (Credential); preliminary multiple subject (Credential); preliminary single subject (Credential); professional clear multiple subject (Credential); professional clear single subject (Credential); special education (MA); teaching (MA); TESOL (Certificate). *Program availability:* Part-time, evening/weekend. *Degree requirements:* For master's, thesis. *Entrance requirements:* For degree, California Basic Educational Skills Test, minimum GPA of 2.5. Additional exam requirements/recommendations for international students: Required—TOEFL (minimum score 550 paper-based), TWE (minimum score 5). Electronic applications accepted. *Faculty research:* Curriculum development, first year teachers, cross-cultural issues in teaching, biliteracy.

Alverno College, School of Professional Studies - Education Division, Milwaukee, WI 53234-3922. Offers adaptive education (MA); administrative leadership (MA); adult education and organizational development (MA); adult educational and instructional design (MA); adult educational and instructional technology (MA); global connections in the humanities (MA); instructional leadership (MA); instructional technology for K-12 settings (MA); professional development (MA); reading education (MA); reading education with adaptive education (MA); science education (MA); special education (MA); teaching in alternative schools (MA). *Accreditation:* NCATE. *Program availability:* Part-time, evening/weekend. *Degree requirements:* For master's, presentation/defense of proposal, conference presentation of inquiry projects. *Entrance requirements:* For master's, bachelor's degree in related field, communication samples from work setting, 3 letters of recommendation. Additional exam requirements/recommendations for international students: Required—TOEFL. Electronic applications accepted. *Expenses:* Contact institution. *Faculty research:* Student self-assessment, self-reflection, integration of curriculum, identifying needs of students in strategic situations and designing appropriate classroom strategies.

American International College, School of Education, Springfield, MA 01109-3189. Offers early childhood education (M Ed, CAGS); education (MA, Ed D), including counseling psychology (MA), educational leadership and supervision (Ed D), professional counseling and supervision (Ed D), teaching and learning (Ed D); elementary education (M Ed, CAGS); middle education/secondary education (M Ed, CAGS); moderate disabilities (M Ed, CAGS); reading specialist (M Ed, CAGS); school adjustment counseling (MAEP, CAGS); school guidance counseling (MAEP, CAGS); school leadership (M Ed, CAGS). *Program availability:* Evening/weekend. *Degree requirements:* For master's and CAGS, practicum/culminating experience. *Entrance requirements:* For master's, Communication and Literacy portion of the Massachusetts Tests for Education Licensure, graduate of accredited four-year college with minimum B-average in undergraduate course work; for CAGS, M Ed or master's degree in field related to licensure from accredited institution. Electronic applications accepted. *Expenses:* Contact institution.

American University, School of Education, Washington, DC 20016-8030. Offers education (Certificate); education policy and leadership (M Ed); international training and education (MA); special education (MA); teacher education (MAT); M Ed/MPA; M Ed/MPP; MAT/MA. *Accreditation:* NCATE. *Program availability:* Part-time, evening/weekend, 100% online. *Faculty:* 17 full-time (13 women), 33 part-time/adjunct (23 women). *Students:* 53 full-time (46 women), 246 part-time (191 women); includes 139 minority (97 Black or African American, non-Hispanic/Latino; 13 Asian, non-Hispanic/Latino; 23 Hispanic/Latino; 6 Two or more races, non-Hispanic/Latino), 5 international. Average age 29. 361 applicants, 88% accepted, 161 enrolled. In 2018, 73 master's, 2 other advanced degrees awarded. *Degree requirements:* For master's, comprehensive exam, thesis or alternative. *Entrance requirements:* For master's, Please visit website: https://www.american.edu/soe/, bachelor's degree, statement of purpose, transcripts, 2 letters of recommendation. Additional exam requirements/recommendations for international students: Required—TOEFL (minimum score 100 iBT). Application fee: $55. Electronic applications accepted. *Expenses: Tuition:* Full-time $30,744; part-time $1642 per credit hour. *Required fees:* $702; $200 per semester. Tuition and fees vary according to course load, degree level and program. *Financial support:* Research assistantships, teaching assistantships, institutionally sponsored loans, scholarships/grants, and unspecified assistantships available. Financial award application deadline: 2/1; financial award applicants required to submit FAFSA. *Unit head:* Dr. Cheryl Holcomb-McCoy, Dean, 202-885-3720, E-mail: educate@american.edu. *Application contact:* Ashleigh Huseth, Senior Coordinator, Admissions & Onboarding, E-mail: ahuseth@american.edu.
Website: https://www.american.edu/cas/education/

American University of Puerto Rico, Program in Education, Bayamon, PR 00960-2037. Offers art education (M Ed); elementary education 4-6 (M Ed); elementary education K-3 (M Ed); general science education (M Ed); physical education (M Ed); special education (M Ed). *Program availability:* Part-time, evening/weekend. *Entrance requirements:* For master's, EXADEP, GRE, or MAT, 2 letters of recommendation, minimum GPA of 2.5.

Andrews University, School of Graduate Studies, School of Education, Department of Graduate Psychology and Counseling, Program in Special Education, Berrien Springs, MI 49104. Offers MS. *Entrance requirements:* Additional exam requirements/recommendations for international students: Required—TOEFL (minimum score 550 paper-based).

Antioch University New England, Graduate School, Department of Applied Psychology, Program in Autism Spectrum Disorders, Keene, NH 03431-3552. Offers applied behavior analysis (Certificate); applied behavior analysis internship (Certificate); autism spectrum disorders (Certificate). *Entrance requirements:* Additional exam requirements/recommendations for international students: Required—TOEFL (minimum score 550 paper-based).

Antioch University New England, Graduate School, Department of Education, Experienced Educators Program, Keene, NH 03431-3552. Offers foundations of education (M Ed), including applied behavioral analysis, autism spectrum disorders, educating for sustainability, next-generation learning using technology, problem-based learning using critical skills, teacher leadership; principal certification (PMC). *Degree requirements:* For master's, thesis, practicum. *Entrance requirements:* For master's, previous course work and work experience in education. Additional exam requirements/recommendations for international students: Required—TOEFL (minimum score 550 paper-based). Electronic applications accepted. *Expenses:* Contact institution. *Faculty research:* Classroom action research, school restructuring, problem-based learning, brain-based learning.

Antioch University New England, Graduate School, Department of Education, Integrated Learning Program, Keene, NH 03431-3552. Offers early childhood education (M Ed); elementary education (M Ed), including arts and humanities, science and environmental education; special education (M Ed). *Degree requirements:* For master's, internship. *Entrance requirements:* For master's, previous course work or work experience in education. Additional exam requirements/recommendations for international students: Required—TOEFL (minimum score 550 paper-based). Electronic applications accepted. *Expenses:* Contact institution. *Faculty research:* Problem-based learning, place-based education, mathematics education, democratic classrooms, art education.

Appalachian State University, Cratis D. Williams School of Graduate Studies, Department of Reading Education and Special Education, Boone, NC 28608. Offers reading education (MA); special education (MA). *Accreditation:* ASHA. *Program availability:* Part-time, evening/weekend, online learning. *Degree requirements:* For master's, comprehensive exam, thesis optional. *Entrance requirements:* For master's, GRE General Test or MAT, 3 letters of recommendation. Additional exam requirements/recommendations for international students: Required—TOEFL (minimum score 570 paper-based; 79 iBT), IELTS (minimum score 6.5). Electronic applications accepted. *Expenses: Tuition, area resident:* Full-time $4839; part-time $237 per credit hour. Tuition, state resident: full-time $4839; part-time $237 per credit hour. Tuition, nonresident: full-time $18,271; part-time $895.50 per credit hour. *Faculty research:* Special education, language arts, reading.

Arcadia University, College of Arts and Sciences, Department of Psychology, Glenside, PA 19038-3295. Offers applied behavior analysis (MAC); autism (MAC); child/family therapy (MAC); community public health (MAC); counseling/international peace and conflict resolution dual degree (MAC); mental health counseling (MAC); trauma (MAC). *Program availability:* Part-time. *Faculty:* 14 full-time (9 women), 11 part-time/adjunct (10 women). *Students:* 37 full-time (33 women), 35 part-time (29 women); includes 23 minority (14 Black or African American, non-Hispanic/Latino; 3 Asian, non-Hispanic/Latino; 4 Hispanic/Latino; 2 Two or more races, non-Hispanic/Latino). In 2018, 25 master's awarded. *Degree requirements:* For master's, practicum. *Entrance requirements:* For master's, test scores are not required of applicants with an earned master's degree or who have a GPA greater than a 3.0. Test scores from the Graduate Record Examination (GRE) or the Miller Analogies Test (MAT), taken within the past five years are required for all other applicants. Additional exam requirements/recommendations for international students: Required—TOEFL. *Application deadline:* Applications are processed on a rolling basis. Application fee: $25. *Expenses:* Contact institution. *Financial support:* Research assistantships, career-related internships or fieldwork, and unspecified assistantships available. Support available to part-time students. Financial award application deadline: 8/15. *Unit head:* Dr. Christina Brown, Chair, 215-572-4695. *Application contact:* 215-572-2925, Fax: 215-572-2126, E-mail: grad@arcadia.edu.

Arcadia University, School of Education, Glenside, PA 19038-3295. Offers art education (M Ed); computer education (CAS); curriculum (CAS); curriculum studies (M Ed); early childhood education (M Ed), including individualized, master teacher, research in child development; educational leadership (M Ed, Ed D, CAS); elementary education (M Ed); English education (MA Ed); environmental education (MA Ed); instructional technology (M Ed); language arts (M Ed); library science (M Ed); mathematics education (M Ed, MA Ed); music education (MA Ed); psychology (MA Ed); reading (M Ed, CAS); science education (M Ed, CAS); secondary education (M Ed, CAS); special education (M Ed, Ed D, CAS); theater arts (MA Ed); written communication (MA Ed). *Accreditation:* NASAD. *Program availability:* Part-time, evening/weekend, online learning. *Faculty:* 14 full-time (10 women). *Students:* 35 full-time (24 women), 299 part-time (243 women); includes 72 minority (49 Black or African American, non-Hispanic/Latino; 1 American Indian or Alaska Native, non-Hispanic/Latino; 12 Asian, non-Hispanic/Latino; 8 Hispanic/Latino; 2 Two or more races, non-Hispanic/Latino), 5 international. In 2018, 152 master's, 8 doctorates awarded. *Entrance requirements:* Additional exam requirements/recommendations for international students: Required—Official results from the TOEFL or IELTS are required. *Application deadline:* Applications are processed on a rolling basis. Application fee: $25. Electronic applications accepted. *Expenses:* Contact institution. *Financial support:* Career-related internships or fieldwork, tuition waivers (partial), and unspecified assistantships available. *Unit head:* Kimberly Dean, Chair, 215-572-8629. *Application contact:* 215-572-2925, Fax: 215-572-2126, E-mail: grad@arcadia.edu.

Arizona State University at the Tempe campus, Mary Lou Fulton Teachers College, Program in Special Education, Phoenix, AZ 85069. Offers autism spectrum disorder (Graduate Certificate); special education (M Ed). *Program availability:* Online learning. *Degree requirements:* For master's, thesis or alternative, applied project, student teaching, interactive Program of Study (iPOS) submitted before completing 50 percent of required credit hours. *Entrance requirements:* For master's, Arizona Educator Proficiency Assessments (AEPA), minimum GPA of 3.0 or equivalent in last 2 years of work leading to bachelor's degree, 3 letters of recommendation, personal statement, resume, IVP fingerprint clearance card (for those seeking Arizona certification). Additional exam requirements/recommendations for international students: Required—TOEFL, IELTS, or PTE. Electronic applications accepted.

Arkansas State University, Graduate School, College of Education and Behavioral Science, Department of Psychology and Counseling, State University, AR 72467. Offers clinical mental health counseling (Graduate Certificate); college student personnel services (MS); dyslexia therapy (Graduate Certificate); psychological science (MS); psychology and counseling (Ed S); rehabilitation counseling (MRC); school counseling (MSE); student affairs (Graduate Certificate). *Accreditation:* ACA (one or more programs are accredited); CORE (one or more programs are accredited); NCATE. *Program availability:* Part-time. *Degree requirements:* For master's and other advanced degree, comprehensive exam, thesis or alternative. *Entrance requirements:* For master's, GRE General Test or MAT (for MSE), appropriate bachelor's degree, interview, letters of reference, official transcripts, immunization records, written statement, 2-3 page autobiography; for other advanced degree, GRE General Test, interview, master's degree, letters of reference, official transcript, personal statement, immunization records. Additional exam requirements/recommendations for international students: Required—TOEFL (minimum score 550 paper-based; 79 iBT), IELTS (minimum score 6), PTE (minimum score 56). Electronic applications accepted.

Special Education

Arkansas State University, Graduate School, College of Education and Behavioral Science, School of Teacher Education and Leadership, State University, AR 72467. Offers community college administration (SCCT); curriculum and instruction (MSE); early childhood education (MSE); early childhood services (MS); educational leadership (MSE, Ed D, Ed S); educational theory and practice (MSE); middle level education (MAT, MSE); reading (MSE, Ed S); special education - gifted, talented, and creative (MSE); special education - instructional specialist grades 4-12 (MSE); special education - instructional specialist grades P-4 (MSE); special education, K-12 (MSE). *Accreditation:* NCATE. *Program availability:* Part-time, online learning. *Degree requirements:* For master's, comprehensive exam, thesis or alternative; for doctorate, comprehensive exam, thesis/dissertation; for other advanced degree, comprehensive exam. *Entrance requirements:* For master's, GRE General Test or MAT, appropriate bachelor's degree, official transcripts, immunization records, letters of reference, interview; for doctorate, GRE General Test or MAT, interview, master's degree, letters of reference, official transcript, personal statement, writing sample, immunization records; for other advanced degree, GRE General Test or MAT, interview, master's degree, official transcript, immunization records, letters of reference, 3 years of teaching experience, teaching license. Additional exam requirements/recommendations for international students: Required—TOEFL (minimum score 550 paper-based; 79 iBT), IELTS (minimum score 6), PTE (minimum score 56). Electronic applications accepted.

Arkansas State University, Graduate School, College of Nursing and Health Professions, Department of Communication Disorders, State University, AR 72467. Offers communication disorders (MCD); dyslexia therapy (Graduate Certificate). *Accreditation:* ASHA. *Program availability:* Part-time. *Degree requirements:* For master's, comprehensive exam, thesis or alternative. *Entrance requirements:* For master's, GRE General Test, appropriate bachelor's degree, letters of recommendation, official transcripts, immunization records. Additional exam requirements/recommendations for international students: Required—TOEFL (minimum score 550 paper-based; 79 iBT), IELTS (minimum score 6), PTE (minimum score 56). Electronic applications accepted. *Expenses:* Contact institution.

Arkansas Tech University, College of Education, Russellville, AR 72801. Offers college student personnel (MS); educational leadership (M Ed, Ed S); instructional technology (M Ed); school counseling and leadership (M Ed); school leadership (Ed D); special education K-12 (M Ed); strength and conditioning studies (MS); teaching (MAT); teaching, learning, and leadership (M Ed). *Accreditation:* NCATE. *Program availability:* Part-time, evening/weekend, 100% online, blended/hybrid learning. *Students:* 90 full-time (52 women), 450 part-time (359 women); includes 100 minority (63 Black or African American, non-Hispanic/Latino; 6 American Indian or Alaska Native, non-Hispanic/Latino; 1 Asian, non-Hispanic/Latino; 15 Hispanic/Latino; 15 Two or more races, non-Hispanic/Latino), 4 international. Average age 34. In 2018, 130 master's, 14 doctorates, 1 other advanced degree awarded. *Degree requirements:* For master's, comprehensive exam, thesis optional, action research project; for doctorate, thesis/dissertation. *Entrance requirements:* Additional exam requirements/recommendations for international students: Required—TOEFL (minimum score 550 paper-based; 79 iBT), IELTS (minimum score 6.5), PTE (minimum score 58). *Application deadline:* For fall admission, 3/1 priority date for domestic students, 5/1 priority date for international students; for spring admission, 10/1 priority date for domestic and international students. Applications are processed on a rolling basis. Application fee: $40 ($90 for international students). Electronic applications accepted. *Expenses: Tuition, area resident:* Full-time $6816; part-time $284 per credit hour. Tuition, state resident: full-time $6816; part-time $284 per credit hour. Tuition, nonresident: full-time $13,632; part-time $568 per credit hour. *International tuition:* $13,632 full-time. *Required fees:* $457.50 per semester. Tuition and fees vary according to course load and degree level. *Financial support:* In 2018–19, research assistantships with full and partial tuition reimbursements (averaging $4,800 per year), teaching assistantships with full and partial tuition reimbursements (averaging $4,800 per year) were awarded; career-related internships or fieldwork, Federal Work-Study, scholarships/grants, health care benefits, and unspecified assistantships also available. Support available to part-time students. Financial award application deadline: 4/15; financial award applicants required to submit FAFSA. *Unit head:* Dr. Linda Bean, Dean, 479-964-3217, E-mail: lbean@atu.edu. *Application contact:* Dr. Jeff Robertson, Interim Dean of Graduate College, 479-968-0398, Fax: 479-964-0542, E-mail: gradcollege@atu.edu.
Website: http://www.atu.edu/education/

Asbury University, School of Graduate and Professional Studies, Wilmore, KY 40390-1198. Offers biology: alternative certificate (MA Ed); chemistry: alternative certificate (MA Ed); English (MA Ed); English as a second language (MA Ed); ESL (MA Ed); French (MA Ed); Latin: alternative certificate (MA Ed); mathematics: alternative certificate (MA Ed); reading/writing endorsement (MA Ed); social studies (MA Ed); social work (MSW), including child and family services; Spanish (MA Ed); special education (MA Ed); special education: alternative certificate (MA Ed); teacher as leader endorsement (MA Ed). *Accreditation:* NCATE. *Program availability:* Part-time. *Degree requirements:* For master's, action research project, portfolio. *Entrance requirements:* For master's, PRAXIS/NTE, minimum GPA of 2.75, letters of recommendation. Additional exam requirements/recommendations for international students: Required—TOEFL (minimum score 550 paper-based). Electronic applications accepted.

Assumption College, Special Education Program, Worcester, MA 01609-1296. Offers positive behavior support (CAGS); special education (MA). *Program availability:* Part-time, evening/weekend. *Degree requirements:* For master's, comprehensive exam, internship, practicum. *Entrance requirements:* For master's, bachelor's degree with minimum GPA of 3.0, three letters of recommendation, official transcripts, personal statement, current resume, teacher certification documents (if certified or licensed); for CAGS, MA or M Ed, minimum one year of full-time employment in educational setting, three letters of recommendation, official transcripts, personal statement, current resume, interview. Additional exam requirements/recommendations for international students: Required—TOEFL (minimum score 540 paper-based; 76 iBT), IELTS (minimum score 6). Electronic applications accepted.

Auburn University, Graduate School, College of Education, Department of Special Education, Rehabilitation, and Counseling, Auburn University, AL 36849. Offers M Ed, MS, PhD. *Accreditation:* CORE; NCATE. *Program availability:* Part-time. *Degree requirements:* For master's, thesis (for some programs); for doctorate, thesis/dissertation. *Entrance requirements:* For master's, GRE General Test; for doctorate, GRE General Test, interview. Electronic applications accepted. *Expenses:* Tuition, state resident: full-time $11,282; part-time $535 per credit hour. Tuition, nonresident: full-time $30,542; part-time $1605 per credit hour. *Required fees:* $826 per semester. Tuition and fees vary according to degree level and program. *Faculty research:* Emotional conflict/behavior disorders, gifted and talented, learning disabilities, mental retardation, multi-handicapped.

Auburn University at Montgomery, College of Education, Department of Counselor, Leadership, and Special Education, Montgomery, AL 36124-4023. Offers counselor education (M Ed, Ed S), including clinical mental health counseling, school counseling; early childhood special education (M Ed); instructional leadership (M Ed, Ed S); special education/collaborative teacher (M Ed, Ed S). *Accreditation:* ACA; NCATE. *Program availability:* Part-time, evening/weekend. *Students:* Average age 34. 76 applicants, 72% accepted, 26 enrolled. In 2018, 37 master's awarded. *Entrance requirements:* For master's, GRE General Test or MAT, certification, BS in teaching; for Ed S, GRE General Test or MAT, certification. Additional exam requirements/recommendations for international students: Recommended—TOEFL (minimum score 500 paper-based; 61 iBT), IELTS (minimum score 5.5), TSE (minimum score 44). *Application deadline:* For fall admission, 7/15 for international students; for spring admission, 11/15 for international students; for summer admission, 4/15 for international students. Applications are processed on a rolling basis. Electronic applications accepted. *Expenses: Tuition, area resident:* Full-time $7146; part-time $4764 per credit hour. Tuition, state resident: full-time $7146; part-time $4764 per credit hour. Tuition, nonresident: full-time $16,056; part-time $10,704 per credit hour. *International tuition:* $16,056 full-time. *Required fees:* $766. One-time fee: $25 full-time. *Financial support:* Career-related internships or fieldwork and scholarships/grants available. Support available to part-time students. Financial award application deadline: 3/1; financial award applicants required to submit FAFSA. *Unit head:* Dr. Samuel Flynt, Head, 334-244-3835, Fax: 334-244-3101, E-mail: sflynt@aum.edu. *Application contact:* Dr. Rhonda Morton, Associate Dean/Graduate Coordinator, 334-244-3287, Fax: 334-244-3978, E-mail: rmorton@aum.edu.
Website: http://education.aum.edu/academic-departments/counselor-leadership-and-special-education

Augustana University, MA in Education Program, Sioux Falls, SD 57197. Offers instructional strategies (MA); reading (MA); special populations (MA); STEM (MA); technology (MA). *Accreditation:* NCATE. *Program availability:* Part-time-only, evening/weekend, online only, 100% online. *Degree requirements:* For master's, thesis. *Entrance requirements:* For master's, appropriate bachelor's degree, minimum GPA of 3.0, teaching certificate. Additional exam requirements/recommendations for international students: Required—TOEFL (minimum score 550 paper-based). Electronic applications accepted. *Expenses:* Contact institution. *Faculty research:* Multicultural education, education of students with autism, well-being in school settings, factors that predict academic hopefulness.

Augusta University, College of Education, Program in Curriculum and Instruction, Augusta, GA 30912. Offers curriculum and instruction (Ed S); elementary education (MAT); foreign language education (MAT); instruction (M Ed); middle grades education (MAT); music education (MAT); secondary education (MAT); special education (MAT). *Degree requirements:* For master's, thesis, portfolio. *Entrance requirements:* For master's, GRE, MAT, minimum GPA of 2.5.

Aurora University, School of Education and Human Performance, Aurora, IL 60506-4892. Offers applied behavioral analysis (MS); bilingual-ESL education (MA); educational leadership with principal endorsement (MA); educational technology (MA); leadership in adult learning higher education (Ed D); leadership in curriculum and instruction (Ed D); leadership in educational administration (Ed D); reading instruction (MA); special education (MA). *Accreditation:* NCATE. *Program availability:* Part-time, evening/weekend, 100% online. *Faculty:* 14 full-time (6 women), 32 part-time/adjunct (17 women). *Students:* 28 full-time (25 women), 537 part-time (359 women); includes 101 minority (25 Black or African American, non-Hispanic/Latino; 8 Asian, non-Hispanic/Latino; 58 Hispanic/Latino; 2 Native Hawaiian or other Pacific Islander, non-Hispanic/Latino; 8 Two or more races, non-Hispanic/Latino), 2 international. Average age 38. 191 applicants, 98% accepted, 133 enrolled. In 2018, 213 master's, 16 doctorates awarded. *Degree requirements:* For master's, student teaching, research seminar, and practicum; for doctorate, comprehensive exam, thesis/dissertation. *Entrance requirements:* For master's, 2 years of teaching experience, valid teaching certificate, resume; for doctorate, appropriate master's degree, two references, curriculum vitae, personal statement, professional project, reflective essay. Additional exam requirements/recommendations for international students: Required—TOEFL (minimum score 550 paper-based; 79 iBT). *Application deadline:* For fall admission, 6/1 for international students; for spring admission, 10/1 for international students. Applications are processed on a rolling basis. Application fee: $0. Electronic applications accepted. *Expenses:* The reported tuition amount is for the program with the greatest enrollment, MA in Educational Leadership with Principal Endorsement. Other programs may require more semester hours, and thus have a greater total cost. The Education doctoral programs are roughly double the amount of the master's programs. *Financial support:* In 2018–19, 31 students received support. Federal Work-Study, scholarships/grants, and unspecified assistantships available. Financial award applicants required to submit FAFSA. *Unit head:* Dr. Jen Buckley, Dean, School of Education and Human Performance, 630-844-1542, Fax: 630-844-6155, E-mail: jbuckley@aurora.edu. *Application contact:* Center for Graduate Studies, 630-947-8955, E-mail: AUadmission@aurora.edu.
Website: http://aurora.edu/education

Averett University, Master in Education Program, Danville, VA 24541-3692. Offers administration and supervision (M Ed); curriculum and instruction (M Ed); special education with endorsement (M Ed); special education with licensure (M Ed). *Program availability:* Part-time, online only, 100% online. *Faculty:* 2 full-time (both women), 14 part-time/adjunct (11 women). *Students:* 141 full-time (108 women), 4 part-time (2 women); includes 31 minority (30 Black or African American, non-Hispanic/Latino; 1 Hispanic/Latino). Average age 37. 106 applicants, 58% accepted, 52 enrolled. In 2018, 52 master's awarded. *Degree requirements:* For master's, 30-credit core curriculum, minimum GPA of 3.0 throughout program, completion of degree requirements within six years from start of program. *Entrance requirements:* For master's, PRAXIS I, GRE, or MAT; writing proficiency test, minimum cumulative GPA of 3.0 over the last 60 hours of undergraduate study toward a baccalaureate degree, three letters of recommendation, Virginia teaching license (or eligibility). Additional exam requirements/recommendations for international students: Required—TOEFL (minimum score 600 paper-based; 100 iBT). *Application deadline:* Applications are processed on a rolling basis. Electronic applications accepted. *Expenses:* Contact institution. *Financial support:* Application deadline: 3/1; applicants required to submit FAFSA. *Unit head:* Dr. Nancy Riddell, Chair of the Education Department; Director of Teacher Education, 434-791-5741, Fax: 434-791-5020, E-mail: nriddell@averett.edu. *Application contact:* Christy Davis, Assistant Director of Admissions, 434-791-7133, E-mail: cdavis@averett.edu.
Website: http://gps.averett.edu/online/education/

Azusa Pacific University, School of Education, Department of Teacher Education, Program in Special Education, Azusa, CA 91702-7000. Offers MA Ed. *Accreditation:* NCATE. *Program availability:* Part-time, evening/weekend. *Degree requirements:* For master's, core exams, oral presentations. *Entrance requirements:* For master's, 12 units of course work in education, minimum GPA of 3.0.

Baldwin Wallace University, Graduate Programs, School of Education, Specialization in Mild/Moderate Educational Needs, Berea, OH 44017-2088. Offers MA Ed. *Accreditation:* NCATE. *Program availability:* Part-time, evening/weekend, 100% online. *Students:* 18 full-time (13 women), 20 part-time (17 women); includes 5 minority (3 Black or African American, non-Hispanic/Latino; 1 Hispanic/Latino; 1 Two or more races, non-Hispanic/Latino). Average age 34. 11 applicants, 82% accepted, 7 enrolled. In 2018, 22 master's awarded. *Degree requirements:* For master's, capstone practicum. *Entrance requirements:* For master's, bachelor's degree in field, MAT or minimum GPA of 3.0. Additional exam requirements/recommendations for international students: Required—

TOEFL (minimum score 550 paper-based; 79 iBT). *Application deadline:* For fall admission, 8/15 priority date for domestic students; for spring admission, 12/15 priority date for domestic students. Applications are processed on a rolling basis. Application fee: $25. Electronic applications accepted. Application fee is waived when completed online. *Expenses:* Partnership tuition - $545 per credit; Non-partnership tuition - $721 per credit. *Financial support:* Career-related internships or fieldwork available. Financial award applicants required to submit FAFSA. *Faculty research:* Adult adjustment of individuals formerly identified as having mild/moderate special education needs, professional development of special educators, teacher beliefs and special education, classroom assessment practices. *Unit head:* Dr. Debra Janas, Coordinator, 440-826-8177, Fax: 440-826-3779, E-mail: djanas@bw.edu. *Application contact:* Amirya Alveranga, Admission Counselor, 440-826-8005, Fax: 440-826-3830, E-mail: aalveran@bw.edu.
Website: http://www.bw.edu/academics/master-of-arts-in-education/maed-mild-moderate/

Ball State University, Graduate School, Teachers College, Department of Educational Studies, Muncie, IN 47306. Offers adult education (MA, Ed D, Certificate), including adult and community education (MA), adult, higher and community education (Ed D); college and university teaching (Certificate); community college leadership (Certificate); community education (Certificate); computer education (Certificate); curriculum and educational technology (MA); diversity studies (Certificate); educational studies (PhD), including educational studies; executive development for public service (MA); middle-level education (Certificate); qualitative research in education (Certificate); secondary education (MA); student affairs administration in higher education (MA), including student affairs administration in higher education. *Accreditation:* NCATE. *Program availability:* Part-time, 100% online, blended/hybrid learning. *Entrance requirements:* For master's, minimum baccalaureate GPA of 2.75 or 3.0 in latter half of baccalaureate; for doctorate, minimum graduate GPA of 3.2. Additional exam requirements/recommendations for international students: Required—TOEFL (minimum score 550 paper-based; 79 iBT), IELTS (minimum score 6.5). Electronic applications accepted.

Ball State University, Graduate School, Teachers College, Department of Special Education, Program in Applied Behavior Analysis, Muncie, IN 47306. Offers applied behavior analysis (MA), including autism. *Program availability:* Part-time, online only, 100% online. *Entrance requirements:* For master's, minimum baccalaureate GPA of 2.75 or 3.0 in latter half of baccalaureate. Additional exam requirements/recommendations for international students: Required—TOEFL (minimum score 550 paper-based; 79 iBT), IELTS (minimum score 6.5). Electronic applications accepted.

Ball State University, Graduate School, Teachers College, Department of Special Education, Program in Special Education, Muncie, IN 47306. Offers special education (MA, Ed D). *Program availability:* Part-time, 100% online, blended/hybrid learning. *Degree requirements:* For doctorate, thesis/dissertation. *Entrance requirements:* For master's, minimum baccalaureate GPA of 2.75 or 3.0 in latter half of baccalaureate; for doctorate, GRE General Test, minimum graduate GPA of 3.2. Additional exam requirements/recommendations for international students: Required—TOEFL (minimum score 550 paper-based; 79 iBT), IELTS (minimum score 6.5). Electronic applications accepted.

Bank Street College of Education, Graduate School, Program in Infant and Family Development and Early Intervention, New York, NY 10025. Offers infant and family development (MS Ed); infant and family early childhood special and general education (MS Ed); infant and family/early childhood special education (Ed M). *Degree requirements:* For master's, thesis. *Entrance requirements:* For master's, interview, essays. Additional exam requirements/recommendations for international students: Required—TOEFL (minimum score 600 paper-based; 100 iBT), IELTS (minimum score 7). Electronic applications accepted. *Faculty research:* Early intervention, early attachment practice in infant and toddler childcare, parenting skills in adolescents.

Bank Street College of Education, Graduate School, Program in Special Education, New York, NY 10025. Offers early childhood special and general education (MS Ed); early childhood special education (Ed M, MS Ed); elementary/childhood special and general education (MS Ed); elementary/childhood special education (MS Ed); elementary/childhood special education certification (Ed M). *Degree requirements:* For master's, thesis. *Entrance requirements:* For master's, interview, essays. Additional exam requirements/recommendations for international students: Required—TOEFL (minimum score 600 paper-based; 100 iBT), IELTS (minimum score 7). Electronic applications accepted. *Faculty research:* Teaching students with disabilities, inclusion, observation and assessment, early intervention, neurodevelopmental assessment, equity and social justice in education.

Barry University, School of Education, Program in Education for Teachers of Students with Hearing Impairments, Miami Shores, FL 33161-6695. Offers MS.

Barry University, School of Education, Program in Exceptional Student Education, Miami Shores, FL 33161-6695. Offers MS, Ed S. *Program availability:* Part-time, evening/weekend. *Degree requirements:* For master's, comprehensive exam; for Ed S, practicum. *Entrance requirements:* For master's, GRE General Test or MAT, minimum GPA of 3.0; for Ed S, GRE General Test, minimum GPA of 3.0. Electronic applications accepted.

Barry University, School of Education, Program in Leadership and Education, Miami Shores, FL 33161-6695. Offers educational technology (PhD); exceptional student education (PhD); higher education administration (PhD); human resource development (PhD); leadership (PhD). *Program availability:* Part-time, evening/weekend. *Degree requirements:* For doctorate, thesis/dissertation. *Entrance requirements:* For doctorate, GRE General Test, minimum GPA of 3.25. Electronic applications accepted.

Bayamón Central University, Graduate Programs, Program in Education, Bayamón, PR 00960-1725. Offers administration and supervision (MA Ed); commercial education (MA Ed); elementary education (K–3) (MA Ed); family counseling (Graduate Certificate); guidance and counseling (MA Ed); pre-elementary teacher (MA Ed); rehabilitation counseling (MA Ed); special education (MA Ed), including attention deficit disorder, education of the autistic, learning disabilities. *Program availability:* Part-time, evening/weekend. *Degree requirements:* For master's, comprehensive exam. *Entrance requirements:* For master's, EXADEP, bachelor's degree in education or related field.

Baylor University, Graduate School, School of Education, Department of Educational Psychology, Waco, TX 76798. Offers educational psychology (MS Ed); exceptionalities (PhD); learning and development (PhD); quantitative methods (MA); school psychology (Ed S). *Accreditation:* NCATE. *Students:* 51 full-time (46 women), 9 part-time (8 women); includes 18 minority (1 Black or African American, non-Hispanic/Latino; 3 Asian, non-Hispanic/Latino; 11 Hispanic/Latino; 3 Two or more races, non-Hispanic/Latino), 4 international. Average age 29. 90 applicants, 33% accepted, 30 enrolled. In 2018, 21 master's, 1 doctorate, 9 other advanced degrees awarded. Terminal master's awarded for partial completion of doctoral program. *Degree requirements:* For master's, thesis optional; for doctorate, comprehensive exam, thesis/dissertation; for Ed S, comprehensive exam, thesis or alternative. *Entrance requirements:* For master's, GRE, minimum GPA of 3.0; for doctorate, GRE General Test, master's degree; for Ed S, GRE General Test. Additional exam requirements/recommendations for international students: Required—TOEFL (minimum score 550 paper-based; 80 iBT), IELTS (minimum score 6.5). *Application deadline:* For fall admission, 2/1 priority date for domestic and international students. Application fee: $80. Electronic applications accepted. *Financial support:* In 2018–19, 42 students received support, including 20 fellowships with full and partial tuition reimbursements available, 22 research assistantships with full and partial tuition reimbursements available; career-related internships or fieldwork, Federal Work-Study, institutionally sponsored loans, scholarships/grants, health care benefits, tuition waivers (full and partial), unspecified assistantships, and stipends also available. Financial award application deadline: 2/1; financial award applicants required to submit FAFSA. *Faculty research:* Individual differences, quantitative methods, gifted and talented, special education, school psychology, autism, applied behavior analysis, learning, human development. *Total annual research expenditures:* $300,000. *Unit head:* Dr. Susan K. Johnsen, Professor and Interim Chair, 254-710-6116, E-mail: susan_johnsen@baylor.edu. *Application contact:* Heather Tindle, Office Manager, 254-710-3112, E-mail: heather_tindle@baylor.edu.
Website: http://www.baylor.edu/soe/EDP/

Bay Path University, Program in Clinical Mental Health Counseling, Longmeadow, MA 01106-2292. Offers clinical mental health counseling (MS), including alcohol and drug abuse counseling, early intervention. Program also offered in Sturbridge and Burlington, MA. *Program availability:* Part-time, blended/hybrid learning. *Students:* 75 full-time (66 women), 83 part-time (75 women); includes 37 minority (21 Black or African American, non-Hispanic/Latino; 1 American Indian or Alaska Native, non-Hispanic/Latino; 14 Hispanic/Latino; 1 Two or more races, non-Hispanic/Latino). Average age 34. *Entrance requirements:* For master's, completed application; official undergraduate and graduate transcripts (a GPA of 3.0 or higher is preferred); original essay of 300-500 words on the topic "Why the MS in Clinical Mental Health Counseling is important to my personal and professional goals"; current resume; 2 recommendations. *Application deadline:* Applications are processed on a rolling basis. Electronic applications accepted. Application fee is waived when completed online. *Expenses:* Contact institution. *Financial support:* Unspecified assistantships available. Financial award applicants required to submit FAFSA. *Unit head:* Dr. Mark Benander, Director, 413-565-1332, E-mail: mbenander@baypath.edu. *Application contact:* Anastasia Spremulli, Assistant Director of Graduate Admissions, 413-565-140, Fax: 413-565-1250, E-mail: aspremulli@baypath.edu.
Website: https://www.baypath.edu/academics/graduate-programs/clinical-mental-health-counseling-ms/

Bay Path University, Program in Education, Longmeadow, MA 01106-2292. Offers MS Ed/Ed S. *Program availability:* Part-time, 100% online. *Students:* 55 full-time (50 women), 168 part-time (149 women); includes 22 minority (6 Black or African American, non-Hispanic/Latino; 3 Asian, non-Hispanic/Latino; 11 Hispanic/Latino; 2 Two or more races, non-Hispanic/Latino). Average age 31. *Application deadline:* Applications are processed on a rolling basis. Electronic applications accepted. Application fee is waived when completed online. *Expenses:* Contact institution. *Financial support:* Unspecified assistantships available. Financial award applicants required to submit FAFSA. *Unit head:* Dr. Ellen Rustico, Program Coordinator, E-mail: erustico@baypath.edu. *Application contact:* Katie Manning, Director of Graduate Admissions, 413-565-1337, Fax: 413-565-1250, E-mail: kmanning@baypath.edu.
Website: http://graduate.baypath.edu/Graduate-Programs/Programs-On-Campus/MS-Programs/Education-Special-Education

Bemidji State University, School of Graduate Studies, Bemidji, MN 56601. Offers biology (MS); education (MS); English (MA, MS); environmental studies (MS); mathematics (MS); mathematics (elementary and middle level education) (MS); special education (M Sp Ed). *Program availability:* Part-time, online learning. *Degree requirements:* For master's, comprehensive exam, thesis (for some programs). *Entrance requirements:* For master's, GRE; GMAT, letters of recommendation, letters of interest. Additional exam requirements/recommendations for international students: Required—TOEFL (minimum score 550 paper-based; 80 iBT). Electronic applications accepted. *Expenses:* Contact institution. *Faculty research:* Human performance, sport, and health: physical education teacher education, continuum models, spiritual health, intellectual health, resiliency, health priorities; psychology: health psychology, college student drinking behavior, micro-aggressions, infant cognition, false memories, leadership assessment; biology: structure and dynamics of forest communities, aquatic and riverine ecology, interaction between animal populations and aquatic environments, cellular motility.

Bethel University, Graduate School, St. Paul, MN 55112-6999. Offers business administration (MBA); classroom management (Certificate); counseling (MA); K-12 education (MA); leadership (Ed D); leadership foundations (Certificate); nurse educator (MS, Certificate); nurse-midwifery (MS); physician assistant (MS); special education (MA); strategic leadership (MA); teaching (MA); teaching and learning (Certificate). *Program availability:* Part-time, evening/weekend, 100% online, blended/hybrid learning. *Faculty:* 23 full-time (17 women), 73 part-time/adjunct (45 women). *Students:* 586 full-time (426 women), 372 part-time (244 women); includes 141 minority (49 Black or African American, non-Hispanic/Latino; 6 American Indian or Alaska Native, non-Hispanic/Latino; 19 Asian, non-Hispanic/Latino; 40 Hispanic/Latino; 2 Native Hawaiian or other Pacific Islander, non-Hispanic/Latino; 25 Two or more races, non-Hispanic/Latino), 25 international. Average age 35. 642 applicants, 39% accepted, 194 enrolled. In 2018, 312 master's, 28 doctorates, 134 other advanced degrees awarded. *Degree requirements:* For master's, comprehensive exam (for some programs), thesis (for some programs); for doctorate, comprehensive exam, thesis/dissertation. *Entrance requirements:* Additional exam requirements/recommendations for international students: Required—TOEFL (minimum score 550 paper-based; 80 iBT), TOEFL (minimum score 550 paper-based, 80 iBT) or IELTS. *Application deadline:* Applications are processed on a rolling basis. Application fee: $0. Electronic applications accepted. *Expenses:* Contact institution. *Financial support:* Teaching assistantships, career-related internships or fieldwork, and scholarships/grants available. Support available to part-time students. Financial award applicants required to submit FAFSA. *Unit head:* Dr. Randy Bergen, Associate Provost, 651-635-8000, Fax: 651-635-8004, E-mail: r-bergen@bethel.edu. *Application contact:* Director of Admissions, 651-635-8000, Fax: 651-635-8004, E-mail: gs@bethel.edu.
Website: https://www.bethel.edu/graduate/

Binghamton University, State University of New York, Graduate School, College of Community and Public Affairs, Department of Teaching, Learning and Educational Leadership, Program in Special Education, Binghamton, NY 13902-6000. Offers MS Ed. *Accreditation:* TEAC. *Program availability:* Part-time, evening/weekend. *Degree requirements:* For master's, portfolio. *Entrance requirements:* For master's, GRE General Test, teaching certification. Additional exam requirements/recommendations for international students: Required—TOEFL (minimum score 550 paper-based; 80 iBT). Electronic applications accepted.

Biola University, School of Education, La Mirada, CA 90639-0001. Offers curriculum and instruction (Certificate); early childhood (MA Ed, MAT); multiple subject (MAT); single subject (MAT); special education (MA Ed, MAT, Certificate). *Program availability:* Part-time, evening/weekend, online learning. *Entrance requirements:* For master's, CBEST, CSET, GRE (waived if cumulative GPA is 3.5 or above or if CBEST and all

CSET subtests are passed). Additional exam requirements/recommendations for international students: Required—TOEFL (minimum score 100 iBT). Electronic applications accepted. *Faculty research:* Early childhood education, elementary education, special education, curriculum development, teacher preparation.

Bloomsburg University of Pennsylvania, School of Graduate Studies, College of Education, Department of Exceptionality Programs, Program in Special Education, Bloomsburg, PA 17815-1301. Offers M Ed, MS, Certificate. *Accreditation:* NCATE. *Degree requirements:* For master's, thesis, minimum QPA of 3.0, practicum. *Entrance requirements:* For master's, teaching certificate, minimum QPA of 2.8, letter of intent, 2 letters of recommendation, interview, professional liability insurance, recent TB screening. Additional exam requirements/recommendations for international students: Required—TOEFL (minimum score 550 paper-based), IELTS. Electronic applications accepted.

Bluffton University, Programs in Education, Bluffton, OH 45817. Offers intervention specialist (MA Ed); leadership (MA Ed); reading (MA Ed). *Accreditation:* NCATE. *Program availability:* Part-time, 100% online, blended/hybrid learning, videoconference. *Faculty:* 2 full-time (both women), 2 part-time/adjunct (1 woman). *Students:* 14 full-time (7 women), 7 part-time (all women). Average age 31. In 2018, 8 master's awarded. *Degree requirements:* For master's, action research project, public presentation. *Entrance requirements:* For master's, PRAXIS I, bachelor's degree, minimum GPA of 3.0. Additional exam requirements/recommendations for international students: Required—TOEFL. *Application deadline:* For fall admission, 8/15 priority date for domestic students, 6/15 priority date for international students; for spring admission, 12/15 priority date for domestic students, 9/15 priority date for international students. Applications are processed on a rolling basis. Electronic applications accepted. *Expenses:* Contact institution. *Financial support:* Unspecified assistantships available. Financial award application deadline: 9/15; financial award applicants required to submit FAFSA. *Unit head:* Dr. Amy K. Mullins, Director of Graduate Programs in Education, 419-358-3457, E-mail: mullinsa@bluffton.edu. *Application contact:* Shelby Koenig, Enrollment Counselor for Graduate Program, 419-358-3022, E-mail: koenigs@bluffton.edu.
Website: https://www.bluffton.edu/ags/index.aspx

Bob Jones University, Graduate Programs, Greenville, SC 29614. Offers accountancy (MS); Bible (MA); Bible translation (MA); Biblical studies (Certificate); business administration (MBA); church history (MA, PhD); church ministries (MA); church music (MM); cinema and video production (MA); counseling (MS); curriculum and instruction (Ed D); divinity (M Div); dramatic production (MA); educational leadership (MS, Ed D, Ed S); elementary education (M Ed, MAT); English (M Ed, MA, MAT); fine arts (MA); graphic design (MA); history (M Ed, MA); illustration (MA); interpretative speech (MA); mathematics (M Ed, MAT); medical missions (Certificate); ministry (MM, D Min); multi-categorical special education (M Ed, MAT); music (M Ed); New Testament interpretation (PhD); Old Testament interpretation (PhD); orchestral instrument performance (MM); organ performance (MM); pastoral studies (MA); personnel services (MS, Ed S); piano pedagogy (MM); piano performance (MM); platform arts (MA); rhetoric and public address (MA); secondary education (M Ed); studio art (MA); teaching Bible (MA); theology (MA, PhD); voice performance (MM); youth ministries (MA); M Div/MM.

Boise State University, College of Education, Department of Early and Special Education, Boise, ID 83725-0399. Offers early and special education (M Ed). *Accreditation:* NCATE. *Program availability:* Part-time. *Degree requirements:* For master's, thesis optional. *Entrance requirements:* For master's, minimum GPA of 3.0. Additional exam requirements/recommendations for international students: Required—TOEFL (minimum score 587 paper-based; 95 iBT), IELTS (minimum score 6.5). Electronic applications accepted.

Boston College, Lynch School of Education and Human Development, Department of Teacher Education, Special Education and Curriculum and Instruction, Chestnut Hill, MA 02467-3800. Offers curriculum and instruction (M Ed, PhD, CAES); early childhood education (M Ed); elementary education (M Ed); law and curriculum and instruction (JD/M Ed); reading specialist (M Ed, CAES); religious education (M Ed, CAES); secondary education (M Ed, MAT, MST), including biology (MST), chemistry (MST), English (MAT), French (MAT), geology (MST), history (MAT), Latin and classical humanities (MAT), mathematics (MST), physics (MST), secondary teaching (M Ed), Spanish (MAT); special needs: moderate disabilities (M Ed, CAES); special needs: severe disabilities (M Ed); JD/M Ed. *Program availability:* Part-time, evening/weekend, 100% online. *Faculty:* 19 full-time (11 women). *Students:* 186 full-time (140 women), 92 part-time (74 women); includes 58 minority (20 Black or African American, non-Hispanic/Latino; 4 Asian, non-Hispanic/Latino; 29 Hispanic/Latino; 5 Two or more races, non-Hispanic/Latino), 33 international. Average age 28. In 2018, 132 master's, 13 doctorates awarded. Terminal master's awarded for partial completion of doctoral program. *Degree requirements:* For master's, comprehensive exam; for doctorate, comprehensive exam, thesis/dissertation. *Entrance requirements:* Additional exam requirements/recommendations for international students: Required—TOEFL. Application fee: $75. Electronic applications accepted. *Financial support:* Fellowships with full and partial tuition reimbursements, research assistantships with full and partial tuition reimbursements, teaching assistantships with full and partial tuition reimbursements, career-related internships or fieldwork, Federal Work-Study, institutionally sponsored loans, scholarships/grants, traineeships, health care benefits, tuition waivers (full and partial), and unspecified assistantships available. Support available to part-time students. Financial award applicants required to submit FAFSA. *Faculty research:* Teacher education, education research and policy, bilingual education, science education, disabilities, urban education. *Unit head:* Dr. Susan Bruce, Chairperson, 617-552-4214, Fax: 617-552-0812. *Application contact:* Jessica Rivers, Assistant Dean of Graduate Admission and Financial Aid, 617-552-4214, Fax: 617-552-0398, E-mail: riversja@bc.edu.
Website: http://www.bc.edu/education

Bowie State University, Graduate Programs, Program in Special Education, Bowie, MD 20715-9465. Offers M Ed. *Accreditation:* NCATE. *Program availability:* Part-time, evening/weekend. *Degree requirements:* For master's, comprehensive exam, thesis optional, research paper. *Entrance requirements:* For master's, teaching experience, 3 professional letters of recommendation. Electronic applications accepted.

Bowling Green State University, Graduate College, College of Education and Human Development, School of Intervention Services, Program in Special Education, Bowling Green, OH 43403. Offers assistive technology (M Ed); autism spectrum disorders (M Ed); general special education (M Ed); intervention specialist: mild/moderate disabilities (M Ed); intervention specialist: moderate/intensive disabilities (M Ed); secondary transition/transition-to-work (M Ed). *Accreditation:* NCATE. *Program availability:* Part-time. *Degree requirements:* For master's, thesis or alternative. *Entrance requirements:* For master's, GRE General Test. Additional exam requirements/recommendations for international students: Required—TOEFL. Electronic applications accepted. *Faculty research:* Reading and special populations, deafness, early childhood, gifted and talented, behavior disorders.

Brandman University, School of Education, Irvine, CA 92618. Offers curriculum and instruction (MAE); educational administration (MAE); educational leadership (MAE); educational leadership and administration (MA); elementary education (MAT); instructional technology: teaching the 21st century learner (MAE); leadership in early childhood education (MAE); organizational leadership (Ed D); school counseling (MA); secondary education (MAT); special education (MA); teaching and learning (MAE).

Brandon University, Faculty of Education, Brandon, MB R7A 6A9, Canada. Offers curriculum and instruction (M Ed, Diploma); educational administration (M Ed, Diploma); guidance and counseling (M Ed, Diploma); special education (M Ed, Diploma). *Degree requirements:* For master's, thesis. *Entrance requirements:* For master's, minimum GPA of 3.0, teaching certificate or equivalent. Additional exam requirements/recommendations for international students: Required—TOEFL. *Faculty research:* Comparative education, environmental studies, parent/school council.

Brenau University, Sydney O. Smith Graduate School, College of Education, Gainesville, GA 30501. Offers early childhood (Ed S); early childhood education (M Ed, MAT); middle grades (Ed S); middle grades education (M Ed, MAT); secondary education (MAT); special education (M Ed, MAT). *Accreditation:* NCATE. *Program availability:* Part-time, evening/weekend, online learning. *Degree requirements:* For master's, thesis optional, comprehensive exam or applied research project, effective portfolio; for Ed S, thesis, applied research project. *Entrance requirements:* For master's, GRE, MAT, interview, minimum GPA of 3.0, 3 references, writing samples; for Ed S, GRE, MAT, master's degree, minimum GPA of 3.0, writing sample, letters of reference. Additional exam requirements/recommendations for international students: Required—TOEFL (minimum score 500 paper-based; 61 iBT); Recommended—IELTS (minimum score 5). Electronic applications accepted. *Expenses:* Contact institution.

Bridgewater State University, College of Graduate Studies, College of Education and Allied Studies, Department of Special Education, Bridgewater, MA 02325. Offers M Ed. *Accreditation:* NCATE. *Program availability:* Part-time, evening/weekend. *Entrance requirements:* For master's, GRE General Test or Massachusetts Test for Educator Licensure.

Brooklyn College of the City University of New York, School of Education, Program in Special Education, Brooklyn, NY 11210-2889. Offers autism spectrum disorders (AC); teacher of students with disabilities (MS Ed), including adolescence education, childhood education, early childhood education. *Program availability:* Part-time. *Entrance requirements:* For master's, LAST, interview; previous course work in education and psychology; minimum GPA of 3.0 in education, 2.8 overall; resume, 2 letters of recommendation; essay. Additional exam requirements/recommendations for international students: Required—TOEFL (minimum score 500 paper-based; 61 iBT). Electronic applications accepted. *Faculty research:* School reform, conflict resolution, curriculum for inclusive settings, urban issues in special education.

Buffalo State College, State University of New York, The Graduate School, School of Education, Department of Exceptional Education, Programs in Special Education, Buffalo, NY 14222-1095. Offers special education (MS Ed); special education: childhood (MS Ed); special education: early childhood (MS Ed). *Accreditation:* NCATE. *Program availability:* Part-time, evening/weekend. *Degree requirements:* For master's, thesis or project. *Entrance requirements:* For master's, minimum GPA of 2.5. Additional exam requirements/recommendations for international students: Required—TOEFL (minimum score 550 paper-based).

Cabrini University, Academic Affairs, Radnor, PA 19087. Offers accounting (M Acc); autism spectrum disorder (M Ed); biological sciences (MS), including civic leadership; criminology and criminal justice (MA); curriculum, instruction, and assessment (M Ed); educational leadership (M Ed, Ed D), including curriculum and instructional leadership (Ed D), preK-12 leadership (Ed D); English as a second language (M Ed); organizational leadership (DBA, PhD); preK to 4 (M Ed); reading specialist (M Ed); secondary education (M Ed), including biology, chemistry, English, English/communication, mathematics, social studies; special education grades 7-12 (M Ed); special education preK-8 (M Ed); teaching and learning (M Ed). *Program availability:* Part-time, evening/weekend. *Degree requirements:* For master's, comprehensive exam (for some programs), thesis (for some programs); for doctorate, comprehensive exam (for some programs), thesis/dissertation. *Entrance requirements:* For master's, professional resume, personal statement, two recommendations, official transcripts; for doctorate, official transcripts, minimum master's GPA of 3.0, two recommendations, interview with admissions committee. Additional exam requirements/recommendations for international students: Required—TOEFL (minimum score 80 iBT). Electronic applications accepted. Application fee is waived when completed online. *Expenses:* Contact institution.

Caldwell University, School of Education, Caldwell, NJ 07006-6195. Offers elementary, secondary or preschool endorsement, special ed, ESL (Postbaccalaureate Certificate). *Program availability:* Part-time, evening/weekend. *Faculty:* 9 full-time (6 women), 18 part-time/adjunct (10 women). *Students:* 35 full-time (29 women), 170 part-time (125 women); includes 45 minority (22 Black or African American, non-Hispanic/Latino; 1 American Indian or Alaska Native, non-Hispanic/Latino; 5 Asian, non-Hispanic/Latino; 14 Hispanic/Latino; 3 Two or more races, non-Hispanic/Latino). Average age 36. 75 applicants, 93% accepted, 42 enrolled. In 2018, 40 master's, 8 doctorates awarded. *Degree requirements:* For master's, comprehensive exam (for some programs), thesis (for some programs); for doctorate, thesis/dissertation. *Entrance requirements:* For master's, PRAXIS, 3 years of work experience (for some programs), prior teaching certification (for some programs); one to two professional references; writing sample (for some programs); personal statement (for some programs); interview (for some programs); bachelor's or graduate degree (for some programs); minimum 3.0 GPA (for some programs); for doctorate, GRE or MAT, 3 years of work experience, prior teaching certification; two letters of recommendation; copy of completed research paper/thesis (or other sample of some type of research writing); resume; interview; master's degree in education or related field; minimum 3.6 GPA in graduate courses; for other advanced degree, PRAXIS (for some programs), bachelor's degree (for some programs); master's degree (for some programs); minimum 3.0 GPA (for some programs); 2 professional references (for some programs); 2 letters of recommendation (for some programs); personal statement; interview; work experience (for some programs); prior certification (for some programs). Additional exam requirements/recommendations for international students: Required—The TOEFL or IELTS is required of international students who were not educated at the Bachelors level in English. Recommended—TOEFL (minimum score 580 paper-based; 92 iBT), IELTS (minimum score 7.5). *Application deadline:* For fall admission, 7/15 for domestic students. Applications are processed on a rolling basis. Application fee: $50. Electronic applications accepted. *Expenses:* $63,450 for full EdD tuition; $77,550 for full PhD tuition; $24,300 for full MA online tuition; $35,820 for full MA tuition. *Financial support:* Unspecified assistantships available. Financial award applicants required to submit FAFSA. *Faculty research:* Curriculum and instruction, secondary education, special education, education and technology, literacy instruction, higher education administration, education leadership. *Unit head:* Dr. Joan Moriarity, Associate Dean, 973-618-3626, E-mail: jmoriarity@caldwell.edu. *Application contact:* Tom Disch, Senior Admissions Counselor, 973-618-3544, E-mail: graduate@caldwell.edu.

California Baptist University, Program in Education, Riverside, CA 92504-3206. Offers educational leadership (MS); educational leadership for faith-based institutions (MS); educational leadership for public institutions (MS); educational technology (MS);

instructional computer applications (MS); international education (MS); leadership and adult learning (MS); leadership and organizational studies (MS); online teaching and learning (MS); reading (MS); science education (MA); special education in mild/moderate disabilities (MS); special education in moderate/severe disabilities (MS); teacher leadership (MS); teaching (MS); teaching and learning (MS). *Program availability:* Part-time, evening/weekend, 100% online, blended/hybrid learning. *Faculty:* 26 full-time (13 women), 28 part-time/adjunct (21 women). *Students:* 201 full-time (164 women), 265 part-time (209 women); includes 226 minority (23 Black or African American, non-Hispanic/Latino; 4 American Indian or Alaska Native, non-Hispanic/Latino; 7 Asian, non-Hispanic/Latino; 169 Hispanic/Latino; 6 Native Hawaiian or other Pacific Islander, non-Hispanic/Latino; 17 Two or more races, non-Hispanic/Latino), 2 international. Average age 39. 145 applicants, 97% accepted, 141 enrolled. In 2018, 253 master's awarded. *Degree requirements:* For master's, comprehensive exam, project, or thesis. *Entrance requirements:* For master's, minimum undergraduate GPA of 2.75; 500-word essay; three letters of recommendation; two prerequisite courses completed with minimum C grade. Additional exam requirements/recommendations for international students: Required—TOEFL (minimum score 80 iBT). *Application deadline:* For fall admission, 8/1 priority date for domestic students, 7/1 for international students; for spring admission, 12/1 priority date for domestic students, 11/1 for international students. Applications are processed on a rolling basis. Application fee: $45. Electronic applications accepted. *Expenses:* $634 per unit. *Financial support:* In 2018–19, 312 students received support. Federal Work-Study and scholarships/grants available. Financial award applicants required to submit CSS PROFILE or FAFSA. *Faculty research:* Leadership development, complexity theory, faith and learning, special education, social and philosophical contexts of education. *Unit head:* Dr. Robin Duncan, Dean, School of Education, 951-552-8948, E-mail: rduncan@calbaptist.edu. *Application contact:* Dr. Shari Farris, Program Director, Online MS in Education, 951-343-2455, E-mail: sfarris@calbaptist.edu.
Website: http://www.calbaptist.edu/mastersined/

California Lutheran University, Graduate Studies, Graduate School of Education, Thousand Oaks, CA 91360-2787. Offers counseling and guidance (MS), including college student personnel, counseling and guidance; educational leadership (MA, Ed D), including educational leadership (K-12) (Ed D), higher education leadership (Ed D); special education (MS); teacher leadership (M Ed); teaching (M Ed). *Accreditation:* NCATE. *Program availability:* Part-time, evening/weekend. *Degree requirements:* For master's, comprehensive exam or thesis; for doctorate, thesis/dissertation. *Entrance requirements:* For master's, GRE General Test, interview, minimum GPA of 3.0. Electronic applications accepted.

California State University, Bakersfield, Division of Graduate Studies, School of Social Sciences and Education, Program in Special Education, Bakersfield, CA 93311. Offers MA. *Accreditation:* NCATE. *Faculty:* 3 full-time (all women), 9 part-time/adjunct (4 women). *Students:* 15 full-time (12 women), 35 part-time (23 women); includes 28 minority (1 Black or African American, non-Hispanic/Latino; 2 Asian, non-Hispanic/Latino; 24 Hispanic/Latino; 1 Two or more races, non-Hispanic/Latino), 1 international. Average age 33. 28 applicants, 71% accepted, 13 enrolled. In 2018, 30 master's awarded. *Degree requirements:* For master's, thesis or alternative, project or culminating exam. *Entrance requirements:* For master's, 3 letters of recommendation, minimum GPA of 2.67, interview. *Application deadline:* Applications are processed on a rolling basis. Application fee: $55. *Unit head:* Dr. Jiwon Hwang, Director, 661-654-3055, Fax: 661-654-2479, E-mail: jhwang4@csub.edu. *Application contact:* Julia Bavier, Admissions and Graduation Advisor, 661-654-3193, Fax: 661-654-2479, E-mail: jbavier@csub.edu.
Website: https://www.csub.edu/specialed/index.html

California State University, Chico, Office of Graduate Studies, College of Communication and Education, School of Education, Chico, CA 95929-0722. Offers curriculum and instruction (MA); teaching English learners and special education advising patterns (MA), including special education, teaching English learners. *Program availability:* Part-time. *Faculty:* 8 full-time (5 women), 12 part-time/adjunct (10 women). *Students:* 15 applicants, 33% accepted, 5 enrolled. In 2018, 40 master's awarded. *Degree requirements:* For master's, thesis or project and comprehensive exam. *Entrance requirements:* For master's, 2 letters of recommendation, department letter of recommendation access waiver form, writing assessment: https://www.csuchico.edu/soe/_assets/documents/csu-chico-ma-educ-applicant-upload-instructions.pdf. Additional exam requirements/recommendations for international students: Required—TOEFL (minimum score 550 paper-based; 80 iBT), IELTS (minimum score 6.5), PTE (minimum score 59). *Application deadline:* For fall admission, 5/1 priority date for domestic and international students; for spring admission, 12/2 priority date for domestic and international students. Application fee: $55. Electronic applications accepted. *Expenses: Tuition, area resident:* Full-time $4622; part-time $3116 per unit. Tuition, state resident: full-time $4622; part-time $3116 per unit. Tuition, nonresident: full-time $10,634. *Required fees:* $2160; $1620 per year. Tuition and fees vary according to class time and program. *Financial support:* Fellowships, research assistantships, teaching assistantships, career-related internships or fieldwork, Federal Work-Study, scholarships/grants, traineeships, health care benefits, unspecified assistantships, and stipends available. Support available to part-time students. Financial award application deadline: 3/2; financial award applicants required to submit FAFSA. *Unit head:* Dr. Rebecca Justeson, Director, 530-898-6421, Fax: 530-898-6177, E-mail: educ@csuchico.edu. *Application contact:* Micah Lehner, Graduate Admission Coordinator, 530-898-5416, Fax: 530-898-3342, E-mail: mlehner@csuchico.edu.
Website: http://www.csuchico.edu/soe/

California State University, Dominguez Hills, College of Education, Division of Teacher Education, Program in Special Education, Carson, CA 90747-0001. Offers early childhood special education (MA). *Program availability:* Part-time, evening/weekend. *Degree requirements:* For master's, comprehensive exam, thesis or alternative. *Entrance requirements:* For master's, minimum GPA of 2.75 in last 60 units, 3 letters of recommendation. Additional exam requirements/recommendations for international students: Required—TOEFL.

California State University, East Bay, Office of Graduate Studies, College of Education and Allied Studies, Department of Educational Psychology, Special Education Program, Hayward, CA 94542-3000. Offers mild-moderate disabilities (MS); moderate-severe disabilities (MS). *Accreditation:* NCATE. *Degree requirements:* For master's, project or thesis. *Entrance requirements:* For master's, GRE or MAT, interview, minimum GPA of 2.5 during previous 2 years of course work. Additional exam requirements/recommendations for international students: Required—TOEFL (minimum score 550 paper-based). Electronic applications accepted.

California State University, Fresno, Division of Research and Graduate Studies, Kremen School of Education and Human Development, Department of Literacy, Early, Bilingual, and Special Education, Fresno, CA 93740-8027. Offers education (MA), including early childhood education, reading/language arts; special education (MA). *Accreditation:* NCATE. *Program availability:* Part-time, evening/weekend. *Degree requirements:* For master's, thesis or alternative. *Entrance requirements:* For master's, GRE General Test, MAT, minimum GPA of 2.75. Additional exam requirements/recommendations for international students: Required—TOEFL. Electronic applications accepted. *Faculty research:* Reading recovery, monitoring/tutoring programs, character and academics, professional ethics, low-performing partnership schools.

California State University, Fullerton, Graduate Studies, College of Education, Department of Special Education, Fullerton, CA 92831-3599. Offers MS. *Accreditation:* NCATE. *Program availability:* Part-time. *Degree requirements:* For master's, comprehensive exam, project or thesis. *Entrance requirements:* For master's, minimum GPA of 2.75.

California State University, Long Beach, Graduate Studies, College of Education, Department of Advanced Studies in Education and Counseling, Long Beach, CA 90840. Offers counseling (MS), including marriage and family therapy, school counseling, student development in higher education; education (MA, Ed D); educational administration (MA, Ed D); educational psychology (MA); special education (MS). *Program availability:* Part-time, evening/weekend. *Entrance requirements:* For master's, GRE General Test, minimum GPA of 2.75. *Application deadline:* For fall admission, 3/1 for domestic students. Applications are processed on a rolling basis. Application fee: $55. Electronic applications accepted. *Expenses: Required fees:* $2628 per term. Tuition and fees vary according to class time, course level, course load, degree level, campus/location and program. *Financial support:* Federal Work-Study, institutionally sponsored loans, and scholarships/grants available. Financial award application deadline: 3/2; financial award applicants required to submit FAFSA. *Unit head:* Dr. Hiromi Masunaga, Chair, 562-985-4517, E-mail: asec@csulb.edu. *Application contact:* Dr. Hiromi Masunaga, Chair, 562-985-4517, E-mail: asec@csulb.edu.
Website: http://www.csulb.edu/college-of-education/advanced-studies-education-and-counseling

California State University, Los Angeles, Graduate Studies, Charter College of Education, Division of Special Education and Counseling, Los Angeles, CA 90032-8530. Offers counseling (MS), including applied behavior analysis, community college counseling, rehabilitation counseling, school counseling, school psychology; special education (MA, PhD). *Accreditation:* ACA. *Program availability:* Part-time, evening/weekend. *Entrance requirements:* For master's, minimum GPA of 2.75 in last 90 units of course work, teaching certificate. Additional exam requirements/recommendations for international students: Required—TOEFL (minimum score 500 paper-based). Electronic applications accepted.

California State University, Northridge, Graduate Studies, Michael D. Eisner College of Education, Department of Special Education, Northridge, CA 91330. Offers early childhood special education (MA); education of the deaf and hard of hearing (MA); educational therapy (MA); mild/moderate disabilities (MA); moderate/severe disabilities (MA). *Accreditation:* NCATE. *Entrance requirements:* For master's, GRE General Test (if cumulative undergraduate GPA less than 3.0). Additional exam requirements/recommendations for international students: Required—TOEFL. *Faculty research:* Teacher training, classroom aide training.

California State University, Sacramento, College of Education, Graduate and Professional Studies in Education, Sacramento, CA 95819. Offers behavioral science and gender equity (MA); child development (MA); counseling (MS); curriculum and instruction (MA); education (Ed D), including K-12 and community college; education leadership and policy studies (MA), including higher education, PreK-12; education specialist (Ed S), including school psychology; educational technology (MA); language and literacy (MA); multicultural education (MA); school psychology (MA); special education (MA); workforce development advocacy (MA). *Program availability:* Part-time, evening/weekend, blended/hybrid learning. *Degree requirements:* For master's, thesis or project; writing proficiency exam; for doctorate, thesis/dissertation. *Entrance requirements:* For master's and doctorate, GRE. Additional exam requirements/recommendations for international students: Required—TOEFL (minimum score 550 paper-based; 80 iBT); Recommended—IELTS (minimum score 7), TSE. Electronic applications accepted. *Expenses:* Contact institution.

California State University, San Marcos, College of Education, Health and Human Services, School of Education, San Marcos, CA 92096-0001. Offers education (MA); educational administration (MA); educational leadership (Ed D); literacy education (MA); special education (MA). *Accreditation:* NCATE (one or more programs are accredited). *Program availability:* Part-time, evening/weekend. *Entrance requirements:* For master's, minimum GPA of 3.0, teaching credentials, 1 year of teaching experience. *Application deadline:* For fall admission, 2/1 priority date for domestic students. Applications are processed on a rolling basis. Application fee: $55. *Financial support:* Applicants required to submit FAFSA. *Faculty research:* Multicultural literature, art as knowledge, poetry and second language acquisition, restructuring K–12 education and improving the training of K–8 science teachers. *Unit head:* Pat Stall, Director, 760-750-4386, E-mail: pstall@csusm.edu. *Application contact:* Dr. Wesley Schultz, Dean of Office of Graduate Studies and Research, 760-750-8045, Fax: 760-750-8045, E-mail: apply@csusm.edu.
Website: http://www.csusm.edu/education/

California State University, Stanislaus, College of Education, Kinesiology and Social Work, MA Program in Education, Turlock, CA 95382. Offers curriculum and instruction (MA), including education technology, elementary education, multilingual education, physical education, reading, secondary education, special education; school administration (MA); school counseling (MA). *Program availability:* Part-time, evening/weekend. *Degree requirements:* For master's, comprehensive exam (for some programs), thesis (for some programs). *Entrance requirements:* For master's, MAT, GRE, or CBEST (varies by concentration), 3 letters of recommendation, personal statement. Additional exam requirements/recommendations for international students: Required—TOEFL (minimum score 550 paper-based). Electronic applications accepted. *Faculty research:* Children's perspectives on historical events, method elementary schools dual language education, K-12 reading programs.

California University of Pennsylvania, School of Graduate Studies and Research, College of Education and Human Services, Department of Special Education, California, PA 15419-1394. Offers autism (M Ed); general special education (M Ed). *Accreditation:* NCATE. *Program availability:* Part-time, evening/weekend. *Degree requirements:* For master's, comprehensive exam, thesis optional. *Entrance requirements:* For master's, MAT, PRAXIS. Additional exam requirements/recommendations for international students: Required—TOEFL (minimum score 550 paper-based; 80 iBT). Electronic applications accepted. *Faculty research:* Case-based instruction, electronic performance support tools, students with disabilities, teacher preparation, No Child Left Behind.

Cambridge College, School of Education, Boston, MA 02129. Offers autism specialist (M Ed); autism/behavior analyst (M Ed); behavior analyst (Post-Master's Certificate); curriculum and instruction (CAGS); early childhood teacher (M Ed); educational leadership (M Ed, Ed D); elementary teacher (M Ed); English as a second language (M Ed, Certificate); general science (M Ed); health education (Post-Master's Certificate); interdisciplinary studies (M Ed); library teacher (M Ed); mathematics education (M Ed); mathematics specialist (Certificate); school administration (M Ed, CAGS); school nurse education (M Ed); teacher of students with moderate disabilities (M Ed); teaching skills and methodologies (M Ed). *Program availability:* Part-time, evening/weekend, online learning. *Degree requirements:* For master's, thesis, internship/practicum (licensure

program only); for doctorate, thesis/dissertation; for other advanced degree, thesis. *Entrance requirements:* For master's, interview, resume, documentation of licensure, 2 professional references; for doctorate, official transcripts, interview, resume, written personal statement/essay, portfolio of scholarly and professional work, 2 professional references, health insurance, immunizations form; for other advanced degree, official transcripts, interview, resume, written personal statement/essay, 2 professional references, health insurance, immunizations form. Additional exam requirements/recommendations for international students: Required—TOEFL (minimum score 550 paper-based; 79 iBT), Michigan English Language Assessment Battery (minimum score 85); Recommended—IELTS (minimum score 6). *Application deadline:* Applications are processed on a rolling basis. Application fee: $30. Electronic applications accepted. *Expenses:* Contact institution. *Financial support:* Career-related internships or fieldwork, Federal Work-Study, and scholarships/grants available. Financial award applicants required to submit FAFSA. *Faculty research:* Adult education, accelerated learning, mathematics education, brain compatible learning, special education and law. *Unit head:* Dr. Mary Garrity, Interim Dean, 617-873-0168, E-mail: mary.garrity@cambridgecollege.edu. *Application contact:* Salvadore Liberto, Interim Assistant Vice President of Enrollment, 800-877-4723, E-mail: admissions@cambridgecollege.edu.
Website: https://www.cambridgecollege.edu/school/school-education

Campbellsville University, School of Education, Campbellsville, KY 42718-2799. Offers education (MA); school counseling (MA); school improvement (MA); special education (MASE); special education-teacher leader (MA); teacher leader (MA); teaching (MAT), including middle grades biology, middle grades chemistry, middle grades English. *Accreditation:* NCATE. *Program availability:* Part-time, evening/weekend, 100% online, blended/hybrid learning. *Faculty:* 16 full-time (10 women), 13 part-time/adjunct (7 women). *Students:* 154 full-time (122 women), 44 part-time (36 women); includes 18 minority (16 Black or African American, non-Hispanic/Latino; 1 Hispanic/Latino; 1 Two or more races, non-Hispanic/Latino), 1 international. Average age 34. 280 applicants, 30% accepted, 72 enrolled. In 2018, 66 master's awarded. *Degree requirements:* For master's, comprehensive exam (for some programs), thesis, research paper. *Entrance requirements:* For master's, GRE or PRAXIS, minimum undergraduate GPA of 2.75, teaching certificate, professional growth plan, letters of recommendation, interview. Additional exam requirements/recommendations for international students: Recommended—TOEFL (minimum score 550 paper-based; 79 iBT), IELTS (minimum score 6). *Application deadline:* Applications are processed on a rolling basis. Application fee: $25. Electronic applications accepted. Application fee is waived when completed online. *Expenses:* $299/credit hour. *Financial support:* Unspecified assistantships available. Financial award applicants required to submit FAFSA. *Faculty research:* Professional development, curriculum development, school governance, assessment, special education. *Unit head:* Dr. Lisa Allen, Dean of School of Education, 270-789-5344, Fax: 270-789-5206, E-mail: lsallen@campbellsville.edu. *Application contact:* Monica Bamwine, Director of Graduate Admissions, 270-789-5221, Fax: 270-789-5071, E-mail: mkbamwine@campbellsville.edu.

Canisius College, Graduate Division, School of Education and Human Services, Department of Graduate Education and Leadership, Buffalo, NY 14208-1098. Offers business and marketing education (MS Ed); college student personnel (MS Ed); deaf education (MS Ed); deaf/adolescent education, grades 7-12 (MS Ed); deaf/childhood education, grades 1-6 (MS Ed); differentiated instruction (MS Ed); education administration (MS); educational administration (MS Ed); educational technologies (Certificate); gifted education extension (Certificate); literacy (MS Ed); reading (Certificate); school building leadership (MS Ed, Certificate); school district leadership (Certificate); teacher leader (Certificate); TESOL (MS Ed). *Accreditation:* NCATE. *Program availability:* Part-time, evening/weekend, 100% online, blended/hybrid learning. *Faculty:* 5 full-time (all women), 21 part-time/adjunct (16 women). *Students:* 79 full-time (66 women), 135 part-time (106 women); includes 45 minority (27 Black or African American, non-Hispanic/Latino; 1 American Indian or Alaska Native, non-Hispanic/Latino; 3 Asian, non-Hispanic/Latino; 9 Hispanic/Latino; 5 Two or more races, non-Hispanic/Latino), 1 international. Average age 32. 83 applicants, 96% accepted, 74 enrolled. In 2018, 94 master's, 47 other advanced degrees awarded. *Entrance requirements:* For master's, GRE (if cumulative GPA less than 2.7), transcripts, two letters of recommendation. Additional exam requirements/recommendations for international students: Required—TOEFL (minimum score 550 paper-based, 79 iBT), IELTS (minimum score 6.5), or CAEL (minimum score 70). *Application deadline:* Applications are processed on a rolling basis. Application fee: $0. Electronic applications accepted. *Expenses: Tuition:* Part-time $820 per credit hour. *Required fees:* $25 per semester. One-time fee: $65 part-time. Tuition and fees vary according to program. *Financial support:* In 2018–19, 206 students received support. Career-related internships or fieldwork, Federal Work-Study, scholarships/grants, tuition waivers (partial), and unspecified assistantships available. Support available to part-time students. Financial award application deadline: 4/30; financial award applicants required to submit FAFSA. *Faculty research:* Asperger's disease, autism, private higher education, reading strategies. *Unit head:* Dr. Anne Marie Tryjankowski, Chair/Associate Professor of Graduate Education and Leadership, 716-888-3715, Fax: 716-888-3142, E-mail: tryjanka@canisius.edu. *Application contact:* Dr. Anne Marie Tryjankowski, Chair/Associate Professor of Graduate Education and Leadership, 716-888-3715, Fax: 716-888-3142, E-mail: tryjanka@canisius.edu.

Canisius College, Graduate Division, School of Education and Human Services, Department of Teacher Education, Buffalo, NY 14208-1098. Offers adolescence education (MS Ed); childhood education (MS Ed); general education (MS Ed); special education (MS), including adolescence special education, advanced special education, childhood education grade 1-6, childhood special education. *Program availability:* Part-time, evening/weekend, 100% online, blended/hybrid learning. *Faculty:* 10 full-time (all women), 16 part-time/adjunct (14 women). *Students:* 69 full-time (50 women), 23 part-time (16 women); includes 10 minority (4 Black or African American, non-Hispanic/Latino; 1 Asian, non-Hispanic/Latino; 4 Hispanic/Latino; 1 Two or more races, non-Hispanic/Latino), 3 international. Average age 26. 85 applicants, 75% accepted, 54 enrolled. In 2018, 32 master's awarded. *Degree requirements:* For master's, research project or thesis, project internship. *Entrance requirements:* For master's, GRE (if cumulative GPA less than 2.7), official transcripts, letters of recommendation. Additional exam requirements/recommendations for international students: Required—TOEFL (minimum score 550 paper-based, 79 iBT), IELTS (minimum score 6.5), or CAEL (minimum score 70). *Application deadline:* Applications are processed on a rolling basis. Application fee: $0. Electronic applications accepted. *Expenses: Tuition:* Part-time $820 per credit hour. *Required fees:* $25 per semester. One-time fee: $65 part-time. Tuition and fees vary according to program. *Financial support:* In 2018–19, 90 students received support. Career-related internships or fieldwork, Federal Work-Study, scholarships/grants, tuition waivers (partial), and unspecified assistantships available. Support available to part-time students. Financial award application deadline: 4/30; financial award applicants required to submit FAFSA. *Unit head:* Dr. Barbara A. Burns, CHAIR/PROFESSOR OF TEACHER EDUCATION, 716-888-3291, Fax: 716-888-2766, E-mail: burns1@canisius.edu. *Application contact:* Dr. Barbara A. Burns, CHAIR/PROFESSOR OF TEACHER EDUCATION, 716-888-3291, Fax: 716-888-2766, E-mail: burns1@canisius.edu.
Website: http://www.canisius.edu/academics/graduate/

Capella University, School of Education, Doctoral Programs in Education, Minneapolis, MN 55402. Offers curriculum and instruction (PhD); educational leadership and management (Ed D); instructional design for online learning (PhD); K-12 studies in education (PhD); leadership for higher education (PhD); leadership in educational administration (PhD); postsecondary and adult education (PhD); professional studies in education (PhD); reading and literacy (Ed D); special education leadership (PhD); training and performance improvement (PhD).

Capella University, School of Education, Master's Programs in Education, Minneapolis, MN 55402. Offers adult education (MS); curriculum and instruction (MS); early childhood education (MS); enrollment management (MS); higher education leadership and management (MS); instructional design for online learning (MS); integrative studies (MS); K-12 studies in education (MS); leadership in educational administration (MS); reading and literacy (MS); special education teaching (MS).

Cardinal Stritch University, College of Education and Leadership, Department of Special Education, Milwaukee, WI 53217-3985. Offers special education (PhD); urban special education (MA). *Accreditation:* NCATE. *Program availability:* Part-time, evening/weekend. *Degree requirements:* For master's, comprehensive exam, thesis, practica; for doctorate, thesis/dissertation. *Entrance requirements:* For master's, 2 letters of recommendation, minimum GPA of 2.75; for doctorate, 3 letters of recommendation, minimum GPA of 3.5. Additional exam requirements/recommendations for international students: Required—TOEFL (minimum score 550 paper-based; 79 iBT), IELTS (minimum score 6.5). Electronic applications accepted. *Expenses:* Contact institution.

Caribbean University, Graduate School, Bayamón, PR 00960-0493. Offers administration and supervision (MA Ed); criminal justice (MA); curriculum and instruction (MA Ed, PhD), including elementary education (MA Ed), English education (MA Ed), history education (MA Ed), mathematics education (MA Ed), primary education (MA Ed), science education (MA Ed), Spanish education (MA Ed); educational technology in instructional systems (MA Ed); gerontology (MSN); human resources (MBA); museology, archiving and art history (MA Ed); neonatal pediatrics (MSN); physical education (MA Ed); special education (MA Ed). *Entrance requirements:* For master's, interview, minimum GPA of 2.5.

Carlow University, College of Learning and Innovation, Program in Education, Pittsburgh, PA 15213-3165. Offers early childhood education (M Ed); education (M Ed); online instructional design and technology (Certificate); special education (M Ed), including early childhood. *Program availability:* Part-time, evening/weekend, 100% online, blended/hybrid learning. *Students:* 41 full-time (33 women), 9 part-time (all women); includes 12 minority (10 Black or African American, non-Hispanic/Latino; 1 Asian, non-Hispanic/Latino; 1 Two or more races, non-Hispanic/Latino). Average age 32. 32 applicants, 100% accepted, 22 enrolled. In 2018, 24 master's, 5 Certificates awarded. *Entrance requirements:* For master's, personal essay; resume or curriculum vitae; two recommendations; official transcripts; interview; minimum undergraduate GPA of 3.0. Additional exam requirements/recommendations for international students: Required—TOEFL (minimum score 550 paper-based). *Application deadline:* Applications are processed on a rolling basis. Electronic applications accepted. *Expenses: Tuition:* Full-time $13,090; part-time $5100 per semester. *Required fees:* $215; $84. Tuition and fees vary according to course load, degree level and program. *Financial support:* Application deadline: 4/1; applicants required to submit FAFSA. *Unit head:* Dr. Keeley Baronak, Chair, Department of Education, 412-578-6135, Fax: 412-578-8816, E-mail: kobaronak@carlow.edu. *Application contact:* Dr. Keeley Baronak, Chair, Department of Education, 412-578-6135, Fax: 412-578-8816, E-mail: kobaronak@carlow.edu.
Website: http://www.carlow.edu/education.aspx

Castleton University, Division of Graduate Studies, Department of Education, Program in Special Education, Castleton, VT 05735. Offers MA Ed, CAGS. *Program availability:* Part-time, evening/weekend. *Degree requirements:* For master's, thesis or alternative; for CAGS, publishable paper. *Entrance requirements:* For master's, GRE General Test, MAT, interview, minimum undergraduate GPA of 3.0; for CAGS, educational research, master's degree, minimum undergraduate GPA of 3.0.

The Catholic University of America, School of Arts and Sciences, Department of Education, Washington, DC 20064. Offers Catholic school leadership (MA); education (Certificate); secondary education (MA); special education (MA), including early childhood, non-categorical. *Accreditation:* NCATE. *Program availability:* Part-time. *Faculty:* 7 full-time (6 women), 7 part-time/adjunct (5 women). *Students:* 12 full-time (11 women), 15 part-time (6 women); includes 3 minority (2 Hispanic/Latino; 1 Two or more races, non-Hispanic/Latino), 2 international. Average age 37. 12 applicants, 75% accepted, 8 enrolled. In 2018, 14 master's awarded. *Degree requirements:* For master's, comprehensive exam, thesis or alternative; for Certificate, action research project. *Entrance requirements:* For master's, GRE General Test or MAT, statement of purpose, official copies of academic transcripts, three letters of recommendation, interview; for Certificate, PRAXIS I, statement of purpose, official copies of academic transcripts, three letters of recommendation, interview. Additional exam requirements/recommendations for international students: Required—TOEFL (minimum score 550 paper-based; 80 iBT). *Application deadline:* For fall admission, 7/15 priority date for domestic students, 7/1 for international students; for spring admission, 11/15 priority date for domestic students, 11/1 for international students. Applications are processed on a rolling basis. Application fee: $55. Electronic applications accepted. *Expenses:* Contact institution. *Financial support:* Fellowships, research assistantships, teaching assistantships, Federal Work-Study, scholarships/grants, tuition waivers (full and partial), and unspecified assistantships available. Financial award application deadline: 2/1; financial award applicants required to submit FAFSA. *Faculty research:* Special education, early childhood education, educational psychology, Catholic school administration, leadership and policy studies, counseling, curriculum and instruction. *Unit head:* Dr. Agnes Cave, Chair, 202-319-5805, Fax: 202-319-5815, E-mail: cave@cua.edu. *Application contact:* Dr. Steven Brown, Director of Graduate Admissions, 202-319-5057, Fax: 202-319-6533, E-mail: cua-admissions@cua.edu.
Website: http://education.cua.edu/

Centenary University, Program in Education, Hackettstown, NJ 07840-2100. Offers education practice (M Ed); educational leadership (MA, Ed D); instructional leadership (MA); reading (M Ed); special education (MA). *Accreditation:* TEAC. *Program availability:* Part-time, evening/weekend, online learning. *Degree requirements:* For master's, thesis. *Entrance requirements:* For master's, interview, minimum undergraduate GPA of 2.8.

Central Connecticut State University, School of Graduate Studies, School of Education and Professional Studies, Department of Special Education and Interventions, New Britain, CT 06050-4010. Offers MS, Certificate. *Program availability:* Part-time, evening/weekend. *Faculty:* 6 full-time (4 women), 13 part-time/adjunct (8 women). *Students:* 67 full-time (56 women), 118 part-time (92 women); includes 32 minority (13 Black or African American, non-Hispanic/Latino; 1 American Indian or Alaska Native, non-Hispanic/Latino; 3 Asian, non-Hispanic/Latino; 13 Hispanic/Latino; 2 Two or more races, non-Hispanic/Latino). Average age 32. 88 applicants, 74% accepted, 41 enrolled. In 2018, 41 master's awarded. *Degree requirements:* For master's, thesis or alternative; for Certificate, qualifying exam. *Entrance requirements:*

For master's, minimum undergraduate GPA of 2.7, teacher certification. Additional exam requirements/recommendations for international students: Required—TOEFL (minimum score 550 paper-based; 79 iBT); Recommended—IELTS (minimum score 6.5). *Application deadline:* For fall admission, 6/1 for domestic students, 5/1 for international students; for spring admission, 11/1 for domestic and international students. Applications are processed on a rolling basis. Application fee: $50. Electronic applications accepted. *Expenses: Tuition, area resident:* Full-time $7027; part-time $388 per credit. Tuition, state resident: full-time $9750; part-time $388 per credit. Tuition, nonresident: full-time $18,102; part-time $388 per credit. *International tuition:* $18,102 full-time. *Required fees:* $266 per semester. *Financial support:* In 2018–19, 16 students received support. Career-related internships or fieldwork, Federal Work-Study, scholarships/grants, and unspecified assistantships available. Support available to part-time students. Financial award application deadline: 3/1; financial award applicants required to submit FAFSA. *Faculty research:* Learning disabilities and language development, consulting teacher practice, occupational and special education, teaching emotionally disturbed students. *Unit head:* Dr. John Foshay, Chair, 860-832-2400, E-mail: FoshayJ@ccsu.edu. *Application contact:* Patricia Gardner, Associate Director of Graduate Studies, 860-832-2350, Fax: 860-832-2362.
Website: http://www.ccsu.edu/sped/

Central Michigan University, College of Graduate Studies, College of Education and Human Services, Department of Counseling and Special Education, Program in Special Education, Mount Pleasant, MI 48859. Offers autism (Graduate Certificate); special education (MA), including the master teacher. *Accreditation:* TEAC. *Program availability:* Part-time. *Degree requirements:* For master's, comprehensive exam (for some programs), thesis or alternative. *Entrance requirements:* For master's, Michigan elementary or secondary provisional, permanent, or life certificate or special education endorsement. Electronic applications accepted. *Faculty research:* Mainstreaming, learning disabled, attention and organization disorders.

Chaminade University of Honolulu, Graduate, Program in Education, Honolulu, HI 96816-1578. Offers child development (M Ed); early childhood education (Montessori) (MAT); early childhood education (PK-3) (MAT); educational leadership (M Ed); elementary education (MAT); instructional leadership (M Ed); Montessori (M Ed); secondary education (MAT); special education (MAT); teacher leader (M Ed). *Program availability:* Part-time, evening/weekend, 100% online, blended/hybrid learning. *Faculty:* 8 full-time (3 women), 11 part-time/adjunct (8 women). *Students:* 80 full-time (57 women), 100 part-time (77 women); includes 113 minority (6 Black or African American, non-Hispanic/Latino; 4 American Indian or Alaska Native, non-Hispanic/Latino; 45 Asian, non-Hispanic/Latino; 6 Hispanic/Latino; 50 Native Hawaiian or other Pacific Islander, non-Hispanic/Latino; 2 Two or more races, non-Hispanic/Latino), 2 international. Average age 35. 53 applicants, 92% accepted, 40 enrolled. In 2018, 92 master's awarded. *Degree requirements:* For master's, thesis or alternative. *Entrance requirements:* For master's, PRAXIS (for MAT), official transcripts, writing sample (for MAT). Additional exam requirements/recommendations for international students: Required—TOEFL (minimum score 550 paper-based; 79 iBT). *Application deadline:* Applications are processed on a rolling basis. Application fee: $40. Electronic applications accepted. *Expenses:* $780 per credit; $93 fee per online course. *Financial support:* Applicants required to submit FAFSA. *Unit head:* Dr. Dale Fryxell, Dean, 808-739-4652, Fax: 808-739-4607, E-mail: edu-office@chaminade.edu. *Application contact:* 808-739-7478, E-mail: gradserv@chaminade.edu.
Website: https://chaminade.edu/academics/education-behavioral-sciences/

Chapman University, Donna Ford Attallah College of Educational Studies, Orange, CA 92866. Offers counseling (MA), including school counseling (MA, Credential); curriculum and instruction (MA), including elementary education, secondary education; education (PhD), including cultural and curricular studies, disability studies, leadership studies, school psychology (PhD, Credential); educational psychology (MA); leadership development (MA); multiple subjects (Credential), including Spanish/English bilingual; pupil personnel services (Credential), including school counseling (MA, Credential), school psychology (PhD, Credential); school psychology (Ed S); single subject (Credential); special education (MA, Credential), including mild/moderate (Credential), moderate/severe (Credential); teaching (MA), including elementary education, secondary education, secondary music education. *Accreditation:* TEAC. *Program availability:* Part-time, evening/weekend. Electronic applications accepted. *Expenses:* Contact institution.

Chatham University, Program in Education, Pittsburgh, PA 15232-2826. Offers early childhood education (MAT); elementary education (MAT); environmental education (K-12) (MAT); secondary art (MAT); secondary biology education (MAT); secondary chemistry education (MAT); secondary English education (MAT); secondary math education (MAT); secondary physics education (MAT); secondary social studies education (MAT); special education (MAT). *Degree requirements:* For master's, thesis, teaching experience. *Entrance requirements:* For master's, minimum GPA of 3.0, sample of written work, recommendation letters. Additional exam requirements/recommendations for international students: Required—TOEFL (minimum score 600 paper-based; 100 iBT), IELTS (minimum score 7), TWE. Electronic applications accepted. Application fee is waived when completed online. *Faculty research:* Gifted education, environmental education, technology in education, writing as learning, class size and achievement.

Chestnut Hill College, School of Graduate Studies, Department of Education, Program in Early Education, Philadelphia, PA 19118-2693. Offers early education (M Ed), including Montessori certificate preparation, preK-4 education, preK-4 education and special education preK-8. *Program availability:* Part-time, evening/weekend. *Degree requirements:* For master's, thesis optional. *Entrance requirements:* For master's, PRAXIS I or proof of teaching certification, writing sample, letters of recommendation, 6 graduate credits with minimum B grade or minimum undergraduate GPA of 3.0. Additional exam requirements/recommendations for international students: Required—TOEFL (minimum score 500 paper-based), IELTS (minimum score 6.0), or TWE (minimum score 22). Electronic applications accepted. *Expenses:* Contact institution. *Faculty research:* Gender issues, early childhood education standardized testing.

Chestnut Hill College, School of Graduate Studies, Department of Education, Program in Reading, Philadelphia, PA 19118-2693. Offers reading specialist (M Ed), including K-12, special education 7-12, special education PreK-8. *Program availability:* Part-time, evening/weekend. *Degree requirements:* For master's, thesis optional. *Entrance requirements:* Additional exam requirements/recommendations for international students: Required—TOEFL (minimum score 500 paper-based) or IELTS (minimum score 6). Electronic applications accepted. *Expenses:* Contact institution. *Faculty research:* Inclusive education, cultural issues in education.

Chestnut Hill College, School of Graduate Studies, Department of Education, Program in Special Education, Philadelphia, PA 19118-2693. Offers special education (M Ed), including 7-12, PreK-8. *Program availability:* Part-time, evening/weekend. *Degree requirements:* For master's, thesis optional. *Entrance requirements:* For master's, PRAXIS I or proof of teaching certification, letters of recommendation, writing sample, 6 graduate credits with minimum B grade if undergraduate GPA less than 3.0. Additional exam requirements/recommendations for international students: Required—TOEFL (minimum score 500 paper-based), IELTS (minimum score 6), or TWE (minimum score 22). Electronic applications accepted. *Expenses:* Contact institution. *Faculty research:* Inclusive education, cultural issues in education.

Chestnut Hill College, School of Graduate Studies, Division of Psychology, Program in Clinical and Counseling Psychology, Philadelphia, PA 19118-2693. Offers clinical and counseling psychology (MS, CAS), including child and adolescent therapy, child and adolescent therapy with autism spectrum disorders, co-occurring disorders, couple and family therapy, diverse and underserved communities, generalist (MS), trauma studies. *Program availability:* Part-time, evening/weekend. *Degree requirements:* For master's, thesis optional, practica. *Entrance requirements:* For master's, GRE General Test, writing sample, letters of recommendation. Additional exam requirements/recommendations for international students: Required—TOEFL (minimum score 500 paper-based), IELTS (minimum score 6.0), or TWE (minimum score 22). Electronic applications accepted. *Expenses:* Contact institution. *Faculty research:* Play therapy, eating disorders, addictions, group psychology and group therapy, health psychology.

Cheyney University of Pennsylvania, Graduate Programs, Program in Special Education, Cheyney, PA 19319. Offers M Ed. *Program availability:* Part-time, evening/weekend. *Degree requirements:* For master's, thesis. *Entrance requirements:* For master's, GRE General Test, MAT, minimum GPA of 2.75. Electronic applications accepted.

Chicago State University, School of Graduate and Professional Studies, College of Education, Department of Special Education, Early Childhood Education and Bilingual Education, Program in Special Education, Chicago, IL 60628. Offers MS Ed. *Accreditation:* NCATE. *Entrance requirements:* For master's, minimum GPA of 2.75. *Faculty research:* Assistive technology, teacher efficiency.

City College of the City University of New York, Graduate School, School of Education, Department of Leadership and Special Education, New York, NY 10031-9198. Offers educational leadership (MS, AC); teacher of students with disabilities in adolescent education (MS Ed); teacher of students with disabilities in childhood education (MS Ed). *Degree requirements:* For master's, thesis, research paper. *Entrance requirements:* For master's, Liberal Arts and Sciences Test (LAST), Content Specialty Test (CST), interview; minimum GPA of 3.0 in major, 2.5 overall. Additional exam requirements/recommendations for international students: Required—TOEFL. *Faculty research:* Dynamics of organizational change, impact of laws on educational policy, leadership development in schools.

City University of Seattle, Graduate Division, Albright School of Education, Seattle, WA 98121. Offers administrator certification (Certificate); curriculum and instruction (M Ed); elementary education (MIT); guidance and counseling (M Ed); leadership (M Ed); reading and literacy (M Ed); school counseling (M Ed); special education (MIT); superintendent certification (Certificate). *Program availability:* Part-time, evening/weekend, online learning. *Degree requirements:* For master's, comprehensive exam (for some programs), thesis (for some programs). *Entrance requirements:* For master's, baccalaureate degree or equivalent from an accredited or otherwise recognized institution. Additional exam requirements/recommendations for international students: Required—TOEFL (minimum score 567 paper-based; 87 iBT); Recommended—IELTS. Electronic applications accepted. *Expenses:* Contact institution.

Claremont Graduate University, Graduate Programs, School of Educational Studies, Claremont, CA 91711-6160. Offers Africana education (Certificate); education and policy (MA, PhD); higher education/student affairs (MA, PhD); human development (MA, PhD); public school administration (MA, PhD); quantitative evaluation (MA, PhD); special education (MA, PhD); teacher education (MA); teaching and learning (MA, PhD); urban leadership (PhD); MBA/PhD. PhD program offered jointly with San Diego State University. *Program availability:* Part-time. Terminal master's awarded for partial completion of doctoral program. *Entrance requirements:* For master's and doctorate, GRE General Test. Additional exam requirements/recommendations for international students: Required—TOEFL (minimum score 75 iBT). Electronic applications accepted. *Faculty research:* Education administration, K-12 and higher education, multicultural education, education policy, diversity in higher education, faculty issues.

Clarion University of Pennsylvania, College of Arts, Education and Sciences, Master of Education Program, Clarion, PA 16214. Offers curriculum and instruction (M Ed); early childhood (M Ed); math education (M Ed); reading (M Ed); science education (M Ed); special education (M Ed); technology (M Ed). *Accreditation:* NCATE. *Program availability:* Part-time, evening/weekend, 100% online, blended/hybrid learning. *Faculty:* 6 full-time (3 women). *Students:* 5 full-time (all women), 85 part-time (73 women); includes 3 minority (2 Black or African American, non-Hispanic/Latino; 1 Two or more races, non-Hispanic/Latino). Average age 30. 57 applicants, 61% accepted, 26 enrolled. In 2018, 51 master's awarded. *Degree requirements:* For master's, comprehensive exam (for some programs), thesis or alternative. *Entrance requirements:* For master's, minimum QPA of 3.0. Additional exam requirements/recommendations for international students: Required—TOEFL (minimum score 550 paper-based; 80 iBT), Or IELTS. Satisfactory completion of a bachelor's degree from an accredited US college or university is also acceptable evidence of English language. *Application deadline:* For fall admission, 8/1 priority date for domestic students, 7/15 priority date for international students; for winter admission, 11/1 priority date for domestic students; for spring admission, 12/1 priority date for domestic students, 11/15 priority date for international students; for summer admission, 4/1 priority date for domestic students. Applications are processed on a rolling basis. Application fee: $40. Electronic applications accepted. *Expenses: Tuition, area resident:* Part-time $516 per credit hour. Tuition, state resident: part-time $516 per credit hour. Tuition, nonresident: part-time $774 per credit hour. *Required fees:* $159 per credit hour. One-time fee: $50 part-time. Tuition and fees vary according to degree level, campus/location and program. *Financial support:* Federal Work-Study, institutionally sponsored loans, and scholarships/grants available. Financial award application deadline: 3/1; financial award applicants required to submit FAFSA. *Unit head:* Dr. John McCullough, Chair, Department of Education, 814-393-2404, Fax: 814-393-2446, E-mail: gradstudies@clarion.edu. *Application contact:* Susan Staub, Graduate Admissions Counselor, 814-393-2337, Fax: 814-393-2722, E-mail: gradstudies@clarion.edu.

Clarion University of Pennsylvania, College of Arts, Education and Sciences, Master's Program in Special Education, Clarion, PA 16214. Offers MS. *Accreditation:* NCATE. *Program availability:* Part-time. *Faculty:* 5 full-time (4 women), 8 part-time/adjunct (6 women). *Students:* 15 full-time (13 women), 9 part-time (8 women); includes 1 minority (Black or African American, non-Hispanic/Latino). Average age 29. 18 applicants, 72% accepted, 13 enrolled. In 2018, 15 master's awarded. *Entrance requirements:* For master's, teacher certification, minimum QPA of 3.0. Additional exam requirements/recommendations for international students: Required—TOEFL (minimum score 550 paper-based; 80 iBT), Or IELTS score of at least 7.0. Bachelor's degree accredited U.S. college or university is acceptable evidence of English language proficiency. *Application deadline:* For fall admission, 8/1 priority date for domestic students, 7/15 priority date for international students; for winter admission, 11/1 priority date for domestic students; for spring admission, 12/1 priority date for domestic students, 11/15 priority date for international students; for summer admission, 4/1 priority date for domestic students. Applications are processed on a rolling basis. Application fee: $40. Electronic applications accepted. *Expenses:* $739.60 per credit.

Financial support: Institutionally sponsored loans and scholarships/grants available. Support available to part-time students. Financial award application deadline: 3/1; financial award applicants required to submit FAFSA. *Unit head:* Dr. Rick Sabousky, Chair, 814-393-2294, Fax: 814-393-1951, E-mail: sabousky@clarion.edu. *Application contact:* Susan Staub, Graduate Admissions Counselor, 814-393-2337, Fax: 814-3932722, E-mail: gradstudies@clarion.edu.

Clark Atlanta University, School of Education, Department of Curriculum and Instruction, Atlanta, GA 30314. Offers special education general curriculum (MA); teaching math and science (MAT). *Program availability:* Part-time. *Degree requirements:* For master's, one foreign language, comprehensive exam. *Entrance requirements:* For master's, GRE General Test, minimum undergraduate GPA of 2.6. Additional exam requirements/recommendations for international students: Required—TOEFL (minimum score 500 paper-based; 61 iBT).

Clemson University, Graduate School, College of Education, Department of Education and Human Development, Clemson, SC 29634. Offers counselor education (M Ed, Ed S), including mental health counseling, school counseling, student affairs (M Ed); learning sciences (PhD); literacy (M Ed); literacy, language and culture (PhD); special education (M Ed, MAT, PhD). *Program availability:* Part-time, evening/weekend, 100% online. *Faculty:* 35 full-time (24 women). *Students:* 103 full-time (87 women), 132 part-time (123 women); includes 37 minority (11 Black or African American, non-Hispanic/Latino; 1 American Indian or Alaska Native, non-Hispanic/Latino; 3 Asian, non-Hispanic/Latino; 11 Hispanic/Latino; 11 Two or more races, non-Hispanic/Latino), 5 international. Average age 29. 435 applicants, 67% accepted, 180 enrolled. In 2018, 51 master's, 3 doctorates, 34 other advanced degrees awarded. *Degree requirements:* For master's, thesis (for some programs); for doctorate, comprehensive exam (for some programs), thesis/dissertation. *Entrance requirements:* For master's and doctorate, GRE General Test, unofficial transcripts, letters of recommendation. Additional exam requirements/recommendations for international students: Required—TOEFL (minimum score 80 paper-based; 80 iBT); Recommended—IELTS (minimum score 6.5), TSE (minimum score 54). *Application deadline:* For fall admission, 4/15 priority date for international students; for spring admission, 10/15 priority date for international students. Applications are processed on a rolling basis. Application fee: $80 ($90 for international students). Electronic applications accepted. *Expenses:* $5198 per semester full-time resident, $10123 per semester full-time non-resident, $556 per credit hour part-time resident, $1109 per credit hour part-time non-resident, online $770 per credit hour, $4938 doctoral programs resident, $10405 doctoral programs non-resident, $1144 full-time graduate assistant, other fees may apply per session. *Financial support:* In 2018–19, 78 students received support, including 5 teaching assistantships with full and partial tuition reimbursements available (averaging $8,759 per year); career-related internships or fieldwork and unspecified assistantships also available. *Faculty research:* Literacy, reading recovery, exceptional children, policy development. *Total annual research expenditures:* $1.3 million. *Unit head:* Dr. Debi Switzer, Department Chair, 864-656-5098, E-mail: debi@clemson.edu. *Application contact:* Julie Jones, Student Services Program Coordinator, 864-656-5096, E-mail: jgambre@clemson.edu.
Website: http://www.clemson.edu/education/departments/education-human-development/index.html

Cleveland State University, College of Graduate Studies, College of Education and Human Services, Department of Teacher Education, Cleveland, OH 44115. Offers art education (M Ed); early childhood education (M Ed); foreign language education (M Ed); middle childhood mathematics and science education (M Ed); special education (M Ed), including mild/moderate disabilities, moderate/intensive disabilities; teaching English to speakers of other languages (M Ed). *Program availability:* Part-time, evening/weekend. *Faculty:* 19 full-time (14 women), 32 part-time/adjunct (27 women). *Students:* 56 full-time (40 women), 344 part-time (278 women); includes 104 minority (74 Black or African American, non-Hispanic/Latino; 1 American Indian or Alaska Native, non-Hispanic/Latino; 5 Asian, non-Hispanic/Latino; 9 Hispanic/Latino; 15 Two or more races, non-Hispanic/Latino), 14 international. Average age 34. 177 applicants, 55% accepted, 68 enrolled. In 2018, 117 master's awarded. *Degree requirements:* For master's, comprehensive exam (for some programs), thesis or alternative. *Entrance requirements:* For master's, GRE General Test or MAT, minimum GPA of 2.75. Additional exam requirements/recommendations for international students: Required—TOEFL (minimum score 550 paper-based; 78 iBT), IELTS (minimum score 6). *Application deadline:* For fall admission, 7/1 priority date for domestic students, 5/15 for international students; for spring admission, 11/15 for domestic students, 11/1 for international students; for summer admission, 4/1 for domestic students, 3/15 for international students. Applications are processed on a rolling basis. Application fee: $30. *Expenses:* Tuition, state resident: full-time $7232.55; part-time $6676 per credit hour. Tuition, nonresident: full-time $12,375. *International tuition:* $18,914 full-time. *Required fees:* $80; $80 $40. Tuition and fees vary according to program. *Financial support:* In 2018–19, 13 research assistantships with full tuition reimbursements (averaging $15,845 per year) were awarded; tuition waivers (partial) and unspecified assistantships also available. Financial award application deadline: 2/15; financial award applicants required to submit FAFSA. *Faculty research:* Early childhood education, literacy education, special education: mild/moderate, moderate/intensive, early childhood intervention specialist), teaching English to speakers of other languages (TESOL). *Total annual research expenditures:* $275,907. *Unit head:* Dr. Tachelle Banks, Department Chairperson, 216-687-4600, Fax: 216-687-5379, E-mail: t.i.banks@csuohio.edu. *Application contact:* Rosalyn Adams, Administrative Coordinator, 216-523-7139, Fax: 216-687-5491, E-mail: r.m.adams@csuohio.edu.
Website: http://www.csuohio.edu/cehs/te/te

Coastal Carolina University, Spadoni College of Education, Conway, SC 29528-6054. Offers education (MAT); educational leadership (M Ed, Ed S); English for speakers of other languages (Certificate); instructional technology (M Ed, Ed S); language, literacy and culture (M Ed); learning and teaching (M Ed); online teaching and training (Certificate); special education (M Ed). *Accreditation:* NCATE. *Program availability:* Part-time, evening/weekend, 100% online, blended/hybrid learning. *Degree requirements:* For master's and other advanced degree, comprehensive exam. *Entrance requirements:* For master's, GRE, GMAT, 2 letters of recommendation, evidence of teacher certification, official transcripts; for other advanced degree, official transcripts, 3 letters of reference, master's degree in related field with minimum overall cumulative GPA of 3.0. Additional exam requirements/recommendations for international students: Required—TOEFL (minimum score 550 paper-based; 79 iBT), IELTS (minimum score 6.5). Electronic applications accepted.

College of Charleston, Graduate School, School of Education, Health, and Human Performance, Department of Foundations, Secondary, and Special Education, Program in Special Education, Charleston, SC 29424-0001. Offers MAT. *Program availability:* Part-time, evening/weekend. *Entrance requirements:* For master's, GRE, minimum GPA of 2.5, 2 letters of recommendation. Additional exam requirements/recommendations for international students: Required—TOEFL (minimum score 81 iBT). Electronic applications accepted.

The College of New Jersey, Office of Graduate and Advancing Education, School of Education, Department of Special Education, Language and Literacy, Program in Special Education, Ewing, NJ 08628. Offers M Ed, MAT. *Accreditation:* NCATE. *Program availability:* Part-time. *Degree requirements:* For master's, comprehensive exam. *Entrance requirements:* For master's, GRE General Test, minimum GPA of 3.0 in field or 2.75 overall. Additional exam requirements/recommendations for international students: Required—TOEFL. Electronic applications accepted.

The College of New Jersey, Office of Graduate and Advancing Education, School of Education, Department of Special Education, Language and Literacy, Program in Special Education with Learning Disabilities, Ewing, NJ 08628. Offers Certificate. *Accreditation:* NCATE. *Program availability:* Part-time. *Entrance requirements:* Additional exam requirements/recommendations for international students: Required—TOEFL. Electronic applications accepted.

The College of New Rochelle, Graduate School, Division of Education, Program in Special Education, New Rochelle, NY 10805-2308. Offers MS Ed. *Program availability:* Part-time. *Degree requirements:* For master's, practicum. *Entrance requirements:* For master's, interview, minimum GPA of 3.0 in field, 2.7 overall.

College of Saint Elizabeth, Program in Education, Morristown, NJ 07960-6989. Offers assistive technology (Certificate); education (MA); ESL (Certificate); Holocaust/genocide education (Certificate); middle school science (Certificate); online teaching in the 21st century (Certificate); teaching (Certificate), including K-12, K-6, teacher of students with disabilities. *Program availability:* Part-time. *Degree requirements:* For master's exam Certificate, thesis. *Entrance requirements:* For master's, certification. Additional exam requirements/recommendations for international students: Required—TOEFL (minimum score 550 paper-based; 79 iBT), IELTS (minimum score 6.5). Electronic applications accepted. Application fee is waived when completed online.

College of St. Joseph, Graduate Programs, Division of Education, Program in Special Education, Rutland, VT 05701-3899. Offers M Ed. *Program availability:* Part-time, evening/weekend. *Degree requirements:* For master's, comprehensive exam. *Entrance requirements:* For master's, PRAXIS I (for initial licensure), official college transcripts; 2 letters of reference; minimum GPA of 3.0 (initial licensure) or 2.7 (nonlicensure); interview. Additional exam requirements/recommendations for international students: Required—TOEFL (minimum score 550 paper-based). Electronic applications accepted. *Faculty research:* Co-teaching, Response to Intervention (RTI).

The College of Saint Rose, Graduate Studies, Thelma P. Lally School of Education, Programs in Special Education, Albany, NY 12203-1419. Offers adolescence education/special education (MS Ed); childhood education/special education (MS Ed); childhood special education (MS Ed); early childhood special education (MS Ed); special education (Certificate); special education professional (MS Ed). *Accreditation:* NCATE. *Students:* 8 full-time (5 women), 7 part-time (4 women). Average age 28. 15 applicants, 47% accepted, 5 enrolled. In 2018, 11 master's awarded. *Degree requirements:* For master's, comprehensive exam (for some programs), thesis or alternative, research project. *Entrance requirements:* For master's, minimum undergraduate GPA of 3.0. Additional exam requirements/recommendations for international students: Required—TOEFL (minimum score 550 paper-based; 80 iBT), IELTS (minimum score 6), PTE (minimum score 56). *Application deadline:* For fall admission, 4/1 priority date for domestic and international students; for spring admission, 10/15 priority date for domestic and international students; for summer admission, 3/15 priority date for domestic and international students. Applications are processed on a rolling basis. Application fee: $40. Electronic applications accepted. *Expenses: Tuition:* Full-time $14,382; part-time $799 per credit hour. *Required fees:* $924; $408 per credit. $286. *Financial support:* Career-related internships or fieldwork, scholarships/grants, tuition waivers (partial), and unspecified assistantships available. Support available to part-time students. Financial award application deadline: 4/15. *Unit head:* Franics Ihle, Chair, 518-337-4885, E-mail: ihlef@strose.edu. *Application contact:* Daniel Gallagher, Assistant Vice President for Graduate Recruitment and Enrollment, 518-485-3390, E-mail: grad@strose.edu.
Website: https://www.strose.edu/special-education/

The College of Saint Rose, Graduate Studies, Thelma P. Lally School of Education, Teacher Education Programs, Albany, NY 12203-1419. Offers adolescence education (MS Ed, Advanced Certificate); adolescence education/special education (Advanced Certificate); childhood education (MS Ed); curriculum and instruction (MS Ed); early childhood education (MS Ed). *Students:* 49 full-time (39 women), 21 part-time (17 women); includes 3 minority (2 Black or African American, non-Hispanic/Latino; 1 Hispanic/Latino). Average age 27. 41 applicants, 66% accepted, 21 enrolled. In 2018, 48 master's, 1 Advanced Certificate awarded. *Entrance requirements:* For master's, minimum undergraduate GPA of 3.0. Additional exam requirements/recommendations for international students: Required—TOEFL (minimum score 550 paper-based; 80 iBT), IELTS (minimum score 6), PTE (minimum score 56). *Application deadline:* For fall admission, 4/1 priority date for domestic and international students; for spring admission, 10/15 priority date for domestic and international students; for summer admission, 3/15 priority date for domestic and international students. Applications are processed on a rolling basis. Application fee: $40. Electronic applications accepted. *Expenses: Tuition:* Full-time $14,382; part-time $799 per credit hour. *Required fees:* $924; $408 per credit. $286. *Financial support:* Career-related internships or fieldwork, scholarships/grants, tuition waivers (partial), and unspecified assistantships available. Support available to part-time students. Financial award application deadline: 4/15. *Unit head:* Dr. Drey Martone, Chair, 518-454-5262, E-mail: martoned@strose.edu. *Application contact:* Daniel Gallagher, Assistant Vice President for Graduate Recruitment and Enrollment, 518-485-3390, Fax: 518-458-5479, E-mail: grad@strose.edu.
Website: https://www.strose.edu/academics/schools/school-of-education/

College of Staten Island of the City University of New York, Graduate Programs, Division of Humanities and Social Sciences, Program in Autism Spectrum Disorders, Staten Island, NY 10314-6600. Offers Advanced Certificate. *Program availability:* Part-time, evening/weekend. *Faculty:* 2. *Students:* 6. 10 applicants, 40% accepted, 3 enrolled. In 2018, 4 Advanced Certificates awarded. *Degree requirements:* For Advanced Certificate, 12 credits. *Entrance requirements:* For degree, bachelor's degree with a 3.0 GPA in either Psychology/Education/Speech-Language Pathology/Science/Letters/Society or a related field or be in a graduate program; 2 letters of recommendation; résumé; cover letter of experience and reasons of interest in the Advanced Certificate. Additional exam requirements/recommendations for international students: Required—TOEFL (minimum score 550 paper-based; 79 iBT), IELTS (minimum score 6.5). *Application deadline:* For fall admission, 5/16 priority date for domestic students, 5/16 for international students; for spring admission, 11/25 priority date for domestic students, 11/25 for international students. Applications are processed on a rolling basis. Application fee: $75. Electronic applications accepted. *Expenses: Tuition, area resident:* Full-time $10,770; part-time $455 per credit. Tuition, state resident: full-time $10,770; part-time $455 per credit. Tuition, nonresident: full-time $19,920; part-time $830 per credit. *International tuition:* $19,920 full-time. *Required fees:* $559.20; $181.10 per semester. Tuition and fees vary according to program. *Faculty research:* Autism spectrum disorder, Interventions to alleviate autism stigma, neurodiversity, computer-mediated interventions, applied behavior analysis. *Unit head:* Dr. Kristen Gillespie-Lynch, Graduate Program Coordinator, 718-982-4121, Fax: 718-982-4114, E-mail: kristen.gillespie@csi.cuny.edu. *Application contact:* Sasha Spence, Associate Director for Graduate Admissions, 718-982-2019, Fax: 718-982-2500, E-mail: sasha.spence@csi.cuny.edu.
Website: http://www.csi.cuny.edu/catalog/graduate/autism-spectrum-disorders-advanced-certificate.htm

College of Staten Island of the City University of New York, Graduate Programs, School of Education, Program in Special Education, Staten Island, NY 10314-6600. Offers special education (MS Ed), including adolescence generalist: grades 7-12, grades 1-6. *Program availability:* Part-time, evening/weekend. *Students:* 130. 58 applicants, 71% accepted, 32 enrolled. In 2018, 42 master's awarded. *Degree requirements:* For master's, comprehensive exam, fieldwork; ten three-credit required courses and one elective for a total of 11 courses (33 credits) or 14 three-credit required courses and a three- to six-credit, field-based requirement for a total of 45-48 credits; research project. *Entrance requirements:* For master's, GRE General Test or an approved equivalent examination, BA/BS or 36 approved credits with a 3.0 GPA, 2 letters of recommendations, 1-2 page statement of experience; must have completed courses for NYS initial certificate in childhood education/early childhood education (Sequence 1); 6 credits each in English, history, math, and science, and 1 year of foreign language (Sequence 2). Additional exam requirements/recommendations for international students: Required—TOEFL (minimum score 550 paper-based; 79 iBT), IELTS (minimum score 6.5). *Application deadline:* For fall admission, 4/25 for domestic and international students; for spring admission, 11/25 for domestic and international students. Applications are processed on a rolling basis. Application fee: $75. Electronic applications accepted. *Expenses: Tuition, area resident:* Full-time $10,770; part-time $455 per credit. Tuition, state resident: full-time $10,770; part-time $455 per credit. Tuition, nonresident: full-time $19,920; part-time $830 per credit. *International tuition:* $19,920 full-time. *Required fees:* $559.20; $181.10 per semester. Tuition and fees vary according to program. *Faculty research:* Disabilities studies, social justice, arts-based research on disabilities, assessment of students with disabilities, technological pedagogical and content knowledge (TPACK) in special education teachers, juvenile justice. *Unit head:* Diane Brescia, 718-982-3877, E-mail: diane.brescia@csi.cuny.edu. *Application contact:* Sasha Spence, Associate Director for Graduate Admissions, 718-982-2019, Fax: 718-982-2500, E-mail: sasha.spence@csi.cuny.edu. Website: https://www.csi.cuny.edu/sites/default/files/pdf/admissions/grad/pdf/Education%20Fact%20Sheet.pdf

Colorado Christian University, Program in Curriculum and Instruction, Lakewood, CO 80226. Offers corporate education (MACI); early childhood educator (MACI); elementary educator (MACI); instructional technology (MACI); master educator (MACI); online course developer (MACI); online teaching and learning (MACI); special education generalist (MACI). *Program availability:* Part-time, evening/weekend. *Degree requirements:* For master's, thesis optional, practicum. *Entrance requirements:* For master's, interviews, letters of recommendation. Additional exam requirements/recommendations for international students: Required—TOEFL. Electronic applications accepted. *Expenses:* Contact institution.

Colorado Mesa University, Center for Teacher Education, Grand Junction, CO 81501-3122. Offers educational leadership (MAEd); English for speakers of other languages (MAEd); exceptional learner/special education (MAEd); teacher education (Graduate Certificate); teacher leader (MAEd). *Accreditation:* NCATE. *Program availability:* Part-time. *Degree requirements:* For master's, comprehensive exam (for some programs), capstone presentation. *Entrance requirements:* For master's, 3 professional letters of recommendation, Colorado teaching license, minimum baccalaureate GPA of 3.0; for Graduate Certificate, minimum baccalaureate GPA of 3.0. Additional exam requirements/recommendations for international students: Required—TOEFL (minimum score 550 paper-based). Electronic applications accepted. *Expenses:* Contact institution. *Faculty research:* K-8 STEM instruction, special education inclusion, elementary math literacy, secondary literacy, elementary/early childhood education literacy.

Colorado State University–Pueblo, College of Education, Engineering and Professional Studies, Education Program, Pueblo, CO 81001-4901. Offers art education (M Ed); foreign language education (M Ed); health and physical education (M Ed); instructional technology (M Ed); linguistically diverse education (M Ed); music education (M Ed); special education (M Ed). *Accreditation:* TEAC. *Program availability:* Part-time. *Degree requirements:* For master's, portfolio. *Entrance requirements:* For master's, 3 recommendations, teaching license. Additional exam requirements/recommendations for international students: Required—TOEFL (minimum score 500 paper-based). Electronic applications accepted. *Faculty research:* Portfolio assessment, math education, science education.

Columbus State University, Graduate Studies, College of Education and Health Professions, Department of Teacher Education, Columbus, GA 31907-5645. Offers curriculum and instruction in accomplished teaching (M Ed); early childhood education (M Ed, MAT, Ed S); middle grades education (M Ed, MAT, Ed S); secondary education (M Ed, MAT, Ed S), including biology (MAT), chemistry (MAT), earth and space science (MAT), English/language arts, general science (M Ed), history (MAT), mathematics, science (Ed S), social science (M Ed, Ed S); special education (M Ed, MAT, Ed S), including general curriculum (M Ed, MAT); teacher leadership (M Ed). *Accreditation:* NCATE. *Program availability:* Part-time, evening/weekend, 100% online, blended/hybrid learning. *Faculty:* 20 full-time (12 women), 20 part-time/adjunct (15 women). *Students:* 110 full-time (84 women), 143 part-time (115 women); includes 105 minority (96 Black or African American, non-Hispanic/Latino; 4 Hispanic/Latino; 5 Two or more races, non-Hispanic/Latino). Average age 33. 147 applicants, 56% accepted, 62 enrolled. In 2018, 112 master's, 11 other advanced degrees awarded. *Degree requirements:* For Ed S, thesis or alternative. *Entrance requirements:* For master's, GRE General Test, minimum undergraduate GPA of 2.75; for Ed S, GRE General Test, minimum undergraduate GPA of 2.75, graduate 3.0. Additional exam requirements/recommendations for international students: Required—TOEFL (minimum score 550 paper-based; 79 iBT). *Application deadline:* For fall admission, 6/30 for domestic students, 5/1 for international students; for spring admission, 11/1 for domestic and international students; for summer admission, 3/1 for domestic and international students. Applications are processed on a rolling basis. Application fee: $50. Electronic applications accepted. *Expenses: Tuition, area resident:* Full-time $4924; part-time $618 per credit hour. Tuition, state resident: full-time $4924; part-time $618 per credit hour. Tuition, nonresident: full-time $19,218; part-time $2403 per credit hour. *International tuition:* $19,218 full-time. *Required fees:* $1870; $802. Tuition and fees vary according to course load, degree level and program. *Financial support:* In 2018–19, 29 students received support, including 7 research assistantships with partial tuition reimbursements available (averaging $3,000 per year); career-related internships or fieldwork, Federal Work-Study, institutionally sponsored loans, scholarships/grants, tuition waivers (partial), and unspecified assistantships also available. Support available to part-time students. Financial award application deadline: 5/1; financial award applicants required to submit FAFSA. *Unit head:* Dr. Jan Burcham, Department Chair, 706-507-8519, Fax: 706-568-3134, E-mail: burcham_jan@columbusstate.edu. *Application contact:* Catrina Smith-Edmond, Assistant Director for Graduate and Global Admission, 706-507-8824, Fax: 706-568-5091, E-mail: smithedmond_catrina@columbusstate.edu. Website: http://te.columbusstate.edu/

Concordia College–New York, Program in Childhood Special Education, Bronxville, NY 10708-1998. Offers MS Ed.

Concordia University, St. Paul, College of Education, St. Paul, MN 55104-5494. Offers classroom instruction (MA Ed), including K-12 reading; differentiated instruction

(MA Ed); early childhood education (MA Ed); education (Ed D); educational leadership (MA Ed); educational technology (MA Ed, Certificate); K-12 principal licensure (Ed S); special education (MA Ed), including autism spectrum disorder, emotional and behavioral disorders, learning disabilities; superintendent (Ed S); teaching (MAT). *Accreditation:* NCATE. *Program availability:* Part-time, evening/weekend, 100% online, blended/hybrid learning. *Faculty:* 13 full-time (9 women), 82 part-time/adjunct (51 women). *Students:* 979 full-time (748 women), 40 part-time (28 women); includes 124 minority (49 Black or African American, non-Hispanic/Latino; 6 American Indian or Alaska Native, non-Hispanic/Latino; 34 Asian, non-Hispanic/Latino; 22 Hispanic/Latino; 1 Native Hawaiian or other Pacific Islander, non-Hispanic/Latino; 12 Two or more races, non-Hispanic/Latino), 11 international. Average age 34. 423 applicants, 99% accepted, 335 enrolled. In 2018, 358 master's, 3 doctorates, 119 other advanced degrees awarded. *Degree requirements:* For master's, thesis (for some programs); for doctorate, thesis/dissertation, capstone projects; for other advanced degree, e-folio review of competencies. *Entrance requirements:* For master's, official transcripts from regionally-accredited institution stating the conferral of a bachelor's degree with minimum cumulative GPA of 3.0; personal statement; professional resume; practitioner in field through work or volunteerism; resume; for doctorate, minimum master's or specialist degree GPA of 3.25; transcript; writing sample; three letters of recommendation; current resume; on-campus interview; for other advanced degree, minimum master's or specialist degree GPA of 3.25; transcript; statement covering employment history and long-term academic and professional goals; two letters of recommendation; interview with program director. Additional exam requirements/recommendations for international students: Recommended—TOEFL (minimum score 547 paper-based; 78 iBT), IELTS (minimum score 6). *Application deadline:* For fall admission, 8/1 for domestic and international students; for spring admission, 12/1 for domestic and international students; for summer admission, 5/1 for domestic and international students. Applications are processed on a rolling basis. Application fee: $0. Electronic applications accepted. *Expenses:* $395 per credit for 30 credits (for MA programs), $440 per credit for 42 credits (for MAT), $415 per credit for 30 credits (for EdS), $615 per credit for 64 credits (for EdD). *Financial support:* In 2018–19, 163 students received support. Federal Work-Study, scholarships/grants, and unspecified assistantships available. Financial award applicants required to submit FAFSA. *Faculty research:* School design for innovative learning practices, equine-assisted instruction, best practices for leadership in early childhood education, mental health needs in K-12 focusing on children of incarcerated parents, competency-based education. *Unit head:* Lonn Maly, Dean, 651-641-8203, E-mail: maly@csp.edu. *Application contact:* Amber Faletti, Director of Enrollment Management, 651-641-8838, Fax: 651-603-6320, E-mail: faletti@csp.edu.

Concordia University Wisconsin, Graduate Programs, School of Education, Mequon, WI 53097-2402. Offers art education (MS Ed); early childhood (MS Ed); educational administration (MS Ed); environmental education (MS Ed); family studies (MS Ed); literacy (MS Ed); school counseling (MS Ed); special education (MS Ed). *Program availability:* Part-time, evening/weekend, online learning. *Degree requirements:* For master's, comprehensive exam, thesis or alternative. *Entrance requirements:* For master's, minimum GPA of 3.0, teaching license. Additional exam requirements/recommendations for international students: Required—TOEFL. *Faculty research:* Motivation, developmental learning, learning styles.

Concord University, Graduate Studies, Athens, WV 24712-1000. Offers educational leadership and supervision (M Ed); health promotion (MA); reading specialist (M Ed); social work (MSW); special education (M Ed); teaching (MAT). *Program availability:* Part-time, evening/weekend, 100% online. *Degree requirements:* For master's, thesis (for some programs). *Entrance requirements:* For master's, GRE or MAT, baccalaureate degree with minimum GPA of 2.5 from regionally-accredited institution; teaching license; 2 letters of recommendation; completed disposition assessment form. Electronic applications accepted.

Converse College, Program in Special Education, Spartanburg, SC 29302. Offers intellectual disabilities (MAT); learning disabilities (MAT); special education (M Ed). *Program availability:* Part-time. *Degree requirements:* For master's, capstone paper. *Entrance requirements:* For master's, NTE or PRAXIS II (M Ed), minimum GPA of 2.75, 2 recommendations. Electronic applications accepted.

Coppin State University, School of Graduate Studies, School of Education, Department of Teaching and Learning, Program in Special Education, Baltimore, MD 21216-3698. Offers M Ed. *Program availability:* Part-time. *Degree requirements:* For master's, 3 hours of capstone experience in urban literacy. *Entrance requirements:* For master's, MAT or GRE, resume, references, teacher certification, 3 years of teaching experience.

Curry College, Graduate Studies, Program in Education, Milton, MA 02186-9984. Offers elementary education (M Ed); foundations (non-license) (M Ed); reading (M Ed, Certificate); special education (M Ed). *Program availability:* Part-time, evening/weekend. *Degree requirements:* For master's, project or thesis. *Entrance requirements:* For master's, interview, recommendations, resume, written statement. Additional exam requirements/recommendations for international students: Required—TOEFL (minimum score 550 paper-based; 80 iBT). *Expenses:* Contact institution. *Faculty research:* Classroom trauma, therapeutic writing, inclusionary practices.

Daemen College, Education Programs, Amherst, NY 14226-3592. Offers adolescence education (MS); childhood education (MS); childhood special education (MS); childhood special-alternative certification (MS); early childhood special-alternative certification (MS). *Accreditation:* TEAC. *Program availability:* Part-time. *Faculty:* 16 full-time (12 women), 19 part-time/adjunct (14 women). *Students:* 233 full-time (210 women), 21 part-time (18 women); includes 4 minority (1 Black or African American, non-Hispanic/Latino; 3 Hispanic/Latino), 1 international. Average age 22. 76 applicants, 93% accepted, 68 enrolled. In 2018, 204 master's awarded. *Degree requirements:* For master's, comprehensive exam, A minimum grade of B earned in all courses, thereby resulting in a minimum cumulative grade point average of 3.00. *Entrance requirements:* For master's, Submit scores from taking the Graduate Record Exam (GRE) by no later than December 16 for fall applicants, no later than May 1 for spring applicants, bachelor's degree, GPA of 3.0 or above, resume, letter of intent, 2 letters of recommendation, interview with department chair. Additional exam requirements/recommendations for international students: Required—TOEFL (minimum score 77 paper-based), IELTS (minimum score 6.5). *Application deadline:* Applications are processed on a rolling basis. Application fee: $25. Electronic applications accepted. Application fee is waived when completed online. *Expenses: Tuition:* Part-time $977 per credit hour. *Required fees:* $125; $14 per credit hour. *Financial support:* Scholarships/grants and unspecified assistantships available. Support available to part-time students. Financial award applicants required to submit FAFSA. *Unit head:* Dr. Elizabeth Heilman, Department Chair, 716-839-8553, E-mail: eheilman@daemen.edu. *Application contact:* Megan Beardi, Senior Assistant Director of Graduate Admissions, 716-566-7861, Fax: 716-839-8229, E-mail: mbeardi@daemen.edu. Website: https://www.daemen.edu/academics/areas-study/education

Dallas Baptist University, Dorothy M. Bush College of Education, Program in Curriculum and Instruction, Dallas, TX 75211-9299. Offers Christian school administration (M Ed); distance learning (M Ed); English as a second language (M Ed);

instructional technology (M Ed); professional life coaching (M Ed); special education (M Ed); supervision (M Ed). *Program availability:* Part-time, evening/weekend, online learning. *Application deadline:* Applications are processed on a rolling basis. Application fee: $25. Electronic applications accepted. Application fee is waived when completed online. *Expenses: Tuition:* Full-time $17,262; part-time $959 per credit hour. *Required fees:* $1000; $500 per semester. Tuition and fees vary according to course load and degree level. *Unit head:* Dr. Neil Dugger, Dean, 214-333-5202, E-mail: neil@dbu.edu. *Application contact:* Karla Hagan, Program Director, 214-333-5831, E-mail: karla@dbu.edu.
Website: http://www3.dbu.edu/graduate/curriculum_instruction.asp

Dallas Baptist University, Dorothy M. Bush College of Education, Program in Special Education, Dallas, TX 75211-9299. Offers diagnostician (M Ed). *Program availability:* Part-time, evening/weekend. *Application deadline:* Applications are processed on a rolling basis. Application fee: $25. Electronic applications accepted. Application fee is waived when completed online. *Expenses: Tuition:* Full-time $17,262; part-time $959 per credit hour. *Required fees:* $1000; $500 per semester. Tuition and fees vary according to course load and degree level. *Unit head:* Dr. Neil Dugger, Dean, 214-333-5202, E-mail: neil@dbu.edu. *Application contact:* Dr. Mary Beth Sanders, Program Director, 214-333-5547, E-mail: marys@dbu.edu.
Website: https://www.dbu.edu/graduate/degree-programs/med-special-education

Delaware State University, Graduate Programs, College of Education, Health and Public Policy, Program in Special Education, Dover, DE 19901-2277. Offers MA. *Program availability:* Part-time, evening/weekend. *Degree requirements:* For master's, comprehensive exam, thesis optional. *Entrance requirements:* For master's, GRE General Test, minimum GPA of 3.0 in field, 2.75 overall. Additional exam requirements/recommendations for international students: Required—TOEFL (minimum score 550 paper-based). Electronic applications accepted. *Faculty research:* Curriculum and instruction, distributive education.

Delta State University, Graduate Programs, College of Education, Division of Teacher Education, Leadership, and Research, Program in Special Education, Cleveland, MS 38733-0001. Offers M Ed. *Accreditation:* NCATE. *Program availability:* Part-time, evening/weekend. *Degree requirements:* For master's, thesis optional, practicum. *Expenses: Tuition, area resident:* Full-time $7076; part-time $393 per credit hour. Tuition, state resident: full-time $7076; part-time $393 per credit hour. Tuition, nonresident: full-time $7076; part-time $393 per credit hour. *International tuition:* $7076 full-time. *Required fees:* $170; $18.90 per credit hour. $9.45 per semester. Part-time tuition and fees vary according to program.

DePaul University, College of Education, Chicago, IL 60614. Offers bilingual-bicultural education (M Ed, MA); counseling (M Ed, MA), including clinical mental health counseling, college student development, school counseling; curriculum studies (M Ed, MA, Ed D); early childhood education (M Ed, MA, Ed D); educational leadership (M Ed, MA, Ed D), including Catholic leadership (M Ed, MA), general (M Ed, MA), higher education (M Ed, MA), physical education (M Ed, MA), principal preparation (M Ed), teacher preparation (M Ed); elementary education (M Ed, MA); middle grades education (M Ed); middle school mathematics education (MS); reading specialist (M Ed, MA); secondary education (M Ed, MA); social and cultural foundations in education (M Ed, MA); special education (M Ed); sport, fitness and recreation leadership (MS); value-creating education for global citizenship (M Ed); world languages education (M Ed, MA). *Program availability:* Part-time, evening/weekend, online learning. *Degree requirements:* For doctorate, thesis/dissertation. Electronic applications accepted.

DeSales University, Division of Liberal Arts and Social Sciences, Center Valley, PA 18034-9568. Offers criminal justice (MCJ); digital forensics (MCJ, Postbaccalaureate Certificate); education (M Ed), including instructional technology, secondary education, special education, teaching English to speakers of other languages; investigative forensics (MCJ, Postbaccalaureate Certificate). *Program availability:* Part-time, 100% online, blended/hybrid learning. *Entrance requirements:* For master's, bachelor's degree from accredited institution, minimum undergraduate GPA of 3.0, personal statement showing potential of graduate work, three letters of recommendation, professional goal statement. Additional exam requirements/recommendations for international students: Required—TOEFL. Electronic applications accepted.

Dominican College, Division of Teacher Education, Orangeburg, NY 10962-1210. Offers education/teaching of individuals with multiple disabilities (MS Ed). *Program availability:* Part-time, evening/weekend, online learning. *Faculty:* 5 part-time/adjunct (all women). *Students:* 4 full-time (all women), 52 part-time (40 women); includes 11 minority (1 Black or African American, non-Hispanic/Latino; 2 Asian, non-Hispanic/Latino; 8 Hispanic/Latino). Average age 33. In 2018, 24 master's awarded. *Degree requirements:* For master's, comprehensive exam (for some programs), thesis. *Entrance requirements:* For master's, 3 letters of recommendation (atleast 1 from a former professor), current resume, Official transcripts (not student copies) of all undergraduate and graduate records, results from GRE/MAT/SAT or ACT scores, interview, State issued teaching certificate & State Certification Exam Scores are Required for TVI program. Additional exam requirements/recommendations for international students: Required—TOEFL (minimum score 90 iBT). *Application deadline:* For fall admission, 8/1 for domestic students, 6/1 for international students. Applications are processed on a rolling basis. Application fee: $50. Electronic applications accepted. *Expenses: Tuition:* Part-time $965 per credit. *Required fees:* $200 per semester. One-time fee: $200. Tuition and fees vary according to course load, degree level and program. *Financial support:* Application deadline: 2/1; applicants required to submit FAFSA. *Unit head:* Dr. Mike Kelly, Director, 845-848-4090, Fax: 845-359-7802, E-mail: mike.kelly@dc.edu. *Application contact:* Heather Karsenty, Assistant Director of Graduate Admissions, 845-848-7908 Ext. 15, Fax: 845-365-3150, E-mail: admissions@dc.edu.

Dominican University, School of Education, River Forest, IL 60305-1099. Offers child life studies (MS); early childhood education (MS); education (MAT); elementary education (MA Ed); English as a second language (MA Ed); reading (MA Ed); secondary education (MAT); special education (MS). *Accreditation:* NCATE. *Program availability:* Part-time, evening/weekend, 100% online, blended/hybrid learning. *Entrance requirements:* For master's, Illinois Test of Basic Skills. Additional exam requirements/recommendations for international students: Required—TOEFL (minimum score 550 paper-based; 79 iBT). *Expenses:* Contact institution. *Faculty research:* Governance of private education institutions, reading and language arts, inclusion, organizational planning, leadership and vision.

Dominican University of California, Programs in Education plus Teacher Preparation, San Rafael, CA 94901-2298. Offers multiple subject (MS); single subject (MS). *Program availability:* Part-time, evening/weekend. *Degree requirements:* For master's, thesis. *Entrance requirements:* Additional exam requirements/recommendations for international students: Required—TOEFL (minimum score 550 paper-based; 80 iBT), IELTS (minimum score 6.5). Electronic applications accepted. *Expenses:* Contact institution.

Drake University, School of Education, Des Moines, IA 50311-4516. Offers applied behavior analysis (MS); counseling (MS); education (PhD); education administration (Ed D); educational leadership (MSE, Ed D); effective teaching (MSE); leadership development (MS); literacy (Ed S); literacy education (MSE); rehabilitation administration (MS); rehabilitation placement (MS); special education (MSE); STEM education (MSE); teacher education (5-12) (MAT); teacher education (K-8) (MST); teacher effectiveness and professional development (MSE). *Program availability:* Part-time, evening/weekend, 100% online, blended/hybrid learning. *Students:* 90 full-time (74 women), 690 part-time (532 women); includes 69 minority (30 Black or African American, non-Hispanic/Latino; 1 American Indian or Alaska Native, non-Hispanic/Latino; 9 Asian, non-Hispanic/Latino; 16 Hispanic/Latino; 13 Two or more races, non-Hispanic/Latino). Average age 34. In 2018, 253 master's, 30 doctorates awarded. *Degree requirements:* For master's and Ed S, comprehensive exam, internships (for some programs); for doctorate, comprehensive exam, thesis/dissertation, internships (for some programs). *Entrance requirements:* For master's, GRE General Test, MAT, or Drake Writing Assessment, resume, 2 letters of recommendation; for doctorate, GRE General Test or MAT, master's degree, 3 letters of recommendation; for Ed S, GRE General Test or MAT. Additional exam requirements/recommendations for international students: Required—TOEFL (minimum score 550 paper-based). *Application deadline:* For fall admission, 7/1 priority date for domestic students, 6/1 priority date for international students; for spring admission, 11/1 priority date for domestic students, 10/1 priority date for international students. Applications are processed on a rolling basis. Application fee: $25. Electronic applications accepted. *Expenses:* Contact institution. *Financial support:* Research assistantships, career-related internships or fieldwork, and unspecified assistantships available. Support available to part-time students. *Faculty research:* Counseling and rehabilitation, behavioral supports, inquiry-based science methods, teacher quality enhancement. *Unit head:* Dr. Janet McMahill, Dean, 515-271-3829, E-mail: janet.mcmahill@drake.edu. *Application contact:* Dr. Janet McMahill, Dean, 515-271-3829, E-mail: janet.mcmahill@drake.edu.
Website: http://www.drake.edu/soe/

Drew University, Caspersen School of Graduate Studies, Madison, NJ 07940-1493. Offers conflict resolution and leadership (Certificate), including community leadership, moderation, peace building; education (M Ed); finance (MA); history and culture (MA, PhD), including American history, book history, British history, European history, intellectual history, Irish history, print culture, public history; K-12 education (MAT), including art, biology, chemistry, elementary education, English, French, Italian, math, secondary education, special education, teacher of students with disabilities; liberal studies (M Litt, D Litt), including history, Irish/Irish-American studies, literature (M Litt, MMH, D Litt, DMH, CMH), religion, spirituality, teaching in the two-year college, writing; medical humanities (MMH, DMH, CMH), including arts, health, healthcare, literature (M Litt, MMH, D Litt, DMH, CMH), scientific research; poetry (MFA). *Program availability:* Part-time, evening/weekend. *Faculty:* 3 full-time (2 women), 27 part-time/adjunct (13 women). *Students:* 66 full-time (38 women), 179 part-time (117 women); includes 37 minority (15 Black or African American, non-Hispanic/Latino; 2 Asian, non-Hispanic/Latino; 15 Hispanic/Latino; 5 Two or more races, non-Hispanic/Latino), 14 international. Average age 42. 157 applicants, 82% accepted, 57 enrolled. In 2018, 34 master's, 24 doctorates, 17 other advanced degrees awarded. Terminal master's awarded for partial completion of doctoral program. *Degree requirements:* For master's and other advanced degree, thesis (for some programs); for doctorate, one foreign language, comprehensive exam (for some programs), thesis/dissertation. *Entrance requirements:* For master's, PRAXIS Core and Subject Area tests (for MAT), GRE/GMAT (for MFin MS in Data Analytics), resume, transcripts, writing sample, personal statement, letters of recommendation; for doctorate, GRE (PhD in history and culture), resume, transcripts, writing sample, personal statement, letters of recommendation; for other advanced degree, resume, transcripts, personal statement. Additional exam requirements/recommendations for international students: Required—TOEFL (minimum score 587 paper-based; 80 iBT), IELTS (minimum score 6), TWE (minimum score 4). *Application deadline:* For fall admission, 8/1 for domestic students, 6/1 for international students; for spring admission, 12/1 for domestic students, 10/1 for international students. Applications are processed on a rolling basis. Application fee: $35. Electronic applications accepted. *Financial support:* Fellowships, research assistantships, teaching assistantships, career-related internships or fieldwork, Federal Work-Study, scholarships/grants, and unspecified assistantships available. Support available to part-time students. Financial award applicants required to submit FAFSA. *Unit head:* Dr. Debra Liebowitz, Provost and Dean of the College of Liberal Arts & Caspersen School of Graduate Studies, 973-4083139, E-mail: dliebowi@drew.edu. *Application contact:* Amo-Augustus Kubeyinje, Associate Vice President for Graduate Enrollment, 973-408-3111, E-mail: akubeyinje@drew.edu.
Website: http://www.drew.edu/caspersen

Drexel University, Goodwin College of Professional Studies, School of Education, Philadelphia, PA 19104-2875. Offers applied behavior analysis (MS); creativity and innovation (MS); education improvement and transformation (MS); educational administration (MS); educational leadership and management (Ed D); educational leadership development and learning technologies (PhD); global and international education (MS); higher education (MS); human resources development (MS); learning technologies (MS); mathematics, learning and teaching (MS); special education (MS); teaching, learning and curriculum (MS). *Program availability:* Part-time, evening/weekend, online learning. *Degree requirements:* For doctorate, thesis/dissertation. *Entrance requirements:* For doctorate, GRE or GMAT. Additional exam requirements/recommendations for international students: Required—TOEFL, IELTS. Electronic applications accepted. Application fee is waived when completed online. *Expenses:* Contact institution. *Faculty research:* Leadership development, mathematics education, literacy, autism, educational technology.

Drury University, Master in Education Program, Springfield, MO 65802. Offers curriculum and instruction (M Ed), including elementary education, middle school education, secondary education; instructional leadership (M Ed); instructional technology (M Ed); integrated learning (M Ed); special education (M Ed); special reading (M Ed). *Accreditation:* NCATE. *Program availability:* Part-time, evening/weekend, 100% online, blended/hybrid learning. *Faculty:* 10 full-time (6 women), 8 part-time/adjunct (6 women). *Students:* 167 full-time (133 women). Average age 32. 92 applicants, 92% accepted, 69 enrolled. In 2018, 44 master's awarded. *Entrance requirements:* For master's, bachelor's degree with minimum GPA of 2.75. Additional exam requirements/recommendations for international students: Recommended—TOEFL (minimum score 80 iBT), IELTS (minimum score 6.5). *Application deadline:* For fall admission, 8/4 priority date for domestic and international students; for spring admission, 1/5 priority date for domestic and international students; for summer admission, 5/26 priority date for domestic and international students. Applications are processed on a rolling basis. Application fee: $25. Electronic applications accepted. *Expenses:* Tuition is $366 per credit hour. Fees are $7 per credit hour. Most M.Ed. degrees are 33 credit hours. *Financial support:* In 2018–19, 5 students received support. Career-related internships or fieldwork, scholarships/grants, and unspecified assistantships available. Financial award application deadline: 6/30; financial award applicants required to submit FAFSA. *Faculty research:* Instructional technology, autism, diversity, and social justice. *Unit head:* Dr. Asikaa Cosgrove, Director, Master in Education Program, 417-873-7806, E-mail: acosgrov@drury.edu. *Application contact:* Dr. Asikaa Cosgrove, Director, Master in Education Program, 417-873-7806, E-mail: acosgrov@drury.edu.
Website: http://www.drury.edu/education-masters

Duquesne University, School of Education, Department of Counseling, Psychology, and Special Education, Program in Special Education, Pittsburgh, PA 15282-0001. Offers cognitive, behavior, physical/health disabilities (MS Ed); community and special education support (MS Ed); special education (PhD); special education 7-12 (MS Ed); special education PreK-8 (MS Ed). *Program availability:* Part-time, evening/weekend. *Faculty:* 7 full-time (5 women). *Students:* 46 full-time (29 women), 8 part-time (6 women); includes 5 minority (1 Black or African American, non-Hispanic/Latino; 2 Hispanic/Latino; 2 Two or more races, non-Hispanic/Latino), 27 international. Average age 29. 43 applicants, 91% accepted, 28 enrolled. In 2018, 8 master's awarded. Terminal master's awarded for partial completion of doctoral program. *Entrance requirements:* For master's, bachelor's degree; for doctorate, GRE, interview, three reference letters. Additional exam requirements/recommendations for international students: Required—TOEFL (minimum score 550 paper-based), IELTS (minimum score 6.5). *Application deadline:* For fall admission, 8/15 for domestic students; for spring admission, 1/2 for domestic students; for summer admission, 5/15 for domestic students. Applications are processed on a rolling basis. Application fee: $0. Electronic applications accepted. *Expenses: Tuition:* Full-time $23,112; part-time $1284 per credit. Tuition and fees vary according to program. *Financial support:* In 2018–19, 8 students received support, including 4 research assistantships with partial tuition reimbursements available (averaging $2,965 per year), 4 teaching assistantships with full tuition reimbursements available (averaging $7,954 per year). Support available to part-time students. Financial award applicants required to submit FAFSA. *Faculty research:* Positive behavior supports, autism, transitions and transition assessments, intersectionality of disability and race, behavior analytic approaches. *Total annual research expenditures:* $116,772. *Unit head:* Dr. Temple Lovelace, Associate Professor/Program Director, 412-396.4159, Fax: 412-396-1340, E-mail: lovelacet@duq.edu. *Application contact:* Kelly McGinley, Graduate Admissions Assistant, 412-396-1559, Fax: 412-396-5585, E-mail: mcginleyk@duq.edu.

D'Youville College, Department of Education, Buffalo, NY 14201-1084. Offers educational leadership (Ed D); elementary education (MS Ed); secondary education (MS Ed); special education (MS Ed). *Program availability:* Part-time, evening/weekend. *Degree requirements:* For master's, one foreign language, comprehensive exam, project or thesis. *Entrance requirements:* For master's, GRE (if GPA less than 2.75), minimum GPA of 3.0. Additional exam requirements/recommendations for international students: Required—TOEFL (minimum score 500 paper-based). Electronic applications accepted. *Faculty research:* Developmental disabilities, multiculturalism, early childhood education.

East Carolina University, Graduate School, College of Education, Department of Special Education, Foundations, and Research, Greenville, NC 27858-4353. Offers assistive technology (Certificate); autism (Certificate); special education (MA Ed, MAT), including behavioral-emotional disabilities (MA Ed), intellectual disabilities (MA Ed), learning disabilities (MA Ed), low-incidence disabilities (MA Ed). *Program availability:* Part-time, evening/weekend, online learning. *Application deadline:* For fall admission, 6/1 priority date for domestic students. *Expenses: Tuition,* area resident: Full-time $4749. Tuition, state resident: full-time $4749. Tuition, nonresident: full-time $17,898. *International tuition:* $17,898 full-time. *Required fees:* $2787. Part-time tuition and fees vary according to course load and program. *Financial support:* Application deadline: 6/1. *Unit head:* Dr. Guili Zhang, Interim Chair, 252-328-4989, E-mail: zhangg@ecu.edu. *Application contact:* Graduate School Admissions, 252-328-6012, Fax: 252-328-6071, E-mail: gradschool@ecu.edu.
Website: http://www.ecu.edu/cs-educ/sefr/index.cfm

Eastern Illinois University, Graduate School, College of Education, Department of Special Education, Charleston, IL 61920. Offers MS Ed. *Accreditation:* NCATE. *Program availability:* Part-time, evening/weekend. *Degree requirements:* For master's, comprehensive exam (for some programs), thesis (for some programs). *Entrance requirements:* For master's, GMAT or GRE. Additional exam requirements/recommendations for international students: Required—TOEFL (minimum score 500 paper-based; 61 iBT), IELTS (minimum score 6). *Application deadline:* For fall admission, 5/15 for domestic and international students; for spring admission, 10/15 for domestic and international students. Applications are processed on a rolling basis. Application fee: $30. Electronic applications accepted. *Expenses:* Tuition, state resident: part-time $299 per credit hour. Tuition, nonresident: part-time $718 per credit hour. *Required fees:* $214.50 per credit hour. *Financial support:* Teaching assistantships with full tuition reimbursements, career-related internships or fieldwork, Federal Work-Study, scholarships/grants, and unspecified assistantships available. Support available to part-time students. Financial award application deadline: 3/1; financial award applicants required to submit FAFSA. *Unit head:* Melissa Jones-Bromenshenkel, Ph.D., Chair, 217-581-5315, Fax: 217-581-7004, E-mail: mljones2@eiu.edu. *Application contact:* Melissa Jones-Bromenshenkel, Ph.D., Chair, 217-581-5315, Fax: 217-581-7004, E-mail: mljones2@eiu.edu.
Website: http://www.eiu.edu/specedgrad/

Eastern Kentucky University, The Graduate School, College of Education, Department of Special Education, Richmond, KY 40475-3102. Offers communication disorders (MA Ed). *Accreditation:* NCATE. *Program availability:* Part-time. *Degree requirements:* For master's, comprehensive exam. *Entrance requirements:* For master's, GRE General Test, MAT, minimum GPA of 2.5. *Faculty research:* Personnel needs in communication disorders, education needs of people who stutter, attention of special ed teacher.

Eastern Mennonite University, Program in Teacher Education, Harrisonburg, VA 22802-2462. Offers curriculum and instruction (MA Ed); diverse needs (MA Ed); literacy (MA Ed); restorative justice in education (MA Ed). *Accreditation:* NCATE. *Program availability:* Part-time. *Degree requirements:* For master's, portfolio, research projects. *Entrance requirements:* For master's, 1 year of teaching experience, interview, minimum undergraduate GPA of 2.75. Additional exam requirements/recommendations for international students: Required—TOEFL (minimum score 550 paper-based). Electronic applications accepted. *Expenses:* Contact institution. *Faculty research:* Effective literacy instruction for middle school English language learners, beginning teacher's emotional experiences, constructivist learning environments, restorative discipline.

Eastern Michigan University, Graduate School, College of Education, Department of Special Education & Communication Sciences and Disorders, Program in Autism Spectrum Disorders, Ypsilanti, MI 48197. Offers MA. *Students:* 4 full-time (3 women), 32 part-time (25 women); includes 4 minority (3 Black or African American, non-Hispanic/Latino; 1 Two or more races, non-Hispanic/Latino). Average age 35. 11 applicants, 82% accepted, 6 enrolled. In 2018, 15 master's awarded. Application fee: $45. *Application contact:* Dr. Sally Burton-Hoyle, Program Coordinator, 734-487-3300, Fax: 734-487-2473, E-mail: sburtonh@emich.edu.

Eastern Michigan University, Graduate School, College of Education, Department of Special Education & Communication Sciences and Disorders, Program in Cognitive Impairment, Ypsilanti, MI 48197. Offers M Ed. *Students:* 11 full-time (9 women), 18 part-time (12 women); includes 3 minority (all Black or African American, non-Hispanic/Latino). Average age 35. 14 applicants, 57% accepted, 4 enrolled. In 2018, 1 master's awarded. Application fee: $45. *Application contact:* Dr. Derrick Fries, Graduate Coordinator, 734-487-3300, Fax: 734-487-2473, E-mail: dfries@emich.edu.

Eastern Michigan University, Graduate School, College of Education, Department of Special Education & Communication Sciences and Disorders, Program in Emotional Impairment, Ypsilanti, MI 48197. Offers M Ed. *Students:* 4 full-time (0 women), 4 part-time (2 women); includes 4 minority (3 Black or African American, non-Hispanic/Latino; 1 Asian, non-Hispanic/Latino). Average age 43. 4 applicants, 50% accepted, 2 enrolled. In 2018, 2 master's awarded. Application fee: $45. *Application contact:* Dr. Derrick Fries, Graduate Coordinator, 734-487-3300, Fax: 734-487-2473, E-mail: dfries@emich.edu.

Eastern Michigan University, Graduate School, College of Education, Department of Special Education & Communication Sciences and Disorders, Program in Learning Disabilities, Ypsilanti, MI 48197. Offers MA. *Students:* 2 full-time (both women), 14 part-time (12 women); includes 3 minority (all Hispanic/Latino), 1 international. Average age 31. 9 applicants, 78% accepted, 6 enrolled. In 2018, 8 master's awarded. Application fee: $45. *Application contact:* Dr. Rhonda Kraai, Advisor, 734-487-2740, Fax: 734-487-2473, E-mail: rkraai@emich.edu.

Eastern Michigan University, Graduate School, College of Education, Department of Special Education & Communication Sciences and Disorders, Program in Physical/Other Health Impairment, Ypsilanti, MI 48197. Offers M Ed. *Students:* 2 part-time (both women). Average age 39. 1 applicant, 100% accepted, 1 enrolled. Application fee: $45. *Application contact:* Dr. Derrick Fries, Graduate Coordinator, 734-487-3300, Fax: 734-487-2473, E-mail: dfries@emich.edu.

Eastern Michigan University, Graduate School, College of Education, Department of Special Education & Communication Sciences and Disorders, Programs in Special Education, Ypsilanti, MI 48197. Offers MA, SPA. *Accreditation:* NCATE. *Program availability:* Part-time, evening/weekend, online learning. *Students:* 5 full-time (4 women), 38 part-time (34 women); includes 6 minority (4 Black or African American, non-Hispanic/Latino; 1 Hispanic/Latino; 1 Two or more races, non-Hispanic/Latino), 2 international. Average age 40. 19 applicants, 89% accepted, 12 enrolled. In 2018, 1 master's, 2 other advanced degrees awarded. *Entrance requirements:* For master's, GRE General Test. Additional exam requirements/recommendations for international students: Required—TOEFL. *Application deadline:* Applications are processed on a rolling basis. Application fee: $45. *Financial support:* Fellowships, research assistantships with full tuition reimbursements, teaching assistantships with full tuition reimbursements, career-related internships or fieldwork, Federal Work-Study, institutionally sponsored loans, scholarships/grants, tuition waivers (partial), and unspecified assistantships available. Support available to part-time students. Financial award applicants required to submit FAFSA. *Application contact:* Dr. Derrick Fries, Advisor, 734-487-3300, Fax: 734-487-2473, E-mail: dfries@emich.edu.

Eastern Michigan University, Graduate School, College of Education, Department of Teacher Education, Program in Urban/Diversity Education, Ypsilanti, MI 48197. Offers MA. *Students:* 1 (woman) part-time. Average age 31. In 2018, 1 master's awarded. Application fee: $45. *Application contact:* Dr. Patricia Williams-Boyd, Advisor, 734-487-3260, Fax: 734-487-2101, E-mail: pwilliams1@emich.edu.

Eastern Nazarene College, Adult and Graduate Studies, Division of Teacher Education, Quincy, MA 02170. Offers administration (M Ed); early childhood education (M Ed, Certificate); elementary education (M Ed, Certificate); English as a second language (Certificate); instructional enrichment and development (Certificate); middle school education (M Ed, Certificate); moderate special needs education (Certificate); principal (Certificate); program development and supervision (Certificate); secondary education (M Ed, Certificate); special education administrator (Certificate); special needs (M Ed); supervisor (Certificate); teacher of reading (M Ed, Certificate). M Ed also available through weekend program for administration, special needs, and teacher of reading only. *Program availability:* Part-time, evening/weekend. *Entrance requirements:* Additional exam requirements/recommendations for international students: Required—TOEFL (minimum score 550 paper-based).

Eastern New Mexico University, Graduate School, College of Education and Technology, Department of Educational Studies, Program in Special Education, Portales, NM 88130. Offers early childhood special education (M Sp Ed); general special education (M Sp Ed); gifted education pedagogy (M Ed); special education pedagogy (M Ed). *Program availability:* Part-time. *Degree requirements:* For master's, comprehensive exam, thesis optional. *Entrance requirements:* For master's, writing assessment, minimum GPA of 3.0, letter of recommendation, photocopy of teaching license or confirmation of entrance into alternative licensure program, special education license or minimum 30 hours of undergraduate course work. Additional exam requirements/recommendations for international students: Required—TOEFL (minimum score 550 paper-based; 79 iBT), IELTS (minimum score 6). Electronic applications accepted. *Expenses: Tuition,* area resident: Full-time $6776. Tuition, state resident: full-time $6776; part-time $282 per credit hour. Tuition, nonresident: full-time $8986; part-time $374 per credit hour. *Required fees:* $60 per semester. One-time fee: $25.

Eastern University, Graduate Education Programs, St. Davids, PA 19087-3696. Offers ESL program specialist (K-12) (Certificate); general supervisor (PreK-12) (Certificate); health and physical education (K-12) (Certificate); middle level (4-8) (Certificate); multicultural education (M Ed); music (K-12) (Certificate); Pre K-4 (Certificate); Pre K-4 with special education (Certificate); reading (M Ed); reading specialist (K-12) (Certificate); reading supervisor (K-12) (Certificate); school counseling (MA, CAGS); school principalship (preK-12) (Certificate); school psychology (MS, CAGS); secondary biology education (7-12) (Certificate); secondary chemistry education (7-12) (Certificate); secondary communication education (7-12) (Certificate); secondary English education (7-12) (Certificate); secondary math education (7-12) (Certificate); secondary social studies education (7-12) (Certificate); special education (M Ed); special education (7-12) (Certificate); special education (Pre K-8) (Certificate); special education supervisor (K-12) (Certificate); TESOL (M Ed); world language (Certificate), including Spanish. *Program availability:* Part-time, evening/weekend, online learning. *Entrance requirements:* Additional exam requirements/recommendations for international students: Required—TOEFL. Electronic applications accepted. Application fee is waived when completed online. *Expenses:* Contact institution.

East Stroudsburg University of Pennsylvania, Graduate and Extended Studies, College of Education, Department of Special Education and Rehabilitation, East Stroudsburg, PA 18301-2999. Offers special education (M Ed). *Program availability:* Part-time, evening/weekend, online learning. *Faculty:* 2 full-time (both women), 1 (woman) part-time/adjunct. *Students:* 13 full-time (12 women), 69 part-time (56 women); includes 7 minority (2 Black or African American, non-Hispanic/Latino; 1 Asian, non-Hispanic/Latino; 3 Hispanic/Latino; 1 Two or more races, non-Hispanic/Latino). Average age 32. 31 applicants, 81% accepted, 21 enrolled. In 2018, 11 master's awarded. *Degree requirements:* For master's, comprehensive exam. *Entrance requirements:* For master's, PRAXIS/teacher certification, letter of recommendation, Pennsylvania Department of Education requirements. Additional exam requirements/recommendations for international students: Recommended—TOEFL (minimum score 560 paper-based; 83 iBT), IELTS. *Application deadline:* For fall admission, 7/31 priority date for domestic students, 6/30 priority date for international students; for spring admission, 11/30 for domestic students, 10/31 for international students. Applications are processed on a rolling basis. Application fee: $50. Electronic applications accepted. *Expenses: Tuition,* area resident: Full-time $9288; part-time $516 per credit. Tuition,

state resident: full-time $9288. Tuition, nonresident: full-time $13,932; part-time $774 per credit. *International tuition:* $13,932 full-time. *Required fees:* $2059; $114 per credit. Tuition and fees vary according to course load and degree level. *Financial support:* Research assistantships with tuition reimbursements, career-related internships or fieldwork, Federal Work-Study, and unspecified assistantships available. Support available to part-time students. Financial award application deadline: 3/1; financial award applicants required to submit FAFSA. *Unit head:* Dr. Gina Scala, Chair, 570-422-3781, Fax: 570-422-3198, E-mail: gscala@esu.edu. *Application contact:* Kevin Quintero, Associate Director, Graduate and Extended Studies, 570-422-3890, Fax: 570-422-2711, E-mail: kquintero@esu.edu.
Website: https://www.esu.edu/special_education_rehabilitation/index.cfm

East Tennessee State University, School of Graduate Studies, College of Education, Department of Educational Foundations and Special Education, Johnson City, TN 37614. Offers community leadership (Post-Master's Certificate), including early childhood special education (M Ed, Post-Master's Certificate), high incidence disabilities (M Ed, Post-Master's Certificate), low incidence disabilities (M Ed, Post-Master's Certificate); special education (M Ed, Post-Master's Certificate), including advanced studies in special education (M Ed), early childhood special education, high incidence disabilities, low incidence disabilities. *Program availability:* Part-time. *Degree requirements:* For master's, thesis (for some programs), practicum, residency, or thesis. *Entrance requirements:* For master's, PRAXIS I or Tennessee teaching license (for special education only), minimum GPA of 3.0 (or complete probationary period with no grade lower than B for first 9 graduate hours for early childhood education), 2-page essay outlining past experience with individuals with disabilities and goals for acquiring an advanced degree in special education; for Post-Master's Certificate, bachelor's or master's degree in early childhood or related field; two years of experience working with young children (preferred). Additional exam requirements/recommendations for international students: Required—TOEFL (minimum score 550 paper-based; 79 iBT). *Faculty research:* Teaching students with significant disabilities, problem-solving in toddlers, children and their development and learning, connecting classroom environment to student engagement in PreK-3, bilingual education in Ecuador, positive discipline/behavior support programs, early childhood relationships, international and comparative special education.

Edinboro University of Pennsylvania, Department of Counseling, School Psychology and Special Education, Edinboro, PA 16444. Offers counseling (MA), including art therapy, clinical mental health counseling, college counseling, rehabilitation counseling, school counseling; educational psychology (M Ed); school psychology (Ed S); special education (M Ed), including autism, behavior management. *Accreditation:* ACA. *Program availability:* Part-time, evening/weekend. *Degree requirements:* For master's, thesis or alternative, competency exam; for Ed S, thesis or alternative. *Entrance requirements:* For master's and Ed S, GRE or MAT, minimum QPA of 2.5. Electronic applications accepted.

Elmhurst College, Graduate Programs, Program in Early Childhood Special Education, Elmhurst, IL 60126-3296. Offers M Ed. *Program availability:* Part-time, evening/weekend. *Faculty:* 3 full-time (all women), 1 (woman) part-time/adjunct. *Students:* 3 full-time (all women), 5 part-time (all women); includes 3 minority (1 Black or African American, non-Hispanic/Latino; 2 Asian, non-Hispanic/Latino). Average age 29. 21 applicants. In 2018, 8 master's awarded. *Entrance requirements:* For master's, 3 recommendations, resume, statement of purpose. Additional exam requirements/recommendations for international students: Required—TOEFL (minimum score 550 paper-based; 79 iBT), IELTS (minimum score 6.5). *Application deadline:* Applications are processed on a rolling basis. Application fee: $0. Electronic applications accepted. *Expenses:* $490 per semester hour. *Financial support:* In 2018–19, 5 students received support. Fellowships and scholarships/grants available. Support available to part-time students. Financial award applicants required to submit FAFSA. *Unit head:* Dr. Therese Wehman, Director, 630-617-3231, E-mail: theresew@elmhurst.edu. *Application contact:* Timothy J. Panfil, Senior Director of Graduate Admission and Enrollment Management, 630-617-3300 Ext. 3256, Fax: 630-617-6471, E-mail: panfilt@elmhurst.edu.
Website: http://www.elmhurst.edu/ecse

Elmhurst College, Graduate Programs, Program in Special Education, Elmhurst, IL 60126-3296. Offers MS Ed. *Program availability:* Part-time, evening/weekend. *Faculty:* 3 full-time (all women), 3 part-time/adjunct (2 women). *Students:* 8 part-time (7 women); includes 1 minority (Hispanic/Latino). Average age 27. In 2018, 2 master's awarded. *Entrance requirements:* For master's, 3 recommendations, resume, statement of purpose. Additional exam requirements/recommendations for international students: Required—TOEFL (minimum score 550 paper-based; 79 iBT), IELTS (minimum score 6.5). *Application deadline:* Applications are processed on a rolling basis. Application fee: $0. Electronic applications accepted. *Expenses:* $490 per semester hour. *Financial support:* In 2018–19, 1 student received support. Scholarships/grants available. Support available to part-time students. Financial award applicants required to submit FAFSA. *Unit head:* Lisa Burke, Department Chair of Education, 630-617-5197, E-mail: lisab@elmhurst.edu. *Application contact:* Timothy J. Panfil, Senior Director of Graduate Admission and Enrollment Management, 630-617-3300 Ext. 3256, Fax: 630-617-6471, E-mail: panfilt@elmhurst.edu.
Website: http://www.elmhurst.edu/admission/graduate/se

Elms College, Division of Education, Chicopee, MA 01013-2839. Offers early childhood education (MAT); education (M Ed, CAGS); elementary education (MAT); English as a second language (MAT); reading (MAT); secondary education (MAT), including biology education, English education, Spanish education; special education (MAT). *Program availability:* Part-time, evening/weekend. *Faculty:* 5 full-time (all women), 6 part-time/adjunct (5 women). *Students:* 3 full-time (all women), 117 part-time (94 women); includes 12 minority (1 Black or African American, non-Hispanic/Latino; 2 Asian, non-Hispanic/Latino; 9 Hispanic/Latino). Average age 34. 27 applicants, 96% accepted, 23 enrolled. In 2018, 34 master's, 3 other advanced degrees awarded. *Degree requirements:* For master's, thesis (for some programs). *Entrance requirements:* For master's, Massachusetts Educators Certification Test, minimum GPA of 3.0; for CAGS, master's degree in education. Additional exam requirements/recommendations for international students: Required—TOEFL. *Application deadline:* For fall admission, 7/1 priority date for domestic students; for spring admission, 11/1 priority date for domestic students. Applications are processed on a rolling basis. Application fee: $30. *Expenses:* *Tuition:* Full-time $14,328; part-time $796 per credit. *Required fees:* $200. Tuition and fees vary according to degree level and program. *Financial support:* In 2018–19, 2 teaching assistantships with partial tuition reimbursements were awarded. Financial award applicants required to submit FAFSA. *Unit head:* Dr. Mary Janeczek, Chair, Division of Education, 413-594-2761, Fax: 413-592-4871, E-mail: janeczeke@elms.edu. *Application contact:* Nancy Davis, Director, Office of Graduate and Continuing Education Admissions, 413-265-2239, E-mail: davisn@elms.edu.

Emmanuel College, Graduate and Professional Programs, Graduate Programs in Education, Boston, MA 02115. Offers moderate learning disabilities (Certificate); urban education (M Ed). *Program availability:* Part-time, evening/weekend. *Degree requirements:* For master's, 36 credits, including 6-credit practicum. *Entrance requirements:* For master's, transcripts from all regionally-accredited institutions attended (showing proof of bachelor's degree completion), 2 letters of recommendation, essay, resume. Additional exam requirements/recommendations for international students: Required—TOEFL. Electronic applications accepted. *Expenses:* Contact institution.

Emporia State University, Program in Special Education, Emporia, KS 66801-5415. Offers behavior disorders (MS); gifted, talented, and creative (MS); interrelated special education (MS). *Accreditation:* NCATE. *Program availability:* Part-time. *Degree requirements:* For master's, comprehensive exam or thesis, practicum. *Entrance requirements:* For master's, GRE General Test or MAT, essay exam, appropriate bachelor's degree, teacher certification, letters of recommendation. Additional exam requirements/recommendations for international students: Required—TOEFL (minimum score 520 paper-based; 68 iBT). Electronic applications accepted.

Endicott College, Van Loan School of Graduate and Professional Studies, Program in Autism and Applied Behavior Analysis, Beverly, MA 01915-2096. Offers applied behavior analysis (M Ed, PhD); autism (Certificate); autism and applied behavior analysis (M Ed). *Program availability:* Part-time, evening/weekend, 100% online, blended/hybrid learning. *Degree requirements:* For master's, thesis; for doctorate, thesis/dissertation, qualifying examination. *Entrance requirements:* For master's, MAT or GRE, undergraduate transcript, two recommendations, personal statement. Additional exam requirements/recommendations for international students: Required—TOEFL. Electronic applications accepted. *Expenses:* Contact institution. *Faculty research:* ABA intervention for autism, behavioral assessment, evidence-based treatments.

Endicott College, Van Loan School of Graduate and Professional Studies, Special Education and Applied Behavior Analysis Program, Beverly, MA 01915-2096. Offers applied behavior analysis (M Ed, Post-Master's Certificate); special education (M Ed). *Program availability:* Part-time, evening/weekend, 100% online, blended/hybrid learning. *Degree requirements:* For master's, comprehensive exam, thesis, practicum. *Entrance requirements:* For master's, MAT or GRE, Massachusetts teaching certificate, letters of recommendation, undergraduate transcript, essay. Additional exam requirements/recommendations for international students: Required—TOEFL. Electronic applications accepted. *Expenses:* Contact institution. *Faculty research:* Evidence-based treatments, developmental disabilities, challenging behaviors, staff training/management, behavioral assessments.

Fairfield University, Graduate School of Education and Allied Professions, Fairfield, CT 06824. Offers applied behavior analysis (ATC); applied psychology (MA); clinical mental health counseling (MA, CAS); educational technology (MA); elementary education (MA, CAS); family studies (MA); integration of spirituality and religion in counseling (ATC); marriage and family therapy (MA); reading and language development (Sixth Year Certificate); school counseling (MA, CAS); school psychology (MA, CAS); school-based marriage and family therapy (ATC); secondary education (MA); special education (MA, CAS); substance abuse counseling (ATC); teaching (Certificate); teaching and foundations (MA, CAS); TESOL, world languages, and bilingual education (MA, CAS). *Accreditation:* NCATE. *Program availability:* Part-time, evening/weekend. *Degree requirements:* For master's, comprehensive exam. *Entrance requirements:* For master's, minimum GPA of 3.0, 2 recommendations, resume. Additional exam requirements/recommendations for international students: Required—TOEFL (minimum score 550 paper-based; 84 iBT) or IELTS (minimum score 7.5). Electronic applications accepted. *Expenses:* Contact institution. *Faculty research:* Reading and literacy, writing, social justice and inequality in education, addictions and mental health issues, therapeutic relationships and clinical supervision.

Fairleigh Dickinson University, Metropolitan Campus, University College: Arts, Sciences, and Professional Studies, Peter Sammartino School of Education, Program in Learning Disabilities, Teaneck, NJ 07666-1914. Offers MA. *Accreditation:* TEAC.

Fairmont State University, Programs in Education, Fairmont, WV 26554. Offers digital media, new literacies and learning (M Ed); education (MAT); exercise science, fitness and wellness (M Ed); professional studies (M Ed); reading (M Ed); special education (M Ed). *Accreditation:* NCATE. *Program availability:* Part-time, evening/weekend, 100% online. *Entrance requirements:* For master's, GRE. Additional exam requirements/recommendations for international students: Required—TOEFL (minimum score 80 iBT), IELTS (minimum score 6.5). Electronic applications accepted.

Ferris State University, College of Education and Human Services, School of Education, Big Rapids, MI 49307. Offers curriculum and instruction (M Ed), including special education, subject area; training and development (MSCTE). *Program availability:* Part-time, evening/weekend, blended/hybrid learning. *Faculty:* 7 full-time (4 women), 1 (woman) part-time/adjunct. *Students:* 4 full-time (3 women), 39 part-time (23 women); includes 7 minority (3 Black or African American, non-Hispanic/Latino; 2 Hispanic/Latino; 2 Two or more races, non-Hispanic/Latino), 2 international. Average age 38. 14 applicants, 93% accepted, 7 enrolled. In 2018, 18 master's awarded. *Degree requirements:* For master's, thesis, Capstone project. *Entrance requirements:* For master's, minimum undergraduate GPA of 3.0. Additional exam requirements/recommendations for international students: Required—TOEFL (minimum score 550 paper-based; 79 iBT), IELTS (minimum score 6.5), TOEFL (minimum score 550 paper-based, 79 iBT) or IELTS 6.5. *Application deadline:* For fall admission, 7/1 priority date for domestic and international students; for spring admission, 11/1 priority date for domestic and international students; for summer admission, 3/1 priority date for domestic and international students. Applications are processed on a rolling basis. Application fee: $0 ($30 for international students). Electronic applications accepted. Application fee is waived when completed online. *Financial support:* In 2018–19, 7 students received support. Career-related internships or fieldwork and scholarships/grants available. Support available to part-time students. Financial award applicants required to submit FAFSA. *Faculty research:* Game based education, needs of students with disabilities in post-secondary education, elementary education students with reading difficulties. *Unit head:* Leonard Johnson, Interim Dean, 231-591-3648, Fax: 231-591-2043, E-mail: LeonardJohnson@ferris.edu. *Application contact:* Liza Ing, Graduate Program Coordinator, 231-591-5362, Fax: 231-591-2043, E-mail: lizaIng@ferris.edu.
Website: http://www.ferris.edu/education/education/

Fitchburg State University, Division of Graduate and Continuing Education, Program in Special Education, Fitchburg, MA 01420-2697. Offers guided studies: dyslexia specialist (M Ed); guided studies: individualized (M Ed); guided studies: professional (M Ed); moderate disabilities: initial licensure (5-12) (M Ed); moderate disabilities: initial licensure (PK-8) (M Ed); teacher of students with severe disabilities (M Ed). *Accreditation:* NCATE. *Program availability:* Part-time, evening/weekend. *Degree requirements:* For master's, internship. *Entrance requirements:* Additional exam requirements/recommendations for international students: Required—TOEFL (minimum score 550 paper-based; 79 iBT). Electronic applications accepted. *Expenses:* Contact institution.

Flagler College, Program in Deaf Education, St. Augustine, FL 32085-1027. Offers MA.

Florida Atlantic University, College of Education, Department of Exceptional Student Education, Boca Raton, FL 33431-0991. Offers M Ed, Ed D. *Accreditation:* NCATE. *Program availability:* Part-time, evening/weekend. *Faculty:* 14 full-time (7 women). *Students:* 13 full-time (12 women), 34 part-time (31 women); includes 18 minority (7 Black or African American, non-Hispanic/Latino; 1 Asian, non-Hispanic/Latino; 8

Hispanic/Latino; 2 Two or more races, non-Hispanic/Latino). Average age 32. 39 applicants, 67% accepted, 18 enrolled. In 2018, 18 master's, 6 doctorates awarded. *Degree requirements:* For master's, thesis optional, internship; for doctorate, comprehensive exam, thesis/dissertation, internship. *Entrance requirements:* For master's, GRE General Test, minimum GPA of 3.0 during previous 2 years; for doctorate, GRE General Test, 3 years of teaching experience, interview. Additional exam requirements/recommendations for international students: Required—TOEFL (minimum score 500 paper-based; 61 iBT), IELTS (minimum score 6). *Application deadline:* For fall admission, 7/1 for domestic students, 2/15 for international students; for spring admission, 11/1 for domestic students, 7/15 for international students. Applications are processed on a rolling basis. Application fee: $30. Electronic applications accepted. *Expenses: Tuition, area resident:* Full-time $7400; part-time $369.82 per credit. Tuition, state resident: full-time $7400; part-time $369.82 per credit. Tuition, nonresident: full-time $20,496; part-time $1024.81 per credit. *Financial support:* Fellowships, research assistantships, teaching assistantships with partial tuition reimbursements, career-related internships or fieldwork, Federal Work-Study, scholarships/grants, tuition waivers (partial), and unspecified assistantships available. Support available to part-time students. Financial award applicants required to submit FAFSA. *Faculty research:* Instructional design, assessment, educational reform, behavioral research, social integration. *Unit head:* Ellen Ismalon, 561-297-3284, E-mail: eismalon@fau.edu. *Application contact:* Ellen Ismalon, 561-297-3284, E-mail: eismalon@fau.edu.
Website: http://www.coe.fau.edu/academicdepartments/ese/

Florida Gulf Coast University, College of Education, Program in Curriculum and Instruction, Fort Myers, FL 33965-6565. Offers elementary education (M Ed); English education (M Ed); English speakers of other languages endorsement (M Ed); gifted education (M Ed); mathematics education (M Ed); middle school education (M Ed); reading education (M Ed); science education (M Ed); social science education (M Ed); special education (M Ed). *Program availability:* Part-time, evening/weekend, online learning. *Degree requirements:* For master's, final project or portfolio. *Entrance requirements:* For master's, GRE General Test, MAT, minimum undergraduate GPA of 3.0 in last 2 years. Additional exam requirements/recommendations for international students: Required—TOEFL (minimum score 550 paper-based). Electronic applications accepted. *Faculty research:* Internet in schools, technology in pre-service and in-service teacher training.

Florida Gulf Coast University, College of Education, Program in Special Education, Fort Myers, FL 33965-6565. Offers behavior disorders (M Ed); mental retardation (M Ed); specific learning disabilities (M Ed); varying exceptionalities (M Ed). *Program availability:* Part-time, evening/weekend. *Degree requirements:* For master's, thesis or alternative. *Entrance requirements:* For master's, GRE General Test, MAT, minimum GPA of 3.0. Additional exam requirements/recommendations for international students: Required—TOEFL (minimum score 550 paper-based). Electronic applications accepted. *Faculty research:* Inclusion, interacting with families, alternative certification.

Florida International University, College of Arts, Sciences, and Education, Department of Teaching and Learning, Miami, FL 33199. Offers art education (MA, MS); curriculum and instruction (MS, Ed D, PhD, Ed S), including curriculum development (MS), elementary education (MS), English education (MS), learning technologies (MS), mathematics education (MS), modern language education (MS), physical education (MS), science education (MS), social studies education (MS), special education (MS); early childhood education (MS); exceptional student education (Ed D); foreign language education (MS), including foreign language education, teaching English to speakers of other languages (TESOL); language, literacy and culture (PhD); mathematics, science, and learning technologies (PhD); physical education (MS), including sport and fitness; reading education (MS). *Program availability:* Part-time, evening/weekend. *Faculty:* 64 full-time (43 women), 104 part-time/adjunct (76 women). *Students:* 169 full-time (144 women), 155 part-time (130 women); includes 260 minority (53 Black or African American, non-Hispanic/Latino; 7 Asian, non-Hispanic/Latino; 193 Hispanic/Latino; 7 Two or more races, non-Hispanic/Latino), 13 international. Average age 33. 184 applicants, 62% accepted, 87 enrolled. In 2018, 153 master's, 10 doctorates awarded. *Degree requirements:* For doctorate, comprehensive exam, thesis/dissertation. *Entrance requirements:* For master's, GRE General Test, Florida General Knowledge Test or Florida College Level Academic Skills Test; for doctorate and Ed S, GRE General Test. Additional exam requirements/recommendations for international students: Required—TOEFL (minimum score 550 paper-based; 80 iBT), IELTS (minimum score 6.3). *Application deadline:* For fall admission, 6/1 priority date for domestic students, 4/1 for international students; for winter admission, 10/1 priority date for domestic students, 9/1 for international students; for spring admission, 3/1 priority date for domestic students, 2/1 for international students. Applications are processed on a rolling basis. Application fee: $30. Electronic applications accepted. *Financial support:* Research assistantships and teaching assistantships available. *Unit head:* Dr. Maria Fernandez, Chair, 305-348-0193, Fax: 305-348-2086, E-mail: Maria.Fernandez9@fiu.edu. *Application contact:* Nanett Rojas, Manager, Admissions Operations, 305-348-7464, Fax: 305-348-7441, E-mail: gradadm@fiu.edu.
Website: https://tl.fiu.edu/

Florida Memorial University, School of Education, Miami-Dade, FL 33054. Offers elementary education (MS); exceptional student education (MS); reading (MS). *Degree requirements:* For master's, comprehensive exam or thesis, field and clinical experiences, exit exam. *Entrance requirements:* For master's, GRE, CLAST, PRAXIS I, baccalaureate or graduate degree with minimum GPA of 3.0 in last 60 hours, 3 recommendations. Additional exam requirements/recommendations for international students: Recommended—TOEFL.

Fontbonne University, Graduate Programs, St. Louis, MO 63105-3098. Offers accounting (MBA, MS); art (MA); art (K-12) (MAT); business (MBA); computer science (MS); deaf education (MA); early intervention in deaf education (MA); education (MA), including autism spectrum disorders, curriculum and instruction, diverse learners, early childhood education, reading, special education; elementary education (MAT); family and consumer sciences (MA), including multidisciplinary health communication studies; fine arts (MFA); instructional design and technology (MS); management and leadership (MM); middle school education (MAT); secondary education (MAT); special education (MAT); speech-language pathology (MS); supply chain management (MS); theatre (MA). *Accreditation:* ASHA. *Program availability:* Part-time, evening/weekend, online learning. *Degree requirements:* For master's, comprehensive exam (for some programs), thesis (for some programs). *Entrance requirements:* Additional exam requirements/recommendations for international students: Required—TOEFL (minimum score 500 paper-based; 65 iBT). Electronic applications accepted.

Fordham University, Graduate School of Education, Division of Curriculum and Teaching, New York, NY 10023. Offers curriculum and teaching (MSE); early childhood education (MSE); elementary education (MST); special education (MSE, Adv C); teaching English as a second language (MSE). *Accreditation:* NCATE. *Program availability:* Part-time, evening/weekend. *Degree requirements:* For Adv C, thesis. *Entrance requirements:* Additional exam requirements/recommendations for international students: Required—TOEFL (minimum score 577 paper-based; 90 iBT), IELTS (minimum score 7). Electronic applications accepted.

Fort Hays State University, Graduate School, College of Education, Department of Special Education, Hays, KS 67601-4099. Offers MS. *Accreditation:* NCATE. *Degree requirements:* For master's, comprehensive exam, thesis optional. *Entrance requirements:* Additional exam requirements/recommendations for international students: Required—TOEFL (minimum score 550 paper-based). Electronic applications accepted. *Faculty research:* Severe behavior disorders, early childhood language, multicultural speech.

Framingham State University, Graduate Studies, Program in Special Education, Framingham, MA 01701-9101. Offers M Ed. *Program availability:* Part-time, evening/weekend. *Entrance requirements:* For master's, MAT, interview.

Francis Marion University, Graduate Programs, School of Education, Florence, SC 29502-0547. Offers learning disabilities (M Ed, MAT). *Accreditation:* NCATE. *Program availability:* Part-time. *Degree requirements:* For master's, comprehensive exam (for some programs), thesis (for some programs), supervised internship (for MAT). *Entrance requirements:* For master's, GRE General Test, MAT, NTE, or PRAXIS II, official transcripts; two letters of recommendation. Additional exam requirements/recommendations for international students: Required—TOEFL (minimum score 550 paper-based; 79 iBT). *Faculty research:* Identification and alternate assessment of at-risk students.

Franklin Pierce University, Graduate and Professional Studies, Rindge, NH 03461-0060. Offers curriculum and instruction (M Ed); elementary education (MS Ed); emerging network technologies (Graduate Certificate); energy and sustainability studies (MBA, Graduate Certificate); health administration (MBA, Graduate Certificate); human resource management (MBA, Graduate Certificate); information technology (MBA); leadership (MBA); nursing education (MS); nursing leadership (MS); physical therapy (DPT); physician assistant studies (MPAS); special education (M Ed); sports management (MBA). *Accreditation:* APTA. *Program availability:* Part-time, 100% online, blended/hybrid learning. *Degree requirements:* For master's, concentrated original research projects; student teaching; fieldwork and/or internship; leadership project; PRAXIS I and II (for M Ed); for doctorate, concentrated original research projects, clinical fieldwork and/or internship, leadership project. *Entrance requirements:* For master's, minimum GPA of 2.5, 3 letters of recommendation; competencies in accounting, economics, statistics, and computer skills through life experience or undergraduate coursework (for MBA); certification/e-portfolio, minimum C grade in all education courses (for M Ed); license to practice as RN (for MS); for doctorate, GRE, 80 hours of observation/work in PT settings; completion of anatomy, chemistry, physics, and statistics; minimum GPA of 3.0. Additional exam requirements/recommendations for international students: Required—TOEFL (minimum score 550 paper-based; 61 iBT). Electronic applications accepted. *Faculty research:* Evidence-based practice in sports physical therapy, human resource management in economic crisis, leadership in nursing, innovation in sports facility management, differentiated learning and understanding by design.

Freed-Hardeman University, Program in Education, Henderson, TN 38340-2399. Offers curriculum and instruction (M Ed); school counseling (M Ed), including administration and supervision, special education; school leadership (Ed S). *Accreditation:* NCATE. *Program availability:* Part-time, evening/weekend. *Degree requirements:* For master's, comprehensive exam, thesis optional; for Ed S, thesis. *Entrance requirements:* For master's, GRE General Test or NTE; for Ed S, 3 years of teaching experience. Additional exam requirements/recommendations for international students: Required—TOEFL (minimum score 500 paper-based).

Fresno Pacific University, Graduate Programs, School of Education, Division of Special Education, Fresno, CA 93702-4709. Offers MA. *Program availability:* Part-time, evening/weekend. *Degree requirements:* For master's, thesis or alternative. *Entrance requirements:* Additional exam requirements/recommendations for international students: Required—TOEFL (minimum score 550 paper-based).

Frostburg State University, College of Education, Department of Educational Professions, Program in Special Education, Frostburg, MD 21532-1099. Offers M Ed. *Accreditation:* NCATE. *Program availability:* Part-time, evening/weekend. *Degree requirements:* For master's, thesis or alternative, PRAXIS II (special education section). *Entrance requirements:* For master's, teaching certificate. Additional exam requirements/recommendations for international students: Required—TOEFL. Electronic applications accepted.

Furman University, Graduate Division, Department of Education, Greenville, SC 29613. Offers curriculum and instruction (MA); early childhood education (MA); educational leadership (Ed S); English as a second language (MA); literacy (MA); school leadership (MA); special education (MA). *Accreditation:* NCATE. *Program availability:* Part-time, online learning. *Degree requirements:* For master's, comprehensive exam (for some programs), thesis or alternative. *Entrance requirements:* For master's, PRAXIS II. *Expenses: Tuition:* Full-time $27,500; part-time $7290 per credit. Tuition and fees vary according to program. *Faculty research:* Literacy, pedagogy and practice, social justice, advanced leadership, achievement in high poverty schools.

Gallaudet University, The Graduate School, Washington, DC 20002-3625. Offers American Sign Language/English bilingual early childhood deaf education: birth to 5 (Certificate); audiology (Au D); clinical psychology (PhD); deaf and hard of hearing infants, toddlers, and their families (Certificate); deaf education (MA, Ed S); deaf history (Certificate); deaf studies (Certificate); educating deaf students with disabilities (Certificate); education: teacher preparation (MA), including deaf education, early childhood education and deaf education, elementary education and deaf education, secondary education and deaf education; educational neuroscience (PhD); hearing, speech and language sciences (MS, PhD); international development (MA); interpretation (MA, PhD), including combined interpreting practice and research (MA), interpreting research (MA); linguistics (MA, PhD); mental health counseling (MA); peer mentoring (Certificate); public administration (MPA); school counseling (MA); school psychology (Psy S); sign language teaching (MA); social work (MSW); speech-language pathology (MS). *Program availability:* Part-time. Terminal master's awarded for partial completion of doctoral program. *Degree requirements:* For master's, comprehensive exam (for some programs), thesis optional; for doctorate, comprehensive exam, thesis/dissertation. *Entrance requirements:* For master's and doctorate, GRE General Test or MAT, letters of recommendation, interviews, goals statement, American Sign Language proficiency interview, written English competency. Additional exam requirements/recommendations for international students: Required—TOEFL. Electronic applications accepted. *Faculty research:* Signing math dictionaries, telecommunications access, cancer genetics, linguistics, visual language and visual learning, integrated quantum materials, deaf legal discourse, advance recruitment and retention in geosciences.

George Fox University, College of Education, Graduate Teaching and Leading Program, Newberg, OR 97132-2697. Offers administrative leadership (Ed S); continuing administrator license (Certificate); educational leadership (M Ed); educational technology (M Ed); English for speakers of other languages (M Ed); ESOL (Certificate); initial administrator license (Certificate); reading (M Ed, Certificate); special education (M Ed); teaching (MAT). *Accreditation:* NCATE. *Program availability:* Part-time, evening/weekend, online learning. *Degree requirements:* For master's, thesis (for some programs). *Entrance requirements:* For master's, minimum undergraduate GPA of 3.0

during previous 2 years of course work, resume, 3 professional recommendations on university forms, official transcripts. Additional exam requirements/recommendations for international students: Required—TOEFL (minimum score 577 paper-based; 90 iBT). Electronic applications accepted. *Expenses:* Contact institution.

George Mason University, College of Education and Human Development, Program in Special Education, Fairfax, VA 22030. Offers M Ed, Certificate. *Program availability:* Part-time, evening/weekend, 100% online. *Faculty:* 26 full-time (22 women), 46 part-time/adjunct (40 women). *Students:* 62 full-time (57 women), 670 part-time (555 women); includes 237 minority (94 Black or African American, non-Hispanic/Latino; 66 Asian, non-Hispanic/Latino; 65 Hispanic/Latino; 1 Native Hawaiian or other Pacific Islander, non-Hispanic/Latino; 11 Two or more races, non-Hispanic/Latino), 10 international. Average age 34. 357 applicants, 95% accepted, 253 enrolled. In 2018, 220 master's awarded. *Entrance requirements:* For master's, bachelor's degree from regionally-accredited institution with minimum GPA of 3.0 cumulative or in last 60 credits of undergraduate study (or PRAXIS I, SAT, ACT or VCLA); 2 official transcripts; 2 letters of recommendation; goals statement. Additional exam requirements/recommendations for international students: Required—TOEFL (minimum score 575 paper-based; 88 iBT), IELTS (minimum score 6.5), PTE (minimum score 59). *Application deadline:* For fall admission, 4/2 priority date for domestic and international students; for spring admission, 11/1 for domestic and international students. Application fee: $75 ($80 for international students). Electronic applications accepted. *Expenses:* $489 per credit in-state tuition; $1,346.75 per credit out-of-state tuition (discounted to $689 per credit). *Financial support:* In 2018–19, 1 student received support, including 1 teaching assistantship (averaging $10,388 per year); career-related internships or fieldwork, Federal Work-Study, and scholarships/grants also available. Financial award application deadline: 3/1; financial award applicants required to submit FAFSA. *Faculty research:* Adapted captions through interactive video, DEVISE Project (multi-sensory virtual learning environment), KIHd System Project (teachers utilizing Kellar Institute handheld data system and Literary Online). *Unit head:* Pam Baker, Director, 703-993-1787, Fax: 703-993-3681, E-mail: pbaker5@gmu.edu. *Application contact:* Jancy Templeton, Advisor, 703-993-2387, Fax: 703-993-3681, E-mail: jtemple1@gmu.edu.
Website: http://gse.gmu.edu/programs/sped/

George Mason University, College of Education and Human Development, Programs in Curriculum and Instruction, Fairfax, VA 22030. Offers assistive technology (M Ed); designing digital learning in schools (M Ed); early childhood education (M Ed); early childhood education for diverse learners (M Ed); elementary education (M Ed); English as a second language (M Ed); gifted child education (M Ed); literacy (M Ed), including PK-12 classroom teachers, reading specialist; literacy leadership for diverse schools (M Ed), including K-12 reading; physical education (M Ed); science K-12 (M Ed); secondary education (M Ed), including biology, chemistry, earth science, English, history/social science, math, physics; special education (M Ed); teacher leadership (M Ed); transformative teaching (M Ed). *Program availability:* Part-time, evening/weekend, 100% online, blended/hybrid learning. *Faculty:* 48 full-time (40 women), 28 part-time/adjunct (20 women). *Students:* 165 full-time (147 women), 697 part-time (579 women); includes 243 minority (47 Black or African American, non-Hispanic/Latino; 3 American Indian or Alaska Native, non-Hispanic/Latino; 88 Asian, non-Hispanic/Latino; 85 Hispanic/Latino; 4 Native Hawaiian or other Pacific Islander, non-Hispanic/Latino; 16 Two or more races, non-Hispanic/Latino), 26 international. Average age 34. 450 applicants, 93% accepted, 315 enrolled. In 2018, 421 master's awarded. *Entrance requirements:* For master's, PRAXIS Core (for some programs), 2 letters of recommendation, interview, program goals statement; 9 hours of complete licensure endorsement requirements (for elementary education); minimum GPA of 3.0 in applicant's last 60 hours of undergraduate coursework (for secondary education); at least 1 year of teaching experience (for literacy). Additional exam requirements/recommendations for international students: Required—TOEFL (minimum score 575 paper-based; 88 iBT), IELTS (minimum score 6.5), PTE (minimum score 59). *Application deadline:* For fall admission, 4/2 priority date for domestic and international students; for spring admission, 11/1 for domestic and international students. Application fee: $75 ($80 for international students). Electronic applications accepted. *Financial support:* In 2018–19, 4 students received support, including 1 fellowship, 3 teaching assistantships (averaging $3,745 per year); career-related internships or fieldwork, Federal Work-Study, scholarships/grants, unspecified assistantships, and health care benefits (for full-time research or teaching assistantship recipients) also available. Support available to part-time students. Financial award application deadline: 3/1; financial award applicants required to submit FAFSA. *Faculty research:* Teacher preparation and professional development; adaptive teaching; wonder in science teacher preparation; literacy (digital, adolescent); site based course instruction. *Unit head:* Rebecca Fox, Professor and Academic Program Coordinator, 703-993-4123, E-mail: rfox@gmu.edu. *Application contact:* Rebecca Fox, Professor and Academic Program Coordinator, 703-993-4123, E-mail: rfox@gmu.edu.
Website: http://gse.gmu.edu/programs/gsemasters

Georgetown College, Department of Education, Georgetown, KY 40324-1696. Offers reading and writing (MA Ed); special education (MA Ed); teaching (MA Ed). *Accreditation:* NCATE. *Program availability:* Part-time. *Degree requirements:* For master's, portfolio. *Entrance requirements:* For master's, teaching certificate, minimum GPA of 2.7 or GRE General Test.

The George Washington University, Graduate School of Education and Human Development, Department of Counseling and Human Development, Washington, DC 20052. Offers clinical mental health counseling (MA); counseling (PhD, Ed S); counseling culturally and linguistically diverse persons (MA Ed/HD, Certificate); forensic rehabilitation counseling (Graduate Certificate); job development and placement (Graduate Certificate); rehabilitation counseling (MA Ed/HD), including autism spectrum disorder, substance abuse and psychiatric disabilities, traumatic brain injury; school counseling (MA Ed, Graduate Certificate). *Accreditation:* ACA (one or more programs are accredited). *Program availability:* Part-time, evening/weekend. *Faculty:* 14 full-time (9 women). *Students:* 110 full-time (94 women), 80 part-time (63 women); includes 63 minority (21 Black or African American, non-Hispanic/Latino; 2 American Indian or Alaska Native, non-Hispanic/Latino; 16 Asian, non-Hispanic/Latino; 19 Hispanic/Latino; 5 Two or more races, non-Hispanic/Latino), 14 international. Average age 31. 297 applicants, 60% accepted, 66 enrolled. In 2018, 49 master's, 7 doctorates, 2 other advanced degrees awarded. *Degree requirements:* For master's and other advanced degree, comprehensive exam; for doctorate, comprehensive exam, thesis/dissertation. *Entrance requirements:* For master's, GRE General Test or MAT, minimum GPA of 2.75; for doctorate, GRE General Test or MAT, interview, minimum GPA of 3.3; for other advanced degree, GRE General Test or MAT, minimum GPA of 3.3. *Application deadline:* For fall admission, 1/15 priority date for domestic students; for spring admission, 10/1 for domestic students. Applications are processed on a rolling basis. Application fee: $75. *Financial support:* In 2018–19, 58 students received support. Fellowships, research assistantships, teaching assistantships, career-related internships or fieldwork, Federal Work-Study, and tuition waivers (full and partial) available. Financial award application deadline: 1/15. *Faculty research:* Multiculturalism and counseling, models of adult development. *Unit head:* Dr. Kenneth C. Hergenrather, Chair, 202-994-1334, E-mail: hergenkc@gwu.edu. *Application contact:* Sarah Lang, Director of Graduate Admissions, 202-994-1447, Fax: 202-994-7207, E-mail: slang@gwu.edu.

The George Washington University, Graduate School of Education and Human Development, Department of Special Education and Disability Studies, Program in Bilingual Special Education, Washington, DC 20052. Offers MA Ed, Certificate. *Unit head:* Michael Feuer, Dean, 202-994-6161, E-mail: mjfeuer@gwu.edu. *Application contact:* Sarah Lang, Director of Graduate Admissions, 202-994-1447, Fax: 202-994-7207, E-mail: slang@gwu.edu.

The George Washington University, Graduate School of Education and Human Development, Department of Special Education and Disability Studies, Program in Early Childhood Special Education, Washington, DC 20052. Offers infant special education (MA Ed/HD). *Accreditation:* NCATE. *Students:* 13 full-time (all women), 4 part-time (all women); includes 4 minority (2 Black or African American, non-Hispanic/Latino; 1 Asian, non-Hispanic/Latino; 1 Two or more races, non-Hispanic/Latino), 10 international. Average age 29. 31 applicants, 77% accepted, 7 enrolled. In 2018, 10 master's awarded. *Entrance requirements:* For master's, GRE General Test or MAT, minimum GPA of 2.75. *Application deadline:* For fall admission, 1/15 priority date for domestic students; for spring admission, 10/1 for domestic students. Applications are processed on a rolling basis. Application fee: $75. *Financial support:* In 2018–19, 19 students received support. Fellowships, career-related internships or fieldwork, Federal Work-Study, and tuition waivers (full) available. Financial award application deadline: 1/15; financial award applicants required to submit FAFSA. *Faculty research:* Computer-assisted instruction and learning, disabled learner assessment of preschool, handicapped children. *Unit head:* Dr. Marian H. Jarrett, Faculty Coordinator, 202-994-1509, E-mail: mjarrett@gwu.edu. *Application contact:* Sarah Lang, Director of Graduate Admissions, 202-994-1447, Fax: 202-994-7207, E-mail: slang@gwu.edu.

The George Washington University, Graduate School of Education and Human Development, Department of Special Education and Disability Studies, Program in Secondary Special Education and Transition Services, Washington, DC 20052. Offers adolescents with emotional and behavioral disabilities (MA Ed/HD); adolescents with learning disabilities (MA Ed/HD); brain injury special education (MA Ed/HD); brain injury specialist (MA Ed/HD); interdisciplinary transition services (MA Ed/HD). *Students:* 34 part-time (28 women); includes 8 minority (4 Black or African American, non-Hispanic/Latino; 4 Hispanic/Latino). Average age 37. 15 applicants, 73% accepted, 9 enrolled. In 2018, 14 master's awarded. *Unit head:* Michael Feuer, Dean, 202-994-6161, E-mail: mjfeuer@gwu.edu. *Application contact:* Sarah Lang, Director of Graduate Admissions, 202-994-1447, Fax: 202-994-7207, E-mail: slang@gwu.edu.
Website: http://gsehd.gwu.edu/

The George Washington University, Graduate School of Education and Human Development, Department of Special Education and Disability Studies, Program in Special Education, Washington, DC 20052. Offers Ed D, Ed S. *Accreditation:* NCATE. *Students:* 11 full-time (10 women), 40 part-time (34 women); includes 20 minority (11 Black or African American, non-Hispanic/Latino; 2 Asian, non-Hispanic/Latino; 6 Hispanic/Latino; 1 Two or more races, non-Hispanic/Latino), 7 international. Average age 40. 22 applicants, 64% accepted, 9 enrolled. In 2018, 3 doctorates, 2 other advanced degrees awarded. *Degree requirements:* For doctorate, comprehensive exam, thesis/dissertation; for Ed S, comprehensive exam. *Entrance requirements:* For doctorate and Ed S, GRE General Test or MAT, interview, minimum GPA of 3.3. *Application deadline:* For fall admission, 1/15 priority date for domestic students; for spring admission, 10/1 for domestic students. Applications are processed on a rolling basis. Application fee: $75. *Financial support:* In 2018–19, 46 students received support. Fellowships, research assistantships, career-related internships or fieldwork, Federal Work-Study, and tuition waivers (partial) available. Financial award application deadline: 1/15; financial award applicants required to submit FAFSA. *Unit head:* Dr. Carol Kochhar, Faculty Coordinator, 202-994-1536, E-mail: kochhar@gwu.edu. *Application contact:* Sarah Lang, Director of Graduate Admissions, 202-994-1447, Fax: 202-994-7207, E-mail: slang@gwu.edu.

The George Washington University, Graduate School of Education and Human Development, Department of Special Education and Disability Studies, Program in Special Education for Children with Emotional and Behavioral Disabilities, Washington, DC 20052. Offers MA Ed/HD. *Accreditation:* NCATE. *Students:* 7 full-time (all women), 3 part-time (2 women); all minorities (6 Black or African American, non-Hispanic/Latino; 2 Asian, non-Hispanic/Latino; 2 Hispanic/Latino). Average age 32. 25 applicants, 56% accepted, 8 enrolled. In 2018, 6 master's awarded. *Entrance requirements:* For master's, PRAXIS, interview, minimum GPA of 2.75, two recommendations. *Application deadline:* For fall admission, 1/15 priority date for domestic students. Applications are processed on a rolling basis. Application fee: $75. *Financial support:* Fellowships, career-related internships or fieldwork, and Federal Work-Study available. Financial award application deadline: 1/15; financial award applicants required to submit FAFSA. *Faculty research:* Action research on the act of teaching emotionally disturbed students, teacher training. *Unit head:* Elisabeth Rice, Program Coordinator, 202-994-1535, E-mail: ehess@gwu.edu. *Application contact:* Sarah Lang, Director of Admission, 202-994-1447, Fax: 202-994-7207, E-mail: slang@gwu.edu.

The George Washington University, Graduate School of Education and Human Development, Department of Special Education and Disability Studies, Program in Special Education for Culturally and Linguistically Diverse Persons, Washington, DC 20052. Offers MA Ed/HD, Certificate. *Students:* 4 full-time (3 women), 47 part-time (42 women); includes 18 minority (4 Black or African American, non-Hispanic/Latino; 3 Asian, non-Hispanic/Latino; 10 Hispanic/Latino; 1 Two or more races, non-Hispanic/Latino), 1 international. Average age 33. 37 applicants, 81% accepted, 16 enrolled. In 2018, 13 master's, 1 Certificate awarded. *Unit head:* Doran Gresham, Assistant Professor, 202-994-2780, E-mail: dgresham@gwu.edu. *Application contact:* Doran Gresham, Assistant Professor, 202-994-2780, E-mail: dgresham@gwu.edu.

The George Washington University, Graduate School of Education and Human Development, Department of Special Education and Disability Studies, Program in Transition Special Education, Washington, DC 20052. Offers Teaching Certificate. *Accreditation:* NCATE. *Program availability:* Evening/weekend. *Students:* 5 part-time (all women). Average age 41. 6 applicants, 50% accepted, 1 enrolled. In 2018, 7 Teaching Certificates awarded. *Entrance requirements:* For degree, GRE General Test or MAT, interview, minimum GPA of 2.75. *Application deadline:* For fall admission, 1/15 priority date for domestic students; for spring admission, 10/1 for domestic students. Applications are processed on a rolling basis. Application fee: $75. *Financial support:* Fellowships, research assistantships, career-related internships or fieldwork, Federal Work-Study, tuition waivers (full and partial), and stipends available. Financial award application deadline: 1/15. *Faculty research:* Computer applications for transition, transition follow-up research, curriculum-based vocational assessment, traumatic brain injury. *Unit head:* Dr. Lynda West, Coordinator, 202-994-1533, E-mail: lwest@gwu.edu. *Application contact:* Sarah Lang, Director of Graduate Admissions, 202-994-1447, Fax: 202-994-7207, E-mail: slang@gwu.edu.

Georgia College & State University, Graduate School, The John H. Lounsbury College of Education, Program in Special Education, Milledgeville, GA 31061. Offers M Ed, MAT, Ed S. *Accreditation:* NCATE. *Program availability:* Part-time, evening/

weekend, blended/hybrid learning. *Degree requirements:* For master's, comprehensive exam, complete program within 6 years, minimum GPA of 3.0; for Ed S, comprehensive exam, complete program within 4 years, electronic portfolio presentation, minimum GPA of 3.0. *Entrance requirements:* For master's, GACE (for MAT), 2 professional recommendations, transcript, immunization verification, resume; minimum undergraduate GPA of 2.75 or 3 years' teaching experience (for M Ed); for Ed S, certification in special education, transcript, 2 letters of recommendation from professional references, resume, statement of purpose. Electronic applications accepted. *Expenses:* Contact institution.

Georgian Court University, School of Arts and Sciences, Lakewood, NJ 08701-2697. Offers applied behavior analysis (MA); autism spectrum disorders (Certificate); clinical mental health counseling (MA); criminal justice and human rights (MS); holistic health studies (MA, Certificate); homeland security (Certificate); instructional technology (CPC); mercy spirituality (Certificate); parish business management (Certificate); professional counselor (Certificate); school psychology (MA, Certificate); theology (MA, Certificate). *Program availability:* Part-time, evening/weekend. *Faculty:* 15 full-time (9 women), 11 part-time/adjunct (9 women). *Students:* 90 full-time (84 women), 99 part-time (67 women); includes 28 minority (9 Black or African American, non-Hispanic/Latino; 1 Asian, non-Hispanic/Latino; 14 Hispanic/Latino; 4 Two or more races, non-Hispanic/Latino), 2 international. Average age 34. 138 applicants, 59% accepted, 60 enrolled. In 2018, 68 master's, 19 other advanced degrees awarded. *Degree requirements:* For master's, comprehensive exam (for some programs), thesis (for some programs). *Entrance requirements:* For master's, GRE, GMAT, or NTE/PRAXIS, 3 letters of recommendation. Additional exam requirements/recommendations for international students: Required—TOEFL (minimum score 550 paper-based; 79 iBT). *Application deadline:* For fall admission, 8/15 for domestic students, 5/1 for international students; for spring admission, 1/15 for domestic students, 10/1 for international students. Applications are processed on a rolling basis. Application fee: $40. Electronic applications accepted. *Expenses: Tuition:* Full-time $856; part-time $856 per credit hour. *Required fees:* $968; $496 per unit. $248 per semester. Tuition and fees vary according to campus/location and program. *Financial support:* Scholarships/grants, health care benefits, and unspecified assistantships available. Financial award application deadline: 4/15; financial award applicants required to submit FAFSA. *Unit head:* Dr. Mary Chinery, Dean, 732-987-2493, Fax: 732-987-2007, E-mail: mchinery@georgian.edu. *Application contact:* Patrick Givens, Director of Graduate and Professional Studies Admissions, 732-987-2736, Fax: 732-987-2000, E-mail: gps@georgian.edu.
Website: https://georgian.edu/academics/school-of-arts-sciences/

Georgian Court University, School of Education, Lakewood, NJ 08701-2697. Offers administration and leadership (MA); autism spectrum disorders (Certificate); education (M Ed, MAT); instructional technology (M Mat SE, MA, Certificate). *Accreditation:* TEAC. *Program availability:* Part-time, evening/weekend. *Faculty:* 10 full-time (6 women), 28 part-time/adjunct (17 women). *Students:* 32 full-time (25 women), 396 part-time (324 women); includes 84 minority (35 Black or African American, non-Hispanic/Latino; 10 Asian, non-Hispanic/Latino; 36 Hispanic/Latino; 3 Two or more races, non-Hispanic/Latino). Average age 34. 323 applicants, 67% accepted, 148 enrolled. In 2018, 152 master's, 4 other advanced degrees awarded. *Degree requirements:* For master's, comprehensive exam (for some programs), thesis (for some programs). *Entrance requirements:* For master's, GRE, GMAT or NTE/PRAXIS, 3 letters of recommendation. Additional exam requirements/recommendations for international students: Required—TOEFL (minimum score 550 paper-based; 79 iBT). *Application deadline:* For fall admission, 8/15 priority date for domestic students, 5/1 for international students; for spring admission, 1/15 priority date for domestic students, 10/1 for international students. Applications are processed on a rolling basis. Application fee: $40. Electronic applications accepted. *Expenses: Tuition:* Full-time $856; part-time $856 per credit hour. *Required fees:* $968; $496 per unit. $248 per semester. Tuition and fees vary according to campus/location and program. *Financial support:* Scholarships/grants, health care benefits, and unspecified assistantships available. Financial award application deadline: 4/15; financial award applicants required to submit FAFSA. *Unit head:* Dr. Christopher Campisano, Dean of School of Education, 732-987-2729, E-mail: ccampisano@georgian.edu. *Application contact:* Patrick Givens, Director of Graduate and Professional Studies Admissions, 732-987-2736, Fax: 732-987-2000, E-mail: gps@georgian.edu.
Website: https://georgian.edu/academics/school-of-education/

Georgia Southern University, Jack N. Averitt College of Graduate Studies, College of Education, Department of Elementary and Special Education, Program in Special Education, Statesboro, GA 30460. Offers M Ed, MAT, Ed S. *Accreditation:* NCATE. *Program availability:* Part-time, evening/weekend, online only, 100% online. *Degree requirements:* For master's, portfolio, transition point assessments, exit assessment; for Ed S, field based research projects, assessments. *Entrance requirements:* For master's, GACE Basic Skills and Content Assessments (for MAT), minimum cumulative GPA of 2.5. Additional exam requirements/recommendations for international students: Required—TOEFL (minimum score 550 paper-based; 80 iBT), IELTS (minimum score 6). Electronic applications accepted. *Expenses: Tuition, area resident:* Part-time $3324 per semester. Tuition, state resident: full-time $5814; part-time $3324 per semester. Tuition, nonresident: full-time $23,204; part-time $13,260 per semester. *Required fees:* $2092; $2092. Tuition and fees vary according to course load, degree level, campus/location and program. *Faculty research:* Learning disorders, behavior disorders, education of the mentally retarded, PBIS, STEM education.

Georgia Southwestern State University, School of Education, Americus, GA 31709-4693. Offers early childhood education (M Ed, Ed S); middle grades education (Ed S); middle grades language arts (M Ed); middle grades mathematics (M Ed); special education (M Ed). *Accreditation:* NCATE. *Degree requirements:* For master's, minimum cumulative GPA of 3.0; maximum of 6 credit hours with C grade; no courses with D grade; degree completed within 7 calendar years; for Ed S, minimum GPA of 3.25 in all courses with no grade less than a B; degree must be completed within 7 calendar years from date of initial enrollment in graduate work. *Entrance requirements:* For master's, undergraduate degree from accredited institution; professional Georgia Teaching Certificate or eligibility; minimum undergraduate GPA of 2.75 as reported on official final transcripts from all accredited institutions attended; 2 confidential Administrative Recommendation Forms; for Ed S, master's degree from accredited college or university; professional Georgia Teaching Certificate or eligibility; minimum graduate GPA of 3.0 as reported on official final graduate transcripts from all accredited institutions attended; 2 confidential Administrative Recommendation Forms. Electronic applications accepted. *Expenses:* Contact institution.

Georgia State University, College of Education and Human Development, Department of Learning Sciences, Program in Education of Students with Exceptionalities, Atlanta, GA 30302-3083. Offers autism spectrum disorders (PhD); behavior disorders (PhD); communication disorders (PhD); early childhood special education (PhD); learning disabilities (PhD); mental retardation (PhD); orthopedic impairments (PhD); sensory impairments (PhD). *Accreditation:* NCATE. *Program availability:* Part-time, evening/weekend. Application fee: $50. Electronic applications accepted. *Expenses: Tuition, area resident:* Full-time $9360; part-time $390 per credit hour. Tuition, state resident: full-time $9360; part-time $390 per credit hour. Tuition, nonresident: full-time $30,024;

part-time $1251 per credit hour. *International tuition:* $30,024 full-time. *Required fees:* $2128. *Financial support:* Fellowships, research assistantships, scholarships/grants, health care benefits, and unspecified assistantships available. *Faculty research:* Academic and behavioral supports for students with emotional/behavior disorders; academic interventions for learning disabilities; cultural, socioeconomic, and linguistic diversity; language and literacy development, disorders, and instruction. *Unit head:* Dr. Brendan Calandra, Chair, 404-413-8420, Fax: 404-413-8420, E-mail: bcalandra@gsu.edu. *Application contact:* Sandy Vaughn, Senior Administrative Coordinator, 404-413-8318, Fax: 404-413-8043, E-mail: svaughn@gsu.edu.
Website: https://education.gsu.edu/program/phd-education-students-exceptionalities/

Gonzaga University, School of Education, Spokane, WA 99258. Offers clinical mental health counseling (MA); educational leadership (M Ed, Ed D); elementary education (MIT); marriage and family counseling (MA); school counseling (MA); secondary education (MIT); special education (M Ed, MIT); sport and athletic administration (MA). *Accreditation:* NCATE. *Program availability:* Part-time, evening/weekend, 100% online, blended/hybrid learning. *Degree requirements:* For master's, comprehensive exam. *Entrance requirements:* For master's, GRE, MAT, and/or Washington Educator Skills Test-Basic (WEST-B), Washington Educator Skills Test-Endorsements (WEST-E), official transcripts from all colleges or universities attended, interview, two letters of recommendation, resume, essay, minimum GPA of 3.0. Additional exam requirements/recommendations for international students: Required—TOEFL (minimum score 580 paper-based, 88 iBT) or IELTS (minimum score 6.5). Electronic applications accepted. *Expenses:* Contact institution.

Gordon College, Graduate Education Program, Wenham, MA 01984-1899. Offers early childhood (M Ed); educational leadership (M Ed, Ed S); elementary education (M Ed); English as a second language (M Ed, Ed S); math specialist (M Ed); mathematics specialist (Ed S); middle school education (M Ed); moderate disabilities (M Ed); Montessori education (M Ed); reading (M Ed, Ed S); secondary education (M Ed). *Program availability:* Part-time, evening/weekend. *Degree requirements:* For master's, action research or clinical experience (for most programs); for Ed S, action research or clinical experience (for some programs). *Entrance requirements:* For master's, minimum undergraduate GPA of 3.0; 2 official undergraduate transcripts; professional resume; 3 recommendation letters (one professional reference, one academic reference, one personal reference); 500-700 word statement of purpose; for Ed S, minimum master's GPA of 3.3; 2 official transcripts from undergraduate and graduate schools; professional resume; 3 recommendation letters (one professional reference, one academic reference, one personal reference); 500-700 word statement of purpose. Additional exam requirements/recommendations for international students: Required—TOEFL (minimum score 550 paper-based, 80 iBT) or IELTS (minimum score 6.5). *Expenses:* Contact institution. *Faculty research:* Reading, early childhood development, English language learners, universal design for learning.

Goucher College, Graduate Programs in Education, Baltimore, MD 21204-2794. Offers at-risk and diverse learners (M Ed, Certificate); athletic program leadership and administration (M Ed, Certificate); elementary education (MAT); literacy strategies for content learning (M Ed); middle school (M Ed, Certificate); Montessori studies (M Ed); reading instruction (M Ed, Certificate); reducing student, classroom, and school disruption (M Ed); school improvement leadership (M Ed); secondary education (MAT); special education (MAT), including elementary education; special education for certified elementary and secondary teachers (M Ed); teacher as leader in technology (M Ed). *Program availability:* Part-time, evening/weekend. *Degree requirements:* For master's, thesis (M Ed), final presentation (MAT). *Entrance requirements:* For master's, minimum GPA of 3.0. Additional exam requirements/recommendations for international students: Required—TOEFL (minimum score 550 paper-based; 80 iBT), IELTS (minimum score 7). Electronic applications accepted. *Expenses:* Contact institution. *Faculty research:* Urban education, middle school, school improvement, teacher education, at-risk student achievement.

Governors State University, College of Education, Program in Multi-Categorical Special Education, University Park, IL 60484. Offers MA. *Accreditation:* NCATE. *Program availability:* Part-time. *Faculty:* 19 full-time (12 women), 20 part-time/adjunct (13 women). *Students:* 3 full-time (2 women), 8 part-time (7 women); includes 7 minority (6 Black or African American, non-Hispanic/Latino; 1 Asian, non-Hispanic/Latino). Average age 37. In 2018, 4 master's awarded. *Application deadline:* For fall admission, 4/1 for domestic students. Applications are processed on a rolling basis. Application fee: $50. Electronic applications accepted. *Financial support:* Application deadline: 5/1; applicants required to submit FAFSA. *Unit head:* Timothy Harrington, Chair, Division of Education, 708-534-5000 Ext. 4361, E-mail: tharrington2@govst.edu. *Application contact:* Timothy Harrington, Chair, Division of Education, 708-534-5000 Ext. 4361, E-mail: tharrington2@govst.edu.

Graceland University, Gleazer School of Education, Independence, MO 64050. Offers curriculum and instruction: collaborative learning and teaching (M Ed); differentiated instruction (M Ed); instructional leadership (M Ed); literacy instruction (M Ed); management in a quality classroom (M Ed); special education (M Ed); technology integration (M Ed). *Accreditation:* NCATE. *Program availability:* Part-time, 100% online. *Students:* 70 full-time (58 women), 36 part-time (34 women); includes 4 minority (1 Black or African American, non-Hispanic/Latino; 1 Asian, non-Hispanic/Latino; 1 Hispanic/Latino; 1 Two or more races, non-Hispanic/Latino). Average age 34. 29 applicants, 21% accepted, 1 enrolled. In 2018, 76 master's awarded. *Degree requirements:* For master's, action research capstone. *Entrance requirements:* For master's, minimum GPA of 3.0, teaching certificate, current teaching contract and license, two letters of reference, statement of professional goals, verification of ongoing access to computer technology, including email and Internet. Additional exam requirements/recommendations for international students: Required—TOEFL (minimum score 550 paper-based; 80 iBT). *Application deadline:* For winter admission, 11/1 for domestic students; for spring admission, 2/1 priority date for domestic students; for summer admission, 7/1 for domestic students. Applications are processed on a rolling basis. Application fee: $50. Electronic applications accepted. *Expenses:* Tuition, material fee, university tech fee, program support fee. *Financial support:* Tuition waivers (partial) available. Financial award applicants required to submit FAFSA. *Faculty research:* Literacy, technology, faculty mentoring, adult literacy, e-learning, online teaching. *Unit head:* Dr. Michele Dickey-Kotz, Dean, 641-784-5202, E-mail: dickey@graceland.edu. *Application contact:* Susan Freeze, Admissions Representative, 816-423-4676, Fax: 816-833-2990, E-mail: sfreeze1@graceland.edu.
Website: http://www.graceland.edu/education

Grambling State University, School of Graduate Studies and Research, College of Education, Department of Curriculum and Instruction, Grambling, LA 71245. Offers curriculum and instruction (MS); special education (M Ed). *Program availability:* Part-time. *Degree requirements:* For master's, comprehensive exam, thesis (for some programs). *Entrance requirements:* Additional exam requirements/recommendations for international students: Required—TOEFL (minimum score 500 paper-based; 62 iBT).

Grand Canyon University, College of Education, Phoenix, AZ 85017-1097. Offers autism spectrum disorders (MA); curriculum and instruction (MA); early childhood education (M Ed); educational administration (M Ed); educational leadership (M Ed); elementary education (M Ed); gifted education (MA); instructional technology (MS); K-12

leadership (Ed S); reading (MA); secondary education (M Ed); secondary humanities education (M Ed); secondary STEM education (M Ed); special education (M Ed); teaching and learning (Ed D); teaching English to speakers of other languages (MA). *Program availability:* Part-time, evening/weekend, online learning. *Degree requirements:* For master's, publishable research paper (M Ed), e-portfolio. *Entrance requirements:* For master's, undergraduate degree from accredited, GCU-approved college, university, or program with minimum GPA 2.8. Additional exam requirements/recommendations for international students: Required—TOEFL (minimum score 550 paper-based; 79 iBT), IELTS (minimum score 6). Electronic applications accepted.

Grand Valley State University, College of Education, Program in Special Education, Allendale, MI 49401-9403. Offers cognitive impairment (M Ed); early childhood developmental delay (M Ed); emotional impairment (M Ed); learning disabilities (M Ed); special education (M Ed). *Accreditation:* NCATE. *Program availability:* Part-time, evening/weekend. *Students:* 4 full-time (3 women), 66 part-time (55 women); includes 4 minority (3 Hispanic/Latino; 1 Two or more races, non-Hispanic/Latino), 2 international. Average age 33. 16 applicants, 88% accepted, 9 enrolled. In 2018, 23 master's awarded. *Entrance requirements:* For master's, GRE General Test or minimum GPA of 3.0, last 60 credits from regionally-accredited college/university, 3 letters of recommendation. Additional exam requirements/recommendations for international students: Required—TOEFL (minimum iBT score of 80), IELTS (6.5), or Michigan English Language Assessment Battery (77). *Application deadline:* Applications are processed on a rolling basis. Application fee: $30. Electronic applications accepted. *Expenses:* $677 per credit hour, 33 credit hours. *Financial support:* In 2018–19, 11 students received support, including 11 fellowships; career-related internships or fieldwork, Federal Work-Study, scholarships/grants, and unspecified assistantships also available. *Faculty research:* Evaluation of special education program effects, adaptive behavior assessment, language development, writing disorders, comparative effects of presentation methods. *Unit head:* Dr. Amy Schelling, Director of Special Education, 616-331-6243, Fax: 616-331-6294, E-mail: schellia@gvsu.edu. *Application contact:* Annukka Thelen, Director, Student Information and Services Center, 616-331-6205, Fax: 616-331-6217, E-mail: thelenan@gvsu.edu.

Greensboro College, Program in Education, Greensboro, NC 27401-1875. Offers elementary education (M Ed); special education (M Ed). *Program availability:* Part-time, evening/weekend. *Degree requirements:* For master's, thesis. *Entrance requirements:* For master's, GRE, teacher license, 2 years of teaching experience, 2 letters of recommendation. Additional exam requirements/recommendations for international students: Required—TOEFL (minimum score 550 paper-based). Electronic applications accepted.

Gwynedd Mercy University, School of Education, Gwynedd Valley, PA 19437-0901. Offers education (Ed D); educational administration (MS); master teacher (MS); school counseling (MS); special education (MS). *Program availability:* Part-time, evening/weekend, 100% online. *Degree requirements:* For master's, thesis, internship, practicum. *Entrance requirements:* For master's, GRE or MAT; PRAXIS I, minimum GPA of 3.0. *Expenses:* Contact institution. *Faculty research:* Learning and the brain, reading literacy, ethics and moral judgment, leadership, teaching and multicultural education.

Harding University, Cannon-Clary College of Education, Searcy, AR 72149-0001. Offers advanced studies in teaching and learning (M Ed); art (MSE); behavioral science (MSE); counseling (MS, Ed S); early childhood special education (M Ed, MSE); education (MSE); educational leadership (M Ed, Ed S); elementary education (M Ed); English (MSE); French (MSE); history/social science (MSE); kinesiology (MSE); math (MSE); reading (M Ed); secondary education (M Ed); Spanish (MSE); teaching (MAT); teaching English as a second language (MSE). *Accreditation:* NCATE. *Program availability:* Part-time, evening/weekend. *Degree requirements:* For master's, comprehensive exam (for some programs), thesis optional, portfolio(s); for Ed S, comprehensive exam, portfolio, project. *Entrance requirements:* For master's, GRE, MAT, PRAXIS; for Ed S, MAT or GRE. Additional exam requirements/recommendations for international students: Required—TOEFL (minimum score 550 paper-based; 79 iBT). *Faculty research:* Reading, comprehension, school violence, educational technology, behavior, college choice, differentiated instruction, brain-based teaching.

Hebrew College, Shoolman Graduate School of Jewish Education, Newton Centre, MA 02459. Offers early childhood Jewish education (Certificate); Jewish day school education (Certificate); Jewish education (MJ Ed); Jewish family education (Certificate); Jewish special education (Certificate); Jewish youth education, informal education and camping (Certificate). *Program availability:* Part-time, evening/weekend, online learning. *Degree requirements:* For master's, one foreign language. *Entrance requirements:* For master's, GRE, interview. Additional exam requirements/recommendations for international students: Required—TOEFL.

Henderson State University, Graduate Studies, Teachers College, Department of Advanced Instructional Studies, Arkadelphia, AR 71999-0001. Offers developmental therapy (MSE); dyslexia therapy (Graduate Certificate); education (MAT); educational technology leadership (Graduate Certificate); English as a second language (MSE, Graduate Certificate); instructional facilitator (MSE, Graduate Certificate); middle level education (MAT); special education (K-12) (MAT, MSE); special education/early childhood (MAT). *Accreditation:* NCATE. *Program availability:* Part-time. *Entrance requirements:* For master's, GRE General Test or MAT, minimum GPA of 2.7, teacher certification. Additional exam requirements/recommendations for international students: Required—TOEFL (minimum score 600 paper-based); Recommended—IELTS (minimum score 6.5).

Heritage University, Graduate Programs in Education, Program in Professional Studies, Toppenish, WA 98948-9599. Offers bilingual education/ESL (M Ed); biology (M Ed); English and literature (M Ed); reading/literacy (M Ed); special education (M Ed). *Program availability:* Part-time, evening/weekend. *Degree requirements:* For master's, comprehensive exam (for some programs), thesis (for some programs).

High Point University, Norcross Graduate School, High Point, NC 27268. Offers athletic training (MSAT); business administration (MBA); educational leadership (M Ed, Ed D); elementary education (M Ed, MAT); pharmacy (Pharm D); physical therapy (DPT); physician assistant studies (MPAS); secondary mathematics (M Ed, MAT); special education (M Ed); strategic communication (MA). *Accreditation:* NCATE. *Program availability:* Part-time, evening/weekend. *Degree requirements:* For master's, comprehensive exam (for some programs), thesis (for some programs). *Entrance requirements:* For master's, GMAT (MBA), GRE, MAT, minimum GPA of 3.0. Additional exam requirements/recommendations for international students: Required—TOEFL (minimum score 550 paper-based). Electronic applications accepted.

Hofstra University, School of Education, Specialized Programs in Education, Hempstead, NY 11549. Offers applied behavior analysis (Advanced Certificate); childhood special education (MS Ed); early childhood special education (MS Ed, Advanced Certificate); educational and policy leadership (Ed D); educational leadership (Advanced Certificate); educational leadership and policy studies (MS Ed), including K-12; elementary special education (MS Ed); gifted education (Advanced Certificate); health education (MS); health professions pedagogy and leadership (MS); higher education leadership and policy studies (MS Ed); inclusive early childhood special education (MS Ed); inclusive elementary special education (MS Ed); inclusive secondary special education (MS Ed); literacy studies (MA, MS Ed, Ed D, Advanced Certificate); pedagogy for health professions (Advanced Certificate); physical education (MS); school district business leader (Advanced Certificate); secondary education generalist - students with disabilities 7-12 (MS Ed); secondary special education generalist - secondary education (MS Ed); special education (MS Ed, Advanced Certificate); special education assessment and diagnosis (Advanced Certificate); special education early childhood intervention (MS Ed); special education: international perspectives (MS Ed); teaching students with severe or multiple disabilities (Advanced Certificate). *Program availability:* Part-time, evening/weekend, blended/hybrid learning. *Students:* 126 full-time (91 women), 230 part-time (175 women); includes 90 minority (40 Black or African American, non-Hispanic/Latino; 4 American Indian or Alaska Native, non-Hispanic/Latino; 11 Asian, non-Hispanic/Latino; 32 Hispanic/Latino; 3 Two or more races, non-Hispanic/Latino), 4 international. Average age 32. 215 applicants, 90% accepted, 117 enrolled. In 2018, 130 master's, 9 doctorates, 23 other advanced degrees awarded. *Degree requirements:* For master's, one foreign language, comprehensive exam (for some programs), thesis (for some programs), electronic portfolio, capstone course, internship, practicum, student teaching, seminars, minimum GPA of 3.0; for doctorate, one foreign language, comprehensive exam, thesis/dissertation, qualifying hearing. *Entrance requirements:* For master's, GRE, interview, letters of recommendation, portfolio, essay, certification; for doctorate, GRE or MAT, interview, resume, essay, master's degree, 3 letters of recommendation, writing sample; for Advanced Certificate, GRE, interview, letters of recommendation, essay, professional experience, resume, master's degree. Additional exam requirements/recommendations for international students: Required—TOEFL (minimum score 550 paper-based; 80 iBT). *Application deadline:* Applications are processed on a rolling basis. Application fee: $75. Electronic applications accepted. *Financial support:* In 2018–19, 208 students received support, including 105 fellowships with full and partial tuition reimbursements available (averaging $3,948 per year), 12 research assistantships with full and partial tuition reimbursements available (averaging $6,573 per year); career-related internships or fieldwork, Federal Work-Study, institutionally sponsored loans, scholarships/grants, traineeships, tuition waivers (full and partial), unspecified assistantships, and scholarships and endowed scholarships also available. Support available to part-time students. Financial award applicants required to submit FAFSA. *Faculty research:* Water quality and income inequality; girls and stem; new media literacies; applied behavior analysis; k-12 leadership development. *Unit head:* Dr. Alan Flurkey, Chairperson, 516-463-5237, E-mail: alan.d.flurkey@hofstra.edu. *Application contact:* Sunil Samuel, Assistant Vice President of Admissions, 516-463-4723, Fax: 516-463-4664, E-mail: graduateadmission@hofstra.edu.
Website: http://www.hofstra.edu/education/

Holy Family University, Graduate and Professional Programs, School of Education, Master of Education Programs, Philadelphia, PA 19114. Offers early elementary education (PreK-Grade 4) (M Ed); education leadership (M Ed); general education (M Ed); reading specialist (M Ed); special education (M Ed); TESOL and literacy (M Ed). *Program availability:* Part-time. *Degree requirements:* For master's, thesis optional. Electronic applications accepted.

Holy Names University, Graduate Division, Department of Education, Oakland, CA 94619-1699. Offers educational therapy (Certificate); mild/moderate disabilities (Ed S); multiple subject teaching (Credential); single subject teaching (Credential); urban education: educational therapy (M Ed); urban education: K-12 education (M Ed); urban education: special education (M Ed). *Program availability:* Part-time. *Students:* 28 full-time (18 women), 63 part-time (45 women); includes 48 minority (22 Black or African American, non-Hispanic/Latino; 1 American Indian or Alaska Native, non-Hispanic/Latino; 3 Asian, non-Hispanic/Latino; 21 Hispanic/Latino; 1 Two or more races, non-Hispanic/Latino), 5 international. Average age 35. 69 applicants, 86% accepted, 34 enrolled. In 2018, 11 master's, 33 Certificates awarded. *Degree requirements:* For master's, comprehensive exam, research paper, thesis or project. *Entrance requirements:* For master's, minimum undergraduate GPA of 2.6 overall, 3.0 in major; personal statement; two recommendations; interview. Additional exam requirements/recommendations for international students: Required—TOEFL (minimum score 550 paper-based; 79 iBT). *Application deadline:* For fall admission, 8/1 priority date for domestic students, 7/15 for international students; for spring admission, 12/1 priority date for domestic students, 12/1 for international students; for summer admission, 5/1 priority date for domestic students, 5/1 for international students. Applications are processed on a rolling basis. Application fee: $65. Electronic applications accepted. Application fee is waived when completed online. *Expenses: Required fees:* $1003. *Financial support:* Career-related internships or fieldwork, Federal Work-Study, scholarships/grants, and unspecified assistantships available. Support available to part-time students. Financial award application deadline: 3/2; financial award applicants required to submit FAFSA. *Faculty research:* Cognitive development, language development, learning handicaps. *Unit head:* Dr. Kimberly Mayfield, Chair, 510-436-1396, Fax: 510-436-1325, E-mail: mayfield@hnu.edu. *Application contact:* Graduate Admission, 800-430-1321, Fax: 510-436-1325, E-mail: graduateadmissions@hnu.edu.
Website: http://www.hnu.edu/academics/graduatePrograms/education.html

Hood College, Graduate School, Department of Education, Frederick, MD 21701-8575. Offers curriculum and instruction (MS), including elementary education, elementary science and mathematics education, secondary education, special education; education, multidisciplinary studies (MS); educational leadership (MS, Certificate); reading specialization (MS); STEM education (Certificate). *Accreditation:* NCATE. *Program availability:* Part-time-only, evening/weekend. *Faculty:* 5 full-time (3 women), 32 part-time/adjunct (24 women). *Students:* 3 full-time (all women), 306 part-time (253 women); includes 65 minority (22 Black or African American, non-Hispanic/Latino; 9 Asian, non-Hispanic/Latino; 17 Hispanic/Latino; 17 Two or more races, non-Hispanic/Latino), 3 international. Average age 33. 80 applicants, 99% accepted, 45 enrolled. In 2018, 59 master's, 47 other advanced degrees awarded. *Degree requirements:* For master's, action research project, portfolio (for reading specialization); for Certificate, STEM capstone activity. *Entrance requirements:* For master's, minimum GPA of 2.75, teaching certification, writing sample during interview, letter of recommendation from principal (for educational leadership program only). Additional exam requirements/recommendations for international students: Required—TOEFL (minimum score 575 paper-based; 89 iBT), IELTS (minimum score 6.5). *Application deadline:* For fall admission, 8/15 priority date for domestic students, 8/5 for international students; for spring admission, 12/1 priority date for domestic students, 12/1 for international students; for summer admission, 5/1 priority date for domestic students, 4/15 for international students. Applications are processed on a rolling basis. Application fee: $50 ($100 for international students). Electronic applications accepted. *Expenses: Tuition:* Full-time $17,640; part-time $4410 per semester. *Required fees:* $125 per semester. Tuition and fees vary according to degree level and program. *Financial support:* Tuition waivers (partial) and unspecified assistantships available. Financial award applicants required to submit FAFSA. *Faculty research:* Leadership, action research, brain research, learning styles. *Unit head:* Dr. April M. Boulton, Dean of the Graduate School, 301-696-3612, E-mail: gofurther@hood.edu. *Application contact:* Tanith Fowler Corsi, Assistant Director of Graduate Admissions, 301-696-3603, E-mail: gofurther@hood.edu.
Website: https://www.hood.edu/academics/departments/department-education/programs-offered

Houston Baptist University, College of Education and Behavioral Sciences, Programs in Education, Houston, TX 77074-3298. Offers bilingual education (M Ed); counselor education (M Ed); curriculum and instruction (M Ed); curriculum and instruction (EC-6 bilingual) (M Ed); curriculum and instruction in all-level art, Spanish, music, or physical education (M Ed); curriculum and instruction in EC-6 and special education (EC-12) (M Ed); curriculum and instruction in instructional technology (M Ed); curriculum and instruction in mathematics, science, or social studies (4-8) (M Ed); curriculum and instruction with EC-6 generalist (M Ed); curriculum and instruction with English language arts and reading (4-8) (M Ed); educational administration (M Ed); educational diagnostician (M Ed); executive educational leadership (Ed D); higher education in business management (M Ed); higher education in Christian studies (M Ed); higher education in counseling (M Ed); higher education in educational technology (M Ed); reading (M Ed); special educational leadership (Ed D). *Program availability:* Part-time, evening/weekend, 100% online, blended/hybrid learning. *Degree requirements:* For master's, comprehensive exam; for doctorate, thesis/dissertation. *Entrance requirements:* For master's, minimum GPA of 2.75, two recommendations, resume, bachelor's degree conferred transcript; interview (for non-certified teachers); for doctorate, GRE, 5 letters of recommendation. Additional exam requirements/recommendations for international students: Required—TOEFL (minimum score 80 iBT), IELTS (minimum score 6.5). Electronic applications accepted. Application fee is waived when completed online. *Expenses:* Contact institution. *Faculty research:* Autism and inclusion, integrating technology into instruction, school change and leadership trust.

Howard University, School of Education, Department of Curriculum and Instruction, Program in Special Education, Washington, DC 20059-0002. Offers M Ed. *Accreditation:* NCATE. *Program availability:* Part-time. *Degree requirements:* For master's, comprehensive exam, thesis (for some programs), expository writing exam, internships, practicum. *Entrance requirements:* For master's, minimum GPA of 2.7. Additional exam requirements/recommendations for international students: Required—TOEFL (minimum score 550 paper-based; 79 iBT). Electronic applications accepted.

Hunter College of the City University of New York, Graduate School, School of Education, Department of Special Education, New York, NY 10065-5085. Offers blind and visually impaired (MS Ed); severe/multiple disabilities (MS Ed). *Accreditation:* NCATE. *Degree requirements:* For master's, comprehensive exam, thesis, student teaching practica, clinical teaching lab courses, New York State Teacher Certification Exams. *Entrance requirements:* For master's, minimum GPA of 2.8. Additional exam requirements/recommendations for international students: Required—TOEFL, TWE. *Faculty research:* Mathematics learning disabilities; street behavior; assessment; bilingual special education; families, diversity, and disabilities.

Idaho State University, Graduate School, College of Education, Department of Teaching and Educational Studies, Pocatello, ID 83209-8059. Offers deaf education (M Ed); elementary education (M Ed); human exceptionality (M Ed); literacy (M Ed); music education (M Ed); secondary education (M Ed). *Program availability:* Part-time. *Degree requirements:* For master's, comprehensive exam, thesis (for some programs), oral thesis defense or written comprehensive exam and oral exam. *Entrance requirements:* For master's, GRE or MAT, minimum undergraduate GPA of 3.0, bachelor's degree, professional experience in an educational context. Additional exam requirements/recommendations for international students: Required—TOEFL (minimum score 550 paper-based; 80 iBT). Electronic applications accepted. *Faculty research:* Literacy, school psychology, special education.

Illinois State University, Graduate School, College of Education, Department of Special Education, Normal, IL 61790. Offers MS, MS Ed, Ed D, Certificate. *Accreditation:* NCATE. *Faculty:* 35 full-time (33 women), 33 part-time/adjunct (30 women). *Students:* 8 full-time (7 women), 108 part-time (98 women); includes 8 minority (5 Black or African American, non-Hispanic/Latino; 2 Hispanic/Latino; 1 Two or more races, non-Hispanic/Latino), 1 international. Average age 34. 48 applicants, 90% accepted, 21 enrolled. In 2018, 11 master's, 2 doctorates, 43 other advanced degrees awarded. *Degree requirements:* For master's, thesis; for doctorate, variable foreign language requirement, comprehensive exam, thesis/dissertation, 2 terms of residency. *Entrance requirements:* For master's, GRE General Test, minimum GPA of 3.0 in last 60 hours; for doctorate, GRE General Test. *Application deadline:* Applications are processed on a rolling basis. Application fee: $40. *Expenses: Tuition, area resident:* Full-time $7264.62. Tuition, state resident: full-time $9466. Tuition, nonresident: full-time $17,290. *International tuition:* $15,089.40 full-time. *Required fees:* $1481.04. *Financial support:* In 2018-19, 13 research assistantships were awarded; tuition waivers (full and partial) and unspecified assistantships also available. Financial award application deadline: 4/1. *Faculty research:* Center for adult learning leadership, promoting a learning community, autism spectrum professional development and technical assistance project, preparing qualified personnel to provide early intervention for children who are deaf. *Unit head:* Dr. Stacey Jones Bock, Department Chair, 309-438-8981, E-mail: sjbock@ilstu.edu. *Application contact:* Dr. Craig Blum, Graduate Coordinator, 309-438-2165, E-mail: cblum@ilstu.edu.

Immaculata University, College of Graduate Studies, Program in Educational Leadership, Immaculata, PA 19345. Offers educational leadership (MA, Ed D); principal (Certificate); secondary education (Certificate); supervisor of special education (Certificate). *Program availability:* Part-time, evening/weekend. *Degree requirements:* For master's, comprehensive exam, thesis optional; for doctorate, comprehensive exam, thesis/dissertation. *Entrance requirements:* For master's, GRE or MAT, minimum GPA of 3.0; for doctorate, GRE General Test or MAT, minimum GPA of 3.5. Additional exam requirements/recommendations for international students: Required—TOEFL. Electronic applications accepted. *Faculty research:* Cooperative learning, school-based management, whole language, performance assessment.

Indiana University Bloomington, School of Education, Department of Curriculum and Instruction, Bloomington, IN 47405-7000. Offers art education (MS, Ed D, PhD); curriculum studies (Ed D, PhD); elementary education (MS, Ed D, PhD, Ed S); mathematics education (MS, Ed D, PhD); science education (MS, Ed D, PhD); secondary education (MS, Ed D, PhD); social studies education (MS, PhD); special education (PhD, Ed S). *Accreditation:* NCATE. *Program availability:* Part-time, evening/weekend. Terminal master's awarded for partial completion of doctoral program. *Degree requirements:* For doctorate, thesis/dissertation; for Ed S, comprehensive exam or project. *Entrance requirements:* For master's, doctorate, and Ed S, GRE General Test. Electronic applications accepted.

Indiana University of Pennsylvania, School of Graduate Studies and Research, College of Education and Communications, Department of Communication Disorders, Special Education, and Disability Services, Program in Special Education, Indiana, PA 15705. Offers M Ed. *Accreditation:* NCATE. *Program availability:* Part-time. *Faculty:* 9 full-time (8 women), 2 part-time/adjunct (both women). *Students:* 2 full-time (both women), 8 part-time (7 women); includes 1 minority (Hispanic/Latino). Average age 27. 7 applicants, 71% accepted, 2 enrolled. In 2018, 5 master's awarded. *Degree requirements:* For master's, comprehensive exam, thesis optional. *Entrance requirements:* For master's, 2 letters of recommendation. Additional exam requirements/recommendations for international students: Required—TOEFL (minimum score 540 paper-based). *Application deadline:* For fall admission, 3/1 for domestic students; for spring admission, 7/1 for domestic students. Applications are processed on a rolling basis. Application fee: $50. Electronic applications accepted. *Expenses:* Tuition, state resident: full-time $12,384; part-time $516 per credit hour. Tuition, nonresident: full-time $18,576; part-time $774 per credit hour. *Required fees:* $4454; $186 per credit hour. $65 per semester. Tuition and fees vary according to program and reciprocity agreements. *Financial support:* In 2018-19, 1 research assistantship with tuition reimbursement (averaging $4,500 per year) was awarded; career-related internships or fieldwork, Federal Work-Study, scholarships/grants, and unspecified assistantships also available. Support available to part-time students. Financial award application deadline: 4/15; financial award applicants required to submit FAFSA. *Unit head:* Dr. Mariha Shields, Graduate Coordinator, 724-357-5686, E-mail: M.K.Shields@iup.edu. *Application contact:* Dr. Mariha Shields, Graduate Coordinator, 724-357-5686, E-mail: M.K.Shields@iup.edu.
Website: http://www.iup.edu/grad/edex/default.aspx

Indiana University-Purdue University Indianapolis, School of Education, Indianapolis, IN 46202-5155. Offers curriculum and instruction (MS); early childhood (MS); educational leadership (MS, Certificate); English as a second language (Certificate); kindergarten (Certificate); language education (MS); reading (Certificate); school counseling (MS); special education (MS, Certificate). *Program availability:* Part-time, evening/weekend. Terminal master's awarded for partial completion of doctoral program. *Degree requirements:* For master's, thesis optional. *Entrance requirements:* For master's, GRE General Test, minimum GPA of 2.5; for Certificate, official transcripts. Additional exam requirements/recommendations for international students: Required—TOEFL (minimum score 60 iBT), IELTS (minimum score 5.5). Electronic applications accepted. *Expenses:* Contact institution. *Faculty research:* Educational policies and school leaders' responses to these; issues of intersectionality in the experiences of African American lesbian, gay, and bisexual students attending historically black colleges and universities and those who belong to black Greek-letter organizations; students' experiential knowledge and their evolving disciplinary-specific literacy and understanding; innovative program development; urban ESL teacher preparation; target-based instructional coaching.

Indiana University South Bend, School of Education, South Bend, IN 46615. Offers addiction counseling (MS Ed); alcohol and drug counseling (Graduate Certificate); clinical mental health counseling (MS Ed); educational leadership (MS Ed); elementary education (MS Ed); marriage, couple, and family counseling (MS Ed); school counseling (MS Ed); secondary education (MS Ed); special education (MAT, MS Ed), including intense intervention (MS Ed), mild intervention (MS Ed). *Accreditation:* NCATE. *Program availability:* Part-time, evening/weekend. *Degree requirements:* For master's, thesis or alternative, exit project. *Entrance requirements:* For master's, letters of recommendation, GRE or minimum GPA of 3.0. Additional exam requirements/recommendations for international students: Required—TOEFL. Electronic applications accepted. *Expenses:* Contact institution. *Faculty research:* Professional dispositions, early childhood literacy, online learning, program assessments, problem-based learning.

Inter American University of Puerto Rico, Barranquitas Campus, Program in Education, Barranquitas, PR 00794. Offers curriculum and teaching (M Ed), including biology, English as a second language, history, Spanish; educational leadership and management (MA); elementary education (M Ed); information and library service technology (M Ed); special education (MA). *Accreditation:* TEAC. *Program availability:* Part-time, evening/weekend. *Degree requirements:* For master's, 2 foreign languages, comprehensive exam, thesis (for some programs). *Entrance requirements:* For master's, GRE or EXADEP, bachelor's degree or its equivalent from accredited institution, official academic transcript from institution that conferred bachelor's degree, minimum GPA of 2.5, two recommendation letters, interview (for some programs), essay (for some programs). Electronic applications accepted. *Expenses:* Contact institution.

Inter American University of Puerto Rico, Fajardo Campus, Graduate Programs, Fajardo, PR 00738-7003. Offers computer science (MS); educational management and leadership (MA Ed); general business (MBA); human resources (MBA); management information systems (MBA); marketing (MBA); special education (MA Ed). *Program availability:* Online learning.

Inter American University of Puerto Rico, Metropolitan Campus, Graduate Programs, Program in Special Education, San Juan, PR 00919-1293. Offers MA. *Degree requirements:* For master's, comprehensive exam. *Entrance requirements:* For master's, GRE or EXADEP, interview. Electronic applications accepted.

Inter American University of Puerto Rico, San Germán Campus, Graduate Studies Center, Program in Special Education, San Germán, PR 00683-5008. Offers MA. *Accreditation:* TEAC. *Program availability:* Part-time, evening/weekend. *Degree requirements:* For master's, comprehensive exam. *Entrance requirements:* For master's, GRE General Test or EXADEP, minimum GPA of 3.0. *Expenses: Tuition:* Full-time $212; part-time $212 per credit. *Required fees:* $366 per semester. One-time fee: $31. Tuition and fees vary according to degree level and program.

Iona College, School of Arts and Science, Department of Education, New Rochelle, NY 10801-1890. Offers adolescence education: biology (MS Ed, MST); adolescence education: English (MS Ed); adolescence education: mathematics (MST); adolescence education: social studies (MS Ed, MST); adolescence education: Spanish (MS Ed); adolescence special education 5-12 (MST); childhood and special education (MST); early childhood and childhood (MST); educational leadership (MS Ed). *Accreditation:* NCATE. *Program availability:* Part-time, evening/weekend. *Faculty:* 7 full-time (5 women), 9 part-time/adjunct (5 women). *Students:* 33 full-time (30 women), 26 part-time (20 women); includes 21 minority (6 Black or African American, non-Hispanic/Latino; 1 Asian, non-Hispanic/Latino; 13 Hispanic/Latino; 1 Two or more races, non-Hispanic/Latino). Average age 25. 39 applicants, 87% accepted, 14 enrolled. In 2018, 20 master's awarded. *Degree requirements:* For master's, thesis or alternative. *Entrance requirements:* For master's, minimum GPA of 3.0, NY State teaching certificate and bachelor's degree (for MS Ed). Additional exam requirements/recommendations for international students: Required—TOEFL (minimum score 550 paper-based; 80 iBT), IELTS (minimum score 6.5). *Application deadline:* For fall admission, 8/1 priority date for domestic students, 5/1 priority date for international students; for spring admission, 1/1 priority date for domestic students, 9/1 priority date for international students. Applications are processed on a rolling basis. Electronic applications accepted. *Expenses: Tuition:* Full-time $14,064; part-time $7032 per credit. *Required fees:* $245 per semester. One-time fee: $250. Tuition and fees vary according to program. *Financial support:* In 2018-19, 2 students received support. Unspecified assistantships available. Support available to part-time students. Financial award application deadline: 4/15; financial award applicants required to submit FAFSA. *Faculty research:* Engaging teacher educators in scientific process, cross-national comparisons of mathematics teaching, questioning strategies in the classroom, research methods, literacy development. *Unit head:* Malissa Scheuring Leipold, EdD, Chair, 914-633-2210, Fax: 914-633-2281, E-mail: mleipold@iona.edu. *Application contact:* Christopher Kash, Assistant Director of Graduate Admissions, 914-633-2403, E-mail: ckash@iona.edu.
Website: http://www.iona.edu/Academics/School-of-Arts-Science/Departments/Education/Graduate-Programs.aspx

Special Education

Iowa State University of Science and Technology, Department of Education, Ames, IA 50011. Offers curriculum and instructional technology (M Ed, MS, PhD); elementary education (M Ed, MS); historical, philosophical, and comparative studies in education (M Ed, MS); special education (M Ed, MS, PhD). *Degree requirements:* For master's, thesis or alternative; for doctorate, thesis/dissertation. *Entrance requirements:* For master's and doctorate, GRE General Test. Additional exam requirements/recommendations for international students: Required—TOEFL (minimum score 560 paper-based; 83 iBT), IELTS (minimum score 6.5). Electronic applications accepted.

Jackson State University, Graduate School, College of Education and Human Development, Department of Special Education, Jackson, MS 39217. Offers special education (MS Ed, Ed S). *Accreditation:* NCATE. *Program availability:* Part-time, evening/weekend, online only, 100% online, blended/hybrid learning. *Degree requirements:* For master's, comprehensive exam, thesis or alternative. *Entrance requirements:* For master's, GRE General Test. Additional exam requirements/recommendations for international students: Required—TOEFL (minimum score 520 paper-based; 67 iBT). Electronic applications accepted. *Expenses:* Contact institution.

Jacksonville State University, Graduate Studies, School of Education, Program in Special Education, Jacksonville, AL 36265-1602. Offers MS Ed. *Accreditation:* NCATE. *Degree requirements:* For master's, comprehensive exam, thesis (for some programs). *Entrance requirements:* For master's, GRE General Test or MAT. Additional exam requirements/recommendations for international students: Required—TOEFL (minimum score 500 paper-based; 61 iBT). Electronic applications accepted.

James Madison University, The Graduate School, College of Education, Program in Special Education, Harrisonburg, VA 22807. Offers adapted curriculum (MAT); autism (M Ed); behavior specialist (M Ed); early childhood special education (MAT); general curriculum K-12 special education (MAT); gifted education (M Ed); inclusive early childhood special education (MAT); instructional specialist (M Ed); K-12 special education (MAT); visual impairments (MAT). *Accreditation:* NCATE. *Program availability:* Part-time. *Students:* 28 full-time (23 women), 9 part-time (5 women); includes 7 minority (3 Black or African American, non-Hispanic/Latino; 2 Hispanic/Latino; 2 Two or more races, non-Hispanic/Latino). Average age 30. In 2018, 25 master's awarded. Application fee: $60. Electronic applications accepted. *Expenses:* Tuition, state resident: full-time $10,848. Tuition, nonresident: full-time $27,888. *Required fees:* $1128. *Financial support:* In 2018–19, 6 students received support. Fellowships, Federal Work-Study, and assistantships (averaging $7911) available. Financial award application deadline: 3/1; financial award applicants required to submit FAFSA. *Unit head:* Dr. David A. Slykhuis, Interim Department Head, 540-568-4314, E-mail: slykhuda@jmu.edu. *Application contact:* Lynette D. Michael, Director of Graduate Admissions, 540-568-6131 Ext. 6395, Fax: 540-568-7860, E-mail: michaeld@jmu.edu.
Website: http://www.jmu.edu/coe/efex/index.shtml

Johnson & Wales University, Graduate Studies, MAT Program in Teacher Education, Providence, RI 02903-3703. Offers business education and secondary special education (MAT); culinary arts education (MAT); elementary education and elementary special education (MAT). *Program availability:* Part-time, evening/weekend. *Entrance requirements:* For master's, MAT, minimum GPA of 2.75. Additional exam requirements/recommendations for international students: Required—TOEFL (minimum score 550 paper-based) or IELTS (recommended). *Faculty research:* Secondary education, student teaching, educational reform, evaluation procedures.

Kansas State University, Graduate School, College of Education, Department of Special Education, Counseling and Student Affairs, Manhattan, KS 66506. Offers academic advising (MS, Certificate); counseling and student development (MS), including college student development, school counseling; special education (MS, Ed D); special education, counseling, and student affairs (PhD). *Accreditation:* ACA; NCATE. *Program availability:* Part-time, online learning. *Degree requirements:* For master's, comprehensive exam; for doctorate, comprehensive exam, thesis/dissertation. *Entrance requirements:* For master's, minimum undergraduate GPA of 3.0; for doctorate, GRE General Test, minimum GPA of 3.0 in last 60 hours. Additional exam requirements/recommendations for international students: Required—TOEFL. Electronic applications accepted. *Faculty research:* Counseling supervision, academic advising, career development, student development, universal design for learning, autism, learning disabilities.

Kean University, College of Education, Program in Special Education, Union, NJ 07083. Offers MA. *Accreditation:* NCATE. *Program availability:* Part-time. *Faculty:* 9 full-time (all women). *Students:* 11 full-time (9 women), 52 part-time (38 women); includes 21 minority (12 Black or African American, non-Hispanic/Latino; 2 Asian, non-Hispanic/Latino; 7 Hispanic/Latino). Average age 34. 27 applicants, 100% accepted, 23 enrolled. In 2018, 31 master's awarded. *Degree requirements:* For master's, comprehensive exam, thesis, portfolio, two semesters of advanced seminar. *Entrance requirements:* For master's, GRE General Test or MAT, minimum GPA of 3.0, New Jersey Standard Instructional Certificate or Certificate of Eligibility with Advanced Standing, 2 letters of recommendation, transcripts. Additional exam requirements/recommendations for international students: Required—TOEFL (minimum score 550 paper-based; 79 iBT), IELTS (minimum score 6.5). *Application deadline:* For fall admission, 6/30 for domestic and international students; for spring admission, 12/1 for domestic and international students. Applications are processed on a rolling basis. Application fee: $75. Electronic applications accepted. *Expenses:* Tuition, state resident: full-time $15,025; part-time $733.50 per credit. Tuition, nonresident: full-time $19,890; part-time $884.50 per credit. *Required fees:* $2107.50; $89.50 per credit. Tuition and fees vary according to course level, course load, degree level and program. *Financial support:* Scholarships/grants and unspecified assistantships available. Financial award applicants required to submit FAFSA. *Unit head:* Dr. Randi Sarokoff, Program Coordinator, 908-737-3849, E-mail: rsarokoff@kean.edu. *Application contact:* Brittany Gerstenhaber, Admissions Counselor, 908-737-7100, E-mail: gradadmissions@kean.edu.
Website: http://grad.kean.edu/masters-programs/special-education-autism-and-developmental-disabilities

Kennesaw State University, Bagwell College of Education, MAT Program, Kennesaw, GA 30144. Offers art education (MAT); secondary English (MAT); secondary mathematics (MAT); secondary science (MAT); special education (MAT); teaching English to speakers of other languages (MAT). *Program availability:* Part-time, evening/weekend. *Students:* 44 full-time (36 women), 10 part-time (6 women); includes 15 minority (10 Black or African American, non-Hispanic/Latino; 4 Hispanic/Latino; 1 Two or more races, non-Hispanic/Latino). Average age 32. 3 applicants. In 2018, 32 master's awarded. *Entrance requirements:* For master's, GRE, GACE I (state certificate exam), minimum GPA of 2.75, 2 recommendations, resume. Additional exam requirements/recommendations for international students: Required—TOEFL (minimum score 550 paper-based; 80 iBT), IELTS (minimum score 6.5). *Application deadline:* For fall admission, 6/1 for domestic and international students; for spring admission, 3/1 for domestic and international students; for summer admission, 4/15 for domestic and international students. Applications are processed on a rolling basis. Application fee: $60. Electronic applications accepted. *Expenses: Tuition, area resident:* Full-time $6960; part-time $290 per credit hour. Tuition, state resident: full-time $6960; part-time $290 per credit hour. Tuition, nonresident: full-time $25,080; part-time $1045 per credit

hour. *International tuition:* $25,080 full-time. *Required fees:* $2006; $1706 per semester. $853 per semester. *Financial support:* Research assistantships with tuition reimbursements and unspecified assistantships available. Financial award application deadline: 4/1; financial award applicants required to submit FAFSA. *Unit head:* Director, 470-578-3093. *Application contact:* Admissions Counselor, 470-578-4377, Fax: 470-578-9172, E-mail: ksugrad@kennesaw.edu.

Kennesaw State University, Bagwell College of Education, Program in Special Education, Kennesaw, GA 30144. Offers M Ed, Ed D, Ed S. *Program availability:* Part-time-only, evening/weekend, online only, 100% online, blended/hybrid learning. *Students:* 1 (woman) full-time, 42 part-time (39 women); includes 15 minority (11 Black or African American, non-Hispanic/Latino; 2 Asian, non-Hispanic/Latino; 2 Hispanic/Latino). Average age 34. In 2018, 9 master's, 1 doctorate, 3 other advanced degrees awarded. *Entrance requirements:* Additional exam requirements/recommendations for international students: Required—TOEFL (minimum score 80 iBT), IELTS (minimum score 6.5). *Application deadline:* For summer admission, 4/1 for domestic students. Applications are processed on a rolling basis. Application fee: $60. Electronic applications accepted. *Expenses: Tuition, area resident:* Full-time $6960; part-time $290 per credit hour. Tuition, state resident: full-time $6960; part-time $290 per credit hour. Tuition, nonresident: full-time $25,080; part-time $1045 per credit hour. *International tuition:* $25,080 full-time. *Required fees:* $2006; $1706 per semester. $853 per semester. *Application contact:* Admission Counselor, 470-578-4377, Fax: 470-578-9172, E-mail: ksugrad@kennesaw.edu.

Kent State University, College of Education, Health and Human Services, School of Lifespan Development and Educational Sciences, Program in Special Education, Kent, OH 44242-0001. Offers deaf education (M Ed); early childhood education (M Ed); educational interpreter K-12 (M Ed); general special education (M Ed); mild/moderate intervention (M Ed); special education (PhD, Ed S); transition to work (M Ed). *Accreditation:* NCATE. *Faculty:* 12 full-time (8 women), 11 part-time/adjunct (all women). *Students:* 56 full-time (46 women), 45 part-time (42 women); includes 11 minority (8 Black or African American, non-Hispanic/Latino; 1 Asian, non-Hispanic/Latino; 2 Native Hawaiian or other Pacific Islander, non-Hispanic/Latino), 3 international. 81 applicants, 26% accepted. In 2018, 35 master's, 4 doctorates awarded. *Degree requirements:* For doctorate, comprehensive exam, thesis/dissertation. *Entrance requirements:* For master's, minimum undergraduate GPA of 2.75, moral character form, 2 letters of reference, goals statement; for doctorate and Ed S, GRE General Test, goals statement, 2 letters of reference, interview, resume. Additional exam requirements/recommendations for international students: Required—TOEFL (minimum score 550 paper-based; 80 iBT). *Application deadline:* Applications are processed on a rolling basis. Application fee: $45 ($60 for international students). Electronic applications accepted. *Expenses:* Tuition, state resident: full-time $11,766; part-time $536 per credit. Tuition, nonresident: full-time $21,952; part-time $999 per credit. *International tuition:* $21,952 full-time. Tuition and fees vary according to course load. *Financial support:* In 2018–19, 6 research assistantships with full tuition reimbursements (averaging $9,667 per year) were awarded; teaching assistantships with full tuition reimbursements, career-related internships or fieldwork, Federal Work-Study, institutionally sponsored loans, scholarships/grants, health care benefits, unspecified assistantships, and 1 administrative assistantship (averaging $8,500 per year) also available. Support available to part-time students. Financial award application deadline: 4/1; financial award applicants required to submit FAFSA. *Faculty research:* Social/emotional needs of gifted, inclusion transition services, early intervention/ecobehavioral assessments, applied behavioral analysis. *Unit head:* Sonya Wisdom, Coordinator, 330-672-0452, E-mail: swisdom@kent.edu. *Application contact:* Cheryl Slusarczyk, Academic Program Director, Office of Graduate Student Services, 330-672-2576, Fax: 330-672-9162, E-mail: ogs@kent.edu.
Website: http://www.kent.edu/ehhs/ldes/sped

Lamar University, College of Graduate Studies, College of Education and Human Development, Department of Counseling, Beaumont, TX 77710. Offers clinical mental health counseling (M Ed); school counseling (M Ed); special education (M Ed). *Accreditation:* ACA. *Faculty:* 16 full-time (13 women), 20 part-time/adjunct (16 women). *Students:* 185 full-time (171 women), 808 part-time (742 women); includes 472 minority (208 Black or African American, non-Hispanic/Latino; 10 American Indian or Alaska Native, non-Hispanic/Latino; 1 Asian, non-Hispanic/Latino; 229 Hispanic/Latino; 19 Native Hawaiian or other Pacific Islander, non-Hispanic/Latino; 5 Two or more races, non-Hispanic/Latino). Average age 37. 1,265 applicants, 74% accepted, 359 enrolled. In 2018, 640 master's awarded. *Entrance requirements:* Additional exam requirements/recommendations for international students: Required—TOEFL (minimum score 550 paper-based; 79 iBT), IELTS (minimum score 6.5). *Application deadline:* Applications are processed on a rolling basis. Application fee: $25 ($50 for international students). Electronic applications accepted. *Expenses:* Contact institution. *Financial support:* In 2018–19, 19 students received support. Fellowships, research assistantships, teaching assistantships, career-related internships or fieldwork, scholarships/grants, and unspecified assistantships available. Financial award applicants required to submit FAFSA. *Total annual research expenditures:* $2,750. *Unit head:* Dr. Wendy Greenidge, Interim Department Chair, 409-880-8978, Fax: 409-880-2263. *Application contact:* Celeste Contreas, Director, Admissions and Academic Services, 409-880-8888, Fax: 409-880-7419, E-mail: gradmissions@lamar.edu.
Website: https://www.lamar.edu/education/counseling/index.html

Lamar University, College of Graduate Studies, College of Fine Arts and Communication, Department of Deaf Studies and Deaf Education, Beaumont, TX 77710. Offers MS, Ed D. *Accreditation:* ASHA. *Program availability:* Part-time, evening/weekend. *Faculty:* 12 full-time (7 women). *Students:* 21 full-time (13 women), 13 part-time (7 women); includes 12 minority (2 Black or African American, non-Hispanic/Latino; 2 Asian, non-Hispanic/Latino; 8 Hispanic/Latino), 6 international. Average age 36. 24 applicants, 83% accepted, 11 enrolled. In 2018, 7 master's, 5 doctorates awarded. *Degree requirements:* For master's, thesis optional; for doctorate, thesis/dissertation. *Entrance requirements:* For master's, GRE General Test, performance IQ score of 115 (for deaf students), minimum GPA of 2.5; for doctorate, GRE General Test, performance IQ score of 115 (for deaf students). Additional exam requirements/recommendations for international students: Required—TOEFL (minimum score 550 paper-based; 79 iBT), IELTS (minimum score 6.5). *Application deadline:* Applications are processed on a rolling basis. Application fee: $25 ($50 for international students). Electronic applications accepted. *Expenses:* Tuition, state resident: full-time $6234; part-time $346 per credit hour. Tuition, nonresident: full-time $6852; part-time $761 per credit hour. *International tuition:* $6852 full-time. *Required fees:* $1940; $327 per credit hour. Tuition and fees vary according to course load, campus/location, program and reciprocity agreements. *Financial support:* In 2018–19, 6 students received support, including 27 fellowships; research assistantships also available. Financial award applicants required to submit FAFSA. *Faculty research:* Multicultural and deaf teacher training, central auditory processing, voice sign language. *Unit head:* Dr. Diane Clark, Chair, 409-880-8170, Fax: 409-880-2265. *Application contact:* Celeste Contreas, Director, Admissions and Academic Services, 409-880-8888, Fax: 409-880-7419, E-mail: gradmissions@lamar.edu.
Website: http://fineartscomm.lamar.edu/deaf-studies-deaf-education

Lancaster Bible College, Graduate School, Lancaster, PA 17601-5036. Offers adult ministries (MA); Bible (MA); children and family ministry (MA); church planting (MA); consulting resource teacher (M Ed); elementary school counseling (M Ed); leadership (PhD); leadership studies (MA); marriage and family counseling (MA); mental health counseling (MA); pastoral studies (MA); secondary school counseling (M Ed); sports ministry (MA); student ministry (MA); town and country ministry (MA). *Program availability:* Part-time, evening/weekend. *Faculty:* 8 full-time (1 woman), 5 part-time/ adjunct (1 woman). *Students:* 94 full-time (47 women), 89 part-time (45 women); includes 21 minority (15 Black or African American, non-Hispanic/Latino; 5 Asian, non-Hispanic/Latino; 1 Hispanic/Latino). Average age 36. *Degree requirements:* For master's, comprehensive exam (for some programs), thesis (for some programs). *Entrance requirements:* For master's, bachelor's degree with a minimum of 30 credits of course work in Bible, minimum undergraduate GPA of 3.0, interview. Additional exam requirements/recommendations for international students: Required—TOEFL. *Application deadline:* Applications are processed on a rolling basis. Application fee: $25. *Financial support:* In 2018–19, 31 students received support. Teaching assistantships, scholarships/grants, and unspecified assistantships available. Support available to part-time students. Financial award application deadline: 6/1; financial award applicants required to submit FAFSA. *Unit head:* Dr. Gary Bredfeldt, Associate Vice President/ Dean of iLead Center, 717-560-8297, Fax: 717-560-8236. *Application contact:* Mark Wilson, Admissions Counselor, 717-560-8229, E-mail: mwilson@lbc.edu.

La Salle University, School of Arts and Sciences, Program in Education, Philadelphia, PA 19141-1199. Offers autism spectrum disorders (MA, Certificate); bilingual/bicultural studies (MA); classroom management (MA); dual early childhood and special education (MA); dual middle-level science and math and special education (MA); education (MA); English (MA); English as a second language (Certificate); history (MA); instructional coach (Certificate); instructional leadership (MA); reading specialist (MA, Certificate); secondary education (MA); special education (MA, Certificate). *Program availability:* Part-time, evening/weekend. *Degree requirements:* For master's, comprehensive exam. *Entrance requirements:* For master's, MAT or GRE, 2 letters of recommendation; for Certificate, GMAT or GRE, 2 letters of recommendation. Additional exam requirements/ recommendations for international students: Required—TOEFL. Electronic applications accepted. Application fee is waived when completed online. *Expenses:* Contact institution.

Lasell College, Graduate and Professional Studies in Education, Newton, MA 02466-2709. Offers curriculum, leadership, and inclusion (M Ed); elementary education (M Ed); special education (M Ed), including moderate disabilities; teaching bilingual/English learners with disabilities (Graduate Certificate). *Program availability:* Part-time-only, evening/weekend, blended/hybrid learning. *Faculty:* 1 (woman) full-time, 5 part-time/ adjunct (4 women). *Students:* 4 full-time (3 women), 45 part-time (37 women); includes 4 minority (3 Asian, non-Hispanic/Latino; 1 Hispanic/Latino). Average age 28. 23 applicants, 70% accepted, 10 enrolled. In 2018, 22 master's awarded. *Degree requirements:* For master's, minimum GPA of 3.0; practicum. *Entrance requirements:* For master's, Massachusetts Tests for Educator Licensure (MTEL) Curriculum and Literacy foundations of reading and writing subtest, one-page personal statement, 2 letters of recommendation, resume, bachelor's degree transcript. Additional exam requirements/recommendations for international students: Required—TOEFL (minimum score 550 paper-based, 79 iBT) or IELTS (minimum score 6). *Application deadline:* For fall admission, 8/31 priority date for domestic students, 6/30 priority date for international students; for spring admission, 12/31 priority date for domestic students, 10/31 priority date for international students. Applications are processed on a rolling basis. Electronic applications accepted. *Expenses:* Tuition: Part-time $600 per credit. *Required fees:* $40 per course. *Financial support:* Federal Work-Study, scholarships/grants, and tuition discounts available. Support available to part-time students. Financial award application deadline: 8/31; financial award applicants required to submit FAFSA. *Faculty research:* Inclusion, English language learners, literacy, and urban education; teacher inquiry; universal design for learning, deaf-blindness, and visual impairments; social and emotional learning; educational law, applied behavior analysis, and classroom management. *Unit head:* Eric Turner, Vice President of Graduate and Professional Studies, 617-243-2071, Fax: 617-243-2450, E-mail: gradinfo@lasell.edu. *Application contact:* Adrienne Franciosi, Director of Graduate Enrollment, 617-243-2214, Fax: 617-243-2450, E-mail: gradinfo@lasell.edu.
Website: http://www.lasell.edu/academics/graduate-and-professional-studies/programs-of-study/master-of-education.html

Lee University, Program in Education, Cleveland, TN 37320-3450. Offers art (MAT); curriculum and instruction (M Ed, Ed S); early childhood (MAT); educational leadership (M Ed, Ed S); elementary education (MAT); English and math (MAT); English and science (MAT); English and social studies (MAT); higher education administration (MS); history (MAT); history and economics (MAT); math and science (MAT); math and social studies (MAT); middle grades (MAT); science and social studies (MASW); secondary education (MAT); Spanish (MAT); special education (M Ed, MAT); TESOL (MAT). *Accreditation:* NCATE. *Program availability:* Part-time. *Faculty:* 13 full-time (5 women), 13 part-time/adjunct (7 women). *Students:* 32 full-time (26 women), 73 part-time (49 women); includes 13 minority (10 Black or African American, non-Hispanic/Latino; 3 Two or more races, non-Hispanic/Latino), 3 international. Average age 30. 56 applicants, 73% accepted, 34 enrolled. In 2018, 60 master's, 3 other advanced degrees awarded. *Degree requirements:* For master's, variable foreign language requirement, thesis optional, internship. *Entrance requirements:* For master's, MAT or GRE General Test, minimum undergraduate GPA of 2.75, 3 letters of recommendation, interview, writing sample, official transcripts, background check; for Ed S, minimum undergraduate and master's GPA of 2.75, official transcripts for undergraduate and master's degrees. Additional exam requirements/recommendations for international students: Required—TOEFL (minimum score 61 iBT). *Application deadline:* For fall admission, 6/1 priority date for domestic and international students; for spring admission, 11/1 priority date for domestic and international students; for summer admission, 4/1 priority date for domestic and international students. Applications are processed on a rolling basis. Application fee: $25. Electronic applications accepted. *Financial support:* In 2018–19, 43 students received support. Career-related internships or fieldwork, Federal Work-Study, institutionally sponsored loans, scholarships/grants, and unspecified assistantships available. Financial award application deadline: 3/1; financial award applicants required to submit FAFSA. *Unit head:* Dr. William Kamm, Director, 423-614-8544, E-mail: wkamm@leeuniversity.edu. *Application contact:* Jeffery McGirt, Director of Graduate Enrollment, 423-614-8691, Fax: 423-614-8317, E-mail: jmcgirt@leeuniversity.edu.
Website: http://www.leeuniversity.edu/academics/graduate/education

Lehigh University, College of Education, Program in Special Education, Bethlehem, PA 18015. Offers M Ed, PhD. *Program availability:* Part-time. *Faculty:* 4 full-time (all women), 4 part-time/adjunct (all women). *Students:* 12 full-time (10 women), 35 part-time (29 women); includes 7 minority (2 Black or African American, non-Hispanic/Latino; 1 Asian, non-Hispanic/Latino; 3 Hispanic/Latino; 1 Two or more races, non-Hispanic/Latino), 6 international. Average age 28. 24 applicants, 63% accepted, 12 enrolled. In 2018, 17 master's, 3 doctorates awarded. *Degree requirements:* For doctorate, comprehensive exam, thesis/dissertation, qualifying exam. *Entrance requirements:* For master's, minimum GPA of 3.0, 2 academic letters of recommendation, essay, transcripts; for doctorate, GRE General Test, minimum GPA of 3.0, 2 academic letters of

recommendation, essay, transcripts. Additional exam requirements/recommendations for international students: Required—TOEFL (minimum score 600 paper-based; 93 iBT), IELTS (minimum score 6.5), TOEFL (minimum iBT score of 93) or IELTS (6.5). *Application deadline:* For fall admission, 7/15 for domestic and international students; for spring admission, 12/15 for domestic and international students; for summer admission, 4/15 for domestic and international students. Application fee: $65. Electronic applications accepted. *Expenses:* $565 per credit. *Financial support:* In 2018–19, 18 students received support, including 14 research assistantships with full and partial tuition reimbursements available (averaging $15,932 per year); fellowships, scholarships/grants, and unspecified assistantships also available. Financial award application deadline: 1/31. *Faculty research:* Special education, autism spectrum disorder, emotional and behavioral disorders, positive behavior support, early childhood special education, ADHD, intellectual disability, intensive instruction, language development, learning disabilities. *Total annual research expenditures:* $528,413. *Unit head:* Dr. Minyi Dennis, Director, 610-758-4793, Fax: 610-758-6223, E-mail: mis210@lehigh.edu. *Application contact:* Donna Toothman, Coordinator, 610-758-3230, Fax: 610-758-3243, E-mail: djt2@lehigh.edu.
Website: https://ed.lehigh.edu/academics/programs/special-education

Lehman College of the City University of New York, School of Education, Department of Counseling, Leadership, Literacy, and Special Education, Bronx, NY 10468-1589. Offers counselor education/school counseling (MS Ed); literacy studies (MS Ed); special education (MS Ed), including bilingual special education, early childhood special education. *Program availability:* Part-time, evening/weekend. *Faculty research:* Battered women, whole language classrooms, parent education, mainstreaming.

Lehman College of the City University of New York, School of Education, Department of Counseling, Leadership, Literacy, and Special Education, Program in Special Education, Option in Bilingual Special Education, Bronx, NY 10468-1589. Offers MS Ed. *Accreditation:* NCATE. *Entrance requirements:* For master's, minimum GPA of 3.0.

Lehman College of the City University of New York, School of Education, Department of Counseling, Leadership, Literacy, and Special Education, Program in Special Education, Option in Early Childhood Special Education, Bronx, NY 10468-1589. Offers MS Ed. *Accreditation:* NCATE. *Entrance requirements:* For master's, minimum GPA of 3.0.

Le Moyne College, Department of Education, Syracuse, NY 13214. Offers adolescent education (MS Ed, MST); adolescent education/special education (MS Ed, MST); adolescent English (MST), including grades 7-12; adolescent English/special education (MST), including grades 7-12; adolescent foreign language (MST), including grades 7-12; adolescent history (MST), including grades 7-12; childhood education (MS Ed); childhood education/special education (MS Ed); elementary education (MS Ed); general education (MS Ed); inclusive childhood education (MST); literacy education (MS Ed), including birth to grade 6, grades 5-12; school building leader (MS Ed); school building leadership (CAS); school district business leader (MS Ed, CAS); school district leader (MS Ed); school district leadership (CAS); secondary education (MS Ed); special education (MS Ed); teaching English to speakers of other languages (MS Ed); urban studies (MS Ed). *Accreditation:* TEAC. *Program availability:* Part-time, evening/weekend. *Faculty:* 7 full-time (5 women), 16 part-time/adjunct (11 women). *Students:* 35 full-time (28 women), 119 part-time (84 women); includes 14 minority (5 Black or African American, non-Hispanic/Latino; 1 Asian, non-Hispanic/Latino; 7 Hispanic/Latino; 1 Two or more races, non-Hispanic/Latino), 1 international. Average age 30. 123 applicants, 89% accepted, 96 enrolled. In 2018, 66 master's, 48 CASs awarded. Terminal master's awarded for partial completion of doctoral program. *Degree requirements:* For master's, thesis. *Entrance requirements:* For master's, bachelor's degree with minimum undergraduate GPA of 3.0, 2 letters of recommendation, transcripts. Additional exam requirements/recommendations for international students: Required—TOEFL (minimum score 79 iBT); Recommended—IELTS (minimum score 6.5). *Application deadline:* For fall admission, 4/1 priority date for domestic and international students; for spring admission, 10/1 priority date for domestic and international students; for summer admission, 3/1 priority date for domestic and international students. Applications are processed on a rolling basis. Electronic applications accepted. *Expenses:* $734 per credit hour; wellness fee $70 per semester for full-time graduate students taking 9+ credit hours; technology fee $75 per semester for full-time graduate students taking 9+ credit hours; $25 per semester for part-time students; $1,470 per credit hour (for ED.D.). *Financial support:* In 2018–19, 44 students received support. Career-related internships or fieldwork, scholarships/grants, and health care benefits available. Support available to part-time students. Financial award applicants required to submit FAFSA. *Faculty research:* Minority teachers, special education, multiculturalism, literacy, technology, media literacy learning, autism, school district organization, service-learning, higher level problem solving, teacher leadership. *Unit head:* Dr. Stephen C. Fleury, Chair, Department of Education, 315-445-4376, Fax: 315-445-4744, E-mail: fleurysc@lemoyne.edu. *Application contact:* Jody F Manning, Assistant Director for Graduate Admission, 315-445-5444, Fax: 315-445-6092, E-mail: manninjf@lemoyne.edu.
Website: http://www.lemoyne.edu/education

Lesley University, Graduate School of Education, Cambridge, MA 02138-2790. Offers arts, community, and education (M Ed); autism studies (Certificate); curriculum and instruction (M Ed, CAGS); early childhood education (M Ed); ecological teaching and learning (MS); educational studies (PhD), including adult learning, educational leadership, individually designed; elementary education (M Ed); emergent technologies for educators (Certificate); ESLArts: language learning through the arts (M Ed); high school education (M Ed); individually designed (M Ed); integrated teaching through the arts (M Ed); literacy for K-8 classroom teachers (M Ed); mathematics education (M Ed); middle school education (M Ed); moderate disabilities (M Ed); online learning (Certificate); reading (CAGS); science in education (M Ed); severe disabilities (M Ed); special needs (CAGS); specialist teacher of reading (M Ed); teacher of visual art (M Ed); technology in education (M Ed, CAGS). *Accreditation:* TEAC. *Program availability:* Part-time, evening/weekend, online learning. *Degree requirements:* For master's, practicum; for doctorate, thesis/dissertation. *Entrance requirements:* For master's, Massachusetts Tests for Educator Licensure (MTEL), transcripts, statement of purpose, recommendations; interview (for special education); for doctorate, GRE General Test, transcripts, statement of purpose, recommendations, interview, master's degree, resume; for other advanced degree, interview, master's degree. Additional exam requirements/recommendations for international students: Required—TOEFL (minimum score 550 paper-based; 80 iBT). Electronic applications accepted. *Faculty research:* Assessment in literacy, mathematics and science; autism spectrum disorders; instructional technology and online learning; multicultural education and English language learners.

Lewis & Clark College, Graduate School of Education and Counseling, Department of Teacher Education, Program in Special Education, Portland, OR 97219-7899. Offers M Ed. *Accreditation:* NCATE. *Program availability:* Part-time, evening/weekend. *Entrance requirements:* For master's, minimum GPA of 2.75. Additional exam requirements/recommendations for international students: Required—TOEFL (minimum score 575 paper-based). Electronic applications accepted.

Lewis University, College of Education, Program in Early Childhood Special Education, Romeoville, IL 60446. Offers MA. *Program availability:* Part-time. *Students:* 14 full-time (all women), 8 part-time (7 women); includes 8 minority (all Hispanic/Latino). Average age 33. *Degree requirements:* For master's, comprehensive exam. *Entrance requirements:* For master's, writing exam, Test of Academic Proficiency/Basic Skills Test/ACT/SAT, bachelor's degree, minimum undergraduate GPA of 2.75, two letters of recommendation, professional educator license, interview. Additional exam requirements/recommendations for international students: Required—TOEFL (minimum score 550 paper-based; 79 iBT), IELTS (minimum score 6). *Application deadline:* For fall admission, 5/1 priority date for international students; for spring admission, 11/1 priority date for international students. Application fee: $40. Electronic applications accepted. *Financial support:* Federal Work-Study and unspecified assistantships available. Financial award application deadline: 5/1; financial award applicants required to submit FAFSA. *Unit head:* Dr. Rebecca Pruitt, Program Director. *Application contact:* Kathy Lisak, Graduate Admission Counselor, 815-836-5610, E-mail: grad@lewisu.edu.
Website: http://www.lewisu.edu/academics/grad-education/earlychildhood/index.htm

Lewis University, College of Education, Program in Special Education, Romeoville, IL 60446. Offers MA. *Program availability:* Part-time. *Students:* 31 part-time (25 women); includes 4 minority (1 Black or African American, non-Hispanic/Latino; 1 Asian, non-Hispanic/Latino; 2 Hispanic/Latino), 1 international. Average age 31. *Degree requirements:* For master's, comprehensive exam, departmental qualifying exam. *Entrance requirements:* For master's, writing exam, Test of Academic Proficiency/Basic Skills Test/ACT/SAT, bachelor's degree, minimum GPA of 2.75, 2 letters of recommendation. Additional exam requirements/recommendations for international students: Required—TOEFL (minimum score 550 paper-based; 80 iBT), IELTS (minimum score 6). *Application deadline:* For fall admission, 5/1 priority date for international students; for spring admission, 11/15 priority date for international students. Applications are processed on a rolling basis. Application fee: $40. Electronic applications accepted. *Financial support:* Federal Work-Study, scholarships/grants, and unspecified assistantships available. Financial award application deadline: 5/1; financial award applicants required to submit FAFSA. *Unit head:* Dr. Mary Fisher, Program Director. *Application contact:* Kathy Lisak, Graduate Admission Counselor, 815-836-5610, E-mail: grad@lewisu.edu.

Lincoln University, The School of Adult & Continuing Education, Philadelphia, PA 19104. Offers counseling (MSC); early childhood education (M Ed), including PreK-4; early childhood education and special education (M Ed); educational leadership (M Ed), including principal certification; finance (MBA); human resources management (MBA); human services delivery (MAHS). *Program availability:* Part-time, evening/weekend. *Faculty:* 8 full-time (3 women), 22 part-time/adjunct (12 women). *Students:* 192 full-time (154 women), 62 part-time (40 women); includes 230 minority (218 Black or African American, non-Hispanic/Latino; 9 Hispanic/Latino; 3 Two or more races, non-Hispanic/Latino), 3 international. Average age 33. 278 applicants, 58% accepted, 94 enrolled. In 2018, 105 master's awarded. *Degree requirements:* For master's, comprehensive exam, thesis or alternative, capstone, grant proposal. *Entrance requirements:* For master's, GRE/GMAT (Optional), Official academic transcript(s), letters of recommendation, personal statement, resume, supervisor's evaluation form, Application fee. Additional exam requirements/recommendations for international students: Required—TOEFL (minimum score 500 paper-based; 71 iBT); Recommended—IELTS (minimum score 6.5). *Application deadline:* For fall admission, 8/19 for domestic and international students; for spring admission, 12/30 for domestic and international students. Applications are processed on a rolling basis. Application fee: $50. Electronic applications accepted. *Financial support:* Scholarships/grants available. Financial award application deadline: 4/1; financial award applicants required to submit FAFSA. *Unit head:* Dr. Patricia Joseph, Dean of Faculty, 484-365-7659, E-mail: joseph@lincoln.edu. *Application contact:* Jernice Lea, Director, Student Services and Admissions, 215-590-8231, Fax: 215-387-3859, E-mail: jlea@lincoln.edu.
Website: http://www.lincoln.edu/admissions/graduate-admissions

Lipscomb University, College of Education, Nashville, TN 37204-3951. Offers applied behavior analysis (MS, Certificate); coaching for learning (M Ed, Certificate, Ed S); educational leadership (M Ed, Ed S); English language learning (M Ed, Ed S); instructional coaching (M Ed, Certificate, Ed S); instructional practice (M Ed); learning organizations and strategic change (Ed D); literacy coaching (Certificate, Ed S); reading specialty (M Ed, Ed S); school counseling (M Ed, Ed S); special education (M Ed); teaching, learning, and leading (M Ed); technology integration (M Ed, Ed S); technology integration specialist (Certificate). *Accreditation:* NCATE. *Program availability:* Part-time, evening/weekend, 100% online. *Degree requirements:* For master's, comprehensive exam, portfolio, research project and presentation; for doctorate, practical capstone project in experiential setting. *Entrance requirements:* For master's, MAT (minimum score 31) or GRE General Test (minimum score 294), 2 reference letters, goals statement, writing sample, interview; for doctorate, MAT or GRE General Test, 3 reference letters, artifact of demonstrated academic excellence, written personal statements, interview. Additional exam requirements/recommendations for international students: Required—TOEFL (minimum score 570 paper-based; 80 iBT). Electronic applications accepted. *Expenses:* Contact institution. *Faculty research:* Facilitative learning styles, leadership, student assessment, interactive multimedia inclusion, learning organizations and strategic change.

London Metropolitan University, Graduate Programs, London, United Kingdom. Offers applied psychology (M Sc); architecture (MA); biomedical science (M Sc); blood science (M Sc); cancer pharmacology (M Sc); computer networking and cyber security (M Sc); computing and information systems (M Sc); conference interpreting (MA); counter-terrorism studies (M Sc); creative, digital and professional writing (MA); crime, violence and prevention (M Sc); criminology (M Sc); curating contemporary art (MA); data analytics (M Sc); digital media (MA); early childhood studies (MA); education (MA, Ed D); financial services law, regulation and compliance (LL M); food science (M Sc); forensic psychology (M Sc); health and social care management and policy (M Sc); human nutrition (M Sc); human resource management (MA); human rights and international conflict (MA); information technology (M Sc); intelligence and security studies (M Sc); international oil, gas and energy law (LL M); international relations (MA); interpreting (MA); learning and teaching in higher education (MA); legal practice (LL M); media and entertainment law (LL M); organizational and consumer psychology (M Sc); psychological therapy (M Sc); psychology of mental health (M Sc); public health (M Sc); public policy and management (MPA); security studies (M Sc); social work (M Sc); spatial planning and urban design (MA); sports therapy (M Sc); supporting older children and young people with dyslexia (MA); teaching languages (MA), including Arabic, English; translation (MA); woman and child abuse (MA).

Long Island University–Brentwood Campus, Graduate Programs, Brentwood, NY 11717. Offers childhood education (MS), including grades 1-6; childhood education/literacy B-6 (MS); childhood education/special education (grades 1-6) (MS); clinical mental health counseling (MS, Advanced Certificate); criminal justice (MS); early childhood education (MS); educational leadership (MS Ed); family nurse practitioner (MS, Advanced Certificate); health administration (MPA); library and information science (MS); literacy (B-6) (MS Ed); school counselor (MS, Advanced Certificate); social work (MSW); special education (MS Ed); students with disabilities generalist (grades 7-12) (Advanced Certificate). *Program availability:* Part-time. *Entrance requirements:* For master's and Advanced Certificate, GRE. Additional exam requirements/recommendations for international students: Required—TOEFL or IELTS. Electronic applications accepted.

Long Island University–Hudson, Graduate School, Purchase, NY 10577. Offers autism (Advanced Certificate); bilingual education (Advanced Certificate); childhood education (MS Ed); crisis management (Advanced Certificate); early childhood education (MS Ed); educational leadership (MS Ed); health administration (MPA); literacy (MS Ed); marriage and family therapy (MS); mental health counseling (MS, Advanced Certificate), including credentialed alcoholism and substance abuse counselor (MS); middle childhood and adolescence education (MS Ed); pharmaceutics (MS), including cosmetic science, industrial pharmacy; public administration (MPA); school counseling (MS Ed, Advanced Certificate); school psychology (MS Ed); special education (MS Ed); TESOL (MS Ed); TESOL (all grades) (Advanced Certificate). *Program availability:* Part-time, evening/weekend. *Entrance requirements:* Additional exam requirements/recommendations for international students: Required—TOEFL. Electronic applications accepted. *Expenses:* Contact institution.

Long Island University–LIU Brooklyn, School of Education, Brooklyn, NY 11201-8423. Offers adolescence urban education (MS Ed); applied behavior analysis (Advanced Certificate); bilingual education (Advanced Certificate); bilingual education in urban setting (MS Ed); bilingual school counselor (MS Ed, Advanced Certificate); childhood urban education (MS Ed); childhood/early childhood education (MS Ed); childhood/early childhood urban education (MS Ed); early childhood urban education (MS Ed, Advanced Certificate); educational leadership (Advanced Certificate); marriage and family therapy (MS, Advanced Certificate); mental health counseling (MS, Advanced Certificate); school building district leader (Advanced Certificate); school counselor (MS Ed, Advanced Certificate); school psychologist (MS Ed); teaching students with disabilities (MS Ed); teaching urban children with disabilities (MS Ed); TESOL (MS Ed, Advanced Certificate). *Accreditation:* TEAC. *Program availability:* Part-time, evening/weekend, 100% online. *Entrance requirements:* For master's, GRE. Additional exam requirements/recommendations for international students: Required—TOEFL (minimum score 527 paper-based, 75 iBT), IELTS, or PTE. Electronic applications accepted. *Faculty research:* Diversity issues in education and mental health care, inclusion - disability studies, sustainability, teacher professional development.

Long Island University–LIU Post, College of Education, Information and Technology, Brookville, NY 11548-1300. Offers adolescence education (MS); adolescence education 7-12 (MS); archives and records management (AC); art education (MS); childhood education (MS); childhood education/literacy B-6 (MS); childhood education/special education (MS); clinical mental health counseling (MS, AC); early childhood education (MS); early childhood education/childhood education (MS); educational leadership (AC); educational technology (MS); information studies (PhD); interdisciplinary educational studies (Ed D); middle childhood education (MS); music education (MS); public library administration (AC); school counselor (MS); special education (MS Ed); speech-language pathology (MA); students with disabilities, 7-12 generalist (AC); TESOL (MA). *Accreditation:* ASHA; TEAC. *Program availability:* Part-time, 100% online, blended/hybrid learning. Terminal master's awarded for partial completion of doctoral program. *Degree requirements:* For master's, variable foreign language requirement, comprehensive exam (for some programs), thesis optional; for doctorate, comprehensive exam, thesis/dissertation. *Entrance requirements:* For master's and AC, GRE (for some programs). Additional exam requirements/recommendations for international students: Required—TOEFL (minimum score 550 paper-based, 75 iBT), IELTS, or PTE. Electronic applications accepted. *Faculty research:* Sleep; use of technology to develop executive function by students with disabilities; early childhood literacy development through play; social justice through education; using a structured protocol to discuss Bad News.

Long Island University–Riverhead, Graduate Programs, Riverhead, NY 11901. Offers applied behavior analysis (Advanced Certificate); childhood education (MS), including grades 1-6; cybersecurity policy (Advanced Certificate); homeland security management (MS, Advanced Certificate); literacy education (MS); literacy education B-6 (MS); teaching students with disabilities (MS), including grades 1-6; TESOL (Advanced Certificate). *Accreditation:* TEAC. *Program availability:* Part-time. *Entrance requirements:* Additional exam requirements/recommendations for international students: Required—TOEFL or IELTS. Electronic applications accepted. *Expenses:* Contact institution.

Longwood University, College of Graduate and Professional Studies, College of Education and Human Services, Farmville, VA 23909. Offers education (MS), including algebra and middle school mathematics, counselor education, elementary and middle school mathematics, elementary education, elementary education initial licensure, health and physical education, special education general curriculum, special education initial licensure; reading, literacy and learning (M Ed); school librarianship (M Ed); social work and communication sciences and disorders (MS), including communication sciences and disorders. *Accreditation:* NCATE. *Program availability:* Part-time, evening/weekend. *Degree requirements:* For master's, comprehensive exam (for some programs), thesis optional, professional portfolio, internship, clinical experience, or practicum. *Entrance requirements:* For master's, PRAXIS I (for initial teaching licensure programs); GRE (for some programs), bachelor's degree from regionally-accredited institution, 2 recommendations (3 for some programs), minimum 500-word personal essay, official transcripts, minimum GPA of 2.75, valid teaching license (for some programs). Additional exam requirements/recommendations for international students: Required—TOEFL (minimum score 570 paper-based), IELTS (minimum score 6.5). Electronic applications accepted. *Expenses:* Contact institution.

Loras College, Graduate Division, Program in Education with an Emphasis in Special Education, Dubuque, IA 52004-0178. Offers instructional strategist I K-6 and 7-12 (MA). *Program availability:* Part-time, evening/weekend. *Degree requirements:* For master's, comprehensive exam, thesis optional. *Entrance requirements:* For master's, minimum cumulative undergraduate GPA of 3.0.

Louisiana Tech University, Graduate School, College of Education, Ruston, LA 71272. Offers counseling and guidance (MA), including clinical mental health counseling, human services, orientation and mobility; counseling psychology (PhD); curriculum and instruction (M Ed); cyber education (Graduate Certificate); dynamics of domestic and family violence (Graduate Certificate); early childhood education - PreK-3 (MAT); educational leadership (M Ed, Ed D); elementary education and special education mild/moderate grades 1-5 (MAT); higher education administration (Graduate Certificate); industrial/organizational psychology (MA, PhD); kinesiology (MS); middle school education (MAT), including mathematics; orientation and mobility (Graduate Certificate); rehabilitation teaching for the blind (Graduate Certificate); secondary education (MAT), including agriculture, biology, business, chemistry, English; special education: visually impaired (MAT); teacher leader education (Graduate Certificate); visual impairments - blind education (Graduate Certificate). *Accreditation:* NCATE. *Program availability:* Part-time. *Degree requirements:* For master's, thesis; for doctorate, thesis/dissertation. *Entrance requirements:* For master's and doctorate, GRE General Test. Additional exam requirements/recommendations for international students: Required—TOEFL (minimum score 550 paper-based; 80 iBT), IELTS (minimum score 6.5). Electronic applications

accepted. *Faculty research:* Blindness and the best methods for increasing independence for individuals who are blind or visually impaired; educating and investigating factors contributing to improvements in human performance across the lifespan and a reduction in injury rates during training.

Loyola Marymount University, School of Education, Program in Special Education, Los Angeles, CA 90045. Offers MA. *Unit head:* Morgan Friedman, Acting Director, Special Education, E-mail: Morgan.Friedman@lmu.edu. *Application contact:* Ammar Dalal, Assistant Vice Provost for Graduate Enrollment, 310-338-2721, Fax: 310-338-6086, E-mail: graduateinfo@lmu.edu.
Website: http://soe.lmu.edu/academics/specialeducation

Loyola University Chicago, School of Education, Program in Teaching and Learning, Chicago, IL 60660. Offers elementary education (M Ed); English language teaching and learning (M Ed); secondary education (M Ed); special education (M Ed). *Accreditation:* NCATE. *Faculty:* 18 full-time (12 women), 33 part-time/adjunct (29 women). *Students:* 5 full-time (all women), 30 part-time (21 women); includes 11 minority (2 Asian, non-Hispanic/Latino; 9 Hispanic/Latino). Average age 28. 28 applicants, 61% accepted, 12 enrolled. In 2018, 20 master's awarded. *Entrance requirements:* For master's, Illinois Basic Skills Test, 3 letters of recommendation, minimum GPA of 3.0, resume. Additional exam requirements/recommendations for international students: Required—TOEFL (minimum score 550 paper-based; 79 iBT). *Application deadline:* For summer admission, 3/1 priority date for domestic and international students. Application fee: $50. Electronic applications accepted. Application fee is waived when completed online. *Expenses:* Contact institution. *Financial support:* In 2018–19, 12 fellowships with partial tuition reimbursements were awarded; institutionally sponsored loans, scholarships/grants, and unspecified assistantships also available. Support available to part-time students. Financial award application deadline: 2/1; financial award applicants required to submit FAFSA. *Faculty research:* Positive behavior support, school reform, school improvement. *Unit head:* Dr. Hank Bohanon, Program Chair, 312-915-7009, E-mail: hbohano@luc.edu. *Application contact:* Dr. Hank Bohanon, Program Chair, 312-915-7009, E-mail: hbohano@luc.edu.

Lynn University, Donald E. and Helen L. Ross College of Education, Boca Raton, FL 33431-5598. Offers educational leadership (M Ed, Ed D), including K-12 (Ed D); school administration K-12 (M Ed); exceptional student education (M Ed), including school administration K-12. *Program availability:* Part-time, evening/weekend, online learning. *Faculty:* 6 full-time (4 women), 8 part-time/adjunct (7 women). *Students:* 38 full-time (30 women), 85 part-time (63 women); includes 50 minority (33 Black or African American, non-Hispanic/Latino; 1 Asian, non-Hispanic/Latino; 15 Hispanic/Latino; 1 Two or more races, non-Hispanic/Latino), 5 international. Average age 38. 78 applicants, 65% accepted, 41 enrolled. In 2018, 13 master's, 14 doctorates awarded. *Degree requirements:* For master's, comprehensive exam, thesis (for some programs), completion of degree in maximum of four calendar years; minimum cumulative GPA of 3.0 and B grade or higher in each course; orientation seminar (one credit); minimum of 40 credits; FTCE ESE K-12 Exam; for doctorate, thesis/dissertation, mid-program review; minimum cumulative GPA of 3.25 and B grade or higher in each course. *Entrance requirements:* For master's, bachelor's degree from accredited institution, minimum undergraduate GPA of 3.0, official undergraduate and graduate transcripts of all academic coursework attempted, current resume, statement of professional goals, writing sample, 2 recent letters of recommendation; for doctorate, professional practice statement that identifies applicant's goals and explains how Lynn's program will help attain them, official transcript showing conferral of master's degree, 2 letters of recommendation from previous professors or employers, current resume, interview. Additional exam requirements/recommendations for international students: Required—TOEFL (minimum score 550 paper-based; 80 iBT), IELTS (minimum score 6.5). *Application deadline:* For fall admission, 8/18 for domestic students, 8/4 for international students; for spring admission, 12/15 for domestic students, 12/1 for international students; for summer admission, 4/17 for domestic students, 4/3 for international students. Applications are processed on a rolling basis. Application fee: $45. Electronic applications accepted. *Expenses:* 850 per credit hour. *Financial support:* In 2018–19, 85 students received support. Career-related internships or fieldwork, Federal Work-Study, scholarships/grants, tuition waivers (partial), and unspecified assistantships available. Support available to part-time students. Financial award application deadline: 3/1; financial award applicants required to submit FAFSA. *Faculty research:* Student achievement, students with learning differences, teacher and student retention, student motivation and cognition, neuroscience leadership and learning. *Unit head:* Dr. Kathleen Weigel, Dean, College of Education, 561-237-7441, E-mail: kweigel@lynn.edu. *Application contact:* Steven Pruitt, Director of Graduate and Undergraduate Evening Admission, 561-237-7834, Fax: 561-237-7100, E-mail: spruitt@lynn.edu.
Website: http://www.lynn.edu/academics/colleges/education

Madonna University, Programs in Education, Livonia, MI 48150-1173. Offers Catholic school leadership (MSA); educational leadership (MSA); learning disabilities (MAT); literacy education (MAT); teaching and learning (MAT). *Accreditation:* NCATE. *Program availability:* Part-time, evening/weekend. *Degree requirements:* For master's, thesis or alternative. Electronic applications accepted. *Expenses: Tuition:* Full-time $15,030; part-time $835 per credit hour. Tuition and fees vary according to degree level and program.

Malone University, Graduate Program in Education, Canton, OH 44709. Offers curriculum and instruction (MA); curriculum, instruction, and professional development (MA); educational leadership (principal license) (MA); intervention specialist (MA). *Accreditation:* NCATE. *Program availability:* Part-time, evening/weekend. *Degree requirements:* For master's, research project. *Entrance requirements:* For master's, minimum GPA of 3.0, teaching license. Additional exam requirements/recommendations for international students: Required—TOEFL (minimum score 550 paper-based; 79 iBT). *Faculty research:* Educational leadership styles: Jesus as master teacher, assessment accommodations for English language learners, preparing culturally proficient teachers, using naturally occurring text in the classroom to meet the syntactic needs of students with learning disabilities, using tablet instructional technology to meet the needs of students with disabilities.

Manhattan College, Graduate Programs, School of Education and Health, Program in Special Education, Riverdale, NY 10471. Offers adolescence education students with disabilities generalist extension in English or math or social studies - grades 7-12 (MS Ed); bilingual education (Advanced Certificate); dual childhood/students with disabilities - grades 1-6 (MS Ed); students with disabilities - grades 1-6 (MS Ed). *Program availability:* Part-time, evening/weekend. *Degree requirements:* For master's, thesis, internship (if not certified). *Entrance requirements:* For master's, GRE, minimum GPA of 3.0. Additional exam requirements/recommendations for international students: Required—TOEFL (minimum score 550 paper-based; 80 iBT), IELTS (minimum score 6). Electronic applications accepted. Application fee is waived when completed online. *Expenses:* Contact institution.

Manhattanville College, School of Education, Jump Start Program, Purchase, NY 10577-2132. Offers childhood education and special education (grades 1-6) (MPS); early childhood education (birth-grade 2) (MAT); education (Advanced Certificate); English and special education (grades 5-12) (MPS); mathematics and special education (grades 5-12) (MPS); science and special education (grades 5-12) (MPS); social studies and special education (grades 5-12) (MPS); Spanish (grades 7-12) (MAT); tesol -

teaching English as a second language (all grades) (MPS). *Program availability:* Part-time, evening/weekend. *Faculty:* 11 full-time (7 women), 78 part-time/adjunct (50 women). *Students:* 3 full-time (2 women), 16 part-time (11 women); includes 5 minority (1 Black or African American, non-Hispanic/Latino; 3 Hispanic/Latino; 1 Native Hawaiian or other Pacific Islander, non-Hispanic/Latino). Average age 31. 48 applicants, 54% accepted, 22 enrolled. In 2018, 23 master's, 1 other advanced degree awarded. *Degree requirements:* For master's, comprehensive exam (for some programs), thesis (for some programs), student teaching, research seminars, portfolios, internships, writing assessment; for Advanced Certificate, comprehensive exam (for some programs). *Entrance requirements:* For master's, for programs leading to certification, candidates must submit scores from GRE or MAT(miller analogies test), minimum undergraduate GPA of 3.0, all transcripts from all colleges and universities attended, 2 letters of recommendation, interview, essay (2-3 page personal statement that describes reasons for choosing education as profession and personal philosophy of education), proof of immunization (for those born after 1957). Additional exam requirements/recommendations for international students: Required—TOEFL (minimum score 600 paper-based; 110 iBT); Recommended—IELTS (minimum score 8). *Application deadline:* Applications are processed on a rolling basis. Application fee: $75. Electronic applications accepted. *Expenses:* 935 per credit. *Financial support:* Teaching assistantships, career-related internships or fieldwork, Federal Work-Study, institutionally sponsored loans, scholarships/grants, and unspecified assistantships available. Financial award application deadline: 3/15; financial award applicants required to submit FAFSA. *Faculty research:* Early childhood and technology, professional development schools and community schools, students with emotional difficulties, literacy and adolescents, mindfulness, changing suburbs institute, and community schools, studying the effects of the environment on special populations, the most difficult cases, students who are presented with multiple challenges: learning, behavioral and ACE experiences who see criminal behavior as a way to cope; working on giving them the tools they need to succeed. *Unit head:* Dr. Shelley Wepner, Dean, 914-323-3153, E-mail: Shelly.Wepner@mville.edu. *Application contact:* Alissa Wilson, Director, SOE Graduate Enrollment Management, 914-323-3150, Fax: 914-694-1732, E-mail: edschool@mville.edu
Website: http://www.mville.edu/programs/jump-start

Manhattanville College, School of Education, Program in Childhood Education, Purchase, NY 10577-2132. Offers childhood education (grades 1-6) (MAT); childhood education (grades 1-6) and special education: childhood (grades 1-6) (MPS); early childhood (birth-grade 2) & childhood ed (grades 1-6) (MAT); special ed early childhood and childhood (birth-grade 6) (MPS); special education childhood (grades 1-6) (MPS); special education: childhood (grades 1-6) (Certificate); special education: early childhood (birth-grade 2) and childhood (grades 1-6) (Certificate). *Program availability:* Part-time, evening/weekend. *Faculty:* 5 full-time (4 women), 3 part-time/adjunct (all women). *Students:* 4 full-time (3 women), 27 part-time (25 women); includes 6 minority (1 Black or African American, non-Hispanic/Latino; 1 Asian, non-Hispanic/Latino; 4 Hispanic/Latino). Average age 25. 18 applicants, 56% accepted, 8 enrolled. In 2018, 15 master's awarded. *Degree requirements:* For master's, comprehensive exam (for some programs), thesis (for some programs), student teaching, research seminars, portfolios, internships, writing assessment; for Certificate, comprehensive exam (for some programs). *Entrance requirements:* For master's, for programs leading to certification, candidates must submit scores from GRE or MAT(Miller Analogies Test), minimum undergraduate GPA of 3.0, all transcripts from all colleges and universities attended, 2 letters of recommendation, interview, essay (2-3 page personal statement that describes reasons for choosing education as profession and personal philosophy of education), proof of immunization (for those born after 1957). Additional exam requirements/recommendations for international students: Required—TOEFL (minimum score 600 paper-based; 110 iBT); Recommended—IELTS (minimum score 8). *Application deadline:* Applications are processed on a rolling basis. Application fee: $75. Electronic applications accepted. *Expenses:* 935 per credit. *Financial support:* Teaching assistantships, career-related internships or fieldwork, Federal Work-Study, institutionally sponsored loans, scholarships/grants, and unspecified assistantships available. Financial award application deadline: 3/15; financial award applicants required to submit FAFSA. *Faculty research:* Early childhood and technology, professional development schools and community schools. *Unit head:* Dr. Shelley Wepner, Dean, 914-323-3153, Fax: 914-323-5493, E-mail: Shelley.Wepner@mville.edu. *Application contact:* Alissa Wilson, Director, SOE Graduate Enrollment Management, 914-323-3150, Fax: 914-694-1732, E-mail: edschool@mville.edu.
Website: http://www.mville.edu/programs/childhood-education

Manhattanville College, School of Education, Program in Early Childhood Education, Purchase, NY 10577-2132. Offers early childhood (birth-grade 2) & childhood ed (grades 1-6) (MAT); early childhood (birth-grade 2) and special education: early childhood (birth-grade 2) (MPS); early childhood education (birth-grade 2) (MAT); special ed early childhood and childhood (birth-grade 6) (MPS); special education: early childhood (birth-grade 2) (MPS, Certificate); special education: early childhood (birth-grade 2) and childhood (grades 1-6) (Certificate). *Program availability:* Part-time, evening/weekend. *Faculty:* 1 (woman) full-time, 5 part-time/adjunct (all women). *Students:* 6 full-time (all women), 18 part-time (17 women); includes 2 minority (1 Black or African American, non-Hispanic/Latino; 1 Hispanic/Latino). Average age 29. 13 applicants, 69% accepted, 5 enrolled. In 2018, 13 master's awarded. *Degree requirements:* For master's, comprehensive exam (for some programs), thesis (for some programs), student teaching, research seminars, portfolios, internships, writing assessment; for Certificate, comprehensive exam (for some programs). *Entrance requirements:* For master's, for programs leading to certification, candidates must submit scores from GRE or MAT(Miller Analogies Test), minimum undergraduate GPA of 3.0, all transcripts from all colleges and universities attended, 2 letters of recommendation, interview, essay (2-3 page personal statement that describes reasons for choosing education as profession and personal philosophy of education), proof of immunization (for those born after 1957). Additional exam requirements/recommendations for international students: Required—TOEFL (minimum score 600 paper-based; 110 iBT); Recommended—IELTS (minimum score 8). *Application deadline:* Applications are processed on a rolling basis. Application fee: $75. Electronic applications accepted. *Expenses:* 935 per credit. *Financial support:* Teaching assistantships, career-related internships or fieldwork, Federal Work-Study, institutionally sponsored loans, scholarships/grants, and unspecified assistantships available. Financial award application deadline: 3/15; financial award applicants required to submit FAFSA. *Faculty research:* Early childhood and technology. *Unit head:* Dr. Shelley Wepner, Dean, 914-323-3153, Fax: 914-323-5493, E-mail: Shelley.Wepner@mville.edu. *Application contact:* Alissa Wilson, Director, SOE Graduate Enrollment Management, 914-323-3150, Fax: 914-694-1732, E-mail: edschool@mville.edu.
Website: http://www.mville.edu/programs/early-childhood-education

Manhattanville College, School of Education, Program in Literacy Education, Purchase, NY 10577-2132. Offers literacy (birth-grade 6) and special education childhood (grades 1-6) (MPS); literacy 5-12; special education generalist 7-12; special ed specialist 7-12 (MPS); literacy specialist (birth-grade 6) (MPS); literacy specialist (grades 5-12) (MPS); science of reading: multisensory instruction – the rose institute for learning and literacy (Advanced Certificate). *Program availability:* Part-time, evening/

weekend. *Faculty:* 3 full-time (all women), 15 part-time/adjunct (14 women). *Students:* 2 full-time (both women), 8 part-time (all women). Average age 26. 6 applicants, 50% accepted, 1 enrolled. In 2018, 8 master's, 11 Advanced Certificates awarded. *Degree requirements:* For master's, comprehensive exam (for some programs), thesis (for some programs), student teaching, research seminars, portfolios, internships, writing assessment; for Advanced Certificate, comprehensive exam (for some programs). *Entrance requirements:* For master's, for programs leading to certification, candidates must submit scores from GRE or MAT(Miller Analogies Test), minimum undergraduate GPA of 3.0, all transcripts from all colleges and universities attended, 2 letters of recommendation, interview, essay (2-3 page personal statement that describes reasons for choosing education as profession and personal philosophy of education), proof of immunization (for those born after 1957). Additional exam requirements/recommendations for international students: Required—TOEFL (minimum score 600 paper-based; 110 iBT); Recommended—IELTS (minimum score 8). *Application deadline:* Applications are processed on a rolling basis. Application fee: $75. Electronic applications accepted. *Expenses:* 935 per credit. *Financial support:* Teaching assistantships, career-related internships or fieldwork, Federal Work-Study, institutionally sponsored loans, scholarships/grants, and unspecified assistantships available. Financial award application deadline: 3/15; financial award applicants required to submit FAFSA. *Faculty research:* Power of story for literacy development, English learners. *Total annual research expenditures:* $800. *Unit head:* Dr. Shelley Wepner, Dean, 914-323-3153, Fax: 914-323-5493, E-mail: Shelley.Wepner@mville.edu. *Application contact:* Alissa Wilson, Director, SOE Graduate Enrollment Management, 914-323-3150, Fax: 914-694-1732, E-mail: edschool@mville.edu.
Website: http://www.mville.edu/programs/literacy-education

Manhattanville College, School of Education, Program in Middle Childhood/Adolescence Education (Grades 5-12), Purchase, NY 10577-2132. Offers biology and special education (MPS); chemistry and special education (MPS); education for sustainability (Advanced Certificate); English and special education (MPS); literacy and special education (MPS); literacy specialist (MPS); math and special education (MPS); mathematics (Advanced Certificate); middle childhood/adolescence ed science (biology or chemistry grades 5-12) or (physics grades 7-12) (MAT); middle childhood/adolescence education (grades 5-12) English (MAT, Advanced Certificate); middle childhood/adolescence education (grades 5-12) mathematics (MAT, Advanced Certificate); middle childhood/adolescence education (grades 5-12) science (biology chemistry, physics, earth science) (Advanced Certificate); middle childhood/adolescence education (grades 5-12) social studies (MAT, Advanced Certificate); physics (MAT, Advanced Certificate); social studies (MAT); social studies and special education (MPS); special education generalist (MPS). *Program availability:* Part-time, evening/weekend. *Faculty:* 3 full-time (2 women), 9 part-time/adjunct (4 women). *Students:* 11 full-time (6 women), 17 part-time (12 women); includes 3 minority (1 Black or African American, non-Hispanic/Latino; 2 Hispanic/Latino). Average age 31. 17 applicants, 71% accepted, 7 enrolled. In 2018, 8 master's, 3 other advanced degrees awarded. *Degree requirements:* For master's, comprehensive exam (for some programs), thesis (for some programs), student teaching, research seminars, portfolios, internships, writing assessment; for Advanced Certificate, comprehensive exam (for some programs). *Entrance requirements:* For master's, for programs leading to certification, candidates must submit scores from GRE or MAT(Miller Analogies Test), minimum undergraduate GPA of 3.0, all transcripts from all colleges and universities attended, 2 letters of recommendation, interview, essay (2-3 page personal statement that describes reasons for choosing education as profession and personal philosophy of education), proof of immunization (for those born after 1957). Additional exam requirements/recommendations for international students: Required—TOEFL (minimum score 600 paper-based; 110 iBT); Recommended—IELTS (minimum score 8). *Application deadline:* Applications are processed on a rolling basis. Application fee: $75. Electronic applications accepted. *Expenses:* 935 per credit. *Financial support:* Teaching assistantships, career-related internships or fieldwork, Federal Work-Study, institutionally sponsored loans, scholarships/grants, and unspecified assistantships available. Financial award application deadline: 3/15; financial award applicants required to submit FAFSA. *Faculty research:* Education for sustainability. *Unit head:* Dr. Shelley Wepner, Dean, 914-323-3153, Fax: 914-323-5493, E-mail: Shelley.Wepner@mville.edu. *Application contact:* Alissa Wilson, Director, Graduate Admissions, 914-323-3150, Fax: 914-694-1732, E-mail: edschool@mville.edu.
Website: http://www.mville.edu/programs#/search/19

Manhattanville College, School of Education, Program in Special Education, Purchase, NY 10577-2132. Offers childhood education (grades 1-6) and special education: childhood (grades 1-6) (MPS); early childhood (birth-grade 2) and special education: early childhood (birth-grade 2) (MPS); English (5-9 and 7-12); special ed generalist (7-12); se English (7-12) (MPS); literacy (birth-grade 6) and special education childhood (grades 1-6) (MPS); literacy 5-12; special education generalist 7-12; special ed specialist 7-12 (MPS); math (5-9 and 7-12); special ed generalist (7-12); se math (7-12) (MPS); science: biology or chemistry (5-9 and 7-12); special ed generalist (7-12); se science (7-12) (MPS); social studies (5-9 and 7-12); special ed generalist (7-12); se soc.st. (7-12) (MPS); special ed early childhood and childhood (birth-grade 6) (MPS); special education childhood (grades 1-6) (MPS); special education: childhood (grades 1-6) (Certificate); special education: early childhood (birth-grade 2) (MPS, Certificate); special education: early childhood (birth-grade 2) and childhood (grades 1-6) (Certificate); special education: grades 7-12 generalist (MPS, Certificate). *Program availability:* Part-time, evening/weekend. *Faculty:* 5 full-time (3 women), 35 part-time/adjunct (23 women). *Students:* 45 full-time (36 women), 179 part-time (152 women); includes 31 minority (6 Black or African American, non-Hispanic/Latino; 4 Asian, non-Hispanic/Latino; 19 Hispanic/Latino; 2 Native Hawaiian or other Pacific Islander, non-Hispanic/Latino), 1 international. Average age 28. 76 applicants, 68% accepted, 40 enrolled. In 2018, 99 master's, 2 Certificates awarded. *Degree requirements:* For master's, comprehensive exam (for some programs), thesis (for some programs), student teaching, research seminars, portfolios, internships, writing assessment; for Certificate, comprehensive exam (for some programs). *Entrance requirements:* For master's, for programs leading to certification, candidates must submit scores from GRE or MAT(Miller Analogies Test), minimum undergraduate GPA of 3.0, all transcripts from all colleges and universities attended, 2 letters of recommendation, interview, essay (2-3 page personal statement that describes reasons for choosing education as profession and personal philosophy of education), proof of immunization (for those born after 1957). Additional exam requirements/recommendations for international students: Required—TOEFL (minimum score 600 paper-based; 110 iBT); Recommended—IELTS (minimum score 8). *Application deadline:* Applications are processed on a rolling basis. Application fee: $75. Electronic applications accepted. *Expenses:* 935 per credit. *Financial support:* Teaching assistantships, career-related internships or fieldwork, Federal Work-Study, institutionally sponsored loans, scholarships/grants, and unspecified assistantships available. Financial award application deadline: 3/15; financial award applicants required to submit FAFSA. *Faculty research:* Students with emotional difficulties, literacy and adolescents, mindfulness, studying the effects of the environment on special populations, the most difficult cases, students who are presented with multiple challenges: learning, behavioral and ACE experiences who see criminal behavior as a way to cope; working on giving them the tools they need to succeed emotionally and cognitively despite the odds stacked against them. *Unit head:* Dr. Shelley Wepner, Dean, 914-323-3153, Fax: 914-323-5493, E-mail: Shelley.Wepner@mville.edu. *Application contact:* Alissa Wilson, Director, SOE Graduate Enrollment Management, 914-323-3150, Fax: 914-694-1732, E-mail: edschool@mville.edu.
Website: http://www.mville.edu/programs/special-education

Mansfield University of Pennsylvania, Graduate Studies, Department of Education and Special Education, Mansfield, PA 16933. Offers elementary education (M Ed); secondary education (MS); special education (M Ed). *Accreditation:* NCATE (one or more programs are accredited). *Program availability:* Part-time, evening/weekend, online learning. *Degree requirements:* For master's, comprehensive exam, thesis optional. *Entrance requirements:* For master's, minimum GPA of 3.0. Additional exam requirements/recommendations for international students: Required—TOEFL (minimum score 550 paper-based). Electronic applications accepted.

Marian University, School of Education, Fond du Lac, WI 54935-4699. Offers curriculum and instruction leadership (PhD); educational administration (PhD); educational leadership (MAE); educational technology (MAE); leadership studies (PhD); special education (MAE); teacher education (MAE). *Accreditation:* NCATE. *Program availability:* Part-time, evening/weekend, online learning. *Degree requirements:* For master's, exam, field-based experience project, portfolio; for doctorate, comprehensive exam, thesis/dissertation, field-based experience. *Entrance requirements:* For master's, minimum GPA of 3.0, BA in education or related field, teaching license; for doctorate, GRE, MAT, resume, 2 writing samples, interview. Additional exam requirements/recommendations for international students: Required—TOEFL (minimum score 525 paper-based; 70 iBT). *Faculty research:* At-risk youth, multicultural issues, values in education, teaching/learning strategies.

Marshall University, Academic Affairs Division, College of Education and Professional Development, Program in Special Education, Huntington, WV 25755. Offers MA. *Accreditation:* NCATE. *Program availability:* Part-time, evening/weekend. *Degree requirements:* For master's, thesis optional, comprehensive or oral assessment, research project. *Entrance requirements:* For master's, GRE General Test or MAT, minimum GPA of 3.0. *Faculty research:* Teaching the severely handicapped, career/vocational education, education of the gifted.

Martin Luther College, Graduate Studies, New Ulm, MN 56073. Offers early childhood director (MS Ed Admin); educational technology (MS Ed); instruction (MS Ed); leadership (MS Ed); principal (MS Ed Admin); special education (MS Ed). *Program availability:* Part-time, evening/weekend, online only, 100% online. *Faculty:* 13 full-time (2 women), 31 part-time/adjunct (10 women). *Students:* 1 full-time (0 women), 86 part-time (26 women); includes 1 minority (Two or more races, non-Hispanic/Latino), 1 international. Average age 38. 35 applicants, 100% accepted, 35 enrolled. In 2018, 26 master's awarded. *Degree requirements:* For master's, capstone project or comprehensive exam. *Entrance requirements:* For master's, undergraduate degree in education from an accredited college or university, minimum undergraduate GPA of 3.0. Additional exam requirements/recommendations for international students: Required—TOEFL (minimum score 550 paper-based; 80 iBT); Recommended—IELTS (minimum score 6.5). *Application deadline:* Applications are processed on a rolling basis. Application fee: $35. Electronic applications accepted. *Financial support:* In 2018–19, 1 student received support. Scholarships/grants available. Financial award application deadline: 9/1. *Faculty research:* Principal effectiveness, principal support, cognitive load in math instruction, reading strategies in multigrade classrooms, mentor provided professional development for new teachers. *Unit head:* John E. Meyer, Director of Graduate Studies, 507-354-8221 Ext. 398, E-mail: meyerjd@mlc-wels.edu. *Application contact:* John E. Meyer, Director of Graduate Studies, 507-354-8221 Ext. 398, E-mail: meyerjd@mlc-wels.edu.
Website: https://mlc-wels.edu/graduate-studies/

Mary Baldwin University, Graduate Studies, Programs in Education, Staunton, VA 24401-3610. Offers applied behavior analysis (MS); autism spectrum disorders (M Ed); elementary education (M Ed, MAT); English as a second language (M Ed); environment-based learning (M Ed); gifted education (M Ed); higher education (MS); leadership (M Ed); middle grades education (MAT); reading education (M Ed); special education (M Ed). *Accreditation:* TEAC.

Marygrove College, Graduate Studies, Detroit, MI 48221-2599. Offers autism spectrum disorders (M Ed, Certificate); curriculum instruction and assessment (MAT); educational leadership (MA); educational technology (M Ed); effective teaching in the 21st century-classroom focus (MAT); effective teaching in the 21st century-technology focus (MAT); human resource management (MA, Certificate); mathematics 6-8 (MAT); mathematics K-5 (MAT); reading and literacy K-6 (MAT); reading specialist (M Ed); school administrator (Certificate); social justice (MA); special education (MAT); special education - learning disabilities (M Ed); teaching - pre-elementary education (M Ed); teaching - pre-secondary education (M Ed). *Program availability:* Part-time, evening/weekend, 100% online, blended/hybrid learning. *Entrance requirements:* For master's, all official bachelor's transcripts. Additional exam requirements/recommendations for international students: Required—TOEFL (minimum score 550 paper-based; 80 iBT). Electronic applications accepted.

Marymount University, School of Sciences, Mathematics, and Education, Program in Education, Arlington, VA 22207-4299. Offers curriculum and instruction (M Ed); elementary education (M Ed); professional studies (M Ed); secondary education (M Ed); special education: general curriculum (M Ed). *Accreditation:* NCATE. *Program availability:* Part-time, evening/weekend. *Faculty:* 7 full-time (all women), 8 part-time/adjunct (6 women). *Students:* 42 full-time (29 women), 103 part-time (80 women); includes 31 minority (8 Black or African American, non-Hispanic/Latino; 11 Asian, non-Hispanic/Latino; 10 Hispanic/Latino; 1 Native Hawaiian or other Pacific Islander, non-Hispanic/Latino; 1 Two or more races, non-Hispanic/Latino), 12 international. Average age 36. 44 applicants, 100% accepted, 30 enrolled. In 2018, 61 master's awarded. *Degree requirements:* For master's, thesis or alternative, capstone/internship. *Entrance requirements:* For master's, PRAXIS MATH or SAT/ACT, and Virginia Communication and Literacy Assessment (VCLA), 2 letters of recommendation, resume, interview, minimum undergraduate GPA of 2.75 or 3.25 in the last 60 hours. Additional exam requirements/recommendations for international students: Required—TOEFL (minimum score 600 paper-based; 96 iBT), IELTS (minimum score 6.5), PTE (minimum score 58). *Application deadline:* For fall admission, 7/16 priority date for domestic and international students; for spring admission, 11/16 priority date for domestic and international students. Applications are processed on a rolling basis. Application fee: $40. Electronic applications accepted. *Expenses:* $770 per credit. *Financial support:* In 2018–19, 3 students received support. Research assistantships, teaching assistantships, career-related internships or fieldwork, scholarships/grants, and unspecified assistantships available. Support available to part-time students. Financial award application deadline: 3/1; financial award applicants required to submit FAFSA. *Unit head:* Dr. Lisa Turissini, Chair, Education, 703-526-1668, E-mail: lisa.turissini@marymount.edu. *Application contact:* Rebecca Esposito, Senior Associate Director, Graduate Admissions, 703-284-5901, Fax: 703-527-3815, E-mail: grad.admissions@marymount.edu.
Website: https://www.marymount.edu/Academics/School-of-Sciences-Mathematics-and-Education/Graduate-Programs/Education-(M-Ed-)

Marywood University, Academic Affairs, Reap College of Education and Human Development, Department of Education, Program in Special Education, Scranton, PA 18509-1598. Offers MS. *Accreditation:* NCATE. *Program availability:* Part-time. Electronic applications accepted.

Marywood University, Academic Affairs, Reap College of Education and Human Development, Department of Education, Program in Special Education Administration and Supervision, Scranton, PA 18509-1598. Offers MS. *Accreditation:* NCATE. *Program availability:* Part-time. Electronic applications accepted.

Massachusetts College of Liberal Arts, Graduate Programs, North Adams, MA 01247-4100. Offers business (MBA); educational administration (M Ed); educational leadership (CAGS); instruction and curriculum (M Ed); instructional technology (M Ed); physical education and health (M Ed); reading (M Ed); special education (M Ed). *Program availability:* Part-time, evening/weekend. *Degree requirements:* For master's, thesis. *Entrance requirements:* For master's, writing sample.

McDaniel College, Graduate and Professional Studies, Program in Deaf Education, Westminster, MD 21157-4390. Offers MS. *Accreditation:* NCATE. *Program availability:* Part-time. *Degree requirements:* For master's, comprehensive exam, thesis optional. *Entrance requirements:* For master's, American Sign Language Proficiency Interview (ASLPI); English Proficiency Essay (EPE). Additional exam requirements/recommendations for international students: Required—TOEFL (minimum score 79 iBT), IELTS (minimum score 6). Electronic applications accepted. *Faculty research:* Mainstreaming of multi-handicapped children.

McDaniel College, Graduate and Professional Studies, Program in Special Education, Westminster, MD 21157-4390. Offers MS. *Accreditation:* NCATE. *Program availability:* Part-time, evening/weekend. *Degree requirements:* For master's, comprehensive exam, thesis optional. *Entrance requirements:* For master's, PRAXIS, 3 recommendations. Additional exam requirements/recommendations for international students: Required—TOEFL (minimum score 79 iBT), IELTS (minimum score 6). Electronic applications accepted.

McKendree University, Graduate Programs, Programs in Education, Lebanon, IL 62254-1299. Offers curriculum design and instruction (Ed D, Ed S); educational administration and leadership (MA Ed); educational studies (MA Ed); higher education administrative services (MA Ed); music education (MA Ed); reading (MA Ed); special education (MA Ed); teacher leadership (MA Ed); teaching certification (MA Ed). *Accreditation:* NCATE. *Program availability:* Part-time, evening/weekend, online learning. *Entrance requirements:* For master's, official transcripts from all institutions previously attended, minimum GPA of 3.0, resume, references; for doctorate, GRE (within the past 5 years), master's degree in education and Ed S, or the equivalent, from regionally-accredited institution; official transcripts from all institutions previously attended; curriculum vitae/resume; essay/personal statement; two years of teaching/professional experience; for Ed S, GRE (within the past 5 years), master's degree in education from regionally-accredited institution of higher education; official transcripts from all institutions previously attended; curriculum vitae/resume; essay/personal statement; two years of teaching/professional experience. Additional exam requirements/recommendations for international students: Required—TOEFL. Electronic applications accepted.

McNeese State University, Doré School of Graduate Studies, Burton College of Education, Department of Education Professions, Program in Curriculum and Instruction, Lake Charles, LA 70609. Offers academically gifted education (M Ed); elementary education (M Ed); reading (M Ed); secondary education (M Ed); special education (M Ed). *Program availability:* Evening/weekend. *Entrance requirements:* For master's, GRE, teaching certificate.

McNeese State University, Doré School of Graduate Studies, Burton College of Education, Department of Education Professions, Program in Special Education, Mild/Moderate for Elementary Education Grades 1-5, Lake Charles, LA 70609. Offers Postbaccalaureate Certificate. *Entrance requirements:* For degree, PRAXIS, 2 letters of recommendation, autobiography.

Medaille College, Program in Education, Buffalo, NY 14214-2695. Offers adolescent education (MS Ed); curriculum and instruction (MS Ed); education preparation (MS Ed); literacy (MS Ed); special education (MS). *Accreditation:* TEAC. *Program availability:* Part-time, evening/weekend. *Degree requirements:* For master's, comprehensive exam (for some programs), thesis or alternative. *Entrance requirements:* For master's, minimum undergraduate GPA of 2.7. Additional exam requirements/recommendations for international students: Required—TOEFL (minimum score 550 paper-based). Electronic applications accepted. *Faculty research:* Curriculum planning, truancy, tracking minority students, curriculum design, mentoring students.

Mercyhurst University, Graduate Studies, Program in Special Education, Erie, PA 16546. Offers applied behavior analysis (MS); autism (MS); generalist (MS); higher education leadership and disabilities (MS). *Program availability:* Part-time, evening/weekend. *Degree requirements:* For master's, thesis optional. *Entrance requirements:* For master's, GRE or PRAXIS I, interview, resume, essay, three professional references, transcripts. Additional exam requirements/recommendations for international students: Required—TOEFL. Electronic applications accepted. *Faculty research:* College-age learning disabled program, teacher preparation/collaboration, applied behavior analysis, special education policy issues.

Meredith College, School of Education, Health and Human Sciences, Raleigh, NC 27607-5298. Offers academically and intellectually gifted (M Ed); elementary education (M Ed, MAT); English as a second language (M Ed, MAT); health and physical education (MAT); nutrition, health and human performance (MS, Postbaccalaureate Certificate), including dietetic internship (Postbaccalaureate Certificate), nutrition (MS); psychology (MA), including industrial/organizational psychology; reading (M Ed); special education (MAT); special education (general curriculum) (M Ed). *Accreditation:* NCATE. *Program availability:* Part-time, evening/weekend. *Students:* 97 full-time (89 women), 76 part-time (73 women); includes 39 minority (17 Black or African American, non-Hispanic/Latino; 1 American Indian or Alaska Native, non-Hispanic/Latino; 9 Asian, non-Hispanic/Latino; 10 Hispanic/Latino; 2 Two or more races, non-Hispanic/Latino). Average age 28. In 2018, 56 master's, 36 other advanced degrees awarded. *Degree requirements:* For master's, thesis optional. *Entrance requirements:* For master's, GRE General Test or MAT, minimum GPA of 2.5, teaching license, recommendations. Additional exam requirements/recommendations for international students: Required—TOEFL. *Application deadline:* For fall admission, 7/1 priority date for domestic students; for spring admission, 11/1 priority date for domestic students. Applications are processed on a rolling basis. Application fee: $50. Electronic applications accepted. *Expenses:* $575 per credit hour for masters degree in education, $725 (for MS. PSY.IO degree), $20,295 (for pre-health post-baccalaureate certificate), $13,600 (for dietetic internship). *Financial support:* Career-related internships or fieldwork, institutionally sponsored loans, and tuition waivers (partial) available. Support available to part-time students. Financial award application deadline: 2/15; financial award applicants required to submit FAFSA. *Unit head:* Dr. Monica McKinney, Graduate Program Manager, 919-760-8056, Fax: 919-760-2303, E-mail: mckinneym@meredith.edu. *Application contact:* Dr. Monica McKinney, Graduate Program Manager, 919-760-8056, Fax: 919-760-2303, E-mail: mckinneym@meredith.edu. Website: https://www.meredith.edu/school-of-education-health-and-human-sciences

Messiah College, Program in Education, Mechanicsburg, PA 17055. Offers curriculum and instruction (M Ed); special education (M Ed); teaching English to speakers of other languages (M Ed). *Program availability:* Part-time, online learning. Electronic applications accepted. *Faculty research:* Socio-cultural perspectives on education, TESOL, autism, special education.

Metropolitan College of New York, Program in Childhood/Special Education, New York, NY 10006. Offers dual childhood 1-6 special education (MS). *Accreditation:* NCATE. *Entrance requirements:* For master's, GRE or MAT, minimum GPA of 3.0, 2 letters of reference, interview, resume. Additional exam requirements/recommendations for international students: Required—TOEFL (minimum score 550 paper-based; 80 iBT), IELTS (minimum score 6.5). Electronic applications accepted. *Expenses:* Contact institution. *Faculty research:* Classroom management, learner autonomy, teacher research, math and gender, intelligence.

Metropolitan State University, School of Urban Education, St. Paul, MN 55106-5000. Offers curriculum, pedagogy and schooling (MS); English as a second language (MS); secondary education (MS), including English teaching, life sciences teaching, mathematics teaching, social studies teaching; special education (MS).

Metropolitan State University of Denver, School of Education, Denver, CO 80204. Offers elementary education (MAT); special education (MAT). *Expenses:* Contact institution.

Michigan State University, The Graduate School, College of Education, Department of Counseling, Educational Psychology and Special Education, East Lansing, MI 48824. Offers counseling (MA); educational psychology and educational technology (PhD); educational technology (MA); measurement and quantitative methods (PhD); rehabilitation counseling (MA); rehabilitation counselor education (PhD); school psychology (MA, PhD, Ed S); special education (MA, PhD). *Accreditation:* APA (one or more programs are accredited); CORE (one or more programs are accredited). *Program availability:* Part-time. *Entrance requirements:* Additional exam requirements/recommendations for international students: Required—TOEFL. Electronic applications accepted.

Middle Tennessee State University, College of Graduate Studies, College of Education, Department of Elementary and Special Education, Major in Special Education, Murfreesboro, TN 37132. Offers M Ed. *Accreditation:* NCATE. *Program availability:* Part-time, evening/weekend, online learning. *Degree requirements:* For master's, comprehensive exam. *Entrance requirements:* For master's, GRE, MAT or PRAXIS. Additional exam requirements/recommendations for international students: Required—TOEFL (minimum score 525 paper-based; 71 iBT) or IELTS (minimum score 6). Electronic applications accepted.

Midwestern State University, Billie Doris McAda Graduate School, West College of Education, Program in Special Education, Wichita Falls, TX 76308. Offers M Ed. *Program availability:* Part-time, evening/weekend. *Degree requirements:* For master's, comprehensive exam. *Entrance requirements:* For master's, GRE General Test, MAT, or GMAT, Texas teacher certificate or equivalent minimum GPA of 3.0 in previous education courses. Additional exam requirements/recommendations for international students: Required—TOEFL (minimum score 550 paper-based). Electronic applications accepted. *Faculty research:* Fragile-X syndrome, phenylketonuria and other causes of handicapping conditions, autism, social development of students with disabilities.

Millersville University of Pennsylvania, College of Graduate Studies and Adult Learning, College of Education and Human Services, Department of Early, Middle, and Exceptional Education, Program in Special Education: 7-12 Option, Millersville, PA 17551-0302. Offers M Ed. *Program availability:* Part-time, evening/weekend, online only, 100% online. *Faculty:* 10 full-time (6 women), 13 part-time/adjunct (9 women). *Students:* 1 full-time (0 women). Average age 27. *Degree requirements:* For master's, thesis (for some programs). *Entrance requirements:* For master's, GRE or MAT, teaching certificate; interview; 3 current professional letters of recommendation. Additional exam requirements/recommendations for international students: Required—TOEFL, IELTS (minimum score 6), PTE (minimum score 60). *Application deadline:* Applications are processed on a rolling basis. Application fee: $40. Electronic applications accepted. *Expenses: Tuition, area resident:* full-time $9288; part-time $516 per credit. Tuition, state resident: full-time $9288; part-time $516 per credit. Tuition, nonresident: full-time $13,932; part-time $774 per credit. *International tuition:* $13,932 full-time. *Required fees:* $2623.50; $145.75 per credit. Tuition and fees vary according to course load, degree level and program. *Financial support:* Unspecified assistantships available. Financial award application deadline: 3/15; financial award applicants required to submit FAFSA. *Faculty research:* Co-teaching, needs of new teachers, use of popular culture in education. *Unit head:* Dr. Rich Mehrenberg, Department Chair, 717-871-7344, E-mail: richard.mehrenberg@millersville.edu. *Application contact:* Dr. James A. Delle, Acting Dean of College of Graduate Studies and Adult Learning/Associate Provost, Academic Administration, 717-871-7462, E-mail: James.Delle@millersville.edu. Website: https://www.millersville.edu/edfoundations/m_ed_sped.php

Millersville University of Pennsylvania, College of Graduate Studies and Adult Learning, College of Education and Human Services, Department of Early, Middle, and Exceptional Education, Program in Special Education: PreK-8 Option, Millersville, PA 17551-0302. Offers M Ed. *Program availability:* Part-time, evening/weekend, online only, 100% online. *Faculty:* 10 full-time (6 women), 13 part-time/adjunct (9 women). *Students:* 1 full-time (0 women), 4 part-time (all women). Average age 27. 2 applicants, 100% accepted, 1 enrolled. In 2018, 1 master's awarded. *Degree requirements:* For master's, thesis (for some programs). *Entrance requirements:* For master's, GRE or MAT, Teaching certificate, interview, 3 current professional letters of recommendation. Additional exam requirements/recommendations for international students: Required—TOEFL, IELTS (minimum score 6), PTE (minimum score 60). *Application deadline:* Applications are processed on a rolling basis. Application fee: $40. Electronic applications accepted. *Expenses: Tuition, area resident:* full-time $9288; part-time $516 per credit. Tuition, state resident: full-time $9288; part-time $516 per credit. Tuition, nonresident: full-time $13,932; part-time $774 per credit. *International tuition:* $13,932 full-time. *Required fees:* $2623.50; $145.75 per credit. Tuition and fees vary according to course load, degree level and program. *Financial support:* Unspecified assistantships available. Financial award application deadline: 3/15; financial award applicants required to submit FAFSA. *Faculty research:* Co-teaching, needs of new teachers, use of popular culture in education. *Unit head:* Dr. Rich Mehrenberg, Department Chair, 717-871-7344, E-mail: richard.mehrenberg@millersville.edu. *Application contact:* Dr. James A. Delle, Acting Dean of College of Graduate Studies and Adult Learning/Associate Provost, Academic Administration, 717-871-7462, E-mail: James.Delle@millersville.edu. Website: https://www.millersville.edu/edfoundations/m_ed_sped.php

Milligan College, Area of Education, Milligan College, TN 37682. Offers combined preK-3/K-5 education (M Ed); educational leadership (Ed D); educational specialist (Ed S); K-5 education (M Ed); middle grades education (M Ed); preK-3 education (M Ed); preK-3 special education (M Ed); secondary education (M Ed). *Accreditation:* NCATE. *Program availability:* Part-time, 100% online, blended/hybrid learning. *Faculty:* 5 full-time (3 women), 6 part-time/adjunct (3 women). *Students:* 38 full-time (31 women), 8 part-time (4 women); includes 2 minority (1 Hispanic/Latino; 1 Two or more races, non-Hispanic/Latino), 1 international. Average age 35. 36 applicants, 97% accepted, 32

enrolled. In 2018, 18 master's awarded. *Degree requirements:* For master's, thesis, portfolio, research project; for doctorate, thesis/dissertation, portfolio, research project. *Entrance requirements:* For master's, MAT, GRE General Test, ACT, SAT, or PRAXIS, undergraduate degree and supporting transcripts, professional recommendations, interview; for doctorate, MAT or GRE, master's degree and supporting transcripts, demonstrated scholastic ability, recognized leadership role within education, professional recommendations, essay/personal statement, portfolio (professional development plan, evidence of ability, knowledge and qualities), interview. Additional exam requirements/recommendations for international students: Required—TOEFL (minimum score 550 paper-based, 79 iBT) or IELTS (6.5). *Application deadline:* For fall admission, 8/1 priority date for domestic students, 6/1 for international students; for spring admission, 11/15 priority date for domestic students, 12/1 for international students; for summer admission, 4/1 for domestic students. Applications are processed on a rolling basis. Application fee: $30. Electronic applications accepted. *Expenses:* $365 per hour (for masters); $485 per hour (for doctoral); $375 fees per semester; $75 one-time records fee. *Financial support:* Scholarships/grants available. Financial award application deadline: 12/1; financial award applicants required to submit FAFSA. *Faculty research:* Assessment; school mental health; literacy; technology; educator preparation. *Unit head:* Dr. Angela Hilton-Prillhart, Area Chair of Education, 423-461-8769, Fax: 423-461-3103, E-mail: anhilton-prillhart@milligan.edu. *Application contact:* Melissa Dillow, Graduate Admissions Recruiter, Education, 423-461-8306, Fax: 423-461-8982, E-mail: msdillow@milligan.edu.
Website: http://www.Milligan.edu/GPS

Minnesota State University Mankato, College of Graduate Studies and Research, College of Education, Department of Special Education, Mankato, MN 56001. Offers emotional and behavioral disorders (MS, Certificate); learning disabilities (MS, Certificate). *Accreditation:* NCATE. *Program availability:* Part-time, online learning. *Degree requirements:* For master's, comprehensive exam, thesis or alternative. *Entrance requirements:* For master's, Council for Exceptional Children pre-program assessment, minimum GPA of 3.2 during previous 2 years. Additional exam requirements/recommendations for international students: Required—TOEFL. Electronic applications accepted.

Minot State University, Graduate School, Program in Special Education, Minot, ND 58707-0002. Offers deaf/hard of hearing education (MS); specific learning disabilities (MS). *Accreditation:* NCATE. *Degree requirements:* For master's, comprehensive exam (for some programs), thesis (for some programs). *Entrance requirements:* For master's, minimum GPA of 2.75, bachelor's degree in education or related field, teacher licensure (for some concentrations). Additional exam requirements/recommendations for international students: Required—TOEFL (minimum score 79 iBT), IELTS (minimum score 6).

Misericordia University, College of Health Sciences and Education, Program in Education, Dallas, PA 18612-1098. Offers instructional technology (MS); reading specialist (MS); special education (MS). *Program availability:* Part-time, evening/weekend. *Entrance requirements:* For master's, minimum undergraduate GPA of 3.0. Additional exam requirements/recommendations for international students: Required—TOEFL. Electronic applications accepted.

Mississippi College, Graduate School, School of Education, Department of Teacher Education and Leadership, Clinton, MS 39058. Offers art (M Ed); biological science (M Ed); business education (M Ed); computer science (M Ed); dyslexia therapy (M Ed); educational leadership (M Ed, Ed D, Ed S); elementary education (M Ed, Ed S); English (M Ed); higher education administration (MS); mathematics (M Ed); secondary education (M Ed); social studies (history) (M Ed); teaching arts (M Ed). *Program availability:* Part-time, online learning. *Degree requirements:* For master's, comprehensive exam, thesis optional. *Entrance requirements:* For master's, NTE. Additional exam requirements/recommendations for international students: Recommended—TOEFL, IELTS. Electronic applications accepted.

Mississippi State University, College of Education, Department of Curriculum, Instruction and Special Education, Mississippi State, MS 39762. Offers early childhood education (PhD); elementary education (MS, PhD, Ed S), including early childhood education (MS), general elementary education (MS), middle level education (MS); general curriculum and instruction (PhD); reading education (PhD); secondary education (MAT, MS, PhD, Ed S); special education (MAT, MS, PhD, Ed S). *Accreditation:* NCATE. *Program availability:* Part-time, evening/weekend. *Faculty:* 20 full-time (14 women), 1 (woman) part-time/adjunct. *Students:* 24 full-time (16 women), 151 part-time (109 women); includes 44 minority (38 Black or African American, non-Hispanic/Latino; 3 American Indian or Alaska Native, non-Hispanic/Latino; 1 Hispanic/Latino; 2 Two or more races, non-Hispanic/Latino), 3 international. Average age 32. 65 applicants, 65% accepted, 38 enrolled. In 2018, 57 master's, 3 doctorates, 1 other advanced degree awarded. *Degree requirements:* For master's, comprehensive exam; for doctorate, thesis/dissertation; for Ed S, comprehensive exam, thesis or alternative. *Entrance requirements:* For master's, GRE, minimum GPA of 2.75 in junior and senior year, eligibility for initial teacher certification; for doctorate, GRE, minimum GPA of 3.4 on previous graduate work; for Ed S, GRE, minimum GPA of 3.2 on master's degree. Additional exam requirements/recommendations for international students: Required—TOEFL (minimum score 550 paper-based; 79 iBT); Recommended—IELTS (minimum score 6.5). *Application deadline:* For fall admission, 3/1 priority date for domestic students, 5/1 for international students; for spring admission, 9/1 priority date for domestic students, 9/1 for international students. Applications are processed on a rolling basis. Application fee: $60 ($80 for international students). Electronic applications accepted. *Expenses:* Tuition, state resident: full-time $8450; part-time $360.59 per credit hour. Tuition, nonresident: full-time $23,140; part-time $969.09 per credit hour. *Required fees:* $110. One-time fee: $55 full-time. Part-time tuition and fees vary according to course load, degree level, campus/location and reciprocity agreements. *Financial support:* In 2018–19, 5 research assistantships with partial tuition reimbursements (averaging $11,453 per year), 1 teaching assistantship (averaging $11,700 per year) were awarded; Federal Work-Study, institutionally sponsored loans, scholarships/grants, and unspecified assistantships also available. Financial award application deadline: 4/1; financial award applicants required to submit FAFSA. *Faculty research:* Early childhood education, reading, rural schools, multicultural education, use of technology in instruction. *Unit head:* Dr. Linda Cornelious, Professor and Head, 662-325-3747, Fax: 662-325-7857, E-mail: lcornelious@colled.msstate.edu. *Application contact:* Robbie Salters, Admissions and Enrollment Assistant, 662-325-7400, E-mail: rsalters@grad.msstate.edu.
Website: http://www.cise.msstate.edu/

Missouri State University, Graduate College, College of Education, Department of Counseling, Leadership, and Special Education, Program in Special Education, Springfield, MO 65897. Offers MS Ed. *Program availability:* Part-time, evening/weekend, 100% online, blended/hybrid learning. *Faculty:* 7 full-time (6 women), 3 part-time/adjunct (2 women). *Students:* 4 full-time (all women), 66 part-time (52 women); includes 2 minority (1 Black or African American, non-Hispanic/Latino; 1 Two or more races, non-Hispanic/Latino), 1 international. Average age 26. 46 applicants, 98% accepted. In 2018, 21 master's awarded. *Degree requirements:* For master's, comprehensive exam, thesis or alternative. *Entrance requirements:* For master's, GRE or minimum GPA of 3.0, teaching certificate. Additional exam requirements/recommendations for international students: Required—TOEFL (minimum score 550 paper-based; 79 iBT), IELTS (minimum score 6). *Application deadline:* For fall admission, 7/20 priority date for domestic students, 5/1 for international students; for spring admission, 12/20 priority date for domestic students, 9/1 for international students; for summer admission, 5/20 priority date for domestic students. Applications are processed on a rolling basis. Application fee: $55 ($60 for international students). Electronic applications accepted. Tuition and fees vary according to class time, course level, course load, degree level, campus/location, program and student level. *Financial support:* Federal Work-Study, institutionally sponsored loans, scholarships/grants, and unspecified assistantships available. Financial award application deadline: 1/31; financial award applicants required to submit FAFSA. *Unit head:* Dr. James Satterfield, Department Head, 417-836-5392, Fax: 417-836-4918, E-mail: spe@missouristate.edu. *Application contact:* Lakan Drinker, Director, Graduate Enrollment Management, 417-836-5300, Fax: 417-836-5980, E-mail: lakandrinker@missouristate.edu.
Website: http://education.missouristate.edu/sped/

Missouri Western State University, Program in Assessment, St. Joseph, MO 64507-2294. Offers K-12 cross-categorical special education (MAS); TESOL (Graduate Certificate). *Program availability:* Part-time. *Students:* 1 (woman) full-time, 33 part-time (32 women); includes 3 minority (2 American Indian or Alaska Native, non-Hispanic/Latino; 1 Asian, non-Hispanic/Latino). Average age 40. 16 applicants, 100% accepted, 8 enrolled. In 2018, 12 master's, 4 other advanced degrees awarded. *Entrance requirements:* For master's, minimum GPA of 2.75. Additional exam requirements/recommendations for international students: Recommended—TOEFL (minimum score 79 iBT), IELTS (minimum score 6). *Application deadline:* For fall admission, 7/15 for domestic and international students; for spring admission, 11/1 for domestic and international students; for summer admission, 4/29 for domestic and international students. Applications are processed on a rolling basis. Application fee: $45 ($50 for international students). Electronic applications accepted. *Expenses: Tuition, area resident:* Part-time $359.39 per credit hour. Tuition, state resident: part-time $359.39 per credit hour. Tuition, nonresident: part-time $643.39 per credit hour. Tuition and fees vary according to program. *Financial support:* Scholarships/grants and unspecified assistantships available. Support available to part-time students. *Unit head:* Dr. Susan Bashinski, Dean of Graduate Programs, 816-271-4394, E-mail: graduate@missouriwestern.edu. *Application contact:* Dr. Susan Bashinski, Dean of Graduate Programs, 816-271-4394, Fax: 816-271-4525, E-mail: graduate@missouriwestern.edu.
Website: https://www.missouriwestern.edu/graduate/

Molloy College, Graduate Education Program, Rockville Centre, NY 11571-5002. Offers adolescent education in biology (MS); adolescent special education (Advanced Certificate); bilingual extension (Advanced Certificate); childhood education (MS); childhood special education (Advanced Certificate); early childhood education (MS); educational technology (MS); English (MS); mathematics (MS); social studies (MS); Spanish (MS); special education on both childhood and adolescent levels (MS); teaching English to speakers of other languages (TESOL) in grades pre-K to 12 (MS); TESOL (Advanced Certificate). *Accreditation:* NCATE. *Program availability:* Part-time, evening/weekend. *Faculty:* 24 full-time (22 women), 26 part-time/adjunct (19 women). *Students:* 106 full-time (78 women), 203 part-time (154 women); includes 65 minority (14 Black or African American, non-Hispanic/Latino; 5 Asian, non-Hispanic/Latino; 41 Hispanic/Latino; 5 Two or more races, non-Hispanic/Latino). Average age 41. 147 applicants, 63% accepted, 79 enrolled. In 2018, 120 master's, 1 other advanced degree awarded. *Entrance requirements:* Additional exam requirements/recommendations for international students: Required—TOEFL (minimum score 550 paper-based; 79 iBT). *Application deadline:* Applications are processed on a rolling basis. Application fee: $60. Electronic applications accepted. *Expenses: Tuition:* Full-time $20,790; part-time $1155 per credit. *Required fees:* $1060; $900. Tuition and fees vary according to course load and degree level. *Financial support:* Application deadline: 3/1; applicants required to submit FAFSA. *Faculty research:* English Language Learners; social emotional needs of students; gifted education; cultural diversity; collaborative teaching methods. *Unit head:* Joanne O'Brien, Dean, 516-323-3116, E-mail: jobrien@molloy.edu. *Application contact:* Faye Hood, Assistant Director for Admissions, 516-323-4009, E-mail: fhood@molloy.edu.

Monmouth University, Graduate Studies, School of Education, West Long Branch, NJ 07764-1898. Offers applied behavior analysis (Certificate); autism (Certificate); director of school counseling services (Post-Master's Certificate); early childhood (M Ed); educational leadership (Ed D); elementary education (MAT), including elementary level, secondary level; English as a second language (M Ed); learning disabilities teacher-consultant (Post-Master's Certificate); literacy (MS Ed); school counseling (MS Ed); special education (MS Ed), including autism, learning disabilities teacher-consultant, teacher of students with disabilities, teaching in inclusive settings; speech-language pathology (MS Ed); student affairs and college counseling (MS Ed); supervisor (Post-Master's Certificate); teaching English to speakers of other languages (Certificate). *Accreditation:* NCATE. *Program availability:* Part-time, evening/weekend, 100% online, blended/hybrid learning. *Faculty:* 29 full-time (23 women), 32 part-time/adjunct (24 women). *Students:* 214 full-time (187 women), 148 part-time (127 women); includes 60 minority (13 Black or African American, non-Hispanic/Latino; 2 Asian, non-Hispanic/Latino; 40 Hispanic/Latino; 5 Two or more races, non-Hispanic/Latino). Average age 27. In 2018, 108 master's, 9 other advanced degrees awarded. *Entrance requirements:* For master's, GRE taken within last 5 years (for MS Ed in speech-language pathology); SAT (minimum combined score of 1660 in 3 sections), ACT (23), GRE (minimum score of 4.0 on analytical writing section and minimum combined score of 310 on quantitative and verbal sections), or passing scores on 3 parts of Core Academic Skills Educators, minimum GPA of 3.0 in major; 2 letters of recommendation (for some programs); resume, personal statement or essay (depending on program). Additional exam requirements/recommendations for international students: Required—TOEFL (minimum score 550 paper-based; 79 iBT), IELTS (minimum score 6), Michigan English Language Assessment Battery (minimum score 77) or Certificate of Advanced English (minimum score 160). *Application deadline:* For fall admission, 7/15 priority date for domestic students, 7/1 for international students; for spring admission, 12/1 priority date for domestic students, 11/1 for international students; for summer admission, 5/1 for domestic students. Applications are processed on a rolling basis. Application fee: $50. Electronic applications accepted. *Expenses: Tuition:* Part-time $1233 per credit. *Required fees:* $178 per term. *Financial support:* In 2018–19, 290 students received support. Institutionally sponsored loans, scholarships/grants, and unspecified assistantships available. Support available to part-time students. Financial award applicants required to submit FAFSA. *Faculty research:* Multicultural literacy, science and mathematics teaching strategies, teacher as reflective practitioner, children with disabilities. *Unit head:* Dr. John E. Henning, Dean, 732-263-5513, Fax: 732-263-5277, E-mail: kodonnel@monmouth.edu. *Application contact:* Kirsten Sneeringer, Graduate Admission Counselor, 732-571-3452, Fax: 732-263-5123, E-mail: gradadm@monmouth.edu.
Website: http://www.monmouth.edu/academics/schools/education/default.asp

Montana State University Billings, College of Education, Department of Educational Theory and Practice, Program in Special Education, Billings, MT 59101. Offers advanced studies (MS Sp Ed); applied behavior analysis (MS Sp Ed); generalist

(MS Sp Ed). *Accreditation:* NCATE. *Program availability:* Part-time. *Degree requirements:* For master's, thesis or professional paper and/or field experience. *Entrance requirements:* For master's, GRE General Test or MAT, minimum GPA of 3.0. Additional exam requirements/recommendations for international students: Required—TOEFL (minimum score 79 iBT), IELTS (minimum score 6.5). Electronic applications accepted.

Montclair State University, The Graduate School, College of Education and Human Services, Program in Inclusive Early Childhood Education, Montclair, NJ 07043-1624. Offers M Ed. *Degree requirements:* For master's, comprehensive exam, thesis or alternative. *Entrance requirements:* For master's, GRE General Test, interview, 2 letters of recommendation. Additional exam requirements/recommendations for international students: Required—TOEFL (minimum score 83 iBT), IELTS (minimum score 6.5). Electronic applications accepted.

Morehead State University, Graduate School, College of Education, Department of Early Childhood, Elementary and Special Education, Morehead, KY 40351. Offers learning and behavioral disorders P-12 (MAT); moderate and severe disabilities P-12 (MAT). *Program availability:* Part-time, evening/weekend. *Degree requirements:* For master's, thesis. *Entrance requirements:* For master's, GRE or PRAXIS II content exam, minimum overall undergraduate GPA of 2.5. Additional exam requirements/ recommendations for international students: Required—TOEFL (minimum score 500 paper-based). Electronic applications accepted.

Morehead State University, Graduate School, College of Education, Department of Foundational and Graduate Studies in Education, Morehead, KY 40351. Offers adult and higher education (MA, Ed S); certified professional counselor (Ed S); counseling P-12 (MA); curriculum and instruction (Ed S); educational technology (MA Ed); instructional leadership (Ed S); school administration (MA); school counseling (Ed S); teacher leader business and marketing content (MA Ed); teacher leader business and marketing technology (MA Ed); teacher leader educational technology (MA Ed); teacher leader English (MA Ed); teacher leader gifted education (MA Ed); teacher leader IECE certification (MA Ed); teacher leader interdisciplinary education P-5 (MA Ed); teacher leader middle grades (MA Ed); teacher leader non IECE certification (MA Ed); teacher leader reading/writing - non-certification (MA Ed); teacher leader reading/writing certification (MA Ed); teacher leader school communication - certification (MA Ed); teacher leader school communication - non-certification (MA Ed); teacher leader social studies (MA Ed); teacher leader special education (MA Ed). *Accreditation:* NCATE. *Program availability:* Part-time, evening/weekend. *Degree requirements:* For master's, thesis optional, oral and/or written comprehensive exams; for Ed S, thesis, oral exam. *Entrance requirements:* For master's, GRE General Test, minimum overall undergraduate GPA of 2.5; for Ed S, GRE General Test, interview, master's degree, minimum GPA of 3.5, work experience. Additional exam requirements/ recommendations for international students: Required—TOEFL (minimum score 500 paper-based). Electronic applications accepted. *Faculty research:* Character education, school accountability, computer applications for school administrators.

Morningside College, Graduate Programs, Sharon Walker School of Education, Sioux City, IA 51106. Offers professional educator (MAT); special education (MAT), including instructional strategist: mild/moderate (7-12), instructional strategist: mild/moderate (K-6), K-12 instructional strategist: behavior disorders/learning disabilities, K-12 instructional strategist: mental disabilities. *Program availability:* Part-time, online only, 100% online. *Entrance requirements:* For master's, writing sample. Electronic applications accepted. *Expenses:* Contact institution.

Mount Mercy University, Program in Education, Cedar Rapids, IA 52402-4797. Offers reading (MA Ed); special education (MA Ed); teacher leadership (MA Ed). *Entrance requirements:* For master's, minimum cumulative GPA of 3.0, 2 letters of recommendation, resume, valid teaching license. Additional exam requirements/recommendations for international students: Required—TOEFL (minimum score 570 paper-based; 88 iBT). Electronic applications accepted.

Mount St. Joseph University, Graduate Education Program, Cincinnati, OH 45233-1670. Offers adolescent to young adult education (MA); dyslexia (Certificate); inclusive early childhood education (MA); middle childhood education (MA); multicultural special education (MA); reading science (MA). *Accreditation:* TEAC. *Program availability:* Part-time, evening/weekend, 100% online, blended/hybrid learning. *Degree requirements:* For master's, comprehensive exam, thesis, research project, student teaching, clinical and field-based experiences. *Entrance requirements:* For master's, GRE (if GPA is below 3.0), letter of intent, 2 referrals, background check, interview, resume, minimum undergraduate GPA of 3.0. Additional exam requirements/recommendations for international students: Required—TOEFL (minimum score 560 paper-based; 83 iBT). Electronic applications accepted. *Expenses:* Contact institution. *Faculty research:* Foreign and second language learning problems/reading disabilities, multicultural/ bilingual special education, science education, pedagogical content knowledge, early childhood, response to intervention.

Mount Saint Mary College, Division of Education, Newburgh, NY 12550-3494. Offers adolescence and special education (MS Ed); childhood education (MS Ed); literacy education (MS Ed); middle school (7-9) (MS Ed). *Accreditation:* NCATE. *Program availability:* Part-time, evening/weekend. *Faculty:* 7 full-time (6 women), 7 part-time/ adjunct (all women). *Students:* 19 full-time (14 women), 78 part-time (64 women); includes 7 minority (5 Hispanic/Latino; 1 Native Hawaiian or other Pacific Islander, non-Hispanic/Latino; 1 Two or more races, non-Hispanic/Latino). Average age 28. 31 applicants, 61% accepted, 17 enrolled. In 2018, 28 master's awarded. *Entrance requirements:* Additional exam requirements/recommendations for international students: Required—TOEFL (minimum score 80 iBT). *Application deadline:* Applications are processed on a rolling basis. Application fee: $45. Electronic applications accepted. Application fee is waived when completed online. *Expenses:* Tuition: Full-time $14,454; part-time $803 per credit. *Required fees:* $172; $86 per semester. *Financial support:* In 2018–19, 17 students received support. Institutionally sponsored loans, scholarships/ grants, and unspecified assistantships available. Financial award application deadline: 4/15; financial award applicants required to submit FAFSA. *Faculty research:* Learning and teaching styles, computers in special education, language development. *Unit head:* Dr. Vicki Caruana, Graduate Coordinator, 845-569-3530, Fax: 845-569-3551, E-mail: Victoria.caruana@msmc.edu. *Application contact:* Eileen Bardney, Director of Admissions, 845-569-3254, Fax: 845-569-3438, E-mail: Eileen.Bardney@msmc.edu. Website: http://www.msmc.edu/Academics/Graduate_Programs/ Master_of_Science_in_Education

Mount Saint Vincent University, Graduate Programs, Faculty of Education, Program in Educational Psychology, Halifax, NS B3M 2J6, Canada. Offers education of the blind or visually impaired (M Ed); education of the deaf or hard of hearing (M Ed); educational psychology (MA-R); evaluation (M Ed); human relations (M Ed). *Program availability:* Part-time, evening/weekend, online learning. *Degree requirements:* For master's, thesis (for some programs). *Entrance requirements:* For master's, bachelor's degree in related field, 1 year of teaching experience. Electronic applications accepted. *Faculty research:* Personality measurement, values reasoning, aggression and sexuality, power and control, quantitative and qualitative research methodologies.

Murray State University, College of Education and Human Services, Department of Adolescent, Career, and Special Education, Murray, KY 42071. Offers career and technical education (MS); middle school teacher leader (MA Ed); secondary teacher leader (MA Ed); special education (MA Ed), including mild learning and behavior disorders, moderate to severe disabilities (P-12), teacher leader in special education learning and behavior disorders; teacher education and professional development (Ed S). *Accreditation:* NCATE. *Program availability:* Part-time. *Entrance requirements:* For master's and Ed S, GRE or GMAT, minimum university GPA of 2.75. Additional exam requirements/recommendations for international students: Required—TOEFL (minimum score 527 paper-based; 71 iBT). Electronic applications accepted.

National Louis University, National College of Education, Chicago, IL 60603. Offers administration and supervision (M Ed, Ed D, CAS, Ed S); curriculum and instruction (M Ed, MS Ed, CAS); early childhood administration (M Ed, CAS); early childhood education (M Ed, MAT, MS Ed, CAS); education (Ed D); educational psychology/human learning and development (M Ed, MS Ed, CAS, Ed S); elementary education (MAT); interdisciplinary curriculum and instruction (M Ed); mathematics education (M Ed, MS Ed, CAS); middle grades education (MAT); reading and language (M Ed, MS Ed, CAS); school psychology (M Ed, Ed S); science education (M Ed, MS Ed, CAS); secondary education (MAT); special education (M Ed, MAT, CAS); technology in education (M Ed, CAS). *Accreditation:* NCATE. *Program availability:* Part-time, evening/ weekend. *Degree requirements:* For doctorate, comprehensive exam, thesis/ dissertation. *Entrance requirements:* For master's, MAT or GRE, minimum GPA of 3.0; for doctorate, GRE General Test, minimum GPA of 3.25, interview, resume, writing sample, 4 recommendations. Additional exam requirements/recommendations for international students: Required—TOEFL (minimum score 550 paper-based; 79 iBT).

National University, Sanford College of Education, La Jolla, CA 92037-1011. Offers advanced teaching practices (MS); applied behavior analysis (MS); applied school leadership (MS); e-teaching and learning (Certificate); education (MA); educational administration (MS); educational and instructional technology (MS); educational counseling (MS); higher education administration (MS); inspired teaching and learning (M Ed); school psychology (MS); special education (MA, MS). *Program availability:* Part-time, evening/weekend, 100% online, blended/hybrid learning. *Degree requirements:* For master's, thesis (for some programs). *Entrance requirements:* For master's, interview, minimum GPA of 2.5. Additional exam requirements/recommendations for international students: Required—TOEFL (minimum score 550 paper-based; 79 iBT), IELTS (minimum score 6). Electronic applications accepted. *Expenses: Tuition:* Full-time $10,320; part-time $430 per unit. Tuition and fees vary according to degree level. *Faculty research:* Teacher education, special education, educational effectiveness, teaching abroad, school counseling.

National University College, Graduate Programs, Bayamón, PR 00960. Offers digital marketing (MBA); general business (MBA); special education (M Ed).

Neumann University, Graduate Program in Education, Aston, PA 19014-1298. Offers education (MS), including administrative certification (school principal PK-12), autism, early elementary education, secondary education, special education. *Program availability:* Part-time, evening/weekend, 100% online, blended/hybrid learning. *Entrance requirements:* For master's, official transcripts from all institutions attended, letter of intent, three professional references, copy of any teaching certifications. Additional exam requirements/recommendations for international students: Required—TOEFL (minimum score 70 iBT). Electronic applications accepted. *Expenses:* Contact institution.

New England College, Program in Education, Henniker, NH 03242-3293. Offers higher education administration (MS, Ed D); K-12 leadership (Ed D); literacy and language arts (M Ed); meeting the needs of all learners/special education (M Ed); teacher leadership/ school reform (M Ed). *Program availability:* Part-time, evening/weekend.

New Jersey City University, Debra Cannon Partridge Wolfe College of Education, Department of Special Education, Jersey City, NJ 07305-1597. Offers MA. *Accreditation:* TEAC. *Program availability:* Part-time, evening/weekend. *Entrance requirements:* Additional exam requirements/recommendations for international students: Required—TOEFL (minimum score 79 iBT). *Faculty research:* Mainstreaming the handicapped child and the autistic child.

New Mexico Highlands University, Graduate Studies, School of Education, Las Vegas, NM 87701. Offers curriculum and instruction (MA); educational leadership (MA); professional counseling (MA); special education (MA). *Accreditation:* NCATE. *Program availability:* Part-time. *Degree requirements:* For master's, comprehensive exam, thesis or alternative. *Entrance requirements:* For master's, minimum undergraduate GPA of 3.0. Additional exam requirements/recommendations for international students: Required—TOEFL (minimum score 540 paper-based). *Faculty research:* Middle school curriculum, integrated computer applications for pre-service classroom teachers, adolescent literacy, narrative cognitive modes in New Mexico multicultural setting, math and math education.

New York University, Steinhardt School of Culture, Education, and Human Development, Department of Teaching and Learning, Program in Early Childhood and Childhood Education, New York, NY 10012. Offers childhood education (MA); early childhood education (MA); early childhood education/early childhood special education (MA). *Accreditation:* TEAC. *Program availability:* Part-time. *Degree requirements:* For master's, thesis (for some programs). *Entrance requirements:* Additional exam requirements/recommendations for international students: Required—TOEFL (minimum score 100 iBT). Electronic applications accepted. *Faculty research:* Teacher evaluation and beliefs about teaching, early literacy development, language arts, child development and education, cultural differences.

New York University, Steinhardt School of Culture, Education, and Human Development, Department of Teaching and Learning, Program in Special Education, New York, NY 10012-1019. Offers childhood (MA); early childhood (MA). *Accreditation:* TEAC. *Program availability:* Part-time. *Entrance requirements:* Additional exam requirements/recommendations for international students: Required—TOEFL (minimum score 100 iBT). Electronic applications accepted. *Faculty research:* Special education referrals, attention deficit disorders in children, mainstreaming, curriculum-based assessment and program implementation, special education policy.

Niagara University, Graduate Division of Education, Concentration in Teacher Education, Niagara University, NY 14109. Offers early childhood and childhood education (MS Ed, Certificate); early childhood special education (MS); middle and adolescence education (MS Ed); special education (MS Ed), including 1-6, 7-12; special education (grades 1-12) (Certificate); teaching English to speakers of other languages (MS Ed, Certificate). *Accreditation:* NCATE. *Students:* 106 full-time (75 women), 105 part-time (90 women); includes 15 minority (5 Black or African American, non-Hispanic/ Latino; 2 American Indian or Alaska Native, non-Hispanic/Latino; 2 Asian, non-Hispanic/ Latino; 2 Hispanic/Latino; 4 Two or more races, non-Hispanic/Latino), 40 international. Average age 28. In 2018, 81 master's, 21 other advanced degrees awarded. *Entrance requirements:* For master's, GRE General Test or Academic Literacy Skills Test (ALST). Additional exam requirements/recommendations for international students: Required—TOEFL (minimum score 550 paper-based; 79 iBT), IELTS (minimum score 6). *Application deadline:* For fall admission, 8/1 for domestic students. Applications are

processed on a rolling basis. Electronic applications accepted. *Expenses:* Contact institution. *Financial support:* Research assistantships with tuition reimbursements, teaching assistantships with tuition reimbursements, career-related internships or fieldwork, Federal Work-Study, scholarships/grants, and unspecified assistantships available. Support available to part-time students. Financial award application deadline: 4/15; financial award applicants required to submit FAFSA. *Unit head:* Dr. Chandra Foote, Dean, College of Education, 716-286-8549, E-mail: cjf@niagara.edu. *Application contact:* Evan Pierce, Associate Director, Graduate Studies, 716-286-8327, E-mail: epierce@niagara.edu.
Website: http://www.niagara.edu/teacher-education

Norfolk State University, School of Graduate Studies, School of Education, Department of Special Education, Norfolk, VA 23504. Offers severe disabilities (MA). *Accreditation:* NCATE. *Program availability:* Part-time. *Degree requirements:* For master's, thesis or alternative. *Entrance requirements:* For master's, minimum GPA of 3.0 in major, 2.5 overall.

North Carolina Central University, School of Education, Special Education Program, Durham, NC 27707-3129. Offers emotional disabilities (M Ed, MAT); learning disabilities (M Ed, MAT); visual impairment (M Ed, MAT). *Accreditation:* NCATE. *Program availability:* Part-time, evening/weekend. *Degree requirements:* For master's, comprehensive exam, thesis or alternative. *Entrance requirements:* For master's, GRE, minimum GPA of 3.0 in major, 2.5 overall. Additional exam requirements/recommendations for international students: Required—TOEFL.

North Carolina State University, Graduate School, College of Education, Department of Teacher Education and Learning Sciences, Program in Special Education, Raleigh, NC 27695. Offers M Ed, MS. *Accreditation:* NCATE. *Degree requirements:* For master's, thesis optional. *Entrance requirements:* For master's, GRE General Test, MAT, minimum GPA of 3.0 in major. Electronic applications accepted. *Faculty research:* Nature of disabilities, intervention research.

Northeastern Illinois University, College of Graduate Studies and Research, Daniel L. Goodwin College of Education, Program in Learning Behavior Specialist I, Chicago, IL 60625. Offers MA. *Entrance requirements:* For master's, bachelor's degree, minimum GPA of 2.75, two professional letters of recommendation. Electronic applications accepted.

Northeastern Illinois University, College of Graduate Studies and Research, Daniel L. Goodwin College of Education, Program in Learning Behavior Specialist II, Chicago, IL 60625. Offers MS. *Entrance requirements:* For master's, Illinois Test of Basic Skills (or equivalent), bachelor's degree; minimum GPA of 2.75 undergraduate, 3.0 graduate; writing sample; interview. Electronic applications accepted.

Northeastern State University, College of Education, Department of Curriculum and Instruction, Program in Special Education-Autism Spectrum Disorders, Tahlequah, OK 74464-2399. Offers M Ed. *Program availability:* Part-time. *Faculty:* 15 full-time (11 women), 2 part-time/adjunct (0 women). *Students:* 12 full-time (11 women), 32 part-time (27 women); includes 17 minority (5 American Indian or Alaska Native, non-Hispanic/Latino; 2 Asian, non-Hispanic/Latino; 2 Hispanic/Latino; 8 Two or more races, non-Hispanic/Latino), 1 international. Average age 36. In 2018, 17 master's awarded. *Degree requirements:* For master's, thesis. *Entrance requirements:* For master's, MAT or GRE. Additional exam requirements/recommendations for international students: Required—TOEFL. *Application deadline:* For fall admission, 6/1 priority date for domestic students. Applications are processed on a rolling basis. Application fee: $0 ($25 for international students). Electronic applications accepted. *Expenses: Tuition, area resident:* Full-time $4500; part-time $250 per credit hour. Tuition, state resident: full-time $4500; part-time $250 per credit hour. Tuition, nonresident: full-time $9999; part-time $555.50 per credit hour. *International tuition:* $9999 full-time. *Required fees:* $601.20; $33.40 per credit hour. *Financial support:* Teaching assistantships available. Financial award application deadline: 3/1. *Unit head:* Jarilyn Haney, Program Chair, 918-449-3786, E-mail: haneyjw@nsuok.edu. *Application contact:* Josh McCollum, Graduate Coordinator, 918-444-2093, E-mail: mccolluj@nsuok.edu.

Northeastern University, College of Professional Studies, Boston, MA 02115-5096. Offers applied nutrition (MS); college athletics administration (MSL); commerce and economic development (MS); corporate and organizational communication (MS); criminal justice (MS); digital media (MPS); elearning and instructional design (M Ed); elementary education (MAT); geographic information technology (MPS); global studies and international relations (MS); higher education administration (M Ed); homeland security (MA); human services (MS); informatics (MPS); leadership (MS); learning analytics (M Ed); learning and instruction (M Ed); nonprofit management (MS); professional sports administration (MSL); project management (MS); regulatory affairs for drugs, biologics, and medical devices (MS); respiratory care leadership (MS); special education (M Ed); technical communication (MS). *Program availability:* Part-time, evening/weekend, 100% online, blended/hybrid learning. Electronic applications accepted. *Expenses:* Contact institution.

Northern Arizona University, College of Education, Department of Educational Specialties, Flagstaff, AZ 86011. Offers autism spectrum disorders (Certificate); bilingual/multicultural education (M Ed), including bilingual, ESL; career and technical education (M Ed, Certificate); educational technology (M Ed, Certificate); English as a second language (Certificate); positive behavior support (Certificate); special education (M Ed), including early childhood special education, mild/moderate disabilities. *Program availability:* Part-time, 100% online, blended/hybrid learning. *Degree requirements:* For master's, variable foreign language requirement, comprehensive exam (for some programs), thesis (for some programs); for Certificate, comprehensive exam (for some programs). *Entrance requirements:* Additional exam requirements/recommendations for international students: Required—TOEFL (minimum score 80 iBT), IELTS (minimum score 6.5). Electronic applications accepted.

Northern Illinois University, Graduate School, College of Education, Department of Special and Early Education, De Kalb, IL 60115-2854. Offers curriculum and instruction (MS Ed); early childhood education (MS Ed); elementary education (MS Ed); special education (MS Ed). *Program availability:* Part-time, evening/weekend. *Faculty:* 22 full-time (14 women), 2 part-time/adjunct (both women). *Students:* 43 full-time (33 women), 87 part-time (70 women); includes 22 minority (5 Black or African American, non-Hispanic/Latino; 1 Asian, non-Hispanic/Latino; 12 Hispanic/Latino; 4 Two or more races, non-Hispanic/Latino), 3 international. Average age 32. 75 applicants, 77% accepted, 37 enrolled. In 2018, 41 master's awarded. *Degree requirements:* For master's, comprehensive exam, thesis optional. *Entrance requirements:* For master's, GRE General Test or MAT, minimum undergraduate GPA of 2.75. Additional exam requirements/recommendations for international students: Required—TOEFL (minimum score 550 paper-based). *Application deadline:* For fall admission, 6/1 for domestic students, 5/1 for international students; for spring admission, 11/1 for domestic students, 10/1 for international students. Applications are processed on a rolling basis. Application fee: $40. Electronic applications accepted. *Financial support:* In 2018–19, 17 research assistantships with full tuition reimbursements were awarded; fellowships with full tuition reimbursements, teaching assistantships with full tuition reimbursements, career-related internships or fieldwork, Federal Work-Study, scholarships/grants, tuition waivers (full), and unspecified assistantships also available. Support available to part-time students. Financial award applicants required to submit FAFSA. *Faculty research:* Teacher certification, stress reduction during student teaching, teaching history, portfolios in student teaching. *Unit head:* Gregory Conderman, Chair, 815-753-1619, E-mail: seed@niu.edu. *Application contact:* Gail Myers, Clerk, Graduate Advising, 815-753-0381, E-mail: gmyers@niu.edu.
Website: http://www.cedu.niu.edu/seed/

Northern Kentucky University, Office of Graduate Programs, College of Education and Human Services, Program in Teaching, Highland Heights, KY 41099. Offers education (Certificate); special education (Certificate); teaching (MAT). *Degree requirements:* For master's, comprehensive exam, thesis optional. *Entrance requirements:* For master's, GRE. Additional exam requirements/recommendations for international students: Required—TOEFL (minimum score 79 iBT); Recommended—IELTS (minimum score 6.5). Electronic applications accepted. *Faculty research:* Teacher education, classroom management.

Northern Michigan University, Office of Graduate Education and Research, College of Health Sciences and Professional Studies, School of Education, Leadership and Public Service, Marquette, MI 49855-5301. Offers administration and supervision (MAE); instruction (MAE); learning disabilities (MAE); postsecondary biology education (MS); reading education (MAE), including reading, reading specialist. *Accreditation:* TEAC. *Program availability:* Part-time, online learning. *Degree requirements:* For master's, thesis (for some programs). *Entrance requirements:* For master's, minimum GPA of 3.0. Additional exam requirements/recommendations for international students: Required—TOEFL (minimum score 550 paper-based; 79 iBT), IELTS (minimum score 6.5). Electronic applications accepted.

Northern Vermont University–Johnson, Program in Education, Johnson, VT 05656. Offers applied behavior analysis (MA Ed); curriculum and instruction (MA Ed); foundations of education (MA Ed); special education (MA Ed). *Program availability:* Part-time. *Degree requirements:* For master's, thesis or alternative, exit interview. *Entrance requirements:* For master's, interview. Additional exam requirements/recommendations for international students: Required—TOEFL. Electronic applications accepted.

Northern Vermont University–Lyndon, Graduate Programs in Education, Department of Education, Lyndonville, VT 05851. Offers curriculum and instruction (M Ed); reading specialist (M Ed); special education (M Ed); teaching and counseling (M Ed). *Program availability:* Part-time, evening/weekend. *Degree requirements:* For master's, exam or major field project. *Entrance requirements:* Additional exam requirements/recommendations for international students: Recommended—TOEFL (minimum score 500 paper-based).

Northwest Christian University, School of Education and Counseling, Eugene, OR 97401-3745. Offers clinical mental health counseling (MA); elementary teaching (MAT); English for speakers of other languages (MAT); physical education (MAT); school counseling (MA); secondary teaching (MAT); special education (MAT). *Program availability:* Part-time, evening/weekend, online learning. *Degree requirements:* For master's, thesis (for some programs). *Entrance requirements:* For master's, GRE or MAT, minimum undergraduate GPA of 3.0, interview, 2-3 page statement of purpose, two letters of recommendation, resume, background check. Additional exam requirements/recommendations for international students: Required—TOEFL (minimum score 550 paper-based; 80 iBT). Electronic applications accepted. *Expenses:* Contact institution.

Northwestern State University of Louisiana, Graduate Studies and Research, College of Education and Human Development, Program in Special Education, Natchitoches, LA 71497. Offers M Ed, MAT. *Degree requirements:* For master's, comprehensive exam, thesis (for some programs). *Entrance requirements:* For master's, GRE General Test. Additional exam requirements/recommendations for international students: Required—TOEFL. Electronic applications accepted.

Northwestern State University of Louisiana, Graduate Studies and Research, College of Education and Human Development, Programs in Educational Leadership and Instruction, Natchitoches, LA 71497. Offers counseling (Ed S); educational leadership (M Ed, Ed S); educational technology (Ed S); elementary teaching (Ed S); reading (Ed S); secondary teaching (Ed S); special education (Ed S). *Accreditation:* NASAD. *Degree requirements:* For master's, comprehensive exam, thesis (for some programs). *Entrance requirements:* For master's and Ed S, GRE General Test. Additional exam requirements/recommendations for international students: Required—TOEFL. Electronic applications accepted.

Northwest Missouri State University, Graduate School, School of Education, Maryville, MO 64468-6001. Offers early childhood education (MS Ed); education leadership (MS Ed), including elementary, K-12, secondary; educational leadership (Ed S), including elementary school principalship, secondary school principalship, superintendency; educational leadership and policy analysis (Ed D); elementary education (MS Ed); elementary mathematics (MS Ed); higher education leadership (MS); middle school education (MS Ed); reading (MS Ed); special education (MS Ed); teacher leadership (MS Ed); teaching English language learners (MS Ed). *Accreditation:* NCATE. *Program availability:* Part-time. *Faculty:* 26 full-time (16 women). *Students:* 109 full-time (87 women), 385 part-time (270 women); includes 30 minority (10 Black or African American, non-Hispanic/Latino; 2 American Indian or Alaska Native, non-Hispanic/Latino; 3 Asian, non-Hispanic/Latino; 12 Hispanic/Latino; 1 Native Hawaiian or other Pacific Islander, non-Hispanic/Latino; 2 Two or more races, non-Hispanic/Latino), 1 international. Average age 33. 210 applicants, 72% accepted, 142 enrolled. In 2018, 71 master's, 11 other advanced degrees awarded. *Degree requirements:* For master's, comprehensive exam; for Ed S, comprehensive exam, thesis. *Entrance requirements:* For master's, GRE General Test, writing sample; for Ed S, minimum graduate GPA of 3.25. Additional exam requirements/recommendations for international students: Required—TOEFL (minimum score 550 paper-based). *Application deadline:* For fall admission, 7/1 for domestic and international students; for spring admission, 11/15 for domestic and international students. Applications are processed on a rolling basis. Application fee: $0 ($75 for international students). Electronic applications accepted. *Expenses:* $389.11 in-state and $653.92 out-of-state per credit hour. *Financial support:* Research assistantships with full tuition reimbursements, teaching assistantships with full tuition reimbursements, and unspecified assistantships available. Financial award application deadline: 4/1; financial award applicants required to submit FAFSA. *Unit head:* Dr. Tim Wall, Director, 660-562-1179, E-mail: timwall@nwmissouri.edu. *Application contact:* Dr. Tim Wall, Director, 660-562-1179, E-mail: timwall@nwmissouri.edu.
Website: https://www.nwmissouri.edu/education/index.htm

Northwest Nazarene University, Graduate Education Program, Nampa, ID 83686-5897. Offers curriculum and instruction (M Ed); educational leadership (M Ed, Ed D, PhD, Ed S), including building administrator (M Ed, Ed S), director of special education (Ed S), leadership and organizational development (Ed S), superintendent (Ed S). *Accreditation:* ACA (one or more programs are accredited); NCATE. *Program availability:* Part-time, online only, 100% online, 2-week face-to-face residency (for doctoral programs). *Faculty:* 4 full-time (3 women), 18 part-time/adjunct (7 women). *Students:* 128 full-time (83 women), 59 part-time (37 women); includes 22 minority (3 Black or African American, non-Hispanic/Latino; 1 Asian, non-Hispanic/Latino; 3

Hispanic/Latino; 15 Two or more races, non-Hispanic/Latino), 1 international. Average age 44. 124 applicants, 84% accepted, 87 enrolled. In 2018, 37 master's, 18 doctorates, 28 other advanced degrees awarded. *Degree requirements:* For master's, comprehensive exam (for some programs), action research project; for doctorate, thesis/dissertation, Dissertation; for Ed S, comprehensive exam, research project. *Entrance requirements:* For master's, minimum undergraduate GPA of 3.0 overall or during final 30 semester credits, undergraduate degree, valid teaching certificate; for doctorate, Ed S or equivalent, minimum GPA of 3.5; for Ed S, undergraduate degree, valid teaching certificate. Additional exam requirements/recommendations for international students: Recommended—TOEFL. *Application deadline:* Applications are processed on a rolling basis. Application fee: $50. Electronic applications accepted. *Expenses:* Masters: $475 per credit, $95 technology fee per semester; EDS: $505 per credit, $95 technology fee per semester; PHD/EDD: $565 per credit, $520 dissertation fee, $95 technology fee per semester. *Financial support:* Application deadline: 1/15; applicants required to submit FAFSA. *Faculty research:* Action research, cooperative learning, accountability, institutional accreditation, personalized learning K-12. *Unit head:* Dr. Heidi Curtis, Chair, 208-467-8250, E-mail: hlcurtis@nnu.edu. *Application contact:* Charlene Brown, Admissions Counselor, 208-467-8492, Fax: 208-467-8384, E-mail: gradeducationinfo@nnu.edu.
Website: http://www.nnu.edu/graded/

Notre Dame College, Graduate Programs, South Euclid, OH 44121-4293. Offers mild/moderate needs (M Ed); reading (M Ed); security policy studies (MA, Graduate Certificate); technology (M Ed). *Program availability:* Part-time, evening/weekend. *Degree requirements:* For master's, thesis. *Entrance requirements:* For master's, GRE General Test, MAT, minimum undergraduate GPA of 2.75, valid teaching certificate, bachelor's degree in an education-related field from accredited college or university, official transcripts of most recent college work. *Faculty research:* Cognitive psychology, teaching critical thinking in the classroom.

Notre Dame de Namur University, Division of Academic Affairs, School of Education and Psychology, Program in Special Education, Belmont, CA 94002-1908. Offers MA. *Program availability:* Part-time, evening/weekend. *Students:* 8 full-time (5 women), 27 part-time (18 women); includes 18 minority (2 Black or African American, non-Hispanic/Latino; 2 Asian, non-Hispanic/Latino; 12 Hispanic/Latino; 2 Native Hawaiian or other Pacific Islander, non-Hispanic/Latino), 1 international. Average age 31. *Degree requirements:* For master's, thesis optional, capstone course. *Entrance requirements:* For master's, interview, minimum GPA of 2.5. Additional exam requirements/recommendations for international students: Required—TOEFL (minimum score 550 paper-based; 79 iBT). *Application deadline:* For fall admission, 8/1 priority date for domestic students; for spring admission, 12/1 priority date for domestic students. Applications are processed on a rolling basis. Application fee: $60. Electronic applications accepted. *Expenses:* Tuition: Full-time $16,596; part-time $11,064 per semester. *Required fees:* $130; $130 per unit. $65 per semester. Tuition and fees vary according to program. *Financial support:* Career-related internships or fieldwork and scholarships/grants available. Financial award applicants required to submit FAFSA. *Unit head:* Sungho Park, Program Director, Special Education, 650-508-3762, E-mail: spark1@ndnu.edu. *Application contact:* Sungho Park, Program Director, Special Education, 650-508-3762, E-mail: spark1@ndnu.edu.

Nyack College, School of Education, Nyack, NY 10960. Offers childhood education (MS); childhood special education (MS); TESOL (MAT, MS). *Program availability:* Part-time, evening/weekend, 100% online, blended/hybrid learning. *Students:* 28 full-time (24 women), 22 part-time (19 women); includes 21 minority (10 Black or African American, non-Hispanic/Latino; 1 American Indian or Alaska Native, non-Hispanic/Latino; 3 Asian, non-Hispanic/Latino; 6 Hispanic/Latino; 1 Two or more races, non-Hispanic/Latino), 4 international. Average age 32. In 2018, 17 master's awarded. *Degree requirements:* For master's, comprehensive exam, clinical experience. *Entrance requirements:* For master's, GRE, transcripts, autobiography and statement on reasons for pursuing graduate study in education, recommendations, 6 credits of language, evidence of computer literacy, introductory course in psychology. Additional exam requirements/recommendations for international students: Required—TOEFL (minimum score 550 paper-based; 80 iBT), GRE. *Application deadline:* Applications are processed on a rolling basis. Application fee: $30. Electronic applications accepted. *Expenses:* $725/credit. *Financial support:* Scholarships/grants available. Financial award applicants required to submit FAFSA. *Unit head:* Dr. JoAnn Looney, Dean, 845-675-4538. *Application contact:* Dr. JoAnn Looney, Dean, 845-675-4538.
Website: http://www.nyack.edu/edu

Oakland University, Graduate Study and Lifelong Learning, School of Education and Human Services, Department of Human Development and Child Studies, Program in Special Education, Rochester, MI 48309-4401. Offers applied behavior analysis (Graduate Certificate); autism spectrum disorder (Graduate Certificate); emotional impairment (Graduate Certificate); special education (M Ed), including applied behavior analysis, autism spectrum disorder, emotional impairment, specific learning disabilities; specific learning disabilities (Graduate Certificate). *Accreditation:* TEAC. *Entrance requirements:* For master's, minimum GPA of 3.0, interview. Additional exam requirements/recommendations for international students: Required—TOEFL (minimum score 550 paper-based). Electronic applications accepted.

The Ohio State University, Graduate School, College of Arts and Sciences, Division of Social and Behavioral Sciences, Department of Psychology, Columbus, OH 43210. Offers behavioral neuroscience (PhD); clinical psychology (PhD); cognitive psychology (PhD); developmental psychology (PhD); intellectual and developmental disabilities psychology (PhD); quantitative psychology (PhD); social psychology (PhD). *Accreditation:* APA. *Faculty:* 53. *Students:* 157 full-time (92 women). Average age 27. In 2018, 21 doctorates awarded. *Entrance requirements:* For doctorate, GRE General Test. Additional exam requirements/recommendations for international students: Required—TOEFL (minimum score 600 paper-based; 100 iBT); Recommended—IELTS (minimum score 8). *Application deadline:* For fall admission, 12/1 for domestic and international students. Applications are processed on a rolling basis. Application fee: $60 ($70 for international students). Electronic applications accepted. *Financial support:* Fellowships, research assistantships, and teaching assistantships available. *Unit head:* Dr. Charles Emery, Chair, 614-688-3061, E-mail: emery.33@osu.edu. *Application contact:* Graduate and Professional Admissions, 614-292-9444, Fax: 614-292-3895, E-mail: gpadmissions@osu.edu.
Website: http://psychology.osu.edu/

Ohio University, Graduate College, Gladys W. and David H. Patton College of Education and Human Services, Department of Teacher Education, Athens, OH 45701-2979. Offers adolescent to young adult education (M Ed); curriculum and instruction (M Ed, PhD); early childhood/special education (M Ed); intervention specialist/mild-moderate needs (M Ed); intervention specialist/moderate-intensive needs (M Ed); middle childhood education (M Ed); reading education (M Ed). *Program availability:* Part-time, evening/weekend. *Degree requirements:* For master's, thesis or alternative; for doctorate, comprehensive exam, thesis/dissertation. *Entrance requirements:* For master's, GRE General Test or MAT (if GPA is below 2.9); for doctorate, GRE General Test, minimum GPA of 3.4, work experience. Additional exam requirements/recommendations for international students: Required—TOEFL (minimum score 550

paper-based; 80 iBT) or IELTS (minimum score 6.5). Electronic applications accepted. *Faculty research:* Cognition literacy, character education, teacher's education reform, disabilities.

Old Dominion University, Darden College of Education, Program in Special Education, Norfolk, VA 23529. Offers adapted curriculum K-12 (MS Ed); early childhood special education (MS Ed); general curriculum K-12 (MS Ed); special education (PhD). *Accreditation:* NCATE. *Program availability:* Part-time, evening/weekend, 100% online, blended/hybrid learning. *Degree requirements:* For master's, comprehensive exam, thesis or alternative, VCLA; for doctorate, comprehensive exam, thesis/dissertation. *Entrance requirements:* For master's, GRE General Test or MAT, PRAXIS Core Academic Skills for Educator Tests, minimum GPA of 2.8; for doctorate, GRE General Test or MAT. Additional exam requirements/recommendations for international students: Recommended—TOEFL (minimum score 550 paper-based). Electronic applications accepted. Application fee is waived when completed online. *Expenses:* Contact institution. *Faculty research:* Inclusion, autism spectrum disorder, functional behavioral assessment, infant, preschool, and school-age children and youth with disabilities, distance learning.

Ottawa University, Graduate Studies-Arizona, Program in Education, Ottawa, KS 66067-3399. Offers community college counseling (MA); curriculum and instruction (MA); early childhood (MA); education intervention (MA); education leadership (MA); education technology (MA); Montessori early childhood education (MA); Montessori elementary education (MA); professional development (MA); school guidance counseling (MA); special education - cross categorical (MA). Programs offered in Mesa, Phoenix, Tempe and West Valley, AZ. *Accreditation:* NCATE. *Program availability:* Part-time. *Degree requirements:* For master's, thesis or alternative. *Entrance requirements:* For master's, minimum undergraduate GPA of 3.0, copy of current state certification or teaching license. Additional exam requirements/recommendations for international students: Required—TOEFL (minimum score 550 paper-based). Electronic applications accepted. *Expenses:* Contact institution.

Pace University, School of Education, New York, NY 10038. Offers adolescent education (MST), including biology, chemistry, earth science, English, foreign languages, mathematics, physics, social studies; childhood education (MST); early childhood development, learning and intervention (MST); educational technology studies (MS); inclusive adolescent education (MST), including biology, chemistry, earth science, English, foreign languages, mathematics, physics, social studies; integrated instruction for educational technology (Certificate); integrated instruction for literacy and technology (Certificate); literacy (MS Ed); special education (MS Ed). *Accreditation:* NCATE. *Program availability:* Part-time, evening/weekend, 100% online, blended/hybrid learning. *Faculty:* 19 full-time (13 women), 86 part-time/adjunct (49 women). *Students:* 98 full-time (82 women), 542 part-time (391 women); includes 256 minority (116 Black or African American, non-Hispanic/Latino; 2 American Indian or Alaska Native, non-Hispanic/Latino; 45 Asian, non-Hispanic/Latino; 83 Hispanic/Latino; 10 Two or more races, non-Hispanic/Latino), 4 international. Average age 30. 223 applicants, 89% accepted, 130 enrolled. In 2018, 269 master's, 12 other advanced degrees awarded. *Degree requirements:* For master's and Certificate, certification exams. *Entrance requirements:* For master's, GRE (for initial certification programs only), teaching certificate (for MS Ed in literacy and special education programs only). Additional exam requirements/recommendations for international students: Required—TOEFL (minimum score 88 iBT), IELTS or PTE. *Application deadline:* For fall admission, 8/1 priority date for domestic students, 6/1 for international students; for spring admission, 12/1 priority date for domestic students, 10/1 for international students. Applications are processed on a rolling basis. Application fee: $70. Electronic applications accepted. *Expenses:* Contact institution. *Financial support:* In 2018–19, 17 students received support, including 17 research assistantships with partial tuition reimbursements available (averaging $6,020 per year); career-related internships or fieldwork, Federal Work-Study, scholarships/grants, and unspecified assistantships also available. Financial award application deadline: 9/1; financial award applicants required to submit FAFSA. *Faculty research:* STEM education, TESOL, teacher education, special education, language and literary development. *Total annual research expenditures:* $1.4 million. *Unit head:* Dr. Harriet Feldman, Dean, School of Education, 914-773-3829, E-mail: hfeldman@pace.edu. *Application contact:* Susan Ford-Goldschein, Director of Graduate Admissions, 212-346-1531, Fax: 212-346-1585, E-mail: graduateadmission@pace.edu.
Website: http://www.pace.edu/school-of-education

Pacific Oaks College, Graduate School, Program in Education, Pasadena, CA 91103. Offers preliminary education specialist (MA); preliminary multiple subject (MA). *Program availability:* Online learning. *Degree requirements:* For master's, practicum. *Entrance requirements:* For master's, bachelor's degree from accredited college or university.

Pacific University, College of Education, Forest Grove, OR 97116-1797. Offers early childhood education (MAT); education (MAE); elementary education (MAT); ESOL (MAT); high school education (MAT); middle school education (MAT); special education (MAT); speech-language pathology (MS); STEM education (MAT); talented and gifted (M Ed); visual function in learning (M Ed). *Accreditation:* ASHA; NCATE. *Program availability:* Part-time, evening/weekend. *Degree requirements:* For master's, research project. *Entrance requirements:* For master's, California Basic Educational Skills Test, PRAXIS II, minimum undergraduate GPA of 2.75, 3.0 graduate. Additional exam requirements/recommendations for international students: Required—TOEFL. Electronic applications accepted. *Expenses:* Contact institution. *Faculty research:* Defining a culturally competent classroom, technology in the K-12 classroom, Socratic seminars, social studies education.

Penn State University Park, Graduate School, College of Education, Department of Educational Psychology, Counseling, and Special Education, University Park, PA 16802. Offers counselor education (M Ed, D Ed, PhD, Certificate); educational psychology (MS, PhD, Certificate); school psychology (M Ed, MS, PhD, Certificate); special education (M Ed, MS, PhD).

Piedmont College, School of Education, Demorest, GA 30535. Offers art education (MAT); curriculum and instruction (Ed D, Ed S); early childhood education (MA, MAT); middle grades education (MA, MAT); music education (MAT); secondary education (MA, MAT); special education (MA, MAT). *Program availability:* Part-time, evening/weekend. *Students:* 496 full-time (416 women), 650 part-time (560 women); includes 185 minority (137 Black or African American, non-Hispanic/Latino; 2 American Indian or Alaska Native, non-Hispanic/Latino; 13 Asian, non-Hispanic/Latino; 31 Hispanic/Latino; 1 Native Hawaiian or other Pacific Islander, non-Hispanic/Latino; 1 Two or more races, non-Hispanic/Latino). Average age 37. 483 applicants, 89% accepted, 372 enrolled. In 2018, 275 master's, 10 doctorates, 229 other advanced degrees awarded. *Degree requirements:* For master's, thesis, field experience in the classroom teaching; for doctorate, thesis/dissertation. *Entrance requirements:* For master's, GRE General Test, MAT; for Ed S, minimum graduate GPA of 3.5, valid teaching certificate. Additional exam requirements/recommendations for international students: Required—TOEFL (minimum score 550 paper-based). *Application deadline:* For fall admission, 7/15 for domestic students; for spring admission, 12/1 for domestic students. Applications are processed on a rolling basis. Electronic applications accepted. *Expenses: Tuition:* Full-time $9738; part-time $541 per credit. *Required fees:* $200 per semester. *Financial support:* Career-related internships or fieldwork, Federal Work-Study, and unspecified

assistantships available. Support available to part-time students. Financial award applicants required to submit FAFSA. *Unit head:* Dr. R.D. Nordgren, Dean, 706-778-3000 Ext. 1201, Fax: 706-776-9608, E-mail: rdnordgren@piedmont.edu. *Application contact:* Kathleen Carter, Director of Graduate Enrollment Management, 706-778-8500 Ext. 1181, Fax: 706-778-0150, E-mail: kanderson@piedmont.edu.

Pittsburg State University, Graduate School, College of Education, Department of Teaching and Leadership, Advanced Studies in Leadership Program, Pittsburg, KS 66762. Offers advanced studies in leadership (Ed S), including general school administration, special education. *Program availability:* Part-time, online only, 100% online. *Degree requirements:* For Ed S, thesis optional. *Entrance requirements:* Additional exam requirements/recommendations for international students: Required—TOEFL (minimum score 520 paper-based; 68 iBT), IELTS (minimum score 6), PTE (minimum score 47). Electronic applications accepted. *Expenses:* Contact institution.

Pittsburg State University, Graduate School, College of Education, Department of Teaching and Leadership, Program in Special Education, Pittsburg, KS 66762. Offers MAT, MS. *Accreditation:* NCATE. *Program availability:* Part-time, online only, 100% online. Terminal master's awarded for partial completion of doctoral program. *Degree requirements:* For master's, thesis or alternative. *Entrance requirements:* For master's, PPST. Additional exam requirements/recommendations for international students: Required—TOEFL (minimum score 520 paper-based; 68 iBT), IELTS (minimum score 6), PTE (minimum score 47). Electronic applications accepted. *Expenses:* Contact institution.

Point Loma Nazarene University, School of Education, Program in Special Education, San Diego, CA 92106-2899. Offers MA. *Program availability:* Part-time, evening/weekend. *Entrance requirements:* For master's, letters of recommendation, essay, interview. Additional exam requirements/recommendations for international students: Required—TOEFL. Electronic applications accepted. *Expenses:* Contact institution. *Faculty research:* Co-teaching, inclusion, teacher preparation, intern teacher support.

Point Park University, School of Arts and Sciences, Department of Education, Pittsburgh, PA 15222-1984. Offers adult learning and training (MA); athletic coaching (M Ed); curriculum and instruction (MA); educational administration (MA); leadership and administration (Ed D); secondary education (M Ed); special education grades 7-12 (M Ed); special education PreK-grade 8 (M Ed). *Program availability:* Part-time, evening/weekend, 100% online, blended/hybrid learning. *Degree requirements:* For master's, comprehensive exam (for some programs), thesis or alternative. *Entrance requirements:* For master's, minimum GPA of 3.0, resume, 2 letters of recommendation. Additional exam requirements/recommendations for international students: Required—TOEFL. Electronic applications accepted.

Prescott College, Graduate Programs, Program in Education, Prescott, AZ 86301. Offers early childhood education (MA); early childhood special education (MA); education (MA); elementary education (MA); environmental education leadership and administration (MA); equine-assisted learning (MA); school guidance counseling (MA); secondary education (MA); special education: learning disabilities (MA); special education: mental retardation (MA); special education: serious emotional disabilities (MA); student-directed independent study (MA); sustainability education (PhD). *Program availability:* Part-time, online learning. *Degree requirements:* For master's, thesis, fieldwork or internship, practicum; for doctorate, thesis/dissertation. *Entrance requirements:* For master's, 2 letters of recommendation, resume; for doctorate, 3 letters of recommendation, resume, official transcripts, personal statement, program proposal. Additional exam requirements/recommendations for international students: Required—TOEFL (minimum score 500 paper-based). Electronic applications accepted.

Providence College, Program in Special Education, Providence, RI 02918. Offers special education (M Ed), including elementary teaching, secondary teaching. *Program availability:* Part-time, evening/weekend. *Degree requirements:* For master's, comprehensive exam, portfolio. *Entrance requirements:* Additional exam requirements/recommendations for international students: Required—TOEFL (minimum score 577 paper-based; 90 iBT).

Purdue University Fort Wayne, College of Professional Studies, School of Education, Fort Wayne, IN 46805-1499. Offers couple and family counseling (MS Ed); educational leadership (MS Ed); elementary education (MS Ed); school counseling (MS Ed); secondary education (MS Ed); special education (MS Ed, Certificate). *Accreditation:* NCATE. *Program availability:* Part-time. *Entrance requirements:* For master's, minimum GPA of 2.5, three professional letters of recommendation. Additional exam requirements/recommendations for international students: Required—TOEFL (minimum score 550 paper-based; 79 iBT). *Faculty research:* International faculty, gender in Burmese refugee narratives, planning effective instruction.

Purdue University Global, School of Teacher Education, Davenport, IA 52807. Offers education (M Ed); secondary education (M Ed); teaching and learning (MA); teaching literacy and language: grades 6-12 (MA); teaching literacy and language: grades K-6 (MA); teaching mathematics: grades 6-8 (MA); teaching mathematics: grades 9-12 (MA); teaching mathematics: grades K-5 (MA); teaching science: grades 6-12 (MA); teaching science: grades K-6 (MA); teaching students with special needs (MA); teaching with technology (MA). *Program availability:* Part-time, evening/weekend, online learning. *Entrance requirements:* Additional exam requirements/recommendations for international students: Required—TOEFL (minimum score 550 paper-based; 80 iBT).

Purdue University Northwest, Graduate Studies Office, School of Education, Program in Special Education, Hammond, IN 46323-2094. Offers MS Ed.

Queens College of the City University of New York, Division of Education, Department of Educational and Community Programs, Queens, NY 11367-1597. Offers bilingual pupil personnel (AC); counselor education (MS Ed); mental health counseling (MS); school building leader (AC); school district leader (AC); school psychologist (MS Ed); special education-childhood education (AC); special education-early childhood (MS Ed); teacher of special education 1-6 (MS Ed); teacher of special education birth-2 (MS Ed); teaching students with disabilities, grades 7-12 (MS Ed, AC). *Program availability:* Part-time. *Faculty:* 19 full-time (13 women), 53 part-time/adjunct (31 women). *Students:* 90 full-time (83 women), 380 part-time (316 women); includes 217 minority (42 Black or African American, non-Hispanic/Latino; 1 American Indian or Alaska Native, non-Hispanic/Latino; 53 Asian, non-Hispanic/Latino; 114 Hispanic/Latino; 7 Two or more races, non-Hispanic/Latino), 6 international. Average age 29. 470 applicants, 65% accepted, 236 enrolled. In 2018, 164 master's, 59 other advanced degrees awarded. *Degree requirements:* For master's, Research project; for AC, internship, research project. *Entrance requirements:* For master's, minimum GPA of 3.0. Additional exam requirements/recommendations for international students: Required—TOEFL, IELTS. *Application deadline:* For fall admission, 3/1 for domestic students. Applications are processed on a rolling basis. Application fee: $125. Electronic applications accepted. *Financial support:* Fellowships available. Financial award application deadline: 4/1; financial award applicants required to submit FAFSA. *Unit head:* Dr. Emilia Lopez, Chair, 718-997-5250, E-mail: emilia.lopez@qc.cuny.edu. *Application contact:* Elizabeth D'Amico-Ramirez, Assistant Director of Graduate Admissions, 718-997-5203, E-mail: elizabeth.damicoramirez@qc.cuny.edu.

Radford University, College of Graduate Studies and Research, Program in Special Education, Radford, VA 24142. Offers MS, Certificate. *Accreditation:* NCATE. *Program availability:* Part-time, evening/weekend. *Faculty:* 10 full-time (9 women), 6 part-time/adjunct (5 women). *Students:* 16 full-time (15 women), 75 part-time (62 women); includes 17 minority (11 Black or African American, non-Hispanic/Latino; 1 Asian, non-Hispanic/Latino; 1 Hispanic/Latino; 4 Two or more races, non-Hispanic/Latino), 1 international. Average age 33. 34 applicants, 94% accepted, 27 enrolled. In 2018, 37 master's awarded. *Degree requirements:* For master's, comprehensive exam. *Entrance requirements:* For master's, minimum GPA of 2.75, 3 letters of reference, resume, personal essay, official transcripts. Additional exam requirements/recommendations for international students: Required—TOEFL (minimum score 550 paper-based; 79 iBT), IELTS (minimum score 6.5). *Application deadline:* For fall admission, 4/1 priority date for domestic students, 12/1 for international students; for spring admission, 11/1 priority date for domestic students, 7/1 for international students. Applications are processed on a rolling basis. Application fee: $50. Electronic applications accepted. *Expenses: Tuition, area resident:* Full-time $8915; part-time $371 per credit hour. Tuition, state resident: full-time $8915; part-time $371 per credit hour. Tuition, nonresident: full-time $17,441. *Required fees:* $3288; $138 per credit hour. *Financial support:* In 2018–19, 6 students received support. Research assistantships, teaching assistantships, career-related internships or fieldwork, scholarships/grants, and unspecified assistantships available. Support available to part-time students. Financial award application deadline: 3/1; financial award applicants required to submit FAFSA. *Unit head:* Dr. Elizabeth Altieri, Special Education Graduate Program Coordinator, 540-831-5590, E-mail: ealtieri@radford.edu. *Application contact:* Dr. Elizabeth Altieri, Special Education Graduate Program Coordinator, 540-831-5590, E-mail: ealtieri@radford.edu.
Website: http://www.radford.edu/content/cehd/home/teacher-ed/programs/special-educationms.html

Ramapo College of New Jersey, Master of Arts in Special Education Program, Mahwah, NJ 07430-1680. Offers MA. *Program availability:* Part-time, evening/weekend. *Faculty:* 1 (woman) full-time, 2 part-time/adjunct (both women). *Students:* 50 part-time (45 women); includes 6 minority (1 Asian, non-Hispanic/Latino; 4 Hispanic/Latino; 1 Two or more races, non-Hispanic/Latino). Average age 29. 41 applicants, 90% accepted, 25 enrolled. In 2018, 19 master's awarded. *Degree requirements:* For master's, thesis, field internship, applied capstone research component. *Entrance requirements:* For master's, official transcript of baccalaureate degree from accredited institution with minimum recommended GPA of 3.0; personal statement; 2 letters of recommendation; resume; state-issued teaching certificate. Additional exam requirements/recommendations for international students: Required—TOEFL (minimum score 550 paper-based; 79 iBT); Recommended—IELTS (minimum score 6). *Application deadline:* For fall admission, 5/1 for domestic and international students. Applications are processed on a rolling basis. Application fee: $65. Electronic applications accepted. *Expenses:* Tuition, state resident: part-time $706.15 per credit. Tuition, nonresident: part-time $706.15 per credit. *Required fees:* $57.50 per credit. *Financial support:* Career-related internships or fieldwork available. Financial award application deadline: 3/1; financial award applicants required to submit FAFSA. *Faculty research:* Differentiated instruction, inclusion, charter schools, technology integration in content areas, infusing literacy strategies in education, undergraduate and graduate students working with school based kids with autism. *Unit head:* Dr. Julie Norflus-Good, Director, 201-684-7246, E-mail: jgood@ramapo.edu. *Application contact:* Karen Viviani, Graduate Program Assistant, 201-684-7638, Fax: 201-684-7983, E-mail: kdroubi@ramapo.edu.
Website: http://www.ramapo.edu/mase/

Randolph College, Programs in Education, Lynchburg, VA 24503. Offers curriculum and instruction (MAT); special education-learning disabilities (M Ed, MAT). *Accreditation:* TEAC. *Entrance requirements:* For master's, minimum GPA of 3.0 in prerequisite education coursework, 2.7 in major or field of interest (MAT); teaching license (M Ed); 2 recommendations; interview.

Regent University, Graduate School, School of Education, Virginia Beach, VA 23464-9800. Offers education (M Ed, Ed D, PhD), including adult education (Ed D, PhD, Ed S), advanced educational leadership (Ed D, PhD, Ed S), character education (Ed D, PhD, Ed S), Christian education leadership (Ed D, PhD, Ed S), Christian school administration (M Ed), curriculum and instruction (Ed D, PhD, Ed S), curriculum and instruction - adult education (M Ed), curriculum and instruction - Christian school (M Ed), curriculum and instruction - gifted and talented (M Ed), curriculum and instruction - STEM education (M Ed), curriculum and instruction - teacher leader (M Ed), discipleship for ministry (M Ed), educational leadership (M Ed), educational psychology (Ed D, PhD, Ed S), educational technology and online learning (Ed D, PhD, Ed S), elementary education (M Ed), exceptional education executive leadership (Ed D, PhD, Ed S), higher education (Ed D, PhD, Ed S), higher education leadership and management (Ed D, PhD, Ed S), instructional design and technology (M Ed), K-12 school leadership (Ed D, PhD, Ed S), K-12 special education (M Ed), leadership in mathematics education (M Ed), reading specialist (M Ed), special education (Ed D, PhD, Ed S), student affairs (M Ed), TESOL - adult education (M Ed), TESOL - K-12 (M Ed); educational specialist (Ed S), including adult education (Ed D, PhD, Ed S), advanced educational leadership (Ed D, PhD, Ed S), character education (Ed D, PhD, Ed S), Christian education leadership (Ed D, PhD, Ed S), curriculum and instruction (Ed D, PhD, Ed S), educational psychology (Ed D, PhD, Ed S), educational technology and online learning (Ed D, PhD, Ed S), exceptional education executive leadership (Ed D, PhD, Ed S), higher education (Ed D, PhD, Ed S), higher education leadership and management (Ed D, PhD, Ed S), K-12 school leadership (Ed D, PhD, Ed S), special education (Ed D, PhD, Ed S). *Accreditation:* TEAC. *Program availability:* Part-time, evening/weekend, 100% online, blended/hybrid learning. *Degree requirements:* For master's, thesis or alternative; for doctorate, comprehensive exam, thesis/dissertation. *Entrance requirements:* For master's, Virginia Communication and Literacy Assessment (VCLA), PRAXIS, college transcripts, writing sample, interview; for doctorate, GRE, writing sample, resume, transcripts, interview. Additional exam requirements/recommendations for international students: Required—TOEFL (minimum score 577 paper-based). Electronic applications accepted. *Expenses:* Contact institution. *Faculty research:* Christian school administration, curriculum and instruction, educational technology and online learning, higher education, special education.

Regis College, Department of Education, Weston, MA 02493. Offers elementary teacher (M Ed); higher education leadership (Ed D); special education (M Ed). *Program availability:* Part-time, evening/weekend. *Degree requirements:* For doctorate, thesis/dissertation, capstone project. *Entrance requirements:* For master's, GRE or MAT, personal statement, recommendations, resume/curriculum vitae, official transcripts, interview; for doctorate, personal statement, recommendations, resume/curriculum vitae, official transcripts, presentation/interview. Additional exam requirements/recommendations for international students: Required—TOEFL (minimum score 560 paper-based; 79 iBT); Recommended—IELTS (minimum score 6.5). *Application deadline:* Applications are processed on a rolling basis. Application fee: $65. Electronic applications accepted. *Financial support:* Federal Work-Study, scholarships/grants, and unspecified assistantships available. Financial award applicants required to submit FAFSA. *Unit head:* Dr. Priscilla Boerger, Department Chair/Graduate Program Director, 781-768-7422, E-mail: priscilla.boerger@regiscollege.edu. *Application contact:* Dr. Priscilla Boerger, Department Chair/Graduate Program Director, 781-768-7422, E-mail: priscilla.boerger@regiscollege.edu.

Regis University, College of Contemporary Liberal Studies, Denver, CO 80221-1099. Offers creative writing (MFA); criminology (M Sc); curriculum, instruction and assessment (M Ed); education - teacher leadership (M Ed); educational leadership (M Ed); elementary education (M Ed); literacy (Certificate); reading (M Ed); secondary education (M Ed); special education (M Ed); teacher academic leadership (Certificate); teacher leadership (MA); teacher/educational leadership (M Ed); teaching the linguistically diverse (M Ed). *Program availability:* Part-time, evening/weekend, 100% online, blended/hybrid learning. *Degree requirements:* For master's, thesis (for some programs). *Entrance requirements:* For master's, official transcript reflecting baccalaureate degree awarded from regionally-accredited college or university, work experience, resume, letters of recommendation. Additional exam requirements/recommendations for international students: Required—TOEFL (minimum score 550 paper-based; 82 iBT). Electronic applications accepted. *Expenses:* Contact institution.

Rhode Island College, School of Graduate Studies, Feinstein School of Education and Human Development, Department of Special Education, Providence, RI 02908-1991. Offers autism education (CGS); severe intellectual disabilities (CGS); special education (M Ed). *Accreditation:* NCATE. *Program availability:* Part-time, evening/weekend. *Faculty:* 5 full-time (4 women), 6 part-time/adjunct (all women). *Students:* 10 full-time (all women), 52 part-time (51 women); includes 5 minority (1 Black or African American, non-Hispanic/Latino; 2 Hispanic/Latino; 2 Two or more races, non-Hispanic/Latino). Average age 32. In 2018, 34 master's awarded. *Degree requirements:* For master's, comprehensive assessment/assignment. *Entrance requirements:* For master's, GRE General Test or MAT, undergraduate transcripts; minimum undergraduate GPA of 3.0; 3 letters of recommendation; for CGS, GRE or MAT, master's degree or equivalent, teaching certificate, 3 letters of recommendation, interview. Additional exam requirements/recommendations for international students: Required—TOEFL (minimum score 550 paper-based; 80 iBT). *Application deadline:* For fall admission, 3/1 for domestic students; for spring admission, 11/1 for domestic students. Applications are processed on a rolling basis. Application fee: $50. Electronic applications accepted. *Expenses: Tuition, area resident:* Part-time $407 per credit. Tuition, nonresident: part-time $792 per credit. *Required fees:* $29 per credit. $100 per semester. *Financial support:* Teaching assistantships with full tuition reimbursements, career-related internships or fieldwork, Federal Work-Study, scholarships/grants, health care benefits, and unspecified assistantships available. Support available to part-time students. Financial award application deadline: 5/15; financial award applicants required to submit FAFSA. *Unit head:* Dr. Ying Hui-Michael, Chair, 401-456-8024, E-mail: yhui@ric.edu. *Application contact:* Dr. Ying Hui-Michael, Chair, 401-456-8024, E-mail: yhui@ric.edu. Website: http://www.ric.edu/specialeducation/Pages/default.aspx

Rider University, College of Education and Human Services, Program in Special Education, Lawrenceville, NJ 08648-3001. Offers special education (MA); teacher of students with disabilities (Certificate). *Program availability:* Part-time, evening/weekend. *Students:* 3 full-time (2 women), 39 part-time (26 women); includes 4 minority (2 Black or African American, non-Hispanic/Latino; 1 Asian, non-Hispanic/Latino; 1 Hispanic/Latino). Average age 42. 11 applicants, 82% accepted, 8 enrolled. In 2018, 12 master's, 9 other advanced degrees awarded. *Entrance requirements:* For master's, letters of reference, resume, NJ teaching license, interview. Additional exam requirements/recommendations for international students: Required—TOEFL (minimum score 540 paper-based; 79 iBT). *Application deadline:* For fall admission, 5/1 priority date for domestic students, 6/1 priority date for international students; for spring admission, 11/1 priority date for domestic and international students. Applications are processed on a rolling basis. Application fee: $50. Electronic applications accepted. *Expenses: Tuition:* Full-time $850; part-time $850 per credit hour. *Required fees:* $50; $50 per course. Tuition and fees vary according to program. *Financial support:* Applicants required to submit FAFSA. *Faculty research:* Collaboration/inclusive, practice, service learning, transition. *Unit head:* Dr. Diane Casale-Giannola, Professor, 609-896-5078, E-mail: dgiannola@rider.edu. *Application contact:* Jamie L Mitchell, Director of Graduate Admissions, 609-896-5036, Fax: 609-895-5680, E-mail: jmitchell@rider.edu.

Rivier University, School of Graduate Studies, Department of Education, Nashua, NH 03060. Offers curriculum and instruction (M Ed); early childhood education (M Ed); educational administration (M Ed); educational studies (M Ed); elementary education (M Ed); elementary education and general special education (M Ed); emotional and behavioral disorders (M Ed); general social education (M Ed); leadership and learning (Ed D, CAGS); learning disabilities (M Ed); learning disabilities and reading (M Ed); mental health counseling (MA); reading (M Ed); school counseling (M Ed). *Program availability:* Part-time, evening/weekend. *Degree requirements:* For master's, comprehensive exam (for some programs), internships. *Entrance requirements:* For master's, GRE General Test or MAT.

Roberts Wesleyan College, Graduate Teacher Education Programs, Rochester, NY 14624-1997. Offers adolescence and special education (M Ed); childhood and special education (M Ed); literacy education (M Ed); special education (M Ed). *Program availability:* Part-time, evening/weekend. *Degree requirements:* For master's, thesis. Electronic applications accepted.

Rochester Institute of Technology, Graduate Enrollment Services, National Technical Institute for the Deaf, Research and Teacher Education Department, MS Program in Secondary Education for the Deaf and Hard of Hearing, Rochester, NY 14623-5603. Offers MS. *Program availability:* Part-time, evening/weekend, blended/hybrid learning. *Students:* 17 full-time (12 women); includes 2 minority (1 Asian, non-Hispanic/Latino; 1 Hispanic/Latino), 5 international. Average age 27. 13 applicants, 54% accepted, 7 enrolled. In 2018, 11 master's awarded. *Degree requirements:* For master's, Student Teaching and Professional Portfolio. *Entrance requirements:* For master's, GRE required for students with a GPA below 3.25, minimum cumulative GPA of 2.8, expository essay, interview, two letters of recommendation, Sign Language Self-Assessment. *Application deadline:* For fall admission, 6/1 priority date for domestic and international students. Applications are processed on a rolling basis. Application fee: $65. Electronic applications accepted. *Financial support:* Fellowships with partial tuition reimbursements, research assistantships with partial tuition reimbursements, teaching assistantships with partial tuition reimbursements, career-related internships or fieldwork, scholarships/grants, and unspecified assistantships available. Support available to part-time students. Financial award applicants required to submit FAFSA. *Faculty research:* Effective use of technology and online learning in teaching deaf students; strategies for inclusive instruction/deaf students with other disabilities; effective literacy instruction strategies for DHH readers; single case experimental design methods; STEM language, literacy and learning; deaf studies; international deaf education; stereotype threat effects on mathematical performance. *Unit head:* Dr. Gerald C. Bateman, Director, 585-475-6480, E-mail: gcbnmp@rit.edu. *Application contact:* Diane Ellison, Senior Associate Vice President, Graduate Enrollment Services, 585-475-2229, Fax: 585-475-7164, E-mail: gradinfo@rit.edu.
Website: https://www.rit.edu/study/secondary-education-students-who-are-deaf-or-hard-hearing-ms

Rockford University, Graduate Studies, Department of Education, Program in Special Education, Rockford, IL 61108-2393. Offers MAT. *Program availability:* Part-time, evening/weekend. *Degree requirements:* For master's, thesis optional. *Entrance requirements:* For master's, GRE General Test, 3 letters of recommendation. Additional exam requirements/recommendations for international students: Required—TOEFL (minimum score 550 paper-based; 79 iBT). Electronic applications accepted.

Roosevelt University, Graduate Division, College of Education, Program in Special Education, Chicago, IL 60605. Offers MA. Electronic applications accepted.

Rowan University, Graduate School, College of Education, Department of Interdisciplinary and Inclusive Education, Autism Spectrum Disorders Certificate of Graduate Study Program, Glassboro, NJ 08028-1701. Offers CGS. Electronic applications accepted.

Rowan University, Graduate School, College of Education, Department of Interdisciplinary and Inclusive Education, Program in Learning Disabilities, Glassboro, NJ 08028-1701. Offers MA, CGS. *Accreditation:* NCATE. *Program availability:* Part-time, evening/weekend. *Degree requirements:* For master's, comprehensive exam, thesis. *Entrance requirements:* For master's, GRE General Test, minimum GPA of 2.8, 1 year of teaching experience. Additional exam requirements/recommendations for international students: Required—TOEFL. Electronic applications accepted.

Rowan University, Graduate School, College of Education, Department of Interdisciplinary and Inclusive Education, Program in Special Education, Glassboro, NJ 08028-1701. Offers MA, CGS. *Accreditation:* NCATE. *Program availability:* Part-time, evening/weekend. *Degree requirements:* For master's, comprehensive exam, thesis. *Entrance requirements:* For master's, GRE General Test, minimum GPA of 2.8. Additional exam requirements/recommendations for international students: Required—TOEFL. Electronic applications accepted.

Rowan University, Graduate School, College of Education, Department of Interdisciplinary and Inclusive Education, Teacher of Students with Disabilities Post-Baccalaureate Certification Program, Glassboro, NJ 08028-1701. Offers Postbaccalaureate Certificate. *Program availability:* Part-time, online learning. *Entrance requirements:* For degree, official transcripts from all colleges attended; current professional resume; two letters of recommendation; minimum cumulative undergraduate GPA of 2.75; essay; BA or BS. Electronic applications accepted.

Rutgers University–New Brunswick, Graduate School of Education, Department of Educational Psychology, Program in Special Education, Piscataway, NJ 08854-8097. Offers Ed M, Ed D. *Program availability:* Part-time, evening/weekend. *Degree requirements:* For doctorate, thesis/dissertation, residency. *Entrance requirements:* For master's, GRE General Test, 3 letters of recommendation; for doctorate, GRE General Test, 3 letters of recommendation, master's degree. Additional exam requirements/recommendations for international students: Required—TOEFL (minimum score 550 paper-based; 83 iBT). Electronic applications accepted. *Faculty research:* Pre- and in-service teacher education, teacher development, inclusion, early identification and intervention of reading disabilities, special education law and social policy.

Sage Graduate School, Esteves School of Education, Program in Childhood Special Education, Troy, NY 12180-4115. Offers MS Ed. *Accreditation:* NCATE. *Program availability:* Part-time, evening/weekend. *Faculty:* 2 full-time (both women), 9 part-time/adjunct (5 women). *Students:* 5 full-time (4 women), 3 part-time (2 women); includes 1 minority (Asian, non-Hispanic/Latino). Average age 24. 16 applicants, 56% accepted, 3 enrolled. In 2018, 2 master's awarded. *Degree requirements:* For master's, thesis optional. *Entrance requirements:* For master's, bachelor's degree in a liberal arts or sciences area or the equivalent. Additional exam requirements/recommendations for international students: Required—TOEFL (minimum score 550 paper-based). *Application deadline:* Applications are processed on a rolling basis. Application fee: $30. Electronic applications accepted. *Financial support:* Fellowships, research assistantships, scholarships/grants, and unspecified assistantships available. Financial award application deadline: 3/1; financial award applicants required to submit FAFSA. *Faculty research:* Effective behavioral strategies for classroom instruction. *Unit head:* Dr. John Pelizza, Dean, Esteves School of Education, 518-244-2051, Fax: 518-244-2334, E-mail: pelizj@sage.edu. *Application contact:* Kathleen Gormley, Chair & Professor of Education, 518-244-2403, Fax: 518-244-2334, E-mail: gormlk@sage.edu.

Sage Graduate School, Esteves School of Education, Program in Literacy/Childhood Special Education, Troy, NY 12180-4115. Offers MS Ed. *Accreditation:* NCATE. *Program availability:* Part-time, evening/weekend. *Faculty:* 2 full-time (both women), 9 part-time/adjunct (5 women). *Students:* 2 part-time (both women). Average age 29. 2 applicants, 50% accepted, 1 enrolled. In 2018, 3 master's awarded. *Entrance requirements:* For master's, MAT (minimum score of 350), GRE (minimum scores: 145 verbal; 145 quantitative; 3.5 analytical writing), application, minimum cumulative GPA of 3.0, current teacher certification, interview with appropriate advisor. Additional exam requirements/recommendations for international students: Required—TOEFL (minimum score 550 paper-based). *Application deadline:* Applications are processed on a rolling basis. Application fee: $30. Electronic applications accepted. *Financial support:* Fellowships, research assistantships, scholarships/grants, and unspecified assistantships available. Financial award application deadline: 3/1; financial award applicants required to submit FAFSA. *Faculty research:* Commonalities in the roles of reading specialists and resource/consultant teachers. *Unit head:* Dr. John Pelizza, Dean, Esteves School of Education, 518-244-2051, Fax: 518-244-2334, E-mail: pelizj@sage.edu. *Application contact:* Kathleen Gormley, Chair and Professor of Education, 518-244-2403, Fax: 518-244-2334, E-mail: gormlk@sage.edu.

Sage Graduate School, Esteves School of Education, Program in Special Education, Troy, NY 12180-4115. Offers MS Ed. *Program availability:* Part-time, evening/weekend. *Faculty:* 2 full-time (both women), 9 part-time/adjunct (5 women). *Students:* 3 part-time (2 women). Average age 25. 5 applicants, 60% accepted, 2 enrolled. In 2018, 2 master's awarded. *Entrance requirements:* For master's, interview with advisor, assessment of writing skills, New York state initial certification in childhood education or closely-related field. Additional exam requirements/recommendations for international students: Required—TOEFL (minimum score 550 paper-based). *Application deadline:* Applications are processed on a rolling basis. Application fee: $30. Electronic applications accepted. *Financial support:* Fellowships, research assistantships, scholarships/grants, and unspecified assistantships available. Financial award application deadline: 3/1; financial award applicants required to submit FAFSA. *Unit head:* Dr. John Pelizza, Dean, Esteves School of Education, 518-244-2051, Fax: 518-244-2334, E-mail: pelizj@sage.edu. *Application contact:* Kathleen Gormley, Chair & Professor of Education, 518-244-2403, Fax: 518-244-2334, E-mail: gormlk@sage.edu.

Saginaw Valley State University, College of Education, Program in Special Education, University Center, MI 48710. Offers MAT. *Program availability:* Part-time, evening/weekend. *Students:* 3 full-time (all women), 55 part-time (44 women); includes 4 minority (1 Black or African American, non-Hispanic/Latino; 2 Hispanic/Latino; 1 Two or more races, non-Hispanic/Latino). Average age 34. 12 applicants, 83% accepted, 9 enrolled. In 2018, 1 master's awarded. *Degree requirements:* For master's, capstone course and practicum or thesis. *Entrance requirements:* For master's, minimum GPA of 3.0, teacher certification. Additional exam requirements/recommendations for international students: Required—TOEFL (minimum score 550 paper-based; 79 iBT). *Application deadline:* For fall admission, 7/15 for international students; for winter admission, 11/15 for international students; for spring admission, 4/15 for international students. Applications are processed on a rolling basis. Application fee: $30 ($90 for international students). Electronic applications accepted. *Expenses: Tuition, area resident:* Full-time $6225;

part-time $623 per credit hour. Tuition, state resident: full-time $6225; part-time $623 per credit hour. Tuition, nonresident: full-time $14,215; part-time $1185 per credit hour. *International tuition:* $14,215 full-time. *Required fees:* $263; $14.60 per credit hour. Tuition and fees vary according to degree level. *Financial support:* Federal Work-Study and scholarships/grants available. Support available to part-time students. Financial award applicants required to submit FAFSA. *Unit head:* Dr. Dottie Millar, Professor, Teacher Education, 989-964-4958, Fax: 989-964-4563, E-mail: coeconnect@svsu.edu. *Application contact:* Jenna Briggs, Director, Graduate and International Admissions, 989-964-6096, Fax: 989-964-2788, E-mail: gradadm@svsu.edu.

St. Bonaventure University, School of Graduate School, School of Education, Inclusive Special Education, St. Bonaventure, NY 14778-2284. Offers gifted education (MS Ed, Adv C); gifted education and students with disabilities (MS Ed). *Program availability:* Part-time, evening/weekend. *Faculty:* 2 full-time (both women), 3 part-time/adjunct (1 woman). *Students:* 2 full-time (1 woman), 12 part-time (9 women); includes 2 minority (1 Hispanic/Latino; 1 Two or more races, non-Hispanic/Latino). Average age 26. 6 applicants, 100% accepted, 3 enrolled. In 2018, 10 master's awarded. *Degree requirements:* For master's, comprehensive exam, internship, portfolio; for Adv C, practicum, portfolio. *Entrance requirements:* For master's, GRE or MAT, disabilities or special education teaching certification (or letter of eligibility); interview; transcripts from all colleges previously attended; 2 letters of recommendation; writing sample; for Adv C, teaching certification (or letter of eligibility); interview; transcripts from all colleges previously attended; 2 references; master's degree; writing sample. Additional exam requirements/recommendations for international students: Required—TOEFL (minimum score 550 paper-based; 79 iBT). *Application deadline:* For fall admission, 3/15 priority date for domestic students, 2/1 priority date for international students; for spring admission, 10/15 priority date for domestic students, 7/1 priority date for international students. Applications are processed on a rolling basis. Application fee: $0. Electronic applications accepted. *Expenses:* $755.00 per credit hour; $100 one time fee. *Financial support:* Scholarships/grants, health care benefits, and unspecified assistantships available. Financial award application deadline: 4/15; financial award applicants required to submit FAFSA. *Faculty research:* Differentiated instruction, Teacher education and curriculum, specializing in authentic and responsive pedagogy for diverse learners, history of education. *Unit head:* Dr. Rene' Hauser, Director, 716-375-4078, Fax: 716-375-2360, E-mail: rhauser@sbu.edu. *Application contact:* Matthew Retchless, Director of Graduate Admissions, 716-375-2021, Fax: 716-375-4015, E-mail: gradsch@sbu.edu. Website: http://www.sbu.edu/academics/post-master's-in-differentiated-instruction

St. Cloud State University, School of Graduate Studies, School of Education, Department of Special Education, St. Cloud, MN 56301-4498. Offers developmental and cognitive disabilities (MS). *Accreditation:* NCATE. *Degree requirements:* For master's, thesis or alternative. *Entrance requirements:* For master's, GRE General Test, minimum GPA of 2.75. Additional exam requirements/recommendations for international students: Required—Michigan English Language Assessment Battery; Recommended—TOEFL (minimum score 550 paper-based), IELTS (minimum score 6.5). Electronic applications accepted.

St. John Fisher College, Ralph C. Wilson Jr. School of Education, Program in Adolescence Education and Special Education, Rochester, NY 14618-3597. Offers adolescence education: biology with special education (MS Ed); adolescence education: chemistry with special education (MS Ed); adolescence education: English with special education (MS Ed); adolescence education: French with special education (MS Ed); adolescence education: math with special education (MS Ed); adolescence education: physics with special education (MS Ed); adolescence education: social studies with special education (MS Ed); adolescence education: Spanish with special education (MS Ed). *Program availability:* Part-time, evening/weekend. *Faculty:* 8 full-time (6 women), 2 part-time/adjunct (both women). *Students:* 13 full-time (4 women), 2 part-time (1 woman); includes 2 minority (1 Black or African American, non-Hispanic/Latino; 1 Two or more races, non-Hispanic/Latino). Average age 27. 24 applicants, 58% accepted, 4 enrolled. In 2018, 9 master's awarded. *Degree requirements:* For master's, field experiences, student teaching. *Entrance requirements:* For master's, LAST, 2 letters of recommendation, personal statement, current resume. Additional exam requirements/recommendations for international students: Required—TOEFL (minimum score 575 paper-based; 80 iBT). *Application deadline:* Applications are processed on a rolling basis. Application fee: $30. Electronic applications accepted. *Expenses:* Contact institution. *Financial support:* Scholarships/grants available. Financial award applicants required to submit FAFSA. *Faculty research:* Arts and humanities, urban schools, constructivist learning, at-risk students, mentoring. *Unit head:* Dr. Susan Hildenbrand, Program Director, 585-385-7297, E-mail: shildenbrand@sjfc.edu. *Application contact:* Michelle Gosier, Director of Transfer and Graduate Admissions, 585-385-8064, E-mail: mgosier@sjfc.edu.

St. John Fisher College, Ralph C. Wilson Jr. School of Education, Program in Childhood Education/Special Education, Rochester, NY 14618-3597. Offers childhood education (MS); childhood education/special education (Certificate). *Program availability:* Part-time, evening/weekend. *Faculty:* 8 full-time (6 women), 2 part-time/adjunct (both women). *Students:* 14 full-time (11 women), 4 part-time (2 women); includes 1 minority (Hispanic/Latino). Average age 28. 27 applicants, 48% accepted, 6 enrolled. In 2018, 14 master's awarded. *Degree requirements:* For master's, field experience, student teaching. *Entrance requirements:* For master's, LAST, 2 letters of recommendation, personal statement, current resume. Additional exam requirements/recommendations for international students: Required—TOEFL (minimum score 575 paper-based; 80 iBT). *Application deadline:* Applications are processed on a rolling basis. Application fee: $30. Electronic applications accepted. *Expenses:* Contact institution. *Financial support:* Scholarships/grants available. Financial award applicants required to submit FAFSA. *Faculty research:* Professional development, science assessment, multi-cultural, educational technology. *Unit head:* Dr. Susan Hildenbrand, Program Director, 585-385-7297, E-mail: shildenbrand@sjfc.edu. *Application contact:* Michelle Gosier, Associate Director of Transfer and Graduate Admissions, 585-385-8064, E-mail: mgosier@sjfc.edu. Website: https://www.sjfc.edu/graduate-programs/ms-in-childhood-special-education/

St. John's University, The School of Education, Department of Education Specialties, Program in Special Education, Queens, NY 11439. Offers childhood and childhood special education (MS Ed); teaching children with disabilities in adolescent education (Adv C); teaching children with disabilities in adolescent education (7-12) (MS Ed); teaching children with disabilities in childhood education (Adv C); teaching children with disabilities in childhood education (1-6) (MS Ed); teaching students with disabilities and early childhood education (B-2) (MS Ed). *Program availability:* Part-time, evening/weekend, 100% online. *Degree requirements:* For master's and Adv C, comprehensive exam, minimum overall GPA of 3.0 at time of graduation, 150 hours of practicum in-field experience in a special needs setting, teaching portfolio. *Entrance requirements:* For master's, GRE, MAT, or PRAXIS, statement of goals (personal essay), official undergraduate transcripts, initial teaching certification; for Adv C, initial teaching certification, first master's transcripts, statement of purpose. Additional exam requirements/recommendations for international students: Required—TOEFL, IELTS. Electronic applications accepted. *Faculty research:* Evidence-based practices for prevention of peer victimization/abuse; autism and intellectual disabilities; interpersonal

decision making, empowerment and self-determination skills; academic motivation, literacy skill development, language and communication skills among adolescents with learning disabilities.

St. Joseph's College, Long Island Campus, Programs in Education, Field in Special Education, Patchogue, NY 11772-2399. Offers MA. *Program availability:* Part-time, evening/weekend. *Faculty:* 9 full-time (7 women), 10 part-time/adjunct (4 women). *Students:* 14 full-time (12 women), 94 part-time (74 women); includes 10 minority (1 Asian, non-Hispanic/Latino; 8 Hispanic/Latino; 1 Two or more races, non-Hispanic/Latino). Average age 25. 79 applicants, 82% accepted, 44 enrolled. In 2018, 69 master's awarded. *Entrance requirements:* For master's, Application, $25 application fee, official transcripts, two letters of recommendation, current resume, copy of NYS teacher certifications, interview. Additional exam requirements/recommendations for international students: Required—TOEFL (minimum score 80 iBT). *Application deadline:* Applications are processed on a rolling basis. Application fee: $25. Electronic applications accepted. *Expenses:* Tuition: Full-time $18,450; part-time $1025 per credit. *Required fees:* $414. *Financial support:* In 2018–19, 42 students received support. Federal Work-Study available. *Unit head:* Joan Silver, Associate Professor/Director of MA in Childhood and Adolescence Education with an annotation in Severe and Multiple Disabilities, 631-687-1219, E-mail: jsilver@sjcny.edu. *Application contact:* Joan Silver, Associate Professor/Director of MA in Childhood and Adolescence Education with an annotation in Severe and Multiple Disabilities, 631-687-1219, E-mail: jsilver@sjcny.edu.

St. Joseph's College, Long Island Campus, Programs in Education, Field of Literacy and Cognition, Patchogue, NY 11772-2399. Offers literacy 5-12 (MA); literacy and cognition birth-6 (MA); literacy birth-12 (MA); literacy/cognition and special education (MA). *Program availability:* Part-time, evening/weekend. *Faculty:* 2 part-time/adjunct (both women). *Students:* 6 full-time (5 women), 91 part-time (86 women); includes 13 minority (1 Black or African American, non-Hispanic/Latino; 1 American Indian or Alaska Native, non-Hispanic/Latino; 1 Asian, non-Hispanic/Latino; 7 Hispanic/Latino; 3 Two or more races, non-Hispanic/Latino). Average age 25. 64 applicants, 88% accepted, 38 enrolled. In 2018, 63 master's awarded. *Entrance requirements:* For master's, Application, $25 application fee, official transcripts, two letters of recommendation, current resume, copy of NYS teacher certifications, interview. Additional exam requirements/recommendations for international students: Required—TOEFL (minimum score 80 iBT). *Application deadline:* Applications are processed on a rolling basis. Application fee: $25. Electronic applications accepted. *Expenses:* Tuition: Full-time $18,450; part-time $1025 per credit. *Required fees:* $414. *Financial support:* In 2018–19, 43 students received support. *Unit head:* Karen Megay-Nespoli, Associate Professor/Director of MA in Literacy and Cognition, 631-687-1212, E-mail: kmegay-nespoli@sjcny.edu. *Application contact:* Karen Megay-Nespoli, Associate Professor/Director of MA in Literacy and Cognition, 631-687-1212, E-mail: kmegay-nespoli@sjcny.edu.

St. Joseph's College, New York, Programs in Education, Field of Special Education, Brooklyn, NY 11205-3688. Offers severe and multiple disabilities (MA). *Program availability:* Part-time, evening/weekend. *Faculty:* 3 full-time (all women). *Students:* 14 part-time (12 women); includes 2 minority (both Hispanic/Latino). Average age 23. 12 applicants, 67% accepted, 7 enrolled. In 2018, 8 master's awarded. *Entrance requirements:* For master's, GRE, PRAXIS or MAT, Application, $25 application fee, official transcripts, two letters of recommendation, current resume, copy of NYS teacher certifications. Additional exam requirements/recommendations for international students: Required—TOEFL (minimum score 80 iBT). *Application deadline:* Applications are processed on a rolling basis. Application fee: $25. Electronic applications accepted. *Expenses:* Tuition: Full-time $18,450; part-time $1025 per credit. *Required fees:* $414. *Financial support:* In 2018–19, 10 students received support. *Unit head:* Susan Straut-Collard, Professor/Associate Chair/Director of the MA in Childhood and Adolescence Special Education, 718-940-5689, E-mail: sstrautcollard@sjcny.edu. *Application contact:* Susan Straut-Collard, Professor/Associate Chair/Director of the MA in Childhood and Adolescence Special Education, 718-940-5689, E-mail: sstrautcollard@sjcny.edu.

Saint Joseph's University, College of Arts and Sciences, Graduate Programs in Education, Philadelphia, PA 19131-1395. Offers curriculum supervisor (Certificate); educational leadership (MS, Ed D); elementary education (MS, Certificate); elementary/middle school education (Certificate); organizational development and leadership (MS); principal (Certificate); professional education (MS); reading specialist (MS, Certificate); reading supervisor (Certificate); secondary education (MS, Certificate); special education (MS); special education 7-12 (Certificate); special education PK-8 (Certificate); superintendent's letter of eligibility (Certificate); supervisor of special education (Certificate); teacher of the deaf and hard of hearing (Certificate). *Program availability:* Part-time, evening/weekend, blended/hybrid learning. *Degree requirements:* For master's, thesis or alternative; for doctorate, comprehensive exam, thesis/dissertation. *Entrance requirements:* For master's, 2 letters of recommendation, minimum GPA of 3.0, official transcripts, personal statement; for doctorate, GRE, master's degree from accredited institution, minimum graduate GPA of 3.5, computer competence, interview with program director. Additional exam requirements/recommendations for international students: Required—TOEFL (minimum score 550 paper-based; 80 iBT), IELTS (minimum score 6.5), PTE (minimum score 60). Electronic applications accepted. *Expenses:* Contact institution. *Faculty research:* Factors predicting early mathematics skills for low income children, early child care and development, preschool quality, parent communication and home-school collaboration issues, education of terminally ill children, preparing literacy teachers for urban schools.

Saint Louis University, Graduate Programs, School of Education, Department of Educational Studies, St. Louis, MO 63103. Offers curriculum and instruction (MA, Ed D, PhD); educational foundations (MA, Ed D, PhD); special education (MA); teaching (MAT). *Accreditation:* NCATE. *Program availability:* Part-time. *Degree requirements:* For master's, comprehensive exam; for doctorate, comprehensive exam, thesis/dissertation, preliminary oral and written exams. *Entrance requirements:* For master's, GRE General Test or MAT, letters of recommendation, resume; for doctorate, GRE General Test, letters of recommendation, resumé, goal statement, transcripts. Additional exam requirements/recommendations for international students: Required—TOEFL (minimum score 525 paper-based). Electronic applications accepted. *Faculty research:* Teacher preparation, multicultural issues, children with special needs, qualitative research in education, inclusion.

Saint Mary's College of California, Kalmanovitz School of Education, Program in Special Education, Moraga, CA 94575. Offers M Ed. *Program availability:* Part-time. *Degree requirements:* For master's, thesis or project. *Entrance requirements:* For master's, writing proficiency exam, interview, minimum GPA of 3.0, teaching experience. *Faculty research:* Consultation model, impact of gifted model on special education.

Saint Mary's University of Minnesota, Schools of Graduate and Professional Programs, Graduate School of Education, Educational Administration Program, Winona, MN 55987-1399. Offers educational administration (Certificate, Ed S), including director of special education, K-12 principal, superintendent. *Unit head:* Dr. William Bjorum, Director, 612-728-5126, Fax: 612-728-5121, E-mail: wbjorum@smumn.edu. *Application contact:* Laurie Roy, Director of Admissions for Graduate and Professional Programs, 612-728-5158, Fax: 612-728-5121, E-mail: lroy@smumn.edu. Website: https://www.smumn.edu/academics/graduate/education/programs/ed.s.-in-educational-administration

Saint Mary's University of Minnesota, Schools of Graduate and Professional Programs, Graduate School of Education, Special Education Program, Winona, MN 55987-1399. Offers behavioral disorders (Certificate); learning disabilities (Certificate); special education (MA). *Program availability:* Part-time, evening/weekend, online learning. *Unit head:* Dr. Judith Nagel, Director, 612-238-4565, E-mail: jnagel@smumn.edu. *Application contact:* Laurie Roy, Director of Admission of Schools of Graduate and Professional Programs, 507-457-8606, Fax: 612-728-5121, E-mail: lroy@smumn.edu.
Website: http://www.smumn.edu/graduate-home/areas-of-study/graduate-school-of-education/ma-in-special-education

Saint Michael's College, Graduate Programs, Program in Education, Colchester, VT 05439. Offers arts in education (CAGS); literacy (M Ed); school leadership (CAGS); special education (M Ed). *Program availability:* Part-time, evening/weekend. *Degree requirements:* For master's, thesis. *Entrance requirements:* For master's, minimum GPA of 3.0, official transcripts, essay, interview. Electronic applications accepted. *Expenses: Tuition:* Part-time $590 per credit. *Faculty research:* Integrative curriculum, moral and spiritual dimensions of education, learning styles, multiple intelligences, integrating technology into the curriculum.

Saint Peter's University, Graduate Programs in Education, Program in Special Education, Jersey City, NJ 07306-5997. Offers literacy (MA Ed). *Program availability:* Part-time, evening/weekend. *Degree requirements:* For master's, comprehensive exam. *Entrance requirements:* For master's, GRE or MAT. Additional exam requirements/recommendations for international students: Required—TOEFL. Electronic applications accepted.

St. Thomas Aquinas College, Division of Teacher Education, Sparkill, NY 10976. Offers adolescence education (MST); childhood and special education (MST); childhood education (MST); educational leadership (MS Ed); reading (MS Ed, PMC); special education (MS Ed, PMC); teaching (MS Ed), including elementary education, middle school education, secondary education. *Accreditation:* NCATE. *Program availability:* Part-time, evening/weekend. *Degree requirements:* For master's, comprehensive exam, comprehensive professional portfolio; for PMC, action research project. *Entrance requirements:* For master's, New York State Qualifying Exam, GRE General Test or minimum GPA of 3.0, teaching certificate; for PMC, GRE General Test or minimum GPA of 3.0. Electronic applications accepted. *Faculty research:* Computer applications in education, adolescent special education students, literacy development, inclusive practices for special education students.

St. Thomas University, School of Leadership Studies, Institute for Education, Miami Gardens, FL 33054-6459. Offers earth/space science (Certificate); educational administration (MS, Certificate); educational leadership (Ed D); elementary education (MS); ESOL (Certificate); gifted education (Certificate); instructional technology (MS, Certificate); professional/studies (Certificate); reading (MS, Certificate); special education (MS). *Program availability:* Part-time, evening/weekend. *Degree requirements:* For master's, comprehensive exam; for doctorate, comprehensive exam, thesis/dissertation. *Entrance requirements:* For master's, interview, minimum GPA of 3.0 or GRE; for doctorate, GRE or MAT. Additional exam requirements/recommendations for international students: Required—TOEFL (minimum score 550 paper-based; 79 iBT). Electronic applications accepted.

Saint Vincent College, Program in Education, Latrobe, PA 15650-2690. Offers curriculum and instruction (MS); instructional design and technology (MS); school administration and supervision (MS); special education (MS). *Program availability:* Part-time, evening/weekend. *Degree requirements:* For master's, comprehensive exam. *Entrance requirements:* For master's, GRE (if undergraduate GPA less than 3.0). Additional exam requirements/recommendations for international students: Required—TOEFL (minimum score 550 paper-based). *Faculty research:* Assessment and instructional technology.

Saint Xavier University, Graduate Studies, School of Education, Chicago, IL 60655-3105. Offers counseling (MA); curriculum and instruction (MA); early childhood education (MA); educational administration (MA); elementary education (MA); individualized studies (MA), including educational technology, English as a second language (ESL), ISTEM (integrative science, technology, engineering, and math), science education; music education (MA); reading (MA); secondary education (MA); Spanish education (MA); special education (MA); teaching and leadership (MA). *Accreditation:* NCATE. *Program availability:* Part-time, evening/weekend. *Degree requirements:* For master's, thesis or project. *Entrance requirements:* For master's, minimum GPA of 3.0. *Expenses:* Contact institution.

Salem College, Graduate Studies, Winston-Salem, NC 27101. Offers art education (MAT); elementary education (M Ed, MAT); language and literacy (M Ed); middle school education (MAT); organ (MM); piano (MM); school counseling (M Ed); second language studies (MAT); secondary education (MAT); special education (M Ed, MAT). *Accreditation:* NCATE. *Program availability:* Part-time, evening/weekend, online learning. *Degree requirements:* For master's, practicum (MAT), action research project (M Ed). *Entrance requirements:* For master's, minimum GPA of 3.0, two academic/professional recommendations, acceptable criminal background check. Additional exam requirements/recommendations for international students: Recommended—TOEFL. Electronic applications accepted. *Faculty research:* Teacher professional development, adolescent literacy, instructional technology.

Salem State University, School of Graduate Studies, Program in Special Education, Salem, MA 01970-5353. Offers M Ed. *Accreditation:* NCATE. *Program availability:* Part-time, evening/weekend. *Entrance requirements:* For master's, GRE, MAT. Additional exam requirements/recommendations for international students: Required—TOEFL (minimum score 550 paper-based; 80 iBT) or IELTS (minimum score 5.5).

Salus University, College of Education and Rehabilitation, Elkins Park, PA 19027-1598. Offers education of children and youth with visual and multiple impairments (M Ed, Certificate); low vision rehabilitation (MS, Certificate); occupational therapy (MS); orientation and mobility therapy (MS, Certificate); speech-language pathology (MS); vision rehabilitation therapy (MS, Certificate); OD/MS. *Accreditation:* AOTA. *Program availability:* Part-time, online learning. *Entrance requirements:* For master's, GRE or MAT, letters of reference (3), interviews (2). Additional exam requirements/recommendations for international students: Required—TOEFL, TWE. *Expenses:* Contact institution. *Faculty research:* Knowledge utilization, technology transfer.

Samford University, Orlean Beeson School of Education, Birmingham, AL 35229. Offers educational leadership (MSE, Ed D); elementary education (MS Ed, MSE); gifted (MSE); instructional design and technology (MSE); instructional leadership (MSE, Ed S); secondary education (MSE); special education (MSE). *Accreditation:* NCATE. *Program availability:* Part-time, evening/weekend, 100% online, blended/hybrid learning. *Faculty:* 12 full-time (10 women), 16 part-time/adjunct (11 women). *Students:* 156 full-time (111 women), 101 part-time (73 women); includes 106 minority (100 Black or African American, non-Hispanic/Latino; 1 American Indian or Alaska Native, non-Hispanic/Latino; 5 Two or more races, non-Hispanic/Latino), 1 international. Average age 37. 107 applicants, 94% accepted, 65 enrolled. In 2018, 94 master's, 40 doctorates, 11 other advanced degrees awarded. *Degree requirements:* For master's and Ed S, comprehensive exam; for doctorate, comprehensive exam, thesis/dissertation. *Entrance requirements:* For master's, GRE, MAT, PRAXIS II, interview, transcripts, essay, recommendations, teaching certification; for doctorate, resume, transcripts, interview, essay, recommendations; for Ed S, teaching certification, transcripts, essay, interview, recommendations. Additional exam requirements/recommendations for international students: Required—TOEFL (minimum score 90 iBT); Recommended—IELTS (minimum score 6.5). *Application deadline:* For fall admission, 7/15 for domestic and international students; for winter admission, 11/15 for domestic and international students; for spring admission, 11/15 for domestic and international students; for summer admission, 4/15 for domestic and international students. Applications are processed on a rolling basis. Application fee: $35. Electronic applications accepted. *Expenses:* $862 Per Hour $100 School of Education $175 Technology Fee $100 Per Fully Online Class. *Financial support:* In 2018–19, 173 students received support. Scholarships/grants available. Financial award application deadline: 2/15; financial award applicants required to submit FAFSA. *Faculty research:* Principal leadership's and teacher organizational commitment mentoring, professional development, and middle grades leadership coaching and administrator effectiveness character development programs in schools teacher efficacy related STEM and professional growth. *Unit head:* Dr. Howard Finch, Interim Dean, 205-726-2745, E-mail: hfinch@samford.edu. *Application contact:* Brooke Karr, Graduate Admissions Office Coordinator, 205-729-2783, E-mail: kbgilrea@samford.edu.
Website: http://www.samford.edu/education

Sam Houston State University, College of Education, Department of Language, Literacy, and Special Populations, Huntsville, TX 77341. Offers international literacy (M Ed); reading (M Ed); special education (M Ed, MA), including low incidence disabilities and autism. *Program availability:* Part-time, evening/weekend, online learning. *Degree requirements:* For master's, comprehensive exam (for some programs), thesis optional, comprehensive portfolio; for doctorate, comprehensive exam, thesis/dissertation. *Entrance requirements:* For master's, GRE General Test, MAT, writing sample, recommendations; for doctorate, GRE General Test, MAT, master's degree, personal statement, recommendations. Additional exam requirements/recommendations for international students: Required—TOEFL (minimum score 550 paper-based; 79 iBT), IELTS (minimum score 6.5). Electronic applications accepted.

San Diego State University, Graduate and Research Affairs, College of Education, Department of Administration, Rehabilitation and Post-Secondary Education, San Diego, CA 92182. Offers educational leadership in post-secondary education (MA); rehabilitation counseling (MS), including deafness. *Program availability:* Evening/weekend, online learning. *Degree requirements:* For master's, comprehensive exam (for some programs), thesis (for some programs). *Entrance requirements:* For master's, GRE General Test, letters of reference. Additional exam requirements/recommendations for international students: Required—TOEFL. Electronic applications accepted. *Faculty research:* Rehabilitation in cultural diversity, distance learning technology.

San Diego State University, Graduate and Research Affairs, College of Education, Department of Special Education, San Diego, CA 92182. Offers MA. *Accreditation:* NCATE. *Program availability:* Evening/weekend. *Entrance requirements:* For master's, GRE General Test, letters of reference. Additional exam requirements/recommendations for international students: Required—TOEFL. Electronic applications accepted.

San Francisco State University, Division of Graduate Studies, College of Education, Department of Special Education, San Francisco, CA 94132-1722. Offers augmentative and alternative communication (AC); autism spectrum (AC); early childhood practices (AC); education specialist (Credential); orientation and mobility (Credential); special education (MA, PhD). PhD offered jointly with University of California, Berkeley. *Accreditation:* NCATE. *Unit head:* Dr. Yvonne Bui, Chair, 415-338-2503, Fax: 415-338-0566, E-mail: ybui@sfsu.edu. *Application contact:* Jeanne Oh, Academic Office Coordinator, 415-338-2501, Fax: 415-338-0566, E-mail: joh2@sfsu.edu.
Website: http://sped.sfsu.edu/home

San Ignacio University, Graduate Programs, Doral, FL 33178. Offers business administration (MBA), including human resources management, international business, marketing management; education (M Ed), including early childhood education, educational leadership, special education; hospitality management (MA), including gastronomy and restaurant management, tourism management.

San Jose State University, Program in Special Education, San Jose, CA 95192-0001. Offers MA. *Accreditation:* NCATE. *Program availability:* Evening/weekend. Electronic applications accepted.

Seattle University, College of Education, Program in Special Education, Seattle, WA 98122-1090. Offers M Ed, MA, Certificate. *Faculty:* 1 (woman) full-time, 1 (woman) part-time/adjunct. *Students:* 7 part-time (6 women). Average age 37. 11 applicants, 18% accepted, 1 enrolled. In 2018, 1 master's awarded. *Entrance requirements:* For master's, GRE, MAT or minimum GPA of 3.0, 1 year of K-12 teaching experience; for Certificate, master's degree, minimum GPA of 3.0, 1 year of K-12 teaching experience. *Application deadline:* For fall admission, 8/20 priority date for domestic students; for winter admission, 11/20 priority date for domestic students; for spring admission, 2/20 priority date for domestic students. *Financial support:* In 2018–19, 2 students received support. *Unit head:* Dr. Katherine Schlick Noe, Director, 206-296-5768, E-mail: kschlnoe@seattleu.edu. *Application contact:* Janet Shandley, Associate Dean of Graduate Admissions, 206-296-5900, Fax: 206-298-5656, E-mail: grad_admissions@seattleu.edu.
Website: https://www.seattleu.edu/education/specialed

Seton Hall University, College of Education and Human Services, Department of Educational Studies, South Orange, NJ 07079-2697. Offers instructional design and technology (MA); special education (MA). *Program availability:* Part-time, evening/weekend, blended/hybrid learning. *Degree requirements:* For master's, comprehensive exam, capstone project. *Entrance requirements:* For master's, GRE or MAT, PRAXIS (for certification candidates), minimum GPA of 2.75. Electronic applications accepted. *Expenses:* Contact institution. *Faculty research:* Special education, applied behavioral analysis, educational technology.

Seton Hill University, Master of Arts Program in Special Education, Greensburg, PA 15601. Offers MA. *Program availability:* Part-time, evening/weekend, blended/hybrid learning. *Entrance requirements:* For master's, 3 letters of recommendation, copy of teacher's certification, transcripts, resume, letter of intent. Additional exam requirements/recommendations for international students: Required—TOEFL (minimum score 600 paper-based; 100 iBT), IELTS (minimum score 6.5). *Application deadline:* Applications are processed on a rolling basis. Application fee: $0. Electronic applications accepted. *Financial support:* Scholarships/grants and tuition discounts available. Financial award application deadline: 8/15; financial award applicants required to submit FAFSA.
Website: http://www.setonhill.edu/academics/graduate_programs/special_education

Shippensburg University of Pennsylvania, School of Graduate Studies, College of Education and Human Services, Department of Educational Leadership and Special Education, Shippensburg, PA 17257-2299. Offers educational leadership (M Ed, Ed D); special education (M Ed). *Accreditation:* NCATE. *Program availability:* Part-time,

evening/weekend, blended/hybrid learning. *Faculty:* 5 full-time (0 women), 4 part-time/adjunct (3 women). *Students:* 8 full-time (7 women), 101 part-time (60 women); includes 8 minority (4 Black or African American, non-Hispanic/Latino; 1 Asian, non-Hispanic/Latino; 3 Two or more races, non-Hispanic/Latino), 5 international. Average age 35. 81 applicants, 64% accepted, 40 enrolled. In 2018, 31 master's, 2 doctorates awarded. *Degree requirements:* For master's, candidacy, thesis, or practicum; for doctorate, comprehensive exam, thesis/dissertation, candidacy exam; 24 credits (six 4-credit residencies) of field-based courses leading to the superintendent's letter of eligibility. *Entrance requirements:* For master's, GRE or MAT (if GPA is less than 2.75), 2 years of successful teaching experience; 3 letters of reference; interview; statement of purpose; writing sample; personal goals statement; resume; two recommendation forms; Education Leadership Certification as a teacher with at least 2 years of teaching experience.; for doctorate, resume; three letters of recommendation; 500-1000 word goals statement; teaching certifications and endorsements currently held; experience as public school administrator or supervisor that requires an administrative/supervisory certificate. Additional exam requirements/recommendations for international students: Required—TOEFL (minimum score 550 paper-based; 68 iBT), IELTS (minimum score 6), TOEFL (minimum score 550 paper-based, 68 iBT) or IELTS (minimum score 6). *Application deadline:* For fall admission, 2/1 for domestic students, 4/30 for international students; for spring admission, 7/1 for domestic students, 9/30 for international students. Applications are processed on a rolling basis. Application fee: $45. Electronic applications accepted. *Expenses:* Tuition, state resident: part-time $516 per credit. Tuition, nonresident: part-time $750 per credit. *Required fees:* $149 per credit. *Financial support:* In 2018–19, 2 students received support. Career-related internships or fieldwork, scholarships/grants, unspecified assistantships, and resident hall director and student payroll positions available. Support available to part-time students. Financial award application deadline: 3/1; financial award applicants required to submit FAFSA. *Unit head:* Dr. Thomas C. Gibbon, Departmental Chair, 717-477-1498, Fax: 717-477-4036, E-mail: tcgibb@ship.edu. *Application contact:* Maya T. Mapp, Director of Admissions, 717-477-1231, Fax: 717-477-4016, E-mail: mtmap@ship.edu.
Website: http://www.ship.edu/else/

Siena Heights University, Graduate College, Adrian, MI 49221-1796. Offers clinical mental health counseling (MA); educational leadership (Specialist); leadership (MA), including health care leadership, organizational leadership; teacher education (MA), including early childhood education, early childhood education: Montessori, education leadership: principal, elementary education: reading K-12, leadership: higher education, secondary education: reading K-12, special education: cognitive impairment, special education: learning disabilities. *Program availability:* Part-time, evening/weekend. *Faculty:* 10 full-time (6 women), 16 part-time/adjunct (6 women). *Students:* 34 full-time (20 women), 183 part-time (126 women); includes 64 minority (38 Black or African American, non-Hispanic/Latino; 2 American Indian or Alaska Native, non-Hispanic/Latino; 4 Asian, non-Hispanic/Latino; 14 Hispanic/Latino; 6 Two or more races, non-Hispanic/Latino). Average age 36. 97 applicants, 41% accepted, 30 enrolled. In 2018, 72 master's awarded. *Degree requirements:* For master's, thesis, Presentation. *Entrance requirements:* For master's, Minimum GPA of 3.0, current resume, essay, all post-secondary transcripts, 3 letters of reference, conviction disclosure form; copy of teaching certificate (for some education programs); for Specialist, Master's degree, minimum GPA of 3.0, current resume, essay, all post-secondary transcripts, 3 letters of reference, conviction disclosure form; copy of teaching certificate (for some education programs). Additional exam requirements/recommendations for international students: Recommended—TOEFL, IELTS, TWE, TSE. *Application deadline:* Applications are processed on a rolling basis. Application fee: $50. Electronic applications accepted. *Expenses: Tuition:* Full-time $11,340; part-time $7560 per year. *Required fees:* $454; $454 per unit. $227 per semester. One-time fee: $100. Tuition and fees vary according to program. *Financial support:* In 2018–19, 55 students received support. Scholarships/grants, tuition waivers (full and partial), unspecified assistantships, and State of Michigan Scholarships/Grants available. Support available to part-time students. Financial award application deadline: 9/1; financial award applicants required to submit FAFSA. *Unit head:* Dr. Cheryl Betz, Dean, College for Professional Studies and Graduate College, 517-264-7234, Fax: 517-264-7714, E-mail: cbetz@sienaheights.edu. *Application contact:* Elizabeth Brooks, Assistant Director, 517-264-7165, Fax: 517-264-7714, E-mail: ebrooks@sienaheights.edu.
Website: http://www.sienaheights.edu

Simmons University, Gwen Ifill College of Media, Arts, and Humanities, Boston, MA 02115. Offers behavior analysis (MS, PhD, Ed S); children's literature (MA); dietetics (Certificate); elementary education (MAT); English (MA); gender/cultural studies (MA); history (MA); nutrition and health promotion (MS); physical therapy (DPT); public health (MPH); public policy (MPP); special education: moderate and severe disabilities (MS Ed); sports nutrition (Certificate); writing for children (MFA). *Program availability:* Part-time. *Faculty:* 16 full-time (13 women), 4 part-time/adjunct (3 women). *Students:* 5 full-time (all women), 70 part-time (61 women); includes 12 minority (2 Black or African American, non-Hispanic/Latino; 4 Asian, non-Hispanic/Latino; 4 Hispanic/Latino; 2 Two or more races, non-Hispanic/Latino). Average age 29. 84 applicants, 79% accepted, 32 enrolled. In 2018, 24 master's awarded. *Degree requirements:* For master's, thesis optional. *Entrance requirements:* For master's, GRE, bachelor's degree from accredited college or university; minimum B average (preferred). Additional exam requirements/recommendations for international students: Required—TOEFL (minimum score 600 paper-based; 100 iBT). *Application deadline:* For fall admission, 8/1 for domestic and international students; for spring admission, 12/15 for domestic and international students; for summer admission, 5/1 for domestic and international students. Applications are processed on a rolling basis. Application fee: $35. Electronic applications accepted. *Expenses:* $1,085 per credit hour plus fees. *Financial support:* In 2018–19, 14 students received support, including 1 fellowship (averaging $15,360 per year), 13 teaching assistantships (averaging $2,000 per year); scholarships/grants also available. Financial award applicants required to submit FAFSA. *Faculty research:* Film and media studies, postcolonial literature, critical theory, arts and culture. *Unit head:* Dr. Brian Norman, Dean, 617-521-2472, E-mail: brian.norman@simmons.edu. *Application contact:* Patricia Flaherty, Director, Graduate Studies Admission, 617-521-3902, Fax: 617-521-3058, E-mail: gsa@simmons.edu.
Website: https://www.simmons.edu/academics/colleges-schools-departments/ifill

Slippery Rock University of Pennsylvania, Graduate Studies (Recruitment), College of Education, Department of Special Education, Slippery Rock, PA 16057-1383. Offers autism (M Ed); master teacher (M Ed), including birth to grade 8, grades 7 to 12; special education (Ed D); supervision (M Ed); technology for online instruction (M Ed). *Accreditation:* NCATE. *Program availability:* Part-time, evening/weekend, 100% online. *Faculty:* 12 full-time (6 women). *Students:* 45 full-time (36 women), 232 part-time (191 women); includes 12 minority (2 Black or African American, non-Hispanic/Latino; 1 American Indian or Alaska Native, non-Hispanic/Latino; 1 Asian, non-Hispanic/Latino; 2 Hispanic/Latino; 6 Two or more races, non-Hispanic/Latino). Average age 30. 197 applicants, 84% accepted, 96 enrolled. In 2018, 108 master's, 12 doctorates awarded. *Degree requirements:* For master's, thesis optional. *Entrance requirements:* For master's, minimum GPA of 3.0, official transcripts, teaching certification. Additional exam requirements/recommendations for international students: Required—TOEFL (minimum score 550 paper-based; 80 iBT). *Application deadline:* For fall admission, 3/1 priority date for domestic students, 5/1 priority date for international students; for spring admission, 10/1 priority date for domestic students, 9/1 priority date for international students. Applications are processed on a rolling basis. Application fee: $25 ($30 for international students). Electronic applications accepted. *Expenses:* Contact institution. *Financial support:* In 2018–19, 15 students received support. Career-related internships or fieldwork, Federal Work-Study, institutionally sponsored loans, scholarships/grants, tuition waivers (partial), and unspecified assistantships available. Support available to part-time students. Financial award application deadline: 5/1; financial award applicants required to submit FAFSA. *Unit head:* Dr. Rachel Barger-Anderson, Graduate Coordinator, 724-738-2873, Fax: 724-738-4395, E-mail: rachel.barger-ander@sru.edu. *Application contact:* Brandi Weber-Mortimer, Director of Graduate Admissions, 724-738-2051, Fax: 724-738-2146, E-mail: graduate.admissions@sru.edu.
Website: http://www.sru.edu/academics/colleges-and-departments/coe/departments/special-education/graduate-programs

Sonoma State University, School of Education, Rohnert Park, CA 94928-3609. Offers administrative services (Credential); curriculum, teaching, and learning (MA); early childhood education (MA); education specialist (Credential); educational leadership (MA); multiple subject (Credential); reading and literacy (MA, Credential); single subject (Credential); special education (MA). *Accreditation:* NCATE. *Program availability:* Part-time, evening/weekend. *Entrance requirements:* For master's, minimum GPA of 2.5. Additional exam requirements/recommendations for international students: Required—TOEFL (minimum score 500 paper-based).

South Carolina State University, College of Graduate and Professional Studies, Department of Education, Orangeburg, SC 29117-0001. Offers early childhood education (MAT); education (M Ed); elementary education (M Ed, MAT); English (MAT); general science/biology (MAT); mathematics (MAT); secondary education (M Ed), including biology education, business education, counselor education, English education, home economics education, industrial education, mathematics education, science education, social studies education; special education (M Ed), including emotionally handicapped, learning disabilities, mentally handicapped. *Accreditation:* NCATE. *Program availability:* Part-time, evening/weekend. *Faculty:* 17 full-time (6 women), 12 part-time/adjunct (5 women). *Students:* 42 full-time (32 women), 93 part-time (64 women); includes 121 minority (119 Black or African American, non-Hispanic/Latino; 2 Asian, non-Hispanic/Latino), 2 international. Average age 40. 50 applicants, 98% accepted, 39 enrolled. In 2018, 9 master's awarded. *Degree requirements:* For master's, thesis optional, departmental qualifying exam. *Entrance requirements:* For master's, GRE General Test, NTE, interview, teaching certificate. *Application deadline:* For fall admission, 6/15 priority date for domestic students, 6/15 for international students; for spring admission, 11/1 for domestic and international students. Application fee: $25. Electronic applications accepted. *Expenses: Tuition, area resident:* Full-time $9928; part-time $552 per credit hour. Tuition, state resident: full-time $9928. Tuition, nonresident: full-time $21,038; part-time $1169 per credit hour. *Required fees:* $1532; $85 per credit hour. *Financial support:* Fellowships, career-related internships or fieldwork, Federal Work-Study, and scholarships/grants available. Financial award application deadline: 6/1. *Unit head:* Dr. Charlie Spell, Chair, Department of Education, 803-536-8963, Fax: 803-516-4568, E-mail: cspell@scsu.edu. *Application contact:* Curtis Foskey, Coordinator of Graduate Studies, 803-536-8419, Fax: 803-536-8812, E-mail: cfoskey@scsu.edu.

Southeastern Louisiana University, College of Education, Department of Teaching and Learning, Hammond, LA 70402. Offers curriculum and instruction (M Ed); elementary education (MAT); special education (M Ed); special education: early interventionist (MAT). *Accreditation:* NCATE. *Program availability:* Part-time. *Faculty:* 10 full-time (9 women). *Students:* 23 full-time (18 women), 118 part-time (102 women); includes 20 minority (14 Black or African American, non-Hispanic/Latino; 3 Hispanic/Latino; 3 Two or more races, non-Hispanic/Latino), 1 international. Average age 37. 78 applicants, 71% accepted, 40 enrolled. In 2018, 12 master's awarded. *Degree requirements:* For master's, comprehensive exam (for some programs), thesis (for some programs), action research project, oral defense of research project, portfolio, teaching certificate, minimum cumulative GPA of 3.0. *Entrance requirements:* For master's, GRE (verbal and quantitative), PRAXIS (for MAT), Prospective Education Candidate (PEC) self-assessment survey; competency on a technology performance assessment in education or three-hour graduate-level technology course; orientation seminar. Additional exam requirements/recommendations for international students: Required—TOEFL (minimum score 500 paper-based; 61 iBT). *Application deadline:* For fall admission, 7/15 priority date for domestic students, 6/1 priority date for international students; for spring admission, 12/1 priority date for domestic students, 10/1 priority date for international students. Applications are processed on a rolling basis. Application fee: $20 ($30 for international students). Electronic applications accepted. *Expenses: Tuition, area resident:* Full-time $6684. Tuition, state resident: full-time $6684. Tuition, nonresident: full-time $19,162. *Required fees:* $2097. *Financial support:* In 2018–19, 7 students received support, including 1 fellowship with tuition reimbursement available (averaging $3,500 per year); career-related internships or fieldwork, Federal Work-Study, institutionally sponsored loans, scholarships/grants, and unspecified assistantships also available. Support available to part-time students. Financial award application deadline: 5/1; financial award applicants required to submit FAFSA. *Faculty research:* Early childhood education, STEM education, literacy, special education early intervention, math education. *Total annual research expenditures:* $404,225. *Unit head:* Dr. Colleen Klein-Ezell, Department Head, 985-549-2221, Fax: 985-549-5009, E-mail: colleen.klein-ezell@southeastern.edu. *Application contact:* Dr. Colleen Klein-Ezell, Department Head, 985-549-2221, Fax: 985-549-5009, E-mail: colleen.klein-ezell@southeastern.edu.
Website: http://www.southeastern.edu/acad_research/depts/teach_lrn/index.html

Southeast Missouri State University, School of Graduate Studies, Department of Elementary, Early and Special Education, Program in Exceptional Child Education, Cape Girardeau, MO 63701-4799. Offers MA. *Accreditation:* NCATE. *Program availability:* Part-time, evening/weekend, 100% online. *Faculty:* 11 full-time (9 women), 1 (woman) part-time/adjunct. *Students:* 4 full-time (3 women), 45 part-time (all women); includes 1 minority (Hispanic/Latino). Average age 33. 17 applicants, 100% accepted, 17 enrolled. In 2018, 18 master's awarded. *Degree requirements:* For master's, action research project and presentation. *Entrance requirements:* For master's, state licensure exam or GRE, minimum GPA of 2.75; teaching certificate. Additional exam requirements/recommendations for international students: Required—TOEFL (minimum score 95 iBT), IELTS (minimum score 7), PTE. *Application deadline:* For fall admission, 8/1 for domestic students, 6/1 for international students; for spring admission, 11/21 for domestic students, 10/1 for international students; for summer admission, 5/15 for domestic students. Applications are processed on a rolling basis. Application fee: $30 ($40 for international students). Electronic applications accepted. *Expenses:* Contact institution. *Financial support:* Career-related internships or fieldwork, Federal Work-Study, scholarships/grants, traineeships, tuition waivers (full), and unspecified assistantships available. Financial award application deadline: 6/30; financial award applicants required to submit FAFSA. *Faculty research:* Instructional and assistive technology, teacher candidate professional dispositions, autism spectrum disorder, grow your own programs. *Unit head:* Dr. Julie Ray, Department of Elementary, Early, and Special Education Chair/Professor, 573-651-2444, E-mail: jaray@semo.edu. *Application contact:* Dr. Nancy Aguinaga, Professor, 573-651-2122, E-mail: naguinaga@semo.edu.
Website: http://www.semo.edu/eese/

Southern Connecticut State University, School of Graduate Studies, School of Education, Program in Special Education, New Haven, CT 06515-1355. Offers MS Ed. *Program availability:* Part-time, evening/weekend. *Degree requirements:* For master's, thesis or alternative. *Entrance requirements:* For master's, interview. Electronic applications accepted.

Southern Illinois University Carbondale, Graduate School, College of Education and Human Services, Department of Educational Psychology and Special Education, Program in Special Education, Carbondale, IL 62901-4701. Offers special education (MS Ed, PhD), including behavior (MS Ed), curriculum (MS Ed), early childhood special education (MS Ed), special education supervision (MS Ed). *Accreditation:* NCATE. *Program availability:* Part-time. *Degree requirements:* For master's, thesis. *Entrance requirements:* For master's, GRE General Test, minimum GPA of 2.7. Additional exam requirements/recommendations for international students: Required—TOEFL. *Faculty research:* Applied and action research; scientific methods used to evaluate effectiveness of products and programs for the handicapped; scientific methods used to develop generalizations about instructional, motivational, and learning processes of the handicapped.

Southern Illinois University Edwardsville, Graduate School, School of Education, Health, and Human Behavior, Department of Special Education and Communication Disorders, Program in Special Education, Edwardsville, IL 62026. Offers MS Ed, Post-Master's Certificate. *Program availability:* Part-time, evening/weekend. *Degree requirements:* For master's, thesis or alternative, final project. *Entrance requirements:* Additional exam requirements/recommendations for international students: Required—TOEFL (minimum score 550 paper-based; 79 iBT), IELTS (minimum score 6.5). Electronic applications accepted.

Southern Methodist University, Simmons School of Education and Human Development, Department of Teaching and Learning, Dallas, TX 75275. Offers bilingual education (MBE); education (M Ed, PhD); English as a second language (M Ed); gifted and talented (M Ed); literacy studies (M Ed); special education (M Ed). *Program availability:* Part-time, evening/weekend. Terminal master's awarded for partial completion of doctoral program. *Degree requirements:* For master's, comprehensive exam, minimum GPA of 3.0; for doctorate, thesis/dissertation, qualifying exams, major area paper, evidence of teaching competency, dissemination of research (e.g., conference presentation), professional portfolio. *Entrance requirements:* For master's, minimum GPA of 3.0 or GRE, 3 letters of recommendation; for doctorate, GRE, minimum GPA of 3.3, 3 years of full-time teaching, 3 letters of recommendation, interview. Additional exam requirements/recommendations for international students: Required—TOEFL. Electronic applications accepted. *Faculty research:* Reading intervention, mathematics intervention, bilingual education, new literacies.

Southern New Hampshire University, School of Education, Manchester, NH 03106-1045. Offers curriculum and instruction (M Ed), including dyslexia studies and language-based learning disabilities, educational leadership, reading, special education, technology integration; dyslexia studies and language-based learning disabilities (Certificate); early childhood and special education (M Ed); educational leadership (M Ed, Ed D); educational studies (M Ed); elementary and special education (M Ed); field based education (M Ed); higher education administration (MS); teaching English as a foreign language (MS). *Program availability:* Part-time, evening/weekend, online learning. *Degree requirements:* For master's, comprehensive exam (for some programs), thesis or alternative. *Entrance requirements:* For master's, PRAXIS I, minimum GPA of 2.75. Additional exam requirements/recommendations for international students: Required—TOEFL (minimum score 550 paper-based). Electronic applications accepted. *Expenses:* Contact institution.

Southern Oregon University, Graduate Studies, School of Education, Ashland, OR 97520. Offers elementary education (MA Ed, MS Ed), including classroom teacher, early childhood, handicapped learner, reading, supervision; secondary education (MA Ed, MS Ed), including classroom teacher, handicapped learner, reading, supervision; teaching (MAT). *Program availability:* Online learning. *Degree requirements:* For master's, thesis optional. *Entrance requirements:* For master's, GRE General Test, minimum cumulative GPA of 3.0 in the last 90 quarter credits (60 semester credits) of undergraduate coursework. Additional exam requirements/recommendations for international students: Required—TOEFL (minimum score 540 paper-based; 76 iBT), IELTS (minimum score 6), ELPT (minimum score 964) or ELS (minimum score 112). Electronic applications accepted.

Southwestern College, Education Programs, Winfield, KS 67156-2499. Offers curriculum and instruction (M Ed); early childhood education (M Ed); educational leadership (Ed D), including higher education leadership, PK-12 education leadership; special education (M Ed), including high-incidence disabilities, low-incidence disabilities; teaching (MA). *Accreditation:* NCATE. *Program availability:* Part-time, evening/weekend, 100% online, blended/hybrid learning. *Faculty:* 7 full-time (5 women), 14 part-time/adjunct (12 women). *Students:* 6 full-time (5 women), 79 part-time (54 women); includes 11 minority (4 Black or African American, non-Hispanic/Latino; 2 American Indian or Alaska Native, non-Hispanic/Latino; 1 Asian, non-Hispanic/Latino; 3 Hispanic/Latino; 1 Two or more races, non-Hispanic/Latino), 4 international. Average age 38. 31 applicants, 74% accepted, 18 enrolled. In 2018, 24 master's, 8 doctorates awarded. *Degree requirements:* For master's, practicum, portfolio; for doctorate, thesis/dissertation, professional portfolio. *Entrance requirements:* For master's, baccalaureate degree, minimum GPA of 3.0, valid teaching certificate (for special education); for doctorate, GRE if no master's degree, baccalaureate degree with minimum GPA of 3.25 and current teaching experience, or master's degree with minimum GPA of 3.5. Additional exam requirements/recommendations for international students: Required—TOEFL (minimum score 60 paper-based; 70 iBT), IELTS (minimum score 5.5). *Application deadline:* Applications are processed on a rolling basis. Application fee: $40. Electronic applications accepted. *Expenses:* Masters programs are $606 per credit hour, $535 per online credit hour; doctorate program is $639 per credit hour. *Financial support:* In 2018–19, 13 students received support. Unspecified assistantships and employee tuition waivers available. Financial award applicants required to submit FAFSA. *Unit head:* J.K. Campbell, Education Division Chair, 620-229-6115, E-mail: JK.Campbell@sckans.edu. *Application contact:* Jen Caughron, Director of Enrollment Services & Marketing, 888-684-5335 Ext. 3312, Fax: 888-684-5218, E-mail: jennifer.caughron@sckans.edu.
Website: http://www.sckans.edu/graduate/education-med/

Southwestern Oklahoma State University, College of Professional and Graduate Studies, School of Behavioral Sciences and Education, Specialization in Special Education, Weatherford, OK 73096-3098. Offers M Ed. M Ed distance learning degree program offered to Oklahoma residents only. *Accreditation:* NCATE. *Program availability:* Part-time, evening/weekend. *Degree requirements:* For master's, exam. *Entrance requirements:* For master's, GRE General Test or minimum undergraduate GPA of 3.0. Additional exam requirements/recommendations for international students: Required—TOEFL (minimum score 550 paper-based), IELTS (minimum score 6.5).

Southwest Minnesota State University, Department of Education, Marshall, MN 56258. Offers ESL (MS); math (MS); reading (MS); special education (MS), including developmental disabilities, early childhood education, emotional behavioral disorders,

learning disabilities; teaching, learning and leadership (MS). *Program availability:* Part-time, evening/weekend, online learning. *Entrance requirements:* Additional exam requirements/recommendations for international students: Required—TOEFL or IELTS; Recommended—TOEFL (minimum score 550 paper-based; 80 iBT), IELTS.

Spalding University, Graduate Studies, College of Education, Programs in Education, Louisville, KY 40203-2188. Offers art teacher education (MAT); business teacher education (MAT); elementary school education (MAT); foreign language (MAT); high school education (MAT); middle school education (MAT); secondary education (MAT); special education (learning and behavioral disorders) (MAT); student guidance counselor (MA); teacher leader (M Ed). *Accreditation:* NCATE. *Program availability:* Part-time, evening/weekend. *Entrance requirements:* For master's, GRE General Test or MAT, interview, letters of recommendation, resume. Additional exam requirements/recommendations for international students: Required—TOEFL (minimum score 535 paper-based). Electronic applications accepted. *Faculty research:* Instructional technology, achievement gap, classroom management, assessment.

Spring Arbor University, School of Education, Spring Arbor, MI 49283-9799. Offers education (MAE); reading (MAR); special education (MSE). *Accreditation:* TEAC. *Program availability:* Part-time, evening/weekend, online learning. *Degree requirements:* For master's, thesis. *Entrance requirements:* For master's, official transcripts from all institutions attended, including evidence of an earned bachelor's degree from regionally-accredited college or university with minimum cumulative GPA of 3.0 for the last two years of the bachelor's degree; two professional letters of recommendation. Additional exam requirements/recommendations for international students: Required—TOEFL (minimum score 600 paper-based). Electronic applications accepted.

Springfield College, Graduate Programs, Programs in Education, Springfield, MA 01109-3797. Offers early childhood education (M Ed); educational studies (M Ed); elementary education (M Ed); secondary education (M Ed); special education (M Ed, CAGS). *Program availability:* Part-time, evening/weekend. *Entrance requirements:* For master's, Massachusetts Tests for Educator Licensure (MTEL). Additional exam requirements/recommendations for international students: Required—TOEFL (minimum score 550 paper-based); Recommended—IELTS (minimum score 7). Electronic applications accepted. *Expenses:* Contact institution.

State University of New York at New Paltz, Graduate and Extended Learning School, School of Education, Program of Educational Administration, Program in Special Education, New Paltz, NY 12561. Offers adolescence special education (7-12) (MS Ed); adolescence special education and literacy (MS Ed); childhood special education (1-6) (MS Ed); childhood special education and literacy (MS Ed); early childhood special education (B-2) (MS Ed). *Accreditation:* NCATE. *Program availability:* Part-time, evening/weekend. *Faculty:* 4 full-time (3 women), 1 (woman) part-time/adjunct. *Students:* 14 full-time (11 women), 34 part-time (26 women); includes 4 minority (all Hispanic/Latino). 26 applicants, 85% accepted, 21 enrolled. In 2018, 15 master's awarded. *Entrance requirements:* For master's, minimum GPA of 3.0 (3.2 for special education and literacy programs), New York state teaching certificate. Additional exam requirements/recommendations for international students: Required—TOEFL (minimum score 550 paper-based; 80 iBT), IELTS (minimum score 6.5). *Application deadline:* For fall admission, 3/15 priority date for domestic students, 3/15 for international students; for spring admission, 11/1 for domestic and international students. Application fee: $50. Electronic applications accepted. *Financial support:* Application deadline: 8/1. *Unit head:* Dr. Jane Sileo, Coordinator, 845-257-2835, E-mail: sileoj@newpaltz.edu. *Application contact:* Vika Shock, Director of Graduate Admissions, 845-257-3286, E-mail: gradstudies@newpaltz.edu.
Website: http://www.newpaltz.edu/schoolofed/department-of-teaching—learning/special_ed.html

State University of New York at Oswego, Graduate Studies, School of Education, Department of Curriculum and Instruction, Oswego, NY 13126. Offers adolescence education (MST); art education (MAT); childhood education (MST); curriculum and instruction (MS Ed); literacy education (MS Ed); special education (MS Ed). *Program availability:* Part-time, evening/weekend. *Degree requirements:* For master's, comprehensive exam (for some programs), thesis optional. *Entrance requirements:* For master's, GRE General Test, minimum GPA of 2.7, provisional teaching certificate. Additional exam requirements/recommendations for international students: Required—TOEFL (minimum score 560 paper-based). *Faculty research:* Classroom applications for microcomputers; classroom questioning, wait-time, and achievement; values clarification and academic achievement.

State University of New York at Plattsburgh, School of Education, Health, and Human Services, Program in Teacher Education: Special Education, Plattsburgh, NY 12901-2681. Offers birth to grade 2 (MS Ed); birth to grade 6 (MS Ed); grades 1 to 6 (MS Ed); grades 7 to 12 (MS Ed). *Accreditation:* TEAC. *Program availability:* Part-time, evening/weekend. *Entrance requirements:* For master's, minimum GPA of 2.75. Additional exam requirements/recommendations for international students: Required—TOEFL. *Faculty research:* Inclusion behavior management technology, applied behavior analysis.

State University of New York College at Cortland, Graduate Studies, School of Education, Programs in Teaching Students with Disabilities, Cortland, NY 13045. Offers MS Ed. *Accreditation:* NCATE. *Program availability:* Part-time, evening/weekend. *Degree requirements:* For master's, one foreign language, comprehensive exam, thesis (for some programs). *Entrance requirements:* For master's, provisional certification. Additional exam requirements/recommendations for international students: Required—TOEFL.

State University of New York College at Oneonta, Graduate Programs, Division of Education, Department of Educational Psychology, Counseling and Special Education, Oneonta, NY 13820-4015. Offers school counselor K-12 (MS Ed, CAS); special education (MS Ed). *Accreditation:* NCATE. *Program availability:* Part-time, evening/weekend. *Degree requirements:* For master's, comprehensive exam. *Entrance requirements:* For master's, GRE General Test.

State University of New York College at Potsdam, School of Education and Professional Studies, Program in Special Education, Potsdam, NY 13676. Offers adolescence (grades 7-12) (MS Ed); childhood (grades 1-6) (MS Ed); early childhood (birth-grade 2) (MS Ed). *Accreditation:* NCATE. *Program availability:* Part-time. *Degree requirements:* For master's, culminating experience. *Entrance requirements:* For master's, minimum GPA of 3.0 in last 60 hours of course work. Additional exam requirements/recommendations for international students: Required—TOEFL (minimum score 550 paper-based; 80 iBT), IELTS (minimum score 6). Electronic applications accepted.

Stephen F. Austin State University, Graduate School, James I. Perkins College of Education, Department of Human Services, Nacogdoches, TX 75962. Offers counseling (MA); school psychology (MA); special education (M Ed); speech-language pathology (MS). *Accreditation:* ACA (one or more programs are accredited); ASHA (one or more programs are accredited); CORE; NCATE. *Degree requirements:* For master's, comprehensive exam, thesis (for some programs). *Entrance requirements:* For master's, GRE General Test, minimum GPA of 2.8. Additional exam requirements/recommendations for international students: Required—TOEFL.

Stonehill College, Program in Special Education, Easton, MA 02357. Offers special education (MA), including moderate disabilities. *Program availability:* Part-time, evening/weekend. *Entrance requirements:* For master's, Mass Teacher for Educator Licensure Exam for Communication and Literacy Test. Additional exam requirements/recommendations for international students: Required—TOEFL (minimum score 90 iBT). *Application deadline:* Applications are processed on a rolling basis. Electronic applications accepted. Application fee is waived when completed online. *Expenses:* Contact institution. *Financial support:* Applicants required to submit FAFSA. *Unit head:* Elizabeth Ann Stringer-Keefe, 508-565-1000, E-mail: stringerkeefe@stonehill.edu. *Application contact:* Melissa Ratliff, Dean of Graduate Admission, 508-5651877, Fax: 508-565-1601, E-mail: mratliff@stonehill.edu.
Website: https://www.stonehill.edu/academics/graduate/special-ed/

Syracuse University, School of Education, MS Program in Early Childhood Special Education, Syracuse, NY 13244. Offers MS. *Program availability:* Part-time. *Entrance requirements:* For master's, GRE, baccalaureate degree from regionally-accredited college/university, strong teacher and/or employer recommendations, personal statement, experience working with children. Additional exam requirements/recommendations for international students: Required—TOEFL (minimum score 100 iBT). *Application deadline:* For fall admission, 1/15 priority date for domestic and international students; for spring admission, 10/15 priority date for domestic and international students; for summer admission, 1/15 priority date for domestic and international students. Applications are processed on a rolling basis. Application fee: $75. Electronic applications accepted. *Financial support:* Fellowships with full tuition reimbursements, research assistantships, teaching assistantships, career-related internships or fieldwork, and scholarships/grants available. Financial award application deadline: 1/15; financial award applicants required to submit FAFSA. *Faculty research:* Teaching children with diverse backgrounds and abilities, home-based itinerant teaching, early childhood special education, general preschool teaching, teacher consulting. *Unit head:* Dr. Benjamin Dotger, Department Chair, 315-443-2685, E-mail: bdotger@syr.edu. *Application contact:* Speranza Migliore, Graduate Admissions Recruiter, 315-443-2505, E-mail: gradrcrt@syr.edu.
Website: http://soe.syr.edu/academic/teaching_and_leadership/graduate/masters/early_childhood_special_education/default.aspx

Syracuse University, School of Education, MS Program in Inclusive Special Education (Grades 1-6), Syracuse, NY 13244. Offers MS. *Program availability:* Part-time. In 2018, 6 master's awarded. *Entrance requirements:* For master's, GRE, baccalaureate degree from regionally-accredited college/university, initial New York State certification in childhood education, three letters of recommendation, personal statement, transcripts. Additional exam requirements/recommendations for international students: Required—TOEFL (minimum score 100 iBT). *Application deadline:* For fall admission, 1/15 priority date for domestic and international students; for spring admission, 10/15 priority date for domestic and international students. Applications are processed on a rolling basis. Application fee: $75. Electronic applications accepted. *Financial support:* Fellowships with full tuition reimbursements, research assistantships, teaching assistantships, career-related internships or fieldwork, and scholarships/grants available. Financial award application deadline: 1/15; financial award applicants required to submit FAFSA. *Faculty research:* Creating safe and peaceful schools, adapting instruction for diverse student needs, early intervention for children's reading problems, teaching children with autism, augmentative and alternative communication in inclusive classrooms. *Unit head:* Dr. Christine Ashby, Assistant Professor/Inclusive Master's Program Coordinator, 315-443-8689, E-mail: ceashby@syr.edu. *Application contact:* Speranza Migliore, Graduate Admissions Recruiter, 315-443-2505, E-mail: gradrcrt@syr.edu.
Website: http://soe.syr.edu/academic/teaching_and_leadership/graduate/masters/inclusive_special_education_grades_1_6/default.aspx

Syracuse University, School of Education, MS Program in Inclusive Special Education (Grades 7-12), Syracuse, NY 13244. Offers MS. *Program availability:* Part-time. *Students:* Average age 29. In 2018, 2 master's awarded. *Entrance requirements:* For master's, GRE, baccalaureate degree from regionally-accredited college/university, recommendation letters, personal statement, experience working with youth. Additional exam requirements/recommendations for international students: Required—TOEFL (minimum score 100 iBT). *Application deadline:* For fall admission, 1/15 priority date for domestic and international students; for spring admission, 10/15 priority date for domestic and international students. Applications are processed on a rolling basis. Application fee: $75. Electronic applications accepted. *Financial support:* Fellowships with full tuition reimbursements, research assistantships, teaching assistantships, career-related internships or fieldwork, and scholarships/grants available. Financial award application deadline: 1/15; financial award applicants required to submit FAFSA. *Faculty research:* Students with disabilities, inclusive education and disability studies, extensive placements in schools, adapting instruction for diverse student needs, assistive technologies. *Unit head:* Dr. Christine Ashby, Assistant Professor, 315-443-8689, E-mail: ceashby@syr.edu. *Application contact:* Speranza Migliore, Graduate Admissions Recruiter, 315-443-2505, E-mail: gradrcrt@syr.edu.
Website: http://soe.syr.edu/academic/teaching_and_leadership/graduate/masters/inclusive_special_education_grades_7_12/default.aspx

Syracuse University, School of Education, MS Program in Inclusive Special Education: Severe/Multiple Disabilities, Syracuse, NY 13244. Offers MS. *Program availability:* Part-time. *Students:* Average age 27. *Entrance requirements:* For master's, GRE, baccalaureate degree from regionally-accredited college/university, New York State initial certification in students with disabilities, strong professor and/or employer recommendations, personal statement, interview. Additional exam requirements/recommendations for international students: Required—TOEFL (minimum score 100 iBT). *Application deadline:* For fall admission, 1/15 priority date for domestic and international students; for spring admission, 10/15 priority date for domestic and international students. Applications are processed on a rolling basis. Application fee: $75. Electronic applications accepted. *Financial support:* Fellowships with full tuition reimbursements, research assistantships, teaching assistantships, career-related internships or fieldwork, and scholarships/grants available. Financial award application deadline: 1/15. *Faculty research:* Teaching children and adolescents with autism, augmentation of communication in the inclusive classroom, families of students with disabilities, positive approaches to challenging behaviors, creating safe and peaceful schools. *Unit head:* Dr. Gail Ensher, Program Coordinator, 315-443-9650, E-mail: glensher@syr.edu. *Application contact:* Speranza Migliore, Graduate Admissions Recruiter, 315-443-2505, E-mail: gradrcrt@syr.edu.
Website: http://soe.syr.edu/academic/teaching_and_leadership/graduate/masters/inclusive_special_education_grades_1_6/admissions.aspx

Syracuse University, School of Education, PhD Program in Special Education, Syracuse, NY 13244. Offers PhD. *Program availability:* Part-time. *Degree requirements:* For doctorate, comprehensive exam, thesis/dissertation. *Entrance requirements:* For doctorate, GRE General Test, master's degree, interview, writing sample, disability experience (preferred), three letters of recommendation. Additional exam requirements/recommendations for international students: Required—TOEFL (minimum score 100 iBT). *Application deadline:* For fall admission, 10/15 priority date for domestic and international students. Applications are processed on a rolling basis. Application fee: $75. Electronic applications accepted. *Financial support:* Fellowships with full tuition reimbursements, research assistantships, teaching assistantships, career-related internships or fieldwork, and institutionally sponsored loans available. Support available to part-time students. Financial award application deadline: 1/15. *Faculty research:* Curriculum development and field-based projects, psychoeducational evaluation and planning, perspectives on learning disabilities, teaching children and adolescents with autism, positive approaches to challenging behavior. *Unit head:* Dr. Beth Ferri, Program Director, 315-443-1465, E-mail: baferri@syr.edu. *Application contact:* Speranza Migliore, Graduate Admissions Recruiter, 315-443-2505, E-mail: gradrcrt@syr.edu.
Website: http://soe.syr.edu/academic/teaching_and_leadership/graduate/PhD/special_education/default.aspx

Tarleton State University, College of Graduate Studies, College of Education, Department of Curriculum and Instruction, Stephenville, TX 76402. Offers curriculum and instruction (M Ed); educational diagnostician (M Ed); elementary education (M Ed); instructional design and technology (M Ed); instructional leadership (M Ed); secondary education (M Ed); special education (M Ed); technology applications (M Ed); technology director (M Ed). *Program availability:* Part-time, evening/weekend. *Faculty:* 11 full-time (10 women), 4 part-time/adjunct (1 woman). *Students:* 16 full-time (14 women), 158 part-time (143 women). Average age 40. 54 applicants, 87% accepted, 41 enrolled. In 2018, 46 master's awarded. *Degree requirements:* For master's, comprehensive exam, thesis (for some programs). *Entrance requirements:* For master's, GRE General Test, minimum GPA of 3.0. Additional exam requirements/recommendations for international students: Required—TOEFL (minimum score 520 paper-based; 69 iBT); Recommended—IELTS (minimum score 6), TSE (minimum score 50). *Application deadline:* For fall admission, 8/15 priority date for domestic students; for spring admission, 1/7 for domestic students. Applications are processed on a rolling basis. Application fee: $50 ($130 for international students). Electronic applications accepted. *Expenses:* Contact institution. *Financial support:* Research assistantships, teaching assistantships, career-related internships or fieldwork, Federal Work-Study, and institutionally sponsored loans available. Support available to part-time students. Financial award application deadline: 5/1; financial award applicants required to submit FAFSA. *Unit head:* Dr. Amber Lynn Diaz, Department Head, 254-968-0730, E-mail: adiaz@tarleton.edu. *Application contact:* Information Contact, 254-968-9104, Fax: 254-968-9670, E-mail: gradoffice@tarleton.edu.
Website: http://www.tarleton.edu/cimasters/

Teachers College, Columbia University, Department of Curriculum and Teaching, New York, NY 10027-6696. Offers curriculum and teaching (Ed M, MA, Ed D); curriculum and teaching: elementary education (MA); curriculum and teaching: secondary education (MA); early childhood education (MA, Ed D); early childhood education: special education (MA); elementary education-gifted extension (MA); elementary inclusive education (MA); gifted education (MA); literacy specialist (MA); secondary inclusive education (MA); special inclusive elementary education (MA). *Program availability:* Part-time, evening/weekend. *Students:* 88 full-time (77 women), 264 part-time (239 women); includes 129 minority (45 Black or African American, non-Hispanic/Latino; 1 American Indian or Alaska Native, non-Hispanic/Latino; 41 Asian, non-Hispanic/Latino; 28 Hispanic/Latino; 14 Two or more races, non-Hispanic/Latino), 48 international. Average age 30. 460 applicants, 73% accepted, 149 enrolled. Terminal master's awarded for partial completion of doctoral program. *Unit head:* Prof. Daniel Friedrich, Chair, 212-678-3263, E-mail: friedrich@exchange.tc.columbia.edu. *Application contact:* Kelly Sutton-Skinner, Director of Admission & New Student Enrollment, E-mail: kms2237@tc.columbia.edu.

Teachers College, Columbia University, Department of Health and Behavior Studies, New York, NY 10027-6696. Offers applied behavior analysis (MA, PhD); applied educational psychology: school psychology (Ed M, PhD); behavioral nutrition (PhD), including nutrition (Ed D, PhD); community health education (MS); community nutrition education (Ed M), including community nutrition education; education of deaf and hard of hearing (MA, PhD); health education (MA, Ed D); hearing impairment (Ed D); intellectual disability/autism (MA, Ed D, PhD); nursing education (Ed D, Advanced Certificate); nutrition and education (MS); nutrition and exercise physiology (MS); nutrition and public health (MS); nutrition education (Ed D), including nutrition (Ed D, PhD); physical disabilities (Ed D); reading specialist (MA); severe or multiple disabilities (MA); special education (Ed M, MA, Ed D); teaching of sign language (MA). *Program availability:* Part-time, evening/weekend. *Students:* 157 full-time (145 women), 344 part-time (310 women); includes 169 minority (46 Black or African American, non-Hispanic/Latino; 2 American Indian or Alaska Native, non-Hispanic/Latino; 55 Asian, non-Hispanic/Latino; 57 Hispanic/Latino; 9 Two or more races, non-Hispanic/Latino), 64 international. Average age 31. 495 applicants, 64% accepted, 171 enrolled. Terminal master's awarded for partial completion of doctoral program. *Unit head:* Prof. Dolores Perin, Chair, 212-678-3091, E-mail: dp111@tc.columbia.edu. *Application contact:* Kelly Sutton-Skinner, Director of Admission & New Student Enrollment, E-mail: kms2237@tc.columbia.edu.
Website: http://www.tc.columbia.edu/health-and-behavior-studies/

Teachers College of San Joaquin, Master's Program in Education, Stockton, CA 95206. Offers early education (M Ed); educational inquiry (M Ed); educational leadership and school development (M Ed); science, technology, engineering, and mathematics (M Ed); special education (M Ed). *Expenses: Tuition:* Full-time $5520. Tuition and fees vary according to course load and program.

Tennessee State University, The School of Graduate Studies and Research, College of Education, Department of Teaching and Learning, Nashville, TN 37209-1561. Offers curriculum and instruction (M Ed, Ed D); elementary education (M Ed); special education (M Ed). *Accreditation:* NCATE. *Degree requirements:* For doctorate, thesis/dissertation. *Entrance requirements:* For master's, GRE General Test, GRE Subject Test, or MAT, minimum GPA of 2.5; for doctorate, GRE General Test, GRE Subject Test, or MAT, minimum GPA of 3.25. Electronic applications accepted. *Faculty research:* Multicultural education, teacher education reform, whole language, interactive video teaching, English as a second language.

Tennessee Technological University, College of Graduate Studies, College of Education, Department of Curriculum and Instruction, Program in Special Education, Cookeville, TN 38505. Offers MA, Ed S. *Accreditation:* NCATE. *Program availability:* Part-time. *Faculty:* 6 full-time (3 women). *Students:* 3 full-time (all women), 21 part-time (16 women). 12 applicants, 75% accepted, 6 enrolled. *Degree requirements:* For master's and Ed S, comprehensive exam, thesis or alternative. *Entrance requirements:* For master's and Ed S, MAT or GRE. Additional exam requirements/recommendations for international students: Required—TOEFL (minimum score 527 paper-based; 71 iBT), IELTS (minimum score 5.5), PTE (minimum score 48), or TOEIC (Test of English as an International Communication). *Application deadline:* For fall admission, 8/1 for domestic students, 5/1 for international students; for spring admission, 12/1 for domestic students, 10/1 for international students; for summer admission, 5/1 for domestic students, 2/1 for international students. Applications are processed on a rolling basis. Application fee: $35 ($40 for international students). Electronic applications accepted. *Financial support:* Fellowships, research assistantships, teaching assistantships, and career-related internships or fieldwork available. Financial award application deadline: 4/1. *Unit head:* Dr. Jeremy Wendt, Chairperson, 931-372-3181, Fax: 931-372-6270, E-mail: jwendt@tntech.edu. *Application contact:* Shelia K. Kendrick, Coordinator of Graduate Studies, 931-372-3808, Fax: 931-372-3497, E-mail: skendrick@tntech.edu.

Texas A&M International University, Office of Graduate Studies and Research, College of Education, Department of Professional Programs, Laredo, TX 78041. Offers educational administration (MS Ed); generic special education (MS Ed); school counseling (MS). *Entrance requirements:* Additional exam requirements/recommendations for international students: Required—TOEFL (minimum score 550 paper-based; 79 iBT).

Texas A&M University, College of Education and Human Development, Department of Educational Psychology, College Station, TX 77843. Offers bilingual education (M Ed, MS); counseling psychology (PhD); educational psychology (M Ed, MS, PhD); educational technology (M Ed); school psychology (PhD); special education (M Ed, MS). *Accreditation:* APA (one or more programs are accredited). *Program availability:* Part-time, evening/weekend, blended/hybrid learning. *Faculty:* 47. *Students:* 146 full-time (118 women), 244 part-time (204 women); includes 146 minority (22 Black or African American, non-Hispanic/Latino; 2 American Indian or Alaska Native, non-Hispanic/Latino; 18 Asian, non-Hispanic/Latino; 92 Hispanic/Latino; 1 Native Hawaiian or other Pacific Islander, non-Hispanic/Latino; 11 Two or more races, non-Hispanic/Latino), 50 international. Average age 33. 142 applicants, 50% accepted, 49 enrolled. In 2018, 152 master's, 23 doctorates awarded. *Degree requirements:* For master's, thesis optional; for doctorate, thesis/dissertation. *Entrance requirements:* For master's and doctorate, GRE General Test. Additional exam requirements/recommendations for international students: Required—TOEFL (minimum score 550 paper-based; 80 iBT), IELTS (minimum score 6), PTE (minimum score 53). *Application deadline:* For fall admission, 12/1 for domestic students; for spring admission, 10/15 for domestic students. Application fee: $50 ($90 for international students). Electronic applications accepted. *Expenses:* Contact institution. *Financial support:* In 2018–19, 125 students received support, including 3 fellowships with tuition reimbursements available (averaging $19,520 per year), 106 research assistantships with tuition reimbursements available (averaging $15,181 per year), 19 teaching assistantships with tuition reimbursements available (averaging $9,322 per year); career-related internships or fieldwork, institutionally sponsored loans, scholarships/grants, traineeships, health care benefits, tuition waivers (full and partial), and unspecified assistantships also available. Support available to part-time students. Financial award application deadline: 3/15; financial award applicants required to submit FAFSA. *Unit head:* Dr. Victor Willson, Department Head, 979-845-1394, E-mail: v-willson@tamu.edu. *Application contact:* Kristie Stramaski, Senior Academic Advisor, 979-845-1833, E-mail: epsyadvisor@tamu.edu.
Website: http://epsy.tamu.edu

Texas A&M University–Commerce, College of Education and Human Services, Commerce, TX 75429. Offers counseling (M Ed, MS, PhD); early childhood education (M Ed, MS); educational administration (M Ed, MS, Ed D); educational psychology (PhD); educational technology leadership (M Ed, MS); educational technology library science (M Ed, MS); elementary education (M Ed); health, kinesiology and sports studies (MS); higher education (MS, Ed D); psychology (MS); reading (M Ed, MS); school psychology (SSP); secondary education (M Ed, MS); social work (MSW); special education (M Ed, MS); supervision, curriculum and instruction-elementary education (Ed D); training and development (MS). *Program availability:* Part-time, evening/weekend, 100% online, blended/hybrid learning. *Faculty:* 95 full-time (59 women), 29 part-time/adjunct (22 women). *Students:* 356 full-time (295 women), 1,262 part-time (992 women); includes 683 minority (349 Black or African American, non-Hispanic/Latino; 9 American Indian or Alaska Native, non-Hispanic/Latino; 30 Asian, non-Hispanic/Latino; 238 Hispanic/Latino; 57 Two or more races, non-Hispanic/Latino), 9 international. Average age 37. 951 applicants, 42% accepted, 304 enrolled. In 2018, 532 master's, 51 doctorates awarded. *Degree requirements:* For master's, comprehensive exam, thesis optional, departmental qualifying exams (for some programs); for doctorate, comprehensive exam, thesis/dissertation, departmental qualifying exam; for SSP, comprehensive exam. *Entrance requirements:* For master's, GRE General Test, official transcripts, letters of recommendation, resume, statement of goals; for doctorate, GRE General Test, letters of recommendation, statement of goals, writing samples, writing sessions, resumes. Additional exam requirements/recommendations for international students: Required—TOEFL (minimum score 550 paper-based; 79 iBT), IELTS (minimum score 6), PTE (minimum score 53). *Application deadline:* For fall admission, 6/1 priority date for international students; for spring admission, 10/15 priority date for international students; for summer admission, 3/15 priority date for international students. Applications are processed on a rolling basis. Application fee: $50 ($75 for international students). Electronic applications accepted. *Expenses: Tuition, area resident:* Full-time $3630. Tuition, state resident: full-time $3630. Tuition, nonresident: full-time $11,100. *International tuition:* $11,100 full-time. *Required fees:* $2794. Tuition and fees vary according to course load, degree level and program. *Financial support:* In 2018–19, 116 students received support, including 94 research assistantships with partial tuition reimbursements available (averaging $3,863 per year), 38 teaching assistantships with partial tuition reimbursements available (averaging $4,728 per year); career-related internships or fieldwork, Federal Work-Study, institutionally sponsored loans, scholarships/grants, health care benefits, and unspecified assistantships also available. Financial award application deadline: 5/1; financial award applicants required to submit FAFSA. *Faculty research:* Cognitive and bilingual education, positive behavioral intervention, literacy, math readiness. *Total annual research expenditures:* $1.1 million. *Unit head:* Dr. Madeline Justice, Interim Dean, 903-886-5181, Fax: 903-886-5905, E-mail: madeline.justice@tamuc.edu. *Application contact:* Vicky Turner, Doctoral Degree and Special Programs Coordinator, 903-886-5167, E-mail: vicky.turner@tamuc.edu.
Website: http://www.tamuc.edu/academics/graduateSchool/programs/education/default.aspx

Texas A&M University–Corpus Christi, College of Graduate Studies, College of Education and Human Development, Program in Special Education, Corpus Christi, TX 78412. Offers MS. *Program availability:* Part-time, evening/weekend. *Degree requirements:* For master's, comprehensive exam. *Entrance requirements:* For master's, minimum GPA of 3.0 in last 60 hours; essay (approximately 300-400 words in length). Additional exam requirements/recommendations for international students: Required—TOEFL (minimum score 550 paper-based; 79 iBT), IELTS (minimum score 6.5). Electronic applications accepted.

Texas A&M University–Kingsville, College of Graduate Studies, College of Education and Human Performance, Department of Teacher and Bilingual Education, Program in Special Education, Kingsville, TX 78363. Offers M Ed. *Program availability:* Part-time, evening/weekend. *Degree requirements:* For master's, variable foreign language requirement, comprehensive exam, thesis (for some programs). *Entrance requirements:* For master's, GRE, MAT, GMAT. Additional exam requirements/recommendations for international students: Required—TOEFL (minimum score 550 paper-based; 79 iBT). Electronic applications accepted.

Texas A&M University–San Antonio, Department of Educator and Leadership Preparation, San Antonio, TX 78224. Offers bilingual education (MS); early childhood education (M Ed); educational administration (MA); reading specialization (MS); special education (M Ed), including educational diagnostician. *Program availability:* Part-time, evening/weekend, online learning. *Degree requirements:* For master's, comprehensive exam, thesis or alternative. *Entrance requirements:* For master's, GRE (Quantitative and Verbal) or MAT. Additional exam requirements/recommendations for international students: Required—TOEFL (minimum score 550 paper-based; 79 iBT), IELTS (minimum score 6). Electronic applications accepted. *Faculty research:* Equity in education, biliteracy practices among Latina and immigrants, academic achievement of low socio-economic students, equity practices in instruction and educational leadership in diverse settings, racial identity development and multicultural education.

Texas A&M University–Texarkana, Graduate Studies and Research, College of Education and Liberal Arts, Texarkana, TX 75503. Offers adult education (MS); curriculum and instruction (M Ed); education (MS); educational administration (M Ed); English (MA); instructional technology (MS); interdisciplinary studies (MA, MS); special education (MS). *Program availability:* Part-time, evening/weekend. *Degree requirements:* For master's, comprehensive exam (for some programs), thesis optional. *Entrance requirements:* For master's, minimum GPA of 2.5 on last 60 hours of bachelor's degree. Additional exam requirements/recommendations for international students: Required—TOEFL. Electronic applications accepted.

Texas Christian University, College of Education, Master's Programs in Education, Fort Worth, TX 76129-0002. Offers counseling (M Ed); curriculum and instruction (M Ed), including curriculum studies, language and literacy, math education, science education; education (MAT); educational leadership (M Ed); special education (M Ed). *Program availability:* Part-time, evening/weekend. *Faculty:* 29 full-time (21 women), 3 part-time/adjunct (1 woman). *Students:* 124 full-time (94 women), 14 part-time (12 women); includes 52 minority (14 Black or African American, non-Hispanic/Latino; 2 American Indian or Alaska Native, non-Hispanic/Latino; 3 Asian, non-Hispanic/Latino; 28 Hispanic/Latino; 5 Two or more races, non-Hispanic/Latino), 1 international. Average age 28. 172 applicants, 69% accepted, 86 enrolled. In 2018, 62 master's awarded. *Degree requirements:* For master's, comprehensive exam (for some programs), thesis (for some programs). *Entrance requirements:* For master's, GRE General Test; Pre-Admission Content Test (for MAT). Additional exam requirements/recommendations for international students: Required—TOEFL (minimum score 550 paper-based; 80 iBT), IELTS (minimum score 6.5). *Application deadline:* For fall admission, 3/1 for domestic and international students; for spring admission, 11/16 for domestic and international students; for summer admission, 3/1 for domestic and international students. Application fee: $60. Electronic applications accepted. *Financial support:* In 2018–19, 135 students received support, including 3 research assistantships with full tuition reimbursements available (averaging $15,000 per year), 33 teaching assistantships with full tuition reimbursements available (averaging $15,000 per year); career-related internships or fieldwork, scholarships/grants, health care benefits, and unspecified assistantships also available. Support available to part-time students. Financial award application deadline: 3/1. *Unit head:* Dr. Jan Lacina, Interim Dean, 817-257-6786, Fax: 817-257-7466, E-mail: j.lacina@tcu.edu. *Application contact:* Lori Kimball, Graduate Studies Coordinator, 817-257-7661, Fax: 817-257-7466, E-mail: l.kimball@tcu.edu.
Website: http://coe.tcu.edu/graduate-overview/

Texas State University, The Graduate College, College of Education, Program in Special Education, San Marcos, TX 78666. Offers M Ed. *Program availability:* Part-time. *Faculty:* 15 full-time (12 women), 2 part-time/adjunct (both women). *Students:* 52 full-time (48 women), 23 part-time (20 women); includes 37 minority (10 Black or African American, non-Hispanic/Latino; 2 Asian, non-Hispanic/Latino; 25 Hispanic/Latino). Average age 27. 93 applicants, 66% accepted, 34 enrolled. In 2018, 21 master's awarded. *Degree requirements:* For master's, comprehensive exam. *Entrance requirements:* For master's, baccalaureate degree from regionally-accredited institution with minimum GPA of 2.75 in last 60 hours of course work, statement of purpose, resume (include license, certificates, teaching experience), 2 letters of recommendation from those familiar with professional work (at least one supervisor). Additional exam requirements/recommendations for international students: Required—IELTS (minimum score 6.5), TOEFL (minimum iBT scores: 22 listening, 22 reading, 24 speaking, 21 writing). *Application deadline:* For fall admission, 2/1 priority date for domestic and international students; for spring admission, 10/15 for domestic students, 10/1 for international students; for summer admission, 4/15 for domestic students, 3/15 for international students. Applications are processed on a rolling basis. Application fee: $55 ($90 for international students). Electronic applications accepted. *Expenses:* Tuition, state resident: full-time $8102; part-time $4051 per semester. Tuition, nonresident: full-time $18,229; part-time $9115 per semester. *International tuition:* $18,229 full-time. *Required fees:* $2116; $120 per credit hour. Tuition and fees vary according to course load. *Financial support:* In 2018–19, 41 students received support, including 8 research assistantships (averaging $12,991 per year), 1 teaching assistantship (averaging $13,337 per year); fellowships, career-related internships or fieldwork, Federal Work-Study, institutionally sponsored loans, scholarships/grants, and unspecified assistantships also available. Support available to part-time students. Financial award application deadline: 1/15; financial award applicants required to submit FAFSA. *Faculty research:* Historical literacy research for students with and at risk for learning disabilities; comparing students with and without reading difficulties on reading comprehension assessments; the effects of a structured classroom management system in special education classrooms. *Total annual research expenditures:* $300,782. *Unit head:* Dr. Glenna Billingsley, Graduate Adviser, 512-245-3110, Fax: 512-245-7911, E-mail: gb28@txstate.edu. *Application contact:* Dr. Andrea Golato, Dean of Graduate School, 512-245-2581, Fax: 512-245-8365, E-mail: gradcollege@txstate.edu.
Website: http://www.education.txstate.edu/ci/degrees-certifications/graduate/special-education.html

Texas Tech University, Graduate School, College of Education, Department of Educational Psychology and Leadership, Lubbock, TX 79409-1071. Offers counselor education (M Ed, PhD); educational leadership (M Ed, Ed D, PhD); educational psychology (M Ed, PhD); higher education administration (M Ed, Ed D); higher education research (PhD); instructional technology (M Ed, Ed D); special education (M Ed, Ed D, PhD). *Accreditation:* ACA; NCATE. *Program availability:* Part-time, evening/weekend, 100% online, blended/hybrid learning. *Faculty:* 65 full-time (29 women), 3 part-time/adjunct (all women). *Students:* 261 full-time (184 women), 624 part-time (482 women); includes 325 minority (88 Black or African American, non-Hispanic/Latino; 3 American Indian or Alaska Native, non-Hispanic/Latino; 12 Asian, non-Hispanic/Latino; 192 Hispanic/Latino; 1 Native Hawaiian or other Pacific Islander, non-Hispanic/Latino; 29 Two or more races, non-Hispanic/Latino), 39 international. Average age 36. 437 applicants, 73% accepted, 252 enrolled. In 2018, 278 master's, 40 doctorates awarded. Terminal master's awarded for partial completion of doctoral program. *Degree requirements:* For master's, comprehensive exam, thesis optional; for doctorate, comprehensive exam, thesis/dissertation. *Entrance requirements:* For master's, GRE (for some programs); for doctorate, GRE. Additional exam requirements/recommendations for international students: Required—TOEFL (minimum score 550 paper-based; 79 iBT). *Application deadline:* For fall admission, 6/1 priority date for domestic students, 1/15 priority date for international students; for spring admission, 9/1 priority date for domestic students, 6/15 priority date for international students. Applications are processed on a rolling basis. Application fee: $65. Electronic applications accepted. *Expenses:* Contact institution. *Financial support:* In 2018–19, 493 students received support, including 489 fellowships (averaging $3,305 per year), 61 research assistantships (averaging $12,558 per year), 5 teaching assistantships (averaging $13,161 per year); scholarships/grants and unspecified assistantships also

available. Support available to part-time students. Financial award application deadline: 1/3; financial award applicants required to submit FAFSA. *Faculty research:* Cognitive, motivational, and developmental processes in learning; counseling education; instructional technology; generic special education and sensory impairment; community college administration; K-12 school administration. *Total annual research expenditures:* $204,930. *Unit head:* Dr. Hansel Burley, Professor, Department Chair, 806-834-5135, Fax: 806-742-2179, E-mail: hansel.burley@ttu.edu. *Application contact:* Pam Smith, Admissions Advisor, 806-834-2969, Fax: 806-742-2179, E-mail: pam.smith@ttu.edu. Website: www.educ.ttu.edu/

Texas Woman's University, Graduate School, College of Professional Education, Department of Teacher Education, Denton, TX 76204. Offers educational administration (M Ed, MA); special education (M Ed, PhD), including educational diagnostician (M Ed), intervention specialist (M Ed); teaching, learning, and curriculum (M Ed, MA). *Program availability:* Part-time, 100% online, blended/hybrid learning. *Faculty:* 24 full-time (19 women), 24 part-time/adjunct (17 women). *Students:* 35 full-time (30 women), 170 part-time (153 women); includes 81 minority (18 Black or African American, non-Hispanic/Latino; 1 American Indian or Alaska Native, non-Hispanic/Latino; 4 Asian, non-Hispanic/Latino; 52 Hispanic/Latino; 6 Two or more races, non-Hispanic/Latino), 1 international. Average age 35. 79 applicants, 70% accepted, 43 enrolled. In 2018, 49 master's, 4 doctorates awarded. *Degree requirements:* For master's, comprehensive exam, thesis, professional paper (M Ed), internship for some; for doctorate, comprehensive exam, thesis/dissertation, residency, portfolio. *Entrance requirements:* For master's, minimum GPA of 3.0 on last 60 undergraduate hours, 2 letters of reference, resume, copy of certifications, teacher service record, statement of intent, interview (for MAT); for doctorate, minimum GPA of 3.0, 3 letters of reference, resume, copy of certifications, teacher service record, statement of intent, interview. Additional exam requirements/recommendations for international students: Required—TOEFL (minimum score 550 paper-based; 79 iBT); Recommended—IELTS (minimum score 6.5), TSE (minimum score 53). *Application deadline:* For fall admission, 7/15 priority date for domestic students, 3/1 priority date for international students; for spring admission, 11/1 priority date for domestic students, 7/1 priority date for international students; for summer admission, 4/1 priority date for domestic and international students. Application fee: $50 ($75 for international students). Electronic applications accepted. *Expenses:* $1,517 in-state resident per 3 hour course, $2,783 out-of-state resident per 3 hour course. *Financial support:* In 2018–19, 42 students received support, including 1 teaching assistantship; research assistantships, career-related internships or fieldwork, Federal Work-Study, institutionally sponsored loans, scholarships/grants, traineeships, health care benefits, and unspecified assistantships also available. Support available to part-time students. Financial award application deadline: 3/1; financial award applicants required to submit FAFSA. *Faculty research:* Experiential learning, classroom management, learning disabilities, staff and professional development, technology in the classroom. *Unit head:* Dr. Diane Myers, Chair, 940-898-2271, Fax: 940-898-2270, E-mail: teachereducation@twu.edu. *Application contact:* Korie Hawkins, Associate Director of Admissions, Graduate Recruitment, 940-898-3188, Fax: 940-898-3081, E-mail: admissions@twu.edu.
Website: http://www.twu.edu/teacher-education/

Touro College, Graduate School of Education, New York, NY 10010. Offers education and special education (MS); instructional technology (MS); mathematics education (MS); school leadership (MS); teaching English to speakers of other languages (MS); teaching literacy (MS). *Accreditation:* TEAC. *Program availability:* Part-time, evening/weekend, online learning. *Entrance requirements:* Additional exam requirements/recommendations for international students: Required—TOEFL (minimum score 83 iBT), IELTS (minimum score 6.5). *Faculty research:* Equity assistance, language development, scholarly communications, Latin American studies and cultural sensitivity, behavior management techniques and strategies in special education.

Towson University, College of Education, Program in Special Education, Towson, MD 21252-0001. Offers special education (M Ed); teacher as leader in autism spectrum disorder (M Ed). *Accreditation:* NCATE. *Program availability:* Part-time, evening/weekend. *Degree requirements:* For master's, thesis optional. *Entrance requirements:* For master's, letter of recommendation, bachelor's degree, professional teacher certification, minimum GPA of 3.0. Electronic applications accepted. *Expenses:* Tuition, area resident: Full-time $9196; part-time $418 per unit. Tuition, state resident: full-time $9196; part-time $418 per unit. Tuition, nonresident: full-time $19,030; part-time $865 per unit. *International tuition:* $19,030 full-time. *Required fees:* $3102; $141 per year. $423 per term. Tuition and fees vary according to campus/location and program.

Towson University, College of Education, Program in Teaching, Towson, MD 21252-0001. Offers early childhood education (MAT); elementary education (MAT); secondary education (MAT); special education (MAT). *Entrance requirements:* For master's, ACT, GRE, PRAXIS I or SAT, 2 letters of reference, resume, minimum GPA of 3.0, essay. Electronic applications accepted. *Expenses: Tuition, area resident:* Full-time $9196; part-time $418 per unit. Tuition, state resident: full-time $9196; part-time $418 per unit. Tuition, nonresident: full-time $19,030; part-time $865 per unit. *International tuition:* $19,030 full-time. *Required fees:* $3102; $141 per year. $423 per term. Tuition and fees vary according to campus/location and program.

Towson University, College of Health Professions, Program in Autism Studies, Towson, MD 21252-0001. Offers Postbaccalaureate Certificate. *Entrance requirements:* For degree, bachelor's degree with minimum GPA of 3.0, 30 hours of human service activity as part of field experience, volunteer or paid work in the last five years. Electronic applications accepted. *Expenses: Tuition, area resident:* Full-time $9196; part-time $418 per unit. Tuition, state resident: full-time $9196; part-time $418 per unit. Tuition, nonresident: full-time $19,030; part-time $865 per unit. *International tuition:* $19,030 full-time. *Required fees:* $3102; $141 per year. $423 per term. Tuition and fees vary according to campus/location and program.

Trevecca Nazarene University, Graduate Education Program, Nashville, TN 37210-2877. Offers accountability and instructional leadership (Ed S); curriculum and instruction for Christian school educators (M Ed); curriculum and instruction K-12 (M Ed); educational leadership (M Ed); English second language (M Ed); library and information science (MLI Sc); special education: visual impairments (M Ed); teaching (MAT), including teaching 6-12, teaching K-5. *Accreditation:* NCATE. *Program availability:* Part-time, evening/weekend, online learning. *Degree requirements:* For master's, comprehensive exam, exit assessment/e-portfolio. *Entrance requirements:* For master's, GRE or MAT; PRAXIS (for MAT), minimum GPA of 3.0, official transcript from regionally-accredited institution, references, interview, writing sample, at least 3 years' successful teaching experience (for M Ed in educational leadership); for Ed S, GRE or MAT, master's degree with minimum GPA of 3.0, official transcript from regionally accredited institution, at least 3 years' successful teaching experience, interview, writing sample, background and fingerprinting check, recommendations. Additional exam requirements/recommendations for international students: Required—TOEFL (minimum score 550 paper-based). Electronic applications accepted. *Expenses:* Contact institution.

Trinity Baptist College, Graduate Programs, Jacksonville, FL 32221. Offers Bible (MA); curriculum and instruction (M Ed); educational leadership (M Ed); special education (M Ed). *Program availability:* Online learning. *Entrance requirements:* For

master's, GRE (for M Ed), 2 letters of recommendation; minimum GPA of 2.5 (for M Min), 3.0 (for M Ed); goals essay; official transcripts.

Trinity Christian College, Program in Special Education, Palos Heights, IL 60463-0929. Offers MA. *Program availability:* Evening/weekend. *Degree requirements:* For master's, project. *Entrance requirements:* For master's, valid teaching license, official transcripts, two letters of recommendation. Electronic applications accepted.

Trinity Washington University, School of Education, Washington, DC 20017-1094. Offers clinical mental health counseling (MA); early childhood education (MAT); educating for change (M Ed); educational administration (MSA); elementary education (MAT); reading (M Ed); school counseling (MA); secondary education (MAT), including English, social studies; special education (MAT). *Accreditation:* NCATE. *Program availability:* Part-time, evening/weekend. *Degree requirements:* For master's, thesis (for some programs), capstone project(s). *Entrance requirements:* For master's, PRAXIS I, minimum GPA of 2.8. Additional exam requirements/recommendations for international students: Required—TOEFL (minimum score 550 paper-based). *Faculty research:* Technology, literacy, special education, organizations, inclusion models.

Tusculum University, Program in Curriculum and Instruction, Greeneville, TN 37743-9997. Offers special education (MA Ed). *Program availability:* Evening/weekend. *Degree requirements:* For master's, thesis or alternative. *Entrance requirements:* For master's, NTE, PRAXIS II, GRE, MAT, 3 years of work experience, minimum GPA of 3.0, bachelor's degree. Additional exam requirements/recommendations for international students: Required—TOEFL (minimum score 540 paper-based; 73 iBT).

Union College, Graduate Programs, Department of Education, Program in Special Education, Barbourville, KY 40906-1499. Offers MA. *Degree requirements:* For master's, thesis optional. *Entrance requirements:* For master's, GRE General Test, NTE.

Universidad del Este, Graduate School, Carolina, PR 00984. Offers accounting (MBA); adult education (M Ed); agribusiness (MBA); criminal justice and criminology (MA); curriculum and instruction - early education (M Ed); curriculum and instruction - elementary (M Ed); curriculum and instruction - English (M Ed); curriculum and instruction - Spanish (M Ed); human resources (MBA); information security management (MBA); information technology and Web business development (MBA); management (MBA); public policy (MPA); social work (MA), including clinical social work; special education (M Ed); strategic leadership (MBA).

Universidad del Turabo, Graduate Programs, Programs in Education, Program in Special Education, Gurabo, PR 00778-3030. Offers M Ed. *Program availability:* Part-time, evening/weekend. *Entrance requirements:* For master's, GRE, EXADEP, GMAT, interview, official transcript, essay, recommendation letters. Electronic applications accepted.

Universidad Iberoamericana, Graduate School, Santo Domingo D.N., Dominican Republic. Offers business administration (MBA, PMBA); constitutional law (LL M); dentistry (DMD); educational management (MA); integrated marketing communication (MA); psychopedagogical intervention (M Ed); real estate law (LL M); strategic management of human talent (MM).

Universidad Metropolitana, School of Education, Program in Special Education, San Juan, PR 00928-1150. Offers M Ed. *Degree requirements:* For master's, thesis or alternative. Electronic applications accepted.

Université de Sherbrooke, Faculty of Education, Program in Special Education, Sherbrooke, QC J1K 2R1, Canada. Offers M Ed, Diploma. *Program availability:* Part-time, evening/weekend. *Degree requirements:* For master's, thesis.

University at Buffalo, the State University of New York, Graduate School, Graduate School of Education, Department of Learning and Instruction, Buffalo, NY 14260. Offers biology education (Ed M, Certificate); chemistry education (Ed M, Certificate); childhood education (Ed M); childhood education with bilingual extension (Ed M); college teaching (Advanced Certificate); curriculum, instruction and the science of learning (PhD); early childhood education (Ed M); early childhood education with bilingual extension (Ed M); earth science education (Ed M, Certificate); education and technology (Ed M); education studies (Ed M); educational technology and new literacies (Certificate); educational technology and new literacies (Advanced Certificate); elementary education (Ed D); English education (Ed M, Certificate); English education studies (Ed M); English for speakers of other languages (Ed M); foreign and second language education (PhD); French education (Ed M, Certificate); German education (Ed M, Certificate); gifted education (Certificate); Latin education (Ed M, Certificate); literacy education studies (Ed M); literacy specialist (Ed M); literacy teaching and learning (Certificate); mathematics education (Ed M, Certificate); music education (Ed M, Certificate); music education studies (Ed M); music learning theory (Advanced Certificate); online education (Advanced Certificate); physics education (Ed M, Certificate); science and the public (Ed M); social studies education (Ed M, Certificate); Spanish education (Ed M, Certificate); special education (PhD); teaching English to speakers of other languages (Ed M). *Program availability:* Part-time, evening/weekend, 100% online. *Faculty:* 31 full-time (22 women), 41 part-time/adjunct (27 women). *Students:* 161 full-time (107 women), 369 part-time (260 women); includes 76 minority (26 Black or African American, non-Hispanic/Latino; 3 American Indian or Alaska Native, non-Hispanic/Latino; 30 Asian, non-Hispanic/Latino; 14 Hispanic/Latino; 3 Two or more races, non-Hispanic/Latino), 41 international. Average age 34. 368 applicants, 70% accepted, 179 enrolled. In 2018, 100 master's, 26 doctorates, 19 other advanced degrees awarded. *Degree requirements:* For master's, comprehensive exam; for doctorate, thesis/dissertation, research analysis exam, research experience. *Entrance requirements:* For master's, letters of reference; for doctorate, GRE General Test or MAT, interview, writing sample, letters of recommendation. Additional exam requirements/recommendations for international students: Required—TOEFL (minimum score 600 paper-based; 96 iBT), IELTS (minimum score 6.5), PTE (minimum score 55). *Application deadline:* For fall admission, 2/1 priority date for domestic and international students; for spring admission, 11/15 priority date for domestic students, 10/1 for international students. Applications are processed on a rolling basis. Application fee: $50. Electronic applications accepted. *Financial support:* In 2018–19, 42 fellowships (averaging $5,181 per year), 44 research assistantships with tuition reimbursements (averaging $10,908 per year) were awarded; teaching assistantships, career-related internships or fieldwork, Federal Work-Study, institutionally sponsored loans, scholarships/grants, tuition waivers (full and partial), and unspecified assistantships also available. Financial award application deadline: 2/28; financial award applicants required to submit FAFSA. *Faculty research:* Science assessment, foreign language teaching and learning, early learning, new literacies, gender and education. *Total annual research expenditures:* $413,233. *Unit head:* Dr. Julie Gorlewski, Department Chair, 716-645-2455, Fax: 716-645-3161, E-mail: jgorlews@buffalo.edu. *Application contact:* Renad Aref, Assistant Director of Admission Recruitment, 716-645-2110, Fax: 716-645-7937, E-mail: gseinfo@buffalo.edu.
Website: http://ed.buffalo.edu/teaching.html

The University of Alabama, Graduate School, College of Education, Department of Special Education and Multiple Abilities, Tuscaloosa, AL 35487. Offers collaborative special education (M Ed, Ed S); early intervention (M Ed, Ed S); gifted and talented

education (M Ed, Ed S); multiple abilities (M Ed); special education (Ed D, PhD). *Program availability:* Part-time, evening/weekend. Terminal master's awarded for partial completion of doctoral program. *Degree requirements:* For master's, comprehensive exam, thesis optional; for doctorate, one foreign language, comprehensive exam, thesis/dissertation. *Entrance requirements:* For master's, GRE, minimum undergraduate GPA of 3.0, teaching certificate, 3 letters of recommendation; for doctorate, GRE, 3 years of teaching experience, minimum undergraduate GPA of 3.25. Additional exam requirements/recommendations for international students: Required—TOEFL. Electronic applications accepted. *Faculty research:* Gifted education, mild disabilities, early intervention, severe disabilities, behavior disorders.

The University of Alabama at Birmingham, School of Education, Program in Special Education, Birmingham, AL 35294. Offers MA Ed. *Accreditation:* NCATE. *Degree requirements:* For master's, thesis optional. *Entrance requirements:* For master's, GRE General Test or NTE, minimum GPA of 3.0. Electronic applications accepted. *Expenses: Tuition, area resident:* Full-time $8100; part-time $8100 per year. Tuition, state resident: full-time $8100. Tuition, nonresident: full-time $19,188; part-time $19,188 per year. Tuition and fees vary according to program.

The University of Alabama in Huntsville, School of Graduate Studies, College of Education, Huntsville, AL 35899. Offers autism spectrum disorders (M Ed, Graduate Certificate); biology (MAT); chemistry (MAT); differentiated instruction in elementary education (M Ed); English language arts (MAT); English speakers of other languages (M Ed, MAT); history (MAT); mathematics (MAT); physics (MAT); reading education (M Ed); secondary education (M Ed). *Program availability:* Part-time. *Faculty:* 13 full-time (10 women). *Students:* 38 full-time (30 women), 39 part-time (37 women); includes 17 minority (10 Black or African American, non-Hispanic/Latino; 3 American Indian or Alaska Native, non-Hispanic/Latino; 2 Asian, non-Hispanic/Latino; 2 Two or more races, non-Hispanic/Latino). Average age 33. 47 applicants, 83% accepted, 29 enrolled. In 2018, 31 master's awarded. *Degree requirements:* For master's, comprehensive exam, thesis or alternative, oral and written. *Entrance requirements:* For master's, GRE General Test, minimum GPA of 3.0. Additional exam requirements/recommendations for international students: Required—TOEFL (minimum score 500 paper-based; 80 iBT), IELTS (minimum score 6.5). *Application deadline:* For fall admission, 7/15 priority date for domestic students, 4/1 priority date for international students; for spring admission, 11/30 priority date for domestic students, 9/1 priority date for international students. Applications are processed on a rolling basis. Application fee: $50. Electronic applications accepted. *Expenses: Tuition, area resident:* Full-time $10,632; part-time $412 per credit hour. Tuition, state resident: full-time $10,632. Tuition, nonresident: full-time $23,604; part-time $412 per credit hour. *Required fees:* $582; $582. Tuition and fees vary according to course load and program. *Financial support:* In 2018–19, 2 students received support, including 1 teaching assistantship with full tuition reimbursement available (averaging $4,500 per year); career-related internships or fieldwork, Federal Work-Study, institutionally sponsored loans, scholarships/grants, health care benefits, tuition waivers (full and partial), and unspecified assistantships also available. Support available to part-time students. Financial award application deadline: 4/1; financial award applicants required to submit FAFSA. *Unit head:* Dr. Beth Nason Quick, Dean, 256-824-2325, E-mail: beth.quick@uah.edu. *Application contact:* Kim Gray, Graduate Studies Admissions Coordinator, 256-824-6002, Fax: 256-824-6405, E-mail: deangrad@uah.edu.
Website: http://www.uah.edu/education/

University of Alaska Anchorage, School of Education, Program in Special Education, Anchorage, AK 99508. Offers early childhood special education (M Ed); special education (M Ed, Certificate). *Program availability:* Part-time. *Degree requirements:* For master's, comprehensive exam (for some programs), thesis or alternative. *Entrance requirements:* For master's, GRE or MAT, interview, minimum GPA of 2.75. Additional exam requirements/recommendations for international students: Required—TOEFL (minimum score 550 paper-based). *Faculty research:* Mild disabilities, substance abuse issues for educators, partnerships to improve at-risk youth, analysis of planning models for teachers in special education.

University of Alaska Fairbanks, School of Education, Program in Education, Fairbanks, AK 99775. Offers special education (M Ed). *Program availability:* Part-time, evening/weekend, 100% online, blended/hybrid learning. *Faculty:* 7 full-time (5 women). *Students:* 39 full-time (27 women), 88 part-time (76 women); includes 27 minority (8 American Indian or Alaska Native, non-Hispanic/Latino; 1 Asian, non-Hispanic/Latino; 9 Hispanic/Latino; 1 Native Hawaiian or other Pacific Islander, non-Hispanic/Latino; 8 Two or more races, non-Hispanic/Latino), 3 international. Average age 37. 58 applicants, 53% accepted, 28 enrolled. In 2018, 43 master's awarded. *Degree requirements:* For master's, oral defense of project or thesis OR comprehensive exam. *Entrance requirements:* For master's, GRE General Test, PRAXIS I, PRAXIS II, bachelor's degree from accredited institution with minimum cumulative undergraduate and major GPA of 3.0, statement of academic goals, 3 letters of reference, resume. Additional exam requirements/recommendations for international students: Required—TOEFL (minimum score 550 paper-based; 79 iBT), IELTS (minimum score 6.5). *Application deadline:* For fall admission, 3/1 for domestic and international students; for spring admission, 10/1 for domestic and international students. Applications are processed on a rolling basis. Application fee: $60. Electronic applications accepted. *Expenses: Tuition, area resident:* Full-time $8802; part-time $5868 per credit hour. Tuition, state resident: full-time $8802; part-time $5868 per credit hour. Tuition, nonresident: full-time $18,504; part-time $12,336 per credit hour. *International tuition:* $18,504 full-time. *Required fees:* $1416; $944 per credit hour. $472 per semester. Tuition and fees vary according to course load and program. *Financial support:* Scholarships/grants and unspecified assistantships available. Financial award application deadline: 6/1; financial award applicants required to submit FAFSA. *Faculty research:* Environmental and place-based education, critical pedagogy and language and literacy, cross-cultural studies and Indigenous methodologies. *Unit head:* Dr. Amy Vinlove, Director, 907-474-7341, E-mail: uaf-soe-school@alaska.edu. *Application contact:* Samara taber, Director of Admissions, 907-474-7500, Fax: 907-474-7097, E-mail: uaf-admissions@alaska.edu.
Website: https://sites.google.com/a/alaska.edu/uaf-soe-graduate/

University of Alaska Southeast, Graduate Programs, Program in Education, Juneau, AK 99801. Offers educational leadership (M Ed); elementary education (MAT); learning design and technology (M Ed); mathematics education (M Ed); reading specialist (M Ed); secondary education (MAT); special education (M Ed, MAT). *Accreditation:* NCATE. *Program availability:* Part-time, evening/weekend, online learning. *Degree requirements:* For master's, comprehensive exam or project, portfolio. *Entrance requirements:* For master's, PRAXIS, minimum GPA of 3.0, writing sample, letters of recommendation. Electronic applications accepted. *Faculty research:* Applied classroom research, culturally responsive practices, action research, teaching effectiveness.

University of Alberta, Faculty of Graduate Studies and Research, Department of Educational Psychology, Edmonton, AB T6G 2E1, Canada. Offers counseling psychology (M Ed, PhD); educational psychology (M Ed, PhD); instructional technology (M Ed); school counseling (M Ed); school psychology (M Ed, PhD); special education (M Ed, PhD); special education-deafness studies (M Ed); teaching English as a second language (M Ed). *Program availability:* Part-time. *Degree requirements:* For master's, thesis optional; for doctorate, comprehensive exam, thesis/dissertation. *Entrance requirements:* For master's and doctorate, minimum GPA of 3.0. Additional exam requirements/recommendations for international students: Required—TOEFL. *Faculty research:* Human learning, development and assessment.

The University of Arizona, College of Education, Department of Disability and Psychoeducational Studies, Program in Special Education, Tucson, AZ 85721. Offers cross-categorical special education (MA); deaf and hard of hearing (MA); learning disabilities (MA); severe and multiple disabilities (MA); special education (PhD); visual impairment (MA). *Program availability:* Part-time. *Entrance requirements:* Additional exam requirements/recommendations for international students: Required—TOEFL (minimum score 550 paper-based; 79 iBT). Electronic applications accepted.

University of Arkansas, Graduate School, College of Education and Health Professions, Department of Curriculum and Instruction, Program in Special Education, Fayetteville, AR 72701. Offers M Ed, MAT. *Accreditation:* NCATE. *Program availability:* Part-time, evening/weekend, online learning. In 2018, 12 master's awarded. *Entrance requirements:* For master's, GRE General Test or MAT. *Application deadline:* For fall admission, 8/1 for domestic students, 4/1 for international students; for spring admission, 12/1 for domestic students, 10/1 for international students; for summer admission, 4/15 for domestic students, 3/1 for international students. Applications are processed on a rolling basis. Application fee: $60. Electronic applications accepted. *Financial support:* Fellowships, research assistantships, teaching assistantships, career-related internships or fieldwork, and Federal Work-Study available. Support available to part-time students. Financial award application deadline: 4/1; financial award applicants required to submit FAFSA. *Unit head:* Dr. Cheryl Murphy, Department Head, 479-575-5111, Fax: 479-575-2492, E-mail: cmurphy@uark.edu. *Application contact:* Dr. Suzanne Kucharczyk, Program Coordinator, 479-575-6210, E-mail: suzannek@uark.edu.
Website: https://sped.uark.edu

University of Arkansas at Little Rock, Graduate School, College of Education and Health Professions, Department of Counseling, Adult and Rehabilitation Education, Little Rock, AR 72204-1099. Offers adult education (M Ed); counselor education (M Ed); rehabilitation counseling (MA, Graduate Certificate); rehabilitation for the blind: orientation and mobility (MA). *Accreditation:* CORE; NCATE. *Program availability:* Part-time. *Entrance requirements:* For master's, interview, minimum GPA of 2.75. *Faculty research:* Low vision, orientation and mobility instruction.

University of Arkansas at Little Rock, Graduate School, College of Education and Health Professions, Department of Teacher Education, Program in Special Education, Little Rock, AR 72204-1099. Offers M Ed. *Accreditation:* NCATE. *Program availability:* Part-time, evening/weekend. *Degree requirements:* For master's, comprehensive exam, portfolio or thesis. *Entrance requirements:* For master's, interview, minimum GPA of 2.75, GRE General Test or teaching certificate.

The University of British Columbia, Faculty of Education, Department of Educational and Counseling Psychology, and Special Education, Vancouver, BC V6T 1Z4, Canada. Offers counseling psychology (M Ed, MA, PhD); guidance studies (Diploma); human development, learning and culture (M Ed, MA, PhD); measurement, evaluation, and research methodology (M Ed, MA, PhD); school psychology (M Ed, MA, PhD); special education (M Ed, MA, PhD, Diploma). *Program availability:* Part-time. *Degree requirements:* For master's, thesis (for some programs); for doctorate, comprehensive exam, thesis/dissertation. *Entrance requirements:* For master's, GRE General Test (for MA in counseling psychology); for doctorate, GRE General Test. Additional exam requirements/recommendations for international students: Required—TOEFL. Electronic applications accepted. *Expenses:* Contact institution. *Faculty research:* Women, family, social problems, career transition, stress and coping problems.

University of California, Berkeley, Graduate Division, School of Education, Program in Special Education, Berkeley, CA 94720. Offers PhD. Program held jointly with San Francisco State University. *Degree requirements:* For doctorate, thesis/dissertation, oral qualifying exam. *Entrance requirements:* For doctorate, GRE General Test, minimum undergraduate GPA of 3.0 during last 2 years, 3 letters of recommendation. Electronic applications accepted.

University of California, Berkeley, Graduate Division, School of Education, Programs in Education, Berkeley, CA 94720. Offers development in mathematics and science (MA); education in mathematics, science, and technology (MA, PhD); human development and education (MA, PhD); leadership education (MA); special education (PhD); teacher education (MA); MA/Credential; PhD/Credential; PhD/MA. Terminal master's awarded for partial completion of doctoral program. *Degree requirements:* For master's, exam or thesis; for doctorate, thesis/dissertation, oral qualifying exam. *Entrance requirements:* For master's and doctorate, GRE General Test, minimum GPA of 3.0 during last 2 years of undergraduate course work. Electronic applications accepted. *Faculty research:* Human development, social and moral educational psychology, developmental teacher preparation.

University of California, Los Angeles, Graduate Division, Graduate School of Education and Information Studies, Program in Special Education, Los Angeles, CA 90095. Offers PhD. Program offered jointly with California State University, Los Angeles. *Degree requirements:* For doctorate, thesis/dissertation, oral and written qualifying exams. *Entrance requirements:* For doctorate, GRE General Test, minimum undergraduate GPA of 3.0. Additional exam requirements/recommendations for international students: Required—TOEFL (minimum score 560 paper-based; 87 iBT). Electronic applications accepted.

University of California, Riverside, Graduate Division, Graduate School of Education, Riverside, CA 92521. Offers applied behavior analysis (M Ed); diversity and equity (M Ed); education policy analysis and leadership (PhD); education specialist (Credential); education, society, and culture (MA, PhD); educational psychology (MA, PhD); general education (M Ed); higher education administration and policy (M Ed, PhD); multiple subject (Credential); research, evaluation, measurement and statistics (MA); school psychology (PhD); single subject (Credential); special education (M Ed, PhD); special education and autism (MA); TESOL (M Ed). Terminal master's awarded for partial completion of doctoral program. *Degree requirements:* For master's, comprehensive exams or thesis (MA), case study or analytical report (M Ed); for doctorate, comprehensive exam, thesis/dissertation, written and oral qualifying exams, college teaching practicum. *Entrance requirements:* For master's, GRE General Test (for MA); CBEST and CSET (for M Ed in general education only), UCR Extension TESOL certificate (for M Ed with TESOL emphasis only); for doctorate, GRE General Test, writing sample; for Credential, CBEST, CSET. Additional exam requirements/recommendations for international students: Required—TOEFL (minimum score 550 paper-based; 80 iBT), IELTS (minimum score 7). Electronic applications accepted. *Faculty research:* Responsiveness to intervention, faculty core, response to intervention of English language learners, advanced modeling techniques, study on social capital, trust, and motivation.

University of Central Arkansas, Graduate School, College of Education, Department of Early Childhood and Special Education, Program in Special Education, Conway, AR 72035-0001. Offers collaborative instructional specialist (ages 0-8) (MSE); collaborative instructional specialist (grades 4-12) (MSE); special education instructional specialist grades 4-12 (Graduate Certificate); special education instructional specialist P-4

(Graduate Certificate). *Accreditation:* NCATE. *Program availability:* Part-time, evening/weekend, online learning. *Degree requirements:* For master's, comprehensive exam, thesis optional. *Entrance requirements:* For master's, GRE General Test, minimum GPA of 2.7. Additional exam requirements/recommendations for international students: Required—TOEFL (minimum score 550 paper-based; 80 iBT).

University of Central Arkansas, Graduate School, College of Education, Department of Leadership Studies, Conway, AR 72035-0001. Offers college student personnel (MS); district-level administration (PMC); educational leadership - district level (Ed S); instructional technology (MS); library media and information technology (MS); school counseling (MS); school leadership (MS); school-based leadership adult education program administration (PMC); school-based leadership building administration (PMC); school-based leadership curriculum administration (PMC); school-based leadership gifted and talented program administration (PMC); school-based leadership special education program administration (PMC). *Accreditation:* NCATE. *Program availability:* Part-time, evening/weekend, online learning. *Degree requirements:* For master's and other advanced degree, comprehensive exam. *Entrance requirements:* For master's, GRE. Additional exam requirements/recommendations for international students: Required—TOEFL (minimum score 80 iBT). Electronic applications accepted. *Expenses:* Contact institution.

University of Central Florida, College of Community Innovation and Education, School of Teacher Education, Program in Exceptional Student Education, Orlando, FL 32816. Offers autism spectrum disorders (Certificate); exceptional student education (M Ed); exceptional student education K-12 (MA); intervention specialist (Certificate); pre-kindergarten disabilities (Certificate). *Accreditation:* NCATE. *Program availability:* Part-time, evening/weekend. *Students:* 14 full-time (13 women), 174 part-time (158 women); includes 81 minority (33 Black or African American, non-Hispanic/Latino; 1 Asian, non-Hispanic/Latino; 44 Hispanic/Latino; 3 Two or more races, non-Hispanic/Latino), 1 international. Average age 38. 85 applicants, 82% accepted, 49 enrolled. In 2018, 61 master's, 56 other advanced degrees awarded. *Degree requirements:* For master's, comprehensive exam, thesis or alternative. *Entrance requirements:* For master's, GRE General Test. Additional exam requirements/recommendations for international students: Required—TOEFL. *Application deadline:* For fall admission, 7/15 for domestic students; for spring admission, 11/15 for domestic students; for summer admission, 4/1 for domestic students. Application fee: $30. Electronic applications accepted. *Financial support:* Career-related internships or fieldwork, Federal Work-Study, institutionally sponsored loans, and unspecified assistantships available. Financial award application deadline: 3/1; financial award applicants required to submit FAFSA. *Unit head:* Dr. Mary Little, Program Coordinator, 407-823-3275, E-mail: mary.little@ucf.edu. *Application contact:* Associate Director, Graduate Admissions, 407-823-2766, Fax: 407-823-6442, E-mail: gradadmissions@ucf.edu.
Website: http://education.ucf.edu/exed/

University of Central Missouri, The Graduate School, Warrensburg, MO 64093. Offers accountancy (MA); accounting (MBA); applied mathematics (MS); aviation safety (MA); biology (MS); business administration (MBA); career and technical education leadership (MS); college student personnel administration (MS); communication (MA); computer science (MS); counseling (MS); criminal justice (MS); educational leadership (Ed D); educational technology (MS); elementary and early childhood education (MSE); English (MA); environmental studies (MA); finance (MBA); history (MA); human services/educational technology (Ed S); human services/learning resources (Ed S); human services/professional counseling (Ed S); industrial hygiene (MS); industrial management (MS); information systems (MBA); information technology (MS); kinesiology (MS); library science and information services (MS); literacy education (MSE); marketing (MBA); mathematics (MS); music (MA); occupational safety management (MS); psychology (MS); rural family nursing (MS); school administration (MSE); social gerontology (MS); sociology (MA); special education (MSE); speech language pathology (MS); superintendency (Ed S); teaching (MAT); teaching English as a second language (MA); technology (MS); technology management (PhD); theatre (MA). *Accreditation:* ASHA. *Program availability:* Part-time, 100% online, blended/hybrid learning. *Degree requirements:* For master's and Ed S, comprehensive exam (for some programs), thesis (for some programs). *Entrance requirements:* Additional exam requirements/recommendations for international students: Required—TOEFL (minimum score 550 paper-based; 79 iBT). Electronic applications accepted.

University of Central Oklahoma, The Jackson College of Graduate Studies, College of Education and Professional Studies, Donna Nigh Department of Advanced Professional and Special Services, Edmond, OK 73034-5209. Offers educational leadership (M Ed); library media education (M Ed); reading (M Ed); school counseling (M Ed); special education (M Ed), including mild/moderate disabilities, severe-profound/multiple disabilities; speech-language pathology (MS). *Accreditation:* ASHA. *Program availability:* Part-time. *Degree requirements:* For master's, comprehensive exam (for some programs), thesis (for some programs). *Entrance requirements:* Additional exam requirements/recommendations for international students: Required—TOEFL (minimum score 550 paper-based; 79 iBT), IELTS (minimum score 6.5). Electronic applications accepted.

University of Cincinnati, Graduate School, College of Education, Criminal Justice, and Human Services, School of Education, Program in Special Education, Cincinnati, OH 45221. Offers M Ed, Ed D. *Accreditation:* NCATE. *Program availability:* Part-time. *Degree requirements:* For master's, thesis or alternative; for doctorate, thesis/dissertation. *Entrance requirements:* For master's, GRE General Test; for doctorate, GRE General Test, GRE Subject Test. Additional exam requirements/recommendations for international students: Required—TOEFL (minimum score 550 paper-based), TWE (minimum score 4.5), OEPT. Electronic applications accepted.

University of Colorado Colorado Springs, College of Education, Colorado Springs, CO 80918. Offers counseling and human services (MA); curriculum and instruction (MA); educational leadership (MA); educational leadership, research and policy (PhD); special education (MA); teaching English to speakers of other languages (MA). *Accreditation:* ACA; NCATE. *Program availability:* Part-time, evening/weekend, 100% online, blended/hybrid learning. *Faculty:* 31 full-time (22 women), 61 part-time/adjunct (47 women). *Students:* 208 full-time (149 women), 351 part-time (256 women); includes 136 minority (30 Black or African American, non-Hispanic/Latino; 1 American Indian or Alaska Native, non-Hispanic/Latino; 12 Asian, non-Hispanic/Latino; 64 Hispanic/Latino; 29 Two or more races, non-Hispanic/Latino), 8 international. Average age 36. 230 applicants, 80% accepted, 101 enrolled. In 2018, 186 master's, 9 doctorates awarded. *Degree requirements:* For master's, comprehensive exam, thesis or alternative, microcomputer proficiency; for doctorate, comprehensive exam, thesis/dissertation, research lab. *Entrance requirements:* For master's, GRE General Test (recommended but not required), career goal statement, professional references; for doctorate, GRE General Test. Additional exam requirements/recommendations for international students: Recommended—TOEFL (minimum score 90 iBT), IELTS (minimum score 6.5). *Application deadline:* For fall admission, 1/28 priority date for domestic and international students; for spring admission, 11/1 priority date for domestic and international students. Applications are processed on a rolling basis. Application fee: $60 ($100 for international students). Electronic applications accepted. *Expenses:* Tuition and fees vary by program, course load, and residency type. Please visit the University of Colorado Colorado Springs Student Financial Services website to estimate current program costs: https://www.uccs.edu/bursar/index.php/estimate-your-bill. *Financial support:* In 2018–19, 15 students received support. Career-related internships or fieldwork, Federal Work-Study, scholarships/grants, and unspecified assistantships available. Support available to part-time students. Financial award application deadline: 3/1; financial award applicants required to submit FAFSA. *Faculty research:* Linguistically diverse education (LDE), educational policy, evidence-based reading and writing instruction, relational and social aggression, positive behavior supports, inclusive schooling, K-12 education policy. *Total annual research expenditures:* $607,967. *Unit head:* Dr. Valerie Martin Conley, Dean, 719-255-4133, E-mail: vmconley@uccs.edu. *Application contact:* The College of Education Student Resource Office, 719-255-4996, E-mail: education@uccs.edu.
Website: https://www.uccs.edu/coe/

University of Colorado Denver, School of Education and Human Development, Early Childhood Education Program, Denver, CO 80217. Offers early childhood education (MA); special education (MA). *Accreditation:* NCATE. *Program availability:* Part-time, evening/weekend, online learning. *Degree requirements:* For master's, comprehensive exam, fieldwork, practica, 40 credit hours. *Entrance requirements:* For master's, GRE or MAT (if GPA is below 2.75), minimum GPA of 2.75, resume, three letters of recommendation, documented experience with young children, transcripts from all previous colleges/universities attended. Additional exam requirements/recommendations for international students: Required—TOEFL (minimum score 537 paper-based; 75 iBT); Recommended—IELTS (minimum score 6.5). Electronic applications accepted. *Expenses:* Tuition, state resident: full-time $6786; part-time $337 per credit hour. Tuition, nonresident: full-time $22,590; part-time $1255 per credit hour. *Required fees:* $1231; $137 per credit hour. Tuition and fees vary according to program and reciprocity agreements. *Faculty research:* Early childhood growth and development, faculty development, adult learning, gender and equity issues, research methodology.

University of Colorado Denver, School of Education and Human Development, Program in Educational Leadership and Innovation, Denver, CO 80217. Offers educational studies and research (PhD), including administrative leadership and policy, early childhood special education, math education, research, assessment and evaluation, science education, urban ecologies. *Program availability:* Part-time, evening/weekend. *Degree requirements:* For doctorate, comprehensive exam, thesis/dissertation, 75 credit hours (for PhD). *Entrance requirements:* For doctorate, GRE or equivalent, resume or curriculum vitae, letters of recommendation, master's degree or equivalent, completion of basic or advanced statistics course with minimum B grade. Additional exam requirements/recommendations for international students: Required—TOEFL (minimum score 537 paper-based; 75 iBT); Recommended—IELTS (minimum score 6.5). Electronic applications accepted. *Expenses:* Tuition, state resident: full-time $6786; part-time $337 per credit hour. Tuition, nonresident: full-time $22,590; part-time $1255 per credit hour. *Required fees:* $1231; $137 per credit hour. Tuition and fees vary according to program and reciprocity agreements. *Faculty research:* Administrative leadership and policy studies, early childhood education, research in diversity, paraprofessionals in education, urban schools lab.

University of Colorado Denver, School of Education and Human Development, Program in Education and Human Development, Denver, CO 80217. Offers administrative leadership and policy (PhD); assessment (MA); early childhood special education/early childhood education (PhD); family science and human development (PhD); human development and family relations (MA); learning (MA); mathematics education (PhD); research and evaluation methods (MA); research, assessment and evaluation (PhD); science education (PhD); urban ecologies (PhD). MA program also offered in partnership with Boulder Journey School, Friends School and Stanley British Primary School. *Program availability:* Part-time, evening/weekend. *Degree requirements:* For master's, comprehensive exam, 9 hours of core courses embedded within a minimum of 36 to 38 hours of relevant coursework, including an educational psychology practicum, independent study project or thesis (recommended). *Entrance requirements:* For master's, GRE if undergraduate GPA below 2.75, resume, three letters of recommendation, transcripts. Additional exam requirements/recommendations for international students: Required—TOEFL (minimum score 537 paper-based; 75 iBT); Recommended—IELTS (minimum score 6.5). Electronic applications accepted. *Expenses:* Contact institution. *Faculty research:* Crisis response and intervention, school violence prevention, immigrant experience, educational environments for English language learners, culturally competent assessment and intervention, child and youth suicide.

University of Colorado Denver, School of Education and Human Development, Teacher Education Programs, Denver, CO 80217. Offers elementary linguistically diverse education (MA); elementary math and science education (MA); elementary math education (MA); elementary reading and writing (MA); elementary science education (MA); secondary English education (MA); secondary linguistically diverse education (MA); secondary math education (MA); secondary reading and writing (MA); secondary science education (MA); special education (MA). *Accreditation:* NCATE. *Program availability:* Part-time, evening/weekend. *Degree requirements:* For master's, comprehensive exam. *Entrance requirements:* For master's, GRE or MAT (for those with GPA below 2.75), transcripts, resume, letters of recommendation. Additional exam requirements/recommendations for international students: Required—TOEFL (minimum score 537 paper-based; 75 iBT); Recommended—IELTS (minimum score 6.5). Electronic applications accepted. *Expenses:* Tuition, state resident: full-time $6786; part-time $337 per credit hour. Tuition, nonresident: full-time $22,590; part-time $1255 per credit hour. *Required fees:* $1231; $137 per credit hour. Tuition and fees vary according to program and reciprocity agreements. *Faculty research:* Linguistically diverse education/ESL, elementary reading and writing, elementary teacher education, secondary teacher education, special education.

University of Denver, Morgridge College of Education, Denver, CO 80208. Offers child, family and school psychology (MA, PhD, Ed S); counseling psychology (MA, PhD); curriculum and instruction (MA, Ed D, PhD); curriculum instruction and teaching (Certificate); early childhood special education (MA, Certificate); educational leadership and policy studies (MA, Ed D, PhD, Certificate); higher education (Ed D, PhD); library and information science (MLIS); research methods and statistics (MA, PhD). *Accreditation:* ALA; APA (one or more programs are accredited). *Program availability:* Part-time, evening/weekend, online learning. *Faculty:* 49 full-time (35 women), 33 part-time/adjunct (20 women). *Students:* 509 full-time (400 women), 365 part-time (277 women); includes 236 minority (53 Black or African American, non-Hispanic/Latino; 6 American Indian or Alaska Native, non-Hispanic/Latino; 28 Asian, non-Hispanic/Latino; 116 Hispanic/Latino; 33 Two or more races, non-Hispanic/Latino), 56 international. Average age 31. 1,372 applicants, 57% accepted, 382 enrolled. In 2018, 258 master's, 41 doctorates, 162 other advanced degrees awarded. Terminal master's awarded for partial completion of doctoral program. *Degree requirements:* For master's, comprehensive exam (for some programs); for doctorate, comprehensive exam (for some programs), thesis/dissertation. *Entrance requirements:* For master's, GRE General Test or GMAT, bachelors degree; transcripts; two letters of recommendation; personal statement; resume; for doctorate, GRE General Test or GMAT, Masters degree; transcripts; two letters of recommendation; personal statement(s); resume. Additional exam requirements/recommendations for international

students: Required—TOEFL (minimum score 550 paper-based; 80 iBT). *Application deadline:* Applications are processed on a rolling basis. Application fee: $65. Electronic applications accepted. *Expenses:* $33,183 per year full-time. *Financial support:* In 2018–19, 690 students received support, including 29 research assistantships with tuition reimbursements available (averaging $11,465 per year), 9 teaching assistantships with tuition reimbursements available (averaging $2,527 per year); career-related internships or fieldwork, Federal Work-Study, institutionally sponsored loans, scholarships/grants, and unspecified assistantships also available. Support available to part-time students. Financial award application deadline: 2/15; financial award applicants required to submit FAFSA. *Faculty research:* Early childhood education, educational leadership, access and opportunity to postsecondary education, marriage and family therapy, data management and archival research. *Total annual research expenditures:* $2.3 million. *Unit head:* Dr. Karen Riley, Dean, 303-871-3665, E-mail: karen.riley@du.edu. *Application contact:* Jodi Dye, Director of Admissions, 303-871-2510, E-mail: jodi.dye@du.edu.
Website: http://morgridge.du.edu

University of Detroit Mercy, College of Liberal Arts and Education, Detroit, MI 48221. Offers addiction counseling (MA); addiction studies (Certificate); clinical mental health counseling (MA); clinical psychology (MA, PhD); computer and information systems (MS); criminal justice (MA); curriculum and instruction (MA); economics (MA); educational administration (MA); financial economics (MA); industrial/organizational psychology (MA); information assurance (MS); intelligence analysis (MA); liberal studies (MALS); religious studies (MA); school counseling (MA, Certificate); school psychology (Spec); security administration (MS); special education: emotionally impaired/behaviorally disordered (MA); special education: learning disabilities (MA). *Program availability:* Part-time, evening/weekend. *Degree requirements:* For doctorate, departmental qualifying exam. *Faculty research:* Psychology of aging, history of technology, Renaissance humanism, U.S. and Japanese economic relations.

University of Florida, Graduate School, College of Education, School of Special Education, School Psychology and Early Childhood Studies, Gainesville, FL 32611. Offers early childhood education (M Ed, MAE); school psychology (M Ed, MAE, Ed D, PhD, Ed S); special education (M Ed, MAE, Ed D, PhD, Ed S). *Accreditation:* NCATE. *Program availability:* Part-time, evening/weekend, online learning. *Degree requirements:* For master's, comprehensive exam (for some programs), thesis (MAE); for doctorate, comprehensive exam, thesis/dissertation. *Entrance requirements:* For master's and doctorate, GRE General Test, minimum GPA of 3.0; for Ed S, GRE General Test. Additional exam requirements/recommendations for international students: Required—TOEFL (minimum score 550 paper-based; 80 iBT), IELTS (minimum score 6). Electronic applications accepted. *Faculty research:* Teacher quality/teacher education, early childhood, autism, academic and behavioral assessment and interventions.

University of Georgia, College of Education, Department of Communication Sciences and Special Education, Athens, GA 30602. Offers communication science and disorders (M Ed, MA, PhD, Ed S); special education (Ed D). *Accreditation:* ASHA (one or more programs are accredited). Terminal master's awarded for partial completion of doctoral program. *Degree requirements:* For master's, comprehensive exam (for some programs), thesis (for some programs); for doctorate, thesis/dissertation. *Entrance requirements:* For master's, doctorate, and Ed S, GRE General Test. Additional exam requirements/recommendations for international students: Required—TOEFL. Electronic applications accepted.

University of Guam, Office of Graduate Studies, School of Education, Program in Special Education, Mangilao, GU 96923. Offers M Ed. *Degree requirements:* For master's, comprehensive oral and written exams, special project or thesis. *Entrance requirements:* For master's, GRE General Test. Additional exam requirements/recommendations for international students: Required—TOEFL. *Faculty research:* Mainstreaming, multiculturalism.

University of Hawaii at Manoa, Office of Graduate Education, College of Education, Department of Special Education, Honolulu, HI 96822. Offers M Ed. *Accreditation:* NCATE. *Program availability:* Part-time. *Degree requirements:* For master's, thesis optional. *Entrance requirements:* For master's, GRE General Test, interview, minimum GPA of 3.0. Additional exam requirements/recommendations for international students: Required—TOEFL (minimum score 580 paper-based; 92 iBT), IELTS (minimum score 5). *Faculty research:* Mild/moderate/severe disabilities, early childhood interventions, inclusion, transition.

University of Hawaii at Manoa, Office of Graduate Education, College of Education, PhD in Education Program, Honolulu, HI 96822. Offers curriculum and instruction (PhD); educational administration (PhD); educational foundations (PhD); educational policy studies (PhD); educational psychology (PhD); exceptionalities (PhD); kinesiology (PhD); learning design and technology (PhD). *Program availability:* Part-time, evening/weekend. *Degree requirements:* For doctorate, thesis/dissertation. *Entrance requirements:* For doctorate, GRE General Test, sample of written work. Additional exam requirements/recommendations for international students: Required—TOEFL (minimum score 600 paper-based; 100 iBT), IELTS (minimum score 7).

University of Houston, College of Education, Department of Psychological, Health and Learning Sciences, Houston, TX 77204. Offers administration and supervision - higher education (M Ed); counseling (M Ed); counseling psychology (PhD); educational psychology (M Ed); school psychology (PhD); school psychology and individual differences (PhD); special education (M Ed). None. *Accreditation:* NCATE. *Program availability:* Part-time, evening/weekend, 100% online, blended/hybrid learning. *Faculty:* 31 full-time (23 women), 3 part-time/adjunct (1 woman). *Students:* 163 full-time (135 women), 51 part-time (43 women); includes 106 minority (35 Black or African American, non-Hispanic/Latino; 1 American Indian or Alaska Native, non-Hispanic/Latino; 18 Asian, non-Hispanic/Latino; 46 Hispanic/Latino; 6 Two or more races, non-Hispanic/Latino), 17 international. Average age 29. 216 applicants, 58% accepted, 60 enrolled. In 2018, 39 master's, 18 doctorates awarded. Terminal master's awarded for partial completion of doctoral program. *Degree requirements:* For master's, comprehensive exam or thesis; for doctorate, comprehensive exam, thesis/dissertation. *Entrance requirements:* For master's, GRE, transcripts, 3 letters of recommendation, curriculum vita, goal statement; for doctorate, GRE, transcripts, 3 letters of recommendation, curriculum vita, goal statement, writing sample, interview. Additional exam requirements/recommendations for international students: Required—TOEFL (minimum score 550 paper-based; 79 iBT). *Application deadline:* For fall admission, 1/15 for domestic and international students; for spring admission, 9/15 for domestic and international students. Applications are processed on a rolling basis. Application fee: $80 ($75 for international students). Electronic applications accepted. Application fee is waived when completed online. *Financial support:* In 2018–19, 10 students received support, including 5 fellowships with full tuition reimbursements available (averaging $2,000 per year), 8 research assistantships with full tuition reimbursements available (averaging $8,664 per year), 56 teaching assistantships with full tuition reimbursements available (averaging $8,760 per year); career-related internships or fieldwork, Federal Work-Study, institutionally sponsored loans, scholarships/grants, health care benefits, and unspecified assistantships also available. Support available to part-time students. Financial award application deadline: 2/1. *Faculty research:* Evidence-based assessment and intervention, multicultural issues in psychology, social and cultural context of learning, systemic barriers to college, motivational aspects of self-regulated learning. *Total annual research expenditures:* $1.9 million. *Unit head:* Dr. Nathan Grant Smith, Interim Department Chair, 713-743-7648, Fax: 713-743-4996, E-mail: ngsmith@uh.edu. *Application contact:* Bridgette Jones, Director of Student Affairs, 713-743-2978, E-mail: bajones5@uh.edu.
Website: http://www.uh.edu/education/departments/phls/

University of Houston–Victoria, School of Education, Health Professions and Human Development, Victoria, TX 77901-4450. Offers administration and supervision (M Ed); adult and higher education (M Ed); counselor education (M Ed); curriculum and instruction (M Ed); dyslexia education (Certificate); educational technology (M Ed); special education (M Ed). *Program availability:* Part-time, evening/weekend, online learning. *Degree requirements:* For master's, comprehensive exam, project or thesis. *Entrance requirements:* For master's, GRE General Test. Additional exam requirements/recommendations for international students: Required—TOEFL. Electronic applications accepted. *Expenses: Tuition, area resident:* Full-time $6154; part-time $3077 per semester. Tuition, state resident: full-time $6154; part-time $3077 per semester. Tuition, nonresident: full-time $13,624; part-time $6812 per semester. *International tuition:* $13,624 full-time. *Required fees:* $1405; $847 per semester. $423 per semester. Tuition and fees vary according to program. *Faculty research:* Reading and language arts education, evaluation and diagnosis of special children's abilities.

University of Idaho, College of Graduate Studies, College of Education, Health and Human Sciences, Department of Curriculum and Instruction, Moscow, ID 83844-3082. Offers career and technology education (M Ed); curriculum and instruction (M Ed, Ed S); special education (M Ed). *Faculty:* 28 full-time (19 women). *Students:* 30 full-time (24 women), 37 part-time (29 women). Average age 37. In 2018, 32 master's awarded. *Entrance requirements:* For master's, minimum GPA of 3.0. Additional exam requirements/recommendations for international students: Required—TOEFL (minimum score 79 iBT). *Application deadline:* For fall admission, 8/1 for domestic students; for spring admission, 12/15 for domestic students. Applications are processed on a rolling basis. Application fee: $60. Electronic applications accepted. *Expenses:* Tuition, state resident: full-time $7266.44; part-time $474.50 per credit hour. Tuition, nonresident: full-time $24,902; part-time $1453.50 per credit hour. *Required fees:* $2085.56; $45.50 per credit hour. *Financial support:* Research assistantships and teaching assistantships available. Financial award applicants required to submit FAFSA.
Website: http://www.uidaho.edu/ed/ci

University of Illinois at Chicago, College of Education, Department of Special Education, Chicago, IL 60607-7128. Offers M Ed, PhD. *Program availability:* Part-time. Terminal master's awarded for partial completion of doctoral program. *Degree requirements:* For doctorate, thesis/dissertation. *Entrance requirements:* For master's, minimum GPA of 2.75; for doctorate, GRE General Test, minimum GPA of 2.75. Additional exam requirements/recommendations for international students: Required—TOEFL. Electronic applications accepted. *Faculty research:* Teaching and learning for special learners, individual differences.

University of Illinois at Urbana–Champaign, Graduate College, College of Education, Department of Special Education, Champaign, IL 61820. Offers Ed M, MS, Ed D, PhD, CAS. *Program availability:* Part-time, online learning.

The University of Iowa, Graduate College, College of Education, Department of Teaching and Learning, Program in Special Education, Iowa City, IA 52242-1316. Offers MA, PhD. *Degree requirements:* For master's, thesis optional, exam; for doctorate, comprehensive exam, thesis/dissertation. *Entrance requirements:* For master's and doctorate, GRE General Test, minimum GPA of 3.0. Additional exam requirements/recommendations for international students: Required—TOEFL (minimum score 550 paper-based; 81 iBT). Electronic applications accepted.

The University of Kansas, Graduate Studies, School of Education, Department of Special Education, Lawrence, KS 66045. Offers autism spectrum disorder (Certificate); early childhood unified (MS Ed); special and inclusive education leadership (Certificate); special education (PhD). *Accreditation:* NCATE. *Program availability:* Part-time, online learning. *Students:* 60 full-time (50 women), 295 part-time (257 women); includes 51 minority (17 Black or African American, non-Hispanic/Latino; 12 Asian, non-Hispanic/Latino; 12 Hispanic/Latino; 1 Native Hawaiian or other Pacific Islander, non-Hispanic/Latino; 9 Two or more races, non-Hispanic/Latino), 19 international. Average age 34. 189 applicants, 77% accepted, 123 enrolled. In 2018, 136 master's, 7 doctorates, 34 other advanced degrees awarded. *Entrance requirements:* For master's, minimum GPA of 3.0, official transcripts, 3 letters of reference, professional resume; for doctorate, GRE General Test, official transcripts, 3 letters of reference, professional resume, professional writing sample. Additional exam requirements/recommendations for international students: Required—TOEFL, IELTS. *Application deadline:* For fall admission, 8/1 for domestic students; for spring admission, 12/13 for domestic students. Application fee: $65 ($85 for international students). Electronic applications accepted. *Financial support:* Fellowships, research assistantships, teaching assistantships, Federal Work-Study, scholarships/grants, and unspecified assistantships available. Support available to part-time students. Financial award application deadline: 2/21; financial award applicants required to submit FAFSA. *Faculty research:* Autism spectrum disorders, learning disabilities research, leadership development, qualitative research and evaluation. *Unit head:* Michael L. Wehmeyer, Chair, 785-864-0723, E-mail: wehmeyer@ku.edu. *Application contact:* Shaunna Price, Graduate Admission Contact, 785-864-4342, E-mail: shaunna.price@ku.edu.
Website: http://specialedu.ku.edu/

University of Kentucky, Graduate School, College of Education, Program in Special Education, Lexington, KY 40506-0032. Offers early childhood (MS Ed); rehabilitation counseling (MRC, PhD); special education (MS Ed, PhD). *Accreditation:* CORE; NCATE. Terminal master's awarded for partial completion of doctoral program. *Degree requirements:* For master's, comprehensive exam, thesis optional; for doctorate, comprehensive exam, thesis/dissertation. *Entrance requirements:* For master's, GRE General Test, minimum undergraduate GPA of 2.75; for doctorate, GRE General Test, minimum graduate GPA of 3.0. Additional exam requirements/recommendations for international students: Required—TOEFL (minimum score 550 paper-based). Electronic applications accepted. *Faculty research:* Applied behavior analysis applications in special education, single subject research design in classroom settings, transition research across life span, rural special education personnel.

University of La Verne, LaFetra College of Education, Program in Special Education, La Verne, CA 91750-4443. Offers mild/moderate education specialist (Credential); special education studies (MS). *Entrance requirements:* For master's, bachelor's degree, minimum undergraduate GPA of 3.0. *Expenses:* Contact institution.

University of La Verne, Regional and Online Campuses, Graduate Credential Program in Education, California Statewide Campus, La Verne, CA 91750-4443. Offers administration services (preliminary) (Credential); education specialist: mild/moderate (Credential); English (Certificate); multiple subject teaching (Credential); pupil personnel services: school counseling (Credential); single subject teaching (Credential); special education (MS); special emphasis (M Ed). *Accreditation:* NCATE. *Program availability:* Part-time. *Entrance requirements:* For degree, California Basic Educational Skills Test, minimum undergraduate GPA of 2.75, 3 letters of recommendation, interview. *Expenses:* Contact institution.

Special Education

University of La Verne, Regional and Online Campuses, Graduate Programs, High Desert Campus, Victorville, CA 92392. Offers business administration for experienced professionals (MBA); educational (special emphasis) (M Ed); educational counseling (MS); leadership and management (MS); multiple subject (elementary) (Credential); preliminary administrative services (Credential); pupil personnel services (Credential); single subject (secondary) (Credential). *Expenses:* Contact institution.

University of La Verne, Regional and Online Campuses, Graduate Programs, Kern County Campus, Bakersfield, CA 93301. Offers business administration for experienced professionals (MBA-EP); education (special emphasis) (M Ed); educational counseling (MS); educational leadership (M Ed); health administration (MHA); leadership and management (MS); mild/moderate education specialist (Credential); multiple subject (elementary) (Credential); organizational leadership (Ed D); preliminary administrative services (Credential); single subject (secondary) (Credential); special education studies (MS). *Program availability:* Part-time, evening/weekend. *Expenses:* Contact institution.

University of La Verne, Regional and Online Campuses, Master's Programs in Education, California Statewide Campus, La Verne, CA 91750-4443. Offers administration services (preliminary) (Credential); education specialist: mild/moderate (Credential); educational counseling (MS); educational leadership (M Ed); multiple subject teaching (Credential); pupil personnel services: school counseling (Credential); single subject teaching (Credential); special education studies (MS); special emphasis (M Ed). *Accreditation:* NCATE. *Entrance requirements:* For master's, California Basic Educational Skills Test, 3 letters of recommendation, teaching credential. *Expenses:* Contact institution.

University of Louisiana at Lafayette, College of Education, Department of Educational Curriculum and Instruction, Program in Curriculum and Instruction, Lafayette, LA 70504. Offers instructional specialist (M Ed); K-8 mathematics education (M Ed); non-public school administration (M Ed); special education diagnostics (M Ed); teacher researcher (M Ed). *Accreditation:* NCATE. *Entrance requirements:* For master's, GRE General Test, teaching certificate. Additional exam requirements/recommendations for international students: Required—TOEFL (minimum score 550 paper-based). Electronic applications accepted.

University of Louisiana at Monroe, Graduate School, College of Arts, Education, and Sciences, School of Education, Program in Special Education, Monroe, LA 71209-0001. Offers MAT. *Accreditation:* NCATE. *Program availability:* Part-time, evening/weekend. *Faculty:* 11 full-time (7 women). *Students:* 3 full-time (all women), 16 part-time (11 women); includes 3 minority (2 Black or African American, non-Hispanic/Latino; 1 Hispanic/Latino). Average age 30. 6 applicants, 50% accepted, 3 enrolled. In 2018, 10 master's awarded. *Entrance requirements:* For master's, GRE General Test, minimum GPA of 2.5. Additional exam requirements/recommendations for international students: Required—TOEFL (minimum score 500 paper-based; 61 iBT). *Application deadline:* For fall admission, 8/22 priority date for domestic students, 7/1 for international students; for winter admission, 12/12 priority date for domestic students; for spring admission, 1/17 for domestic students, 11/1 for international students. Applications are processed on a rolling basis. Application fee: $20 ($30 for international students). Electronic applications accepted. *Financial support:* In 2018–19, 5 students received support. Research assistantships, career-related internships or fieldwork, Federal Work-Study, and unspecified assistantships available. Financial award application deadline: 4/1; financial award applicants required to submit FAFSA.

University of Louisville, Graduate School, College of Education and Human Development, Departments of Early Childhood and Elementary Education, Middle and Secondary Education, and Special Education, Louisville, KY 40292-0001. Offers art education (MAT); autism and applied behavior analysis (Certificate); curriculum and instruction (PhD); early elementary education (MAT); exercise physiology (MS); health and physical education (MAT); health professions education (Certificate); higher education (MA); human resources and organization development (MS); instructional technology (M Ed); interdisciplinary early childhood education (MAT); middle school education (MAT); music education (MAT); secondary education (MAT); special education (MAT); sport administration (MS); teacher leadership (M Ed). *Program availability:* Part-time, evening/weekend, 100% online, blended/hybrid learning. *Faculty:* 97 full-time (64 women), 131 part-time/adjunct (86 women). *Students:* 109 full-time (72 women), 139 part-time (87 women); includes 43 minority (18 Black or African American, non-Hispanic/Latino; 6 Asian, non-Hispanic/Latino; 10 Hispanic/Latino; 9 Two or more races, non-Hispanic/Latino), 9 international. Average age 29. 108 applicants, 75% accepted, 59 enrolled. In 2018, 64 master's awarded. Terminal master's awarded for partial completion of doctoral program. *Degree requirements:* For master's, comprehensive exam (for some programs), thesis optional; for doctorate, comprehensive exam (for some programs), thesis/dissertation. *Entrance requirements:* For master's, GRE (for most programs), PRAXIS (for educator preparation programs), professional statement, recommendation letters, resume, transcripts; for doctorate and Certificate, GRE, professional statement, recommendation letters, resume, transcripts. Additional exam requirements/recommendations for international students: Required—TOEFL (minimum score 550 paper-based; 79 iBT); Recommended—IELTS (minimum score 6.5). *Application deadline:* For fall admission, 6/1 priority date for domestic students, 5/1 priority date for international students; for spring admission, 10/1 for domestic students, 11/1 priority date for international students; for summer admission, 3/1 priority date for domestic students, 4/1 priority date for international students. Application fee: $65. *Expenses: Tuition, area resident:* Full-time $6500; part-time $723 per credit hour. *Tuition, state resident:* full-time $6500. *Tuition, nonresident:* full-time $13,557; part-time $1507 per credit hour. Tuition and fees vary according to course load and program. *Financial support:* In 2018–19, 144 students received support, including fellowships with full tuition reimbursements available (averaging $21,024 per year), research assistantships with full tuition reimbursements available (averaging $21,024 per year), teaching assistantships with full tuition reimbursements available (averaging $21,024 per year); Federal Work-Study, scholarships/grants, health care benefits, tuition waivers (full), and unspecified assistantships also available. Financial award application deadline: 3/1; financial award applicants required to submit FAFSA. *Faculty research:* Children's early reading and writing development, crelevance of basic facts in elementary mathematics instruction, clinical model of teacher education, cultural and linguistic context of diverse learners, and STEM-integrated curriculum design and development. STEM teaching and learning, content literacy for English language learners, social justice in teacher education, adolescent literacy, mathematics teacher development. Classroom and behavior management; moderate/severe disabilities, autism. *Unit head:* Dr. Amy Lingo, Interim Dean, 502-852-3235, Fax: 502-852-1464, E-mail: cehdinfo@louisville.edu. *Application contact:* Dr. Margaret Pentecost, Assistant Dean for Graduate Student Success, 502-852-6437, Fax: 502-852-1417, E-mail: gedadm@louisville.edu.
Website: http://louisville.edu/delphi

University of Lynchburg, Graduate Studies, M Ed Program in Special Education, Lynchburg, VA 24501-3199. Offers M Ed. *Program availability:* Part-time, evening/weekend. *Degree requirements:* For master's, comprehensive exam, internship; practicum. *Entrance requirements:* For master's, GRE, minimum GPA of 3.0 (preferred), official transcripts (bachelor's, others as relevant), three letters of recommendation, career goals statement. Additional exam requirements/recommendations for

international students: Required—TOEFL (minimum score 550 paper-based; 80 iBT), IELTS (minimum score 6). Electronic applications accepted. Application fee is waived when completed online. *Expenses:* Contact institution.

University of Maine, Graduate School, College of Education and Human Development, School of Learning and Teaching, Orono, ME 04469. Offers counselor education (M Ed, MA, MS, CAS); early childhood teacher (CGS); education (PhD), including counselor education, literacy education, prevention and intervention studies; elementary education (M Ed, CAS); individualized education (M Ed); literacy education (CAS); response to intervention for behavior (CGS); secondary education (M Ed, CAS); social studies education (M Ed); special education (M Ed, CAS). *Program availability:* Part-time. *Faculty:* 21 full-time (12 women), 37 part-time/adjunct (29 women). *Students:* 113 full-time (96 women), 224 part-time (191 women); includes 11 minority (3 Black or African American, non-Hispanic/Latino; 4 American Indian or Alaska Native, non-Hispanic/Latino; 1 Asian, non-Hispanic/Latino; 2 Hispanic/Latino; 1 Two or more races, non-Hispanic/Latino), 3 international. Average age 37. 195 applicants, 99% accepted, 147 enrolled. In 2018, 82 master's, 2 doctorates, 49 other advanced degrees awarded. *Degree requirements:* For master's, thesis (for some programs); for doctorate, comprehensive exam, thesis/dissertation. *Entrance requirements:* For master's, GRE General Test, MAT. Additional exam requirements/recommendations for international students: Required—TOEFL (minimum score 550 paper-based; 80 iBT), IELTS (minimum score 6.5). *Application deadline:* For fall admission, 2/1 priority date for domestic students. Applications are processed on a rolling basis. Application fee: $65. Electronic applications accepted. *Financial support:* In 2018–19, 22 students received support, including 8 teaching assistantships with full tuition reimbursements available (averaging $1,600 per year); Federal Work-Study, scholarships/grants, and unspecified assistantships also available. Financial award application deadline: 3/1. *Faculty research:* Gender and leadership, virtual reality, using writing to improve performance in athletics, digital citizenship, professional development for special and general education. *Total annual research expenditures:* $2.1 million. *Unit head:* Dr. Jim Artesani, Associate Dean of Accreditation and Graduate Affairs, 207-581-4061. *Application contact:* Scott G. Delcourt, Assistant Vice President for Graduate Studies and Senior Associate Dean, 207-581-3291, Fax: 207-581-3232, E-mail: graduate@maine.edu.
Website: http://umaine.edu/edhd/

University of Manitoba, Faculty of Graduate Studies, Faculty of Education, Department of Educational Administration, Foundations and Psychology, Winnipeg, MB R3T 2N2, Canada. Offers adult and post-secondary education (M Ed); educational administration (M Ed); guidance and counseling (M Ed); inclusive special education (M Ed); social foundations of education (M Ed). *Degree requirements:* For master's, thesis or alternative.

University of Mary, Liffrig Family School of Education and Behavioral Sciences, Department of Education, Bismarck, ND 58504-9652. Offers curriculum, instruction and assessment (M Ed); education (Ed D); elementary administration (M Ed); reading (M Ed); secondary administration (M Ed); special education strategist (M Ed). *Program availability:* Part-time. *Degree requirements:* For master's, portfolio or thesis. *Entrance requirements:* For master's, interview, letters of reference, minimum GPA of 2.5. Additional exam requirements/recommendations for international students: Required—TOEFL (minimum score 500 paper-based; 71 iBT). Electronic applications accepted.

University of Maryland Eastern Shore, Graduate Programs, Department of Education, Program in Special Education, Princess Anne, MD 21853. Offers M Ed. *Accreditation:* NCATE. *Degree requirements:* For master's, comprehensive exam, seminar paper, internship. *Entrance requirements:* For master's, PRAXIS I, interview, minimum GPA of 3.0. Additional exam requirements/recommendations for international students: Required—TOEFL (minimum score 80 iBT). Electronic applications accepted.

University of Massachusetts Amherst, Graduate School, College of Education, Program in Education, Amherst, MA 01003. Offers bilingual, English as a second language, and multicultural education (M Ed, Ed S); child study and early education (M Ed); children, families and schools (Ed D, Ed S); early childhood and elementary teacher education (M Ed); educational leadership (M Ed); educational policy and leadership (Ed D); higher education (M Ed); international education (M Ed); language, literacy and culture (Ed D); learning, media and technology (M Ed, Ed S); mathematics, science, and learning technologies (Ed D); reading and writing (M Ed); research, educational measurement and psychometrics (Ed D); school counselor education (M Ed, Ed S); school psychology (Ed S); science education (Ed S); secondary teacher education (M Ed); social justice education (M Ed, Ed D, Ed S); special education (M Ed, Ed D, Ed S); teacher education and school improvement (Ed D, Ed S). *Accreditation:* NCATE. *Program availability:* Part-time, online learning. Terminal master's awarded for partial completion of doctoral program. *Degree requirements:* For doctorate, comprehensive exam, thesis/dissertation. *Entrance requirements:* Additional exam requirements/recommendations for international students: Required—TOEFL (minimum score 550 paper-based; 80 iBT), IELTS (minimum score 6.5). Electronic applications accepted.

University of Massachusetts Boston, College of Education and Human Development, Program in Special Education, Boston, MA 02125-3393. Offers M Ed. *Program availability:* Part-time, evening/weekend. *Students:* 4 full-time (all women), 33 part-time (24 women); includes 4 minority (all Hispanic/Latino). Average age 28. 18 applicants, 94% accepted, 9 enrolled. In 2018, 16 master's awarded. *Entrance requirements:* For master's, GRE General Test or MAT, minimum GPA of 2.75. *Application deadline:* For fall admission, 7/1 for domestic students; for spring admission, 11/1 for domestic students. Application fee: $60 ($100 for international students). Electronic applications accepted. *Expenses: Tuition, area resident:* Full-time $17,896. *Tuition, state resident:* full-time $17,896. *Tuition, nonresident:* full-time $34,932. *International tuition:* $34,932 full-time. *Required fees:* $355. *Financial support:* Research assistantships, teaching assistantships, career-related internships or fieldwork, Federal Work-Study, and unspecified assistantships available. Support available to part-time students. Financial award application deadline: 3/1; financial award applicants required to submit FAFSA. *Faculty research:* Inclusionary learning, cross-cultural special needs, special education restructuring. *Unit head:* Dr. Christopher Denning, Graduate Program Director, 617-287.6539, E-mail: christopher.denning@umb.edu. *Application contact:* Graduate Admissions Coordinator, 617-287-6400, Fax: 617-287-6236, E-mail: graduate.admissions@umb.edu.

University of Massachusetts Dartmouth, Graduate School, College of Arts and Sciences, Department of Psychology, North Dartmouth, MA 02747-2300. Offers autism studies (Graduate Certificate); psychology - applied behavioral analysis (MA, Post-Master's Certificate); psychology - clinical (MA); psychology - research (MA). *Program availability:* Part-time. *Faculty:* 19 full-time (11 women), 7 part-time/adjunct (4 women). *Students:* 37 full-time (27 women), 54 part-time (47 women); includes 15 minority (3 Black or African American, non-Hispanic/Latino; 2 Asian, non-Hispanic/Latino; 7 Hispanic/Latino; 3 Two or more races, non-Hispanic/Latino), 3 international. Average age 28. 104 applicants, 50% accepted, 32 enrolled. In 2018, 32 master's, 1 other advanced degree awarded. *Degree requirements:* For master's, thesis (for some programs), thesis. *Entrance requirements:* For master's, GRE (recommended, not required), statement of purpose (minimum of 300 words), resume, 3 letters of recommendation, official transcripts. Clinical Psych requires acknowdgement of

conditions of a competency/fitness and full participation policy; for other advanced degree, statement of purpose (minimum of 300 words), resume, 3 letters of recommendation, official transcripts. Additional exam requirements/recommendations for international students: Required—TOEFL (minimum score 550 paper-based; 79 iBT), IELTS (minimum score 6.5). *Application deadline:* For fall admission, 8/15 priority date for domestic students, 7/15 for international students. Application fee: $60. Electronic applications accepted. *Financial support:* In 2018–19, 1 research assistantship (averaging $12,000 per year), 2 teaching assistantships (averaging $14,000 per year) were awarded; Federal Work-Study, tuition waivers (full and partial), and unspecified assistantships also available. Financial award application deadline: 3/1; financial award applicants required to submit FAFSA. *Faculty research:* Health inequities, language and cognitive development, interethnic dating and marriage, executive function and implicit learning in deaf children, behavioral medicine. *Total annual research expenditures:* $188,000. *Unit head:* Mahzad Hojjat, Graduate Program Director, Research Psychology, 508-999-8951, E-mail: mhojjat@umassd.edu. *Application contact:* Scott Webster, Director of Graduate Studies & Admissions, 508-999-8604, Fax: 508-999-8183, E-mail: graduate@umassd.edu.
Website: http://www.umassd.edu/cas/psychology

University of Memphis, Graduate School, College of Education, Department of Instruction and Curriculum Leadership, Memphis, TN 38152. Offers advanced studies in teaching and learning (M Ed); applied behavior analysis (Graduate Certificate); autism studies (Graduate Certificate); early childhood education (MAT, MS, Ed D); elementary education (MAT); instruction and curriculum (MS, Ed D); instruction design and technology (MS, Ed D); instructional design and technology (Graduate Certificate); literacy, leadership, and coaching (Graduate Certificate); reading (MS, Ed D); school library information specialist (Graduate Certificate); secondary education (MAT); special education (MAT, MS, Ed D); STEM teacher leadership (Graduate Certificate); urban education (Graduate Certificate). *Accreditation:* NCATE (one or more programs are accredited). *Program availability:* Part-time. *Students:* 62 full-time (45 women), 412 part-time (326 women); includes 209 minority (179 Black or African American, non-Hispanic/Latino; 1 American Indian or Alaska Native, non-Hispanic/Latino; 5 Asian, non-Hispanic/Latino; 17 Hispanic/Latino; 7 Two or more races, non-Hispanic/Latino), 4 international. Average age 35. 195 applicants, 91% accepted, 143 enrolled. In 2018, 122 master's, 13 doctorates, 29 other advanced degrees awarded. Terminal master's awarded for partial completion of doctoral program. *Degree requirements:* For master's, comprehensive exam, thesis or alternative; for doctorate, comprehensive exam, thesis/dissertation. *Entrance requirements:* For master's, GRE General Test, PRAXIS, minimum GPA of 2.5, letters of reference; for doctorate, GRE General Test, GRE Subject Test, 2 years of teaching experience, letters of reference, statement of purpose, interview. Additional exam requirements/recommendations for international students: Required—TOEFL (minimum score 550 paper-based; 79 iBT). *Application deadline:* For fall admission, 4/1 priority date for domestic students; for spring admission, 10/1 priority date for domestic students; for summer admission, 2/1 priority date for domestic students. Applications are processed on a rolling basis. Application fee: $35 ($60 for international students). Electronic applications accepted. *Expenses: Tuition, area resident:* Full-time $10,240; part-time $503 per credit hour. *Tuition, state resident:* full-time $10,464. *Tuition, nonresident:* full-time $20,224; part-time $991 per credit hour. *Required fees:* $850; $106 per credit hour. *Financial support:* Research assistantships with full tuition reimbursements, teaching assistantships with full tuition reimbursements, career-related internships or fieldwork, Federal Work-Study, institutionally sponsored loans, scholarships/grants, traineeships, and unspecified assistantships available. Support available to part-time students. Financial award application deadline: 2/1; financial award applicants required to submit FAFSA. *Faculty research:* Effective urban teachers, preparation and retention of urban teachers, technology utilization in schools, field-based teacher preparation programs, effective use of online instruction. *Unit head:* Dr. Christian Mueller, Chair, 901-678-2365, E-mail: cemuellr@memphis.edu. *Application contact:* Dr. Lee Allen, Director of Graduate Programs, 901-678-4073, E-mail: allenlee@memphis.edu.
Website: http://www.memphis.edu/icl/

University of Miami, Graduate School, School of Education and Human Development, Department of Teaching and Learning, Program in Early Childhood Special Education, Coral Gables, FL 33124. Offers MS Ed, Ed S. *Program availability:* Part-time, evening/weekend. *Faculty:* 4 full-time (3 women), 6 part-time/adjunct (all women). *Students:* 13 part-time (12 women); includes 10 minority (2 Black or African American, non-Hispanic/Latino; 8 Hispanic/Latino). Average age 35. In 2018, 13 master's awarded. *Degree requirements:* For master's, electronic portfolio. *Entrance requirements:* For master's, GRE General Test. Additional exam requirements/recommendations for international students: Required—TOEFL (minimum score 550 paper-based; 80 iBT); Recommended—IELTS (minimum score 6.5). *Application deadline:* Applications are processed on a rolling basis. Application fee: $75. Electronic applications accepted. *Financial support:* Scholarships/grants available. Financial award application deadline: 3/1; financial award applicants required to submit FAFSA. *Unit head:* Dr. Elizabeth Harry, Professor, 305-284-4961, Fax: 305-284-6998, E-mail: bharry@miami.edu. *Application contact:* Lois Heffernan, Graduate Admissions Coordinator, 305-284-2167, E-mail: lheffernan@miami.edu.
Website: http://www.education.miami.edu

University of Miami, Graduate School, School of Education and Human Development, Department of Teaching and Learning, Program in Teaching and Learning, Coral Gables, FL 33124. Offers language and literacy learning in multilingual settings (PhD); science, technology, engineering and mathematics (stem) (PhD); special education (PhD). *Faculty:* 14 full-time (10 women), 9 part-time/adjunct (all women). *Students:* 18 full-time (12 women); includes 8 minority (2 Black or African American, non-Hispanic/Latino; 1 Asian, non-Hispanic/Latino; 4 Hispanic/Latino; 1 Two or more races, non-Hispanic/Latino), 6 international. Average age 36. 15 applicants, 33% accepted, 3 enrolled. In 2018, 4 doctorates awarded. *Degree requirements:* For doctorate, thesis/dissertation, electronic portfolio. *Entrance requirements:* For doctorate, GRE General Test. Additional exam requirements/recommendations for international students: Required—TOEFL (minimum score 550 paper-based; 80 iBT); Recommended—IELTS (minimum score 6.5). *Application deadline:* For fall admission, 6/30 for domestic students, 10/1 for international students. Application fee: $75. Electronic applications accepted. *Financial support:* Fellowships, research assistantships, teaching assistantships, health care benefits, tuition waivers (full and partial), and unspecified assistantships available. Financial award application deadline: 3/1; financial award applicants required to submit FAFSA. *Faculty research:* Teacher education, multicultural education, special education, second language acquisition, math and science education. *Unit head:* Dr. Matthew Deroo, Assistant Professor and Program Director, 305-284-5217, Fax: 305-284-6998, E-mail: deroomat@miami.edu. *Application contact:* Lois Heffernan, Graduate Admission Coordinator, 305-284-2167, Fax: 305-284-9395, E-mail: lheffernan@miami.edu.
Website: http://www.education.miami.edu

University of Minnesota, Twin Cities Campus, Graduate School, College of Education and Human Development, Department of Educational Psychology, Program in Special Education, Minneapolis, MN 55455-0213. Offers M Ed, MA, PhD. *Students:* 103 full-time (83 women), 16 part-time (12 women); includes 15 minority (3 Black or African American, non-Hispanic/Latino; 6 Asian, non-Hispanic/Latino; 4 Hispanic/Latino; 2 Two or more races, non-Hispanic/Latino), 13 international. Average age 30. 106 applicants, 59% accepted, 51 enrolled. In 2018, 50 master's, 4 doctorates awarded. Application fee: $75 ($95 for international students). *Unit head:* Dr. Kristen McMaster, Chair, 612-624-6083, Fax: 612-624-8241, E-mail: mcmas004@umn.edu. *Application contact:* Dr. Panayiota Kendeou, Director of Graduate Studies, 612-626-7814, E-mail: kend0040@umn.edu.
Website: http://www.cehd.umn.edu/EdPsych/Programs/SpecialEd/

University of Mississippi, Graduate School, School of Education, University, MS 38677. Offers counselor education (M Ed, PhD); counselor education - play therapy (Ed S); early childhood (M Ed); educational leadership K-12 (M Ed, Ed D, PhD, Ed S); elementary education (M Ed, Ed D, Ed S); higher education/student personnel (Ed D, PhD); literacy education (M Ed); math education (Ed D); secondary education (M Ed, PhD, Ed S); special education (M Ed, PhD, Ed S); teacher corporations (MA); teacher education (MA). *Accreditation:* NCATE. *Faculty:* 59 full-time (35 women), 34 part-time/adjunct (26 women). *Students:* 169 full-time (137 women), 461 part-time (329 women); includes 199 minority (185 Black or African American, non-Hispanic/Latino; 3 Asian, non-Hispanic/Latino; 7 Hispanic/Latino; 4 Two or more races, non-Hispanic/Latino), 5 international. Average age 33. In 2018, 180 master's, 57 doctorates, 37 other advanced degrees awarded. *Entrance requirements:* For master's, GRE General Test, minimum GPA of 3.0; for doctorate, GRE General Test. Additional exam requirements/recommendations for international students: Required—TOEFL. *Application deadline:* Applications are processed on a rolling basis. Application fee: $50. Electronic applications accepted. *Financial support:* Scholarships/grants available. Financial award application deadline: 3/1; financial award applicants required to submit FAFSA. *Unit head:* Dr. David Rock, Dean, 662-915-7063, Fax: 662-915-7249, E-mail: soe@olemiss.edu. *Application contact:* Temeka Smith, Graduate Activities Specialist for Admissions, 662-915-7474, Fax: 662-915-7577, E-mail: gschool@olemiss.edu.

University of Missouri, Office of Research and Graduate Studies, College of Education, Department of Special Education, Columbia, MO 65211. Offers administration and supervision of special education (PhD). *Accreditation:* TEAC. *Program availability:* Part-time, evening/weekend, online learning. *Entrance requirements:* For doctorate, GRE General Test, letters of recommendation. Additional exam requirements/recommendations for international students: Required—TOEFL.

University of Missouri–Kansas City, School of Education, Kansas City, MO 64110-2499. Offers administration (Ed D); counseling and guidance (MA, Ed S), including mental health counseling (Ed S), school counseling (Ed S); counseling psychology (PhD); curriculum and instruction (MA, Ed S), including language and literacy (Ed S); education (PhD), including higher education administration, PK-12 education administration; educational administration (MA, Ed S), including advanced principal (Ed S), beginning principal (Ed S), district-level administration (Ed S); reading education (MA); special education (MA). PhD in education offered through the School of Graduate Studies. *Accreditation:* NCATE. *Program availability:* Part-time, evening/weekend. *Degree requirements:* For doctorate, thesis/dissertation, internship, practicum. *Entrance requirements:* For master's, GRE, minimum GPA of 2.75, 2 letters of reference, written statement of purpose; for doctorate, GRE, minimum GPA of 3.0; for Ed S, minimum GPA of 3.0. Additional exam requirements/recommendations for international students: Required—TOEFL (minimum score 550 paper-based; 80 iBT). *Faculty research:* Urban education, inquiry-based field study, theories of counseling and psychotherapy, school literacy, educational technology.

University of Missouri–St. Louis, College of Education, Department of Educator Preparation, Innovation and Research, St. Louis, MO 63121. Offers elementary education (M Ed), including early childhood, general, reading; secondary education (M Ed), including curriculum and instruction, general, middle level education, reading, teaching English to speakers of other languages (TESOL); special education (M Ed), including autism and developmental disabilities, early childhood special education. *Program availability:* Part-time, evening/weekend. *Degree requirements:* For master's, comprehensive exam. *Entrance requirements:* Additional exam requirements/recommendations for international students: Recommended—TOEFL (minimum score 550 paper-based; 79 iBT), IELTS (minimum score 6.5). Electronic applications accepted.

University of Nebraska at Kearney, College of Education, Department of Educational Administration, Kearney, NE 68849-0001. Offers curriculum supervisor of academic area (MA Ed); school principalship 7-12 (MA Ed); school principalship PK-8 (MA Ed); school superintendent (Ed S); supervisor of special education (MA Ed). *Accreditation:* NCATE. *Program availability:* Part-time, evening/weekend, online only, 100% online. *Degree requirements:* For master's and Ed S, comprehensive exam, thesis optional. *Entrance requirements:* For master's, letters of recommendation, resume, letter of interest; for Ed S, letters of recommendation, resume, essay. Additional exam requirements/recommendations for international students: Recommended—TOEFL (minimum score 550 paper-based; 79 iBT), IELTS (minimum score 6.5). Electronic applications accepted. *Faculty research:* Leadership and organizational behavior.

University of Nebraska at Kearney, College of Education, Department of Teacher Education, Kearney, NE 68849-0001. Offers curriculum and instruction (MA Ed), including early childhood education, elementary education, English as a second language, instructional effectiveness, reading/special education, secondary education; instructional technology (MS Ed), including information technology, instructional technology, school librarian; reading PK-12 (MA Ed); special education (MA Ed), including advanced practitioner: assistive technology specialist, advanced practitioner: behavioral interventionist, advanced practitioner: inclusive collaboration specialist, gifted, teacher education. *Program availability:* Part-time, evening/weekend, online only, 100% online. *Degree requirements:* For master's, comprehensive exam, thesis optional. *Entrance requirements:* For master's, portfolio or GRE. Additional exam requirements/recommendations for international students: Recommended—TOEFL (minimum score 550 paper-based; 79 iBT), IELTS (minimum score 6.5). Electronic applications accepted. *Expenses:* Contact institution.

University of Nebraska at Kearney, College of Education, Kinesiology and Sport Sciences Department, Kearney, NE 68849-0001. Offers general physical education (MA Ed), including recreation and leisure, sports administration; physical education exercise science (MA Ed); physical education master teacher (MA Ed), including pedagogy, special populations. *Program availability:* Part-time, evening/weekend, 100% online. *Degree requirements:* For master's, comprehensive exam, thesis optional. *Entrance requirements:* For master's, GRE General Test (for some programs), personal statement. Additional exam requirements/recommendations for international students: Recommended—TOEFL (minimum score 550 paper-based; 79 iBT), IELTS (minimum score 6.5). Electronic applications accepted. *Faculty research:* Ergonomic aids, nutrition, motor development, sports pedagogy, applied behavior analysis, physical activity and wellness, athletic training, therapeutic Interventions, exercise physiology, endocrinology and metabolism.

University of Nebraska at Omaha, Graduate Studies, College of Education, Department of Special Education and Communication Disorders, Omaha, NE 68182. Offers special education (MS); speech-language pathology (MS). *Accreditation:* ASHA;

NCATE. *Program availability:* Part-time, evening/weekend. *Degree requirements:* For master's, comprehensive exam, thesis (for some programs). *Entrance requirements:* For master's, minimum GPA of 3.0, statement of purpose, 2 letters of recommendation, copy of teaching certificate. Additional exam requirements/recommendations for international students: Required—TOEFL, IELTS, PTE. Electronic applications accepted.

University of Nebraska–Lincoln, Graduate College, College of Education and Human Sciences, Department of Special Education and Communication Disorders, Program in Special Education, Lincoln, NE 68588. Offers M Ed, MA, Ed S. *Accreditation:* NCATE; TEAC. *Degree requirements:* For master's, thesis optional. *Entrance requirements:* For master's, GRE. Additional exam requirements/recommendations for international students: Required—TOEFL (minimum score 500 paper-based). Electronic applications accepted.

University of Nebraska–Lincoln, Graduate College, College of Education and Human Sciences, Department of Teaching, Learning and Teacher Education, Lincoln, NE 68588. Offers adult and continuing education (MA); educational studies (Ed D, PhD), including special education (Ed D); teaching, learning and teacher education (M Ed, MA, MST, Ed D, PhD); vocational and adult education (M Ed, MA). *Accreditation:* NCATE. *Degree requirements:* For master's, thesis optional. *Entrance requirements:* Additional exam requirements/recommendations for international students: Required—TOEFL (minimum score 550 paper-based). Electronic applications accepted. *Faculty research:* Teacher education, instructional leadership, literacy education, technology, improvement of school curriculum.

University of Nevada, Las Vegas, Graduate College, College of Education, Department of Educational and Clinical Studies, Las Vegas, NV 89154-3066. Offers addiction studies (Advanced Certificate); counselor education (M Ed, MS), including clinical mental health (MS), school counseling (M Ed); early childhood education (M Ed); early childhood special education (Certificate), including infancy, preschool; English language learning (M Ed); mental health counseling (Advanced Certificate); special education (M Ed, PhD); PhD/JD. *Program availability:* Part-time. *Degree requirements:* For master's, comprehensive exam (for some programs); for doctorate, comprehensive exam, thesis/dissertation; for other advanced degree, final project. *Entrance requirements:* For master's, bachelor's degree; letter of recommendation; statement of purpose; for doctorate, GRE General Test, statement of purpose; writing sample; 3 letters of recommendation. Additional exam requirements/recommendations for international students: Required—TOEFL (minimum score 550 paper-based; 80 iBT), IELTS (minimum score 7). Electronic applications accepted. *Expenses:* Contact institution. *Faculty research:* Multicultural issues in counseling, academic interventions for students with disabilities, establishment of pro-social skills in young children with severe disabilities, inclusive strategies for students with disabilities, language and literacy for English language learners.

University of Nevada, Reno, Graduate School, College of Education, Department of Curriculum, Teaching and Learning, Reno, NV 89557. Offers curriculum and instruction (PhD); curriculum, teaching and learning (Ed D, PhD); elementary education (M Ed, MA, MS); secondary education (M Ed, MA, MS); special education and disability studies (PhD). *Degree requirements:* For master's, thesis optional; for doctorate, thesis/dissertation. *Entrance requirements:* For master's, GRE General Test, minimum GPA of 2.75; for doctorate, GRE General Test, minimum GPA of 3.0. Additional exam requirements/recommendations for international students: Required—TOEFL (minimum score 500 paper-based; 61 iBT), IELTS (minimum score 6). Electronic applications accepted. *Faculty research:* Education, curricula, pedagogy.

University of Nevada, Reno, Graduate School, College of Education, Department of Educational Specialties, Program in Special Education, Reno, NV 89557. Offers M Ed, MA, MS, Ed D, PhD. Terminal master's awarded for partial completion of doctoral program. *Degree requirements:* For master's, thesis optional; for doctorate, thesis/dissertation. *Entrance requirements:* For master's, minimum GPA of 2.75; for doctorate, GRE General Test, minimum GPA of 3.0. Additional exam requirements/recommendations for international students: Required—TOEFL (minimum score 500 paper-based; 61 iBT), IELTS (minimum score 6). Electronic applications accepted. *Faculty research:* Learning disabilities, equity and diversity in educational settings.

University of New Hampshire, Graduate School, College of Liberal Arts, Department of Education, Program in Early Childhood Education, Durham, NH 03824. Offers early childhood education (M Ed); early childhood education: special needs (M Ed). *Program availability:* Part-time. *Entrance requirements:* For master's, PRAXIS, Department of Education background check. Additional exam requirements/recommendations for international students: Required—TOEFL (minimum score 550 paper-based; 80 iBT). Electronic applications accepted.

University of New Hampshire, Graduate School, College of Liberal Arts, Department of Education, Program in Special Education, Durham, NH 03824. Offers special education (M Ed); special education administration (Postbaccalaureate Certificate). *Program availability:* Part-time. *Entrance requirements:* For master's, PRAXIS, Department of Education background check. Additional exam requirements/recommendations for international students: Required—TOEFL (minimum score 550 paper-based; 80 iBT). Electronic applications accepted.

University of New Mexico, Graduate Studies, College of Education, Program in Intensive Social, Language and Behavioral Needs, Albuquerque, NM 87131-2039. Offers Graduate Certificate. *Program availability:* Part-time, evening/weekend. *Students:* Average age 44. 5 applicants, 80% accepted, 3 enrolled. In 2018, 1 Graduate Certificate awarded. *Entrance requirements:* Additional exam requirements/recommendations for international students: Required—TOEFL (minimum score 550 paper-based). *Application deadline:* For fall admission, 3/31 priority date for domestic students, 3/1 for international students; for spring admission, 9/30 priority date for domestic students, 8/1 for international students. Applications are processed on a rolling basis. Application fee: $50. Electronic applications accepted. *Financial support:* Fellowships available. Financial award application deadline: 3/1; financial award applicants required to submit FAFSA. *Unit head:* Prof. Ruth Luckasson, Chair, 505-266-6510, Fax: 505-277-6929, E-mail: ruthl@unm.edu. *Application contact:* Jo Sanchez, Information Contact, 505-277-5018, Fax: 505-277-8679, E-mail: jsanchez@unm.edu.
Website: http://coe.unm.edu

University of New Mexico, Graduate Studies, College of Education, Program in Special Education, Albuquerque, NM 87131-2039. Offers intellectual disability and severe disabilities (MA); learning and behavioral exceptionalities (MA); special education (Ed D, PhD, Ed S). *Accreditation:* NCATE. *Program availability:* Part-time, evening/weekend. *Students:* Average age 37. 24 applicants, 50% accepted, 12 enrolled. In 2018, 37 master's, 6 doctorates, 4 other advanced degrees awarded. *Degree requirements:* For master's, comprehensive exam, thesis optional; for doctorate, comprehensive exam, thesis/dissertation, screening, proposal hearing. *Entrance requirements:* For master's, minimum GPA of 3.2; for doctorate, minimum GPA of 3.2, 2 years of relevant experience; for Ed S, special education degree, 2 years of teaching experience with people with disabilities, writing sample, minimum GPA of 3.2. *Application deadline:* For fall admission, 3/31 priority date for domestic students; for spring admission, 9/30 priority date for domestic students. Applications are processed on a rolling basis. Application fee: $50. Electronic applications accepted. *Financial support:* Fellowships, research assistantships, teaching assistantships, career-related internships or fieldwork, Federal Work-Study, scholarships/grants, traineeships, health care benefits, unspecified assistantships, and stipends available. Support available to part-time students. Financial award application deadline: 3/1; financial award applicants required to submit FAFSA. *Faculty research:* Mathematics instruction, bilingual special education, inclusive education, autism, reading instruction for students with cognitive disabilities, alternative assessment, human rights and disability, applied behavior analysis, bilingualism, language and literacy, mathematics, science instruction, special education. *Unit head:* Prof. Ruth Luckasson, Chair, 505-277-6510, Fax: 505-277-6929, E-mail: luckasson@unm.edu. *Application contact:* Della Gallegos, Information Contact, 505-277-5018, Fax: 505-277-8679, E-mail: dgalle06@unm.edu.
Website: http://coe.unm.edu/departments-programs/es/special-education-program/index.html

University of New Orleans, Graduate School, College of Liberal Arts, Education and Human Development, Department of Curriculum, Instruction, and Special Education, New Orleans, LA 70148. Offers curriculum and instruction (M Ed); teaching (MAT). *Accreditation:* NCATE. *Program availability:* Evening/weekend. *Entrance requirements:* For master's, GRE General Test. Additional exam requirements/recommendations for international students: Required—TOEFL (minimum score 550 paper-based; 79 iBT). Electronic applications accepted. *Faculty research:* Inclusion, transition, early childhood, mild/moderate, severe/profound.

University of North Alabama, College of Education, Department of Elementary Education, Collaborative Teacher Special Education Program, Florence, AL 35632-0001. Offers MA Ed. *Accreditation:* NCATE. *Program availability:* Part-time, 100% online. *Degree requirements:* For master's, comprehensive exam. *Entrance requirements:* For master's, GRE, MAT, or NTE, minimum GPA of 2.5, Alabama Class B Certificate or equivalent, teaching experience. Additional exam requirements/recommendations for international students: Required—TOEFL (minimum score 79 iBT), IELTS (minimum score 6), PTE (minimum score 54). Electronic applications accepted.

University of North Alabama, College of Education, Department of Secondary Education, Program in Secondary Education, Florence, AL 35632-0001. Offers secondary education (MA Ed); special education (MA Ed). *Accreditation:* NCATE. *Program availability:* Part-time, 100% online, blended/hybrid learning. *Degree requirements:* For master's, comprehensive exam. *Entrance requirements:* For master's, GRE, MAT, or NTE, minimum GPA of 2.5, Alabama Class B Certificate or equivalent, teaching experience. Additional exam requirements/recommendations for international students: Required—TOEFL (minimum score 79 iBT), IELTS (minimum score 6), PTE (minimum score 54). Electronic applications accepted.

The University of North Carolina at Charlotte, Cato College of Education, Department of Special Education and Child Development, Charlotte, NC 28223-0001. Offers academically or intellectually gifted (Graduate Certificate); autism spectrum disorders (Graduate Certificate); child and family development: birth through kindergarten (Graduate Certificate); child and family studies: early education (M Ed); special education (M Ed, PhD, Graduate Certificate), including academically or intellectually gifted (M Ed). *Program availability:* Part-time, 100% online, blended/hybrid learning. *Students:* 16 full-time (11 women), 64 part-time (61 women); includes 16 minority (13 Black or African American, non-Hispanic/Latino; 1 Hispanic/Latino; 2 Two or more races, non-Hispanic/Latino), 3 international. Average age 32. 65 applicants, 78% accepted, 32 enrolled. In 2018, 16 master's, 6 doctorates, 33 other advanced degrees awarded. *Entrance requirements:* For master's, GRE or MAT, personal statement, letters of recommendation; for doctorate, GRE or MAT, 2 official transcripts of all academic work attempted since high school indicating minimum GPA of 3.5 in graduate degree program; at least 3 references of someone who knows applicant's current work and/or academic achievements in previous degree work; two-page essay; current resume or curriculum vitae; writing sample; documentation of teaching; for Graduate Certificate, undergraduate degree from regionally-accredited four-year institution; minimum cumulative undergraduate GPA of 3.0; three recommendations from persons knowledgeable of applicant's interaction with children and families; statement of purpose; clear criminal background check. Additional exam requirements/recommendations for international students: Required—TOEFL (minimum score 523 paper-based; 70 iBT), IELTS (minimum score 6), TOEFL (minimum score 523 paper-based, 70 iBT) or IELTS (6). *Application deadline:* Applications are processed on a rolling basis. Application fee: $75. Electronic applications accepted. Tuition and fees vary according to course load and program. *Financial support:* Research assistantships, teaching assistantships, career-related internships or fieldwork, institutionally sponsored loans, scholarships/grants, and unspecified assistantships available. Support available to part-time students. Financial award application deadline: 3/1; financial award applicants required to submit FAFSA. *Total annual research expenditures:* $3.9 million. *Unit head:* Dr. Belva Collins, Chair, 704-687-8828, E-mail: belva.collins@uncc.edu. *Application contact:* Kathy B. Giddings, Director of Graduate Admissions, 704-687-5503, Fax: 704-687-1668, E-mail: gradadm@uncc.edu.
Website: http://spcd.uncc.edu/

The University of North Carolina at Charlotte, Cato College of Education, Interdisciplinary Education Programs, Charlotte, NC 28223-0001. Offers art education (Graduate Certificate); child and family development: early childhood education (MAT); curriculum and instruction (PhD); elementary education (MAT); foreign language education (MAT); middle grades education (MAT); secondary education (MAT); special education (MAT); teaching (Graduate Certificate); teaching English as a second language (MAT); theatre education (Graduate Certificate). *Program availability:* Part-time, 100% online, blended/hybrid learning. *Students:* 70 full-time (55 women), 511 part-time (414 women); includes 228 minority (160 Black or African American, non-Hispanic/Latino; 1 American Indian or Alaska Native, non-Hispanic/Latino; 11 Asian, non-Hispanic/Latino; 38 Hispanic/Latino; 18 Two or more races, non-Hispanic/Latino), 8 international. Average age 34. 343 applicants, 92% accepted, 219 enrolled. In 2018, 69 master's, 13 doctorates, 161 other advanced degrees awarded. *Entrance requirements:* For master's, GRE or MAT, bachelor's degree, or its U.S. equivalent, from regionally-accredited college or university; minimum overall GPA of 3.0 on all previous work beyond high school; statement of purpose (essay); at least three recommendation forms; for doctorate, GRE or MAT, bachelor's degree (or its U.S. equivalent) from regionally-accredited college or university; minimum overall GPA of 3.5 in master's degree program; for Graduate Certificate, bachelor's degree from regionally-accredited university; minimum GPA of 2.75 on all post-secondary work attempted; transcripts; personal statement outlining why the applicant seeks admission to the program. Additional exam requirements/recommendations for international students: Required—TOEFL (minimum score 523 paper-based; 70 iBT), IELTS (minimum score 6), TOEFL (minimum score 523 paper-based, 70 iBT) or IELTS (6). *Application deadline:* Applications are processed on a rolling basis. Application fee: $75. Electronic applications accepted. Tuition and fees vary according to course load and program. *Financial support:* Career-related internships or fieldwork, institutionally sponsored loans, scholarships/grants, and unspecified assistantships available. Support available to part-time students. Financial award application deadline: 3/1; financial award applicants required to submit FAFSA. *Unit head:* Dr. Ellen McIntyre, Dean, 704-687-

8722, E-mail: ellen.mcintyre@uncc.edu. *Application contact:* Kathy B. Giddings, Director of Graduate Admissions, 704-687-5503, Fax: 704-687-1668, E-mail: gradadm@uncc.edu.
Website: http://education.uncc.edu/academic-programs

The University of North Carolina at Greensboro, Graduate School, School of Education, Department of Specialized Education Services, Greensboro, NC 27412-5001. Offers cross-categorical special education (M Ed); interdisciplinary studies in special education (M Ed); leadership early care and education (Certificate); special education (M Ed, PhD). *Degree requirements:* For master's, thesis or alternative. *Entrance requirements:* For master's, GRE General Test. Additional exam requirements/recommendations for international students: Required—TOEFL. Electronic applications accepted.

The University of North Carolina Wilmington, Watson College of Education, Department of Early Childhood, Elementary, Middle, Literacy and Special Education, Wilmington, NC 28403-3297. Offers educational leadership, policy, and advocacy (M Ed); elementary education (M Ed, MAT); language and literacy (M Ed); middle grades education (MAT). *Accreditation:* NCATE. *Program availability:* Part-time, blended/hybrid learning. *Degree requirements:* For master's, thesis or alternative, exit portfolio, oral presentation, internship, research project (depending on specialization). *Entrance requirements:* For master's, 3 letters of recommendations, NC Class A teacher license in related field, education statement of interest essay. Additional exam requirements/recommendations for international students: Required—TOEFL (minimum score 550 paper-based; 79 iBT), IELTS (minimum score 6.5). Electronic applications accepted.

University of North Dakota, Graduate School, College of Education and Human Development, Program in Special Education, Grand Forks, ND 58202. Offers M Ed, MS. *Accreditation:* NCATE. *Program availability:* Part-time, online learning. *Degree requirements:* For master's, comprehensive exam, thesis or alternative. *Entrance requirements:* For master's, minimum GPA of 3.0. Additional exam requirements/recommendations for international students: Required—TOEFL (minimum score 550 paper-based; 79 iBT), IELTS (minimum score 6.5). Electronic applications accepted. *Faculty research:* Visual, emotional, and mental disabilities; early childhood.

University of Northern Colorado, Graduate School, College of Education and Behavioral Sciences, Department of American Sign Language and Interpreting Studies, Greeley, CO 80639. Offers teaching American Sign Language (MA).

University of Northern Colorado, Graduate School, College of Education and Behavioral Sciences, School of Special Education, Greeley, CO 80639. Offers deaf/hard of hearing (MA); early childhood special education (MA); gifted and talented (MA); special education (MA, PhD); visual impairment (MA). *Program availability:* Part-time, evening/weekend, online learning. *Degree requirements:* For master's, comprehensive exam, thesis or alternative; for doctorate, comprehensive exam, thesis/dissertation. *Entrance requirements:* For master's, letters of recommendation, interview; for doctorate, GRE General Test, resume. Electronic applications accepted.

University of Northern Colorado, Graduate School, College of Education and Behavioral Sciences, School of Teacher Education, Program in Teaching Diverse Learners, Greeley, CO 80639. Offers MA. *Program availability:* Online learning.

University of Northern Iowa, Graduate College, College of Education, Department of Special Education, MAE Program in Special Education, Cedar Falls, IA 50614. Offers career/vocational programming and transition (MAE); consultant (MAE); field specialization (MAE).

University of North Florida, College of Education and Human Services, Department of Exceptional, Deaf, and Interpreter Education, Jacksonville, FL 32224. Offers American Sign Language (MS); American Sign Language/English interpreting (M Ed); applied behavior analysis (M Ed); autism (M Ed); deaf education (M Ed); disability services (M Ed); exceptional student education (M Ed). *Accreditation:* NCATE. *Program availability:* Part-time, evening/weekend. *Faculty:* 11 full-time (7 women), 3 part-time/adjunct (all women). *Students:* 25 full-time (22 women), 35 part-time (29 women); includes 9 minority (2 Black or African American, non-Hispanic/Latino; 2 Hispanic/Latino; 5 Two or more races, non-Hispanic/Latino), 5 international. Average age 30. 41 applicants, 59% accepted, 18 enrolled. In 2018, 18 master's awarded. *Entrance requirements:* For master's, GRE General Test, minimum GPA of 3.0 in last 60 hours, interview, 3 letters of recommendation. Additional exam requirements/recommendations for international students: Required—TOEFL (minimum score 500 paper-based). *Application deadline:* For fall admission, 3/31 priority date for domestic students, 5/1 for international students; for spring admission, 12/1 priority date for domestic students, 10/1 for international students; for summer admission, 3/31 priority date for domestic students, 2/1 for international students. Application fee: $30. Electronic applications accepted. *Expenses: Tuition, area resident:* Part-time $408.10 per credit hour. *Tuition, state resident:* part-time $408.10 per credit hour. *Tuition, nonresident:* part-time $932.61 per credit hour. *Required fees:* $111.81 per credit hour. Tuition and fees vary according to course load, campus/location and program. *Financial support:* In 2018–19, 8 students received support, including 2 research assistantships (averaging $2,639 per year); teaching assistantships, career-related internships or fieldwork, Federal Work-Study, scholarships/grants, tuition waivers (partial), and unspecified assistantships also available. Support available to part-time students. Financial award application deadline: 4/1; financial award applicants required to submit FAFSA. *Faculty research:* Transportation, energy, communications, healthcare, nano-science and engineering, unmanned aircraft systems, biomedical applications. *Total annual research expenditures:* $98,616. *Unit head:* Dr. Janice Seabrooks-Blackmore, Chair, 904-620-2930, Fax: 904-620-3895, E-mail: janice.seabrooks-blackmore@unf.edu. *Application contact:* Dr. Amanda Pascale, Director, The Graduate School, 904-620-1360, Fax: 904-620-1362, E-mail: graduateschool@unf.edu.
Website: http://www.unf.edu/coehs/edie/

University of North Texas, Toulouse Graduate School, Denton, TX 76203-5459. Offers accounting (MS); applied anthropology (MA, MS); applied behavior analysis (Certificate); applied geography (MA); applied technology and performance improvement (M Ed, MS); art education (MA); art history (MA); arts leadership (Certificate); audiology (Au D); behavior analysis (MS); behavioral science (PhD); biochemistry and molecular biology (MS); biology (MA, MS); biomedical engineering (MS); business analysis (MS); chemistry (MS); clinical health psychology (PhD); communication studies (MA, MS); computer engineering (MS); computer science (MS); counseling (M Ed, MS), including clinical mental health counseling (MS), college and university counseling, elementary school counseling, secondary school counseling; creative writing (MA); criminal justice (MS); curriculum and instruction (M Ed); decision sciences (MBA); design (MA, MFA), including fashion design (MFA), innovation studies, interior design (MFA); early childhood studies (MS); economics (MS); educational leadership (M Ed, Ed D); educational psychology (MS, PhD), including family studies (MS), gifted and talented (MS), human development (MS), learning and cognition (MS), research, measurement and evaluation (MS); electrical engineering (MS); emergency management (MPA); engineering technology (MS); English (MA); English as a second language (MA); environmental science (MS); finance (MBA, MS); financial management (MPA); French (MA); health services management (MBA); higher education (M Ed,

Ed D); history (MA, MS); hospitality management (MS); human resources management (MPA); information science (MS); information systems (PhD); information technologies (MBA); interdisciplinary studies (MA, MS); international studies (MA); international sustainable tourism (MS); jazz studies (MM); journalism (MA, MJ, Graduate Certificate), including interactive and virtual digital communication (Graduate Certificate), narrative journalism (Graduate Certificate), public relations (Graduate Certificate); kinesiology (MS); linguistics (MA); local government management (MPA); logistics (PhD); logistics and supply chain management (MBA); long-term care, senior housing, and aging services (MA); management (PhD); marketing (MBA); mathematics (MA, MS); mechanical and energy engineering (MS, PhD); music (MA), including ethnomusicology, music theory, musicology, performance; music composition (PhD); music education (MM Ed, PhD); nonprofit management (MPA); operations and supply chain management (MBA); performance (MM, DMA); philosophy (MA); political science (MA); professional and technical communication (MA); radio, television and film (MA, MFA); rehabilitation counseling (Certificate); sociology (MA); Spanish (MA); special education (M Ed); speech-language pathology (MA); strategic management (MBA); studio art (MFA); teaching (M Ed); MBA/MS. *Program availability:* Part-time, evening/weekend, online learning. Terminal master's awarded for partial completion of doctoral program. *Degree requirements:* For master's, variable foreign language requirement, comprehensive exam (for some programs), thesis (for some programs); for doctorate, variable foreign language requirement, comprehensive exam (for some programs), thesis/dissertation; for other advanced degree, variable foreign language requirement, comprehensive exam (for some programs). *Entrance requirements:* For master's and doctorate, GRE, GMAT. Additional exam requirements/recommendations for international students: Required—TOEFL (minimum score 550 paper-based; 79 iBT). Electronic applications accepted.

University of Oklahoma, Jeannine Rainbolt College of Education, Department of Educational Psychology, Norman, OK 73019. Offers instructional psychology and technology (M Ed, PhD), including educational psychology (M Ed), instructional design and technology (M Ed), instructional psychology and technology (PhD), integrating technology in teaching (M Ed); professional counseling (M Ed), including professional counseling; special education (M Ed, PhD), including applied behavior analysis (M Ed), higher education and community support (PhD), higher education professor (PhD), school instruction and leadership (PhD), secondary transition education (M Ed). *Accreditation:* NCATE. *Program availability:* Part-time, 100% online, blended/hybrid learning. Terminal master's awarded for partial completion of doctoral program. *Degree requirements:* For master's, comprehensive exam (for some programs), thesis (for some programs); for doctorate, comprehensive exam (for some programs), thesis/dissertation. *Entrance requirements:* For doctorate, GRE. Additional exam requirements/recommendations for international students: Required—TOEFL (minimum score 79 iBT) or IELTS (minimum score 6.5). Electronic applications accepted. *Expenses:* Tuition, state resident: full-time $5683.20; part-time $236.80 per credit hour. Tuition, nonresident: full-time $20,342; part-time $847.60 per credit hour. International tuition: $20,342.40 full-time. *Required fees:* $2894.20; $110.05 per credit hour. $126.50 per semester. Tuition and fees vary according to course load and program. *Faculty research:* Diversity Issues in counseling; qualitative and mixed-methods research; high-stakes assessments and related educational policy; self-determination and post-secondary outcomes; reading, writing, spelling, and mathematics interventions.

University of Oklahoma Health Sciences Center, Graduate College, College of Allied Health, Department of Communication Sciences and Disorders, Oklahoma City, OK 73190. Offers audiology (MS, Au D, PhD); communication sciences and disorders (Certificate), including reading, speech-language pathology; education of the deaf (MS); speech-language pathology (MS, PhD). *Accreditation:* ASHA (one or more programs are accredited). *Program availability:* Part-time. Terminal master's awarded for partial completion of doctoral program. *Degree requirements:* For master's, comprehensive exam, thesis optional; for doctorate, one foreign language, comprehensive exam, thesis/dissertation. *Entrance requirements:* For master's and doctorate, GRE General Test, 3 letters of recommendation. Additional exam requirements/recommendations for international students: Required—TOEFL (minimum score 550 paper-based). *Faculty research:* Event-related potentials, cleft palate, fluency disorders, language disorders, hearing and speech science.

University of Oregon, Graduate School, College of Education, Eugene, OR 97403. Offers communication disorders and sciences (MA, MS, PhD); counseling psychology (PhD); couples and family therapy (MS); critical and sociocultural studies in education (PhD); curriculum and teacher education (MA, MS); educational leadership (MS, D Ed, PhD); prevention science (M Ed, MS, PhD); school psychology (MS, PhD); special education (M Ed, MA, MS, PhD). *Accreditation:* ASHA. *Program availability:* Part-time. Terminal master's awarded for partial completion of doctoral program. *Degree requirements:* For master's, exam, paper, or project; for doctorate, comprehensive exam, thesis/dissertation. *Entrance requirements:* Additional exam requirements/recommendations for international students: Required—TOEFL. *Faculty research:* Basic and applied research in teaching, learning and habilitation in all settings, schooling effectiveness.

University of Phoenix–Bay Area Campus, College of Education, San Jose, CA 95134-1805. Offers administration and supervision (MA Ed); adult education and training (MA Ed); early childhood education (MA Ed); education (Ed S); educational leadership (Ed D); elementary teacher education (MA Ed); higher education administration (PhD); secondary teacher education (MA Ed); special education (MA Ed); teacher leadership (MA Ed). *Program availability:* Evening/weekend, online learning. *Degree requirements:* For master's, thesis (for some programs). *Entrance requirements:* For master's, minimum undergraduate GPA of 2.5, 3 years of work experience. Additional exam requirements/recommendations for international students: Required—TOEFL (minimum score 550 paper-based; 79 iBT). Electronic applications accepted.

University of Phoenix–Hawaii Campus, College of Education, Honolulu, HI 96813-3800. Offers administration and supervision (MA Ed); curriculum and instruction (MA Ed); elementary education (MA Ed); secondary education (MA Ed); special education (MA Ed); teacher education for elementary licensure (MA Ed). *Program availability:* Evening/weekend. *Degree requirements:* For master's, thesis (for some programs). *Entrance requirements:* For master's, minimum undergraduate GPA of 2.5, 3 years of work experience. Additional exam requirements/recommendations for international students: Required—TOEFL (minimum score 550 paper-based; 79 iBT). Electronic applications accepted.

University of Phoenix–Online Campus, College of Education, Phoenix, AZ 85034-7209. Offers administration and supervision (MAEd, Certificate); adult education and training (MAEd); curriculum and instruction (MAEd), including computer education, curriculum and instruction, English as a second language, language arts, mathematics, reading; early childhood education (MAEd); educational studies (MAEd); elementary teacher education (MAEd), including early childhood, elementary teacher education, high school middle level, middle level; principal licensure (Certificate); secondary teacher education (MAEd); special education (MAEd, Certificate); teacher education (MAEd), including middle level generalist; teacher education middle level mathematics (MAEd), including middle level mathematics; teacher education middle level science (MAEd), including middle level science; teacher education secondary mathematics

(MAEd); teacher education secondary science (MAEd); teacher leadership (MAEd); teachers of English learners (Certificate); transition to teaching (Certificate), including elementary education, secondary education. *Program availability:* Evening/weekend, online learning. *Entrance requirements:* Additional exam requirements/recommendations for international students: Required—TOEFL, TOEIC (Test of English as an International Communication), Berlitz Online English Proficiency Exam, PTE, or IELTS. Electronic applications accepted. *Expenses:* Contact institution.

University of Phoenix–Phoenix Campus, College of Education, Tempe, AZ 85282-2371. Offers administration and supervision (MA Ed); adult education and training (MA Ed); curriculum and instruction reading (MA Ed); early childhood education (MA Ed); education studies (MA Ed); elementary teacher education (MA Ed); secondary teacher education (MA Ed); special education (MA Ed); teacher leadership (MA Ed). *Program availability:* Evening/weekend, online learning. *Entrance requirements:* Additional exam requirements/recommendations for international students: Required—TOEFL, TOEIC (Test of English as an International Communication), Berlitz Online English Proficiency Exam, PTE, or IELTS. Electronic applications accepted. *Expenses:* Contact institution.

University of Pittsburgh, School of Education, Department of Instruction and Learning, Program in Special Education, Pittsburgh, PA 15260. Offers applied behavior analysis (M Ed); early intervention (M Ed, PhD); general special education (M Ed, Ed D); special education teacher preparation (M Ed); vision studies (M Ed, PhD). *Program availability:* Part-time, evening/weekend. *Degree requirements:* For master's, thesis; for doctorate, thesis/dissertation. *Entrance requirements:* For master's, PRAXIS I; for doctorate, GRE General Test. Additional exam requirements/recommendations for international students: Required—TOEFL.

University of Portland, School of Education, Portland, OR 97203-5798. Offers education (MA, MAT); educational leadership (M Ed); English for speakers of other languages (M Ed); initial administrator licensure (M Ed); neuroeducation (M Ed, Ed D); organizational leadership and development (Ed D); reading (M Ed); school leadership and development (Ed D); special education (M Ed). *Accreditation:* NCATE. *Program availability:* Part-time, evening/weekend. *Students:* 32 full-time (30 women), 239 part-time (187 women); includes 33 minority (7 Black or African American, non-Hispanic/Latino; 3 American Indian or Alaska Native, non-Hispanic/Latino; 13 Asian, non-Hispanic/Latino; 1 Native Hawaiian or other Pacific Islander, non-Hispanic/Latino; 9 Two or more races, non-Hispanic/Latino). Average age 34. 92 applicants, 60% accepted, 42 enrolled. In 2018, 57 master's, 16 doctorates awarded. *Degree requirements:* For doctorate, thesis/dissertation. *Entrance requirements:* For master's, minimum GPA of 3.0, teaching certificate, letters of recommendation, resume, statement of goals, official transcripts; for doctorate, 2 letters of recommendation, resume, essays, official transcripts. Additional exam requirements/recommendations for international students: Required—TOEFL (minimum score 550 paper-based; 80 iBT), IELTS (minimum score 7). *Application deadline:* For fall admission, 7/15 priority date for domestic and international students; for spring admission, 12/15 priority date for domestic and international students; for summer admission, 4/15 for domestic and international students. Applications are processed on a rolling basis. Electronic applications accepted. *Expenses:* MAT degree - $995/credit hour; EDD and Educational Specialist - $813/credit hour; all other degrees and certificates - $663/credit hour. *Financial support:* Fellowships, Federal Work-Study, and scholarships/grants available. Support available to part-time students. Financial award application deadline: 3/1; financial award applicants required to submit FAFSA. *Faculty research:* Multicultural education, supervision/leadership. *Unit head:* Dr. Bruce Weitzel, Associate Dean, 503-943-7135, E-mail: soed@up.edu. *Application contact:* Caitlin Biddulph, Graduate Programs and Admissions Specialist, 503-943-7107, E-mail: biddulph@up.edu.
Website: http://education.up.edu/default.aspx?cid-4318&pid-5590

University of Puerto Rico–Medical Sciences Campus, Graduate School of Public Health, Department of Human Development, Program in Developmental Disabilities-Early Intervention, San Juan, PR 00936-5067. Offers Certificate. *Program availability:* Part-time, evening/weekend.

University of Puerto Rico–Río Piedras, College of Education, Program in Special and Differentiated Education, San Juan, PR 00931-3300. Offers M Ed. *Degree requirements:* For master's, thesis. *Entrance requirements:* For master's, GRE or PAEG, interview, minimum GPA of 3.0, letter of recommendation.

University of Rhode Island, Graduate School, Alan Shawn Feinstein College of Education and Professional Studies, School of Education, Kingston, RI 02881. Offers education (PhD); reading (MA); special education (MA). *Accreditation:* NCATE. *Program availability:* Part-time, evening/weekend. *Faculty:* 19 full-time (13 women). *Students:* 53 full-time (35 women), 151 part-time (124 women); includes 28 minority (13 Black or African American, non-Hispanic/Latino; 3 American Indian or Alaska Native, non-Hispanic/Latino; 4 Asian, non-Hispanic/Latino; 5 Hispanic/Latino; 3 Two or more races, non-Hispanic/Latino), 6 international. 79 applicants, 71% accepted, 44 enrolled. In 2018, 54 master's, 6 doctorates awarded. *Entrance requirements:* For master's, 2 letters of recommendation; personal statement; two official transcripts; interview and minimum undergraduate GPA of 3.0 (for special education applicants); for doctorate, GRE, 3 letters of recommendation, resume, personal statement, two copies of official transcripts. Additional exam requirements/recommendations for international students: Required—TOEFL. Application fee: $65. Electronic applications accepted. *Expenses: Tuition, area resident:* Full-time $13,226; part-time $735 per credit. Tuition, state resident: full-time $13,226; part-time $735 per credit. Tuition, nonresident: full-time $25,854; part-time $1436 per credit. *International tuition:* $25,854 full-time. *Required fees:* $1698; $50 per credit. $35 per semester. One-time fee: $165. *Financial support:* In 2018–19, 1 research assistantship with tuition reimbursement (averaging $9,040 per year), 4 teaching assistantships with tuition reimbursements (averaging $15,776 per year) were awarded. Financial award applicants required to submit FAFSA. *Unit head:* Dr. David Byrd, Director, School of Education, 401-874-5484, Fax: 401-874-5471, E-mail: dbyrd@uri.edu. *Application contact:* Dr. David Byrd, Director, School of Education, 401-874-5484, Fax: 401-874-5471, E-mail: dbyrd@uri.edu.
Website: https://web.uri.edu/education/

University of Rio Grande, Graduate School, Rio Grande, OH 45674. Offers athletic coaching leadership (M Ed); educational leadership (M Ed); integrated arts (M Ed); intervention specialist in early childhood (M Ed); intervention specialist in mild/moderate (M Ed). *Accreditation:* NCATE. *Program availability:* Part-time. *Degree requirements:* For master's, final research project, portfolio. *Entrance requirements:* For master's, minimum GPA of 2.7 in major, 2.5 overall. Additional exam requirements/recommendations for international students: Required—TOEFL. *Faculty research:* Interagency collaboration, reading and mathematics, learning styles, college access, literacy.

University of St. Francis, College of Education, Joliet, IL 60435-6169. Offers educational leadership (MS, Ed D); elementary education (M Ed); reading (MS); secondary education (M Ed), including English education, math education, science education, social studies education, visual arts education; special education (M Ed); teaching and learning (MS); TESOL (Certificate). *Accreditation:* NCATE. *Program availability:* Part-time, evening/weekend, 100% online, blended/hybrid learning. *Faculty:* 11 full-time (8 women), 58 part-time/adjunct (38 women). *Students:* 43 full-time (35 women), 453 part-time (354 women); includes 110 minority (48 Black or African American, non-Hispanic/Latino; 7 Asian, non-Hispanic/Latino; 52 Hispanic/Latino; 3 Two or more races, non-Hispanic/Latino), 3 international. Average age 37. 300 applicants, 66% accepted, 164 enrolled. In 2018, 151 master's, 42 doctorates, 4 other advanced degrees awarded. *Degree requirements:* For master's, comprehensive exam; for doctorate, thesis/dissertation. *Entrance requirements:* Additional exam requirements/recommendations for international students: Required—TOEFL (minimum score 550 paper-based; 79 iBT), IELTS (minimum score 6). *Application deadline:* Applications are processed on a rolling basis. Electronic applications accepted. Application fee is waived when completed online. *Expenses:* Contact institution. *Financial support:* In 2018–19, 33 students received support. Scholarships/grants and tuition waivers (partial) available. Support available to part-time students. Financial award applicants required to submit FAFSA. *Unit head:* Dr. John Gambro, Dean, 815-740-3456, E-mail: jgambro@stfrancis.edu. *Application contact:* Sandee Sloka, Director Adult & Graduate Admissions, 800-735-7500, E-mail: ssloka@stfrancis.edu.
Website: https://www.stfrancis.edu/education/

University of Saint Francis, Graduate School, Department of Education, Fort Wayne, IN 46808-3994. Offers secondary education (MAT); special education (MS Ed), including intense intervention, mild intervention. *Accreditation:* NCATE. *Program availability:* Part-time, evening/weekend, online only, 100% online. *Faculty:* 2 full-time (1 woman), 3 part-time/adjunct (all women). *Students:* 3 full-time (2 women), 27 part-time (18 women); includes 3 minority (1 Black or African American, non-Hispanic/Latino; 1 Hispanic/Latino; 1 Two or more races, non-Hispanic/Latino). Average age 33. 19 applicants, 95% accepted, 18 enrolled. In 2018, 12 master's awarded. *Expenses: Tuition:* Full-time $22,440; part-time $935 per credit hour. *Required fees:* $330 per semester. Tuition and fees vary according to degree level, campus/location and program. *Unit head:* Mary Riepenhoff, Chair of the Department of Education, 260-399-7700 Ext. 8409, E-mail: mriepenhoff@sf.edu. *Application contact:* Kyle Richardson, Associate Director of Enrollment Services for Adult Learning, 260-399-7700 Ext. 6310, Fax: 260-399-8152, E-mail: krichardson@sf.edu.
Website: https://admissions.sf.edu/graduate/

University of Saint Joseph, Program in Special Education, West Hartford, CT 06117-2700. Offers autism spectrum disorders (Graduate Certificate); special education (MA). *Program availability:* Part-time, evening/weekend. *Degree requirements:* For master's, thesis. Electronic applications accepted. Application fee is waived when completed online.

University of Saint Mary, Graduate Programs, Program in Special Education, Leavenworth, KS 66048-5082. Offers MA. *Program availability:* Part-time, evening/weekend. *Entrance requirements:* For master's, bachelor's degree, minimum undergraduate GPA of 2.75, two letters of recommendation, teaching certification, essay. *Application deadline:* Applications are processed on a rolling basis. Application fee: $25. Electronic applications accepted. *Expenses:* Contact institution. *Financial support:* Applicants required to submit FAFSA. *Unit head:* Dr. Cheryl Reding, Unit Head of Education, 913-758-6159, E-mail: cheryl.reding@stmary.edu. *Application contact:* Dr. Cheryl Reding, Unit Head of Education, 913-758-6159, E-mail: cheryl.reding@stmary.edu.
Website: http://www.stmary.edu/success/Grad-Program/Master-of-Arts-Special-Education.aspx

University of St. Thomas, College of Education, Leadership and Counseling, Department of Special Education, St. Paul, MN 55105-1096. Offers MA, Certificate, Ed S. *Accreditation:* NCATE. *Program availability:* Part-time-only, evening/weekend, online only, 100% online, blended/hybrid learning. *Degree requirements:* For master's, thesis; for other advanced degree, professional portfolio. *Entrance requirements:* For master's, minimum GPA of 3.0 or MAT; for other advanced degree, MAT or minimum GPA of 2.75. Additional exam requirements/recommendations for international students: Required—TOEFL (minimum score 550 paper-based; 80 iBT). Electronic applications accepted. *Expenses:* Contact institution. *Faculty research:* Reading and math fluency, inclusion curriculum for developmental disorders, parent involvement in positive behavior supports, children's friendships, preschool inclusion.

University of St. Thomas, School of Education and Human Services, Houston, TX 77006-4696. Offers all level education (M Ed); bilingual/dual language (M Ed); Catholic school teaching (M Ed); Catholic/private school leadership (M Ed); counselor education (M Ed); curriculum and instruction (M Ed); education (Ed D); educational leadership (M Ed); elementary teaching (M Ed); English as a second language (M Ed); exceptionality/educational diagnostician (M Ed); exceptionality/special education (M Ed); generalist (M Ed); reading (M Ed); secondary teaching (M Ed); teaching (MAT). *Accreditation:* TEAC. *Program availability:* Part-time, evening/weekend, online learning. *Degree requirements:* For master's, thesis, field experience. *Entrance requirements:* For master's, GRE or MAT if GPA is below 3.0, bachelor's degree; minimum GPA of 2.75 in bachelor's degree or last 60 credit hours; official transcripts from all institutions; goal statement of 250-300 words; 1 reference. Additional exam requirements/recommendations for international students: Required—TOEFL (minimum score 94 iBT), IELTS (minimum score 7), PTE (minimum score 53). Electronic applications accepted. *Expenses:* Contact institution. *Faculty research:* Leadership, diversity, personality traits, second language acquisition.

University of San Diego, School of Leadership and Education Sciences, Department of Learning and Teaching, San Diego, CA 92110-2492. Offers curriculum and instruction (M Ed), including inclusive learning, literacy and digital learning, school leadership, steam (science, technology, engineering, arts, and mathematics); inclusive learning (M Ed); literacy and digital learning (M Ed); school leadership (M Ed); special education (M Ed); STEAM (science, technology, engineering, arts, and mathematics) (M Ed); TESOL, literacy and culture (M Ed). *Program availability:* Part-time, evening/weekend. *Faculty:* 9 full-time (7 women), 34 part-time/adjunct (26 women). *Students:* 136 full-time (102 women), 223 part-time (177 women); includes 130 minority (17 Black or African American, non-Hispanic/Latino; 21 Asian, non-Hispanic/Latino; 74 Hispanic/Latino; 3 Native Hawaiian or other Pacific Islander, non-Hispanic/Latino; 15 Two or more races, non-Hispanic/Latino), 10 international. Average age 33. 391 applicants, 85% accepted, 190 enrolled. In 2018, 201 master's awarded. *Degree requirements:* For master's, thesis (for some programs), international experience. *Entrance requirements:* For master's, California Basic Educational Skills Test, California Subject Examination for Teachers. Additional exam requirements/recommendations for international students: Required—TOEFL (minimum score 580 paper-based; 83 iBT), TWE. *Application deadline:* Applications are processed on a rolling basis. Application fee: $45. Electronic applications accepted. *Financial support:* In 2018–19, 127 students received support. Career-related internships or fieldwork, Federal Work-Study, institutionally sponsored loans, scholarships/grants, and stipends available. Financial award application deadline: 4/1; financial award applicants required to submit FAFSA. *Faculty research:* Action research methodology, cultural studies, instructional theories and practices, second language acquisition, school reform. *Unit head:* Dr. Reyes Quezada, Chair, 619-260-7655, E-mail: rquezada@sandiego.edu. *Application contact:* Erika Garwood, Associate Director of Graduate Admissions, 619-260-4524, Fax: 619-260-4158, E-mail: grads@sandiego.edu.
Website: http://www.sandiego.edu/soles/learning-and-teaching/

University of San Francisco, School of Education, Department of Learning and Instruction, San Francisco, CA 94117. Offers digital technologies for teaching and learning (MA); learning and instruction (MA, Ed D); special education (MA, Ed D); teaching reading (MA). *Program availability:* Part-time, evening/weekend. *Students:* 34 full-time (25 women), 11 part-time (8 women); includes 12 minority (4 Black or African American, non-Hispanic/Latino; 3 Asian, non-Hispanic/Latino; 5 Hispanic/Latino), 11 international. Average age 40. 24 applicants, 96% accepted, 16 enrolled. In 2018, 9 doctorates awarded. *Degree requirements:* For doctorate, thesis/dissertation. *Entrance requirements:* Additional exam requirements/recommendations for international students: Required—TOEFL, IELTS, PTE. *Application deadline:* For fall admission, 3/1 priority date for domestic and international students; for spring admission, 11/1 priority date for domestic and international students. Applications are processed on a rolling basis. Application fee: $55 ($65 for international students). Electronic applications accepted. *Financial support:* In 2018–19, 13 students received support. Fellowships, research assistantships, and teaching assistantships available. Financial award application deadline: 3/2; financial award applicants required to submit FAFSA. *Unit head:* Dr. Kevin Oh, Chair, 415-422-2099. *Application contact:* Peter Cole, Admission Coordinator, 415-422-5467, E-mail: schoolofeducation@usfca.edu.

University of Saskatchewan, College of Graduate and Postdoctoral Studies, College of Education, Department of Educational Psychology and Special Education, Saskatoon, SK S7N 5A2, Canada. Offers measurement and evaluation (M Ed, PhD); school and counseling psychology (M Ed, PhD); special education (M Ed, PhD). *Degree requirements:* For master's, thesis (for some programs); for doctorate, comprehensive exam (for some programs), thesis/dissertation. *Entrance requirements:* Additional exam requirements/recommendations for international students: Required—TOEFL (minimum score 80 iBT); Recommended—IELTS (minimum score 6.5). Electronic applications accepted.

The University of Scranton, Panuska College of Professional Studies, Department of Education, Program in Special Education, Scranton, PA 18510. Offers MS. *Program availability:* Part-time. *Degree requirements:* For master's, comprehensive exam (for some programs), thesis (for some programs), capstone experience. *Entrance requirements:* For master's, GRE General Test accepted but not required, minimum GPA of 3.0, three letters of reference. Additional exam requirements/recommendations for international students: Required—TOEFL (minimum score 500 paper-based; 80 iBT), IELTS (minimum score 6.5). Electronic applications accepted. Application fee is waived when completed online.

University of South Alabama, College of Education and Professional Studies, Department of Leadership and Teacher Education, Mobile, AL 36688. Offers art education (M Ed); early childhood education (M Ed); educational leadership (M Ed, Ed D); elementary education (M Ed); reading education (M Ed); science education (M Ed); secondary education (M Ed); special education (M Ed). *Accreditation:* NCATE. *Program availability:* Part-time. *Degree requirements:* For master's, comprehensive exam, thesis (for some programs); for doctorate, comprehensive exam, thesis/dissertation. *Entrance requirements:* For master's, GRE General Test or MAT, minimum GPA of 3.0; for doctorate, GRE, minimum graduate GPA of 3.25, 3 years of experience in field, 3 letters of recommendation, interview, official transcripts. Additional exam requirements/recommendations for international students: Required—TOEFL. Electronic applications accepted.

University of South Carolina, The Graduate School, College of Education, Department of Educational Studies, Program in Special Education, Columbia, SC 29208. Offers M Ed, MAT, PhD. *Accreditation:* NCATE. *Program availability:* Part-time. *Degree requirements:* For master's, comprehensive exam; for doctorate, one foreign language, comprehensive exam, thesis/dissertation. *Entrance requirements:* For master's, GRE General Test, MAT, interview, sample of written work; for doctorate, GRE General Test or MAT, interview, sample of written work. *Faculty research:* Strategy training, transition, technology, rural special education, behavior management.

University of South Carolina Upstate, Graduate Programs, Spartanburg, SC 29303-4999. Offers early childhood education (M Ed); elementary education (M Ed); informatics (MS); special education: visual impairment (M Ed). *Accreditation:* NCATE. *Program availability:* Part-time, evening/weekend. *Degree requirements:* For master's, professional portfolio. *Entrance requirements:* For master's, GRE General Test or MAT, interview, minimum undergraduate GPA of 2.5, teaching certificate, 2 letters of recommendation. *Faculty research:* Promoting university diversity awareness, rough and tumble play, social justice education, American Indian literatures and cultures, diversity and multicultural education, science teaching strategy.

University of South Dakota, Graduate School, School of Education, Division of Curriculum and Instruction, Program in Special Education, Vermillion, SD 57069. Offers special education (MA), including advanced specialist in disabilities, early childhood special education, multicategorical special education K-12. *Accreditation:* NCATE. *Program availability:* Part-time, online learning. *Degree requirements:* For master's, comprehensive exam, thesis or alternative. *Entrance requirements:* For master's, GRE General Test, MAT, minimum GPA of 2.7. Additional exam requirements/recommendations for international students: Required—TOEFL (minimum score 550 paper-based; 79 iBT). Electronic applications accepted.

University of South Dakota, Graduate School, School of Education, Division of Educational Leadership, Vermillion, SD 57069. Offers educational administration (MA, Ed D, Ed S), including adult and higher education (MA, Ed D), curriculum director, director of special education (Ed D, Ed S), preK-12 principal, school district superintendent (Ed D, Ed S). *Accreditation:* NCATE. *Program availability:* Part-time, evening/weekend, 100% online, blended/hybrid learning. *Degree requirements:* For master's and Ed S, comprehensive exam, thesis or alternative; for doctorate, comprehensive exam, thesis/dissertation. *Entrance requirements:* For master's, GRE General Test, MAT, minimum GPA of 2.7; for doctorate, minimum GPA of 2.7. Additional exam requirements/recommendations for international students: Required—TOEFL (minimum score 550 paper-based; 79 iBT). Electronic applications accepted.

University of Southern Maine, College of Management and Human Service, School of Education and Human Development, Program in Special Education, Portland, ME 04103. Offers gifted and talented education (CGS); special education (MS); teaching all students (CGS). *Accreditation:* TEAC. *Program availability:* Part-time, evening/weekend. *Degree requirements:* For master's, thesis or alternative, portfolio. *Entrance requirements:* For master's, proof of teacher certification. Additional exam requirements/recommendations for international students: Required—TOEFL (minimum score 550 paper-based; 79 iBT). Electronic applications accepted. *Faculty research:* Special education, gifted and talented education, diversity education, positive behavioral interventions and supports.

University of Southern Mississippi, College of Education and Human Sciences, Department of Curriculum, Instruction and Special Education, Hattiesburg, MS 39406-0001. Offers elementary education (M Ed, PhD); instructional technology (MS); instructional technology and design (PhD); secondary education (MAT); special education (M Ed, PhD). *Program availability:* Part-time, online learning. *Degree requirements:* For master's, comprehensive exam, thesis (for some programs); for doctorate, comprehensive exam, thesis/dissertation. *Entrance requirements:* For master's, GRE General Test, MAT, minimum GPA of 3.0; for doctorate, GRE General Test, minimum GPA of 3.5. Additional exam requirements/recommendations for international students: Required—TOEFL, IELTS. *Faculty research:* Mathematical problem solving, integrative curriculum, writing process, teacher education models.

University of South Florida, Innovative Education, Tampa, FL 33620-9951. Offers adult, career and higher education (Graduate Certificate), including college teaching, leadership in developing human resources, leadership in higher education; Africana studies (Graduate Certificate), including diasporas and health disparities, genocide and human rights; aging studies (Graduate Certificate), including gerontology; art research (Graduate Certificate), including museum studies; business foundations (Graduate Certificate); chemical and biomedical engineering (Graduate Certificate), including materials science and engineering, water, health and sustainability; child and family studies (Graduate Certificate), including positive behavior support; civil and industrial engineering (Graduate Certificate), including transportation systems analysis; community and family health (Graduate Certificate), including maternal and child health, social marketing and public health, violence and injury: prevention and intervention, women's health; criminology (Graduate Certificate), including criminal justice administration; data science for public administration (Graduate Certificate); digital humanities (Graduate Certificate); educational measurement and research (Graduate Certificate), including evaluation; English (Graduate Certificate), including comparative literary studies, creative writing, professional and technical communication; entrepreneurship (Graduate Certificate); environmental health (Graduate Certificate), including safety management; epidemiology and biostatistics (Graduate Certificate), including applied biostatistics, biostatistics, concepts and tools of epidemiology, epidemiology, epidemiology of infectious diseases; geography, environment and planning (Graduate Certificate), including community development, environmental policy and management, geographical information systems; geology (Graduate Certificate), including hydrogeology; global health (Graduate Certificate), including disaster management, global health and Latin American and Caribbean studies, global health practice, humanitarian assistance, infection control; government and international affairs (Graduate Certificate), including Cuban studies, globalization studies; health policy and management (Graduate Certificate), including health management and leadership, public health policy and programs; hearing specialist: early intervention (Graduate Certificate); industrial and management systems engineering (Graduate Certificate), including systems engineering, technology management; information studies (Graduate Certificate), including school library media specialist; information systems/decision sciences (Graduate Certificate), including analytics and business intelligence; instructional technology (Graduate Certificate), including distance education, Florida digital/virtual educator, instructional design, multimedia design, Web design; internal medicine, bioethics and medical humanities (Graduate Certificate), including biomedical ethics; Latin American and Caribbean studies (Graduate Certificate); leadership for coastal resiliency planning (Graduate Certificate); mass communications (Graduate Certificate), including multimedia journalism; mathematics and statistics (Graduate Certificate), including mathematics; medicine (Graduate Certificate), including aging and neuroscience, bioinformatics, biotechnology, brain fitness and memory management, clinical investigation, hand and upper limb rehabilitation, health informatics, health sciences, integrative weight management, intellectual property, medicine and gender, metabolic and nutritional medicine, metabolic cardiology, pharmacy sciences; national and competitive intelligence (Graduate Certificate); nursing (Graduate Certificate), including simulation based academic fellowship in advanced pain management; psychological and social foundations (Graduate Certificate), including career counseling, college teaching, diversity in education, mental health counseling, school counseling; public affairs (Graduate Certificate), including nonprofit management, public management, research administration; public health (Graduate Certificate), including assessing chemical toxicity and public health risks, health equity, pharmacoepidemiology, public health generalist, toxicology, translational research in adolescent behavioral health; public health practices (Graduate Certificate), including planning for healthy communities; rehabilitation and mental health counseling (Graduate Certificate), including integrative mental health care, marriage and family therapy, rehabilitation technology; secondary education (Graduate Certificate), including ESOL, foreign language education: culture and content, foreign language education: professional; social work (Graduate Certificate), including geriatric social work/clinical gerontology; special education (Graduate Certificate), including autism spectrum disorder, disabilities education: severe/profound; world languages (Graduate Certificate), including teaching English as a second language (TESL) or foreign language. *Expenses:* Tuition, state resident: full-time $6350. Tuition, nonresident: full-time $19,048. *International tuition:* $19,048 full-time. *Required fees:* $2079. *Unit head:* Dr. Cynthia DeLuca, Associate Vice President and Assistant Vice Provost, 813-974-3077, Fax: 813-974-7061, E-mail: deluca@usf.edu. *Application contact:* Owen Hooper, Director, Summer and Alternative Calendar Programs, 813-974-6917, E-mail: hooper@usf.edu.
Website: http://www.usf.edu/innovative-education/

The University of Tennessee, Graduate School, College of Education, Health and Human Sciences, Program in Education, Knoxville, TN 37996. Offers art education (MS); counseling education (PhD); cultural studies in education (PhD); curriculum (MS, Ed S); curriculum, educational research and evaluation (Ed D, PhD); early childhood education (PhD); early childhood special education (MS); education of deaf and hard of hearing (MS); educational administration and policy studies (Ed D, PhD); educational administration and supervision (Ed S); educational psychology (Ed D, PhD); elementary education (MS, Ed S); elementary teaching (MS); English education (MS, Ed S); exercise science (PhD); foreign language/ESL education (MS, Ed S); instructional technology (MS, Ed D, PhD, Ed S); literacy, language and ESL education (PhD); literacy, language education, and ESL education (Ed D); mathematics education (MS, Ed S); modified and comprehensive special education (MS); reading education (MS, Ed S); school counseling (Ed S); school psychology (PhD, Ed S); science education (MS, Ed S); secondary teaching (MS); social foundations (MS); social science education (MS, Ed S); socio-cultural foundations of sports and education (PhD); special education (Ed S); teacher education (Ed D, PhD). *Accreditation:* NCATE. *Program availability:* Part-time, evening/weekend. *Degree requirements:* For master's and Ed S, thesis optional; for doctorate, variable foreign language requirement, thesis/dissertation. *Entrance requirements:* For master's, minimum GPA of 2.7; for doctorate and Ed S, GRE General Test, minimum GPA of 2.7. Additional exam requirements/recommendations for international students: Required—TOEFL. Electronic applications accepted.

The University of Tennessee at Chattanooga, School of Education, Chattanooga, TN 37403. Offers counseling (M Ed), including community counseling, school counseling; education (M Ed, Post-Master's Certificate), including elementary education (M Ed), school leadership (Post-Master's Certificate); elementary education (M Ed); learning and leadership (Ed D), including educational leadership; school leadership (Post-Master's Certificate); school leadership: principal licensure (Ed S); secondary education (M Ed); special education (M Ed). *Accreditation:* ACA; NCATE. *Program availability:* Part-time. *Degree requirements:* For master's, comprehensive exam, thesis optional, culminating experience; for other advanced degree, internship. *Entrance requirements:* For master's, GRE General Test, PPST 1, teaching certificate; for other advanced

degree, two letters of recommendation, graduate degree in education, teaching certificate with three years of experience. Additional exam requirements/ recommendations for international students: Required—TOEFL (minimum score 550 paper-based; 79 iBT), IELTS (minimum score 6). Electronic applications accepted. *Expenses:* Contact institution. *Faculty research:* School counseling, community counseling, elementary and secondary education, school leadership and administration.

The University of Tennessee at Martin, Graduate Programs, College of Education, Health and Behavioral Sciences, Program in Teaching, Martin, TN 38238. Offers curriculum and instruction (MS Ed), including 7-12, K-6; initial licensure (MS Ed), including elementary education, secondary education; initial licensure k-8 (MS Ed), including library service, special education; interdisciplinary (MS Ed). *Program availability:* Part-time, online only, 100% online. *Students:* 24 full-time (20 women), 126 part-time (90 women); includes 19 minority (11 Black or African American, non-Hispanic/ Latino; 3 Hispanic/Latino; 5 Two or more races, non-Hispanic/Latino). Average age 34. 69 applicants, 58% accepted, 21 enrolled. In 2018, 28 master's awarded. *Degree requirements:* For master's, comprehensive exam. *Entrance requirements:* For master's, GRE General Test, minimum GPA of 2.5, teaching license. Additional exam requirements/recommendations for international students: Required—TOEFL (minimum score 525 paper-based; 71 iBT). *Application deadline:* For fall admission, 7/27 for domestic and international students; for spring admission, 12/17 for domestic and international students; for summer admission, 5/10 for domestic and international students. Applications are processed on a rolling basis. Application fee: $30 ($130 for international students). Electronic applications accepted. *Expenses: Tuition, area resident:* Full-time $8918; part-time $495 per credit hour. Tuition, state resident: full-time $8918; part-time $485 per credit hour. Tuition, nonresident: full-time $14,958; part-time $831 per credit hour. *International tuition:* $22,862 full-time. *Required fees:* $1446; $81 per credit hour. Part-time tuition and fees vary according to course load. *Financial support:* In 2018–19, 26 students received support, including 1 research assistantship with full tuition reimbursement available (averaging $6,283 per year), 5 teaching assistantships with full tuition reimbursements available (averaging $7,464 per year); scholarships/grants and tuition waivers also available. Financial award application deadline: 2/1; financial award applicants required to submit FAFSA. *Faculty research:* Special education, science/math/technology, school reform, reading. *Unit head:* Cynthia West, Dean, 731-881-7125, Fax: 731-881-7975, E-mail: cwest@utm.edu. *Application contact:* Jolene L. Cunningham, Student Services Specialist, 731-881-7012, Fax: 731-881-7499, E-mail: jcunningham@utm.edu.

The University of Texas at Austin, Graduate School, College of Education, Department of Special Education, Austin, TX 78712-1111. Offers autism and developmental disabilities (Ed D, PhD); autism and developmental disability (M Ed, MA); early childhood special education (M Ed, MA, Ed D, PhD); learning disabilities (Ed D, PhD); learning disabilities/behavior disorders (M Ed, MA); multicultural special education (M Ed, MA, Ed D, PhD); rehabilitation counselor (M Ed); rehabilitation counselor education (Ed D, PhD); special education administration (Ed D, PhD). *Accreditation:* CORE. *Program availability:* Part-time, evening/weekend, online learning. *Degree requirements:* For master's, thesis or alternative; for doctorate, thesis/dissertation. *Entrance requirements:* For master's and doctorate, GRE General Test. *Faculty research:* Anchored instruction, reading disabilities, multicultural/bilingual.

The University of Texas at El Paso, Graduate School, College of Education, Department of Educational Psychology and Special Services, El Paso, TX 79968-0001. Offers educational diagnostics (M Ed); guidance and counseling (M Ed); special education (M Ed). *Program availability:* Part-time, evening/weekend. *Degree requirements:* For master's, thesis optional. *Entrance requirements:* For master's, minimum GPA of 3.0. Additional exam requirements/recommendations for international students: Required—TOEFL. Electronic applications accepted.

The University of Texas at San Antonio, College of Education and Human Development, Department of Interdisciplinary Learning and Teaching, San Antonio, TX 78249-0617. Offers education (MA), including curriculum and instruction, early childhood and elementary education, instructional technology, reading and literacy, special education; interdisciplinary learning and teaching (PhD). *Program availability:* Part-time, evening/weekend. *Degree requirements:* For master's, comprehensive exam, thesis optional, 36 hours of course work without thesis (33 with thesis); for doctorate, comprehensive exam, thesis/dissertation, minimum of 60 semester credit hours. *Entrance requirements:* For master's, bachelor's degree with minimum GPA of 3.0 in last 60 hours of coursework; 18 hours of undergraduate coursework in education or related field; for doctorate, GRE, transcripts from all colleges and universities attended, professional vitae demonstrating experience in work environment where education was primary professional emphasis, 3 letters of recommendation, statement of purpose, minimum GPA of 3.5. Additional exam requirements/recommendations for international students: Required—TOEFL (minimum score 550 paper-based; 79 iBT), IELTS (minimum score 6.5). Electronic applications accepted. *Faculty research:* Explorations of science, learning and teaching, family involvement in early childhood, culturally-responsive literacy instruction in diverse settings, STEM education, autism spectrum disorder.

The University of Texas at Tyler, College of Education and Psychology, School of Education, Tyler, TX 75799-0001. Offers early childhood education (M Ed, MA); reading (M Ed, MA); special education (M Ed, MA). *Program availability:* Part-time, evening/ weekend. *Students:* 4 full-time (3 women), 30 part-time (all women); includes 4 minority (3 Black or African American, non-Hispanic/Latino; 1 Hispanic/Latino), 2 international. Average age 37. 13 applicants, 100% accepted, 6 enrolled. In 2018, 14 master's awarded. *Degree requirements:* For master's, comprehensive exam, thesis (for some programs), research project. *Entrance requirements:* For master's, GRE General Test. Additional exam requirements/recommendations for international students: Required—TOEFL. *Application deadline:* For fall admission, 8/17 priority date for domestic students, 7/1 priority date for international students; for spring admission, 12/21 priority date for domestic students, 11/1 priority date for international students. Applications are processed on a rolling basis. Application fee: $25 ($50 for international students). Electronic applications accepted. *Financial support:* In 2018–19, 2 research assistantships (averaging $12,000 per year) were awarded; scholarships/grants also available. Financial award application deadline: 7/1. *Faculty research:* Improving quality in childcare settings, play and creativity, teacher interactions, effects of modeling on early childhood teachers, biofeedback, literacy instruction. *Unit head:* Dr. Wes Hickey, Dean, 903-565-5669, E-mail: whickey@uttyler.edu. *Application contact:* Dr. Wes Hickey, Dean, 903-565-5669, E-mail: whickey@uttyler.edu.
Website: http://www.uttyler.edu/education/

The University of Texas Health Science Center at San Antonio, Joe R. and Teresa Lozano Long School of Medicine, San Antonio, TX 78229-3900. Offers deaf education and hearing (MS); medicine (MD); MPH/MD. *Accreditation:* LCME/AMA. *Degree requirements:* For master's, comprehensive exam, practicum assignments. *Entrance requirements:* For master's, minimum GPA of 3.0, interview, 3 professional letters of recommendation; for doctorate, MCAT. Electronic applications accepted. *Expenses:* Contact institution. *Faculty research:* Geriatrics, diabetes, cancer, AIDS, obesity.

The University of Texas of the Permian Basin, Office of Graduate Studies, School of Education, Program in Special Education, Odessa, TX 79762-0001. Offers MA. *Degree requirements:* For master's, comprehensive exam (for some programs), thesis (for some programs). *Entrance requirements:* For master's, GRE General Test. Additional exam requirements/recommendations for international students: Required—TOEFL (minimum score 550 paper-based).

The University of Texas Rio Grande Valley, College of Education and P-16 Integration, Department of Human Development and School Services, Edinburg, TX 78539. Offers early childhood education (M Ed); early childhood special education (M Ed); school psychology (MA); special education (M Ed). *Program availability:* Part-time, evening/weekend. *Degree requirements:* For master's, comprehensive exam (for some programs). *Entrance requirements:* For master's, minimum GPA of 3.0. Additional exam requirements/recommendations for international students: Required—TOEFL (minimum score 550 paper-based; 79 iBT), IELTS (minimum score 6.5). Electronic applications accepted. *Expenses: Tuition, area resident:* Full-time $6888. Tuition, state resident: full-time $6888. Tuition, nonresident: full-time $14,484. *International tuition:* $14,484 full-time. *Required fees:* $1468. *Faculty research:* Special education, assessment practice, behavior interventions, mental retardation, early childhood.

University of the Cumberlands, Graduate Programs in Education, Williamsburg, KY 40769-1372. Offers all grades (P-12) (M Ed); business and marketing (MA Ed, MAT); counselor education and supervision (Ed D); director of pupil personnel (Certificate); director of special education (Certificate); educational administration and supervision (Ed S); educational leadership (Ed D); elementary education (MA Ed, MAT); instructional leadership - principalship (MA Ed); instructional leadership - school principal (Certificate); middle school education (MA Ed, MAT); reading and writing (MA Ed); school counseling (MA Ed); school superintendent (Certificate); secondary education (MA Ed, MAT); special education (MAT); supervisor of instruction (Certificate); teacher leader (MA Ed). *Program availability:* Part-time, evening/weekend, online learning. *Degree requirements:* For master's, comprehensive exam. Electronic applications accepted.

University of the Pacific, Gladys L. Benerd School of Education, Stockton, CA 95211-0197. Offers curriculum and instruction (MA, Ed D); education (M Ed); educational administration and leadership (MA, Ed D); educational and school psychology (MA, Ed D); educational entrepreneurship (MA); school psychology (Ed S); special education (MA); teacher education (MA). *Accreditation:* NCATE. *Degree requirements:* For doctorate, thesis/dissertation. *Entrance requirements:* For master's, GRE General Test; for doctorate, GRE General Test, GRE Subject Test. Additional exam requirements/ recommendations for international students: Required—TOEFL.

University of the Southwest, Graduate Programs, Hobbs, NM 88240-9129. Offers business administration (MBA); curriculum and instruction (MSE); curriculum and instruction: bilingual (MSE); curriculum and instruction: TESOL (MSE); early childhood education (MSE); educational administration (MSE); mental health counseling (MSE); school counseling (MSE); special education (MSE); sports management (MBA). *Program availability:* Part-time, evening/weekend, online learning. *Degree requirements:* For master's, comprehensive exam, thesis (for some programs). *Entrance requirements:* Additional exam requirements/recommendations for international students: Recommended—TOEFL. Electronic applications accepted.

The University of Toledo, College of Graduate Studies, Judith Herb College of Education, Department of Curriculum and Instruction, Toledo, OH 43606-3390. Offers art education (ME); career and technical education (ME, Ed S); curriculum and instruction (ME, PhD, Ed S); early childhood education (Ed S); education and anthropology (MAE); education and biology (MES); education and chemistry (MES); education and classics (MAE); education and economics (MAE); education and English (MAE); education and French (MAE); education and geology (MES); education and German (MAE); education and history (MAE); education and mathematics (MAE, MES); education and physics (MES); education and political science (MAE); education and sociology (MAE); education and Spanish (MAE); educational media (PhD); educational technology (ME); educational technology: virtual educator (Certificate); elementary education (PhD); English as a second language (MAE); gifted and talented education (PhD); middle childhood education (ME); secondary education (ME, PhD); special education (PhD). *Accreditation:* NCATE. *Program availability:* Part-time, evening/ weekend. *Degree requirements:* For master's, comprehensive exam, thesis or alternative; for doctorate, comprehensive exam, thesis/dissertation; for other advanced degree, thesis optional. *Entrance requirements:* For master's, doctorate, and other advanced degree, minimum cumulative GPA of 2.7 for all previous academic work, letters of recommendation. Additional exam requirements/recommendations for international students: Required—TOEFL (minimum score 550 paper-based; 80 iBT). Electronic applications accepted.

The University of Toledo, College of Graduate Studies, Judith Herb College of Education, Department of Early Childhood, Physical and Special Education, Toledo, OH 43606-3390. Offers early childhood education (ME); physical education (ME); special education (ME). *Program availability:* Part-time. *Degree requirements:* For master's, thesis. *Entrance requirements:* For master's, minimum cumulative GPA of 2.7 for all previous academic work, letters of recommendation. Additional exam requirements/ recommendations for international students: Required—TOEFL (minimum score 550 paper-based; 80 iBT). Electronic applications accepted.

University of Vermont, Graduate College, College of Education and Social Services, Program in Early Childhood Special Education, Burlington, VT 05405. Offers M Ed. *Program availability:* Part-time, evening/weekend. *Entrance requirements:* Additional exam requirements/recommendations for international students: Required—TOEFL (minimum iBT score of 90) or IELTS (6.5). Electronic applications accepted.

University of Vermont, Graduate College, College of Education and Social Services, Program in Special Education, Grades K-12, Burlington, VT 05405. Offers M Ed. *Accreditation:* NCATE. *Degree requirements:* For master's, thesis or alternative. *Entrance requirements:* For master's, license (or eligible for licensure). Additional exam requirements/recommendations for international students: Required—TOEFL (minimum score 550 paper-based, 90 iBT) or IELTS (6.5). Electronic applications accepted.

University of Victoria, Faculty of Graduate Studies, Faculty of Education, Department of Educational Psychology and Leadership Studies, Victoria, BC V8W 2Y2, Canada. Offers aboriginal communities counseling (M Ed); counseling (M Ed, MA); educational psychology (M Ed, MA, PhD), including counseling psychology (M Ed, MA), leadership studies (PhD), learning and development (MA, PhD), measurement and evaluation, special education (M Ed, MA); leadership studies (M Ed, MA). *Program availability:* Part-time. *Degree requirements:* For master's, thesis (for some programs), comprehensive exam (M Ed); for doctorate, comprehensive exam, thesis/dissertation, candidacy exam. *Entrance requirements:* For master's, 2 years of work experience in a relevant field; for doctorate, GRE, 2 years of work experience in a relevant field, minimum B average. Additional exam requirements/recommendations for international students: Required—TOEFL (minimum score 575 paper-based), IELTS (minimum score 7). *Faculty research:* Learning and development (child, adolescent and adult), special education and exceptional children.

University of Virginia, Curry School of Education, Department of Curriculum, Instruction, and Special Education, Program in Special Education, Charlottesville, VA 22903. Offers M Ed, Ed D, Ed S. *Accreditation:* TEAC. *Entrance requirements:* For

master's, doctorate, and Ed S, GRE General Test, 2 letters of recommendation. Additional exam requirements/recommendations for international students: Required—TOEFL (minimum score 600 paper-based; 90 iBT), IELTS (minimum score 7). Electronic applications accepted.

University of Virginia, Curry School of Education, Program in Education, Charlottesville, VA 22903. Offers administration and supervision (PhD); applied developmental science (PhD); counselor education (PhD); curriculum and instruction (PhD); early childhood special education (MT); education evaluation (PhD); educational psychology (PhD); educational research (PhD); elementary education (MT); English education (MT, PhD); foreign language education (MT); higher education (PhD); instructional technology (PhD); kinesiology (MT, PhD); math education (PhD); reading education (PhD); research, statistics and evaluation (PhD); school psychology (PhD); science education (PhD); social studies education (MT, PhD); special education (PhD); world languages education (MT). *Degree requirements:* For master's, comprehensive exam (for some programs), field project; for doctorate, comprehensive exam, thesis/dissertation. *Entrance requirements:* For doctorate, GRE General Test. Additional exam requirements/recommendations for international students: Required—TOEFL (minimum score 600 paper-based; 90 iBT), IELTS (minimum score 7). Electronic applications accepted.

University of Washington, Graduate School, College of Education, Program in Special Education, Seattle, WA 98195. Offers early childhood special education (M Ed); emotional and behavioral disabilities (M Ed); learning disabilities (M Ed); low-incidence disabilities (M Ed); special education (Ed D, PhD). *Degree requirements:* For master's, thesis optional; for doctorate, thesis/dissertation. *Entrance requirements:* For master's and doctorate, GRE General Test, minimum GPA of 3.0. Additional exam requirements/recommendations for international students: Required—TOEFL.

University of Washington, Tacoma, Graduate Programs, Program in Education, Tacoma, WA 98402-3100. Offers education (M Ed); educational administration (principal or program administrator certification) (M Ed); elementary education teacher certification (M Ed); elementary education/special education teacher certification (M Ed); secondary science or math teacher certification (M Ed). *Program availability:* Part-time, evening/weekend. *Degree requirements:* For master's, culminating project. *Entrance requirements:* For master's, WEST-B, WEST-E (teacher certification programs only), official sealed transcript from every college/university attended, personal goal statement, letters of recommendation, copy of valid teaching certificate. Additional exam requirements/recommendations for international students: Required—TOEFL (minimum score 580 paper-based; 92 iBT). Electronic applications accepted. *Faculty research:* Global learning communities for English/Chinese languages, evaluation of mathematics and reading intervention programs, response to intervention, school-wide behavioral and emotional support, mathematics education and culturally responsive mathematics education.

The University of West Alabama, School of Graduate Studies, College of Education, Program in Special Education, Livingston, AL 35470. Offers collaborative special education 6-12 (Ed S); collaborative special education K-6 (Ed S); special education collaborative teacher 6-12 (M Ed); special education collaborative teacher K-6 (M Ed). *Accreditation:* NCATE. *Program availability:* Part-time, evening/weekend, 100% online. *Faculty:* 5 full-time (all women), 31 part-time/adjunct (20 women). *Students:* 270 full-time (232 women), 11 part-time (10 women); includes 70 minority (62 Black or African American, non-Hispanic/Latino; 1 American Indian or Alaska Native, non-Hispanic/Latino; 4 Hispanic/Latino; 1 Native Hawaiian or other Pacific Islander, non-Hispanic/Latino; 2 Two or more races, non-Hispanic/Latino), 2 international. Average age 35. 91 applicants, 96% accepted, 69 enrolled. In 2018, 77 master's, 15 Ed Ss awarded. *Degree requirements:* For master's, comprehensive exam, thesis optional; for Ed S, comprehensive exam. *Entrance requirements:* For master's, GRE, minimum GPA of 2.75, verification of background clearance/fingerprints, valid bachelor's-level Professional Educator Certificate in any teaching area. Additional exam requirements/recommendations for international students: Required—TOEFL (minimum score 500 paper-based; 61 iBT). *Application deadline:* Applications are processed on a rolling basis. Application fee: $40. Electronic applications accepted. *Expenses: Tuition, area resident:* Full-time $9100. Tuition, state resident: full-time $9100. Tuition, nonresident: full-time $19,200. *Required fees:* $1890; $130. *Financial support:* Teaching assistantships, Federal Work-Study, scholarships/grants, and unspecified assistantships available. Support available to part-time students. Financial award application deadline: 3/1; financial award applicants required to submit FAFSA. *Unit head:* Dr. Jodie Winship, Chair of College of Education, 205-652-5415, Fax: 205-652-3706, E-mail: jwinship@uwa.edu. *Application contact:* Dr. B. J. Kimbrough, Dean of Graduate Studies, 205-652-3647, Fax: 205-652-3670, E-mail: bkimbrough@uwa.edu.

The University of Western Ontario, School of Graduate and Postdoctoral Studies, Faculty of Social Science, Faculty of Education, Program in Educational Studies, London, ON N6A 3K7, Canada. Offers curriculum studies (M Ed); educational policy studies (M Ed); educational psychology/special education (M Ed). *Program availability:* Part-time. *Faculty research:* Reflective practice, gender and schooling, feminist pedagogy, narrative inquiry, second language, multiculturalism in Canada, education and law.

University of West Florida, College of Education and Professional Studies, Department of Teacher Education and Educational Leadership, Program in Exceptional Student Education, Pensacola, FL 32514-5750. Offers applied behavior analysis (MA); special and alternative education (MA). *Accreditation:* NCATE. *Program availability:* Part-time, evening/weekend, online learning. *Entrance requirements:* For master's, GRE (minimum score 450 verbal) or MAT (minimum score 396) if bachelor's GPA less than 3.0, state teaching certification; letter of intent; two professional references. Additional exam requirements/recommendations for international students: Required—TOEFL (minimum score 550 paper-based). *Faculty research:* Memory, semantic structure, remedial programming.

University of West Georgia, College of Education, Carrollton, GA 30118. Offers business education (M Ed); early childhood education (M Ed, Ed S); educational leadership (M Ed, Ed S); media (M Ed, Ed S); professional counseling (M Ed, Ed S); professional counseling and supervision (Ed D); reading instruction (M Ed); school improvement (Ed D); secondary education (M Ed); special education (M Ed, Ed S), including teaching (M Ed); speech language pathology (M Ed); teaching (MAT). *Accreditation:* NCATE. *Program availability:* Part-time, evening/weekend, 100% online, blended/hybrid learning. *Faculty:* 39 full-time (23 women). *Students:* 368 full-time (316 women), 1,140 part-time (960 women); includes 460 minority (376 Black or African American, non-Hispanic/Latino; 1 American Indian or Alaska Native, non-Hispanic/Latino; 11 Asian, non-Hispanic/Latino; 44 Hispanic/Latino; 28 Two or more races, non-Hispanic/Latino), 6 international. Average age 35. 625 applicants, 77% accepted, 401 enrolled. In 2018, 399 master's, 25 doctorates, 273 other advanced degrees awarded. *Entrance requirements:* Additional exam requirements/recommendations for international students: Required—TOEFL (minimum score 523 paper-based; 69 iBT); Recommended—IELTS (minimum score 6.5). *Application deadline:* For fall admission, 7/21 for domestic students, 6/1 for international students; for spring admission, 11/30 for domestic students, 10/15 for international students; for summer admission, 4/15 for domestic students, 3/30 for international students. Applications are processed on a rolling basis. Application fee: $40. Electronic applications accepted. Tuition and fees vary according to course load, degree level, campus/location and program. *Financial support:* Fellowships, research assistantships, teaching assistantships, career-related internships or fieldwork, Federal Work-Study, institutionally sponsored loans, scholarships/grants, and unspecified assistantships available. Support available to part-time students. Financial award application deadline: 4/1; financial award applicants required to submit FAFSA. *Unit head:* Dr. Diane Hoff, Dean, College of Education, 678-839-6570, Fax: 678-839-6098, E-mail: dhoff@westga.edu. *Application contact:* Dr. Toby Ziglar, Assistant Dean of the Graduate School, 678-839-1394, Fax: 678-839-1395, E-mail: graduate@westga.edu.
Website: http://www.westga.edu/education/

University of Wisconsin–Eau Claire, College of Education and Human Sciences, Program in Special Education, Eau Claire, WI 54702-4004. Offers MSE. *Program availability:* Part-time. *Degree requirements:* For master's, comprehensive exam, thesis, research paper, or written exam; oral exam. *Entrance requirements:* For master's, minimum GPA of 2.75. Additional exam requirements/recommendations for international students: Required—TOEFL (minimum score 79 iBT).

University of Wisconsin–La Crosse, School of Education, La Crosse, WI 54601-3742. Offers English language arts elementary (Graduate Certificate); professional development in education (ME-PD); reading (MS Ed); special education (MS Ed). *Program availability:* Part-time, evening/weekend. *Entrance requirements:* For master's, GRE. Additional exam requirements/recommendations for international students: Required—TOEFL (minimum score 550 paper-based; 79 iBT). Electronic applications accepted.

University of Wisconsin–Madison, Graduate School, School of Education, Department of Rehabilitation Psychology and Special Education, Program in Special Education, Madison, WI 53706-1380. Offers MA, MS, PhD. *Degree requirements:* For doctorate, thesis/dissertation. Electronic applications accepted.

University of Wisconsin–Milwaukee, Graduate School, School of Education, Department of Exceptional Education, Milwaukee, WI 53201-0413. Offers autism spectrum disorders (Graduate Certificate); exceptional education (MS); transition for students with disabilities (Graduate Certificate); urban education (PhD), including adult, continuing and higher education leadership, art education, curriculum and instruction, exceptional education, mathematics education, multicultural studies, social foundations of education. *Program availability:* Part-time. *Students:* 38 full-time (29 women), 67 part-time (50 women); includes 39 minority (23 Black or African American, non-Hispanic/Latino; 1 American Indian or Alaska Native, non-Hispanic/Latino; 6 Asian, non-Hispanic/Latino; 1 Hispanic/Latino; 8 Two or more races, non-Hispanic/Latino), 2 international. Average age 40. 47 applicants, 40% accepted, 11 enrolled. In 2018, 13 master's, 14 doctorates, 4 other advanced degrees awarded. *Entrance requirements:* Additional exam requirements/recommendations for international students: Required—TOEFL (minimum score 550 paper-based; 79 iBT), IELTS (minimum score 6.5). *Application deadline:* For fall admission, 1/1 priority date for domestic students; for spring admission, 9/1 for domestic students. Application fee: $56 ($96 for international students). Electronic applications accepted. *Financial support:* Fellowships, research assistantships, teaching assistantships, career-related internships or fieldwork, health care benefits, and unspecified assistantships available. Support available to part-time students. Financial award application deadline: 4/15; financial award applicants required to submit FAFSA. *Faculty research:* Emotional disturbance, hearing impairment, learning disabilities, mental retardation. *Application contact:* General Information Contact, 414-229-4721, E-mail: soeinfo@uwm.edu.
Website: http://uwm.edu/education/academics/exceptional-edu-department/

University of Wisconsin–Oshkosh, Graduate Studies, College of Education and Human Services, Department of Special Education, Oshkosh, WI 54901. Offers cross-categorical (MSE); early childhood: exceptional education needs (MSE); non-licensure (MSE). *Program availability:* Part-time, evening/weekend. *Degree requirements:* For master's, comprehensive exam (for some programs), thesis or alternative, field report. *Entrance requirements:* For master's, interview, minimum GPA of 3.0, teaching license, letters of recommendation. Additional exam requirements/recommendations for international students: Required—TOEFL (minimum score 550 paper-based; 79 iBT). Electronic applications accepted. *Faculty research:* Private agency contributions to the disabled, graduation requirements for exceptional education needs students, direct instruction in spelling for learning disabled, effects of behavioral parent training, secondary education programming issues.

University of Wisconsin–Stevens Point, College of Professional Studies, School of Education, Program in Education—General/Special, Stevens Point, WI 54481-3897. Offers MSE. *Program availability:* Part-time. *Degree requirements:* For master's, comprehensive exam, thesis or alternative. *Entrance requirements:* For master's, minimum undergraduate GPA of 3.0, 2 years' teaching experience, letters of recommendation, teacher certification. *Faculty research:* Curriculum and instruction, early childhood special education, standards-based education.

University of Wisconsin–Superior, Graduate Division, Department of Teacher Education, Program in Special Education, Superior, WI 54880-4500. Offers emotional/behavior disabilities (MSE); learning disabilities (MSE). *Program availability:* Part-time, evening/weekend, online learning. *Degree requirements:* For master's, research project. *Entrance requirements:* For master's, minimum GPA of 2.75, teaching certificate. Electronic applications accepted.

University of Wisconsin–Whitewater, School of Graduate Studies, College of Education and Professional Studies, Department of Special Education, Whitewater, WI 53190-1790. Offers cross categorical licensure (MSE); professional development (MSE); special education (Postbaccalaureate Certificate). *Accreditation:* NCATE. *Program availability:* Part-time, evening/weekend, online learning. *Degree requirements:* For master's, thesis or alternative. *Entrance requirements:* Additional exam requirements/recommendations for international students: Required—TOEFL (minimum score 550 paper-based; 80 iBT), IELTS (minimum score 6). Electronic applications accepted.

University of Wyoming, College of Education, Program in Special Education, Laramie, WY 82071. Offers MA, PhD, Ed S. *Degree requirements:* For master's, comprehensive exam, thesis. *Entrance requirements:* For master's, GRE, 2 years teaching experience, 3 letters of recommendation, writing sample. *Expenses: Tuition, area resident:* Full-time $6504; part-time $271 per credit hour. Tuition, state resident: full-time $6504; part-time $271 per credit hour. Tuition, nonresident: full-time $19,464; part-time $811 per credit hour. *International tuition:* $19,464 full-time. *Required fees:* $1410.94; $343.82 per semester. $343.82 per semester. Tuition and fees vary according to course load, program and reciprocity agreements. *Faculty research:* Self-determination; transition; digital learning; severe disabilities; response to intervention.

Utah State University, School of Graduate Studies, Emma Eccles Jones College of Education and Human Services, Department of Special Education and Rehabilitation, Logan, UT 84322. Offers disability disciplines (PhD); rehabilitation counseling (MRC); special education (M Ed, MS, Ed S). *Program availability:* Part-time, online learning. *Degree requirements:* For master's, thesis (for some programs), internships (for some programs); for doctorate, comprehensive exam, thesis/dissertation. *Entrance requirements:* For master's and doctorate, GRE General Test, minimum GPA of 3.0.

Additional exam requirements/recommendations for international students: Required—TOEFL (minimum score 550 paper-based). Electronic applications accepted. *Faculty research:* Applied behavior analysis, effective instructional practices, early childhood teacher training research, distance education, multicultural rehabilitation.

Valdosta State University, Department of Communication Sciences and Disorders, Valdosta, GA 31698. Offers communication disorders (M Ed); communication sciences and disorders (SLPD); special education (MAT, Ed S). *Accreditation:* ASHA. *Degree requirements:* For master's, comprehensive exam. *Entrance requirements:* For master's, GRE or MAT. Additional exam requirements/recommendations for international students: Required—TOEFL. Electronic applications accepted.

Vanderbilt University, PhD Program in Special Education, Nashville, TN 37240-1001. Offers PhD. *Faculty:* 16 full-time (10 women). *Students:* 145 full-time (134 women), 10 part-time (all women); includes 28 minority (1 Black or African American, non-Hispanic/Latino; 7 Asian, non-Hispanic/Latino; 10 Hispanic/Latino; 10 Two or more races, non-Hispanic/Latino), 9 international. Average age 27. 62 applicants, 23% accepted, 13 enrolled. In 2018, 5 doctorates awarded. *Degree requirements:* For doctorate, thesis/dissertation, qualifying examinations. *Entrance requirements:* For doctorate, GRE. Additional exam requirements/recommendations for international students: Required—TOEFL (minimum score 570 paper-based; 88 iBT). *Application deadline:* For fall admission, 12/1 for domestic and international students. Application fee: $0. Electronic applications accepted. *Expenses:* Contact institution. *Financial support:* Fellowships with full tuition reimbursements, research assistantships with full tuition reimbursements, teaching assistantships with full tuition reimbursements, Federal Work-Study, institutionally sponsored loans, traineeships, and health care benefits available. Financial award application deadline: 1/15; financial award applicants required to submit CSS PROFILE or FAFSA. *Faculty research:* Early language and social skills development, learning and behavior disorders, autism and developmental/intellectual disabilities, low vision and blindness, giftedness and diversity. *Unit head:* Dr. Joseph Wehby, Chair, 615-322-8150, Fax: 615-343-1570, E-mail: joseph.wehby@vanderbilt.edu. *Application contact:* Dr. Robert Hodapp, Director of Graduate Studies, 615-322-8150, Fax: 615-343-1570, E-mail: robert.hodapp@vanderbilt.edu.

Virginia Commonwealth University, Graduate School, School of Education, Doctoral Program in Education, Richmond, VA 23284-9005. Offers art education (PhD); counselor education and supervision (PhD); curriculum, culture and change (PhD); educational leadership (PhD); educational psychology (PhD); leadership (Ed D); research and evaluation (PhD); special education and disability leadership (PhD); sport leadership (PhD); urban services leadership (PhD). *Accreditation:* NCATE. *Program availability:* Part-time. *Degree requirements:* For doctorate, thesis/dissertation. *Entrance requirements:* For doctorate, GRE (for PhD), MAT (for Ed D), interview, master's degree, writing sample. Additional exam requirements/recommendations for international students: Required—TOEFL (minimum score 600 paper-based; 100 iBT). Electronic applications accepted.

Virginia Commonwealth University, Graduate School, School of Education, Program in Special Education, Richmond, VA 23284-9005. Offers early childhood (M Ed); general education (M Ed); severe disabilities (M Ed). *Accreditation:* NCATE. *Degree requirements:* For master's, comprehensive exam. *Entrance requirements:* For master's, GRE General Test or MAT. Additional exam requirements/recommendations for international students: Required—TOEFL (minimum score 600 paper-based; 100 iBT). Electronic applications accepted.

Viterbo University, Graduate Programs in Education, La Crosse, WI 54601-4797. Offers cross-categorical special education (Certificate); director of instruction (Certificate); director of special education and pupil services (Certificate); early childhood (Certificate); education (MAE); literacy coaching (Certificate); PreK-12 principal/supervisor of special education (Certificate); principal (Certificate); reading specialist endorsement (Certificate); reading teacher (Certificate); reading teacher 5-12 endorsement (Certificate); reading teacher K-8 endorsement (Certificate); superintendent (Certificate); talented and gifted endorsement (Certificate); Wisconsin school business administrator (Certificate). Weekend courses available in summer. *Accreditation:* NCATE. *Program availability:* Part-time, evening/weekend. *Degree requirements:* For master's, comprehensive exam, thesis, 30 credits of course work. *Entrance requirements:* For master's, BS, transcripts, teaching license, written narrative. Electronic applications accepted. *Expenses:* Contact institution.

Wagner College, Division of Graduate Studies, Education Department, Program in Childhood Education/Students with Disabilities, Staten Island, NY 10301-4495. Offers childhood education (MS Ed). *Program availability:* Part-time, evening/weekend. *Degree requirements:* For master's, thesis (for some programs), passage of New York State certification exams before student teaching. *Entrance requirements:* For master's, GRE, minimum GPA of 3.0, interview, recommendations. Additional exam requirements/recommendations for international students: Required—TOEFL (minimum score 550 paper-based; 79 iBT), IELTS (minimum score 6.5). Electronic applications accepted. *Expenses:* Contact institution.

Wagner College, Division of Graduate Studies, Education Department, Program in Early Childhood Education/Students with Disabilities (Birth-Grade 2), Staten Island, NY 10301-4495. Offers MS Ed. *Program availability:* Part-time, evening/weekend. *Degree requirements:* For master's, thesis. *Entrance requirements:* For master's, minimum GPA of 3.0, valid initial NY State Certificate or equivalent, interview, recommendations. Additional exam requirements/recommendations for international students: Recommended—TOEFL (minimum score 550 paper-based; 79 iBT), IELTS (minimum score 6.5). Electronic applications accepted. *Expenses:* Contact institution.

Wagner College, Division of Graduate Studies, Education Department, Program in Secondary Education/Students with Disabilities, Staten Island, NY 10301-4495. Offers secondary education 7-12 (MS Ed), including language arts, languages other than English, mathematics and technology, science and technology, social studies. *Program availability:* Evening/weekend. *Degree requirements:* For master's, thesis (for some programs), completion of state certification exams before student teaching. *Entrance requirements:* For master's, GRE, minimum GPA of 3.0, interview, recommendations. Additional exam requirements/recommendations for international students: Required—TOEFL (minimum score 550 paper-based; 79 iBT), IELTS (minimum score 6.5). Electronic applications accepted. *Expenses:* Contact institution.

Walden University, Graduate Programs, Richard W. Riley College of Education and Leadership, Minneapolis, MN 55401. Offers adult education (Post-Master's Certificate); adult learning (Graduate Certificate); college teaching and learning (Graduate Certificate); community college leadership (Ed D); curriculum, instruction and assessment (Ed D, Ed S, Graduate Certificate); developmental education (Graduate Certificate); early childhood administration, management, and leadership (Graduate Certificate); early childhood education (Ed D, Ed S); early childhood public policy and advocacy (Graduate Certificate); early childhood studies (MS), including administration, management and leadership, early childhood public policy and advocacy, teaching adults in the early childhood field, teaching and diversity in early childhood education; education (MS, PhD), including adolescent literacy and learning (MS), curriculum, instruction, and assessment (grades K-12) (MS), curriculum, instruction, assessment, and evaluation (PhD), early childhood leadership and advocacy (PhD), early childhood special education (PhD), educational leadership (MS), educational leadership and administration (principal preparation) (MS), educational technology and design (PhD), elementary reading and literacy (PreK-6) (MS), elementary reading and mathematics (grades K-6) (MS), global and comparative education (PhD), higher education leadership management and policy (PhD), integrating technology in the classroom (grades K-12) (MS), learning, instruction and innovation (PhD), mathematics (grades 5-8) (MS), mathematics (grades K-6) (MS), mathematics and science (grades K-8) (MS), organizational research, assessment, and evaluation (PhD), reading and literacy with a reading K-12 endorsement (MS), reading literacy assessment and evaluation (PhD), science (grades K-8) (MS), special education (non-licensure) (grades K-12) (MS), teacher leadership (grades K-12) (MS), teaching English language learners (grades K-12) (MS); educational administration and leadership (Ed D); educational leadership and administration (principal preparation) (Ed S); educational technology (Ed D, Ed S, Post Master's Certificate); elementary reading and literacy (Graduate Certificate); engaging culturally diverse learners (Graduate Certificate); enrollment management and institutional marketing (Graduate Certificate); higher education (MS), including adult learning, college teaching and learning, enrollment management and institutional marketing, global higher education, leadership for student success, online and distance learning; higher education and adult learning (Ed D); higher education leadership and management (Ed D); higher education leadership for student success (Graduate Certificate); instructional design and technology (MS, Postbaccalaureate Certificate), including general program (MS), online learning (MS), training and performance improvement (MS); integrating technology in the classroom (Graduate Certificate); mathematics 5-8 (Graduate Certificate); mathematics K-6 (Graduate Certificate); online teaching for adult educators (Graduate Certificate); reading, literacy, and assessment (Ed D, Ed S); science K-8 (Graduate Certificate); special education (Ed D, Ed S, Graduate Certificate); special education (K-age 21) (MAT); teacher leadership (Graduate Certificate); teaching adults English as a second language (Graduate Certificate); teaching adults in the early childhood field (Graduate Certificate); teaching and diversity in early childhood education (Graduate Certificate); teaching English language learners (grades K-12) (Graduate Certificate); teaching K-12 students online (Graduate Certificate). *Accreditation:* NCATE. *Program availability:* Part-time, evening/weekend, online only, 100% online. *Degree requirements:* For doctorate, thesis/dissertation (for some programs), residency; for other advanced degree, residency (for some programs). *Entrance requirements:* For master's, bachelor's degree or higher; minimum GPA of 2.5; official transcripts; goal statement (for some programs); access to computer and Internet; for doctorate, master's degree or higher; three years of related professional or academic experience (preferred); minimum GPA of 3.0; goal statement and current resume (for select programs); official transcripts; access to computer and Internet; for other advanced degree, relevant work experience; access to computer and Internet. Additional exam requirements/recommendations for international students: Required—TOEFL (minimum score 550 paper-based, 79 iBT), IELTS (minimum score 6.5), Michigan English Language Assessment Battery (minimum score 82), or PTE (minimum score 53). Electronic applications accepted.

Walla Walla University, Graduate Studies, School of Education and Psychology, College Place, WA 99324. Offers curriculum and instruction (M Ed, MAT); educational leadership (M Ed, MAT); literacy instruction (M Ed, MAT); special education (M Ed, MAT). *Program availability:* Part-time. *Entrance requirements:* For master's, GRE General Test, minimum GPA of 2.75. Additional exam requirements/recommendations for international students: Required—TOEFL (minimum score 550 paper-based; 79 iBT). Electronic applications accepted. *Faculty research:* Admissions/retention, instructional psychology, moral development, teaching of reading.

Washburn University, College of Arts and Sciences, Department of Education, Topeka, KS 66621. Offers curriculum and instruction (M Ed); educational leadership (M Ed); reading (M Ed); special education (M Ed). *Accreditation:* NCATE. *Program availability:* Part-time. *Degree requirements:* For master's, comprehensive exam, thesis or alternative, portfolio, comprehensive paper, or action research project. *Entrance requirements:* For master's, department exam, GRE General Test, or MAT, minimum GPA of 3.0 in graduate coursework or last 60 hours of undergraduate coursework. Additional exam requirements/recommendations for international students: Required—TOEFL (minimum score 80 iBT). *Faculty research:* Reading/literature/literacy, foundations, special education, diversity, teaching and technology.

Washington State University, College of Education, Department of Teaching and Learning, Pullman, WA 99164-2132. Offers cultural studies and social thought in education (PhD); curriculum and instruction (Ed M, MA); English language learners (Ed M, MA); language, literacy and technology (PhD); literacy education (Ed M, MA); mathematics education (PhD); special education (Ed M, MA, PhD); teacher leadership (Ed D); teaching (MIT), including elementary education, secondary education. Programs offered at the Pullman, Spokane, Tri-cities, Vancouver and Global (online) campuses. *Program availability:* Part-time, online learning. *Degree requirements:* For master's, comprehensive exam, thesis, oral or written exam; for doctorate, comprehensive exam, thesis/dissertation, oral and written exam. *Entrance requirements:* For master's, GRE General Test, minimum GPA of 3.0, 3 letters of recommendation, letter of intent, transcripts, resume/curriculum vitae; for doctorate, GRE General Test, minimum GPA of 3.0, 3 letters of recommendation, letter of intent, transcripts, writing sample, resume/curriculum vitae. Additional exam requirements/recommendations for international students: Required—TOEFL (minimum score 550 paper-based; 80 iBT). Electronic applications accepted. *Faculty research:* Intersection of gender, youth cultures and schooling; examination of ideology of power in children's literature; early childhood special education; analyzing pre-service and in-service teacher development; second language acquisition.

Washington University in St. Louis, School of Medicine, Program in Audiology and Communication Sciences, St. Louis, MO 63110. Offers audiology (Au D); deaf education (MS); speech and hearing sciences (PhD). *Accreditation:* ASHA (one or more programs are accredited). *Faculty:* 22 full-time (12 women), 18 part-time/adjunct (12 women). *Students:* 72 full-time (69 women). Average age 23. 140 applicants, 24% accepted, 26 enrolled. In 2018, 12 master's, 14 doctorates awarded. *Degree requirements:* For master's, comprehensive exam, thesis, independent study project, oral exam; for doctorate, comprehensive exam, thesis/dissertation, capstone project. *Entrance requirements:* For master's and doctorate, GRE General Test, minimum B average in previous college/university coursework (recommended). Additional exam requirements/recommendations for international students: Required—TOEFL (minimum score 100 iBT). *Application deadline:* For fall admission, 2/15 for domestic and international students. Application fee: $25. Electronic applications accepted. *Expenses:* Contact institution. *Financial support:* In 2018–19, 72 students received support, including 72 fellowships with full and partial tuition reimbursements available (averaging $18,500 per year), 6 teaching assistantships with partial tuition reimbursements available (averaging $2,000 per year); Federal Work-Study, scholarships/grants, traineeships, health care benefits, tuition waivers (partial), and unspecified assistantships also available. Financial award application deadline: 2/15; financial award applicants required to submit FAFSA. *Faculty research:* Audiology, deaf education, speech and hearing sciences, sensory neuroscience. *Unit head:* Dr. William W. Clark, Program Director, 314-747-0104, Fax: 314-747-0105. *Application contact:* Beth Elliott, Director, Finance and Student/Academic Affairs, 314-747-0104, Fax: 314-747-0105, E-mail: elliottb@wustl.edu.
Website: http://pacs.wustl.edu/

Wayland Baptist University, Graduate Programs, Program in Education, Plainview, TX 79072-6998. Offers education administration (M Ed); education diagnostics (M Ed); education literacy (M Ed); elementary certification (M Ed); English (M Ed); English as a second language (M Ed); higher education administration (M Ed); human resources (M Ed); instructional leadership (M Ed); instructional technology (M Ed); leadership training and development (M Ed); science education (M Ed); secondary certification (M Ed); social studies (M Ed); special education (M Ed); sports administration and management (M Ed). *Program availability:* Part-time, evening/weekend, 100% online. *Degree requirements:* For master's, comprehensive exam, capstone course. *Entrance requirements:* For master's, GRE, GMAT or MAT. Additional exam requirements/recommendations for international students: Required—TOEFL (minimum score 500 paper-based; 61 iBT). Electronic applications accepted.

Waynesburg University, Graduate and Professional Studies, Canonsburg, PA 15370. Offers business (MBA), including energy management, finance, health systems, human resources, leadership, market development; counseling (MA), including addictions counseling, clinical mental health; counselor education and supervision (PhD); criminal investigation (MA); education (M Ed), including autism, curriculum and instruction, educational leadership, online teaching; nursing (MSN), including administration, education, informatics; nursing practice (DNP); special education (M Ed); technology (M Ed); MSN/MBA. *Accreditation:* AACN. *Program availability:* Part-time, evening/weekend. *Degree requirements:* For doctorate, thesis/dissertation. *Entrance requirements:* Additional exam requirements/recommendations for international students: Required—TOEFL. Electronic applications accepted.

Wayne State College, School of Education and Counseling, Department of Counseling and Special Education, Program in Special Education, Wayne, NE 68787. Offers MSE. *Accreditation:* NCATE. *Program availability:* Part-time, evening/weekend. *Degree requirements:* For master's, comprehensive exam, thesis. *Entrance requirements:* For master's, GRE General Test, minimum GPA of 3.0. Additional exam requirements/recommendations for international students: Required—TOEFL (minimum score 550 paper-based). Electronic applications accepted.

Wayne State University, College of Education, Division of Teacher Education, Detroit, MI 48202. Offers art education (M Ed); bilingual/bicultural education (Certificate); curriculum and instruction (Ed D, PhD, Ed S), including English as a second language (MAT, Ed D, Ed S), K-12 curriculum (PhD); elementary education (MAT), including bilingual/bicultural education (M Ed, MAT), early childhood education (M Ed, MAT), English as a second language (MAT, Ed D, Ed S), foreign language education, science education (M Ed, MAT), special education (M Ed, MAT); elementary mathematics specialist (Certificate); English as a second language (Certificate); reading (M Ed, Ed S); reading, language and literature (Ed D); secondary education (MAT), including bilingual/bicultural education (M Ed, MAT), early childhood education (M Ed, MAT), English as a second language (MAT, Ed D, Ed S), English education, foreign language education, mathematics education (M Ed, MAT), science education (M Ed, MAT), social studies education (M Ed, MAT); special education (MAT), including career and technical education; teaching and learning (M Ed), including bilingual/bicultural education (M Ed, MAT), early childhood education (M Ed, MAT), elementary education, foreign language, mathematics education (M Ed, MAT), science education (M Ed, MAT), social studies education (M Ed, MAT), special education (M Ed, MAT). *Program availability:* Part-time, evening/weekend. *Faculty:* 20. *Students:* 121 full-time (94 women), 251 part-time (209 women); includes 116 minority (83 Black or African American, non-Hispanic/Latino; 3 American Indian or Alaska Native, non-Hispanic/Latino; 3 Asian, non-Hispanic/Latino; 14 Hispanic/Latino; 13 Two or more races, non-Hispanic/Latino), 11 international. Average age 37. 171 applicants, 23% accepted, 32 enrolled. In 2018, 112 master's, 8 doctorates, 11 other advanced degrees awarded. *Degree requirements:* For master's, thesis (for some programs), essay or project (for some M Ed programs), professional field experience (for MAT programs); for doctorate, comprehensive exam, thesis/dissertation. *Entrance requirements:* For master's, undergraduate degree, verification of participation in group work with children, Michigan State Police criminal background check, negative tb test, personal statement (for MAT programs); for all other master's programs: undergraduate degree, personal statement; for doctorate, minimum undergraduate GPA of 3.0, graduate 3.5; interview; curriculum vitae; references; writing sample; letter of application; master's degree (for most programs); for other advanced degree, education specialist certificate: undergraduate with GPA of 2.5 or better and master's degree with GPA of 2.75 or better; personal statement. Additional exam requirements/recommendations for international students: Required—TOEFL (minimum score 550 paper-based; 79 iBT); Recommended—IELTS (minimum score 6.5), TWE (minimum score 5.5), TSE (minimum score 58). *Application deadline:* Applications are processed on a rolling basis. Application fee: $50. Electronic applications accepted. *Financial support:* In 2018–19, 85 students received support, including 3 fellowships (averaging $14,275 per year); research assistantships with tuition reimbursements available, Federal Work-Study, scholarships/grants, and unspecified assistantships also available. Support available to part-time students. Financial award applicants required to submit FAFSA. *Faculty research:* Improving students' skill achievement in mathematics, improving elementary children's understanding of informational text, teachers' use of their pedagogical and mathematical knowledge in the interactive work of teaching, the intersection of identity construction in teaching and learning, identifying effective methods of literacy instruction and assessments for bilingual students in elementary language arts classrooms. *Unit head:* Dr. Roland Coloma, Assistant Dean for Teacher Education, 313-577-0902, E-mail: rscoloma@wayne.edu. *Application contact:* Dr. Mary L. Waker, Graduate Admissions Officer, 313-577-1601, Fax: 313-577-7904, E-mail: m.waker@wayne.edu.
Website: http://coe.wayne.edu/ted/index.php

Webster University, School of Education, Department of Multidisciplinary Studies, St. Louis, MO 63119-3194. Offers applied educational psychology (MA, Ed S); communication arts (MA); early childhood education (MA, MAT); education and innovation (MA); educational technology (MET); elementary education (MAT); mathematics for educators (MA); middle school education (MAT); multidisciplinary studies (MAT); multimodal literacy for global impact (MA); reading (MA); secondary school education (MAT); special education (MA, MAT); teaching English as a second language (MA); transformative learning in the global community (Ed S). *Program availability:* Part-time. *Entrance requirements:* For master's, minimum GPA of 2.5. Additional exam requirements/recommendations for international students: Required—TOEFL. *Expenses: Tuition:* Full-time $22,500; part-time $750 per credit hour. Tuition and fees vary according to degree level, campus/location and program.

West Chester University of Pennsylvania, College of Education and Social Work, Department of Special Education, West Chester, PA 19383. Offers autism (Certificate); special education (Teaching Certificate); special education (M Ed); universal design for learning and assistive technology (Certificate). *Accreditation:* NCATE. *Program availability:* Part-time, 100% online. *Degree requirements:* For master's, minimum GPA of 3.0, action research; for other advanced degree, minimum GPA of 3.0; modified student teaching. *Entrance requirements:* For master's, GRE if GPA is below 3.0, two letters of recommendation; for other advanced degree, GRE if GPA is below 3.0. Additional exam requirements/recommendations for international students: Required—TOEFL or IELTS. Electronic applications accepted. *Faculty research:* Instructional strategies for students with moderate to severe disabilities; family involvement for families of students with disabilities; instructional strategies for students with autism; math instruction for students with learning disabilities; transitions for students with disabilities; behavior management for students with behavior disorders.

Western Connecticut State University, Division of Graduate Studies, School of Professional Studies, Department of Education and Educational Psychology, Special Education Option, Danbury, CT 06810-6885. Offers MS. *Program availability:* Part-time. *Students:* 8 part-time (6 women). Average age 28. *Entrance requirements:* For master's, minimum GPA of 2.8, teaching certificate. Additional exam requirements/recommendations for international students: Recommended—TOEFL (minimum score 550 paper-based; 79 iBT), IELTS (minimum score 6). *Application deadline:* For fall admission, 8/5 priority date for domestic students; for spring admission, 1/5 priority date for domestic students. Applications are processed on a rolling basis. Application fee: $50. *Financial support:* Scholarships/grants available. Financial award application deadline: 5/1; financial award applicants required to submit FAFSA. *Faculty research:* Education and development of exceptional, gifted, talented, and disabled students in a regular (mainstream) classroom. *Unit head:* Dr. Pauline Goolkasian, Graduate Coordinator, 203-837-8510, Fax: 203-837-8413, E-mail: goolkasianp@wcsu.edu. *Application contact:* Dr. Chris Shankle, Associate Director of Graduate Studies, 203-837-9005, Fax: 203-837-8326, E-mail: shanklec@wcsu.edu.

Western Governors University, Teachers College, Salt Lake City, UT 84107. Offers curriculum and instruction (MS); educational leadership (MS); elementary education (MAT, Postbaccalaureate Certificate); English education (5-12) (MAT); English language learning (PreK-12) (MA); instructional design (M Ed); learning and technology (M Ed); mathematics (5-12) (MAT); mathematics (5-9) (MAT); mathematics education (5-12) (MA); mathematics education (5-9) (MA); mathematics education (K-6) (MA); science (5-12) (MAT); science education (5-12) (MA), including biology, chemistry, earth science, physics; science education (5-9) (MA); special education (MS). *Accreditation:* NCATE. *Program availability:* Evening/weekend, online learning. *Degree requirements:* For master's, capstone project. *Entrance requirements:* For master's and Postbaccalaureate Certificate, transcripts. Additional exam requirements/recommendations for international students: Required—TOEFL (minimum score 450 paper-based; 80 iBT). Electronic applications accepted. Application fee is waived when completed online. *Expenses:* Contact institution.

Western Illinois University, School of Graduate Studies, College of Education and Human Services, Department of Curriculum and Instruction, Program in Special Education, Macomb, IL 61455-1390. Offers MS Ed. *Accreditation:* NCATE. *Program availability:* Part-time. *Students:* 25 part-time (22 women); includes 1 minority (Two or more races, non-Hispanic/Latino). Average age 34. 7 applicants, 100% accepted, 6 enrolled. In 2018, 7 master's awarded. *Degree requirements:* For master's, comprehensive exam, thesis or alternative. *Entrance requirements:* For master's, teacher certification. Additional exam requirements/recommendations for international students: Required—TOEFL (minimum score 550 paper-based; 80 iBT). *Application deadline:* Applications are processed on a rolling basis. Application fee: $30. Electronic applications accepted. *Financial support:* Applicants required to submit FAFSA. *Unit head:* Dr. Eric Sheffield, Chairperson, 309-298-1961. *Application contact:* Dr. Mark Mossman, Associate Provost and Director of Graduate Studies, 309-298-1806, Fax: 309-298-2345, E-mail: grad-office@wiu.edu.
Website: http://www.wiu.edu/coehs/curriculum_and_instruction/prospective_students/spedgrad.php

Western Kentucky University, Graduate School, College of Education and Behavioral Sciences, School of Teacher Education, Bowling Green, KY 42101. Offers elementary education (MAE, Ed S); exceptional education: learning and behavioral disorders (MAE); instructional design (MS); interdisciplinary early childhood education (MAE); library media education (MS); literacy education (MAE); middle grades education (MAE); secondary education (MAE, Ed S); special education: moderate and severe disabilities (MAE). *Program availability:* Part-time, evening/weekend, online learning. *Degree requirements:* For master's, comprehensive exam. *Entrance requirements:* For master's, GRE General Test. Additional exam requirements/recommendations for international students: Required—TOEFL (minimum score 555 paper-based; 79 iBT). *Faculty research:* Teacher preparation in moderate/severe disabilities.

Western Michigan University, Graduate College, College of Education and Human Development, Department of Special Education and Literacy Studies, Kalamazoo, MI 49008. Offers literacy studies (MA); special education (MA, Ed D), including clinical teacher (MA); teaching children with visual impairments (MA).

Western New Mexico University, Graduate Division, School of Education, Silver City, NM 88062-0680. Offers bilingual education (MAT); educational leadership (MA); elementary education (MAT); reading (MAT); secondary education (MAT); special education (MAT); TESOL (teaching English to speakers of other languages) (MAT). *Accreditation:* NCATE. *Program availability:* Part-time, online learning. *Degree requirements:* For master's, comprehensive exam. *Entrance requirements:* For master's, minimum GPA of 3.0 in last 64 hours of undergraduate study. Additional exam requirements/recommendations for international students: Required—TOEFL (minimum score 550 paper-based; 79 iBT). Electronic applications accepted. *Faculty research:* International education, electronic reading assessment, developing STEM teachers.

Western Oregon University, Graduate Programs, College of Education, Division of Special Education, Program in Deaf Education, Monmouth, OR 97361. Offers MS Ed. *Accreditation:* NCATE. *Program availability:* Part-time, evening/weekend. *Degree requirements:* For master's, thesis, portfolio. *Entrance requirements:* For master's, California Basic Educational Skills Test or PRAXIS, GRE General Test or MAT, interview, minimum GPA of 3.0, teaching license. Additional exam requirements/recommendations for international students: Required—TOEFL (minimum score 550 paper-based; 79 iBT), IELTS (minimum score 6.5). *Faculty research:* Effects of infant massage on the interactions between high-risk infants and their caregivers, work sample methodology.

Western Oregon University, Graduate Programs, College of Education, Division of Special Education, Special Education Program, Monmouth, OR 97361. Offers MS Ed. *Program availability:* Part-time, evening/weekend. *Degree requirements:* For master's, comprehensive exam (for some programs), thesis optional, oral exam, portfolio, written exam. *Entrance requirements:* For master's, California Basic Educational Skills Test or PRAXIS, GRE General Test or MAT, interview, minimum GPA of 3.0, teaching license. Additional exam requirements/recommendations for international students: Required—TOEFL (minimum score 550 paper-based; 79 iBT), IELTS (minimum score 6.5). *Faculty research:* Interpreter teacher training, hearing disabilities, mental retardation.

Westfield State University, College of Graduate and Continuing Education, Department of Education, Program in Special Education, Westfield, MA 01086. Offers moderate disabilities, 5-12 (M Ed); moderate disabilities, preK-8 (M Ed). *Accreditation:* NCATE. *Program availability:* Part-time, evening/weekend. *Degree requirements:* For master's, comprehensive exam, practicum. *Entrance requirements:* For master's, GRE General Test or MAT, minimum undergraduate GPA of 2.8. Additional exam requirements/recommendations for international students: Recommended—TOEFL (minimum score 550 paper-based; 79 iBT).

Special Education

West Liberty University, College of Education and Human Performance, West Liberty, WV 26074. Offers community education research and leadership (MA Ed); innovative instruction (MA Ed); leadership in disability services (MA Ed); leadership studies (MA Ed); multi-categorical special education (MA Ed); reading specialist (MA Ed); sports leadership and coaching (MA Ed). *Accreditation:* NCATE. *Program availability:* Part-time, evening/weekend. *Degree requirements:* For master's, capstone experience. *Entrance requirements:* For master's, minimum GPA of 2.5 or 3.0 (depending on track). Additional exam requirements/recommendations for international students: Required—TOEFL. Electronic applications accepted.

Westminster College, Graduate School, Program in Special Education and Reading Specialist, New Wilmington, PA 16172-0001. Offers M Ed. *Program availability:* Part-time, evening/weekend. *Degree requirements:* For master's, comprehensive exam, portfolio. *Entrance requirements:* For master's, minimum GPA of 3.0.

West Virginia University, College of Education and Human Services, Morgantown, WV 26506. Offers audiology (Au D); autism spectrum disorder (MA); clinical rehabilitation and mental health counseling (MS); communication science and disorders (PhD); counseling (MA); counseling psychology (PhD); curriculum and instruction (Ed D); early childhood education (MA); early intervention/ early childhood special education (MA); education (PhD); educational leadership (MA); educational leadership/ public school administration (Ed D); educational leadership/public school administration (MA); educational psychology (MA, Ed D); elementary education (MA); gifted education (MA); higher education administration (MA, Ed D); higher education curriculum and teaching (MA); institutional design and technology (MA); instructional design and technology (Ed D); literacy education (MA); secondary education (MA); secondary education/ English (MA); special education (Ed D); speech pathology (MS). *Accreditation:* ASHA; NCATE. *Program availability:* Part-time, evening/weekend, online learning. *Students:* 392 full-time (325 women), 337 part-time (285 women); includes 44 minority (16 Black or African American, non-Hispanic/Latino; 16 Hispanic/Latino; 12 Two or more races, non-Hispanic/Latino), 11 international. In 2018, 303 master's, 6 doctorates awarded. *Degree requirements:* For master's, content exams; for doctorate, comprehensive exam, thesis/ dissertation. *Entrance requirements:* Additional exam requirements/recommendations for international students: Required—TOEFL (minimum score 500 paper-based; 61 iBT). *Application deadline:* For fall admission, 8/1 for domestic students; for spring admission, 1/1 for domestic students; for summer admission, 5/1 for domestic students. Application fee: $60. Electronic applications accepted. *Financial support:* Fellowships, research assistantships, teaching assistantships, career-related internships or fieldwork, Federal Work-Study, institutionally sponsored loans, health care benefits, tuition waivers (full and partial), and administrative assistantships available. Financial award applicants required to submit FAFSA. *Faculty research:* Internet training and integration for teachers, rural education, teacher preparation, organization of schools, evaluation of personnel. *Unit head:* Dr. Tracy L. Morris, Interim Dean, 304-293-0816, Fax: 304-293-7565, E-mail: Tracy.Morris@mail.wvu.edu. *Application contact:* Dr. Melissa Luna, Associate Dean for Research, 304-293-2174, Fax: 304-293-3802, E-mail: Melissa.Luna@mail.wvu.edu.
Website: http://cehs.wvu.edu/

Whitworth University, School of Education, Graduate Studies in Education, Program in Special Education, Spokane, WA 99251-0001. Offers MAT. *Accreditation:* NCATE. *Program availability:* Part-time, evening/weekend. *Degree requirements:* For master's, comprehensive exam, internship, practicum, research project, or thesis. *Entrance requirements:* For master's, GRE General Test, MAT. Additional exam requirements/ recommendations for international students: Required—TOEFL.

Wichita State University, Graduate School, College of Applied Studies, School of Education, Wichita, KS 67260. Offers learning and instructional design (M Ed); special education (M Ed), including early childhood (M Ed, MAT), gifted, high incidence, low incidence; teaching (MAT), including early childhood (M Ed, MAT), middle level/ secondary, transition to teaching. *Accreditation:* NCATE. *Program availability:* Part-time, evening/weekend, 100% online, blended/hybrid learning. *Entrance requirements:* For master's, MAT, minimum GPA of 2.75. *Unit head:* Dr. Edward Robeck, Department Head, 316-978-3322, E-mail: edward.robeck@wichita.edu. *Application contact:* Jordan Oleson, Admission Coordinator, 316-978-3095, Fax: 316-978-3253, E-mail: jordan.oleson@wichita.edu.

Widener University, School of Human Service Professions, Center for Education, Chester, PA 19013-5792. Offers adult education (M Ed); counseling in higher education (M Ed); counselor education (M Ed); early childhood education (M Ed); educational foundations (M Ed); educational leadership (M Ed); educational psychology (M Ed); elementary education (M Ed); English and language arts (M Ed); health education (M Ed); higher education leadership (Ed D); home and school visitor (M Ed); human sexuality (M Ed, PhD); mathematics education (M Ed); middle school education (M Ed); principalship (M Ed); reading and language arts (Ed D); reading education (M Ed); school administration (Ed D); science education (M Ed); social studies education (M Ed); special education (M Ed); technology education (M Ed). *Accreditation:* NCATE. *Program availability:* Part-time, evening/weekend. Terminal master's awarded for partial completion of doctoral program. *Degree requirements:* For doctorate, thesis/ dissertation. *Entrance requirements:* For master's, minimum GPA of 2.5; for doctorate, GRE or MAT, minimum GPA of 2.0 (undergraduate), 3.5 (graduate). Electronic applications accepted. *Expenses:* Contact institution. *Faculty research:* Reading and cognition, adult education, technology education, educational leadership, special education.

Wilkes University, College of Graduate and Professional Studies, School of Education, Wilkes-Barre, PA 18766-0002. Offers educational development and strategies (MS Ed); educational leadership (MS Ed, Ed D); effective teaching (MS Ed); instructional media (MS Ed); instructional technology (MS Ed); international school leadership (MS Ed); international teaching and learning (MS Ed); literacy (MS Ed); middle level education (MS Ed); online teaching (MS Ed); school business leadership (MS Ed); special education (MS Ed); teaching English to speakers of other languages (MS Ed). *Program availability:* Part-time, evening/weekend, 100% online, blended/hybrid learning. *Students:* 87 full-time (67 women), 1,418 part-time (1,078 women); includes 87 minority (13 Black or African American, non-Hispanic/Latino; 1 American Indian or Alaska Native, non-Hispanic/Latino; 11 Asian, non-Hispanic/Latino; 40 Hispanic/Latino; 22 Two or more races, non-Hispanic/Latino). Average age 35. In 2018, 611 master's, 9 doctorates awarded. *Entrance requirements:* Additional exam requirements/recommendations for international students: Required—TOEFL (minimum score 550 paper-based; 79 iBT). *Application deadline:* Applications are processed on a rolling basis. Application fee: $45 ($65 for international students). Electronic applications accepted. *Expenses:* Contact institution. *Financial support:* Unspecified assistantships available. Financial award application deadline: 3/1; financial award applicants required to submit FAFSA. *Unit head:* Dr. Rhonda Rabbitt, Dean, 570-408-4680, Fax: 570-408-7872, E-mail: rhonda.rabbitt@wilkes.edu. *Application contact:* Stephanie Wasmanski, Associate Director of Graduate Admissions, 570-408-5535, Fax: 570-408-7846, E-mail: stephanie.wasmanski@wilkes.edu.
Website: http://www.wilkes.edu/academics/graduate-programs/masters-programs/graduate-education/index.aspx

William Carey University, School of Education, Hattiesburg, MS 39401. Offers art education (M Ed); art of teaching (M Ed); elementary education (M Ed, Ed S); English education (M Ed); gifted education (M Ed); history and social science (M Ed); mild/ moderate disabilities (M Ed); secondary education (M Ed). *Accreditation:* NCATE. *Program availability:* Part-time. *Degree requirements:* For master's, comprehensive exam. *Entrance requirements:* For master's, GRE, MAT, minimum GPA of 2.5, Class A teacher's license. Additional exam requirements/recommendations for international students: Required—TOEFL (minimum score 550 paper-based).

William Paterson University of New Jersey, College of Education, Wayne, NJ 07470-8420. Offers curriculum and learning (M Ed); early childhood education (Certificate); educational leadership (M Ed); educational media specialist (Certificate); elementary education (MAT, Certificate); elementary education subject area (Certificate); higher education administration (MA); learning disabilities consultant (Certificate); literacy (M Ed); middle level education (M Ed); middle school education subject area (Certificate); professional counseling (M Ed); reading specialist (Certificate); school library media specialist (Certificate); school principal (Certificate); school supervisor (Certificate); secondary education (MAT); special education (M Ed); teacher of students with disabilities (Certificate). *Accreditation:* NCATE. *Program availability:* Part-time, evening/weekend. *Students:* Average age 35. 347 applicants, 87% accepted, 226 enrolled. In 2018, 136 master's awarded. *Degree requirements:* For master's, comprehensive exam, thesis (for some programs), exit interview (for some programs); practicum/internship; minimum GPA of 3.0 (for some programs); exit portfolio (for some programs). *Entrance requirements:* For master's, GRE/MAT, minimum GPA of 2.75; teaching certificate; essay; interview; 2 letters of recommendation; personal statement. Additional exam requirements/recommendations for international students: Required—TOEFL (minimum score 550 paper-based; 79 iBT), IELTS (minimum score 6). *Application deadline:* For fall admission, 6/1 for domestic students, 3/1 for international students; for spring admission, 11/1 for domestic students, 10/1 for international students. Applications are processed on a rolling basis. Application fee: $50. Electronic applications accepted. *Expenses: Tuition, area resident:* Full-time $14,714; part-time $727 per credit. Tuition, state resident: full-time $14,714; part-time $727 per credit. Tuition, nonresident: full-time $22,952; part-time $727 per credit. *International tuition:* $22,952 full-time. *Required fees:* $4 per semester. Tuition and fees vary according to course load, degree level and program. *Financial support:* In 2018–19, 8,416 students received support. Career-related internships or fieldwork, Federal Work-Study, scholarships/grants, and unspecified assistantships available. Support available to part-time students. Financial award application deadline: 3/15; financial award applicants required to submit FAFSA. *Faculty research:* Code switching and creative writing, language instruction, teacher evaluation, preschools, history of educational theories. *Total annual research expenditures:* $311,226. *Unit head:* Dr. Dorothy Feola, Dean, 973-720-2138, Fax: 973-720-3647, E-mail: feolad@wpunj.edu. *Application contact:* Liana Fornarotto, Director of Education Enrollment and Certification, 973-720-2206, Fax: 973-720-2989, E-mail: fornarottol@wpunj.edu.
Website: http://www.wpunj.edu/coe

Wilmington College, Department of Education, Wilmington, OH 45177. Offers reading (M Ed); special education (M Ed). *Accreditation:* TEAC. *Program availability:* Part-time. *Degree requirements:* For master's, comprehensive exam. *Entrance requirements:* For master's, GRE or MAT, minimum GPA of 3.0, 2 letters of recommendation. Additional exam requirements/recommendations for international students: Required—TOEFL. *Faculty research:* Reading instruction, special education practices, conflict resolution in the schools, models of higher education for teachers.

Wilmington University, College of Education, New Castle, DE 19720-6491. Offers applied technology in education (M Ed); career and technical education (M Ed); educational leadership (Ed D); elementary and secondary school counseling (M Ed); elementary studies (M Ed); ESOL literacy (M Ed); higher education leadership (Ed D); instruction: gifted and talented (M Ed); instruction: teacher of reading (M Ed); instruction: teaching and learning (M Ed); organizational leadership (Ed D); school leadership (M Ed); secondary education (MAT); special education (M Ed). *Accreditation:* NCATE. *Program availability:* Part-time, evening/weekend. *Entrance requirements:* For master's, 2 letters of recommendation, interview. Additional exam requirements/recommendations for international students: Required—TOEFL (minimum score 500 paper-based). Electronic applications accepted.

Wilson College, Graduate Programs, Chambersburg, PA 17201-1285. Offers accounting (M Acc); choreography and visual art (MFA); education (M Ed); educational technology (MET); healthcare administration (MHA); humanities (MA), including art and culture, critical/cultural theory, English language and literature, women's studies; management (MSM); nursing (MSN), including nursing education, nursing leadership and management; special education (MSE). *Program availability:* Evening/weekend. *Degree requirements:* For master's, project. *Entrance requirements:* For master's, PRAXIS, minimum undergraduate cumulative GPA of 3.0, 2 letters of recommendation, current certification for eligibility to teach in grades K-12, resume, personal interview. Electronic applications accepted.

Winona State University, College of Education, Department of Special Education, Winona, MN 55987. Offers special education (MS), including developmental disabilities, learning disabilities. *Program availability:* Part-time, evening/weekend. *Degree requirements:* For master's, comprehensive exam, thesis.

Winston-Salem State University, MAT Program, Winston-Salem, NC 27110-0003. Offers middle grades education (MAT); special education (MAT). *Accreditation:* NCATE. *Program availability:* Part-time, evening/weekend, online learning. *Entrance requirements:* For master's, GRE, MAT, NC teacher licensure. Electronic applications accepted. *Faculty research:* Action research on issues in elementary classroom.

Winthrop University, College of Education, Program in Special Education, Rock Hill, SC 29733. Offers M Ed. *Accreditation:* NCATE. *Program availability:* Part-time. *Students:* 14 part-time (all women); includes 3 minority (all Black or African American, non-Hispanic/Latino). Average age 28. *Entrance requirements:* For master's, PRAXIS, South Carolina Class III Teaching Certificate, sample of written work. Additional exam requirements/recommendations for international students: Required—TOEFL (minimum score 550 paper-based; 79 iBT), IELTS (minimum score 6). *Application deadline:* For fall admission, 7/15 priority date for domestic students; for spring admission, 12/1 for domestic students. Applications are processed on a rolling basis. Application fee: $50. Electronic applications accepted. *Expenses:* Tuition, state resident: full-time $15,166; part-time $635 per credit hour. Tuition, nonresident: full-time $29,214. *Required fees:* $500; $180 per semester. *Financial support:* Career-related internships or fieldwork, Federal Work-Study, scholarships/grants, and unspecified assistantships available. Support available to part-time students. Financial award application deadline: 2/1; financial award applicants required to submit FAFSA. *Unit head:* Dr. Lisa Harris, Graduate Program Advisor, 803-323-2453, E-mail: harrisl@winthrop.edu. *Application contact:* 800-411-7041, Fax: 803-323-2292, E-mail: gradschool@winthrop.edu.
Website: http://www.winthrop.edu/graduateschool

Worcester State University, Graduate School, Department of Education, Program in Moderate Disabilities, Worcester, MA 01602-2597. Offers M Ed, Postbaccalaureate Certificate. *Program availability:* Part-time, evening/weekend. *Faculty:* 4 full-time (all

women), 14 part-time/adjunct (8 women). *Students:* 17 part-time (12 women). Average age 35. 3 applicants, 100% accepted, 2 enrolled. In 2018, 11 master's, 8 other advanced degrees awarded. *Degree requirements:* For master's, comprehensive exam (for some programs), thesis optional, For a detail list in Degree Completion requirements please see the graduate catalog at catalog.worcester.edu. *Entrance requirements:* For master's, GRE General Test or MAT, For a detail list of entrance requirements please see the graduate catalog at catalog.worcester.edu; for Postbaccalaureate Certificate, MTEL (Communication and Literacy, Foundations of Reading, and General Curriculum), bachelor's degree with minimum GPA of 2.7. Additional exam requirements/recommendations for international students: Required—TOEFL (minimum score 550 paper-based; 79 iBT), IELTS (minimum score 6). *Application deadline:* For fall admission, 3/1 for domestic and international students; for spring admission, 11/1 for domestic and international students; for summer admission, 3/1 for domestic and international students. Applications are processed on a rolling basis. Application fee: $50. Electronic applications accepted. *Expenses: Tuition, area resident:* Full-time $3042; part-time $169 per credit hour. Tuition, state resident: full-time $3042; part-time $169 per credit hour. Tuition, nonresident: full-time $3042; part-time $169 per credit hour. *International tuition:* $3042 full-time. *Required fees:* $2754; $153 per credit hour. *Financial support:* Career-related internships or fieldwork, scholarships/grants, and unspecified assistantships available. Financial award application deadline: 3/1; financial award applicants required to submit FAFSA. *Unit head:* Dr. Sue Foo, Program Coordinator, 508-929-8071, Fax: 508-929-8164, E-mail: sfoo@worcester.edu. *Application contact:* Sara Grady, Associate Dean for Graduate Studies and Professional Development, 508-929-8130, Fax: 508-929-8100, E-mail: sara.grady@worcester.edu.

Wright State University, Graduate School, College of Education and Human Services, Department of Teacher Education, Programs in Intervention Specialist, Dayton, OH 45435. Offers intervention specialist (M Ed). *Accreditation:* NCATE. *Degree requirements:* For master's, thesis (for some programs). *Entrance requirements:* For master's, GRE General Test, MAT. Additional exam requirements/recommendations for international students: Required—TOEFL.

Xavier University, College of Professional Sciences, School of Education, Department of Secondary and Special Education, Cincinnati, OH 45207. Offers secondary education (M Ed); special education (M Ed). *Entrance requirements:* Additional exam requirements/recommendations for international students: Required—TOEFL (minimum score 550 paper-based; 79 iBT). Application fee is waived when completed online. *Expenses:* Contact institution.

Youngstown State University, College of Graduate Studies, Beeghly College of Education, Department of Teacher Education, Youngstown, OH 44555-0001. Offers content area concentration (MS Ed); curriculum and instruction (MS Ed); literacy (MS Ed); special education (MS Ed), including special education. *Accreditation:* NCATE. *Program availability:* Part-time, evening/weekend. *Degree requirements:* For master's, comprehensive exam. *Entrance requirements:* For master's, GRE, MAT, or teaching certificate; minimum GPA of 2.7. Additional exam requirements/recommendations for international students: Required—TOEFL. *Faculty research:* Multicultural literacy, hands-on mathematics teaching, integrated instruction, reading comprehension, emergent curriculum.

Urban Education

Alvernia University, School of Graduate Studies, Program in Education, Reading, PA 19607-1799. Offers urban education (M Ed). *Program availability:* Part-time, evening/weekend. *Degree requirements:* For master's, thesis optional. *Entrance requirements:* For master's, GRE or MAT (alumni excluded). Electronic applications accepted.

Bakke Graduate University, Programs in Pastoral Ministry and Business, Dallas, TX 75243-7039. Offers business administration (MBA); church and ministry multiplication (D Min); global urban leadership (MA); leadership (D Min); ministry in complex contexts (D Min); social and civic entrepreneurship (MA); theology of work (D Min); theology reflection (D Min); transformational leadership (DTL); urban youth ministry (D Min). *Program availability:* Part-time, online learning. *Degree requirements:* For master's, thesis; for doctorate, thesis/dissertation. *Entrance requirements:* For master's, 2 years of ministry experience, BA in Biblical studies or theology; for doctorate, 3 years of ministry experience, M Div. Additional exam requirements/recommendations for international students: Required—TOEFL. Electronic applications accepted. *Faculty research:* Theological systems, church management, worship.

Brown University, Graduate School, Department of Education, Program in Urban Education Policy, Providence, RI 02912. Offers AM. *Entrance requirements:* For master's, GRE General Test, official transcripts, 3 letters of recommendation, personal statement. Additional exam requirements/recommendations for international students: Required—TOEFL. Electronic applications accepted. *Faculty research:* Mayoral control of school systems.

Buffalo State College, State University of New York, The Graduate School, School of Education, Department of Social and Psychological Foundations of Education, Buffalo, NY 14222-1095. Offers urban education (MS). *Program availability:* Part-time, evening/weekend. *Degree requirements:* For master's, comprehensive exam, thesis (for some programs). *Entrance requirements:* Additional exam requirements/recommendations for international students: Required—TOEFL (minimum score 550 paper-based).

Cardinal Stritch University, College of Education and Leadership, Department of Education, Milwaukee, WI 53217-3985. Offers educational leadership (MS); higher education student affairs leadership (MS); leadership for the advancement of learning and service (Ed D, PhD); leadership for the advancement of learning and service in higher education (Ed D, PhD); teaching (MAT); urban education (MA). *Accreditation:* NCATE. *Program availability:* Part-time, evening/weekend, 100% online, blended/hybrid learning. *Degree requirements:* For master's, comprehensive exam, thesis (for some programs), research project, faculty recommendation; for doctorate, thesis/dissertation, practica, field experience. *Entrance requirements:* For master's, 2 letters of recommendation, minimum GPA of 3.0; for doctorate, minimum GPA of 3.5 in master's coursework, 3 letters of recommendation. Additional exam requirements/recommendations for international students: Required—TOEFL (minimum score 550 paper-based; 79 iBT), IELTS (minimum score 6.5). Electronic applications accepted. *Expenses:* Contact institution.

Cheyney University of Pennsylvania, Graduate Programs, Program in Urban Education, Cheyney, PA 19319. Offers M Ed. *Program availability:* Part-time, evening/weekend. *Degree requirements:* For master's, thesis or alternative. Electronic applications accepted.

Claremont Graduate University, Graduate Programs, School of Educational Studies, Claremont, CA 91711-6160. Offers Africana education (Certificate); education and policy (MA, PhD); higher education/student affairs (MA, PhD); human development (MA, PhD); public school administration (MA, PhD); quantitative evaluation (MA, PhD); special education (MA, PhD); teacher education (MA); teaching and learning (MA, PhD); urban leadership (PhD); MBA/PhD. PhD program offered jointly with San Diego State University. *Program availability:* Part-time. Terminal master's awarded for partial completion of doctoral program. *Entrance requirements:* For master's and doctorate, GRE General Test. Additional exam requirements/recommendations for international students: Required—TOEFL (minimum score 75 iBT). Electronic applications accepted. *Faculty research:* Education administration, K-12 and higher education, multicultural education, education policy, diversity in higher education, faculty issues.

Cleveland State University, College of Graduate Studies, College of Education and Human Services, Program in Urban Education, Cleveland, OH 44115. Offers PhD. *Program availability:* Part-time. *Faculty:* 19 full-time (10 women), 12 part-time/adjunct (7 women). *Students:* 37 full-time (28 women), 55 part-time (41 women); includes 33 minority (25 Black or African American, non-Hispanic/Latino; 1 Asian, non-Hispanic/Latino; 6 Hispanic/Latino; 1 Two or more races, non-Hispanic/Latino), 5 international. Average age 40. In 2018, 12 doctorates awarded. *Degree requirements:* For doctorate, one foreign language, comprehensive exam, thesis/dissertation. *Entrance requirements:* For doctorate, GRE General Test, minimum graduate GPA of 3.25. Additional exam requirements/recommendations for international students: Required—TOEFL (minimum score 550 paper-based; 78 iBT), IELTS (minimum score 6). *Application deadline:* For fall admission, 2/1 for domestic and international students. Application fee: $30. *Expenses:* Tuition, state resident: full-time $7232.55; part-time $6676 per credit hour. Tuition, nonresident: full-time $12,375. *International tuition:* $18,914 full-time. *Required fees:* $80; $80 $40. Tuition and fees vary according to program. *Financial support:* In 2018–19, 16 students received support, including 12 research assistantships with tuition reimbursements available (averaging $10,325 per year), 4 teaching assistantships with tuition reimbursements available (averaging $10,325 per year); tuition waivers (full and partial) and tuition grants with hourly work assignments also available. Financial award application deadline: 4/30; financial award applicants required to submit FAFSA. *Faculty research:* Equity issues (race, ethnicity, and gender), education development consequences for special needs of urban populations, urban education programming, counseling the violent or aggressive adolescent. *Unit head:* Dr. Graham Stead, Director, 216-875-9869, Fax: 216-875-9697, E-mail: g.b.stead@csuohio.edu. *Application contact:* Rita M. Grabowski, Administrative Coordinator, 216-687-4697, Fax: 216-875-9697, E-mail: r.grabowski@csuohio.edu.
Website: http://www.csuohio.edu/cehs/doc/doc

College of Mount Saint Vincent, School of Professional and Graduate Studies, Department of Teacher Education, Riverdale, NY 10471-1093. Offers instructional technology and global perspectives (Certificate); middle level education (Certificate); multicultural studies (Certificate); teaching English to speakers of other languages (MS Ed); urban and multicultural education (MS Ed). *Accreditation:* TEAC. *Program availability:* Part-time. *Degree requirements:* For master's, comprehensive exam. *Entrance requirements:* For master's, interview, New York teaching certificate. Additional exam requirements/recommendations for international students: Required—TOEFL.

Eastern Michigan University, Graduate School, College of Education, Department of Teacher Education, Program in Urban/Diversity Education, Ypsilanti, MI 48197. Offers MA. *Students:* 1 (woman) part-time. Average age 31. In 2018, 1 master's awarded. Application fee: $45. *Application contact:* Dr. Patricia Williams-Boyd, Advisor, 734-487-3260, Fax: 734-487-2101, E-mail: pwilliams1@emich.edu.

Eastern Michigan University, Graduate School, College of Education, Department of Teacher Education, Programs in Curriculum and Instruction, Ypsilanti, MI 48197. Offers advanced teaching and learning (MA); early literacy instruction (Graduate Certificate); instructional leadership (MA); learning, motivation and creativity (Graduate Certificate); literacy coaching (Graduate Certificate); online teaching (Certificate); secondary literacy instruction (Graduate Certificate); urban and diversity education (MA). *Students:* 1 (woman) full-time, 28 part-time (21 women); includes 11 minority (3 Black or African American, non-Hispanic/Latino; 1 Asian, non-Hispanic/Latino; 4 Hispanic/Latino; 3 Two or more races, non-Hispanic/Latino). Average age 31. 7 applicants, 71% accepted, 3 enrolled. In 2018, 5 master's awarded. Application fee: $45. *Application contact:* Dr. Virginia Harder, Graduate Coordinator/Advisor, 734-487-2729, Fax: 734-487-2101, E-mail: vharder1@emich.edu.

Emmanuel College, Graduate and Professional Programs, Graduate Programs in Education, Boston, MA 02115. Offers moderate learning disabilities (Certificate); urban education (M Ed). *Program availability:* Part-time, evening/weekend. *Degree requirements:* For master's, 36 credits, including 6-credit practicum. *Entrance requirements:* For master's, transcripts from all regionally-accredited institutions attended (showing proof of bachelor's degree completion), 2 letters of recommendation, essay, resume. Additional exam requirements/recommendations for international students: Required—TOEFL. Electronic applications accepted. *Expenses:* Contact institution.

Florida International University, College of Arts, Sciences, and Education, Department of Leadership and Professional Studies, Miami, FL 33199. Offers adult education and human resource development (MS, Ed D); counseling (MS), including rehabilitation counseling, school counseling; counselor education (MS), including clinical mental health counseling; educational administration and supervision (Ed D); educational leadership (MS, Certificate, Ed S); higher education (Ed D); higher education administration (MS); international and comparative education (MS); recreation and sport management (MS), including recreation and sport management, recreational therapy; school psychology (Ed S); urban education (MS), including instruction in urban settings, learning technologies, multicultural/bilingual, multicultural/TESOL, urban education. *Program availability:* Part-time, evening/weekend. *Faculty:* 64 full-time (43 women), 104 part-time/adjunct (76 women). *Students:* 258 full-time (196 women), 217 part-time (155 women); includes 387 minority (118 Black or African American, non-Hispanic/Latino; 8 Asian, non-Hispanic/Latino; 249 Hispanic/Latino; 12 Two or more races, non-Hispanic/Latino), 11 international. Average age 31. 345 applicants, 57% accepted, 126 enrolled. In 2018, 172 master's, 11 doctorates awarded. *Entrance requirements:* For master's, minimum GPA of 3.0; for doctorate and other advanced degree, GRE General Test. Additional exam requirements/recommendations for

international students: Required—TOEFL (minimum score 550 paper-based; 80 iBT), IELTS (minimum score 6.3). *Application deadline:* For fall admission, 6/1 priority date for domestic students, 4/1 for international students; for winter admission, 10/1 priority date for domestic students, 9/1 for international students; for spring admission, 3/1 priority date for domestic students, 2/1 for international students. Applications are processed on a rolling basis. Application fee: $30. Electronic applications accepted. *Financial support:* Fellowships, research assistantships, teaching assistantships, Federal Work-Study, and tuition waivers (full and partial) available. Support available to part-time students. Financial award applicants required to submit FAFSA. *Unit head:* Dr. Benjamin Baez, Chair, 305-348-3214, Fax: 305-348-1515, E-mail: benjamin.baez@fiu.edu. *Application contact:* Nanett Rojas, Manager, Admissions Operations, 305-348-7464, Fax: 305-348-7441, E-mail: gradadm@fiu.edu.
Website: http://education.fiu.edu

Georgia State University, College of Education and Human Development, Department of Early Childhood Education, Atlanta, GA 30302-3083. Offers early childhood and elementary education (PhD); early childhood education (M Ed, Ed S); mathematics education (M Ed); urban education (M Ed). *Accreditation:* NCATE. *Program availability:* Part-time, evening/weekend. *Faculty:* 20 full-time (17 women), 1 (woman) part-time/adjunct. *Students:* 82 full-time (74 women), 30 part-time (27 women); includes 69 minority (48 Black or African American, non-Hispanic/Latino; 3 Asian, non-Hispanic/Latino; 11 Hispanic/Latino; 7 Two or more races, non-Hispanic/Latino), 3 international. Average age 31. 116 applicants, 70% accepted, 77 enrolled. In 2018, 36 master's, 6 doctorates awarded. *Entrance requirements:* For master's, GRE, undergraduate diploma; for doctorate and Ed S, GRE, master's degree. *Application deadline:* Applications are processed on a rolling basis. Application fee: $50. Electronic applications accepted. *Expenses: Tuition, area resident:* Full-time $9360; part-time $390 per credit hour. Tuition, state resident: full-time $9360; part-time $390 per credit hour. Tuition, nonresident: full-time $30,024; part-time $1251 per credit hour. *International tuition:* $30,024 full-time. *Required fees:* $2128. *Financial support:* In 2018–19, fellowships with full tuition reimbursements (averaging $24,000 per year), research assistantships with tuition reimbursements (averaging $4,000 per year), teaching assistantships with full tuition reimbursements (averaging $2,000 per year) were awarded; career-related internships or fieldwork, Federal Work-Study, institutionally sponsored loans, scholarships/grants, traineeships, health care benefits, tuition waivers (partial), and unspecified assistantships also available. Support available to part-time students. Financial award applicants required to submit FAFSA. *Faculty research:* Teacher development; language arts/literacy education; mathematics education; intersection of science, urban, and multicultural education; diversity in education.
Website: http://ecee.education.gsu.edu/

Georgia State University, College of Education and Human Development, Department of Educational Policy Studies, Program in Educational Leadership, Atlanta, GA 30302-3083. Offers educational leadership (M Ed, Ed D, Ed S); urban teacher leadership (M Ed). *Accreditation:* NCATE. *Program availability:* Part-time. *Entrance requirements:* For master's, GRE; for doctorate and Ed S, GRE, MAT. *Application deadline:* Applications are processed on a rolling basis. Application fee: $50. Electronic applications accepted. *Expenses: Tuition, area resident:* Full-time $9360; part-time $390 per credit hour. Tuition, state resident: full-time $9360; part-time $390 per credit hour. Tuition, nonresident: full-time $30,024; part-time $1251 per credit hour. *International tuition:* $30,024 full-time. *Required fees:* $2128. *Financial support:* Fellowships, research assistantships, teaching assistantships, career-related internships or fieldwork, scholarships/grants, health care benefits, tuition waivers, and unspecified assistantships available. Support available to part-time students. Financial award application deadline: 3/15. *Faculty research:* Practices with diverse populations, leadership and success, the cohort model of instruction, technology in the schools, instructional supervision and academic coaching. *Unit head:* Dr. Jennifer Esposito, Interim Department Chair, 404-413-8281, Fax: 404-413-8003, E-mail: jesposito@gsu.edu. *Application contact:* Aishah Cowan, Administrative Academic Specialist, 404-413-8273, Fax: 404-413-8033, E-mail: acowan@gsu.edu.
Website: https://education.gsu.edu/program/med-educational-leadership/

The Graduate Center, City University of New York, Graduate Studies, Program in Urban Education, New York, NY 10016-4039. Offers PhD. *Entrance requirements:* For doctorate, GRE General Test. Additional exam requirements/recommendations for international students: Required—TOEFL. Electronic applications accepted.

Grand View University, Graduate Studies, Des Moines, IA 50316-1599. Offers athletic training (MS); clinical nurse leader (MSN, Post Master's Certificate); nursing education (MSN, Post Master's Certificate); organizational leadership (MS); sport management (MS); teacher leadership (M Ed); urban education (M Ed). *Program availability:* Part-time, evening/weekend. *Degree requirements:* For master's, completion of all required coursework in common core and selected track with minimum cumulative GPA of 3.0 and no more than two grades of C. *Entrance requirements:* For master's, GRE, GMAT, or essay, minimum undergraduate GPA of 3.0, professional resume, 3 letters of recommendation, interview. Additional exam requirements/recommendations for international students: Required—TOEFL (minimum score 550 paper-based). Electronic applications accepted.

Holy Names University, Graduate Division, Department of Education, Oakland, CA 94619-1699. Offers educational therapy (Certificate); mild/moderate disabilities (Ed S); multiple subject teaching (Credential); single subject teaching (Credential); urban education: educational therapy (M Ed); urban education: K-12 education (M Ed); urban education: special education (M Ed). *Program availability:* Part-time. *Students:* 28 full-time (18 women), 63 part-time (45 women); includes 48 minority (22 Black or African American, non-Hispanic/Latino; 1 American Indian or Alaska Native, non-Hispanic/Latino; 3 Asian, non-Hispanic/Latino; 21 Hispanic/Latino; 1 Two or more races, non-Hispanic/Latino), 5 international. Average age 35. 69 applicants, 86% accepted, 34 enrolled. In 2018, 11 master's, 33 Certificates awarded. *Degree requirements:* For master's, comprehensive exam, research paper, thesis or project. *Entrance requirements:* For master's, minimum undergraduate GPA of 2.6 overall, 3.0 in major; personal statement; two recommendations; interview. Additional exam requirements/recommendations for international students: Required—TOEFL (minimum score 550 paper-based; 79 iBT). *Application deadline:* For fall admission, 8/1 priority date for domestic students, 7/15 for international students; for spring admission, 12/1 priority date for domestic students, 12/1 for international students; for summer admission, 5/1 priority date for domestic students, 5/1 for international students. Applications are processed on a rolling basis. Application fee: $65. Electronic applications accepted. Application fee is waived when completed online. *Expenses: Required fees:* $1003. *Financial support:* Career-related internships or fieldwork, Federal Work-Study, scholarships/grants, and unspecified assistantships available. Support available to part-time students. Financial award application deadline: 3/2; financial award applicants required to submit FAFSA. *Faculty research:* Cognitive development, language development, learning handicaps. *Unit head:* Dr. Kimberly Mayfield, Chair, 510-436-1396, Fax: 510-436-1325, E-mail: mayfield@hnu.edu. *Application contact:* Graduate Admission, 800-430-1321, Fax: 510-436-1325, E-mail: graduateadmissions@hnu.edu.
Website: http://www.hnu.edu/academics/graduatePrograms/education.html

Langston University, School of Education and Behavioral Sciences, Langston, OK 73050. Offers bilingual/multicultural (M Ed); elementary education (M Ed); English as a second language (M Ed); rehabilitation counseling (M Sc); urban education (M Ed). *Accreditation:* CORE; NCATE (one or more programs are accredited). *Program availability:* Part-time. *Degree requirements:* For master's, comprehensive exam, thesis optional. *Entrance requirements:* For master's, GRE, writing skills test, minimum GPA of 2.5, 3 letters of recommendation. Additional exam requirements/recommendations for international students: Required—TOEFL, TWE. *Faculty research:* Bilingual/multicultural education, financing post-secondary education.

Long Island University–LIU Brooklyn, School of Education, Brooklyn, NY 11201-8423. Offers adolescence urban education (MS Ed); applied behavior analysis (Advanced Certificate); bilingual education (Advanced Certificate); bilingual education in urban setting (MS Ed); bilingual school counselor (MS Ed, Advanced Certificate); childhood urban education (MS Ed); childhood/early childhood education (MS Ed); childhood/early childhood urban education (MS Ed); early childhood urban education (MS Ed, Advanced Certificate); educational leadership (Advanced Certificate); marriage and family therapy (MS, Advanced Certificate); mental health counseling (MS, Advanced Certificate); school building district leader (Advanced Certificate); school counselor (MS Ed, Advanced Certificate); school psychologist (MS Ed); teaching students with disabilities (MS Ed); teaching urban children with disabilities (MS Ed); TESOL (MS Ed, Advanced Certificate). *Accreditation:* TEAC. *Program availability:* Part-time, evening/weekend, 100% online. *Entrance requirements:* For master's, GRE. Additional exam requirements/recommendations for international students: Required—TOEFL (minimum score 527 paper-based, 75 iBT), IELTS, or PTE. Electronic applications accepted. *Faculty research:* Diversity issues in education and mental health care, inclusion - disability studies, sustainability, teacher professional development.

Loyola Marymount University, School of Education, JD/MA Program in Urban Education, Los Angeles, CA 90045. Offers JD/MA. *Unit head:* Dr. Edmundo Litton, Chair, Department of Specialized Programs in Urban Education, 310-338-1859, E-mail: elitton@lmu.edu. *Application contact:* Ammar Dalal, Assistant Vice Provost for Graduate Enrollment, 310-338-2721, Fax: 310-338-6086, E-mail: graduateinfo@lmu.edu.
Website: http://lls.edu/admissionsaid/degreeprograms/jdprograms/majdprogram

Loyola Marymount University, School of Education, Program in Literacy Instruction for Urban Environments, Los Angeles, CA 90045. Offers MA. *Unit head:* Dr. Candace Poindexter, Director, Literacy and Educational Studies, 310-338-7314, E-mail: cpoindex@lmu.edu. *Application contact:* Ammar Dalal, Assistant Vice Provost for Graduate Enrollment, 310-338-2721, Fax: 310-338-6086, E-mail: graduateinfo@lmu.edu.
Website: http://soe.lmu.edu/academics/literacyinstructionforurbanenvironmentsonline

Loyola Marymount University, School of Education, Program in Urban Education, Los Angeles, CA 90045. Offers MA. *Unit head:* Dr. Yvette Lapayese, Chair, Department of Specialized Programs in Urban Education, 310-338-3773, E-mail: ylapayes@lmu.edu. *Application contact:* Ammar Dalal, Assistant Vice Provost for Graduate Enrollment, 310-338-2721, Fax: 310-338-6086, E-mail: graduateinfo@lmu.edu.
Website: http://soe.lmu.edu

Manhattanville College, School of Education, Jump Start Program, Purchase, NY 10577-2132. Offers childhood education and special education (grades 1-6) (MPS); early childhood education (birth-grade 2) (MAT); education (Advanced Certificate); English and special education (grades 5-12) (MPS); mathematics and special education (grades 5-12) (MPS); science and special education (grades 5-12) (MPS); social studies and special education (grades 5-12) (MPS); Spanish (grades 7-12) (MAT); tesol - teaching English as a second language (all grades) (MPS). *Program availability:* Part-time, evening/weekend. *Faculty:* 11 full-time (7 women), 78 part-time/adjunct (50 women). *Students:* 3 full-time (2 women), 16 part-time (11 women); includes 5 minority (1 Black or African American, non-Hispanic/Latino; 3 Hispanic/Latino; 1 Native Hawaiian or other Pacific Islander, non-Hispanic/Latino). Average age 31. 48 applicants, 54% accepted, 22 enrolled. In 2018, 23 master's, 1 other advanced degree awarded. *Degree requirements:* For master's, comprehensive exam (for some programs), thesis (for some programs), student teaching, research seminars, portfolios, internships, writing assessment; for Advanced Certificate, comprehensive exam (for some programs). *Entrance requirements:* For master's, for programs leading to certification, candidates must submit scores from GRE or MAT(miller analogies test), minimum undergraduate GPA of 3.0, all transcripts from all colleges and universities attended, 2 letters of recommendation, interview, essay (2-3 page personal statement that describes reasons for choosing education as profession and personal philosophy of education), proof of immunization (for those born after 1957). Additional exam requirements/recommendations for international students: Required—TOEFL (minimum score 600 paper-based; 110 iBT); Recommended—IELTS (minimum score 8). *Application deadline:* Applications are processed on a rolling basis. Application fee: $75. Electronic applications accepted. *Expenses:* 935 per credit. *Financial support:* Teaching assistantships, career-related internships or fieldwork, Federal Work-Study, institutionally sponsored loans, scholarships/grants, and unspecified assistantships available. Financial award application deadline: 3/15; financial award applicants required to submit FAFSA. *Faculty research:* Early childhood and technology, professional development schools and community schools, students with emotional difficulties, literacy and adolescents, mindfulness, changing suburbs institute, and community schools, studying the effects of the environment on special populations, the most difficult cases, students who are presented with multiple challenges: learning, behavioral and ACE experiences who see criminal behavior as a way to cope; working on giving them the tools they need to succeed. *Unit head:* Dr. Shelley Wepner, Dean, 914-323-3153, E-mail: Shelly.Wepner@mville.edu. *Application contact:* Alissa Wilson, Director, SOE Graduate Enrollment Management, 914-323-3150, Fax: 914-694-1732, E-mail: edschool@mville.edu.
Website: http://www.mville.edu/programs/jump-start

Metropolitan State University, School of Urban Education, St. Paul, MN 55106-5000. Offers curriculum, pedagogy and schooling (MS); English as a second language (MS); secondary education (MS), including English teaching, life sciences teaching, mathematics teaching, social studies teaching; special education (MS).

Morgan State University, School of Graduate Studies, School of Education and Urban Studies, Department of Advanced Studies, Leadership and Policy, Program in Urban Educational Leadership, Baltimore, MD 21251. Offers Ed D. *Accreditation:* NCATE. *Program availability:* Part-time, evening/weekend. *Faculty research:* Multicultural education, cooperative learning, psychology of cognition.

New Jersey City University, Debra Cannon Partridge Wolfe College of Education, Department of Educational Leadership and Counseling, Jersey City, NJ 07305-1597. Offers counselor education (MA); educational administration and supervision (MA); urban education (MA). *Accreditation:* TEAC. *Program availability:* Part-time, evening/weekend. *Entrance requirements:* Additional exam requirements/recommendations for international students: Required—TOEFL (minimum score 79 iBT).

New Jersey City University, Debra Cannon Partridge Wolfe College of Education, Department of Modern Languages, Jersey City, NJ 07305-1597. Offers urban education world language (MA).

Norfolk State University, School of Graduate Studies, School of Education, Department of Secondary Education and School Leadership, Program in Urban Education/Administration, Norfolk, VA 23504. Offers teaching (MA). *Accreditation:* NCATE. *Program availability:* Part-time. *Entrance requirements:* For master's, GRE General Test, PRAXIS I, minimum GPA of 3.0 in major, 2.5 overall.

Northeastern Illinois University, College of Graduate Studies and Research, Daniel L. Goodwin College of Education, Program in Inner City Studies, Chicago, IL 60625. Offers MA. *Program availability:* Part-time, evening/weekend. *Degree requirements:* For master's, comprehensive exam, thesis or alternative. *Entrance requirements:* For master's, minimum GPA of 2.75. Additional exam requirements/recommendations for international students: Required—TOEFL (minimum score 550 paper-based; 79 iBT). Electronic applications accepted.

Providence College, Program in Urban Teaching, Providence, RI 02918. Offers M Ed. *Program availability:* Part-time, evening/weekend. *Entrance requirements:* Additional exam requirements/recommendations for international students: Required—TOEFL (minimum score 577 paper-based; 90 iBT).

Teachers College, Columbia University, Department of Organization and Leadership, New York, NY 10027-6696. Offers adult education guided intensive study (Ed D); adult learning and leadership (Ed M, MA, Ed D); educational leadership (Ed D); higher and postsecondary education (MA, Ed D); leadership, policy and politics (Ed D); nurse executive (MA, Ed D), including administration studies (MA), professorial studies (MA); private school leadership (Ed M, MA); public school building leadership (Ed M, MA); social and organizational psychology (MA); urban education leaders (Ed D); MA/MBA. *Program availability:* Part-time, evening/weekend. *Students:* 249 full-time (165 women), 427 part-time (299 women); includes 275 minority (99 Black or African American, non-Hispanic/Latino; 75 Asian, non-Hispanic/Latino; 82 Hispanic/Latino; 1 Native Hawaiian or other Pacific Islander, non-Hispanic/Latino; 18 Two or more races, non-Hispanic/Latino), 84 international. Average age 34. 770 applicants, 59% accepted, 267 enrolled. *Unit head:* Prof. Bill Baldwin, Chair, 212-678-3043, E-mail: wjb12@tc.columbia.edu. *Application contact:* Kelly Sutton-Skinner, Director of Admission & New Student Enrollment, E-mail: kms2237@tc.columbia.edu.

Temple University, College of Education, Department of Teaching and Learning, Philadelphia, PA 19122-6096. Offers career and technical education (Ed M), including business, computing, and information technology, industrial education, marketing education; middle grades education (Ed M), including math and language arts, math and science, science and language arts; secondary education (Ed M), including English, math, social studies; teaching English to speakers of other languages (MS Ed); urban education (Ed M). *Program availability:* Part-time, evening/weekend. *Faculty:* 27 full-time (19 women), 71 part-time/adjunct (51 women). *Students:* 181 full-time (126 women), 128 part-time (78 women); includes 71 minority (25 Black or African American, non-Hispanic/Latino; 1 American Indian or Alaska Native, non-Hispanic/Latino; 20 Asian, non-Hispanic/Latino; 19 Hispanic/Latino; 1 Native Hawaiian or other Pacific Islander, non-Hispanic/Latino; 5 Two or more races, non-Hispanic/Latino), 12 international. 234 applicants, 67% accepted, 103 enrolled. In 2018, 148 master's awarded. *Degree requirements:* For master's, thesis (for some programs). *Entrance requirements:* For master's, statement of goals, 2 letters of recommendation. Additional exam requirements/recommendations for international students: Required—TOEFL (minimum score 79 iBT), IELTS, PTE, one of three is required. Application fee: $60. Electronic applications accepted. *Financial support:* Fellowships, research assistantships, teaching assistantships, career-related internships or fieldwork, Federal Work-Study, scholarships/grants, health care benefits, and unspecified assistantships available. Financial award applicants required to submit FAFSA. *Faculty research:* Career & technical education, early childhood education, middle grades education, secondary education, special education. *Unit head:* Matthew Tincani, Prof. of Applied Behavior Analysis and Dept. Chairperson, 215-204-8073, E-mail: matthew.tincani@temple.edu. *Application contact:* Stacey Sanginette, Academic Coordinator, 215-204-6143, E-mail: stacey.sangtinette@temple.edu.
Website: http://education.temple.edu/tl

University of Chicago, Graham School of Continuing Liberal and Professional Studies, Urban Teacher Education Program, Chicago, IL 60637. Offers MAT. *Degree requirements:* For master's, exams; student teaching. *Entrance requirements:* For master's, ACT or TAP, 3 letters of recommendation, statement of purpose, transcripts, resume or curriculum vitae. Electronic applications accepted. *Expenses:* Contact institution.

University of Houston–Downtown, College of Public Service, Department of Urban Education, Houston, TX 77002. Offers curriculum and instruction (MAT). *Program availability:* Part-time, evening/weekend. *Degree requirements:* For master's, capstone course with completed project, position paper, grant proposal, empirical study, curriculum development/revision, or advanced technology project presented at annual Graduate Project Exhibition. *Entrance requirements:* For master's, GRE, personal statement, 3 recommendation forms. Additional exam requirements/recommendations for international students: Required—TOEFL (minimum score 550 paper-based; 80 iBT). Electronic applications accepted. *Expenses:* Contact institution.

University of Illinois at Chicago, College of Education, Department of Educational Policy Studies, Chicago, IL 60607-7128. Offers policy studies (M Ed); policy studies in urban education (PhD); urban education leadership (Ed D). *Faculty research:* Social foundations of education, educational organizations and leadership, education policy analysis, understanding and addressing educational problems in urban contexts.

University of Massachusetts Boston, College of Education and Human Development, Program in Urban Education, Leadership, and Policy Studies, Boston, MA 02125-3393. Offers Ed D, PhD. *Program availability:* Part-time, evening/weekend. *Faculty:* 11 full-time (7 women), 10 part-time/adjunct (6 women). *Students:* 1 (woman) full-time, 43 part-time (29 women); includes 19 minority (8 Black or African American, non-Hispanic/Latino; 10 Hispanic/Latino; 1 Two or more races, non-Hispanic/Latino), 3 international. Average age 38. 18 applicants, 33% accepted, 3 enrolled. In 2018, 3 doctorates awarded. *Entrance requirements:* For doctorate, GRE General Test or MAT, minimum GPA of 2.75. *Application deadline:* For summer admission, 3/1 for domestic students. Application fee: $60 ($100 for international students). Electronic applications accepted. *Expenses: Tuition, area resident:* Full-time $17,896. Tuition, state resident: full-time $17,896. Tuition, nonresident: full-time $34,932. *International tuition:* $34,932 full-time. *Required fees:* $355. *Financial support:* Research assistantships, teaching assistantships, career-related internships or fieldwork, Federal Work-Study, and unspecified assistantships available. Support available to part-time students. Financial award application deadline: 3/1; financial award applicants required to submit FAFSA. *Faculty research:* School reform, race and culture in schools, race and higher education, language, literacy and writing. *Unit head:* Dr. Wenfan Yan, Graduate Program Director, 617-287.4873, E-mail: WenFan.Yan@umb.edu. *Application contact:* Graduate Admissions Coordinator, 617-287-6400, Fax: 617-287-6236, E-mail: graduate.admissions@umb.edu.

University of Memphis, Graduate School, College of Education, Department of Instruction and Curriculum Leadership, Memphis, TN 38152. Offers advanced studies in teaching and learning (M Ed); applied behavior analysis (Graduate Certificate); autism studies (Graduate Certificate); early childhood education (MAT, MS, Ed D); elementary education (MAT); instruction and curriculum (MS, Ed D); instruction design and technology (MS, Ed D); instructional design and technology (Graduate Certificate); literacy, leadership, and coaching (Graduate Certificate); reading (MS, Ed D); school library information specialist (Graduate Certificate); secondary education (MAT); special education (MAT, MS, Ed D); STEM teacher leadership (Graduate Certificate); urban education (Graduate Certificate). *Accreditation:* NCATE (one or more programs are accredited). *Program availability:* Part-time. *Students:* 62 full-time (45 women), 412 part-time (326 women); includes 209 minority (179 Black or African American, non-Hispanic/Latino; 1 American Indian or Alaska Native, non-Hispanic/Latino; 5 Asian, non-Hispanic/Latino; 17 Hispanic/Latino; 7 Two or more races, non-Hispanic/Latino), 4 international. Average age 35. 195 applicants, 91% accepted, 143 enrolled. In 2018, 122 master's, 13 doctorates, 29 other advanced degrees awarded. Terminal master's awarded for partial completion of doctoral program. *Degree requirements:* For master's, comprehensive exam, thesis or alternative; for doctorate, comprehensive exam, thesis/dissertation. *Entrance requirements:* For master's, GRE General Test, PRAXIS, minimum GPA of 2.5, letters of reference; for doctorate, GRE General Test, GRE Subject Test, 2 years of teaching experience, letters of reference, statement of purpose, interview. Additional exam requirements/recommendations for international students: Required—TOEFL (minimum score 550 paper-based; 79 iBT). *Application deadline:* For fall admission, 4/1 priority date for domestic students; for spring admission, 10/1 priority date for domestic students; for summer admission, 2/1 priority date for domestic students. Applications are processed on a rolling basis. Application fee: $35 ($60 for international students). Electronic applications accepted. *Expenses: Tuition, area resident:* Full-time $10,240; part-time $503 per credit hour. Tuition, state resident: full-time $10,464. Tuition, nonresident: full-time $20,224; part-time $991 per credit hour. *Required fees:* $850; $106 per credit hour. *Financial support:* Research assistantships with full tuition reimbursements, teaching assistantships with full tuition reimbursements, career-related internships or fieldwork, Federal Work-Study, institutionally sponsored loans, scholarships/grants, traineeships, and unspecified assistantships available. Support available to part-time students. Financial award application deadline: 2/1; financial award applicants required to submit FAFSA. *Faculty research:* Effective urban teachers, preparation and retention of urban teachers, technology utilization in schools, field-based teacher preparation programs, effective use of online instruction. *Unit head:* Dr. Christian Mueller, Chair, 901-678-2365, E-mail: cemuellr@memphis.edu. *Application contact:* Dr. Lee Allen, Director of Graduate Programs, 901-678-4073, E-mail: allenlee@memphis.edu.
Website: http://www.memphis.edu/icl/

University of Michigan–Dearborn, College of Education, Health, and Human Services, Doctoral Program in Education, Dearborn, MI 48126. Offers curriculum and practice (Ed D); educational leadership (Ed D); metropolitan education (Ed D). *Program availability:* Part-time, evening/weekend. *Faculty:* 5 full-time (3 women), 1 part-time/adjunct (0 women). *Students:* 2 full-time (both women), 19 part-time (12 women); includes 9 minority (8 Black or African American, non-Hispanic/Latino; 1 Hispanic/Latino). Average age 44. 9 applicants, 44% accepted, 3 enrolled. In 2018, 5 doctorates awarded. *Degree requirements:* For doctorate, thesis/dissertation. *Entrance requirements:* For doctorate, GRE (taken within the last 5 years), master's degree with minimum GPA of 3.3, 3 letters of recommendation (1 from faculty), 3 years' professional and/or teaching experience. Additional exam requirements/recommendations for international students: Required—TOEFL (minimum score 560 paper-based; 84 iBT), IELTS (minimum score 6.5). *Application deadline:* For fall admission, 3/1 for domestic and international students. Application fee: $60. Electronic applications accepted. *Expenses:* $12,140 per academic year (typical full-time in-state); $20,708 per academic year (typical full-time out-of-state). *Financial support:* In 2018–19, 6 students received support. Scholarships/grants available. Financial award application deadline: 3/1; financial award applicants required to submit FAFSA. *Faculty research:* Urban education, educational leadership, assessment and evaluation, research methods, science education. *Unit head:* Dr. Chris Burke, Director, 313-593-5319, E-mail: cjfburke@umich.edu. *Application contact:* Office of Graduate Studies, 313-583-6321, E-mail: umd-graduatestudies@umich.edu.
Website: http://umdearborn.edu/cehhs/cehhs_edd/

University of Michigan–Dearborn, College of Education, Health, and Human Services, Master of Arts Program in Community Based Education, Dearborn, MI 48126. Offers MA. *Program availability:* Part-time, evening/weekend. *Faculty:* 1 full-time (0 women), 1 part-time/adjunct (0 women). *Students:* 7 part-time (6 women); includes 3 minority (all Black or African American, non-Hispanic/Latino). Average age 33. 5 applicants, 80% accepted, 2 enrolled. *Degree requirements:* For master's, essay. *Entrance requirements:* Additional exam requirements/recommendations for international students: Required—TOEFL (minimum score 560 paper-based; 84 iBT), IELTS (minimum score 6.5). *Application deadline:* For fall admission, 8/1 for domestic students, 5/1 for international students; for winter admission, 12/1 for domestic students, 9/1 for international students; for spring admission, 4/1 for domestic students, 1/1 for international students. Applications are processed on a rolling basis. Application fee: $60. Electronic applications accepted. *Expenses:* $12,140 per academic year (typical full-time in-state); $20,708 per academic year (typical full-time out-of-state). *Financial support:* In 2018–19, 4 students received support. Scholarships/grants available. Financial award application deadline: 3/1; financial award applicants required to submit FAFSA. *Faculty research:* Community based education, ecojustice education, multicultural education, place based education, urban education. *Unit head:* Dr. Paul Fossum, Director, Master's Programs, 313-583-6415, E-mail: pfossum@umich.edu. *Application contact:* Office of Graduate Studies, 313-583-6321, E-mail: umd-graduatestudies@umich.edu.
Website: https://umdearborn.edu/cehhs/graduate-programs/areas-study/ma-community-based-education

University of Nebraska at Omaha, Graduate Studies, College of Education, Department of Teacher Education, Program in Secondary Education, Omaha, NE 68182. Offers instruction in urban schools (Certificate); secondary education (MS). *Accreditation:* NCATE. *Program availability:* Part-time, evening/weekend. *Degree requirements:* For master's, comprehensive exam, thesis (for some programs). *Entrance requirements:* For master's, minimum GPA of 3.0, transcripts. Additional exam requirements/recommendations for international students: Required—TOEFL, IELTS, PTE. Electronic applications accepted.

University of Pennsylvania, Graduate School of Education, Teach for America Program, Philadelphia, PA 19104. Offers MS Ed. Program designed for Teach For America corps members teaching in Philadelphia public and charter schools. *Program availability:* Evening/weekend. *Students:* 1 (woman) full-time. 70 applicants, 96% accepted, 58 enrolled. In 2018, 5 master's awarded. *Entrance requirements:* For master's, bachelor's degree; Teach for America placement. Additional exam requirements/recommendations for international students: Required—TOEFL, IELTS. *Application deadline:* Applications are processed on a rolling basis. Application fee: $75. Electronic applications accepted. *Unit head:* Program Director, 215-746-4855. *Application contact:* Program Director, 215-746-4855.
Website: http://www.gse.upenn.edu/exec-ed/tfa

University of San Francisco, School of Education, Department of Teacher Education, San Francisco, CA 94117. Offers digital media and learning (MA); teaching (MA); teaching reading (MA); teaching urban education and social justice (MA). *Program availability:* Part-time. *Students:* 377 full-time (280 women), 51 part-time (43 women); includes 228 minority (28 Black or African American, non-Hispanic/Latino; 62 Asian, non-Hispanic/Latino; 121 Hispanic/Latino; 1 Native Hawaiian or other Pacific Islander, non-Hispanic/Latino; 16 Two or more races, non-Hispanic/Latino), 22 international. Average age 29. 536 applicants, 70% accepted, 182 enrolled. In 2018, 212 master's awarded. *Entrance requirements:* Additional exam requirements/recommendations for international students: Required—TOEFL, IELTS, PTE. *Application deadline:* For fall admission, 3/1 priority date for domestic and international students; for spring admission, 10/15 priority date for domestic students, 10/1 for international students. Applications are processed on a rolling basis. Electronic applications accepted. *Financial support:* Applicants required to submit FAFSA. *Unit head:* Dr. Noah Borrero, Chair, 415-422-6481. *Application contact:* Peter Cole, Admission Coordinator, 415-422-5467, E-mail: schoolofeducation@usfca.edu.
Website: https://www.usfca.edu/catalog/graduate/school-of-education/programs-teacher-education

University of Southern California, Graduate School, Rossier School of Education, Doctor of Education Programs, Los Angeles, CA 90089. Offers educational psychology (Ed D); higher education administration (Ed D); K-12 leadership in urban school settings (Ed D); teacher education in multicultural societies (Ed D). *Program availability:* Part-time, evening/weekend. *Degree requirements:* For doctorate, thesis/dissertation. *Entrance requirements:* For doctorate, GRE. Additional exam requirements/recommendations for international students: Required—TOEFL (minimum score 100 iBT). Electronic applications accepted. *Faculty research:* Data-driven decision-making in K-12 schools and districts; examination of college and university leadership and management in U. S. and Asia; studies in facilitating student learning; organizational change and the role of leaders; leadership, diversity, learning and accountability.

University of Wisconsin–Milwaukee, Graduate School, School of Education, Department of Curriculum and Instruction, Milwaukee, WI 53201-0413. Offers curriculum and instruction (MS), including cross-curricular focus, early childhood education, English education, mathematics education, middle childhood/early adolescence education, reading education, science education, urban social studies education. *Program availability:* Part-time. *Students:* 19 full-time (15 women), 56 part-time (49 women); includes 15 minority (3 Black or African American, non-Hispanic/Latino; 1 American Indian or Alaska Native, non-Hispanic/Latino; 3 Asian, non-Hispanic/Latino; 1 Hispanic/Latino; 7 Two or more races, non-Hispanic/Latino), 2 international. Average age 33. 27 applicants, 44% accepted, 11 enrolled. In 2018, 20 master's awarded. *Entrance requirements:* Additional exam requirements/recommendations for international students: Required—TOEFL (minimum score 550 paper-based; 79 iBT), IELTS (minimum score 6.5). *Application deadline:* For fall admission, 1/1 priority date for domestic students; for spring admission, 9/1 for domestic students. Application fee: $56 ($96 for international students). Electronic applications accepted. *Financial support:* Fellowships, research assistantships, teaching assistantships, career-related internships or fieldwork, health care benefits, unspecified assistantships, and project assistantships available. Support available to part-time students. Financial award application deadline: 4/15; financial award applicants required to submit FAFSA. *Application contact:* General Information Contact, 414-229-4721, E-mail: soeinfo@uwm.edu.
Website: http://uwm.edu/education/academics/curriculum-instruction-department/

University of Wisconsin–Milwaukee, Graduate School, School of Education, Department of Exceptional Education, Milwaukee, WI 53201-0413. Offers autism spectrum disorders (Graduate Certificate); exceptional education (MS); transition for students with disabilities (Graduate Certificate); urban education (PhD), including adult, continuing and higher education leadership, art education, curriculum and instruction, exceptional education, mathematics education, multicultural studies, social foundations of education. *Program availability:* Part-time. *Students:* 38 full-time (29 women), 67 part-time (50 women); includes 39 minority (23 Black or African American, non-Hispanic/Latino; 1 American Indian or Alaska Native, non-Hispanic/Latino; 6 Asian, non-Hispanic/Latino; 1 Hispanic/Latino; 8 Two or more races, non-Hispanic/Latino), 2 international. Average age 40. 47 applicants, 40% accepted, 11 enrolled. In 2018, 13 master's, 14 doctorates, 4 other advanced degrees awarded. *Entrance requirements:* Additional exam requirements/recommendations for international students: Required—TOEFL (minimum score 550 paper-based; 79 iBT), IELTS (minimum score 6.5). *Application deadline:* For fall admission, 1/1 priority date for domestic students; for spring admission, 9/1 for domestic students. Application fee: $56 ($96 for international students). Electronic applications accepted. *Financial support:* Fellowships, research assistantships, teaching assistantships, career-related internships or fieldwork, health care benefits, and unspecified assistantships available. Support available to part-time students. Financial award application deadline: 4/15; financial award applicants required to submit FAFSA. *Faculty research:* Emotional disturbance, hearing impairment, learning disabilities, mental retardation. *Application contact:* General Information Contact, 414-229-4721, E-mail: soeinfo@uwm.edu.
Website: http://uwm.edu/education/academics/exceptional-edu-department/

Virginia Commonwealth University, Graduate School, School of Education, Doctoral Program in Education, Richmond, VA 23284-9005. Offers art education (PhD); counselor education and supervision (PhD); curriculum, culture and change (PhD); educational leadership (PhD); educational psychology (PhD); leadership (Ed D); research and evaluation (PhD); special education and disability leadership (PhD); sport leadership (PhD); urban services leadership (PhD). *Accreditation:* NCATE. *Program availability:* Part-time. *Degree requirements:* For doctorate, thesis/dissertation. *Entrance requirements:* For doctorate, GRE (for PhD), MAT (for Ed D), interview, master's degree, writing sample. Additional exam requirements/recommendations for international students: Required—TOEFL (minimum score 600 paper-based; 100 iBT). Electronic applications accepted.

Section 26
Subject Areas

This section contains a directory of institutions offering graduate work in subject areas. Additional information about programs listed in the directory may be obtained by writing directly to the dean of a graduate school or chair of a department at the address given in the directory.

For programs offering related work, see also in this book *Administration, Instruction, and Theory; Business Administration and Management; Education; Instructional Levels; Leisure Studies and Recreation; Physical Education and Kinesiology;* and *Special Focus.* In the other guides in this series:

Graduate Programs in the Humanities, Arts & Social Sciences

See *Art and Art History; Family and Consumer Sciences; Language and Literature; Performing Arts; Psychology and Counseling (School Psychology); Public, Regional, and Industrial Affairs (Urban Studies); Religious Studies;* and *Social Sciences*

Graduate Programs in the Biological/Biomedical Sciences & Health-Related Medical Professions

See *Health-Related Professions*

Graduate Programs in the Physical Sciences, Mathematics, Agricultural Sciences, the Environment & Natural Resources

See *Mathematical Sciences*

Graduate Programs in Engineering & Applied Sciences

See *Computer Science and Information Technology*

CONTENTS

Program Directories

Agricultural Education

Alcorn State University, School of Graduate Studies, School of Education and Psychology, Lorman, MS 39096-7500. Offers agricultural education (MS Ed); elementary education (MAT, MS Ed, Ed S); guidance and counseling (MS Ed); industrial education (MS Ed); secondary education (MAT, MS Ed), including health and physical education (MS Ed), NCAA compliance and academic progress reporting (MS Ed); special education (MS Ed). *Accreditation:* NCATE. *Degree requirements:* For master's, thesis optional.

Arkansas State University, Graduate School, College of Agriculture and Technology, State University, AR 72467. Offers agricultural education (SCCT); agriculture (MSA); vocational-technical administration (SCCT). *Program availability:* Part-time. *Degree requirements:* For master's, comprehensive exam, thesis or alternative; for SCCT, comprehensive exam. *Entrance requirements:* For master's, GRE General Test or MAT, appropriate bachelor's degree, official transcripts, immunization records; for SCCT, GRE General Test or MAT, interview, master's degree, official transcript, immunization records. Additional exam requirements/recommendations for international students: Required—TOEFL (minimum score 550 paper-based; 79 iBT), IELTS (minimum score 6), PTE (minimum score 56). Electronic applications accepted.

California Polytechnic State University, San Luis Obispo, College of Agriculture, Food and Environmental Sciences, Department of Agricultural Education and Communication, San Luis Obispo, CA 93407. Offers MAE. *Program availability:* Part-time. *Faculty:* 4 full-time (2 women), 1 (woman) part-time/adjunct. *Students:* 25 full-time (17 women), 3 part-time (2 women); includes 7 minority (5 Hispanic/Latino; 2 Two or more races, non-Hispanic/Latino). Average age 25. 26 applicants, 85% accepted, 18 enrolled. In 2018, 21 master's awarded. *Degree requirements:* For master's, comprehensive exam. *Entrance requirements:* For master's, GRE. Additional exam requirements/recommendations for international students: Required—TOEFL (minimum score 80 iBT). *Application deadline:* For fall admission, 4/1 for domestic and international students; for winter admission, 10/1 for domestic and international students; for spring admission, 2/1 for domestic students, 1/1 for international students. Applications are processed on a rolling basis. Application fee: $55. Electronic applications accepted. *Expenses: Tuition, area resident:* Full-time $7176; part-time $4164 per year. Tuition, state resident: full-time $10,965. Tuition, nonresident: full-time $10,965. *Required fees:* $6336; $3711. *Financial support:* Fellowships, research assistantships, teaching assistantships, career-related internships or fieldwork, institutionally sponsored loans, scholarships/grants, health care benefits, and unspecified assistantships available. Financial award application deadline: 3/2; financial award applicants required to submit FAFSA. *Faculty research:* Agricultural education with emphasis on public school teaching. *Unit head:* Dr. Robert Flores, Department Head, 805-756-2169, E-mail: rflores@calpoly.edu. *Application contact:* Dr. Ann De Lay, Graduate Coordinator, 805-756-7272, E-mail: adelay@calpoly.edu.
Website: http://aged.calpoly.edu/

California State University, Chico, Office of Graduate Studies, College of Agriculture, Chico, CA 95929-0722. Offers agricultural education (MS). *Students:* 1 full-time (0 women). 3 applicants, 67% accepted. In 2018, 10 master's awarded. *Degree requirements:* For master's, thesis or alternative, the culminating activity can be in the form of thesis, project or oral exam. *Entrance requirements:* For master's, GRE or MAT, 3 letters of recommendation, three departmental recommendation forms, statement of purpose. Additional exam requirements/recommendations for international students: Required—TOEFL (minimum score 550 paper-based; 80 iBT), IELTS (minimum score 6.5), PTE (minimum score 59). *Application deadline:* For fall admission, 6/1 priority date for domestic students, 7/1 priority date for international students. Application fee: $55. Electronic applications accepted. *Expenses: Tuition, area resident:* Full-time $4622; part-time $3116 per unit. Tuition, state resident: full-time $4622; part-time $3116 per unit. Tuition, nonresident: full-time $10,634. *Required fees:* $2160; $1620 per year. Tuition and fees vary according to class time and program. *Financial support:* Fellowships, research assistantships, teaching assistantships, career-related internships or fieldwork, Federal Work-Study, scholarships/grants, traineeships, health care benefits, unspecified assistantships, and stipends available. Support available to part-time students. Financial award application deadline: 3/2; financial award applicants required to submit FAFSA. *Unit head:* Mollie Aschenbrener, MS Education Coordinator, 530-898-4568, Fax: 530-898-5844, E-mail: maschenbrener@csuchico.edu. *Application contact:* Micah Lehner, Graduate Admissions Coordinator, 530-898-5416, Fax: 530-898-3342, E-mail: mlehner@csuchico.edu.
Website: http://www.csuchico.edu/ag/

Clemson University, Graduate School, College of Agriculture, Forestry and Life Sciences, Department of Agricultural Sciences, Clemson, SC 29634. Offers agricultural education (M Ag Ed); applied economics (PhD); applied economics and statistics (MS). *Program availability:* Part-time. *Faculty:* 18 full-time (3 women). *Students:* 20 full-time (14 women), 12 part-time (6 women); includes 2 minority (both Black or African American, non-Hispanic/Latino). Average age 29. 39 applicants, 64% accepted, 15 enrolled. In 2018, 30 master's awarded. *Degree requirements:* For master's, thesis optional; for doctorate, comprehensive exam, thesis/dissertation. *Entrance requirements:* For master's and doctorate, GRE General Test, unofficial transcripts, letters of recommendation. Additional exam requirements/recommendations for international students: Required—TOEFL (minimum score 80 paper-based; 80 iBT), IELTS (minimum score 6.5), PTE (minimum score 5). *Application deadline:* For fall admission, 6/1 for domestic students, 7/1 for international students; for spring admission, 10/1 for domestic students, 11/1 for international students. Applications are processed on a rolling basis. Application fee: $80 ($90 for international students). Electronic applications accepted. *Expenses:* $5898 per semester full-time resident, $11623 per semester full-time non-resident, $724 per credit hour part-time resident, $1451 per credit hour part-time non-resident, online $955 per credit hour, $4938 doctoral programs resident, $10405 doctoral programs non-resident, $1144 full-time graduate assistant, other fees may apply per session. *Financial support:* In 2018–19, 17 students received support, including 2 fellowships with full and partial tuition reimbursements available (averaging $8,750 per year), 2 research assistantships with full and partial tuition reimbursements available (averaging $12,000 per year), 5 teaching assistantships with full and partial tuition reimbursements available (averaging $13,188 per year); career-related internships or fieldwork and unspecified assistantships also available. Financial award application deadline: 6/1. *Faculty research:* Agricultural education, agricultural economics, agricultural statistics, agribusiness. *Total annual research expenditures:* $427,800. *Unit head:* Dr. Charles Privette, Department Chair, 864-656-6247, E-mail: privett@clemson.edu. *Application contact:* Dr. Charles Privette, Department Chair, 864-656-6247, E-mail: privett@clemson.edu.
Website: http://www.clemson.edu/cafls/departments/agricultural-sciences/index.html

Colorado State University, College of Agricultural Sciences, Programs in Agricultural Sciences and Extension Education, Fort Collins, CO 80523. Offers agricultural sciences

(M Agr); extension education (M Ext Ed). *Program availability:* Part-time, evening/weekend, online only, 100% online. *Degree requirements:* For master's, professional paper (for some programs); internship. *Entrance requirements:* For master's, minimum GPA of 3.0, bachelor's degree. Additional exam requirements/recommendations for international students: Required—TOEFL (minimum score 550 paper-based; 80 iBT), IELTS (minimum score 6.5). Electronic applications accepted. *Expenses:* Contact institution.

Cornell University, Graduate School, Graduate Fields of Agriculture and Life Sciences, Field of Education, Ithaca, NY 14853. Offers adult and extension education (MPS, MS, PhD); learning, teaching, and social policy (MPS, MS, PhD); mathematics 7-12 (MS). Terminal master's awarded for partial completion of doctoral program. *Degree requirements:* For master's, thesis (MS); for doctorate, comprehensive exam, thesis/dissertation. *Entrance requirements:* For master's and doctorate, GRE General Test, sample of written work (recommended), 2 letters of recommendation. Additional exam requirements/recommendations for international students: Required—TOEFL (minimum score 550 paper-based; 77 iBT). Electronic applications accepted. *Faculty research:* Moral development and professional ethics, public issues education and community development, socio/political issues in public education, teacher education and curriculum in agricultural science and mathematics, extension research.

Eastern Kentucky University, The Graduate School, College of Education, Department of Curriculum and Instruction, Program in Secondary and Higher Education, Richmond, KY 40475-3102. Offers secondary education (MA Ed), including agricultural education, art education, biological sciences education, business education, English education, geography education, history education, home economics education, industrial education, mathematical sciences education, physical education, school health education. *Accreditation:* NCATE. *Program availability:* Part-time. *Entrance requirements:* For master's, GRE General Test, minimum GPA of 2.5.

Iowa State University of Science and Technology, Department of Agricultural Education and Studies, Ames, IA 50011. Offers MS, PhD. *Entrance requirements:* For master's and doctorate, resume. Additional exam requirements/recommendations for international students: Required—TOEFL (minimum score 550 paper-based; 79 iBT), IELTS (minimum score 6.5). Electronic applications accepted. *Faculty research:* Agricultural extension education, teaching, learning processes, distance education, international education, adult education.

Ithaca College, School of Humanities and Sciences, Program in Agriculture Education, Ithaca, NY 14850. Offers MAT. *Faculty:* 14 full-time (7 women). *Students:* 5 full-time (4 women). Average age 27. 6 applicants, 100% accepted, 5 enrolled. In 2018, 3 master's awarded. *Degree requirements:* For master's, one foreign language, student teaching, portfolio, teacher inquiry project. *Entrance requirements:* Additional exam requirements/recommendations for international students: Required—TOEFL (minimum score 550 paper-based; 80 iBT). *Application deadline:* For fall admission, 3/19 for domestic and international students. Applications are processed on a rolling basis. Application fee: $40. Electronic applications accepted. *Expenses:* Contact institution. *Financial support:* In 2018–19, 5 students received support, including 5 research assistantships (averaging $10,901 per year); career-related internships or fieldwork, Federal Work-Study, and scholarships/grants also available. Support available to part-time students. Financial award application deadline: 3/1; financial award applicants required to submit FAFSA. *Unit head:* Dr. Peter Martin, Chair, 607-274-1076, E-mail: pmartin@ithaca.edu. *Application contact:* Nicole Eversley Bradwell, Director, Office of Admission, 800-429-4274, Fax: 607-274-1263, E-mail: admission@ithaca.edu.
Website: http://www.ithaca.edu/gradprograms/education/programs/aded

Kansas State University, Graduate School, College of Agriculture, Department of Communications and Agricultural Education, Manhattan, KS 66506. Offers agricultural education and communication (MS). *Program availability:* Part-time, online learning. *Degree requirements:* For master's, comprehensive exam, thesis or alternative. *Entrance requirements:* For master's, GRE if GPA on last 60 undergraduate credits is less than 3.0. Electronic applications accepted. *Faculty research:* Curriculum development, instructional design, strategic communications, risk and crisis communications.

Louisiana State University and Agricultural & Mechanical College, Graduate School, College of Human Sciences and Education, School of Human Resource Education and Workforce Development, Baton Rouge, LA 70803. Offers agriculture and extension education and youth development (MS, PhD); career and technical education (MS, PhD); comprehensive vocational education (MS, PhD); extension and international education (MS, PhD); human resource and leadership development (MS, PhD); industrial education (MS); vocational agriculture education (MS, PhD); vocational business education (MS); vocational home economics education (MS). *Accreditation:* NCATE.

Mississippi State University, College of Agriculture and Life Sciences, School of Human Sciences, Mississippi State, MS 39762. Offers agriculture and extension education (MS), including communication, leadership; agriculture science (PhD), including agriculture and extension education; fashion design and merchandising (MS), including design and product development, merchandising; human development and family studies (MS, PhD). *Accreditation:* NCATE (one or more programs are accredited). *Program availability:* Part-time. *Faculty:* 21 full-time (12 women). *Students:* 30 full-time (28 women), 51 part-time (35 women); includes 17 minority (13 Black or African American, non-Hispanic/Latino; 1 Hispanic/Latino; 3 Two or more races, non-Hispanic/Latino), 4 international. Average age 34. 26 applicants, 62% accepted, 16 enrolled. In 2018, 8 master's, 12 doctorates awarded. *Degree requirements:* For master's, thesis optional, comprehensive oral or written exam. *Entrance requirements:* For master's, GRE, minimum GPA of 2.75 in last 4 semesters of course work; for doctorate, minimum GPA of 3.0 on prior graduate work. Additional exam requirements/recommendations for international students: Required—TOEFL (minimum score 477 paper-based; 53 iBT); Recommended—IELTS (minimum score 4.5). *Application deadline:* For fall admission, 7/1 for domestic students, 5/1 for international students; for spring admission, 11/1 for domestic students, 9/1 for international students. Applications are processed on a rolling basis. Application fee: $60 ($80 for international students). Electronic applications accepted. *Expenses:* Tuition, state resident: full-time $8450; part-time $360.59 per credit hour. Tuition, nonresident: full-time $23,140; part-time $969.09 per credit hour. *Required fees:* $110. One-time fee: $55 full-time. Part-time tuition and fees vary according to course load, degree level, campus/location and reciprocity agreements. *Financial support:* In 2018–19, 14 research assistantships (averaging $12,575 per year) were awarded; Federal Work-Study, institutionally sponsored loans, and unspecified assistantships also available. Financial award application deadline: 4/1; financial award applicants required to submit FAFSA. *Faculty research:* Animal welfare, agroscience, information technology, learning styles, problem solving. *Unit head:* Dr. Michael

Newman, Professor and Director, 662-325-2950, E-mail: mnewman@humansci.msstate.edu. *Application contact:* Ryan King, Admissions and Enrollment Assistant, 662-325-8951, E-mail: rjk101@grad.msstate.edu.
Website: http://www.humansci.msstate.edu

Montana State University, The Graduate School, College of Agriculture, Division of Agricultural Education, Bozeman, MT 59717. Offers MS. *Program availability:* Part-time, online learning. *Degree requirements:* For master's, comprehensive exam. *Entrance requirements:* For master's, GRE General Test. Additional exam requirements/recommendations for international students: Required—TOEFL (minimum score 550 paper-based). Electronic applications accepted. *Faculty research:* Extension systems, youth leadership, agricultural, adult and youth education in agriculture, international agricultural education, enzymology of vitamins, coenzymes and metal ions, steroid metabolism, protein structure, impact of wolves on big game hunting demand, prescription drug price dispersion in heterogeneous markets, divorce risk and the labor force participation of women with and without children, the economics of terraces in the Peruvian Andes.

Murray State University, Hutson School of Agriculture, Murray, KY 42071. Offers agriculture (MS), including agribusiness economics, agriculture education, sustainable agriculture, veterinary hospital management; veterinary hospital management (Certificate). *Program availability:* Part-time, 100% online, blended/hybrid learning. *Entrance requirements:* For master's, GRE or GMAT, minimum university GPA of 2.75. Additional exam requirements/recommendations for international students: Required—TOEFL (minimum score 527 paper-based; 71 iBT). Electronic applications accepted.

North Carolina Agricultural and Technical State University, The Graduate College, College of Agriculture and Environmental Sciences, Department of Agribusiness, Applied Economics, and Agriscience Education, Greensboro, NC 27411. Offers agribusiness and food industry management (MS); agricultural education (MS). *Accreditation:* NCATE. *Program availability:* Part-time, evening/weekend. *Degree requirements:* For master's, comprehensive exam, thesis or alternative, qualifying exam. *Entrance requirements:* For master's, GRE General Test, minimum GPA of 3.0. *Faculty research:* Aid for small farmers, agricultural technology resources, labor force mobility, agrology.

North Dakota State University, College of Graduate and Interdisciplinary Studies, College of Human Development and Education, School of Education, Program in Agricultural Education, Fargo, ND 58102. Offers M Ed, MS. *Accreditation:* NCATE. *Program availability:* Part-time. *Degree requirements:* For master's, comprehensive exam, thesis or alternative. *Entrance requirements:* Additional exam requirements/recommendations for international students: Required—TOEFL (minimum score 525 paper-based; 71 iBT). *Faculty research:* Vocational and cooperative extension education, rural leadership, rural education, international extension.

Northwest Missouri State University, Graduate School, School of Agricultural Sciences, Maryville, MO 64468-6001. Offers agricultural economics (MBA); agricultural education (MS Ed); agriculture (MS); teaching: agriculture (MS Ed). *Program availability:* Part-time. *Faculty:* 6 full-time (1 woman). *Students:* 9 full-time (7 women), 4 international. Average age 23. 8 applicants, 63% accepted, 4 enrolled. In 2018, 1 master's awarded. *Degree requirements:* For master's, comprehensive exam, thesis (for some programs). *Entrance requirements:* For master's, GRE General Test, minimum undergraduate GPA of 2.5, writing sample. Additional exam requirements/recommendations for international students: Required—TOEFL (minimum score 550 paper-based). *Application deadline:* For fall admission, 7/1 for domestic and international students; for spring admission, 11/15 for domestic and international students. Applications are processed on a rolling basis. Application fee: $0 ($75 for international students). Electronic applications accepted. *Expenses: Tuition, area resident:* Full-time $4551; part-time $252.86 per credit hour. Tuition, state resident: full-time $4551; part-time $252.86 per credit hour. Tuition, nonresident: full-time $9103; part-time $505.72 per credit hour. *International tuition:* $9103 full-time. *Required fees:* $2668; $148.20 per credit hour. Tuition and fees vary according to program. *Financial support:* Research assistantships with full tuition reimbursements, teaching assistantships with full tuition reimbursements, and unspecified assistantships available. Financial award application deadline: 4/1; financial award applicants required to submit FAFSA. *Unit head:* Rodney Barr, Director, 660-562-1620. *Application contact:* Rodney Barr, Director, 660-562-1620.
Website: http://www.nwmissouri.edu/ag/

The Ohio State University, Graduate School, College of Food, Agricultural, and Environmental Sciences, Department of Agricultural Communication, Education and Leadership, Program in Agricultural and Extension Education, Columbus, OH 43210. Offers MS. *Program availability:* Part-time, online learning. *Students:* 14. Average age 27. In 2018, 8 master's awarded. *Entrance requirements:* For master's, GRE. Additional exam requirements/recommendations for international students: Required—TOEFL (minimum score 550 paper-based; 79 iBT), Michigan English Language Assessment Battery (minimum score 82); Recommended—IELTS (minimum score 7). *Application deadline:* For fall admission, 1/1 priority date for domestic students, 12/1 priority date for international students; for spring admission, 11/11 for domestic and international students; for summer admission, 3/1 for domestic and international students. Applications are processed on a rolling basis. Application fee: $60 ($70 for international students). Electronic applications accepted. *Financial support:* Institutionally sponsored loans available. Support available to part-time students. *Unit head:* Dr. Scott Scheer, Graduate Studies Chair, 614-292-6758, E-mail: scheer.9@osu.edu. *Application contact:* Graduate and Professional Admissions, 614-292-9444, Fax: 614-292-3895, E-mail: gpadmissions@osu.edu.
Website: http://acel.osu.edu/

Oklahoma State University, College of Agricultural Science and Natural Resources, Department of Agricultural Education, Communications and Leadership, Stillwater, OK 74078. Offers M Ag, MS, PhD. *Program availability:* Online learning. *Faculty:* 12 full-time (3 women), 3 part-time/adjunct (2 women). *Students:* 17 full-time (15 women), 36 part-time (24 women); includes 6 minority (1 Black or African American, non-Hispanic/Latino; 3 American Indian or Alaska Native, non-Hispanic/Latino; 2 Hispanic/Latino), 3 international. Average age 29. 25 applicants, 84% accepted, 17 enrolled. In 2018, 18 master's, 1 doctorate awarded. *Entrance requirements:* For master's and doctorate, GRE or GMAT. Additional exam requirements/recommendations for international students: Required—TOEFL (minimum score 550 paper-based; 79 iBT). *Application deadline:* For fall admission, 3/1 priority date for international students; for spring admission, 8/1 priority date for international students. Applications are processed on a rolling basis. Application fee: $40 ($75 for international students). Electronic applications accepted. *Expenses: Tuition, area resident:* Full-time $4148. Tuition, state resident: full-time $4148. Tuition, nonresident: full-time $10,517. *International tuition:* $10,517 full-time. *Required fees:* $4394; $2929 per credit hour. Tuition and fees vary according to course load and program. *Financial support:* Research assistantships, teaching assistantships, career-related internships or fieldwork, Federal Work-Study, scholarships/grants, health care benefits, tuition waivers (partial), and unspecified assistantships available. Support available to part-time students. Financial award application deadline: 3/1; financial award applicants required to submit FAFSA. *Faculty research:* Teaching in and learning about agriculture, agriculture teacher evaluation,

evaluation of information dissemination delivery methods, agricultural literacy curriculum model development, distance education delivery methods. *Unit head:* Dr. Robert Terry, Department Head, 405-744-8036, Fax: 405-744-5176, E-mail: rob.terry@okstate.edu. *Application contact:* Dr. Sheryl Tucker, Dean, 405-744-6368, Fax: 405-744-0355, E-mail: gradi@okstate.edu.
Website: http://aged.okstate.edu/

Oregon State University, College of Agricultural Sciences, Program in Agricultural Education, Corvallis, OR 97331. Offers leadership and communication in agriculture (MS). *Program availability:* Part-time. *Entrance requirements:* Additional exam requirements/recommendations for international students: Required—TOEFL (minimum score 80 iBT), IELTS (minimum score 6.5).

Oregon State University, College of Education, Program in Education, Corvallis, OR 97331. Offers agricultural education (PhD); language equity and education policy (PhD); mathematics education (MS); science education (MS); science/mathematics education (PhD). *Program availability:* Part-time, 100% online, blended/hybrid learning. Terminal master's awarded for partial completion of doctoral program. *Degree requirements:* For master's, variable foreign language requirement, thesis (for some programs); for doctorate, variable foreign language requirement, thesis/dissertation. *Entrance requirements:* Additional exam requirements/recommendations for international students: Required—TOEFL (minimum score 575 paper-based). *Faculty research:* School administration, educational foundations, research methodology, education policy development, higher education administration.

Penn State University Park, Graduate School, College of Agricultural Sciences, Department of Agricultural Economics, Sociology, and Education, University Park, PA 16802. Offers agricultural and extension education (M Ed, MS, PhD, Certificate); applied youth, family and community education (M Ed); energy, environmental, and food economics (MS, PhD); rural sociology (MS, PhD).

Purdue University, Graduate School, College of Agriculture, Department of Youth Development and Agricultural Education, West Lafayette, IN 47907. Offers MA, PhD. *Faculty:* 10 full-time (6 women). *Students:* 17 full-time (11 women), 8 part-time (6 women); includes 7 minority (5 Black or African American, non-Hispanic/Latino; 1 Asian, non-Hispanic/Latino; 1 Two or more races, non-Hispanic/Latino), 5 international. Average age 30. 10 applicants, 40% accepted, 4 enrolled. In 2018, 7 master's, 2 doctorates awarded. *Degree requirements:* For doctorate, comprehensive exam. *Entrance requirements:* For master's and doctorate, GRE General Test (minimum combined score of 1000), minimum undergraduate GPA of 3.0 or equivalent. Additional exam requirements/recommendations for international students: Required—TOEFL (minimum score 550 paper-based; 77 iBT), TWE with minimum score of 5 (recommended for MA, required for PhD). *Application deadline:* For fall admission, 3/15 priority date for domestic students, 3/1 for international students; for spring admission, 10/15 priority date for domestic students, 8/1 for international students; for summer admission, 3/15 for domestic students, 1/1 for international students. Applications are processed on a rolling basis. Application fee: $60 ($75 for international students). Electronic applications accepted. *Unit head:* Mark A. Russell, Head, 765-494-8423, E-mail: mrussell@purdue.edu. *Application contact:* Brenda Pickett, Graduate Contact, 765-494-8439, E-mail: bpicket@purdue.edu.
Website: https://ag.purdue.edu/ydae

Purdue University, Graduate School, College of Education, Department of Curriculum and Instruction, West Lafayette, IN 47907. Offers agricultural and extension education (MS, MS Ed, PhD, Ed S); art education (PhD); career and technical education (MS Ed, PhD, Ed S); curriculum studies (MS Ed, PhD, Ed S); educational technology (MS Ed, PhD, Ed S); elementary education (MS Ed); family and consumer sciences education (MS Ed, PhD, Ed S); foreign language education (MS Ed, PhD, Ed S); industrial technology (PhD, Ed S); language arts (MS Ed, PhD, Ed S); literacy (MS Ed, PhD, Ed S); mathematics education (MS, MS Ed, PhD, Ed S); science education (MS, MS Ed, PhD, Ed S); social studies education (MS Ed, PhD, Ed S). *Accreditation:* NCATE. *Program availability:* Part-time, evening/weekend, online learning. *Faculty:* 34 full-time (24 women), 3 part-time/adjunct (1 woman). *Students:* 75 full-time (52 women), 357 part-time (271 women); includes 83 minority (29 Black or African American, non-Hispanic/Latino; 1 American Indian or Alaska Native, non-Hispanic/Latino; 14 Asian, non-Hispanic/Latino; 29 Hispanic/Latino; 1 Native Hawaiian or other Pacific Islander, non-Hispanic/Latino; 9 Two or more races, non-Hispanic/Latino), 43 international. Average age 36. 169 applicants, 83% accepted, 102 enrolled. In 2018, 141 master's, 15 doctorates awarded. *Degree requirements:* For master's, thesis optional; for doctorate, thesis/dissertation, oral and written exams; for Ed S, oral presentation, project. *Entrance requirements:* For master's, GRE General Test (if undergraduate GPA is below 3.0), minimum undergraduate GPA of 3.0 or equivalent; for doctorate, GRE General Test (minimum combined verbal and quantitative score of 1000, 300 for new scoring), minimum undergraduate GPA of 3.0 or equivalent; master's degree with minimum GPA of 3.0 or equivalent; for Ed S, GRE General Test (minimum combined verbal and quantitative score of 1000, 300 for new scoring), minimum undergraduate GPA of 3.0 or equivalent; master's degree. Additional exam requirements/recommendations for international students: Required—TOEFL (minimum score 550 paper-based; 77 iBT). *Application deadline:* For fall admission, 12/15 for domestic students, 3/1 for international students; for spring admission, 9/15 for domestic students, 8/1 for international students. Application fee: $60 ($75 for international students). Electronic applications accepted. *Financial support:* Fellowships with full tuition reimbursements, research assistantships with full tuition reimbursements, teaching assistantships with full tuition reimbursements, career-related internships or fieldwork, and tuition waivers (full) available. Support available to part-time students. Financial award application deadline: 3/1; financial award applicants required to submit FAFSA. *Faculty research:* Literacy acquisition and development, teacher beliefs and knowledge, recruitment and retention of underrepresented students, economic education, literacy discourse. *Unit head:* Janet M. Alsup, Head, 765-494-9667, E-mail: alsupj@purdue.edu. *Application contact:* Heather Brinkman, Graduate Contact, 765-494-2345, E-mail: hbrinkma@purdue.edu.
Website: http://www.edci.purdue.edu/

Saint Leo University, Graduate Studies in Public Safety Administration, Saint Leo, FL 33574-6665. Offers criminal justice (MS, DCJ), including behavioral studies (MS), corrections (MS), criminal investigation (MS), criminal justice (MS), emergency and disaster management (MS), forensic science (MS), legal studies (MS); emergency and disaster management (MS), including emergency and disaster management, fire science. *Program availability:* Part-time, evening/weekend, 100% online, blended/hybrid learning. *Faculty:* 8 full-time (3 women), 29 part-time/adjunct (7 women). *Students:* 3 full-time (1 woman), 800 part-time (492 women); includes 400 minority (281 Black or African American, non-Hispanic/Latino; 3 American Indian or Alaska Native, non-Hispanic/Latino; 8 Asian, non-Hispanic/Latino; 90 Hispanic/Latino; 1 Native Hawaiian or other Pacific Islander, non-Hispanic/Latino; 17 Two or more races, non-Hispanic/Latino), 1 international. Average age 37. 300 applicants, 86% accepted, 195 enrolled. In 2018, 235 master's awarded. *Degree requirements:* For master's, comprehensive project. *Entrance requirements:* For master's, official transcripts, bachelor's degree from regionally-accredited university with minimum GPA of 3.0. Additional exam requirements/recommendations for international students: Required—TOEFL (minimum score 550 paper-based; 78 iBT). *Application deadline:* For fall admission, 7/1 priority

date for domestic and international students; for spring admission, 11/1 priority date for domestic and international students. Applications are processed on a rolling basis. Application fee: $80. Electronic applications accepted. *Expenses:* Master's $575 per credit, Doctorate $750 per credit. *Financial support:* In 2018–19, 21 students received support. Scholarships/grants and tuition remission for Saint Leo employees and their dependents available. Financial award application deadline: 3/1; financial award applicants required to submit FAFSA. *Faculty research:* Emergency management, fire science, community policing. *Unit head:* Dr. Robert Diemer, Director of Graduate Studies in Safety Administration, 352-588-8974, Fax: 352-588-8660, E-mail: graduatepublicsafety@saintleo.edu. *Application contact:* Mark Russum, Assistant Vice President, Enrollment, 800-707-8846, Fax: 352-588-7873, E-mail: grad.admissions@saintleo.edu.
Website: https://www.saintleo.edu/criminal-justice-master-degree

South Dakota State University, Graduate School, College of Education and Human Sciences, Department of Teaching, Learning and Leadership, Brookings, SD 57007. Offers agricultural education (MS); curriculum and instruction (M Ed); educational administration (M Ed). *Program availability:* Part-time, evening/weekend, online learning. *Degree requirements:* For master's, portfolio, oral exam. *Entrance requirements:* For master's, minimum GPA of 2.75. Additional exam requirements/recommendations for international students: Required—TOEFL (minimum score 550 paper-based; 80 iBT). *Faculty research:* Inclusion school climate, K-12 reform and restructuring, rural development, ESL, leadership.

State University of New York at Oswego, Graduate Studies, School of Education, Department of Vocational Teacher Preparation, Oswego, NY 13126. Offers agriculture (MS Ed); business and marketing (MS Ed); family and consumer sciences (MS Ed); health careers (MS Ed); technical education (MS Ed); trade education (MS Ed). *Accreditation:* NCATE. *Program availability:* Part-time, evening/weekend. *Degree requirements:* For master's, comprehensive exam, thesis or alternative. *Entrance requirements:* Additional exam requirements/recommendations for international students: Required—TOEFL (minimum score 560 paper-based).

Tennessee State University, The School of Graduate Studies and Research, College of Agriculture, Human and Natural Sciences, Nashville, TN 37209-1561. Offers agricultural sciences (MS), including agribusiness, agricultural and extension education, animal science, plant and soil science; biological sciences (MS, PhD); biotechnology (PhD); chemistry (MS). *Program availability:* Part-time, evening/weekend. *Degree requirements:* For master's, thesis. *Entrance requirements:* For master's, GRE General Test, GRE Subject Test, MAT. *Faculty research:* Small farm economics, ornamental horticulture, beef cattle production, rural elderly.

Texas A&M University, College of Agriculture and Life Sciences, Department of Agricultural Leadership, Education and Communications, College Station, TX 77843. Offers agricultural development (M Agr); agricultural education (Ed D); agricultural leadership, education and communication (M Ed, MS). *Program availability:* Part-time, blended/hybrid learning. *Faculty:* 21 full-time (9 women). *Students:* 48 full-time (41 women), 58 part-time (39 women); includes 20 minority (5 Black or African American, non-Hispanic/Latino; 1 American Indian or Alaska Native, non-Hispanic/Latino; 1 Asian, non-Hispanic/Latino; 13 Hispanic/Latino), 2 international. Average age 33. 34 applicants, 65% accepted, 17 enrolled. In 2018, 31 master's, 9 doctorates awarded. Terminal master's awarded for partial completion of doctoral program. *Degree requirements:* For master's, comprehensive exam, thesis (for some programs); for doctorate, comprehensive exam, thesis/dissertation. *Entrance requirements:* For master's, GRE General Test, letters of reference, curriculum vitae; for doctorate, GRE General Test, 3 years of professional experience, letters of reference, curriculum vitae. Additional exam requirements/recommendations for international students: Required—TOEFL (minimum score 550 paper-based; 80 iBT), IELTS (minimum score 6), PTE (minimum score 53). *Application deadline:* For fall admission, 3/15 priority date for domestic students; for spring admission, 10/15 for domestic students. Application fee: $50 ($90 for international students). Electronic applications accepted. *Expenses:* Contact institution. *Financial support:* In 2018–19, 60 students received support, including 8 fellowships with tuition reimbursements available (averaging $5,877 per year), 7 research assistantships with tuition reimbursements available (averaging $10,979 per year), 24 teaching assistantships with tuition reimbursements available (averaging $12,007 per year); career-related internships or fieldwork, institutionally sponsored loans, scholarships/grants, traineeships, health care benefits, tuition waivers (full and partial), and unspecified assistantships also available. Support available to part-time students. Financial award application deadline: 3/15; financial award applicants required to submit FAFSA. *Faculty research:* Planning and needs assessment, instructional design, delivery strategies, evaluation and accountability, distance education. *Unit head:* Dr. Jack Elliot, Department Head, 979-862-3003, E-mail: jelliot@tamu.edu. *Application contact:* Clarice Fulton, Graduate Program Coordinator, 979-862-7180, E-mail: cfulton@tamu.edu.
Website: http://alec.tamu.edu/

Texas State University, The Graduate College, College of Applied Arts, Program in Agricultural Education, San Marcos, TX 78666. Offers M Ed. *Program availability:* Part-time, evening/weekend. *Faculty:* 10 full-time (2 women), 1 (woman) part-time/adjunct. *Students:* 5 full-time (all women), 3 part-time (1 woman); includes 3 minority (all Hispanic/Latino). Average age 30. 9 applicants, 67% accepted, 1 enrolled. In 2018, 3 master's awarded. *Degree requirements:* For master's, comprehensive exam, thesis (for some programs). *Entrance requirements:* For master's, baccalaureate degree from regionally-accredited university in agriculture or closely-related field with minimum GPA of 2.75 in last 60 hours of course work; 3 letters of reference (2 from academia). Additional exam requirements/recommendations for international students: Required—TOEFL (minimum score 550 paper-based; 78 iBT), IELTS (minimum score 6.5). *Application deadline:* For fall admission, 6/15 for domestic students, 6/1 for international students; for spring admission, 10/15 for domestic students, 10/1 for international students; for summer admission, 4/15 for domestic students, 3/15 for international students. Applications are processed on a rolling basis. Application fee: $55 ($90 for international students). Electronic applications accepted. *Expenses:* Tuition, state resident: full-time $8102; part-time $4051 per semester. Tuition, nonresident: full-time $18,229; part-time $9115 per semester. *International tuition:* $18,229 full-time. *Required fees:* $2116; $120 per credit hour. Tuition and fees vary according to course load. *Financial support:* In 2018–19, 16 students received support, including 7 research assistantships (averaging $12,850 per year), 7 teaching assistantships (averaging $13,146 per year); career-related internships or fieldwork, Federal Work-Study, institutionally sponsored loans, and scholarships/grants also available. Support available to part-time students. Financial award application deadline: 1/15; financial award applicants required to submit FAFSA. *Faculty research:* Production economics, economic development, agricultural finance, international trade, goat and small ruminant production, ruminant physiology, animal endocrinology and technology, horticultural therapy, service-learning, composting, invasive species, aquaculture and fisheries economics, arid lands agriculture and sustainability, urban agriculture, evaluation of potential oxidation/reducation modulation using both in-vitro and in-vivo models. *Total annual research expenditures:* $332,907. *Unit head:* Dr. Madan M Dey, Chair Department of Agriculture, 512-245-2130, E-mail: mmd120@txstate.edu. *Application contact:* Dr. Andrea Golato, Dean of the Graduate College, 512-245-2581, Fax: 512-245-8365, E-mail: gradcollege@txstate.edu.
Website: http://ag.txstate.edu/

Texas Tech University, Graduate School, College of Agricultural Sciences and Natural Resources, Department of Agricultural Education and Communications, Lubbock, TX 79409-2131. Offers agricultural communications (MS); agricultural communications and education (PhD); agricultural education (MS, Ed D). *Program availability:* Part-time, evening/weekend, 100% online. *Faculty:* 14 full-time (7 women), 2 part-time/adjunct (0 women). *Students:* 44 full-time (34 women), 47 part-time (34 women); includes 10 minority (1 Black or African American, non-Hispanic/Latino; 6 Hispanic/Latino; 3 Two or more races, non-Hispanic/Latino), 10 international. Average age 30. 29 applicants, 79% accepted, 19 enrolled. In 2018, 22 master's, 7 doctorates awarded. Terminal master's awarded for partial completion of doctoral program. *Degree requirements:* For master's, variable foreign language requirement, comprehensive exam, thesis optional; for doctorate, variable foreign language requirement, comprehensive exam, thesis/dissertation, experience plan. *Entrance requirements:* For master's and doctorate, GRE. Additional exam requirements/recommendations for international students: Required—TOEFL (minimum score 550 paper-based; 79 iBT). *Application deadline:* For fall admission, 6/1 priority date for domestic students, 1/15 priority date for international students; for spring admission, 9/1 priority date for domestic students, 6/15 priority date for international students. Applications are processed on a rolling basis. Application fee: $65. Electronic applications accepted. *Expenses:* Contact institution. *Financial support:* In 2018–19, 54 students received support, including 43 fellowships (averaging $3,415 per year), 31 research assistantships (averaging $15,197 per year), 10 teaching assistantships (averaging $11,291 per year); institutionally sponsored loans and scholarships/grants also available. Financial award application deadline: 4/15; financial award applicants required to submit FAFSA. *Faculty research:* Sustainable agriculture, food safety, international development, use of technology in agriculture, improvement of teaching and pedagogy. *Total annual research expenditures:* $429,575. *Unit head:* Dr. Steve Fraze, Garrison Professor and Department Chair, 806-742-2816, Fax: 806-742-2880, E-mail: steven.fraze@ttu.edu. *Application contact:* Dr. Courtney Meyers, Associate Professor and Graduate Coordinator, 806-834-4364, Fax: 806-742-2880, E-mail: courtney.meyers@ttu.edu.
Website: www.aged.ttu.edu

The University of Arizona, College of Agriculture and Life Sciences, Department of Agricultural Education, Tucson, AZ 85721. Offers MAE, MS, Graduate Certificate. *Degree requirements:* For master's, thesis. *Entrance requirements:* For master's, teaching/extension experience or equivalent, minimum GPA of 3.0, 2 letters of recommendation. Additional exam requirements/recommendations for international students: Required—TOEFL (minimum score 550 paper-based; 79 iBT). Electronic applications accepted. *Faculty research:* Career placement, learning styles, noise impact on learning, computer technology, vocational education.

University of Arkansas, Graduate School, Dale Bumpers College of Agricultural, Food and Life Sciences, Department of Agricultural Education, Communications and Technology, Fayetteville, AR 72701. Offers agricultural and extension education (MS). *Accreditation:* NCATE. *Students:* 11 applicants, 100% accepted. In 2018, 10 master's awarded. *Application deadline:* For fall admission, 8/1 for domestic students, 4/1 for international students; for spring admission, 12/1 for domestic students, 10/1 for international students; for summer admission, 4/15 for domestic students, 3/1 for international students. Applications are processed on a rolling basis. Application fee: $60. Electronic applications accepted. *Financial support:* In 2018–19, 3 research assistantships, 4 teaching assistantships were awarded; fellowships, career-related internships or fieldwork, and Federal Work-Study also available. Support available to part-time students. Financial award application deadline: 4/1; financial award applicants required to submit FAFSA. *Unit head:* Dr. George William Wardlow, Department Head, 479-575-2038, E-mail: wardlow@uark.edu. *Application contact:* Dr. Donna Graham, Graduate Coordinator, 479-575-6346, E-mail: dgraham@uark.edu.
Website: https://agricultural-education-communications-and-technology.uark.edu/index.php

University of Connecticut, Graduate School, Neag School of Education, Department of Curriculum and Instruction, Storrs, CT 06269. Offers agriculture (MA), including agriculture education; agriculture education (PhD); bilingual and bicultural education (MA, PhD); elementary education (MA, PhD); English education (MA, PhD); history and social sciences education (MA, PhD); mathematics education (MA, PhD); music education (MA); reading education (MA, PhD); science education (MA, PhD); secondary education (MA, PhD); world languages education (MA, PhD). *Accreditation:* NCATE. Terminal master's awarded for partial completion of doctoral program. *Degree requirements:* For master's, comprehensive exam, thesis or alternative; for doctorate, thesis/dissertation. *Entrance requirements:* For doctorate, GRE General Test. Additional exam requirements/recommendations for international students: Required—TOEFL (minimum score 550 paper-based). Electronic applications accepted.

University of Delaware, College of Agriculture and Natural Resources, Department of Food and Resource Economics, Agricultural Education Program, Newark, DE 19716. Offers MA.

University of Florida, Graduate School, College of Agricultural and Life Sciences, Department of Agricultural Education and Communication, Gainesville, FL 32611. Offers agricultural education and communication (MS, PhD); tropical conservation and development (MS, PhD). *Program availability:* Part-time, evening/weekend, online learning. *Degree requirements:* For master's, comprehensive exam (for some programs), thesis (for some programs); for doctorate, comprehensive exam, thesis/dissertation. *Entrance requirements:* For master's and doctorate, GRE General Test, minimum GPA of 3.0. Additional exam requirements/recommendations for international students: Required—TOEFL (minimum score 550 paper-based; 80 iBT), IELTS (minimum score 6). Electronic applications accepted. *Faculty research:* Teaching and learning in formal and non-formal settings, program evaluation and development, leadership development in agriculture and natural resources, public issues education in agriculture and natural resources.

University of Illinois at Urbana–Champaign, Graduate College, College of Agricultural, Consumer and Environmental Sciences, Agricultural Education Program, Champaign, IL 61820. Offers MS. *Program availability:* Part-time, online learning.

University of Missouri, Office of Research and Graduate Studies, College of Agriculture, Food and Natural Resources, Department of Agricultural Education, Columbia, MO 65211. Offers MS, PhD. *Accreditation:* TEAC. *Entrance requirements:* For master's, minimum GPA of 3.0 for last 60 hours of undergraduate coursework; for doctorate, GRE (preferred minimum score of 1000), minimum GPA of 3.5 on prior graduate course work; minimum of 3 years of full-time appropriate teaching or other professional experience; correspondence with one department faculty member in proposed area of concentration. *Faculty research:* Program and professional development, evaluation, teaching and learning theories and practices, educational methods, organization and administration, leadership and communication.

University of Missouri, Office of Research and Graduate Studies, College of Education, Department of Learning, Teaching and Curriculum, Columbia, MO 65211.

Offers agricultural education (M Ed, PhD, Ed S); art education (M Ed, PhD, Ed S); business and office education (M Ed, PhD, Ed S); early childhood education (M Ed, PhD, Ed S); elementary education (M Ed, PhD, Ed S); English education (M Ed, PhD, Ed S); foreign language education (M Ed, PhD, Ed S); health education and promotion (M Ed, PhD); learning and instruction (M Ed); marketing education (M Ed, PhD, Ed S); mathematics education (M Ed, PhD, Ed S); music education (M Ed, PhD, Ed S); reading education (M Ed, PhD, Ed S); science education (M Ed, PhD, Ed S); social studies education (M Ed, PhD, Ed S); vocational education (M Ed, PhD, Ed S). *Program availability:* Part-time. Terminal master's awarded for partial completion of doctoral program. *Entrance requirements:* For master's and Ed S, GRE General Test or MAT, minimum GPA of 3.0; for doctorate, GRE General Test, minimum GPA of 3.0. Additional exam requirements/recommendations for international students: Required—TOEFL.

University of Nebraska–Lincoln, Graduate College, College of Agricultural Sciences and Natural Resources, Department of Agricultural Leadership, Education and Communication, Lincoln, NE 68588. Offers leadership development (MS); leadership education (MS); teaching and extension education (MS). *Accreditation:* TEAC. *Degree requirements:* For master's, thesis optional. *Entrance requirements:* For master's, resume. Additional exam requirements/recommendations for international students: Required—TOEFL (minimum score 550 paper-based). Electronic applications accepted. *Faculty research:* Teaching and instruction, extension education, leadership and human resource development, international agricultural education.

University of Puerto Rico–Mayagüez, Graduate Studies, College of Agricultural Sciences, Department of Agricultural Education, Mayagüez, PR 00681-9000. Offers agricultural education (MS); agricultural extension (MS). *Accreditation:* NCATE. *Program availability:* Part-time. *Degree requirements:* For master's, comprehensive exam, thesis. *Entrance requirements:* For master's, BA in home economics; BS in agricultural education, agriculture, home economics, or equivalent. Electronic applications accepted. *Faculty research:* Curricular development and supervision, youth education, rural sociology.

The University of Tennessee, Graduate School, College of Agricultural Sciences and Natural Resources, Department of Agricultural Economics, Knoxville, TN 37996. Offers agricultural education (MS); agricultural extension education (MS). *Accreditation:* NCATE. *Program availability:* Part-time, online learning. *Degree requirements:* For master's, thesis or alternative. *Entrance requirements:* For master's, minimum GPA of 2.7. Additional exam requirements/recommendations for international students: Required—TOEFL. Electronic applications accepted.

University of Wisconsin–River Falls, Outreach and Graduate Studies, College of Agriculture, Food, and Environmental Sciences, Department of Agricultural Education, River Falls, WI 54022. Offers MS. *Program availability:* Part-time. *Degree requirements:* For master's, comprehensive exam, thesis (for some programs). *Entrance requirements:* For master's, minimum GPA of 2.75. Additional exam requirements/recommendations

for international students: Required—TOEFL (minimum score 500 paper-based; 65 iBT), IELTS (minimum score 5.5). Electronic applications accepted.

Utah State University, School of Graduate Studies, College of Agriculture and Applied Sciences, School of Applied Sciences, Technology and Education, Logan, UT 84322. Offers agricultural extension and education (MS); family and consumer sciences education and extension (MS); technology and engineering education (MS). *Program availability:* Part-time, online learning. *Degree requirements:* For master's, comprehensive exam (for some programs), thesis (for some programs). *Entrance requirements:* For master's, GRE General Test, MAT, BS in agricultural education, agricultural extension, or related agricultural or science discipline; minimum GPA of 3.0. Additional exam requirements/recommendations for international students: Required—TOEFL. *Faculty research:* Extension and adult education; structures and environment; low-input agriculture; farm safety, systems, and mechanizations.

West Virginia University, Davis College of Agriculture, Forestry and Consumer Sciences, Morgantown, WV 26506. Offers agricultural and extension education (MS, PhD); agriculture and resource management (MS); agriculture, natural resources and design (M Agr); agronomy (MS); animal and food science (PhD); animal physiology (MS); applied and environmental microbiology (MS); design and merchandising (MS); entomology (MS); forest resource science (PhD); forestry (MSF); genetics and developmental biology (MS, PhD); horticulture (MS); human and community development (PhD); landscape architecture (MLA); natural resource economics (PhD); nutritional and food science (MS); plant and soil science (PhD); plant pathology (MS); recreation, parks and tourism resources (MS); reproductive physiology (MS, PhD); wildlife and fisheries resources (PhD). *Accreditation:* ASLA. *Program availability:* Part-time. *Students:* 188 full-time (86 women), 47 part-time (30 women); includes 22 minority (5 Black or African American, non-Hispanic/Latino; 5 Asian, non-Hispanic/Latino; 8 Hispanic/Latino; 4 Two or more races, non-Hispanic/Latino), 60 international. In 2018, 56 master's, 14 doctorates awarded. *Degree requirements:* For master's, thesis; for doctorate, thesis/dissertation. *Entrance requirements:* Additional exam requirements/recommendations for international students: Required—TOEFL (minimum score 550 paper-based). *Application deadline:* For fall admission, 6/1 priority date for domestic students, 6/1 for international students; for spring admission, 1/5 for domestic and international students. Applications are processed on a rolling basis. Application fee: $60. Electronic applications accepted. *Financial support:* Fellowships, research assistantships, teaching assistantships, career-related internships or fieldwork, Federal Work-Study, institutionally sponsored loans, tuition waivers (full and partial), and unspecified assistantships available. Financial award application deadline: 2/1; financial award applicants required to submit FAFSA. *Faculty research:* Reproductive physiology, soil and water quality, human nutrition, aquaculture, wildlife management. *Unit head:* Dr. Ken Blemings, Interim Dean, 304-293-2395, Fax: 304-293-3740, E-mail: ken.blemings@mail.wvu.edu. *Application contact:* Dr. J. Todd Petty, Associate Dean, 304-293-2278, Fax: 304-293-3740, E-mail: jtpetty@mail.wvu.edu. Website: https://www.davis.wvu.edu

Art Education

Academy of Art University, Graduate Programs, School of Art Education, San Francisco, CA 94105-3410. Offers MA, MAT. *Program availability:* Part-time, 100% online. *Degree requirements:* For master's, final review. *Entrance requirements:* For master's, statement of intent; resume; portfolio/reel; official college transcripts. Electronic applications accepted.

Adelphi University, College of Education & Health Sciences, College of Education and Health Services, Garden City, NY 11530-0701. Offers MA. *Program availability:* Part-time. *Students:* 4 full-time (all women), 9 part-time (all women); includes 1 minority (Hispanic/Latino). Average age 31. 21 applicants, 62% accepted, 9 enrolled. In 2018, 3 master's awarded. *Entrance requirements:* For master's, 2 letters of recommendation, visual arts portfolio, essay. Additional exam requirements/recommendations for international students: Required—TOEFL (minimum score 550 paper-based; 80 iBT), IELTS (minimum score 6.5). *Application deadline:* For fall admission, 3/1 for international students; for spring admission, 11/1 for international students. Application fee: $50. Electronic applications accepted. *Expenses:* Contact institution. *Financial support:* Research assistantships, teaching assistantships, career-related internships or fieldwork, institutionally sponsored loans, scholarships/grants, traineeships, and unspecified assistantships available. Support available to part-time students. Financial award application deadline: 1/1; financial award applicants required to submit FAFSA. *Unit head:* Courtney Lee Weida, Director, 516-877-4105, E-mail: cweida@adelphi.edu. *Application contact:* Courtney Lee Weida, Director, 516-877-4105, E-mail: cweida@adelphi.edu.

Alabama Agricultural and Mechanical University, School of Graduate Studies, College of Education, Humanities, and Behavioral Sciences, Department of Visual, Performing, and Communication Arts, Huntsville, AL 35811. Offers art education (MS); music education (M Ed). *Accreditation:* NCATE. *Program availability:* Part-time, evening/weekend. *Degree requirements:* For master's, comprehensive exam. *Entrance requirements:* For master's, GRE General Test. Additional exam requirements/recommendations for international students: Required—TOEFL (minimum score 500 paper-based; 61 iBT). Electronic applications accepted. *Faculty research:* Jazz and black music, Alabama folk music.

American University of Puerto Rico, Program in Education, Bayamon, PR 00960-2037. Offers art education (M Ed); elementary education 4-6 (M Ed); elementary education K-3 (M Ed); general science education (M Ed); physical education (M Ed); special education (M Ed). *Program availability:* Part-time, evening/weekend. *Entrance requirements:* For master's, EXADEP, GRE, or MAT, 2 letters of recommendation, minimum GPA of 2.5.

Arcadia University, School of Education, Glenside, PA 19038-3295. Offers art education (M Ed); computer education (CAS); curriculum (CAS); curriculum studies (M Ed); early childhood education (M Ed), including individualized, master teacher, research in child development; educational leadership (M Ed, Ed D, CAS); elementary education (M Ed); English education (MA Ed); environmental education (MA Ed); instructional technology (M Ed); language arts (M Ed); library science (M Ed); mathematics education (M Ed, MA Ed); music education (MA Ed); psychology (MA Ed); reading (M Ed, CAS); science education (M Ed, CAS); secondary education (M Ed, CAS); special education (M Ed, Ed D, CAS); theater arts (MA Ed); written communication (MA Ed). *Accreditation:* NASAD. *Program availability:* Part-time, evening/weekend, online learning. *Faculty:* 14 full-time (10 women). *Students:* 35 full-time (24 women), 299 part-time (243 women); includes 72 minority (49 Black or African American, non-Hispanic/Latino; 1 American Indian or Alaska Native, non-Hispanic/

Latino; 12 Asian, non-Hispanic/Latino; 8 Hispanic/Latino; 2 Two or more races, non-Hispanic/Latino), 5 international. In 2018, 152 master's, 8 doctorates awarded. *Entrance requirements:* Additional exam requirements/recommendations for international students: Required—Official results from the TOEFL or IELTS are required. *Application deadline:* Applications are processed on a rolling basis. Application fee: $25. Electronic applications accepted. *Expenses:* Contact institution. *Financial support:* Career-related internships or fieldwork, tuition waivers (partial), and unspecified assistantships available. *Unit head:* Kimberly Dean, Chair, 215-572-8629. *Application contact:* 215-572-2925, Fax: 215-572-2126, E-mail: grad@arcadia.edu.

Arizona State University at the Tempe campus, Herberger Institute for Design and the Arts, School of Art, Tempe, AZ 85287-1505. Offers art education (MA); art history (MA); ceramics (MFA); design, environment and the arts (PhD), including history, theory and criticism; drawing (MFA); fibers (MFA); intermedia (MFA); metals (MFA); museum studies (MFA); painting (MFA); printmaking (MFA); sculpture (MFA); wood (MFA); MFA/MA. Terminal master's awarded for partial completion of doctoral program. *Degree requirements:* For master's, thesis/exhibition (MFA, MA in art education); interactive Program of Study (iPOS) submitted before completing 50 percent of required credit hours; for doctorate, comprehensive exam, thesis/dissertation, interactive Program of Study (iPOS) submitted before completing 50 percent of required credit hours. *Entrance requirements:* For master's, GRE or MAT, minimum GPA of 3.0 or equivalent in last 2 years of work leading to bachelor's degree; for doctorate, GRE, master's degree in architecture, graphic design, industrial design, interior design, landscape architecture, or art history or equivalent standing; statement of purpose; 3 letters of recommendation; indication of potential faculty mentor; sample of written work. Additional exam requirements/recommendations for international students: Required—TOEFL, IELTS, or PTE. Electronic applications accepted.

Art Academy of Cincinnati, Program in Art Education, Cincinnati, OH 45202. Offers MAAE. Offered during summer only. *Accreditation:* NASAD. *Program availability:* Part-time. *Degree requirements:* For master's, thesis, portfolio/exhibit. *Entrance requirements:* For master's, 2 letters of recommendation, portfolio, artist statement, undergraduate transcript. Additional exam requirements/recommendations for international students: Required—TOEFL (minimum score 550 paper-based; 80 iBT). Electronic applications accepted.

Boston University, College of Fine Arts, School of Visual Arts, Boston, MA 02215. Offers sculpture (MFA); studio teaching (MA). *Faculty:* 17 full-time, 4 part-time/adjunct. *Students:* 155 full-time (133 women), 3 part-time (all women); includes 19 minority (3 Black or African American, non-Hispanic/Latino; 5 Asian, non-Hispanic/Latino; 10 Hispanic/Latino; 1 Two or more races, non-Hispanic/Latino), 41 international. Average age 30. 365 applicants, 27% accepted, 21 enrolled. In 2018, 89 master's awarded. *Entrance requirements:* For master's, portfolio. Additional exam requirements/recommendations for international students: Required—TOEFL (minimum score 90 iBT), IELTS (minimum score 7). *Application deadline:* For fall admission, 2/1 for domestic and international students. Applications are processed on a rolling basis. Application fee: $95. *Expenses:* Contact institution. *Financial support:* In 2018–19, 36 students received support. Fellowships, teaching assistantships, scholarships/grants, and unspecified assistantships available. Financial award application deadline: 2/1. *Unit head:* Lynne Allen, Director, 617-353-3371. *Application contact:* Jessica Caccamo, Assistant Director of Admissions, 617-353-3371, E-mail: visuarts@bu.edu.

Bowling Green State University, Graduate College, College of Arts and Sciences, School of Art, Bowling Green, OH 43403. Offers 2-D studio art (MA, MFA); 3-D studio art

(MA, MFA); art education (MA); art history (MA); computer art (MA); design (MFA); digital arts (MFA); graphics (MFA). *Accreditation:* NASAD. *Program availability:* Part-time. *Degree requirements:* For master's, thesis or alternative, final exhibit (MFA). *Entrance requirements:* For master's, GRE General Test (for MA), slide portfolio (15-20 slides). Additional exam requirements/recommendations for international students: Required—TOEFL. Electronic applications accepted. *Faculty research:* Computer animation and virtual reality, Spanish still-life painting from 1600 to 1800, art and psychotherapy, Japanese wood-firing techniques in ceramics, non-toxic printmaking technologies.

Bridgewater State University, College of Graduate Studies, College of Humanities and Social Sciences, Department of Art, Bridgewater, MA 02325. Offers MAT. *Accreditation:* NASAD. *Program availability:* Part-time, evening/weekend. *Degree requirements:* For master's, comprehensive exam. *Entrance requirements:* For master's, GRE General Test.

Brigham Young University, Graduate Studies, College of Fine Arts and Communications, Department of Art, Provo, UT 84602-6414. Offers art education (MA); studio arts (MFA). Art education applications accepted biennially. *Accreditation:* NASAD. *Faculty:* 13 full-time (2 women). *Students:* 26 full-time (18 women); includes 4 minority (3 Asian, non-Hispanic/Latino; 1 Hispanic/Latino). Average age 36. 25 applicants, 40% accepted, 8 enrolled. In 2018, 11 master's awarded. *Degree requirements:* For master's, comprehensive exam, thesis, selected project (for MFA); curriculum project (for art education). *Entrance requirements:* For master's, minimum GPA of 3.0 (for MFA, MA in art education), portfolio submitted on a flash drive (for MFA); writing samples (for MA). Additional exam requirements/recommendations for international students: Required—TOEFL (minimum score 580 paper-based), TOEFL (minimum score 580 paper-based, 85 iBT) or IELTS (7); Recommended—IELTS (minimum score 7). *Application deadline:* For fall admission, 2/1 for domestic and international students. Application fee: $50. Electronic applications accepted. *Financial support:* In 2018–19, 15 students received support, including 8 teaching assistantships with partial tuition reimbursements available; scholarships/grants also available. Financial award application deadline: 2/1. *Faculty research:* Methodology-standards-assessment, exploration of art making processes, new genre, installation, photography, theory and critical studies, art history. *Unit head:* Prof. Gary C. Barton, Chair, 801-422-4429, Fax: 801-422-0695, E-mail: garold_barton@byu.edu. *Application contact:* Sharon Lyn Heelis, Secretary, 801-422-4429, Fax: 801-422-0695, E-mail: sharon_heelis@byu.edu.
Website: http://art.byu.edu

Brooklyn College of the City University of New York, School of Education, Program in Early Childhood Education, Brooklyn, NY 11210-2889. Offers art teacher (K-12) (MA); birth-grade 2 (MS Ed). *Program availability:* Part-time, evening/weekend. *Entrance requirements:* For master's, LAST, bachelor's degree in early childhood education, resume, 2 letters of recommendation, essay. Additional exam requirements/recommendations for international students: Required—TOEFL (minimum score 500 paper-based; 61 iBT). Electronic applications accepted. *Faculty research:* Children's narrations, language acquisition, culture and education.

Buffalo State College, State University of New York, The Graduate School, School of Arts and Humanities, Department of Art and Design, Buffalo, NY 14222-1095. Offers art education (MS Ed). *Accreditation:* NASAD; NCATE. *Program availability:* Part-time, evening/weekend. *Degree requirements:* For master's, thesis or alternative, project. *Entrance requirements:* For master's, New York teaching certificate, interview, minimum GPA of 3.0. Additional exam requirements/recommendations for international students: Required—TOEFL (minimum score 550 paper-based).

California State University, Long Beach, Graduate Studies, College of the Arts, Department of Art, Long Beach, CA 90840. Offers art education (MA); studio art (MFA). *Accreditation:* NASAD. *Program availability:* Part-time. *Degree requirements:* For master's, thesis (for some programs). *Entrance requirements:* For master's, minimum GPA of 3.0 in last 60 hours. *Application deadline:* For fall admission, 1/15 for domestic students. Applications are processed on a rolling basis. Application fee: $55. Electronic applications accepted. *Expenses: Required fees:* $2628 per term. Tuition and fees vary according to class time, course level, course load, degree level, campus/location and program. *Financial support:* Federal Work-Study, institutionally sponsored loans, and scholarships/grants available. Financial award application deadline: 3/2; financial award applicants required to submit FAFSA. *Unit head:* Prof. Aubry Mintz, Chair, 562-985-4376, Fax: 562-985-1650, E-mail: aubry.mintz@csulb.edu. *Application contact:* Rebecca Sittler Schrock, Graduate Advisor, 562-985-7910, Fax: 562-985-7910, E-mail: Rebecca.Sittler@csulb.edu.
Website: http://art.csulb.edu/home/?cat=1

California State University, Los Angeles, Graduate Studies, College of Arts and Letters, Department of Art, Los Angeles, CA 90032-8530. Offers art (MA), including art education, art history, art therapy, ceramics, metals, and textiles, design (MA, MFA), painting, sculpture, and graphic arts, photography; fine arts (MFA), including crafts, design (MA, MFA), studio arts. *Accreditation:* NASAD (one or more programs are accredited). *Program availability:* Part-time, evening/weekend. *Degree requirements:* For master's, comprehensive exam, project or thesis. *Entrance requirements:* For master's, portfolio. Additional exam requirements/recommendations for international students: Required—TOEFL (minimum score 500 paper-based). Electronic applications accepted. *Faculty research:* The artist and the book, conceptual art, ceramic processes, computer graphics, architectural graphics.

California State University, Northridge, Graduate Studies, Mike Curb College of Arts, Media, and Communication, Department of Art, Northridge, CA 91330. Offers art education (MA); art history (MA); studio art (MA, MFA); visual communications (MA, MFA). *Accreditation:* NASAD.

Carthage College, Division of Teacher Education, Kenosha, WI 53140. Offers classroom guidance and counseling (M Ed); creative arts (M Ed); gifted and talented children (M Ed); language arts (M Ed); modern language (M Ed); natural sciences (M Ed); reading (M Ed, Certificate); social sciences (M Ed); teacher leadership (M Ed). *Program availability:* Part-time, evening/weekend. *Degree requirements:* For master's, thesis optional. *Entrance requirements:* For master's, MAT, minimum B average, letters of reference.

Case Western Reserve University, School of Graduate Studies, Department of Art History and Art, Program in Art Education, Cleveland, OH 44106. Offers MA. Programs offered jointly with The Cleveland Museum of Art. *Accreditation:* TEAC. *Program availability:* Part-time. *Faculty:* 8 full-time (7 women), 2 part-time/adjunct (both women). *Students:* 4 full-time (all women); includes 2 minority (1 Hispanic/Latino; 1 Two or more races, non-Hispanic/Latino). Average age 26. 5 applicants, 60% accepted, 3 enrolled. In 2018, 3 master's awarded. *Degree requirements:* For master's, thesis, art exhibit. *Entrance requirements:* For master's, NTE, interview, portfolio, three letters of recommendation. Additional exam requirements/recommendations for international students: Required—TOEFL (minimum score 577 paper-based; 90 iBT); Recommended—IELTS (minimum score 7). *Application deadline:* For fall admission, 3/1 for domestic students; for spring admission, 11/1 for domestic students. Applications are processed on a rolling basis. Application fee: $50. Electronic applications accepted. *Expenses: Tuition:* Full-time $45,168; part-time $1939 per credit hour. *Required fees:* $36; $18 per semester. $18 per semester. *Financial support:* Health care benefits available. Financial award applicants required to submit FAFSA. *Faculty research:* Visual and aesthetic education, ethnographic arts, multiculturalism. *Unit head:* Tim Shuckerow, Director of Art Education and Art Studio, 216-368-2714, Fax: 216-368-2715, E-mail: tim.shuckerow@case.edu. *Application contact:* Dawn Rohm, Department Assistant, 216-368-2714, Fax: 216-368-4681, E-mail: dawn.rohm@case.edu.
Website: http://arthistory.case.edu/graduate/art-education/

Central Connecticut State University, School of Graduate Studies, College of Liberal Arts and Social Sciences, Department of Art, New Britain, CT 06050-4010. Offers art education (MS, Certificate). *Program availability:* Part-time, evening/weekend. *Faculty:* 5 full-time (2 women). *Students:* 13 full-time (10 women), 16 part-time (13 women); includes 1 minority (Hispanic/Latino). Average age 33. 18 applicants, 67% accepted, 11 enrolled. In 2018, 5 master's, 8 other advanced degrees awarded. *Degree requirements:* For master's, thesis or alternative, exhibit or special project; for Certificate, qualifying exam. *Entrance requirements:* For master's, portfolio, essay. Additional exam requirements/recommendations for international students: Required—TOEFL (minimum score 550 paper-based; 79 iBT); Recommended—IELTS (minimum score 6.5). *Application deadline:* For fall admission, 6/1 for domestic students, 5/1 for international students; for spring admission, 11/1 for domestic and international students. Applications are processed on a rolling basis. Application fee: $50. Electronic applications accepted. *Expenses: Tuition, area resident:* Full-time $7027; part-time $388 per credit. Tuition, state resident: full-time $9750; part-time $388 per credit. Tuition, nonresident: full-time $18,102; part-time $388 per credit. *International tuition:* $18,102 full-time. *Required fees:* $266 per semester. *Financial support:* In 2018–19, 3 students received support. Career-related internships or fieldwork, Federal Work-Study, scholarships/grants, and unspecified assistantships available. Support available to part-time students. Financial award application deadline: 3/1; financial award applicants required to submit FAFSA. *Faculty research:* Visual arts. *Unit head:* Prof. Rachel Siporin, Chair, 860-832-2620, E-mail: siporinr@ccsu.edu. *Application contact:* Patricia Gardner, Associate Director of Graduate Studies, 860-832-2350, Fax: 860-832-2362.
Website: http://www.ccsu.edu/art/

Chatham University, Program in Education, Pittsburgh, PA 15232-2826. Offers early childhood education (MAT); elementary education (MAT); environmental education (K-12) (MAT); secondary art (MAT); secondary biology education (MAT); secondary chemistry education (MAT); secondary English education (MAT); secondary math education (MAT); secondary physics education (MAT); secondary social studies education (MAT); special education (MAT). *Degree requirements:* For master's, thesis, teaching experience. *Entrance requirements:* For master's, minimum GPA of 3.0, sample of written work, recommendation letters. Additional exam requirements/recommendations for international students: Required—TOEFL (minimum score 600 paper-based; 100 iBT), IELTS (minimum score 7), TWE. Electronic applications accepted. Application fee is waived when completed online. *Faculty research:* Gifted education, environmental education, technology in education, writing as learning, class size and achievement.

Cleveland State University, College of Graduate Studies, College of Education and Human Services, Department of Teacher Education, Cleveland, OH 44115. Offers art education (M Ed); early childhood education (M Ed); foreign language education (M Ed); middle childhood mathematics and science education (M Ed); special education (M Ed), including mild/moderate disabilities, moderate/intensive disabilities; teaching English to speakers of other languages (M Ed). *Program availability:* Part-time, evening/weekend. *Faculty:* 19 full-time (14 women), 32 part-time/adjunct (27 women). *Students:* 56 full-time (40 women), 344 part-time (278 women); includes 104 minority (74 Black or African American, non-Hispanic/Latino; 1 American Indian or Alaska Native, non-Hispanic/Latino; 5 Asian, non-Hispanic/Latino; 9 Hispanic/Latino; 15 Two or more races, non-Hispanic/Latino), 14 international. Average age 34. 177 applicants, 55% accepted, 68 enrolled. In 2018, 117 master's awarded. *Degree requirements:* For master's, comprehensive exam (for some programs), thesis or alternative. *Entrance requirements:* For master's, GRE General Test or MAT, minimum GPA of 2.75. Additional exam requirements/recommendations for international students: Required—TOEFL (minimum score 550 paper-based; 78 iBT), IELTS (minimum score 6). *Application deadline:* For fall admission, 7/1 priority date for domestic students, 5/15 for international students; for spring admission, 11/15 for domestic students, 11/1 for international students; for summer admission, 4/1 for domestic students, 3/15 for international students. Applications are processed on a rolling basis. Application fee: $30. *Expenses:* Tuition, state resident: full-time $7232.55; part-time $6676 per credit hour. Tuition, nonresident: full-time $12,375. *International tuition:* $18,914 full-time. *Required fees:* $80; $80 $40. Tuition and fees vary according to program. *Financial support:* In 2018–19, 13 research assistantships with full tuition reimbursements (averaging $15,845 per year) were awarded; tuition waivers (partial) and unspecified assistantships also available. Financial award application deadline: 2/15; financial award applicants required to submit FAFSA. *Faculty research:* Early childhood education, literacy education, special education: mild/moderate, moderate/intensive, early childhood intervention specialist), teaching English to speakers of other languages (TESOL). *Total annual research expenditures:* $275,907. *Unit head:* Dr. Tachelle Banks, Department Chairperson, 216-687-4600, Fax: 216-687-5379, E-mail: t.i.banks@csuohio.edu. *Application contact:* Rosalyn Adams, Administrative Coordinator, 216-523-7139, Fax: 216-687-5491, E-mail: r.m.adams@csuohio.edu.
Website: http://www.csuohio.edu/cehs/te/te

The College of New Rochelle, Graduate School, Division of Education, Program in Art Education, New Rochelle, NY 10805-2308. Offers MS. *Program availability:* Part-time, evening/weekend. *Degree requirements:* For master's, thesis. *Entrance requirements:* For master's, interview, minimum GPA of 3.0 in field, 2.7 overall, portfolio. *Faculty research:* Developmental stages in art, assessment and evaluation, curriculum development, multicultural education, art museum education.

The Colorado College, Education Department, Program in Secondary Education, Colorado Springs, CO 80903-3294. Offers art teaching (K-12) (MAT); English teaching (MAT); foreign language teaching (MAT); mathematics teaching (MAT); music teaching (MAT); science teaching (MAT); social studies teaching (MAT). *Degree requirements:* For master's, thesis, internship. Electronic applications accepted.

Colorado State University–Pueblo, College of Education, Engineering and Professional Studies, Education Program, Pueblo, CO 81001-4901. Offers art education (M Ed); foreign language education (M Ed); health and physical education (M Ed); instructional technology (M Ed); linguistically diverse education (M Ed); music education (M Ed); special education (M Ed). *Accreditation:* TEAC. *Program availability:* Part-time. *Degree requirements:* For master's, portfolio. *Entrance requirements:* For master's, 3 recommendations, teaching license. Additional exam requirements/recommendations for international students: Required—TOEFL (minimum score 500 paper-based). Electronic applications accepted. *Faculty research:* Portfolio assessment, math education, science education.

Columbus State University, Graduate Studies, College of the Arts, Department of Art, Columbus, GA 31907-5645. Offers art education (M Ed, MAT). *Accreditation:* NASAD; NCATE. *Program availability:* Part-time, evening/weekend. *Faculty:* 1 full-time (0 women). *Students:* 1 (woman) full-time, 5 part-time (3 women); includes 2 minority (both

Black or African American, non-Hispanic/Latino). Average age 27. 8 applicants, 63% accepted, 3 enrolled. In 2018, 2 master's awarded. *Degree requirements:* For master's, comprehensive exam, exhibit. *Entrance requirements:* For master's, portfolio, interview. Additional exam requirements/recommendations for international students: Required—TOEFL (minimum score 550 paper-based; 79 iBT). *Application deadline:* For fall admission, 6/30 for domestic students, 5/1 for international students; for spring admission, 11/1 for domestic and international students; for summer admission, 3/1 for domestic and international students. Applications are processed on a rolling basis. Application fee: $50. Electronic applications accepted. *Expenses: Tuition, area resident:* Full-time $4924; part-time $618 per credit hour. Tuition, state resident: full-time $4924; part-time $618 per credit hour. Tuition, nonresident: full-time $19,218; part-time $2403 per credit hour. *International tuition:* $19,218 full-time. *Required fees:* $1870; $802. Tuition and fees vary according to course load, degree level and program. *Financial support:* In 2018–19, 1 student received support, including 1 research assistantship; career-related internships or fieldwork, Federal Work-Study, institutionally sponsored loans, scholarships/grants, tuition waivers (partial), and unspecified assistantships also available. Support available to part-time students. Financial award application deadline: 5/1; financial award applicants required to submit FAFSA. *Unit head:* Prof. Joe Sanders, Department Chair, 706-507-8302, E-mail: sanders_joe@columbusstate.edu. *Application contact:* Catrina Smith-Edmond, Assistant Director for Graduate and Global Admission, 706-507-8824, Fax: 706-568-5091, E-mail: smithedmond_catrina@columbusstate.edu. Website: http://art.columbusstate.edu/

Concordia University, College of Education, Portland, OR 97211-6099. Offers administrative leadership (Ed D); career and technical education (M Ed); curriculum and instruction (M Ed), including adolescent literacy, early childhood education, educational technology leadership, English for speakers of other languages, environmental education, health and physical education, mathematics, methods and curriculum, reading interventionist, science, social studies, STEAM education, teacher leadership, the inclusive classroom, trauma and resilience in educational settings; educational administration (M Ed); educational leadership (M Ed); elementary education (MAT); higher education (Ed D); instructional leadership (Ed D); professional leadership, inquiry, and transformation (Ed D); secondary education (MAT); transformational leadership (Ed D). *Program availability:* Part-time, online learning. *Degree requirements:* For master's, comprehensive exam, work samples/portfolio. *Entrance requirements:* For master's, California Basic Educational Skills Test or PRAXIS I, minimum undergraduate GPA of 2.8, graduate 3.0; 2 letters of recommendation. Additional exam requirements/recommendations for international students: Required—TOEFL (minimum score 525 paper-based). Electronic applications accepted. *Faculty research:* Learner-centered classroom, brain-based learning, future of online learning.

Concordia University, School of Graduate Studies, Faculty of Fine Arts, Department of Art Education, Montréal, QC H3G 1M8, Canada. Offers art education (MA, PhD), including art in education (MA). *Degree requirements:* For master's, thesis (for some programs), practicum; for doctorate, comprehensive exam, thesis/dissertation. *Entrance requirements:* For master's, teaching experience; for doctorate, teaching or related professional experience. *Faculty research:* Vernacular culture, museum education, psychotic art, adults and families.

Concordia University Wisconsin, Graduate Programs, School of Education, Mequon, WI 53097-2402. Offers art education (MS Ed); early childhood (MS Ed); educational administration (MS Ed); environmental education (MS Ed); family studies (MS Ed); literacy (MS Ed); school counseling (MS Ed); special education (MS Ed). *Program availability:* Part-time, evening/weekend, online learning. *Degree requirements:* For master's, comprehensive exam, thesis or alternative. *Entrance requirements:* For master's, minimum GPA of 3.0, teaching license. Additional exam requirements/recommendations for international students: Required—TOEFL. *Faculty research:* Motivation, developmental learning, learning styles.

Converse College, Program in Art Education, Spartanburg, SC 29302. Offers M Ed, MAT. *Accreditation:* NASAD.

Delaware State University, Graduate Programs, College of Education, Health and Public Policy, Program in Art Education, Dover, DE 19901-2277. Offers MA. *Entrance requirements:* Additional exam requirements/recommendations for international students: Required—TOEFL (minimum score 550 paper-based). Electronic applications accepted.

East Carolina University, Graduate School, College of Fine Arts and Communication, School of Art and Design, Greenville, NC 27858-4353. Offers art education (MA Ed); ceramics (MFA); graphic design (MFA); illustration (MFA); metal design (MFA); painting and drawing (MFA); photography (MFA); printmaking (MFA); sculpture (MFA); textile design (MFA); wood design (MFA). *Accreditation:* NASAD (one or more programs are accredited). *Program availability:* Part-time, evening/weekend. *Application deadline:* For fall admission, 2/1 for domestic students; for spring admission, 10/1 for domestic students. *Expenses: Tuition, area resident:* Full-time $4749. Tuition, state resident: full-time $4749. Tuition, nonresident: full-time $17,898. *International tuition:* $17,898 full-time. *Required fees:* $2787. Part-time tuition and fees vary according to course load and program. *Financial support:* Application deadline: 6/1. *Unit head:* Dr. Kate Bukowski, Director, 252-328-6665, E-mail: bukowskik16@ecu.edu. *Application contact:* Graduate School Admissions, 252-328-6012, E-mail: gradschool@ecu.edu. Website: http://www.ecu.edu/soad/

Eastern Illinois University, Graduate School, College of Liberal Arts and Sciences, Department of Art, Charleston, IL 61920. Offers art (MA); art education (MA); community arts (MA). *Accreditation:* NASAD. *Program availability:* Part-time, evening/weekend, online learning. *Degree requirements:* For master's, comprehensive exam (for some programs), thesis (for some programs). *Entrance requirements:* For master's, GMAT or GRE. Additional exam requirements/recommendations for international students: Required—TOEFL (minimum score 500 paper-based; 61 iBT), IELTS (minimum score 6). Electronic applications accepted. *Expenses:* Tuition, state resident: part-time $299 per credit hour. Tuition, nonresident: part-time $718 per credit hour. *Required fees:* $214.50 per credit hour.

Eastern Kentucky University, The Graduate School, College of Education, Department of Curriculum and Instruction, Program in Secondary and Higher Education, Richmond, KY 40475-3102. Offers secondary education (MA Ed), including agricultural education, art education, biological sciences education, business education, English education, geography education, history education, home economics education, industrial education, mathematical sciences education, physical education, school health education. *Accreditation:* NCATE. *Program availability:* Part-time. *Entrance requirements:* For master's, GRE General Test, minimum GPA of 2.5.

Eastern Michigan University, Graduate School, College of Arts and Sciences, School of Art and Design, Program in Visual Art Education, Ypsilanti, MI 48197. Offers MA. *Program availability:* Part-time, evening/weekend, online learning. *Students:* 4 part-time (2 women). Average age 35. 3 applicants, 67% accepted. In 2018, 1 master's awarded. *Entrance requirements:* Additional exam requirements/recommendations for international students: Required—TOEFL. *Application deadline:* Applications are processed on a rolling basis. Application fee: $45. *Financial support:* Fellowships with tuition reimbursements, research assistantships with full tuition reimbursements,

teaching assistantships with full tuition reimbursements, career-related internships or fieldwork, Federal Work-Study, institutionally sponsored loans, scholarships/grants, and unspecified assistantships available. Support available to part-time students. Financial award applicants required to submit FAFSA. *Application contact:* Michael Reedy, Advisor, 734-487-1268, Fax: 734-487-2324, E-mail: mreedy@emich.edu.

Edinboro University of Pennsylvania, Department of Art, Edinboro, PA 16444. Offers art education (MA); fine arts (MFA), including ceramics (MA, MFA), metals/jewelry, painting (MA, MFA), printmaking (MA, MFA), sculpture (MA, MFA); studio art (MA), including ceramics (MA, MFA), jewelry/metals, painting (MA, MFA), printmaking (MA, MFA), sculpture (MA, MFA). *Accreditation:* NASAD. *Program availability:* Evening/ weekend. *Degree requirements:* For master's, comprehensive exam, thesis or alternative, competency exam, exhibit, portfolio. *Entrance requirements:* For master's, GRE or MAT, interview, minimum QPA of 2.5, portfolio. Electronic applications accepted.

Fitchburg State University, Division of Graduate and Continuing Education, Program in Arts Education, Fitchburg, MA 01420-2697. Offers arts education (M Ed); fine arts director (Certificate). *Accreditation:* NCATE. *Program availability:* Part-time, evening/ weekend. *Entrance requirements:* Additional exam requirements/recommendations for international students: Required—TOEFL (minimum score 550 paper-based; 79 iBT). Electronic applications accepted. *Expenses:* Contact institution.

Florida International University, College of Arts, Sciences, and Education, Department of Teaching and Learning, Miami, FL 33199. Offers art education (MA, MS); curriculum and instruction (MS, Ed D, PhD, Ed S), including curriculum development (MS), elementary education (MS), English education (MS), learning technologies (MS), mathematics education (MS), modern language education (MS), physical education (MS), science education (MS), social studies education (MS), special education (MS); early childhood education (MS); exceptional student education (Ed D); foreign language education (MS), including foreign language education, teaching English to speakers of other languages (TESOL); language, literacy and culture (PhD); mathematics, science, and learning technologies (PhD); physical education (MS), including sport and fitness; reading education (MS). *Program availability:* Part-time, evening/weekend. *Faculty:* 64 full-time (43 women), 104 part-time/adjunct (76 women). *Students:* 169 full-time (144 women), 155 part-time (130 women); includes 260 minority (53 Black or African American, non-Hispanic/Latino; 7 Asian, non-Hispanic/Latino; 193 Hispanic/Latino; 7 Two or more races, non-Hispanic/Latino), 13 international. Average age 33. 184 applicants, 62% accepted, 87 enrolled. In 2018, 153 master's, 10 doctorates awarded. *Degree requirements:* For doctorate, comprehensive exam, thesis/dissertation. *Entrance requirements:* For master's, GRE General Test, Florida General Knowledge Test or Florida College Level Academic Skills Test; for doctorate and Ed S, GRE General Test. Additional exam requirements/recommendations for international students: Required—TOEFL (minimum score 550 paper-based; 80 iBT), IELTS (minimum score 6.3). *Application deadline:* For fall admission, 6/1 priority date for domestic students, 4/1 for international students; for winter admission, 10/1 priority date for domestic students, 9/1 for international students; for spring admission, 3/1 priority date for domestic students, 2/1 for international students. Applications are processed on a rolling basis. Application fee: $30. Electronic applications accepted. *Financial support:* Research assistantships and teaching assistantships available. *Unit head:* Dr. Maria Fernandez, Chair, 305-348-0193, Fax: 305-348-2086, E-mail: Maria.Fernandez9@ fiu.edu. *Application contact:* Nanett Rojas, Manager, Admissions Operations, 305-348-7464, Fax: 305-348-7441, E-mail: gradadm@fiu.edu. Website: https://tl.fiu.edu/

Florida State University, The Graduate School, College of Fine Arts, Department of Art Education, Tallahassee, FL 32306. Offers art education (MA, MS, Ed D, PhD); art therapy (PhD); arts administration (PhD). *Accreditation:* NASAD (one or more programs are accredited). *Program availability:* Part-time, evening/weekend, 100% online. *Faculty:* 10 full-time (7 women), 4 part-time/adjunct (all women). *Students:* 66 full-time (65 women), 28 part-time (23 women); includes 32 minority (7 Black or African American, non-Hispanic/Latino; 1 American Indian or Alaska Native, non-Hispanic/Latino; 6 Asian, non-Hispanic/Latino; 2 Hispanic/Latino; 16 Two or more races, non-Hispanic/Latino), 6 international. Average age 31. 95 applicants, 48% accepted, 28 enrolled. In 2018, 30 master's, 6 doctorates awarded. *Degree requirements:* For master's, comprehensive exam, thesis (for some programs); for doctorate, thesis/dissertation. *Entrance requirements:* For master's, GRE (can apply for waiver with GPA greater than 3.0, there is no GRE waiver available for the Art Therapy Program); minimum GPA of 3.0 in last 2 years; for doctorate, GRE. Additional exam requirements/recommendations for international students: Required—TOEFL (minimum score 550 paper-based; 80 iBT), Students can take the TOEFL or IELTS; Recommended—IELTS (minimum score 6.5), TSE (minimum score 55). *Application deadline:* For fall admission, 1/15 priority date for domestic and international students; for spring admission, 10/1 priority date for domestic and international students. Application fee: $30. Electronic applications accepted. *Expenses: Tuition, area resident:* Part-time $479.32 per credit hour. Tuition and fees vary according to campus/location and program. *Financial support:* In 2018–19, 22 students received support, including 18 research assistantships with full tuition reimbursements available (averaging $6,350 per year), 4 teaching assistantships with full tuition reimbursements available (averaging $8,750 per year); fellowships, career-related internships or fieldwork, Federal Work-Study, scholarships/grants, health care benefits, tuition waivers (full), and unspecified assistantships also available. Financial award application deadline: 1/15; financial award applicants required to submit FAFSA. *Faculty research:* Teaching and learning in art, museum education, art therapy, arts administration, discipline-based art education. *Unit head:* Victoria Cole, Program Associate, 850-644-2147, E-mail: vcole@fsu.edu. *Application contact:* Vicki Barr, Academic Support Assistant, 850-644-5473, Fax: 850-644-6067, E-mail: vbarr@ fsu.edu. Website: http://arted.fsu.edu/

Fontbonne University, Graduate Programs, St. Louis, MO 63105-3098. Offers accounting (MBA, MS); art (MA); art (K-12) (MAT); business (MBA); computer science (MS); deaf education (MA); early intervention in deaf education (MA); education (MA), including autism spectrum disorders, curriculum and instruction, diverse learners, early childhood education, reading, special education; elementary education (MAT); family and consumer sciences (MA), including multidisciplinary health communication studies; fine arts (MFA); instructional design and technology (MS); management and leadership (MM); middle school education (MAT); secondary education (MAT); special education (MAT); speech-language pathology (MS); supply chain management (MS); theatre (MA). *Accreditation:* ASHA. *Program availability:* Part-time, evening/weekend, online learning. *Degree requirements:* For master's, comprehensive exam (for some programs), thesis (for some programs). *Entrance requirements:* Additional exam requirements/recommendations for international students: Required—TOEFL (minimum score 500 paper-based; 65 iBT). Electronic applications accepted.

Framingham State University, Graduate Studies, Program in Art, Framingham, MA 01701-9101. Offers M Ed. *Accreditation:* NASAD.

George Mason University, College of Visual and Performing Arts, Program in Art Education, Fairfax, VA 22030. Offers MAT. *Faculty:* 3 full-time (2 women), 2 part-time/ adjunct (both women). *Students:* 5 full-time (all women), 15 part-time (12 women);

includes 8 minority (7 Asian, non-Hispanic/Latino; 1 Hispanic/Latino). Average age 30. 9 applicants, 67% accepted, 5 enrolled. In 2018, 7 master's awarded. *Degree requirements:* For master's, thesis or alternative, capstone. *Entrance requirements:* Additional exam requirements/recommendations for international students: Required—TOEFL (minimum score 575 paper-based; 88 iBT), IELTS (minimum score 6.5), PTE (minimum score 59). *Application deadline:* For fall admission, 4/1 for domestic and international students. Application fee: $75 ($80 for international students). Electronic applications accepted. *Financial support:* Career-related internships or fieldwork, Federal Work-Study, and scholarships/grants available. Financial award application deadline: 3/1; financial award applicants required to submit FAFSA. *Faculty research:* Maker spaces and technology; data visualization; teacher preparation licensure; cognition and child development in the arts. *Unit head:* Mary Del Popolo, Program Director, 703-993-8562, Fax: 703-993-8798, E-mail: mdelpopo@gmu.edu. *Application contact:* Nikki Brugnoli-Whipkey, Administrative Assistant for Graduate Study, 703-993-5792, Fax: 703-993-8798, E-mail: nbrugnol@gmu.edu.
Website: http://arteducation.gmu.edu/

The George Washington University, Columbian College of Arts and Sciences, Corcoran School of the Arts and Design, Washington, DC 20007. Offers art and the book (MA); art education (MA, MAT); decorative arts and design history (MA); exhibition design (MA); interior design (MA); new media photojournalism (MA). MA in decorative arts and design history offered in partnership with Smithsonian Associates. *Accreditation:* NASAD. *Program availability:* Part-time. *Entrance requirements:* Additional exam requirements/recommendations for international students: Required—TOEFL (minimum score 95 iBT).

Georgia State University, College of Arts, Ernest G. Welch School of Art and Design, Program in Art Education, Atlanta, GA 30302-3083. Offers MA Ed. *Accreditation:* NASAD. *Program availability:* Part-time. *Entrance requirements:* For master's, GRE. Additional exam requirements/recommendations for international students: Required—TOEFL. Application fee: $50. Electronic applications accepted. *Expenses: Tuition, area resident:* Full-time $9360; part-time $390 per credit hour. Tuition, state resident: full-time $9360; part-time $390 per credit hour. Tuition, nonresident: full-time $30,024; part-time $1251 per credit hour. *International tuition:* $30,024 full-time. *Required fees:* $2128. *Financial support:* Tuition waivers (full) and unspecified assistantships available. Financial award application deadline: 4/15; financial award applicants required to submit FAFSA. *Faculty research:* Critical theories, museum education, instructional technology, multi-culture and interdisciplinary art education, Chinese art history. *Unit head:* Joseph Peragine, Director, Welch School of Art and Design, 404-413-5229, E-mail: jperagine@gsu.edu. *Application contact:* Joseph Peragine, Director, Welch School of Art and Design, 404-413-5229, E-mail: jperagine@gsu.edu.
Website: http://artdesign.gsu.edu/graduate/admissions/masters-of-art-education/

Harding University, Cannon-Clary College of Education, Searcy, AR 72149-0001. Offers advanced studies in teaching and learning (M Ed); art (MSE); behavioral science (MSE); counseling (MS, Ed S); early childhood special education (M Ed, MSE); education (MSE); educational leadership (M Ed, Ed S); elementary education (M Ed); English (MSE); French (MSE); history/social science (MSE); kinesiology (MSE); math (MSE); reading (M Ed); secondary education (M Ed); Spanish (MSE); teaching (MAT); teaching English as a second language (MSE). *Accreditation:* NCATE. *Program availability:* Part-time, evening/weekend. *Degree requirements:* For master's, comprehensive exam (for some programs), thesis optional, portfolio(s); for Ed S, comprehensive exam, portfolio, project. *Entrance requirements:* For master's, GRE, MAT, PRAXIS; for Ed S, MAT or GRE. Additional exam requirements/recommendations for international students: Required—TOEFL (minimum score 550 paper-based; 79 iBT). *Faculty research:* Reading, comprehension, school violence, educational technology, behavior, college choice, differentiated instruction, brain-based teaching.

Harvard University, Harvard Graduate School of Education, Master's Programs in Education, Cambridge, MA 02138. Offers arts in education (Ed M); education policy and management (Ed M); higher education (Ed M); human development and psychology (Ed M); international education policy (Ed M); language and literacy (Ed M); learning and teaching (Ed M); mind, brain, and education (Ed M); prevention science and practice (Ed M); school leadership (Ed M); special studies (Ed M); teacher education (Ed M); technology, innovation, and education (Ed M). *Program availability:* Part-time. *Entrance requirements:* For master's, GRE General Test, statement of purpose, 3 letters of recommendation, resume, official transcripts. Additional exam requirements/recommendations for international students: Required—TOEFL (minimum score 613 paper-based; 104 iBT), TWE (minimum score 5). Electronic applications accepted. *Faculty research:* Learning and development, educational leadership and organizations, education policy analysis.

Hofstra University, School of Education, Programs in Teacher Education, Hempstead, NY 11549. Offers bilingual education (MA); bilingual extension (Advanced Certificate); business education (MS Ed); curriculum studies (MS Ed); early childhood and childhood education (MS Ed); early childhood education (MA, MS Ed); educational technology (Advanced Certificate); elementary education (MA, MS Ed); English education (MS Ed); family and consumer science (MS Ed); fine arts and music education (Advanced Certificate); fine arts education (MS Ed); foreign language and TESOL (MS Ed); foreign language education (MA, MS Ed); languages other than English and teaching English as a second language (MA); learning and teaching (Ed D); mathematics education (MA, MS Ed); middle childhood extension (Advanced Certificate); music education (MA, MS Ed); science education (MA); secondary education (Advanced Certificate); social studies education (MA, MS Ed); teaching languages other than English and TESOL (MS Ed); technology for learning (MA); TESOL (MS Ed, Advanced Certificate); TESOL with specialization in STEM (MA); work based learning extension (Advanced Certificate). *Program availability:* Part-time, evening/weekend, blended/hybrid learning. *Students:* 138 full-time (94 women), 109 part-time (78 women); includes 66 minority (16 Black or African American, non-Hispanic/Latino; 17 Asian, non-Hispanic/Latino; 31 Hispanic/Latino; 2 Native Hawaiian or other Pacific Islander, non-Hispanic/Latino), 6 international. Average age 29. 217 applicants, 86% accepted, 113 enrolled. In 2018, 105 master's, 11 doctorates, 25 other advanced degrees awarded. *Degree requirements:* For master's, comprehensive exam, thesis (for some programs), exit project, student teaching, fieldwork, electronic portfolio, curriculum project, minimum GPA of 3.0; for doctorate, dissertation; for Advanced Certificate, 3 foreign languages, comprehensive exam (for some programs), thesis project. *Entrance requirements:* For master's, GRE, 2 letters of recommendation, portfolio, teacher certification (MA), interview, essay; for doctorate, GMAT, GRE, LSAT, or MAT; for Advanced Certificate, 2 letters of recommendation, essay, interview and/or portfolio, teaching certificate. Additional exam requirements/recommendations for international students: Required—TOEFL (minimum score 550 paper-based; 80 iBT). *Application deadline:* Applications are processed on a rolling basis. Application fee: $75. Electronic applications accepted. *Financial support:* In 2018–19, 86 students received support, including 51 fellowships with full and partial tuition reimbursements available (averaging $5,080 per year), 2 research assistantships with full and partial tuition reimbursements available (averaging $3,470 per year); career-related internships or fieldwork, Federal Work-Study, institutionally sponsored loans, scholarships/grants, traineeships, tuition waivers (full and partial), unspecified assistantships, and scholarships and endowed scholarships also available. Support available to part-time students. Financial award applicants required to submit FAFSA. *Faculty research:* Impact of memory on learning; brain function, cognitive-development, learning, and achievement; student activism and civic education; using children's literature to promote diversity; 2nd language acquisition. *Unit head:* Dr. Alan Singer, Chairperson, 516-463-5853, Fax: 516-463-6275, E-mail: alan.j.singer@hofstra.edu. *Application contact:* Sunil Samuel, Assistant Vice President of Admissions, 516-463-4723, Fax: 516-463-4664, E-mail: graduateadmission@hofstra.edu.
Website: http://www.hofstra.edu/education/

Indiana University Bloomington, School of Education, Department of Curriculum and Instruction, Bloomington, IN 47405-7000. Offers art education (MS, Ed D, PhD); curriculum studies (Ed D, PhD); elementary education (MS, Ed D, PhD, Ed S); mathematics education (MS, Ed D, PhD); science education (MS, Ed D, PhD); secondary education (MS, Ed D, PhD); social studies education (MS, PhD); special education (PhD, Ed S). *Accreditation:* NCATE. *Program availability:* Part-time, evening/weekend. Terminal master's awarded for partial completion of doctoral program. *Degree requirements:* For doctorate, thesis/dissertation; for Ed S, comprehensive exam or project. *Entrance requirements:* For master's, doctorate, and Ed S, GRE General Test. Electronic applications accepted.

James Madison University, The Graduate School, College of Visual and Performing Arts, School of Art, Design and Art History, Harrisonburg, VA 22807. Offers art education (MA); studio art (MA, MFA), including ceramics (MFA), drawing/painting (MFA), intermedia (MFA), metal/jewelry (MFA), photography (MFA), sculpture (MFA). *Accreditation:* NASAD. *Program availability:* Part-time. *Students:* 6 full-time (4 women), 1 (woman) part-time. Average age 30. In 2018, 3 master's awarded. Electronic applications accepted. *Expenses:* Tuition, state resident: full-time $10,848. Tuition, nonresident: full-time $27,888. *Required fees:* $1128. *Financial support:* In 2018–19, 6 students received support, including 1 teaching assistantship with full tuition reimbursement available (averaging $9,284 per year); Federal Work-Study and assistantships (averaging $7911) also available. Financial award application deadline: 3/1; financial award applicants required to submit FAFSA. *Unit head:* Dr. Kathy A. Schwartz, Director of School of Art, Design and Art History, 540-568-6216, E-mail: schwarka@jmu.edu. *Application contact:* Lynette D. Michael, Director of Graduate Student Admissions, 540-568-6131 Ext. 6395, Fax: 540-568-7860, E-mail: michaeld@jmu.edu.
Website: http://www.jmu.edu/artandarthistory/

Kean University, College of Liberal Arts, Program in Fine Arts Education, Union, NJ 07083. Offers MA. *Accreditation:* NASAD. *Program availability:* Part-time. *Faculty:* 3 full-time (2 women). *Students:* 3 full-time (all women), 16 part-time (11 women); includes 6 minority (1 Black or African American, non-Hispanic/Latino; 1 Asian, non-Hispanic/Latino; 3 Hispanic/Latino; 1 Native Hawaiian or other Pacific Islander, non-Hispanic/Latino), 1 international. Average age 36. 2 applicants, 100% accepted, 2 enrolled. In 2018, 9 master's awarded. *Degree requirements:* For master's, thesis (for some programs), exhibition, 3 years of teaching experience (for supervision), PRAXIS and fieldwork (for initial teaching certification). *Entrance requirements:* For master's, studio portfolio, proficiencies in academic writing, dialogue skills, minimum GPA of 3.0, interview, 2 letters of recommendation, official transcripts from all institutions attended. Additional exam requirements/recommendations for international students: Required—TOEFL (minimum score 550 paper-based; 79 iBT), IELTS (minimum score 6.5). *Application deadline:* For fall admission, 6/30 for domestic and international students; for spring admission, 12/1 for domestic and international students. Applications are processed on a rolling basis. Application fee: $75. Electronic applications accepted. *Expenses:* Tuition, state resident: full-time $15,025; part-time $733.50 per credit. Tuition, nonresident: full-time $19,890; part-time $884.50 per credit. *Required fees:* $2107.50; $89.50 per credit. Tuition and fees vary according to course level, course load, degree level and program. *Financial support:* Scholarships/grants and unspecified assistantships available. Financial award applicants required to submit FAFSA. *Unit head:* Dr. Joseph Amorino, Program Coordinator, 908-737-4403, Fax: 908-737-4377, E-mail: jamorino@kean.edu. *Application contact:* Amy Clark, Program Assistant, 908-737-7100, E-mail: gradadmissions@kean.edu.
Website: http://grad.kean.edu/masters-programs/initial-teaching-certification

Kennesaw State University, Bagwell College of Education, MAT Program, Kennesaw, GA 30144. Offers art education (MAT); secondary English (MAT); secondary mathematics (MAT); secondary science (MAT); special education (MAT); teaching English to speakers of other languages (MAT). *Program availability:* Part-time, evening/weekend. *Students:* 44 full-time (36 women), 10 part-time (6 women); includes 15 minority (10 Black or African American, non-Hispanic/Latino; 4 Hispanic/Latino; 1 Two or more races, non-Hispanic/Latino). Average age 32. 3 applicants. In 2018, 32 master's awarded. *Entrance requirements:* For master's, GRE, GACE I (state certificate exam), minimum GPA of 2.75, 2 recommendations, resume. Additional exam requirements/recommendations for international students: Required—TOEFL (minimum score 550 paper-based; 80 iBT), IELTS (minimum score 6.5). *Application deadline:* For fall admission, 6/1 for domestic and international students; for spring admission, 3/1 for domestic and international students; for summer admission, 4/15 for domestic and international students. Applications are processed on a rolling basis. Application fee: $60. Electronic applications accepted. *Expenses: Tuition, area resident:* Full-time $6960; part-time $290 per credit hour. Tuition, state resident: full-time $6960; part-time $290 per credit hour. Tuition, nonresident: full-time $25,080; part-time $1045 per credit hour. *International tuition:* $25,080 full-time. *Required fees:* $2006; $1706 per semester. $853 per semester. *Financial support:* Research assistantships with tuition reimbursements and unspecified assistantships available. Financial award application deadline: 4/1; financial award applicants required to submit FAFSA. *Unit head:* Director, 470-578-3093. *Application contact:* Admissions Counselor, 470-578-4377, Fax: 470-578-9172, E-mail: ksugrad@kennesaw.edu.

Kent State University, College of the Arts, School of Art, Kent, OH 44242-0001. Offers art education (MA); art history (MA); crafts (MA), including glass (MA, MFA); fine arts (MA), including fashion; studio art (MFA), including ceramics, drawing, glass (MA, MFA), jewelry, metals and enameling, painting, print media and photography, sculpture, textiles. *Accreditation:* NASAD (one or more programs are accredited). *Program availability:* Part-time, 100% online, blended/hybrid learning. *Faculty:* 17 full-time (10 women), 1 (woman) part-time/adjunct. *Students:* 34 full-time (23 women), 27 part-time (24 women); includes 1 minority (Black or African American, non-Hispanic/Latino), 1 international. Average age 31. 41 applicants, 73% accepted, 16 enrolled. In 2018, 22 master's awarded. *Degree requirements:* For master's, comprehensive exam, thesis (for some programs), 1 foreign language (for art history); final project (for crafts and fine arts). *Entrance requirements:* For master's, transcripts, goal statement, 3 letters of recommendation, curriculum vitae, portfolio, artist statement. Additional exam requirements/recommendations for international students: Required—TOEFL (minimum score 550 paper-based, 79 iBT), Michigan English Language Assessment Battery (minimum score 77), IELTS (minimum score 6.5) or PTE (minimum score 58). *Application deadline:* For fall admission, 2/2 priority date for domestic students, 2/2 for international students; for spring admission, 10/15 for domestic and international students. Applications are processed on a rolling basis. Application fee: $45 ($70 for international students). Electronic applications accepted. *Expenses:* Tuition, state

resident: full-time $11,766; part-time $536 per credit. Tuition, nonresident: full-time $21,952; part-time $999 per credit. *International tuition:* $21,952 full-time. Tuition and fees vary according to course load. *Financial support:* Career-related internships or fieldwork, scholarships/grants, and unspecified assistantships available. Financial award application deadline: 3/16. *Unit head:* Marie Bukowski, Director, 330-672-2192, E-mail: mbukows1@kent.edu. *Application contact:* Peter Christian Johnson, Graduate Coordinator and Associate Professor Ceramics, 330-672-3360, E-mail: pjohns35@kent.edu.
Website: http://www.kent.edu/art

Kutztown University of Pennsylvania, College of Visual and Performing Arts, Program in Art Education, Kutztown, PA 19530-0730. Offers M Ed. *Accreditation:* NASAD; NCATE. *Program availability:* Part-time. *Faculty:* 3 full-time (all women), 3 part-time/adjunct (all women). *Students:* 14 full-time (11 women), 47 part-time (42 women); includes 3 minority (1 Black or African American, non-Hispanic/Latino; 1 Hispanic/Latino; 1 Two or more races, non-Hispanic/Latino). Average age 31. 44 applicants, 95% accepted, 22 enrolled. In 2018, 14 master's awarded. *Degree requirements:* For master's, comprehensive exam, thesis optional. *Entrance requirements:* For master's, PRAXIS II, valid instructional I or II teaching certificate, or GRE, minimum undergraduate GPA of 3.0, 3 letters of recommendation. Additional exam requirements/recommendations for international students: Required—TOEFL (minimum score 550 paper-based, 79 iBT), IELTS (minimum score 6.5), or PTE (minimum score 53). *Application deadline:* For fall admission, 8/1 for domestic and international students; for spring admission, 12/1 for domestic and international students. Application fee: $35. Electronic applications accepted. *Expenses:* Tuition, state resident: part-time $516 per credit. Tuition, nonresident: part-time $774 per credit. *Required fees:* $119 per credit. One-time fee: $50 part-time. Tuition and fees vary according to degree level. *Financial support:* Career-related internships or fieldwork, Federal Work-Study, and unspecified assistantships available. Financial award application deadline: 3/1; financial award applicants required to submit FAFSA. *Faculty research:* Teaching of art history, child development in art, aesthetics and criticism curriculum, multicultural education, assessment in art. *Unit head:* Dr. Julia Hovanec, Department Chair, 610-683-4815, E-mail: hovanec@kutztown.edu. *Application contact:* Dr. Julia Hovanec, Department Chair, 610-683-4815, E-mail: hovanec@kutztown.edu.
Website: https://www.kutztown.edu/academics/graduate-programs/art-education.htm

Lake Forest College, Master of Arts in Teaching Program, Lake Forest, IL 60045. Offers elementary education (MAT); K-12 French (MAT); K-12 music (MAT); K-12 Spanish (MAT); K-12 visual art (MAT); secondary biology (MAT); secondary chemistry (MAT); secondary English (MAT); secondary history (MAT); secondary mathematics (MAT). *Degree requirements:* For master's, comprehensive exam, portfolio. *Entrance requirements:* For master's, GRE.

Lehman College of the City University of New York, School of Arts and Humanities, Department of Art, Bronx, NY 10468-1589. Offers art education (MA); art studio (MA, MFA). *Program availability:* Part-time, evening/weekend. *Entrance requirements:* For master's, 33 undergraduate credits in art, interview, portfolio. *Faculty research:* Graphic art, modern and contemporary art, sculpture, primitive and pre-Columbian art, medieval art.

Lesley University, Graduate School of Education, Cambridge, MA 02138-2790. Offers arts, community, and education (M Ed); autism studies (Certificate); curriculum and instruction (M Ed, CAGS); early childhood education (M Ed); ecological teaching and learning (MS); educational studies (PhD), including adult learning, educational leadership, individually designed; elementary education (M Ed); emergent technologies for educators (Certificate); ESLArts: language learning through the arts (M Ed); high school education (M Ed); individually designed (M Ed); integrated teaching through the arts (M Ed); literacy for K-8 classroom teachers (M Ed); mathematics education (M Ed); middle school education (M Ed); moderate disabilities (M Ed); online learning (Certificate); reading (CAGS); science in education (M Ed); severe disabilities (M Ed); special needs (CAGS); specialist teacher of reading (M Ed); teacher of visual art (M Ed); technology in education (M Ed, CAGS). *Accreditation:* TEAC. *Program availability:* Part-time, evening/weekend, online learning. *Degree requirements:* For master's, practicum; for doctorate, thesis/dissertation. *Entrance requirements:* For master's, Massachusetts Tests for Educator Licensure (MTEL), transcripts, statement of purpose, recommendations; interview (for special education); for doctorate, GRE General Test, transcripts, statement of purpose, recommendations, interview, master's degree, resume; for other advanced degree, interview, master's degree. Additional exam requirements/recommendations for international students: Required—TOEFL (minimum score 550 paper-based; 80 iBT). Electronic applications accepted. *Faculty research:* Assessment in literacy, mathematics and science; autism spectrum disorders; instructional technology and online learning; multicultural education and English language learners.

Long Island University–LIU Post, College of Education, Information and Technology, Brookville, NY 11548-1300. Offers adolescence education (MS); adolescence education 7-12 (MS); archives and records management (AC); art education (MS); childhood education (MS); childhood education/literacy B-6 (MS); childhood education/special education (MS); clinical mental health counseling (MS, AC); early childhood education (MS); early childhood education/childhood education (MS); educational leadership (AC); educational technology (MS); information studies (PhD); interdisciplinary educational studies (Ed D); middle childhood education (MS); music education (MS); public library administration (AC); school counselor (MS); special education (MS Ed); speech-language pathology (MA); students with disabilities, 7-12 generalist (AC); TESOL (MA). *Accreditation:* ASHA; TEAC. *Program availability:* Part-time, 100% online, blended/hybrid learning. Terminal master's awarded for partial completion of doctoral program. *Degree requirements:* For master's, variable foreign language requirement, comprehensive exam (for some programs), thesis optional; for doctorate, comprehensive exam, thesis/dissertation. *Entrance requirements:* For master's and AC, GRE (for some programs). Additional exam requirements/recommendations for international students: Required—TOEFL (minimum score 550 paper-based, 75 iBT), IELTS, or PTE. Electronic applications accepted. *Faculty research:* Sleep; use of technology to develop executive function by students with disabilities; early childhood literacy development through play; social justice through education; using a structured protocol to discuss Bad News.

Manhattanville College, School of Education, Program in Visual Arts Education, Purchase, NY 10577-2132. Offers visual arts education(all grades) (MAT, Certificate). *Program availability:* Part-time, evening/weekend. *Faculty:* 1 (woman) part-time/adjunct. *Students:* 5 full-time (all women), 7 part-time (5 women). Average age 30. 6 applicants, 67% accepted, 4 enrolled. In 2018, 7 master's awarded. *Degree requirements:* For master's, comprehensive exam (for some programs), thesis (for some programs), student teaching, research seminars, portfolios, internships, writing assessment; for Certificate, comprehensive exam (for some programs). *Entrance requirements:* For master's, for programs leading to certification, candidates must submit scores from GRE or MAT(Miller Analogies Test), minimum undergraduate GPA of 3.0, all transcripts from all colleges and universities attended, 2 letters of recommendation, interview, essay (2-3 page personal statement that describes reasons for choosing education as profession and personal philosophy of education), Electronic art portfolio, proof of immunization (for

those born after 1957). Additional exam requirements/recommendations for international students: Required—TOEFL (minimum score 600 paper-based; 110 iBT); Recommended—IELTS (minimum score 8). *Application deadline:* Applications are processed on a rolling basis. Application fee: $75. Electronic applications accepted. *Expenses:* 935 per credit. *Financial support:* Teaching assistantships, career-related internships or fieldwork, Federal Work-Study, institutionally sponsored loans, scholarships/grants, and unspecified assistantships available. Financial award application deadline: 3/15; financial award applicants required to submit FAFSA. *Unit head:* Dr. Shelley Wepner, Dean, 914-323-3153, Fax: 914-323-5493, E-mail: Shelley.Wepner@mville.edu. *Application contact:* Alissa Wilson, Director, SOE Graduate Enrollment Management, 914-323-3150, Fax: 914-694-1732, E-mail: edschool@mville.edu.
Website: http://www.mville.edu/programs/visual-art-education

Mansfield University of Pennsylvania, Graduate Studies, Department of Art, Mansfield, PA 16933. Offers art education (M Ed). *Program availability:* Part-time. *Degree requirements:* For master's, thesis optional. *Entrance requirements:* For master's, minimum GPA of 3.0, portfolio. Additional exam requirements/recommendations for international students: Required—TOEFL (minimum score 550 paper-based). Electronic applications accepted.

Maryland Institute College of Art, Graduate Studies, MA Program in Art Education, Baltimore, MD 21201. Offers MA. Program offered in summer only. *Accreditation:* NASAD. *Degree requirements:* For master's, thesis, exhibition and documentation. *Entrance requirements:* For master's, portfolio, bachelor's degree in any field. Additional exam requirements/recommendations for international students: Required—TOEFL (minimum score 550 paper-based; 80 iBT), IELTS (minimum score 6.5). Electronic applications accepted. *Expenses:* Contact institution.

Maryland Institute College of Art, Graduate Studies, MAT Program, Baltimore, MD 21201. Offers MAT. *Degree requirements:* For master's, thesis, student teaching, thesis exhibition, thesis writing. *Entrance requirements:* For master's, PRAXIS I, portfolio, writing samples. Additional exam requirements/recommendations for international students: Required—TOEFL (minimum score 550 paper-based; 80 iBT), IELTS (minimum score 6.5). Electronic applications accepted.

Marywood University, Academic Affairs, Insalaco College of Creative and Performing Arts, Art Department, Program in Art Education, Scranton, PA 18509-1598. Offers MA. *Accreditation:* NASAD; NCATE. Electronic applications accepted.

Massachusetts College of Art and Design, Graduate Programs, Program in Art Education, Boston, MA 02115-5882. Offers art education (M Ed, MAT); art teacher preparation (Postbaccalaureate Certificate). *Accreditation:* NASAD. *Entrance requirements:* For master's and Postbaccalaureate Certificate, portfolio, college transcripts, resume, statement of purpose, letters of reference, interview. Additional exam requirements/recommendations for international students: Required—TOEFL (minimum score 550 paper-based; 85 iBT); Recommended—IELTS (minimum score 6). Electronic applications accepted. *Expenses:* Contact institution. *Faculty research:* Cognitive and developmental psychology, research methodologies and synthesis, embodied aesthetics, neuro-aesthetics and neuro-philosophy, interactive art.

McNeese State University, Doré School of Graduate Studies, Burton College of Education, Department of Education Professions, Program in Multiple Levels Grades K-12, Lake Charles, LA 70609. Offers multiple levels grades K-12 (Postbaccalaureate Certificate), including art, health and physical education, music - instrumental, music - vocal. *Entrance requirements:* For degree, PRAXIS, 2 letters of recommendation, autobiography.

Miami University, College of Creative Arts, Department of Art, Oxford, OH 45056. Offers art education (MA); studio art (MFA). *Accreditation:* NASAD (one or more programs are accredited). *Faculty:* 21 full-time (9 women). *Students:* 18 full-time (14 women); includes 2 minority (1 Black or African American, non-Hispanic/Latino; 1 Hispanic/Latino), 1 international. Average age 29. In 2018, 4 master's awarded. *Unit head:* Rob Robbins, Chair and Professor, 513-529-2900, E-mail: art@miamioh.edu. *Application contact:* Rob Robbins, Chair and Professor, 513-529-2900, E-mail: art@miamioh.edu.
Website: http://www.MiamiOH.edu/art

Minnesota State University Mankato, College of Graduate Studies and Research, College of Arts and Humanities, Department of Art, Mankato, MN 56001. Offers art (MA); art education (MAT). *Accreditation:* NASAD (one or more programs are accredited). *Program availability:* Part-time. *Degree requirements:* For master's, one foreign language, comprehensive exam, thesis or alternative. *Entrance requirements:* For master's, portfolio, three letters of reference. Additional exam requirements/recommendations for international students: Required—TOEFL. Electronic applications accepted.

Mississippi College, Graduate School, School of Education, Department of Teacher Education and Leadership, Clinton, MS 39058. Offers art (M Ed); biological science (M Ed); business education (M Ed); computer science (M Ed); dyslexia therapy (M Ed); educational leadership (M Ed, Ed D, Ed S); elementary education (M Ed, Ed S); English (M Ed); higher education administration (MS); mathematics (M Ed); secondary education (M Ed); social studies (history) (M Ed); teaching arts (M Ed). *Program availability:* Part-time, online learning. *Degree requirements:* For master's, comprehensive exam, thesis optional. *Entrance requirements:* For master's, NTE. Additional exam requirements/recommendations for international students: Recommended—TOEFL, IELTS. Electronic applications accepted.

Montclair State University, The Graduate School, College of Education and Human Services, MAT Program in Teaching, Montclair, NJ 07043-1624. Offers art (MAT); biology (MAT); chemistry (MAT); earth science (MAT); English (MAT); French (MAT); health and physical education (MAT); health education (MAT); mathematics (MAT); music (MAT); physical education (MAT); physical science (MAT); social studies (MAT); Spanish (MAT); teacher of English as a second language (MAT). *Degree requirements:* For master's, comprehensive exam, thesis or alternative. *Entrance requirements:* For master's, interview, 2 letters of recommendation. Additional exam requirements/recommendations for international students: Required—TOEFL (minimum score 83 iBT), IELTS (minimum score 6.5). Electronic applications accepted.

Moore College of Art & Design, Program in Art Education, Philadelphia, PA 19103. Offers MA. *Program availability:* Part-time. *Degree requirements:* For master's, thesis, field practicum. *Entrance requirements:* For master's, minimum GPA of 3.0, on-site interview, portfolio, 3 letters of recommendation, resume.

Morehead State University, Graduate School, Caudill College of Arts, Humanities and Social Sciences, Department of Art and Design, Morehead, KY 40351. Offers art education (MA); graphic design (MA); studio art (MA). *Accreditation:* NASAD. *Program availability:* Part-time, evening/weekend. *Degree requirements:* For master's, comprehensive exam, thesis (for some programs), oral exam during exhibition. *Entrance requirements:* For master's, GRE General Test, minimum undergraduate GPA of 3.0 in major, 2.5 overall; portfolio; bachelor's degree in art. Additional exam requirements/recommendations for international students: Required—TOEFL (minimum score 500 paper-based). Electronic applications accepted. *Faculty research:* Computer art, painting, drawing, ceramics, photography.

Art Education

Nazareth College of Rochester, Graduate Studies, Department of Art, Program in Art Education, Rochester, NY 14618. Offers MS Ed. *Accreditation:* TEAC. *Program availability:* Part-time. *Entrance requirements:* For master's, GRE (for speech-language pathology); GRE or MAT (for education programs), minimum GPA of 3.0, portfolio review. Additional exam requirements/recommendations for international students: Required—TOEFL (minimum score 550 paper-based, 79 iBT) or IELTS (6.5). Electronic applications accepted.

New Hampshire Institute of Art, Graduate Studies, Manchester, NH 03104. Offers art education (MA); creative writing (MFA); photography (MFA); teaching visual arts (MAT); visual arts (MFA). *Accreditation:* NASAD. *Degree requirements:* For master's, thesis, corresponding exhibition and artist talk. *Entrance requirements:* For master's, writing sample or visual art portfolio; curriculum vitae; transcripts; letters of recommendation. Additional exam requirements/recommendations for international students: Required—TOEFL (minimum score 550 paper-based; 80 iBT), IELTS (minimum score 6.5). Electronic applications accepted. *Expenses:* Contact institution. *Faculty research:* Fine arts - visual arts, photography, creative writing; art education.

New Jersey City University, William J. Maxwell College of Arts and Sciences, Department of Art, Jersey City, NJ 07305-1597. Offers art (MFA); art education (MA); studio art (MFA). *Accreditation:* NASAD. *Program availability:* Part-time, evening/weekend. *Degree requirements:* For master's, thesis or alternative, exhibit. *Entrance requirements:* For master's, portfolio. Additional exam requirements/recommendations for international students: Required—TOEFL (minimum score 79 iBT).

New York University, Steinhardt School of Culture, Education, and Human Development, Department of Art and Art Professions, Program in Art Education, New York, NY 10003-5799. Offers art, education, and community practice (MA); teachers of art, all grades (MA); teaching art/social studies 7-12 (MA), including 5-6 extension. *Accreditation:* TEAC. *Program availability:* Part-time. *Entrance requirements:* For master's, portfolio. Additional exam requirements/recommendations for international students: Required—TOEFL (minimum score 100 iBT). Electronic applications accepted. *Faculty research:* Multicultural aesthetic inquiry, urban art education, feminism, equity and social justice.

New York University, Steinhardt School of Culture, Education, and Human Development, Department of Teaching and Learning, Program in Social Studies Education, New York, NY 10012. Offers teaching art/social studies 7-12 (MA), including 5-6 extension; teaching social studies 7-12 (MA). *Accreditation:* TEAC. *Program availability:* Part-time, evening/weekend. *Entrance requirements:* Additional exam requirements/recommendations for international students: Required—TOEFL (minimum score 100 iBT). Electronic applications accepted. *Faculty research:* Social studies education reform, ethnography and oral history, civic education, labor history and social studies curriculum, material culture.

The Ohio State University, Graduate School, College of Arts and Sciences, Division of Arts and Humanities, Department of Arts Administration, Education and Policy, Columbus, OH 43210. Offers art education (MA); arts administration, education and policy (PhD); arts policy and administration (MA). *Accreditation:* NASAD; NCATE. *Program availability:* Online learning. *Faculty:* 11. *Students:* 72 (61 women). Average age 30. In 2018, 7 master's, 7 doctorates awarded. Terminal master's awarded for partial completion of doctoral program. *Degree requirements:* For master's, thesis; for doctorate, thesis/dissertation. *Entrance requirements:* For master's, GRE; for doctorate, GRE General Test. Additional exam requirements/recommendations for international students: Required—TOEFL (minimum score 600 paper-based; 100 iBT); Recommended—IELTS (minimum score 8). *Application deadline:* For fall admission, 11/30 priority date for domestic and international students; for winter admission, 12/1 for domestic students, 11/1 for international students; for spring admission, 11/30 priority date for domestic and international students. Applications are processed on a rolling basis. Application fee: $60 ($70 for international students). Electronic applications accepted. *Financial support:* Fellowships with tuition reimbursements, research assistantships with tuition reimbursements, teaching assistantships with tuition reimbursements, career-related internships or fieldwork, Federal Work-Study, institutionally sponsored loans, and unspecified assistantships available. Support available to part-time students. Financial award applicants required to submit FAFSA. *Unit head:* Dr. Karen Hutzel, Chair and Associate Professor, 614-292-9852, E-mail: hutzel.4@osu.edu. *Application contact:* Graduate Admissions, 614-292-9444, Fax: 614-292-3895, E-mail: gradadmissions@osu.edu.
Website: http://aaep.osu.edu/

Penn State University Park, Graduate School, College of Arts and Architecture, School of Visual Arts, University Park, PA 16802. Offers art (MFA); art education (MS, PhD, Certificate).

Piedmont College, School of Education, Demorest, GA 30535. Offers art education (MAT); curriculum and instruction (Ed D, Ed S); early childhood education (MA, MAT); middle grades education (MA, MAT); music education (MAT); secondary education (MA, MAT); special education (MA, MAT). *Program availability:* Part-time, evening/weekend. *Students:* 496 full-time (416 women), 650 part-time (560 women); includes 185 minority (137 Black or African American, non-Hispanic/Latino; 2 American Indian or Alaska Native, non-Hispanic/Latino; 13 Asian, non-Hispanic/Latino; 31 Hispanic/Latino; 1 Native Hawaiian or other Pacific Islander, non-Hispanic/Latino; 1 Two or more races, non-Hispanic/Latino). Average age 37. 483 applicants, 89% accepted, 372 enrolled. In 2018, 275 master's, 10 doctorates, 229 other advanced degrees awarded. *Degree requirements:* For master's, thesis, field experience in the classroom teaching; for doctorate, thesis/dissertation. *Entrance requirements:* For master's, GRE General Test, MAT; for Ed S, minimum graduate GPA of 3.5, valid teaching certificate. Additional exam requirements/recommendations for international students: Required—TOEFL (minimum score 550 paper-based). *Application deadline:* For fall admission, 7/15 for domestic students; for spring admission, 12/1 for domestic students. Applications are processed on a rolling basis. Electronic applications accepted. *Expenses: Tuition:* Full-time $9738; part-time $541 per credit. *Required fees:* $200 per semester. *Financial support:* Career-related internships or fieldwork, Federal Work-Study, and unspecified assistantships available. Support available to part-time students. Financial award applicants required to submit FAFSA. *Unit head:* Dr. R.D. Nordgren, Dean, 706-778-3000 Ext. 1201, Fax: 706-776-9608, E-mail: rdnordgren@piedmont.edu. *Application contact:* Kathleen Carter, Director of Graduate Enrollment Management, 706-778-8500 Ext. 1181, Fax: 706-778-0150, E-mail: kanderson@piedmont.edu.

Plymouth State University, College of Graduate Studies, Graduate Studies in Education, Program in Teaching, Plymouth, NH 03264-1595. Offers art education (MAT). *Program availability:* Evening/weekend.

Pratt Institute, School of Art, Program in Art and Design Education, Brooklyn, NY 11205-3899. Offers MA, MS, Adv C. *Accreditation:* NASAD. *Program availability:* Part-time. *Students:* 23 full-time (19 women), 4 part-time (all women); includes 14 minority (4 Black or African American, non-Hispanic/Latino; 3 Asian, non-Hispanic/Latino; 5 Hispanic/Latino; 2 Two or more races, non-Hispanic/Latino), 2 international. Average age 25. 21 applicants, 100% accepted, 13 enrolled. In 2018, 11 master's, 1 other advanced degree awarded. *Degree requirements:* For master's, thesis. *Entrance requirements:* For master's, portfolio. Additional exam requirements/recommendations for international students: Required—TOEFL (minimum score 600 paper-based; 100 iBT). *Application deadline:* For fall admission, 1/5 for domestic and international students; for spring admission, 10/1 for domestic and international students. Application fee: $50 ($90 for international students). Electronic applications accepted. *Expenses: Tuition:* Full-time $33,246; part-time $1847 per credit. *Required fees:* $1980. *Financial support:* Career-related internships or fieldwork, Federal Work-Study, institutionally sponsored loans, scholarships/grants, health care benefits, and unspecified assistantships available. Support available to part-time students. Financial award application deadline: 2/1; financial award applicants required to submit FAFSA. *Unit head:* Heather Lewis, Chairperson, 718-636-3637, Fax: 718-636-3632, E-mail: hlewis@pratt.edu. *Application contact:* Natalie Capannelli, Director of Graduate Admissions, 718-636-3551, Fax: 718-399-4242, E-mail: ncapanne@pratt.edu.
Website: https://www.pratt.edu/academics/school-of-art/graduate-school-of-art/art-and-design-education-grad/

Purdue University, Graduate School, College of Education, Department of Curriculum and Instruction, West Lafayette, IN 47907. Offers agricultural and extension education (MS, MS Ed, PhD, Ed S); art education (PhD); career and technical education (MS Ed, PhD, Ed S); curriculum studies (MS Ed, PhD, Ed S); educational technology (MS Ed, PhD, Ed S); elementary education (MS Ed); family and consumer sciences education (MS Ed, PhD, Ed S); foreign language education (MS Ed, PhD, Ed S); industrial technology (PhD, Ed S); language arts (MS Ed, PhD, Ed S); literacy (MS Ed, PhD, Ed S); mathematics education (MS, MS Ed, PhD, Ed S); science education (MS, MS Ed, PhD, Ed S); social studies education (MS Ed, PhD, Ed S). *Accreditation:* NCATE. *Program availability:* Part-time, evening/weekend, online learning. *Faculty:* 34 full-time (24 women), 3 part-time/adjunct (1 woman). *Students:* 75 full-time (52 women), 357 part-time (271 women); includes 83 minority (29 Black or African American, non-Hispanic/Latino; 1 American Indian or Alaska Native, non-Hispanic/Latino; 14 Asian, non-Hispanic/Latino; 29 Hispanic/Latino; 1 Native Hawaiian or other Pacific Islander, non-Hispanic/Latino; 9 Two or more races, non-Hispanic/Latino), 43 international. Average age 36. 169 applicants, 83% accepted, 102 enrolled. In 2018, 141 master's, 15 doctorates awarded. *Degree requirements:* For master's, thesis optional; for doctorate, thesis/dissertation, oral and written exams; for Ed S, oral presentation, project. *Entrance requirements:* For master's, GRE General Test (if undergraduate GPA is below 3.0), minimum undergraduate GPA of 3.0 or equivalent; for doctorate, GRE General Test (minimum combined verbal and quantitative score of 1000, 300 for new scoring), minimum undergraduate GPA of 3.0 or equivalent; master's degree with minimum GPA of 3.0 or equivalent; for Ed S, GRE General Test (minimum combined verbal and quantitative score of 1000, 300 for new scoring), minimum undergraduate GPA of 3.0 or equivalent; master's degree. Additional exam requirements/recommendations for international students: Required—TOEFL (minimum score 550 paper-based; 77 iBT). *Application deadline:* For fall admission, 12/15 for domestic students, 3/1 for international students; for spring admission, 9/15 for domestic students, 8/1 for international students. Application fee: $60 ($75 for international students). Electronic applications accepted. *Financial support:* Fellowships with full tuition reimbursements, research assistantships with full tuition reimbursements, teaching assistantships with full tuition reimbursements, career-related internships or fieldwork, and tuition waivers (full) available. Support available to part-time students. Financial award application deadline: 3/1; financial award applicants required to submit FAFSA. *Faculty research:* Literacy acquisition and development, teacher beliefs and knowledge, recruitment and retention of underrepresented students, economic education, literacy discourse. *Unit head:* Janet M. Alsup, Head, 765-494-9667, E-mail: alsupj@purdue.edu. *Application contact:* Heather Brinkman, Graduate Contact, 765-494-2345, E-mail: hbrinkma@purdue.edu.
Website: http://www.edci.purdue.edu/

Purdue University, Graduate School, College of Liberal Arts, Department of Art and Design, West Lafayette, IN 47907. Offers art education (MA, PhD); industrial design (MFA); interior design (MFA); visual communications design (MFA). *Accreditation:* NASAD; NAST. *Program availability:* Part-time. *Students:* 21 full-time (9 women); includes 1 minority (Asian, non-Hispanic/Latino), 17 international. Average age 28. 76 applicants, 36% accepted, 6 enrolled. In 2018, 5 master's awarded. *Degree requirements:* For master's, terminal exhibit, project, or thesis. *Entrance requirements:* For master's, GRE General Test (for art education), minimum undergraduate GPA of 3.0 or equivalent; 9 undergraduate hours in an art or design history; BA in art (for MA in art education); for doctorate, GRE General Test (minimum scores 600 in verbal and 1000 total), master's degree in art education or art with teaching certification; 3 years of teaching experience at the K-12 level. Additional exam requirements/recommendations for international students: Required—TOEFL (minimum score 550 paper-based; 77 iBT). *Application deadline:* For fall admission, 2/1 for domestic students, 2/1 priority date for international students. Applications are processed on a rolling basis. Application fee: $60 ($75 for international students). Electronic applications accepted. *Financial support:* Teaching assistantships with tuition reimbursements and career-related internships or fieldwork available. Support available to part-time students. Financial award applicants required to submit FAFSA. *Faculty research:* Design, fine arts, photography, acting, directing, theatre technology. *Unit head:* Arne R. Flaten, Head of the Graduate Program, 765-494-3056, E-mail: aflaten@purdue.edu. *Application contact:* Sara J. Unser, Graduate Contact, 765-494-8662, E-mail: sunser@purdue.edu.
Website: https://www.cla.purdue.edu/vpa/ad/

Queens College of the City University of New York, Division of Education, Department of Secondary Education and Youth Services, Queens, NY 11367-1597. Offers adolescent biology (MAT); art (MS Ed); biology (MS Ed, AC); chemistry (MS Ed, AC); earth sciences (MS Ed, AC); English (MS Ed, AC); French (MS Ed); Italian (MS Ed, AC); literacy education (MS Ed); mathematics (MS Ed, AC); music (MS Ed, AC); physics (MS Ed, AC); social studies (MS Ed, AC); Spanish (MS Ed, AC). *Program availability:* Part-time, evening/weekend. *Faculty:* 22 full-time (14 women), 35 part-time/adjunct (24 women). *Students:* 33 full-time (19 women), 358 part-time (228 women); includes 182 minority (15 Black or African American, non-Hispanic/Latino; 62 Asian, non-Hispanic/Latino; 91 Hispanic/Latino; 4 Native Hawaiian or other Pacific Islander, non-Hispanic/Latino; 10 Two or more races, non-Hispanic/Latino), 13 international. Average age 29. 216 applicants, 74% accepted, 109 enrolled. In 2018, 108 master's, 35 other advanced degrees awarded. *Degree requirements:* For master's, research project. *Entrance requirements:* For master's, GRE, minimum GPA of 3.0. Additional exam requirements/recommendations for international students: Required—TOEFL, IELTS. *Application deadline:* For fall admission, 4/1 for domestic students; for spring admission, 11/1 for domestic students. Applications are processed on a rolling basis. Application fee: $125. Electronic applications accepted. *Financial support:* Career-related internships or fieldwork available. Financial award application deadline: 4/1; financial award applicants required to submit FAFSA. *Faculty research:* Self regulated learning, teacher learning, assessment and teaching, language diversity, teaching and learning history. *Unit head:* Dr. Eleanor Armour-Thomas, Chairperson, 718-997-5150, E-mail: eleanor.armour-thomas@qc.cuny.edu. *Application contact:* Elizabeth D'Amico-Ramirez, Assistant Director of Graduate Admissions, 718-997-5203, E-mail: elizabeth.damicoramirez@qc.cuny.edu.

Rhode Island College, School of Graduate Studies, Faculty of Arts and Sciences, Department of Art, Providence, RI 02908-1991. Offers art education (MA, MAT); media studies (MA). *Accreditation:* NASAD (one or more programs are accredited). *Program*

availability: Part-time, evening/weekend. *Faculty:* 5 full-time (3 women), 2 part-time/adjunct (0 women). *Students:* 6 part-time (4 women). Average age 41. In 2018, 1 master's awarded. *Degree requirements:* For master's, thesis. *Entrance requirements:* For master's, GRE General Test, portfolio (MA), 3 letters of recommendation, interview. Additional exam requirements/recommendations for international students: Required—TOEFL (minimum score 550 paper-based; 80 iBT). *Application deadline:* For fall admission, 3/1 for domestic students. Applications are processed on a rolling basis. Application fee: $50. Electronic applications accepted. *Expenses: Tuition, area resident:* Part-time $407 per credit. Tuition, nonresident: part-time $792 per credit. *Required fees:* $29 per credit. $100 per semester. *Financial support:* Teaching assistantships, career-related internships or fieldwork, Federal Work-Study, scholarships/grants, health care benefits, and unspecified assistantships available. Support available to part-time students. Financial award application deadline: 5/15; financial award applicants required to submit FAFSA. *Unit head:* Prof. Douglas Bosch, Chair, 401-456-8054. *Application contact:* Prof. Douglas Bosch, Chair, 401-456-8054.
Website: http://www.ric.edu/art/Pages/M.A.T.-in-Art-Education.aspx

Rhode Island School of Design, Department of Teaching and Learning in Art and Design, Providence, RI 02903-2784. Offers art education (MAT). *Accreditation:* NASAD. *Students:* 11 full-time (all women); includes 3 minority (2 Asian, non-Hispanic/Latino; 1 Hispanic/Latino), 4 international. Average age 25. 26 applicants, 69% accepted, 11 enrolled. In 2018, 21 master's awarded. *Degree requirements:* For master's, thesis, exhibition. *Entrance requirements:* For master's, portfolio, statement of purpose, 3 letters of recommendation. Additional exam requirements/recommendations for international students: Required—TOEFL (minimum score 580 paper-based; 93 iBT), IELTS (minimum score 6.5), Duolingo. *Application deadline:* For fall admission, 1/10 for domestic and international students. Application fee: $60. Electronic applications accepted. *Expenses: Tuition:* Full-time $49,900. *Required fees:* $1060. *Financial support:* Fellowships, research assistantships, teaching assistantships, Federal Work-Study, scholarships/grants, and unspecified assistantships available. Financial award application deadline: 2/1; financial award applicants required to submit FAFSA. *Unit head:* Paul Sproll, Department Head and Graduate Program Director, 401-454-6695, Fax: 401-454-6694, E-mail: teachlearn@risd.edu. *Application contact:* Molly Pettengill, Associate Director for Graduate Recruitment, 401-454-6312, Fax: 401-454-6309, E-mail: mpetteng@risd.edu.
Website: http://www.risd.edu/academics/tlad/

Rochester Institute of Technology, Graduate Enrollment Services, College of Imaging Arts and Sciences, School of Art, MST Program in Visual Arts-All Grades, Rochester, NY 14623-5603. Offers MST. *Accreditation:* NASAD; TEAC. *Students:* 6 full-time (5 women); includes 1 minority (Two or more races, non-Hispanic/Latino). Average age 29. 12 applicants, 92% accepted, 6 enrolled. In 2018, 10 master's awarded. *Entrance requirements:* For master's, portfolio and artist's statement, resume, personal statement. Additional exam requirements/recommendations for international students: Required—TOEFL (minimum score 550 paper-based; 79 iBT), IELTS (minimum score 6.5), PTE (minimum score 58). *Application deadline:* For fall admission, 2/15 priority date for domestic and international students. Applications are processed on a rolling basis. Application fee: $65. Electronic applications accepted. *Expenses:* Contact institution. *Financial support:* In 2018–19, 10 students received support. Scholarships/grants and unspecified assistantships available. Financial award applicants required to submit FAFSA. *Faculty research:* Innovation and creativity in teaching and learning. *Unit head:* Lauren Ramich, Graduate Program Director, 585-475-7140, E-mail: larfaa@rit.edu. *Application contact:* Diane Ellison, Senior Associate Vice President, Graduate Enrollment Services, 585-475-2229, Fax: 585-475-7164, E-mail: gradinfo@rit.edu.
Website: https://www.rit.edu/study/visual-arts-all-grades-art-education-mst

Rocky Mountain College of Art + Design, Program in Education, Leadership + Emerging Technologies, Lakewood, CO 80214. Offers MA. *Accreditation:* NASAD. *Program availability:* Online learning.

Saint Michael's College, Graduate Programs, Program in Education, Colchester, VT 05439. Offers arts in education (CAGS); literacy (M Ed); school leadership (CAGS); special education (M Ed). *Program availability:* Part-time, evening/weekend. *Degree requirements:* For master's, thesis. *Entrance requirements:* For master's, minimum GPA of 3.0, official transcripts, essay, interview. Electronic applications accepted. *Expenses: Tuition:* Part-time $590 per credit. *Faculty research:* Integrative curriculum, moral and spiritual dimensions of education, learning styles, multiple intelligences, integrating technology into the curriculum.

Salem College, Graduate Studies, Winston-Salem, NC 27101. Offers art education (MAT); elementary education (M Ed, MAT); language and literacy (M Ed); middle school education (MAT); organ (MM); piano (MM); school counseling (M Ed); second language studies (MAT); secondary education (MAT); special education (M Ed, MAT). *Accreditation:* NCATE. *Program availability:* Part-time, evening/weekend, online learning. *Degree requirements:* For master's, practicum (MAT), action research project (M Ed). *Entrance requirements:* For master's, minimum GPA of 3.0, two academic/professional recommendations, acceptable criminal background check. Additional exam requirements/recommendations for international students: Recommended—TOEFL. Electronic applications accepted. *Faculty research:* Teacher professional development, adolescent literacy, instructional technology.

Salem State University, School of Graduate Studies, Program in Art, Salem, MA 01970-5353. Offers MAT. *Accreditation:* NASAD. *Program availability:* Part-time, evening/weekend. *Entrance requirements:* For master's, GRE or MAT. Additional exam requirements/recommendations for international students: Required—TOEFL (minimum score 550 paper-based; 80 iBT) or IELTS (minimum score 5.5).

School of Visual Arts, Graduate Programs, Art Education Department, New York, NY 10011. Offers MAT. *Program availability:* Part-time. *Degree requirements:* For master's, thesis, 60 credits; minimum cumulative GPA of 3.0; residency of two academic years. *Entrance requirements:* For master's, Liberal Arts and Sciences Test (strongly recommended), CD with 15 to 20 images (jpeg or tiff formats, and at least 600x500 pixels); 30 credits each in studio art and liberal arts and sciences; 12 credits in art history; coursework in language other than English; personal interview. Additional exam requirements/recommendations for international students: Required—TOEFL (minimum score 550 paper-based; 79 iBT). Electronic applications accepted. *Faculty research:* Teaching art to children in pre-kindergarten through grade 12.

Simon Fraser University, Office of Graduate Studies and Postdoctoral Fellows, Faculty of Education, Program in Arts Education, Burnaby, BC V5A 1S6, Canada. Offers M Ed, MA, Ed D, PhD. *Program availability:* Part-time, evening/weekend. *Degree requirements:* For master's, comprehensive exam (for some programs), thesis (for some programs); for doctorate, comprehensive exam (for some programs), thesis/dissertation (for some programs). *Entrance requirements:* For master's, minimum GPA of 3.0 (on scale of 4.33) or 3.33 based on last 60 credits of undergraduate courses; for doctorate, minimum GPA of 3.5 (on scale of 4.33). Additional exam requirements/recommendations for international students: Recommended—TOEFL (minimum score 580 paper-based; 93 iBT), IELTS (minimum score 7), TWE (minimum score 5). *Faculty research:* Drama education, poetic and performative inquiry, the integration of the arts in education, art therapy, arts-based narrative and arts-informed research methodologies.

Southern Connecticut State University, School of Graduate Studies, School of Arts and Sciences, Department of Art, New Haven, CT 06515-1355. Offers art education (MS). *Program availability:* Part-time, evening/weekend. *Degree requirements:* For master's, thesis or alternative. *Entrance requirements:* For master's, interview. Electronic applications accepted.

Southwestern Oklahoma State University, College of Arts and Sciences, Department of Art, Communication and Theatre, Weatherford, OK 73096-3098. Offers art education (M Ed). *Program availability:* Part-time. *Degree requirements:* For master's, exam. *Entrance requirements:* For master's, GRE General Test or minimum undergraduate GPA of 3.0. Additional exam requirements/recommendations for international students: Required—TOEFL (minimum score 550 paper-based), IELTS (minimum score 6.5).

Spalding University, Graduate Studies, College of Education, Programs in Education, Louisville, KY 40203-2188. Offers art teacher education (MAT); business teacher education (MAT); elementary school education (MAT); foreign language (MAT); high school education (MAT); middle school education (MAT); secondary education (MAT); special education (learning and behavioral disorders) (MAT); student guidance counselor (MA); teacher leader (M Ed). *Accreditation:* NCATE. *Program availability:* Part-time, evening/weekend. *Entrance requirements:* For master's, GRE General Test or MAT, interview, letters of recommendation, resume. Additional exam requirements/recommendations for international students: Required—TOEFL (minimum score 535 paper-based). Electronic applications accepted. *Faculty research:* Instructional technology, achievement gap, classroom management, assessment.

State University of New York at Oswego, Graduate Studies, School of Education, Department of Curriculum and Instruction, Oswego, NY 13126. Offers adolescence education (MST); art education (MAT); childhood education (MST); curriculum and instruction (MS Ed); literacy education (MS Ed); special education (MS Ed). *Program availability:* Part-time, evening/weekend. *Degree requirements:* For master's, comprehensive exam (for some programs), thesis optional. *Entrance requirements:* For master's, GRE General Test, minimum GPA of 2.7, provisional teaching certificate. Additional exam requirements/recommendations for international students: Required—TOEFL (minimum score 560 paper-based). *Faculty research:* Classroom applications for microcomputers; classroom questioning, wait-time, and achievement; values clarification and academic achievement.

Stephen F. Austin State University, Graduate School, College of Fine Arts, School of Art, Nacogdoches, TX 75962. Offers art (MA); art education (MAAE); design (MFA); drawing (MFA); filmmaking (MFA); painting (MFA); sculpture (MFA). *Accreditation:* NASAD. *Program availability:* Part-time. *Degree requirements:* For master's, comprehensive exam, thesis, exhibit. *Entrance requirements:* For master's, GRE General Test, portfolio. Additional exam requirements/recommendations for international students: Required—TOEFL. *Faculty research:* Printmaking, jewelry, photography, ceramics, art history.

Sul Ross State University, College of Arts and Sciences, Department of Fine Arts and Communication, Alpine, TX 79832. Offers art history (MA); studio art (MA), including art education. *Program availability:* Part-time. *Degree requirements:* For master's, oral or written exam. *Entrance requirements:* For master's, GRE General Test, minimum GPA of 2.5 in last 60 hours of undergraduate work. *Faculty research:* Ceramic sculpture, watercolor, wood sculpture, rock art.

Syracuse University, School of Education, MS Program in Art Education, Syracuse, NY 13244. Offers MS. *Program availability:* Part-time. *Entrance requirements:* For master's, GRE, strong teacher and/or employer recommendations, portfolio review. Additional exam requirements/recommendations for international students: Required—TOEFL (minimum score 100 iBT). *Application deadline:* For fall admission, 1/15 for domestic and international students. Application fee: $75 ($0 for international students). Electronic applications accepted. *Financial support:* Fellowships with full tuition reimbursements, research assistantships, teaching assistantships, career-related internships or fieldwork, and scholarships/grants available. Financial award application deadline: 1/15. *Faculty research:* Art educational practice, arts and design practices as a means for personal agency and social responsibility, developing art and design curricula for teaching and learning in multiple contexts, interdisciplinary research promoting creative leadership and entrepreneurship. *Unit head:* Dr. James Haywood Rolling, Jr., Director, 315-443-2355, E-mail: jrolling@syr.edu. *Application contact:* Speranza Migliore, Graduate Admissions Recruiter, 315-443-2505, E-mail: gradrcrt@syr.edu.
Website: http://soe.syr.edu/academic/teaching_and_leadership/graduate/masters/art_education/preparation/default.aspx

Teachers College, Columbia University, Department of Arts and Humanities, New York, NY 10027. Offers applied linguistics (MA, Ed D); art and art education (Ed M, MA, Ed D, Ed DCT); arts administration (MA); bilingual and bicultural education (MA); global competence (Certificate); history and education (Ed D, PhD); music and music education (Ed DCT); philosophy and education (MA, Ed D, PhD); social studies education (Ed M, PhD); teaching English to speakers of other languages (Ed M); teaching of English and English education (Ed M, MA, Ed D, PhD), including English education (Ed M, Ed D, PhD), teaching of English (MA); teaching of social studies (MA); TESOL (MA, Ed D). *Program availability:* Part-time, evening/weekend. *Students:* 267 full-time (216 women), 569 part-time (400 women); includes 235 minority (62 Black or African American, non-Hispanic/Latino; 2 American Indian or Alaska Native, non-Hispanic/Latino; 88 Asian, non-Hispanic/Latino; 69 Hispanic/Latino; 14 Two or more races, non-Hispanic/Latino), 229 international. Average age 31. 1,075 applicants, 56% accepted, 342 enrolled. Terminal master's awarded for partial completion of doctoral program. *Financial support:* Fellowships, research assistantships, teaching assistantships, career-related internships or fieldwork, Federal Work-Study, institutionally sponsored loans, tuition waivers (full and partial), and unspecified assistantships available. Support available to part-time students. *Unit head:* Prof. ZhaoHong Han, Department Chair, E-mail: zhh2@tc.columbia.edu. *Application contact:* Kelly Sutton-Skinner, Director of Admissions & New Student Enrollment, E-mail: kms2237@tc.columbia.edu.

Temple University, Tyler School of Art and Architecture, Department of Art Education and Community Arts Practices, Philadelphia, PA 19122-6096. Offers art education (Ed M). *Program availability:* Part-time. *Faculty:* 7 full-time (4 women), 7 part-time/adjunct (5 women). *Students:* 9 full-time (7 women), 9 part-time (7 women); includes 4 minority (1 Black or African American, non-Hispanic/Latino; 3 Hispanic/Latino). 8 applicants, 63% accepted, 3 enrolled. In 2018, 2 master's awarded. *Degree requirements:* For master's, thesis (for some programs), artwork review, internship (if seeking teaching certification). *Entrance requirements:* For master's, GRE or MAT, portfolio, 40 credits in studio art, 9 credits in art history, 3 letters of recommendation, statement of goals, resume. Additional exam requirements/recommendations for international students: Required—TOEFL (minimum score 79 iBT), IELTS (minimum score 6.5), PTE (minimum score 53), one of three is required. *Application deadline:* For fall admission, 1/6 for domestic students; for spring admission, 11/1 for domestic students. Application fee: $60. Electronic applications accepted. *Financial support:* Fellowships, teaching assistantships, Federal Work-Study, health care benefits, and unspecified assistantships available. Financial award applicants required to submit FAFSA. *Faculty research:* Intersections of art education and art therapy, game design

and game play as collaborative art forms and learning tools, integration of social justice video games in art classrooms to support 21st century learning, relations between the perceptual and the social as a political endeavor. *Unit head:* Lisa Kay, Chair, 215-777-9763, E-mail: lisakay@temple.edu. *Application contact:* Lauren O'Neill, Director of Admissions, 215-777-9159, E-mail: tyleradmissions@temple.edu.
Website: https://tyler.temple.edu/programs/art-education

Texas Tech University, Graduate School, J.T. and Margaret Talkington College of Visual and Performing Arts, School of Art, Lubbock, TX 79409-2081. Offers art (MFA); art education (MAE); art history (MA). *Accreditation:* NASAD (one or more programs are accredited). *Program availability:* Part-time, blended/hybrid learning. *Faculty:* 32 full-time (16 women), 5 part-time/adjunct (3 women). *Students:* 32 full-time (24 women), 14 part-time (12 women); includes 17 minority (1 Black or African American, non-Hispanic/Latino; 1 Asian, non-Hispanic/Latino; 13 Hispanic/Latino; 2 Two or more races, non-Hispanic/Latino), 1 international. Average age 34. 23 applicants, 65% accepted, 13 enrolled. In 2018, 12 master's awarded. *Degree requirements:* For master's, variable foreign language requirement, comprehensive exam, thesis (for some programs), Exhibition as Exam (for MFA). *Entrance requirements:* For master's, GRE (for MA). Additional exam requirements/recommendations for international students: Required—TOEFL (minimum score 550 paper-based; 79 iBT), IELTS (minimum score 6.5). *Application deadline:* For fall admission, 6/1 priority date for domestic students, 1/15 priority date for international students; for spring admission, 9/1 priority date for domestic students, 6/15 priority date for international students. Applications are processed on a rolling basis. Application fee: $65. Electronic applications accepted. *Expenses:* Contact institution. *Financial support:* In 2018–19, 46 students received support, including 45 fellowships (averaging $4,252 per year), 31 teaching assistantships (averaging $9,584 per year); research assistantships, Federal Work-Study, institutionally sponsored loans, scholarships/grants, health care benefits, tuition waivers (partial), and unspecified assistantships also available. Financial award application deadline: 1/15; financial award applicants required to submit FAFSA. *Faculty research:* Contemporary Chicano/a art; Art in Medicine; Art and Food; Engineering and Art; Ecology, Environment and Art. *Total annual research expenditures:* $73,285. *Unit head:* Prof. Robin D. Germany, Interim Department Chairperson, 806-834-6440, E-mail: robin.d.germany@ttu.edu. *Application contact:* Linda Rumbelow, Academic Advisor, 806-742-3825 Ext. 222, E-mail: linda.rumbelow@ttu.edu.
Website: www.art.ttu.edu

Texas Woman's University, Graduate School, College of Arts and Sciences, School of the Arts, Department of Visual Arts, Denton, TX 76204. Offers art (MA, MAT, MFA), including art education (MA, MAT), art history (MA), ceramics (MFA), graphic design (MA), intermedia (MFA), painting (MFA), photography (MFA), sculpture (MFA). MFA degrees are granted through the Federation of North Texas Area Universities (The University of North Texas, Texas A&M Commerce, and Texas Woman's University). *Faculty:* 6 full-time (4 women). *Students:* 13 full-time (10 women), 9 part-time (7 women); includes 12 minority (1 American Indian or Alaska Native, non-Hispanic/Latino; 1 Asian, non-Hispanic/Latino; 8 Hispanic/Latino; 2 Two or more races, non-Hispanic/Latino). Average age 37. 22 applicants, 45% accepted, 9 enrolled. In 2018, 5 master's awarded. *Degree requirements:* For master's, comprehensive exam, thesis (for some programs), exhibit (MFA), oral exam, thesis or professional paper (MA). *Entrance requirements:* For master's, portfolio, interview, current curriculum vitae, letter of intent, 3 letters of recommendation, artist statement, 2 research papers (for art history or art education). Additional exam requirements/recommendations for international students: Required—TOEFL (minimum score 550 paper-based; 79 iBT); Recommended—IELTS (minimum score 6.5), TSE (minimum score 53). *Application deadline:* For fall admission, 2/15 for domestic and international students; for spring admission, 11/15 for domestic and international students. Application fee: $50 ($75 for international students). Electronic applications accepted. *Expenses:* Contact institution. *Financial support:* In 2018–19, 12 students received support, including 10 teaching assistantships (averaging $4,988 per year); career-related internships or fieldwork, Federal Work-Study, institutionally sponsored loans, scholarships/grants, traineeships, health care benefits, and unspecified assistantships also available. Support available to part-time students. Financial award application deadline: 3/1; financial award applicants required to submit FAFSA. *Faculty research:* Art education and electronic technology,one-of-a kind art books, new media. *Unit head:* Dr. Vagner Whitehead, Chair, 940-898-2530, Fax: 940-898-2496, E-mail: visualarts@twu.edu. *Application contact:* Korie Hawkins, Associate Director of Admissions, Graduate Recruitment, 940-898-3188, Fax: 940-898-3081, E-mail: admissions@twu.edu.
Website: http://www.twu.edu/visual-arts/

Towson University, College of Fine Arts and Communication, Program in Art Education, Towson, MD 21252-0001. Offers M Ed. *Accreditation:* NCATE. *Program availability:* Part-time, evening/weekend. *Degree requirements:* For master's, thesis optional. *Entrance requirements:* For master's, bachelor's degree and/or certification in art education, minimum GPA of 3.0, resume. Electronic applications accepted. *Expenses: Tuition, area resident:* Full-time $9196; part-time $418 per unit. Tuition, state resident: full-time $9196; part-time $418 per unit. Tuition, nonresident: full-time $19,030; part-time $865 per unit. *International tuition:* $19,030 full-time. *Required fees:* $3102; $141 per year. $423 per term. Tuition and fees vary according to campus/location and program.

Towson University, College of Fine Arts and Communication, Program in Arts Integration, Towson, MD 21252-0001. Offers Postbaccalaureate Certificate. Program offered jointly with Johns Hopkins University, University of Maryland, College Park and University of Maryland, Baltimore County. *Entrance requirements:* For degree, bachelor's degree, minimum GPA of 3.0 (based upon last 60 credits of study); teaching experience (preferred). Electronic applications accepted. *Expenses: Tuition, area resident:* Full-time $9196; part-time $418 per unit. Tuition, state resident: full-time $9196; part-time $418 per unit. Tuition, nonresident: full-time $19,030; part-time $865 per unit. *International tuition:* $19,030 full-time. *Required fees:* $3102; $141 per year. $423 per term. Tuition and fees vary according to campus/location and program.

Towson University, College of Fine Arts and Communication, Program in Interdisciplinary Arts Infusion, Towson, MD 21252-0001. Offers MA. Electronic applications accepted. *Expenses: Tuition, area resident:* Full-time $9196; part-time $418 per unit. Tuition, state resident: full-time $9196; part-time $418 per unit. Tuition, nonresident: full-time $19,030; part-time $865 per unit. *International tuition:* $19,030 full-time. *Required fees:* $3102; $141 per year. $423 per term. Tuition and fees vary according to campus/location and program.

Tufts University, Graduate School of Arts and Sciences, Department of Education, Medford, MA 02155. Offers art education (MAT); education (MA, MAT, MS, PhD), including educational studies (MA), elementary education (MAT), middle and secondary education (MAT), museum education (MA), secondary education (MA), STEM education (MS, PhD); school psychology (MA, Ed S). *Program availability:* Part-time. *Degree requirements:* For master's, thesis optional; for doctorate, thesis/dissertation. *Entrance requirements:* For master's and doctorate, GRE General Test. Additional exam requirements/recommendations for international students: Required—TOEFL (minimum score 550 paper-based; 80 iBT), IELTS (minimum score 6.5). Electronic applications accepted. *Expenses:* Contact institution.

Tufts University, School of the Museum of Fine Arts at Tufts University, Boston, MA 02115. Offers art education (MAT); studio art (MFA, Postbaccalaureate Certificate), including museum studies (MFA). Terminal master's awarded for partial completion of doctoral program. *Degree requirements:* For master's, thesis, thesis exhibition. *Entrance requirements:* For master's, BFA (preferred) or bachelor's degree or equivalent in related area; portfolio; for Postbaccalaureate Certificate, portfolio, BFA or equivalent. Additional exam requirements/recommendations for international students: Required—TOEFL (minimum score 85 iBT), IELTS (minimum score 6.5). Electronic applications accepted. *Expenses:* Contact institution. *Faculty research:* Public art commissions, National Endowment for the Arts grant recipients, international group and solo exhibitions.

The University of Akron, Graduate School, College of Education, Department of Curricular and Instructional Studies, Program in P-12 Multi-Age Education, Akron, OH 44325. Offers art education (MS); drama/theatre (MS). *Entrance requirements:* Additional exam requirements/recommendations for international students: Required—TOEFL (minimum score 79 iBT), IELTS (minimum score 6.5).

The University of Alabama at Birmingham, School of Education, Program in Arts Education, Birmingham, AL 35294. Offers MA Ed. *Accreditation:* NCATE. *Program availability:* Part-time. *Degree requirements:* For master's, thesis optional. *Entrance requirements:* For master's, MAT (minimum score 388 scaled, 35 raw) or GRE (minimum score 385). Electronic applications accepted. *Expenses: Tuition, area resident:* Full-time $8100; part-time $8100 per year. Tuition, state resident: full-time $8100. Tuition, nonresident: full-time $19,188; part-time $19,188 per year. Tuition and fees vary according to program.

The University of Arizona, College of Fine Arts, School of Art, Program in Art Education, Tucson, AZ 85721. Offers MA. *Accreditation:* NASAD. *Degree requirements:* For master's, thesis. *Entrance requirements:* For master's, portfolio, resume, autobiography, 3 letters of reference, writing sample. Additional exam requirements/recommendations for international students: Required—TOEFL (minimum score 550 paper-based; 79 iBT). Electronic applications accepted. *Faculty research:* Artistic styles, visual perception, integration of arts into elementary curricula, aesthetics of the vanishing roadsides of America.

The University of Arizona, College of Fine Arts, School of Art, Program in Art History and Education, Tucson, AZ 85721. Offers PhD. *Degree requirements:* For doctorate, thesis/dissertation. *Entrance requirements:* Additional exam requirements/recommendations for international students: Required—TOEFL (minimum score 550 paper-based; 79 iBT). Electronic applications accepted.

University of Arkansas at Little Rock, Graduate School, College of Arts, Letters, and Sciences, Department of Art, Little Rock, AR 72204-1099. Offers art education (MA); art history (MA); studio art (MA). *Accreditation:* NASAD. *Program availability:* Part-time. *Degree requirements:* For master's, 4 foreign languages, oral exam, oral defense of thesis or exhibit. *Entrance requirements:* For master's, portfolio review or term paper evaluation, minimum GPA of 2.7.

The University of British Columbia, Faculty of Education, Department of Curriculum and Pedagogy, Vancouver, BC V6T 1Z4, Canada. Offers art education (M Ed, MA); curriculum studies (M Ed, MA, PhD); home economics education (M Ed, MA); mathematics education (M Ed, MA); media and technology studies education (M Ed, MA); music education (M Ed, MA); physical education (M Ed, MA); science education (M Ed, MA); social studies education (M Ed, MA). *Program availability:* Part-time, online learning. *Degree requirements:* For master's, thesis (MA); for doctorate, comprehensive exam, thesis/dissertation. *Entrance requirements:* Additional exam requirements/recommendations for international students: Required—TOEFL, IELTS. Electronic applications accepted. *Expenses:* Contact institution. *Faculty research:* School subjects, teaching and learning.

University of Central Florida, College of Community Innovation and Education, School of Teacher Education, Orlando, FL 32816. Offers applied learning and instruction (MA); curriculum and instruction (M Ed); elementary education (M Ed, MA); exceptional student education (M Ed, MA, Certificate), including autism spectrum disorders (Certificate), exceptional student education (M Ed), exceptional student education K-12 (MA), intervention specialist (Certificate), pre-kindergarten disabilities (Certificate), severe or profound disabilities (Certificate), special education (Certificate); K-8 mathematics and science education (M Ed, Certificate); reading education (M Ed, Certificate); teacher education (MAT), including art education, English language, mathematics education, middle school mathematics, middle school science, science education, social science education; world languages education - English for speakers of other languages (ESOL) (Certificate); world languages education - languages other than English (LOTE) (Certificate). *Program availability:* Part-time, evening/weekend. *Degree requirements:* For Certificate, thesis or alternative. *Entrance requirements:* For degree, GRE General Test, minimum GPA of 3.0. Additional exam requirements/recommendations for international students: Required—TOEFL. Electronic applications accepted.

University of Cincinnati, Graduate School, College of Design, Architecture, Art, and Planning, School of Art, Program in Art Education, Cincinnati, OH 45221. Offers MA. *Accreditation:* NASAD; NCATE. *Entrance requirements:* For master's, MAT. Electronic applications accepted.

University of Denver, University College, Denver, CO 80208. Offers arts and culture (MA, Certificate); communication management (MS, Certificate), including translation studies (Certificate), world history and culture (Certificate); environmental policy and management (MS); geographic information systems (MS); global affairs (MA, Certificate), including human capital in organizations (Certificate), philanthropic leadership (Certificate), project management (Certificate), strategic innovation and change (Certificate); healthcare leadership (MS); information communications and technology (MS); leadership and organizations (MS); professional creative writing (MA, Certificate), including emergency planning and response (Certificate), organizational security (Certificate); security management (MS, Certificate); strategic human resources (Certificate). *Program availability:* Part-time, evening/weekend, 100% online, blended/hybrid learning. *Faculty:* 4 full-time (2 women), 108 part-time/adjunct (51 women). *Students:* 51 full-time (26 women), 1,291 part-time (733 women); includes 337 minority (112 Black or African American, non-Hispanic/Latino; 6 American Indian or Alaska Native, non-Hispanic/Latino; 46 Asian, non-Hispanic/Latino; 132 Hispanic/Latino; 3 Native Hawaiian or other Pacific Islander, non-Hispanic/Latino; 38 Two or more races, non-Hispanic/Latino), 75 international. Average age 34. 834 applicants, 87% accepted, 423 enrolled. In 2018, 443 master's, 232 other advanced degrees awarded. *Degree requirements:* For master's, capstone project. *Entrance requirements:* For master's, baccalaureate degree, transcripts, two letters of recommendation, personal statement, resume, writing sample (Master of Arts in Professional Creative Writing). Additional exam requirements/recommendations for international students: Required—TOEFL (minimum score 550 paper-based; 80 iBT). *Application deadline:* For fall admission, 6/19 priority date for domestic students, 6/14 priority date for international students; for winter admission, 10/25 priority date for domestic students, 9/27 priority date for international students; for spring admission, 2/7 priority date for domestic students, 1/10 priority date for international students; for summer admission, 4/24 priority date for domestic

students, 3/27 priority date for international students. Applications are processed on a rolling basis. Application fee: $75. Electronic applications accepted. *Expenses:* $8,280 per year half-time. *Financial support:* In 2018–19, 38 students received support. Teaching assistantships available. Financial award applicants required to submit FAFSA. *Unit head:* Dr. Michael McGuire, Dean, 303-871-3518, E-mail: michael.mcguire@du.edu. *Application contact:* Admission Team, 303-871-2291, E-mail: ucoladm@du.edu.
Website: http://universitycollege.du.edu/

University of Florida, Graduate School, College of The Arts, School of Art and Art History, Gainesville, FL 32611. Offers art (MA), including digital arts and sciences; art education (MA); art history (MA, PhD); museology (MA), including historic preservation. *Accreditation:* NASAD. *Program availability:* Online learning. *Degree requirements:* For master's, project or thesis (MFA); 1 foreign language (MA in art history); for doctorate, 2 foreign languages, comprehensive exam, thesis/dissertation. *Entrance requirements:* For master's, GRE General Test, portfolio (MFA), writing sample (MA), minimum GPA 3.0; for doctorate, GRE General Test, minimum GPA of 3.0. Additional exam requirements/recommendations for international students: Required—TOEFL (minimum score 550 paper-based; 80 iBT), IELTS (minimum score 6). Electronic applications accepted. *Faculty research:* Studio production, art historical studies of style context.

University of Illinois at Urbana–Champaign, Graduate College, College of Fine and Applied Arts, School of Art and Design, Program in Art Education, Champaign, IL 61820. Offers Ed M, MA, PhD. *Accreditation:* NASAD.

University of Indianapolis, Graduate Programs, School of Education, Indianapolis, IN 46227-3697. Offers art education (MAT); biology (MAT); chemistry (MAT); curriculum and instruction (MA); earth sciences (MAT); education (MA, MAT); educational leadership (MA); elementary education (MA); English (MAT); French (MAT); math (MAT); physical education (MAT); physics (MAT); secondary education (MA), including art education, education, English education, social studies education; social studies (MAT); Spanish (MAT). *Accreditation:* NCATE. *Program availability:* Part-time, evening/weekend. *Entrance requirements:* For master's, GRE Subject Test, PRAXIS I, minimum GPA of 2.5, 3 letters of recommendation, interview. Additional exam requirements/recommendations for international students: Required—TOEFL (minimum score 550 paper-based). *Faculty research:* Assessment of teacher education, perceptions of prospective teachers by parents.

The University of Iowa, Graduate College, College of Education, Department of Teaching and Learning, Program in Education, Iowa City, IA 52242-1316. Offers art education (MA); developmental reading (MA); elementary education (MA); English education (MA, MAT); foreign and second language education (MAT); foreign language education (MA); foreign language/ESL education (PhD); language, literacy and culture (PhD); mathematics education (MA, MAT, PhD); music education (MM, PhD); science education (MA); secondary education (MA); social studies (MA, PhD). *Degree requirements:* For master's, thesis optional, exam; for doctorate, comprehensive exam, thesis/dissertation. *Entrance requirements:* For master's and doctorate, GRE General Test, minimum GPA of 3.0. Additional exam requirements/recommendations for international students: Required—TOEFL (minimum score 550 paper-based; 81 iBT). Electronic applications accepted.

The University of Kansas, Graduate Studies, College of Liberal Arts and Sciences, Department of Visual Art, Program in Visual Art Education, Lawrence, KS 66045. Offers MA. *Program availability:* Part-time. *Students:* 2 full-time (both women). Average age 25. 4 applicants, 75% accepted, 1 enrolled. In 2018, 1 master's awarded. *Entrance requirements:* For master's, portfolio, 3 letters of recommendation, minimum GPA of 3.0. Additional exam requirements/recommendations for international students: Required—TOEFL, IELTS, TOEFL (minimum score 570 paper-based) or IELTS (minimum score 6.5). *Application deadline:* For fall admission, 5/1 for domestic and international students; for spring admission, 12/1 for domestic and international students. Application fee: $65 ($85 for international students). Electronic applications accepted. *Financial support:* Teaching assistantships, Federal Work-Study, scholarships/grants, and unspecified assistantships available. *Faculty research:* Emphasizing a balance of studio, art history, and education courses. *Unit head:* Marshall Maude, Associate Chair, E-mail: maude@ku.edu. *Application contact:* Julia Reilly, Graduate Admissions Contact, 785-864-9488, E-mail: juliareilly@ku.edu.
Website: http://art.ku.edu/programs/visual_art_education/

University of Kentucky, Graduate School, College of Fine Arts, Program in Art Education, Lexington, KY 40506-0032. Offers MA. *Degree requirements:* For master's, comprehensive exam, thesis optional. *Entrance requirements:* For master's, GRE General Test, minimum undergraduate GPA of 2.75. Additional exam requirements/recommendations for international students: Required—TOEFL (minimum score 550 paper-based). Electronic applications accepted. *Faculty research:* Multicultural art education, women's issues in art education, lifelong learning in the arts, the artist-teacher, art teaching as a form of art, place and art, children's home art and creativity as a basis for school art instruction.

University of Louisville, Graduate School, College of Education and Human Development, Departments of Early Childhood and Elementary Education, Middle and Secondary Education, and Special Education, Louisville, KY 40292-0001. Offers art education (MAT); autism and applied behavior analysis (Certificate); curriculum and instruction (PhD); early elementary education (MAT); exercise physiology (MS); health and physical education (MAT); health professions education (Certificate); higher education (MA); human resources and organization development (MS); instructional technology (M Ed); interdisciplinary early childhood education (MAT); middle school education (MAT); music education (MAT); secondary education (MAT); special education (MAT); sport administration (MS); teacher leadership (M Ed). *Program availability:* Part-time, evening/weekend, 100% online, blended/hybrid learning. *Faculty:* 97 full-time (64 women), 131 part-time/adjunct (86 women). *Students:* 109 full-time (72 women), 139 part-time (87 women); includes 43 minority (18 Black or African American, non-Hispanic/Latino; 6 Asian, non-Hispanic/Latino; 10 Hispanic/Latino; 9 Two or more races, non-Hispanic/Latino), 9 international. Average age 29. 108 applicants, 75% accepted, 59 enrolled. In 2018, 64 master's awarded. Terminal master's awarded for partial completion of doctoral program. *Degree requirements:* For master's, comprehensive exam (for some programs), thesis optional; for doctorate, comprehensive exam (for some programs), thesis/dissertation. *Entrance requirements:* For master's, GRE (for most programs), PRAXIS (for educator preparation programs), professional statement, recommendation letters, resume, transcripts; for doctorate and Certificate, GRE, professional statement, recommendation letters, resume, transcripts. Additional exam requirements/recommendations for international students: Required—TOEFL (minimum score 550 paper-based; 79 iBT); Recommended—IELTS (minimum score 6.5). *Application deadline:* For fall admission, 6/1 priority date for domestic students, 5/1 priority date for international students; for spring admission, 10/1 for domestic students, 11/1 priority date for international students; for summer admission, 3/1 priority date for domestic students, 4/1 priority date for international students. Application fee: $65. *Expenses: Tuition, area resident:* Full-time $6500; part-time $723 per credit hour. *Tuition, state resident:* full-time $6500. *Tuition, nonresident:* full-time $13,557; part-time $1507 per credit hour. Tuition and fees vary according to course load and program. *Financial support:* In 2018–19, 144 students received support, including

fellowships with full tuition reimbursements available (averaging $21,024 per year), research assistantships with full tuition reimbursements available (averaging $21,024 per year), teaching assistantships with full tuition reimbursements available (averaging $21,024 per year); Federal Work-Study, scholarships/grants, health care benefits, tuition waivers (full), and unspecified assistantships also available. Financial award application deadline: 3/1; financial award applicants required to submit FAFSA. *Faculty research:* Children's early reading and writing development, crelevance of basic facts in elementary mathematics instruction, clinical model of teacher education, cultural and linguistic context of diverse learners, and STEM-integrated curriculum design and development. STEM teaching and learning, content literacy for English language learners, social justice in teacher education, adolescent literacy, mathematics teacher development. Classroom and behavior management; moderate/severe disabilities, autism. *Unit head:* Dr. Amy Lingo, Interim Dean, 502-852-3235, Fax: 502-852-1464, E-mail: cehdinfo@louisville.edu. *Application contact:* Dr. Margaret Pentecost, Assistant Dean for Graduate Student Success, 502-852-6437, Fax: 502-852-1417, E-mail: gedadm@louisville.edu.
Website: http://louisville.edu/delphi

University of Maryland, Baltimore County, The Graduate School, College of Arts, Humanities and Social Sciences, Department of Education, Program in Teaching, Baltimore, MD 21250. Offers early childhood education (MAT); elementary education (MAT); teaching (MAT), including art, biology, chemistry, choral music, classical foreign language, dance, earth/space science, English, instrumental music, mathematics, modern foreign language, physical science, physics, social studies, theatre. *Program availability:* Part-time, evening/weekend. *Degree requirements:* For master's, comprehensive exam (for some programs), thesis (for some programs). *Entrance requirements:* For master's, PRAXIS Core Examination or GRE (minimum score of 1000), minimum GPA of 3.0. Additional exam requirements/recommendations for international students: Required—TOEFL. Electronic applications accepted. *Faculty research:* STEM teacher education, culturally sensitive pedagogy, ESOL/bilingual education, early childhood education, language, literacy and culture.

University of Massachusetts Amherst, Graduate School, College of Humanities and Fine Arts, Department of Art, Amherst, MA 01003. Offers art (MA, MFA), including art education (MA), studio art (MFA). *Program availability:* Part-time. *Degree requirements:* For master's, comprehensive exam (for some programs), thesis (for some programs). *Entrance requirements:* For master's, portfolio. Additional exam requirements/recommendations for international students: Required—TOEFL (minimum score 550 paper-based; 80 iBT), IELTS (minimum score 6.5). Electronic applications accepted.

University of Massachusetts Dartmouth, Graduate School, College of Visual and Performing Arts, Department of Art Education, Art History and Media Studies, North Dartmouth, MA 02747-2300. Offers MAE. *Accreditation:* NASAD. *Program availability:* Part-time. *Faculty:* 7 full-time (6 women), 2 part-time/adjunct (both women). *Students:* 2 full-time (both women), 25 part-time (19 women); includes 1 minority (Hispanic/Latino). Average age 32. 4 applicants, 100% accepted, 2 enrolled. In 2018, 3 master's awarded. *Degree requirements:* For master's, thesis. *Entrance requirements:* For master's, MTEL (per program description), statement of purpose (minimum of 300 words), resume, 2 letters of recommendation, official transcripts, portfolio (20 images representing applicant's original art work, process of thinking, implementation of concepts and studio production). Copy of MA Tests for Educator Licensure (MTEL). Additional exam requirements/recommendations for international students: Required—TOEFL (minimum score 550 paper-based; 79 iBT), IELTS (minimum score 6.5). *Application deadline:* For fall admission, 8/1 priority date for domestic students, 7/1 priority date for international students; for spring admission, 10/15 priority date for domestic students, 9/15 priority date for international students. Application fee: $60. Electronic applications accepted. *Financial support:* Application deadline: 3/1; applicants required to submit FAFSA. *Faculty research:* Contemporary art, design and architectural history, curatorial studies, film studies, theory of photography. *Unit head:* Cathy Smilan, Graduate Program Director, 508-910-6594, Fax: 508-999-8901, E-mail: csmilan@umassd.edu. *Application contact:* Scott Webster, Director of Graduate Studies, 508-999-8604, Fax: 508-999-8183, E-mail: graduate@umassd.edu.
Website: http://www.umassd.edu/cvpa/programs

University of Minnesota, Twin Cities Campus, Graduate School, College of Education and Human Development, Department of Curriculum and Instruction, Program in Teaching, Minneapolis, MN 55455-0213. Offers teaching (M Ed), including arts in education, elementary education, English education, mathematics, science, second language education, social studies. *Students:* 249 full-time (182 women), 101 part-time (59 women); includes 57 minority (5 Black or African American, non-Hispanic/Latino; 16 Asian, non-Hispanic/Latino; 25 Hispanic/Latino; 11 Two or more races, non-Hispanic/Latino), 12 international. Average age 28. 383 applicants, 79% accepted, 261 enrolled. In 2018, 292 master's awarded. Application fee: $75 ($95 for international students). *Unit head:* Dr. Mark Vagle, Chair, 612-625-4006, Fax: 612-624-8277, E-mail: mvagle@umn.edu. *Application contact:* Dr. Mark Vagle, Chair, 612-625-4006, Fax: 612-624-8277, E-mail: mvagle@umn.edu.
Website: http://www.cehd.umn.edu/ci/

University of Missouri, Office of Research and Graduate Studies, College of Education, Department of Learning, Teaching and Curriculum, Columbia, MO 65211. Offers agricultural education (M Ed, PhD, Ed S); art education (M Ed, PhD, Ed S); business and office education (M Ed, PhD, Ed S); early childhood education (M Ed, PhD, Ed S); elementary education (M Ed, PhD, Ed S); English education (M Ed, PhD, Ed S); foreign language education (M Ed, PhD, Ed S); health education and promotion (M Ed, PhD); learning and instruction (M Ed); marketing education (M Ed, PhD, Ed S); mathematics education (M Ed, PhD, Ed S); music education (M Ed, PhD, Ed S); reading education (M Ed, PhD, Ed S); science education (M Ed, PhD, Ed S); social studies education (M Ed, PhD, Ed S); vocational education (M Ed, PhD, Ed S). *Program availability:* Part-time. Terminal master's awarded for partial completion of doctoral program. *Entrance requirements:* For master's and Ed S, GRE General Test or MAT, minimum GPA of 3.0; for doctorate, GRE General Test, minimum GPA of 3.0. Additional exam requirements/recommendations for international students: Required—TOEFL.

University of Montana, Graduate School, College of Visual and Performing Arts, Creative Pulse: Master's in Integrated Arts and Education, Missoula, MT 59812. Offers MA. *Degree requirements:* For master's, field project.

University of Nebraska at Kearney, College of Fine Arts and Humanities, Department of Art and Design, Kearney, NE 68849-0001. Offers art education (MA Ed), including classroom education, museum education. *Accreditation:* NCATE. *Program availability:* Part-time, evening/weekend, 100% online. *Degree requirements:* For master's, comprehensive exam, thesis optional. *Entrance requirements:* For master's, two letters of recommendation, resume, statement of purpose, 24 undergraduate hours of art/art history/art education. Additional exam requirements/recommendations for international students: Recommended—TOEFL (minimum score 550 paper-based; 79 iBT), IELTS (minimum score 6.5). Electronic applications accepted. *Faculty research:* Fibers, art education, kiln design construction and low-fire glaze, relationship between environment and photography, digital arts, graphic design, three-dimensional design, atomic testing imagery.

Art Education

University of New Mexico, Graduate Studies, College of Education, Program in Art Education, Albuquerque, NM 87131-2039. Offers MA. *Accreditation:* NCATE. *Program availability:* Part-time, evening/weekend. *Students:* Average age 44. 8 applicants, 63% accepted, 4 enrolled. In 2018, 16 master's awarded. *Degree requirements:* For master's, comprehensive exam, thesis optional, participation in art exhibit. *Entrance requirements:* For master's, letter of intent, resume, 3 letters of recommendation, portfolio of 10 samples of art work. Additional exam requirements/recommendations for international students: Required—TOEFL. *Application deadline:* For fall admission, 3/30 for domestic and international students; for spring admission, 10/30 for domestic and international students. Application fee: $50. Electronic applications accepted. *Financial support:* Fellowships, research assistantships with full tuition reimbursements, teaching assistantships, Federal Work-Study, institutionally sponsored loans, scholarships/grants, and unspecified assistantships available. Financial award application deadline: 3/1; financial award applicants required to submit FAFSA. *Faculty research:* Studio in art education, visual culture, curricular issues regarding gender and sexual identity, archetypal thought in art education, teacher preparation. *Unit head:* Prof. Ruth Luckasson, Chair, 505-277-6510, Fax: 505-277-6929, E-mail: ruthl@unm.edu. *Application contact:* Katherine Vazquez, Information Contact, 505-277-4112, Fax: 505-277-0576, E-mail: arted@unm.edu.
Website: http://www.unm.edu/~arted

The University of North Carolina at Charlotte, Cato College of Education, Interdisciplinary Education Programs, Charlotte, NC 28223-0001. Offers art education (Graduate Certificate); child and family development: early childhood education (MAT); curriculum and instruction (PhD); elementary education (MAT); foreign language education (MAT); middle grades education (MAT); secondary education (MAT); special education (MAT); teaching (Graduate Certificate); teaching English as a second language (MAT); theatre education (Graduate Certificate). *Program availability:* Part-time, 100% online, blended/hybrid learning. *Students:* 70 full-time (55 women), 511 part-time (414 women); includes 228 minority (160 Black or African American, non-Hispanic/Latino; 1 American Indian or Alaska Native, non-Hispanic/Latino; 11 Asian, non-Hispanic/Latino; 38 Hispanic/Latino; 18 Two or more races, non-Hispanic/Latino), 8 international. Average age 34. 343 applicants, 92% accepted, 219 enrolled. In 2018, 69 master's, 13 doctorates, 161 other advanced degrees awarded. *Entrance requirements:* For master's, GRE or MAT, bachelor's degree, or its U.S. equivalent, from regionally-accredited college or university; minimum overall GPA of 3.0 on all previous work beyond high school; statement of purpose (essay); at least three recommendation forms; for doctorate, GRE or MAT, bachelor's degree (or its U.S. equivalent) from regionally-accredited college or university; minimum overall GPA of 3.5 in master's degree program; for Graduate Certificate, bachelor's degree from regionally-accredited university; minimum GPA of 2.75 on all post-secondary work attempted; transcripts; personal statement outlining why the applicant seeks admission to the program. Additional exam requirements/recommendations for international students: Required—TOEFL (minimum score 523 paper-based; 70 iBT), IELTS (minimum score 6), TOEFL (minimum score 523 paper-based, 70 iBT) or IELTS (6). *Application deadline:* Applications are processed on a rolling basis. Application fee: $75. Electronic applications accepted. Tuition and fees vary according to course load and program. *Financial support:* Career-related internships or fieldwork, institutionally sponsored loans, scholarships/grants, and unspecified assistantships available. Support available to part-time students. Financial award application deadline: 3/1; financial award applicants required to submit FAFSA. *Unit head:* Dr. Ellen McIntyre, Dean, 704-687-8722, E-mail: ellen.mcintyre@uncc.edu. *Application contact:* Kathy B. Giddings, Director of Graduate Admissions, 704-687-5503, Fax: 704-687-1668, E-mail: gradadm@uncc.edu.
Website: http://education.uncc.edu/academic-programs

The University of North Carolina at Pembroke, The Graduate School, Department of Art, Pembroke, NC 28372-1510. Offers art (MAT); art education (MA). *Program availability:* Part-time, evening/weekend. *Degree requirements:* For master's, comprehensive exam, capstone show. *Entrance requirements:* For master's, GRE or MAT, minimum GPA of 3.0 in major or 2.5 overall. Additional exam requirements/recommendations for international students: Required—TOEFL. *Expenses:* Contact institution.

University of Northern Colorado, Graduate School, College of Performing and Visual Arts, School of Art and Design, Greeley, CO 80639. Offers art education (MA); art history (MA); studio art (MA). *Accreditation:* NASAD. *Program availability:* Part-time. *Degree requirements:* For master's, comprehensive exam, thesis. *Entrance requirements:* For master's, GRE General Test, portfolio, 3 letters of recommendation, minimum undergraduate GPA of 3.0. Electronic applications accepted.

University of Northern Iowa, Graduate College, College of Humanities, Arts and Sciences, Department of Art, Cedar Falls, IA 50614. Offers art education (MA). *Program availability:* Part-time, evening/weekend. *Degree requirements:* For master's, comprehensive exam (for some programs), thesis or alternative. *Entrance requirements:* For master's, minimum GPA of 3.0, portfolio. Additional exam requirements/recommendations for international students: Required—TOEFL (minimum score 500 paper-based; 61 iBT). Electronic applications accepted.

University of North Texas, Toulouse Graduate School, Denton, TX 76203-5459. Offers accounting (MS); applied anthropology (MA, MS); applied behavior analysis (Certificate); applied geography (MA); applied technology and performance improvement (M Ed, MS); art education (MA); art history (MA); arts leadership (Certificate); audiology (Au D); behavior analysis (MS); behavioral science (PhD); biochemistry and molecular biology (MS); biology (MA, MS); biomedical engineering (MS); business analysis (MS); chemistry (MS); clinical health psychology (PhD); communication studies (MA, MS); computer engineering (MS); computer science (MS); counseling (M Ed, MS), including clinical mental health counseling (MS), college and university counseling, elementary school counseling, secondary school counseling; creative writing (MA); criminal justice (MS); curriculum and instruction (M Ed); decision sciences (MBA); design (MA, MFA), including fashion design (MFA), innovation studies, interior design (MFA); early childhood studies (MS); economics (MS); educational leadership (M Ed, Ed D); educational psychology (MS, PhD), including family studies (MS), gifted and talented (MS), human development (MS), learning and cognition (MS), research, measurement and evaluation (MS); electrical engineering (MS); emergency management (MPA); engineering technology (MS); English (MA); English as a second language (MA); environmental science (MS); finance (MBA, MS); financial management (MPA); French (MA); health services management (MBA); higher education (M Ed, Ed D); history (MA, MS); hospitality management (MS); human resources management (MPA); information science (MS); information systems (PhD); information technologies (MBA); interdisciplinary studies (MA, MS); international studies (MA); international sustainable tourism (MS); jazz studies (MM); journalism (MA, MJ, Graduate Certificate), including interactive and virtual digital communication (Graduate Certificate), narrative journalism (Graduate Certificate), public relations (Graduate Certificate); kinesiology (MS); linguistics (MA); local government management (MPA); logistics (PhD); logistics and supply chain management (MBA); long-term care, senior housing, and aging services (MA); management (PhD); marketing (MBA); mathematics (MA, MS); mechanical and energy engineering (MS, PhD); music (MA), including ethnomusicology,

music theory, musicology, performance; music composition (PhD); music education (MM Ed, PhD); nonprofit management (MPA); operations and supply chain management (MBA); performance (MM, DMA); philosophy (MA); political science (MA); professional and technical communication (MA); radio, television and film (MA, MFA); rehabilitation counseling (Certificate); sociology (MA); Spanish (MA); special education (M Ed); speech-language pathology (MA); strategic management (MBA); studio art (MFA); teaching (M Ed); MBA/MS. *Program availability:* Part-time, evening/weekend, online learning. Terminal master's awarded for partial completion of doctoral program. *Degree requirements:* For master's, variable foreign language requirement, comprehensive exam (for some programs), thesis (for some programs); for doctorate, variable foreign language requirement, comprehensive exam (for some programs), thesis/dissertation; for other advanced degree, variable foreign language requirement, comprehensive exam (for some programs). *Entrance requirements:* For master's and doctorate, GRE, GMAT. Additional exam requirements/recommendations for international students: Required—TOEFL (minimum score 550 paper-based; 79 iBT). Electronic applications accepted.

University of Rio Grande, Graduate School, Rio Grande, OH 45674. Offers athletic coaching leadership (M Ed); educational leadership (M Ed); integrated arts (M Ed); intervention specialist in early childhood (M Ed); intervention specialist in mild/moderate (M Ed). *Accreditation:* NCATE. *Program availability:* Part-time. *Degree requirements:* For master's, final research project, portfolio. *Entrance requirements:* For master's, minimum GPA of 2.7 in major, 2.5 overall. Additional exam requirements/recommendations for international students: Required—TOEFL. *Faculty research:* Interagency collaboration, reading and mathematics, learning styles, college access, literacy.

University of St. Francis, College of Education, Joliet, IL 60435-6169. Offers educational leadership (MS, Ed D); elementary education (M Ed); reading (MS); secondary education (M Ed), including English education, math education, science education, social studies education, visual arts education; special education (M Ed); teaching and learning (MS); TESOL (Certificate). *Accreditation:* NCATE. *Program availability:* Part-time, evening/weekend, 100% online, blended/hybrid learning. *Faculty:* 11 full-time (8 women), 58 part-time/adjunct (38 women). *Students:* 43 full-time (35 women), 453 part-time (354 women); includes 110 minority (48 Black or African American, non-Hispanic/Latino; 7 Asian, non-Hispanic/Latino; 52 Hispanic/Latino; 3 Two or more races, non-Hispanic/Latino), 3 international. Average age 37. 300 applicants, 66% accepted, 164 enrolled. In 2018, 151 master's, 42 doctorates, 4 other advanced degrees awarded. *Degree requirements:* For master's, comprehensive exam; for doctorate, thesis/dissertation. *Entrance requirements:* Additional exam requirements/recommendations for international students: Required—TOEFL (minimum score 550 paper-based; 79 iBT), IELTS (minimum score 6). *Application deadline:* Applications are processed on a rolling basis. Electronic applications accepted. Application fee is waived when completed online. *Expenses:* Contact institution. *Financial support:* In 2018–19, 33 students received support. Scholarships/grants and tuition waivers (partial) available. Support available to part-time students. Financial award applicants required to submit FAFSA. *Unit head:* Dr. John Gambro, Dean, 815-740-3456, E-mail: jgambro@stfrancis.edu. *Application contact:* Sandee Sloka, Director Adult & Graduate Admissions, 800-735-7500, E-mail: ssloka@stfrancis.edu.
Website: https://www.stfrancis.edu/education/

University of South Alabama, College of Education and Professional Studies, Department of Leadership and Teacher Education, Mobile, AL 36688. Offers art education (M Ed); early childhood education (M Ed); educational leadership (M Ed, Ed D); elementary education (M Ed); reading education (M Ed); science education (M Ed); secondary education (M Ed); special education (M Ed). *Accreditation:* NCATE. *Program availability:* Part-time. *Degree requirements:* For master's, comprehensive exam, thesis (for some programs); for doctorate, comprehensive exam, thesis/dissertation. *Entrance requirements:* For master's, GRE General Test or MAT, minimum GPA of 3.0; for doctorate, GRE, minimum graduate GPA of 3.25, 3 years of experience in field, 3 letters of recommendation, interview, official transcripts. Additional exam requirements/recommendations for international students: Required—TOEFL. Electronic applications accepted.

University of South Carolina, The Graduate School, College of Arts and Sciences, Department of Art, Program in Art Education, Columbia, SC 29208. Offers IMA, MA, MAT. IMA and MAT offered in cooperation with the College of Education. *Accreditation:* NCATE. *Degree requirements:* For master's, comprehensive exam, thesis (for some programs). *Entrance requirements:* For master's, GRE General Test or MAT, portfolio. Additional exam requirements/recommendations for international students: Required—TOEFL. Electronic applications accepted. *Faculty research:* Teaching art at the primary and secondary levels of education.

University of South Carolina, The Graduate School, College of Education, Department of Instruction and Teacher Education, Program in Secondary Education, Columbia, SC 29208. Offers art education (IMA, MAT); business education (IMA, MAT); English (MAT); foreign language (MAT); health education (MAT); mathematics (MAT); science (IMA, MAT); secondary (Ed D); secondary education (MT, PhD); social studies (MAT); theatre and speech (MAT). IMA and MT offered jointly with the subject areas. *Accreditation:* NCATE. *Degree requirements:* For master's, comprehensive exam, thesis (for some programs), foreign language (MA); for doctorate, one foreign language, comprehensive exam, thesis/dissertation. *Entrance requirements:* For master's, GRE General Test or MAT, teaching certificate (IMA, M Ed), interview; for doctorate, GRE General Test or MAT, interview. *Faculty research:* Middle school programs, professional development, school collaboration.

University of South Dakota, Graduate School, College of Fine Arts, Department of Art, Vermillion, SD 57069. Offers art education (MFA); ceramics (MFA); graphic design (MFA); painting (MFA); photography (MFA); printmaking (MFA); sculpture (MFA). *Accreditation:* NASAD. *Degree requirements:* For master's, thesis or alternative. *Entrance requirements:* For master's, portfolio, minimum GPA of 2.7. Additional exam requirements/recommendations for international students: Required—TOEFL (minimum score 550 paper-based; 79 iBT). Electronic applications accepted.

The University of Tennessee, Graduate School, College of Education, Health and Human Sciences, Program in Education, Knoxville, TN 37996. Offers art education (MS); counseling education (PhD); cultural studies in education (PhD); curriculum (MS, Ed S); curriculum, educational research and evaluation (Ed D, PhD); early childhood education (PhD); early childhood special education (MS); education of deaf and hard of hearing (MS); educational administration and policy studies (Ed D, PhD); educational administration and supervision (Ed S); educational psychology (Ed D, PhD); elementary education (MS, Ed S); elementary teaching (MS); English education (MS, Ed S); exercise science (PhD); foreign language/ESL education (MS, Ed S); instructional technology (MS, Ed D, PhD, Ed S); literacy, language and ESL education (PhD); literacy, language education, and ESL education (Ed D); mathematics education (MS, Ed S); modified and comprehensive special education (MS); reading education (MS, Ed S); school counseling (Ed S); school psychology (PhD, Ed S); science education (MS, Ed S); secondary teaching (MS); social foundations (MS); social science education (MS, Ed S); socio-cultural foundations of sports and education (PhD); special education (Ed S); teacher education (Ed D, PhD). *Accreditation:* NCATE. *Program availability:*

Part-time, evening/weekend. *Degree requirements:* For master's and Ed S, thesis optional; for doctorate, variable foreign language requirement, thesis/dissertation. *Entrance requirements:* For master's, minimum GPA of 2.7; for doctorate and Ed S, GRE General Test, minimum GPA of 2.7. Additional exam requirements/recommendations for international students: Required—TOEFL. Electronic applications accepted.

The University of Texas at Austin, Graduate School, College of Fine Arts, Department of Art and Art History, Program in Art Education, Austin, TX 78712-1111. Offers MA. *Accreditation:* NASAD. *Program availability:* Part-time. *Degree requirements:* For master's, thesis, oral and written exam. *Entrance requirements:* For master's, GRE General Test, 2 samples of written work, 10 slides of art work. Electronic applications accepted. *Faculty research:* Museum education; community-based, environmental, and multicultural art education; interdisciplinary art education, elementary and secondary art education.

The University of Texas at El Paso, Graduate School, College of Liberal Arts, Department of Art, El Paso, TX 79968-0001. Offers art education (MA); studio art (MA). *Program availability:* Part-time, evening/weekend. *Degree requirements:* For master's, thesis optional. *Entrance requirements:* For master's, minimum GPA of 3.0, digital portfolio, letters of recommendation. Additional exam requirements/recommendations for international students: Required—TOEFL; Recommended—IELTS. Electronic applications accepted.

The University of the Arts, College of Art, Media and Design, Department of Art and Education, Philadelphia, PA 19102-4944. Offers visual arts (MAT), including art education. *Accreditation:* NASAD. *Program availability:* Part-time. *Degree requirements:* For master's, student teaching (MAT); thesis (MA). *Entrance requirements:* For master's, portfolio, official transcripts from each undergraduate or graduate school attended, three letters of recommendation, one- to two-page statement of professional plans and goals, personal interview, writing sample. Additional exam requirements/recommendations for international students: Required—TOEFL (minimum score 580 paper-based, 92 iBT) or IELTS (minimum score 6.5). *Faculty research:* Using technology and visual arts concepts to develop critical and creative thinking skills.

The University of Toledo, College of Graduate Studies, Judith Herb College of Education, Department of Curriculum and Instruction, Toledo, OH 43606-3390. Offers art education (ME); career and technical education (ME, Ed S); curriculum and instruction (ME, PhD, Ed S); early childhood education (Ed S); education and anthropology (MAE); education and biology (MES); education and chemistry (MES); education and classics (MAE); education and economics (MAE); education and English (MAE); education and French (MAE); education and geology (MES); education and German (MAE); education and history (MAE); education and mathematics (MAE, MES); education and physics (MES); education and political science (MAE); education and sociology (MAE); education and Spanish (MAE); educational media (PhD); educational technology (ME); educational technology: virtual educator (Certificate); elementary education (PhD); English as a second language (MAE); gifted and talented education (PhD); middle childhood education (ME); secondary education (ME, PhD); special education (PhD). *Accreditation:* NCATE. *Program availability:* Part-time, evening/weekend. *Degree requirements:* For master's, comprehensive exam, thesis or alternative; for doctorate, comprehensive exam, thesis/dissertation; for other advanced degree, thesis optional. *Entrance requirements:* For master's, doctorate, and other advanced degree, minimum cumulative GPA of 2.7 for all previous academic work, letters of recommendation. Additional exam requirements/recommendations for international students: Required—TOEFL (minimum score 550 paper-based; 80 iBT). Electronic applications accepted.

University of Utah, Graduate School, College of Fine Arts, Department of Art and Art History, Salt Lake City, UT 84112-0380. Offers art history (MA); ceramics (MFA); community-based art education (MFA); drawing (MFA); graphic design (MFA); painting (MFA); photography/digital imaging (MFA); printmaking (MFA); sculpture/intermedia (MFA). *Faculty:* 18 full-time (8 women), 28 part-time/adjunct (13 women). *Students:* 6 full-time (3 women), 1 (woman) part-time; includes 1 minority (Asian, non-Hispanic/Latino). Average age 33. 48 applicants, 31% accepted, 3 enrolled. In 2018, 3 master's awarded. *Degree requirements:* For master's, variable foreign language requirement, comprehensive exam (for some programs), thesis or alternative, exhibit and final project paper (for MFA). *Entrance requirements:* For master's, CD portfolio (MFA), writing sample (MA), curriculum vitae, letters of recommendation, letter of intent. Additional exam requirements/recommendations for international students: Required—TOEFL (minimum score 575 paper-based; 75 iBT). *Application deadline:* For fall admission, 1/15 priority date for domestic and international students. Application fee: $55 ($65 for international students). Electronic applications accepted. *Expenses:* Contact institution. *Financial support:* In 2018–19, 6 students received support, including 2 fellowships, 6 research assistantships with partial tuition reimbursements available, 34 teaching assistantships with partial tuition reimbursements available; Federal Work-Study, institutionally sponsored loans, scholarships/grants, tuition waivers (partial), unspecified assistantships, and stipends also available. Financial award application deadline: 1/15; financial award applicants required to submit FAFSA. *Faculty research:* Studio art, European art history, Asian art history, Latin American art history, twentieth-century/contemporary art history. *Total annual research expenditures:* $54,906. *Unit head:* Prof. Brian Snapp, Chair, 801-581-8677, Fax: 801-585-6171, E-mail: b.snapp@utah.edu. *Application contact:* Prof. Kim Martinez, Director of Graduate Studies, 801-581-8677, Fax: 801-585-6171, E-mail: kim.martinez@art.utah.edu.
Website: http://www.art.utah.edu/

University of Victoria, Faculty of Graduate Studies, Faculty of Education, Department of Curriculum and Instruction, Victoria, BC V8W 2Y2, Canada. Offers art education (M Ed, PhD); curriculum studies (M Ed, MA, PhD); early childhood education (M Ed, PhD); educational studies (PhD); language and literacy (M Ed, MA, PhD); mathematics (M Ed, MA, PhD); music education (M Ed, MA, PhD); science (M Ed, MA, PhD); social studies (M Ed, MA); social, cultural and foundational studies (MA, PhD); technology and environmental education (PhD). *Program availability:* Part-time. *Degree requirements:* For master's, thesis, project (M Ed); for doctorate, comprehensive exam, thesis/dissertation. *Entrance requirements:* For master's, minimum B average. Additional exam requirements/recommendations for international students: Required—TOEFL (minimum score 575 paper-based), IELTS (minimum score 7). Electronic applications accepted. *Faculty research:* Elementary and secondary English, language arts, curriculum theory and practice, educational media and technology, educational administration and leadership, history and philosophy of education.

University of Wisconsin–Milwaukee, Graduate School, Peck School of the Arts, Milwaukee, WI 53201-0413. Offers art education (MS); chamber music (CAS); conducting (MM); dance (MFA); design entrepreneurship and innovation (MA); film, video, animation, and new genres (MFA); music education (MM); music history and literature (MM); performance (MM); string pedagogy (MM); studio art (MA, MFA); theory and composition (MM). *Program availability:* Part-time. *Students:* 85 full-time (52 women), 18 part-time (12 women); includes 15 minority (1 Black or African American, non-Hispanic/Latino; 2 Asian, non-Hispanic/Latino; 3 Hispanic/Latino; 1 Native Hawaiian or other Pacific Islander, non-Hispanic/Latino; 8 Two or more races, non-Hispanic/Latino), 22 international. Average age 31. 140 applicants, 36% accepted, 37 enrolled. In 2018, 39 master's, 2 other advanced degrees awarded. *Degree requirements:* For master's, comprehensive exam, thesis or alternative. *Entrance requirements:* For master's, portfolio. Additional exam requirements/recommendations for international students: Required—TOEFL (minimum score 550 paper-based; 79 iBT), IELTS (minimum score 6.5). *Application deadline:* For fall admission, 1/1 priority date for domestic students; for spring admission, 9/1 for domestic students. Application fee: $56 ($96 for international students). Electronic applications accepted. *Financial support:* Teaching assistantships, career-related internships or fieldwork, Federal Work-Study, health care benefits, unspecified assistantships, and project assistantships available. Support available to part-time students. Financial award application deadline: 4/15; financial award applicants required to submit FAFSA. *Unit head:* Scott Emmons, Dean, 414-229-4762, E-mail: semm@uwm.edu. *Application contact:* Arts Student Services, 414-229-4763, E-mail: uwmpsoa@uwm.edu.
Website: http://uwm.edu/arts/

University of Wisconsin–Milwaukee, Graduate School, School of Education, Department of Exceptional Education, Milwaukee, WI 53201-0413. Offers autism spectrum disorders (Graduate Certificate); exceptional education (MS); transition for students with disabilities (Graduate Certificate); urban education (PhD), including adult, continuing and higher education leadership, art education, curriculum and instruction, exceptional education, mathematics education, multicultural studies, social foundations of education. *Program availability:* Part-time. *Students:* 38 full-time (29 women), 67 part-time (50 women); includes 39 minority (23 Black or African American, non-Hispanic/Latino; 1 American Indian or Alaska Native, non-Hispanic/Latino; 6 Asian, non-Hispanic/Latino; 1 Hispanic/Latino; 8 Two or more races, non-Hispanic/Latino), 2 international. Average age 40. 47 applicants, 40% accepted, 11 enrolled. In 2018, 13 master's, 14 doctorates, 4 other advanced degrees awarded. *Entrance requirements:* Additional exam requirements/recommendations for international students: Required—TOEFL (minimum score 550 paper-based; 79 iBT), IELTS (minimum score 6.5). *Application deadline:* For fall admission, 1/1 priority date for domestic students; for spring admission, 9/1 for domestic students. Application fee: $56 ($96 for international students). Electronic applications accepted. *Financial support:* Fellowships, research assistantships, teaching assistantships, career-related internships or fieldwork, health care benefits, and unspecified assistantships available. Support available to part-time students. Financial award application deadline: 4/15; financial award applicants required to submit FAFSA. *Faculty research:* Emotional disturbance, hearing impairment, learning disabilities, mental retardation. *Application contact:* General Information Contact, 414-229-4721, E-mail: soeinfo@uwm.edu.
Website: http://uwm.edu/education/academics/exceptional-edu-department/

University of Wisconsin–Superior, Graduate Division, Department of Visual Arts, Superior, WI 54880-4500. Offers art education (MA); art history (MA); art therapy (MA); studio arts (MA). *Program availability:* Part-time. *Degree requirements:* For master's, comprehensive exam, exhibit. *Entrance requirements:* For master's, minimum GPA of 2.75, portfolio. Electronic applications accepted.

Vermont College of Fine Arts, Graduate Studies in Art and Design Education, Montpelier, VT 05602. Offers MA, MAT. *Degree requirements:* For master's, thesis. *Entrance requirements:* For master's, SAT, GRE, PRAXIS, bachelor's degree. Electronic applications accepted. *Expenses:* Contact institution.

Virginia Commonwealth University, Graduate School, School of Education, Doctoral Program in Education, Richmond, VA 23284-9005. Offers art education (PhD); counselor education and supervision (PhD); curriculum, culture and change (PhD); educational leadership (PhD); educational psychology (PhD); leadership (Ed D); research and evaluation (PhD); special education and disability leadership (PhD); sport leadership (PhD); urban services leadership (PhD). *Accreditation:* NCATE. *Program availability:* Part-time. *Degree requirements:* For doctorate, thesis/dissertation. *Entrance requirements:* For doctorate, GRE (for PhD), MAT (for Ed D), interview, master's degree, writing sample. Additional exam requirements/recommendations for international students: Required—TOEFL (minimum score 600 paper-based; 100 iBT). Electronic applications accepted.

Virginia Commonwealth University, Graduate School, School of the Arts, Department of Art Education, Richmond, VA 23284-9005. Offers MAE, PhD. *Accreditation:* NASAD. *Degree requirements:* For master's, thesis optional. *Entrance requirements:* For master's, GRE if GPA is below 3.0, portfolio. Additional exam requirements/recommendations for international students: Required—TOEFL (minimum score 600 paper-based; 100 iBT). Electronic applications accepted. *Faculty research:* Teaching methods.

Wayne State University, College of Education, Division of Teacher Education, Detroit, MI 48202. Offers art education (M Ed); bilingual/bicultural education (Certificate); curriculum and instruction (Ed D, PhD, Ed S), including English as a second language (MAT, Ed D, Ed S), K-12 curriculum (PhD); elementary education (MAT), including bilingual/bicultural education (M Ed, MAT), early childhood education (M Ed, MAT), English as a second language (MAT, Ed D, Ed S), foreign language education, science education (M Ed, MAT), special education (M Ed, MAT); elementary mathematics specialist (Certificate); English as a second language (Certificate); reading (M Ed, Ed S); reading, language and literature (Ed D); secondary education (MAT), including bilingual/bicultural education (M Ed, MAT), early childhood education (M Ed, MAT), English as a second language (MAT, Ed D, Ed S), English education, foreign language education, mathematics education (M Ed, MAT), science education (M Ed, MAT), social studies education (M Ed, MAT); special education (MAT), including career and technical education; teaching and learning (M Ed), including bilingual/bicultural education (M Ed, MAT), early childhood education (M Ed, MAT), elementary education, foreign language, mathematics education (M Ed, MAT), science education (M Ed, MAT), social studies education (M Ed, MAT), special education (M Ed, MAT). *Program availability:* Part-time, evening/weekend. *Faculty:* 20. *Students:* 121 full-time (94 women), 251 part-time (209 women); includes 116 minority (83 Black or African American, non-Hispanic/Latino; 3 American Indian or Alaska Native, non-Hispanic/Latino; 3 Asian, non-Hispanic/Latino; 14 Hispanic/Latino; 13 Two or more races, non-Hispanic/Latino), 11 international. Average age 37. 171 applicants, 23% accepted, 32 enrolled. In 2018, 112 master's, 8 doctorates, 11 other advanced degrees awarded. *Degree requirements:* For master's, thesis (for some programs), essay or project (for some M Ed programs), professional field experience (for MAT programs); for doctorate, comprehensive exam, thesis/dissertation. *Entrance requirements:* For master's, undergraduate degree, verification of participation in group work with children, Michigan State Police criminal background check, negative tb test, personal statement (for MAT programs); for all other master's programs: undergraduate degree, personal statement; for doctorate, minimum undergraduate GPA of 3.0, graduate 3.5; interview; curriculum vitae; references; writing sample; letter of application; master's degree (for most programs); for other advanced degree, education specialist certificate: undergraduate with GPA of 2.5 or better and master's degree with GPA of 2.75 or better; personal statement. Additional exam requirements/recommendations for international students: Required—TOEFL (minimum score 550 paper-based; 79 iBT); Recommended—IELTS (minimum score 6.5), TWE (minimum score 5.5), TSE (minimum score 58). *Application deadline:* Applications are processed on a rolling basis. Application fee: $50. Electronic applications accepted. *Financial support:* In 2018–19, 85 students received support, including 3 fellowships

(averaging $14,275 per year); research assistantships with tuition reimbursements available, Federal Work-Study, scholarships/grants, and unspecified assistantships also available. Support available to part-time students. Financial award applicants required to submit FAFSA. *Faculty research:* Improving students' skill achievement in mathematics, improving elementary children's understanding of informational text, teachers' use of their pedagogical and mathematical knowledge in the interactive work of teaching, the intersection of identity construction in teaching and learning, identifying effective methods of literacy instruction and assessments for bilingual students in elementary language arts classrooms. *Unit head:* Dr. Roland Coloma, Assistant Dean for Teacher Education, 313-577-0902, E-mail: rscoloma@wayne.edu. *Application contact:* Dr. Mary L. Waker, Graduate Admissions Officer, 313-577-1601, Fax: 313-577-7904, E-mail: m.waker@wayne.edu.
Website: http://coe.wayne.edu/ted/index.php

Western Kentucky University, Graduate School, Potter College of Arts and Letters, Department of Art, Bowling Green, KY 42101. Offers art education (MA Ed). *Accreditation:* NASAD; NCATE. *Program availability:* Part-time, evening/weekend. *Degree requirements:* For master's, comprehensive exam, final exam. *Entrance requirements:* For master's, GRE General Test, minimum GPA of 2.75. Additional exam requirements/recommendations for international students: Required—TOEFL (minimum score 555 paper-based; 79 iBT). *Faculty research:* Nineteenth century Kentucky women artists.

Western Michigan University, Graduate College, College of Fine Arts, Gwen Frostic School of Art, Kalamazoo, MI 49008. Offers art education (MA). *Accreditation:* NASAD. *Degree requirements:* For master's, thesis or alternative.

West Virginia University, College of Creative Arts, Morgantown, WV 26506. Offers acting (MFA); art education (MA); art history (MA); ceramics (MFA); collaborative piano (MM, DMA); composition (MM, DMA); conducting (MM, DMA); costume design and technology (MFA); graphic design (MFA); intermedia and photography (MFA); jazz pedagogy (MM); lighting design and technology (MFA); music (PhD); music education (MM, PhD); music industry (MA); music theory (MM); musicology (MA); painting and printmaking (MFA); performance (MM, DMA); piano pedagogy (MM); scenic design and technology (MFA); sculpture (MFA); studio art (MA); technical direction (MFA); vocal pedagogy and performance (DMA). *Program availability:* Part-time. *Students:* 110 full-time (58 women), 30 part-time (15 women); includes 15 minority (5 Black or African American, non-Hispanic/Latino; 4 Asian, non-Hispanic/Latino; 6 Hispanic/Latino), 29 international. In 2018, 29 master's, 14 doctorates awarded. *Degree requirements:* For master's, thesis, recitals; for doctorate, comprehensive exam, thesis/dissertation, recitals (DMA). *Entrance requirements:* For doctorate, minimum GPA of 3.0, audition. Additional exam requirements/recommendations for international students: Required—TOEFL. *Application deadline:* For fall admission, 3/1 priority date for domestic students, 2/15 for international students; for spring admission, 11/1 for domestic students, 9/15 for

international students. Applications are processed on a rolling basis. Application fee: $60. Electronic applications accepted. *Financial support:* Research assistantships, teaching assistantships, career-related internships or fieldwork, Federal Work-Study, institutionally sponsored loans, scholarships/grants, health care benefits, tuition waivers (partial), and administrative assistantships available. Financial award applicants required to submit FAFSA. *Faculty research:* Professional directing, consulting, acting design, music education, jazz history. *Unit head:* Dr. Keith Jackson, Dean, 304-293-4351, Fax: 304-293-6896, E-mail: Keith.jackson@mail.wvu.edu. *Application contact:* Dr. Keith Jackson, Dean, 304-293-4351, Fax: 304-293-6896, E-mail: Keith.jackson@mail.wvu.edu.

William Carey University, School of Education, Hattiesburg, MS 39401. Offers art education (M Ed); art of teaching (M Ed); elementary education (M Ed, Ed S); English education (M Ed); gifted education (M Ed); history and social science (M Ed); mild/moderate disabilities (M Ed); secondary education (M Ed). *Accreditation:* NCATE. *Program availability:* Part-time. *Degree requirements:* For master's, comprehensive exam. *Entrance requirements:* For master's, GRE, MAT, minimum GPA of 2.5, Class A teacher's license. Additional exam requirements/recommendations for international students: Required—TOEFL (minimum score 550 paper-based).

Winthrop University, College of Visual and Performing Arts, Department of Art, Rock Hill, SC 29733. Offers art (MFA); art administration (MA); art education (MA). *Accreditation:* NASAD. *Program availability:* Part-time. *Students:* 2 full-time (both women), 31 part-time (26 women); includes 9 minority (6 Black or African American, non-Hispanic/Latino; 2 Hispanic/Latino; 1 Two or more races, non-Hispanic/Latino). Average age 37. In 2018, 3 master's awarded. *Degree requirements:* For master's, comprehensive exam (for some programs), thesis (for some programs), documented exhibit, oral exam. *Entrance requirements:* For master's, GRE General Test or MAT, PRAXIS (for MA), minimum GPA of 3.0, resume, slide portfolio, teaching certificate (MA). Additional exam requirements/recommendations for international students: Required—TOEFL (minimum score 550 paper-based; 79 iBT), IELTS (minimum score 6). *Application deadline:* For fall admission, 3/1 priority date for domestic students; for spring admission, 9/1 for domestic students. Applications are processed on a rolling basis. Application fee: $50. Electronic applications accepted. *Expenses:* Tuition, state resident: full-time $15,166; part-time $635 per credit hour. Tuition, nonresident: full-time $29,214. *Required fees:* $500; $180 per semester. *Financial support:* Research assistantships with full tuition reimbursements, Federal Work-Study, scholarships/grants, and unspecified assistantships available. Support available to part-time students. Financial award application deadline: 2/1; financial award applicants required to submit FAFSA. *Unit head:* Anne Fiala, Interim Chair, 803-323-2653, E-mail: fialaa@winthrop.edu. *Application contact:* 800-411-7041, Fax: 803-323-2292, E-mail: graduatestu@winthrop.edu.
Website: http://www.winthrop.edu/cvpa/finearts

Business Education

Alabama Agricultural and Mechanical University, School of Graduate Studies, College of Education, Humanities, and Behavioral Sciences, Department of Educational Leadership and Secondary Education, Huntsville, AL 35811. Offers biology (M Ed); business/marketing education (M Ed, Ed S); chemistry (M Ed); collaborative teacher secondary education (M Ed, Ed S); education (M Ed, Ed S); English language arts (M Ed); family/consumer science education (M Ed, Ed S); general science (M Ed); general social science (M Ed); mathematics (M Ed, Ed S); physics (M Ed, Ed S); technology education (M Ed). *Accreditation:* NCATE. *Program availability:* Evening/weekend. *Degree requirements:* For master's, comprehensive exam; for Ed S, thesis. *Entrance requirements:* For master's, GRE General Test. Additional exam requirements/recommendations for international students: Required—TOEFL (minimum score 500 paper-based; 61 iBT). Electronic applications accepted. *Faculty research:* World peace through education, computer-assisted instruction.

Arkansas State University, Graduate School, College of Business, Department of Computer and Information Technology, State University, AR 72467. Offers business administration education (SCCT); business technology education (SCCT). *Program availability:* Part-time. *Entrance requirements:* Additional exam requirements/recommendations for international students: Required—TOEFL (minimum score 550 paper-based; 79 iBT), IELTS (minimum score 6), PTE (minimum score 56). Electronic applications accepted. *Expenses:* Contact institution.

Ball State University, Graduate School, Miller College of Business, Department of Information Systems and Operations Management, Muncie, IN 47306. Offers business education (MA); information systems security management (Certificate). *Accreditation:* NCATE (one or more programs are accredited). *Program availability:* Part-time, online only, 100% online. *Entrance requirements:* For master's, minimum baccalaureate GPA of 2.75 or 3.0 in latter half of baccalaureate. Additional exam requirements/recommendations for international students: Required—TOEFL (minimum score 550 paper-based; 79 iBT), IELTS (minimum score 6.5). Electronic applications accepted. *Expenses:* Contact institution.

Bloomsburg University of Pennsylvania, School of Graduate Studies, Zeigler College of Business, Program in Business Education, Bloomsburg, PA 17815-1301. Offers M Ed. *Program availability:* Part-time, evening/weekend. *Degree requirements:* For master's, thesis optional, student teaching, minimum QPA of 3.0. *Entrance requirements:* For master's, PRAXIS, minimum QPA of 3.0, 2 letters of recommendation, personal statement, resume. Additional exam requirements/recommendations for international students: Required—TOEFL, IELTS. Electronic applications accepted.

Bowling Green State University, Graduate College, College of Education and Human Development, School of Teaching and Learning, Program in Workforce Education and Development, Bowling Green, OH 43403. Offers M Ed. *Accreditation:* NCATE. *Program availability:* Part-time. *Degree requirements:* For master's, thesis or alternative. *Entrance requirements:* For master's, GRE General Test. Additional exam requirements/recommendations for international students: Required—TOEFL. Electronic applications accepted. *Faculty research:* School to work, workforce education, marketing education, contextual teaching and learning.

Buffalo State College, State University of New York, The Graduate School, School of Education, Department of Career and Technical Education, Buffalo, NY 14222-1095. Offers business and marketing education (MS Ed); career and technical education (MS Ed); technology education (MS Ed). *Accreditation:* NCATE. *Program availability:* Part-time, evening/weekend. *Degree requirements:* For master's, thesis or project. *Entrance requirements:* For master's, minimum GPA of 2.5 in last 60 hours, New York

teaching certificate. Additional exam requirements/recommendations for international students: Required—TOEFL (minimum score 550 paper-based).

Canisius College, Graduate Division, School of Education and Human Services, Department of Graduate Education and Leadership, Buffalo, NY 14208-1098. Offers business and marketing education (MS Ed); college student personnel (MS Ed); deaf education (MS Ed); deaf/adolescent education, grades 7-12 (MS Ed); deaf/childhood education, grades 1-6 (MS Ed); differentiated instruction (MS Ed); education administration (MS); educational administration (MS Ed); educational technologies (Certificate); gifted education extension (Certificate); literacy (MS Ed); reading (Certificate); school building leadership (MS Ed, Certificate); school district leadership (Certificate); teacher leader (Certificate); TESOL (MS Ed). *Accreditation:* NCATE. *Program availability:* Part-time, evening/weekend, 100% online, blended/hybrid learning. *Faculty:* 5 full-time (all women), 21 part-time/adjunct (16 women). *Students:* 79 full-time (66 women), 135 part-time (106 women); includes 45 minority (27 Black or African American, non-Hispanic/Latino; 1 American Indian or Alaska Native, non-Hispanic/Latino; 3 Asian, non-Hispanic/Latino; 9 Hispanic/Latino; 5 Two or more races, non-Hispanic/Latino), 1 international. Average age 32. 83 applicants, 96% accepted, 74 enrolled. In 2018, 94 master's, 47 other advanced degrees awarded. *Entrance requirements:* For master's, GRE (if cumulative GPA less than 2.7), transcripts, two letters of recommendation. Additional exam requirements/recommendations for international students: Required—TOEFL (minimum score 550 paper-based, 79 iBT), IELTS (minimum score 6.5), or CAEL (minimum score 70). *Application deadline:* Applications are processed on a rolling basis. Application fee: $0. Electronic applications accepted. *Expenses: Tuition:* Part-time $820 per credit hour. *Required fees:* $25 per semester. One-time fee: $65 part-time. Tuition and fees vary according to program. *Financial support:* In 2018–19, 206 students received support. Career-related internships or fieldwork, Federal Work-Study, scholarships/grants, tuition waivers (partial), and unspecified assistantships available. Support available to part-time students. Financial award application deadline: 4/30; financial award applicants required to submit FAFSA. *Faculty research:* Asperger's disease, autism, private higher education, reading strategies. *Unit head:* Dr. Anne Marie Tryjankowski, Chair/Associate Professor of Graduate Education and Leadership, 716-888-3715, Fax: 716-888-3142, E-mail: tryjanka@canisius.edu. *Application contact:* Dr. Anne Marie Tryjankowski, Chair/Associate Professor of Graduate Education and Leadership, 716-888-3715, Fax: 716-888-3142, E-mail: tryjanka@canisius.edu.

Capella University, School of Business and Technology, Doctoral Programs in Business, Minneapolis, MN 55402. Offers accounting (DBA, PhD); business intelligence (DBA); finance (DBA, PhD); general business management (PhD); human resource management (DBA, PhD); leadership (DBA, PhD); management education (PhD); marketing (DBA, PhD); project management (DBA, PhD); strategy and innovation (DBA, PhD). *Accreditation:* ACBSP.

Chadron State College, School of Professional and Graduate Studies, Department of Education, Chadron, NE 69337. Offers business (MA Ed); community counseling (MA Ed); educational administration (MS Ed, Sp Ed); elementary education (MS Ed); history (MA Ed); language and literature (MA Ed); secondary administration (MS Ed); secondary education (MS Ed). *Accreditation:* NCATE. *Program availability:* Part-time, evening/weekend, online learning. *Degree requirements:* For master's, thesis optional. *Entrance requirements:* For master's, GRE General Test, GRE Writing Test, minimum GPA of 2.75 or 12 graduate hours at CSC with minimum GPA of 3.25. Additional exam requirements/recommendations for international students: Required—TOEFL. Electronic applications accepted. *Faculty research:* Rural education, technology, mental health.

Clemson University, Graduate School, College of Business, Clemson, SC 29634. Offers MA, MBA, MP Acc, MS, PhD. *Program availability:* Part-time, evening/weekend, 100% online. *Faculty:* 156 full-time (53 women), 27 part-time/adjunct (6 women). *Students:* 317 full-time (151 women), 442 part-time (152 women); includes 117 minority (49 Black or African American, non-Hispanic/Latino; 6 American Indian or Alaska Native, non-Hispanic/Latino; 19 Asian, non-Hispanic/Latino; 28 Hispanic/Latino; 2 Native Hawaiian or other Pacific Islander, non-Hispanic/Latino; 13 Two or more races, non-Hispanic/Latino), 75 international. Average age 31. 873 applicants, 80% accepted, 440 enrolled. In 2018, 333 master's, 16 doctorates awarded. Terminal master's awarded for partial completion of doctoral program. *Degree requirements:* For master's, thesis optional; for doctorate, thesis/dissertation. *Entrance requirements:* For master's and doctorate, GRE General Test, GMAT, unofficial transcripts, letters of recommendation. Additional exam requirements/recommendations for international students: Required—TOEFL (minimum score 80 paper-based; 80 iBT), IELTS (minimum score 6.5), PTE (minimum score 54). *Application deadline:* For fall admission, 4/15 for international students; for spring admission, 10/15 for international students. Applications are processed on a rolling basis. *Application fee:* $80 ($90 for international students). Electronic applications accepted. *Expenses:* Full-Time tuition per semester: $5300 in-state, $11035 out-of-state; Part-Time tuition per credit hour: $724 in-state, $1451 out-of-state; Full-Time fees: $598; Part-Time fees: $20 per credit hour plus $48 - $477 per semester; Online programs tuition per credit hour: $955; Online programs fees: $20 per credit hour plus $28 per semester; Doctoral base academic fee per semester: $4938 in-state, $10405 out-of-state; Full-Time Graduate Assistant fee per semester: $1144; Graduate Insurance Rates: $923 Fall, $1258 Spring/Summer (Graduate Assistant receives $860 subsidy per semester); MBA Program substantially higher. *Financial support:* In 2018–19, 128 students received support, including 17 fellowships with partial tuition reimbursements available (averaging $4,118 per year), 8 research assistantships with partial tuition reimbursements available (averaging $20,790 per year), 31 teaching assistantships with partial tuition reimbursements available (averaging $19,975 per year); career-related internships or fieldwork and unspecified assistantships also available. *Faculty research:* Entrepreneurship, marketing, price theory, information systems, operations management. *Total annual research expenditures:* $173,533. *Unit head:* Wendy York, Dean, 864-656-3178, E-mail: BIZDEAN@clemson.edu. *Application contact:* Dr. Gregory Pickett, Senior Associate Dean, 864-656-3975, E-mail: pgregor@clemson.edu.
Website: http://www.clemson.edu/business/index.html

Colorado Christian University, Program in Curriculum and Instruction, Lakewood, CO 80226. Offers corporate education (MACI); early childhood educator (MACI); elementary educator (MACI); instructional technology (MACI); master educator (MACI); online course developer (MACI); online teaching and learning (MACI); special education generalist (MACI). *Program availability:* Part-time, evening/weekend. *Degree requirements:* For master's, thesis optional, practicum. *Entrance requirements:* For master's, interviews, letters of recommendation. Additional exam requirements/recommendations for international students: Required—TOEFL. Electronic applications accepted. *Expenses:* Contact institution.

East Carolina University, Graduate School, College of Education, Department of Interdisciplinary Professions, Greenville, NC 27858-4353. Offers adult education (MA Ed); business and marketing education (MA Ed); community college instruction (Certificate); counselor education (MS); education in the healthcare professions (Certificate); library science (MLS); student affairs in higher education (Certificate); vocational education (MS). *Accreditation:* ACA; ALA; NCATE. *Program availability:* Part-time, evening/weekend. *Application deadline:* For fall admission, 5/15 priority date for domestic students. *Expenses:* Tuition, area resident: Full-time $4749. Tuition, state resident: full-time $4749. Tuition, nonresident: full-time $17,898. *International tuition:* $17,898 full-time. *Required fees:* $2787. Part-time tuition and fees vary according to course load and program. *Financial support:* Application deadline: 6/1. *Unit head:* Dr. Scott Glass, Professor, 252-328-5670, E-mail: glassj@ecu.edu. *Application contact:* Graduate School Admissions, 252-328-6012, Fax: 252-328-6071, E-mail: gradschool@ecu.edu.
Website: http://www.ecu.edu/cs-educ/idp/index.cfm

Eastern Kentucky University, The Graduate School, College of Education, Department of Curriculum and Instruction, Program in Secondary and Higher Education, Richmond, KY 40475-3102. Offers secondary education (MA Ed), including agricultural education, art education, biological sciences education, business education, English education, geography education, history education, home economics education, industrial education, mathematical sciences education, physical education, school health education. *Accreditation:* NCATE. *Program availability:* Part-time. *Entrance requirements:* For master's, GRE General Test, minimum GPA of 2.5.

Florida Agricultural and Mechanical University, Division of Graduate Studies, Research, and Continuing Education, College of Education, Department of Vocational Education, Tallahassee, FL 32307-3200. Offers business education (MBE); industrial education (MS Ed); technology education (M Ed). *Accreditation:* NCATE. *Degree requirements:* For master's, thesis (for some programs). *Entrance requirements:* For master's, GRE General Test, minimum GPA of 3.0. Additional exam requirements/recommendations for international students: Required—TOEFL.

Hofstra University, School of Education, Programs in Teacher Education, Hempstead, NY 11549. Offers bilingual education (MA); bilingual extension (Advanced Certificate); business education (MS Ed); curriculum studies (MS Ed); early childhood and childhood education (MS Ed); early childhood education (MA, MS Ed); educational technology (Advanced Certificate); elementary education (MA, MS Ed); English education (MS Ed); family and consumer science (MS Ed); fine arts and music education (Advanced Certificate); fine arts education (MS Ed); foreign language and TESOL (MS Ed); foreign language education (MA, MS Ed); languages other than English and teaching English as a second language (MA); learning and teaching (Ed D); mathematics education (MA, MS Ed); middle childhood extension (Advanced Certificate); music education (MA, MS Ed); science education (MA); secondary education (Advanced Certificate); social studies education (MA, MS Ed); teaching languages other than English and TESOL (MS Ed); technology for learning (MA); TESOL (MS Ed, Advanced Certificate); TESOL with specialization in STEM (MA); work based learning extension (Advanced Certificate). *Program availability:* Part-time, evening/weekend, blended/hybrid learning. *Students:* 138 full-time (94 women), 109 part-time (78 women); includes 66 minority (16 Black or African American, non-Hispanic/Latino; 17 Asian, non-Hispanic/Latino; 31 Hispanic/Latino; 2 Native Hawaiian or other Pacific Islander, non-Hispanic/Latino), 6 international. Average age 29. 217 applicants, 86% accepted, 113 enrolled. In 2018, 105 master's, 11 doctorates, 25 other advanced degrees awarded. *Degree requirements:* For master's, comprehensive exam, thesis (for some programs), exit project, student teaching, fieldwork, electronic portfolio, curriculum project, minimum GPA of 3.0; for doctorate, dissertation; for Advanced Certificate, 3 foreign languages, comprehensive exam (for some programs), thesis project. *Entrance requirements:* For master's, GRE, 2 letters of recommendation, portfolio, teacher certification (MA), interview, essay; for doctorate, GMAT, GRE, LSAT, or MAT; for Advanced Certificate, 2 letters of recommendation, essay, interview and/or portfolio, teaching certificate. Additional exam requirements/recommendations for international students: Required—TOEFL (minimum score 550 paper-based; 80 iBT). *Application deadline:* Applications are processed on a rolling basis. Application fee: $75. Electronic applications accepted. *Financial support:* In 2018–19, 86 students received support, including 51 fellowships with full and partial tuition reimbursements available (averaging $5,080 per year), 2 research assistantships with full and partial tuition reimbursements available (averaging $3,470 per year); career-related internships or fieldwork, Federal Work-Study, institutionally sponsored loans, scholarships/grants, traineeships, tuition waivers (full and partial), unspecified assistantships, and scholarships and endowed scholarships also available. Support available to part-time students. Financial award applicants required to submit FAFSA. *Faculty research:* Impact of memory on learning; brain function, cognitive-development, learning, and achievement; student activism and civic education; using children's literature to promote diversity; 2nd language acquisition. *Unit head:* Dr. Alan Singer, Chairperson, 516-463-5853, Fax: 516-463-6275, E-mail: alan.j.singer@hofstra.edu. *Application contact:* Sunil Samuel, Assistant Vice President of Admissions, 516-463-4723, Fax: 516-463-4664, E-mail: graduateadmission@hofstra.edu.
Website: http://www.hofstra.edu/education/

Indiana University of Pennsylvania, School of Graduate Studies and Research, College of Education and Communications, Department of Adult and Community Education, Program in Business/Business Specialist, Indiana, PA 15705. Offers M Ed. *Program availability:* Part-time. *Faculty:* 2 full-time (both women). *Students:* 1 (woman) part-time. Average age 56. 3 applicants, 67% accepted, 3 enrolled. *Degree requirements:* For master's, thesis optional. *Entrance requirements:* For master's, GMAT or GRE. Additional exam requirements/recommendations for international students: Required—TOEFL (minimum score 540 paper-based). *Application deadline:* Applications are processed on a rolling basis. Application fee: $50. Electronic applications accepted. *Expenses:* Tuition, state resident: full-time $12,384; part-time $516 per credit hour. Tuition, nonresident: full-time $18,576; part-time $774 per credit hour. *Required fees:* $4454; $186 per credit hour. $65 per semester. Tuition and fees vary according to program and reciprocity agreements. *Financial support:* Research assistantships with tuition reimbursements, career-related internships or fieldwork, Federal Work-Study, scholarships/grants, and unspecified assistantships available. Financial award application deadline: 4/15; financial award applicants required to submit FAFSA. *Unit head:* Prof. Jacqueline McGinty, Coordinator, 724-357-2470, E-mail: jacqueline.mcginty@iup.edu. *Application contact:* Prof. Jacqueline McGinty, Coordinator, 724-357-2470, E-mail: jacqueline.mcginty@iup.edu.
Website: http://www.iup.edu/ace/grad/default.aspx

Inter American University of Puerto Rico, Metropolitan Campus, Graduate Programs, Program in Commercial Education, San Juan, PR 00919-1293. Offers MA.

Inter American University of Puerto Rico, San Germán Campus, Graduate Studies Center, Program in Business Education, San Germán, PR 00683-5008. Offers MA. *Accreditation:* TEAC. *Program availability:* Part-time, evening/weekend. *Degree requirements:* For master's, comprehensive exam. *Entrance requirements:* For master's, GRE General Test or EXADEP, minimum GPA of 3.0. *Expenses: Tuition:* Full-time $212; part-time $212 per credit. *Required fees:* $366 per semester. One-time fee: $31. Tuition and fees vary according to degree level and program.

Johnson & Wales University, Graduate Studies, MAT Program in Teacher Education, Providence, RI 02903-3703. Offers business education and secondary special education (MAT); culinary arts education (MAT); elementary education and elementary special education (MAT). *Program availability:* Part-time, evening/weekend. *Entrance requirements:* For master's, MAT, minimum GPA of 2.75. Additional exam requirements/recommendations for international students: Required—TOEFL (minimum score 550 paper-based) or IELTS (recommended). *Faculty research:* Secondary education, student teaching, educational reform, evaluation procedures.

Lock Haven University of Pennsylvania, The Stephen Poorman College of Business, Information Systems, and Human Services, Lock Haven, PA 17745-2390. Offers clinical mental health counseling (MS); sport science (MS). *Program availability:* Online learning. *Degree requirements:* For master's, thesis. *Entrance requirements:* For master's, minimum undergraduate GPA of 3.0. Additional exam requirements/recommendations for international students: Required—TOEFL. Electronic applications accepted.

Louisiana State University and Agricultural & Mechanical College, Graduate School, College of Human Sciences and Education, School of Human Resource Education and Workforce Development, Baton Rouge, LA 70803. Offers agriculture and extension education and youth development (MS, PhD); career and technical education (MS, PhD); comprehensive vocational education (MS, PhD); extension and international education (MS, PhD); human resource and leadership development (MS, PhD); industrial education (MS); vocational agriculture education (MS, PhD); vocational business education (MS); vocational home economics education (MS). *Accreditation:* NCATE.

Manhattanville College, School of Professional Studies, Purchase, NY 10577-2132. Offers business leadership (Advanced Certificate). *Program availability:* Part-time, evening/weekend. *Faculty:* 27 part-time/adjunct (10 women). *Students:* 82 full-time (43 women), 24 part-time (12 women); includes 39 minority (9 Black or African American, non-Hispanic/Latino; 1 American Indian or Alaska Native, non-Hispanic/Latino; 2 Asian, non-Hispanic/Latino; 25 Hispanic/Latino; 2 Two or more races, non-Hispanic/Latino), 11 international. Average age 30. 120 applicants, 40% accepted, 30 enrolled. In 2018, 60 master's awarded. *Degree requirements:* For master's, thesis (for some programs), final project, internship, portfolio. *Entrance requirements:* For master's, scores of GRE and GMAT are optional, personal essay, transcripts, 2 letters of recommendation (academic or professional), resume, health form with proof of immunization (for those born after 1957). Additional exam requirements/recommendations for international students: Required—TOEFL (minimum score 563 paper-based; 85 iBT), exams TOEFL, IELTS, or ITEP are required; minimum IBT TOEFL score is 85, minimum IELTS score is 7 and minimum ITEP score is B2; Recommended—IELTS (minimum score 7). *Application deadline:* Applications are processed on a rolling basis. Application fee: $75. Electronic applications accepted. *Expenses:* 935 per credit. *Financial support:* Federal Work-Study, institutionally sponsored loans, scholarships/grants, and unspecified assistantships available. Financial award application deadline: 3/15; financial award applicants required to submit FAFSA. *Faculty research:* Corporate culture, authentic leadership, emotional intelligence, workplace civility, and workplace bullying. *Unit head:* Laura Persky, Associate Dean, 914-323-5188, E-mail: Laura.Persky@mville.edu. *Application contact:* Monika Pottgen, Assistant Director of Recruitment and Admissions, 914-323-5150, E-mail: sps@mville.edu.
Website: http://www.mville.edu/SPS

Maryville University of Saint Louis, The John E. Simon School of Business, St. Louis, MO 63141-7299. Offers accounting (MBA, MS, Certificate); business studies (Certificate); cybersecurity (MBA, MS, Certificate); financial services (MBA, Certificate); health administration (MBA); healthcare administration (Certificate); human resource management (MBA); human resources management (Certificate); information technology (MBA); information technology management (Certificate); management (MBA, Certificate); management and leadership (MA); marketing (MBA, Certificate); project management (MBA, Certificate); sport business management (MBA); supply

chain management (Certificate); supply chain management/logistics (MBA). *Accreditation:* ACBSP. *Program availability:* Part-time, 100% online, blended/hybrid learning. *Faculty:* 5 full-time (1 woman), 77 part-time/adjunct (19 women). *Students:* 338 full-time (166 women), 739 part-time (356 women); includes 310 minority (161 Black or African American, non-Hispanic/Latino; 6 American Indian or Alaska Native, non-Hispanic/Latino; 59 Asian, non-Hispanic/Latino; 57 Hispanic/Latino; 27 Two or more races, non-Hispanic/Latino), 30 international. Average age 33. In 2018, 143 master's awarded. *Degree requirements:* For master's, capstone course (for MBA). *Entrance requirements:* Additional exam requirements/recommendations for international students: Required—TOEFL (minimum score 563 paper-based; 85 iBT). *Application deadline:* Applications are processed on a rolling basis. Electronic applications accepted. *Expenses:* Tuition varies by program. *Financial support:* Career-related internships or fieldwork, Federal Work-Study, tuition waivers (partial), and campus employment available. Financial award application deadline: 4/1; financial award applicants required to submit FAFSA. *Unit head:* Tammy Gocial, Interim Dean, 314-529-9401, Fax: 314-529-9975, E-mail: tgocial@maryville.edu. *Application contact:* Chris Gourdine, Assistant Dean Business Administration, 314-529-6861, Fax: 314-529-9975, E-mail: cgourdine@maryville.edu.
Website: http://www.maryville.edu/bu/business-administration-masters/

Middle Tennessee State University, College of Graduate Studies, Jennings A. Jones College of Business, Department of Business Communication and Entrepreneurship, Murfreesboro, TN 37132. Offers business education (MBE). *Program availability:* Part-time, evening/weekend, online learning. *Degree requirements:* For master's, comprehensive exam. *Entrance requirements:* For master's, GRE or MAT. Additional exam requirements/recommendations for international students: Required—TOEFL (minimum score 525 paper-based; 71 iBT) or IELTS (minimum score 6). Electronic applications accepted.

Milwaukee School of Engineering, MBA Program in Education Leadership, Milwaukee, WI 53202-3109. Offers MBA. *Program availability:* Part-time, evening/weekend. *Degree requirements:* For master's, thesis or alternative. *Entrance requirements:* For master's, GRE or GMAT if college GPA is less than 3.5, teaching license, three years of full-time classroom teaching experience, two letters of recommendation, Professional Educator License or eligibility, personal interview. Additional exam requirements/recommendations for international students: Required—TOEFL (minimum score 90 iBT), IELTS (minimum score 7). Electronic applications accepted.

Mississippi College, Graduate School, School of Business, Clinton, MS 39058. Offers accounting (Certificate); business administration (MBA), including accounting; business education (M Ed); finance (MBA, Certificate); JD/MBA. *Accreditation:* ACBSP. *Program availability:* Part-time, evening/weekend. *Degree requirements:* For master's, comprehensive exam, thesis optional. *Entrance requirements:* For master's, GMAT, minimum GPA of 2.5, 24 hours of undergraduate course work in business. Additional exam requirements/recommendations for international students: Recommended—TOEFL, IELTS. Electronic applications accepted.

Mississippi College, Graduate School, School of Education, Department of Teacher Education and Leadership, Clinton, MS 39058. Offers art (M Ed); biological science (M Ed); business education (M Ed); computer science (M Ed); dyslexia therapy (M Ed); educational leadership (M Ed, Ed D, Ed S); elementary education (M Ed, Ed S); English (M Ed); higher education administration (MS); mathematics (M Ed); secondary education (M Ed); social studies (history) (M Ed); teaching arts (M Ed). *Program availability:* Part-time, online learning. *Degree requirements:* For master's, comprehensive exam, thesis optional. *Entrance requirements:* For master's, NTE. Additional exam requirements/recommendations for international students: Recommended—TOEFL, IELTS. Electronic applications accepted.

Morehead State University, Graduate School, College of Education, Department of Foundational and Graduate Studies in Education, Morehead, KY 40351. Offers adult and higher education (MA, Ed S); certified professional counselor (Ed S); counseling P-12 (MA); curriculum and instruction (Ed S); educational technology (MA Ed); instructional leadership (Ed S); school administration (MA); school counseling (Ed S); teacher leader business and marketing content (MA Ed); teacher leader business and marketing technology (MA Ed); teacher leader educational technology (MA Ed); teacher leader English (MA Ed); teacher leader gifted education (MA Ed); teacher leader IECE certification (MA Ed); teacher leader interdisciplinary education P-5 (MA Ed); teacher leader middle grades (MA Ed); teacher leader non IECE certification (MA Ed); teacher leader reading/writing - non-certification (MA Ed); teacher leader reading/writing certification (MA Ed); teacher leader school communication - certification (MA Ed); teacher leader school communication - non-certification (MA Ed); teacher leader social studies (MA Ed); teacher leader special education (MA Ed). *Accreditation:* NCATE. *Program availability:* Part-time, evening/weekend. *Degree requirements:* For master's, thesis optional, oral and/or written comprehensive exams; for Ed S, thesis, oral exam. *Entrance requirements:* For master's, GRE General Test, minimum overall undergraduate GPA of 2.5; for Ed S, GRE General Test, interview, master's degree, minimum GPA of 3.5, work experience. Additional exam requirements/recommendations for international students: Required—TOEFL (minimum score 500 paper-based). Electronic applications accepted. *Faculty research:* Character education, school accountability, computer applications for school administrators.

Morehead State University, Graduate School, College of Education, Department of Middle Grades and Secondary Education, Morehead, KY 40351. Offers business and marketing education (MAT); English/language arts 5-9 (MAT); French (MAT); health P-12 (MAT); mathematics 5-9 (MAT); physical education P-12 (MAT); science 5-9 (MAT); secondary biology (MAT); secondary chemistry (MAT); secondary earth science (MAT); secondary English (MAT); secondary math (MAT); secondary physics (MAT); secondary social studies (MAT); social studies 5-9 (MAT); Spanish (MAT). *Program availability:* Part-time, evening/weekend. *Degree requirements:* For master's, portfolio. *Entrance requirements:* For master's, GRE or PRAXIS II content exam, minimum overall undergraduate GPA of 2.5. Additional exam requirements/recommendations for international students: Required—TOEFL (minimum score 500 paper-based). Electronic applications accepted.

New York University, Steinhardt School of Culture, Education, and Human Development, Department of Administration, Leadership, and Technology, Program in Business Education, New York, NY 10012. Offers business and workplace education (MA, Advanced Certificate); workplace learning (Advanced Certificate). *Accreditation:* TEAC. *Program availability:* Part-time. *Entrance requirements:* For degree, master's degree. Additional exam requirements/recommendations for international students: Required—TOEFL (minimum score 100 iBT). Electronic applications accepted. *Faculty research:* Applications of technology to instruction, workplace and corporate education, adult learning.

North Carolina Agricultural and Technical State University, The Graduate College, College of Business and Economics, Greensboro, NC 27411. Offers accounting (MBA); business education (MAT); human resources management (MBA); supply chain systems (MBA).

North Carolina State University, Graduate School, College of Education, Department of Teacher Education and Learning Sciences, Program in Business and Marketing Education, Raleigh, NC 27695. Offers M Ed, MS. *Entrance requirements:* For master's, MAT or GRE, minimum GPA of 3.0, teaching license, 3 letters of reference.

Nova Southeastern University, H. Wayne Huizenga College of Business and Entrepreneurship, Fort Lauderdale, FL 33314-7796. Offers accounting (M Acc); business (MBA); business intelligence/analytics (MBA); complex health systems (MBA); enterprise informatics (MBA); entrepreneurship (MBA); finance (MBA); human resource management (MBA); international business (MBA); management (MBA); marketing (MBA); process improvement (MBA); public administration (MPA); real estate development (MS); sport revenue generation (MBA); supply chain management (MBA). *Accreditation:* NASPAA. *Program availability:* Part-time, evening/weekend, 100% online, blended/hybrid learning. *Entrance requirements:* For master's, GMAT or GRE (depending on undergraduate GPA), official transcripts from all schools attended while in pursuit of bachelor's degree; minimum GPA of 2.5 from regionally-accredited institution. Additional exam requirements/recommendations for international students: Required—TOEFL (minimum score 550 paper-based; 79 iBT), IELTS (minimum score 6), PTE (minimum score 54). Electronic applications accepted. *Expenses:* Contact institution. *Faculty research:* Entrepreneurship and venture capital, ethics and social responsibility, global commerce and cultures, business process management.

Old Dominion University, Darden College of Education, Programs in STEM Education and Professional Studies, Norfolk, VA 23529. Offers community college teaching (MS); human resources training (PhD); technology education (PhD). *Accreditation:* NCATE (one or more programs are accredited). *Program availability:* Part-time, evening/weekend, mix of synchronous and asynchronous study. Terminal master's awarded for partial completion of doctoral program. *Degree requirements:* For master's, comprehensive exam, thesis optional, writing exam, candidacy exam; for doctorate, comprehensive exam, thesis/dissertation, writing exam, candidacy exam. *Entrance requirements:* For master's, GRE General Test or MAT, minimum GPA of 2.8, 2 letters of reference; for doctorate, GRE, minimum GPA of 3.0, 3 letters of reference. Additional exam requirements/recommendations for international students: Required—TOEFL. Electronic applications accepted. *Faculty research:* Training and development, STEM education, visualization, leadership, technology literacy.

Pontifical Catholic University of Puerto Rico, College of Education, Doctoral Program in Business Teacher Education, Ponce, PR 00717-0777. Offers PhD. *Degree requirements:* For doctorate, thesis/dissertation. *Entrance requirements:* For doctorate, EXADEP, GRE General Test or MAT, 3 letters of recommendation.

Pontifical Catholic University of Puerto Rico, College of Education, Master's Program in Business Teacher Education, Ponce, PR 00717-0777. Offers M Ed. *Degree requirements:* For master's, comprehensive exam, thesis (for some programs). *Entrance requirements:* For master's, GRE, 2 letters of recommendation, interview, minimum GPA of 2.75.

Regis University, College of Business and Economics, Denver, CO 80221-1099. Offers accounting (MS); executive leadership (Certificate); finance (MS); finance and accounting (MBA); health industry leadership (MBA); human resource management and leadership (MSOL); management (MBA); marketing (MBA); nonprofit leadership (Post-Graduate Certificate); nonprofit management (MNM); nonprofit organizational capacity building (Certificate); operations management (MBA); organizational leadership and management (MSOL); project leadership and management (MS, MSOL); strategic business management (Certificate); strategic human resource integration (Certificate); strategic management (MBA). Programs offered at Colorado Springs Campus, Northwest Denver Campus, Southeast Denver Campus, Fort Collins Campus, Broomfield Campus, Henderson (Nevada) Campus, and Summerlin (Nevada) Campus. *Program availability:* Part-time, evening/weekend, 100% online, blended/hybrid learning. *Degree requirements:* For master's, thesis (for some programs), capstone or final research project. *Entrance requirements:* For master's, official transcript reflecting baccalaureate degree awarded from regionally-accredited college or university, interview, 2 years of full-time related work experience, resume, letters of recommendation. Additional exam requirements/recommendations for international students: Required—TOEFL (minimum score 550 paper-based; 82 iBT). Electronic applications accepted. *Expenses:* Contact institution. *Faculty research:* Impact of information technology on small business regulation of accounting, international project financing, mineral development, delivery of healthcare to rural indigenous communities.

Salve Regina University, Program in Management, Newport, RI 02840-4192. Offers business studies (CGS); human resource management (CGS); innovation and strategic management (MS); management (CGS); nonprofit management (CGS); social entrepreneurship (CGS). *Program availability:* Part-time, evening/weekend, online learning. *Entrance requirements:* For master's, GMAT, GRE General Test, or MAT. Additional exam requirements/recommendations for international students: Required—TOEFL (minimum score 600 paper-based; 100 iBT). Electronic applications accepted. *Expenses: Tuition:* Full-time $10,530; part-time $585 per credit. *Required fees:* $60 per term. Tuition and fees vary according to course level, course load, degree level and program.

South Carolina State University, College of Graduate and Professional Studies, Department of Education, Orangeburg, SC 29117-0001. Offers early childhood education (MAT); education (M Ed); elementary education (M Ed, MAT); English (MAT); general science/biology (MAT); mathematics (MAT); secondary education (M Ed), including biology education, business education, counselor education, English education, home economics education, industrial education, mathematics education, science education, social studies education; special education (M Ed), including emotionally handicapped, learning disabilities, mentally handicapped. *Accreditation:* NCATE. *Program availability:* Part-time, evening/weekend. *Faculty:* 17 full-time (6 women), 12 part-time/adjunct (5 women). *Students:* 42 full-time (32 women), 93 part-time (64 women); includes 121 minority (119 Black or African American, non-Hispanic/Latino; 2 Asian, non-Hispanic/Latino), 2 international. Average age 40. 50 applicants, 98% accepted, 39 enrolled. In 2018, 9 master's awarded. *Degree requirements:* For master's, thesis optional, departmental qualifying exam. *Entrance requirements:* For master's, GRE General Test, NTE, interview, teaching certificate. *Application deadline:* For fall admission, 6/15 priority date for domestic students, 6/15 for international students; for spring admission, 11/1 for domestic and international students. Application fee: $25. Electronic applications accepted. *Expenses: Tuition, area resident:* Full-time $9928; part-time $552 per credit hour. Tuition, state resident: full-time $9928. Tuition, nonresident: full-time $21,038; part-time $1169 per credit hour. *Required fees:* $1532; $85 per credit hour. *Financial support:* Fellowships, career-related internships or fieldwork, Federal Work-Study, and scholarships/grants available. Financial award application deadline: 6/1. *Unit head:* Dr. Charlie Spell, Chair, Department of Education, 803-536-8963, Fax: 803-516-4568, E-mail: cspell@scsu.edu. *Application contact:* Curtis Foskey, Coordinator of Graduate Studies, 803-536-8419, Fax: 803-536-8812, E-mail: cfoskey@scsu.edu.

Spalding University, Graduate Studies, College of Education, Programs in Education, Louisville, KY 40203-2188. Offers art teacher education (MAT); business teacher education (MAT); elementary school education (MAT); foreign language (MAT); high

school education (MAT); middle school education (MAT); secondary education (MAT); special education (learning and behavioral disorders) (MAT); student guidance counselor (MA); teacher leader (M Ed). *Accreditation:* NCATE. *Program availability:* Part-time, evening/weekend. *Entrance requirements:* For master's, GRE General Test or MAT, interview, letters of recommendation, resume. Additional exam requirements/recommendations for international students: Required—TOEFL (minimum score 535 paper-based). Electronic applications accepted. *Faculty research:* Instructional technology, achievement gap, classroom management, assessment.

State University of New York at Oswego, Graduate Studies, School of Education, Department of Vocational Teacher Preparation, Oswego, NY 13126. Offers agriculture (MS Ed); business and marketing (MS Ed); family and consumer sciences (MS Ed); health careers (MS Ed); technical education (MS Ed); trade education (MS Ed). *Accreditation:* NCATE. *Program availability:* Part-time, evening/weekend. *Degree requirements:* For master's, comprehensive exam, thesis or alternative. *Entrance requirements:* Additional exam requirements/recommendations for international students: Required—TOEFL (minimum score 560 paper-based).

Temple University, College of Education, Department of Teaching and Learning, Philadelphia, PA 19122-6096. Offers career and technical education (Ed M), including business, computing, and information technology, industrial education, marketing education; middle grades education (Ed M), including math and language arts, math and science, science and language arts; secondary education (Ed M), including English, math, social studies; teaching English to speakers of other languages (MS Ed); urban education (Ed M). *Program availability:* Part-time, evening/weekend. *Faculty:* 27 full-time (19 women), 71 part-time/adjunct (51 women). *Students:* 181 full-time (126 women), 128 part-time (78 women); includes 71 minority (25 Black or African American, non-Hispanic/Latino; 1 American Indian or Alaska Native, non-Hispanic/Latino; 20 Asian, non-Hispanic/Latino; 19 Hispanic/Latino; 1 Native Hawaiian or other Pacific Islander, non-Hispanic/Latino; 5 Two or more races, non-Hispanic/Latino), 12 international. 234 applicants, 67% accepted, 103 enrolled. In 2018, 148 master's awarded. *Degree requirements:* For master's, thesis (for some programs). *Entrance requirements:* For master's, statement of goals, 2 letters of recommendation. Additional exam requirements/recommendations for international students: Required—TOEFL (minimum score 79 iBT), IELTS, PTE, one of three is required. Application fee: $60. Electronic applications accepted. *Financial support:* Fellowships, research assistantships, teaching assistantships, career-related internships or fieldwork, Federal Work-Study, scholarships/grants, health care benefits, and unspecified assistantships available. Financial award applicants required to submit FAFSA. *Faculty research:* Career & technical education, early childhood education, middle grades education, secondary education, special education. *Unit head:* Matthew Tincani, Prof. of Applied Behavior Analysis and Dept. Chairperson, 215-204-8073, E-mail: matthew.tincani@temple.edu. *Application contact:* Stacey Sanginette, Academic Coordinator, 215-204-6143, E-mail: stacey.sangtinette@temple.edu.
Website: http://education.temple.edu/tl

Thomas College, Graduate School, Programs in Business, Waterville, ME 04901-5097. Offers business (MBA); computer technology education (MS); education (MS); human resource management (MBA). *Program availability:* Part-time, evening/weekend. *Entrance requirements:* For master's, GMAT, GRE, MAT or minimum GPA of 3.3 in first 3 graduate-level courses. Additional exam requirements/recommendations for international students: Recommended—TOEFL.

University of Delaware, Alfred Lerner College of Business and Economics, Department of Economics, Newark, DE 19716. Offers economic education (PhD); economics (MA, MS, PhD); economics for entrepreneurship and educators (MA); MA/MBA. *Program availability:* Part-time. *Degree requirements:* For master's, comprehensive exam, thesis (for some programs), mathematics review exam, research project; for doctorate, comprehensive exam, thesis/dissertation, field exam. *Entrance requirements:* For master's, GMAT or GRE General Test, minimum GPA of 2.5; for doctorate, GRE General Test, minimum GPA of 3.5 in graduate economics course work. Additional exam requirements/recommendations for international students: Required—TOEFL (minimum score 550 paper-based). Electronic applications accepted. *Faculty research:* Applied quantitative economics, industrial organization, resource economics, monetary economics, labor economics.

University of Georgia, College of Education, Department of Career and Information Studies, Athens, GA 30602. Offers learning, design, and technology (M Ed, PhD, Ed S), including instructional design and development (M Ed, Ed S); workforce education (MAT, Ed D), including business education (MAT). *Accreditation:* NCATE. *Entrance requirements:* For master's, GRE General Test, MAT; for doctorate, GRE General Test; for Ed S, GRE General Test or MAT. Electronic applications accepted.

University of Missouri, Office of Research and Graduate Studies, College of Education, Department of Learning, Teaching and Curriculum, Columbia, MO 65211. Offers agricultural education (M Ed, PhD, Ed S); art education (M Ed, PhD, Ed S); business and office education (M Ed, PhD, Ed S); early childhood education (M Ed, PhD, Ed S); elementary education (M Ed, PhD, Ed S); English education (M Ed, PhD, Ed S); foreign language education (M Ed, PhD, Ed S); health education and promotion (M Ed, PhD); learning and instruction (M Ed); marketing education (M Ed, PhD, Ed S); mathematics education (M Ed, PhD, Ed S); music education (M Ed, PhD, Ed S); reading education (M Ed, PhD, Ed S); science education (M Ed, PhD, Ed S); social studies education (M Ed, PhD, Ed S); vocational education (M Ed, PhD, Ed S). *Program availability:* Part-time. Terminal master's awarded for partial completion of doctoral program. *Entrance requirements:* For master's and Ed S, GRE General Test or MAT, minimum GPA of 3.0; for doctorate, GRE General Test, minimum GPA of 3.0. Additional exam requirements/recommendations for international students: Required—TOEFL.

The University of North Carolina at Charlotte, College of Computing and Informatics, Program in Computing and Information Systems, Charlotte, NC 28223-0001. Offers computing and information systems (PhD), including bioinformatics, business information systems and operations management, computer science, interdisciplinary, software and information systems. *Students:* 99 full-time (27 women), 18 part-time (5 women); includes 4 minority (1 Black or African American, non-Hispanic/Latino; 1 Asian, non-Hispanic/Latino; 1 Hispanic/Latino; 1 Two or more races, non-Hispanic/Latino), 90 international. Average age 30. 86 applicants, 33% accepted, 15 enrolled. In 2018, 17 doctorates awarded. *Entrance requirements:* For doctorate, GRE or GMAT, baccalaureate degree, minimum GPA of 3.0 on courses related to the chosen field of PhD study, essay, reference letters. Additional exam requirements/recommendations for international students: Required—TOEFL (minimum score 523 paper-based; 70 iBT), IELTS (minimum score 6), TOEFL (minimum score 523 paper-based, 70 iBT) or IELTS (6). *Application deadline:* Applications are processed on a rolling basis. Application fee: $75. Electronic applications accepted. Tuition and fees vary according to course load and program. *Financial support:* Career-related internships or fieldwork, institutionally sponsored loans, scholarships/grants, health care benefits, and unspecified assistantships available. Support available to part-time students. Financial award applicants required to submit FAFSA. *Unit head:* Dr. Fatma Mili, Dean, 704-687-8450. *Application contact:* Kathy B. Giddings, Director of Graduate Admissions, 704-687-5503, Fax: 704-687-1668, E-mail: gradadm@uncc.edu.

University of South Carolina, The Graduate School, College of Education, Department of Instruction and Teacher Education, Program in Secondary Education, Columbia, SC 29208. Offers art education (IMA, MAT); business education (IMA, MAT); English (MAT); foreign language (MAT); health education (MAT); mathematics (MAT); science (IMA, MAT); secondary (Ed D); secondary education (MT, PhD); social studies (MAT); theatre and speech (MAT). IMA and MT offered jointly with the subject areas. *Accreditation:* NCATE. *Degree requirements:* For master's, comprehensive exam, thesis (for some programs), foreign language (MA); for doctorate, one foreign language, comprehensive exam, thesis/dissertation. *Entrance requirements:* For master's, GRE General Test or MAT, teaching certificate (IMA, M Ed), interview; for doctorate, GRE General Test or MAT, interview. *Faculty research:* Middle school programs, professional development, school collaboration.

University of the Cumberlands, Graduate Programs in Education, Williamsburg, KY 40769-1372. Offers all grades (P-12) (M Ed); business and marketing (MA Ed, MAT); counselor education and supervision (Ed D); director of pupil personnel (Certificate); director of special education (Certificate); educational administration and supervision (Ed S); educational leadership (Ed D); elementary education (MA Ed, MAT); instructional leadership - principalship (MA Ed); instructional leadership - school principal (Certificate); middle school education (MA Ed, MAT); reading and writing (MA Ed); school counseling (MA Ed); school superintendent (Certificate); secondary education (MA Ed, MAT); special education (MAT); supervisor of instruction (Certificate); teacher leader (MA Ed). *Program availability:* Part-time, evening/weekend, online learning. *Degree requirements:* For master's, comprehensive exam. Electronic applications accepted.

The University of Toledo, College of Graduate Studies, Judith Herb College of Education, Department of Curriculum and Instruction, Toledo, OH 43606-3390. Offers art education (ME); career and technical education (ME, Ed S); curriculum and instruction (ME, PhD, Ed S); early childhood education (Ed S); education and anthropology (MAE); education and biology (MES); education and chemistry (MES); education and classics (MAE); education and economics (MAE); education and English (MAE); education and French (MAE); education and geology (MES); education and German (MAE); education and history (MAE); education and mathematics (MAE, MES); education and physics (MES); education and political science (MAE); education and sociology (MAE); education and Spanish (MAE); educational media (PhD); educational technology (ME); educational technology: virtual educator (Certificate); elementary education (PhD); English as a second language (MAE); gifted and talented education (PhD); middle childhood education (ME); secondary education (ME, PhD); special education (PhD). *Accreditation:* NCATE. *Program availability:* Part-time, evening/weekend. *Degree requirements:* For master's, comprehensive exam, thesis or alternative; for doctorate, comprehensive exam, thesis/dissertation; for other advanced degree, thesis optional. *Entrance requirements:* For master's, doctorate, and other advanced degree, minimum cumulative GPA of 2.7 for all previous academic work, letters of recommendation. Additional exam requirements/recommendations for international students: Required—TOEFL (minimum score 550 paper-based; 80 iBT). Electronic applications accepted.

University of West Georgia, College of Education, Carrollton, GA 30118. Offers business education (M Ed); early childhood education (M Ed, Ed S); educational leadership (M Ed, Ed S); media (M Ed, Ed S); professional counseling (M Ed, Ed S); professional counseling and supervision (Ed D); reading instruction (M Ed); school improvement (Ed D); secondary education (M Ed); special education (M Ed, Ed S), including teaching (M Ed); speech language pathology (M Ed); teaching (MAT). *Accreditation:* NCATE. *Program availability:* Part-time, evening/weekend, 100% online, blended/hybrid learning. *Faculty:* 39 full-time (23 women). *Students:* 368 full-time (316 women), 1,140 part-time (960 women); includes 460 minority (376 Black or African American, non-Hispanic/Latino; 1 American Indian or Alaska Native, non-Hispanic/Latino; 11 Asian, non-Hispanic/Latino; 44 Hispanic/Latino; 28 Two or more races, non-Hispanic/Latino), 6 international. Average age 35. 625 applicants, 77% accepted, 401 enrolled. In 2018, 399 master's, 25 doctorates, 273 other advanced degrees awarded. *Entrance requirements:* Additional exam requirements/recommendations for international students: Required—TOEFL (minimum score 523 paper-based; 69 iBT); Recommended—IELTS (minimum score 6.5). *Application deadline:* For fall admission, 7/21 for domestic students, 6/1 for international students; for spring admission, 11/30 for domestic students, 10/15 for international students; for summer admission, 4/15 for domestic students, 3/30 for international students. Applications are processed on a rolling basis. Application fee: $40. Electronic applications accepted. Tuition and fees vary according to course load, degree level, campus/location and program. *Financial support:* Fellowships, research assistantships, teaching assistantships, career-related internships or fieldwork, Federal Work-Study, institutionally sponsored loans, scholarships/grants, and unspecified assistantships available. Support available to part-time students. Financial award application deadline: 4/1; financial award applicants required to submit FAFSA. *Unit head:* Dr. Diane Hoff, Dean, College of Education, 678-839-6570, Fax: 678-839-6098, E-mail: dhoff@westga.edu. *Application contact:* Dr. Toby Ziglar, Assistant Dean of the Graduate School, 678-839-1394, Fax: 678-839-1395, E-mail: graduate@westga.edu.
Website: http://www.westga.edu/education/

University of Wisconsin–Whitewater, School of Graduate Studies, College of Business and Economics, Program in Business and Marketing Education, Whitewater, WI 53190-1790. Offers MS. *Accreditation:* NCATE. *Program availability:* Part-time, evening/weekend, online learning. *Degree requirements:* For master's, thesis or alternative. *Entrance requirements:* For master's, interview, teaching license. Additional exam requirements/recommendations for international students: Required—TOEFL (minimum score 550 paper-based; 80 iBT), IELTS (minimum score 6). Electronic applications accepted.

Utah State University, School of Graduate Studies, Emma Eccles Jones College of Education and Human Services, Doctoral Program in Education, Logan, UT 84322. Offers business information systems (Ed D, PhD); curriculum and instruction (Ed D, PhD); research and evaluation (PhD). *Degree requirements:* For doctorate, comprehensive exam, thesis/dissertation. *Entrance requirements:* For doctorate, GRE General Test, minimum GPA of 3.0, master's degree. Additional exam requirements/recommendations for international students: Required—TOEFL. Electronic applications accepted. *Faculty research:* Language and literacy development, math and science education, instructional technology, hearing problems/deafness, domestic violence and animal abuse.

Washington State University, College of Education, Department of Educational Leadership, Sports Studies, and Educational/Counseling Psychology, Pullman, WA 99164-2136. Offers counseling psychology (PhD); educational leadership (Ed M, MA, Ed D, PhD); educational psychology (MA, PhD); sport management (MA). Programs also offered at the Spokane, Tri-Cities, Vancouver and Global (online) campuses. *Program availability:* Part-time, online learning. *Degree requirements:* For master's, comprehensive exam (for some programs), thesis (for some programs), oral or written exam; for doctorate, comprehensive exam, thesis/dissertation, oral and written exam, internship. *Entrance requirements:* For master's and doctorate, GRE General Test, minimum GPA of 3.0, 3 letters of recommendation, transcripts showing all college or

university course work, statement of professional objectives, current curriculum vitae/resume. Additional exam requirements/recommendations for international students: Required—TOEFL (minimum score 550 paper-based; 80 iBT). Electronic applications accepted. *Faculty research:* Multicultural counseling and career development, educational and psychological measurement issues, business decision-making process and power relationships, leadership practices and processes as suffused with and constituted by emotion work.

Wayne State College, School of Education and Counseling, Department of Educational Foundations and Leadership, Program in Curriculum and Instruction, Wayne, NE 68787. Offers alternative education (MSE); business and information technology education (MSE); communication arts education (MSE); early childhood education (MSE); elementary education (MSE); English as a second language (MSE); English education (MSE); family and consumer sciences education (MSE); industrial technology and vocational education (MSE); learning communities (MSE); mathematics education

(MSE); music education (MSE); science education (MSE); social science education (MSE). *Accreditation:* NCATE. *Program availability:* Part-time, evening/weekend. *Degree requirements:* For master's, comprehensive exam, thesis optional. *Entrance requirements:* For master's, GRE General Test. Additional exam requirements/recommendations for international students: Required—TOEFL (minimum score 550 paper-based).

West Chester University of Pennsylvania, College of Business and Public Management, School of Business, West Chester, PA 19383. Offers business analytics (Certificate); business education (MBA). *Accreditation:* AACSB. *Program availability:* Part-time, evening/weekend, online only, 100% online. *Degree requirements:* For master's, minimum GPA of 3.0. *Entrance requirements:* For master's, GMAT or GRE, statement of professional goals, resume, three letters of recommendation, transcripts. Additional exam requirements/recommendations for international students: Required—TOEFL or IELTS. Electronic applications accepted.

Computer Education

Arcadia University, School of Education, Glenside, PA 19038-3295. Offers art education (M Ed); computer education (CAS); curriculum (CAS); curriculum studies (M Ed); early childhood education (M Ed), including individualized, master teacher, research in child development; educational leadership (M Ed, Ed D, CAS); elementary education (M Ed); English education (MA Ed); environmental education (MA Ed); instructional technology (M Ed); language arts (M Ed); library science (M Ed); mathematics education (M Ed, MA Ed); music education (MA Ed); psychology (MA Ed); reading (M Ed, CAS); science education (M Ed, CAS); secondary education (M Ed, CAS); special education (M Ed, Ed D, CAS); theater arts (MA Ed); written communication (MA Ed). *Accreditation:* NASAD. *Program availability:* Part-time, evening/weekend, online learning. *Faculty:* 14 full-time (10 women). *Students:* 35 full-time (24 women), 299 part-time (243 women); includes 72 minority (49 Black or African American, non-Hispanic/Latino; 1 American Indian or Alaska Native, non-Hispanic/Latino; 12 Asian, non-Hispanic/Latino; 8 Hispanic/Latino; 2 Two or more races, non-Hispanic/Latino), 5 international. In 2018, 152 master's, 8 doctorates awarded. *Entrance requirements:* Additional exam requirements/recommendations for international students: Required—Official results from the TOEFL or IELTS are required. *Application deadline:* Applications are processed on a rolling basis. Application fee: $25. Electronic applications accepted. *Expenses:* Contact institution. *Financial support:* Career-related internships or fieldwork, tuition waivers (partial), and unspecified assistantships available. *Unit head:* Kimberly Dean, Chair, 215-572-8629. *Application contact:* 215-572-2925, Fax: 215-572-2126, E-mail: grad@arcadia.edu.

Ball State University, Graduate School, Teachers College, Department of Educational Studies, Muncie, IN 47306. Offers adult education (MA, Ed D, Certificate), including adult and community education (MA), adult, higher and community education (Ed D); college and university teaching (Certificate); community college leadership (Certificate); community education (Certificate); computer education (Certificate); curriculum and educational technology (MA); diversity studies (Certificate); educational studies (PhD), including educational studies; executive development for public service (MA); middle-level education (Certificate); qualitative research in education (Certificate); secondary education (MA); student affairs administration in higher education (MA), including student affairs administration in higher education. *Accreditation:* NCATE. *Program availability:* Part-time, 100% online, blended/hybrid learning. *Entrance requirements:* For master's, minimum baccalaureate GPA of 2.75 or 3.0 in latter half of baccalaureate; for doctorate, minimum graduate GPA of 3.2. Additional exam requirements/recommendations for international students: Required—TOEFL (minimum score 550 paper-based; 79 iBT), IELTS (minimum score 6.5). Electronic applications accepted.

Eastern Washington University, Graduate Studies, College of Science, Technology, Engineering and Mathematics, Department of Computer Science, Cheney, WA 99004-2431. Offers computer science (MS). *Program availability:* Part-time. *Degree requirements:* For master's, comprehensive exam, thesis or alternative. *Entrance requirements:* For master's, minimum GPA of 3.0. Additional exam requirements/recommendations for international students: Required—TOEFL (minimum score 580 paper-based; 92 iBT), IELTS (minimum score 7), PTE (minimum score 63). Electronic applications accepted.

Illinois Institute of Technology, Graduate College, College of Science, Department of Computer Science, Chicago, IL 60616. Offers business (MCS); computational intelligence (MCS); computer science (MCS, MS, PhD); cyber-physical systems (MCS); data analytics (MCS); data science (MAS); database systems (MCS); distributed and cloud computing (MCS); education (MCS); finance (MCS); information security and assurance (MCS); networking and communications (MCS); software engineering (MCS); telecommunications and software engineering (MAS); MS/MAS. *Program availability:* Part-time, evening/weekend, online learning. Terminal master's awarded for partial completion of doctoral program. *Degree requirements:* For master's, thesis optional; for doctorate, comprehensive exam, thesis/dissertation. *Entrance requirements:* For master's, GRE General Test with minimum scores of 298 Quantitative and Verbal, 3.0 Analytical Writing (for MS); GRE General Test with minimum scores of 292 Quantitative and Verbal, 2.5 Analytical Writing (for MAS), minimum undergraduate GPA of 3.0; for doctorate, GRE General Test (minimum scores: 304 Quantitative and Verbal, 3.5 Analytical Writing), minimum undergraduate GPA of 3.0. Additional exam requirements/recommendations for international students: Required—TOEFL (minimum score 523 paper-based; 70 iBT). Electronic applications accepted. *Faculty research:* Parallel and distributed processing, high-performance computing, computational linguistics, information retrieval, data mining, grid computing.

Kent State University, College of Education, Health and Human Services, School of Lifespan Development and Educational Sciences, Kent, OH 44242-0001. Offers clinical mental health counseling (M Ed); counseling (Ed S); counseling and human development services (PhD); educational psychology (M Ed, MA); human development and family studies (MA); instructional technology (M Ed, PhD), including computer technology (M Ed), educational psychology (PhD), general instructional technology (M Ed); rehabilitation counseling (M Ed); school counseling (M Ed); school psychology (PhD, Ed S); special education (M Ed, PhD, Ed S), including deaf education (M Ed), early childhood education (M Ed), educational interpreter K-12 (M Ed), general special education (M Ed), gifted education (M Ed), mild/moderate intervention (M Ed), moderate/intensive intervention (M Ed), special education (PhD, Ed S), transition to work (M Ed). *Program availability:* Part-time, evening/weekend. *Faculty:* 71 full-time (37 women), 80 part-time/adjunct (61 women). *Students:* 341 full-time (272 women), 238 part-time (193 women); includes 66 minority (40 Black or African American, non-Hispanic/Latino; 5 American Indian or Alaska Native, non-Hispanic/Latino; 5 Asian, non-

Hispanic/Latino; 8 Hispanic/Latino; 7 Native Hawaiian or other Pacific Islander, non-Hispanic/Latino; 1 Two or more races, non-Hispanic/Latino), 16 international. 461 applicants, 35% accepted. In 2018, 162 master's, 21 doctorates, 14 other advanced degrees awarded. *Degree requirements:* For master's, thesis optional; for doctorate, comprehensive exam, thesis/dissertation. *Entrance requirements:* For master's, doctorate, and Ed S, GRE General Test. Additional exam requirements/recommendations for international students: Required—TOEFL (minimum score 550 paper-based; 80 iBT). *Application deadline:* Applications are processed on a rolling basis. Application fee: $45 ($60 for international students). Electronic applications accepted. *Expenses:* Tuition, state resident: full-time $11,766; part-time $536 per credit. Tuition, nonresident: full-time $21,952; part-time $999 per credit. *International tuition:* $21,952 full-time. Tuition and fees vary according to course load. *Financial support:* In 2018–19, 35 research assistantships with full tuition reimbursements (averaging $10,000 per year), 8 teaching assistantships with full tuition reimbursements (averaging $12,000 per year) were awarded; Federal Work-Study, scholarships/grants, unspecified assistantships, and 16 administrative assistantships (averaging $9,594 per year) also available. Financial award application deadline: 4/1. *Unit head:* Dr. Mary Dellmann-Jenkins, Director, 330-672-6958, E-mail: mdellman@kent.edu. *Application contact:* Cheryl Slusarczyk, Academic Program Director, Office of Graduate Student Services, 330-672-2576, Fax: 330-672-9162, E-mail: ogs@kent.edu. Website: http://www.kent.edu/ehhs/ldes/

Lesley University, Graduate School of Education, Cambridge, MA 02138-2790. Offers arts, community, and education (M Ed); autism studies (Certificate); curriculum and instruction (M Ed, CAGS); early childhood education (M Ed); ecological teaching and learning (MS); educational studies (PhD), including adult learning, educational leadership, individually designed; elementary education (M Ed); emergent technologies for educators (Certificate); ESLArts: language learning through the arts (M Ed); high school education (M Ed); individually designed (M Ed); integrated teaching through the arts (M Ed); literacy for K-8 classroom teachers (M Ed); mathematics education (M Ed); middle school education (M Ed); moderate disabilities (M Ed); online learning (Certificate); reading (CAGS); science in education (M Ed); severe disabilities (M Ed); special needs (CAGS); specialist teacher of reading (M Ed); teacher of visual art (M Ed); technology in education (M Ed, CAGS). *Accreditation:* TEAC. *Program availability:* Part-time, evening/weekend, online learning. *Degree requirements:* For master's, practicum; for doctorate, thesis/dissertation. *Entrance requirements:* For master's, Massachusetts Tests for Educator Licensure (MTEL), transcripts, statement of purpose, recommendations; interview (for special education); for doctorate, GRE General Test, transcripts, statement of purpose, recommendations, interview, master's degree, resume; for other advanced degree, interview, master's degree. Additional exam requirements/recommendations for international students: Required—TOEFL (minimum score 550 paper-based; 80 iBT). Electronic applications accepted. *Faculty research:* Assessment in literacy, mathematics and science; autism spectrum disorders; instructional technology and online learning; multicultural education and English language learners.

Mississippi College, Graduate School, College of Arts and Sciences, School of Science and Mathematics, Department of Engineering, Computer Science, and Physics, Clinton, MS 39058. Offers computer science (M Ed, MS); cybersecurity and information assurance (MS). *Program availability:* Part-time. *Degree requirements:* For master's, comprehensive exam, thesis or alternative. *Entrance requirements:* For master's, GRE. Additional exam requirements/recommendations for international students: Recommended—TOEFL, IELTS.

Mississippi College, Graduate School, School of Education, Department of Teacher Education and Leadership, Clinton, MS 39058. Offers art (M Ed); biological science (M Ed); business education (M Ed); computer science (M Ed); dyslexia therapy (M Ed); educational leadership (M Ed, Ed D, Ed S); elementary education (M Ed, Ed S); English (M Ed); higher education administration (MS); mathematics (M Ed); secondary education (M Ed); social studies (history) (M Ed); teaching arts (M Ed). *Program availability:* Part-time, online learning. *Degree requirements:* For master's, comprehensive exam, thesis optional. *Entrance requirements:* For master's, NTE. Additional exam requirements/recommendations for international students: Recommended—TOEFL, IELTS. Electronic applications accepted.

Ohio University, Graduate College, Gladys W. and David H. Patton College of Education and Human Services, Department of Educational Studies, Athens, OH 45701-2979. Offers computer education and technology (M Ed); educational administration (M Ed, Ed D); educational research and evaluation (M Ed, PhD); instructional technology (PhD). *Program availability:* Part-time, evening/weekend, online learning. *Degree requirements:* For master's, thesis or alternative; for doctorate, comprehensive exam, thesis/dissertation. *Entrance requirements:* For master's, GRE General Test (if GPA less than 2.9); for doctorate, GRE General Test, GRE Subject Test, minimum GPA of 2.9, work experience, 3 letters of reference, autobiography. Additional exam requirements/recommendations for international students: Required—TOEFL (minimum score 550 paper-based; 80 iBT) or IELTS (minimum score 6.5). Electronic applications accepted. *Faculty research:* Race, class and gender; computer programs; development and organization theory; evaluation/development of instruments, leadership.

Teachers College, Columbia University, Department of Mathematics, Science and Technology, New York, NY 10027-6696. Offers biology 7-12 (MA); chemistry 7-12 (MA); communication and education (MA, Ed D); computing in education (MA); earth science 7-12 (MA); instructional technology and media (Ed M, MA, Ed D); mathematics

education (Ed M, MA, Ed D, Ed DCT, PhD); physics 7-12 (MA); science and dental education (MA); science education (Ed M, MS, Ed DCT, PhD); supervisor/teacher of science education (MA); technology specialist (MA). *Program availability:* Part-time, evening/weekend, online learning. *Students:* 155 full-time (114 women), 254 part-time (162 women); includes 136 minority (44 Black or African American, non-Hispanic/Latino; 1 American Indian or Alaska Native, non-Hispanic/Latino; 59 Asian, non-Hispanic/Latino; 23 Hispanic/Latino; 9 Two or more races, non-Hispanic/Latino), 140 international. Average age 31. 484 applicants, 60% accepted, 138 enrolled. Terminal master's awarded for partial completion of doctoral program. *Unit head:* Prof. Erica Walker, Chair, 212-678-8246, E-mail: ewalker@tc.columbia.edu. *Application contact:* Kelly Sutton Skinner, Director of Admission & New Student Enrollment, E-mail: kms2237@tc.columbia.edu.
Website: http://www.tc.columbia.edu/mathematics-science-and-technology/

Thomas College, Graduate School, Programs in Business, Waterville, ME 04901-5097. Offers business (MBA); computer technology education (MS); education (MS); human resource management (MBA). *Program availability:* Part-time, evening/weekend. *Entrance requirements:* For master's, GMAT, GRE, MAT or minimum GPA of 3.3 in first 3 graduate-level courses. Additional exam requirements/recommendations for international students: Recommended—TOEFL.

University of Bridgeport, School of Education, Department of Education, Bridgeport, CT 06604. Offers education (MS); educational management (Ed D, Diploma), including intermediate administrator or supervisor (Diploma), leadership (Ed D); elementary education (MS, Diploma), including early childhood education, elementary education; middle school education (MS); music education (MS); remedial reading and language arts (Diploma); secondary education (MS, Diploma), including computer specialist (Diploma), international education (Diploma), reading specialist, secondary education. *Program availability:* Part-time, evening/weekend. *Degree requirements:* For master's, final exam, final project, or thesis; for doctorate, comprehensive exam, thesis/dissertation; for Diploma, thesis or alternative, final project. *Entrance requirements:* For master's, minimum undergraduate QPA of 2.67; for doctorate, GRE, MAT; for Diploma, GRE General Test or MAT, minimum graduate QPA of 3.0. Additional exam requirements/recommendations for international students: Recommended—TOEFL (minimum score 550 paper-based; 80 iBT), IELTS (minimum score 6.5). Electronic applications accepted. *Expenses:* Contact institution.

University of Illinois at Chicago, Program in Learning Sciences, Chicago, IL 60607-7128. Offers PhD.

University of Phoenix–Central Valley Campus, College of Education, Fresno, CA 93720-1552. Offers curriculum and instruction (MA Ed); curriculum and instruction-computer education (MA Ed); elementary teacher education (MA Ed); secondary teacher education (MA Ed).

University of Phoenix–Online Campus, College of Education, Phoenix, AZ 85034-7209. Offers administration and supervision (MAEd, Certificate); adult education and training (MAEd); curriculum and instruction (MAEd), including computer education, curriculum and instruction, English as a second language, language arts, mathematics, reading; early childhood education (MAEd); educational studies (MAEd); elementary teacher education (MAEd), including early childhood, elementary teacher education, high school middle level, middle level; principal licensure (Certificate); secondary teacher education (MAEd); special education (MAEd, Certificate); teacher education (MAEd), including middle level generalist; teacher education middle level mathematics (MAEd), including middle level mathematics; teacher education middle level science (MAEd), including middle level science; teacher education secondary mathematics (MAEd); teacher education secondary science (MAEd); teacher leadership (MAEd); teachers of English learners (Certificate); transition to teaching (Certificate), including elementary education, secondary education. *Program availability:* Evening/weekend, online learning. *Entrance requirements:* Additional exam requirements/recommendations for international students: Required—TOEFL, TOEIC (Test of English as an International Communication), Berlitz Online English Proficiency Exam, PTE, or IELTS. Electronic applications accepted. *Expenses:* Contact institution.

University of Phoenix–San Diego Campus, College of Education, San Diego, CA 92123. Offers curriculum and instruction (MA Ed), including computer education, curriculum and instruction, English as a second language; elementary teacher education (MA Ed); secondary teacher education (MA Ed). *Program availability:* Evening/weekend. *Degree requirements:* For master's, thesis (for some programs). *Entrance requirements:* For master's, 3 years of work experience, minimum undergraduate GPA of 3.0. Additional exam requirements/recommendations for international students: Required—TOEFL (minimum score 550 paper-based; 79 iBT). Electronic applications accepted.

Counselor Education

Acadia University, Faculty of Professional Studies, School of Education, Program in Counseling, Wolfville, NS B4P 2R6, Canada. Offers M Ed. *Program availability:* Part-time. *Entrance requirements:* For master's, B Ed, minimum B average in undergraduate course work, 2 years of teaching or related experience. Additional exam requirements/recommendations for international students: Required—TOEFL (minimum score 580 paper-based; 93 iBT), IELTS (minimum score 6.5). *Faculty research:* Computer-assisted supervision, rural/remote school counseling, non-custodial fathers, spirituality, counseling relationships.

Adams State University, Office of Graduate Studies, Department of Counselor Education, Alamosa, CO 81101. Offers counselor education (MA), including clinical mental health counseling, school counseling; counselor education and supervision (PhD). *Accreditation:* ACA (one or more programs are accredited). *Program availability:* Part-time. *Degree requirements:* For master's, internship, qualifying exam. *Entrance requirements:* For master's, GRE General Test or MAT, minimum undergraduate GPA of 2.75.

Adler Graduate School, Program in Adlerian Counseling and Psychotherapy, Richfield, MN 55423. Offers Adlerian studies (MA); art therapy (MA); clinical mental health counseling (MA); co-occurring substance use and mental health disorders (MA); marriage and family therapy (MA); school counseling (MA). *Program availability:* Part-time, evening/weekend. *Degree requirements:* For master's, thesis or alternative, 500-700 hour internship (depending on license choice). *Entrance requirements:* For master's, interview, official transcripts, minimum cumulative GPA of 3.0. Electronic applications accepted. *Expenses:* Contact institution.

Adler University, Graduate Programs, PhD in Counselor Education and Supervision Program, Chicago, IL 60602. Offers PhD. *Program availability:* Evening/weekend, online learning.

Alabama Agricultural and Mechanical University, School of Graduate Studies, College of Education, Humanities, and Behavioral Sciences, Department of Social Work, Psychology and Counseling, Huntsville, AL 35811. Offers psychology and counseling (MS, Ed S), including clinical psychology (MS), counseling psychology (MS), guidance and counseling, rehabilitation counseling (MS), school counseling (MS), school psychology (MS), school psychometry (MS); social work (MSW). *Accreditation:* CORE; NCATE. *Program availability:* Part-time, evening/weekend. *Degree requirements:* For master's, comprehensive exam. *Entrance requirements:* For master's, GRE General Test. Additional exam requirements/recommendations for international students: Required—TOEFL (minimum score 500 paper-based; 61 iBT). *Faculty research:* Increasing numbers of minorities in special education and speech-language pathology.

Alabama State University, College of Education, Department of Instructional Support Programs, Montgomery, AL 36101-0271. Offers counselor education (M Ed, MS, Ed S), including general counseling (MS, Ed S), school counseling (M Ed, Ed S); educational administration (M Ed), including instructional leadership; educational leadership, policy and law (PhD); library education media (Ed S). *Program availability:* Part-time, evening/weekend. *Faculty:* 11 full-time (6 women), 7 part-time/adjunct (5 women). *Students:* 27 full-time (17 women), 85 part-time (58 women); includes 182 minority (181 Black or African American, non-Hispanic/Latino; 1 Hispanic/Latino). Average age 41. 70 applicants, 54% accepted, 12 enrolled. In 2018, 14 master's, 6 doctorates, 1 other advanced degree awarded. Terminal master's awarded for partial completion of doctoral program. *Degree requirements:* For master's and Ed S, comprehensive exam; for doctorate, thesis/dissertation. *Entrance requirements:* For master's, GRE General Test, MAT, writing competency test, bachelor's degree or its equivalent from accredited college or university with minimum GPA of 2.5; for Ed S, GRE General Test, MAT, writing competency test, minimum GPA of 3.25. Additional exam requirements/recommendations for international students: Required—TOEFL (minimum score 500 paper-based). *Application deadline:* For fall admission, 4/15 for domestic and international students; for spring admission, 11/15 for domestic and international students; for summer admission, 3/15 for domestic and international students. Applications are processed on a rolling basis. Application fee: $25. Electronic applications accepted. *Expenses:* Contact institution. *Financial support:* In 2018–19, 3 students received support. Fellowships, research assistantships, teaching assistantships, Federal Work-Study, scholarships/grants, tuition waivers (partial), and unspecified assistantships available. Financial award application deadline: 6/30; financial award applicants required to submit FAFSA. *Unit head:* Dr. Kecia Asley, Chair, Instructional Leadership/Educational Leadership, Policy, & Law, 334-229-8828, Fax: 334-229-6831, E-mail: kashley@alasu.edu. *Application contact:* Dr. Ed Brown, Dean of Graduate Studies, 334-229-4275, Fax: 334-229-4928, E-mail: ebrown@alasu.edu.
Website: http://www.alasu.edu/academics/colleges—departments/college-of-education/instructional-support-programs/index.aspx

Albany State University, College of Education, Albany, GA 31705-2717. Offers early childhood education (M Ed); educational leadership (Ed S); health and physical education (M Ed); middle grades education (M Ed); school counseling (M Ed); special education (M Ed). *Accreditation:* NCATE. *Program availability:* Part-time, evening/weekend, online learning. *Degree requirements:* For master's, comprehensive exam, internship, GACE Content Exam. *Entrance requirements:* For master's, GRE or MAT. Electronic applications accepted. *Faculty research:* GACE preparation, STEM (science, technology, engineering, and mathematics), technology education, special education, professional teacher development, health implications liberation philosophy, NET-Q, learning community, disabled or at-risk students.

Alcorn State University, School of Graduate Studies, School of Education and Psychology, Lorman, MS 39096-7500. Offers agricultural education (MS Ed); elementary education (MAT, MS Ed, Ed S); guidance and counseling (MS Ed); industrial education (MS Ed); secondary education (MAT, MS Ed), including health and physical education (MS Ed), NCAA compliance and academic progress reporting (MS Ed); special education (MS Ed). *Accreditation:* NCATE. *Degree requirements:* For master's, thesis optional.

Alfred University, Graduate School, Counseling and School Psychology Program, Alfred, NY 14802-1205. Offers mental health counseling (MS Ed); school counseling (MS Ed, CAS); school psychology (MA, Psy D, CAS). *Accreditation:* APA. *Degree requirements:* For master's, internship; for doctorate, thesis/dissertation, internship. *Entrance requirements:* For master's and doctorate, GRE General Test. Additional exam requirements/recommendations for international students: Required—TOEFL (minimum score 590 paper-based; 90 iBT), IELTS (minimum score 6.5). Electronic applications accepted. *Faculty research:* Family processes, alternative assessment approaches, behavior disorders in children, parent involvement, school psychology training issues.

Alliant International University–San Francisco, California School of Professional Psychology, Program in Clinical Counseling, San Francisco, CA 94133. Offers MA. *Degree requirements:* For master's, comprehensive exam, project. *Entrance requirements:* For master's, minimum GPA of 3.0, recommendations, essay, interview. Additional exam requirements/recommendations for international students: Required—TOEFL (minimum score 550 paper-based; 80 iBT), TWE (minimum score 5). Electronic applications accepted. *Faculty research:* Systems of privilege and oppression, multicultural and social justice advocacy competence, rural issues, LGBTQ affirmative therapy and identity development, college student mental health.

Amberton University, Graduate School, Programs in Counseling, Garland, TX 75041-5595. Offers marriage and family therapy (MA); professional counseling (MA); school counseling (MA). *Entrance requirements:* For master's, minimum GPA of 3.0.

American International College, School of Education, Springfield, MA 01109-3189. Offers early childhood education (M Ed, CAGS); education (MA, Ed D), including counseling psychology (MA), educational leadership and supervision (Ed D), professional counseling and supervision (Ed D), teaching and learning (Ed D); elementary education (M Ed, CAGS); middle education/secondary education (M Ed, CAGS); moderate disabilities (M Ed, CAGS); reading specialist (M Ed, CAGS); school adjustment counseling (MAEP, CAGS); school guidance counseling (MAEP, CAGS); school leadership (M Ed, CAGS). *Program availability:* Evening/weekend. *Degree requirements:* For master's and CAGS, practicum/culminating experience. *Entrance requirements:* For master's, Communication and Literacy portion of the Massachusetts

Tests for Education Licensure, graduate of accredited four-year college with minimum B- average in undergraduate course work; for CAGS, M Ed or master's degree in field related to licensure from accredited institution. Electronic applications accepted. *Expenses:* Contact institution.

Amridge University, Graduate and Professional Programs, Montgomery, AL 36117. Offers Biblical studies (MA, PhD); Christian ministry (MS); family therapy (D Min); human services (MS); leadership and management (MS); marriage and family therapy (M Div, MA, PhD); ministerial leadership (M Div, MS); New Testament studies (MA); Old Testament studies (MA); professional counseling (M Div, MA, PhD); theology (M Div, D Min). *Program availability:* Part-time, evening/weekend, online learning. *Degree requirements:* For master's, one foreign language, comprehensive exam (for some programs), thesis (for some programs); for doctorate, one foreign language, comprehensive exam (for some programs), thesis/dissertation (for some programs). *Entrance requirements:* For master's, official transcript showing an earned 4-year BA or BS from regionally- or nationally-accredited institution; for doctorate, official transcript showing earned graduate degree from regionally- or nationally-accredited institution; writing sample (e.g. career monograph, published journal article, term paper from master's degree or doctoral dissertation); interview. Additional exam requirements/recommendations for international students: Required—TOEFL (minimum score 79 iBT). Electronic applications accepted. *Faculty research:* Technology and mental healthcare, resilience in black families, theology and congregational ministry.

Angelo State University, College of Graduate Studies and Research, College of Education, Department of Curriculum and Instruction, San Angelo, TX 76909. Offers curriculum and instruction (MA); educational administration (M Ed); guidance and counseling (M Ed); student development and leadership in higher education (M Ed). *Program availability:* Part-time, evening/weekend, online learning. *Students:* 360 full-time (307 women), 456 part-time (364 women); includes 312 minority (93 Black or African American, non-Hispanic/Latino; 3 American Indian or Alaska Native, non-Hispanic/Latino; 7 Asian, non-Hispanic/Latino; 193 Hispanic/Latino; 1 Native Hawaiian or other Pacific Islander, non-Hispanic/Latino; 15 Two or more races, non-Hispanic/Latino). Average age 35. *Application deadline:* For fall admission, 7/15 priority date for domestic students, 6/10 for international students; for spring admission, 12/1 priority date for domestic students, 11/1 for international students. Application fee: $40 ($50 for international students). *Expenses: Tuition, area resident:* Full-time $3964; part-time $220 per credit hour. Tuition, state resident: full-time $3964; part-time $220 per credit hour. Tuition, nonresident: full-time $11,434; part-time $635 per credit hour. *International tuition:* $11,434 full-time. *Unit head:* Dr. Kim Livengood, Chair, 325-942-2647, Fax: 325-942-2039, E-mail: kim.livengood@angelo.edu. *Application contact:* Dr. Kim Livengood, Chair, 325-942-2647, Fax: 325-942-2039, E-mail: kim.livengood@angelo.edu.
Website: http://www.angelo.edu/dept/ci/

Antioch University Seattle, Program in Counseling, Therapy and Wellness, Seattle, WA 98121. Offers clinical mental health counseling (MA); counselor education and supervision (PhD); couple and family therapy (MA).

Appalachian State University, Cratis D. Williams School of Graduate Studies, Department of Human Development and Psychological Counseling, Boone, NC 28608. Offers clinical mental health counseling (MA); college student development (MA); marriage and family therapy (MA); school counseling (MA). *Accreditation:* AAMFT/COAMFTE; ACA; NCATE. *Program availability:* Part-time. *Degree requirements:* For master's, comprehensive exam (for some programs), thesis optional, internships. *Entrance requirements:* For master's, GRE General Test, 3 letters of recommendation. Additional exam requirements/recommendations for international students: Required—TOEFL (minimum score 570 paper-based; 79 iBT), IELTS (minimum score 6.5). Electronic applications accepted. *Expenses: Tuition, area resident:* Full-time $4839; part-time $237 per credit hour. Tuition, state resident: full-time $4839; part-time $237 per credit hour. Tuition, nonresident: full-time $18,271; part-time $895.50 per credit hour. *Faculty research:* Multicultural counseling, addictions counseling, play therapy, expressive arts, child and adolescent therapy, sexual abuse counseling.

Argosy University, Atlanta, Georgia School of Professional Psychology, Atlanta, GA 30328. Offers clinical psychology (MA, Psy D, Postdoctoral Respecialization Certificate), including child and family psychology (Psy D), general adult clinical (Psy D), health psychology (Psy D), neuropsychology/geropsychology (Psy D); community counseling (MA), including marriage and family therapy; counselor education and supervision (Ed D); forensic psychology (MA); industrial organizational psychology (MA); marriage and family therapy (Certificate); sport-exercise psychology (MA). *Accreditation:* APA.

Argosy University, Chicago, Illinois School of Professional Psychology, Program in Counseling Psychology, Chicago, IL 60601. Offers counselor education and supervision (Ed D). *Accreditation:* ACA. *Program availability:* Online learning.

Argosy University, Northern Virginia, American School of Professional Psychology, Arlington, VA 22209. Offers clinical psychology (MA, Psy D), including child and family psychology (Psy D), diversity and multicultural psychology (Psy D), forensic psychology (Psy D), health and neuropsychology (Psy D); community counseling (MA); counseling psychology (Ed D), including counselor education and supervision; counselor education and supervision (Ed D); forensic psychology (MA).

Argosy University, Tampa, College of Education, Tampa, FL 33607. Offers community college executive leadership (Ed D); educational leadership (MA Ed, Ed D, Ed S), including higher education administration (Ed D), K-12 education (Ed D); school counseling (MA); teaching and learning (MA Ed, Ed D, Ed S), including higher education (Ed D), K-12 education (Ed D).

Argosy University, Tampa, Florida School of Professional Psychology, Tampa, FL 33607. Offers clinical psychology (MA, Psy D), including clinical psychology; counselor education and supervision (Ed D); industrial organizational psychology (MA); marriage and family therapy (MA); mental health counseling (MA).

Arizona State University at the Tempe campus, School of Letters and Sciences, Program in Counseling, Tempe, AZ 85287-0811. Offers MC. *Accreditation:* ACA. *Degree requirements:* For master's, comprehensive exam (for some programs), thesis (for some programs), interactive Program of Study (iPOS) submitted before completing 50 percent of required credit hours. *Entrance requirements:* For master's, GRE, minimum GPA of 3.0 or equivalent in last 2 years of work leading to bachelor's degree; 3 letters of recommendation; 3-5 page personal statement with information on significant life experiences, professional experiences and goals. Additional exam requirements/recommendations for international students: Required—TOEFL, IELTS, or PTE. Electronic applications accepted.

Arkansas State University, Graduate School, College of Education and Behavioral Science, Department of Psychology and Counseling, State University, AR 72467. Offers clinical mental health counseling (Graduate Certificate); college student personnel services (MS); dyslexia therapy (Graduate Certificate); psychological science (MS); psychology and counseling (Ed S); rehabilitation counseling (MRC); school counseling (MSE); student affairs (Graduate Certificate). *Accreditation:* ACA (one or more programs are accredited); CORE (one or more programs are accredited); NCATE. *Program availability:* Part-time. *Degree requirements:* For master's and other advanced degree, comprehensive exam, thesis or alternative. *Entrance requirements:* For master's, GRE General Test or MAT (for MSE), appropriate bachelor's degree, interview, letters of reference, official transcripts, immunization records, written statement, 2-3 page autobiography; for other advanced degree, GRE General Test, interview, master's degree, letters of reference, official transcript, personal statement, immunization records. Additional exam requirements/recommendations for international students: Required—TOEFL (minimum score 550 paper-based; 79 iBT), IELTS (minimum score 6), PTE (minimum score 56). Electronic applications accepted.

Arkansas Tech University, College of Education, Russellville, AR 72801. Offers college student personnel (MS); educational leadership (M Ed, Ed S); instructional technology (M Ed); school counseling and leadership (M Ed); school leadership (Ed D); special education K-12 (M Ed); strength and conditioning studies (MS); teaching (MAT); teaching, learning, and leadership (M Ed). *Accreditation:* NCATE. *Program availability:* Part-time, evening/weekend, 100% online, blended/hybrid learning. *Students:* 90 full-time (52 women), 450 part-time (359 women); includes 100 minority (63 Black or African American, non-Hispanic/Latino; 6 American Indian or Alaska Native, non-Hispanic/Latino; 1 Asian, non-Hispanic/Latino; 15 Hispanic/Latino; 15 Two or more races, non-Hispanic/Latino), 4 international. Average age 34. In 2018, 130 master's, 14 doctorates, 1 other advanced degree awarded. *Degree requirements:* For master's, comprehensive exam, thesis optional, action research project; for doctorate, thesis/dissertation. *Entrance requirements:* Additional exam requirements/recommendations for international students: Required—TOEFL (minimum score 550 paper-based; 79 iBT), IELTS (minimum score 6.5), PTE (minimum score 58). *Application deadline:* For fall admission, 3/1 priority date for domestic students, 5/1 priority date for international students; for spring admission, 10/1 priority date for domestic and international students. Applications are processed on a rolling basis. Application fee: $40 ($90 for international students). Electronic applications accepted. *Expenses: Tuition, area resident:* Full-time $6816; part-time $284 per credit hour. Tuition, state resident: full-time $6816; part-time $284 per credit hour. Tuition, nonresident: full-time $13,632; part-time $568 per credit hour. *International tuition:* $13,632 full-time. *Required fees:* $457.50 per semester. Tuition and fees vary according to course load and degree level. *Financial support:* In 2018–19, research assistantships with full and partial tuition reimbursements (averaging $4,800 per year), teaching assistantships with full and partial tuition reimbursements (averaging $4,800 per year) were awarded; career-related internships or fieldwork, Federal Work-Study, scholarships/grants, health care benefits, and unspecified assistantships also available. Support available to part-time students. Financial award application deadline: 4/15; financial award applicants required to submit FAFSA. *Unit head:* Dr. Linda Bean, Dean, 479-964-3217, E-mail: lbean@atu.edu. *Application contact:* Dr. Jeff Robertson, Interim Dean of Graduate College, 479-968-0398, Fax: 479-964-0542, E-mail: gradcollege@atu.edu.
Website: http://www.atu.edu/education/

Ashland Theological Seminary, Graduate Programs, Ashland, OH 44805. Offers Biblical studies (MA); Christian ministries (MACM), including Black church studies (MACM, D Min), general Christian ministries, leadership, spiritual formation (MACM, D Min); clinical mental health counseling (MA); counseling (MAC); historical and theological studies (MA), including Anabaptism and Pietism, Christian theology, church history, New Testament, Old Testament; ministry (D Min), including Black church studies (MACM, D Min), chaplaincy (M Div, D Min), independent design, spiritual formation (MACM, D Min), transformational leadership; pastoral ministry (M Div), including chaplaincy (M Div, D Min), general ministry. MAC program offered in Detroit, MI. *Accreditation:* ATS. *Program availability:* Part-time. *Degree requirements:* For master's, 2 foreign languages, comprehensive exam (for some programs), thesis (for some programs); for doctorate, thesis/dissertation. *Entrance requirements:* For master's, bachelor's degree from accredited institution with minimum undergraduate GPA of 2.75; for doctorate, M Div, minimum undergraduate GPA of 3.0. Additional exam requirements/recommendations for international students: Required—TOEFL (minimum score 500 paper-based; 65 iBT). Electronic applications accepted. *Faculty research:* Semitic languages and linguistics, rhetorical and social-scientific criticism, Anabaptist studies, inner spiritual healing, African-American clergy in film and literature.

Athabasca University, Program in Counseling, Athabasca, AB T9S 3A3, Canada. Offers applied psychology (Post Master's Certificate); art therapy (MC); career counseling (MC); counseling (Advanced Certificate); counseling psychology (MC); school counseling (MC).

Auburn University at Montgomery, College of Education, Department of Counselor, Leadership, and Special Education, Montgomery, AL 36124-4023. Offers counselor education (M Ed, Ed S), including clinical mental health counseling, school counseling; early childhood special education (M Ed); instructional leadership (M Ed, Ed S); special education/collaborative teacher (M Ed, Ed S). *Accreditation:* ACA; NCATE. *Program availability:* Part-time, evening/weekend. *Students:* Average age 34. 76 applicants, 72% accepted, 26 enrolled. In 2018, 37 master's awarded. *Entrance requirements:* For master's, GRE General Test or MAT, certification, BS in teaching; for Ed S, GRE General Test or MAT, certification. Additional exam requirements/recommendations for international students: Recommended—TOEFL (minimum score 500 paper-based; 61 iBT), IELTS (minimum score 5.5), TSE (minimum score 44). *Application deadline:* For fall admission, 7/15 for international students; for spring admission, 11/15 for international students; for summer admission, 4/15 for international students. Applications are processed on a rolling basis. Electronic applications accepted. *Expenses: Tuition, area resident:* Full-time $7146; part-time $4764 per credit hour. Tuition, state resident: full-time $7146; part-time $4764 per credit hour. Tuition, nonresident: full-time $16,056; part-time $10,704 per credit hour. *International tuition:* $16,056 full-time. *Required fees:* $766. One-time fee: $25 full-time. *Financial support:* Career-related internships or fieldwork and scholarships/grants available. Support available to part-time students. Financial award application deadline: 3/1; financial award applicants required to submit FAFSA. *Unit head:* Dr. Samuel Flynt, Head, 334-244-3835, Fax: 334-244-3101, E-mail: sflynt@aum.edu. *Application contact:* Dr. Rhonda Morton, Associate Dean/Graduate Coordinator, 334-244-3287, Fax: 334-244-3978, E-mail: rmorton@aum.edu.
Website: http://education.aum.edu/academic-departments/counselor-leadership-and-special-education

Augusta University, College of Education, Department of Counselor Education, Leadership, and Research, Augusta, GA 30912. Offers counselor education (M Ed, Ed S), including clinical mental health counseling (M Ed), school counselor (M Ed). *Accreditation:* ACA; NCATE. *Program availability:* Part-time, evening/weekend. *Degree requirements:* For master's, comprehensive exam; for Ed S, comprehensive exam, thesis. *Entrance requirements:* For master's, GRE, MAT, minimum GPA of 2.5; for Ed S, GRE, MAT. *Faculty research:* Restructuring schools, financing education, student transition.

Austin Peay State University, College of Graduate Studies, College of Behavioral and Health Sciences, Department of Psychological Science and Counseling, Clarksville, TN 37044. Offers industrial-organizational psychology (MS); mental health counseling (MS), including clinical mental health, school counseling; school counseling (MS). *Program availability:* Part-time, online learning. *Faculty:* 10 full-time (6 women), 2 part-time/adjunct (both women). *Students:* 49 full-time (40 women), 40 part-time (29 women);

includes 25 minority (12 Black or African American, non-Hispanic/Latino; 1 American Indian or Alaska Native, non-Hispanic/Latino; 1 Asian, non-Hispanic/Latino; 6 Hispanic/Latino; 5 Two or more races, non-Hispanic/Latino). Average age 30. 59 applicants, 75% accepted, 38 enrolled. In 2018, 18 master's awarded. *Degree requirements:* For master's, comprehensive exam, thesis (for some programs). *Entrance requirements:* For master's, GRE General Test, minimum undergraduate GPA of 2.5, 3 letters of recommendation, bachelor's degree. Additional exam requirements/recommendations for international students: Required—TOEFL (minimum score 500 paper-based). *Application deadline:* For fall admission, 8/21 priority date for domestic students. Applications are processed on a rolling basis. Application fee: $45 ($55 for international students). Electronic applications accepted. *Expenses: Tuition, area resident:* Part-time $450 per credit hour. Tuition, state resident: full-time $5987; part-time $450 per credit hour. Tuition, nonresident: full-time $8757; part-time $806 per credit hour. *Required fees:* $1583; $79.15 per credit hour. *Financial support:* Research assistantships with full tuition reimbursements, career-related internships or fieldwork, Federal Work-Study, institutionally sponsored loans, scholarships/grants, and unspecified assistantships available. Support available to part-time students. Financial award application deadline: 7/1; financial award applicants required to submit FAFSA. *Unit head:* Dr. Nicole Knickmeyer, Chair, 931-221-7232, Fax: 931-221-6267, E-mail: knickmeyer@apsu.edu. *Application contact:* Megan Mitchell, Coordinator of Graduate Admissions, 800-859-4723, Fax: 931-221-7641, E-mail: gradadmissions@apsu.edu.
Website: http://www.apsu.edu/psychology/index.php

Azusa Pacific University, School of Education, Department of School Counseling and School Psychology, Program in Educational Counseling, Azusa, CA 91702-7000. Offers MA Ed.

Ball State University, Graduate School, College of Health, Department of Counseling Psychology, Social Psychology, and Counseling, Program in Counseling Psychology, Muncie, IN 47306. Offers counseling (MA), including clinical mental health counseling, mental health counseling, rehabilitation counseling, school counseling; counseling psychology (PhD). *Accreditation:* ACA; APA. *Program availability:* Part-time. *Degree requirements:* For doctorate, thesis/dissertation. *Entrance requirements:* For master's, GRE General Test (minimum scores 144 quantitative, 153 verbal), minimum baccalaureate GPA of 2.75 or 3.0 in latter half of baccalaureate, minimum GPA of 3.0 in psychology coursework, three letters of recommendation; for doctorate, GRE General Test, interview, minimum graduate GPA of 3.2, resume. Additional exam requirements/recommendations for international students: Required—TOEFL (minimum score 550 paper-based; 79 iBT), IELTS (minimum score 6.5). Electronic applications accepted.

Barry University, School of Education, Program in Counseling, Miami Shores, FL 33161-6695. Offers MS, PhD, Ed S. *Accreditation:* ACA. *Program availability:* Part-time, evening/weekend. *Degree requirements:* For master's, comprehensive exam. *Entrance requirements:* For master's, GRE General Test or MAT, minimum GPA of 3.0; for doctorate, GRE, minimum GPA of 3.25; for Ed S, GRE General Test, minimum GPA of 3.0.

Barry University, School of Education, Program in Mental Health Counseling, Miami Shores, FL 33161-6695. Offers MS, Ed S. *Accreditation:* ACA. *Program availability:* Part-time, evening/weekend. *Degree requirements:* For master's, comprehensive exam, scholarly paper; for Ed S, comprehensive exam. *Entrance requirements:* For master's, GRE General Test or MAT, minimum GPA of 3.0; for Ed S, GRE General Test, minimum GPA of 3.0. Electronic applications accepted.

Barry University, School of Education, Program in School Counseling, Miami Shores, FL 33161-6695. Offers MS, Ed S. *Accreditation:* ACA (one or more programs are accredited). *Program availability:* Part-time, evening/weekend. *Degree requirements:* For master's, comprehensive exam, scholarly paper; for Ed S, comprehensive exam. *Entrance requirements:* For master's, GRE General Test or MAT, minimum GPA of 3.0; for Ed S, GRE General Test, minimum GPA of 3.0. Electronic applications accepted.

Bayamón Central University, Graduate Programs, Program in Education, Bayamón, PR 00960-1725. Offers administration and supervision (MA Ed); commercial education (MA Ed); elementary education (K–3) (MA Ed); family counseling (Graduate Certificate); guidance and counseling (MA Ed); pre-elementary teacher (MA Ed); rehabilitation counseling (MA Ed); special education (MA Ed), including attention deficit disorder, education of the autistic, learning disabilities. *Program availability:* Part-time, evening/weekend. *Degree requirements:* For master's, comprehensive exam. *Entrance requirements:* For master's, EXADEP, bachelor's degree in education or related field.

Becker College, Program in Mental Health Counseling, Worcester, MA 01609. Offers community mental health (MA); school consultation (MA). *Entrance requirements:* For master's, GRE, interview, official transcript, three letters of recommendation, essay. Electronic applications accepted.

Bellevue University, Graduate School, College of Arts and Sciences, Bellevue, NE 68005-3098. Offers clinical counseling (MS); healthcare administration (MHA); human services (MA); international security and intelligence studies (MS); managerial communication (MA). *Program availability:* Online learning.

Bloomsburg University of Pennsylvania, School of Graduate Studies, College of Education, Department of Teaching and Learning, Program in Educational Leadership, Bloomsburg, PA 17815-1301. Offers college student affairs (M Ed); PreK-12 curriculum and instruction (M Ed); PreK-12 school counseling (M Ed); PreK-12 school principal (M Ed). *Degree requirements:* For master's, practicum. *Entrance requirements:* For master's, 3 letters of recommendation, resume, minimum QPA of 3.0, personal statement, interview. Additional exam requirements/recommendations for international students: Required—TOEFL, IELTS. Electronic applications accepted.

Bob Jones University, Graduate Programs, Greenville, SC 29614. Offers accountancy (MS); Bible (MA); Bible translation (MA); Biblical studies (Certificate); business administration (MBA); church history (MA, PhD); church ministries (MA); church music (MM); cinema and video production (MA); counseling (MS); curriculum and instruction (Ed D); divinity (M Div); dramatic production (MA); educational leadership (MS, Ed D, Ed S); elementary education (M Ed, MAT); English (M Ed, MA, MAT); fine arts (MA); graphic design (MA); history (M Ed, MA); illustration (MA); interpretative speech (MA); mathematics (M Ed, MAT); medical missions (Certificate); ministry (MM, D Min); multi-categorical special education (M Ed, MAT); music (M Ed); New Testament interpretation (PhD); Old Testament interpretation (PhD); orchestral instrument performance (MM); organ performance (MM); pastoral studies (MA); personnel services (MS, Ed S); piano pedagogy (MM); piano performance (MM); platform arts (MA); rhetoric and public address (MA); secondary education (M Ed); studio art (MA); teaching Bible (MA); theology (MA, PhD); voice performance (MM); youth ministries (MA); M Div/MM.

Boise State University, College of Education, Department of Counselor Education, Boise, ID 83725-0399. Offers MA, Graduate Certificate. *Accreditation:* ACA. *Program availability:* Part-time. *Degree requirements:* For master's, comprehensive exam, comprehensive portfolio, video-recorded evidence of skill. *Entrance requirements:* For master's, minimum GPA of 3.0. Additional exam requirements/recommendations for international students: Required—TOEFL (minimum score 550 paper-based; 80 iBT), IELTS (minimum score 6). Electronic applications accepted.

Bowie State University, Graduate Programs, Program in Guidance and Counseling, Bowie, MD 20715-9465. Offers M Ed. *Program availability:* Part-time, evening/weekend. *Degree requirements:* For master's, comprehensive exam, thesis optional, research paper. *Entrance requirements:* For master's, teaching experience, minimum GPA of 2.5, 3 recommendations. Electronic applications accepted.

Bowling Green State University, Graduate College, College of Education and Human Development, School of Intervention Services, Program in Clinical Mental Health Counseling, Bowling Green, OH 43403. Offers clinical mental health counseling (MA); school counseling (M Ed). *Accreditation:* ACA; NCATE. *Program availability:* Part-time. *Degree requirements:* For master's, thesis or alternative. *Entrance requirements:* For master's, GRE General Test. Additional exam requirements/recommendations for international students: Required—TOEFL. Electronic applications accepted. *Faculty research:* Perfectionism, multicultural counseling, suicide, ethics and legal issues related to counseling, play therapy.

Bradley University, The Graduate School, College of Education and Health Sciences, Department of Leadership in Education, Nonprofits and Counseling, Peoria, IL 61625-0002. Offers counseling (MA), including clinical mental health counseling, professional school counseling; leadership in educational administration (MA); nonprofit leadership (MA). *Accreditation:* ACA; NCATE. *Program availability:* Part-time, evening/weekend, blended/hybrid learning. *Faculty:* 11 full-time (6 women), 10 part-time/adjunct (6 women). *Students:* 83 full-time (68 women), 166 part-time (137 women); includes 50 minority (26 Black or African American, non-Hispanic/Latino; 2 American Indian or Alaska Native, non-Hispanic/Latino; 4 Asian, non-Hispanic/Latino; 14 Hispanic/Latino; 4 Two or more races, non-Hispanic/Latino), 3 international. Average age 33. 181 applicants, 97% accepted, 54 enrolled. In 2018, 58 master's awarded. *Degree requirements:* For master's, comprehensive exam, thesis optional. *Entrance requirements:* For master's, GRE General Test or MAT, interview, 3 letters of recommendation. Additional exam requirements/recommendations for international students: Required—TOEFL (minimum score 550 paper-based; 79 iBT), IELTS (minimum score 6.5). *Application deadline:* For fall admission, 5/15 priority date for domestic and international students; for spring admission, 10/15 priority date for domestic and international students. Applications are processed on a rolling basis. Application fee: $40 ($50 for international students). Electronic applications accepted. *Expenses: Tuition:* Part-time $890 per credit. *Required fees:* $50 per unit. *Financial support:* In 2018–19, 67 students received support, including 1 fellowship with full tuition reimbursement available (averaging $16,020 per year), 12 research assistantships with full tuition reimbursements available (averaging $14,388 per year); career-related internships or fieldwork, scholarships/grants, tuition waivers (partial), and unspecified assistantships also available. Support available to part-time students. Financial award application deadline: 4/1. *Unit head:* Dean Cantu, Associate Dean and Director, Professor, 309-677-3190, E-mail: dcantu@bradley.edu. *Application contact:* Rachel Webb, Director of On-Campus Graduate Admissions & International Student and Scholar Services, 309-677-2375, E-mail: rkwebb@bradley.edu.
Website: http://www.bradley.edu/academic/departments/lenc/

Brandman University, School of Education, Irvine, CA 92618. Offers curriculum and instruction (MAE); educational administration (MAE); educational leadership (MAE); educational leadership and administration (MA); elementary education (MAT); instructional technology: teaching the 21st century learner (MAE); leadership in early childhood education (MAE); organizational leadership (Ed D); school counseling (MA); secondary education (MAT); special education (MA); teaching and learning (MAE).

Brandon University, Faculty of Education, Brandon, MB R7A 6A9, Canada. Offers curriculum and instruction (M Ed, Diploma); educational administration (M Ed, Diploma); guidance and counseling (M Ed, Diploma); special education (M Ed, Diploma). *Degree requirements:* For master's, thesis. *Entrance requirements:* For master's, minimum GPA of 3.0, teaching certificate or equivalent. Additional exam requirements/recommendations for international students: Required—TOEFL. *Faculty research:* Comparative education, environmental studies, parent/school council.

Bridgewater State University, College of Graduate Studies, College of Education and Allied Studies, Department of Secondary Education and Professional Programs, Program in Counseling, Bridgewater, MA 02325. Offers M Ed, CAGS. *Accreditation:* ACA; NCATE. *Program availability:* Part-time, evening/weekend. *Entrance requirements:* For master's, GRE General Test.

Brooklyn College of the City University of New York, School of Education, Program in School Counseling, Brooklyn, NY 11210-2889. Offers MS Ed. *Accreditation:* ACA. *Program availability:* Part-time. *Degree requirements:* For master's, comprehensive exam, internship. *Entrance requirements:* For master's, interview, 2 letters of recommendation, resume, essay. Additional exam requirements/recommendations for international students: Required—TOEFL (minimum score 500 paper-based; 61 iBT). Electronic applications accepted. *Faculty research:* Urban school counseling, parent involvement, multicultural competence and counselor training.

Buena Vista University, School of Education, Storm Lake, IA 50588. Offers curriculum and instruction (M Ed), including effective teaching, TESL; school guidance and counseling (MS Ed). Program offered in summer only. *Program availability:* Part-time, evening/weekend, online learning. *Degree requirements:* For master's, thesis, fieldwork/practicum, capstone portfolio. *Entrance requirements:* For master's, Analytical Writing Assessment (in-house), minimum undergraduate GPA of 2.75. Electronic applications accepted. *Faculty research:* Reading, curriculum, educational psychology, special education.

California Baptist University, Program in School Counseling, Riverside, CA 92504-3206. Offers MS. *Program availability:* Part-time. *Faculty:* 2 full-time (both women), 10 part-time/adjunct (5 women). *Students:* 2 full-time (1 woman), 59 part-time (46 women); includes 35 minority (1 Black or African American, non-Hispanic/Latino; 1 Asian, non-Hispanic/Latino; 30 Hispanic/Latino; 3 Two or more races, non-Hispanic/Latino). Average age 34. 23 applicants, 87% accepted, 20 enrolled. In 2018, 18 master's awarded. *Degree requirements:* For master's, 100 hours of introductory fieldwork, 600 hours of field experience/internship, PRAXIS. *Entrance requirements:* For master's, California Basic Educational Skills Test (CBEST), minimum GPA of 3.0, completion of prerequisite courses with minimum C grade, three letters of recommendation, 500-word essay. Additional exam requirements/recommendations for international students: Required—TOEFL (minimum score 80 iBT). *Application deadline:* For fall admission, 8/1 priority date for domestic students, 7/7 priority date for international students; for spring admission, 12/1 priority date for domestic students, 11/1 priority date for international students. Applications are processed on a rolling basis. Application fee: $45. Electronic applications accepted. *Expenses:* $634 per unit. *Financial support:* In 2018–19, 30 students received support. Federal Work-Study and scholarships/grants available. Financial award applicants required to submit CSS PROFILE or FAFSA. *Faculty research:* Cultural competence, behavioral assessment, school neuropsychology, learning handicapped, cognitive development. *Unit head:* Dr. Robin Duncan, Dean, School of Education, 951-552-8948, E-mail: rduncan@calbaptist.edu. *Application contact:* Daniel Robinson, Program Director, School Counseling, 951-552-8351, E-mail: darobinson@calbaptist.edu.
Website: http://www.calbaptist.edu/academics/schools-colleges/school-education/programs/graduate/master-science-school-counseling/

California Lutheran University, Graduate Studies, Graduate School of Education, Thousand Oaks, CA 91360-2787. Offers counseling and guidance (MS), including college student personnel, counseling and guidance; educational leadership (MA, Ed D), including educational leadership (K-12) (Ed D), higher education leadership (Ed D); special education (MS); teacher leadership (M Ed); teaching (M Ed). *Accreditation:* NCATE. *Program availability:* Part-time, evening/weekend. *Degree requirements:* For master's, comprehensive exam or thesis; for doctorate, thesis/dissertation. *Entrance requirements:* For master's, GRE General Test, interview, minimum GPA of 3.0. Electronic applications accepted.

California State University, Bakersfield, Division of Graduate Studies, School of Social Sciences and Education, Program in Counseling, Bakersfield, CA 93311. Offers school counseling (MS); student affairs (MS). *Accreditation:* NCATE. *Faculty:* 1 (woman) full-time, 7 part-time/adjunct (5 women). *Students:* 69 full-time (53 women), 3 part-time (2 women); includes 59 minority (2 Black or African American, non-Hispanic/Latino; 1 American Indian or Alaska Native, non-Hispanic/Latino; 1 Asian, non-Hispanic/Latino; 55 Hispanic/Latino), 4 international. Average age 28. 81 applicants, 47% accepted, 37 enrolled. In 2018, 31 master's awarded. *Degree requirements:* For master's, thesis or alternative, culminating projects. *Entrance requirements:* For master's, CBEST (for school counseling). *Application deadline:* Applications are processed on a rolling basis. Application fee: $55. *Financial support:* In 2018–19, fellowships (averaging $1,850 per year) were awarded; Federal Work-Study, scholarships/grants, and tuition waivers (full and partial) also available. Financial award application deadline: 3/2; financial award applicants required to submit FAFSA. *Unit head:* Dr. Yvonne Oritz-Bush, Director, 661-654-3193, Fax: 661-654-2479, E-mail: yortiz_bush@csub.edu. *Application contact:* Martha Manriquez, Graduate Student Center Coordinator, 661-654-2786, Fax: 661-654-2791, E-mail: gsc@csub.edu.
Website: https://www.csub.edu/sse/departments/advancededucationalstudies/educational_counseling/index.html

California State University, Dominguez Hills, College of Education, Division of Graduate Education, Program in Counseling, Carson, CA 90747-0001. Offers college counseling (MS); school counseling (MS). *Program availability:* Part-time, evening/weekend. *Degree requirements:* For master's, comprehensive exam. *Entrance requirements:* For master's, minimum GPA of 3.0. Additional exam requirements/recommendations for international students: Required—TOEFL. *Faculty research:* Social development.

California State University, East Bay, Office of Graduate Studies, College of Education and Allied Studies, Department of Educational Psychology, Counseling Program, Hayward, CA 94542-3000. Offers MS. *Accreditation:* NCATE. *Degree requirements:* For master's, comprehensive exam, project or thesis. *Entrance requirements:* For master's, GRE or MAT, interview, minimum GPA of 2.5 during previous 2 years of course work. Additional exam requirements/recommendations for international students: Required—TOEFL (minimum score 550 paper-based). Electronic applications accepted.

California State University, Fresno, Division of Research and Graduate Studies, Kremen School of Education and Human Development, Department of Counselor Education and Rehabilitation, Program in Student Affairs and College Counseling, Fresno, CA 93740-8027. Offers MS. *Accreditation:* NCATE. *Program availability:* Part-time, evening/weekend. *Degree requirements:* For master's, thesis or alternative. *Entrance requirements:* For master's, GRE General Test, MAT, minimum GPA of 3.0. Additional exam requirements/recommendations for international students: Required—TOEFL. Electronic applications accepted.

California State University, Fullerton, Graduate Studies, College of Health and Human Development, Department of Counseling, Fullerton, CA 92831-3599. Offers MS. *Accreditation:* ACA; NCATE. *Program availability:* Part-time. *Degree requirements:* For master's, comprehensive exam, project or thesis. *Entrance requirements:* For master's, minimum GPA of 3.0 in behavioral science and for undergraduate degree.

California State University, Long Beach, Graduate Studies, College of Education, Department of Advanced Studies in Education and Counseling, Long Beach, CA 90840. Offers counseling (MS), including marriage and family therapy, school counseling, student development in higher education; education (MA, Ed D); educational administration (MA, Ed D); educational psychology (MA); special education (MS). *Program availability:* Part-time, evening/weekend. *Entrance requirements:* For master's, GRE General Test, minimum GPA of 2.75. *Application deadline:* For fall admission, 3/1 for domestic students. Applications are processed on a rolling basis. Application fee: $55. Electronic applications accepted. *Expenses: Required fees:* $2628 per term. Tuition and fees vary according to class time, course level, course load, degree level, campus/location and program. *Financial support:* Federal Work-Study, institutionally sponsored loans, and scholarships/grants available. Financial award application deadline: 3/2; financial award applicants required to submit FAFSA. *Unit head:* Dr. Hiromi Masunaga, Chair, 562-985-4517, E-mail: asec@csulb.edu. *Application contact:* Dr. Hiromi Masunaga, Chair, 562-985-4517, E-mail: asec@csulb.edu.
Website: http://www.csulb.edu/college-of-education/advanced-studies-education-and-counseling

California State University, Los Angeles, Graduate Studies, Charter College of Education, Division of Special Education and Counseling, Los Angeles, CA 90032-8530. Offers counseling (MS), including applied behavior analysis, community college counseling, rehabilitation counseling, school counseling, school psychology; special education (MA, PhD). *Accreditation:* ACA. *Program availability:* Part-time, evening/weekend. *Entrance requirements:* For master's, minimum GPA of 2.75 in last 90 units of course work, teaching certificate. Additional exam requirements/recommendations for international students: Required—TOEFL (minimum score 500 paper-based). Electronic applications accepted.

California State University, Northridge, Graduate Studies, Michael D. Eisner College of Education, Department of Educational Psychology and Counseling, Northridge, CA 91330. Offers counseling (MS), including career counseling, college counseling and student services, marriage and family therapy, school counseling, school psychology; educational psychology (MA Ed), including development, learning, and instruction, early childhood education. *Accreditation:* ACA (one or more programs are accredited); NCATE. *Program availability:* Part-time, evening/weekend. *Entrance requirements:* For master's, GRE General Test or minimum GPA of 3.0. Additional exam requirements/recommendations for international students: Required—TOEFL.

California State University, Sacramento, College of Education, Graduate and Professional Studies in Education, Sacramento, CA 95819. Offers behavioral science and gender equity (MA); child development (MA); counseling (MS); curriculum and instruction (MA); education (Ed D), including K-12 and community college; education leadership and policy studies (MA), including higher education, PreK-12; education specialist (Ed S), including school psychology; educational technology (MA); language and literacy (MA); multicultural education (MA); school psychology (MA); special education (MA); workforce development advocacy (MA). *Program availability:* Part-time, evening/weekend, blended/hybrid learning. *Degree requirements:* For master's, thesis or project; writing proficiency exam; for doctorate, thesis/dissertation. *Entrance requirements:* For master's and doctorate, GRE. Additional exam requirements/recommendations for international students: Required—TOEFL (minimum score 550 paper-based; 80 iBT); Recommended—IELTS (minimum score 7), TSE. Electronic applications accepted. *Expenses:* Contact institution.

California State University, San Bernardino, Graduate Studies, College of Education, Program in Counseling and Guidance, San Bernardino, CA 92407. Offers counseling and guidance (MS); rehabilitation counseling (MA). *Accreditation:* NCATE. *Program availability:* Part-time, evening/weekend. *Students:* 130 full-time (100 women), 4 part-time (3 women); includes 107 minority (11 Black or African American, non-Hispanic/Latino; 6 Asian, non-Hispanic/Latino; 88 Hispanic/Latino; 1 Native Hawaiian or other Pacific Islander, non-Hispanic/Latino; 1 Two or more races, non-Hispanic/Latino), 2 international. Average age 29. 91 applicants, 57% accepted, 48 enrolled. In 2018, 37 master's awarded. *Degree requirements:* For master's, comprehensive exam, thesis or alternative. *Entrance requirements:* Additional exam requirements/recommendations for international students: Required—TOEFL. *Application deadline:* For fall admission, 7/16 for domestic students. Application fee: $55. *Unit head:* Dr. Lorraine Hedtke, Program Coordinator, 909-537-7640, E-mail: lhedtke@csusb.edu. *Application contact:* Dr. Dorota Huizinga, Dean of Graduate Studies, 909-537-3064, E-mail: dorota.huizinga@csusb.edu.

California State University, Stanislaus, College of Education, Kinesiology and Social Work, MA Program in Education, Turlock, CA 95382. Offers curriculum and instruction (MA), including education technology, elementary education, multilingual education, physical education, reading, secondary education, special education; school administration (MA); school counseling (MA). *Program availability:* Part-time, evening/weekend. *Degree requirements:* For master's, comprehensive exam (for some programs), thesis (for some programs). *Entrance requirements:* For master's, MAT, GRE, or CBEST (varies by concentration), 3 letters of recommendation, personal statement. Additional exam requirements/recommendations for international students: Required—TOEFL (minimum score 550 paper-based). Electronic applications accepted. *Faculty research:* Children's perspectives on historical events, method elementary schools dual language education, K-12 reading programs.

California University of Pennsylvania, School of Graduate Studies and Research, College of Education and Human Services, Department of Counselor Education, California, PA 15419-1394. Offers clinical mental health counseling (MS); school counseling (M Ed). *Accreditation:* ACA; NCATE. *Program availability:* Part-time, evening/weekend. *Degree requirements:* For master's, comprehensive exam, thesis optional. *Entrance requirements:* For master's, MAT, minimum GPA of 3.0, resume, letters of reference. Additional exam requirements/recommendations for international students: Required—TOEFL (minimum score 550 paper-based; 80 iBT). Electronic applications accepted. *Faculty research:* Mind-body theories and practice, grief issues, career development, supervision, sports counseling.

Cambridge College, School of Psychology and Counseling, Boston, MA 02129. Offers alcohol and drug counseling (Certificate); behavioral health care management (CAGS); marriage and family therapy (M Ed); mental health and school counseling (M Ed); mental health counseling (M Ed); psychological studies (M Ed); rehabilitation counseling (Certificate); school adjustment and mental health counseling (M Ed); school adjustment counseling for mental health counselors (Certificate); school counseling (M Ed); trauma studies (Certificate). *Program availability:* Part-time, evening/weekend. *Degree requirements:* For master's and other advanced degree, thesis, practicum/internship. *Entrance requirements:* For master's, resume, 2 professional references; for other advanced degree, official transcripts, documents for transfer credit evaluation, resume, written personal statement/essay, 2 professional references, health insurance, immunizations form. Additional exam requirements/recommendations for international students: Required—TOEFL (minimum score 550 paper-based; 79 iBT), Michigan English Language Assessment Battery (minimum score 85); Recommended—IELTS (minimum score 6). *Application deadline:* Applications are processed on a rolling basis. Application fee: $50 ($100 for international students). Electronic applications accepted. *Expenses:* Contact institution. *Financial support:* Career-related internships or fieldwork, Federal Work-Study, and scholarships/grants available. Financial award applicants required to submit FAFSA. *Faculty research:* Trauma, drug and alcohol counseling, cross-cultural issues, school counseling, trauma in schools. *Unit head:* Dr. Niti Seth, Dean, 617-873-0208, Fax: 617-349-3561, E-mail: niti.seth@cambridgecollege.edu. *Application contact:* Salvadore Liberto, Interim Assistant Vice President of Enrollment, 800-877-4723, E-mail: admissions@cambridgecollege.edu.
Website: https://www.cambridgecollege.edu/school/school-psychology-counseling

Campbell University, Graduate and Professional Programs, School of Education, Buies Creek, NC 27506. Offers elementary education (M Ed); interdisciplinary studies (M Ed); middle grades education (M Ed); physical education (M Ed); school administration (MSA); school counseling (M Ed); secondary education (M Ed). *Accreditation:* NCATE. *Program availability:* Part-time, evening/weekend. *Degree requirements:* For master's, comprehensive exam. *Entrance requirements:* For master's, GRE General Test, minimum GPA of 2.7. *Faculty research:* Spiritual values and wellness issues in counseling, stress and professional burnout among counselors, thinking strategies, leadership, adaptive technology.

Canisius College, Graduate Division, School of Education and Human Services, Programs in Counseling and Human Services, Buffalo, NY 14208-1098. Offers community mental health counseling (MS); counseling and human services (MS); school agency counseling (MS). *Accreditation:* ACA. *Program availability:* Part-time, evening/weekend. *Faculty:* 5 full-time (2 women), 10 part-time/adjunct (7 women). *Students:* 64 full-time (54 women), 40 part-time (36 women); includes 20 minority (8 Black or African American, non-Hispanic/Latino; 2 Asian, non-Hispanic/Latino; 5 Hispanic/Latino; 5 Two or more races, non-Hispanic/Latino), 3 international. Average age 28. 76 applicants, 84% accepted, 28 enrolled. In 2018, 38 master's awarded. *Degree requirements:* For master's, thesis, research project, internship. *Entrance requirements:* For master's, GRE/GMAT (if cumulative GPA less than 3.0), official transcripts, two letters of recommendation, interview, Bachelors Degree, Resume. Additional exam requirements/recommendations for international students: Required—TOEFL (minimum score 550 paper-based, 79 iBT), IELTS (minimum score 6.5), or CAEL (minimum score 70). *Application deadline:* Applications are processed on a rolling basis. Application fee: $0. Electronic applications accepted. *Expenses: Tuition:* Part-time $820 per credit hour. *Required fees:* $25 per semester. One-time fee: $65 part-time. Tuition and fees vary according to program. *Financial support:* In 2018–19, 95 students received support. Career-related internships or fieldwork, Federal Work-Study, scholarships/grants, tuition waivers (partial), and unspecified assistantships available. Support available to part-time students. Financial award application deadline: 4/30; financial award applicants required to submit FAFSA. *Faculty research:* Impact of trauma on adults, long term psych-social impact on police officers. *Unit head:* Dr. Holly D'Angelis, Chair, 716-888-3187, Fax: 716-888-3299, E-mail: tanigosh@canisius.edu. *Application contact:* Dr. Holly D'Angelis, Chair, 716-888-3187, Fax: 716-888-3299, E-mail: tanigosh@canisius.edu.
Website: http://www.canisius.edu/masters-counseling/

Capella University, Harold Abel School of Social and Behavioral Science, Doctoral Programs in Counseling, Minneapolis, MN 55402. Offers general counselor education and supervision (PhD); general social work (DSW). *Accreditation:* ACA.

Capella University, Harold Abel School of Social and Behavioral Science, Master's Programs in Counseling, Minneapolis, MN 55402. Offers child and adolescent development (MS); general addiction counseling (MS); general marriage and family counseling/therapy (MS); general mental health counseling (MS); general school counseling (MS).

Carson-Newman University, Graduate Program in Education, Jefferson City, TN 37760. Offers curriculum and instruction (M Ed); educational leadership (M Ed); elementary education (MAT); school counseling (MS); secondary education (MAT); teaching English as a second language (MATESL). *Accreditation:* NCATE. *Program availability:* Part-time, evening/weekend, 100% online, blended/hybrid learning. *Faculty:* 20 full-time (11 women), 16 part-time/adjunct (13 women). *Students:* 14 full-time (8 women), 401 part-time (294 women); includes 45 minority (34 Black or African American, non-Hispanic/Latino; 1 American Indian or Alaska Native, non-Hispanic/Latino; 4 Hispanic/Latino; 1 Native Hawaiian or other Pacific Islander, non-Hispanic/Latino; 5 Two or more races, non-Hispanic/Latino). Average age 36. 223 applicants, 100% accepted, 199 enrolled. In 2018, 211 master's awarded. *Degree requirements:* For master's, thesis or alternative. *Entrance requirements:* For master's, PRAXIS II or GRE with minimum score of 290 on the verbal and quantitative components (for MAT), minimum GPA of 3.0 in major, 2.5 overall. Additional exam requirements/recommendations for international students: Recommended—TOEFL (minimum score 79 iBT), IELTS (minimum score 6.5), TSE (minimum score 53). *Application deadline:* For fall admission, 7/15 priority date for domestic students. Applications are processed on a rolling basis. Application fee: $50. *Expenses: Tuition:* Full-time $9036; part-time $502 per credit hour. *Required fees:* $900; $25 per credit hour. $300 per semester. One-time fee: $150. *Financial support:* Federal Work-Study and unspecified assistantships available. Financial award applicants required to submit FAFSA. *Unit head:* Dr. Kim Hawkins, Chair, 865-471-3314, E-mail: khawkins@cn.edu. *Application contact:* Nilma Stewart, Graduate Admissions and Services Adviser, 865-471-3230, Fax: 865-471-3875, E-mail: adults@cn.edu.
Website: http://www.cn.edu/adult-graduate-studies

Carson-Newman University, Program in Counseling, Jefferson City, TN 37760. Offers MSC. *Accreditation:* ACA. *Program availability:* Part-time, evening/weekend. *Faculty:* 3 full-time (2 women), 1 part-time/adjunct (0 women). *Students:* 33 full-time (29 women), 22 part-time (21 women); includes 3 minority (2 Black or African American, non-Hispanic/Latino; 1 Hispanic/Latino), 2 international. Average age 30. 13 applicants, 100% accepted, 11 enrolled. In 2018, 18 master's awarded. *Entrance requirements:* Additional exam requirements/recommendations for international students: Recommended—TOEFL (minimum score 79 iBT), IELTS (minimum score 6.5), TSE (minimum score 53). *Application deadline:* Applications are processed on a rolling basis. Application fee: $50. *Expenses: Tuition:* Full-time $9036; part-time $502 per credit hour. *Required fees:* $900; $25 per credit hour. $300 per semester. One-time fee: $150. *Financial support:* Federal Work-Study and tuition waivers (full and partial) available. Financial award applicants required to submit FAFSA. *Unit head:* Dr. Michael L. Bundy, Director, 865-471-2087, E-mail: mbundy@cn.edu. *Application contact:* Nilma Stewart, Graduate Admissions and Services Adviser, 865-471-3230, Fax: 865-471-3875, E-mail: adults@cn.edu.
Website: http://www.cn.edu/graduate-adult-studies/programs/graduate-studies-in-counseling

Carthage College, Division of Teacher Education, Kenosha, WI 53140. Offers classroom guidance and counseling (M Ed); creative arts (M Ed); gifted and talented children (M Ed); language arts (M Ed); modern language (M Ed); natural sciences (M Ed); reading (M Ed, Certificate); social sciences (M Ed); teacher leadership (M Ed). *Program availability:* Part-time, evening/weekend. *Degree requirements:* For master's, thesis optional. *Entrance requirements:* For master's, MAT, minimum B average, letters of reference.

Central Connecticut State University, School of Graduate Studies, School of Education and Professional Studies, Department of Counselor Education and Family Therapy, New Britain, CT 06050-4010. Offers marriage and family therapy (MS); professional counseling (MS, AC, Certificate); school counseling (MS); student development in higher education (MS). *Accreditation:* AAMFT/COAMFTE; ACA. *Program availability:* Part-time, evening/weekend. *Faculty:* 9 full-time (7 women), 27 part-time/adjunct (21 women). *Students:* 168 full-time (128 women), 198 part-time (160 women); includes 140 minority (50 Black or African American, non-Hispanic/Latino; 6 Asian, non-Hispanic/Latino; 70 Hispanic/Latino; 1 Native Hawaiian or other Pacific Islander, non-Hispanic/Latino; 13 Two or more races, non-Hispanic/Latino), 1 international. Average age 34. 180 applicants, 58% accepted, 78 enrolled. In 2018, 86 master's, 6 other advanced degrees awarded. *Degree requirements:* For master's, comprehensive exam, thesis or alternative; for other advanced degree, qualifying exam. *Entrance requirements:* For master's, minimum undergraduate GPA of 2.7, essay, interview, letters of recommendation. Additional exam requirements/recommendations for international students: Required—TOEFL (minimum score 550 paper-based; 79 iBT); Recommended—IELTS (minimum score 6.5). *Application deadline:* For fall admission, 2/1 for domestic and international students; for summer admission, 2/1 for domestic and international students. Applications are processed on a rolling basis. Application fee: $50. Electronic applications accepted. *Expenses: Tuition, area resident:* Full-time $7027; part-time $388 per credit. Tuition, state resident: full-time $9750; part-time $388 per credit. Tuition, nonresident: full-time $18,102; part-time $388 per credit. *International tuition:* $18,102 full-time. *Required fees:* $266 per semester. *Financial support:* In 2018–19, 72 students received support. Career-related internships or fieldwork, Federal Work-Study, scholarships/grants, and unspecified assistantships available. Support available to part-time students. Financial award application deadline: 3/1; financial award applicants required to submit FAFSA. *Faculty research:* Elementary and secondary school counseling, marriage and family therapy, rehabilitation counseling, counseling in higher educational settings. *Unit head:* Dr. Cherie King, Chair, 860-832-2154, E-mail: kingche@ccsu.edu. *Application contact:* Patricia Gardner, Associate Director of Graduate Studies, 860-832-2350, Fax: 860-832-2362.
Website: http://www.ccsu.edu/ceft/

Central Methodist University, College of Graduate and Extended Studies, Fayette, MO 65248-1198. Offers clinical counseling (MS); clinical nurse leader (MSN); education (M Ed); music education (MME); nurse educator (MSN). *Program availability:* Part-time, evening/weekend, online learning. *Degree requirements:* For master's, thesis. *Entrance requirements:* For master's, GRE General Test, minimum GPA of 2.75. Electronic applications accepted.

Central Michigan University, Central Michigan University Global Campus, Program in Counseling, Mount Pleasant, MI 48859. Offers professional counseling (MA); school counseling (MA). *Accreditation:* TEAC. *Program availability:* Part-time, evening/weekend. *Entrance requirements:* For master's, MAT, minimum GPA of 2.7. Additional exam requirements/recommendations for international students: Required—TOEFL. Electronic applications accepted.

Central Michigan University, College of Graduate Studies, College of Education and Human Services, Department of Counseling and Special Education, Program in Counseling, Mount Pleasant, MI 48859. Offers counseling (MA), including professional counseling, school counseling. *Accreditation:* TEAC. *Program availability:* Part-time. *Degree requirements:* For master's, comprehensive exam, thesis or alternative. *Entrance requirements:* For master's, MAT, eligible for Michigan Teacher Certification (for school counseling). Electronic applications accepted. *Faculty research:* School counseling, professional counseling.

Chadron State College, School of Professional and Graduate Studies, Department of Education, Chadron, NE 69337. Offers business (MA Ed); community counseling (MA Ed); educational administration (MS Ed, Sp Ed); elementary education (MS Ed); history (MA Ed); language and literature (MA Ed); secondary administration (MS Ed); secondary education (MS Ed). *Accreditation:* NCATE. *Program availability:* Part-time, evening/weekend, online learning. *Degree requirements:* For master's, thesis optional. *Entrance requirements:* For master's, GRE General Test, GRE Writing Test, minimum GPA of 2.75 or 12 graduate hours at CSC with minimum GPA of 3.25. Additional exam requirements/recommendations for international students: Required—TOEFL. Electronic applications accepted. *Faculty research:* Rural education, technology, mental health.

Chapman University, Donna Ford Attallah College of Educational Studies, Orange, CA 92866. Offers counseling (MA), including school counseling (MA, Credential); curriculum and instruction (MA), including elementary education, secondary education; education (PhD), including cultural and curricular studies, disability studies, leadership studies, school psychology (PhD, Credential); educational psychology (MA); leadership development (MA); multiple subjects (Credential), including Spanish/English bilingual; pupil personnel services (Credential), including school counseling (MA, Credential), school psychology (PhD, Credential); school psychology (Ed S); single subject (Credential); special education (MA, Credential), including mild/moderate (Credential), moderate/severe (Credential); teaching (MA), including elementary education, secondary education, secondary music education. *Accreditation:* TEAC. *Program availability:* Part-time, evening/weekend. Electronic applications accepted. *Expenses:* Contact institution.

Chicago State University, School of Graduate and Professional Studies, College of Arts and Sciences, Department of Psychology, Chicago, IL 60628. Offers counseling (MA), including bilingual specialization, clinical mental health counseling, school counseling. *Accreditation:* ACA; NCATE. *Degree requirements:* For master's, comprehensive exam, thesis optional. *Entrance requirements:* For master's, minimum GPA of 3.0 for last 60 semester hours of course work or essay; interview.

The Citadel, The Military College of South Carolina, Citadel Graduate College, School of Humanities and Social Sciences, Department of Psychology, Charleston, SC 29409. Offers psychology (MA), including clinical counseling; school psychology (Ed S). *Program availability:* Part-time, evening/weekend. *Degree requirements:* For master's, comprehensive exam, practicum; internship (written and oral presentation of a case study as part of internship); for Ed S, comprehensive exam, thesis (for some programs), practicum, internship. *Entrance requirements:* For master's, GRE (minimum combined score of 297, 150 on verbal reasoning and 141 on quantitative reasoning) or MAT (minimum score of 410), minimum undergraduate GPA of 3.0; 12 credit hours in psychology or minimum score on GRE Subject Test in psychology of 600; 2 letters of recommendation; for Ed S, GRE (minimum combined score of 297, 150 on verbal reasoning and 147 on quantitative reasoning) or MAT (minimum score of 410), minimum undergraduate or graduate GPA of 3.0; 2 letters of recommendation. Additional exam requirements/recommendations for international students: Required—TOEFL (minimum score 550 paper-based; 79 iBT). Electronic applications accepted. *Expenses:* Tuition, state resident: part-time $595 per credit hour. Tuition, nonresident: part-time $1020 per credit hour. *Required fees:* $90 per term.

The Citadel, The Military College of South Carolina, Citadel Graduate College, Zucker Family School of Education, Charleston, SC 29409. Offers elementary/secondary school administration and supervision (M Ed); elementary/secondary school counseling (M Ed); interdisciplinary STEM education (M Ed); literacy education (M Ed, Graduate Certificate); middle grades (MAT), including English, mathematics, science, social studies; physical education (grades K-12) (MAT); school superintendency (Ed S); secondary education (MAT), including biology, English, mathematics, social studies; student affairs (Graduate Certificate); student affairs and college counseling (M Ed). *Accreditation:* NCATE. *Program availability:* Part-time, evening/weekend, 100% online, blended/hybrid learning. *Degree requirements:* For master's, comprehensive exam (for some programs). *Entrance requirements:* For master's, GRE (minimum combined verbal and quantitative score of 290) or MAT (minimum score 396). Additional exam requirements/recommendations for international students: Required—TOEFL (minimum score 550 paper-based; 79 iBT). Electronic applications accepted. *Expenses:* Tuition, state resident: part-time $595 per credit hour. Tuition, nonresident: part-time $1020 per credit hour. *Required fees:* $90 per term.

City University of Seattle, Graduate Division, Albright School of Education, Seattle, WA 98121. Offers administrator certification (Certificate); curriculum and instruction (M Ed); elementary education (MIT); guidance and counseling (M Ed); leadership (M Ed); reading and literacy (M Ed); school counseling (M Ed); special education (MIT); superintendent certification (Certificate). *Program availability:* Part-time, evening/weekend, online learning. *Degree requirements:* For master's, comprehensive exam (for some programs), thesis (for some programs). *Entrance requirements:* For master's, baccalaureate degree or equivalent from an accredited or otherwise recognized institution. Additional exam requirements/recommendations for international students: Required—TOEFL (minimum score 567 paper-based; 87 iBT); Recommended—IELTS. Electronic applications accepted. *Expenses:* Contact institution.

Clark Atlanta University, School of Education, Department of Counseling and Psychological Studies, Atlanta, GA 30314. Offers MA. *Accreditation:* ACA. *Program availability:* Part-time. *Degree requirements:* For master's, comprehensive exam. *Entrance requirements:* For master's, GRE General Test, minimum undergraduate GPA of 2.6. Additional exam requirements/recommendations for international students: Required—TOEFL (minimum score 500 paper-based; 61 iBT). Electronic applications accepted.

Clarks Summit University, Online Master's Programs, South Abington Township, PA 18411. Offers Bible (MA); counseling (MA, MS); curriculum and instruction (M Ed); educational administration (M Ed); literature (MA); organizational leadership (MA). *Program availability:* Part-time, evening/weekend, online learning. *Entrance requirements:* Additional exam requirements/recommendations for international students: Required—TOEFL (minimum score 500 paper-based).

Clemson University, Graduate School, College of Education, Department of Education and Human Development, Clemson, SC 29634. Offers counselor education (M Ed, Ed S), including mental health counseling, school counseling, student affairs (M Ed); learning sciences (PhD); literacy (M Ed); literacy, language and culture (PhD); special education (M Ed, MAT, PhD). *Program availability:* Part-time, evening/weekend, 100% online. *Faculty:* 35 full-time (24 women). *Students:* 103 full-time (87 women), 132 part-time (123 women); includes 37 minority (11 Black or African American, non-Hispanic/Latino; 1 American Indian or Alaska Native, non-Hispanic/Latino; 3 Asian, non-Hispanic/Latino; 11 Hispanic/Latino; 11 Two or more races, non-Hispanic/Latino), 5 international. Average age 29. 435 applicants, 67% accepted, 180 enrolled. In 2018, 51 master's, 3 doctorates, 34 other advanced degrees awarded. *Degree requirements:* For master's,

thesis (for some programs); for doctorate, comprehensive exam (for some programs), thesis/dissertation. *Entrance requirements:* For master's and doctorate, GRE General Test, unofficial transcripts, letters of recommendation. Additional exam requirements/recommendations for international students: Required—TOEFL (minimum score 80 paper-based; 80 iBT); Recommended—IELTS (minimum score 6.5), TSE (minimum score 54). *Application deadline:* For fall admission, 4/15 priority date for international students; for spring admission, 10/15 priority date for international students. Applications are processed on a rolling basis. Application fee: $80 ($90 for international students). Electronic applications accepted. *Expenses:* $5198 per semester full-time resident, $10123 per semester full-time non-resident, $556 per credit hour part-time resident, $1109 per credit hour part-time non-resident, online $770 per credit hour, $4938 doctoral programs resident, $10405 doctoral programs non-resident, $1144 full-time graduate assistant, other fees may apply per session. *Financial support:* In 2018–19, 78 students received support, including 5 teaching assistantships with full and partial tuition reimbursements available (averaging $8,759 per year); career-related internships or fieldwork and unspecified assistantships also available. *Faculty research:* Literacy, reading recovery, exceptional children, policy development. *Total annual research expenditures:* $1.3 million. *Unit head:* Dr. Debi Switzer, Department Chair, 864-656-5098, E-mail: debi@clemson.edu. *Application contact:* Julie Jones, Student Services Program Coordinator, 864-656-5096, E-mail: jgambre@clemson.edu.
Website: http://www.clemson.edu/education/departments/education-human-development/index.html

Cleveland State University, College of Graduate Studies, College of Education and Human Services, Department of Counseling, Administration, Supervision and Adult Learning (CASAL), Cleveland, OH 44115. Offers adult learning and development (M Ed); counselor education (PhD); early childhood mental health counseling (Certificate); educational administration and supervision (M Ed). *Accreditation:* ACA (one or more programs are accredited). *Program availability:* Part-time, evening/weekend. *Faculty:* 15 full-time (8 women), 19 part-time/adjunct (10 women). *Students:* 134 full-time (118 women), 259 part-time (195 women); includes 131 minority (93 Black or African American, non-Hispanic/Latino; 2 American Indian or Alaska Native, non-Hispanic/Latino; 4 Asian, non-Hispanic/Latino; 23 Hispanic/Latino; 9 Two or more races, non-Hispanic/Latino), 11 international. Average age 33. 57 applicants, 93% accepted, 51 enrolled. In 2018, 119 master's, 1 other advanced degree awarded. *Degree requirements:* For master's, comprehensive exam (for some programs), thesis optional, internship. *Entrance requirements:* For master's, GRE General Test or MAT, letter of recommendation and minimum GPA of 2.75 (for counseling); 2 letters of recommendation and interviews (for organizational leadership). Additional exam requirements/recommendations for international students: Required—TOEFL (minimum score 550 paper-based; 78 iBT), IELTS (minimum score 6). *Application deadline:* For fall admission, 6/21 for domestic students, 5/15 for international students; for spring admission, 8/31 for domestic students, 11/1 for international students. Application fee: $40. Electronic applications accepted. *Expenses:* Tuition, state resident: full-time $7232.55; part-time $6676 per credit hour. Tuition, nonresident: full-time $12,375. *International tuition:* $18,914 full-time. *Required fees:* $80; $80 $40. Tuition and fees vary according to program. *Financial support:* In 2018–19, 19 students received support, including 10 research assistantships with tuition reimbursements available (averaging $11,882 per year), 5 teaching assistantships with tuition reimbursements available (averaging $11,882 per year); scholarships/grants and unspecified assistantships also available. Support available to part-time students. *Faculty research:* Education law, career development, bullying, psychopharmacology, counseling and spirituality. *Total annual research expenditures:* $225,821. *Unit head:* Dr. R. Elliott Ingersoll, Chair/Professor, 216-687-4582, Fax: 216-687-5378, E-mail: r.ingersoll@csuohio.edu. *Application contact:* Deborah L. Brown, Interim Assistant Director, Graduate Admissions, 216-523-7572, Fax: 216-687-5400, E-mail: d.l.brown@csuohio.edu.
Website: http://www.csuohio.edu/cehs/departments/CASAL/casal_dept.html

The College at Brockport, State University of New York, School of Education, Health, and Human Services, Department of Counselor Education, Brockport, NY 14420-2997. Offers college counseling (MS Ed, CAS); mental health counseling (MS, CAS); school counseling (MS Ed, CAS); school counselor supervision (CAS). *Accreditation:* ACA (one or more programs are accredited). *Program availability:* Part-time. *Faculty:* 7 full-time (3 women), 4 part-time/adjunct (all women). *Students:* 26 full-time (22 women), 104 part-time (73 women); includes 8 minority (7 Black or African American, non-Hispanic/Latino; 1 Hispanic/Latino). 91 applicants, 45% accepted, 25 enrolled. In 2018, 39 master's, 6 other advanced degrees awarded. *Degree requirements:* For master's, thesis, internship. *Entrance requirements:* For master's, group interview, letters of recommendation, written objectives, audio response; for CAS, master's degree, New York state school counselor certificate. Additional exam requirements/recommendations for international students: Required—TOEFL (minimum score 550 paper-based; 79 iBT), IELTS (minimum score 6.5). *Application deadline:* For fall admission, 2/1 priority date for domestic and international students; for spring admission, 9/1 priority date for domestic and international students; for summer admission, 2/1 priority date for domestic and international students. Application fee: $80. Electronic applications accepted. *Expenses:* Tuition, state resident: part-time $471 per credit. Tuition, nonresident: part-time $963 per credit. *Financial support:* In 2018–19, 1 fellowship with full tuition reimbursement (averaging $7,500 per year), 1 teaching assistantship with full tuition reimbursement (averaging $6,000 per year) were awarded; Federal Work-Study, scholarships/grants, and unspecified assistantships also available. Support available to part-time students. Financial award application deadline: 3/15; financial award applicants required to submit FAFSA. *Faculty research:* Gender and diversity issues; counseling outcomes; spirituality; school, college and mental health counseling; obesity. *Unit head:* Dr. Robert Dobmeier, Chair, 585-395-5090, Fax: 585-395-2366, E-mail: rdobmeie@brockport.edu. *Application contact:* Danielle A. Welch, Graduate Admissions Counselor, 585-395-5465, Fax: 585-395-2515.
Website: https://www.brockport.edu/academics/counselor_education/

The College of New Jersey, Office of Graduate and Advancing Education, School of Education, Department of Counselor Education, Program in Community Counseling: Human Services Specialization, Ewing, NJ 08628. Offers MA. *Accreditation:* ACA. *Program availability:* Part-time. *Degree requirements:* For master's, comprehensive exam. *Entrance requirements:* For master's, GRE General Test, minimum GPA of 3.0 in field or 2.75 overall, interview. Additional exam requirements/recommendations for international students: Required—TOEFL. Electronic applications accepted.

The College of New Jersey, Office of Graduate and Advancing Education, School of Education, Department of Counselor Education, Program in School Counseling, Ewing, NJ 08628. Offers MA. *Accreditation:* ACA; NCATE. *Program availability:* Part-time. *Degree requirements:* For master's, comprehensive exam. *Entrance requirements:* For master's, GRE General Test, minimum GPA of 3.0 in field or 2.75 overall, interview. Additional exam requirements/recommendations for international students: Required—TOEFL. Electronic applications accepted.

College of St. Joseph, Graduate Programs, Division of Psychology and Human Services, Rutland, VT 05701-3899. Offers alcohol and substance abuse counseling (MS); clinical mental health counseling (MS); clinical psychology (MS); community counseling (MS); school guidance counseling (MS). *Program availability:* Part-time, evening/weekend. *Degree requirements:* For master's, comprehensive exam, thesis optional. *Entrance requirements:* For master's, official college transcripts; 2 letters of reference. Additional exam requirements/recommendations for international students: Required—TOEFL (minimum score 550 paper-based). Electronic applications accepted.

The College of Saint Rose, Graduate Studies, Thelma P. Lally School of Education, Programs in Clinical Mental Health Counseling, Albany, NY 12203-1419. Offers clinical mental health counseling (Certificate); school counseling (MS Ed, Certificate), including mental health counseling (MS Ed). *Students:* 28 full-time (24 women), 24 part-time (22 women); includes 11 minority (5 Black or African American, non-Hispanic/Latino; 2 Asian, non-Hispanic/Latino; 1 Hispanic/Latino; 3 Two or more races, non-Hispanic/Latino). Average age 28. 28 applicants, 71% accepted, 11 enrolled. In 2018, 22 master's, 1 Certificate awarded. *Entrance requirements:* For master's, minimum undergraduate GPA of 3.0. Additional exam requirements/recommendations for international students: Required—TOEFL (minimum score 550 paper-based; 80 iBT), IELTS (minimum score 6), PTE (minimum score 56). *Application deadline:* For fall admission, 4/1 for domestic and international students; for spring admission, 10/15 priority date for domestic and international students; for summer admission, 3/15 for domestic and international students. Applications are processed on a rolling basis. Application fee: $40. Electronic applications accepted. *Expenses: Tuition:* Full-time $14,382; part-time $799 per credit hour. *Required fees:* $924; $408 per credit. $286. *Financial support:* Career-related internships or fieldwork, scholarships/grants, tuition waivers (partial), and unspecified assistantships available. Support available to part-time students. Financial award application deadline: 4/15. *Unit head:* Claudia Lingertat-Putnam, Chair, 518-337-4311, E-mail: lingertc@strose.edu. *Application contact:* Daniel Gallagher, Assistant Vice President for Graduate Recruitment and Enrollment, 518-485-3390, Fax: 518-458-5479, E-mail: grad@strose.edu.
Website: https://www.strose.edu/counseling/

The College of William and Mary, School of Education, Program in Counselor Education, Williamsburg, VA 23187-8795. Offers family counseling (M Ed); school counseling (M Ed). *Accreditation:* ACA; NCATE. *Program availability:* Part-time, evening/weekend, 100% online with required residency. *Faculty:* 11 full-time (3 women), 4 part-time/adjunct (3 women). *Students:* 67 full-time (51 women), 48 part-time (35 women); includes 17 minority (3 Black or African American, non-Hispanic/Latino; 1 American Indian or Alaska Native, non-Hispanic/Latino; 4 Asian, non-Hispanic/Latino; 6 Hispanic/Latino; 3 Two or more races, non-Hispanic/Latino), 10 international. Average age 31. 202 applicants, 51% accepted, 52 enrolled. In 2018, 23 master's, 6 doctorates awarded. *Degree requirements:* For doctorate, comprehensive exam, thesis/dissertation. *Entrance requirements:* For master's, GRE, minimum GPA of 3.0; for doctorate, GRE, minimum GPA of 3.5. Additional exam requirements/recommendations for international students: Required—TOEFL (minimum score 100 iBT), IELTS (minimum score 7). *Application deadline:* For fall admission, 1/15 for domestic and international students. Application fee: $50. Electronic applications accepted. *Expenses:* Contact institution. *Financial support:* In 2018–19, 31 students received support, including 26 research assistantships with full tuition reimbursements available (averaging $19,190 per year); scholarships/grants also available. Financial award application deadline: 1/15; financial award applicants required to submit FAFSA. *Faculty research:* Sexuality, multicultural education, addiction counseling, transpersonal psychology, measurement and evaluation in counseling. *Unit head:* Dr. Charles R. Adams, Department Chair, 757-221-2338, E-mail: crmcad@wm.edu. *Application contact:* Dorothy Smith Osborne, Assistant Dean for Academic Programs and Student Services, 757-221-2317, E-mail: dsosbo@wm.edu.
Website: http://education.wm.edu

Colorado State University, College of Health and Human Sciences, School of Education, Fort Collins, CO 80523-1588. Offers adult education and training (M Ed); counseling and career development (MA); education and human resources (M Ed); education, equity, and transformation (PhD); higher education leadership (PhD); organizational learning, performance, and change (M Ed, PhD); student affairs in higher education (MS). *Accreditation:* ACA; TEAC. *Program availability:* Part-time, online only, 100% online, blended/hybrid learning. *Degree requirements:* For master's, thesis optional, professional portfolio or capstone project; for doctorate, comprehensive exam, thesis/dissertation. *Entrance requirements:* For master's, bachelor's degree; minimum GPA of 3.0 in last degree earned; for doctorate, GRE; GRE or GMAT (for organizational learning, performance and change only), master's degree; minimum GPA of 3.0 in last degree earned. Additional exam requirements/recommendations for international students: Required—TOEFL (minimum score 550 paper-based; 80 iBT), IELTS (minimum score 6.5), PTE (minimum score 58). Electronic applications accepted. *Expenses:* Contact institution. *Faculty research:* Diversity, equity, and inclusion; STEM education; higher education; occupational learning, performance, and change; teacher education.

Columbia International University, Columbia Graduate School, Columbia, SC 29203. Offers Bible teaching (MABT); counseling (MACN); early childhood and elementary education (MAT); educational administration (M Ed); educational leadership (PhD); instruction and learning (M Ed); teaching English as a foreign language (Certificate); teaching English as a foreign language and intercultural studies (MATF). *Program availability:* Part-time, evening/weekend, online learning. *Degree requirements:* For master's, internships, professional project. *Entrance requirements:* For master's, MAT; GRE (for some programs), minimum GPA of 2.7. Additional exam requirements/recommendations for international students: Required—TOEFL. Electronic applications accepted.

Columbus State University, Graduate Studies, College of Education and Health Professions, Department of Counseling, Foundations, and Leadership, Columbus, GA 31907-5645. Offers clinical mental health counseling (MS); curriculum and leadership (Ed D), including curriculum, educational leadership, higher education (M Ed, Ed D); educational leadership (M Ed, Ed S), including higher education (M Ed, Ed D); school counseling (M Ed, Ed S). *Accreditation:* ACA; NCATE. *Program availability:* Part-time, evening/weekend, 100% online, blended/hybrid learning. *Faculty:* 13 full-time (5 women), 17 part-time/adjunct (8 women). *Students:* 66 full-time (50 women), 209 part-time (158 women); includes 145 minority (124 Black or African American, non-Hispanic/Latino; 5 Asian, non-Hispanic/Latino; 10 Hispanic/Latino; 6 Two or more races, non-Hispanic/Latino), 1 international. Average age 39. 168 applicants, 48% accepted, 54 enrolled. In 2018, 44 master's, 25 doctorates, 129 other advanced degrees awarded. *Degree requirements:* For master's, thesis, exit exam; for doctorate, comprehensive exam, thesis/dissertation; for Ed S, thesis or alternative. *Entrance requirements:* For master's, GRE General Test, minimum undergraduate GPA of 2.75; for doctorate, GRE General Test, minimum graduate GPA of 3.5, four years of professional service; for Ed S, GRE General Test, minimum undergraduate GPA of 2.75, graduate 3.0. Additional exam requirements/recommendations for international students: Required—TOEFL (minimum score 550 paper-based; 79 iBT). *Application deadline:* For fall admission, 6/30 for domestic and international students; for spring admission, 11/1 for domestic and international students; for summer admission, 3/1 for domestic and international students. Applications are processed on a rolling basis. Application fee: $50. Electronic applications accepted. *Expenses: Tuition, area resident:* Full-time

$4924; part-time $618 per credit hour. Tuition, state resident: full-time $4924; part-time $618 per credit hour. Tuition, nonresident: full-time $19,218; part-time $2403 per credit hour. *International tuition:* $19,218 full-time. *Required fees:* $1870; $802. Tuition and fees vary according to course load, degree level and program. *Financial support:* In 2018–19, 30 students received support, including 6 research assistantships with partial tuition reimbursements available (averaging $3,000 per year); career-related internships or fieldwork, Federal Work-Study, institutionally sponsored loans, scholarships/grants, tuition waivers (partial), and unspecified assistantships also available. Support available to part-time students. Financial award application deadline: 5/1; financial award applicants required to submit FAFSA. *Unit head:* Dr. Tom Hackett, Department Chair, 706-507-8968, Fax: 706-569-3134, E-mail: hackett_paul@columbusstate.edu. *Application contact:* Catrina Smith-Edmond, Assistant Director for Graduate and Global Admission, 706-507-8824, Fax: 706-568-5091, E-mail: smithedmond_catrina@columbusstate.edu.
Website: http://cfl.columbusstate.edu/

Concordia University Chicago, College of Graduate Studies, Program in School Counseling, River Forest, IL 60305-1499. Offers MA. *Accreditation:* ACA; NCATE. *Program availability:* Part-time, evening/weekend. *Degree requirements:* For master's, comprehensive exam, thesis optional. *Entrance requirements:* For master's, minimum GPA of 2.9. Additional exam requirements/recommendations for international students: Required—TOEFL (minimum score 550 paper-based). Electronic applications accepted. *Faculty research:* Development of comprehensive school counseling education, training of school counselors for parochial schools.

Concordia University Irvine, School of Education, Irvine, CA 92612-3299. Offers curriculum and instruction (MA); education and preliminary teaching credential (M Ed); educational administration and preliminary administrative services credential (MA); educational technology (MA); school counseling with pupil personnel services credential (MA). *Program availability:* Part-time, evening/weekend, online learning. *Degree requirements:* For master's, action research project. *Entrance requirements:* For master's, California Basic Educational Skills Test, California Subject Examinations for Teachers (M Ed and MA in educational administration and preliminary administrative services credential), official college transcript(s), signed statement of intent, two references, copy of credential. Additional exam requirements/recommendations for international students: Required—TOEFL. Electronic applications accepted. *Expenses:* Contact institution.

Concordia University Wisconsin, Graduate Programs, School of Education, Mequon, WI 53097-2402. Offers art education (MS Ed); early childhood (MS Ed); educational administration (MS Ed); environmental education (MS Ed); family studies (MS Ed); literacy (MS Ed); school counseling (MS Ed); special education (MS Ed). *Program availability:* Part-time, evening/weekend, online learning. *Degree requirements:* For master's, comprehensive exam, thesis or alternative. *Entrance requirements:* For master's, minimum GPA of 3.0, teaching license. Additional exam requirements/recommendations for international students: Required—TOEFL. *Faculty research:* Motivation, developmental learning, learning styles.

Creighton University, Graduate School, College of Arts and Sciences, Department of Education, Program in School Counseling and Preventive Mental Health, Omaha, NE 68178-0001. Offers elementary school guidance (MS); secondary school guidance (MS). *Program availability:* Part-time, online only, 100% online, blended/hybrid learning. *Faculty:* 3 full-time (1 woman). *Students:* 35 full-time (33 women), 54 part-time (46 women); includes 9 minority (2 Black or African American, non-Hispanic/Latino; 2 American Indian or Alaska Native, non-Hispanic/Latino; 1 Asian, non-Hispanic/Latino; 2 Hispanic/Latino; 2 Native Hawaiian or other Pacific Islander, non-Hispanic/Latino), 1 international. Average age 31. In 2018, 28 master's awarded. *Degree requirements:* For master's, comprehensive exam. *Entrance requirements:* For master's, resume, 3 letters of recommendation, personal statement, background check. Additional exam requirements/recommendations for international students: Required—TOEFL (minimum score 90 iBT). *Application deadline:* For fall admission, 7/1 for domestic students, 3/1 for international students; for winter admission, 10/1 for domestic students, 7/1 for international students; for spring admission, 3/1 for domestic students, 9/1 for international students; for summer admission, 3/1 for domestic and international students. Application fee: $50. Electronic applications accepted. *Financial support:* Scholarships/grants available. Support available to part-time students. Financial award applicants required to submit FAFSA. *Unit head:* Dr. Jeffrey Smith, Associate Professor of Education, 402-280-2413, E-mail: JeffreySmith@creighton.edu. *Application contact:* Lindsay Johnson, Director of Graduate and Adult Recruitment, 402-280-2703, Fax: 402-280-2423, E-mail: gradschool@creighton.edu.

Dallas Baptist University, Dorothy M. Bush College of Education, Program in School Counseling, Dallas, TX 75211-9299. Offers M Ed. *Program availability:* Part-time, evening/weekend. *Application deadline:* Applications are processed on a rolling basis. Application fee: $25. Electronic applications accepted. Application fee is waived when completed online. *Expenses: Tuition:* Full-time $17,262; part-time $959 per credit hour. *Required fees:* $1000; $500 per semester. Tuition and fees vary according to course load and degree level. *Unit head:* Dr. Neil Dugger, Dean, 214-333-5202, E-mail: neil@dbu.edu. *Application contact:* Dr. Bonnie Bond, Program Director, 214-333-6838, E-mail: bonnie@dbu.edu.
Website: https://www.dbu.edu/graduate/degree-programs/med-school-counseling

Delta State University, Graduate Programs, College of Education, Division of Counselor Education and Psychology, Cleveland, MS 38733-0001. Offers counseling (M Ed). *Accreditation:* ACA (one or more programs are accredited); NCATE. *Program availability:* Part-time, evening/weekend. *Degree requirements:* For master's, thesis optional, practicum. Electronic applications accepted. *Expenses: Tuition, area resident:* Full-time $7076; part-time $393 per credit hour. Tuition, state resident: full-time $7076; part-time $393 per credit hour. Tuition, nonresident: full-time $7076; part-time $393 per credit hour. *International tuition:* $7076 full-time. *Required fees:* $170; $18.90 per credit hour. $9.45 per semester. Part-time tuition and fees vary according to program.

Delta State University, Graduate Programs, College of Education, Division of Teacher Education, Leadership, and Research, Program in Professional Studies, Cleveland, MS 38733-0001. Offers counselor education (Ed D); elementary education (Ed D); higher education (Ed D). *Program availability:* Part-time, evening/weekend. *Degree requirements:* For doctorate, thesis/dissertation. *Entrance requirements:* For doctorate, GRE General Test. *Expenses: Tuition, area resident:* Full-time $7076; part-time $393 per credit hour. Tuition, state resident: full-time $7076; part-time $393 per credit hour. Tuition, nonresident: full-time $7076; part-time $393 per credit hour. *International tuition:* $7076 full-time. *Required fees:* $170; $18.90 per credit hour. $9.45 per semester. Part-time tuition and fees vary according to program.

DePaul University, College of Education, Chicago, IL 60614. Offers bilingual-bicultural education (M Ed, MA); counseling (M Ed, MA), including clinical mental health counseling, college student development, school counseling; curriculum studies (M Ed, MA, Ed D); early childhood education (M Ed, MA, Ed D); educational leadership (M Ed, MA, Ed D), including Catholic leadership (M Ed, MA), general (M Ed, MA), higher education (M Ed, MA), physical education (M Ed, MA), principal preparation (M Ed), teacher preparation (M Ed); elementary education (M Ed, MA); middle grades education (M Ed); middle school mathematics education (MS); reading specialist (M Ed, MA); secondary education (M Ed, MA); social and cultural foundations in education (M Ed, MA); special education (M Ed); sport, fitness and recreation leadership (MS); value-creating education for global citizenship (M Ed); world languages education (M Ed, MA). *Program availability:* Part-time, evening/weekend, online learning. *Degree requirements:* For doctorate, thesis/dissertation. Electronic applications accepted.

Doane University, Program in Counseling, Crete, NE 68333-2430. Offers MAC. *Program availability:* Evening/weekend. *Faculty:* 2 full-time (1 woman), 15 part-time/adjunct (11 women). *Students:* 47 full-time (39 women), 17 part-time (14 women); includes 9 minority (2 Black or African American, non-Hispanic/Latino; 1 American Indian or Alaska Native, non-Hispanic/Latino; 4 Hispanic/Latino; 2 Two or more races, non-Hispanic/Latino). Average age 34. In 2018, 21 master's awarded. *Degree requirements:* For master's, thesis. *Entrance requirements:* For master's, minimum GPA of 3.0. Additional exam requirements/recommendations for international students: Required—TOEFL. *Application deadline:* Applications are processed on a rolling basis. Application fee: $25. Electronic applications accepted. *Expenses:* Contact institution. *Financial support:* Unspecified assistantships available. Financial award application deadline: 6/1; financial award applicants required to submit FAFSA. *Unit head:* Associate Dean/Director of the Counseling Program, 402-466-4774, Fax: 402-466-4228. *Application contact:* Jean Kilnoski, Assistant Dean, 402-466-4774, Fax: 404-466-4228, E-mail: jean.kilnoski@doane.edu.
Website: http://www.doane.edu/master-of-arts-in-counseling-0

Drake University, School of Education, Des Moines, IA 50311-4516. Offers applied behavior analysis (MS); counseling (MS); education (PhD); education administration (Ed D); educational leadership (MSE, Ed D); effective teaching (MSE); leadership development (MS); literacy (Ed S); literacy education (MSE); rehabilitation administration (MS); rehabilitation placement (MS); special education (MSE); STEM education (MSE); teacher education (5-12) (MAT); teacher education (K-8) (MST); teacher effectiveness and professional development (MSE). *Program availability:* Part-time, evening/weekend, 100% online, blended/hybrid learning. *Students:* 90 full-time (74 women), 690 part-time (532 women); includes 69 minority (30 Black or African American, non-Hispanic/Latino; 1 American Indian or Alaska Native, non-Hispanic/Latino; 9 Asian, non-Hispanic/Latino; 16 Hispanic/Latino; 13 Two or more races, non-Hispanic/Latino). Average age 34. In 2018, 253 master's, 30 doctorates awarded. *Degree requirements:* For master's and Ed S, comprehensive exam, internships (for some programs); for doctorate, comprehensive exam, thesis/dissertation, internships (for some programs). *Entrance requirements:* For master's, GRE General Test, MAT, or Drake Writing Assessment, resume, 2 letters of recommendation; for doctorate, GRE General Test or MAT, master's degree, 3 letters of recommendation; for Ed S, GRE General Test or MAT. Additional exam requirements/recommendations for international students: Required—TOEFL (minimum score 550 paper-based). *Application deadline:* For fall admission, 7/1 priority date for domestic students, 6/1 priority date for international students; for spring admission, 11/1 priority date for domestic students, 10/1 priority date for international students. Applications are processed on a rolling basis. Application fee: $25. Electronic applications accepted. *Expenses:* Contact institution. *Financial support:* Research assistantships, career-related internships or fieldwork, and unspecified assistantships available. Support available to part-time students. *Faculty research:* Counseling and rehabilitation, behavioral supports, inquiry-based science methods, teacher quality enhancement. *Unit head:* Dr. Janet McMahill, Dean, 515-271-3829, E-mail: janet.mcmahill@drake.edu. *Application contact:* Dr. Janet McMahill, Dean, 515-271-3829, E-mail: janet.mcmahill@drake.edu.
Website: http://www.drake.edu/soe/

Duquesne University, School of Education, Department of Counseling, Psychology, and Special Education, Program in Counselor Education, Pittsburgh, PA 15282-0001. Offers clinical mental health counseling (MS Ed, Post-Master's Certificate); counselor education and supervision (Ed D); counselor licensure (Post-Master's Certificate); marriage and family counseling (MS Ed); school counseling (MS Ed). *Accreditation:* ACA (one or more programs are accredited). *Program availability:* Part-time, evening/weekend. *Faculty:* 8 full-time (3 women). *Students:* 179 full-time (131 women), 8 part-time (6 women); includes 46 minority (22 Black or African American, non-Hispanic/Latino; 1 American Indian or Alaska Native, non-Hispanic/Latino; 3 Asian, non-Hispanic/Latino; 10 Hispanic/Latino; 10 Two or more races, non-Hispanic/Latino), 7 international. Average age 29. 106 applicants, 92% accepted, 53 enrolled. In 2018, 52 master's, 11 doctorates awarded. *Degree requirements:* For master's, thesis optional; for doctorate, thesis/dissertation. *Entrance requirements:* For master's, letters of recommendation, essay, interview, bachelor's degree; for doctorate, GRE, letters of recommendation, essay, interview, master's degree; for Post-Master's Certificate, GRE, letters of recommendation, essay, interview, bachelor's/master's degree. Additional exam requirements/recommendations for international students: Required—TOEFL (minimum score 550 paper-based), IELTS (minimum score 6.5). *Application deadline:* For fall admission, 4/2 for domestic students; for spring admission, 9/1 for domestic students. Applications are processed on a rolling basis. Application fee: $0. Electronic applications accepted. *Expenses: Tuition:* Full-time $23,112; part-time $1284 per credit. Tuition and fees vary according to program. *Financial support:* In 2018–19, 21 students received support, including 15 research assistantships with full and partial tuition reimbursements available (averaging $2,422 per year), 6 teaching assistantships with full and partial tuition reimbursements available (averaging $2,422 per year); Federal Work-Study also available. Support available to part-time students. Financial award applicants required to submit FAFSA. *Faculty research:* Trauma counseling, counseling supervision, purpose and meaning, Internet addictions, bullying and relational aggression. *Unit head:* Dr. Jered Kolbert, Professor/Director, 412-396-4471, Fax: 412-396-1340, E-mail: kolbertj@duq.edu. *Application contact:* Kelly McGinley, Graduate Admissions Assistant, 412-396-1559, Fax: 412-396-5585, E-mail: mcginleyk@duq.edu.

East Carolina University, Graduate School, College of Allied Health Sciences, Department of Addictions and Rehabilitation Studies, Greenville, NC 27858-4353. Offers clinical counseling (MS); military and trauma counseling (Certificate); rehabilitation and career counseling (MS); rehabilitation counseling (Certificate); rehabilitation counseling and administration (PhD); substance abuse counseling (Certificate); vocational evaluation (Certificate). *Accreditation:* CORE. *Program availability:* Part-time, evening/weekend. *Students:* 82 full-time (64 women), 55 part-time (43 women); includes 39 minority (28 Black or African American, non-Hispanic/Latino; 1 American Indian or Alaska Native, non-Hispanic/Latino; 2 Asian, non-Hispanic/Latino; 5 Hispanic/Latino; 3 Two or more races, non-Hispanic/Latino). Average age 33. 51 applicants, 73% accepted, 31 enrolled. In 2018, 19 master's, 5 doctorates, 34 other advanced degrees awarded. *Degree requirements:* For master's, comprehensive exam, thesis or alternative, internship; for doctorate, thesis/dissertation, internship. *Entrance requirements:* For master's and doctorate, GRE General Test or MAT. Additional exam requirements/recommendations for international students: Recommended—TOEFL (minimum score 78 iBT), IELTS (minimum score 6.5). *Application deadline:* For fall admission, 3/1 priority date for domestic students; for spring admission, 10/1 priority date for domestic students. Applications are processed on a rolling basis. Application fee: $75. Electronic applications accepted. *Expenses: Tuition, area resident:* Full-time $4749. Tuition, state resident: full-time $4749. Tuition, nonresident: full-time $17,898. *International tuition:* $17,898 full-time. *Required fees:* $2787. Part-time tuition and fees

vary according to course load and program. *Financial support:* Research assistantships with partial tuition reimbursements, teaching assistantships with partial tuition reimbursements, Federal Work-Study, scholarships/grants, and unspecified assistantships available. Support available to part-time students. Financial award application deadline: 3/1; financial award applicants required to submit FAFSA. *Unit head:* Dr. Paul Toriello, Chair, 252-744-6292, E-mail: toriellop@ecu.edu. *Application contact:* Graduate School Admissions, 252-328-6013, Fax: 252-328-6071, E-mail: gradschool@ecu.edu.
Website: http://www.ecu.edu/rehb/

East Carolina University, Graduate School, College of Education, Department of Interdisciplinary Professions, Greenville, NC 27858-4353. Offers adult education (MA Ed); business and marketing education (MA Ed); community college instruction (Certificate); counselor education (MS); education in the healthcare professions (Certificate); library science (MLS); student affairs in higher education (Certificate); vocational education (MS). *Accreditation:* ACA; ALA; NCATE. *Program availability:* Part-time, evening/weekend. *Application deadline:* For fall admission, 5/15 priority date for domestic students. *Expenses: Tuition, area resident:* Full-time $4749. Tuition, state resident: full-time $4749. Tuition, nonresident: full-time $17,898. *International tuition:* $17,898 full-time. *Required fees:* $2787. Part-time tuition and fees vary according to course load and program. *Financial support:* Application deadline: 6/1. *Unit head:* Dr. Scott Glass, Professor, 252-328-5670, E-mail: glassj@ecu.edu. *Application contact:* Graduate School Admissions, 252-328-6012, Fax: 252-328-6071, E-mail: gradschool@ecu.edu.
Website: http://www.ecu.edu/cs-educ/idp/index.cfm

Eastern Illinois University, Graduate School, College of Education, Department of Counseling and Higher Education, Charleston, IL 61920. Offers college student affairs (MS); counseling (MS). *Accreditation:* ACA; NCATE. *Program availability:* Part-time, evening/weekend, online learning. *Degree requirements:* For master's, comprehensive exam (for some programs), thesis (for some programs). *Entrance requirements:* For master's, GMAT or GRE. Additional exam requirements/recommendations for international students: Required—TOEFL (minimum score 500 paper-based; 61 iBT), IELTS (minimum score 6). *Application deadline:* For fall admission, 5/15 for domestic and international students; for spring admission, 10/15 for domestic and international students. Applications are processed on a rolling basis. Application fee: $30. Electronic applications accepted. *Expenses:* Tuition, state resident: part-time $299 per credit hour. Tuition, nonresident: part-time $718 per credit hour. *Required fees:* $214.50 per credit hour. *Financial support:* Research assistantships with full tuition reimbursements, career-related internships or fieldwork, Federal Work-Study, scholarships/grants, and unspecified assistantships available. Support available to part-time students. Financial award application deadline: 3/1; financial award applicants required to submit FAFSA. *Unit head:* Richard Roberts, Ph.D., Chair, 217-581-2400, Fax: 217-581-7800, E-mail: rlroberts@eiu.edu. *Application contact:* Richard Roberts, Ph.D., Chair, 217-581-2400, Fax: 217-581-7800, E-mail: rlroberts@eiu.edu.
Website: https://www.eiu.edu/che/

Eastern Kentucky University, The Graduate School, College of Education, Department of Counseling and Educational Leadership, Richmond, KY 40475-3102. Offers human services (MA); instructional leadership (MA Ed); mental health counseling (MA); school counseling (MA Ed). *Accreditation:* ACA (one or more programs are accredited); NCATE. *Program availability:* Part-time, online learning. *Entrance requirements:* For master's, GRE General Test, minimum GPA of 2.5.

Eastern Mennonite University, Master of Arts in Counseling Program, Harrisonburg, VA 22802-2462. Offers MA, M Div/MA. *Accreditation:* ACA (one or more programs are accredited); ACIPE. *Program availability:* Part-time. *Degree requirements:* For master's, practicum, internship. *Entrance requirements:* For master's, minimum GPA of 3.0. Additional exam requirements/recommendations for international students: Required—TOEFL (minimum score 550 paper-based; 79 iBT). Electronic applications accepted. *Expenses:* Contact institution. *Faculty research:* Career and gender, empathy and consciousness, emotion theory, education models.

Eastern Michigan University, Graduate School, College of Education, Department of Leadership and Counseling, Programs in Counseling, Ypsilanti, MI 48197. Offers clinical mental health counseling (MA); college counseling (MA); helping interventions in a multicultural society (Graduate Certificate); school counseling (MA); school counselor licensure (Post Master's Certificate). *Program availability:* Part-time, evening/weekend. *Students:* 30 full-time (25 women), 42 part-time (35 women); includes 22 minority (12 Black or African American, non-Hispanic/Latino; 1 Asian, non-Hispanic/Latino; 4 Hispanic/Latino; 5 Two or more races, non-Hispanic/Latino), 1 international. Average age 28. 79 applicants, 62% accepted, 33 enrolled. In 2018, 24 master's, 23 other advanced degrees awarded. *Degree requirements:* For master's, comprehensive exam, internship. *Entrance requirements:* Additional exam requirements/recommendations for international students: Required—TOEFL. *Application deadline:* For fall admission, 5/1 for domestic and international students; for winter admission, 9/15 for domestic and international students; for spring admission, 2/10 for domestic and international students. Applications are processed on a rolling basis. Application fee: $45. *Financial support:* Fellowships, research assistantships with full tuition reimbursements, teaching assistantships with full tuition reimbursements, career-related internships or fieldwork, Federal Work-Study, institutionally sponsored loans, scholarships/grants, tuition waivers (partial), and unspecified assistantships available. Support available to part-time students. Financial award applicants required to submit FAFSA. *Application contact:* Dr. Irene Ametrano, Coordinator of Advising for Programs in Counseling, 734-487-0255, Fax: 734-487-4608, E-mail: iametrano@emich.edu.

Eastern New Mexico University, Graduate School, College of Education and Technology, Department of Educational Studies, Program in Counseling, Portales, NM 88130. Offers MA. *Program availability:* Part-time. *Degree requirements:* For master's, comprehensive exam, thesis optional, 48-hour course work including a 600-hour internship in field placement. *Entrance requirements:* For master's, minimum GPA of 3.0, 3 letters of recommendation, interview. Additional exam requirements/recommendations for international students: Required—TOEFL (minimum score 550 paper-based; 79 iBT), IELTS (minimum score 6). Electronic applications accepted. *Expenses: Tuition, area resident:* Full-time $6776. Tuition, state resident: full-time $6776; part-time $282 per credit hour. Tuition, nonresident: full-time $8986; part-time $374 per credit hour. *Required fees:* $60 per semester. One-time fee: $25.

Eastern New Mexico University, Graduate School, College of Education and Technology, Department of Educational Studies, Program in School Counseling, Portales, NM 88130. Offers M Ed. *Program availability:* Part-time. *Degree requirements:* For master's, comprehensive exam, thesis optional, 48-hour curriculum, 600-hour internship in field placement. *Entrance requirements:* For master's, minimum GPA of 3.0, three letters of recommendation, interview. Additional exam requirements/recommendations for international students: Required—TOEFL (minimum score 550 paper-based; 79 iBT), IELTS (minimum score 6). Electronic applications accepted. *Expenses: Tuition, area resident:* Full-time $6776. Tuition, state resident: full-time $6776; part-time $282 per credit hour. Tuition, nonresident: full-time $8986; part-time $374 per credit hour. *Required fees:* $60 per semester. One-time fee: $25.

Eastern Washington University, Graduate Studies, College of Social Sciences, Department of Psychology, Program in School Counseling, Cheney, WA 99004-2431. Offers applied psychology (MS); school counseling (MS). *Accreditation:* ACA. *Entrance requirements:* Additional exam requirements/recommendations for international students: Required—TOEFL (minimum score 580 paper-based; 92 iBT), IELTS (minimum score 7).

East Tennessee State University, School of Graduate Studies, College of Education, Department of Counseling and Human Services, Johnson City, TN 37614. Offers clinical mental health counseling (MA); college counseling/student affairs higher education (MA); couples and family therapy (MA); human services (MS); school counseling (MA). *Accreditation:* ACA; NCATE. *Program availability:* Part-time. *Degree requirements:* For master's, comprehensive exam, thesis optional, internship, student teaching, culminating experience. *Entrance requirements:* For master's, GRE General Test, minimum GPA of 3.0, three letters of recommendation, interview, 2-3 page essay detailing experiences that have shaped pursuit of degree, resume. Additional exam requirements/recommendations for international students: Required—TOEFL (minimum score 550 paper-based; 79 iBT). Electronic applications accepted. *Faculty research:* Intervention and assistance with at-risk and under-served youth and high conflict families; service and social justice; women and girls' issues in counseling; counseling competence with LGBTQ individuals; counselor education and supervision.

Edinboro University of Pennsylvania, Department of Counseling, School Psychology and Special Education, Edinboro, PA 16444. Offers counseling (MA), including art therapy, clinical mental health counseling, college counseling, rehabilitation counseling, school counseling; educational psychology (M Ed); school psychology (Ed S); special education (M Ed), including autism, behavior management. *Accreditation:* ACA. *Program availability:* Part-time, evening/weekend. *Degree requirements:* For master's, thesis or alternative, competency exam; for Ed S, thesis or alternative. *Entrance requirements:* For master's and Ed S, GRE or MAT, minimum QPA of 2.5. Electronic applications accepted.

Emporia State University, Program in School Counseling, Emporia, KS 66801-5415. Offers MS. *Accreditation:* ACA; NCATE. *Program availability:* Part-time. *Degree requirements:* For master's, comprehensive exam or thesis, practicum. *Entrance requirements:* For master's, GRE or MAT, essay exam, appropriate bachelor's degree, interview, letters of recommendation. Electronic applications accepted.

Evangel University, School Counseling Program, Springfield, MO 65802. Offers MS. *Program availability:* Part-time, evening/weekend. *Degree requirements:* For master's, comprehensive exam. *Entrance requirements:* For master's, MAT (preferred) or GRE. Additional exam requirements/recommendations for international students: Required—TOEFL (minimum score 550 paper-based). Electronic applications accepted.

Fairfield University, Graduate School of Education and Allied Professions, Fairfield, CT 06824. Offers applied behavior analysis (ATC); applied psychology (MA); clinical mental health counseling (MA, CAS); educational technology (MA); elementary education (MA, CAS); family studies (MA); integration of spirituality and religion in counseling (ATC); marriage and family therapy (MA); reading and language development (Sixth Year Certificate); school counseling (MA, CAS); school psychology (MA, CAS); school-based marriage and family therapy (ATC); secondary education (MA); special education (MA, CAS); substance abuse counseling (ATC); teaching (Certificate); teaching and foundations (MA, CAS); TESOL, world languages, and bilingual education (MA, CAS). *Accreditation:* NCATE. *Program availability:* Part-time, evening/weekend. *Degree requirements:* For master's, comprehensive exam. *Entrance requirements:* For master's, minimum GPA of 3.0, 2 recommendations, resume. Additional exam requirements/recommendations for international students: Required—TOEFL (minimum score 550 paper-based; 84 iBT) or IELTS (minimum score 7.5). Electronic applications accepted. *Expenses:* Contact institution. *Faculty research:* Reading and literacy, writing, social justice and inequality in education, addictions and mental health issues, therapeutic relationships and clinical supervision.

Faulkner University, College of Education, Montgomery, AL 36109-3398. Offers counseling (MS); curriculum and instruction (M Ed); elementary education (M Ed); school counseling (M Ed). *Program availability:* Part-time, evening/weekend, 100% online, blended/hybrid learning. *Degree requirements:* For master's, 5+ hours in clinical training (for MS, M Ed in school counseling). *Entrance requirements:* For master's, MAT (minimum score of 370) or GRE (minimum score of 280) taken within last five years, bachelor's degree from regionally-accredited college or university; official transcripts from all colleges and universities attended; 3 letters of recommendation; goal statement (approximately 600 words); minimum cumulative GPA of 2.75 in undergraduate courses, 3.0 in graduate courses. Additional exam requirements/recommendations for international students: Required—TOEFL (minimum score 500 paper-based). Electronic applications accepted. *Expenses:* Contact institution.

Fitchburg State University, Division of Graduate and Continuing Education, Program in Interdisciplinary Studies, Fitchburg, MA 01420-2697. Offers applied communications (CAGS); counseling/psychology (CAGS); individualized track (CAGS); reading specialist (CAGS). *Program availability:* Part-time, evening/weekend. *Entrance requirements:* Additional exam requirements/recommendations for international students: Required—TOEFL (minimum score 550 paper-based; 79 iBT). Electronic applications accepted. *Expenses:* Contact institution.

Fitchburg State University, Division of Graduate and Continuing Education, Programs in Counseling, Fitchburg, MA 01420-2697. Offers clinical mental health counseling (MS); school guidance counseling (MS). *Accreditation:* NCATE. *Program availability:* Part-time, evening/weekend. *Entrance requirements:* Additional exam requirements/recommendations for international students: Required—TOEFL (minimum score 550 paper-based; 79 iBT). Electronic applications accepted. *Expenses:* Contact institution.

Florida Agricultural and Mechanical University, Division of Graduate Studies, Research, and Continuing Education, College of Education, Department of Educational Leadership and Human Services, Tallahassee, FL 32307-3200. Offers administration and supervision (M Ed, MS, PhD); adult education (M Ed, MS); educational leadership (PhD); guidance and counseling (M Ed, MS). *Accreditation:* NCATE. *Degree requirements:* For master's, thesis (for some programs); for doctorate, thesis/dissertation. *Entrance requirements:* For master's, GRE General Test, minimum GPA of 3.0. Additional exam requirements/recommendations for international students: Required—TOEFL.

Florida Atlantic University, College of Education, Department of Counselor Education, Boca Raton, FL 33431-0991. Offers MS, PhD. *Accreditation:* ACA; NCATE. *Program availability:* Part-time, evening/weekend. *Faculty:* 10 full-time (6 women), 5 part-time/adjunct (2 women). *Students:* 88 full-time (80 women), 83 part-time (72 women); includes 88 minority (35 Black or African American, non-Hispanic/Latino; 2 Asian, non-Hispanic/Latino; 47 Hispanic/Latino; 4 Two or more races, non-Hispanic/Latino), 2 international. Average age 32. 177 applicants, 28% accepted, 41 enrolled. In 2018, 20 master's, 5 doctorates awarded. *Entrance requirements:* For master's, GRE General Test, minimum GPA of 3.0 during previous 2 years. Additional exam requirements/recommendations for international students: Required—TOEFL (minimum score 500 paper-based; 61 iBT), IELTS (minimum score 6). *Application deadline:* For fall admission, 3/1 for domestic students, 2/1 for international students; for spring

admission, 9/15 for domestic students, 7/1 for international students. Applications are processed on a rolling basis. Application fee: $30. *Expenses: Tuition, area resident:* Full-time $7400; part-time $369.82 per credit. Tuition, state resident: full-time $7400; part-time $369.82 per credit. Tuition, nonresident: full-time $20,496; part-time $1024.81 per credit. *Financial support:* Research assistantships with partial tuition reimbursements, teaching assistantships, career-related internships or fieldwork, scholarships/grants, and unspecified assistantships available. *Faculty research:* Brief therapy, psychological type, marriage and family counseling, international programs, integrated services. *Unit head:* Dr. Paul Peluso, Chair, 561-297-3625, Fax: 561-297-2309, E-mail: ppeluso@fau.edu. *Application contact:* Dr. Paul Peluso, Chair, 561-297-3625, Fax: 561-297-2309, E-mail: ppeluso@fau.edu.
Website: http://www.coe.fau.edu/academicdepartments/ce/

Florida International University, College of Arts, Sciences, and Education, Department of Leadership and Professional Studies, Miami, FL 33199. Offers adult education and human resource development (MS, Ed D); counseling (MS), including rehabilitation counseling, school counseling; counselor education (MS), including clinical mental health counseling; educational administration and supervision (Ed D); educational leadership (MS, Certificate, Ed S); higher education (Ed D); higher education administration (MS); international and comparative education (MS); recreation and sport management (MS), including recreation and sport management, recreational therapy; school psychology (Ed S); urban education (MS), including instruction in urban settings, learning technologies, multicultural/bilingual, multicultural/TESOL, urban education. *Program availability:* Part-time, evening/weekend. *Faculty:* 64 full-time (43 women), 104 part-time/adjunct (76 women). *Students:* 258 full-time (196 women), 217 part-time (155 women); includes 387 minority (118 Black or African American, non-Hispanic/Latino; 8 Asian, non-Hispanic/Latino; 249 Hispanic/Latino; 12 Two or more races, non-Hispanic/Latino), 11 international. Average age 31. 345 applicants, 57% accepted, 126 enrolled. In 2018, 172 master's, 11 doctorates awarded. *Entrance requirements:* For master's, minimum GPA of 3.0; for doctorate and other advanced degree, GRE General Test. Additional exam requirements/recommendations for international students: Required—TOEFL (minimum score 550 paper-based; 80 iBT), IELTS (minimum score 6.3). *Application deadline:* For fall admission, 6/1 priority date for domestic students, 4/1 for international students; for winter admission, 10/1 priority date for domestic students, 9/1 for international students; for spring admission, 3/1 priority date for domestic students, 2/1 for international students. Applications are processed on a rolling basis. Application fee: $30. Electronic applications accepted. *Financial support:* Fellowships, research assistantships, teaching assistantships, Federal Work-Study, and tuition waivers (full and partial) available. Support available to part-time students. Financial award applicants required to submit FAFSA. *Unit head:* Dr. Benjamin Baez, Chair, 305-348-3214, Fax: 305-348-1515, E-mail: benjamin.baez@fiu.edu. *Application contact:* Nanett Rojas, Manager, Admissions Operations, 305-348-7464, Fax: 305-348-7441, E-mail: gradadm@fiu.edu.
Website: http://education.fiu.edu

Fordham University, Graduate School of Education, Division of Psychological and Educational Services, New York, NY 10023. Offers counseling and personnel services (MSE); counseling psychology (PhD); school psychology (PhD). *Accreditation:* APA (one or more programs are accredited); NCATE. *Program availability:* Part-time, evening/weekend. Terminal master's awarded for partial completion of doctoral program. *Degree requirements:* For master's, comprehensive exam (for some programs); for doctorate, comprehensive exam (for some programs), thesis/dissertation. *Entrance requirements:* For doctorate, GRE General Test. Additional exam requirements/recommendations for international students: Required—TOEFL (minimum score 577 paper-based; 90 iBT), IELTS (minimum score 7). Electronic applications accepted.

Fort Hays State University, Graduate School, College of Education, Department of Educational Administration and Counseling, Program in Counseling, Hays, KS 67601-4099. Offers MS. *Accreditation:* NCATE. *Program availability:* Part-time. *Degree requirements:* For master's, comprehensive exam, thesis or alternative. *Entrance requirements:* For master's, GRE General Test or MAT, minimum undergraduate GPA of 3.0 in last 60 hours. Additional exam requirements/recommendations for international students: Required—TOEFL (minimum score 550 paper-based). Electronic applications accepted. *Faculty research:* Career education, evaluation and plans, counseling the disabled, marriage and family parenting, underemployment and work in the family.

Fort Valley State University, College of Graduate Studies and Extended Education, Department of Counseling Psychology, Fort Valley, GA 31030. Offers guidance and counseling (Ed S); mental health counseling (MS); rehabilitation counseling (MS). *Program availability:* Part-time. *Degree requirements:* For master's, comprehensive exam (for some programs), thesis optional. *Entrance requirements:* For master's and Ed S, GRE General Test or MAT.

Freed-Hardeman University, Program in Counseling, Henderson, TN 38340-2399. Offers MS. *Program availability:* Part-time, evening/weekend. *Degree requirements:* For master's, comprehensive exam, practicum. *Entrance requirements:* For master's, GRE General Test or MAT. Additional exam requirements/recommendations for international students: Required—TOEFL (minimum score 500 paper-based).

Freed-Hardeman University, Program in Education, Henderson, TN 38340-2399. Offers curriculum and instruction (M Ed); school counseling (M Ed), including administration and supervision, special education; school leadership (Ed S). *Accreditation:* NCATE. *Program availability:* Part-time, evening/weekend. *Degree requirements:* For master's, comprehensive exam, thesis optional; for Ed S, thesis. *Entrance requirements:* For master's, GRE General Test or NTE; for Ed S, 3 years of teaching experience. Additional exam requirements/recommendations for international students: Required—TOEFL (minimum score 500 paper-based).

Fresno Pacific University, Graduate Programs, School of Education, Division of Pupil Personnel Services, Program in School Counseling, Fresno, CA 93702-4709. Offers MA. *Program availability:* Part-time, evening/weekend. *Degree requirements:* For master's, thesis or alternative. *Entrance requirements:* Additional exam requirements/recommendations for international students: Required—TOEFL (minimum score 550 paper-based). *Expenses:* Contact institution.

Frostburg State University, College of Education, Department of Educational Professions, Program in School Counseling, Frostburg, MD 21532-1099. Offers M Ed. *Accreditation:* NCATE. *Program availability:* Part-time, evening/weekend. *Degree requirements:* For master's, comprehensive exam, thesis or alternative. *Entrance requirements:* For master's, GRE General Test or MAT, interview. Additional exam requirements/recommendations for international students: Required—TOEFL. Electronic applications accepted.

Gallaudet University, The Graduate School, Washington, DC 20002-3625. Offers American Sign Language/English bilingual early childhood deaf education: birth to 5 (Certificate); audiology (Au D); clinical psychology (PhD); deaf and hard of hearing infants, toddlers, and their families (Certificate); deaf education (MA, Ed S); deaf history (Certificate); deaf studies (Certificate); educating deaf students with disabilities (Certificate); education: teacher preparation (MA), including deaf education, early childhood education and deaf education, elementary education and deaf education,

secondary education and deaf education; educational neuroscience (PhD); hearing, speech and language sciences (MS, PhD); international development (MA); interpretation (MA, PhD), including combined interpreting practice and research (MA), interpreting research (MA); linguistics (MA, PhD); mental health counseling (MA); peer mentoring (Certificate); public administration (MPA); school counseling (MA); school psychology (Psy S); sign language teaching (MA); social work (MSW); speech-language pathology (MS). *Program availability:* Part-time. Terminal master's awarded for partial completion of doctoral program. *Degree requirements:* For master's, comprehensive exam (for some programs), thesis optional; for doctorate, comprehensive exam, thesis/dissertation. *Entrance requirements:* For master's and doctorate, GRE General Test or MAT, letters of recommendation, interviews, goals statement, American Sign Language proficiency interview, written English competency. Additional exam requirements/recommendations for international students: Required—TOEFL. Electronic applications accepted. *Faculty research:* Signing math dictionaries, telecommunications access, cancer genetics, linguistics, visual language and visual learning, integrated quantum materials, deaf legal discourse, advance recruitment and retention in geosciences.

Geneva College, Master of Arts in Counseling Program, Beaver Falls, PA 15010-3599. Offers clinical mental health counseling (MA); marriage and family counseling (MA); school counseling (MA). *Accreditation:* ACA. *Program availability:* Part-time, evening/weekend. *Degree requirements:* For master's, comprehensive exam, 60 credits including practicum and internship. *Entrance requirements:* For master's, minimum GPA of 3.0 (preferred), 3 letters of recommendation, essay on career goals, resume of educational and professional experiences. Additional exam requirements/recommendations for international students: Required—TOEFL. Electronic applications accepted. *Expenses:* Contact institution. *Faculty research:* Blended family counseling; premarital and newlywed couples; religion in clinical supervision; conceptual mapping in research, supervision, and clinical work.

George Fox University, College of Education, Graduate Department of Counseling, Newberg, OR 97132-2697. Offers clinical mental health counseling (MA); marriage, couple and family counseling (MA, Certificate); school counseling (MA, Certificate); school psychology (Ed S). *Program availability:* Part-time. *Degree requirements:* For master's, clinical project. *Entrance requirements:* For master's, MAT or GRE, bachelor's degree from regionally-accredited college or university, minimum cumulative GPA of 3.0, 1 professional and 1 academic reference, resume, on-campus interview, official transcripts. Additional exam requirements/recommendations for international students: Required—TOEFL (minimum score 577 paper-based; 90 iBT), IELTS (minimum score 7). Electronic applications accepted. *Expenses:* Contact institution.

George Mason University, College of Education and Human Development, Program in Counseling and Development, Fairfax, VA 22030. Offers M Ed. *Accreditation:* NCATE. *Program availability:* Part-time. *Faculty:* 6 full-time (5 women), 11 part-time/adjunct (8 women). *Students:* 54 full-time (47 women), 84 part-time (72 women); includes 67 minority (22 Black or African American, non-Hispanic/Latino; 20 Asian, non-Hispanic/Latino; 21 Hispanic/Latino; 4 Two or more races, non-Hispanic/Latino), 4 international. Average age 31. 93 applicants, 51% accepted, 28 enrolled. In 2018, 48 master's awarded. *Degree requirements:* For master's, thesis (for some programs), degree must be completed within six years of enrollment. *Entrance requirements:* For master's, bachelor's degree from regionally-accredited institution with minimum GPA of 3.0 overall or in last 60 credit hours; 2 copies of official transcripts; expanded goals statement; 2 letters of recommendation; 12 credits of undergraduate behavioral sciences; 1000 hours of counseling or related experience. Additional exam requirements/recommendations for international students: Required—TOEFL (minimum score 575 paper-based; 88 iBT), IELTS (minimum score 6.5), PTE (minimum score 59). *Application deadline:* For fall admission, 2/1 for domestic and international students; for spring admission, 10/1 for domestic and international students. Application fee: $75 ($80 for international students). Electronic applications accepted. *Expenses:* $489 per credit in-state tuition; $1,346.75 per credit out-of-state tuition (discounted to $689 per credit). *Financial support:* In 2018–19, 5 students received support, including 4 research assistantships with tuition reimbursements available (averaging $11,990 per year), 1 teaching assistantship; career-related internships or fieldwork, Federal Work-Study, scholarships/grants, unspecified assistantships, and health care benefits (for full-time research or teaching assistantship recipients) also available. Support available to part-time students. Financial award application deadline: 3/1; financial award applicants required to submit FAFSA. *Faculty research:* Leadership, multiculturalism, social justice, and advocacy; global well-being; social psychological, physical, and spiritual health of individuals, families, communities, and organizations. *Unit head:* Fred Bemak, Academic Program Coordinator, 703-993-3941, Fax: 703-993-5577, E-mail: fbemak@gmu.edu. *Application contact:* Fred Bemak, Academic Program Coordinator, 703-993-3941, Fax: 703-993-5577, E-mail: fbemak@gmu.edu.
Website: http://gse.gmu.edu/programs/counseling/

The George Washington University, Graduate School of Education and Human Development, Department of Counseling and Human Development, Program in Counseling, Washington, DC 20052. Offers PhD, Ed S. *Accreditation:* ACA (one or more programs are accredited); NCATE. *Program availability:* Part-time, evening/weekend. *Students:* 13 full-time (all women), 33 part-time (26 women); includes 18 minority (6 Black or African American, non-Hispanic/Latino; 1 American Indian or Alaska Native, non-Hispanic/Latino; 6 Asian, non-Hispanic/Latino; 3 Hispanic/Latino; 2 Two or more races, non-Hispanic/Latino), 4 international. Average age 33. 59 applicants, 42% accepted, 9 enrolled. In 2018, 7 doctorates awarded. *Degree requirements:* For doctorate, comprehensive exam, thesis/dissertation; for Ed S, comprehensive exam. *Entrance requirements:* For doctorate, GRE General Test, interview, minimum GPA of 3.3; for Ed S, GRE General Test or MAT, minimum GPA of 3.3. *Application deadline:* For fall admission, 1/15 priority date for domestic students; for spring admission, 10/1 for domestic students. Applications are processed on a rolling basis. Application fee: $75. *Financial support:* Fellowships, research assistantships, teaching assistantships, career-related internships or fieldwork, Federal Work-Study, and tuition waivers (partial) available. Financial award application deadline: 1/15; financial award applicants required to submit FAFSA. *Faculty research:* Values in counseling, religion and counseling. *Unit head:* Dr. Pat Schwallie-Giddis, Director, 202-994-6856, E-mail: drpat@gwu.edu. *Application contact:* Sarah Lang, Director of Graduate Admissions, 202-994-1447, Fax: 202-994-7207, E-mail: slang@gwu.edu.

The George Washington University, Graduate School of Education and Human Development, Department of Counseling and Human Development, Program in School Counseling, Washington, DC 20052. Offers MA Ed, Graduate Certificate. *Students:* 38 full-time (34 women), 5 part-time (all women); includes 13 minority (7 Black or African American, non-Hispanic/Latino; 1 Asian, non-Hispanic/Latino; 4 Hispanic/Latino; 1 Two or more races, non-Hispanic/Latino), 1 international. Average age 29. 61 applicants, 74% accepted, 20 enrolled. In 2018, 17 master's awarded. *Unit head:* Dr. Pat Schwallie-Giddis, Chair, 202-994-6856, E-mail: drpat@gwu.edu. *Application contact:* Sarah Lang, Director of Graduate Admissions, 202-994-1447, Fax: 202-994-7207, E-mail: slang@gwu.edu.

Georgian Court University, School of Arts and Sciences, Lakewood, NJ 08701-2697. Offers applied behavior analysis (MA); autism spectrum disorders (Certificate); clinical mental health counseling (MA); criminal justice and human rights (MS); holistic health

studies (MA, Certificate); homeland security (Certificate); instructional technology (CPC); mercy spirituality (Certificate); parish business management (Certificate); professional counselor (Certificate); school psychology (MA, Certificate); theology (MA, Certificate). *Program availability:* Part-time, evening/weekend. *Faculty:* 15 full-time (9 women), 11 part-time/adjunct (9 women). *Students:* 90 full-time (84 women), 99 part-time (67 women); includes 28 minority (9 Black or African American, non-Hispanic/Latino; 1 Asian, non-Hispanic/Latino; 14 Hispanic/Latino; 4 Two or more races, non-Hispanic/Latino), 2 international. Average age 34. 138 applicants, 59% accepted, 60 enrolled. In 2018, 68 master's, 19 other advanced degrees awarded. *Degree requirements:* For master's, comprehensive exam (for some programs), thesis (for some programs). *Entrance requirements:* For master's, GRE, GMAT, or NTE/PRAXIS, 3 letters of recommendation. Additional exam requirements/recommendations for international students: Required—TOEFL (minimum score 550 paper-based; 79 iBT). *Application deadline:* For fall admission, 8/15 for domestic students, 5/1 for international students; for spring admission, 1/15 for domestic students, 10/1 for international students. Applications are processed on a rolling basis. Application fee: $40. Electronic applications accepted. *Expenses: Tuition:* Full-time $856; part-time $856 per credit hour. *Required fees:* $968; $496 per unit. $248 per semester. Tuition and fees vary according to campus/location and program. *Financial support:* Scholarships/grants, health care benefits, and unspecified assistantships available. Financial award application deadline: 4/15; financial award applicants required to submit FAFSA. *Unit head:* Dr. Mary Chinery, Dean, 732-987-2493, Fax: 732-987-2007, E-mail: mchinery@georgian.edu. *Application contact:* Patrick Givens, Director of Graduate and Professional Studies Admissions, 732-987-2736, Fax: 732-987-2000, E-mail: gps@georgian.edu.
Website: https://georgian.edu/academics/school-of-arts-sciences/

Georgia Southern University, Jack N. Averitt College of Graduate Studies, College of Education, Department of Leadership, Technology, and Human Development, Program in Counselor Education, Statesboro, GA 30460. Offers mental health counseling (M Ed); school counseling (M Ed). *Accreditation:* ACA; NCATE. *Program availability:* Part-time, evening/weekend. *Degree requirements:* For master's, comprehensive exam, transition point assessments. *Entrance requirements:* For master's, minimum GPA of 2.5, letters of recommendation, interview. Additional exam requirements/recommendations for international students: Required—TOEFL (minimum score 550 paper-based; 80 iBT), IELTS (minimum score 6). Electronic applications accepted. *Expenses: Tuition, area resident:* Part-time $3324 per semester. Tuition, state resident: full-time $5814; part-time $3324 per semester. Tuition, nonresident: full-time $23,204; part-time $13,260 per semester. *Required fees:* $2092; $2092. Tuition and fees vary according to course load, degree level, campus/location and program. *Faculty research:* School counseling, test development, gender equity, career counseling, mental health counseling, best practices for preparing counselors.

Georgia State University, College of Education and Human Development, Department of Counseling and Psychological Services, Program in School Counseling, Atlanta, GA 30302-3083. Offers M Ed, Ed S. *Accreditation:* ACA (one or more programs are accredited); NCATE. *Entrance requirements:* For master's, GRE, goal statement, resume, 3 letters of recommendation, transcripts. Additional exam requirements/recommendations for international students: Required—TOEFL. Application fee: $50. Electronic applications accepted. *Expenses: Tuition, area resident:* Full-time $9360; part-time $390 per credit hour. Tuition, state resident: full-time $9360; part-time $390 per credit hour. Tuition, nonresident: full-time $30,024; part-time $1251 per credit hour. *International tuition:* $30,024 full-time. *Required fees:* $2128. *Financial support:* Research assistantships, teaching assistantships, career-related internships or fieldwork, institutionally sponsored loans, scholarships/grants, health care benefits, and unspecified assistantships available. Financial award application deadline: 4/1. *Faculty research:* Mattering, adolescent counseling, school counselor identity, group leadership of school counselors, play therapy. *Unit head:* Dr. Brian Dew, Chairperson, 404-413-8168, Fax: 404-413-8013, E-mail: bdew@gsu.edu. *Application contact:* CPS Admissions Office, 404-413-8200, E-mail: nkeita@gsu.edu.
Website: https://education.gsu.edu/cps/

Grambling State University, School of Graduate Studies and Research, College of Education, Department of Educational Leadership, Grambling, LA 71245. Offers developmental education (MS, Ed D, PMC), including curriculum and instructional design (Ed D), English (MS), guidance and counseling (MS), higher education administration and management (Ed D), mathematics (MS), reading (MS), science (MS), student development and personnel services (Ed D); educational leadership (M Ed). *Program availability:* Part-time, evening/weekend. *Degree requirements:* For master's, comprehensive exam, thesis (for some programs); for doctorate, comprehensive exam, thesis/dissertation. *Entrance requirements:* For master's, GRE, minimum GPA of 2.5 on last degree; for doctorate, GRE (minimum score 1000, 500 on Verbal), master's degree, minimum GPA of 3.0 on last degree. Additional exam requirements/recommendations for international students: Required—TOEFL (minimum score 500 paper-based; 62 iBT). Electronic applications accepted.

Gwynedd Mercy University, School of Education, Gwynedd Valley, PA 19437-0901. Offers education (Ed D); educational administration (MS); master teacher (MS); school counseling (MS); special education (MS). *Program availability:* Part-time, evening/weekend, 100% online. *Degree requirements:* For master's, thesis, internship, practicum. *Entrance requirements:* For master's, GRE or MAT; PRAXIS I, minimum GPA of 3.0. *Expenses:* Contact institution. *Faculty research:* Learning and the brain, reading literacy, ethics and moral judgment, leadership, teaching and multicultural education.

Hampton University, School of Liberal Arts and Education, Program in Counseling, Hampton, VA 23668. Offers college student development (MA); community agency counseling (MA); counseling (Ed S); counselor education and supervision (PhD); pastoral counseling (MA); school counseling (MA). *Accreditation:* ACA; NCATE. *Program availability:* Part-time, evening/weekend, online learning. *Students:* 42 full-time (35 women), 12 part-time (11 women); includes 49 minority (48 Black or African American, non-Hispanic/Latino; 1 Asian, non-Hispanic/Latino). Average age 35. 35 applicants, 63% accepted, 17 enrolled. In 2018, 9 master's, 1 doctorate, 5 other advanced degrees awarded. *Degree requirements:* For master's, comprehensive exam; for doctorate, comprehensive exam, thesis/dissertation. *Entrance requirements:* For master's, GRE General Test, personal statement, two letters of recommendation; for doctorate, GRE General Test, personal statement, writing sample, three letters of recommendation; for Ed S, personal statement, two letters of recommendation. Additional exam requirements/recommendations for international students: Required—TOEFL, TOEFL (minimum score 525 paper-based) or IELTS (6.5). *Application deadline:* For fall admission, 6/1 priority date for domestic students, 4/1 priority date for international students; for winter admission, 9/1 priority date for international students; for spring admission, 11/1 priority date for domestic students, 9/1 for international students; for summer admission, 4/1 priority date for domestic students, 2/1 priority date for international students. Applications are processed on a rolling basis. Application fee: $35. Electronic applications accepted. *Financial support:* Fellowships, research assistantships, teaching assistantships, career-related internships or fieldwork, Federal Work-Study, institutionally sponsored loans, scholarships/grants, tuition waivers, unspecified assistantships, and grant funding provided 10k when students enrolled in

the required internships available. Support available to part-time students. Financial award application deadline: 6/30; financial award applicants required to submit FAFSA. *Faculty research:* Personality development, temperament, post-traumatic stress disorder, continuum of normal to abnormal personality. *Unit head:* Dr. Richard Mason, Chairperson, 757-728-6160, E-mail: richard.mason@hamptonu.edu. *Application contact:* Dr. Richard Mason, Chairperson, 757-728-6160, E-mail: richard.mason@hamptonu.edu.
Website: http://edhd.hamptonu.edu/counseling/

Harding University, Cannon-Clary College of Education, Searcy, AR 72149-0001. Offers advanced studies in teaching and learning (M Ed); art (MSE); behavioral science (MSE); counseling (MS, Ed S); early childhood special education (M Ed, MSE); education (MSE); educational leadership (M Ed, Ed S); elementary education (M Ed); English (MSE); French (MSE); history/social science (MSE); kinesiology (MSE); math (MSE); reading (M Ed); secondary education (M Ed); Spanish (MSE); teaching (MAT); teaching English as a second language (MSE). *Accreditation:* NCATE. *Program availability:* Part-time, evening/weekend. *Degree requirements:* For master's, comprehensive exam (for some programs), thesis optional, portfolio(s); for Ed S, comprehensive exam, portfolio, project. *Entrance requirements:* For master's, GRE, MAT, PRAXIS; for Ed S, MAT or GRE. Additional exam requirements/recommendations for international students: Required—TOEFL (minimum score 550 paper-based; 79 iBT). *Faculty research:* Reading, comprehension, school violence, educational technology, behavior, college choice, differentiated instruction, brain-based teaching.

Hardin-Simmons University, Graduate School, College of Human Sciences and Educational Studies, Department of Counseling and Human Development, Abilene, TX 79698-0001. Offers M Ed. *Program availability:* Part-time. *Students:* 11 full-time (6 women), 7 part-time (3 women); includes 4 minority (3 Black or African American, non-Hispanic/Latino; 1 Asian, non-Hispanic/Latino), 2 international. Average age 28. 9 applicants, 78% accepted, 4 enrolled. In 2018, 10 master's awarded. *Degree requirements:* For master's, comprehensive exam, practicum. *Entrance requirements:* For master's, minimum undergraduate GPA of 3.0 in major, 2.7 overall; interview; 3 letters of recommendation; resume. Additional exam requirements/recommendations for international students: Required—TOEFL (minimum score 550 paper-based; 79 iBT). *Application deadline:* For fall admission, 8/15 priority date for domestic students, 4/1 for international students; for spring admission, 1/5 priority date for domestic students, 9/1 for international students. Applications are processed on a rolling basis. Application fee: $50. Electronic applications accepted. *Expenses: Tuition:* Full-time $750; part-time $750 per credit hour. *Required fees:* $1300; $880 per credit. Tuition and fees vary according to degree level and program. *Financial support:* Fellowships, career-related internships or fieldwork, and scholarships/grants available. Support available to part-time students. Financial award application deadline: 6/30; financial award applicants required to submit FAFSA. *Unit head:* Dr. Scott Brown, Program Director, 325-670-1865, Fax: 325-670-5859, E-mail: robert.s.brown@hsutx.edu. *Application contact:* Dr. Nancy Kucinski, Dean of Graduate Studies, 325-670-1298, Fax: 325-670-1564, E-mail: gradoff@hsutx.edu.
Website: http://www.hsutx.edu/academics/irvin/graduate/counseling

Henderson State University, Graduate Studies, Teachers College, Department of Counselor Education, Arkadelphia, AR 71999-0001. Offers clinical mental health counseling (MS); developmental therapy (MS, Graduate Certificate); secondary school counseling (MSE). *Accreditation:* NCATE. *Program availability:* Part-time. *Entrance requirements:* For master's, GRE General Test or MAT, letters of recommendation, minimum GPA of 2.7, teacher certification. Additional exam requirements/recommendations for international students: Required—TOEFL (minimum score 600 paper-based); Recommended—IELTS (minimum score 6.5).

Heritage University, Graduate Programs in Education, Program in Counseling, Toppenish, WA 98948-9599. Offers M Ed. *Program availability:* Part-time. *Degree requirements:* For master's, comprehensive exam. *Entrance requirements:* For master's, interview, letters of recommendation, at least 9 semester-credits of behavioral sciences.

Hofstra University, School of Health Professions and Human Services, Programs in Counseling, Hempstead, NY 11549. Offers counseling (MS Ed, PD); creative arts therapy (MA); interdisciplinary transition specialist (Advanced Certificate); marriage and family therapy (MA); mental health counseling (MA, Advanced Certificate); rehabilitation administration (PD); rehabilitation counseling (MS Ed, Advanced Certificate); rehabilitation counseling in mental health (MS Ed, Advanced Certificate). *Accreditation:* ACA. *Program availability:* Part-time, evening/weekend. *Students:* 100 full-time (89 women), 66 part-time (57 women); includes 55 minority (22 Black or African American, non-Hispanic/Latino; 10 Asian, non-Hispanic/Latino; 20 Hispanic/Latino; 2 Native Hawaiian or other Pacific Islander, non-Hispanic/Latino; 1 Two or more races, non-Hispanic/Latino), 2 international. Average age 29. 136 applicants, 73% accepted, 54 enrolled. In 2018, 59 master's, 3 other advanced degrees awarded. *Degree requirements:* For master's, comprehensive exam (for some programs), thesis (for some programs), internship, practicum, student teaching, seminars, minimum GPA of 3.0. *Entrance requirements:* For master's, GRE, interview, letters of recommendation, portfolio, essay, professional experience, certification; for other advanced degree, GRE, interview, letters of recommendation, essay, professional experience, resume, master's degree. Additional exam requirements/recommendations for international students: Required—TOEFL (minimum score 550 paper-based; 80 iBT). *Application deadline:* Applications are processed on a rolling basis. Application fee: $75. Electronic applications accepted. *Financial support:* In 2018–19, 75 students received support, including 45 fellowships with full and partial tuition reimbursements available (averaging $3,643 per year), 5 research assistantships with full and partial tuition reimbursements available (averaging $7,038 per year); career-related internships or fieldwork, Federal Work-Study, institutionally sponsored loans, scholarships/grants, traineeships, tuition waivers (full and partial), unspecified assistantships, and scholarships and endowed scholarships also available. Support available to part-time students. Financial award applicants required to submit FAFSA. *Faculty research:* Couple and family therapy infidelity; creative arts impact on Parkinson's disease; LGBTQ+ inclusion; substance abuse/opioid addiction; racial identity, multicultural issues, white privilege, Latinos, school counseling and the intensity of the high school curriculum. *Unit head:* Dr. Jamie Mitus, Chairperson, 516-463-5759, E-mail: jamie.s.mitus@hofstra.edu. *Application contact:* Sunil Samuel, Assistant Vice President of Admissions, 516-463-4723, Fax: 516-463-4664, E-mail: graduateadmission@hofstra.edu.
Website: http://www.hofstra.edu/academics/colleges/healthscienceshumanservices/

Houston Baptist University, College of Education and Behavioral Sciences, Programs in Education, Houston, TX 77074-3298. Offers bilingual education (M Ed); counselor education (M Ed); curriculum and instruction (M Ed); curriculum and instruction (EC-6 bilingual) (M Ed); curriculum and instruction in all-level art, Spanish, music, or physical education (M Ed); curriculum and instruction in EC-6 and special education (EC-12) (M Ed); curriculum and instruction in instructional technology (M Ed); curriculum and instruction in mathematics, science, or social studies (4-8) (M Ed); curriculum and instruction with EC-6 generalist (M Ed); curriculum and instruction with English language arts and reading (4-8) (M Ed); educational administration (M Ed); educational diagnostician (M Ed); executive educational leadership (Ed D); higher education in business management (M Ed); higher education in Christian studies (M Ed); higher

education in counseling (M Ed); higher education in educational technology (M Ed); reading (M Ed); special educational leadership (Ed D). *Program availability:* Part-time, evening/weekend, 100% online, blended/hybrid learning. *Degree requirements:* For master's, comprehensive exam; for doctorate, thesis/dissertation. *Entrance requirements:* For master's, minimum GPA of 2.75, two recommendations, resume, bachelor's degree conferred transcript; interview (for non-certified teachers); for doctorate, GRE, 5 letters of recommendation. Additional exam requirements/recommendations for international students: Required—TOEFL (minimum score 80 iBT), IELTS (minimum score 6.5). Electronic applications accepted. Application fee is waived when completed online. *Expenses:* Contact institution. *Faculty research:* Autism and inclusion, integrating technology into instruction, school change and leadership trust.

Howard University, School of Education, Department of Human Development and Psychoeducational Studies, Program in School Psychology and Counseling Services, Washington, DC 20059-0002. Offers M Ed. *Accreditation:* NCATE. *Program availability:* Part-time. *Degree requirements:* For master's, comprehensive exam, expository writing exam, practicum. *Entrance requirements:* Additional exam requirements/recommendations for international students: Required—TOEFL (minimum score 550 paper-based; 79 iBT). Electronic applications accepted. *Faculty research:* Law and forensic evaluation, juvenile justice, ethics, clinical assessment, personality disorders, substance abuse.

Hunter College of the City University of New York, Graduate School, School of Education, Department of Educational Foundations and Counseling, Program in School Counseling, New York, NY 10065-5085. Offers MS Ed. *Accreditation:* ACA; NCATE. *Degree requirements:* For master's, thesis, internship, practicum, research seminar. *Entrance requirements:* For master's, interview, minimum GPA of 2.7. Additional exam requirements/recommendations for international students: Required—TOEFL, TWE.

Husson University, Graduate Programs in Counseling and Human Relations, Bangor, ME 04401-2999. Offers clinical mental health counseling (MS); human relations (MS); school counseling (MS). *Accreditation:* ACA. *Program availability:* Part-time, evening/weekend. *Degree requirements:* For master's, comprehensive exam (for some programs), thesis optional. *Entrance requirements:* For master's, BS with minimum GPA of 3.0, letters of recommendation, interview. Additional exam requirements/recommendations for international students: Required—TOEFL (minimum score 550 paper-based; 80 iBT), IELTS (minimum score 6.5). Electronic applications accepted. *Expenses:* Contact institution. *Faculty research:* Challenges and rewards of counseling practice in rural, small town and neighborhood settings.

Idaho State University, Graduate School, College of Health Professions, Department of Counseling, Pocatello, ID 83209-8120. Offers counseling (M Coun, Ed S), including marriage and family counseling (M Coun), mental health counseling (M Coun), school counseling (M Coun), student affairs and college counseling (M Coun); counselor education and counseling (PhD). *Accreditation:* ACA (one or more programs are accredited). *Program availability:* Part-time. *Degree requirements:* For master's, comprehensive exam, thesis, 4 semesters resident graduate study, practicum/internship; for doctorate, comprehensive exam, thesis/dissertation, 3 semesters internship, 4 consecutive semesters doctoral-level study on campus; for Ed S, comprehensive exam, thesis, case studies, oral exam. *Entrance requirements:* For master's, GRE General Test, MAT, minimum GPA of 3.0, bachelors degree, interview, 3 letters of recommendation; for doctorate, GRE General Test, MAT, minimum graduate GPA of 3.0, resume, interview, counseling license, master's degree; for Ed S, GRE General Test, minimum graduate GPA of 3.0, master's degree in counseling, 3 letters of recommendation, 2 years work experience. Additional exam requirements/recommendations for international students: Required—TOEFL (minimum score 600 paper-based; 80 iBT). Electronic applications accepted. *Faculty research:* Group counseling, multicultural counseling, family counseling, child therapy, supervision.

Indiana State University, College of Graduate and Professional Studies, Bayh College of Education, Department of Communication Disorders and Counseling, School, and Educational Psychology, Terre Haute, IN 47809. Offers clinical mental health counseling (MS); communication disorders (MS); school counseling (M Ed); school psychology (PhD, Ed S); MA/MS. *Accreditation:* ACA; ASHA; NCATE. *Program availability:* Part-time, evening/weekend. *Degree requirements:* For master's, thesis optional; for doctorate, thesis/dissertation, research tools proficiency tests. *Entrance requirements:* For master's, GRE General Test or MAT, minimum undergraduate GPA of 2.75; for doctorate, GRE General Test, master's degree, minimum undergraduate GPA of 3.5. Electronic applications accepted. *Faculty research:* Vocational development supervision.

Indiana University Bloomington, School of Education, Department of Counseling and Educational Psychology, Bloomington, IN 47405-1006. Offers counseling (MS, PhD, Ed S); counselor education (MS, Ed S); educational psychology (MS, PhD); inquiry methodology (PhD); learning and developmental sciences (MS, PhD); school psychology (PhD, Ed S). *Accreditation:* ACA (one or more programs are accredited); APA (one or more programs are accredited); NCATE. Terminal master's awarded for partial completion of doctoral program. *Degree requirements:* For master's, thesis optional; for doctorate, thesis/dissertation; for Ed S, comprehensive exam or project. *Entrance requirements:* For master's, doctorate, and Ed S, GRE General Test. Additional exam requirements/recommendations for international students: Required—TOEFL. Electronic applications accepted. *Faculty research:* Counseling psychology, inquiry methodology, school psychology, learning sciences, human development, educational psychology.

Indiana University of Pennsylvania, School of Graduate Studies and Research, College of Education and Communications, Department of Counseling, Program in School Counseling, Indiana, PA 15705. Offers M Ed. *Accreditation:* ACA. *Program availability:* Part-time. *Faculty:* 10 full-time (9 women), 6 part-time/adjunct (3 women). *Students:* 22 full-time (15 women), 23 part-time (21 women); includes 10 minority (7 Black or African American, non-Hispanic/Latino; 1 Hispanic/Latino; 2 Two or more races, non-Hispanic/Latino). Average age 29. 33 applicants, 55% accepted, 15 enrolled. In 2018, 19 master's awarded. *Entrance requirements:* Additional exam requirements/recommendations for international students: Required—TOEFL (minimum score 540 paper-based). *Application deadline:* Applications are processed on a rolling basis. Application fee: $50. Electronic applications accepted. *Expenses:* Tuition, state resident: full-time $12,384; part-time $516 per credit hour. Tuition, nonresident: full-time $18,576; part-time $774 per credit hour. *Required fees:* $4454; $186 per credit hour. $65 per semester. Tuition and fees vary according to program and reciprocity agreements. *Financial support:* In 2018–19, 5 research assistantships with tuition reimbursements (averaging $3,500 per year) were awarded; fellowships with full tuition reimbursements, career-related internships or fieldwork, Federal Work-Study, scholarships/grants, and unspecified assistantships also available. Financial award application deadline: 4/15; financial award applicants required to submit FAFSA. *Unit head:* Dr. Claire Dandeneau, Chairperson/Graduate Coordinator, 724-357-2306, E-mail: candean@iup.edu. *Application contact:* Dr. Claire Dandeneau, Chairperson/Graduate Coordinator, 724-357-2306, E-mail: candean@iup.edu.
Website: http://www.iup.edu/grad/schoolcounseling/default.aspx

Indiana University–Purdue University Indianapolis, School of Education, Indianapolis, IN 46202-5155. Offers curriculum and instruction (MS); early childhood (MS); educational leadership (MS, Certificate); English as a second language (Certificate); kindergarten (Certificate); language education (MS); reading (Certificate); school counseling (MS); special education (MS, Certificate). *Program availability:* Part-time, evening/weekend. Terminal master's awarded for partial completion of doctoral program. *Degree requirements:* For master's, thesis optional. *Entrance requirements:* For master's, GRE General Test, minimum GPA of 2.5; for Certificate, official transcripts. Additional exam requirements/recommendations for international students: Required—TOEFL (minimum score 60 iBT), IELTS (minimum score 5.5). Electronic applications accepted. *Expenses:* Contact institution. *Faculty research:* Educational policies and school leaders' responses to these; issues of intersectionality in the experiences of African American lesbian, gay, and bisexual students attending historically black colleges and universities and those who belong to black Greek-letter organizations; students' experiential knowledge and their evolving disciplinary-specific literacy and understanding; innovative program development; urban ESL teacher preparation; target-based instructional coaching.

Indiana University South Bend, School of Education, South Bend, IN 46615. Offers addiction counseling (MS Ed); alcohol and drug counseling (Graduate Certificate); clinical mental health counseling (MS Ed); educational leadership (MS Ed); elementary education (MS Ed); marriage, couple, and family counseling (MS Ed); school counseling (MS Ed); secondary education (MS Ed); special education (MAT, MS Ed), including intense intervention (MS Ed), mild intervention (MS Ed). *Accreditation:* NCATE. *Program availability:* Part-time, evening/weekend. *Degree requirements:* For master's, thesis or alternative, exit project. *Entrance requirements:* For master's, letters of recommendation, GRE or minimum GPA of 3.0. Additional exam requirements/recommendations for international students: Required—TOEFL. Electronic applications accepted. *Expenses:* Contact institution. *Faculty research:* Professional dispositions, early childhood literacy, online learning, program assessments, problem-based learning.

Indiana University Southeast, School of Education, New Albany, IN 47150. Offers counselor education (MS Ed); elementary education (MS Ed); secondary education (MS Ed). *Accreditation:* NCATE. *Program availability:* Part-time, evening/weekend. *Entrance requirements:* For master's, minimum undergraduate GPA of 2.5, graduate 3.0. Electronic applications accepted. *Faculty research:* Learning styles, technology, constructivism, group process, innovative math strategies.

Indiana Wesleyan University, Graduate School, College of Arts and Sciences, Marion, IN 46953. Offers addictions counseling (MS); clinical mental health counseling (MS); community counseling (MS); marriage and family therapy (MS); school counseling (MS); student development counseling and administration (MS). *Accreditation:* ACA. *Program availability:* Part-time. *Degree requirements:* For master's, thesis or alternative. *Entrance requirements:* For master's, GRE General Test. Additional exam requirements/recommendations for international students: Required—TOEFL. Electronic applications accepted. *Expenses:* Contact institution. *Faculty research:* Community counseling, multicultural counseling, addictions.

Inter American University of Puerto Rico, Arecibo Campus, Programs in Education, Arecibo, PR 00614-4050. Offers administration and educational supervision (MA Ed); counseling and guidance (MA Ed); curriculum and teaching (MA Ed), including biology education, English as a second language, history education, math education, Spanish; elementary education (MA Ed). *Accreditation:* TEAC. *Degree requirements:* For master's, comprehensive exam, thesis optional. *Entrance requirements:* For master's, GRE, EXADEP, bachelor's degree in education or teaching license (administration and supervision) or courses in education and psychology (counseling and guidance), minimum GPA of 2.5 in last 60 credits.

Inter American University of Puerto Rico, Metropolitan Campus, Graduate Programs, Program in Education, San Juan, PR 00919-1293. Offers curriculum and instruction (Ed D); educational administration (Ed D); guidance and counseling (MA, Ed D); special education administration (Ed D). *Accreditation:* TEAC. *Degree requirements:* For doctorate, comprehensive exam, thesis/dissertation. *Entrance requirements:* For doctorate, GRE, MAT, or EXADEP. Electronic applications accepted.

Inter American University of Puerto Rico, San Germán Campus, Graduate Studies Center, Program in Counseling and Guidance, San Germán, PR 00683-5008. Offers education: counseling (MA, PhD). *Accreditation:* TEAC. *Program availability:* Part-time, evening/weekend. *Degree requirements:* For master's, comprehensive exam. *Entrance requirements:* For master's, GRE General Test or EXADEP, minimum GPA of 3.0. *Expenses: Tuition:* Full-time $212; part-time $212 per credit. *Required fees:* $366 per semester. One-time fee: $31. Tuition and fees vary according to degree level and program.

Iowa State University of Science and Technology, Department of Educational Leadership and Policy Studies, Ames, IA 50011. Offers counselor education (M Ed, MS); educational administration (M Ed, MS); educational leadership (PhD); higher education (M Ed, MS); organizational learning and human resource development (M Ed, MS); research and evaluation (MS); student affairs (MS). *Degree requirements:* For master's, thesis or alternative; for doctorate, thesis/dissertation. *Entrance requirements:* For master's and doctorate, GRE General Test. Additional exam requirements/recommendations for international students: Required—TOEFL (minimum score 560 paper-based; 83 iBT), IELTS (minimum score 6.5). Electronic applications accepted.

Jackson State University, Graduate School, College of Education and Human Development, Department of Counseling, Rehabilitation and Psychometric Services, Jackson, MS 39217. Offers clinical mental health (MS); rehabilitation counseling (MS); school counseling (MS Ed). *Accreditation:* ACA; CORE (one or more programs are accredited); NCATE. *Program availability:* Part-time, evening/weekend, 100% online, blended/hybrid learning. *Degree requirements:* For master's, comprehensive exam, thesis. *Entrance requirements:* For master's, GRE General Test. Additional exam requirements/recommendations for international students: Required—TOEFL (minimum score 520 paper-based; 67 iBT). Electronic applications accepted. *Expenses:* Contact institution.

Jacksonville State University, Graduate Studies, School of Education, Program in Guidance and Counseling, Jacksonville, AL 36265-1602. Offers MS. *Accreditation:* ACA; NCATE. *Program availability:* Part-time, evening/weekend. *Degree requirements:* For master's, comprehensive exam, thesis (for some programs). *Entrance requirements:* For master's, GRE General Test or MAT. Additional exam requirements/recommendations for international students: Required—TOEFL (minimum score 500 paper-based; 61 iBT). Electronic applications accepted.

John Brown University, Graduate Counseling Programs, Siloam Springs, AR 72761-2121. Offers clinical mental health counseling (MS); marriage and family therapy (MS); play therapy (Graduate Certificate); school counseling (MS). *Accreditation:* NCATE. *Program availability:* Part-time, evening/weekend. *Degree requirements:* For master's, practica or internships. *Entrance requirements:* For master's, GRE (minimum score of 300), recommendation forms from three people, 200-word essay describing professional plans and reason for seeking acceptance. Additional exam requirements/recommendations for international students: Required—TOEFL (minimum score 550 paper-based; 79 iBT). Electronic applications accepted. *Expenses:* Contact institution.

Counselor Education

John Carroll University, Graduate Studies, Program in Clinical Mental Health Counseling, University Heights, OH 44118. Offers clinical counseling (Certificate); community counseling (MA). *Accreditation:* ACA. *Program availability:* Part-time, evening/weekend. *Degree requirements:* For master's, internship, practicum. *Entrance requirements:* Additional exam requirements/recommendations for international students: Required—TOEFL. *Application deadline:* For fall admission, 5/1 priority date for domestic students; for summer admission, 2/1 priority date for domestic students. Applications are processed on a rolling basis. Electronic applications accepted. *Expenses: Tuition:* Full-time $13,140; part-time $730 per credit hour. Tuition and fees vary according to program. *Financial support:* Scholarships/grants and unspecified assistantships available. Financial award applicants required to submit FAFSA. *Faculty research:* Child and adolescent development, HIV, hypnosis, wellness, women's issues. *Unit head:* Dr. Nathan Gehlert, Chair, 216-397-4697, Fax: 216-397-3045, E-mail: ngehlert@jcu.edu. *Application contact:* Colleen K. Sommerfeld, Assistant Dean for Graduate Admission & Retention, 216-397-4902, Fax: 216-397-1835, E-mail: csommerfeld@jcu.edu.
Website: http://sites.jcu.edu/counselingdepartment/pages/programs-of-study/clinical-mental-health-counseling/

John Carroll University, Graduate Studies, Program in School Counseling, University Heights, OH 44118. Offers M Ed. *Accreditation:* ACA; NCATE. *Program availability:* Part-time, evening/weekend. *Entrance requirements:* Additional exam requirements/recommendations for international students: Required—TOEFL. *Application deadline:* For fall admission, 5/1 priority date for domestic students; for summer admission, 2/1 priority date for domestic students. Applications are processed on a rolling basis. Electronic applications accepted. *Expenses: Tuition:* Full-time $13,140; part-time $730 per credit hour. Tuition and fees vary according to program. *Financial support:* Scholarships/grants and unspecified assistantships available. Financial award applicants required to submit FAFSA. *Unit head:* Dr. Nathan Gehlert, Chair, 216-397-4697, E-mail: ngehlert@jcu.edu. *Application contact:* Colleen K. Sommerfeld, Assistant Dean for Graduate Admission & Retention, 216-397-4902, Fax: 216-397-1835, E-mail: csommerfeld@jcu.edu.
Website: http://sites.jcu.edu/counselingdepartment/pages/learn-more-about-our-program/

Johnson University, Graduate and Professional Programs, Knoxville, TN 37998-1001. Offers biblical interpretation (Graduate Certificate); business administration (MBA); Christian ministries (Graduate Certificate); clinical mental health counseling (MA); educational technology (MA); intercultural studies (MA); leadership (MBA); leadership studies (PhD); New Testament (MA); nonprofit management (MBA); school counseling (MA); spiritual formation and leadership (Graduate Certificate); strategic ministry (MA); teacher education (MA). *Program availability:* Part-time, evening/weekend, 100% online, blended/hybrid learning. *Degree requirements:* For master's, variable foreign language requirement, comprehensive exam, thesis (for some programs), internships; for doctorate, variable foreign language requirement, comprehensive exam, thesis/dissertation, internships. *Entrance requirements:* For master's, PRAXIS for MA in teacher education); MAT (for counseling); GRE or GMAT (for MBA), interview, 3 references, transcripts, essay, minimum GPA of 2.5 or 3.0 (depending on program); for doctorate, GRE or MAT (taken not less than 5 years prior), interview, 3 references, transcripts, essay, minimum GPA of 3.0; for Graduate Certificate, interview, 3 references, transcripts, essay, minimum GPA of 3.0. Additional exam requirements/recommendations for international students: Required—TOEFL (minimum score 527 paper-based; 71 iBT). Electronic applications accepted. *Expenses:* Contact institution.

Kansas State University, Graduate School, College of Education, Department of Special Education, Counseling and Student Affairs, Manhattan, KS 66506. Offers academic advising (MS, Certificate); counseling and student development (MS), including college student development, school counseling; special education (MS, Ed D); special education, counseling, and student affairs (PhD). *Accreditation:* ACA; NCATE. *Program availability:* Part-time, online learning. *Degree requirements:* For master's, comprehensive exam; for doctorate, comprehensive exam, thesis/dissertation. *Entrance requirements:* For master's, minimum undergraduate GPA of 3.0; for doctorate, GRE General Test, minimum GPA of 3.0 in last 60 hours. Additional exam requirements/recommendations for international students: Required—TOEFL. Electronic applications accepted. *Faculty research:* Counseling supervision, academic advising, career development, student development, universal design for learning, autism, learning disabilities.

Kean University, Nathan Weiss Graduate College, Program in Counselor Education, Union, NJ 07083. Offers alcohol and drug abuse counseling (MA); clinical mental health counseling (MA); school counseling (MA). *Accreditation:* ACA; NCATE. *Program availability:* Part-time. *Faculty:* 11 full-time (8 women). *Students:* 135 full-time (100 women), 159 part-time (126 women); includes 133 minority (62 Black or African American, non-Hispanic/Latino; 1 American Indian or Alaska Native, non-Hispanic/Latino; 8 Asian, non-Hispanic/Latino; 56 Hispanic/Latino; 6 Two or more races, non-Hispanic/Latino), 2 international. Average age 33. 201 applicants, 41% accepted, 52 enrolled. In 2018, 69 master's awarded. *Degree requirements:* For master's, practicum, internship, portfolio. *Entrance requirements:* For master's, minimum GPA of 3.0, 2 letters of recommendation, personal statement, resume. Additional exam requirements/recommendations for international students: Required—TOEFL (minimum score 550 paper-based; 79 iBT), IELTS (minimum score 6.5). *Application deadline:* For fall admission, 3/1 for domestic and international students; for spring admission, 11/1 for domestic and international students. Applications are processed on a rolling basis. Application fee: $75. Electronic applications accepted. *Expenses:* Tuition, state resident: full-time $15,025; part-time $733.50 per credit. Tuition, nonresident: full-time $19,890; part-time $884.50 per credit. *Required fees:* $2107.50; $89.50 per credit. Tuition and fees vary according to course level, course load, degree level and program. *Financial support:* Scholarships/grants and unspecified assistantships available. Financial award applicants required to submit FAFSA. *Unit head:* Dr. J. Barry Mascari, Program Coordinator, 908-737-5954, E-mail: jmascari@kean.edu. *Application contact:* Pedro Lopes, Admissions Counselor, 908-737-7100, E-mail: gradadmissions@kean.edu.
Website: http://grad.kean.edu/counseling

Kent State University, College of Education, Health and Human Services, School of Lifespan Development and Educational Sciences, Counselor Education and Supervision, Kent, OH 44242-0001. Offers PhD. *Accreditation:* ACA; NCATE. *Faculty:* 9 full-time (5 women), 12 part-time/adjunct (8 women). *Students:* 61 full-time (41 women), 13 part-time (7 women); includes 11 minority (8 Black or African American, non-Hispanic/Latino; 2 Asian, non-Hispanic/Latino; 1 Two or more races, non-Hispanic/Latino), 3 international. 31 applicants, 39% accepted. In 2018, 7 doctorates awarded. *Degree requirements:* For doctorate, comprehensive exam, thesis/dissertation. *Entrance requirements:* For doctorate, GRE General Test, preliminary written exam, 2 letters of reference, resume, interview. Additional exam requirements/recommendations for international students: Required—TOEFL (minimum score 550 paper-based; 80 iBT). *Application deadline:* For fall admission, 2/1 for domestic students. Application fee: $45 ($60 for international students). Electronic applications accepted. *Expenses:* Tuition, state resident: full-time $11,766; part-time $536 per credit. Tuition, nonresident: full-time

$21,952; part-time $999 per credit. *International tuition:* $21,952 full-time. Tuition and fees vary according to course load. *Financial support:* In 2018–19, 7 research assistantships with full tuition reimbursements (averaging $12,000 per year), 5 teaching assistantships with full tuition reimbursements (averaging $12,000 per year) were awarded; career-related internships or fieldwork, Federal Work-Study, institutionally sponsored loans, scholarships/grants, health care benefits, unspecified assistantships, and 4 administrative assistantships (averaging $12,000 per year) also available. Support available to part-time students. Financial award application deadline: 4/1; financial award applicants required to submit FAFSA. *Faculty research:* Family/child therapy, clinical supervision, group work, experiential training methods. *Unit head:* Dr. Cassandra Storlie, Coordinator, 330-672-0693, Fax: 330-672-2472, E-mail: cstorlie@kent.edu. *Application contact:* Cheryl Slusarczyk, Academic Program Director, Office of Graduate Student Services, 330-672-2576, Fax: 330-672-9162, E-mail: ogs@kent.edu.

Kent State University, College of Education, Health and Human Services, School of Lifespan Development and Educational Sciences, Program in Counseling, Kent, OH 44242-0001. Offers Ed S. *Accreditation:* ACA. *Faculty:* 9 full-time (5 women), 12 part-time/adjunct (8 women). *Students:* 7 part-time (6 women). 9 applicants, 44% accepted. In 2018, 2 Ed Ss awarded. *Entrance requirements:* For degree, 2 letters of reference, goals statement, interview. Additional exam requirements/recommendations for international students: Required—TOEFL (minimum score 550 paper-based; 80 iBT). *Application deadline:* Applications are processed on a rolling basis. Application fee: $45 ($60 for international students). Electronic applications accepted. *Expenses:* Tuition, state resident: full-time $11,766; part-time $536 per credit. Tuition, nonresident: full-time $21,952; part-time $999 per credit. *International tuition:* $21,952 full-time. Tuition and fees vary according to course load. *Financial support:* Research assistantships, teaching assistantships, Federal Work-Study, scholarships/grants, and unspecified assistantships available. *Unit head:* Dr. Lynne Guillot Miller, Coordinator, 330-672-0697, E-mail: lguillot@kent.edu. *Application contact:* Cheryl Slusarczyk, Academic Program Director, Office of Graduate Student Services, 330-672-2576, Fax: 330-672-9162, E-mail: ogs@kent.edu.
Website: https://www.kent.edu/ehhs/ldes/ces

Kent State University, College of Education, Health and Human Services, School of Lifespan Development and Educational Sciences, Program in School Counseling, Kent, OH 44242-0001. Offers M Ed. *Accreditation:* ACA; NCATE. *Faculty:* 9 full-time (5 women), 12 part-time/adjunct (8 women). *Students:* 21 full-time (19 women), 28 part-time (25 women); includes 6 minority (5 Black or African American, non-Hispanic/Latino; 1 Hispanic/Latino), 2 international. 53 applicants, 32% accepted. In 2018, 30 master's awarded. *Entrance requirements:* For master's, minimum undergraduate GPA of 2.75, 2 letters of reference, goals statement, moral character statement, interview. Additional exam requirements/recommendations for international students: Required—TOEFL (minimum score 550 paper-based; 80 iBT). *Application deadline:* Applications are processed on a rolling basis. Application fee: $45 ($60 for international students). Electronic applications accepted. *Expenses:* Tuition, state resident: full-time $11,766; part-time $536 per credit. Tuition, nonresident: full-time $21,952; part-time $999 per credit. *International tuition:* $21,952 full-time. Tuition and fees vary according to course load. *Financial support:* In 2018–19, 2 research assistantships with full tuition reimbursements (averaging $8,500 per year) were awarded; Federal Work-Study, scholarships/grants, and unspecified assistantships also available. Financial award application deadline: 4/1; financial award applicants required to submit FAFSA. *Faculty research:* Appraisal, diagnosis, group work. *Unit head:* Dr. Lynne Guilott Miller, Coordinator, 330-672-0697, E-mail: jmcgloth@kent.edu. *Application contact:* Cheryl Slusarczyk, Academic Program Director, Office of Graduate Student Services, 330-672-2576, Fax: 330-672-9162, E-mail: ogs@kent.edu.

Kutztown University of Pennsylvania, College of Education, Program in School Counseling, Kutztown, PA 19530-0730. Offers MS. *Accreditation:* ACA; NCATE. *Program availability:* Part-time, evening/weekend. *Faculty:* 5 full-time (3 women). *Students:* 40 full-time (36 women), 29 part-time (21 women); includes 13 minority (4 Black or African American, non-Hispanic/Latino; 1 Asian, non-Hispanic/Latino; 7 Hispanic/Latino; 1 Two or more races, non-Hispanic/Latino). Average age 27. 48 applicants, 81% accepted, 25 enrolled. In 2018, 13 master's awarded. *Degree requirements:* For master's, comprehensive exam, thesis optional. *Entrance requirements:* For master's, GRE General Test, 3 letters of recommendation, minimum undergraduate GPA of 3.0, psychobiographical statement, resume. Additional exam requirements/recommendations for international students: Required—TOEFL (minimum score 550 paper-based, 79 iBT), IELTS (minimum score 6.5), or PTE (minimum score 53). *Application deadline:* For fall admission, 3/1 for domestic and international students; for spring admission, 10/1 for domestic and international students. Application fee: $35. Electronic applications accepted. *Expenses:* Tuition, state resident: part-time $516 per credit. Tuition, nonresident: part-time $774 per credit. *Required fees:* $119 per credit. One-time fee: $50 part-time. Tuition and fees vary according to degree level. *Financial support:* Career-related internships or fieldwork, Federal Work-Study, and unspecified assistantships available. Financial award application deadline: 3/1; financial award applicants required to submit FAFSA. *Faculty research:* Family addictions, family roles. *Unit head:* Dr. Helen S. Hamlet, Department Chair, 610-683-4204, Fax: 610-683-1585, E-mail: hamlet@kutztown.edu. *Application contact:* Dr. Helen S. Hamlet, Department Chair, 610-683-4204, Fax: 610-683-1585, E-mail: hamlet@kutztown.edu.
Website: https://www.kutztown.edu/academics/graduate-programs/counseling.htm

Lakeland University, Graduate Studies Division, Program in Counseling, Plymouth, WI 53073. Offers MA.

Lamar University, College of Graduate Studies, College of Education and Human Development, Department of Counseling, Beaumont, TX 77710. Offers clinical mental health counseling (M Ed); school counseling (M Ed); special education (M Ed). *Accreditation:* ACA. *Faculty:* 16 full-time (13 women), 20 part-time/adjunct (16 women). *Students:* 185 full-time (171 women), 808 part-time (742 women); includes 472 minority (208 Black or African American, non-Hispanic/Latino; 10 American Indian or Alaska Native, non-Hispanic/Latino; 1 Asian, non-Hispanic/Latino; 229 Hispanic/Latino; 19 Native Hawaiian or other Pacific Islander, non-Hispanic/Latino; 5 Two or more races, non-Hispanic/Latino). Average age 37. 1,265 applicants, 74% accepted, 359 enrolled. In 2018, 640 master's awarded. *Entrance requirements:* Additional exam requirements/recommendations for international students: Required—TOEFL (minimum score 550 paper-based; 79 iBT), IELTS (minimum score 6.5). *Application deadline:* Applications are processed on a rolling basis. Application fee: $25 ($50 for international students). Electronic applications accepted. *Expenses:* Contact institution. *Financial support:* In 2018–19, 19 students received support. Fellowships, research assistantships, teaching assistantships, career-related internships or fieldwork, scholarships/grants, and unspecified assistantships available. Financial award applicants required to submit FAFSA. *Total annual research expenditures:* $2,750. *Unit head:* Dr. Wendy Greenidge, Interim Department Chair, 409-880-8978, Fax: 409-880-2263. *Application contact:* Celeste Contreas, Director, Admissions and Academic Services, 409-880-8888, Fax: 409-880-7419, E-mail: gradmissions@lamar.edu.
Website: https://www.lamar.edu/education/counseling/index.html

Lancaster Bible College, Graduate School, Lancaster, PA 17601-5036. Offers adult ministries (MA); Bible (MA); children and family ministry (MA); church planting (MA);

consulting resource teacher (M Ed); elementary school counseling (M Ed); leadership (PhD); leadership studies (MA); marriage and family counseling (MA); mental health counseling (MA); pastoral studies (MA); secondary school counseling (M Ed); sports ministry (MA); student ministry (MA); town and country ministry (MA). *Program availability:* Part-time, evening/weekend. *Faculty:* 8 full-time (1 woman), 5 part-time/adjunct (1 woman). *Students:* 94 full-time (47 women), 89 part-time (45 women); includes 21 minority (15 Black or African American, non-Hispanic/Latino; 5 Asian, non-Hispanic/Latino; 1 Hispanic/Latino). Average age 36. *Degree requirements:* For master's, comprehensive exam (for some programs), thesis (for some programs). *Entrance requirements:* For master's, bachelor's degree with a minimum of 30 credits of course work in Bible, minimum undergraduate GPA of 3.0, interview. Additional exam requirements/recommendations for international students: Required—TOEFL. *Application deadline:* Applications are processed on a rolling basis. Application fee: $25. *Financial support:* In 2018–19, 31 students received support. Teaching assistantships, scholarships/grants, and unspecified assistantships available. Support available to part-time students. Financial award application deadline: 6/1; financial award applicants required to submit FAFSA. *Unit head:* Dr. Gary Bredfeldt, Associate Vice President/Dean of iLead Center, 717-560-8297, Fax: 717-560-8236. *Application contact:* Mark Wilson, Admissions Counselor, 717-560-8229, E-mail: mwilson@lbc.edu.

La Sierra University, School of Education, Department of School Psychology and Counseling, Riverside, CA 92505. Offers counseling (MA); educational psychology (Ed S); school psychology (Ed S). *Program availability:* Part-time, evening/weekend. *Degree requirements:* For master's, thesis optional; for Ed S, practicum (educational psychology). *Entrance requirements:* For master's, California Basic Educational Skills Test, NTE, minimum GPA of 3.0; for Ed S, minimum GPA of 3.3. *Faculty research:* Equivalent score scales, self perception.

Lee University, Graduate Studies in Counseling, Cleveland, TN 37320-3450. Offers holistic child development (MS); marriage and family studies (MS); marriage and family therapy (MS); school counseling (MS). *Program availability:* Part-time, 100% online. *Faculty:* 8 full-time (4 women), 2 part-time/adjunct (0 women). *Students:* 89 full-time (71 women), 29 part-time (19 women); includes 26 minority (8 Black or African American, non-Hispanic/Latino; 17 Hispanic/Latino; 1 Two or more races, non-Hispanic/Latino), 5 international. Average age 30. 50 applicants, 76% accepted, 31 enrolled. In 2018, 46 master's awarded. *Degree requirements:* For master's, variable foreign language requirement, comprehensive exam (for some programs), thesis (for some programs), internship. *Entrance requirements:* For master's, GRE General Test or MAT (waived if undergraduate GPA is greater than 3.0 or if applicant already has a graduate degree), minimum undergraduate GPA of 3.0, 3 letters of recommendation, interview, official transcripts, essay. Additional exam requirements/recommendations for international students: Required—TOEFL (minimum score 61 iBT). *Application deadline:* For fall admission, 4/1 priority date for domestic and international students; for spring admission, 11/1 priority date for domestic and international students. Applications are processed on a rolling basis. Application fee: $25. Electronic applications accepted. *Financial support:* In 2018–19, 46 students received support. Career-related internships or fieldwork, Federal Work-Study, institutionally sponsored loans, scholarships/grants, and unspecified assistantships available. Financial award application deadline: 3/1; financial award applicants required to submit FAFSA. *Unit head:* Dr. Trevor Milliron, Director, 423-614-8126, Fax: 423-614-8124, E-mail: tmilliron@leeuniversity.edu. *Application contact:* Jeffery McGirt, Director of Graduate Enrollment, 423-614-8691, Fax: 423-614-8317, E-mail: jmcgirt@leeuniversity.edu.
Website: http://www.leeuniversity.edu/academics/graduate/counseling/

Lehigh University, College of Education, Program in Counseling Psychology, Bethlehem, PA 18015. Offers counseling and human services (M Ed); counseling psychology (PhD); international counseling (M Ed, Certificate); school counseling (M Ed). *Accreditation:* APA (one or more programs are accredited). *Program availability:* Part-time. *Faculty:* 8 full-time (5 women), 12 part-time/adjunct (9 women). *Students:* 61 full-time (55 women), 33 part-time (27 women); includes 18 minority (3 Black or African American, non-Hispanic/Latino; 5 Asian, non-Hispanic/Latino; 10 Hispanic/Latino), 18 international. Average age 29. 155 applicants, 39% accepted, 32 enrolled. In 2018, 42 master's, 5 doctorates awarded. *Degree requirements:* For master's, thesis (for some programs); for doctorate, comprehensive exam, thesis/dissertation. *Entrance requirements:* For master's, minimum GPA of 3.0, 2 letters of recommendation, essay, transcript; for doctorate, GRE General Test, 2 letters of recommendation, transcript, essay, GRE; for Certificate, minimum GPA of 3.0 (undergraduate), 3.5 (graduate). Additional exam requirements/recommendations for international students: Required—TOEFL (minimum score 600 paper-based; 93 iBT), Either TOEFL or IELTS is required of international students for whom English is not their main language; Recommended—IELTS. *Application deadline:* For fall admission, 2/1 for domestic and international students. Application fee: $65. Electronic applications accepted. Application fee is waived when completed online. *Expenses:* $565 per credit hour. *Financial support:* In 2018–19, 28 students received support, including 2 fellowships (averaging $22,250 per year), 6 research assistantships with full and partial tuition reimbursements available (averaging $16,059 per year); scholarships/grants and unspecified assistantships also available. Financial award application deadline: 2/15; financial award applicants required to submit FAFSA. *Faculty research:* Maternal/infant attachment, multicultural training and counseling, career development and health interventions, intersection of identities, community based participatory research, trauma informed schools, gerontology, multicultural competence, south Asian-Asian American concerns, sexual assault prevention, LGBTQ, intimate partner violence, feminist theory and therapy, sexual and reproductive health, women's health, culture and health, prevention, minority student development, educational access. *Total annual research expenditures:* $419,624. *Unit head:* Dr. Grace Caskie, Director, 610-758-6094, Fax: 610-758-3227, E-mail: caskie@lehigh.edu. *Application contact:* Dominique Jones, Coordinator, Counseling Psychology, 610-758-3250, Fax: 610-758-6223, E-mail: dvj218@lehigh.edu.
Website: https://ed.lehigh.edu/academics/programs/counseling-psychology

Lehman College of the City University of New York, School of Education, Department of Counseling, Leadership, Literacy, and Special Education, Program in Counselor Education/School Counseling, Bronx, NY 10468-1589. Offers MS Ed. *Accreditation:* ACA; NCATE. *Program availability:* Part-time, evening/weekend. *Degree requirements:* For master's, thesis. *Entrance requirements:* For master's, minimum GPA of 2.7. *Faculty research:* Crisis intervention, domestic violence, alcohol abuse, gender issues.

Lenoir-Rhyne University, Graduate Programs, School of Counseling and Human Services, Program in School Counseling, Hickory, NC 28601. Offers MA. *Program availability:* Part-time, evening/weekend. *Degree requirements:* For master's, comprehensive exam, thesis optional. *Entrance requirements:* For master's, GRE General Test, minimum undergraduate GPA of 2.7, graduate 3.0; writing sample. Additional exam requirements/recommendations for international students: Required—TOEFL (minimum score 600 paper-based). Electronic applications accepted. *Expenses:* Contact institution.

Lewis University, College of Arts and Sciences, Program in School Counseling, Romeoville, IL 60446. Offers MA. *Program availability:* Part-time, evening/weekend. *Students:* 43 full-time (31 women), 30 part-time (25 women); includes 7 minority (1 Black or African American, non-Hispanic/Latino; 1 Asian, non-Hispanic/Latino; 4 Hispanic/Latino; 1 Two or more races, non-Hispanic/Latino). Average age 28. *Degree requirements:* For master's, comprehensive exam, internship; practicum. *Entrance requirements:* For master's, Test of Academic Proficiency/Basic Skills Test/ACT/SAT, bachelor's degree, two letters of recommendation, interview, minimum GPA of 2.75. Additional exam requirements/recommendations for international students: Required—TOEFL (minimum score 550 paper-based; 79 iBT), IELTS (minimum score 6). *Application deadline:* For fall admission, 5/1 priority date for international students; for spring admission, 11/15 priority date for international students. Applications are processed on a rolling basis. Application fee: $40. Electronic applications accepted. *Financial support:* Federal Work-Study, scholarships/grants, tuition waivers (full and partial), and unspecified assistantships available. Financial award application deadline: 5/1; financial award applicants required to submit FAFSA. *Unit head:* Dr. Judith Zito, Program Director. *Application contact:* Linda Campbell, Graduate Admission Counselor, 815-836-5610, E-mail: grad@lewisu.edu.

Liberty University, School of Behavioral Sciences, Lynchburg, VA 24515. Offers applied psychology (MA), including developmental psychology (MA, MS), industrial/organizational psychology (MA, MS); clinical mental health counseling (MA); community care and counseling (Ed D), including marriage and family counseling, pastoral care and counseling, traumatology; counselor education and supervision (PhD); human services counseling (MA), including addictions and recovery, business, child and family law, Christian ministries, criminal justice, crisis response and trauma, executive leadership, health and wellness, life coaching, marriage and family, military resilience; marriage and family counseling (MA); marriage and family therapy (MA); military resilience (Certificate); pastoral counseling (MA), including addictions and recovery, community chaplaincy, crisis response and trauma, discipleship and church ministry, leadership, life coaching, marriage and family, marriage and family studies, military resilience, parenting and child/adolescent, pastoral counseling, theology; professional counseling (MA); psychology (MS), including developmental psychology (MA, MS), industrial/organizational psychology (MA, MS); school counseling (M Ed). *Program availability:* Part-time, online learning. *Students:* 3,163 full-time (2,537 women), 4,813 part-time (3,790 women); includes 2,399 minority (1,847 Black or African American, non-Hispanic/Latino; 39 American Indian or Alaska Native, non-Hispanic/Latino; 77 Asian, non-Hispanic/Latino; 244 Hispanic/Latino; 13 Native Hawaiian or other Pacific Islander, non-Hispanic/Latino; 179 Two or more races, non-Hispanic/Latino), 129 international. Average age 39. 8,226 applicants, 38% accepted, 1752 enrolled. In 2018, 2,420 master's, 21 doctorates, 79 other advanced degrees awarded. *Application deadline:* Applications are processed on a rolling basis. Application fee: $50. Electronic applications accepted. *Expenses: Tuition:* Full-time $10,851; part-time $562 per credit hour. *Financial support:* In 2018–19, 1,003 students received support. Teaching assistantships and Federal Work-Study available. Financial award applicants required to submit FAFSA. *Unit head:* Dr. Ronald Hawkins, Founding Dean, School of Behavioral Sciences, E-mail: provost@liberty.edu. *Application contact:* Jay Bridge, Director of Admissions, 800-424-9595, Fax: 800-628-7977, E-mail: gradadmissions@liberty.edu.
Website: https://www.liberty.edu/behavioral-sciences/

Lincoln Memorial University, Carter and Moyers School of Education, Harrogate, TN 37752-1901. Offers administration and supervision (M Ed, Ed S); counseling and guidance (M Ed); curriculum and instruction (M Ed, Ed D, Ed S); English (M Ed); executive leadership (Ed D); higher education administration (Ed D); human resource development (Ed D); leadership and administration (Ed D). *Program availability:* Part-time, evening/weekend, online learning. *Degree requirements:* For master's, comprehensive exam, thesis optional; for Ed S, comprehensive exam. *Entrance requirements:* For master's, PRAXIS, NTE, GRE, MAT, letters of recommendation; for Ed S, graduate transcripts. Additional exam requirements/recommendations for international students: Recommended—TOEFL. *Faculty research:* Brain compatible teaching and learning; poverty in Appalachia; leadership for change; ethics, moral responsibility and social justice; human and organizational learning.

Lincoln University, Graduate Studies, Jefferson City, MO 65101. Offers business administration (MBA); counseling (M Ed); environmental science (MS); higher education (MA); history (MA); natural sciences (MS); school teaching middle school with certification (M Ed); school teaching-elementary (M Ed); school teaching-secondary (M Ed); sociology (MA); sociology/criminal justice (MA); sustainable agriculture (MS). *Program availability:* Part-time, evening/weekend, 100% online, blended/hybrid learning. *Students:* 37 full-time (23 women), 52 part-time (25 women); includes 26 minority (24 Black or African American, non-Hispanic/Latino; 1 Asian, non-Hispanic/Latino; 1 Two or more races, non-Hispanic/Latino), 11 international. Average age 34. 67 applicants, 52% accepted, 29 enrolled. In 2018, 48 master's awarded. *Degree requirements:* For master's, comprehensive exam, thesis optional. *Entrance requirements:* For master's, GRE, MAT, or GMAT, minimum GPA of 2.75 overall, 3.0 in courses related to specialization; 3 letters of recommendation; minimum C average in English composition; personal statement of purpose. Additional exam requirements/recommendations for international students: Required—TOEFL (minimum score 500 paper-based; 61 iBT), IELTS (minimum score 5.5), Michigan English Language Assessment Battery (minimum score 80). *Application deadline:* For fall admission, 7/1 priority date for domestic students, 5/1 priority date for international students; for spring admission, 11/1 priority date for domestic students, 10/1 priority date for international students; for summer admission, 6/1 priority date for domestic students. Applications are processed on a rolling basis. Application fee: $30. Electronic applications accepted. *Expenses: Tuition, area resident:* Full-time $6984; part-time $291 per credit. Tuition, state resident: full-time $6984; part-time $291 per credit. Tuition, nonresident: full-time $12,996; part-time $541.50 per credit. *International tuition:* $12,996 full-time. *Required fees:* $1242.20. *Financial support:* In 2018–19, 9 research assistantships with tuition reimbursements (averaging $4,050 per year) were awarded; fellowships with tuition reimbursements, Federal Work-Study, scholarships/grants, and unspecified assistantships also available. Support available to part-time students. Financial award application deadline: 3/1; financial award applicants required to submit FAFSA. *Unit head:* Dr. Benjamin Arnold, Assistant Vice President of Academic Affairs, 573-681-5247, Fax: 573-681-5106, E-mail: gradschool@lincolnu.edu. *Application contact:* Sarah Robinett, Administrative Assistant, 573-681-5247, Fax: 573-681-5106, E-mail: gradschool@lincolnu.edu.
Website: http://www.lincolnu.edu/web/graduate-studies/graduate-studies

Lindenwood University–Belleville, Graduate Programs, Belleville, IL 62226. Offers business administration (MBA); communications (MA), including digital and multimedia, media management, promotions, training and development; counseling (MA); criminal justice administration (MS); education (MA); healthcare administration (MS); human resource management (MS); school administration (MA); teaching (MAT).

Lindsey Wilson College, School of Professional Counseling, Columbia, KY 42728. Offers counseling and human development (M Ed); counselor education and supervision (PhD). *Accreditation:* ACA (one or more programs are accredited). *Program availability:* Part-time, evening/weekend, online learning.

Loma Linda University, School of Behavioral Health, Department of Counseling and Family Sciences, Loma Linda, CA 92350. Offers child life specialist (MS); clinical mediation (Certificate); counseling (MS); drug and alcohol counseling (Certificate); family life education (Certificate); marital and family therapy (DMFT); school counseling

(Certificate). *Degree requirements:* For master's, comprehensive exam, thesis optional; for doctorate, comprehensive exam, thesis/dissertation (for some programs). *Entrance requirements:* For master's, minimum GPA of 3.0; for doctorate, GRE. Additional exam requirements/recommendations for international students: Required—TOEFL (minimum score 550 paper-based). Electronic applications accepted.

Long Island University–Brentwood Campus, Graduate Programs, Brentwood, NY 11717. Offers childhood education (MS), including grades 1-6; childhood education/literacy B-6 (MS); childhood education/special education (grades 1-6) (MS); clinical mental health counseling (MS, Advanced Certificate); criminal justice (MS); early childhood education (MS); educational leadership (MS Ed); family nurse practitioner (MS, Advanced Certificate); health administration (MPA); library and information science (MS); literacy (B-6) (MS Ed); school counselor (MS, Advanced Certificate); social work (MSW); special education (MS Ed); students with disabilities generalist (grades 7-12) (Advanced Certificate). *Program availability:* Part-time. *Entrance requirements:* For master's and Advanced Certificate, GRE. Additional exam requirements/recommendations for international students: Required—TOEFL or IELTS. Electronic applications accepted.

Long Island University–Hudson, Graduate School, Purchase, NY 10577. Offers autism (Advanced Certificate); bilingual education (Advanced Certificate); childhood education (MS Ed); crisis management (Advanced Certificate); early childhood education (MS Ed); educational leadership (MS Ed); health administration (MPA); literacy (MS Ed); marriage and family therapy (MS); mental health counseling (MS, Advanced Certificate), including credentialed alcoholism and substance abuse counselor (MS); middle childhood and adolescence education (MS Ed); pharmaceutics (MS), including cosmetic science, industrial pharmacy; public administration (MPA); school counseling (MS Ed, Advanced Certificate); school psychology (MS Ed); special education (MS Ed); TESOL (MS Ed); TESOL (all grades) (Advanced Certificate). *Program availability:* Part-time, evening/weekend. *Entrance requirements:* Additional exam requirements/recommendations for international students: Required—TOEFL. Electronic applications accepted. *Expenses:* Contact institution.

Long Island University–LIU Brooklyn, School of Education, Brooklyn, NY 11201-8423. Offers adolescence urban education (MS Ed); applied behavior analysis (Advanced Certificate); bilingual education (Advanced Certificate); bilingual education in urban setting (MS Ed); bilingual school counselor (MS Ed, Advanced Certificate); childhood urban education (MS Ed); childhood/early childhood education (MS Ed); childhood/early childhood urban education (MS Ed); early childhood urban education (MS Ed, Advanced Certificate); educational leadership (Advanced Certificate); marriage and family therapy (MS, Advanced Certificate); mental health counseling (MS, Advanced Certificate); school building district leader (Advanced Certificate); school counselor (MS Ed, Advanced Certificate); school psychologist (MS Ed); teaching students with disabilities (MS Ed); teaching urban children with disabilities (MS Ed); TESOL (MS Ed, Advanced Certificate). *Accreditation:* TEAC. *Program availability:* Part-time, evening/weekend, 100% online. *Entrance requirements:* For master's, GRE. Additional exam requirements/recommendations for international students: Required—TOEFL (minimum score 527 paper-based, 75 iBT), IELTS, or PTE. Electronic applications accepted. *Faculty research:* Diversity issues in education and mental health care, inclusion - disability studies, sustainability, teacher professional development.

Longwood University, College of Graduate and Professional Studies, College of Education and Human Services, Farmville, VA 23909. Offers education (MS), including algebra and middle school mathematics, counselor education, elementary and middle school mathematics, elementary education, elementary education initial licensure, health and physical education, special education general curriculum, special education initial licensure; reading, literacy and learning (M Ed); school librarianship (M Ed); social work and communication sciences and disorders (MS), including communication sciences and disorders. *Accreditation:* NCATE. *Program availability:* Part-time, evening/weekend. *Degree requirements:* For master's, comprehensive exam (for some programs), thesis optional, professional portfolio, internship, clinical experience, or practicum. *Entrance requirements:* For master's, PRAXIS I (for initial teaching licensure programs); GRE (for some programs), bachelor's degree from regionally-accredited institution, 2 recommendations (3 for some programs), minimum 500-word personal essay, official transcripts, minimum GPA of 2.75, valid teaching license (for some programs). Additional exam requirements/recommendations for international students: Required—TOEFL (minimum score 570 paper-based), IELTS (minimum score 6.5). Electronic applications accepted. *Expenses:* Contact institution.

Louisiana State University and Agricultural & Mechanical College, Graduate School, College of Human Sciences and Education, Department of Educational Theory, Policy and Practice, Baton Rouge, LA 70803. Offers counseling (M Ed, MA, Ed S); educational administration (M Ed, MA, PhD, Ed S); educational technology (MA); elementary education (M Ed, MAT); higher education (PhD); research methodology (PhD); secondary education (M Ed, MAT). *Accreditation:* ACA (one or more programs are accredited); NCATE.

Louisiana State University in Shreveport, College of Business, Education, and Human Development, Program in Counseling, Shreveport, LA 71115-2399. Offers MS. *Degree requirements:* For master's, comprehensive exam, internship (600 clock hours). *Entrance requirements:* For master's, GRE, references, interview. Additional exam requirements/recommendations for international students: Required—TOEFL (minimum score 550 paper-based; 61 iBT). Electronic applications accepted.

Loyola Marymount University, School of Education, Program in Guidance and Counseling, Los Angeles, CA 90045. Offers MA. *Unit head:* Dr. Sheri Atwater, Director, Counseling Program, E-mail: sheri.atwater@lmu.edu. *Application contact:* Ammar Dalal, Assistant Vice Provost for Graduate Enrollment, 310-338-2721, Fax: 310-338-6086, E-mail: graduateinfo@lmu.edu.
Website: http://soe.lmu.edu/academics/counseling

Loyola Marymount University, School of Education, Program in School Counseling, Los Angeles, CA 90045. Offers MA. *Unit head:* Dr. Sheri Atwater, Director, Counseling Program, E-mail: sheri.atwater@lmu.edu. *Application contact:* Ammar Dalal, Assistant Vice Provost for Graduate Enrollment, 310-338-2721, Fax: 310-338-6086, E-mail: graduateinfo@lmu.edu.
Website: http://soe.lmu.edu/academics/counseling

Loyola University Chicago, School of Education, Program in School Counseling, Chicago, IL 60660. Offers M Ed, Certificate. *Accreditation:* NCATE. *Program availability:* Part-time. *Faculty:* 5 full-time (2 women), 5 part-time/adjunct (4 women). *Students:* 15 full-time (12 women), 1 (woman) part-time; includes 5 minority (1 Black or African American, non-Hispanic/Latino; 2 Asian, non-Hispanic/Latino; 2 Hispanic/Latino). Average age 26. 24 applicants, 83% accepted, 5 enrolled. In 2018, 9 master's awarded. *Entrance requirements:* For master's, GRE General Test, minimum GPA of 3.0, letters of recommendation, resume. Additional exam requirements/recommendations for international students: Required—TOEFL (minimum score 550 paper-based; 79 iBT). *Application deadline:* For fall admission, 1/1 for domestic and international students. Application fee: $50. Electronic applications accepted. Application fee is waived when completed online. *Expenses:* Contact institution. *Financial support:* Career-related internships or fieldwork, institutionally sponsored loans, and scholarships/grants available. Support available to part-time students. Financial award application deadline: 2/1; financial award applicants required to submit FAFSA. *Faculty research:* Career development, group counseling, family therapy, child and adolescent development, multicultural counseling. *Unit head:* Dr. Eunju Yoon, Program Chair, 312-915-6461, E-mail: eyoon@luc.edu. *Application contact:* Dr. Eunju Yoon, Program Chair, 312-915-6461, E-mail: eyoon@luc.edu.

Loyola University Maryland, Graduate Programs, School of Education, Program in School Counseling, Baltimore, MD 21210-2699. Offers M Ed, MA, CAS. *Accreditation:* ACA; NCATE. *Program availability:* Part-time. *Degree requirements:* For master's, thesis. *Entrance requirements:* For master's, essay, transcript, 2 letters of recommendation. Additional exam requirements/recommendations for international students: Required—TOEFL (minimum score 550 paper-based), IELTS (minimum score 7). Electronic applications accepted. *Expenses:* Contact institution.

Malone University, Graduate Program in Counseling and Human Development, Canton, OH 44709. Offers clinical counseling (MA); school counseling (MA). *Accreditation:* ACA; NCATE. *Program availability:* Part-time, evening/weekend. *Entrance requirements:* For master's, minimum undergraduate GPA of 3.0. Additional exam requirements/recommendations for international students: Required—TOEFL (minimum score 550 paper-based; 79 iBT). *Faculty research:* Spirituality and clinical counseling supervision, ethical and legal issues in counseling regarding supervision, resilience in adolescent offenders, protective factors for suicidal clients.

Manhattan College, Graduate Programs, School of Education and Health, Program in School Counseling, Riverdale, NY 10471. Offers bilingual pupil personnel services (Professional Diploma); school counseling (MA, Professional Diploma). *Program availability:* Part-time, evening/weekend. *Degree requirements:* For master's, thesis, internship. *Entrance requirements:* For master's, minimum GPA of 3.0. Additional exam requirements/recommendations for international students: Required—TOEFL. Electronic applications accepted. *Expenses:* Contact institution. *Faculty research:* Cognitive development, college and career readiness, group counseling, cultural attitudes, bullying, family social environments.

Marian University, Master of Science in Counseling Program, Indianapolis, IN 46222-1997. Offers clinical mental health counseling (MS); school counseling (MS). *Program availability:* Part-time. *Degree requirements:* For master's, 60 credit hours plus 1000 hours of supervised practicum (for clinical mental health counseling track); 48 credit hours plus 700 hours of supervised practicum (for school counseling track). *Entrance requirements:* For master's, GRE (preferred scores: combined 295, verbal 150, quantitative 145, writing 4), bachelor's degree (in related field preferred); minimum undergraduate and major GPA of 3.0; completion of undergraduate psychology courses in development, abnormal psychology, statistics or research methods; official transcripts from all postsecondary institutions attended; personal statement; 3 letters of recommendation; resume; interview. Additional exam requirements/recommendations for international students: Required—TOEFL (minimum score 550 paper-based; 79 iBT). Electronic applications accepted. Application fee is waived when completed online. *Expenses:* Contact institution.

Marquette University, Graduate School, College of Education, Department of Counselor Education and Counseling Psychology, Milwaukee, WI 53201-1881. Offers clinical mental health counseling (MS); community counseling (MA); counseling psychology (PhD); school counseling (MA). *Accreditation:* ACA. *Program availability:* Part-time. Terminal master's awarded for partial completion of doctoral program. *Degree requirements:* For master's, comprehensive exam, thesis (for some programs); for doctorate, thesis/dissertation, qualifying exam. *Entrance requirements:* For master's, GRE General Test or MAT, official transcripts from all current and previous colleges/universities except Marquette, three letters of recommendation, statement of purpose; for doctorate, GRE General Test, MAT, sample of written work, official transcripts from all current and previous colleges/universities except Marquette, three letters of recommendation, statement of purpose, resume/curriculum vitae. Additional exam requirements/recommendations for international students: Required—TOEFL (minimum score 530 paper-based). *Faculty research:* Ethical and legal issues in education, anxiety disorders, multicultural counseling, child psychopathology, group counseling and dynamics.

Marshall University, Academic Affairs Division, College of Education and Professional Development, Program in Counseling, Huntington, WV 25755. Offers MA. *Accreditation:* NCATE. *Program availability:* Part-time, evening/weekend. *Degree requirements:* For master's, thesis optional, comprehensive or oral assessment. *Entrance requirements:* For master's, GRE General Test, MAT.

Marymount University, School of Sciences, Mathematics, and Education, Program in Counseling, Arlington, VA 22207-4299. Offers clinical mental health counseling (MA); counseling with forensic and legal studies (MA/MA); pastoral counseling (MA); school counseling (MA); MA/MA. *Accreditation:* ACA (one or more programs are accredited). *Program availability:* Part-time, evening/weekend. *Faculty:* 10 full-time (8 women), 3 part-time/adjunct (all women). *Students:* 114 full-time (95 women), 39 part-time (34 women); includes 48 minority (21 Black or African American, non-Hispanic/Latino; 5 Asian, non-Hispanic/Latino; 18 Hispanic/Latino; 4 Two or more races, non-Hispanic/Latino), 1 international. Average age 29. 112 applicants, 87% accepted, 65 enrolled. In 2018, 50 master's awarded. *Degree requirements:* For master's, thesis or alternative, capstone/internship. *Entrance requirements:* For master's, GRE, 2 letters of recommendation, interview, resume, personal statement. Additional exam requirements/recommendations for international students: Required—TOEFL (minimum score 600 paper-based; 96 iBT), IELTS (minimum score 6.5), PTE (minimum score 58). *Application deadline:* For fall admission, 1/15 priority date for domestic and international students. Applications are processed on a rolling basis. Application fee: $40. Electronic applications accepted. *Expenses: Tuition:* Full-time $18,900; part-time $1050 per credit. *Required fees:* $396; $22 per credit hour. One-time fee: $270. Tuition and fees vary according to program. *Financial support:* In 2018–19, 9 students received support. Research assistantships, teaching assistantships, career-related internships or fieldwork, scholarships/grants, and unspecified assistantships available. Support available to part-time students. Financial award application deadline: 3/1; financial award applicants required to submit FAFSA. *Unit head:* Dr. Lisa Jackson-Cherry, Chair, Counseling, 703-284-1633, E-mail: lisa.jackson-cherry@marymount.edu. *Application contact:* Rebecca Esposito, Senior Associate Director, Graduate Admissions, 703-284-5901, Fax: 703-527-3815, E-mail: grad.admissions@marymount.edu.
Website: https://www.marymount.edu/Academics/School-of-Sciences-Mathematics-and-Education/Graduate-Programs/Counseling-(M-A-)

Marywood University, Academic Affairs, Reap College of Education and Human Development, Department of Psychology and Counseling, Program in Counselor Education, Scranton, PA 18509-1598. Offers MS. *Program availability:* Part-time. Electronic applications accepted.

McDaniel College, Graduate and Professional Studies, Program in Counseling, Westminster, MD 21157-4390. Offers MS. *Program availability:* Part-time, evening/weekend. *Degree requirements:* For master's, thesis optional, internship. *Entrance requirements:* For master's, 3 letters of reference; interview with program faculty. Additional exam requirements/recommendations for international students: Required—TOEFL (minimum score 79 iBT), IELTS (minimum score 6). Electronic applications accepted. *Expenses:* Contact institution.

McNeese State University, Doré School of Graduate Studies, Burton College of Education, Department of Education Professions, Program in School Counseling, Lake Charles, LA 70609. Offers M Ed. *Accreditation:* ACA; NCATE. *Program availability:* Evening/weekend. *Entrance requirements:* For master's, GRE, 18 hours in professional education.

Mercer University, Graduate Studies, Cecil B. Day Campus, Penfield College, Atlanta, GA 30341. Offers certified rehabilitation counseling (MS); clinical mental health (MS); counselor education and supervision (PhD); criminal justice and public safety leadership (MS); health informatics (MS); human services (MS), including child and adolescent services, gerontology services; organizational leadership (MS), including leadership for the health care professional, leadership for the nonprofit organization, organizational development and change; school counseling (MS). *Program availability:* Part-time, evening/weekend, 100% online, blended/hybrid learning. *Degree requirements:* For master's, comprehensive exam (for some programs), thesis (for some programs); for doctorate, thesis/dissertation. *Entrance requirements:* For master's, GRE or MAT, Georgia Professional Standards Commission (GPSC) Certification at the SC-5 level; for doctorate, GRE or MAT. Additional exam requirements/recommendations for international students: Recommended—TOEFL (minimum score 550 paper-based; 80 iBT), IELTS (minimum score 6.5). Electronic applications accepted. Application fee is waived when completed online. *Expenses:* Contact institution. *Faculty research:* Marriage and families issues, leadership and ethics, cyber-bullying, trauma, narrative counseling and theory.

Mercy College, School of Social and Behavioral Sciences, Dobbs Ferry, NY 10522-1189. Offers counseling (MS, Certificate), including counseling (MS), family counseling (Certificate); health services management (MPA, MS); marriage and family therapy (MS); mental health counseling (MS); psychology (MS); school counseling (Certificate); school psychology (MS). *Program availability:* Part-time, evening/weekend, 100% online, blended/hybrid learning. *Students:* 210 full-time (179 women), 285 part-time (248 women); includes 361 minority (162 Black or African American, non-Hispanic/Latino; 11 Asian, non-Hispanic/Latino; 182 Hispanic/Latino; 1 Native Hawaiian or other Pacific Islander, non-Hispanic/Latino; 5 Two or more races, non-Hispanic/Latino), 5 international. Average age 32. 401 applicants, 40% accepted, 112 enrolled. In 2018, 157 master's awarded. *Degree requirements:* For master's, comprehensive exam (for some programs), thesis (for some programs), Capstone project and internship or fieldwork required for most programs. *Entrance requirements:* For master's, transcript(s); two letters of recommendation; resume; essay; interview. Additional exam requirements/recommendations for international students: Required—TOEFL (minimum score 600 paper-based; 71 iBT), IELTS (minimum score 8). *Application deadline:* Applications are processed on a rolling basis. Application fee: $40. Electronic applications accepted. *Expenses: Tuition:* Full-time $15,696; part-time $872 per credit. *Required fees:* $642; $161 per term. Tuition and fees vary according to course load, degree level and program. *Financial support:* Career-related internships or fieldwork, Federal Work-Study, scholarships/grants, and unspecified assistantships available. Support available to part-time students. Financial award applicants required to submit FAFSA. *Unit head:* Dr. Karol Dean, Dean, School of Social and Behavioral Sciences, 914-674-7517, Fax: 914-674-7413, E-mail: kdean@mercy.edu. *Application contact:* Allison Gurdineer, Executive Director of Admissions, 877-637-2946, Fax: 914-674-7382, E-mail: admissions@mercy.edu.
Website: https://www.mercy.edu/social-and-behavioral-sciences/

Messiah College, Program in Counseling, Mechanicsburg, PA 17055. Offers clinical mental health counseling (MAC); counseling (CAGS); marriage, couple, and family counseling (MAC); school counseling (MAC). *Accreditation:* ACA. *Program availability:* Part-time, online learning. *Entrance requirements:* For master's, minimum undergraduate cumulative GPA of 3.0, 2 recommendations, resume or curriculum vitae, interview; for CAGS, bachelor's degree, minimum undergraduate cumulative GPA of 3.0, essay, two recommendations, resume or curriculum vitae, interview. Electronic applications accepted.

Michigan State University, The Graduate School, College of Education, Department of Counseling, Educational Psychology and Special Education, East Lansing, MI 48824. Offers counseling (MA); educational psychology and educational technology (PhD); educational technology (MA); measurement and quantitative methods (PhD); rehabilitation counseling (MA); rehabilitation counselor education (PhD); school psychology (MA, PhD, Ed S); special education (MA, PhD). *Accreditation:* APA (one or more programs are accredited); CORE (one or more programs are accredited). *Program availability:* Part-time. *Entrance requirements:* Additional exam requirements/recommendations for international students: Required—TOEFL. Electronic applications accepted.

Middle Tennessee State University, College of Graduate Studies, College of Education, Department of Educational Leadership, Program in Professional Counseling, Murfreesboro, TN 37132. Offers mental health counseling (M Ed); school counseling (M Ed). *Accreditation:* ACA; NCATE. *Program availability:* Part-time, evening/weekend, online learning. *Degree requirements:* For master's, comprehensive exam, thesis. *Entrance requirements:* For master's, GRE or MAT. Additional exam requirements/recommendations for international students: Required—TOEFL (minimum score 525 paper-based; 71 iBT) or IELTS (minimum score 6). Electronic applications accepted.

Midwestern State University, Billie Doris McAda Graduate School, West College of Education, Program in Counseling, Wichita Falls, TX 76308. Offers counseling (MA); human resource development (MA); school counseling (M Ed); training and development (MA). *Program availability:* Part-time, evening/weekend. *Degree requirements:* For master's, comprehensive exam, thesis (for some programs). *Entrance requirements:* For master's, GRE General Test, MAT, or GMAT, valid teaching certificate (M Ed). Additional exam requirements/recommendations for international students: Required—TOEFL (minimum score 550 paper-based). Electronic applications accepted. *Faculty research:* Social development of students with disabilities, autism, criminal justice counseling, conflict resolution issues, leadership.

Midwest University, Graduate Programs, Wentzville, MO 63385. Offers asset management/investment/real estate (MBA); Christian counseling (D Min); Christian education (D Min); counseling (MA), including marriage and family counseling, school counseling; divinity (M Div); education (MA), including brain and gifted education, Christian education; global business management (MBA); global leadership (MBA); leadership (PhD), including brain and gifted educational leadership, entrepreneurial leadership, international aviation leadership, organizational leadership, political leadership; mission studies (D Min); music (MM, DMA); pastoral theology (D Min); public policy/administration (MBA); teaching English to speakers of other languages (MA). *Program availability:* Part-time, online learning. *Degree requirements:* For master's, thesis (for some programs); for doctorate, thesis/dissertation. *Entrance requirements:* Additional exam requirements/recommendations for international students: Recommended—TOEFL (minimum score 550 paper-based).

Milligan College, Area of Counselor Education Programs, Milligan College, TN 37682. Offers clinical mental health counseling (MSC); counseling ministry (Graduate Certificate); school counseling (MSC). *Program availability:* Part-time. *Faculty:* 3 full-time (all women), 2 part-time/adjunct (1 woman). *Students:* 21 full-time (15 women), 3 part-time (all women); includes 2 minority (1 Black or African American, non-Hispanic/Latino; 1 Two or more races, non-Hispanic/Latino). Average age 31. 24 applicants, 88% accepted, 13 enrolled. In 2018, 15 master's awarded. *Degree requirements:* For master's, thesis or alternative. *Entrance requirements:* For master's, GRE General Test if undergraduate GPA is less than 3.0, undergraduate degree and supporting transcripts, essay/personal statement, professional recommendations, interview. Additional exam requirements/recommendations for international students: Required—TOEFL (minimum score 550 paper-based, 79 iBT) or IELTS (6.5). *Application deadline:* For fall admission, 8/1 for domestic students, 6/1 for international students. Applications are processed on a rolling basis. Application fee: $30. Electronic applications accepted. *Expenses:* $450 per credit hour; $375 fees per semester; $75 one time records fee. *Financial support:* Scholarships/grants available. Financial award application deadline: 12/1; financial award applicants required to submit FAFSA. *Faculty research:* Parent-child interaction therapy/autism; childhood developmental trauma/childhood sexual abuse; poverty and homelessness; social justice advocacy and multicultural competencies; school based mental health. *Unit head:* Dr. Rebecca Sapp, Director of Master of Science in Counseling Program, 423-461-3071, E-mail: rlsapp@milligan.edu. *Application contact:* Stacy Shankle, Graduate Admissions Recruiter, Healthcare Programs, 423-461-8424, Fax: 423-461-8789, E-mail: srshankle@milligan.edu.

Minnesota State University Mankato, College of Graduate Studies and Research, College of Education, Department of Counseling and Student Personnel, Mankato, MN 56001. Offers college student affairs (MS); counselor education and supervision (Ed D); mental health counseling (MS); professional school counseling (K-12) (MS). *Accreditation:* ACA (one or more programs are accredited); NCATE. *Degree requirements:* For master's, comprehensive exam, thesis or alternative. *Entrance requirements:* For master's, GRE General Test or MAT (if GPA less than 3.0 for last 2 years), minimum GPA of 3.0 during previous 2 years, 3 letters of reference. Additional exam requirements/recommendations for international students: Required—TOEFL. Electronic applications accepted.

Minnesota State University Moorhead, Graduate and Extended Learning, College of Education and Human Services, Moorhead, MN 56563. Offers counseling and student affairs (MS); educational leadership (MS, Ed D, Ed S). *Accreditation:* ASHA; NCATE. *Program availability:* Part-time, evening/weekend, 100% online, blended/hybrid learning. *Students:* 129 full-time (105 women), 425 part-time (300 women); includes 32 minority (8 Black or African American, non-Hispanic/Latino; 4 American Indian or Alaska Native, non-Hispanic/Latino; 6 Asian, non-Hispanic/Latino; 7 Hispanic/Latino; 7 Two or more races, non-Hispanic/Latino), 1 international. Average age 33. 154 applicants, 77% accepted. In 2018, 198 master's, 29 other advanced degrees awarded. *Degree requirements:* For master's, comprehensive exam (for some programs), thesis, final oral defense; for doctorate, comprehensive exam (for some programs), thesis/dissertation, final oral defense. *Entrance requirements:* For master's, GRE, essay, letter of intent, letters of reference, teaching license, teaching verification, minimum cumulative GPA of 3.0; for doctorate, official transcripts; letter of intent; resume or curriculum vitae; master's degree; personal essay. Additional exam requirements/recommendations for international students: Required—TOEFL (minimum score 550 paper-based); Recommended—IELTS (minimum score 6.5). *Application deadline:* For fall admission, 7/1 priority date for domestic students; for spring admission, 11/15 priority date for domestic students. Applications are processed on a rolling basis. Application fee: $35. Electronic applications accepted. Tuition and fees vary according to course load, degree level, program and reciprocity agreements. *Financial support:* Federal Work-Study and unspecified assistantships available. Financial award application deadline: 10/1; financial award applicants required to submit FAFSA. *Unit head:* Dr. Ok-Hee Lee, Dean, 218-477-2095, E-mail: okheelee@mnstate.edu. *Application contact:* Karla Wenger, Office Manager, 218-477-2344, Fax: 218-477-2482, E-mail: wengerk@mnstate.edu.
Website: http://www.mnstate.edu/cehs/

Mississippi College, Graduate School, School of Education, Department of Psychology and Counseling, Clinton, MS 39058. Offers counseling (Ed S); marriage and family counseling (MS); mental health counseling (MS); school counseling (M Ed). *Program availability:* Part-time. *Degree requirements:* For master's and Ed S, comprehensive exam, thesis optional. *Entrance requirements:* For master's, GRE or NTE. Additional exam requirements/recommendations for international students: Recommended—TOEFL, IELTS. Electronic applications accepted.

Mississippi State University, College of Education, Department of Counseling, Educational Psychology, and Foundations, Mississippi State, MS 39762. Offers clinical mental health (MS); college counseling (MS); counseling/mental health (PhD); counseling/school psychology (PhD); counselor education (Ed S); educational psychology/general educational psychology (PhD); educational psychology/school psychology (PhD); general educational psychology (MS); psychometry (MS); rehabilitation counseling (MS); school counseling (MS); school psychology (Ed S); student affairs (MS). *Accreditation:* ACA (one or more programs are accredited); APA; CORE (one or more programs are accredited); NCATE. *Program availability:* Part-time, blended/hybrid learning. *Faculty:* 17 full-time (12 women), 2 part-time/adjunct (both women). *Students:* 94 full-time (81 women), 54 part-time (44 women); includes 50 minority (39 Black or African American, non-Hispanic/Latino; 2 Asian, non-Hispanic/Latino; 8 Hispanic/Latino; 1 Two or more races, non-Hispanic/Latino), 6 international. Average age 29. 90 applicants, 63% accepted, 45 enrolled. In 2018, 33 master's, 6 doctorates, 6 other advanced degrees awarded. Terminal master's awarded for partial completion of doctoral program. *Degree requirements:* For master's, comprehensive exam, thesis optional; for doctorate, thesis/dissertation, comprehensive oral and written exam. *Entrance requirements:* For master's, GRE (taken within the last five years), BS with minimum GPA of 2.75 on last 60 hours; for doctorate, GRE, MS from CACREP- or CORE-accredited program in counseling; for Ed S, GRE, MS in counseling or related field, minimum GPA of 3.3 on all graduate work. Additional exam requirements/recommendations for international students: Required—TOEFL (minimum score 550 paper-based; 79 iBT); Recommended—IELTS (minimum score 6.5). *Application deadline:* For fall admission, 2/1 priority date for domestic and international students. Applications are processed on a rolling basis. Application fee: $60 ($80 for international students). Electronic applications accepted. *Expenses:* Tuition, state resident: full-time $8450; part-time $360.59 per credit hour. Tuition, nonresident: full-time $23,140; part-time $969.09 per credit hour. *Required fees:* $110. One-time fee: $55 full-time. Part-time tuition and fees vary according to course load, degree level, campus/location and reciprocity agreements. *Financial support:* In 2018–19, 6 research assistantships (averaging $10,050 per year), 6 teaching assistantships with full tuition reimbursements (averaging $8,401 per year) were awarded; career-related internships or fieldwork, Federal Work-Study, institutionally sponsored loans, and unspecified assistantships also available. Financial award application deadline: 2/1; financial award applicants required to submit FAFSA. *Faculty research:* HIV/AIDS in college population, substance abuse in youth and college students, ADHD and conduct disorders in youth, assessment and identification of early childhood disabilities, assessment and vocational transition of the disabled. *Unit head:* Dr. Daniel Gadke, Professor and Interim Head, 662-325-3426, Fax: 662-325-3263, E-mail: dgadke@colled.msstate.edu. *Application contact:* Ryan King, Admissions and Enrollment Assistant, 662-325-8951, E-mail: rjk101@grad.msstate.edu.
Website: http://www.cep.msstate.edu/

Counselor Education

Missouri Baptist University, Graduate Programs, St. Louis, MO 63141-8660. Offers business administration (MBA); Christian ministries (MACM); counseling (MAC); education (MSE); education administration (MEA); educational leadership (MSE, Ed S); teaching (MAT).

Missouri State University, Graduate College, College of Education, Department of Counseling, Leadership, and Special Education, Program in Counseling, Springfield, MO 65897. Offers mental health counseling (MS). *Accreditation:* ACA. *Program availability:* Part-time, evening/weekend. *Faculty:* 9 full-time (6 women), 3 part-time/adjunct (2 women). *Students:* 75 full-time (59 women), 37 part-time (30 women); includes 17 minority (8 Black or African American, non-Hispanic/Latino; 6 Hispanic/Latino; 3 Two or more races, non-Hispanic/Latino), 2 international. Average age 24. 35 applicants, 31% accepted. In 2018, 32 master's awarded. *Degree requirements:* For master's, comprehensive exam, thesis or alternative. *Entrance requirements:* For master's, GRE or MAT, minimum GPA of 2.75. Additional exam requirements/recommendations for international students: Required—TOEFL (minimum score 550 paper-based; 79 iBT), IELTS (minimum score 6). *Application deadline:* For fall admission, 2/1 priority date for domestic students, 1/1 priority date for international students; for spring admission, 10/1 priority date for domestic students, 9/1 priority date for international students. Application fee: $55 ($60 for international students). Electronic applications accepted. Tuition and fees vary according to class time, course level, course load, degree level, campus/location, program and student level. *Financial support:* Federal Work-Study, institutionally sponsored loans, scholarships/grants, and unspecified assistantships available. Financial award application deadline: 1/31; financial award applicants required to submit FAFSA. *Unit head:* Dr. James Satterfield, Department Head, 417-836-5392, Fax: 417-836-4918, E-mail: clse@missouristate.edu. *Application contact:* Lakan Drinker, Director, Graduate Enrollment Management, 417-836-5300, Fax: 417-836-6200, E-mail: lakandrinker@missouristate.edu.
Website: http://education.missouristate.edu/clse/

Montana State University Billings, College of Education, Department of Educational Theory and Practice, Option in School Counseling, Billings, MT 59101. Offers M Ed. *Accreditation:* NCATE. *Program availability:* Part-time. *Degree requirements:* For master's, thesis or professional paper and/or field experience. *Entrance requirements:* For master's, GRE General Test or MAT, minimum GPA of 3.0, letters of recommendation, resume, letter of intent. Additional exam requirements/recommendations for international students: Required—TOEFL (minimum score 79 iBT), IELTS (minimum score 6.5). Electronic applications accepted.

Montana State University–Northern, Graduate Programs, Option in Counselor Education, Havre, MT 59501-7751. Offers M Ed. *Program availability:* Part-time, evening/weekend. *Degree requirements:* For master's, comprehensive exam, thesis optional, oral exams, internship. *Entrance requirements:* For master's, GRE General Test or MAT, minimum major and overall GPA of 3.0. Electronic applications accepted.

Montclair State University, The Graduate School, College of Education and Human Services, Doctoral Program in Counselor Education, Montclair, NJ 07043-1624. Offers PhD. *Accreditation:* ACA. *Program availability:* Part-time, evening/weekend. *Degree requirements:* For doctorate, comprehensive exam, thesis/dissertation. *Entrance requirements:* For doctorate, GRE General Test, interview, 3 letters of recommendation. Additional exam requirements/recommendations for international students: Required—TOEFL (minimum score 83 iBT), IELTS (minimum score 6.5). Electronic applications accepted.

Montclair State University, The Graduate School, College of Education and Human Services, Program in Counseling, Montclair, NJ 07043-1624. Offers MA. *Accreditation:* ACA. *Program availability:* Part-time, evening/weekend. *Degree requirements:* For master's, comprehensive exam, thesis or alternative. *Entrance requirements:* For master's, GRE General Test, interview, 2 letters of recommendation. Additional exam requirements/recommendations for international students: Required—TOEFL (minimum score 83 iBT), IELTS (minimum score 6.5). Electronic applications accepted.

Morehead State University, Graduate School, College of Education, Department of Foundational and Graduate Studies in Education, Morehead, KY 40351. Offers adult and higher education (MA, Ed S); certified professional counselor (Ed S); counseling P-12 (MA); curriculum and instruction (Ed S); educational technology (MA Ed); instructional leadership (Ed S); school administration (MA); school counseling (Ed S); teacher leader business and marketing content (MA Ed); teacher leader business and marketing technology (MA Ed); teacher leader educational technology (MA Ed); teacher leader English (MA Ed); teacher leader gifted education (MA Ed); teacher leader IECE certification (MA Ed); teacher leader interdisciplinary education P-5 (MA Ed); teacher leader middle grades (MA Ed); teacher leader non IECE certification (MA Ed); teacher leader reading/writing - non-certification (MA Ed); teacher leader reading/writing certification (MA Ed); teacher leader school communication - certification (MA Ed); teacher leader school communication - non-certification (MA Ed); teacher leader social studies (MA Ed); teacher leader special education (MA Ed). *Accreditation:* NCATE. *Program availability:* Part-time, evening/weekend. *Degree requirements:* For master's, thesis optional, oral and/or written comprehensive exams; for Ed S, thesis, oral exam. *Entrance requirements:* For master's, GRE General Test, minimum overall undergraduate GPA of 2.5; for Ed S, GRE General Test, interview, master's degree, minimum GPA of 3.5, work experience. Additional exam requirements/recommendations for international students: Required—TOEFL (minimum score 500 paper-based). Electronic applications accepted. *Faculty research:* Character education, school accountability, computer applications for school administrators.

Mount Mary University, Graduate Programs, Program in Counseling, Milwaukee, WI 53222-4597. Offers clinical mental health counseling (MS, Certificate); clinical rehabilitation counseling (MS, Certificate); school counseling (MS, Certificate); vocational rehabilitation counseling (MS, Certificate). *Accreditation:* ACA. *Program availability:* Part-time, evening/weekend. *Degree requirements:* For master's, comprehensive exam, thesis or alternative. *Entrance requirements:* For master's, minimum GPA of 3.0. Additional exam requirements/recommendations for international students: Required—TOEFL (minimum score 550 paper-based; 80 iBT); Recommended—IELTS (minimum score 6.5). Electronic applications accepted. *Expenses:* Contact institution. *Faculty research:* Cognitive behavioral interventions for depression, eating disorders and compliance, trauma-informed care.

Murray State University, College of Education and Human Services, Department of Educational Studies, Leadership and Counseling, Murray, KY 42071. Offers college advising (Certificate); education administration (MA Ed); human development and leadership (MS, Certificate); library media (MA Ed); middle school teacher leader (MA Ed); P-20 and community leadership (Ed D); postsecondary education administration (MA Ed); school counseling (MA Ed); school guidance and counseling (Ed S); secondary teacher leader (MA Ed). *Program availability:* Part-time, evening/weekend, 100% online, blended/hybrid learning. *Entrance requirements:* For master's and other advanced degree, GRE or GMAT, minimum university GPA of 2.75. Additional exam requirements/recommendations for international students: Required—TOEFL (minimum score 527 paper-based; 71 iBT). Electronic applications accepted.

Naropa University, Graduate Programs, Program in Clinical Mental Health Counseling, Concentration in Mindfulness-based Transpersonal Counseling, Boulder, CO 80302-6697. Offers MA. *Degree requirements:* For master's, internship, counseling practicum. *Entrance requirements:* For master's, interview, statement of interest, essay, professional experience, resume, 2 letters of recommendation, transcripts. Additional exam requirements/recommendations for international students: Required—TOEFL (minimum score 550 paper-based; 80 iBT). Electronic applications accepted. *Expenses:* Contact institution.

National Louis University, College of Arts and Sciences, Chicago, IL 60603. Offers adult education (Ed D); counseling and human services (MS); language and academic development (M Ed, Certificate); psychology (MA, PhD, Certificate); public policy (MA); written communication (MS, Certificate). *Program availability:* Part-time, evening/weekend, online learning. *Degree requirements:* For master's and Certificate, comprehensive exam (for some programs), thesis (for some programs); for doctorate, thesis/dissertation. *Entrance requirements:* For master's, MAT or GRE, 3 professional or academic references, interview, minimum GPA of 3.0; for doctorate, GRE General Test, MAT, or Watson-Glaser Critical Thinking Appraisal, three professional or academic references, statement of academic and professional goals, 3 years of experience in field, interview, master's degree, resume, writing sample; for Certificate, GRE, MAT, or Watson-Glaser Critical Thinking Appraisal, three professional or academic references, statement of academic and professional goals, interview, minimum GPA of 3.0. Additional exam requirements/recommendations for international students: Required—Department of Language Studies Assessment or TOEFL (minimum score 550 paper-based; 79 iBT). Electronic applications accepted.

National University, Sanford College of Education, La Jolla, CA 92037-1011. Offers advanced teaching practices (MS); applied behavior analysis (MS); applied school leadership (MS); e-teaching and learning (Certificate); education (MA); educational administration (MS); educational and instructional technology (MS); educational counseling (MS); higher education administration (MS); inspired teaching and learning (M Ed); school psychology (MS); special education (MA, MS). *Program availability:* Part-time, evening/weekend, 100% online, blended/hybrid learning. *Degree requirements:* For master's, thesis (for some programs). *Entrance requirements:* For master's, interview, minimum GPA of 2.5. Additional exam requirements/recommendations for international students: Required—TOEFL (minimum score 550 paper-based; 79 iBT), IELTS (minimum score 6). Electronic applications accepted. *Expenses: Tuition:* Full-time $10,320; part-time $430 per unit. Tuition and fees vary according to degree level. *Faculty research:* Teacher education, special education, educational effectiveness, teaching abroad, school counseling.

New Jersey City University, Debra Cannon Partridge Wolfe College of Education, Department of Educational Leadership and Counseling, Counselor Education Program, Jersey City, NJ 07305-1597. Offers MA. *Accreditation:* ACA. *Program availability:* Part-time, evening/weekend. *Entrance requirements:* Additional exam requirements/recommendations for international students: Required—TOEFL (minimum score 79 iBT).

New Mexico Highlands University, Graduate Studies, School of Education, Las Vegas, NM 87701. Offers curriculum and instruction (MA); educational leadership (MA); professional counseling (MA); special education (MA). *Accreditation:* NCATE. *Program availability:* Part-time. *Degree requirements:* For master's, comprehensive exam, thesis or alternative. *Entrance requirements:* For master's, minimum undergraduate GPA of 3.0. Additional exam requirements/recommendations for international students: Required—TOEFL (minimum score 540 paper-based). *Faculty research:* Middle school curriculum, integrated computer applications for pre-service classroom teachers, adolescent literacy, narrative cognitive modes in New Mexico multicultural setting, math and math education.

New York Institute of Technology, School of Interdisciplinary Studies and Education, Department of School Counseling, Old Westbury, NY 11568-8000. Offers bilingual school counseling (Advanced Certificate); school counseling (MS); student behavior management (Advanced Certificate). *Accreditation:* ACA. *Program availability:* Part-time, blended/hybrid learning. *Faculty:* 1 full-time (0 women), 13 part-time/adjunct (10 women). *Students:* 21 full-time (19 women), 33 part-time (27 women); includes 35 minority (14 Black or African American, non-Hispanic/Latino; 1 Asian, non-Hispanic/Latino; 19 Hispanic/Latino; 1 Two or more races, non-Hispanic/Latino). Average age 37. 77 applicants, 57% accepted, 30 enrolled. In 2018, 16 master's, 1 other advanced degree awarded. *Degree requirements:* For master's, internship, practicum. *Entrance requirements:* For master's, minimum undergraduate GPA of 3.0; BS or equivalent with academic background in psychology, education, sociology, law, or related behavioral science, or work experience in school, social agency, hospital, criminal justice, or community action program; goal statement; 3 letters of reference; signed candidate statement of understanding. Additional exam requirements/recommendations for international students: Required—TOEFL (minimum score 79 iBT), IELTS (minimum score 6), PTE (minimum score 53). *Application deadline:* Applications are processed on a rolling basis. Application fee: $50. Electronic applications accepted. *Expenses: Tuition:* Full-time $1285; part-time $1285 per credit. *Required fees:* $215; $175 per unit. Tuition and fees vary according to course load, degree level and campus/location. *Financial support:* Career-related internships or fieldwork, Federal Work-Study, scholarships/grants, tuition waivers (full and partial), and unspecified assistantships available. Support available to part-time students. Financial award application deadline: 2/15; financial award applicants required to submit FAFSA. *Faculty research:* School counselor accountability, school counselor-principal relationship, comprehensive school counseling program design and evaluation, cultural competence, college and career readiness. *Unit head:* Dr. Carol Dahir, Department Chair, 516-686-7616, Fax: 516-686-7655, E-mail: cdahir@nyit.edu. *Application contact:* Alice Dolitsky, Director, Graduate Admissions, 516-686-7520, Fax: 516-686-1116, E-mail: admissions@nyit.edu.
Website: http://www.nyit.edu/degrees/school_counseling

New York University, Steinhardt School of Culture, Education, and Human Development, Department of Applied Psychology, Programs in Counseling, New York, NY 10012. Offers counseling and guidance (MA, Advanced Certificate), including bilingual school counseling K-12 (MA), school counseling K-12 (MA); counseling for mental health and wellness (MA); counseling psychology (PhD); LGBT health, education, and social services (Advanced Certificate); Advanced Certificate/MPH; MA/Advanced Certificate. *Accreditation:* APA (one or more programs are accredited). *Program availability:* Part-time. *Entrance requirements:* For doctorate, GRE General Test, interview. Additional exam requirements/recommendations for international students: Required—TOEFL (minimum score 100 iBT). Electronic applications accepted. *Faculty research:* Sexual and gender identities, group dynamics, psychopathy and personality, multicultural assessment, working people's lives.

Niagara University, Graduate Division of Education, Concentration in Mental Health Counseling, Niagara University, NY 14109. Offers MS, Certificate. *Accreditation:* ACA. *Program availability:* Part-time. *Students:* 36 full-time (31 women), 9 part-time (7 women); includes 5 minority (2 Black or African American, non-Hispanic/Latino; 3 Hispanic/Latino), 14 international. Average age 27. In 2018, 10 master's awarded. *Entrance requirements:* For master's, GRE General Test or MAT. Additional exam requirements/recommendations for international students: Required—TOEFL (minimum score 550 paper-based; 79 iBT), IELTS (minimum score 6). *Application deadline:* For fall admission, 8/1 for domestic students. Applications are processed on a rolling basis.

Electronic applications accepted. *Expenses:* Contact institution. *Financial support:* Research assistantships with tuition reimbursements, teaching assistantships with tuition reimbursements, career-related internships or fieldwork, Federal Work-Study, scholarships/grants, and unspecified assistantships available. Support available to part-time students. Financial award application deadline: 4/15; financial award applicants required to submit FAFSA. *Unit head:* Dr. Jennifer Beebe, Associate Professor, 716-286-8182, E-mail: jbeebe@niagara.edu. *Application contact:* Evan Pierce, Associate Director, Graduate Studies, 716-286-8327, E-mail: epierce@niagara.edu. Website: http://www.niagara.edu/mental-health-counseling

Niagara University, Graduate Division of Education, Concentration in School Counseling, Niagara University, NY 14109. Offers MS Ed, Certificate. *Accreditation:* NCATE. *Program availability:* Part-time, evening/weekend. *Students:* 19 full-time (18 women), 10 part-time (9 women); includes 6 minority (4 Black or African American, non-Hispanic/Latino; 1 Hispanic/Latino; 1 Two or more races, non-Hispanic/Latino). Average age 28. In 2018, 16 master's, 3 Certificates awarded. *Entrance requirements:* For master's, GRE General Test or MAT; for Certificate, GRE General Test, GRE Subject Test or MAT. Additional exam requirements/recommendations for international students: Required—TOEFL (minimum score 550 paper-based; 79 iBT), IELTS (minimum score 6). *Application deadline:* For fall admission, 8/1 for domestic students. Applications are processed on a rolling basis. Electronic applications accepted. *Expenses:* Contact institution. *Financial support:* Research assistantships with tuition reimbursements, teaching assistantships with tuition reimbursements, career-related internships or fieldwork, Federal Work-Study, scholarships/grants, and unspecified assistantships available. Support available to part-time students. Financial award application deadline: 4/15; financial award applicants required to submit FAFSA. *Unit head:* Dr. Jennifer Beebe, Associate Professor of Counseling, 716-286-8182, E-mail: jbeebe@niagara.edu. *Application contact:* Evan Pierce, Associate Director, Graduate Studies, 716-286-8327, E-mail: epierce@niagara.edu. Website: http://www.niagara.edu/school-counseling

Nicholls State University, Graduate Studies, College of Education, Department of Psychology, Counseling and Family Studies, Thibodaux, LA 70310. Offers clinical mental health counseling (MA); school counseling (M Ed); school psychology (SSP). *Accreditation:* NCATE. *Program availability:* Part-time, evening/weekend. *Degree requirements:* For master's, comprehensive exam; for SSP, comprehensive exam, internship. *Entrance requirements:* For master's, GRE General Test. Electronic applications accepted.

North Carolina Agricultural and Technical State University, The Graduate College, College of Education, Department of Counseling, Greensboro, NC 27411. Offers mental health counseling (MS); rehabilitation counseling and rehabilitation counselor education (PhD); school counseling (MS). *Accreditation:* ACA. *Program availability:* Part-time, evening/weekend. *Degree requirements:* For master's, comprehensive exam, thesis, qualifying exam. *Entrance requirements:* For master's, GRE General Test, minimum GPA of 3.0.

North Carolina Central University, School of Education, Program in Counselor Education, Durham, NC 27707-3129. Offers career counseling (MA); clinical mental health counseling (MA); school counseling (MA). *Accreditation:* ACA; NCATE. *Program availability:* Part-time, evening/weekend. *Degree requirements:* For master's, comprehensive exam, thesis or alternative. *Entrance requirements:* For master's, GRE, minimum GPA of 3.0 in major, 2.5 overall. Additional exam requirements/recommendations for international students: Required—TOEFL.

North Carolina State University, Graduate School, College of Education, Department of Teacher Education and Learning Sciences, Program in Counselor Education, Raleigh, NC 27695. Offers M Ed, MS, PhD. *Accreditation:* ACA. *Degree requirements:* For master's, thesis (for some programs). *Entrance requirements:* For master's, GRE or MAT. Electronic applications accepted. *Faculty research:* Career development, retention of at-risk students in higher education, psycho-social development, multicultural issues, cognitive-developmental interventions.

North Dakota State University, College of Graduate and Interdisciplinary Studies, College of Human Development and Education, School of Education, Program in Counselor Education, Fargo, ND 58102. Offers clinical mental health counseling (M Ed, MS); counselor education and supervision (PhD); school counseling (M Ed, MS). *Accreditation:* ACA; NCATE. *Program availability:* Part-time, online learning. *Degree requirements:* For master's, comprehensive exam, thesis or alternative; for doctorate, comprehensive exam, thesis/dissertation. *Entrance requirements:* For master's, GRE, MAT, interview. Additional exam requirements/recommendations for international students: Required—TOEFL. *Faculty research:* Supervision, program assessment, multicultural issues.

Northeastern Illinois University, College of Graduate Studies and Research, Daniel L. Goodwin College of Education, Program in School Counseling, Chicago, IL 60625. Offers MA. *Accreditation:* ACA.

Northern Arizona University, College of Education, Department of Educational Psychology, Flagstaff, AZ 86011. Offers clinical mental health counseling (MA); combined counseling/school psychology (PhD), including counseling psychology; counseling (M Ed), including school counseling, student affairs; human relations (M Ed); psychology of human development and learning (Graduate Certificate); school psychology (Ed S). *Program availability:* Part-time, 100% online, blended/hybrid learning. Terminal master's awarded for partial completion of doctoral program. *Degree requirements:* For master's, variable foreign language requirement, comprehensive exam (for some programs), thesis (for some programs); for doctorate, variable foreign language requirement, comprehensive exam (for some programs), thesis/dissertation (for some programs); for other advanced degree, comprehensive exam (for some programs). *Entrance requirements:* Additional exam requirements/recommendations for international students: Required—TOEFL (minimum score 80 iBT), IELTS (minimum score 6.5). Electronic applications accepted.

Northern Illinois University, Graduate School, College of Education, Department of Counseling, Adult and Higher Education, De Kalb, IL 60115-2854. Offers adult and higher education (MS Ed, Ed D); counseling (MS Ed, Ed D). *Accreditation:* ACA. *Program availability:* Part-time, evening/weekend. *Faculty:* 19 full-time (11 women), 2 part-time/adjunct (1 woman). *Students:* 129 full-time (94 women), 225 part-time (158 women); includes 150 minority (68 Black or African American, non-Hispanic/Latino; 8 American Indian or Alaska Native, non-Hispanic/Latino; 12 Asian, non-Hispanic/Latino; 50 Hispanic/Latino; 12 Two or more races, non-Hispanic/Latino), 7 international. Average age 36. 158 applicants, 61% accepted, 67 enrolled. In 2018, 58 master's, 19 doctorates awarded. Terminal master's awarded for partial completion of doctoral program. *Degree requirements:* For master's, comprehensive exam, thesis optional; for doctorate, thesis/dissertation, candidacy exam, dissertation defense. *Entrance requirements:* For master's, GRE General Test or MAT, minimum undergraduate GPA of 2.75, interview (for counseling); for doctorate, GRE General Test, minimum undergraduate GPA of 2.75, 3.2 graduate; interview (for counseling). Additional exam requirements/recommendations for international students: Required—TOEFL (minimum score 550 paper-based). *Application deadline:* For fall admission, 6/1 for domestic students, 5/1 for international students; for spring admission, 11/1 for domestic students,

10/1 for international students. Applications are processed on a rolling basis. Application fee: $40. Electronic applications accepted. *Financial support:* In 2018–19, 15 research assistantships with full tuition reimbursements, 7 teaching assistantships with full tuition reimbursements were awarded; fellowships with full tuition reimbursements, career-related internships or fieldwork, Federal Work-Study, scholarships/grants, tuition waivers (full), and staff assistantships also available. Support available to part-time students. Financial award applicants required to submit FAFSA. *Unit head:* Dr. Suzanne Degges-White, Interim Chair, 815-753-1448, E-mail: cahe@niu.edu. *Application contact:* Graduate School Office, 815-753-0395, E-mail: gradsch@niu.edu. Website: http://www.cedu.niu.edu/cahe/index.html

Northern Kentucky University, Office of Graduate Programs, College of Education and Human Services, Program in School Counseling, Highland Heights, KY 41099. Offers MA. *Accreditation:* ACA. *Program availability:* Part-time, evening/weekend. *Degree requirements:* For master's, portfolio, practicum, internship. *Entrance requirements:* For master's, GRE or MAT, official transcript(s), two essays, three letters of reference, professional resume, KY Statement of Eligibility or teaching certificate, criminal background check, interview. Additional exam requirements/recommendations for international students: Required—TOEFL (minimum score 79 iBT); Recommended—IELTS (minimum score 6.5). Electronic applications accepted. *Faculty research:* Counselor wellness, counseling preferences and expectations, creativity in counseling, integrating mindfulness-based approaches into counseling, evidence-based school counseling.

Northern State University, MS Ed Program in Counseling, Aberdeen, SD 57401-7198. Offers clinical mental health counseling (MS Ed); school counseling (MS Ed). *Accreditation:* ACA; NCATE. *Program availability:* Part-time, online learning. *Degree requirements:* For master's, comprehensive exam, thesis optional. *Entrance requirements:* For master's, minimum GPA of 2.75. Additional exam requirements/recommendations for international students: Required—TOEFL (minimum score 550 paper-based; 78 iBT), IELTS (minimum score 6). Electronic applications accepted.

Northern Vermont University–Johnson, Program in Counseling, Johnson, VT 05656. Offers addictions counseling (MA); clinical mental health counseling (MA); general counseling (MA); school counseling (MA). *Program availability:* Part-time. *Degree requirements:* For master's, comprehensive exam. *Entrance requirements:* For master's, interview. Additional exam requirements/recommendations for international students: Required—TOEFL. Electronic applications accepted.

Northern Vermont University–Lyndon, Graduate Programs in Education, Department of Education, Lyndonville, VT 05851. Offers curriculum and instruction (M Ed); reading specialist (M Ed); special education (M Ed); teaching and counseling (M Ed). *Program availability:* Part-time, evening/weekend. *Degree requirements:* For master's, exam or major field project. *Entrance requirements:* Additional exam requirements/recommendations for international students: Recommended—TOEFL (minimum score 500 paper-based).

Northwest Christian University, School of Education and Counseling, Eugene, OR 97401-3745. Offers clinical mental health counseling (MA); elementary teaching (MAT); English for speakers of other languages (MAT); physical education (MAT); school counseling (MA); secondary teaching (MAT); special education (MAT). *Program availability:* Part-time, evening/weekend, online learning. *Degree requirements:* For master's, thesis (for some programs). *Entrance requirements:* For master's, GRE or MAT, minimum undergraduate GPA of 3.0, interview, 2-3 page statement of purpose, two letters of recommendation, resume, background check. Additional exam requirements/recommendations for international students: Required—TOEFL (minimum score 550 paper-based; 80 iBT). Electronic applications accepted. *Expenses:* Contact institution.

Northwestern Oklahoma State University, School of Professional Studies, Program in School Counseling, Alva, OK 73717-2799. Offers M Ed. *Accreditation:* NCATE. *Program availability:* Part-time. *Degree requirements:* For master's, thesis optional, portfolio. *Entrance requirements:* For master's, GRE General Test or MAT, minimum GPA of 2.75.

Northwestern State University of Louisiana, Graduate Studies and Research, College of Education and Human Development, Program in School Counseling, Natchitoches, LA 71497. Offers MA. *Accreditation:* ACA. *Degree requirements:* For master's, comprehensive exam, thesis (for some programs). *Entrance requirements:* For master's, GRE General Test. Additional exam requirements/recommendations for international students: Required—TOEFL. Electronic applications accepted.

Northwestern State University of Louisiana, Graduate Studies and Research, College of Education and Human Development, Programs in Educational Leadership and Instruction, Natchitoches, LA 71497. Offers counseling (Ed S); educational leadership (M Ed, Ed S); educational technology (Ed S); elementary teaching (Ed S); reading (Ed S); secondary teaching (Ed S); special education (Ed S). *Accreditation:* NASAD. *Degree requirements:* For master's, comprehensive exam, thesis (for some programs). *Entrance requirements:* For master's and Ed S, GRE General Test. Additional exam requirements/recommendations for international students: Required—TOEFL. Electronic applications accepted.

Northwest Nazarene University, Program in Counselor Education, Nampa, ID 83686-5897. Offers clinical counseling (MS); marriage and family counseling (MS); school counseling (MS). *Program availability:* Part-time, evening/weekend. *Faculty:* 5 full-time (3 women), 28 part-time/adjunct (15 women). *Students:* Average age 35. 47 applicants, 66% accepted, 25 enrolled. In 2018, 49 master's awarded. *Degree requirements:* For master's, comprehensive exam. *Entrance requirements:* For master's, GRE (if GPA less than 3.0), minimum GPA of 3.0, BA, 2 letters of recommendation, definition of counseling writing sample, background check, group evaluation, role play, dispositions rubric score. Additional exam requirements/recommendations for international students: Required—TOEFL (minimum score 85 paper-based), WES. *Application deadline:* For fall admission, 2/15 for domestic and international students; for spring admission, 9/15 for domestic and international students. Application fee: $50. Electronic applications accepted. *Expenses: Tuition:* Full-time $6744; part-time $3372 per credit. *Required fees:* $190; $190 per unit. $95 per semester. Tuition and fees vary according to course load, degree level and program. *Financial support:* Applicants required to submit FAFSA. *Faculty research:* Lay Therapy, gatekeeping in higher ed, trauma and grief, spirituality. *Unit head:* Dr. Lori Fairgrieve, Chair, 208-467-8343. *Application contact:* Christy Gilliam, Graduate Admissions Counselor, 208-467-8853, E-mail: cgilliam@nnu.edu.

Nova Southeastern University, College of Psychology, Fort Lauderdale, FL 33314-7796. Offers clinical mental health counseling (MS); clinical psychology (PhD, Psy D); counseling (MS); experimental psychology (MS); forensic psychology (MS); general psychology (MS); school counseling (MS); school psychology (Psy D, Psy S); substance abuse counseling (MS); substance abuse counseling and education (MS). *Accreditation:* APA (one or more programs are accredited). *Program availability:* 100% online, blended/hybrid learning. Terminal master's awarded for partial completion of doctoral program. *Degree requirements:* For master's, comprehensive exam, 3 practica; for doctorate, thesis/dissertation, clinical internship, competency exam; for Psy S, comprehensive exam, internship. *Entrance requirements:* For master's and Psy S, GRE General Test, letters of recommendation, research/personal statement, interview; for

doctorate, GRE General Test, GRE Subject Test (recommended), minimum undergraduate GPA of 3.0, letters of recommendation, research/personal statement, interview, curriculum vitae/resume. Additional exam requirements/recommendations for international students: Required—TOEFL (minimum score 550 paper-based). Electronic applications accepted. *Expenses:* Contact institution. *Faculty research:* Clinical health psychology, multicultural/diversity psychology, clinical neuropsychology, clinical child psychology, family violence.

Nyack College, Alliance Graduate School of Counseling, Nyack, NY 10960. Offers marriage and family therapy (MA); mental health counseling (MA). *Program availability:* Part-time, evening/weekend, 100% online. *Students:* 74 full-time (60 women), 134 part-time (107 women); includes 172 minority (68 Black or African American, non-Hispanic/Latino; 1 American Indian or Alaska Native, non-Hispanic/Latino; 46 Asian, non-Hispanic/Latino; 50 Hispanic/Latino; 7 Two or more races, non-Hispanic/Latino), 7 international. Average age 37. In 2018, 62 master's awarded. *Degree requirements:* For master's, comprehensive exam, counselor-in-training therapy, internship, CPCE exam. *Entrance requirements:* For master's, Millon Clinical Multiaxial Inventory-3, Minnesota Multiphasic Personality Inventory-2, transcripts, statement of Christian life and experience, statement of support systems. Additional exam requirements/recommendations for international students: Required—TOEFL (minimum score 550 paper-based; 80 iBT). *Application deadline:* For fall admission, 8/1 for domestic students, 2/15 for international students; for spring admission, 12/15 for domestic students, 7/15 for international students. Applications are processed on a rolling basis. Application fee: $30. Electronic applications accepted. *Expenses:* $800/credit. *Financial support:* Career-related internships or fieldwork and scholarships/grants available. Financial award applicants required to submit FAFSA. *Unit head:* Dr. Antoinette Gines-Rivera, Director, 646-378-6160. *Application contact:* Chastity Crespo, Admissions Associate, 646-378-6199, E-mail: admissions.grad@nyack.edu.
Website: http://www.nyack.edu/agsc

Ohio University, Graduate College, Gladys W. and David H. Patton College of Education and Human Services, Department of Counseling and Higher Education, Athens, OH 45701-2979. Offers college student personnel (M Ed); community/agency counseling (M Ed); counselor education (PhD); higher education (PhD); rehabilitation counseling (M Ed); school counseling (M Ed). *Accreditation:* ACA; CORE. *Program availability:* Part-time, evening/weekend. *Degree requirements:* For master's, comprehensive exam (for some programs), thesis or alternative; for doctorate, comprehensive exam, thesis/dissertation. *Entrance requirements:* For master's, GRE General Test or MAT (if GPA less than 2.9), 3 letters of reference; for doctorate, GRE General Test, work experience, minimum GPA of 3.4. Additional exam requirements/recommendations for international students: Required—TOEFL (minimum score 550 paper-based; 80 iBT) or IELTS (minimum score 6.5). Electronic applications accepted. *Faculty research:* Youth violence, gender studies, student affairs, chemical dependency, disabilities issues.

Oklahoma City University, Petree College of Arts and Sciences, Oklahoma City, OK 73106-1402. Offers applied behavioral studies (M Ed); applied sociology: nonprofit leadership (MA); creative writing (MFA); criminology (MS); early childhood education (M Ed); elementary education (M Ed); general studies (MLA); leadership/management (MLA); moving image arts (MFA); professional counseling (M Ed); teaching (MA); teaching English to speakers of other languages (MA). *Program availability:* Part-time, evening/weekend. *Degree requirements:* For master's, capstone/practicum. *Entrance requirements:* For master's, bachelor's degree from accredited institution with minimum GPA of 3.0, essay, recommendation letters. Additional exam requirements/recommendations for international students: Required—TOEFL (minimum score 550 paper-based; 80 iBT). Electronic applications accepted. *Expenses:* Contact institution.

Old Dominion University, Darden College of Education, Counseling Program, Norfolk, VA 23529. Offers clinical mental health counseling (MS Ed); college counseling (MS Ed); counseling (Ed S); counselor education (PhD); school counseling (MS Ed). *Accreditation:* ACA. *Program availability:* Part-time, evening/weekend. *Degree requirements:* For master's and Ed S, comprehensive exam; for doctorate, comprehensive exam, thesis/dissertation. *Entrance requirements:* For master's and Ed S, GRE General Test, resume, essay, transcripts, recommendations; for doctorate, GRE General Test, resume, interview, essay, transcripts, recommendations. Additional exam requirements/recommendations for international students: Required—TOEFL. Electronic applications accepted. *Expenses:* Contact institution. *Faculty research:* Group counseling, counselor education, career counseling, spirituality and counseling, school counseling, LGBT counseling, legal and ethical issues.

Oregon State University, College of Education, Program in Counseling, Corvallis, OR 97331. Offers clinical mental health counseling (M Coun); counseling (PhD); school counseling (M Coun). *Accreditation:* ACA (one or more programs are accredited); NCATE. *Program availability:* Part-time, blended/hybrid learning. *Degree requirements:* For master's, thesis or alternative; for doctorate, one foreign language, thesis/dissertation. *Entrance requirements:* For master's, minimum GPA of 3.0 in last 90 hours; for doctorate, GRE or MAT, master's degree, minimum GPA of 3.0 in last 90 hours of course work, 2 years of teaching experience. Additional exam requirements/recommendations for international students: Required—TOEFL (minimum score 575 paper-based). *Faculty research:* Counseling and guidance improvement in social services agencies, elementary and secondary schools.

Ottawa University, Graduate Studies-Arizona, Program in Education, Ottawa, KS 66067-3399. Offers community college counseling (MA); curriculum and instruction (MA); early childhood (MA); education intervention (MA); education leadership (MA); education technology (MA); Montessori early childhood education (MA); Montessori elementary education (MA); professional development (MA); school guidance counseling (MA); special education - cross categorical (MA). Programs offered in Mesa, Phoenix, Tempe and West Valley, AZ. *Accreditation:* NCATE. *Program availability:* Part-time. *Degree requirements:* For master's, thesis or alternative. *Entrance requirements:* For master's, minimum undergraduate GPA of 3.0, copy of current state certification or teaching license. Additional exam requirements/recommendations for international students: Required—TOEFL (minimum score 550 paper-based). Electronic applications accepted. *Expenses:* Contact institution.

Our Lady of the Lake University, College of Professional Studies, Program in School Counseling, San Antonio, TX 78207-4689. Offers M Ed. *Program availability:* Part-time, online only, 100% online. *Faculty:* 3 full-time (2 women), 4 part-time/adjunct (3 women). *Students:* 66 full-time (60 women), 16 part-time (14 women); includes 56 minority (9 Black or African American, non-Hispanic/Latino; 1 American Indian or Alaska Native, non-Hispanic/Latino; 46 Hispanic/Latino). Average age 32. 15 applicants, 87% accepted, 8 enrolled. In 2018, 20 master's awarded. *Degree requirements:* For master's, comprehensive exam, practicum. *Entrance requirements:* For master's, official transcripts, personal statement, reference form, FERPA Consent to Release Education Records and Information form, current teaching license. Additional exam requirements/recommendations for international students: Required—TOEFL. *Application deadline:* For fall admission, 6/15 priority date for domestic and international students; for spring admission, 11/15 priority date for domestic and international students; for summer admission, 4/15 priority date for domestic students, 4/15 for international students. Applications are processed on a rolling basis. Application fee: $40 ($50 for international students). Electronic applications accepted. Application fee is waived when completed online. *Expenses: Tuition:* Full-time $16,326; part-time $907 per credit. *Financial support:* In 2018–19, 1 student received support. Federal Work-Study, scholarships/grants, unspecified assistantships, and tuition discounts available. Support available to part-time students. Financial award application deadline: 5/1; financial award applicants required to submit FAFSA. *Faculty research:* Multicultural issues, career counseling, counselor identity, ethics. *Unit head:* Dr. Alycia Maurer, Education Department Chair, 210-434-6711 Ext. 7152, E-mail: admaurer@ollusa.edu. *Application contact:* Office of Graduate Admissions, 210-431-3995 Ext. 2314, Fax: 210-431-3945, E-mail: gradadm@lake.ollusa.edu.
Website: http://onlineprograms.ollusa.edu/med-school-counseling

Palm Beach Atlantic University, School of Education and Behavioral Studies, West Palm Beach, FL 33416-4708. Offers counseling psychology (MS), including addictions/mental health, general counseling, marriage and family therapy, mental health counseling, school guidance counseling. *Program availability:* Part-time, evening/weekend. *Faculty:* 9 full-time (2 women), 12 part-time/adjunct (9 women). *Students:* 182 full-time (149 women), 69 part-time (56 women); includes 130 minority (53 Black or African American, non-Hispanic/Latino; 3 Asian, non-Hispanic/Latino; 60 Hispanic/Latino; 14 Two or more races, non-Hispanic/Latino), 5 international. Average age 35. In 2018, 101 master's awarded. *Entrance requirements:* For master's, GRE or MAT, minimum GPA of 3.0; essay. Additional exam requirements/recommendations for international students: Required—TOEFL (minimum score 550 paper-based; 79 iBT). *Application deadline:* Applications are processed on a rolling basis. Application fee: $50. Electronic applications accepted. *Expenses: Tuition:* Part-time $767 per credit. Tuition and fees vary according to program. *Financial support:* In 2018–19, 63 students received support. Career-related internships or fieldwork, scholarships/grants, and employee education grants available. Financial award application deadline: 5/1; financial award applicants required to submit FAFSA. *Faculty research:* Group dynamics, phenomenology, spirituality, multicultural psychology. *Unit head:* Dr. Chelly Templeton, Dean, 561-803-2353. *Application contact:* Graduate Admissions, 888-468-6722, E-mail: grad@pba.edu.
Website: http://learn-well.pba.edu/academics/ms-mental-health-counseling.html

Penn State University Park, Graduate School, College of Education, Department of Educational Psychology, Counseling, and Special Education, University Park, PA 16802. Offers counselor education (M Ed, D Ed, PhD, Certificate); educational psychology (MS, PhD, Certificate); school psychology (M Ed, MS, PhD, Certificate); special education (M Ed, MS, PhD).

Phillips Graduate University, Master's Program in Psychology, Chatsworth, CA 91311. Offers art therapy (MA); marriage and family therapy (MA); school counseling (MA); school psychology (MA). *Program availability:* Evening/weekend. *Degree requirements:* For master's, comprehensive exam, thesis. *Entrance requirements:* For master's, minimum GPA of 2.5. Electronic applications accepted. *Faculty research:* Integration of interpersonal psychological theory, systems approach, firsthand experiential learning.

Pittsburg State University, Graduate School, College of Education, Department of Psychology and Counseling, Program in Counselor Education, Pittsburg, KS 66762. Offers school counseling (MS). *Accreditation:* NCATE. *Degree requirements:* For master's, thesis or alternative. *Entrance requirements:* For master's, GRE General Test, minimum GPA of 2.8. Additional exam requirements/recommendations for international students: Required—TOEFL (minimum score 550 paper-based; 79 iBT), IELTS (minimum score 6.5), PTE (minimum score 53). Electronic applications accepted. *Expenses:* Contact institution.

Plymouth State University, College of Graduate Studies, Graduate Studies in Education, Programs in Counseling, Plymouth, NH 03264-1595. Offers addictions treatment (MS); couples and family therapy (MS); play therapy (MS). *Accreditation:* ACA; NCATE. *Program availability:* Part-time, evening/weekend. *Entrance requirements:* For master's, MAT, minimum GPA of 3.0.

Point Loma Nazarene University, School of Education, Program in Education, San Diego, CA 92106-2899. Offers counseling and guidance (MA); educational administration (MA); leadership in learning (MA). *Program availability:* Part-time, evening/weekend. *Entrance requirements:* For master's, interview, letters of recommendation, essay. Additional exam requirements/recommendations for international students: Required—TOEFL. Electronic applications accepted. *Expenses:* Contact institution.

Pontifical Catholic University of Puerto Rico, College of Education, Program in Counselor Education, Ponce, PR 00717-0777. Offers M Ed. *Degree requirements:* For master's, comprehensive exam, thesis (for some programs). *Entrance requirements:* For master's, GRE, 2 letters of recommendation, interview, minimum GPA of 2.75.

Prairie View A&M University, College of Education, Department of Educational Leadership and Counseling, Prairie View, TX 77446. Offers M Ed, MA, MS Ed, PhD. *Accreditation:* NCATE. *Program availability:* Part-time, evening/weekend. *Faculty:* 13 full-time (5 women), 2 part-time/adjunct (1 woman). *Students:* 31 full-time (19 women), 167 part-time (129 women); includes 188 minority (177 Black or African American, non-Hispanic/Latino; 11 Hispanic/Latino), 4 international. Average age 37. 46 applicants, 83% accepted, 30 enrolled. In 2018, 87 master's, 4 doctorates awarded. *Degree requirements:* For master's, thesis optional; for doctorate, comprehensive exam, thesis/dissertation. *Entrance requirements:* For master's, GRE General Test, 3 letters of reference, minimum undergraduate GPA of 2.5; for doctorate, GRE General Test, 3 letters of reference. Additional exam requirements/recommendations for international students: Required—TOEFL (minimum score 550 paper-based; 79 iBT). *Application deadline:* For fall admission, 5/1 priority date for domestic students, 5/1 for international students; for spring admission, 10/1 priority date for domestic students, 9/1 for international students; for summer admission, 3/1 for domestic students, 2/1 for international students. Applications are processed on a rolling basis. Application fee: $50. Electronic applications accepted. *Expenses: Tuition, area resident:* Full-time $3172; part-time $317 per credit. Tuition, state resident: full-time $3172; part-time $317 per credit. Tuition, nonresident: full-time $7965; part-time $796 per credit. *Required fees:* $4847; $485 per credit. *Financial support:* Career-related internships or fieldwork available. Support available to part-time students. Financial award application deadline: 4/1; financial award applicants required to submit FAFSA. *Faculty research:* Mentoring, personality assessment, holistic/humanistic education. *Unit head:* Dr. Maduakolam Ireh, Department Head, 936-261-3565, Fax: 936-261-3617, E-mail: maireh@pvamu.edu. *Application contact:* Pauline Walker, Administrative Assistant II, Research and Graduate Studies, 936-261-3521, Fax: 936-261-3529, E-mail: gradadmissions@pvamu.edu.

Prescott College, Graduate Programs, Program in Education, Prescott, AZ 86301. Offers early childhood education (MA); early childhood special education (MA); education (MA); elementary education (MA); environmental education leadership and administration (MA); equine-assisted learning (MA); school guidance counseling (MA); secondary education (MA); special education: learning disabilities (MA); special education: mental retardation (MA); special education: serious emotional disabilities (MA); student-directed independent study (MA); sustainability education (PhD). *Program availability:* Part-time, online learning. *Degree requirements:* For master's, thesis,

fieldwork or internship, practicum; for doctorate, thesis/dissertation. *Entrance requirements:* For master's, 2 letters of recommendation, resume; for doctorate, 3 letters of recommendation, resume, official transcripts, personal statement, program proposal. Additional exam requirements/recommendations for international students: Required—TOEFL (minimum score 500 paper-based). Electronic applications accepted.

Providence College, Program in Counseling, Providence, RI 02918. Offers M Ed. *Program availability:* Part-time, evening/weekend. *Degree requirements:* For master's, comprehensive exam, portfolio. *Entrance requirements:* Additional exam requirements/recommendations for international students: Required—TOEFL (minimum score 577 paper-based; 90 iBT).

Purdue University Fort Wayne, College of Professional Studies, School of Education, Fort Wayne, IN 46805-1499. Offers couple and family counseling (MS Ed); educational leadership (MS Ed); elementary education (MS Ed); school counseling (MS Ed); secondary education (MS Ed); special education (MS Ed, Certificate). *Accreditation:* NCATE. *Program availability:* Part-time. *Entrance requirements:* For master's, minimum GPA of 2.5, three professional letters of recommendation. Additional exam requirements/recommendations for international students: Required—TOEFL (minimum score 550 paper-based; 79 iBT). *Faculty research:* International faculty, gender in Burmese refugee narratives, planning effective instruction.

Purdue University Northwest, Graduate Studies Office, School of Education, Program in Counseling, Hammond, IN 46323-2094. Offers human services (MS Ed); mental health counseling (MS Ed); school counseling (MS Ed). *Accreditation:* ACA. *Entrance requirements:* Additional exam requirements/recommendations for international students: Required—TOEFL.

Queens College of the City University of New York, Division of Education, Department of Educational and Community Programs, Queens, NY 11367-1597. Offers bilingual pupil personnel (AC); counselor education (MS Ed); mental health counseling (MS); school building leader (AC); school district leader (AC); school psychologist (MS Ed); special education-childhood education (AC); special education-early childhood (MS Ed); teacher of special education 1-6 (MS Ed); teacher of special education birth-2 (MS Ed); teaching students with disabilities, grades 7-12 (MS Ed, AC). *Program availability:* Part-time. *Faculty:* 19 full-time (13 women), 53 part-time/adjunct (31 women). *Students:* 90 full-time (83 women), 380 part-time (316 women); includes 217 minority (42 Black or African American, non-Hispanic/Latino; 1 American Indian or Alaska Native, non-Hispanic/Latino; 53 Asian, non-Hispanic/Latino; 114 Hispanic/Latino; 7 Two or more races, non-Hispanic/Latino), 6 international. Average age 29. 470 applicants, 65% accepted, 236 enrolled. In 2018, 164 master's, 59 other advanced degrees awarded. *Degree requirements:* For master's, Research project; for AC, internship, research project. *Entrance requirements:* For master's, minimum GPA of 3.0. Additional exam requirements/recommendations for international students: Required—TOEFL, IELTS. *Application deadline:* For fall admission, 3/1 for domestic students. Applications are processed on a rolling basis. Application fee: $125. Electronic applications accepted. *Financial support:* Fellowships available. Financial award application deadline: 4/1; financial award applicants required to submit FAFSA. *Unit head:* Dr. Emilia Lopez, Chair, 718-997-5250, E-mail: emilia.lopez@qc.cuny.edu. *Application contact:* Elizabeth D'Amico-Ramirez, Assistant Director of Graduate Admissions, 718-997-5203, E-mail: elizabeth.damicoramirez@qc.cuny.edu.

Quincy University, Master of Science in Education Counseling Program, Quincy, IL 62301-2699. Offers clinical mental health counseling (MS Ed); college student personnel (MS Ed); school counseling (MS Ed). *Program availability:* Part-time, evening/weekend. *Degree requirements:* For master's, comprehensive exam, practicum, internship. *Entrance requirements:* For master's, MAT or GRE. Additional exam requirements/recommendations for international students: Required—TOEFL (minimum score 550 paper-based; 79 iBT). Electronic applications accepted.

Radford University, College of Graduate Studies and Research, Program in Counselor Education, Radford, VA 24142. Offers MS. *Accreditation:* ACA; NCATE. *Program availability:* Part-time, evening/weekend. *Faculty:* 5 full-time (3 women), 2 part-time/adjunct (both women). *Students:* 53 full-time (45 women), 8 part-time (7 women); includes 11 minority (5 Black or African American, non-Hispanic/Latino; 1 American Indian or Alaska Native, non-Hispanic/Latino; 5 Two or more races, non-Hispanic/Latino). Average age 26. 46 applicants, 89% accepted, 22 enrolled. In 2018, 26 master's awarded. *Degree requirements:* For master's, comprehensive exam, thesis optional. *Entrance requirements:* For master's, GRE or MAT, minimum GPA of 2.75, 3 letters of reference, personal essay, resume, official transcripts. Additional exam requirements/recommendations for international students: Required—TOEFL (minimum score 550 paper-based; 79 iBT), IELTS (minimum score 6.5). *Application deadline:* For fall admission, 2/15 priority date for domestic students, 12/1 for international students; for spring admission, 7/1 for international students; for summer admission, 2/15 priority date for domestic students. Applications are processed on a rolling basis. Application fee: $50. Electronic applications accepted. *Expenses:* Tuition, area resident: Full-time $8915; part-time $371 per credit hour. Tuition, state resident: full-time $8915; part-time $371 per credit hour. Tuition, nonresident: full-time $17,441. *Required fees:* $3288; $138 per credit hour. *Financial support:* In 2018–19, 5 students received support, including 3 teaching assistantships (averaging $11,000 per year); career-related internships or fieldwork, scholarships/grants, and unspecified assistantships also available. Support available to part-time students. Financial award application deadline: 3/1; financial award applicants required to submit FAFSA. *Unit head:* Dr. Alan Forrest, Chair, 540-831-5214, Fax: 540-831-6755, E-mail: vgoad4@radford.edu. *Application contact:* Dr. Alan Forrest, Chair, 540-831-5214, Fax: 540-831-6755, E-mail: vgoad4@radford.edu.
Website: http://www.radford.edu/content/cehd/home/counselor-education.html

Regent University, Graduate School, School of Psychology and Counseling, Virginia Beach, VA 23464-9800. Offers clinical mental health counseling (MA); clinical psychology (Psy D); counseling and psychological studies - clinical (PhD); counseling and psychological studies - research (PhD); counseling studies (CAGS); counselor education and supervision (PhD); general psychology (MS); human services (MA), including addictions counseling, Biblical counseling, Christian counseling, conflict and mediation ministry, criminal justice and ministry, grief counseling, human services counseling, human services for student affairs, life coaching, marriage and family ministry, trauma and crisis counseling; marriage, couple, and family counseling (MA); pastoral counseling (MA); school counseling (MA); M Div/MA; M Ed/MA; MBA/MA. *Accreditation:* ACA; APA (one or more programs are accredited). *Program availability:* Part-time, evening/weekend, 100% online, blended/hybrid learning. *Degree requirements:* For master's, thesis or alternative, internship, practicum, written competency exam; for doctorate, thesis/dissertation or alternative. *Entrance requirements:* For master's, GRE General Test (including writing exam) or MAT, minimum undergraduate GPA of 3.0, resume, transcripts, writing sample, personal goals statement; for doctorate, GRE General Test (including writing exam), minimum undergraduate GPA of 3.0, graduate 3.5; writing sample; 3 recommendations; resume; college transcripts; personal goals statement. Additional exam requirements/recommendations for international students: Required—TOEFL (minimum score 577 paper-based). Electronic applications accepted. *Expenses:* Contact institution. *Faculty research:* Marriage enrichment, clinical psychology, troubled youth, faith and learning, trauma.

Regis University, Rueckert-Hartman College for Health Professions, Denver, CO 80221-1099. Offers advanced practice nurse (DNP); counseling (MA); counseling children and adolescents (Post-Graduate Certificate); counseling military families (Post-Graduate Certificate); depth psychotherapy (Post-Graduate Certificate); fellowship in orthopedic manual physical therapy (Certificate); health care business management (Certificate); health care quality and patient safety (Certificate); health industry leadership (MBA); health services administration (MS); marriage and family therapy (MA, Post-Graduate Certificate); neonatal nurse practitioner (MSN); nursing education (MSN); nursing leadership (MSN); occupational therapy (OTD); pharmacy (Pharm D); physical therapy (DPT). *Accreditation:* ACPE. *Program availability:* Part-time, evening/weekend, 100% online, blended/hybrid learning. *Degree requirements:* For master's, thesis (for some programs), internship. *Entrance requirements:* For master's, official transcript reflecting baccalaureate degree awarded from regionally-accredited college or university. Additional exam requirements/recommendations for international students: Required—TOEFL (minimum score 550 paper-based; 82 iBT). Electronic applications accepted. *Expenses:* Contact institution. *Faculty research:* Normal and pathological balance and gait research, normal/pathological upper limb motor control/biomechanics, exercise energy/metabolism research, optical treatment protocols for therapeutic modalities.

Rhode Island College, School of Graduate Studies, Feinstein School of Education and Human Development, Department of Counseling, Educational Leadership, and School Psychology, Providence, RI 02908-1991. Offers advanced counseling (CGS); agency counseling (MA); clinical mental health counseling (MS); co-occurring disorders (MA, CGS); educational leadership (M Ed); mental health counseling (CAGS); school counseling (MA); school psychology (CAGS); teacher leadership (CGS). *Accreditation:* ACA; NCATE. *Program availability:* Part-time, evening/weekend. *Faculty:* 12 full-time (9 women), 5 part-time/adjunct (4 women). *Students:* 45 full-time (35 women), 47 part-time (39 women); includes 12 minority (2 Black or African American, non-Hispanic/Latino; 10 Hispanic/Latino). Average age 30. In 2018, 13 master's, 27 other advanced degrees awarded. *Degree requirements:* For master's and other advanced degree, comprehensive exam (for some programs), thesis (for some programs). *Entrance requirements:* For master's, GRE General Test or MAT, undergraduate transcripts; minimum undergraduate GPA of 3.0; for other advanced degree, GRE or MAT (for most programs), undergraduate transcripts; minimum undergraduate GPA of 3.0; 3 letters of recommendation; current resume. Additional exam requirements/recommendations for international students: Required—TOEFL (minimum score 550 paper-based; 80 iBT). *Application deadline:* For fall admission, 3/1 for domestic students; for spring admission, 11/1 for domestic students. Applications are processed on a rolling basis. Application fee: $50. Electronic applications accepted. *Expenses:* Tuition, area resident: Part-time $407 per credit. Tuition, nonresident: part-time $792 per credit. *Required fees:* $29 per credit. $100 per semester. *Financial support:* Teaching assistantships, career-related internships or fieldwork, Federal Work-Study, scholarships/grants, health care benefits, and unspecified assistantships available. Support available to part-time students. Financial award application deadline: 5/15; financial award applicants required to submit FAFSA. *Unit head:* Dr. John Eagle, Chair, 401-456-8023. *Application contact:* Dr. John Eagle, Chair, 401-456-8023.
Website: http://www.ric.edu/counselingEducationalLeadershipSchoolPsychology/index.php

Richmont Graduate University, School of Counseling, Atlanta, GA 30339. Offers clinical mental health counseling (MA); marriage and family therapy (MA). *Accreditation:* ACA. *Program availability:* Part-time, evening/weekend. *Degree requirements:* For master's, comprehensive exam, thesis optional. *Entrance requirements:* For master's, GRE or MAT. Electronic applications accepted.

Rider University, College of Education and Human Services, Program in Counseling Services, Lawrenceville, NJ 08648-3001. Offers clinical mental health counseling (MA); director of counseling services (Ed S); school counseling (MA, Certificate, Ed S). *Accreditation:* ACA; NCATE. *Program availability:* Part-time, evening/weekend. *Students:* 63 full-time (55 women), 66 part-time (55 women); includes 41 minority (15 Black or African American, non-Hispanic/Latino; 1 American Indian or Alaska Native, non-Hispanic/Latino; 6 Asian, non-Hispanic/Latino; 19 Hispanic/Latino). Average age 30. 85 applicants, 59% accepted, 27 enrolled. In 2018, 35 master's, 16 other advanced degrees awarded. *Degree requirements:* For master's, comprehensive exam, research project; for other advanced degree, specialty seminar. *Entrance requirements:* For master's, GRE or MAT, interview, resume, 2 letters of recommendation; for other advanced degree, GRE or MAT. Additional exam requirements/recommendations for international students: Required—TOEFL (minimum score 540 paper-based; 79 iBT). *Application deadline:* For fall admission, 2/1 priority date for domestic students, 6/1 priority date for international students; for spring admission, 10/1 priority date for domestic students, 11/1 priority date for international students. Applications are processed on a rolling basis. Application fee: $50. Electronic applications accepted. *Expenses:* Tuition: Full-time $850; part-time $850 per credit hour. *Required fees:* $50; $50 per course. Tuition and fees vary according to program. *Financial support:* Applicants required to submit FAFSA. *Faculty research:* Diversity in counseling. *Unit head:* C. Emmanuel Ahia, Director, Ed S Counseling Services, 609-896-5339, E-mail: eahia@rider.edu. *Application contact:* Jamie L Mitchell, Director of Graduate Admissions, 609-896-5036, Fax: 609-895-5680, E-mail: jmitchell@rider.edu.

Rivier University, School of Graduate Studies, Department of Education, Nashua, NH 03060. Offers curriculum and instruction (M Ed); early childhood education (M Ed); educational administration (M Ed); educational studies (M Ed); elementary education (M Ed); elementary education and general special education (M Ed); emotional and behavioral disorders (M Ed); general social education (M Ed); leadership and learning (Ed D, CAGS); learning disabilities (M Ed); learning disabilities and reading (M Ed); mental health counseling (MA); reading (M Ed); school counseling (M Ed). *Program availability:* Part-time, evening/weekend. *Degree requirements:* For master's, comprehensive exam (for some programs), internships. *Entrance requirements:* For master's, GRE General Test or MAT.

Roberts Wesleyan College, Graduate Psychology Programs, Rochester, NY 14624-1997. Offers clinical/school psychology (Psy D); school counseling (MS); school psychology (MS). *Program availability:* Part-time, evening/weekend. *Degree requirements:* For master's, comprehensive exam, PRAXIS II (for school psychology). *Entrance requirements:* For master's, GRE. Electronic applications accepted. Application fee is waived when completed online. *Faculty research:* Counselor supervision, forgiveness, community health psychology, applied research in group process.

Rollins College, Hamilton Holt School, Master of Arts in Counseling Program, Winter Park, FL 32789-4499. Offers clinical mental health counseling (MA). *Accreditation:* ACA. *Program availability:* Part-time, evening/weekend. *Degree requirements:* For master's, satisfactory completion of pre-practicum, practicum, and internship (1,000 hours total). *Entrance requirements:* For master's, GRE General Test or MAT, official transcripts, minimum GPA of 3.0, three letters of recommendation, essay, current resume. Additional exam requirements/recommendations for international students: Required—TOEFL (minimum score 550 paper-based; 80 iBT). *Expenses:* Contact institution.

Counselor Education

Rosemont College, Schools of Graduate and Professional Studies, Counseling Psychology Program, Rosemont, PA 19010-1699. Offers human services (MA); school counseling (MA). *Program availability:* Part-time, evening/weekend. *Degree requirements:* For master's, thesis or alternative, practicum. *Entrance requirements:* For master's, minimum undergraduate GPA of 3.0, 3 letters of recommendation. Additional exam requirements/recommendations for international students: Required—TOEFL. Electronic applications accepted. Application fee is waived when completed online. *Expenses:* Contact institution. *Faculty research:* Addictions counseling.

Rowan University, Graduate School, College of Education, Department of Educational Services and Leadership, Program in Counseling in Educational Settings, Glassboro, NJ 08028-1701. Offers MA. *Accreditation:* ACA. *Program availability:* Part-time, evening/weekend. *Degree requirements:* For master's, thesis. *Entrance requirements:* For master's, GRE General Test, minimum GPA of 2.8, 1 year of teaching experience. Additional exam requirements/recommendations for international students: Required—TOEFL. Electronic applications accepted.

Rutgers University–New Brunswick, Graduate School of Education, Department of Educational Psychology, Programs in School Counseling and Counseling Psychology, Piscataway, NJ 08854-8097. Offers Ed M. *Accreditation:* ACA. *Program availability:* Part-time, evening/weekend. *Entrance requirements:* For master's, GRE General Test, 3 letters of recommendation. Additional exam requirements/recommendations for international students: Required—TOEFL (minimum score 550 paper-based; 83 iBT). Electronic applications accepted. *Faculty research:* Children and family in cross-cultural context, attachment theory, multicultural counseling, therapy relationship.

Sage Graduate School, Esteves School of Education, Professional School Counseling Program, Troy, NY 12180-4115. Offers MS, Post Master's Certificate. *Accreditation:* NCATE. *Program availability:* Part-time, evening/weekend. *Faculty:* 2 full-time (both women), 9 part-time/adjunct (5 women). *Students:* 41 full-time (30 women), 6 part-time (all women); includes 9 minority (3 Black or African American, non-Hispanic/Latino; 1 American Indian or Alaska Native, non-Hispanic/Latino; 1 Asian, non-Hispanic/Latino; 2 Hispanic/Latino; 2 Two or more races, non-Hispanic/Latino). Average age 25. 52 applicants, 54% accepted, 13 enrolled. In 2018, 20 master's, 7 other advanced degrees awarded. *Entrance requirements:* For master's, application, minimum GPA of 3.0, current resume, essay, official transcripts, 2 letters of recommendation. Applicants must have earned at least 9 credits in Social Science and have completed the following pre-requisite courses: Statistics, Educational Foundations and Developmental Psychology. Additional exam requirements/recommendations for international students: Required—TOEFL (minimum score 550 paper-based). *Application deadline:* Applications are processed on a rolling basis. Application fee: $30. *Financial support:* Fellowships, research assistantships, scholarships/grants, and unspecified assistantships available. Financial award application deadline: 3/1; financial award applicants required to submit FAFSA. *Faculty research:* Roles and responsibilities of guidance personnel, projections of need for guidance counselors. *Unit head:* Dr. John Pelizza, Dean, Esteves School of Education, 518-244-2051, Fax: 518-244-2334, E-mail: pelizj@sage.edu. *Application contact:* Peter Stapleton, Assistant Professor, PEP, Esteves School of Education, 518-244-6883, Fax: 518-244-2334, E-mail: staplp@sage.edu.

St. Bonaventure University, School of Graduate School, School of Education, Program in Counselor Education, St. Bonaventure, NY 14778-2284. Offers community mental health counseling (MS Ed); rehabilitation counseling (MS Ed); school counseling (MS Ed); school counselor (Adv C). *Accreditation:* ACA. *Program availability:* Part-time, evening/weekend, 100% online. *Faculty:* 5 full-time (3 women), 7 part-time/adjunct (5 women). *Students:* 23 full-time (18 women), 132 part-time (105 women); includes 35 minority (14 Black or African American, non-Hispanic/Latino; 1 American Indian or Alaska Native, non-Hispanic/Latino; 2 Asian, non-Hispanic/Latino; 12 Hispanic/Latino; 6 Two or more races, non-Hispanic/Latino). Average age 31. 106 applicants, 100% accepted, 68 enrolled. In 2018, 27 master's, 6 Adv Cs awarded. *Degree requirements:* For master's, comprehensive exam, thesis optional, internship, portfolio; for Adv C, internship. *Entrance requirements:* For master's, statement of intent/writing sample; transcripts from all colleges previously attended; two references; interview; minimum undergraduate GPA of 3.0; for Adv C, interview, writing sample, minimum undergraduate GPA of 3.0, two letters of recommendation, master's degree, transcripts from all colleges previously attended. Additional exam requirements/recommendations for international students: Required—TOEFL (minimum score 550 paper-based; 79 iBT). *Application deadline:* For fall admission, 3/15 priority date for domestic students, 2/1 priority date for international students; for spring admission, 10/15 priority date for domestic students, 7/1 priority date for international students. Applications are processed on a rolling basis. Application fee: $0. Electronic applications accepted. *Financial support:* Scholarships/grants, health care benefits, and unspecified assistantships available. Financial award application deadline: 4/15; financial award applicants required to submit FAFSA. *Faculty research:* Therapeutic relationship, live supervision and the impacts for counseling interns and their clients. *Unit head:* Dr. LaToya Pierce, Director, 716-375-2038, Fax: 716-375-2360, E-mail: lpierce@sbu.edu. *Application contact:* Matthew Retchless, Director of Graduate Admissions, 716-375-2021, Fax: 716-375-4015, E-mail: gradsch@sbu.edu.
Website: http://www.sbu.edu/academics/msed-in-school-counseling

St. Cloud State University, School of Graduate Studies, School of Education, Department of Educational Leadership and Higher Education, Program in College Counseling and Student Development, St. Cloud, MN 56301-4498. Offers MS. *Degree requirements:* For master's, comprehensive exam, thesis or alternative. *Entrance requirements:* For master's, GRE General Test, minimum GPA of 2.75. Additional exam requirements/recommendations for international students: Required—Michigan English Language Assessment Battery; Recommended—TOEFL (minimum score 550 paper-based), IELTS (minimum score 6.5). Electronic applications accepted.

St. John's University, The School of Education, Department of Counselor Education, Program in School Counseling, Queens, NY 11439. Offers MS Ed, Adv C. Master's program admits in fall only; Advanced Certificate in spring only. *Accreditation:* ACA (one or more programs are accredited). *Entrance requirements:* For master's, 2 letters of recommendation, interview; for Adv C, official master's transcripts, statement of purpose. Electronic applications accepted. *Faculty research:* Counseling/client engagement; counseling accountability; pipe-line mentoring from grade 4 to college; stress, coping and resilience for children and adults; helping parents deal with aggressive children; effects of bullying and cyber bullying with adolescents; creative connections through the arts.

Saint Mary's College of California, Kalmanovitz School of Education, Program in Counseling, Moraga, CA 94575. Offers career counseling (MA); college student services (Credential); general counseling (MA); marriage and family therapy (MA); pupil personnel services (Credential), including school counseling, school psychology; school counseling (MA); school psychology (MA). *Program availability:* Part-time, evening/weekend. *Degree requirements:* For master's, thesis or alternative. *Entrance requirements:* For master's, interview, minimum GPA of 3.0. *Faculty research:* Counselor training effectiveness, multicultural development, empathy, the interface of spirituality and psychotherapy, gender issues.

St. Mary's University, Graduate Studies, Program in Counselor Education and Supervision, San Antonio, TX 78228. Offers PhD. *Accreditation:* ACA. *Program availability:* Part-time, evening/weekend. *Students:* 16 full-time (13 women), 37 part-time (26 women); includes 21 minority (7 Black or African American, non-Hispanic/Latino; 1 American Indian or Alaska Native, non-Hispanic/Latino; 3 Asian, non-Hispanic/Latino; 10 Hispanic/Latino), 12 international. Average age 41. 24 applicants, 67% accepted, 12 enrolled. In 2018, 5 doctorates awarded. *Degree requirements:* For doctorate, comprehensive exam, thesis/dissertation, internship. *Entrance requirements:* For doctorate, GRE General Test, master's degree in counseling or related area from accredited college or university; recommendations from past employers relating to professional counseling experience, as well as from faculties of previous undergraduate/graduate studies; recommendation from Graduate Admissions Committee. Additional exam requirements/recommendations for international students: Required—TOEFL (minimum score 550 paper-based; 80 iBT), IELTS (minimum score 6). *Application deadline:* For fall admission, 7/1 for domestic students; for spring admission, 11/15 for domestic students; for summer admission, 4/1 for domestic students. Applications are processed on a rolling basis. Application fee: $0. Electronic applications accepted. *Expenses: Tuition:* Full-time $16,830; part-time $935 per credit hour. *Required fees:* $1055. Tuition and fees vary according to program. *Financial support:* Fellowships, research assistantships, career-related internships or fieldwork, Federal Work-Study, institutionally sponsored loans, scholarships/grants, health care benefits, and unspecified assistantships available. Financial award application deadline: 3/31; financial award applicants required to submit FAFSA. *Faculty research:* Palliative care, neuroscience of psychology and religion, cranial electrotherapy, EEG biofeedback. *Unit head:* Dr. Melanie Harper, Program Director, 210-438-6400, E-mail: mharper@stmarytx.edu. *Application contact:* Kim Thornton, Director of Graduate Admission, 210-436-3101, E-mail: kthornton@stmarytx.edu.
Website: https://www.stmarytx.edu/academics/programs/doctor-counselor-education-supervision/

Saint Peter's University, Graduate Programs in Education, Program in School Counseling, Jersey City, NJ 07306-5997. Offers MA, Certificate.

St. Thomas University, Biscayne College, Department of Social Sciences and Counseling, Program in Guidance and Counseling, Miami Gardens, FL 33054-6459. Offers MS, Post-Master's Certificate. *Program availability:* Part-time, evening/weekend. *Degree requirements:* For master's, comprehensive exam. *Entrance requirements:* For master's, interview, minimum GPA of 3.0 or GRE. Additional exam requirements/recommendations for international students: Required—TOEFL (minimum score 550 paper-based; 79 iBT). Electronic applications accepted.

Saint Xavier University, Graduate Studies, School of Education, Program in Counseling, Chicago, IL 60655-3105. Offers MA. *Degree requirements:* For master's, practicum, internship. *Entrance requirements:* For master's, 3 letters of recommendation, interview. Additional exam requirements/recommendations for international students: Required—TOEFL. Electronic applications accepted.

Salem College, Graduate Studies, Winston-Salem, NC 27101. Offers art education (MAT); elementary education (M Ed, MAT); language and literacy (M Ed); middle school education (MAT); organ (MM); piano (MM); school counseling (M Ed); second language studies (MAT); secondary education (MAT); special education (M Ed, MAT). *Accreditation:* NCATE. *Program availability:* Part-time, evening/weekend, online learning. *Degree requirements:* For master's, practicum (MAT), action research project (M Ed). *Entrance requirements:* For master's, minimum GPA of 3.0, two academic/professional recommendations, acceptable criminal background check. Additional exam requirements/recommendations for international students: Recommended—TOEFL. Electronic applications accepted. *Faculty research:* Teacher professional development, adolescent literacy, instructional technology.

Salem State University, School of Graduate Studies, Program in School Counseling, Salem, MA 01970-5353. Offers M Ed. *Accreditation:* NCATE. *Program availability:* Part-time, evening/weekend. *Entrance requirements:* For master's, GRE or MAT. Additional exam requirements/recommendations for international students: Required—TOEFL (minimum score 550 paper-based; 80 iBT) or IELTS (minimum score 5.5).

Sam Houston State University, College of Education, Department of Counseling, Huntsville, TX 77341. Offers M Ed, MA, PhD. *Accreditation:* NCATE. *Program availability:* Part-time, online learning. *Degree requirements:* For master's, thesis optional; for doctorate, comprehensive exam, thesis/dissertation. *Entrance requirements:* For master's, GRE General Test, 3.0 GPA, Three References, Essay, Face-to-Face interview; for doctorate, On-site interview, on-site professional presentation, and on-site writing prompt, Personal statement, Five References, Master's Degree with 3.5 GPA. Additional exam requirements/recommendations for international students: Required—TOEFL (minimum score 550 paper-based; 79 iBT), IELTS (minimum score 6.5). Electronic applications accepted. *Faculty research:* Family counseling, career counseling, business emergent counseling.

San Diego State University, Graduate and Research Affairs, College of Education, Department of Counseling and School Psychology, San Diego, CA 92182. Offers MS. *Accreditation:* NCATE. *Program availability:* Evening/weekend. *Degree requirements:* For master's, comprehensive exam (for some programs), thesis (for some programs). *Entrance requirements:* For master's, GRE General Test, interview, letters of reference. Additional exam requirements/recommendations for international students: Required—TOEFL. Electronic applications accepted. *Faculty research:* Multicultural and cross-cultural counseling and training, AIDS counseling.

San Jose State University, Program in Counselor Education, San Jose, CA 95192-0001. Offers MA. *Accreditation:* NCATE. *Program availability:* Evening/weekend. *Degree requirements:* For master's, thesis or alternative. Electronic applications accepted.

Santa Clara University, School of Education and Counseling Psychology, Santa Clara, CA 95053. Offers alternative and correctional education (Certificate); counseling (MA); counseling psychology (MA); educational leadership (MA); interdisciplinary education (MA); teaching + clear teaching certificate for catholic school teachers (MAT); teaching + teaching credential (mattc) - multiple subjects (MAT); teaching + teaching credential (mattc) - single subjects (MAT). *Program availability:* Part-time, online learning. *Faculty:* 31 full-time (19 women), 35 part-time/adjunct (24 women). *Students:* 291 full-time (235 women), 298 part-time (238 women); includes 301 minority (15 Black or African American, non-Hispanic/Latino; 1 American Indian or Alaska Native, non-Hispanic/Latino; 87 Asian, non-Hispanic/Latino; 146 Hispanic/Latino; 52 Two or more races, non-Hispanic/Latino), 44 international. Average age 31. 219 applicants, 79% accepted, 143 enrolled. In 2018, 223 master's awarded. *Entrance requirements:* For master's, Statement of purpose, resume or cv, official transcript; other requirements vary by degree. Additional exam requirements/recommendations for international students: Required—TOEFL (minimum score 90 iBT), IELTS (minimum score 6.5), A TOEFL score of 90 or above or IELTS score of 6.5 or above is required for international students. *Application deadline:* For fall admission, 9/23 for domestic students; for winter admission, 1/6 for domestic students. Applications are processed on a rolling basis. Application fee: $50. Electronic applications accepted. *Financial support:* Fellowships, Federal Work-Study, and scholarships/grants available. Support available to part-time

students. Financial award applicants required to submit FAFSA. *Unit head:* Dr. Sabrina Zirkel, Dean, 408-551-3074, Fax: 408-554-4367, E-mail: szirkel@scu.edu. *Application contact:* Victoria Rodriguez, Graduate Admissions Advisor, 408-554-4723, Fax: 408-554-4367, E-mail: vlrodriguez@scu.edu.
Website: http://www.scu.edu/ecp/

Seattle Pacific University, Master of Education in School Counseling Program, Seattle, WA 98119-1997. Offers M Ed, Certificate. *Accreditation:* ACA; NCATE. *Program availability:* Part-time. *Students:* 53 full-time (46 women), 34 part-time (27 women); includes 23 minority (2 Black or African American, non-Hispanic/Latino; 1 American Indian or Alaska Native, non-Hispanic/Latino; 12 Asian, non-Hispanic/Latino; 4 Hispanic/Latino; 1 Native Hawaiian or other Pacific Islander, non-Hispanic/Latino; 3 Two or more races, non-Hispanic/Latino), 4 international. Average age 29. 65 applicants, 71% accepted, 24 enrolled. In 2018, 19 master's awarded. *Degree requirements:* For master's, year-long internship. *Entrance requirements:* For master's, GRE General Test or MAT, copy of teaching certificate; official transcript(s) from each college/university attended; resume; personal statement, including long-term professional goals (maximum of 500 words); 2 letters of recommendation. Additional exam requirements/recommendations for international students: Required—TOEFL (minimum score 550 paper-based), IELTS (minimum score 7). *Application deadline:* For fall admission, 4/1 priority date for domestic students. Application fee: $50. Electronic applications accepted. *Expenses:* Contact institution. *Financial support:* Scholarships/grants available. Financial award applicants required to submit FAFSA. *Unit head:* Dr. June Hyun, Chair, 206-281-2671, Fax: 206-281-2756, E-mail: jhyun@spu.edu. *Application contact:* Dr. June Hyun, Chair, 206-281-2671, Fax: 206-281-2756, E-mail: jhyun@spu.edu.
Website: http://spu.edu/academics/school-of-education/graduate-programs/masters-programs/school-counseling-med/program-outline

Seattle Pacific University, PhD in Counselor Education Program, Seattle, WA 98119-1997. Offers PhD. *Students:* 7 part-time (5 women); includes 3 minority (2 Asian, non-Hispanic/Latino; 1 Two or more races, non-Hispanic/Latino). Average age 35. 1 applicant, 100% accepted, 1 enrolled. In 2018, 1 doctorate awarded. *Entrance requirements:* For doctorate, GRE (minimum revised score of 153 Verbal, 152 Quantitative, taken within five years of application; minimum combined score of 1200 on old test), official transcripts, personal statement, four recent letters of recommendation, writing sample, resume. *Application deadline:* For fall admission, 8/15 for domestic students; for winter admission, 11/15 for domestic students; for spring admission, 2/15 for domestic students; for summer admission, 5/15 for domestic students. Application fee: $50. *Unit head:* Munyi Shea, Chair, 206-281-2369, E-mail: mshea@spu.edu. *Application contact:* Munyi Shea, Chair, 206-281-2369, E-mail: mshea@spu.edu.
Website: https://spu.edu/academics/school-of-education/graduate-programs/doctoral-programs/doctor-of-philosophy-counselor-education-phd

Seattle University, College of Education, Program in Counseling and School Psychology, Seattle, WA 98122-1090. Offers MA, Certificate, Ed S. *Accreditation:* ACA; NCATE. *Program availability:* Part-time, evening/weekend. *Faculty:* 15 full-time (8 women), 13 part-time/adjunct (8 women). *Students:* 118 full-time (107 women), 94 part-time (79 women); includes 76 minority (10 Black or African American, non-Hispanic/Latino; 3 American Indian or Alaska Native, non-Hispanic/Latino; 21 Asian, non-Hispanic/Latino; 30 Hispanic/Latino; 1 Native Hawaiian or other Pacific Islander, non-Hispanic/Latino; 11 Two or more races, non-Hispanic/Latino), 2 international. Average age 29. 239 applicants, 42% accepted, 60 enrolled. In 2018, 47 master's, 25 other advanced degrees awarded. *Degree requirements:* For master's, comprehensive exam. *Entrance requirements:* For master's, interview; GRE, MAT, or minimum GPA of 3.0; related work experience. Additional exam requirements/recommendations for international students: Required—TOEFL. *Application deadline:* For fall admission, 7/1 for domestic students; for winter admission, 10/20 for domestic students; for spring admission, 1/20 for domestic students. Application fee: $55. *Financial support:* In 2018-19, 52 students received support. *Unit head:* Hutch Haney, Director, 206-296-5750, E-mail: schpsy@seattleu.edu. *Application contact:* Janet Shandley, Associate Dean of Graduate Admissions, 206-296-5900, Fax: 206-298-5656, E-mail: grad_admissions@seattleu.edu.
Website: https://www.seattleu.edu/education/psychology/

Seton Hall University, College of Education and Human Services, Department of Professional Psychology and Family Therapy, Program in Counseling Psychology, South Orange, NJ 07079-2697. Offers counseling psychology (PhD); school counseling (MA). *Accreditation:* APA. *Degree requirements:* For doctorate, comprehensive exam, thesis/dissertation, internship. *Entrance requirements:* For master's and doctorate, GRE, interview. *Faculty research:* Vocational indecision, coping skills, cognitive behavioral interventions, vocational development.

Shippensburg University of Pennsylvania, School of Graduate Studies, College of Education and Human Services, Department of Counseling, Shippensburg, PA 17257-2299. Offers college counseling (MS); college student personnel (MS); counselor education and supervision (Ed D); mental health counseling (MS); school counseling (M Ed). *Accreditation:* ACA (one or more programs are accredited); NCATE. *Program availability:* Part-time, evening/weekend, online only, blended/hybrid learning. *Faculty:* 6 full-time (2 women), 6 part-time/adjunct (all women). *Students:* 79 full-time (70 women), 37 part-time (28 women); includes 27 minority (16 Black or African American, non-Hispanic/Latino; 3 Asian, non-Hispanic/Latino; 7 Hispanic/Latino; 1 Two or more races, non-Hispanic/Latino), 3 international. Average age 29. 103 applicants, 40% accepted, 28 enrolled. In 2018, 45 master's awarded. *Degree requirements:* For master's, fieldwork, research project, internship, candidacy; for doctorate, thesis/dissertation, practicum, internship. *Entrance requirements:* For master's, GRE or MAT (for MS if GPA is less than 2.75), minimum GPA of 2.75 (3.0 for M Ed), resume, 3 letter of recommendation forms, one year of relevant work experience, on-campus interview, autobiographical statement; for doctorate, master's degree in counseling or related discipline; resume; three recommendation letters (1 each from employer, clinical supervisor, and prior graduate school faculty member); personal essay; interview with department chair. Additional exam requirements/recommendations for international students: Required—TOEFL (minimum score 550 paper-based; 68 iBT), IELTS (minimum score 6), TOEFL (minimum score 550 paper-based; 68 iBT) or IELTS (minimum score 6). *Application deadline:* Applications are processed on a rolling basis. Application fee: $45. Electronic applications accepted. *Expenses:* Tuition, state resident: part-time $516 per credit. Tuition, nonresident: part-time $750 per credit. *Required fees:* $149 per credit. *Financial support:* In 2018-19, 50 students received support. Career-related internships or fieldwork, scholarships/grants, unspecified assistantships, and resident hall director and student payroll positions available. Support available to part-time students. Financial award application deadline: 3/1; financial award applicants required to submit FAFSA. *Unit head:* Dr. Kurt L. Kraus, Departmental Chair and Program Coordinator, 717-477-1603, Fax: 717-477-4056, E-mail: klkrau@ship.edu. *Application contact:* Maya T. Mapp, Director of Admissions, 717-477-1231, Fax: 717-477-4016, E-mail: mtmapp@ship.edu.
Website: http://www.ship.edu/counsel/

Simon Fraser University, Office of Graduate Studies and Postdoctoral Fellows, Faculty of Education, Program in Counseling Psychology, Burnaby, BC V5A 1S6, Canada.

Offers M Ed, MA. *Program availability:* Part-time, evening/weekend. *Degree requirements:* For master's, comprehensive exam (for some programs), thesis (for some programs), practicum. *Entrance requirements:* For master's, minimum GPA of 3.0 (on scale of 4.33) or 3.33 based on last 60 credits of undergraduate courses. Additional exam requirements/recommendations for international students: Recommended—TOEFL (minimum score 580 paper-based; 93 iBT), IELTS (minimum score 7), TWE (minimum score 5). Electronic applications accepted. *Faculty research:* Cultural and personal dimensions in psychological development, and psychology of working; and career development, social justice and multicultural competence issues, traumatic stress studies, counselor education.

Slippery Rock University of Pennsylvania, Graduate Studies (Recruitment), College of Education, Department of Counseling and Development, Slippery Rock, PA 16057-1383. Offers clinical mental health (MA); school counseling (M Ed); student affairs in higher education (MA); student affairs in higher education with college counseling (MA). *Accreditation:* ACA (one or more programs are accredited); NCATE. *Program availability:* Part-time, evening/weekend. *Faculty:* 8 full-time (5 women), 1 (woman) part-time/adjunct. *Students:* 86 full-time (68 women), 23 part-time (16 women); includes 13 minority (7 Black or African American, non-Hispanic/Latino; 1 Asian, non-Hispanic/Latino; 5 Hispanic/Latino), 1 international. Average age 26. 126 applicants, 58% accepted, 44 enrolled. In 2018, 36 master's awarded. *Degree requirements:* For master's, comprehensive exam, thesis (for some programs). *Entrance requirements:* For master's, GRE General Test or MAT, official transcripts, personal statement, three letters of recommendation, interview. Additional exam requirements/recommendations for international students: Required—TOEFL (minimum score 550 paper-based; 80 iBT). *Application deadline:* For fall admission, 1/15 priority date for domestic and international students. Applications are processed on a rolling basis. Application fee: $25 ($30 for international students). Electronic applications accepted. *Expenses:* Contact institution. *Financial support:* In 2018-19, 55 students received support. Career-related internships or fieldwork, Federal Work-Study, institutionally sponsored loans, scholarships/grants, tuition waivers (partial), and unspecified assistantships available. Support available to part-time students. Financial award application deadline: 5/1; financial award applicants required to submit FAFSA. *Unit head:* Dr. Stacy Jacob, Graduate Coordinator, 724-738-2758, Fax: 724-738-4859, E-mail: stacy.jacob@sru.edu. *Application contact:* Brandi Weber-Mortimer, Director of Graduate Admissions, 724-738-2051, Fax: 724-738-2146, E-mail: graduate.admissions@sru.edu.
Website: http://www.sru.edu/academics/colleges-and-departments/coe/departments/counseling-and-development

South Carolina State University, College of Graduate and Professional Studies, Department of Education, Orangeburg, SC 29117-0001. Offers early childhood education (MAT); education (M Ed); elementary education (M Ed, MAT); English (MAT); general science/biology (MAT); mathematics (MAT); secondary education (M Ed), including biology education, business education, counselor education, English education, home economics education, industrial education, mathematics education, science education, social studies education; special education (M Ed), including emotionally handicapped, learning disabilities, mentally handicapped. *Accreditation:* NCATE. *Program availability:* Part-time, evening/weekend. *Faculty:* 17 full-time (6 women), 12 part-time/adjunct (5 women). *Students:* 42 full-time (32 women), 93 part-time (64 women); includes 121 minority (119 Black or African American, non-Hispanic/Latino; 2 Asian, non-Hispanic/Latino), 2 international. Average age 40. 50 applicants, 98% accepted, 39 enrolled. In 2018, 9 master's awarded. *Degree requirements:* For master's, thesis optional, departmental qualifying exam. *Entrance requirements:* For master's, GRE General Test, NTE, interview, teaching certificate. *Application deadline:* For fall admission, 6/15 priority date for domestic students, 6/15 for international students; for spring admission, 11/1 for domestic and international students. Application fee: $25. Electronic applications accepted. *Expenses:* Tuition, area resident: Full-time $9928; part-time $552 per credit hour. Tuition, state resident: full-time $9928. Tuition, nonresident: full-time $21,038; part-time $1169 per credit hour. *Required fees:* $1532; $85 per credit hour. *Financial support:* Fellowships, career-related internships or fieldwork, Federal Work-Study, and scholarships/grants available. Financial award application deadline: 6/1. *Unit head:* Dr. Charlie Spell, Chair, Department of Education, 803-536-8963, Fax: 803-516-4568, E-mail: cspell@scsu.edu. *Application contact:* Curtis Foskey, Coordinator of Graduate Studies, 803-536-8419, Fax: 803-536-8812, E-mail: cfoskey@scsu.edu.

South Carolina State University, College of Graduate and Professional Studies, Department of Human Services, Orangeburg, SC 29117-0001. Offers counselor education (M Ed); rehabilitation counseling (MA). *Accreditation:* CORE. *Program availability:* Part-time, evening/weekend. *Faculty:* 8 full-time (6 women), 7 part-time/adjunct (6 women). *Students:* 88 full-time (70 women), 23 part-time (18 women); includes 104 minority (all Black or African American, non-Hispanic/Latino). Average age 32. 31 applicants, 90% accepted, 28 enrolled. In 2018, 31 master's awarded. *Degree requirements:* For master's, comprehensive exam (for some programs), departmental qualifying exam, internship. *Entrance requirements:* For master's, GRE, MAT, minimum GPA of 2.7. *Application deadline:* For fall admission, 6/15 priority date for domestic students, 6/15 for international students; for spring admission, 11/1 for domestic and international students. Application fee: $25. Electronic applications accepted. *Expenses:* Tuition, area resident: Full-time $9928; part-time $552 per credit hour. Tuition, state resident: full-time $9928. Tuition, nonresident: full-time $21,038; part-time $1169 per credit hour. *Required fees:* $1532; $85 per credit hour. *Financial support:* Fellowships, career-related internships or fieldwork, scholarships/grants, and unspecified assistantships available. Financial award application deadline: 6/1. *Unit head:* Dr. Michelle Maultsby-Priester, Interim Chair, Department of Human Services, 803-536-7075, Fax: 803-533-3636, E-mail: mmaultsb@scsu.edu. *Application contact:* Curtis Foskey, Coordinator of Graduate Admissions, 803-536-8419, Fax: 803-536-8812, E-mail: cfoskey@scsu.edu.

South Dakota State University, Graduate School, College of Education and Human Sciences, Department of Counseling and Human Development, Brookings, SD 57007. Offers counseling and human resource development (M Ed, MS); human sciences (MS). *Accreditation:* ACA (one or more programs are accredited); NCATE. *Program availability:* Part-time, evening/weekend. *Degree requirements:* For master's, comprehensive exam, thesis (for some programs), oral exams. *Entrance requirements:* For master's, minimum GPA of 2.75. Additional exam requirements/recommendations for international students: Required—TOEFL (minimum score 525 paper-based; 71 iBT). *Faculty research:* Rural mental health, family issues, character education, student affairs, solution focused therapy.

Southeastern Louisiana University, College of Nursing and Health Sciences, Department of Health and Human Sciences, Hammond, LA 70402. Offers communication sciences and disorders (MS); counseling (MS). *Accreditation:* ACA; ASHA; NCATE. *Program availability:* Part-time. *Faculty:* 16 full-time (15 women). *Students:* 96 full-time (90 women), 53 part-time (48 women); includes 40 minority (13 Black or African American, non-Hispanic/Latino; 1 Asian, non-Hispanic/Latino; 14 Hispanic/Latino; 1 Native Hawaiian or other Pacific Islander, non-Hispanic/Latino; 11 Two or more races, non-Hispanic/Latino), 1 international. Average age 28. 179 applicants, 53% accepted, 19 enrolled. In 2018, 48 master's awarded. *Degree*

requirements: For master's, comprehensive exam (for some programs), thesis (for some programs), 25 clock hours of clinical observation (for communication sciences and disorders). *Entrance requirements:* For master's, Counseling: GRE minumum 279; Child Life: GRE; Communication Sciences and Disorders: GRE verbal 138, quantitative 138, writing 3.0, Counseling: minimum GPA of 2.8; Child Life: minimum GPA of 3.25; Communication Sciences and Disorders: minimum 2.75 GPA. Additional exam requirements/recommendations for international students: Required—TOEFL (minimum score 500 paper-based; 61 iBT). *Application deadline:* For fall admission, 3/1 priority date for domestic students, 6/1 priority date for international students; for spring admission, 10/1 priority date for domestic and international students. Applications are processed on a rolling basis. Application fee: $20 ($30 for international students). Electronic applications accepted. *Expenses: Tuition, area resident:* Full-time $6684. Tuition, state resident: full-time $6684. Tuition, nonresident: full-time $19,162. *Required fees:* $2097. *Financial support:* In 2018–19, 84 students received support, including 1 fellowship with tuition reimbursement available (averaging $3,500 per year), 1 research assistantship with tuition reimbursement available (averaging $5,070 per year); career-related internships or fieldwork, Federal Work-Study, institutionally sponsored loans, scholarships/grants, and unspecified assistantships also available. Support available to part-time students. Financial award application deadline: 5/1; financial award applicants required to submit FAFSA. *Faculty research:* Animal assisted therapy and affects on reading outcomes in children, interprofessional education and interprofessional practice, aphasia, play therapy/creative interventions with all populations, school counseling-related issues. *Total annual research expenditures:* $21,657. *Unit head:* Dr. Jacqueline Guendouzi, Department Head, 985-549-2309, Fax: 985-549-3758, E-mail: jguendouzi@southeastern.edu. *Application contact:* Office of Admissions, 985-549-5637, Fax: 985-549-5632, E-mail: admissions@southeastern.edu.
Website: http://www.southeastern.edu/acad_research/depts/hhs/index.html

Southeastern Oklahoma State University, School of Behavioral Sciences, Durant, OK 74701-0609. Offers clinical mental health counseling (MS). *Accreditation:* ACA. *Program availability:* Part-time, evening/weekend. *Degree requirements:* For master's, comprehensive exam, thesis optional. *Entrance requirements:* For master's, GRE General Test, minimum GPA of 3.0 in last 60 hours or 2.75 overall. Additional exam requirements/recommendations for international students: Required—TOEFL (minimum score 550 paper-based; 79 iBT). Electronic applications accepted.

Southeastern Oklahoma State University, School of Education, Durant, OK 74701-0609. Offers math specialist (M Ed); reading specialist (M Ed); school administration (M Ed); school counseling (M Ed). *Accreditation:* NCATE. *Program availability:* Part-time, evening/weekend. *Degree requirements:* For master's, comprehensive exam, thesis optional, portfolio (M Ed). *Entrance requirements:* For master's, GRE General Test (for school counseling), minimum GPA of 3.0 in last 60 hours or 2.75 overall. Additional exam requirements/recommendations for international students: Required—TOEFL (minimum score 550 paper-based; 79 iBT). Electronic applications accepted.

Southeastern University, College of Behavioral and Social Sciences, Lakeland, FL 33801-6099. Offers human services (MA); international community development (MA); marriage and family counseling (MS); professional counseling (MS); school counseling (MS); social work (MSW). *Program availability:* Evening/weekend. Electronic applications accepted.

Southeast Missouri State University, School of Graduate Studies, Leadership, Middle and Secondary Education, Counseling Program, Cape Girardeau, MO 63701-4799. Offers career counseling (MA); mental health counseling (MA); school counseling (MA). *Accreditation:* ACA; NCATE. *Program availability:* Part-time, evening/weekend. *Faculty:* 5 full-time (4 women), 2 part-time/adjunct (both women). *Students:* 35 full-time (29 women), 23 part-time (19 women); includes 7 minority (6 Black or African American, non-Hispanic/Latino; 1 American Indian or Alaska Native, non-Hispanic/Latino), 1 international. Average age 33. 45 applicants, 78% accepted, 26 enrolled. In 2018, 16 master's, 7 other advanced degrees awarded. *Degree requirements:* For master's and Ed S, comprehensive exam, thesis or alternative. *Entrance requirements:* For master's, personal essay, interview, minimum GPA of 3.0; for Ed S, minimum graduate GPA of 3.7. Additional exam requirements/recommendations for international students: Required—TOEFL (minimum score 550 paper-based; 79 iBT), IELTS (minimum score 6), PTE (minimum score 53). *Application deadline:* For fall admission, 3/1 for domestic and international students; for spring admission, 11/21 for domestic students, 10/1 for international students; for summer admission, 3/1 for domestic students. Applications are processed on a rolling basis. Application fee: $30 ($40 for international students). Electronic applications accepted. *Expenses:* Contact institution. *Financial support:* In 2018–19, 9 students received support. Career-related internships or fieldwork, Federal Work-Study, scholarships/grants, traineeships, tuition waivers (full), and unspecified assistantships available. Financial award application deadline: 6/30; financial award applicants required to submit FAFSA. *Faculty research:* School counseling, mental health, career and family counseling, social justice and spirituality in counseling. *Unit head:* Dr. Melissia A. Odegard-Koester, Department Chair, 573-651-2835, E-mail: moedegard@semo.edu. *Application contact:* Dr. Janice Ward, Program Coordinator/Associate Professor, 573-651-2137, Fax: 573-986-6512, E-mail: jward@semo.edu.
Website: http://www.semo.edu/eduleadcounsel/

Southern Adventist University, School of Education and Psychology, Collegedale, TN 37315-0370. Offers clinical mental health counseling (MS); instructional leadership (MS Ed); literacy education (MS Ed); outdoor education (MS Ed); professional school counseling (MS). *Accreditation:* NCATE. *Program availability:* Part-time, evening/weekend, 100% online, blended/hybrid learning. *Faculty:* 11 full-time (8 women), 11 part-time/adjunct (5 women). *Students:* 42 full-time (32 women), 40 part-time (29 women). 13 applicants, 38% accepted, 4 enrolled. *Degree requirements:* For master's, comprehensive exam (for some programs), thesis optional, portfolio (MS) portfolio (MS Ed in outdoor education). *Entrance requirements:* For master's, interview (MS); 9 semester hours of upper-division course work in psychology or related field, including 1 course in psychology research or statistics; 9 semester hours of education (MS Ed). Additional exam requirements/recommendations for international students: Required—TOEFL (minimum score 100 iBT). *Application deadline:* For fall admission, 7/1 priority date for domestic students, 6/1 priority date for international students; for winter admission, 11/1 priority date for domestic students, 10/1 priority date for international students; for spring admission, 4/1 priority date for domestic students, 3/1 priority date for international students. Applications are processed on a rolling basis. Application fee: $40. Electronic applications accepted. *Financial support:* Scholarships/grants and unspecified assistantships available. Support available to part-time students. Financial award application deadline: 4/1; financial award applicants required to submit FAFSA. *Faculty research:* Millennials, spiritual self-awareness, parenting styles, attitudes toward student mental health issues, reliance on social media. *Unit head:* Dr. Tammy Overstreet, Dean, 423-236-2444, Fax: 423-236-1765, E-mail: toverstreet@southern.edu. *Application contact:* Mikhaile Spence, Graduate Program Manager, 423-236-2496, Fax: 423-236-1765, E-mail: maspence@southern.edu.
Website: https://www.southern.edu/academics/edpsych.html

Southern Arkansas University–Magnolia, School of Graduate Studies, Magnolia, AR 71753. Offers agriculture (MS); business administration (MBA), including agribusiness, social entrepreneurship, supply chain management; clinical and mental health

counseling (MS); computer and information sciences (MS), including cyber security and privacy, data science, information technology; gifted and talented (M Ed), including curriculum and instruction, educational administration and supervision, gifted and talented P-8/7-12, instructional specialist P-4; higher, adult and lifelong education (M Ed); kinesiology (M Ed), including coaching; library media and information specialist (M Ed); public administration (MPA); school counseling K-12 (M Ed); student affairs and college counseling (M Ed); teaching (MAT). *Accreditation:* NCATE. *Program availability:* Part-time, 100% online, blended/hybrid learning. *Faculty:* 36 full-time (21 women), 32 part-time/adjunct (15 women). *Students:* 164 full-time (77 women), 762 part-time (510 women); includes 192 minority (163 Black or African American, non-Hispanic/Latino; 7 American Indian or Alaska Native, non-Hispanic/Latino; 13 Asian, non-Hispanic/Latino; 1 Hispanic/Latino; 8 Two or more races, non-Hispanic/Latino), 213 international. Average age 28. 363 applicants, 100% accepted, 237 enrolled. In 2018, 716 master's awarded. *Degree requirements:* For master's, comprehensive exam (for some programs), thesis optional. *Entrance requirements:* For master's, GRE, MAT or GMAT, minimum GPA of 2.5. Additional exam requirements/recommendations for international students: Required—TOEFL (minimum score 550 paper-based), IELTS (minimum score 6). *Application deadline:* For fall admission, 8/1 for domestic and international students; for spring admission, 12/1 for domestic students, 11/15 for international students; for summer admission, 4/1 for domestic students, 5/10 for international students. Applications are processed on a rolling basis. Application fee: $25 ($90 for international students). Electronic applications accepted. *Expenses: Tuition, area resident:* Full-time $5130; part-time $3420 per year. Tuition, state resident: full-time $5130; part-time $3420 per year. Tuition, nonresident: full-time $7866; part-time $5244 per year. *International tuition:* $7866 full-time. *Required fees:* $1052; $710 per unit. Tuition and fees vary according to course load. *Financial support:* Career-related internships or fieldwork, Federal Work-Study, scholarships/grants, tuition waivers (full), and unspecified assistantships available. Financial award applicants required to submit FAFSA. *Faculty research:* Alternative certification for teachers, supervision of instruction, instructional leadership, counseling. *Unit head:* Dr. Kim Bloss, Dean, School of Graduate Studies, 870-235-4150, Fax: 870-235-5227, E-mail: kkbloss@saumag.edu. *Application contact:* Talia Jett, Admissions Coordinator, 870-2355450, Fax: 870-235-5227, E-mail: taliajett@saumag.edu.
Website: http://www.saumag.edu/graduate

Southern Connecticut State University, School of Graduate Studies, School of Education, Department of Counseling and School Psychology, New Haven, CT 06515-1355. Offers community counseling (MS); counseling (Diploma); school counseling (MS); school psychology (MS, Diploma). *Accreditation:* ACA (one or more programs are accredited); NCATE. *Program availability:* Part-time, evening/weekend. *Degree requirements:* For master's, comprehensive exam. *Entrance requirements:* For master's, interview, previous course work in behavioral sciences, minimum QPA of 2.7. Electronic applications accepted.

Southern Methodist University, Simmons School of Education and Human Development, Department of Dispute Resolution and Counseling, Dallas, TX 75275. Offers counseling (MS); dispute resolution (MA, Graduate Certificate); healthcare collaboration and conflict engagement (Graduate Certificate). *Program availability:* Part-time. *Entrance requirements:* For master's, minimum undergraduate GPA of 2.75 (for dispute resolution), 3.0 (for counseling); 3 letters of recommendation. Additional exam requirements/recommendations for international students: Required—TOEFL. Electronic applications accepted.

Southern University and Agricultural and Mechanical College, Graduate School, College of Humanities and Interdisciplinary Studies, School of Education, Department of Counseling and Educational Leadership, Baton Rouge, LA 70813. Offers administration and supervision (M Ed); counselor education (MA); educational leadership (M Ed); mental health counseling (MA). *Accreditation:* ACA; NCATE. *Degree requirements:* For master's, comprehensive exam, thesis optional. *Entrance requirements:* For master's, GRE General Test. Additional exam requirements/recommendations for international students: Required—TOEFL (minimum score 525 paper-based). *Faculty research:* Mental health, computer assisted programs, families relations, head start improvements, careers.

Southwestern Oklahoma State University, College of Professional and Graduate Studies, School of Behavioral Sciences and Education, Specialization in Community Counseling, Weatherford, OK 73096-3098. Offers MS. *Accreditation:* NCATE. *Program availability:* Part-time, evening/weekend, online learning. *Degree requirements:* For master's, exam. *Entrance requirements:* For master's, GRE General Test or minimum undergraduate GPA of 3.0. Additional exam requirements/recommendations for international students: Required—TOEFL (minimum score 550 paper-based), IELTS (minimum score 6.5).

Southwestern Oklahoma State University, College of Professional and Graduate Studies, School of Behavioral Sciences and Education, Specialization in School Counseling, Weatherford, OK 73096-3098. Offers M Ed. M Ed distance learning degree program offered to Oklahoma residents only. *Accreditation:* NCATE. *Program availability:* Part-time, evening/weekend, online learning. *Degree requirements:* For master's, exam. *Entrance requirements:* For master's, GRE General Test or minimum undergraduate GPA of 3.0, portfolio. Additional exam requirements/recommendations for international students: Required—TOEFL (minimum score 550 paper-based), IELTS (minimum score 6.5).

Spalding University, Graduate Studies, College of Education, Programs in Education, Louisville, KY 40203-2188. Offers art teacher education (MAT); business teacher education (MAT); elementary school education (MAT); foreign language (MAT); high school education (MAT); middle school education (MAT); secondary education (MAT); special education (learning and behavioral disorders) (MAT); student guidance counselor (MA); teacher leader (M Ed). *Accreditation:* NCATE. *Program availability:* Part-time, evening/weekend. *Entrance requirements:* For master's, GRE General Test or MAT, interview, letters of recommendation, resume. Additional exam requirements/recommendations for international students: Required—TOEFL (minimum score 535 paper-based). Electronic applications accepted. *Faculty research:* Instructional technology, achievement gap, classroom management, assessment.

Springfield College, Graduate Programs, Programs in Psychology, Springfield, MA 01109-3797. Offers athletic counseling (MS, CAGS); clinical mental health counseling (M Ed, CAGS); counseling psychology (Psy D); general counseling (M Ed); industrial/organizational psychology (M Ed, CAGS); school counseling (M Ed, CAGS); student personnel administration in higher education (M Ed, CAGS). *Accreditation:* APA. *Program availability:* Part-time. *Degree requirements:* For master's, research project, portfolio; for doctorate, dissertation project, 1500 hours of counseling psychology practicum, full-year internship. *Entrance requirements:* For doctorate, GRE. Additional exam requirements/recommendations for international students: Required—TOEFL (minimum score 550 paper-based); Recommended—IELTS (minimum score 7). Electronic applications accepted.

State University of New York at New Paltz, Graduate and Extended Learning School, School of Liberal Arts and Sciences, Department of Psychology, New Paltz, NY 12561. Offers clinical mental health counseling (MS); mental health counseling (AC);

psychological science (MS); school counseling (MS); trauma and disaster mental health (AC). *Program availability:* Part-time, evening/weekend. *Faculty:* 16 full-time (10 women), 4 part-time/adjunct (2 women). *Students:* 68 full-time (55 women), 25 part-time (18 women); includes 20 minority (3 Black or African American, non-Hispanic/Latino; 1 Asian, non-Hispanic/Latino; 13 Hispanic/Latino; 1 Native Hawaiian or other Pacific Islander, non-Hispanic/Latino; 2 Two or more races, non-Hispanic/Latino). 97 applicants, 64% accepted, 38 enrolled. In 2018, 31 master's, 5 other advanced degrees awarded. *Degree requirements:* For master's, comprehensive exam, thesis. *Entrance requirements:* For master's, GRE General Test, minimum GPA of 3.0. Additional exam requirements/recommendations for international students: Required—TOEFL (minimum score 550 paper-based; 80 iBT), IELTS (minimum score 6.5). *Application deadline:* For fall admission, 2/1 priority date for domestic and international students; for spring admission, 11/15 priority date for domestic and international students. Application fee: $50. Electronic applications accepted. *Financial support:* In 2018–19, 6 teaching assistantships with partial tuition reimbursements (averaging $5,000 per year) were awarded. Financial award application deadline: 8/1. *Faculty research:* Disaster mental health, women's objectification, mate selection, cultural psychology, achievement motivation. *Unit head:* Dr. Jonathan Raskin, Chair, 845-257-3471, E-mail: raskinj@newpaltz.edu. *Application contact:* Vika Shock, Director of Graduate Admissions, 845-257-3286, E-mail: gradstudies@newpaltz.edu.
Website: http://www.newpaltz.edu/psychology/

State University of New York at Plattsburgh, School of Education, Health, and Human Services, Department of Counselor Education, Plattsburgh, NY 12901-2681. Offers clinical mental health counseling (MS, Advanced Certificate); school counselor (MS Ed, CAS); student affairs counseling (MS). *Accreditation:* ACA (one or more programs are accredited); TEAC. *Program availability:* Part-time. *Entrance requirements:* For master's, GRE General Test or MAT, minimum GPA of 2.8. Additional exam requirements/recommendations for international students: Required—TOEFL. *Faculty research:* Campus violence, program accreditation, substance abuse, vocational assessment, group counseling, divorce.

State University of New York College at Oneonta, Graduate Programs, Division of Education, Department of Educational Psychology, Counseling and Special Education, Oneonta, NY 13820-4015. Offers school counselor K-12 (MS Ed, CAS); special education (MS Ed). *Accreditation:* NCATE. *Program availability:* Part-time, evening/weekend. *Degree requirements:* For master's, comprehensive exam. *Entrance requirements:* For master's, GRE General Test.

Stephen F. Austin State University, Graduate School, James I. Perkins College of Education, Department of Human Services, Nacogdoches, TX 75962. Offers counseling (MA); school psychology (MA); special education (M Ed); speech-language pathology (MS). *Accreditation:* ACA (one or more programs are accredited); ASHA (one or more programs are accredited); CORE; NCATE. *Degree requirements:* For master's, comprehensive exam, thesis (for some programs). *Entrance requirements:* For master's, GRE General Test, minimum GPA of 2.8. Additional exam requirements/recommendations for international students: Required—TOEFL.

Stephens College, Division of Graduate and Continuing Studies, Columbia, MO 65215-0002. Offers counseling (M Ed), including addictions counseling, clinical mental health counseling, school counseling; health information administration (Postbaccalaureate Certificate); physician assistant studies (MPAS); TV and screenwriting (MFA). *Program availability:* Part-time, evening/weekend, online learning. *Entrance requirements:* For master's, minimum GPA of 3.0 in last 60 hours. Additional exam requirements/recommendations for international students: Required—TOEFL (minimum score 79 iBT). Electronic applications accepted. *Faculty research:* Educational psychology, outcomes assessment.

Stetson University, College of Arts and Sciences, Division of Education, Department of Counselor Education, DeLand, FL 32723. Offers MS. *Accreditation:* ACA. *Program availability:* Evening/weekend. *Faculty:* 6 full-time (5 women), 4 part-time/adjunct (3 women). *Students:* 90 full-time (72 women), 6 part-time (5 women); includes 31 minority (5 Black or African American, non-Hispanic/Latino; 3 American Indian or Alaska Native, non-Hispanic/Latino; 13 Hispanic/Latino; 10 Two or more races, non-Hispanic/Latino), 6 international. Average age 30. 52 applicants, 58% accepted, 21 enrolled. In 2018, 26 master's awarded. *Entrance requirements:* For master's, GRE or MAT, transcripts, three letters of recommendation, group interview. Additional exam requirements/recommendations for international students: Required—TOEFL (minimum score 90 iBT), IELTS (minimum score 7). *Application deadline:* For fall admission, 8/1 priority date for domestic students; for spring admission, 1/1 priority date for domestic students; for summer admission, 5/1 priority date for domestic students. Applications are processed on a rolling basis. Application fee: $50. Electronic applications accepted. *Expenses:* $890 per credit hour. *Financial support:* In 2018–19, 30 students received support. Federal Work-Study, scholarships/grants, unspecified assistantships, and tuition waivers (for staff and dependents) available. Support available to part-time students. Financial award applicants required to submit FAFSA. *Faculty research:* Play therapy, trauma, spirituality and wellness in counseling, gatekeeping and supervision in counselor education, reproductive health in counseling, LBGTQ+ issues in counseling. *Unit head:* Dr. Leila Roach, Chair, 386-822-8992. *Application contact:* Jamie Vanderlip, Director of Admissions for Graduate, Transfer and Adult Programs, 386-822-7100, Fax: 386-822-7112, E-mail: jlvander@stetson.edu.

Suffolk University, College of Arts and Sciences, Department of Psychology, Boston, MA 02108-2770. Offers clinical psychology (PhD); college admission counseling (Certificate); mental health counseling (MS); school counseling (MS). *Accreditation:* APA. *Faculty:* 9 full-time (5 women). *Students:* 37 full-time (34 women), 24 part-time (22 women); includes 12 minority (2 Black or African American, non-Hispanic/Latino; 4 Asian, non-Hispanic/Latino; 3 Hispanic/Latino; 3 Two or more races, non-Hispanic/Latino), 2 international. Average age 28. 249 applicants, 25% accepted, 17 enrolled. In 2018, 11 master's, 7 doctorates, 1 other advanced degree awarded. Terminal master's awarded for partial completion of doctoral program. *Degree requirements:* For master's, practicum, internship; for doctorate, thesis/dissertation, practicum. *Entrance requirements:* For doctorate, GRE General Test or MAT, 2 letters of recommendation, resume. Additional exam requirements/recommendations for international students: Required—TOEFL (minimum score 550 paper-based; 80 iBT). *Application deadline:* For fall admission, 12/1 for domestic and international students. Applications are processed on a rolling basis. Application fee: $50. Electronic applications accepted. *Expenses:* Contact institution. *Financial support:* In 2018–19, 42 students received support, including 14 fellowships (averaging $3,435 per year); career-related internships or fieldwork, Federal Work-Study, institutionally sponsored loans, scholarships/grants, and unspecified assistantships also available. Support available to part-time students. Financial award application deadline: 4/1; financial award applicants required to submit FAFSA. *Faculty research:* Assessing exposure in the context of a family-based cognitive behavioral treatment for pediatric OCD, a mindfulness approach to designing and testing the efficacy of a new sexual revictimization prevention program for college women, olfaction and decision-making in substance-dependent individuals, the role of experiential avoidance in Generalized Anxiety Disorder, ego development as a predictor of dogmatism and intolerance in the political right and left. *Unit head:* Dr. Amy Marks, Chairperson, 617-573-8017, E-mail: akmarks@suffolk.edu. *Application contact:* Mara Marzocchi, Associate Director of Graduate Admissions, 617-573-8302, Fax: 617-305-1733, E-mail: grad.admission@suffolk.edu.
Website: http://www.suffolk.edu/college/graduate/69299.php

Sul Ross State University, College of Professional Studies, Department of Education, Program in Counseling, Alpine, TX 79832. Offers M Ed. *Program availability:* Part-time, evening/weekend. *Degree requirements:* For master's, thesis optional. *Entrance requirements:* For master's, GMAT or GRE General Test, minimum GPA of 2.5 in last 60 hours of undergraduate work.

Sul Ross State University, Rio Grande College of Sul Ross State University, Alpine, TX 79832. Offers business administration (MBA); teacher education (M Ed), including bilingual education, counseling, educational diagnostics, elementary education, general education, reading, school administration, secondary education. *Program availability:* Part-time, evening/weekend, online learning. *Degree requirements:* For master's, comprehensive exam, thesis optional, minimum GPA of 3.0. *Entrance requirements:* For master's, GMAT or GRE General Test, minimum GPA of 2.5 in last 60 hours of undergraduate work. Additional exam requirements/recommendations for international students: Required—TOEFL.

Syracuse University, School of Education, MS Program in Student Affairs Counseling, Syracuse, NY 13244. Offers MS. *Program availability:* Part-time. *Students:* Average age 28. *Entrance requirements:* For master's, GRE or MAT, baccalaureate degree from regionally-accredited college/university, three letters of recommendation, personal statement, transcripts, interview. Additional exam requirements/recommendations for international students: Required—TOEFL (minimum score 100 iBT). *Application deadline:* For fall admission, 6/15 priority date for domestic and international students; for spring admission, 10/15 priority date for domestic and international students; for summer admission, 1/15 priority date for domestic and international students. Applications are processed on a rolling basis. Application fee: $75. Electronic applications accepted. *Financial support:* Fellowships with full tuition reimbursements, research assistantships, teaching assistantships, career-related internships or fieldwork, and scholarships/grants available. Financial award application deadline: 1/15. *Faculty research:* Group work in counseling, theories of counseling and psychotherapy, social and cultural dimensions of counseling, life-span human development, assessment in counseling. *Unit head:* Dr. Derek Seward, Professor/Chair of the Department of Counseling and Human Service, 315-443-2266, E-mail: dxseward@syr.edu. *Application contact:* Speranza Migliore, Graduate Admissions Recruiter, 315-443-2505, E-mail: gradrcrt@syr.edu.
Website: http://soe.syr.edu/academic/counseling_and_human_services/graduate/masters/student_affairs_counseling/default.aspx

Syracuse University, School of Education, PhD Program in Counseling and Counselor Education, Syracuse, NY 13244. Offers PhD. *Accreditation:* ACA. *Program availability:* Part-time. *Degree requirements:* For doctorate, comprehensive exam, thesis/dissertation. *Entrance requirements:* For doctorate, GRE including Writing/Analytic Test, master's degree in counseling or rehabilitation counseling, personal interview, three letters of recommendation, transcripts of all undergraduate and graduate study, personal statement. Additional exam requirements/recommendations for international students: Required—TOEFL (minimum score 600 paper-based; 100 iBT), IELTS (minimum score 7). *Application deadline:* For fall admission, 11/1 for domestic and international students. Applications are processed on a rolling basis. Application fee: $75. Electronic applications accepted. *Financial support:* Fellowships with full tuition reimbursements, research assistantships, teaching assistantships with full tuition reimbursements, career-related internships or fieldwork, and scholarships/grants available. Financial award application deadline: 1/15; financial award applicants required to submit FAFSA. *Faculty research:* Clinical supervision, college mental health counseling, counseling people with disabilities, the future professoriate, social justice and urban youth. *Unit head:* Dr. Derek Seward, Chair, 315-443-2266, Fax: 315-443-5732, E-mail: dxseward@syr.edu. *Application contact:* Speranza Migliore, Graduate Admissions Recruiter, 315-443-2505, E-mail: gradrcrt@syr.edu.
Website: http://soe.syr.edu/academic/counseling_and_human_services/graduate/phd/default.aspx

Texas A&M International University, Office of Graduate Studies and Research, College of Education, Department of Professional Programs, Laredo, TX 78041. Offers educational administration (MS Ed); generic special education (MS Ed); school counseling (MS). *Entrance requirements:* Additional exam requirements/recommendations for international students: Required—TOEFL (minimum score 550 paper-based; 79 iBT).

Texas A&M University–Central Texas, Graduate Studies and Research, Killeen, TX 76549. Offers accounting (MS); business administration (MBA); clinical mental health counseling (MS); criminal justice (MCJ); curriculum and instruction (M Ed); educational administration (M Ed); educational psychology - experimental psychology (MS); history (MA); human resource management (MS); information systems (MS); liberal studies (MS); management and leadership (MS); marriage and family therapy (MS); mathematics (MS); political science (MA); school counseling (M Ed); school psychology (Ed S).

Texas A&M University–Commerce, College of Education and Human Services, Commerce, TX 75429. Offers counseling (M Ed, MS, PhD); early childhood education (M Ed, MS); educational administration (M Ed, MS, Ed D); educational psychology (PhD); educational technology leadership (M Ed, MS); educational technology library science (M Ed, MS); elementary education (M Ed); health, kinesiology and sports studies (MS); higher education (MS, Ed D); psychology (MS); reading (M Ed, MS); school psychology (SSP); secondary education (M Ed, MS); social work (MSW); special education (M Ed, MS); supervision, curriculum and instruction-elementary education (Ed D); training and development (MS). *Program availability:* Part-time, evening/weekend, 100% online, blended/hybrid learning. *Faculty:* 95 full-time (59 women), 29 part-time/adjunct (22 women). *Students:* 356 full-time (295 women), 1,262 part-time (992 women); includes 683 minority (349 Black or African American, non-Hispanic/Latino; 9 American Indian or Alaska Native, non-Hispanic/Latino; 30 Asian, non-Hispanic/Latino; 238 Hispanic/Latino; 57 Two or more races, non-Hispanic/Latino), 9 international. Average age 37. 951 applicants, 42% accepted, 304 enrolled. In 2018, 532 master's, 51 doctorates awarded. *Degree requirements:* For master's, comprehensive exam, thesis optional, departmental qualifying exams (for some programs); for doctorate, comprehensive exam, thesis/dissertation, departmental qualifying exam; for SSP, comprehensive exam. *Entrance requirements:* For master's, GRE General Test, official transcripts, letters of recommendation, resume, statement of goals; for doctorate, GRE General Test, letters of recommendation, statement of goals, writing samples, writing sessions, resumes. Additional exam requirements/recommendations for international students: Required—TOEFL (minimum score 550 paper-based; 79 iBT), IELTS (minimum score 6), PTE (minimum score 53). *Application deadline:* For fall admission, 6/1 priority date for international students; for spring admission, 10/15 priority date for international students; for summer admission, 3/15 priority date for international students. Applications are processed on a rolling basis. Application fee: $50 ($75 for international students). Electronic applications accepted. *Expenses: Tuition, area resident:* Full-time $3630. Tuition, state resident: full-time $3630. Tuition, nonresident: full-time $11,100. *International tuition:* $11,100 full-time. *Required fees:* $2794. Tuition

and fees vary according to course load, degree level and program. *Financial support:* In 2018–19, 116 students received support, including 94 research assistantships with partial tuition reimbursements available (averaging $3,863 per year), 38 teaching assistantships with partial tuition reimbursements available (averaging $4,728 per year); career-related internships or fieldwork, Federal Work-Study, institutionally sponsored loans, scholarships/grants, health care benefits, and unspecified assistantships also available. Financial award application deadline: 5/1; financial award applicants required to submit FAFSA. *Faculty research:* Cognitive and bilingual education, positive behavioral intervention, literacy, math readiness. *Total annual research expenditures:* $1.1 million. *Unit head:* Dr. Madeline Justice, Interim Dean, 903-886-5181, Fax: 903-886-5905, E-mail: madeline.justice@tamuc.edu. *Application contact:* Vicky Turner, Doctoral Degree and Special Programs Coordinator, 903-886-5167, E-mail: vicky.turner@tamuc.edu.
Website: http://www.tamuc.edu/academics/graduateSchool/programs/education/default.aspx

Texas A&M University–Corpus Christi, College of Graduate Studies, College of Education and Human Development, Programs in Counseling, Corpus Christi, TX 78412. Offers MS, PhD. *Accreditation:* ACA. *Program availability:* Part-time, evening/weekend. *Degree requirements:* For master's, comprehensive exam; for doctorate, comprehensive exam, thesis/dissertation. *Entrance requirements:* For master's, minimum GPA of 3.0 in last 60 hours, essay (approximately 500-700 words in length), 3 letters of recommendation, interview; for doctorate, GRE (taken within 5 years), master's degree, essay (2 pages), resume, 3 reference forms, interview. Additional exam requirements/recommendations for international students: Required—TOEFL (minimum score 550 paper-based; 79 iBT), IELTS (minimum score 6.5). Electronic applications accepted.

Texas A&M University–Kingsville, College of Graduate Studies, College of Education and Human Performance, Department of Educational Leadership and Counseling, Program in Counseling and Guidance, Kingsville, TX 78363. Offers MA, MS. MS offered jointly with University of North Texas. *Program availability:* Part-time, evening/weekend. *Degree requirements:* For master's, variable foreign language requirement, comprehensive exam, thesis (for some programs). *Entrance requirements:* For master's, GRE, MAT, GMAT, minimum GPA of 2.6. Additional exam requirements/recommendations for international students: Required—TOEFL (minimum score 550 paper-based; 79 iBT). Electronic applications accepted. *Faculty research:* Diagnostician requirements for certification, teaching methods for adult learners.

Texas A&M University–San Antonio, Department of Counseling, Health and Kinesiology, San Antonio, TX 78224. Offers clinical mental health counseling (MA); counseling and guidance (MA); kinesiology (MS); marriage and family counseling (MA). *Program availability:* Part-time, evening/weekend, online learning. *Degree requirements:* For master's, comprehensive exam, thesis or alternative. *Entrance requirements:* For master's, MAT or GRE (composite quantitative and verbal). Additional exam requirements/recommendations for international students: Required—TOEFL (minimum score 550 paper-based; 79 iBT), IELTS (minimum score 6). Electronic applications accepted.

Texas Christian University, College of Education, Doctoral Programs in Education, Fort Worth, TX 76129-0002. Offers counseling and counselor education (PhD); curriculum studies (PhD); educational leadership (Ed D); higher educational leadership (Ed D); science education (PhD); MBA/Ed D. *Program availability:* Part-time, evening/weekend. *Faculty:* 29 full-time (21 women), 3 part-time/adjunct (1 woman). *Students:* 80 full-time (57 women), 26 part-time (13 women); includes 41 minority (15 Black or African American, non-Hispanic/Latino; 6 Asian, non-Hispanic/Latino; 17 Hispanic/Latino; 3 Two or more races, non-Hispanic/Latino), 6 international. Average age 39. 109 applicants, 50% accepted, 23 enrolled. In 2018, 12 doctorates awarded. *Degree requirements:* For doctorate, comprehensive exam, thesis/dissertation. *Entrance requirements:* For doctorate, GRE General Test. Additional exam requirements/recommendations for international students: Required—TOEFL (minimum score 550 paper-based; 80 iBT), IELTS (minimum score 6.5). *Application deadline:* For fall admission, 2/1 for domestic and international students; for winter admission, 2/1 for domestic and international students; for spring admission, 11/16 for domestic and international students. Application fee: $60. Electronic applications accepted. *Financial support:* In 2018–19, 66 students received support, including 1 fellowship with full tuition reimbursement available (averaging $18,500 per year), 8 research assistantships with full tuition reimbursements available (averaging $18,500 per year), 6 teaching assistantships with full tuition reimbursements available (averaging $18,500 per year); career-related internships or fieldwork, scholarships/grants, health care benefits, and unspecified assistantships also available. Support available to part-time students. Financial award application deadline: 2/1. *Unit head:* Dr. Jan Lacina, Interim Dean, 817-257-6786, Fax: 817-257-7466, E-mail: j.lacina@tcu.edu. *Application contact:* Lori Kimball, Graduate Studies Coordinator, 817-257-7661, Fax: 817-257-7466, E-mail: l.kimball@tcu.edu.
Website: http://coe.tcu.edu/graduate-overview/

Texas Christian University, College of Education, Master's Programs in Education, Fort Worth, TX 76129-0002. Offers counseling (M Ed); curriculum and instruction (M Ed), including curriculum studies, language and literacy, math education, science education; education (MAT); educational leadership (M Ed); special education (M Ed). *Program availability:* Part-time, evening/weekend. *Faculty:* 29 full-time (21 women), 3 part-time/adjunct (1 woman). *Students:* 124 full-time (94 women), 14 part-time (12 women); includes 52 minority (14 Black or African American, non-Hispanic/Latino; 2 American Indian or Alaska Native, non-Hispanic/Latino; 3 Asian, non-Hispanic/Latino; 28 Hispanic/Latino; 5 Two or more races, non-Hispanic/Latino), 1 international. Average age 28. 172 applicants, 69% accepted, 86 enrolled. In 2018, 62 master's awarded. *Degree requirements:* For master's, comprehensive exam (for some programs), thesis (for some programs). *Entrance requirements:* For master's, GRE General Test; Pre-Admission Content Test (for MAT). Additional exam requirements/recommendations for international students: Required—TOEFL (minimum score 550 paper-based; 80 iBT), IELTS (minimum score 6.5). *Application deadline:* For fall admission, 3/1 for domestic and international students; for spring admission, 11/16 for domestic and international students; for summer admission, 3/1 for domestic and international students. Application fee: $60. Electronic applications accepted. *Financial support:* In 2018–19, 135 students received support, including 3 research assistantships with full tuition reimbursements available (averaging $15,000 per year), 33 teaching assistantships with full tuition reimbursements available (averaging $15,000 per year); career-related internships or fieldwork, scholarships/grants, health care benefits, and unspecified assistantships also available. Support available to part-time students. Financial award application deadline: 3/1. *Unit head:* Dr. Jan Lacina, Interim Dean, 817-257-6786, Fax: 817-257-7466, E-mail: j.lacina@tcu.edu. *Application contact:* Lori Kimball, Graduate Studies Coordinator, 817-257-7661, Fax: 817-257-7466, E-mail: l.kimball@tcu.edu.
Website: http://coe.tcu.edu/graduate-overview/

Texas Southern University, College of Education, Department of Counselor Education, Houston, TX 77004-4584. Offers counseling (M Ed); counselor education (Ed D). *Program availability:* Part-time, evening/weekend. *Degree requirements:* For master's, one foreign language, comprehensive exam; for doctorate, comprehensive exam, thesis/dissertation. *Entrance requirements:* For master's, GRE General Test, minimum GPA of 2.5; for doctorate, GRE General Test or MAT, master's degree, minimum B+ average. Additional exam requirements/recommendations for international students: Required—TOEFL. Electronic applications accepted. *Faculty research:* Clinical and urban psychology.

Texas State University, The Graduate College, College of Education, Program in Professional Counseling, San Marcos, TX 78666. Offers clinical mental health counseling (MA); marriage and family counseling (MA); school counseling (MA). *Accreditation:* ACA. *Program availability:* Part-time. *Faculty:* 13 full-time (11 women), 6 part-time/adjunct (all women). *Students:* 105 full-time (89 women), 103 part-time (87 women); includes 51 minority (7 Black or African American, non-Hispanic/Latino; 6 Asian, non-Hispanic/Latino; 32 Hispanic/Latino; 6 Two or more races, non-Hispanic/Latino). Average age 31. 137 applicants, 45% accepted, 31 enrolled. In 2018, 51 master's awarded. *Degree requirements:* For master's, comprehensive exam, thesis optional, internship. *Entrance requirements:* For master's, Official GRE (general test only) required with competitive scores in the verbal and quantitative reasoning sections, baccalaureate degree from regionally-accredited institution with minimum GPA of 3.0 in last 60 hours of undergraduate work; resume; statement of purpose addressing professional goals, reasoning for specified emphasis (i.e., community, school, marital), strengths and weaknesses, and perspective on diversity; 3 references. Additional exam requirements/recommendations for international students: Required—TOEFL (minimum iBT scores: 22 listening, 22 reading, 24 speaking, 21 writing). *Application deadline:* For fall admission, 2/1 priority date for domestic and international students; for spring admission, 10/1 for domestic and international students; for summer admission, 2/15 for domestic and international students. Applications are processed on a rolling basis. Application fee: $55 ($90 for international students). Electronic applications accepted. *Expenses:* Tuition, state resident: full-time $8102; part-time $4051 per semester. Tuition, nonresident: full-time $18,229; part-time $9115 per semester. *International tuition:* $18,229 full-time. *Required fees:* $2116; $120 per credit hour. Tuition and fees vary according to course load. *Financial support:* In 2018–19, 87 students received support, including 17 research assistantships (averaging $9,328 per year); teaching assistantships, Federal Work-Study, institutionally sponsored loans, and scholarships/grants also available. Support available to part-time students. Financial award application deadline: 1/15; financial award applicants required to submit FAFSA. *Faculty research:* Examining the role of Teachers and Externalizing Behavior Problems; Creativity in counseling, stress management, blended families; Messages to New Survivors by Longer-Term Survivors of Intimate Partner Violence; Promoting Girls' leadership in secondary schools; Collaborative Approaches to Infusing Neuroscience Principles in Counseling and Psychotherapy. *Unit head:* Dr. Kathy Ybanez-Llorente, Graduate Advisor, 512-2452579, Fax: 512-245-8872, E-mail: profcounadm@txstate.edu. *Application contact:* Dr. Andrea Golato, Dean of Graduate School, 512-245-2581, Fax: 512-245-8365, E-mail: gradcollege@txstate.edu.
Website: http://www.gradcollege.txstate.edu/programs/counseling.html

Texas Tech University, Graduate School, College of Education, Department of Educational Psychology and Leadership, Lubbock, TX 79409-1071. Offers counselor education (M Ed, PhD); educational leadership (M Ed, Ed D, PhD); educational psychology (M Ed, PhD); higher education administration (M Ed, Ed D); higher education research (PhD); instructional technology (M Ed, Ed D); special education (M Ed, Ed D, PhD). *Accreditation:* ACA; NCATE. *Program availability:* Part-time, evening/weekend, 100% online, blended/hybrid learning. *Faculty:* 65 full-time (29 women), 3 part-time/adjunct (all women). *Students:* 261 full-time (184 women), 624 part-time (482 women); includes 325 minority (88 Black or African American, non-Hispanic/Latino; 3 American Indian or Alaska Native, non-Hispanic/Latino; 12 Asian, non-Hispanic/Latino; 192 Hispanic/Latino; 1 Native Hawaiian or other Pacific Islander, non-Hispanic/Latino; 29 Two or more races, non-Hispanic/Latino), 39 international. Average age 36. 437 applicants, 73% accepted, 252 enrolled. In 2018, 278 master's, 40 doctorates awarded. Terminal master's awarded for partial completion of doctoral program. *Degree requirements:* For master's, comprehensive exam, thesis optional; for doctorate, comprehensive exam, thesis/dissertation. *Entrance requirements:* For master's, GRE (for some programs); for doctorate, GRE. Additional exam requirements/recommendations for international students: Required—TOEFL (minimum score 550 paper-based; 79 iBT). *Application deadline:* For fall admission, 6/1 priority date for domestic students, 1/15 priority date for international students; for spring admission, 9/1 priority date for domestic students, 6/15 priority date for international students. Applications are processed on a rolling basis. Application fee: $65. Electronic applications accepted. *Expenses:* Contact institution. *Financial support:* In 2018–19, 493 students received support, including 489 fellowships (averaging $3,305 per year), 61 research assistantships (averaging $12,558 per year), 5 teaching assistantships (averaging $13,161 per year); scholarships/grants and unspecified assistantships also available. Support available to part-time students. Financial award application deadline: 1/3; financial award applicants required to submit FAFSA. *Faculty research:* Cognitive, motivational, and developmental processes in learning; counseling education; instructional technology; generic special education and sensory impairment; community college administration; K-12 school administration. *Total annual research expenditures:* $204,930. *Unit head:* Dr. Hansel Burley, Professor, Department Chair, 806-834-5135, Fax: 806-742-2179, E-mail: hansel.burley@ttu.edu. *Application contact:* Pam Smith, Admissions Advisor, 806-834-2969, Fax: 806-742-2179, E-mail: pam.smith@ttu.edu.
Website: www.educ.ttu.edu/

Texas Woman's University, Graduate School, College of Professional Education, Department of Family Sciences, Denton, TX 76204. Offers child development (MS); child life (MS); counseling and development (MS); early childhood development and education (PhD); early childhood education (M Ed); family studies (MS, PhD); family therapy (MS, PhD). *Accreditation:* ACA (one or more programs are accredited). *Program availability:* Part-time, evening/weekend, 100% online, blended/hybrid learning. *Faculty:* 25 full-time (18 women), 19 part-time/adjunct (16 women). *Students:* 180 full-time (172 women), 247 part-time (229 women); includes 176 minority (86 Black or African American, non-Hispanic/Latino; 11 Asian, non-Hispanic/Latino; 68 Hispanic/Latino; 11 Two or more races, non-Hispanic/Latino), 9 international. Average age 32. 203 applicants, 69% accepted, 100 enrolled. In 2018, 101 master's, 18 doctorates awarded. *Degree requirements:* For master's, comprehensive exam (for some programs), thesis (for some programs), thesis, professional paper, portfolio, or coursework; practicums (for some programs); for doctorate, comprehensive exam, thesis/dissertation, seminars, qualifying exam, dissertation. *Entrance requirements:* For master's, minimum GPA of 3.0 (3.25 for family therapy), letter of intent, curriculum vitae/resume, interview, writing sample, letter of recommendation,; for doctorate, minimum GPA of 3.5 (3.35 for family studies) on all prior graduate work, curriculum vitae/resume, letter of intent. Additional exam requirements/recommendations for international students: Required—TOEFL (minimum score 550 paper-based; 79 iBT); Recommended—IELTS (minimum score 6.5), TSE (minimum score 53). *Application deadline:* For fall admission, 3/15 for domestic students, 3/1 priority date for international students; for spring admission, 9/15 for domestic students, 7/1 priority date for international students. Application fee: $50 ($75 for international students). Electronic applications accepted. *Expenses: Tuition, area resident:* Full-time $4852; part-time $270 per semester hour. Tuition, state resident: full-time $4852; part-time $270 per semester hour. Tuition, nonresident: full-time $12,322; part-time $685 per semester hour. *International tuition:* $12,322 full-time.

Required fees: $2714; $113 per semester hour. $296 per semester. Tuition and fees vary according to course level, course load, degree level, campus/location and program. *Financial support:* In 2018–19, 106 students received support, including 1 research assistantship, 17 teaching assistantships (averaging $10,232 per year); career-related internships or fieldwork, Federal Work-Study, institutionally sponsored loans, scholarships/grants, traineeships, health care benefits, and unspecified assistantships also available. Support available to part-time students. Financial award application deadline: 3/1; financial award applicants required to submit FAFSA. *Faculty research:* Parenting/parent education, play therapy, healthy relationships, child development, technology integration. *Unit head:* Ron Hovis, Interim Chair, 940-898-2685, Fax: 940-898-2676, E-mail: famsci@twu.edu. *Application contact:* Korie Hawkins, Associate Director of Admissions, Graduate Recruitment, 940-898-3188, Fax: 940-898-3081, E-mail: admissions@twu.edu.
Website: http://www.twu.edu/family-sciences/

Trevecca Nazarene University, Graduate Counseling Program, Nashville, TN 37210-2877. Offers clinical counseling: teaching and supervision (PhD); clinical mental health counseling (MA); marriage and family counseling/therapy (MMFC/T). *Accreditation:* ACA. *Program availability:* Part-time, evening/weekend. *Degree requirements:* For master's, comprehensive exam; for doctorate, comprehensive exam, thesis/dissertation. *Entrance requirements:* For master's, MAT (minimum score of 380) or GRE (minimum score of 290 combined verbal and quantitative), minimum GPA of 2.7, official transcript from regionally accredited institution, 2 reference assessment forms; for doctorate, GRE (minimum scores: 300 combined verbal and quantitative, 3.5 analytical writing), minimum GPA of 3.25, official transcript of master's degree from regionally accredited institution, 3 recommendation forms, 400-word letter of intent, professional vita, interview. Additional exam requirements/recommendations for international students: Required—TOEFL (minimum score 600 paper-based; 100 iBT). Electronic applications accepted. *Expenses:* Contact institution.

Trinity Washington University, School of Education, Washington, DC 20017-1094. Offers clinical mental health counseling (MA); early childhood education (MAT); educating for change (M Ed); educational administration (MSA); elementary education (MAT); reading (M Ed); school counseling (MA); secondary education (MAT), including English, social studies; special education (MAT). *Accreditation:* NCATE. *Program availability:* Part-time, evening/weekend. *Degree requirements:* For master's, thesis (for some programs), capstone project(s). *Entrance requirements:* For master's, PRAXIS I, minimum GPA of 2.8. Additional exam requirements/recommendations for international students: Required—TOEFL (minimum score 550 paper-based). *Faculty research:* Technology, literacy, special education, organizations, inclusion models.

Troy University, Graduate School, College of Education, Program in Counseling and Psychology, Troy, AL 36082. Offers community counseling (MS). *Accreditation:* ACA; CORE; NCATE. *Program availability:* Part-time, evening/weekend. *Faculty:* 39 full-time (18 women), 23 part-time/adjunct (14 women). *Students:* 287 full-time (237 women), 336 part-time (277 women); includes 207 minority (181 Black or African American, non-Hispanic/Latino; 3 American Indian or Alaska Native, non-Hispanic/Latino; 1 Asian, non-Hispanic/Latino; 11 Hispanic/Latino; 1 Native Hawaiian or other Pacific Islander, non-Hispanic/Latino; 10 Two or more races, non-Hispanic/Latino), 7 international. Average age 35. 251 applicants, 93% accepted, 144 enrolled. In 2018, 203 master's, 17 other advanced degrees awarded. *Degree requirements:* For master's, comprehensive exam, thesis. *Entrance requirements:* For master's, GRE (minimum score of 850 on old exam or 290 on new exam), GMAT (minimum score of 380), or MAT (minimum score of 385), bachelor's degree; minimum undergraduate GPA of 2.5 or 3.0 on last 30 semester hours, letter of recommendation. Additional exam requirements/recommendations for international students: Required—TOEFL (minimum score 523 paper-based; 70 iBT), IELTS (minimum score 6). *Application deadline:* Applications are processed on a rolling basis. Application fee: $50. Electronic applications accepted. *Expenses: Tuition, area resident:* Full-time $425; part-time $425 per credit hour. Tuition, state resident: full-time $425; part-time $425 per credit hour. Tuition, nonresident: full-time $850; part-time $850 per credit hour. *International tuition:* $850 full-time. *Required fees:* $50 per semester. Tuition and fees vary according to campus/location and program. *Financial support:* Fellowships, career-related internships or fieldwork, and scholarships/grants available. Support available to part-time students. *Unit head:* Dr. Lynn Boyd, Associate Professor, Chair Counseling and Psychology, 334-670-3350, Fax: 334-670-3291, E-mail: lynnboyd@troy.edu. *Application contact:* Jessica A. Kimbro, Assistant Director of Graduate Programs, 334-670-3189, E-mail: jacord@troy.edu.

Troy University, Graduate School, College of Education, Program in School Counseling, Troy, AL 36082. Offers MS, Ed S. *Accreditation:* ACA; CORE; NCATE. *Program availability:* Part-time, evening/weekend. *Faculty:* 22 full-time (12 women), 13 part-time/adjunct (8 women). *Students:* 8 full-time (4 women), 32 part-time (30 women); includes 25 minority (all Black or African American, non-Hispanic/Latino). Average age 34. 11 applicants, 91% accepted, 7 enrolled. In 2018, 22 master's awarded. *Degree requirements:* For master's, comprehensive exam, thesis. *Entrance requirements:* For master's, GRE (minimum score of 850 on old exam or 290 on new exam), GMAT (minimum score of 380), or MAT (minimum score of 385), bachelor's degree, minimum undergraduate GPA of 2.5 or 3.0 on last 30 semester hours, letter of recommendation, teaching certification, 2 years of teaching experience. Additional exam requirements/recommendations for international students: Required—TOEFL (minimum score 523 paper-based; 70 iBT), IELTS (minimum score 6). *Application deadline:* Applications are processed on a rolling basis. Application fee: $50. Electronic applications accepted. *Expenses: Tuition, area resident:* Full-time $425; part-time $425 per credit hour. Tuition, state resident: full-time $425; part-time $425 per credit hour. Tuition, nonresident: full-time $850; part-time $850 per credit hour. *International tuition:* $850 full-time. *Required fees:* $50 per semester. Tuition and fees vary according to campus/location and program. *Financial support:* Fellowships, career-related internships or fieldwork, and scholarships/grants available. Support available to part-time students. *Unit head:* Dr. Lynn Boyd, Associate Professor, Chair, School Counseling, 334-670-3350, Fax: 334-670-3291, E-mail: lynnboyd@troy.edu. *Application contact:* Jessica A. Kimbro, Assistant Director of Graduate Programs, 334-670-3189, E-mail: jacord@troy.edu.
Website: https://www.troy.edu/academics/academic-programs/college-education-programs.php

Universidad del Turabo, Graduate Programs, Programs in Education, Program in Counseling, Gurabo, PR 00778-3030. Offers M Ed. *Program availability:* Part-time, evening/weekend. *Entrance requirements:* For master's, GRE, EXADEP, GMAT, interview, official transcript, essay, recommendation letters. Electronic applications accepted.

Université de Moncton, Faculty of Education, Graduate Studies in Education, Moncton, NB E1A 3E9, Canada. Offers educational psychology (M Ed, MA Ed); guidance (M Ed, MA Ed); school administration (M Ed, MA Ed); teaching (M Ed, MA Ed). *Program availability:* Part-time. *Degree requirements:* For master's, proficiency in English and French. *Entrance requirements:* For master's, minimum GPA of 3.0. *Faculty research:* Guidance, ethnolinguistic vitality, children's rights, ecological education, entrepreneurship.

Université Laval, Faculty of Education, Department of Foundations and Interventions in Education, Programs in Orientation Sciences, Québec, QC G1K 7P4, Canada. Offers MA, PhD. Terminal master's awarded for partial completion of doctoral program. *Degree requirements:* For master's, thesis (for some programs); for doctorate, comprehensive exam, thesis/dissertation. *Entrance requirements:* For master's, English test (comprehension of written English), knowledge of French; for doctorate, oral exam (subject of thesis), knowledge of French and English. Electronic applications accepted. *Faculty research:* Counseling psychology, psychological education, vocational guidance, growth and development.

University at Buffalo, the State University of New York, Graduate School, Graduate School of Education, Department of Counseling, School, and Educational Psychology, Buffalo, NY 14260. Offers applied statistical analysis (Advanced Certificate); counseling/school psychology (PhD); counselor education (PhD); education studies (Ed M); educational psychology (MA, PhD); mental health counseling (MS, Certificate); mindful counseling for wellness and engagement (Advanced Certificate); rehabilitation counseling (MS, Advanced Certificate); school counseling (Ed M, Certificate). *Accreditation:* CORE (one or more programs are accredited). *Program availability:* Part-time, 100% online. *Faculty:* 21 full-time (11 women), 23 part-time/adjunct (18 women). *Students:* 163 full-time (132 women), 137 part-time (111 women); includes 55 minority (25 Black or African American, non-Hispanic/Latino; 11 Asian, non-Hispanic/Latino; 15 Hispanic/Latino; 4 Two or more races, non-Hispanic/Latino), 15 international. Average age 32. 355 applicants, 57% accepted, 147 enrolled. In 2018, 66 master's, 13 doctorates, 62 other advanced degrees awarded. *Degree requirements:* For master's, comprehensive exam (for some programs), thesis (for some programs); for doctorate, comprehensive exam, thesis/dissertation. *Entrance requirements:* For master's, GRE General Test, interview, letters of reference; for doctorate, GRE General Test, interview, letters of reference, writing sample. Additional exam requirements/recommendations for international students: Required—TOEFL (minimum score 600 paper-based; 79 iBT), IELTS (minimum score 6.5), PTE (minimum score 55). *Application deadline:* For fall admission, 2/1 priority date for domestic and international students. Application fee: $50. Electronic applications accepted. *Financial support:* In 2018–19, 22 fellowships (averaging $7,823 per year), 41 research assistantships with tuition reimbursements (averaging $10,876 per year) were awarded; teaching assistantships, career-related internships or fieldwork, Federal Work-Study, institutionally sponsored loans, scholarships/grants, tuition waivers (full and partial), and unspecified assistantships also available. Financial award application deadline: 2/1; financial award applicants required to submit FAFSA. *Faculty research:* Multicultural counseling, class size effects, good work in counseling, eating disorders, outcome assessment, change agents and therapeutic factors in group counseling. *Total annual research expenditures:* $1.3 million. *Unit head:* Dr. Myles Faith, Department Chair, 716-645-1124, Fax: 716-645-6616, E-mail: mfaith@buffalo.edu. *Application contact:* Renad Aref, Assistant Director of Admission Recruitment, 716-645-2110, Fax: 716-645-7937, E-mail: gseinfo@buffalo.edu.
Website: http://gse.buffalo.edu/csep

The University of Akron, Graduate School, College of Health Professions, School of Counseling, Program in Counselor Education and Supervision, Akron, OH 44325. Offers PhD. *Accreditation:* ACA. *Degree requirements:* For doctorate, comprehensive exam, thesis/dissertation, written and oral exams. *Entrance requirements:* For doctorate, GRE, minimum GPA of 3.25 on all completed graduate coursework, three letters of recommendation, professional resume, interview. Additional exam requirements/recommendations for international students: Required—TOEFL (minimum score 79 iBT), IELTS (minimum score 6.5). Electronic applications accepted.

The University of Akron, Graduate School, College of Health Professions, School of Counseling, Program in School Counseling, Akron, OH 44325. Offers MA, MS. *Accreditation:* ACA; NCATE. *Degree requirements:* For master's, comprehensive exam. *Entrance requirements:* For master's, minimum GPA of 2.75, three letters of recommendation, Bureau of Criminal Investigation clearance, interview. Additional exam requirements/recommendations for international students: Required—TOEFL (minimum score 79 iBT), IELTS (minimum score 6.5). Electronic applications accepted.

The University of Alabama, Graduate School, College of Education, Department of Educational Studies in Psychology, Research Methodology and Counseling, Tuscaloosa, AL 35487. Offers MA, Ed D, PhD, Ed S. *Accreditation:* ACA (one or more programs are accredited); CORE; NCATE. *Program availability:* Part-time. *Degree requirements:* For master's, comprehensive exam, thesis optional; for doctorate, comprehensive exam, thesis/dissertation; for Ed S, comprehensive exam. *Entrance requirements:* For master's and doctorate, GRE General Test, MAT, or NTE, minimum GPA of 3.0; for Ed S, minimum GPA of 3.0 during previous 2 years. Additional exam requirements/recommendations for international students: Required—TOEFL (minimum score 550 paper-based), IELTS (minimum score 6.5). Electronic applications accepted. *Faculty research:* Moral development, positive psychology, children's fears, digital storytelling.

The University of Alabama at Birmingham, School of Education, Program in Counseling, Birmingham, AL 35294. Offers MA. *Accreditation:* ACA; CORE; NCATE. *Degree requirements:* For master's, comprehensive exam, thesis optional, practicum, internship. *Entrance requirements:* For master's, GRE General Test or MAT, minimum GPA of 2.75, interview. Electronic applications accepted. *Expenses: Tuition, area resident:* Full-time $8100; part-time $8100 per year. Tuition, state resident: full-time $8100. Tuition, nonresident: full-time $19,188; part-time $19,188 per year. Tuition and fees vary according to program.

University of Alaska Fairbanks, School of Education, Program in Counseling, Fairbanks, AK 99775-7520. Offers community counseling (M Ed). *Program availability:* Part-time, evening/weekend, 100% online, blended/hybrid learning. *Faculty:* 1 (woman) full-time. *Students:* 17 part-time (13 women). Average age 38. 5 applicants, 40% accepted, 1 enrolled. In 2018, 6 master's, 4 other advanced degrees awarded. Terminal master's awarded for partial completion of doctoral program. *Degree requirements:* For master's, comprehensive exam, oral defense of project or thesis. *Entrance requirements:* For master's, bachelor's degree from accredited institution with minimum cumulative undergraduate and major GPA of 3.0, 3 letters of recommendation, statement of academic goals, resume, interview; for Graduate Certificate, master's degree from accredited institution with minimum GPA of 3.0. Additional exam requirements/recommendations for international students: Required—TOEFL (minimum score 550 paper-based; 79 iBT), IELTS (minimum score 6.5). *Application deadline:* For fall admission, 3/1 for domestic and international students; for spring admission, 10/1 for domestic students, 9/1 for international students. Applications are processed on a rolling basis. Application fee: $60. Electronic applications accepted. *Expenses: Tuition, area resident:* Full-time $8802; part-time $5868 per credit hour. Tuition, state resident: full-time $8802; part-time $5868 per credit hour. Tuition, nonresident: full-time $18,504; part-time $12,336 per credit hour. *International tuition:* $18,504 full-time. *Required fees:* $1416; $944 per credit hour. $472 per semester. Tuition and fees vary according to course load and program. *Financial support:* Scholarships/grants and unspecified assistantships available. Financial award application deadline: 7/1; financial award applicants required to submit FAFSA. *Unit head:* Dr. Amy Vinlove, Director, 907-474-7701, E-mail: alvinlove@alaska.edu. *Application contact:* Samara Taber, Director of Admissions, 907-474-7500, E-mail: uaf-admissions@alaska.edu.

Counselor Education

University of Alberta, Faculty of Graduate Studies and Research, Department of Educational Psychology, Edmonton, AB T6G 2E1, Canada. Offers counseling psychology (M Ed, PhD); educational psychology (M Ed, PhD); instructional technology (M Ed); school counseling (M Ed); school psychology (M Ed, PhD); special education (M Ed, PhD); special education-deafness studies (M Ed); teaching English as a second language (M Ed). *Program availability:* Part-time. *Degree requirements:* For master's, thesis optional; for doctorate, comprehensive exam, thesis/dissertation. *Entrance requirements:* For master's and doctorate, minimum GPA of 3.0. Additional exam requirements/recommendations for international students: Required—TOEFL. *Faculty research:* Human learning, development and assessment.

The University of Arizona, College of Education, Department of Disability and Psychoeducational Studies, Program in School Counseling, Tucson, AZ 85721. Offers MA. *Accreditation:* ACA. *Program availability:* Part-time. *Degree requirements:* For master's, presentation or thesis. *Entrance requirements:* Additional exam requirements/recommendations for international students: Required—TOEFL (minimum score 550 paper-based; 79 iBT). Electronic applications accepted.

University of Arkansas, Graduate School, College of Education and Health Professions, Department of Rehabilitation, Human Resources and Communication Disorders, Program in Counselor Education, Fayetteville, AR 72701. Offers MS, PhD. *Accreditation:* ACA; NCATE. *Program availability:* Part-time, evening/weekend. *Students:* 130 part-time (96 women); includes 30 minority (9 Black or African American, non-Hispanic/Latino; 4 American Indian or Alaska Native, non-Hispanic/Latino; 2 Asian, non-Hispanic/Latino; 10 Hispanic/Latino; 5 Two or more races, non-Hispanic/Latino), 3 international. In 2018, 5 doctorates awarded. *Entrance requirements:* For master's, GRE General Test or MAT; for doctorate, GRE General Test. *Application deadline:* For fall admission, 8/1 for domestic students, 4/1 for international students; for spring admission, 12/1 for domestic students, 10/1 for international students; for summer admission, 4/15 for domestic students, 3/1 for international students. Applications are processed on a rolling basis. Application fee: $60. Electronic applications accepted. *Financial support:* In 2018–19, 15 research assistantships, 2 teaching assistantships were awarded; fellowships with tuition reimbursements, career-related internships or fieldwork, and Federal Work-Study also available. Support available to part-time students. Financial award application deadline: 4/1; financial award applicants required to submit FAFSA. *Unit head:* Dr. Matthew Ganio, Department Head, 479-575-2956, E-mail: msganio@uark.edu. *Application contact:* Paul Calleja, Assistant Dept. head - HHPR, Graduate Coordinator, 479-575-2854, Fax: 479-575-5778, E-mail: pcallej@uark.edu.
Website: http://cned.uark.edu

University of Arkansas at Little Rock, Graduate School, College of Education and Health Professions, Department of Counseling, Adult and Rehabilitation Education, Program in Counselor Education, Little Rock, AR 72204-1099. Offers M Ed. *Program availability:* Part-time, evening/weekend. *Degree requirements:* For master's, comprehensive exam, portfolio or thesis; PRAXIS II. *Entrance requirements:* For master's, minimum GPA of 2.75, teaching certificate, interview, current resume.

University of Central Arkansas, Graduate School, College of Education, Department of Leadership Studies, Program in School Counseling, Conway, AR 72035-0001. Offers MS. *Accreditation:* NCATE. *Program availability:* Part-time, evening/weekend, online learning. *Degree requirements:* For master's, comprehensive exam, thesis optional. *Entrance requirements:* For master's, GRE General Test, minimum GPA of 2.7. Additional exam requirements/recommendations for international students: Required—TOEFL (minimum score 550 paper-based). Electronic applications accepted.

University of Central Florida, College of Community Innovation and Education, Department of Counselor Education and School Psychology, Program in Counselor Education, Orlando, FL 32816. Offers M Ed, MA, Certificate, Ed S. *Accreditation:* ACA. *Program availability:* Part-time, evening/weekend. *Students:* 163 full-time (133 women), 59 part-time (49 women); includes 82 minority (21 Black or African American, non-Hispanic/Latino; 9 Asian, non-Hispanic/Latino; 45 Hispanic/Latino; 7 Two or more races, non-Hispanic/Latino), 3 international. Average age 27. 222 applicants, 55% accepted, 74 enrolled. In 2018, 60 master's, 17 other advanced degrees awarded. *Degree requirements:* For master's, comprehensive exam, thesis or alternative. *Entrance requirements:* For master's, GRE General Test, minimum GPA of 3.0, letters of recommendation, resume, goal statement. Additional exam requirements/recommendations for international students: Required—TOEFL. *Application deadline:* For fall admission, 2/15 for domestic students; for spring admission, 9/1 for domestic students. Application fee: $30. Electronic applications accepted. *Financial support:* In 2018–19, 22 students received support, including 4 fellowships with partial tuition reimbursements available (averaging $950 per year), 13 research assistantships with partial tuition reimbursements available (averaging $8,824 per year), 7 teaching assistantships with partial tuition reimbursements available (averaging $6,568 per year); career-related internships or fieldwork, Federal Work-Study, institutionally sponsored loans, tuition waivers (partial), and unspecified assistantships also available. Financial award application deadline: 3/1; financial award applicants required to submit FAFSA. *Unit head:* Dr. W. Bryce Hagedorn, Program Coordinator, 407-823-2401, E-mail: bryce.hagedorn@ucf.edu. *Application contact:* Associate Director, Graduate Admissions, 407-823-2766, Fax: 407-823-6442, E-mail: gradadmissions@ucf.edu.
Website: http://education.ucf.edu/counselored/

University of Central Missouri, The Graduate School, Warrensburg, MO 64093. Offers accountancy (MA); accounting (MBA); applied mathematics (MS); aviation safety (MA); biology (MS); business administration (MBA); career and technical education leadership (MS); college student personnel administration (MS); communication (MA); computer science (MS); counseling (MS); criminal justice (MS); educational leadership (Ed D); educational technology (MS); elementary and early childhood education (MSE); English (MA); environmental studies (MA); finance (MBA); history (MA); human services/educational technology (Ed S); human services/learning resources (Ed S); human services/professional counseling (Ed S); industrial hygiene (MS); industrial management (MS); information systems (MBA); information technology (MS); kinesiology (MS); library science and information services (MS); literacy education (MSE); marketing (MBA); mathematics (MS); music (MA); occupational safety management (MS); psychology (MS); rural family nursing (MS); school administration (MSE); social gerontology (MS); sociology (MA); special education (MSE); speech language pathology (MS); superintendency (Ed S); teaching (MAT); teaching English as a second language (MA); technology (MS); technology management (PhD); theatre (MA). *Accreditation:* ASHA. *Program availability:* Part-time, 100% online, blended/hybrid learning. *Degree requirements:* For master's and Ed S, comprehensive exam (for some programs), thesis (for some programs). *Entrance requirements:* Additional exam requirements/recommendations for international students: Required—TOEFL (minimum score 550 paper-based; 79 iBT). Electronic applications accepted.

University of Central Oklahoma, The Jackson College of Graduate Studies, College of Education and Professional Studies, Donna Nigh Department of Advanced Professional and Special Services, Edmond, OK 73034-5209. Offers educational leadership (M Ed); library media education (M Ed); reading (M Ed); school counseling (M Ed); special education (M Ed), including mild/moderate disabilities, severe-profound/multiple disabilities; speech-language pathology (MS). *Accreditation:* ASHA. *Program availability:* Part-time. *Degree requirements:* For master's, comprehensive exam (for some programs), thesis (for some programs). *Entrance requirements:* Additional exam requirements/recommendations for international students: Required—TOEFL (minimum score 550 paper-based; 79 iBT), IELTS (minimum score 6.5). Electronic applications accepted.

University of Cincinnati, Graduate School, College of Education, Criminal Justice, and Human Services, School of Human Services, Counseling Program, Cincinnati, OH 45221. Offers counselor education (Ed D); mental health (MA); school counseling (M Ed); substance abuse prevention (Graduate Certificate). *Accreditation:* ACA (one or more programs are accredited); NCATE. *Program availability:* Part-time. Terminal master's awarded for partial completion of doctoral program. *Degree requirements:* For master's, comprehensive exam, thesis or alternative; for doctorate, comprehensive exam, thesis/dissertation. *Entrance requirements:* For master's and doctorate, GRE General Test, interview. Additional exam requirements/recommendations for international students: Required—TOEFL (minimum score 620 paper-based). Electronic applications accepted. *Faculty research:* Group work, career development, ecology, prevention, multicultural.

University of Colorado Colorado Springs, College of Education, Colorado Springs, CO 80918. Offers counseling and human services (MA); curriculum and instruction (MA); educational leadership (MA); educational leadership, research and policy (PhD); special education (MA); teaching English to speakers of other languages (MA). *Accreditation:* ACA; NCATE. *Program availability:* Part-time, evening/weekend, 100% online, blended/hybrid learning. *Faculty:* 31 full-time (22 women), 61 part-time/adjunct (47 women). *Students:* 208 full-time (149 women), 351 part-time (256 women); includes 136 minority (30 Black or African American, non-Hispanic/Latino; 1 American Indian or Alaska Native, non-Hispanic/Latino; 12 Asian, non-Hispanic/Latino; 64 Hispanic/Latino; 29 Two or more races, non-Hispanic/Latino), 8 international. Average age 36. 230 applicants, 80% accepted, 101 enrolled. In 2018, 186 master's, 9 doctorates awarded. *Degree requirements:* For master's, comprehensive exam, thesis or alternative, microcomputer proficiency; for doctorate, comprehensive exam, thesis/dissertation, research lab. *Entrance requirements:* For master's, GRE General Test (recommended but not required), career goal statement, professional references; for doctorate, GRE General Test. Additional exam requirements/recommendations for international students: Recommended—TOEFL (minimum score 90 iBT), IELTS (minimum score 6.5). *Application deadline:* For fall admission, 1/28 priority date for domestic and international students; for spring admission, 11/1 priority date for domestic and international students. Applications are processed on a rolling basis. Application fee: $60 ($100 for international students). Electronic applications accepted. *Expenses:* Tuition and fees vary by program, course load, and residency type. Please visit the University of Colorado Colorado Springs Student Financial Services website to estimate current program costs: https://www.uccs.edu/bursar/index.php/estimate-your-bill. *Financial support:* In 2018–19, 15 students received support. Career-related internships or fieldwork, Federal Work-Study, scholarships/grants, and unspecified assistantships available. Support available to part-time students. Financial award application deadline: 3/1; financial award applicants required to submit FAFSA. *Faculty research:* Linguistically diverse education (LDE), educational policy, evidence-based reading and writing instruction, relational and social aggression, positive behavior supports, inclusive schooling, K-12 education policy. Total annual research expenditures: $607,967. *Unit head:* Dr. Valerie Martin Conley, Dean, 719-255-4133, E-mail: vmconley@uccs.edu. *Application contact:* The College of Education Student Resource Office, 719-255-4996, E-mail: education@uccs.edu.
Website: https://www.uccs.edu/coe/

University of Colorado Denver, School of Education and Human Development, Program in Counseling Psychology and Counselor Education, Denver, CO 80217. Offers counseling (MA), including clinical mental health counseling, couple and family counseling, multicultural counseling, school counseling; school counseling (MA). *Accreditation:* ACA; NCATE. *Program availability:* Part-time, evening/weekend. *Entrance requirements:* For master's, GRE or MAT (unless applicant already holds a graduate degree), letters of recommendation, interview, resume, transcripts from all colleges/universities attended. *Expenses:* Tuition, state resident: full-time $6786; part-time $337 per credit hour. Tuition, nonresident: full-time $22,590; part-time $1255 per credit hour. *Required fees:* $1231; $137 per credit hour. Tuition and fees vary according to program and reciprocity agreements. *Faculty research:* Spiritual issues in counseling, multicultural and diversity issues in counseling, adolescent suicide, career development.

University of Connecticut, Graduate School, Neag School of Education, Department of Educational Psychology, Program in Counseling Psychology, Storrs, CT 06269. Offers counseling psychology (PhD); school counseling (MA). *Accreditation:* ACA. Terminal master's awarded for partial completion of doctoral program. *Degree requirements:* For master's, comprehensive exam, thesis or alternative; for doctorate, thesis/dissertation. *Entrance requirements:* For doctorate, GRE General Test. Additional exam requirements/recommendations for international students: Required—TOEFL (minimum score 550 paper-based). Electronic applications accepted.

University of Dayton, Department of Counselor Education and Human Services, Dayton, OH 45469. Offers clinical mental health counseling (MS Ed); college student personnel (MS Ed); higher education administration (MS Ed); human services (MS Ed); school counseling (MS Ed); school psychology (MS Ed, Ed S). *Accreditation:* ACA; NCATE. *Program availability:* Part-time. *Degree requirements:* For master's, thesis (for some programs); for Ed S, thesis (for some programs), professional portfolio. *Entrance requirements:* For master's, MAT or GRE (if GPA less than 2.75), essays (for some programs). Additional exam requirements/recommendations for international students: Required—TOEFL (minimum score 550 paper-based; 80 iBT). Electronic applications accepted. *Expenses:* Contact institution. *Faculty research:* Student school bonding, traumatic brain injuries, wellness and counseling, creativity in education.

University of Florida, Graduate School, College of Education, School of Human Development and Organizational Studies in Education, Gainesville, FL 32611. Offers counseling and counselor education (Ed D, PhD), including counseling and counselor education, marriage and family counseling, mental health counseling, school counseling and guidance; educational leadership (M Ed, MAE, Ed D, PhD, Ed S), including educational leadership (Ed D, PhD), educational policy (Ed D, PhD); higher education administration (Ed D, PhD), including education policy (Ed D), educational policy, higher education administration; marriage and family counseling (M Ed, MAE, Ed D, PhD, Ed S); mental health counseling (M Ed, MAE, Ed D, PhD, Ed S); research and evaluation methodology (M Ed, MAE, Ed D, PhD); school counseling and guidance (M Ed, MAE, Ed D, PhD, Ed S); student personnel in higher education (M Ed, MAE). *Accreditation:* ACA (one or more programs are accredited); NCATE. *Program availability:* Part-time, online learning. Terminal master's awarded for partial completion of doctoral program. *Degree requirements:* For master's, thesis optional; for doctorate, comprehensive exam, thesis/dissertation. *Entrance requirements:* For master's and doctorate, GRE General Test, minimum GPA of 3.0 (undergraduate), 3.5 (graduate); for Ed S, GRE General Test. Additional exam requirements/recommendations for international students: Required—TOEFL (minimum score 550 paper-based; 80 iBT), IELTS (minimum score 6). Electronic applications accepted.

University of Georgia, College of Education, Department of Counseling and Human Development Services, Athens, GA 30602. Offers college student affairs administration (M Ed, PhD); professional school counseling (Ed S). *Accreditation:* ACA (one or more programs are accredited); APA (one or more programs are accredited); NCATE. *Degree requirements:* For master's, thesis (MA); for doctorate, variable foreign language requirement, thesis/dissertation. *Entrance requirements:* For master's, GRE General Test or MAT; for doctorate, GRE General Test. Electronic applications accepted.

University of Guam, Office of Graduate Studies, School of Education, Program in Counseling, Mangilao, GU 96923. Offers MA. *Degree requirements:* For master's, comprehensive oral and written exams, special project or thesis. *Entrance requirements:* For master's, GRE General Test. Additional exam requirements/recommendations for international students: Required—TOEFL. *Faculty research:* Drugs in the local schools, standardized teaching procedures in the elementary school, how to address the dropout problems.

University of Holy Cross, Graduate Programs, New Orleans, LA 70131-7399. Offers biomedical sciences (MS); Catholic theology (MA); counseling (MA, PhD), including community counseling (MA), marriage and family counseling (MA), school counseling (MA); educational leadership (M Ed); executive leadership (Ed D); management (MS), including healthcare management, operations management; teaching and learning (M Ed). *Accreditation:* ACA; NCATE. *Program availability:* Part-time, evening/weekend, online learning. *Degree requirements:* For master's, thesis. *Entrance requirements:* For master's, GRE General Test, minimum GPA of 2.7.

University of Houston–Clear Lake, School of Education, Program in Foundations and Professional Studies, Houston, TX 77058-1002. Offers counseling (MS); instructional technology (MS); multicultural studies (MS). *Program availability:* Part-time, evening/weekend. *Degree requirements:* For master's, thesis optional. *Entrance requirements:* For master's, GRE or minimum GPA of 3.0 in last 60 hours. Additional exam requirements/recommendations for international students: Required—TOEFL (minimum score 550 paper-based). Electronic applications accepted.

University of Houston–Victoria, School of Education, Health Professions and Human Development, Victoria, TX 77901-4450. Offers administration and supervision (M Ed); adult and higher education (M Ed); counselor education (M Ed); curriculum and instruction (M Ed); dyslexia education (Certificate); educational technology (M Ed); special education (M Ed). *Program availability:* Part-time, evening/weekend, online learning. *Degree requirements:* For master's, comprehensive exam, project or thesis. *Entrance requirements:* For master's, GRE General Test. Additional exam requirements/recommendations for international students: Required—TOEFL. Electronic applications accepted. *Expenses: Tuition, area resident:* Full-time $6154; part-time $3077 per semester. Tuition, state resident: full-time $6154; part-time $3077 per semester. Tuition, nonresident: full-time $13,624; part-time $6812 per semester. *International tuition:* $13,624 full-time. *Required fees:* $1405; $847 per semester. $423 per semester. Tuition and fees vary according to program. *Faculty research:* Reading and language arts education, evaluation and diagnosis of special children's abilities.

University of Idaho, College of Graduate Studies, College of Education, Health and Human Sciences, Department of Leadership and Counseling, Boise, ID 83702. Offers adult/organizational learning and leadership (Ed S); educational leadership (Ed S); rehabilitation counseling and human services (M Ed); school counseling (M Ed, MS). *Faculty:* 14. *Students:* 32 full-time (19 women), 123 part-time (68 women). Average age 37. In 2018, 53 master's, 22 other advanced degrees awarded. *Entrance requirements:* For master's, minimum GPA of 3.0, writing sample. Additional exam requirements/recommendations for international students: Required—TOEFL (minimum score 79 iBT). *Application deadline:* Applications are processed on a rolling basis. Application fee: $60. Electronic applications accepted. *Expenses:* Tuition, state resident: full-time $7266.44; part-time $474.50 per credit hour. Tuition, nonresident: full-time $24,902; part-time $1453.50 per credit hour. *Required fees:* $2085.56; $45.50 per credit hour. *Financial support:* Applicants required to submit FAFSA. *Unit head:* Dr. Kathy Canfield-Davis, Chair, 208-364-4047, E-mail: lead@uidaho.edu. *Application contact:* Dr. Kathy Canfield-Davis, Chair, 208-364-4047, E-mail: lead@uidaho.edu.
Website: https://www.uidaho.edu/ed/lc

University of Illinois at Urbana–Champaign, Graduate College, College of Education, Department of Educational Psychology, Champaign, IL 61820. Offers Ed M, MA, MS, PhD, CAS. *Accreditation:* APA (one or more programs are accredited). *Program availability:* Part-time, online learning.

The University of Iowa, Graduate College, College of Education, Department of Rehabilitation and Counselor Education, Iowa City, IA 52242-1316. Offers counselor education and supervision (PhD); couple and family therapy (PhD); rehabilitation and mental health counseling (MA); rehabilitation counselor education (PhD); school counseling (MA). *Accreditation:* ACA (one or more programs are accredited); CORE (one or more programs are accredited). *Degree requirements:* For master's, thesis optional, exam; for doctorate, comprehensive exam, thesis/dissertation. *Entrance requirements:* For master's and doctorate, GRE General Test, minimum GPA of 3.0. Additional exam requirements/recommendations for international students: Required—TOEFL (minimum score 550 paper-based; 81 iBT). Electronic applications accepted.

University of La Verne, LaFetra College of Education, Program in Educational Counseling, La Verne, CA 91750-4443. Offers educational counseling (MS); pupil personnel services (Credential); school psychology (MS). *Program availability:* Part-time. *Entrance requirements:* For master's, California Basic Educational Skills Test, minimum undergraduate GPA of 2.75, graduate 3.0; interview; 1 year's experience working with children; 3 letters of reference. Additional exam requirements/recommendations for international students: Required—TOEFL (minimum score 550 paper-based). *Expenses:* Contact institution.

University of La Verne, Regional and Online Campuses, Graduate Credential Program in Education, California Statewide Campus, La Verne, CA 91750-4443. Offers administration services (preliminary) (Credential); education specialist: mild/moderate (Credential); English (Certificate); multiple subject teaching (Credential); pupil personnel services: school counseling (Credential); single subject teaching (Credential); special education (MS); special emphasis (M Ed). *Accreditation:* NCATE. *Program availability:* Part-time. *Entrance requirements:* For degree, California Basic Educational Skills Test, minimum undergraduate GPA of 2.75, 3 letters of recommendation, interview. *Expenses:* Contact institution.

University of La Verne, Regional and Online Campuses, Graduate Programs, High Desert Campus, Victorville, CA 92392. Offers business administration for experienced professionals (MBA); educational (special emphasis) (M Ed); educational counseling (MS); leadership and management (MS); multiple subject (elementary) (Credential); preliminary administrative services (Credential); pupil personnel services (Credential); single subject (secondary) (Credential). *Expenses:* Contact institution.

University of La Verne, Regional and Online Campuses, Graduate Programs, Kern County Campus, Bakersfield, CA 93301. Offers business administration for experienced professionals (MBA-EP); education (special emphasis) (M Ed); educational counseling (MS); educational leadership (M Ed); health administration (MHA); leadership and management (MS); mild/moderate education specialist (Credential); multiple subject (elementary) (Credential); organizational leadership (Ed D); preliminary administrative services (Credential); single subject (secondary) (Credential); special education studies (MS). *Program availability:* Part-time, evening/weekend. *Expenses:* Contact institution.

University of La Verne, Regional and Online Campuses, Graduate Programs, Orange County Campus, Irvine, CA 92840. Offers business administration for experienced professionals (MBA); educational counseling (MS); educational leadership (M Ed); health administration (MHA); leadership and management (MS); preliminary administrative services (Credential); pupil personnel services (Credential). *Program availability:* Part-time. *Expenses:* Contact institution.

University of La Verne, Regional and Online Campuses, Graduate Programs, San Fernando Valley Campus, Burbank, CA 91505. Offers business administration for experienced professionals (MBA-EP); educational counseling (MS); educational leadership (M Ed); leadership and management (MS); preliminary administrative services (Credential); pupil personnel services (Credential). *Program availability:* Part-time, evening/weekend. *Expenses:* Contact institution.

University of La Verne, Regional and Online Campuses, Graduate Programs, Ventura County/Point Mugu Naval Air Station Campuses, Oxnard, CA 93036. Offers business administration for experienced professionals (MS); educational counseling (MS); educational leadership (M Ed); leadership and management (MS); multiple subject (elementary) (Credential); pupil personnel services (Credential); single subject (secondary) (Credential). *Program availability:* Part-time, evening/weekend. *Expenses:* Contact institution.

University of La Verne, Regional and Online Campuses, Master's Programs in Education, California Statewide Campus, La Verne, CA 91750-4443. Offers administration services (preliminary) (Credential); education specialist: mild/moderate (Credential); educational counseling (MS); educational leadership (M Ed); multiple subject teaching (Credential); pupil personnel services: school counseling (Credential); single subject teaching (Credential); special education studies (MS); special emphasis (M Ed). *Accreditation:* NCATE. *Entrance requirements:* For master's, California Basic Educational Skills Test, 3 letters of recommendation, teaching credential. *Expenses:* Contact institution.

University of Lethbridge, School of Graduate Studies, Lethbridge, AB T1K 3M4, Canada. Offers addictions counseling (M Sc); agricultural biotechnology (M Sc); agricultural studies (M Sc, MA); anthropology (MA); archaeology (M Sc, MA); art (MA, MFA); biochemistry (M Sc); biological sciences (M Sc); biomolecular science (PhD); biosystems and biodiversity (PhD); Canadian studies (MA); chemistry (M Sc); computer science (M Sc); computer science and geographical information science (M Sc); counseling (MC); counseling psychology (M Ed); dramatic arts (MA); earth, space, and physical science (PhD); economics (MA); education (MA, PhD); educational leadership (M Ed); English (MA); environmental science (M Sc); evolution and behavior (PhD); exercise science (M Sc); French (MA); French/German (MA); French/Spanish (MA); general education (M Ed); geography (M Sc, MA); German (MA); health sciences (M Sc); individualized multidisciplinary (M Sc, MA); kinesiology (M Sc, MA); management (M Sc), including accounting, finance, human resource management and labor relations, information systems, international management, marketing, policy and strategy; mathematics (M Sc); music (M Mus, MA); Native American studies (MA); neuroscience (M Sc, PhD); new media (MA, MFA); nursing (M Sc, MN); philosophy (MA); physics (M Sc); political science (MA); psychology (M Sc, MA); religious studies (MA); sociology (MA); theatre and dramatic arts (MFA); theoretical and computational science (PhD); urban and regional studies (MA); women and gender studies (MA). *Program availability:* Part-time, evening/weekend. *Degree requirements:* For master's, thesis (for some programs); for doctorate, comprehensive exam, thesis/dissertation. *Entrance requirements:* For master's, GMAT (for M Sc in management), bachelor's degree in related field, minimum GPA of 3.0 during previous 20 graded semester courses, 2 years' teaching or related experience (M Ed); for doctorate, master's degree, minimum graduate GPA of 3.5. Additional exam requirements/recommendations for international students: Required—TOEFL (minimum score 580 paper-based; 93 iBT). Electronic applications accepted. *Faculty research:* Movement and brain plasticity, gibberellin physiology, photosynthesis, carbon cycling, molecular properties of main-group ring components.

University of Louisiana at Lafayette, College of Education, Department of Counselor Education, Lafayette, LA 70504. Offers MS. *Accreditation:* ACA. *Entrance requirements:* For master's, GRE General Test, minimum GPA of 2.75. Additional exam requirements/recommendations for international students: Required—TOEFL (minimum score 550 paper-based). Electronic applications accepted.

University of Louisiana at Monroe, Graduate School, College of Health Sciences, Programs in Counseling Studies, Monroe, LA 71209-0001. Offers clinical mental health counseling (MS); school counseling (MS). *Accreditation:* ACA; NCATE. *Program availability:* Part-time, evening/weekend, online learning. *Faculty:* 3 full-time (all women). *Students:* 36 full-time (32 women), 13 part-time (10 women); includes 13 minority (11 Black or African American, non-Hispanic/Latino; 1 Hispanic/Latino; 1 Two or more races, non-Hispanic/Latino). Average age 33. 18 applicants, 94% accepted, 13 enrolled. In 2018, 18 master's awarded. *Degree requirements:* For master's, comprehensive exam, thesis. *Entrance requirements:* For master's, GRE General Test, minimum GPA of 2.8 in last 60 hours. Additional exam requirements/recommendations for international students: Required—TOEFL (minimum score 500 paper-based; 61 iBT). *Application deadline:* For fall admission, 8/24 priority date for domestic students, 7/1 for international students; for winter admission, 12/14 priority date for domestic students; for spring admission, 1/19 for domestic students, 11/1 for international students. Applications are processed on a rolling basis. Application fee: $20 ($30 for international students). Electronic applications accepted. *Financial support:* In 2018–19, 9 students received support. Career-related internships or fieldwork, Federal Work-Study, and unspecified assistantships available. Financial award application deadline: 4/1; financial award applicants required to submit FAFSA. *Unit head:* Dr. David Hale, Director, 318-342-1349, E-mail: dhale@ulm.edu. *Application contact:* Dr. David Hale, Director, 318-342-1349, E-mail: dhale@ulm.edu.
Website: http://www.ulm.edu/counseling/

University of Louisville, Graduate School, College of Education and Human Development, Department of Counseling and Human Development, Louisville, KY 40292-0001. Offers counseling and personnel services (M Ed, PhD), including art therapy (M Ed), college student personnel, counseling psychology, counselor education and supervision (PhD), educational psychology, measurement, and evaluation (PhD), mental health counseling (M Ed), school counseling (M Ed). *Accreditation:* APA; NCATE. *Program availability:* Part-time, evening/weekend, 100% online, blended/hybrid learning. *Students:* 136 full-time (109 women), 53 part-time (38 women); includes 40 minority (26 Black or African American, non-Hispanic/Latino; 1 American Indian or Alaska Native, non-Hispanic/Latino; 1 Asian, non-Hispanic/Latino; 8 Hispanic/Latino; 4 Two or more races, non-Hispanic/Latino), 4 international. Average age 29. 180 applicants, 47% accepted, 54 enrolled. In 2018, 39 master's awarded. Terminal master's awarded for partial completion of doctoral program. *Degree requirements:* For master's, comprehensive exam (for some programs), thesis optional; for doctorate, comprehensive exam (for some programs), thesis/dissertation. *Entrance requirements:*

For master's, GRE (for most programs), PRAXIS (for educator preparation programs), professional statement, recommendation letters, resume, transcripts; for doctorate, GRE, professional statement, recommendation letters, resume, transcripts. Additional exam requirements/recommendations for international students: Required—TOEFL (minimum score 550 paper-based; 79 iBT); Recommended—IELTS (minimum score 6.5). *Application deadline:* For fall admission, 6/1 priority date for domestic students, 5/1 priority date for international students; for spring admission, 10/1 priority date for domestic students, 11/1 priority date for international students; for summer admission, 3/1 priority date for domestic students, 4/1 priority date for international students. Application fee: $65. *Expenses: Tuition, area resident:* Full-time $6500; part-time $723 per credit hour. Tuition, state resident: full-time $6500. Tuition, nonresident: full-time $13,557; part-time $1507 per credit hour. Tuition and fees vary according to course load and program. *Financial support:* In 2018–19, 95 students received support, including 5 fellowships with full tuition reimbursements available (averaging $21,024 per year), 32 research assistantships with full tuition reimbursements available (averaging $21,024 per year), 18 teaching assistantships with full tuition reimbursements available (averaging $21,024 per year); Federal Work-Study, scholarships/grants, health care benefits, and unspecified assistantships also available. Financial award application deadline: 3/1; financial award applicants required to submit FAFSA. *Faculty research:* Mental health services and under-served populations; health disparities and outcomes; well-being identity development; measurement and evaluation; college student personnel. *Unit head:* Dr. Mark M. Leach, Chair and Professor, 502-852-6884, E-mail: ecpy@louisville.edu. *Application contact:* Dr. Margaret Pentecost, Assistant Dean for Graduate Student Success, 502-852-2628, Fax: 502-852-1417, E-mail: gedadm@louisville.edu.
Website: http://www.louisville.edu/education/departments/ecpy

University of Lynchburg, Graduate Studies, M Ed Program in School Counseling, Lynchburg, VA 24501-3199. Offers M Ed. *Accreditation:* ACA. *Program availability:* Part-time, evening/weekend. *Degree requirements:* For master's, counseling internship. *Entrance requirements:* For master's, GRE, minimum GPA of 3.0 (preferred), official transcripts (bachelor's, others as relevant), three letters of recommendation, career goals statement, personal interview. Additional exam requirements/recommendations for international students: Required—TOEFL (minimum score 550 paper-based; 80 iBT), IELTS (minimum score 6). Electronic applications accepted. Application fee is waived when completed online. *Expenses:* Contact institution.

University of Manitoba, Faculty of Graduate Studies, Faculty of Education, Department of Educational Administration, Foundations and Psychology, Winnipeg, MB R3T 2N2, Canada. Offers adult and post-secondary education (M Ed); educational administration (M Ed); guidance and counseling (M Ed); inclusive special education (M Ed); social foundations of education (M Ed). *Degree requirements:* For master's, thesis or alternative.

University of Mary Hardin-Baylor, Graduate Studies in Counseling, Belton, TX 76513. Offers clinical and mental health counseling (MA); marriage, family and child counseling (MA); non-clinical professional studies (MA). *Accreditation:* ACA. *Program availability:* Part-time, evening/weekend. *Degree requirements:* For master's, comprehensive exam. *Entrance requirements:* For master's, GRE General Test with minimum cumulative score of 300 on verbal and quantitative portions and 3.0 on analytical section (if overall undergraduate GPA is below a 3.0), minimum cumulative undergraduate GPA of 2.75 or 3.0 on last 60 hours of course work; three letters of recommendation; interview with departmental graduate admissions committee. Additional exam requirements/recommendations for international students: Required—TOEFL (minimum score 60 iBT), IELTS (minimum score 4.5). Electronic applications accepted. *Faculty research:* Teaching mindfulness skills as part of an interdisciplinary training protocol for doctor of physical therapy students; using symbolic art cards and oracle cards in supervision as a method for teaching appropriate self-disclosure, clinical reflection and counselor development reflection; understanding integral breath therapy.

University of Maryland, College Park, Academic Affairs, College of Education, Department of Counseling, Higher Education and Special Education, College Park, MD 20742. Offers college student personnel (M Ed, MA); college student personnel administration (PhD); community counseling (CAGS); community/career counseling (M Ed, MA); counseling and personnel services (M Ed, MA, PhD), including art therapy (M Ed), college student personnel (M Ed), counseling and personnel services (PhD), counseling psychology (M Ed), mental health counseling (M Ed), school counseling (M Ed); counseling psychology (PhD); counselor education (PhD); rehabilitation counseling (M Ed, MA, AGSC); school counseling (M Ed, MA); school psychology (M Ed, MA, PhD). *Accreditation:* APA (one or more programs are accredited); NCATE. *Program availability:* Part-time, evening/weekend, online learning. *Degree requirements:* For master's, thesis (for some programs); for doctorate, thesis/dissertation. *Entrance requirements:* For master's, GRE General Test or MAT, minimum GPA of 3.0, 3 letters of recommendation; for doctorate, GRE General Test or MAT, minimum GPA of 3.5, 3 letters of recommendation. Additional exam requirements/recommendations for international students: Required—TOEFL. Electronic applications accepted. *Faculty research:* Educational psychology, counseling, health.

University of Maryland Eastern Shore, Graduate Programs, Department of Education, Program in Guidance and Counseling, Princess Anne, MD 21853. Offers M Ed. *Program availability:* Evening/weekend. *Degree requirements:* For master's, comprehensive exam, practicum, seminar paper. *Entrance requirements:* For master's, interview, minimum GPA of 3.0. Additional exam requirements/recommendations for international students: Required—TOEFL (minimum score 80 iBT). Electronic applications accepted.

University of Massachusetts Amherst, Graduate School, College of Education, Program in Education, Amherst, MA 01003. Offers bilingual, English as a second language, and multicultural education (M Ed, Ed S); child study and early education (M Ed); children, families and schools (Ed D, Ed S); early childhood and elementary teacher education (M Ed); educational leadership (M Ed); educational policy and leadership (Ed D); higher education (M Ed); international education (M Ed); language, literacy and culture (Ed D); learning, media and technology (M Ed, Ed S); mathematics, science, and learning technologies (Ed D); reading and writing (M Ed); research, educational measurement and psychometrics (Ed D); school counselor education (M Ed, Ed S); school psychology (Ed S); science education (Ed S); secondary teacher education (M Ed); social justice education (M Ed, Ed D, Ed S); special education (M Ed, Ed D, Ed S); teacher education and school improvement (Ed D, Ed S). *Accreditation:* NCATE. *Program availability:* Part-time, online learning. Terminal master's awarded for partial completion of doctoral program. *Degree requirements:* For doctorate, comprehensive exam, thesis/dissertation. *Entrance requirements:* Additional exam requirements/recommendations for international students: Required—TOEFL (minimum score 550 paper-based; 80 iBT), IELTS (minimum score 6.5). Electronic applications accepted.

University of Massachusetts Boston, College of Education and Human Development, Program in School Counseling, Boston, MA 02125-3393. Offers M Ed. *Students:* 51 full-time (41 women), 8 part-time (7 women); includes 9 minority (5 Black or African American, non-Hispanic/Latino; 2 Hispanic/Latino; 2 Two or more races, non-Hispanic/Latino). Average age 30. 61 applicants, 84% accepted, 32 enrolled. In 2018, 22 master's awarded. *Application deadline:* For fall admission, 1/2 for domestic students. Application fee: $60 ($100 for international students). Electronic applications accepted. *Expenses: Tuition, area resident:* Full-time $17,896. Tuition, state resident: full-time $17,896. Tuition, nonresident: full-time $34,932. *International tuition:* $34,932 full-time. *Required fees:* $355. *Unit head:* Dr. Amy L Cook, Assistant Professor in Counseling and School Psychology, 617-287.7585, E-mail: amy.cook@umb.edu. *Application contact:* Graduate Admissions Coordinator, 617-287-6400, Fax: 617-287-6236, E-mail: graduate.admissions@umb.edu.

University of Memphis, Graduate School, College of Education, Department of Counseling, Educational Psychology and Research, Memphis, TN 38152. Offers counseling (MS, Ed D), including clinical mental health counseling (MS), clinical rehabilitation counseling (MS), rehabilitation counseling (MS), school counseling (MS); counseling psychology (PhD); educational psychology and research (MS, PhD), including educational psychology, educational research. *Accreditation:* ACA (one or more programs are accredited); APA (one or more programs are accredited); CORE (one or more programs are accredited); NCATE. *Program availability:* Blended/hybrid learning. *Students:* 137 full-time (114 women), 126 part-time (96 women); includes 96 minority (75 Black or African American, non-Hispanic/Latino; 6 Asian, non-Hispanic/Latino; 10 Hispanic/Latino; 5 Two or more races, non-Hispanic/Latino), 5 international. Average age 33. 103 applicants, 61% accepted, 59 enrolled. In 2018, 30 master's, 19 doctorates awarded. *Degree requirements:* For master's, comprehensive exam, thesis or alternative, internship; for doctorate, comprehensive exam, thesis/dissertation, practicum, internship, residency, scholarly work. *Entrance requirements:* For master's, GRE General Test or MAT, minimum GPA of 2.5, letters of reference, interview; for doctorate, GRE General Test, master's degree or equivalent, letters of reference, interview, curriculum vitae, personal statement. Additional exam requirements/recommendations for international students: Required—TOEFL (minimum score 550 paper-based; 79 iBT). *Application deadline:* For fall admission, 10/1 priority date for domestic students; for spring admission, 4/1 priority date for domestic students. Applications are processed on a rolling basis. Application fee: $35 ($60 for international students). Electronic applications accepted. *Expenses: Tuition, area resident:* Full-time $10,240; part-time $503 per credit hour. Tuition, state resident: full-time $10,464. Tuition, nonresident: full-time $20,224; part-time $991 per credit hour. *Required fees:* $850; $106 per credit hour. *Financial support:* Fellowships with full tuition reimbursements, research assistantships with full tuition reimbursements, teaching assistantships with full tuition reimbursements, career-related internships or fieldwork, Federal Work-Study, scholarships/grants, and unspecified assistantships available. Financial award application deadline: 2/1; financial award applicants required to submit FAFSA. *Faculty research:* Anger management, aging and disability, supervision, multicultural counseling. *Unit head:* Dr. Steve West, Chair, 901-678-2841, Fax: 901-678-5114, E-mail: slwest@memphis.edu. *Application contact:* Stormey Warren, Graduate Programs, 901-678-2363, Fax: 901-678-4778, E-mail: shutsell@memphis.edu.
Website: http://www.memphis.edu/cepr/

University of Miami, Graduate School, School of Education and Human Development, Department of Educational and Psychological Studies, Program in Counseling, Coral Gables, FL 33124. Offers counseling and research (MS Ed); Latino mental health (Certificate); marriage and family therapy (MS Ed); mental health counseling (MS Ed). *Program availability:* Part-time, evening/weekend. *Faculty:* 6 full-time (2 women). *Students:* 27 full-time (21 women), 3 part-time (all women); includes 11 minority (all Hispanic/Latino), 8 international. Average age 26. 57 applicants, 53% accepted, 12 enrolled. In 2018, 21 master's awarded. *Degree requirements:* For master's, comprehensive exam, personal growth experience, 15-practicum credit hours. *Entrance requirements:* For master's, GRE General Test. Additional exam requirements/recommendations for international students: Required—TOEFL (minimum score 550 paper-based; 80 iBT); Recommended—IELTS (minimum score 6.5). *Application deadline:* Applications are processed on a rolling basis. Application fee: $75. Electronic applications accepted. *Financial support:* Career-related internships or fieldwork, institutionally sponsored loans, and tuition waivers (partial) available. Support available to part-time students. Financial award application deadline: 3/1; financial award applicants required to submit FAFSA. *Faculty research:* Cocaine recidivism, HIV, non-traditional families, health psychology, diversity. *Unit head:* Dr. Anabel Bejarano, Assistant Professor of Professional Practice/Program Director, 305-284-4829, Fax: 305-284-3003, E-mail: bejarano@miami.edu. *Application contact:* Lois Heffernan, Graduate Admissions Coordinator, 305-284-2167, Fax: 305-284-9395, E-mail: lheffernan@miami.edu.
Website: http://www.education.miami.edu

University of Minnesota, Twin Cities Campus, Graduate School, College of Education and Human Development, Department of Educational Psychology, Program in Counseling and Student Personnel Psychology, Minneapolis, MN 55455-0213. Offers MA. *Students:* 63 full-time (46 women), 3 part-time (all women); includes 8 minority (3 Asian, non-Hispanic/Latino; 2 Hispanic/Latino; 3 Two or more races, non-Hispanic/Latino), 9 international. Average age 26. 64 applicants, 67% accepted, 29 enrolled. In 2018, 34 master's awarded. Application fee: $75 ($95 for international students). *Unit head:* Dr. Kristen McMaster, Chair, 612-624-6083, Fax: 612-624-8241, E-mail: mcmas004@umn.edu. *Application contact:* Dr. Panayiota Kendeou, Director of Graduate Studies, 612-626-7814, E-mail: kend0040@umn.edu.
Website: http://www.cehd.umn.edu/EdPsych/Programs/CSPP/default.html

University of Mississippi, Graduate School, School of Education, University, MS 38677. Offers counselor education (M Ed, PhD); counselor education - play therapy (Ed S); early childhood (M Ed); educational leadership K-12 (M Ed, Ed D, PhD, Ed S); elementary education (M Ed, Ed D, Ed S); higher education/student personnel (Ed D, PhD); literacy education (M Ed); math education (Ed D); secondary education (M Ed, PhD, Ed S); special education (M Ed, PhD, Ed S); teacher corporations (MA); teacher education (MA). *Accreditation:* NCATE. *Faculty:* 59 full-time (35 women), 34 part-time/adjunct (26 women). *Students:* 169 full-time (137 women), 461 part-time (329 women); includes 199 minority (185 Black or African American, non-Hispanic/Latino; 3 Asian, non-Hispanic/Latino; 7 Hispanic/Latino; 4 Two or more races, non-Hispanic/Latino), 5 international. Average age 33. In 2018, 180 master's, 57 doctorates, 37 other advanced degrees awarded. *Entrance requirements:* For master's, GRE General Test, minimum GPA of 3.0; for doctorate, GRE General Test. Additional exam requirements/recommendations for international students: Required—TOEFL. *Application deadline:* Applications are processed on a rolling basis. Application fee: $50. Electronic applications accepted. *Financial support:* Scholarships/grants available. Financial award application deadline: 3/1; financial award applicants required to submit FAFSA. *Unit head:* Dr. David Rock, Dean, 662-915-7063, Fax: 662-915-7249, E-mail: soe@olemiss.edu. *Application contact:* Temeka Smith, Graduate Activities Specialist for Admissions, 662-915-7474, Fax: 662-915-7577, E-mail: gschool@olemiss.edu.

University of Missouri–Kansas City, School of Education, Kansas City, MO 64110-2499. Offers administration (Ed D); counseling and guidance (MA, Ed S), including mental health counseling (Ed S), school counseling (Ed S); counseling psychology (PhD); curriculum and instruction (MA, Ed S), including language and literacy (Ed S); education (PhD), including higher education administration, PK-12 education administration; educational administration (MA, Ed S), including advanced principal (Ed S), beginning principal (Ed S), district-level administration (Ed S); reading education

(MA); special education (MA). PhD in education offered through the School of Graduate Studies. *Accreditation:* NCATE. *Program availability:* Part-time, evening/weekend. *Degree requirements:* For doctorate, thesis/dissertation, internship, practicum. *Entrance requirements:* For master's, GRE, minimum GPA of 2.75, 2 letters of reference, written statement of purpose; for doctorate, GRE, minimum GPA of 3.0; for Ed S, minimum GPA of 3.0. Additional exam requirements/recommendations for international students: Required—TOEFL (minimum score 550 paper-based; 80 iBT). *Faculty research:* Urban education, inquiry-based field study, theories of counseling and psychotherapy, school literacy, educational technology.

University of Missouri–St. Louis, College of Education, Interdisciplinary Doctoral Programs, St. Louis, MO 63121. Offers counseling (PhD); educational leadership and policy studies (PhD); educational psychology (PhD); leadership in educational practice (Ed D); teaching-learning processes (PhD). *Degree requirements:* For doctorate, thesis/dissertation. *Entrance requirements:* For doctorate, GRE General Test, 3 letters of recommendation; personal interview. Additional exam requirements/recommendations for international students: Recommended—TOEFL (minimum score 550 paper-based; 79 iBT), IELTS (minimum score 6.5). Electronic applications accepted. *Faculty research:* Higher education law and policy, gender and higher education, student retention, lifelong learning orientation, school counselor's role in violence prevention.

University of Montana, Graduate School, Phyllis J. Washington College of Education and Human Sciences, Department of Counselor Education, Missoula, MT 59812. Offers clinical mental health counseling (MA); counseling and supervision (Ed D); counselor education (Ed S); intercultural youth and family development (MA); school counseling (MA). *Accreditation:* ACA. *Degree requirements:* For doctorate, thesis/dissertation. *Entrance requirements:* For master's, doctorate, and Ed S, GRE General Test. Additional exam requirements/recommendations for international students: Required—TOEFL.

University of Montevallo, College of Education, Program in Counseling, Montevallo, AL 35115. Offers M Ed. *Accreditation:* ACA; NCATE. *Program availability:* Part-time, evening/weekend. *Students:* 50 full-time (41 women), 51 part-time (37 women); includes 23 minority (17 Black or African American, non-Hispanic/Latino; 3 Hispanic/Latino; 3 Two or more races, non-Hispanic/Latino). In 2018, 43 master's awarded. *Entrance requirements:* For master's, GRE General Test or MAT, minimum undergraduate GPA of 2.75 in last 60 hours or 2.5 overall, interview. Additional exam requirements/recommendations for international students: Required—TOEFL (minimum score 550 paper-based). *Application deadline:* For fall admission, 7/15 for domestic students; for spring admission, 11/15 for domestic students. Application fee: $30. *Expenses: Tuition, area resident:* Full-time $10,512. Tuition, state resident: full-time $10,512. Tuition, nonresident: full-time $22,464. *International tuition:* $22,464 full-time. *Financial support:* Federal Work-Study, scholarships/grants, and unspecified assistantships available. *Unit head:* Dr. Charlotte Daughhetee, Chair, 205-665-6358, E-mail: daughc@montevallo.edu. *Application contact:* Colleen Kennedy, Graduate Program Assistant, 205-665-6350, E-mail: ckennedy@montevallo.edu.
Website: http://www.montevallo.edu/education/college-of-education/traditional-masters-degrees/counseling/

University of Nebraska at Kearney, College of Education, Department of Counseling and School Psychology, Kearney, NE 68849-0001. Offers clinical mental health counseling (MS Ed); school counseling (MS Ed), including elementary, secondary; school psychology (Ed S); student affairs (MS Ed). *Accreditation:* ACA; NCATE. *Program availability:* Part-time, evening/weekend, 100% online. *Degree requirements:* For master's, comprehensive exam, thesis optional; for Ed S, thesis. *Entrance requirements:* For master's and Ed S, personal statement, recommendations, resume, interview. Additional exam requirements/recommendations for international students: Recommended—TOEFL (minimum score 550 paper-based; 79 iBT), IELTS (minimum score 6.5). Electronic applications accepted. *Faculty research:* Multicultural counseling and diversity issues, team decision-making, adult development, women's issues, brief therapy.

University of Nebraska at Omaha, Graduate Studies, College of Education, Department of Counseling, Omaha, NE 68182. Offers MA, MS. *Accreditation:* ACA (one or more programs are accredited); NCATE. *Program availability:* Part-time, evening/weekend. *Degree requirements:* For master's, comprehensive exam, thesis (for some programs). *Entrance requirements:* For master's, GRE General Test, MAT, interview, minimum GPA of 3.0, 3 letters of recommendation, transcripts. Additional exam requirements/recommendations for international students: Required—TOEFL, IELTS, PTE. Electronic applications accepted.

University of Nevada, Las Vegas, Graduate College, College of Education, Department of Educational and Clinical Studies, Las Vegas, NV 89154-3066. Offers addiction studies (Advanced Certificate); counselor education (M Ed, MS), including clinical mental health (MS), school counseling (M Ed); early childhood education (M Ed); early childhood special education (Certificate), including infancy, preschool; English language learning (M Ed); mental health counseling (Advanced Certificate); special education (M Ed, PhD); PhD/JD. *Program availability:* Part-time. *Degree requirements:* For master's, comprehensive exam (for some programs); for doctorate, comprehensive exam, thesis/dissertation; for other advanced degree, final project. *Entrance requirements:* For master's, bachelor's degree; letter of recommendation; statement of purpose; for doctorate, GRE General Test, statement of purpose; writing sample; 3 letters of recommendation. Additional exam requirements/recommendations for international students: Required—TOEFL (minimum score 550 paper-based; 80 iBT), IELTS (minimum score 7). Electronic applications accepted. *Expenses:* Contact institution. *Faculty research:* Multicultural issues in counseling, academic interventions for students with disabilities, establishment of pro-social skills in young children with severe disabilities, inclusive strategies for students with disabilities, language and literacy for English language learners.

University of Nevada, Reno, Graduate School, College of Education, Department of Counseling and Educational Psychology, Reno, NV 89557. Offers M Ed, MA, MS, Ed D, PhD, Ed S. *Accreditation:* ACA (one or more programs are accredited); NCATE. Terminal master's awarded for partial completion of doctoral program. *Degree requirements:* For master's, comprehensive exam, thesis optional; for doctorate, comprehensive exam, thesis/dissertation, qualifying exam. *Entrance requirements:* For master's, GRE, minimum GPA of 2.75; for doctorate, GRE, minimum GPA of 3.0. Additional exam requirements/recommendations for international students: Required—TOEFL (minimum score 500 paper-based; 61 iBT), IELTS (minimum score 6). Electronic applications accepted. *Faculty research:* Marriage and family counseling, substance abuse attitudes of teachers, current supply of counseling educators, HIV-positive services for patients, family counseling for youth at risk.

University of New Mexico, Graduate Studies, College of Education, Program in Counselor Education, Albuquerque, NM 87131-2039. Offers counseling (MA); counselor education (PhD). *Accreditation:* ACA (one or more programs are accredited); NCATE. *Program availability:* Part-time. *Students:* Average age 33. 69 applicants, 26% accepted, 16 enrolled. In 2018, 30 master's, 3 doctorates awarded. *Degree requirements:* For master's, comprehensive exam; for doctorate, comprehensive exam, thesis/dissertation. *Entrance requirements:* For master's, 3 letters of recommendation, personal statement; for doctorate, GRE General Test, 3 letters of recommendation, writing sample, personal statement. Additional exam requirements/recommendations for international students: Required—TOEFL. *Application deadline:* For fall admission, 11/1 for domestic and international students; for spring admission, 9/15 for domestic and international students. Application fee: $50. Electronic applications accepted. *Financial support:* Unspecified assistantships available. Financial award application deadline: 3/1; financial award applicants required to submit FAFSA. *Faculty research:* Counselor education and supervision, school counseling, LGBTQQI, crisis and trauma, multiculturalism. *Unit head:* Dr. Jean Keim, Program Coordinator, 505-277-4535, Fax: 505-277-8361, E-mail: divbse@unm.edu. *Application contact:* Cynthia Salas, Department Administrator, 505-277-4535, Fax: 505-277-8361, E-mail: divbse@unm.edu.
Website: https://coe.unm.edu/departments-programs/ifce/counselor-education/index.html

University of New Orleans, Graduate School, College of Liberal Arts, Education and Human Development, Department of Educational Leadership, Counseling, and Foundations, Program in Counselor Education, New Orleans, LA 70148. Offers counseling (M Ed); counselor education (PhD). *Accreditation:* ACA (one or more programs are accredited); NCATE. *Program availability:* Evening/weekend. Terminal master's awarded for partial completion of doctoral program. *Degree requirements:* For master's, thesis (for some programs); for doctorate, variable foreign language requirement, thesis/dissertation. *Entrance requirements:* For master's and doctorate, GRE General Test. Additional exam requirements/recommendations for international students: Required—TOEFL (minimum score 550 paper-based; 79 iBT). Electronic applications accepted.

University of North Alabama, College of Education, Department of Counselor Education, Florence, AL 35632-0001. Offers clinical mental health counseling (MA); counseling (MA Ed). *Accreditation:* ACA; NCATE. *Program availability:* Part-time. *Degree requirements:* For master's, comprehensive exam. *Entrance requirements:* For master's, GRE, MAT, or NTE, minimum GPA of 2.5, Alabama Class B Certificate or equivalent, teaching experience. Additional exam requirements/recommendations for international students: Required—TOEFL (minimum score 79 iBT), IELTS (minimum score 6), PTE (minimum score 54). Electronic applications accepted.

The University of North Carolina at Chapel Hill, Graduate School, School of Education, Program in School Counseling, Chapel Hill, NC 27599. Offers M Ed. *Accreditation:* ACA; NCATE. *Degree requirements:* For master's, comprehensive exam. *Entrance requirements:* For master's, GRE General Test, minimum GPA of 3.0 during last 2 years of undergraduate course work. Additional exam requirements/recommendations for international students: Required—TOEFL (minimum score 550 paper-based). Electronic applications accepted. *Faculty research:* Career counseling, development and assessment, multicultural counseling, measurement.

The University of North Carolina at Charlotte, Cato College of Education, Department of Counseling, Charlotte, NC 28223-0001. Offers counseling (MA); counselor education and supervision (PhD); play therapy (Postbaccalaureate Certificate); school counseling (Post-Master's Certificate); substance abuse counseling (Postbaccalaureate Certificate). *Accreditation:* ACA. *Program availability:* Part-time, evening/weekend. *Students:* 121 full-time (105 women), 96 part-time (76 women); includes 70 minority (44 Black or African American, non-Hispanic/Latino; 4 Asian, non-Hispanic/Latino; 19 Hispanic/Latino; 3 Two or more races, non-Hispanic/Latino), 4 international. Average age 31. 263 applicants, 46% accepted, 72 enrolled. In 2018, 45 master's, 10 doctorates, 16 other advanced degrees awarded. Terminal master's awarded for partial completion of doctoral program. *Entrance requirements:* For master's, GRE or MAT, bachelor's degree from regionally-accredited university, minimum overall GPA of 3.0, brief statement of purpose, professional references, official transcripts; for doctorate, GRE or MAT, master's degree in counseling from a CACREP-accredited program with minimum cumulative GPA of 3.5; one year of experience as a professional counselor (preferred); letters of reference; essay; interview; for other advanced degree, statement of purpose, three reference letters. Additional exam requirements/recommendations for international students: Required—TOEFL (minimum score 523 paper-based; 70 iBT), IELTS (minimum score 6), TOEFL (minimum score 523 paper-based, 70 iBT) or IELTS (6). *Application deadline:* Applications are processed on a rolling basis. Application fee: $75. Electronic applications accepted. Tuition and fees vary according to course load and program. *Financial support:* Research assistantships, teaching assistantships, career-related internships or fieldwork, institutionally sponsored loans, scholarships/grants, and unspecified assistantships available. Support available to part-time students. Financial award application deadline: 3/1; financial award applicants required to submit FAFSA. *Total annual research expenditures:* $10,000. *Unit head:* Dr. Henry L. Harris, Chair, 704-687-8960, E-mail: hharris2@uncc.edu. *Application contact:* Kathy B. Giddings, Director of Graduate Admissions, 704-687-5503, Fax: 704-687-1668, E-mail: gradadm@uncc.edu.
Website: http://counseling.uncc.edu/

The University of North Carolina at Greensboro, Graduate School, School of Education, Department of Counseling and Educational Development, Greensboro, NC 27412-5001. Offers advanced school counseling (PMC); counseling and counselor education (PhD); counseling and educational development (MS); couple and family counseling (PMC); school counseling (PMC); MS/Ed S. *Accreditation:* ACA (one or more programs are accredited); NCATE. *Degree requirements:* For master's, comprehensive exam, practicum, internship; for doctorate, comprehensive exam, thesis/dissertation. *Entrance requirements:* For master's, doctorate, and PMC, GRE General Test. Additional exam requirements/recommendations for international students: Required—TOEFL. Electronic applications accepted. *Faculty research:* Gerontology, invitational theory, career development, marriage and family therapy, drug and alcohol abuse prevention.

The University of North Carolina at Pembroke, The Graduate School, School of Education, Programs in Counseling, Pembroke, NC 28372-1510. Offers clinical mental health counseling (MA Ed); professional school counseling (MA Ed). *Accreditation:* NCATE. *Program availability:* Part-time, evening/weekend. *Degree requirements:* For master's, comprehensive exam, thesis optional. *Entrance requirements:* For master's, GRE General Test or MAT, minimum GPA of 3.0 in major, 2.5 overall. Additional exam requirements/recommendations for international students: Required—TOEFL.

University of Northern Colorado, Graduate School, College of Education and Behavioral Sciences, Department of Applied Psychology and Counselor Education, Program in Counselor Education and Supervision, Greeley, CO 80639. Offers PhD. *Accreditation:* ACA. *Program availability:* Part-time. *Degree requirements:* For doctorate, comprehensive exam, thesis/dissertation. *Entrance requirements:* For doctorate, GRE General Test, 3 letters of recommendation.

University of Northern Colorado, Graduate School, College of Education and Behavioral Sciences, Department of Applied Psychology and Counselor Education, Program in School Counseling, Greeley, CO 80639. Offers MA. *Accreditation:* ACA. *Program availability:* Part-time. Electronic applications accepted.

University of Northern Iowa, Graduate College, College of Social and Behavioral Sciences, School of Applied Human Sciences, MA Program in Counseling, Cedar Falls, IA 50614. Offers mental health counseling (MA); school counseling (MA). *Accreditation:*

ACA. *Program availability:* Part-time, evening/weekend. *Degree requirements:* For master's, comprehensive exam, thesis or alternative. *Entrance requirements:* For master's, minimum GPA of 3.0. Additional exam requirements/recommendations for international students: Required—TOEFL (minimum score 500 paper-based; 61 iBT). Electronic applications accepted.

University of North Florida, College of Education and Human Services, Department of Leadership, School Counseling and Sport Management, Jacksonville, FL 32224. Offers counselor education (M Ed), including school counseling; educational leadership (M Ed, Ed D), including athletic administration (M Ed), educational leadership, educational technology (M Ed), instructional leadership (M Ed). *Program availability:* Part-time, evening/weekend. *Faculty:* 19 full-time (13 women), 3 part-time/adjunct (1 woman). *Students:* 73 full-time (58 women), 228 part-time (179 women); includes 111 minority (66 Black or African American, non-Hispanic/Latino; 7 Asian, non-Hispanic/Latino; 26 Hispanic/Latino; 1 Native Hawaiian or other Pacific Islander, non-Hispanic/Latino; 11 Two or more races, non-Hispanic/Latino), 8 international. Average age 38. 184 applicants, 58% accepted, 74 enrolled. In 2018, 77 master's, 20 doctorates awarded. *Degree requirements:* For doctorate, thesis/dissertation. *Entrance requirements:* For master's, GRE General Test, minimum GPA of 3.0 in last 60 hours, interview, 3 letters of recommendation; for doctorate, GRE General Test, master's degree, interview, 3 letters of recommendation, writing sample. Additional exam requirements/recommendations for international students: Required—TOEFL (minimum score 500 paper-based). *Application deadline:* For fall admission, 5/1 priority date for domestic students, 5/1 for international students. Application fee: $30. Electronic applications accepted. *Expenses: Tuition, area resident:* Part-time $408.10 per credit hour. Tuition, state resident: part-time $408.10 per credit hour. Tuition, nonresident: part-time $932.61 per credit hour. *Required fees:* $111.81 per credit hour. Tuition and fees vary according to course load, campus/location and program. *Financial support:* In 2018–19, 42 students received support, including 1 research assistantship (averaging $8,096 per year), 1 teaching assistantship (averaging $5,824 per year); career-related internships or fieldwork, Federal Work-Study, scholarships/grants, tuition waivers (partial), and unspecified assistantships also available. Support available to part-time students. Financial award application deadline: 4/1; financial award applicants required to submit FAFSA. *Faculty research:* Counseling: ethics; lesbian, bisexual and transgender issues; educational leadership: school culture and climate; educational assessment and accountability; school safety and student discipline. *Total annual research expenditures:* $12,024. *Unit head:* Dr. Liz Gregg, Chair, 904-620-5199, E-mail: liz.gregg@unf.edu. *Application contact:* Dr. Amanda Pascale, Director, The Graduate School, 904-620-1360, Fax: 904-620-1362, E-mail: graduateschool@unf.edu.
Website: http://www.unf.edu/coehs/lscsm/

University of North Texas, Toulouse Graduate School, Denton, TX 76203-5459. Offers accounting (MS); applied anthropology (MA, MS); applied behavior analysis (Certificate); applied geography (MA); applied technology and performance improvement (M Ed, MS); art education (MA); art history (MA); arts leadership (Certificate); audiology (Au D); behavior analysis (MS); behavioral science (PhD); biochemistry and molecular biology (MS); biology (MA, MS); biomedical engineering (MS); business analysis (MS); chemistry (MS); clinical health psychology (PhD); communication studies (MA, MS); computer engineering (MS); computer science (MS); counseling (M Ed, MS), including clinical mental health counseling (MS), college and university counseling, elementary school counseling, secondary school counseling; creative writing (MA); criminal justice (MS); curriculum and instruction (M Ed); decision sciences (MBA); design (MA, MFA), including fashion design (MFA), innovation studies, interior design (MFA); early childhood studies (MS); economics (MS); educational leadership (M Ed, Ed D); educational psychology (MS, PhD), including family studies (MS), gifted and talented (MS), human development (MS), learning and cognition (MS), research, measurement and evaluation (MS); electrical engineering (MS); emergency management (MPA); engineering technology (MS); English (MA); English as a second language (MA); environmental science (MS); finance (MBA, MS); financial management (MPA); French (MA); health services management (MBA); higher education (M Ed, Ed D); history (MA, MS); hospitality management (MS); human resources management (MPA); information science (MS); information systems (PhD); information technologies (MBA); interdisciplinary studies (MA, MS); international studies (MA); international sustainable tourism (MS); jazz studies (MM); journalism (MA, MJ, Graduate Certificate), including interactive and virtual digital communication (Graduate Certificate), narrative journalism (Graduate Certificate), public relations (Graduate Certificate); kinesiology (MS); linguistics (MA); local government management (MPA); logistics (PhD); logistics and supply chain management (MBA); long-term care, senior housing, and aging services (MA); management (PhD); marketing (MBA); mathematics (MA, MS); mechanical and energy engineering (MS, PhD); music (MA), including ethnomusicology, music theory, musicology, performance; music composition (PhD); music education (MM Ed, PhD); nonprofit management (MPA); operations and supply chain management (MBA); performance (MM, DMA); philosophy (MA); political science (MA); professional and technical communication (MA); radio, television and film (MA, MFA); rehabilitation counseling (Certificate); sociology (MA); Spanish (MA); special education (M Ed); speech-language pathology (MA); strategic management (MBA); studio art (MFA); teaching (M Ed); MBA/MS. *Program availability:* Part-time, evening/weekend, online learning. Terminal master's awarded for partial completion of doctoral program. *Degree requirements:* For master's, variable foreign language requirement, comprehensive exam (for some programs), thesis (for some programs); for doctorate, variable foreign language requirement, comprehensive exam (for some programs), thesis/dissertation; for other advanced degree, variable foreign language requirement, comprehensive exam (for some programs). *Entrance requirements:* For master's and doctorate, GRE, GMAT. Additional exam requirements/recommendations for international students: Required—TOEFL (minimum score 550 paper-based; 79 iBT). Electronic applications accepted.

University of North Texas at Dallas, Graduate School, Dallas, TX 75241. Offers accounting (MBA); counseling (M Ed, MS); criminal justice (MS); curriculum and instruction (M Ed); educational administration (M Ed); human resources and organizational behavior (MBA); public leadership (MS); strategic management (MBA).

University of Pennsylvania, Graduate School of Education, Division of Human Development and Quantitative Methods, Program in School and Mental Health Counseling, Philadelphia, PA 19104. Offers MS Ed. *Students:* 67 full-time (51 women); includes 30 minority (13 Black or African American, non-Hispanic/Latino; 6 Asian, non-Hispanic/Latino; 6 Hispanic/Latino; 5 Two or more races, non-Hispanic/Latino), 3 international. Average age 33. 80 applicants, 70% accepted, 48 enrolled. In 2018, 29 master's awarded. Application fee: $80.

University of Phoenix–Las Vegas Campus, College of Human Services, Las Vegas, NV 89135. Offers marriage, family, and child therapy (MSC); mental health counseling (MSC); school counseling (MSC). *Program availability:* Online learning. *Entrance requirements:* For master's, minimum undergraduate GPA of 2.5, 3 years of work experience. Additional exam requirements/recommendations for international students: Required—TOEFL (minimum score 550 paper-based; 79 iBT). Electronic applications accepted.

University of Phoenix–Phoenix Campus, College of Social Sciences, Tempe, AZ 85282-2371. Offers counseling (MS), including clinical mental health counseling, community counseling, counseling, marriage, family and child therapy; psychology (MS). *Program availability:* Evening/weekend, online learning. *Entrance requirements:* Additional exam requirements/recommendations for international students: Required—TOEFL, TOEIC (Test of English as an International Communication), Berlitz Online English Proficiency Exam, PTE, or IELTS. Electronic applications accepted. *Expenses:* Contact institution.

University of Puerto Rico–Río Piedras, College of Education, Program in Guidance and Counseling, San Juan, PR 00931-3300. Offers M Ed, Ed D. *Program availability:* Part-time. *Degree requirements:* For master's, thesis; for doctorate, thesis/dissertation, internship. *Entrance requirements:* For master's, PAEG or GRE, interview, minimum GPA of 3.0, letter of recommendation; for doctorate, GRE or PAEG, master's degree, minimum GPA of 3.0, letter of recommendation (2), interview.

University of Puget Sound, School of Education, Program in Counseling, Tacoma, WA 98416. Offers mental health counseling (M Ed); school counseling (M Ed). *Program availability:* Part-time. *Degree requirements:* For master's, capstone course. *Entrance requirements:* For master's, GRE General Test, interview. Additional exam requirements/recommendations for international students: Required—TOEFL (minimum score 550 paper-based; 90 iBT). Electronic applications accepted. *Expenses:* Contact institution. *Faculty research:* Suicide prevention.

University of Rochester, Margaret Warner Graduate School of Education and Human Development, Doctoral Programs in Education, Rochester, NY 14627. Offers counseling (Ed D); educational administration (Ed D); educational policy and theory (PhD); higher education (PhD); human development in educational context (PhD); teaching, curriculum, and change (PhD). *Expenses: Tuition:* Full-time $52,974; part-time $1654 per credit hour. *Required fees:* $612. One-time fee: $30 part-time. Tuition and fees vary according to campus/location and program.

University of Rochester, Margaret Warner Graduate School of Education and Human Development, Master's Program in Counseling, Rochester, NY 14627. Offers school and community counseling (MS); school counseling (MS). *Expenses: Tuition:* Full-time $52,974; part-time $1654 per credit hour. *Required fees:* $612. One-time fee: $30 part-time. Tuition and fees vary according to campus/location and program.

University of Saint Francis, Graduate School, Department of Behavioral and Social Sciences, Fort Wayne, IN 46808-3994. Offers clinical mental health counseling (MS, Post Master's Certificate); psychology (MS); school counseling (MS Ed). *Program availability:* Part-time, evening/weekend. *Faculty:* 5 full-time (2 women), 1 (woman) part-time/adjunct. *Students:* 18 full-time (13 women), 6 part-time (5 women); includes 5 minority (3 Black or African American, non-Hispanic/Latino; 1 Asian, non-Hispanic/Latino; 1 Hispanic/Latino). Average age 29. 16 applicants, 88% accepted, 9 enrolled. In 2018, 19 master's awarded. *Expenses: Tuition:* Full-time $22,440; part-time $935 per credit hour. *Required fees:* $330 per semester. Tuition and fees vary according to degree level, campus/location and program. *Unit head:* Dr. John Brinkman, Chair of Department of Behavioral and Social Sciences, 260-399-7700 Ext. 8425, E-mail: jbrinkman@sf.edu. *Application contact:* Kyle Richardson, Associate Director of Enrollment Services for Adult Learning, 260-399-7700 Ext. 6310, Fax: 260-399-8152, E-mail: krichardson@sf.edu.
Website: https://admissions.sf.edu/graduate/

University of Saint Joseph, Department of Counseling and Applied Behavioral Studies, West Hartford, CT 06117-2700. Offers clinical mental health counseling (MA); school counseling (MA). *Accreditation:* ACA. *Program availability:* Part-time, evening/weekend. *Degree requirements:* For master's, comprehensive exam, thesis optional. *Entrance requirements:* For master's, 2 letters of recommendation. Electronic applications accepted. Application fee is waived when completed online.

University of St. Thomas, School of Education and Human Services, Houston, TX 77006-4696. Offers all level education (M Ed); bilingual/dual language (M Ed); Catholic school teaching (M Ed); Catholic/private school leadership (M Ed); counselor education (M Ed); curriculum and instruction (M Ed); education (Ed D); educational leadership (M Ed); elementary teaching (M Ed); English as a second language (M Ed); exceptionality/educational diagnostician (M Ed); exceptionality/special education (M Ed); generalist (M Ed); reading (M Ed); secondary teaching (M Ed); teaching (MAT). *Accreditation:* TEAC. *Program availability:* Part-time, evening/weekend, online learning. *Degree requirements:* For master's, thesis, field experience. *Entrance requirements:* For master's, GRE or MAT if GPA is below 3.0, bachelor's degree; minimum GPA of 2.75 in bachelor's degree or last 60 credit hours; official transcripts from all institutions; goal statement of 250-300 words; 1 reference. Additional exam requirements/recommendations for international students: Required—TOEFL (minimum score 94 iBT), IELTS (minimum score 7), PTE (minimum score 53). Electronic applications accepted. *Expenses:* Contact institution. *Faculty research:* Leadership, diversity, personality traits, second language acquisition.

University of San Diego, School of Leadership and Education Sciences, Department of Counseling and Marital and Family Therapy, San Diego, CA 92110-2492. Offers clinical mental health counseling (MA); marital and family therapy (MA); school counseling (MA). *Accreditation:* ACA. *Program availability:* Part-time, evening/weekend. *Faculty:* 13 full-time (7 women), 26 part-time/adjunct (17 women). *Students:* 179 full-time (160 women), 49 part-time (43 women); includes 119 minority (11 Black or African American, non-Hispanic/Latino; 20 Asian, non-Hispanic/Latino; 67 Hispanic/Latino; 21 Two or more races, non-Hispanic/Latino), 5 international. Average age 27. 377 applicants, 49% accepted, 95 enrolled. In 2018, 71 master's awarded. *Degree requirements:* For master's, comprehensive exam, international experience. *Entrance requirements:* For master's, GRE or GMAT (minimum overall score in 50th percentile), group interview with faculty. Additional exam requirements/recommendations for international students: Required—TOEFL (minimum score 580 paper-based; 83 iBT), TWE. *Application deadline:* For fall admission, 1/13 priority date for domestic and international students. Applications are processed on a rolling basis. Application fee: $45. Electronic applications accepted. *Financial support:* In 2018–19, 195 students received support. Career-related internships or fieldwork, Federal Work-Study, institutionally sponsored loans, scholarships/grants, unspecified assistantships, and stipends available. Support available to part-time students. Financial award application deadline: 4/1; financial award applicants required to submit FAFSA. *Faculty research:* Action research, collaboration between family therapists and medical professionals, family therapy training and supervision, multicultural counseling, school counseling. *Unit head:* Dr. Ann Garland, Director, 619-260-7879, E-mail: agarland@sandiego.edu. *Application contact:* Erika Garwood, Director of Admissions and Enrollment, 619-260-4524, Fax: 619-260-4158, E-mail: grads@sandiego.edu.
Website: http://www.sandiego.edu/soles/counseling-and-marital-and-family-therapy//

University of San Francisco, School of Education, Department of Counseling Psychology, San Francisco, CA 94117. Offers counseling (MA), including educational counseling, life transitions counseling, marital and family therapy. *Program availability:* Part-time. *Students:* 294 full-time (243 women), 60 part-time (51 women); includes 213 minority (28 Black or African American, non-Hispanic/Latino; 2 American Indian or Alaska Native, non-Hispanic/Latino; 54 Asian, non-Hispanic/Latino; 115 Hispanic/Latino;

14 Two or more races, non-Hispanic/Latino), 4 international. Average age 29. 353 applicants, 73% accepted, 146 enrolled. In 2018, 108 master's awarded. *Entrance requirements:* Additional exam requirements/recommendations for international students: Required—TOEFL, IELTS, PTE. *Application deadline:* For fall admission, 3/1 priority date for domestic students, 3/1 for international students; for spring admission, 10/15 priority date for domestic students, 10/15 for international students. Applications are processed on a rolling basis. Application fee: $55 ($65 for international students). Electronic applications accepted. *Financial support:* Fellowships, research assistantships, and teaching assistantships available. Financial award application deadline: 3/2; financial award applicants required to submit FAFSA. *Unit head:* Dr. Christine Yeh, Chair, 415-422-6868. *Application contact:* Peter Cole, Admission Coordinator, 415-422-5467, E-mail: schoolofeducation@usfca.edu.

The University of Scranton, Panuska College of Professional Studies, Department of Counseling and Human Services, Program in School Counseling, Scranton, PA 18510. Offers MS. *Accreditation:* ACA; NCATE. *Program availability:* Part-time, evening/weekend. *Degree requirements:* For master's, comprehensive exam (for some programs), thesis (for some programs), capstone experience. *Entrance requirements:* For master's, minimum GPA of 3.0, three letters of reference. Additional exam requirements/recommendations for international students: Required—TOEFL (minimum score 500 paper-based; 80 iBT), IELTS (minimum score 6.5). Electronic applications accepted.

University of South Africa, College of Human Sciences, Pretoria, South Africa. Offers adult education (M Ed); African languages (MA, PhD); African politics (MA, PhD); Afrikaans (MA, PhD); ancient history (MA, PhD); ancient Near Eastern studies (MA, PhD); anthropology (MA, PhD); applied linguistics (MA); Arabic (MA, PhD); archaeology (MA); art history (MA); Biblical archaeology (MA); Biblical studies (M Th, D Th, PhD); Christian spirituality (M Th, D Th); church history (M Th, D Th); classical studies (MA, PhD); clinical psychology (MA); communication (MA, PhD); comparative education (M Ed, Ed D); consulting psychology (D Admin, D Com, PhD); curriculum studies (M Ed, Ed D); development studies (M Admin, MA, D Admin, PhD); didactics (M Ed, Ed D); education (M Tech); education management (M Ed, Ed D); educational psychology (M Ed); English (MA); environmental education (M Ed); French (MA, PhD); German (MA, PhD); Greek (MA); guidance and counseling (M Ed); health studies (MA, PhD), including health sciences education (MA), health services management (MA), medical and surgical nursing science (critical care general) (MA), midwifery and neonatal nursing science (MA), trauma and emergency care (MA); history (MA, PhD); history of education (Ed D); inclusive education (M Ed, Ed D); information and communications technology policy and regulation (MA); information science (MA, MIS, PhD); international politics (MA, PhD); Islamic studies (MA, PhD); Italian (MA, PhD); Judaica (MA, PhD); linguistics (MA, PhD); mathematical education (M Ed); mathematics education (MA); missiology (M Th, D Th); modern Hebrew (MA, PhD); musicology (MA, MMus, D Mus, PhD); natural science education (M Ed); New Testament (M Th, D Th); Old Testament (D Th); pastoral therapy (M Th, D Th); philosophy (MA); philosophy of education (M Ed, Ed D); politics (MA, PhD); Portuguese (MA, PhD); practical theology (M Th, D Th); psychology (MA, MS, PhD); psychology of education (M Ed, Ed D); public health (MA); religious studies (MA, D Th, PhD); Romance languages (MA); Russian (MA, PhD); Semitic languages (MA, PhD); social behavior studies in HIV/AIDS (MA); social science (mental health) (MA); social science in development studies (MA); social science in psychology (MA); social science in social work (MA); social science in sociology (MA); social work (MSW, DSW, PhD); socio-education (M Ed, Ed D); sociolinguistics (MA); sociology (MA, PhD); Spanish (MA, PhD); systematic theology (M Th, D Th); TESOL (teaching English to speakers of other languages) (MA); theological ethics (M Th, D Th); theory of literature (MA, PhD); urban ministries (D Th); urban ministry (M Th).

University of South Alabama, College of Education and Professional Studies, Department of Counseling and Instructional Sciences, Mobile, AL 36688. Offers clinical mental health counseling (MS); educational media (M Ed); educational media and technology (MS); instructional design and development (MS, PhD); instructional leadership (Ed S); school counseling (M Ed). *Accreditation:* NCATE. *Program availability:* Part-time. *Degree requirements:* For master's, comprehensive exam; for doctorate, comprehensive exam, thesis/dissertation. *Entrance requirements:* For master's, GRE General Test or MAT, minimum GPA of 3.0, three letters of recommendation; for doctorate, GRE, three letters of recommendation, master's degree in field or completion of prerequisites, resume. Additional exam requirements/recommendations for international students: Required—TOEFL (minimum score 525 paper-based; 71 iBT). Electronic applications accepted. *Faculty research:* Agency counseling, rehabilitation counseling, school psychometry, juvenile delinquency, mixed methods research.

University of South Carolina, The Graduate School, College of Education, Department of Educational Studies, Program in Counseling Education, Columbia, SC 29208. Offers PhD, Ed S. *Accreditation:* ACA (one or more programs are accredited); NCATE. *Program availability:* Part-time. *Degree requirements:* For doctorate, one foreign language, comprehensive exam, thesis/dissertation; for Ed S, comprehensive exam. *Entrance requirements:* For doctorate, GRE General Test or MAT, interview, resume, references; for Ed S, GRE General Test or MAT, interview, resum&e, transcripts, letter of intent, references. Electronic applications accepted. *Faculty research:* Multicultural counseling, children's fears, career development, family counseling.

University of South Dakota, Graduate School, School of Education, Division of Counseling and Psychology in Education, Vermillion, SD 57069. Offers counseling (MA, PhD, Ed S); human development and educational psychology (MA, PhD, Ed S); mental health counseling (Certificate); school psychology (PhD, Ed S). *Accreditation:* ACA (one or more programs are accredited); NCATE. *Program availability:* Part-time. *Degree requirements:* For master's and other advanced degree, comprehensive exam, thesis or alternative; for doctorate, comprehensive exam, thesis/dissertation. *Entrance requirements:* For master's and doctorate, GRE General Test, minimum GPA of 3.0. Additional exam requirements/recommendations for international students: Required—TOEFL (minimum score 550 paper-based; 79 iBT). Electronic applications accepted.

University of Southern California, Graduate School, Rossier School of Education, Master's Programs in Education, Los Angeles, CA 90089-4038. Offers educational counseling (ME); marriage, family and child counseling (MMFT); postsecondary administration and student affairs [PASA] (ME); school counseling (ME); teaching (online) (MAT); teaching and teaching credential (MAT); teaching English to speakers of other languages (MAT). *Program availability:* Part-time, evening/weekend, online learning. *Degree requirements:* For master's, thesis optional. *Entrance requirements:* For master's, GRE (for all programs except MAT). Additional exam requirements/recommendations for international students: Required—TOEFL (minimum score 100 iBT). Electronic applications accepted. *Faculty research:* College access and equity, preparing teachers for culturally diverse populations, sociocultural basis of learning as mediated by instruction with focus on reading and literacy in English learners, social and political aspects of teaching and learning English, school counselor development and training.

University of Southern Maine, College of Management and Human Service, School of Education and Human Development, Program in Counselor Education, Portland, ME 04103. Offers clinical mental health counseling (MS); counseling (CAS); culturally responsive practices in education and human development (CGS); mental health rehabilitation technician/community (CGS); rehabilitation counseling (MS); school counseling (MS); substance abuse counseling (CGS). *Accreditation:* ACA (one or more programs are accredited); CORE; TEAC. *Program availability:* Part-time, evening/weekend. *Degree requirements:* For master's, comprehensive exam, thesis or alternative; for other advanced degree, thesis or alternative. *Entrance requirements:* For master's, GRE General Test or MAT, interview; for other advanced degree, master's degree. Additional exam requirements/recommendations for international students: Required—TOEFL (minimum score 550 paper-based; 79 iBT). Electronic applications accepted. *Faculty research:* Counselor licensure, group dynamics, counseling theories, healthy adaptation, counselor educator well-being.

University of Southern Mississippi, College of Education and Human Sciences, School of Child and Family Sciences, Hattiesburg, MS 39406-0001. Offers child and family studies (MS); marriage and family therapy (MS); school counseling (M Ed). *Accreditation:* AAMFT/COAMFTE (one or more programs are accredited). *Program availability:* Part-time, online learning. *Degree requirements:* For master's, comprehensive exam, thesis optional. *Entrance requirements:* For master's, GRE General Test, minimum GPA of 2.75 on last 60 hours. Additional exam requirements/recommendations for international students: Required—TOEFL. Electronic applications accepted. *Faculty research:* School food service, teen pregnancy, diet and cholesterol metabolism.

University of South Florida, College of Education, Department of Educational and Psychological Studies, Tampa, FL 33620-9951. Offers college student affairs (M Ed); counselor education (MA, PhD, Ed S); interdisciplinary education (PhD, Ed S); school psychology (PhD, Ed S). *Faculty:* 27 full-time (14 women). *Students:* 133 full-time (92 women), 113 part-time (81 women); includes 64 minority (23 Black or African American, non-Hispanic/Latino; 6 Asian, non-Hispanic/Latino; 27 Hispanic/Latino; 1 Native Hawaiian or other Pacific Islander, non-Hispanic/Latino; 7 Two or more races, non-Hispanic/Latino), 29 international. Average age 32. 205 applicants, 57% accepted, 85 enrolled. In 2018, 49 master's, 11 doctorates awarded. *Degree requirements:* For master's, comprehensive exam, thesis (for some programs); for doctorate, comprehensive exam, thesis/dissertation (for some programs). *Entrance requirements:* For master's, GRE may be required, Letters of recommendation, personal statement, interview, resume; CLAST/GKT may be required; for doctorate, GRE may be required, 3.5 master's GPA; letter of intent; resume; letters of reference. Additional exam requirements/recommendations for international students: Required—TOEFL. Application fee: $30. *Expenses:* Tuition, state resident: full-time $6350. Tuition, nonresident: full-time $19,048. *International tuition:* $19,048 full-time. *Required fees:* $2079. *Financial support:* In 2018–19, 1 student received support. *Faculty research:* College student affairs, counselor education, educational psychology, school psychology, social foundations. *Total annual research expenditures:* $10.8 million. *Unit head:* Dr. Barabara Shircliff, Chair, 813-974-4001, E-mail: shirclif@usf.edu. *Application contact:* Dr. Barbara Shircliff, Chair, 813-974-4001, E-mail: shirclif@usf.edu.

University of South Florida, College of Education, Department of Leadership, Counseling, Adult, Career and Higher Education, Tampa, FL 33620-9951. Offers adult education (MA, Ed D, PhD, Ed S); career and technical education (MA); career and workforce education (PhD); higher education/community college teaching (MA, Ed D, PhD); vocational education (Ed S). *Faculty:* 19 full-time (11 women). *Students:* 107 full-time (81 women), 275 part-time (185 women); includes 143 minority (67 Black or African American, non-Hispanic/Latino; 2 American Indian or Alaska Native, non-Hispanic/Latino; 10 Asian, non-Hispanic/Latino; 56 Hispanic/Latino; 8 Two or more races, non-Hispanic/Latino), 14 international. Average age 36. 188 applicants, 54% accepted, 73 enrolled. In 2018, 51 master's, 8 doctorates, 3 other advanced degrees awarded. *Entrance requirements:* For master's, GRE may be required, goals statement; letters of recommendation; proof of educational or professional experience; prerequisites, if needed; for doctorate, GRE may be required, letters of recommendation; masters degree in appropriate field; optional interview; evidence of professional experience; personal statement. Additional exam requirements/recommendations for international students: Required—TOEFL. Application fee: $30. *Expenses:* Tuition, state resident: full-time $6350. Tuition, nonresident: full-time $19,048. *International tuition:* $19,048 full-time. *Required fees:* $2079. *Financial support:* In 2018–19, 19 students received support. *Total annual research expenditures:* $40,520. *Unit head:* Dr. Judith Ponticell, Chair, 813-974-4897, Fax: 813-974-5423, E-mail: jponticell@usf.edu. *Application contact:* Dr. Judith Ponticell, Chair, 813-974-4897, Fax: 813-974-5423, E-mail: jponticell@usf.edu.
Website: http://www.coedu.usf.edu/main/departments/ache/ache.html

University of South Florida, Innovative Education, Tampa, FL 33620-9951. Offers adult, career and higher education (Graduate Certificate), including college teaching, leadership in developing human resources, leadership in higher education; Africana studies (Graduate Certificate), including diasporas and health disparities, genocide and human rights; aging studies (Graduate Certificate), including gerontology; art research (Graduate Certificate), including museum studies; business foundations (Graduate Certificate); chemical and biomedical engineering (Graduate Certificate), including materials science and engineering, water, health and sustainability; child and family studies (Graduate Certificate), including positive behavior support; civil and industrial engineering (Graduate Certificate), including transportation systems analysis; community and family health (Graduate Certificate), including maternal and child health, social marketing and public health, violence and injury: prevention and intervention, women's health; criminology (Graduate Certificate), including criminal justice administration; data science for public administration (Graduate Certificate); digital humanities (Graduate Certificate); educational measurement and research (Graduate Certificate), including evaluation; English (Graduate Certificate), including comparative literary studies, creative writing, professional and technical communication; entrepreneurship (Graduate Certificate); environmental health (Graduate Certificate), including safety management; epidemiology and biostatistics (Graduate Certificate), including applied biostatistics, biostatistics, concepts and tools of epidemiology, epidemiology, epidemiology of infectious diseases; geography, environment and planning (Graduate Certificate), including community development, environmental policy and management, geographical information systems; geology (Graduate Certificate), including hydrogeology; global health (Graduate Certificate), including disaster management, global health and Latin American and Caribbean studies, global health practice, humanitarian assistance, infection control; government and international affairs (Graduate Certificate), including Cuban studies, globalization studies; health policy and management (Graduate Certificate), including health management and leadership, public health policy and programs; hearing specialist: early intervention (Graduate Certificate); industrial and management systems engineering (Graduate Certificate), including systems engineering, technology management; information studies (Graduate Certificate), including school library media specialist; information systems/decision sciences (Graduate Certificate), including analytics and business intelligence; instructional technology (Graduate Certificate), including distance education, Florida digital/virtual educator, instructional design, multimedia design, Web design; internal medicine, bioethics and medical humanities (Graduate Certificate), including biomedical ethics; Latin American and Caribbean studies (Graduate Certificate); leadership for coastal resiliency planning (Graduate Certificate); mass communications (Graduate

Certificate), including multimedia journalism; mathematics and statistics (Graduate Certificate), including mathematics; medicine (Graduate Certificate), including aging and neuroscience, bioinformatics, biotechnology, brain fitness and memory management, clinical investigation, hand and upper limb rehabilitation, health informatics, health sciences, integrative weight management, intellectual property, medicine and gender, metabolic and nutritional medicine, metabolic cardiology, pharmacy sciences; national and competitive intelligence (Graduate Certificate); nursing (Graduate Certificate), including simulation based academic fellowship in advanced pain management; psychological and social foundations (Graduate Certificate), including career counseling, college teaching, diversity in education, mental health counseling, school counseling; public affairs (Graduate Certificate), including nonprofit management, public management, research administration; public health (Graduate Certificate), including assessing chemical toxicity and public health risks, health equity, pharmacoepidemiology, public health generalist, toxicology, translational research in adolescent behavioral health; public health practices (Graduate Certificate), including planning for healthy communities; rehabilitation and mental health counseling (Graduate Certificate), including integrative mental health care, marriage and family therapy, rehabilitation technology; secondary education (Graduate Certificate), including ESOL, foreign language education: culture and content, foreign language education: professional; social work (Graduate Certificate), including geriatric social work/clinical gerontology; special education (Graduate Certificate), including autism spectrum disorder, disabilities education: severe/profound; world languages (Graduate Certificate), including teaching English as a second language (TESL) or foreign language. *Expenses:* Tuition, state resident: full-time $6350. Tuition, nonresident: full-time $19,048. *International tuition:* $19,048 full-time. *Required fees:* $2079. *Unit head:* Dr. Cynthia DeLuca, Associate Vice President and Assistant Vice Provost, 813-974-3077, Fax: 813-974-7061, E-mail: deluca@usf.edu. *Application contact:* Owen Hooper, Director, Summer and Alternative Calendar Programs, 813-974-6917, E-mail: hooper@usf.edu.
Website: http://www.usf.edu/innovative-education/

The University of Tennessee, Graduate School, College of Education, Health and Human Sciences, Department of Educational Psychology and Counseling, Knoxville, TN 37996. Offers adult education (MS); applied educational psychology (MS); collaborative learning (Ed D); college student personnel (MS); mental health counseling (MS); rehabilitation counseling (MS); school counseling (MS). *Accreditation:* ACA (one or more programs are accredited); CORE (one or more programs are accredited); NCATE. *Program availability:* Part-time, evening/weekend. *Degree requirements:* For master's, thesis optional. *Entrance requirements:* For master's, GRE General Test, minimum GPA of 2.7. Additional exam requirements/recommendations for international students: Required—TOEFL. Electronic applications accepted.

The University of Tennessee, Graduate School, College of Education, Health and Human Sciences, Program in Education, Knoxville, TN 37996. Offers art education (MS); counseling education (PhD); cultural studies in education (PhD); curriculum (MS, Ed S); curriculum, educational research and evaluation (Ed D, PhD); early childhood education (PhD); early childhood special education (MS); education of deaf and hard of hearing (MS); educational administration and policy studies (Ed D, PhD); educational administration and supervision (Ed S); educational psychology (Ed D, PhD); elementary education (MS, Ed S); elementary teaching (MS); English education (MS, Ed S); exercise science (PhD); foreign language/ESL education (MS, Ed S); instructional technology (MS, Ed D, PhD, Ed S); literacy, language and ESL education (PhD); literacy, language education, and ESL education (Ed D); mathematics education (MS, Ed S); modified and comprehensive special education (MS); reading education (MS, Ed S); school counseling (Ed S); school psychology (PhD, Ed S); science education (MS, Ed S); secondary teaching (MS); social foundations (MS); social science education (MS, Ed S); socio-cultural foundations of sports and education (PhD); special education (Ed S); teacher education (Ed D, PhD). *Accreditation:* NCATE. *Program availability:* Part-time, evening/weekend. *Degree requirements:* For master's and Ed S, thesis optional; for doctorate, variable foreign language requirement, thesis/dissertation. *Entrance requirements:* For master's, minimum GPA of 2.7; for doctorate and Ed S, GRE General Test, minimum GPA of 2.7. Additional exam requirements/recommendations for international students: Required—TOEFL. Electronic applications accepted.

The University of Tennessee at Chattanooga, Program in Counseling, Chattanooga, TN 37403. Offers mental health (M Ed); school counseling (M Ed, Post Master's Certificate). *Degree requirements:* For master's, comprehensive exam, internship. *Entrance requirements:* For master's, MAT or GRE, 2 letters of reference, interview; for Post Master's Certificate, graduate degree in counseling, 2 letters of reference. Additional exam requirements/recommendations for international students: Required—TOEFL (minimum score 550 paper-based; 79 iBT), IELTS (minimum score 6). Electronic applications accepted. *Faculty research:* Play therapy; clinical supervision; technology in marital infidelity; female inmates and recidivism; grief, loss and trauma in children.

The University of Tennessee at Chattanooga, School of Education, Chattanooga, TN 37403. Offers counseling (M Ed), including community counseling, school counseling; education (M Ed, Post-Master's Certificate), including elementary education (M Ed); school leadership (Post-Master's Certificate); elementary education (M Ed); learning and leadership (Ed D), including educational leadership; school leadership (Post-Master's Certificate); school leadership: principal licensure (Ed S); secondary education (M Ed); special education (M Ed). *Accreditation:* ACA; NCATE. *Program availability:* Part-time. *Degree requirements:* For master's, comprehensive exam, thesis optional, culminating experience; for other advanced degree, internship. *Entrance requirements:* For master's, GRE General Test, PPST 1, teaching certificate; for other advanced degree, two letters of recommendation, graduate degree in education, teaching certificate with three years of experience. Additional exam requirements/recommendations for international students: Required—TOEFL (minimum score 550 paper-based; 79 iBT), IELTS (minimum score 6). Electronic applications accepted. *Expenses:* Contact institution. *Faculty research:* School counseling, community counseling, elementary and secondary education, school leadership and administration.

The University of Tennessee at Martin, Graduate Programs, College of Education, Health and Behavioral Sciences, Program in Counseling, Martin, TN 38238. Offers addictions counseling (MS Ed); community counseling (MS Ed); school counseling (MS Ed); student affairs and college counseling (MS Ed). *Accreditation:* NCATE. *Program availability:* Part-time, online only, 100% online. *Students:* 18 full-time (16 women), 56 part-time (53 women); includes 12 minority (11 Black or African American, non-Hispanic/Latino; 1 Hispanic/Latino). Average age 34. 56 applicants, 36% accepted, 18 enrolled. In 2018, 16 master's awarded. *Degree requirements:* For master's, comprehensive exam. *Entrance requirements:* For master's, GRE General Test, minimum GPA of 2.5, resume, letters of reference. Additional exam requirements/recommendations for international students: Required—TOEFL (minimum score 525 paper-based; 71 iBT). *Application deadline:* For fall admission, 7/27 priority date for domestic and international students; for spring admission, 12/17 priority date for domestic and international students; for summer admission, 5/10 priority date for domestic and international students. Applications are processed on a rolling basis. Application fee: $30 ($130 for international students). Electronic applications accepted.

Expenses: Tuition, area resident: Full-time $8918; part-time $495 per credit hour. Tuition, state resident: full-time $8918; part-time $485 per credit hour. Tuition, nonresident: full-time $14,958; part-time $831 per credit hour. *International tuition:* $22,862 full-time. *Required fees:* $1446; $81 per credit hour. Part-time tuition and fees vary according to course load. *Financial support:* In 2018–19, 13 students received support, including 1 teaching assistantship with full tuition reimbursement available (averaging $6,283 per year); research assistantships with full tuition reimbursements available, scholarships/grants, and tuition waivers (full and partial) also available. Financial award application deadline: 2/1; financial award applicants required to submit FAFSA. *Unit head:* Cynthia West, Dean, 731-881-7125, Fax: 731-881-7975, E-mail: cwest@utm.edu. *Application contact:* Jolene L. Cunningham, Student Services Specialist, 731-881-7012, Fax: 731-881-7499, E-mail: jcunningham@utm.edu.

The University of Texas at Austin, Graduate School, College of Education, Department of Educational Psychology, Austin, TX 78712-1111. Offers academic educational psychology (M Ed, MA); counseling psychology (PhD); counselor education (M Ed); human development, culture and learning sciences (PhD); program evaluation (MA); quantitative methods (M Ed, MA, PhD); school psychology (MA, PhD). *Accreditation:* APA (one or more programs are accredited). *Degree requirements:* For master's, thesis optional; for doctorate, thesis/dissertation. *Entrance requirements:* For master's and doctorate, GRE General Test, 3 letters of recommendation. Additional exam requirements/recommendations for international students: Required—TOEFL.

The University of Texas at El Paso, Graduate School, College of Education, Department of Educational Psychology and Special Services, El Paso, TX 79968-0001. Offers educational diagnostics (M Ed); guidance and counseling (M Ed); special education (M Ed). *Program availability:* Part-time, evening/weekend. *Degree requirements:* For master's, thesis optional. *Entrance requirements:* For master's, minimum GPA of 3.0. Additional exam requirements/recommendations for international students: Required—TOEFL. Electronic applications accepted.

The University of Texas at San Antonio, College of Education and Human Development, Department of Counseling, San Antonio, TX 78207. Offers counselor education and supervision (PhD); school counseling (M Ed). *Accreditation:* ACA. *Program availability:* Part-time, evening/weekend. *Degree requirements:* For master's, comprehensive exam, thesis; for doctorate, comprehensive exam, thesis/dissertation. *Entrance requirements:* For master's, minimum GPA of 3.0 during last 60 hours of undergraduate study; two-page narrative statement; for doctorate, GRE, minimum GPA of 3.0 in master's-level courses in counseling or in related mental health field; resume; three letters of recommendation; statement of purpose; interview. Additional exam requirements/recommendations for international students: Required—TOEFL (minimum score 550 paper-based; 79 iBT), IELTS (minimum score 6.5). Electronic applications accepted. *Expenses:* Contact institution. *Faculty research:* Creativity in counseling, non-suicidal self-injury, family violence, counselor preparation and supervision, technology, ethics, cognitive complexity, counseling outcome research, trauma, body image resiliency.

The University of Texas of the Permian Basin, Office of Graduate Studies, School of Education, Program in Counseling, Odessa, TX 79762-0001. Offers MA. *Degree requirements:* For master's, comprehensive exam (for some programs), thesis (for some programs). *Entrance requirements:* For master's, GRE General Test. Additional exam requirements/recommendations for international students: Required—TOEFL (minimum score 550 paper-based).

The University of Texas Rio Grande Valley, College of Education and P-16 Integration, Department of Counseling, Edinburg, TX 78539. Offers clinical mental health counseling (M Ed); school counseling (M Ed). *Program availability:* Part-time. *Entrance requirements:* For master's, minimum GPA of 3.0 on undergraduate coursework. Additional exam requirements/recommendations for international students: Required—TOEFL (minimum score 550 paper-based; 79 iBT), IELTS (minimum score 6.5). Electronic applications accepted. *Expenses: Tuition, area resident:* Full-time $6888. Tuition, state resident: full-time $6888. Tuition, nonresident: full-time $14,484. *International tuition:* $14,484 full-time. *Required fees:* $1468. *Faculty research:* Counseling, mental health.

University of the Cumberlands, Graduate Programs in Education, Williamsburg, KY 40769-1372. Offers all grades (P-12) (M Ed); business and marketing (MA Ed, MAT); counselor education and supervision (Ed D); director of pupil personnel (Certificate); director of special education (Certificate); educational administration and supervision (Ed S); educational leadership (Ed D); elementary education (MA Ed, MAT); instructional leadership - principalship (MA Ed); instructional leadership - school principal (Certificate); middle school education (MA Ed, MAT); reading and writing (MA Ed); school counseling (MA Ed); school superintendent (Certificate); secondary education (MA Ed, MAT); special education (MAT); supervisor of instruction (Certificate); teacher leader (MA Ed). *Program availability:* Part-time, evening/weekend, online learning. *Degree requirements:* For master's, comprehensive exam. Electronic applications accepted.

University of the Southwest, Graduate Programs, Hobbs, NM 88240-9129. Offers business administration (MBA); curriculum and instruction (MSE); curriculum and instruction: bilingual (MSE); curriculum and instruction: TESOL (MSE); early childhood education (MSE); educational administration (MSE); mental health counseling (MSE); school counseling (MSE); special education (MSE); sports management (MBA). *Program availability:* Part-time, evening/weekend, online learning. *Degree requirements:* For master's, comprehensive exam, thesis (for some programs). *Entrance requirements:* Additional exam requirements/recommendations for international students: Recommended—TOEFL. Electronic applications accepted.

The University of Toledo, College of Graduate Studies, College of Health and Human Services, School of Intervention and Wellness, Toledo, OH 43606-3390. Offers counselor education (MA, PhD); school psychology (Ed S); speech-language pathology (MA). *Accreditation:* ACA (one or more programs are accredited); NCATE. *Degree requirements:* For master's, seminar paper. *Entrance requirements:* For master's, GRE General Test, interview, minimum GPA of 3.0. Electronic applications accepted. *Faculty research:* Training and supervision, ethics and standards, therapist development, multicultural issues, substance abuse screening.

The University of Toledo, College of Graduate Studies, College of Social Justice and Human Service, Department of School Psychology, Higher Education and Counselor Education, Toledo, OH 43606-3390. Offers counselor education (MA, PhD); higher education (ME, PhD, Certificate); school psychology (MA, Ed S). *Program availability:* Part-time. *Degree requirements:* For master's, comprehensive exam, thesis or alternative; for doctorate, comprehensive exam, thesis/dissertation; for other advanced degree, thesis optional. *Entrance requirements:* For master's, doctorate, and other advanced degree, minimum cumulative GPA of 2.7 for all previous academic work, letters of recommendation. Additional exam requirements/recommendations for international students: Required—TOEFL (minimum score 550 paper-based; 80 iBT). Electronic applications accepted.

University of Utah, Graduate School, College of Education, Department of Educational Psychology, Salt Lake City, UT 84112. Offers clinical mental health counseling (M Ed); counseling psychology (PhD); elementary education (M Ed); instructional design and

educational technology (M Ed); instructional design and technology (MS); learning and cognition (MS, PhD); reading and literacy (M Ed, PhD); school counseling (M Ed); school psychology (M Ed, PhD, Ed S); statistics (M Stat). *Accreditation:* APA (one or more programs are accredited). *Faculty:* 20 full-time (12 women), 50 part-time/adjunct (34 women). *Students:* 127 full-time (93 women), 92 part-time (63 women); includes 33 minority (1 Black or African American, non-Hispanic/Latino; 7 Asian, non-Hispanic/Latino; 18 Hispanic/Latino; 1 Native Hawaiian or other Pacific Islander, non-Hispanic/Latino; 6 Two or more races, non-Hispanic/Latino), 5 international. Average age 32. 296 applicants, 27% accepted, 73 enrolled. In 2018, 68 master's, 10 doctorates, 3 other advanced degrees awarded. Terminal master's awarded for partial completion of doctoral program. *Degree requirements:* For master's, thesis (for some programs); for doctorate, thesis/dissertation. *Entrance requirements:* For master's and doctorate, GRE General Test, minimum GPA of 3.0. Additional exam requirements/recommendations for international students: Required—TOEFL (minimum score 80 iBT). *Application deadline:* For fall admission, 12/15 for domestic and international students; for winter admission, 11/1 for domestic and international students; for spring admission, 3/15 for domestic and international students. Application fee: $55 ($65 for international students). Electronic applications accepted. *Expenses:* Contact institution. *Financial support:* In 2018–19, 72 students received support, including 6 fellowships with full and partial tuition reimbursements available (averaging $17,000 per year), 14 research assistantships with full and partial tuition reimbursements available (averaging $15,750 per year), 27 teaching assistantships with full and partial tuition reimbursements available (averaging $15,500 per year); career-related internships or fieldwork, scholarships/grants, traineeships, health care benefits, and unspecified assistantships also available. Financial award application deadline: 4/1; financial award applicants required to submit FAFSA. *Faculty research:* Autism, computer technology and instruction, cognitive behavior, aging, group counseling. *Total annual research expenditures:* $620,935. *Unit head:* Dr. Anne E. Cook, Chair, 801-581-7148, Fax: 801-581-5566, E-mail: anne.cook@utah.edu. *Application contact:* JoLynn N. Yates, Academic Coordinator, 801-581-7148, Fax: 801-581-5566, E-mail: jo.yates@utah.edu.
Website: http://www.ed.utah.edu/edps/

University of Vermont, Graduate College, College of Education and Social Services, Counseling Program, Burlington, VT 05405. Offers counseling (MS), including clinical mental health, school counseling. *Accreditation:* ACA; NCATE. *Entrance requirements:* For master's, resume. Additional exam requirements/recommendations for international students: Required—TOEFL (minimum score 550 paper-based, 90 iBT) or IELTS (6.5). Electronic applications accepted. *Faculty research:* Women and tenure, counseling children and adolescents.

University of Victoria, Faculty of Graduate Studies, Faculty of Education, Department of Educational Psychology and Leadership Studies, Victoria, BC V8W 2Y2, Canada. Offers aboriginal communities counseling (M Ed); counseling (M Ed, MA); educational psychology (M Ed, MA, PhD), including counseling psychology (M Ed, MA), leadership studies (PhD), learning and development (MA, PhD), measurement and evaluation, special education (M Ed, MA); leadership studies (M Ed, MA). *Program availability:* Part-time. *Degree requirements:* For master's, thesis (for some programs), comprehensive exam (M Ed); for doctorate, comprehensive exam, thesis/dissertation, candidacy exam. *Entrance requirements:* For master's, 2 years of work experience in a relevant field; for doctorate, GRE, 2 years of work experience in a relevant field, minimum B average. Additional exam requirements/recommendations for international students: Required—TOEFL (minimum score 575 paper-based), IELTS (minimum score 7). *Faculty research:* Learning and development (child, adolescent and adult), special education and exceptional children.

University of Virginia, Curry School of Education, Department of Human Services, Program in Counselor Education, Charlottesville, VA 22903. Offers M Ed, Ed D, Ed S. *Accreditation:* ACA (one or more programs are accredited). *Entrance requirements:* For master's and doctorate, GRE General Test, 2 letters of recommendation; for Ed S, GRE General Test. Additional exam requirements/recommendations for international students: Required—TOEFL (minimum score 600 paper-based; 90 iBT), IELTS. Electronic applications accepted.

University of Virginia, Curry School of Education, Program in Education, Charlottesville, VA 22903. Offers administration and supervision (PhD); applied developmental science (PhD); counselor education (PhD); curriculum and instruction (PhD); early childhood special education (MT); education evaluation (PhD); educational psychology (PhD); educational research (PhD); elementary education (MT); English education (MT, PhD); foreign language education (MT); higher education (PhD); instructional technology (PhD); kinesiology (MT, PhD); math education (PhD); reading education (PhD); research, statistics and evaluation (PhD); school psychology (PhD); science education (PhD); social studies education (MT, PhD); special education (PhD); world languages education (MT). *Degree requirements:* For master's, comprehensive exam (for some programs), field project; for doctorate, comprehensive exam, thesis/dissertation. *Entrance requirements:* For doctorate, GRE General Test. Additional exam requirements/recommendations for international students: Required—TOEFL (minimum score 600 paper-based; 90 iBT), IELTS (minimum score 7). Electronic applications accepted.

The University of West Alabama, School of Graduate Studies, College of Education, Program in Continuing Education, Livingston, AL 35470. Offers counseling and psychology (MSCE); general (MSCE); library media (MSCE). *Accreditation:* NCATE. *Program availability:* Part-time, evening/weekend, 100% online. *Faculty:* 10 full-time (8 women), 53 part-time/adjunct (35 women). *Students:* 157 full-time (133 women), 2 part-time (both women); includes 105 minority (102 Black or African American, non-Hispanic/Latino; 1 Hispanic/Latino; 2 Two or more races, non-Hispanic/Latino), 2 international. Average age 35. 44 applicants, 98% accepted, 35 enrolled. In 2018, 57 master's awarded. *Degree requirements:* For master's, comprehensive exam, thesis optional. *Entrance requirements:* For master's, GRE, minimum GPA of 2.75. Additional exam requirements/recommendations for international students: Required—TOEFL (minimum score 500 paper-based; 61 iBT). *Application deadline:* Applications are processed on a rolling basis. Application fee: $40. Electronic applications accepted. *Expenses: Tuition, area resident:* full-time $9100. Tuition, state resident: full-time $9100. Tuition, nonresident: full-time $19,200. *Required fees:* $1890; $130. *Financial support:* Teaching assistantships, Federal Work-Study, scholarships/grants, and unspecified assistantships available. Support available to part-time students. Financial award application deadline: 3/1; financial award applicants required to submit FAFSA. *Unit head:* Dr. Jodie Winship, Chair of College of Education, 205-652-5415, E-mail: jwinship@uwa.edu. *Application contact:* Dr. B. J. Kimbrough, Dean of Graduate Studies, 205-652-3647, Fax: 205-652-3670, E-mail: bkimbrough@uwa.edu.

The University of West Alabama, School of Graduate Studies, College of Education, Program in School Counseling, Livingston, AL 35470. Offers guidance and counseling (MS); school counseling (M Ed, Ed S). *Accreditation:* NCATE. *Program availability:* Part-time, evening/weekend, 100% online. *Faculty:* 5 full-time (all women), 13 part-time/adjunct (8 women). *Students:* 373 full-time (347 women), 5 part-time (4 women); includes 126 minority (119 Black or African American, non-Hispanic/Latino; 3 American Indian or Alaska Native, non-Hispanic/Latino; 1 Hispanic/Latino; 3 Two or more races, non-Hispanic/Latino), 5 international. Average age 36. 120 applicants, 91% accepted,

78 enrolled. In 2018, 119 master's, 27 other advanced degrees awarded. *Degree requirements:* For master's, comprehensive exam, thesis optional; for Ed S, comprehensive exam. *Entrance requirements:* For master's, GRE, minimum GPA of 2.75, verification of background clearance/fingerprints, essay, three academic references, resume. Additional exam requirements/recommendations for international students: Required—TOEFL (minimum score 500 paper-based; 61 iBT). *Application deadline:* Applications are processed on a rolling basis. Application fee: $40. Electronic applications accepted. *Expenses: Tuition, area resident:* Full-time $9100. Tuition, state resident: full-time $9100. Tuition, nonresident: full-time $19,200. *Required fees:* $1890; $130. *Financial support:* Teaching assistantships, Federal Work-Study, scholarships/grants, and unspecified assistantships available. Support available to part-time students. Financial award application deadline: 3/1; financial award applicants required to submit FAFSA. *Unit head:* Dr. Jodie Winship, Chair of College of Education, 205-652-5415, Fax: 205-652-3706, E-mail: jwinship@uwa.edu. *Application contact:* Dr. B. J. Kimbrough, Dean of Graduate Studies, 205-652-3647, Fax: 205-652-3670, E-mail: bkimbrough@uwa.edu.

University of West Georgia, College of Education, Carrollton, GA 30118. Offers business education (M Ed); early childhood education (M Ed, Ed S); educational leadership (M Ed, Ed S); media (M Ed, Ed S); professional counseling (M Ed, Ed S); professional counseling and supervision (Ed D); reading instruction (M Ed); school improvement (Ed D); secondary education (M Ed); special education (M Ed, Ed S), including teaching (M Ed); speech language pathology (M Ed); teaching (MAT). *Accreditation:* NCATE. *Program availability:* Part-time, evening/weekend, 100% online, blended/hybrid learning. *Faculty:* 39 full-time (23 women). *Students:* 368 full-time (316 women), 1,140 part-time (960 women); includes 460 minority (376 Black or African American, non-Hispanic/Latino; 1 American Indian or Alaska Native, non-Hispanic/Latino; 11 Asian, non-Hispanic/Latino; 44 Hispanic/Latino; 28 Two or more races, non-Hispanic/Latino), 6 international. Average age 35. 625 applicants, 77% accepted, 401 enrolled. In 2018, 399 master's, 25 doctorates, 273 other advanced degrees awarded. *Entrance requirements:* Additional exam requirements/recommendations for international students: Required—TOEFL (minimum score 523 paper-based; 69 iBT); Recommended—IELTS (minimum score 6.5). *Application deadline:* For fall admission, 7/21 for domestic students, 6/1 for international students; for spring admission, 11/30 for domestic students, 10/15 for international students; for summer admission, 4/15 for domestic students, 3/30 for international students. Applications are processed on a rolling basis. Application fee: $40. Electronic applications accepted. Tuition and fees vary according to course load, degree level, campus/location and program. *Financial support:* Fellowships, research assistantships, teaching assistantships, career-related internships or fieldwork, Federal Work-Study, institutionally sponsored loans, scholarships/grants, and unspecified assistantships available. Support available to part-time students. Financial award application deadline: 4/1; financial award applicants required to submit FAFSA. *Unit head:* Dr. Diane Hoff, Dean, College of Education, 678-839-6570, Fax: 678-839-6098, E-mail: dhoff@westga.edu. *Application contact:* Dr. Toby Ziglar, Assistant Dean of the Graduate School, 678-839-1394, Fax: 678-839-1395, E-mail: graduate@westga.edu.
Website: http://www.westga.edu/education/

University of Wisconsin–Madison, Graduate School, School of Education, Department of Counseling Psychology, Program in Counseling, Madison, WI 53706-1380. Offers MS. *Entrance requirements:* For master's, GRE General Test. Electronic applications accepted.

University of Wisconsin–Oshkosh, Graduate Studies, College of Education and Human Services, Department of Professional Counseling, Oshkosh, WI 54901. Offers counseling (MSE). *Accreditation:* ACA. *Program availability:* Part-time, evening/weekend. *Degree requirements:* For master's, thesis optional, practicum. *Entrance requirements:* For master's, MAT, interview, minimum GPA of 3.0, letters of recommendation. Additional exam requirements/recommendations for international students: Required—TOEFL (minimum score 550 paper-based; 79 iBT). Electronic applications accepted. *Faculty research:* Gender issues, grief and loss, addictions, career development, close relationships.

University of Wisconsin–River Falls, Outreach and Graduate Studies, College of Education and Professional Studies, Department of Counseling and School Psychology, River Falls, WI 54022. Offers counseling (MSE); school psychology (MSE, Ed S). *Accreditation:* ACA. *Program availability:* Part-time. *Entrance requirements:* For master's, minimum GPA of 2.75, resume, 3 letters of reference, vita. Additional exam requirements/recommendations for international students: Required—TOEFL (minimum score 500 paper-based; 65 iBT), IELTS (minimum score 5.5). Electronic applications accepted.

University of Wisconsin–Superior, Graduate Division, Department of Counseling and Psychological Professions, Superior, WI 54880-4500. Offers community counseling (MSE); human relations (MSE); school counseling (MSE). *Program availability:* Part-time, evening/weekend. *Degree requirements:* For master's, position paper, practicum. *Entrance requirements:* For master's, GRE and/or MAT, minimum GPA of 2.75. Electronic applications accepted. *Faculty research:* Women and power, intrafamily dynamics.

University of Wyoming, College of Education, Programs in Counselor Education, Laramie, WY 82071. Offers community mental health (MS); counselor education and supervision (PhD); school counseling (MS); student affairs (MS). *Accreditation:* ACA (one or more programs are accredited). *Degree requirements:* For master's, comprehensive exam (for some programs), thesis optional; for doctorate, thesis/dissertation, video demonstration. *Entrance requirements:* For master's, interview, background check; for doctorate, video tape session, interview, writing sample, master's degree, background check. Additional exam requirements/recommendations for international students: Required—TOEFL. *Expenses: Tuition, area resident:* Full-time $6504; part-time $271 per credit hour. Tuition, state resident: full-time $6504; part-time $271 per credit hour. Tuition, nonresident: full-time $19,464; part-time $811 per credit hour. International tuition: $19,464 full-time. *Required fees:* $1410.94; $343.82 per semester. $343.82 per semester. Tuition and fees vary according to course load, program and reciprocity agreements. *Faculty research:* Wyoming SAGE photovoice project; accountable school counseling programs; GLBT issues; addictions; play therapy-early childhood mental health.

Utah State University, School of Graduate Studies, Emma Eccles Jones College of Education and Human Services, Department of Psychology, Logan, UT 84322. Offers clinical/counseling/school psychology (PhD); research and evaluation methodology (PhD); school counseling (MS); school psychology (MS). *Accreditation:* APA (one or more programs are accredited). *Program availability:* Part-time, evening/weekend, online learning. Terminal master's awarded for partial completion of doctoral program. *Degree requirements:* For master's, thesis (for some programs); for doctorate, thesis/dissertation. *Entrance requirements:* For master's, GRE General Test (school psychology), MAT (school counseling), minimum GPA of 3.5; for doctorate, GRE General Test, minimum GPA of 3.5. Additional exam requirements/recommendations for international students: Required—TOEFL. *Faculty research:* Hearing loss detection in infancy, ADHD, eating disorders, domestic violence, neuropsychology, bilingual/Spanish speaking students/parents.

Counselor Education

Valdosta State University, Department of Psychology, Counseling, and Family Therapy, Valdosta, GA 31698. Offers industrial/organizational psychology (MS); marriage and family therapy (MS); school counseling (M Ed, Ed S). *Accreditation:* AAMFT/COAMFTE. *Program availability:* Part-time, evening/weekend, 100% online, blended/hybrid learning. *Degree requirements:* For master's, thesis or alternative, comprehensive written and/or oral exams; for Ed S, thesis. *Entrance requirements:* For master's, GRE General Test or MAT, GACE; for Ed S, GRE General Test or MAT. Additional exam requirements/recommendations for international students: Required—TOEFL (minimum score 523 paper-based); Recommended—IELTS. Electronic applications accepted. *Expenses:* Contact institution.

Villanova University, Graduate School of Liberal Arts and Sciences, Department of Education and Counseling, Villanova, PA 19085-1699. Offers elementary school counseling (MS), including counseling and human relations; teacher leadership (MA). *Program availability:* Part-time, evening/weekend. *Degree requirements:* For master's, comprehensive exam. *Entrance requirements:* For master's, GRE or MAT, minimum GPA of 3.0, statement of goals. Electronic applications accepted.

Virginia Commonwealth University, Graduate School, School of Education, Doctoral Program in Education, Richmond, VA 23284-9005. Offers art education (PhD); counselor education and supervision (PhD); curriculum, culture and change (PhD); educational leadership (PhD); educational psychology (PhD); leadership (Ed D); research and evaluation (PhD); special education and disability leadership (PhD); sport leadership (PhD); urban services leadership (PhD). *Accreditation:* NCATE. *Program availability:* Part-time. *Degree requirements:* For doctorate, thesis/dissertation. *Entrance requirements:* For doctorate, GRE (for PhD), MAT (for Ed D), interview, master's degree, writing sample. Additional exam requirements/recommendations for international students: Required—TOEFL (minimum score 600 paper-based; 100 iBT). Electronic applications accepted.

Virginia Commonwealth University, Graduate School, School of Education, Program in Counselor Education, Richmond, VA 23284-9005. Offers college student development and counseling (M Ed); school counseling (M Ed). *Accreditation:* ACA; NCATE. *Entrance requirements:* For master's, GRE General Test or MAT. Additional exam requirements/recommendations for international students: Required—TOEFL (minimum score 600 paper-based; 100 iBT). Electronic applications accepted.

Virginia Polytechnic Institute and State University, Graduate School, College of Liberal Arts and Human Sciences, Blacksburg, VA 24061. Offers career and technical education (MS Ed, Ed S); communication (MA); counselor education (MA); creative writing (MFA); curriculum and instruction (MA Ed, Ed S); educational leadership and policy studies (Ed S); educational research and evaluation (PhD); English (MA); social, political, ethical, and cultural thought (PhD); Ed D/PhD. *Faculty:* 420 full-time (221 women), 1 (woman) part-time/adjunct. *Students:* 603 full-time (428 women), 359 part-time (237 women); includes 189 minority (107 Black or African American, non-Hispanic/Latino; 4 American Indian or Alaska Native, non-Hispanic/Latino; 24 Asian, non-Hispanic/Latino; 27 Hispanic/Latino; 2 Native Hawaiian or other Pacific Islander, non-Hispanic/Latino; 25 Two or more races, non-Hispanic/Latino), 84 international. Average age 33. 856 applicants, 48% accepted, 262 enrolled. In 2018, 270 master's, 63 doctorates awarded. *Degree requirements:* For master's, comprehensive exam (for some programs), thesis (for some programs); for doctorate, comprehensive exam (for some programs), thesis/dissertation (for some programs). *Entrance requirements:* For master's and doctorate, GRE/GMAT. Additional exam requirements/recommendations for international students: Required—TOEFL (minimum score 90 iBT). *Application deadline:* For fall admission, 8/1 for domestic students, 4/1 for international students; for spring admission, 1/1 for domestic students, 9/1 for international students. Applications are processed on a rolling basis. Application fee: $75. Electronic applications accepted. *Expenses:* Tuition, state resident: full-time $15,510; part-time $739.50 per credit hour. Tuition, nonresident: full-time $29,629; part-time $1490.25 per credit hour. *Required fees:* $2804; $550 per semester. Tuition and fees vary according to course load, campus/location and program. *Financial support:* In 2018–19, 4 fellowships with full tuition reimbursements (averaging $23,122 per year), 28 research assistantships with full tuition reimbursements (averaging $15,605 per year), 245 teaching assistantships with full tuition reimbursements (averaging $16,046 per year) were awarded; scholarships/grants and unspecified assistantships also available. Financial award application deadline: 3/1; financial award applicants required to submit FAFSA. *Total annual research expenditures:* $7.5 million. *Unit head:* Dr. Laura Belmonte, Dean, 540-231-6779, Fax: 540-231-7157, E-mail: belmonte@vt.edu. *Application contact:* Chelsea Blanchet, Executive Assistant, 540-231-6779, Fax: 540-231-7157, E-mail: bchels1@vt.edu.
Website: http://www.liberalarts.vt.edu/

Virginia State University, College of Graduate Studies, College of Education, Department of School and Community Counseling, Petersburg, VA 23806-0001. Offers M Ed, MS. *Accreditation:* NCATE. *Degree requirements:* For master's, thesis optional.

Wake Forest University, Graduate School of Arts and Sciences, Counseling Program, Winston-Salem, NC 27109. Offers MA, M Div/MA. *Accreditation:* ACA. *Entrance requirements:* For master's, GRE General Test. Additional exam requirements/recommendations for international students: Required—TOEFL (minimum score 79 iBT). Electronic applications accepted.

Walden University, Graduate Programs, School of Counseling, Minneapolis, MN 55401. Offers addiction counseling (MS), including addictions and public health, child and adolescent counseling, family studies and interventions, forensic counseling, general program, military families and culture, trauma and crisis counseling; clinical mental health counseling (MS), including addiction counseling, forensic counseling, military families and culture, trauma and crisis counseling; counselor education and supervision (PhD), including consultation, counseling and social change, forensic mental health counseling, leadership and program evaluation, trauma and crisis; marriage, couple, and family counseling (MS), including addiction counseling, career counseling, forensic counseling, military families and culture, trauma and crisis counseling; school counseling (MS), including addiction counseling, career counseling, crisis and trauma, military families and culture. *Accreditation:* ACA. *Program availability:* Part-time, evening/weekend, online only, 100% online. *Degree requirements:* For master's, residency, field experience, professional development plan, licensure plan; for doctorate, thesis/dissertation, residency, practicum, internship. *Entrance requirements:* For master's, bachelor's degree or higher; minimum GPA of 2.5; official transcripts; goal statement (for some programs); access to computer and Internet; for doctorate, master's degree or higher; three years of related professional or academic experience (preferred); minimum GPA of 3.0; goal statement and current resume (for select programs); official transcripts; access to computer and Internet. Additional exam requirements/recommendations for international students: Required—TOEFL (minimum score 550 paper-based, 79 iBT), IELTS (minimum score 6.5), Michigan English Language Assessment Battery (minimum score 82), or PTE (minimum score 53). Electronic applications accepted.

Walsh University, Graduate Programs, Program in Counseling and Human Development, North Canton, OH 44720-3396. Offers clinical mental health counseling (MA); school counseling (MA); student affairs in higher education (MA). *Accreditation:* ACA. *Program availability:* Part-time, evening/weekend. *Degree requirements:* For master's, comprehensive exam, internship, practicum. *Entrance requirements:* For master's, GRE (minimum score of 145 verbal and 146 quantitative) or MAT (minimum score of 397), interview, minimum GPA of 3.0, writing sample, reference forms, notarized affidavit of good moral conduct. Additional exam requirements/recommendations for international students: Required—TOEFL (minimum score 500 paper-based; 61 iBT). Electronic applications accepted. Application fee is waived when completed online. *Expenses:* Contact institution. *Faculty research:* Supervision of clinical mental health, clinical mental health practice/issues, clinical mental health skills development, advocacy, teaching and professional development, career development, refugee development in US, supervision in student affairs, offender treatment, domestic violence issues, alcohol and drug treatment issues, Professional identity and advocacy in school counseling, Efficacy in counseling clinic.

Waynesburg University, Graduate and Professional Studies, Canonsburg, PA 15370. Offers business (MBA), including energy management, finance, health systems, human resources, leadership, market development; counseling (MA), including addictions counseling, clinical mental health; counselor education and supervision (PhD); criminal investigation (MA); education (M Ed), including autism, curriculum and instruction, educational leadership, online teaching; nursing (MSN), including administration, education, informatics; nursing practice (DNP); special education (M Ed); technology (M Ed); MSN/MBA. *Accreditation:* AACN. *Program availability:* Part-time, evening/weekend. *Degree requirements:* For doctorate, thesis/dissertation. *Entrance requirements:* Additional exam requirements/recommendations for international students: Required—TOEFL. Electronic applications accepted.

Wayne State College, School of Education and Counseling, Department of Counseling and Special Education, Program in Guidance and Counseling, Wayne, NE 68787. Offers counseling (MSE); counselor education (MSE); school counseling (MSE). *Accreditation:* ACA; NCATE. *Program availability:* Part-time, evening/weekend. *Degree requirements:* For master's, comprehensive exam, thesis optional. *Entrance requirements:* For master's, GRE General Test, minimum GPA of 3.0. Additional exam requirements/recommendations for international students: Required—TOEFL (minimum score 550 paper-based). Electronic applications accepted.

Wayne State University, College of Education, Division of Theoretical and Behavioral Foundations, Detroit, MI 48202. Offers applied behavior analysis (Certificate); counseling (M Ed, MA, Ed D, Ed S); counseling psychology (MA, PhD); education evaluation and research (M Ed, Ed D); educational psychology (M Ed, PhD), including learning and instruction sciences (PhD); rehabilitation counseling and community inclusion (MA); school and community psychology (MA, Certificate). *Accreditation:* ACA (one or more programs are accredited); CORE (one or more programs are accredited). *Program availability:* Part-time, evening/weekend. *Faculty:* 9. *Students:* 168 full-time (136 women), 200 part-time (171 women); includes 128 minority (82 Black or African American, non-Hispanic/Latino; 2 American Indian or Alaska Native, non-Hispanic/Latino; 8 Asian, non-Hispanic/Latino; 12 Hispanic/Latino; 24 Two or more races, non-Hispanic/Latino), 14 international. Average age 32. 340 applicants, 24% accepted, 66 enrolled. In 2018, 103 master's, 6 doctorates, 18 other advanced degrees awarded. *Degree requirements:* For master's, thesis (for some programs); for doctorate, comprehensive exam, thesis/dissertation. *Entrance requirements:* For master's, GRE, interview, personal statement, portfolio (only art therapy); references; program application; for doctorate, GRE, departmental writing exam, interview, curriculum vitae, references, master's degree in closely-related field with minimum GPA of 3.5, demonstration of counseling skills (for Ed D in counseling); autobiographical statement; letter of application; personal statement; for other advanced degree, education specialist certificate: GRE, education specialist certificate: master's degree in counseling or closely related field and licensure; personal statement; recommendations; autobiographical statement; interview. Additional exam requirements/recommendations for international students: Required—TOEFL (minimum score 550 paper-based; 79 iBT); Recommended—IELTS (minimum score 6.5), TWE (minimum score 5.5), TSE (minimum score 58). *Application deadline:* Applications are processed on a rolling basis. Application fee: $50. Electronic applications accepted. *Expenses:* Contact institution. *Financial support:* In 2018–19, 86 students received support, including 2 research assistantships with tuition reimbursements available (averaging $19,267 per year); fellowships, teaching assistantships, Federal Work-Study, scholarships/grants, health care benefits, and unspecified assistantships also available. Support available to part-time students. Financial award applicants required to submit FAFSA. *Faculty research:* Adolescents at risk, supervision of counseling. *Unit head:* Dr. Cheryl Somers, Assistant Dean, 313-577-1670, E-mail: c.somers@wayne.edu. *Application contact:* Dr. Mary L Waker, Graduate Admissions Officer, 313-577-1601, Fax: 313-577-7904, E-mail: m.waker@wayne.edu.
Website: http://coe.wayne.edu/tbf/index.php

West Chester University of Pennsylvania, College of Education and Social Work, Department of Counselor Education, West Chester, PA 19383. Offers clinical mental health counseling (MS); counseling (Certificate); higher education counseling (Post Master's Certificate); higher education counseling/student affairs (MS, Certificate); school counseling (M Ed). *Accreditation:* ACA; NCATE. *Program availability:* Part-time, evening/weekend. *Degree requirements:* For master's, comprehensive exam. *Entrance requirements:* For master's, minimum GPA of 3.0, three letters of reference. Additional exam requirements/recommendations for international students: Required—TOEFL or IELTS. Electronic applications accepted. *Faculty research:* Bullying in the schools, adolescent cognitive development, counseling pedagogy, motivational interviewing.

Western Connecticut State University, Division of Graduate Studies, School of Professional Studies, Department of Education and Educational Psychology, Program in School Counseling, Danbury, CT 06810-6885. Offers MS. *Accreditation:* ACA. *Program availability:* Part-time. *Students:* 11 full-time (9 women), 77 part-time (65 women). Average age 33. *Entrance requirements:* For master's, PRAXIS I, minimum GPA of 2.8, 3 letters of reference, essay, 6 hours of psychology. Additional exam requirements/recommendations for international students: Recommended—TOEFL (minimum score 550 paper-based; 79 iBT), IELTS (minimum score 6). *Application deadline:* For fall admission, 8/5 priority date for domestic students; for spring admission, 1/5 priority date for domestic students. Applications are processed on a rolling basis. Application fee: $50. *Financial support:* Application deadline: 5/1; applicants required to submit FAFSA. *Faculty research:* The effect of affective factors on cognition and learning, statistics and research methods, interviewing, individual and multicultural counseling. *Unit head:* Dr. Gabe Lomas, Coordinator, 203-837-8512, Fax: 203-837-8413, E-mail: lomasg@wcsu.edu. *Application contact:* Dr. Chris Shankle, Associate Director of Graduate Studies, 203-837-9005, Fax: 203-837-8326, E-mail: shanklec@wcsu.edu.

Western Illinois University, School of Graduate Studies, College of Education and Human Services, Department of Counselor Education, Macomb, IL 61455-1390. Offers counseling (MS Ed). *Accreditation:* ACA. *Program availability:* Part-time. *Students:* 23 full-time (20 women), 43 part-time (36 women); includes 15 minority (8 Black or African American, non-Hispanic/Latino; 7 Hispanic/Latino). Average age 31. 35 applicants, 63% accepted, 11 enrolled. In 2018, 23 master's awarded. *Degree requirements:* For master's, thesis or alternative. *Entrance requirements:* For master's, GRE, interview. Additional exam requirements/recommendations for international students: Required—

TOEFL (minimum score 550 paper-based; 80 iBT). Application fee: $30. Electronic applications accepted. *Financial support:* Unspecified assistantships available. Financial award applicants required to submit FAFSA. *Unit head:* Dr. Holly Nikels, Chairperson, 309-762-1876. *Application contact:* Dr. Mark Mossman, Assistant Director of Graduate Studies, 309-298-1806, Fax: 309-298-2345, E-mail: grad-office@wiu.edu. Website: http://wiu.edu/counselored

Western Kentucky University, Graduate School, College of Education and Behavioral Sciences, Department of Counseling and Student Affairs, Bowling Green, KY 42101. Offers counseling (MA Ed), including marriage and family therapy, mental health counseling; school counseling (P-12) (MA Ed); student affairs in higher education (MA Ed). *Accreditation:* ACA; NCATE. *Program availability:* Part-time, evening/weekend. *Degree requirements:* For master's, comprehensive exam, thesis optional. *Entrance requirements:* For master's, GRE General Test. Additional exam requirements/recommendations for international students: Required—TOEFL (minimum score 555 paper-based; 79 iBT). *Faculty research:* Counselor education, research for residential workers.

Western Michigan University, Graduate College, College of Education and Human Development, Department of Counselor Education and Counseling Psychology, Kalamazoo, MI 49008. Offers counseling psychology (MA, PhD); counselor education (MA, PhD), including counselor education (MA). *Accreditation:* ACA (one or more programs are accredited); APA (one or more programs are accredited); CORE; NCATE. *Degree requirements:* For doctorate, thesis/dissertation.

Western Washington University, Graduate School, College of Humanities and Social Sciences, Department of Psychology, Program in School Counseling, Bellingham, WA 98225-5996. Offers M Ed. *Accreditation:* ACA. *Degree requirements:* For master's, comprehensive exam. *Entrance requirements:* For master's, GRE General Test, minimum GPA of 3.0 in last 60 semester hours or last 90 quarter hours. Additional exam requirements/recommendations for international students: Required—TOEFL (minimum score 567 paper-based). Electronic applications accepted.

Westfield State University, College of Graduate and Continuing Education, Department of Psychology, Program in Counseling, Westfield, MA 01086. Offers forensic mental health counseling (MA); mental health counseling (MA); school adjustment counseling (MA); school guidance counseling (MA). *Program availability:* Part-time, evening/weekend. *Degree requirements:* For master's, comprehensive exam, practicum. *Entrance requirements:* For master's, GRE General Test, MAT, minimum undergraduate GPA of 3.0. Additional exam requirements/recommendations for international students: Recommended—TOEFL (minimum score 550 paper-based; 79 iBT).

Westminster College, Graduate School, Program in School Counseling, New Wilmington, PA 16172-0001. Offers clinical mental health counseling (MA); school counselor (M Ed). *Program availability:* Part-time, evening/weekend. *Degree requirements:* For master's, comprehensive exam (for M Ed). *Entrance requirements:* For master's, minimum GPA of 3.0, two recommendations.

West Texas A&M University, College of Education and Social Sciences, Department of Education, Program in Counseling, Canyon, TX 79015. Offers MA. *Program availability:* Part-time. *Degree requirements:* For master's, comprehensive exam. *Entrance requirements:* For master's, GRE General Test, interview, 12 semester hours in education and/or psychology, approval from the Counselor Admissions Committee. Additional exam requirements/recommendations for international students: Required—TOEFL (minimum score 550 paper-based). Electronic applications accepted.

West Virginia University, College of Education and Human Services, Morgantown, WV 26506. Offers audiology (Au D); autism spectrum disorder (MA); clinical rehabilitation and mental health counseling (MS); communication science and disorders (PhD); counseling (MA); counseling psychology (PhD); curriculum and instruction (Ed D); early childhood education (MA); early intervention/ early childhood special education (MA); education (PhD); educational leadership (MA); educational leadership/ public school administration (Ed D); educational leadership/public school administration (MA); educational psychology (MA, Ed D); elementary education (MA); gifted education (MA); higher education administration (MA, Ed D); higher education curriculum and teaching (MA); institutional design and technology (MA); instructional design and technology (Ed D); literacy education (MA); secondary education (MA); secondary education/ English (MA); special education (Ed D); speech pathology (MS). *Accreditation:* ASHA; NCATE. *Program availability:* Part-time, evening/weekend, online learning. *Students:* 392 full-time (325 women), 337 part-time (285 women); includes 44 minority (16 Black or African American, non-Hispanic/Latino; 16 Hispanic/Latino; 12 Two or more races, non-Hispanic/Latino), 11 international. In 2018, 303 master's, 6 doctorates awarded. *Degree requirements:* For master's, content exams; for doctorate, comprehensive exam, thesis/dissertation. *Entrance requirements:* Additional exam requirements/recommendations for international students: Required—TOEFL (minimum score 500 paper-based; 61 iBT). *Application deadline:* For fall admission, 8/1 for domestic students; for spring admission, 1/1 for domestic students; for summer admission, 5/1 for domestic students. Application fee: $60. Electronic applications accepted. *Financial support:* Fellowships, research assistantships, teaching assistantships, career-related internships or fieldwork, Federal Work-Study, institutionally sponsored loans, health care benefits, tuition waivers (full and partial), and administrative assistantships available. Financial award applicants required to submit FAFSA. *Faculty research:* Internet training and integration for teachers, rural education, teacher preparation, organization of schools, evaluation of personnel. *Unit head:* Dr. Tracy L. Morris, Interim Dean, 304-293-0816, Fax: 304-293-7565, E-mail: Tracy.Morris@mail.wvu.edu. *Application contact:* Dr. Melissa Luna, Associate Dean for Research, 304-293-2174, Fax: 304-293-3802, E-mail: Melissa.Luna@mail.wvu.edu. Website: http://cehs.wvu.edu/

Whitworth University, School of Education, Graduate Studies in Education, Program in Counseling, Spokane, WA 99251-0001. Offers school counselors (M Ed); social agency/ church setting (M Ed). *Accreditation:* NCATE. *Program availability:* Part-time, evening/weekend. *Degree requirements:* For master's, comprehensive exam, internship, practicum, research project, or thesis. *Entrance requirements:* For master's, GRE General Test, MAT. *Faculty research:* Church counseling service support.

Wichita State University, Graduate School, College of Applied Studies, Department of Counseling, Educational Leadership, Educational and School Psychology, Wichita, KS 67260. Offers counseling (M Ed); educational leadership (M Ed, Ed D); educational psychology (M Ed); school psychology (Ed S). *Accreditation:* NCATE. *Program availability:* Part-time, evening/weekend. Application fee: $50 ($65 for international students). *Unit head:* Dr. Jody Fiorini, Department Head, 316-978-3325, Fax: 316-978-3102, E-mail: jody.fiorini@wichita.edu. *Application contact:* Jordan Oleson, Admissions Coordinator, 316-978-3095, Fax: 316-978-3253, E-mail: jordan.oleson@wichita.edu. Website: http://www.wichita.edu/cles

Widener University, School of Human Service Professions, Center for Education, Chester, PA 19013-5792. Offers adult education (M Ed); counseling in higher education (M Ed); counselor education (M Ed); early childhood education (M Ed); educational foundations (M Ed); educational leadership (M Ed); educational psychology (M Ed); elementary education (M Ed); English and language arts (M Ed); health education (M Ed);

higher education leadership (Ed D); home and school visitor (M Ed); human sexuality (M Ed, PhD); mathematics education (M Ed); middle school education (M Ed); principalship (M Ed); reading and language arts (Ed D); reading education (M Ed); school administration (Ed D); science education (M Ed); social studies education (M Ed); special education (M Ed); technology education (M Ed). *Accreditation:* NCATE. *Program availability:* Part-time, evening/weekend. Terminal master's awarded for partial completion of doctoral program. *Degree requirements:* For doctorate, thesis/dissertation. *Entrance requirements:* For master's, minimum GPA of 2.5; for doctorate, GRE or MAT, minimum GPA of 2.0 (undergraduate), 3.5 (graduate). Electronic applications accepted. *Expenses:* Contact institution. *Faculty research:* Reading and cognition, adult education, technology education, educational leadership, special education.

William Paterson University of New Jersey, College of Education, Wayne, NJ 07470-8420. Offers curriculum and learning (M Ed); early childhood education (Certificate); educational leadership (M Ed); educational media specialist (Certificate); elementary education (MAT, Certificate); elementary education subject area (Certificate); higher education administration (MA); learning disabilities consultant (Certificate); literacy (M Ed); middle level education (M Ed); middle school education subject area (Certificate); professional counseling (M Ed); reading specialist (Certificate); school library media specialist (Certificate); school principal (Certificate); school supervisor (Certificate); secondary education (MAT); special education (M Ed); teacher of students with disabilities (Certificate). *Accreditation:* NCATE. *Program availability:* Part-time, evening/weekend. *Students:* Average age 35. 347 applicants, 87% accepted, 226 enrolled. In 2018, 136 master's awarded. *Degree requirements:* For master's, comprehensive exam, thesis (for some programs), exit interview (for some programs); practicum/internship; minimum GPA of 3.0 (for some programs); exit portfolio (for some programs). *Entrance requirements:* For master's, GRE/MAT, minimum GPA of 2.75; teaching certificate; essay; interview; 2 letters of recommendation; personal statement. Additional exam requirements/recommendations for international students: Required—TOEFL (minimum score 550 paper-based; 79 iBT), IELTS (minimum score 6). *Application deadline:* For fall admission, 6/1 for domestic students, 3/1 for international students; for spring admission, 11/1 for domestic students, 10/1 for international students. Applications are processed on a rolling basis. Application fee: $50. Electronic applications accepted. *Expenses: Tuition, area resident:* Full-time $14,714; part-time $727 per credit. Tuition, state resident: full-time $14,714; part-time $727 per credit. Tuition, nonresident: full-time $22,952; part-time $727 per credit. *International tuition:* $22,952 full-time. *Required fees:* $4 per semester. Tuition and fees vary according to course load, degree level and program. *Financial support:* In 2018–19, 8,416 students received support. Career-related internships or fieldwork, Federal Work-Study, scholarships/grants, and unspecified assistantships available. Support available to part-time students. Financial award application deadline: 3/15; financial award applicants required to submit FAFSA. *Faculty research:* Code switching and creative writing, language instruction, teacher evaluation, preschools, history of educational theories. *Total annual research expenditures:* $311,226. *Unit head:* Dr. Dorothy Feola, Dean, 973-720-2138, Fax: 973-720-3647, E-mail: feolad@wpunj.edu. *Application contact:* Liana Fornarotto, Director of Education Enrollment and Certification, 973-720-2206, Fax: 973-720-2989, E-mail: fornarottol@wpunj.edu. Website: http://www.wpunj.edu/coe

Wilmington University, College of Education, New Castle, DE 19720-6491. Offers applied technology in education (M Ed); career and technical education (M Ed); educational leadership (Ed D); elementary and secondary school counseling (M Ed); elementary studies (M Ed); ESOL literacy (M Ed); higher education leadership (Ed D); instruction: gifted and talented (M Ed); instruction: teacher of reading (M Ed); instruction: teaching and learning (M Ed); organizational leadership (Ed D); school leadership (M Ed); secondary education (MAT); special education (M Ed). *Accreditation:* NCATE. *Program availability:* Part-time, evening/weekend. *Entrance requirements:* For master's, 2 letters of recommendation, interview. Additional exam requirements/recommendations for international students: Required—TOEFL (minimum score 500 paper-based). Electronic applications accepted.

Winona State University, College of Education, Department of Counselor Education, Winona, MN 55987. Offers addiction counseling (Certificate); clinical mental health counseling (MS); human services (MS); school counseling (MS). *Accreditation:* ACA (one or more programs are accredited); NCATE. *Program availability:* Part-time, evening/weekend. *Degree requirements:* For master's, thesis or alternative. *Entrance requirements:* For master's, letters of reference, interview, group activity, on-site writing. Electronic applications accepted.

Winthrop University, College of Education, Program in Counseling and Development, Rock Hill, SC 29733. Offers agency counseling (M Ed); school counseling (M Ed). *Accreditation:* ACA; NCATE. *Program availability:* Part-time. *Students:* 90 full-time (75 women), 83 part-time (65 women); includes 59 minority (46 Black or African American, non-Hispanic/Latino; 9 Hispanic/Latino; 4 Two or more races, non-Hispanic/Latino), 1 international. Average age 26. In 2018, 26 master's awarded. *Degree requirements:* For master's, comprehensive exam. *Entrance requirements:* For master's, GRE General Test or MAT, interview. Additional exam requirements/recommendations for international students: Required—TOEFL (minimum score 550 paper-based; 79 iBT), IELTS (minimum score 6). *Application deadline:* For fall admission, 2/1 for domestic students. Application fee: $50. Electronic applications accepted. *Expenses:* Tuition, state resident: full-time $15,166; part-time $635 per credit hour. Tuition, nonresident: full-time $29,214. *Required fees:* $500; $180 per semester. *Financial support:* Research assistantships with full tuition reimbursements, career-related internships or fieldwork, Federal Work-Study, scholarships/grants, and unspecified assistantships available. Support available to part-time students. Financial award application deadline: 2/1; financial award applicants required to submit FAFSA. *Unit head:* Dr. Jennifer Jordan, Unit Head, 803-323-2456, E-mail: jordanje@winthrop.edu. *Application contact:* 800-411-7041, Fax: 803-323-2292, E-mail: gradschool@winthrop.edu. Website: http://www.winthrop.edu/coe/csdv

Wright State University, Graduate School, College of Education and Human Services, Department of Human Services, Programs in Counseling, Dayton, OH 45435. Offers counseling (MA, MS), including business and industrial management; pupil personnel services (M Ed), including school counseling. *Accreditation:* ACA (one or more programs are accredited); NCATE. *Degree requirements:* For master's, comprehensive exam, thesis (for some programs). *Entrance requirements:* For master's, GRE General Test, MAT, interview. Additional exam requirements/recommendations for international students: Required—TOEFL.

Xavier University, College of Professional Sciences, School of Education, Department of Counseling, Cincinnati, OH 45207. Offers clinical mental health counseling (MA); school counseling (MA). *Program availability:* Part-time, evening/weekend. *Degree requirements:* For master's, internship. *Entrance requirements:* For master's, GRE or MAT, minimum GPA of 3.0; 2 letters of recommendation; resume; official transcript; statement of purpose. Additional exam requirements/recommendations for international students: Required—TOEFL (minimum score 550 paper-based; 79 iBT). Electronic applications accepted. Application fee is waived when completed online. *Expenses:* Contact institution. *Faculty research:* Supervision, ethics, consultation, self-injury, bullying.

Xavier University of Louisiana, Graduate School, Programs in Education, New Orleans, LA 70125. Offers counseling (MA); curriculum and instruction (MA), including special interest - non certification; educational leadership (MA). *Accreditation:* NCATE. *Program availability:* Part-time, evening/weekend. *Faculty:* 7 full-time (5 women), 2 part-time/adjunct (both women). *Students:* 96 full-time (84 women), 51 part-time (42 women); includes 139 minority (138 Black or African American, non-Hispanic/Latino; 1 Hispanic/Latino). Average age 31. 77 applicants, 100% accepted, 77 enrolled. In 2018, 70 master's awarded. *Degree requirements:* For master's, comprehensive exam, thesis or alternative. *Entrance requirements:* For master's, GRE General Test, MAT /Praxis I & II, minimum GPA of 2.5. Additional exam requirements/recommendations for international students: Required—TOEFL. *Application deadline:* For fall admission, 7/1 for domestic students, 3/1 priority date for international students; for spring admission, 12/1 for domestic students, 9/15 priority date for international students; for summer admission, 3/1 for domestic students. Applications are processed on a rolling basis. Application fee: $30. Electronic applications accepted. *Expenses: Tuition:* Full-time $2652; part-time $1326 per credit hour. *Required fees:* $531; $323 per semester. $258 per semester. Tuition and fees vary according to degree level and program. *Financial support:* Career-related internships or fieldwork and tuition waivers (partial) available. Support available to part-time students. Financial award application deadline: 6/30; financial award applicants required to submit FAFSA. *Unit head:* Dr. Judith Miranti, Chair, Division of Education, 504-520-7536, Fax: 504-520-7909, E-mail: jmiranti@xula.edu. *Application contact:* Yiraliz Beltran, Program Manager, 504-520-7487, Fax: 504-520-7896, E-mail: ybeltran@xula.edu.

Youngstown State University, College of Graduate Studies, Beeghly College of Education, Department of Counseling, School Psychology and Educational Leadership, Youngstown, OH 44555-0001. Offers counseling (MS Ed); educational administration (MS Ed); educational leadership (Ed D); school psychology (Ed S). *Accreditation:* NCATE. *Program availability:* Part-time, evening/weekend. *Degree requirements:* For master's, comprehensive exam; for doctorate, comprehensive exam, thesis/dissertation. *Entrance requirements:* For master's, GRE, MAT, or teaching certificate; minimum GPA of 2.7; for doctorate, GRE General Test, GRE Subject Test, interview, minimum GPA of 3.5. Additional exam requirements/recommendations for international students: Required—TOEFL. *Faculty research:* Administrative theory, computer applications, education law, school and community relations, finance principalship.

Developmental Education

East Tennessee State University, School of Graduate Studies, School of Continuing Studies and Academic Outreach, Johnson City, TN 37614. Offers archival studies (Postbaccalaureate Certificate); liberal studies (MALS); reinforcing education through artistic learning (Postbaccalaureate Certificate); strategic leadership (MPS); training and development (MPS). *Program availability:* Part-time, online learning. *Degree requirements:* For master's, comprehensive exam, thesis (for some programs), professional project. *Entrance requirements:* For master's, GRE General Test, minimum GPA of 2.75, professional portfolio, three letters of recommendation, interview, writing sample; for Postbaccalaureate Certificate, minimum GPA of 2.5, three letters of recommendation, interview. Additional exam requirements/recommendations for international students: Required—TOEFL (minimum score 550 paper-based; 79 iBT). Electronic applications accepted. *Faculty research:* Appalachian studies, women's and gender studies, interdisciplinary theory, regional and Southern cultures.

Ferris State University, College of Education and Human Services, School of Education, Big Rapids, MI 49307. Offers curriculum and instruction (M Ed), including special education, subject area; training and development (MSCTE). *Program availability:* Part-time, evening/weekend, blended/hybrid learning. *Faculty:* 7 full-time (4 women), 1 (woman) part-time/adjunct. *Students:* 4 full-time (3 women), 39 part-time (23 women); includes 7 minority (3 Black or African American, non-Hispanic/Latino; 2 Hispanic/Latino; 2 Two or more races, non-Hispanic/Latino), 2 international. Average age 38. 14 applicants, 93% accepted, 7 enrolled. In 2018, 18 master's awarded. *Degree requirements:* For master's, thesis, Capstone project. *Entrance requirements:* For master's, minimum undergraduate GPA of 3.0. Additional exam requirements/recommendations for international students: Required—TOEFL (minimum score 550 paper-based; 79 iBT), IELTS (minimum score 6.5), TOEFL (minimum score 550 paper-based, 79 iBT) or IELTS 6.5. *Application deadline:* For fall admission, 7/1 priority date for domestic and international students; for spring admission, 11/1 priority date for domestic and international students; for summer admission, 3/1 priority date for domestic and international students. Applications are processed on a rolling basis. Application fee: $0 ($30 for international students). Electronic applications accepted. Application fee is waived when completed online. *Financial support:* In 2018–19, 7 students received support. Career-related internships or fieldwork and scholarships/grants available. Support available to part-time students. Financial award applicants required to submit FAFSA. *Faculty research:* Game based education, needs of students with disabilities in post-secondary education, elementary education students with reading difficulties. *Unit head:* Leonard Johnson, Interim Dean, 231-591-3648, Fax: 231-591-2043, E-mail: LeonardJohnson@ferris.edu. *Application contact:* Liza Ing, Graduate Program Coordinator, 231-591-5362, Fax: 231-591-2043, E-mail: lizaIng@ferris.edu. Website: http://www.ferris.edu/education/education/

Grambling State University, School of Graduate Studies and Research, College of Education, Department of Educational Leadership, Grambling, LA 71245. Offers developmental education (MS, Ed D, PMC), including curriculum and instructional design (Ed D), English (MS), guidance and counseling (MS), higher education administration and management (Ed D), mathematics (MS), reading (MS), science (MS), student development and personnel services (Ed D); educational leadership (M Ed). *Program availability:* Part-time, evening/weekend. *Degree requirements:* For master's, comprehensive exam, thesis (for some programs); for doctorate, comprehensive exam, thesis/dissertation. *Entrance requirements:* For master's, GRE, minimum GPA of 2.5 on last degree; for doctorate, GRE (minimum score 1000, 500 on Verbal), master's degree, minimum GPA of 3.0 on last degree. Additional exam requirements/recommendations for international students: Required—TOEFL (minimum score 500 paper-based; 62 iBT). Electronic applications accepted.

Instituto Tecnológico y de Estudios Superiores de Monterrey, Campus Ciudad Obregón, Programs in Education, Program in Cognitive Development, Ciudad Obregón, Mexico. Offers ME.

National Louis University, College of Arts and Sciences, Chicago, IL 60603. Offers adult education (Ed D); counseling and human services (MS); language and academic development (M Ed, Certificate); psychology (MA, PhD, Certificate); public policy (MA); written communication (MS, Certificate). *Program availability:* Part-time, evening/weekend, online learning. *Degree requirements:* For master's and Certificate, comprehensive exam (for some programs), thesis (for some programs); for doctorate, thesis/dissertation. *Entrance requirements:* For master's, MAT or GRE, 3 professional or academic references, interview, minimum GPA of 3.0; for doctorate, GRE General Test, MAT, or Watson-Glaser Critical Thinking Appraisal, three professional or academic references, statement of academic and professional goals, 3 years of experience in field, interview, master's degree, resume, writing sample; for Certificate, GRE, MAT, or Watson-Glaser Critical Thinking Appraisal, three professional or academic references, statement of academic and professional goals, interview, minimum GPA of 3.0. Additional exam requirements/recommendations for international students: Required—Department of Language Studies Assessment or TOEFL (minimum score 550 paper-based; 79 iBT). Electronic applications accepted.

Penn State Harrisburg, Graduate School, School of Behavioral Sciences and Education, Middletown, PA 17057. Offers adult education in the health and medical professions (Certificate); applied behavior analysis (MA); applied clinical psychology (MA); applied psychological research (MA); community psychology and social change

(MA); English as a second language (ESL) program specialist and leadership (Certificate); health education (M Ed); lifelong learning and adult education (M Ed, D Ed); literacy education (M Ed); literacy leadership (Certificate); psychology: applications in clinical psychology (Certificate); psychology: health psychology (Certificate); teaching and curriculum (M Ed); training and development (M Ed, Certificate). *Program availability:* Part-time, evening/weekend.

Rutgers University–New Brunswick, Graduate School of Education, Department of Educational Psychology, Program in Learning, Cognition and Development, Piscataway, NJ 08854-8097. Offers Ed M. *Program availability:* Part-time, evening/weekend. *Entrance requirements:* For master's, GRE General Test, 3 letters of recommendation. Additional exam requirements/recommendations for international students: Required—TOEFL (minimum score 550 paper-based; 83 iBT). Electronic applications accepted. *Faculty research:* Cognitive development, gender roles, cognition and instruction, peer learning, infancy and early childhood.

Sam Houston State University, College of Education, Department of Educational Leadership, Huntsville, TX 77341. Offers administration (M Ed); developmental education administration (Ed D); educational leadership (Ed D); higher education administration (MA); higher education leadership (Ed D); instructional leadership (M Ed, MA). *Program availability:* Part-time, evening/weekend, online learning. *Degree requirements:* For master's, comprehensive exam (for some programs), thesis (for some programs); for doctorate, comprehensive exam, thesis/dissertation. *Entrance requirements:* For master's, GRE General Test, references, personal essay, resume, professional statement; for doctorate, GRE General Test, master's degree, references, personal essay, resume. Additional exam requirements/recommendations for international students: Required—TOEFL (minimum score 550 paper-based; 79 iBT), IELTS (minimum score 6.5). Electronic applications accepted.

Texas State University, The Graduate College, College of Education, Program in Developmental Education, San Marcos, TX 78666. Offers MA, PhD. *Program availability:* Part-time. *Faculty:* 8 full-time (4 women). *Students:* 26 full-time (20 women), 18 part-time (17 women); includes 20 minority (3 Black or African American, non-Hispanic/Latino; 1 Asian, non-Hispanic/Latino; 15 Hispanic/Latino; 1 Two or more races, non-Hispanic/Latino), 2 international. Average age 40. 19 applicants, 63% accepted, 8 enrolled. In 2018, 4 master's, 7 doctorates awarded. *Degree requirements:* For master's, comprehensive exam, thesis optional; for doctorate, comprehensive exam, thesis/dissertation. *Entrance requirements:* For master's, baccalaureate degree from regionally-accredited institution with minimum GPA of 2.75 on last 60 hours of undergraduate work, statement of purpose, 3 letters of reference from individuals with knowledge of the candidate as a student or professional; for doctorate, GRE (general test only) required with competitive scores in the verbal reasoning, quantitative reasoning, and analytical writing sections., baccalaureate and master's degrees from regionally-accredited institution in area relevant to developmental education with minimum graduate GPA of 3.0; statement of purpose; resume; 3 letters of recommendation addressing the applicant's professional and academic background. Additional exam requirements/recommendations for international students: Required—TOEFL (minimum score 550 paper-based; 78 iBT), IELTS (minimum score 6.5). *Application deadline:* For fall admission, 1/15 priority date for domestic and international students; for spring admission, 10/15 for domestic students, 10/1 for international students; for summer admission, 4/15 for domestic students, 3/15 for international students. Application fee: $55 ($90 for international students). Electronic applications accepted. *Expenses:* Tuition, state resident: full-time $8102; part-time $4051 per semester. Tuition, nonresident: full-time $18,229; part-time $9115 per semester. *International tuition:* $18,229 full-time. *Required fees:* $2116; $120 per credit hour. Tuition and fees vary according to course load. *Financial support:* In 2018–19, 31 students received support, including 12 research assistantships (averaging $26,661 per year), 8 teaching assistantships (averaging $27,820 per year); scholarships/grants and unspecified assistantships also available. Financial award application deadline: 1/15; financial award applicants required to submit FAFSA. *Faculty research:* Adult student transition to postsecondary models, developmental and basic literacy instruction, and the impact of developmental education professional development on instruction; reading, developmental education, learning strategies, disciplinary literacy; cognitive, metacognitive, motivational, affective, and behavioral factors that underlie effective and efficient learning in postsecondary education. *Total annual research expenditures:* $108,121. *Unit head:* Dr. Sonya Armstrong, Doctoral Program Director, 512-245-7789, E-mail: sla113@txstate.edu. *Application contact:* Dr. Andrea Golato, Dean of Graduate School, 512-245-2581, Fax: 512-245-8365, E-mail: gradcollege@txstate.edu. Website: http://www.gradcollege.txstate.edu/programs/developmental-ed-phd.html

The University of Iowa, Graduate College, College of Education, Department of Teaching and Learning, Program in Education, Iowa City, IA 52242-1316. Offers art education (MA); developmental reading (MA); elementary education (MA); English education (MA, MAT); foreign and second language education (MAT); foreign language education (MA); foreign language/ESL education (PhD); language, literacy and culture (PhD); mathematics education (MA, MAT, PhD); music education (MM, PhD); science education (MA); secondary education (MA); social studies (MA, PhD). *Degree requirements:* For master's, thesis optional, exam; for doctorate, comprehensive exam, thesis/dissertation. *Entrance requirements:* For master's and doctorate, GRE General

Test, minimum GPA of 3.0. Additional exam requirements/recommendations for international students: Required—TOEFL (minimum score 550 paper-based; 81 iBT). Electronic applications accepted.

Walden University, Graduate Programs, Richard W. Riley College of Education and Leadership, Minneapolis, MN 55401. Offers adult education (Post-Master's Certificate); adult learning (Graduate Certificate); college teaching and learning (Graduate Certificate); community college leadership (Ed D); curriculum, instruction and assessment (Ed D, Ed S, Graduate Certificate); developmental education (Graduate Certificate); early childhood administration, management, and leadership (Graduate Certificate); early childhood education (Ed D, Ed S); early childhood public policy and advocacy (Graduate Certificate); early childhood studies (MS), including administration, management and leadership, early childhood public policy and advocacy, teaching adults in the early childhood field, teaching and diversity in early childhood education; education (MS, PhD), including adolescent literacy and learning (MS), curriculum, instruction, and assessment (grades K-12) (MS), curriculum, instruction, assessment, and evaluation (PhD), early childhood leadership and advocacy (PhD), early childhood special education (PhD), educational leadership (MS), educational leadership and administration (principal preparation) (MS), educational technology and design (PhD), elementary reading and literacy (PreK-6) (MS), elementary reading and mathematics (grades K-6) (MS), global and comparative education (PhD), higher education leadership management and policy (PhD), integrating technology in the classroom (grades K-12) (MS), learning, instruction and innovation (PhD), mathematics (grades 5-8) (MS), mathematics (grades K-6) (MS), mathematics and science (grades K-8) (MS), organizational research, assessment, and evaluation (PhD), reading and literacy with a reading K-12 endorsement (MS), reading literacy assessment and evaluation (PhD), science (grades K-8) (MS), special education (non-licensure) (grades K-12) (MS), teacher leadership (grades K-12) (MS), teaching English language learners (grades K-12) (MS); educational administration and leadership (Ed D); educational leadership and administration (principal preparation) (Ed S); educational technology (Ed D, Ed S, Post Master's Certificate); elementary reading and literacy (Graduate Certificate); engaging culturally diverse learners (Graduate Certificate); enrollment management and institutional marketing (Graduate Certificate); higher education (MS), including adult learning, college teaching and learning, enrollment management and institutional marketing, global higher education, leadership for student success, online and distance learning; higher education and adult learning (Ed D); higher education leadership and management (Ed D); higher education leadership for student success (Graduate Certificate); instructional design and technology (MS, Postbaccalaureate Certificate), including general program (MS), online learning (MS), training and performance improvement (MS); integrating technology in the classroom (Graduate Certificate); mathematics 5-8 (Graduate Certificate); mathematics K-6 (Graduate Certificate); online teaching for adult educators (Graduate Certificate); reading, literacy, and assessment (Ed D, Ed S); science K-8 (Graduate Certificate); special education (Ed D, Ed S, Graduate Certificate); special education (K-age 21) (MAT); teacher leadership (Graduate Certificate); teaching adults English as a second language (Graduate Certificate); teaching adults in the early childhood field (Graduate Certificate); teaching and diversity in early childhood education (Graduate Certificate); teaching English language learners (grades K-12) (Graduate Certificate); teaching K-12 students online (Graduate Certificate). *Accreditation:* NCATE. *Program availability:* Part-time, evening/weekend, online only, 100% online. *Degree requirements:* For doctorate, thesis/dissertation (for some programs), residency; for other advanced degree, residency (for some programs). *Entrance requirements:* For master's, bachelor's degree or higher; minimum GPA of 2.5; official transcripts; goal statement (for some programs); access to computer and Internet; for doctorate, master's degree or higher; three years of related professional or academic experience (preferred); minimum GPA of 3.0; goal statement and current resume (for select programs); official transcripts; access to computer and Internet; for other advanced degree, relevant work experience; access to computer and Internet. Additional exam requirements/recommendations for international students: Required—TOEFL (minimum score 550 paper-based, 79 iBT), IELTS (minimum score 6.5), Michigan English Language Assessment Battery (minimum score 82), or PTE (minimum score 53). Electronic applications accepted.

English Education

Alabama Agricultural and Mechanical University, School of Graduate Studies, College of Education, Humanities, and Behavioral Sciences, Department of Educational Leadership and Secondary Education, Huntsville, AL 35811. Offers biology (M Ed); business/marketing education (M Ed, Ed S); chemistry (M Ed); collaborative teacher secondary education (M Ed, Ed S); education (M Ed, Ed S); English language arts (M Ed); family/consumer science education (M Ed, Ed S); general science (M Ed); general social science (M Ed); mathematics (M Ed, Ed S); physics (M Ed, Ed S); technology education (M Ed). *Accreditation:* NCATE. *Program availability:* Evening/weekend. *Degree requirements:* For master's, comprehensive exam; for Ed S, thesis. *Entrance requirements:* For master's, GRE General Test. Additional exam requirements/recommendations for international students: Required—TOEFL (minimum score 500 paper-based; 61 iBT). Electronic applications accepted. *Faculty research:* World peace through education, computer-assisted instruction.

Alabama State University, College of Education, Department of Curriculum and Instruction, Montgomery, AL 36101-0271. Offers early childhood education (Ed S); secondary education (M Ed), including biology education, English language arts education, history education, math education, music education, reading education, social science education. *Program availability:* Part-time, evening/weekend, online only, 100% online. *Faculty:* 7 full-time (4 women), 7 part-time/adjunct (4 women). *Students:* 22 full-time (19 women), 58 part-time (49 women); includes 235 minority (234 Black or African American, non-Hispanic/Latino; 1 Hispanic/Latino), 5 international. Average age 36. 45 applicants, 33% accepted, 6 enrolled. In 2018, 34 master's awarded. *Degree requirements:* For master's, comprehensive exam, thesis optional; for Ed S, comprehensive exam, thesis. *Entrance requirements:* For master's, GRE General Test, MAT, writing competency test; for Ed S, writing competency test, GRE, MAT. Additional exam requirements/recommendations for international students: Required—TOEFL (minimum score 500 paper-based). *Application deadline:* For fall admission, 4/15 for domestic and international students; for spring admission, 11/15 for domestic and international students; for summer admission, 3/15 for domestic and international students. Applications are processed on a rolling basis. Application fee: $25. Electronic applications accepted. *Expenses:* Contact institution. *Financial support:* Fellowships, teaching assistantships, career-related internships or fieldwork, scholarships/grants, tuition waivers (partial), and unspecified assistantships available. Financial award application deadline: 6/30; financial award applicants required to submit FAFSA. *Unit head:* Dr. Joyce Johnson, Acting Chairperson, 334-229-4485, Fax: 334-229-5603, E-mail: jjohnson@alasu.edu. *Application contact:* Dr. Ed Brown, Dean of Graduate Studies, 334-229-4274, Fax: 334-229-4928, E-mail: ebrown@alasu.edu.
Website: http://www.alasu.edu/academics/colleges—departments/college-of-education/curriculum—instruction/index.aspx

Albany State University, College of Arts and Humanities, Albany, GA 31705-2717. Offers criminal justice (MS); English education (M Ed); public administration (MPA), including community and economic development, criminal justice administration, health administration and policy, human resources management, public management, public policy, water resources management and policy; social work (MSW). *Accreditation:* NASPAA. *Program availability:* Part-time. *Degree requirements:* For master's, comprehensive exam, professional portfolio (for MPA), internship, capstone report. *Entrance requirements:* For master's, GRE, MAT, minimum GPA of 3.0, official transcript, pre-medical record/certificate of immunization, letters of reference. Electronic applications accepted. *Faculty research:* HIV prevention for minority students.

Andrews University, School of Graduate Studies, College of Arts and Sciences, Department of English, Berrien Springs, MI 49104. Offers MA, MAT. *Program availability:* Part-time. *Degree requirements:* For master's, one foreign language, thesis optional. *Entrance requirements:* For master's, GRE Subject Test. Additional exam requirements/recommendations for international students: Required—TOEFL (minimum score 550 paper-based). *Faculty research:* Shakespearean studies.

Andrews University, School of Graduate Studies, School of Education, Department of Teaching, Learning, and Curriculum, Berrien Springs, MI 49104. Offers curriculum and instruction (MA, Ed D, PhD, Ed S); elementary education (MAT); secondary education (MAT), including biology, education, English, English as a second language, French, history, physics; teacher education (MAT). *Entrance requirements:* For master's, GRE Subject Test. Additional exam requirements/recommendations for international students: Required—TOEFL (minimum score 550 paper-based).

Anna Maria College, Graduate Division, Program in Education, Paxton, MA 01612. Offers early childhood education (M Ed); education (CAGS); elementary education (M Ed); English language arts (M Ed); visual arts (M Ed). *Program availability:* Part-time, evening/weekend. *Entrance requirements:* For master's, bachelor's degree in liberal arts or sciences, minimum GPA of 3.0. Additional exam requirements/recommendations for international students: Required—TOEFL (minimum score 500 paper-based). Electronic applications accepted.

Appalachian State University, Cratis D. Williams School of Graduate Studies, Department of Curriculum and Instruction, Boone, NC 28608. Offers curriculum specialist (MA); educational media (MA); elementary education (MA); middle grades education (MA), including language arts, mathematics, science, social studies. *Accreditation:* NCATE. *Program availability:* Part-time, evening/weekend, online learning. *Degree requirements:* For master's, comprehensive exam, thesis or alternative. *Entrance requirements:* For master's, GRE General Test or MAT, 3 letters of recommendation. Additional exam requirements/recommendations for international students: Required—TOEFL (minimum score 570 paper-based; 79 iBT), IELTS (minimum score 6.5). Electronic applications accepted. *Expenses: Tuition, area resident:* Full-time $4839; part-time $237 per credit hour. Tuition, state resident: full-time $4839; part-time $237 per credit hour. Tuition, nonresident: full-time $18,271; part-time $895.50 per credit hour. *Faculty research:* Media literacy, elementary teaching, curriculum development, online learning environments.

Arcadia University, School of Education, Glenside, PA 19038-3295. Offers art education (M Ed); computer education (CAS); curriculum (CAS); curriculum studies (M Ed); early childhood education (M Ed), including individualized, master teacher, research in child development; educational leadership (M Ed, Ed D, CAS); elementary education (M Ed); English education (MA Ed); environmental education (MA Ed); instructional technology (M Ed); language arts (M Ed); library science (M Ed); mathematics education (M Ed, MA Ed); music education (MA Ed); psychology (MA Ed); reading (M Ed, CAS); science education (M Ed, CAS); secondary education (M Ed, CAS); special education (M Ed, Ed D, CAS); theater arts (MA Ed); written communication (MA Ed). *Accreditation:* NASAD. *Program availability:* Part-time, evening/weekend, online learning. *Faculty:* 14 full-time (10 women). *Students:* 35 full-time (24 women), 299 part-time (243 women); includes 72 minority (49 Black or African American, non-Hispanic/Latino; 1 American Indian or Alaska Native, non-Hispanic/Latino; 12 Asian, non-Hispanic/Latino; 8 Hispanic/Latino; 2 Two or more races, non-Hispanic/Latino), 5 international. In 2018, 152 master's, 8 doctorates awarded. *Entrance requirements:* Additional exam requirements/recommendations for international students: Required—Official results from the TOEFL or IELTS are required. *Application deadline:* Applications are processed on a rolling basis. Application fee: $25. Electronic applications accepted. *Expenses:* Contact institution. *Financial support:* Career-related internships or fieldwork, tuition waivers (partial), and unspecified assistantships available. *Unit head:* Kimberly Dean, Chair, 215-572-8629. *Application contact:* 215-572-2925, Fax: 215-572-2126, E-mail: grad@arcadia.edu.

Arkansas State University, Graduate School, College of Humanities and Social Sciences, Department of English and Philosophy, State University, AR 72467. Offers English (MA); English education (MSE, SCCT). *Program availability:* Part-time. *Degree requirements:* For master's, variable foreign language requirement, comprehensive exam, thesis or alternative, preliminary exam; for SCCT, comprehensive exam. *Entrance requirements:* For master's, GRE General Test or MAT, appropriate bachelor's degree, official transcript, valid teaching certificate (for MSE), immunization records; for SCCT, GRE General Test or MAT, interview, master's degree, official transcript, immunization records. Additional exam requirements/recommendations for international students: Required—TOEFL (minimum score 550 paper-based; 79 iBT), IELTS (minimum score 6), PTE (minimum score 56). Electronic applications accepted.

Arkansas Tech University, College of Arts and Humanities, Russellville, AR 72801. Offers applied sociology (MS); English (M Ed, MA); history (MA); liberal arts (MLA); multi-media journalism (MA); psychology (MS); teaching English as a second language (MA). *Program availability:* Part-time, 100% online, blended/hybrid learning. *Students:* 34 full-time (21 women), 150 part-time (108 women); includes 38 minority (10 Black or African American, non-Hispanic/Latino; 4 Asian, non-Hispanic/Latino; 20 Hispanic/Latino; 4 Two or more races, non-Hispanic/Latino), 11 international. Average age 34. In 2018, 75 master's awarded. *Degree requirements:* For master's, comprehensive exam (for some programs), thesis (for some programs), project. *Entrance requirements:*

Additional exam requirements/recommendations for international students: Required—TOEFL (minimum score 550 paper-based; 79 iBT), IELTS (minimum score 6.5), PTE (minimum score 58). *Application deadline:* For fall admission, 3/1 priority date for domestic students, 5/1 priority date for international students; for spring admission, 10/1 priority date for domestic and international students. Applications are processed on a rolling basis. Application fee: $40 ($90 for international students). Electronic applications accepted. *Expenses: Tuition, area resident:* Full-time $6816; part-time $284 per credit hour. Tuition, state resident: full-time $6816; part-time $284 per credit hour. Tuition, nonresident: full-time $13,632; part-time $568 per credit hour. *International tuition:* $13,632 full-time. *Required fees:* $457.50 per semester. Tuition and fees vary according to course load and degree level. *Financial support:* In 2018–19, research assistantships with full and partial tuition reimbursements (averaging $4,800 per year), teaching assistantships with full and partial tuition reimbursements (averaging $4,800 per year) were awarded; career-related internships or fieldwork, Federal Work-Study, scholarships/grants, health care benefits, and unspecified assistantships also available. Support available to part-time students. Financial award application deadline: 4/15; financial award applicants required to submit FAFSA. *Unit head:* Dr. Wayne Powell, Dean, 479-968-0274, Fax: 479-964-0812, E-mail: wpowell4@atu.edu. *Application contact:* Dr. Jeff Robertson, Interim Dean of Graduate College, 479-968-0398, Fax: 479-964-0542, E-mail: gradcollege@atu.edu.
Website: http://www.atu.edu/humanities/

Binghamton University, State University of New York, Graduate School, College of Community and Public Affairs, Department of Teaching, Learning and Educational Leadership, Program in Adolescence Education, Binghamton, NY 13902-6000. Offers biology education (MAT, MS Ed); chemistry education (MAT, MS Ed); earth science education (MAT, MS Ed); English education (MAT, MS Ed); French education (MAT, MS Ed); mathematical sciences education (MAT, MS Ed); physics (MAT, MS Ed); social studies (MAT, MS Ed); Spanish education (MAT, MS Ed). *Accreditation:* TEAC. *Program availability:* Part-time, evening/weekend. *Degree requirements:* For master's, portfolio. *Entrance requirements:* For master's, GRE General Test, teaching certification. Additional exam requirements/recommendations for international students: Required—TOEFL (minimum score 550 paper-based; 80 iBT). Electronic applications accepted.

Bloomsburg University of Pennsylvania, School of Graduate Studies, College of Education, Department of Teaching and Learning, Program in Middle Level Education Grades 4-8, Bloomsburg, PA 17815-1301. Offers language arts (M Ed); math (M Ed); science (M Ed); social studies (M Ed). *Accreditation:* NCATE. *Degree requirements:* For master's, thesis optional, practicum, student teaching. *Entrance requirements:* For master's, MAT, GRE, or PRAXIS, minimum QPA of 3.0, teaching certificate, U.S. citizenship, related undergraduate coursework, professional liability insurance, recent TB test. Additional exam requirements/recommendations for international students: Required—TOEFL (minimum score 550 paper-based), IELTS. Electronic applications accepted.

Bob Jones University, Graduate Programs, Greenville, SC 29614. Offers accountancy (MS); Bible (MA); Bible translation (MA); Biblical studies (Certificate); business administration (MBA); church history (MA, PhD); church ministries (MA); church music (MM); cinema and video production (MA); counseling (MS); curriculum and instruction (Ed D); divinity (M Div); dramatic production (MA); educational leadership (MS, Ed D, Ed S); elementary education (M Ed, MAT); English (M Ed, MA, MAT); fine arts (MA); graphic design (MA); history (M Ed, MA); illustration (MA); interpretative speech (MA); mathematics (M Ed, MAT); medical missions (Certificate); ministry (MM, D Min); multi-categorical special education (M Ed, MAT); music (M Ed); New Testament interpretation (PhD); Old Testament interpretation (PhD); orchestral instrument performance (MM); organ performance (MM); pastoral studies (MA); personnel services (MS, Ed S); piano pedagogy (MM); piano performance (MM); platform arts (MA); rhetoric and public address (MA); secondary education (M Ed); studio art (MA); teaching Bible (MA); theology (MA, PhD); voice performance (MM); youth ministries (MA); M Div/MM.

Boise State University, College of Arts and Sciences, Department of English, Boise, ID 83725-0399. Offers English literature (MA); English, rhetoric and composition (MA); teaching English language (MA); technical communication (MA). *Program availability:* Part-time. *Degree requirements:* For master's, thesis (for some programs). *Entrance requirements:* For master's, GRE General Test, minimum GPA of 3.0. Additional exam requirements/recommendations for international students: Required—TOEFL (minimum score 550 paper-based; 80 iBT), IELTS (minimum score 6). Electronic applications accepted.

Boston College, Lynch School of Education and Human Development, Department of Teacher Education, Special Education and Curriculum and Instruction, Chestnut Hill, MA 02467-3800. Offers curriculum and instruction (M Ed, PhD, CAES); early childhood education (M Ed); elementary education (M Ed); law and curriculum and instruction (JD/M Ed); reading specialist (M Ed, CAES); religious education (M Ed, CAES); secondary education (M Ed, MAT, MST), including biology (MST), chemistry (MST), English (MAT), French (MAT), geology (MST), history (MAT), Latin and classical humanities (MAT), mathematics (MST), physics (MST), secondary teaching (M Ed), Spanish (MAT); special needs: moderate disabilities (M Ed, CAES); special needs: severe disabilities (M Ed); JD/M Ed. *Program availability:* Part-time, evening/weekend, 100% online. *Faculty:* 19 full-time (11 women). *Students:* 186 full-time (140 women), 92 part-time (74 women); includes 58 minority (20 Black or African American, non-Hispanic/Latino; 4 Asian, non-Hispanic/Latino; 29 Hispanic/Latino; 5 Two or more races, non-Hispanic/Latino), 33 international. Average age 28. In 2018, 132 master's, 13 doctorates awarded. Terminal master's awarded for partial completion of doctoral program. *Degree requirements:* For master's, comprehensive exam; for doctorate, comprehensive exam, thesis/dissertation. *Entrance requirements:* Additional exam requirements/recommendations for international students: Required—TOEFL. Application fee: $75. Electronic applications accepted. *Financial support:* Fellowships with full and partial tuition reimbursements, research assistantships with full and partial tuition reimbursements, teaching assistantships with full and partial tuition reimbursements, career-related internships or fieldwork, Federal Work-Study, institutionally sponsored loans, scholarships/grants, traineeships, health care benefits, tuition waivers (full and partial), and unspecified assistantships available. Support available to part-time students. Financial award applicants required to submit FAFSA. *Faculty research:* Teacher education, education research and policy, bilingual education, science education, disabilities, urban education. *Unit head:* Dr. Susan Bruce, Chairperson, 617-552-4214, Fax: 617-552-0812. *Application contact:* Jessica Rivers, Assistant Dean of Graduate Admission and Financial Aid, 617-552-4214, Fax: 617-552-0398, E-mail: riversja@bc.edu.
Website: http://www.bc.edu/education

Brooklyn College of the City University of New York, School of Education, Program in Adolescence Science Education and Special Subjects, Brooklyn, NY 11210-2889. Offers adolescence science education (MAT); biology teacher (7-12) (MA); chemistry teacher (7-12) (MA); earth science teacher (7-12) (MAT); English teacher (7-12) (MA); French teacher (7-12) (MA); mathematics teacher (7-12) (MA); music teacher (MA); physics teacher (7-12) (MA); social studies teacher (7-12) (MA); Spanish teacher (7-12) (MA). *Program availability:* Part-time, evening/weekend. *Degree requirements:* For master's, comprehensive exam (for some programs), thesis (for some programs). *Entrance requirements:* For master's, LAST, previous course work in education, resume, 2 letters of recommendation, essay. Additional exam requirements/recommendations for international students: Required—TOEFL (minimum score 500 paper-based; 61 iBT). Electronic applications accepted. *Faculty research:* Interdisciplinary education, semiotics, discourse analysis, autobiography, teacher identity.

Brown University, Graduate School, Department of Education, Program in Teaching, Providence, RI 02912. Offers elementary education (MAT); English (MAT); history/social studies (MAT); science (MAT); secondary education (MAT). *Degree requirements:* For master's, student teaching, portfolio. *Entrance requirements:* For master's, GRE General Test, transcript, personal statement, 3 letters of recommendation, interview, writing sample (English applicants only). Additional exam requirements/recommendations for international students: Required—TOEFL (minimum score 577 paper-based). Electronic applications accepted. *Faculty research:* Literacy, English language learners, diversity, special education, biodiversity.

Buffalo State College, State University of New York, The Graduate School, School of Arts and Humanities, Department of English, Buffalo, NY 14222-1095. Offers English (MA); secondary education (MS Ed), including English. *Program availability:* Part-time, evening/weekend. *Degree requirements:* For master's, thesis or project, 1 foreign language (MS Ed). *Entrance requirements:* For master's, minimum GPA of 2.75, 36 hours in English, New York teaching certificate (MS Ed). Additional exam requirements/recommendations for international students: Required—TOEFL (minimum score 550 paper-based).

California Baptist University, Program in English, Riverside, CA 92504-3206. Offers English pedagogy (MA); literature (MA); teaching English to speakers of other languages (TESOL) (MA). *Program availability:* Part-time. *Faculty:* 17 full-time (11 women). *Students:* 1 (woman) full-time, 19 part-time (12 women); includes 14 minority (8 Black or African American, non-Hispanic/Latino; 6 Hispanic/Latino). Average age 33. 2 applicants, 100% accepted, 2 enrolled. In 2018, 6 master's awarded. *Degree requirements:* For master's, comprehensive exam, project, or thesis. *Entrance requirements:* For master's, GRE (for applicants with a GPA below 2.75) or CSET, minimum undergraduate GPA of 2.75; 18 semester hours of course work in English beyond freshman level; three recommendations; essay; demonstration of writing; interview. Additional exam requirements/recommendations for international students: Required—TOEFL (minimum score 80 iBT). *Application deadline:* For fall admission, 8/1 priority date for domestic students, 7/1 for international students; for spring admission, 12/1 priority date for domestic students, 11/1 for international students. Applications are processed on a rolling basis. Application fee: $45. Electronic applications accepted. *Expenses:* $607 per unit. *Financial support:* In 2018–19, 9 students received support. Federal Work-Study and scholarships/grants available. Financial award applicants required to submit CSS PROFILE or FAFSA. *Faculty research:* Classical mythology and folklore, multicultural literature, genre studies, science fiction and fantasy literature, intercultural rhetoric. *Unit head:* Dr. Lisa Hernandez, Dean, College of Arts and Sciences, 951-343-4767, E-mail: lihernandez@calbaptist.edu. *Application contact:* Dr. Laura Veltman, Director, MA in English, 951-343-4649, E-mail: lveltman@calbaptist.edu.
Website: http://www.calbaptist.edu/maenglish/

California State University, Northridge, Graduate Studies, Michael D. Eisner College of Education, Department of Secondary Education, Northridge, CA 91330. Offers educational technology (MA); English education (MA); mathematics education (MA); secondary science education (MA); teaching and learning (MA). *Accreditation:* NCATE. *Program availability:* Part-time. *Degree requirements:* For master's, thesis optional. *Entrance requirements:* For master's, GRE General Test or minimum GPA of 3.0. Additional exam requirements/recommendations for international students: Required—TOEFL.

Campbellsville University, School of Education, Campbellsville, KY 42718-2799. Offers education (MA); school counseling (MA); school improvement (MA); special education (MASE); special education-teacher leader (MA); teacher leader (MA); teaching (MAT), including middle grades biology, middle grades chemistry, middle grades English. *Accreditation:* NCATE. *Program availability:* Part-time, evening/weekend, 100% online, blended/hybrid learning. *Faculty:* 16 full-time (10 women), 13 part-time/adjunct (7 women). *Students:* 154 full-time (122 women), 44 part-time (36 women); includes 18 minority (16 Black or African American, non-Hispanic/Latino; 1 Hispanic/Latino; 1 Two or more races, non-Hispanic/Latino), 1 international. Average age 34. 280 applicants, 30% accepted, 72 enrolled. In 2018, 66 master's awarded. *Degree requirements:* For master's, comprehensive exam (for some programs), thesis, research paper. *Entrance requirements:* For master's, GRE or PRAXIS, minimum undergraduate GPA of 2.75, teaching certificate, professional growth plan, letters of recommendation, interview. Additional exam requirements/recommendations for international students: Recommended—TOEFL (minimum score 550 paper-based; 79 iBT), IELTS (minimum score 6). *Application deadline:* Applications are processed on a rolling basis. Application fee: $25. Electronic applications accepted. Application fee is waived when completed online. *Expenses:* $299/credit hour. *Financial support:* Unspecified assistantships available. Financial award applicants required to submit FAFSA. *Faculty research:* Professional development, curriculum development, school governance, assessment, special education. *Unit head:* Dr. Lisa Allen, Dean of School of Education, 270-789-5344, Fax: 270-789-5206, E-mail: lsallen@campbellsville.edu. *Application contact:* Monica Bamwine, Director of Graduate Admissions, 270-789-5221, Fax: 270-789-5071, E-mail: mkbamwine@campbellsville.edu.

Caribbean University, Graduate School, Bayamón, PR 00960-0493. Offers administration and supervision (MA Ed); criminal justice (MA); curriculum and instruction (MA Ed, PhD), including elementary education (MA Ed), English education (MA Ed), history education (MA Ed), mathematics education (MA Ed), primary education (MA Ed), science education (MA Ed), Spanish education (MA Ed); educational technology in instructional systems (MA Ed); gerontology (MSN); human resources (MBA); museology, archiving and art history (MA Ed); neonatal pediatrics (MSN); physical education (MA Ed); special education (MA Ed). *Entrance requirements:* For master's, interview, minimum GPA of 2.5.

Carthage College, Division of Teacher Education, Kenosha, WI 53140. Offers classroom guidance and counseling (M Ed); creative arts (M Ed); gifted and talented children (M Ed); language arts (M Ed); modern language (M Ed); natural sciences (M Ed); reading (M Ed, Certificate); social sciences (M Ed); teacher leadership (M Ed). *Program availability:* Part-time, evening/weekend. *Degree requirements:* For master's, thesis optional. *Entrance requirements:* For master's, MAT, minimum B average, letters of reference.

Central Connecticut State University, School of Graduate Studies, College of Liberal Arts and Social Sciences, Department of English, New Britain, CT 06050-4010. Offers English (MA); English education (MAT). *Program availability:* Part-time, evening/weekend. *Faculty:* 8 full-time (6 women). *Students:* 17 full-time (12 women), 40 part-time (33 women); includes 16 minority (3 Black or African American, non-Hispanic/Latino; 1 American Indian or Alaska Native, non-Hispanic/Latino; 3 Asian, non-Hispanic/Latino; 8 Hispanic/Latino; 1 Two or more races, non-Hispanic/Latino), 1 international. Average age 35. 25 applicants, 88% accepted, 18 enrolled. In 2018, 22 master's, 4 other

advanced degrees awarded. *Degree requirements:* For master's, comprehensive exam, thesis or alternative; for Certificate, qualifying exam. *Entrance requirements:* For master's, minimum undergraduate GPA of 3.0, writing sample, letters of recommendation, essay. Additional exam requirements/recommendations for international students: Required—TOEFL (minimum score 550 paper-based; 79 iBT); Recommended—IELTS (minimum score 6.5). *Application deadline:* For fall admission, 6/1 for domestic students, 5/1 for international students; for spring admission, 11/1 for domestic and international students. Applications are processed on a rolling basis. Application fee: $50. Electronic applications accepted. *Expenses: Tuition, area resident:* Full-time $7027; part-time $388 per credit. Tuition, state resident: full-time $9750; part-time $388 per credit. Tuition, nonresident: full-time $18,102; part-time $388 per credit. *International tuition:* $18,102 full-time. *Required fees:* $266 per semester. *Financial support:* In 2018–19, 11 students received support. Career-related internships or fieldwork, Federal Work-Study, scholarships/grants, and unspecified assistantships available. Support available to part-time students. Financial award application deadline: 3/1; financial award applicants required to submit FAFSA. *Unit head:* Dr. Stephen Cohen, Chair, 860-832-2795, E-mail: cohens@ccsu.edu. *Application contact:* Patricia Gardner, Associate Director of Graduate Studies, 860-832-2350, Fax: 860-832-2362. Website: http://www.ccsu.edu/english

Chadron State College, School of Professional and Graduate Studies, Department of Education, Chadron, NE 69337. Offers business (MA Ed); community counseling (MA Ed); educational administration (MS Ed, Sp Ed); elementary education (MS Ed); history (MA Ed); language and literature (MA Ed); secondary administration (MS Ed); secondary education (MS Ed). *Accreditation:* NCATE. *Program availability:* Part-time, evening/weekend, online learning. *Degree requirements:* For master's, thesis optional. *Entrance requirements:* For master's, GRE General Test, GRE Writing Test, minimum GPA of 2.75 or 12 graduate hours at CSC with minimum GPA of 3.25. Additional exam requirements/recommendations for international students: Required—TOEFL. Electronic applications accepted. *Faculty research:* Rural education, technology, mental health.

Chatham University, Program in Education, Pittsburgh, PA 15232-2826. Offers early childhood education (MAT); elementary education (MAT); environmental education (K-12) (MAT); secondary art (MAT); secondary biology education (MAT); secondary chemistry education (MAT); secondary English education (MAT); secondary math education (MAT); secondary physics education (MAT); secondary social studies education (MAT); special education (MAT). *Degree requirements:* For master's, thesis, teaching experience. *Entrance requirements:* For master's, minimum GPA of 3.0, sample of written work, recommendation letters. Additional exam requirements/recommendations for international students: Required—TOEFL (minimum score 600 paper-based; 100 iBT), IELTS (minimum score 7), TWE. Electronic applications accepted. Application fee is waived when completed online. *Faculty research:* Gifted education, environmental education, technology in education, writing as learning, class size and achievement.

The Citadel, The Military College of South Carolina, Citadel Graduate College, Zucker Family School of Education, Charleston, SC 29409. Offers elementary/secondary school administration and supervision (M Ed); elementary/secondary school counseling (M Ed); interdisciplinary STEM education (M Ed); literacy education (M Ed, Graduate Certificate); middle grades (MAT), including English, mathematics, science, social studies; physical education (grades K-12) (MAT); school superintendency (Ed S); secondary education (MAT), including biology, English, mathematics, social studies; student affairs (Graduate Certificate); student affairs and college counseling (M Ed). *Accreditation:* NCATE. *Program availability:* Part-time, evening/weekend, 100% online, blended/hybrid learning. *Degree requirements:* For master's, comprehensive exam (for some programs). *Entrance requirements:* For master's, GRE (minimum combined verbal and quantitative score of 290) or MAT (minimum score 396). Additional exam requirements/recommendations for international students: Required—TOEFL (minimum score 550 paper-based; 79 iBT). Electronic applications accepted. *Expenses:* Tuition, state resident: part-time $595 per credit hour. Tuition, nonresident: part-time $1020 per credit hour. *Required fees:* $90 per term.

City College of the City University of New York, Graduate School, School of Education, Department of Secondary Education, New York, NY 10031-9198. Offers adolescent mathematics education (MA, AC); English education (MA); middle school mathematics education (MS); science education (MA); social studies education (AC). *Accreditation:* NCATE. *Entrance requirements:* For master's, Liberal Arts and Sciences Test (LAST), Content Specialty Test (CST). Additional exam requirements/recommendations for international students: Required—TOEFL.

Clayton State University, School of Graduate Studies, College of Arts and Sciences, Program in Education, Morrow, GA 30260-0285. Offers biology (MAT); English (MAT); history (MAT); mathematics (MAT). *Accreditation:* NCATE. *Entrance requirements:* For master's, GRE, GACE, 2 official copies of transcripts, 3 recommendation letters, statement of purpose. Additional exam requirements/recommendations for international students: Required—TOEFL (minimum score 550 paper-based). Electronic applications accepted. *Expenses: Tuition, area resident:* Full-time $3528; part-time $2352 per year. Tuition, state resident: full-time $3528; part-time $2352 per year. Tuition, nonresident: full-time $13,176; part-time $8784 per year. *International tuition:* $13,176 full-time. *Required fees:* $1474; $1474 per unit. Tuition and fees vary according to campus/location and program.

The College at Brockport, State University of New York, School of Education, Health, and Human Services, Department of Education and Human Development, Brockport, NY 14420-2997. Offers adolescence education (MS Ed), including adolescence biology education, adolescence chemistry education, adolescence English, adolescence mathematics, adolescence physics, adolescence physics education, adolescence social studies education; bilingual education (MS Ed, AGC); childhood curriculum specialist (MS Ed); inclusive generalist education (MS Ed, AGC, Advanced Certificate), including biology (MS Ed, AGC), chemistry (MS Ed), English (MS Ed, Advanced Certificate), mathematics (MS Ed, Advanced Certificate), science (MS Ed, Advanced Certificate), social studies (MS Ed, Advanced Certificate); literacy education B-12 (MS Ed). *Accreditation:* NCATE. *Faculty:* 12 full-time (7 women), 10 part-time/adjunct (6 women). *Students:* 60 full-time (39 women), 227 part-time (157 women); includes 9 minority (1 Asian, non-Hispanic/Latino; 8 Hispanic/Latino). 135 applicants, 71% accepted, 59 enrolled. In 2018, 107 master's, 13 AGCs awarded. *Degree requirements:* For master's, thesis or alternative. *Entrance requirements:* For master's, minimum GPA of 3.0, letters of recommendation, interview (for some programs); statement of objectives, current resume. Additional exam requirements/recommendations for international students: Required—TOEFL (minimum score 550 paper-based; 79 iBT), IELTS (minimum score 6.5). *Application deadline:* For fall admission, 3/15 priority date for domestic and international students; for spring admission, 10/15 priority date for domestic and international students; for summer admission, 3/15 priority date for domestic and international students. Application fee: $80. Electronic applications accepted. *Expenses:* Tuition, state resident: part-time $471 per credit. Tuition, nonresident: part-time $963 per credit. *Financial support:* In 2018–19, 1 fellowship with full tuition reimbursement (averaging $7,500 per year), 1 teaching assistantship with full tuition reimbursement (averaging $6,000 per year) were awarded; Federal Work-Study, scholarships/grants, and unspecified assistantships also available. Support available to part-time students. Financial award application deadline: 3/15; financial award applicants required to submit FAFSA. *Faculty research:* Educational assessment, literacy education, inclusive education, teacher preparation, qualitative methodology. *Unit head:* Dr. Janka Szilagyi, Chairperson, 585-395-5945, Fax: 585-395-2172, E-mail: jszilagy@brockport.edu. *Application contact:* Buffie Edick, Graduate Program Director, 585-395-2326, Fax: 585-395-2172, E-mail: bedick@brockport.edu. Website: https://www.brockport.edu/academics/education_human_development/department.html

College of St. Joseph, Graduate Programs, Division of Education, Program in Secondary Education, Rutland, VT 05701-3899. Offers English (M Ed); social studies (M Ed). *Program availability:* Part-time, evening/weekend. *Degree requirements:* For master's, comprehensive exam. *Entrance requirements:* For master's, PRAXIS I, official college transcripts; 2 letters of reference; minimum GPA of 3.0 (initial licensure) or 2.7 (nonlicensure); interview. Additional exam requirements/recommendations for international students: Required—TOEFL (minimum score 550 paper-based). Electronic applications accepted.

College of Staten Island of the City University of New York, Graduate Programs, School of Education, Program in Adolescence Education, Staten Island, NY 10314-6600. Offers adolescence education (MS Ed), including biology, English, mathematics, social studies. *Program availability:* Part-time, evening/weekend. *Students:* 76. 34 applicants, 59% accepted, 14 enrolled. In 2018, 28 master's awarded. *Degree requirements:* For master's, thesis, educational research project supervised by faculty; Sequence 1 consists of a minimum of 33-38 graduate credits among 11 courses. Sequence 2 consists of a minimum of 46-53 graduate credits. *Entrance requirements:* For master's, The candidate must also take the General Test of the Graduate Record Examination (GRE) or an approved equivalent examination and request the submission of official scores to the College. The CSI Code is 2778. Applicants should apply directly to the Educational Testing Service (ETS) to take the examination., relevant bachelor's degree, minimum overall GPA of 3.0, two letters of recommendation, one- or two-page personal statement. Additional exam requirements/recommendations for international students: Required—TOEFL (minimum score 550 paper-based; 79 iBT), IELTS (minimum score 6.5). *Application deadline:* For fall admission, 4/25 for domestic and international students; for spring admission, 11/25 for domestic and international students. Applications are processed on a rolling basis. Application fee: $75. Electronic applications accepted. *Expenses: Tuition, area resident:* Full-time $10,770; part-time $455 per credit. Tuition, state resident: full-time $10,770; part-time $455 per credit. Tuition, nonresident: full-time $19,920; part-time $830 per credit. *International tuition:* $19,920 full-time. *Required fees:* $559.20; $181.10 per semester. Tuition and fees vary according to program. *Faculty research:* Social Studies curriculum and Pedagogy; Civics Education; Teacher effectiveness and student achievement; Teacher knowledge, Knowledge transfer from college to classroom. *Unit head:* Diane Brescia, 718-982-3877, E-mail: diane.brescia@csi.cuny.edu. *Application contact:* Sasha Spence, Associate Director for Graduate Admissions, 718-982-2019, Fax: 718-982-2500, E-mail: sasha.spence@csi.cuny.edu.
Website: https://www.csi.cuny.edu/academics-and-research/divisions-and-schools/school-education/programs-and-courses/adolescence-graduate

The Colorado College, Education Department, Program in Secondary Education, Colorado Springs, CO 80903-3294. Offers art teaching (K-12) (MAT); English teaching (MAT); foreign language teaching (MAT); mathematics teaching (MAT); music teaching (MAT); science teaching (MAT); social studies teaching (MAT). *Degree requirements:* For master's, thesis, internship. Electronic applications accepted.

Columbus State University, Graduate Studies, College of Education and Health Professions, Department of Teacher Education, Columbus, GA 31907-5645. Offers curriculum and instruction in accomplished teaching (M Ed); early childhood education (M Ed, MAT, Ed S); middle grades education (M Ed, MAT, Ed S); secondary education (M Ed, MAT, Ed S), including biology (MAT), chemistry (MAT), earth and space science (MAT), English/language arts, general science (M Ed), history (MAT), mathematics, science (Ed S), social science (M Ed, Ed S); special education (M Ed, MAT, Ed S), including general curriculum (M Ed, MAT); teacher leadership (M Ed). *Accreditation:* NCATE. *Program availability:* Part-time, evening/weekend, 100% online, blended/hybrid learning. *Faculty:* 20 full-time (12 women), 20 part-time/adjunct (15 women). *Students:* 110 full-time (84 women), 143 part-time (115 women); includes 105 minority (96 Black or African American, non-Hispanic/Latino; 4 Hispanic/Latino; 5 Two or more races, non-Hispanic/Latino). Average age 33. 147 applicants, 56% accepted, 62 enrolled. In 2018, 112 master's, 11 other advanced degrees awarded. *Degree requirements:* For Ed S, thesis or alternative. *Entrance requirements:* For master's, GRE General Test, minimum undergraduate GPA of 2.75; for Ed S, GRE General Test, minimum undergraduate GPA of 2.75, graduate 3.0. Additional exam requirements/recommendations for international students: Required—TOEFL (minimum score 550 paper-based; 79 iBT). *Application deadline:* For fall admission, 6/30 for domestic students, 5/1 for international students; for spring admission, 11/1 for domestic and international students; for summer admission, 3/1 for domestic and international students. Applications are processed on a rolling basis. Application fee: $50. Electronic applications accepted. *Expenses: Tuition, area resident:* Full-time $4924; part-time $618 per credit hour. Tuition, state resident: full-time $4924; part-time $618 per credit hour. Tuition, nonresident: full-time $19,218; part-time $2403 per credit hour. *International tuition:* $19,218 full-time. *Required fees:* $1870; $802. Tuition and fees vary according to course load, degree level and program. *Financial support:* In 2018–19, 29 students received support, including 7 research assistantships with partial tuition reimbursements available (averaging $3,000 per year); career-related internships or fieldwork, Federal Work-Study, institutionally sponsored loans, scholarships/grants, tuition waivers (partial), and unspecified assistantships also available. Support available to part-time students. Financial award application deadline: 5/1; financial award applicants required to submit FAFSA. *Unit head:* Dr. Jan Burcham, Department Chair, 706-507-8519, Fax: 706-568-3134, E-mail: burcham_jan@columbusstate.edu. *Application contact:* Catrina Smith-Edmond, Assistant Director for Graduate and Global Admission, 706-507-8824, Fax: 706-568-5091, E-mail: smithedmond_catrina@columbusstate.edu.
Website: http://te.columbusstate.edu/

Converse College, Program in Secondary Education, Spartanburg, SC 29302. Offers biology (MAT); chemistry (MAT); English (M Ed, MAT); mathematics (M Ed, MAT); natural sciences (M Ed); social sciences (M Ed, MAT). *Program availability:* Part-time. *Degree requirements:* For master's, capstone paper. *Entrance requirements:* For master's, NTE or PRAXIS II (M Ed), minimum GPA of 2.75, 2 recommendations. Electronic applications accepted.

Delta State University, Graduate Programs, College of Arts and Sciences, Division of Languages and Literature, Cleveland, MS 38733-0001. Offers secondary education (M Ed), including English. *Program availability:* Part-time. *Degree requirements:* For master's, thesis or alternative. *Expenses: Tuition, area resident:* Full-time $7076; part-time $393 per credit hour. Tuition, state resident: full-time $7076; part-time $393 per credit hour. Tuition, nonresident: full-time $7076; part-time $393 per credit hour. *International tuition:* $7076 full-time. *Required fees:* $170; $18.90 per credit hour. $9.45 per semester. Part-time tuition and fees vary according to program.

English Education

Duquesne University, School of Education, Department of Instruction and Leadership, Program in Secondary Education, Pittsburgh, PA 15282-0001. Offers biology (MS Ed); chemistry (MS Ed); English (MS Ed); K-12 education (MS Ed), including Latin; mathematics (MS Ed); physics (MS Ed); social studies (MS Ed). *Program availability:* Part-time, evening/weekend. *Faculty:* 5 full-time (4 women). *Students:* 20 full-time (12 women); includes 3 minority (1 Black or African American, non-Hispanic/Latino; 1 Hispanic/Latino; 1 Two or more races, non-Hispanic/Latino). Average age 24. 20 applicants, 85% accepted, 13 enrolled. In 2018, 14 master's awarded. *Entrance requirements:* For master's, two letters of recommendation, letter of intent, interview, bachelor's degree. Additional exam requirements/recommendations for international students: Required—TOEFL (minimum score 550 paper-based), IELTS (minimum score 7). *Application deadline:* For fall admission, 9/1 for domestic students; for spring admission, 1/2 for domestic students. Applications are processed on a rolling basis. Application fee: $0. Electronic applications accepted. *Expenses: Tuition:* Full-time $23,112; part-time $1284 per credit. Tuition and fees vary according to program. *Financial support:* In 2018–19, 1 student received support, including 1 teaching assistantship with full tuition reimbursement available; Federal Work-Study also available. Support available to part-time students. Financial award applicants required to submit FAFSA. *Faculty research:* Factors that create highly effective teachers; how to best support teachers to support students in reform-oriented environments; urban education; models of teacher leadership; improving instruction in mathematics/science/social studies/English. *Total annual research expenditures:* $120,139. *Unit head:* Dr. Melissa Boston, Associate Dean for Teacher Education/Professor, 412-396.6109, Fax: 412-396-5585, E-mail: bostonm@duq.edu. *Application contact:* Kelly McGinley, Graduate Admissions Assistant, 412-396-1559, Fax: 412-396-5585, E-mail: mcginleyk@duq.edu.
Website: http://www.duq.edu/academics/schools/education/graduate-programs-education/ms-ed-secondary-education

East Carolina University, Graduate School, Thomas Harriot College of Arts and Sciences, Department of English, Greenville, NC 27858-4353. Offers creative writing (MA); English studies (MA); linguistics (MA); literature (MA); multicultural and transnational literatures (MA, Certificate); professional communication (Certificate); rhetoric and composition (MA); rhetoric, writing, and professional communication (PhD); teaching English in the two-year college (Certificate); teaching English to speakers of other languages (MA, Certificate); technical and professional communication (MA). *Program availability:* Part-time, evening/weekend, online learning. *Application deadline:* For fall admission, 7/31 priority date for domestic students, 2/1 priority date for international students; for spring admission, 11/30 priority date for domestic students, 10/1 priority date for international students. *Expenses: Tuition, area resident:* Full-time $4749. Tuition, state resident: full-time $4749. Tuition, nonresident: full-time $17,898. *International tuition:* $17,898 full-time. *Required fees:* $2787. Part-time tuition and fees vary according to course load and program. *Financial support:* Application deadline: 3/1. *Unit head:* Dr. Marianne Montgomery, Chair, 252-328-6041, E-mail: montgomerym@ecu.edu. *Application contact:* Graduate School Admissions, 252-328-6012, Fax: 252-328-6071, E-mail: gradschool@ecu.edu.
Website: http://www.ecu.edu/cs-cas/engl/

Eastern Kentucky University, The Graduate School, College of Education, Department of Curriculum and Instruction, Program in Secondary and Higher Education, Richmond, KY 40475-3102. Offers secondary education (MA Ed), including agricultural education, art education, biological sciences education, business education, English education, geography education, history education, home economics education, industrial education, mathematical sciences education, physical education, school health education. *Accreditation:* NCATE. *Program availability:* Part-time. *Entrance requirements:* For master's, GRE General Test, minimum GPA of 2.5.

Eastern Michigan University, Graduate School, College of Arts and Sciences, Department of English Language and Literature, Program in English Studies for Teachers, Ypsilanti, MI 48197. Offers MA. *Program availability:* Part-time, evening/weekend. *Students:* 3 part-time (2 women); includes 1 minority (Black or African American, non-Hispanic/Latino). Average age 35. In 2018, 1 master's awarded. *Entrance requirements:* Additional exam requirements/recommendations for international students: Required—TOEFL. Application fee: $45. *Financial support:* Research assistantships with full tuition reimbursements, teaching assistantships with full tuition reimbursements, career-related internships or fieldwork, Federal Work-Study, institutionally sponsored loans, scholarships/grants, and unspecified assistantships available. Support available to part-time students. *Application contact:* Dr. John Staunton, Program Advisor, 734-487-0135, Fax: 734-487-9744, E-mail: jstaunto@emich.edu.

Eastern University, Graduate Education Programs, St. Davids, PA 19087-3696. Offers ESL program specialist (K-12) (Certificate); general supervisor (PreK-12) (Certificate); health and physical education (K-12) (Certificate); middle level (4-8) (Certificate); multicultural education (M Ed); music (K-12) (Certificate); Pre K-4 (Certificate); Pre K-4 with special education (Certificate); reading (M Ed); reading specialist (K-12) (Certificate); reading supervisor (K-12) (Certificate); school counseling (MA, CAGS); school principalship (preK-12) (Certificate); school psychology (MS, CAGS); secondary biology education (7-12) (Certificate); secondary chemistry education (7-12) (Certificate); secondary communication education (7-12) (Certificate); secondary English education (7-12) (Certificate); secondary math education (7-12) (Certificate); secondary social studies education (7-12) (Certificate); special education (M Ed); special education (7-12) (Certificate); special education (Pre K-8) (Certificate); special education supervisor (K-12) (Certificate); TESOL (M Ed); world language (Certificate), including Spanish. *Program availability:* Part-time, evening/weekend, online learning. *Entrance requirements:* Additional exam requirements/recommendations for international students: Required—TOEFL. Electronic applications accepted. Application fee is waived when completed online. *Expenses:* Contact institution.

Elms College, Division of Education, Chicopee, MA 01013-2839. Offers early childhood education (MAT); education (M Ed, CAGS); elementary education (MAT); English as a second language (MAT); reading (MAT); secondary education (MAT), including biology education, English education, Spanish education; special education (MAT). *Program availability:* Part-time, evening/weekend. *Faculty:* 5 full-time (all women), 6 part-time/adjunct (5 women). *Students:* 3 full-time (all women), 117 part-time (94 women); includes 12 minority (1 Black or African American, non-Hispanic/Latino; 2 Asian, non-Hispanic/Latino; 9 Hispanic/Latino). Average age 34. 27 applicants, 96% accepted, 23 enrolled. In 2018, 34 master's, 3 other advanced degrees awarded. *Degree requirements:* For master's, thesis (for some programs). *Entrance requirements:* For master's, Massachusetts Educators Certification Test, minimum GPA of 3.0; for CAGS, master's degree in education. Additional exam requirements/recommendations for international students: Required—TOEFL. *Application deadline:* For fall admission, 7/1 priority date for domestic students; for spring admission, 11/1 priority date for domestic students. Applications are processed on a rolling basis. Application fee: $30. *Expenses: Tuition:* Full-time $14,328; part-time $796 per credit. *Required fees:* $200. Tuition and fees vary according to degree level and program. *Financial support:* In 2018–19, 2 teaching assistantships with partial tuition reimbursements were awarded. Financial award applicants required to submit FAFSA. *Unit head:* Dr. Mary Janeczek, Chair, Division of Education, 413-594-2761, Fax: 413-592-4871, E-mail: janeczeke@elms.edu. *Application contact:* Nancy Davis, Director, Office of Graduate and Continuing Education Admissions, 413-265-2239, E-mail: davisn@elms.edu.

Fitchburg State University, Division of Graduate and Continuing Education, Programs in English and Teaching English (Secondary Level), Fitchburg, MA 01420-2697. Offers MA, MAT, Certificate. *Accreditation:* NCATE. *Program availability:* Part-time, evening/weekend. *Entrance requirements:* Additional exam requirements/recommendations for international students: Required—TOEFL (minimum score 550 paper-based; 79 iBT). Electronic applications accepted. *Expenses:* Contact institution.

Florida Agricultural and Mechanical University, Division of Graduate Studies, Research, and Continuing Education, College of Education, Program in Secondary Education and Foundation, Tallahassee, FL 32307-3200. Offers biology (M Ed); chemistry (MS Ed); English (MS Ed); history (MS Ed); math (MS Ed); physics (MS Ed). *Accreditation:* NCATE. *Degree requirements:* For master's, thesis (for some programs). *Entrance requirements:* For master's, GRE General Test, minimum GPA of 3.0. Additional exam requirements/recommendations for international students: Required—TOEFL.

Florida Gulf Coast University, College of Education, Program in Curriculum and Instruction, Fort Myers, FL 33965-6565. Offers elementary education (M Ed); English education (M Ed); English speakers of other languages endorsement (M Ed); gifted education (M Ed); mathematics education (M Ed); middle school education (M Ed); reading education (M Ed); science education (M Ed); social science education (M Ed); special education (M Ed). *Program availability:* Part-time, evening/weekend, online learning. *Degree requirements:* For master's, final project or portfolio. *Entrance requirements:* For master's, GRE General Test, MAT, minimum undergraduate GPA of 3.0 in last 2 years. Additional exam requirements/recommendations for international students: Required—TOEFL (minimum score 550 paper-based). Electronic applications accepted. *Faculty research:* Internet in schools, technology in pre-service and in-service teacher training.

Florida International University, College of Arts, Sciences, and Education, Department of Teaching and Learning, Miami, FL 33199. Offers art education (MA, MS); curriculum and instruction (MS, Ed D, PhD, Ed S), including curriculum development (MS), elementary education (MS), English education (MS), learning technologies (MS), mathematics education (MS), modern language education (MS), physical education (MS), science education (MS), social studies education (MS), special education (MS); early childhood education (MS); exceptional student education (Ed D); foreign language education (MS), including foreign language education, teaching English to speakers of other languages (TESOL); language, literacy and culture (PhD); mathematics, science, and learning technologies (PhD); physical education (MS), including sport and fitness; reading education (MS). *Program availability:* Part-time, evening/weekend. *Faculty:* 64 full-time (43 women), 104 part-time/adjunct (76 women). *Students:* 169 full-time (144 women), 155 part-time (130 women); includes 260 minority (53 Black or African American, non-Hispanic/Latino; 7 Asian, non-Hispanic/Latino; 193 Hispanic/Latino; 7 Two or more races, non-Hispanic/Latino), 13 international. Average age 33. 184 applicants, 62% accepted, 87 enrolled. In 2018, 153 master's, 10 doctorates awarded. *Degree requirements:* For doctorate, comprehensive exam, thesis/dissertation. *Entrance requirements:* For master's, GRE General Test, Florida General Knowledge Test or Florida College Level Academic Skills Test; for doctorate and Ed S, GRE General Test. Additional exam requirements/recommendations for international students: Required—TOEFL (minimum score 550 paper-based; 80 iBT), IELTS (minimum score 6.3). *Application deadline:* For fall admission, 6/1 priority date for domestic students, 4/1 for international students; for winter admission, 10/1 priority date for domestic students, 9/1 for international students; for spring admission, 3/1 priority date for domestic students, 2/1 for international students. Applications are processed on a rolling basis. Application fee: $30. Electronic applications accepted. *Financial support:* Research assistantships and teaching assistantships available. *Unit head:* Dr. Maria Fernandez, Chair, 305-348-0193, Fax: 305-348-2086, E-mail: Maria.Fernandez9@fiu.edu. *Application contact:* Nanett Rojas, Manager, Admissions Operations, 305-348-7464, Fax: 305-348-7441, E-mail: gradadm@fiu.edu.
Website: https://tl.fiu.edu/

Florida State University, The Graduate School, College of Education, School of Teacher Education, Tallahassee, FL 32306. Offers curriculum and instruction (MS, PhD, Ed S), including reading and language arts (Ed S); teaching English to speakers of other languages (Certificate). *Program availability:* Part-time, evening/weekend, 100% online, blended/hybrid learning, asynchronous, minimal on-campus study. *Faculty:* 30 full-time (23 women), 8 part-time/adjunct (7 women). *Students:* 90 full-time (66 women), 66 part-time (51 women); includes 56 minority (12 Black or African American, non-Hispanic/Latino; 19 Asian, non-Hispanic/Latino; 15 Hispanic/Latino; 10 Two or more races, non-Hispanic/Latino), 32 international. Average age 32. 146 applicants, 56% accepted, 52 enrolled. In 2018, 50 master's, 15 doctorates, 2 other advanced degrees awarded. Terminal master's awarded for partial completion of doctoral program. *Degree requirements:* For master's and other advanced degree, comprehensive exam, thesis optional; for doctorate, comprehensive exam, thesis/dissertation, diagnostic exam, preliminary exam, prospectus defense, dissertation defense. *Entrance requirements:* For master's, doctorate, and other advanced degree, GRE General Test, minimum upper-division GPA of 3.0. Additional exam requirements/recommendations for international students: Required—TOEFL (minimum score 550 paper-based, 80 iBT), Michigan English Language Assessment Battery (minimum score 77), IELTS (minimum score 6.5) or PTE (minimum score 55). *Application deadline:* For fall admission, 6/17 for domestic students; for spring admission, 10/18 for domestic students; for summer admission, 2/11 for domestic students. Application fee: $30. Electronic applications accepted. *Expenses: Tuition, area resident:* Part-time $479.32 per credit hour. Tuition and fees vary according to campus/location and program. *Financial support:* Fellowships, research assistantships, teaching assistantships, scholarships/grants, tuition waivers (full and partial), and unspecified assistantships available. Financial award application deadline: 1/15; financial award applicants required to submit FAFSA. *Faculty research:* Identifying effective intervention strategies to improve reading skills; improving literacy teaching and learning through technology; understanding of student sense making, problem solving, the history and structure of STEM disciplines, and teacher education to support the development of ambitious instruction that supports the STEM learning of all students; examining practices of international education; identifying ways to support the professional development of teachers. *Unit head:* Dr. Sherry Southerland, Professor/Department Chair, 850-644-6885, Fax: 850-644-2725, E-mail: ssoutherland@admin.fsu.edu. *Application contact:* Britni DeZerga, Academic Program Specialist, 850-644-2122, Fax: 850-644-7736, E-mail: bpurvis@fsu.edu.
Website: http://education.fsu.edu

Gardner-Webb University, Graduate School, Department of English, Boiling Springs, NC 28017. Offers English (MA); English education (MA). *Program availability:* Part-time, evening/weekend. *Degree requirements:* For master's, comprehensive exam. *Entrance requirements:* For master's, GRE General Test, MAT, or NTE; PRAXIS, minimum GPA of 2.5. Electronic applications accepted. *Expenses:* Contact institution.

George Mason University, College of Education and Human Development, Programs in Curriculum and Instruction, Fairfax, VA 22030. Offers assistive technology (M Ed);

designing digital learning in schools (M Ed); early childhood education (M Ed); early childhood education for diverse learners (M Ed); elementary education (M Ed); English as a second language (M Ed); gifted child education (M Ed); literacy (M Ed), including PK-12 classroom teachers, reading specialist; literacy leadership for diverse schools (M Ed), including K-12 reading; physical education (M Ed); science K-12 (M Ed); secondary education (M Ed), including biology, chemistry, earth science, English, history/social science, math, physics; special education (M Ed); teacher leadership (M Ed); transformative teaching (M Ed). *Program availability:* Part-time, evening/weekend, 100% online, blended/hybrid learning. *Faculty:* 48 full-time (40 women), 28 part-time/adjunct (20 women). *Students:* 165 full-time (147 women), 697 part-time (579 women); includes 243 minority (47 Black or African American, non-Hispanic/Latino; 3 American Indian or Alaska Native, non-Hispanic/Latino; 88 Asian, non-Hispanic/Latino; 85 Hispanic/Latino; 4 Native Hawaiian or other Pacific Islander, non-Hispanic/Latino; 16 Two or more races, non-Hispanic/Latino), 26 international. Average age 34. 450 applicants, 93% accepted, 315 enrolled. In 2018, 421 master's awarded. *Entrance requirements:* For master's, PRAXIS Core (for some programs), 2 letters of recommendation, interview, program goals statement; 9 hours of complete licensure endorsement requirements (for elementary education); minimum GPA of 3.0 in applicant's last 60 hours of undergraduate coursework (for secondary education); at least 1 year of teaching experience (for literacy). Additional exam requirements/recommendations for international students: Required—TOEFL (minimum score 575 paper-based; 88 iBT), IELTS (minimum score 6.5), PTE (minimum score 59). *Application deadline:* For fall admission, 4/2 priority date for domestic and international students; for spring admission, 11/1 for domestic and international students. Application fee: $75 ($80 for international students). Electronic applications accepted. *Financial support:* In 2018–19, 4 students received support, including 1 fellowship, 3 teaching assistantships (averaging $3,745 per year); career-related internships or fieldwork, Federal Work-Study, scholarships/grants, unspecified assistantships, and health care benefits (for full-time research or teaching assistantship recipients) also available. Support available to part-time students. Financial award application deadline: 3/1; financial award applicants required to submit FAFSA. *Faculty research:* Teacher preparation and professional development; adaptive teaching; wonder in science teacher preparation; literacy (digital, adolescent); site based course instruction. *Unit head:* Rebecca Fox, Professor and Academic Program Coordinator, 703-993-4123, E-mail: rfox@gmu.edu. *Application contact:* Rebecca Fox, Professor and Academic Program Coordinator, 703-993-4123, E-mail: rfox@gmu.edu.
Website: http://gse.gmu.edu/programs/gsemasters

George Mason University, College of Humanities and Social Sciences, Department of English, Fairfax, VA 22030. Offers college teaching (Certificate), including higher education pedagogy; creative writing (MFA), including fiction, nonfiction writing, poetry; English (MA), including cultural studies, linguistics, literature, professional writing and rhetoric, teaching of writing and literature; English pedagogy (Certificate); folklore studies (Certificate); linguistics (PhD); writing and rhetoric (PhD). *Program availability:* Part-time. *Faculty:* 86 full-time (47 women), 38 part-time/adjunct (26 women). *Students:* 116 full-time (81 women), 112 part-time (83 women); includes 37 minority (7 Black or African American, non-Hispanic/Latino; 1 American Indian or Alaska Native, non-Hispanic/Latino; 6 Asian, non-Hispanic/Latino; 12 Hispanic/Latino; 1 Native Hawaiian or other Pacific Islander, non-Hispanic/Latino; 10 Two or more races, non-Hispanic/Latino), 18 international. Average age 33. 152 applicants, 79% accepted, 57 enrolled. In 2018, 67 master's, 1 doctorate, 16 other advanced degrees awarded. *Degree requirements:* For master's, thesis (for some programs), proficiency in a foreign language by course work or translation test; for doctorate, comprehensive exam, thesis/dissertation, 2 papers. *Entrance requirements:* For master's, official transcripts; expanded goals statement; writing sample; portfolio; 2 letters of recommendation; resume; for doctorate, GRE (for linguistics), expanded goals statement; 2 letters of recommendation (writing and rhetoric); 3 letters of recommendation (linguistics); writing sample; introductory course in linguistics; official transcripts; master's degree in relevant field; for Certificate, official transcripts; expanded goals statement; 2 letters of recommendation; writing sample; resume. Additional exam requirements/recommendations for international students: Required—TOEFL (minimum score 575 paper-based; 88 iBT), IELTS (minimum score 6.5), PTE (minimum score 59). *Application deadline:* For fall admission, 3/15 for domestic and international students; for spring admission, 10/15 for domestic and international students. Application fee: $75 ($80 for international students). Electronic applications accepted. *Financial support:* In 2018–19, 81 students received support, including 8 research assistantships with tuition reimbursements available (averaging $20,666 per year), 74 teaching assistantships with tuition reimbursements available (averaging $14,714 per year); career-related internships or fieldwork, Federal Work-Study, scholarships/grants, unspecified assistantships, and health care benefits (for full-time research or teaching assistantship recipients) also available. Support available to part-time students. Financial award application deadline: 3/1; financial award applicants required to submit FAFSA. *Faculty research:* Literature, professional writing and editing, writing of fiction or poetry. *Total annual research expenditures:* $68,592. *Unit head:* Debra Lattanzi-Shutika, Chair, 703-993-1170, Fax: 703-993-1161, E-mail: dshutika@gmu.edu. *Application contact:* Alex Walsh, Graduate Admissions Coordinator, 703-993-1185, Fax: 703-993-1161, E-mail: awalsh7@gmu.edu.
Website: http://english.gmu.edu

Georgia Southwestern State University, School of Education, Americus, GA 31709-4693. Offers early childhood education (M Ed, Ed S); middle grades education (Ed S); middle grades language arts (M Ed); middle grades mathematics (M Ed); special education (M Ed). *Accreditation:* NCATE. *Degree requirements:* For master's, minimum cumulative GPA of 3.0; maximum of 6 credit hours with C grade; no courses with D grade; degree completed within 7 calendar years; for Ed S, minimum GPA of 3.25 in all courses with no grade less than a B; degree must be completed within 7 calendar years from date of initial enrollment in graduate work. *Entrance requirements:* For master's, undergraduate degree from accredited institution; professional Georgia Teaching Certificate or eligibility; minimum undergraduate GPA of 2.75 as reported on official final transcripts from all accredited institutions attended; 2 confidential Administrative Recommendation Forms; for Ed S, master's degree from accredited college or university; professional Georgia Teaching Certificate or eligibility; minimum graduate GPA of 3.0 as reported on official final graduate transcripts from all accredited institutions attended; 2 confidential Administrative Recommendation Forms. Electronic applications accepted. *Expenses:* Contact institution.

Georgia State University, College of Education and Human Development, Department of Middle and Secondary Education, Atlanta, GA 30302-3083. Offers curriculum and instruction (Ed D); English education (MAT); mathematics education (M Ed, MAT); middle level education (MAT); reading, language and literacy education (M Ed, MAT), including reading instruction (M Ed); science education (M Ed, MAT), including biology (MAT), broad field science (MAT), chemistry (MAT), earth science (MAT), physics (MAT); social studies education (M Ed, MAT), including economics (MAT), geography (MAT), history (MAT), political science (MAT); teaching and learning (PhD), including language and literacy, mathematics education, music education, science education, social studies education, teaching and teacher education. *Accreditation:* NCATE. *Program availability:* Part-time, evening/weekend, online learning. *Faculty:* 19 full-time (15 women), 9 part-time/adjunct (7 women). *Students:* 217 full-time (136 women), 203 part-time (140 women); includes 229 minority (156 Black or African American, non-Hispanic/Latino; 23 Asian, non-Hispanic/Latino; 31 Hispanic/Latino; 19 Two or more races, non-Hispanic/Latino), 3 international. Average age 34. 149 applicants, 60% accepted, 70 enrolled. In 2018, 112 master's, 23 doctorates awarded. *Entrance requirements:* For master's, GRE; GACE I (for initial teacher preparation programs), baccalaureate degree or equivalent, resume, goals statement, two letters of recommendation, minimum undergraduate GPA of 2.5; proof of initial teacher certification in the content area (for M Ed); for doctorate, GRE, resume, goals statement, writing sample, two letters of recommendation, minimum graduate GPA of 3.3, interview. *Application deadline:* For fall admission, 1/15 priority date for domestic and international students; for spring admission, 10/1 for domestic and international students. Application fee: $50. Electronic applications accepted. *Expenses: Tuition, area resident:* Full-time $9360; part-time $390 per credit hour. Tuition, state resident: full-time $9360; part-time $390 per credit hour. Tuition, nonresident: full-time $30,024; part-time $1251 per credit hour. *International tuition:* $30,024 full-time. *Required fees:* $2128. *Financial support:* In 2018–19, fellowships with full tuition reimbursements (averaging $19,667 per year), research assistantships with full tuition reimbursements (averaging $5,436 per year), teaching assistantships with full tuition reimbursements (averaging $2,779 per year) were awarded; career-related internships or fieldwork, Federal Work-Study, scholarships/grants, health care benefits, tuition waivers (full and partial), and unspecified assistantships also available. Financial award application deadline: 3/15. *Faculty research:* Teacher education in language and literacy, mathematics, science, and social studies in urban middle and secondary school settings; learning technologies in school, community, and corporate settings; multicultural education and education for social justice; urban education; international education. *Unit head:* Dr. Gertrude Marilyn Tinker Sachs, Chair, 404-413-8384, Fax: 404-413-8063, E-mail: gtinkersachs@gsu.edu. *Application contact:* Shaleen Tibbs, Administrative Specialist, 404-413-8385, Fax: 404-413-8063, E-mail: stibbs@gsu.edu.
Website: http://mse.education.gsu.edu/

Grand Valley State University, College of Education, Program in Reading and Language Arts, Allendale, MI 49401-9403. Offers M Ed. *Accreditation:* NCATE. *Program availability:* Part-time, evening/weekend. *Students:* 1 (woman) part-time. Average age 44. *Entrance requirements:* For master's, GRE General Test or minimum GPA of 3.0; last 60 credits from regionally-accredited college/university; 3 letters of recommendation. Additional exam requirements/recommendations for international students: Required—TOEFL (minimum iBT score of 80), IELTS (6.5), or Michigan English Language Assessment Battery (77). *Application deadline:* Applications are processed on a rolling basis. Application fee: $30. Electronic applications accepted. *Expenses:* $677 per credit hour, K-12 Reading and Language Arts Specialist endorsement is 36 credits, Elementary/ Secondary Reading and Language Arts endorsement is 33 credits. *Financial support:* Career-related internships or fieldwork, Federal Work-Study, scholarships/grants, and unspecified assistantships available. *Faculty research:* Culture of literacy, literacy acquisition, assessment, content area literacy, writing pedagogy. *Unit head:* Dr. Elizabeth Stolle, Graduate Program Director, 616-331-6242, Fax: 616-331-6516, E-mail: stollee@gvsu.edu. *Application contact:* Annukka Thelen, Director, Student Information and Services Center, 616-331-6205, Fax: 616-331-6217, E-mail: thelenan@gvsu.edu.

Hampton University, School of Liberal Arts and Education, Program in Teaching, Hampton, VA 23668. Offers English education 6-12 (MT); mathematics education 6-12 (MT). *Program availability:* Part-time. *Students:* 2 full-time (both women); both minorities (both Black or African American, non-Hispanic/Latino). Average age 30. 2 applicants, 50% accepted, 1 enrolled. In 2018, 1 master's awarded. *Entrance requirements:* For master's, GRE General Test. Additional exam requirements/recommendations for international students: Required—TOEFL (minimum score 525 paper-based) or IELTS (6.5). *Application deadline:* For fall admission, 6/1 priority date for domestic students, 4/1 for international students; for spring admission, 11/1 priority date for domestic students, 9/1 for international students; for summer admission, 4/1 priority date for domestic students, 2/1 priority date for international students. Applications are processed on a rolling basis. Application fee: $35. Electronic applications accepted. *Financial support:* Application deadline: 6/30; applicants required to submit FAFSA. *Unit head:* Dr. Martha Jallim-Hall, Program Coordinator, 757-727-5793. *Application contact:* Dr. Martha Jallim-Hall, Program Coordinator, 757-727-5793.

Harding University, Cannon-Clary College of Education, Searcy, AR 72149-0001. Offers advanced studies in teaching and learning (M Ed); art (MSE); behavioral science (MSE); counseling (MS, Ed S); early childhood special education (M Ed, MSE); education (MSE); educational leadership (M Ed, Ed S); elementary education (M Ed); English (MSE); French (MSE); history/social science (MSE); kinesiology (MSE); math (MSE); reading (M Ed); secondary education (M Ed); Spanish (MSE); teaching (MAT); teaching English as a second language (MSE). *Accreditation:* NCATE. *Program availability:* Part-time, evening/weekend. *Degree requirements:* For master's, comprehensive exam (for some programs), thesis optional, portfolio(s); for Ed S, comprehensive exam, portfolio, project. *Entrance requirements:* For master's, GRE, MAT, PRAXIS; for Ed S, MAT or GRE. Additional exam requirements/recommendations for international students: Required—TOEFL (minimum score 550 paper-based; 79 iBT). *Faculty research:* Reading, comprehension, school violence, educational technology, behavior, college choice, differentiated instruction, brain-based teaching.

Hofstra University, School of Education, Programs in Teacher Education, Hempstead, NY 11549. Offers bilingual education (MA); bilingual extension (Advanced Certificate); business education (MS Ed); curriculum studies (MS Ed); early childhood and childhood education (MS Ed); early childhood education (MA, MS Ed); educational technology (Advanced Certificate); elementary education (MA, MS Ed); English education (MS Ed); family and consumer science (MS Ed); fine arts and music education (Advanced Certificate); fine arts education (MS Ed); foreign language and TESOL (MS Ed); foreign language education (MA, MS Ed); languages other than English and teaching English as a second language (MA); learning and teaching (Ed D); mathematics education (MA, MS Ed); middle childhood extension (Advanced Certificate); music education (MA, MS Ed); science education (MA); secondary education (Advanced Certificate); social studies education (MA, MS Ed); teaching languages other than English and TESOL (MS Ed); technology for learning (MA); TESOL (MS Ed, Advanced Certificate); TESOL with specialization in STEM (MA); work based learning extension (Advanced Certificate). *Program availability:* Part-time, evening/weekend, blended/hybrid learning. *Students:* 138 full-time (94 women), 109 part-time (78 women); includes 66 minority (16 Black or African American, non-Hispanic/Latino; 17 Asian, non-Hispanic/Latino; 31 Hispanic/Latino; 2 Native Hawaiian or other Pacific Islander, non-Hispanic/Latino), 6 international. Average age 29. 217 applicants, 86% accepted, 113 enrolled. In 2018, 105 master's, 11 doctorates, 25 other advanced degrees awarded. *Degree requirements:* For master's, comprehensive exam, thesis (for some programs), exit project, student teaching, fieldwork, electronic portfolio, curriculum project, minimum GPA of 3.0; for doctorate, dissertation; for Advanced Certificate, 3 foreign languages, comprehensive exam (for some programs), thesis project. *Entrance requirements:* For master's, GRE, 2 letters of recommendation, portfolio, teacher certification (MA), interview, essay; for doctorate, GMAT, GRE, LSAT, or MAT; for Advanced Certificate, 2 letters of recommendation, essay, interview and/or portfolio, teaching certificate. Additional exam requirements/recommendations for international students: Required—TOEFL (minimum

score 550 paper-based; 80 iBT). *Application deadline:* Applications are processed on a rolling basis. Application fee: $75. Electronic applications accepted. *Financial support:* In 2018–19, 86 students received support, including 51 fellowships with full and partial tuition reimbursements available (averaging $5,080 per year), 2 research assistantships with full and partial tuition reimbursements available (averaging $3,470 per year); career-related internships or fieldwork, Federal Work-Study, institutionally sponsored loans, scholarships/grants, traineeships, tuition waivers (full and partial), unspecified assistantships, and scholarships and endowed scholarships also available. Support available to part-time students. Financial award applicants required to submit FAFSA. *Faculty research:* Impact of memory on learning; brain function, cognitive-development, learning, and achievement; student activism and civic education; using children's literature to promote diversity; 2nd language acquisition. *Unit head:* Dr. Alan Singer, Chairperson, 516-463-5853, Fax: 516-463-6275, E-mail: alan.j.singer@hofstra.edu. *Application contact:* Sunil Samuel, Assistant Vice President of Admissions, 516-463-4723, Fax: 516-463-4664, E-mail: graduateadmission@hofstra.edu.
Website: http://www.hofstra.edu/education/

Houston Baptist University, School of Christian Thought, Program in Divinity, Houston, TX 77074-3298. Offers Biblical languages (M Div); English languages (M Div). *Program availability:* Part-time, evening/weekend. *Entrance requirements:* For master's, bachelor's degree conferred transcript, resume, essay/personal statement. Additional exam requirements/recommendations for international students: Required—TOEFL (minimum score 80 iBT), IELTS (minimum score 6.5). Electronic applications accepted. Application fee is waived when completed online. *Expenses:* Contact institution.

Hunter College of the City University of New York, Graduate School, School of Education, Programs in Secondary Education, Concentration in English Education, New York, NY 10065-5085. Offers MA. *Accreditation:* NCATE. *Degree requirements:* For master's, thesis, professional teaching portfolio, New York State Teacher Certification Exam, research project. *Entrance requirements:* For master's, minimum GPA of 2.8, 2 letters of reference, minimum of 21 credits in English. Additional exam requirements/recommendations for international students: Required—TOEFL, TWE.

Indiana University of Pennsylvania, School of Graduate Studies and Research, College of Humanities and Social Sciences, Department of English, PhD Program in Composition and Teaching English to Speakers of Other Languages, Indiana, PA 15705. Offers PhD. *Program availability:* Part-time. *Faculty:* 22 full-time (9 women). *Students:* 15 full-time (11 women), 81 part-time (50 women); includes 10 minority (2 Black or African American, non-Hispanic/Latino; 6 Asian, non-Hispanic/Latino; 2 Hispanic/Latino), 39 international. Average age 37. 2 applicants, 100% accepted, 1 enrolled. In 2018, 17 doctorates awarded. *Degree requirements:* For doctorate, one foreign language, comprehensive exam, thesis/dissertation. *Entrance requirements:* For doctorate, 2 letters of recommendation. Additional exam requirements/recommendations for international students: Required—TOEFL (minimum score 600 paper-based). *Application deadline:* For fall admission, 2/1 priority date for domestic students; for summer admission, 11/1 priority date for domestic students. Applications are processed on a rolling basis. Application fee: $50. Electronic applications accepted. *Expenses:* Contact institution. *Financial support:* In 2018–19, 7 fellowships with full tuition reimbursements (averaging $1,093 per year), 8 research assistantships with tuition reimbursements (averaging $6,916 per year), 6 teaching assistantships with partial tuition reimbursements (averaging $22,389 per year) were awarded; career-related internships or fieldwork, Federal Work-Study, scholarships/grants, and unspecified assistantships also available. Support available to part-time students. Financial award application deadline: 4/15; financial award applicants required to submit FAFSA. *Unit head:* Dr. Gloria Park, Graduate Coordinator, 724-357-3095, E-mail: gloria.park@iup.edu. *Application contact:* Dr. Gloria Park, Graduate Coordinator, 724-357-3095, E-mail: gloria.park@iup.edu.
Website: http://www.iup.edu/english/grad/composition-tesol-phd/default.aspx

Iona College, School of Arts and Science, Department of Education, New Rochelle, NY 10801-1890. Offers adolescence education: biology (MS Ed, MST); adolescence education: English (MS Ed); adolescence education: mathematics (MST); adolescence education: social studies (MS Ed, MST); adolescence education: Spanish (MS Ed); adolescence special education 5-12 (MST); childhood and special education (MST); early childhood and childhood (MST); educational leadership (MS Ed). *Accreditation:* NCATE. *Program availability:* Part-time, evening/weekend. *Faculty:* 7 full-time (5 women), 9 part-time/adjunct (5 women). *Students:* 33 full-time (30 women), 26 part-time (20 women); includes 21 minority (6 Black or African American, non-Hispanic/Latino; 1 Asian, non-Hispanic/Latino; 13 Hispanic/Latino; 1 Two or more races, non-Hispanic/Latino). Average age 25. 39 applicants, 87% accepted, 14 enrolled. In 2018, 20 master's awarded. *Degree requirements:* For master's, thesis or alternative. *Entrance requirements:* For master's, minimum GPA of 3.0, NY State teaching certificate and bachelor's degree (for MS Ed). Additional exam requirements/recommendations for international students: Required—TOEFL (minimum score 550 paper-based; 80 iBT), IELTS (minimum score 6.5). *Application deadline:* For fall admission, 8/1 priority date for domestic students, 5/1 priority date for international students; for spring admission, 1/1 priority date for domestic students, 9/1 priority date for international students. Applications are processed on a rolling basis. Electronic applications accepted. *Expenses: Tuition:* Full-time $14,064; part-time $7032 per credit. *Required fees:* $245 per semester. One-time fee: $250. Tuition and fees vary according to program. *Financial support:* In 2018–19, 2 students received support. Unspecified assistantships available. Support available to part-time students. Financial award application deadline: 4/15; financial award applicants required to submit FAFSA. *Faculty research:* Engaging teacher educators in scientific process, cross-national comparisons of mathematics teaching, questioning strategies in the classroom, research methods, literacy development. *Unit head:* Malissa Scheuring Leipold, EdD, Chair, 914-633-2210, Fax: 914-633-2281, E-mail: mleipold@iona.edu. *Application contact:* Christopher Kash, Assistant Director of Graduate Admissions, 914-633-2403, E-mail: ckash@iona.edu.
Website: http://www.iona.edu/Academics/School-of-Arts-Science/Departments/Education/Graduate-Programs.aspx

Ithaca College, School of Humanities and Sciences, Program in Adolescence Education, Ithaca, NY 14850. Offers English (MAT). *Faculty:* 14 full-time (7 women). *Students:* 6 full-time (2 women); includes 1 minority (Hispanic/Latino). Average age 30. 12 applicants, 83% accepted, 6 enrolled. In 2018, 7 master's awarded. *Degree requirements:* For master's, one foreign language, student teaching, portfolio, teacher inquiry project. *Entrance requirements:* Additional exam requirements/recommendations for international students: Required—TOEFL (minimum score 550 paper-based; 80 iBT). *Application deadline:* For fall admission, 3/19 for domestic and international students. Applications are processed on a rolling basis. Application fee: $40. Electronic applications accepted. *Expenses:* Contact institution. *Financial support:* In 2018–19, 6 students received support, including 6 research assistantships (averaging $12,112 per year); career-related internships or fieldwork, Federal Work-Study, and scholarships/grants also available. Support available to part-time students. Financial award application deadline: 3/1; financial award applicants required to submit FAFSA. *Unit head:* Dr. Peter Martin, Chair, 607-274-1076, E-mail: pmartin@ithaca.edu. *Application contact:* Nicole Eversley Bradwell, Director, Office of Admission, 800-429-4274, Fax: 607-274-1263, E-mail: admission@ithaca.edu.
Website: http://www.ithaca.edu/gradprograms/education/programs/aded

Jackson State University, Graduate School, College of Liberal Arts, Department of English and Modern Foreign Languages, Jackson, MS 39217. Offers English (MA); teaching English (MAT). *Program availability:* Part-time, evening/weekend. *Degree requirements:* For master's, comprehensive exam, thesis or alternative. *Entrance requirements:* For master's, GRE General Test. Additional exam requirements/recommendations for international students: Required—TOEFL (minimum score 520 paper-based; 67 iBT). Electronic applications accepted. *Expenses:* Contact institution.

Kansas State University, Graduate School, College of Education, Department of Curriculum and Instruction, Manhattan, KS 66506. Offers curriculum and instruction (Ed D, PhD); digital teaching and learning (MS); educational computing, design and online learning (MS); elementary/middle level curriculum and instruction (MS); online learning (Certificate); reading specialist endorsement (MS); reading/language arts (MS); teacher leader/school improvement (MS); teaching and learning (Certificate). *Accreditation:* NCATE. *Program availability:* Part-time, online learning. *Degree requirements:* For master's, comprehensive exam, portfolio, project, report or thesis; for doctorate, comprehensive exam, thesis/dissertation, preliminary exam; for Certificate, comprehensive exam, portfolio. *Entrance requirements:* For master's, minimum GPA of 3.0, 3 letters of recommendation; for doctorate, GRE, minimum GPA of 3.0, 3 letters of recommendation, evidence of scholarly writing; for Certificate, minimum GPA of 3.0, letters of recommendation. Additional exam requirements/recommendations for international students: Required—TOEFL (minimum score 550 paper-based; 80 iBT) or IELTS. Electronic applications accepted. *Faculty research:* Literacy and technology, critical race theory and diversity, achievement gaps, school improvement, teacher education.

Kennesaw State University, Bagwell College of Education, MAT Program, Kennesaw, GA 30144. Offers art education (MAT); secondary English (MAT); secondary mathematics (MAT); secondary science (MAT); special education (MAT); teaching English to speakers of other languages (MAT). *Program availability:* Part-time, evening/weekend. *Students:* 44 full-time (36 women), 10 part-time (6 women); includes 15 minority (10 Black or African American, non-Hispanic/Latino; 4 Hispanic/Latino; 1 Two or more races, non-Hispanic/Latino). Average age 32. 3 applicants. In 2018, 32 master's awarded. *Entrance requirements:* For master's, GRE, GACE I (state certificate exam), minimum GPA of 2.75, 2 recommendations, resume. Additional exam requirements/recommendations for international students: Required—TOEFL (minimum score 550 paper-based; 80 iBT), IELTS (minimum score 6.5). *Application deadline:* For fall admission, 6/1 for domestic and international students; for spring admission, 3/1 for domestic and international students; for summer admission, 4/15 for domestic and international students. Applications are processed on a rolling basis. Application fee: $60. Electronic applications accepted. *Expenses: Tuition, area resident:* Full-time $6960; part-time $290 per credit hour. Tuition, state resident: full-time $6960; part-time $290 per credit hour. Tuition, nonresident: full-time $25,080; part-time $1045 per credit hour. *International tuition:* $25,080 full-time. *Required fees:* $2006; $1706 per semester. $853 per semester. *Financial support:* Research assistantships with tuition reimbursements and unspecified assistantships available. Financial award application deadline: 4/1; financial award applicants required to submit FAFSA. *Unit head:* Director, 470-578-3093. *Application contact:* Admissions Counselor, 470-578-4377, Fax: 470-578-9172, E-mail: ksugrad@kennesaw.edu.

Kent State University, College of Arts and Sciences, Department of English, Kent, OH 44242-0001. Offers creative writing (MFA); English (MA, PhD); English for teachers (MA); literature and writing (MA); rhetoric and composition (PhD); teaching English as a second language (MA). MFA program offered jointly with Cleveland State University, The University of Akron, and Youngstown State University as a consortium. Students must also apply through NEOMFA. *Program availability:* Part-time. *Faculty:* 21 full-time (9 women). *Students:* 98 full-time (62 women), 20 part-time (11 women); includes 9 minority (3 Black or African American, non-Hispanic/Latino; 1 Asian, non-Hispanic/Latino; 2 Hispanic/Latino; 3 Two or more races, non-Hispanic/Latino), 21 international. Average age 35. 75 applicants, 28% accepted, 21 enrolled. In 2018, 18 master's, 7 doctorates awarded. *Degree requirements:* For master's, one foreign language, thesis (for some programs), final portfolio, final exam, or thesis (for MA in teaching English as a second language); for doctorate, one foreign language, comprehensive exam, thesis/dissertation. *Entrance requirements:* For master's, GRE General Test, goal statement, 3 letters of recommendation, 8-15 page writing sample relevant to the field of study (waived for MA in English for teachers concentration), transcripts; for doctorate, GRE General Test, statement of purpose, 3 letters of recommendation, 8-15 page writing sample relevant to field of study, transcripts. Additional exam requirements/recommendations for international students: Required—TOEFL (minimum score 587 paper-based, 94 iBT), Michigan English Language Assessment Battery (minimum score 82), IELTS (minimum score 7.0) or PTE (minimum score 65). *Application deadline:* For fall admission, 1/15 for domestic and international students. Applications are processed on a rolling basis. Application fee: $45 ($70 for international students). Electronic applications accepted. *Expenses:* Tuition, state resident: full-time $11,766; part-time $536 per credit. Tuition, nonresident: full-time $21,952; part-time $999 per credit. *International tuition:* $21,952 full-time. Tuition and fees vary according to course load. *Financial support:* Fellowships with full tuition reimbursements, teaching assistantships with full tuition reimbursements, and unspecified assistantships available. Financial award application deadline: 1/15. *Unit head:* Dr. Robert Trogdon, Chair, 330-672-2676, E-mail: rtrogdon@kent.edu. *Application contact:* Wesley Raabe, Graduate Studies Coordinator, 330-672-1723, E-mail: wraabe@kent.edu.
Website: http://www.kent.edu/english/

Kutztown University of Pennsylvania, College of Education, Program in Secondary Education, Kutztown, PA 19530-0730. Offers biology (M Ed); curriculum and instruction (M Ed); English (M Ed); mathematics (M Ed); middle level (M Ed); social studies (M Ed); teaching (M Ed); transformational teaching and learning (Ed D). *Accreditation:* NCATE. *Program availability:* Part-time, evening/weekend, 100% online, blended/hybrid learning. *Faculty:* 5 full-time (3 women), 3 part-time/adjunct (0 women). *Students:* 25 full-time (16 women), 80 part-time (51 women); includes 8 minority (1 Black or African American, non-Hispanic/Latino; 5 Hispanic/Latino; 2 Two or more races, non-Hispanic/Latino), 1 international. Average age 32. 86 applicants, 93% accepted, 45 enrolled. In 2018, 3,531 master's awarded. *Degree requirements:* For master's, comprehensive exam, thesis optional; for doctorate, thesis/dissertation. *Entrance requirements:* For master's, GRE General Test, minimum undergraduate major GPA of 3.0, 3 letters of recommendation, copy of PRAXIS II or valid instructional I or II teaching certificate; for doctorate, master's or specialist degree in education or related field from regionally-accredited institution of higher learning with minimum graduate GPA of 3.25, significant educational experience, employment in an education setting (preferred). Additional exam requirements/recommendations for international students: Required—TOEFL (minimum score 550 paper-based, 79 iBT), IELTS (minimum score 6.5), or PTE (minimum score 53). *Application deadline:* For fall admission, 8/1 for domestic and international students; for spring admission, 12/1 for domestic and international students. Application fee: $35. Electronic applications accepted. *Expenses:* Tuition, state resident: part-time $516 per credit. Tuition, nonresident: part-time $774 per credit. *Required fees:* $119 per credit.

One-time fee: $50 part-time. Tuition and fees vary according to degree level. *Financial support:* Career-related internships or fieldwork, Federal Work-Study, scholarships/grants, and unspecified assistantships available. Financial award application deadline: 3/1; financial award applicants required to submit FAFSA. *Unit head:* Dr. Georgeos Sirrakos, Department Chair, 610-683-4279, Fax: 610-683-1338, E-mail: sirrakos@kutztown.edu. *Application contact:* Dr. Patricia Walsh Coates, Graduate Coordinator, 610-638-4289, Fax: 610-683-1338, E-mail: coates@kutztown.edu.
Website: https://www.kutztown.edu/academcs/graduate-programs/secondary-education.htm

Lake Forest College, Master of Arts in Teaching Program, Lake Forest, IL 60045. Offers elementary education (MAT); K-12 French (MAT); K-12 music (MAT); K-12 Spanish (MAT); K-12 visual art (MAT); secondary biology (MAT); secondary chemistry (MAT); secondary English (MAT); secondary history (MAT); secondary mathematics (MAT). *Degree requirements:* For master's, comprehensive exam, portfolio. *Entrance requirements:* For master's, GRE.

Lehman College of the City University of New York, School of Education, Department of Middle and High School Education, Program in English Education, Bronx, NY 10468-1589. Offers MS Ed. *Accreditation:* NCATE. *Entrance requirements:* For master's, minimum GPA of 3.0 in English, 2.8 overall; teaching certificate.

Le Moyne College, Department of Education, Syracuse, NY 13214. Offers adolescent education (MS Ed, MST); adolescent education/special education (MS Ed, MST); adolescent English (MST), including grades 7-12; adolescent English/special education (MST), including grades 7-12; adolescent foreign language (MST), including grades 7-12; adolescent history (MST), including grades 7-12; childhood education (MS Ed); childhood education/special education (MS Ed); elementary education (MS Ed); general education (MS Ed); inclusive childhood education (MST); literacy education (MS Ed), including birth to grade 6, grades 5-12; school building leader (MS Ed); school building leadership (CAS); school district business leader (MS Ed, CAS); school district leader (MS Ed); school district leadership (CAS); secondary education (MS Ed); special education (MS Ed); teaching English to speakers of other languages (MS Ed); urban studies (MS Ed). *Accreditation:* TEAC. *Program availability:* Part-time, evening/weekend. *Faculty:* 7 full-time (5 women), 16 part-time/adjunct (11 women). *Students:* 35 full-time (28 women), 119 part-time (84 women); includes 14 minority (5 Black or African American, non-Hispanic/Latino; 1 Asian, non-Hispanic/Latino; 7 Hispanic/Latino; 1 Two or more races, non-Hispanic/Latino), 1 international. Average age 30. 123 applicants, 89% accepted, 96 enrolled. In 2018, 66 master's, 48 CASs awarded. Terminal master's awarded for partial completion of doctoral program. *Degree requirements:* For master's, thesis. *Entrance requirements:* For master's, bachelor's degree with minimum undergraduate GPA of 3.0, 2 letters of recommendation, transcripts. Additional exam requirements/recommendations for international students: Required—TOEFL (minimum score 79 iBT); Recommended—IELTS (minimum score 6.5). *Application deadline:* For fall admission, 4/1 priority date for domestic and international students; for spring admission, 10/1 priority date for domestic and international students; for summer admission, 3/1 priority date for domestic and international students. Applications are processed on a rolling basis. Electronic applications accepted. *Expenses:* $734 per credit hour; wellness fee $70 per semester for full-time graduate students taking 9+ credit hours; technology fee $75 per semester for full-time graduate students taking 9+ credit hours, $25 per semester for part-time students; $1,470 per credit hour (for ED.D.). *Financial support:* In 2018–19, 44 students received support. Career-related internships or fieldwork, scholarships/grants, and health care benefits available. Support available to part-time students. Financial award applicants required to submit FAFSA. *Faculty research:* Minority teachers, special education, multiculturalism, literacy, technology, media literacy learning, autism, school district organization, service-learning, higher level problem solving, teacher leadership. *Unit head:* Dr. Stephen C. Fleury, Chair, Department of Education, 315-445-4376, Fax: 315-445-4744, E-mail: fleurysc@lemoyne.edu. *Application contact:* Jody F Manning, Assistant Director for Graduate Admission, 315-445-5444, Fax: 315-445-6092, E-mail: manninjf@lemoyne.edu.
Website: http://www.lemoyne.edu/education

Lewis University, College of Education, Program in Secondary Education, Romeoville, IL 60446. Offers chemistry (MA); English (MA); history (MA); physics (MA); psychology and social science (MA). *Program availability:* Part-time. *Students:* 24 full-time (9 women), 28 part-time (17 women); includes 16 minority (2 Black or African American, non-Hispanic/Latino; 2 Asian, non-Hispanic/Latino; 10 Hispanic/Latino; 2 Two or more races, non-Hispanic/Latino). Average age 27. *Degree requirements:* For master's, comprehensive exam, departmental qualifying exam. *Entrance requirements:* For master's, writing exam, Test of Academic Proficiency/Basic Skills Test/ACT/SAT, bachelor's degree, minimum GPA of 2.75, 2 letters of recommendation. Additional exam requirements/recommendations for international students: Required—TOEFL (minimum score 550 paper-based; 79 iBT), IELTS (minimum score 6). *Application deadline:* For fall admission, 5/1 priority date for international students; for spring admission, 11/15 priority date for international students. Applications are processed on a rolling basis. Application fee: $40. Electronic applications accepted. *Financial support:* Federal Work-Study, scholarships/grants, and unspecified assistantships available. Financial award application deadline: 5/1; financial award applicants required to submit FAFSA. *Unit head:* Dr. Chris Palmi, Program Director. *Application contact:* Kathy Lisak, Graduate Admission Counselor, 815-836-5610, E-mail: grad@lewisu.edu.

Lincoln Memorial University, Carter and Moyers School of Education, Harrogate, TN 37752-1901. Offers administration and supervision (M Ed, Ed S); counseling and guidance (M Ed); curriculum and instruction (M Ed, Ed D, Ed S); English (M Ed); executive leadership (Ed D); higher education administration (Ed D); human resource development (Ed D); leadership and administration (Ed D). *Program availability:* Part-time, evening/weekend, online learning. *Degree requirements:* For master's, comprehensive exam, thesis optional; for Ed S, comprehensive exam. *Entrance requirements:* For master's, PRAXIS, NTE, GRE, MAT, letters of recommendation; for Ed S, graduate transcripts. Additional exam requirements/recommendations for international students: Recommended—TOEFL. *Faculty research:* Brain compatible teaching and learning; poverty in Appalachia; leadership for change; ethics, moral responsibility and social justice; human and organizational learning.

Lipscomb University, College of Education, Nashville, TN 37204-3951. Offers applied behavior analysis (MS, Certificate); coaching for learning (M Ed, Certificate, Ed S); educational leadership (M Ed, Ed S); English language learning (M Ed, Ed S); instructional coaching (M Ed, Certificate, Ed S); instructional practice (M Ed); learning organizations and strategic change (Ed D); literacy coaching (Certificate, Ed S); reading specialty (M Ed, Ed S); school counseling (M Ed, Ed S); special education (M Ed); teaching, learning, and leading (M Ed); technology integration (M Ed, Ed S); technology integration specialist (Certificate). *Accreditation:* NCATE. *Program availability:* Part-time, evening/weekend, 100% online. *Degree requirements:* For master's, comprehensive exam, portfolio, research project and presentation; for doctorate, practical capstone project in experiential setting. *Entrance requirements:* For master's, MAT (minimum score 31) or GRE General Test (minimum score 294), 2 reference letters, goals statement, writing sample, interview; for doctorate, MAT or GRE General Test, 3 reference letters, artifact of demonstrated academic excellence, written personal statements, interview. Additional exam requirements/recommendations for international students: Required—TOEFL (minimum score 570 paper-based; 80 iBT). Electronic applications accepted. *Expenses:* Contact institution. *Faculty research:* Facilitative learning styles, leadership, student assessment, interactive multimedia inclusion, learning organizations and strategic change.

London Metropolitan University, Graduate Programs, London, United Kingdom. Offers applied psychology (M Sc); architecture (MA); biomedical science (M Sc); blood science (M Sc); cancer pharmacology (M Sc); computer networking and cyber security (M Sc); computing and information systems (M Sc); conference interpreting (MA); counter-terrorism studies (M Sc); creative, digital and professional writing (MA); crime, violence and prevention (M Sc); criminology (M Sc); curating contemporary art (MA); data analytics (M Sc); digital media (MA); early childhood studies (MA); education (MA, Ed D); financial services law, regulation and compliance (LL M); food science (M Sc); forensic psychology (M Sc); health and social care management and policy (M Sc); human nutrition (M Sc); human resource management (MA); human rights and international conflict (MA); information technology (M Sc); intelligence and security studies (M Sc); international oil, gas and energy law (LL M); international relations (MA); interpreting (MA); learning and teaching in higher education (MA); legal practice (LL M); media and entertainment law (LL M); organizational and consumer psychology (M Sc); psychological therapy (M Sc); psychology of mental health (M Sc); public health (M Sc); public policy and management (MPA); security studies (M Sc); social work (M Sc); spatial planning and urban design (MA); sports therapy (M Sc); supporting older children and young people with dyslexia (MA); teaching languages (MA), including Arabic, English; translation (MA); woman and child abuse (MA).

Manhattanville College, School of Education, Program in Middle Childhood/Adolescence Education (Grades 5-12), Purchase, NY 10577-2132. Offers biology and special education (MPS); chemistry and special education (MPS); education for sustainability (Advanced Certificate); English and special education (MPS); literacy and special education (MPS); literacy specialist (MPS); math and special education (MPS); mathematics (Advanced Certificate); middle childhood/adolescence ed science (biology or chemistry grades 5-12) or (physics grades 7-12) (MAT); middle childhood/adolescence education (grades 5-12) English (MAT, Advanced Certificate); middle childhood/adolescence education (grades 5-12) mathematics (MAT, Advanced Certificate); middle childhood/adolescence education (grades 5-12) science (biology chemistry, physics, earth science) (Advanced Certificate); middle childhood/adolescence education (grades 5-12) social studies (MAT, Advanced Certificate); physics (MAT, Advanced Certificate); social studies (MAT); social studies and special education (MPS); special education generalist (MPS). *Program availability:* Part-time, evening/weekend. *Faculty:* 3 full-time (2 women), 9 part-time/adjunct (4 women). *Students:* 11 full-time (6 women), 17 part-time (12 women); includes 3 minority (1 Black or African American, non-Hispanic/Latino; 2 Hispanic/Latino). Average age 31. 17 applicants, 71% accepted, 7 enrolled. In 2018, 8 master's, 3 other advanced degrees awarded. *Degree requirements:* For master's, comprehensive exam (for some programs), thesis (for some programs), student teaching, research seminars, portfolios, internships, writing assessment; for Advanced Certificate, comprehensive exam (for some programs). *Entrance requirements:* For master's, for programs leading to certification, candidates must submit scores from GRE or MAT(Miller Analogies Test), minimum undergraduate GPA of 3.0, all transcripts from all colleges and universities attended, 2 letters of recommendation, interview, essay (2-3 page personal statement that describes reasons for choosing education as profession and personal philosophy of education), proof of immunization (for those born after 1957). Additional exam requirements/recommendations for international students: Required—TOEFL (minimum score 600 paper-based; 110 iBT); Recommended—IELTS (minimum score 8). *Application deadline:* Applications are processed on a rolling basis. Application fee: $75. Electronic applications accepted. *Expenses:* 935 per credit. *Financial support:* Teaching assistantships, career-related internships or fieldwork, Federal Work-Study, institutionally sponsored loans, scholarships/grants, and unspecified assistantships available. Financial award application deadline: 3/15; financial award applicants required to submit FAFSA. *Faculty research:* Education for sustainability. *Unit head:* Dr. Shelley Wepner, Dean, 914-323-3153, Fax: 914-323-5493, E-mail: Shelley.Wepner@mville.edu. *Application contact:* Alissa Wilson, Director, Graduate Admissions, 914-323-3150, Fax: 914-694-1732, E-mail: edschool@mville.edu.
Website: http://www.mville.edu/programs#/search/19

Manhattanville College, School of Education, Program in Special Education, Purchase, NY 10577-2132. Offers childhood education (grades 1-6) and special education: childhood (grades 1-6) (MPS); early childhood (birth-grade 2) and special education: early childhood (birth-grade 2) (MPS); English (5-9 and 7-12); special ed generalist (7-12); se English (7-12) (MPS); literacy (birth-grade 6) and special education childhood (grades 1-6) (MPS); literacy 5-12; special education generalist 7-12; special ed specialist 7-12 (MPS); math (5-9 and 7-12); special ed generalist (7-12); se math (7-12) (MPS); science: biology or chemistry (5-9 and 7-12); special ed generalist (7-12); se science (7-12) (MPS); social studies (5-9 and 7-12); special ed generalist (7-12); se soc.st. (7-12) (MPS); special ed early childhood and childhood (birth-grade 6) (MPS); special education childhood (grades 1-6) (MPS); special education: childhood (grades 1-6) (Certificate); special education: early childhood (birth-grade 2) (MPS, Certificate); special education: early childhood (birth-grade 2) and childhood (grades 1-6) (Certificate); special education: grades 7-12 generalist (MPS, Certificate). *Program availability:* Part-time, evening/weekend. *Faculty:* 5 full-time (3 women), 35 part-time/adjunct (23 women). *Students:* 45 full-time (36 women), 179 part-time (152 women); includes 31 minority (6 Black or African American, non-Hispanic/Latino; 4 Asian, non-Hispanic/Latino; 19 Hispanic/Latino; 2 Native Hawaiian or other Pacific Islander, non-Hispanic/Latino), 1 international. Average age 28. 76 applicants, 68% accepted, 40 enrolled. In 2018, 99 master's, 2 Certificates awarded. *Degree requirements:* For master's, comprehensive exam (for some programs), thesis (for some programs), student teaching, research seminars, portfolios, internships, writing assessment; for Certificate, comprehensive exam (for some programs). *Entrance requirements:* For master's, for programs leading to certification, candidates must submit scores from GRE or MAT(Miller Analogies Test), minimum undergraduate GPA of 3.0, all transcripts from all colleges and universities attended, 2 letters of recommendation, interview, essay (2-3 page personal statement that describes reasons for choosing education as profession and personal philosophy of education), proof of immunization (for those born after 1957). Additional exam requirements/recommendations for international students: Required—TOEFL (minimum score 600 paper-based; 110 iBT); Recommended—IELTS (minimum score 8). *Application deadline:* Applications are processed on a rolling basis. Application fee: $75. Electronic applications accepted. *Expenses:* 935 per credit. *Financial support:* Teaching assistantships, career-related internships or fieldwork, Federal Work-Study, institutionally sponsored loans, scholarships/grants, and unspecified assistantships available. Financial award application deadline: 3/15; financial award applicants required to submit FAFSA. *Faculty research:* Students with emotional difficulties, literacy and adolescents, mindfulness, studying the effects of the environment on special populations, the most difficult cases, students who are presented with multiple challenges: learning, behavioral and ACE experiences who see criminal behavior as a way to cope; working on giving them the tools they need to succeed emotionally and cognitively despite the odds stacked against them. *Unit head:* Dr. Shelley Wepner, Dean, 914-323-3153, Fax: 914-323-5493, E-mail:

Shelley.Wepner@mville.edu. *Application contact:* Alissa Wilson, Director, SOE Graduate Enrollment Management, 914-323-3150, Fax: 914-694-1732, E-mail: edschool@mville.edu.
Website: http://www.mville.edu/programs/special-education

Marymount University, School of Design, Arts, and Humanities, Program in English and Humanities, Arlington, VA 22207-4299. Offers English and humanities (MA); teaching English at the community college (Certificate). *Program availability:* Part-time, evening/weekend. *Faculty:* 2 full-time (both women), 1 (woman) part-time/adjunct. *Students:* 4 full-time (2 women), 10 part-time (6 women); includes 6 minority (2 Black or African American, non-Hispanic/Latino; 1 Asian, non-Hispanic/Latino; 2 Hispanic/Latino; 1 Two or more races, non-Hispanic/Latino), 1 international. Average age 32. 9 applicants, 100% accepted, 3 enrolled. In 2018, 3 master's awarded. *Degree requirements:* For master's, thesis, capstone. *Entrance requirements:* For master's, 2 letters of recommendation, resume, bachelor's degree in English or other humanities discipline, writing sample of 8-10 pages, personal statement. Additional exam requirements/recommendations for international students: Required—TOEFL (minimum score 600 paper-based; 96 iBT), IELTS (minimum score 6.5), PTE (minimum score 58). *Application deadline:* For fall admission, 7/16 priority date for domestic and international students; for spring admission, 11/16 priority date for domestic and international students; for summer admission, 4/16 priority date for domestic and international students. Applications are processed on a rolling basis. Application fee: $40. Electronic applications accepted. *Expenses: Tuition:* Full-time $18,900; part-time $1050 per credit. *Required fees:* $396; $22 per credit hour. One-time fee: $270. Tuition and fees vary according to program. *Financial support:* In 2018–19, 2 students received support. Research assistantships, teaching assistantships, career-related internships or fieldwork, scholarships/grants, and unspecified assistantships available. Support available to part-time students. Financial award application deadline: 3/1; financial award applicants required to submit FAFSA. *Unit head:* Dr. Tonya-Marie Howe, Chair, Literature and Languages, 703-284-5762, E-mail: thowe@marymount.edu. *Application contact:* Rebecca Esposito, Senior Associate Director, Graduate Admissions, 703-284-5901, Fax: 703-527-3815, E-mail: grad.admissions@marymount.edu.
Website: https://www.marymount.edu/English-Humanities

Metropolitan State University, School of Urban Education, St. Paul, MN 55106-5000. Offers curriculum, pedagogy and schooling (MS); English as a second language (MS); secondary education (MS), including English teaching, life sciences teaching, mathematics teaching, social studies teaching; special education (MS).

Millersville University of Pennsylvania, College of Graduate Studies and Adult Learning, College of Education and Human Services, Department of Early, Middle, and Exceptional Education, Program in Language and Literacy Education, Millersville, PA 17551-0302. Offers M Ed. *Program availability:* Part-time, evening/weekend. *Faculty:* 10 full-time (6 women), 13 part-time/adjunct (9 women). *Students:* 21 part-time (all women). Average age 31. In 2018, 7 master's awarded. *Degree requirements:* For master's, clinical practicum. *Entrance requirements:* For master's, GRE or MAT if undergraduate cumulative GPA is lower than 3.0, Teaching Certificate. Additional exam requirements/recommendations for international students: Required—TOEFL, IELTS (minimum score 6), PTE (minimum score 60). *Application deadline:* Applications are processed on a rolling basis. Application fee: $40. Electronic applications accepted. *Expenses: Tuition, area resident:* Full-time $9288; part-time $516 per credit. Tuition, state resident: full-time $9288; part-time $516 per credit. Tuition, nonresident: full-time $13,932; part-time $774 per credit. *International tuition:* $13,932 full-time. *Required fees:* $2623.50; $145.75 per credit. Tuition and fees vary according to course load, degree level and program. *Financial support:* Unspecified assistantships available. Financial award application deadline: 3/15; financial award applicants required to submit FAFSA. *Faculty research:* Literacy and technology, children's literature. *Unit head:* Dr. Rich Mehrenberg, Department Chair, 717-871-7344, E-mail: richard.mehrenberg@millersville.edu. *Application contact:* Dr. James A. Delle, Acting Dean of College of Graduate Studies and Adult Learning/Associate Provost, Academic Administration, 717-871-7462, E-mail: James.Delle@millersville.edu.
Website: http://www.millersville.edu/academics/educ/eled/graduate-programs/language-and-literacy.php

Mississippi College, Graduate School, School of Education, Department of Teacher Education and Leadership, Clinton, MS 39058. Offers art (M Ed); biological science (M Ed); business education (M Ed); computer science (M Ed); dyslexia therapy (M Ed); educational leadership (M Ed, Ed D, Ed S); elementary education (M Ed, Ed S); English (M Ed); higher education administration (MS); mathematics (M Ed); secondary education (M Ed); social studies (history) (M Ed); teaching arts (M Ed). *Program availability:* Part-time, online learning. *Degree requirements:* For master's, comprehensive exam, thesis optional. *Entrance requirements:* For master's, NTE. Additional exam requirements/recommendations for international students: Recommended—TOEFL, IELTS. Electronic applications accepted.

Missouri State University, Graduate College, College of Arts and Letters, Department of English, Springfield, MO 65897. Offers applied second language acquisition (MASLA); English (MA); English education (MS Ed); teaching English to speakers of other languages (Certificate); writing (MA). MASLA offered with the Department of Modern and Classical Languages. *Program availability:* Part-time, evening/weekend. *Faculty:* 25 full-time (18 women), 5 part-time/adjunct (2 women). *Students:* 41 full-time (32 women), 73 part-time (66 women); includes 5 minority (2 Hispanic/Latino; 1 Native Hawaiian or other Pacific Islander, non-Hispanic/Latino; 2 Two or more races, non-Hispanic/Latino), 7 international. Average age 24. 97 applicants, 65% accepted, 56 enrolled. In 2018, 29 master's awarded. *Degree requirements:* For master's, one foreign language, comprehensive exam, thesis or alternative. *Entrance requirements:* For master's, GRE (for MA), 9-12 teacher certification (MS Ed); minimum GPA of 3.0 (MA); personal statement (200- to 250-word description of reasons and goals behind interest in English graduate studies); at least two letters of recommendation from individuals able to speak of the applicant's academic achievements and potential; writing sample. Additional exam requirements/recommendations for international students: Required—TOEFL (minimum score 550 paper-based; 79 iBT), IELTS (minimum score 6). *Application deadline:* For fall admission, 3/1 priority date for domestic students, 3/1 for international students; for spring admission, 10/1 priority date for domestic students, 10/1 for international students. Applications are processed on a rolling basis. Application fee: $55 ($60 for international students). Electronic applications accepted. Tuition and fees vary according to class time, course level, course load, degree level, campus/location, program and student level. *Financial support:* In 2018–19, 23 teaching assistantships with full tuition reimbursements (averaging $8,772 per year) were awarded; Federal Work-Study, institutionally sponsored loans, scholarships/grants, and unspecified assistantships also available. Financial award application deadline: 1/31; financial award applicants required to submit FAFSA. *Faculty research:* History of rhetoric, modern poetry, African-American literature, digital writing, teaching English to speakers of other languages. *Unit head:* Dr. Linda Moser, Interim Department Head, 417-836-6565, Fax: 417-836-6940, E-mail: english@missouristate.edu. *Application contact:* Lakan Drinker, Director, Graduate Enrollment Management, 417-836-5330, Fax: 417-836-6200, E-mail: lakandrinker@missouristate.edu.
Website: https://english.missouristate.edu/

Molloy College, Graduate Education Program, Rockville Centre, NY 11571-5002. Offers adolescent education in biology (MS); adolescent special education (Advanced Certificate); bilingual extension (Advanced Certificate); childhood education (MS); childhood special education (Advanced Certificate); early childhood education (MS); educational technology (MS); English (MS); mathematics (MS); social studies (MS); Spanish (MS); special education on both childhood and adolescent levels (MS); teaching English to speakers of other languages (TESOL) in grades pre-K to 12 (MS); TESOL (Advanced Certificate). *Accreditation:* NCATE. *Program availability:* Part-time, evening/weekend. *Faculty:* 24 full-time (22 women), 26 part-time/adjunct (19 women). *Students:* 106 full-time (78 women), 203 part-time (154 women); includes 65 minority (14 Black or African American, non-Hispanic/Latino; 5 Asian, non-Hispanic/Latino; 41 Hispanic/Latino; 5 Two or more races, non-Hispanic/Latino). Average age 41. 147 applicants, 63% accepted, 79 enrolled. In 2018, 120 master's, 1 other advanced degree awarded. *Entrance requirements:* Additional exam requirements/recommendations for international students: Required—TOEFL (minimum score 550 paper-based; 79 iBT). *Application deadline:* Applications are processed on a rolling basis. Application fee: $60. Electronic applications accepted. *Expenses: Tuition:* Full-time $20,790; part-time $1155 per credit. *Required fees:* $1060; $900. Tuition and fees vary according to course load and degree level. *Financial support:* Application deadline: 3/1; applicants required to submit FAFSA. *Faculty research:* English Language Learners; social emotional needs of students; gifted education; cultural diversity; collaborative teaching methods. *Unit head:* Joanne O'Brien, Dean, 516-323-3116, E-mail: jobrien@molloy.edu. *Application contact:* Faye Hood, Assistant Director for Admissions, 516-323-4009, E-mail: fhood@molloy.edu.

Montclair State University, The Graduate School, College of Education and Human Services, MAT Program in Teaching, Montclair, NJ 07043-1624. Offers art (MAT); biology (MAT); chemistry (MAT); earth science (MAT); English (MAT); French (MAT); health and physical education (MAT); health education (MAT); mathematics (MAT); music (MAT); physical education (MAT); physical science (MAT); social studies (MAT); Spanish (MAT); teacher of English as a second language (MAT). *Degree requirements:* For master's, comprehensive exam, thesis or alternative. *Entrance requirements:* For master's, interview, 2 letters of recommendation. Additional exam requirements/recommendations for international students: Required—TOEFL (minimum score 83 iBT), IELTS (minimum score 6.5). Electronic applications accepted.

Montclair State University, The Graduate School, College of Humanities and Social Sciences, Teaching Writing Certificate Program, Montclair, NJ 07043-1624. Offers Certificate. *Program availability:* Part-time, evening/weekend. *Entrance requirements:* For degree, 2 letters of recommendation, essay. Additional exam requirements/recommendations for international students: Required—TOEFL (minimum score 83 iBT), IELTS (minimum score 6.5). Electronic applications accepted. *Faculty research:* Pedagogy in writing.

Morehead State University, Graduate School, College of Education, Department of Foundational and Graduate Studies in Education, Morehead, KY 40351. Offers adult and higher education (MA, Ed S); certified professional counselor (Ed S); counseling P-12 (MA); curriculum and instruction (Ed S); educational technology (MA Ed); instructional leadership (Ed S); school administration (MA); school counseling (Ed S); teacher leader business and marketing content (MA Ed); teacher leader business and marketing technology (MA Ed); teacher leader educational technology (MA Ed); teacher leader English (MA Ed); teacher leader gifted education (MA Ed); teacher leader IECE certification (MA Ed); teacher leader interdisciplinary education P-5 (MA Ed); teacher leader middle grades (MA Ed); teacher leader non IECE certification (MA Ed); teacher leader reading/writing - non-certification (MA Ed); teacher leader reading/writing certification (MA Ed); teacher leader school communication - certification (MA Ed); teacher leader school communication - non-certification (MA Ed); teacher leader social studies (MA Ed); teacher leader special education (MA Ed). *Accreditation:* NCATE. *Program availability:* Part-time, evening/weekend. *Degree requirements:* For master's, thesis optional, oral and/or written comprehensive exams; for Ed S, thesis, oral exam. *Entrance requirements:* For master's, GRE General Test, minimum overall undergraduate GPA of 2.5; for Ed S, GRE General Test, interview, master's degree, minimum GPA of 3.5, work experience. Additional exam requirements/recommendations for international students: Required—TOEFL (minimum score 500 paper-based). Electronic applications accepted. *Faculty research:* Character education, school accountability, computer applications for school administrators.

Morehead State University, Graduate School, College of Education, Department of Middle Grades and Secondary Education, Morehead, KY 40351. Offers business and marketing education (MAT); English/language arts 5-9 (MAT); French (MAT); health P-12 (MAT); mathematics 5-9 (MAT); physical education P-12 (MAT); science 5-9 (MAT); secondary biology (MAT); secondary chemistry (MAT); secondary earth science (MAT); secondary English (MAT); secondary math (MAT); secondary physics (MAT); secondary social studies (MAT); social studies 5-9 (MAT); Spanish (MAT). *Program availability:* Part-time, evening/weekend. *Degree requirements:* For master's, portfolio. *Entrance requirements:* For master's, GRE or PRAXIS II content exam, minimum overall undergraduate GPA of 2.5. Additional exam requirements/recommendations for international students: Required—TOEFL (minimum score 500 paper-based). Electronic applications accepted.

Murray State University, College of Humanities and Fine Arts, Department of English and Philosophy, Murray, KY 42071. Offers creative writing (MFA); English (MA); English pedagogy and technology (DA); gender studies (Certificate); teaching English to speakers of other languages (TESOL) (MA). *Program availability:* Part-time, 100% online, blended/hybrid learning. *Entrance requirements:* For master's, doctorate, and Certificate, GRE or GMAT, minimum university GPA of 2.75. Additional exam requirements/recommendations for international students: Required—TOEFL (minimum score 527 paper-based; 71 iBT). Electronic applications accepted.

National Louis University, National College of Education, Chicago, IL 60603. Offers administration and supervision (M Ed, Ed D, CAS, Ed S); curriculum and instruction (M Ed, MS Ed, CAS); early childhood administration (M Ed, CAS); early childhood education (M Ed, MAT, MS Ed, CAS); education (Ed D); educational psychology/human learning and development (M Ed, MS Ed, CAS, Ed S); elementary education (MAT); interdisciplinary curriculum and instruction (M Ed); mathematics education (M Ed, MS Ed, CAS); middle grades education (MAT); reading and language (M Ed, MS Ed, CAS); school psychology (M Ed, Ed S); science education (M Ed, MS Ed, CAS); secondary education (MAT); special education (M Ed, MAT, CAS); technology in education (M Ed, CAS). *Accreditation:* NCATE. *Program availability:* Part-time, evening/weekend. *Degree requirements:* For doctorate, comprehensive exam, thesis/dissertation. *Entrance requirements:* For master's, MAT or GRE, minimum GPA of 3.0; for doctorate, GRE General Test, minimum GPA of 3.25, interview, resume, writing sample, 4 recommendations. Additional exam requirements/recommendations for international students: Required—TOEFL (minimum score 550 paper-based; 79 iBT).

New Mexico State University, College of Arts and Sciences, Department of English, Las Cruces, NM 88003-8001. Offers creative writing (MFA); English (MA), including creative writing, English studies for teachers, literature, rhetoric and professional communication; rhetoric and professional communication (PhD). *Program availability:* Part-time. *Faculty:* 18 full-time (9 women). *Students:* 49 full-time (31 women), 21 part-

time (15 women); includes 25 minority (3 Black or African American, non-Hispanic/Latino; 2 Asian, non-Hispanic/Latino; 18 Hispanic/Latino; 2 Two or more races, non-Hispanic/Latino), 8 international. Average age 35. 51 applicants, 51% accepted, 15 enrolled. In 2018, 16 master's, 4 doctorates awarded. *Degree requirements:* For master's, one foreign language, thesis (for some programs); for doctorate, comprehensive exam, thesis/dissertation, internship. *Entrance requirements:* For master's and doctorate, sample of written work. Additional exam requirements/recommendations for international students: Required—TOEFL (minimum score 550 paper-based; 79 iBT), IELTS (minimum score 6.5). *Application deadline:* For fall admission, 2/1 for domestic and international students. Application fee: $40 ($50 for international students). Electronic applications accepted. *Expenses: Tuition, area resident:* Full-time $4216.70; part-time $252.70 per credit hour. Tuition, state resident: full-time $4216.70; part-time $252.70 per credit hour. Tuition, nonresident: full-time $12,769; part-time $881.10 per credit hour. *International tuition:* $12,769.30 full-time. *Required fees:* $878.40; $48.80 per credit hour. Full-time tuition and fees vary according to course load and reciprocity agreements. *Financial support:* In 2018–19, 44 students received support, including 4 fellowships (averaging $4,548 per year), 42 teaching assistantships (averaging $17,469 per year); career-related internships or fieldwork, Federal Work-Study, scholarships/grants, traineeships, health care benefits, and unspecified assistantships also available. Support available to part-time students. Financial award application deadline: 3/1. *Faculty research:* Composition research, history and theory of rhetoric, technical/professional communication, creative writing, English and American literature. *Total annual research expenditures:* $4,162. *Unit head:* Dr. Elizabeth Schirmer, Interim Department Head, 575-646-3931, Fax: 575-646-7725, E-mail: eschirme@nmsu.edu. *Application contact:* Dr. Tracey Eileen Miller-Tomlinson, Director of Graduate Studies, 575-646-2213, Fax: 575-646-7725, E-mail: tomlin@nmsu.edu.
Website: http://english.nmsu.edu

New York Institute of Technology, School of Interdisciplinary Studies and Education, Department of Teacher Education, Old Westbury, NY 11568-8000. Offers adolescence education (MS), including math (MAT, MS), science; adolescent education (MAT), including biology, chemistry, English, math (MAT, MS), social studies; childhood education (MS); early childhood (MS). *Program availability:* Part-time, evening/weekend, 100% online, blended/hybrid learning. *Faculty:* 2 full-time (both women), 8 part-time/adjunct (5 women). *Students:* 47 full-time (45 women), 56 part-time (47 women); includes 36 minority (13 Black or African American, non-Hispanic/Latino; 1 American Indian or Alaska Native, non-Hispanic/Latino; 7 Asian, non-Hispanic/Latino; 12 Hispanic/Latino; 1 Native Hawaiian or other Pacific Islander, non-Hispanic/Latino; 2 Two or more races, non-Hispanic/Latino), 3 international. Average age 31. 81 applicants, 53% accepted, 27 enrolled. In 2018, 27 master's awarded. *Entrance requirements:* For master's, GRE or MAT, BS or equivalent; minimum cumulative undergraduate GPA of 3.0; NY state initial certification; BS with major (or minimum 30 credits in a concentration) in biology, chemistry, English, math, physics, or social studies (for MS in childhood, early childhood education, and MAT); interview; personal statement. Additional exam requirements/recommendations for international students: Required—TOEFL (minimum score 79 iBT), IELTS (minimum score 6), PTE (minimum score 53). *Application deadline:* Applications are processed on a rolling basis. Application fee: $50. Electronic applications accepted. *Expenses:* $1285 per credit plus $215 fees per year (full-time) or $175 fees per year (part-time); $1395 per 3-credit education UFT or off-site graduate course. *Financial support:* Career-related internships or fieldwork, Federal Work-Study, scholarships/grants, tuition waivers (full and partial), and unspecified assistantships available. Support available to part-time students. Financial award application deadline: 2/15; financial award applicants required to submit FAFSA. *Faculty research:* Evolving definition of new literacies and its impact on teaching and learning (twenty-first century skills), new literacies practices in teacher education, teachers' professional development, English language and literacy learning through mobile learning, teaching reading to culturally and linguistically diverse children. *Application contact:* Alice Dolitsky, Director, Graduate Admissions, 516-686-7520, Fax: 516-686-1116, E-mail: admissions@nyit.edu.
Website: http://www.nyit.edu/departments/teacher_education

New York University, Steinhardt School of Culture, Education, and Human Development, Department of Music and Performing Arts Professions, Program in Educational Theatre, New York, NY 10012. Offers educational theatre and English 7-12 (MA); educational theatre and social studies 7-12 (MA); educational theatre in colleges and communities (MA, Ed D, PhD); educational theatre, all grades (MA). *Program availability:* Part-time. *Entrance requirements:* For master's, audition; for doctorate, GRE General Test, interview. Additional exam requirements/recommendations for international students: Required—TOEFL (minimum score 100 iBT). Electronic applications accepted. *Faculty research:* Theatre for young audiences, drama in education, applied theatre, arts education assessment, reflective praxis.

New York University, Steinhardt School of Culture, Education, and Human Development, Department of Teaching and Learning, Program in English Education, New York, NY 10012-1019. Offers clinically-based English education, grades 7-12 (MA); English education (PhD, Advanced Certificate); English education, grades 7-12 (MA). *Accreditation:* TEAC. *Program availability:* Part-time. *Entrance requirements:* For doctorate, GRE General Test, interview; for Advanced Certificate, master's degree. Additional exam requirements/recommendations for international students: Required—TOEFL (minimum score 100 iBT). Electronic applications accepted. *Faculty research:* Making meaning of literature, teaching of literature, urban adolescent literacy and equity, literacy development and globalization, digital media and literacy.

North Carolina Agricultural and Technical State University, The Graduate College, College of Arts, Humanities, and Social Sciences, Department of English, Greensboro, NC 27411. Offers English and African-American literature (MA); English education (MAT). *Program availability:* Part-time, evening/weekend. *Degree requirements:* For master's, comprehensive exam, qualifying exam. *Entrance requirements:* For master's, GRE General Test, minimum GPA of 3.0.

Northeastern Illinois University, College of Graduate Studies and Research, Daniel L. Goodwin College of Education, MAT Program in Secondary Education, Chicago, IL 60625. Offers English language arts (MAT); mathematics (MAT); science (MAT); social science (MAT).

Northeastern Illinois University, College of Graduate Studies and Research, Daniel L. Goodwin College of Education, MSI Program in Language Arts - Secondary Education, Chicago, IL 60625-4699. Offers MSI.

Northwest Missouri State University, Graduate School, College of Arts and Sciences, Maryville, MO 64468-6001. Offers biology (MS); elementary mathematics specialist (MS Ed); English (MA); English education (MS Ed); English pedagogy (MA); geographic information science (MS, Certificate); history (MS Ed); mathematics (MS); mathematics education (MS Ed); teaching: science (MS Ed). *Program availability:* Part-time. *Faculty:* 20 full-time (9 women). *Students:* 15 full-time (9 women), 66 part-time (30 women); includes 6 minority (2 Black or African American, non-Hispanic/Latino; 1 American Indian or Alaska Native, non-Hispanic/Latino; 1 Hispanic/Latino; 2 Two or more races, non-Hispanic/Latino), 2 international. Average age 34. 32 applicants, 66% accepted, 19 enrolled. In 2018, 17 master's awarded. *Degree requirements:* For master's, comprehensive exam. *Entrance requirements:* For master's, GRE General Test, writing sample. Additional exam requirements/recommendations for international students: Required—TOEFL (minimum score 550 paper-based). *Application deadline:* For fall admission, 7/1 for domestic and international students; for spring admission, 11/15 for domestic and international students. Applications are processed on a rolling basis. Application fee: $0 ($75 for international students). Electronic applications accepted. *Expenses: Tuition, area resident:* Full-time $4551; part-time $252.86 per credit hour. Tuition, state resident: full-time $4551; part-time $252.86 per credit hour. Tuition, nonresident: full-time $9103; part-time $505.72 per credit hour. *International tuition:* $9103 full-time. *Required fees:* $2668; $148.20 per credit hour. Tuition and fees vary according to program. *Financial support:* Research assistantships with full tuition reimbursements, teaching assistantships with full tuition reimbursements, and administrative assistantships, tutorial assistantships available. Financial award application deadline: 4/1; financial award applicants required to submit FAFSA. *Unit head:* Dr. Michael Steiner, Dean, 660-562-1197. *Application contact:* Dr. Michael Steiner, Dean, 660-562-1197.
Website: https://www.nwmissouri.edu/academics/undergraduate/majors/liberal-arts-sciences.htm

Oregon State University, College of Education, Program in Teaching, Corvallis, OR 97331. Offers clinically based elementary education (MAT); elementary education (MAT); language arts (MAT); mathematics (MAT); music education (MAT); science (MAT); social studies (MAT). *Program availability:* Part-time, blended/hybrid learning. *Entrance requirements:* For master's, CBEST. Additional exam requirements/recommendations for international students: Required—TOEFL (minimum score 575 paper-based). *Expenses:* Contact institution.

Plymouth State University, College of Graduate Studies, Graduate Studies in Education, Program in English Education, Plymouth, NH 03264-1595. Offers M Ed. *Program availability:* Part-time, evening/weekend. *Entrance requirements:* For master's, MAT.

Purdue University, Graduate School, College of Education, Department of Curriculum and Instruction, West Lafayette, IN 47907. Offers agricultural and extension education (MS, MS Ed, PhD, Ed S); art education (PhD); career and technical education (MS Ed, PhD, Ed S); curriculum studies (MS Ed, PhD, Ed S); educational technology (MS Ed, PhD, Ed S); elementary education (MS Ed); family and consumer sciences education (MS Ed, PhD, Ed S); foreign language education (MS Ed, PhD, Ed S); industrial technology (PhD, Ed S); language arts (MS Ed, PhD, Ed S); literacy (MS Ed, PhD, Ed S); mathematics education (MS, MS Ed, PhD, Ed S); science education (MS, MS Ed, PhD, Ed S); social studies education (MS Ed, PhD, Ed S). *Accreditation:* NCATE. *Program availability:* Part-time, evening/weekend, online learning. *Faculty:* 34 full-time (24 women), 3 part-time/adjunct (1 woman). *Students:* 75 full-time (52 women), 357 part-time (271 women); includes 83 minority (29 Black or African American, non-Hispanic/Latino; 1 American Indian or Alaska Native, non-Hispanic/Latino; 14 Asian, non-Hispanic/Latino; 29 Hispanic/Latino; 1 Native Hawaiian or other Pacific Islander, non-Hispanic/Latino; 9 Two or more races, non-Hispanic/Latino), 43 international. Average age 36. 169 applicants, 83% accepted, 102 enrolled. In 2018, 141 master's, 15 doctorates awarded. *Degree requirements:* For master's, thesis optional; for doctorate, thesis/dissertation, oral and written exams; for Ed S, oral presentation, project. *Entrance requirements:* For master's, GRE General Test (if undergraduate GPA is below 3.0), minimum undergraduate GPA of 3.0 or equivalent; for doctorate, GRE General Test (minimum combined verbal and quantitative score of 1000, 300 for new scoring), minimum undergraduate GPA of 3.0 or equivalent; master's degree with minimum GPA of 3.0 or equivalent; for Ed S, GRE General Test (minimum combined verbal and quantitative score of 1000, 300 for new scoring), minimum undergraduate GPA of 3.0 or equivalent; master's degree. Additional exam requirements/recommendations for international students: Required—TOEFL (minimum score 550 paper-based; 77 iBT). *Application deadline:* For fall admission, 12/15 for domestic students, 3/1 for international students; for spring admission, 9/15 for domestic students, 8/1 for international students. Application fee: $60 ($75 for international students). Electronic applications accepted. *Financial support:* Fellowships with full tuition reimbursements, research assistantships with full tuition reimbursements, teaching assistantships with full tuition reimbursements, career-related internships or fieldwork, and tuition waivers (full) available. Support available to part-time students. Financial award application deadline: 3/1; financial award applicants required to submit FAFSA. *Faculty research:* Literacy acquisition and development, teacher beliefs and knowledge, recruitment and retention of underrepresented students, economic education, literacy discourse. *Unit head:* Janet M. Alsup, Head, 765-494-9667, E-mail: alsupj@purdue.edu. *Application contact:* Heather Brinkman, Graduate Contact, 765-494-2345, E-mail: hbrinkma@purdue.edu.
Website: http://www.edci.purdue.edu/

Purdue University Fort Wayne, College of Arts and Sciences, Department of English and Linguistics, Fort Wayne, IN 46805-1499. Offers English (MA, MAT); TENL (teaching English as a new language) (Certificate). *Program availability:* Part-time. *Degree requirements:* For master's, one foreign language, thesis (for some programs), teaching certificate (for MAT). *Entrance requirements:* For master's, GRE General Test, minimum GPA of 3.0, major or minor in English, 3 letters of recommendation; for Certificate, bachelor's degree with minimum GPA of 2.5. Additional exam requirements/recommendations for international students: Required—TOEFL (minimum score 600 paper-based; 79 iBT). *Faculty research:* Hebrew names and the vernacular Savior in Anglo-Saxon England.

Queens College of the City University of New York, Division of Education, Department of Secondary Education and Youth Services, Queens, NY 11367-1597. Offers adolescent biology (MAT); art (MS Ed); biology (MS Ed, AC); chemistry (MS Ed, AC); earth sciences (MS Ed, AC); English (MS Ed, AC); French (MS Ed); Italian (MS Ed, AC); literacy education (MS Ed); mathematics (MS Ed, AC); music (MS Ed, AC); physics (MS Ed, AC); social studies (MS Ed, AC); Spanish (MS Ed, AC). *Program availability:* Part-time, evening/weekend. *Faculty:* 22 full-time (14 women), 35 part-time/adjunct (24 women). *Students:* 33 full-time (19 women), 358 part-time (228 women); includes 182 minority (15 Black or African American, non-Hispanic/Latino; 62 Asian, non-Hispanic/Latino; 91 Hispanic/Latino; 4 Native Hawaiian or other Pacific Islander, non-Hispanic/Latino; 10 Two or more races, non-Hispanic/Latino), 13 international. Average age 29. 216 applicants, 74% accepted, 109 enrolled. In 2018, 108 master's, 35 other advanced degrees awarded. *Degree requirements:* For master's, research project. *Entrance requirements:* For master's, GRE, minimum GPA of 3.0. Additional exam requirements/recommendations for international students: Required—TOEFL, IELTS. *Application deadline:* For fall admission, 4/1 for domestic students; for spring admission, 11/1 for domestic students. Applications are processed on a rolling basis. Application fee: $125. Electronic applications accepted. *Financial support:* Career-related internships or fieldwork available. Financial award application deadline: 4/1; financial award applicants required to submit FAFSA. *Faculty research:* Self regulated learning, teacher learning, assessment and teaching, language diversity, teaching and learning history. *Unit head:* Dr. Eleanor Armour-Thomas, Chairperson, 718-997-5150, E-mail: eleanor.armour-thomas@qc.cuny.edu. *Application contact:* Elizabeth D'Amico-Ramirez, Assistant Director of Graduate Admissions, 718-997-5203, E-mail: elizabeth.damicoramirez@qc.cuny.edu.

English Education

Quinnipiac University, School of Education, Program in Secondary Education, Hamden, CT 06518-1940. Offers biology (MAT); English (MAT); history (MAT); mathematics (MAT); Spanish (MAT). *Accreditation:* NCATE. *Entrance requirements:* For master's, PRAXIS I or PRAXIS Core Academic Skills Exam, minimum GPA of 3.0, interview. Electronic applications accepted. *Faculty research:* Multicultural and urban education/leadership, challenges of teaching diverse learners, scholarship of teaching and learning, technology and teaching, humor and education.

Rhode Island College, School of Graduate Studies, Feinstein School of Education and Human Development, Department of Educational Studies, Providence, RI 02908-1991. Offers advanced studies in teaching and learning (M Ed); English (MAT); French (MAT); history (MAT); math (MAT); secondary education (MAT); Spanish (MAT); teaching English as a second language (M Ed). *Accreditation:* NCATE. *Program availability:* Part-time, evening/weekend. *Faculty:* 12 full-time (9 women), 7 part-time/adjunct (6 women). *Students:* 12 full-time (10 women), 31 part-time (28 women); includes 5 minority (1 Black or African American, non-Hispanic/Latino; 1 Asian, non-Hispanic/Latino; 3 Hispanic/Latino). Average age 33. In 2018, 24 master's awarded. *Degree requirements:* For master's, capstone or comprehensive assessment. *Entrance requirements:* For master's, GRE or MAT (for most programs), minimum undergraduate GPA of 3.0; baccalaureate degree in English, French, history, math or Spanish; 3 letters of recommendation; interview. Additional exam requirements/recommendations for international students: Required—TOEFL (minimum score 550 paper-based; 80 iBT). *Application deadline:* For fall admission, 3/1 for domestic students; for spring admission, 11/1 for domestic students. Applications are processed on a rolling basis. Application fee: $50. Electronic applications accepted. *Expenses: Tuition,* area resident: Part-time $407 per credit. Tuition, nonresident: part-time $792 per credit. *Required fees:* $29 per credit. $100 per semester. *Financial support:* Teaching assistantships, career-related internships or fieldwork, Federal Work-Study, scholarships/grants, health care benefits, and unspecified assistantships available. Support available to part-time students. Financial award application deadline: 5/15; financial award applicants required to submit FAFSA. *Unit head:* Dr. Leslie Bogad, Chair, 401-456-8170. *Application contact:* Dr. Leslie Bogad, Chair, 401-456-8170.
Website: http://www.ric.edu/educationalStudies/Pages/default.aspx

Rowan University, Graduate School, College of Communication and Creative Arts, Writing, Composition, and Rhetoric Certificate of Graduate Study Program, Glassboro, NJ 08028-1701. Offers CGS.

Rutgers University–New Brunswick, Graduate School of Education, Department of Learning and Teaching, Program in English Education, Piscataway, NJ 08854-8097. Offers Ed M. *Program availability:* Part-time. *Degree requirements:* For master's, comprehensive exam or paper. *Entrance requirements:* For master's, GRE General Test, minimum GPA of 3.0. Additional exam requirements/recommendations for international students: Required—TOEFL. Electronic applications accepted.

St. John Fisher College, Ralph C. Wilson Jr. School of Education, Program in Adolescence Education and Special Education, Rochester, NY 14618-3597. Offers adolescence education: biology with special education (MS Ed); adolescence education: chemistry with special education (MS Ed); adolescence education: English with special education (MS Ed); adolescence education: French with special education (MS Ed); adolescence education: math with special education (MS Ed); adolescence education: physics with special education (MS Ed); adolescence education: social studies with special education (MS Ed); adolescence education: Spanish with special education (MS Ed). *Program availability:* Part-time, evening/weekend. *Faculty:* 8 full-time (6 women), 2 part-time/adjunct (both women). *Students:* 13 full-time (4 women), 2 part-time (1 woman); includes 2 minority (1 Black or African American, non-Hispanic/Latino; 1 Two or more races, non-Hispanic/Latino). Average age 27. 24 applicants, 58% accepted, 4 enrolled. In 2018, 9 master's awarded. *Degree requirements:* For master's, field experiences, student teaching. *Entrance requirements:* For master's, LAST, 2 letters of recommendation, personal statement, current resume. Additional exam requirements/recommendations for international students: Required—TOEFL (minimum score 575 paper-based; 80 iBT). *Application deadline:* Applications are processed on a rolling basis. Application fee: $30. Electronic applications accepted. *Expenses:* Contact institution. *Financial support:* Scholarships/grants available. Financial award applicants required to submit FAFSA. *Faculty research:* Arts and humanities, urban schools, constructivist learning, at-risk students, mentoring. *Unit head:* Dr. Susan Hildenbrand, Program Director, 585-385-7297, E-mail: shildenbrand@sjfc.edu. *Application contact:* Michelle Gosier, Director of Transfer and Graduate Admissions, 585-385-8064, E-mail: mgosier@sjfc.edu.

San Francisco State University, Division of Graduate Studies, College of Education, Department of Elementary Education, Program in Language and Literacy Education, San Francisco, CA 94132-1722. Offers language and literacy education (MA); reading (Certificate); reading and literacy leadership (Credential).

Simon Fraser University, Office of Graduate Studies and Postdoctoral Fellows, Faculty of Arts and Social Sciences, Department of English, Burnaby, BC V5A 1S6, Canada. Offers English (MA, PhD); teachers of English (MA). *Program availability:* Part-time. *Degree requirements:* For master's, one foreign language, thesis or alternative; for doctorate, one foreign language, thesis/dissertation, field exams. *Entrance requirements:* For master's, minimum GPA of 3.0 (on scale of 4.33) or 3.33 based on last 60 credits of undergraduate courses; for doctorate, minimum GPA of 3.5 (on scale of 4.33). Additional exam requirements/recommendations for international students: Recommended—TOEFL (minimum score 580 paper-based; 93 iBT), IELTS (minimum score 7), TWE (minimum score 5). Electronic applications accepted. *Faculty research:* Literary criticism, literature and psychoanalysis, Renaissance drama and poetry, Shakespeare, Canadian and American literature.

Slippery Rock University of Pennsylvania, Graduate Studies (Recruitment), College of Education, Department of Secondary Education/Foundations of Education, Slippery Rock, PA 16057-1383. Offers secondary education (M Ed), including English, math/science, social studies. *Accreditation:* NCATE. *Program availability:* Part-time, evening/weekend, 100% online. *Faculty:* 9 full-time (4 women), 1 part-time/adjunct (0 women). *Students:* 45 full-time (36 women), 232 part-time (191 women); includes 2 minority (both Black or African American, non-Hispanic/Latino). Average age 28. 58 applicants, 76% accepted, 28 enrolled. In 2018, 34 master's awarded. *Degree requirements:* For master's, comprehensive exam, thesis (for some programs). *Entrance requirements:* For master's, copy of teaching certification and two letters of recommendation (for some programs). Additional exam requirements/recommendations for international students: Required—TOEFL (minimum score 550 paper-based; 80 iBT). *Application deadline:* For fall admission, 3/1 priority date for domestic students, 5/1 priority date for international students; for spring admission, 10/1 priority date for domestic students, 9/1 priority date for international students. Applications are processed on a rolling basis. Application fee: $25 ($30 for international students). Electronic applications accepted. *Expenses:* Contact institution. *Financial support:* In 2018–19, 9 students received support. Career-related internships or fieldwork, Federal Work-Study, institutionally sponsored loans, scholarships/grants, tuition waivers (partial), and unspecified assistantships available. Support available to part-time students. Financial award application deadline: 5/1; financial award applicants required to submit FAFSA. *Unit head:* Dr. Jeffrey Lehman, Graduate Coordinator, 724-738-2311, Fax: 724-738-4987, E-mail: jeffrey.lehman@

sru.edu. *Application contact:* Brandi Weber-Mortimer, Director of Graduate Studies, 724-738-2051, Fax: 724-738-2146, E-mail: graduate.admissions@sru.edu.
Website: http://www.sru.edu/academics/colleges-and-departments/coe/departments/secondary-education-/-foundations-of-education

Smith College, Graduate and Special Programs, Department of Education and Child Study, Program in Secondary Education, Northampton, MA 01063. Offers secondary education (MAT), including biological sciences education, chemistry education, English education, geology education, government education, history education, mathematics education, physics education. *Program availability:* Part-time. *Students:* 8 full-time (all women), 2 part-time (0 women); includes 2 minority (1 Black or African American, non-Hispanic/Latino; 1 Asian, non-Hispanic/Latino), 2 international. Average age 27. 25 applicants, 84% accepted, 10 enrolled. In 2018, 8 master's awarded. *Entrance requirements:* Additional exam requirements/recommendations for international students: Required—TOEFL (minimum score 595 paper-based; 97 iBT), IELTS (minimum score 7.5). *Application deadline:* For fall admission, 4/15 for domestic students, 1/15 priority date for international students; for spring admission, 12/1 for domestic students. Applications are processed on a rolling basis. Application fee: $60. *Expenses:* The total tuition cost to each M.A.T. student (the full program fee, after 'built-in' scholarship award) is $18,500. *Financial support:* In 2018–19, 9 students received support, including 2 fellowships with full tuition reimbursements available; scholarships/grants and human resources employee benefit also available. Support available to part-time students. Financial award application deadline: 4/15; financial award applicants required to submit CSS PROFILE or FAFSA. *Unit head:* Rosetta Cohen, Graduate Student Advisor, 413-585-3266, E-mail: rcohen@smith.edu. *Application contact:* Ruth Morgan, Program Coordinator, 413-585-3050, Fax: 413-585-3054, E-mail: gradstdy@smith.edu.
Website: http://www.smith.edu/educ/

Smith College, Graduate and Special Programs, Department of English Language and Literature, Northampton, MA 01063. Offers secondary education (MAT), including English education. *Program availability:* Part-time. *Students:* 3 full-time (all women). Average age 29. 11 applicants, 82% accepted, 3 enrolled. In 2018, 3 master's awarded. *Entrance requirements:* Additional exam requirements/recommendations for international students: Required—TOEFL (minimum score 595 paper-based; 97 iBT), IELTS (minimum score 7.5). *Application deadline:* For fall admission, 4/15 for domestic students, 1/15 for international students; for spring admission, 12/1 for domestic students. Applications are processed on a rolling basis. Application fee: $60. *Expenses:* The total tuition cost to each M.A.T. student (the full program fee, after 'built-in' scholarship award) is $18,500. *Financial support:* In 2018–19, 3 students received support. Fellowships and scholarships/grants available. Support available to part-time students. Financial award application deadline: 4/15; financial award applicants required to submit CSS PROFILE or FAFSA. *Unit head:* Craig Davis, Graduate Adviser, 413-585-3327, E-mail: crdavis@smith.edu. *Application contact:* Ruth Morgan, Program Coordinator, 413-585-3050, Fax: 413-585-3054, E-mail: gradstdy@smith.edu.
Website: http://www.smith.edu/english/

South Carolina State University, College of Graduate and Professional Studies, Department of Education, Orangeburg, SC 29117-0001. Offers early childhood education (MAT); education (M Ed); elementary education (M Ed, MAT); English (MAT); general science/biology (MAT); mathematics (MAT); secondary education (M Ed), including biology education, business education, counselor education, English education, home economics education, industrial education, mathematics education, science education, social studies education; special education (M Ed), including emotionally handicapped, learning disabilities, mentally handicapped. *Accreditation:* NCATE. *Program availability:* Part-time, evening/weekend. *Faculty:* 17 full-time (6 women), 12 part-time/adjunct (5 women). *Students:* 42 full-time (32 women), 93 part-time (64 women); includes 121 minority (119 Black or African American, non-Hispanic/Latino; 2 Asian, non-Hispanic/Latino), 2 international. Average age 40. 50 applicants, 98% accepted, 39 enrolled. In 2018, 9 master's awarded. *Degree requirements:* For master's, thesis optional, departmental qualifying exam. *Entrance requirements:* For master's, GRE General Test, NTE, interview, teaching certificate. *Application deadline:* For fall admission, 6/15 priority date for domestic students, 6/15 for international students; for spring admission, 11/1 for domestic and international students. Application fee: $25. Electronic applications accepted. *Expenses: Tuition,* area resident: Full-time $9928; part-time $552 per credit hour. Tuition, state resident: full-time $9928. Tuition, nonresident: full-time $21,038; part-time $1169 per credit hour. *Required fees:* $1532; $85 per credit hour. *Financial support:* Fellowships, career-related internships or fieldwork, Federal Work-Study, and scholarships/grants available. Financial award application deadline: 6/1. *Unit head:* Dr. Charlie Spell, Chair, Department of Education, 803-536-8963, Fax: 803-516-4568, E-mail: cspell@scsu.edu. *Application contact:* Curtis Foskey, Coordinator of Graduate Studies, 803-536-8419, Fax: 803-536-8812, E-mail: cfoskey@scsu.edu.

Southeastern Louisiana University, College of Arts, Humanities and Social Sciences, Department of English, Hammond, LA 70402. Offers creative writing (MA); language and literacy (MA); professional writing (MA); publishing studies (MA). *Program availability:* Part-time. *Faculty:* 18 full-time (8 women). *Students:* 8 full-time (6 women), 16 part-time (14 women); includes 7 minority (2 Black or African American, non-Hispanic/Latino; 1 Hispanic/Latino; 4 Two or more races, non-Hispanic/Latino). Average age 26. 10 applicants, 80% accepted, 6 enrolled. In 2018, 11 master's awarded. *Degree requirements:* For master's, comprehensive exam, thesis optional. *Entrance requirements:* For master's, GRE verbal score of 150 or greater required. Additional exam requirements/recommendations for international students: Required—TOEFL (minimum score 500 paper-based; 61 iBT). *Application deadline:* For fall admission, 7/15 priority date for domestic students, 6/1 priority date for international students; for spring admission, 12/1 priority date for domestic students, 10/1 priority date for international students. Applications are processed on a rolling basis. Application fee: $20 ($30 for international students). Electronic applications accepted. *Expenses: Tuition,* area resident: Full-time $6684. Tuition, state resident: full-time $6684. Tuition, nonresident: full-time $19,162. *Required fees:* $2097. *Financial support:* In 2018–19, 19 students received support, including 8 research assistantships with tuition reimbursements available (averaging $8,494 per year); institutionally sponsored loans, scholarships/grants, and unspecified assistantships also available. Support available to part-time students. Financial award application deadline: 5/1; financial award applicants required to submit FAFSA. *Faculty research:* Digital Humanities, John Donne and Liminality, Film: From Analog to Digital, Animal Studies and Literature, John Ruskin's Juvenalia/Digital Humanities Project. *Total annual research expenditures:* $64,854. *Unit head:* Dr. David Hanson, Department Head, 985-549-2100, Fax: 985-549-5021, E-mail: dhanson@southeastern.edu. *Application contact:* Office of Admissions, 985-549-5637, Fax: 985-549-5632, E-mail: admissions@southeastern.edu.
Website: http://www.southeastern.edu/acad_research/depts/engl

Southern Illinois University Edwardsville, Graduate School, College of Arts and Sciences, Department of English Language and Literature, Program in Teaching of Writing, Edwardsville, IL 62026. Offers MA, Postbaccalaureate Certificate. *Program availability:* Part-time, evening/weekend. *Degree requirements:* For master's, thesis or alternative, final exam. *Entrance requirements:* Additional exam requirements/

recommendations for international students: Required—TOEFL (minimum score 550 paper-based, 79 iBT), IELTS (minimum score 6.5), Michigan Test of English Language Proficiency or PTE. Electronic applications accepted.

State University of New York at Fredonia, College of Liberal Arts and Sciences, Fredonia, NY 14063-1136. Offers biology (MS); English (MA); English education 7-12 (MA); interdisciplinary studies (MA, MS); math education (MS Ed); professional writing (CAS); speech pathology (MS); MA/MS. *Program availability:* Part-time, evening/weekend. *Faculty:* 23 full-time (12 women), 3 part-time/adjunct (1 woman). *Students:* 67 full-time (60 women), 6 part-time (5 women); includes 9 minority (2 Black or African American, non-Hispanic/Latino; 5 Asian, non-Hispanic/Latino; 1 Hispanic/Latino; 1 Two or more races, non-Hispanic/Latino), 9 international. Average age 23. 131 applicants, 77% accepted, 36 enrolled. In 2018, 37 master's, 1 other advanced degree awarded. *Degree requirements:* For master's, comprehensive exam (for some programs), thesis (for some programs). *Entrance requirements:* For master's, GRE. Additional exam requirements/recommendations for international students: Required—TOEFL (minimum score 79 iBT), IELTS (minimum score 6.5). *Application deadline:* For fall admission, 4/1 for domestic and international students; for spring admission, 11/1 for domestic and international students. Applications are processed on a rolling basis. Application fee: $75. Electronic applications accepted. *Expenses:* Tuition, state resident: full-time $6870; part-time $462 per credit hour. Tuition, nonresident: full-time $16,650; part-time $944 per credit hour. *International tuition:* $16,650 full-time. *Required fees:* $25; $2 per credit hour. $1 per semester. *Financial support:* In 2018–19, 17 students received support, including 14 teaching assistantships with full and partial tuition reimbursements available (averaging $5,957 per year); tuition waivers (full and partial) and unspecified assistantships also available. *Faculty research:* Immunology/microbiology, applied human physiology, ecology and evolution, invertebrate biology, molecular biology, biochemistry, physiology, animal behavior, science education, vertebrate physiology, cell biology, plant biology, developmental biology, aquatic ecology, bilingual language acquisition, bilingual language acquisition and disorders, augmentative and alternate communication with ALS, World War I, Zweig, environmental literature, editing, adolescent literature, pedagogy. *Unit head:* Dr. Andy Karafa, Dean, 716-673-3173, Fax: 716-673-3338, E-mail: andy.karafa@gmail.com. *Application contact:* Wendy S. Dunst, Interim Graduate Recruitment and Admissions Associate, 716-673-3808, Fax: 716-673-3712, E-mail: wendy.dunst@fredonia.edu.
Website: http://www.fredonia.edu/clas/

State University of New York at New Paltz, Graduate and Extended Learning School, School of Education, Department of Teaching and Learning, New Paltz, NY 12561. Offers adolescence education: biology (MAT, MS Ed); adolescence education: chemistry (MAT, MS Ed); adolescence education: earth science (MAT, MS Ed); adolescence education: English (MAT, MS Ed); adolescence education: French (MAT, MS Ed); adolescence education: social studies (MAT, MS Ed); adolescence education: Spanish (MAT, MS Ed); second language education (MS Ed, AC), including second language education (MS Ed), teaching English language learners (AC). *Accreditation:* NCATE. *Program availability:* Part-time, evening/weekend. *Faculty:* 21 full-time (16 women), 15 part-time/adjunct (12 women). *Students:* 127 full-time (91 women), 171 part-time (149 women); includes 48 minority (5 Black or African American, non-Hispanic/Latino; 2 Asian, non-Hispanic/Latino; 37 Hispanic/Latino; 4 Two or more races, non-Hispanic/Latino). 152 applicants, 84% accepted, 104 enrolled. In 2018, 135 master's, 19 other advanced degrees awarded. *Degree requirements:* For master's, comprehensive exam (for some programs), portfolio. *Entrance requirements:* For master's, minimum GPA of 3.0, New York state teaching certificate (MS Ed). Additional exam requirements/recommendations for international students: Required—TOEFL (minimum score 550 paper-based; 80 iBT), IELTS (minimum score 6.5). *Application deadline:* For fall admission, 3/1 priority date for domestic students, 3/1 for international students; for spring admission, 10/1 priority date for domestic students, 10/1 for international students. Application fee: $50. Electronic applications accepted. *Financial support:* Application deadline: 8/1. *Unit head:* Dr. Aaron Isabelle, Associate Dean, 845-257-2837, E-mail: isabella@newpaltz.edu. *Application contact:* Vika Shock, Director of Graduate Admissions, 845-257-3285, Fax: 845-257-3284, E-mail: gradstudies@newpaltz.edu.
Website: http://www.newpaltz.edu/secondaryed/

State University of New York at Plattsburgh, School of Education, Health, and Human Services, Program in Teacher Education: Adolescence Education, Plattsburgh, NY 12901-2681. Offers adolescence education (MST); biology 7-12 (MST); chemistry 7-12 (MST); earth science 7-12 (MST); English 7-12 (MST); French 7-12 (MST); mathematics 7-12 (MST); physics 7-12 (MST); social studies 7-12 (MST); Spanish 7-12 (MST). *Accreditation:* TEAC. *Program availability:* Part-time, evening/weekend. *Entrance requirements:* For master's, minimum GPA of 2.75. Additional exam requirements/recommendations for international students: Required—TOEFL.

State University of New York College at Cortland, Graduate Studies, School of Arts and Sciences, Programs in Adolescence Education, Cortland, NY 13045. Offers biology (MAT); chemistry (MAT); English (MAT, MS Ed); mathematics (MAT); mathematics and physics (MS Ed); physics (MAT, MS Ed). *Accreditation:* NCATE. *Program availability:* Part-time, evening/weekend. *Degree requirements:* For master's, one foreign language, comprehensive exam (for some programs), thesis (for some programs). *Entrance requirements:* For master's, GRE General Test.

State University of New York College at Geneseo, Graduate Studies, School of Education, Program in Adolescence Education, Geneseo, NY 14454-1401. Offers English 7-12 (MS Ed); French 7-12 (MS Ed); social studies 7-12 (MS Ed); Spanish 7-12 (MS Ed). *Program availability:* Part-time, evening/weekend. *Degree requirements:* For master's, 2 foreign languages, comprehensive examination, thesis or research project. *Entrance requirements:* For master's, GRE, MAT, EAS, edTPA, PRAXIS, or another substantially equivalent test, proof of New York State initial certification or equivalent certification from another state. Additional exam requirements/recommendations for international students: Required—TOEFL (minimum score 525 paper-based; 71 iBT), IELTS (minimum score 6.5), PTE, iTEP. Electronic applications accepted. *Expenses:* Contact institution.

State University of New York College at Old Westbury, School of Education, Old Westbury, NY 11568-0210. Offers biology (MAT, MS); chemistry (MAT, MS); English language arts (MAT, MS); math (MAT, MS); social studies (MAT, MS); Spanish (MAT, MS). *Program availability:* Part-time, evening/weekend. *Entrance requirements:* For master's, Liberal Arts and Sciences Test, undergraduate degree with at least 30 semester hours of appropriate coursework as defined by the respective discipline; minimum cumulative undergraduate GPA of 3.0; two letters of recommendation (one from an academic source); essay. Additional exam requirements/recommendations for international students: Required—TOEFL (minimum score 550 paper-based); Recommended—IELTS.

State University of New York College at Potsdam, School of Education and Professional Studies, Program in Secondary Education, Potsdam, NY 13676. Offers English education (MST); mathematics education (MST); science education (MST), including biology, chemistry, earth science, physics; social studies education (MST). *Accreditation:* NCATE. *Degree requirements:* For master's, culminating experience. *Entrance requirements:* For master's, minimum GPA of 2.75 in last 60 hours of course work (3.0 for English program). Additional exam requirements/recommendations for international students: Required—TOEFL (minimum score 550 paper-based; 80 iBT), IELTS (minimum score 6). Electronic applications accepted.

Syracuse University, School of Education, MS Program in English Education Preparation (Grades 7-12), Syracuse, NY 13244. Offers MS. *Program availability:* Part-time. *Entrance requirements:* For master's, GRE, baccalaureate degree from regionally-accredited college/university with an English major or a 30-credit major equivalent determined via transcript review, at least nine credits of writing-intensive coursework, strong teacher and/or employer recommendations, personal statement. Additional exam requirements/recommendations for international students: Required—TOEFL (minimum score 100 iBT). *Application deadline:* For fall admission, 1/15 for domestic and international students. Applications are processed on a rolling basis. Application fee: $75. Electronic applications accepted. *Financial support:* Fellowships with full tuition reimbursements, research assistantships, teaching assistantships, career-related internships or fieldwork, and scholarships/grants available. Financial award application deadline: 1/15. *Faculty research:* Educational theory, research in the field of English education, English and textual studies, composition and cultural rhetoric, teaching youth from diverse backgrounds. *Unit head:* Dr. Kelly Chandler-Olcott, Program Coordinator, 315-443-4755, E-mail: kpchandl@syr.edu. *Application contact:* Speranza Migliore, Graduate Admissions Recruiter, 315-443-2505, E-mail: gradrcrt@syr.edu.
Website: http://soe.syr.edu/academic/reading_language_arts/graduate/masters/english_ed_prep_7_12/default.aspx

Teachers College, Columbia University, Department of Arts and Humanities, New York, NY 10027. Offers applied linguistics (MA, Ed D); art and art education (Ed M, MA, Ed D, Ed DCT); arts administration (MA); bilingual and bicultural education (MA); global competence (Certificate); history and education (Ed D, PhD); music and music education (Ed DCT); philosophy and education (MA, Ed D, PhD); social studies education (Ed M, PhD); teaching English to speakers of other languages (Ed M); teaching of English and English education (Ed M, MA, Ed D, PhD), including English education (Ed M, Ed D, PhD), teaching of English (MA); teaching of social studies (MA); TESOL (MA, Ed D). *Program availability:* Part-time, evening/weekend. *Students:* 267 full-time (216 women), 569 part-time (400 women); includes 235 minority (62 Black or African American, non-Hispanic/Latino; 2 American Indian or Alaska Native, non-Hispanic/Latino; 88 Asian, non-Hispanic/Latino; 69 Hispanic/Latino; 14 Two or more races, non-Hispanic/Latino), 229 international. Average age 31. 1,075 applicants, 56% accepted, 342 enrolled. Terminal master's awarded for partial completion of doctoral program. *Financial support:* Fellowships, research assistantships, teaching assistantships, career-related internships or fieldwork, Federal Work-Study, institutionally sponsored loans, tuition waivers (full and partial), and unspecified assistantships available. Support available to part-time students. *Unit head:* Prof. ZhaoHong Han, Department Chair, E-mail: zhh2@tc.columbia.edu. *Application contact:* Kelly Sutton-Skinner, Director of Admissions & New Student Enrollment, E-mail: kms2237@tc.columbia.edu.

Temple University, College of Education, Department of Teaching and Learning, Philadelphia, PA 19122-6096. Offers career and technical education (Ed M), including business, computing, and information technology, industrial education, marketing education; middle grades education (Ed M), including math and language arts, math and science, science and language arts; secondary education (Ed M), including English, math, social studies; teaching English to speakers of other languages (MS Ed); urban education (Ed M). *Program availability:* Part-time, evening/weekend. *Faculty:* 27 full-time (19 women), 71 part-time/adjunct (51 women). *Students:* 181 full-time (126 women), 128 part-time (78 women); includes 71 minority (25 Black or African American, non-Hispanic/Latino; 1 American Indian or Alaska Native, non-Hispanic/Latino; 20 Asian, non-Hispanic/Latino; 19 Hispanic/Latino; 1 Native Hawaiian or other Pacific Islander, non-Hispanic/Latino; 5 Two or more races, non-Hispanic/Latino), 12 international. 234 applicants, 67% accepted, 103 enrolled. In 2018, 148 master's awarded. *Degree requirements:* For master's, thesis (for some programs). *Entrance requirements:* For master's, statement of goals, 2 letters of recommendation. Additional exam requirements/recommendations for international students: Required—TOEFL (minimum score 79 iBT), IELTS, PTE, one of three is required. Application fee: $60. Electronic applications accepted. *Financial support:* Fellowships, research assistantships, teaching assistantships, career-related internships or fieldwork, Federal Work-Study, scholarships/grants, health care benefits, and unspecified assistantships available. Financial award applicants required to submit FAFSA. *Faculty research:* Career & technical education, early childhood education, middle grades education, secondary education, special education. *Unit head:* Matthew Tincani, Prof. of Applied Behavior Analysis and Dept. Chairperson, 215-204-8073, E-mail: matthew.tincani@temple.edu. *Application contact:* Stacey Sanginette, Academic Coordinator, 215-204-6143, E-mail: stacey.sangtinette@temple.edu.
Website: http://education.temple.edu/tl

Texas Woman's University, Graduate School, College of Arts and Sciences, Department of English, Speech, and Foreign Languages, Denton, TX 76204. Offers English (MA, MAT); rhetoric (PhD). *Program availability:* Part-time. *Faculty:* 8 full-time (3 women). *Students:* 6 full-time (5 women), 42 part-time (36 women); includes 10 minority (4 Black or African American, non-Hispanic/Latino; 1 Asian, non-Hispanic/Latino; 2 Hispanic/Latino; 3 Two or more races, non-Hispanic/Latino), 1 international. Average age 37. 21 applicants, 67% accepted, 12 enrolled. In 2018, 4 master's, 6 doctorates awarded. *Degree requirements:* For master's, comprehensive exam (for some programs), thesis (for some programs), professional paper, thesis or coursework; for doctorate, thesis/dissertation, residency for at least 2 consecutive semesters (strongly encouraged), oral defense of dissertation. *Entrance requirements:* For master's, 3 letters of reference, minimum GPA of 3.0 on previous upper-division undergraduate and graduate work, writing sample, statement of purpose; for doctorate, writing sample, 3 letters of reference, interview (for graduate assistants), minimum GPA of 3.0 on previous upper-division and graduate work, statement of purpose. Additional exam requirements/recommendations for international students: Required—TOEFL (minimum score 600 paper-based; 79 iBT); Recommended—IELTS (minimum score 6.5). *Application deadline:* For fall admission, 7/1 priority date for domestic students, 3/1 priority date for international students; for spring admission, 11/1 priority date for domestic students, 7/1 priority date for international students; for summer admission, 4/1 priority date for domestic students, 2/1 priority date for international students. Applications are processed on a rolling basis. Application fee: $50 ($75 for international students). Electronic applications accepted. *Expenses: Tuition, area resident:* Full-time $4852; part-time $270 per semester hour. Tuition, state resident: full-time $4852; part-time $270 per semester hour. Tuition, nonresident: full-time $12,322; part-time $685 per semester hour. *International tuition:* $12,322 full-time. *Required fees:* $2714; $113 per semester hour. $296 per semester. Tuition and fees vary according to course level, course load, degree level, campus/location and program. *Financial support:* In 2018–19, 19 students received support, including 13 teaching assistantships (averaging $12,302 per year); career-related internships or fieldwork, Federal Work-Study, institutionally sponsored loans, scholarships/grants, traineeships, health care benefits, and unspecified assistantships also available. Support available to part-time students. Financial award application deadline: 3/1; financial award applicants required to submit FAFSA. *Faculty research:* American literature, medieval literature, history of the English language, rhetoric, world literature. *Unit head:* Dr. Genevieve West, Chair, 940-898-

2324, Fax: 940-898-2297, E-mail: engspfl@twu.edu. *Application contact:* Korie Hawkins, Associate Director of Admissions, Graduate Recruitment, 940-898-3188, Fax: 940-898-3081, E-mail: admissions@twu.edu.
Website: http://www.twu.edu/english-speech-foreign-languages/

Trinity Washington University, School of Education, Washington, DC 20017-1094. Offers clinical mental health counseling (MA); early childhood education (MAT); educating for change (M Ed); educational administration (MSA); elementary education (MAT); reading (M Ed); school counseling (MA); secondary education (MAT), including English, social studies; special education (MAT). *Accreditation:* NCATE. *Program availability:* Part-time, evening/weekend. *Degree requirements:* For master's, thesis (for some programs), capstone project(s). *Entrance requirements:* For master's, PRAXIS I, minimum GPA of 2.8. Additional exam requirements/recommendations for international students: Required—TOEFL (minimum score 550 paper-based). *Faculty research:* Technology, literacy, special education, organizations, inclusion models.

University at Buffalo, the State University of New York, Graduate School, Graduate School of Education, Department of Learning and Instruction, Buffalo, NY 14260. Offers biology education (Ed M, Certificate); chemistry education (Ed M, Certificate); childhood education (Ed M); childhood education with bilingual extension (Ed M); college teaching (Advanced Certificate); curriculum, instruction and the science of learning (PhD); early childhood education (Ed M); early childhood education with bilingual extension (Ed M); earth science education (Ed M, Certificate); education and technology (Ed M); education studies (Ed M); educational technology and new literacies (Certificate); educational technology and new literacies (Advanced Certificate); elementary education (Ed D); English education (Ed M, Certificate); English education studies (Ed M); English for speakers of other languages (Ed M); foreign and second language education (PhD); French education (Ed M, Certificate); German education (Ed M, Certificate); gifted education (Certificate); Latin education (Ed M, Certificate); literacy education studies (Ed M); literacy specialist (Ed M); literacy teaching and learning (Certificate); mathematics education (Ed M, Certificate); music education (Ed M, Certificate); music education studies (Ed M); music learning theory (Advanced Certificate); online education (Advanced Certificate); physics education (Ed M, Certificate); science and the public (Ed M); social studies education (Ed M, Certificate); Spanish education (Ed M, Certificate); special education (PhD); teaching English to speakers of other languages (Ed M). *Program availability:* Part-time, evening/weekend, 100% online. *Faculty:* 31 full-time (22 women), 41 part-time/adjunct (27 women). *Students:* 161 full-time (107 women), 369 part-time (260 women); includes 76 minority (26 Black or African American, non-Hispanic/Latino; 3 American Indian or Alaska Native, non-Hispanic/Latino; 30 Asian, non-Hispanic/Latino; 14 Hispanic/Latino; 3 Two or more races, non-Hispanic/Latino), 41 international. Average age 34. 368 applicants, 70% accepted, 179 enrolled. In 2018, 100 master's, 26 doctorates, 19 other advanced degrees awarded. *Degree requirements:* For master's, comprehensive exam; for doctorate, thesis/dissertation, research analysis exam, research experience. *Entrance requirements:* For master's, letters of reference; for doctorate, GRE General Test or MAT, interview, writing sample, letters of recommendation. Additional exam requirements/recommendations for international students: Required—TOEFL (minimum score 600 paper-based; 96 iBT), IELTS (minimum score 6.5), PTE (minimum score 55). *Application deadline:* For fall admission, 2/1 priority date for domestic and international students; for spring admission, 11/15 priority date for domestic students, 10/1 for international students. Applications are processed on a rolling basis. Application fee: $50. Electronic applications accepted. *Financial support:* In 2018–19, 42 fellowships (averaging $5,181 per year), 44 research assistantships with tuition reimbursements (averaging $10,908 per year) were awarded; teaching assistantships, career-related internships or fieldwork, Federal Work-Study, institutionally sponsored loans, scholarships/grants, tuition waivers (full and partial), and unspecified assistantships also available. Financial award application deadline: 2/28; financial award applicants required to submit FAFSA. *Faculty research:* Science assessment, foreign language teaching and learning, early learning, new literacies, gender and education. *Total annual research expenditures:* $413,233. *Unit head:* Dr. Julie Gorlewski, Department Chair, 716-645-2455, Fax: 716-645-3161, E-mail: jgorlews@buffalo.edu. *Application contact:* Renad Aref, Assistant Director of Admission Recruitment, 716-645-2110, Fax: 716-645-7937, E-mail: gseinfo@buffalo.edu.
Website: http://ed.buffalo.edu/teaching.html

The University of Akron, Graduate School, College of Education, Department of Curricular and Instructional Studies, Program in Adolescent to Young Adult Education, Akron, OH 44325. Offers chemistry (MS); chemistry and physics (MS); earth science (MS); earth science and chemistry (MS); earth science and physics (MS); integrated language arts (MS); integrated mathematics (MS); integrated social studies (MS); life science (MS); life science and chemistry (MS); life science and earth science (MS); life science and physics (MS); physics (MS). *Accreditation:* NCATE. *Degree requirements:* For master's, comprehensive exam. *Entrance requirements:* For master's, minimum GPA of 3.0. Additional exam requirements/recommendations for international students: Required—TOEFL (minimum score 79 iBT), IELTS (minimum score 6.5). Electronic applications accepted.

The University of Alabama in Huntsville, School of Graduate Studies, College of Arts, Humanities, and Social Sciences, Department of English, Huntsville, AL 35899. Offers education (MA); English (MA); technical writing (Certificate); TESOL (Certificate). *Program availability:* Part-time. *Faculty:* 9 full-time (5 women). *Students:* 13 full-time (7 women), 16 part-time (10 women); includes 7 minority (6 Black or African American, non-Hispanic/Latino; 1 Hispanic/Latino). Average age 34. 8 applicants, 100% accepted, 6 enrolled. In 2018, 11 master's awarded. *Degree requirements:* For master's, one foreign language, comprehensive exam, thesis or alternative, oral and written exams. *Entrance requirements:* For master's and Certificate, GRE General Test, minimum GPA of 3.0. Additional exam requirements/recommendations for international students: Required—TOEFL (minimum score 500 paper-based; 80 iBT), IELTS (minimum score 6.5). *Application deadline:* For fall admission, 7/15 priority date for domestic students, 4/1 priority date for international students; for spring admission, 11/30 priority date for domestic students, 9/1 priority date for international students. Applications are processed on a rolling basis. Application fee: $50. Electronic applications accepted. *Expenses: Tuition, area resident:* Full-time $10,632; part-time $412 per credit hour. Tuition, state resident: full-time $10,632. Tuition, nonresident: full-time $23,604; part-time $412 per credit hour. *Required fees:* $582; $582. Tuition and fees vary according to course load and program. *Financial support:* In 2018–19, 12 students received support, including 10 teaching assistantships with full tuition reimbursements available (averaging $4,500 per year); career-related internships or fieldwork, Federal Work-Study, institutionally sponsored loans, scholarships/grants, health care benefits, tuition waivers (full and partial), and unspecified assistantships also available. Support available to part-time students. Financial award application deadline: 4/1; financial award applicants required to submit FAFSA. *Faculty research:* Fiction and identity, Shakespeare, science fiction, eighteenth-century literature, technical writing. *Unit head:* Dr. Alanna Frost, Chair, 256-824-2373, Fax: 256-824-6949, E-mail: alanna.frost@uah.edu. *Application contact:* Kim Gray, Graduate Studies Admissions Coordinator, 256-824-6002, Fax: 256-824-6405, E-mail: deangrad@uah.edu.
Website: http://www.uah.edu/ahs/departments/english

The University of Alabama in Huntsville, School of Graduate Studies, College of Education, Huntsville, AL 35899. Offers autism spectrum disorders (M Ed, Graduate Certificate); biology (MAT); chemistry (MAT); differentiated instruction in elementary education (M Ed); English language arts (MAT); English speakers of other languages (M Ed, MAT); history (MAT); mathematics (MAT); physics (MAT); reading education (M Ed); secondary education (M Ed). *Program availability:* Part-time. *Faculty:* 13 full-time (10 women). *Students:* 38 full-time (30 women), 39 part-time (37 women); includes 17 minority (10 Black or African American, non-Hispanic/Latino; 3 American Indian or Alaska Native, non-Hispanic/Latino; 2 Asian, non-Hispanic/Latino; 2 Two or more races, non-Hispanic/Latino). Average age 33. 47 applicants, 83% accepted, 29 enrolled. In 2018, 31 master's awarded. *Degree requirements:* For master's, comprehensive exam, thesis or alternative, oral and written. *Entrance requirements:* For master's, GRE General Test, minimum GPA of 3.0. Additional exam requirements/recommendations for international students: Required—TOEFL (minimum score 500 paper-based; 80 iBT), IELTS (minimum score 6.5). *Application deadline:* For fall admission, 7/15 priority date for domestic students, 4/1 priority date for international students; for spring admission, 11/30 priority date for domestic students, 9/1 priority date for international students. Applications are processed on a rolling basis. Application fee: $50. Electronic applications accepted. *Expenses: Tuition, area resident:* Full-time $10,632; part-time $412 per credit hour. Tuition, state resident: full-time $10,632. Tuition, nonresident: full-time $23,604; part-time $412 per credit hour. *Required fees:* $582; $582. Tuition and fees vary according to course load and program. *Financial support:* In 2018–19, 2 students received support, including 1 teaching assistantship with full tuition reimbursement available (averaging $4,500 per year); career-related internships or fieldwork, Federal Work-Study, institutionally sponsored loans, scholarships/grants, health care benefits, tuition waivers (full and partial), and unspecified assistantships also available. Support available to part-time students. Financial award application deadline: 4/1; financial award applicants required to submit FAFSA. *Unit head:* Dr. Beth Nason Quick, Dean, 256-824-2325, E-mail: beth.quick@uah.edu. *Application contact:* Kim Gray, Graduate Studies Admissions Coordinator, 256-824-6002, Fax: 256-824-6405, E-mail: deangrad@uah.edu.
Website: http://www.uah.edu/education/

The University of Arizona, College of Humanities, Department of English, Rhetoric, Composition and the Teaching of English Program, Tucson, AZ 85721. Offers MA, PhD. *Accreditation:* NASM. *Degree requirements:* For master's, one foreign language, comprehensive exam; for doctorate, one foreign language, comprehensive exam, thesis/dissertation. *Entrance requirements:* For doctorate, GRE General Test, 3 letters of recommendation, writing sample. Additional exam requirements/recommendations for international students: Required—TOEFL (minimum score 550 paper-based; 79 iBT). Electronic applications accepted.

University of Arkansas at Pine Bluff, School of Education, Pine Bluff, AR 71601-2799. Offers elementary education (M Ed); secondary education (M Ed), including English education, mathematics education, science education, social studies education; teaching (MAT). *Accreditation:* NCATE. *Program availability:* Part-time, evening/weekend. *Degree requirements:* For master's, comprehensive exam. *Entrance requirements:* For master's, GRE, minimum GPA of 2.75, NTE or Standard Arkansas Teaching Certificate. *Faculty research:* Teacher certification, accreditation, assessment, standards, portfolio development, rehabilitation, technology.

University of Central Florida, College of Community Innovation and Education, School of Teacher Education, Orlando, FL 32816. Offers applied learning and instruction (MA); curriculum and instruction (M Ed); elementary education (M Ed, MA); exceptional student education (M Ed, MA, Certificate), including autism spectrum disorders (Certificate), exceptional student education (M Ed), exceptional student education K-12 (MA), intervention specialist (Certificate), pre-kindergarten disabilities (Certificate), severe or profound disabilities (Certificate), special education (Certificate); K-8 mathematics and science education (M Ed, Certificate); reading education (M Ed, Certificate); teacher education (MAT), including art education, English language, mathematics education, middle school mathematics, middle school science, science education, social science education; world languages education - English for speakers of other languages (ESOL) (Certificate); world languages education - languages other than English (LOTE) (Certificate). *Program availability:* Part-time, evening/weekend. *Degree requirements:* For Certificate, thesis or alternative. *Entrance requirements:* For degree, GRE General Test, minimum GPA of 3.0. Additional exam requirements/recommendations for international students: Required—TOEFL. Electronic applications accepted.

University of Colorado Denver, School of Education and Human Development, Teacher Education Programs, Denver, CO 80217. Offers elementary linguistically diverse education (MA); elementary math and science education (MA); elementary math education (MA); elementary reading and writing (MA); elementary science education (MA); secondary English education (MA); secondary linguistically diverse education (MA); secondary math education (MA); secondary reading and writing (MA); secondary science education (MA); special education (MA). *Accreditation:* NCATE. *Program availability:* Part-time, evening/weekend. *Degree requirements:* For master's, comprehensive exam. *Entrance requirements:* For master's, GRE or MAT (for those with GPA below 2.75), transcripts, resume, letters of recommendation. Additional exam requirements/recommendations for international students: Required—TOEFL (minimum score 537 paper-based; 75 iBT); Recommended—IELTS (minimum score 6.5). Electronic applications accepted. *Expenses:* Tuition, state resident: full-time $6786; part-time $337 per credit hour. Tuition, nonresident: full-time $22,590; part-time $1255 per credit hour. *Required fees:* $1231; $137 per credit hour. Tuition and fees vary according to program and reciprocity agreements. *Faculty research:* Linguistically diverse education/ESL, elementary reading and writing, elementary teacher education, secondary teacher education, special education.

University of Connecticut, Graduate School, Neag School of Education, Department of Curriculum and Instruction, Program in English Education, Storrs, CT 06269. Offers MA, PhD. *Accreditation:* NCATE. Terminal master's awarded for partial completion of doctoral program. *Degree requirements:* For master's, comprehensive exam, thesis or alternative; for doctorate, thesis/dissertation. *Entrance requirements:* For doctorate, GRE General Test. Additional exam requirements/recommendations for international students: Required—TOEFL (minimum score 550 paper-based). Electronic applications accepted.

University of Florida, Graduate School, College of Education, School of Teaching and Learning, Gainesville, FL 32611. Offers curriculum and instruction (M Ed, MAE, Ed D, PhD, Ed S); elementary education (M Ed, MAE); English education (M Ed, MAE); mathematics education (M Ed, MAE); reading education (M Ed, MAE); science education (M Ed, MAE); social studies education (M Ed, MAE). *Accreditation:* NCATE. *Program availability:* Part-time, evening/weekend, online learning. Terminal master's awarded for partial completion of doctoral program. *Degree requirements:* For master's, comprehensive exam (for some programs), thesis (for some programs); for doctorate, comprehensive exam (for some programs), thesis/dissertation (for some programs). *Entrance requirements:* For master's and doctorate, GRE General Test, minimum GPA of 3.0; for Ed S, GRE General Test. Additional exam requirements/recommendations for international students: Required—TOEFL (minimum score 550 paper-based; 80 iBT),

IELTS (minimum score 6). Electronic applications accepted. *Faculty research:* STEM education; curriculum; teaching and teacher education; languages and literacy; schools, culture, and society; theories and processes of learning.

University of Georgia, College of Education, Department of Language and Literacy Education, Athens, GA 30602. Offers English education (M Ed); language and literacy education (PhD). *Accreditation:* NCATE. *Degree requirements:* For doctorate, variable foreign language requirement. *Entrance requirements:* For master's, GRE General Test or MAT; for doctorate, GRE General Test. Additional exam requirements/recommendations for international students: Required—TOEFL (minimum score 550 paper-based). Electronic applications accepted. *Faculty research:* Comprehension, critical literacy, literacy and technology, vocabulary instruction, content area reading.

University of Indianapolis, Graduate Programs, School of Education, Indianapolis, IN 46227-3697. Offers art education (MAT); biology (MAT); chemistry (MAT); curriculum and instruction (MA); earth sciences (MAT); education (MA, MAT); educational leadership (MA); elementary education (MA); English (MAT); French (MAT); math (MAT); physical education (MAT); physics (MAT); secondary education (MA), including art education, education, English education, social studies education; social studies (MAT); Spanish (MAT). *Accreditation:* NCATE. *Program availability:* Part-time, evening/weekend. *Entrance requirements:* For master's, GRE Subject Test, PRAXIS I, minimum GPA of 2.5, 3 letters of recommendation, interview. Additional exam requirements/recommendations for international students: Required—TOEFL (minimum score 550 paper-based). *Faculty research:* Assessment of teacher education, perceptions of prospective teachers by parents.

The University of Iowa, Graduate College, College of Education, Department of Teaching and Learning, Program in Education, Iowa City, IA 52242-1316. Offers art education (MA); developmental reading (MA); elementary education (MA); English education (MA, MAT); foreign and second language education (MAT); foreign language education (MA); foreign language/ESL education (PhD); language, literacy and culture (PhD); mathematics education (MA, MAT, PhD); music education (MM, PhD); science education (MA); secondary education (MA); social studies (MA, PhD). *Degree requirements:* For master's, thesis optional, exam; for doctorate, comprehensive exam, thesis/dissertation. *Entrance requirements:* For master's and doctorate, GRE General Test, minimum GPA of 3.0. Additional exam requirements/recommendations for international students: Required—TOEFL (minimum score 550 paper-based; 81 iBT). Electronic applications accepted.

University of Manitoba, Faculty of Graduate Studies, Faculty of Education, Department of Curriculum, Teaching and Learning, Winnipeg, MB R3T 2N2, Canada. Offers language and literacy (M Ed); second language education (M Ed); studies in curriculum, teaching and learning (M Ed). *Degree requirements:* For master's, thesis or alternative.

University of Maryland, Baltimore County, The Graduate School, College of Arts, Humanities and Social Sciences, Department of Education, Program in Teaching, Baltimore, MD 21250. Offers early childhood education (MAT); elementary education (MAT); teaching (MAT), including art, biology, chemistry, choral music, classical foreign language, dance, earth/space science, English, instrumental music, mathematics, modern foreign language, physical science, physics, social studies, theatre. *Program availability:* Part-time, evening/weekend. *Degree requirements:* For master's, comprehensive exam (for some programs), thesis (for some programs). *Entrance requirements:* For master's, PRAXIS Core Examination or GRE (minimum score of 1000), minimum GPA of 3.0. Additional exam requirements/recommendations for international students: Required—TOEFL. Electronic applications accepted. *Faculty research:* STEM teacher education, culturally sensitive pedagogy, ESOL/bilingual education, early childhood education, language, literacy and culture.

University of Michigan, Rackham Graduate School, Joint PhD Program in English and Education, Ann Arbor, MI 48109. Offers PhD. *Accreditation:* TEAC. *Faculty:* 12 full-time (8 women). *Students:* 25 full-time (19 women); includes 4 minority (2 Asian, non-Hispanic/Latino; 2 Hispanic/Latino). Average age 35. 56 applicants, 14% accepted, 3 enrolled. In 2018, 6 doctorates awarded. *Degree requirements:* For doctorate, one foreign language, comprehensive exam, thesis/dissertation, 3 preliminary exams, oral defense of dissertation. *Entrance requirements:* For doctorate, GRE General Test, master's degree, teaching experience. Additional exam requirements/recommendations for international students: Required—TOEFL. *Application deadline:* For fall admission, 12/30 for domestic and international students. Application fee: $75 ($90 for international students). Electronic applications accepted. *Financial support:* In 2018–19, 24 students received support, including 10 fellowships with full tuition reimbursements available, 6 research assistantships with full tuition reimbursements available, 30 teaching assistantships with full tuition reimbursements available; institutionally sponsored loans, scholarships/grants, health care benefits, and tuition waivers (full) also available. Financial award application deadline: 4/15. *Faculty research:* Literacy, teacher education, discourse analysis, rhetoric and composition studies. *Unit head:* Dr. Anne Ruggles Gere, Chair, 734-763-6643, Fax: 734-936-1606, E-mail: argere@umich.edu. *Application contact:* Jeanie Mahoney Laubenthal, Graduate Coordinator, 734-763-6643, Fax: 734-936-1606, E-mail: laubenth@umich.edu.
Website: https://jpee.lsa.umich.edu/

University of Minnesota, Twin Cities Campus, Graduate School, College of Education and Human Development, Department of Curriculum and Instruction, Program in Teaching, Minneapolis, MN 55455-0213. Offers teaching (M Ed), including arts in education, elementary education, English education, mathematics, science, second language education, social studies. *Students:* 249 full-time (182 women), 101 part-time (59 women); includes 57 minority (5 Black or African American, non-Hispanic/Latino; 16 Asian, non-Hispanic/Latino; 25 Hispanic/Latino; 11 Two or more races, non-Hispanic/Latino), 12 international. Average age 28. 383 applicants, 79% accepted, 261 enrolled. In 2018, 292 master's awarded. Application fee: $75 ($95 for international students). *Unit head:* Dr. Mark Vagle, Chair, 612-625-4006, Fax: 612-624-8277, E-mail: mvagle@umn.edu. *Application contact:* Dr. Mark Vagle, Chair, 612-625-4006, Fax: 612-624-8277, E-mail: mvagle@umn.edu.
Website: http://www.cehd.umn.edu/ci/

University of Missouri, Office of Research and Graduate Studies, College of Education, Department of Learning, Teaching and Curriculum, Columbia, MO 65211. Offers agricultural education (M Ed, PhD, Ed S); art education (M Ed, PhD, Ed S); business and office education (M Ed, PhD, Ed S); early childhood education (M Ed, PhD, Ed S); elementary education (M Ed, PhD, Ed S); English education (M Ed, PhD, Ed S); foreign language education (M Ed, PhD, Ed S); health education and promotion (M Ed, PhD); learning and instruction (M Ed); marketing education (M Ed, PhD, Ed S); mathematics education (M Ed, PhD, Ed S); music education (M Ed, PhD, Ed S); reading education (M Ed, PhD, Ed S); science education (M Ed, PhD, Ed S); social studies education (M Ed, PhD, Ed S); vocational education (M Ed, PhD, Ed S). *Program availability:* Part-time. Terminal master's awarded for partial completion of doctoral program. *Entrance requirements:* For master's and Ed S, GRE General Test or MAT, minimum GPA of 3.0; for doctorate, GRE General Test, minimum GPA of 3.0. Additional exam requirements/recommendations for international students: Required—TOEFL.

University of Montana, Graduate School, College of Humanities and Sciences, Department of English, Program in Teaching, Missoula, MT 59812. Offers MA. *Entrance requirements:* For master's, GRE General Test, sample of written work.

University of New Mexico, Graduate Studies, College of Education, Program in Language, Literacy and Sociocultural Studies, Albuquerque, NM 87131-2039. Offers American Indian education (MA); bilingual education (MA, PhD); educational linguistics (PhD); educational thought and sociocultural studies (MA, PhD); literacy/language arts (MA, PhD); social studies (MA); TESOL (MA, PhD). *Students:* Average age 40. 61 applicants, 38% accepted, 23 enrolled. In 2018, 36 master's, 4 doctorates awarded. *Degree requirements:* For master's, comprehensive exam, thesis optional; for doctorate, comprehensive exam, thesis/dissertation, research skills. *Entrance requirements:* For master's, letter of intent, 3 letters of recommendation, resume, BA/BS, department demographic form, transcripts; for doctorate, writing sample, letter of intent, 3 letters of recommendation, resume, BA/BS, MA, department demographic form, transcripts. Additional exam requirements/recommendations for international students: Required—TOEFL. *Application deadline:* For fall admission, 12/1 for domestic and international students; for spring admission, 9/15 for domestic and international students. Application fee: $50. Electronic applications accepted. *Financial support:* Fellowships, research assistantships, teaching assistantships, career-related internships or fieldwork, institutionally sponsored loans, scholarships/grants, and unspecified assistantships available. Support available to part-time students. Financial award application deadline: 3/1; financial award applicants required to submit FAFSA. *Faculty research:* School reform, professional development, history of education, Native American education, politics of education, feminism and issues of sexual identity, critical race theory, bilingualism, literacy reading, adolescent literature, second language acquisition, critical theory and schooling, indigenous languages. *Unit head:* Dr. Lois M. Meyer, Chair, 505-277-7244, Fax: 505-277-8362, E-mail: lsmeyer@unm.edu. *Application contact:* Debra Schaffer, Administrative Assistant, 505-277-0437, Fax: 505-277-8362, E-mail: schaffer@unm.edu.
Website: http://coe.unm.edu/departments-programs/llss/index.html

The University of North Carolina at Chapel Hill, Graduate School, School of Education, Program in Secondary Education, Chapel Hill, NC 27599. Offers English (Grades 9-12) (MAT); English as a second language (MAT); French (Grades K-12) (MAT); German (Grades K-12) (MAT); Japanese (Grades K-12) (MAT); Latin (Grades 9-12) (MAT); mathematics (Grades 9-12) (MAT); music (Grades K-12) (MAT); science (Grades 9-12) (MAT); social studies (Grades 9-12) (MAT); Spanish (Grades K-12) (MAT). *Accreditation:* NCATE. *Degree requirements:* For master's, comprehensive exam. *Entrance requirements:* For master's, GRE General Test, minimum GPA of 3.0 during last 2 years of undergraduate course work. Additional exam requirements/recommendations for international students: Required—TOEFL (minimum score 550 paper-based). Electronic applications accepted.

The University of North Carolina at Greensboro, Graduate School, College of Arts and Sciences, Department of English, Program in English, Greensboro, NC 27412-5001. Offers American literature (PhD); English (M Ed, MA); English literature (PhD); rhetoric and composition (PhD). *Degree requirements:* For master's, comprehensive exam, thesis or alternative; for doctorate, variable foreign language requirement, thesis/dissertation, preliminary exam. *Entrance requirements:* For master's, GRE General Test, GRE Subject Test, minimum GPA of 3.0; for doctorate, GRE General Test, GRE Subject Test, critical writing sample, minimum GPA of 3.0. Additional exam requirements/recommendations for international students: Required—TOEFL. Electronic applications accepted.

The University of North Carolina at Pembroke, The Graduate School, Department of English, Theatre and Foreign Languages, Pembroke, NC 28372-1510. Offers English education (MA, MAT). *Program availability:* Part-time, evening/weekend. *Degree requirements:* For master's, comprehensive exam, thesis optional. *Entrance requirements:* For master's, GRE, MAT, or NTE, minimum GPA of 3.0 in major or 2.5 overall. Additional exam requirements/recommendations for international students: Required—TOEFL.

University of Northern Colorado, Graduate School, College of Education and Behavioral Sciences, School of Teacher Education, Greeley, CO 80639. Offers curriculum studies (MAT); educational studies (Ed D); elementary education (MAT); English education (MAT); literacy (MA); multilingual education (MA), including TESOL, world languages; teaching diverse learners (MA). *Accreditation:* NCATE. *Program availability:* Part-time, evening/weekend. *Degree requirements:* For master's, comprehensive exam, thesis or alternative; for doctorate, comprehensive exam, thesis/dissertation. *Entrance requirements:* For master's and doctorate, GRE General Test, 3 letters of recommendation. Electronic applications accepted.

University of Northern Iowa, Graduate College, College of Humanities, Arts and Sciences, Department of Languages and Literatures, MA Program in Teaching English in Secondary Schools, Cedar Falls, IA 50614. Offers MA.

University of North Georgia, Master of Arts in Teaching Program, Dahlonega, GA 30597. Offers physical education (MAT); secondary education - English (MAT); secondary education - history (MAT); secondary education - mathematics (MAT); secondary education - middle grades (MAT). *Degree requirements:* For master's, internship, capstone. *Entrance requirements:* For master's, GRE or MAT, GACE I and II, GA pre-service application, lawful presence verification, official transcripts, GA Educator Ethics Program entry assessment. Additional exam requirements/recommendations for international students: Required—TOEFL (minimum score 550 paper-based; 79 iBT), IELTS (minimum score 6.5). Electronic applications accepted. *Expenses:* Contact institution.

University of Oklahoma, Jeannine Rainbolt College of Education, Department of Instructional Leadership and Academic Curriculum, Norman, OK 73072. Offers instructional leadership and academic curriculum (M Ed, PhD), including biomedical education (PhD), early childhood education, elementary education, English education, instructional leadership, mathematics education, reading education, science education, social studies education, world languages education (M Ed); reading specialist (M Ed). *Accreditation:* NCATE. *Program availability:* Part-time. *Faculty:* 26 full-time (12 women), 1 part-time/adjunct (0 women). *Students:* 42 full-time (32 women), 113 part-time (85 women); includes 33 minority (9 Black or African American, non-Hispanic/Latino; 5 American Indian or Alaska Native, non-Hispanic/Latino; 6 Asian, non-Hispanic/Latino; 4 Hispanic/Latino; 1 Native Hawaiian or other Pacific Islander, non-Hispanic/Latino; 8 Two or more races, non-Hispanic/Latino), 9 international. Average age 35. 42 applicants, 79% accepted, 21 enrolled. In 2018, 30 master's, 17 doctorates awarded. Terminal master's awarded for partial completion of doctoral program. *Degree requirements:* For master's, comprehensive exam (for some programs), thesis (for some programs); for doctorate, comprehensive exam (for some programs), thesis/dissertation. *Entrance requirements:* For doctorate, GRE. Additional exam requirements/recommendations for international students: Required—TOEFL (minimum score 79 iBT) or IELTS (minimum score 6.5). Application fee: $50 ($100 for international students). Electronic applications accepted. *Expenses:* Tuition, state resident: full-time $5683.20; part-time $236.80 per credit hour. Tuition, nonresident: full-time $20,342; part-time $847.60 per credit hour. *International tuition:* $20,342.40 full-time. *Required fees:* $2894.20; $110.05 per credit

hour. $126.50 per semester. Tuition and fees vary according to course load and program. *Financial support:* Fellowships, research assistantships, teaching assistantships, scholarships/grants, and unspecified assistantships available. Financial award application deadline: 6/1; financial award applicants required to submit FAFSA. *Faculty research:* Teacher preparation; instruction; curriculum; learning; constructivist theory. *Unit head:* Dr. Stacy Reeder, Chair, 405-325-1498, Fax: 405-325-4061, E-mail: reeder@ou.edu. *Application contact:* Anna Steele, Graduate Programs Officer, 405-325-4525, E-mail: anna.steele@ou.edu.
Website: http://www.ou.edu/education/ilac

University of Pennsylvania, Graduate School of Education, Division of Literacy, Culture, and International Education, Program in Reading/Writing/Literacy, Philadelphia, PA 19104. Offers MS Ed, Ed D, PhD. *Program availability:* Part-time. *Students:* 44 full-time (34 women), 14 part-time (all women); includes 23 minority (11 Black or African American, non-Hispanic/Latino; 4 Asian, non-Hispanic/Latino; 6 Hispanic/Latino; 2 Two or more races, non-Hispanic/Latino), 4 international. Average age 31. 101 applicants, 42% accepted, 23 enrolled. In 2018, 22 master's, 5 doctorates awarded. Application fee: $80. *Financial support:* In 2018–19, 26 students received support.

University of Phoenix–Online Campus, College of Education, Phoenix, AZ 85034-7209. Offers administration and supervision (MAEd, Certificate); adult education and training (MAEd); curriculum and instruction (MAEd), including computer education, curriculum and instruction, English as a second language, language arts, mathematics, reading; early childhood education (MAEd); educational studies (MAEd); elementary teacher education (MAEd), including early childhood, elementary teacher education, high school middle level, middle level; principal licensure (Certificate); secondary teacher education (MAEd); special education (MAEd, Certificate); teacher education (MAEd), including middle level generalist; teacher education middle level mathematics (MAEd), including middle level mathematics; teacher education middle level science (MAEd), including middle level science; teacher education secondary mathematics (MAEd); teacher education secondary science (MAEd); teacher leadership (MAEd); teachers of English learners (Certificate); transition to teaching (Certificate), including elementary education, secondary education. *Program availability:* Evening/weekend, online learning. *Entrance requirements:* Additional exam requirements/recommendations for international students: Required—TOEFL, TOEIC (Test of English as an International Communication), Berlitz Online English Proficiency Exam, PTE, or IELTS. Electronic applications accepted. *Expenses:* Contact institution.

University of Pittsburgh, School of Education, Department of Instruction and Learning, Program in Secondary Education, Pittsburgh, PA 15260. Offers English and communications education (M Ed, MAT); foreign language education (M Ed, MAT); language, literacy and culture education (Ed D, PhD); mathematics education (M Ed, MAT, Ed D, PhD); science education (M Ed, MAT, Ed D, PhD); secondary education (PhD); social studies education (M Ed, MAT); STEM education (Ed D). *Program availability:* Part-time, evening/weekend. *Degree requirements:* For master's, thesis; for doctorate, thesis/dissertation. *Entrance requirements:* For master's, PRAXIS I; for doctorate, GRE General Test. Additional exam requirements/recommendations for international students: Required—TOEFL. Electronic applications accepted.

University of Puerto Rico–Mayagüez, Graduate Studies, College of Arts and Sciences, Department of English, Mayagüez, PR 00681-9000. Offers English education (MA). *Program availability:* Part-time. *Degree requirements:* For master's, one foreign language, comprehensive exam, thesis. *Entrance requirements:* For master's, minimum GPA of 3.0; course work in linguistics or language, American literature, British literature, and structure/grammar or syntax. Additional exam requirements/recommendations for international students: Required—TOEFL (minimum score 550 paper-based; 79 iBT). Electronic applications accepted. *Faculty research:* Multiliteracies and multimodality theorizing and practice, second language writing, Afro-Puerto Rican studies, modern poetry, Puerto Rican culture and folklore.

University of St. Francis, College of Education, Joliet, IL 60435-6169. Offers educational leadership (MS, Ed D); elementary education (M Ed); reading (MS); secondary education (M Ed), including English education, math education, science education, social studies education, visual arts education; special education (M Ed); teaching and learning (MS); TESOL (Certificate). *Accreditation:* NCATE. *Program availability:* Part-time, evening/weekend, 100% online, blended/hybrid learning. *Faculty:* 11 full-time (8 women), 58 part-time/adjunct (38 women). *Students:* 43 full-time (35 women), 453 part-time (354 women); includes 110 minority (48 Black or African American, non-Hispanic/Latino; 7 Asian, non-Hispanic/Latino; 52 Hispanic/Latino; 3 Two or more races, non-Hispanic/Latino), 3 international. Average age 37. 300 applicants, 66% accepted, 164 enrolled. In 2018, 151 master's, 42 doctorates, 4 other advanced degrees awarded. *Degree requirements:* For master's, comprehensive exam; for doctorate, thesis/dissertation. *Entrance requirements:* Additional exam requirements/recommendations for international students: Required—TOEFL (minimum score 550 paper-based; 79 iBT), IELTS (minimum score 6). *Application deadline:* Applications are processed on a rolling basis. Electronic applications accepted. Application fee is waived when completed online. *Expenses:* Contact institution. *Financial support:* In 2018–19, 33 students received support. Scholarships/grants and tuition waivers (partial) available. Support available to part-time students. Financial award applicants required to submit FAFSA. *Unit head:* Dr. John Gambro, Dean, 815-740-3456, E-mail: jgambro@stfrancis.edu. *Application contact:* Sandee Sloka, Director Adult & Graduate Admissions, 800-735-7500, E-mail: ssloka@stfrancis.edu.
Website: https://www.stfrancis.edu/education/

University of South Carolina, The Graduate School, College of Arts and Sciences, Department of English Language and Literature, Columbia, SC 29208. Offers creative writing (MFA); English (MA, PhD); English education (MAT); MLIS/MA. MAT offered in cooperation with the College of Education. *Program availability:* Part-time. *Degree requirements:* For master's, one foreign language, comprehensive exam, thesis; for doctorate, 2 foreign languages, comprehensive exam, thesis/dissertation. *Entrance requirements:* For master's, GRE General Test (MFA), GRE Subject Test (MA, MAT), sample of written work; for doctorate, GRE General Test, GRE Subject Test, sample of written work. Additional exam requirements/recommendations for international students: Required—TOEFL. Electronic applications accepted. *Faculty research:* American literature, British literature, composition and rhetoric, linguistics, speech communication.

University of South Carolina, The Graduate School, College of Education, Department of Instruction and Teacher Education, Program in Secondary Education, Columbia, SC 29208. Offers art education (IMA, MAT); business education (IMA, MAT); English (MAT); foreign language (MAT); health education (MAT); mathematics (MAT); science (IMA, MAT); secondary (Ed D); secondary education (MT, PhD); social studies (MAT); theatre and speech (MAT). IMA and MT offered jointly with the subject areas. *Accreditation:* NCATE. *Degree requirements:* For master's, comprehensive exam, thesis (for some programs), foreign language (MA); for doctorate, one foreign language, comprehensive exam, thesis/dissertation. *Entrance requirements:* For master's, GRE General Test or MAT, teaching certificate (IMA, M Ed), interview; for doctorate, GRE General Test or MAT, interview. *Faculty research:* Middle school programs, professional development, school collaboration.

University of Southern Mississippi, College of Arts and Sciences, Department of English, Hattiesburg, MS 39406-0001. Offers creative writing (MA, PhD); English education (MA); literature (MA, PhD). *Degree requirements:* For master's, one foreign language, comprehensive exam, thesis; for doctorate, 2 foreign languages, comprehensive exam, thesis/dissertation. *Entrance requirements:* For master's, GRE General Test, minimum GPA of 3.0 in field of study, 2.75 in last 2 years; for doctorate, GRE General Test, minimum GPA of 3.5. Additional exam requirements/recommendations for international students: Required—TOEFL, IELTS. Electronic applications accepted. *Faculty research:* English and American literature, critical theory and cultural studies, creative writing.

University of South Florida, St. Petersburg, College of Education, St. Petersburg, FL 33701. Offers educational leadership development (M Ed); elementary education (MA), including math/science; English education (MA); middle grades STEM education (MS); reading education (MA). *Program availability:* Part-time. *Degree requirements:* For master's, comprehensive exam, practicum, internship, comprehensive portfolio. *Entrance requirements:* For master's, State of Florida General Knowledge Test (GKT), Florida Teaching Certificate (for non-initial certification programs), letters of recommendation. Additional exam requirements/recommendations for international students: Required—TOEFL (minimum score 550 paper-based; 79 iBT); Recommended—IELTS. Electronic applications accepted.

University of South Florida Sarasota-Manatee, College of Liberal Arts and Social Sciences, Sarasota, FL 34243. Offers criminal justice (MA); education (MA); educational leadership (M Ed), including curriculum leadership, K-12 public school leadership, non-public/charter school leadership; elementary education (MAT); English education (MA); social work (MSW). *Program availability:* Part-time, 100% online, blended/hybrid learning. *Faculty:* 14 full-time (9 women), 6 part-time/adjunct (5 women). *Students:* 10 full-time (8 women), 46 part-time (40 women); includes 17 minority (6 Black or African American, non-Hispanic/Latino; 7 Hispanic/Latino; 4 Two or more races, non-Hispanic/Latino). Average age 33. 57 applicants, 46% accepted, 24 enrolled. In 2018, 12 master's awarded. *Degree requirements:* For master's, comprehensive exam (for some programs). *Entrance requirements:* For master's, GRE. Additional exam requirements/recommendations for international students: Required—TOEFL (minimum score 550 paper-based; 79 iBT), IELTS (minimum score 6.5). *Application deadline:* For fall admission, 3/1 priority date for domestic students, 3/1 for international students; for spring admission, 10/1 priority date for domestic students, 10/1 for international students. Applications are processed on a rolling basis. Application fee: $30. Electronic applications accepted. *Expenses: Tuition, area resident:* Full-time $8350; part-time $348 per credit hour. Tuition, state resident: full-time $8350; part-time $348 per credit hour. Tuition, nonresident: full-time $19,048; part-time $794 per credit hour. *Required fees:* $1689; $70 per credit hour. $5 per semester. Tuition and fees vary according to program. *Financial support:* Career-related internships or fieldwork, institutionally sponsored loans, scholarships/grants, health care benefits, and unspecified assistantships available. Support available to part-time students. Financial award application deadline: 6/30; financial award applicants required to submit FAFSA. *Faculty research:* Educational leadership, secondary education, elementary education, and criminal justice. *Total annual research expenditures:* $97,764. *Unit head:* Dr. Jane Rose, Dean, 941-359-4469, Fax: 941-359-4778, E-mail: jane.rose@sar.usf.edu. *Application contact:* Brandon Avery, Assistant Director, Admissions, 941-359-4331, E-mail: bavery@sar.usf.edu.

The University of Tennessee, Graduate School, College of Education, Health and Human Sciences, Program in Education, Knoxville, TN 37996. Offers art education (MS); counseling education (PhD); cultural studies in education (PhD); curriculum (MS, Ed S); curriculum, educational research and evaluation (Ed D, PhD); early childhood education (PhD); early childhood special education (MS); education of deaf and hard of hearing (MS); educational administration and policy studies (Ed D, PhD); educational administration and supervision (Ed S); educational psychology (Ed D, PhD); elementary education (MS, Ed S); elementary teaching (MS); English education (MS, Ed S); exercise science (PhD); foreign language/ESL education (MS, Ed S); instructional technology (MS, Ed D, PhD, Ed S); literacy, language and ESL education (PhD); literacy, language education, and ESL education (Ed D); mathematics education (MS, Ed S); modified and comprehensive special education (MS); reading education (MS, Ed S); school counseling (Ed S); school psychology (PhD, Ed S); science education (MS, Ed S); secondary teaching (MS); social foundations (MS); social science education (MS, Ed S); socio-cultural foundations of sports and education (PhD); special education (Ed S); teacher education (Ed D, PhD). *Accreditation:* NCATE. *Program availability:* Part-time, evening/weekend. *Degree requirements:* For master's and Ed S, thesis optional; for doctorate, variable foreign language requirement, thesis/dissertation. *Entrance requirements:* For master's, minimum GPA of 2.7; for doctorate and Ed S, GRE General Test, minimum GPA of 2.7. Additional exam requirements/recommendations for international students: Required—TOEFL. Electronic applications accepted.

The University of Texas at El Paso, Graduate School, College of Liberal Arts, Department of English, El Paso, TX 79968-0001. Offers bilingual professional writing (Certificate); English and American literature (MA); rhetoric and composition (PhD); rhetoric and writing studies (MA); teaching English (MAT). *Program availability:* Part-time, evening/weekend. *Degree requirements:* For master's, thesis optional. *Entrance requirements:* For master's, GRE General Test, minimum GPA of 3.0. Additional exam requirements/recommendations for international students: Required—TOEFL. Electronic applications accepted. *Faculty research:* Literature, creative writing, literary theory.

University of the District of Columbia, College of Arts and Sciences, Program in Teaching, Washington, DC 20008-1175. Offers elementary education (MAT); middle school mathematics (MAT); secondary English language arts (MAT); secondary social studies (MAT).

University of the Sacred Heart, Graduate Programs, Department of Education, San Juan, PR 00914-0383. Offers early childhood education (M Ed); information technology and multimedia (Certificate); instruction systems and education technology (M Ed), including English, information technology and multimedia, instructional design, mathematics, Spanish. *Program availability:* Part-time, evening/weekend. *Degree requirements:* For master's, thesis. *Entrance requirements:* For master's, EXADEP, minimum undergraduate GPA of 2.75, interview.

The University of Toledo, College of Graduate Studies, Judith Herb College of Education, Department of Curriculum and Instruction, Toledo, OH 43606-3390. Offers art education (ME); career and technical education (ME, Ed S); curriculum and instruction (ME, PhD, Ed S); early childhood education (Ed S); education and anthropology (MAE); education and biology (MES); education and chemistry (MES); education and classics (MAE); education and economics (MAE); education and English (MAE); education and French (MAE); education and geology (MES); education and German (MAE); education and history (MAE); education and mathematics (MAE, MES); education and physics (MES); education and political science (MAE); education and sociology (MAE); education and Spanish (MAE); educational media (PhD); educational technology (ME); educational technology: virtual educator (Certificate); elementary education (PhD); English as a second language (MAE); gifted and talented education

(PhD); middle childhood education (ME); secondary education (ME, PhD); special education (PhD). *Accreditation:* NCATE. *Program availability:* Part-time, evening/weekend. *Degree requirements:* For master's, comprehensive exam, thesis or alternative; for doctorate, comprehensive exam, thesis/dissertation; for other advanced degree, thesis optional. *Entrance requirements:* For master's, doctorate, and other advanced degree, minimum cumulative GPA of 2.7 for all previous academic work, letters of recommendation. Additional exam requirements/recommendations for international students: Required—TOEFL (minimum score 550 paper-based; 80 iBT). Electronic applications accepted.

University of Victoria, Faculty of Graduate Studies, Faculty of Education, Department of Curriculum and Instruction, Victoria, BC V8W 2Y2, Canada. Offers art education (M Ed, PhD); curriculum studies (M Ed, MA, PhD); early childhood education (M Ed, PhD); educational studies (PhD); language and literacy (M Ed, MA, PhD); mathematics (M Ed, MA, PhD); music education (M Ed, MA, PhD); science (M Ed, MA, PhD); social studies (M Ed, MA); social, cultural and foundational studies (MA, PhD); technology and environmental education (PhD). *Program availability:* Part-time. *Degree requirements:* For master's, thesis, project (M Ed); for doctorate, comprehensive exam, thesis/dissertation. *Entrance requirements:* For master's, minimum B average. Additional exam requirements/recommendations for international students: Required—TOEFL (minimum score 575 paper-based), IELTS (minimum score 7). Electronic applications accepted. *Faculty research:* Elementary and secondary English, language arts, curriculum theory and practice, educational media and technology, educational administration and leadership, history and philosophy of education.

University of Virginia, Curry School of Education, Department of Curriculum, Instruction, and Special Education, Program in Curriculum and Instruction, Charlottesville, VA 22903. Offers curriculum and instruction (M Ed, Ed S); elementary education (M Ed, Ed D); English education (M Ed, Ed D); foreign language education (M Ed); mathematics education (M Ed, Ed D); science education (Ed D); social studies education (M Ed); MBA/M Ed. *Program availability:* 100% online. *Degree requirements:* For master's, comprehensive exam (for some programs); for doctorate, comprehensive exam, thesis/dissertation; for Ed S, comprehensive exam. *Entrance requirements:* For master's, doctorate, and Ed S, GRE General Test, 2 letters of recommendation. Additional exam requirements/recommendations for international students: Required—TOEFL (minimum score 600 paper-based; 90 iBT), IELTS (minimum score 7). Electronic applications accepted.

University of Virginia, Curry School of Education, Program in Education, Charlottesville, VA 22903. Offers administration and supervision (PhD); applied developmental science (PhD); counselor education (PhD); curriculum and instruction (PhD); early childhood special education (MT); education evaluation (PhD); educational psychology (PhD); educational research (PhD); elementary education (MT); English education (MT, PhD); foreign language education (MT); higher education (PhD); instructional technology (PhD); kinesiology (MT, PhD); math education (PhD); reading education (PhD); research, statistics and evaluation (PhD); school psychology (PhD); science education (PhD); social studies education (MT, PhD); special education (PhD); world languages education (MT). *Degree requirements:* For master's, comprehensive exam (for some programs), field project; for doctorate, comprehensive exam, thesis/dissertation. *Entrance requirements:* For doctorate, GRE General Test. Additional exam requirements/recommendations for international students: Required—TOEFL (minimum score 600 paper-based; 90 iBT), IELTS (minimum score 7). Electronic applications accepted.

University of Washington, Graduate School, College of Arts and Sciences, Department of English, Seattle, WA 98195. Offers creative writing (MFA); English as a second language (MAT); English literature and language (MA, MAT, PhD). *Program availability:* Part-time. Terminal master's awarded for partial completion of doctoral program. *Degree requirements:* For master's, one foreign language, thesis (for some programs); for doctorate, one foreign language, thesis/dissertation. *Entrance requirements:* For master's, GRE General Test, GRE Subject Test (MA and MAT in English), minimum GPA of 3.0; for doctorate, GRE General Test, GRE Subject Test. Additional exam requirements/recommendations for international students: Required—TOEFL. Electronic applications accepted. *Faculty research:* English and American literature, critical theory, creative writing, language theory.

University of Washington, Graduate School, College of Education, Seattle, WA 98195. Offers curriculum and instruction (M Ed, Ed D, PhD), including educational technology, general curriculum (Ed D, PhD), language, literacy, and culture, mathematics education, multicultural education, reading and language arts education (Ed D), science education, social studies education, teaching and curriculum (M Ed); educational leadership and policy studies (M Ed, Ed D, PhD), including administration (Ed D), educational policy, organization, and leadership (M Ed, PhD), higher education, leadership for learning (Ed D), social and cultural foundations of education (M Ed, PhD); educational psychology (M Ed, PhD), including educational psychology (PhD), human development and cognition (M Ed), learning sciences, measurement, statistics and research design (M Ed), school psychology (M Ed); instructional leadership (M Ed); intercollegiate athletic leadership (M Ed); special education (M Ed, Ed D, PhD), including early childhood special education (M Ed), emotional and behavioral disabilities (M Ed), learning disabilities (M Ed), low-incidence disabilities (M Ed), severe disabilities (M Ed), special education (Ed D, PhD); teacher education (MIT). *Accreditation:* APA. *Program availability:* Part-time, evening/weekend. *Degree requirements:* For master's, thesis optional; for doctorate, thesis/dissertation. *Entrance requirements:* For master's and doctorate, GRE General Test, minimum GPA of 3.0. Additional exam requirements/recommendations for international students: Required—TOEFL. Electronic applications accepted. *Faculty research:* School restructuring/effective schools, special education interventions, literacy and writing, technology, school partnerships, teacher preparation.

The University of West Alabama, School of Graduate Studies, College of Education, Program in Secondary Education, Livingston, AL 35470. Offers biology (MAT); English language arts (MAT); high school 6-12 (M Ed); history (MAT); mathematics (MAT); science (MAT); social science (MAT). *Program availability:* Part-time, evening/weekend, 100% online. *Faculty:* 18 full-time (6 women), 8 part-time/adjunct (2 women). *Students:* 232 full-time (165 women), 34 part-time (24 women); includes 53 minority (44 Black or African American, non-Hispanic/Latino; 3 American Indian or Alaska Native, non-Hispanic/Latino; 2 Hispanic/Latino; 4 Two or more races, non-Hispanic/Latino), 3 international. Average age 31. 84 applicants, 93% accepted, 67 enrolled. In 2018, 100 master's awarded. *Degree requirements:* For master's, comprehensive exam, thesis optional. *Entrance requirements:* For master's, GRE, minimum GPA of 2.75, verification of background clearance/fingerprints, valid bachelor's-level Professional Educator Certificate in same teaching field. Additional exam requirements/recommendations for international students: Required—TOEFL (minimum score 500 paper-based; 61 iBT). *Application deadline:* Applications are processed on a rolling basis. Application fee: $40. Electronic applications accepted. *Expenses: Tuition, area resident:* Full-time $9100. Tuition, state resident: full-time $9100. Tuition, nonresident: full-time $19,200. *Required fees:* $1890; $130. *Financial support:* Teaching assistantships, Federal Work-Study, scholarships/grants, and unspecified assistantships available. Support available to part-time students. Financial award application deadline: 3/1; financial award applicants required to submit FAFSA. *Unit head:* Dr. Jodie Winship, Chair of College of Education, 205-652-5415, Fax: 205-652-3706, E-mail: jwinship@uwa.edu. *Application contact:* Dr. B. J. Kimbrough, Dean of Graduate Studies, 205-652-3647, Fax: 205-652-3670, E-mail: bkimbrough@uwa.edu.

University of Wisconsin–La Crosse, School of Education, La Crosse, WI 54601-3742. Offers English language arts elementary (Graduate Certificate); professional development in education (ME-PD); reading (MS Ed); special education (MS Ed). *Program availability:* Part-time, evening/weekend. *Entrance requirements:* For master's, GRE. Additional exam requirements/recommendations for international students: Required—TOEFL (minimum score 550 paper-based; 79 iBT). Electronic applications accepted.

University of Wisconsin–Milwaukee, Graduate School, College of Letters and Science, Department of English, Milwaukee, WI 53201-0413. Offers English (MA, PhD), including creative writing, English language and linguistics, English secondary education, literary and critical studies, literature and cultural theory (PhD), literature and language studies, literature, culture, and media, media, cinema and digital studies, professional and technical communication (MA), professional and technical writing, professional writing (PhD), rhetoric and composition (PhD), rhetoric and writing. *Students:* 82 full-time (46 women), 44 part-time (21 women); includes 9 minority (2 American Indian or Alaska Native, non-Hispanic/Latino; 3 Asian, non-Hispanic/Latino; 1 Hispanic/Latino; 3 Two or more races, non-Hispanic/Latino), 11 international. Average age 34. 161 applicants, 27% accepted, 32 enrolled. In 2018, 13 master's, 9 doctorates awarded. *Degree requirements:* For master's, thesis or alternative; for doctorate, one foreign language, thesis/dissertation. *Entrance requirements:* For master's, GRE General Test, GRE Subject Test; for doctorate, GRE. Additional exam requirements/recommendations for international students: Required—TOEFL (minimum score 550 paper-based; 79 iBT), IELTS (minimum score 6.5). *Application deadline:* For fall admission, 1/1 priority date for domestic students; for spring admission, 9/1 for domestic students. Application fee: $56 ($96 for international students). Electronic applications accepted. *Financial support:* Fellowships, research assistantships, teaching assistantships, career-related internships or fieldwork, unspecified assistantships, and project assistantships available. Support available to part-time students. Financial award application deadline: 4/15; financial award applicants required to submit FAFSA. *Unit head:* Mark Netzloff, Department Chair, 414-229-4511, E-mail: netzloff@uwm.edu. *Application contact:* General Information Contact, 414-229-4982, Fax: 414-229-6967, E-mail: gradschool@uwm.edu.
Website: https://uwm.edu/english/

University of Wisconsin–Milwaukee, Graduate School, School of Education, Department of Curriculum and Instruction, Milwaukee, WI 53201-0413. Offers curriculum and instruction (MS), including cross-curricular focus, early childhood education, English education, mathematics education, middle childhood/early adolescence education, reading education, science education, urban social studies education. *Program availability:* Part-time. *Students:* 19 full-time (15 women), 56 part-time (49 women); includes 15 minority (3 Black or African American, non-Hispanic/Latino; 1 American Indian or Alaska Native, non-Hispanic/Latino; 3 Asian, non-Hispanic/Latino; 1 Hispanic/Latino; 7 Two or more races, non-Hispanic/Latino), 2 international. Average age 33. 27 applicants, 44% accepted, 11 enrolled. In 2018, 20 master's awarded. *Entrance requirements:* Additional exam requirements/recommendations for international students: Required—TOEFL (minimum score 550 paper-based; 79 iBT), IELTS (minimum score 6.5). *Application deadline:* For fall admission, 1/1 priority date for domestic students; for spring admission, 9/1 for domestic students. Application fee: $56 ($96 for international students). Electronic applications accepted. *Financial support:* Fellowships, research assistantships, teaching assistantships, career-related internships or fieldwork, health care benefits, unspecified assistantships, and project assistantships available. Support available to part-time students. Financial award application deadline: 4/15; financial award applicants required to submit FAFSA. *Application contact:* General Information Contact, 414-229-4721, E-mail: soeinfo@uwm.edu.
Website: http://uwm.edu/education/academics/curriculum-instruction-department/

University of Wisconsin–Stevens Point, College of Letters and Science, Department of English, Stevens Point, WI 54481-3897. Offers MST. *Degree requirements:* For master's, thesis or alternative.

Valdosta State University, Department of English, Valdosta, GA 31698. Offers English (MA); English studies for language arts teachers (MA). *Program availability:* Part-time, 100% online, blended/hybrid learning. *Degree requirements:* For master's, one foreign language, thesis, comprehensive written and/or oral exams. *Entrance requirements:* For master's, GRE General Test, minimum GPA of 3.0. Additional exam requirements/recommendations for international students: Required—TOEFL (minimum score 523 paper-based); Recommended—IELTS. Electronic applications accepted. *Expenses:* Contact institution. *Faculty research:* American literature, creative writing.

Valley City State University, Online Graduate Programs, Valley City, ND 58072. Offers elementary education (M Ed); English education (M Ed); library and information technologies (M Ed); teaching (MAT); teaching and technology (M Ed); teaching English language learners (M Ed); technology education (M Ed). *Accreditation:* NCATE. *Program availability:* Part-time, evening/weekend, online only, 100% online. *Faculty:* 20 full-time (11 women), 13 part-time/adjunct (8 women). *Students:* 5 full-time (2 women), 133 part-time (100 women); includes 8 minority (1 Black or African American, non-Hispanic/Latino; 3 American Indian or Alaska Native, non-Hispanic/Latino; 2 Asian, non-Hispanic/Latino; 2 Hispanic/Latino). Average age 36. 23 applicants, 74% accepted, 12 enrolled. In 2018, 47 master's awarded. *Degree requirements:* For master's, action research report, comprehensive portfolio. *Entrance requirements:* For master's, GRE, MAT, PRAXIS II or National Teaching Board for Professional Standards (if GPA is less than 3.0). Additional exam requirements/recommendations for international students: Required—TOEFL (minimum score 525 paper-based; 71 iBT); Recommended—IELTS (minimum score 5.5). *Application deadline:* For fall admission, 7/26 for domestic and international students; for spring admission, 12/13 for domestic and international students; for summer admission, 5/18 for domestic and international students. Applications are processed on a rolling basis. Application fee: $35. Electronic applications accepted. *Expenses:* $396.39 per credit for all students regardless of residency. *Financial support:* In 2018–19, 16 students received support. Scholarships/grants, tuition waivers (full and partial), and unspecified assistantships available. Financial award applicants required to submit FAFSA. *Faculty research:* Universal accessibility, instructional design and technology, gender communication, STEM education in K-12, English language learners. *Unit head:* Dr. Sheri Okland, Dean, 701-845-7184, E-mail: sheri.l.okland@vcsu.edu. *Application contact:* Misty Lindgren, Graduate Studies, 701-845-7303, Fax: 701-845-7190, E-mail: misty.lindgren@vcsu.edu.
Website: http://www.vcsu.edu/graduate

Vanderbilt University, Peabody College, Department of Teaching and Learning, Nashville, TN 37240-1001. Offers elementary education (M Ed); English language learners (M Ed); reading education (M Ed); secondary education (M Ed). *Accreditation:* NCATE. *Program availability:* Part-time. *Faculty:* 47 full-time (34 women), 19 part-time/adjunct (16 women). *Students:* 122 full-time (99 women), 37 part-time (27 women); includes 34 minority (22 Black or African American, non-Hispanic/Latino; 2 American Indian or Alaska Native, non-Hispanic/Latino; 4 Asian, non-Hispanic/Latino; 4 Hispanic/

English Education

Latino; 2 Two or more races, non-Hispanic/Latino), 41 international. Average age 26. 359 applicants, 74% accepted, 106 enrolled. In 2018, 113 master's awarded. *Degree requirements:* For master's, comprehensive exam, thesis optional. *Entrance requirements:* For master's, GRE General Test, MAT. Additional exam requirements/recommendations for international students: Required—TOEFL (minimum score 550 paper-based; 80 iBT). *Application deadline:* For fall admission, 12/31 priority date for domestic and international students; for spring admission, 11/1 priority date for domestic and international students. Applications are processed on a rolling basis. Application fee: $0. Electronic applications accepted. *Expenses: Tuition:* Full-time $47,208; part-time $2026 per credit hour. *Required fees:* $478. *Financial support:* Fellowships with partial tuition reimbursements, research assistantships with partial tuition reimbursements, teaching assistantships with partial tuition reimbursements, Federal Work-Study, institutionally sponsored loans, scholarships/grants, tuition waivers (partial), and unspecified assistantships available. Support available to part-time students. Financial award application deadline: 1/15; financial award applicants required to submit FAFSA. *Faculty research:* Literacy education; science education; math education; learning sciences; diversity studies. *Unit head:* Dr. Deborah Rowe, Chair, 615-322-8100, Fax: 615-322-8999, E-mail: deborah.w.rowe@vanderbilt.edu. *Application contact:* Angela Saylor, Educational Coordinator, 615-322-8092, Fax: 615-322-8999, E-mail: angela.saylor@vanderbilt.edu.

Wagner College, Division of Graduate Studies, Education Department, Program in Secondary Education/Students with Disabilities, Staten Island, NY 10301-4495. Offers secondary education 7-12 (MS Ed), including language arts, languages other than English, mathematics and technology, science and technology, social studies. *Program availability:* Evening/weekend. *Degree requirements:* For master's, thesis (for some programs), completion of state certification exams before student teaching. *Entrance requirements:* For master's, GRE, minimum GPA of 3.0, interview, recommendations. Additional exam requirements/recommendations for international students: Required—TOEFL (minimum score 550 paper-based; 79 iBT), IELTS (minimum score 6.5). Electronic applications accepted. *Expenses:* Contact institution.

Wayland Baptist University, Graduate Programs, Program in Education, Plainview, TX 79072-6998. Offers education administration (M Ed); education diagnostics (M Ed); education literacy (M Ed); elementary certification (M Ed); English (M Ed); English as a second language (M Ed); higher education administration (M Ed); human resources (M Ed); instructional leadership (M Ed); instructional technology (M Ed); leadership training and development (M Ed); science education (M Ed); secondary certification (M Ed); social studies (M Ed); special education (M Ed); sports administration and management (M Ed). *Program availability:* Part-time, evening/weekend, 100% online. *Degree requirements:* For master's, comprehensive exam, capstone course. *Entrance requirements:* For master's, GRE, GMAT or MAT. Additional exam requirements/recommendations for international students: Required—TOEFL (minimum score 500 paper-based; 61 iBT). Electronic applications accepted.

Wayne State College, School of Education and Counseling, Department of Educational Foundations and Leadership, Program in Curriculum and Instruction, Wayne, NE 68787. Offers alternative education (MSE); business and information technology education (MSE); communication arts education (MSE); early childhood education (MSE); elementary education (MSE); English as a second language (MSE); English education (MSE); family and consumer sciences education (MSE); industrial technology and vocational education (MSE); learning communities (MSE); mathematics education (MSE); music education (MSE); science education (MSE); social science education (MSE). *Accreditation:* NCATE. *Program availability:* Part-time, evening/weekend. *Degree requirements:* For master's, comprehensive exam, thesis optional. *Entrance requirements:* For master's, GRE General Test. Additional exam requirements/recommendations for international students: Required—TOEFL (minimum score 550 paper-based).

Wayne State University, College of Education, Division of Teacher Education, Detroit, MI 48202. Offers art education (M Ed); bilingual/bicultural education (Certificate); curriculum and instruction (Ed D, PhD, Ed S), including English as a second language (MAT, Ed D, Ed S), K-12 curriculum (PhD); elementary education (MAT), including bilingual/bicultural education (M Ed, MAT), early childhood education (M Ed, MAT), English as a second language (MAT, Ed D, Ed S), foreign language education, science education (M Ed, MAT), special education (M Ed, MAT); elementary mathematics specialist (Certificate); English as a second language (Certificate); reading (M Ed, Ed S); reading, language and literature (Ed D); secondary education (MAT), including bilingual/bicultural education (M Ed, MAT), early childhood education (M Ed, MAT), English as a second language (MAT, Ed D, Ed S), English education, foreign language education, mathematics education (M Ed, MAT), science education (M Ed, MAT), social studies education (M Ed, MAT); special education (MAT), including career and technical education; teaching and learning (M Ed), including bilingual/bicultural education (M Ed, MAT), early childhood education (M Ed, MAT), elementary education, foreign language, mathematics education (M Ed, MAT), science education (M Ed, MAT), social studies education (M Ed, MAT), special education (M Ed, MAT). *Program availability:* Part-time, evening/weekend. *Faculty:* 20. *Students:* 121 full-time (94 women), 251 part-time (209 women); includes 116 minority (83 Black or African American, non-Hispanic/Latino; 3 American Indian or Alaska Native, non-Hispanic/Latino; 3 Asian, non-Hispanic/Latino; 14 Hispanic/Latino; 13 Two or more races, non-Hispanic/Latino), 11 international. Average age 37. 171 applicants, 23% accepted, 32 enrolled. In 2018, 112 master's, 8 doctorates, 11 other advanced degrees awarded. *Degree requirements:* For master's, thesis (for some programs), essay or project (for some M Ed programs), professional field experience (for MAT programs); for doctorate, comprehensive exam, thesis/dissertation. *Entrance requirements:* For master's, undergraduate degree, verification of participation in group work with children, Michigan State Police criminal background check, negative tb test, personal statement (for MAT programs); for all other master's programs: undergraduate degree, personal statement; for doctorate, minimum undergraduate GPA of 3.0, graduate 3.5; interview; curriculum vitae; references; writing sample; letter of application; master's degree (for most programs); for other advanced degree, education specialist certificate: undergraduate with GPA of 2.5 or better and master's degree with GPA of 2.75 or better; personal statement. Additional exam requirements/recommendations for international students: Required—TOEFL (minimum score 550 paper-based; 79 iBT); Recommended—IELTS (minimum score 6.5), TWE (minimum score 5.5), TSE (minimum score 58). *Application deadline:* Applications are processed on a rolling basis. Application fee: $50. Electronic applications accepted. *Financial support:* In 2018–19, 85 students received support, including 3 fellowships (averaging $14,275 per year); research assistantships with tuition reimbursements available, Federal Work-Study, scholarships/grants, and unspecified assistantships also available. Support available to part-time students. Financial award applicants required to submit FAFSA. *Faculty research:* Improving students' skill achievement in mathematics, improving elementary children's understanding of informational text, teachers' use of their pedagogical and mathematical knowledge in the interactive work of teaching, the intersection of identity construction in teaching and learning, identifying effective methods of literacy instruction and assessments for bilingual students in elementary language arts classrooms. *Unit head:* Dr. Roland Coloma, Assistant Dean for Teacher Education, 313-577-0902, E-mail: rscoloma@wayne.edu. *Application contact:* Dr. Mary L. Waker, Graduate Admissions Officer, 313-577-1601, Fax: 313-577-7904, E-mail: m.waker@wayne.edu.
Website: http://coe.wayne.edu/ted/index.php

West Chester University of Pennsylvania, College of Arts and Humanities, Department of English, West Chester, PA 19383. Offers English (MA), including creative writing, literature, writing, teaching, and criticism; publishing (Certificate); secondary English (Teaching Certificate). *Program availability:* Part-time, evening/weekend. *Degree requirements:* For master's, thesis optional; for other advanced degree, capstone internship and e-portfolio (for Certificate in publishing). *Entrance requirements:* For master's, minimum GPA of 2.8, two letters of recommendation, writing sample, goals statement, official transcripts; for other advanced degree, two letters of recommendation, statement of goals, official transcripts; undergraduate degree (for Certificate); minimum GPA of 2.85 and writing sample (for Teaching Certificate). Additional exam requirements/recommendations for international students: Required—TOEFL or IELTS. Electronic applications accepted. *Faculty research:* Critical theory, cultural studies, literature, rhetoric and composition, creative writing.

Western Governors University, Teachers College, Salt Lake City, UT 84107. Offers curriculum and instruction (MS); educational leadership (MS); elementary education (MAT, Postbaccalaureate Certificate); English education (5-12) (MAT); English language learning (PreK-12) (MA); instructional design (M Ed); learning and technology (M Ed); mathematics (5-12) (MAT); mathematics (5-9) (MAT); mathematics education (5-12) (MA); mathematics education (5-9) (MA); mathematics education (K-6) (MA); science (5-12) (MAT); science education (5-12) (MA), including biology, chemistry, earth science, physics; science education (5-9) (MA); special education (MS). *Accreditation:* NCATE. *Program availability:* Evening/weekend, online learning. *Degree requirements:* For master's, capstone project. *Entrance requirements:* For master's and Postbaccalaureate Certificate, transcripts. Additional exam requirements/recommendations for international students: Required—TOEFL (minimum score 450 paper-based; 80 iBT). Electronic applications accepted. Application fee is waived when completed online. *Expenses:* Contact institution.

Western Kentucky University, Graduate School, Potter College of Arts and Letters, Department of English, Bowling Green, KY 42101. Offers education (MA); English (MA Ed); literature (MA), including American literature, British literature, literary theory, women writers, world literature; teaching English as a second language (MA); writing (MA). *Program availability:* Part-time, evening/weekend. *Degree requirements:* For master's, comprehensive exam, thesis optional, final exam. *Entrance requirements:* For master's, GRE General Test, minimum GPA of 2.75. Additional exam requirements/recommendations for international students: Required—TOEFL (minimum score 555 paper-based; 79 iBT). *Faculty research:* Improving writing, linking teacher knowledge and performance, Victorian women writers, Kentucky women writers, Kentucky poets.

Western Michigan University, Graduate College, College of Arts and Sciences, Department of English, Kalamazoo, MI 49008. Offers creative writing (MFA, PhD); English (MA, PhD); English teaching (MA). *Degree requirements:* For doctorate, one foreign language, thesis/dissertation.

Western New England University, College of Arts and Sciences, Program in English for Teachers, Springfield, MA 01119. Offers MAET. *Program availability:* Part-time, evening/weekend. *Faculty:* 10 full-time (6 women). *Students:* 9 part-time (7 women). Average age 33. 15 applicants, 100% accepted, 11 enrolled. In 2018, 15 master's awarded. *Entrance requirements:* For master's, two letters of recommendation, official transcript, personal statement, resume; provisional or standard state teaching certificate (preferred). Additional exam requirements/recommendations for international students: Required—TOEFL (minimum score 79 iBT). *Application deadline:* Applications are processed on a rolling basis. Application fee: $30. Electronic applications accepted. *Expenses:* Contact institution. *Financial support:* Application deadline: 4/15; applicants required to submit FAFSA. *Unit head:* Dr. Saeed Ghahramani, Dean, 413-782-1218, Fax: 413-796-2118, E-mail: sghahram@wne.edu. *Application contact:* Matthew Fox, Executive Director of Graduate Admissions, 413-782-1410, Fax: 413-782-1777, E-mail: study@wne.edu. Website: http://www1.wne.edu/academics/graduate/ma-english-teachers.cfm

West Virginia University, College of Education and Human Services, Morgantown, WV 26506. Offers audiology (Au D); autism spectrum disorder (MA); clinical rehabilitation and mental health counseling (MS); communication science and disorders (PhD); counseling (MA); counseling psychology (PhD); curriculum and instruction (Ed D); early childhood education (MA); early intervention/ early childhood special education (MA); education (PhD); educational leadership (MA); educational leadership/ public school administration (Ed D); educational leadership/public school administration (MA); educational psychology (MA, Ed D); elementary education (MA); gifted education (MA); higher education administration (MA, Ed D); higher education curriculum and teaching (MA); institutional design and technology (MA); instructional design and technology (Ed D); literacy education (MA); secondary education (MA); secondary education/English (MA); special education (Ed D); speech pathology (MS). *Accreditation:* ASHA; NCATE. *Program availability:* Part-time, evening/weekend, online learning. *Students:* 392 full-time (325 women), 337 part-time (285 women); includes 44 minority (16 Black or African American, non-Hispanic/Latino; 16 Hispanic/Latino; 12 Two or more races, non-Hispanic/Latino), 11 international. In 2018, 303 master's, 6 doctorates awarded. *Degree requirements:* For master's, content exams; for doctorate, comprehensive exam, thesis/dissertation. *Entrance requirements:* Additional exam requirements/recommendations for international students: Required—TOEFL (minimum score 500 paper-based; 61 iBT). *Application deadline:* For fall admission, 8/1 for domestic students; for spring admission, 1/1 for domestic students; for summer admission, 5/1 for domestic students. Application fee: $60. Electronic applications accepted. *Financial support:* Fellowships, research assistantships, teaching assistantships, career-related internships or fieldwork, Federal Work-Study, institutionally sponsored loans, health care benefits, tuition waivers (full and partial), and administrative assistantships available. Financial award applicants required to submit FAFSA. *Faculty research:* Internet training and integration for teachers, rural education, teacher preparation, organization of schools, evaluation of personnel. *Unit head:* Dr. Tracy L. Morris, Interim Dean, 304-293-0816, Fax: 304-293-7565, E-mail: Tracy.Morris@mail.wvu.edu. *Application contact:* Dr. Melissa Luna, Associate Dean for Research, 304-293-2174, Fax: 304-293-3802, E-mail: Melissa.Luna@mail.wvu.edu. Website: http://cehs.wvu.edu/

Widener University, School of Human Service Professions, Center for Education, Chester, PA 19013-5792. Offers adult education (M Ed); counseling in higher education (M Ed); counselor education (M Ed); early childhood education (M Ed); educational foundations (M Ed); educational leadership (M Ed); educational psychology (M Ed); elementary education (M Ed); English and language arts (M Ed); health education (M Ed); higher education leadership (Ed D); home and school visitor (M Ed); human sexuality (M Ed, PhD); mathematics education (M Ed); middle school education (M Ed); principalship (M Ed); reading and language arts (Ed D); reading education (M Ed); school administration (Ed D); science education (M Ed); social studies education (M Ed); special education (M Ed); technology education (M Ed). *Accreditation:* NCATE. *Program availability:* Part-time, evening/weekend. Terminal master's awarded for partial completion of doctoral program. *Degree requirements:* For doctorate, thesis/dissertation. *Entrance requirements:* For master's, minimum GPA of 2.5; for doctorate, GRE or MAT, minimum GPA of 2.0 (undergraduate), 3.5 (graduate). Electronic applications accepted. *Expenses:* Contact institution. *Faculty research:* Reading and cognition, adult education, technology education, educational leadership, special education.

William Carey University, School of Education, Hattiesburg, MS 39401. Offers art education (M Ed); art of teaching (M Ed); elementary education (M Ed, Ed S); English education (M Ed); gifted education (M Ed); history and social science (M Ed); mild/moderate disabilities (M Ed); secondary education (M Ed). *Accreditation:* NCATE. *Program availability:* Part-time. *Degree requirements:* For master's, comprehensive exam. *Entrance requirements:* For master's, GRE, MAT, minimum GPA of 2.5, Class A teacher's license. Additional exam requirements/recommendations for international students: Required—TOEFL (minimum score 550 paper-based).

William Jessup University, Program in Teaching, Rocklin, CA 95765. Offers single subject English (MAT); single subject math (MAT). *Program availability:* Evening/weekend.

Worcester State University, Graduate School, Program in English, Worcester, MA 01602-2597. Offers MA. *Program availability:* Part-time, evening/weekend. *Faculty:* 4 full-time (2 women). *Students:* 1 (woman) full-time, 8 part-time (6 women); includes 1 minority (Two or more races, non-Hispanic/Latino). Average age 48. 4 applicants, 100% accepted, 3 enrolled. In 2018, 2 master's awarded. *Degree requirements:* For master's, comprehensive exam, thesis, For a detail list in Degree Completion requirements please see the graduate catalog at catalog.worcester.edu. *Entrance requirements:* For master's, GRE General Test or MAT, For a detail list of entrance requirements please see the graduate catalog at catalog.worcester.edu. Additional exam requirements/recommendations for international students: Required—TOEFL (minimum score 550 paper-based; 79 iBT), IELTS (minimum score 6). *Application deadline:* For fall admission, 3/1 for domestic and international students; for spring admission, 11/1 for domestic and international students; for summer admission, 3/1 for domestic and international students. Applications are processed on a rolling basis. Application fee: $50. Electronic applications accepted. *Expenses: Tuition, area resident:* Full-time $3042; part-time $169 per credit hour. Tuition, state resident: full-time $3042; part-time $169 per credit hour. Tuition, nonresident: full-time $3042; part-time $169 per credit hour. *International tuition:* $3042 full-time. *Required fees:* $2754; $153 per credit hour. *Financial support:* Career-related internships or fieldwork, scholarships/grants, and unspecified assistantships available. Financial award application deadline: 3/1; financial award applicants required to submit FAFSA. *Unit head:* Dr. Donald Vescio, Program Coordinator, 508-929-8444, Fax: 508-929-8174, E-mail: dvescio@worcester.edu. *Application contact:* Sara Grady, Associate Dean, Graduate Studies and Professional Development, 508-929-8130, Fax: 508-929-8100, E-mail: sara.grady@worcester.edu.

Environmental Education

Alaska Pacific University, Graduate Programs, Environmental Science Department, Program in Outdoor and Environmental Education, Anchorage, AK 99508-4672. Offers MSOEE. *Program availability:* Part-time. *Degree requirements:* For master's, thesis. *Entrance requirements:* For master's, MAT or GRE, minimum GPA of 3.0. Additional exam requirements/recommendations for international students: Required—TOEFL (minimum score 550 paper-based).

Antioch University New England, Graduate School, Department of Environmental Studies, Program in Environmental Education, Keene, NH 03431-3552. Offers MS. *Degree requirements:* For master's, practicum. *Entrance requirements:* For master's, previous undergraduate course work in biology, chemistry, and mathematics; resume; 3 letters of recommendation. Additional exam requirements/recommendations for international students: Required—TOEFL (minimum score 550 paper-based). Electronic applications accepted. *Expenses:* Contact institution. *Faculty research:* Sustainability, natural resources inventory.

Arcadia University, School of Education, Glenside, PA 19038-3295. Offers art education (M Ed); computer education (CAS); curriculum (CAS); curriculum studies (M Ed); early childhood education (M Ed), including individualized, master teacher, research in child development; educational leadership (M Ed, Ed D, CAS); elementary education (M Ed); English education (MA Ed); environmental education (MA Ed); instructional technology (M Ed); language arts (M Ed); library science (M Ed); mathematics education (M Ed, MA Ed); music education (MA Ed); psychology (MA Ed); reading (M Ed, CAS); science education (M Ed, CAS); secondary education (M Ed, CAS); special education (M Ed, Ed D, CAS); theater arts (MA Ed); written communication (MA Ed). *Accreditation:* NASAD. *Program availability:* Part-time, evening/weekend, online learning. *Faculty:* 14 full-time (10 women). *Students:* 35 full-time (24 women), 299 part-time (243 women); includes 72 minority (49 Black or African American, non-Hispanic/Latino; 1 American Indian or Alaska Native, non-Hispanic/Latino; 12 Asian, non-Hispanic/Latino; 8 Hispanic/Latino; 2 Two or more races, non-Hispanic/Latino), 5 international. In 2018, 152 master's, 8 doctorates awarded. *Entrance requirements:* Additional exam requirements/recommendations for international students: Required—Official results from the TOEFL or IELTS are required. *Application deadline:* Applications are processed on a rolling basis. Application fee: $25. Electronic applications accepted. *Expenses:* Contact institution. *Financial support:* Career-related internships or fieldwork, tuition waivers (partial), and unspecified assistantships available. *Unit head:* Kimberly Dean, Chair, 215-572-8629. *Application contact:* 215-572-2925, Fax: 215-572-2126, E-mail: grad@arcadia.edu.

Ball State University, Graduate School, College of Sciences and Humanities, Department of Natural Resources and Environmental Management, Muncie, IN 47306. Offers emergency management and homeland security (Certificate); natural resources and environmental management (MA, MS). *Program availability:* Part-time. *Degree requirements:* For master's, thesis (for some programs). *Entrance requirements:* For master's, GRE General Test, minimum baccalaureate GPA of 2.75 or 3.0 in latter half of baccalaureate, two letters of reference. Additional exam requirements/recommendations for international students: Required—TOEFL (minimum score 550 paper-based; 79 iBT), IELTS (minimum score 6.5). Electronic applications accepted. *Faculty research:* Acid rain, indoor air pollution, land reclamation.

Brooklyn College of the City University of New York, School of Education, Program in Childhood Education, Brooklyn, NY 11210-2889. Offers bilingual education (MS Ed); liberal arts (MS Ed); mathematics (MS Ed); science and environmental education (MS Ed). *Program availability:* Part-time, evening/weekend. *Entrance requirements:* For master's, LAST, interview, previous course work in education, writing sample, resume, 2 letters of recommendation. Additional exam requirements/recommendations for international students: Required—TOEFL (minimum score 500 paper-based; 61 iBT). Electronic applications accepted. *Faculty research:* Emotional intelligence, multiculturalism, arts immersion, the Holocaust.

Chatham University, Program in Education, Pittsburgh, PA 15232-2826. Offers early childhood education (MAT); elementary education (MAT); environmental education (K-12) (MAT); secondary art (MAT); secondary biology education (MAT); secondary chemistry education (MAT); secondary English education (MAT); secondary math education (MAT); secondary physics education (MAT); secondary social studies education (MAT); special education (MAT). *Degree requirements:* For master's, thesis, teaching experience. *Entrance requirements:* For master's, minimum GPA of 3.0, sample of written work, recommendation letters. Additional exam requirements/recommendations for international students: Required—TOEFL (minimum score 600 paper-based; 100 iBT), IELTS (minimum score 7), TWE. Electronic applications accepted. Application fee is waived when completed online. *Faculty research:* Gifted education, environmental education, technology in education, writing as learning, class size and achievement.

Concordia University, College of Education, Portland, OR 97211-6099. Offers administrative leadership (Ed D); career and technical education (M Ed); curriculum and instruction (M Ed), including adolescent literacy, early childhood education, educational technology leadership, English for speakers of other languages, environmental education, health and physical education, mathematics, methods and curriculum, reading interventionist, science, social studies, STEAM education, teacher leadership, the inclusive classroom, trauma and resilience in educational settings; educational administration (M Ed); educational leadership (M Ed); elementary education (MAT); higher education (Ed D); instructional leadership (Ed D); professional leadership, inquiry, and transformation (Ed D); secondary education (MAT); transformational leadership (Ed D). *Program availability:* Part-time, online learning. *Degree requirements:* For master's, comprehensive exam, work samples/portfolio. *Entrance requirements:* For master's, California Basic Educational Skills Test or PRAXIS I, minimum undergraduate GPA of 2.8, graduate 3.0; 2 letters of recommendation. Additional exam requirements/recommendations for international students: Required—TOEFL (minimum score 525 paper-based). Electronic applications accepted. *Faculty research:* Learner-centered classroom, brain-based learning, future of online learning.

Concordia University Wisconsin, Graduate Programs, School of Education, Mequon, WI 53097-2402. Offers art education (MS Ed); early childhood (MS Ed); educational administration (MS Ed); environmental education (MS Ed); family studies (MS Ed); literacy (MS Ed); school counseling (MS Ed); special education (MS Ed). *Program availability:* Part-time, evening/weekend, online learning. *Degree requirements:* For master's, comprehensive exam, thesis or alternative. *Entrance requirements:* For master's, minimum GPA of 3.0, teaching license. Additional exam requirements/recommendations for international students: Required—TOEFL. *Faculty research:* Motivation, developmental learning, learning styles.

Florida Atlantic University, College of Education, Department of Teaching and Learning, Boca Raton, FL 33431-0991. Offers elementary education (M Ed); environmental education (M Ed); instructional technology (M Ed); reading education (M Ed); secondary education (M Ed). *Accreditation:* NCATE. *Program availability:* Part-time, evening/weekend. *Faculty:* 16 full-time (12 women), 1 part-time/adjunct (0 women). *Students:* 30 full-time (21 women), 45 part-time (36 women); includes 27 minority (14 Black or African American, non-Hispanic/Latino; 3 Asian, non-Hispanic/Latino; 8 Hispanic/Latino; 2 Two or more races, non-Hispanic/Latino), 6 international. Average age 30. 71 applicants, 58% accepted, 28 enrolled. In 2018, 23 master's awarded. *Entrance requirements:* For master's, GRE General Test, minimum GPA of 3.0 in last 2 years of undergraduate course work. Additional exam requirements/recommendations for international students: Required—TOEFL (minimum score 500 paper-based; 61 iBT), IELTS (minimum score 6). *Application deadline:* For fall admission, 7/1 for domestic students, 2/15 for international students; for spring admission, 11/1 for domestic students, 7/15 for international students. Applications are processed on a rolling basis. Application fee: $30. *Expenses: Tuition, area resident:* Full-time $7400; part-time $369.82 per credit. Tuition, state resident: full-time $7400; part-time $369.82 per credit. Tuition, nonresident: full-time $20,496; part-time $1024.81 per credit. *Financial support:* Fellowships with partial tuition reimbursements, research assistantships with partial tuition reimbursements, teaching assistantships with partial tuition reimbursements, career-related internships or fieldwork, scholarships/grants, and unspecified assistantships available. *Faculty research:* Technology, teaching English to speakers of other languages, math teaching, electronic portfolio assessment, global perspectives through social studies. *Unit head:* Dr. Barbara Ridener, Chairperson, 561-297-3588, E-mail: bridener@fau.edu. *Application contact:* Dr. Debora Shepherd, Associate Dean, 561-296-3570, E-mail: dshep@fau.edu.
Website: http://www.coe.fau.edu/academicdepartments/tl/

Goshen College, Merry Lea Environmental Learning Center, Goshen, IN 46526-4794. Offers MA. *Accreditation:* NCATE. *Degree requirements:* For master's, thesis. *Entrance requirements:* For master's, resume, official transcripts, three letters of reference. Additional exam requirements/recommendations for international students: Required—TOEFL (minimum score 600 paper-based; 100 iBT), IELTS (minimum score 6.5). Electronic applications accepted. *Faculty research:* Environmental education, climate change, climate justice, landscape ecology, invasive species.

Hamline University, School of Education, St. Paul, MN 55104-1284. Offers education (MA Ed, Ed D); English as a second language (MA); literacy education (MA); natural science and environmental education (MA Ed); teaching (MAT); teaching English to speakers of other languages (MA). *Accreditation:* NCATE (one or more programs are accredited). *Program availability:* Part-time, evening/weekend, 100% online, blended/hybrid learning. *Degree requirements:* For master's, thesis (for some programs), thesis or capstone project; for doctorate, comprehensive exam, thesis/dissertation. *Entrance requirements:* For master's, official transcripts, essay, letters of recommendation, minimum GPA of 3.0 from bachelor's work; resume and/or writing samples (for some programs); for doctorate, personal statement, master's degree with minimum GPA of 3.0, letters of recommendation, writing sample. Additional exam requirements/recommendations for international students: Required—TOEFL (minimum score 550 paper-based; 80 iBT), IELTS (minimum score 6.5). Electronic applications accepted. *Expenses:* Contact institution. *Faculty research:* Adult basic education, service-learning, teacher dispositions, diversity, technology.

Instituto Tecnologico de Santo Domingo, Graduate School, Area of Basic And Environmental Sciences, Santo Domingo, Dominican Republic. Offers environmental science (M En S), including environmental education, environmental management, marine resources, natural resources management; mathematics (MS, PhD); renewable energy technology (MS, Certificate).

Mary Baldwin University, Graduate Studies, Programs in Education, Staunton, VA 24401-3610. Offers applied behavior analysis (MS); autism spectrum disorders (M Ed); elementary education (M Ed, MAT); English as a second language (M Ed); environment-based learning (M Ed); gifted education (M Ed); higher education (MS); leadership (M Ed); middle grades education (MAT); reading education (M Ed); special education (M Ed). *Accreditation:* TEAC.

Montclair State University, The Graduate School, College of Science and Mathematics, Program in Environmental Studies, Montclair, NJ 07043-1624. Offers environmental education (MA); environmental management (MA); environmental science (MA). *Program availability:* Part-time, evening/weekend. *Degree requirements:* For master's, thesis. *Entrance requirements:* For master's, GRE General Test, 2 letters of recommendation, essay. Additional exam requirements/recommendations for international students: Required—TOEFL (minimum score 83 iBT), IELTS (minimum score 6.5). Electronic applications accepted. *Faculty research:* Environmental geochemistry/remediation/forensics, environmental law and policy, regional climate modeling, remote sensing, Cenozoic marine sediment records from polar regions, sustainability science.

New York University, Steinhardt School of Culture, Education, and Human Development, Department of Teaching and Learning, Program in Environmental Conservation Education, New York, NY 10012. Offers MA. *Accreditation:* TEAC. *Program availability:* Part-time. *Entrance requirements:* Additional exam requirements/recommendations for international students: Required—TOEFL (minimum score 100 iBT). Electronic applications accepted. *Faculty research:* Environmental ethics, values and policy, philosophy and geography.

Oregon State University, Interdisciplinary/Institutional Programs, Program in Environmental Sciences, Corvallis, OR 97331. Offers biogeochemistry (MA, MS, PSM, PhD); ecology (MA, MS, PSM, PhD); environmental education (MA, MS, PhD); quantitative analysis (PSM); social science (MA, MS, PSM, PhD); water resources (MA, MS, PhD). *Program availability:* Part-time. *Degree requirements:* For master's, variable foreign language requirement, thesis; for doctorate, thesis/dissertation. *Entrance requirements:* For master's and doctorate, GRE. Additional exam requirements/recommendations for international students: Required—TOEFL (minimum score 80 iBT), IELTS (minimum score 6.5).

Prescott College, Graduate Programs, Program in Education, Prescott, AZ 86301. Offers early childhood education (MA); early childhood special education (MA); education (MA); elementary education (MA); environmental education leadership and administration (MA); equine-assisted learning (MA); school guidance counseling (MA); secondary education (MA); special education: learning disabilities (MA); special education: mental retardation (MA); special education: serious emotional disabilities (MA); student-directed independent study (MA); sustainability education (PhD). *Program availability:* Part-time, online learning. *Degree requirements:* For master's, thesis, fieldwork or internship, practicum; for doctorate, thesis/dissertation. *Entrance requirements:* For master's, 2 letters of recommendation, resume; for doctorate, 3 letters of recommendation, resume, official transcripts, personal statement, program proposal. Additional exam requirements/recommendations for international students: Required—TOEFL (minimum score 500 paper-based). Electronic applications accepted.

Royal Roads University, Graduate Studies, Environment and Sustainability Program, Victoria, BC V9B 5Y2, Canada. Offers environment and management (M Sc, MA); environment and sustainability (MAIS); environmental education and communication (MA, G Dip, Graduate Certificate); MA/MS. *Program availability:* Blended/hybrid learning. *Degree requirements:* For master's, thesis. *Entrance requirements:* For master's, 5-7 years of related work experience. Electronic applications accepted. *Expenses: Tuition, area resident:* Full-time $27,000 Canadian dollars. Tuition, state resident: full-time $27,000 Canadian dollars. Tuition, nonresident: full-time $33,000 Canadian dollars. *Required fees:* $662 Canadian dollars. *Faculty research:* Sustainable development, atmospheric processes, sustainable communities, chemical fate and transport of persistent organic pollutants, educational technology.

Slippery Rock University of Pennsylvania, Graduate Studies (Recruitment), College of Health, Environment, and Science, Department of Parks, Conservation and Recreation Therapy, Slippery Rock, PA 16057-1383. Offers environmental education (M Ed); park and resource management (MS). *Program availability:* Part-time, evening/weekend, online only, 100% online. *Faculty:* 2 full-time (1 woman), 2 part-time/adjunct (1 woman). *Students:* 4 full-time (3 women), 69 part-time (44 women); includes 5 minority (1 Black or African American, non-Hispanic/Latino; 3 Hispanic/Latino; 1 Two or more races, non-Hispanic/Latino). Average age 33. 44 applicants, 73% accepted, 20 enrolled. In 2018, 34 master's awarded. *Degree requirements:* For master's, comprehensive exam (for some programs), thesis (for some programs), internship. *Entrance requirements:* For master's, official transcripts, minimum GPA of 2.75, personal statement. Additional exam requirements/recommendations for international students: Required—TOEFL (minimum score 550 paper-based; 80 iBT). *Application deadline:* For fall admission, 3/1 priority date for domestic students, 5/1 priority date for international students; for spring admission, 10/1 priority date for domestic students, 9/1 priority date for international students. Applications are processed on a rolling basis. Application fee: $25 ($30 for international students). Electronic applications accepted. *Expenses:* Contact institution. *Financial support:* In 2018–19, 4 students received support. Career-related internships or fieldwork, Federal Work-Study, institutionally sponsored loans, scholarships/grants, tuition waivers (partial), and unspecified assistantships available. Support available to part-time students. Financial award application deadline: 5/1; financial award applicants required to submit FAFSA. *Unit head:* Dr. John Lisco, Graduate Coordinator, 724-738-2596, Fax: 724-738-2938, E-mail: john.lisco@sru.edu. *Application contact:* Brandi Weber-Mortimer, Director of Graduate Admissions, 724-738-2051, Fax: 724-738-2146, E-mail: graduate.admissions@sru.edu.
Website: http://www.sru.edu/academics/colleges-and-departments/ches/departments/parks-and-recreation

Southern Connecticut State University, School of Graduate Studies, School of Arts and Sciences, Department of Environment, Geography and Marine Sciences, New Haven, CT 06515-1355. Offers environmental education (MS); science education (MS, Diploma). *Accreditation:* NCATE. *Program availability:* Part-time, evening/weekend. *Degree requirements:* For master's, thesis or alternative. *Entrance requirements:* For master's, interview; for Diploma, master's degree. Electronic applications accepted.

Southern Oregon University, Graduate Studies, Program in Environmental Education, Ashland, OR 97520. Offers MS. *Program availability:* Part-time, online learning. *Degree requirements:* For master's, thesis (for some programs), comprehensive exam (for MA). *Entrance requirements:* For master's, GRE General Test, minimum cumulative GPA of 3.0 in the last 90 quarter credits (60 semester credits) of undergraduate coursework. Additional exam requirements/recommendations for international students: Required—TOEFL (minimum score 540 paper-based; 76 iBT), IELTS (minimum score 6), ELPT (minimum score 964) or ELS (minimum score 112). Electronic applications accepted.

State University of New York College at Cortland, Graduate Studies, School of Professional Studies, Department of Recreation, Parks and Leisure Studies, Cortland, NY 13045. Offers outdoor education (MS, MS Ed); recreation management (MS, MS Ed); therapeutic recreation (MS, MS Ed). *Program availability:* Part-time, evening/weekend. *Degree requirements:* For master's, comprehensive exam, thesis (for some programs). *Entrance requirements:* Additional exam requirements/recommendations for international students: Required—TOEFL.

Université du Québec à Montréal, Graduate Programs, Program in Education, Montréal, QC H3C 3P8, Canada. Offers education (M Ed, MA, PhD); education of the environmental sciences (Diploma). PhD offered jointly with Université du Québec à Chicoutimi, Université du Québec à Rimouski, Université du Québec à Trois-Rivières, Université du Québec en Outaouais, and Université du Québec en Abitibi-Témiscamingue. *Program availability:* Part-time. *Degree requirements:* For master's, thesis (for some programs); for doctorate, thesis/dissertation. *Entrance requirements:* For master's and Diploma, appropriate bachelor's degree or equivalent, proficiency in French; for doctorate, appropriate master's degree or equivalent, proficiency in French.

University of Florida, Graduate School, College of Agricultural and Life Sciences, Department of Wildlife Ecology and Conservation, Gainesville, FL 32611. Offers environmental education and communications (Certificate); wildlife ecology and conservation (MS, PhD), including geographic information systems, tropical conservation and development, wetland sciences. *Degree requirements:* For master's, comprehensive exam, thesis optional; for doctorate, comprehensive exam, thesis/dissertation. *Entrance requirements:* For master's and doctorate, GRE General Test (minimum 34th percentile for Quantitative), minimum GPA of 3.3. Additional exam requirements/recommendations for international students: Required—TOEFL (minimum score 550 paper-based; 80 iBT), IELTS (minimum score 6). Electronic applications accepted. *Faculty research:* Conservation biology, spatial ecology, wildlife conservation and management, wetlands ecology and conservation, human dimensions in wildlife conservation.

University of South Africa, College of Human Sciences, Pretoria, South Africa. Offers adult education (M Ed); African languages (MA, PhD); African politics (MA, PhD); Afrikaans (MA, PhD); ancient history (MA, PhD); ancient Near Eastern studies (MA, PhD); anthropology (MA, PhD); applied linguistics (MA); Arabic (MA, PhD); archaeology (MA); art history (MA); Biblical archaeology (MA); Biblical studies (M Th, D Th, PhD); Christian spirituality (M Th, D Th); church history (M Th, D Th); classical studies (MA, PhD); clinical psychology (MA); communication (MA, PhD); comparative education (M Ed, Ed D); consulting psychology (D Admin, D Com, PhD); curriculum studies (M Ed, Ed D); development studies (M Admin, MA, D Admin, PhD); didactics (M Ed, Ed D); education (M Tech); education management (M Ed, Ed D); educational psychology (M Ed); English (MA); environmental education (M Ed); French (MA, PhD); German (MA, PhD); Greek (MA); guidance and counseling (M Ed); health studies (MA, PhD), including health sciences education (MA), health services management (MA), medical and surgical nursing science (critical care general) (MA), midwifery and neonatal nursing science (MA), trauma and emergency care (MA); history (MA, PhD); history of education (Ed D); inclusive education (M Ed, Ed D); information and communications technology policy and regulation (MA); information science (MA, MIS, PhD); international politics (MA, PhD); Islamic studies (MA, PhD); Italian (MA, PhD); Judaica (MA, PhD); linguistics (MA, PhD); mathematical education (M Ed); mathematics education (MA); missiology (M Th, D Th); modern Hebrew (MA, PhD); musicology (MA, MMus, D Mus, PhD); natural science education (M Ed); New Testament (M Th, D Th); Old Testament (D Th); pastoral therapy (M Th, D Th); philosophy (MA); philosophy of education (M Ed, Ed D); politics (MA, PhD); Portuguese (MA, PhD); practical theology (M Th, D Th); psychology (MA, MS, PhD); psychology of education (M Ed, Ed D); public health (MA); religious studies (MA, D Th, PhD); Romance languages (MA); Russian (MA, PhD); Semitic languages (MA, PhD); social behavior studies in HIV/AIDS (MA); social science (mental health) (MA); social science in development studies (MA); social science in psychology (MA); social science in social work (MA); social science in sociology (MA); social work (MSW, DSW, PhD); socio-education (M Ed, Ed D); sociolinguistics (MA); sociology (MA, PhD); Spanish (MA, PhD); systematic theology (M Th, D Th); TESOL (teaching English to speakers of other languages) (MA); theological ethics (M Th, D Th); theory of literature (MA, PhD); urban ministries (D Th); urban ministry (M Th).

University of Victoria, Faculty of Graduate Studies, Faculty of Education, Department of Curriculum and Instruction, Victoria, BC V8W 2Y2, Canada. Offers art education (M Ed, PhD); curriculum studies (M Ed, MA, PhD); early childhood education (M Ed, PhD); educational studies (PhD); language and literacy (M Ed, MA, PhD); mathematics (M Ed, MA, PhD); music education (M Ed, MA, PhD); science (M Ed, MA, PhD); social studies (M Ed, MA); social, cultural and foundational studies (MA, PhD); technology and environmental education (PhD). *Program availability:* Part-time. *Degree requirements:* For master's, thesis, project (M Ed); for doctorate, comprehensive exam, thesis/dissertation. *Entrance requirements:* For master's, minimum B average. Additional exam requirements/recommendations for international students: Required—TOEFL (minimum score 575 paper-based), IELTS (minimum score 7). Electronic applications accepted. *Faculty research:* Elementary and secondary English, language arts, curriculum theory and practice, educational media and technology, educational administration and leadership, history and philosophy of education.

Western Washington University, Graduate School, Huxley College of the Environment, Department of Environmental Studies, Program in Environmental Education, Bellingham, WA 98225-5996. Offers M Ed. *Program availability:* Part-time. *Degree requirements:* For master's, comprehensive exam, thesis optional. *Entrance requirements:* For master's, GRE or MAT, minimum GPA of 3.0 in last 60 semester hours. Additional exam requirements/recommendations for international students: Required—TOEFL (minimum score 567 paper-based). Electronic applications accepted. *Faculty research:* Role of wilderness in national park history; history of the conservation movement and sense of place in environmental education; environmental care and responsibility; conservation psychology and environmental education.

Foreign Languages Education

Andrews University, School of Graduate Studies, School of Education, Department of Teaching, Learning, and Curriculum, Berrien Springs, MI 49104. Offers curriculum and instruction (MA, Ed D, PhD, Ed S); elementary education (MAT); secondary education (MAT), including biology, education, English, English as a second language, French, history, physics; teacher education (MAT). *Entrance requirements:* For master's, GRE Subject Test. Additional exam requirements/recommendations for international students: Required—TOEFL (minimum score 550 paper-based).

Appalachian State University, Cratis D. Williams School of Graduate Studies, Department of Languages, Literatures and Cultures, Boone, NC 28608. Offers romance languages (MA), including French teaching, Spanish teaching. *Program availability:* Part-time, online learning. *Degree requirements:* For master's, one foreign language, comprehensive exam, thesis optional. *Entrance requirements:* For master's, GRE General Test, 3 letters of recommendation. Additional exam requirements/recommendations for international students: Required—TOEFL (minimum score 570 paper-based; 79 iBT) or IELTS (minimum score 6.5). Electronic applications accepted. *Expenses: Tuition, area resident:* Full-time $4839; part-time $237 per credit hour. Tuition, state resident: full-time $4839; part-time $237 per credit hour. Tuition, nonresident: full-time $18,271; part-time $895.50 per credit hour. *Faculty research:* French and Spanish literature, Latin American culture, teaching foreign languages.

Arizona State University at the Tempe campus, College of Liberal Arts and Sciences, School of International Letters and Cultures, Program in Spanish, Tempe, AZ 85287-0202. Offers cultural studies (PhD); linguistics (MA), including second language acquisition/applied linguistics, sociolinguistics; literature (PhD); literature and culture (MA). *Program availability:* Part-time. Terminal master's awarded for partial completion of doctoral program. *Degree requirements:* For master's, thesis, oral defense; written comprehensive exam (literature and culture); portfolio review (linguistics); interactive Program of Study (iPOS) submitted before completing 50 percent of required credit hours; for doctorate, comprehensive exam, thesis/dissertation, interactive Program of Study (iPOS) submitted before completing 50 percent of required credit hours. *Entrance requirements:* For master's, GRE (recommended), BA in Spanish or close equivalent from accredited institution with minimum GPA of 3.5, 3 letters of recommendation, personal statement, academic writing sample; for doctorate, GRE (recommended), MA in Spanish or equivalent from accredited institution with minimum GPA of 3.75, 3 letters of recommendation, personal statement, academic writing sample. Additional exam requirements/recommendations for international students: Required—TOEFL (minimum score 550 paper-based; 83 iBT), IELTS (minimum score 6.5). Electronic applications accepted.

Augusta University, College of Education, Program in Curriculum and Instruction, Augusta, GA 30912. Offers curriculum and instruction (Ed S); elementary education (MAT); foreign language education (MAT); instruction (M Ed); middle grades education (MAT); music education (MAT); secondary education (MAT); special education (MAT). *Degree requirements:* For master's, thesis, portfolio. *Entrance requirements:* For master's, GRE, MAT, minimum GPA of 2.5.

Binghamton University, State University of New York, Graduate School, College of Community and Public Affairs, Department of Teaching, Learning and Educational Leadership, Program in Adolescence Education, Binghamton, NY 13902-6000. Offers biology education (MAT, MS Ed); chemistry education (MAT, MS Ed); earth science education (MAT, MS Ed); English education (MAT, MS Ed); French education (MAT, MS Ed); mathematical sciences education (MAT, MS Ed); physics (MAT, MS Ed); social studies (MAT, MS Ed); Spanish education (MAT, MS Ed). *Accreditation:* TEAC. *Program availability:* Part-time, evening/weekend. *Degree requirements:* For master's, portfolio. *Entrance requirements:* For master's, GRE General Test, teaching certification. Additional exam requirements/recommendations for international students: Required—TOEFL (minimum score 550 paper-based; 80 iBT). Electronic applications accepted.

Boston College, Lynch School of Education and Human Development, Department of Teacher Education, Special Education and Curriculum and Instruction, Chestnut Hill, MA 02467-3800. Offers curriculum and instruction (M Ed, PhD, CAES); early childhood education (M Ed); elementary education (M Ed); law and curriculum and instruction (JD/M Ed); reading specialist (M Ed, CAES); religious education (M Ed, CAES); secondary education (M Ed, MAT, MST), including biology (MST), chemistry (MST), English (MAT), French (MAT), geology (MST), history (MAT), Latin and classical humanities (MAT), mathematics (MST), physics (MST), secondary teaching (M Ed), Spanish (MAT); special needs: moderate disabilities (M Ed, CAES); special needs: severe disabilities (M Ed); JD/M Ed. *Program availability:* Part-time, evening/weekend, 100% online. *Faculty:* 19 full-time (11 women). *Students:* 186 full-time (140 women), 92 part-time (74 women); includes 58 minority (20 Black or African American, non-Hispanic/Latino; 4 Asian, non-Hispanic/Latino; 29 Hispanic/Latino; 5 Two or more races, non-Hispanic/Latino), 33 international. Average age 28. In 2018, 132 master's, 13 doctorates awarded. Terminal master's awarded for partial completion of doctoral program. *Degree requirements:* For master's, comprehensive exam; for doctorate, comprehensive exam, thesis/dissertation. *Entrance requirements:* Additional exam requirements/recommendations for international students: Required—TOEFL. Application fee: $75. Electronic applications accepted. *Financial support:* Fellowships with full and partial tuition reimbursements, research assistantships with full and partial tuition reimbursements, teaching assistantships with full and partial tuition reimbursements, career-related internships or fieldwork, Federal Work-Study, institutionally sponsored loans, scholarships/grants, traineeships, health care benefits, tuition waivers (full and partial), and unspecified assistantships available. Support available to part-time students. Financial award applicants required to submit FAFSA. *Faculty research:* Teacher education, education research and policy, bilingual education, science education, disabilities, urban education. *Unit head:* Dr. Susan Bruce, Chairperson, 617-552-4214, Fax: 617-552-0812. *Application contact:* Jessica Rivers, Assistant Dean of Graduate Admission and Financial Aid, 617-552-4214, Fax: 617-552-0398, E-mail: riversja@bc.edu.
Website: http://www.bc.edu/education

Brandeis University, Graduate School of Arts and Sciences, Teaching Chinese at the College Level, Waltham, MA 02454-9110. Offers MA. *Faculty:* 9 full-time (5 women), 9 part-time/adjunct (all women). *Students:* 7 full-time (6 women); includes 1 minority (Asian, non-Hispanic/Latino), 5 international. Average age 30. 12 applicants, 83% accepted, 7 enrolled. In 2018, 5 master's awarded. *Degree requirements:* For master's, one foreign language. *Entrance requirements:* For master's, transcripts, letters of recommendation, resume, video of teaching in the classroom, statement of purpose. Additional exam requirements/recommendations for international students: Required—TOEFL, IELTS, PTE. *Application deadline:* For fall admission, 1/15 priority date for domestic students. Applications are processed on a rolling basis. Application fee: $75. Electronic applications accepted. *Financial support:* In 2018–19, 4 teaching assistantships (averaging $3,200 per year) were awarded; scholarships/grants also available. *Unit head:* Dr. Yu Feng, Director of Graduate Studies, 781-736-2961, E-mail: yfeng@brandeis.edu. *Application contact:* Dr. Yu Feng, Director of Graduate Studies, 781-736-2961, E-mail: yfeng@brandeis.edu.
Website: http://www.brandeis.edu/gsas/programs/chinese.html

Brigham Young University, Graduate Studies, College of Humanities, Department of Spanish and Portuguese, Provo, UT 84602. Offers Portuguese (MA), including Luso-Brazilian literatures, Portuguese linguistics, Portuguese pedagogy; Spanish (MA), including Hispanic linguistics, Hispanic literatures, Spanish pedagogy. *Faculty:* 31 full-time (6 women). *Students:* 44 full-time (27 women), 13 part-time (6 women); includes 25 minority (1 Black or African American, non-Hispanic/Latino; 1 Asian, non-Hispanic/Latino; 22 Hispanic/Latino; 1 Native Hawaiian or other Pacific Islander, non-Hispanic/Latino). Average age 31. 22 applicants, 59% accepted, 13 enrolled. In 2018, 29 master's awarded. *Degree requirements:* For master's, 2 foreign languages, comprehensive exam, thesis, 1 semester of teaching. *Entrance requirements:* For master's, minimum GPA of 3.5 in Spanish or Portuguese, 3.3 overall. Additional exam requirements/recommendations for international students: Required—TOEFL (minimum score 580 paper-based; 85 iBT), IELTS (minimum score 6), PTE (minimum score 53). *Application deadline:* For fall admission, 2/1 for domestic and international students. Application fee: $50. Electronic applications accepted. *Expenses:* Regular student for the 2 years: $13,728; professional track student total for 3 years: $13,728. *Financial support:* In 2018–19, 35 students received support, including 87 teaching assistantships (averaging $3,400 per year); research assistantships, institutionally sponsored loans, scholarships/grants, tuition waivers (partial), and unspecified assistantships also available. Support available to part-time students. *Faculty research:* Mexican prose; Latin American theater; literature; phonetics, and phonology; pedagogy; classical Portuguese literature. *Unit head:* Dr. Jeffrey S. Turley, Chair, 801-422-7019, Fax: 801-422-0308, E-mail: jeffrey_turley@byu.edu. *Application contact:* Holly A. Price, Graduate Program Manager, 801-422-2196, Fax: 801-422-0308, E-mail: holly_price@byu.edu.
Website: http://spanport.byu.edu/

Brooklyn College of the City University of New York, School of Education, Program in Adolescence Science Education and Special Subjects, Brooklyn, NY 11210-2889. Offers adolescence science education (MAT); biology teacher (7-12) (MA); chemistry teacher (7-12) (MA); earth science teacher (7-12) (MAT); English teacher (7-12) (MA); French teacher (7-12) (MA); mathematics teacher (7-12) (MA); music teacher (MA); physics teacher (7-12) (MA); social studies teacher (7-12) (MA); Spanish teacher (7-12) (MA). *Program availability:* Part-time, evening/weekend. *Degree requirements:* For master's, comprehensive exam (for some programs), thesis (for some programs). *Entrance requirements:* For master's, LAST, previous course work in education, resume, 2 letters of recommendation, essay. Additional exam requirements/recommendations for international students: Required—TOEFL (minimum score 500 paper-based; 61 iBT). Electronic applications accepted. *Faculty research:* Interdisciplinary education, semiotics, discourse analysis, autobiography, teacher identity.

California State University, Sacramento, College of Arts and Letters, Department of World Languages and Literatures, Sacramento, CA 95819. Offers MA. *Program availability:* Part-time. *Degree requirements:* For master's, comprehensive exam, thesis or project. *Entrance requirements:* For master's, interview, minimum GPA of 3.0 during previous 2 years of course work. Additional exam requirements/recommendations for international students: Required—TOEFL (minimum score 550 paper-based; 80 iBT). Electronic applications accepted. *Expenses:* Contact institution.

Caribbean University, Graduate School, Bayamón, PR 00960-0493. Offers administration and supervision (MA Ed); criminal justice (MA); curriculum and instruction (MA Ed, PhD), including elementary education (MA Ed), English education (MA Ed), history education (MA Ed), mathematics education (MA Ed), primary education (MA Ed), science education (MA Ed), Spanish education (MA Ed); educational technology in instructional systems (MA Ed); gerontology (MSN); human resources (MBA); museology, archiving and art history (MA Ed); neonatal pediatrics (MSN); physical education (MA Ed); special education (MA Ed). *Entrance requirements:* For master's, interview, minimum GPA of 2.5.

Central Connecticut State University, School of Graduate Studies, College of Liberal Arts and Social Sciences, Department of Modern Languages, New Britain, CT 06050-4010. Offers modern language (MA, Certificate), including French, German (Certificate), Italian, Spanish (MA); Spanish (MS, Certificate). *Program availability:* Part-time, evening/weekend. *Faculty:* 6 full-time (5 women). *Students:* 22 part-time (18 women); includes 12 minority (1 Black or African American, non-Hispanic/Latino; 11 Hispanic/Latino). Average age 40. 25 applicants, 76% accepted, 11 enrolled. In 2018, 5 master's, 1 other advanced degree awarded. *Degree requirements:* For master's, one foreign language, comprehensive exam, thesis or alternative; for Certificate, qualifying exam. *Entrance requirements:* For master's, minimum undergraduate GPA of 2.7, 24 credits of undergraduate courses in each language in which graduate work will be undertaken. Additional exam requirements/recommendations for international students: Required—TOEFL (minimum score 550 paper-based; 79 iBT); Recommended—IELTS (minimum score 6.5). *Application deadline:* For fall admission, 6/1 for domestic students, 5/1 for international students; for spring admission, 11/1 for domestic and international students. Applications are processed on a rolling basis. Application fee: $50. Electronic applications accepted. *Expenses: Tuition, area resident:* Full-time $7027; part-time $388 per credit. Tuition, state resident: full-time $9750; part-time $388 per credit. Tuition, nonresident: full-time $18,102; part-time $388 per credit. *International tuition:* $18,102 full-time. *Required fees:* $266 per semester. *Financial support:* In 2018–19, 2 students received support. Career-related internships or fieldwork, Federal Work-Study, scholarships/grants, and unspecified assistantships available. Support available to part-time students. Financial award application deadline: 3/1; financial award applicants required to submit FAFSA. *Faculty research:* Quebecois literature, Caribbean literature, modern French/Spanish drama, Puerto Rican novel and drama. *Unit head:* Dr. Carmela Pesca, Chair, 860-832-2875, E-mail: pescac@ccsu.edu. *Application contact:* Patricia Gardner, Associate Director of Graduate Studies, 860-832-2350, Fax: 860-832-2362.
Website: http://www.ccsu.edu/modlang/

Cleveland State University, College of Graduate Studies, College of Education and Human Services, Department of Teacher Education, Cleveland, OH 44115. Offers art education (M Ed); early childhood education (M Ed); foreign language education (M Ed); middle childhood mathematics and science education (M Ed); special education (M Ed), including mild/moderate disabilities, moderate/intensive disabilities; teaching English to speakers of other languages (M Ed). *Program availability:* Part-time, evening/weekend. *Faculty:* 19 full-time (14 women), 32 part-time/adjunct (27 women). *Students:* 56 full-time (40 women), 344 part-time (278 women); includes 104 minority (74 Black or African American, non-Hispanic/Latino; 1 American Indian or Alaska Native, non-Hispanic/

Latino; 5 Asian, non-Hispanic/Latino; 9 Hispanic/Latino; 15 Two or more races, non-Hispanic/Latino), 14 international. Average age 34. 177 applicants, 55% accepted, 68 enrolled. In 2018, 117 master's awarded. *Degree requirements:* For master's, comprehensive exam (for some programs), thesis or alternative. *Entrance requirements:* For master's, GRE General Test or MAT, minimum GPA of 2.75. Additional exam requirements/recommendations for international students: Required—TOEFL (minimum score 550 paper-based; 78 iBT), IELTS (minimum score 6). *Application deadline:* For fall admission, 7/1 priority date for domestic students, 5/15 for international students; for spring admission, 11/15 for domestic students, 11/1 for international students; for summer admission, 4/1 for domestic students, 3/15 for international students. Applications are processed on a rolling basis. Application fee: $30. *Expenses:* Tuition, state resident: full-time $7232.55; part-time $6676 per credit hour. Tuition, nonresident: full-time $12,375. *International tuition:* $18,914 full-time. *Required fees:* $80; $80 $40. Tuition and fees vary according to program. *Financial support:* In 2018–19, 13 research assistantships with full tuition reimbursements (averaging $15,845 per year) were awarded; tuition waivers (partial) and unspecified assistantships also available. Financial award application deadline: 2/15; financial award applicants required to submit FAFSA. *Faculty research:* Early childhood education, literacy education, special education: mild/moderate, moderate/intensive, early childhood intervention specialist), teaching English to speakers of other languages (TESOL). *Total annual research expenditures:* $275,907. *Unit head:* Dr. Tachelle Banks, Department Chairperson, 216-687-4600, Fax: 216-687-5379, E-mail: t.i.banks@csuohio.edu. *Application contact:* Rosalyn Adams, Administrative Coordinator, 216-523-7139, Fax: 216-687-5491, E-mail: r.m.adams@csuohio.edu.
Website: http://www.csuohio.edu/cehs/te/te

College of Charleston, Graduate School, School of Education, Health, and Human Performance, Program in Languages, Charleston, SC 29424-0001. Offers M Ed. *Program availability:* Part-time, evening/weekend. *Degree requirements:* For master's, comprehensive exam or portfolio. *Entrance requirements:* For master's, minimum GPA of 2.5. Additional exam requirements/recommendations for international students: Required—TOEFL (minimum score 81 iBT). Electronic applications accepted.

The Colorado College, Education Department, Program in Secondary Education, Colorado Springs, CO 80903-3294. Offers art teaching (K-12) (MAT); English teaching (MAT); foreign language teaching (MAT); mathematics teaching (MAT); music teaching (MAT); science teaching (MAT); social studies teaching (MAT). *Degree requirements:* For master's, thesis, internship. Electronic applications accepted.

Colorado State University–Pueblo, College of Education, Engineering and Professional Studies, Education Program, Pueblo, CO 81001-4901. Offers art education (M Ed); foreign language education (M Ed); health and physical education (M Ed); instructional technology (M Ed); linguistically diverse education (M Ed); music education (M Ed); special education (M Ed). *Accreditation:* TEAC. *Program availability:* Part-time. *Degree requirements:* For master's, portfolio. *Entrance requirements:* For master's, 3 recommendations, teaching license. Additional exam requirements/recommendations for international students: Required—TOEFL (minimum score 500 paper-based). Electronic applications accepted. *Faculty research:* Portfolio assessment, math education, science education.

Columbia University, Graduate School of Arts and Sciences, New York, NY 10027. Offers African-American studies (MA); American studies (MA); anthropology (MA, PhD); art history and archaeology (MA, PhD); astronomy (PhD); biological sciences (PhD); biotechnology (MA); chemical physics (PhD); chemistry (PhD); classical studies (MA, PhD); classics (MA, PhD); climate and society (MA); conservation biology (MA); earth and environmental sciences (PhD); East Asia: regional studies (MA); East Asian languages and cultures (MA, PhD); ecology, evolution and environmental biology (MA), including conservation biology; ecology, evolution, and environmental biology (PhD), including ecology and evolutionary biology, evolutionary primatology; economics (MA, PhD); English and comparative literature (MA, PhD); French and Romance philology (MA, PhD); Germanic languages (MA, PhD); global French studies (MA); global thought (MA); Hispanic cultural studies (MA); history (PhD); history and literature (MA); human rights studies (MA); Islamic studies (MA); Italian (MA, PhD); Japanese pedagogy (MA); Jewish studies (MA); Latin America and the Caribbean: regional studies (MA); Latin American and Iberian cultures (PhD); mathematics (MA, PhD), including finance (MA); medieval and Renaissance studies (MA); Middle Eastern, South Asian, and African studies (MA, PhD); modern art: critical and curatorial studies (MA); modern European studies (MA); museum anthropology (MA); music (DMA, PhD); oral history (MA); philosophical foundations of physics (MA); philosophy (MA, PhD); physics (PhD); political science (MA, PhD); psychology (PhD); quantitative methods in the social sciences (MA); religion (MA, PhD); Russia, Eurasia and East Europe: regional studies (MA); Russian translation (MA); Slavic cultures (MA); Slavic languages (MA, PhD); sociology (MA, PhD); South Asian studies (MA); statistics (MA, PhD); theatre (PhD). Dual-degree programs require admission to both Graduate School of Arts and Sciences and another Columbia school. *Program availability:* Part-time. Terminal master's awarded for partial completion of doctoral program. *Degree requirements:* For master's, variable foreign language requirement, comprehensive exam (for some programs), thesis (for some programs); for doctorate, variable foreign language requirement, comprehensive exam (for some programs), thesis/dissertation. *Entrance requirements:* For master's and doctorate, GRE General Test, GRE Subject Test (for some programs). Additional exam requirements/recommendations for international students: Required—TOEFL, IELTS. Electronic applications accepted.

Concordia College, Program in Education, Moorhead, MN 56562. Offers world language instruction (M Ed). *Degree requirements:* For master's, thesis/seminar. *Entrance requirements:* For master's, 2 professional references, 1 personal reference.

Cornell University, Graduate School, Graduate Fields of Arts and Sciences, Field of Linguistics, Ithaca, NY 14853. Offers applied linguistics (MA, PhD); East Asian linguistics (MA, PhD); English linguistics (MA, PhD); general linguistics (MA, PhD); Germanic linguistics (MA, PhD); Indo-European linguistics (MA, PhD); phonetics (MA, PhD); phonological theory (MA, PhD); Romance linguistics (MA, PhD); second language acquisition (MA, PhD); semantics (MA, PhD); Slavic linguistics (MA, PhD); sociolinguistics (MA, PhD); South Asian linguistics (MA, PhD); Southeast Asian linguistics (MA, PhD); syntactic theory (MA, PhD). Terminal master's awarded for partial completion of doctoral program. *Degree requirements:* For master's, one foreign language, thesis; for doctorate, one foreign language, comprehensive exam, thesis/dissertation. *Entrance requirements:* For master's and doctorate, GRE General Test, 2 letters of recommendation. Additional exam requirements/recommendations for international students: Required—TOEFL (minimum score 600 paper-based; 77 iBT). Electronic applications accepted. *Faculty research:* Phonology and phonetics, syntax and semantics, historical linguistics, philosophy of language, language acquisition.

Delaware State University, Graduate Programs, Department of English and Foreign Languages, Dover, DE 19901-2277. Offers French (MA); Spanish (MA). *Entrance requirements:* Additional exam requirements/recommendations for international students: Required—TOEFL (minimum score 550 paper-based). Electronic applications accepted.

DePaul University, College of Education, Chicago, IL 60614. Offers bilingual-bicultural education (M Ed, MA); counseling (M Ed, MA), including clinical mental health counseling, college student development, school counseling; curriculum studies (M Ed, MA, Ed D); early childhood education (M Ed, MA, Ed D); educational leadership (M Ed, MA, Ed D), including Catholic leadership (M Ed, MA), general (M Ed, MA), higher education (M Ed, MA), physical education (M Ed, MA), principal preparation (M Ed), teacher preparation (M Ed); elementary education (M Ed, MA); middle grades education (M Ed); middle school mathematics education (MS); reading specialist (M Ed, MA); secondary education (M Ed, MA); social and cultural foundations in education (M Ed, MA); special education (M Ed); sport, fitness and recreation leadership (MS); value-creating education for global citizenship (M Ed); world languages education (M Ed, MA). *Program availability:* Part-time, evening/weekend, online learning. *Degree requirements:* For doctorate, thesis/dissertation. Electronic applications accepted.

Duquesne University, School of Education, Department of Instruction and Leadership, Program in Secondary Education, Pittsburgh, PA 15282-0001. Offers biology (MS Ed); chemistry (MS Ed); English (MS Ed); K-12 education (MS Ed), including Latin; mathematics (MS Ed); physics (MS Ed); social studies (MS Ed). *Program availability:* Part-time, evening/weekend. *Faculty:* 5 full-time (4 women). *Students:* 20 full-time (12 women); includes 3 minority (1 Black or African American, non-Hispanic/Latino; 1 Hispanic/Latino; 1 Two or more races, non-Hispanic/Latino). Average age 24. 20 applicants, 85% accepted, 13 enrolled. In 2018, 14 master's awarded. *Entrance requirements:* For master's, two letters of recommendation, letter of intent, interview, bachelor's degree. Additional exam requirements/recommendations for international students: Required—TOEFL (minimum score 550 paper-based), IELTS (minimum score 7). *Application deadline:* For fall admission, 9/1 for domestic students; for spring admission, 1/2 for domestic students. Applications are processed on a rolling basis. Application fee: $0. Electronic applications accepted. *Expenses: Tuition:* Full-time $23,112; part-time $1284 per credit. Tuition and fees vary according to program. *Financial support:* In 2018–19, 1 student received support, including 1 teaching assistantship with full tuition reimbursement available; Federal Work-Study also available. Support available to part-time students. Financial award applicants required to submit FAFSA. *Faculty research:* Factors that create highly effective teachers; how to best support teachers to support students in reform-oriented environments; urban education; models of teacher leadership; improving instruction in mathematics/science/social studies/English. *Total annual research expenditures:* $120,139. *Unit head:* Dr. Melissa Boston, Associate Dean for Teacher Education/Professor, 412-396.6109, Fax: 412-396-5585, E-mail: bostonm@duq.edu. *Application contact:* Kelly McGinley, Graduate Admissions Assistant, 412-396-1559, Fax: 412-396-5585, E-mail: mcginleyk@duq.edu.
Website: http://www.duq.edu/academics/schools/education/graduate-programs-education/ms-ed-secondary-education

Eastern Michigan University, Graduate School, College of Arts and Sciences, Department of World Languages, Programs in World Languages, Ypsilanti, MI 48197. Offers MA, Graduate Certificate. *Program availability:* Part-time, evening/weekend, online learning. *Students:* 11 part-time (9 women); includes 7 minority (1 Black or African American, non-Hispanic/Latino; 1 Asian, non-Hispanic/Latino; 5 Hispanic/Latino). Average age 48. 8 applicants, 50% accepted, 3 enrolled. In 2018, 5 master's awarded. *Degree requirements:* For master's, one foreign language, thesis optional. *Entrance requirements:* Additional exam requirements/recommendations for international students: Required—TOEFL. *Application deadline:* Applications are processed on a rolling basis. Application fee: $45. *Financial support:* Fellowships, research assistantships with full tuition reimbursements, teaching assistantships with full tuition reimbursements, career-related internships or fieldwork, Federal Work-Study, institutionally sponsored loans, scholarships/grants, tuition waivers (partial), and unspecified assistantships available. Support available to part-time students. Financial award applicants required to submit FAFSA. *Application contact:* Dr. Genevieve Peden, Program Advisor, 734-487-1498, Fax: 734-487-3411, E-mail: gpeden@emich.edu.

Eastern University, Graduate Education Programs, St. Davids, PA 19087-3696. Offers ESL program specialist (K-12) (Certificate); general supervisor (PreK-12) (Certificate); health and physical education (K-12) (Certificate); middle level (4-8) (Certificate); multicultural education (M Ed); music (K-12) (Certificate); Pre K-4 (Certificate); Pre K-4 with special education (Certificate); reading (M Ed); reading specialist (K-12) (Certificate); reading supervisor (K-12) (Certificate); school counseling (MA, CAGS); school principalship (preK-12) (Certificate); school psychology (MS, CAGS); secondary biology education (7-12) (Certificate); secondary chemistry education (7-12) (Certificate); secondary communication education (7-12) (Certificate); secondary English education (7-12) (Certificate); secondary math education (7-12) (Certificate); secondary social studies education (7-12) (Certificate); special education (M Ed); special education (7-12) (Certificate); special education (Pre K-8) (Certificate); special education supervisor (K-12) (Certificate); TESOL (M Ed); world language (Certificate), including Spanish. *Program availability:* Part-time, evening/weekend, online learning. *Entrance requirements:* Additional exam requirements/recommendations for international students: Required—TOEFL. Electronic applications accepted. Application fee is waived when completed online. *Expenses:* Contact institution.

Elms College, Division of Education, Chicopee, MA 01013-2839. Offers early childhood education (MAT); education (M Ed, CAGS); elementary education (MAT); English as a second language (MAT); reading (MAT); secondary education (MAT), including biology education, English education, Spanish education; special education (MAT). *Program availability:* Part-time, evening/weekend. *Faculty:* 5 full-time (all women), 6 part-time/adjunct (5 women). *Students:* 3 full-time (all women), 117 part-time (94 women); includes 12 minority (1 Black or African American, non-Hispanic/Latino; 2 Asian, non-Hispanic/Latino; 9 Hispanic/Latino). Average age 34. 27 applicants, 96% accepted, 23 enrolled. In 2018, 34 master's, 3 other advanced degrees awarded. *Degree requirements:* For master's, thesis (for some programs). *Entrance requirements:* For master's, Massachusetts Educators Certification Test, minimum GPA of 3.0; for CAGS, master's degree in education. Additional exam requirements/recommendations for international students: Required—TOEFL. *Application deadline:* For fall admission, 7/1 priority date for domestic students; for spring admission, 11/1 priority date for domestic students. Applications are processed on a rolling basis. Application fee: $30. *Expenses: Tuition:* Full-time $14,328; part-time $796 per credit. *Required fees:* $200. Tuition and fees vary according to degree level and program. *Financial support:* In 2018–19, 2 teaching assistantships with partial tuition reimbursements were awarded. Financial award applicants required to submit FAFSA. *Unit head:* Dr. Mary Janeczek, Chair, Division of Education, 413-594-2761, Fax: 413-592-4871, E-mail: janeczeke@elms.edu. *Application contact:* Nancy Davis, Director, Office of Graduate and Continuing Education Admissions, 413-265-2239, E-mail: davisn@elms.edu.

Florida International University, College of Arts, Sciences, and Education, Department of Teaching and Learning, Miami, FL 33199. Offers art education (MA, MS); curriculum and instruction (MS, Ed D, PhD, Ed S), including curriculum development (MS), elementary education (MS), English education (MS), learning technologies (MS), mathematics education (MS), modern language education (MS), physical education (MS), science education (MS), social studies education (MS), special education (MS); early childhood education (MS); exceptional student education (Ed D); foreign language

education (MS), including foreign language education, teaching English to speakers of other languages (TESOL); language, literacy and culture (PhD); mathematics, science, and learning technologies (PhD); physical education (MS), including sport and fitness; reading education (MS). *Program availability:* Part-time, evening/weekend. *Faculty:* 64 full-time (43 women), 104 part-time/adjunct (76 women). *Students:* 169 full-time (144 women), 155 part-time (130 women); includes 260 minority (53 Black or African American, non-Hispanic/Latino; 7 Asian, non-Hispanic/Latino; 193 Hispanic/Latino; 7 Two or more races, non-Hispanic/Latino), 13 international. Average age 33. 184 applicants, 62% accepted, 87 enrolled. In 2018, 153 master's, 10 doctorates awarded. *Degree requirements:* For doctorate, comprehensive exam, thesis/dissertation. *Entrance requirements:* For master's, GRE General Test, Florida General Knowledge Test or Florida College Level Academic Skills Test; for doctorate and Ed S, GRE General Test. Additional exam requirements/recommendations for international students: Required—TOEFL (minimum score 550 paper-based; 80 iBT), IELTS (minimum score 6.3). *Application deadline:* For fall admission, 6/1 priority date for domestic students, 4/1 for international students; for winter admission, 10/1 priority date for domestic students, 9/1 for international students; for spring admission, 3/1 priority date for domestic students, 2/1 for international students. Applications are processed on a rolling basis. Application fee: $30. Electronic applications accepted. *Financial support:* Research assistantships and teaching assistantships available. *Unit head:* Dr. Maria Fernandez, Chair, 305-348-0193, Fax: 305-348-2086, E-mail: Maria.Fernandez9@fiu.edu. *Application contact:* Nanett Rojas, Manager, Admissions Operations, 305-348-7464, Fax: 305-348-7441, E-mail: gradadm@fiu.edu.
Website: https://tl.fiu.edu/

George Mason University, College of Humanities and Social Sciences, Department of Modern and Classical Languages, Fairfax, VA 22030. Offers foreign languages (MA), including French, Spanish, Spanish and French, Spanish/bilingual-multicultural education. *Faculty:* 35 full-time (25 women), 39 part-time/adjunct (31 women). *Students:* 7 full-time (all women), 13 part-time (7 women); includes 11 minority (1 Black or African American, non-Hispanic/Latino; 10 Hispanic/Latino). Average age 34. 7 applicants, 100% accepted, 3 enrolled. In 2018, 10 master's awarded. *Degree requirements:* For master's, one foreign language, thesis optional, take-home exit exam. *Entrance requirements:* For master's, goals statement, language proficiency statement. Additional exam requirements/recommendations for international students: Required—TOEFL (minimum score 575 paper-based; 88 iBT), IELTS (minimum score 6.5), PTE (minimum score 59). *Application deadline:* For fall admission, 4/15 for domestic students. Application fee: $75 ($80 for international students). Electronic applications accepted. *Financial support:* In 2018–19, 6 students received support, including 6 teaching assistantships with tuition reimbursements available (averaging $5,720 per year); career-related internships or fieldwork, Federal Work-Study, scholarships/grants, unspecified assistantships, and health care benefits (for full-time research or teaching assistantship recipients) also available. Support available to part-time students. Financial award application deadline: 3/1; financial award applicants required to submit FAFSA. *Faculty research:* Film and media studies; literary analysis, criticism, and theory; applied linguistics and pedagogy, sociolinguistics, interdisciplinary approaches. *Unit head:* Rei Berroa, Chair, 703-993-1220, Fax: 703-993-1245, E-mail: rberroa@gmu.edu. *Application contact:* Jen Barnard, Office Manager, 703-993-1230, Fax: 703-993-1245, E-mail: jbarnard@gmu.edu.
Website: http://mcl.gmu.edu/

The George Washington University, Graduate School of Education and Human Development, Department of Curriculum and Pedagogy, Program in Secondary Education, Washington, DC 20052. Offers Arabic (M Ed); Italian (M Ed); math (M Ed); physics (M Ed); Russian (M Ed). Programs also offered in Arlington and Ashburn, VA. *Accreditation:* NCATE. *Students:* 7 full-time (3 women), 23 part-time (13 women); includes 10 minority (5 Black or African American, non-Hispanic/Latino; 2 American Indian or Alaska Native, non-Hispanic/Latino; 1 Hispanic/Latino; 1 Native Hawaiian or other Pacific Islander, non-Hispanic/Latino; 1 Two or more races, non-Hispanic/Latino). Average age 33. 55 applicants, 69% accepted, 16 enrolled. In 2018, 17 master's awarded. *Entrance requirements:* For master's, GRE General Test or MAT, interview, minimum GPA of 2.75. *Application deadline:* For fall admission, 1/15 priority date for domestic students; for spring admission, 10/1 for domestic students. Applications are processed on a rolling basis. Application fee: $75. *Financial support:* Fellowships, career-related internships or fieldwork, Federal Work-Study, tuition waivers (full and partial), and stipends available. Financial award application deadline: 1/15; financial award applicants required to submit FAFSA. *Unit head:* Prof. Curtis Pyke, Chair, 202-994-4516, E-mail: cpyke@gwu.edu. *Application contact:* Sarah Lang, Director of Graduate Admissions, 202-994-1447, Fax: 202-994-7207, E-mail: slang@gwu.edu.

Georgia Southern University, Jack N. Averitt College of Graduate Studies, College of Education, Department of Elementary and Special Education, Program in Spanish P-12 Education, Statesboro, GA 30458. Offers MAT. *Program availability:* Part-time. *Degree requirements:* For master's, key assessments. *Entrance requirements:* For master's, GACE. Additional exam requirements/recommendations for international students: Required—TOEFL (minimum score 80 iBT). *Expenses: Tuition, area resident:* Part-time $3324 per semester. Tuition, state resident: full-time $5814; part-time $3324 per semester. Tuition, nonresident: full-time $23,204; part-time $13,260 per semester. *Required fees:* $2092; $2092. Tuition and fees vary according to course load, degree level, campus/location and program. *Faculty research:* P-12 preparation of Spanish language education professionals.

Georgia State University, College of Arts and Sciences, Department of World Languages and Cultures, Atlanta, GA 30302-3083. Offers French (MA), including applied linguistics and pedagogy, French studies, literature and culture; Latin American studies (Certificate); Spanish (MA); translation and interpretation (Certificate), including interpretation, translation. *Program availability:* Part-time. *Faculty:* 11 full-time (6 women), 1 (woman) part-time/adjunct. *Students:* 31 full-time (23 women), 7 part-time (4 women); includes 24 minority (13 Black or African American, non-Hispanic/Latino; 1 Asian, non-Hispanic/Latino; 10 Hispanic/Latino), 5 international. Average age 37. 29 applicants, 72% accepted, 16 enrolled. In 2018, 7 master's, 1 other advanced degree awarded. *Entrance requirements:* For master's, GRE, statement of purpose, writing sample in the target language, 2 letters of recommendation, official transcripts; for Certificate, entrance examination involving translating one passage from English to the target language and one passage from the target language to English, 3 letters of recommendation, resume/curriculum vitae, official transcripts. Additional exam requirements/recommendations for international students: Required—TOEFL (minimum score 79 iBT). *Application deadline:* For fall admission, 3/15 priority date for domestic and international students; for spring admission, 11/15 priority date for domestic and international students. Application fee: $50. Electronic applications accepted. *Expenses: Tuition, area resident:* Full-time $9360; part-time $390 per credit hour. Tuition, state resident: full-time $9360; part-time $390 per credit hour. Tuition, nonresident: full-time $30,024; part-time $1251 per credit hour. *International tuition:* $30,024 full-time. *Required fees:* $2128. *Financial support:* Applicants required to submit FAFSA. *Faculty research:* French literature and culture, Francophone literature and culture, Latin American literature and culture, Spanish literature and culture, Hispanic linguistics. *Unit head:* Dr. Fernando Reati, Department Chair, 404-413-5984, Fax: 404-413-5982, E-mail: freati@gsu.edu. *Application contact:* Amber Amari, Director, Graduate and Scheduling Services, 404-413-5037, E-mail: aamari@gsu.edu.
Website: http://wlc.gsu.edu/

Harding University, Cannon-Clary College of Education, Searcy, AR 72149-0001. Offers advanced studies in teaching and learning (M Ed); art (MSE); behavioral science (MSE); counseling (MS, Ed S); early childhood special education (M Ed, MSE); education (MSE); educational leadership (M Ed, Ed S); elementary education (M Ed); English (MSE); French (MSE); history/social science (MSE); kinesiology (MSE); math (MSE); reading (M Ed); secondary education (M Ed); Spanish (MSE); teaching (MAT); teaching English as a second language (MSE). *Accreditation:* NCATE. *Program availability:* Part-time, evening/weekend. *Degree requirements:* For master's, comprehensive exam (for some programs), thesis optional, portfolio(s); for Ed S, comprehensive exam, portfolio, project. *Entrance requirements:* For master's, GRE, MAT, PRAXIS; for Ed S, MAT or GRE. Additional exam requirements/recommendations for international students: Required—TOEFL (minimum score 550 paper-based; 79 iBT). *Faculty research:* Reading, comprehension, school violence, educational technology, behavior, college choice, differentiated instruction, brain-based teaching.

Hofstra University, School of Education, Programs in Teacher Education, Hempstead, NY 11549. Offers bilingual education (MA); bilingual extension (Advanced Certificate); business education (MS Ed); curriculum studies (MS Ed); early childhood and childhood education (MS Ed); early childhood education (MA, MS Ed); educational technology (Advanced Certificate); elementary education (MA, MS Ed); English education (MS Ed); family and consumer science (MS Ed); fine arts and music education (Advanced Certificate); fine arts education (MS Ed); foreign language and TESOL (MS Ed); foreign language education (MA, MS Ed); languages other than English and teaching English as a second language (MA); learning and teaching (Ed D); mathematics education (MA, MS Ed); middle childhood extension (Advanced Certificate); music education (MA, MS Ed); science education (MA); secondary education (Advanced Certificate); social studies education (MA, MS Ed); teaching languages other than English and TESOL (MS Ed); technology for learning (MA); TESOL (MS Ed, Advanced Certificate); TESOL with specialization in STEM (MA); work based learning extension (Advanced Certificate). *Program availability:* Part-time, evening/weekend, blended/hybrid learning. *Students:* 138 full-time (94 women), 109 part-time (78 women); includes 66 minority (16 Black or African American, non-Hispanic/Latino; 17 Asian, non-Hispanic/Latino; 31 Hispanic/Latino; 2 Native Hawaiian or other Pacific Islander, non-Hispanic/Latino), 6 international. Average age 29. 217 applicants, 86% accepted, 113 enrolled. In 2018, 105 master's, 11 doctorates, 25 other advanced degrees awarded. *Degree requirements:* For master's, comprehensive exam, thesis (for some programs), exit project, student teaching, fieldwork, electronic portfolio, curriculum project, minimum GPA of 3.0; for doctorate, dissertation; for Advanced Certificate, 3 foreign languages, comprehensive exam (for some programs), thesis project. *Entrance requirements:* For master's, GRE, 2 letters of recommendation, portfolio, teacher certification (MA), interview, essay; for doctorate, GMAT, GRE, LSAT, or MAT; for Advanced Certificate, 2 letters of recommendation, essay, interview and/or portfolio, teaching certificate. Additional exam requirements/recommendations for international students: Required—TOEFL (minimum score 550 paper-based; 80 iBT). *Application deadline:* Applications are processed on a rolling basis. Application fee: $75. Electronic applications accepted. *Financial support:* In 2018–19, 86 students received support, including 51 fellowships with full and partial tuition reimbursements available (averaging $5,080 per year), 2 research assistantships with full and partial tuition reimbursements available (averaging $3,470 per year); career-related internships or fieldwork, Federal Work-Study, institutionally sponsored loans, scholarships/grants, traineeships, tuition waivers (full and partial), unspecified assistantships, and scholarships and endowed scholarships also available. Support available to part-time students. Financial award applicants required to submit FAFSA. *Faculty research:* Impact of memory on learning; brain function, cognitive-development, learning, and achievement; student activism and civic education; using children's literature to promote diversity; 2nd language acquisition. *Unit head:* Dr. Alan Singer, Chairperson, 516-463-5853, Fax: 516-463-6275, E-mail: alan.j.singer@hofstra.edu. *Application contact:* Sunil Samuel, Assistant Vice President of Admissions, 516-463-4723, Fax: 516-463-4664, E-mail: graduateadmission@hofstra.edu.
Website: http://www.hofstra.edu/education/

Hunter College of the City University of New York, Graduate School, School of Education, Programs in Secondary Education, Concentration in French Education, New York, NY 10065-5085. Offers MA. *Accreditation:* NCATE. *Degree requirements:* For master's, thesis, professional teaching portfolio, New York State Teacher Certification Exam. *Entrance requirements:* For master's, 24 credits in French; minimum GPA of 3.0 in French, 2.8 overall; 2 letters of reference; interview. Additional exam requirements/recommendations for international students: Required—TOEFL, TWE.

Hunter College of the City University of New York, Graduate School, School of Education, Programs in Secondary Education, Concentration in Italian Education, New York, NY 10065-5085. Offers MA. *Accreditation:* NCATE. *Degree requirements:* For master's, thesis, professional teaching portfolio, New York State Teacher Certification Exam, research project. *Entrance requirements:* For master's, minimum GPA of 3.0 in Italian, 2.8 overall; 24 credits of course work in Italian; 2 letters of reference; interview. Additional exam requirements/recommendations for international students: Required—TOEFL, TWE.

Hunter College of the City University of New York, Graduate School, School of Education, Programs in Secondary Education, Concentration in Spanish Education, New York, NY 10065-5085. Offers MA. *Accreditation:* NCATE. *Degree requirements:* For master's, thesis, professional teaching portfolio, New York State Teacher Certification Exam. *Entrance requirements:* For master's, minimum GPA of 3.0 in Spanish, 2.8 overall; 24 credits of course work in Spanish; 2 letters of reference; interview. Additional exam requirements/recommendations for international students: Required—TOEFL, TWE.

Indiana State University, College of Graduate and Professional Studies, College of Arts and Sciences, Department of Languages, Literatures, and Linguistics, Terre Haute, IN 47809. Offers applied linguistics/teaching English as a second language (MA); language education (PhD); Spanish/teaching English as a second language (MA); TESL/TEFL (CAS). *Degree requirements:* For master's, comprehensive exam. Electronic applications accepted.

Indiana University Bloomington, University Graduate School, College of Arts and Sciences, Department of French and Italian, Bloomington, IN 47405. Offers French (MA, PhD), including French and Francophone studies (MA), French instruction (MA), French linguistics; Italian (MA, PhD). *Program availability:* Part-time. Terminal master's awarded for partial completion of doctoral program. *Degree requirements:* For master's, variable foreign language requirement, comprehensive exam (for some programs), thesis or alternative; for doctorate, variable foreign language requirement, comprehensive exam, thesis/dissertation. *Entrance requirements:* For master's, GRE General Test, BA or equivalent undergraduate preparation in French or Italian; for doctorate, GRE General Test, MA from degree program at IU; MA in the specific field. Additional exam requirements/recommendations for international students: Required—TOEFL (minimum score 550 paper-based; 79 iBT), GRE General Test (recommended). Electronic applications accepted. *Faculty research:* French and Italian literature, French linguistics, including the novel and political theory, literature and fine arts, literary theory,

postcolonialism, French-Creole studies, French literature of Africa and its Diaspora, humanism, Medieval folklore and mythology, humor in Medieval and Renaissance literature, emigration, second language acquisition, syntax, sociolinguistics, phonology, lexicography, media and cultural studies, cinema, drama.

Indiana University Bloomington, University Graduate School, College of Arts and Sciences, Department of Germanic Studies, Bloomington, IN 47405-7000. Offers German philology and linguistics (PhD); German studies (MA, PhD), including German (MA), German literature and culture (MA), German literature and linguistics (MA); medieval German studies (PhD); teaching German (MAT). *Degree requirements:* For master's, one foreign language, project; for doctorate, one foreign language, comprehensive exam, thesis/dissertation. *Entrance requirements:* For master's, GRE General Test, BA in German or equivalent; for doctorate, GRE General Test, MA in German or equivalent. Additional exam requirements/recommendations for international students: Required—TOEFL. Electronic applications accepted. *Faculty research:* German and other European literature: medieval to modern/postmodern, German and culture studies, Germanic philology, literary theory, literature and the other arts.

Indiana University Bloomington, University Graduate School, College of Arts and Sciences, School of Global and International Studies, Department of East Asian Languages and Cultures, Bloomington, IN 47408. Offers Chinese (MA, PhD); Chinese language pedagogy (MA); East Asian studies (MA); Japanese (MA, PhD); Japanese language pedagogy (MA). *Program availability:* Part-time. *Degree requirements:* For master's, one foreign language, thesis; for doctorate, 2 foreign languages, comprehensive exam, thesis/dissertation. *Entrance requirements:* Additional exam requirements/recommendations for international students: Required—TOEFL (minimum score 93 iBT). Electronic applications accepted. *Faculty research:* Modern East Asian history; politics and society; traditional Chinese thought and society; medieval and premodern Japanese history, literature and society; modern Chinese and Japanese film and literature; Chinese, Japanese, Korean language and linguistics.

Indiana University–Purdue University Indianapolis, School of Education, Indianapolis, IN 46202-5155. Offers curriculum and instruction (MS); early childhood (MS); educational leadership (MS, Certificate); English as a second language (Certificate); kindergarten (Certificate); language education (MS); reading (Certificate); school counseling (MS); special education (MS, Certificate). *Program availability:* Part-time, evening/weekend. Terminal master's awarded for partial completion of doctoral program. *Degree requirements:* For master's, thesis optional. *Entrance requirements:* For master's, GRE General Test, minimum GPA of 2.5; for Certificate, official transcripts. Additional exam requirements/recommendations for international students: Required—TOEFL (minimum score 60 iBT), IELTS (minimum score 5.5). Electronic applications accepted. *Expenses:* Contact institution. *Faculty research:* Educational policies and school leaders' responses to these; issues of intersectionality in the experiences of African American lesbian, gay, and bisexual students attending historically black colleges and universities and those who belong to black Greek-letter organizations; students' experiential knowledge and their evolving disciplinary-specific literacy and understanding; innovative program development; urban ESL teacher preparation; target-based instructional coaching.

Inter American University of Puerto Rico, Arecibo Campus, Programs in Education, Arecibo, PR 00614-4050. Offers administration and educational supervision (MA Ed); counseling and guidance (MA Ed); curriculum and teaching (MA Ed), including biology education, English as a second language, history education, math education, Spanish; elementary education (MA Ed). *Accreditation:* TEAC. *Degree requirements:* For master's, comprehensive exam, thesis optional. *Entrance requirements:* For master's, GRE, EXADEP, bachelor's degree in education or teaching license (administration and supervision) or courses in education and psychology (counseling and guidance), minimum GPA of 2.5 in last 60 credits.

Inter American University of Puerto Rico, Barranquitas Campus, Program in Education, Barranquitas, PR 00794. Offers curriculum and teaching (M Ed), including biology, English as a second language, history, Spanish; educational leadership and management (MA); elementary education (M Ed); information and library service technology (M Ed); special education (MA). *Accreditation:* TEAC. *Program availability:* Part-time, evening/weekend. *Degree requirements:* For master's, 2 foreign languages, comprehensive exam, thesis (for some programs). *Entrance requirements:* For master's, GRE or EXADEP, bachelor's degree or its equivalent from accredited institution, official academic transcript from institution that conferred bachelor's degree, minimum GPA of 2.5, two recommendation letters, interview (for some programs), essay (for some programs). Electronic applications accepted. *Expenses:* Contact institution.

Inter American University of Puerto Rico, Metropolitan Campus, Graduate Programs, Program in Spanish Education, San Juan, PR 00919-1293. Offers MA.

Iona College, School of Arts and Science, Department of Education, New Rochelle, NY 10801-1890. Offers adolescence education: biology (MS Ed, MST); adolescence education: English (MS Ed); adolescence education: mathematics (MST); adolescence education: social studies (MS Ed, MST); adolescence education: Spanish (MS Ed); adolescence special education 5-12 (MST); childhood and special education (MST); early childhood and childhood (MST); educational leadership (MS Ed). *Accreditation:* NCATE. *Program availability:* Part-time, evening/weekend. *Faculty:* 7 full-time (5 women), 9 part-time/adjunct (5 women). *Students:* 33 full-time (30 women), 26 part-time (20 women); includes 21 minority (6 Black or African American, non-Hispanic/Latino; 1 Asian, non-Hispanic/Latino; 13 Hispanic/Latino; 1 Two or more races, non-Hispanic/Latino). Average age 25. 39 applicants, 87% accepted, 14 enrolled. In 2018, 20 master's awarded. *Degree requirements:* For master's, thesis or alternative. *Entrance requirements:* For master's, minimum GPA of 3.0, NY State teaching certificate and bachelor's degree (for MS Ed). Additional exam requirements/recommendations for international students: Required—TOEFL (minimum score 550 paper-based; 80 iBT), IELTS (minimum score 6.5). *Application deadline:* For fall admission, 8/1 priority date for domestic students, 5/1 priority date for international students; for spring admission, 1/1 priority date for domestic students, 9/1 priority date for international students. Applications are processed on a rolling basis. Electronic applications accepted. *Expenses: Tuition:* Full-time $14,064; part-time $7032 per credit. *Required fees:* $245 per semester. One-time fee: $250. Tuition and fees vary according to program. *Financial support:* In 2018–19, 2 students received support. Unspecified assistantships available. Support available to part-time students. Financial award application deadline: 4/15; financial award applicants required to submit FAFSA. *Faculty research:* Engaging teacher educators in scientific process, cross-national comparisons of mathematics teaching, questioning strategies in the classroom, research methods, literacy development. *Unit head:* Malissa Scheuring Leipold, EdD, Chair, 914-633-2210, Fax: 914-633-2281, E-mail: mleipold@iona.edu. *Application contact:* Christopher Kash, Assistant Director of Graduate Admissions, 914-633-2403, E-mail: ckash@iona.edu.
Website: http://www.iona.edu/Academics/School-of-Arts-Science/Departments/Education/Graduate-Programs.aspx

James Madison University, The Graduate School, College of Education, Program in Education, Harrisonburg, VA 22807. Offers early childhood education (preK-3) (MAT); educational leadership (M Ed); educational technology (M Ed); elementary education (MAT); equity and cultural diversity (M Ed); inclusive early childhood education (MAT); K-8 mathematics specialist (M Ed); middle education (MAT); reading education (M Ed); secondary education (MAT); Spanish language and culture for educators (M Ed); TESOL (MAT). *Accreditation:* NCATE. *Program availability:* Part-time, evening/weekend. *Students:* 255 full-time (224 women), 200 part-time (140 women); includes 56 minority (13 Black or African American, non-Hispanic/Latino; 8 Asian, non-Hispanic/Latino; 21 Hispanic/Latino; 14 Two or more races, non-Hispanic/Latino), 1 international. Average age 30. In 2018, 295 master's awarded. Application fee: $60. Electronic applications accepted. *Expenses:* Tuition, state resident: full-time $10,848. Tuition, nonresident: full-time $27,888. *Required fees:* $1128. *Financial support:* In 2018–19, 22 students received support. Teaching assistantships, career-related internships or fieldwork, Federal Work-Study, and assistantships (averaging $7911) available. Financial award application deadline: 3/1; financial award applicants required to submit FAFSA. *Unit head:* Dr. Phillip M. Wishon, Dean, 540-568-6572, E-mail: wishonpm@jmu.edu. *Application contact:* Lynette D. Michael, Director of Graduate Admissions, 540-568-6131 Ext. 6395, Fax: 540-568-7860, E-mail: michaeld@jmu.edu.
Website: http://www.jmu.edu/coe/index.shtml

Kean University, College of Education, Program in Hindi and Urdu Language Pedagogy, Union, NJ 07083. Offers MA. *Program availability:* Blended/hybrid learning. *Faculty:* 2 full-time (0 women). *Students:* 8 part-time (all women); includes 7 minority (all Asian, non-Hispanic/Latino). Average age 44. 13 applicants, 100% accepted, 8 enrolled. In 2018, 5 master's awarded. *Degree requirements:* For master's, thesis/action research project. *Entrance requirements:* For master's, ACTFL OPI and WPT in Hindi or Urdu, bachelor's degree, minimum cumulative GPA of 3.0, official transcripts, professional resume or curriculum vitae, personal statement, two letters of recommendation, interview, teaching experience. Additional exam requirements/recommendations for international students: Required—TOEFL (minimum score 550 paper-based, 79 iBT) or IELTS (6.5). *Application deadline:* For fall admission, 6/30 for domestic and international students. Application fee: $75. Electronic applications accepted. *Expenses:* Tuition, state resident: full-time $15,025; part-time $733.50 per credit. Tuition, nonresident: full-time $19,890; part-time $884.50 per credit. *Required fees:* $2107.50; $89.50 per credit. Tuition and fees vary according to course level, course load, degree level and program. *Financial support:* Scholarships/grants and unspecified assistantships available. Financial award applicants required to submit FAFSA. *Unit head:* Dr. Gail Verdi, 908-737-0550, E-mail: gverdi@kean.edu. *Application contact:* Brittany Gerstenhaber, Admissions Counselor, 908-737-7100, E-mail: grad-adm@kean.edu.

Lamar University, College of Graduate Studies, College of Arts and Sciences, Department of English and Modern Languages, Beaumont, TX 77710. Offers English (MA); teaching Spanish (MA). *Program availability:* Part-time, evening/weekend. *Faculty:* 41 full-time (22 women), 4 part-time/adjunct (3 women). *Students:* 8 full-time (7 women), 23 part-time (21 women); includes 19 minority (2 Black or African American, non-Hispanic/Latino; 17 Hispanic/Latino), 1 international. Average age 35. 20 applicants, 100% accepted, 13 enrolled. In 2018, 11 master's awarded. *Degree requirements:* For master's, one foreign language, thesis optional, practicum. *Entrance requirements:* For master's, GRE General Test, minimum GPA of 2.5 in last 60 hours of undergraduate course work. Additional exam requirements/recommendations for international students: Required—TOEFL (minimum score 550 paper-based; 79 iBT), IELTS (minimum score 6.5). *Application deadline:* Applications are processed on a rolling basis. Application fee: $25 ($50 for international students). Electronic applications accepted. *Expenses:* Tuition, state resident: full-time $6234; part-time $346 per credit hour. Tuition, nonresident: full-time $6852; part-time $761 per credit hour. *International tuition:* $6852 full-time. *Required fees:* $1940; $327 per credit hour. Tuition and fees vary according to course load, campus/location, program and reciprocity agreements. *Financial support:* In 2018–19, 10 students received support, including 4 teaching assistantships (averaging $8,000 per year); career-related internships or fieldwork, Federal Work-Study, and institutionally sponsored loans also available. Support available to part-time students. Financial award applicants required to submit FAFSA. *Faculty research:* British, Renaissance, nineteenth-century, and American literature; creative writing; modern literature; African-American literature. *Unit head:* Dr. Jim Sanderson, Chair, 409-880-8558, Fax: 409-880-8591. *Application contact:* Celeste Contreas, Director, Admissions and Academic Services, 409-880-8888, Fax: 409-880-7419, E-mail: gradmissions@lamar.edu.
Website: http://artssciences.lamar.edu/english-and-modern-languages

Le Moyne College, Department of Education, Syracuse, NY 13214. Offers adolescent education (MS Ed, MST); adolescent education/special education (MS Ed, MST); adolescent English (MST), including grades 7-12; adolescent English/special education (MST), including grades 7-12; adolescent foreign language (MST), including grades 7-12; adolescent history (MST), including grades 7-12; childhood education (MS Ed); childhood education/special education (MS Ed); elementary education (MS Ed); general education (MS Ed); inclusive childhood education (MST); literacy education (MS Ed), including birth to grade 6, grades 5-12; school building leader (MS Ed); school building leadership (CAS); school district business leader (MS Ed, CAS); school district leader (MS Ed); school district leadership (CAS); secondary education (MS Ed); special education (MS Ed); teaching English to speakers of other languages (MS Ed); urban studies (MS Ed). *Accreditation:* TEAC. *Program availability:* Part-time, evening/weekend. *Faculty:* 7 full-time (5 women), 16 part-time/adjunct (11 women). *Students:* 35 full-time (28 women), 119 part-time (84 women); includes 14 minority (5 Black or African American, non-Hispanic/Latino; 1 Asian, non-Hispanic/Latino; 7 Hispanic/Latino; 1 Two or more races, non-Hispanic/Latino), 1 international. Average age 30. 123 applicants, 89% accepted, 96 enrolled. In 2018, 66 master's, 48 CASs awarded. Terminal master's awarded for partial completion of doctoral program. *Degree requirements:* For master's, thesis. *Entrance requirements:* For master's, bachelor's degree with minimum undergraduate GPA of 3.0, 2 letters of recommendation, transcripts. Additional exam requirements/recommendations for international students: Required—TOEFL (minimum score 79 iBT); Recommended—IELTS (minimum score 6.5). *Application deadline:* For fall admission, 4/1 priority date for domestic and international students; for spring admission, 10/1 priority date for domestic and international students; for summer admission, 3/1 priority date for domestic and international students. Applications are processed on a rolling basis. Electronic applications accepted. *Expenses:* $734 per credit hour; wellness fee $70 per semester for full-time graduate students taking 9+ credit hours; technology fee $75 per semester for full-time graduate students taking 9+ credit hours, $25 per semester for part-time students; $1,470 per credit hour (for ED.D.). *Financial support:* In 2018–19, 44 students received support. Career-related internships or fieldwork, scholarships/grants, and health care benefits available. Support available to part-time students. Financial award applicants required to submit FAFSA. *Faculty research:* Minority teachers, special education, multiculturalism, literacy, technology, media literacy learning, autism, school district organization, service-learning, higher level problem solving, teacher leadership. *Unit head:* Dr. Stephen C. Fleury, Chair, Department of Education, 315-445-4376, Fax: 315-445-4744, E-mail: fleurysc@lemoyne.edu. *Application contact:* Jody F Manning, Assistant Director for Graduate Admission, 315-445-5444, Fax: 315-445-6092, E-mail: manninjf@lemoyne.edu.
Website: http://www.lemoyne.edu/education

Lewis University, College of Education, Program in Foreign Language Instruction, Romeoville, IL 60446. Offers MA. *Program availability:* Part-time. *Students:* 3 full-time (all women), 5 part-time (4 women); includes 3 minority (1 Black or African American,

non-Hispanic/Latino; 2 Hispanic/Latino). Average age 28. *Degree requirements:* For master's, comprehensive exam. *Entrance requirements:* For master's, writing exam, Test of Academic Proficiency/Basic Skills Test/ACT/SAT, bachelor's degree, minimum GPA of 2.75, 2 letters of recommendation. Additional exam requirements/recommendations for international students: Required—TOEFL (minimum score 550 paper-based; 79 iBT), IELTS (minimum score 6). *Application deadline:* For fall admission, 5/1 for international students; for spring admission, 11/1 for international students. Application fee: $40. Electronic applications accepted. *Financial support:* Federal Work-Study, scholarships/grants, and unspecified assistantships available. Support available to part-time students. Financial award application deadline: 5/1; financial award applicants required to submit FAFSA. *Unit head:* Dr. Chris Palmi, Program Director. *Application contact:* Kathy Lisak, Graduate Admission Counselor, 815-836-5610, E-mail: grad@lewisu.edu.
Website: http://www.lewisu.edu/academics/mastersforeignlanguage/index.htm

London Metropolitan University, Graduate Programs, London, United Kingdom. Offers applied psychology (M Sc); architecture (MA); biomedical science (M Sc); blood science (M Sc); cancer pharmacology (M Sc); computer networking and cyber security (M Sc); computing and information systems (M Sc); conference interpreting (MA); counter-terrorism studies (M Sc); creative, digital and professional writing (MA); crime, violence and prevention (M Sc); criminology (M Sc); curating contemporary art (MA); data analytics (M Sc); digital media (MA); early childhood studies (MA); education (MA, Ed D); financial services law, regulation and compliance (LL M); food science (M Sc); forensic psychology (M Sc); health and social care management and policy (M Sc); human nutrition (M Sc); human resource management (MA); human rights and international conflict (MA); information technology (M Sc); intelligence and security studies (M Sc); international oil, gas and energy law (LL M); international relations (MA); interpreting (MA); learning and teaching in higher education (MA); legal practice (LL M); media and entertainment law (LL M); organizational and consumer psychology (M Sc); psychological therapy (M Sc); psychology of mental health (M Sc); public health (M Sc); public policy and management (MPA); security studies (M Sc); social work (M Sc); spatial planning and urban design (MA); sports therapy (M Sc); supporting older children and young people with dyslexia (MA); teaching languages (MA), including Arabic, English; translation (MA); woman and child abuse (MA).

Manhattanville College, School of Education, Program in Teaching of Languages Other than English, Purchase, NY 10577-2132. Offers adolescence education (grades 7-12) foreign language(French, Spanish, Italian and Latin) (MAT, Advanced Certificate). *Program availability:* Part-time, evening/weekend. *Faculty:* 2 full-time (1 woman), 1 (woman) part-time/adjunct. *Students:* 2 full-time (both women), 2 part-time (both women). Average age 28. 4 applicants, 75% accepted, 3 enrolled. In 2018, 2 master's awarded. *Degree requirements:* For master's, comprehensive exam (for some programs), thesis (for some programs), student teaching, research seminars, portfolios, internships, writing assessment; for Advanced Certificate, comprehensive exam (for some programs). *Entrance requirements:* For master's, for programs leading to certification, candidates must submit scores from GRE or MAT(Miller Analogies Test), minimum undergraduate GPA of 3.0, all transcripts from all colleges and universities attended, 2 letters of recommendation, interview, essay (2-3 page personal statement that describes reasons for choosing education as profession and personal philosophy of education), proof of immunization (for those born after 1957). Additional exam requirements/recommendations for international students: Required—TOEFL (minimum score 600 paper-based; 110 iBT); Recommended—IELTS (minimum score 8). *Application deadline:* Applications are processed on a rolling basis. Application fee: $75. Electronic applications accepted. *Expenses:* 935 per credit. *Financial support:* Teaching assistantships, career-related internships or fieldwork, Federal Work-Study, institutionally sponsored loans, scholarships/grants, and unspecified assistantships available. Financial award application deadline: 3/15; financial award applicants required to submit FAFSA. *Faculty research:* Changing suburbs institute and community schools. *Unit head:* Dr. Shelley Wepner, Dean, 914-323-3153, Fax: 914-323-5493, E-mail: Shelley.Wepner@mville.edu. *Application contact:* Alissa Wilson, Director, SOE Graduate Enrollment Management, 914-323-3150, Fax: 914-694-1732, E-mail: edschool@mville.edu.
Website: https://www.mville.edu/programs/teaching-languages-other-english

Marquette University, Graduate School, College of Arts and Sciences, Department of Foreign Languages and Literatures, Milwaukee, WI 53201-1881. Offers Spanish (MA). *Program availability:* Part-time, evening/weekend. *Degree requirements:* For master's, one foreign language, comprehensive exam. *Entrance requirements:* For master's, official transcripts from all current and previous colleges/universities except Marquette, three letters of recommendation, tape recording of foreign speaking voice. Additional exam requirements/recommendations for international students: Required—TOEFL. Electronic applications accepted. *Faculty research:* Latin American literature, Afro-Hispanic literature, descriptive Spanish linguistics, inter-American studies, foreign language education.

McGill University, Faculty of Graduate and Postdoctoral Studies, Faculty of Education, Department of Integrated Studies in Education, Montréal, QC H3A 2T5, Canada. Offers culture and values in education (MA, PhD); curriculum studies (MA); educational leadership (MA, Certificate); educational studies (PhD); integrated studies in education (M Ed); second language education (MA, PhD).

Michigan State University, The Graduate School, College of Arts and Letters, Program in Second Language Studies, East Lansing, MI 48824. Offers PhD. *Accreditation:* TEAC. *Entrance requirements:* Additional exam requirements/recommendations for international students: Required—TOEFL, Michigan State University ELT (minimum score 85), Michigan English Language Assessment Battery (minimum score 83). Electronic applications accepted.

Middlebury Institute of International Studies at Monterey, Graduate School of Translation, Interpretation and Language Education, Program in Teaching Foreign Language, Monterey, CA 93940-2691. Offers MATFL. *Degree requirements:* For master's, one foreign language, portfolio, oral defense. *Entrance requirements:* For master's, minimum GPA of 3.0, proficiency in foreign language. Additional exam requirements/recommendations for international students: Required—TOEFL (minimum score 600 paper-based; 100 iBT). Electronic applications accepted.

Middle Tennessee State University, College of Graduate Studies, College of Liberal Arts, Department of Foreign Languages and Literatures, Murfreesboro, TN 37132. Offers foreign languages (MAT), including French, German, Spanish. *Program availability:* Part-time, evening/weekend, online learning. *Degree requirements:* For master's, one foreign language, comprehensive exam, thesis optional. *Entrance requirements:* For master's, GRE. Additional exam requirements/recommendations for international students: Required—TOEFL (minimum score 525 paper-based; 71 iBT) or IELTS (minimum score 6). Electronic applications accepted.

Minnesota State University Mankato, College of Graduate Studies and Research, College of Arts and Humanities, Department of World Languages and Cultures, Program in French, Mankato, MN 56001. Offers French (MS); French education (MS). *Degree requirements:* For master's, one foreign language, comprehensive exam, thesis or alternative. *Entrance requirements:* For master's, minimum GPA of 3.0 during previous 2

years. Additional exam requirements/recommendations for international students: Required—TOEFL. Electronic applications accepted.

Minnesota State University Mankato, College of Graduate Studies and Research, College of Arts and Humanities, Department of World Languages and Cultures, Program in Spanish, Mankato, MN 56001. Offers Spanish (MS); Spanish education (MS); Spanish for the professions (MS). *Degree requirements:* For master's, one foreign language, comprehensive exam, thesis. *Entrance requirements:* For master's, minimum GPA of 3.0 during previous 2 years. Electronic applications accepted.

Mississippi State University, College of Arts and Sciences, Department of Classical and Modern Languages and Literatures, Mississippi State, MS 39762. Offers French (MA). *Program availability:* Part-time. *Faculty:* 13 full-time (4 women). *Students:* 8 full-time (5 women), 2 part-time (both women); includes 3 minority (1 Black or African American, non-Hispanic/Latino; 2 Hispanic/Latino), 2 international. Average age 27. 3 applicants, 67% accepted, 1 enrolled. In 2018, 2 master's awarded. *Degree requirements:* For master's, one foreign language, thesis optional, comprehensive oral or written exam. *Entrance requirements:* For master's, minimum GPA of 2.75 on last two years of undergraduate courses. Additional exam requirements/recommendations for international students: Required—TOEFL (minimum score 525 paper-based; 70 iBT); Recommended—IELTS (minimum score 6). *Application deadline:* For fall admission, 7/1 for domestic students, 5/1 for international students; for spring admission, 11/1 for domestic students, 9/1 for international students. Applications are processed on a rolling basis. Application fee: $60 ($80 for international students). Electronic applications accepted. *Expenses:* Tuition, state resident: full-time $8450; part-time $360.59 per credit hour. Tuition, nonresident: full-time $23,140; part-time $969.09 per credit hour. *Required fees:* $110. One-time fee: $55 full-time. Part-time tuition and fees vary according to course load, degree level, campus/location and reciprocity agreements. *Financial support:* In 2018–19, 9 teaching assistantships (averaging $8,766 per year) were awarded; Federal Work-Study, institutionally sponsored loans, and unspecified assistantships also available. Financial award application deadline: 4/1; financial award applicants required to submit FAFSA. *Faculty research:* French, German, Spanish literature from medieval era to present; gender and cultural studies in French; Spanish-American literature; foreign language methodology; linguistics. *Unit head:* Dr. Peter Corrigan, Professor and Department Head, 662-325-3480, Fax: 662-325-8209, E-mail: pc862@msstate.edu. *Application contact:* Robbie Salters, Admissions and Enrollment Assistant, 662-325-7400, E-mail: rks139@msstate.edu.
Website: http://www.cmll.msstate.edu/

Molloy College, Graduate Education Program, Rockville Centre, NY 11571-5002. Offers adolescent education in biology (MS); adolescent special education (Advanced Certificate); bilingual extension (Advanced Certificate); childhood education (MS); childhood special education (Advanced Certificate); early childhood education (MS); educational technology (MS); English (MS); mathematics (MS); social studies (MS); Spanish (MS); special education on both childhood and adolescent levels (MS); teaching English to speakers of other languages (TESOL) in grades pre-K to 12 (MS); TESOL (Advanced Certificate). *Accreditation:* NCATE. *Program availability:* Part-time, evening/weekend. *Faculty:* 24 full-time (22 women), 26 part-time/adjunct (19 women). *Students:* 106 full-time (78 women), 203 part-time (154 women); includes 65 minority (14 Black or African American, non-Hispanic/Latino; 5 Asian, non-Hispanic/Latino; 41 Hispanic/Latino; 5 Two or more races, non-Hispanic/Latino). Average age 41. 147 applicants, 63% accepted, 79 enrolled. In 2018, 120 master's, 1 other advanced degree awarded. *Entrance requirements:* Additional exam requirements/recommendations for international students: Required—TOEFL (minimum score 550 paper-based; 79 iBT). *Application deadline:* Applications are processed on a rolling basis. Application fee: $60. Electronic applications accepted. *Expenses:* Tuition: Full-time $20,790; part-time $1155 per credit. *Required fees:* $1060; $900. Tuition and fees vary according to course load and degree level. *Financial support:* Application deadline: 3/1; applicants required to submit FAFSA. *Faculty research:* English Language Learners; social emotional needs of students; gifted education; cultural diversity; collaborative teaching methods. *Unit head:* Joanne O'Brien, Dean, 516-323-3116, E-mail: jobrien@molloy.edu. *Application contact:* Faye Hood, Assistant Director for Admissions, 516-323-4009, E-mail: fhood@molloy.edu.

Morehead State University, Graduate School, College of Education, Department of Middle Grades and Secondary Education, Morehead, KY 40351. Offers business and marketing education (MAT); English/language arts 5-9 (MAT); French (MAT); health P-12 (MAT); mathematics 5-9 (MAT); physical education P-12 (MAT); science 5-9 (MAT); secondary biology (MAT); secondary chemistry (MAT); secondary earth science (MAT); secondary English (MAT); secondary math (MAT); secondary physics (MAT); secondary social studies (MAT); social studies 5-9 (MAT); Spanish (MAT). *Program availability:* Part-time, evening/weekend. *Degree requirements:* For master's, portfolio. *Entrance requirements:* For master's, GRE or PRAXIS II content exam, minimum overall undergraduate GPA of 2.5. Additional exam requirements/recommendations for international students: Required—TOEFL (minimum score 500 paper-based). Electronic applications accepted.

New York University, Steinhardt School of Culture, Education, and Human Development, Department of Teaching and Learning, Program in Multilingual/ Multicultural Studies, New York, NY 10012. Offers bilingual education (MA, PhD, Advanced Certificate); foreign language education (MA); teaching English to speakers of other languages (MA, PhD); teaching foreign languages, 7-12 (MA), including Chinese, French, Italian, Japanese, Spanish; teaching French as a foreign language (MA), including teaching English to speakers of other languages; teaching Spanish as a foreign language (MA), including teaching English to speakers of other languages. MA in teaching English to speakers of other languages also offered in collaboration with NYU Shanghai. *Accreditation:* TEAC. *Program availability:* Part-time, evening/weekend. *Entrance requirements:* For doctorate, GRE General Test, interview; for Advanced Certificate, master's degree. Additional exam requirements/recommendations for international students: Required—TOEFL (minimum score 100 iBT). Electronic applications accepted. *Faculty research:* Second language acquisition, cross-cultural communication, technology-enhanced language learning, language variation, action learning.

Northern Arizona University, College of Arts and Letters, Department of Global Languages and Cultures, Flagstaff, AZ 86011. Offers Spanish (MAT); Spanish education (MAT). *Program availability:* Part-time. *Degree requirements:* For master's, variable foreign language requirement, comprehensive exam (for some programs), thesis (for some programs). *Entrance requirements:* Additional exam requirements/ recommendations for international students: Required—TOEFL (minimum score 80 iBT), IELTS (minimum score 7). Electronic applications accepted.

Pace University, School of Education, New York, NY 10038. Offers adolescent education (MST), including biology, chemistry, earth science, English, foreign languages, mathematics, physics, social studies; childhood education (MST); early childhood development, learning and intervention (MST); educational technology studies (MS); inclusive adolescent education (MST), including biology, chemistry, earth science, English, foreign languages, mathematics, physics, social studies; integrated instruction for educational technology (Certificate); integrated instruction for literacy and technology (Certificate); literacy (MS Ed); special education (MS Ed). *Accreditation:* NCATE. *Program availability:* Part-time, evening/weekend, 100% online, blended/hybrid

learning. *Faculty:* 19 full-time (13 women), 86 part-time/adjunct (49 women). *Students:* 98 full-time (82 women), 542 part-time (391 women); includes 256 minority (116 Black or African American, non-Hispanic/Latino; 2 American Indian or Alaska Native, non-Hispanic/Latino; 45 Asian, non-Hispanic/Latino; 83 Hispanic/Latino; 10 Two or more races, non-Hispanic/Latino), 4 international. Average age 30. 223 applicants, 89% accepted, 130 enrolled. In 2018, 269 master's, 12 other advanced degrees awarded. *Degree requirements:* For master's and Certificate, certification exams. *Entrance requirements:* For master's, GRE (for initial certification programs only), teaching certificate (for MS Ed in literacy and special education programs only). Additional exam requirements/recommendations for international students: Required—TOEFL (minimum score 88 iBT), IELTS or PTE. *Application deadline:* For fall admission, 8/1 priority date for domestic students, 6/1 for international students; for spring admission, 12/1 priority date for domestic students, 10/1 for international students. Applications are processed on a rolling basis. Application fee: $70. Electronic applications accepted. *Expenses:* Contact institution. *Financial support:* In 2018–19, 17 students received support, including 17 research assistantships with partial tuition reimbursements available (averaging $6,020 per year); career-related internships or fieldwork, Federal Work-Study, scholarships/grants, and unspecified assistantships also available. Financial award application deadline: 9/1; financial award applicants required to submit FAFSA. *Faculty research:* STEM education, TESOL, teacher education, special education, language and literary development. *Total annual research expenditures:* $1.4 million. *Unit head:* Dr. Harriet Feldman, Dean, School of Education, 914-773-3829, E-mail: hfeldman@pace.edu. *Application contact:* Susan Ford-Goldschein, Director of Graduate Admissions, 212-346-1531, Fax: 212-346-1585, E-mail: graduateadmission@pace.edu.
Website: http://www.pace.edu/school-of-education

Portland State University, Graduate Studies, College of Liberal Arts and Sciences, Department of World Languages and Literatures, Portland, OR 97207-0751. Offers French (MA); German (MA); Japanese (MA); Spanish (MA); world literature and language (MA). *Program availability:* Part-time. *Degree requirements:* For master's, variable foreign language requirement, thesis (for some programs). *Entrance requirements:* For master's, ACTFL, BA in the major language, minimum GPA of 3.0 in all coursework. Additional exam requirements/recommendations for international students: Required—TOEFL (minimum score 550 paper-based; 80 iBT), IELTS (minimum score 6.5). *Faculty research:* Foreign language pedagogy, applied and social linguistics, literary history and criticism.

Purdue University, Graduate School, College of Education, Department of Curriculum and Instruction, West Lafayette, IN 47907. Offers agricultural and extension education (MS, MS Ed, PhD, Ed S); art education (PhD); career and technical education (MS Ed, PhD, Ed S); curriculum studies (MS Ed, PhD, Ed S); educational technology (MS Ed, PhD, Ed S); elementary education (MS Ed); family and consumer sciences education (MS Ed, PhD, Ed S); foreign language education (MS Ed, PhD, Ed S); industrial technology (PhD, Ed S); language arts (MS Ed, PhD, Ed S); literacy (MS Ed, PhD, Ed S); mathematics education (MS, MS Ed, PhD, Ed S); science education (MS, MS Ed, PhD, Ed S); social studies education (MS Ed, PhD, Ed S). *Accreditation:* NCATE. *Program availability:* Part-time, evening/weekend, online learning. *Faculty:* 34 full-time (24 women), 3 part-time/adjunct (1 woman). *Students:* 75 full-time (52 women), 357 part-time (271 women); includes 83 minority (29 Black or African American, non-Hispanic/Latino; 1 American Indian or Alaska Native, non-Hispanic/Latino; 14 Asian, non-Hispanic/Latino; 29 Hispanic/Latino; 1 Native Hawaiian or other Pacific Islander, non-Hispanic/Latino; 9 Two or more races, non-Hispanic/Latino), 43 international. Average age 36. 169 applicants, 83% accepted, 102 enrolled. In 2018, 141 master's, 15 doctorates awarded. *Degree requirements:* For master's, thesis optional; for doctorate, thesis/dissertation, oral and written exams; for Ed S, oral presentation, project. *Entrance requirements:* For master's, GRE General Test (if undergraduate GPA is below 3.0), minimum undergraduate GPA of 3.0 or equivalent; for doctorate, GRE General Test (minimum combined verbal and quantitative score of 1000, 300 for new scoring), minimum undergraduate GPA of 3.0 or equivalent; master's degree with minimum GPA of 3.0 or equivalent; for Ed S, GRE General Test (minimum combined verbal and quantitative score of 1000, 300 for new scoring), minimum undergraduate GPA of 3.0 or equivalent; master's degree. Additional exam requirements/recommendations for international students: Required—TOEFL (minimum score 550 paper-based; 77 iBT). *Application deadline:* For fall admission, 12/15 for domestic students, 3/1 for international students; for spring admission, 9/15 for domestic students, 8/1 for international students. Application fee: $60 ($75 for international students). Electronic applications accepted. *Financial support:* Fellowships with full tuition reimbursements, research assistantships with full tuition reimbursements, teaching assistantships with full tuition reimbursements, career-related internships or fieldwork, and tuition waivers (full) available. Support available to part-time students. Financial award application deadline: 3/1; financial award applicants required to submit FAFSA. *Faculty research:* Literacy acquisition and development, teacher beliefs and knowledge, recruitment and retention of underrepresented students, economic education, literacy discourse. *Unit head:* Janet M. Alsup, Head, 765-494-9667, E-mail: alsupj@purdue.edu. *Application contact:* Heather Brinkman, Graduate Contact, 765-494-2345, E-mail: hbrinkma@purdue.edu.
Website: http://www.edci.purdue.edu/

Purdue University, Graduate School, College of Liberal Arts, School of Languages and Cultures, West Lafayette, IN 47907. Offers French (MA, MAT, PhD), including French (MA, PhD), French education (MAT); German (MA, MAT, PhD), including German (MA, PhD), German education (MAT); Japanese pedagogy (MA); Spanish (MA, MAT, PhD), including Spanish (MA, PhD), Spanish education (MAT). *Faculty:* 34 full-time (16 women), 2 part-time/adjunct (1 woman). *Students:* 34 full-time (22 women), 22 part-time (15 women); includes 8 minority (1 Black or African American, non-Hispanic/Latino; 7 Hispanic/Latino), 36 international. Average age 34. 51 applicants, 22% accepted, 5 enrolled. In 2018, 12 master's, 7 doctorates awarded. Terminal master's awarded for partial completion of doctoral program. *Degree requirements:* For master's, one foreign language; for doctorate, 2 foreign languages, thesis/dissertation. *Entrance requirements:* For master's, GRE General Test (minimum score 600, 160 for new scoring), two writing samples, one in English, one in language (French, German, Japanese, or Spanish); sample recording of English and language of study; for doctorate, GRE General Test (minimum score 600, 160 for new scoring), master's degree with minimum GPA of 3.5 or equivalent; two writing samples, one in English, one in language (French, German, Japanese, or Spanish); sample recording of English and language of study. Additional exam requirements/recommendations for international students: Required—TOEFL (minimum score 550 paper-based; 77 iBT); Recommended—TWE. *Application deadline:* For fall admission, 12/12 for domestic and international students; for spring admission, 10/1 for domestic and international students. Applications are processed on a rolling basis. Application fee: $60 ($75 for international students). Electronic applications accepted. *Financial support:* In 2018–19, fellowships with tuition reimbursements (averaging $15,750 per year), teaching assistantships with tuition reimbursements (averaging $13,463 per year) were awarded. Support available to part-time students. Financial award applicants required to submit FAFSA. *Faculty research:* Linguistics, semiotics, literary criticism, pedagogy. *Unit head:* Jennifer M. William, Head, 765-494-3834, E-mail: jmwilliam@purdue.edu. *Application contact:* Joni L. Hipsher, Graduate Contact, 765-494-3841, E-mail: jlhipshe@purdue.edu.
Website: http://www.cla.purdue.edu/slc/main/

Queens College of the City University of New York, Division of Education, Department of Secondary Education and Youth Services, Queens, NY 11367-1597. Offers adolescent biology (MAT); art (MS Ed); biology (MS Ed, AC); chemistry (MS Ed, AC); earth sciences (MS Ed, AC); English (MS Ed, AC); French (MS Ed); Italian (MS Ed, AC); literacy education (MS Ed); mathematics (MS Ed, AC); music (MS Ed, AC); physics (MS Ed, AC); social studies (MS Ed, AC); Spanish (MS Ed, AC). *Program availability:* Part-time, evening/weekend. *Faculty:* 22 full-time (14 women), 35 part-time/adjunct (24 women). *Students:* 33 full-time (19 women), 358 part-time (228 women); includes 182 minority (15 Black or African American, non-Hispanic/Latino; 62 Asian, non-Hispanic/Latino; 91 Hispanic/Latino; 4 Native Hawaiian or other Pacific Islander, non-Hispanic/Latino; 10 Two or more races, non-Hispanic/Latino), 13 international. Average age 29. 216 applicants, 74% accepted, 109 enrolled. In 2018, 108 master's, 35 other advanced degrees awarded. *Degree requirements:* For master's, research project. *Entrance requirements:* For master's, GRE, minimum GPA of 3.0. Additional exam requirements/recommendations for international students: Required—TOEFL, IELTS. *Application deadline:* For fall admission, 4/1 for domestic students; for spring admission, 11/1 for domestic students. Applications are processed on a rolling basis. Application fee: $125. Electronic applications accepted. *Financial support:* Career-related internships or fieldwork available. Financial award application deadline: 4/1; financial award applicants required to submit FAFSA. *Faculty research:* Self regulated learning, teacher learning, assessment and teaching, language diversity, teaching and learning history. *Unit head:* Dr. Eleanor Armour-Thomas, Chairperson, 718-997-5150, E-mail: eleanor.armour-thomas@qc.cuny.edu. *Application contact:* Elizabeth D'Amico-Ramirez, Assistant Director of Graduate Admissions, 718-997-5203, E-mail: elizabeth.damicoramirez@qc.cuny.edu.

Quinnipiac University, School of Education, Program in Secondary Education, Hamden, CT 06518-1940. Offers biology (MAT); English (MAT); history (MAT); mathematics (MAT); Spanish (MAT). *Accreditation:* NCATE. *Entrance requirements:* For master's, PRAXIS I or PRAXIS Core Academic Skills Exam, minimum GPA of 3.0, interview. Electronic applications accepted. *Faculty research:* Multicultural and urban education/leadership, challenges of teaching diverse learners, scholarship of teaching and learning, technology and teaching, humor and education.

Rhode Island College, School of Graduate Studies, Feinstein School of Education and Human Development, Department of Educational Studies, Providence, RI 02908-1991. Offers advanced studies in teaching and learning (M Ed); English (MAT); French (MAT); history (MAT); math (MAT); secondary education (MAT); Spanish (MAT); teaching English as a second language (M Ed). *Accreditation:* NCATE. *Program availability:* Part-time, evening/weekend. *Faculty:* 12 full-time (9 women), 7 part-time/adjunct (6 women). *Students:* 12 full-time (10 women), 31 part-time (28 women); includes 5 minority (1 Black or African American, non-Hispanic/Latino; 1 Asian, non-Hispanic/Latino; 3 Hispanic/Latino). Average age 33. In 2018, 24 master's awarded. *Degree requirements:* For master's, capstone or comprehensive assessment. *Entrance requirements:* For master's, GRE or MAT (for most programs), minimum undergraduate GPA of 3.0; baccalaureate degree in English, French, history, math or Spanish; 3 letters of recommendation; interview. Additional exam requirements/recommendations for international students: Required—TOEFL (minimum score 550 paper-based; 80 iBT). *Application deadline:* For fall admission, 3/1 for domestic students; for spring admission, 11/1 for domestic students. Applications are processed on a rolling basis. Application fee: $50. Electronic applications accepted. *Expenses: Tuition, area resident:* Part-time $407 per credit. Tuition, nonresident: part-time $792 per credit. *Required fees:* $29 per credit. $100 per semester. *Financial support:* Teaching assistantships, career-related internships or fieldwork, Federal Work-Study, scholarships/grants, health care benefits, and unspecified assistantships available. Support available to part-time students. Financial award application deadline: 5/15; financial award applicants required to submit FAFSA. *Unit head:* Dr. Leslie Bogad, Chair, 401-456-8170. *Application contact:* Dr. Leslie Bogad, Chair, 401-456-8170.
Website: http://www.ric.edu/educationalStudies/Pages/default.aspx

Rider University, College of Education and Human Services, Program in Teaching, Lawrenceville, NJ 08648-3001. Offers bilingual education (MAT); early childhood education (MAT); elementary education (MAT); English as a second language (MAT); secondary education (MAT); world language (MAT). *Students:* 35 full-time (26 women), 88 part-time (67 women); includes 12 minority (1 Black or African American, non-Hispanic/Latino; 1 American Indian or Alaska Native, non-Hispanic/Latino; 2 Asian, non-Hispanic/Latino; 8 Hispanic/Latino). Average age 34. 104 applicants, 67% accepted, 54 enrolled. In 2018, 70 master's awarded. *Entrance requirements:* For master's, Praxis exams, resume,application fee, statement of aims and objectives, official prior college transcripts, interview. Additional exam requirements/recommendations for international students: Required—TOEFL (minimum score 540 paper-based; 79 iBT). *Application deadline:* For fall admission, 5/1 priority date for domestic students, 6/1 priority date for international students; for spring admission, 12/1 priority date for domestic students, 11/1 priority date for international students. Applications are processed on a rolling basis. Application fee: $50. Electronic applications accepted. *Expenses: Tuition:* Full-time $850; part-time $850 per credit hour. *Required fees:* $50; $50 per course. Tuition and fees vary according to program. *Financial support:* Applicants required to submit FAFSA. *Unit head:* Kathleen Pierce, Professor, 609-895-5478, E-mail: kpierce@rider.edu. *Application contact:* Jamie L Mitchell, Director of Graduate Admissions, 609-896-5036, Fax: 609-895-5680, E-mail: jmitchell@rider.edu.

Rivier University, School of Graduate Studies, Department of Modern Languages, Nashua, NH 03060. Offers Spanish (MAT). *Program availability:* Part-time, evening/weekend.

Rutgers University–New Brunswick, Graduate School-New Brunswick, Program in French, Piscataway, NJ 08854-8097. Offers French (MA, PhD); French studies (MAT). *Program availability:* Part-time, evening/weekend. Terminal master's awarded for partial completion of doctoral program. *Degree requirements:* For master's, one foreign language, written and oral exams (MA); for doctorate, 3 foreign languages, thesis/dissertation, qualifying exam. *Entrance requirements:* For master's and doctorate, GRE General Test. *Faculty research:* Literatures in French, literary history and theory, rhetoric and poetics.

Rutgers University–New Brunswick, Graduate School-New Brunswick, Program in Italian, Piscataway, NJ 08854-8097. Offers Italian (MA, PhD); Italian literature and literary criticism (MA); language, literature and culture (MAT). *Program availability:* Part-time, evening/weekend. Terminal master's awarded for partial completion of doctoral program. *Degree requirements:* For master's, one foreign language, comprehensive exam (for some programs), thesis optional; for doctorate, 2 foreign languages, thesis/dissertation, qualifying exam. *Entrance requirements:* For master's and doctorate, GRE General Test. Additional exam requirements/recommendations for international students: Required—TOEFL. *Faculty research:* Literature.

Rutgers University–New Brunswick, Graduate School-New Brunswick, Program in Spanish, Piscataway, NJ 08854-8097. Offers bilingualism and second language acquisition (MA, PhD); Spanish (MA, MAT, PhD); Spanish literature (MA, PhD); translation (MA). *Program availability:* Part-time. *Degree requirements:* For master's, comprehensive exam (for some programs), thesis (for some programs); for doctorate, 2 foreign languages, comprehensive exam, thesis/dissertation. *Entrance requirements:*

For master's and doctorate, GRE General Test. Additional exam requirements/recommendations for international students: Required—TOEFL. Electronic applications accepted. *Faculty research:* Hispanic literature, Luso-Brazilian literature, Spanish linguistics, Spanish translation.

Rutgers University–New Brunswick, Graduate School of Education, Department of Learning and Teaching, Program in Language Education, Piscataway, NJ 08854-8097. Offers English as a second language education (Ed M); language education (Ed M, Ed D). *Program availability:* Part-time. Terminal master's awarded for partial completion of doctoral program. *Degree requirements:* For master's, comprehensive exam; for doctorate, thesis/dissertation, concept paper, qualifying exam. *Entrance requirements:* For master's, GRE General Test, minimum GPA of 3.0; for doctorate, GRE General Test, minimum GPA of 3.5. Additional exam requirements/recommendations for international students: Required—TOEFL. Electronic applications accepted. *Faculty research:* Linguistics, sociolinguistics, cross-cultural/international communication.

Saginaw Valley State University, College of Education, Program in Teaching Chinese as a Foreign Language, University Center, MI 48710. Offers MAT. *Program availability:* Part-time, evening/weekend. *Students:* 12 full-time (7 women), all international. Average age 26. 8 applicants, 100% accepted, 6 enrolled. *Entrance requirements:* For master's, minimum GPA of 3.0. Additional exam requirements/recommendations for international students: Required—TOEFL (minimum score 550 paper-based; 79 iBT). *Application deadline:* For fall admission, 7/15 for international students; for winter admission, 11/15 for international students; for spring admission, 4/15 for international students. Applications are processed on a rolling basis. Application fee: $30 ($90 for international students). Electronic applications accepted. *Expenses:* Tuition, area resident: Full-time $6225; part-time $623 per credit hour. Tuition, state resident: full-time $6225; part-time $623 per credit hour. Tuition, nonresident: full-time $14,215; part-time $1185 per credit hour. *International tuition:* $14,215 full-time. *Required fees:* $263; $14.60 per credit hour. Tuition and fees vary according to degree level. *Financial support:* Federal Work-Study and scholarships/grants available. Support available to part-time students. Financial award application deadline: 4/1; financial award applicants required to submit FAFSA. *Unit head:* Dr. Craig Douglas, Dean, 989-964-4057, Fax: 989-964-4563, E-mail: coeconnect@svsu.edu. *Application contact:* Jenna Briggs, Director, Graduate and International Admissions, 989-964-6096, Fax: 989-964-2788, E-mail: gradadm@svsu.edu.

St. John Fisher College, Ralph C. Wilson Jr. School of Education, Program in Adolescence Education and Special Education, Rochester, NY 14618-3597. Offers adolescence education: biology with special education (MS Ed); adolescence education: chemistry with special education (MS Ed); adolescence education: English with special education (MS Ed); adolescence education: French with special education (MS Ed); adolescence education: math with special education (MS Ed); adolescence education: physics with special education (MS Ed); adolescence education: social studies with special education (MS Ed); adolescence education: Spanish with special education (MS Ed). *Program availability:* Part-time, evening/weekend. *Faculty:* 8 full-time (6 women), 2 part-time/adjunct (both women). *Students:* 13 full-time (4 women), 2 part-time (1 woman); includes 2 minority (1 Black or African American, non-Hispanic/Latino; 1 Two or more races, non-Hispanic/Latino). Average age 27. 24 applicants, 58% accepted, 4 enrolled. In 2018, 9 master's awarded. *Degree requirements:* For master's, field experiences, student teaching. *Entrance requirements:* For master's, LAST, 2 letters of recommendation, personal statement, current resume. Additional exam requirements/recommendations for international students: Required—TOEFL (minimum score 575 paper-based; 80 iBT). *Application deadline:* Applications are processed on a rolling basis. Application fee: $30. Electronic applications accepted. *Expenses:* Contact institution. *Financial support:* Scholarships/grants available. Financial award applicants required to submit FAFSA. *Faculty research:* Arts and humanities, urban schools, constructivist learning, at-risk students, mentoring. *Unit head:* Dr. Susan Hildenbrand, Program Director, 585-385-7297, E-mail: shildenbrand@sjfc.edu. *Application contact:* Michelle Gosier, Director of Transfer and Graduate Admissions, 585-385-8064, E-mail: mgosier@sjfc.edu.

Saint Xavier University, Graduate Studies, School of Education, Chicago, IL 60655-3105. Offers counseling (MA); curriculum and instruction (MA); early childhood education (MA); educational administration (MA); elementary education (MA); individualized studies (MA), including educational technology, English as a second language (ESL), ISTEM (integrative science, technology, engineering, and math), science education; music education (MA); reading (MA); secondary education (MA); Spanish education (MA); special education (MA); teaching and leadership (MA). *Accreditation:* NCATE. *Program availability:* Part-time, evening/weekend. *Degree requirements:* For master's, thesis or project. *Entrance requirements:* For master's, minimum GPA of 3.0. *Expenses:* Contact institution.

Shippensburg University of Pennsylvania, School of Graduate Studies, College of Education and Human Services, Department of Teacher Education, Shippensburg, PA 17257-2299. Offers curriculum and instruction (M Ed), including biology, early childhood education, elementary education, geography/earth science, history, mathematics, middle school education, modern languages; reading (M Ed). *Accreditation:* NCATE. *Program availability:* Part-time, evening/weekend, 100% online, blended/hybrid learning. *Faculty:* 12 full-time (9 women), 2 part-time/adjunct (0 women). *Students:* 10 full-time (8 women), 68 part-time (64 women); includes 7 minority (2 Black or African American, non-Hispanic/Latino; 4 Hispanic/Latino; 1 Two or more races, non-Hispanic/Latino). Average age 31. 41 applicants, 73% accepted, 19 enrolled. In 2018, 34 master's awarded. *Degree requirements:* For master's, comprehensive exam (for some programs), thesis optional, practicum or internship; capstone seminar (for some programs). *Entrance requirements:* For master's, MAT or GRE (if GPA less than 2.75), interview, 3 letters of reference, questionnaire of teaching background and future goals, resume. Additional exam requirements/recommendations for international students: Required—TOEFL (minimum score 550 paper-based; 68 iBT), IELTS (minimum score 6), TOEFL (minimum score 550 paper-based, 68 iBT) or IELTS (minimum score 6). *Application deadline:* For fall admission, 4/1 priority date for domestic students, 4/30 for international students; for spring admission, 9/1 priority date for domestic students, 9/30 for international students; for summer admission, 2/1 priority date for domestic students. Applications are processed on a rolling basis. Application fee: $45. Electronic applications accepted. *Expenses:* Tuition, state resident: part-time $516 per credit. Tuition, nonresident: part-time $750 per credit. *Required fees:* $149 per credit. *Financial support:* In 2018–19, 5 students received support. Career-related internships or fieldwork, scholarships/grants, unspecified assistantships, and resident hall director and student payroll positions available. Support available to part-time students. Financial award application deadline: 3/1; financial award applicants required to submit FAFSA. *Unit head:* Dr. Christine A. Royce, Chairperson, 717-477-1688, Fax: 717-477-4046, E-mail: caroyc@ship.edu. *Application contact:* Maya T. Mapp, Director of Admissions, 717-477-1231, Fax: 717-477-4016, E-mail: mtmapp@ship.edu. Website: http://www.ship.edu/teacher/

Southern Connecticut State University, School of Graduate Studies, School of Arts and Sciences, Department of World Languages and Literatures, New Haven, CT 06515-1355. Offers multicultural-bilingual education/teaching English to speakers of other languages (MS); romance languages (MA). *Program availability:* Part-time, evening/

weekend. *Degree requirements:* For master's, one foreign language, thesis or alternative. *Entrance requirements:* For master's, interview, minimum undergraduate GPA of 2.7. Electronic applications accepted.

Southern Oregon University, Graduate Studies, Department of Foreign Languages and Literatures, Ashland, OR 97520. Offers French language teaching (MA); Spanish language teaching (MA). *Program availability:* Part-time, online learning. *Degree requirements:* For master's, thesis (for some programs). *Entrance requirements:* For master's, GRE General Test, minimum cumulative GPA of 3.0 in the last 90 quarter credits (60 semester credits) of undergraduate coursework. Additional exam requirements/recommendations for international students: Required—TOEFL (minimum score 540 paper-based; 76 iBT), IELTS (minimum score 6), ELPT (minimum score 964) or ELS (minimum score 112). Electronic applications accepted.

Spalding University, Graduate Studies, College of Education, Programs in Education, Louisville, KY 40203-2188. Offers art teacher education (MAT); business teacher education (MAT); elementary school education (MAT); foreign language (MAT); high school education (MAT); middle school education (MAT); secondary education (MAT); special education (learning and behavioral disorders) (MAT); student guidance counselor (MA); teacher leader (M Ed). *Accreditation:* NCATE. *Program availability:* Part-time, evening/weekend. *Entrance requirements:* For master's, GRE General Test or MAT, interview, letters of recommendation, resume. Additional exam requirements/recommendations for international students: Required—TOEFL (minimum score 535 paper-based). Electronic applications accepted. *Faculty research:* Instructional technology, achievement gap, classroom management, assessment.

State University of New York at Plattsburgh, School of Education, Health, and Human Services, Program in Teacher Education: Adolescence Education, Plattsburgh, NY 12901-2681. Offers adolescence education (MST); biology 7-12 (MST); chemistry 7-12 (MST); earth science 7-12 (MST); English 7-12 (MST); French 7-12 (MST); mathematics 7-12 (MST); physics 7-12 (MST); social studies 7-12 (MST); Spanish 7-12 (MST). *Accreditation:* TEAC. *Program availability:* Part-time, evening/weekend. *Entrance requirements:* For master's, minimum GPA of 2.75. Additional exam requirements/recommendations for international students: Required—TOEFL.

State University of New York College at Old Westbury, School of Education, Old Westbury, NY 11568-0210. Offers biology (MAT, MS); chemistry (MAT, MS); English language arts (MAT, MS); math (MAT, MS); social studies (MAT, MS); Spanish (MAT, MS). *Program availability:* Part-time, evening/weekend. *Entrance requirements:* For master's, Liberal Arts and Sciences Test, undergraduate degree with at least 30 semester hours of appropriate coursework as defined by the respective discipline; minimum cumulative undergraduate GPA of 3.0; two letters of recommendation (one from an academic source); essay. Additional exam requirements/recommendations for international students: Required—TOEFL (minimum score 550 paper-based); Recommended—IELTS.

Stony Brook University, State University of New York, School of Professional Development, Stony Brook, NY 11794. Offers coaching (Graduate Certificate); environmental management (MPS); German (MAT); higher education administration (MA, Certificate); human resource management (MS, Graduate Certificate); Italian (MAT); liberal studies (MA); mathematics (MAT); school district business leadership (Advanced Certificate); social studies (MAT); Spanish (MAT). *Program availability:* Part-time, evening/weekend, online learning. *Faculty:* 3 full-time (2 women), 94 part-time/adjunct (40 women). *Students:* 214 full-time (138 women), 1,100 part-time (813 women); includes 313 minority (117 Black or African American, non-Hispanic/Latino; 2 American Indian or Alaska Native, non-Hispanic/Latino; 32 Asian, non-Hispanic/Latino; 140 Hispanic/Latino; 3 Native Hawaiian or other Pacific Islander, non-Hispanic/Latino; 19 Two or more races, non-Hispanic/Latino), 7 international. Average age 33. 483 applicants, 89% accepted, 337 enrolled. In 2018, 315 master's, 178 other advanced degrees awarded. *Entrance requirements:* Additional exam requirements/recommendations for international students: Required—TOEFL (minimum score 85 iBT). *Application deadline:* For fall admission, 1/15 for domestic students, 6/1 for international students; for spring admission, 10/1 for domestic and international students. Applications are processed on a rolling basis. Application fee: $100. *Expenses:* Contact institution. *Financial support:* Fellowships, research assistantships, teaching assistantships, and career-related internships or fieldwork available. Support available to part-time students. *Unit head:* Patricia Malone, Associate Vice President for Professional Education and Assistant Provost for Engaged Learning, 631-632-7512, Fax: 631-632-9046, E-mail: patricia.malone@stonybrook.edu. *Application contact:* Melissa Jordan, Assistant Dean, 631-632-7751, E-mail: melissa.jordan@stonybrook.edu. Website: http://www.stonybrook.edu/spd/

Texas A&M International University, Office of Graduate Studies and Research, College of Arts and Sciences, Department of Humanities, Laredo, TX 78041. Offers English (MA); history and political thought (MA); language, literature and translation (MA). *Degree requirements:* For master's, comprehensive exam (for some programs), thesis (for some programs). *Entrance requirements:* For master's, GRE General Test. Additional exam requirements/recommendations for international students: Required—TOEFL (minimum score 550 paper-based; 79 iBT).

Texas A&M University–Kingsville, College of Graduate Studies, College of Arts and Sciences, Department of Language and Literature, Kingsville, TX 78363. Offers cultural studies (MA); English (MA, MS); Spanish (MA). *Entrance requirements:* Additional exam requirements/recommendations for international students: Required—TOEFL (minimum score 550 paper-based; 79 iBT); Recommended—IELTS. Electronic applications accepted.

Universidad del Este, Graduate School, Carolina, PR 00984. Offers accounting (MBA); adult education (M Ed); agribusiness (MBA); criminal justice and criminology (MA); curriculum and instruction - early education (M Ed); curriculum and instruction - elementary (M Ed); curriculum and instruction - English (M Ed); curriculum and instruction - Spanish (M Ed); human resources (MBA); information security management (MBA); information technology and Web business development (MBA); management (MBA); public policy (MPA); social work (MA), including clinical social work; special education (M Ed); strategic leadership (MBA).

Université du Québec en Outaouais, Graduate Programs, Department of Language Studies, Gatineau, QC J8X 3X7, Canada. Offers second and foreign language teaching (Diploma).

University at Buffalo, the State University of New York, Graduate School, Graduate School of Education, Department of Learning and Instruction, Buffalo, NY 14260. Offers biology education (Ed M, Certificate); chemistry education (Ed M, Certificate); childhood education (Ed M); childhood education with bilingual extension (Ed M); college teaching (Advanced Certificate); curriculum, instruction and the science of learning (PhD); early childhood education (Ed M); early childhood education with bilingual extension (Ed M); earth science education (Ed M, Certificate); education and technology (Ed M); education studies (Ed M); educational technology and new literacies (Certificate); educational technology and new literacies (Advanced Certificate); elementary education (Ed D); English education (Ed M, Certificate); English education studies (Ed M); English for speakers of other languages (Ed M); foreign and second language education (PhD);

French education (Ed M, Certificate); German education (Ed M, Certificate); gifted education (Certificate); Latin education (Ed M, Certificate); literacy education studies (Ed M); literacy specialist (Ed M); literacy teaching and learning (Certificate); mathematics education (Ed M, Certificate); music education (Ed M, Certificate); music education studies (Ed M); music learning theory (Advanced Certificate); online education (Advanced Certificate); physics education (Ed M, Certificate); science and the public (Ed M); social studies education (Ed M, Certificate); Spanish education (Ed M, Certificate); special education (PhD); teaching English to speakers of other languages (Ed M). *Program availability:* Part-time, evening/weekend, 100% online. *Faculty:* 31 full-time (22 women), 41 part-time/adjunct (27 women). *Students:* 161 full-time (107 women), 369 part-time (260 women); includes 76 minority (26 Black or African American, non-Hispanic/Latino; 3 American Indian or Alaska Native, non-Hispanic/Latino; 30 Asian, non-Hispanic/Latino; 14 Hispanic/Latino; 3 Two or more races, non-Hispanic/Latino), 41 international. Average age 34. 368 applicants, 70% accepted, 179 enrolled. In 2018, 100 master's, 26 doctorates, 19 other advanced degrees awarded. *Degree requirements:* For master's, comprehensive exam; for doctorate, thesis/dissertation, research analysis exam, research experience. *Entrance requirements:* For master's, letters of reference; for doctorate, GRE General Test or MAT, interview, writing sample, letters of recommendation. Additional exam requirements/recommendations for international students: Required—TOEFL (minimum score 600 paper-based; 96 iBT), IELTS (minimum score 6.5), PTE (minimum score 55). *Application deadline:* For fall admission, 2/1 priority date for domestic and international students; for spring admission, 11/15 priority date for domestic students, 10/1 for international students. Applications are processed on a rolling basis. Application fee: $50. Electronic applications accepted. *Financial support:* In 2018–19, 42 fellowships (averaging $5,181 per year), 44 research assistantships with tuition reimbursements (averaging $10,908 per year) were awarded; teaching assistantships, career-related internships or fieldwork, Federal Work-Study, institutionally sponsored loans, scholarships/grants, tuition waivers (full and partial), and unspecified assistantships also available. Financial award application deadline: 2/28; financial award applicants required to submit FAFSA. *Faculty research:* Science assessment, foreign language teaching and learning, early learning, new literacies, gender and education. *Total annual research expenditures:* $413,233. *Unit head:* Dr. Julie Gorlewski, Department Chair, 716-645-2455, Fax: 716-645-3161, E-mail: jgorlews@buffalo.edu. *Application contact:* Renad Aref, Assistant Director of Admission Recruitment, 716-645-2110, Fax: 716-645-7937, E-mail: gseinfo@buffalo.edu.
Website: http://ed.buffalo.edu/teaching.html

University of Arkansas at Little Rock, Graduate School, College of Arts, Letters, and Sciences, Department of International and Second Language Studies, Little Rock, AR 72204-1099. Offers second languages (MA). *Degree requirements:* For master's, comprehensive exam, thesis. *Entrance requirements:* For master's, GRE or MAT, bachelor's degree; 3 letters of reference; personal interview; minimum overall undergraduate GPA of 2.75, 3.0 in last 60 hours.

University of California, Irvine, School of Humanities, Department of Spanish and Portuguese, Irvine, CA 92697. Offers Spanish (MA, MAT, PhD). *Students:* 27 full-time (17 women); includes 16 minority (15 Hispanic/Latino; 1 Two or more races, non-Hispanic/Latino), 5 international. Average age 36. 14 applicants, 50% accepted, 4 enrolled. In 2018, 8 doctorates awarded. *Entrance requirements:* For master's and doctorate, GRE General Test, minimum GPA of 3.0. Additional exam requirements/recommendations for international students: Required—TOEFL (minimum score 550 paper-based). *Application deadline:* For fall admission, 1/2 priority date for domestic students, 1/2 for international students. Applications are processed on a rolling basis. Application fee: $105 ($125 for international students). Electronic applications accepted. *Financial support:* Fellowships, teaching assistantships, institutionally sponsored loans, traineeships, health care benefits, and unspecified assistantships available. Financial award application deadline: 3/1; financial award applicants required to submit FAFSA. *Faculty research:* Latin American literature, Spanish literature, Spanish linguistics in Creole studies, Hispanic literature in the U.S., Luso-Brazilian literature. *Unit head:* Luis Aviles, Department Chair, 949-824-7268, Fax: 949-824-2803, E-mail: laviles@uci.edu. *Application contact:* Evelyn Flores, Graduate Program Coordinator, 949-824-8793, Fax: 949-824-2803, E-mail: evelynf@uci.edu.
Website: http://www.hnet.uci.edu/spanishandportuguese/

University of Central Florida, College of Community Innovation and Education, School of Teacher Education, Orlando, FL 32816. Offers applied learning and instruction (MA); curriculum and instruction (M Ed); elementary education (M Ed, MA); exceptional student education (M Ed, MA, Certificate), including autism spectrum disorders (Certificate), exceptional student education (M Ed), exceptional student education K-12 (MA), intervention specialist (Certificate), pre-kindergarten disabilities (Certificate), severe or profound disabilities (Certificate), special education (Certificate); K-8 mathematics and science education (M Ed, Certificate); reading education (M Ed, Certificate); teacher education (MAT), including art education, English language, mathematics education, middle school mathematics, middle school science, science education, social science education; world languages education - English for speakers of other languages (ESOL) (Certificate); world languages education - languages other than English (LOTE) (Certificate). *Program availability:* Part-time, evening/weekend. *Degree requirements:* For Certificate, thesis or alternative. *Entrance requirements:* For degree, GRE General Test, minimum GPA of 3.0. Additional exam requirements/recommendations for international students: Required—TOEFL. Electronic applications accepted.

University of Connecticut, Graduate School, Neag School of Education, Department of Curriculum and Instruction, Program in World Languages Education, Storrs, CT 06269. Offers MA, PhD. *Accreditation:* NCATE. Terminal master's awarded for partial completion of doctoral program. *Degree requirements:* For master's, comprehensive exam, thesis or alternative; for doctorate, thesis/dissertation. *Entrance requirements:* For doctorate, GRE General Test. Additional exam requirements/recommendations for international students: Required—TOEFL (minimum score 550 paper-based). Electronic applications accepted.

University of Dayton, Department of Teacher Education, Dayton, OH 45469. Offers adolescence to young adult education (MS Ed); early childhood leadership and advocacy (MS Ed); interdisciplinary education (MS Ed), including visual arts; interdisciplinary education studies (MS Ed); leadership in educational systems (MS Ed); literacy (MS Ed); mathematics education (MS Ed); middle childhood education (MS Ed); multi-age education (MS Ed), including world languages; music education (MS Ed); teacher as leader (MS Ed); teacher education (MS Ed); technology-enhanced learning (MS Ed); trans-disciplinary early childhood education (MS Ed). *Program availability:* Part-time, 100% online. *Degree requirements:* For master's, variable foreign language requirement, thesis or alternative, internship (for teaching licensure or endorsement). *Entrance requirements:* For master's, GRE (minimum score of 149 verbal, 4 on writing) or MAT (minimum score of 396) if undergraduate GPA was under 2.75, minimum GPA of 2.75, 3 letters of recommendation, personal statement or resume, official transcripts. Additional exam requirements/recommendations for international students: Required—TOEFL (minimum score 550 paper-based; 80 iBT); Recommended—IELTS (minimum score 6.5). Electronic applications accepted. *Expenses:* Contact institution. *Faculty research:* Social emotional learning, culturally responsive teaching, urban teaching, literacy, instructional strategies, pre-service teacher education preparation.

University of Delaware, College of Arts and Sciences, Department of Foreign Languages and Literatures, Newark, DE 19716. Offers foreign languages and literatures (MA), including French, German, Spanish; foreign languages pedagogy (MA), including French, German, Spanish; technical Chinese translation (MA). *Degree requirements:* For master's, one foreign language, comprehensive exam, thesis optional. *Entrance requirements:* For master's, GRE General Test, letters of recommendation, writing sample. Additional exam requirements/recommendations for international students: Required—TOEFL. Electronic applications accepted. *Faculty research:* Medieval to Modern French and Spanish literature, twentieth-century German, French, Spanish literature by women, computer-assisted instruction.

University of Florida, Graduate School, College of Liberal Arts and Sciences, Department of Spanish and Portuguese Studies, Gainesville, FL 32611. Offers Spanish (MA, MAT, PhD). *Program availability:* Part-time. Terminal master's awarded for partial completion of doctoral program. *Degree requirements:* For master's, one foreign language, comprehensive exam, thesis or extended research paper; for doctorate, 2 foreign languages, comprehensive exam, thesis/dissertation, qualifying exam. *Entrance requirements:* For master's and doctorate, GRE General Test, minimum GPA of 3.0. Additional exam requirements/recommendations for international students: Required—TOEFL (minimum score 550 paper-based; 80 iBT), IELTS (minimum score 6). Electronic applications accepted. *Faculty research:* Spanish linguistics; second language acquisition and teaching; Spanish literature, film and culture; Latin American literature, film and culture; Portuguese literature, film and culture.

University of Hawaii at Hilo, Program in Hawaiian and Indigenous Language and Culture Revitalization, Hilo, HI 96720-4091. Offers PhD. *Entrance requirements:* Additional exam requirements/recommendations for international students: Required—TOEFL, IELTS. Electronic applications accepted.

University of Hawaii at Hilo, Program in Hawaiian Language and Literature, Hilo, HI 96720-4091. Offers MA. *Entrance requirements:* Additional exam requirements/recommendations for international students: Required—TOEFL, IELTS. Electronic applications accepted.

University of Hawaii at Hilo, Program in Indigenous Language and Culture Education, Hilo, HI 96720-4091. Offers MA. *Entrance requirements:* Additional exam requirements/recommendations for international students: Required—TOEFL, IELTS. Electronic applications accepted.

University of Hawaii at Manoa, Office of Graduate Education, College of Languages, Linguistics and Literature, Department of Second Language Studies, Honolulu, HI 96822. Offers English as a second language (MA, Graduate Certificate); second language acquisition (PhD). *Program availability:* Part-time. *Degree requirements:* For master's, 2 foreign languages, thesis optional; for doctorate, 2 foreign languages, comprehensive exam, thesis/dissertation. *Entrance requirements:* For master's, GRE General Test, minimum GPA of 3.0; for doctorate, GRE General Test, MA, scholarly publications. Additional exam requirements/recommendations for international students: Required—TOEFL (minimum score 600 paper-based; 100 iBT), IELTS (minimum score 7). *Faculty research:* Second language use, second language analysis, second language pedagogy and testing, second language learning, qualitative and quantitative research methods for second languages.

University of Hawaii at Manoa, Office of Graduate Education, Hawai'inuiakea School of Hawaiian Knowledge, Program in Hawaiian, Honolulu, HI 96822. Offers MA. *Program availability:* Part-time. *Degree requirements:* For master's, thesis optional. *Entrance requirements:* Additional exam requirements/recommendations for international students: Required—TOEFL (minimum score 500 paper-based; 61 iBT), IELTS (minimum score 5).

University of Hawaii at Manoa, Office of Graduate Education, Hawai'inuiakea School of Hawaiian Knowledge, Program in Hawaiian Studies, Honolulu, HI 96822. Offers MA. *Program availability:* Part-time. *Degree requirements:* For master's, thesis optional. *Entrance requirements:* Additional exam requirements/recommendations for international students: Required—TOEFL (minimum score 500 paper-based; 61 iBT), IELTS (minimum score 5).

University of Illinois at Chicago, College of Liberal Arts and Sciences, School of Literatures, Cultural Studies and Linguistics, Chicago, IL 60607-7128. Offers French and Francophone studies (MA); Germanic studies (MA); Hispanic and Italian studies (MAT, PhD), including Hispanic linguistics (PhD), Hispanic literary and cultural studies (PhD), teaching of Spanish (MAT); linguistics (MA), including teaching English to speakers of other languages/applied linguistics; Slavic and Baltic languages and literatures (MA), including Slavic studies (MA, PhD); Slavic and Baltic languages and literatures (PhD), including Slavic studies (MA, PhD). *Program availability:* Part-time. Terminal master's awarded for partial completion of doctoral program. *Degree requirements:* For master's, one foreign language, exam. *Entrance requirements:* For master's, minimum GPA of 2.75. Additional exam requirements/recommendations for international students: Required—TOEFL. Electronic applications accepted. *Faculty research:* International studies, religious (Catholic, Jewish) studies, moving image arts.

University of Illinois at Urbana–Champaign, Graduate College, College of Liberal Arts and Sciences, School of Literatures, Cultures and Linguistics, Department of Spanish, Italian and Portuguese, Champaign, IL 61820. Offers Italian (MA, PhD); Portuguese (MA, PhD); Spanish (MA, PhD).

University of Illinois at Urbana–Champaign, Graduate College, College of Liberal Arts and Sciences, School of Literatures, Cultures and Linguistics, Department of the Classics, Champaign, IL 61820. Offers classical philology (PhD); classics (MA); teaching of Latin (MA).

University of Indianapolis, Graduate Programs, School of Education, Indianapolis, IN 46227-3697. Offers art education (MAT); biology (MAT); chemistry (MAT); curriculum and instruction (MA); earth sciences (MAT); education (MA, MAT); educational leadership (MA); elementary education (MA); English (MAT); French (MAT); math (MAT); physical education (MAT); physics (MAT); secondary education (MA), including art education, education, English education, social studies education; social studies (MAT); Spanish (MAT). *Accreditation:* NCATE. *Program availability:* Part-time, evening/weekend. *Entrance requirements:* For master's, GRE Subject Test, PRAXIS I, minimum GPA of 2.5, 3 letters of recommendation, interview. Additional exam requirements/recommendations for international students: Required—TOEFL (minimum score 550 paper-based). *Faculty research:* Assessment of teacher education, perceptions of prospective teachers by parents.

The University of Iowa, Graduate College, College of Education, Department of Teaching and Learning, Program in Education, Iowa City, IA 52242-1316. Offers art education (MA); developmental reading (MA); elementary education (MA); English education (MA, MAT); foreign and second language education (MAT); foreign language education (MA); foreign language/ESL education (PhD); language, literacy and culture (PhD); mathematics education (MA, MAT, PhD); music education (MM, PhD); science education (MA); secondary education (MA); social studies (MA, PhD). *Degree requirements:* For master's, thesis optional, exam; for doctorate, comprehensive exam,

thesis/dissertation. *Entrance requirements:* For master's and doctorate, GRE General Test, minimum GPA of 3.0. Additional exam requirements/recommendations for international students: Required—TOEFL (minimum score 550 paper-based; 81 iBT). Electronic applications accepted.

The University of Iowa, Graduate College, College of Liberal Arts and Sciences, Program in Second Language Acquisition, Iowa City, IA 52242-1316. Offers PhD. *Degree requirements:* For doctorate, comprehensive exam, thesis/dissertation. *Entrance requirements:* For doctorate, GRE General Test, minimum GPA of 3.0. Additional exam requirements/recommendations for international students: Required—TOEFL (minimum score 600 paper-based; 100 iBT). Electronic applications accepted.

University of Kentucky, Graduate School, College of Arts and Sciences and College of Education, Program in Teaching World Languages, Lexington, KY 40506-0032. Offers MA. *Entrance requirements:* For master's, GRE General Test, minimum undergraduate GPA of 2.75. Additional exam requirements/recommendations for international students: Required—TOEFL (minimum score 550 paper-based). Electronic applications accepted.

University of Maine, Graduate School, College of Liberal Arts and Sciences, Department of Modern Languages and Classics, Orono, ME 04469. Offers French (MA, MAT); Spanish (MAT). *Program availability:* Part-time. *Faculty:* 7 full-time (4 women). *Students:* 4 full-time (all women), 4 part-time (3 women); includes 3 minority (1 Black or African American, non-Hispanic/Latino; 2 Hispanic/Latino). Average age 36. 2 applicants, 100% accepted, 2 enrolled. In 2018, 1 master's awarded. *Degree requirements:* For master's, one foreign language, thesis (for some programs). *Entrance requirements:* For master's, GRE General Test; PRAXIS II (for MAT). Additional exam requirements/recommendations for international students: Required—TOEFL, PRAXIS II. *Application deadline:* For fall admission, 2/1 priority date for domestic and international students. Applications are processed on a rolling basis. Application fee: $65. Electronic applications accepted. *Financial support:* In 2018–19, 3 students received support, including 2 fellowships with full tuition reimbursements available (averaging $15,000 per year), 1 teaching assistantship with full tuition reimbursement available (averaging $15,600 per year); Federal Work-Study and tuition waivers (full and partial) also available. Financial award application deadline: 3/1. *Faculty research:* Contemporary Latin American literature and culture, modern and contemporary Spanish peninsular literature, North American French linguistics, 20th-century Quebec literature and culture, contemporary French philosophy. *Unit head:* Dr. Jane Smith, Chair, 207-581-2075, Fax: 207-581-1832. *Application contact:* Scott G. Delcourt, Assistant Vice President for Graduate Studies/Senior Associate Dean, 207-581-3291, Fax: 207-581-3232, E-mail: graduate@maine.edu. *Website:* https://umaine.edu/mlandc/graduate-programs/

University of Maryland, Baltimore County, The Graduate School, College of Arts, Humanities and Social Sciences, Department of Education, Program in Teaching, Baltimore, MD 21250. Offers early childhood education (MAT); elementary education (MAT); teaching (MAT), including art, biology, chemistry, choral music, classical foreign language, dance, earth/space science, English, instrumental music, mathematics, modern foreign language, physical science, physics, social studies, theatre. *Program availability:* Part-time, evening/weekend. *Degree requirements:* For master's, comprehensive exam (for some programs), thesis (for some programs). *Entrance requirements:* For master's, PRAXIS Core Examination or GRE (minimum score of 1000), minimum GPA of 3.0. Additional exam requirements/recommendations for international students: Required—TOEFL. Electronic applications accepted. *Faculty research:* STEM teacher education, culturally sensitive pedagogy, ESOL/bilingual education, early childhood education, language, literacy and culture.

University of Maryland, College Park, Academic Affairs, College of Arts and Humanities, School of Languages, Literatures, and Cultures, Program in Second Language Acquisition and Application, College Park, MD 20742. Offers second language instruction (PhD); second language learning (PhD); second language measurement and assessment (PhD); second language use (PhD). Electronic applications accepted. *Faculty research:* Second language acquisition, pedagogical perspectives, technological applications, language use in professional contexts.

University of Massachusetts Amherst, Graduate School, College of Humanities and Fine Arts, Department of Languages, Literatures, and Cultures, Program in French and Francophone Studies, Amherst, MA 01003. Offers French (MAT); French and Francophone studies (MA). *Program availability:* Part-time. *Degree requirements:* For master's, thesis or alternative. *Entrance requirements:* For master's, GRE General Test. Additional exam requirements/recommendations for international students: Required—TOEFL (minimum score 550 paper-based; 80 iBT), IELTS (minimum score 6.5). Electronic applications accepted.

University of Michigan, Rackham Graduate School, College of Literature, Science, and the Arts, Department of Classical Studies, Ann Arbor, MI 48109. Offers classical studies (MA, PhD); Greek and Roman history (PhD); Latin (MA); Latin with teaching certification (MAT). *Faculty:* 26 full-time (15 women), 3 part-time/adjunct (2 women). *Students:* 46 full-time (20 women); includes 4 minority (2 Asian, non-Hispanic/Latino; 2 Two or more races, non-Hispanic/Latino), 6 international. Average age 27. 75 applicants, 13% accepted, 9 enrolled. In 2018, 1 master's, 4 doctorates awarded. Terminal master's awarded for partial completion of doctoral program. *Degree requirements:* For master's, one foreign language, comprehensive exam; for doctorate, 4 foreign languages, comprehensive exam, thesis/dissertation, oral defense of dissertation, preliminary exams, qualifying exams. *Entrance requirements:* For master's, 2-3 years of Latin (for the Latin MAT); for doctorate, strict minimum of 3 years of college-level Latin and 2 years of college-level Greek. Additional exam requirements/recommendations for international students: Required—TOEFL (minimum score 560 paper-based). *Application deadline:* For fall admission, 12/15 for domestic and international students. Application fee: $75 ($90 for international students). Electronic applications accepted. *Financial support:* In 2018–19, 46 students received support, including 23 fellowships with full tuition reimbursements available (averaging $20,850 per year), 1 research assistantship with full tuition reimbursement available (averaging $20,850 per year), 15 teaching assistantships with full tuition reimbursements available (averaging $20,850 per year); career-related internships or fieldwork, institutionally sponsored loans, scholarships/grants, traineeships, health care benefits, tuition waivers (full), unspecified assistantships, and summer support also available. Financial award application deadline: 3/15. *Faculty research:* Greek and Latin literature, ancient history, papyrology, archaeology. *Unit head:* Prof. Artemis Leontis, Chair and Professor, 734-764-0360, Fax: 734-763-4959, E-mail: classics@umich.edu. *Application contact:* Sarah Kandell-Gritzmaker, Student Services Coordinator, 734-615-3181, Fax: 734-763-4959, E-mail: skandell@umich.edu. *Website:* http://www.lsa.umich.edu/classics

University of Minnesota, Twin Cities Campus, Graduate School, College of Education and Human Development, Department of Curriculum and Instruction, Program in Teaching, Minneapolis, MN 55455-0213. Offers teaching (M Ed), including arts in education, elementary education, English education, mathematics, science, second language education, social studies. *Students:* 249 full-time (182 women), 101 part-time (59 women); includes 57 minority (5 Black or African American, non-Hispanic/Latino; 16 Asian, non-Hispanic/Latino; 25 Hispanic/Latino; 11 Two or more races, non-

Hispanic/Latino), 12 international. Average age 28. 383 applicants, 79% accepted, 261 enrolled. In 2018, 292 master's awarded. Application fee: $75 ($95 for international students). *Unit head:* Dr. Mark Vagle, Chair, 612-625-4006, Fax: 612-624-8277, E-mail: mvagle@umn.edu. *Application contact:* Dr. Mark Vagle, Chair, 612-625-4006, Fax: 612-624-8277, E-mail: mvagle@umn.edu. *Website:* http://www.cehd.umn.edu/ci/

University of Mississippi, Graduate School, College of Liberal Arts, University, MS 38677-1848. Offers anthropology (MA); biology (MS, PhD); chemistry (MS, DA, PhD); creative writing (MFA); documentary expression (MFA); economics (MA, PhD); English (MA, PhD); experimental psychology (PhD); history (MA, PhD); mathematics (MS, PhD); modern languages (MA); music (MM); philosophy (MA); physics (MA, MS, PhD); political science (MA, PhD); Southern studies (MA); studio art (MFA). *Program availability:* Part-time. *Faculty:* 474 full-time (209 women), 71 part-time/adjunct (38 women). *Students:* 471 full-time (241 women), 80 part-time (39 women); includes 90 minority (43 Black or African American, non-Hispanic/Latino; 14 Asian, non-Hispanic/Latino; 23 Hispanic/Latino; 10 Two or more races, non-Hispanic/Latino), 136 international. *Degree requirements:* For doctorate, thesis/dissertation. *Entrance requirements:* For master's, GRE General Test, minimum GPA of 3.0; for doctorate, GRE General Test. Additional exam requirements/recommendations for international students: Required—TOEFL. *Application deadline:* Applications are processed on a rolling basis. Application fee: $50. Electronic applications accepted. *Financial support:* Fellowships, research assistantships, teaching assistantships, career-related internships or fieldwork, Federal Work-Study, institutionally sponsored loans, scholarships/grants, and unspecified assistantships available. Financial award application deadline: 3/1; financial award applicants required to submit FAFSA. *Unit head:* Dr. Lee Michael Cohen, Dean, 662-915-7177, Fax: 662-915-5792, E-mail: libarts@olemiss.edu. *Application contact:* Tameka Smith, Graduate Activities Specialist for Admissions, 662-915-7474, Fax: 662-915-7577, E-mail: gschool@olemiss.edu. *Website:* ventress@olemiss.edu

University of Missouri, Office of Research and Graduate Studies, College of Education, Department of Learning, Teaching and Curriculum, Columbia, MO 65211. Offers agricultural education (M Ed, PhD, Ed S); art education (M Ed, PhD, Ed S); business and office education (M Ed, PhD, Ed S); early childhood education (M Ed, PhD, Ed S); elementary education (M Ed, PhD, Ed S); English education (M Ed, PhD, Ed S); foreign language education (M Ed, PhD, Ed S); health education and promotion (M Ed, PhD); learning and instruction (M Ed); marketing education (M Ed, PhD, Ed S); mathematics education (M Ed, PhD, Ed S); music education (M Ed, PhD, Ed S); reading education (M Ed, PhD, Ed S); science education (M Ed, PhD, Ed S); social studies education (M Ed, PhD, Ed S); vocational education (M Ed, PhD, Ed S). *Program availability:* Part-time. Terminal master's awarded for partial completion of doctoral program. *Entrance requirements:* For master's and Ed S, GRE General Test or MAT, minimum GPA of 3.0; for doctorate, GRE General Test, minimum GPA of 3.0. Additional exam requirements/recommendations for international students: Required—TOEFL.

University of Nebraska at Kearney, College of Fine Arts and Humanities, Department of Modern Languages, Kearney, NE 68849-0001. Offers Spanish education (MA Ed). *Accreditation:* NCATE. *Program availability:* Part-time, evening/weekend. *Degree requirements:* For master's, comprehensive exam, thesis optional. *Entrance requirements:* For master's, 21 semester hours of upper-level Spanish; two-page Spanish essay; one-page English essay; two letters of recommendation. Additional exam requirements/recommendations for international students: Recommended—TOEFL (minimum score 550 paper-based; 79 iBT), IELTS (minimum score 6.5). Electronic applications accepted. *Faculty research:* Translation theory, Spanish linguistics; symotolistic poetry, critical theory and Marxism, French and Francophone film, themes of culture, nationality and ethnicity.

University of Nebraska at Omaha, Graduate Studies, College of Arts and Sciences, Program in Language Teaching, Omaha, NE 68182. Offers MA. *Program availability:* Part-time, evening/weekend. *Degree requirements:* For master's, comprehensive exam, thesis (for some programs). *Entrance requirements:* For master's, minimum GPA of 3.0, official transcripts, 2 letters of recommendation, oral language sample, writing sample. Additional exam requirements/recommendations for international students: Required—TOEFL, IELTS, PTE. Electronic applications accepted.

The University of North Carolina at Chapel Hill, Graduate School, School of Education, Program in Secondary Education, Chapel Hill, NC 27599. Offers English (Grades 9-12) (MAT); English as a second language (MAT); French (Grades K-12) (MAT); German (Grades K-12) (MAT); Japanese (Grades K-12) (MAT); Latin (Grades 9-12) (MAT); mathematics (Grades 9-12) (MAT); music (Grades K-12) (MAT); science (Grades 9-12) (MAT); social studies (Grades 9-12) (MAT); Spanish (Grades K-12) (MAT). *Accreditation:* NCATE. *Degree requirements:* For master's, comprehensive exam. *Entrance requirements:* For master's, GRE General Test, minimum GPA of 3.0 during last 2 years of undergraduate course work. Additional exam requirements/recommendations for international students: Required—TOEFL (minimum score 550 paper-based). Electronic applications accepted.

The University of North Carolina at Charlotte, Cato College of Education, Interdisciplinary Education Programs, Charlotte, NC 28223-0001. Offers art education (Graduate Certificate); child and family development: early childhood education (MAT); curriculum and instruction (PhD); elementary education (MAT); foreign language education (MAT); middle grades education (MAT); secondary education (MAT); special education (MAT); teaching (Graduate Certificate); teaching English as a second language (MAT); theatre education (Graduate Certificate). *Program availability:* Part-time, 100% online, blended/hybrid learning. *Students:* 70 full-time (55 women), 511 part-time (414 women); includes 228 minority (160 Black or African American, non-Hispanic/Latino; 1 American Indian or Alaska Native, non-Hispanic/Latino; 11 Asian, non-Hispanic/Latino; 38 Hispanic/Latino; 18 Two or more races, non-Hispanic/Latino), 8 international. Average age 34. 343 applicants, 92% accepted, 219 enrolled. In 2018, 69 master's, 13 doctorates, 161 other advanced degrees awarded. *Entrance requirements:* For master's, GRE or MAT, bachelor's degree, or its U.S. equivalent, from regionally-accredited college or university; minimum overall GPA of 3.0 on all previous work beyond high school; statement of purpose (essay); at least three recommendation forms; for doctorate, GRE or MAT, bachelor's degree (or its U.S. equivalent) from regionally-accredited college or university; minimum overall GPA of 3.5 in master's degree program; for Graduate Certificate, bachelor's degree from regionally-accredited university; minimum GPA of 2.75 on all post-secondary work attempted; transcripts; personal statement outlining why the applicant seeks admission to the program. Additional exam requirements/recommendations for international students: Required—TOEFL (minimum score 523 paper-based; 70 iBT), IELTS (minimum score 6), TOEFL (minimum score 523 paper-based, 70 iBT) or IELTS (6). *Application deadline:* Applications are processed on a rolling basis. Application fee: $75. Electronic applications accepted. Tuition and fees vary according to course load and program. *Financial support:* Career-related internships or fieldwork, institutionally sponsored loans, scholarships/grants, and unspecified assistantships available. Support available to part-time students. Financial award application deadline: 3/1; financial award applicants required to submit FAFSA. *Unit head:* Dr. Ellen McIntyre, Dean, 704-687-8722, E-mail: ellen.mcintyre@uncc.edu. *Application contact:* Kathy B. Giddings, Director

of Graduate Admissions, 704-687-5503, Fax: 704-687-1668, E-mail: gradadm@uncc.edu.
Website: http://education.uncc.edu/academic-programs

The University of North Carolina at Greensboro, Graduate School, School of Education, Department of Teacher Education and Higher Education, Greensboro, NC 27412-5001. Offers college teaching and adult learning (Certificate); curriculum and instruction (M Ed), including chemistry education, elementary education, English as a second language, French education, instructional technology, mathematics education, middle grades education, reading education, science education, social studies education, Spanish education; curriculum and teaching (PhD), including higher education, teacher education and development; English as a second language (Certificate); higher education (M Ed); supervision (M Ed). *Accreditation:* NCATE. *Program availability:* Part-time. *Degree requirements:* For doctorate, thesis/dissertation. *Entrance requirements:* For master's and doctorate, GRE General Test. Additional exam requirements/recommendations for international students: Required—TOEFL. Electronic applications accepted. *Faculty research:* Community college literacy program, middle school mathematics/computer mathematics.

University of Northern Colorado, Graduate School, College of Education and Behavioral Sciences, School of Teacher Education, Greeley, CO 80639. Offers curriculum studies (MAT); educational studies (Ed D); elementary education (MAT); English education (MAT); literacy (MA); multilingual education (MA), including TESOL, world languages; teaching diverse learners (MA). *Accreditation:* NCATE. *Program availability:* Part-time, evening/weekend. *Degree requirements:* For master's, comprehensive exam, thesis or alternative; for doctorate, comprehensive exam, thesis/dissertation. *Entrance requirements:* For master's and doctorate, GRE General Test, 3 letters of recommendation. Electronic applications accepted.

University of Northern Iowa, Graduate College, College of Humanities, Arts and Sciences, Department of Languages and Literatures, MA Program in Spanish, Cedar Falls, IA 50614. Offers Spanish (MA); Spanish teaching (MA). *Program availability:* Part-time, evening/weekend. *Degree requirements:* For master's, one foreign language, comprehensive exam, thesis or alternative. *Entrance requirements:* For master's, minimum GPA of 3.0, valid teaching license, documentation of successful teaching experience. Additional exam requirements/recommendations for international students: Required—TOEFL (minimum score 600 paper-based; 100 iBT). Electronic applications accepted.

University of Northern Iowa, Graduate College, College of Humanities, Arts and Sciences, Department of Languages and Literatures, MA Program in TESOL/Spanish, Cedar Falls, IA 50614. Offers MA.

University of Oklahoma, Jeannine Rainbolt College of Education, Department of Instructional Leadership and Academic Curriculum, Norman, OK 73072. Offers instructional leadership and academic curriculum (M Ed, PhD), including biomedical education (PhD), early childhood education, elementary education, English education, instructional leadership, mathematics education, reading education, science education, social studies education, world languages education (M Ed); reading specialist (M Ed). *Accreditation:* NCATE. *Program availability:* Part-time. *Faculty:* 26 full-time (12 women), 1 part-time/adjunct (0 women). *Students:* 42 full-time (32 women), 113 part-time (85 women); includes 33 minority (9 Black or African American, non-Hispanic/Latino; 5 American Indian or Alaska Native, non-Hispanic/Latino; 6 Asian, non-Hispanic/Latino; 4 Hispanic/Latino; 1 Native Hawaiian or other Pacific Islander, non-Hispanic/Latino; 8 Two or more races, non-Hispanic/Latino), 9 international. Average age 35. 42 applicants, 79% accepted, 21 enrolled. In 2018, 30 master's, 17 doctorates awarded. Terminal master's awarded for partial completion of doctoral program. *Degree requirements:* For master's, comprehensive exam (for some programs), thesis (for some programs); for doctorate, comprehensive exam (for some programs), thesis/dissertation. *Entrance requirements:* For doctorate, GRE. Additional exam requirements/recommendations for international students: Required—TOEFL (minimum score 79 iBT) or IELTS (minimum score 6.5). Application fee: $50 ($100 for international students). Electronic applications accepted. *Expenses:* Tuition, state resident: full-time $5683.20; part-time $236.80 per credit hour. Tuition, nonresident: full-time $20,342; part-time $847.60 per credit hour. *International tuition:* $20,342.40 full-time. *Required fees:* $2894.20; $110.05 per credit hour. $126.50 per semester. Tuition and fees vary according to course load and program. *Financial support:* Fellowships, research assistantships, teaching assistantships, scholarships/grants, and unspecified assistantships available. Financial award application deadline: 6/1; financial award applicants required to submit FAFSA. *Faculty research:* Teacher preparation; instruction; curriculum; learning; constructivist theory. *Unit head:* Dr. Stacy Reeder, Chair, 405-325-1498, Fax: 405-325-4061, E-mail: reeder@ou.edu. *Application contact:* Anna Steele, Graduate Programs Officer, 405-325-4525, E-mail: anna.steele@ou.edu.
Website: http://www.ou.edu/education/ilac

University of Pittsburgh, School of Education, Department of Instruction and Learning, Program in Secondary Education, Pittsburgh, PA 15260. Offers English and communications education (M Ed, MAT); foreign language education (M Ed, MAT); language, literacy and culture education (Ed D, PhD); mathematics education (M Ed, MAT, Ed D, PhD); science education (M Ed, MAT, Ed D, PhD); secondary education (PhD); social studies education (M Ed, MAT); STEM education (Ed D). *Program availability:* Part-time, evening/weekend. *Degree requirements:* For master's, thesis; for doctorate, thesis/dissertation. *Entrance requirements:* For master's, PRAXIS I; for doctorate, GRE General Test. Additional exam requirements/recommendations for international students: Required—TOEFL. Electronic applications accepted.

University of Puerto Rico–Río Piedras, College of Education, Program in Curriculum and Teaching, San Juan, PR 00931-3300. Offers biology education (M Ed); chemistry education (M Ed); curriculum and teaching (Ed D); history education (M Ed); mathematics education (M Ed); physics education (M Ed); Spanish education (M Ed). *Program availability:* Part-time. *Degree requirements:* For master's, thesis; for doctorate, thesis/dissertation, internship. *Entrance requirements:* For master's, PAEG or GRE, minimum GPA of 3.0, letter of recommendation; for doctorate, GRE or PAEG, master's degree, minimum GPA of 3.0, letter of recommendation (2), interview. *Faculty research:* Curriculum, math teaching.

University of South Carolina, The Graduate School, College of Arts and Sciences, Department of Languages, Literatures, and Cultures, Columbia, SC 29208. Offers comparative literature (MA, PhD); foreign languages (MAT), including French, German, Spanish; French (MA); German (MA); Spanish (MA). MAT offered in cooperation with the College of Education. *Program availability:* Part-time. *Degree requirements:* For master's, one foreign language, comprehensive exam, thesis optional; for doctorate, 2 foreign languages, comprehensive exam, thesis/dissertation. *Entrance requirements:* For master's and doctorate, GRE General Test, writing sample. Additional exam requirements/recommendations for international students: Required—TOEFL (minimum score 75 iBT). Electronic applications accepted. *Faculty research:* Modern literature, linguistics, literature and culture, medieval literature, literary theory.

University of South Carolina, The Graduate School, College of Education, Department of Instruction and Teacher Education, Program in Secondary Education, Columbia, SC 29208. Offers art education (IMA, MAT); business education (IMA, MAT); English (MAT); foreign language (MAT); health education (MAT); mathematics (MAT); science (IMA, MAT); secondary (Ed D); secondary education (MT, PhD); social studies (MAT); theatre and speech (MAT). IMA and MT offered jointly with the subject areas. *Accreditation:* NCATE. *Degree requirements:* For master's, comprehensive exam, thesis (for some programs), foreign language (MA); for doctorate, one foreign language, comprehensive exam, thesis/dissertation. *Entrance requirements:* For master's, GRE General Test or MAT, teaching certificate (IMA, M Ed), interview; for doctorate, GRE General Test or MAT, interview. *Faculty research:* Middle school programs, professional development, school collaboration.

University of Southern Mississippi, College of Arts and Sciences, Department of World Languages, Hattiesburg, MS 39406-0001. Offers French (MATL); Spanish (MATL); teaching English to speakers of other languages (MATL). *Program availability:* 100% online. *Degree requirements:* For master's, comprehensive exam. *Entrance requirements:* For master's, GRE General Test, minimum GPA of 3.0 in field of study, 2.75 in last 2 years. Additional exam requirements/recommendations for international students: Required—TOEFL, IELTS. Electronic applications accepted.

University of South Florida, Innovative Education, Tampa, FL 33620-9951. Offers adult, career and higher education (Graduate Certificate), including college teaching, leadership in developing human resources, leadership in higher education; Africana studies (Graduate Certificate), including diasporas and health disparities, genocide and human rights; aging studies (Graduate Certificate), including gerontology; art research (Graduate Certificate), including museum studies; business foundations (Graduate Certificate); chemical and biomedical engineering (Graduate Certificate), including materials science and engineering, water, health and sustainability; child and family studies (Graduate Certificate), including positive behavior support; civil and industrial engineering (Graduate Certificate), including transportation systems analysis; community and family health (Graduate Certificate), including maternal and child health, social marketing and public health, violence and injury: prevention and intervention, women's health; criminology (Graduate Certificate), including criminal justice administration; data science for public administration (Graduate Certificate); digital humanities (Graduate Certificate); educational measurement and research (Graduate Certificate), including evaluation; English (Graduate Certificate), including comparative literary studies, creative writing, professional and technical communication; entrepreneurship (Graduate Certificate); environmental health (Graduate Certificate), including safety management; epidemiology and biostatistics (Graduate Certificate), including applied biostatistics, biostatistics, concepts and tools of epidemiology, epidemiology, epidemiology of infectious diseases; geography, environment and planning (Graduate Certificate), including community development, environmental policy and management, geographical information systems; geology (Graduate Certificate), including hydrogeology; global health (Graduate Certificate), including disaster management, global health and Latin American and Caribbean studies, global health practice, humanitarian assistance, infection control; government and international affairs (Graduate Certificate), including Cuban studies, globalization studies; health policy and management (Graduate Certificate), including health management and leadership, public health policy and programs; hearing specialist: early intervention (Graduate Certificate); industrial and management systems engineering (Graduate Certificate), including systems engineering, technology management; information studies (Graduate Certificate), including school library media specialist; information systems/decision sciences (Graduate Certificate), including analytics and business intelligence; instructional technology (Graduate Certificate), including distance education, Florida digital/virtual educator, instructional design, multimedia design, Web design; internal medicine, bioethics and medical humanities (Graduate Certificate), including biomedical ethics; Latin American and Caribbean studies (Graduate Certificate); leadership for coastal resiliency planning (Graduate Certificate); mass communications (Graduate Certificate), including multimedia journalism; mathematics and statistics (Graduate Certificate), including mathematics; medicine (Graduate Certificate), including aging and neuroscience, bioinformatics, biotechnology, brain fitness and memory management, clinical investigation, hand and upper limb rehabilitation, health informatics, health sciences, integrative weight management, intellectual property, medicine and gender, metabolic and nutritional medicine, metabolic cardiology, pharmacy sciences; national and competitive intelligence (Graduate Certificate); nursing (Graduate Certificate), including simulation based academic fellowship in advanced pain management; psychological and social foundations (Graduate Certificate), including career counseling, college teaching, diversity in education, mental health counseling, school counseling; public affairs (Graduate Certificate), including nonprofit management, public management, research administration; public health (Graduate Certificate), including assessing chemical toxicity and public health risks, health equity, pharmacoepidemiology, public health generalist, toxicology, translational research in adolescent behavioral health; public health practices (Graduate Certificate), including planning for healthy communities; rehabilitation and mental health counseling (Graduate Certificate), including integrative mental health care, marriage and family therapy, rehabilitation technology; secondary education (Graduate Certificate), including ESOL, foreign language education: culture and content, foreign language education: professional; social work (Graduate Certificate), including geriatric social work/clinical gerontology; special education (Graduate Certificate), including autism spectrum disorder, disabilities education: severe/profound; world languages (Graduate Certificate), including teaching English as a second language (TESL) or foreign language. *Expenses:* Tuition, state resident: full-time $6350. Tuition, nonresident: full-time $19,048. *International tuition:* $19,048 full-time. *Required fees:* $2079. *Unit head:* Dr. Cynthia DeLuca, Associate Vice President and Assistant Vice Provost, 813-974-3077, Fax: 813-974-7061, E-mail: deluca@usf.edu. *Application contact:* Owen Hooper, Director, Summer and Alternative Calendar Programs, 813-974-6917, E-mail: hooper@usf.edu.
Website: http://www.usf.edu/innovative-education/

The University of Tennessee, Graduate School, College of Education, Health and Human Sciences, Program in Education, Knoxville, TN 37996. Offers art education (MS); counseling education (PhD); cultural studies in education (PhD); curriculum (MS, Ed S); curriculum, educational research and evaluation (Ed D, PhD); early childhood education (PhD); early childhood special education (MS); education of deaf and hard of hearing (MS); educational administration and policy studies (Ed D, PhD); educational administration and supervision (Ed S); educational psychology (Ed D, PhD); elementary education (MS, Ed S); elementary teaching (MS); English education (MS, Ed S); exercise science (PhD); foreign language/ESL education (MS, Ed S); instructional technology (MS, Ed D, PhD, Ed S); literacy, language and ESL education (PhD); literacy, language education, and ESL education (Ed D); mathematics education (MS, Ed S); modified and comprehensive special education (MS); reading education (MS, Ed S); school counseling (Ed S); school psychology (PhD, Ed S); science education (MS, Ed S); secondary teaching (MS); social foundations (MS); social science education (MS, Ed S); socio-cultural foundations of sports and education (PhD); special education (Ed S); teacher education (Ed D, PhD). *Accreditation:* NCATE. *Program availability:* Part-time, evening/weekend. *Degree requirements:* For master's and Ed S, thesis optional; for doctorate, variable foreign language requirement, thesis/dissertation. *Entrance requirements:* For master's, minimum GPA of 2.7; for doctorate and Ed S, GRE General Test, minimum GPA of 2.7. Additional exam requirements/recommendations for international students: Required—TOEFL. Electronic applications accepted.

University of the Sacred Heart, Graduate Programs, Department of Education, San Juan, PR 00914-0383. Offers early childhood education (M Ed); information technology

and multimedia (Certificate); instruction systems and education technology (M Ed), including English, information technology and multimedia, instructional design, mathematics, Spanish. *Program availability:* Part-time, evening/weekend. *Degree requirements:* For master's, thesis. *Entrance requirements:* For master's, EXADEP, minimum undergraduate GPA of 2.75, interview.

The University of Toledo, College of Graduate Studies, Judith Herb College of Education, Department of Curriculum and Instruction, Toledo, OH 43606-3390. Offers art education (ME); career and technical education (ME, Ed S); curriculum and instruction (ME, PhD, Ed S); early childhood education (Ed S); education and anthropology (MAE); education and biology (MES); education and chemistry (MES); education and classics (MAE); education and economics (MAE); education and English (MAE); education and French (MAE); education and geology (MES); education and German (MAE); education and history (MAE); education and mathematics (MAE, MES); education and physics (MES); education and political science (MAE); education and sociology (MAE); education and Spanish (MAE); educational media (PhD); educational technology (ME); educational technology: virtual educator (Certificate); elementary education (PhD); English as a second language (MAE); gifted and talented education (PhD); middle childhood education (ME); secondary education (ME, PhD); special education (PhD). *Accreditation:* NCATE. *Program availability:* Part-time, evening/weekend. *Degree requirements:* For master's, comprehensive exam, thesis or alternative; for doctorate, comprehensive exam, thesis/dissertation; for other advanced degree, thesis optional. *Entrance requirements:* For master's, doctorate, and other advanced degree, minimum cumulative GPA of 2.7 for all previous academic work, letters of recommendation. Additional exam requirements/recommendations for international students: Required—TOEFL (minimum score 550 paper-based; 80 iBT). Electronic applications accepted.

University of Vermont, Graduate College, College of Arts and Sciences, Department of Classics, Burlington, VT 05404. Offers Greek and Latin (MA); Greek and Latin languages (Graduate Certificate); Latin (MAT). *Degree requirements:* For master's, one foreign language, thesis. *Entrance requirements:* For master's, GRE General Test, writing sample (for MA). Additional exam requirements/recommendations for international students: Required—TOEFL (minimum score 550 paper-based, 90 iBT) or IELTS (6.5). Electronic applications accepted. *Faculty research:* Early Greek literature.

University of Victoria, Faculty of Graduate Studies, Faculty of Humanities, Department of French, Victoria, BC V8W 2Y2, Canada. Offers literature (MA); teaching emphasis (MA). *Program availability:* Part-time, evening/weekend. *Degree requirements:* For master's, 2 foreign languages, thesis optional. *Entrance requirements:* For master's, BA in French. Additional exam requirements/recommendations for international students: Required—TOEFL (minimum score 575 paper-based), IELTS (minimum score 7). Electronic applications accepted. *Faculty research:* French-Canadian literature, stylistics, comparative literature, Francophone literature.

University of Virginia, Curry School of Education, Department of Curriculum, Instruction, and Special Education, Program in Curriculum and Instruction, Charlottesville, VA 22903. Offers curriculum and instruction (M Ed, Ed S); elementary education (M Ed, Ed D); English education (M Ed, Ed D); foreign language education (M Ed); mathematics education (M Ed, Ed D); science education (Ed D); social studies education (M Ed); MBA/M Ed. *Program availability:* 100% online. *Degree requirements:* For master's, comprehensive exam (for some programs); for doctorate, comprehensive exam, thesis/dissertation; for Ed S, comprehensive exam. *Entrance requirements:* For master's, doctorate, and Ed S, GRE General Test, 2 letters of recommendation. Additional exam requirements/recommendations for international students: Required—TOEFL (minimum score 600 paper-based; 90 iBT), IELTS (minimum score 7). Electronic applications accepted.

University of Virginia, Curry School of Education, Program in Education, Charlottesville, VA 22903. Offers administration and supervision (PhD); applied developmental science (PhD); counselor education (PhD); curriculum and instruction (PhD); early childhood special education (MT); education evaluation (PhD); educational psychology (PhD); educational research (PhD); elementary education (MT); English education (MT, PhD); foreign language education (MT); higher education (PhD); instructional technology (PhD); kinesiology (MT, PhD); math education (PhD); reading education (PhD); research, statistics and evaluation (PhD); school psychology (PhD); science education (PhD); social studies education (MT, PhD); special education (PhD); world languages education (MT). *Degree requirements:* For master's, comprehensive exam (for some programs), field project; for doctorate, comprehensive exam, thesis/dissertation. *Entrance requirements:* For doctorate, GRE General Test. Additional exam requirements/recommendations for international students: Required—TOEFL (minimum score 600 paper-based; 90 iBT), IELTS (minimum score 7). Electronic applications accepted.

University of Wisconsin–Milwaukee, Graduate School, College of Letters and Science, Department of Foreign Languages and Literature, Milwaukee, WI 53201-0413. Offers foreign languages and literature (MA), including classic Greek, classics, comparative literature, French/Francophone language, literature, and culture, German language, literature, and culture, interpreting, Latin, linguistics, Spanish language, literature, and culture, translation; interpreting (Graduate Certificate); language, literature, and translation (MA, MALLT); translation (Graduate Certificate). *Program availability:* Part-time. *Students:* 10 full-time (7 women), 38 part-time (29 women); includes 9 minority (1 Black or African American, non-Hispanic/Latino; 3 Hispanic/Latino; 1 Native Hawaiian or other Pacific Islander, non-Hispanic/Latino; 4 Two or more races, non-Hispanic/Latino), 3 international. Average age 35. 36 applicants, 69% accepted, 11 enrolled. In 2018, 14 master's awarded. *Degree requirements:* For master's, 2 foreign languages, thesis or alternative. *Entrance requirements:* Additional exam requirements/recommendations for international students: Required—TOEFL (minimum score 550 paper-based; 79 iBT), IELTS (minimum score 6.5). *Application deadline:* For fall admission, 1/1 priority date for domestic students; for spring admission, 9/1 for domestic students. Application fee: $56 ($96 for international students). Electronic applications accepted. *Financial support:* Fellowships, research assistantships, teaching assistantships, career-related internships or fieldwork, health care benefits, unspecified assistantships, and project assistantships available. Support available to part-time students. Financial award application deadline: 4/15; financial award applicants required to submit FAFSA. *Unit head:* Kevin Muse, Department Chair, 414-229-5213, E-mail: kmuse@uwm.edu. *Application contact:* General Information Contact, 414-229-4982, Fax: 414-229-6967, E-mail: gradschool@uwm.edu.
Website: http://uwm.edu/foreign-languages-literature/

Vanderbilt University, Department of French and Italian, Nashville, TN 37240-1001. Offers French (MA, MAT, PhD). *Faculty:* 15 full-time (10 women). *Students:* 14 full-time (8 women); includes 2 minority (1 Hispanic/Latino; 1 Two or more races, non-Hispanic/Latino), 3 international. Average age 29. 19 applicants, 11% accepted, 2 enrolled. In 2018, 2 doctorates awarded. Terminal master's awarded for partial completion of doctoral program. *Degree requirements:* For master's, one foreign language, comprehensive exam; for doctorate, 2 foreign languages, comprehensive exam, thesis/dissertation, final and qualifying exams. *Entrance requirements:* For master's and doctorate, GRE General Test. Additional exam requirements/recommendations for international students: Required—TOEFL (minimum score 570 paper-based; 88 iBT). *Application deadline:* For fall admission, 1/15 for domestic and international students. Electronic applications accepted. *Expenses: Tuition:* Full-time $47,208; part-time $2026 per credit hour. *Required fees:* $478. *Financial support:* Fellowships, teaching assistantships, career-related internships or fieldwork, Federal Work-Study, institutionally sponsored loans, scholarships/grants, and health care benefits available. Financial award application deadline: 1/15; financial award applicants required to submit CSS PROFILE or FAFSA. *Faculty research:* Baudelaire, Rabelais, voyage literature, postcolonial literature, medieval epic. *Unit head:* Dr. Lynn Ramey, Chair, 615-322-6900, Fax: 615-343-6909, E-mail: lynn.ramey@vanderbilt.edu. *Application contact:* Nathalie Debrauwere-Miller, Director of Graduate Studies, 615-322-6900, Fax: 615-343-6909, E-mail: n.debrau@vanderbilt.edu.
Website: http://as.vanderbilt.edu/french-italian/

Wagner College, Division of Graduate Studies, Education Department, Program in Secondary Education/Students with Disabilities, Staten Island, NY 10301-4495. Offers secondary education 7-12 (MS Ed), including language arts, languages other than English, mathematics and technology, science and technology, social studies. *Program availability:* Evening/weekend. *Degree requirements:* For master's, thesis (for some programs), completion of state certification exams before student teaching. *Entrance requirements:* For master's, GRE, minimum GPA of 3.0, interview, recommendations. Additional exam requirements/recommendations for international students: Required—TOEFL (minimum score 550 paper-based; 79 iBT), IELTS (minimum score 6.5). Electronic applications accepted. *Expenses:* Contact institution.

Washington State University, College of Arts and Sciences, Department of Foreign Languages and Cultures, Pullman, WA 99164. Offers MA. Programs offered at the Pullman campus. *Degree requirements:* For master's, comprehensive exam (for some programs), thesis (for some programs), 4 written exams, oral exam, paper. *Entrance requirements:* For master's, three current letters of recommendation; all original transcripts including an official English translation; two writing samples; letter of application stating qualifications and personal goals; brief (3-5 minute) tape recordings of two informal dialogues between applicant and native speaker. Additional exam requirements/recommendations for international students: Required—TOEFL (minimum score 550 paper-based). Electronic applications accepted. *Faculty research:* Spanish and Latin American literature, film, and culture; pedagogy; computer-aided instruction.

Wayne State University, College of Education, Division of Teacher Education, Detroit, MI 48202. Offers art education (M Ed); bilingual/bicultural education (Certificate); curriculum and instruction (Ed D, PhD, Ed S), including English as a second language (MAT, Ed D, Ed S), K-12 curriculum (PhD); elementary education (MAT), including bilingual/bicultural education (M Ed, MAT), early childhood education (M Ed, MAT), English as a second language (MAT, Ed D, Ed S), foreign language education, science education (M Ed, MAT), special education (M Ed, MAT); elementary mathematics specialist (Certificate); English as a second language (Certificate); reading (M Ed, Ed S); reading, language and literature (Ed D); secondary education (MAT), including bilingual/bicultural education (M Ed, MAT), early childhood education (M Ed, MAT), English as a second language (MAT, Ed D, Ed S), English education, foreign language education, mathematics education (M Ed, MAT), science education (M Ed, MAT), social studies education (M Ed, MAT); special education (MAT), including career and technical education; teaching and learning (M Ed), including bilingual/bicultural education (M Ed, MAT), early childhood education (M Ed, MAT), elementary education, foreign language, mathematics education (M Ed, MAT), science education (M Ed, MAT), social studies education (M Ed, MAT), special education (M Ed, MAT). *Program availability:* Part-time, evening/weekend. *Faculty:* 20. *Students:* 121 full-time (94 women), 251 part-time (209 women); includes 116 minority (83 Black or African American, non-Hispanic/Latino; 3 American Indian or Alaska Native, non-Hispanic/Latino; 3 Asian, non-Hispanic/Latino; 14 Hispanic/Latino; 13 Two or more races, non-Hispanic/Latino), 11 international. Average age 37. 171 applicants, 23% accepted, 32 enrolled. In 2018, 112 master's, 8 doctorates, 11 other advanced degrees awarded. *Degree requirements:* For master's, thesis (for some programs), essay or project (for some M Ed programs), professional field experience (for MAT programs); for doctorate, comprehensive exam, thesis/dissertation. *Entrance requirements:* For master's, undergraduate degree, verification of participation in group work with children, Michigan State Police criminal background check, negative tb test, personal statement (for MAT programs); for all other master's programs: undergraduate degree, personal statement; for doctorate, minimum undergraduate GPA of 3.0, graduate 3.5; interview; curriculum vitae; references; writing sample; letter of application; master's degree (for most programs); for other advanced degree, education specialist certificate: undergraduate with GPA of 2.5 or better and master's degree with GPA of 2.75 or better; personal statement. Additional exam requirements/recommendations for international students: Required—TOEFL (minimum score 550 paper-based; 79 iBT); Recommended—IELTS (minimum score 6.5), TWE (minimum score 5.5), TSE (minimum score 58). *Application deadline:* Applications are processed on a rolling basis. Application fee: $50. Electronic applications accepted. *Financial support:* In 2018–19, 85 students received support, including 3 fellowships (averaging $14,275 per year); research assistantships with tuition reimbursements available, Federal Work-Study, scholarships/grants, and unspecified assistantships also available. Support available to part-time students. Financial award applicants required to submit FAFSA. *Faculty research:* Improving students' skill achievement in mathematics, improving elementary children's understanding of informational text, teachers' use of their pedagogical and mathematical knowledge in the interactive work of teaching, the intersection of identity construction in teaching and learning, identifying effective methods of literacy instruction and assessments for bilingual students in elementary language arts classrooms. *Unit head:* Dr. Roland Coloma, Assistant Dean for Teacher Education, 313-577-0902, E-mail: rscoloma@wayne.edu. *Application contact:* Dr. Mary L. Waker, Graduate Admissions Officer, 313-577-1601, Fax: 313-577-7904, E-mail: m.waker@wayne.edu.
Website: http://coe.wayne.edu/ted/index.php

Wayne State University, College of Liberal Arts and Sciences, Department of Classical and Modern Languages, Literatures, and Cultures, Detroit, MI 48202. Offers classics (MA), including ancient Greek and Latin, ancient studies, classics, Latin; German (MA); language learning (MALL), including Arabic (MA, MALL), French (MA, MALL, PhD), German (MALL, PhD), Italian (MA, MALL), Spanish (MA, MALL, PhD); modern languages (PhD), including French (MA, MALL, PhD), German (MALL, PhD), Spanish (MA, MALL, PhD); Near Eastern languages (MA), including Arabic (MA, MALL), Hebrew; Romance languages (MA), including French (MA, MALL, PhD), Italian (MA, MALL), Spanish (MA, MALL, PhD). *Faculty:* 16. *Students:* 22 full-time (17 women), 21 part-time (13 women); includes 9 minority (4 Black or African American, non-Hispanic/Latino; 1 American Indian or Alaska Native, non-Hispanic/Latino; 2 Asian, non-Hispanic/Latino; 2 Hispanic/Latino), 2 international. Average age 36. 27 applicants, 41% accepted, 5 enrolled. In 2018, 6 master's, 4 doctorates awarded. *Degree requirements:* For master's, variable foreign language requirement, comprehensive exam (for some programs), thesis (for some programs); for doctorate, one foreign language, comprehensive exam, thesis/dissertation. *Entrance requirements:* Additional exam requirements/recommendations for international students: Required—TOEFL (minimum score 550 paper-based; 79 iBT), TWE (minimum score 5.5), Michigan English Language Assessment Battery (minimum score 85); Recommended—IELTS (minimum score 6.5). Application fee: $50. Electronic applications accepted. *Financial support:* In 2018–19,

21 students received support, including 3 fellowships with tuition reimbursements available (averaging $17,137 per year), 1 research assistantship (averaging $23,119 per year), 12 teaching assistantships with tuition reimbursements available (averaging $19,267 per year); scholarships/grants, health care benefits, and unspecified assistantships also available. Financial award applicants required to submit FAFSA. *Faculty research:* Classical and modern literature and culture (Greek, Latin, Arabic, Chinese, French, German, Russian, Spanish) including colonial studies and exile and Holocaust studies; critical theory (French, German, Slavic, Spanish); theoretical and applied linguistics (Arabic, Chinese, French, Spanish); area studies (Arabic, Near Eastern, classical, Islamic, and Judaic studies). *Unit head:* Dr. Anne Duggan, Department Chair, 313-577-6244, Fax: 313-577-6243, E-mail: a.duggan@wayne.edu. *Application contact:* Dr. Anne Duggan, Department Chair, 313-577-6244, Fax: 313-577-6243, E-mail: a.duggan@wayne.edu.
Website: http://clas.wayne.edu/languages/

West Chester University of Pennsylvania, College of Arts and Humanities, Department of Languages and Cultures, West Chester, PA 19383. Offers French (Teaching Certificate); German (Teaching Certificate); languages and cultures (MA), including French, German, Spanish; Spanish (Teaching Certificate). *Program availability:* Part-time, evening/weekend, minimal on-campus study. *Degree requirements:* For master's, one foreign language, comprehensive exam, portfolio defended at oral exit exam, capstone project; for Teaching Certificate, one foreign language. *Entrance requirements:* For master's and Teaching Certificate, ACTFL OPI and WPT. Additional exam requirements/recommendations for international students: Required—TOEFL or IELTS. Electronic applications accepted. *Faculty research:* Language structure, literature, film, culture, pedagogy, technology.

Western Kentucky University, Graduate School, Potter College of Arts and Letters, Department of Modern Languages, Bowling Green, KY 42101. Offers French (MA Ed); German (MA Ed); Spanish (MA Ed).

Worcester State University, Graduate School, Program in Spanish, Worcester, MA 01602-2597. Offers MA. *Program availability:* Part-time. *Faculty:* 2 full-time (both women). *Students:* 1 (woman) full-time, 6 part-time (5 women); includes 3 minority (all Hispanic/Latino). Average age 32. 1 applicant, 100% accepted, 1 enrolled. In 2018, 1 master's awarded. *Degree requirements:* For master's, one foreign language, comprehensive exam, thesis (for some programs), For a detail list in Degree Completion requirements please see the graduate catalog at catalog.worcester.edu. *Entrance requirements:* For master's, GRE, MAT, For a detail list of entrance requirements please see the graduate catalog at catalog.worcester.edu. Additional exam requirements/recommendations for international students: Required—TOEFL (minimum score 550 paper-based; 79 iBT), IELTS (minimum score 6). *Application deadline:* For fall admission, 3/1 for domestic and international students; for spring admission, 11/1 for domestic and international students; for summer admission, 3/1 for domestic and international students. Applications are processed on a rolling basis. Application fee: $50. Electronic applications accepted. *Expenses: Tuition, area resident:* Full-time $3042; part-time $169 per credit hour. Tuition, state resident: full-time $3042; part-time $169 per credit hour. Tuition, nonresident: full-time $3042; part-time $169 per credit hour. *International tuition:* $3042 full-time. *Required fees:* $2754; $153 per credit hour. *Financial support:* Career-related internships or fieldwork, scholarships/grants, and unspecified assistantships available. Financial award application deadline: 3/1; financial award applicants required to submit FAFSA. *Unit head:* Dr. Antonio Guijarro-Donadios, Program Coordinator, 508-929-8619, Fax: 508-929-8174, E-mail: aguijarrodonadios@worcester.edu. *Application contact:* Sara Grady, Associate Dean, Graduate Studies and Professional Development, 508-929-8130, Fax: 508-929-8100, E-mail: sara.grady@worcester.edu.

Health Education

Adelphi University, College of Education & Health Sciences, College of Education and Health Sciences, Garden City, NY 11530-0701. Offers community health education (MA, Certificate); school health education (MA). *Program availability:* Part-time, evening/weekend. *Students:* 7 full-time (6 women), 31 part-time (16 women); includes 4 minority (2 Black or African American, non-Hispanic/Latino; 2 Hispanic/Latino), 6 international. Average age 30. 27 applicants, 85% accepted, 14 enrolled. In 2018, 5 master's, 2 other advanced degrees awarded. *Degree requirements:* For master's, internship. *Entrance requirements:* For master's, 3 letters of recommendation, resume, minimum cumulative GPA of 2.75. Additional exam requirements/recommendations for international students: Required—TOEFL (minimum score 550 paper-based; 80 iBT), IELTS (minimum score 6.5). *Application deadline:* Applications are processed on a rolling basis. Application fee: $50. Electronic applications accepted. *Expenses:* Contact institution. *Financial support:* Research assistantships, teaching assistantships, career-related internships or fieldwork, institutionally sponsored loans, scholarships/grants, traineeships, and unspecified assistantships available. Support available to part-time students. Financial award application deadline: 1/1; financial award applicants required to submit FAFSA. *Faculty research:* Alcohol abuse, tobacco cessation, drug abuse, healthy family lives, healthy personal living. *Unit head:* Dr. Emilia Zarco, Chair, 516-877-4261, E-mail: zarco@adelphi.edu. *Application contact:* Dr. Emilia Zarco, Chair, 516-877-4261, E-mail: zarco@adelphi.edu.

Alabama State University, College of Education, Department of Health, Physical Education, and Recreation, Montgomery, AL 36101-0271. Offers health education (M Ed); physical education (M Ed). *Program availability:* Part-time, evening/weekend. *Faculty:* 3 full-time (2 women), 2 part-time/adjunct (1 woman). *Students:* 5 full-time (2 women), 4 part-time (2 women); includes 7 minority (all Black or African American, non-Hispanic/Latino), 1 international. Average age 29. 4 applicants, 75% accepted. In 2018, 3 master's awarded. *Degree requirements:* For master's, comprehensive exam. *Entrance requirements:* For master's, GRE General Test, MAT, writing competency test, bachelor's degree or its equivalent from accredited college or university with minimum GPA of 2.5. Additional exam requirements/recommendations for international students: Required—TOEFL (minimum score 500 paper-based). *Application deadline:* For fall admission, 4/15 for domestic and international students; for spring admission, 11/15 for domestic and international students; for summer admission, 3/15 for domestic and international students. Applications are processed on a rolling basis. Application fee: $25. Electronic applications accepted. *Expenses:* Contact institution. *Financial support:* Fellowships, teaching assistantships, career-related internships or fieldwork, scholarships/grants, tuition waivers (partial), and unspecified assistantships available. Financial award application deadline: 6/30; financial award applicants required to submit FAFSA. *Faculty research:* Risk factors for heart disease in the college-age population, cardiovascular reactivity for the Cold Pressor Test. *Unit head:* Dr. Charlie Gibbons, Chair, Associate Professor of Health Education, 334-229-4504, Fax: 334-229-4928, E-mail: cgibbons@alasu.edu. *Application contact:* Dr. Ed Brown, Dean of Graduate Studies, 334-229-4274, Fax: 334-229-4928, E-mail: ebrown@alasu.edu.
Website: http://www.alasu.edu/academics/colleges—departments/college-of-education/health-physical-education—recreation/index.aspx

Albany State University, College of Education, Albany, GA 31705-2717. Offers early childhood education (M Ed); educational leadership (Ed S); health and physical education (M Ed); middle grades education (M Ed); school counseling (M Ed); special education (M Ed). *Accreditation:* NCATE. *Program availability:* Part-time, evening/weekend, online learning. *Degree requirements:* For master's, comprehensive exam, internship, GACE Content Exam. *Entrance requirements:* For master's, GRE or MAT. Electronic applications accepted. *Faculty research:* GACE preparation, STEM (science, technology, engineering, and mathematics), technology education, special education, professional teacher development, health implications liberation philosophy, NET-Q, learning community, disabled or at-risk students.

Alcorn State University, School of Graduate Studies, School of Education and Psychology, Lorman, MS 39096-7500. Offers agricultural education (MS Ed); elementary education (MAT, MS Ed, Ed S); guidance and counseling (MS Ed); industrial education (MS Ed); secondary education (MAT, MS Ed), including health and physical education (MS Ed), NCAA compliance and academic progress reporting (MS Ed); special education (MS Ed). *Accreditation:* NCATE. *Degree requirements:* For master's, thesis optional.

Allen College, Graduate Programs, Waterloo, IA 50703. Offers adult-gerontology acute care nurse practitioner (MSN); community/public health nursing (MSN); education (MSN); family nurse practitioner (MSN); health sciences (Ed D); leadership in health

care delivery (MSN); leadership in health care informatics (MSN); nursing (DNP); occupational therapy (MS); psychiatric mental health nurse practitioner (MSN). MSN in leadership in healthcare informatics offered in partnership with University of Minnesota. *Accreditation:* AACN; ACEN. *Program availability:* Part-time, 100% online, blended/hybrid learning. *Faculty:* 24 full-time (all women), 8 part-time/adjunct (7 women). *Students:* 106 full-time (91 women), 187 part-time (164 women); includes 22 minority (12 Black or African American, non-Hispanic/Latino; 1 American Indian or Alaska Native, non-Hispanic/Latino; 2 Asian, non-Hispanic/Latino; 3 Hispanic/Latino; 4 Two or more races, non-Hispanic/Latino), 2 international. Average age 33. 352 applicants, 56% accepted, 131 enrolled. In 2018, 73 master's, 2 doctorates awarded. *Entrance requirements:* For master's, minimum GPA of 3.0 in the last 60 hours of undergraduate coursework; for doctorate, minimum GPA of 3.25 in graduate coursework. *Application deadline:* For fall admission, 2/1 priority date for domestic students; for spring admission, 9/1 priority date for domestic students. Applications are processed on a rolling basis. Application fee: $50. Electronic applications accepted. *Expenses:* Contact institution. *Financial support:* In 2018–19, 97 students received support. Federal Work-Study, institutionally sponsored loans, scholarships/grants, and traineeships available. Support available to part-time students. Financial award application deadline: 8/1; financial award applicants required to submit FAFSA. *Faculty research:* Poverty. *Unit head:* Dr. Bob Loch, Provost, 319-226-2040, Fax: 319-226-2070, E-mail: bob.loch@allencollege.edu. *Application contact:* Molly Quinn, Director of Admissions, 319-226-2001, Fax: 319-226-2010, E-mail: molly.quinn@allencollege.edu.
Website: http://www.allencollege.edu/

Arcadia University, College of Health Sciences, Department of Public Health, Glenside, PA 19038-3295. Offers health education (MSHE); public health (MPH). *Faculty:* 5 full-time (all women), 11 part-time/adjunct (8 women). *Students:* 28 full-time (23 women), 13 part-time (12 women); includes 10 minority (3 Black or African American, non-Hispanic/Latino; 4 Asian, non-Hispanic/Latino; 1 Native Hawaiian or other Pacific Islander, non-Hispanic/Latino; 2 Two or more races, non-Hispanic/Latino), 2 international. In 2018, 53 master's awarded. *Entrance requirements:* For master's, GRE or MCAT taken within the last five years; test scores not required for students with an earned graduate degree in a related field per the department's review and approval. Additional exam requirements/recommendations for international students: Required—TOEFL or IELTS results are required for all students for whom English is a second language. Application fee is waived when completed online. *Expenses:* Contact institution. *Unit head:* Dr. Katie DiSantis, Chair, 215-517-2680, E-mail: DiSantisK@arcadia.edu. *Application contact:* Information Contact, 215-572-2910, Fax: 215-572-4049, E-mail: admiss@arcadia.edu.

Arizona State University at the Tempe campus, College of Health Solutions, Program in Behavioral Health, Phoenix, AZ 85004-2135. Offers DBH. *Program availability:* Part-time, evening/weekend, online learning. *Degree requirements:* For doctorate, thesis/dissertation or alternative, 16 hours/week practicum (400 hours total), applied research paper focused on design, implementation and evaluation of a clinical intervention in primary care or related setting, interactive Program of Study (iPOS) submitted before completing 50 percent of required credit hours. *Entrance requirements:* For doctorate, minimum GPA of 3.0 or equivalent in last 2 years of work leading to bachelor's degree; 3 professional reference letters; copy of current clinical license(s) to practice behavioral health; interview. Additional exam requirements/recommendations for international students: Required—TOEFL, IELTS, or PTE. Electronic applications accepted. *Expenses:* Contact institution.

Arkansas State University, Graduate School, College of Nursing and Health Professions, School of Nursing, State University, AR 72467. Offers aging studies (Graduate Certificate); health care management (Graduate Certificate); health sciences (MS); health sciences education (Graduate Certificate); nurse anesthesia (MSN); nursing (MSN); nursing practice (DNP). *Accreditation:* AANA/CANAEP (one or more programs are accredited); ACEN. *Program availability:* Part-time. *Degree requirements:* For master's and Graduate Certificate, comprehensive exam, thesis or alternative; for doctorate, comprehensive exam, thesis/dissertation. *Entrance requirements:* For master's, GRE General Test or MAT, appropriate bachelor's degree, current Arkansas nursing license, CPR certification, physical examination, professional liability insurance, critical care experience, ACLS Certification, PALS Certification, interview, immunization records, personal goal statement, health assessment; for doctorate, GRE or MAT, NCLEX-RN Exam, appropriate master's degree, current Arkansas nursing license, CPR certification, physical examination, professional liability insurance, critical care experience, ACLS Certification, PALS Certification, interview, immunization records,

personal goal statement, health assessment, TB skin test, background check; for Graduate Certificate, GRE or MAT, appropriate bachelor's degree, official transcripts, immunization records, proof of employment in healthcare, TB Skin Test, TB Mask Fit Test, CPR Certification. Additional exam requirements/recommendations for international students: Required—TOEFL (minimum score 550 paper-based; 79 iBT), IELTS (minimum score 6), PTE (minimum score 56). Electronic applications accepted. *Expenses:* Contact institution.

Auburn University, Graduate School, College of Education, School of Kinesiology, Auburn University, AL 36849. Offers exercise science (M Ed). *Accreditation:* NCATE. *Program availability:* Part-time. *Degree requirements:* For master's, thesis (for some programs); for doctorate, thesis/dissertation; for Ed S, exam, field project. *Entrance requirements:* For master's, GRE General Test; for doctorate and Ed S, GRE General Test, interview, master's degree. Electronic applications accepted. *Expenses:* Tuition, state resident: full-time $11,282; part-time $535 per credit hour. Tuition, nonresident: full-time $30,542; part-time $1605 per credit hour. *Required fees:* $826 per semester. Tuition and fees vary according to degree level and program. *Faculty research:* Biomechanics, exercise physiology, motor skill learning, school health, curriculum development.

Austin Peay State University, College of Graduate Studies, College of Behavioral and Health Sciences, Department of Health and Human Performance, Clarksville, TN 37044. Offers public health education (MS); sports and wellness leadership (MS). *Program availability:* Part-time, evening/weekend, online learning. *Faculty:* 8 full-time (4 women), 1 (woman) part-time/adjunct. *Students:* 18 full-time (8 women), 55 part-time (33 women); includes 21 minority (13 Black or African American, non-Hispanic/Latino; 1 Asian, non-Hispanic/Latino; 2 Hispanic/Latino; 5 Two or more races, non-Hispanic/Latino), 2 international. Average age 30. 81 applicants, 84% accepted, 54 enrolled. In 2018, 35 master's awarded. *Degree requirements:* For master's, comprehensive exam, thesis optional. *Entrance requirements:* For master's, GRE General Test, 3 letters of recommendation, minimum undergraduate GPA of 2.5. Additional exam requirements/recommendations for international students: Required—TOEFL (minimum score 500 paper-based). *Application deadline:* For fall admission, 8/21 priority date for domestic students. Applications are processed on a rolling basis. Application fee: $45 ($55 for international students). Electronic applications accepted. *Expenses: Tuition, area resident:* Part-time $450 per credit hour. Tuition, state resident: full-time $5987; part-time $450 per credit hour. Tuition, nonresident: full-time $8757; part-time $806 per credit hour. *Required fees:* $1583; $79.15 per credit hour. *Financial support:* Research assistantships with full tuition reimbursements, career-related internships or fieldwork, Federal Work-Study, institutionally sponsored loans, scholarships/grants, and unspecified assistantships available. Support available to part-time students. Financial award application deadline: 7/1; financial award applicants required to submit FAFSA. *Unit head:* Dr. Marcy Maurer, Chair, 931-221-6105, Fax: 931-221-7040, E-mail: maurerm@apsu.edu. *Application contact:* Megan Mitchell, Coordinator of Graduate Admissions, 931-221-6189, Fax: 931-221-7641, E-mail: mitchellm@apsu.edu.
Website: http://www.apsu.edu/hhp/index.php

Baldwin Wallace University, Graduate Programs, Public Health Program, Berea, OH 44017-2088. Offers health education and disease prevention (MPH); population health leadership and management (MPH). Program offered in partnership with The MetroHealth System. *Program availability:* Part-time, evening/weekend. *Faculty:* 2 full-time (0 women), 1 part-time/adjunct (0 women). *Students:* 20 full-time (16 women), 11 part-time (9 women); includes 12 minority (4 Black or African American, non-Hispanic/Latino; 4 Asian, non-Hispanic/Latino; 2 Hispanic/Latino; 2 Two or more races, non-Hispanic/Latino), 1 international. Average age 38. 25 applicants, 48% accepted, 9 enrolled. *Entrance requirements:* For master's, GRE. Additional exam requirements/recommendations for international students: Required—TOEFL (minimum score 550 paper-based; 100 iBT). *Application deadline:* For fall admission, 7/15 for domestic students. Applications are processed on a rolling basis. *Expenses:* MetroHealth Employees: $36,000 to complete program or $750 per credit hours; MPH Partners (Visiting Nurse Association, Cleveland Clinic, University Hospitals): $43,200 to complete program or $900 per credit hour; Non-Partners: $48,000 to complete program or $1,000 to complete program. *Financial support:* Applicants required to submit FAFSA. *Unit head:* Stephen D. Stahl, Provost, Academic Affairs, 440-826-2251, Fax: 440-826-2329, E-mail: sstahl@bw.edu. *Application contact:* Winnie W. Gerhardt, Director of Transfer, Adult and Graduate Admission, 440-826-8002, E-mail: wgerhard@bw.edu.
Website: http://www.bw.edu/academics/master-public-health/

Baylor University, Graduate School, Robbins College of Health and Human Sciences, Department of Health, Human Performance and Recreation, Waco, TX 76798. Offers athletic training (MS); exercise physiology (MS); kinesiology, exercise nutrition, and health promotion (PhD); sport pedagogy (MS). *Accreditation:* NCATE. *Program availability:* Part-time. *Students:* 72 full-time (40 women), 13 part-time (8 women); includes 20 minority (5 Black or African American, non-Hispanic/Latino; 1 American Indian or Alaska Native, non-Hispanic/Latino; 1 Asian, non-Hispanic/Latino; 7 Hispanic/Latino; 6 Two or more races, non-Hispanic/Latino), 5 international. 109 applicants, 59% accepted, 44 enrolled. In 2018, 35 master's, 2 doctorates awarded. *Degree requirements:* For master's, comprehensive exam, thesis optional; for doctorate, comprehensive exam, thesis/dissertation. *Entrance requirements:* For master's and doctorate, GRE General Test. Additional exam requirements/recommendations for international students: Required—TOEFL (minimum score 550 paper-based; 80 iBT). *Application deadline:* For fall admission, 2/1 priority date for domestic students, 2/1 for international students; for spring admission, 10/1 for domestic and international students. Applications are processed on a rolling basis. Application fee: $25. Electronic applications accepted. *Financial support:* In 2018–19, 60 students received support, including 1 research assistantship with full tuition reimbursement available (averaging $12,700 per year), 33 teaching assistantships with full tuition reimbursements available (averaging $7,650 per year); career-related internships or fieldwork, Federal Work-Study, institutionally sponsored loans, scholarships/grants, tuition waivers (full), and unspecified assistantships also available. Financial award application deadline: 2/1. *Faculty research:* Exercise testing, cardio-metabolic health, resistance exercise and training, nutritional intervention, population health, health promotion, global health epidemiology, coaching, natural resource management, stimulant misuse, diet, microbiome and colon cancer etiology. *Total annual research expenditures:* $250,118. *Unit head:* Dr. Jaeho Shim, Graduate Program Director, 254-710-4009, Fax: 254-710-3527, E-mail: joe_shim@baylor.edu. *Application contact:* Deepa Morris, Graduate Program Coordinator, 254-710-3526, Fax: 254-710-3527, E-mail: deepa_morris@baylor.edu.
Website: http://www.baylor.edu/HHPR/

Benedictine University, Graduate Programs, Program in Public Health, Lisle, IL 60532. Offers administration of health care institutions (MPH); dietetics (MPH); disaster management (MPH); health education (MPH); health information systems (MPH); management information systems (MPH/MS); MBA/MPH; MPH/MS. *Accreditation:* CEPH. *Program availability:* Part-time, evening/weekend, 100% online. *Faculty:* 8 full-time (5 women), 25 part-time/adjunct (15 women). *Students:* 60 full-time (53 women), 544 part-time (415 women); includes 71 minority (26 Black or African American, non-Hispanic/Latino; 3 American Indian or Alaska Native, non-Hispanic/Latino; 27 Asian, non-Hispanic/Latino; 14 Hispanic/Latino; 1 Native Hawaiian or other Pacific Islander, non-Hispanic/Latino), 11 international. Average age 33. 245 applicants, 84% accepted, 201 enrolled. In 2018, 219 master's awarded. *Entrance requirements:* For master's, GRE, MAT, GMAT, LSAT, DAT or other graduate professional exams, official transcript; 2 letters of recommendation from individuals familiar with the applicant's professional or academic work, excluding family or personal friends; essay describing the candidate's career path. Additional exam requirements/recommendations for international students: Required—TOEFL (minimum score 600 paper-based; 79 iBT), IELTS (minimum score 6.5). *Application deadline:* Applications are processed on a rolling basis. Application fee: $40. Electronic applications accepted. *Unit head:* Dr. Susan Cheng, Department Chair and Associate Professor, 630-829-6181, E-mail: scheng@ben.edu. *Application contact:* Dr. Susan Cheng, Department Chair and Associate Professor, 630-829-6181, E-mail: scheng@ben.edu.

Boston University, School of Medicine, Graduate Medical Sciences, Program in Health Sciences Education, Boston, MA 02215. Offers MS. *Unit head:* Dr. Jeff Markuns, Director, E-mail: jmarkuns@bu.edu. *Application contact:* GMS Admissions Office, 617-638-5255, Fax: 617-638-5740, E-mail: askgms@bu.edu.
Website: http://www.bumc.bu.edu/gms/hse/

Brandeis University, The Heller School for Social Policy and Management, Program in Social Policy, Waltham, MA 02454-9110. Offers assets and inequalities (PhD); children, youth and families (PhD); global health and development (PhD); health and behavioral health (PhD). *Degree requirements:* For doctorate, comprehensive exam, thesis/dissertation, qualifying paper, 2-year residency. *Entrance requirements:* For doctorate, GRE General Test, 3 letters of recommendation, statement of purpose, writing sample, at least 3-5 years of professional experience. Additional exam requirements/recommendations for international students: Required—TOEFL (minimum score 600 paper-based; 100 iBT). Electronic applications accepted. *Faculty research:* Health; mental health; substance abuse; children, youth, and families; aging; international and community development; disabilities; work and inequality; hunger and poverty.

California Baptist University, Program in Public Health, Riverside, CA 92504-3206. Offers health education and promotion (MPH); health policy and administration (MPH). *Accreditation:* CEPH. *Program availability:* Part-time, evening/weekend, 100% online, blended/hybrid learning. *Faculty:* 10 full-time (7 women), 3 part-time/adjunct (1 woman). *Students:* 44 full-time (37 women), 34 part-time (28 women); includes 61 minority (12 Black or African American, non-Hispanic/Latino; 9 Asian, non-Hispanic/Latino; 35 Hispanic/Latino; 5 Two or more races, non-Hispanic/Latino), 4 international. Average age 33. 33 applicants, 61% accepted, 20 enrolled. In 2018, 22 master's awarded. *Degree requirements:* For master's, capstone project; practicum. *Entrance requirements:* For master's, minimum undergraduate GPA of 2.75, two recommendations, 500-word essay, resume. Additional exam requirements/recommendations for international students: Required—TOEFL (minimum score 80 iBT). *Application deadline:* For fall admission, 8/1 priority date for domestic students, 7/1 for international students; for spring admission, 12/1 priority date for domestic students, 11/1 for international students. Applications are processed on a rolling basis. Application fee: $45. Electronic applications accepted. *Expenses:* $853 per unit. *Financial support:* In 2018–19, 23 students received support. Federal Work-Study and scholarships/grants available. Financial award applicants required to submit CSS PROFILE or FAFSA. *Faculty research:* Epidemiology, statistical education, exercise and immunity, obesity and chronic disease. *Unit head:* Dr. David Pearson, Dean, College of Health Science, 951-343-4298, E-mail: dpearson@calbaptist.edu. *Application contact:* Dr. Bochi McKinney, Program Director, Online MPH, 951-343-2177, E-mail: omckinney@calbaptist.edu.
Website: http://www.calbaptist.edu/explore-cbu/schools-colleges/college-allied-health/health-sciences/master-public-health/

California State University, Long Beach, Graduate Studies, College of Health and Human Services, Department of Health Science, Long Beach, CA 90840. Offers MPH. *Accreditation:* CEPH; NCATE. *Program availability:* Part-time. *Degree requirements:* For master's, thesis optional. *Entrance requirements:* For master's, GRE, minimum GPA of 3.0 in last 60 units. *Application deadline:* For fall admission, 3/15 for domestic students; for spring admission, 10/1 for domestic students. Applications are processed on a rolling basis. Application fee: $55. Electronic applications accepted. *Expenses: Required fees:* $2628 per term. Tuition and fees vary according to class time, course level, course load, degree level, campus/location and program. *Financial support:* Federal Work-Study, institutionally sponsored loans, and scholarships/grants available. Financial award application deadline: 3/2; financial award applicants required to submit FAFSA. *Unit head:* Terry Robertson, Interim Chair, 562-985-5102. *Application contact:* Toni Espinoza-Ferrel, Graduate Advisor, E-mail: Toni.Espinoza-Ferrel@csulb.edu.
Website: http://web.csulb.edu/colleges/chhs/departments/health-science/

California State University, Northridge, Graduate Studies, College of Health and Human Development, Department of Health Sciences, Northridge, CA 91330. Offers health administration (MS); public health (MPH), including applied epidemiology, community health education. *Accreditation:* CAHME; CEPH. *Entrance requirements:* For master's, GRE General Test or minimum GPA of 3.0. Additional exam requirements/recommendations for international students: Required—TOEFL. *Faculty research:* Labor market needs assessment, health education products, dental hygiene, independent practice prototype.

California State University, Northridge, Graduate Studies, Tseng College, Northridge, CA 91330. Offers business administration (Graduate Certificate); health administration (MPA); health education (MPH); knowledge management (MKM); music industry administration (MA); nonprofit-sector management (Graduate Certificate); public administration (MPA); public sector management and leadership (MPA); social work (MSW); taxation (MS); tourism, hospitality and recreation management (MS). *Entrance requirements:* For master's, GRE (if cumulative undergraduate GPA less than 3.0).

Cambridge College, School of Education, Boston, MA 02129. Offers autism specialist (M Ed); autism/behavior analyst (M Ed); behavior analyst (Post-Master's Certificate); curriculum and instruction (CAGS); early childhood teacher (M Ed); educational leadership (M Ed, Ed D); elementary teacher (M Ed); English as a second language (M Ed, Certificate); general science (M Ed); health education (Post-Master's Certificate); interdisciplinary studies (M Ed); library teacher (M Ed); mathematics education (M Ed); mathematics specialist (Certificate); school administration (M Ed, CAGS); school nurse education (M Ed); teacher of students with moderate disabilities (M Ed); teaching skills and methodologies (M Ed). *Program availability:* Part-time, evening/weekend, online learning. *Degree requirements:* For master's, thesis, internship/practicum (licensure program only); for doctorate, thesis/dissertation; for other advanced degree, thesis. *Entrance requirements:* For master's, interview, resume, documentation of licensure, 2 professional references; for doctorate, official transcripts, interview, resume, written personal statement/essay, portfolio of scholarly and professional work, 2 professional references, health insurance, immunizations form; for other advanced degree, official transcripts, interview, resume, written personal statement/essay, 2 professional references, health insurance, immunizations form. Additional exam requirements/recommendations for international students: Required—TOEFL (minimum score 550 paper-based; 79 iBT), Michigan English Language Assessment Battery (minimum score 85); Recommended—IELTS (minimum score 6). *Application deadline:* Applications are

processed on a rolling basis. Application fee: $30. Electronic applications accepted. *Expenses:* Contact institution. *Financial support:* Career-related internships or fieldwork, Federal Work-Study, and scholarships/grants available. Financial award applicants required to submit FAFSA. *Faculty research:* Adult education, accelerated learning, mathematics education, brain compatible learning, special education and law. *Unit head:* Dr. Mary Garrity, Interim Dean, 617-873-0168, E-mail: mary.garrity@cambridgecollege.edu. *Application contact:* Salvadore Liberto, Interim Assistant Vice President of Enrollment, 800-877-4723, E-mail: admissions@cambridgecollege.edu. Website: https://www.cambridgecollege.edu/school/school-education

Central Washington University, School of Graduate Studies and Research, College of Education and Professional Studies, Department of Physical Education, School Health and Movement Studies, Ellensburg, WA 98926. Offers athletic administration (MS); health and physical education (MS). *Program availability:* Part-time. *Degree requirements:* For master's, comprehensive exam, thesis or alternative. *Entrance requirements:* For master's, minimum GPA of 3.0. Additional exam requirements/recommendations for international students: Required—TOEFL (minimum score 550 paper-based; 79 iBT), IELTS. Electronic applications accepted.

Clark University, Graduate School, Department of International Development, Community, and Environment, Worcester, MA 01610-1477. Offers community and global health (MHS); community development and planning (MA); environmental science and policy (MS); geographic information science for development and environment (MS); international development and social change (MA); MA/MBA; MBA/MS. *Entrance requirements:* For master's, 3 references, resume or curriculum vitae. Additional exam requirements/recommendations for international students: Required—TOEFL (minimum score 575 paper-based; 90 iBT) or IELTS (minimum score 6.5). *Expenses:* Tuition: Full-time $34,110. *Required fees:* $40. Tuition and fees vary according to course load and program. *Faculty research:* Community action research, gender analysis, environmental risk assessment, land-use planning, geographic information systems, HIV and AIDS, global health and social justice, environmental health, climate change and sustainability.

Cleveland State University, College of Graduate Studies, College of Education and Human Services, Department of Health and Human Performance, Cleveland, OH 44115. Offers physical education pedagogy (M Ed); public health (MPH). *Program availability:* Part-time. *Faculty:* 7 full-time (4 women), 3 part-time/adjunct (2 women). *Students:* 29 full-time (17 women), 50 part-time (28 women); includes 31 minority (23 Black or African American, non-Hispanic/Latino; 1 Asian, non-Hispanic/Latino; 1 Hispanic/Latino; 6 Two or more races, non-Hispanic/Latino), 2 international. Average age 29. 103 applicants, 72% accepted, 43 enrolled. In 2018, 30 master's awarded. *Degree requirements:* For master's, comprehensive exam, thesis optional. *Entrance requirements:* For master's, GRE General Test or MAT (if undergraduate GPA less than 2.75), minimum undergraduate GPA of 2.75. Additional exam requirements/recommendations for international students: Required—TOEFL (minimum score 550 paper-based; 78 iBT), IELTS (minimum score 6). *Application deadline:* For fall admission, 7/15 priority date for domestic students; for spring admission, 12/15 priority date for domestic students. Applications are processed on a rolling basis. Application fee: $30. Electronic applications accepted. *Expenses:* Tuition: state resident: full-time $7232.55; part-time $6676 per credit hour. Tuition, nonresident: full-time $12,375. *International tuition:* $18,914 full-time. *Required fees:* $80; $80 $40. Tuition and fees vary according to program. *Financial support:* In 2018–19, 6 research assistantships with tuition reimbursements (averaging $3,480 per year), 1 teaching assistantship with tuition reimbursement (averaging $3,480 per year) were awarded; career-related internships or fieldwork, tuition waivers (full), and unspecified assistantships also available. Financial award application deadline: 3/15; financial award applicants required to submit FAFSA. *Faculty research:* Bone density, marketing fitness centers, motor development of disabled, online learning and survey research. *Unit head:* Dr. Mike Loovis, Associate Professor/Department Chairperson, 216-687-3665, Fax: 216-687-5410, E-mail: e.loovis@csuohio.edu. *Application contact:* David Easler, Director, Graduate Recruitment, 216-687-5047, Fax: 216-687-5400, E-mail: d.easler@csuohio.edu. Website: http://www.csuohio.edu/cehs/departments/HPERD/hperd_dept.html

Cleveland University–Kansas City, Program in Health Education and Promotion, Overland Park, KS 66210. Offers MS. *Program availability:* Part-time. *Entrance requirements:* For master's, professional statement. Additional exam requirements/recommendations for international students: Required—TOEFL (minimum score 550 paper-based; 79 iBT). Electronic applications accepted. *Expenses:* Contact institution.

The College at Brockport, State University of New York, School of Education, Health, and Human Services, Department of Public Health and Health Education, Brockport, NY 14420-2997. Offers community health education (MS Ed); health education (MS Ed), including health education K-12. *Faculty:* 4 full-time (2 women), 3 part-time/adjunct (2 women). *Students:* 23 full-time (13 women), 54 part-time (23 women); includes 1 minority (Hispanic/Latino). 46 applicants, 72% accepted, 28 enrolled. In 2018, 18 master's awarded. *Degree requirements:* For master's, thesis or alternative. *Entrance requirements:* For master's, minimum GPA of 3.0, letters of recommendation. Additional exam requirements/recommendations for international students: Required—TOEFL (minimum score 550 paper-based; 79 iBT), IELTS (minimum score 6.5). *Application deadline:* For fall admission, 3/1 priority date for domestic and international students; for spring admission, 10/1 priority date for domestic and international students; for summer admission, 3/1 priority date for domestic and international students. Application fee: $80. Electronic applications accepted. *Expenses:* Tuition, state resident: part-time $471 per credit. Tuition, nonresident: part-time $963 per credit. *Financial support:* In 2018–19, 1 teaching assistantship with full tuition reimbursement (averaging $6,000 per year) was awarded; Federal Work-Study, scholarships/grants, and unspecified assistantships also available. Support available to part-time students. Financial award application deadline: 3/15; financial award applicants required to submit FAFSA. *Faculty research:* Nutrition, substance use, HIV/AIDS, bioethics, worksite health. *Unit head:* Dr. Darson Rhodes, Graduate Director, 585-395-5901, Fax: 585-395-5246, E-mail: drhodes@brockport.edu. *Application contact:* Danielle A. Welch, Graduate Admissions Counselor, 585-395-5465, Fax: 585-395-2515. Website: https://www.brockport.edu/academics/public_health

College of Saint Mary, Program in Health Professions Education, Omaha, NE 68106. Offers Ed D. *Program availability:* Part-time.

Colorado State University–Pueblo, College of Education, Engineering and Professional Studies, Education Program, Pueblo, CO 81001-4901. Offers art education (M Ed); foreign language education (M Ed); health and physical education (M Ed); instructional technology (M Ed); linguistically diverse education (M Ed); music education (M Ed); special education (M Ed). *Accreditation:* TEAC. *Program availability:* Part-time. *Degree requirements:* For master's, portfolio. *Entrance requirements:* For master's, 3 recommendations, teaching license. Additional exam requirements/recommendations for international students: Required—TOEFL (minimum score 500 paper-based). Electronic applications accepted. *Faculty research:* Portfolio assessment, math education, science education.

Columbus State University, Graduate Studies, College of Education and Health Professions, Kinesiology & Health Sciences, Columbus, GA 31907-5645. Offers exercise science (MS); health and physical education (M Ed, MAT). *Program availability:*

Part-time, evening/weekend. *Faculty:* 5 full-time (3 women). *Students:* 17 full-time (7 women), 14 part-time (8 women); includes 13 minority (8 Black or African American, non-Hispanic/Latino; 1 Asian, non-Hispanic/Latino; 3 Hispanic/Latino; 1 Two or more races, non-Hispanic/Latino). Average age 28. 23 applicants, 65% accepted, 12 enrolled. In 2018, 12 master's awarded. *Degree requirements:* For master's, thesis optional. *Entrance requirements:* For master's, GRE, minimum undergraduate GPA of 2.75. Additional exam requirements/recommendations for international students: Required—TOEFL (minimum score 550 paper-based; 79 iBT). *Application deadline:* For fall admission, 5/1 for domestic students, 4/1 for international students; for spring admission, 11/1 for domestic and international students; for summer admission, 2/1 for domestic students, 3/1 for international students. Applications are processed on a rolling basis. Application fee: $50. Electronic applications accepted. *Expenses: Tuition, area resident:* Full-time $4924; part-time $618 per credit hour. Tuition, state resident: full-time $4924; part-time $618 per credit hour. Tuition, nonresident: full-time $19,218; part-time $2403 per credit hour. *International tuition:* $19,218 full-time. *Required fees:* $1870; $802. Tuition and fees vary according to course load, degree level and program. *Financial support:* In 2018–19, 4 students received support, including 7 research assistantships (averaging $3,000 per year). Financial award application deadline: 5/15; financial award applicants required to submit FAFSA. *Unit head:* Dr. Clay Nicks, Chair, 706-507-8293, E-mail: nicks_clayton@columbusstate.edu. *Application contact:* Catrina Smith-Edmond, Assistant Director for Graduate and Global Admission, 706-507-8824, Fax: 706-568-5091, E-mail: smithedmond_catrina@columbusstate.edu. Website: http://hpex.columbusstate.edu/

Concordia University, College of Education, Portland, OR 97211-6099. Offers administrative leadership (Ed D); career and technical education (M Ed); curriculum and instruction (M Ed), including adolescent literacy, early childhood education, educational technology leadership, English for speakers of other languages, environmental education, health and physical education, mathematics, methods and curriculum, reading interventionist, science, social studies, STEAM education, teacher leadership, the inclusive classroom, trauma and resilience in educational settings; educational administration (M Ed); educational leadership (M Ed); elementary education (MAT); higher education (Ed D); instructional leadership (Ed D); professional leadership, inquiry, and transformation (Ed D); secondary education (MAT); transformational leadership (Ed D). *Program availability:* Part-time, online learning. *Degree requirements:* For master's, comprehensive exam, work samples/portfolio. *Entrance requirements:* For master's, California Basic Educational Skills Test or PRAXIS I, minimum undergraduate GPA of 2.8, graduate 3.0; 2 letters of recommendation. Additional exam requirements/recommendations for international students: Required—TOEFL (minimum score 525 paper-based). Electronic applications accepted. *Faculty research:* Learner-centered classroom, brain-based learning, future of online learning.

Concordia University Wisconsin, Graduate Programs, School of Health Professions, Mequon, WI 53097-2402. Offers MOT, MSRS, MSW, DPT.

Daemen College, Public Health Programs, Amherst, NY 14226-3592. Offers community health education (MPH); epidemiology (MPH); generalist (MPH). *Program availability:* Part-time, evening/weekend. *Faculty:* 4 full-time (2 women), 6 part-time/adjunct (4 women). *Students:* 17 full-time (15 women), 4 part-time (3 women); includes 8 minority (6 Black or African American, non-Hispanic/Latino; 1 Asian, non-Hispanic/Latino; 1 Two or more races, non-Hispanic/Latino), 1 international. Average age 26. 18 applicants, 61% accepted, 9 enrolled. In 2018, 8 master's awarded. *Degree requirements:* For master's, Successful completion of a practicum and capstone; A minimum grade of B- in any course; A maximum of two repeated courses is allowed; Students must maintain an overall minimum cumulative grade point average (GPA) of 3.00. *Entrance requirements:* For master's, bachelor's degree, official transcripts, GPA 3.0 or above (under 3.0 may be submitted on a conditional basis), 2 letters of recommendation, personal statement, interview with MPH faculty. Additional exam requirements/recommendations for international students: Required—TOEFL (minimum score 85 paper-based), IELTS (minimum score 6.5). *Application deadline:* Applications are processed on a rolling basis. Application fee: $25. Electronic applications accepted. Application fee is waived when completed online. *Expenses:* Tuition: Part-time $977 per credit hour. *Required fees:* $125; $14 per credit hour. *Financial support:* Scholarships/grants and unspecified assistantships available. Support available to part-time students. Financial award applicants required to submit FAFSA. *Faculty research:* Childhood obesity, health disparities, social determinants. *Unit head:* Dr. Brian Wrotniak, Director of Masters in Public Health, 716-839-8298, E-mail: bwrotnia@daemen.edu. *Application contact:* Megan Beardi, Senior Assistant Director of Graduate Admissions, 716-566-7861, Fax: 716-839-8229, E-mail: mbeardi@daemen.edu. Website: https://www.daemen.edu/academics/areas-study/public-health

Dalhousie University, Faculty of Health, School of Health and Human Performance, Program in Health Promotion, Halifax, NS B3H 3J5, Canada. Offers MA. *Program availability:* Part-time. *Degree requirements:* For master's, thesis. *Entrance requirements:* Additional exam requirements/recommendations for international students: Required—TOEFL, IELTS, CANTEST, CAEL, or Michigan English Language Assessment Battery. Electronic applications accepted. *Faculty research:* AIDS research, health knowledge of adolescents, evaluating health promotion, program evaluation.

Delta State University, Graduate Programs, College of Education, Division of Health, Physical Education, and Recreation, Cleveland, MS 38733-0001. Offers health, physical education, and recreation (M Ed); sport and human performance (MS). *Program availability:* Part-time, evening/weekend. *Degree requirements:* For master's, thesis optional. *Entrance requirements:* For master's, GRE General Test or MAT, Class A teaching certificate. *Expenses: Tuition, area resident:* Full-time $7076; part-time $393 per credit hour. Tuition, state resident: full-time $7076; part-time $393 per credit hour. Tuition, nonresident: full-time $7076; part-time $393 per credit hour. *International tuition:* $7076 full-time. *Required fees:* $170; $18.90 per credit hour. $9.45 per semester. Part-time tuition and fees vary according to program. *Faculty research:* Blood pressure, body fat, power and reaction time, learning disorders of athletes, effects of walking.

Drew University, Caspersen School of Graduate Studies, Madison, NJ 07940-1493. Offers conflict resolution and leadership (Certificate), including community leadership, moderation, peace building; education (M Ed); finance (MA); history and culture (MA, PhD), including American history, book history, British history, European history, intellectual history, Irish history, print culture, public history; K-12 education (MAT), including art, biology, chemistry, elementary education, English, French, Italian, math, secondary education, special education, teacher of students with disabilities; liberal studies (M Litt, D Litt), including history, Irish/Irish-American studies, literature (M Litt, MMH, D Litt, DMH, CMH), religion, spirituality, teaching in the two-year college, writing; medical humanities (MMH, DMH, CMH), including arts, health, healthcare, literature (M Litt, MMH, D Litt, DMH, CMH), scientific research; poetry (MFA). *Program availability:* Part-time, evening/weekend. *Faculty:* 3 full-time (2 women), 27 part-time/adjunct (13 women). *Students:* 66 full-time (38 women), 179 part-time (117 women); includes 37 minority (15 Black or African American, non-Hispanic/Latino; 2 Asian, non-Hispanic/Latino; 15 Hispanic/Latino; 5 Two or more races, non-Hispanic/Latino), 14 international. Average age 42. 157 applicants, 82% accepted, 57 enrolled. In 2018, 34 master's, 24 doctorates, 17 other advanced degrees awarded. Terminal master's awarded for partial completion of doctoral program. *Degree requirements:* For master's and other advanced degree, thesis

(for some programs); for doctorate, one foreign language, comprehensive exam (for some programs), thesis/dissertation. *Entrance requirements:* For master's, PRAXIS Core and Subject Area tests (for MAT), GRE/GMAT (for MFin MS in Data Analytics), resume, transcripts, writing sample, personal statement, letters of recommendation; for doctorate, GRE (PhD in history and culture), resume, transcripts, writing sample, personal statement, letters of recommendation; for other advanced degree, resume, transcripts, personal statement. Additional exam requirements/recommendations for international students: Required—TOEFL (minimum score 587 paper-based; 80 iBT), IELTS (minimum score 6), TWE (minimum score 4). *Application deadline:* For fall admission, 8/1 for domestic students, 6/1 for international students; for spring admission, 12/1 for domestic students, 10/1 for international students. Applications are processed on a rolling basis. Application fee: $35. Electronic applications accepted. *Financial support:* Fellowships, research assistantships, teaching assistantships, career-related internships or fieldwork, Federal Work-Study, scholarships/grants, and unspecified assistantships available. Support available to part-time students. Financial award applicants required to submit FAFSA. *Unit head:* Dr. Debra Liebowitz, Provost and Dean of the College of Liberal Arts & Caspersen School of Graduate Studies, 973-4083139, E-mail: dliebowi@drew.edu. *Application contact:* Amo-Augustus Kubeyinje, Associate Vice President for Graduate Enrollment, 973-408-3111, E-mail: akubeyinje@drew.edu.
Website: http://www.drew.edu/caspersen

East Carolina University, Graduate School, College of Health and Human Performance, Department of Health Education and Promotion, Greenville, NC 27858-4353. Offers environmental health (MS); health education (MA Ed); health education and promotion (MA). *Accreditation:* NCATE. *Application deadline:* For fall admission, 6/1 priority date for domestic students. *Expenses: Tuition, area resident:* Full-time $4749. Tuition, state resident: full-time $4749. Tuition, nonresident: full-time $17,898. *International tuition:* $17,898 full-time. *Required fees:* $2787. Part-time tuition and fees vary according to course load and program. *Financial support:* Application deadline: 6/1. *Unit head:* Vic Aeby, Associate Professor, 252-328-6000, E-mail: aeby@ecu.edu. *Application contact:* Graduate School Admissions, 252-328-6012, Fax: 252-328-6071, E-mail: gradschool@ecu.edu.
Website: https://hhp.ecu.edu/hep/

Eastern Kentucky University, The Graduate School, College of Education, Department of Curriculum and Instruction, Program in Secondary and Higher Education, Richmond, KY 40475-3102. Offers secondary education (MA Ed), including agricultural education, art education, biological sciences education, business education, English education, geography education, history education, home economics education, industrial education, mathematical sciences education, physical education, school health education. *Accreditation:* NCATE. *Program availability:* Part-time. *Entrance requirements:* For master's, GRE General Test, minimum GPA of 2.5.

Eastern Michigan University, Graduate School, College of Health and Human Services, School of Health Promotion and Human Performance, Programs in Health Education, Ypsilanti, MI 48197. Offers MS, Graduate Certificate. *Program availability:* Part-time, evening/weekend. *Students:* 3 full-time (all women), 10 part-time (6 women); includes 1 minority (Black or African American, non-Hispanic/Latino). Average age 30. 7 applicants, 86% accepted, 3 enrolled. In 2018, 11 master's awarded. *Entrance requirements:* For master's, teaching credential. Additional exam requirements/recommendations for international students: Required—TOEFL. *Application deadline:* For fall admission, 8/1 for domestic students, 5/1 for international students; for winter admission, 12/1 for domestic students, 10/1 for international students; for spring admission, 4/15 for domestic students, 3/1 for international students. Application fee: $45. *Application contact:* Dr. Joan Cowdery, Program Coordinator, 734-487-2811, Fax: 734-487-2024, E-mail: jcowdery@emich.edu.

Eastern University, Department of Nursing, St. Davids, PA 19087-3696. Offers nursing (MSN); school health services (M Ed); school health supervisor (K-12) (Certificate); school nurse (K-12) (Certificate). Electronic applications accepted. Application fee is waived when completed online. *Expenses:* Contact institution.

Eastern University, Graduate Education Programs, St. Davids, PA 19087-3696. Offers ESL program specialist (K-12) (Certificate); general supervisor (PreK-12) (Certificate); health and physical education (K-12) (Certificate); middle level (4-8) (Certificate); multicultural education (M Ed); music (K-12) (Certificate); Pre K-4 (Certificate); Pre K-4 with special education (Certificate); reading (M Ed); reading specialist (K-12) (Certificate); reading supervisor (K-12) (Certificate); school counseling (MA, CAGS); school principalship (preK-12) (Certificate); school psychology (MS, CAGS); secondary biology education (7-12) (Certificate); secondary chemistry education (7-12) (Certificate); secondary communication education (7-12) (Certificate); secondary English education (7-12) (Certificate); secondary math education (7-12) (Certificate); secondary social studies education (7-12) (Certificate); special education (M Ed); special education (7-12) (Certificate); special education (Pre K-8) (Certificate); special education supervisor (K-12) (Certificate); TESOL (M Ed); world language (Certificate), including Spanish. *Program availability:* Part-time, evening/weekend, online learning. *Entrance requirements:* Additional exam requirements/recommendations for international students: Required—TOEFL. Electronic applications accepted. Application fee is waived when completed online. *Expenses:* Contact institution.

East Stroudsburg University of Pennsylvania, Graduate and Extended Studies, College of Health Sciences, Department of Exercise Science, East Stroudsburg, PA 18301-2999. Offers MS. *Program availability:* Part-time, evening/weekend, online learning. *Faculty:* 9 full-time (2 women). *Students:* 53 full-time (20 women), 1 part-time (0 women); includes 3 minority (1 Black or African American, non-Hispanic/Latino; 1 Asian, non-Hispanic/Latino; 1 Native Hawaiian or other Pacific Islander, non-Hispanic/Latino). Average age 23. 21 applicants, 52% accepted. In 2018, 51 master's awarded. *Degree requirements:* For master's, comprehensive exam, thesis or alternative, computer literacy. *Entrance requirements:* For master's, letters of recommendation, resume, professional goals statement. Additional exam requirements/recommendations for international students: Recommended—TOEFL (minimum score 560 paper-based; 83 iBT), IELTS. *Application deadline:* For fall admission, 3/1 priority date for domestic and international students; for spring admission, 11/30 for domestic students, 10/31 for international students. Applications are processed on a rolling basis. Application fee: $50. Electronic applications accepted. *Expenses: Tuition, area resident:* Full-time $9288; part-time $516 per credit. Tuition, state resident: full-time $9288. Tuition, nonresident: full-time $13,932; part-time $774 per credit. *International tuition:* $13,932 full-time. *Required fees:* $2059; $114 per credit. Tuition and fees vary according to course load and degree level. *Financial support:* Research assistantships with tuition reimbursements, Federal Work-Study, and unspecified assistantships available. Support available to part-time students. Financial award application deadline: 3/1; financial award applicants required to submit FAFSA. *Unit head:* Dr. Chad Witmer, Graduate Coordinator, 570-422-3362, E-mail: cwitmer@esu.edu. *Application contact:* Kevin Quintero, Associate Director, Graduate and Extended Studies, 570-422-3890, Fax: 570-422-2711, E-mail: kquintero@esu.edu.
Website: https://www.esu.edu/exercise_science/graduate_programs/exercise_science.cfm

East Stroudsburg University of Pennsylvania, Graduate and Extended Studies, College of Health Sciences, Department of Health Studies, East Stroudsburg, PA 18301-2999. Offers MPH, MS. *Accreditation:* CEPH (one or more programs are accredited). *Program availability:* Part-time, evening/weekend, online learning. *Faculty:* 5 full-time (all women), 1 (woman) part-time/adjunct. *Students:* 16 full-time (15 women), 26 part-time (19 women); includes 10 minority (2 Asian, non-Hispanic/Latino; 5 Hispanic/Latino; 3 Two or more races, non-Hispanic/Latino), 1 international. Average age 31. 29 applicants, 62% accepted, 12 enrolled. In 2018, 19 master's awarded. *Degree requirements:* For master's, oral comprehensive exam. *Entrance requirements:* For master's, GRE General Test, minimum GPA of 3.0 in major, 2.8 overall; undergraduate prerequisites in anatomy and physiology; 3 verifiable letters of recommendation; professional resume. Additional exam requirements/recommendations for international students: Recommended—TOEFL (minimum score 560 paper-based; 83 iBT), IELTS. *Application deadline:* For fall admission, 7/31 priority date for domestic students, 6/30 priority date for international students; for spring admission, 11/30 for domestic students, 10/31 for international students. Applications are processed on a rolling basis. Application fee: $50. Electronic applications accepted. *Expenses: Tuition, area resident:* Full-time $9288; part-time $516 per credit. Tuition, state resident: full-time $9288. Tuition, nonresident: full-time $13,932; part-time $774 per credit. *International tuition:* $13,932 full-time. *Required fees:* $2059; $114 per credit. Tuition and fees vary according to course load and degree level. *Financial support:* Research assistantships with tuition reimbursements, Federal Work-Study, and unspecified assistantships available. Support available to part-time students. Financial award application deadline: 3/1; financial award applicants required to submit FAFSA. *Faculty research:* HIV prevention, wellness, international health issues. *Unit head:* Dr. Kim Razzano, Chair, 570-422-3693, Fax: 570-422-3848, E-mail: krazzano@esu.edu. *Application contact:* Kevin Quintero, Associate Director, Graduate and Extended Studies, 570-422-3890, Fax: 570-422-2711, E-mail: kquintero@esu.edu.
Website: https://www.esu.edu/health_studies/graduate_programs/health_education.cfm

Emory University, Rollins School of Public Health, Department of Behavioral Sciences and Health Education, Atlanta, GA 30322-1100. Offers MPH, PhD. *Accreditation:* CEPH. *Program availability:* Part-time. *Degree requirements:* For master's, comprehensive exam (for some programs), thesis, practicum. *Entrance requirements:* For master's, GRE General Test. Additional exam requirements/recommendations for international students: Required—TOEFL (minimum score 550 paper-based; 80 iBT). Electronic applications accepted.

Fairfield University, Marion Peckham Egan School of Nursing and Health Studies, Fairfield, CT 06824. Offers advanced practice (DNP); family nurse practitioner (MSN, DNP); nurse anesthesia (DNP); nursing leadership (MSN); psychiatric nurse practitioner (MSN, DNP). *Accreditation:* AACN; AANA/CANAEP. *Program availability:* Part-time, evening/weekend. *Degree requirements:* For master's, capstone project. *Entrance requirements:* For master's, minimum QPA of 3.0, RN license, resume, 2 recommendations; for doctorate, MSN (minimum QPA of 3.2) or BSN (minimum QPA of 3.0); critical care nursing experience (for nurse anesthesia DNP candidates). Additional exam requirements/recommendations for international students: Required—TOEFL (minimum score 550 paper-based; 80 iBT) or IELTS (minimum score 6.5). Electronic applications accepted. *Expenses:* Contact institution. *Faculty research:* Aging, spiritual care, palliative and end of life care, psychiatric mental health, pediatric trauma.

Florida State University, The Graduate School, College of Human Sciences, Department of Nutrition, Food and Exercise Sciences, Tallahassee, FL 32306-1493. Offers exercise physiology (MS, PhD); nutrition and food science (MS, PhD), including nutrition education and health promotion (MS); sports nutrition (MS); sports sciences (MS). *Program availability:* Part-time. *Faculty:* 26 full-time (12 women). *Students:* 71 full-time (49 women), 15 part-time (7 women); includes 15 minority (1 Black or African American, non-Hispanic/Latino; 2 Asian, non-Hispanic/Latino; 1 Hispanic/Latino; 11 Two or more races, non-Hispanic/Latino), 12 international. 177 applicants, 37% accepted, 31 enrolled. In 2018, 24 master's, 6 doctorates awarded. *Degree requirements:* For master's, thesis optional; for doctorate, thesis/dissertation, preliminary examination, minimum of 24 credit hours dissertation, dissertation defense. *Entrance requirements:* For master's, GRE General Test, minimum upper-division GPA of 3.0; for doctorate, GRE General Test, minimum upper-division GPA of 3.0 or awarded master's degree. Additional exam requirements/recommendations for international students: Required—TOEFL (minimum score 550 paper-based; 80 iBT). *Application deadline:* For fall admission, 4/1 for domestic and international students; for spring admission, 10/1 for domestic and international students. Applications are processed on a rolling basis. Application fee: $30. Electronic applications accepted. *Expenses: Tuition, area resident:* Part-time $479.32 per credit hour. Tuition and fees vary according to campus/location and program. *Financial support:* In 2018–19, 45 students received support, including 12 research assistantships with full tuition reimbursements available (averaging $25,000 per year), 30 teaching assistantships with full tuition reimbursements available (averaging $25,000 per year); career-related internships or fieldwork, Federal Work-Study, institutionally sponsored loans, scholarships/grants, and unspecified assistantships also available. Financial award application deadline: 2/1; financial award applicants required to submit FAFSA. *Faculty research:* Nutrition and health, sports nutrition, energy and human performance, strength training, functional performance, cardiovascular physiology, sarcopenia, chronic disease and aging, functional food, food safety, food allergy, and food safety/quality detection methods. *Total annual research expenditures:* $1.1 million. *Unit head:* Dr. Chester Ray, Department Chair, 850-644-1850, Fax: 850-645-5000, E-mail: caray@fsu.edu. *Application contact:* Mary-Sue McLemore, Academic Support Assistant, 850-644-1117, E-mail: mmclemore@fsu.edu.
Website: https://humansciences.fsu.edu/nutrition-food-exercise-sciences/students/graduate-programs/

Fort Hays State University, Graduate School, College of Health and Behavioral Sciences, Department of Health and Human Performance, Hays, KS 67601-4099. Offers MS. *Program availability:* Part-time. *Degree requirements:* For master's, comprehensive exam, thesis optional. *Entrance requirements:* For master's, GRE General Test or MAT. Additional exam requirements/recommendations for international students: Required—TOEFL (minimum score 550 paper-based). Electronic applications accepted. *Faculty research:* Isoproterenol hydrochloride and exercise, dehydrogenase and high-density lipoprotein levels in athletics, venous blood parameters to adipose fat.

Georgia College & State University, Graduate School, College of Health Sciences, School of Health and Human Performance, Milledgeville, GA 31061. Offers health and human performance (MS), including health performance, health promotion; kinesiology/health education (MAT). *Accreditation:* NCATE (one or more programs are accredited). *Program availability:* Part-time, 100% online. *Degree requirements:* For master's, thesis (for some programs), completed in 6 years with minimum GPA of 3.0 (for MS); minimum GPA of 3.0 and electronic teaching portfolio (for MAT). *Entrance requirements:* For master's, GRE with minimum score of 297 or MAT with minimum score of 385 (for MS); GRE with minimum score of 297, MAT 385, SAT 1000, ACT 43, or GACE with 250 on each section (for MAT), resume, 3 professional references; minimum GPA of 2.75 in upper-level undergraduate courses and undergraduate statistics course (for MS); minimum GPA of 2.75 on upper-division major courses (for MAT). Electronic applications accepted. *Expenses:* Contact institution.

Georgia Southern University, Jack N. Averitt College of Graduate Studies, Jiann-Ping Hsu College of Public Health, Program in Public Health, Statesboro, GA 30460. Offers

biostatistics (MPH, Dr PH); community health behavior and education (Dr PH); community health education (MPH); environmental health sciences (MPH); epidemiology (MPH); health policy and management (MPH, Dr PH). *Program availability:* Part-time. *Degree requirements:* For master's, thesis optional, practicum; for doctorate, comprehensive exam, thesis/dissertation, preceptorship. *Entrance requirements:* For master's, GRE General Test, minimum GPA of 2.75, 3 letters of recommendation, statement of purpose, resume or curriculum vitae; for doctorate, GRE, GMAT, MCAT, LSAT, minimum GPA of 3.0, 3 letters of recommendation, statement of purpose, resume or curriculum vitae. Additional exam requirements/recommendations for international students: Required—TOEFL (minimum score 537 paper-based; 75 iBT), IELTS (minimum score 6). Electronic applications accepted. *Expenses:* Contact institution. *Faculty research:* Rural public health best practices, health disparity elimination, community initiatives to enhance public health, cost effectiveness analysis, epidemiology of rural public health, environmental health issues, health care system assessment, rural health care, health policy and healthcare financing, survival analysis, nonparametric statistics and resampling methods, micro-arrays and genomics, data imputation techniques and clinical trial methodology.

Georgia State University, College of Education and Human Development, Department of Kinesiology and Health, Program in Health and Physical Education, Atlanta, GA 30302-3083. Offers M Ed. *Program availability:* Part-time, evening/weekend. *Entrance requirements:* For master's, GRE General Test, minimum GPA of 2.5. Application fee: $50. *Expenses: Tuition, area resident:* Full-time $9360; part-time $390 per credit hour. Tuition, state resident: full-time $9360; part-time $390 per credit hour. Tuition, nonresident: full-time $30,024; part-time $1251 per credit hour. *International tuition:* $30,024 full-time. *Required fees:* $2128. *Financial support:* Teaching assistantships and career-related internships or fieldwork available. *Faculty research:* Exercise science, teacher behavior. *Unit head:* Dr. Jacalyn Lea Lund, Chair, 404-413-8051, E-mail: jlund@gsu.edu. *Application contact:* Dr. Rachel Gurvitch, Program Coordinator, 404-413-8374, Fax: 404-413-8053, E-mail: rgurvitch@gsu.edu. Website: https://education.gsu.edu/kh/

Harding University, Cannon-Clary College of Education, Searcy, AR 72149-0001. Offers advanced studies in teaching and learning (M Ed); art (MSE); behavioral science (MSE); counseling (MS, Ed S); early childhood special education (M Ed, MSE); education (MSE); educational leadership (M Ed, Ed S); elementary education (M Ed); English (MSE); French (MSE); history/social science (MSE); kinesiology (MSE); math (MSE); reading (M Ed); secondary education (M Ed); Spanish (MSE); teaching (MAT); teaching English as a second language (MSE). *Accreditation:* NCATE. *Program availability:* Part-time, evening/weekend. *Degree requirements:* For master's, comprehensive exam (for some programs), thesis optional, portfolio(s); for Ed S, comprehensive exam, portfolio, project. *Entrance requirements:* For master's, GRE, MAT, PRAXIS; for Ed S, MAT or GRE. Additional exam requirements/recommendations for international students: Required—TOEFL (minimum score 550 paper-based; 79 iBT). *Faculty research:* Reading, comprehension, school violence, educational technology, behavior, college choice, differentiated instruction, brain-based teaching.

Hofstra University, School of Education, Specialized Programs in Education, Hempstead, NY 11549. Offers applied behavior analysis (Advanced Certificate); childhood special education (MS Ed); early childhood special education (MS Ed, Advanced Certificate); educational and policy leadership (Ed D); educational leadership (Advanced Certificate); educational leadership and policy studies (MS Ed), including K-12; elementary special education (MS Ed); gifted education (Advanced Certificate); health education (MS); health professions pedagogy and leadership (MS); higher education leadership and policy studies (MS Ed); inclusive early childhood special education (MS Ed); inclusive elementary special education (MS Ed); inclusive secondary special education (MS Ed); literacy studies (MA, MS Ed, Ed D, Advanced Certificate); pedagogy for health professions (Advanced Certificate); physical education (MS); school district business leader (Advanced Certificate); secondary education generalist - students with disabilities 7-12 (MS Ed); secondary special education generalist - secondary education (MS Ed); special education (MS Ed, Advanced Certificate); special education assessment and diagnosis (Advanced Certificate); special education early childhood intervention (MS Ed); special education: international perspectives (MS Ed); teaching students with severe or multiple disabilities (Advanced Certificate). *Program availability:* Part-time, evening/weekend, blended/hybrid learning. *Students:* 126 full-time (91 women), 230 part-time (175 women); includes 90 minority (40 Black or African American, non-Hispanic/Latino; 4 American Indian or Alaska Native, non-Hispanic/Latino; 11 Asian, non-Hispanic/Latino; 32 Hispanic/Latino; 3 Two or more races, non-Hispanic/Latino), 4 international. Average age 32. 215 applicants, 90% accepted, 117 enrolled. In 2018, 130 master's, 9 doctorates, 23 other advanced degrees awarded. *Degree requirements:* For master's, one foreign language, comprehensive exam (for some programs), thesis (for some programs), electronic portfolio, capstone course, internship, practicum, student teaching, seminars, minimum GPA of 3.0; for doctorate, one foreign language, comprehensive exam, thesis/dissertation, qualifying hearing. *Entrance requirements:* For master's, GRE, interview, letters of recommendation, portfolio, essay, certification; for doctorate, GRE or MAT, interview, resume, essay, master's degree, 3 letters of recommendation, writing sample; for Advanced Certificate, GRE, interview, letters of recommendation, essay, professional experience, resume, master's degree. Additional exam requirements/recommendations for international students: Required—TOEFL (minimum score 550 paper-based; 80 iBT). *Application deadline:* Applications are processed on a rolling basis. Application fee: $75. Electronic applications accepted. *Financial support:* In 2018–19, 208 students received support, including 105 fellowships with full and partial tuition reimbursements available (averaging $3,948 per year), 12 research assistantships with full and partial tuition reimbursements available (averaging $6,573 per year); career-related internships or fieldwork, Federal Work-Study, institutionally sponsored loans, scholarships/grants, traineeships, tuition waivers (full and partial), unspecified assistantships, and scholarships and endowed scholarships also available. Support available to part-time students. Financial award applicants required to submit FAFSA. *Faculty research:* Water quality and income inequality; girls and stem; new media literacies; applied behavior analysis; k-12 leadership development. *Unit head:* Dr. Alan Flurkey, Chairperson, 516-463-5237, E-mail: alan.d.flurkey@hofstra.edu. *Application contact:* Sunil Samuel, Assistant Vice President of Admissions, 516-463-4723, Fax: 516-463-4664, E-mail: graduateadmission@hofstra.edu. Website: http://www.hofstra.edu/education/

Howard University, Graduate School, Department of Health, Human Performance and Leisure Studies, Washington, DC 20059-0002. Offers exercise physiology (MS); health education (MS); sports studies (MS), including sociology of sports, sports management; urban recreation (MS), including leisure studies. *Program availability:* Part-time, evening/weekend. *Degree requirements:* For master's, comprehensive exam, thesis. *Entrance requirements:* For master's, BS in human performance or related field. Additional exam requirements/recommendations for international students: Recommended—TOEFL. Electronic applications accepted. *Faculty research:* Health promotion, cardiovascular hypertension, physical activity, sport and human rights issues.

Idaho State University, Graduate School, College of Health Professions, Department of Community and Public Health, Program in Health Education, Pocatello, ID 83209-

8109. Offers MHE. *Program availability:* Part-time. *Degree requirements:* For master's, comprehensive exam, thesis or project. *Entrance requirements:* For master's, GRE General Test, previous coursework in statistics, natural sciences, tests and measurements. Additional exam requirements/recommendations for international students: Required—TOEFL (minimum score 600 paper-based). Electronic applications accepted. *Faculty research:* Health and wellness.

Illinois State University, Graduate School, College of Applied Science and Technology, School of Kinesiology and Recreation, Normal, IL 61790. Offers health education (MS). *Faculty:* 35 full-time (20 women), 16 part-time/adjunct (10 women). *Students:* 114 full-time (58 women), 22 part-time (9 women); includes 23 minority (7 Black or African American, non-Hispanic/Latino; 2 Asian, non-Hispanic/Latino; 12 Hispanic/Latino; 2 Two or more races, non-Hispanic/Latino), 10 international. Average age 25. 166 applicants, 54% accepted, 68 enrolled. In 2018, 68 master's awarded. *Degree requirements:* For master's, thesis or alternative. *Entrance requirements:* For master's, GRE General Test, minimum GPA of 2.6 in last 60 hours of course work. *Application deadline:* Applications are processed on a rolling basis. Application fee: $40. *Expenses: Tuition, area resident:* Full-time $7264.62. Tuition, state resident: full-time $9466. Tuition, nonresident: full-time $17,290. *International tuition:* $15,089.40 full-time. *Required fees:* $1481.04. *Financial support:* In 2018–19, 5 research assistantships, 24 teaching assistantships were awarded; career-related internships or fieldwork, Federal Work-Study, tuition waivers (full and partial), and unspecified assistantships also available. Financial award application deadline: 4/1. *Faculty research:* Influences on positive youth development through sport, country-wide health fitness project, graduate practicum in athletic training, perceived exertion and self-selected intensity during resistance exercise in younger and older. *Unit head:* Dr. Dan Elkins, 309-438-8661, E-mail: delkins@IllinoisState.edu. *Application contact:* Dr. Dan Elkins, 309-438-8661, E-mail: delkins@IllinoisState.edu. Website: http://www.kinrec.ilstu.edu/

Indiana State University, College of Graduate and Professional Studies, College of Health and Human Services, Department of Applied Health Sciences, Terre Haute, IN 47809. Offers MS, DHS. *Accreditation:* NCATE (one or more programs are accredited). *Degree requirements:* For master's, thesis or alternative. *Entrance requirements:* For master's, GRE General Test. Electronic applications accepted.

Indiana University Bloomington, School of Public Health, Department of Applied Health Science, Bloomington, IN 47405. Offers behavioral, social, and community health (MPH); family health (MPH); health behavior (PhD); nutrition science (MS); professional health education (MPH); public health administration (MPH); safety management (MS); school and college health education (MS). *Degree requirements:* For master's, thesis optional; for doctorate, comprehensive exam, thesis/dissertation. *Entrance requirements:* For master's, GRE (for MS in nutrition science), 3 recommendations; for doctorate, GRE, 3 recommendations. Additional exam requirements/recommendations for international students: Required—TOEFL (minimum score 550 paper-based; 80 iBT). Electronic applications accepted. *Faculty research:* Cancer education, HIV/AIDS and drug education, public health, parent-child interactions, safety education, obesity, public health policy, public health administration, school health, health education, human development, nutrition, human sexuality, chronic disease, early childhood health.

Indiana University of Pennsylvania, School of Graduate Studies and Research, College of Health and Human Services, Department of Kinesiology, Health, and Sport Science, Program in Health and Physical Education, Indiana, PA 15705. Offers M Ed. *Program availability:* Part-time. *Faculty:* 44 full-time (27 women), 18 part-time/adjunct (12 women). *Students:* 44 full-time (27 women), 18 part-time (12 women); includes 2 minority (both Black or African American, non-Hispanic/Latino). Average age 25. 54 applicants, 81% accepted, 34 enrolled. In 2018, 24 master's awarded. *Entrance requirements:* Additional exam requirements/recommendations for international students: Required—TOEFL (minimum score 540 paper-based). *Application deadline:* Applications are processed on a rolling basis. Application fee: $50. Electronic applications accepted. *Expenses:* Tuition, state resident: full-time $12,384; part-time $516 per credit hour. Tuition, nonresident: full-time $18,576; part-time $774 per credit hour. *Required fees:* $4454; $186 per credit hour. $65 per semester. Tuition and fees vary according to program and reciprocity agreements. *Financial support:* In 2018–19, 6 research assistantships with tuition reimbursements (averaging $3,083 per year) were awarded; career-related internships or fieldwork, Federal Work-Study, scholarships/grants, and unspecified assistantships also available. Support available to part-time students. Financial award application deadline: 4/15; financial award applicants required to submit FAFSA. *Unit head:* Dr. David Wachob, Coordinator, 724-357-3194, E-mail: d.wachob@iup.edu. *Application contact:* Dr. David Wachob, Coordinator, 724-357-3194, E-mail: d.wachob@iup.edu. Website: http://www.iup.edu/grad/healthphysed/default.aspx

Indiana University–Purdue University Indianapolis, School of Health and Rehabilitation Sciences, Indianapolis, IN 46202. Offers health and rehabilitation sciences (PhD); health sciences (MS); nutrition and dietetics (MS); occupational therapy (OTD); physical therapy (DPT); physician assistant (MPAS). *Accreditation:* AOTA. *Program availability:* Part-time, evening/weekend. *Degree requirements:* For master's, thesis (for some programs). *Entrance requirements:* For master's, GRE General Test, minimum GPA of 3.0 (for MS in health sciences, nutrition and dietetics), 3.2 (for MS in occupational therapy), 3.0 cumulative and prerequisite math/science (for MPAS); for doctorate, GRE, minimum cumulative and prerequisite math/science GPA of 3.2. Additional exam requirements/recommendations for international students: Required—TOEFL (minimum score 550 paper-based; 79 iBT), IELTS (minimum score 6.5), PTE (minimum score 54). Electronic applications accepted. *Expenses:* Contact institution. *Faculty research:* Function and mobility across the lifespan, pediatric nutrition, driving and mobility rehabilitation, neurorehabilitation and biomechanics, rehabilitation and integrative therapy.

Inter American University of Puerto Rico, Metropolitan Campus, Graduate Programs, Program in Physical Education, San Juan, PR 00919-1293. Offers teaching of physical education (MA); training and sport performance (MA). *Degree requirements:* For master's, comprehensive exam. *Entrance requirements:* For master's, GRE or EXADEP, interview. Electronic applications accepted.

Inter American University of Puerto Rico, San Germán Campus, Graduate Studies Center, Program in Health and Physical Education, San Germán, PR 00683-5008. Offers MA. *Program availability:* Part-time, evening/weekend. *Degree requirements:* For master's, comprehensive exam. *Entrance requirements:* For master's, GRE General Test or EXADEP, minimum GPA of 3.0. *Expenses: Tuition:* Full-time $212; part-time $212 per credit. *Required fees:* $366 per semester. One-time fee: $31. Tuition and fees vary according to degree level and program.

Ithaca College, School of Health Sciences and Human Performance, Program in Health Education, Ithaca, NY 14850. Offers MS. In 2018, 5 master's awarded. Application fee: $40. *Unit head:* Dr. Stewart Auyash, Chair, 607-274-1312, E-mail: auyash@ithaca.edu. *Application contact:* Nicole Eversley Bradwell, Director, Office of Admission, 800-429-4274, Fax: 607-274-1263, E-mail: admission@ithaca.edu. Website: http://www.ithaca.edu/gradprograms/hppe/programs/healthed

Jackson State University, Graduate School, College of Education and Human Development, Department of Health, Physical Education and Recreation, Jackson, MS 39217. Offers physical education (MS Ed); sport science (MS). *Accreditation:* NCATE. *Program availability:* Part-time, evening/weekend, 100% online, blended/hybrid learning. *Degree requirements:* For master's, comprehensive exam, thesis or alternative. *Entrance requirements:* For master's, GRE General Test. Additional exam requirements/recommendations for international students: Required—TOEFL (minimum score 520 paper-based; 67 iBT). Electronic applications accepted. *Expenses:* Contact institution.

James Madison University, The Graduate School, College of Arts and Letters, Program in Communication and Advocacy, Harrisonburg, VA 22807. Offers environmental communication (MA); health communication (MA); strategic communication (MA). *Program availability:* Part-time, evening/weekend. *Students:* 28 full-time (21 women), 4 part-time (all women); includes 12 minority (6 Black or African American, non-Hispanic/Latino; 1 Asian, non-Hispanic/Latino; 4 Hispanic/Latino; 1 Two or more races, non-Hispanic/Latino), 3 international. Average age 30. In 2018, 11 master's awarded. Application fee: $60. Electronic applications accepted. *Expenses:* Tuition, state resident: full-time $10,848. Tuition, nonresident: full-time $27,888. *Required fees:* $1128. *Financial support:* In 2018–19, 28 students received support, including 7 teaching assistantships with full tuition reimbursements available (averaging $9,284 per year); fellowships, Federal Work-Study, and assistantships (averaging $7911) also available. Financial award application deadline: 3/1; financial award applicants required to submit FAFSA. *Unit head:* Dr. Eric M. Fife, Director of the School of Communication Studies, 540-568-6449, E-mail: fifeem@jmu.edu. *Application contact:* Lynette D. Michael, Director of Graduate Admissions, 540-568-6131 Ext. 6395, Fax: 540-568-7860, E-mail: michaeld@jmu.edu.
Website: http://www.jmu.edu/commstudies/

James Madison University, The Graduate School, College of Health and Behavioral Studies, Program in Kinesiology, Harrisonburg, VA 22807. Offers clinical exercise physiology (MS); exercise physiology (MS); kinesiology (MAT, MS); nutrition and exercise (MS); physical and health education (MAT); sport and recreation leadership (MS). *Program availability:* Part-time, evening/weekend. *Students:* 33 full-time (11 women); includes 3 minority (2 Black or African American, non-Hispanic/Latino; 1 Hispanic/Latino). Average age 30. In 2018, 18 master's awarded. Electronic applications accepted. *Expenses:* Tuition, state resident: full-time $10,848. Tuition, nonresident: full-time $27,888. *Required fees:* $1128. *Financial support:* In 2018–19, 20 students received support, including teaching assistantships with full tuition reimbursements available (averaging $8,837 per year); Federal Work-Study and assistantships (averaging $7911), athletic assistantships (averaging $9284) also available. Financial award application deadline: 3/1; financial award applicants required to submit FAFSA. *Unit head:* Dr. Christopher J. Womack, Department Head, 540-568-6145, E-mail: womackcx@jmu.edu. *Application contact:* Lynette D. Michael, Director of Graduate Admissions, 540-568-6131 Ext. 6395, Fax: 540-568-7860, E-mail: michaeld@jmu.edu. Website: http://www.jmu.edu/kinesiology/

John F. Kennedy University, College of Business and Professional Studies, Program in Holistic Health Education, Pleasant Hill, CA 94523-4817. Offers MA. *Program availability:* Part-time, evening/weekend, 100% online, blended/hybrid learning. *Degree requirements:* For master's, thesis or alternative. *Entrance requirements:* For master's, interview. Additional exam requirements/recommendations for international students: Required—TOEFL.

Johns Hopkins University, Bloomberg School of Public Health, Department of Health, Behavior and Society, Baltimore, MD 21218. Offers genetic counseling (Sc M); health education and health communication (MSPH); social and behavioral sciences (PhD); social factors in health (MHS). *Faculty:* 56 full-time. *Students:* 93 (75 women). 314 applicants, 29% accepted, 30 enrolled. In 2018, 22 master's, 4 doctorates awarded. *Degree requirements:* For master's, comprehensive exam (for some programs), thesis (for some programs); for doctorate, comprehensive exam, thesis/dissertation. *Entrance requirements:* For master's, GRE, curriculum vitae, 3 letters of recommendation; for doctorate, GRE, transcripts, curriculum vitae, 3 recommendation letters. Additional exam requirements/recommendations for international students: Required—TOEFL (minimum score 100 iBT), IELTS (minimum score 7). *Application deadline:* Applications are processed on a rolling basis. Application fee: $135. Electronic applications accepted. *Financial support:* Fellowships, research assistantships, teaching assistantships, career-related internships or fieldwork, Federal Work-Study, scholarships/grants, traineeships, health care benefits, unspecified assistantships, and stipends available. *Faculty research:* Social determinants of health and structural and community-level inventions to improve health, communication and health education, behavioral and social aspects of genetic counseling. *Unit head:* Rajiv Rimal, Chair, 410-502-4076, E-mail: HBS_Admissions@jhu.edu. *Application contact:* Rajiv Rimal, Chair, 410-502-4076, E-mail: HBS_Admissions@jhu.edu.
Website: http://jhsph.edu/dept/hbs

Kansas State University, Graduate School, College of Human Ecology, Department of Food, Nutrition, Dietetics and Health, Manhattan, KS 66506. Offers dietetics (MS); human nutrition (PhD); nutrition, dietetics and sensory sciences (MS); nutritional sciences (PhD); public health nutrition (PhD); public health physical activity (PhD); sensory analysis and consumer behavior (PhD). *Program availability:* Part-time. *Degree requirements:* For master's, thesis or alternative, residency; for doctorate, thesis/dissertation, residency. *Entrance requirements:* For master's, GRE General Test, minimum undergraduate GPA of 3.0; for doctorate, GRE General Test, minimum graduate GPA of 3.0. Additional exam requirements/recommendations for international students: Required—TOEFL (minimum score 550 paper-based; 79 iBT), IELTS (minimum score 6.5). Electronic applications accepted. *Faculty research:* Cancer and immunology, obesity, sensory analysis and consumer behavior, nutrient metabolism, clinical and community interventions.

Keiser University, Master of Science in Education Program, Fort Lauderdale, FL 33309. Offers allied health teaching and leadership (MS Ed); career college administration (MS Ed); leadership (MS Ed); online teaching and learning (MS Ed); teaching and learning (MS Ed). *Program availability:* Part-time, online learning.

Kent State University, College of Education, Health and Human Services, School of Health Sciences, Program in Health Education and Promotion, Kent, OH 44242-0001. Offers M Ed, PhD. *Accreditation:* NCATE. *Faculty:* 6 full-time (5 women), 2 part-time/adjunct (both women). *Students:* 21 full-time (16 women), 11 part-time (9 women); includes 8 minority (7 Black or African American, non-Hispanic/Latino; 1 Asian, non-Hispanic/Latino), 2 international. 20 applicants, 45% accepted. In 2018, 5 master's, 3 doctorates awarded. *Degree requirements:* For doctorate, comprehensive exam, thesis/dissertation. *Entrance requirements:* For master's, 2 letters of reference, goals statement; for doctorate, goals statement, resume, interview. Additional exam requirements/recommendations for international students: Required—TOEFL (minimum score 550 paper-based; 80 iBT). *Application deadline:* Applications are processed on a rolling basis. Application fee: $30 ($60 for international students). Electronic applications accepted. *Expenses:* Tuition, state resident: full-time $11,766; part-time $536 per credit. Tuition, nonresident: full-time $21,952; part-time $999 per credit. *International tuition:* $21,952 full-time. Tuition and fees vary according to course load. *Financial support:* In 2018–19, 1 research assistantship with full tuition reimbursement (averaging $8,500 per year), 6 teaching assistantships with full tuition reimbursements (averaging $10,833 per year) were awarded; Federal Work-Study, scholarships/grants, and unspecified assistantships also available. Financial award application deadline: 4/1; financial award applicants required to submit FAFSA. *Faculty research:* Substance use/abuse, sexuality, community health assessment, epidemiology, HIV/AIDS. *Unit head:* Dr. Laurie Wagner, Coordinator, 330-672-0685, E-mail: lyoo@kent.edu. *Application contact:* Cheryl Slusarczyk, Academic Program Director, Office of Graduate Student Services, 330-672-2586, Fax: 330-672-9162, E-mail: ogs@kent.edu.
Website: http://www.kent.edu/ehhs/hs/hedp

Lake Erie College of Osteopathic Medicine, Professional Programs, Erie, PA 16509-1025. Offers biomedical sciences (Postbaccalaureate Certificate); medical education (MS); osteopathic medicine (DO); pharmacy (Pharm D). *Accreditation:* ACPE; AOsA. *Degree requirements:* For doctorate, comprehensive exam, National Osteopathic Medical Licensing Exam, Levels 1 and 2; for Postbaccalaureate Certificate, comprehensive exam, North American Pharmacist Licensure Examination (NAPLEX). *Entrance requirements:* For doctorate, MCAT, minimum GPA of 3.2, letters of recommendation; for Postbaccalaureate Certificate, PCAT, letters of recommendation, minimum GPA of 3.5. Electronic applications accepted. *Faculty research:* Cardiac smooth and skeletal muscle mechanics, chemotherapeutics and vitamins, osteopathic manipulation.

Lehman College of the City University of New York, School of Health Sciences, Human Services and Nursing, Department of Health Sciences, Program in Health Education and Promotion, Bronx, NY 10468-1589. Offers MA. *Accreditation:* NCATE. *Program availability:* Part-time, evening/weekend. *Degree requirements:* For master's, thesis or alternative. *Entrance requirements:* For master's, minimum GPA of 2.7.

Lehman College of the City University of New York, School of Health Sciences, Human Services and Nursing, Department of Health Sciences, Program in Health N–12 Teacher, Bronx, NY 10468-1589. Offers MS Ed. *Accreditation:* NCATE. *Degree requirements:* For master's, thesis or alternative.

Lock Haven University of Pennsylvania, College of Natural, Behavioral and Health Sciences, Lock Haven, PA 17745-2390. Offers actuarial science (PSM); athletic training (MS); health promotion/education (MHS); healthcare management (MHS); physician assistant (MHS). Program also offered at the Clearfield, Coudersport, and Harrisburg campuses. *Accreditation:* ARC-PA. *Entrance requirements:* For master's, minimum undergraduate GPA of 3.0. Additional exam requirements/recommendations for international students: Required—TOEFL. Electronic applications accepted.

Logan University, College of Health Sciences, Chesterfield, MO 63017. Offers health informatics (MS); health professions education (DHPE); nutrition and human performance (MS); sports science and rehabilitation (MS). *Program availability:* Part-time, online only, 100% online. *Entrance requirements:* For master's, minimum GPA of 2.5; 6 hours of biology and physical science; bachelor's degree and 9 hours of business health administration (for health informatics). Additional exam requirements/recommendations for international students: Required—TOEFL (minimum score 500 paper-based; 79 iBT); Recommended—IELTS (minimum score 6.5). Electronic applications accepted. *Expenses:* Contact institution. *Faculty research:* Ankle injury prevention in high school athletes, low back pain in college football players, short arc banding and low back pain, the effects of enzymes on inflammatory blood markers, gait analysis in high school and college athletes.

Loma Linda University, School of Public Health, Programs in Health Education, Loma Linda, CA 92350. Offers MPH, Dr PH. *Accreditation:* CEPH (one or more programs are accredited). *Degree requirements:* For doctorate, thesis/dissertation. *Entrance requirements:* For doctorate, GRE General Test. Additional exam requirements/recommendations for international students: Required—Michigan English Language Assessment Battery or TOEFL. *Expenses:* Contact institution.

Longwood University, College of Graduate and Professional Studies, College of Education and Human Services, Farmville, VA 23909. Offers education (MS), including algebra and middle school mathematics, counselor education, elementary and middle school mathematics, elementary education, elementary education initial licensure, health and physical education, special education general curriculum, special education initial licensure; reading, literacy and learning (M Ed); school librarianship (M Ed); social work and communication sciences and disorders (MS), including communication sciences and disorders. *Accreditation:* NCATE. *Program availability:* Part-time, evening/weekend. *Degree requirements:* For master's, comprehensive exam (for some programs), thesis optional, professional portfolio, internship, clinical experience, or practicum. *Entrance requirements:* For master's, PRAXIS I (for initial teaching licensure programs); GRE (for some programs), bachelor's degree from regionally-accredited institution, 2 recommendations (3 for some programs), minimum 500-word personal essay, official transcripts, minimum GPA of 2.75, valid teaching license (for some programs). Additional exam requirements/recommendations for international students: Required—TOEFL (minimum score 570 paper-based), IELTS (minimum score 6.5). Electronic applications accepted. *Expenses:* Contact institution.

Marshall University, Academic Affairs Division, College of Information Technology and Engineering, Division of Applied Science and Technology, Program in Safety, Huntington, WV 25755. Offers MS. *Accreditation:* NCATE. *Degree requirements:* For master's, thesis optional, comprehensive assessment.

Marymount University, Malek School of Health Professions, Program in Health Education and Promotion, Arlington, VA 22207-4299. Offers health education and promotion (MS). *Program availability:* Part-time, evening/weekend. *Faculty:* 5 full-time (3 women), 3 part-time/adjunct (all women). *Students:* 16 full-time (8 women), 7 part-time (6 women); includes 4 minority (2 Black or African American, non-Hispanic/Latino; 1 Asian, non-Hispanic/Latino; 1 Two or more races, non-Hispanic/Latino), 8 international. Average age 29. 17 applicants, 100% accepted, 10 enrolled. In 2018, 4 master's awarded. *Degree requirements:* For master's, internship. *Entrance requirements:* For master's, GRE or MAT OR Cumulative GPA of 3.0 OR significant related experience, 2 letters of recommendation, resume, personal statement. Additional exam requirements/recommendations for international students: Required—TOEFL (minimum score 600 paper-based; 96 iBT), IELTS (minimum score 6.5), PTE (minimum score 58). *Application deadline:* Applications are processed on a rolling basis. Application fee: $40. Electronic applications accepted. *Expenses: Tuition:* Full-time $18,900; part-time $1050 per credit. *Required fees:* $396; $22 per credit hour. One-time fee: $270. Tuition and fees vary according to program. *Financial support:* In 2018–19, 1 student received support. Research assistantships, teaching assistantships, career-related internships or fieldwork, scholarships/grants, and unspecified assistantships available. Support available to part-time students. Financial award application deadline: 3/1; financial award applicants required to submit FAFSA. *Unit head:* Dr. Michael Nordvall, Chair, Health and Human Performance, 703-526-6876, E-mail: michael.nordvall@marymount.edu. *Application contact:* Rebecca Esposito, Senior Associate Director, Graduate Admissions, 703-284-5901, Fax: 703-527-3815, E-mail: grad.admissions@marymount.edu.
Website: https://www.marymount.edu/Academics/Malek-School-of-Health-Professions/Graduate-Programs/Health-Education-Promotion-(M-S-)

Health Education

Marywood University, Academic Affairs, Center for Interdisciplinary Studies, Scranton, PA 18509-1598. Offers human development (PhD), including educational administration, health promotion, higher education administration, instructional leadership, social work. *Program availability:* Part-time. Electronic applications accepted. *Expenses:* Contact institution.

Massachusetts College of Liberal Arts, Graduate Programs, North Adams, MA 01247-4100. Offers business (MBA); educational administration (M Ed); educational leadership (CAGS); instruction and curriculum (M Ed); instructional technology (M Ed); physical education and health (M Ed); reading (M Ed); special education (M Ed). *Program availability:* Part-time, evening/weekend. *Degree requirements:* For master's, thesis. *Entrance requirements:* For master's, writing sample.

McNeese State University, Doré School of Graduate Studies, Burton College of Education, Department of Education Professions, Program in Multiple Levels Grades K-12, Lake Charles, LA 70609. Offers multiple levels grades K-12 (Postbaccalaureate Certificate), including art, health and physical education, music - instrumental, music - vocal. *Entrance requirements:* For degree, PRAXIS, 2 letters of recommendation, autobiography.

Meredith College, School of Education, Health and Human Sciences, Raleigh, NC 27607-5298. Offers academically and intellectually gifted (M Ed); elementary education (M Ed, MAT); English as a second language (M Ed, MAT); health and physical education (MAT); nutrition, health and human performance (MS, Postbaccalaureate Certificate), including dietetic internship (Postbaccalaureate Certificate), nutrition (MS); psychology (MA), including industrial/organizational psychology; reading (M Ed); special education (MAT); special education (general curriculum) (M Ed). *Accreditation:* NCATE. *Program availability:* Part-time, evening/weekend. *Students:* 97 full-time (89 women), 76 part-time (73 women); includes 39 minority (17 Black or African American, non-Hispanic/Latino; 1 American Indian or Alaska Native, non-Hispanic/Latino; 9 Asian, non-Hispanic/Latino; 10 Hispanic/Latino; 2 Two or more races, non-Hispanic/Latino). Average age 28. In 2018, 56 master's, 36 other advanced degrees awarded. *Degree requirements:* For master's, thesis optional. *Entrance requirements:* For master's, GRE General Test or MAT, minimum GPA of 2.5, teaching license, recommendations. Additional exam requirements/recommendations for international students: Required—TOEFL. *Application deadline:* For fall admission, 7/1 priority date for domestic students; for spring admission, 11/1 priority date for domestic students. Applications are processed on a rolling basis. Application fee: $50. Electronic applications accepted. *Expenses:* $575 per credit hour for masters degree in education, $725 (for MS. PSY.IO degree), $20,295 (for pre-health post-baccalaureate certificate), $13,600 (for dietetic internship). *Financial support:* Career-related internships or fieldwork, institutionally sponsored loans, and tuition waivers (partial) available. Support available to part-time students. Financial award application deadline: 2/15; financial award applicants required to submit FAFSA. *Unit head:* Dr. Monica McKinney, Graduate Program Manager, 919-760-8056, Fax: 919-760-2303, E-mail: mckinneym@meredith.edu. *Application contact:* Dr. Monica McKinney, Graduate Program Manager, 919-760-8056, Fax: 919-760-2303, E-mail: mckinneym@meredith.edu.
Website: https://www.meredith.edu/school-of-education-health-and-human-sciences

Merrimack College, School of Health Sciences, North Andover, MA 01845-5800. Offers athletic training (MS); community health education (MS); exercise and sport science (MS); health and wellness management (MS). *Program availability:* Part-time, evening/weekend. *Faculty:* 11 full-time (10 women), 2 part-time/adjunct (both women). *Students:* 93 full-time (62 women), 12 part-time (10 women); includes 3 minority (all Black or African American, non-Hispanic/Latino), 4 international. Average age 26. 163 applicants, 92% accepted, 82 enrolled. In 2018, 71 master's awarded. *Degree requirements:* For master's, capstone (for community health education, exercise and sport science, and health and wellness management). *Entrance requirements:* For master's, resume, official college transcripts, personal statement, 2 recommendations. Additional exam requirements/recommendations for international students: Required—TOEFL (minimum score 84 iBT), IELTS (minimum score 6.5), PTE (minimum score 56). *Application deadline:* For fall admission, 8/24 for domestic students, 7/30 for international students; for summer admission, 5/10 for domestic students, 4/10 for international students. Applications are processed on a rolling basis. Application fee: $0. Electronic applications accepted. Application fee is waived when completed online. *Expenses:* School of Health Sciences (all programs except Athletic Training) $28,420; M.S. in Athletic Training $32,980. *Financial support:* Fellowships with partial tuition reimbursements, career-related internships or fieldwork, scholarships/grants, and health care benefits available. Support available to part-time students. Financial award application deadline: 5/1; financial award applicants required to submit FAFSA. *Unit head:* Dr. Janet Blum, Dean, 978-837-5396, E-mail: blumj@merrimack.edu. *Application contact:* Allison Pena, Office of Graduate Studies, 978-837-3563, E-mail: graduate@merrimack.edu.
Website: http://www.merrimack.edu/academics/health-sciences/

Middle Tennessee State University, College of Graduate Studies, College of Behavioral and Health Sciences, Department of Health and Human Performance, Program in Health, Physical Education and Recreation, Murfreesboro, TN 37132. Offers health and human performance (MS); leisure and sport management (MS). *Program availability:* Part-time, evening/weekend, online learning. *Degree requirements:* For master's, comprehensive exam, thesis optional. *Entrance requirements:* For master's, GRE. Additional exam requirements/recommendations for international students: Required—TOEFL (minimum score 525 paper-based; 71 iBT) or IELTS (minimum score 6). *Faculty research:* Kinesiometrics, leisure behavior, health, lifestyles.

Minnesota State University Mankato, College of Graduate Studies and Research, College of Allied Health and Nursing, Department of Health Science, Mankato, MN 56001. Offers community health education (MS); public health education (Postbaccalaureate Certificate); school health education (MS, Postbaccalaureate Certificate). *Program availability:* Part-time. *Degree requirements:* For master's, comprehensive exam, thesis or alternative. *Entrance requirements:* For master's, minimum GPA of 3.0 during previous 2 years; for Postbaccalaureate Certificate, teaching license. Additional exam requirements/recommendations for international students: Required—TOEFL (minimum score 500 paper-based; 61 iBT). Electronic applications accepted.

Mississippi University for Women, Graduate School, College of Nursing and Health Sciences, Columbus, MS 39701-9998. Offers nursing (MSN, DNP, PMC); public health education (MPH); speech-language pathology (MS). *Accreditation:* AACN; ASHA. *Program availability:* Part-time. *Degree requirements:* For master's, comprehensive exam, thesis. *Entrance requirements:* For master's, GRE General Test, bachelor's degree in nursing, previous course work in statistics, proficiency in English.

Montana State University, The Graduate School, College of Education, Health, and Human Development, Department of Health and Human Development, Bozeman, MT 59717. Offers family and consumer sciences (MS). *Accreditation:* ACA. *Program availability:* Part-time, online learning. *Degree requirements:* For master's, comprehensive exam. *Entrance requirements:* For master's, GRE (minimum scores: verbal 480; quantitative 480). Additional exam requirements/recommendations for international students: Required—TOEFL (minimum score 550 paper-based). Electronic applications accepted. *Faculty research:* Community food systems, ethic of care for teachers and coaches, influence of public policy on families and communities, cost effectiveness of early childhood education, exercise metabolism, winter sport performance enhancement, assessment of physical activity.

Montclair State University, The Graduate School, College of Education and Human Services, MAT Program in Teaching, Montclair, NJ 07043-1624. Offers art (MAT); biology (MAT); chemistry (MAT); earth science (MAT); English (MAT); French (MAT); health and physical education (MAT); health education (MAT); mathematics (MAT); music (MAT); physical education (MAT); physical science (MAT); social studies (MAT); Spanish (MAT); teacher of English as a second language (MAT). *Degree requirements:* For master's, comprehensive exam, thesis or alternative. *Entrance requirements:* For master's, interview, 2 letters of recommendation. Additional exam requirements/recommendations for international students: Required—TOEFL (minimum score 83 iBT), IELTS (minimum score 6.5). Electronic applications accepted.

Morehead State University, Graduate School, College of Education, Department of Middle Grades and Secondary Education, Morehead, KY 40351. Offers business and marketing education (MAT); English/language arts 5-9 (MAT); French (MAT); health P-12 (MAT); mathematics 5-9 (MAT); physical education P-12 (MAT); science 5-9 (MAT); secondary biology (MAT); secondary chemistry (MAT); secondary earth science (MAT); secondary English (MAT); secondary math (MAT); secondary physics (MAT); secondary social studies (MAT); social studies 5-9 (MAT); Spanish (MAT). *Program availability:* Part-time, evening/weekend. *Degree requirements:* For master's, portfolio. *Entrance requirements:* For master's, GRE or PRAXIS II content exam, minimum overall undergraduate GPA of 2.5. Additional exam requirements/recommendations for international students: Required—TOEFL (minimum score 500 paper-based). Electronic applications accepted.

New Jersey City University, College of Professional Studies, Department of Health Sciences, Jersey City, NJ 07305-1597. Offers community health education (MS); health administration (MS); school health education (MS). *Program availability:* Part-time, evening/weekend. *Degree requirements:* For master's, thesis or alternative, internship. *Entrance requirements:* Additional exam requirements/recommendations for international students: Required—TOEFL (minimum score 79 iBT).

New Mexico Highlands University, Graduate Studies, College of Arts and Sciences, Department of Exercise and Sport Sciences, Las Vegas, NM 87701. Offers human performance and sport (MA), including human performance and sport sciences, sports administration, teacher education. *Program availability:* Part-time. *Degree requirements:* For master's, comprehensive exam, thesis or alternative. *Entrance requirements:* For master's, minimum undergraduate GPA of 3.0. Additional exam requirements/recommendations for international students: Required—TOEFL (minimum score 540 paper-based). *Faculty research:* Child obesity and physical inactivity, body composition and fitness assessment, motor development, sport marketing, sport finance.

New York Medical College, School of Health Sciences and Practice, Valhalla, NY 10595. Offers behavioral sciences and health promotion (MPH); biostatistics (MS); children with special health care (Graduate Certificate); emergency preparedness (Graduate Certificate); environmental health science (MPH); epidemiology (MPH, MS); global health (Graduate Certificate); health education (Graduate Certificate); health policy and management (MPH, Dr PH); industrial hygiene (Graduate Certificate); pediatric dysphagia (Post-Graduate Certificate); physical therapy (DPT); public health (Graduate Certificate); speech-language pathology (MS). *Accreditation:* ASHA; CEPH. *Program availability:* Part-time, evening/weekend, 100% online, blended/hybrid learning. *Faculty:* 47 full-time (34 women), 239 part-time/adjunct (141 women). *Students:* 245 full-time (181 women), 233 part-time (167 women); includes 208 minority (79 Black or African American, non-Hispanic/Latino; 2 American Indian or Alaska Native, non-Hispanic/Latino; 59 Asian, non-Hispanic/Latino; 57 Hispanic/Latino; 1 Native Hawaiian or other Pacific Islander, non-Hispanic/Latino; 10 Two or more races, non-Hispanic/Latino), 13 international. Average age 27. 484 applicants, 68% accepted, 88 enrolled. In 2018, 113 master's, 47 doctorates awarded. *Degree requirements:* For master's, comprehensive exam (for some programs), thesis (for some programs); for doctorate, thesis/dissertation. *Entrance requirements:* For master's, GRE (for MS in speech-language pathology); for doctorate, GRE (for Doctor of Physical Therapy and Doctor of Public Health). Additional exam requirements/recommendations for international students: Required—TOEFL (minimum score 96 paper-based; 24 iBT), IELTS (minimum score 7). *Application deadline:* For fall admission, 8/1 for domestic students, 4/15 for international students; for spring admission, 12/1 for domestic students; for summer admission, 5/1 for domestic students, 4/15 for international students. Applications are processed on a rolling basis. Application fee: $128 ($120 for international students). Electronic applications accepted. *Expenses:* $1165 per credit, $645 fees. *Financial support:* In 2018–19, 4 students received support. Federal Work-Study, scholarships/grants, unspecified assistantships, and Federal student loans available. Financial award application deadline: 4/30; financial award applicants required to submit FAFSA. *Faculty research:* Disaster medicine, environmental health, health policy, speech-language pathology including dysphagia, biomechanics of human motion in activities of daily living and occupations. *Total annual research expenditures:* $325,000. *Unit head:* Ben Johnson, PhD, Vice Dean, 914-594-4531, E-mail: bjohnson23@nymc.edu. *Application contact:* Irene Bundziak, Assistant to Director of Admissions, 914-594-4905, E-mail: irene_bundziak@nymc.edu.
Website: http://www.nymc.edu/school-of-health-sciences-and-practice-shsp/

Nicholls State University, Graduate Studies, College of Education, Department of Teacher Education, Thibodaux, LA 70310. Offers curriculum and instruction (M Ed); educational leadership (M Ed); elementary education (MAT); human performance education (MAT); middle school education (MAT); secondary education (MAT). *Accreditation:* NCATE. *Program availability:* Part-time, evening/weekend, online learning. *Degree requirements:* For master's, comprehensive exam, portfolio. *Entrance requirements:* For master's, GRE General Test, teaching license. Electronic applications accepted.

Northeastern State University, College of Education, Department of Health and Kinesiology, Tahlequah, OK 74464-2399. Offers MS. *Program availability:* Part-time, evening/weekend. *Faculty:* 15 full-time (10 women), 2 part-time/adjunct (0 women). *Students:* 12 full-time (7 women), 18 part-time (9 women); includes 14 minority (3 Black or African American, non-Hispanic/Latino; 3 American Indian or Alaska Native, non-Hispanic/Latino; 2 Hispanic/Latino; 6 Two or more races, non-Hispanic/Latino), 2 international. Average age 27. In 2018, 18 master's awarded. *Entrance requirements:* For master's, MAT or GRE, minimum GPA of 2.5. Additional exam requirements/recommendations for international students: Required—TOEFL. *Application deadline:* For fall admission, 6/1 for domestic and international students; for winter admission, 11/1 for domestic and international students; for spring admission, 3/1 for domestic students, 2/1 for international students. Applications are processed on a rolling basis. Application fee: $25. Electronic applications accepted. *Expenses: Tuition, area resident:* Full-time $4500; part-time $250 per credit hour. Tuition, state resident: full-time $4500; part-time $250 per credit hour. Tuition, nonresident: full-time $9999; part-time $555.50 per credit hour. *International tuition:* $9999 full-time. *Required fees:* $601.20; $33.40 per credit hour. *Unit head:* Dee Gerlach, Department Chair, 918-444-3929, E-mail: gerlach@nsuok.edu. *Application contact:* Josh McCollum, Graduate Coordinator, 918-444-2093, E-mail: mccolluj@nsuok.edu.
Website: http://academics.nsuok.edu/education/DegreePrograms/GraduatePrograms/HealthandKinesiology.aspx

Northwestern State University of Louisiana, Graduate Studies and Research, Department of Health and Human Performance, Natchitoches, LA 71497. Offers MS. *Degree requirements:* For master's, comprehensive exam, thesis or alternative. *Entrance requirements:* For master's, GRE General Test, minimum undergraduate GPA of 2.5. Additional exam requirements/recommendations for international students: Required—TOEFL. Electronic applications accepted.

Northwest Missouri State University, Graduate School, School of Health Science and Wellness, Maryville, MO 64468-6001. Offers applied health and sport sciences (MS); guidance and counseling (MS Ed); health and physical education (MS Ed); recreation (MS); sport and exercise psychology (MS). *Accreditation:* NCATE. *Program availability:* Part-time. *Faculty:* 15 full-time (7 women). *Students:* 58 full-time (35 women), 27 part-time (17 women); includes 9 minority (7 Black or African American, non-Hispanic/Latino; 1 Hispanic/Latino; 1 Two or more races, non-Hispanic/Latino), 6 international. Average age 26. 50 applicants, 74% accepted, 23 enrolled. In 2018, 54 master's awarded. *Degree requirements:* For master's, comprehensive exam. *Entrance requirements:* For master's, GRE General Test, minimum undergraduate GPA of 2.75, teaching certificate, writing sample. Additional exam requirements/recommendations for international students: Required—TOEFL (minimum score 550 paper-based; 79 iBT). *Application deadline:* For fall admission, 7/1 for domestic and international students; for spring admission, 11/15 for domestic and international students. Applications are processed on a rolling basis. Application fee: $0 ($75 for international students). *Expenses: Tuition, area resident:* Full-time $4551; part-time $252.86 per credit hour. Tuition, state resident: full-time $4551; part-time $252.86 per credit hour. Tuition, nonresident: full-time $9103; part-time $505.72 per credit hour. *International tuition:* $9103 full-time. *Required fees:* $2668; $148.20 per credit hour. Tuition and fees vary according to program. *Financial support:* Teaching assistantships with full tuition reimbursements and unspecified assistantships available. Financial award application deadline: 4/1; financial award applicants required to submit FAFSA. *Unit head:* Dr. Terry Long, Director, School of Health Science and Wellness, 660-562-1706, Fax: 660-562-1483, E-mail: tlong@nwmissouri.edu. *Application contact:* Gina Smith, Office Manager, 660-562-1297, Fax: 660-562-1963, E-mail: smigina@nwmissouri.edu.
Website: http://www.nwmissouri.edu/health/

Nova Southeastern University, Dr. Kiran C. Patel College of Osteopathic Medicine, Fort Lauderdale, FL 33328. Offers biomedical informatics (MS, Graduate Certificate), including biomedical informatics (MS), clinical informatics (Graduate Certificate); public health informatics (Graduate Certificate); disaster and emergency management (MS); medical education (MS); nutrition (MS, Graduate Certificate), including functional nutrition and herbal therapy (Graduate Certificate); osteopathic medicine (DO); public health (MPH, Graduate Certificate), including health education (Graduate Certificate); social medicine (Graduate Certificate); DO/DMD. *Accreditation:* AOsA; CEPH. *Degree requirements:* For master's, comprehensive exam (for MPH); field/special projects; for doctorate, comprehensive exam, COMLEX Board Exams; for Graduate Certificate, thesis or alternative. *Entrance requirements:* For master's, GRE; for doctorate, MCAT, coursework in biology, chemistry, organic chemistry, physics (all with labs), biochemistry, and English. Electronic applications accepted. *Expenses:* Contact institution. *Faculty research:* Teaching strategies, simulated patient use, HIV/AIDS education, minority health issues, immune disorders.

Nova Southeastern University, Halmos College of Natural Sciences and Oceanography, Fort Lauderdale, FL 33314-7796. Offers biological sciences (MS), including health studies; marine biology and oceanography (PhD), including marine biology, oceanography. *Program availability:* Part-time, evening/weekend, blended/hybrid learning. *Degree requirements:* For master's, thesis; for doctorate, comprehensive exam, thesis/dissertation, departmental qualifying exam. *Entrance requirements:* For master's, GRE General Test, 3 letters of recommendation; BS/BA in natural science (for marine biology program); BS/BA in biology (for biological sciences program); minor in the natural sciences or equivalent (for coastal zone management and marine environmental sciences); for doctorate, GRE General Test, master's degree. Additional exam requirements/recommendations for international students: Required—TOEFL (minimum score 550 paper-based); Recommended—IELTS. Electronic applications accepted. *Expenses:* Contact institution. *Faculty research:* Physical and biological oceanography, molecular and microbiology, ecology and evolution, coral reefs, marine ecosystems.

Oklahoma State University, College of Education, Health and Aviation, School of Applied Health and Educational Psychology, Stillwater, OK 74078. Offers applied behavioral studies (Ed D); applied health and educational psychology (MS, PhD, Ed S). *Accreditation:* APA (one or more programs are accredited). *Program availability:* Part-time. *Entrance requirements:* For master's and doctorate, GRE or GMAT. Additional exam requirements/recommendations for international students: Required—TOEFL (minimum score 550 paper-based; 79 iBT). Electronic applications accepted. *Expenses: Tuition, area resident:* Full-time $4148. Tuition, state resident: full-time $4148. Tuition, nonresident: full-time $10,517. *International tuition:* $10,517 full-time. *Required fees:* $4394; $2929 per credit hour. Tuition and fees vary according to course load and program.

Old Dominion University, Darden College of Education, Program in Physical Education, Curriculum and Instruction Emphasis, Norfolk, VA 23529. Offers human movement sciences (PhD), including health and sport pedagogy; physical education (MS Ed), including adapted physical education, coaching education, curriculum and instruction. *Program availability:* Part-time, evening/weekend. *Degree requirements:* For master's, comprehensive exam (for some programs), thesis or alternative, internship, research project. *Entrance requirements:* For master's, GRE, PRAXIS tests (for licensure only), minimum GPA of 2.8 overall, 3.0 in major. Additional exam requirements/recommendations for international students: Required—TOEFL (minimum score 500 paper-based; 97 iBT). Electronic applications accepted. *Faculty research:* Motor development, physical activity and fitness, motivation and learning in physical education, curriculum and instruction, adapted physical education.

Penn State Harrisburg, Graduate School, School of Behavioral Sciences and Education, Middletown, PA 17057. Offers adult education in the health and medical professions (Certificate); applied behavior analysis (MA); applied clinical psychology (MA); applied psychological research (MA); community psychology and social change (MA); English as a second language (ESL) program specialist and leadership (Certificate); health education (M Ed); lifelong learning and adult education (M Ed, D Ed); literacy education (M Ed); literacy leadership (Certificate); psychology: applications in clinical psychology (Certificate); psychology: health psychology (Certificate); teaching and curriculum (M Ed); training and development (M Ed, Certificate). *Program availability:* Part-time, evening/weekend.

Pennsylvania College of Health Sciences, Graduate Programs, Lancaster, PA 17601. Offers administration (MSN); education (MSHS, MSN); healthcare administration (MHA). *Degree requirements:* For master's, internship (for MHA, MSN in administration); practicum (for MSHS, MSN in education).

Pittsburg State University, Graduate School, College of Education, Department of Health, Physical Education and Recreation, Pittsburg, KS 66762. Offers health, human performance, and recreation (MS), including human performance and wellness, sport and leisure service management. *Program availability:* Part-time, online only, 100% online. *Degree requirements:* For master's, thesis or alternative. *Entrance requirements:* For master's, letter of intent. Additional exam requirements/recommendations for international students: Required—TOEFL (minimum score 520 paper-based; 68 iBT), IELTS (minimum score 6), PTE (minimum score 47). Electronic applications accepted. *Expenses:* Contact institution. *Faculty research:* Personality of athletes, fitness activities for children, aerobic conditioning, fitness evaluation.

Plymouth State University, College of Graduate Studies, Graduate Studies in Education, Program in Health Education, Plymouth, NH 03264-1595. Offers eating disorders (M Ed); health education (M Ed); health promotion (MS). *Program availability:* Part-time, evening/weekend. *Entrance requirements:* For master's, MAT, minimum GPA of 3.0.

Prairie View A&M University, College of Education, Department of Health and Kinesiology, Prairie View, TX 77446. Offers M Ed, MS. *Accreditation:* NCATE. *Program availability:* Part-time, evening/weekend. *Faculty:* 4 full-time (all women). *Students:* 31 full-time (19 women), 7 part-time (2 women); all minorities (35 Black or African American, non-Hispanic/Latino; 2 Hispanic/Latino; 1 Two or more races, non-Hispanic/Latino). Average age 27. 23 applicants, 87% accepted, 18 enrolled. In 2018, 10 master's awarded. *Degree requirements:* For master's, thesis. *Entrance requirements:* For master's, GRE General Test. Additional exam requirements/recommendations for international students: Required—TOEFL (minimum score 550 paper-based; 79 iBT). *Application deadline:* For fall admission, 5/1 priority date for domestic and international students; for spring admission, 10/1 priority date for domestic students, 9/1 priority date for international students; for summer admission, 3/1 priority date for domestic students, 2/1 priority date for international students. Applications are processed on a rolling basis. Application fee: $50. Electronic applications accepted. *Expenses: Tuition, area resident:* Full-time $3172; part-time $317 per credit. Tuition, state resident: full-time $3172; part-time $317 per credit. Tuition, nonresident: full-time $7965; part-time $796 per credit. *Required fees:* $4847; $485 per credit. *Financial support:* Career-related internships or fieldwork available. Support available to part-time students. Financial award application deadline: 4/1; financial award applicants required to submit FAFSA. *Unit head:* Dr. Angela Branch-Vital, Department Head, 936-261-3900, Fax: 936-261-3905, E-mail: abranch-vital@pvamu.edu. *Application contact:* Pauline Walker, Administrative Assistant II, Research and Graduate Studies, 936-261-3521, Fax: 936-261-3529, E-mail: gradadmissions@pvamu.edu.

Purdue University, Graduate School, College of Health and Human Sciences, Department of Health and Kinesiology, West Lafayette, IN 47907. Offers athletic training education administration (MS, PhD); biomechanics (MS, PhD); exercise physiology (MS, PhD); health education (MS, PhD); history/philosophy of sport (MS, PhD); motor control and development (MS, PhD); physical education pedagogy (PhD); physical education teacher education (MS); recreation and sport management (MS, PhD); sport and exercise psychology (MS, PhD). *Program availability:* Part-time. *Faculty:* 23 full-time (10 women). *Students:* 29 full-time (13 women), 8 part-time (5 women); includes 3 minority (1 Asian, non-Hispanic/Latino; 1 Hispanic/Latino; 1 Two or more races, non-Hispanic/Latino), 8 international. Average age 26. 61 applicants, 26% accepted, 14 enrolled. In 2018, 14 master's awarded. *Degree requirements:* For master's, thesis optional; for doctorate, comprehensive exam, thesis/dissertation, qualifying examination, preliminary examination. *Entrance requirements:* For master's, GRE General Test (minimum score 1000 combined verbal and quantitative), minimum undergraduate GPA of 3.0 or equivalent; for doctorate, GRE General Test (minimum score 1100 combined verbal and quantitative), minimum undergraduate GPA of 3.0 or equivalent; master's degree with minimum GPA of 3.25 (recommended). Additional exam requirements/recommendations for international students: Required—TOEFL (minimum score 77 iBT); Recommended—TWE. *Application deadline:* For fall admission, 4/30 for domestic and international students; for spring admission, 10/15 for domestic and international students. Applications are processed on a rolling basis. Application fee: $60 ($75 for international students). Electronic applications accepted. *Financial support:* Fellowships with partial tuition reimbursements, research assistantships with partial tuition reimbursements, teaching assistantships with partial tuition reimbursements, and Federal Work-Study available. Support available to part-time students. Financial award applicants required to submit FAFSA. *Faculty research:* Wellness, motivation, teaching effectiveness, learning and development. *Unit head:* Dr. Timothy P. Gavin, Head of the Graduate Program, 765-494-3178, Fax: 765-494-1239, E-mail: gavin1@purdue.edu. *Application contact:* David B. Klenosky, Graduate Contact, 765-494-0865, E-mail: klenosky@purdue.edu.
Website: http://www.purdue.edu/hhs/hk/

Purdue University, Graduate School, College of Health and Human Sciences, Department of Nutrition Science, West Lafayette, IN 47907. Offers animal health (MS, PhD); biochemical and molecular nutrition (MS, PhD); growth and development (MS, PhD); human and clinical nutrition (MS, PhD); public health and education (MS, PhD). *Faculty:* 18 full-time (12 women), 1 part-time/adjunct (0 women). *Students:* 44 full-time (36 women), 2 part-time (1 woman); includes 4 minority (2 Black or African American, non-Hispanic/Latino; 1 Asian, non-Hispanic/Latino; 1 Two or more races, non-Hispanic/Latino), 17 international. Average age 26. 51 applicants, 29% accepted, 11 enrolled. In 2018, 3 master's, 13 doctorates awarded. *Degree requirements:* For master's, thesis; for doctorate, thesis/dissertation. *Entrance requirements:* For master's and doctorate, GRE General Test (minimum scores in verbal and quantitative areas of 1000 or 300 on new scoring), minimum undergraduate GPA of 3.0 or equivalent. Additional exam requirements/recommendations for international students: Required—TOEFL (minimum score 600 paper-based; 77 iBT). *Application deadline:* For fall admission, 1/10 for domestic and international students. Applications are processed on a rolling basis. Application fee: $60 ($75 for international students). Electronic applications accepted. *Financial support:* Fellowships, research assistantships, and teaching assistantships available. Support available to part-time students. Financial award applicants required to submit FAFSA. *Faculty research:* Nutrient requirements, nutrient metabolism, nutrition and disease prevention. *Unit head:* Michele R. Forman, Head, 765-494-9921, E-mail: mforman@purdue.edu. *Application contact:* Kim Buhman, Graduate Contact for Admissions, 765-496-6872, E-mail: kbuhman@purdue.edu.
Website: http://www.cfs.purdue.edu/fn/

Rhode Island College, School of Graduate Studies, Feinstein School of Education and Human Development, Department of Health and Physical Education, Providence, RI 02908-1991. Offers health education (M Ed); physical education (CGS). *Accreditation:* NCATE. *Program availability:* Part-time, evening/weekend. *Faculty:* 1 full-time (0 women), 2 part-time/adjunct (0 women). *Students:* 3 part-time (2 women); includes 1 minority (Hispanic/Latino). Average age 35. In 2018, 1 master's awarded. *Degree requirements:* For master's, comprehensive assessment. *Entrance requirements:* For master's, GRE General Test or MAT, undergraduate transcripts; minimum undergraduate GPA of 3.0; 3 letters of recommendation; for CGS, GRE or MAT (for most programs), undergraduate transcripts; minimum undergraduate GPA of 3.0; 3 letters of recommendation. Additional exam requirements/recommendations for international students: Required—TOEFL (minimum score 550 paper-based; 80 iBT). *Application deadline:* For fall admission, 3/1 for domestic students; for spring admission, 11/1 for domestic students. Applications are processed on a rolling basis. Application

fee: $50. Electronic applications accepted. *Expenses: Tuition, area resident:* Part-time $407 per credit. Tuition, nonresident: part-time $792 per credit. *Required fees:* $29 per credit. $100 per semester. *Financial support:* Teaching assistantships, Federal Work-Study, scholarships/grants, health care benefits, and unspecified assistantships available. Support available to part-time students. Financial award application deadline: 5/15; financial award applicants required to submit FAFSA. *Unit head:* Dr. Carol Cummings, Chair, 401-456-8046. *Application contact:* Dr. Carol Cummings, Chair, 401-456-8046.
Website: http://www.ric.edu/healthphysicaleducation/Pages/default.aspx

Rosalind Franklin University of Medicine and Science, College of Health Professions, Department of Interprofessional Healthcare Studies, Health Professions Education Program, North Chicago, IL 60064-3095. Offers MS.

Rosalind Franklin University of Medicine and Science, College of Health Professions, Department of Nutrition, North Chicago, IL 60064-3095. Offers clinical nutrition (MS); health promotion and wellness (MS); nutrition education (MS). *Program availability:* Part-time, evening/weekend, online learning. *Degree requirements:* For master's, thesis optional, portfolio. *Entrance requirements:* For master's, minimum GPA of 2.75, registered dietitian (RD), professional certificate or license. Additional exam requirements/recommendations for international students: Required—TOEFL. *Expenses:* Contact institution. *Faculty research:* Nutrition education, distance learning, computer-based graduate education, childhood obesity, nutrition medical education.

Rutgers University–Newark, School of Health Related Professions, Department of Interdisciplinary Studies, Program in Health Sciences, Newark, NJ 07102. Offers health sciences (MS, PhD). *Program availability:* Part-time, evening/weekend, online learning. *Degree requirements:* For doctorate, thesis/dissertation. *Entrance requirements:* For master's, BS, 2 reference letters, statement of career goals, curriculum vitae; for doctorate, GRE, interview, writing sample, 3 reference letters, curriculum vitae. Additional exam requirements/recommendations for international students: Required—TOEFL. Electronic applications accepted.

Rutgers University–New Brunswick, School of Public Health, Piscataway, NJ 08854. Offers biostatistics (MPH, MS, Dr PH, PhD); clinical epidemiology (Certificate); environmental and occupational health (MPH, Dr PH, PhD, Certificate); epidemiology (MPH, Dr PH, PhD); general public health (Certificate); health education and behavioral science (MPH, Dr PH, PhD); health systems and policy (MPH, PhD); public health (MPH, Dr PH, PhD); public health preparedness (Certificate); DO/MPH; JD/MPH; MBA/MPH; MD/MPH; MPH/MBA; MPH/MSPA; MS/MPH; Psy D/MPH. *Accreditation:* CEPH. *Program availability:* Part-time, evening/weekend. *Degree requirements:* For master's, thesis, internship; for doctorate, comprehensive exam, thesis/dissertation. *Entrance requirements:* For master's, GRE General Test; for doctorate, GRE General Test, MPH (Dr PH); MA, MPH, or MS (PhD). Additional exam requirements/recommendations for international students: Required—TOEFL. Electronic applications accepted.

Sage Graduate School, Esteves School of Education, Program in School Health Education, Troy, NY 12180-4115. Offers MS. *Accreditation:* NCATE. *Program availability:* Part-time, evening/weekend. *Faculty:* 2 full-time (both women), 9 part-time/adjunct (5 women). *Students:* 6 full-time (5 women), 20 part-time (9 women). Average age 26. 22 applicants, 73% accepted, 8 enrolled. In 2018, 9 master's awarded. *Degree requirements:* For master's, thesis optional. *Entrance requirements:* For master's, interview with advisor, assessment of writing skills. Additional exam requirements/recommendations for international students: Required—TOEFL (minimum score 550 paper-based). *Application deadline:* Applications are processed on a rolling basis. Application fee: $30. Electronic applications accepted. *Financial support:* Fellowships, research assistantships, scholarships/grants, and unspecified assistantships available. Financial award application deadline: 3/1; financial award applicants required to submit FAFSA. *Faculty research:* Policy development in health education and health care. *Unit head:* Dr. John Pelizza, Dean, Esteves School of Education, 518-244-2051, Fax: 518-244-2334, E-mail: pelizj@sage.edu. *Application contact:* John Pelizza, Dean, Esteves School of Education, 518-244-2051, Fax: 518-244-2334, E-mail: pelizj@sage.edu.

Saint Francis University, Health Science Program, Loretto, PA 15940-0600. Offers MHS. *Program availability:* Part-time, evening/weekend, 100% online. *Degree requirements:* For master's, minimum GPA of 2.8. *Entrance requirements:* For master's, undergraduate transcript, letters of reference, minimum QPA of 2.5, resume. Additional exam requirements/recommendations for international students: Recommended—TOEFL (minimum score 80 iBT). Electronic applications accepted. *Expenses:* Contact institution. *Faculty research:* Distance education, health sciences, medical sciences, communication, adult education.

Saint Joseph's College of Maine, Master of Science in Education Program, Standish, ME 04084. Offers adult education and training (MS Ed); Catholic school leadership (MS Ed); health care educator (MS Ed); school educator (MS Ed). Program available by correspondence. *Program availability:* Part-time, online learning. Electronic applications accepted.

San Francisco State University, Division of Graduate Studies, College of Health and Social Sciences, Department of Health Education, San Francisco, CA 94132-1722. Offers community health education (MPH). *Accreditation:* CEPH. *Program availability:* Part-time. *Students:* Average age 36. *Application deadline:* Applications are processed on a rolling basis. *Unit head:* Marty Martinson, Chair, 415-338-1413, Fax: 415-338-0570, E-mail: martym@sfsu.edu. *Application contact:* Vincent Lam, Graduate Coordinator, 415-338-1413, Fax: 415-338-0570, E-mail: vlam@sfsu.edu.
Website: http://healthed.sfsu.edu/graduate

San Francisco State University, Division of Graduate Studies, College of Health and Social Sciences, Department of Sexuality Studies, San Francisco, CA 94132-1722. Offers MA. *Unit head:* Dr. Karen Hossfeld, Chair, 415-338-7059, Fax: 415-338-2653, E-mail: hossfeld@sfsu.edu. *Application contact:* Dr. Alexis Martinez, Graduate Coordinator, 415-338-2269, Fax: 415-338-2653, E-mail: alexisnm@sfsu.edu.
Website: http://sxs.sfsu.edu/

Southeastern Louisiana University, College of Nursing and Health Sciences, Department of Kinesiology and Health Studies, Hammond, LA 70402. Offers health and kinesiology (MS). *Accreditation:* NCATE. *Program availability:* Part-time, evening/weekend. *Faculty:* 9 full-time (3 women). *Students:* 28 full-time (18 women), 20 part-time (14 women); includes 23 minority (14 Black or African American, non-Hispanic/Latino; 2 American Indian or Alaska Native, non-Hispanic/Latino; 4 Hispanic/Latino; 1 Native Hawaiian or other Pacific Islander, non-Hispanic/Latino; 2 Two or more races, non-Hispanic/Latino; 2 international. Average age 26. 35 applicants, 51% accepted, 17 enrolled. In 2018, 16 master's awarded. *Degree requirements:* For master's, comprehensive exam (for some programs), thesis optional. *Entrance requirements:* For master's, GRE (minimum combined Verbal and Quantitative score of 286), 4 hours of human anatomy and physiology. Additional exam requirements/recommendations for international students: Required—TOEFL (minimum score 500 paper-based; 61 iBT). *Application deadline:* For fall admission, 7/15 priority date for domestic students, 6/1 priority date for international students; for spring admission, 12/1 priority date for domestic students, 10/1 priority date for international students. Applications are processed on a rolling basis. Application fee: $20 ($30 for international students). Electronic applications accepted. *Expenses: Tuition, area resident:* Full-time $6684.

Tuition, state resident: full-time $6684. Tuition, nonresident: full-time $19,162. *Required fees:* $2097. *Financial support:* In 2018–19, 25 students received support, including 8 research assistantships with tuition reimbursements available (averaging $8,489 per year), 4 teaching assistantships with tuition reimbursements available (averaging $21,249 per year); career-related internships or fieldwork, Federal Work-Study, institutionally sponsored loans, scholarships/grants, and unspecified assistantships also available. Support available to part-time students. Financial award application deadline: 5/1; financial award applicants required to submit FAFSA. *Faculty research:* Exercise physiology, motor learning, sport and exercise psychology, sport management, health promotion. *Total annual research expenditures:* $9,465. *Unit head:* Dr. Bovorn Sirikul, Interim Department Head, 985-549-2129, Fax: 985-549-5119, E-mail: bsirikul@southeastern.edu. *Application contact:* Office of Admissions, 985-549-5637, Fax: 985-549-5632, E-mail: admissions@southeastern.edu.
Website: http://www.southeastern.edu/acad_research/depts/kin_hs/index.html

Southern Connecticut State University, School of Graduate Studies, School of Health and Human Services, Department of Exercise Science, Program in School Health Education, New Haven, CT 06515-1355. Offers MS. *Accreditation:* NCATE. *Program availability:* Part-time, evening/weekend. *Entrance requirements:* For master's, interview. Electronic applications accepted.

Southern Illinois University Carbondale, Graduate School, College of Education and Human Services, Department of Health Education and Recreation, Program in Community Health Education, Carbondale, IL 62901-4701. Offers MPH, MD/MPH, PhD/MPH. *Accreditation:* CEPH. *Entrance requirements:* Additional exam requirements/recommendations for international students: Required—TOEFL (minimum score 550 paper-based; 80 iBT).

Southern Illinois University Carbondale, Graduate School, College of Education and Human Services, Department of Health Education and Recreation, Program in Health Education, Carbondale, IL 62901-4701. Offers MS Ed, PhD. *Accreditation:* NCATE. *Program availability:* Part-time. *Degree requirements:* For master's, thesis; for doctorate, thesis/dissertation. *Entrance requirements:* For master's, MAT, minimum GPA of 2.7; for doctorate, MAT, minimum GPA of 3.25. Additional exam requirements/recommendations for international students: Required—TOEFL. *Faculty research:* Sexuality education, research design, injury control, program evaluation.

Southern Illinois University Edwardsville, Graduate School, College of Arts and Sciences, Department of Applied Communication Studies, Edwardsville, IL 62026. Offers corporate and organizational communication (MA); health communication (MA); interpersonal communication (MA); public relations (MA). *Program availability:* Part-time, evening/weekend. *Degree requirements:* For master's, comprehensive exam (for some programs), thesis (for some programs), final exam. *Entrance requirements:* Additional exam requirements/recommendations for international students: Required—TOEFL (minimum score 550 paper-based; 79 iBT), IELTS (minimum score 6.5). Electronic applications accepted.

Southern Illinois University Edwardsville, Graduate School, School of Education, Health, and Human Behavior, Edwardsville, IL 62062. Offers MA, MS, MS Ed, Ed D, Ed S, Post-Master's Certificate, Postbaccalaureate Certificate, SD. *Accreditation:* NCATE. *Program availability:* Part-time, evening/weekend. *Degree requirements:* For master's, comprehensive exam (for some programs), thesis (for some programs), final exam, portfolio. *Entrance requirements:* For master's, GRE. Additional exam requirements/recommendations for international students: Required—TOEFL (minimum score 550 paper-based; 79 iBT), IELTS (minimum score 6.5). Electronic applications accepted.

Southwestern Oklahoma State University, College of Professional and Graduate Studies, School of Behavioral Sciences and Education, Specialization in Kinesiology, Weatherford, OK 73096-3098. Offers health and physical education (M Ed); sports management (M Ed). *Program availability:* Part-time. *Degree requirements:* For master's, exam. *Entrance requirements:* For master's, GRE General Test or minimum undergraduate GPA of 3.0. Additional exam requirements/recommendations for international students: Required—TOEFL (minimum score 550 paper-based), IELTS (minimum score 6.5).

State University of New York College at Cortland, Graduate Studies, School of Professional Studies, Department of Health, Cortland, NY 13045. Offers community health (MS); health education (MST). *Accreditation:* NCATE. *Program availability:* Part-time, evening/weekend. *Entrance requirements:* Additional exam requirements/recommendations for international students: Required—TOEFL.

Stony Brook University, State University of New York, Stony Brook Medicine, School of Medicine, Program in Public Health, Stony Brook, NY 11794. Offers community health (MPH); evaluation sciences (MPH); family violence (MPH); health communication (Certificate); health economics (MPH); health education and promotion (Certificate); population health (MPH); substance abuse (MPH). *Accreditation:* CEPH. *Program availability:* Part-time, evening/weekend. *Students:* 45 full-time (33 women), 20 part-time (14 women); includes 29 minority (4 Black or African American, non-Hispanic/Latino; 17 Asian, non-Hispanic/Latino; 8 Hispanic/Latino), 2 international. Average age 29. 130 applicants, 70% accepted, 49 enrolled. In 2018, 31 master's, 1 other advanced degree awarded. *Entrance requirements:* For master's, GRE, 3 references, bachelor's degree from accredited college or university with minimum GPA of 3.0, essays, interview. Additional exam requirements/recommendations for international students: Required—TOEFL (minimum score 90 iBT). *Application deadline:* For fall admission, 7/15 for domestic students. Application fee: $100. Electronic applications accepted. *Expenses:* Contact institution. *Financial support:* Fellowships available. *Faculty research:* Abnormal psychology, academic achievement, broadcast media, communications, communications systems, public health. *Total annual research expenditures:* $1.7 million. *Unit head:* Dr. Lisa A. Benz Scott, Director, 631-444-8811, E-mail: lisa.benzscott@stonybrook.edu. *Application contact:* Joanie Maniaci, Assistant Director for Student Affairs, 631-444-2074, Fax: 631-444-6035, E-mail: joanmarie.maniaci@stonybrook.edu.
Website: http://publichealth.stonybrookmedicine.edu/

Teachers College, Columbia University, Department of Health and Behavior Studies, New York, NY 10027-6696. Offers applied behavior analysis (MA, PhD); applied educational psychology: school psychology (Ed M, PhD); behavioral nutrition (PhD), including nutrition (Ed D, PhD); community health education (MS); community nutrition education (Ed M), including community nutrition education; education of deaf and hard of hearing (MA, PhD); health education (MA, Ed D); hearing impairment (Ed D); intellectual disability/autism (MA, Ed D, PhD); nursing education (Ed D, Advanced Certificate); nutrition and education (MS); nutrition and exercise physiology (MS); nutrition and public health (MS); nutrition education (Ed D), including nutrition (Ed D, PhD); physical disabilities (Ed D); reading specialist (MA); severe or multiple disabilities (MA); special education (Ed M, MA, Ed D); teaching of sign language (MA). *Program availability:* Part-time, evening/weekend. *Students:* 157 full-time (145 women), 344 part-time (310 women); includes 169 minority (46 Black or African American, non-Hispanic/Latino; 2 American Indian or Alaska Native, non-Hispanic/Latino; 55 Asian, non-Hispanic/Latino; 57 Hispanic/Latino; 9 Two or more races, non-Hispanic/Latino), 64 international. Average age 31. 495 applicants, 64% accepted, 171 enrolled. Terminal

master's awarded for partial completion of doctoral program. *Unit head:* Prof. Dolores Perin, Chair, 212-678-3091, E-mail: dp111@tc.columbia.edu. *Application contact:* Kelly Sutton-Skinner, Director of Admission & New Student Enrollment, E-mail: kms2237@tc.columbia.edu.
Website: http://www.tc.columbia.edu/health-and-behavior-studies/

Tennessee Technological University, College of Graduate Studies, College of Education, Department of Exercise Science, Physical Education and Wellness, Cookeville, TN 38505. Offers adapted physical education (MA); elementary/middle school physical education (MA); lifetime wellness (MA); sport management (MA). *Accreditation:* NCATE. *Program availability:* Part-time, online learning. *Faculty:* 7 full-time (0 women). *Students:* 12 full-time (10 women), 45 part-time (22 women); includes 8 minority (3 Black or African American, non-Hispanic/Latino; 1 Asian, non-Hispanic/Latino; 2 Hispanic/Latino; 2 Two or more races, non-Hispanic/Latino), 1 international. 43 applicants, 67% accepted, 22 enrolled. In 2018, 17 master's awarded. *Degree requirements:* For master's, comprehensive exam, thesis or alternative. *Entrance requirements:* For master's, MAT or GRE. Additional exam requirements/recommendations for international students: Required—TOEFL (minimum score 527 paper-based; 71 iBT), IELTS (minimum score 5.5), PTE (minimum score 48), or TOEIC (Test of English as an International Communication). *Application deadline:* For fall admission, 8/1 for domestic students, 5/1 for international students; for spring admission, 12/1 for domestic students, 10/1 for international students; for summer admission, 5/1 for domestic students, 2/1 for international students. Applications are processed on a rolling basis. Application fee: $35 ($40 for international students). Electronic applications accepted. *Financial support:* Fellowships, research assistantships, teaching assistantships, and career-related internships or fieldwork available. Financial award application deadline: 4/1. *Unit head:* Dr. Christy Killman, Chairperson, 931-372-3467, Fax: 931-372-6319, E-mail: ckillman@tntech.edu. *Application contact:* Shelia K. Kendrick, Coordinator of Graduate Studies, 931-372-3808, Fax: 931-372-3497, E-mail: skendrick@tntech.edu.

Texas A&M University, College of Education and Human Development, Department of Health and Kinesiology, College Station, TX 77843. Offers athletic training (MS); health education (MS, PhD); kinesiology (MS, PhD); sports management (MS). *Program availability:* Part-time. *Faculty:* 56. *Students:* 211 full-time (117 women), 80 part-time (41 women); includes 94 minority (35 Black or African American, non-Hispanic/Latino; 3 American Indian or Alaska Native, non-Hispanic/Latino; 5 Asian, non-Hispanic/Latino; 44 Hispanic/Latino; 7 Two or more races, non-Hispanic/Latino), 24 international. Average age 28. 95 applicants, 88% accepted, 60 enrolled. In 2018, 112 master's, 14 doctorates awarded. *Degree requirements:* For master's, thesis (for some programs); for doctorate, comprehensive exam, thesis/dissertation. *Entrance requirements:* For master's and doctorate, GRE General Test. Additional exam requirements/recommendations for international students: Required—TOEFL (minimum score 550 paper-based; 80 iBT), IELTS (minimum score 6), PTE (minimum score 53). *Application deadline:* For fall admission, 1/15 for domestic students; for spring admission, 10/1 for domestic students. Applications are processed on a rolling basis. Application fee: $50 ($90 for international students). Electronic applications accepted. *Expenses:* Contact institution. *Financial support:* In 2018–19, 109 students received support, including 2 fellowships with tuition reimbursements available (averaging $24,073 per year), 41 research assistantships with tuition reimbursements available (averaging $13,093 per year), 68 teaching assistantships with tuition reimbursements available (averaging $11,596 per year); career-related internships or fieldwork, institutionally sponsored loans, scholarships/grants, traineeships, health care benefits, tuition waivers (full and partial), and unspecified assistantships also available. Support available to part-time students. Financial award application deadline: 3/15; financial award applicants required to submit FAFSA. *Unit head:* Dr. Richard Kreider, Head, 979-845-1333, Fax: 979-847-8987, E-mail: rkreider@hlkn.tamu.edu. *Application contact:* Jenny Bilski, Academic Advisor, 979-862-4052, E-mail: jenny.bilski@tamu.edu.
Website: http://hlknweb.tamu.edu/

Texas A&M University–Kingsville, College of Graduate Studies, College of Education and Human Performance, Department of Health and Kinesiology, Kingsville, TX 78363. Offers MA, MS. *Degree requirements:* For master's, variable foreign language requirement, comprehensive exam, thesis (for some programs). *Entrance requirements:* For master's, GRE, MAT, GMAT, essay. Additional exam requirements/recommendations for international students: Required—TOEFL (minimum score 550 paper-based; 79 iBT). Electronic applications accepted.

Texas Southern University, College of Education, Department of Health and Kinesiology, Houston, TX 77004-4584. Offers health education (MS); human performance (MS). *Program availability:* Part-time, evening/weekend. *Degree requirements:* For master's, comprehensive exam, thesis optional. *Entrance requirements:* For master's, GRE General Test, minimum GPA of 2.5. Additional exam requirements/recommendations for international students: Required—TOEFL. Electronic applications accepted.

Texas State University, The Graduate College, College of Education, Program in Public Health Education and Promotion, San Marcos, TX 78666. Offers M Ed. *Program availability:* Part-time, evening/weekend. *Faculty:* 5 full-time (2 women). *Students:* 18 full-time (15 women), 5 part-time (4 women); includes 16 minority (6 Black or African American, non-Hispanic/Latino; 2 Asian, non-Hispanic/Latino; 8 Hispanic/Latino), 1 international. Average age 26. 20 applicants, 75% accepted, 10 enrolled. In 2018, 12 master's awarded. *Degree requirements:* For master's, comprehensive exam, thesis optional. *Entrance requirements:* For master's, baccalaureate degree from regionally-accredited institution with minimum GPA of 2.75 in last 60 hours of course work, 18 hours of health education background courses, statement of purpose; resume/CV; 3 letters of recommendation. Additional exam requirements/recommendations for international students: Required—TOEFL (minimum score 550 paper-based; 78 iBT), IELTS (minimum score 6.5). *Application deadline:* For fall admission, 2/1 priority date for domestic and international students; for spring admission, 10/15 priority date for domestic students, 10/1 for international students; for summer admission, 4/15 for domestic students, 3/15 for international students. Applications are processed on a rolling basis. Application fee: $55 ($90 for international students). Electronic applications accepted. *Expenses:* Tuition, state resident: full-time $8102; part-time $4051 per semester. Tuition, nonresident: full-time $18,229; part-time $9115 per semester. *International tuition:* $18,229 full-time. *Required fees:* $2116; $120 per credit hour. Tuition and fees vary according to course load. *Financial support:* In 2018–19, 12 students received support, including 8 teaching assistantships (averaging $13,044 per year); research assistantships, career-related internships or fieldwork, Federal Work-Study, institutionally sponsored loans, scholarships/grants, and unspecified assistantships also available. Support available to part-time students. Financial award application deadline: 1/15; financial award applicants required to submit FAFSA. *Faculty research:* Urban and rural adolescents' points-of-access for alcohol and tobacco; particulate matter in bars six months after adoption of a smoke-free ordinance; substance abuse prevention, alcohol and energy drinks, tobacco-free and smoke-free advocacy, social ecology of health; socio-ecological influences on obesity and nutrition-related chronic health conditions. *Unit head:* Dr. Ronald Williams, Graduate Advisor, 512-245-2947, E-mail: r_w82@txstate.edu. *Application contact:* Dr. Andrea Golato,

Dean of the Graduate College, 512-245-2581, Fax: 512-245-8365, E-mail: gradcollege@txstate.edu.
Website: http://www.gradcollege.txstate.edu/programs/health-ed.html

Texas Woman's University, Graduate School, College of Health Sciences, School of Health Promotion and Kinesiology, Denton, TX 76204. Offers health studies (MS, PhD), including dental hygiene (MS). *Program availability:* Part-time, evening/weekend, 100% online. *Faculty:* 22 full-time (12 women), 6 part-time/adjunct (3 women). *Students:* 65 full-time (46 women), 170 part-time (139 women); includes 105 minority (53 Black or African American, non-Hispanic/Latino; 10 Asian, non-Hispanic/Latino; 36 Hispanic/Latino; 6 Two or more races, non-Hispanic/Latino), 14 international. Average age 34. 119 applicants, 58% accepted, 45 enrolled. In 2018, 53 master's, 8 doctorates awarded. *Degree requirements:* For master's, comprehensive exam, thesis or alternative, thesis, non-thesis options, or work-site health (for dental hygiene); for doctorate, comprehensive exam, thesis/dissertation, qualifying exam. *Entrance requirements:* For master's, GRE, minimum undergraduate GPA of 3.0 in last 60 credit hours of bachelor's degree, resume/curriculum vitae, 2 letters of recommendation, personal statement letter; for doctorate, GRE, minimum GPA of 3.5 on all master's course work, 2 letters of recommendation, curriculum vitae, essay, writing sample. Additional exam requirements/recommendations for international students: Required—TOEFL (minimum score 575 paper-based; 79 iBT); Recommended—IELTS (minimum score 6.5), TSE (minimum score 53). *Application deadline:* For fall admission, 3/1 for domestic and international students; for spring admission, 7/1 for domestic and international students. Application fee: $50 ($75 for international students). Electronic applications accepted. *Expenses: Tuition, area resident:* Full-time $4852; part-time $270 per semester hour. Tuition, state resident: full-time $4852; part-time $270 per semester hour. Tuition, nonresident: full-time $12,322; part-time $685 per semester hour. *International tuition:* $12,322 full-time. *Required fees:* $2714; $113 per semester hour. $296 per semester. Tuition and fees vary according to course level, course load, degree level, campus/location and program. *Financial support:* In 2018–19, 65 students received support, including 23 teaching assistantships (averaging $10,495 per year); research assistantships, career-related internships or fieldwork, Federal Work-Study, institutionally sponsored loans, scholarships/grants, traineeships, health care benefits, and unspecified assistantships also available. Support available to part-time students. Financial award application deadline: 3/1; financial award applicants required to submit FAFSA. *Faculty research:* Teen pregnancy prevention, eating disorder and obesity prevention, body image issues, adolescent and women's health, chronic disease prevention. *Unit head:* Dr. George King, Chair, 940-898-2860, Fax: 940-898-2859, E-mail: healthstudiesinfo@twu.edu. *Application contact:* Korie Hawkins, Associate Director of Admissions, Graduate Recruitment, 940-898-3188, Fax: 940-898-3081, E-mail: admissions@twu.edu.
Website: http://www.twu.edu/health-studies/

Thomas Jefferson University, Jefferson College of Population Health, Philadelphia, PA 19107. Offers applied health economics and outcomes research (MS, PhD, Certificate); behavioral health science (PhD); health policy (MS, Certificate); healthcare quality and safety (MS, PhD); population health (Certificate); public health (MPH, Certificate). *Program availability:* Part-time, evening/weekend, online learning. Terminal master's awarded for partial completion of doctoral program. *Degree requirements:* For master's, thesis; for doctorate, comprehensive exam, thesis/dissertation. *Entrance requirements:* For master's, GRE or other graduate entrance exam (MCAT, LSAT, DAT, etc.), two letters of recommendation, curriculum vitae, transcripts from all undergraduate and graduate institutions; for doctorate, GRE (taken within the last 5 years), three letters of recommendation, curriculum vitae, transcripts from all undergraduate and graduate institutions. Additional exam requirements/recommendations for international students: Required—TOEFL. Electronic applications accepted. *Faculty research:* Applied health economics and outcomes research, behavioral and health sciences, chronic disease management, health policy, healthcare quality and patient safety, wellness and prevention.

Trident University International, College of Health Sciences, Program in Health Sciences, Cypress, CA 90630. Offers clinical research administration (MS, Certificate); emergency and disaster management (MS, Certificate); environmental health science (Certificate); health care administration (PhD); health care management (MS), including health informatics; health education (MS, Certificate); health informatics (Certificate); health sciences (PhD); international health (MS); international health: educator or researcher option (PhD); international health: practitioner option (PhD); law and expert witness studies (MS, Certificate); public health (MS); quality assurance (Certificate). *Program availability:* Part-time, evening/weekend, online learning. *Degree requirements:* For doctorate, comprehensive exam, thesis/dissertation, defense of dissertation. *Entrance requirements:* For master's, minimum GPA of 2.5 (students with GPA 3.0 or greater may transfer up to 30% of graduate level credits); for doctorate, minimum GPA of 3.4, curriculum vitae, course work in research methods or statistics. Additional exam requirements/recommendations for international students: Required—TOEFL. Electronic applications accepted.

Union College, Graduate Programs, Department of Education, Barbourville, KY 40906-1499. Offers elementary education (MA); health and physical education (MA); middle grades (MA); music education (MA); principalship (MA); reading specialist (MA); secondary education (MA); special education (MA). *Degree requirements:* For master's, thesis optional. *Entrance requirements:* For master's, GRE General Test, NTE.

Union College, Graduate Programs, Department of Health and Physical Education, Barbourville, KY 40906-1499. Offers health (MA Ed). *Degree requirements:* For master's, thesis optional. *Entrance requirements:* For master's, GRE General Test, NTE.

The University of Alabama, Graduate School, College of Human Environmental Sciences, Department of Health Science, Tuscaloosa, AL 35487-0311. Offers health education and promotion (PhD); health studies (MA). *Program availability:* Part-time, online learning. *Degree requirements:* For master's, comprehensive exam, thesis optional; for doctorate, one foreign language, comprehensive exam, thesis/dissertation. *Entrance requirements:* For master's, minimum GPA of 3.0; for doctorate, GRE General Test, minimum GPA of 3.0, prerequisites in health education. Additional exam requirements/recommendations for international students: Required—TOEFL. Electronic applications accepted. *Faculty research:* Program planning, substance abuse prevention, obesity prevention, nutrition, physical activity, athletic training, osteoporosis, health behavior.

University of Arkansas, Graduate School, College of Education and Health Professions, Department of Health, Human Performance and Recreation, Fayetteville, AR 72701. Offers athletic training (MAT); community health promotion (MS, PhD); health science (MS, PhD); kinesiology (MS, PhD); physical education (M Ed, MAT); recreation and sports management (M Ed, Ed D). In 2018, 77 master's, 6 doctorates awarded. *Application deadline:* For fall admission, 8/1 for domestic students, 4/1 for international students; for spring admission, 12/1 for domestic students, 10/1 for international students; for summer admission, 4/15 for domestic students, 3/1 for international students. Applications are processed on a rolling basis. Application fee: $60. Electronic applications accepted. *Financial support:* In 2018–19, 13 research assistantships, 10 teaching assistantships were awarded; fellowships with tuition reimbursements, career-

related internships or fieldwork, and Federal Work-Study also available. Support available to part-time students. Financial award application deadline: 4/1; financial award applicants required to submit FAFSA. *Unit head:* Dr. Matthew Ganio, Department Head, 479-575-2857, E-mail: msganio@uark.edu. *Application contact:* Dr. Paul Calleja, Graduate Coordinator, 479-575-2854, Fax: 479-5778, E-mail: pcallej@uark.edu.
Website: https://hhpr.uark.edu/

University of Arkansas at Little Rock, Graduate School, College of Education and Health Professions, Department of Educational Leadership, Program in Higher Education, Little Rock, AR 72204-1099. Offers administration (MA); college student affairs (MA); health professions teaching and learning (MA); higher education (Ed D); two-year college teaching (MA). *Degree requirements:* For doctorate, comprehensive exam, oral defense of dissertation, residency. *Entrance requirements:* For master's, GRE General Test or MAT, interview, minimum graduate GPA of 3.0; for doctorate, GRE General Test, interview, minimum graduate GPA of 3.5, teaching certificate, three years of work experience.

University of Arkansas at Little Rock, Graduate School, College of Education and Health Professions, Department of Health, Human Performance and Sport Management, Little Rock, AR 72204-1099. Offers exercise science (MS); health education and promotion (MS); sport management (MS). *Program availability:* Part-time, evening/weekend. *Degree requirements:* For master's, directed study or residency. *Entrance requirements:* For master's, GRE General Test, minimum GPA of 3.0, 3 reference letters.

University of Arkansas for Medical Sciences, Fay W. Boozman College of Public Health, Little Rock, AR 72205-7199. Offers biostatistics (MPH); environmental and occupational health (MPH, Certificate); epidemiology (MPH, PhD); health behavior and health education (MPH); health policy and management (MPH); health promotion and prevention research (PhD); health services administration (MHSA); health systems research (PhD); public health (Certificate); public health leadership (Dr PH). *Accreditation:* CAHME; CEPH. *Program availability:* Part-time. *Degree requirements:* For master's, preceptorship, culminating experience, internship; for doctorate, comprehensive exam, capstone. *Entrance requirements:* For master's, GRE, GMAT, LSAT, PCAT, MCAT, DAT; for doctorate, GRE. Additional exam requirements/recommendations for international students: Required—TOEFL (minimum score 80 iBT), IELTS. Electronic applications accepted. *Expenses:* Contact institution. *Faculty research:* Health systems, tobacco prevention control, obesity prevention, environmental and occupational exposure, cancer prevention.

University of Central Arkansas, Graduate School, College of Health and Behavioral Sciences, Department of Health Sciences, Conway, AR 72035-0001. Offers health education (MS). *Program availability:* Part-time, evening/weekend, online learning. *Degree requirements:* For master's, comprehensive exam, thesis optional. *Entrance requirements:* For master's, GRE General Test, minimum GPA of 2.7. Additional exam requirements/recommendations for international students: Required—TOEFL (minimum score 550 paper-based). Electronic applications accepted.

University of Cincinnati, Graduate School, College of Education, Criminal Justice, and Human Services, School of Human Services, Health Promotion and Education Program, Cincinnati, OH 45221. Offers exercise and fitness (MS); health education (PhD); public and community health (MS); public health (MPH). *Accreditation:* NCATE. *Program availability:* Part-time, evening/weekend. *Degree requirements:* For master's, thesis or alternative; for doctorate, thesis/dissertation. *Entrance requirements:* For master's and doctorate, GRE General Test. Additional exam requirements/recommendations for international students: Required—TOEFL (minimum score 580 paper-based). Electronic applications accepted.

University of Colorado Denver, Colorado School of Public Health, Program in Public Health, Aurora, CO 80045. Offers community and behavioral health (MPH, Dr PH). *Accreditation:* CEPH. *Program availability:* Part-time, evening/weekend. *Degree requirements:* For master's, thesis or alternative, 42 credit hours; for doctorate, comprehensive exam, thesis/dissertation, 67 credit hours. *Entrance requirements:* For master's, GRE, MCAT, DAT, LSAT, PCAT, GMAT or master's degree from accredited institution, baccalaureate degree or equivalent; minimum GPA of 3.0; transcripts; references; resume; essay; for doctorate, GRE, MCAT, DAT, LSAT, PCAT or GMAT, MPH or master's or higher degree in related field or equivalent; 2 years of previous work experience in public health; essay; resume. Additional exam requirements/recommendations for international students: Required—TOEFL (minimum score 550 paper-based; 80 iBT). *Expenses:* Tuition, state resident: full-time $6786; part-time $337 per credit hour. Tuition, nonresident: full-time $22,590; part-time $1255 per credit hour. *Required fees:* $1231; $137 per credit hour. Tuition and fees vary according to program and reciprocity agreements. *Faculty research:* Cancer prevention by nutrition, cancer survivorship outcomes, social and cultural factors related to health.

University of Colorado Denver, School of Medicine, Physician Assistant Program, Aurora, CO 80045. Offers child health associate (MPAS), including global health, leadership, education, advocacy, development, and scholarship, pediatric critical and acute care, rural health, urban/underserved populations. *Accreditation:* ARC-PA. *Degree requirements:* For master's, comprehensive exam. *Entrance requirements:* For master's, GRE General Test, minimum GPA of 2.8; 3 letters of recommendation; prerequisite courses in chemistry, biology, general genetics, psychology and statistics; interview. Additional exam requirements/recommendations for international students: Required—TOEFL (minimum score 550 paper-based; 80 iBT). Electronic applications accepted. *Expenses:* Tuition, state resident: full-time $6786; part-time $337 per credit hour. Tuition, nonresident: full-time $22,590; part-time $1255 per credit hour. *Required fees:* $1231; $137 per credit hour. Tuition and fees vary according to program and reciprocity agreements. *Faculty research:* Clinical genetics and genetic counseling, evidence-based medicine, pediatric allergy and asthma, childhood diabetes, standardized patient assessment.

University of Florida, Graduate School, College of Health and Human Performance, Department of Health Education and Behavior, Gainesville, FL 32611. Offers health and human performance (PhD), including health behavior; health communication (Graduate Certificate); health education and behavior (MS). *Accreditation:* NCATE (one or more programs are accredited). *Program availability:* Part-time. Terminal master's awarded for partial completion of doctoral program. *Degree requirements:* For master's, comprehensive exam, thesis (for some programs); for doctorate, comprehensive exam, thesis/dissertation. *Entrance requirements:* For master's and doctorate, GRE General Test (minimum score 293), minimum GPA of 3.0. Additional exam requirements/recommendations for international students: Required—TOEFL (minimum score 550 paper-based; 80 iBT), IELTS (minimum score 6). Electronic applications accepted. *Faculty research:* Community-based participatory research; health disparities issues; health; cancer prevention and control; obesity-related issues; community capacity building; training community health workers; use of community based research principles to design, implement, an evaluate community health worker interventions; obesity; weight management; health literacy; health disparities (ethnic, gender, age, urban/rural); tailored health messages; entertainment education; COPD.

University of Georgia, Biomedical and Health Sciences Institute, Athens, GA 30602. Offers neuroscience (PhD). *Entrance requirements:* For doctorate, GRE, official transcripts, 3 letters of recommendation, statement of interest. Additional exam requirements/recommendations for international students: Required—TOEFL.

University of Georgia, College of Public Health, Department of Health Promotion and Behavior, Athens, GA 30602. Offers MA, MPH, Dr PH, PhD. *Accreditation:* NCATE (one or more programs are accredited). *Degree requirements:* For master's, thesis (MA); for doctorate, thesis/dissertation. *Entrance requirements:* For master's, GRE General Test or MAT; for doctorate, GRE General Test. Electronic applications accepted.

University of Houston, College of Liberal Arts and Social Sciences, Department of Health and Human Performance, Houston, TX 77204. Offers exercise science (MS); human nutrition (MS); human space exploration sciences (MS); kinesiology (PhD); physical education (M Ed). *Accreditation:* NCATE (one or more programs are accredited). *Program availability:* Part-time, evening/weekend. *Degree requirements:* For master's, comprehensive exam (for some programs), thesis (for some programs); for doctorate, comprehensive exam, thesis/dissertation, qualifying exam, candidacy paper. *Entrance requirements:* For master's, GRE (minimum 35th percentile on each section), minimum cumulative GPA of 3.0; for doctorate, GRE (minimum 35th percentile on each section), minimum cumulative GPA of 3.3. Additional exam requirements/recommendations for international students: Required—TOEFL (minimum score 550 paper-based; 79 iBT). Electronic applications accepted. *Faculty research:* Biomechanics, exercise physiology, obesity, nutrition, space exploration science.

University of Illinois at Chicago, College of Medicine, Graduate Programs in Medicine, Department of Medical Education, Chicago, IL 60607-7128. Offers MHPE. *Program availability:* Part-time. *Degree requirements:* For master's, thesis. *Entrance requirements:* For master's, GRE General Test. Additional exam requirements/recommendations for international students: Required—TOEFL. Electronic applications accepted.

University of Illinois at Springfield, Graduate Programs, College of Public Affairs and Administration, Program in Public Health, Springfield, IL 62703-5407. Offers community health education (Graduate Certificate); emergency preparedness and homeland security (Graduate Certificate); environmental health (MPH, Graduate Certificate); environmental risk assessment (Graduate Certificate); epidemiology (Graduate Certificate); public health (MPH). *Program availability:* Part-time, evening/weekend, 100% online. *Faculty:* 7 full-time (5 women). *Students:* 39 full-time (27 women), 40 part-time (32 women); includes 19 minority (11 Black or African American, non-Hispanic/Latino; 3 Asian, non-Hispanic/Latino; 3 Hispanic/Latino; 2 Two or more races, non-Hispanic/Latino), 25 international. Average age 31. 87 applicants, 48% accepted, 17 enrolled. In 2018, 29 master's, 10 other advanced degrees awarded. *Degree requirements:* For master's, comprehensive exam, internship. *Entrance requirements:* For master's, GRE, minimum undergraduate GPA of 3.0, 3 letters of recommendation, essay addressing the areas outlined on the department application form, current vitae. Additional exam requirements/recommendations for international students: Required—TOEFL (minimum score 500 paper-based; 61 iBT). *Application deadline:* Applications are processed on a rolling basis. Application fee: $60 ($75 for international students). Electronic applications accepted. *Financial support:* In 2018–19, research assistantships with full tuition reimbursements (averaging $10,384 per year), teaching assistantships with full tuition reimbursements (averaging $10,303 per year) were awarded; fellowships, career-related internships or fieldwork, Federal Work-Study, scholarships/grants, health care benefits, and unspecified assistantships also available. Support available to part-time students. Financial award application deadline: 11/15; financial award applicants required to submit FAFSA. *Unit head:* Dr. Josiah Alamu, Program Administrator, 217-206-7874, Fax: 217-206-7279, E-mail: jalam3@uis.edu. *Application contact:* Dr. Josiah Alamu, Program Administrator, 217-206-7874, Fax: 217-206-7279, E-mail: jalam3@uis.edu.
Website: http://www.uis.edu/publichealth/

The University of Kansas, University of Kansas Medical Center, School of Nursing, Kansas City, KS 66045. Offers adult/gerontological clinical nurse specialist (PMC); adult/gerontological nurse practitioner (PMC); health care informatics (PMC); health professions educator (PMC); nurse midwife (PMC); nursing (MS, DNP, PhD); organizational leadership (PMC); psychiatric/mental health nurse practitioner (PMC); public health nursing (PMC). *Accreditation:* AACN; ACNM/ACME. *Program availability:* Part-time, 100% online, blended/hybrid learning. *Faculty:* 56. *Students:* 55 full-time (49 women), 273 part-time (246 women); includes 62 minority (16 Black or African American, non-Hispanic/Latino; 2 American Indian or Alaska Native, non-Hispanic/Latino; 21 Asian, non-Hispanic/Latino; 9 Hispanic/Latino; 14 Two or more races, non-Hispanic/Latino), 1 international. Average age 36. 76 applicants, 93% accepted, 60 enrolled. In 2018, 19 master's, 28 doctorates, 7 other advanced degrees awarded. Terminal master's awarded for partial completion of doctoral program. *Degree requirements:* For master's, comprehensive exam, thesis (for some programs), general oral exam; for doctorate, thesis/dissertation or alternative, comprehensive oral exam (for DNP); comprehensive written and oral exam, or three publications (for PhD). *Entrance requirements:* For master's, bachelor's degree in nursing, minimum GPA of 3.0, 1 year of clinical experience, RN license in KS and MO; for doctorate, GRE General Test (for PhD only), bachelor's degree in nursing, minimum GPA of 3.5, RN license in KS and MO. Additional exam requirements/recommendations for international students: Required—TOEFL. *Application deadline:* For fall admission, 4/1 for domestic and international students; for spring admission, 9/1 for domestic and international students. Application fee: $75. Electronic applications accepted. *Financial support:* In 2018–19, 5 research assistantships with tuition reimbursements (averaging $20,000 per year), 30 teaching assistantships with tuition reimbursements (averaging $20,000 per year) were awarded; scholarships/grants and traineeships also available. Financial award application deadline: 3/1; financial award applicants required to submit FAFSA. *Faculty research:* Breastfeeding practices of teen mothers, national database of nursing quality indicators, caregiving of families of patients using technology in the home, simulation in nursing education, diaphragm fatigue. *Total annual research expenditures:* $3 million. *Unit head:* Dr. Sally Maliski, Dean, 913-588-1601, Fax: 913-588-1660, E-mail: smaliski@kumc.edu. *Application contact:* Dr. Pamela K. Barnes, Associate Dean, Student Affairs, 913-588-1619, Fax: 913-588-1615, E-mail: pbarnes2@kumc.edu.
Website: http://nursing.kumc.edu

University of Louisville, Graduate School, College of Education and Human Development, Department of Educational Leadership, Evaluation and Organizational Development, Louisville, KY 40292-0001. Offers educational leadership and organizational development (Ed D, PhD), including evaluation (PhD), human resource development (PhD), P-12 administration (PhD), post-secondary administration (PhD), sport administration (MA, PhD); health professions education (Certificate); higher education administration (MA), including sport administration (MA, PhD); human resources and organization development (MS), including health professions education, human resource leadership, workplace learning and performance; P-12 educational administration (Ed S), including principalship, supervisor of instruction. *Accreditation:* NCATE. *Program availability:* Part-time, evening/weekend, 100% online, blended/hybrid learning. *Students:* 200 full-time (82 women), 474 part-time (262 women); includes 218 minority (127 Black or African American, non-Hispanic/Latino; 1 American Indian or Alaska Native, non-Hispanic/Latino; 18 Asian, non-Hispanic/Latino; 46 Hispanic/Latino; 2 Native Hawaiian or other Pacific Islander, non-Hispanic/Latino; 24 Two or more races,

non-Hispanic/Latino), 5 international. Average age 36. 257 applicants, 77% accepted, 170 enrolled. In 2018, 111 master's, 10 doctorates, 22 other advanced degrees awarded. Terminal master's awarded for partial completion of doctoral program. *Degree requirements:* For master's, comprehensive exam (for some programs), thesis (for some programs); for doctorate, comprehensive exam (for some programs), thesis/dissertation. *Entrance requirements:* For master's, GRE (for most programs), PRAXIS (for educator preparation programs), professional statement, recommendation letters, resume, transcripts; for doctorate and other advanced degree, GRE, professional statement, recommendation letters, resume, transcripts. Additional exam requirements/recommendations for international students: Required—TOEFL (minimum score 550 paper-based; 79 iBT); Recommended—IELTS (minimum score 6.5). *Application deadline:* For fall admission, 6/1 priority date for domestic students, 5/1 priority date for international students; for spring admission, 10/1 priority date for domestic students, 11/1 priority date for international students; for summer admission, 3/1 for domestic students, 4/1 priority date for international students. Application fee: $65. *Expenses: Tuition, area resident:* Full-time $6500; part-time $723 per credit hour. Tuition, state resident: full-time $6500. Tuition, nonresident: full-time $13,557; part-time $1507 per credit hour. Tuition and fees vary according to course load and program. *Financial support:* In 2018–19, 144 students received support, including fellowships (averaging $21,024 per year), research assistantships with full tuition reimbursements available (averaging $21,024 per year), teaching assistantships with full tuition reimbursements available (averaging $21,024 per year); Federal Work-Study, scholarships/grants, health care benefits, tuition waivers (full), and unspecified assistantships also available. Financial award application deadline: 3/1; financial award applicants required to submit FAFSA. *Faculty research:* Human resources and organizational development; career, technical, health professions, and economic education; health professions education; community and military partnerships; higher education. *Unit head:* Dr. Sharron Kerrick, Chair, 502-852-6475, E-mail: lead@louisville.edu. *Application contact:* Dr. Margaret Pentecost, Assistant Dean for Graduate Student Success, 502-852-6437, Fax: 502-852-1417, E-mail: gedadm@louisville.edu.
Website: http://louisville.edu/education/departments/eleod

University of Louisville, Graduate School, College of Education and Human Development, Department of Health and Sport Sciences, Louisville, KY 40292-0001. Offers community health education (M Ed); exercise physiology (MS), including health and sport sciences, strength and conditioning; health and physical education (MAT); sport administration (MS). *Program availability:* Part-time, evening/weekend, 100% online, blended/hybrid learning. *Students:* 32 full-time (10 women), 5 part-time (3 women); includes 9 minority (7 Black or African American, non-Hispanic/Latino; 2 Two or more races, non-Hispanic/Latino). Average age 28. 41 applicants, 66% accepted, 21 enrolled. In 2018, 21 master's awarded. Terminal master's awarded for partial completion of doctoral program. *Degree requirements:* For master's, comprehensive exam (for some programs), thesis optional. *Entrance requirements:* For master's, GRE (for most programs), PRAXIS (for educator preparation programs), professional statement, recommendation letters, resume, transcripts. Additional exam requirements/recommendations for international students: Required—TOEFL (minimum score 550 paper-based; 79 iBT); Recommended—IELTS (minimum score 6.5). *Application deadline:* For fall admission, 6/1 priority date for domestic students, 5/1 priority date for international students; for spring admission, 10/1 priority date for domestic students, 11/1 priority date for international students; for summer admission, 3/1 priority date for domestic students, 4/1 priority date for international students. Application fee: $65. *Expenses: Tuition, area resident:* Full-time $6500; part-time $723 per credit hour. Tuition, state resident: full-time $6500. Tuition, nonresident: full-time $13,557; part-time $1507 per credit hour. Tuition and fees vary according to course load and program. *Financial support:* In 2018–19, 15 students received support, including fellowships with full tuition reimbursements available (averaging $21,024 per year), research assistantships (averaging $21,024 per year); teaching assistantships with full tuition reimbursements available, Federal Work-Study, scholarships/grants, health care benefits, tuition waivers (full), and unspecified assistantships also available. Financial award application deadline: 3/1; financial award applicants required to submit FAFSA. *Faculty research:* Sport administration, exercise science, exercise physiology, physical and health education, youth sport development. *Unit head:* Dr. Dylan Naeger, Interim Chair, 502-852-6645, E-mail: hss@louisville.edu. *Application contact:* Dr. Margaret Pentecost, Director of Grad Assistant Dean for Graduate Student Success Graduate Student Services, 502-852-6437, Fax: 502-852-1465, E-mail: gedadm@louisville.edu.
Website: http://www.louisville.edu/education/departments/hss

University of Louisville, Graduate School, College of Education and Human Development, Departments of Early Childhood and Elementary Education, Middle and Secondary Education, and Special Education, Louisville, KY 40292-0001. Offers art education (MAT); autism and applied behavior analysis (Certificate); curriculum and instruction (PhD); early elementary education (MAT); exercise physiology (MS); health and physical education (MAT); health professions education (Certificate); higher education (MA); human resources and organization development (MS); instructional technology (M Ed); interdisciplinary early childhood education (MAT); middle school education (MAT); music education (MAT); secondary education (MAT); special education (MAT); sport administration (MS); teacher leadership (M Ed). *Program availability:* Part-time, evening/weekend, 100% online, blended/hybrid learning. *Faculty:* 97 full-time (64 women), 131 part-time/adjunct (86 women). *Students:* 109 full-time (72 women), 139 part-time (87 women); includes 43 minority (18 Black or African American, non-Hispanic/Latino; 6 Asian, non-Hispanic/Latino; 10 Hispanic/Latino; 9 Two or more races, non-Hispanic/Latino), 9 international. Average age 29. 108 applicants, 75% accepted, 59 enrolled. In 2018, 64 master's awarded. Terminal master's awarded for partial completion of doctoral program. *Degree requirements:* For master's, comprehensive exam (for some programs), thesis optional; for doctorate, comprehensive exam (for some programs), thesis/dissertation. *Entrance requirements:* For master's, GRE (for most programs), PRAXIS (for educator preparation programs), professional statement, recommendation letters, resume, transcripts; for doctorate and Certificate, GRE, professional statement, recommendation letters, resume, transcripts. Additional exam requirements/recommendations for international students: Required—TOEFL (minimum score 550 paper-based; 79 iBT); Recommended—IELTS (minimum score 6.5). *Application deadline:* For fall admission, 6/1 priority date for domestic students, 5/1 priority date for international students; for spring admission, 10/1 for domestic students, 11/1 priority date for international students; for summer admission, 3/1 priority date for domestic students, 4/1 priority date for international students. Application fee: $65. *Expenses: Tuition, area resident:* Full-time $6500; part-time $723 per credit hour. Tuition, state resident: full-time $6500. Tuition, nonresident: full-time $13,557; part-time $1507 per credit hour. Tuition and fees vary according to course load and program. *Financial support:* In 2018–19, 144 students received support, including fellowships with full tuition reimbursements available (averaging $21,024 per year), research assistantships with full tuition reimbursements available (averaging $21,024 per year), teaching assistantships with full tuition reimbursements available (averaging $21,024 per year); Federal Work-Study, scholarships/grants, health care benefits, tuition waivers (full), and unspecified assistantships also available. Financial award application deadline: 3/1; financial award applicants required to submit FAFSA. *Faculty research:* Children's early reading and writing development, crelevance of basic facts in elementary mathematics instruction, clinical model of teacher education, cultural and linguistic context of diverse learners, and STEM-integrated curriculum design and development. STEM teaching and learning, content literacy for English language learners, social justice in teacher education, adolescent literacy, mathematics teacher development. Classroom and behavior management; moderate/severe disabilities, autism. *Unit head:* Dr. Amy Lingo, Interim Dean, 502-852-3235, Fax: 502-852-1464, E-mail: cehdinfo@louisville.edu. *Application contact:* Dr. Margaret Pentecost, Assistant Dean for Graduate Student Success, 502-852-6437, Fax: 502-852-1417, E-mail: gedadm@louisville.edu.
Website: http://louisville.edu/delphi

University of Maryland, College Park, Academic Affairs, School of Public Health, Department of Behavioral and Community Health, College Park, MD 20742. Offers community health education (MPH); public/community health (PhD). *Accreditation:* CEPH. *Program availability:* Part-time, evening/weekend. *Degree requirements:* For master's, thesis optional; for doctorate, comprehensive exam, thesis/dissertation. *Entrance requirements:* For master's, GRE General Test, minimum GPA of 3.0, 3 letters of recommendation; for doctorate, GRE General Test, minimum GPA of 3.5, 3 letters of recommendation. Additional exam requirements/recommendations for international students: Required—TOEFL. Electronic applications accepted. *Faculty research:* Controlling stress and tension, women's health, aging and public policy, adolescent health, long-term care.

University of Massachusetts Amherst, Graduate School, School of Public Health and Health Sciences, Department of Public Health, Amherst, MA 01003. Offers biostatistics (MPH, MS, PhD); community health education (MPH, MS, PhD); environmental health sciences (MPH, MS, PhD); epidemiology (MPH, MS, PhD); health policy and management (MPH, MS, PhD); nutrition (MPH, PhD); public health practice (MPH); MPH/MPPA. *Accreditation:* CEPH. *Program availability:* Part-time, evening/weekend, online learning. Terminal master's awarded for partial completion of doctoral program. *Degree requirements:* For master's, thesis (for some programs); for doctorate, comprehensive exam, thesis/dissertation. *Entrance requirements:* For master's and doctorate, GRE General Test. Additional exam requirements/recommendations for international students: Required—TOEFL (minimum score 550 paper-based; 80 iBT), IELTS (minimum score 6.5). Electronic applications accepted.

University of Michigan, School of Public Health, Department of Health Behavior and Health Education, Ann Arbor, MI 48109. Offers MPH, PhD, MPH/MSW. PhD offered through the Rackham Graduate School. *Accreditation:* CEPH (one or more programs are accredited). Terminal master's awarded for partial completion of doctoral program. *Degree requirements:* For doctorate, oral defense of dissertation, preliminary exam. *Entrance requirements:* For master's, GRE General Test (preferred); MCAT; for doctorate, GRE General Test. Additional exam requirements/recommendations for international students: Required—TOEFL (minimum score 100 iBT). Electronic applications accepted. *Faculty research:* Empowerment theory; structure, culture, and health; health disparities; community-based participatory research; health and medical decision-making.

University of Michigan–Flint, College of Health Sciences, Program in Public Health, Flint, MI 48502-1950. Offers health administration (MPH); health education (MPH). *Program availability:* Part-time. *Faculty:* 17 full-time (12 women), 34 part-time/adjunct (18 women). *Students:* 19 full-time (16 women), 26 part-time (22 women); includes 13 minority (7 Black or African American, non-Hispanic/Latino; 1 American Indian or Alaska Native, non-Hispanic/Latino; 2 Asian, non-Hispanic/Latino; 3 Hispanic/Latino), 9 international. Average age 32. 63 applicants, 56% accepted, 15 enrolled. In 2018, 22 master's awarded. *Entrance requirements:* For master's, bachelor's degree from accredited institution with sufficient preparation in algebra to succeed in epidemiology and biostatistics; minimum overall undergraduate GPA of 3.0; completion of BIO 104 or an equivalent course in anatomy and physiology. Additional exam requirements/recommendations for international students: Required—TOEFL (minimum score 84 iBT), IELTS (minimum score 6.5). *Application deadline:* For fall admission, 8/1 for domestic students, 5/1 for international students; for winter admission, 11/15 for domestic students, 9/1 for international students; for spring admission, 3/15 for domestic students, 1/1 for international students. Applications are processed on a rolling basis. Application fee: $55. Electronic applications accepted. *Expenses:* Contact institution. *Financial support:* Federal Work-Study, scholarships/grants, and unspecified assistantships available. Support available to part-time students. Financial award application deadline: 3/1; financial award applicants required to submit FAFSA. *Unit head:* Dr. Shan Parker, Director, 810-762-3172, E-mail: shanpark@umflint.edu. *Application contact:* Matt Bohlen, Director of Graduate Admissions, 810-762-3171, Fax: 810-766-6789, E-mail: mbohlen@umflint.edu.
Website: http://www.umflint.edu/graduateprograms/public-health-mph

University of Missouri, Office of Research and Graduate Studies, College of Education, Department of Learning, Teaching and Curriculum, Columbia, MO 65211. Offers agricultural education (M Ed, PhD, Ed S); art education (M Ed, PhD, Ed S); business and office education (M Ed, PhD, Ed S); early childhood education (M Ed, PhD, Ed S); elementary education (M Ed, PhD, Ed S); English education (M Ed, PhD, Ed S); foreign language education (M Ed, PhD, Ed S); health education and promotion (M Ed, PhD); learning and instruction (M Ed); marketing education (M Ed, PhD, Ed S); mathematics education (M Ed, PhD, Ed S); music education (M Ed, PhD, Ed S); reading education (M Ed, PhD, Ed S); science education (M Ed, PhD, Ed S); social studies education (M Ed, PhD, Ed S); vocational education (M Ed, PhD, Ed S). *Program availability:* Part-time. Terminal master's awarded for partial completion of doctoral program. *Entrance requirements:* For master's and Ed S, GRE General Test or MAT, minimum GPA of 3.0; for doctorate, GRE General Test, minimum GPA of 3.0. Additional exam requirements/recommendations for international students: Required—TOEFL.

University of Missouri–Kansas City, School of Medicine, Kansas City, MO 64110-2499. Offers health professions education (MS); MD/PhD. *Accreditation:* LCME/AMA. *Degree requirements:* For doctorate, one foreign language, United States Medical Licensing Exam Step 1 and 2. *Entrance requirements:* For doctorate, interview. *Expenses:* Contact institution. *Faculty research:* Cardiovascular disease, women's and children's health, trauma and infectious diseases, neurological, metabolic disease.

University of Montana, Graduate School, Phyllis J. Washington College of Education and Human Sciences, Department of Health and Human Performance, Missoula, MT 59812. Offers community health (MS); exercise science (MS); health and human performance generalist (MS). *Program availability:* Part-time. *Entrance requirements:* For master's, GRE General Test. Additional exam requirements/recommendations for international students: Required—TOEFL. *Faculty research:* Exercise physiology, performance psychology, nutrition, pre-employment physical screening, program evaluation.

University of Nebraska at Omaha, Graduate Studies, College of Education, School of Health and Kinesiology, Omaha, NE 68182. Offers athletic training (MA); exercise science (PhD); health, physical education, and recreation (MA, MS). *Program availability:* Part-time, evening/weekend. *Degree requirements:* For master's, comprehensive exam, thesis (for some programs). *Entrance requirements:* For master's, GRE; entrance exam, minimum GPA of 3.0, official transcripts, statement of purpose, 2

letters of recommendation; for doctorate, GRE, minimum GPA of 3.2, official transcripts, statement of purpose, 3 letters of recommendation, resume, writing sample. Additional exam requirements/recommendations for international students: Required—TOEFL, IELTS, PTE. Electronic applications accepted.

University of New Mexico, Graduate Studies, College of Education, Program in Health Education, Albuquerque, NM 87131-2039. Offers community health education (MS). *Accreditation:* NCATE. *Program availability:* Part-time. *Students:* Average age 32. 8 applicants, 75% accepted, 6 enrolled. In 2018, 11 master's awarded. *Degree requirements:* For master's, comprehensive exam, thesis optional. *Entrance requirements:* For master's, 3 letters of reference, resume, minimum cumulative GPA of 3.0 in last 2 years of bachelor's degree, letter of intent. Additional exam requirements/recommendations for international students: Required—TOEFL (minimum score 550 paper-based). *Application deadline:* For fall admission, 6/15 priority date for domestic students; for spring admission, 11/1 priority date for domestic students. Applications are processed on a rolling basis. Application fee: $50. Electronic applications accepted. *Financial support:* Fellowships, teaching assistantships with full tuition reimbursements, career-related internships or fieldwork, institutionally sponsored loans, scholarships/grants, and health care benefits available. Financial award application deadline: 3/1; financial award applicants required to submit FAFSA. *Faculty research:* Alcohol and families, health behaviors and sexuality, multicultural health behavior, health promotion policy, school/community-based prevention, health and aging. *Unit head:* Dr. Elias Duryea, Coordinator, 505-277-5151, Fax: 505-277-6227, E-mail: duryea@unm.edu. *Application contact:* Carol Catania, Graduate Coordinator, 505-277-5151, Fax: 505-277-6227, E-mail: catania@unm.edu.

The University of North Carolina at Pembroke, The Graduate School, School of Education, Department of Health and Human Performance, Pembroke, NC 28372-1510. Offers health/physical education (MAT); physical education (MA), including exercise/sports administration, physical education advanced licensure. *Program availability:* Part-time, evening/weekend. *Degree requirements:* For master's, comprehensive exam, thesis optional. *Entrance requirements:* For master's, MAT or GRE, minimum GPA of 3.0 in major, 2.5 overall. Additional exam requirements/recommendations for international students: Required—TOEFL.

University of Northern Colorado, Graduate School, College of Natural and Health Sciences, School of Human Sciences, Program in Public Health, Greeley, CO 80639. Offers community health education (MPH); global health and community health education (MPH); healthy aging and community health education (MPH). *Degree requirements:* For master's, comprehensive exam, thesis or alternative. *Entrance requirements:* For master's, GRE General Test, 2 letters of recommendation. Electronic applications accepted.

University of Northern Iowa, Graduate College, College of Education, School of Kinesiology, Allied Health and Human Services, MA Program in Health Education, Cedar Falls, IA 50614. Offers community health education (MA); health promotion/fitness management (MA); school health education (MA). *Program availability:* Part-time, evening/weekend. *Degree requirements:* For master's, comprehensive exam, thesis or alternative. *Entrance requirements:* For master's, minimum GPA of 3.0. Additional exam requirements/recommendations for international students: Required—TOEFL (minimum score 500 paper-based; 61 iBT). Electronic applications accepted.

University of Oklahoma Health Sciences Center, Graduate College, College of Allied Health, Department of Allied Health Sciences, Oklahoma City, OK 73190. Offers PhD. *Degree requirements:* For doctorate, one foreign language, comprehensive exam, thesis/dissertation optional. *Entrance requirements:* For doctorate, GRE General Test, 3 letters of recommendation, master's degree. Additional exam requirements/recommendations for international students: Required—TOEFL (minimum score 550 paper-based).

University of Phoenix–Online Campus, College of Health Sciences and Nursing, Phoenix, AZ 85034-7209. Offers family nurse practitioner (Certificate); health care (Certificate); health care education (Certificate); health care informatics (Certificate); informatics (MSN); nursing (MSN); nursing and health care education (MSN); MSN/MBA; MSN/MHA. *Accreditation:* AACN. *Program availability:* Evening/weekend, online learning. *Entrance requirements:* Additional exam requirements/recommendations for international students: Required—TOEFL, TOEIC (Test of English as an International Communication), Berlitz Online English Proficiency Exam, PTE, or IELTS. Electronic applications accepted. *Expenses:* Contact institution.

University of Pittsburgh, Graduate School of Public Health, Department of Infectious Diseases and Microbiology, Pittsburgh, PA 15261. Offers infectious diseases and microbiology (MS, PhD); management, intervention, and community practice (MPH); pathogenesis, eradication, and laboratory practice (MPH). *Program availability:* Part-time. Terminal master's awarded for partial completion of doctoral program. *Degree requirements:* For master's, thesis, comprehensive exam (for MS); for doctorate, comprehensive exam, thesis/dissertation, preliminary exam, dissertation defense. *Entrance requirements:* For master's, GRE General Test, MCAT, or DAT, minimum GPA of 3.0, 6 credits of behavioral science; for doctorate, GRE General Test, MCAT, DAT, minimum GPA of 3.0; research experience; knowledge of biology or microbiology, chemistry, and algebra. Additional exam requirements/recommendations for international students: Required—TOEFL (minimum score 550 paper-based, 80 iBT) or IELTS (minimum score 6.5). Electronic applications accepted. *Expenses:* Contact institution. *Faculty research:* Development of HIV vaccines, complications of antiretroviral therapy, emerging infections, herpes viruses.

University of Puerto Rico–Medical Sciences Campus, Graduate School of Public Health, Department of Social Sciences, Program in Public Health Education, San Juan, PR 00936-5067. Offers MPHE. *Program availability:* Part-time, evening/weekend. *Degree requirements:* For master's, thesis. *Entrance requirements:* For master's, GRE, previous course work in education, social sciences, algebra, and natural sciences.

University of Rhode Island, Graduate School, College of Health Sciences, Department of Kinesiology, Kingston, RI 02881. Offers cultural studies of sport and physical culture (MS); exercise science (MS); psychosocial/behavioral aspects of physical activity (MS). *Accreditation:* NCATE. *Program availability:* Part-time. *Faculty:* 16 full-time (11 women). *Students:* 13 full-time (5 women), 2 part-time (1 woman), 1 international. 18 applicants, 100% accepted, 8 enrolled. In 2018, 5 master's awarded. *Entrance requirements:* Additional exam requirements/recommendations for international students: Required—TOEFL. *Application deadline:* For fall admission, 7/15 for domestic students, 2/1 for international students; for spring admission, 11/15 for domestic students, 7/15 for international students. Application fee: $65. Electronic applications accepted. *Expenses:* Tuition, area resident: Full-time $13,226; part-time $735 per credit. Tuition, state resident: full-time $13,226; part-time $735 per credit. Tuition, nonresident: full-time $25,854; part-time $1436 per credit. International tuition: $25,854 full-time. *Required fees:* $1698; $50 per credit. $35 per semester. One-time fee: $165. *Financial support:* In 2018–19, 1 research assistantship (averaging $8,862 per year), 6 teaching assistantships with tuition reimbursements (averaging $16,247 per year) were awarded. Financial award application deadline: 2/1; financial award applicants required to submit FAFSA. *Unit head:* Dr. Disa Hatfield, Interim Chair, 401-874-5183, E-mail: doch@uri.edu. *Application contact:* Dr. Matthew Delmonico, Graduate Program Director, 401-874-5440, E-mail: delmonico@uri.edu. Website: http://web.uri.edu/kinesiology/

University of St. Augustine for Health Sciences, Graduate Programs, Master of Health Science Program, San Marcos, CA 92069. Offers athletic training (MHS); executive leadership (MHS); informatics (MHS); teaching and learning (MHS). *Program availability:* Online learning. *Degree requirements:* For master's, comprehensive project.

University of St. Augustine for Health Sciences, Graduate Programs, Post Professional Programs, San Marcos, CA 92069. Offers health science (DH Sc); health sciences education (Ed D); occupational therapy (TOTD); physical therapy (TDPT). *Program availability:* Part-time, online learning. *Entrance requirements:* For doctorate, GRE General Test, master's degree in related field. Additional exam requirements/recommendations for international students: Required—TOEFL.

University of South Africa, College of Human Sciences, Pretoria, South Africa. Offers adult education (M Ed); African languages (MA, PhD); African politics (MA, PhD); Afrikaans (MA, PhD); ancient history (MA, PhD); ancient Near Eastern studies (MA, PhD); anthropology (MA, PhD); applied linguistics (MA); Arabic (MA, PhD); archaeology (MA); art history (MA); Biblical archaeology (MA); Biblical studies (M Th, D Th, PhD); Christian spirituality (M Th, D Th); church history (M Th, D Th); classical studies (MA, PhD); clinical psychology (MA); communication (MA, PhD); comparative education (M Ed, Ed D); consulting psychology (D Admin, D Com, PhD); curriculum studies (M Ed, Ed D); development studies (M Admin, MA, D Admin, PhD); didactics (M Ed, Ed D); education (M Tech); education management (M Ed, Ed D); educational psychology (M Ed); English (MA); environmental education (M Ed); French (MA, PhD); German (MA, PhD); Greek (MA); guidance and counseling (M Ed); health studies (MA, PhD), including health sciences education (MA), health services management (MA), medical and surgical nursing science (critical care general) (MA), midwifery and neonatal nursing science (MA), trauma and emergency care (MA); history (MA, PhD); history of education (Ed D); inclusive education (M Ed, Ed D); information and communications technology policy and regulation (MA); information science (MA, MIS, PhD); international politics (MA, PhD); Islamic studies (MA, PhD); Italian (MA, PhD); Judaica (MA, PhD); linguistics (MA, PhD); mathematical education (M Ed); mathematics education (MA); missiology (M Th, D Th); modern Hebrew (MA, PhD); musicology (MA, MMus, D Mus, PhD); natural science education (M Ed); New Testament (M Th, D Th); Old Testament (D Th); pastoral therapy (M Th, D Th); philosophy (MA); philosophy of education (M Ed, Ed D); politics (MA, PhD); Portuguese (MA, PhD); practical theology (M Th, D Th); psychology (MA, MS, PhD); psychology of education (M Ed, Ed D); public health (MA); religious studies (MA, D Th, PhD); Romance languages (MA); Russian (MA, PhD); Semitic languages (MA, PhD); social behavior studies in HIV/AIDS (MA); social science (mental health) (MA); social science in development studies (MA); social science in psychology (MA); social science in social work (MA); social science in sociology (MA); social work (MSW, DSW, PhD); socio-education (M Ed, Ed D); sociolinguistics (MA); sociology (MA, PhD); Spanish (MA, PhD); systematic theology (M Th, D Th); TESOL (teaching English to speakers of other languages) (MA); theological ethics (M Th, D Th); theory of literature (MA, PhD); urban ministries (D Th); urban ministry (M Th).

University of South Alabama, College of Education and Professional Studies, Department of Health, Kinesiology, and Sport, Mobile, AL 36688. Offers exercise science (MS); health education (M Ed, MS); physical education (M Ed); sport management (MS). *Accreditation:* NCATE (one or more programs are accredited). *Program availability:* Part-time. *Degree requirements:* For master's, comprehensive exam, thesis optional. *Entrance requirements:* For master's, GRE General Test or MAT, Alabama Class B certificate or the equivalent (for students seeking the master's-level/Class A certification). Additional exam requirements/recommendations for international students: Required—TOEFL. Electronic applications accepted.

University of South Carolina, The Graduate School, Arnold School of Public Health, Department of Health Promotion, Education, and Behavior, Columbia, SC 29208. Offers health education (MAT); health promotion, education, and behavior (MPH, MS, MSPH, Dr PH, PhD); school health education (Certificate); MSW/MPH. MAT offered in cooperation with the College of Education. *Accreditation:* CEPH (one or more programs are accredited); NCATE (one or more programs are accredited). *Program availability:* Part-time. *Degree requirements:* For master's, comprehensive exam, thesis or alternative, practicum (MPH), project (MS); for doctorate, comprehensive exam, thesis/dissertation. *Entrance requirements:* For master's and doctorate, GRE General Test. Additional exam requirements/recommendations for international students: Required—TOEFL (minimum score 570 paper-based; 75 iBT). Electronic applications accepted. *Faculty research:* Health disparities and inequalities in communities, global health and nutrition, cancer and HIV/AIDS prevention, health communication, policy and program design.

University of South Carolina, The Graduate School, College of Education, Department of Instruction and Teacher Education, Program in Secondary Education, Columbia, SC 29208. Offers art education (IMA, MAT); business education (IMA, MAT); English (MAT); foreign language (MAT); health education (MAT); mathematics (MAT); science (IMA, MAT); secondary (Ed D); secondary education (MT, PhD); social studies (MAT); theatre and speech (MAT). IMA and MT offered jointly with the subject areas. *Accreditation:* NCATE. *Degree requirements:* For master's, comprehensive exam, thesis (for some programs), foreign language (MA); for doctorate, one foreign language, comprehensive exam, thesis/dissertation. *Entrance requirements:* For master's, GRE General Test or MAT, teaching certificate (IMA, M Ed), interview; for doctorate, GRE General Test or MAT, interview. *Faculty research:* Middle school programs, professional development, school collaboration.

University of Southern California, Keck School of Medicine and Graduate School, Graduate Programs in Medicine, Department of Preventive Medicine, Master of Public Health Program, Los Angeles, CA 90032. Offers biostatistics and epidemiology (MPH); child and family health (MPH); community health promotion (MPH); environmental health (MPH); geohealth (MPH); global health leadership (MPH); health communication (MPH); health services and policy (MPH). *Accreditation:* CEPH. *Program availability:* Part-time, evening/weekend, 100% online. *Faculty:* 38 full-time (30 women), 10 part-time/adjunct (6 women). *Students:* 213 full-time (164 women), 108 part-time (81 women); includes 195 minority (55 Black or African American, non-Hispanic/Latino; 2 American Indian or Alaska Native, non-Hispanic/Latino; 82 Asian, non-Hispanic/Latino; 56 Hispanic/Latino), 39 international. Average age 28. 460 applicants, 69% accepted, 77 enrolled. In 2018, 130 master's awarded. *Degree requirements:* For master's, practicum, final report, oral presentation. *Entrance requirements:* For master's, GRE General Test, MCAT, GMAT, minimum GPA of 3.0. Additional exam requirements/recommendations for international students: Required—TOEFL (minimum score 600 paper-based; 90 iBT). *Application deadline:* For fall admission, 12/1 priority date for domestic students, 5/1 priority date for international students; for spring admission, 9/1 priority date for domestic and international students; for summer admission, 3/1 for domestic and international students. Applications are processed on a rolling basis. Application fee: $135. Electronic applications accepted. *Financial support:* Career-related internships or fieldwork, Federal Work-Study, institutionally sponsored loans, and scholarships/grants available. Support available to part-time students. Financial award application deadline: 5/4; financial award applicants required to submit CSS PROFILE or FAFSA. *Faculty research:* Cancer and heart disease epidemiology and prevention, mass media and

health communication, effects of air pollution on health, tobacco control, global health. *Total annual research expenditures:* $9.6 million. *Unit head:* Dr. Louise A. Rohrbach, Director, 323-442-8237, Fax: 323-442-8297, E-mail: rohrbac@usc.edu. *Application contact:* Valerie Burris, Admissions Counselor, 323-442-7257, Fax: 323-442-8297, E-mail: valeriem@usc.edu.
Website: https://preventivemedicine.usc.edu/education/graduate-programs/mph/

University of South Florida, Taneja College of Pharmacy, Tampa, FL 33620-9951. Offers pharmaceutical nanotechnology (MS), including biomedical engineering, drug discovery, delivery, development and manufacturing; pharmacy (Pharm D), including pharmacy and health education. *Accreditation:* ACPE. *Faculty:* 32 full-time (18 women), 1 part-time/adjunct (0 women). *Students:* 398 full-time (234 women), 7 part-time (3 women); includes 180 minority (33 Black or African American, non-Hispanic/Latino; 72 Asian, non-Hispanic/Latino; 59 Hispanic/Latino; 2 Native Hawaiian or other Pacific Islander, non-Hispanic/Latino; 14 Two or more races, non-Hispanic/Latino; 13 international. Average age 25. 465 applicants, 44% accepted, 112 enrolled. In 2018, 11 master's, 91 doctorates awarded. *Degree requirements:* For master's, comprehensive exam, thesis optional, capstone or thesis; for doctorate, internship/field experience. *Entrance requirements:* For master's, GRE, MCAT or DAT, Bachelor's preferably in biomedical, biological, chemical sciences or engineering; 2 letters of recommendation; resume; professional statement; interview; for doctorate, PCAT, minimum GPA of 2.75 overall (preferred); completion of 72 prerequisite credit hours; U.S. citizenship or permanent resident; interviews; criminal background check and drug screen. Additional exam requirements/recommendations for international students: Required—TOEFL (minimum score 550 paper-based; 79 iBT), IELTS (minimum score 6.5). *Application deadline:* For fall admission, 6/1 for domestic and international students; for spring admission, 10/15 for domestic students, 9/15 for international students; for summer admission, 2/15 for domestic and international students. Electronic applications accepted. *Expenses:* Tuition, state resident: full-time $6350. Tuition, nonresident: full-time $19,048. *International tuition:* $19,048 full-time. *Required fees:* $2079. *Financial support:* In 2018–19, 159 students received support. *Total annual research expenditures:* $1.4 million. *Unit head:* James Lambert, 813-974-4562, E-mail: jlambert2@usf.edu. *Application contact:* Dr. Amy Schwartz, Associate Dean, 813-974-2251, E-mail: aschwar1@health.usf.edu.

The University of Tennessee, Graduate School, College of Education, Health and Human Sciences, Program in Health Promotion and Health Education, Knoxville, TN 37996. Offers MS. *Program availability:* Part-time. *Degree requirements:* For master's, thesis optional. *Entrance requirements:* For master's, minimum GPA of 2.7. Additional exam requirements/recommendations for international students: Required—TOEFL. Electronic applications accepted.

The University of Tennessee, Graduate School, College of Education, Health and Human Sciences, Program in Safety, Knoxville, TN 37996. Offers MS. *Accreditation:* NCATE. *Program availability:* Part-time. *Degree requirements:* For master's, thesis optional. *Entrance requirements:* For master's, minimum GPA of 2.7. Additional exam requirements/recommendations for international students: Required—TOEFL. Electronic applications accepted.

The University of Texas at Austin, Graduate School, College of Education, Department of Kinesiology and Health Education, Austin, TX 78712-1111. Offers behavioral health (PhD); exercise and sport psychology (M Ed, MA); exercise science (M Ed, MS, PhD); health education (M Ed, MS, Ed D, PhD). *Program availability:* Part-time. Terminal master's awarded for partial completion of doctoral program. *Degree requirements:* For master's, thesis (for some programs); for doctorate, thesis/dissertation. *Entrance requirements:* For master's and doctorate, GRE General Test. Additional exam requirements/recommendations for international students: Required—TOEFL. Electronic applications accepted. *Faculty research:* Health promotion, human performance and exercise biochemistry, motor behavior and biomechanics, sport management, aging and pediatric development.

The University of Texas at San Antonio, College of Education and Human Development, Department of Kinesiology, Health, and Nutrition, San Antonio, TX 78249-0617. Offers health and kinesiology (MS). *Program availability:* Part-time, evening/weekend. *Degree requirements:* For master's, comprehensive exam, thesis optional. *Entrance requirements:* For master's, bachelor's degree with minimum GPA of 3.0 in last 60 hours of coursework; resume; statement of purpose; two letters of recommendation. Additional exam requirements/recommendations for international students: Required—TOEFL (minimum score 550 paper-based; 79 iBT), IELTS (minimum score 6.5). Electronic applications accepted. *Expenses:* Contact institution. *Faculty research:* Childhood obesity, health disparities, community health, exercise physiology, sport psychology.

The University of Texas at Tyler, College of Nursing and Health Sciences, Department of Health and Kinesiology, Tyler, TX 75799-0001. Offers health and kinesiology (M Ed, MA); health sciences (MS); kinesiology (MS). *Accreditation:* TEAC. *Program availability:* Part-time, online learning. *Students:* Average age 29. 44 applicants, 100% accepted, 27 enrolled. In 2018, 13 master's awarded. *Degree requirements:* For master's, comprehensive exam (for some programs), thesis (for some programs). *Entrance requirements:* Additional exam requirements/recommendations for international students: Required—TOEFL. *Application deadline:* For fall admission, 8/17 priority date for domestic students, 7/1 priority date for international students; for spring admission, 12/21 priority date for domestic students, 11/1 priority date for international students. Applications are processed on a rolling basis. Application fee: $25 ($50 for international students). Electronic applications accepted. *Financial support:* In 2018–19, 2 teaching assistantships (averaging $6,000 per year) were awarded; research assistantships, Federal Work-Study, and scholarships/grants also available. Financial award application deadline: 7/1. *Faculty research:* Osteoporosis, muscle soreness, economy of locomotion, adoption of rehabilitation programs, effect of inactivity and aging on muscle blood vessels, territoriality. *Unit head:* Dr. David Criswell, Chair, 903-566-7178, E-mail: dcriswell@uttyler.edu. *Application contact:* Dr. David Criswell, Chair, 903-566-7178, E-mail: dcriswell@uttyler.edu.
Website: https://www.uttyler.edu/hkdept/

The University of Toledo, College of Graduate Studies, College of Health and Human Services, School of Population Health, Toledo, OH 43606-3390. Offers health education (PhD); occupational health-industrial hygiene (MS); public health (MPH).

The University of Toledo, College of Graduate Studies, College of Medicine and Life Sciences, Department of Public Health and Preventative Medicine, Toledo, OH 43606-3390. Offers biostatistics and epidemiology (Certificate); contemporary gerontological practice (Certificate); environmental and occupational health and safety (MPH); epidemiology (Certificate); global public health (Certificate); health promotion and education (MPH); industrial hygiene (MSOH); medical and health science teaching and learning (Certificate); occupational health (Certificate); public health administration (MPH); public health and emergency response (Certificate); public health epidemiology (MPH); public health nutrition (MPH); MD/MPH. *Program availability:* Part-time, evening/weekend. *Degree requirements:* For master's, thesis or alternative. *Entrance requirements:* For master's, GRE, minimum undergraduate GPA of 3.0, three letters of recommendation, statement of purpose, transcripts from all prior institutions attended,

resume; for Certificate, minimum undergraduate GPA of 3.0, three letters of recommendation, statement of purpose, transcripts from all prior institutions attended, resume. Additional exam requirements/recommendations for international students: Required—TOEFL (minimum score 550 paper-based; 80 iBT), IELTS (minimum score 6.5). Electronic applications accepted.

University of Utah, Graduate School, College of Health, Health Promotion and Education Program, Salt Lake City, UT 84112. Offers M Phil, MS, PhD. *Program availability:* Part-time. *Faculty:* 5 full-time (2 women), 9 part-time/adjunct (5 women). *Students:* 38 full-time (32 women), 3 part-time (1 woman); includes 5 minority (1 Black or African American, non-Hispanic/Latino; 1 American Indian or Alaska Native, non-Hispanic/Latino; 2 Asian, non-Hispanic/Latino; 1 Hispanic/Latino), 2 international. Average age 29. 26 applicants, 69% accepted, 16 enrolled. In 2018, 24 master's, 3 doctorates awarded. *Degree requirements:* For master's, comprehensive exam, thesis or alternative, field experience; for doctorate, comprehensive exam, thesis/dissertation, field experience. *Entrance requirements:* For master's, GRE, minimum GPA of 3.0; for doctorate, GRE, minimum GPA of 3.2. Additional exam requirements/recommendations for international students: Required—TOEFL (minimum score 550 paper-based; 80 iBT). *Application deadline:* For fall admission, 1/15 for domestic and international students. Application fee: $55 ($65 for international students). Electronic applications accepted. *Expenses: Tuition, area resident:* Full-time $7190.66; part-time $2112.48 per year. Tuition, state resident: full-time $7190.66. Tuition, nonresident: full-time $25,195. *Required fees:* $558; $555.04 per unit. Tuition and fees vary according to course level, course load, degree level, program and student level. *Financial support:* In 2018–19, 11 students received support, including 3 research assistantships with full tuition reimbursements available (averaging $14,500 per year), 6 teaching assistantships with full tuition reimbursements available (averaging $14,500 per year); health care benefits and unspecified assistantships also available. Financial award application deadline: 3/1; financial award applicants required to submit FAFSA. *Faculty research:* Health behavior and counseling, health service administration, evaluation of health programs. *Unit head:* Dr. Tim Brusseau, Program Director, 801-581-7558, Fax: 801-585-3992, E-mail: tim.brusseau@utah.edu. *Application contact:* Dr. Maria Newton, Director of Graduate Studies, 801-581-7558, Fax: 801-585-3992, E-mail: maria.newton@health.utah.edu.
Website: http://www.health.utah.edu/healthed/index.htm

University of Waterloo, Graduate Studies and Postdoctoral Affairs, Faculty of Applied Health Sciences, School of Public Health and Health Systems, Waterloo, ON N2L 3G1, Canada. Offers health evaluation (MHE); health informatics (MHI); health studies and gerontology (M Sc, PhD); public health (MPH). *Program availability:* Part-time. *Degree requirements:* For master's, thesis; for doctorate, comprehensive exam, thesis/dissertation. *Entrance requirements:* For master's, honors degree, minimum B average, resume, writing sample; for doctorate, GRE (recommended), master's degree, minimum B average, resume, writing sample. Additional exam requirements/recommendations for international students: Required—TOEFL, IELTS, PTE. *Application deadline:* For fall admission, 2/1 for domestic and international students. Application fee: $125 Canadian dollars. Electronic applications accepted. *Financial support:* In 2018–19, teaching assistantships (averaging $6,141 per year) were awarded; research assistantships, career-related internships or fieldwork, Federal Work-Study, institutionally sponsored loans, scholarships/grants, and university-sponsored bursaries also available. *Faculty research:* Population health, health promotion and disease prevention, healthy aging, health policy, planning and evaluation, health information management and health informatics, aging, health and well-being, work and health.
Website: https://uwaterloo.ca/public-health-and-health-systems/

University of Wisconsin–La Crosse, College of Science and Health, Department of Health Education and Health Promotion, Program in Community Health Education, La Crosse, WI 54601-3742. Offers community health education (MS); public health (MPH). *Accreditation:* CEPH. *Degree requirements:* For master's, thesis. *Entrance requirements:* For master's, GRE General Test, GRE Subject Test (for MPH), 3 letters of recommendation. Additional exam requirements/recommendations for international students: Required—TOEFL (minimum score 550 paper-based; 79 iBT). Electronic applications accepted.

University of Wisconsin–La Crosse, College of Science and Health, Department of Health Education and Health Promotion, Program in School Health Education, La Crosse, WI 54601-3742. Offers MS. *Entrance requirements:* For master's, GRE General Test, minimum GPA of 2.85. Additional exam requirements/recommendations for international students: Required—TOEFL (minimum score 550 paper-based; 79 iBT). Electronic applications accepted. *Faculty research:* Adolescent health issues, health education, human sexuality, mental health, stress management, comprehensive school health pedagogy (curriculum, instructional methodology and assessment), PK-12 health literacy, K-12 education, relationship management, substance use and abuse, skill development within health education.

University of Wyoming, College of Health Sciences, Division of Kinesiology and Health, Laramie, WY 82071. Offers MS. *Accreditation:* NCATE. *Program availability:* Part-time, online learning. *Degree requirements:* For master's, comprehensive exam (for some programs), thesis (for some programs). *Entrance requirements:* For master's, GRE General Test, minimum GPA of 3.0. Additional exam requirements/recommendations for international students: Required—TOEFL. Electronic applications accepted. *Expenses:* Tuition, area resident: Full-time $6504; part-time $271 per credit hour. Tuition, state resident: full-time $6504; part-time $271 per credit hour. Tuition, nonresident: full-time $19,464; part-time $811 per credit hour. *International tuition:* $19,464 full-time. *Required fees:* $1410.94; $343.82 per semester. $343.82 per semester. Tuition and fees vary according to course load, program and reciprocity agreements. *Faculty research:* Teacher effectiveness, effects of exercising on heart function, physiological responses of overtraining, psychological benefits of physical activity, health behavior.

Utah State University, School of Graduate Studies, Emma Eccles Jones College of Education and Human Services, Department of Kinesiology and Health Science, Logan, UT 84322. Offers fitness promotion (MS); health and human movement (MS); pathokinesiology (PhD); physical and sport education (M Ed); public health (MPH). *Program availability:* Part-time, evening/weekend, online learning. *Degree requirements:* For master's, thesis (for some programs). *Entrance requirements:* For master's, GRE General Test or MAT, minimum GPA of 3.0. Additional exam requirements/recommendations for international students: Required—TOEFL. *Faculty research:* Sport psychology intervention, motor learning biomechanics, pedagogy, physiology.

Virginia State University, College of Graduate Studies, College of Natural and Health Sciences, Department of Psychology, Petersburg, VA 23806-0001. Offers behavioral and community health sciences (PhD); clinical health psychology (PhD); clinical psychology (MS); general psychology (MS). *Degree requirements:* For master's, one foreign language, thesis. *Entrance requirements:* For master's, GRE General Test.

Walden University, Graduate Programs, School of Health Sciences, Minneapolis, MN 55401. Offers clinical research administration (MS, Graduate Certificate); health education and promotion (MS, PhD), including behavioral health (PhD), disease surveillance (PhD), emergency preparedness (MS), general (MHA, MS), global health (PhD), health policy (PhD), health policy and advocacy (MS), population health (PhD);

health informatics (MS); health services (PhD), including community health, healthcare administration, leadership, public health policy, self-designed; healthcare administration (MHA, DHA), including general (MHA, MS); leadership and organizational development (MHA); public health (MPH, Dr PH, PhD, Graduate Certificate), including community health education (PhD), epidemiology (PhD); systems policy (MHA). *Program availability:* Part-time, evening/weekend, online only, 100% online. *Degree requirements:* For doctorate, thesis/dissertation, residency. *Entrance requirements:* For master's, bachelor's degree or higher; minimum GPA of 2.5; official transcripts; goal statement (for some programs); access to computer and Internet; for doctorate, master's degree or higher; three years of related professional or academic experience (preferred); minimum GPA of 3.0; goal statement and current resume (for select programs); official transcripts; access to computer and Internet; for Graduate Certificate, relevant work experience; access to computer and Internet. Additional exam requirements/recommendations for international students: Required—TOEFL (minimum score 550 paper-based, 79 iBT), IELTS (minimum score 6.5), Michigan English Language Assessment Battery (minimum score 82), or PTE (minimum score 53). Electronic applications accepted.

Washburn University, School of Applied Studies, Department of Allied Health, Topeka, KS 66621. Offers health care education (MHS). *Program availability:* Part-time. *Degree requirements:* For master's, internship, practicum. *Entrance requirements:* For master's, bachelor's degree, two years of professional work experience in a health care environment, official transcripts, minimum cumulative GPA of 3.0 in last 60 hours, personal statement, resume, college algebra course with grade no lower than a C. Additional exam requirements/recommendations for international students: Required—TOEFL (minimum score 80 iBT).

Wayne State University, College of Education, Division of Kinesiology, Health and Sports Studies, Detroit, MI 48202. Offers athletic training (MSAT); health education (M Ed); kinesiology (M Ed, PhD), including exercise and sport science (PhD), physical education and physical activity leadership (PhD); sports administration (MA). *Program availability:* Part-time, evening/weekend. *Faculty:* 9. *Students:* 76 full-time (47 women), 110 part-time (56 women); includes 73 minority (53 Black or African American, non-Hispanic/Latino; 4 Asian, non-Hispanic/Latino; 8 Hispanic/Latino; 8 Two or more races, non-Hispanic/Latino), 9 international. Average age 30. 163 applicants, 60% accepted, 69 enrolled. In 2018, 70 master's, 4 doctorates awarded. *Degree requirements:* For master's, thesis (for some programs); for doctorate, comprehensive exam, thesis/dissertation. *Entrance requirements:* For master's, minimum undergraduate GPA of 3.0; undergraduate degree directly relating to the field of specialization being applied for or one accompanied by extensive educational background in closely-related field; teaching certificates in specific areas (for some programs); for doctorate, minimum undergraduate GPA of 3.0; undergraduate degree directly relating to the field of specialization being applied for or one accompanied by extensive educational background in closely-related field. Additional exam requirements/recommendations for international students: Required—TOEFL (minimum score 550 paper-based; 79 iBT); Recommended—IELTS (minimum score 6.5), TWE (minimum score 5.5), TSE (minimum score 58). *Application deadline:* Applications are processed on a rolling basis. Application fee: $50. Electronic applications accepted. *Financial support:* In 2018–19, 51 students received support. Fellowships with tuition reimbursements available, research assistantships with tuition reimbursements available, teaching assistantships with tuition reimbursements available, scholarships/grants, health care benefits, and unspecified assistantships available. Support available to part-time students. Financial award applicants required to submit FAFSA. *Faculty research:* Exercise and sport science, nutrition and physical activity interventions, school and community health, obesity prevention. *Unit head:* Dr. Nate McCaughtry, Assistant Dean, Division of Kinesiology, Health and Sport Studies/Director, Center for School Health, 313-577-0014, Fax: 313-577-5002, E-mail: aj4391@wayne.edu. *Application contact:* Heather Ladanyi, Manager, 313-577-1191, E-mail: eb3703@wayne.edu.
Website: http://coe.wayne.edu/kinesiology/index.php

Wayne State University, School of Medicine, Office of Biomedical Graduate Programs, Detroit, MI 48201. Offers anatomy and cell biology (MS, PhD); basic medical sciences (MS); biochemistry and molecular biology (MS, PhD); cancer biology (MS, PhD); clinical and translational science (Graduate Certificate); family medicine and public health sciences (MPH, Graduate Certificate), including public health practice; genetic counseling (MS); immunology and microbiology (MS, PhD); medical physics (MS, PhD, Graduate Certificate); medical research (MS); molecular medicine and genomics (MS, PhD), including molecular genetics and genomics; pathology (PhD); pharmacology (MS, PhD); physiology (MS, PhD), including physiology, reproductive sciences (PhD); psychiatry and behavioral neurosciences (PhD), including translational neuroscience; MD/MPH; MD/PhD; MPH/MA; MSW/MPH. *Accreditation:* CEPH. *Program availability:* Part-time, evening/weekend. *Students:* 289 full-time (162 women), 104 part-time (64 women); includes 115 minority (26 Black or African American, non-Hispanic/Latino; 2 American Indian or Alaska Native, non-Hispanic/Latino; 67 Asian, non-Hispanic/Latino; 9 Hispanic/Latino; 1 Native Hawaiian or other Pacific Islander, non-Hispanic/Latino; 10 Two or more races, non-Hispanic/Latino), 30 international. Average age 27. 1,255 applicants, 21% accepted, 174 enrolled. In 2018, 70 master's, 25 doctorates, 10 other advanced degrees awarded. Terminal master's awarded for partial completion of doctoral program. *Degree requirements:* For master's, thesis (for some programs); for doctorate, thesis/dissertation. *Entrance requirements:* For master's, GRE or equivalent graduate standardized test (MCAT, DAT, etc.) where applicable; for doctorate, GRE or MCAT where applicable; for Graduate Certificate, GRE. Additional exam requirements/recommendations for international students: Required—TOEFL (minimum score 550 paper-based; 100 iBT), Michigan English Language Assessment Battery (minimum score 85); Recommended—IELTS (minimum score 6.5), TWE (minimum score 5.5). *Application deadline:* For fall admission, 2/1 for domestic and international students. Applications are processed on a rolling basis. Application fee: $50. Electronic applications accepted. *Expenses:* $845.26 per credit hour tuition; $54.56 Student service fee per credit hour & $315.70 registration fee per term. *Financial support:* In 2018–19, 177 students received support, including 64 fellowships with full tuition reimbursements available (averaging $24,388 per year), 79 research assistantships with full tuition reimbursements available (averaging $26,894 per year); scholarships/grants, traineeships, and health care benefits also available. Financial award applicants required to submit FAFSA. *Faculty research:* Cancer biology, neurosciences, vision sciences, molecular biology, pathology, physiology, pharmacology, public health, medical physics. *Unit head:* Dr. Daniel A. Walz, Associate Dean for Biomedical Graduate Programs, 313-577-1455, Fax: 313-577-8796, E-mail: gradprogs@med.wayne.edu. *Application contact:* Dr. Daniel A. Walz, Associate Dean for Biomedical Graduate Programs, 313-577-1455, Fax: 313-577-8796, E-mail: gradprogs@med.wayne.edu.
Website: https://gradprograms.med.wayne.edu/

Western Illinois University, School of Graduate Studies, College of Education and Human Services, Department of Health Sciences and Social Work, Macomb, IL 61455-1390. Offers health sciences (MS), including public health, school health. *Accreditation:* NCATE. *Program availability:* Part-time. *Students:* 37 full-time (25 women), 18 part-time (14 women); includes 17 minority (11 Black or African American, non-Hispanic/Latino; 6 Hispanic/Latino), 20 international. Average age 31. 38 applicants, 82% accepted, 12 enrolled. In 2018, 12 master's awarded. *Degree requirements:* For master's, comprehensive exam, thesis or alternative. *Entrance requirements:* Additional exam requirements/recommendations for international students: Required—TOEFL (minimum score 550 paper-based; 80 iBT). *Application deadline:* Applications are processed on a rolling basis. Application fee: $30. Electronic applications accepted. *Financial support:* Unspecified assistantships available. Financial award applicants required to submit FAFSA. *Unit head:* Dr. Lorette Oden, Chairperson, 309-298-1076. *Application contact:* Dr. Mark Mossman, Associate Provost and Director of Graduate Studies, 309-298-1806, Fax: 309-298-2345, E-mail: grad-office@wiu.edu.
Website: http://www.wiu.edu/coehs/health_sciences/

Western Michigan University, Graduate College, College of Health and Human Services, Department of Interdisciplinary Health and Human Services, Kalamazoo, MI 49008. Offers interdisciplinary health services (PhD).

Western Oregon University, Graduate Programs, College of Education, Division of Teacher Education, Program in Secondary Education, Monmouth, OR 97361. Offers bilingual education (MS Ed); health (MS Ed); humanities (MAT, MS Ed); initial licensure (MAT); mathematics (MAT, MS Ed); science (MAT, MS Ed); social science (MAT, MS Ed). *Accreditation:* NCATE. *Program availability:* Part-time, evening/weekend. *Degree requirements:* For master's, thesis optional, written exam. *Entrance requirements:* For master's, minimum GPA of 3.0, teaching license. Additional exam requirements/recommendations for international students: Required—TOEFL (minimum score 550 paper-based; 79 iBT), IELTS (minimum score 6.5). *Faculty research:* Literacy, science in primary grades, geography education, retention, teacher burnout.

Western University of Health Sciences, College of Health Sciences, Program in Health Sciences, Pomona, CA 91766-1854. Offers MS. *Program availability:* Blended/hybrid learning. *Faculty:* 3 full-time (all women), 4 part-time/adjunct (all women). *Students:* 16 full-time (13 women), 6 part-time (all women); includes 16 minority (4 Black or African American, non-Hispanic/Latino; 2 Asian, non-Hispanic/Latino; 7 Hispanic/Latino; 3 Two or more races, non-Hispanic/Latino), 1 international. Average age 36. 15 applicants, 40% accepted, 4 enrolled. In 2018, 10 master's awarded. *Degree requirements:* For master's, thesis (for some programs). *Entrance requirements:* For master's, GRE (minimum score of 3.5 on analytical writing), bachelor's degree (preferred); minimum undergraduate GPA of 2.7, graduate 3.0; letters of recommendation; statement of purpose; current curriculum vitae. Additional exam requirements/recommendations for international students: Required—TOEFL (minimum score 450 paper-based). *Application deadline:* For fall admission, 6/30 priority date for domestic students, 6/30 for international students. Applications are processed on a rolling basis. Application fee: $35. Electronic applications accepted. *Expenses:* $636.00 per unit. *Financial support:* In 2018–19, 5 students received support. Scholarships/grants available. Financial award application deadline: 3/2; financial award applicants required to submit FAFSA. *Faculty research:* Women's health, community based participatory research, global health, central Asia health and politics. *Unit head:* Dr. Gail Evans Grayson, Chair, 909-706-3796, Fax: 909-469-5407, E-mail: gevans@westernu.edu. *Application contact:* Susan Hanson, Executive Director of Admissions for the College of Osteopathic Medicine of the Pacific and for Health Professions Education, 909-469-5335, Fax: 909-469-5570, E-mail: admissions@westernu.edu.
Website: http://prospective.westernu.edu/health-sciences/welcome-3/

Widener University, School of Human Service Professions, Center for Education, Chester, PA 19013-5792. Offers adult education (M Ed); counseling in higher education (M Ed); counselor education (M Ed); early childhood education (M Ed); educational foundations (M Ed); educational leadership (M Ed); educational psychology (M Ed); elementary education (M Ed); English and language arts (M Ed); health education (M Ed); higher education leadership (Ed D); home and school visitor (M Ed); human sexuality (M Ed, PhD); mathematics education (M Ed); middle school education (M Ed); principalship (M Ed); reading and language arts (Ed D); reading education (M Ed); school administration (Ed D); science education (M Ed); social studies education (M Ed); special education (M Ed); technology education (M Ed). *Accreditation:* NCATE. *Program availability:* Part-time, evening/weekend. Terminal master's awarded for partial completion of doctoral program. *Degree requirements:* For doctorate, thesis/dissertation. *Entrance requirements:* For master's, minimum GPA of 2.5; for doctorate, GRE or MAT, minimum GPA of 2.0 (undergraduate), 3.5 (graduate). Electronic applications accepted. *Expenses:* Contact institution. *Faculty research:* Reading and cognition, adult education, technology education, educational leadership, special education.

Worcester State University, Graduate School, Department of Education, Worcester, MA 01602-2597. Offers adult English as a esl (Postbaccalaureate Certificate); curriculum and instruction (Ed S); early childhood education (M Ed); education (M Ed); elementary education (M Ed); English as a second language (M Ed, Postbaccalaureate Certificate); middle school education (M Ed); middle/secondary school education (Postbaccalaureate Certificate); moderate disabilities (M Ed, Postbaccalaureate Certificate); reading (M Ed, Postbaccalaureate Certificate); reading specialist (Postbaccalaureate Certificate); school leadership and education administration (M Ed); school psychology (M Ed, Ed S); secondary education (M Ed, Ed S, Postbaccalaureate Certificate). *Faculty:* 10 full-time (9 women), 23 part-time/adjunct (11 women). *Students:* 38 full-time (33 women), 281 part-time (212 women); includes 30 minority (4 Black or African American, non-Hispanic/Latino; 3 American Indian or Alaska Native, non-Hispanic/Latino; 2 Asian, non-Hispanic/Latino; 16 Hispanic/Latino; 5 Two or more races, non-Hispanic/Latino), 2 international. Average age 41. 102 applicants, 98% accepted, 88 enrolled. In 2018, 132 master's, 52 Ed Ss awarded. *Degree requirements:* For master's, comprehensive exam (for some programs), thesis (for some programs). For a detail list of degree completion requirements please see the graduate catalog at catalog.worcester.edu. *Entrance requirements:* For master's, GRE General Test, MAT or GMAT, teaching certificate. For a detail list of entrance requirements please see the graduate catalog at catalog.worcester.edu. Additional exam requirements/recommendations for international students: Required—TOEFL (minimum score 550 paper-based; 79 iBT), PTE. *Application deadline:* For fall admission, 3/1 for domestic and international students; for spring admission, 11/1 for domestic and international students; for summer admission, 3/1 for domestic and international students. Applications are processed on a rolling basis. Application fee: $50. Electronic applications accepted. *Expenses: Tuition, area resident:* Full-time $3042; part-time $169 per credit hour. *Tuition, state resident:* Full-time $3042; part-time $169 per credit hour. Tuition, nonresident: full-time $3042; part-time $169 per credit hour. *International tuition:* $3042 full-time. *Required fees:* $2754; $153 per credit hour. *Financial support:* Career-related internships or fieldwork, scholarships/grants, and unspecified assistantships available. Support available to part-time students. Financial award application deadline: 3/1; financial award applicants required to submit FAFSA. *Unit head:* Dr. Sara Young, Graduate Program Coordinator, 508-929-8246, Fax: 508-929-8164, E-mail: syoung3@worcester.edu. *Application contact:* Sara Grady, Associate Dean of Graduate and Continuing Education, 508-929-8130, Fax: 508-929-8100, E-mail: sara.grady@worcester.edu.

Wright State University, Boonshoft School of Medicine, Department of Population and Public Health Sciences, Dayton, OH 45435. Offers health promotion and education (MPH). *Accreditation:* CEPH.

Home Economics Education

Alabama Agricultural and Mechanical University, School of Graduate Studies, College of Education, Humanities, and Behavioral Sciences, Department of Educational Leadership and Secondary Education, Huntsville, AL 35811. Offers biology (M Ed); business/marketing education (M Ed, Ed S); chemistry (M Ed); collaborative teacher secondary education (M Ed, Ed S); education (M Ed, Ed S); English language arts (M Ed); family/consumer science education (M Ed, Ed S); general science (M Ed); general social science (M Ed); mathematics (M Ed, Ed S); physics (M Ed, Ed S); technology education (M Ed). *Accreditation:* NCATE. *Program availability:* Evening/weekend. *Degree requirements:* For master's, comprehensive exam; for Ed S, thesis. *Entrance requirements:* For master's, GRE General Test. Additional exam requirements/recommendations for international students: Required—TOEFL (minimum score 500 paper-based; 61 iBT). Electronic applications accepted. *Faculty research:* World peace through education, computer-assisted instruction.

Central Washington University, School of Graduate Studies and Research, College of Education and Professional Studies, Department of Family and Consumer Sciences, Ellensburg, WA 98926. Offers career and technical education (MS); family and child life (MS); family and consumer sciences education (MS). *Program availability:* Part-time. *Entrance requirements:* For master's, minimum GPA of 3.0. Additional exam requirements/recommendations for international students: Required—TOEFL (minimum score 550 paper-based; 79 iBT). Electronic applications accepted.

Eastern Kentucky University, The Graduate School, College of Education, Department of Curriculum and Instruction, Program in Secondary and Higher Education, Richmond, KY 40475-3102. Offers secondary education (MA Ed), including agricultural education, art education, biological sciences education, business education, English education, geography education, history education, home economics education, industrial education, mathematical sciences education, physical education, school health education. *Accreditation:* NCATE. *Program availability:* Part-time. *Entrance requirements:* For master's, GRE General Test, minimum GPA of 2.5.

Louisiana State University and Agricultural & Mechanical College, Graduate School, College of Human Sciences and Education, School of Human Resource Education and Workforce Development, Baton Rouge, LA 70803. Offers agriculture and extension education and youth development (MS, PhD); career and technical education (MS, PhD); comprehensive vocational education (MS, PhD); extension and international education (MS, PhD); human resource and leadership development (MS, PhD); industrial education (MS); vocational agriculture education (MS, PhD); vocational business education (MS); vocational home economics education (MS). *Accreditation:* NCATE.

Montana State University, The Graduate School, College of Education, Health, and Human Development, Department of Health and Human Development, Bozeman, MT 59717. Offers family and consumer sciences (MS). *Accreditation:* ACA. *Program availability:* Part-time, online learning. *Degree requirements:* For master's, comprehensive exam. *Entrance requirements:* For master's, GRE (minimum scores: verbal 480; quantitative 480). Additional exam requirements/recommendations for international students: Required—TOEFL (minimum score 550 paper-based). Electronic applications accepted. *Faculty research:* Community food systems, ethic of care for teachers and coaches, influence of public policy on families and communities, cost effectiveness of early childhood education, exercise metabolism, winter sport performance enhancement, assessment of physical activity.

Purdue University, Graduate School, College of Education, Department of Curriculum and Instruction, West Lafayette, IN 47907. Offers agricultural and extension education (MS, MS Ed, PhD, Ed S); art education (PhD); career and technical education (MS Ed, PhD, Ed S); curriculum studies (MS Ed, PhD, Ed S); educational technology (MS Ed, PhD, Ed S); elementary education (MS Ed); family and consumer sciences education (MS Ed, PhD, Ed S); foreign language education (MS Ed, PhD, Ed S); industrial technology (PhD, Ed S); language arts (MS Ed, PhD, Ed S); literacy (MS Ed, PhD, Ed S); mathematics education (MS, MS Ed, PhD, Ed S); science education (MS, MS Ed, PhD, Ed S); social studies education (MS Ed, PhD, Ed S). *Accreditation:* NCATE. *Program availability:* Part-time, evening/weekend, online learning. *Faculty:* 34 full-time (24 women), 3 part-time/adjunct (1 woman). *Students:* 75 full-time (52 women), 357 part-time (271 women); includes 83 minority (29 Black or African American, non-Hispanic/Latino; 1 American Indian or Alaska Native, non-Hispanic/Latino; 14 Asian, non-Hispanic/Latino; 29 Hispanic/Latino; 1 Native Hawaiian or other Pacific Islander, non-Hispanic/Latino; 9 Two or more races, non-Hispanic/Latino), 43 international. Average age 36. 169 applicants, 83% accepted, 102 enrolled. In 2018, 141 master's, 15 doctorates awarded. *Degree requirements:* For master's, thesis optional; for doctorate, thesis/dissertation, oral and written exams; for Ed S, oral presentation, project. *Entrance requirements:* For master's, GRE General Test (if undergraduate GPA is below 3.0), minimum undergraduate GPA of 3.0 or equivalent; for doctorate, GRE General Test (minimum combined verbal and quantitative score of 1000, 300 for new scoring), minimum undergraduate GPA of 3.0 or equivalent; master's degree with minimum GPA of 3.0 or equivalent; for Ed S, GRE General Test (minimum combined verbal and quantitative score of 1000, 300 for new scoring), minimum undergraduate GPA of 3.0 or equivalent; master's degree. Additional exam requirements/recommendations for international students: Required—TOEFL (minimum score 550 paper-based; 77 iBT). *Application deadline:* For fall admission, 12/15 for domestic students, 3/1 for international students; for spring admission, 9/15 for domestic students, 8/1 for international students. Application fee: $60 ($75 for international students). Electronic applications accepted. *Financial support:* Fellowships with full tuition reimbursements, research assistantships with full tuition reimbursements, teaching assistantships with full tuition reimbursements, career-related internships or fieldwork, and tuition waivers (full) available. Support available to part-time students. Financial award application deadline: 3/1; financial award applicants required to submit FAFSA. *Faculty research:* Literacy acquisition and development, teacher beliefs and knowledge, recruitment and retention of underrepresented students, economic education, literacy discourse. *Unit head:* Janet M. Alsup, Head, 765-494-9667, E-mail: alsupj@purdue.edu. *Application contact:* Heather Brinkman, Graduate Contact, 765-494-2345, E-mail: hbrinkma@purdue.edu. Website: http://www.edci.purdue.edu/

South Carolina State University, College of Graduate and Professional Studies, Department of Education, Orangeburg, SC 29117-0001. Offers early childhood education (MAT); education (M Ed); elementary education (M Ed, MAT); English (MAT); general science/biology (MAT); mathematics (MAT); secondary education (M Ed), including biology education, business education, counselor education, English education, home economics education, industrial education, mathematics education, science education, social studies education; special education (M Ed), including

emotionally handicapped, learning disabilities, mentally handicapped. *Accreditation:* NCATE. *Program availability:* Part-time, evening/weekend. *Faculty:* 17 full-time (6 women), 12 part-time/adjunct (5 women). *Students:* 42 full-time (32 women), 93 part-time (64 women); includes 121 minority (119 Black or African American, non-Hispanic/Latino; 2 Asian, non-Hispanic/Latino), 2 international. Average age 40. 50 applicants, 98% accepted, 39 enrolled. In 2018, 9 master's awarded. *Degree requirements:* For master's, thesis optional, departmental qualifying exam. *Entrance requirements:* For master's, GRE General Test, NTE, interview, teaching certificate. *Application deadline:* For fall admission, 6/15 priority date for domestic students, 6/15 for international students; for spring admission, 11/1 for domestic and international students. Application fee: $25. Electronic applications accepted. *Expenses: Tuition, area resident:* Full-time $9928; part-time $552 per credit hour. Tuition, state resident: full-time $9928. Tuition, nonresident: full-time $21,038; part-time $1169 per credit hour. *Required fees:* $1532; $85 per credit hour. *Financial support:* Fellowships, career-related internships or fieldwork, Federal Work-Study, and scholarships/grants available. Financial award application deadline: 6/1. *Unit head:* Dr. Charlie Spell, Chair, Department of Education, 803-536-8963, Fax: 803-516-4568, E-mail: cspell@scsu.edu. *Application contact:* Curtis Foskey, Coordinator of Graduate Studies, 803-536-8419, Fax: 803-536-8812, E-mail: cfoskey@scsu.edu.

Texas Tech University, Graduate School, College of Human Sciences, Program in Family and Consumer Sciences Education, Lubbock, TX 79409-1161. Offers MS, PhD. *Program availability:* Part-time, evening/weekend, 100% online, blended/hybrid learning. *Students:* 4 full-time (3 women), 50 part-time (45 women); includes 7 minority (2 Black or African American, non-Hispanic/Latino; 4 Hispanic/Latino; 1 Two or more races, non-Hispanic/Latino). Average age 38. 13 applicants, 85% accepted, 8 enrolled. In 2018, 2 master's, 1 doctorate awarded. *Degree requirements:* For master's, comprehensive exam, thesis or alternative; for doctorate, comprehensive exam, thesis/dissertation. *Entrance requirements:* Additional exam requirements/recommendations for international students: Required—TOEFL (minimum score 550 paper-based; 79 iBT). *Application deadline:* For fall admission, 6/1 priority date for domestic students, 1/15 priority date for international students; for spring admission, 9/1 priority date for domestic students, 6/15 priority date for international students. Applications are processed on a rolling basis. Application fee: $65. Electronic applications accepted. *Expenses:* Contact institution. *Financial support:* In 2018–19, 23 students received support, including 23 fellowships (averaging $3,299 per year); research assistantships, teaching assistantships, and scholarships/grants also available. Financial award application deadline: 1/15; financial award applicants required to submit FAFSA. *Faculty research:* Content literacy, Implementation of Programs of Study, Instructional Practices for Working with Limited English Proficiency Students in FCS, Mobile technologies with FCS Instruction. *Total annual research expenditures:* $47,243. *Unit head:* Dr. Karen Alexander, Program Chair, Graduate Program Coordinator, Associate Professor, CCFCS Interim Director, 806-834-2212, Fax: 806-742-1849, E-mail: karen.alexander@ttu.edu. *Application contact:* Ashlee Murden, FCSE Business Coordinator, 806-834-4140, Fax: 806-742-1849, E-mail: ashlee.murden@ttu.edu. Website: www.depts.ttu.edu/hs/fcse/

The University of British Columbia, Faculty of Education, Department of Curriculum and Pedagogy, Vancouver, BC V6T 1Z4, Canada. Offers art education (M Ed, MA); curriculum studies (M Ed, MA, PhD); home economics education (M Ed, MA); mathematics education (M Ed, MA); media and technology studies education (M Ed, MA); music education (M Ed, MA); physical education (M Ed, MA); science education (M Ed, MA); social studies education (M Ed, MA). *Program availability:* Part-time, online learning. *Degree requirements:* For master's, thesis (MA); for doctorate, comprehensive exam, thesis/dissertation. *Entrance requirements:* Additional exam requirements/recommendations for international students: Required—TOEFL, IELTS. Electronic applications accepted. *Expenses:* Contact institution. *Faculty research:* School subjects, teaching and learning.

University of Nebraska–Lincoln, Graduate College, College of Education and Human Sciences, Department of Child, Youth and Family Studies, Lincoln, NE 68588. Offers child development/early childhood education (MS, PhD); child, youth and family studies (MS); family and consumer sciences education (MS, PhD); family financial planning (MS); family science (MS, PhD); gerontology (PhD); human sciences (PhD), including child, youth and family studies, gerontology, medical family therapy; marriage and family therapy (MS); medical family therapy (PhD); youth development (MS). *Accreditation:* AAMFT/COAMFTE (one or more programs are accredited). *Program availability:* Online learning. *Degree requirements:* For master's, thesis optional. *Entrance requirements:* For master's, GRE. Additional exam requirements/recommendations for international students: Required—TOEFL (minimum score 550 paper-based). Electronic applications accepted. *Faculty research:* Marriage and family therapy, child development/early childhood education, family financial management.

Utah State University, School of Graduate Studies, College of Agriculture and Applied Sciences, School of Applied Sciences, Technology and Education, Logan, UT 84322. Offers agricultural extension and education (MS); family and consumer sciences education and extension (MS); technology and engineering education (MS). *Program availability:* Part-time, online learning. *Degree requirements:* For master's, comprehensive exam (for some programs), thesis (for some programs). *Entrance requirements:* For master's, GRE General Test, MAT, BS in agricultural education, agricultural extension, or related agricultural or science discipline; minimum GPA of 3.0. Additional exam requirements/recommendations for international students: Required—TOEFL. *Faculty research:* Extension and adult education; structures and environment; low-input agriculture; farm safety, systems, and mechanizations.

Wayne State College, School of Education and Counseling, Department of Educational Foundations and Leadership, Program in Curriculum and Instruction, Wayne, NE 68787. Offers alternative education (MSE); business and information technology education (MSE); communication arts education (MSE); early childhood education (MSE); elementary education (MSE); English as a second language (MSE); English education (MSE); family and consumer sciences education (MSE); industrial technology and vocational education (MSE); learning communities (MSE); mathematics education (MSE); music education (MSE); science education (MSE); social science education (MSE). *Accreditation:* NCATE. *Program availability:* Part-time, evening/weekend. *Degree requirements:* For master's, comprehensive exam, thesis optional. *Entrance requirements:* For master's, GRE General Test. Additional exam requirements/recommendations for international students: Required—TOEFL (minimum score 550 paper-based).

Mathematics Education

Adams State University, Office of Graduate Studies, Department of Teacher Education, Alamosa, CO 81101. Offers teacher education (MA), including adaptive leadership, curriculum and instruction, curriculum and instruction-STEM, educational leadership. *Program availability:* Part-time, online learning. *Degree requirements:* For master's, qualifying exam. *Entrance requirements:* For master's, GRE General Test or MAT, minimum undergraduate GPA of 3.0.

Alabama Agricultural and Mechanical University, School of Graduate Studies, College of Education, Humanities, and Behavioral Sciences, Department of Educational Leadership and Secondary Education, Huntsville, AL 35811. Offers biology (M Ed); business/marketing education (M Ed, Ed S); chemistry (M Ed); collaborative teacher secondary education (M Ed, Ed S); education (M Ed, Ed S); English language arts (M Ed); family/consumer science education (M Ed, Ed S); general science (M Ed); general social science (M Ed); mathematics (M Ed, Ed S); physics (M Ed, Ed S); technology education (M Ed). *Accreditation:* NCATE. *Program availability:* Evening/weekend. *Degree requirements:* For master's, comprehensive exam; for Ed S, thesis. *Entrance requirements:* For master's, GRE General Test. Additional exam requirements/recommendations for international students: Required—TOEFL (minimum score 500 paper-based; 61 iBT). Electronic applications accepted. *Faculty research:* World peace through education, computer-assisted instruction.

Alabama State University, College of Education, Department of Curriculum and Instruction, Montgomery, AL 36101-0271. Offers early childhood education (Ed S); secondary education (M Ed), including biology education, English language arts education, history education, math education, music education, reading education, social science education. *Program availability:* Part-time, evening/weekend, online only, 100% online. *Faculty:* 7 full-time (4 women), 7 part-time/adjunct (4 women). *Students:* 22 full-time (19 women), 58 part-time (49 women); includes 235 minority (234 Black or African American, non-Hispanic/Latino; 1 Hispanic/Latino), 5 international. Average age 36. 45 applicants, 33% accepted, 6 enrolled. In 2018, 34 master's awarded. *Degree requirements:* For master's, comprehensive exam, thesis optional; for Ed S, comprehensive exam, thesis. *Entrance requirements:* For master's, GRE General Test, MAT, writing competency test; for Ed S, writing competency test, GRE, MAT. Additional exam requirements/recommendations for international students: Required—TOEFL (minimum score 500 paper-based). *Application deadline:* For fall admission, 4/15 for domestic and international students; for spring admission, 11/15 for domestic and international students; for summer admission, 3/15 for domestic and international students. Applications are processed on a rolling basis. Application fee: $25. Electronic applications accepted. *Expenses:* Contact institution. *Financial support:* Fellowships, teaching assistantships, career-related internships or fieldwork, scholarships/grants, tuition waivers (partial), and unspecified assistantships available. Financial award application deadline: 6/30; financial award applicants required to submit FAFSA. *Unit head:* Dr. Joyce Johnson, Acting Chairperson, 334-229-4485, Fax: 334-229-5603, E-mail: jjohnson@alasu.edu. *Application contact:* Dr. Ed Brown, Dean of Graduate Studies, 334-229-4274, Fax: 334-229-4928, E-mail: ebrown@alasu.edu.
Website: http://www.alasu.edu/academics/colleges—departments/college-of-education/curriculum—instruction/index.aspx

American University of Beirut, Graduate Programs, Faculty of Arts and Sciences, Beirut 1107 2020, Lebanon. Offers anthropology (MA); Arab and Middle Eastern history (PhD); Arabic language and literature (MA, PhD); archaeology (MA); art history and curating (MA); biology (MS); cell and molecular biology (PhD); chemistry (MS); clinical psychology (MA); computational sciences (MS); computer science (MS); economics (MA); education (MA), including administration and policy studies, elementary education, mathematics education, psychology school guidance, psychology test and measurements, science education, teaching English as a foreign language; English language (MA); English literature (MA); environmental policy planning (MS); financial economics (MAFE); general psychology (MA); geology (MS); history (MA); Islamic studies (MA); mathematics (MS); media studies (MA); Middle East studies (MA); philosophy (MA); physics (MS); political studies (MA); public administration (MA); public policy and international affairs (MA); sociology (MA); theoretical physics (PhD). *Program availability:* Part-time. *Faculty:* 187 full-time (64 women), 27 part-time/adjunct (15 women). *Students:* 292 full-time (215 women), 216 part-time (148 women). Average age 27. 422 applicants, 64% accepted, 124 enrolled. In 2018, 90 master's, 3 doctorates awarded. *Degree requirements:* For master's, comprehensive exam, thesis (for some programs), project; for doctorate, comprehensive exam, thesis/dissertation (for some programs). *Entrance requirements:* For master's, GRE General Test (for archaeology, clinical psychology, general psychology, economics, financial economics and biology); for doctorate, GRE General Test for all PhD programs, GRE Subject Test for theoretical physics. Additional exam requirements/recommendations for international students: Required—TOEFL (minimum score 583 paper-based; 97 iBT), IELTS (minimum score 7). *Application deadline:* For fall admission, 3/18 for domestic students; for spring admission, 11/5 for domestic students. Application fee: $50. Electronic applications accepted. *Expenses:* MA/MS: Humanities and social sciences=$912/credit. Sciences=$943/credit. Financial economics=$986/credit. Thesis: Humanities/social sciences=$6565 and sciences=$6865. *Financial support:* In 2018–19, 227 fellowships with full tuition reimbursements, 17 research assistantships with full tuition reimbursements, 83 teaching assistantships with full tuition reimbursements were awarded; scholarships/grants, tuition waivers (full and partial), and unspecified assistantships also available. Financial award application deadline: 3/18. *Faculty research:* Sciences: Physics: High energy, Particle, Polymer and Soft Matter, Thermal, Plasma; String Theory, Mathematical physics, Astrophysics (stellar evolution, planet and galaxy formation and evolution, astrophysical dynamics), Solid State physics/thin films, Spintronics, Magnetic properties of materials, Mineralogy, Petrology, and Geochemistry of Hard Rocks, Geophysics and Petrophysics, Hydrogeology, Micropaleontology, Sedimentology, and Stratigraphy, Structural Geology and Geotectonics, Renewable en. *Total annual research expenditures:* $4.3 million. *Unit head:* Dr. Nadia Maria El Cheikh, Dean, Faculty of Arts and Sciences, 961-1-350000 Ext. 3800, Fax: 961-1-744461, E-mail: nmcheikh@aub.edu.lb. *Application contact:* Adriana Michelle Zanaty, Curriculum and Graduate Studies Officer, 961-1-350000 Ext. 3833, Fax: 961-1-744461, E-mail: az48@aub.edu.lb.
Website: https://www.aub.edu.lb/fas/Pages/default.aspx

Appalachian State University, Cratis D. Williams School of Graduate Studies, Department of Curriculum and Instruction, Boone, NC 28608. Offers curriculum specialist (MA); educational media (MA); elementary education (MA); middle grades education (MA), including language arts, mathematics, science, social studies. *Accreditation:* NCATE. *Program availability:* Part-time, evening/weekend, online learning. *Degree requirements:* For master's, comprehensive exam, thesis or alternative. *Entrance requirements:* For master's, GRE General Test or MAT, 3 letters of recommendation. Additional exam requirements/recommendations for international students: Required—TOEFL (minimum score 570 paper-based; 79 iBT), IELTS (minimum score 6.5). Electronic applications accepted. *Expenses: Tuition, area resident:* Full-time $4839; part-time $237 per credit hour. Tuition, state resident: full-time $4839; part-time $237 per credit hour. Tuition, nonresident: full-time $18,271; part-time $895.50 per credit hour. *Faculty research:* Media literacy, elementary teaching, curriculum development, online learning environments.

Arcadia University, School of Education, Glenside, PA 19038-3295. Offers art education (M Ed); computer education (CAS); curriculum (CAS); curriculum studies (M Ed); early childhood education (M Ed), including individualized, master teacher, research in child development; educational leadership (M Ed, Ed D, CAS); elementary education (M Ed); English education (MA Ed); environmental education (MA Ed); instructional technology (M Ed); language arts (M Ed); library science (M Ed); mathematics education (M Ed, MA Ed); music education (MA Ed); psychology (MA Ed); reading (M Ed, CAS); science education (M Ed, CAS); secondary education (M Ed, CAS); special education (M Ed, Ed D, CAS); theater arts (MA Ed); written communication (MA Ed). *Accreditation:* NASAD. *Program availability:* Part-time, evening/weekend, online learning. *Faculty:* 14 full-time (10 women). *Students:* 35 full-time (24 women), 299 part-time (243 women); includes 72 minority (49 Black or African American, non-Hispanic/Latino; 1 American Indian or Alaska Native, non-Hispanic/Latino; 12 Asian, non-Hispanic/Latino; 8 Hispanic/Latino; 2 Two or more races, non-Hispanic/Latino), 5 international. In 2018, 152 master's, 8 doctorates awarded. *Entrance requirements:* Additional exam requirements/recommendations for international students: Required—Official results from the TOEFL or IELTS are required. *Application deadline:* Applications are processed on a rolling basis. Application fee: $25. Electronic applications accepted. *Expenses:* Contact institution. *Financial support:* Career-related internships or fieldwork, tuition waivers (partial), and unspecified assistantships available. *Unit head:* Kimberly Dean, Chair, 215-572-8629. *Application contact:* 215-572-2925, Fax: 215-572-2126, E-mail: grad@arcadia.edu.

Arizona State University at the Tempe campus, College of Liberal Arts and Sciences, School of Mathematical and Statistical Sciences, Tempe, AZ 85287-1804. Offers applied mathematics (PhD); mathematics (MA, PhD); mathematics education (PhD); statistics (MS, PhD, Graduate Certificate). *Program availability:* Part-time. Terminal master's awarded for partial completion of doctoral program. *Degree requirements:* For master's, thesis or alternative, interactive Program of Study (iPOS) submitted before completing 50 percent of required credit hours; for doctorate, comprehensive exam, thesis/dissertation, interactive Program of Study (iPOS) submitted before completing 50 percent of required credit hours. *Entrance requirements:* For master's and doctorate, GRE General Test, minimum GPA of 3.0 or equivalent in last 2 years of work leading to bachelor's degree. Additional exam requirements/recommendations for international students: Required—TOEFL, IELTS, or PTE. Electronic applications accepted. *Expenses:* Contact institution.

Arkansas State University, Graduate School, College of Sciences and Mathematics, Department of Mathematics and Statistics, State University, AR 72467. Offers mathematics (MS); mathematics education (MSE). *Program availability:* Part-time. *Degree requirements:* For master's, comprehensive exam, thesis or alternative. *Entrance requirements:* For master's, GRE General Test or MAT, appropriate bachelor's degree, official transcripts, immunization records, valid teaching certificate (for MSE). Additional exam requirements/recommendations for international students: Required—TOEFL (minimum score 550 paper-based; 79 iBT), IELTS (minimum score 6), PTE (minimum score 56). Electronic applications accepted.

Asbury University, School of Graduate and Professional Studies, Wilmore, KY 40390-1198. Offers biology: alternative certificate (MA Ed); chemistry: alternative certificate (MA Ed); English (MA Ed); English as a second language (MA Ed); ESL (MA Ed); French (MA Ed); Latin: alternative certificate (MA Ed); mathematics: alternative certificate (MA Ed); reading/writing endorsement (MA Ed); social studies (MA Ed); social work (MSW), including child and family services; Spanish (MA Ed); special education (MA Ed); special education: alternative certificate (MA Ed); teacher as leader endorsement (MA Ed). *Accreditation:* NCATE. *Program availability:* Part-time. *Degree requirements:* For master's, action research project, portfolio. *Entrance requirements:* For master's, PRAXIS/NTE, minimum GPA of 2.75, letters of recommendation. Additional exam requirements/recommendations for international students: Required—TOEFL (minimum score 550 paper-based). Electronic applications accepted.

Aurora University, School of Arts and Sciences, Aurora, IL 60506-4892. Offers homeland security (MS); mathematics (MS); mathematics and science education for elementary teachers (MA); mathematics education (MA); science education (MA). *Program availability:* Part-time, evening/weekend, 100% online. *Faculty:* 3 full-time (1 woman), 10 part-time/adjunct (4 women). *Students:* 9 full-time (4 women), 76 part-time (52 women); includes 13 minority (6 Black or African American, non-Hispanic/Latino; 1 Asian, non-Hispanic/Latino; 5 Hispanic/Latino; 1 Two or more races, non-Hispanic/Latino). Average age 36. 54 applicants, 98% accepted, 24 enrolled. In 2018, 6 master's awarded. *Degree requirements:* For master's, research seminars, capstone project. *Entrance requirements:* For master's, bachelor's degree in mathematics or in some other field with extensive course work in mathematics (for MS in mathematics). Additional exam requirements/recommendations for international students: Required—TOEFL (minimum score 550 paper-based; 79 iBT). *Application deadline:* For fall admission, 6/1 for international students; for spring admission, 10/1 for international students. Applications are processed on a rolling basis. Application fee: $0. Electronic applications accepted. *Expenses:* Contact institution. *Financial support:* In 2018–19, 2 students received support. Federal Work-Study, scholarships/grants, and unspecified assistantships available. Financial award applicants required to submit FAFSA. *Unit head:* Dr. Frank Buscher, Vice President for Academic Affairs, 630-844-5252, E-mail: fbuscher@aurora.edu. *Application contact:* Center for Graduate Studies, 630-947-8955, E-mail: AUadmission@aurora.edu.

Austin Peay State University, College of Graduate Studies, College of Science, Technology, Engineering and Mathematics, Professional Science Master's Program, Clarksville, TN 37044. Offers data management and analysis (MS, PSM); information assurance and security (MS, PSM); mathematical finance (MS, PSM); mathematics instruction (MS); predictive analytics (MS, PSM). *Program availability:* Part-time, online learning. *Faculty:* 7 full-time (0 women), 1 part-time/adjunct (0 women). *Students:* 48 full-time (11 women), 72 part-time (29 women); includes 22 minority (9 Black or African American, non-Hispanic/Latino; 5 Asian, non-Hispanic/Latino; 4 Hispanic/Latino; 4 Two or more races, non-Hispanic/Latino), 41 international. Average age 32. 76 applicants, 88% accepted, 41 enrolled. In 2018, 16 master's awarded. *Entrance requirements:* For master's, GRE, minimum undergraduate GPA of 2.5. Additional exam requirements/recommendations for international students: Required—TOEFL (minimum score 500 paper-based). *Application deadline:* For fall admission, 8/21 priority date for domestic

students. Applications are processed on a rolling basis. Application fee: $45 ($55 for international students). Electronic applications accepted. *Expenses: Tuition, area resident:* Part-time $450 per credit hour. Tuition, state resident: full-time $5987; part-time $450 per credit hour. Tuition, nonresident: full-time $8757; part-time $806 per credit hour. *Required fees:* $1583; $79.15 per credit hour. *Financial support:* Research assistantships with full tuition reimbursements, career-related internships or fieldwork, Federal Work-Study, institutionally sponsored loans, scholarships/grants, and unspecified assistantships available. Support available to part-time students. Financial award application deadline: 7/1; financial award applicants required to submit FAFSA. *Unit head:* Dr. Matt Jones, Graduate Coordinator, 931-221-7814, E-mail: gradpsm@apsu.edu. *Application contact:* Megan Mitchell, Coordinator of Graduate Admissions, 800-859-4723, Fax: 931-221-7641, E-mail: gradadmissions@apsu.edu. Website: http://www.apsu.edu/csci/masters_degrees/index.php

Ball State University, Graduate School, College of Sciences and Humanities, Department of Mathematical Sciences, Program in Mathematics Education, Muncie, IN 47306. Offers mathematics education (MA), including elementary and middle school mathematics, elementary and middle school mathematics specialist, secondary mathematics. *Program availability:* Part-time, 100% online, blended/hybrid learning. *Entrance requirements:* For master's, minimum baccalaureate GPA of 2.75 or 3.0 in latter half of baccalaureate. Additional exam requirements/recommendations for international students: Required—TOEFL (minimum score 550 paper-based; 79 iBT), IELTS (minimum score 6.5). Electronic applications accepted.

Bank Street College of Education, Graduate School, Programs in Educational Leadership, New York, NY 10025. Offers early childhood leadership (MS Ed); educational leadership (MS Ed); leadership for educational change (Ed M, MS Ed); leadership in community-based learning (MS Ed); leadership in mathematics education (MS Ed); leadership in museum education (MS Ed); leadership in the arts: creative writing (MS Ed); leadership in the arts: visual arts (MS Ed). *Degree requirements:* For master's, thesis. *Entrance requirements:* For master's, interview, essays, minimum of 2 years experience as a classroom teacher. Additional exam requirements/recommendations for international students: Required—TOEFL (minimum score 600 paper-based; 100 iBT), IELTS (minimum score 7). Electronic applications accepted. *Faculty research:* Leadership in urban schools, leadership in small schools, mathematics in elementary schools, professional development in early childhood, leadership in arts education, leadership in special education, museum leadership, community-based leadership.

Bard College, Master of Arts in Teaching Program, Annandale-on-Hudson, NY 12504. Offers secondary education (MAT), including biology, history, literature, mathematics, Spanish; MS/MAT. *Program availability:* Part-time. *Degree requirements:* For master's, year-long teaching residencies in area middle and high schools. *Entrance requirements:* For master's, GRE General Test, resume, 3 letters of recommendation, personal statement, official transcripts. Additional exam requirements/recommendations for international students: Required—TOEFL. Electronic applications accepted. Application fee is waived when completed online.

Bemidji State University, School of Graduate Studies, Bemidji, MN 56601. Offers biology (MS); education (MS); English (MA, MS); environmental studies (MS); mathematics (MS); mathematics (elementary and middle level education) (MS); special education (M Sp Ed). *Program availability:* Part-time, online learning. *Degree requirements:* For master's, comprehensive exam, thesis (for some programs). *Entrance requirements:* For master's, GRE; GMAT, letters of recommendation, letters of interest. Additional exam requirements/recommendations for international students: Required—TOEFL (minimum score 550 paper-based; 80 iBT). Electronic applications accepted. *Expenses:* Contact institution. *Faculty research:* Human performance, sport, and health: physical education teacher education, continuum models, spiritual health, intellectual health, resiliency, health priorities; psychology: health psychology, college student drinking behavior, micro-aggressions, infant cognition, false memories, leadership assessment; biology: structure and dynamics of forest communities, aquatic and riverine ecology, interaction between animal populations and aquatic environments, cellular motility.

Binghamton University, State University of New York, Graduate School, College of Community and Public Affairs, Department of Teaching, Learning and Educational Leadership, Program in Adolescence Education, Binghamton, NY 13902-6000. Offers biology education (MAT, MS Ed); chemistry education (MAT, MS Ed); earth science education (MAT, MS Ed); English education (MAT, MS Ed); French education (MAT, MS Ed); mathematical sciences education (MAT, MS Ed); physics (MAT, MS Ed); social studies (MAT, MS Ed); Spanish education (MAT, MS Ed). *Accreditation:* TEAC. *Program availability:* Part-time, evening/weekend. *Degree requirements:* For master's, portfolio. *Entrance requirements:* For master's, GRE General Test, teaching certification. Additional exam requirements/recommendations for international students: Required—TOEFL (minimum score 550 paper-based; 80 iBT). Electronic applications accepted.

Bloomsburg University of Pennsylvania, School of Graduate Studies, College of Education, Department of Teaching and Learning, Program in Middle Level Education Grades 4-8, Bloomsburg, PA 17815-1301. Offers language arts (M Ed); math (M Ed); science (M Ed); social studies (M Ed). *Accreditation:* NCATE. *Degree requirements:* For master's, thesis optional, practicum, student teaching. *Entrance requirements:* For master's, MAT, GRE, or PRAXIS, minimum QPA of 3.0, teaching certificate, U.S. citizenship, related undergraduate coursework, professional liability insurance, recent TB test. Additional exam requirements/recommendations for international students: Required—TOEFL (minimum score 550 paper-based), IELTS. Electronic applications accepted.

Bob Jones University, Graduate Programs, Greenville, SC 29614. Offers accountancy (MS); Bible (MA); Bible translation (MA); Biblical studies (Certificate); business administration (MBA); church history (MA, PhD); church ministries (MA); church music (MM); cinema and video production (MA); counseling (MS); curriculum and instruction (Ed D); divinity (M Div); dramatic production (MA); educational leadership (MS, Ed D, Ed S); elementary education (M Ed, MAT); English (M Ed, MA, MAT); fine arts (MA); graphic design (MA); history (M Ed, MA); illustration (MA); interpretative speech (MA); mathematics (M Ed, MAT); medical missions (Certificate); ministry (MM, D Min); multi-categorical special education (M Ed, MAT); music (M Ed); New Testament interpretation (PhD); Old Testament interpretation (PhD); orchestral instrument performance (MM); organ performance (MM); pastoral studies (MA); personnel services (MS, Ed S); piano pedagogy (MM); piano performance (MM); platform arts (MA); rhetoric and public address (MA); secondary education (M Ed); studio art (MA); teaching Bible (MA); theology (MA, PhD); voice performance (MM); youth ministries (MA); M Div/MM.

Boise State University, College of Arts and Sciences, Department of Mathematics, Boise, ID 83725-0399. Offers mathematics (MS); mathematics education (MS). *Program availability:* Part-time. *Degree requirements:* For master's, thesis optional. *Entrance requirements:* For master's, GRE General Test. Additional exam requirements/recommendations for international students: Required—TOEFL (minimum score 550 paper-based; 80 iBT), IELTS (minimum score 6). Electronic applications accepted.

Boston College, Lynch School of Education and Human Development, Department of Teacher Education, Special Education and Curriculum and Instruction, Chestnut Hill,

MA 02467-3800. Offers curriculum and instruction (M Ed, PhD, CAES); early childhood education (M Ed); elementary education (M Ed); law and curriculum and instruction (JD/M Ed); reading specialist (M Ed, CAES); religious education (M Ed, CAES); secondary education (M Ed, MAT, MST), including biology (MST), chemistry (MST), English (MAT), French (MAT), geology (MST), history (MAT), Latin and classical humanities (MAT), mathematics (MST), physics (MST), secondary teaching (M Ed), Spanish (MAT); special needs: moderate disabilities (M Ed, CAES); special needs: severe disabilities (M Ed); JD/M Ed. *Program availability:* Part-time, evening/weekend, 100% online. *Faculty:* 19 full-time (11 women). *Students:* 186 full-time (140 women), 92 part-time (74 women); includes 58 minority (20 Black or African American, non-Hispanic/Latino; 4 Asian, non-Hispanic/Latino; 29 Hispanic/Latino; 5 Two or more races, non-Hispanic/Latino), 33 international. Average age 28. In 2018, 132 master's, 13 doctorates awarded. Terminal master's awarded for partial completion of doctoral program. *Degree requirements:* For master's, comprehensive exam; for doctorate, comprehensive exam, thesis/dissertation. *Entrance requirements:* Additional exam requirements/recommendations for international students: Required—TOEFL. Application fee: $75. Electronic applications accepted. *Financial support:* Fellowships with full and partial tuition reimbursements, research assistantships with full and partial tuition reimbursements, teaching assistantships with full and partial tuition reimbursements, career-related internships or fieldwork, Federal Work-Study, institutionally sponsored loans, scholarships/grants, traineeships, health care benefits, tuition waivers (full and partial), and unspecified assistantships available. Support available to part-time students. Financial award applicants required to submit FAFSA. *Faculty research:* Teacher education, education research and policy, bilingual education, science education, disabilities, urban education. *Unit head:* Dr. Susan Bruce, Chairperson, 617-552-4214, Fax: 617-552-0812. *Application contact:* Jessica Rivers, Assistant Dean of Graduate Admission and Financial Aid, 617-552-4214, Fax: 617-552-0398, E-mail: riversja@bc.edu. Website: http://www.bc.edu/education

Bowling Green State University, Graduate College, College of Arts and Sciences, Department of Mathematics and Statistics, Bowling Green, OH 43403. Offers mathematics (MA, MAT, PhD); statistics (PhD). *Program availability:* Part-time. *Degree requirements:* For master's, thesis or alternative; for doctorate, comprehensive exam, thesis/dissertation. *Entrance requirements:* For master's and doctorate, GRE General Test. Additional exam requirements/recommendations for international students: Required—TOEFL. Electronic applications accepted. *Faculty research:* Statistics and probability, algebra, analysis.

Bridgewater State University, College of Graduate Studies, Bartlett College of Science and Mathematics, Department of Mathematics, Bridgewater, MA 02325. Offers MAT. *Program availability:* Part-time, evening/weekend. *Entrance requirements:* For master's, GRE General Test.

Brigham Young University, Graduate Studies, College of Physical and Mathematical Sciences, Department of Mathematics Education, Provo, UT 84602-1001. Offers MA. *Program availability:* Part-time. *Faculty:* 8 full-time (2 women). *Students:* 12 full-time (10 women), 5 part-time (4 women). Average age 27. 14 applicants, 79% accepted, 9 enrolled. In 2018, 5 master's awarded. *Degree requirements:* For master's, comprehensive exam, project or thesis. *Entrance requirements:* For master's, GRE General Test, teaching certificate, bachelor's degree in math education or equivalent. Additional exam requirements/recommendations for international students: Required—TOEFL. *Application deadline:* For fall admission, 3/1 priority date for domestic and international students; for summer admission, 3/1 priority date for domestic and international students. Application fee: $50. Electronic applications accepted. *Financial support:* In 2018–19, 17 students received support, including 3 research assistantships (averaging $20,000 per year), 10 teaching assistantships (averaging $14,000 per year); scholarships/grants also available. Financial award application deadline: 3/1. *Faculty research:* Understanding the characteristics of high-quality mathematics instruction, teaching mathematics for social justice, applying mathematics to science and engineering, technology in teaching and learning mathematics, how preservice teachers learn to teach mathematics, discourse and literacy in mathematics classrooms, how national policy influences mathematics teachers. *Total annual research expenditures:* $150,000. *Unit head:* Dr. Blake E. Peterson, Chair, 801-422-7784, E-mail: blake@byu.edu. *Application contact:* Kathy Lee Garrett, Administrative Assistant, 801-422-1840, E-mail: kathylee@mathed.byu.edu. Website: https://mathed.byu.edu/

Brooklyn College of the City University of New York, School of Education, Program in Adolescence Science Education and Special Subjects, Brooklyn, NY 11210-2889. Offers adolescence science education (MAT); biology teacher (7-12) (MA); chemistry teacher (7-12) (MA); earth science teacher (7-12) (MAT); English teacher (7-12) (MA); French teacher (7-12) (MA); mathematics teacher (7-12) (MA); music teacher (MA); physics teacher (7-12) (MA); social studies teacher (7-12) (MA); Spanish teacher (7-12) (MA). *Program availability:* Part-time, evening/weekend. *Degree requirements:* For master's, comprehensive exam (for some programs), thesis (for some programs). *Entrance requirements:* For master's, LAST, previous course work in education, resume, 2 letters of recommendation, essay. Additional exam requirements/recommendations for international students: Required—TOEFL (minimum score 500 paper-based; 61 iBT). Electronic applications accepted. *Faculty research:* Interdisciplinary education, semiotics, discourse analysis, autobiography, teacher identity.

Brooklyn College of the City University of New York, School of Education, Program in Childhood Education, Brooklyn, NY 11210-2889. Offers bilingual education (MS Ed); liberal arts (MS Ed); mathematics (MS Ed); science and environmental education (MS Ed). *Program availability:* Part-time, evening/weekend. *Entrance requirements:* For master's, LAST, interview, previous course work in education, writing sample, resume, 2 letters of recommendation. Additional exam requirements/recommendations for international students: Required—TOEFL (minimum score 500 paper-based; 61 iBT). Electronic applications accepted. *Faculty research:* Emotional intelligence, multiculturalism, arts immersion, the Holocaust.

Brooklyn College of the City University of New York, School of Education, Program in Middle Childhood Mathematics Education, Brooklyn, NY 11210-2889. Offers MS Ed. *Entrance requirements:* For master's, LAST, 2 letters of recommendation, essay, resume. Additional exam requirements/recommendations for international students: Required—TOEFL (minimum score 500 paper-based; 61 iBT). Electronic applications accepted.

Buffalo State College, State University of New York, The Graduate School, School of Natural and Social Sciences, Department of Mathematics, Buffalo, NY 14222-1095. Offers mathematics education (MS Ed). *Accreditation:* NCATE. *Program availability:* Part-time, evening/weekend. *Degree requirements:* For master's, thesis or alternative. *Entrance requirements:* For master's, 18 undergraduate hours in upper-level mathematics, minimum GPA of 2.5 in undergraduate math courses. Additional exam requirements/recommendations for international students: Required—TOEFL (minimum score 550 paper-based).

California State University, Chico, Office of Graduate Studies, College of Natural Sciences, Program in Mathematics Education, Chico, CA 95929-0722. Offers

mathematics in education (MS). *Program availability:* Part-time. *Faculty:* 3 full-time (1 woman). In 2018, 1 master's awarded. *Degree requirements:* For master's, thesis or project. *Entrance requirements:* For master's, GRE, Apply for even years only, 2020, 2022, 2024. Two letters of recommendation, statement of purpose, letter of recommendation access waiver form, writing assessment, teaching credential in mathematics, GPA of 3.0 on last 60 units. Additional exam requirements/ recommendations for international students: Required—TOEFL (minimum score 550 paper-based; 80 iBT), IELTS (minimum score 6.5), PTE (minimum score 59). *Application deadline:* For fall admission, 6/1 priority date for domestic and international students. Application fee: $55. Electronic applications accepted. *Expenses: Tuition, area resident:* Full-time $4622; part-time $3116 per unit. Tuition, state resident: full-time $4622; part-time $3116 per unit. Tuition, nonresident: full-time $10,634. *Required fees:* $2160; $1620 per year. Tuition and fees vary according to class time and program. *Financial support:* Fellowships, research assistantships, teaching assistantships, career-related internships or fieldwork, Federal Work-Study, scholarships/grants, traineeships, health care benefits, unspecified assistantships, and stipends available. Support available to part-time students. Financial award application deadline: 3/2; financial award applicants required to submit FAFSA. *Unit head:* Dr. LaDawn Haws, Chair, 530-898-6111, Fax: 530-898-3097, E-mail: math@csuchico.edu. *Application contact:* Micah Lehner, Graduate Admissions Coordinator, 530-898-5416, Fax: 530-898-3342, E-mail: mlehner@csuchico.edu.
Website: http://catalog.csuchico.edu/viewer/15/MATH/MATHNONEMS.html

California State University, East Bay, Office of Graduate Studies, College of Science, Department of Mathematics, Hayward, CA 94542-3000. Offers mathematics teaching (MS); pure mathematics (MS). *Program availability:* Part-time, evening/weekend. *Degree requirements:* For master's, comprehensive exam or thesis. *Entrance requirements:* For master's, minimum GPA of 3.0 in field. Additional exam requirements/ recommendations for international students: Required—TOEFL (minimum score 550 paper-based). Electronic applications accepted.

California State University, Fresno, Division of Research and Graduate Studies, College of Science and Mathematics, Department of Mathematics, Fresno, CA 93740-8027. Offers mathematics (MA); mathematics teaching (MA). *Program availability:* Part-time. *Degree requirements:* For master's, thesis or alternative. *Entrance requirements:* For master's, GRE General Test. Additional exam requirements/recommendations for international students: Required—TOEFL. Electronic applications accepted. *Faculty research:* Diagnostic testing project.

California State University, Fullerton, Graduate Studies, College of Education, Department of Secondary Education, Fullerton, CA 92831-3599. Offers teacher instruction (MS); teaching foundational mathematics (MS). *Program availability:* Part-time.

California State University, Fullerton, Graduate Studies, College of Natural Science and Mathematics, Department of Mathematics, Fullerton, CA 92831-3599. Offers applied mathematics (MA); mathematics education (MA). *Program availability:* Part-time. *Entrance requirements:* For master's, minimum GPA of 2.5 in last 60 units of course work, major in mathematics or related field.

California State University, Long Beach, Graduate Studies, College of Natural Sciences and Mathematics, Department of Mathematics and Statistics, Long Beach, CA 90840. Offers mathematics (MS), including applied mathematics, applied statistics, mathematics education for secondary school teachers. *Program availability:* Part-time. *Degree requirements:* For master's, comprehensive exam or thesis. *Application deadline:* For fall admission, 6/1 for domestic students; for spring admission, 11/1 for domestic students. Applications are processed on a rolling basis. Application fee: $55. Electronic applications accepted. *Expenses: Required fees:* $2628 per term. Tuition and fees vary according to class time, course level, course load, degree level, campus/ location and program. *Financial support:* Teaching assistantships, Federal Work-Study, institutionally sponsored loans, scholarships/grants, and traineeships available. Financial award application deadline: 3/2; financial award applicants required to submit FAFSA. *Faculty research:* Algebra, functional analysis, partial differential equations, operator theory, numerical analysis. *Unit head:* Dr. Tangan Gao, Chair, 562-985-4721, Fax: 562-985-8227, E-mail: tangan.gao@csulb.edu. *Application contact:* Dr. Tangan Gao, Chair, 562-985-4721, Fax: 562-985-8227, E-mail: tangan.gao@csulb.edu.

California State University, Northridge, Graduate Studies, Michael D. Eisner College of Education, Department of Secondary Education, Northridge, CA 91330. Offers educational technology (MA); English education (MA); mathematics education (MA); secondary science education (MA); teaching and learning (MA). *Accreditation:* NCATE. *Program availability:* Part-time. *Degree requirements:* For master's, thesis optional. *Entrance requirements:* For master's, GRE General Test or minimum GPA of 3.0. Additional exam requirements/ recommendations for international students: Required—TOEFL.

California State University, San Bernardino, Graduate Studies, College of Natural Sciences, Program in Mathematics, San Bernardino, CA 92407. Offers mathematics (MA); teaching mathematics (MAT). *Program availability:* Part-time. *Faculty:* 7 full-time (3 women). *Students:* 4 full-time (2 women), 33 part-time (17 women); includes 24 minority (1 Black or African American, non-Hispanic/Latino; 1 Asian, non-Hispanic/ Latino; 21 Hispanic/Latino; 1 Two or more races, non-Hispanic/Latino), 2 international. Average age 29. 23 applicants, 52% accepted, 10 enrolled. In 2018, 15 master's awarded. *Degree requirements:* For master's, advancement to candidacy. *Entrance requirements:* Additional exam requirements/recommendations for international students: Required—TOEFL. *Application deadline:* For fall admission, 7/16 for domestic students; for winter admission, 10/16 for domestic students; for spring admission, 1/22 for domestic students. Application fee: $55. *Faculty research:* Mathematics education, technology in education, algebra, combinatorics, real analysis. *Unit head:* Corey Dunn, Coordinator, 909-537-5368, E-mail: cmdunn@csusb.edu. *Application contact:* Dr. Dorota Huizinga, Assistant Dean of Graduate Studies, 909-537-3064, E-mail: dorota.huizinga@csusb.edu.

California University of Pennsylvania, School of Graduate Studies and Research, College of Education and Human Services, Department of Childhood Education, California, PA 15419-1394. Offers early childhood education (M Ed); elementary education (M Ed); STEM education (M Ed). *Accreditation:* NCATE. *Program availability:* Part-time, evening/weekend. *Degree requirements:* For master's, comprehensive exam, thesis optional. *Entrance requirements:* For master's, MAT, PRAXIS, minimum GPA of 3.0, state police clearances. Additional exam requirements/recommendations for international students: Required—TOEFL (minimum score 550 paper-based; 80 iBT). Electronic applications accepted. *Faculty research:* English as a second language, adult literacy, emerging literacy, diagnosis and remediation, phonemic awareness.

Cambridge College, School of Education, Boston, MA 02129. Offers autism specialist (M Ed); autism/behavior analyst (M Ed); behavior analyst (Post-Master's Certificate); curriculum and instruction (CAGS); early childhood teacher (M Ed); educational leadership (M Ed, Ed D); elementary teacher (M Ed); English as a second language (M Ed, Certificate); general science (M Ed); health education (Post-Master's Certificate); interdisciplinary studies (M Ed); library teacher (M Ed); mathematics education (M Ed); mathematics specialist (Certificate); school administration (M Ed, CAGS); school nurse education (M Ed); teacher of students with moderate disabilities (M Ed); teaching skills and methodologies (M Ed). *Program availability:* Part-time, evening/weekend, online learning. *Degree requirements:* For master's, thesis, internship/practicum (licensure program only); for doctorate, thesis/dissertation; for other advanced degree, thesis. *Entrance requirements:* For master's, interview, resume, documentation of licensure, 2 professional references; for doctorate, official transcripts, interview, resume, written personal statement/essay, portfolio of scholarly and professional work, 2 professional references, health insurance, immunizations form; for other advanced degree, official transcripts, interview, resume, written personal statement/essay, 2 professional references, health insurance, immunizations form. Additional exam requirements/ recommendations for international students: Required—TOEFL (minimum score 550 paper-based; 79 iBT), Michigan English Language Assessment Battery (minimum score 85); Recommended—IELTS (minimum score 6). *Application deadline:* Applications are processed on a rolling basis. Application fee: $30. Electronic applications accepted. *Expenses:* Contact institution. *Financial support:* Career-related internships or fieldwork, Federal Work-Study, and scholarships/grants available. Financial award applicants required to submit FAFSA. *Faculty research:* Adult education, accelerated learning, mathematics education, brain compatible learning, special education and law. *Unit head:* Dr. Mary Garrity, Interim Dean, 617-873-0168, E-mail: mary.garrity@cambridgecollege.edu. *Application contact:* Salvadore Liberto, Interim Assistant Vice President of Enrollment, 800-877-4723, E-mail: admissions@cambridgecollege.edu.
Website: https://www.cambridgecollege.edu/school/school-education

Caribbean University, Graduate School, Bayamón, PR 00960-0493. Offers administration and supervision (MA Ed); criminal justice (MA); curriculum and instruction (MA Ed, PhD), including elementary education (MA Ed), English education (MA Ed), history education (MA Ed), mathematics education (MA Ed), primary education (MA Ed), science education (MA Ed), Spanish education (MA Ed); educational technology in instructional systems (MA Ed); gerontology (MSN); human resources (MBA); museology, archiving and art history (MA Ed); neonatal pediatrics (MSN); physical education (MA Ed); special education (MA Ed). *Entrance requirements:* For master's, interview, minimum GPA of 2.5.

Central Michigan University, College of Graduate Studies, College of Science and Engineering, Department of Mathematics, Mount Pleasant, MI 48859. Offers mathematics (MA, PhD), including teaching of college mathematics (PhD). *Program availability:* Part-time. *Degree requirements:* For master's, thesis or alternative; for doctorate, thesis/dissertation. *Entrance requirements:* For master's, minimum GPA of 2.7, 20 hours of course work in mathematics; for doctorate, GRE, minimum GPA of 3.0, 20 hours of course work in mathematics. Electronic applications accepted. *Faculty research:* Combinatorics, approximation theory, applied mathematics, statistics, functional analysis and operator theory.

Chatham University, Program in Education, Pittsburgh, PA 15232-2826. Offers early childhood education (MAT); elementary education (MAT); environmental education (K-12) (MAT); secondary art (MAT); secondary biology education (MAT); secondary chemistry education (MAT); secondary English education (MAT); secondary math education (MAT); secondary physics education (MAT); secondary social studies education (MAT); special education (MAT). *Degree requirements:* For master's, thesis, teaching experience. *Entrance requirements:* For master's, minimum GPA of 3.0, sample of written work, recommendation letters. Additional exam requirements/ recommendations for international students: Required—TOEFL (minimum score 600 paper-based; 100 iBT), IELTS (minimum score 7), TWE. Electronic applications accepted. Application fee is waived when completed online. *Faculty research:* Gifted education, environmental education, technology in education, writing as learning, class size and achievement.

The Citadel, The Military College of South Carolina, Citadel Graduate College, Zucker Family School of Education, Charleston, SC 29409. Offers elementary/ secondary school administration and supervision (M Ed); elementary/secondary school counseling (M Ed); interdisciplinary STEM education (M Ed); literacy education (M Ed, Graduate Certificate); middle grades (MAT), including English, mathematics, science, social studies; physical education (grades K-12) (MAT); school superintendency (Ed S); secondary education (MAT), including biology, English, mathematics, social studies; student affairs (Graduate Certificate); student affairs and college counseling (M Ed). *Accreditation:* NCATE. *Program availability:* Part-time, evening/weekend, 100% online, blended/hybrid learning. *Degree requirements:* For master's, comprehensive exam (for some programs). *Entrance requirements:* For master's, GRE (minimum combined verbal and quantitative score of 290) or MAT (minimum score 396). Additional exam requirements/recommendations for international students: Required—TOEFL (minimum score 550 paper-based; 79 iBT). Electronic applications accepted. *Expenses:* Tuition, state resident: part-time $595 per credit hour. Tuition, nonresident: part-time $1020 per credit hour. *Required fees:* $90 per term.

City College of the City University of New York, Graduate School, School of Education, Department of Secondary Education, New York, NY 10031-9198. Offers adolescent mathematics education (MA, AC); English education (MA); middle school mathematics education (MS); science education (MA); social studies education (AC). *Accreditation:* NCATE. *Entrance requirements:* For master's, Liberal Arts and Sciences Test (LAST), Content Specialty Test (CST). Additional exam requirements/ recommendations for international students: Required—TOEFL.

Clarion University of Pennsylvania, College of Arts, Education and Sciences, Master of Education Program, Clarion, PA 16214. Offers curriculum and instruction (M Ed); early childhood (M Ed); math education (M Ed); reading (M Ed); science education (M Ed); special education (M Ed); technology (M Ed). *Accreditation:* NCATE. *Program availability:* Part-time, evening/weekend, 100% online, blended/hybrid learning. *Faculty:* 6 full-time (3 women). *Students:* 5 full-time (all women), 85 part-time (73 women); includes 3 minority (2 Black or African American, non-Hispanic/Latino; 1 Two or more races, non-Hispanic/Latino). Average age 30. 57 applicants, 61% accepted, 26 enrolled. In 2018, 51 master's awarded. *Degree requirements:* For master's, comprehensive exam (for some programs), thesis or alternative. *Entrance requirements:* For master's, minimum QPA of 3.0. Additional exam requirements/recommendations for international students: Required—TOEFL (minimum score 550 paper-based; 80 iBT), Or IELTS. Satisfactory completion of a bachelor's degree from an accredited US college or university is also acceptable evidence of English language. *Application deadline:* For fall admission, 8/1 priority date for domestic students, 7/15 priority date for international students; for winter admission, 11/1 priority date for domestic students; for spring admission, 12/1 priority date for domestic students, 11/15 priority date for international students; for summer admission, 4/1 priority date for domestic students. Applications are processed on a rolling basis. Application fee: $40. Electronic applications accepted. *Expenses: Tuition, area resident:* Part-time $516 per credit hour. Tuition, state resident: part-time $516 per credit hour. Tuition, nonresident: part-time $774 per credit hour. *Required fees:* $159 per credit hour. One-time fee: $50 part-time. Tuition and fees vary according to degree level, campus/location and program. *Financial support:* Federal Work-Study, institutionally sponsored loans, and scholarships/grants available. Financial award application deadline: 3/1; financial award applicants required to submit FAFSA. *Unit head:* Dr. John McCullough, Chair, Department of Education, 814-393-2404, Fax: 814-393-2446, E-mail: gradstudies@clarion.edu. *Application contact:* Susan Staub, Graduate Admissions Counselor, 814-393-2337, Fax: 814-393-2722, E-mail: gradstudies@clarion.edu.

Clark Atlanta University, School of Education, Department of Curriculum and Instruction, Atlanta, GA 30314. Offers special education general curriculum (MA); teaching math and science (MAT). *Program availability:* Part-time. *Degree requirements:* For master's, one foreign language, comprehensive exam. *Entrance requirements:* For master's, GRE General Test, minimum undergraduate GPA of 2.6. Additional exam requirements/recommendations for international students: Required—TOEFL (minimum score 500 paper-based; 61 iBT).

Clayton State University, School of Graduate Studies, College of Arts and Sciences, Program in Education, Morrow, GA 30260-0285. Offers biology (MAT); English (MAT); history (MAT); mathematics (MAT). *Accreditation:* NCATE. *Entrance requirements:* For master's, GRE, GACE, 2 official copies of transcripts, 3 recommendation letters, statement of purpose. Additional exam requirements/recommendations for international students: Required—TOEFL (minimum score 550 paper-based). Electronic applications accepted. *Expenses: Tuition, area resident:* Full-time $3528; part-time $2352 per year. Tuition, state resident: full-time $3528; part-time $2352 per year. Tuition, nonresident: full-time $13,176; part-time $8784 per year. *International tuition:* $13,176 full-time. *Required fees:* $1474; $1474 per unit. Tuition and fees vary according to campus/location and program.

Clemson University, Graduate School, College of Education, Department of Teaching and Learning, Clemson, SC 29634. Offers curriculum and instruction (PhD); middle level education (MAT); secondary math and science (MAT); STEAM education (Certificate); teaching and learning (M Ed). *Program availability:* Part-time, evening/weekend, 100% online. *Faculty:* 16 full-time (13 women). *Students:* 40 full-time (36 women), 198 part-time (171 women); includes 32 minority (10 Black or African American, non-Hispanic/Latino; 1 American Indian or Alaska Native, non-Hispanic/Latino; 3 Asian, non-Hispanic/Latino; 12 Hispanic/Latino; 1 Native Hawaiian or other Pacific Islander, non-Hispanic/Latino; 5 Two or more races, non-Hispanic/Latino), 8 international. Average age 31. 257 applicants, 77% accepted, 163 enrolled. In 2018, 38 master's, 5 doctorates awarded. *Degree requirements:* For master's, comprehensive exam; for doctorate, comprehensive exam, thesis/dissertation. *Entrance requirements:* For master's, doctorate, and Certificate, GRE General Test, unofficial transcripts, letters of recommendation. Additional exam requirements/recommendations for international students: Required—TOEFL (minimum score 80 paper-based; 80 iBT); Recommended—IELTS (minimum score 6.5), TSE (minimum score 54). *Application deadline:* For fall admission, 4/15 for international students; for spring admission, 10/15 for international students. Applications are processed on a rolling basis. Application fee: $80 ($90 for international students). Electronic applications accepted. *Expenses:* $5198 per semester full-time resident, $10123 per semester full-time non-resident, $556 per credit hour part-time resident, $1109 per credit hour part-time non-resident, online $770 per credit hour, $4938 doctoral programs resident, $10405 doctoral programs non-resident, $1144 full-time graduate assistant, other fees may apply per session; MAT Programs: $5898 per semester full-time resident, $11623 per semester full-time non-resident, $724 per credit hour part-time resident, $1451 per credit hour part-time non-resident, online $955 per credit hour, $1144 full-time graduate assistant, other fees may apply per session. *Financial support:* In 2018–19, 8 students received support, including 9 fellowships with full and partial tuition reimbursements available (averaging $3,414 per year), 3 research assistantships with full and partial tuition reimbursements available (averaging $17,500 per year), 28 teaching assistantships with full and partial tuition reimbursements available (averaging $18,020 per year); career-related internships or fieldwork also available. *Faculty research:* STEAM education, inquiry-based instruction, cultural hegemony and mathematics, equity and ethics, teacher effectiveness. *Total annual research expenditures:* $1.3 million. *Unit head:* Dr. Jeff Marshall, Department Chair, 864-656-2059, E-mail: marsha9@clemson.edu. *Application contact:* Julie Jones, Student Services Manager, 864-656-5096, E-mail: jgambre@clemson.edu.
Website: http://www.clemson.edu/education/departments/teaching-learning/index.html

Cleveland State University, College of Graduate Studies, College of Education and Human Services, Department of Teacher Education, Cleveland, OH 44115. Offers art education (M Ed); early childhood education (M Ed); foreign language education (M Ed); middle childhood mathematics and science education (M Ed); special education (M Ed), including mild/moderate disabilities, moderate/intensive disabilities; teaching English to speakers of other languages (M Ed). *Program availability:* Part-time, evening/weekend. *Faculty:* 19 full-time (14 women), 32 part-time/adjunct (27 women). *Students:* 56 full-time (40 women), 344 part-time (278 women); includes 104 minority (74 Black or African American, non-Hispanic/Latino; 1 American Indian or Alaska Native, non-Hispanic/Latino; 5 Asian, non-Hispanic/Latino; 9 Hispanic/Latino; 15 Two or more races, non-Hispanic/Latino), 14 international. Average age 34. 177 applicants, 55% accepted, 68 enrolled. In 2018, 117 master's awarded. *Degree requirements:* For master's, comprehensive exam (for some programs), thesis or alternative. *Entrance requirements:* For master's, GRE General Test or MAT, minimum GPA of 2.75. Additional exam requirements/recommendations for international students: Required—TOEFL (minimum score 550 paper-based; 78 iBT), IELTS (minimum score 6). *Application deadline:* For fall admission, 7/1 priority date for domestic students, 5/15 for international students; for spring admission, 11/15 for domestic students, 11/1 for international students; for summer admission, 4/1 for domestic students, 3/15 for international students. Applications are processed on a rolling basis. Application fee: $30. *Expenses:* Tuition, state resident: full-time $7232.55; part-time $6676 per credit hour. Tuition, nonresident: full-time $12,375. *International tuition:* $18,914 full-time. *Required fees:* $80; $80 $40. Tuition and fees vary according to program. *Financial support:* In 2018–19, 13 research assistantships with full tuition reimbursements (averaging $15,845 per year) were awarded; tuition waivers (partial) and unspecified assistantships also available. Financial award application deadline: 2/15; financial award applicants required to submit FAFSA. *Faculty research:* Early childhood education, literacy education, special education: mild/moderate, moderate/intensive, early childhood intervention specialist), teaching English to speakers of other languages (TESOL). *Total annual research expenditures:* $275,907. *Unit head:* Dr. Tachelle Banks, Department Chairperson, 216-687-4600, Fax: 216-687-5379, E-mail: t.i.banks@csuohio.edu. *Application contact:* Rosalyn Adams, Administrative Coordinator, 216-523-7139, Fax: 216-687-5491, E-mail: r.m.adams@csuohio.edu.
Website: http://www.csuohio.edu/cehs/te/te

The College at Brockport, State University of New York, School of Education, Health, and Human Services, Department of Education and Human Development, Brockport, NY 14420-2997. Offers adolescence education (MS Ed), including adolescence biology education, adolescence chemistry education, adolescence English, adolescence mathematics, adolescence physics, adolescence physics education, adolescence social studies education; bilingual education (MS Ed, AGC); childhood curriculum specialist (MS Ed); inclusive generalist education (MS Ed, AGC, Advanced Certificate), including biology (MS Ed, AGC), chemistry (MS Ed), English (MS Ed, Advanced Certificate), mathematics (MS Ed, Advanced Certificate), science (MS Ed, Advanced Certificate), social studies (MS Ed, Advanced Certificate); literacy education B-12 (MS Ed). *Accreditation:* NCATE. *Faculty:* 12 full-time (7 women), 10 part-time/adjunct (6 women). *Students:* 60 full-time (39 women), 227 part-time (157 women); includes 9 minority (1 Asian, non-Hispanic/Latino; 8 Hispanic/Latino). 135 applicants, 71% accepted, 59 enrolled. In 2018, 107 master's, 13 AGCs awarded. *Degree requirements:* For master's, thesis or alternative. *Entrance requirements:* For master's, minimum GPA of 3.0, letters of recommendation, interview (for some programs); statement of objectives, current resume. Additional exam requirements/recommendations for international students: Required—TOEFL (minimum score 550 paper-based; 79 iBT), IELTS (minimum score 6.5). *Application deadline:* For fall admission, 3/15 priority date for domestic and international students; for spring admission, 10/15 priority date for domestic and international students; for summer admission, 3/15 priority date for domestic and international students. Application fee: $80. Electronic applications accepted. *Expenses:* Tuition, state resident: part-time $471 per credit. Tuition, nonresident: part-time $963 per credit. *Financial support:* In 2018–19, 1 fellowship with full tuition reimbursement (averaging $7,500 per year), 1 teaching assistantship with full tuition reimbursement (averaging $6,000 per year) were awarded; Federal Work-Study, scholarships/grants, and unspecified assistantships also available. Support available to part-time students. Financial award application deadline: 3/15; financial award applicants required to submit FAFSA. *Faculty research:* Educational assessment, literacy education, inclusive education, teacher preparation, qualitative methodology. *Unit head:* Dr. Janka Szilagyi, Chairperson, 585-395-5945, Fax: 585-395-2172, E-mail: jszilagy@brockport.edu. *Application contact:* Buffie Edick, Graduate Program Director, 585-395-2326, Fax: 585-395-2172, E-mail: bedick@brockport.edu.
Website: https://www.brockport.edu/academics/education_human_development/department.html

College of Charleston, Graduate School, School of Education, Health, and Human Performance, Program in Science and Mathematics for Teachers, Charleston, SC 29424-0001. Offers M Ed. *Accreditation:* NCATE. *Program availability:* Part-time, evening/weekend. *Degree requirements:* For master's, capstone project. *Entrance requirements:* For master's, GRE or PRAXIS, 2 letters of recommendation, copy of teaching certificate. Additional exam requirements/recommendations for international students: Required—TOEFL (minimum score 81 iBT). Electronic applications accepted.

College of Staten Island of the City University of New York, Graduate Programs, School of Education, Program in Adolescence Education, Staten Island, NY 10314-6600. Offers adolescence education (MS Ed), including biology, English, mathematics, social studies. *Program availability:* Part-time, evening/weekend. *Students:* 76. 34 applicants, 59% accepted, 14 enrolled. In 2018, 28 master's awarded. *Degree requirements:* For master's, thesis, educational research project supervised by faculty; Sequence 1 consists of a minimum of 33-38 graduate credits among 11 courses. Sequence 2 consists of a minimum of 46-53 graduate credits. *Entrance requirements:* For master's, The candidate must also take the General Test of the Graduate Record Examination (GRE) or an approved equivalent examination and request the submission of official scores to the College. The CSI Code is 2778. Applicants should apply directly to the Educational Testing Service (ETS) to take the examination., relevant bachelor's degree, minimum overall GPA of 3.0, two letters of recommendation, one- or two-page personal statement. Additional exam requirements/recommendations for international students: Required—TOEFL (minimum score 550 paper-based; 79 iBT), IELTS (minimum score 6.5). *Application deadline:* For fall admission, 4/25 for domestic and international students; for spring admission, 11/25 for domestic and international students. Applications are processed on a rolling basis. Application fee: $75. Electronic applications accepted. *Expenses: Tuition, area resident:* Full-time $10,770; part-time $455 per credit. Tuition, state resident: full-time $10,770; part-time $455 per credit. Tuition, nonresident: full-time $19,920; part-time $830 per credit. *International tuition:* $19,920 full-time. *Required fees:* $559.20; $181.10 per semester. Tuition and fees vary according to program. *Faculty research:* Social Studies curriculum and Pedagogy; Civics Education; Teacher effectiveness and student achievement; Teacher knowledge, Knowledge transfer from college to classroom. *Unit head:* Diane Brescia, 718-982-3877, E-mail: diane.brescia@csi.cuny.edu. *Application contact:* Sasha Spence, Associate Director for Graduate Admissions, 718-982-2019, Fax: 718-982-2500, E-mail: sasha.spence@csi.cuny.edu.
Website: https://www.csi.cuny.edu/academics-and-research/divisions-and-schools/school-education/programs-and-courses/adolescence-graduate

The Colorado College, Education Department, Program in Secondary Education, Colorado Springs, CO 80903-3294. Offers art teaching (K-12) (MAT); English teaching (MAT); foreign language teaching (MAT); mathematics teaching (MAT); music teaching (MAT); science teaching (MAT); social studies teaching (MAT). *Degree requirements:* For master's, thesis, internship. Electronic applications accepted.

Columbus State University, Graduate Studies, College of Education and Health Professions, Department of Teacher Education, Columbus, GA 31907-5645. Offers curriculum and instruction in accomplished teaching (M Ed); early childhood education (M Ed, MAT, Ed S); middle grades education (M Ed, MAT, Ed S); secondary education (M Ed, MAT, Ed S), including biology (MAT), chemistry (MAT), earth and space science (MAT), English/language arts, general science (M Ed), history (MAT), mathematics, science (Ed S), social science (M Ed, Ed S); special education (M Ed, MAT, Ed S), including general curriculum (M Ed, MAT); teacher leadership (M Ed). *Accreditation:* NCATE. *Program availability:* Part-time, evening/weekend, 100% online, blended/hybrid learning. *Faculty:* 20 full-time (12 women), 20 part-time/adjunct (15 women). *Students:* 110 full-time (84 women), 143 part-time (115 women); includes 105 minority (96 Black or African American, non-Hispanic/Latino; 4 Hispanic/Latino; 5 Two or more races, non-Hispanic/Latino). Average age 33. 147 applicants, 56% accepted, 62 enrolled. In 2018, 112 master's, 11 other advanced degrees awarded. *Degree requirements:* For Ed S, thesis or alternative. *Entrance requirements:* For master's, GRE General Test, minimum undergraduate GPA of 2.75; for Ed S, GRE General Test, minimum undergraduate GPA of 2.75, graduate 3.0. Additional exam requirements/recommendations for international students: Required—TOEFL (minimum score 550 paper-based; 79 iBT). *Application deadline:* For fall admission, 6/30 for domestic students, 5/1 for international students; for spring admission, 11/1 for domestic and international students; for summer admission, 3/1 for domestic and international students. Applications are processed on a rolling basis. Application fee: $50. Electronic applications accepted. *Expenses: Tuition, area resident:* Full-time $4924; part-time $618 per credit hour. Tuition, state resident: full-time $4924; part-time $618 per credit hour. Tuition, nonresident: full-time $19,218; part-time $2403 per credit hour. *International tuition:* $19,218 full-time. *Required fees:* $1870; $802. Tuition and fees vary according to course load, degree level and program. *Financial support:* In 2018–19, 29 students received support, including 7 research assistantships with partial tuition reimbursements available (averaging $3,000 per year); career-related internships or fieldwork, Federal Work-Study, institutionally sponsored loans, scholarships/grants, tuition waivers (partial), and unspecified assistantships also available. Support available to part-time students. Financial award application deadline: 5/1; financial award applicants required to submit FAFSA. *Unit head:* Dr. Jan Burcham, Department Chair, 706-507-8519, Fax: 706-568-3134, E-mail: burcham_jan@columbusstate.edu. *Application contact:* Catrina Smith-Edmond, Assistant Director for Graduate and Global Admission, 706-507-8824, Fax: 706-568-5091, E-mail: smithedmond_catrina@columbusstate.edu.
Website: http://te.columbusstate.edu/

Concordia University, College of Education, Portland, OR 97211-6099. Offers administrative leadership (Ed D); career and technical education (M Ed); curriculum and instruction (M Ed), including adolescent literacy, early childhood education, educational technology leadership, English for speakers of other languages, environmental

education, health and physical education, mathematics, methods and curriculum, reading interventionist, science, social studies, STEAM education, teacher leadership, the inclusive classroom, trauma and resilience in educational settings; educational administration (M Ed); educational leadership (M Ed); elementary education (MAT); higher education (Ed D); instructional leadership (Ed D); professional leadership, inquiry, and transformation (Ed D); secondary education (MAT); transformational leadership (Ed D). *Program availability:* Part-time, online learning. *Degree requirements:* For master's, comprehensive exam, work samples/portfolio. *Entrance requirements:* For master's, California Basic Educational Skills Test or PRAXIS I, minimum undergraduate GPA of 2.8, graduate 3.0; 2 letters of recommendation. Additional exam requirements/recommendations for international students: Required—TOEFL (minimum score 525 paper-based). Electronic applications accepted. *Faculty research:* Learner-centered classroom, brain-based learning, future of online learning.

Concordia University, School of Graduate Studies, Faculty of Arts and Science, Department of Mathematics and Statistics, Montréal, QC H3G 1M8, Canada. Offers mathematics (PhD); mathematics and statistics (M Sc, MA); teaching of mathematics (MTM). *Degree requirements:* For master's, thesis optional; for doctorate, comprehensive exam, thesis/dissertation. *Entrance requirements:* For master's, honors degree in mathematics or equivalent. *Faculty research:* Number theory, computational algebra, mathematical physics, differential geometry, dynamical systems and statistics.

Converse College, Program in Middle Level Education, Spartanburg, SC 29302. Offers language arts/English (MAT); mathematics (MAT); middle level education (M Ed); science (MAT); social studies (MAT).

Converse College, Program in Secondary Education, Spartanburg, SC 29302. Offers biology (MAT); chemistry (MAT); English (M Ed, MAT); mathematics (M Ed, MAT); natural sciences (M Ed); social sciences (M Ed, MAT). *Program availability:* Part-time. *Degree requirements:* For master's, capstone paper. *Entrance requirements:* For master's, NTE or PRAXIS II (M Ed), minimum GPA of 2.75, 2 recommendations. Electronic applications accepted.

Cornell University, Graduate School, Graduate Fields of Agriculture and Life Sciences, Field of Education, Ithaca, NY 14853. Offers adult and extension education (MPS, MS, PhD); learning, teaching, and social policy (MPS, MS, PhD); mathematics 7-12 (MS). Terminal master's awarded for partial completion of doctoral program. *Degree requirements:* For master's, thesis (MS); for doctorate, comprehensive exam, thesis/dissertation. *Entrance requirements:* For master's and doctorate, GRE General Test, sample of written work (recommended), 2 letters of recommendation. Additional exam requirements/recommendations for international students: Required—TOEFL (minimum score 550 paper-based; 77 iBT). Electronic applications accepted. *Faculty research:* Moral development and professional ethics, public issues education and community development, socio/political issues in public education, teacher education and curriculum in agricultural science and mathematics, extension research.

Delaware State University, Graduate Programs, Department of Mathematics, Program in Mathematics Education, Dover, DE 19901-2277. Offers MS. *Entrance requirements:* Additional exam requirements/recommendations for international students: Required—TOEFL (minimum score 550 paper-based). Electronic applications accepted.

DePaul University, College of Science and Health, Chicago, IL 60604-2287. Offers applied mathematics (MS); applied statistics (MS); biological sciences (MA, MS); chemistry (MS); environmental science (MS); mathematics education (MA); mathematics for teaching (MS); nursing (MS); nursing practice (DNP); physics (MS); polymer and coatings science (MS); psychology (MS); pure mathematics (MS); science education (MS); MA/PhD. *Accreditation:* AACN. Electronic applications accepted.

Drake University, School of Education, Des Moines, IA 50311-4516. Offers applied behavior analysis (MS); counseling (MS); education (PhD); education administration (Ed D); educational leadership (MSE, Ed D); effective teaching (MSE); leadership development (MS); literacy (Ed S); literacy education (MSE); rehabilitation administration (MS); rehabilitation placement (MS); special education (MSE); STEM education (MSE); teacher education (5-12) (MAT); teacher education (K-8) (MST); teacher effectiveness and professional development (MSE). *Program availability:* Part-time, evening/weekend, 100% online, blended/hybrid learning. *Students:* 90 full-time (74 women), 690 part-time (532 women); includes 69 minority (30 Black or African American, non-Hispanic/Latino; 1 American Indian or Alaska Native, non-Hispanic/Latino; 9 Asian, non-Hispanic/Latino; 16 Hispanic/Latino; 13 Two or more races, non-Hispanic/Latino). Average age 34. In 2018, 253 master's, 30 doctorates awarded. *Degree requirements:* For master's and Ed S, comprehensive exam, internships (for some programs); for doctorate, comprehensive exam, thesis/dissertation, internships (for some programs). *Entrance requirements:* For master's, GRE General Test, MAT, or Drake Writing Assessment, resume, 2 letters of recommendation; for doctorate, GRE General Test or MAT, master's degree, 3 letters of recommendation; for Ed S, GRE General Test or MAT. Additional exam requirements/recommendations for international students: Required—TOEFL (minimum score 550 paper-based). *Application deadline:* For fall admission, 7/1 priority date for domestic students, 6/1 priority date for international students; for spring admission, 11/1 priority date for domestic students, 10/1 priority date for international students. Applications are processed on a rolling basis. Application fee: $25. Electronic applications accepted. *Expenses:* Contact institution. *Financial support:* Research assistantships, career-related internships or fieldwork, and unspecified assistantships available. Support available to part-time students. *Faculty research:* Counseling and rehabilitation, behavioral supports, inquiry-based science methods, teacher quality enhancement. *Unit head:* Dr. Janet McMahill, Dean, 515-271-3829, E-mail: janet.mcmahill@drake.edu. *Application contact:* Dr. Janet McMahill, Dean, 515-271-3829, E-mail: janet.mcmahill@drake.edu.
Website: http://www.drake.edu/soe/

Duquesne University, School of Education, Department of Instruction and Leadership, Program in Secondary Education, Pittsburgh, PA 15282-0001. Offers biology (MS Ed); chemistry (MS Ed); English (MS Ed); K-12 education (MS Ed), including Latin; mathematics (MS Ed); physics (MS Ed); social studies (MS Ed). *Program availability:* Part-time, evening/weekend. *Faculty:* 5 full-time (4 women). *Students:* 20 full-time (12 women); includes 3 minority (1 Black or African American, non-Hispanic/Latino; 1 Hispanic/Latino; 1 Two or more races, non-Hispanic/Latino). Average age 24. 20 applicants, 85% accepted, 13 enrolled. In 2018, 14 master's awarded. *Entrance requirements:* For master's, two letters of recommendation, letter of intent, interview, bachelor's degree. Additional exam requirements/recommendations for international students: Required—TOEFL (minimum score 550 paper-based), IELTS (minimum score 7). *Application deadline:* For fall admission, 9/1 for domestic students; for spring admission, 1/2 for domestic students. Applications are processed on a rolling basis. Application fee: $0. Electronic applications accepted. *Expenses: Tuition:* Full-time $23,112; part-time $1284 per credit. Tuition and fees vary according to program. *Financial support:* In 2018–19, 1 student received support, including 1 teaching assistantship with full tuition reimbursement available; Federal Work-Study also available. Support available to part-time students. Financial award applicants required to submit FAFSA. *Faculty research:* Factors that create highly effective teachers; how to best support teachers to support students in reform-oriented environments; urban education; models of teacher leadership; improving instruction in mathematics/science/social studies/English. *Total annual research expenditures:* $120,139. *Unit head:* Dr. Melissa Boston, Associate Dean for Teacher Education/Professor, 412-396.6109, Fax: 412-396-5585, E-mail: bostonm@duq.edu. *Application contact:* Kelly McGinley, Graduate Admissions Assistant, 412-396-1559, Fax: 412-396-5585, E-mail: mcginleyk@duq.edu.
Website: http://www.duq.edu/academics/schools/education/graduate-programs-education/ms-ed-secondary-education

East Carolina University, Graduate School, College of Education, Department of Mathematics, Science, and Instructional Technology Education, Greenville, NC 27858-4353. Offers distance learning and administration (Certificate); elementary mathematics education (Certificate); instructional technology (MA Ed, MS); mathematics education (MA Ed); science education (MA Ed, MAT); special endorsement in computer education (Certificate). *Program availability:* Part-time, evening/weekend. *Application deadline:* For fall admission, 6/1 priority date for domestic students. *Expenses: Tuition, area resident:* Full-time $4749. Tuition, state resident: full-time $4749. Tuition, nonresident: full-time $17,898. *International tuition:* $17,898 full-time. *Required fees:* $2787. Part-time tuition and fees vary according to course load and program. *Financial support:* Application deadline: 6/1. *Unit head:* Dr. Ron Preston, Director of Students, 252-737-9355, E-mail: prestonr@ecu.edu. *Application contact:* Graduate School Admissions, 252-328-6012, Fax: 252-328-6071, E-mail: gradschool@ecu.edu.
Website: http://www.ecu.edu/cs-educ/msite/

Eastern Illinois University, Graduate School, College of Liberal Arts and Sciences, Department of Mathematics and Computer Science, Charleston, IL 61920. Offers elementary/middle school mathematics education (MA); mathematics (MA); secondary mathematics education (MA). *Program availability:* Part-time, evening/weekend. *Degree requirements:* For master's, comprehensive exam (for some programs), thesis (for some programs). *Entrance requirements:* For master's, GMAT or GRE. Additional exam requirements/recommendations for international students: Required—TOEFL (minimum score 500 paper-based; 61 iBT), IELTS (minimum score 6). Electronic applications accepted. *Expenses:* Tuition, state resident: part-time $299 per credit hour. Tuition, nonresident: part-time $718 per credit hour. *Required fees:* $214.50 per credit hour.

Eastern Kentucky University, The Graduate School, College of Education, Department of Curriculum and Instruction, Program in Secondary and Higher Education, Richmond, KY 40475-3102. Offers secondary education (MA Ed), including agricultural education, art education, biological sciences education, business education, English education, geography education, history education, home economics education, industrial education, mathematical sciences education, physical education, school health education. *Accreditation:* NCATE. *Program availability:* Part-time. *Entrance requirements:* For master's, GRE General Test, minimum GPA of 2.5.

Eastern University, Graduate Education Programs, St. Davids, PA 19087-3696. Offers ESL program specialist (K-12) (Certificate); general supervisor (PreK-12) (Certificate); health and physical education (K-12) (Certificate); middle level (4-8) (Certificate); multicultural education (M Ed); music (K-12) (Certificate); Pre K-4 (Certificate); Pre K-4 with special education (Certificate); reading (M Ed); reading specialist (K-12) (Certificate); reading supervisor (K-12) (Certificate); school counseling (MA, CAGS); school principalship (preK-12) (Certificate); school psychology (MS, CAGS); secondary biology education (7-12) (Certificate); secondary chemistry education (7-12) (Certificate); secondary communication education (7-12) (Certificate); secondary English education (7-12) (Certificate); secondary math education (7-12) (Certificate); secondary social studies education (7-12) (Certificate); special education (M Ed); special education (7-12) (Certificate); special education (Pre K-8) (Certificate); special education supervisor (K-12) (Certificate); TESOL (M Ed); world language (Certificate), including Spanish. *Program availability:* Part-time, evening/weekend, online learning. *Entrance requirements:* Additional exam requirements/recommendations for international students: Required—TOEFL. Electronic applications accepted. Application fee is waived when completed online. *Expenses:* Contact institution.

Elizabeth City State University, Department of Mathematics and Computer Science, Master of Science in Mathematics Program, Elizabeth City, NC 27909-7806. Offers applied mathematics (MS); community college teaching (MS); mathematics education (MS); remote sensing (MS). *Program availability:* Part-time, evening/weekend. *Degree requirements:* For master's, thesis. *Entrance requirements:* For master's, MAT and/or GRE, minimum GPA of 3.0, 3 letters of recommendation, two official transcripts from all undergraduate/graduate schools attended, typewritten one-page request for entry into program that includes description of student's educational preparation. Additional exam requirements/recommendations for international students: Required—TOEFL (minimum score 550 paper-based, 80 iBT) or IELTS (minimum score 6.5). Electronic applications accepted. *Faculty research:* Oceanic temperature effects, mathematics strategies in elementary schools, multimedia, Antarctic temperature mapping, computer networks, water quality, remote sensing, polar ice, satellite imagery.

Fitchburg State University, Division of Graduate and Continuing Education, Program in Middle School Education, Fitchburg, MA 01420-2697. Offers English (M Ed); general science (M Ed); history (M Ed); math (M Ed). *Accreditation:* NCATE. *Program availability:* Part-time, evening/weekend. *Entrance requirements:* Additional exam requirements/recommendations for international students: Required—TOEFL (minimum score 550 paper-based; 79 iBT). Electronic applications accepted. *Expenses:* Contact institution.

Florida Agricultural and Mechanical University, Division of Graduate Studies, Research, and Continuing Education, College of Education, Program in Secondary Education and Foundation, Tallahassee, FL 32307-3200. Offers biology (M Ed); chemistry (MS Ed); English (MS Ed); history (MS Ed); math (MS Ed); physics (MS Ed). *Accreditation:* NCATE. *Degree requirements:* For master's, thesis (for some programs). *Entrance requirements:* For master's, GRE General Test, minimum GPA of 3.0. Additional exam requirements/recommendations for international students: Required—TOEFL.

Florida Gulf Coast University, College of Education, Program in Curriculum and Instruction, Fort Myers, FL 33965-6565. Offers elementary education (M Ed); English education (M Ed); English speakers of other languages endorsement (M Ed); gifted education (M Ed); mathematics education (M Ed); middle school education (M Ed); reading education (M Ed); science education (M Ed); social science education (M Ed); special education (M Ed). *Program availability:* Part-time, evening/weekend, online learning. *Degree requirements:* For master's, final project or portfolio. *Entrance requirements:* For master's, GRE General Test, MAT, minimum undergraduate GPA of 3.0 in last 2 years. Additional exam requirements/recommendations for international students: Required—TOEFL (minimum score 550 paper-based). Electronic applications accepted. *Faculty research:* Internet in schools, technology in pre-service and in-service teacher training.

Florida International University, College of Arts, Sciences, and Education, Department of Teaching and Learning, Miami, FL 33199. Offers art education (MA, MS); curriculum and instruction (MS, Ed D, PhD, Ed S), including curriculum development (MS), elementary education (MS), English education (MS), learning technologies (MS), mathematics education (MS), modern language education (MS), physical education (MS), science education (MS), social studies education (MS), special education (MS);

early childhood education (MS); exceptional student education (Ed D); foreign language education (MS), including foreign language education, teaching English to speakers of other languages (TESOL); language, literacy and culture (PhD); mathematics, science, and learning technologies (PhD); physical education (MS), including sport and fitness; reading education (MS). *Program availability:* Part-time, evening/weekend. *Faculty:* 64 full-time (43 women), 104 part-time/adjunct (76 women). *Students:* 169 full-time (144 women), 155 part-time (130 women); includes 260 minority (53 Black or African American, non-Hispanic/Latino; 7 Asian, non-Hispanic/Latino; 193 Hispanic/Latino; 7 Two or more races, non-Hispanic/Latino), 13 international. Average age 33. 184 applicants, 62% accepted, 87 enrolled. In 2018, 153 master's, 10 doctorates awarded. *Degree requirements:* For doctorate, comprehensive exam, thesis/dissertation. *Entrance requirements:* For master's, GRE General Test, Florida General Knowledge Test or Florida College Level Academic Skills Test; for doctorate and Ed S, GRE General Test. Additional exam requirements/recommendations for international students: Required—TOEFL (minimum score 550 paper-based; 80 iBT), IELTS (minimum score 6.3). *Application deadline:* For fall admission, 6/1 priority date for domestic students, 4/1 for international students; for winter admission, 10/1 priority date for domestic students, 9/1 for international students; for spring admission, 3/1 priority date for domestic students, 2/1 for international students. Applications are processed on a rolling basis. Application fee: $30. Electronic applications accepted. *Financial support:* Research assistantships and teaching assistantships available. *Unit head:* Dr. Maria Fernandez, Chair, 305-348-0193, Fax: 305-348-2086, E-mail: Maria.Fernandez9@fiu.edu. *Application contact:* Nanett Rojas, Manager, Admissions Operations, 305-348-7464, Fax: 305-348-7441, E-mail: gradadm@fiu.edu.
Website: https://tl.fiu.edu/

Framingham State University, Graduate Studies, Program in Mathematics, Framingham, MA 01701-9101. Offers M Ed. *Entrance requirements:* For master's, GRE General Test, minimum GPA of 3.0.

Fresno Pacific University, Graduate Programs, School of Education, Program in STEM Education, Fresno, CA 93702-4709. Offers MA Ed. *Program availability:* Part-time, evening/weekend. *Degree requirements:* For master's, thesis or alternative. *Entrance requirements:* Additional exam requirements/recommendations for international students: Required—TOEFL (minimum score 550 paper-based). *Expenses:* Contact institution.

George Mason University, College of Education and Human Development, Programs in Curriculum and Instruction, Fairfax, VA 22030. Offers assistive technology (M Ed); designing digital learning in schools (M Ed); early childhood education (M Ed); early childhood education for diverse learners (M Ed); elementary education (M Ed); English as a second language (M Ed); gifted child education (M Ed); literacy (M Ed), including PK-12 classroom teachers, reading specialist; literacy leadership for diverse schools (M Ed), including K-12 reading; physical education (M Ed); science K-12 (M Ed); secondary education (M Ed), including biology, chemistry, earth science, English, history/social science, math, physics; special education (M Ed); teacher leadership (M Ed); transformative teaching (M Ed). *Program availability:* Part-time, evening/weekend, 100% online, blended/hybrid learning. *Faculty:* 48 full-time (40 women), 28 part-time/adjunct (20 women). *Students:* 165 full-time (147 women), 697 part-time (579 women); includes 243 minority (47 Black or African American, non-Hispanic/Latino; 3 American Indian or Alaska Native, non-Hispanic/Latino; 88 Asian, non-Hispanic/Latino; 85 Hispanic/Latino; 4 Native Hawaiian or other Pacific Islander, non-Hispanic/Latino; 16 Two or more races, non-Hispanic/Latino), 26 international. Average age 34. 450 applicants, 93% accepted, 315 enrolled. In 2018, 421 master's awarded. *Entrance requirements:* For master's, PRAXIS Core (for some programs), 2 letters of recommendation, interview, program goals statement; 9 hours of complete licensure endorsement requirements (for elementary education); minimum GPA of 3.0 in applicant's last 60 hours of undergraduate coursework (for secondary education); at least 1 year of teaching experience (for literacy). Additional exam requirements/recommendations for international students: Required—TOEFL (minimum score 575 paper-based; 88 iBT), IELTS (minimum score 6.5), PTE (minimum score 59). *Application deadline:* For fall admission, 4/2 priority date for domestic and international students; for spring admission, 11/1 for domestic and international students. Application fee: $75 ($80 for international students). Electronic applications accepted. *Financial support:* In 2018–19, 4 students received support, including 1 fellowship, 3 teaching assistantships (averaging $3,745 per year); career-related internships or fieldwork, Federal Work-Study, scholarships/grants, unspecified assistantships, and health care benefits (for full-time research or teaching assistantship recipients) also available. Support available to part-time students. Financial award application deadline: 3/1; financial award applicants required to submit FAFSA. *Faculty research:* Teacher preparation and professional development; adaptive teaching; wonder in science teacher preparation; literacy (digital, adolescent); site based course instruction. *Unit head:* Rebecca Fox, Professor and Academic Program Coordinator, 703-993-4123, E-mail: rfox@gmu.edu. *Application contact:* Rebecca Fox, Professor and Academic Program Coordinator, 703-993-4123, E-mail: rfox@gmu.edu.
Website: http://gse.gmu.edu/programs/gsemasters

The George Washington University, Graduate School of Education and Human Development, Department of Curriculum and Pedagogy, Program in Secondary Education, Washington, DC 20052. Offers Arabic (M Ed); Italian (M Ed); math (M Ed); physics (M Ed); Russian (M Ed). Programs also offered in Arlington and Ashburn, VA. *Accreditation:* NCATE. *Students:* 7 full-time (3 women), 23 part-time (13 women); includes 10 minority (5 Black or African American, non-Hispanic/Latino; 2 American Indian or Alaska Native, non-Hispanic/Latino; 1 Hispanic/Latino; 1 Native Hawaiian or other Pacific Islander, non-Hispanic/Latino; 1 Two or more races, non-Hispanic/Latino). Average age 33. 55 applicants, 69% accepted, 16 enrolled. In 2018, 17 master's awarded. *Entrance requirements:* For master's, GRE General Test or MAT, interview, minimum GPA of 2.75. *Application deadline:* For fall admission, 1/15 priority date for domestic students; for spring admission, 10/1 for domestic students. Applications are processed on a rolling basis. Application fee: $75. *Financial support:* Fellowships, career-related internships or fieldwork, Federal Work-Study, tuition waivers (full and partial), and stipends available. Financial award application deadline: 1/15; financial award applicants required to submit FAFSA. *Unit head:* Prof. Curtis Pyke, Chair, 202-994-4516, E-mail: cpyke@gwu.edu. *Application contact:* Sarah Lang, Director of Graduate Admissions, 202-994-1447, Fax: 202-994-7207, E-mail: slang@gwu.edu.

Georgia Southwestern State University, School of Education, Americus, GA 31709-4693. Offers early childhood education (M Ed, Ed S); middle grades education (Ed S); middle grades language arts (M Ed); middle grades mathematics (M Ed); special education (M Ed). *Accreditation:* NCATE. *Degree requirements:* For master's, minimum cumulative GPA of 3.0; maximum of 6 credit hours with C grade; no courses with D grade; degree completed within 7 calendar years; for Ed S, minimum GPA of 3.25 in all courses with no grade less than a B; degree must be completed within 7 calendar years from date of initial enrollment in graduate work. *Entrance requirements:* For master's, undergraduate degree from accredited institution; professional Georgia Teaching Certificate or eligibility; minimum undergraduate GPA of 2.75 as reported on official final transcripts from all accredited institutions attended; 2 confidential Administrative Recommendation Forms; for Ed S, master's degree from accredited college or university; professional Georgia Teaching Certificate or eligibility; minimum graduate GPA of 3.0 as reported on official final graduate transcripts from all accredited institutions attended; 2 confidential Administrative Recommendation Forms. Electronic applications accepted. *Expenses:* Contact institution.

Georgia State University, College of Education and Human Development, Department of Early Childhood Education, Atlanta, GA 30302-3083. Offers early childhood and elementary education (PhD); early childhood education (M Ed, Ed S); mathematics education (M Ed); urban education (M Ed). *Accreditation:* NCATE. *Program availability:* Part-time, evening/weekend. *Faculty:* 20 full-time (17 women), 1 (woman) part-time/adjunct. *Students:* 82 full-time (74 women), 30 part-time (27 women); includes 69 minority (48 Black or African American, non-Hispanic/Latino; 3 Asian, non-Hispanic/Latino; 11 Hispanic/Latino; 7 Two or more races, non-Hispanic/Latino), 3 international. Average age 31. 116 applicants, 70% accepted, 77 enrolled. In 2018, 36 master's, 6 doctorates awarded. *Entrance requirements:* For master's, GRE, undergraduate diploma; for doctorate and Ed S, GRE, master's degree. *Application deadline:* Applications are processed on a rolling basis. Application fee: $50. Electronic applications accepted. *Expenses: Tuition, area resident:* Full-time $9360; part-time $390 per credit hour. Tuition, state resident: full-time $9360; part-time $390 per credit hour. Tuition, nonresident: full-time $30,024; part-time $1251 per credit hour. *International tuition:* $30,024 full-time. *Required fees:* $2128. *Financial support:* In 2018–19, fellowships with full tuition reimbursements (averaging $24,000 per year), research assistantships with tuition reimbursements (averaging $4,000 per year), teaching assistantships with full tuition reimbursements (averaging $2,000 per year) were awarded; career-related internships or fieldwork, Federal Work-Study, institutionally sponsored loans, scholarships/grants, traineeships, health care benefits, tuition waivers (partial), and unspecified assistantships also available. Support available to part-time students. Financial award applicants required to submit FAFSA. *Faculty research:* Teacher development; language arts/literacy education; mathematics education; intersection of science, urban, and multicultural education; diversity in education.
Website: http://ecee.education.gsu.edu/

Georgia State University, College of Education and Human Development, Department of Middle and Secondary Education, Atlanta, GA 30302-3083. Offers curriculum and instruction (Ed D); English education (MAT); mathematics education (M Ed, MAT); middle level education (MAT); reading, language and literacy education (M Ed, MAT), including reading instruction (M Ed); science education (M Ed, MAT), including biology (MAT), broad field science (MAT), chemistry (MAT), earth science (MAT), physics (MAT); social studies education (M Ed, MAT), including economics (MAT), geography (MAT), history (MAT), political science (MAT); teaching and learning (PhD), including language and literacy, mathematics education, music education, science education, social studies education, teaching and teacher education. *Accreditation:* NCATE. *Program availability:* Part-time, evening/weekend, online learning. *Faculty:* 19 full-time (15 women), 9 part-time/adjunct (7 women). *Students:* 217 full-time (136 women), 203 part-time (140 women); includes 229 minority (156 Black or African American, non-Hispanic/Latino; 23 Asian, non-Hispanic/Latino; 31 Hispanic/Latino; 19 Two or more races, non-Hispanic/Latino), 3 international. Average age 34. 149 applicants, 60% accepted, 70 enrolled. In 2018, 112 master's, 23 doctorates awarded. *Entrance requirements:* For master's, GRE; GACE I (for initial teacher preparation programs), baccalaureate degree or equivalent, resume, goals statement, two letters of recommendation, minimum undergraduate GPA of 2.5; proof of initial teacher certification in the content area (for M Ed); for doctorate, GRE, resume, goals statement, writing sample, two letters of recommendation, minimum graduate GPA of 3.3, interview. *Application deadline:* For fall admission, 1/15 priority date for domestic and international students; for spring admission, 10/1 for domestic and international students. Application fee: $50. Electronic applications accepted. *Expenses: Tuition, area resident:* Full-time $9360; part-time $390 per credit hour. Tuition, state resident: full-time $9360; part-time $390 per credit hour. Tuition, nonresident: full-time $30,024; part-time $1251 per credit hour. *International tuition:* $30,024 full-time. *Required fees:* $2128. *Financial support:* In 2018–19, fellowships with full tuition reimbursements (averaging $19,667 per year), research assistantships with full tuition reimbursements (averaging $5,436 per year), teaching assistantships with full tuition reimbursements (averaging $2,779 per year) were awarded; career-related internships or fieldwork, Federal Work-Study, scholarships/grants, health care benefits, tuition waivers (full and partial), and unspecified assistantships also available. Financial award application deadline: 3/15. *Faculty research:* Teacher education in language and literacy, mathematics, science, and social studies in urban middle and secondary school settings; learning technologies in school, community, and corporate settings; multicultural education and education for social justice; urban education; international education. *Unit head:* Dr. Gertrude Marilyn Tinker Sachs, Chair, 404-413-8384, Fax: 404-413-8063, E-mail: gtinkersachs@gsu.edu. *Application contact:* Shaleen Tibbs, Administrative Specialist, 404-413-8385, Fax: 404-413-8063, E-mail: stibbs@gsu.edu.
Website: http://mse.education.gsu.edu/

Gordon College, Graduate Education Program, Wenham, MA 01984-1899. Offers early childhood (M Ed); educational leadership (M Ed, Ed S); elementary education (M Ed); English as a second language (M Ed, Ed S); math specialist (M Ed); mathematics specialist (Ed S); middle school education (M Ed); moderate disabilities (M Ed); Montessori education (M Ed); reading (M Ed, Ed S); secondary education (M Ed). *Program availability:* Part-time, evening/weekend. *Degree requirements:* For master's, action research or clinical experience (for most programs); for Ed S, action research or clinical experience (for some programs). *Entrance requirements:* For master's, minimum undergraduate GPA of 3.0; 2 official undergraduate transcripts; professional resume; 3 recommendation letters (one professional reference, one academic reference, one personal reference); 500-700 word statement of purpose; for Ed S, minimum master's GPA of 3.3; 2 official transcripts from undergraduate and graduate schools; professional resume; 3 recommendation letters (one professional reference, one academic reference, one personal reference); 500-700 word statement of purpose. Additional exam requirements/recommendations for international students: Required—TOEFL (minimum score 550 paper-based, 80 iBT) or IELTS (minimum score 6.5). *Expenses:* Contact institution. *Faculty research:* Reading, early childhood development, English language learners, universal design for learning.

Grambling State University, School of Graduate Studies and Research, College of Education, Department of Educational Leadership, Grambling, LA 71245. Offers developmental education (MS, Ed D, PMC), including curriculum and instructional design (Ed D), English (MS), guidance and counseling (MS), higher education administration and management (Ed D), mathematics (MS), reading (MS), science (MS), student development and personnel services (Ed D); educational leadership (M Ed). *Program availability:* Part-time, evening/weekend. *Degree requirements:* For master's, comprehensive exam, thesis (for some programs); for doctorate, comprehensive exam, thesis/dissertation. *Entrance requirements:* For master's, GRE, minimum GPA of 2.5 on last degree; for doctorate, GRE (minimum score 1000, 500 on Verbal), master's degree, minimum GPA of 3.0 on last degree. Additional exam requirements/recommendations for international students: Required—TOEFL (minimum score 500 paper-based; 62 iBT). Electronic applications accepted.

Mathematics Education

Hampton University, School of Liberal Arts and Education, Program in Teaching, Hampton, VA 23668. Offers English education 6-12 (MT); mathematics education 6-12 (MT). *Program availability:* Part-time. *Students:* 2 full-time (both women); both minorities (both Black or African American, non-Hispanic/Latino). Average age 30. 2 applicants, 50% accepted, 1 enrolled. In 2018, 1 master's awarded. *Entrance requirements:* For master's, GRE General Test. Additional exam requirements/recommendations for international students: Required—TOEFL (minimum score 525 paper-based) or IELTS (6.5). *Application deadline:* For fall admission, 6/1 priority date for domestic students, 4/1 for international students; for spring admission, 11/1 priority date for domestic students, 9/1 for international students; for summer admission, 4/1 priority date for domestic students, 2/1 priority date for international students. Applications are processed on a rolling basis. Application fee: $35. Electronic applications accepted. *Financial support:* Application deadline: 6/30; applicants required to submit FAFSA. *Unit head:* Dr. Martha Jallim-Hall, Program Coordinator, 757-727-5793. *Application contact:* Dr. Martha Jallim-Hall, Program Coordinator, 757-727-5793.

Harding University, Cannon-Clary College of Education, Searcy, AR 72149-0001. Offers advanced studies in teaching and learning (M Ed); art (MSE); behavioral science (MSE); counseling (MS, Ed S); early childhood special education (M Ed, MSE); education (MSE); educational leadership (M Ed, Ed S); elementary education (M Ed); English (MSE); French (MSE); history/social science (MSE); kinesiology (MSE); math (MSE); reading (M Ed); secondary education (M Ed); Spanish (MSE); teaching (MAT); teaching English as a second language (MSE). *Accreditation:* NCATE. *Program availability:* Part-time, evening/weekend. *Degree requirements:* For master's, comprehensive exam (for some programs), thesis optional, portfolio(s); for Ed S, comprehensive exam, portfolio, project. *Entrance requirements:* For master's, GRE, MAT, PRAXIS; for Ed S, MAT or GRE. Additional exam requirements/recommendations for international students: Required—TOEFL (minimum score 550 paper-based; 79 iBT). *Faculty research:* Reading, comprehension, school violence, educational technology, behavior, college choice, differentiated instruction, brain-based teaching.

Harvard University, Extension School, Cambridge, MA 02138-3722. Offers applied sciences (CAS); biotechnology (ALM); educational technologies (ALM); educational technology (CET); English for graduate and professional studies (DGP); environmental management (ALM, CEM); information technology (ALM); journalism (ALM); liberal arts (ALM); management (ALM, CM); mathematics for teaching (ALM); museum studies (ALM); premedical studies (Diploma); publication and communication (CPC). *Program availability:* Part-time, evening/weekend. *Degree requirements:* For master's, thesis. *Entrance requirements:* For master's, 3 completed graduate courses with grade of B or higher. Additional exam requirements/recommendations for international students: Required—TOEFL (minimum score 600 paper-based), TWE (minimum score 5). *Expenses:* Contact institution.

High Point University, Norcross Graduate School, High Point, NC 27268. Offers athletic training (MSAT); business administration (MBA); educational leadership (M Ed, Ed D); elementary education (M Ed, MAT); pharmacy (Pharm D); physical therapy (DPT); physician assistant studies (MPAS); secondary mathematics (M Ed, MAT); special education (M Ed); strategic communication (MA). *Accreditation:* NCATE. *Program availability:* Part-time, evening/weekend. *Degree requirements:* For master's, comprehensive exam (for some programs), thesis (for some programs). *Entrance requirements:* For master's, GMAT (MBA), GRE, MAT, minimum GPA of 3.0. Additional exam requirements/recommendations for international students: Required—TOEFL (minimum score 550 paper-based). Electronic applications accepted.

Hofstra University, School of Education, Programs in Teacher Education, Hempstead, NY 11549. Offers bilingual education (MA); bilingual extension (Advanced Certificate); business education (MS Ed); curriculum studies (MS Ed); early childhood and childhood education (MS Ed); early childhood education (MA, MS Ed); educational technology (Advanced Certificate); elementary education (MA, MS Ed); English education (MS Ed); family and consumer science (MS Ed); fine arts and music education (Advanced Certificate); fine arts education (MS Ed); foreign language and TESOL (MS Ed); foreign language education (MA, MS Ed); languages other than English and teaching English as a second language (MA); learning and teaching (Ed D); mathematics education (MA, MS Ed); middle childhood extension (Advanced Certificate); music education (MA, MS Ed); science education (MA); secondary education (Advanced Certificate); social studies education (MA, MS Ed); teaching languages other than English and TESOL (MS Ed); technology for learning (MA); TESOL (MS Ed, Advanced Certificate); TESOL with specialization in STEM (MA); work based learning extension (Advanced Certificate). *Program availability:* Part-time, evening/weekend, blended/hybrid learning. *Students:* 138 full-time (94 women), 109 part-time (78 women); includes 66 minority (16 Black or African American, non-Hispanic/Latino; 17 Asian, non-Hispanic/Latino; 31 Hispanic/Latino; 2 Native Hawaiian or other Pacific Islander, non-Hispanic/Latino), 6 international. Average age 29. 217 applicants, 86% accepted, 113 enrolled. In 2018, 105 master's, 11 doctorates, 25 other advanced degrees awarded. *Degree requirements:* For master's, comprehensive exam, thesis (for some programs), exit project, student teaching, fieldwork, electronic portfolio, curriculum project, minimum GPA of 3.0; for doctorate, dissertation; for Advanced Certificate, 3 foreign languages, comprehensive exam (for some programs), thesis project. *Entrance requirements:* For master's, GRE, 2 letters of recommendation, portfolio, teacher certification (MA), interview, essay; for doctorate, GMAT, GRE, LSAT, or MAT; for Advanced Certificate, 2 letters of recommendation, essay, interview and/or portfolio, teaching certificate. Additional exam requirements/recommendations for international students: Required—TOEFL (minimum score 550 paper-based; 80 iBT). *Application deadline:* Applications are processed on a rolling basis. Application fee: $75. Electronic applications accepted. *Financial support:* In 2018–19, 86 students received support, including 51 fellowships with full and partial tuition reimbursements available (averaging $5,080 per year), 2 research assistantships with full and partial tuition reimbursements available (averaging $3,470 per year); career-related internships or fieldwork, Federal Work-Study, institutionally sponsored loans, scholarships/grants, traineeships, tuition waivers (full and partial), unspecified assistantships, and scholarships and endowed scholarships also available. Support available to part-time students. Financial award applicants required to submit FAFSA. *Faculty research:* Impact of memory on learning; brain function, cognitive-development, learning, and achievement; student activism and civic education; using children's literature to promote diversity; 2nd language acquisition. *Unit head:* Dr. Alan Singer, Chairperson, 516-463-5853, Fax: 516-463-6275, E-mail: alan.j.singer@hofstra.edu. *Application contact:* Sunil Samuel, Assistant Vice President of Admissions, 516-463-4723, Fax: 516-463-4664, E-mail: graduateadmission@hofstra.edu. Website: http://www.hofstra.edu/education/

Hood College, Graduate School, Department of Education, Frederick, MD 21701-8575. Offers curriculum and instruction (MS), including elementary education, elementary science and mathematics education, secondary education, special education; education, multidisciplinary studies (MS); educational leadership (MS, Certificate); reading specialization (MS); STEM education (Certificate). *Accreditation:* NCATE. *Program availability:* Part-time-only, evening/weekend. *Faculty:* 5 full-time (3 women), 32 part-time/adjunct (24 women). *Students:* 3 full-time (all women), 306 part-time (253 women); includes 65 minority (22 Black or African American, non-Hispanic/Latino; 9 Asian, non-Hispanic/Latino; 17 Hispanic/Latino; 17 Two or more races, non-Hispanic/

Latino), 3 international. Average age 33. 80 applicants, 99% accepted, 45 enrolled. In 2018, 59 master's, 47 other advanced degrees awarded. *Degree requirements:* For master's, action research project, portfolio (for reading specialization); for Certificate, STEM capstone activity. *Entrance requirements:* For master's, minimum GPA of 2.75, teaching certification, writing sample during interview, letter of recommendation from principal (for educational leadership program only). Additional exam requirements/recommendations for international students: Required—TOEFL (minimum score 575 paper-based; 89 iBT), IELTS (minimum score 6.5). *Application deadline:* For fall admission, 8/15 priority date for domestic students, 8/5 for international students; for spring admission, 12/1 priority date for domestic students, 12/1 for international students; for summer admission, 5/1 priority date for domestic students, 4/15 for international students. Applications are processed on a rolling basis. Application fee: $50 ($100 for international students). Electronic applications accepted. *Expenses: Tuition:* Full-time $17,640; part-time $4410 per semester. *Required fees:* $125 per semester. Tuition and fees vary according to degree level and program. *Financial support:* Tuition waivers (partial) and unspecified assistantships available. Financial award applicants required to submit FAFSA. *Faculty research:* Leadership, action research, brain research, learning styles. *Unit head:* Dr. April M. Boulton, Dean of the Graduate School, 301-696-3612, E-mail: gofurther@hood.edu. *Application contact:* Tanith Fowler Corsi, Assistant Director of Graduate Admissions, 301-696-3603, E-mail: gofurther@hood.edu.
Website: https://www.hood.edu/academics/departments/department-education/programs-offered

Hood College, Graduate School, Program in Secondary Mathematics Education, Frederick, MD 21701-8575. Offers high school (MS); middle school (MS); secondary mathematics education (Certificate). *Program availability:* Part-time-only, evening/weekend. *Faculty:* 1 (woman) full-time, 2 part-time/adjunct (both women). *Students:* 20 part-time (13 women); includes 3 minority (1 Black or African American, non-Hispanic/Latino; 2 Hispanic/Latino). Average age 33. 6 applicants, 100% accepted, 4 enrolled. In 2018, 3 master's awarded. *Degree requirements:* For master's, exitfolio, capstone/research project. *Entrance requirements:* For master's, minimum GPA of 2.75, initial teacher certification, essay. Additional exam requirements/recommendations for international students: Required—TOEFL (minimum score 575 paper-based; 89 iBT), IELTS (minimum score 6.5). *Application deadline:* For fall admission, 8/15 priority date for domestic students, 8/15 for international students; for spring admission, 12/1 priority date for domestic students, 12/1 for international students; for summer admission, 5/1 priority date for domestic students, 4/15 for international students. Applications are processed on a rolling basis. Application fee: $50 ($100 for international students). Electronic applications accepted. *Expenses: Tuition:* Full-time $17,640; part-time $4410 per semester. *Required fees:* $125 per semester. Tuition and fees vary according to degree level and program. *Financial support:* Tuition waivers (partial) and unspecified assistantships available. Financial award applicants required to submit FAFSA. *Unit head:* Dr. April M. Boulton, Dean of the Graduate School, 301-696-3600, E-mail: gofurther@hood.edu. *Application contact:* Tanith Fowler Corsi, Assistant Director of Graduate Admissions, 301-696-3603, E-mail: gofurther@hood.edu.
Website: http://www.hood.edu/graduate

Hunter College of the City University of New York, Graduate School, School of Arts and Sciences, Department of Mathematics and Statistics, New York, NY 10065-5085. Offers adolescent mathematics education (MA); applied mathematics (MA); bioinformatics (MA); pure mathematics (MA); statistics (MA). *Program availability:* Part-time, evening/weekend. *Degree requirements:* For master's, one foreign language, comprehensive exam, thesis (for some programs). *Entrance requirements:* For master's, GRE General Test, 24 credits in mathematics. Additional exam requirements/recommendations for international students: Required—TOEFL. *Faculty research:* Data analysis, dynamical systems, computer graphics, topology, statistical decision theory.

Hunter College of the City University of New York, Graduate School, School of Education, Programs in Secondary Education, Concentration in Mathematics Education, New York, NY 10065-5085. Offers MA. *Accreditation:* NCATE. *Degree requirements:* For master's, thesis, professional teaching portfolio, New York State Teacher Certification Exam, research project. *Entrance requirements:* For master's, minimum GPA of 2.8 overall, 2.7 in mathematics courses; 24 credits of course work in mathematics. Additional exam requirements/recommendations for international students: Required—TOEFL, TWE.

Idaho State University, Graduate School, College of Science and Engineering, Department of Mathematics and Statistics, Pocatello, ID 83209-8085. Offers mathematics (MS, DA); mathematics for secondary teachers (MA). *Program availability:* Part-time. *Degree requirements:* For master's, comprehensive exam, thesis (for some programs), oral and written exams; for doctorate, comprehensive exam, thesis/dissertation, teaching internships. *Entrance requirements:* For master's, GRE General Test, GRE Subject Test, course work in modern algebra, differential equations, advanced calculus, introductory analysis; for doctorate, GRE General Test, GRE Subject Test, minimum graduate GPA of 3.5, MS in mathematics, teaching experience, 3 letters of recommendation. Additional exam requirements/recommendations for international students: Required—TOEFL (minimum score 550 paper-based; 80 iBT). Electronic applications accepted. *Faculty research:* Algebra, analysis geometry, statistics, applied mathematics.

Illinois Institute of Technology, Graduate College, College of Science, Department of Mathematics and Science Education, Chicago, IL 60616. Offers mathematics education (MAS, PhD); science education (MAS, PhD). *Degree requirements:* For master's, comprehensive exam (for some programs), thesis optional; for doctorate, comprehensive exam, thesis/dissertation. *Entrance requirements:* For master's, GRE General Test (minimum score 900 quantitative and verbal; 2.5 analytical writing), minimum undergraduate GPA of 3.0; two-page professional statement of goals/objectives; curriculum vita; three letters of recommendation; for doctorate, GRE General Test (minimum score 1000 quantitative and verbal; 3.0 analytical writing), minimum GPA of 3.0, 3 years of teaching experience. Additional exam requirements/recommendations for international students: Required—TOEFL (minimum score 600 paper-based; 80 iBT). Electronic applications accepted. *Faculty research:* Informal science/math education, curriculum development, integration of science/math disciplines and across disciplines, instructional methods, students' and teachers' conceptions of scientific/mathematical inquiry and the nature of science/math, instructional models, evaluation, and research design.

Illinois State University, Graduate School, College of Arts and Sciences, Department of Mathematics, Program in Mathematics Education, Normal, IL 61790. Offers MA, PhD. *Faculty:* 47 full-time (26 women), 14 part-time/adjunct (5 women). *Students:* 1 (woman) full-time, 2 part-time (both women); includes 1 minority (Black or African American, non-Hispanic/Latino). Average age 30. 109 applicants, 94% accepted, 3 enrolled. In 2018, 2 doctorates awarded. *Degree requirements:* For doctorate, variable foreign language requirement, comprehensive exam, thesis/dissertation, 2 terms of residency. *Entrance requirements:* For doctorate, GRE General Test. *Application deadline:* Applications are processed on a rolling basis. Application fee: $40. *Expenses: Tuition, area resident:* Full-time $7264.62. Tuition, state resident: full-time $9466. Tuition, nonresident: full-time $17,290. International tuition: $15,089.40 full-time. *Required fees:* $1481.04. *Financial*

support: In 2018–19, 30 teaching assistantships were awarded. Financial award application deadline: 4/1. *Unit head:* Dr. George Seelinger, Department Chair, 309-438-8781, E-mail: gfseeli@IllinoisState.edu. *Application contact:* Dr. Amin Bahmainian, 309-438-7707, E-mail: mbahman@IllinoisState.edu.
Website: http://www.math.ilstu.edu/dept/academicprograms/phd.html

Indiana University Bloomington, School of Education, Department of Curriculum and Instruction, Bloomington, IN 47405-7000. Offers art education (MS, Ed D, PhD); curriculum studies (Ed D, PhD); elementary education (MS, Ed D, PhD, Ed S); mathematics education (MS, Ed D, PhD); science education (MS, Ed D, PhD); secondary education (MS, Ed D, PhD); social studies education (MS, PhD); special education (PhD, Ed S). *Accreditation:* NCATE. *Program availability:* Part-time, evening/weekend. Terminal master's awarded for partial completion of doctoral program. *Degree requirements:* For doctorate, thesis/dissertation; for Ed S, comprehensive exam or project. *Entrance requirements:* For master's, doctorate, and Ed S, GRE General Test. Electronic applications accepted.

Indiana University Bloomington, University Graduate School, College of Arts and Sciences, Department of Mathematics, Bloomington, IN 47405. Offers applied mathematics (MA); mathematical physics (PhD); mathematics education (MAT); pure mathematics (MA, PhD). Terminal master's awarded for partial completion of doctoral program. *Degree requirements:* For doctorate, one foreign language, thesis/dissertation. *Entrance requirements:* For master's and doctorate, GRE General Test, GRE Subject Test. Additional exam requirements/recommendations for international students: Required—TOEFL. Electronic applications accepted. *Expenses:* Contact institution. *Faculty research:* Topology, geometry, algebra, applied mathematics, analysis.

Indiana University of Pennsylvania, School of Graduate Studies and Research, College of Natural Sciences and Mathematics, Department of Mathematics, Program in Elementary and Middle School Mathematics Education, Indiana, PA 15705. Offers M Ed. *Accreditation:* NCATE. *Program availability:* Part-time. *Faculty:* 11 full-time (4 women). *Students:* 1 (woman) full-time, 6 part-time (4 women); includes 1 minority (Hispanic/Latino), 1 international. Average age 26. 3 applicants, 67% accepted, 3 enrolled. In 2018, 6 master's awarded. *Entrance requirements:* For master's, 2 letters of recommendation. Additional exam requirements/recommendations for international students: Required—TOEFL (minimum score 540 paper-based). *Application deadline:* Applications are processed on a rolling basis. Application fee: $50. Electronic applications accepted. *Expenses:* Tuition, state resident: full-time $12,384; part-time $516 per credit hour. Tuition, nonresident: full-time $18,576; part-time $774 per credit hour. *Required fees:* $4454; $186 per credit hour. $65 per semester. Tuition and fees vary according to program and reciprocity agreements. *Financial support:* Research assistantships, career-related internships or fieldwork, and Federal Work-Study available. Support available to part-time students. Financial award application deadline: 4/15; financial award applicants required to submit FAFSA. *Unit head:* Dr. Valerie Long, Graduate Coordinator, 724-357-4060, E-mail: vlong@iup.edu. *Application contact:* Dr. Valerie Long, Graduate Coordinator, 724-357-4060, E-mail: vlong@iup.edu.
Website: http://www.iup.edu/grad/mathed/default.aspx

Indiana University of Pennsylvania, School of Graduate Studies and Research, College of Natural Sciences and Mathematics, Department of Mathematics, Program in Secondary Mathematics Education, Indiana, PA 15705. Offers M Ed. *Accreditation:* NCATE. *Program availability:* Part-time. *Faculty:* 11 full-time (4 women). *Students:* 1 (woman) full-time, 13 part-time (9 women). Average age 33. 8 applicants, 100% accepted, 4 enrolled. In 2018, 7 master's awarded. *Entrance requirements:* For master's, 2 letters of recommendation. Additional exam requirements/recommendations for international students: Required—TOEFL (minimum score 540 paper-based). *Application deadline:* Applications are processed on a rolling basis. Application fee: $50. Electronic applications accepted. *Expenses:* Tuition, state resident: full-time $12,384; part-time $516 per credit hour. Tuition, nonresident: full-time $18,576; part-time $774 per credit hour. *Required fees:* $4454; $186 per credit hour. $65 per semester. Tuition and fees vary according to program and reciprocity agreements. *Financial support:* Fellowships, research assistantships, career-related internships or fieldwork, Federal Work-Study, scholarships/grants, and unspecified assistantships available. Support available to part-time students. Financial award application deadline: 4/15; financial award applicants required to submit FAFSA. *Unit head:* Dr. Valerie Long, Graduate Coordinator, 724-357-4060, E-mail: vlong@iup.edu. *Application contact:* Dr. Valerie Long, Graduate Coordinator, 724-357-4060, E-mail: vlong@iup.edu.
Website: http://www.iup.edu/math/grad/mathematics-education-med/

Indiana University–Purdue University Indianapolis, School of Science, Department of Mathematical Sciences, Indianapolis, IN 46202-3216. Offers mathematics (MS, PhD), including applied mathematics, applied statistics (MS), mathematical statistics (PhD), mathematics, mathematics education (MS). *Program availability:* Part-time, evening/weekend. *Degree requirements:* For master's, thesis optional; for doctorate, one foreign language, comprehensive exam, thesis/dissertation. *Entrance requirements:* For doctorate, GRE General Test (recommended). Additional exam requirements/recommendations for international students: Required—TOEFL (minimum score 79 iBT), IELTS (minimum score 6.5), GRE General Test. Electronic applications accepted. *Faculty research:* Mathematical physics, integral systems, partial differential equations, noncommutative geometry, biomathematics, computational neurosciences.

Instituto Tecnológico y de Estudios Superiores de Monterrey, Campus Ciudad Obregón, Programs in Education, Program in Mathematics, Ciudad Obregón, Mexico. Offers ME.

Inter American University of Puerto Rico, Arecibo Campus, Programs in Education, Arecibo, PR 00614-4050. Offers administration and educational supervision (MA Ed); counseling and guidance (MA Ed); curriculum and teaching (MA Ed), including biology education, English as a second language, history education, math education, Spanish; elementary education (MA Ed). *Accreditation:* TEAC. *Degree requirements:* For master's, comprehensive exam, thesis optional. *Entrance requirements:* For master's, GRE, EXADEP, bachelor's degree in education or teaching license (administration and supervision) or courses in education and psychology (counseling and guidance), minimum GPA of 2.5 in last 60 credits.

Inter American University of Puerto Rico, Metropolitan Campus, Graduate Programs, Program in Teaching of Math, San Juan, PR 00919-1293. Offers MA.

Inter American University of Puerto Rico, Ponce Campus, Graduate School, Mercedita, PR 00715-1602. Offers accounting (MBA); biology (M Ed); chemistry (M Ed); criminal justice (MA); elementary education (M Ed); English as a Second Language (M Ed); finance (MBA); history (M Ed); human resources (MBA); marketing (MBA); mathematics (M Ed); Spanish (M Ed). *Entrance requirements:* For master's, minimum GPA of 2.5.

Inter American University of Puerto Rico, San Germán Campus, Graduate Studies Center, Program in Mathematics Education, San Germán, PR 00683-5008. Offers applied mathematics (MA). *Program availability:* Part-time, evening/weekend. *Degree requirements:* For master's, comprehensive exam. *Entrance requirements:* For master's, EXADEP or GRE General Test, minimum GPA of 3.0. *Expenses:* Tuition: Full-time $212; part-time $212 per credit. *Required fees:* $366 per semester. One-time fee: $31. Tuition and fees vary according to degree level and program.

Iona College, School of Arts and Science, Department of Education, New Rochelle, NY 10801-1890. Offers adolescence education: biology (MS Ed, MST); adolescence education: English (MS Ed); adolescence education: mathematics (MST); adolescence education: social studies (MS Ed, MST); adolescence education: Spanish (MS Ed); adolescence special education 5-12 (MST); childhood and special education (MST); early childhood and childhood (MST); educational leadership (MS Ed). *Accreditation:* NCATE. *Program availability:* Part-time, evening/weekend. *Faculty:* 7 full-time (5 women), 9 part-time/adjunct (5 women). *Students:* 33 full-time (30 women), 26 part-time (20 women); includes 21 minority (6 Black or African American, non-Hispanic/Latino; 1 Asian, non-Hispanic/Latino; 13 Hispanic/Latino; 1 Two or more races, non-Hispanic/Latino). Average age 25. 39 applicants, 87% accepted, 14 enrolled. In 2018, 20 master's awarded. *Degree requirements:* For master's, thesis or alternative. *Entrance requirements:* For master's, minimum GPA of 3.0, NY State teaching certificate and bachelor's degree (for MS Ed). Additional exam requirements/recommendations for international students: Required—TOEFL (minimum score 550 paper-based; 80 iBT), IELTS (minimum score 6.5). *Application deadline:* For fall admission, 8/1 priority date for domestic students, 5/1 priority date for international students; for spring admission, 1/1 priority date for domestic students, 9/1 priority date for international students. Applications are processed on a rolling basis. Electronic applications accepted. *Expenses:* Tuition: Full-time $14,064; part-time $7032 per credit. *Required fees:* $245 per semester. One-time fee: $250. Tuition and fees vary according to program. *Financial support:* In 2018–19, 2 students received support. Unspecified assistantships available. Support available to part-time students. Financial award application deadline: 4/15; financial award applicants required to submit FAFSA. *Faculty research:* Engaging teacher educators in scientific process, cross-national comparisons of mathematics teaching, questioning strategies in the classroom, research methods, literacy development. *Unit head:* Malissa Scheuring Leipold, EdD, Chair, 914-633-2210, Fax: 914-633-2281, E-mail: mleipold@iona.edu. *Application contact:* Christopher Kash, Assistant Director of Graduate Admissions, 914-633-2403, E-mail: ckash@iona.edu.
Website: http://www.iona.edu/Academics/School-of-Arts-Science/Departments/Education/Graduate-Programs.aspx

Iowa State University of Science and Technology, Department of Mathematics, Ames, IA 50011. Offers applied mathematics (MS, PhD); mathematics (MS, PhD); school mathematics (MSM). *Degree requirements:* For master's, thesis or alternative; for doctorate, thesis/dissertation. *Entrance requirements:* For master's and doctorate, GRE General Test. Additional exam requirements/recommendations for international students: Required—TOEFL (minimum score 550 paper-based; 79 iBT), IELTS (minimum score 6.5). Electronic applications accepted.

Iowa State University of Science and Technology, Program in School Mathematics, Ames, IA 50011. Offers MSM. *Entrance requirements:* For master's, official academic transcripts, resume, three letters of recommendation, statement of purpose. Additional exam requirements/recommendations for international students: Required—TOEFL (minimum score 550 paper-based; 79 iBT), IELTS (minimum score 6.5). Electronic applications accepted.

Jackson State University, Graduate School, College of Science, Engineering and Technology, Department of Mathematics and Statistical Sciences, Jackson, MS 39217. Offers applied mathematics (MS); mathematics education (MST); pure mathematics (MS). *Program availability:* Part-time, evening/weekend. *Degree requirements:* For master's, comprehensive exam, thesis (for some programs). *Entrance requirements:* For master's, GRE General Test. Additional exam requirements/recommendations for international students: Required—TOEFL (minimum score 520 paper-based; 67 iBT).

James Madison University, The Graduate School, College of Education, Program in Education, Harrisonburg, VA 22807. Offers early childhood education (preK-3) (MAT); educational leadership (M Ed); educational technology (M Ed); elementary education (MAT); equity and cultural diversity (M Ed); inclusive early childhood education (MAT); K-8 mathematics specialist (M Ed); middle education (MAT); reading education (M Ed); secondary education (MAT); Spanish language and culture for educators (M Ed); TESOL (MAT). *Accreditation:* NCATE. *Program availability:* Part-time, evening/weekend. *Students:* 255 full-time (224 women), 200 part-time (140 women); includes 56 minority (13 Black or African American, non-Hispanic/Latino; 8 Asian, non-Hispanic/Latino; 21 Hispanic/Latino; 14 Two or more races, non-Hispanic/Latino), 1 international. Average age 30. In 2018, 295 master's awarded. Application fee: $60. Electronic applications accepted. *Expenses:* Tuition, state resident: full-time $10,848. Tuition, nonresident: full-time $27,888. *Required fees:* $1128. *Financial support:* In 2018–19, 22 students received support. Teaching assistantships, career-related internships or fieldwork, Federal Work-Study, and assistantships (averaging $7911) available. Financial award application deadline: 3/1; financial award applicants required to submit FAFSA. *Unit head:* Dr. Phillip M. Wishon, Dean, 540-568-6572, E-mail: wishonpm@jmu.edu. *Application contact:* Lynette D. Michael, Director of Graduate Admissions, 540-568-6131 Ext. 6395, Fax: 540-568-7860, E-mail: michaeld@jmu.edu.
Website: http://www.jmu.edu/coe/index.shtml

James Madison University, The Graduate School, College of Education, Program in Mathematics Education, Harrisonburg, VA 22807. Offers K-8 math specialist (M Ed); mathematics (M Ed). *Students:* Average age 27. Electronic applications accepted. *Expenses:* Tuition, state resident: full-time $10,848. Tuition, nonresident: full-time $27,888. *Required fees:* $1128. *Financial support:* Fellowships available. Financial award application deadline: 3/1; financial award applicants required to submit FAFSA. *Unit head:* Dr. Steven L. Purcell, Department Head, 540-568-6793. *Application contact:* Lynette D. Michael, Director of Graduate Admissions and Student Records, 540-568-6131 Ext. 6395, Fax: 540-568-7860, E-mail: michaeld@jmu.edu.
Website: http://www.jmu.edu/coe/msme/index.shtml

James Madison University, The Graduate School, College of Science and Mathematics, Program in Mathematics, Harrisonburg, VA 22807. Offers M Ed. *Program availability:* Part-time. *Students:* 1 (woman) full-time, 23 part-time (17 women); includes 1 minority (Asian, non-Hispanic/Latino). Average age 30. In 2018, 2 master's awarded. Electronic applications accepted. *Expenses:* Tuition, state resident: full-time $10,848. Tuition, nonresident: full-time $27,888. *Required fees:* $1128. *Financial support:* Federal Work-Study and unspecified assistantships available. Financial award application deadline: 3/1; financial award applicants required to submit FAFSA. *Unit head:* Dr. David C. Carothers, Department Head, 540-568-6184, E-mail: carothdc@jmu.edu. *Application contact:* Lynette D. Michael, Director of Graduate Admissions, 540-568-6395, Fax: 540-568-7860, E-mail: michaeld@jmu.edu.
Website: http://www.jmu.edu/mathstat/

Kennesaw State University, Bagwell College of Education, MAT Program, Kennesaw, GA 30144. Offers art education (MAT); secondary English (MAT); secondary mathematics (MAT); secondary science (MAT); special education (MAT); teaching English to speakers of other languages (MAT). *Program availability:* Part-time, evening/weekend. *Students:* 44 full-time (36 women), 10 part-time (6 women); includes 15 minority (10 Black or African American, non-Hispanic/Latino; 4 Hispanic/Latino; 1 Two or more races, non-Hispanic/Latino). Average age 32. 3 applicants. In 2018, 32 master's awarded. *Entrance requirements:* For master's, GRE, GACE I (state certificate exam), minimum GPA of 2.75, 2 recommendations, resume. Additional exam requirements/recommendations for international students: Required—TOEFL (minimum score 550

paper-based; 80 iBT), IELTS (minimum score 6.5). *Application deadline:* For fall admission, 6/1 for domestic and international students; for spring admission, 3/1 for domestic and international students; for summer admission, 4/15 for domestic and international students. Applications are processed on a rolling basis. Application fee: $60. Electronic applications accepted. *Expenses: Tuition, area resident:* Full-time $6960; part-time $290 per credit hour. Tuition, state resident: full-time $6960; part-time $290 per credit hour. Tuition, nonresident: full-time $25,080; part-time $1045 per credit hour. *International tuition:* $25,080 full-time. *Required fees:* $2006; $1706 per semester. $853 per semester. *Financial support:* Research assistantships with tuition reimbursements and unspecified assistantships available. Financial award application deadline: 4/1; financial award applicants required to submit FAFSA. *Unit head:* Director, 470-578-3093. *Application contact:* Admissions Counselor, 470-578-4377, Fax: 470-578-9172, E-mail: ksugrad@kennesaw.edu.

Kent State University, College of Arts and Sciences, Department of Mathematical Sciences, Kent, OH 44242-0001. Offers applied mathematics (MA, MS, PhD); mathematics for secondary teachers (MA); pure mathematics (MA, MS, PhD). *Program availability:* Part-time. *Faculty:* 23 full-time (7 women). *Students:* 84 full-time (33 women), 39 part-time (17 women); includes 7 minority (2 Black or African American, non-Hispanic/Latino; 4 Asian, non-Hispanic/Latino; 1 Hispanic/Latino), 43 international. Average age 31. 66 applicants, 79% accepted, 12 enrolled. In 2018, 16 master's, 10 doctorates awarded. *Degree requirements:* For master's, comprehensive exam (for some programs), thesis (for some programs); for doctorate, comprehensive exam, thesis/dissertation. *Entrance requirements:* For master's, bachelor's degree with proficiency in numerical analysis and statistics, goal statement, resume or vita, 3 letters of recommendation; for doctorate, official transcript(s), goal statement, three letters of recommendation, resume or vita, passage of the departmental qualifying examination at the master's level. Additional exam requirements/recommendations for international students: Required—TOEFL (minimum score 525 paper-based, 71 iBT), Michigan English Language Assessment Battery (minimum score 74), IELTS (minimum score 6.0) or PTE (minimum score 50). *Application deadline:* For fall admission, 5/1 for domestic and international students; for spring admission, 10/1 for domestic and international students; for summer admission, 2/1 for domestic and international students. Applications are processed on a rolling basis. Application fee: $45 ($70 for international students). Electronic applications accepted. *Expenses:* Tuition, state resident: full-time $11,766; part-time $536 per credit. Tuition, nonresident: full-time $21,952; part-time $999 per credit. *International tuition:* $21,952 full-time. Tuition and fees vary according to course load. *Financial support:* Fellowships with full tuition reimbursements, research assistantships with full tuition reimbursements, teaching assistantships with full tuition reimbursements, scholarships/grants, and unspecified assistantships available. Financial award application deadline: 1/31. *Unit head:* Dr. Andrew Tonge, Professor and Chair, 330-672-9046, E-mail: atonge@kent.edu. *Application contact:* Artem Zvavitch, Professor and Graduate Coordinator, 330-672-3316, E-mail: zvavitch@math.kent.edu. Website: http://www.kent.edu/math/

Lake Forest College, Master of Arts in Teaching Program, Lake Forest, IL 60045. Offers elementary education (MAT); K-12 French (MAT); K-12 music (MAT); K-12 Spanish (MAT); K-12 visual art (MAT); secondary biology (MAT); secondary chemistry (MAT); secondary English (MAT); secondary history (MAT); secondary mathematics (MAT). *Degree requirements:* For master's, comprehensive exam, portfolio. *Entrance requirements:* For master's, GRE.

Lebanon Valley College, Program in Science Education, Annville, PA 17003-1400. Offers integrative STEM education (Certificate); STEM education (MSE). *Program availability:* Part-time-only, evening/weekend, 100% online, blended/hybrid learning. *Degree requirements:* For master's, thesis or capstone project. *Entrance requirements:* For master's, baccalaureate degree, minimum GPA of 3.0, teacher certification, 3 letters of recommendation, transcripts, goal statement. Additional exam requirements/recommendations for international students: Required—TOEFL (minimum score 80 iBT). Electronic applications accepted. *Expenses:* Contact institution. *Faculty research:* Teacher quality and student achievement, STEM reform, STEM education, effective teaching.

Lee University, Program in Education, Cleveland, TN 37320-3450. Offers art (MAT); curriculum and instruction (M Ed, Ed S); early childhood (MAT); educational leadership (M Ed, Ed S); elementary education (MAT); English and math (MAT); English and science (MAT); English and social studies (MAT); higher education administration (MS); history (MAT); history and economics (MAT); math and science (MAT); math and social studies (MAT); middle grades (MAT); science and social studies (MASW); secondary education (MAT); Spanish (MAT); special education (M Ed, MAT); TESOL (MAT). *Accreditation:* NCATE. *Program availability:* Part-time. *Faculty:* 13 full-time (5 women), 13 part-time/adjunct (7 women). *Students:* 32 full-time (26 women), 73 part-time (49 women); includes 13 minority (10 Black or African American, non-Hispanic/Latino; 3 Two or more races, non-Hispanic/Latino), 3 international. Average age 30. 56 applicants, 73% accepted, 34 enrolled. In 2018, 60 master's, 3 other advanced degrees awarded. *Degree requirements:* For master's, variable foreign language requirement, thesis optional, internship. *Entrance requirements:* For master's, MAT or GRE General Test, minimum undergraduate GPA of 2.75, 3 letters of recommendation, interview, writing sample, official transcripts, background check; for Ed S, minimum undergraduate and master's GPA of 2.75, official transcripts for undergraduate and master's degrees. Additional exam requirements/recommendations for international students: Required—TOEFL (minimum score 61 iBT). *Application deadline:* For fall admission, 6/1 priority date for domestic and international students; for spring admission, 11/1 priority date for domestic and international students; for summer admission, 4/1 priority date for domestic and international students. Applications are processed on a rolling basis. Application fee: $25. Electronic applications accepted. *Financial support:* In 2018—19, 43 students received support. Career-related internships or fieldwork, Federal Work-Study, institutionally sponsored loans, scholarships/grants, and unspecified assistantships available. Financial award application deadline: 3/1; financial award applicants required to submit FAFSA. *Unit head:* Dr. William Kamm, Director, 423-614-8544, E-mail: wkamm@leeuniversity.edu. *Application contact:* Jeffery McGirt, Director of Graduate Enrollment, 423-614-8691, Fax: 423-614-8317, E-mail: jmcgirt@leeuniversity.edu. Website: http://www.leeuniversity.edu/academics/graduate/education

Lehman College of the City University of New York, School of Education, Department of Middle and High School Education, Program in Mathematics Education, Bronx, NY 10468-1589. Offers MA. *Accreditation:* NCATE. *Program availability:* Part-time, evening/weekend. *Degree requirements:* For master's, comprehensive exam or thesis. *Entrance requirements:* For master's, 18 credits in mathematics, 12 credits in education. *Faculty research:* Mathematical problem solving, Piagetian cognitive theory.

Lesley University, Graduate School of Education, Cambridge, MA 02138-2790. Offers arts, community, and education (M Ed); autism studies (Certificate); curriculum and instruction (M Ed, CAGS); early childhood education (M Ed); ecological teaching and learning (MS); educational studies (PhD), including adult learning, educational leadership, individually designed; elementary education (M Ed); emergent technologies for educators (Certificate); ESLArts: language learning through the arts (M Ed); high school education (M Ed); individually designed (M Ed); integrated teaching through the

arts (M Ed); literacy for K-8 classroom teachers (M Ed); mathematics education (M Ed); middle school education (M Ed); moderate disabilities (M Ed); online learning (Certificate); reading (CAGS); science in education (M Ed); severe disabilities (M Ed); special needs (CAGS); specialist teacher of reading (M Ed); teacher of visual art (M Ed); technology in education (M Ed, CAGS). *Accreditation:* TEAC. *Program availability:* Part-time, evening/weekend, online learning. *Degree requirements:* For master's, practicum; for doctorate, thesis/dissertation. *Entrance requirements:* For master's, Massachusetts Tests for Educator Licensure (MTEL), transcripts, statement of purpose, recommendations; interview (for special education); for doctorate, GRE General Test, transcripts, statement of purpose, recommendations, interview, master's degree, resume; for other advanced degree, interview, master's degree. Additional exam requirements/recommendations for international students: Required—TOEFL (minimum score 550 paper-based; 80 iBT). Electronic applications accepted. *Faculty research:* Assessment in literacy, mathematics and science; autism spectrum disorders; instructional technology and online learning; multicultural education and English language learners.

Longwood University, College of Graduate and Professional Studies, College of Education and Human Services, Farmville, VA 23909. Offers education (MS), including algebra and middle school mathematics, counselor education, elementary and middle school mathematics, elementary education, elementary education initial licensure, health and physical education, special education general curriculum, special education initial licensure; reading, literacy and learning (M Ed); school librarianship (M Ed); social work and communication sciences and disorders (MS), including communication sciences and disorders. *Accreditation:* NCATE. *Program availability:* Part-time, evening/weekend. *Degree requirements:* For master's, comprehensive exam (for some programs), thesis optional, professional portfolio, internship, clinical experience, or practicum. *Entrance requirements:* For master's, PRAXIS I (for initial teaching licensure programs); GRE (for some programs), bachelor's degree from regionally-accredited institution, 2 recommendations (3 for some programs), minimum 500-word personal essay, official transcripts, minimum GPA of 2.75, valid teaching license (for some programs). Additional exam requirements/recommendations for international students: Required—TOEFL (minimum score 570 paper-based), IELTS (minimum score 6.5). Electronic applications accepted. *Expenses:* Contact institution.

Loyola Marymount University, Frank R. Seaver College of Science and Engineering, Program in Teaching Mathematics, Los Angeles, CA 90045. Offers MAT. *Unit head:* Christina Eubanks-Turner, Graduate Program Director, Mathematics for Teaching, 310-338-5107, E-mail: abargagl@lmu.edu. *Application contact:* Ammar Dalal, Assistant Vice Provost for Graduate Enrollment, 310-338-2721, Fax: 310-338-6086, E-mail: graduateinfo@lmu.edu. Website: http://cse.lmu.edu/graduateprograms/teachingmathematics

Manhattanville College, School of Education, Program in Middle Childhood/Adolescence Education (Grades 5-12), Purchase, NY 10577-2132. Offers biology and special education (MPS); chemistry and special education (MPS); education for sustainability (Advanced Certificate); English and special education (MPS); literacy and special education (MPS); literacy specialist (MPS); math and special education (MPS); mathematics (Advanced Certificate); middle childhood/adolescence ed science (biology or chemistry grades 5-12) or (physics grades 7-12) (MAT); middle childhood/adolescence education (grades 5-12) English (MAT, Advanced Certificate); middle childhood/adolescence education (grades 5-12) mathematics (MAT, Advanced Certificate); middle childhood/adolescence education (grades 5-12) science (biology chemistry, physics, earth science) (Advanced Certificate); middle childhood/adolescence education (grades 5-12) social studies (MAT, Advanced Certificate); physics (MAT, Advanced Certificate); social studies (MAT); social studies and special education (MPS); special education generalist (MPS). *Program availability:* Part-time, evening/weekend. *Faculty:* 3 full-time (2 women), 9 part-time/adjunct (4 women). *Students:* 11 full-time (6 women), 17 part-time (12 women); includes 3 minority (1 Black or African American, non-Hispanic/Latino; 2 Hispanic/Latino). Average age 31. 17 applicants, 71% accepted, 7 enrolled. In 2018, 8 master's, 3 other advanced degrees awarded. *Degree requirements:* For master's, comprehensive exam (for some programs), thesis (for some programs), student teaching, research seminars, portfolios, internships, writing assessment; for Advanced Certificate, comprehensive exam (for some programs). *Entrance requirements:* For master's, for programs leading to certification, candidates must submit scores from GRE or MAT(Miller Analogies Test), minimum undergraduate GPA of 3.0, all transcripts from all colleges and universities attended, 2 letters of recommendation, interview, essay (2-3 page personal statement that describes reasons for choosing education as profession and personal philosophy of education), proof of immunization (for those born after 1957). Additional exam requirements/recommendations for international students: Required—TOEFL (minimum score 600 paper-based; 110 iBT); Recommended—IELTS (minimum score 8). *Application deadline:* Applications are processed on a rolling basis. Application fee: $75. Electronic applications accepted. *Expenses:* 935 per credit. *Financial support:* Teaching assistantships, career-related internships or fieldwork, Federal Work-Study, institutionally sponsored loans, scholarships/grants, and unspecified assistantships available. Financial award application deadline: 3/15; financial award applicants required to submit FAFSA. *Faculty research:* Education for sustainability. *Unit head:* Dr. Shelley Wepner, Dean, 914-323-3153, Fax: 914-323-5493, E-mail: Shelley.Wepner@mville.edu. *Application contact:* Alissa Wilson, Director, Graduate Admissions, 914-323-3150, Fax: 914-694-1732, E-mail: edschool@mville.edu. Website: http://www.mville.edu/programs#/search/19

Manhattanville College, School of Education, Program in Special Education, Purchase, NY 10577-2132. Offers childhood education (grades 1-6) and special education: childhood (grades 1-6) (MPS); early childhood (birth-grade 2) and special education: early childhood (birth-grade 2) (MPS); English (5-9 and 7-12); special ed generalist (7-12); se English (7-12) (MPS); literacy (birth-grade 6) and special education childhood (grades 1-6) (MPS); literacy 5-12; special education generalist 7-12; special ed specialist 7-12 (MPS); math (5-9 and 7-12); special ed generalist (7-12); se math (7-12) (MPS); science: biology or chemistry (5-9 and 7-12); special ed generalist (7-12); se science (7-12) (MPS); social studies (5-9 and 7-12); special ed generalist (7-12); se soc.st. (7-12) (MPS); special ed early childhood and childhood (birth-grade 6) (MPS); special education childhood (grades 1-6) (MPS); special education: childhood (grades 1-6) (Certificate); special education: early childhood (birth-grade 2) (MPS, Certificate); special education: early childhood (birth-grade 2) and childhood (grades 1-6) (Certificate); special education: grades 7-12 generalist (MPS, Certificate). *Program availability:* Part-time, evening/weekend. *Faculty:* 5 full-time (3 women), 35 part-time/adjunct (23 women). *Students:* 45 full-time (36 women), 179 part-time (152 women); includes 31 minority (6 Black or African American, non-Hispanic/Latino; 4 Asian, non-Hispanic/Latino; 19 Hispanic/Latino; 2 Native Hawaiian or other Pacific Islander, non-Hispanic/Latino, 1 international. Average age 28. 76 applicants, 68% accepted, 40 enrolled. In 2018, 99 master's, 2 Certificates awarded. *Degree requirements:* For master's, comprehensive exam (for some programs), thesis (for some programs), student teaching, research seminars, portfolios, internships, writing assessment; for Certificate, comprehensive exam (for some programs). *Entrance requirements:* For master's, for programs leading to certification, candidates must submit scores from GRE or MAT(Miller Analogies Test), minimum undergraduate GPA of 3.0, all transcripts from

all colleges and universities attended, 2 letters of recommendation, interview, essay (2-3 page personal statement that describes reasons for choosing education as profession and personal philosophy of education), proof of immunization (for those born after 1957). Additional exam requirements/recommendations for international students: Required—TOEFL (minimum score 600 paper-based; 110 iBT); Recommended—IELTS (minimum score 8). *Application deadline:* Applications are processed on a rolling basis. Application fee: $75. Electronic applications accepted. *Expenses:* 935 per credit. *Financial support:* Teaching assistantships, career-related internships or fieldwork, Federal Work-Study, institutionally sponsored loans, scholarships/grants, and unspecified assistantships available. Financial award application deadline: 3/15; financial award applicants required to submit FAFSA. *Faculty research:* Students with emotional difficulties, literacy and adolescents, mindfulness, studying the effects of the environment on special populations, the most difficult cases, students who are presented with multiple challenges: learning, behavioral and ACE experiences who see criminal behavior as a way to cope; working on giving them the tools they need to succeed emotionally and cognitively despite the odds stacked against them. *Unit head:* Dr. Shelley Wepner, Dean, 914-323-3153, Fax: 914-323-5493, E-mail: Shelley.Wepner@mville.edu. *Application contact:* Alissa Wilson, Director, SOE Graduate Enrollment Management, 914-323-3150, Fax: 914-694-1732, E-mail: edschool@mville.edu.
Website: http://www.mville.edu/programs/special-education

Marquette University, Graduate School, College of Arts and Sciences, Department of Mathematics, Statistics, and Computer Science, Milwaukee, WI 53201-1881. Offers bioinformatics (MS); computational sciences (MS, PhD); computing (MS); mathematics education (MS). *Program availability:* Part-time, evening/weekend, online learning. Terminal master's awarded for partial completion of doctoral program. *Degree requirements:* For master's, thesis (for some programs), essay with oral presentation; for doctorate, comprehensive exam, thesis/dissertation, qualifying examination. *Entrance requirements:* For master's, official transcripts from all current and previous colleges/ universities except Marquette, three letters of recommendation; for doctorate, GRE General Test, official transcripts from all current and previous colleges/universities except Marquette, three letters of recommendation. Additional exam requirements/ recommendations for international students: Required—TOEFL (minimum score 530 paper-based). Electronic applications accepted. *Faculty research:* Models of physiological systems, mathematical immunology, computational group theory, mathematical logic, computational science.

McDaniel College, Graduate and Professional Studies, Program in Elementary and Secondary Education, Westminster, MD 21157-4390. Offers elementary education (MS); elementary STEM instructional leader (Postbaccalaureate Certificate); equity and excellence in education (Postbaccalaureate Certificate); learning technology specialist (Postbaccalaureate Certificate); secondary education (MS). *Accreditation:* NCATE. *Program availability:* Part-time, evening/weekend. *Degree requirements:* For master's, comprehensive exam (for some programs), thesis optional. *Entrance requirements:* For master's, PRAXIS, 2 references. Additional exam requirements/recommendations for international students: Required—TOEFL (minimum score 79 iBT), IELTS (minimum score 6). Electronic applications accepted.

McNeese State University, Doré School of Graduate Studies, Burton College of Education, Department of Education Professions, Program in Middle School Education Grades 4-8, Lake Charles, LA 70609. Offers middle school education grades 4-8 (Postbaccalaureate Certificate), including mathematics, science. *Entrance requirements:* For degree, PRAXIS, 2 letters of recommendation, autobiography.

Metropolitan State University, School of Urban Education, St. Paul, MN 55106-5000. Offers curriculum, pedagogy and schooling (MS); English as a second language (MS); secondary education (MS), including English teaching, life sciences teaching, mathematics teaching, social studies teaching; special education (MS).

Miami University, College of Arts and Science, Department of Mathematics, Oxford, OH 45056. Offers MA, MAT, MS. *Faculty:* 30 full-time (8 women). *Students:* 19 full-time (8 women), 8 part-time (7 women); includes 1 minority (Hispanic/Latino), 8 international. Average age 26. In 2018, 12 master's awarded. *Unit head:* Dr. Patrick Dowling, Department Chair, 513-529-5831, E-mail: dowlinpn@miamioh.edu. *Application contact:* Dr. Paul Larson, Director of Graduate Studies, 513-529-9248, E-mail: larsonpb@ miamioh.edu.
Website: http://www.MiamiOH.edu/mathematics

Michigan State University, The Graduate School, College of Natural Science, Department of Mathematics, East Lansing, MI 48824. Offers applied mathematics (MS, PhD); industrial mathematics (MS); mathematics (MAT, MS, PhD). *Entrance requirements:* Additional exam requirements/recommendations for international students: Required—TOEFL. Electronic applications accepted.

Michigan State University, The Graduate School, College of Natural Science and College of Education, Program in Mathematics Education, East Lansing, MI 48824. Offers PhD.

Middle Tennessee State University, College of Graduate Studies, College of Basic and Applied Sciences, Department of Mathematical Sciences, Murfreesboro, TN 37132. Offers mathematics (MS, MST). *Program availability:* Part-time, evening/weekend, online learning. *Degree requirements:* For master's, comprehensive exam, thesis optional. *Entrance requirements:* For master's, GRE General Test or MAT. Additional exam requirements/recommendations for international students: Required—TOEFL (minimum score 525 paper-based; 71 iBT) or IELTS (minimum score 6). Electronic applications accepted.

Middle Tennessee State University, College of Graduate Studies, Interdisciplinary Program in Mathematics and Science Education, Murfreesboro, TN 37132. Offers PhD. *Program availability:* Part-time, evening/weekend, online learning. *Entrance requirements:* For doctorate, GRE. Additional exam requirements/recommendations for international students: Required—TOEFL (minimum score 525 paper-based; 71 iBT) or IELTS (minimum score 6). Electronic applications accepted.

Millersville University of Pennsylvania, College of Graduate Studies and Adult Learning, College of Education and Human Services, Department of Educational Foundations, Millersville, PA 17551-0302. Offers assessment, curriculum and teaching - online teaching (M Ed), including online instruction; assessment, curriculum and teaching - stem education (M Ed), including integrative stem education; educational leadership (Ed D); leadership for teaching and learning (M Ed). Doctor of Educational Leadership: Collaborative program with Shippensburg University. *Program availability:* Part-time, evening/weekend, 100% online, blended/hybrid learning. *Faculty:* 10 full-time (9 women), 10 part-time/adjunct (6 women). *Students:* 1 full-time (0 women), 78 part-time (53 women); includes 5 minority (3 Black or African American, non-Hispanic/Latino; 2 Hispanic/Latino). Average age 34. 42 applicants, 98% accepted, 21 enrolled. In 2018, 21 master's, 2 doctorates awarded. *Degree requirements:* For master's, comprehensive exam (for some programs), thesis (for some programs), graded portfolio and portfolio defense; for doctorate, comprehensive exam, thesis/dissertation. *Entrance requirements:* For master's, GRE or MAT, only if undergraduate cumulative GPA is lower than 2.8, Interview (Leadership for Teaching and Learning), Teaching Certificate; for doctorate, teaching certificate, resume, letter of sponsorship, 3-5 years of professional experience as specified by PDE CSPG #96. Additional exam requirements/ recommendations for international students: Required—TOEFL, IELTS (minimum score 6), PTE (minimum score 60). *Application deadline:* Applications are processed on a rolling basis. Application fee: $40. Electronic applications accepted. *Expenses: Tuition, area resident:* Full-time $9288; part-time $516 per credit. Tuition, state resident: full-time $9288; part-time $516 per credit. Tuition, nonresident: full-time $13,932; part-time $774 per credit. *International tuition:* $13,932 full-time. *Required fees:* $2623.50; $145.75 per credit. Tuition and fees vary according to course load, degree level and program. *Financial support:* Unspecified assistantships available. Financial award application deadline: 3/15; financial award applicants required to submit FAFSA. *Faculty research:* Instructional technology, poverty research, support for LGBTQ educators and students, diversifying the teaching workforce, inclusive education. *Total annual research expenditures:* $741,634. *Unit head:* Dr. Timothy E. Mahoney, Chair, 717-871-7202, E-mail: timothy.mahoney@millersville.edu. *Application contact:* Dr. James A. Delle, Acting Dean of College of Graduate Studies and Adult Learning/Associate Provost, Academic Administration, 717-871-7462, E-mail: James.Delle@millersville.edu.
Website: http://www.millersville.edu/edfoundations/

Minnesota State University Mankato, College of Graduate Studies and Research, College of Science, Engineering and Technology, Department of Mathematics and Statistics, Program in Mathematics, Mankato, MN 56001. Offers mathematics (MA); mathematics education (MS). *Degree requirements:* For master's, one foreign language, comprehensive exam (for some programs), thesis or alternative. *Entrance requirements:* For master's, GRE General Test, minimum GPA of 3.0 during previous 2 years. Additional exam requirements/recommendations for international students: Required—TOEFL. Electronic applications accepted.

Minot State University, Graduate School, Department of Mathematics and Computer Science, Minot, ND 58707-0002. Offers mathematics (MAT). *Degree requirements:* For master's, thesis or alternative. *Entrance requirements:* For master's, GRE General Test, minimum GPA of 2.75, undergraduate major in mathematics, teaching certificate. Additional exam requirements/recommendations for international students: Required—TOEFL (minimum score 79 iBT), IELTS (minimum score 6). *Faculty research:* Mathematics education.

Mississippi College, Graduate School, School of Education, Department of Teacher Education and Leadership, Clinton, MS 39058. Offers art (M Ed); biological science (M Ed); business education (M Ed); computer science (M Ed); dyslexia therapy (M Ed); educational leadership (M Ed, Ed D, Ed S); elementary education (M Ed, Ed S); English (M Ed); higher education administration (MS); mathematics (M Ed); secondary education (M Ed); social studies (history) (M Ed); teaching arts (M Ed). *Program availability:* Part-time, online learning. *Degree requirements:* For master's, comprehensive exam, thesis optional. *Entrance requirements:* For master's, NTE. Additional exam requirements/recommendations for international students: Recommended—TOEFL, IELTS. Electronic applications accepted.

Missouri State University, Graduate College, College of Natural and Applied Sciences, Department of Mathematics, Springfield, MO 65897. Offers mathematics (MS); natural and applied science (MNAS), including mathematics (MNAS, MS Ed); secondary education (MS Ed), including mathematics (MNAS, MS Ed). *Program availability:* Part-time. *Faculty:* 21 full-time (4 women). *Students:* 13 full-time (4 women), 15 part-time (10 women); includes 2 minority (1 American Indian or Alaska Native, non-Hispanic/Latino; 1 Hispanic/Latino), 6 international. Average age 24. 18 applicants, 56% accepted. In 2018, 11 master's awarded. *Degree requirements:* For master's, comprehensive exam, thesis or alternative. *Entrance requirements:* For master's, GRE (MS, MNAS), minimum undergraduate GPA of 3.0 (MS, MNAS), 9-12 teacher certification (MS Ed). Additional exam requirements/recommendations for international students: Required—TOEFL (minimum score 550 paper-based; 79 iBT), IELTS (minimum score 6). *Application deadline:* For fall admission, 7/20 priority date for domestic students, 5/1 for international students; for spring admission, 12/20 priority date for domestic students, 9/1 for international students. Applications are processed on a rolling basis. Application fee: $55 ($60 for international students). Electronic applications accepted. Tuition and fees vary according to class time, course level, course load, degree level, campus/location, program and student level. *Financial support:* In 2018–19, 11 teaching assistantships with full tuition reimbursements (averaging $10,672 per year) were awarded; Federal Work-Study, institutionally sponsored loans, scholarships/grants, and unspecified assistantships also available. Financial award application deadline: 1/31; financial award applicants required to submit FAFSA. *Faculty research:* Harmonic analysis, commutative algebra, number theory, K-theory, probability. *Unit head:* Dr. William Bray, Department Head, 417-836-5112, Fax: 417-836-6966, E-mail: mathematics@ missouristate.edu. *Application contact:* Lakan Drinker, Director, Graduate Enrollment Management, 417-836-5330, Fax: 417-836-6200, E-mail: lakandrinker@ missouristate.edu.
Website: http://math.missouristate.edu/

Missouri University of Science and Technology, Department of Mathematics and Statistics, Rolla, MO 65401. Offers applied mathematics (MS); mathematics (MST, PhD), including mathematics (PhD), mathematics education (MST), statistics (PhD). Terminal master's awarded for partial completion of doctoral program. *Degree requirements:* For master's, thesis or alternative; for doctorate, one foreign language, thesis/dissertation. *Entrance requirements:* For master's and doctorate, GRE General Test, GRE Subject Test. Additional exam requirements/recommendations for international students: Required—TOEFL (minimum score 550 paper-based). Electronic applications accepted. *Expenses:* Tuition, state resident: full-time $7545.60; part-time $419.20 per credit hour. Tuition, nonresident: full-time $22,169; part-time $1231.60 per credit hour. *International tuition:* $23,518.80 full-time. *Required fees:* $4523.05. Full-time tuition and fees vary according to course load, campus/location, program and reciprocity agreements. *Faculty research:* Analysis, differential equations, topology, statistics.

Molloy College, Graduate Education Program, Rockville Centre, NY 11571-5002. Offers adolescent education in biology (MS); adolescent special education (Advanced Certificate); bilingual extension (Advanced Certificate); childhood education (MS); childhood special education (Advanced Certificate); early childhood education (MS); educational technology (MS); English (MS); mathematics (MS); social studies (MS); Spanish (MS); special education on both childhood and adolescent levels (MS); teaching English to speakers of other languages (TESOL) in grades pre-K to 12 (MS); TESOL (Advanced Certificate). *Accreditation:* NCATE. *Program availability:* Part-time, evening/weekend. *Faculty:* 24 full-time (22 women), 26 part-time/adjunct (19 women). *Students:* 106 full-time (78 women), 203 part-time (154 women); includes 65 minority (14 Black or African American, non-Hispanic/Latino; 5 Asian, non-Hispanic/Latino; 41 Hispanic/Latino; 5 Two or more races, non-Hispanic/Latino). Average age 41. 147 applicants, 63% accepted, 79 enrolled. In 2018, 120 master's, 1 other advanced degree awarded. *Entrance requirements:* Additional exam requirements/recommendations for international students: Required—TOEFL (minimum score 550 paper-based; 79 iBT). *Application deadline:* Applications are processed on a rolling basis. Application fee: $60. Electronic applications accepted. *Expenses: Tuition:* Full-time $20,790; part-time $1155 per credit. *Required fees:* $1060; $900. Tuition and fees vary according to course load and degree level. *Financial support:* Application deadline: 3/1; applicants required to submit FAFSA. *Faculty research:* English Language Learners; social emotional needs of

students; gifted education; cultural diversity; collaborative teaching methods. *Unit head:* Joanne O'Brien, Dean, 516-323-3116, E-mail: jobrien@molloy.edu. *Application contact:* Faye Hood, Assistant Director for Admissions, 516-323-4009, E-mail: fhood@molloy.edu.

Montana State University, The Graduate School, College of Letters and Science, Department of Mathematical Sciences, Bozeman, MT 59717. Offers mathematics (MS, PhD), including mathematics education option (MS); statistics (MS, PhD). *Program availability:* Part-time, online learning. *Degree requirements:* For master's, comprehensive exam, thesis (for some programs); for doctorate, comprehensive exam, thesis/dissertation. *Entrance requirements:* For master's and doctorate, GRE General Test. Additional exam requirements/recommendations for international students: Required—TOEFL (minimum score 550 paper-based). Electronic applications accepted. *Faculty research:* Applied mathematics, dynamical systems, statistics, mathematics education, mathematical and computational biology.

Montclair State University, The Graduate School, College of Education and Human Services, MAT Program in Teaching, Montclair, NJ 07043-1624. Offers art (MAT); biology (MAT); chemistry (MAT); earth science (MAT); English (MAT); French (MAT); health and physical education (MAT); health education (MAT); mathematics (MAT); music (MAT); physical education (MAT); physical science (MAT); social studies (MAT); Spanish (MAT); teacher of English as a second language (MAT). *Degree requirements:* For master's, comprehensive exam, thesis or alternative. *Entrance requirements:* For master's, interview, 2 letters of recommendation. Additional exam requirements/recommendations for international students: Required—TOEFL (minimum score 83 iBT), IELTS (minimum score 6.5). Electronic applications accepted.

Montclair State University, The Graduate School, College of Science and Mathematics, Program in Mathematics, Montclair, NJ 07043-1624. Offers mathematics education (MS); pure and applied mathematics (MS). *Program availability:* Part-time, evening/weekend. *Degree requirements:* For master's, comprehensive exam. *Entrance requirements:* For master's, GRE General Test, 2 letters of recommendation, essay. Additional exam requirements/recommendations for international students: Required—TOEFL (minimum score 83 iBT), IELTS (minimum score 6.5). Electronic applications accepted. *Faculty research:* Computation, applied analysis.

Montclair State University, The Graduate School, College of Science and Mathematics, Program in Mathematics Education, Montclair, NJ 07043-1624. Offers Ed D. *Degree requirements:* For doctorate, thesis/dissertation. *Entrance requirements:* For doctorate, GRE General Test, 2 letters of recommendation, essay. Additional exam requirements/recommendations for international students: Required—TOEFL (minimum score 83 iBT), IELTS (minimum score 6.5). Electronic applications accepted. *Faculty research:* Teacher development, student thinking.

Montclair State University, The Graduate School, College of Science and Mathematics, Program in Teaching Middle Grades Mathematics, Montclair, NJ 07043-1624. Offers MA. *Program availability:* Part-time, evening/weekend. *Degree requirements:* For master's, comprehensive exam, thesis or alternative. *Entrance requirements:* For master's, GRE General Test, 2 letters of recommendation, essay. Additional exam requirements/recommendations for international students: Required—TOEFL (minimum score 83 iBT), IELTS (minimum score 6.5). Electronic applications accepted. *Faculty research:* Teacher knowledge, curriculum.

Montclair State University, The Graduate School, College of Science and Mathematics, Teaching Middle Grades Mathematics Certificate Program, Montclair, NJ 07043-1624. Offers Certificate.

Morehead State University, Graduate School, College of Education, Department of Middle Grades and Secondary Education, Morehead, KY 40351. Offers business and marketing education (MAT); English/language arts 5-9 (MAT); French (MAT); health P-12 (MAT); mathematics 5-9 (MAT); physical education P-12 (MAT); science 5-9 (MAT); secondary biology (MAT); secondary chemistry (MAT); secondary earth science (MAT); secondary English (MAT); secondary math (MAT); secondary physics (MAT); secondary social studies (MAT); social studies 5-9 (MAT); Spanish (MAT). *Program availability:* Part-time, evening/weekend. *Degree requirements:* For master's, portfolio. *Entrance requirements:* For master's, GRE or PRAXIS II content exam, minimum overall undergraduate GPA of 2.5. Additional exam requirements/recommendations for international students: Required—TOEFL (minimum score 500 paper-based). Electronic applications accepted.

Morgan State University, School of Graduate Studies, School of Education and Urban Studies, Department of Advanced Studies, Leadership and Policy, Program in Mathematics Education, Baltimore, MD 21251. Offers MS, Ed D. *Degree requirements:* For doctorate, comprehensive exam, thesis/dissertation. *Entrance requirements:* For doctorate, GRE General Test or MAT. Additional exam requirements/recommendations for international students: Required—TOEFL (minimum score 550 paper-based).

Mount Holyoke College, Professional and Graduate Education (PaGE), South Hadley, MA 01075. Offers initial teacher licensure (MAT); mathematics teaching (MAMT); teacher leadership (MATL). *Program availability:* Part-time, evening/weekend, blended/hybrid learning. *Faculty:* 48 part-time/adjunct (38 women). *Students:* 16 full-time (15 women), 111 part-time (91 women); includes 23 minority (5 Black or African American, non-Hispanic/Latino; 2 Asian, non-Hispanic/Latino; 10 Hispanic/Latino; 6 Two or more races, non-Hispanic/Latino), 7 international. Average age 36. 86 applicants, 91% accepted, 50 enrolled. In 2018, 32 master's awarded. *Degree requirements:* For master's, practicum (for MAT); capstone project (for MATL); capstone portfolio (for MAMT); internship required for some programs. *Entrance requirements:* For master's, Communication & Literacy (both subtests) MTEL for Initial Licensure students, bachelor's degree; subject area knowledge in desired teaching discipline; personal statement; essay; official transcripts; two letters of recommendation; history of effective classroom teaching (for MATL). Additional exam requirements/recommendations for international students: Required—TOEFL (minimum score 100 paper-based), IELTS (minimum score 7). *Application deadline:* For fall admission, 8/1 for domestic and international students; for winter admission, 12/1 for domestic and international students; for spring admission, 1/15 for domestic and international students; for summer admission, 5/15 for domestic and international students. Applications are processed on a rolling basis. Application fee: $50. Electronic applications accepted. Application fee is waived when completed online. *Expenses: Tuition:* Full-time $27,900; part-time $775 per credit hour. One-time fee: $150. Tuition and fees vary according to course level, course load, program and student level. *Financial support:* In 2018–19, 134 students received support, including 5 fellowships with partial tuition reimbursements available (averaging $3,390 per year); scholarships/grants and unspecified assistantships also available. Financial award applicants required to submit FAFSA. *Faculty research:* Mathematics education; educational leadership; special education and inclusivity; equity and advocacy in education; professional development for teachers. *Unit head:* Dr. Tiffany Espinosa, Executive Director of Professional and Graduate Education, 413-538-3478, Fax: 413-538-3098, E-mail: tespinos@mtholyoke.edu. *Application contact:* Dr. Tiffany Espinosa, Executive Director of Professional and Graduate Education, 413-538-3478, Fax: 413-538-3098, E-mail: tespinos@mtholyoke.edu.
Website: https://www.mtholyoke.edu/professional-graduate

Murray State University, Jesse D. Jones College of Science, Engineering and Technology, Department of Mathematics and Statistics, Murray, KY 42071. Offers mathematics (MA, MS); mathematics teacher leader (MAT). *Program availability:* Part-time. *Entrance requirements:* For master's, GRE or GMAT, minimum university GPA of 2.75. Additional exam requirements/recommendations for international students: Required—TOEFL (minimum score 527 paper-based; 71 iBT). Electronic applications accepted.

National Louis University, National College of Education, Chicago, IL 60603. Offers administration and supervision (M Ed, Ed D, CAS, Ed S); curriculum and instruction (M Ed, MS Ed, CAS); early childhood administration (M Ed, CAS); early childhood education (M Ed, MAT, MS Ed, CAS); education (Ed D); educational psychology/human learning and development (M Ed, MS Ed, CAS, Ed S); elementary education (MAT); interdisciplinary curriculum and instruction (M Ed); mathematics education (M Ed, MS Ed, CAS); middle grades education (MAT); reading and language (M Ed, MS Ed, CAS); school psychology (M Ed, Ed S); science education (M Ed, MS Ed, CAS); secondary education (MAT); special education (M Ed, MAT, CAS); technology in education (M Ed, CAS). *Accreditation:* NCATE. *Program availability:* Part-time, evening/weekend. *Degree requirements:* For doctorate, comprehensive exam, thesis/dissertation. *Entrance requirements:* For master's, MAT or GRE, minimum GPA of 3.0; for doctorate, GRE General Test, minimum GPA of 3.25, interview, resume, writing sample, 4 recommendations. Additional exam requirements/recommendations for international students: Required—TOEFL (minimum score 550 paper-based; 79 iBT).

National University, College of Letters and Sciences, La Jolla, CA 92037-1011. Offers biology (MS); counseling psychology (MA), including licensed professional clinical counseling, marriage and family therapy; creative writing (MFA); English (MA); film studies (MA); forensic and crime scene investigations (Certificate); forensic sciences (MFS); human behavior (MA); mathematics for educators (MS); performance psychology (MA); strategic communications (MA). *Program availability:* Part-time, evening/weekend, 100% online, blended/hybrid learning. *Degree requirements:* For master's, thesis (for some programs). *Entrance requirements:* For master's, interview, minimum GPA of 2.5. Additional exam requirements/recommendations for international students: Required—TOEFL (minimum score 550 paper-based; 79 iBT), IELTS (minimum score 6). Electronic applications accepted. *Expenses: Tuition:* Full-time $10,320; part-time $430 per unit. Tuition and fees vary according to degree level.

New Jersey City University, William J. Maxwell College of Arts and Sciences, Department of Mathematics, Jersey City, NJ 07305-1597. Offers mathematics education (MA). *Accreditation:* TEAC. *Program availability:* Part-time, evening/weekend. *Degree requirements:* For master's, comprehensive exam, thesis optional. *Entrance requirements:* Additional exam requirements/recommendations for international students: Required—TOEFL (minimum score 79 iBT).

New York Institute of Technology, School of Interdisciplinary Studies and Education, Department of Instructional Technology, Old Westbury, NY 11568-8000. Offers emerging technologies for trainers (Advanced Certificate); instructional design for global e-learning (Advanced Certificate); instructional technology (MS), including educators, trainers; STEM education (Advanced Certificate). *Program availability:* Part-time, evening/weekend, 100% online, blended/hybrid learning. *Faculty:* 2 full-time (1 woman), 13 part-time/adjunct (5 women). *Students:* 1 full-time (0 women), 80 part-time (51 women); includes 22 minority (8 Black or African American, non-Hispanic/Latino; 5 Asian, non-Hispanic/Latino; 7 Hispanic/Latino; 2 Two or more races, non-Hispanic/Latino). Average age 33. 56 applicants, 63% accepted, 25 enrolled. In 2018, 54 master's, 6 other advanced degrees awarded. *Entrance requirements:* For master's, bachelor's degree; minimum undergraduate GPA of 3.0; demonstrated proficiency in basic uses of instructional technologies; initial/provisional or permanent/professional NY state certification in any teaching area; for Advanced Certificate, BS; minimum undergraduate GPA of 3.0; demonstrated proficiency in basic uses of instructional technologies. Additional exam requirements/recommendations for international students: Required—TOEFL (minimum score 79 iBT), IELTS (minimum score 6), PTE (minimum score 53). *Application deadline:* Applications are processed on a rolling basis. Application fee: $50. Electronic applications accepted. *Expenses:* $1285 per credit plus $215 fees per year (full-time) or $175 fees per year (part-time); $1395 per three-credit education UFT or off-site graduate course. *Financial support:* Career-related internships or fieldwork, scholarships/grants, health care benefits, tuition waivers (full and partial), and unspecified assistantships available. Support available to part-time students. Financial award application deadline: 2/15; financial award applicants required to submit FAFSA. *Faculty research:* Integration of information and communication technologies (ICTs) and media literacy education into learning environments; urban K-12 teachers' effective use of technology to enhance student achievement; instructional design and transdisciplinary curriculum studies for online instruction; STEM and computing partnerships for K-12 teachers; experiential, collaborative, and performance-based approaches to pedagogy and technology integration in the K-12 classroom. *Unit head:* Dr. Melda Yildiz, Department Chair, 516-686-1053, Fax: 516-686-7655, E-mail: myildiz@nyit.edu. *Application contact:* Alice Dolitsky, Director, Graduate Admissions, 516-686-7520, Fax: 516-686-1116, E-mail: admissions@nyit.edu.
Website: http://www.nyit.edu/departments_instructional_technology

New York Institute of Technology, School of Interdisciplinary Studies and Education, Department of Teacher Education, Old Westbury, NY 11568-8000. Offers adolescence education (MS), including math (MAT, MS), science; adolescent education (MAT), including biology, chemistry, English, math (MAT, MS), social studies; childhood education (MS); early childhood (MS). *Program availability:* Part-time, evening/weekend, 100% online, blended/hybrid learning. *Faculty:* 2 full-time (both women), 8 part-time/adjunct (5 women). *Students:* 47 full-time (45 women), 56 part-time (47 women); includes 36 minority (13 Black or African American, non-Hispanic/Latino; 1 American Indian or Alaska Native, non-Hispanic/Latino; 7 Asian, non-Hispanic/Latino; 12 Hispanic/Latino; 1 Native Hawaiian or other Pacific Islander, non-Hispanic/Latino; 2 Two or more races, non-Hispanic/Latino), 3 international. Average age 31. 81 applicants, 53% accepted, 27 enrolled. In 2018, 27 master's awarded. *Entrance requirements:* For master's, GRE or MAT, BS or equivalent; minimum cumulative undergraduate GPA of 3.0; NY state initial certification; BS with major (or minimum 30 credits in a concentration) in biology, chemistry, English, math, physics, or social studies (for MS in childhood, early childhood education, and MAT); interview; personal statement. Additional exam requirements/recommendations for international students: Required—TOEFL (minimum score 79 iBT), IELTS (minimum score 6), PTE (minimum score 53). *Application deadline:* Applications are processed on a rolling basis. Application fee: $50. Electronic applications accepted. *Expenses:* $1285 per credit plus $215 fees per year (full-time) or $175 fees per year (part-time); $1395 per 3-credit education UFT or off-site graduate course. *Financial support:* Career-related internships or fieldwork, Federal Work-Study, scholarships/grants, tuition waivers (full and partial), and unspecified assistantships available. Support available to part-time students. Financial award application deadline: 2/15; financial award applicants required to submit FAFSA. *Faculty research:* Evolving definition of new literacies and its impact on teaching and learning (twenty-first century skills), new literacies practices in teacher education, teachers' professional development, English language and literacy learning through mobile learning, teaching reading to culturally and linguistically diverse children. *Application*

contact: Alice Dolitsky, Director, Graduate Admissions, 516-686-7520, Fax: 516-686-1116, E-mail: admissions@nyit.edu.
Website: http://www.nyit.edu/departments/teacher_education

New York University, Steinhardt School of Culture, Education, and Human Development, Department of Teaching and Learning, Program in Mathematics Education, New York, NY 10012. Offers MA. *Accreditation:* TEAC. *Program availability:* Part-time, evening/weekend. *Entrance requirements:* Additional exam requirements/recommendations for international students: Required—TOEFL (minimum score 100 iBT). Electronic applications accepted. *Faculty research:* Race, gender and mathematics learning; developing mathematical concepts through activity; innovative secondary school mathematics materials.

North Carolina Agricultural and Technical State University, The Graduate College, College of Science and Technology, Department of Mathematics, Greensboro, NC 27411. Offers applied mathematics (MS), including secondary education; mathematics (MAT). *Accreditation:* NCATE (one or more programs are accredited). *Program availability:* Part-time, evening/weekend. *Degree requirements:* For master's, comprehensive exam, thesis or alternative, qualifying exam. *Entrance requirements:* For master's, GRE General Test, minimum GPA of 3.0.

North Carolina State University, Graduate School, College of Education, Department of Science, Technology, Engineering, and Mathematics Education, Program in Mathematics Education, Raleigh, NC 27695. Offers M Ed, MS, PhD. *Accreditation:* NCATE. *Program availability:* Part-time. *Degree requirements:* For master's, thesis (for some programs), oral exam; for doctorate, one foreign language, thesis/dissertation, oral and written exams. *Entrance requirements:* For master's, GRE General Test or MAT, minimum GPA of 3.0; for doctorate, GRE General Test, minimum GPA of 3.0, interview. Electronic applications accepted. *Faculty research:* Teacher education using technology, curriculum development, scientific visualization, problem solving.

North Dakota State University, College of Graduate and Interdisciplinary Studies, College of Engineering, Doctoral Program in Engineering, Fargo, ND 58102. Offers environmental and conservation science (PhD); materials and nanotechnology (PhD); natural resource management (PhD); STEM education (PhD); transportation and logistics (PhD). *Degree requirements:* For doctorate, comprehensive exam, thesis/ dissertation. *Entrance requirements:* For doctorate, bachelor's degree in engineering, minimum GPA of 3.0. Additional exam requirements/recommendations for international students: Required—TOEFL. Electronic applications accepted. *Expenses:* Contact institution.

North Dakota State University, College of Graduate and Interdisciplinary Studies, Program in STEM Education, Fargo, ND 58102. Offers PhD. Electronic applications accepted.

Northeastern Illinois University, College of Graduate Studies and Research, College of Arts and Sciences, Program in Secondary Education Mathematics, Chicago, IL 60625-4699. Offers MS.

Northeastern Illinois University, College of Graduate Studies and Research, Daniel L. Goodwin College of Education, MAT Program in Secondary Education, Chicago, IL 60625. Offers English language arts (MAT); mathematics (MAT); science (MAT); social science (MAT).

Northeastern State University, College of Science and Health Professions, Program in Mathematics Education, Tahlequah, OK 74464-2399. Offers M Ed. *Faculty:* 5 full-time (1 woman). *Students:* 8 full-time (6 women), 19 part-time (16 women); includes 7 minority (3 American Indian or Alaska Native, non-Hispanic/Latino; 1 Asian, non-Hispanic/Latino; 3 Two or more races, non-Hispanic/Latino). Average age 38. In 2018, 7 master's awarded. *Entrance requirements:* For master's, GRE or MAT, minimum GPA of 2.5. Additional exam requirements/recommendations for international students: Required— TOEFL. *Application deadline:* For fall admission, 8/19 for domestic students; for spring admission, 1/7 for domestic students. Applications are processed on a rolling basis. Application fee: $25. Electronic applications accepted. *Expenses: Tuition, area resident:* Full-time $4500; part-time $250 per credit hour. *Tuition, state resident:* full-time $4500; part-time $250 per credit hour. *Tuition, nonresident:* full-time $9999; part-time $555.50 per credit hour. *International tuition:* $9999 full-time. *Required fees:* $601.20; $33.40 per credit hour. *Unit head:* Dr. Darryl Linde, Department Chair, 918-444-3809, E-mail: linded@nsuok.edu. *Application contact:* Josh McCollum, Graduate Coordinator, 918-444-2093, E-mail: mccolluj@nsuok.edu.
Website: http://academics.nsuok.edu/mathematics/DegreesMajors/Graduate/MEdMathematicsEducation.aspx

Northern Arizona University, College of Environment, Forestry, and Natural Sciences, Department of Mathematics and Statistics, Flagstaff, AZ 86011. Offers applied statistics (Graduate Certificate); mathematics (MS); mathematics education (MS); statistics (MS); teaching introductory community college mathematics (Graduate Certificate). *Program availability:* Part-time. *Degree requirements:* For master's, variable foreign language requirement, comprehensive exam (for some programs), thesis (for some programs); for Graduate Certificate, comprehensive exam (for some programs). *Entrance requirements:* Additional exam requirements/recommendations for international students: Required—TOEFL (minimum score 80 iBT), IELTS (minimum score 6.5), TOEFL minimum iBT score of 89 (for MS and Graduate Certificate). Electronic applications accepted.

Northwest Missouri State University, Graduate School, College of Arts and Sciences, Maryville, MO 64468-6001. Offers biology (MS); elementary mathematics specialist (MS Ed); English (MA); English education (MS Ed); English pedagogy (MA); geographic information science (MS, Certificate); history (MS Ed); mathematics (MS); mathematics education (MS Ed); teaching: science (MS Ed). *Program availability:* Part-time. *Faculty:* 20 full-time (9 women). *Students:* 15 full-time (9 women), 66 part-time (30 women); includes 6 minority (2 Black or African American, non-Hispanic/Latino; 1 American Indian or Alaska Native, non-Hispanic/Latino; 1 Hispanic/Latino; 2 Two or more races, non-Hispanic/Latino), 2 international. Average age 34. 32 applicants, 66% accepted, 19 enrolled. In 2018, 17 master's awarded. *Degree requirements:* For master's, comprehensive exam. *Entrance requirements:* For master's, GRE General Test, writing sample. Additional exam requirements/recommendations for international students: Required—TOEFL (minimum score 550 paper-based). *Application deadline:* For fall admission, 7/1 for domestic and international students; for spring admission, 11/15 for domestic and international students. Applications are processed on a rolling basis. Application fee: $0 ($75 for international students). Electronic applications accepted. *Expenses: Tuition, area resident:* Full-time $4551; part-time $252.86 per credit hour. *Tuition, state resident:* full-time $4551; part-time $252.86 per credit hour. *Tuition, nonresident:* full-time $9103; part-time $505.72 per credit hour. *International tuition:* $9103 full-time. *Required fees:* $2668; $148.20 per credit hour. Tuition and fees vary according to program. *Financial support:* Research assistantships with full tuition reimbursements, teaching assistantships with full tuition reimbursements, and administrative assistantships, tutorial assistantships available. Financial award application deadline: 4/1; financial award applicants required to submit FAFSA. *Unit head:* Dr. Michael Steiner, Dean, 660-562-1197. *Application contact:* Dr. Michael Steiner, Dean, 660-562-1197.

Website: https://www.nwmissouri.edu/academics/undergraduate/majors/liberal-arts-sciences.htm

Northwest Missouri State University, Graduate School, School of Education, Maryville, MO 64468-6001. Offers early childhood education (MS Ed); education leadership (MS Ed), including elementary, K-12, secondary; educational leadership (Ed S), including elementary school principalship, secondary school principalship, superintendency; educational leadership and policy analysis (Ed D); elementary education (MS Ed); elementary mathematics (MS Ed); higher education leadership (MS); middle school education (MS Ed); reading (MS Ed); special education (MS Ed); teacher leadership (MS Ed); teaching English language learners (MS Ed). *Accreditation:* NCATE. *Program availability:* Part-time. *Faculty:* 26 full-time (16 women). *Students:* 109 full-time (87 women), 385 part-time (270 women); includes 30 minority (10 Black or African American, non-Hispanic/Latino; 2 American Indian or Alaska Native, non-Hispanic/Latino; 3 Asian, non-Hispanic/Latino; 12 Hispanic/Latino; 1 Native Hawaiian or other Pacific Islander, non-Hispanic/Latino; 2 Two or more races, non-Hispanic/Latino), 1 international. Average age 33. 210 applicants, 72% accepted, 142 enrolled. In 2018, 71 master's, 11 other advanced degrees awarded. *Degree requirements:* For master's, comprehensive exam; for Ed S, comprehensive exam, thesis. *Entrance requirements:* For master's, GRE General Test, writing sample; for Ed S, minimum graduate GPA of 3.25. Additional exam requirements/recommendations for international students: Required—TOEFL (minimum score 550 paper-based). *Application deadline:* For fall admission, 7/1 for domestic and international students; for spring admission, 11/15 for domestic and international students. Applications are processed on a rolling basis. Application fee: $0 ($75 for international students). Electronic applications accepted. *Expenses:* $389.11 in-state and $653.92 out-of-state per credit hour. *Financial support:* Research assistantships with full tuition reimbursements, teaching assistantships with full tuition reimbursements, and unspecified assistantships available. Financial award application deadline: 4/1; financial award applicants required to submit FAFSA. *Unit head:* Dr. Tim Wall, Director, 660-562-1179, E-mail: timwall@nwmissouri.edu. *Application contact:* Dr. Tim Wall, Director, 660-562-1179, E-mail: timwall@nwmissouri.edu.
Website: https://www.nwmissouri.edu/education/index.htm

The Ohio State University, Graduate School, College of Arts and Sciences, Division of Natural and Mathematical Sciences, Department of Mathematics, Columbus, OH 43210. Offers actuarial and quantitative risk management (MAQRM); computational sciences (MMS); mathematical biosciences (MMS); mathematics (PhD); mathematics for educators (MMS). *Faculty:* 61. *Students:* 150 full-time (32 women); includes 16 minority (9 Asian, non-Hispanic/Latino; 5 Hispanic/Latino; 2 Two or more races, non-Hispanic/Latino), 84 international. Average age 26. In 2018, 24 master's, 21 doctorates awarded. *Degree requirements:* For master's, thesis optional; for doctorate, one foreign language, thesis/dissertation. *Entrance requirements:* For master's, GRE General Test; for doctorate, GRE General Test (recommended), GRE Subject Test (mathematics). Additional exam requirements/recommendations for international students: Required— TOEFL (minimum score 550 paper-based; 79 iBT), Michigan English Language Assessment Battery (minimum score 82); Recommended—IELTS (minimum score 7). *Application deadline:* For fall admission, 12/15 priority date for domestic and international students. Applications are processed on a rolling basis. Application fee: $60 ($70 for international students). Electronic applications accepted. *Financial support:* Fellowships, research assistantships, teaching assistantships, Federal Work-Study, institutionally sponsored loans, and unspecified assistantships available. Support available to part-time students. *Unit head:* Dr. Jean-Francois Lafont, Chair, 614-292-7173, E-mail: lafont.1@osu.edu. *Application contact:* Erin Anthony, Graduate Studies Coordinator, 614-292-6274, Fax: 614-292-1479, E-mail: grad-info@math.osu.edu.
Website: http://www.math.osu.edu/

Oregon State University, College of Education, Program in Education, Corvallis, OR 97331. Offers agricultural education (PhD); language equity and education policy (PhD); mathematics education (MS); science education (MS); science/mathematics education (PhD). *Program availability:* Part-time, 100% online, blended/hybrid learning. Terminal master's awarded for partial completion of doctoral program. *Degree requirements:* For master's, variable foreign language requirement, thesis (for some programs); for doctorate, variable foreign language requirement, thesis/dissertation. *Entrance requirements:* Additional exam requirements/recommendations for international students: Required—TOEFL (minimum score 575 paper-based). *Faculty research:* School administration, educational foundations, research methodology, education policy development, higher education administration.

Oregon State University, College of Science, Program in Mathematics, Corvallis, OR 97331. Offers differential geometry (MA, MS, PhD); financial and actuarial mathematics (MA, MS, PhD); mathematical biology (MA, MS, PhD); mathematics education (MS, PhD); number theory (MA, MS, PhD); numerical analysis (MA, MS, PhD); probability (MA). Terminal master's awarded for partial completion of doctoral program. *Degree requirements:* For master's, thesis or alternative; for doctorate, thesis/dissertation, qualifying exams. *Entrance requirements:* For master's and doctorate, GRE. Additional exam requirements/recommendations for international students: Required—TOEFL (minimum score 100 iBT). Electronic applications accepted.

Plymouth State University, College of Graduate Studies, Graduate Studies in Education, Program in Mathematics Education, Plymouth, NH 03264-1595. Offers M Ed. *Program availability:* Part-time, evening/weekend. *Degree requirements:* For master's, comprehensive exam, thesis optional, internship or practicum. *Entrance requirements:* For master's, MAT, minimum GPA of 3.0.

Portland State University, Graduate Studies, College of Liberal Arts and Sciences, Fariborz Maseeh Department of Mathematics and Statistics, Portland, OR 97207-0751. Offers applied statistics (Certificate); mathematical sciences (PhD); mathematics education (PhD); mathematics for middle school (Certificate); mathematics for teachers (MS); statistics (MS); MA/MS. *Degree requirements:* For master's, comprehensive exam, thesis or alternative, 2 written examinations; for doctorate, thesis/dissertation, preliminary and comprehensive examinations. *Entrance requirements:* For master's, GRE General Test, GRE Subject Test, minimum GPA of 3.0 in upper-division course work or 2.75 cumulative undergraduate; for doctorate, GRE General Test. Additional exam requirements/recommendations for international students: Required—TOEFL (minimum score 550 paper-based; 80 iBT). *Faculty research:* Algebra, topology, statistical distribution theory, control theory, statistical robustness.

Providence College, Program in Teaching Mathematics, Providence, RI 02918. Offers MA. *Program availability:* Part-time, evening/weekend. *Entrance requirements:* Additional exam requirements/recommendations for international students: Required— TOEFL (minimum score 577 paper-based; 90 iBT). *Expenses:* Contact institution.

Purdue University, Graduate School, College of Education, Department of Curriculum and Instruction, West Lafayette, IN 47907. Offers agricultural and extension education (MS, MS Ed, PhD, Ed S); art education (PhD); career and technical education (MS Ed, PhD, Ed S); curriculum studies (MS Ed, PhD, Ed S); educational technology (MS Ed, PhD, Ed S); elementary education (MS Ed); family and consumer sciences education (MS Ed, PhD, Ed S); foreign language education (MS Ed, PhD, Ed S); industrial technology (PhD, Ed S); language arts (MS Ed, PhD, Ed S); literacy (MS Ed, PhD,

Ed S); mathematics education (MS, MS Ed, PhD, Ed S); science education (MS, MS Ed, PhD, Ed S); social studies education (MS Ed, PhD, Ed S). *Accreditation:* NCATE. *Program availability:* Part-time, evening/weekend, online learning. *Faculty:* 34 full-time (24 women), 3 part-time/adjunct (1 woman). *Students:* 75 full-time (52 women), 357 part-time (271 women); includes 83 minority (29 Black or African American, non-Hispanic/Latino; 1 American Indian or Alaska Native, non-Hispanic/Latino; 14 Asian, non-Hispanic/Latino; 29 Hispanic/Latino; 1 Native Hawaiian or other Pacific Islander, non-Hispanic/Latino; 9 Two or more races, non-Hispanic/Latino), 43 international. Average age 36. 169 applicants, 83% accepted, 102 enrolled. In 2018, 141 master's, 15 doctorates awarded. *Degree requirements:* For master's, thesis optional; for doctorate, thesis/dissertation, oral and written exams; for Ed S, oral presentation, project. *Entrance requirements:* For master's, GRE General Test (if undergraduate GPA is below 3.0), minimum undergraduate GPA of 3.0 or equivalent; for doctorate, GRE General Test (minimum combined verbal and quantitative score of 1000, 300 for new scoring), minimum undergraduate GPA of 3.0 or equivalent; master's degree with minimum GPA of 3.0 or equivalent; for Ed S, GRE General Test (minimum combined verbal and quantitative score of 1000, 300 for new scoring), minimum undergraduate GPA of 3.0 or equivalent; master's degree. Additional exam requirements/recommendations for international students: Required—TOEFL (minimum score 550 paper-based; 77 iBT). *Application deadline:* For fall admission, 12/15 for domestic students, 3/1 for international students; for spring admission, 9/15 for domestic students, 8/1 for international students. Application fee: $60 ($75 for international students). Electronic applications accepted. *Financial support:* Fellowships with full tuition reimbursements, research assistantships with full tuition reimbursements, teaching assistantships with full tuition reimbursements, career-related internships or fieldwork, and tuition waivers (full) available. Support available to part-time students. Financial award application deadline: 3/1; financial award applicants required to submit FAFSA. *Faculty research:* Literacy acquisition and development, teacher beliefs and knowledge, recruitment and retention of underrepresented students, economic education, literacy discourse. *Unit head:* Janet M. Alsup, Head, 765-494-9667, E-mail: alsupj@purdue.edu. *Application contact:* Heather Brinkman, Graduate Contact, 765-494-2345, E-mail: hbrinkma@purdue.edu.
Website: http://www.edci.purdue.edu/

Purdue University Fort Wayne, College of Arts and Sciences, Department of Mathematical Sciences, Fort Wayne, IN 46805-1499. Offers applied mathematics (MS); applied statistics (Certificate); mathematics (MS); operations research (MS); teaching (MAT). *Program availability:* Part-time, evening/weekend. *Entrance requirements:* For master's, minimum GPA of 3.0, major or minor in mathematics, three letters of recommendation. Additional exam requirements/recommendations for international students: Required—TOEFL (minimum score 550 paper-based; 79 iBT); Recommended—TWE. Electronic applications accepted. *Faculty research:* Eves' Theorem, paired-placements for student teaching, holomorphic maps.

Purdue University Global, School of Teacher Education, Davenport, IA 52807. Offers education (M Ed); secondary education (M Ed); teaching and learning (MA); teaching literacy and language: grades 6-12 (MA); teaching literacy and language: grades K-6 (MA); teaching mathematics: grades 6-8 (MA); teaching mathematics: grades 9-12 (MA); teaching mathematics: grades K-5 (MA); teaching science: grades 6-12 (MA); teaching science: grades K-6 (MA); teaching students with special needs (MA); teaching with technology (MA). *Program availability:* Part-time, evening/weekend, online learning. *Entrance requirements:* Additional exam requirements/recommendations for international students: Required—TOEFL (minimum score 550 paper-based; 80 iBT).

Purdue University Northwest, Graduate Studies Office, School of Engineering, Mathematics, and Science, Department of Mathematics, Computer Science, and Statistics, Hammond, IN 46323-2094. Offers computer science (MS); mathematics (MAT, MS). *Program availability:* Part-time. *Entrance requirements:* Additional exam requirements/recommendations for international students: Required—TOEFL. *Faculty research:* Topology, analysis, algebra, mathematics education.

Queens College of the City University of New York, Division of Education, Department of Secondary Education and Youth Services, Queens, NY 11367-1597. Offers adolescent biology (MAT); art (MS Ed); biology (MS Ed, AC); chemistry (MS Ed, AC); earth sciences (MS Ed, AC); English (MS Ed, AC); French (MS Ed); Italian (MS Ed, AC); literacy education (MS Ed); mathematics (MS Ed, AC); music (MS Ed, AC); physics (MS Ed, AC); social studies (MS Ed, AC); Spanish (MS Ed, AC). *Program availability:* Part-time, evening/weekend. *Faculty:* 22 full-time (14 women), 35 part-time/adjunct (24 women). *Students:* 33 full-time (19 women), 358 part-time (228 women); includes 182 minority (15 Black or African American, non-Hispanic/Latino; 62 Asian, non-Hispanic/Latino; 91 Hispanic/Latino; 4 Native Hawaiian or other Pacific Islander, non-Hispanic/Latino; 10 Two or more races, non-Hispanic/Latino), 13 international. Average age 29. 216 applicants, 74% accepted, 109 enrolled. In 2018, 108 master's, 35 other advanced degrees awarded. *Degree requirements:* For master's, research project. *Entrance requirements:* For master's, GRE, minimum GPA of 3.0. Additional exam requirements/recommendations for international students: Required—TOEFL, IELTS. *Application deadline:* For fall admission, 4/1 for domestic students; for spring admission, 11/1 for domestic students. Applications are processed on a rolling basis. Application fee: $125. Electronic applications accepted. *Financial support:* Career-related internships or fieldwork available. Financial award application deadline: 4/1; financial award applicants required to submit FAFSA. *Faculty research:* Self regulated learning, teacher learning, assessment and teaching, language diversity, teaching and learning history. *Unit head:* Dr. Eleanor Armour-Thomas, Chairperson, 718-997-5150, E-mail: eleanor.armour-thomas@qc.cuny.edu. *Application contact:* Elizabeth D'Amico-Ramirez, Assistant Director of Graduate Admissions, 718-997-5203, E-mail: elizabeth.damicoramirez@qc.cuny.edu.

Quinnipiac University, School of Education, Program in Secondary Education, Hamden, CT 06518-1940. Offers biology (MAT); English (MAT); history (MAT); mathematics (MAT); Spanish (MAT). *Accreditation:* NCATE. *Entrance requirements:* For master's, PRAXIS I or PRAXIS Core Academic Skills Exam, minimum GPA of 3.0, interview. Electronic applications accepted. *Faculty research:* Multicultural and urban education/leadership, challenges of teaching diverse learners, scholarship of teaching and learning, technology and teaching, humor and education.

Radford University, College of Graduate Studies and Research, Program in Education, Radford, VA 24142. Offers early childhood education (MS); mathematics education (MS). *Accreditation:* NCATE. *Program availability:* Part-time, evening/weekend. *Faculty:* 28 full-time (21 women), 8 part-time/adjunct (6 women). *Students:* 39 full-time (28 women), 65 part-time (48 women); includes 10 minority (6 Black or African American, non-Hispanic/Latino; 1 Asian, non-Hispanic/Latino; 1 Hispanic/Latino; 2 Two or more races, non-Hispanic/Latino). Average age 31. 40 applicants, 93% accepted, 29 enrolled. In 2018, 42 master's awarded. *Degree requirements:* For master's, comprehensive exam. *Entrance requirements:* For master's, GRE (waived for any applicant with advanced degree), minimum GPA of 3.0, 2 letters of professional reference, personal statement, resume, official transcripts. Additional exam requirements/recommendations for international students: Required—TOEFL (minimum score 550 paper-based; 79 iBT), IELTS (minimum score 6.5). *Application deadline:* For fall admission, 2/15 priority date for domestic students, 12/1 for international students; for spring admission, 7/1 for international students. Applications are processed on a rolling basis. Application fee: $50. Electronic applications accepted. *Expenses: Tuition, area resident:* Full-time $8915; part-time $371 per credit hour. Tuition, state resident: full-time $8915; part-time $371 per credit hour. Tuition, nonresident: full-time $17,441. *Required fees:* $3288; $138 per credit hour. *Financial support:* In 2018–19, 5 students received support. Research assistantships, career-related internships or fieldwork, scholarships/grants, and unspecified assistantships available. Support available to part-time students. Financial award application deadline: 3/1; financial award applicants required to submit FAFSA. *Unit head:* Dr. Wendy Eckenrod-Green, Coordinator, 540-831-5302, E-mail: stel@radford.edu. *Application contact:* Dr. Wendy Eckenrod-Green, Coordinator, 540-831-5302, E-mail: stel@radford.edu.
Website: http://www.radford.edu/content/cehd/home/teacher-ed/programs/education-master.html

Rhode Island College, School of Graduate Studies, Feinstein School of Education and Human Development, Department of Educational Studies, Providence, RI 02908-1991. Offers advanced studies in teaching and learning (M Ed); English (MAT); French (MAT); history (MAT); math (MAT); secondary education (MAT); Spanish (MAT); teaching English as a second language (M Ed). *Accreditation:* NCATE. *Program availability:* Part-time, evening/weekend. *Faculty:* 12 full-time (9 women), 7 part-time/adjunct (6 women). *Students:* 12 full-time (10 women), 31 part-time (28 women); includes 5 minority (1 Black or African American, non-Hispanic/Latino; 1 Asian, non-Hispanic/Latino; 3 Hispanic/Latino). Average age 33. In 2018, 24 master's awarded. *Degree requirements:* For master's, capstone or comprehensive assessment. *Entrance requirements:* For master's, GRE or MAT (for most programs), minimum undergraduate GPA of 3.0; baccalaureate degree in English, French, history, math or Spanish; 3 letters of recommendation; interview. Additional exam requirements/recommendations for international students: Required—TOEFL (minimum score 550 paper-based; 80 iBT). *Application deadline:* For fall admission, 3/1 for domestic students; for spring admission, 11/1 for domestic students. Applications are processed on a rolling basis. Application fee: $50. Electronic applications accepted. *Expenses: Tuition, area resident:* Part-time $407 per credit. Tuition, nonresident: part-time $792 per credit. *Required fees:* $29 per credit. $100 per semester. *Financial support:* Teaching assistantships, career-related internships or fieldwork, Federal Work-Study, scholarships/grants, health care benefits, and unspecified assistantships available. Support available to part-time students. Financial award application deadline: 5/15; financial award applicants required to submit FAFSA. *Unit head:* Dr. Leslie Bogad, Chair, 401-456-8170. *Application contact:* Dr. Leslie Bogad, Chair, 401-456-8170.
Website: http://www.ric.edu/educationalStudies/Pages/default.aspx

Rowan University, Graduate School, College of Education, Department of Science, Technology, Engineering, Art and Math Education, Glassboro, NJ 08028-1701. Offers educational technology (CGS); STEM education (MA). *Program availability:* Part-time, evening/weekend. *Degree requirements:* For master's, thesis. *Entrance requirements:* For master's, GRE General Test. Additional exam requirements/recommendations for international students: Required—TOEFL. Electronic applications accepted.

Rowan University, Graduate School, College of Science and Mathematics, Department of Mathematics, Program in Middle Grades Math Education, Glassboro, NJ 08028-1701. Offers CGS. Electronic applications accepted.

Rutgers University–Camden, Graduate School of Arts and Sciences, Program in Mathematical Sciences, Camden, NJ 08102. Offers industrial mathematics (MBS); industrial/applied mathematics (MS); mathematical computer science (MS); pure mathematics (MS); teaching in mathematical sciences (MS). *Program availability:* Part-time, evening/weekend. *Degree requirements:* For master's, comprehensive exam, thesis optional, survey paper, 30 credits. *Entrance requirements:* For master's, GRE, BS/BA in math or related subject, 2 letters of recommendation. Additional exam requirements/recommendations for international students: Required—TOEFL (minimum score 550 paper-based), IELTS. Electronic applications accepted. *Faculty research:* Differential geometry, dynamical systems, vertex operator algebra, automorphic forms, CR-structures.

Rutgers University–New Brunswick, Graduate School of Education, Department of Learning and Teaching, Program in Mathematics Education, Piscataway, NJ 08854-8097. Offers Ed M, Ed D. *Program availability:* Part-time. Terminal master's awarded for partial completion of doctoral program. *Degree requirements:* For master's, comprehensive exam (for some programs); for doctorate, thesis/dissertation, qualifying exam. *Entrance requirements:* For master's, GRE General Test, minimum GPA of 3.0; for doctorate, GRE General Test, minimum GPA of 3.5. Additional exam requirements/recommendations for international students: Required—TOEFL. Electronic applications accepted.

Rutgers University–New Brunswick, Graduate School of Education, Doctoral Program in Education, New Brunswick, NJ 08901. Offers educational policy (PhD); educational psychology (PhD); literacy education (PhD); mathematics education (PhD). *Program availability:* Part-time. *Degree requirements:* For doctorate, thesis/dissertation, qualifying exam. *Entrance requirements:* For doctorate, GRE General Test, GRE Subject Test (mathematics education). Additional exam requirements/recommendations for international students: Required—TOEFL (minimum score 575 paper-based; 83 iBT). Electronic applications accepted. *Faculty research:* Literacy education, math education, educational psychology, educational policy, learning sciences.

St. John Fisher College, Ralph C. Wilson Jr. School of Education, Program in Adolescence Education and Special Education, Rochester, NY 14618-3597. Offers adolescence education: biology with special education (MS Ed); adolescence education: chemistry with special education (MS Ed); adolescence education: English with special education (MS Ed); adolescence education: French with special education (MS Ed); adolescence education: math with special education (MS Ed); adolescence education: physics with special education (MS Ed); adolescence education: social studies with special education (MS Ed); adolescence education: Spanish with special education (MS Ed). *Program availability:* Part-time, evening/weekend. *Faculty:* 8 full-time (6 women), 2 part-time/adjunct (both women). *Students:* 13 full-time (4 women), 2 part-time (1 woman); includes 2 minority (1 Black or African American, non-Hispanic/Latino; 1 Two or more races, non-Hispanic/Latino). Average age 27. 24 applicants, 58% accepted, 4 enrolled. In 2018, 9 master's awarded. *Degree requirements:* For master's, field experiences, student teaching. *Entrance requirements:* For master's, LAST, 2 letters of recommendation, personal statement, current resume. Additional exam requirements/recommendations for international students: Required—TOEFL (minimum score 575 paper-based; 80 iBT). *Application deadline:* Applications are processed on a rolling basis. Application fee: $30. Electronic applications accepted. *Expenses:* Contact institution. *Financial support:* Scholarships/grants available. Financial award applicants required to submit FAFSA. *Faculty research:* Arts and humanities, urban schools, constructivist learning, at-risk students, mentoring. *Unit head:* Dr. Susan Hildenbrand, Program Director, 585-385-7297, E-mail: shildenbrand@sjfc.edu. *Application contact:* Michelle Gosier, Director of Transfer and Graduate Admissions, 585-385-8064, E-mail: mgosier@sjfc.edu.

St. John Fisher College, School of Arts and Sciences, Program in Applied Data Science, Rochester, NY 14618-3597. Offers MS. *Program availability:* Part-time, evening/weekend. *Faculty:* 2 full-time (0 women). *Students:* 13 part-time (6 women);

includes 4 minority (2 Black or African American, non-Hispanic/Latino; 2 Asian, non-Hispanic/Latino). Average age 28. 26 applicants, 100% accepted, 13 enrolled. *Degree requirements:* For master's, directed research project. *Entrance requirements:* For master's, 2 letters of recommendation, personal statement, current resume. Additional exam requirements/recommendations for international students: Required—TOEFL (minimum score 575 paper-based; 80 iBT). Application fee: $30. *Expenses: Tuition:* Full-time $950; part-time $950 per credit hour. *Required fees:* $15; $15 per semester. *Financial support:* Scholarships/grants available. *Unit head:* Dr. Bernard Ricca, Director, 585-899-3866, E-mail: bricca@sjfc.edu. *Application contact:* Michelle Gosier, Director of Transfer and Graduate Admissions, 585-385-8064, E-mail: mgosier@sjfc.edu.

Website: https://www.sjfc.edu/graduate-programs/ms-in-applied-data-science/

St. John's University, The School of Education, Department of Curriculum and Instruction, PhD in Curriculum and Instruction Program, Queens, NY 11439. Offers early childhood (PhD); global education (PhD); STEM education (PhD); teaching, learning, and knowing (PhD). *Program availability:* Part-time-only. *Degree requirements:* For doctorate, comprehensive exam, thesis/dissertation. *Entrance requirements:* For doctorate, teacher certification (or equivalent), at least three years' teaching experience or the equivalent in informal learning environments, master's degree. Additional exam requirements/recommendations for international students: Required—TOEFL. Electronic applications accepted. *Faculty research:* Literacies, early childhood, STEM, school culture, global education.

Saint Peter's University, Graduate Programs in Education, Jersey City, NJ 07306-5997. Offers director of school counseling services (Certificate); educational leadership (MA Ed, Ed D); higher education (MHE, Ed D), including educational leadership (Ed D), general administration (MHE); middle school mathematics (Certificate); professional/associate counselor (Certificate); reading (MA Ed); school business administrator (Certificate); school counseling (MA, Certificate); special education (MA Ed, Certificate), including applied behavioral analysis (MA Ed), literacy (MA Ed), teacher of students with disabilities (Certificate); teaching (MA Ed, Certificate), including 6-8 middle school education, K-12 secondary education, K-5 elementary education. *Accreditation:* TEAC. *Program availability:* Part-time, evening/weekend. *Degree requirements:* For master's, comprehensive exam; for doctorate, comprehensive exam, thesis/dissertation. *Entrance requirements:* For master's and doctorate, GRE or MAT. Additional exam requirements/recommendations for international students: Required—TOEFL. Electronic applications accepted.

Salem State University, School of Graduate Studies, Program in Middle School Education, Salem, MA 01970-5353. Offers humanities (M Ed); math/science (MAT). *Program availability:* Part-time, evening/weekend. *Entrance requirements:* For master's, GRE or MAT. Additional exam requirements/recommendations for international students: Required—TOEFL (minimum score 550 paper-based; 80 iBT) or IELTS (minimum score 5.5).

Salem State University, School of Graduate Studies, Program in Middle School Math, Salem, MA 01970-5353. Offers MAT. *Program availability:* Part-time, evening/weekend. *Entrance requirements:* For master's, GRE or MAT. Additional exam requirements/recommendations for international students: Required—TOEFL (minimum score 550 paper-based; 80 iBT) or IELTS (minimum score 5.5).

Salisbury University, Program in Mathematics Education, Salisbury, MD 21801-6837. Offers mathematics (MSME), including high school, middle school. *Program availability:* Part-time. *Faculty:* 2 full-time (1 woman). *Students:* 1 (woman) full-time, 11 part-time (10 women). Average age 26. 7 applicants, 100% accepted, 6 enrolled. In 2018, 1 master's awarded. *Degree requirements:* For master's, capstone experience. *Entrance requirements:* For master's, transcripts from colleges and universities attended; personal statement; two letters of recommendation. Additional exam requirements/recommendations for international students: Required—TOEFL (minimum score 550 paper-based; 79 iBT), IELTS (minimum score 6.5). *Application deadline:* For fall admission, 8/15 priority date for domestic and international students; for spring admission, 10/1 priority date for domestic and international students. Applications are processed on a rolling basis. Application fee: $65. Electronic applications accepted. *Expenses:* Resident - $412 per credit hour; Non-resident - $746 per credit hour; Fees - $108. *Financial support:* In 2018–19, 1 teaching assistantship with full tuition reimbursement (averaging $8,000 per year) was awarded; career-related internships or fieldwork and scholarships/grants also available. Support available to part-time students. Financial award application deadline: 3/1; financial award applicants required to submit FAFSA. *Faculty research:* Multiplicative reasoning of children; the mathematics of games; probabilistic reasoning of middle grade children; fractional reasoning of children; pre-service teacher education. *Unit head:* Dr. Jennifer Bergner, Graduate Program Director, 410-677-5429, E-mail: jabergner@salisbury.edu. *Application contact:* Dr. Jennifer Bergner, Graduate Program Director, 410-677-5429, E-mail: jabergner@salisbury.edu.

Website: https://www.salisbury.edu/explore-academics/programs/graduate-degree-programs/mathematics-education-masters/

San Diego State University, Graduate and Research Affairs, College of Sciences, Department of Mathematics and Statistics, San Diego, CA 92182. Offers applied mathematics (MS); mathematics (MA); mathematics and science education (PhD); statistics (MS). PhD offered jointly wtih University of California, San Diego. *Program availability:* Part-time. *Degree requirements:* For doctorate, thesis/dissertation. *Entrance requirements:* For master's, GRE General Test; for doctorate, GRE, minimum GPA of 3.25 in last 30 undergraduate semester units, minimum graduate GPA of 3.5, MSE recommendation form, 3 letters of recommendation. Additional exam requirements/recommendations for international students: Required—TOEFL. Electronic applications accepted. *Faculty research:* Teacher education in mathematics.

San Francisco State University, Division of Graduate Studies, College of Education, Department of Elementary Education, Program in Mathematics Education, San Francisco, CA 94132-1722. Offers MA. *Accreditation:* NCATE. *Unit head:* Dr. Stephanie Sisk-Hilton, Chair, 415-338-1562, Fax: 415-338-0567, E-mail: stephsh@sfsu.edu. *Application contact:* Dr. Maria Zavala, MA Program Coordinator, 415-405-0465, Fax: 415-338-0567, E-mail: mza@sfsu.edu.

Website: https://eed.sfsu.edu/

San Francisco State University, Division of Graduate Studies, College of Education, Department of Secondary Education, San Francisco, CA 94132-1722. Offers mathematics education (MA); secondary education (MA, Credential). *Accreditation:* NCATE. *Unit head:* Dr. Maika Watanabe, Chair, 415-338-1622, Fax: 415-338-0914, E-mail: watanabe@sfsu.edu. *Application contact:* Marisol Del Rio, Administrative Office Coordinator, 415-338-7649, Fax: 415-338-0914, E-mail: seced@sfsu.edu.

Website: http://secondaryed.sfsu.edu/

Seattle Pacific University, Program in Teaching Mathematics and Science, Seattle, WA 98119-1997. Offers MTMS. *Students:* 11 full-time (4 women), 2 part-time (both women); includes 2 minority (1 Asian, non-Hispanic/Latino; 1 Two or more races, non-Hispanic/Latino). Average age 33. 38 applicants, 55% accepted, 13 enrolled. In 2018, 15 master's awarded. *Degree requirements:* For master's, internship. *Application deadline:* For fall admission, 8/15 for domestic students; for winter admission, 11/15 for

domestic students; for spring admission, 2/15 for domestic students; for summer admission, 5/15 for domestic students. *Unit head:* David W. Dento, Graduate Teacher Education Chair, 206-281-2504, E-mail: dentod@spu.edu. *Application contact:* David W. Dento, Graduate Teacher Education Chair, 206-281-2504, E-mail: dentod@spu.edu. Website: http://spu.edu/academics/school-of-education/graduate-programs/masters-programs/master-in-teaching-mathematics-and-science

Shippensburg University of Pennsylvania, School of Graduate Studies, College of Education and Human Services, Department of Teacher Education, Shippensburg, PA 17257-2299. Offers curriculum and instruction (M Ed), including biology, early childhood education, elementary education, geography/earth science, history, mathematics, middle school education, modern languages; reading (M Ed). *Accreditation:* NCATE. *Program availability:* Part-time, evening/weekend, 100% online, blended/hybrid learning. *Faculty:* 12 full-time (9 women), 2 part-time/adjunct (0 women). *Students:* 10 full-time (8 women), 68 part-time (64 women); includes 7 minority (2 Black or African American, non-Hispanic/Latino; 4 Hispanic/Latino; 1 Two or more races, non-Hispanic/Latino). Average age 31. 41 applicants, 73% accepted, 19 enrolled. In 2018, 34 master's awarded. *Degree requirements:* For master's, comprehensive exam (for some programs), thesis optional, practicum or internship; capstone seminar (for some programs). *Entrance requirements:* For master's, MAT or GRE (if GPA less than 2.75), interview, 3 letters of reference, questionnaire of teaching background and future goals, resume. Additional exam requirements/recommendations for international students: Required—TOEFL (minimum score 550 paper-based; 68 iBT), IELTS (minimum score 6), TOEFL (minimum score 550 paper-based, 68 iBT) or IELTS (minimum score 6). *Application deadline:* For fall admission, 4/1 priority date for domestic students, 4/30 for international students; for spring admission, 9/1 priority date for domestic students, 9/30 for international students; for summer admission, 2/1 priority date for domestic students. Applications are processed on a rolling basis. Application fee: $45. Electronic applications accepted. *Expenses:* Tuition, state resident: part-time $516 per credit. Tuition, nonresident: part-time $750 per credit. *Required fees:* $149 per credit. *Financial support:* In 2018–19, 5 students received support. Career-related internships or fieldwork, scholarships/grants, unspecified assistantships, and resident hall director and student payroll positions available. Support available to part-time students. Financial award application deadline: 3/1; financial award applicants required to submit FAFSA. *Unit head:* Dr. Christine A. Royce, Chairperson, 717-477-1688, Fax: 717-477-4046, E-mail: caroyc@ship.edu. *Application contact:* Maya T. Mapp, Director of Admissions, 717-477-1231, Fax: 717-477-4016, E-mail: mtmapp@ship.edu. Website: http://www.ship.edu/teacher/

Simon Fraser University, Office of Graduate Studies and Postdoctoral Fellows, Faculty of Education, Program in Mathematics Education, Burnaby, BC V5A 1S6, Canada. Offers mathematics education (PhD); secondary mathematics education (M Ed, M Sc). *Program availability:* Part-time, evening/weekend. *Degree requirements:* For master's, comprehensive exam (for some programs), thesis; for doctorate, comprehensive exam, thesis/dissertation. *Entrance requirements:* For master's, minimum GPA of 3.0 (on scale of 4.33) or 3.33 based on last 60 credits of undergraduate courses; for doctorate, minimum GPA of 3.5 (on scale of 4.33). Additional exam requirements/recommendations for international students: Recommended—TOEFL (minimum score 580 paper-based; 93 iBT), IELTS (minimum score 7), TWE (minimum score 5). Electronic applications accepted. *Faculty research:* Historical and psychological development of mathematical thinking, math anxiety and concept formation, mathematical problem solving, numeracy, instructional design, cognition in mathematics thinking and learning, undergraduate math education.

Slippery Rock University of Pennsylvania, Graduate Studies (Recruitment), College of Education, Department of Elementary Education and Early Childhood, Slippery Rock, PA 16057-1383. Offers instructional coach (M Ed); K-12 reading (M Ed); K-12 science and math (M Ed); reading specialist (M Ed). *Accreditation:* NCATE. *Program availability:* Part-time, evening/weekend, online only, 100% online. *Faculty:* 5 full-time (all women). *Students:* 6 full-time (all women), 115 part-time (107 women); includes 3 minority (1 Asian, non-Hispanic/Latino; 2 Hispanic/Latino). Average age 29. 106 applicants, 83% accepted, 45 enrolled. In 2018, 73 master's awarded. *Degree requirements:* For master's, comprehensive exam (for some programs), thesis optional. *Entrance requirements:* For master's, minimum GPA of 3.0, resume, teaching certification, transcripts, letters of recommendation (depending on program). Additional exam requirements/recommendations for international students: Required—TOEFL (minimum score 550 paper-based; 80 iBT). *Application deadline:* For fall admission, 3/1 priority date for domestic students, 5/1 priority date for international students; for spring admission, 10/1 priority date for domestic students, 9/1 priority date for international students. Applications are processed on a rolling basis. Application fee: $25 ($30 for international students). Electronic applications accepted. *Expenses:* Contact institution. *Financial support:* Career-related internships or fieldwork, Federal Work-Study, institutionally sponsored loans, scholarships/grants, tuition waivers (partial), and unspecified assistantships available. Support available to part-time students. Financial award application deadline: 5/1; financial award applicants required to submit FAFSA. *Unit head:* Dr. Suzanne Rose, Graduate Coordinator, 724-738-2042, Fax: 724-738-2779, E-mail: suzanne.rose@sru.edu. *Application contact:* Brandi Weber-Mortimer, Director of Graduate Admissions, 724-738-2051, Fax: 724-738-2146, E-mail: graduate.admissions@sru.edu.

Website: http://www.sru.edu/academics/colleges-and-departments/coe/departments/elementary-education-/-early-childhood/graduate-programs

Slippery Rock University of Pennsylvania, Graduate Studies (Recruitment), College of Education, Department of Secondary Education/Foundations of Education, Slippery Rock, PA 16057-1383. Offers secondary education (M Ed), including English, math/science, social studies. *Accreditation:* NCATE. *Program availability:* Part-time, evening/weekend, 100% online. *Faculty:* 9 full-time (4 women), 1 part-time/adjunct (0 women). *Students:* 45 full-time (36 women), 232 part-time (191 women); includes 2 minority (both Black or African American, non-Hispanic/Latino). Average age 28. 58 applicants, 76% accepted, 28 enrolled. In 2018, 34 master's awarded. *Degree requirements:* For master's, comprehensive exam, thesis (for some programs). *Entrance requirements:* For master's, copy of teaching certification and two letters of recommendation (for some programs). Additional exam requirements/recommendations for international students: Required—TOEFL (minimum score 550 paper-based; 80 iBT). *Application deadline:* For fall admission, 3/1 priority date for domestic students, 5/1 priority date for international students; for spring admission, 10/1 priority date for domestic students, 9/1 priority date for international students. Applications are processed on a rolling basis. Application fee: $25 ($30 for international students). Electronic applications accepted. *Expenses:* Contact institution. *Financial support:* In 2018–19, 9 students received support. Career-related internships or fieldwork, Federal Work-Study, institutionally sponsored loans, scholarships/grants, tuition waivers (partial), and unspecified assistantships available. Support available to part-time students. Financial award application deadline: 5/1; financial award applicants required to submit FAFSA. *Unit head:* Dr. Jeffrey Lehman, Graduate Coordinator, 724-738-2311, Fax: 724-738-4987, E-mail: jeffrey.lehman@sru.edu. *Application contact:* Brandi Weber-Mortimer, Director of Graduate Studies, 724-738-2051, Fax: 724-738-2146, E-mail: graduate.admissions@sru.edu.

Website: http://www.sru.edu/academics/colleges-and-departments/coe/departments/secondary-education-/-foundations-of-education

Smith College, Graduate and Special Programs, Department of Education and Child Study, Program in Secondary Education, Northampton, MA 01063. Offers secondary education (MAT), including biological sciences education, chemistry education, English education, geology education, government education, history education, mathematics education, physics education. *Program availability:* Part-time. *Students:* 8 full-time (all women), 2 part-time (0 women); includes 2 minority (1 Black or African American, non-Hispanic/Latino; 1 Asian, non-Hispanic/Latino), 2 international. Average age 27. 25 applicants, 84% accepted, 10 enrolled. In 2018, 8 master's awarded. *Entrance requirements:* Additional exam requirements/recommendations for international students: Required—TOEFL (minimum score 595 paper-based; 97 iBT), IELTS (minimum score 7.5). *Application deadline:* For fall admission, 4/15 for domestic students, 1/15 priority date for international students; for spring admission, 12/1 for domestic students. Applications are processed on a rolling basis. Application fee: $60. *Expenses:* The total tuition cost to each M.A.T. student (the full program fee, after 'built-in' scholarship award) is $18,500. *Financial support:* In 2018–19, 9 students received support, including 2 fellowships with full tuition reimbursements available; scholarships/grants and human resources employee benefit also available. Support available to part-time students. Financial award application deadline: 4/15; financial award applicants required to submit CSS PROFILE or FAFSA. *Unit head:* Rosetta Cohen, Graduate Student Advisor, 413-585-3266, E-mail: rcohen@smith.edu. *Application contact:* Ruth Morgan, Program Coordinator, 413-585-3050, Fax: 413-585-3054, E-mail: gradstdy@smith.edu.
Website: http://www.smith.edu/educ/

Smith College, Graduate and Special Programs, Department of Mathematics, Northampton, MA 01063. Offers secondary education (MAT), including mathematics education. *Program availability:* Part-time. *Students:* 3 applicants, 67% accepted. *Entrance requirements:* Additional exam requirements/recommendations for international students: Required—TOEFL (minimum score 595 paper-based; 97 iBT), IELTS (minimum score 7.5). *Application deadline:* For fall admission, 11/1 for domestic students, 1/15 for international students; for spring admission, 4/15 for domestic students. Applications are processed on a rolling basis. Application fee: $60. *Expenses:* The total tuition cost to each M.A.T. student (the full program fee, after automatic scholarship award) is $18,500. *Financial support:* Fellowships and scholarships/grants available. Support available to part-time students. Financial award application deadline: 4/15; financial award applicants required to submit CSS PROFILE or FAFSA. *Unit head:* Julianna Tymoczko, Program Director, 413-585-3775, E-mail: jtymoczko@smith.edu. *Application contact:* Ruth Morgan, Program Coordinator, 413-585-3050, Fax: 413-585-3054, E-mail: gradstdy@smith.edu.
Website: http://www.math.smith.edu/

South Carolina State University, College of Graduate and Professional Studies, Department of Education, Orangeburg, SC 29117-0001. Offers early childhood education (MAT); education (M Ed); elementary education (M Ed, MAT); English (MAT); general science/biology (MAT); mathematics (MAT); secondary education (M Ed), including biology education, business education, counselor education, English education, home economics education, industrial education, mathematics education, science education, social studies education; special education (M Ed), including emotionally handicapped, learning disabilities, mentally handicapped. *Accreditation:* NCATE. *Program availability:* Part-time, evening/weekend. *Faculty:* 17 full-time (6 women), 12 part-time/adjunct (5 women). *Students:* 42 full-time (32 women), 93 part-time (64 women); includes 121 minority (119 Black or African American, non-Hispanic/Latino; 2 Asian, non-Hispanic/Latino), 2 international. Average age 40. 50 applicants, 98% accepted, 39 enrolled. In 2018, 9 master's awarded. *Degree requirements:* For master's, thesis optional, departmental qualifying exam. *Entrance requirements:* For master's, GRE General Test, NTE, interview, teaching certificate. *Application deadline:* For fall admission, 6/15 priority date for domestic students, 6/15 for international students; for spring admission, 11/1 for domestic and international students. Application fee: $25. Electronic applications accepted. *Expenses: Tuition, area resident:* Full-time $9928; part-time $552 per credit hour. Tuition, state resident: full-time $9928. Tuition, nonresident: full-time $21,038; part-time $1169 per credit hour. *Required fees:* $1532; $85 per credit hour. *Financial support:* Fellowships, career-related internships or fieldwork, Federal Work-Study, and scholarships/grants available. Financial award application deadline: 6/1. *Unit head:* Dr. Charlie Spell, Chair, Department of Education, 803-536-8963, Fax: 803-516-4568, E-mail: cspell@scsu.edu. *Application contact:* Curtis Foskey, Coordinator of Graduate Studies, 803-536-8419, Fax: 803-536-8812, E-mail: cfoskey@scsu.edu.

Southeastern Oklahoma State University, School of Education, Durant, OK 74701-0609. Offers math specialist (M Ed); reading specialist (M Ed); school administration (M Ed); school counseling (M Ed). *Accreditation:* NCATE. *Program availability:* Part-time, evening/weekend. *Degree requirements:* For master's, comprehensive exam, thesis optional, portfolio (M Ed). *Entrance requirements:* For master's, GRE General Test (for school counseling), minimum GPA of 3.0 in last 60 hours or 2.75 overall. Additional exam requirements/recommendations for international students: Required—TOEFL (minimum score 550 paper-based; 79 iBT). Electronic applications accepted.

Southern Illinois University Edwardsville, Graduate School, College of Arts and Sciences, Department of Mathematics and Statistics, Program in Postsecondary Mathematics Education, Edwardsville, IL 62026. Offers MS. *Program availability:* Part-time. *Degree requirements:* For master's, thesis (for some programs), special project. *Entrance requirements:* Additional exam requirements/recommendations for international students: Required—TOEFL (minimum score 550 paper-based, 79 iBT), IELTS (minimum score 6.5), Michigan Test of English Language Proficiency or PTE. Electronic applications accepted.

Southern University and Agricultural and Mechanical College, Graduate School, College of Sciences and Engineering, Department of Science/Mathematics Education, Baton Rouge, LA 70813. Offers PhD. *Accreditation:* NCATE. *Degree requirements:* For doctorate, thesis/dissertation. *Entrance requirements:* For doctorate, GRE General Test. Additional exam requirements/recommendations for international students: Required—TOEFL (minimum score 525 paper-based). *Faculty research:* Performance assessment in science/mathematics education, equity in science/mathematics education, technology and distance learning, science/mathematics concept formation, cognitive themes, problem solving in science/mathematics education.

Southwestern Oklahoma State University, College of Professional and Graduate Studies, School of Behavioral Sciences and Education, Program in Mathematics, Weatherford, OK 73096-3098. Offers M Ed. *Program availability:* Part-time. *Degree requirements:* For master's, exam. *Entrance requirements:* For master's, GRE General Test or minimum undergraduate GPA of 3.0. Additional exam requirements/recommendations for international students: Required—TOEFL (minimum score 550 paper-based), IELTS (minimum score 6.5).

Southwest Minnesota State University, Department of Education, Marshall, MN 56258. Offers ESL (MS); math (MS); reading (MS); special education (MS), including developmental disabilities, early childhood education, emotional behavioral disorders, learning disabilities; teaching, learning and leadership (MS). *Program availability:* Part-time, evening/weekend, online learning. *Entrance requirements:* Additional exam requirements/recommendations for international students: Required—TOEFL or IELTS; Recommended—TOEFL (minimum score 550 paper-based; 80 iBT), IELTS.

State University of New York at Fredonia, College of Liberal Arts and Sciences, Fredonia, NY 14063-1136. Offers biology (MS); English (MA); English education 7-12 (MA); interdisciplinary studies (MA, MS); math education (MS Ed); professional writing (CAS); speech pathology (MS); MA/MS. *Program availability:* Part-time, evening/weekend. *Faculty:* 23 full-time (12 women), 3 part-time/adjunct (1 woman). *Students:* 67 full-time (60 women), 6 part-time (5 women); includes 9 minority (2 Black or African American, non-Hispanic/Latino; 5 Asian, non-Hispanic/Latino; 1 Hispanic/Latino; 1 Two or more races, non-Hispanic/Latino), 9 international. Average age 23. 131 applicants, 77% accepted, 36 enrolled. In 2018, 37 master's, 1 other advanced degree awarded. *Degree requirements:* For master's, comprehensive exam (for some programs), thesis (for some programs). *Entrance requirements:* For master's, GRE. Additional exam requirements/recommendations for international students: Required—TOEFL (minimum score 79 iBT), IELTS (minimum score 6.5). *Application deadline:* For fall admission, 4/1 for domestic and international students; for spring admission, 11/1 for domestic and international students. Applications are processed on a rolling basis. Application fee: $75. Electronic applications accepted. *Expenses:* Tuition, state resident: full-time $6870; part-time $462 per credit hour. Tuition, nonresident: full-time $16,650; part-time $944 per credit hour. *International tuition:* $16,650 full-time. *Required fees:* $25; $2 per credit hour. $1 per semester. *Financial support:* In 2018–19, 17 students received support, including 14 teaching assistantships with full and partial tuition reimbursements available (averaging $5,957 per year); tuition waivers (full and partial) and unspecified assistantships also available. *Faculty research:* Immunology/microbiology, applied human physiology, ecology and evolution, invertebrate biology, molecular biology, biochemistry, physiology, animal behavior, science education, vertebrate physiology, cell biology, plant biology, developmental biology, aquatic ecology, bilingual language acquisition, bilingual language acquisition and disorders, augmentative and alternate communication with ALS, World War I, Zweig, environmental literature, editing, adolescent literature, pedagogy. *Unit head:* Dr. Andy Karafa, Dean, 716-673-3173, Fax: 716-673-3338, E-mail: andy.karafa@gmail.com. *Application contact:* Wendy S. Dunst, Interim Graduate Recruitment and Admissions Associate, 716-673-3808, Fax: 716-673-3712, E-mail: wendy.dunst@fredonia.edu.
Website: http://www.fredonia.edu/clas/

State University of New York at Plattsburgh, School of Education, Health, and Human Services, Program in Teacher Education: Adolescence Education, Plattsburgh, NY 12901-2681. Offers adolescence education (MST); biology 7-12 (MST); chemistry 7-12 (MST); earth science 7-12 (MST); English 7-12 (MST); French 7-12 (MST); mathematics 7-12 (MST); physics 7-12 (MST); social studies 7-12 (MST); Spanish 7-12 (MST). *Accreditation:* TEAC. *Program availability:* Part-time, evening/weekend. *Entrance requirements:* For master's, minimum GPA of 2.75. Additional exam requirements/recommendations for international students: Required—TOEFL.

State University of New York College at Cortland, Graduate Studies, School of Arts and Sciences, Programs in Adolescence Education, Cortland, NY 13045. Offers biology (MAT); chemistry (MAT); English (MAT, MS Ed); mathematics (MAT); mathematics and physics (MS Ed); physics (MAT, MS Ed). *Accreditation:* NCATE. *Program availability:* Part-time, evening/weekend. *Degree requirements:* For master's, one foreign language, comprehensive exam (for some programs), thesis (for some programs). *Entrance requirements:* For master's, GRE General Test.

State University of New York College at Old Westbury, School of Education, Old Westbury, NY 11568-0210. Offers biology (MAT, MS); chemistry (MAT, MS); English language arts (MAT, MS); math (MAT, MS); social studies (MAT, MS); Spanish (MAT, MS). *Program availability:* Part-time, evening/weekend. *Entrance requirements:* For master's, Liberal Arts and Sciences Test, undergraduate degree with at least 30 semester hours of appropriate coursework as defined by the respective discipline; minimum cumulative undergraduate GPA of 3.0; two letters of recommendation (one from an academic source); essay. Additional exam requirements/recommendations for international students: Required—TOEFL (minimum score 550 paper-based); Recommended—IELTS.

State University of New York College at Potsdam, School of Education and Professional Studies, Program in Secondary Education, Potsdam, NY 13676. Offers English education (MST); mathematics education (MST); science education (MST), including biology, chemistry, earth science, physics; social studies education (MST). *Accreditation:* NCATE. *Degree requirements:* For master's, culminating experience. *Entrance requirements:* For master's, minimum GPA of 2.75 in last 60 hours of course work (3.0 for English program). Additional exam requirements/recommendations for international students: Required—TOEFL (minimum score 550 paper-based; 80 iBT), IELTS (minimum score 6). Electronic applications accepted.

Stephen F. Austin State University, Graduate School, College of Sciences and Mathematics, Department of Mathematics and Statistics, Nacogdoches, TX 75962. Offers mathematics (MS); mathematics education (MS); statistics (MS). *Degree requirements:* For master's, comprehensive exam, thesis optional. *Entrance requirements:* For master's, GRE General Test, minimum GPA of 2.8 in last 60 hours, 2.5 overall. Additional exam requirements/recommendations for international students: Required—TOEFL. *Faculty research:* Kernel type estimators, fractal mappings, spline curve fitting, robust regression continua theory.

Stevenson University, Master of Arts in Teaching Program, Stevenson, MD 21153. Offers secondary biology (MAT); secondary chemistry (MAT); secondary mathematics (MAT). *Program availability:* Part-time, blended/hybrid learning. *Faculty:* 5 part-time/adjunct (all women). *Students:* 13 part-time (9 women); includes 5 minority (1 Black or African American, non-Hispanic/Latino; 2 Asian, non-Hispanic/Latino; 2 Hispanic/Latino). Average age 31. 8 applicants, 75% accepted, 6 enrolled. *Degree requirements:* For master's, internship, portfolio, action research project. *Entrance requirements:* For master's, PRAXIS, GRE, SAT, or ACT, official transcripts from each college or university attended verifying completion of baccalaureate degree in a science or math discipline from regionally-accredited institution. *Application deadline:* Applications are processed on a rolling basis. Electronic applications accepted. *Expenses:* Contact institution. *Financial support:* Unspecified assistantships available. Financial award applicants required to submit FAFSA. *Unit head:* Dr. Anne P. Davis, Dean, Stevenson University Online. *Application contact:* Amanda Millar, Director, Admissions, 443-352-4243, Fax: 443-352-4440, E-mail: amillar@stevenson.edu.
Website: http://www.stevenson.edu/online/academics/online-graduate-programs/master-arts-teaching/

Stony Brook University, State University of New York, School of Professional Development, Stony Brook, NY 11794. Offers coaching (Graduate Certificate); environmental management (MPS); German (MAT); higher education administration (MA, Certificate); human resource management (MS, Graduate Certificate); Italian (MAT); liberal studies (MA); mathematics (MAT); school district business leadership (Advanced Certificate); social studies (MAT); Spanish (MAT). *Program availability:* Part-time, evening/weekend, online learning. *Faculty:* 3 full-time (2 women), 94 part-time/adjunct (40 women). *Students:* 214 full-time (138 women), 1,100 part-time (813 women); includes 313 minority (117 Black or African American, non-Hispanic/Latino; 2 American

Indian or Alaska Native, non-Hispanic/Latino; 32 Asian, non-Hispanic/Latino; 140 Hispanic/Latino; 3 Native Hawaiian or other Pacific Islander, non-Hispanic/Latino; 19 Two or more races, non-Hispanic/Latino), 7 international. Average age 33. 483 applicants, 89% accepted, 337 enrolled. In 2018, 315 master's, 178 other advanced degrees awarded. *Entrance requirements:* Additional exam requirements/recommendations for international students: Required—TOEFL (minimum score 85 iBT). *Application deadline:* For fall admission, 1/15 for domestic students, 6/1 for international students; for spring admission, 10/1 for domestic and international students. Applications are processed on a rolling basis. Application fee: $100. *Expenses:* Contact institution. *Financial support:* Fellowships, research assistantships, teaching assistantships, and career-related internships or fieldwork available. Support available to part-time students. *Unit head:* Patricia Malone, Associate Vice President for Professional Education and Assistant Provost for Engaged Learning, 631-632-7512, Fax: 631-632-9046, E-mail: patricia.malone@stonybrook.edu. *Application contact:* Melissa Jordan, Assistant Dean, 631-632-7751, E-mail: melissa.jordan@stonybrook.edu.
Website: http://www.stonybrook.edu/spd/

Syracuse University, College of Arts and Sciences, Department of Mathematics, Syracuse, NY 13244. Offers math education (PhD); mathematics (MS, PhD); mathematics education (MS). *Program availability:* Part-time. In 2018, 11 master's, 3 doctorates awarded. Terminal master's awarded for partial completion of doctoral program. *Degree requirements:* For doctorate, 2 foreign languages, comprehensive exam, thesis/dissertation. *Entrance requirements:* For master's and doctorate, GRE General Test, GRE Subject Test (recommended), brief (about 500 words) statement indicating why applicant wishes to pursue graduate study and why Syracuse is a good fit, curriculum vitae or resume, transcripts from each post-secondary institution, three letters of recommendation. Additional exam requirements/recommendations for international students: Required—TOEFL (minimum score 100 iBT). *Application deadline:* For fall admission, 1/20 priority date for domestic and international students. Application fee: $75. Electronic applications accepted. *Financial support:* Teaching assistantships, scholarships/grants, and tuition waivers available. Financial award applicants required to submit FAFSA. *Faculty research:* Pure mathematics, numerical mathematics, computing statistics. *Unit head:* Dr. Uday Banerjee, Chair, 315-443-1471, E-mail: banerjee@syr.edu. *Application contact:* Graham Leuschke, Professor and Associate Chair for Graduate Affairs, 315-443-1500, E-mail: gjleusch@syr.edu.
Website: http://math.syr.edu

Syracuse University, School of Education, Programs in Mathematics Education, Syracuse, NY 13244. Offers MS, PhD. *Program availability:* Part-time. *Students:* Average age 30. *Degree requirements:* For master's, thesis or alternative; for doctorate, comprehensive exam, thesis/dissertation. *Entrance requirements:* For master's, GRE or MAT, baccalaureate degree from regionally-accredited college/university, transcripts, personal essay; for doctorate, GRE, master's degree, transcripts. Additional exam requirements/recommendations for international students: Required—TOEFL (minimum score 100 iBT). *Application deadline:* For fall admission, 1/15 priority date for domestic and international students; for spring admission, 10/15 priority date for domestic and international students. Applications are processed on a rolling basis. Application fee: $75. Electronic applications accepted. *Financial support:* Fellowships with full tuition reimbursements, research assistantships, teaching assistantships, career-related internships or fieldwork, and scholarships/grants available. Financial award application deadline: 1/15. *Unit head:* Dr. Joanna Masingila, Dean and Professor, 315-443-4751, E-mail: jomasing@syr.edu. *Application contact:* Speranza Migliore, Graduate Admissions Recruiter, 315-443-2505, E-mail: gradrcrt@syr.edu.
Website: http://soe.syr.edu/academic/teaching_and_leadership/graduate/masters/mathematics_education/

Teachers College, Columbia University, Department of Mathematics, Science and Technology, New York, NY 10027-6696. Offers biology 7-12 (MA); chemistry 7-12 (MA); communication and education (MA, Ed D); computing in education (MA); earth science 7-12 (MA); instructional technology and media (Ed M, MA, Ed D); mathematics education (Ed M, MA, Ed D, Ed DCT, PhD); physics 7-12 (MA); science and dental education (MA); science education (Ed M, MS, Ed DCT, PhD); supervisor/teacher of science education (MA); technology specialist (MA). *Program availability:* Part-time, evening/weekend, online learning. *Students:* 155 full-time (114 women), 254 part-time (162 women); includes 136 minority (44 Black or African American, non-Hispanic/Latino; 1 American Indian or Alaska Native, non-Hispanic/Latino; 59 Asian, non-Hispanic/Latino; 23 Hispanic/Latino; 9 Two or more races, non-Hispanic/Latino), 140 international. Average age 31. 484 applicants, 60% accepted, 138 enrolled. Terminal master's awarded for partial completion of doctoral program. *Unit head:* Prof. Erica Walker, Chair, 212-678-8246, E-mail: ewalker@tc.columbia.edu. *Application contact:* Kelly Sutton Skinner, Director of Admission & New Student Enrollment, E-mail: kms2237@tc.columbia.edu.
Website: http://www.tc.columbia.edu/mathematics-science-and-technology/

Teachers College of San Joaquin, Master's Program in Education, Stockton, CA 95206. Offers early education (M Ed); educational inquiry (M Ed); educational leadership and school development (M Ed); science, technology, engineering, and mathematics (M Ed); special education (M Ed). *Expenses: Tuition:* Full-time $5520. Tuition and fees vary according to course load and program.

Temple University, College of Education, Department of Teaching and Learning, Philadelphia, PA 19122-6096. Offers career and technical education (Ed M), including business, computing, and information technology, industrial education, marketing education; middle grades education (Ed M), including math and language arts, math and science, science and language arts; secondary education (Ed M), including English, math, social studies; teaching English to speakers of other languages (MS Ed); urban education (Ed M). *Program availability:* Part-time, evening/weekend. *Faculty:* 27 full-time (19 women), 71 part-time/adjunct (51 women). *Students:* 181 full-time (126 women), 128 part-time (78 women); includes 71 minority (25 Black or African American, non-Hispanic/Latino; 1 American Indian or Alaska Native, non-Hispanic/Latino; 20 Asian, non-Hispanic/Latino; 19 Hispanic/Latino; 1 Native Hawaiian or other Pacific Islander, non-Hispanic/Latino; 5 Two or more races, non-Hispanic/Latino), 12 international. 234 applicants, 67% accepted, 103 enrolled. In 2018, 148 master's awarded. *Degree requirements:* For master's, thesis (for some programs). *Entrance requirements:* For master's, statement of goals, 2 letters of recommendation. Additional exam requirements/recommendations for international students: Required—TOEFL (minimum score 79 iBT), IELTS, PTE, one of three is required. Application fee: $60. Electronic applications accepted. *Financial support:* Fellowships, research assistantships, teaching assistantships, career-related internships or fieldwork, Federal Work-Study, scholarships/grants, health care benefits, and unspecified assistantships available. Financial award applicants required to submit FAFSA. *Faculty research:* Career & technical education, early childhood education, middle grades education, secondary education, special education. *Unit head:* Matthew Tincani, Prof. of Applied Behavior Analysis and Dept. Chairperson, 215-204-8073, E-mail: matthew.tincani@temple.edu. *Application contact:* Stacey Sanginette, Academic Coordinator, 215-204-6143, E-mail: stacey.sangtinette@temple.edu.
Website: http://education.temple.edu/tl

Tennessee Technological University, College of Graduate Studies, College of Education, Department of Curriculum and Instruction, Program in STEM Education, Cookeville, TN 38505. Offers MA, Ed S. *Program availability:* Part-time, evening/weekend. *Students:* 2 full-time (both women), 4 part-time (3 women); includes 1 minority (Two or more races, non-Hispanic/Latino). 3 applicants, 100% accepted, 3 enrolled. *Degree requirements:* For master's, comprehensive exam, thesis or alternative. *Entrance requirements:* For master's, GRE, MAT. Additional exam requirements/recommendations for international students: Required—TOEFL (minimum score 527 paper-based; 71 iBT), IELTS (minimum score 5.5) or PTE (48). *Application deadline:* For fall admission, 8/1 for domestic students, 5/1 for international students; for spring admission, 2/1 for domestic students, 10/1 for international students; for summer admission, 5/1 for domestic students, 2/1 for international students. Applications are processed on a rolling basis. Application fee: $35 ($40 for international students). Electronic applications accepted. *Financial support:* Application deadline: 4/1. *Unit head:* Dr. Jeremy Wendt, Chairperson, 931-372-3181, E-mail: jwendt@tntech.edu. *Application contact:* Shelia K. Kendrick, Coordinator of Graduate Studies, 931-372-3808, Fax: 931-372-3497, E-mail: skendrick@tntech.edu.

Texas Christian University, College of Education, Master's Programs in Education, Fort Worth, TX 76129-0002. Offers counseling (M Ed); curriculum and instruction (M Ed), including curriculum studies, language and literacy, math education, science education; education (MAT); educational leadership (M Ed); special education (M Ed). *Program availability:* Part-time, evening/weekend. *Faculty:* 29 full-time (21 women), 3 part-time/adjunct (1 woman). *Students:* 124 full-time (94 women), 14 part-time (12 women); includes 52 minority (14 Black or African American, non-Hispanic/Latino; 2 American Indian or Alaska Native, non-Hispanic/Latino; 3 Asian, non-Hispanic/Latino; 28 Hispanic/Latino; 5 Two or more races, non-Hispanic/Latino), 1 international. Average age 28. 172 applicants, 69% accepted, 86 enrolled. In 2018, 62 master's awarded. *Degree requirements:* For master's, comprehensive exam (for some programs), thesis (for some programs). *Entrance requirements:* For master's, GRE General Test; Pre-Admission Content Test (for MAT). Additional exam requirements/recommendations for international students: Required—TOEFL (minimum score 550 paper-based; 80 iBT), IELTS (minimum score 6.5). *Application deadline:* For fall admission, 3/1 for domestic and international students; for spring admission, 11/16 for domestic and international students; for summer admission, 3/1 for domestic and international students. Application fee: $60. Electronic applications accepted. *Financial support:* In 2018–19, 135 students received support, including 3 research assistantships with full tuition reimbursements available (averaging $15,000 per year), 33 teaching assistantships with full tuition reimbursements available (averaging $15,000 per year); career-related internships or fieldwork, scholarships/grants, health care benefits, and unspecified assistantships also available. Support available to part-time students. Financial award application deadline: 3/1. *Unit head:* Dr. Jan Lacina, Interim Dean, 817-257-6786, Fax: 817-257-7466, E-mail: j.lacina@tcu.edu. *Application contact:* Lori Kimball, Graduate Studies Coordinator, 817-257-7661, Fax: 817-257-7466, E-mail: l.kimball@tcu.edu.
Website: http://coe.tcu.edu/graduate-overview/

Texas State University, The Graduate College, College of Science and Engineering, PhD Program in Mathematics Education, San Marcos, TX 78666. Offers PhD. *Program availability:* Part-time. *Faculty:* 16 full-time (7 women). *Students:* 19 full-time (14 women), 7 part-time (5 women); includes 2 minority (1 Hispanic/Latino; 1 Two or more races, non-Hispanic/Latino), 7 international. Average age 34. 18 applicants, 33% accepted, 4 enrolled. In 2018, 4 doctorates awarded. *Degree requirements:* For doctorate, comprehensive exam, thesis/dissertation. *Entrance requirements:* For doctorate, official GRE (general test only) required with competitive scores in the verbal reasoning and quantitative reasoning sections, baccalaureate degree from regionally-accredited university with minimum GPA of 3.0 on last 60 undergraduate semester hours, 500-word statement of purpose, current curriculum vitae, 3 letters of recommendation, interview with faculty, 2 years of teaching experience. Additional exam requirements/recommendations for international students: Required—TOEFL (minimum score 550 paper-based; 78 iBT), IELTS (minimum score 6.5). *Application deadline:* For fall admission, 1/10 for domestic and international students; for spring admission, 8/10 for domestic and international students. Application fee: $55 ($90 for international students). Electronic applications accepted. *Expenses:* Tuition, state resident: full-time $8102; part-time $4051 per semester. Tuition, nonresident: full-time $18,229; part-time $9115 per semester. *International tuition:* $18,229 full-time. *Required fees:* $2116; $120 per credit hour. Tuition and fees vary according to course load. *Financial support:* In 2018–19, 20 students received support, including 3 research assistantships (averaging $27,820 per year), 17 teaching assistantships (averaging $27,759 per year); Federal Work-Study, institutionally sponsored loans, scholarships/grants, health care benefits, and unspecified assistantships also available. Support available to part-time students. Financial award application deadline: 1/15; financial award applicants required to submit FAFSA. *Faculty research:* The impact of mathematical modeling tasks on students' mathematical thinking; mathematical practices, inquiry-oriented instruction, and proof-oriented mathematics; modeling students' constructions of quantities (e.g., angularity, length, etc.), how these constructions change over time, and how they vary across contexts; constructions of coordinate systems and their spatial and quantitative reasoning within coordinate systems. *Total annual research expenditures:* $110,017. *Unit head:* Dr. Alexander White, PhD Program Director, 512-245-2551, E-mail: mathgrad@txstate.edu. *Application contact:* Dr. Andrea Golato, Dean of the Graduate College, 512-245-2581, Fax: 512-245-8365, E-mail: gradcollege@txstate.edu.
Website: http://www.math.txstate.edu/math-ed/

Texas Woman's University, Graduate School, College of Arts and Sciences, Department of Mathematics and Computer Science, Denton, TX 76204. Offers emphasis in mathematics or computer science (MAT); informatics (MS); mathematics (MS); mathematics teaching (MS). *Program availability:* Part-time, evening/weekend, blended/hybrid learning. *Faculty:* 11 full-time (7 women), 1 part-time/adjunct (0 women). *Students:* 17 full-time (13 women), 71 part-time (49 women); includes 53 minority (22 Black or African American, non-Hispanic/Latino; 16 Asian, non-Hispanic/Latino; 13 Hispanic/Latino; 2 Two or more races, non-Hispanic/Latino), 2 international. Average age 36. 37 applicants, 78% accepted, 24 enrolled. In 2018, 23 master's awarded. *Degree requirements:* For master's, comprehensive exam, thesis (for some programs), professional paper, capstone or thesis (depending on degree). *Entrance requirements:* For master's, minimum GPA of 3.0 in last 60 undergraduate credit hours, 2 semesters of calculus, 2 additional advanced math courses, 2 letters of reference (for MS in mathematics, mathematics teaching); minimum GPA of 3.0, statement of intent, resume, 2 letters of recommendation (for MS in informatics). Additional exam requirements/recommendations for international students: Required—TOEFL (minimum score 79 iBT); Recommended—IELTS (minimum score 6.5), TSE (minimum score 53). *Application deadline:* Applications are processed on a rolling basis. Application fee: $50 ($75 for international students). Electronic applications accepted. *Expenses: Tuition, area resident:* Full-time $4852; part-time $270 per semester hour. Tuition, state resident: full-time $4852; part-time $270 per semester hour. Tuition, nonresident: full-time $12,322; part-time $685 per semester hour. *International tuition:* $12,322 full-time. *Required fees:* $2714; $113 per semester hour. $296 per semester. Tuition and fees vary according to course level, course load, degree level, campus/location and program. *Financial support:* In 2018–19, 16 students received support, including 12 teaching

assistantships (averaging $10,987 per year); career-related internships or fieldwork, Federal Work-Study, institutionally sponsored loans, scholarships/grants, traineeships, health care benefits, and unspecified assistantships also available. Support available to part-time students. Financial award application deadline: 3/1; financial award applicants required to submit FAFSA. *Faculty research:* Optimal control theory and differential games, information security, statistics and modern approaches, knot theory, math and computer science education. *Unit head:* Dr. Don E. Edwards, Chair, 940-898-2166, Fax: 940-898-2179, E-mail: mathcs@twu.edu. *Application contact:* Korie Hawkins, Associate Director of Admissions, Graduate Recruitment, 940-898-3188, Fax: 940-898-3081, E-mail: admissions@twu.edu.
Website: http://www.twu.edu/math-computer-science/

Touro College, Graduate School of Education, New York, NY 10010. Offers education and special education (MS); instructional technology (MS); mathematics education (MS); school leadership (MS); teaching English to speakers of other languages (MS); teaching literacy (MS). *Accreditation:* TEAC. *Program availability:* Part-time, evening/weekend, online learning. *Entrance requirements:* Additional exam requirements/recommendations for international students: Required—TOEFL (minimum score 83 iBT), IELTS (minimum score 6.5). *Faculty research:* Equity assistance, language development, scholarly communications, Latin American studies and cultural sensitivity, behavior management techniques and strategies in special education.

Towson University, Jess and Mildred Fisher College of Science and Mathematics, Program in Mathematics Education, Towson, MD 21252-0001. Offers MS. *Accreditation:* NCATE. *Program availability:* Part-time, evening/weekend. *Entrance requirements:* For master's, undergraduate degree in mathematics or elementary education, current certification for teaching secondary school or elementary school mathematics, minimum GPA of 3.0. Electronic applications accepted. *Expenses: Tuition, area resident:* Full-time $9196; part-time $418 per unit. Tuition, state resident: full-time $9196; part-time $418 per unit. Tuition, nonresident: full-time $19,030; part-time $865 per unit. *International tuition:* $19,030 full-time. *Required fees:* $3102; $141 per year. $423 per term. Tuition and fees vary according to campus/location and program.

Tufts University, Graduate School of Arts and Sciences, Department of Education, Program in Education, Medford, MA 02155. Offers educational studies (MA); elementary education (MAT); middle and secondary education (MAT); museum education (MA); secondary education (MA); STEM education (MS, PhD). *Program availability:* Part-time. *Degree requirements:* For master's, thesis optional. *Entrance requirements:* For master's, GRE General Test, portfolio (for art education only); for doctorate, GRE General Test, writing sample. Additional exam requirements/recommendations for international students: Required—TOEFL (minimum score 550 paper-based; 80 iBT), IELTS (minimum score 6.5). Electronic applications accepted. *Expenses:* Contact institution.

Universidad Autonoma de Guadalajara, Graduate Programs, Guadalajara, Mexico. Offers administrative law and justice (LL M); advertising and corporate communications (MA); architecture (M Arch); business (MBA); computational science (MCC); education (Ed M, Ed D); English-Spanish translation (MA); entrepreneurship and management (MBA); integrated management of digital animation (MA); international business (MIB); international corporate law (LL M); Internet technologies (MS); manufacturing systems (MMS); occupational health (MS); philosophy (MA, PhD); power electronics (MS); quality systems (MQS); renewable energy (MS); social evaluation of projects (MBA); strategic market research (MBA); tax law (MA); teaching mathematics (MA).

University at Buffalo, the State University of New York, Graduate School, Graduate School of Education, Department of Learning and Instruction, Buffalo, NY 14260. Offers biology education (Ed M, Certificate); chemistry education (Ed M, Certificate); childhood education (Ed M); childhood education with bilingual extension (Ed M); college teaching (Advanced Certificate); curriculum, instruction and the science of learning (PhD); early childhood education (Ed M); early childhood education with bilingual extension (Ed M); earth science education (Ed M, Certificate); education and technology (Ed M); education studies (Ed M); educational technology and new literacies (Certificate); educational technology and new literacies (Advanced Certificate); elementary education (Ed D); English education (Ed M, Certificate); English education studies (Ed M); English for speakers of other languages (Ed M); foreign and second language education (PhD); French education (Ed M, Certificate); German education (Ed M, Certificate); gifted education (Certificate); Latin education (Ed M, Certificate); literacy education studies (Ed M); literacy specialist (Ed M); literacy teaching and learning (Certificate); mathematics education (Ed M, Certificate); music education (Ed M, Certificate); music education studies (Ed M); music learning theory (Advanced Certificate); online education (Advanced Certificate); physics education (Ed M, Certificate); science and the public (Ed M); social studies education (Ed M, Certificate); Spanish education (Ed M, Certificate); special education (PhD); teaching English to speakers of other languages (Ed M). *Program availability:* Part-time, evening/weekend, 100% online. *Faculty:* 31 full-time (22 women), 41 part-time/adjunct (27 women). *Students:* 161 full-time (107 women), 369 part-time (260 women); includes 76 minority (26 Black or African American, non-Hispanic/Latino; 3 American Indian or Alaska Native, non-Hispanic/Latino; 30 Asian, non-Hispanic/Latino; 14 Hispanic/Latino; 3 Two or more races, non-Hispanic/Latino), 41 international. Average age 34. 368 applicants, 70% accepted, 179 enrolled. In 2018, 100 master's, 26 doctorates, 19 other advanced degrees awarded. *Degree requirements:* For master's, comprehensive exam; for doctorate, thesis/dissertation, research analysis exam, research experience. *Entrance requirements:* For master's, letters of reference; for doctorate, GRE General Test or MAT, interview, writing sample, letters of recommendation. Additional exam requirements/recommendations for international students: Required—TOEFL (minimum score 600 paper-based; 96 iBT), IELTS (minimum score 6.5), PTE (minimum score 55). *Application deadline:* For fall admission, 2/1 priority date for domestic and international students; for spring admission, 11/15 priority date for domestic students, 10/1 for international students. Applications are processed on a rolling basis. Application fee: $50. Electronic applications accepted. *Financial support:* In 2018–19, 42 fellowships (averaging $5,181 per year), 44 research assistantships with tuition reimbursements (averaging $10,908 per year) were awarded; teaching assistantships, career-related internships or fieldwork, Federal Work-Study, institutionally sponsored loans, scholarships/grants, tuition waivers (full and partial), and unspecified assistantships also available. Financial award application deadline: 2/28; financial award applicants required to submit FAFSA. *Faculty research:* Science assessment, foreign language teaching and learning, early learning, new literacies, gender and education. *Total annual research expenditures:* $413,233. *Unit head:* Dr. Julie Gorlewski, Department Chair, 716-645-2455, Fax: 716-645-3161, E-mail: jgorlews@buffalo.edu. *Application contact:* Renad Aref, Assistant Director of Admission Recruitment, 716-645-2110, Fax: 716-645-7937, E-mail: gseinfo@buffalo.edu.
Website: http://ed.buffalo.edu/teaching.html

The University of Akron, Graduate School, College of Education, Department of Curricular and Instructional Studies, Program in Adolescent to Young Adult Education, Akron, OH 44325. Offers chemistry and physics (MS); earth science (MS); earth science and chemistry (MS); earth science and physics (MS); integrated language arts (MS); integrated mathematics (MS); integrated social studies (MS); life science (MS); life science and chemistry (MS); life science and earth science (MS); life science and physics (MS); physics (MS). *Accreditation:* NCATE. *Degree requirements:* For master's, comprehensive exam. *Entrance requirements:* For master's, minimum GPA of 3.0. Additional exam requirements/recommendations for international students: Required—TOEFL (minimum score 79 iBT), IELTS (minimum score 6.5). Electronic applications accepted.

The University of Alabama in Huntsville, School of Graduate Studies, College of Education, Huntsville, AL 35899. Offers autism spectrum disorders (M Ed, Graduate Certificate); biology (MAT); chemistry (MAT); differentiated instruction in elementary education (M Ed); English language arts (MAT); English speakers of other languages (M Ed, MAT); history (MAT); mathematics (MAT); physics (MAT); reading education (M Ed); secondary education (M Ed). *Program availability:* Part-time. *Faculty:* 13 full-time (10 women). *Students:* 38 full-time (30 women), 39 part-time (37 women); includes 17 minority (10 Black or African American, non-Hispanic/Latino; 3 American Indian or Alaska Native, non-Hispanic/Latino; 2 Asian, non-Hispanic/Latino; 2 Two or more races, non-Hispanic/Latino). Average age 33. 47 applicants, 83% accepted, 29 enrolled. In 2018, 31 master's awarded. *Degree requirements:* For master's, comprehensive exam, thesis or alternative, oral and written. *Entrance requirements:* For master's, GRE General Test, minimum GPA of 3.0. Additional exam requirements/recommendations for international students: Required—TOEFL (minimum score 500 paper-based; 80 iBT), IELTS (minimum score 6.5). *Application deadline:* For fall admission, 7/15 priority date for domestic students, 4/1 priority date for international students; for spring admission, 11/30 priority date for domestic students, 9/1 priority date for international students. Applications are processed on a rolling basis. Application fee: $50. Electronic applications accepted. *Expenses: Tuition, area resident:* Full-time $10,632; part-time $412 per credit hour. Tuition, state resident: full-time $10,632. Tuition, nonresident: full-time $23,604; part-time $412 per credit hour. *Required fees:* $582; $582. Tuition and fees vary according to course load and program. *Financial support:* In 2018–19, 2 students received support, including 1 teaching assistantship with full tuition reimbursement available (averaging $4,500 per year); career-related internships or fieldwork, Federal Work-Study, institutionally sponsored loans, scholarships/grants, health care benefits, tuition waivers (full and partial), and unspecified assistantships also available. Support available to part-time students. Financial award application deadline: 4/1; financial award applicants required to submit FAFSA. *Unit head:* Dr. Beth Nason Quick, Dean, 256-824-2325, E-mail: beth.quick@uah.edu. *Application contact:* Kim Gray, Graduate Studies Admissions Coordinator, 256-824-6002, Fax: 256-824-6405, E-mail: deangrad@uah.edu.
Website: http://www.uah.edu/education/

The University of Alabama in Huntsville, School of Graduate Studies, College of Science, Department of Mathematical Sciences, Huntsville, AL 35899. Offers applied mathematics (PhD); education (MA); mathematics (MA, MS). PhD offered jointly with The University of Alabama (Tuscaloosa) and The University of Alabama at Birmingham. *Program availability:* Part-time. *Faculty:* 7 full-time. *Students:* 18 full-time (4 women), 12 part-time (4 women); includes 5 minority (3 Black or African American, non-Hispanic/Latino; 2 Asian, non-Hispanic/Latino), 2 international. Average age 31. 25 applicants, 80% accepted, 10 enrolled. In 2018, 6 master's, 3 doctorates awarded. *Degree requirements:* For master's, comprehensive exam, thesis or alternative, oral and written exams; for doctorate, comprehensive exam, thesis/dissertation, oral and written exams. *Entrance requirements:* For master's and doctorate, GRE General Test, minimum GPA of 3.0. Additional exam requirements/recommendations for international students: Required—TOEFL (minimum score 550 paper-based; 80 iBT), IELTS (minimum score 6.5). *Application deadline:* For fall admission, 7/15 priority date for domestic students, 4/1 priority date for international students; for spring admission, 11/30 priority date for domestic students, 9/1 priority date for international students. Applications are processed on a rolling basis. Application fee: $50. Electronic applications accepted. *Expenses: Tuition, area resident:* Full-time $10,632; part-time $412 per credit hour. Tuition, state resident: full-time $10,632. Tuition, nonresident: full-time $23,604; part-time $412 per credit hour. *Required fees:* $582; $582. Tuition and fees vary according to course load and program. *Financial support:* In 2018–19, 7 students received support, including 6 teaching assistantships with full tuition reimbursements available (averaging $6,000 per year); career-related internships or fieldwork, Federal Work-Study, institutionally sponsored loans, scholarships/grants, health care benefits, and unspecified assistantships also available. Support available to part-time students. Financial award application deadline: 4/1; financial award applicants required to submit FAFSA. *Faculty research:* Combinatorics and graph theory, computational mathematics, differential equations and applications, mathematical biology, probability and stochastic processes. *Unit head:* Dr. Toka Diagana, Professor and Chair, 256-824-6470, Fax: 256-824-6173, E-mail: mathchair@uah.edu. *Application contact:* Kim Gray, Graduate Studies Admissions Coordinator, 256-824-6002, Fax: 256-824-6405, E-mail: deangrad@uah.edu.
Website: http://www.math.uah.edu/

University of Alaska Southeast, Graduate Programs, Program in Education, Juneau, AK 99801. Offers educational leadership (M Ed); elementary education (MAT); learning design and technology (M Ed); mathematics education (M Ed); reading specialist (M Ed); secondary education (MAT); special education (M Ed, MAT). *Accreditation:* NCATE. *Program availability:* Part-time, evening/weekend, online learning. *Degree requirements:* For master's, comprehensive exam or project, portfolio. *Entrance requirements:* For master's, PRAXIS, minimum GPA of 3.0, writing sample, letters of recommendation. Electronic applications accepted. *Faculty research:* Applied classroom research, culturally responsive practices, action research, teaching effectiveness.

The University of Arizona, College of Science, Department of Mathematics, Program in Secondary Mathematics Education, Tucson, AZ 85721. Offers MA. *Program availability:* Part-time. *Degree requirements:* For master's, thesis, internships, colloquium, business courses. *Entrance requirements:* For master's, GRE, minimum GPA of 3.0, statement of purpose. Additional exam requirements/recommendations for international students: Required—TOEFL (minimum score 550 paper-based). *Faculty research:* Algebra, coding theory, graph theory, combinatorics, probability.

University of Arkansas, Graduate School, J. William Fulbright College of Arts and Sciences, Department of Mathematical Sciences, Program in Secondary Mathematics, Fayetteville, AR 72701. Offers MA. *Accreditation:* NCATE. In 2018, 1 master's awarded. *Application deadline:* For fall admission, 8/1 for domestic students, 4/1 for international students; for spring admission, 12/1 for domestic students, 10/1 for international students; for summer admission, 4/15 for domestic students, 3/1 for international students. Applications are processed on a rolling basis. Application fee: $60. Electronic applications accepted. *Financial support:* In 2018–19, 1 teaching assistantship was awarded; fellowships, research assistantships, career-related internships or fieldwork, and Federal Work-Study also available. Support available to part-time students. Financial award application deadline: 4/1; financial award applicants required to submit FAFSA. *Unit head:* Dr. Mark Arnold, Statistics and Analytics Director, 479-575-7701, E-mail: arnold@uark.edu. *Application contact:* Giovanni Petris, Director of Statistics Program, 479-575-6324, E-mail: gpetris@uark.edu.
Website: https://catalog.uark.edu/undergraduatecatalog/collegesandschools/jwilliamfulbrightcollegeofartsandsciences/statisticsstat/

University of Arkansas at Pine Bluff, School of Education, Pine Bluff, AR 71601-2799. Offers elementary education (M Ed); secondary education (M Ed), including English education, mathematics education, science education, social studies education; teaching (MAT). *Accreditation:* NCATE. *Program availability:* Part-time, evening/weekend. *Degree requirements:* For master's, comprehensive exam. *Entrance requirements:* For master's, GRE, minimum GPA of 2.75, NTE or Standard Arkansas Teaching Certificate. *Faculty research:* Teacher certification, accreditation, assessment, standards, portfolio development, rehabilitation, technology.

The University of British Columbia, Faculty of Education, Department of Curriculum and Pedagogy, Vancouver, BC V6T 1Z4, Canada. Offers art education (M Ed, MA); curriculum studies (M Ed, MA, PhD); home economics education (M Ed, MA); mathematics education (M Ed, MA); media and technology studies education (M Ed, MA); music education (M Ed, MA); physical education (M Ed, MA); science education (M Ed, MA); social studies education (M Ed, MA). *Program availability:* Part-time, online learning. *Degree requirements:* For master's, thesis (MA); for doctorate, comprehensive exam, thesis/dissertation. *Entrance requirements:* Additional exam requirements/recommendations for international students: Required—TOEFL, IELTS. Electronic applications accepted. *Expenses:* Contact institution. *Faculty research:* School subjects, teaching and learning.

University of California, Berkeley, Graduate Division, School of Education, Group in Science and Mathematics Education, Berkeley, CA 94720. Offers PhD, MA/Credential. Electronic applications accepted.

University of California, Berkeley, Graduate Division, School of Education, Programs in Education, Berkeley, CA 94720. Offers development in mathematics and science (MA); education in mathematics, science, and technology (MA, PhD); human development and education (MA, PhD); leadership education (MA); special education (PhD); teacher education (MA); MA/Credential; PhD/Credential; PhD/MA. Terminal master's awarded for partial completion of doctoral program. *Degree requirements:* For master's, exam or thesis; for doctorate, thesis/dissertation, oral qualifying exam. *Entrance requirements:* For master's and doctorate, GRE General Test, minimum GPA of 3.0 during last 2 years of undergraduate course work. Electronic applications accepted. *Faculty research:* Human development, social and moral educational psychology, developmental teacher preparation.

University of California, San Diego, Graduate Division, Program in Mathematics and Science Education, La Jolla, CA 92093. Offers PhD. Program offered jointly with San Diego State University. *Students:* 1 full-time (0 women), 14 part-time (9 women). In 2018, 4 doctorates awarded. *Degree requirements:* For doctorate, thesis/dissertation, teaching practicum. *Entrance requirements:* For doctorate, GRE General Test, minimum GPA of 3.25. Additional exam requirements/recommendations for international students: Required—TOEFL (minimum score 550 paper-based; 80 iBT), IELTS (minimum score 7). Electronic applications accepted. *Financial support:* Scholarships/grants and stipends available. Financial award applicants required to submit FAFSA. *Faculty research:* Effective teaching of rational numbers, teacher development, development of number sense and estimation. *Unit head:* Gabriele Wienhausen, Chair, 858-534-3105, E-mail: gwienhausen@ucsd.edu. *Application contact:* Sherry Seethaler, Graduate Coordinator, 858-534-4656, E-mail: sseethaler@ucsd.edu. Website: http://sci.sdsu.edu/CRMSE/msed/

University of Central Arkansas, Graduate School, College of Natural Sciences and Math, Department of Mathematics, Conway, AR 72035-0001. Offers applied mathematics (MS); math education (MA). *Program availability:* Part-time. *Degree requirements:* For master's, comprehensive exam, thesis optional. *Entrance requirements:* For master's, GRE General Test, minimum GPA of 2.7. Additional exam requirements/recommendations for international students: Required—TOEFL (minimum score 550 paper-based; 80 iBT). Electronic applications accepted.

University of Central Florida, College of Community Innovation and Education, School of Teacher Education, Program in K-8 Mathematics and Science Education, Orlando, FL 32816. Offers M Ed, Certificate. *Accreditation:* NCATE. *Program availability:* Part-time. *Students:* 1 full-time (0 women), 50 part-time (46 women); includes 19 minority (8 Black or African American, non-Hispanic/Latino; 11 Hispanic/Latino). Average age 36. 2 applicants, 100% accepted, 1 enrolled. In 2018, 7 master's awarded. *Entrance requirements:* Additional exam requirements/recommendations for international students: Required—TOEFL. *Application deadline:* For summer admission, 4/15 for domestic students. Application fee: $30. Electronic applications accepted. *Financial support:* In 2018–19, 1 student received support, including 2 research assistantships with partial tuition reimbursements available (averaging $5,702 per year). Financial award application deadline: 3/1; financial award applicants required to submit FAFSA. *Unit head:* Dr. Malcolm Butler, Program Coordinator, 407-823-3272, E-mail: malcolm.butler@ucf.edu. *Application contact:* Associate Director, Graduate Admissions, 407-823-2766, Fax: 407-823-6442, E-mail: gradadmissions@ucf.edu. Website: http://education.ucf.edu/mathed/

University of Central Florida, College of Community Innovation and Education, School of Teacher Education, Program in Teacher Education, Orlando, FL 32816. Offers MAT. *Accreditation:* NCATE. *Program availability:* Part-time, evening/weekend. *Students:* 130 full-time (94 women), 96 part-time (79 women); includes 64 minority (25 Black or African American, non-Hispanic/Latino; 12 Asian, non-Hispanic/Latino; 23 Hispanic/Latino; 4 Two or more races, non-Hispanic/Latino), 23 international. Average age 33. 214 applicants, 52% accepted, 75 enrolled. In 2018, 41 master's awarded. *Entrance requirements:* For master's, Florida Teacher Certification Examination/General Knowledge Test or GRE General Test. Additional exam requirements/recommendations for international students: Required—TOEFL. *Application deadline:* For spring admission, 12/1 for domestic students; for summer admission, 4/15 for domestic students. Application fee: $30. Electronic applications accepted. *Financial support:* In 2018–19, 80 students received support, including 28 fellowships (averaging $5,518 per year), 41 research assistantships (averaging $8,487 per year), 58 teaching assistantships (averaging $11,573 per year); career-related internships or fieldwork, Federal Work-Study, institutionally sponsored loans, tuition waivers (partial), and unspecified assistantships also available. Financial award application deadline: 3/1; financial award applicants required to submit FAFSA. *Unit head:* Dr. Michael Hynes, Director, 407-823-2005, E-mail: mychael.hynes@ucf.edu. *Application contact:* Associate Director, Graduate Admissions, 407-823-2766, Fax: 407-823-6442, E-mail: gradadmissions@ucf.edu. Website: http://www.graduatecatalog.ucf.edu/programs/program.aspx?id-9727&program-Teacher%20Education%20MAT

University of Cincinnati, Graduate School, McMicken College of Arts and Sciences, Department of Mathematical Sciences, Cincinnati, OH 45221. Offers applied mathematics (MS, PhD); mathematics education (MAT); pure mathematics (MS, PhD); statistics (MS, PhD). *Program availability:* Part-time. *Faculty:* 39 full-time (4 women), 12 part-time/adjunct (4 women). *Students:* 44 full-time (24 women), 19 part-time (9 women); includes 28 minority (2 Black or African American, non-Hispanic/Latino; 25 Asian, non-Hispanic/Latino; 1 Hispanic/Latino), 42 international. 91 applicants, 35% accepted, 27 enrolled. In 2018, 5 master's, 4 doctorates awarded. Terminal master's awarded for partial completion of doctoral program. *Degree requirements:* For master's, comprehensive exam, thesis or alternative; for doctorate, comprehensive exam, thesis/

dissertation. *Entrance requirements:* For master's and doctorate, GRE. Additional exam requirements/recommendations for international students: Required—TOEFL, IELTS. *Application deadline:* For fall admission, 2/1 priority date for domestic and international students. Applications are processed on a rolling basis. Application fee: $65. Electronic applications accepted. *Financial support:* In 2018–19, 51 students received support, including 2 fellowships with full tuition reimbursements available (averaging $13,500 per year), 2 research assistantships with full tuition reimbursements available (averaging $13,000 per year), 26 teaching assistantships with full tuition reimbursements available (averaging $18,500 per year); career-related internships or fieldwork, scholarships/grants, and unspecified assistantships also available. Support available to part-time students. Financial award application deadline: 2/1. *Faculty research:* Algebra, analysis, differential equations, numerical analysis, statistics. *Unit head:* Dr. Shuang Zhang, Professor and Department Head, 513-556-4052, Fax: 513-556-3417, E-mail: zhangs@ucmail.uc.edu. *Application contact:* Kamellia Smith, Program Coordinator, 513-5564053, Fax: 513-556-3417, E-mail: kamellia.smith@uc.edu. Website: https://www.artsci.uc.edu/departments/math.html

University of Colorado Denver, College of Liberal Arts and Sciences, Department of Mathematical and Statistical Sciences, Denver, CO 80217. Offers applied mathematics (MS, PhD), including applied mathematics, applied probability (MS), applied statistics (MS), computational biology (PhD), computational mathematics (PhD), discrete mathematics, finite geometry (PhD), mathematics education (PhD), mathematics of engineering and science (MS), numerical analysis, operations research (MS), optimization and operations research (PhD), probability (PhD), statistics (PhD). *Program availability:* Part-time. *Degree requirements:* For master's, comprehensive exam, thesis optional, 30 hours of course work with minimum GPA of 3.0; for doctorate, comprehensive exam, thesis/dissertation, 42 hours of course work with minimum GPA of 3.25. *Entrance requirements:* For master's, GRE General Test; GRE Subject Test in math (recommended), 30 hours of course work in mathematics (24 of which must be upper-division mathematics), bachelor's degree with minimum GPA of 3.0; for doctorate, GRE General Test; GRE Subject Test in math (recommended), 30 hours of course work in mathematics (24 of which must be upper-division mathematics), master's degree with minimum GPA of 3.25. Additional exam requirements/recommendations for international students: Required—TOEFL (minimum score 537 paper-based; 75 iBT); Recommended—IELTS (minimum score 6.5). Electronic applications accepted. *Expenses:* Tuition, state resident: full-time $6786; part-time $337 per credit hour. Tuition, nonresident: full-time $22,590; part-time $1255 per credit hour. *Required fees:* $1231; $137 per credit hour. Tuition and fees vary according to program and reciprocity agreements. *Faculty research:* Computational mathematics, computational biology, discrete mathematics and geometry, probability and statistics, optimization.

University of Colorado Denver, School of Education and Human Development, Program in Educational Leadership and Innovation, Denver, CO 80217. Offers educational studies and research (PhD), including administrative leadership and policy, early childhood special education, math education, research, assessment and evaluation, science education, urban ecologies. *Program availability:* Part-time, evening/weekend. *Degree requirements:* For doctorate, comprehensive exam, thesis/dissertation, 75 credit hours (for PhD). *Entrance requirements:* For doctorate, GRE or equivalent, resume or curriculum vitae, letters of recommendation, master's degree or equivalent, completion of basic or advanced statistics course with minimum B grade. Additional exam requirements/recommendations for international students: Required—TOEFL (minimum score 537 paper-based; 75 iBT); Recommended—IELTS (minimum score 6.5). Electronic applications accepted. *Expenses:* Tuition, state resident: full-time $6786; part-time $337 per credit hour. Tuition, nonresident: full-time $22,590; part-time $1255 per credit hour. *Required fees:* $1231; $137 per credit hour. Tuition and fees vary according to program and reciprocity agreements. *Faculty research:* Administrative leadership and policy studies, early childhood education, research in diversity, paraprofessionals in education, urban schools lab.

University of Colorado Denver, School of Education and Human Development, Program in Education and Human Development, Denver, CO 80217. Offers administrative leadership and policy (PhD); assessment (MA); early childhood special education/early childhood education (PhD); family science and human development (PhD); human development and family relations (MA); learning (MA); mathematics education (PhD); research and evaluation methods (MA); research, assessment and evaluation (PhD); science education (PhD); urban ecologies (PhD). MA program also offered in partnership with Boulder Journey School, Friends School and Stanley British Primary School. *Program availability:* Part-time, evening/weekend. *Degree requirements:* For master's, comprehensive exam, 9 hours of core courses embedded within a minimum of 36 to 38 hours of relevant coursework, including an educational psychology practicum, independent study project or thesis (recommended). *Entrance requirements:* For master's, GRE if undergraduate GPA below 2.75, resume, three letters of recommendation, transcripts. Additional exam requirements/recommendations for international students: Required—TOEFL (minimum score 537 paper-based; 75 iBT); Recommended—IELTS (minimum score 6.5). Electronic applications accepted. *Expenses:* Contact institution. *Faculty research:* Crisis response and intervention, school violence prevention, immigrant experience, educational environments for English language learners, culturally competent assessment and intervention, child and youth suicide.

University of Colorado Denver, School of Education and Human Development, Program in Mathematics Education, Denver, CO 80217. Offers MS Ed. *Degree requirements:* For master's, thesis or alternative, 36 semester hours. *Entrance requirements:* For master's, GRE or MAT, resume or curriculum vitae, three letters of recommendation, transcripts from all colleges/universities attended. Additional exam requirements/recommendations for international students: Required—TOEFL (minimum score 75 iBT). Electronic applications accepted. *Expenses:* Tuition, state resident: full-time $6786; part-time $337 per credit hour. Tuition, nonresident: full-time $22,590; part-time $1255 per credit hour. *Required fees:* $1231; $137 per credit hour. Tuition and fees vary according to program and reciprocity agreements.

University of Colorado Denver, School of Education and Human Development, Teacher Education Programs, Denver, CO 80217. Offers elementary linguistically diverse education (MA); elementary math and science education (MA); elementary math education (MA); elementary reading and writing (MA); elementary science education (MA); secondary English education (MA); secondary linguistically diverse education (MA); secondary math education (MA); secondary reading and writing (MA); secondary science education (MA); special education (MA). *Accreditation:* NCATE. *Program availability:* Part-time, evening/weekend. *Degree requirements:* For master's, comprehensive exam. *Entrance requirements:* For master's, GRE or MAT (for those with GPA below 2.75), transcripts, resume, letters of recommendation. Additional exam requirements/recommendations for international students: Required—TOEFL (minimum score 537 paper-based; 75 iBT); Recommended—IELTS (minimum score 6.5). Electronic applications accepted. *Expenses:* Tuition, state resident: full-time $6786; part-time $337 per credit hour. Tuition, nonresident: full-time $22,590; part-time $1255 per credit hour. *Required fees:* $1231; $137 per credit hour. Tuition and fees vary according to program and reciprocity agreements. *Faculty research:* Linguistically diverse education/ESL, elementary reading and writing, elementary teacher education, secondary teacher education, special education.

Mathematics Education

University of Connecticut, Graduate School, Neag School of Education, Department of Curriculum and Instruction, Program in Mathematics Education, Storrs, CT 06269. Offers MA, PhD. *Accreditation:* NCATE. Terminal master's awarded for partial completion of doctoral program. *Degree requirements:* For master's, comprehensive exam; for doctorate, thesis/dissertation. *Entrance requirements:* For doctorate, GRE General Test. Additional exam requirements/recommendations for international students: Required—TOEFL (minimum score 550 paper-based). Electronic applications accepted.

University of Dayton, Department of Teacher Education, Dayton, OH 45469. Offers adolescence to young adult education (MS Ed); early childhood leadership and advocacy (MS Ed); interdisciplinary education (MS Ed), including visual arts; interdisciplinary education studies (MS Ed); leadership in educational systems (MS Ed); literacy (MS Ed); mathematics education (MS Ed); middle childhood education (MS Ed); multi-age education (MS Ed), including world languages; music education (MS Ed); teacher as leader (MS Ed); teacher education (MS Ed); technology-enhanced learning (MS Ed); trans-disciplinary early childhood education (MS Ed). *Program availability:* Part-time, 100% online. *Degree requirements:* For master's, variable foreign language requirement, thesis or alternative, internship (for teaching licensure or endorsement). *Entrance requirements:* For master's, GRE (minimum score of 149 verbal, 4 on writing) or MAT (minimum score of 396) if undergraduate GPA was under 2.75, minimum GPA of 2.75, 3 letters of recommendation, personal statement or resume, official transcripts. Additional exam requirements/recommendations for international students: Required—TOEFL (minimum score 550 paper-based; 80 iBT); Recommended—IELTS (minimum score 6.5). Electronic applications accepted. *Expenses:* Contact institution. *Faculty research:* Social emotional learning, culturally responsive teaching, urban teaching, literacy, instructional strategies, pre-service teacher education preparation.

University of Detroit Mercy, College of Engineering and Science, Detroit, MI 48221. Offers chemistry (MS); civil and environmental engineering (DE); electrical and computer engineering (ME); electrical engineering (DE); engineering management (M Eng Mgt); environmental engineering (MEE); mechanical engineering (MME, DE); product development (MS); software engineering (MSSE); teaching of mathematics (MATM). *Program availability:* Part-time, evening/weekend. *Degree requirements:* For doctorate, thesis/dissertation. Electronic applications accepted. Application fee is waived when completed online. *Expenses:* Contact institution.

University of Florida, Graduate School, College of Education, School of Teaching and Learning, Gainesville, FL 32611. Offers curriculum and instruction (M Ed, MAE, Ed D, PhD, Ed S); elementary education (M Ed, MAE); English education (M Ed, MAE); mathematics education (M Ed, MAE); reading education (M Ed, MAE); science education (M Ed, MAE); social studies education (M Ed, MAE). *Accreditation:* NCATE. *Program availability:* Part-time, evening/weekend, online learning. Terminal master's awarded for partial completion of doctoral program. *Degree requirements:* For master's, comprehensive exam (for some programs), thesis (for some programs); for doctorate, comprehensive exam (for some programs), thesis/dissertation (for some programs). *Entrance requirements:* For master's and doctorate, GRE General Test, minimum GPA of 3.0; for Ed S, GRE General Test. Additional exam requirements/recommendations for international students: Required—TOEFL (minimum score 550 paper-based; 80 iBT), IELTS (minimum score 6). Electronic applications accepted. *Faculty research:* STEM education; curriculum; teaching and teacher education; languages and literacy; schools, culture, and society; theories and processes of learning.

University of Georgia, College of Education, Department of Mathematics and Science Education, Athens, GA 30602. Offers mathematics education (M Ed, PhD, Ed S).

University of Illinois at Chicago, College of Liberal Arts and Sciences, Department of Mathematics, Statistics, and Computer Science, Program in Secondary School Mathematics, Chicago, IL 60607-7128. Offers MST. *Program availability:* Part-time. *Degree requirements:* For master's, comprehensive exam. *Entrance requirements:* For master's, GRE General Test, minimum GPA of 2.75. Additional exam requirements/recommendations for international students: Required—TOEFL. Electronic applications accepted.

University of Illinois at Chicago, Program in Learning Sciences, Chicago, IL 60607-7128. Offers PhD.

University of Illinois at Urbana–Champaign, Graduate College, College of Liberal Arts and Sciences, Department of Mathematics, Champaign, IL 61820. Offers applied mathematics (MS); applied mathematics: actuarial science (MS); mathematics (MS, PhD); teaching of mathematics (MS).

University of Indianapolis, Graduate Programs, School of Education, Indianapolis, IN 46227-3697. Offers art education (MAT); biology (MAT); chemistry (MAT); curriculum and instruction (MA); earth sciences (MAT); education (MA, MAT); educational leadership (MA); elementary education (MA); English (MAT); French (MAT); math (MAT); physical education (MAT); physics (MAT); secondary education (MA), including art education, education, English education, social studies education; social studies (MAT); Spanish (MAT). *Accreditation:* NCATE. *Program availability:* Part-time, evening/weekend. *Entrance requirements:* For master's, GRE Subject Test, PRAXIS I, minimum GPA of 2.5, 3 letters of recommendation, interview. Additional exam requirements/recommendations for international students: Required—TOEFL (minimum score 550 paper-based). *Faculty research:* Assessment of teacher education, perceptions of prospective teachers by parents.

The University of Iowa, Graduate College, College of Education, Department of Teaching and Learning, Program in Education, Iowa City, IA 52242-1316. Offers art education (MA); developmental reading (MA); elementary education (MA); English education (MA, MAT); foreign and second language education (MAT); foreign language education (MA); foreign language/ESL education (PhD); language, literacy and culture (PhD); mathematics education (MA, MAT, PhD); music education (MM, PhD); science education (MA); secondary education (MA); social studies (MA, PhD). *Degree requirements:* For master's, thesis optional, exam; for doctorate, comprehensive exam, thesis/dissertation. *Entrance requirements:* For master's and doctorate, GRE General Test, minimum GPA of 3.0. Additional exam requirements/recommendations for international students: Required—TOEFL (minimum score 550 paper-based; 81 iBT). Electronic applications accepted.

University of Louisiana at Lafayette, College of Education, Department of Educational Curriculum and Instruction, Program in Curriculum and Instruction, Lafayette, LA 70504. Offers instructional specialist (M Ed); K-8 mathematics education (M Ed); non-public school administration (M Ed); special education diagnostics (M Ed); teacher researcher (M Ed). *Accreditation:* NCATE. *Entrance requirements:* For master's, GRE General Test, teaching certificate. Additional exam requirements/recommendations for international students: Required—TOEFL (minimum score 550 paper-based). Electronic applications accepted.

University of Maryland, Baltimore County, The Graduate School, College of Arts, Humanities and Social Sciences, Department of Education, Master of Arts in Education Program, Baltimore, MD 21250. Offers K-8 mathematics instructional leadership (MAE); K-8 science education (MAE); K-8 STEM education (MAE); secondary mathematics education (MAE); secondary science education (MAE); secondary STEM education (MAE). *Program availability:* Part-time-only, evening/weekend, 100% online, blended/hybrid learning. *Degree requirements:* For master's, comprehensive exam (for some programs), thesis (for some programs). Electronic applications accepted. *Expenses:* Contact institution.

University of Maryland, Baltimore County, The Graduate School, College of Arts, Humanities and Social Sciences, Department of Education, Program in Teaching, Baltimore, MD 21250. Offers early childhood education (MAT); elementary education (MAT); teaching (MAT), including art, biology, chemistry, choral music, classical foreign language, dance, earth/space science, English, instrumental music, mathematics, modern foreign language, physical science, physics, social studies, theatre. *Program availability:* Part-time, evening/weekend. *Degree requirements:* For master's, comprehensive exam (for some programs), thesis (for some programs). *Entrance requirements:* For master's, PRAXIS Core Examination or GRE (minimum score of 1000), minimum GPA of 3.0. Additional exam requirements/recommendations for international students: Required—TOEFL. Electronic applications accepted. *Faculty research:* STEM teacher education, culturally sensitive pedagogy, ESOL/bilingual education, early childhood education, language, literacy and culture.

University of Massachusetts Dartmouth, Graduate School, College of Arts and Sciences, School of Education, Department of STEM Education and Teacher Development, North Dartmouth, MA 02747-2300. Offers English as a second language (Postbaccalaureate Certificate); mathematics education (PhD); middle school education (MAT); secondary school education (MAT). *Program availability:* Part-time. *Faculty:* 9 full-time (6 women), 3 part-time/adjunct (2 women). *Students:* 21 full-time (18 women), 100 part-time (53 women); includes 20 minority (3 Black or African American, non-Hispanic/Latino; 2 Asian, non-Hispanic/Latino; 11 Hispanic/Latino; 4 Two or more races, non-Hispanic/Latino), 3 international. Average age 34. 63 applicants, 90% accepted, 45 enrolled. In 2018, 68 master's, 1 doctorate, 1 other advanced degree awarded. *Degree requirements:* For doctorate, thesis/dissertation. *Entrance requirements:* For master's, Statement of Purpose, Resume, Official Transcripts, copy of MA MTELs, 2 letters of recommendation, Proof of License (for Professional Licensure Program); for doctorate, GRE Score, Statement of Purpose, Resume, Official transcripts, 3 letters of recommendation; for Postbaccalaureate Certificate, Statement of Purpose, Resume, Official Transcripts, 2 letters of recommendation, MTEL Score Report. Additional exam requirements/recommendations for international students: Required—TOEFL (minimum score 550 paper-based; 79 iBT), IELTS (minimum score 6.5). *Application deadline:* For fall admission, 1/15 priority date for domestic students, 12/15 priority date for international students; for spring admission, 12/15 priority date for domestic students, 11/15 priority date for international students. Application fee: $60. Electronic applications accepted. *Financial support:* In 2018–19, 1 fellowship (averaging $18,000 per year), 3 research assistantships (averaging $10,897 per year), 6 teaching assistantships (averaging $8,017 per year) were awarded; tuition waivers (full) and doctoral support also available. Financial award application deadline: 3/1; financial award applicants required to submit FAFSA. *Faculty research:* Mindfulness in education, literacies, assessment of teacher knowledge, curriculum tools for supporting mathematics learning. *Total annual research expenditures:* $1.8 million. *Unit head:* Traci Almeida, Coordinator of Graduate Admissions and Licensure, 508-999-8098, Fax: 508-910-8183, E-mail: talmeida@umassd.edu. *Application contact:* Scott Webster, Director of Graduate Studies and Admissions, 508-999-8604, Fax: 508-999-8183, E-mail: graduate@umassd.edu.
Website: http://www.umassd.edu/cas/schoolofeducation/departments/stemeducationandteacherdevelopment/

University of Memphis, Graduate School, College of Arts and Sciences, Department of Mathematical Sciences, Memphis, TN 38152. Offers applied mathematics (MS); applied statistics (PhD); mathematics (MS, PhD); statistics (MS); teaching of mathematics (MS). *Program availability:* Part-time. *Students:* 35 full-time (11 women), 41 part-time (13 women); includes 33 minority (14 Black or African American, non-Hispanic/Latino; 12 Asian, non-Hispanic/Latino; 5 Hispanic/Latino; 2 Two or more races, non-Hispanic/Latino), 22 international. Average age 34. 35 applicants, 83% accepted, 17 enrolled. In 2018, 10 master's, 5 doctorates awarded. Terminal master's awarded for partial completion of doctoral program. *Degree requirements:* For master's, comprehensive exam, thesis or alternative; for doctorate, one foreign language, comprehensive exam, thesis/dissertation, qualifying exam, final exam. *Entrance requirements:* For master's, GRE General Test, minimum GPA of 2.5, undergraduate degree in math or statistics, two letters of recommendation; for doctorate, GRE General Test, minimum GPA of 2.5, three letters of recommendation. Additional exam requirements/recommendations for international students: Required—TOEFL (minimum score 550 paper-based; 79 iBT). *Application deadline:* For fall admission, 8/1 for domestic students, 5/1 priority date for international students; for spring admission, 12/1 for domestic students, 9/1 priority date for international students. Applications are processed on a rolling basis. Application fee: $35 ($60 for international students). Electronic applications accepted. *Expenses: Tuition, area resident:* Full-time $10,240; part-time $503 per credit hour. Tuition, state resident: full-time $10,464. Tuition, nonresident: full-time $20,224; part-time $991 per credit hour. *Required fees:* $850; $106 per credit hour. *Financial support:* Fellowships with full tuition reimbursements, research assistantships with full tuition reimbursements, teaching assistantships with full tuition reimbursements, career-related internships or fieldwork, Federal Work-Study, scholarships/grants, and unspecified assistantships available. Financial award application deadline: 2/1; financial award applicants required to submit FAFSA. *Faculty research:* Combinatorics, ergodic theory, graph theory, Ramsey theory, applied statistics. *Unit head:* Dr. Irena Lasiecka, Chair, 901-678-2482, Fax: 901-678-2480, E-mail: lasiecka@memphis.edu. *Application contact:* Dr. Fernanda Botelho, Graduate Advising Coordinator, 901-678-3131, Fax: 901-678-2480, E-mail: mbotelho@memphis.edu.
Website: https://www.memphis.edu/msci

University of Miami, Graduate School, School of Education and Human Development, Department of Teaching and Learning, Program in Teaching and Learning, Coral Gables, FL 33124. Offers language and literacy learning in multilingual settings (PhD); science, technology, engineering and mathematics (stem) (PhD); special education (PhD). *Faculty:* 14 full-time (10 women), 9 part-time/adjunct (all women). *Students:* 18 full-time (12 women); includes 8 minority (2 Black or African American, non-Hispanic/Latino; 1 Asian, non-Hispanic/Latino; 4 Hispanic/Latino; 1 Two or more races, non-Hispanic/Latino), 6 international. Average age 36. 15 applicants, 33% accepted, 3 enrolled. In 2018, 4 doctorates awarded. *Degree requirements:* For doctorate, thesis/dissertation, electronic portfolio. *Entrance requirements:* For doctorate, GRE General Test. Additional exam requirements/recommendations for international students: Required—TOEFL (minimum score 550 paper-based; 80 iBT); Recommended—IELTS (minimum score 6.5). *Application deadline:* For fall admission, 6/30 for domestic students, 10/1 for international students. Application fee: $75. Electronic applications accepted. *Financial support:* Fellowships, research assistantships, teaching assistantships, health care benefits, tuition waivers (full and partial), and unspecified assistantships available. Financial award application deadline: 3/1; financial award applicants required to submit FAFSA. *Faculty research:* Teacher education, multicultural education, special education, second language acquisition, math and science education. *Unit head:* Dr. Matthew Deroo, Assistant Professor and Program Director, 305-284-5217, Fax: 305-284-6998, E-mail: deroomat@miami.edu. *Application contact:* Lois

Heffernan, Graduate Admission Coordinator, 305-284-2167, Fax: 305-284-9395, E-mail: lheffernan@miami.edu.
Website: http://www.education.miami.edu

University of Minnesota, Twin Cities Campus, Graduate School, College of Education and Human Development, Department of Curriculum and Instruction, Minneapolis, MN 55455-0213. Offers art education (M Ed, MA, PhD); curriculum and instruction (M Ed, MA, PhD); elementary education (MA, PhD); English education (PhD); language and immersion education (Certificate); learning technologies (MA, PhD); literacy education (MA, PhD); second language education (MA, PhD); social studies education (MA, PhD); STEM education (MA, PhD); teaching (M Ed), including mathematics, science, social studies, teaching; teaching English to speakers of other languages (MA); technology enhanced learning (Certificate). *Faculty:* 33 full-time (18 women). *Students:* 414 full-time (293 women), 247 part-time (170 women); includes 129 minority (16 Black or African American, non-Hispanic/Latino; 3 American Indian or Alaska Native, non-Hispanic/Latino; 38 Asian, non-Hispanic/Latino; 47 Hispanic/Latino; 25 Two or more races, non-Hispanic/Latino), 57 international. Average age 31. 610 applicants, 69% accepted, 349 enrolled. In 2018, 338 master's, 21 doctorates, 41 other advanced degrees awarded. Application fee: $75 ($95 for international students). *Financial support:* In 2018–19, 9 fellowships, 35 research assistantships with full tuition reimbursements (averaging $11,380 per year), 85 teaching assistantships with full tuition reimbursements (averaging $11,180 per year) were awarded. *Faculty research:* Teaching and learning; influence of cultural, linguistic, social, political, and technological factors on teaching, learning and educational research; relationship between educational practice and a democratic and just society; urban education; immigrant education, racial justice and education. *Total annual research expenditures:* $3.9 million. *Unit head:* Dr. Mark Vagle, Chair, 612-625-4006, E-mail: mvagle@umn.edu. *Application contact:* Dr. Mark Vagle, Chair, 612-625-4006, E-mail: mvagle@umn.edu.
Website: http://www.cehd.umn.edu/ci

University of Mississippi, Graduate School, School of Education, University, MS 38677. Offers counselor education (M Ed, PhD); counselor education - play therapy (Ed S); early childhood (M Ed); educational leadership K-12 (M Ed, Ed D, PhD, Ed S); elementary education (M Ed, Ed D, Ed S); higher education/student personnel (Ed D, PhD); literacy education (M Ed); math education (Ed D); secondary education (M Ed, PhD, Ed S); special education (M Ed, PhD, Ed S); teacher corporations (MA); teacher education (MA). *Accreditation:* NCATE. *Faculty:* 59 full-time (35 women), 34 part-time/adjunct (26 women). *Students:* 169 full-time (137 women), 461 part-time (329 women); includes 199 minority (185 Black or African American, non-Hispanic/Latino; 3 Asian, non-Hispanic/Latino; 7 Hispanic/Latino; 4 Two or more races, non-Hispanic/Latino), 5 international. Average age 33. In 2018, 180 master's, 57 doctorates, 37 other advanced degrees awarded. *Entrance requirements:* For master's, GRE General Test, minimum GPA of 3.0; for doctorate, GRE General Test. Additional exam requirements/recommendations for international students: Required—TOEFL. *Application deadline:* Applications are processed on a rolling basis. Application fee: $50. Electronic applications accepted. *Financial support:* Scholarships/grants available. Financial award application deadline: 3/1; financial award applicants required to submit FAFSA. *Unit head:* Dr. David Rock, Dean, 662-915-7063, Fax: 662-915-7249, E-mail: soe@olemiss.edu. *Application contact:* Temeka Smith, Graduate Activities Specialist for Admissions, 662-915-7474, Fax: 662-915-7577, E-mail: gschool@olemiss.edu.

University of Missouri, Office of Research and Graduate Studies, College of Education, Department of Learning, Teaching and Curriculum, Columbia, MO 65211. Offers agricultural education (M Ed, PhD, Ed S); art education (M Ed, PhD, Ed S); business and office education (M Ed, PhD, Ed S); early childhood education (M Ed, PhD, Ed S); elementary education (M Ed, PhD, Ed S); English education (M Ed, PhD, Ed S); foreign language education (M Ed, PhD, Ed S); health education and promotion (M Ed, PhD); learning and instruction (M Ed); marketing education (M Ed, PhD, Ed S); mathematics education (M Ed, PhD, Ed S); music education (M Ed, PhD, Ed S); reading education (M Ed, PhD, Ed S); science education (M Ed, PhD, Ed S); social studies education (M Ed, PhD, Ed S); vocational education (M Ed, PhD, Ed S). *Program availability:* Part-time. Terminal master's awarded for partial completion of doctoral program. *Entrance requirements:* For master's and Ed S, GRE General Test or MAT, minimum GPA of 3.0; for doctorate, GRE General Test, minimum GPA of 3.0. Additional exam requirements/recommendations for international students: Required—TOEFL.

University of Montana, Graduate School, College of Humanities and Sciences, Department of Mathematical Sciences, Missoula, MT 59812. Offers mathematics (MA, PhD), including college mathematics teaching (PhD), mathematical sciences research (PhD); mathematics education (MA). *Program availability:* Part-time. Terminal master's awarded for partial completion of doctoral program. *Degree requirements:* For doctorate, thesis/dissertation. *Entrance requirements:* For master's and doctorate, GRE General Test. Additional exam requirements/recommendations for international students: Required—TOEFL (minimum score 525 paper-based).

University of Nebraska at Kearney, College of Natural and Social Sciences, Department of Biology, Kearney, NE 68849. Offers biology (MS); science/math education (MA Ed). *Program availability:* Part-time, evening/weekend, 100% online. *Degree requirements:* For master's, comprehensive exam, thesis optional. *Entrance requirements:* For master's, GRE (for thesis option and for online program applicants if undergraduate GPA is below 2.75), letter of interest. Additional exam requirements/recommendations for international students: Recommended—TOEFL (minimum score 550 paper-based; 79 iBT), IELTS (minimum score 6.5). Electronic applications accepted. *Expenses:* Contact institution. *Faculty research:* Pollution injury, molecular biology-viral gene expression, prairie range condition modeling, evolution of symbiotic nitrogen fixation, geographic information systems (GIS), molecular genetics of aging.

University of Nevada, Reno, Graduate School, College of Science, Department of Mathematics and Statistics, Reno, NV 89557. Offers mathematics (MS); teaching mathematics (MATM). *Degree requirements:* For master's, thesis optional. *Entrance requirements:* For master's, GRE General Test, minimum GPA of 2.75. Additional exam requirements/recommendations for international students: Required—TOEFL (minimum score 500 paper-based; 61 iBT), IELTS (minimum score 6). Electronic applications accepted. *Faculty research:* Operator algebra, nonlinear systems, differential equations.

University of New Hampshire, Graduate School, College of Engineering and Physical Sciences, Department of Mathematics and Statistics, Durham, NH 03824. Offers applied mathematics (PhD); industrial statistics (Certificate); mathematics (MS, MST, PhD); mathematics education (PhD); mathematics: applied mathematics (MS); mathematics: statistics (MS, PhD). Terminal master's awarded for partial completion of doctoral program. *Entrance requirements:* Additional exam requirements/recommendations for international students: Required—TOEFL (minimum score 550 paper-based; 80 iBT). Electronic applications accepted.

The University of North Carolina at Chapel Hill, Graduate School, School of Education, Program in Secondary Education, Chapel Hill, NC 27599. Offers English (Grades 9-12) (MAT); English as a second language (MAT); French (Grades K-12) (MAT); German (Grades K-12) (MAT); Japanese (Grades K-12) (MAT); Latin (Grades 9-12) (MAT); mathematics (Grades 9-12) (MAT); music (Grades K-12) (MAT); science (Grades 9-12) (MAT); social studies (Grades 9-12) (MAT); Spanish (Grades K-12) (MAT). *Accreditation:* NCATE. *Degree requirements:* For master's, comprehensive exam. *Entrance requirements:* For master's, GRE General Test, minimum GPA of 3.0 during last 2 years of undergraduate course work. Additional exam requirements/recommendations for international students: Required—TOEFL (minimum score 550 paper-based). Electronic applications accepted.

The University of North Carolina at Greensboro, Graduate School, School of Education, Department of Teacher Education and Higher Education, Greensboro, NC 27412-5001. Offers college teaching and adult learning (Certificate); curriculum and instruction (M Ed), including chemistry education, elementary education, English as a second language, French education, instructional technology, mathematics education, middle grades education, reading education, science education, social studies education, Spanish education; curriculum and teaching (PhD), including higher education, teacher education and development; English as a second language (Certificate); higher education (M Ed); supervision (M Ed). *Accreditation:* NCATE. *Program availability:* Part-time. *Degree requirements:* For doctorate, thesis/dissertation. *Entrance requirements:* For master's and doctorate, GRE General Test. Additional exam requirements/recommendations for international students: Required—TOEFL. Electronic applications accepted. *Faculty research:* Community college literacy program, middle school mathematics/computer mathematics.

The University of North Carolina at Pembroke, The Graduate School, Department of Mathematics and Computer Science, Pembroke, NC 28372-1510. Offers mathematics education (MA). *Program availability:* Part-time, evening/weekend. *Degree requirements:* For master's, comprehensive exam, thesis optional. *Entrance requirements:* For master's, GRE General Test or MAT, bachelor's degree in mathematics or mathematics education; minimum GPA of 3.0 in major, 2.5 overall. Additional exam requirements/recommendations for international students: Required—TOEFL.

University of Northern Colorado, Graduate School, College of Natural and Health Sciences, School of Mathematical Sciences, Greeley, CO 80639. Offers educational mathematics (PhD); mathematical teaching (MA); mathematics (MA). *Program availability:* Part-time. *Degree requirements:* For master's, comprehensive exam, thesis or alternative; for doctorate, comprehensive exam, thesis/dissertation. *Entrance requirements:* For master's, GRE General Test (for liberal arts), 3 letters of recommendation; for doctorate, GRE General Test, 3 letters of recommendation. Electronic applications accepted.

University of Northern Iowa, Graduate College, College of Humanities, Arts and Sciences, Department of Mathematics, MA Program in Mathematics, Cedar Falls, IA 50614. Offers community college teaching (MA); mathematics (MA); secondary teaching (MA).

University of Northern Iowa, Graduate College, College of Humanities, Arts and Sciences, Department of Mathematics, MA Program in Mathematics for the Middle Grades, Cedar Falls, IA 50614. Offers MA.

University of North Georgia, Master of Arts in Teaching Program, Dahlonega, GA 30597. Offers physical education (MAT); secondary education - English (MAT); secondary education - history (MAT); secondary education - mathematics (MAT); secondary education - middle grades (MAT). *Degree requirements:* For master's, internship, capstone. *Entrance requirements:* For master's, GRE or MAT, GACE I and II, GA pre-service application, lawful presence verification, official transcripts, GA Educator Ethics Program entry assessment. Additional exam requirements/recommendations for international students: Required—TOEFL (minimum score 550 paper-based; 79 iBT), IELTS (minimum score 6.5). Electronic applications accepted. *Expenses:* Contact institution.

University of North Georgia, Program in Middle Grades Math and Science, Dahlonega, GA 30597. Offers M Ed. *Program availability:* Part-time, evening/weekend, online only, 100% online. *Degree requirements:* For master's, teaching practicum. *Entrance requirements:* For master's, baccalaureate degree from regionally-accredited, four-year institution with minimum cumulative GPA of 2.75; employment as teacher in middle grades classroom working with students at least 20 hours per week; clear/renewable teaching certificate in middle grades math or science in the state of Georgia or equivalent. Additional exam requirements/recommendations for international students: Required—TOEFL (minimum score 550 paper-based; 79 iBT), IELTS (minimum score 6.5). Electronic applications accepted. *Expenses:* Contact institution.

University of Oklahoma, Jeannine Rainbolt College of Education, Department of Instructional Leadership and Academic Curriculum, Norman, OK 73072. Offers instructional leadership and academic curriculum (M Ed, PhD), including biomedical education (PhD), early childhood education, elementary education, English education, instructional leadership, mathematics education, reading education, science education, social studies education, world languages education (M Ed); reading specialist (M Ed). *Accreditation:* NCATE. *Program availability:* Part-time. *Faculty:* 26 full-time (12 women), 1 part-time/adjunct (0 women). *Students:* 42 full-time (32 women), 113 part-time (85 women); includes 33 minority (9 Black or African American, non-Hispanic/Latino; 5 American Indian or Alaska Native, non-Hispanic/Latino; 6 Asian, non-Hispanic/Latino; 4 Hispanic/Latino; 1 Native Hawaiian or other Pacific Islander, non-Hispanic/Latino; 8 Two or more races, non-Hispanic/Latino), 9 international. Average age 35. 42 applicants, 79% accepted, 21 enrolled. In 2018, 30 master's, 17 doctorates awarded. Terminal master's awarded for partial completion of doctoral program. *Degree requirements:* For master's, comprehensive exam (for some programs), thesis (for some programs); for doctorate, comprehensive exam (for some programs), thesis/dissertation. *Entrance requirements:* For doctorate, GRE. Additional exam requirements/recommendations for international students: Required—TOEFL (minimum score 79 iBT) or IELTS (minimum score 6.5). Application fee: $50 ($100 for international students). Electronic applications accepted. *Expenses:* Tuition, state resident: full-time $5683.20; part-time $236.80 per credit hour. Tuition, nonresident: full-time $20,342; part-time $847.60 per credit hour. *International tuition:* $20,342.40 full-time. *Required fees:* $2894.20; $110.05 per credit hour. $126.50 per semester. Tuition and fees vary according to course load and program. *Financial support:* Fellowships, research assistantships, teaching assistantships, scholarships/grants, and unspecified assistantships available. Financial award application deadline: 6/1; financial award applicants required to submit FAFSA. *Faculty research:* Teacher preparation; instruction; curriculum; learning; constructivist theory. *Unit head:* Dr. Stacy Reeder, Chair, 405-325-1498, Fax: 405-325-4061, E-mail: reeder@ou.edu. *Application contact:* Anna Steele, Graduate Programs Officer, 405-325-4525, E-mail: anna.steele@ou.edu.
Website: http://www.ou.edu/education/ilac

University of Phoenix–Online Campus, College of Education, Phoenix, AZ 85034-7209. Offers administration and supervision (MAEd, Certificate); adult education and training (MAEd); curriculum and instruction (MAEd), including computer education, curriculum and instruction, English as a second language, language arts, mathematics, reading; early childhood education (MAEd); educational studies (MAEd); elementary teacher education (MAEd), including early childhood, elementary teacher education, high school middle level, middle level; principal licensure (Certificate); secondary teacher education (MAEd); special education (MAEd, Certificate); teacher education (MAEd), including middle level generalist; teacher education middle level mathematics

(MAEd), including middle level mathematics; teacher education middle level science (MAEd), including middle level science; teacher education secondary mathematics (MAEd); teacher education secondary science (MAEd); teacher leadership (MAEd); teachers of English learners (Certificate); transition to teaching (Certificate), including elementary education, secondary education. *Program availability:* Evening/weekend, online learning. *Entrance requirements:* Additional exam requirements/recommendations for international students: Required—TOEFL, TOEIC (Test of English as an International Communication), Berlitz Online English Proficiency Exam, PTE, or IELTS. Electronic applications accepted. *Expenses:* Contact institution.

University of Pittsburgh, School of Education, Department of Instruction and Learning, Program in Secondary Education, Pittsburgh, PA 15260. Offers English and communications education (M Ed, MAT); foreign language education (M Ed, MAT); language, literacy and culture education (Ed D, PhD); mathematics education (M Ed, MAT, Ed D, PhD); science education (M Ed, MAT, Ed D, PhD); secondary education (PhD); social studies education (M Ed, MAT); STEM education (Ed D). *Program availability:* Part-time, evening/weekend. *Degree requirements:* For master's, thesis; for doctorate, thesis/dissertation. *Entrance requirements:* For master's, PRAXIS I; for doctorate, GRE General Test. Additional exam requirements/recommendations for international students: Required—TOEFL. Electronic applications accepted.

University of Puerto Rico–Mayagüez, Graduate Studies, College of Arts and Sciences, Department of Mathematical Sciences, Mayagüez, PR 00681-9000. Offers applied mathematics (MS); pre-college math education (MS); pure mathematics (MS); scientific computing (MS); statistics (MS). *Program availability:* Part-time. *Degree requirements:* For master's, one foreign language, comprehensive exam, thesis. *Entrance requirements:* For master's, undergraduate degree in mathematics or its equivalent. Electronic applications accepted. *Faculty research:* Automata theory, linear algebra, logic.

University of Puerto Rico–Río Piedras, College of Education, Program in Curriculum and Teaching, San Juan, PR 00931-3300. Offers biology education (M Ed); chemistry education (M Ed); curriculum and teaching (Ed D); history education (M Ed); mathematics education (M Ed); physics education (M Ed); Spanish education (M Ed). *Program availability:* Part-time. *Degree requirements:* For master's, thesis; for doctorate, thesis/dissertation, internship. *Entrance requirements:* For master's, PAEG or GRE, minimum GPA of 3.0, letter of recommendation; for doctorate, GRE or PAEG, master's degree, minimum GPA of 3.0, letter of recommendation (2), interview. *Faculty research:* Curriculum, math teaching.

University of St. Francis, College of Education, Joliet, IL 60435-6169. Offers educational leadership (MS, Ed D); elementary education (M Ed); reading (MS); secondary education (M Ed), including English education, math education, science education, social studies education, visual arts education; special education (M Ed); teaching and learning (MS); TESOL (Certificate). *Accreditation:* NCATE. *Program availability:* Part-time, evening/weekend, 100% online, blended/hybrid learning. *Faculty:* 11 full-time (8 women), 58 part-time/adjunct (38 women). *Students:* 43 full-time (35 women), 453 part-time (354 women); includes 110 minority (48 Black or African American, non-Hispanic/Latino; 7 Asian, non-Hispanic/Latino; 52 Hispanic/Latino; 3 Two or more races, non-Hispanic/Latino), 3 international. Average age 37. 300 applicants, 66% accepted, 164 enrolled. In 2018, 151 master's, 42 doctorates, 4 other advanced degrees awarded. *Degree requirements:* For master's, comprehensive exam; for doctorate, thesis/dissertation. *Entrance requirements:* Additional exam requirements/recommendations for international students: Required—TOEFL (minimum score 550 paper-based; 79 iBT), IELTS (minimum score 6). *Application deadline:* Applications are processed on a rolling basis. Electronic applications accepted. Application fee is waived when completed online. *Expenses:* Contact institution. *Financial support:* In 2018–19, 33 students received support. Scholarships/grants and tuition waivers (partial) available. Support available to part-time students. Financial award applicants required to submit FAFSA. *Unit head:* Dr. John Gambro, Dean, 815-740-3456, E-mail: jgambro@stfrancis.edu. *Application contact:* Sandee Sloka, Director Adult & Graduate Admissions, 800-735-7500, E-mail: ssloka@stfrancis.edu.
Website: https://www.stfrancis.edu/education/

University of South Africa, College of Human Sciences, Pretoria, South Africa. Offers adult education (M Ed); African languages (MA, PhD); African politics (MA, PhD); Afrikaans (MA, PhD); ancient history (MA, PhD); ancient Near Eastern studies (MA, PhD); anthropology (MA, PhD); applied linguistics (MA); Arabic (MA, PhD); archaeology (MA); art history (MA); Biblical archaeology (MA); Biblical studies (M Th, D Th, PhD); Christian spirituality (M Th, D Th); church history (M Th, D Th); classical studies (MA, PhD); clinical psychology (MA); communication (MA, PhD); comparative education (M Ed, Ed D); consulting psychology (D Admin, D Com, PhD); curriculum studies (M Ed, Ed D); development studies (M Admin, MA, D Admin, PhD); didactics (M Ed, Ed D); education (M Tech); education management (M Ed, Ed D); educational psychology (M Ed); English (MA); environmental education (M Ed); French (MA, PhD); German (MA, PhD); Greek (MA); guidance and counseling (M Ed); health studies (MA, PhD), including health sciences education (MA), health services management (MA), medical and surgical nursing science (critical care general) (MA), midwifery and neonatal nursing science (MA), trauma and emergency care (MA); history (MA, PhD); history of education (Ed D); inclusive education (M Ed, Ed D); information and communications technology policy and regulation (MA); information science (MA, MIS, PhD); international politics (MA, PhD); Islamic studies (MA, PhD); Italian (MA, PhD); Judaica (MA, PhD); linguistics (MA, PhD); mathematical education (M Ed); mathematics education (MA); missiology (M Th, D Th); modern Hebrew (MA, PhD); musicology (MA, MMus, D Mus, PhD); natural science education (M Ed); New Testament (M Th, D Th); Old Testament (D Th); pastoral therapy (M Th, D Th); philosophy (MA); philosophy of education (M Ed, Ed D); politics (MA, PhD); Portuguese (MA, PhD); practical theology (M Th, D Th); psychology (MA, MS, PhD); psychology of education (M Ed, Ed D); public health (MA); religious studies (MA, D Th, PhD); Romance languages (MA); Russian (MA, PhD); Semitic languages (MA, PhD); social behavior studies in HIV/AIDS (MA); social science (mental health) (MA); social science in development studies (MA); social science in psychology (MA); social science in social work (MA); social science in sociology (MA); social work (MSW, DSW, PhD); socio-education (M Ed, Ed D); sociolinguistics (MA); sociology (MA, PhD); Spanish (MA, PhD); systematic theology (M Th, D Th); TESOL (teaching English to speakers of other languages) (MA); theological ethics (M Th, D Th); theory of literature (MA, PhD); urban ministries (D Th); urban ministry (M Th).

University of South Africa, Institute for Science and Technology Education, Pretoria, South Africa. Offers mathematics, science and technology education (M Sc, PhD).

University of South Carolina, The Graduate School, College of Arts and Sciences, Department of Mathematics, Columbia, SC 29208. Offers mathematics (MA, MS, PhD); mathematics education (M Math, MAT). MAT offered in cooperation with the College of Education. *Program availability:* Part-time. Terminal master's awarded for partial completion of doctoral program. *Degree requirements:* For master's, comprehensive exam, thesis (for some programs); for doctorate, one foreign language, comprehensive exam, thesis/dissertation, admission to candidacy exam, residency. *Entrance requirements:* For master's and doctorate, GRE General Test. Additional exam requirements/recommendations for international students: Required—TOEFL (minimum score 600 paper-based; 100 iBT). Electronic applications accepted. *Faculty research:* Computational mathematics, analysis (classical/modern), discrete mathematics, algebra, number theory.

University of South Carolina, The Graduate School, College of Education, Department of Instruction and Teacher Education, Program in Secondary Education, Columbia, SC 29208. Offers art education (IMA, MAT); business education (IMA, MAT); English (MAT); foreign language (MAT); health education (MAT); mathematics (MAT); science (IMA, MAT); secondary (Ed D); secondary education (MT, PhD); social studies (MAT); theatre and speech (MAT). IMA and MT offered jointly with the subject areas. *Accreditation:* NCATE. *Degree requirements:* For master's, comprehensive exam, thesis (for some programs), foreign language (MA); for doctorate, one foreign language, comprehensive exam, thesis/dissertation. *Entrance requirements:* For master's, GRE General Test or MAT, teaching certificate (IMA, M Ed), interview; for doctorate, GRE General Test or MAT, interview. *Faculty research:* Middle school programs, professional development, school collaboration.

University of South Dakota, Graduate School, School of Education, Division of Curriculum and Instruction, Program in Elementary Education, Vermillion, SD 57069. Offers elementary education (MA), including early childhood education, English language learning, reading specialist/literacy coach, science, technology and math (STEM). *Accreditation:* NCATE. *Program availability:* Part-time, 100% online, blended/hybrid learning. *Degree requirements:* For master's, comprehensive exam, thesis or alternative. *Entrance requirements:* For master's, GRE General Test, MAT, minimum GPA of 2.7. Additional exam requirements/recommendations for international students: Required—TOEFL (minimum score 550 paper-based; 79 iBT). Electronic applications accepted.

University of South Dakota, Graduate School, School of Education, Division of Curriculum and Instruction, Program in Secondary Education, Vermillion, SD 57069. Offers secondary education (MA), including English language learning, science, technology and math (STEM), secondary education plus certification. *Accreditation:* NCATE. *Program availability:* Part-time, online learning. *Degree requirements:* For master's, comprehensive exam, thesis or alternative. *Entrance requirements:* For master's, GRE General Test, MAT, minimum GPA of 2.7. Additional exam requirements/recommendations for international students: Required—TOEFL (minimum score 550 paper-based; 79 iBT). Electronic applications accepted.

University of Southern Indiana, Graduate Studies, Pott College of Science, Engineering, and Education, Department of Teacher Education, Program in Secondary Education, Evansville, IN 47712-3590. Offers secondary education (MSE), including mathematics teaching. *Accreditation:* NCATE. *Program availability:* Part-time, evening/weekend. *Entrance requirements:* For master's, PRAXIS II, bachelor's degree with minimum cumulative GPA of 2.75 from college or university accredited by NCATE or comparable association; minimum GPA of 3.0 in all courses taken at graduate level at all schools attended; teaching license. Additional exam requirements/recommendations for international students: Required—TOEFL (minimum score 550 paper-based; 79 iBT), IELTS (minimum score 6). Electronic applications accepted.

University of South Florida, St. Petersburg, College of Education, St. Petersburg, FL 33701. Offers educational leadership development (M Ed); elementary education (MA), including math/science; English education (MA); middle grades STEM education (MS); reading education (MA). *Program availability:* Part-time. *Degree requirements:* For master's, comprehensive exam, practicum, internship, comprehensive portfolio. *Entrance requirements:* For master's, State of Florida General Knowledge Test (GKT), Florida Teaching Certificate (for non-initial certification programs), letters of recommendation. Additional exam requirements/recommendations for international students: Required—TOEFL (minimum score 550 paper-based; 79 iBT); Recommended—IELTS. Electronic applications accepted.

The University of Tennessee, Graduate School, College of Education, Health and Human Sciences, Program in Education, Knoxville, TN 37996. Offers art education (MS); counseling education (PhD); cultural studies in education (PhD); curriculum (MS, Ed S); curriculum, educational research and evaluation (Ed D, PhD); early childhood education (PhD); early childhood special education (MS); education of deaf and hard of hearing (MS); educational administration and policy studies (Ed D, PhD); educational administration and supervision (Ed S); educational psychology (Ed D, PhD); elementary education (MS, Ed S); elementary teaching (MS); English education (MS, Ed S); exercise science (PhD); foreign language/ESL education (MS, Ed S); instructional technology (MS, Ed D, PhD, Ed S); literacy, language and ESL education (PhD); literacy, language education, and ESL education (Ed D); mathematics education (MS, Ed S); modified and comprehensive special education (MS); reading education (MS, Ed S); school counseling (Ed S); school psychology (PhD, Ed S); science education (MS, Ed S); secondary teaching (MS); social foundations (MS); social science education (MS, Ed S); socio-cultural foundations of sports and education (PhD); special education (Ed S); teacher education (Ed D, PhD). *Accreditation:* NCATE. *Program availability:* Part-time, evening/weekend. *Degree requirements:* For master's and Ed S, thesis optional; for doctorate, variable foreign language requirement, thesis/dissertation. *Entrance requirements:* For master's, minimum GPA of 2.7; for doctorate and Ed S, GRE General Test, minimum GPA of 2.7. Additional exam requirements/recommendations for international students: Required—TOEFL. Electronic applications accepted.

The University of Tennessee at Chattanooga, Program in Mathematics, Chattanooga, TN 37403. Offers applied mathematics (MS); applied statistics (MS); mathematics education (MS); pre-professional mathematics (MS). *Program availability:* Part-time. *Degree requirements:* For master's, internship or thesis. *Entrance requirements:* For master's, GRE (if applying for an assistantship), two letters of recommendation. Additional exam requirements/recommendations for international students: Required—TOEFL (minimum score 550 paper-based; 61 iBT), IELTS (minimum score 6). Electronic applications accepted. *Expenses:* Contact institution.

The University of Texas at Arlington, Graduate School, College of Education, Department of Curriculum and Instruction, Arlington, TX 76019. Offers curriculum and instruction (M Ed), including literacy studies, mathematics education, mind, brain, and education, science education; teaching (with certification) (M Ed T). *Accreditation:* NCATE. *Program availability:* Part-time, evening/weekend, online learning. *Degree requirements:* For master's, comprehensive exam (for some programs), comprehensive activity, research project. *Entrance requirements:* For master's, GRE General Test, minimum undergraduate GPA of 3.0 in last 60 hours of course work, writing sample, 3 letters of recommendation. Additional exam requirements/recommendations for international students: Required—TOEFL (minimum score 550 paper-based). Electronic applications accepted.

The University of Texas at Arlington, Graduate School, College of Science, Department of Mathematics, Arlington, TX 76019. Offers applied math (MS); mathematics (PhD); mathematics education (MA). *Program availability:* Part-time, evening/weekend. *Degree requirements:* For master's, comprehensive exam, thesis or alternative; for doctorate, comprehensive exam, thesis/dissertation, preliminary examinations. *Entrance requirements:* For master's, GRE General Test (minimum score 350 verbal, 650 quantitative); for doctorate, GRE General Test (minimum score 350 verbal, 700 quantitative), 30 hours of graduate course work in mathematics, minimum

GPA of 3.0 in last 60 hours of course work. Additional exam requirements/recommendations for international students: Required—TOEFL (minimum score 550 paper-based; 79 iBT). Electronic applications accepted. *Faculty research:* Algebra, combinatorics and geometry, applied mathematics and mathematical biology, computational mathematics, mathematics education, probability and statistics.

The University of Texas at Dallas, School of Natural Sciences and Mathematics, Department of Science/Mathematics Education, Richardson, TX 75080. Offers mathematics education (MAT); science education (MAT). *Program availability:* Part-time, evening/weekend, online learning. *Faculty:* 3 full-time (1 woman), 2 part-time/adjunct (1 woman). *Students:* 9 full-time (6 women), 23 part-time (17 women); includes 17 minority (2 Black or African American, non-Hispanic/Latino; 9 Asian, non-Hispanic/Latino; 4 Hispanic/Latino; 2 Two or more races, non-Hispanic/Latino), 3 international. Average age 31. 21 applicants, 57% accepted, 8 enrolled. In 2018, 9 master's awarded. *Degree requirements:* For master's, thesis optional. *Entrance requirements:* For master's, GRE General Test, minimum GPA of 3.0 in upper-level coursework in field. Additional exam requirements/recommendations for international students: Required—TOEFL (minimum score 550 paper-based). *Application deadline:* For fall admission, 7/15 for domestic students, 5/1 priority date for international students; for spring admission, 11/15 for domestic students, 9/1 priority date for international students. Applications are processed on a rolling basis. Application fee: $50 ($100 for international students). Electronic applications accepted. *Expenses: Tuition, area resident:* Full-time $13,458. Tuition, state resident: full-time $13,458. Tuition, nonresident: full-time $26,852. *International tuition:* $26,852 full-time. Tuition and fees vary according to course load. *Financial support:* In 2018–19, 4 students received support, including 1 research assistantship with partial tuition reimbursement available (averaging $22,800 per year), 3 teaching assistantships with partial tuition reimbursements available (averaging $17,100 per year); fellowships, career-related internships or fieldwork, Federal Work-Study, institutionally sponsored loans, scholarships/grants, and unspecified assistantships also available. Support available to part-time students. Financial award application deadline: 4/30; financial award applicants required to submit FAFSA. *Faculty research:* Innovative science/math education programs. *Unit head:* Dr. Mary Urquhart Kelly, Department Head, 972-883-2496, Fax: 972-883-6796, E-mail: scimathed@utdallas.edu. *Application contact:* Dr. Mary Urquhart Kelly, Department Head, 972-883-2496, Fax: 972-883-6796, E-mail: scimathed@utdallas.edu.
Website: http://www.utdallas.edu/sme/

The University of Texas at San Antonio, College of Sciences, Department of Mathematics, San Antonio, TX 78249-0617. Offers applied mathematics (MS), including industrial mathematics; mathematics (MS); mathematics education (MS). *Program availability:* Part-time, evening/weekend. *Degree requirements:* For master's, comprehensive exam (for some programs), thesis or alternative. *Entrance requirements:* For master's, GRE General Test, minimum GPA of 3.0 in last 60 hours. Additional exam requirements/recommendations for international students: Required—TOEFL (minimum score 550 paper-based; 79 iBT), IELTS (minimum score 6.5). Electronic applications accepted. *Faculty research:* Differential equations, functional analysis, numerical analysis, number theory, logic.

University of the District of Columbia, College of Arts and Sciences, Program in Teaching, Washington, DC 20008-1175. Offers elementary education (MAT); middle school mathematics (MAT); secondary English language arts (MAT); secondary social studies (MAT).

University of the Incarnate Word, School of Mathematics, Science, and Engineering, San Antonio, TX 78209-6397. Offers applied statistics (MS); biology (MA, MS); mathematics (MA), including teaching; multidisciplinary sciences (MA); nutrition (MS). *Program availability:* Part-time, evening/weekend. *Faculty:* 6 full-time (4 women), 1 (woman) part-time/adjunct. *Students:* 30 full-time (24 women), 9 part-time (7 women); includes 20 minority (1 Black or African American, non-Hispanic/Latino; 1 American Indian or Alaska Native, non-Hispanic/Latino; 1 Asian, non-Hispanic/Latino; 17 Hispanic/Latino), 5 international. 34 applicants, 88% accepted, 13 enrolled. In 2018, 10 master's awarded. *Degree requirements:* For master's, comprehensive exam (for some programs), thesis optional, capstone. *Entrance requirements:* For master's, GRE, recommendation letter. Additional exam requirements/recommendations for international students: Required—TOEFL (minimum score 560 paper-based; 83 iBT). *Application deadline:* Applications are processed on a rolling basis. Application fee: $20. Electronic applications accepted. *Expenses: Tuition:* Full-time $22,560; part-time $940 per credit hour. *Required fees:* $2484; $94 per credit hour. Tuition and fees vary according to degree level, program and student level. *Financial support:* Research assistantships, Federal Work-Study, scholarships/grants, tuition waivers (partial), and unspecified assistantships available. Financial award applicants required to submit FAFSA. *Faculty research:* Neural morphallaxis in lumbriculus variegatus, igneous and metamorphic petrology, applied cloud and precipitation physics, DNA-protein interactions, evolution of adenoviruses and picornaviruses. *Unit head:* Dr. Carlos A. Garcia, Dean, 210-829-2717, Fax: 210-829-3153, E-mail: cagarci9@uiwtx.edu. *Application contact:* Jessica Delarosa, Associate Director of Admissions, 210-8296005, Fax: 210-829-3921, E-mail: admis@uiwtx.edu.
Website: https://www.uiw.edu/smse/index.html

University of the Sacred Heart, Graduate Programs, Department of Education, San Juan, PR 00914-0383. Offers early childhood education (M Ed); information technology and multimedia (Certificate); instruction systems and education technology (M Ed), including English, information technology and multimedia, instructional design, mathematics, Spanish. *Program availability:* Part-time, evening/weekend. *Degree requirements:* For master's, thesis. *Entrance requirements:* For master's, EXADEP, minimum undergraduate GPA of 2.75, interview.

University of the Virgin Islands, College of Science and Mathematics, St. Thomas, VI 00802. Offers marine and environmental science (MS); mathematics for secondary teachers (MA). *Faculty:* 5 full-time (4 women), 7 part-time/adjunct (2 women). *Students:* 16 full-time (13 women), 19 part-time (13 women); includes 10 minority (4 Black or African American, non-Hispanic/Latino; 1 American Indian or Alaska Native, non-Hispanic/Latino; 2 Hispanic/Latino; 1 Native Hawaiian or other Pacific Islander, non-Hispanic/Latino; 2 Two or more races, non-Hispanic/Latino), 1 international. Average age 27. In 2018, 8 master's awarded. *Degree requirements:* For master's, comprehensive exam, thesis. *Entrance requirements:* For master's, GRE, minimum GPA of 2.5. Additional exam requirements/recommendations for international students: Required—TOEFL (minimum score 550 paper-based). *Application deadline:* For fall admission, 4/30 for domestic and international students; for spring admission, 10/30 for domestic and international students. Application fee: $30. Electronic applications accepted. *Expenses:* Tuition, state resident: full-time $6948; part-time $386 per credit. Tuition, nonresident: full-time $13,230; part-time $735 per credit. *International tuition:* $13,230 full-time. *Required fees:* $508. *Financial support:* Fellowships, research assistantships, teaching assistantships, career-related internships or fieldwork, and scholarships/grants available. Financial award application deadline: 4/15; financial award applicants required to submit FAFSA. *Unit head:* Dr. Sandra Romano, Dean, 340-693-1230, Fax: 340-693-1245, E-mail: sromano@uvi.edu. *Application contact:* Charmaine Smith, Director of Admissions, 340-690-4070, E-mail: csmith@uvi.edu.

The University of Toledo, College of Graduate Studies, Judith Herb College of Education, Department of Curriculum and Instruction, Toledo, OH 43606-3390. Offers art education (ME); career and technical education (ME, Ed S); curriculum and instruction (ME, PhD, Ed S); early childhood education (Ed S); education and anthropology (MAE); education and biology (MES); education and chemistry (MES); education and classics (MAE); education and economics (MAE); education and English (MAE); education and French (MAE); education and geology (MES); education and German (MAE); education and history (MAE); education and mathematics (MAE, MES); education and physics (MES); education and political science (MAE); education and sociology (MAE); education and Spanish (MAE); educational media (PhD); educational technology (ME); educational technology: virtual educator (Certificate); elementary education (PhD); English as a second language (MAE); gifted and talented education (PhD); middle childhood education (ME); secondary education (ME, PhD); special education (PhD). *Accreditation:* NCATE. *Program availability:* Part-time, evening/weekend. *Degree requirements:* For master's, comprehensive exam, thesis or alternative; for doctorate, comprehensive exam, thesis/dissertation; for other advanced degree, thesis optional. *Entrance requirements:* For master's, doctorate, and other advanced degree, minimum cumulative GPA of 2.7 for all previous academic work, letters of recommendation. Additional exam requirements/recommendations for international students: Required—TOEFL (minimum score 550 paper-based; 80 iBT). Electronic applications accepted.

University of Utah, Graduate School, College of Science, Department of Mathematics, Salt Lake City, UT 84112-0090. Offers mathematics (MA, MS, PhD); mathematics teaching (MS); statistics (M Stat). *Program availability:* Part-time. *Faculty:* 45 full-time (4 women), 17 part-time/adjunct (6 women). *Students:* 112 full-time (40 women), 26 part-time (12 women); includes 7 minority (1 Black or African American, non-Hispanic/Latino; 6 Asian, non-Hispanic/Latino), 40 international. Average age 28. 288 applicants, 20% accepted, 25 enrolled. In 2018, 9 master's, 16 doctorates awarded. Terminal master's awarded for partial completion of doctoral program. *Degree requirements:* For master's, comprehensive exam, thesis or alternative, written or oral exam; for doctorate, comprehensive exam, thesis/dissertation, written and oral exam. *Entrance requirements:* For master's and doctorate, GRE Subject Test in math (recommended), Minimum undergraduate GPA of 3.0. Additional exam requirements/recommendations for international students: Required—TOEFL (minimum score 550 paper-based; 80 iBT), GRE (recommended). *Application deadline:* For fall admission, 1/1 for domestic and international students; for spring admission, 11/1 for domestic and international students; for summer admission, 3/15 for domestic and international students. Application fee: $55 ($65 for international students). Electronic applications accepted. *Expenses: Tuition, area resident:* Full-time $7190.66; part-time $2112.48 per year. Tuition, state resident: full-time $7190.66. Tuition, nonresident: full-time $25,195. *Required fees:* $558; $555.04 per unit. Tuition and fees vary according to course level, course load, degree level, program and student level. *Financial support:* In 2018–19, 106 students received support, including 1 fellowship (averaging $20,000 per year), 22 research assistantships with full tuition reimbursements available (averaging $20,000 per year), 73 teaching assistantships with full tuition reimbursements available (averaging $20,000 per year); health care benefits and unspecified assistantships also available. Financial award application deadline: 1/1; financial award applicants required to submit FAFSA. *Faculty research:* Algebraic geometry, applied mathematics, commutative algebra, data science, geometry and topology, materials and microstructure, mathematical biology, number theory, probability, statistics. *Total annual research expenditures:* $4.7 million. *Unit head:* Dr. Davar Khoshnvesian, Chair, 801-581-7870, E-mail: chair@math.utah.edu. *Application contact:* Dr. Elena Cherkaev, Director of Graduate Studies, 801-581-7315, Fax: 801-581-6841, E-mail: elena@math.utah.edu.
Website: http://www.math.utah.edu/

University of Victoria, Faculty of Graduate Studies, Faculty of Education, Department of Curriculum and Instruction, Victoria, BC V8W 2Y2, Canada. Offers art education (M Ed, PhD); curriculum studies (M Ed, MA, PhD); early childhood education (M Ed, PhD); educational studies (PhD); language and literacy (M Ed, MA, PhD); mathematics (M Ed, MA, PhD); music education (M Ed, MA, PhD); science (M Ed, MA, PhD); social studies (M Ed, MA); social, cultural and foundational studies (MA, PhD); technology and environmental education (PhD). *Program availability:* Part-time. *Degree requirements:* For master's, thesis, project (M Ed); for doctorate, comprehensive exam, thesis/dissertation. *Entrance requirements:* For master's, minimum B average. Additional exam requirements/recommendations for international students: Required—TOEFL (minimum score 575 paper-based), IELTS (minimum score 7). Electronic applications accepted. *Faculty research:* Elementary and secondary English, language arts, curriculum theory and practice, educational media and technology, educational administration and leadership, history and philosophy of education.

University of Virginia, Curry School of Education, Department of Curriculum, Instruction, and Special Education, Program in Curriculum and Instruction, Charlottesville, VA 22903. Offers curriculum and instruction (M Ed, Ed S); elementary education (M Ed, Ed D); English education (M Ed, Ed D); foreign language education (M Ed); mathematics education (M Ed, Ed D); science education (Ed D); social studies education (M Ed); MBA/M Ed. *Program availability:* 100% online. *Degree requirements:* For master's, comprehensive exam (for some programs); for doctorate, comprehensive exam, thesis/dissertation; for Ed S, comprehensive exam. *Entrance requirements:* For master's, doctorate, and Ed S, GRE General Test, 2 letters of recommendation. Additional exam requirements/recommendations for international students: Required—TOEFL (minimum score 600 paper-based; 90 iBT), IELTS (minimum score 7). Electronic applications accepted.

University of Virginia, Curry School of Education, Program in Education, Charlottesville, VA 22903. Offers administration and supervision (PhD); applied developmental science (PhD); counselor education (PhD); curriculum and instruction (PhD); early childhood special education (MT); education evaluation (PhD); educational psychology (PhD); educational research (PhD); elementary education (MT); English education (MT, PhD); foreign language education (MT); higher education (PhD); instructional technology (PhD); kinesiology (MT, PhD); math education (PhD); reading education (PhD); research, statistics and evaluation (PhD); school psychology (PhD); science education (PhD); social studies education (MT, PhD); special education (PhD); world languages education (MT). *Degree requirements:* For master's, comprehensive exam (for some programs), field project; for doctorate, comprehensive exam, thesis/dissertation. *Entrance requirements:* For doctorate, GRE General Test. Additional exam requirements/recommendations for international students: Required—TOEFL (minimum score 600 paper-based; 90 iBT), IELTS (minimum score 7). Electronic applications accepted.

University of Washington, Graduate School, College of Education, Seattle, WA 98195. Offers curriculum and instruction (M Ed, Ed D, PhD), including educational technology, general curriculum (Ed D, PhD), language, literacy, and culture, mathematics education, multicultural education, reading and language arts education (Ed D), science education, social studies education, teaching and curriculum (M Ed); educational leadership and policy studies (M Ed, Ed D, PhD), including administration (Ed D), educational policy, organization, and leadership (M Ed, PhD), higher education, leadership for learning

(Ed D), social and cultural foundations of education (M Ed, PhD); educational psychology (M Ed, PhD), including educational psychology (PhD); human development and cognition (M Ed), learning sciences, measurement, statistics and research design (M Ed), school psychology (M Ed); instructional leadership (M Ed); intercollegiate athletic leadership (M Ed); special education (M Ed, Ed D, PhD), including early childhood special education (M Ed), emotional and behavioral disabilities (M Ed), learning disabilities (M Ed), low-incidence disabilities (M Ed), severe disabilities (M Ed), special education (Ed D, PhD); teacher education (MIT). *Accreditation:* APA. *Program availability:* Part-time, evening/weekend. *Degree requirements:* For master's, thesis optional; for doctorate, thesis/dissertation. *Entrance requirements:* For master's and doctorate, GRE General Test, minimum GPA of 3.0. Additional exam requirements/recommendations for international students: Required—TOEFL. Electronic applications accepted. *Faculty research:* School restructuring/effective schools, special education interventions, literacy and writing, technology, school partnerships, teacher preparation.

University of Washington, Tacoma, Graduate Programs, Program in Education, Tacoma, WA 98402-3100. Offers education (M Ed); educational administration (principal or program administrator certification) (M Ed); elementary education teacher certification (M Ed); elementary education/special education teacher certification (M Ed); secondary science or math teacher certification (M Ed). *Program availability:* Part-time, evening/weekend. *Degree requirements:* For master's, culminating project. *Entrance requirements:* For master's, WEST-B, WEST-E (teacher certification programs only), official sealed transcript from every college/university attended, personal goal statement, letters of recommendation, copy of valid teaching certificate. Additional exam requirements/recommendations for international students: Required—TOEFL (minimum score 580 paper-based; 92 iBT). Electronic applications accepted. *Faculty research:* Global learning communities for English/Chinese languages, evaluation of mathematics and reading intervention programs, response to intervention, school-wide behavioral and emotional support, mathematics education and culturally responsive mathematics education.

The University of West Alabama, School of Graduate Studies, College of Education, Program in Secondary Education, Livingston, AL 35470. Offers biology (MAT); English language arts (MAT); high school 6-12 (M Ed); history (MAT); mathematics (MAT); science (MAT); social science (MAT). *Program availability:* Part-time, evening/weekend, 100% online. *Faculty:* 18 full-time (6 women), 8 part-time/adjunct (2 women). *Students:* 232 full-time (165 women), 34 part-time (24 women); includes 53 minority (44 Black or African American, non-Hispanic/Latino; 3 American Indian or Alaska Native, non-Hispanic/Latino; 2 Hispanic/Latino; 4 Two or more races, non-Hispanic/Latino), 3 international. Average age 31. 84 applicants, 93% accepted, 67 enrolled. In 2018, 100 master's awarded. *Degree requirements:* For master's, comprehensive exam, thesis optional. *Entrance requirements:* For master's, GRE, minimum GPA of 2.75, verification of background clearance/fingerprints, valid bachelor's-level Professional Educator Certificate in same teaching field. Additional exam requirements/recommendations for international students: Required—TOEFL (minimum score 500 paper-based; 61 iBT). *Application deadline:* Applications are processed on a rolling basis. Application fee: $40. Electronic applications accepted. *Expenses: Tuition, area resident:* Full-time $9100. Tuition, state resident: full-time $9100. Tuition, nonresident: full-time $19,200. *Required fees:* $1890; $130. *Financial support:* Teaching assistantships, Federal Work-Study, scholarships/grants, and unspecified assistantships available. Support available to part-time students. Financial award application deadline: 3/1; financial award applicants required to submit FAFSA. *Unit head:* Dr. Jodie Winship, Chair of College of Education, 205-652-5415, Fax: 205-652-3706, E-mail: jwinship@uwa.edu. *Application contact:* Dr. B. J. Kimbrough, Dean of Graduate Studies, 205-652-3647, Fax: 205-652-3670, E-mail: bkimbrough@uwa.edu.

University of Wisconsin–Milwaukee, Graduate School, School of Education, Department of Curriculum and Instruction, Milwaukee, WI 53201-0413. Offers curriculum and instruction (MS), including cross-curricular focus, early childhood education, English education, mathematics education, middle childhood/early adolescence education, reading education, science education, urban social studies education. *Program availability:* Part-time. *Students:* 19 full-time (15 women), 56 part-time (49 women); includes 15 minority (3 Black or African American, non-Hispanic/Latino; 1 American Indian or Alaska Native, non-Hispanic/Latino; 3 Asian, non-Hispanic/Latino; 1 Hispanic/Latino; 7 Two or more races, non-Hispanic/Latino), 2 international. Average age 33. 27 applicants, 44% accepted, 11 enrolled. In 2018, 20 master's awarded. *Entrance requirements:* Additional exam requirements/recommendations for international students: Required—TOEFL (minimum score 550 paper-based; 79 iBT), IELTS (minimum score 6.5). *Application deadline:* For fall admission, 1/1 priority date for domestic students; for spring admission, 9/1 for domestic students. Application fee: $56 ($96 for international students). Electronic applications accepted. *Financial support:* Fellowships, research assistantships, teaching assistantships, career-related internships or fieldwork, health care benefits, unspecified assistantships, and project assistantships available. Support available to part-time students. Financial award application deadline: 4/15; financial award applicants required to submit FAFSA. *Application contact:* General Information Contact, 414-229-4721, E-mail: soeinfo@uwm.edu.
Website: http://uwm.edu/education/academics/curriculum-instruction-department/

University of Wisconsin–Milwaukee, Graduate School, School of Education, Department of Exceptional Education, Milwaukee, WI 53201-0413. Offers autism spectrum disorders (Graduate Certificate); exceptional education (MS); transition for students with disabilities (Graduate Certificate); urban education (PhD), including adult, continuing and higher education leadership, art education, curriculum and instruction, exceptional education, mathematics education, multicultural studies, social foundations of education. *Program availability:* Part-time. *Students:* 38 full-time (29 women), 67 part-time (50 women); includes 39 minority (23 Black or African American, non-Hispanic/Latino; 1 American Indian or Alaska Native, non-Hispanic/Latino; 6 Asian, non-Hispanic/Latino; 1 Hispanic/Latino; 8 Two or more races, non-Hispanic/Latino), 2 international. Average age 40. 47 applicants, 40% accepted, 11 enrolled. In 2018, 13 master's, 14 doctorates, 4 other advanced degrees awarded. *Entrance requirements:* Additional exam requirements/recommendations for international students: Required—TOEFL (minimum score 550 paper-based; 79 iBT), IELTS (minimum score 6.5). *Application deadline:* For fall admission, 1/1 priority date for domestic students; for spring admission, 9/1 for domestic students. Application fee: $56 ($96 for international students). Electronic applications accepted. *Financial support:* Fellowships, research assistantships, teaching assistantships, career-related internships or fieldwork, health care benefits, and unspecified assistantships available. Support available to part-time students. Financial award application deadline: 4/15; financial award applicants required to submit FAFSA. *Faculty research:* Emotional disturbance, hearing impairment, learning disabilities, mental retardation. *Application contact:* General Information Contact, 414-229-4721, E-mail: soeinfo@uwm.edu.
Website: http://uwm.edu/education/academics/exceptional-edu-department/

University of Wisconsin–Oshkosh, Graduate Studies, College of Letters and Science, Department of Mathematics, Oshkosh, WI 54901. Offers mathematics education (MS). *Program availability:* Part-time. *Degree requirements:* For master's, comprehensive exam, thesis optional. *Entrance requirements:* For master's, 30 undergraduate credits in

mathematics. Additional exam requirements/recommendations for international students: Required—TOEFL (minimum score 550 paper-based; 79 iBT). Electronic applications accepted. *Faculty research:* Problem solving, number theory, discrete mathematics, statistics.

University of Wisconsin–River Falls, Outreach and Graduate Studies, College of Arts and Science, Program in Mathematics, River Falls, WI 54022. Offers mathematics education (MSE). *Program availability:* Part-time. *Degree requirements:* For master's, thesis (for some programs). *Entrance requirements:* For master's, minimum GPA of 2.75. Additional exam requirements/recommendations for international students: Required—TOEFL (minimum score 500 paper-based; 65 iBT), IELTS (minimum score 5.5). Electronic applications accepted.

University of Wyoming, College of Arts and Sciences, Department of Mathematics and Statistics, Laramie, WY 82071. Offers applied statistics (MS); mathematics (MA, MAT, MS, MST, PhD). *Program availability:* Part-time. Terminal master's awarded for partial completion of doctoral program. *Degree requirements:* For master's, comprehensive exam, thesis, qualifying exam; for doctorate, comprehensive exam, thesis/dissertation, preliminary exam. *Entrance requirements:* For master's and doctorate, GRE General Test, minimum GPA of 3.0. Additional exam requirements/recommendations for international students: Required—TOEFL (minimum score 540 paper-based; 76 iBT). *Expenses: Tuition, area resident:* Full-time $6504; part-time $271 per credit hour. Tuition, state resident: full-time $6504; part-time $271 per credit hour. Tuition, nonresident: full-time $19,464; part-time $811 per credit hour. International tuition: $19,464 full-time. *Required fees:* $1410.94; $343.82 per semester. $343.82 per semester. Tuition and fees vary according to course load, program and reciprocity agreements. *Faculty research:* Numerical analysis, classical analysis, mathematical modeling, algebraic combinations.

Utah Valley University, Program in Education, Orem, UT 84058-5999. Offers educational technology (M Ed); elementary mathematics (M Ed); elementary STEM (M Ed); English as a second language (M Ed); reading (M Ed); teachers as leaders (M Ed). *Accreditation:* TEAC. *Program availability:* Part-time. *Degree requirements:* For master's, project. *Entrance requirements:* For master's, GRE, 3 letters of recommendation, interview, essay. Additional exam requirements/recommendations for international students: Required—TOEFL (minimum score 83 iBT). Electronic applications accepted. *Expenses:* Contact institution.

Wagner College, Division of Graduate Studies, Education Department, Program in Secondary Education/Students with Disabilities, Staten Island, NY 10301-4495. Offers secondary education 7-12 (MS Ed), including language arts, languages other than English, mathematics and technology, science and technology, social studies. *Program availability:* Evening/weekend. *Degree requirements:* For master's, thesis (for some programs), completion of state certification exams before student teaching. *Entrance requirements:* For master's, GRE, minimum GPA of 3.0, interview, recommendations. Additional exam requirements/recommendations for international students: Required—TOEFL (minimum score 550 paper-based; 79 iBT), IELTS (minimum score 6.5). Electronic applications accepted. *Expenses:* Contact institution.

Walden University, Graduate Programs, Richard W. Riley College of Education and Leadership, Minneapolis, MN 55401. Offers adult education (Post-Master's Certificate); adult learning (Graduate Certificate); college teaching and learning (Graduate Certificate); community college leadership (Ed D); curriculum, instruction and assessment (Ed D, Ed S, Graduate Certificate); developmental education (Graduate Certificate); early childhood administration, management, and leadership (Graduate Certificate); early childhood education (Ed D, Ed S); early childhood public policy and advocacy (Graduate Certificate); early childhood studies (MS), including administration, management and leadership, early childhood public policy and advocacy, teaching adults in the early childhood field, teaching and diversity in early childhood education; education (MS, PhD), including adolescent literacy and learning (MS), curriculum, instruction, and assessment (grades K-12) (MS), curriculum, instruction, assessment, and evaluation (PhD), early childhood leadership and advocacy (PhD), early childhood special education (PhD), educational leadership (MS), educational leadership and administration (principal preparation) (MS), educational technology and design (PhD), elementary reading and literacy (PreK-6) (MS), elementary reading and mathematics (grades K-6) (MS), global and comparative education (PhD), higher education leadership management and policy (PhD), integrating technology in the classroom (grades K-12) (MS), learning, instruction and innovation (PhD), mathematics (grades 5-8) (MS), mathematics (grades K-6) (MS), mathematics and science (grades K-8) (MS), organizational research, assessment, and evaluation (PhD), reading and literacy with a reading K-12 endorsement (MS), reading literacy assessment and evaluation (PhD), science (grades K-8) (MS), special education (non-licensure) (grades K-12) (MS), teacher leadership (grades K-12) (MS), teaching English language learners (grades K-12) (MS); educational administration and leadership (Ed D); educational leadership and administration (principal preparation) (Ed S); educational technology (Ed D, Ed S, Post Master's Certificate); elementary reading and literacy (Graduate Certificate); engaging culturally diverse learners (Graduate Certificate); enrollment management and institutional marketing (Graduate Certificate); higher education (MS), including adult learning, college teaching and learning, enrollment management and institutional marketing, global higher education, leadership for student success, online and distance learning; higher education and adult learning (Ed D); higher education leadership and management (Ed D); higher education leadership for student success (Graduate Certificate); instructional design and technology (MS, Postbaccalaureate Certificate), including general program (MS), online learning (MS), training and performance improvement (MS); integrating technology in the classroom (Graduate Certificate); mathematics 5-8 (Graduate Certificate); mathematics K-6 (Graduate Certificate); online teaching for adult educators (Graduate Certificate); reading, literacy, and assessment (Ed D, Ed S); science K-8 (Graduate Certificate); special education (Ed D, Ed S, Graduate Certificate); special education (K-age 21) (MAT); teacher leadership (Graduate Certificate); teaching adults English as a second language (Graduate Certificate); teaching adults in the early childhood field (Graduate Certificate); teaching and diversity in early childhood education (Graduate Certificate); teaching English language learners (grades K-12) (Graduate Certificate); teaching K-12 students online (Graduate Certificate). *Accreditation:* NCATE. *Program availability:* Part-time, evening/weekend, online only, 100% online. *Degree requirements:* For doctorate, thesis/dissertation (for some programs), residency; for other advanced degree, residency (for some programs). *Entrance requirements:* For master's, bachelor's degree or higher; minimum GPA of 2.5; official transcripts; goal statement (for some programs); access to computer and Internet; for doctorate, master's degree or higher; three years of related professional or academic experience (preferred); minimum GPA of 3.0; goal statement and current resume (for select programs); official transcripts; access to computer and Internet; for other advanced degree, relevant work experience; access to computer and Internet. Additional exam requirements/recommendations for international students: Required—TOEFL (minimum score 550 paper-based; 79 iBT), IELTS (minimum score 6.5), Michigan English Language Assessment Battery (minimum score 82), or PTE (minimum score 53). Electronic applications accepted.

Washington State University, College of Arts and Sciences, Department of Mathematics, Pullman, WA 99164. Offers applied mathematics (MS, PhD); mathematics

(MS, PhD); mathematics teaching (MS, PhD). Programs offered at the Pullman campus. *Program availability:* Part-time. Terminal master's awarded for partial completion of doctoral program. *Degree requirements:* For master's, comprehensive exam (for some programs), thesis or alternative, oral exam, project; for doctorate, 2 foreign languages, comprehensive exam, thesis/dissertation, oral exam, written exam. *Entrance requirements:* For master's and doctorate, minimum GPA of 3.0, 3 letters of recommendation. Additional exam requirements/recommendations for international students: Required—TOEFL (minimum score 600 paper-based; 100 iBT) or IELTS (minimum score 7). Electronic applications accepted. *Faculty research:* Computational mathematics, operations research, modeling in the natural sciences, applied statistics.

Washington State University, College of Education, Department of Teaching and Learning, Pullman, WA 99164-2132. Offers cultural studies and social thought in education (PhD); curriculum and instruction (Ed M, MA); English language learners (Ed M, MA); language, literacy and technology (PhD); literacy education (Ed M, MA); mathematics education (PhD); special education (Ed M, MA, PhD); teacher leadership (Ed D); teaching (MIT), including elementary education, secondary education. Programs offered at the Pullman, Spokane, Tri-cities, Vancouver and Global (online) campuses. *Program availability:* Part-time, online learning. *Degree requirements:* For master's, comprehensive exam, thesis, oral or written exam; for doctorate, comprehensive exam, thesis/dissertation, oral and written exam. *Entrance requirements:* For master's, GRE General Test, minimum GPA of 3.0, 3 letters of recommendation, letter of intent, transcripts, resume/curriculum vitae; for doctorate, GRE General Test, minimum GPA of 3.0, 3 letters of recommendation, letter of intent, transcripts, writing sample, resume/ curriculum vitae. Additional exam requirements/recommendations for international students: Required—TOEFL (minimum score 550 paper-based; 80 iBT). Electronic applications accepted. *Faculty research:* Intersection of gender, youth cultures and schooling; examination of ideology of power in children's literature; early childhood special education; analyzing pre-service and in-service teacher development; second language acquisition.

Wayne State College, School of Education and Counseling, Department of Educational Foundations and Leadership, Program in Curriculum and Instruction, Wayne, NE 68787. Offers alternative education (MSE); business and information technology education (MSE); communication arts education (MSE); early childhood education (MSE); elementary education (MSE); English as a second language (MSE); English education (MSE); family and consumer sciences education (MSE); industrial technology and vocational education (MSE); learning communities (MSE); mathematics education (MSE); music education (MSE); science education (MSE); social science education (MSE). *Accreditation:* NCATE. *Program availability:* Part-time, evening/weekend. *Degree requirements:* For master's, comprehensive exam, thesis optional. *Entrance requirements:* For master's, GRE General Test. Additional exam requirements/ recommendations for international students: Required—TOEFL (minimum score 550 paper-based).

Wayne State University, College of Education, Division of Teacher Education, Detroit, MI 48202. Offers art education (M Ed); bilingual/bicultural education (Certificate); curriculum and instruction (Ed D, PhD, Ed S), including English as a second language (MAT, Ed D, Ed S), K-12 curriculum (PhD); elementary education (MAT), including bilingual/bicultural education (M Ed, MAT), early childhood education (M Ed, MAT), English as a second language (MAT, Ed D, Ed S), foreign language education, science education (M Ed, MAT), special education (M Ed, MAT); elementary mathematics specialist (Certificate); English as a second language (Certificate); reading (M Ed, Ed S); reading, language and literature (Ed D); secondary education (MAT), including bilingual/ bicultural education (M Ed, MAT), early childhood education (M Ed, MAT), English as a second language (MAT, Ed D, Ed S), English education, foreign language education, mathematics education (M Ed, MAT), science education (M Ed, MAT), social studies education (M Ed, MAT); special education (MAT), including career and technical education; teaching and learning (M Ed), including bilingual/bicultural education (M Ed, MAT), early childhood education (M Ed, MAT), elementary education, foreign language, mathematics education (M Ed, MAT), science education (M Ed, MAT), social studies education (M Ed, MAT), special education (M Ed, MAT). *Program availability:* Part-time, evening/weekend. *Faculty:* 20. *Students:* 121 full-time (94 women), 251 part-time (209 women); includes 116 minority (83 Black or African American, non-Hispanic/Latino; 3 American Indian or Alaska Native, non-Hispanic/Latino; 3 Asian, non-Hispanic/Latino; 14 Hispanic/Latino; 13 Two or more races, non-Hispanic/Latino), 11 international. Average age 37. 171 applicants, 23% accepted, 32 enrolled. In 2018, 112 master's, 8 doctorates, 11 other advanced degrees awarded. *Degree requirements:* For master's, thesis (for some programs), essay or project (for some M Ed programs), professional field experience (for MAT programs); for doctorate, comprehensive exam, thesis/ dissertation. *Entrance requirements:* For master's, undergraduate degree, verification of participation in group work with children, Michigan State Police criminal background check, negative tb test, personal statement (for MAT programs); for all other master's programs: undergraduate degree, personal statement; for doctorate, minimum undergraduate GPA of 3.0, graduate 3.5; interview; curriculum vitae; references; writing sample; letter of application; master's degree (for most programs); for other advanced degree, education specialist certificate: undergraduate with GPA of 2.5 or better and master's degree with GPA of 2.75 or better; personal statement. Additional exam requirements/recommendations for international students: Required—TOEFL (minimum score 550 paper-based; 79 iBT); Recommended—IELTS (minimum score 6.5), TWE (minimum score 5.5), TSE (minimum score 58). *Application deadline:* Applications are processed on a rolling basis. Application fee: $50. Electronic applications accepted. *Financial support:* In 2018–19, 85 students received support, including 3 fellowships (averaging $14,275 per year); research assistantships with tuition reimbursements available, Federal Work-Study, scholarships/grants, and unspecified assistantships also available. Support available to part-time students. Financial award applicants required to submit FAFSA. *Faculty research:* Improving students' skill achievement in mathematics, improving elementary children's understanding of informational text, teachers' use of their pedagogical and mathematical knowledge in the interactive work of teaching, the intersection of identity construction in teaching and learning, identifying effective methods of literacy instruction and assessments for bilingual students in elementary language arts classrooms. *Unit head:* Dr. Roland Coloma, Assistant Dean for Teacher Education, 313-577-0902, E-mail: rscoloma@wayne.edu. *Application contact:* Dr. Mary L. Waker, Graduate Admissions Officer, 313-577-1601, Fax: 313-577-7904, E-mail: m.waker@wayne.edu.
Website: http://coe.wayne.edu/ted/index.php

Webster University, School of Education, Department of Multidisciplinary Studies, St. Louis, MO 63119-3194. Offers applied educational psychology (MA, Ed S); communication arts (MA); early childhood education (MA, MAT); education and innovation (MA); educational technology (MET); elementary education (MAT); mathematics for educators (MA); middle school education (MAT); multidisciplinary studies (MAT); multimodal literacy for global impact (MA); reading (MA); secondary school education (MAT); special education (MA, MAT); teaching English as a second language (MA); transformative learning in the global community (Ed S). *Program availability:* Part-time. *Entrance requirements:* For master's, minimum GPA of 2.5. Additional exam requirements/recommendations for international students: Required—

TOEFL. *Expenses: Tuition:* Full-time $22,500; part-time $750 per credit hour. Tuition and fees vary according to degree level, campus/location and program.

West Chester University of Pennsylvania, College of the Sciences and Mathematics, Department of Mathematics, West Chester, PA 19383. Offers applied and computational mathematics (MS); applied statistics (MS, Certificate); mathematics (MA, Teaching Certificate); mathematics education (MA). *Program availability:* Part-time, evening/ weekend. *Degree requirements:* For master's, comprehensive exam or thesis (for MA). *Entrance requirements:* For master's, GMAT or GRE General Test (for MA in mathematics, may be waived under certain circumstances), interview (for MA in mathematics); for other advanced degree, GMAT or GRE General Test (for Certificate in, applied statistics). Additional exam requirements/recommendations for international students: Required—TOEFL or IELTS. Electronic applications accepted. *Faculty research:* Teachers teaching with technology in service training program, biostatistics, hierarchical linear models, clustered binary outcome data, mathematics biology, stochastic analysis.

Western Governors University, Teachers College, Salt Lake City, UT 84107. Offers curriculum and instruction (MS); educational leadership (MS); elementary education (MAT, Postbaccalaureate Certificate); English education (5-12) (MAT); English language learning (PreK-12) (MA); instructional design (M Ed); learning and technology (M Ed); mathematics (5-12) (MAT); mathematics (5-9) (MAT); mathematics education (5-12) (MA); mathematics education (5-9) (MA); mathematics education (K-6) (MA); science (5-12) (MAT); science education (5-12) (MA), including biology, chemistry, earth science, physics; science education (5-9) (MA); special education (MS). *Accreditation:* NCATE. *Program availability:* Evening/weekend, online learning. *Degree requirements:* For master's, capstone project. *Entrance requirements:* For master's and Postbaccalaureate Certificate, transcripts. Additional exam requirements/ recommendations for international students: Required—TOEFL (minimum score 450 paper-based; 80 iBT). Electronic applications accepted. Application fee is waived when completed online. *Expenses:* Contact institution.

Western Michigan University, Graduate College, College of Arts and Sciences, Department of Mathematics, Kalamazoo, MI 49008. Offers applied and computational mathematics (MS); mathematics education (MA, PhD), including collegiate mathematics education (PhD). *Degree requirements:* For doctorate, one foreign language, thesis/ dissertation.

Western New England University, College of Arts and Sciences, Program in Mathematics for Teachers, Springfield, MA 01119. Offers MAMT. *Program availability:* Part-time, evening/weekend. *Faculty:* 14 full-time (6 women). *Students:* 14 part-time (7 women); includes 1 minority (Asian, non-Hispanic/Latino). Average age 37. 18 applicants, 100% accepted, 5 enrolled. In 2018, 9 master's awarded. *Entrance requirements:* For master's, two letters of recommendation, official transcript, personal statement, resume. Additional exam requirements/recommendations for international students: Required—TOEFL (minimum score 79 iBT). *Application deadline:* Applications are processed on a rolling basis. Application fee: $30. Electronic applications accepted. *Expenses:* Contact institution. *Financial support:* Application deadline: 4/15; applicants required to submit FAFSA. *Unit head:* Dr. David Mazur, Chair and Professor of Mathematics, 413-782-1696, E-mail: dmazur@wne.edu. *Application contact:* Matthew Fox, Executive Director of Graduate Admissions, 413-782-1410, Fax: 413-782-1777, E-mail: study@wne.edu.
Website: http://www1.wne.edu/academics/graduate/ma-mathematics-teachers.cfm

Western Oregon University, Graduate Programs, College of Education, Division of Teacher Education, Program in Secondary Education, Monmouth, OR 97361. Offers bilingual education (MS Ed); health (MS Ed); humanities (MAT, MS Ed); initial licensure (MAT); mathematics (MAT, MS Ed); science (MAT, MS Ed); social science (MAT, MS Ed). *Accreditation:* NCATE. *Program availability:* Part-time, evening/weekend. *Degree requirements:* For master's, thesis optional, written exam. *Entrance requirements:* For master's, minimum GPA of 3.0, teaching license. Additional exam requirements/recommendations for international students: Required—TOEFL (minimum score 550 paper-based; 79 iBT), IELTS (minimum score 6.5). *Faculty research:* Literacy, science in primary grades, geography education, retention, teacher burnout.

Westfield State University, College of Graduate and Continuing Education, Department of Education, Westfield, MA 01086. Offers early childhood education (M Ed); elementary education (M Ed); reading specialist (M Ed); secondary education (M Ed), including biology teacher education, chemistry teacher education, general science teacher education, history teacher education, mathematics teacher education, physical education teacher education; special education (M Ed), including moderate disabilities, 5-12, moderate disabilities, preK-8; vocational technical education (M Ed). *Accreditation:* NCATE. *Program availability:* Part-time, evening/weekend. *Degree requirements:* For master's, comprehensive exam, practicum. *Entrance requirements:* For master's, GRE General Test or MAT, minimum undergraduate GPA of 2.8. Additional exam requirements/recommendations for international students: Recommended—TOEFL (minimum score 550 paper-based; 79 iBT). *Faculty research:* Collaborative teacher education, developmental early childhood education.

Westfield State University, College of Graduate and Continuing Education, Department of Education, Programs in Secondary Education, Program in Mathematics Teacher Education, Westfield, MA 01086. Offers secondary education-mathematics (M Ed). *Program availability:* Part-time, evening/weekend. *Degree requirements:* For master's, comprehensive exam, thesis (for some programs). *Entrance requirements:* For master's, GRE General Test or MAT, minimum undergraduate GPA of 2.8. Additional exam requirements/recommendations for international students: Recommended— TOEFL (minimum score 550 paper-based; 79 iBT).

Widener University, School of Human Service Professions, Center for Education, Chester, PA 19013-5792. Offers adult education (M Ed); counseling in higher education (M Ed); counselor education (M Ed); early childhood education (M Ed); educational foundations (M Ed); educational leadership (M Ed); educational psychology (M Ed); elementary education (M Ed); English and language arts (M Ed); health education (M Ed); higher education leadership (Ed D); home and school visitor (M Ed); human sexuality (M Ed, PhD); mathematics education (M Ed); middle school education (M Ed); principalship (M Ed); reading and language arts (Ed D); reading education (M Ed); school administration (Ed D); science education (M Ed); social studies education (M Ed); special education (M Ed); technology education (M Ed). *Accreditation:* NCATE. *Program availability:* Part-time, evening/weekend. Terminal master's awarded for partial completion of doctoral program. *Degree requirements:* For doctorate, thesis/ dissertation. *Entrance requirements:* For master's, minimum GPA of 2.5; for doctorate, GRE or MAT, minimum GPA of 2.0 (undergraduate), 3.5 (graduate). Electronic applications accepted. *Expenses:* Contact institution. *Faculty research:* Reading and cognition, adult education, technology education, educational leadership, special education.

William Jessup University, Program in Teaching, Rocklin, CA 95765. Offers single subject English (MAT); single subject math (MAT). *Program availability:* Evening/ weekend.

Wright State University, Graduate School, College of Science and Mathematics, Interdisciplinary Program in Science and Mathematics, Dayton, OH 45435. Offers PhD.

Youngstown State University, College of Graduate Studies, College of Science, Technology, Engineering and Mathematics, Department of Mathematics and Statistics, Youngstown, OH 44555-0001. Offers actuarial science (MS); applied mathematics (MS); computer science (MS); mathematics (MS); secondary/community college mathematics (MS); statistics (MS). *Program availability:* Part-time. *Degree requirements:* For master's, comprehensive exam, thesis optional. *Entrance requirements:* For master's, minimum GPA of 2.7 in computer science and mathematics. Additional exam requirements/recommendations for international students: Required—TOEFL. *Faculty research:* Regression analysis, numerical analysis, statistics, Markov chain, topology and fuzzy sets.

Museum Education

Bank Street College of Education, Graduate School, Program in Museum Education, New York, NY 10025. Offers museum education (MS Ed); museum education: elementary education certification (MS Ed). *Degree requirements:* For master's, thesis. *Entrance requirements:* For master's, interview, essays. Additional exam requirements/recommendations for international students: Required—TOEFL (minimum score 600 paper-based; 100 iBT), IELTS (minimum score 7). Electronic applications accepted. *Faculty research:* Equitable access and openness to diversity in museum settings, exhibition display and development, museum and school partnerships.

Bank Street College of Education, Graduate School, Programs in Educational Leadership, New York, NY 10025. Offers early childhood leadership (MS Ed); educational leadership (MS Ed); leadership for educational change (Ed M, MS Ed); leadership in community-based learning (MS Ed); leadership in mathematics education (MS Ed); leadership in museum education (MS Ed); leadership in the arts: creative writing (MS Ed); leadership in the arts: visual arts (MS Ed). *Degree requirements:* For master's, thesis. *Entrance requirements:* For master's, interview, essays, minimum of 2 years experience as a classroom teacher. Additional exam requirements/recommendations for international students: Required—TOEFL (minimum score 600 paper-based; 100 iBT), IELTS (minimum score 7). Electronic applications accepted. *Faculty research:* Leadership in urban schools, leadership in small schools, mathematics in elementary schools, professional development in early childhood, leadership in arts education, leadership in special education, museum leadership, community-based leadership.

City College of the City University of New York, Graduate School, Division of Humanities and the Arts, Department of Art, Programs in Art History and Museum Studies, New York, NY 10031-9198. Offers art history (MA); art museum education (MA); museum studies (MA). *Program availability:* Part-time. *Degree requirements:* For master's, one foreign language, thesis. *Entrance requirements:* For master's, minimum GPA of 3.0, portfolio, art history paper. Additional exam requirements/recommendations for international students: Required—TOEFL (minimum score 577 paper-based; 90 iBT). Electronic applications accepted. *Faculty research:* Egyptian, Greek, medieval, Romanesque, and Ottoman art.

Eastern Michigan University, Graduate School, College of Arts and Sciences, Department of Sociology, Anthropology and Criminology, Program in Cultural Museum Studies, Ypsilanti, MI 48197. Offers Graduate Certificate. *Program availability:* Part-time, evening/weekend, online learning. *Students:* 1 (woman) part-time. Average age 58. 3 applicants, 33% accepted. In 2018, 2 Graduate Certificates awarded. *Entrance requirements:* Additional exam requirements/recommendations for international students: Required—TOEFL. *Application deadline:* Applications are processed on a rolling basis. Application fee: $45. *Financial support:* Fellowships, research assistantships with full tuition reimbursements, teaching assistantships with full tuition reimbursements, career-related internships or fieldwork, Federal Work-Study, institutionally sponsored loans, scholarships/grants, tuition waivers (partial), and unspecified assistantships available. Support available to part-time students. Financial award applicants required to submit FAFSA. *Application contact:* Dr. Liza Cerroni-Long, Advisor, 734-487-0012, Fax: 734-487-9666, E-mail: liza.cerroni-long@emich.edu.

The George Washington University, Graduate School of Education and Human Development, Department of Educational Leadership, Program in Museum Education, Washington, DC 20052. Offers MAT. *Students:* 15 full-time (14 women); includes 3 minority (1 Hispanic/Latino; 2 Two or more races, non-Hispanic/Latino), 1 international. Average age 27. 34 applicants, 88% accepted, 15 enrolled. In 2018, 15 master's awarded. *Entrance requirements:* For master's, GRE General Test or MAT, minimum GPA of 2.75. *Application deadline:* For fall admission, 1/15 priority date for domestic students; for spring admission, 10/1 for domestic students. Applications are processed on a rolling basis. Application fee: $75. *Financial support:* In 2018–19, 7 students received support. Fellowships, career-related internships or fieldwork, Federal Work-Study, and tuition waivers available. Financial award application deadline: 1/15; financial award applicants required to submit FAFSA. *Unit head:* Michael Feuer, Dean, 202-994-6161, E-mail: mjfeuer@gwu.edu. *Application contact:* Sarah Lang, Director of Graduate Admissions, 202-994-1447, Fax: 202-994-7207, E-mail: slang@gwu.edu. Website: http://gsehd.gwu.edu/MEP

Tufts University, Graduate School of Arts and Sciences, Department of Education, Program in Education, Medford, MA 02155. Offers educational studies (MA); elementary education (MAT); middle and secondary education (MAT); museum education (MA); secondary education (MA); STEM education (MS, PhD). *Program availability:* Part-time. *Degree requirements:* For master's, thesis optional. *Entrance requirements:* For master's, GRE General Test, portfolio (for art education only); for doctorate, GRE General Test, writing sample. Additional exam requirements/recommendations for international students: Required—TOEFL (minimum score 550 paper-based; 80 iBT), IELTS (minimum score 6.5). Electronic applications accepted. *Expenses:* Contact institution.

University of Nebraska at Kearney, College of Fine Arts and Humanities, Department of Art and Design, Kearney, NE 68849-0001. Offers art education (MA Ed), including classroom education, museum education. *Accreditation:* NCATE. *Program availability:* Part-time, evening/weekend, 100% online. *Degree requirements:* For master's, comprehensive exam, thesis optional. *Entrance requirements:* For master's, two letters of recommendation, resume, statement of purpose, 24 undergraduate hours of art/art history/art education. Additional exam requirements/recommendations for international students: Recommended—TOEFL (minimum score 550 paper-based; 79 iBT), IELTS (minimum score 6.5). Electronic applications accepted. *Faculty research:* Fibers, art education, kiln design construction and low-fire glaze, relationship between environment and photography, digital arts, graphic design, three-dimensional design, atomic testing imagery.

The University of the Arts, College of Art, Media and Design, Department of Museum Studies, Philadelphia, PA 19102-4944. Offers museum education (MA); museum exhibition planning and design (MFA); museum studies (MA). *Accreditation:* NASAD. *Degree requirements:* For master's, thesis, internship. *Entrance requirements:* For master's, official transcripts, three letters of recommendation, personal interview; academic writing sample and examples of work (for museum communication); two examples of academic and professional writing (for museum education); portfolio and/or writing samples (for museum exhibition planning and design). Additional exam requirements/recommendations for international students: Required—TOEFL (minimum score 580 paper-based, 92 iBT) or IELTS (minimum score 6.5).

Music Education

Acadia University, Faculty of Professional Studies, School of Education, Program in Curriculum Studies, Wolfville, NS B4P 2R6, Canada. Offers curriculum studies (M Ed); interprofessional health practice (M Ed); music education (M Ed). *Program availability:* Part-time. *Entrance requirements:* For master's, B Ed or the equivalent, minimum B average in undergraduate course work, 2 years of teaching experience. Additional exam requirements/recommendations for international students: Required—TOEFL (minimum score 580 paper-based; 93 iBT), IELTS (minimum score 6.5). *Faculty research:* Literacy development, postmodern philosophy and curriculum theory, historiography, philosophy of education, learning and technology.

Adams State University, Office of Graduate Studies, Department of Music, Alamosa, CO 81101. Offers music education (MA).

Alabama Agricultural and Mechanical University, School of Graduate Studies, College of Education, Humanities, and Behavioral Sciences, Department of Visual, Performing, and Communication Arts, Huntsville, AL 35811. Offers art education (MS); music education (M Ed). *Accreditation:* NCATE. *Program availability:* Part-time, evening/weekend. *Degree requirements:* For master's, comprehensive exam. *Entrance requirements:* For master's, GRE General Test. Additional exam requirements/recommendations for international students: Required—TOEFL (minimum score 500 paper-based; 61 iBT). Electronic applications accepted. *Faculty research:* Jazz and black music, Alabama folk music.

Alabama State University, College of Education, Department of Curriculum and Instruction, Montgomery, AL 36101-0271. Offers early childhood education (Ed S); secondary education (M Ed), including biology education, English language arts education, history education, math education, music education, reading education, social science education. *Program availability:* Part-time, evening/weekend, online only, 100% online. *Faculty:* 7 full-time (4 women), 7 part-time/adjunct (4 women). *Students:* 22 full-time (19 women), 58 part-time (49 women); includes 235 minority (234 Black or African American, non-Hispanic/Latino; 1 Hispanic/Latino), 5 international. Average age 36. 45 applicants, 33% accepted, 6 enrolled. In 2018, 34 master's awarded. *Degree requirements:* For master's, comprehensive exam, thesis optional; for Ed S, comprehensive exam, thesis. *Entrance requirements:* For master's, GRE General Test, MAT, writing competency test; for Ed S, writing competency test, GRE, MAT. Additional exam requirements/recommendations for international students: Required—TOEFL (minimum score 500 paper-based). *Application deadline:* For fall admission, 4/15 for domestic and international students; for spring admission, 11/15 for domestic and international students; for summer admission, 3/15 for domestic and international students. Applications are processed on a rolling basis. Application fee: $25. Electronic applications accepted. *Expenses:* Contact institution. *Financial support:* Fellowships, teaching assistantships, career-related internships or fieldwork, scholarships/grants, tuition waivers (partial), and unspecified assistantships available. Financial award application deadline: 6/30; financial award applicants required to submit FAFSA. *Unit head:* Dr. Joyce Johnson, Acting Chairperson, 334-229-4485, Fax: 334-229-5603, E-mail: jjohnson@alasu.edu. *Application contact:* Dr. Ed Brown, Dean of Graduate Studies, 334-229-4274, Fax: 334-229-4928, E-mail: ebrown@alasu.edu. Website: http://www.alasu.edu/academics/colleges—departments/college-of-education/curriculum—instruction/index.aspx

Anderson University, South Carolina School of the Arts, Anderson, SC 29621-4035. Offers music education (MM). *Program availability:* Online learning. *Degree requirements:* For master's, comprehensive exam. *Expenses:* Contact institution. *Financial support:* Scholarships/grants available. *Unit head:* David Larson, Dean, 864-231-2002, E-mail: dlarson@andersonuniversity.edu. *Application contact:* David Larson, Dean, 864-231-2002, E-mail: dlarson@andersonuniversity.edu. Website: http://www.andersonuniversity.edu/school-of-the-arts

Arcadia University, School of Education, Glenside, PA 19038-3295. Offers art education (M Ed); computer education (CAS); curriculum (CAS); curriculum studies (M Ed); early childhood education (M Ed), including individualized, master teacher, research in child development; educational leadership (M Ed, Ed D, CAS); elementary education (M Ed); English education (MA Ed); environmental education (MA Ed); instructional technology (M Ed); language arts (M Ed); library science (M Ed); mathematics education (M Ed, MA Ed); music education (MA Ed); psychology (MA Ed); reading (M Ed, CAS); science education (M Ed, CAS); secondary education (M Ed,

CAS); special education (M Ed, Ed D, CAS); theater arts (MA Ed); written communication (MA Ed). *Accreditation:* NASAD. *Program availability:* Part-time, evening/weekend, online learning. *Faculty:* 14 full-time (10 women). *Students:* 35 full-time (24 women), 299 part-time (243 women); includes 72 minority (49 Black or African American, non-Hispanic/Latino; 1 American Indian or Alaska Native, non-Hispanic/Latino; 12 Asian, non-Hispanic/Latino; 8 Hispanic/Latino; 2 Two or more races, non-Hispanic/Latino), 5 international. In 2018, 152 master's, 8 doctorates awarded. *Entrance requirements:* Additional exam requirements/recommendations for international students: Required—Official results from the TOEFL or IELTS are required. *Application deadline:* Applications are processed on a rolling basis. Application fee: $25. Electronic applications accepted. *Expenses:* Contact institution. *Financial support:* Career-related internships or fieldwork, tuition waivers (partial), and unspecified assistantships available. *Unit head:* Kimberly Dean, Chair, 215-572-8629. *Application contact:* 215-572-2925, Fax: 215-572-2126, E-mail: grad@arcadia.edu.

Arizona State University at the Tempe campus, Herberger Institute for Design and the Arts, School of Music, Tempe, AZ 85287-0405. Offers composition (MM, DMA); conducting (DMA); ethnomusicology (MA); interdisciplinary digital media/performance (DMA); music education (MM, PhD); music history and literature (MA); music therapy (MM); performance (MM, DMA). *Accreditation:* NASM. Terminal master's awarded for partial completion of doctoral program. *Degree requirements:* For master's, thesis (for some programs), interactive Program of Study (iPOS) submitted before completing 50 percent of required credit hours; for doctorate, comprehensive exam, thesis/dissertation, interactive Program of Study (iPOS) submitted before completing 50 percent of required credit hours. *Entrance requirements:* For master's, minimum GPA of 3.0 or equivalent in last 2 years of work leading to bachelor's degree, 3 letters of recommendation, resume; for doctorate, GRE or MAT, minimum GPA of 3.0 or equivalent in last 2 years of work leading to bachelor's degree, 3 letters of recommendation, curriculum vitae, statement of intent. Additional exam requirements/recommendations for international students: Required—TOEFL, IELTS, or PTE. Electronic applications accepted.

Arkansas State University, Graduate School, College of Fine Arts, Department of Music, State University, AR 72467. Offers music education (MME, SCCT); music performance (MM). *Accreditation:* NASM (one or more programs are accredited). *Program availability:* Part-time. *Degree requirements:* For master's, 2 foreign languages, comprehensive exam, thesis or alternative; for SCCT, comprehensive exam. *Entrance requirements:* For master's, GRE General Test or MAT, university entrance exam, appropriate bachelor's degree, audition, letters of recommendation, teaching experience, official transcripts, immunization records, valid teaching certificate; for SCCT, GRE General Test or MAT, interview, master's degree, official transcript, immunization records, letters of recommendation. Additional exam requirements/recommendations for international students: Required—TOEFL (minimum score 550 paper-based; 79 iBT), IELTS (minimum score 6), PTE (minimum score 56). Electronic applications accepted.

Augusta University, College of Education, Program in Curriculum and Instruction, Augusta, GA 30912. Offers curriculum and instruction (Ed S); elementary education (MAT); foreign language education (MAT); instruction (M Ed); middle grades education (MAT); music education (MAT); secondary education (MAT); special education (MAT). *Degree requirements:* For master's, thesis, portfolio. *Entrance requirements:* For master's, GRE, MAT, minimum GPA of 2.5.

Austin Peay State University, College of Graduate Studies, College of Arts and Letters, Department of Music, Clarksville, TN 37044. Offers music education (M Mu); music performance (M Mu). *Accreditation:* NASM. *Program availability:* Part-time. *Faculty:* 16 full-time (6 women), 4 part-time/adjunct (2 women). *Students:* 30 full-time (16 women), 3 part-time (1 woman); includes 6 minority (4 Black or African American, non-Hispanic/Latino; 2 Hispanic/Latino), 2 international. Average age 26. 26 applicants, 92% accepted, 19 enrolled. In 2018, 6 master's awarded. *Degree requirements:* For master's, comprehensive exam, thesis optional. *Entrance requirements:* For master's, GRE General Test, diagnostic exams, audition, interview, bachelor's degree, 3 letters of recommendation. Additional exam requirements/recommendations for international students: Required—TOEFL (minimum score 500 paper-based). *Application deadline:* For fall admission, 8/21 priority date for domestic students. Applications are processed on a rolling basis. Application fee: $45 ($55 for international students). Electronic applications accepted. *Expenses: Tuition, area resident:* Part-time $450 per credit hour. Tuition, state resident: full-time $5987; part-time $450 per credit hour. Tuition, nonresident: full-time $8757; part-time $806 per credit hour. *Required fees:* $1583; $79.15 per credit hour. *Financial support:* Research assistantships with full tuition reimbursements, career-related internships or fieldwork, Federal Work-Study, institutionally sponsored loans, scholarships/grants, and unspecified assistantships available. Support available to part-time students. Financial award application deadline: 7/1; financial award applicants required to submit FAFSA. *Unit head:* Dr. Eric Branscome, Chair, 931-221-7811, Fax: 931-221-7529, E-mail: branscomee@apsu.edu. *Application contact:* Megan Mitchell, Coordinator of Graduate Admissions, 931-221-6189, Fax: 931-221-7641, E-mail: mitchellm@apsu.edu.
Website: http://www.apsu.edu/music/

Azusa Pacific University, College of Music and the Arts, Azusa, CA 91702-7000. Offers composition (M Mus); conducting (M Mus); education (M Mus); modern art history, theory, and criticism (MA); music entrepreneurial studies (MA); performance (M Mus); screenwriting (MA); visual art (MFA). *Accreditation:* NASAD; NASM. *Program availability:* Part-time, evening/weekend. *Degree requirements:* For master's, recital. *Entrance requirements:* For master's, interview, audition. Additional exam requirements/recommendations for international students: Required—TOEFL (minimum score 550 paper-based).

Ball State University, Graduate School, College of Fine Arts, School of Music, Muncie, IN 47306. Offers music (MA, MM, DA, Artist Diploma), including conducting (MM, DA), music education (MA, MM, DA), music history and musicology (MA, MM, DA), music performance (MA, MM, DA), music theory (MA), music theory and composition (DA), piano chamber music/accompanying (MM, DA), piano performance and pedagogy (MM), woodwinds (MM). *Accreditation:* NASM; NCATE (one or more programs are accredited). *Degree requirements:* For doctorate, thesis/dissertation. *Entrance requirements:* For master's, placement tests in history and theory, minimum baccalaureate GPA of 2.75 or 3.0 in latter half of baccalaureate, resume, audition; for doctorate, GRE General Test, minimum graduate GPA of 3.2, interview, audition, resume, three professional letters of reference. Additional exam requirements/recommendations for international students: Required—TOEFL (minimum score 550 paper-based; 79 iBT), IELTS (minimum score 6.5). Electronic applications accepted. *Expenses:* Contact institution.

Bob Jones University, Graduate Programs, Greenville, SC 29614. Offers accountancy (MS); Bible (MA); Bible translation (MA); Biblical studies (Certificate); business administration (MBA); church history (MA, PhD); church ministries (MA); church music (MM); cinema and video production (MA); counseling (MS); curriculum and instruction (Ed D); divinity (M Div); dramatic production (MA); educational leadership (MS, Ed D, Ed S); elementary education (M Ed, MAT); English (M Ed, MA, MAT); fine arts (MA); graphic design (MA); history (M Ed, MA); illustration (MA); interpretative speech (MA); mathematics (M Ed, MAT); medical missions (Certificate); ministry (MM, D Min); multi-categorical special education (M Ed, MAT); music (M Ed); New Testament interpretation (PhD); Old Testament interpretation (PhD); orchestral instrument performance (MM); organ performance (MM); pastoral studies (MA); personnel services (MS, Ed S); piano pedagogy (MM); piano performance (MM); platform arts (MA); rhetoric and public address (MA); secondary education (M Ed); studio art (MA); teaching Bible (MA); theology (MA, PhD); voice performance (MM); youth ministries (MA); M Div/MM.

Boise State University, College of Arts and Sciences, Department of Music, Boise, ID 83725-0399. Offers music education (MM); music performance (MM). *Accreditation:* NASM. *Program availability:* Part-time. *Degree requirements:* For master's, thesis optional. *Entrance requirements:* For master's, minimum GPA of 3.0, performance demonstration. Additional exam requirements/recommendations for international students: Required—TOEFL (minimum score 550 paper-based; 80 iBT), IELTS (minimum score 6). Electronic applications accepted.

Boston University, College of Fine Arts, School of Music, Program in Music Education, Boston, MA 02215. Offers MM, DMA. *Accreditation:* NASM. *Program availability:* Part-time, 100% online. *Faculty:* 9 full-time (3 women). *Students:* 341 full-time (182 women), 3 part-time (0 women); includes 56 minority (20 Black or African American, non-Hispanic/Latino; 9 Asian, non-Hispanic/Latino; 18 Hispanic/Latino; 1 Native Hawaiian or other Pacific Islander, non-Hispanic/Latino; 8 Two or more races, non-Hispanic/Latino), 19 international. Average age 35. 36 applicants, 56% accepted, 7 enrolled. In 2018, 97 master's, 22 doctorates awarded. *Degree requirements:* For master's, thesis; for doctorate, 2 foreign languages, thesis/dissertation. *Entrance requirements:* Additional exam requirements/recommendations for international students: Required—TOEFL (minimum score 90 iBT), IELTS (minimum score 7). *Application deadline:* For fall admission, 12/1 priority date for domestic and international students. Application fee: $95. Electronic applications accepted. *Expenses:* Contact institution. *Financial support:* Fellowships, teaching assistantships, scholarships/grants, and unspecified assistantships available. Financial award application deadline: 12/1. *Unit head:* Shiela Kibbe, Director, 617-353-8789, Fax: 617-353-7455, E-mail: cfamusic@bu.edu. *Application contact:* Katie Luellen, Assistant Director, School of Music Admissions and Student Affairs, 617-353-3341, E-mail: arts@bu.edu.

Bowling Green State University, Graduate College, College of Musical Arts, Bowling Green, OH 43403. Offers composition (MM); contemporary music (DMA), including composition, performance; ethnomusicology (MM); music education (MM), including choral music education, comprehensive music education, instrumental music education; music history (MM); music theory (MM); performance (MM). *Accreditation:* NASM. *Program availability:* Part-time. *Degree requirements:* For master's, thesis or alternative, recitals; for doctorate, comprehensive exam, thesis/dissertation. *Entrance requirements:* For master's, GRE General Test, diagnostic placement exams in music history and theory, audition, interview. Additional exam requirements/recommendations for international students: Required—TOEFL. Electronic applications accepted. *Faculty research:* Ethnomusicology.

Brandon University, School of Music, Brandon, MB R7A 6A9, Canada. Offers composition (M Mus); music education (M Mus); performance and literature (M Mus), including clarinet, conducting, jazz, low brass, piano, strings, trumpet. *Program availability:* Part-time. *Degree requirements:* For master's, comprehensive exam (for some programs), thesis (for some programs), 2 recitals. *Entrance requirements:* For master's, B Mus. Additional exam requirements/recommendations for international students: Required—TOEFL (minimum score 580 paper-based), IELTS (minimum score 7). Electronic applications accepted. *Expenses:* Contact institution. *Faculty research:* Composition, evaluation and assessment, performance anxiety, philosophy of music, teacher education.

Brigham Young University, Graduate Studies, College of Fine Arts and Communications, School of Music, Provo, UT 84602-1001. Offers composition (MM); conducting, choral (MM); music education (MA, MM); performance (MM). *Accreditation:* NASM. *Faculty:* 51 full-time (10 women), 61 part-time/adjunct (39 women). *Students:* 25 full-time (13 women), 16 part-time (7 women); includes 8 minority (1 American Indian or Alaska Native, non-Hispanic/Latino; 3 Asian, non-Hispanic/Latino; 3 Hispanic/Latino; 1 Native Hawaiian or other Pacific Islander, non-Hispanic/Latino). Average age 29. 44 applicants, 45% accepted, 17 enrolled. In 2018, 13 master's awarded. *Degree requirements:* For master's, variable foreign language requirement, comprehensive exam (for some programs), thesis (for some programs), composition, project, recital, or thesis (for some programs). *Entrance requirements:* For master's, School of Music Entrance Exam, minimum GPA of 3.0, undergraduate degree in music, supplemental material and/or audition. Additional exam requirements/recommendations for international students: Required—TOEFL (minimum score 580 paper-based; 85 iBT), IELTS (minimum score 7), E3PT, TOEFL, or IELTS are accepted; only one is required to show English proficiency for non-native English speakers. *Application deadline:* For fall admission, 12/15 priority date for domestic and international students. Application fee: $50. Electronic applications accepted. *Expenses:* $3540 full-time LDS semester, $7080 full-time non-LDS semester, $458 private instruction class fee. *Financial support:* In 2018–19, 41 students received support, including 41 research assistantships (averaging $3,000 per year), 41 teaching assistantships (averaging $3,500 per year); career-related internships or fieldwork, institutionally sponsored loans, scholarships/grants, tuition waivers (partial), and unspecified assistantships also available. Support available to part-time students. Financial award application deadline: 12/15; financial award applicants required to submit FAFSA. *Faculty research:* Secondary general music methods; music listening; History of Western music in China; interdisciplinary performance: art and music; oboe, bassoon, and piano repertoire database. *Unit head:* Dr. Kirt R. Saville, Director, 801-422-6304, Fax: 801-422-0533, E-mail: kirt_saville@byu.edu. *Application contact:* Dr. A. Claudine Bigelow, Associate Director, Graduate Studies, 801-422-1315, E-mail: claudine_bigelow@byu.edu.
Website: https://music.byu.edu

Brooklyn College of the City University of New York, School of Education, Program in Adolescence Science Education and Special Subjects, Brooklyn, NY 11210-2889. Offers adolescence science education (MAT); biology teacher (7-12) (MA); chemistry teacher (7-12) (MA); earth science teacher (7-12) (MAT); English teacher (7-12) (MA); French teacher (7-12) (MA); mathematics teacher (7-12) (MA); music teacher (MA); physics teacher (7-12) (MA); social studies teacher (7-12) (MA); Spanish teacher (7-12) (MA). *Program availability:* Part-time, evening/weekend. *Degree requirements:* For master's, comprehensive exam (for some programs), thesis (for some programs). *Entrance requirements:* For master's, LAST, previous course work in education, resume, 2 letters of recommendation, essay. Additional exam requirements/recommendations for international students: Required—TOEFL (minimum score 500 paper-based; 61 iBT). Electronic applications accepted. *Faculty research:* Interdisciplinary education, semiotics, discourse analysis, autobiography, teacher identity.

Brooklyn College of the City University of New York, School of Visual, Media and Performing Arts, Conservatory of Music, Brooklyn, NY 11210-2889. Offers composition (MM); music teacher (MA); musicology (MA); performance (MM). *Program availability:* Part-time. *Degree requirements:* For master's, one foreign language, comprehensive exam, thesis. *Entrance requirements:* For master's, placement exam, 36 credits in music, audition, completed composition, writing sample. Additional exam requirements/

recommendations for international students: Required—TOEFL (minimum score 550 paper-based; 79 iBT). Electronic applications accepted. *Faculty research:* American music, computer music.

Butler University, Jordan College of the Arts, Indianapolis, IN 46208-3485. Offers composition (MM); conducting (MM), including choral, instrumental; music education (MM); musicology (MA); performance (MM); piano pedagogy (MM). *Accreditation:* NASM. *Program availability:* Part-time. *Faculty:* 21 full-time (4 women), 7 part-time/adjunct (4 women). *Students:* 19 full-time (8 women), 22 part-time (9 women); includes 9 minority (3 Black or African American, non-Hispanic/Latino; 1 Asian, non-Hispanic/Latino; 3 Hispanic/Latino; 2 Two or more races, non-Hispanic/Latino), 2 international. Average age 27. 48 applicants, 79% accepted, 18 enrolled. In 2018, 12 master's awarded. *Degree requirements:* For master's, variable foreign language requirement, comprehensive exam, thesis (for some programs). *Entrance requirements:* For master's, GRE General Test (for MA in musicology), audition, interview, three letters of recommendation, transcripts, sample works. Additional exam requirements/recommendations for international students: Required—TOEFL (minimum score 550 paper-based; 79 iBT), IELTS (minimum score 6). *Application deadline:* For fall admission, 2/1 for domestic and international students; for spring admission, 12/15 for domestic and international students; for summer admission, 4/15 for domestic and international students. Applications are processed on a rolling basis. Application fee: $0. Electronic applications accepted. Application fee is waived when completed online. *Expenses:* Contact institution. *Financial support:* In 2018–19, 20 students received support. Scholarships/grants, tuition waivers (full and partial), and unspecified assistantships available. Financial award application deadline: 7/15; financial award applicants required to submit FAFSA. *Faculty research:* Music neuroscience; woodwind pedagogy and repertoire; Johannes Kepler and Carolus Luython; music criticism in early 20th-century Germany and Austria; Arabic choral music; pedagogy of music theory. *Unit head:* Wendy Meaden, Associate Dean, 317-940-9229, E-mail: wmeaden@butler.edu. *Application contact:* Diane Dubord, Graduate Student Services Specialist, 317-940-8107, E-mail: ddubord@butler.edu.
Website: http://www.butler.edu/jca/

California Baptist University, Program in Music, Riverside, CA 92504-3206. Offers conducting (MM); music education (MM); performance (MM). *Accreditation:* NASM. *Program availability:* Part-time. *Faculty:* 16 full-time (3 women), 11 part-time/adjunct (5 women). *Students:* 18 full-time (6 women), 3 part-time (1 woman); includes 9 minority (5 Black or African American, non-Hispanic/Latino; 4 Hispanic/Latino), 8 international. Average age 31. 2 applicants, 100% accepted, 2 enrolled. In 2018, 5 master's awarded. *Degree requirements:* For master's, comprehensive exam or thesis. *Entrance requirements:* For master's, minimum undergraduate GPA of 2.75; bachelor's degree in music; three recommendations; comprehensive essay; interview/audition. Additional exam requirements/recommendations for international students: Required—TOEFL (minimum score 80 iBT). *Application deadline:* For fall admission, 8/1 priority date for domestic students, 7/1 for international students; for spring admission, 12/1 priority date for domestic students, 11/1 for international students. Applications are processed on a rolling basis. Application fee: $45. Electronic applications accepted. *Expenses:* $635 per unit. *Financial support:* In 2018–19, 9 students received support. Federal Work-Study and scholarships/grants available. Financial award applicants required to submit CSS PROFILE or FAFSA. *Faculty research:* Choral conducting, church music, choir building, hymnology, music technology. *Unit head:* Dr. Joseph Bolin, Dean, School of Music, 951-343-4714, Fax: 951-343-4570, E-mail: jbolin@calbaptist.edu. *Application contact:* Dr. Lance Beaumont, Associate Dean for Graduate Studies and Program Development, 951-552-8162, E-mail: lbeaumont@calbaptist.edu.
Website: http://www.calbaptist.edu/masterofmusic/

California State University, Fresno, Division of Research and Graduate Studies, College of Arts and Humanities, Department of Music, Fresno, CA 93740-8027. Offers music (MA); music education (MA); performance (MA). *Accreditation:* NASM. *Program availability:* Part-time. *Degree requirements:* For master's, thesis or alternative. *Entrance requirements:* For master's, GRE General Test, BA in music, minimum GPA of 3.0. Additional exam requirements/recommendations for international students: Required—TOEFL. Electronic applications accepted. *Faculty research:* Technology transfer, folk art.

California State University, Fullerton, Graduate Studies, College of the Arts, Department of Music, Fullerton, CA 92831-3599. Offers music education (MA); performance (MM). *Accreditation:* NASM. *Program availability:* Part-time. *Degree requirements:* For master's, comprehensive exam, project or thesis. *Entrance requirements:* For master's, audition, major in music or related field, minimum GPA of 2.5 in last 60 units of course work.

California State University, Los Angeles, Graduate Studies, College of Arts and Letters, Department of Music, Los Angeles, CA 90032-8530. Offers music composition (MM); music education (MA); musicology (MA); performance (MM). *Accreditation:* NASM. *Program availability:* Part-time, evening/weekend. *Degree requirements:* For master's, comprehensive exam, project or thesis. *Entrance requirements:* For master's, audition. Additional exam requirements/recommendations for international students: Required—TOEFL (minimum score 500 paper-based). Electronic applications accepted. *Faculty research:* Gregorian semiology, Baroque opera.

California State University, Northridge, Graduate Studies, Mike Curb College of Arts, Media, and Communication, Department of Music, Northridge, CA 91330. Offers composition (MM); conducting (MM); music education (MA); performance (MM). *Accreditation:* NASM. *Degree requirements:* For master's, thesis. *Entrance requirements:* For master's, audition, GRE General Test or minimum GPA of 3.0. Additional exam requirements/recommendations for international students: Required—TOEFL.

Campbellsville University, School of Music, Campbellsville, KY 42718-2799. Offers music (MA); music education (MM), including conducting, instrumental performance, vocal performance and pedagogy; musicology (MA); worship (MA). *Accreditation:* NASM. *Program availability:* Part-time, 100% online, blended/hybrid learning. *Faculty:* 12 full-time (5 women), 8 part-time/adjunct (5 women). *Students:* 16 full-time (10 women), 4 part-time (1 woman); includes 1 minority (Black or African American, non-Hispanic/Latino), 4 international. Average age 29. 22 applicants, 59% accepted, 6 enrolled. In 2018, 6 master's awarded. *Degree requirements:* For master's, comprehensive exam, thesis (for some programs), paper or recital. *Entrance requirements:* For master's, GRE General Test or PRAXIS, minimum GPA of 2.75, college transcripts. Additional exam requirements/recommendations for international students: Required—TOEFL (minimum score 550 paper-based; 79 iBT); Recommended—IELTS (minimum score 6). *Application deadline:* Applications are processed on a rolling basis. Application fee: $25. Electronic applications accepted. Application fee is waived when completed online. *Expenses:* $399/credit hour. This program completes generally 15 credit hours in an academic year, due to being on 16-week semesters. *Financial support:* Unspecified assistantships available. Financial award application deadline: 6/1; financial award applicants required to submit FAFSA. *Unit head:* Dr. Tony Cunha, Dean of School of Music, 270-789-5240, Fax: 270-789-5524, E-mail: aocunha@campbellsville.edu. *Application contact:* Monica Bamwine, Director of Graduate Admissions, 270-789-5221, Fax: 270-789-5071, E-mail: mkbamwine@campbellsville.edu.
Website: http://www.campbellsville.edu/music

Capital University, Conservatory of Music, Columbus, OH 43209-2394. Offers music education (MM), including instrumental emphasis, Kodály emphasis. Program offered only in summer. *Accreditation:* NASM. *Program availability:* Part-time. *Degree requirements:* For master's, comprehensive exam, thesis or alternative, chamber performance exam. *Entrance requirements:* For master's, music theory exam, minimum undergraduate GPA of 3.0. Additional exam requirements/recommendations for international students: Required—TOEFL (minimum score 550 paper-based; 80 iBT). Electronic applications accepted. *Expenses:* Contact institution. *Faculty research:* Folk song research, Kodály method, performance, composition.

Carnegie Mellon University, College of Fine Arts, School of Music, Pittsburgh, PA 15213-3891. Offers collaborative piano (MM); composition (MM); instrumental performance (MM); music and technology (MS); music education (MM); vocal performance (MM). *Accreditation:* NASM. *Program availability:* Part-time. *Degree requirements:* For master's, comprehensive exam, recital. *Entrance requirements:* For master's, audition. *Faculty research:* Computer music, music history.

Case Western Reserve University, School of Graduate Studies, Department of Music, Program in Music Education, Cleveland, OH 44106. Offers MA, PhD. *Accreditation:* NASM; TEAC. *Faculty:* 18 full-time (7 women), 17 part-time/adjunct (8 women). *Students:* 8 full-time (6 women), 10 part-time (8 women). Average age 31. 5 applicants, 60% accepted, 3 enrolled. In 2018, 1 master's, 1 doctorate awarded. *Degree requirements:* For master's, comprehensive exam (for some programs), thesis (for some programs); for doctorate, comprehensive exam, thesis/dissertation. *Entrance requirements:* For master's, GRE, resume, PDF of teaching license/certificate, audition/interview, writing sample, 1 year of teaching; for doctorate, GRE, resume, PDF of teaching license/certificate, audition/interview, writing sample, 3 years of teaching. Additional exam requirements/recommendations for international students: Required—TOEFL (minimum score 577 paper-based; 90 iBT); Recommended—IELTS (minimum score 7). *Application deadline:* For fall admission, 1/15 priority date for domestic students. Application fee: $50. Electronic applications accepted. *Expenses: Tuition:* Full-time $45,168; part-time $1939 per credit hour. *Required fees:* $36; $18 per semester. $18 per semester. *Financial support:* Fellowships, teaching assistantships, career-related internships or fieldwork, health care benefits, tuition waivers (full), unspecified assistantships, and stipends available. Financial award application deadline: 1/15; financial award applicants required to submit CSS PROFILE or FAFSA. *Faculty research:* Psychology of music, creative thinking, computer applications, educational psychology. *Unit head:* David J. Rothenberg, Associate Professor/Department Chair, 216-368-6046, Fax: 216-368-6557, E-mail: music@case.edu. *Application contact:* Laura Stauffer, Department Administrator, 216-368-0117, Fax: 216-368-6557, E-mail: music@case.edu.
Website: http://music.case.edu/

The Catholic University of America, Benjamin T. Rome School of Music, Washington, DC 20064. Offers cello (Artist Diploma); chamber music (piano) (MM, DMA); composition (MM, DMA), including concert music (MM), stage music (MM); music (MAT); musicology (MA, PhD); orchestral conducting (MM, DMA, Artist Diploma); orchestral instruments/guitar (MM, DMA); piano (Artist Diploma); piano pedagogy (MM, DMA); piano performance (MM, DMA); sacred music (MMSM, DMA); violin (Artist Diploma); vocal accompanying (MM, DMA); vocal pedagogy (MM, DMA); vocal performance (MM, DMA); voice (Artist Diploma); MA/MSLIS. MA/MSLIS offered in partnership with Department of Library and Information Science. *Accreditation:* NASM. *Program availability:* Part-time. *Faculty:* 17 full-time (4 women), 46 part-time/adjunct (17 women). *Students:* 40 full-time (29 women), 90 part-time (55 women); includes 36 minority (10 Black or African American, non-Hispanic/Latino; 13 Asian, non-Hispanic/Latino; 8 Hispanic/Latino; 5 Two or more races, non-Hispanic/Latino), 28 international. Average age 33. 137 applicants, 61% accepted, 49 enrolled. In 2018, 12 master's, 10 doctorates awarded. *Degree requirements:* For master's, variable foreign language requirement, comprehensive exam (for some programs), thesis (for some programs), final recital (for some programs); for doctorate, variable foreign language requirement, comprehensive exam (for some programs), thesis/dissertation (for some programs), final recital (for some programs); for Artist Diploma, variable foreign language requirement, final recital (for some programs). *Entrance requirements:* For master's, music theory and music history placement examinations, statement of purpose, 2 letters of recommendation, minimum undergraduate B average, audition (for all performance degrees), official copy of academic transcript showing completed and conferred BM; for doctorate, music theory and music history placement examinations, 2 letters of recommendation, minimum B average in all previous course work and degrees, official copies of academic transcripts showing completion and conferral of all previous degrees, audition (for all performance degrees); for Artist Diploma, music theory and music history placement examinations, statement of purpose, 2 letters of recommendation, minimum B average in all previous course work and degrees, BM, audition, official copies of academic transcripts showing completion and conferral of all previous degrees. Additional exam requirements/recommendations for international students: Required—TOEFL (minimum score 550 paper-based; 80 iBT). *Application deadline:* For fall admission, 7/15 priority date for domestic students, 7/1 for international students; for spring admission, 11/15 priority date for domestic students, 11/1 for international students. Applications are processed on a rolling basis. Application fee: $55. Electronic applications accepted. *Expenses:* Contact institution. *Financial support:* Fellowships, research assistantships, teaching assistantships, Federal Work-Study, scholarships/grants, tuition waivers (full and partial), and unspecified assistantships available. Financial award application deadline: 2/1; financial award applicants required to submit FAFSA. *Faculty research:* Composition, sacred music, orchestral instruments, piano and vocal performance, piano and vocal pedagogy. *Unit head:* Jacqueline Leary-Warsaw, Dean, 202-319-5417, Fax: 202-319-6280, E-mail: cua-music@cua.edu. *Application contact:* Dr. Steven Brown, Director of Graduate Admissions, 202-319-5247, Fax: 202-319-6174, E-mail: cua-graduatestudies@cua.edu.
Website: https://music.catholic.edu/

Central Connecticut State University, School of Graduate Studies, College of Liberal Arts and Social Sciences, Department of Music, New Britain, CT 06050-4010. Offers music education (MS, Certificate). *Accreditation:* NASM. *Program availability:* Part-time, evening/weekend. *Faculty:* 1 full-time (0 women). *Students:* 2 full-time (1 woman), 1 part-time (0 women). Average age 33. 9 applicants, 56% accepted. In 2018, 4 master's, 1 other advanced degree awarded. *Degree requirements:* For master's, comprehensive exam, thesis or alternative, special project; for Certificate, qualifying exam. *Entrance requirements:* For master's, theory examination, audition, minimum undergraduate GPA of 2.7, essay, portfolio, evidence of proficiency in technology. Additional exam requirements/recommendations for international students: Required—TOEFL (minimum score 550 paper-based; 79 iBT); Recommended—IELTS (minimum score 6.5). *Application deadline:* For fall admission, 6/1 for domestic students, 4/1 for international students; for spring admission, 11/1 for domestic and international students. Applications are processed on a rolling basis. Application fee: $50. Electronic applications accepted. *Expenses: Tuition, area resident:* Full-time $7027; part-time $388 per credit. Tuition, state resident: full-time $9750; part-time $388 per credit. Tuition,

nonresident: full-time $18,102; part-time $388 per credit. *International tuition:* $18,102 full-time. *Required fees:* $266 per semester. *Financial support:* Career-related internships or fieldwork, Federal Work-Study, scholarships/grants, and unspecified assistantships available. Support available to part-time students. Financial award application deadline: 3/1. *Faculty research:* Applied music. *Unit head:* Dr. Carlotta Parr, Chair, 860-832-2912, E-mail: parrc@ccsu.edu. *Application contact:* Patricia Gardner, Associate Director of Graduate Studies, 860-832-2350, Fax: 860-832-2362. Website: http://www.ccsu.edu/music/

Central Methodist University, College of Graduate and Extended Studies, Fayette, MO 65248-1198. Offers clinical counseling (MS); clinical nurse leader (MSN); education (M Ed); music education (MME); nurse educator (MSN). *Program availability:* Part-time, evening/weekend, online learning. *Degree requirements:* For master's, thesis. *Entrance requirements:* For master's, GRE General Test, minimum GPA of 2.75. Electronic applications accepted.

Central Michigan University, College of Graduate Studies, College of the Arts and Media, School of Music, Mount Pleasant, MI 48859. Offers composition (MM); conducting (MM); music education (MM); performance (MM). *Accreditation:* NASM. *Program availability:* Part-time. *Degree requirements:* For master's, thesis or alternative. Electronic applications accepted. *Faculty research:* Music education, music composition, conducting, music performance.

Central Washington University, School of Graduate Studies and Research, College of Arts and Humanities, Department of Music, Ellensburg, WA 98926. Offers composition (MM); conducting (MM); music education (MM); pedagogy (MM); performance (MM). *Accreditation:* NASM. *Entrance requirements:* For master's, minimum GPA of 3.0. Additional exam requirements/recommendations for international students: Required—TOEFL (minimum score 550 paper-based; 79 iBT) or IELTS (minimum score 6.5). Electronic applications accepted.

Cleveland State University, College of Graduate Studies, College of Liberal Arts and Social Sciences, Department of Music, Cleveland, OH 44115. Offers composition (MM); music education (MM). *Accreditation:* NASM. *Program availability:* Part-time, evening/weekend. *Faculty:* 9 full-time (2 women), 19 part-time/adjunct (6 women). *Students:* 8 full-time (2 women), 13 part-time (5 women); includes 4 minority (1 Black or African American, non-Hispanic/Latino; 3 Hispanic/Latino), 4 international. Average age 26. 34 applicants, 91% accepted, 19 enrolled. In 2018, 15 master's awarded. *Entrance requirements:* For master's, departmental assessment in music history, minimum undergraduate GPA of 2.75, audition on primary instrument, or submission of composition portfolio or written samples (for music education). Additional exam requirements/recommendations for international students: Required—TOEFL (minimum score 550 paper-based; 78 iBT). *Application deadline:* For fall admission, 7/1 priority date for domestic students, 5/15 for international students; for spring admission, 11/15 for domestic students, 11/1 for international students; for summer admission, 4/1 for domestic students, 3/15 for international students. Applications are processed on a rolling basis. Application fee: $40. Electronic applications accepted. *Expenses:* Tuition, state resident: full-time $7232.55; part-time $6676 per credit hour. Tuition, nonresident: full-time $12,375. *International tuition:* $18,914 full-time. *Required fees:* $80; $80 $40. Tuition and fees vary according to program. *Financial support:* In 2018–19, 14 students received support. Scholarships/grants, tuition waivers (partial), and unspecified assistantships available. Financial award application deadline: 3/15; financial award applicants required to submit FAFSA. *Faculty research:* Performance, music education, music composition. *Total annual research expenditures:* $26. *Unit head:* Dr. John Perrine, Chairperson/Associate Professor, 216-687-3959, Fax: 216-687-9279, E-mail: j.m.perrine@csuohio.edu. *Application contact:* Kate Bill, Music Admission Specialist, 216-687-5039, Fax: 216-687-9279, E-mail: m.c.bill@csuohio.edu. Website: http://www.csuohio.edu/music/

College of Charleston, Graduate School, School of Education, Health, and Human Performance, Department of Foundations, Secondary, and Special Education, Program in Performing Arts Education, Charleston, SC 29424-0001. Offers MAT. *Accreditation:* NASM. *Program availability:* Part-time, evening/weekend. *Entrance requirements:* For master's, GRE, minimum GPA of 2.5 overall, 3.0 in last 60 hours of undergraduate coursework; 2 letters of recommendation; audition/interview. Additional exam requirements/recommendations for international students: Required—TOEFL (minimum score 81 iBT). Electronic applications accepted.

The Colorado College, Education Department, Program in Secondary Education, Colorado Springs, CO 80903-3294. Offers art teaching (K-12) (MAT); English teaching (MAT); foreign language teaching (MAT); mathematics teaching (MAT); music teaching (MAT); science teaching (MAT); social studies teaching (MAT). *Degree requirements:* For master's, thesis, internship. Electronic applications accepted.

Colorado State University–Pueblo, College of Education, Engineering and Professional Studies, Education Program, Pueblo, CO 81001-4901. Offers art education (M Ed); foreign language education (M Ed); health and physical education (M Ed); instructional technology (M Ed); linguistically diverse education (M Ed); music education (M Ed); special education (M Ed). *Accreditation:* TEAC. *Program availability:* Part-time. *Degree requirements:* For master's, portfolio. *Entrance requirements:* For master's, 3 recommendations, teaching license. Additional exam requirements/recommendations for international students: Required—TOEFL (minimum score 500 paper-based). Electronic applications accepted. *Faculty research:* Portfolio assessment, math education, science education.

Columbus State University, Graduate Studies, College of the Arts, Schwob School of Music, Columbus, GA 31907-5645. Offers music (Artist Diploma); music education (MM); music performance (MM). *Accreditation:* NASM; NCATE (one or more programs are accredited). *Program availability:* Part-time. *Faculty:* 23 full-time (9 women), 5 part-time/adjunct (3 women). *Students:* 44 full-time (16 women), 10 part-time (3 women); includes 16 minority (5 Black or African American, non-Hispanic/Latino; 5 Asian, non-Hispanic/Latino; 5 Hispanic/Latino; 1 Native Hawaiian or other Pacific Islander, non-Hispanic/Latino), 16 international. Average age 27. 55 applicants, 64% accepted, 27 enrolled. In 2018, 14 master's, 15 Artist Diplomas awarded. *Degree requirements:* For master's, exit exam. *Entrance requirements:* For master's, audition, letters of recommendation, undergraduate degree in music with minimum GPA of 2.5. Additional exam requirements/recommendations for international students: Required—TOEFL (minimum score 550 paper-based; 79 iBT). *Application deadline:* For fall admission, 6/30 for domestic students, 5/1 for international students; for spring admission, 11/1 for domestic and international students; for summer admission, 3/1 for domestic and international students. Applications are processed on a rolling basis. Application fee: $50. Electronic applications accepted. *Expenses:* Tuition, area resident: Full-time $4924; part-time $618 per credit hour. Tuition, state resident: full-time $4924; part-time $618 per credit hour. Tuition, nonresident: full-time $19,218; part-time $2403 per credit hour. *International tuition:* $19,218 full-time. *Required fees:* $1870; $802. Tuition and fees vary according to course load, degree level and program. *Financial support:* In 2018–19, 45 students received support, including 30 research assistantships with partial tuition reimbursements available (averaging $3,000 per year); career-related internships or fieldwork, Federal Work-Study, institutionally sponsored loans, scholarships/grants, tuition waivers (partial), and unspecified assistantships also available. Support available

to part-time students. Financial award application deadline: 5/1; financial award applicants required to submit FAFSA. *Unit head:* Dr. Edwin Scott Harris, Director, 706-507-8419, E-mail: harris_scott@columbusstate.edu. *Application contact:* Catrina Smith-Edmond, Assistant Director for Graduate and Global Admission, 706-507-8824, Fax: 706-568-5091, E-mail: smithedmond_catrina@columbusstate.edu. Website: http://music.columbusstate.edu/

Conservatorio de Musica de Puerto Rico, Program in Music Education, San Juan, PR 00907. Offers MM Ed. *Entrance requirements:* For master's, EXADEP, 3 letters of recommendation, audition, bachelor's degree in music education, interview, minimum GPA of 2.5, performance video, teaching video. Additional exam requirements/recommendations for international students: Required—TOEFL.

Converse College, Petrie School of Music, Spartanburg, SC 29302. Offers music education (M Mus); performance (M Mus). *Accreditation:* NASM. *Program availability:* Part-time, evening/weekend. *Degree requirements:* For master's, variable foreign language requirement, comprehensive exam, thesis (for some programs), recitals. *Entrance requirements:* For master's, NTE (music education), audition, 3 letters of recommendation. Additional exam requirements/recommendations for international students: Required—TOEFL. Electronic applications accepted. *Faculty research:* Chamber music, opera, performance, composition, recording.

DePaul University, School of Music, Chicago, IL 60614. Offers composition (MM); jazz studies (MM); music education (MM); music performance (MM); performance (Certificate). *Accreditation:* NASM (one or more programs are accredited). *Program availability:* Part-time, evening/weekend. *Degree requirements:* For master's, comprehensive exam. *Entrance requirements:* For master's, bachelor's degree in music or related field, minimum GPA of 3.0, auditions (performance), scores (composition); for Certificate, master's degree in performance or related field, auditions (for performance majors). Additional exam requirements/recommendations for international students: Required—TOEFL (minimum score 550 paper-based; 80 iBT). Electronic applications accepted. *Expenses:* Contact institution.

Duquesne University, Mary Pappert School of Music, Pittsburgh, PA 15282-0001. Offers music education (MM). *Accreditation:* NASM. *Program availability:* Part-time. *Faculty:* 26 full-time (9 women), 77 part-time/adjunct (22 women). *Students:* 67 full-time (32 women), 6 part-time (4 women); includes 6 minority (1 Black or African American, non-Hispanic/Latino; 2 Asian, non-Hispanic/Latino; 3 Hispanic/Latino), 36 international. Average age 27. 68 applicants, 99% accepted, 32 enrolled. In 2018, 23 master's, 4 ADs awarded. *Degree requirements:* For master's, comprehensive exam, thesis (for some programs), recital (music performance); for AD, recital. *Entrance requirements:* For master's, audition, minimum undergraduate QPA of 3.0 in music, portfolio of original compositions, or music education experience; for AD, audition. Additional exam requirements/recommendations for international students: Required—TOEFL (minimum score 550 paper-based; 79 iBT), IELTS (minimum score 6.5). *Application deadline:* For fall admission, 7/1 for domestic and international students; for spring admission, 12/1 for domestic and international students. Applications are processed on a rolling basis. Application fee: $50. Electronic applications accepted. Application fee is waived when completed online. *Expenses:* $1,600/credit hour. *Financial support:* In 2018–19, 64 students received support. Scholarships/grants and unspecified assistantships available. Financial award application deadline: 4/1. *Faculty research:* Assessment of music education and professional dispositions; music philosophy; curricular design, pedagogy, and assessment; music composition; music performance. *Unit head:* Dr. Seth Beckman, Dean/Professor, 412-396-6082, Fax: 412-396-1524, E-mail: beckmans@duq.edu. *Application contact:* Thomas Carsecka, Director of Music Admissions, 412-396-5983, Fax: 412-396-5719, E-mail: carseckat@duq.edu. Website: http://duq.edu/music

East Carolina University, Graduate School, College of Fine Arts and Communication, School of Music, Greenville, NC 27858-4353. Offers advanced performance studies (Certificate); composition (MM); music education (MM), including choral conducting, instrumental conducting, music theory/composition, music therapy, performance, Suzuki pedagogy; music therapy (MM); Suzuki pedagogy (Certificate); theory (MM); woodwind specialist (MM), including accompanying, choral conducting, instrumental, instrumental conducting, jazz studies, keyboard, organ, piano pedagogy, Suzuki string pedagogy, vocal pedagogy, voice, woodwind specialist. *Accreditation:* NASM. *Program availability:* Part-time. *Application deadline:* For fall admission, 6/1 priority date for domestic students. *Expenses: Tuition, area resident:* Full-time $4749. Tuition, state resident: full-time $4749. Tuition, nonresident: full-time $17,898. *International tuition:* $17,898 full-time. *Required fees:* $2787. Part-time tuition and fees vary according to course load and program. *Financial support:* Application deadline: 6/1. *Unit head:* Christopher Ulffers, Director, 252-328-4270, E-mail: ulffersj@ecu.edu. *Application contact:* Graduate School Admissions, 252-328-6012, Fax: 252-328-6071, E-mail: gradschool@ecu.edu. Website: http://www.ecu.edu/music/

Eastern Illinois University, Graduate School, College of Liberal Arts and Sciences, Department of Music, Charleston, IL 61920. Offers composition (MA); conducting (MA); music education (MA); performance (MA). *Accreditation:* NASM. *Program availability:* Part-time, evening/weekend, online learning. *Degree requirements:* For master's, comprehensive exam (for some programs), thesis (for some programs). *Entrance requirements:* For master's, personal statement, resume, three letters of recommendation. Additional exam requirements/recommendations for international students: Required—TOEFL (minimum score 500 paper-based; 61 iBT), IELTS (minimum score 6). Electronic applications accepted. *Expenses:* Tuition, state resident: part-time $299 per credit hour. Tuition, nonresident: part-time $718 per credit hour. *Required fees:* $214.50 per credit hour.

Eastern Kentucky University, The Graduate School, College of Education, Department of Curriculum and Instruction, Richmond, KY 40475-3102. Offers elementary education (MA Ed), including early elementary education, reading; library science (MA Ed); music education (MA Ed); secondary and higher education (MA Ed), including secondary education; teaching (MAT). *Accreditation:* NCATE. *Program availability:* Part-time. *Degree requirements:* For master's, portfolio is part of exam. *Entrance requirements:* For master's, GRE General Test, PRAXIS II (KY), minimum GPA of 2.5. *Faculty research:* Technology in education, reading instruction, e-portfolios, induction to teacher education, dispositions of teachers.

Eastern Washington University, Graduate Studies, College of Arts, Letters and Education, Department of Music, Cheney, WA 99004-2431. Offers composition (MA); instrumental/vocal performance (MA); jazz pedagogy (MA); liberal arts (MA); music education (MA). *Accreditation:* NASM. *Program availability:* Part-time. *Degree requirements:* For master's, comprehensive exam, thesis or alternative. *Entrance requirements:* For master's, GRE General Test, minimum GPA of 3.0. Additional exam requirements/recommendations for international students: Required—TOEFL (minimum score 580 paper-based; 92 iBT), IELTS (minimum score 7), TWE, PTE (minimum score 63). Electronic applications accepted.

Five Towns College, Graduate Programs, Dix Hills, NY 11746-6055. Offers childhood education (MS Ed); composition and arranging (DMA); jazz/commercial music (MM); music education (MM, DMA); music history and literature (DMA); music performance (DMA). *Program availability:* Part-time. *Degree requirements:* For master's, thesis,

exams, major composition or capstone project, recital; for doctorate, comprehensive exam, thesis/dissertation, final oral exam. *Entrance requirements:* For master's, audition (for MM); New York state teaching certification (for MS Ed); personal statement, two letters of recommendation; for doctorate, 3 letters of recommendation, audition, essay. Additional exam requirements/recommendations for international students: Required—TOEFL (minimum score 520 paper-based; 85 iBT); Recommended—IELTS (minimum score 7). Electronic applications accepted. *Faculty research:* Teaching methods, teaching strategies and techniques, analysis of modern music, jazz.

Florida International University, College of Communication, Architecture and The Arts, School of Music, Miami, FL 33199. Offers music (MM); music education (MS). *Accreditation:* NASM. *Program availability:* Part-time, evening/weekend. *Faculty:* 27 full-time (6 women), 30 part-time/adjunct (10 women). *Students:* 28 full-time (13 women), 15 part-time (5 women); includes 32 minority (6 Black or African American, non-Hispanic/Latino; 25 Hispanic/Latino; 1 Two or more races, non-Hispanic/Latino), 4 international. Average age 32. 38 applicants, 74% accepted, 18 enrolled. In 2018, 12 master's awarded. *Degree requirements:* For master's, thesis (for some programs). *Entrance requirements:* For master's, GRE (depending on program), statement of intent; 2 letters of recommendation; audition, interview and/or writing sample (depending on the area). Additional exam requirements/recommendations for international students: Required—TOEFL (minimum score 550 paper-based; 80 iBT). *Application deadline:* For fall admission, 6/1 for domestic students, 4/1 for international students; for spring admission, 10/1 for domestic students, 9/1 for international students. Applications are processed on a rolling basis. Application fee: $30. Electronic applications accepted. *Financial support:* Institutionally sponsored loans and scholarships/grants available. Financial award application deadline: 3/1; financial award applicants required to submit FAFSA. *Unit head:* Joel Galand, Program Director, 305-348-7078, E-mail: Joel.Galand@fiu.edu. *Application contact:* Nanett Rojas, Manager, Admissions Operations, 305-348-7464, Fax: 305-348-7441, E-mail: gradadm@fiu.edu.
Website: http://carta.fiu.edu/music/

George Mason University, College of Visual and Performing Arts, School of Music, Program in Music, Fairfax, VA 22030. Offers composition (MM); conducting (MM); jazz studies (MM); music education (MM); pedagogy (MM); performance (MM). *Accreditation:* NASM. *Faculty:* 21 full-time (10 women), 35 part-time/adjunct (9 women). *Students:* 30 full-time (13 women), 28 part-time (9 women); includes 15 minority (5 Black or African American, non-Hispanic/Latino; 5 Asian, non-Hispanic/Latino; 3 Hispanic/Latino; 2 Two or more races, non-Hispanic/Latino), 8 international. Average age 30. 51 applicants, 76% accepted, 23 enrolled. In 2018, 19 master's awarded. *Entrance requirements:* For master's, expanded goals statement; 2 letters of recommendation; official transcript. Additional exam requirements/recommendations for international students: Required—TOEFL (minimum score 575 paper-based; 88 iBT), IELTS (minimum score 6.5), PTE (minimum score 59). Application fee: $75 ($80 for international students). Electronic applications accepted. *Financial support:* Career-related internships or fieldwork, Federal Work-Study, scholarships/grants, and unspecified assistantships available. Financial award application deadline: 3/1; financial award applicants required to submit FAFSA. *Unit head:* Dr. Linda Apple Monson, Managing Director, 703-993-3580, Fax: 703-993-1394, E-mail: lmonson@gmu.edu. *Application contact:* Dr. Lisa A. Billingham, Director of Graduate Studies, 703-993-3778, Fax: 703-993-1394, E-mail: lbillin1@gmu.edu.
Website: http://music.gmu.edu

Georgia College & State University, Graduate School, College of Arts and Sciences, Department of Music, Milledgeville, GA 31061. Offers MM Ed. *Accreditation:* NASM. *Program availability:* Part-time, evening/weekend, online only, 100% online. *Degree requirements:* For master's, comprehensive exam, publication or presentation of a capstone project. *Entrance requirements:* For master's, bachelor's degree in music education, 3 letters of recommendation, interview, resume, video recorded lesson or rehearsal with written lesson plan, transcript. Electronic applications accepted. *Expenses:* Contact institution.

Georgia Southern University, Jack N. Averitt College of Graduate Studies, College of Arts and Humanities, Program in Music, Statesboro, GA 30460. Offers composition (MM); conducting (MM); music education (MM); music technology (MM); performance (MM). *Accreditation:* NASM. *Program availability:* Part-time, evening/weekend. *Degree requirements:* For master's, comprehensive exam, recital or final project. *Entrance requirements:* For master's, minimum GPA of 2.5, audition, letters of recommendation. Additional exam requirements/recommendations for international students: Required—TOEFL (minimum score 550 paper-based; 80 iBT), IELTS (minimum score 6). Electronic applications accepted. *Expenses: Tuition, area resident:* Part-time $3324 per semester. Tuition, state resident: full-time $5814; part-time $3324 per semester. Tuition, nonresident: full-time $23,204; part-time $13,260 per semester. *Required fees:* $2092; $2092. Tuition and fees vary according to course load, degree level, campus/location and program. *Faculty research:* Performance, conducting, composition, technology, education.

Georgia State University, College of Education and Human Development, Department of Middle and Secondary Education, Atlanta, GA 30302-3083. Offers curriculum and instruction (Ed D); English education (MAT); mathematics education (M Ed, MAT); middle level education (MAT); reading, language and literacy education (M Ed, MAT), including reading instruction (M Ed); science education (M Ed, MAT), including biology (MAT), broad field science (MAT), chemistry (MAT), earth science (MAT), physics (MAT); social studies education (M Ed, MAT), including economics (MAT), geography (MAT), history (MAT), political science (MAT); teaching and learning (PhD), including language and literacy, mathematics education, music education, science education, social studies education, teaching and teacher education. *Accreditation:* NCATE. *Program availability:* Part-time, evening/weekend, online learning. *Faculty:* 19 full-time (15 women), 9 part-time/adjunct (7 women). *Students:* 217 full-time (136 women), 203 part-time (140 women); includes 229 minority (156 Black or African American, non-Hispanic/Latino; 23 Asian, non-Hispanic/Latino; 31 Hispanic/Latino; 19 Two or more races, non-Hispanic/Latino), 3 international. Average age 34. 149 applicants, 60% accepted, 70 enrolled. In 2018, 112 master's, 23 doctorates awarded. *Entrance requirements:* For master's, GRE; GACE I (for initial teacher preparation programs), baccalaureate degree or equivalent, resume, goals statement, two letters of recommendation, minimum undergraduate GPA of 2.5; proof of initial teacher certification in the content area (for M Ed); for doctorate, GRE, resume, goals statement, writing sample, two letters of recommendation, minimum graduate GPA of 3.3, interview. *Application deadline:* For fall admission, 1/15 priority date for domestic and international students; for spring admission, 10/1 for domestic and international students. Application fee: $50. Electronic applications accepted. *Expenses: Tuition, area resident:* Full-time $9360; part-time $390 per credit hour. Tuition, state resident: full-time $9360; part-time $390 per credit hour. Tuition, nonresident: full-time $30,024; part-time $1251 per credit hour. *International tuition:* $30,024 full-time. *Required fees:* $2128. *Financial support:* In 2018–19, fellowships with full tuition reimbursements (averaging $19,667 per year), research assistantships with full tuition reimbursements (averaging $5,436 per year), teaching assistantships with full tuition reimbursements (averaging $2,779 per year) were awarded; career-related internships or fieldwork, Federal Work-Study, scholarships/grants, health care benefits, tuition waivers (full and partial), and unspecified assistantships also available. Financial award application deadline: 3/15. *Faculty research:* Teacher education in language and literacy, mathematics, science, and social studies in urban middle and secondary school settings; learning technologies in school, community, and corporate settings; multicultural education and education for social justice; urban education; international education. *Unit head:* Dr. Gertrude Marilyn Tinker Sachs, Chair, 404-413-8384, Fax: 404-413-8063, E-mail: gtinkersachs@gsu.edu. *Application contact:* Shaleen Tibbs, Administrative Specialist, 404-413-8385, Fax: 404-413-8063, E-mail: stibbs@gsu.edu.
Website: http://mse.education.gsu.edu/

Gordon College, Graduate Music Education Program, Wenham, MA 01984-1899. Offers MM Ed. *Accreditation:* NASM. *Program availability:* Part-time. *Degree requirements:* For master's, comprehensive exam, thesis or alternative, field-based experience, capstone research project. *Entrance requirements:* For master's, music theory and music history diagnostic exams, 15-20 minute video-recorded demonstration of current classroom teaching; letter of introduction; at least one year of teaching experience; initial license in music (for professional licensure); professional resume; 3-4 page essay; two letters of recommendation; two official transcripts. Additional exam requirements/recommendations for international students: Required—TOEFL (minimum score 550 paper-based with minimum of 50 on each test area), Oral Proficiency Interview. *Expenses:* Contact institution. *Faculty research:* Medium-high security prison education through choral music instruction; healthy vocal development in adolescents; healthy use of the singing voice; national common music assessment initiative; choral literature and techniques to incorporate the new national standards for music education.

Hardin-Simmons University, Graduate School, College of Fine Arts, Abilene, TX 79698-0001. Offers church music (MM); music education (MM); music performance (MM); theory and composition (MM). *Accreditation:* NASM. *Program availability:* Part-time. *Faculty:* 12 full-time (4 women), 2 part-time/adjunct (0 women). *Students:* 1 (woman) full-time, 5 part-time (2 women); includes 4 minority (1 Black or African American, non-Hispanic/Latino; 1 Hispanic/Latino; 2 Two or more races, non-Hispanic/Latino). Average age 31. 7 applicants, 71% accepted, 1 enrolled. In 2018, 1 master's awarded. *Degree requirements:* For master's, comprehensive exam, thesis (for some programs). *Entrance requirements:* For master's, minimum undergraduate GPA of 3.0 in major, 2.7 overall; writing sample; demonstrated knowledge in chosen area. Additional exam requirements/recommendations for international students: Required—TOEFL (minimum score 550 paper-based; 79 iBT). *Application deadline:* For fall admission, 8/15 priority date for domestic students, 4/1 for international students; for spring admission, 1/5 priority date for domestic students, 9/1 for international students. Applications are processed on a rolling basis. Application fee: $50. Electronic applications accepted. *Expenses: Tuition:* Full-time $750; part-time $750 per credit hour. *Required fees:* $1300; $880 per credit. Tuition and fees vary according to degree level and program. *Financial support:* Fellowships, career-related internships or fieldwork, and scholarships/grants available. Support available to part-time students. Financial award application deadline: 6/30; financial award applicants required to submit FAFSA. *Unit head:* Dr. Robert Tucker, Dean, College of Fine Arts, 325-670-1498, E-mail: robert.l.tucker@hsutx.edu. *Application contact:* Dr. Nancy Kucinski, Dean of Graduate Studies, 325-670-1298, Fax: 325-670-1564, E-mail: gradoff@hsutx.edu.
Website: http://www.hsutx.edu/academics/cofa/

Hebrew College, Program in Jewish Studies, Newton Centre, MA 02459. Offers Jewish liturgical music (Certificate); Jewish music education (Certificate); Jewish studies (MA). *Program availability:* Part-time, evening/weekend, online learning. *Degree requirements:* For master's, one foreign language. *Entrance requirements:* For master's, GRE, interview. Additional exam requirements/recommendations for international students: Required—TOEFL.

Heidelberg University, Master of Music Education Program, Tiffin, OH 44883-2462. Offers MME. Program offered in summer only. *Accreditation:* NASM. *Program availability:* Part-time. In 2018, 1 master's awarded. *Entrance requirements:* For master's, bachelor's degree in music education; minimum cumulative GPA of 2.9; 3 letters of recommendation; copy of U.S. teaching license in music education. *Application deadline:* For fall admission, 6/1 for domestic students. Applications are processed on a rolling basis. Application fee: $0. Electronic applications accepted. Application fee is waived when completed online. *Expenses: Tuition:* Part-time $575 per semester hour. *Financial support:* Unspecified assistantships available. Financial award applicants required to submit FAFSA. *Unit head:* Dr. Carol Dusdieker, Director, 419-448-2080, E-mail: cdusdiek@heidelberg.edu. *Application contact:* Katie Zeyen, Graduate Studies Coordinator, 419-448-2602, Fax: 419-448-2565, E-mail: kzeyen@heidelberg.edu.
Website: https://www.heidelberg.edu/academics/programs/master-music-education

Hofstra University, School of Education, Programs in Teacher Education, Hempstead, NY 11549. Offers bilingual education (MA); bilingual extension (Advanced Certificate); business education (MS Ed); curriculum studies (MS Ed); early childhood and childhood education (MS Ed); early childhood education (MA, MS Ed); educational technology (Advanced Certificate); elementary education (MA, MS Ed); English education (MS Ed); family and consumer science (MS Ed); fine arts and music education (Advanced Certificate); fine arts education (MS Ed); foreign language and TESOL (MS Ed); foreign language education (MA, MS Ed); languages other than English and teaching English as a second language (MA); learning and teaching (Ed D); mathematics education (MA, MS Ed); middle childhood extension (Advanced Certificate); music education (MA, MS Ed); science education (MA); secondary education (Advanced Certificate); social studies education (MA, MS Ed); teaching languages other than English and TESOL (MS Ed); technology for learning (MA); TESOL (MS Ed, Advanced Certificate); TESOL with specialization in STEM (MA); work based learning extension (Advanced Certificate). *Program availability:* Part-time, evening/weekend, blended/hybrid learning. *Students:* 138 full-time (94 women), 109 part-time (78 women); includes 66 minority (16 Black or African American, non-Hispanic/Latino; 17 Asian, non-Hispanic/Latino; 31 Hispanic/Latino; 2 Native Hawaiian or other Pacific Islander, non-Hispanic/Latino), 6 international. Average age 29. 217 applicants, 86% accepted, 113 enrolled. In 2018, 105 master's, 11 doctorates, 25 other advanced degrees awarded. *Degree requirements:* For master's, comprehensive exam, thesis (for some programs), exit project, student teaching, fieldwork, electronic portfolio, curriculum project, minimum GPA of 3.0; for doctorate, dissertation; for Advanced Certificate, 3 foreign languages, comprehensive exam (for some programs), thesis project. *Entrance requirements:* For master's, GRE, 2 letters of recommendation, portfolio, teacher certification (MA), interview, essay; for doctorate, GMAT, GRE, LSAT, or MAT; for Advanced Certificate, 2 letters of recommendation, essay, interview and/or portfolio, teaching certificate. Additional exam requirements/recommendations for international students: Required—TOEFL (minimum score 550 paper-based; 80 iBT). *Application deadline:* Applications are processed on a rolling basis. Application fee: $75. Electronic applications accepted. *Financial support:* In 2018–19, 86 students received support, including 51 fellowships with full and partial tuition reimbursements available (averaging $5,080 per year), 2 research assistantships with full and partial tuition reimbursements available (averaging $3,470 per year); career-related internships or fieldwork, Federal Work-Study, institutionally sponsored loans, scholarships/grants, traineeships, tuition waivers (full and partial), unspecified assistantships, and scholarships and endowed scholarships also available. Support available to part-time students. Financial award applicants required to submit FAFSA.

Faculty research: Impact of memory on learning; brain function, cognitive-development, learning, and achievement; student activism and civic education; using children's literature to promote diversity; 2nd language acquisition. *Unit head:* Dr. Alan Singer, Chairperson, 516-463-5853, Fax: 516-463-6275, E-mail: alan.j.singer@hofstra.edu. *Application contact:* Sunil Samuel, Assistant Vice President of Admissions, 516-463-4723, Fax: 516-463-4664, E-mail: graduateadmission@hofstra.edu.
Website: http://www.hofstra.edu/education/

Holy Names University, Graduate Division, Department of Music, Oakland, CA 94619-1699. Offers Kodaly (Certificate); music education with Kodaly emphasis (MM); piano pedagogy (MM); vocal pedagogy (MM). *Students:* 1 (woman) full-time, 14 part-time (10 women); includes 5 minority (1 Black or African American, non-Hispanic/Latino; 2 Asian, non-Hispanic/Latino; 1 Native Hawaiian or other Pacific Islander, non-Hispanic/Latino; 1 Two or more races, non-Hispanic/Latino). Average age 37. 10 applicants, 60% accepted, 4 enrolled. In 2018, 4 master's, 2 Certificates awarded. *Degree requirements:* For master's, comprehensive exam, recital. *Entrance requirements:* For master's, audition; minimum undergraduate GPA of 2.6 overall, 3.0 in major. Additional exam requirements/recommendations for international students: Required—TOEFL (minimum score 550 paper-based; 79 iBT). *Application deadline:* For fall admission, 8/1 priority date for domestic students, 7/15 for international students; for spring admission, 12/1. priority date for domestic students, 12/1 for international students; for summer admission, 5/1 priority date for domestic students, 5/1 for international students. Applications are processed on a rolling basis. Application fee: $65. Electronic applications accepted. *Expenses: Required fees:* $1003. *Financial support:* Career-related internships or fieldwork, Federal Work-Study, scholarships/grants, and unspecified assistantships available. Support available to part-time students. Financial award application deadline: 3/2; financial award applicants required to submit FAFSA. *Faculty research:* Performance practice with special interest in Baroque, Romantic, and twentieth-century instrumental and vocal music; choral pedagogy; Hungarian music education. *Unit head:* Dr. Steven Hofer, Chair of Music Department, 510-436-1244, E-mail: hofer@hnu.edu. *Application contact:* 800-430-1321, Fax: 510-436-1325, E-mail: graduateadmissions@hnu.edu.

Howard University, Graduate School, Division of Fine Arts, Department of Music, Washington, DC 20059-0002. Offers applied music (MM); instrument (MM Ed); jazz studies (MM); organ (MM Ed); piano (MM Ed); voice (MM Ed). *Accreditation:* NASM. *Program availability:* Part-time. *Degree requirements:* For master's, comprehensive exam, thesis or alternative, departmental qualifying exam, recital. *Entrance requirements:* For master's, minimum GPA of 3.0, bachelor's degree in music or music education. Additional exam requirements/recommendations for international students: Required—TOEFL.

Hunter College of the City University of New York, Graduate School, School of Education, Program in Music Education, New York, NY 10065-5085. Offers MA. *Accreditation:* NCATE. *Degree requirements:* For master's, one foreign language, comprehensive exam, thesis, professional teaching portfolio, New York State Teacher Certification Exams. *Entrance requirements:* For master's, minimum GPA of 2.8, 2 letters of reference. Additional exam requirements/recommendations for international students: Required—TOEFL, TWE.

Idaho State University, Graduate School, College of Education, Department of Teaching and Educational Studies, Pocatello, ID 83209-8059. Offers deaf education (M Ed); elementary education (M Ed); human exceptionality (M Ed); literacy (M Ed); music education (M Ed); secondary education (M Ed). *Program availability:* Part-time. *Degree requirements:* For master's, comprehensive exam, thesis (for some programs), oral thesis defense or written comprehensive exam and oral exam. *Entrance requirements:* For master's, GRE or MAT, minimum undergraduate GPA of 3.0, bachelor's degree, professional experience in an educational context. Additional exam requirements/recommendations for international students: Required—TOEFL (minimum score 550 paper-based; 80 iBT). Electronic applications accepted. *Faculty research:* Literacy, school psychology, special education.

Indiana State University, College of Graduate and Professional Studies, College of Arts and Sciences, School of Music, Terre Haute, IN 47809. Offers conducting (MM); music education (MM); music performance (MM). *Accreditation:* NASM. *Degree requirements:* For master's, comprehensive exam, thesis, qualifying exam. Electronic applications accepted.

Indiana University of Pennsylvania, School of Graduate Studies and Research, College of Fine Arts, Department of Music, Program in Music Education, Indiana, PA 15705. Offers MA. *Faculty:* 13 full-time (3 women), 1 (woman) part-time/adjunct. *Students:* 16 part-time (10 women). Average age 26. 8 applicants, 100% accepted, 5 enrolled. In 2018, 3 master's awarded. *Application deadline:* Applications are processed on a rolling basis. Application fee: $50. Electronic applications accepted. *Expenses:* Tuition, state resident: full-time $12,384; part-time $516 per credit hour. Tuition, nonresident: full-time $18,576; part-time $774 per credit hour. *Required fees:* $4454; $186 per credit hour. $65 per semester. Tuition and fees vary according to program and reciprocity agreements. *Financial support:* Federal Work-Study and scholarships/grants available. *Unit head:* Dr. Matthew Baumer, Coordinator, 724-357-5646, E-mail: mbaumer@iup.edu. *Application contact:* Dr. Matthew Baumer, Coordinator, 724-357-5646, E-mail: mbaumer@iup.edu.
Website: http://www.iup.edu/music/grad/music-education-ma/

Inter American University of Puerto Rico, Metropolitan Campus, Graduate Programs, Program in Music Education, San Juan, PR 00919-1293. Offers MM.

Inter American University of Puerto Rico, San Germán Campus, Graduate Studies Center, Program in Music Education, San Germán, PR 00683-5008. Offers music (MA); music teacher education (MA). *Accreditation:* TEAC. *Program availability:* Part-time, evening/weekend. *Expenses: Tuition:* Full-time $212; part-time $212 per credit. *Required fees:* $366 per semester. One-time fee: $31. Tuition and fees vary according to degree level and program.

Ithaca College, School of Music, Programs in Music and Music Education, Ithaca, NY 14850. Offers composition (MM); music education (MS); performance (MM). *Accreditation:* NASM. *Program availability:* Part-time. *Faculty:* 62 full-time (20 women), 3 part-time/adjunct (all women). *Students:* 20 full-time (9 women), 23 part-time (11 women); includes 11 minority (2 Black or African American, non-Hispanic/Latino; 6 Asian, non-Hispanic/Latino; 3 Hispanic/Latino), 6 international. Average age 24. 99 applicants, 53% accepted, 19 enrolled. In 2018, 27 master's awarded. *Degree requirements:* For master's, thesis (for some programs). *Entrance requirements:* For master's, GRE (for Music Education applicants). Additional exam requirements/recommendations for international students: Required—TOEFL (minimum score 550 paper-based; 80 iBT). *Application deadline:* For fall admission, 12/1 for domestic and international students. Applications are processed on a rolling basis. Application fee: $40. Electronic applications accepted. *Expenses:* Contact institution. *Financial support:* In 2018–19, 42 students received support, including 41 teaching assistantships (averaging $10,447 per year); career-related internships or fieldwork, Federal Work-Study, and scholarships/grants also available. Support available to part-time students. Financial award application deadline: 12/1; financial award applicants required to submit FAFSA. *Unit head:* Dr. Les Black, Chair, Graduate Studies in Music, 607-274-7997,

E-mail: lblack@ithaca.edu. *Application contact:* Nicole Eversley Bradwell, Director, Office of Admission, 800-429-4274, Fax: 607-274-1263, E-mail: admission@ithaca.edu.
Website: http://www.ithaca.edu/gradprograms/music

Jackson State University, Graduate School, College of Liberal Arts, Department of Music, Jackson, MS 39217. Offers music education (MM Ed). *Accreditation:* NASM. *Program availability:* Part-time, evening/weekend. *Degree requirements:* For master's, comprehensive exam, thesis or alternative. *Entrance requirements:* For master's, GRE General Test. Additional exam requirements/recommendations for international students: Required—TOEFL (minimum score 520 paper-based; 67 iBT).

James Madison University, The Graduate School, College of Visual and Performing Arts, Master of Music Program, Harrisonburg, VA 22807. Offers composition (MM); conducting (MM); music education (MM); performance (MM). *Accreditation:* NASM. *Program availability:* Part-time. *Students:* 19 full-time (7 women), 7 part-time (5 women); includes 6 minority (4 Black or African American, non-Hispanic/Latino; 1 Hispanic/Latino; 1 Two or more races, non-Hispanic/Latino), 2 international. Average age 30. In 2018, 6 master's awarded. Electronic applications accepted. *Expenses:* Tuition, state resident: full-time $10,848. Tuition, nonresident: full-time $27,888. *Required fees:* $1128. *Financial support:* In 2018–19, 13 students received support, including 1 teaching assistantship with full tuition reimbursement available (averaging $8,837 per year); fellowships, Federal Work-Study, and assistantships (averaging $7911) also available. Financial award application deadline: 3/1; financial award applicants required to submit FAFSA. *Unit head:* Dr. Jeffrey Bush, Director of the School of Music, 540-568-3614, E-mail: bushje@jmu.edu. *Application contact:* Lynette D. Michael, Director of Graduate Admissions, 540-568-6131 Ext. 6395, Fax: 540-568-7860, E-mail: michaeld@jmu.edu.
Website: http://www.jmu.edu/music/

Kent State University, College of the Arts, Hugh A. Glauser School of Music, Kent, OH 44242-0001. Offers conducting (MM), including choral conducting; ethnomusicology (MA); music composition (MA); music education (MM, PhD); music theory (MA); music theory-composition (PhD); performance (MM), including chamber music. *Accreditation:* NASM. *Program availability:* Part-time, 100% online. *Faculty:* 29 full-time (8 women), 24 part-time/adjunct (16 women). *Students:* 70 full-time (35 women), 160 part-time (104 women); includes 22 minority (11 Black or African American, non-Hispanic/Latino; 2 Asian, non-Hispanic/Latino; 3 Hispanic/Latino; 1 Native Hawaiian or other Pacific Islander, non-Hispanic/Latino; 5 Two or more races, non-Hispanic/Latino), 30 international. Average age 31. 91 applicants, 85% accepted, 57 enrolled. In 2018, 82 master's, 2 doctorates awarded. *Degree requirements:* For master's, comprehensive exam (for some programs), thesis (for some programs), capstone project or thesis (for MM in music education); for doctorate, comprehensive exam, thesis/dissertation. *Entrance requirements:* For master's, transcripts; minimum GPA of 3.0; 3 letters of recommendation; goal statement; resume; writing sample (for MA in ethnomusicology); portfolio of original composition (for MA in composition); audition (for MM in conducting, performance); prior degree, teaching certificate, and 1 year of teaching experience (for MM in music education); for doctorate, writing sample; 3 letters of recommendation; curriculum vitae/resume; transcripts; minimum GPA of 3.0; prior degree in music education, teaching license, statement of purpose, video of teaching sample, 3 years of teaching, and interview (for music education); goal statement and 3 original compositions (for music theory-composition). Additional exam requirements/recommendations for international students: Required—TOEFL (minimum score 525 paper-based, 71 iBT), Michigan English Language Assessment Battery (minimum score 74), IELTS (minimum score 6.0) or PTE (minimum score 50). *Application deadline:* For fall admission, 2/9 priority date for domestic and international students. Applications are processed on a rolling basis. Application fee: $45 ($70 for international students). Electronic applications accepted. *Expenses:* Tuition, state resident: full-time $11,766; part-time $536 per credit. Tuition, nonresident: full-time $21,952; part-time $999 per credit. *International tuition:* $21,952 full-time. Tuition and fees vary according to course load. *Financial support:* Teaching assistantships with full and partial tuition reimbursements, scholarships/grants, and unspecified assistantships available. Financial award application deadline: 4/1. *Unit head:* Jane Dressler, Interim Director and Voice-Professor, 330-672-9239, E-mail: jdressle@kent.edu. *Application contact:* Michael Chunn, Graduate Coordinator/Trumpet Professor, 330-672-9234, Fax: 330-672-7837, E-mail: mchunn@kent.edu.
Website: http://www.kent.edu/music/

Kutztown University of Pennsylvania, College of Visual and Performing Arts, Program in Music Education, Kutztown, PA 19530-0730. Offers M Ed. *Program availability:* Part-time, evening/weekend, 100% online, blended/hybrid learning. *Faculty:* 5 full-time (2 women), 2 part-time/adjunct (1 woman). *Students:* 4 full-time (2 women), 17 part-time (11 women); includes 1 minority (Two or more races, non-Hispanic/Latino). Average age 33. 9 applicants, 100% accepted, 5 enrolled. *Entrance requirements:* For master's, official transcripts from previous colleges or universities (non-KU), resume, and digital recording of teaching or two reference letters. Additional exam requirements/recommendations for international students: Required—TOEFL (minimum score 550 paper-based or 79 iBT) or IELTS (minimum score 6.5) or PTE (minimum score 53). *Application deadline:* For fall admission, 8/1 for domestic and international students; for spring admission, 12/1 for domestic and international students. Application fee: $35. Electronic applications accepted. *Expenses:* Tuition, state resident: part-time $516 per credit. Tuition, nonresident: part-time $774 per credit. *Required fees:* $119 per credit. One-time fee: $50 part-time. Tuition and fees vary according to degree level. *Financial support:* Career-related internships or fieldwork, Federal Work-Study, unspecified assistantships, and graduate assistantship includes stipend and full tuition waiver available. Financial award application deadline: 3/1; financial award applicants required to submit FAFSA. *Unit head:* Dr. Jeremy Justeson, Department Chair, 610-683-4551, Fax: 610-683-1506, E-mail: justeson@kutztown.edu. *Application contact:* Fran Melchionne, Department Secretary, 610-683-4550, E-mail: melchionne@kutztown.edu.
Website: https://www.kutztown.edu/academics/graduate-programs/music-education.htm

Lake Forest College, Master of Arts in Teaching Program, Lake Forest, IL 60045. Offers elementary education (MAT); K-12 French (MAT); K-12 music (MAT); K-12 Spanish (MAT); K-12 visual art (MAT); secondary biology (MAT); secondary chemistry (MAT); secondary English (MAT); secondary history (MAT); secondary mathematics (MAT). *Degree requirements:* For master's, comprehensive exam, portfolio. *Entrance requirements:* For master's, GRE.

Lebanon Valley College, Program in Music Education, Annville, PA 17003-1400. Offers MME. *Accreditation:* NASM. *Program availability:* Part-time-only, evening/weekend. *Degree requirements:* For master's, thesis or project. *Entrance requirements:* For master's, teaching certification, 2 years of teaching experience, bachelor's degree, current resume, professional statement. Additional exam requirements/recommendations for international students: Required—TOEFL (minimum score 80 iBT). Electronic applications accepted. *Expenses:* Contact institution. *Faculty research:* Modern band, popular music pedagogy.

Lee University, Program in Music, Cleveland, TN 37320-3450. Offers conducting (MM); music education (MM); music performance (MM); religious studies (MCM); sacred music (MCM). *Accreditation:* NASM. *Program availability:* Part-time, online only, 100% online.

Faculty: 24 full-time (6 women), 6 part-time/adjunct (4 women). *Students:* 18 full-time (8 women), 6 part-time (4 women); includes 3 minority (all Asian, non-Hispanic/Latino), 5 international. Average age 26. 15 applicants, 93% accepted, 10 enrolled. In 2018, 12 master's awarded. *Degree requirements:* For master's, variable foreign language requirement, comprehensive exam, thesis, internship. *Entrance requirements:* For master's, placement exercises in music theory, music history, diction, and piano proficiency, audition, resume, interview, minimum GPA of 2.75, official transcripts, essay, 3 recommendations, immunization forms. Additional exam requirements/recommendations for international students: Required—TOEFL (minimum score 61 iBT). *Application deadline:* For fall admission, 4/1 priority date for domestic and international students; for spring admission, 10/1 priority date for domestic and international students. Applications are processed on a rolling basis. Application fee: $25. Electronic applications accepted. *Financial support:* In 2018–19, 26 students received support. Career-related internships or fieldwork, Federal Work-Study, institutionally sponsored loans, scholarships/grants, and unspecified assistantships available. Financial award application deadline: 3/1; financial award applicants required to submit FAFSA. *Unit head:* Dr. Brad J. Moffett, Director, 423-614-8240, Fax: 423-614-8245, E-mail: gradmusic@leeuniversity.edu. *Application contact:* Jeffery McGirt, Director of Graduate Enrollment, 423-614-8691, Fax: 423-614-8317, E-mail: jmcgirt@leeuniversity.edu.
Website: http://www.leeuniversity.edu/academics/graduate/music

Lehman College of the City University of New York, School of Arts and Humanities, Department of Music, Multimedia, Theatre and Dance, Bronx, NY 10468-1589. Offers applied music and music teaching (MAT). *Accreditation:* NCATE. *Program availability:* Part-time, evening/weekend. *Entrance requirements:* For master's, audition. *Faculty research:* Music, music education.

Liberty University, School of Music, Lynchburg, VA 24515. Offers ethnomusicology (MA); music and worship (MA); music education (MA); worship studies (MA, DWS), including ethnomusicology (MA), leadership (MA), pastoral counseling (MA), worship techniques (MA). *Accreditation:* NASM. *Program availability:* Part-time, online learning. *Students:* 118 full-time (48 women), 187 part-time (92 women); includes 73 minority (49 Black or African American, non-Hispanic/Latino; 6 Asian, non-Hispanic/Latino; 15 Hispanic/Latino; 3 Two or more races, non-Hispanic/Latino), 16 international. Average age 37. 429 applicants, 29% accepted, 56 enrolled. In 2018, 48 master's, 6 doctorates awarded. *Entrance requirements:* For master's, minimum GPA of 3.0; interview; letter of recommendation; statement of purpose; bachelor's/master's degree in music, worship, or related field, or 5 years of experience. Additional exam requirements/recommendations for international students: Required—TOEFL (minimum score 600 paper-based; 100 iBT). *Application deadline:* Applications are processed on a rolling basis. Application fee: $50. Electronic applications accepted. *Expenses:* Tuition: Full-time $10,851; part-time $562 per credit hour. *Financial support:* In 2018–19, 619 students received support. Federal Work-Study available. Financial award applicants required to submit FAFSA. *Unit head:* Dr. Vernon Whaley, Dean, 434-592-3463, E-mail: vwhaley@liberty.edu. *Application contact:* Jay Bridge, Director of Admissions, 800-424-9595, Fax: 800-628-7977, E-mail: gradadmissions@liberty.edu.
Website: https://www.liberty.edu/music/

Long Island University–LIU Post, College of Education, Information and Technology, Brookville, NY 11548-1300. Offers adolescence education (MS); adolescence education 7-12 (MS); archives and records management (AC); art education (MS); childhood education (MS); childhood education/literacy B-6 (MS); childhood education/special education (MS); clinical mental health counseling (MS, AC); early childhood education (MS); early childhood education/childhood education (MS); educational leadership (AC); educational technology (MS); information studies (PhD); interdisciplinary educational studies (Ed D); middle childhood education (MS); music education (MS); public library administration (AC); school counselor (MS); special education (MS Ed); speech-language pathology (MA); students with disabilities, 7-12 generalist (AC); TESOL (MA). *Accreditation:* ASHA; TEAC. *Program availability:* Part-time, 100% online, blended/hybrid learning. Terminal master's awarded for partial completion of doctoral program. *Degree requirements:* For master's, variable foreign language requirement, comprehensive exam (for some programs), thesis optional; for doctorate, comprehensive exam, thesis/dissertation. *Entrance requirements:* For master's and AC, GRE (for some programs). Additional exam requirements/recommendations for international students: Required—TOEFL (minimum score 550 paper-based, 75 iBT), IELTS, or PTE. Electronic applications accepted. *Faculty research:* Sleep; use of technology to develop executive function by students with disabilities; early childhood literacy development through play; social justice through education; using a structured protocol to discuss Bad News.

Louisiana State University and Agricultural & Mechanical College, Graduate School, College of Music and Dramatic Arts, School of Music, Baton Rouge, LA 70803. Offers music (MM, DMA, PhD); music education (PhD). *Accreditation:* NASM.

Loyola University Maryland, Graduate Programs, School of Education, Program in Kodaly Music Education, Baltimore, MD 21210-2699. Offers M Ed. *Entrance requirements:* For master's, essay, letter of recommendation, resume, transcript. Additional exam requirements/recommendations for international students: Required—TOEFL (minimum score 80 iBT), IELTS (minimum score 7). Electronic applications accepted. *Expenses:* Contact institution.

Manhattanville College, School of Education, Program in Music Education, Purchase, NY 10577-2132. Offers music education (all grades) (MAT). *Program availability:* Part-time, evening/weekend. *Faculty:* 1 full-time (0 women), 3 part-time/adjunct (0 women). *Students:* 4 full-time (3 women), 1 part-time (0 women). Average age 23. 3 applicants, 33% accepted, 1 enrolled. In 2018, 4 master's awarded. *Degree requirements:* For master's, comprehensive exam (for some programs), thesis (for some programs), student teaching, research seminars, portfolios, internships, writing assessment; for Advanced Certificate, comprehensive exam (for some programs). *Entrance requirements:* For master's, one-hour written music theory exam (including analysis, figured bass realization, and general fundamentals); one-hour written music history and literature exam (covering significant musical developments, compositions, and key figures from Renaissance-present); for programs leading to certification, candidates must submit scores from GRE or MAT, audition (performance of 3 compositions from different periods of music on major performing medium, test of sight-reading skills at piano, test of sight-singing skills, and test of skills involving the harmonization of a melody at piano); minimum GPA of 3.0, transcripts, 2 letters of recommendation, interview, essay, proof of immunization. Additional exam requirements/recommendations for international students: Required—TOEFL (minimum score 600 paper-based; 110 iBT); Recommended—IELTS (minimum score 8). *Application deadline:* Applications are processed on a rolling basis. Application fee: $75. Electronic applications accepted. *Expenses:* 935 per credit. *Financial support:* Teaching assistantships, career-related internships or fieldwork, Federal Work-Study, institutionally sponsored loans, scholarships/grants, and unspecified assistantships available. Financial award application deadline: 3/15; financial award applicants required to submit FAFSA. *Unit head:* Dr. Shelley Wepner, Dean, 914-323-3153, Fax: 914-323-5493, E-mail: Shelley.Wepner@mville.edu. *Application contact:* Alissa Wilson, Director, SOE Graduate Enrollment Management, 914-323-3150, Fax: 914-694-1732, E-mail: edschool@mville.edu.
Website: http://www.mville.edu/programs/music-education-graduate

Marywood University, Academic Affairs, Insalaco College of Creative and Performing Arts, Music, Theatre and Dance Department, Scranton, PA 18509-1598. Offers music education (MA). *Accreditation:* NASM. *Program availability:* Part-time. Electronic applications accepted.

McGill University, Faculty of Graduate and Postdoctoral Studies, Schulich School of Music, Montréal, QC H3A 2T5, Canada. Offers composition (M Mus, D Mus, PhD); music education (MA, PhD); music technology (MA, PhD); musicology (MA, PhD); performance (M Mus); performance studies (D Mus); sound recording (M Mus, PhD); theory (MA, PhD).

McKendree University, Graduate Programs, Programs in Education, Lebanon, IL 62254-1299. Offers curriculum design and instruction (Ed D, Ed S); educational administration and leadership (MA Ed); educational studies (MA Ed); higher education administrative services (MA Ed); music education (MA Ed); reading (MA Ed); special education (MA Ed); teacher leadership (MA Ed); teaching certification (MA Ed). *Accreditation:* NCATE. *Program availability:* Part-time, evening/weekend, online learning. *Entrance requirements:* For master's, official transcripts from all institutions previously attended, minimum GPA of 3.0, resume, references; for doctorate, GRE (within the past 5 years), master's degree in education and Ed S, or the equivalent, from regionally-accredited institution; official transcripts from all institutions previously attended; curriculum vitae/resume; essay/personal statement; two years of teaching/professional experience; for Ed S, GRE (within the past 5 years), master's degree in education from regionally-accredited institution of higher education; official transcripts from all institutions previously attended; curriculum vitae/resume; essay/personal statement; two years of teaching/professional experience. Additional exam requirements/recommendations for international students: Required—TOEFL. Electronic applications accepted.

McNeese State University, Doré School of Graduate Studies, Burton College of Education, Department of Education Professions, Program in Multiple Levels Grades K-12, Lake Charles, LA 70609. Offers multiple levels grades K-12 (Postbaccalaureate Certificate), including art, health and physical education, music - instrumental, music - vocal. *Entrance requirements:* For degree, PRAXIS, 2 letters of recommendation, autobiography.

Miami University, College of Creative Arts, Department of Music, Oxford, OH 45056. Offers music education (MM); music performance (MM). *Accreditation:* NASM. *Faculty:* 26 full-time (10 women). *Students:* 20 full-time (13 women); includes 5 minority (4 Asian, non-Hispanic/Latino; 1 Hispanic/Latino), 6 international. Average age 24. In 2018, 8 master's awarded. *Unit head:* Dr. Chris Tanner, Interim Chair, 513-529-3082, E-mail: tannerc@miamioh.edu. *Application contact:* Dr. Brenda Mitchell, Associate Professor of Music/Director of Graduate Studies, 513-529-1228, E-mail: mitchebs@miamioh.edu.
Website: http://www.miamioh.edu/music

Michigan State University, The Graduate School, College of Music, East Lansing, MI 48824. Offers collaborative piano (M Mus); jazz studies (M Mus); music (PhD); music composition (M Mus, DMA); music conducting (M Mus, DMA); music education (M Mus); music performance (M Mus, DMA); music theory (M Mus); music therapy (M Mus); musicology (MA); piano pedagogy (M Mus). *Accreditation:* NASM. *Entrance requirements:* Additional exam requirements/recommendations for international students: Required—TOEFL. Electronic applications accepted.

Minnesota State University Mankato, College of Graduate Studies and Research, College of Arts and Humanities, Department of Music, Mankato, MN 56001. Offers choral conducting (MM); music education (MAT); piano performance (MM); wind band conducting (MM). *Accreditation:* NASM. *Degree requirements:* For master's, comprehensive exam, thesis or alternative. *Entrance requirements:* For master's, minimum GPA of 3.0 during previous 2 years, audition or test. Additional exam requirements/recommendations for international students: Required—TOEFL. Electronic applications accepted.

Mississippi College, Graduate School, College of Arts and Sciences, School of Christian Studies and the Arts, Department of Music, Clinton, MS 39058. Offers applied music performance (MM); conducting (MM); music education (MM); music performance: organ (MM); vocal pedagogy (MM). *Accreditation:* NASM. *Program availability:* Part-time, evening/weekend. *Degree requirements:* For master's, comprehensive exam, recital. *Entrance requirements:* For master's, GRE, minimum GPA of 2.5. Additional exam requirements/recommendations for international students: Recommended—TOEFL, IELTS. Electronic applications accepted.

Montclair State University, The Graduate School, College of Education and Human Services, MAT Program in Teaching, Montclair, NJ 07043-1624. Offers art (MAT); biology (MAT); chemistry (MAT); earth science (MAT); English (MAT); French (MAT); health and physical education (MAT); health education (MAT); mathematics (MAT); music (MAT); physical education (MAT); physical science (MAT); social studies (MAT); Spanish (MAT); teacher of English as a second language (MAT). *Degree requirements:* For master's, comprehensive exam, thesis or alternative. *Entrance requirements:* For master's, interview, 2 letters of recommendation. Additional exam requirements/recommendations for international students: Required—TOEFL (minimum score 83 iBT), IELTS (minimum score 6.5). Electronic applications accepted.

Montclair State University, The Graduate School, College of the Arts, John J. Cali School of Music, Program in Music, Montclair, NJ 07043-1624. Offers music education (MA); music therapy (MA); performance (MA); theory/composition (MA). *Program availability:* Part-time, evening/weekend. *Degree requirements:* For master's, thesis. *Entrance requirements:* For master's, GRE General Test, 2 letters of recommendation, essay. Additional exam requirements/recommendations for international students: Required—TOEFL (minimum score 83 iBT), IELTS (minimum score 6.5). Electronic applications accepted.

Morehead State University, Graduate School, Caudill College of Arts, Humanities and Social Sciences, Department of Music, Theatre and Dance, Morehead, KY 40351. Offers music education (MM); music performance (MM). *Accreditation:* NASM. *Program availability:* Part-time, evening/weekend. *Degree requirements:* For master's, comprehensive exam, oral and written exams. *Entrance requirements:* For master's, music entrance exam, BA in music with minimum GPA of 3.0, 2.5 overall; audition. Additional exam requirements/recommendations for international students: Required—TOEFL (minimum score 550 paper-based). Electronic applications accepted. *Faculty research:* Musical instrument digital interface (MIDI) applications, tonal concepts of euphonium and baritone horn, digital synthesis, computer-assisted instruction in music, musical composition.

Murray State University, College of Humanities and Fine Arts, Department of Music, Murray, KY 42071. Offers music education (MME). *Accreditation:* NASM. *Program availability:* Part-time. *Entrance requirements:* For master's, GRE or GMAT, minimum university GPA of 2.75. Additional exam requirements/recommendations for international students: Required—TOEFL (minimum score 527 paper-based; 71 iBT). Electronic applications accepted.

Nazareth College of Rochester, Graduate Studies, Department of Music, Program in Music Education, Rochester, NY 14618. Offers MS Ed. *Accreditation:* NASM; TEAC. *Program availability:* Part-time, evening/weekend. *Entrance requirements:* For master's, audition, minimum GPA of 3.0. Additional exam requirements/recommendations for international students: Required—TOEFL or IELTS.

Nebraska Christian College of Hope International University, Graduate Programs, Papillion, NE 68046. Offers biblical studies (M Div); business as mission/social entrepreneurship (MBA); children, youth, and family (M Div); church planting (M Div); counseling psychology (MS); educational administration (MA); elementary education (M Ed); general management (MBA); gifted and talented education (M Ed); intercultural studies (M Div); international development (MBA); marketing management (MBA); ministry (MA); ministry and leadership (M Div); music education (M Ed); non-profit management (MBA); pastoral care (M Div); secondary education (M Ed); spiritual formation (M Div); worship ministry (M Div).

New Jersey City University, William J. Maxwell College of Arts and Sciences, Department of Music, Dance and Theatre, Jersey City, NJ 07305-1597. Offers music education (MA); performance (MM). *Accreditation:* NASM. *Program availability:* Part-time, evening/weekend. *Degree requirements:* For master's, thesis optional, recital. *Entrance requirements:* Additional exam requirements/recommendations for international students: Required—TOEFL (minimum score 79 iBT).

New Mexico State University, College of Arts and Sciences, Department of Music, Las Cruces, NM 88003-8001. Offers conducting (MM); music education (MM); performance (MM). *Accreditation:* NASM. *Program availability:* Part-time-only, online learning. *Faculty:* 15 full-time (5 women), 3 part-time/adjunct (0 women). *Students:* 10 full-time (8 women), 12 part-time (3 women); includes 14 minority (1 Black or African American, non-Hispanic/Latino; 13 Hispanic/Latino), 4 international. Average age 33. 12 applicants, 58% accepted, 5 enrolled. In 2018, 10 master's awarded. *Degree requirements:* For master's, comprehensive exam, thesis (for some programs), recital. *Entrance requirements:* For master's, 2 initial review courses, audition, bachelor's degree or equivalent from an accredited institution. Additional exam requirements/recommendations for international students: Required—TOEFL (minimum score 550 paper-based; 79 iBT), IELTS (minimum score 6.5). *Application deadline:* For fall admission, 7/1 priority date for domestic students; for spring admission, 11/1 for domestic students; for summer admission, 3/1 for domestic students. Applications are processed on a rolling basis. Application fee: $40 ($50 for international students). Electronic applications accepted. *Expenses: Tuition, area resident:* Full-time $4216.70; part-time $252.70 per credit hour. Tuition, state resident: full-time $4216.70; part-time $252.70 per credit hour. Tuition, nonresident: full-time $12,769; part-time $881.10 per credit hour. *International tuition:* $12,769.30 full-time. *Required fees:* $878.40; $48.80 per credit hour. Full-time tuition and fees vary according to course load and reciprocity agreements. *Financial support:* In 2018–19, 13 students received support, including 1 fellowship (averaging $792 per year), 7 teaching assistantships (averaging $14,541 per year); career-related internships or fieldwork, Federal Work-Study, scholarships/grants, traineeships, health care benefits, and unspecified assistantships also available. Support available to part-time students. Financial award application deadline: 3/1. *Faculty research:* Music education, contemporary wind band literature, performance, music history, composition. *Total annual research expenditures:* $3,284. *Unit head:* Dr. Lon W. Chaffin, Department Head, 575-646-2421, Fax: 575-646-8199, E-mail: lchaffin@nmsu.edu. *Application contact:* Dr. James Shearer, Coordinator of Graduate Studies, 575-646-2601, Fax: 575-646-8199, E-mail: jshearer@nmsu.edu.
Website: http://music.nmsu.edu

New York University, Steinhardt School of Culture, Education, and Human Development, Department of Music and Performing Arts Professions, Program in Music Education, New York, NY 10012. Offers MA, Ed D, PhD. *Accreditation:* TEAC. *Program availability:* Part-time. *Entrance requirements:* For master's, audition; for doctorate, GRE General Test, interview. Additional exam requirements/recommendations for international students: Required—TOEFL (minimum score 100 iBT). Electronic applications accepted. *Faculty research:* Music education philosophy; community music education; integrated curriculum; multiple intelligences; technology in arts education; cognition, emotion, and music.

New York University, Steinhardt School of Culture, Education, and Human Development, Department of Music and Performing Arts Professions, Program in Music Performance and Composition, New York, NY 10012. Offers instrumental performance (MM), including instrumental performance, jazz instrumental performance; music performance and composition (PhD), including music performance and composition; music theory and composition (MM), including composition for film and multimedia, composition for music theater, computer music composition, music theory and composition, songwriting; piano performance (MM), including collaborative piano, solo piano; vocal pedagogy (Advanced Certificate); vocal performance (MM), including classical voice, musical theatre performance. *Program availability:* Part-time. *Entrance requirements:* For master's, audition; for doctorate, GRE General Test, audition, interview. Additional exam requirements/recommendations for international students: Required—TOEFL (minimum score 100 iBT). Electronic applications accepted. *Faculty research:* Aesthetics, performance analysis, twentieth century music, music methodologies for arts criticism and analysis.

Norfolk State University, School of Graduate Studies, School of Liberal Arts, Department of Music, Norfolk, VA 23504. Offers music (MM); music education (MM); performance (MM); theory and composition (MM). *Accreditation:* NASM. *Program availability:* Part-time. *Degree requirements:* For master's, thesis or alternative. *Entrance requirements:* For master's, minimum GPA of 2.7, letters of recommendation. Additional exam requirements/recommendations for international students: Required—TOEFL.

North Dakota State University, College of Graduate and Interdisciplinary Studies, College of Arts, Humanities and Social Sciences, Challey School of Music, Fargo, ND 58102. Offers conducting (MM, DMA); music education (MM); performance (MM, DMA). *Accreditation:* NASM. *Degree requirements:* For master's, 2 foreign languages, comprehensive exam, thesis or alternative, recitals; for doctorate, 2 foreign languages, comprehensive exam, thesis/dissertation or alternative, recitals. *Entrance requirements:* For master's and doctorate, music history, music theory, performance audition. Additional exam requirements/recommendations for international students: Required—TOEFL (minimum score 525 paper-based; 71 iBT). Electronic applications accepted. *Faculty research:* Performance, conducting.

Northeastern Illinois University, College of Graduate Studies and Research, College of Arts and Sciences, Program in Music, Chicago, IL 60625. Offers music (MA), including applied music pedagogy. *Accreditation:* NASM. *Program availability:* Part-time, evening/weekend. *Degree requirements:* For master's, comprehensive exam, thesis optional. *Entrance requirements:* For master's, departmental exam, audition, minimum GPA of 2.75. Additional exam requirements/recommendations for international students: Required—TOEFL (minimum score 550 paper-based; 79 iBT). Electronic applications accepted. *Faculty research:* World music, computers as applied instruments, vocal pedagogy, vocal interpretation, jazz repertory.

Northern State University, MME Program in Music Education, Aberdeen, SD 57401-7198. Offers MME. *Accreditation:* NASM. *Program availability:* Part-time, online learning. *Entrance requirements:* For master's, minimum GPA of 2.75. Additional exam requirements/recommendations for international students: Required—TOEFL (minimum score 550 paper-based; 78 iBT), IELTS (minimum score 6). Electronic applications accepted.

Northwestern University, Henry and Leigh Bienen School of Music, Department of Music Performance, Evanston, IL 60208. Offers brass performance (MM, DMA); conducting (MM, DMA); jazz studies (MM); percussion performance (MM, DMA); performance (MM); piano pedagogy (MME); piano performance (MM, DMA); piano performance and collaborative arts (MM, DMA); piano performance and pedagogy (MM, DMA); string performance (MM, DMA); voice and opera performance (MM, DMA); woodwind performance (MM, DMA). *Accreditation:* NASM. *Degree requirements:* For master's, recital; for doctorate, comprehensive exam, thesis/dissertation, 3 recitals. *Entrance requirements:* For master's, audition, prescreening auditions where required; for doctorate, audition, preliminary tapes. Additional exam requirements/recommendations for international students: Required—TOEFL (minimum score 80 iBT).

Northwestern University, Henry and Leigh Bienen School of Music, Department of Music Studies, Evanston, IL 60208. Offers composition (DMA); music education (MME, PhD); music theory and cognition (PhD); musicology (MM, PhD); theory (MM). PhD admissions and degree offered through The Graduate School. *Accreditation:* NASM. *Degree requirements:* For doctorate, comprehensive exam, thesis/dissertation. *Entrance requirements:* For master's, portfolio or research papers; for doctorate, GRE General Test (for PhD), portfolio, research papers. Additional exam requirements/recommendations for international students: Required—TOEFL (minimum score 600 paper-based; 80 iBT). *Faculty research:* Music cognition, cognitive learning, aesthetic education, computer music, technology in education.

Oakland University, School of Music, Theatre and Dance, Rochester, MI 48309-4401. Offers music (MM); music education (PhD). *Accreditation:* NASM. *Entrance requirements:* For master's, minimum GPA of 3.0. Additional exam requirements/recommendations for international students: Required—TOEFL (minimum score 550 paper-based). Electronic applications accepted. *Expenses:* Contact institution.

Ohio University, Graduate College, College of Fine Arts, School of Music, Athens, OH 45701-2979. Offers accompanying (MM); composition (MM); conducting (MM); history/literature (MM); music education (MM); music therapy (MM); performance (MM, Certificate); performance/pedagogy (MM); theory (MM). *Accreditation:* NASM. *Program availability:* Part-time, evening/weekend, online learning. *Degree requirements:* For master's, comprehensive exam, thesis (for some programs), oral exam. *Entrance requirements:* For master's, audition, interview, portfolio, recordings (varies by program). Additional exam requirements/recommendations for international students: Required—TOEFL (minimum score 550 paper-based; 80 iBT) or IELTS (minimum score 6.5). Electronic applications accepted.

Oklahoma State University, College of Arts and Sciences, Michael and Anne Greenwood School of Music, Stillwater, OK 74078. Offers pedagogy and performance (MM). *Accreditation:* NASM. *Faculty:* 33 full-time (14 women), 9 part-time/adjunct (2 women). *Students:* 21 full-time (9 women), 6 part-time (2 women); includes 2 minority (1 Black or African American, non-Hispanic/Latino; 1 Asian, non-Hispanic/Latino), 4 international. Average age 26. 37 applicants, 49% accepted, 13 enrolled. In 2018, 7 master's awarded. *Entrance requirements:* For master's, GRE, audition. Additional exam requirements/recommendations for international students: Required—TOEFL (minimum score 550 paper-based; 79 iBT). *Application deadline:* For fall admission, 3/1 priority date for international students; for spring admission, 8/1 priority date for international students. Applications are processed on a rolling basis. Application fee: $40 ($75 for international students). Electronic applications accepted. *Expenses: Tuition, area resident:* Full-time $4148. Tuition, state resident: full-time $4148. Tuition, nonresident: full-time $10,517. *International tuition:* $10,517 full-time. *Required fees:* $4394; $2929 per credit hour. Tuition and fees vary according to course load and program. *Financial support:* Teaching assistantships, career-related internships or fieldwork, Federal Work-Study, scholarships/grants, health care benefits, tuition waivers (partial), and unspecified assistantships available. Support available to part-time students. Financial award application deadline: 3/1; financial award applicants required to submit FAFSA. *Faculty research:* Discovery and presentation of music literature of other countries, transportation of ancient music literature to modern notation. *Unit head:* Dr. Howard Potter, Department Head, 405-744-8997, Fax: 405-744-9324, E-mail: osumusic@okstate.edu. *Application contact:* Dr. Sheryl Tucker, Dean, 405-744-6368, Fax: 405-744-0355, E-mail: gradi@okstate.edu.
Website: http://music.okstate.edu/

Old Dominion University, College of Arts and Letters, Master of Music Education Program, Norfolk, VA 23529. Offers applied studies or conducting (MME); pedagogy (MME); research (MME). *Accreditation:* NASM. *Program availability:* Part-time, evening/weekend. *Degree requirements:* For master's, comprehensive exam, thesis (for some programs), performance recital (for applied studies or conducting), ePortfolio (for pedagogy). *Entrance requirements:* For master's, music theory exam, diagnostic examination, GRE or MAT, baccalaureate degree in music education, music theory, music history, or applied music; audition (for applied music areas). Additional exam requirements/recommendations for international students: Required—TOEFL. Electronic applications accepted. *Expenses:* Contact institution. *Faculty research:* Performance, composition, conducting, music education research.

Oregon State University, College of Education, Program in Teaching, Corvallis, OR 97331. Offers clinically based elementary education (MAT); elementary education (MAT); language arts (MAT); mathematics (MAT); music education (MAT); science (MAT); social studies (MAT). *Program availability:* Part-time, blended/hybrid learning. *Entrance requirements:* For master's, CBEST. Additional exam requirements/recommendations for international students: Required—TOEFL (minimum score 575 paper-based). *Expenses:* Contact institution.

Penn State University Park, Graduate School, College of Arts and Architecture, School of Music, University Park, PA 16802. Offers composition-theory (M Mus); conducting (M Mus); music (MA); music education (MME, PhD, Certificate); pedagogy and performance (M Mus); performance (M Mus); piano performance (DMA). *Accreditation:* NASM.

Piedmont College, School of Education, Demorest, GA 30535. Offers art education (MAT); curriculum and instruction (Ed D, Ed S); early childhood education (MA, MAT); middle grades education (MA, MAT); music education (MAT); secondary education (MA, MAT); special education (MA, MAT). *Program availability:* Part-time, evening/weekend. *Students:* 496 full-time (416 women), 650 part-time (560 women); includes 185 minority (137 Black or African American, non-Hispanic/Latino; 2 American Indian or Alaska Native, non-Hispanic/Latino; 13 Asian, non-Hispanic/Latino; 31 Hispanic/Latino; 1 Native Hawaiian or other Pacific Islander, non-Hispanic/Latino; 1 Two or more races, non-Hispanic/Latino). Average age 37. 483 applicants, 89% accepted, 372 enrolled. In 2018, 275 master's, 10 doctorates, 229 other advanced degrees awarded. *Degree requirements:* For master's, thesis, field experience in the classroom teaching; for doctorate, thesis/dissertation. *Entrance requirements:* For master's, GRE General Test, MAT; for Ed S, minimum graduate GPA of 3.5, valid teaching certificate. Additional

exam requirements/recommendations for international students: Required—TOEFL (minimum score 550 paper-based). *Application deadline:* For fall admission, 7/15 for domestic students; for spring admission, 12/1 for domestic students. Applications are processed on a rolling basis. Electronic applications accepted. *Expenses: Tuition:* Full-time $9738; part-time $541 per credit. *Required fees:* $200 per semester. *Financial support:* Career-related internships or fieldwork, Federal Work-Study, and unspecified assistantships available. Support available to part-time students. Financial award applicants required to submit FAFSA. *Unit head:* Dr. R.D. Nordgren, Dean, 706-778-3000 Ext. 1201, Fax: 706-776-9608, E-mail: rdnordgren@piedmont.edu. *Application contact:* Kathleen Carter, Director of Graduate Enrollment Management, 706-778-8500 Ext. 1181, Fax: 706-778-0150, E-mail: kanderson@piedmont.edu.

Pittsburg State University, Graduate School, College of Arts and Sciences, Department of Music, Pittsburg, KS 66762. Offers conducting (MM), including choral, instrumental - orchestral, instrumental - wind, organ, piano, voice; education (MM), including instrumental, vocal; performance (MM), including harpsichord, percussion, strings, winds. *Accreditation:* NASM. *Degree requirements:* For master's, thesis or alternative. *Entrance requirements:* Additional exam requirements/recommendations for international students: Required—TOEFL (minimum score 520 paper-based; 68 iBT), IELTS (minimum score 6), PTE (minimum score 47). Electronic applications accepted. *Expenses:* Contact institution.

Plymouth State University, College of Graduate Studies, Graduate Studies in Education, Program in Music Education, Plymouth, NH 03264-1595. Offers M Ed. *Program availability:* Evening/weekend.

Queens College of the City University of New York, Arts and Humanities Division, Aaron Copland School of Music, Queens, NY 11367. Offers classical performance (MM, Advanced Diploma); jazz studies (MM); music (MA); music education (MS Ed, Advanced Certificate). *Program availability:* Part-time. *Faculty:* 25 full-time (7 women), 74 part-time/adjunct (28 women). *Students:* 21 full-time (6 women), 153 part-time (75 women); includes 60 minority (8 Black or African American, non-Hispanic/Latino; 1 American Indian or Alaska Native, non-Hispanic/Latino; 22 Asian, non-Hispanic/Latino; 22 Hispanic/Latino; 7 Two or more races, non-Hispanic/Latino), 33 international. Average age 30. 72 applicants, 63% accepted, 19 enrolled. In 2018, 50 master's, 5 other advanced degrees awarded. *Degree requirements:* For master's, comprehensive exam (for some programs), thesis (for some programs), Graduation Recital for MM Performance Classical Programs. *Entrance requirements:* For master's, For Master of Music (Classical), all applicants must pass the Theory Quiz, Audition, bachelor's degree in music, minimum GPA of 3.0; for other advanced degree, For all classical music performance certificates, all applicants are required to audition. Additional exam requirements/recommendations for international students: Required—TOEFL (minimum score 550 paper-based; 79 iBT), IELTS (minimum score 6). *Application deadline:* For fall admission, 4/1 for domestic students; for spring admission, 11/1 for domestic students. Applications are processed on a rolling basis. Application fee: $125. Electronic applications accepted. *Financial support:* In 2018–19, 20 students received support. Career-related internships or fieldwork, Federal Work-Study, institutionally sponsored loans, and scholarships/grants available. Financial award application deadline: 4/1; financial award applicants required to submit FAFSA. *Faculty research:* For the Master of Arts program: Music of J. S. Bach (Anson-Cartwright), 19th-century opera (Henson, Rothstein), 17th-century opera (Wilbourne), Life and music of Maurice Ravel (Orenstein), Rhythm and meter (Rothstein). *Unit head:* Michael Lipsey, Chair, 718-997-3800, E-mail: Michael.Lipsey@qc.cuny.edu. *Application contact:* Elizabeth D'Amico-Ramirez, Assistant Director of Graduate Admissions, 718-997-5203, E-mail: elizabeth.damicoramirez@qc.cuny.edu.
Website: http://qcpages.qc.cuny.edu/music/

Queens College of the City University of New York, Division of Education, Department of Secondary Education and Youth Services, Queens, NY 11367-1597. Offers adolescent biology (MAT); art (MS Ed); biology (MS Ed, AC); chemistry (MS Ed, AC); earth sciences (MS Ed, AC); English (MS Ed, AC); French (MS Ed); Italian (MS Ed, AC); literacy education (MS Ed); mathematics (MS Ed, AC); music (MS Ed, AC); physics (MS Ed, AC); social studies (MS Ed, AC); Spanish (MS Ed, AC). *Program availability:* Part-time, evening/weekend. *Faculty:* 22 full-time (14 women), 35 part-time/adjunct (24 women). *Students:* 33 full-time (19 women), 358 part-time (228 women); includes 182 minority (15 Black or African American, non-Hispanic/Latino; 62 Asian, non-Hispanic/Latino; 91 Hispanic/Latino; 4 Native Hawaiian or other Pacific Islander, non-Hispanic/Latino; 10 Two or more races, non-Hispanic/Latino), 13 international. Average age 29. 216 applicants, 74% accepted, 109 enrolled. In 2018, 108 master's, 35 other advanced degrees awarded. *Degree requirements:* For master's, research project. *Entrance requirements:* For master's, GRE, minimum GPA of 3.0. Additional exam requirements/recommendations for international students: Required—TOEFL, IELTS. *Application deadline:* For fall admission, 4/1 for domestic students; for spring admission, 11/1 for domestic students. Applications are processed on a rolling basis. Application fee: $125. Electronic applications accepted. *Financial support:* Career-related internships or fieldwork available. Financial award application deadline: 4/1; financial award applicants required to submit FAFSA. *Faculty research:* Self regulated learning, teacher learning, assessment and teaching, language diversity, teaching and learning history. *Unit head:* Dr. Eleanor Armour-Thomas, Chairperson, 718-997-5150, E-mail: eleanor.armour-thomas@qc.cuny.edu. *Application contact:* Elizabeth D'Amico-Ramirez, Assistant Director of Graduate Admissions, 718-997-5203, E-mail: elizabeth.damicoramirez@qc.cuny.edu.

Rhode Island College, School of Graduate Studies, Faculty of Arts and Sciences, Department of Music, Theatre, and Dance, Providence, RI 02908-1991. Offers music education (MAT, MM Ed). *Program availability:* Part-time, evening/weekend. *Faculty:* 6 full-time (1 woman), 3 part-time/adjunct (2 women). *Students:* 3 part-time (2 women). Average age 25. In 2018, 1 master's awarded. *Degree requirements:* For master's, comprehensive exam, thesis, final project (MFA). *Entrance requirements:* For master's, GRE General Test or MAT; exams in music education, theory, history and literature, audition, 3 letters of recommendation, evidence of musicianship, interview. Additional exam requirements/recommendations for international students: Required—TOEFL (minimum score 550 paper-based; 80 iBT). *Application deadline:* For fall admission, 3/1 for domestic students; for spring admission, 11/1 for domestic students. Applications are processed on a rolling basis. Application fee: $50. Electronic applications accepted. *Expenses: Tuition, area resident:* Part-time $407 per credit. Tuition, nonresident: part-time $792 per credit. *Required fees:* $29 per credit. $100 per semester. *Financial support:* Teaching assistantships, Federal Work-Study, scholarships/grants, health care benefits, and unspecified assistantships available. Support available to part-time students. Financial award application deadline: 5/15; financial award applicants required to submit FAFSA. *Unit head:* Prof. Ian Greitzer, Chair, 401-456-9883. *Application contact:* Prof. Ian Greitzer, Chair, 401-456-9883.
Website: http://www.ric.edu/mtd/Pages/Master-of-Arts-in-Teaching-Music.aspx

Rider University, Westminster Choir College, Program in Music Education, Lawrenceville, NJ 08648-3001. Offers MME. *Program availability:* Part-time, 100% online. *Students:* 1 full-time (0 women), 2 part-time (both women); includes 2 minority (1 Asian, non-Hispanic/Latino; 1 Hispanic/Latino). Average age 37. 4 applicants, 50% accepted. In 2018, 6 master's awarded. *Entrance requirements:* For master's, audition, interview, repertoire list, 2 letters of reference, resume, personal statement, official transcripts. Additional exam requirements/recommendations for international students: Required—TOEFL (minimum score 540 paper-based; 79 iBT). *Application deadline:* Applications are processed on a rolling basis. Application fee: $50. Electronic applications accepted. *Expenses: Tuition:* Full-time $850; part-time $850 per credit hour. *Required fees:* $50; $50 per course. Tuition and fees vary according to program. *Financial support:* Application deadline: 3/1; applicants required to submit FAFSA. *Unit head:* Frank Abrahams, Dean, 609-921-7100 Ext. 8229, E-mail: abrahams@rider.edu. *Application contact:* Kimberly Apadula, Assistant Director, WCC Admissions, 609-921-7100, Fax: 609-921-2538, E-mail: wccadmission@rider.edu.

Rider University, Westminster Choir College, Programs in Music, Lawrenceville, NJ 08648-3001. Offers American and public musicology (MM); choral conducting (MM); composition (MM); organ performance (MM); piano accompanying and coaching (MM); piano pedagogy and performance (MM); piano performance (MM); sacred music (MM); voice pedagogy and performance (MM, MVP). *Program availability:* Part-time. *Students:* 58 full-time (35 women), 11 part-time (8 women); includes 8 minority (1 Black or African American, non-Hispanic/Latino; 2 Asian, non-Hispanic/Latino; 1 Hispanic/Latino; 4 Two or more races, non-Hispanic/Latino), 9 international. Average age 28. 164 applicants, 65% accepted, 46 enrolled. In 2018, 54 master's awarded. *Degree requirements:* For master's, variable foreign language requirement, departmental qualifying exam. *Entrance requirements:* For master's, audition, interview, repertoire list, 2 letters of reference, resume, Applications must be received at least three weeks in advance of the requested audition date, official transcripts, personal statement. Additional exam requirements/recommendations for international students: Required—TOEFL (minimum score 540 paper-based; 79 iBT). *Application deadline:* Applications are processed on a rolling basis. Application fee: $50. Electronic applications accepted. *Expenses: Tuition:* Full-time $850; part-time $850 per credit hour. *Required fees:* $50; $50 per course. Tuition and fees vary according to program. *Financial support:* Application deadline: 3/1; applicants required to submit FAFSA. *Unit head:* Marshall Onofrio, Dean, 609-921-7100 Ext. 8206, Fax: 609-683-8856, E-mail: monofrio@rider.edu. *Application contact:* Kimberly Apadula, Assistant Director, WCC Admissions, 609-921-7100, Fax: 609-921-2538, E-mail: wccadmission@rider.edu.

Rutgers University–New Brunswick, Mason Gross School of the Arts, Music Department, New Brunswick, NJ 08901. Offers collaborative piano (MM, DMA); conducting: choral (MM, DMA); conducting: instrumental (MM, DMA); conducting: orchestral (MM, DMA); jazz studies (MM); music (DMA, AD); music education (MM, DMA); music performance (MM). *Accreditation:* NASM. *Degree requirements:* For doctorate, one foreign language. *Entrance requirements:* For master's and doctorate, audition. Additional exam requirements/recommendations for international students: Required—TOEFL (minimum score 550 paper-based), IELTS (minimum score 7). Electronic applications accepted. *Faculty research:* Performance, twentieth-century music, jazz, music education.

Saint Xavier University, Graduate Studies, School of Education, Chicago, IL 60655-3105. Offers counseling (MA); curriculum and instruction (MA); early childhood education (MA); educational administration (MA); elementary education (MA); individualized studies (MA), including educational technology, English as a second language (ESL), ISTEM (integrative science, technology, engineering, and math), science education; music education (MA); reading (MA); secondary education (MA); Spanish education (MA); special education (MA); teaching and leadership (MA). *Accreditation:* NCATE. *Program availability:* Part-time, evening/weekend. *Degree requirements:* For master's, thesis or project. *Entrance requirements:* For master's, minimum GPA of 3.0. *Expenses:* Contact institution.

Samford University, School of the Arts, Birmingham, AL 35229. Offers church music (MM), including conducting, performance, thesis; instrumental performance (MM); piano performance and pedagogy (MM); vocal performance (MM); vocal/choral or instrumental music (MME). *Accreditation:* NASM. *Program availability:* Part-time. *Faculty:* 10 full-time (4 women), 4 part-time/adjunct (2 women). *Students:* 12 full-time (8 women), 4 part-time (3 women); includes 2 minority (both Black or African American, non-Hispanic/Latino), 2 international. Average age 26. 9 applicants, 89% accepted, 3 enrolled. In 2018, 4 master's awarded. *Degree requirements:* For master's, comprehensive exam, thesis/dissertation varies; recital. *Entrance requirements:* For master's, placement examinations, 3 letters of recommendation, audition. Additional exam requirements/recommendations for international students: Required—TOEFL (minimum score 550 paper-based; 79 iBT). *Application deadline:* For fall admission, 1/17 for domestic and international students; for spring admission, 10/18 for domestic and international students. Applications are processed on a rolling basis. Application fee: $35. Electronic applications accepted. *Expenses: Tuition:* Full-time $17,255; part-time $837 per credit. *Required fees:* $610; $305 per term. Tuition and fees vary according to course load, degree level, program and student level. *Financial support:* In 2018–19, 13 students received support. Scholarships/grants available. Financial award application deadline: 2/15; financial award applicants required to submit FAFSA. *Unit head:* Dr. Joseph Hopkin, Dean of the School of the Arts/Professor, 205-726-2778, E-mail: jhopkins@samford.edu. *Application contact:* Dr. Mark Lackey, Assistant Professor, 205-726-4623, Fax: 205-726-2615, E-mail: mlckey@samford.edu.
Website: http://www.samford.edu/arts/

San Diego State University, Graduate and Research Affairs, College of Professional Studies and Fine Arts, School of Music and Dance, San Diego, CA 92182. Offers composition (acoustic and electronic) (MM); conducting (MM); ethnomusicology (MA); jazz studies (MM); musicology (MA); performance (MM); piano pedagogy (MA); theory (MA). *Degree requirements:* For master's, comprehensive exam (for some programs), thesis (for some programs). *Entrance requirements:* For master's, GRE General Test, bachelor's degree in related field, 2 letters of reference. Additional exam requirements/recommendations for international students: Required—TOEFL. Electronic applications accepted.

San Francisco Conservatory of Music, Graduate Division, San Francisco, CA 94102. Offers brass (MM), including bass trombone, horn, tenor trombone, trumpet, tuba; chamber music (MM, Artist Certificate), including cello (MM, Artist Certificate, Artist Diploma), piano (MM, Artist Certificate, Artist Diploma), preformed string quartet, viola (MM, Artist Certificate, Artist Diploma), violin (MM, Artist Certificate, Artist Diploma); composition (MM); conducting (MM); guitar (MM); harp (MM); historical performance (MM), including harpsichord (MM, MM); percussion (MM), including percussion; piano (MM, MM, Artist Diploma), including collaborative piano (MM), harpsichord (MM, MM), organ (MM), piano (MM, Artist Certificate, Artist Diploma); strings (MM, Artist Diploma), including cello (MM, Artist Certificate, Artist Diploma), double bass (MM), viola (MM, Artist Certificate, Artist Diploma), violin (MM, Artist Certificate, Artist Diploma); voice (MM, Postgraduate Diploma); woodwinds (MM), including bassoon, clarinet, flute, oboe. *Degree requirements:* For master's and other advanced degree, variable foreign language requirement, 1-2 recitals, 1-3 juried performances. *Entrance requirements:* For master's and other advanced degree, recommendations, transcripts, audition. Additional exam requirements/recommendations for international students: Required—TOEFL (minimum score 500 paper-based; 80 iBT). Electronic applications accepted. *Expenses:* Contact institution.

San Francisco State University, Division of Graduate Studies, College of Liberal and Creative Arts, School of Music, San Francisco, CA 94132-1722. Offers chamber music (MM); classical performance (MM); composition (MA); conducting (MM); music education (MA); music history (MA). *Accreditation:* NASM. *Unit head:* Dr. Cyrus Ginwala, Director, 415-338-7613, E-mail: cginwala@sfsu.edu. *Application contact:* Dr. Benjamin Sabey, Graduate Coordinator, E-mail: sabey@sfsu.edu.
Website: http://music.sfsu.edu/

Southern Illinois University Edwardsville, Graduate School, College of Arts and Sciences, Department of Music, Program in Music, Edwardsville, IL 62026. Offers music education (MM); music performance (MM). *Accreditation:* NASM. *Program availability:* Part-time. *Degree requirements:* For master's, one foreign language, thesis (for some programs), recital. *Entrance requirements:* Additional exam requirements/recommendations for international students: Required—TOEFL (minimum score 550 paper-based; 79 iBT), IELTS (minimum score 6.5). Electronic applications accepted.

Southern Illinois University Edwardsville, Graduate School, College of Arts and Sciences, Department of Music, Program in Piano Pedagogy, Edwardsville, IL 62026. Offers Postbaccalaureate Certificate. *Program availability:* Part-time. *Entrance requirements:* Additional exam requirements/recommendations for international students: Required—TOEFL (minimum score 550 paper-based; 79 iBT), IELTS (minimum score 6.5). Electronic applications accepted.

Southern Illinois University Edwardsville, Graduate School, College of Arts and Sciences, Department of Music, Program in Vocal Pedagogy, Edwardsville, IL 62026. Offers Postbaccalaureate Certificate. *Program availability:* Part-time. *Entrance requirements:* Additional exam requirements/recommendations for international students: Required—TOEFL (minimum score 550 paper-based; 79 iBT), IELTS (minimum score 6.5). Electronic applications accepted.

Southern Methodist University, Meadows School of the Arts, Division of Music, Dallas, TX 75275. Offers composition (MM); conducting (MM), including choral, instrumental; music education (MM); musicology (MM); performance (MM), including organ, piano, piano performance and pedagogy, voice; theory pedagogy (MM). *Accreditation:* NASM. *Program availability:* Part-time. *Degree requirements:* For master's, variable foreign language requirement, comprehensive exam, project, recital, or thesis. *Entrance requirements:* For master's, placement exams in music history and theory, audition; bachelor's degree in music or equivalent; minimum GPA of 3.0; research paper in history/theory/education. Additional exam requirements/recommendations for international students: Required—TOEFL (minimum score 550 paper-based; 80 iBT). Electronic applications accepted. *Faculty research:* Music perception and cognition, computer-based instruction, music medicine and therapy, theoretical and historical analysis-medieval to contemporary.

Southwestern Oklahoma State University, College of Arts and Sciences, Department of Music, Weatherford, OK 73096-3098. Offers music education (MM); music performance (MM); music therapy (MM). *Accreditation:* NASM. *Program availability:* Part-time. *Degree requirements:* For master's, comprehensive exam, recital (music performance). *Entrance requirements:* For master's, minimum GPA of 2.5. Additional exam requirements/recommendations for international students: Required—TOEFL (minimum score 550 paper-based), IELTS (minimum score 6.5).

State University of New York at Fredonia, School of Music, Fredonia, NY 14063-1136. Offers music education (MM); music performance (MM); music theory/composition (MM); music therapy (MM). *Accreditation:* NASM. *Program availability:* Part-time. *Faculty:* 40 full-time (17 women), 15 part-time/adjunct (9 women). *Students:* 44 full-time (28 women), 18 part-time (13 women); includes 5 minority (2 Black or African American, non-Hispanic/Latino; 1 Asian, non-Hispanic/Latino; 1 Hispanic/Latino; 1 Two or more races, non-Hispanic/Latino), 16 international. Average age 25. 63 applicants, 59% accepted, 24 enrolled. In 2018, 87 master's awarded. *Degree requirements:* For master's, comprehensive exam (for some programs), thesis or final project/recital. *Entrance requirements:* For master's, audition. Additional exam requirements/recommendations for international students: Required—TOEFL (minimum score 79 iBT), IELTS (minimum score 6.5). *Application deadline:* For fall admission, 4/1 priority date for domestic and international students; for spring admission, 11/1 priority date for domestic students, 11/1 for international students. Applications are processed on a rolling basis. Application fee: $75. Electronic applications accepted. *Expenses:* Tuition, state resident: full-time $6870; part-time $462 per credit hour. Tuition, nonresident: full-time $16,650; part-time $944 per credit hour. *International tuition:* $16,650 full-time. *Required fees:* $25; $2 per credit hour. $1 per semester. *Financial support:* In 2018–19, 14 students received support. Unspecified assistantships available. Financial award application deadline: 3/15; financial award applicants required to submit FAFSA. *Faculty research:* Schenkerian analysis, early American Music, music pedagogy, music therapy, professional performance. *Unit head:* Dr. Melvin Unger, Director, School of Music, 716-673-3151, E-mail: melvin.unger@fredonia.edu. *Application contact:* Dr. Barry Kilpatrick, Admissions Coordinator, School of Music, 716-673-4635, E-mail: barry.kilpatrick@fredonia.edu.
Website: http://www.fredonia.edu/music/

State University of New York College at Potsdam, Crane School of Music, Potsdam, NY 13676. Offers music education (MM); music performance (MM). *Program availability:* Part-time. *Degree requirements:* For master's, variable foreign language requirement, thesis (for some programs). *Entrance requirements:* For master's, audition, minimum GPA of 3.0. Additional exam requirements/recommendations for international students: Required—TOEFL (minimum score 550 paper-based; 80 iBT), IELTS (minimum score 6). Electronic applications accepted.

Syracuse University, College of Visual and Performing Arts, MM Program in Voice Pedagogy, Syracuse, NY 13244. Offers MM. *Entrance requirements:* For master's, audition, three letters of recommendation, academic transcript, personal statement/essay, resume. Additional exam requirements/recommendations for international students: Required—TOEFL (minimum score 100 iBT). *Application deadline:* For fall admission, 2/1 priority date for domestic and international students. Application fee: $75. Electronic applications accepted. *Financial support:* Fellowships with full tuition reimbursements and teaching assistantships available. Financial award application deadline: 1/1; financial award applicants required to submit FAFSA. *Faculty research:* Voice pedagogy, voice science, pedagogical issues, repertoire, diction, career planning methods, voice study, performance, experience in teaching. *Unit head:* Prof. Kathleen Roland-Silverstein, Assistant Professor, Applied Music and Performance, 315-443-5898, E-mail: krolands@syr.edu. *Application contact:* Caitlin Jarvis, Graduate Recruitment Specialist, 315-443-2769, E-mail: admissg@syr.edu.
Website: http://vpa.syr.edu/academics/setnor/graduate/voice-pedagogy/

Syracuse University, School of Education, MM/MS Programs in Music Education, Syracuse, NY 13244. Offers MM, MS. *Accreditation:* NASM. *Program availability:* Part-time. *Students:* Average age 23. *Entrance requirements:* For master's, GRE, bachelor's degree in music from institution accredited by the National Association of Schools of Music (NASM). Additional exam requirements/recommendations for international students: Required—TOEFL (minimum score 100 iBT). *Application deadline:* For fall admission, 1/15 priority date for domestic and international students; for spring admission, 10/15 priority date for domestic and international students; for summer admission, 4/1 priority date for domestic and international students. Applications are processed on a rolling basis. Application fee: $75. Electronic applications accepted. *Financial support:* Fellowships with full tuition reimbursements, research assistantships, teaching assistantships, career-related internships or fieldwork, and scholarships/grants available. Financial award application deadline: 1/15. *Faculty research:* Developing optimal teaching competencies, artistry and musicianship, philosophical perspectives of music, theoretical and historical perspectives of music and music education. *Unit head:* Dr. Benjamin Dotger, Department Chair, 315-443-2685, E-mail: bdotger@syr.edu. *Application contact:* Speranza Migliore, Graduate Admissions Recruiter, 315-443-2505, E-mail: gradrcrt@syr.edu.
Website: http://soe.syr.edu/academic/teaching_and_leadership/graduate/masters/music_education/default.aspx

Tarleton State University, College of Graduate Studies, College of Liberal and Fine Arts, Department of Fine Arts, Stephenville, TX 76402. Offers music education (MM). *Accreditation:* NASM. *Program availability:* Part-time, evening/weekend. *Faculty:* 2 full-time (1 woman), 1 (woman) part-time/adjunct. *Students:* 29 part-time (16 women). Average age 33. 5 applicants, 100% accepted, 5 enrolled. In 2018, 5 master's awarded. *Degree requirements:* For master's, comprehensive exam, thesis optional. *Entrance requirements:* For master's, GRE, minimum GPA of 3.0. Additional exam requirements/recommendations for international students: Required—TOEFL (minimum score 520 paper-based; 69 iBT); Recommended—IELTS (minimum score 6), TSE (minimum score 50). *Application deadline:* For fall admission, 8/15 priority date for domestic students; for spring admission, 1/7 for domestic students. Applications are processed on a rolling basis. Application fee: $50 ($130 for international students). Electronic applications accepted. *Expenses:* Contact institution. *Financial support:* Research assistantships, institutionally sponsored loans, and scholarships/grants available. Financial award application deadline: 5/1; financial award applicants required to submit FAFSA. *Unit head:* Dr. Vicky Johnson, Department Head, 254-968-9245, E-mail: vjohnson@tarleton.edu. *Application contact:* Information Contact, 254-968-9104, Fax: 254-968-9670, E-mail: gradoffice@tarleton.edu.

Teachers College, Columbia University, Department of Arts and Humanities, New York, NY 10027. Offers applied linguistics (MA, Ed D); art and art education (Ed M, MA, Ed D, Ed DCT); arts administration (MA); bilingual and bicultural education (MA); global competence (Certificate); history and education (Ed D, PhD); music and music education (Ed DCT); philosophy and education (MA, Ed D, PhD); social studies education (Ed M, PhD); teaching English to speakers of other languages (Ed M); teaching of English and English education (Ed M, MA, Ed D, PhD), including English education (Ed M, Ed D, PhD), teaching of English (MA); teaching of social studies (MA); TESOL (MA, Ed D). *Program availability:* Part-time, evening/weekend. *Students:* 267 full-time (216 women), 569 part-time (400 women); includes 235 minority (62 Black or African American, non-Hispanic/Latino; 2 American Indian or Alaska Native, non-Hispanic/Latino; 88 Asian, non-Hispanic/Latino; 69 Hispanic/Latino; 14 Two or more races, non-Hispanic/Latino), 229 international. Average age 31. 1,075 applicants, 56% accepted, 342 enrolled. Terminal master's awarded for partial completion of doctoral program. *Financial support:* Fellowships, research assistantships, teaching assistantships, career-related internships or fieldwork, Federal Work-Study, institutionally sponsored loans, tuition waivers (full and partial), and unspecified assistantships available. Support available to part-time students. *Unit head:* Prof. ZhaoHong Han, Department Chair, E-mail: zhh2@tc.columbia.edu. *Application contact:* Kelly Sutton-Skinner, Director of Admissions & New Student Enrollment, E-mail: kms2237@tc.columbia.edu.

Temple University, Center for the Performing and Cinematic Arts, Boyer College of Music and Dance, Department of Music, Philadelphia, PA 19122-6096. Offers choral conducting (MM); collaborative piano/chamber music (MM); collaborative piano/opera coaching (MM); composition (MM, PhD); instrumental conducting (MM); music education (MM, PhD); music history (MM); music performance (MM, DMA), including instrumental studies (MM), keyboard (DMA), keyboard studies (MM), voice (DMA), voice and opera (MM); music studies (PhD); music theory (MM, PhD); music therapy (MMT, PhD); musicology (MM, PhD); opera (MM); piano pedagogy (MM); string pedagogy (MM). *Accreditation:* NASM. *Program availability:* Part-time, evening/weekend, online learning. *Faculty:* 44 full-time (21 women), 43 part-time/adjunct (16 women). *Students:* 194 full-time (106 women), 45 part-time (27 women); includes 30 minority (12 Black or African American, non-Hispanic/Latino; 3 Asian, non-Hispanic/Latino; 7 Hispanic/Latino; 8 Two or more races, non-Hispanic/Latino), 76 international. 412 applicants, 44% accepted, 79 enrolled. In 2018, 68 master's, 11 doctorates awarded. Terminal master's awarded for partial completion of doctoral program. *Degree requirements:* For doctorate, thesis/dissertation (for some programs). *Entrance requirements:* Additional exam requirements/recommendations for international students: Required—TOEFL, IELTS, PTE, one of three is required. *Application deadline:* For fall admission, 1/1 for international students; for spring admission, 11/1 for international students. Applications are processed on a rolling basis. Application fee: $60. Electronic applications accepted. *Expenses:* Contact institution. *Financial support:* Fellowships with tuition reimbursements, research assistantships with tuition reimbursements, teaching assistantships with tuition reimbursements, career-related internships or fieldwork, Federal Work-Study, scholarships/grants, health care benefits, and unspecified assistantships available. Financial award application deadline: 3/1; financial award applicants required to submit FAFSA. *Unit head:* Dr. Robert Stroker, Dean, 215-204-8598, Fax: 215-204-4957, E-mail: rstroker@temple.edu. *Application contact:* James Short, Assistant Dean, Undergraduate and Graduate Admissions, 215-204-8301, Fax: 215-204-8598, E-mail: james.short@temple.edu.
Website: http://www.temple.edu/boyer/academicprograms/

Tennessee Technological University, College of Graduate Studies, College of Education, Department of Curriculum and Instruction, Program in Music, Cookeville, TN 38505. Offers MA. *Accreditation:* NASM. *Program availability:* Part-time, evening/weekend. *Students:* 2 full-time (1 woman), 3 part-time (1 woman); includes 1 minority (Two or more races, non-Hispanic/Latino). 1 applicant, 100% accepted, 1 enrolled. *Degree requirements:* For master's, comprehensive exam, thesis or alternative. *Entrance requirements:* For master's, MAT or GRE. Additional exam requirements/recommendations for international students: Required—TOEFL (minimum score 527 paper-based; 71 iBT), IELTS (minimum score 5.5), PTE (minimum score 48), or TOEIC (Test of English as an International Communication). *Application deadline:* For fall admission, 8/1 for domestic students, 5/1 for international students; for spring admission, 12/1 for domestic students, 10/1 for international students; for summer admission, 5/1 for domestic students, 2/1 for international students. Applications are processed on a rolling basis. Application fee: $35 ($40 for international students). Electronic applications accepted. *Financial support:* Career-related internships or fieldwork available. Financial award application deadline: 4/1; financial award applicants required to submit FAFSA. *Unit head:* Dr. Jeremy Wendt, Chairperson, 931-372-3181, Fax: 931-372-6270, E-mail: jwendt@tntech.edu. *Application contact:* Shelia K. Kendrick, Coordinator of Graduate Studies, 931-372-3808, Fax: 931-372-3497, E-mail: skendrick@tntech.edu.

Texas A&M University–Commerce, College of Humanities, Social Sciences and Arts, Commerce, TX 75429. Offers applied criminology (MS); applied linguistics (MA, MS); art

(MA, MFA); computational linguistics (Graduate Certificate); creative writing (Graduate Certificate); criminal justice management (Graduate Certificate); criminal justice studies (Graduate Certificate); English (MA, MS, PhD); film studies (Graduate Certificate); history (MA, MS); history of Christianity (Graduate Certificate); Holocaust studies (Graduate Certificate); homeland security (Graduate Certificate); music (MM); music performance (MM); political science (MA, MS); public history (Graduate Certificate); sociology (MS); Spanish (MA); studies in children's and adolescent literature and culture (Graduate Certificate); teaching English to speakers of other languages (Graduate Certificate); theater (MA, MS); world history (Graduate Certificate). *Program availability:* Part-time. *Faculty:* 50 full-time (26 women), 11 part-time/adjunct (2 women). *Students:* 125 full-time (83 women), 393 part-time (278 women); includes 197 minority (75 Black or African American, non-Hispanic/Latino; 2 American Indian or Alaska Native, non-Hispanic/Latino; 13 Asian, non-Hispanic/Latino; 92 Hispanic/Latino; 1 Native Hawaiian or other Pacific Islander, non-Hispanic/Latino; 14 Two or more races, non-Hispanic/Latino), 16 international. Average age 37. 261 applicants, 46% accepted, 106 enrolled. In 2018, 124 master's, 8 doctorates awarded. *Degree requirements:* For master's, one foreign language, comprehensive exam, thesis (for some programs); for doctorate, one foreign language, comprehensive exam, thesis/dissertation, departmental qualifying exam. *Entrance requirements:* For master's, GRE General Test, official transcripts, letters of recommendation, resume, statement of goals; for doctorate, GRE General Test, official transcripts, letters of recommendation, statement of goals, writing samples, writing sessions, resumes. Additional exam requirements/recommendations for international students: Required—TOEFL (minimum score 550 paper-based; 79 iBT), IELTS (minimum score 6), PTE (minimum score 53). *Application deadline:* For fall admission, 6/1 priority date for international students; for spring admission, 10/15 priority date for international students; for summer admission, 3/15 priority date for international students. Applications are processed on a rolling basis. Application fee: $50 ($75 for international students). Electronic applications accepted. *Expenses: Tuition, area resident:* Full-time $3630. Tuition, state resident: full-time $3630. Tuition, nonresident: full-time $11,100. *International tuition:* $11,100 full-time. *Required fees:* $2794. Tuition and fees vary according to course load, degree level and program. *Financial support:* In 2018–19, 39 students received support, including 18 research assistantships with partial tuition reimbursements available (averaging $3,231 per year), 136 teaching assistantships with partial tuition reimbursements available (averaging $4,053 per year); Federal Work-Study, institutionally sponsored loans, scholarships/grants, health care benefits, and unspecified assistantships also available. Financial award application deadline: 5/1; financial award applicants required to submit FAFSA. *Unit head:* Dr. William F. Kuracina, Interim Dean, 903-886-5166, Fax: 903-886-5774, E-mail: william.kuracina@tamuc.edu. *Application contact:* Vicky Turner, Doctoral Degree and Special Programs Coordinator, 903-886-5167, E-mail: vicky.turner@tamuc.edu.
Website: http://www.tamuc.edu/academics/colleges/humanitiesSocialSciencesArts/

Texas A&M University–Kingsville, College of Graduate Studies, College of Arts and Sciences, Department of Music, Program in Music Education, Kingsville, TX 78363. Offers elementary music (MM); instrumental (MM); vocal (MM).

Texas Christian University, College of Fine Arts, School of Music, Doctoral Programs in Music, Fort Worth, TX 76129. Offers composition (DMA), including music history; conducting (DMA), including music history, music theory; performance (DMA), including music history, music theory, piano pedagogy; piano pedagogy (DMA). *Accreditation:* NASM. *Faculty:* 43 full-time (10 women), 15 part-time/adjunct (7 women). *Students:* 9 full-time (3 women), 6 part-time (1 woman); includes 1 minority (Two or more races, non-Hispanic/Latino), 5 international. Average age 33. 44 applicants, 25% accepted, 2 enrolled. In 2018, 3 doctorates awarded. *Degree requirements:* For doctorate, comprehensive exam, thesis/dissertation. *Entrance requirements:* For doctorate, GRE General Test, Music Theory and Music History Diagnostic Exams. Additional exam requirements/recommendations for international students: Required—TOEFL (minimum score 100 iBT). *Application deadline:* For spring admission, 12/1 for domestic and international students. Application fee: $80. Electronic applications accepted. *Financial support:* In 2018–19, 15 students received support, including 10 research assistantships with full tuition reimbursements available (averaging $10,000 per year); career-related internships or fieldwork, institutionally sponsored loans, scholarships/grants, tuition waivers (full and partial), and unspecified assistantships also available. Financial award application deadline: 12/1; financial award applicants required to submit CSS PROFILE or FAFSA. *Faculty research:* Music in media, time usage in secondary instrumental classroom, vocal health and pedagogy, musician health and wellness, piano pedagogy. *Unit head:* Dr. Kristen A. Queen, Interim Director, 817-257-6606, Fax: 817-257-5818, E-mail: k.queen@tcu.edu. *Application contact:* Donna Smolik, TCU College of Fine Arts Graduate Office, 817-257-7603, Fax: 817-257-5672, E-mail: cfagradinfo@tcu.edu.
Website: http://www.music.tcu.edu

Texas Christian University, College of Fine Arts, School of Music, Master's Programs in Music, Fort Worth, TX 76129-0002. Offers conducting (M Mus); music education (MM Ed). *Faculty:* 43 full-time (10 women), 15 part-time/adjunct (7 women). *Students:* 39 full-time (16 women), 1 part-time (0 women); includes 6 minority (4 Hispanic/Latino; 2 Two or more races, non-Hispanic/Latino), 11 international. Average age 24. 62 applicants, 47% accepted, 20 enrolled. In 2018, 21 master's awarded. *Degree requirements:* For master's, comprehensive exam. *Entrance requirements:* For master's, GRE General Test for some programs, Music Theory Diagnostic Exam. Additional exam requirements/recommendations for international students: Required—TOEFL (minimum score 80 iBT). *Application deadline:* For fall admission, 2/15 for domestic and international students. Application fee: $80. Electronic applications accepted. *Financial support:* In 2018–19, 60 students received support, including 60 research assistantships with full tuition reimbursements available (averaging $6,000 per year); career-related internships or fieldwork, institutionally sponsored loans, scholarships/grants, tuition waivers (full and partial), and unspecified assistantships also available. Financial award application deadline: 2/15; financial award applicants required to submit CSS PROFILE or FAFSA. *Faculty research:* Music in media, time usage in secondary instrumental music classes, vocal health and pedagogy, musician health and wellness, piano pedagogy. *Unit head:* Dr. Kristen A. Queen, Interim Director, 817-257-6606, Fax: 817-257-5818, E-mail: music@tcu.edu. *Application contact:* Donna Smolik, TCU College of Fine Arts Graduate Office, 817-257-7603, Fax: 817-257-5672, E-mail: cfagradinfo@tcu.edu.
Website: http://www.music.tcu.edu

Texas State University, The Graduate College, College of Fine Arts and Communication, Program in Music Education, San Marcos, TX 78666. Offers MM. *Accreditation:* NASM. *Program availability:* Part-time. *Faculty:* 5 full-time (3 women), 1 part-time/adjunct (0 women). *Students:* 1 full-time (0 women), 4 part-time (2 women); includes 1 minority (Hispanic/Latino). Average age 31. 5 applicants, 40% accepted, 1 enrolled. In 2018, 6 master's awarded. *Degree requirements:* For master's, comprehensive exam. *Entrance requirements:* For master's, baccalaureate degree in music from regionally-accredited institution with minimum GPA of 2.75 in last 60 hours of undergraduate course work, certificate to teach public school music, statement of purpose, resume, 3 letters of reference, music portfolio. Additional exam requirements/recommendations for international students: Required—TOEFL (minimum score 550 paper-based; 78 iBT), IELTS (minimum score 6). *Application deadline:* For fall admission, 1/15 priority date for domestic and international students; for spring admission, 10/15 for domestic students, 10/1 for international students; for summer admission, 4/15 for domestic students, 3/15 for international students. Applications are processed on a rolling basis. Application fee: $55 ($90 for international students). Electronic applications accepted. *Expenses:* Tuition, state resident: full-time $8102; part-time $4051 per semester. Tuition, nonresident: full-time $18,229; part-time $9115 per semester. *International tuition:* $18,229 full-time. *Required fees:* $2116; $120 per credit hour. Tuition and fees vary according to course load. *Financial support:* In 2018–19, 1 student received support, including 1 teaching assistantship (averaging $6,501 per year); career-related internships or fieldwork, Federal Work-Study, institutionally sponsored loans, scholarships/grants, and unspecified assistantships also available. Support available to part-time students. Financial award application deadline: 1/15; financial award applicants required to submit FAFSA. *Unit head:* Dr. Ludim Pedroza, Graduate Advisor, 512-245-3405, Fax: 512-245-8181, E-mail: lp27@txstate.edu. *Application contact:* Dr. Andrea Golato, Dean of Graduate School, 512-245-2581, Fax: 512-245-8365, E-mail: gradcollege@txstate.edu.
Website: http://www.finearts.txstate.edu/music/

Texas Tech University, Graduate School, J.T. and Margaret Talkington College of Visual and Performing Arts, School of Music, Lubbock, TX 79409-2033. Offers music (MM, DMA); music education (MM Ed). *Accreditation:* NASM. *Program availability:* Part-time. *Faculty:* 56 full-time (24 women), 7 part-time/adjunct (4 women). *Students:* 110 full-time (42 women), 18 part-time (7 women); includes 20 minority (4 Black or African American, non-Hispanic/Latino; 14 Hispanic/Latino; 2 Two or more races, non-Hispanic/Latino), 48 international. Average age 29. 106 applicants, 59% accepted, 40 enrolled. In 2018, 26 master's, 28 doctorates awarded. *Degree requirements:* For master's, thesis or alternative; for doctorate, comprehensive exam (for some programs), thesis/dissertation. *Entrance requirements:* For master's, Performance audition or portfolio presentation, BM or BME or BA; for doctorate, BM, MM or comparable experience and accomplishment. Additional exam requirements/recommendations for international students: Required—TOEFL (minimum score 550 paper-based; 79 iBT). *Application deadline:* For fall admission, 6/1 priority date for domestic students, 1/15 priority date for international students; for spring admission, 9/1 priority date for domestic students, 6/15 priority date for international students. Applications are processed on a rolling basis. Application fee: $65. Electronic applications accepted. *Expenses:* Contact institution. *Financial support:* In 2018–19, 154 students received support, including 139 fellowships (averaging $3,246 per year), 98 teaching assistantships (averaging $10,669 per year); research assistantships, career-related internships or fieldwork, Federal Work-Study, institutionally sponsored loans, scholarships/grants, health care benefits, tuition waivers (partial), and unspecified assistantships also available. Financial award application deadline: 4/15; financial award applicants required to submit FAFSA. *Faculty research:* Professional Performance Practice -Historically informed and contemporary; World music & Vernacular Music Center; 18th and 19th century European Music, Vocal health and Peak Performance; Resonance and Neuroscience Wellness (RENEW). *Total annual research expenditures:* $8,528. *Unit head:* Prof. Kim Walker, Director, 806-834-7420, E-mail: kim.walker@ttu.edu. *Application contact:* Emily Gifford, Graduate Student Coordinator, 806-834-5076, Fax: 806-742-2294, E-mail: emily.gifford@ttu.edu.
Website: www.depts.ttu.edu/music

Texas Woman's University, Graduate School, College of Arts and Sciences, School of the Arts, Department of Music and Theatre, Denton, TX 76204. Offers drama (MA); music (MA), including music education, music therapy, pedagogy, performance. *Accreditation:* NASM. *Program availability:* Part-time. *Faculty:* 16 full-time (7 women), 11 part-time/adjunct (7 women). *Students:* 57 full-time (43 women), 40 part-time (29 women); includes 31 minority (7 Black or African American, non-Hispanic/Latino; 3 Asian, non-Hispanic/Latino; 19 Hispanic/Latino; 2 Two or more races, non-Hispanic/Latino), 8 international. Average age 30. 40 applicants, 88% accepted, 25 enrolled. In 2018, 21 master's awarded. *Degree requirements:* For master's, comprehensive exam, thesis (for some programs), project, recital, professional paper or thesis (for music education). *Entrance requirements:* For master's, music history/theory placement exam (for music only), audition and/or design portfolio, interview, resume, writing sample (for drama only), letter of intent, minimum undergraduate GPA of 3.0. Additional exam requirements/recommendations for international students: Required—TOEFL (minimum score 550 paper-based; 79 iBT); Recommended—IELTS (minimum score 6.5), TSE (minimum score 53). *Application deadline:* For fall admission, 7/31 for domestic students; for spring admission, 11/30 for domestic students; for summer admission, 4/30 for domestic students. Applications are processed on a rolling basis. Application fee: $50 ($75 for international students). Electronic applications accepted. *Expenses:* Music: $1,577 in-state resident per 3 hour course, $2,843 out-of-state resident per 3 hour course. *Financial support:* In 2018–19, 40 students received support, including 10 teaching assistantships (averaging $5,986 per year); career-related internships or fieldwork, Federal Work-Study, institutionally sponsored loans, scholarships/grants, traineeships, health care benefits, and unspecified assistantships also available. Support available to part-time students. Financial award application deadline: 3/1; financial award applicants required to submit FAFSA. *Faculty research:* Musical development in early childhood, script analysis, pedagogical development of the singing voice, music therapy, music and neuroscience technology. *Unit head:* Dr. Pamela Youngblood, Chair of Music and Theatre, 940-898-2500, Fax: 940-898-2494, E-mail: music@twu.edu. *Application contact:* Korie Hawkins, Associate Director of Admissions, Graduate Recruitment, 940-898-3188, Fax: 940-898-3081, E-mail: admissions@twu.edu.

Towson University, College of Fine Arts and Communication, Program in Music Education, Towson, MD 21252-0001. Offers MS. *Accreditation:* NASM; NCATE. *Program availability:* Part-time, evening/weekend. *Degree requirements:* For master's, thesis optional. *Entrance requirements:* For master's, placement examination in music history and music theory, bachelor's degree in music education or certification as public school music teacher, minimum GPA of 3.0. Electronic applications accepted. *Expenses: Tuition, area resident:* Full-time $9196; part-time $418 per unit. Tuition, state resident: full-time $9196; part-time $418 per unit. Tuition, nonresident: full-time $19,030; part-time $865 per unit. *International tuition:* $19,030 full-time. *Required fees:* $3102; $141 per year. $423 per term. Tuition and fees vary according to campus/location and program.

Union College, Graduate Programs, Department of Education, Barbourville, KY 40906-1499. Offers elementary education (MA); health and physical education (MA); middle grades (MA); music education (MA); principalship (MA); reading specialist (MA); secondary education (MA); special education (MA). *Degree requirements:* For master's, thesis optional. *Entrance requirements:* For master's, GRE General Test, NTE.

Université Laval, Faculty of Music, Programs in Music, Québec, QC G1K 7P4, Canada. Offers composition (M Mus); instrumental didactics (M Mus); interpretation (M Mus); music education (M Mus, PhD); musicology (M Mus, PhD). Terminal master's awarded for partial completion of doctoral program. *Degree requirements:* For master's, thesis (for some programs); for doctorate, comprehensive exam, thesis/dissertation. *Entrance requirements:* For master's, English exam, audition, knowledge of French; for doctorate, English exam, knowledge of French, third language. Electronic applications accepted.

University at Buffalo, the State University of New York, Graduate School, Graduate School of Education, Department of Learning and Instruction, Buffalo, NY 14260. Offers biology education (Ed M, Certificate); chemistry education (Ed M, Certificate); childhood education (Ed M); childhood education with bilingual extension (Ed M); college teaching (Advanced Certificate); curriculum, instruction and the science of learning (PhD); early childhood education (Ed M); early childhood education with bilingual extension (Ed M); earth science education (Ed M, Certificate); education and technology (Ed M); education studies (Ed M); educational technology and new literacies (Certificate); educational technology and new literacies (Advanced Certificate); elementary education (Ed D); English education (Ed M, Certificate); English education studies (Ed M); English for speakers of other languages (Ed M); foreign and second language education (PhD); French education (Ed M, Certificate); German education (Ed M, Certificate); gifted education (Certificate); Latin education (Ed M, Certificate); literacy education studies (Ed M); literacy specialist (Ed M); literacy teaching and learning (Certificate); mathematics education (Ed M, Certificate); music education (Ed M, Certificate); music education studies (Ed M); music learning theory (Advanced Certificate); online education (Advanced Certificate); physics education (Ed M, Certificate); science and the public (Ed M); social studies education (Ed M, Certificate); Spanish education (Ed M, Certificate); special education (PhD); teaching English to speakers of other languages (Ed M). *Program availability:* Part-time, evening/weekend, 100% online. *Faculty:* 31 full-time (22 women), 41 part-time/adjunct (27 women). *Students:* 161 full-time (107 women), 369 part-time (260 women); includes 76 minority (26 Black or African American, non-Hispanic/Latino; 3 American Indian or Alaska Native, non-Hispanic/Latino; 30 Asian, non-Hispanic/Latino; 14 Hispanic/Latino; 3 Two or more races, non-Hispanic/Latino), 41 international. Average age 34. 368 applicants, 70% accepted, 179 enrolled. In 2018, 100 master's, 26 doctorates, 19 other advanced degrees awarded. *Degree requirements:* For master's, comprehensive exam; for doctorate, thesis/dissertation, research analysis exam, research experience. *Entrance requirements:* For master's, letters of reference; for doctorate, GRE General Test or MAT, interview, writing sample, letters of recommendation. Additional exam requirements/recommendations for international students: Required—TOEFL (minimum score 600 paper-based; 96 iBT), IELTS (minimum score 6.5), PTE (minimum score 55). *Application deadline:* For fall admission, 2/1 priority date for domestic and international students; for spring admission, 11/15 priority date for domestic students, 10/1 for international students. Applications are processed on a rolling basis. Application fee: $50. Electronic applications accepted. *Financial support:* In 2018–19, 42 fellowships (averaging $5,181 per year), 44 research assistantships with tuition reimbursements (averaging $10,908 per year) were awarded; teaching assistantships, career-related internships or fieldwork, Federal Work-Study, institutionally sponsored loans, scholarships/grants, tuition waivers (full and partial), and unspecified assistantships also available. Financial award application deadline: 2/28; financial award applicants required to submit FAFSA. *Faculty research:* Science assessment, foreign language teaching and learning, early learning, new literacies, gender and education. *Total annual research expenditures:* $413,233. *Unit head:* Dr. Julie Gorlewski, Department Chair, 716-645-2455, Fax: 716-645-3161, E-mail: jgorlews@buffalo.edu. *Application contact:* Renad Aref, Assistant Director of Admission Recruitment, 716-645-2110, Fax: 716-645-7937, E-mail: gseinfo@buffalo.edu.
Website: http://ed.buffalo.edu/teaching.html

The University of Akron, Graduate School, Buchtel College of Arts and Sciences, School of Music, Program in Music Education, Akron, OH 44325. Offers MM. *Accreditation:* NCATE. *Degree requirements:* For master's, comprehensive exam, thesis optional. *Entrance requirements:* For master's, minimum GPA of 2.75, interview, three letters of recommendation. Additional exam requirements/recommendations for international students: Required—TOEFL (minimum score 79 iBT), IELTS (minimum score 6.5). Electronic applications accepted.

The University of Alabama, Graduate School, College of Arts and Sciences, School of Music, Tuscaloosa, AL 35487. Offers arranging (MM); choral conducting (MM, DMA); church music (MM); composition (MM, DMA); music education (MA, PhD); musicology (MM); performance (MM, DMA); theory (MM); wind conducting (MM, DMA). *Accreditation:* NASM. *Degree requirements:* For master's, variable foreign language requirement, comprehensive exam (for some programs), thesis (for some programs), recital; for doctorate, variable foreign language requirement, comprehensive exam, thesis/dissertation, oral exam; recital (for some majors). *Entrance requirements:* For master's and doctorate, audition exam, audition in the major instrument or area. Additional exam requirements/recommendations for international students: Required—PTE (minimum score 59), TOEFL (minimum score 550 paper-based, 79 iBT) or IELTS (minimum score 6.5). Electronic applications accepted. *Faculty research:* Performance practice, musicology, theory, composition.

The University of Alabama, Graduate School, College of Education, Department of Music Education, Tuscaloosa, AL 35487-0366. Offers choral music education (MA); instrumental music education (MA); music education (Ed D, PhD, Ed S). *Accreditation:* NASM. *Program availability:* Part-time. *Degree requirements:* For master's, comprehensive exam, thesis optional; for doctorate, comprehensive exam, thesis/dissertation, oral exam (for PhD). *Entrance requirements:* For master's, GRE or MAT, video of teaching, letters of recommendation; for doctorate, GRE or MAT, interview, writing sample, video of teaching, letters of recommendation; for Ed S, GRE or MAT. Additional exam requirements/recommendations for international students: Required—TOEFL (minimum score 550 paper-based). Electronic applications accepted. *Faculty research:* Elementary music, music for students with special needs, choral music.

The University of Arizona, College of Fine Arts, School of Music, Program in Music, Tucson, AZ 85721. Offers composition (MM); ethnomusicology (MM); music education (MM, PhD); music theory (MM, PhD); musicology (MM); performance (MM), including conducting - choral, conducting - instrumental, instrumental, keyboard, piano accompanying, piano and dance accompanying, vocal. *Entrance requirements:* Additional exam requirements/recommendations for international students: Required—TOEFL (minimum score 550 paper-based; 79 iBT). Electronic applications accepted. *Faculty research:* Music in general education, psychology of music learning, innovation in string music education, Zarzuela, Franz Liszt's work.

University of Bridgeport, School of Education, Department of Education, Bridgeport, CT 06604. Offers education (MS); educational management (Ed D, Diploma), including intermediate administrator or supervisor (Diploma), leadership (Ed D); elementary education (MS, Diploma), including early childhood education, elementary education; middle school education (MS); music education (MS); remedial reading and language arts (Diploma); secondary education (MS, Diploma), including computer specialist (Diploma), international education (Diploma), reading specialist, secondary education. *Program availability:* Part-time, evening/weekend. *Degree requirements:* For master's, final exam, final project, or thesis; for doctorate, comprehensive exam, thesis/dissertation; for Diploma, thesis or alternative, final project. *Entrance requirements:* For master's, minimum undergraduate QPA of 2.67; for doctorate, GRE, MAT; for Diploma, GRE General Test or MAT, minimum graduate QPA of 3.0. Additional exam requirements/recommendations for international students: Recommended—TOEFL (minimum score 550 paper-based; 80 iBT), IELTS (minimum score 6.5). Electronic applications accepted. *Expenses:* Contact institution.

The University of British Columbia, Faculty of Education, Department of Curriculum and Pedagogy, Vancouver, BC V6T 1Z4, Canada. Offers art education (M Ed, MA); curriculum studies (M Ed, MA, PhD); home economics education (M Ed, MA); mathematics education (M Ed, MA); media and technology studies education (M Ed, MA); music education (M Ed, MA); physical education (M Ed, MA); science education (M Ed, MA); social studies education (M Ed, MA). *Program availability:* Part-time, online learning. *Degree requirements:* For master's, thesis (MA); for doctorate, comprehensive exam, thesis/dissertation. *Entrance requirements:* Additional exam requirements/recommendations for international students: Required—TOEFL, IELTS. Electronic applications accepted. *Expenses:* Contact institution. *Faculty research:* School subjects, teaching and learning.

University of Central Arkansas, Graduate School, College of Fine Arts and Communication, Department of Music, Conway, AR 72035-0001. Offers choral conducting (MM); instrumental conducting (MM); music (PC); music education (MM); music theory (MM); performance (MM). *Accreditation:* NASM. *Program availability:* Part-time. *Degree requirements:* For master's, comprehensive exam, thesis optional. *Entrance requirements:* For master's, GRE General Test, minimum GPA of 2.7. Additional exam requirements/recommendations for international students: Required—TOEFL (minimum score 550 paper-based). Electronic applications accepted.

University of Central Oklahoma, The Jackson College of Graduate Studies, College of Fine Arts and Design, Department of Music, Edmond, OK 73034-5209. Offers jazz studies (MM), including music production, performance; music (MM), including collaborative piano, composition, conducting, instrumental performance, music education, musical theatre, piano pedagogy, piano performance, vocal pedagogy, vocal performance. *Accreditation:* NASM. *Program availability:* Part-time. *Degree requirements:* For master's, comprehensive exam, recital or project. *Entrance requirements:* For master's, interview, audition. Additional exam requirements/recommendations for international students: Required—TOEFL (minimum score 550 paper-based; 79 iBT), IELTS (minimum score 6.5). Electronic applications accepted.

University of Cincinnati, Graduate School, College-Conservatory of Music, Division of Music Education, Cincinnati, OH 45221. Offers MM. *Accreditation:* NASM; NCATE. *Degree requirements:* For master's, comprehensive exam, paper or thesis. *Entrance requirements:* For master's, GRE General Test, interview. Additional exam requirements/recommendations for international students: Required—TOEFL (minimum score 520 paper-based). Electronic applications accepted. *Faculty research:* Choral, orchestral, and wind conducting; Kodaly; Orff-Schulwerk; jazz studies; string education.

University of Colorado Boulder, Graduate School, College of Music, Boulder, CO 80309. Offers composition (M Mus, D Mus A); conducting (M Mus); instrumental conducting and literature (D Mus A); literature and performance of choral music (D Mus A); music education (M Mus Ed, PhD), including choral or wind instrument conducting (M Mus Ed), general (M Mus Ed), Kodaly concepts (M Mus Ed), piano pedagogy (M Mus Ed), primary instruments (M Mus Ed), secondary instruments (M Mus Ed), voice pedagogy (M Mus Ed); music theory (M Mus); performance (M Mus, D Mus A); performance and pedagogy (M Mus, D Mus A). *Accreditation:* NASM. Terminal master's awarded for partial completion of doctoral program. *Degree requirements:* For master's, variable foreign language requirement, comprehensive exam, thesis or alternative, recital; for doctorate, variable foreign language requirement, thesis/dissertation. *Entrance requirements:* For master's, GRE General Test, GRE Subject Test (music literature), minimum undergraduate GPA of 2.75; for doctorate, GRE General Test, GRE Subject Test, audition, sample of research. Electronic applications accepted. Application fee is waived when completed online. *Faculty research:* Music; instrumental music; performing arts; chamber music; musicology/music theory.

University of Connecticut, Graduate School, Neag School of Education, Department of Curriculum and Instruction, Storrs, CT 06269. Offers agriculture (MA), including agriculture education; agriculture education (PhD); bilingual and bicultural education (MA, PhD); elementary education (MA, PhD); English education (MA, PhD); history and social sciences education (MA, PhD); mathematics education (MA, PhD); music education (MA); reading education (MA, PhD); science education (MA, PhD); secondary education (MA, PhD); world languages education (MA, PhD). *Accreditation:* NCATE. Terminal master's awarded for partial completion of doctoral program. *Degree requirements:* For master's, comprehensive exam, thesis or alternative; for doctorate, thesis/dissertation. *Entrance requirements:* For doctorate, GRE General Test. Additional exam requirements/recommendations for international students: Required—TOEFL (minimum score 550 paper-based). Electronic applications accepted.

University of Dayton, Department of Teacher Education, Dayton, OH 45469. Offers adolescence to young adult education (MS Ed); early childhood leadership and advocacy (MS Ed); interdisciplinary education (MS Ed), including visual arts; interdisciplinary education studies (MS Ed); leadership in educational systems (MS Ed); literacy (MS Ed); mathematics education (MS Ed); middle childhood education (MS Ed); multi-age education (MS Ed), including world languages; music education (MS Ed); teacher as leader (MS Ed); teacher education (MS Ed); technology-enhanced learning (MS Ed); trans-disciplinary early childhood education (MS Ed). *Program availability:* Part-time, 100% online. *Degree requirements:* For master's, variable foreign language requirement, thesis or alternative, internship (for teaching licensure or endorsement). *Entrance requirements:* For master's, GRE (minimum score of 149 verbal, 4 on writing) or MAT (minimum score of 396) if undergraduate GPA was under 2.75, minimum GPA of 2.75, 3 letters of recommendation, personal statement or resume, official transcripts. Additional exam requirements/recommendations for international students: Required—TOEFL (minimum score 550 paper-based; 80 iBT); Recommended—IELTS (minimum score 6.5). Electronic applications accepted. *Expenses:* Contact institution. *Faculty research:* Social emotional learning, culturally responsive teaching, urban teaching, literacy, instructional strategies, pre-service teacher education preparation.

University of Delaware, College of Arts and Sciences, Department of Music, Newark, DE 19716. Offers composition (MM); music education (MM); performance (MM). *Accreditation:* NASM. *Program availability:* Part-time. *Entrance requirements:* For master's, audition. Additional exam requirements/recommendations for international students: Required—TOEFL. Electronic applications accepted. *Faculty research:* Teaching of music.

University of Denver, Division of Arts, Humanities and Social Sciences, Lamont School of Music, Denver, CO 80208. Offers composition (MM); composition - jazz emphasis (MM); conducting (MM, Certificate); jazz studies (Certificate); music theory (MA); musicology (MA); orchestral studies (Certificate); pedagogy (MM); performance (MM, Certificate); performance - jazz emphasis (MM); Suzuki teaching (Certificate). *Accreditation:* NASM. *Program availability:* Part-time. *Faculty:* 30 full-time (9 women), 33 part-time/adjunct (16 women). *Students:* 20 full-time (8 women), 89 part-time (36 women); includes 20 minority (4 Black or African American, non-Hispanic/Latino; 3 Asian, non-Hispanic/Latino; 7 Hispanic/Latino; 6 Two or more races, non-Hispanic/Latino), 14 international. Average age 28. 162 applicants, 80% accepted, 59 enrolled. In 2018, 26 master's awarded. *Degree requirements:* For master's, one foreign language, comprehensive exam, recital or project (for performance), thesis (for musicology, music theory, piano pedagogy). *Entrance requirements:* For master's, GRE General Test (for

MA only), bachelor's degree, transcripts, personal statement, resume, three letters of recommendation, pre-screen audition (for performance), portfolio (for composition), essay or research paper (for MA only); for Certificate, bachelor's degree, transcripts, personal statement, resume, letters of recommendation, pre-screen video recording or music audition. Additional exam requirements/recommendations for international students: Required—TOEFL (minimum score 550 paper-based; 80 iBT). *Application deadline:* For fall admission, 1/15 priority date for domestic and international students. Applications are processed on a rolling basis. Application fee: $65. Electronic applications accepted. *Expenses:* $33,183 per year full-time. *Financial support:* In 2018–19, 92 students received support, including 40 teaching assistantships with tuition reimbursements available (averaging $6,031 per year); career-related internships or fieldwork, Federal Work-Study, institutionally sponsored loans, scholarships/grants, tuition waivers, and unspecified assistantships also available. Support available to part-time students. Financial award application deadline: 2/15; financial award applicants required to submit FAFSA. *Faculty research:* Performance, jazz studies and commercial music, musicology, music theory, composition, music pedagogy, music recording and production. *Unit head:* Dr. Nancy Cochran, Professor and Director, 303-871-6986, E-mail: nancy.cochran@du.edu. *Application contact:* Stephen Campbell, Director of Admission, 303-871-6973, E-mail: stephen.l.campbell@du.edu.
Website: http://www.du.edu/ahss/lamont/index.html

University of Florida, Graduate School, College of The Arts, School of Music, Gainesville, FL 32611. Offers choral conducting (MM); composition (MM, PhD); electronic music (MM); ethnomusicology (MM); instrumental conducting (MM); music (MM, PhD); music education (MM, PhD), including choral conducting (MM), composition (MM), electronic music (MM), ethnomusicology (MM), instrumental conducting (MM), music education (MM), music history and literature (MM), music theory (MM), performance (MM), piano pedagogy (MM); music history and literature (MM, PhD); music theory (MM); performance (MM); sacred music (MM). *Accreditation:* NASM. *Degree requirements:* For master's, variable foreign language requirement, comprehensive exam, thesis, recital; for doctorate, thesis/dissertation. *Entrance requirements:* For master's and doctorate, GRE General Test, audition, minimum GPA of 3.0. Additional exam requirements/recommendations for international students: Required—TOEFL (minimum score 550 paper-based; 80 iBT), IELTS (minimum score 6). Electronic applications accepted.

University of Georgia, Franklin College of Arts and Sciences, Hugh Hodgson School of Music, Athens, GA 30602. Offers composition (MM, DMA); conducting (MM, DMA); music (PhD); music education (MM Ed, Ed D); musicology (MA); performance (MM, DMA). Ed D offered jointly with College of Education. *Accreditation:* NASM. *Degree requirements:* For master's, variable foreign language requirement, thesis (MA); for doctorate, variable foreign language requirement, thesis/dissertation. *Entrance requirements:* For master's and doctorate, GRE General Test. Electronic applications accepted.

University of Hartford, The Hartt School, West Hartford, CT 06117-1599. Offers choral conducting (MM Ed); composition (MM, DMA, Artist Diploma, Diploma); conducting (MM, DMA, Artist Diploma, Diploma), including choral (MM, Diploma), instrumental (MM, Diploma); early childhood education (MM Ed); instrumental conducting (MM Ed); Kodály (MM Ed); music (CAGS); music education (DMA, PhD); music history (MM); music theory (MM); pedagogy (MM Ed); performance (MM, MM Ed, DMA, Artist Diploma, Diploma); research (MM Ed); technology (MM Ed). *Program availability:* Part-time. *Degree requirements:* For master's, variable foreign language requirement, thesis (for some programs), recital; for doctorate, variable foreign language requirement, thesis/dissertation (for some programs), recital; for other advanced degree, recital. *Entrance requirements:* For master's, audition, letters of recommendation; for doctorate, proficiency exam, audition, interview, research paper; for other advanced degree, audition. Additional exam requirements/recommendations for international students: Required—TOEFL. Electronic applications accepted. *Expenses:* Contact institution.

University of Houston, Kathrine G. McGovern College of the Arts, Moores School of Music, Houston, TX 77204. Offers accompanying and chamber music (MM); applied music (MM); composition (MM); music education (DMA); music theory (MM); performance (DMA). *Accreditation:* NASM. *Program availability:* Part-time. *Degree requirements:* For master's, one foreign language, comprehensive exam, recital; for doctorate, one foreign language, comprehensive exam, thesis/dissertation. *Entrance requirements:* For master's, audition, resume, 3 letters of recommendation; for doctorate, writing sample, audition, statement of purpose, resume. Additional exam requirements/recommendations for international students: Required—TOEFL (minimum score 550 paper-based; 79 iBT), IELTS (minimum score 6.5). Electronic applications accepted. *Faculty research:* Twentieth century music, Baroque music, history of music theory, music analysis.

University of Illinois at Urbana–Champaign, Graduate College, College of Fine and Applied Arts, School of Music, Champaign, IL 61820. Offers music (M Mus, AD, DMA); music education (MME, PhD); musicology (PhD). *Accreditation:* NASM.

The University of Iowa, Graduate College, College of Education, Department of Teaching and Learning, Program in Education, Iowa City, IA 52242-1316. Offers art education (MA); developmental reading (MA); elementary education (MA); English education (MA, MAT); foreign and second language education (MAT); foreign language education (MA); foreign language/ESL education (PhD); language, literacy and culture (PhD); mathematics education (MA, MAT, PhD); music education (MM, PhD); science education (MA); secondary education (MA); social studies (MA, PhD). *Degree requirements:* For master's, thesis optional, exam; for doctorate, comprehensive exam, thesis/dissertation. *Entrance requirements:* For master's and doctorate, GRE General Test, minimum GPA of 3.0. Additional exam requirements/recommendations for international students: Required—TOEFL (minimum score 550 paper-based; 81 iBT). Electronic applications accepted.

The University of Kansas, Graduate Studies, School of Music, Program in Music Education, Lawrence, KS 66045. Offers MME, PhD. *Accreditation:* NASM. *Program availability:* Part-time. *Students:* 17 full-time (10 women), 7 part-time (6 women); includes 2 minority (1 Asian, non-Hispanic/Latino; 1 Hispanic/Latino). Average age 34. 16 applicants, 88% accepted, 13 enrolled. In 2018, 7 master's, 3 doctorates awarded. *Entrance requirements:* For master's, GRE General Test, minimum undergraduate GPA of 3.0, video, letters of reference, transcripts; for doctorate, GRE General Test, MEMT Diagnostic Exam, minimum graduate GPA of 3.5, video, reference letters, transcripts, writing sample, proof of professional experience. Additional exam requirements/recommendations for international students: Required—TOEFL, IELTS. *Application deadline:* For fall admission, 12/1 priority date for domestic students, 12/15 priority date for international students. Application fee: $65 ($85 for international students). Electronic applications accepted. *Financial support:* Fellowships, research assistantships, teaching assistantships, institutionally sponsored loans, scholarships/grants, and unspecified assistantships available. Financial award application deadline: 12/15; financial award applicants required to submit FAFSA. *Faculty research:* Philosophy of music and music education; choral/voice pedagogy, choir acoustics; classroom management, teacher stress; the child voice, children's choirs; string pedagogy, history of string education in American public school systems. *Unit head:* Dr. Martin Bergee, Dean, 785-864-9746, E-mail: mbergee@ku.edu. *Application contact:* Lois Elmer, Administrative Professional, 785-864-2862, Fax: 785-864-9640, E-mail: elmer@ku.edu.
Website: http://music.ku.edu/memt

University of Kentucky, Graduate School, College of Fine Arts, Program in Music, Lexington, KY 40506-0032. Offers composition (MM, DMA); conducting (MM, DMA); music education (MM, PhD); music theory (MA, PhD); music therapy (MM); musicology (MA, PhD); performance (MM, DMA); sacred music (MM). *Accreditation:* NASM. *Program availability:* Part-time, evening/weekend. *Degree requirements:* For master's, variable foreign language requirement, comprehensive exam, thesis (for some programs); for doctorate, variable foreign language requirement, comprehensive exam, thesis/dissertation. *Entrance requirements:* For master's, GRE General Test, minimum undergraduate GPA of 2.75; for doctorate, GRE General Test, minimum undergraduate GPA of 2.75, graduate 3.0. Additional exam requirements/recommendations for international students: Required—TOEFL (minimum score 550 paper-based). Electronic applications accepted. *Faculty research:* Musicology, music theory, jazz, music education, performance and conducting.

University of Louisiana at Lafayette, College of the Arts, School of Music, Lafayette, LA 70504. Offers conducting (MM); music education (MM); performance (MM); performance pedagogy (MM); theory/composition (MM). *Accreditation:* NASM. *Entrance requirements:* For master's, GRE General Test, minimum GPA of 2.75. Additional exam requirements/recommendations for international students: Required—TOEFL (minimum score 550 paper-based). Electronic applications accepted. *Faculty research:* Nineteenth-century American music, trumpet pedagogy, fifteenth-century Renaissance polyphony, Charles Ives.

University of Louisville, Graduate School, College of Education and Human Development, Departments of Early Childhood and Elementary Education, Middle and Secondary Education, and Special Education, Louisville, KY 40292-0001. Offers art education (MAT); autism and applied behavior analysis (Certificate); curriculum and instruction (PhD); early elementary education (MAT); exercise physiology (MS); health and physical education (MAT); health professions education (Certificate); higher education (MA); human resources and organization development (MS); instructional technology (M Ed); interdisciplinary early childhood education (MAT); middle school education (MAT); music education (MAT); secondary education (MAT); special education (MAT); sport administration (MS); teacher leadership (M Ed). *Program availability:* Part-time, evening/weekend, 100% online, blended/hybrid learning. *Faculty:* 97 full-time (64 women), 131 part-time/adjunct (86 women). *Students:* 109 full-time (72 women), 139 part-time (87 women); includes 43 minority (18 Black or African American, non-Hispanic/Latino; 6 Asian, non-Hispanic/Latino; 10 Hispanic/Latino; 9 Two or more races, non-Hispanic/Latino), 9 international. Average age 29. 108 applicants, 75% accepted, 59 enrolled. In 2018, 64 master's awarded. Terminal master's awarded for partial completion of doctoral program. *Degree requirements:* For master's, comprehensive exam (for some programs), thesis optional; for doctorate, comprehensive exam (for some programs), thesis/dissertation. *Entrance requirements:* For master's, GRE (for most programs), PRAXIS (for educator preparation programs), professional statement, recommendation letters, resume, transcripts; for doctorate and Certificate, GRE, professional statement, recommendation letters, resume, transcripts. Additional exam requirements/recommendations for international students: Required—TOEFL (minimum score 550 paper-based; 79 iBT); Recommended—IELTS (minimum score 6.5). *Application deadline:* For fall admission, 6/1 priority date for domestic students, 5/1 priority date for international students; for spring admission, 10/1 for domestic students, 11/1 priority date for international students; for summer admission, 3/1 priority date for domestic students, 4/1 priority date for international students. Application fee: $65. *Expenses: Tuition, area resident:* Full-time $6500; part-time $723 per credit hour. Tuition, state resident: full-time $6500. Tuition, nonresident: full-time $13,557; part-time $1507 per credit hour. Tuition and fees vary according to course load and program. *Financial support:* In 2018–19, 144 students received support, including fellowships with full tuition reimbursements available (averaging $21,024 per year), research assistantships with full tuition reimbursements available (averaging $21,024 per year), teaching assistantships with full tuition reimbursements available (averaging $21,024 per year); Federal Work-Study, scholarships/grants, health care benefits, tuition waivers (full), and unspecified assistantships also available. Financial award application deadline: 3/1; financial award applicants required to submit FAFSA. *Faculty research:* Children's early reading and writing development, crelevance of basic facts in elementary mathematics instruction, clinical model of teacher education, cultural and linguistic context of diverse learners, and STEM-integrated curriculum design and development. STEM teaching and learning, content literacy for English language learners, social justice in teacher education, adolescent literacy, mathematics teacher development. Classroom and behavior management; moderate/severe disabilities, autism. *Unit head:* Dr. Amy Lingo, Interim Dean, 502-852-3235, Fax: 502-852-1464, E-mail: cehdinfo@louisville.edu. *Application contact:* Dr. Margaret Pentecost, Assistant Dean for Graduate Student Success, 502-852-6437, Fax: 502-852-1417, E-mail: gedadm@louisville.edu.
Website: http://louisville.edu/delphi

University of Louisville, Graduate School, School of Music, Louisville, KY 40292-0001. Offers composition (MM); electronic composition (MM); music education (MME); music history and literature (MM); music performance (MM), including choral conducting, instrumental, jazz composition, jazz performance, orchestral conducting, organ performance, piano pedagogy, piano performance, string pedagogy, vocal performance, wind band performance, wind conducting; music theory (MM). *Accreditation:* NASM. *Program availability:* Part-time, evening/weekend. *Faculty:* 42 full-time (13 women), 37 part-time/adjunct (17 women). *Students:* 54 full-time (20 women), 4 part-time (1 woman); includes 10 minority (2 Black or African American, non-Hispanic/Latino; 1 American Indian or Alaska Native, non-Hispanic/Latino; 4 Asian, non-Hispanic/Latino; 2 Hispanic/Latino; 1 Two or more races, non-Hispanic/Latino), 8 international. Average age 27. 87 applicants, 63% accepted, 32 enrolled. In 2018, 23 master's awarded. *Degree requirements:* For master's, variable foreign language requirement, comprehensive exam, thesis (for some programs), recital (for performance), paper or thesis (for music education), major composition (for composition). *Entrance requirements:* For master's, music history and theory entrance exams, jazz history and theory entrance exam (for jazz majors), audition, portfolio. Additional exam requirements/recommendations for international students: Required—TOEFL (minimum score 550 paper-based; 79 iBT); Recommended—IELTS (minimum score 6.5). Application fee: $65. Electronic applications accepted. *Expenses:* 26700. *Financial support:* In 2018–19, 52 students received support, including 1 fellowship with full tuition reimbursement available (averaging $12,000 per year), 12 teaching assistantships with full tuition reimbursements available (averaging $12,000 per year); Federal Work-Study, scholarships/grants, health care benefits, tuition waivers (full), and unspecified assistantships also available. Financial award application deadline: 3/1. *Faculty research:* Composition, musicology, performance, pedagogy, analysis and theoretical application. *Total annual research expenditures:* $50,000. *Unit head:* Dr. Teresa L. Reed, Dean, 502-852-6907, Fax: 502-852-0520, E-mail: teresa.reed@louisville.edu. *Application contact:* Laura Angermeier, Admissions Counselor/Senior Advising Counselor, 502-852-1623, Fax: 502-852-0520, E-mail: leange01@louisville.edu.
Website: http://www.louisville.edu/music/

University of Maryland, Baltimore County, The Graduate School, College of Arts, Humanities and Social Sciences, Department of Education, Program in Teaching, Baltimore, MD 21250. Offers early childhood education (MAT); elementary education (MAT); teaching (MAT), including art, biology, chemistry, choral music, classical foreign language, dance, earth/space science, English, instrumental music, mathematics, modern foreign language, physical science, physics, social studies, theatre. *Program availability:* Part-time, evening/weekend. *Degree requirements:* For master's, comprehensive exam (for some programs), thesis (for some programs). *Entrance requirements:* For master's, PRAXIS Core Examination or GRE (minimum score of 1000), minimum GPA of 3.0. Additional exam requirements/recommendations for international students: Required—TOEFL. Electronic applications accepted. *Faculty research:* STEM teacher education, culturally sensitive pedagogy, ESOL/bilingual education, early childhood education, language, literacy and culture.

University of Maryland, College Park, Academic Affairs, College of Arts and Humanities, School of Music, Program in Music, College Park, MD 20742. Offers M Ed, MA, MM, DMA, Ed D, PhD. *Accreditation:* NASM. *Entrance requirements:* For master's, GRE General Test (for ethnomusicology, historical musicology and music theory), 3 letters of recommendation, audition/interview. Additional exam requirements/recommendations for international students: Required—TOEFL.

University of Massachusetts Amherst, Graduate School, College of Humanities and Fine Arts, Department of Music and Dance, Amherst, MA 01003. Offers collaborative piano (MM); composition (MM); conducting (MM); jazz composition/arranging (MM); music education (MM, PhD); music history (MM); music theory (PhD); performance (MM). *Accreditation:* NASM. *Program availability:* Part-time. Terminal master's awarded for partial completion of doctoral program. *Degree requirements:* For master's, thesis or alternative; for doctorate, comprehensive exam, thesis/dissertation. *Entrance requirements:* For master's and doctorate, placement tests, original scores, research, audition or tape. Additional exam requirements/recommendations for international students: Required—TOEFL (minimum score 550 paper-based; 80 iBT), IELTS (minimum score 6.5). Electronic applications accepted.

University of Massachusetts Lowell, College of Fine Arts, Humanities and Social Sciences, Department of Music, Lowell, MA 01854. Offers music education (MM). *Accreditation:* NASM. *Program availability:* Part-time. *Degree requirements:* For master's, one foreign language, thesis. *Entrance requirements:* For master's, MAT, audition. Electronic applications accepted.

University of Memphis, Graduate School, College of Communication and Fine Arts, Rudi E. Scheidt School of Music, Memphis, TN 38152. Offers composition (M Mu, DMA); conducting (M Mu, DMA); jazz and studio music (M Mu); music education (M Mu, PhD); music theory (DCC); musicology (PhD); Orff-Schulwerk (M Mu); pedagogy (M Mu); performance (M Mu, DMA). *Accreditation:* NASM. *Program availability:* Part-time. *Students:* 63 full-time (21 women), 58 part-time (28 women); includes 30 minority (12 Black or African American, non-Hispanic/Latino; 3 Asian, non-Hispanic/Latino; 11 Hispanic/Latino; 4 Two or more races, non-Hispanic/Latino), 13 international. Average age 31. 105 applicants, 77% accepted, 39 enrolled. In 2018, 20 master's, 7 doctorates awarded. Terminal master's awarded for partial completion of doctoral program. *Degree requirements:* For master's, variable foreign language requirement, comprehensive exam, thesis or alternative; for doctorate, one foreign language, comprehensive exam, thesis/dissertation, qualifying exam. *Entrance requirements:* For master's, audition; for doctorate, GRE General Test or MAT, proficiency exam, audition, work sample, master's degree. Additional exam requirements/recommendations for international students: Required—TOEFL (minimum score 550 paper-based; 79 iBT). *Application deadline:* For fall admission, 8/1 for domestic students; for spring admission, 12/1 for domestic students. Applications are processed on a rolling basis. Application fee: $35 ($60 for international students). Electronic applications accepted. *Expenses: Tuition, area resident:* Full-time $10,240; part-time $503 per credit hour. Tuition, state resident: full-time $10,464. Tuition, nonresident: full-time $20,224; part-time $991 per credit hour. *Required fees:* $850; $106 per credit hour. *Financial support:* Research assistantships with tuition reimbursements, teaching assistantships with tuition reimbursements, Federal Work-Study, scholarships/grants, and unspecified assistantships available. Financial award application deadline: 2/1; financial award applicants required to submit FAFSA. *Faculty research:* Spanish Renaissance, twentieth-century music, Project OPTIMUS, composition, musical performance, regional music, performance, performance practice, composition. *Unit head:* John Chiego, Director, 901-678-3764, Fax: 901-678-3096, E-mail: jchiego@memphis.edu. *Application contact:* Dr. Kevin Sanders, Associate Director of Graduate Studies, 901-678-3742, Fax: 901-678-3096, E-mail: kmsnders@memphis.edu.
Website: http://www.memphis.edu/music/

University of Miami, Graduate School, Frost School of Music, Department of Music Education and Music Therapy, Coral Gables, FL 33124. Offers music education (MM, PhD, Spec M); music therapy (MM). *Accreditation:* NASM. *Degree requirements:* For master's, thesis; for doctorate, thesis/dissertation, 2 research tools; for Spec M, thesis, research project. *Entrance requirements:* For master's and doctorate, GRE General Test. Additional exam requirements/recommendations for international students: Required—TOEFL (minimum score 550 paper-based; 59 iBT). Electronic applications accepted. *Faculty research:* Motivation, quantitative research, early childhood, instrumental music, elementary music.

University of Michigan, Rackham Graduate School, School of Music, Theatre, and Dance, Program in Music Education, Ann Arbor, MI 48109-2085. Offers MM, PhD, Spec M. *Accreditation:* NASM; TEAC. *Degree requirements:* For doctorate, thesis/dissertation, oral and preliminary exams. *Entrance requirements:* For doctorate, MAT, writing sample, portfolio. Additional exam requirements/recommendations for international students: Required—TOEFL. Electronic applications accepted.

University of Minnesota, Duluth, Graduate School, School of Fine Arts, Department of Music, Duluth, MN 55812-2496. Offers music education (MM); performance (MM). *Accreditation:* NASM. *Program availability:* Part-time. *Degree requirements:* For master's, comprehensive exam, thesis (for some programs), recital (MM in performance). *Entrance requirements:* For master's, audition, minimum GPA of 3.0, sample of written work, interview, bachelor's degree in music, video of teaching. Additional exam requirements/recommendations for international students: Required—TOEFL (minimum score 550 paper-based). *Faculty research:* Band composition, music aesthetics, learning theory, value theory, music advocacy.

University of Missouri, Office of Research and Graduate Studies, College of Education, Department of Learning, Teaching and Curriculum, Columbia, MO 65211. Offers agricultural education (M Ed, PhD, Ed S); art education (M Ed, PhD, Ed S); business and office education (M Ed, PhD, Ed S); early childhood education (M Ed, PhD, Ed S); elementary education (M Ed, PhD, Ed S); English education (M Ed, PhD, Ed S); foreign language education (M Ed, PhD, Ed S); health education and promotion (M Ed, PhD); learning and instruction (M Ed); marketing education (M Ed, PhD, Ed S); mathematics education (M Ed, PhD, Ed S); music education (M Ed, PhD, Ed S); reading education (M Ed, PhD, Ed S); science education (M Ed, PhD, Ed S); social studies education (M Ed, PhD, Ed S); vocational education (M Ed, PhD, Ed S). *Program availability:* Part-time. Terminal master's awarded for partial completion of doctoral

program. *Entrance requirements:* For master's and Ed S, GRE General Test or MAT, minimum GPA of 3.0; for doctorate, GRE General Test, minimum GPA of 3.0. Additional exam requirements/recommendations for international students: Required—TOEFL.

University of Missouri–Kansas City, Conservatory of Music and Dance, Kansas City, MO 64110-2499. Offers composition (MM, DMA); conducting (MM, DMA); music (MA); music education (MME, PhD); music history and literature (MM); music theory (MM); music therapy (MA); performance (MM, DMA). PhD (interdisciplinary) offered through the School of Graduate Studies. *Accreditation:* NASM. *Program availability:* Part-time. *Degree requirements:* For master's, variable foreign language requirement, comprehensive exam, thesis (for some programs); for doctorate, variable foreign language requirement, comprehensive exam, thesis/dissertation or alternative. *Entrance requirements:* For master's, minimum GPA of 3.0 in major, auditions (for MM in performance); for doctorate, minimum graduate GPA of 3.5, auditions (for DMA in performance), portfolio of compositions. Additional exam requirements/recommendations for international students: Required—TOEFL (minimum score 550 paper-based; 80 iBT). *Faculty research:* Electro-acoustic composition, affective music responses, American music theatre, Russian choral music, music therapy and Alzheimer's.

University of Nebraska at Kearney, College of Fine Arts and Humanities, Department of Music, Kearney, NE 68849-0001. Offers music education (MA Ed). *Accreditation:* NASM; NCATE. *Program availability:* Part-time, evening/weekend, 100% online. *Degree requirements:* For master's, comprehensive exam, thesis optional. *Entrance requirements:* For master's, undergraduate degree in music, resume, philosophy of teaching, three letters of recommendation. Additional exam requirements/recommendations for international students: Recommended—TOEFL (minimum score 550 paper-based; 79 iBT), IELTS (minimum score 6.5). Electronic applications accepted. *Faculty research:* Contemporary American music, musical theater, opera, woodwind performance and pedagogy, percussion pedagogy, historic and contemporary American piano, dramatic mezzo-soprano, violin performance, piano performance and pedagogy, music composition, opera, healing effects of music, Chamber music, diction.

University of Nebraska–Lincoln, Graduate College, College of Fine and Performing Arts, School of Music, Lincoln, NE 68588. Offers composition (MM, DMA); conducting (MM, DMA); music education (MM, PhD); music history (MM); music theory (MM); performance (MM, DMA); piano pedagogy (MM); woodwind specialties (MM). *Accreditation:* NASM. *Degree requirements:* For master's, thesis optional; for doctorate, comprehensive exam, thesis/dissertation. *Entrance requirements:* For master's and doctorate, audition. Additional exam requirements/recommendations for international students: Required—TOEFL. Electronic applications accepted. *Faculty research:* Mozart, Tchaikovsky, Josquin des Prez, practice of J.S. Bach's organ works, instructional strategies in music education.

University of New Mexico, Graduate Studies, College of Fine Arts, Program in Music, Albuquerque, NM 87131-0001. Offers collaborative piano (M Mu); conducting (M Mu); music education (M Mu); music history and literature (M Mu); performance (M Mu); theory and composition (M Mu). *Accreditation:* NASM. *Program availability:* Part-time. *Students:* Average age 29. 75 applicants, 76% accepted, 36 enrolled. In 2018, 30 master's awarded. *Degree requirements:* For master's, variable foreign language requirement, comprehensive exam, thesis (for some programs), recital (for some programs). *Entrance requirements:* For master's, placement exams in music history and theory. Additional exam requirements/recommendations for international students: Required—TOEFL (minimum score 550 paper-based). *Application deadline:* For fall admission, 7/1 for domestic students, 5/1 for international students; for spring admission, 11/1 for domestic students, 10/1 for international students. Applications are processed on a rolling basis. Application fee: $50. Electronic applications accepted. *Financial support:* Research assistantships, teaching assistantships, Federal Work-Study, scholarships/grants, and unspecified assistantships available. Support available to part-time students. Financial award application deadline: 2/1; financial award applicants required to submit FAFSA. *Faculty research:* Opera, twentieth-century and contemporary music, performance, conducting. *Unit head:* Dr. Steven Block, Chair, 505-277-2127, Fax: 505-277-4202, E-mail: sblock@unm.edu. *Application contact:* Colleen M. Sheinberg, Graduate Coordinator, 505-277-8401, Fax: 505-277-4202, E-mail: colleens@unm.edu.
Website: http://music.unm.edu/

The University of North Carolina at Chapel Hill, Graduate School, School of Education, Program in Secondary Education, Chapel Hill, NC 27599. Offers English (Grades 9-12) (MAT); English as a second language (MAT); French (Grades K-12) (MAT); German (Grades K-12) (MAT); Japanese (Grades K-12) (MAT); Latin (Grades 9-12) (MAT); mathematics (Grades 9-12) (MAT); music (Grades K-12) (MAT); science (Grades 9-12) (MAT); social studies (Grades 9-12) (MAT); Spanish (Grades K-12) (MAT). *Accreditation:* NCATE. *Degree requirements:* For master's, comprehensive exam. *Entrance requirements:* For master's, GRE General Test, minimum GPA of 3.0 during last 2 years of undergraduate course work. Additional exam requirements/recommendations for international students: Required—TOEFL (minimum score 550 paper-based). Electronic applications accepted.

The University of North Carolina at Greensboro, Graduate School, School of Music, Theatre and Dance, Greensboro, NC 27412-5001. Offers composition (MM); dance (MA, MFA); education (MM); music education (PhD); performance (MM, DMA); theatre (M Ed, MFA), including acting (MFA), design (MFA), directing (MFA), theatre education (M Ed), theatre for youth (MFA); theory (MM). *Accreditation:* NASM. *Degree requirements:* For master's, variable foreign language requirement, thesis (for some programs), recital; for doctorate, comprehensive exam, thesis/dissertation, diagnostic exam, recital. *Entrance requirements:* For master's, GRE General Test, NTE, audition; for doctorate, GRE General Test, GRE Subject Test (music), audition. Additional exam requirements/recommendations for international students: Required—TOEFL. Electronic applications accepted.

University of North Dakota, Graduate School, College of Arts and Sciences, Department of Music, Grand Forks, ND 58202. Offers music (MM); music education (PhD). *Accreditation:* NASM. *Program availability:* Part-time. *Degree requirements:* For master's, comprehensive exam, thesis or alternative. *Entrance requirements:* For master's, minimum GPA of 3.0. Additional exam requirements/recommendations for international students: Required—TOEFL (minimum score 550 paper-based; 79 iBT), IELTS (minimum score 6.5). Electronic applications accepted.

University of Northern Colorado, Graduate School, College of Performing and Visual Arts, School of Music, Greeley, CO 80639. Offers collaborative piano (MM, DA); composition (DA); conducting (MM, DA); instrumental performance (MM); jazz studies (MM, DA); music education (MM, DA); music history and literature (MM, DA); music theory and composition (MM); performance (DA); vocal performance (MM). *Accreditation:* NASM; NCATE (one or more programs are accredited). *Program availability:* Part-time. *Degree requirements:* For master's, comprehensive exam, thesis or alternative; for doctorate, comprehensive exam, thesis/dissertation. *Entrance requirements:* For master's, audition; for doctorate, GRE General Test, audition, 3 letters of recommendation. Electronic applications accepted.

Music Education

University of Northern Iowa, Graduate College, College of Humanities, Arts and Sciences, School of Music, MM Program in Jazz Pedagogy, Cedar Falls, IA 50614. Offers MM. *Degree requirements:* For master's, comprehensive exam. *Entrance requirements:* For master's, audition, interview, essay.

University of Northern Iowa, Graduate College, College of Humanities, Arts and Sciences, School of Music, MM Program in Music Education, Cedar Falls, IA 50614. Offers MM. *Accreditation:* NASM. *Program availability:* Part-time, evening/weekend. *Degree requirements:* For master's, comprehensive exam, thesis or alternative. *Entrance requirements:* For master's, written diagnostic exam in theory, music history, expository writing skills, and in the area of claimed competency, portfolio, tape recordings of compositions, in-person auditions, minimum GPA of 3.0. Additional exam requirements/recommendations for international students: Required—TOEFL (minimum score 500 paper-based; 61 iBT). Electronic applications accepted.

University of Northern Iowa, Graduate College, College of Humanities, Arts and Sciences, School of Music, MM Program in Piano Performance and Pedagogy, Cedar Falls, IA 50614. Offers MM.

University of North Texas, Toulouse Graduate School, Denton, TX 76203-5459. Offers accounting (MS); applied anthropology (MA, MS); applied behavior analysis (Certificate); applied geography (MA); applied technology and performance improvement (M Ed, MS); art education (MA); art history (MA); arts leadership (Certificate); audiology (Au D); behavior analysis (MS); behavioral science (PhD); biochemistry and molecular biology (MS); biology (MA, MS); biomedical engineering (MS); business analysis (MS); chemistry (MS); clinical health psychology (PhD); communication studies (MA, MS); computer engineering (MS); computer science (MS); counseling (M Ed, MS), including clinical mental health counseling (MS), college and university counseling, elementary school counseling, secondary school counseling; creative writing (MA); criminal justice (MS); curriculum and instruction (M Ed); decision sciences (MBA); design (MA, MFA), including fashion design (MFA), innovation studies, interior design (MFA); early childhood studies (MS); economics (MS); educational leadership (M Ed, Ed D); educational psychology (MS, PhD), including family studies (MS), gifted and talented (MS), human development (MS), learning and cognition (MS), research, measurement and evaluation (MS); electrical engineering (MS); emergency management (MPA); engineering technology (MS); English (MA); English as a second language (MA); environmental science (MS); finance (MBA, MS); financial management (MPA); French (MA); health services management (MBA); higher education (M Ed, Ed D); history (MA, MS); hospitality management (MS); human resources management (MPA); information science (MS); information systems (PhD); information technologies (MBA); interdisciplinary studies (MA, MS); international studies (MA); international sustainable tourism (MS); jazz studies (MM); journalism (MA, MJ, Graduate Certificate), including interactive and virtual digital communication (Graduate Certificate), narrative journalism (Graduate Certificate), public relations (Graduate Certificate); kinesiology (MS); linguistics (MA); local government management (MPA); logistics (PhD); logistics and supply chain management (MBA); long-term care, senior housing, and aging services (MA); management (PhD); marketing (MBA); mathematics (MA, MS); mechanical and energy engineering (MS, PhD); music (MA), including ethnomusicology, music theory, musicology, performance; music composition (PhD); music education (MM Ed, PhD); nonprofit management (MPA); operations and supply chain management (MBA); performance (MM, DMA); philosophy (MA); political science (MA); professional and technical communication (MA); radio, television and film (MA, MFA); rehabilitation counseling (Certificate); sociology (MA); Spanish (MA); special education (M Ed); speech-language pathology (MA); strategic management (MBA); studio art (MFA); teaching (M Ed); MBA/MS. *Program availability:* Part-time, evening/weekend, online learning. Terminal master's awarded for partial completion of doctoral program. *Degree requirements:* For master's, variable foreign language requirement, comprehensive exam (for some programs), thesis (for some programs); for doctorate, variable foreign language requirement, comprehensive exam (for some programs), thesis/dissertation; for other advanced degree, variable foreign language requirement, comprehensive exam (for some programs). *Entrance requirements:* For master's and doctorate, GRE, GMAT. Additional exam requirements/recommendations for international students: Required—TOEFL (minimum score 550 paper-based; 79 iBT). Electronic applications accepted.

University of Oklahoma, Weitzenhoffer Family College of Fine Arts, School of Music, Norman, OK 73019. Offers choral conducting (M Mus), including church music (M Mus, DMA), standard; composition (M Mus); conducting (M Mus Ed, DMA), including choral (M Mus Ed), choral conducting (DMA), church music (M Mus, DMA), instrumental (M Mus Ed), orchestral conducting (DMA), wind conducting (DMA); general (M Mus Ed), including Kodaly concepts (M Mus Ed, PhD), vocal/general; instrumental (M Mus Ed), including primary instrument, secondary instrument; instrumental conducting (M Mus); music composition (DMA); music education (PhD), including choral or wind instrument conducting, general, Kodaly concepts (M Mus Ed, PhD), piano pedagogy; music performance (Graduate Certificate); music theory (M Mus); musicology (M Mus); organ (M Mus, DMA), including church music, organ - standard (DMA), organ technology (M Mus), standard (M Mus); piano (M Mus, DMA), including performance, performance and pedagogy; piano pedagogy (M Mus Ed); voice (M Mus, DMA), including opera (M Mus), performance; wind/percussion/string (M Mus); wind/percussion/string instruments (DMA), including performance (M Mus, DMA). *Accreditation:* NASM. *Faculty:* 53 full-time (15 women). *Students:* 97 full-time (47 women), 65 part-time (26 women); includes 22 minority (3 Black or African American, non-Hispanic/Latino; 3 American Indian or Alaska Native, non-Hispanic/Latino; 3 Asian, non-Hispanic/Latino; 8 Hispanic/Latino; 5 Two or more races, non-Hispanic/Latino), 30 international. Average age 29. 157 applicants, 56% accepted, 47 enrolled. In 2018, 37 master's, 10 doctorates awarded. *Degree requirements:* For master's, variable foreign language requirement, comprehensive exam (for some programs), thesis (for some programs), final recital (for M Mus performance, conducting, and composition degrees); for doctorate, variable foreign language requirement, comprehensive exam, thesis/dissertation, three recitals and/or workshops (two recitals for DMA in composition); for Graduate Certificate, variable foreign language requirement, two recitals. *Entrance requirements:* For master's, bachelor's degree in music, music education, or the equivalent; transcripts; resume; personal statement; 3 letters of recommendation; audition and/or other practical application materials as appropriate to intended degree; sample of scholarly writing (for M Mus in musicology and in music theory); for doctorate, master's degree in music, music education, or the equivalent; transcripts; resume; personal statement; 3 letters of recommendation; sample of scholarly writing; audition and/or other practical application materials as appropriate to intended degree; for Graduate Certificate, bachelor's degree in music, music education, or the equivalent; transcripts; resume; personal statement; 3 letters of recommendation; audition. Additional exam requirements/recommendations for international students: Required—TOEFL (minimum score 79 iBT) or IELTS (minimum score 6.5). *Application deadline:* For fall admission, 2/1 for domestic and international students; for spring admission, 10/1 for domestic students, 9/1 for international students; for summer admission, 2/1 for domestic and international students. Applications are processed on a rolling basis. Application fee: $50 ($100 for international students). Electronic applications accepted. *Expenses:* Tuition, state resident: full-time $5683.20; part-time $236.80 per credit hour. Tuition, nonresident: full-time $20,342; part-time $847.60 per credit hour. *International tuition:* $20,342.40 full-time. *Required fees:* $2894.20; $110.05 per credit hour. $126.50 per semester. Tuition and fees vary according to course load and program. *Financial support:* Fellowships, research assistantships, teaching assistantships, health care benefits, tuition waivers, and unspecified assistantships available. Financial award application deadline: 6/1; financial award applicants required to submit FAFSA. *Faculty research:* Piano pedagogy, performance practice, music education, musicology, music theory. *Unit head:* Dr. Roland Barrett, Director, 405-325-2081, Fax: 405-325-7574, E-mail: rcbarrett@ou.edu. *Application contact:* Jan Russell, Graduate Admissions and Recruiting Advisor, 405-325-5393, Fax: 405-325-7574, E-mail: jrussell@ou.edu.
Website: http://music.ou.edu

University of Oregon, Graduate School, School of Music, Program in Music Education, Eugene, OR 97403. Offers M Mus, DMA, PhD. *Accreditation:* NASM. *Program availability:* Part-time. Terminal master's awarded for partial completion of doctoral program. *Degree requirements:* For master's, variable foreign language requirement, thesis (for some programs); for doctorate, one foreign language, comprehensive exam, thesis/dissertation. *Entrance requirements:* For master's, minimum GPA of 3.0, videotape or interview; for doctorate, GRE General Test, minimum GPA of 3.0, videotape or interview. Additional exam requirements/recommendations for international students: Required—TOEFL. *Faculty research:* Psalms of DeLasso, stress and muscular tension in stringed instrument performance, piano music of Stravinsky, learning aptitudes in elementary music.

University of Ottawa, Faculty of Graduate and Postdoctoral Studies, Faculty of Arts, Department of Music, Ottawa, ON K1N 6N5, Canada. Offers music (M Mus, MA); orchestral studies (Certificate); piano pedagogy research (Certificate). *Degree requirements:* For master's, thesis optional. *Entrance requirements:* For master's, honors degree or equivalent, minimum B+ average. Electronic applications accepted. *Faculty research:* Performance, theory, musicology.

University of Rhode Island, Graduate School, College of Arts and Sciences, Department of Music, Kingston, RI 02881. Offers music education (MM), including composition, conducting, performance, thesis; music performance (MM), including composition, conducting, voice or instrument. Program offered in partnership with School of Education. *Accreditation:* NASM. *Program availability:* Part-time. *Faculty:* 13 full-time (7 women). *Students:* 9 full-time (3 women), 1 (woman) part-time; includes 1 minority (Black or African American, non-Hispanic/Latino). 4 applicants, 100% accepted, 1 enrolled. In 2018, 4 master's awarded. *Entrance requirements:* For master's, 2 letters of recommendation, audition. Additional exam requirements/recommendations for international students: Required—TOEFL. *Application deadline:* For fall admission, 7/15 for domestic students, 2/1 for international students; for spring admission, 11/15 for domestic students, 7/15 for international students. Application fee: $65. Electronic applications accepted. *Expenses: Tuition, area resident:* Full-time $13,226; part-time $735 per credit. Tuition, state resident: full-time $13,226; part-time $735 per credit. Tuition, nonresident: full-time $25,854; part-time $1436 per credit. *International tuition:* $25,854 full-time. *Required fees:* $1698; $50 per credit. $35 per semester. One-time fee: $165. *Financial support:* In 2018–19, 3 teaching assistantships with tuition reimbursements (averaging $13,293 per year) were awarded. Financial award application deadline: 2/1; financial award applicants required to submit FAFSA. *Unit head:* Dr. Mark Conley, Chair, 401-874-2431, E-mail: mconley@uri.edu. *Application contact:* Dr. Joe Parillo, Director of Graduate Studies, 401-874-2431, E-mail: jmparillo@uri.edu.
Website: https://web.uri.edu/music/

University of Rochester, Eastman School of Music, Programs in Music Education, Rochester, NY 14627. Offers MA, MM, DMA, PhD. *Expenses: Tuition:* Full-time $52,974; part-time $1654 per credit hour. *Required fees:* $612. One-time fee: $30 part-time. Tuition and fees vary according to campus/location and program.

University of St. Thomas, College of Arts and Sciences, Graduate Programs in Music Education, St. Paul, MN 55105-1096. Offers choral (MA); instrumental (MA); Kodaly (MA); leadership in music education (Ed D); Orff Schulwerk (MA); piano pedagogy (MA). *Accreditation:* NASM; NCATE. *Program availability:* Part-time. *Degree requirements:* For master's, comprehensive exam, thesis, music history theory and diagnostic exam, piano recital (for piano pedagogy students), oral exam. *Entrance requirements:* For master's, performance assessment hearing, interview. Additional exam requirements/recommendations for international students: Required—TOEFL (minimum score 550 paper-based; 80 iBT). Electronic applications accepted. *Expenses:* Contact institution. *Faculty research:* Kodaly, choral, piano pedagogy, Orff, instrumental, world music.

University of South Alabama, College of Arts and Sciences, Department of Music, Mobile, AL 36688. Offers collaborative keyboard (MM); music education (MM); performance (MM). *Degree requirements:* For master's, comprehensive exam, final project. *Entrance requirements:* For master's, GRE/GMAT, undergraduate degree in music with minimum GPA of 3.0, official transcript, resume, 3 recommendation letters; teaching certificate (for music education). Additional exam requirements/recommendations for international students: Required—TOEFL (minimum score 525 paper-based; 71 iBT). Electronic applications accepted.

University of South Carolina, The Graduate School, School of Music, Columbia, SC 29208. Offers composition (MM, DMA); conducting (MM, DMA); jazz studies (MM); music education (MM Ed, PhD); music history (MM); music performance (Certificate); music theory (MM); opera theater (MM); performance (MM, DMA); piano pedagogy (MM, DMA). *Accreditation:* NASM. *Program availability:* Part-time. *Degree requirements:* For master's, 5 foreign languages, comprehensive exam, thesis (for some programs); for doctorate, one foreign language, comprehensive exam, thesis/dissertation; for Certificate, recitals. *Entrance requirements:* For master's and doctorate, GRE General Test or MAT, music diagnostic exam. Additional exam requirements/recommendations for international students: Required—TOEFL (minimum score 570 paper-based). Electronic applications accepted. *Expenses:* Contact institution. *Faculty research:* Music skills in pre-school children, evaluation of school performing ensembles.

University of South Dakota, Graduate School, College of Fine Arts, Department of Music, Vermillion, SD 57069. Offers collaborative piano (MM); conducting (MM); history of musical instruments (MM); music education (MM); music history (MM); music performance (MM). *Accreditation:* NASM. *Degree requirements:* For master's, thesis or alternative. *Entrance requirements:* For master's, minimum GPA of 2.7, audition or performance tape. Additional exam requirements/recommendations for international students: Required—TOEFL (minimum score 550 paper-based; 79 iBT). Electronic applications accepted.

University of Southern California, Graduate School, Thornton School of Music, Los Angeles, CA 90089. Offers brass performance (MM, DMA, Graduate Certificate); choral and sacred music (MM, DMA); classical guitar (MM, DMA, Graduate Certificate); composition (MM, DMA); early music (MA, DMA); harp performance (MM, DMA, Graduate Certificate); historical musicology (PhD); jazz studies (MM, DMA, Graduate Certificate); keyboard collaborative arts (MM, DMA, Graduate Certificate); music education (MM, DMA); organ performance (MM, DMA, Graduate Certificate); percussion performance (MM, DMA, Graduate Certificate); piano performance (MM, DMA, Graduate Certificate); scoring for motion pictures and television (Graduate Certificate); strings performance (MM, DMA, Graduate Certificate); studio jazz guitar (MM, DMA,

Graduate Certificate); teaching music (MA); vocal arts (classical voice/opera) (MM, DMA, Graduate Certificate); woodwind performance (MM, DMA, Graduate Certificate). *Program availability:* Part-time, evening/weekend. Terminal master's awarded for partial completion of doctoral program. *Degree requirements:* For master's, variable foreign language requirement, comprehensive exam (for some programs), thesis (for some programs); for doctorate, variable foreign language requirement, comprehensive exam, thesis/dissertation (for some programs). *Entrance requirements:* For master's, GRE (for MA in early music and MM in music education); for doctorate, GRE (for DMA). Additional exam requirements/recommendations for international students: Required—TOEFL (minimum score 560 paper-based; 83 iBT). Electronic applications accepted. *Expenses:* Contact institution. *Faculty research:* Early Modern musical improvisation and composition, maternal sound stimulation of the premature infant, physiological characteristics of jazz guitarists, the musical experience of the very young child, electronic music.

University of Southern Maine, College of Arts, Humanities, and Social Sciences, School of Music, Portland, ME 04103. Offers composition (MM); conducting (MM); jazz studies (MM); music education (MM); performance (MM). *Accreditation:* NASM.

University of Southern Mississippi, College of Arts and Sciences, School of Music, Hattiesburg, MS 39406-0001. Offers conducting (DMA); music education (MME); performance and pedagogy (DMA); piano accompanying (MM); theory (MM); woodwind performance and pedagogy (MM). *Accreditation:* NASM. *Program availability:* Blended/hybrid learning. Terminal master's awarded for partial completion of doctoral program. *Degree requirements:* For master's, comprehensive exam, thesis (for some programs); for doctorate, comprehensive exam, thesis/dissertation. *Entrance requirements:* For master's, GRE General Test, minimum GPA of 2.75 in last 60 hours; for doctorate, GRE General Test, minimum GPA of 3.5. Additional exam requirements/recommendations for international students: Required—TOEFL, IELTS. *Faculty research:* Music theory, composition, music performance.

University of South Florida, College of The Arts, School of Music, Tampa, FL 33620-9951. Offers music (MM, PhD), including chamber music (MM), choral conducting (MM), composition (MM), electro-acoustic music (MM), instrumental conducting (MM), jazz composition (MM), jazz performance (MM), music education (PhD), performance (MM), piano pedagogy (MM), theory (MM); music education (MA). *Accreditation:* NASM. *Program availability:* Part-time, evening/weekend. *Faculty:* 23 full-time (7 women), 1 part-time/adjunct (0 women). *Students:* 58 full-time (27 women), 18 part-time (9 women); includes 11 minority (3 Black or African American, non-Hispanic/Latino; 3 Hispanic/Latino; 5 Two or more races, non-Hispanic/Latino), 29 international. Average age 28. 76 applicants, 55% accepted, 28 enrolled. In 2018, 34 master's, 2 doctorates awarded. *Degree requirements:* For master's, comprehensive exam, thesis optional; for doctorate, comprehensive exam, thesis/dissertation. *Entrance requirements:* For master's, minimum GPA of 3.0 in upper-division courses and music courses for bachelor's degree; resume; three letters of recommendation; at least 2 years of K-12 music teaching experience (for MA in music education); audition or interview (for MM); for doctorate, GRE General Test, master's degree from accredited institution with minimum GPA of 3.5, 3.0 in upper-division undergraduate courses; at least 2 years of K-12 music teaching experience; interview with faculty; 3 letters of recommendation; academic writing sample; curriculum vitae; personal goals statement; 15-20 minute video of applicant teaching music. Additional exam requirements/recommendations for international students: Required—TOEFL, TOEFL (minimum score 550 paper-based; 79 iBT) or IELTS (minimum score 6.5). *Application deadline:* For fall admission, 2/15 priority date for domestic students, 2/1 for international students; for spring admission, 10/15 for domestic students, 9/15 for international students; for summer admission, 2/15 for domestic students, 1/15 for international students. Application fee: $30. Electronic applications accepted. *Expenses:* Tuition, state resident: full-time $6350. Tuition, nonresident: full-time $19,048. *International tuition:* $19,048 full-time. *Required fees:* $2079. *Financial support:* In 2018–19, 40 students received support, including 1 research assistantship with tuition reimbursement available (averaging $15,724 per year), 46 teaching assistantships with tuition reimbursements available (averaging $10,099 per year); unspecified assistantships also available. Financial award application deadline: 2/15. *Faculty research:* Music education: alternate methods, community collaboration, contemporary changes, early childhood, general music, international perspectives, multicultural issues, technology, teacher behaviors, philosophy, psychology, sociology; music: chamber music, composition, conducting, jazz studies, music performance, music theory, pedagogy, electronic music. *Total annual research expenditures:* $149,061. *Unit head:* Dr. Karen Bryan, Director, 813-974-2311, Fax: 813-974-8721, E-mail: kmbryan@usf.edu. *Application contact:* Dr. David Williams, Associate Director/Associate Professor of Music Education, 813-974-9166, Fax: 813-974-8721, E-mail: davidw@usf.edu.
Website: http://music.arts.usf.edu/

The University of Tennessee, Graduate School, College of Arts and Sciences, School of Music, Knoxville, TN 37996. Offers accompanying (MM); choral conducting (MM); composition (MM); instrumental conducting (MM); jazz (MM); music education (MM); music theory (MM); musicology (MM); performance (MM); piano pedagogy and literature (MM). *Accreditation:* NASM. *Program availability:* Part-time. *Degree requirements:* For master's, thesis (for some programs). *Entrance requirements:* For master's, audition, minimum GPA of 2.7. Additional exam requirements/recommendations for international students: Required—TOEFL. Electronic applications accepted.

The University of Tennessee at Chattanooga, Program in Music, Chattanooga, TN 37403. Offers music education (MM); performance (MM). *Accreditation:* NASM. *Degree requirements:* For master's, comprehensive exam, thesis or alternative, recital. *Entrance requirements:* For master's, GRE General Test, bachelor's degree in music. Additional exam requirements/recommendations for international students: Required—TOEFL (minimum score 550 paper-based; 79 iBT), IELTS (minimum score 6). Electronic applications accepted. *Expenses:* Contact institution. *Faculty research:* Music education, conducting, opera, vocal instruction, orchestras.

The University of Texas at Arlington, Graduate School, College of Liberal Arts, Department of Music, Arlington, TX 76019. Offers education (MM); performance (MM). *Accreditation:* NASM. *Program availability:* Part-time, evening/weekend. *Degree requirements:* For master's, comprehensive exam, thesis optional. *Entrance requirements:* For master's, GRE, 3 letters of recommendation, minimum GPA of 3.0 in last 60 hours of course work. Additional exam requirements/recommendations for international students: Required—TOEFL (minimum score 550 paper-based). Electronic applications accepted.

The University of Texas at Austin, Graduate School, College of Fine Arts, Sarah and Ernest Butler School of Music, Austin, TX 78712-1111. Offers band and wind conducting (M Music, DMA); brass/woodwind/percussion (MM, DMA); chamber music (MM); choral conducting (MM, DMA); collaborative piano (MM, DMA); composition (MM, DMA), including composition, jazz, jazz (DMA); ethnomusicology (MM, PhD); literature and pedagogy (MM); music and human learning (MM, PhD); music and human learning (DMA), including jazz (MM, DMA), piano pedagogy; musicology (MM, PhD); opera performance (MM, DMA); orchestral conducting (MM, DMA); organ (MM), including sacred music; organ performance (MM, DMA); performance (MM), including jazz (MM, DMA); performance (DMA), including jazz (MM, DMA); piano (DMA), including jazz (MM, DMA); piano literature and pedagogy (MM); piano performance (MM, DMA); string performance (MM, DMA); theory (MM, PhD); vocal performance (MM, DMA); voice (DMA), including opera; voice performance pedagogy (DMA); woodwind, brass, percussion performance (MM). *Accreditation:* NASM. *Program availability:* Part-time. *Degree requirements:* For master's, one foreign language, comprehensive exam, thesis (for some programs), recital (performance or composition majors); for doctorate, one foreign language, comprehensive exam, thesis/dissertation (for some programs), recital (for performance or composition majors). *Entrance requirements:* For master's and doctorate, GRE General Test (except for performance or composition majors), audition (performance majors). Electronic applications accepted.

The University of Texas at El Paso, Graduate School, College of Liberal Arts, Department of Music, El Paso, TX 79968-0001. Offers music education (MM); music performance (MM). *Accreditation:* NASM. *Program availability:* Part-time, evening/weekend. *Degree requirements:* For master's, thesis optional. *Entrance requirements:* For master's, audition, interview, letters of recommendation. Additional exam requirements/recommendations for international students: Required—TOEFL; Recommended—IELTS. Electronic applications accepted.

The University of the Arts, College of Performing Arts, School of Music, Division of Music Education, Philadelphia, PA 19102-4944. Offers MAT, MM. MM program offered in conjunction with Villanova University's Summer Music Studies program with summer enrollment only and priority application date of January 1. *Program availability:* Part-time. *Degree requirements:* For master's, student teaching (for MAT); thesis/project (for MM). *Entrance requirements:* For master's, official transcripts, three letters of recommendation, personal interview, undergraduate degree with minimum cumulative GPA of 3.0, DVD/CD or link to uploaded film on YouTube or related site (or VHS video tape for MM), live or taped performance audition (for MAT). Additional exam requirements/recommendations for international students: Required—TOEFL (minimum score 580 paper-based, 92 iBT) or IELTS (minimum score 6.5).

University of the Pacific, Conservatory of Music, Stockton, CA 95211-0197. Offers music education (MM); music therapy (MA). *Entrance requirements:* For master's, GRE General Test. Additional exam requirements/recommendations for international students: Required—TOEFL.

The University of Toledo, College of Graduate Studies, College of Communication and the Arts, Toledo, OH 43606-3390. Offers ME, MME, MMP, Certificate. *Accreditation:* NASM. *Degree requirements:* For master's, comprehensive exam, diagnostic theory and history exam. *Entrance requirements:* For master's, GRE if GPA is less than 3.0, minimum cumulative point-hour ratio of 2.7 for all previous academic work, audition. Additional exam requirements/recommendations for international students: Required—TOEFL (minimum score 550 paper-based; 80 iBT). Electronic applications accepted.

University of Toronto, School of Graduate Studies, Faculty of Music, Toronto, ON M5S 1A1, Canada. Offers composition (M Mus, DMA); ethnomusicology (MA, PhD); jazz (M Mus); music education (MA, PhD); musicology/theory (MA, PhD); opera (M Mus); performance (M Mus, DMA). *Program availability:* Part-time. *Degree requirements:* For master's, comprehensive exam (for some programs), oral examination (M Mus in composition), 1 foreign language (MA); for doctorate, recital of original works (DMA), thesis (PhD). *Entrance requirements:* For master's, BM in area of specialization with minimum B average in final 2 years, original compositions (M Mus in composition); for doctorate, master's degree in area of specialization, minimum B+ average, at least 2 extended compositions (DMA). Additional exam requirements/recommendations for international students: Required—TOEFL (minimum score 580 paper-based; 93 iBT), TWE (minimum score 5). Electronic applications accepted.

University of Utah, Graduate School, College of Fine Arts, School of Music, Salt Lake City, UT 84112. Offers choral conducting (M Mus, DMA); collaborative piano (M Mus); composition (M Mus, PhD); instrumental conducting (M Mus, DMA); instrumental performance (M Mus, DMA); jazz studies (M Mus); music education (M Mus, PhD); music history and literature (M Mus); musicology (MA); organ performance (M Mus); piano performance (M Mus, DMA); piano performance and pedagogy (M Mus); string performance and pedagogy (M Mus); theory (M Mus); vocal performance (DMA). *Accreditation:* NASM. *Faculty:* 27 full-time (7 women), 55 part-time/adjunct (22 women). *Students:* 75 full-time (40 women), 21 part-time (8 women); includes 20 minority (4 Asian, non-Hispanic/Latino; 12 Hispanic/Latino; 1 Native Hawaiian or other Pacific Islander, non-Hispanic/Latino; 3 Two or more races, non-Hispanic/Latino), 18 international. Average age 32. 121 applicants, 55% accepted, 31 enrolled. In 2018, 18 master's, 12 doctorates awarded. *Degree requirements:* For master's, thesis or alternative; for doctorate, comprehensive exam (for some programs), thesis/dissertation (for some programs). *Entrance requirements:* For master's, placement exams, minimum GPA of 3.0, audition, bachelor's degree in music; for doctorate, placement exams, minimum GPA of 3.0, audition, master's degree in music. Additional exam requirements/recommendations for international students: Required—TOEFL (minimum score 85 iBT), IELTS (minimum score 6.5), We require either a TOEFL score of 85 or above OR an IELTS score of 6.5 or above. *Application deadline:* For fall admission, 2/15 for domestic students, 1/15 for international students; for spring admission, 10/1 for domestic students, 9/1 for international students; for summer admission, 3/15 for domestic students, 2/15 for international students. Applications are processed on a rolling basis. Application fee: $55 ($65 for international students). Electronic applications accepted. *Expenses:* Contact institution. *Financial support:* In 2018–19, 62 students received support, including 52 teaching assistantships with full and partial tuition reimbursements available (averaging $10,875 per year); scholarships/grants, health care benefits, tuition waivers (full and partial), and unspecified assistantships also available. Financial award application deadline: 2/15. *Faculty research:* Music education, conducting, musicology, composition, performance. *Total annual research expenditures:* $25,000. *Unit head:* Miguel Chuaqui, Director, 801-585-3720, E-mail: m.chauqui@utah.edu. *Application contact:* Cassie Wagstaff, Academic Coordinator, 801-585-6972, Fax: 801-581-5683, E-mail: cassandra.wagstaff@utah.edu.
Website: http://www.music.utah.edu/

University of Victoria, Faculty of Graduate Studies, Faculty of Education, Department of Curriculum and Instruction, Victoria, BC V8W 2Y2, Canada. Offers art education (M Ed, PhD); curriculum studies (M Ed, MA, PhD); early childhood education (M Ed, PhD); educational studies (PhD); language and literacy (M Ed, MA, PhD); mathematics (M Ed, MA, PhD); music education (M Ed, MA, PhD); science (M Ed, MA, PhD); social studies (M Ed, MA); social, cultural and foundational studies (MA, PhD); technology and environmental education (PhD). *Program availability:* Part-time. *Degree requirements:* For master's, thesis, project (M Ed); for doctorate, comprehensive exam, thesis/dissertation. *Entrance requirements:* For master's, minimum B average. Additional exam requirements/recommendations for international students: Required—TOEFL (minimum score 575 paper-based), IELTS (minimum score 7). Electronic applications accepted. *Faculty research:* Elementary and secondary English, language arts, curriculum theory and practice, educational media and technology, educational administration and leadership, history and philosophy of education.

University of Washington, Graduate School, College of Arts and Sciences, School of Music, Concentration in Music Education, Seattle, WA 98195. Offers MA, PhD. *Degree requirements:* For doctorate, thesis/dissertation. *Entrance requirements:* For master's,

GRE General Test, GRE Subject Test, minimum GPA of 3.0; for doctorate, GRE General Test, GRE Subject Test, minimum GPA of 3.0, sample of scholarly writing, videotape of teaching, 1 year of teaching experience. Additional exam requirements/recommendations for international students: Required—TOEFL. Electronic applications accepted. *Faculty research:* Multiethnic issues in music instruction, affective responses to music.

University of West Georgia, College of Arts and Humanities, Carrollton, GA 30118. Offers English (MA); history (MA); museum studies (Postbaccalaureate Certificate); music performance (M Mus); music teacher education (M Mus); public history (Postbaccalaureate Certificate). *Program availability:* Part-time, evening/weekend, 100% online, blended/hybrid learning. *Faculty:* 67 full-time (36 women). *Students:* 22 full-time (11 women), 71 part-time (48 women); includes 13 minority (7 Black or African American, non-Hispanic/Latino; 1 American Indian or Alaska Native, non-Hispanic/Latino; 1 Asian, non-Hispanic/Latino; 1 Hispanic/Latino; 3 Two or more races, non-Hispanic/Latino). Average age 30. 44 applicants, 95% accepted, 32 enrolled. In 2018, 24 master's, 8 other advanced degrees awarded. *Entrance requirements:* Additional exam requirements/recommendations for international students: Required—TOEFL (minimum score 523 paper-based; 69 iBT); Recommended—IELTS (minimum score 6.5). *Application deadline:* For fall admission, 8/1 for domestic students, 6/1 for international students; for spring admission, 11/15 for domestic students, 10/15 for international students; for summer admission, 5/15 for domestic students, 3/30 for international students. Applications are processed on a rolling basis. Application fee: $40. Electronic applications accepted. Tuition and fees vary according to course load, degree level, campus/location and program. *Financial support:* Fellowships, research assistantships, teaching assistantships, career-related internships or fieldwork, Federal Work-Study, institutionally sponsored loans, scholarships/grants, and unspecified assistantships available. Support available to part-time students. Financial award application deadline: 4/1; financial award applicants required to submit FAFSA. *Unit head:* Dr. Pauline D. Gagnon, Dean of Arts and Humanities, Interim Dean COSM, 678-839-5450, Fax: 678-839-5451, E-mail: pgagnon@westga.edu. *Application contact:* Dr. Toby Ziglar, Assistant Dean of the Graduate School, 678-839-1394, Fax: 678-839-1395, E-mail: graduate@westga.edu.
Website: http://www.westga.edu/coah

University of Wisconsin–Madison, Graduate School, College of Letters and Science, School of Music, Program in Music Education, Madison, WI 53706-1380. Offers curriculum and instruction (MS, PhD); music education (MM). *Accreditation:* NASM. *Degree requirements:* For doctorate, 2 foreign languages, thesis/dissertation. *Entrance requirements:* For doctorate, GRE General Test.

University of Wisconsin–Milwaukee, Graduate School, Peck School of the Arts, Milwaukee, WI 53201-0413. Offers art education (MS); chamber music (CAS); conducting (MM); dance (MFA); design entrepreneurship and innovation (MA); film, video, animation, and new genres (MFA); music education (MM); music history and literature (MM); performance (MM); string pedagogy (MM); studio art (MA, MFA); theory and composition (MM). *Program availability:* Part-time. *Students:* 85 full-time (52 women), 18 part-time (12 women); includes 15 minority (1 Black or African American, non-Hispanic/Latino; 2 Asian, non-Hispanic/Latino; 3 Hispanic/Latino; 1 Native Hawaiian or other Pacific Islander, non-Hispanic/Latino; 8 Two or more races, non-Hispanic/Latino), 22 international. Average age 31. 140 applicants, 36% accepted, 37 enrolled. In 2018, 39 master's, 2 other advanced degrees awarded. *Degree requirements:* For master's, comprehensive exam, thesis or alternative. *Entrance requirements:* For master's, portfolio. Additional exam requirements/recommendations for international students: Required—TOEFL (minimum score 550 paper-based; 79 iBT), IELTS (minimum score 6.5). *Application deadline:* For fall admission, 1/1 priority date for domestic students; for spring admission, 9/1 for domestic students. Application fee: $56 ($96 for international students). Electronic applications accepted. *Financial support:* Teaching assistantships, career-related internships or fieldwork, Federal Work-Study, health care benefits, unspecified assistantships, and project assistantships available. Support available to part-time students. Financial award application deadline: 4/15; financial award applicants required to submit FAFSA. *Unit head:* Scott Emmons, Dean, 414-229-4762, E-mail: semm@uwm.edu. *Application contact:* Arts Student Services, 414-229-4763, E-mail: uwmpsoa@uwm.edu.
Website: http://uwm.edu/arts/

University of Wisconsin–Stevens Point, College of Fine Arts and Communication, Department of Music, Stevens Point, WI 54481-3897. Offers elementary/secondary music education (MM Ed); studio pedagogy (MM Ed); Suzuki talent education (MM Ed). *Accreditation:* NASM. *Program availability:* Part-time. *Degree requirements:* For master's, thesis or alternative. *Entrance requirements:* For master's, teaching certificate. *Faculty research:* Music education, music composition, music performance.

University of Wyoming, College of Arts and Sciences, Department of Music, Laramie, WY 82071. Offers music education (MME); performance (MM). *Accreditation:* NASM. *Degree requirements:* For master's, comprehensive exam, thesis or alternative. *Entrance requirements:* For master's, minimum GPA of 3.0. Additional exam requirements/recommendations for international students: Required—TOEFL (minimum score 540 paper-based). Electronic applications accepted. *Expenses: Tuition, area resident:* Full-time $6504; part-time $271 per credit hour. Tuition, state resident: full-time $6504; part-time $271 per credit hour. Tuition, nonresident: full-time $19,464; part-time $811 per credit hour. *International tuition:* $19,464 full-time. *Required fees:* $1410.94; $343.82 per semester. $343.82 per semester. Tuition and fees vary according to course load, program and reciprocity agreements.

Utah State University, School of Graduate Studies, Caine College of the Arts, Department of Music, Logan, UT 84322. Offers guitar performance (MM); piano performance and pedagogy (MM).

VanderCook College of Music, Master of Music Education Program, Chicago, IL 60616-3731. Offers MM Ed. *Accreditation:* NASM. *Program availability:* Part-time. *Faculty:* 11 full-time (6 women), 66 part-time/adjunct (17 women). *Students:* 115 full-time (57 women), 25 part-time (12 women); includes 17 minority (10 Black or African American, non-Hispanic/Latino; 4 Asian, non-Hispanic/Latino; 1 Hispanic/Latino; 2 Two or more races, non-Hispanic/Latino). Average age 30. In 2018, 38 master's awarded. *Degree requirements:* For master's, thesis, written comprehensive exam or professional teaching portfolio. *Entrance requirements:* For master's, minimum of one year of teaching experience, or its equivalent, in music; official transcripts; 3 letters of recommendation; bachelor's degree in music education from accredited college or university or minimum of 60 credits in undergraduate music and music education coursework. Additional exam requirements/recommendations for international students: Required—TOEFL (minimum score 500 paper-based; 70 iBT). *Application deadline:* For fall admission, 4/1 for domestic and international students; for spring admission, 11/1 for domestic and international students. Applications are processed on a rolling basis. Application fee: $50. *Financial support:* Federal Work-Study, scholarships/grants, and unspecified assistantships available. Financial award application deadline: 5/1; financial award applicants required to submit FAFSA. *Faculty research:* Teaching outcomes. *Unit head:* Dr. Robert L. Sinclair, Dean of Graduate Studies, 312-788-1144, Fax: 312-225-5211, E-mail: rsinclair@vandercook.edu. *Application contact:* Cindy Tovar, Director of Admissions and Alumni Relations, 312-788-1122, Fax: 312-225-5211, E-mail: ctovar@vandercook.edu.
Website: http://www.vandercook.edu/admissions/graduate

Virginia Commonwealth University, Graduate School, School of the Arts, Department of Music, Richmond, VA 23284-9005. Offers music education (MM). *Accreditation:* NASM. *Degree requirements:* For master's, departmental qualifying exam, recital. *Entrance requirements:* For master's, department examination, audition or tapes, portfolio. Additional exam requirements/recommendations for international students: Required—TOEFL (minimum score 600 paper-based; 100 iBT). Electronic applications accepted. *Faculty research:* Composition, conducting, education, performance.

Wayne State College, School of Education and Counseling, Department of Educational Foundations and Leadership, Program in Curriculum and Instruction, Wayne, NE 68787. Offers alternative education (MSE); business and information technology education (MSE); communication arts education (MSE); early childhood education (MSE); elementary education (MSE); English as a second language (MSE); English education (MSE); family and consumer sciences education (MSE); industrial technology and vocational education (MSE); learning communities (MSE); mathematics education (MSE); music education (MSE); science education (MSE); social science education (MSE). *Accreditation:* NCATE. *Program availability:* Part-time, evening/weekend. *Degree requirements:* For master's, comprehensive exam, thesis optional. *Entrance requirements:* For master's, GRE General Test. Additional exam requirements/recommendations for international students: Required—TOEFL (minimum score 550 paper-based).

Wayne State University, College of Fine, Performing and Communication Arts, Department of Music, Detroit, MI 48202. Offers composition/theory (MA, MM); conducting (MA, MM); jazz performance (MA, MM); music education (MA, MM); orchestral studies (Certificate); performance (MA, MM). *Accreditation:* NASM. *Faculty:* 5. *Students:* 14 full-time (3 women), 5 part-time (1 woman); includes 2 minority (both Two or more races, non-Hispanic/Latino), 4 international. Average age 31. 31 applicants, 39% accepted, 8 enrolled. In 2018, 10 master's awarded. *Degree requirements:* For master's, thesis (for some programs), oral examination (for some programs), recital with program notes (for some programs). *Entrance requirements:* For master's, diagnostic exam in theory and history, undergraduate degree in same field as desired field of graduate study or equivalent in course work, private study, or experience; audition/interview; for Certificate, undergraduate degree in same field as desired field of graduate study or equivalent in course work, private study, or experience; audition/interview. Additional exam requirements/recommendations for international students: Required—TOEFL (minimum score 550 paper-based; 79 iBT), Michigan English Language Assessment Battery (minimum score 85); Recommended—IELTS (minimum score 6.5), TWE (minimum score 5.5). *Application deadline:* Applications are processed on a rolling basis. Application fee: $50. Electronic applications accepted. *Expenses:* Contact institution. *Financial support:* In 2018–19, 17 students received support, including 1 research assistantship (averaging $23,119 per year), 1 teaching assistantship (averaging $19,267 per year); career-related internships or fieldwork, institutionally sponsored loans, and scholarships/grants also available. Support available to part-time students. Financial award applicants required to submit FAFSA. *Faculty research:* Teacher training, pedagogy, musicology, composition/theory, conducting/performance practice. *Unit head:* Dr. Norah Duncan, Professor and Chair, 313-577-1775, E-mail: norah.duncan@wayne.edu. *Application contact:* Dr. Norah Duncan, Professor and Chair, 313-577-1775, E-mail: norah.duncan@wayne.edu.
Website: http://music.wayne.edu/

Webster University, Leigh Gerdine College of Fine Arts, Department of Music, St. Louis, MO 63119-3194. Offers church music (MM); composition (MM); jazz studies (MM); music (MA); music education (MM); organ (MM); performance (MM); piano (MM); voice (MM). *Accreditation:* NASM. *Entrance requirements:* Additional exam requirements/recommendations for international students: Required—TOEFL. *Expenses: Tuition:* Full-time $22,500; part-time $750 per credit hour. Tuition and fees vary according to degree level, campus/location and program.

West Chester University of Pennsylvania, School of Music, Department of Applied Music, West Chester, PA 19383. Offers performance (MM), including conducting, instrumental, keyboard, voice; piano pedagogy (MM, Certificate). *Program availability:* Part-time, evening/weekend. *Degree requirements:* For master's, comprehensive exam, thesis optional, recital. *Entrance requirements:* For master's and Certificate, School of Music Graduate Placement Test (GPT), audition, interview. Additional exam requirements/recommendations for international students: Required—TOEFL or IELTS. Electronic applications accepted. *Faculty research:* Performance, historical perspective, pedagogy.

West Chester University of Pennsylvania, School of Music, Department of Music Education, West Chester, PA 19383. Offers Kodaly methodology (Certificate); music education (MM, Teaching Certificate), including Kodaly methodology (MM), music technology (MM), Orff-Schulwerk (MM), performance (MM); music technology (Certificate); Orff-Schulwerk (Certificate). *Accreditation:* NASM; NCATE. *Program availability:* Part-time, evening/weekend. *Degree requirements:* For master's, comprehensive exam, thesis (for some programs), recital (performance option only). *Entrance requirements:* For master's, School of Music Graduate Placement Test (GPT), audition (performance track only), interview; for other advanced degree, audition, interview. Additional exam requirements/recommendations for international students: Required—TOEFL or IELTS. Electronic applications accepted. *Faculty research:* Music education in other cultures, educational advocacy and pedagogy, research in music education, special needs learners in music education, developing music listening skills.

Western Connecticut State University, Division of Graduate Studies, School of Visual and Performing Arts, Department of Music, Danbury, CT 06810-6885. Offers music education (MS). *Accreditation:* NASM. *Program availability:* Part-time. *Students:* 4 part-time (3 women). Average age 29. *Entrance requirements:* For master's, minimum GPA of 2.8, teaching certificate. Additional exam requirements/recommendations for international students: Recommended—TOEFL (minimum score 550 paper-based; 79 iBT), IELTS (minimum score 6). *Application deadline:* For fall admission, 8/5 priority date for domestic students; for spring admission, 1/5 for domestic students. Applications are processed on a rolling basis. Application fee: $50. *Financial support:* Application deadline: 5/1; applicants required to submit FAFSA. *Faculty research:* Ear training. *Unit head:* Kevin Isaacs, Graduate Coordinator, 203-837-8355, Fax: 203-837-8630, E-mail: isaacsk@wcsu.edu. *Application contact:* Dr. Chris Shankle, Associate Director of Graduate Studies, 203-837-9005, Fax: 203-837-8326, E-mail: shanklec@wcsu.edu.

Western Kentucky University, Graduate School, Potter College of Arts and Letters, Department of Music, Bowling Green, KY 42101. Offers MA Ed. *Accreditation:* NASM; NCATE. *Program availability:* Part-time, evening/weekend. *Degree requirements:* For master's, comprehensive exam, written exam. *Entrance requirements:* For master's, GRE General Test, minimum GPA of 3.0. Additional exam requirements/recommendations for international students: Required—TOEFL (minimum score 555 paper-based; 79 iBT). *Faculty research:* Music education, music technology, performance.

Western Michigan University, Graduate College, College of Fine Arts, School of Music, Kalamazoo, MI 49008. Offers music (MA); music composition (MM); music conducting (MM); music education (MM); music performance (MM); music therapy (MM). *Accreditation:* NASM.

West Virginia University, College of Creative Arts, Morgantown, WV 26506. Offers acting (MFA); art education (MA); art history (MA); ceramics (MFA); collaborative piano (MM, DMA); composition (MM, DMA); conducting (MM, DMA); costume design and technology (MFA); graphic design (MFA); intermedia and photography (MFA); jazz pedagogy (MM); lighting design and technology (MFA); music (PhD); music education (MM, PhD); music industry (MA); music theory (MM); musicology (MA); painting and printmaking (MFA); performance (MM, DMA); piano pedagogy (MM); scenic design and technology (MFA); sculpture (MFA); studio art (MA); technical direction (MFA); vocal pedagogy and performance (DMA). *Program availability:* Part-time. *Students:* 110 full-time (58 women), 30 part-time (15 women); includes 15 minority (5 Black or African American, non-Hispanic/Latino; 4 Asian, non-Hispanic/Latino; 6 Hispanic/Latino), 29 international. In 2018, 29 master's, 14 doctorates awarded. *Degree requirements:* For master's, thesis, recitals; for doctorate, comprehensive exam, thesis/dissertation, recitals (DMA). *Entrance requirements:* For doctorate, minimum GPA of 3.0, audition. Additional exam requirements/recommendations for international students: Required—TOEFL. *Application deadline:* For fall admission, 3/1 priority date for domestic students, 2/15 for international students; for spring admission, 11/1 for domestic students, 9/15 for international students. Applications are processed on a rolling basis. Application fee: $60. Electronic applications accepted. *Financial support:* Research assistantships, teaching assistantships, career-related internships or fieldwork, Federal Work-Study, institutionally sponsored loans, scholarships/grants, health care benefits, tuition waivers (partial), and administrative assistantships available. Financial award applicants required to submit FAFSA. *Faculty research:* Professional directing, consulting, acting design, music education, jazz history. *Unit head:* Dr. Keith Jackson, Dean, 304-293-4351, Fax: 304-293-6896, E-mail: Keith.jackson@mail.wvu.edu. *Application contact:* Dr. Keith Jackson, Dean, 304-293-4351, Fax: 304-293-6896, E-mail: Keith.jackson@mail.wvu.edu.

Wichita State University, Graduate School, College of Fine Arts, School of Music, Wichita, KS 67260. Offers music (MM); music education (MME). *Accreditation:* NASM. *Program availability:* Part-time. *Unit head:* Dr. Aleks Sternfeld-Dunn, Director, 316-978-6272, Fax: 316-978-3625, E-mail: aleks.sternfeld-dunn@wichita.edu. *Application contact:* Jordan Oleson, Admissions Coordinator, 316-978-3095, Fax: 316-978-3253, E-mail: jordan.oleson@wichita.edu.
Website: http://www.wichita.edu/music

Winthrop University, College of Visual and Performing Arts, Department of Music, Rock Hill, SC 29733. Offers conducting (MM); music education (MME); performance (MM). *Accreditation:* NASM. *Program availability:* Part-time. *Students:* 2 full-time (1 woman), 3 part-time (1 woman); includes 1 minority (Black or African American, non-Hispanic/Latino). Average age 32. In 2018, 1 master's awarded. *Degree requirements:* For master's, comprehensive exam (for some programs), oral and written exams, recital (MM). *Entrance requirements:* For master's, GRE General Test, audition, minimum GPA of 3.0, 2 recitals. Additional exam requirements/recommendations for international students: Required—TOEFL (minimum score 550 paper-based; 79 iBT), IELTS (minimum score 6). *Application deadline:* For fall admission, 7/15 priority date for domestic students; for spring admission, 12/1 for domestic students. Applications are processed on a rolling basis. Application fee: $50. Electronic applications accepted. *Expenses:* Tuition, state resident: full-time $15,166; part-time $635 per credit hour. Tuition, nonresident: full-time $29,214. *Required fees:* $500; $180 per semester. *Financial support:* Research assistantships with full tuition reimbursements, Federal Work-Study, scholarships/grants, and unspecified assistantships available. Support available to part-time students. Financial award application deadline: 2/1; financial award applicants required to submit FAFSA. *Unit head:* Donald Rogers, Graduate Program Director, 803-323-2255, E-mail: rogersd@winthrop.edu. *Application contact:* Donald Rogers, Graduate Program Director, 803-323-2255, E-mail: rogersd@winthrop.edu.
Website: http://www.winthrop.edu/cvpa/music

Wright State University, Graduate School, College of Liberal Arts, Department of Music, Dayton, OH 45435. Offers MM. *Accreditation:* NASM. *Program availability:* Part-time. *Degree requirements:* For master's, thesis or alternative, oral exam. *Entrance requirements:* For master's, theory placement test, BA in music. Additional exam requirements/recommendations for international students: Required—TOEFL. *Faculty research:* General music, current needs, role of teacher, expectations in music education.

Youngstown State University, College of Graduate Studies, Cliffe College of Creative Arts and Communication, Dana School of Music, Youngstown, OH 44555-0001. Offers jazz studies (MM); music education (MM); music history and literature (MM); music theory and composition (MM); performance (MM). *Accreditation:* NASM. *Program availability:* Part-time, evening/weekend. *Degree requirements:* For master's, one foreign language, thesis optional, final qualifying exam. *Entrance requirements:* For master's, audition; GRE General Test or minimum GPA of 2.7. Additional exam requirements/recommendations for international students: Required—TOEFL. *Faculty research:* Teaching education, use of computers, conducting.

Reading Education

Abilene Christian University, Graduate Programs, College of Education and Human Services, Teaching and Learning Program, Abilene, TX 79699. Offers initial certification (M Ed); reading teacher (M Ed). *Faculty:* 9 part-time/adjunct (7 women). *Students:* 14 part-time (all women); includes 2 minority (1 Black or African American, non-Hispanic/Latino; 1 Hispanic/Latino). 21 applicants, 67% accepted, 14 enrolled. In 2018, 13 master's awarded. *Entrance requirements:* Additional exam requirements/recommendations for international students: Required—TOEFL (minimum score 80 iBT), IELTS (minimum score 6), PTE. *Application deadline:* For fall admission, 11/15 for domestic students. Application fee: $65. Electronic applications accepted. *Expenses:* $1000 per hour. *Financial support:* In 2018–19, 13 students received support. Scholarships/grants available. Financial award application deadline: 4/1; financial award applicants required to submit FAFSA. *Unit head:* Dr. Andrew Huddleston, Director, 325-674-2112, Fax: 325-674-2123, E-mail: aph97a@acu.edu. *Application contact:* Graduate Admissions, 325-674-6911, E-mail: gradinfo@acu.edu.
Website: http://www.acu.edu/graduate/academics/teaching-and-learning.html

Adelphi University, College of Education & Health Sciences, College of Education and Health Sciences, Garden City, NY 11530-0701. Offers birth-grade 12 (MS); birth-grade 6 (MS); grades 5-12 (MS). *Program availability:* Part-time, evening/weekend. *Students:* 6 full-time (all women), 12 part-time (11 women); includes 2 minority (both Black or African American, non-Hispanic/Latino). Average age 30. 16 applicants, 69% accepted, 5 enrolled. In 2018, 4 master's awarded. *Entrance requirements:* For master's, letters of recommendation, resume, minimum grade point average of 3.0, personal essay. Additional exam requirements/recommendations for international students: Required—TOEFL (minimum score 550 paper-based; 80 iBT), IELTS (minimum score 6.5). *Application deadline:* Applications are processed on a rolling basis. Application fee: $50. Electronic applications accepted. *Expenses:* Contact institution. *Financial support:* Research assistantships, teaching assistantships, career-related internships or fieldwork, institutionally sponsored loans, scholarships/grants, traineeships, and unspecified assistantships available. Support available to part-time students. Financial award application deadline: 1/1; financial award applicants required to submit FAFSA. *Faculty research:* Assessment and intervention, literacy education and development, higher and teacher education, human and adult development, achieving styles and human motivation. *Unit head:* Dr. Evelyn O'Connor, Director, Literacy, 516-877-4173, E-mail: eoconnor@adelphi.edu. *Application contact:* Dr. Evelyn O'Connor, Director, Literacy, 516-877-4173, E-mail: eoconnor@adelphi.edu.

Alabama Agricultural and Mechanical University, School of Graduate Studies, College of Education, Humanities, and Behavioral Sciences, Department of Reading, Elementary, Early Childhood and Special Education, Huntsville, AL 35811. Offers early childhood education (MS Ed, Ed S); elementary education (MS Ed, Ed S); reading/literacy (PhD); special education collaborative teacher training (MS Ed, Ed S). *Accreditation:* NCATE. *Program availability:* Evening/weekend. *Degree requirements:* For master's, comprehensive exam; for Ed S, thesis. *Entrance requirements:* For master's, GRE General Test. Additional exam requirements/recommendations for international students: Required—TOEFL (minimum score 500 paper-based; 61 iBT). Electronic applications accepted. *Faculty research:* Multicultural education, learning styles, diagnostic-prescriptive instruction.

Alabama State University, College of Education, Department of Curriculum and Instruction, Montgomery, AL 36101-0271. Offers early childhood education (Ed S); secondary education (M Ed), including biology education, English language arts education, history education, math education, music education, reading education, social science education. *Program availability:* Part-time, evening/weekend, online only, 100% online. *Faculty:* 7 full-time (4 women), 7 part-time/adjunct (4 women). *Students:* 22 full-time (19 women), 58 part-time (49 women); includes 235 minority (234 Black or African American, non-Hispanic/Latino; 1 Hispanic/Latino), 5 international. Average age 36. 45 applicants, 33% accepted, 6 enrolled. In 2018, 34 master's awarded. *Degree requirements:* For master's, comprehensive exam, thesis optional; for Ed S, comprehensive exam, thesis. *Entrance requirements:* For master's, GRE General Test, MAT, writing competency test; for Ed S, writing competency test, GRE, MAT. Additional exam requirements/recommendations for international students: Required—TOEFL (minimum score 500 paper-based). *Application deadline:* For fall admission, 4/15 for domestic and international students; for spring admission, 11/15 for domestic and international students; for summer admission, 3/15 for domestic and international students. Applications are processed on a rolling basis. Application fee: $25. Electronic applications accepted. *Expenses:* Contact institution. *Financial support:* Fellowships, teaching assistantships, career-related internships or fieldwork, scholarships/grants, tuition waivers (partial), and unspecified assistantships available. Financial award application deadline: 6/30; financial award applicants required to submit FAFSA. *Unit head:* Dr. Joyce Johnson, Acting Chairperson, 334-229-4485, Fax: 334-229-5603, E-mail: jjohnson@alasu.edu. *Application contact:* Dr. Ed Brown, Dean of Graduate Studies, 334-229-4274, Fax: 334-229-4928, E-mail: ebrown@alasu.edu.
Website: http://www.alasu.edu/academics/colleges—departments/college-of-education/curriculum—instruction/index.aspx

Alfred University, Graduate School, Division of Education, Alfred, NY 14802-1205. Offers college student development (MS Ed); literacy (MS Ed). *Accreditation:* TEAC. *Program availability:* Part-time. *Entrance requirements:* For master's, Liberal Arts and Sciences Test (LAST), Assessment of Teaching Skills (written) (ATS-W), Content Specialty Test (CST). Additional exam requirements/recommendations for international students: Required—TOEFL (minimum score 590 paper-based; 90 iBT), IELTS (minimum score 6.5). Electronic applications accepted.

Alverno College, School of Professional Studies - Education Division, Milwaukee, WI 53234-3922. Offers adaptive education (MA); administrative leadership (MA); adult education and organizational development (MA); adult educational and instructional design (MA); adult educational and instructional technology (MA); global connections in the humanities (MA); instructional leadership (MA); instructional technology for K-12 settings (MA); professional development (MA); reading education (MA); reading education with adaptive education (MA); science education (MA); special education (MA); teaching in alternative schools (MA). *Accreditation:* NCATE. *Program availability:* Part-time, evening/weekend. *Degree requirements:* For master's, presentation/defense of proposal, conference presentation of inquiry projects. *Entrance requirements:* For master's, bachelor's degree in related field, communication samples from work setting, 3 letters of recommendation. Additional exam requirements/recommendations for international students: Required—TOEFL. Electronic applications accepted. *Expenses:* Contact institution. *Faculty research:* Student self-assessment, self-reflection, integration of curriculum, identifying needs of students in strategic situations and designing appropriate classroom strategies.

American International College, School of Education, Springfield, MA 01109-3189. Offers early childhood education (M Ed, CAGS); education (MA, Ed D), including counseling psychology (MA), educational leadership and supervision (Ed D), professional counseling and supervision (Ed D), teaching and learning (Ed D); elementary education (M Ed, CAGS); middle education/secondary education (M Ed, CAGS); moderate disabilities (M Ed, CAGS); reading specialist (M Ed, CAGS); school adjustment counseling (MAEP, CAGS); school guidance counseling (MAEP, CAGS); school leadership (M Ed, CAGS). *Program availability:* Evening/weekend. *Degree requirements:* For master's and CAGS, practicum/culminating experience. *Entrance requirements:* For master's, Communication and Literacy portion of the Massachusetts Tests for Education Licensure, graduate of accredited four-year college with minimum B-average in undergraduate course work; for CAGS, M Ed or master's degree in field related to licensure from accredited institution. Electronic applications accepted. *Expenses:* Contact institution.

Appalachian State University, Cratis D. Williams School of Graduate Studies, Department of Reading Education and Special Education, Boone, NC 28608. Offers reading education (MA); special education (MA). *Accreditation:* ASHA. *Program availability:* Part-time, evening/weekend, online learning. *Degree requirements:* For master's, comprehensive exam, thesis optional. *Entrance requirements:* For master's,

GRE General Test or MAT, 3 letters of recommendation. Additional exam requirements/recommendations for international students: Required—TOEFL (minimum score 570 paper-based; 79 iBT), IELTS (minimum score 6.5). Electronic applications accepted. *Expenses: Tuition, area resident:* Full-time $4839; part-time $237 per credit hour. Tuition, state resident: full-time $4839; part-time $237 per credit hour. Tuition, nonresident: full-time $18,271; part-time $895.50 per credit hour. *Faculty research:* Special education, language arts, reading.

Arcadia University, School of Education, Glenside, PA 19038-3295. Offers art education (M Ed); computer education (CAS); curriculum (CAS); curriculum studies (M Ed); early childhood education (M Ed), including individualized, master teacher, research in child development; educational leadership (M Ed, Ed D, CAS); elementary education (M Ed); English education (MA Ed); environmental education (MA Ed); instructional technology (M Ed); language arts (M Ed); library science (M Ed); mathematics education (M Ed, MA Ed); music education (MA Ed); psychology (MA Ed); reading (M Ed, CAS); science education (M Ed, CAS); secondary education (M Ed, CAS); special education (M Ed, Ed D, CAS); theater arts (MA Ed); written communication (MA Ed). *Accreditation:* NASAD. *Program availability:* Part-time, evening/weekend, online learning. *Faculty:* 14 full-time (10 women). *Students:* 35 full-time (24 women), 299 part-time (243 women); includes 72 minority (49 Black or African American, non-Hispanic/Latino; 1 American Indian or Alaska Native, non-Hispanic/Latino; 12 Asian, non-Hispanic/Latino; 8 Hispanic/Latino; 2 Two or more races, non-Hispanic/Latino), 5 international. In 2018, 152 master's, 8 doctorates awarded. *Entrance requirements:* Additional exam requirements/recommendations for international students: Required—Official results from the TOEFL or IELTS are required. *Application deadline:* Applications are processed on a rolling basis. Application fee: $25. Electronic applications accepted. *Expenses:* Contact institution. *Financial support:* Career-related internships or fieldwork, tuition waivers (partial), and unspecified assistantships available. *Unit head:* Kimberly Dean, Chair, 215-572-8629. *Application contact:* 215-572-2925, Fax: 215-572-2126, E-mail: grad@arcadia.edu.

Arkansas State University, Graduate School, College of Education and Behavioral Science, School of Teacher Education and Leadership, State University, AR 72467. Offers community college administration (SCCT); curriculum and instruction (MSE); early childhood education (MSE); early childhood services (MS); educational leadership (MSE, Ed D, Ed S); educational theory and practice (MSE); middle level education (MAT, MSE); reading (MSE, Ed S); special education - gifted, talented, and creative (MSE); special education - instructional specialist grades 4-12 (MSE); special education - instructional specialist grades P-4 (MSE); special education, K-12 (MSE). *Accreditation:* NCATE. *Program availability:* Part-time, online learning. *Degree requirements:* For master's, comprehensive exam, thesis or alternative; for doctorate, comprehensive exam, thesis/dissertation; for other advanced degree, comprehensive exam. *Entrance requirements:* For master's, GRE General Test or MAT, appropriate bachelor's degree, official transcripts, immunization records, letters of reference, interview; for doctorate, GRE General Test or MAT, interview, master's degree, letters of reference, official transcript, personal statement, writing sample, immunization records; for other advanced degree, GRE General Test or MAT, interview, master's degree, official transcript, immunization records, letters of reference, 3 years of teaching experience, teaching license. Additional exam requirements/recommendations for international students: Required—TOEFL (minimum score 550 paper-based; 79 iBT), IELTS (minimum score 6), PTE (minimum score 56). Electronic applications accepted.

Asbury University, School of Graduate and Professional Studies, Wilmore, KY 40390-1198. Offers biology: alternative certificate (MA Ed); chemistry: alternative certificate (MA Ed); English (MA Ed); English as a second language (MA Ed); ESL (MA Ed); French (MA Ed); Latin: alternative certificate (MA Ed); mathematics: alternative certificate (MA Ed); reading/writing endorsement (MA Ed); social studies (MA Ed); social work (MSW), including child and family services; Spanish (MA Ed); special education (MA Ed); special education: alternative certificate (MA Ed); teacher as leader endorsement (MA Ed). *Accreditation:* NCATE. *Program availability:* Part-time. *Degree requirements:* For master's, action research project, portfolio. *Entrance requirements:* For master's, PRAXIS/NTE, minimum GPA of 2.75, letters of recommendation. Additional exam requirements/recommendations for international students: Required—TOEFL (minimum score 550 paper-based). Electronic applications accepted.

Augustana University, MA in Education Program, Sioux Falls, SD 57197. Offers instructional strategies (MA); reading (MA); special populations (MA); STEM (MA); technology (MA). *Accreditation:* NCATE. *Program availability:* Part-time-only, evening/weekend, online only, 100% online. *Degree requirements:* For master's, thesis. *Entrance requirements:* For master's, appropriate bachelor's degree, minimum GPA of 3.0, teaching certificate. Additional exam requirements/recommendations for international students: Required—TOEFL (minimum score 550 paper-based). Electronic applications accepted. *Expenses:* Contact institution. *Faculty research:* Multicultural education, education of students with autism, well-being in school settings, factors that predict academic hopefulness.

Aurora University, School of Education and Human Performance, Aurora, IL 60506-4892. Offers applied behavioral analysis (MS); bilingual-ESL education (MA); educational leadership with principal endorsement (MA); educational technology (MA); leadership in adult learning higher education (Ed D); leadership in curriculum and instruction (Ed D); leadership in educational administration (Ed D); reading instruction (MA); special education (MA). *Accreditation:* NCATE. *Program availability:* Part-time, evening/weekend, 100% online. *Faculty:* 14 full-time (6 women), 32 part-time/adjunct (17 women). *Students:* 28 full-time (25 women), 537 part-time (359 women); includes 101 minority (25 Black or African American, non-Hispanic/Latino; 8 Asian, non-Hispanic/Latino; 58 Hispanic/Latino; 2 Native Hawaiian or other Pacific Islander, non-Hispanic/Latino; 8 Two or more races, non-Hispanic/Latino), 2 international. Average age 38. 191 applicants, 98% accepted, 133 enrolled. In 2018, 213 master's, 16 doctorates awarded. *Degree requirements:* For master's, student teaching, research seminar, and practicum; for doctorate, comprehensive exam, thesis/dissertation. *Entrance requirements:* For master's, 2 years of teaching experience, valid teaching certificate, resume; for doctorate, appropriate master's degree, two references, curriculum vitae, personal statement, professional project, reflective essay. Additional exam requirements/recommendations for international students: Required—TOEFL (minimum score 550 paper-based; 79 iBT). *Application deadline:* For fall admission, 6/1 for international students; for spring admission, 10/1 for international students. Applications are processed on a rolling basis. Application fee: $0. Electronic applications accepted. *Expenses:* The reported tuition amount is for the program with the greatest enrollment, MA in Educational Leadership with Principal Endorsement. Other programs may require more semester hours, and thus have a greater total cost. The Education doctoral programs are roughly double the amount of the master's programs. *Financial support:* In 2018–19, 31 students received support. Federal Work-Study, scholarships/grants, and unspecified assistantships available. Financial award applicants required to submit FAFSA. *Unit head:* Dr. Jen Buckley, Dean, School of Education and Human Performance, 630-844-1542, Fax: 630-844-6155, E-mail: jbuckley@aurora.edu. *Application contact:* Center for Graduate Studies, 630-947-8955, E-mail: AUadmission@aurora.edu.
Website: http://aurora.edu/education

Baldwin Wallace University, Graduate Programs, School of Education, Specialization in Literacy, Berea, OH 44017-2088. Offers MA Ed. *Accreditation:* NCATE. *Program availability:* Part-time, evening/weekend, blended/hybrid learning. *Students:* 7 full-time (all women), 23 part-time (all women); includes 4 minority (3 Black or African American, non-Hispanic/Latino; 1 Two or more races, non-Hispanic/Latino). Average age 30. 12 applicants, 67% accepted, 6 enrolled. In 2018, 10 master's awarded. *Degree requirements:* For master's, capstone practicum. *Entrance requirements:* For master's, bachelor's degree in field, MAT or minimum GPA of 3.0. Additional exam requirements/recommendations for international students: Required—TOEFL (minimum score 550 paper-based; 79 iBT). *Application deadline:* For fall admission, 8/15 priority date for domestic students; for spring admission, 12/15 priority date for domestic students. Applications are processed on a rolling basis. Application fee: $25. Electronic applications accepted. Application fee is waived when completed online. *Expenses:* $545 per credit partnership tuition, $721 per credit non-partnership tuition. *Financial support:* Career-related internships or fieldwork available. Financial award applicants required to submit FAFSA. *Faculty research:* Metacognition and the reading process, language acquisition, genres and the reader response theory, cultural responsiveness, content area literacy. *Unit head:* Dr. Rochelle Berndt, Chair, 440-826-2168, Fax: 440-826-3779, E-mail: kkaye@bw.edu. *Application contact:* Amirya Alveranga, Admission Counselor, 440-826-8005, Fax: 440-826-3830, E-mail: aalveran@bw.edu.
Website: http://www.bw.edu/academics/master-of-arts-in-education/maed-in-literacy/

Ball State University, Graduate School, Teachers College, Department of Elementary Education, Muncie, IN 47306. Offers early childhood administration (Certificate); elementary education (MAE, Ed D, PhD); enhanced teaching practices for elementary teachers (Certificate); literacy instruction (Certificate). *Accreditation:* NCATE. *Program availability:* Part-time, 100% online. *Entrance requirements:* For master's, minimum baccalaureate GPA of 2.75 or 3.0 in latter half of baccalaureate; for doctorate, GRE General Test, minimum graduate GPA of 3.2. Additional exam requirements/recommendations for international students: Required—TOEFL (minimum score 550 paper-based; 79 iBT), IELTS (minimum score 6.5). Electronic applications accepted.

Bank Street College of Education, Graduate School, Program in Reading and Literacy, New York, NY 10025. Offers advanced literacy specialization (Ed M); reading and literacy (MS Ed); teaching literacy (MS Ed); teaching literacy and childhood general education (MS Ed). *Degree requirements:* For master's, thesis. *Entrance requirements:* For master's, interview, essays. Additional exam requirements/recommendations for international students: Required—TOEFL (minimum score 600 paper-based; 100 iBT), IELTS (minimum score 7). Electronic applications accepted. *Faculty research:* Language development, children's literature, whole language, the reading and writing processes, reading difficulties in multicultural classrooms.

Barry University, School of Education, Program in Curriculum and Instruction, Miami Shores, FL 33161-6695. Offers accomplished teacher (Ed S); culture, language and literacy (TESOL) (PhD); curriculum evaluation and research (PhD); early childhood (Ed S); early childhood education (PhD); elementary (Ed S); elementary education (PhD); ESOL (Ed S); gifted (Ed S); Montessori (Ed S); PKP/elementary (Ed S); reading (Ed S); reading, language and cognition (PhD). *Entrance requirements:* For doctorate, GRE, minimum GPA of 3.25.

Barry University, School of Education, Program in Reading, Miami Shores, FL 33161-6695. Offers MS, Ed S. *Program availability:* Part-time, evening/weekend. *Degree requirements:* For master's, comprehensive exam, practicum; for Ed S, practicum. *Entrance requirements:* For master's, GRE General Test or MAT, minimum GPA of 3.0, course work in children's literature; for Ed S, GRE General Test, minimum GPA of 3.0. Electronic applications accepted.

Belhaven University, School of Education, Jackson, MS 39202-1789. Offers education (M Ed, MAT); educational leadership (Ed D, Ed S); reading literacy (M Ed). *Program availability:* Part-time, evening/weekend, 100% online, blended/hybrid learning. *Faculty:* 8 full-time (6 women), 24 part-time/adjunct (20 women). *Students:* 11 full-time (7 women), 452 part-time (360 women); includes 262 minority (244 Black or African American, non-Hispanic/Latino; 1 American Indian or Alaska Native, non-Hispanic/Latino; 3 Asian, non-Hispanic/Latino; 3 Hispanic/Latino; 11 Two or more races, non-Hispanic/Latino), 1 international. Average age 36. 299 applicants, 49% accepted, 103 enrolled. In 2018, 65 master's, 5 other advanced degrees awarded. *Degree requirements:* For master's, comprehensive exam, portfolio; for doctorate, thesis/dissertation. *Entrance requirements:* For master's, PRAXIS I and II, minimum GPA of 2.8; for doctorate, MAT or GRE, master's degree in education or related field with minimum GPA of 3.0; essay; three professional letters of recommendation; minimum three years' experience in a PK-12 education context. *Application deadline:* Applications are processed on a rolling basis. Application fee: $25. Electronic applications accepted. *Expenses:* $525 per credit hour, $75 technology fee per course. *Financial support:* Applicants required to submit FAFSA. *Unit head:* Dr. David Hand, Dean, 601-965-7020, E-mail: dhand@belhaven.edu. *Application contact:* Sean Kirnan, Assistant Vice President for Adult and Graduate Enrollment and Student Services, 601-968-8727, Fax: 601-968-5953, E-mail: gradadmission@belhaven.edu.

Bellarmine University, Annsley Frazier Thornton School of Education, Louisville, KY 40205. Offers education and district leadership (Ed D); education and social change (PhD); elementary education (MA Ed, MAT); leadership in higher education (PhD); middle school education (MA Ed, MAT); principalship (Ed S); reading and writing (MA Ed); secondary education (MAT); teacher leadership (MA Ed). *Accreditation:* NCATE. *Program availability:* Part-time, evening/weekend. *Faculty:* 14 full-time (7 women), 17 part-time/adjunct (11 women). *Students:* 27 full-time (19 women), 205 part-time (156 women); includes 74 minority (53 Black or African American, non-Hispanic/Latino; 6 Asian, non-Hispanic/Latino; 7 Hispanic/Latino; 8 Two or more races, non-Hispanic/Latino). Average age 34. 155 applicants, 71% accepted, 95 enrolled. In 2018, 69 master's, 10 doctorates, 30 other advanced degrees awarded. *Degree requirements:* For master's, comprehensive exam (for some programs), thesis (for some programs); for doctorate, comprehensive exam (for some programs), thesis/dissertation; for Ed S, comprehensive exam (for some programs). *Entrance requirements:* For master's, GRE, baccalaureate degree from accredited institution; minimum cumulative GPA of 2.75; recommendations from employers, supervisors, or professors attesting to applicant's potential as graduate student; statement of intent to pursue graduate degree; for doctorate, GRE, minimum GPA of 3.5 in all graduate coursework; baccalaureate and master's degrees in education or fields directly relevant to education; three letters of recommendation; two essays (no more than 1,000 words each); resume or curriculum vitae; interview; for Ed S, master's degree in education; valid teaching certificate; three years of experience in teaching; three recommendations; minimum GPA of 3.0 in all graduate work; interview; essays; personal goal statement. Additional exam requirements/recommendations for international students: Required—TOEFL (minimum score 80 iBT), IELTS (minimum score 6), TOEFL (minimum score 550 paper-based, 68 iBT), IELTS (minimum score 6), or Michigan English Language Assessment Battery. *Application deadline:* For fall admission, 8/1 priority date for domestic and international students; for spring admission, 12/1 priority date for domestic and international students; for summer admission, 4/10 priority date for domestic and international students. Applications are processed on a rolling basis. Application fee: $40. Electronic applications accepted. *Expenses:* Doctor of Education: $855 per credit hour;

Educational Specialist: $410 per credit hour; Master of Arts in Education: $410 per credit hour; Master of Arts in Teaching: $665 per credit hour; Master of Arts in Teaching, undergraduate content courses: $410 per credit hour; Master of Education in Higher Education Leadership and Social Justice: $665 per credit hour; Ph.D., Social Change: $855 per credit hour; Ph.D., Leadership in Higher Education: $855 per credit hour; Rank I Programs: $410 per credit hour. *Financial support:* Scholarships/grants available. Financial award applicants required to submit FAFSA. *Faculty research:* Literacy, service-learning, dispositions, educational technology, special education. *Unit head:* Dr. Elizabeth Dinkins, Dean, 502-272-7958, Fax: 502-272-8189, E-mail: edinkins@bellarmine.edu. *Application contact:* Sarah Schuble, Assistant Director of Graduate Student Enrollment, 502-272-8271, Fax: 502-272-8002, E-mail: sschuble@bellarmine.edu.
Website: http://www.bellarmine.edu/education/graduate

Berry College, Graduate Programs, Graduate Programs in Education, Program in Middle-Grades Education and Reading, Mount Berry, GA 30149. Offers middle grades education (MAT); middle-grades education (M Ed); reading (M Ed). *Accreditation:* NCATE. *Program availability:* Part-time. *Degree requirements:* For master's, thesis, portfolio, oral exams. *Entrance requirements:* For master's, GRE General Test or MAT, minimum GPA of 2.5. Additional exam requirements/recommendations for international students: Required—TOEFL (minimum score 550 paper-based). *Application deadline:* For fall admission, 7/26 for domestic students, 5/1 for international students; for spring admission, 12/1 for domestic students, 10/1 for international students. Applications are processed on a rolling basis. Application fee: $25 ($30 for international students). Electronic applications accepted. *Expenses:* Contact institution. *Financial support:* Research assistantships with full tuition reimbursements, scholarships/grants, tuition waivers (partial), and unspecified assistantships available. Support available to part-time students. Financial award application deadline: 3/1; financial award applicants required to submit FAFSA. *Unit head:* Dr. Jacqueline McDowell, Dean, 706-236-1717, Fax: 706-238-5827, E-mail: jmcdowell@berry.edu. *Application contact:* Admissions, 706-236-2215, Fax: 706-290-2178, E-mail: admissions@berry.edu.

Binghamton University, State University of New York, Graduate School, College of Community and Public Affairs, Department of Teaching, Learning and Educational Leadership, Program in Literacy Education, Binghamton, NY 13902-6000. Offers MS Ed. *Accreditation:* TEAC. *Program availability:* Part-time, evening/weekend. *Degree requirements:* For master's, thesis. *Entrance requirements:* For master's, GRE General Test, teaching certification. Additional exam requirements/recommendations for international students: Required—TOEFL (minimum score 550 paper-based; 80 iBT). Electronic applications accepted.

Bloomsburg University of Pennsylvania, School of Graduate Studies, College of Education, Department of Teaching and Learning, Program in Reading, Bloomsburg, PA 17815-1301. Offers M Ed. *Degree requirements:* For master's, thesis, PRAXIS II. *Entrance requirements:* For master's, baccalaureate degree, letter of intent, two letters of recommendation, teaching certificate. Additional exam requirements/recommendations for international students: Required—TOEFL, IELTS. Electronic applications accepted.

Blue Mountain College, Program in Literacy/Reading (K-12), Blue Mountain, MS 38610. Offers M Ed. *Program availability:* Part-time, evening/weekend. *Degree requirements:* For master's, comprehensive exam. *Entrance requirements:* For master's, PRAXIS, GRE or MAT, official transcripts, bachelor's degree in a field of education from an accredited university or college, permanent teaching license, three recommendations. Additional exam requirements/recommendations for international students: Required—TOEFL (minimum score 550 paper-based). Electronic applications accepted.

Bluffton University, Programs in Education, Bluffton, OH 45817. Offers intervention specialist (MA Ed); leadership (MA Ed); reading (MA Ed). *Accreditation:* NCATE. *Program availability:* Part-time, 100% online, blended/hybrid learning, videoconference. *Faculty:* 2 full-time (both women), 2 part-time/adjunct (1 woman). *Students:* 14 full-time (7 women), 7 part-time (all women). Average age 31. In 2018, 8 master's awarded. *Degree requirements:* For master's, action research project, public presentation. *Entrance requirements:* For master's, PRAXIS I, bachelor's degree, minimum GPA of 3.0. Additional exam requirements/recommendations for international students: Required—TOEFL. *Application deadline:* For fall admission, 8/15 priority date for domestic students, 6/15 priority date for international students; for spring admission, 12/15 priority date for domestic students, 9/15 priority date for international students. Applications are processed on a rolling basis. Electronic applications accepted. *Expenses:* Contact institution. *Financial support:* Unspecified assistantships available. Financial award application deadline: 9/15; financial award applicants required to submit FAFSA. *Unit head:* Dr. Amy K. Mullins, Director of Graduate Programs in Education, 419-358-3457, E-mail: mullinsa@bluffton.edu. *Application contact:* Shelby Koenig, Enrollment Counselor for Graduate Program, 419-358-3022, E-mail: koenigs@bluffton.edu.
Website: https://www.bluffton.edu/ags/index.aspx

Boise State University, College of Education, Department of Literacy, Language and Culture, Boise, ID 83725-0399. Offers bilingual education (M Ed); English as a new language (M Ed); literacy (MA). *Accreditation:* NCATE. *Program availability:* Part-time, evening/weekend. *Degree requirements:* For master's, thesis optional. *Entrance requirements:* For master's, minimum GPA of 3.0. Additional exam requirements/recommendations for international students: Required—TOEFL (minimum score 550 paper-based; 80 iBT), IELTS (minimum score 6). Electronic applications accepted.

Boston College, Lynch School of Education and Human Development, Department of Teacher Education, Special Education and Curriculum and Instruction, Chestnut Hill, MA 02467-3800. Offers curriculum and instruction (M Ed, PhD, CAES); early childhood education (M Ed); elementary education (M Ed); law and curriculum and instruction (JD/M Ed); reading specialist (M Ed, CAES); religious education (M Ed, CAES); secondary education (M Ed, MAT, MST), including biology (MST), chemistry (MST), English (MAT), French (MAT), geology (MST), history (MAT), Latin and classical humanities (MAT), mathematics (MST), physics (MST), secondary teaching (M Ed), Spanish (MAT); special needs: moderate disabilities (M Ed, CAES); special needs: severe disabilities (M Ed); JD/M Ed. *Program availability:* Part-time, evening/weekend, 100% online. *Faculty:* 19 full-time (11 women). *Students:* 186 full-time (140 women), 92 part-time (74 women); includes 58 minority (20 Black or African American, non-Hispanic/Latino; 4 Asian, non-Hispanic/Latino; 29 Hispanic/Latino; 5 Two or more races, non-Hispanic/Latino), 33 international. Average age 28. In 2018, 132 master's, 13 doctorates awarded. Terminal master's awarded for partial completion of doctoral program. *Degree requirements:* For master's, comprehensive exam; for doctorate, comprehensive exam, thesis/dissertation. *Entrance requirements:* Additional exam requirements/recommendations for international students: Required—TOEFL. Application fee: $75. Electronic applications accepted. *Financial support:* Fellowships with full and partial tuition reimbursements, research assistantships with full and partial tuition reimbursements, teaching assistantships with full and partial tuition reimbursements, career-related internships or fieldwork, Federal Work-Study, institutionally sponsored loans, scholarships/grants, traineeships, health care benefits, tuition waivers (full and partial), and unspecified assistantships available. Support available to part-time students. Financial award applicants required to submit FAFSA. *Faculty research:* Teacher education, education research and policy, bilingual education, science education, disabilities, urban education. *Unit head:* Dr. Susan Bruce, Chairperson, 617-552-4214, Fax: 617-552-0812. *Application contact:* Jessica Rivers, Assistant Dean of Graduate Admission and Financial Aid, 617-552-4214, Fax: 617-552-0398, E-mail: riversja@bc.edu.
Website: http://www.bc.edu/education

Bowie State University, Graduate Programs, Program in Reading Education, Bowie, MD 20715-9465. Offers M Ed. *Accreditation:* NCATE. *Program availability:* Part-time, evening/weekend. *Degree requirements:* For master's, comprehensive exam, thesis optional, research paper. *Entrance requirements:* For master's, minimum GPA of 2.5, teaching certificate, teaching experience. *Faculty research:* Literacy education, multicultural education.

Bowling Green State University, Graduate College, College of Education and Human Development, School of Teaching and Learning, Program in Reading, Bowling Green, OH 43403. Offers M Ed, Ed S. *Accreditation:* NCATE. *Program availability:* Part-time. *Degree requirements:* For master's, thesis or alternative; for Ed S, practicum or field experience. *Entrance requirements:* For master's and Ed S, GRE General Test. Additional exam requirements/recommendations for international students: Required—TOEFL. Electronic applications accepted. *Faculty research:* Children's literature, attention deficit disorder (ADD)/reading correlation, content area reading, reading instruction, reading/writing connection.

Bridgewater State University, College of Graduate Studies, College of Education and Allied Studies, Department of Elementary and Early Childhood Education, Program in Reading, Bridgewater, MA 02325. Offers M Ed, CAGS. *Accreditation:* NCATE. *Program availability:* Part-time, evening/weekend. *Entrance requirements:* For master's, GRE General Test, 1 year of teaching experience.

Buffalo State College, State University of New York, The Graduate School, School of Education, Department of Elementary Education, Literacy, and Educational Leadership, Program in Literacy Specialist, Buffalo, NY 14222-1095. Offers literacy specialist (birth-grade 12) (MS Ed). *Accreditation:* NCATE. *Program availability:* Part-time, evening/weekend. *Degree requirements:* For master's, project. *Entrance requirements:* For master's, minimum GPA of 3.0 in last 60 hours. Additional exam requirements/recommendations for international students: Required—TOEFL (minimum score 550 paper-based).

Cabrini University, Academic Affairs, Radnor, PA 19087. Offers accounting (M Acc); autism spectrum disorder (M Ed); biological sciences (MS), including civic leadership; criminology and criminal justice (MA); curriculum, instruction, and assessment (M Ed); educational leadership (M Ed, Ed D), including curriculum and instructional leadership (Ed D), preK-12 leadership (Ed D); English as a second language (M Ed); organizational leadership (DBA, PhD); preK to 4 (M Ed); reading specialist (M Ed); secondary education (M Ed), including biology, chemistry, English, English/communication, mathematics, social studies; special education grades 7-12 (M Ed); special education preK-8 (M Ed); teaching and learning (M Ed). *Program availability:* Part-time, evening/weekend. *Degree requirements:* For master's, comprehensive exam (for some programs), thesis (for some programs); for doctorate, comprehensive exam (for some programs), thesis/dissertation. *Entrance requirements:* For master's, professional resume, personal statement, two recommendations, official transcripts; for doctorate, official transcripts, minimum master's GPA of 3.0, two recommendations, interview with admissions committee. Additional exam requirements/recommendations for international students: Required—TOEFL (minimum score 80 iBT). Electronic applications accepted. Application fee is waived when completed online. *Expenses:* Contact institution.

California Baptist University, Program in Education, Riverside, CA 92504-3206. Offers educational leadership (MS); educational leadership for faith-based institutions (MS); educational leadership for public institutions (MS); educational technology (MS); instructional computer applications (MS); international education (MS); leadership and adult learning (MS); leadership and organizational studies (MS); online teaching and learning (MS); reading (MS); science education (MA); special education in mild/moderate disabilities (MS); special education in moderate/severe disabilities (MS); teacher leadership (MS); teaching (MS); teaching and learning (MS). *Program availability:* Part-time, evening/weekend, 100% online, blended/hybrid learning. *Faculty:* 26 full-time (13 women), 28 part-time/adjunct (21 women). *Students:* 201 full-time (164 women), 265 part-time (209 women); includes 226 minority (23 Black or African American, non-Hispanic/Latino; 4 American Indian or Alaska Native, non-Hispanic/Latino; 7 Asian, non-Hispanic/Latino; 169 Hispanic/Latino; 6 Native Hawaiian or other Pacific Islander, non-Hispanic/Latino; 17 Two or more races, non-Hispanic/Latino), 2 international. Average age 39. 145 applicants, 97% accepted, 141 enrolled. In 2018, 253 master's awarded. *Degree requirements:* For master's, comprehensive exam, project, or thesis. *Entrance requirements:* For master's, minimum undergraduate GPA of 2.75; 500-word essay; three letters of recommendation; two prerequisite courses completed with minimum C grade. Additional exam requirements/recommendations for international students: Required—TOEFL (minimum score 80 iBT). *Application deadline:* For fall admission, 8/1 priority date for domestic students, 7/1 for international students; for spring admission, 12/1 priority date for domestic students, 11/1 for international students. Applications are processed on a rolling basis. Application fee: $45. Electronic applications accepted. *Expenses:* $634 per unit. *Financial support:* In 2018–19, 312 students received support. Federal Work-Study and scholarships/grants available. Financial award applicants required to submit CSS PROFILE or FAFSA. *Faculty research:* Leadership development, complexity theory, faith and learning, special education, social and philosophical contexts of education. *Unit head:* Dr. Robin Duncan, Dean, School of Education, 951-552-8948, E-mail: rduncan@calbaptist.edu. *Application contact:* Dr. Shari Farris, Program Director, Online MS in Education, 951-343-2455, E-mail: sfarris@calbaptist.edu.
Website: http://www.calbaptist.edu/mastersined/

California State University, East Bay, Office of Graduate Studies, College of Education and Allied Studies, Department of Teacher Education, Hayward, CA 94542-3000. Offers education (MS), including curriculum, early childhood education, educational technology and leadership, reading instruction. *Program availability:* Online learning. *Degree requirements:* For master's, project or thesis. *Entrance requirements:* For master's, minimum GPA of 3.0 in field, 2.5 overall; teaching experience; baccalaureate degree; 3 letters of recommendation. Additional exam requirements/recommendations for international students: Required—TOEFL (minimum score 550 paper-based), IELTS. Electronic applications accepted. *Faculty research:* Online, pedagogy, writing, learning, teaching.

California State University, Fresno, Division of Research and Graduate Studies, Kremen School of Education and Human Development, Department of Literacy, Early, Bilingual, and Special Education, Fresno, CA 93740-8027. Offers education (MA), including early childhood education, reading/language arts; special education (MA). *Accreditation:* NCATE. *Program availability:* Part-time, evening/weekend. *Degree requirements:* For master's, thesis or alternative. *Entrance requirements:* For master's, GRE General Test, MAT, minimum GPA of 2.75. Additional exam requirements/recommendations for international students: Required—TOEFL. Electronic applications

accepted. *Faculty research:* Reading recovery, monitoring/tutoring programs, character and academics, professional ethics, low-performing partnership schools.

California State University, Fullerton, Graduate Studies, College of Education, Department of Literacy and Reading Education, Fullerton, CA 92831-3599. Offers MS. *Program availability:* Part-time.

California State University, Northridge, Graduate Studies, Michael D. Eisner College of Education, Department of Elementary Education, Northridge, CA 91330. Offers curriculum and instruction (MA); language and literacy (MA); multilingual/multicultural education (MA). *Accreditation:* NCATE. *Program availability:* Part-time, evening/weekend. *Degree requirements:* For master's, comprehensive exam. *Entrance requirements:* For master's, GRE General Test or minimum GPA of 3.0. Additional exam requirements/recommendations for international students: Required—TOEFL.

California State University, Sacramento, College of Education, Graduate and Professional Studies in Education, Sacramento, CA 95819. Offers behavioral science and gender equity (MA); child development (MA); counseling (MS); curriculum and instruction (MA); education (Ed D), including K-12 and community college; education leadership and policy studies (MA), including higher education, PreK-12; education specialist (Ed S), including school psychology; educational technology (MA); language and literacy (MA); multicultural education (MA); school psychology (MA); special education (MA); workforce development advocacy (MA). *Program availability:* Part-time, evening/weekend, blended/hybrid learning. *Degree requirements:* For master's, thesis or project; writing proficiency exam; for doctorate, thesis/dissertation. *Entrance requirements:* For master's and doctorate, GRE. Additional exam requirements/recommendations for international students: Required—TOEFL (minimum score 550 paper-based; 80 iBT); Recommended—IELTS (minimum score 7), TSE. Electronic applications accepted. *Expenses:* Contact institution.

California State University, San Marcos, College of Education, Health and Human Services, School of Education, San Marcos, CA 92096-0001. Offers education (MA); educational administration (MA); educational leadership (Ed D); literacy education (MA); special education (MA). *Accreditation:* NCATE (one or more programs are accredited). *Program availability:* Part-time, evening/weekend. *Entrance requirements:* For master's, minimum GPA of 3.0, teaching credentials, 1 year of teaching experience. *Application deadline:* For fall admission, 2/1 priority date for domestic students. Applications are processed on a rolling basis. Application fee: $55. *Financial support:* Applicants required to submit FAFSA. *Faculty research:* Multicultural literature, art as knowledge, poetry and second language acquisition, restructuring K–12 education and improving the training of K–8 science teachers. *Unit head:* Pat Stall, Director, 760-750-4386, E-mail: pstall@csusm.edu. *Application contact:* Dr. Wesley Schultz, Dean of Office of Graduate Studies and Research, 760-750-8045, Fax: 760-750-8045, E-mail: apply@csusm.edu.
Website: http://www.csusm.edu/education/

California State University, Stanislaus, College of Education, Kinesiology and Social Work, MA Program in Education, Turlock, CA 95382. Offers curriculum and instruction (MA), including education technology, elementary education, multilingual education, physical education, reading, secondary education, special education; school administration (MA); school counseling (MA). *Program availability:* Part-time, evening/weekend. *Degree requirements:* For master's, comprehensive exam (for some programs), thesis (for some programs). *Entrance requirements:* For master's, MAT, GRE, or CBEST (varies by concentration), 3 letters of recommendation, personal statement. Additional exam requirements/recommendations for international students: Required—TOEFL (minimum score 550 paper-based). Electronic applications accepted. *Faculty research:* Children's perspectives on historical events, method elementary schools dual language education, K-12 reading programs.

California University of Pennsylvania, School of Graduate Studies and Research, College of Education and Human Services, Program in Reading Specialist, California, PA 15419-1394. Offers M Ed. *Accreditation:* NCATE. *Program availability:* Part-time, evening/weekend. *Degree requirements:* For master's, comprehensive exam, thesis optional, practicum. *Entrance requirements:* For master's, MAT, PRAXIS, minimum GPA of 3.0, teaching certificate. Additional exam requirements/recommendations for international students: Required—TOEFL (minimum score 550 paper-based; 80 iBT). Electronic applications accepted. *Faculty research:* Online education in reading supervision, phonetics education, remedial reading, injury and reading remediation in brain patients.

Canisius College, Graduate Division, School of Education and Human Services, Department of Graduate Education and Leadership, Buffalo, NY 14208-1098. Offers business and marketing education (MS Ed); college student personnel (MS Ed); deaf education (MS Ed); deaf/adolescent education, grades 7-12 (MS Ed); deaf/childhood education, grades 1-6 (MS Ed); differentiated instruction (MS Ed); education administration (MS); educational administration (MS Ed); educational technologies (Certificate); gifted education extension (Certificate); literacy (MS Ed); reading (Certificate); school building leadership (MS Ed, Certificate); school district leadership (Certificate); teacher leader (Certificate); TESOL (MS Ed). *Accreditation:* NCATE. *Program availability:* Part-time, evening/weekend, 100% online, blended/hybrid learning. *Faculty:* 5 full-time (all women), 21 part-time/adjunct (16 women). *Students:* 79 full-time (66 women), 135 part-time (106 women); includes 45 minority (27 Black or African American, non-Hispanic/Latino; 1 American Indian or Alaska Native, non-Hispanic/Latino; 3 Asian, non-Hispanic/Latino; 9 Hispanic/Latino; 5 Two or more races, non-Hispanic/Latino), 1 international. Average age 32. 83 applicants, 96% accepted, 74 enrolled. In 2018, 94 master's, 47 other advanced degrees awarded. *Entrance requirements:* For master's, GRE (if cumulative GPA less than 2.7), transcripts, two letters of recommendation. Additional exam requirements/recommendations for international students: Required—TOEFL (minimum score 550 paper-based, 79 iBT), IELTS (minimum score 6.5), or CAEL (minimum score 70). *Application deadline:* Applications are processed on a rolling basis. Application fee: $0. Electronic applications accepted. *Expenses: Tuition:* Part-time $820 per credit hour. *Required fees:* $25 per semester. One-time fee: $65 part-time. Tuition and fees vary according to program. *Financial support:* In 2018–19, 206 students received support. Career-related internships or fieldwork, Federal Work-Study, scholarships/grants, tuition waivers (partial), and unspecified assistantships available. Support available to part-time students. Financial award application deadline: 4/30; financial award applicants required to submit FAFSA. *Faculty research:* Asperger's disease, autism, private higher education, reading strategies. *Unit head:* Dr. Anne Marie Tryjankowski, Chair/Associate Professor of Graduate Education and Leadership, 716-888-3715, Fax: 716-888-3142, E-mail: tryjanka@canisius.edu. *Application contact:* Dr. Anne Marie Tryjankowski, Chair/Associate Professor of Graduate Education and Leadership, 716-888-3715, Fax: 716-888-3142, E-mail: tryjanka@canisius.edu.

Capella University, School of Education, Doctoral Programs in Education, Minneapolis, MN 55402. Offers curriculum and instruction (PhD); educational leadership and management (Ed D); instructional design for online learning (PhD); K-12 studies in education (PhD); leadership for higher education (PhD); leadership in educational administration (PhD); postsecondary and adult education (PhD); professional studies in education (PhD); reading and literacy (Ed D); special education leadership (PhD); training and performance improvement (PhD).

Capella University, School of Education, Master's Programs in Education, Minneapolis, MN 55402. Offers adult education (MS); curriculum and instruction (MS); early childhood education (MS); enrollment management (MS); higher education leadership and management (MS); instructional design for online learning (MS); integrative studies (MS); K-12 studies in education (MS); leadership in educational administration (MS); reading and literacy (MS); special education teaching (MS).

Cardinal Stritch University, College of Education and Leadership, Department of Literacy, Milwaukee, WI 53217-3985. Offers language and literacy (MA, PhD). *Accreditation:* NCATE. *Program availability:* Part-time, evening/weekend. *Degree requirements:* For master's, comprehensive exam, thesis, faculty recommendation, research project; for doctorate, thesis/dissertation. *Entrance requirements:* For master's, 2 letters of recommendation, minimum GPA of 2.75; for doctorate, 3 letters of recommendation, minimum GPA of 3.5. Additional exam requirements/recommendations for international students: Required—TOEFL (minimum score 550 paper-based; 79 iBT), IELTS (minimum score 6.5). Electronic applications accepted. *Expenses:* Contact institution.

Carthage College, Division of Teacher Education, Kenosha, WI 53140. Offers classroom guidance and counseling (M Ed); creative arts (M Ed); gifted and talented children (M Ed); language arts (M Ed); modern language (M Ed); natural sciences (M Ed); reading (M Ed, Certificate); social sciences (M Ed); teacher leadership (M Ed). *Program availability:* Part-time, evening/weekend. *Degree requirements:* For master's, thesis optional. *Entrance requirements:* For master's, MAT, minimum B average, letters of reference.

Castleton University, Division of Graduate Studies, Department of Education, Program in Language Arts and Reading, Castleton, VT 05735. Offers MA Ed, CAGS. *Program availability:* Part-time, evening/weekend. *Degree requirements:* For master's, thesis or alternative; for CAGS, publishable paper, written exams. *Entrance requirements:* For master's, GRE General Test, MAT, interview, minimum undergraduate GPA of 3.0; for CAGS, educational research, master's degree, minimum undergraduate GPA of 3.0.

Centenary University, Program in Education, Hackettstown, NJ 07840-2100. Offers education practice (M Ed); educational leadership (MA, Ed D); instructional leadership (MA); reading (M Ed); special education (MA). *Accreditation:* TEAC. *Program availability:* Part-time, evening/weekend, online learning. *Degree requirements:* For master's, thesis. *Entrance requirements:* For master's, interview, minimum undergraduate GPA of 2.8.

Central Connecticut State University, School of Graduate Studies, School of Education and Professional Studies, Department of Literacy, Elementary, and Early Childhood Education, New Britain, CT 06050-4010. Offers MS, AC, Sixth Year Certificate. *Program availability:* Part-time, evening/weekend. *Faculty:* 5 full-time (4 women), 5 part-time/adjunct (all women). *Students:* 9 full-time (8 women), 100 part-time (97 women); includes 7 minority (6 Hispanic/Latino; 1 Two or more races, non-Hispanic/Latino). Average age 30. 62 applicants, 77% accepted, 32 enrolled. In 2018, 29 master's, 9 other advanced degrees awarded. *Degree requirements:* For master's, comprehensive exam, thesis or alternative; for other advanced degree, qualifying exam. *Entrance requirements:* For master's, minimum undergraduate GPA of 2.7, teacher certification, interview, essay, letters of recommendation; for other advanced degree, master's degree, essay, teacher certification, interview, letters of recommendation. Additional exam requirements/recommendations for international students: Required—TOEFL (minimum score 550 paper-based; 79 iBT); Recommended—IELTS (minimum score 6.5). *Application deadline:* For fall admission, 6/1 for domestic students, 5/1 for international students; for spring admission, 11/1 for domestic and international students. Applications are processed on a rolling basis. Application fee: $50. Electronic applications accepted. *Expenses: Tuition, area resident:* Full-time $7027; part-time $388 per credit. Tuition, state resident: full-time $9750; part-time $388 per credit. Tuition, nonresident: full-time $18,102; part-time $388 per credit. *International tuition:* $18,102 full-time. *Required fees:* $266 per semester. *Financial support:* In 2018–19, 6 students received support. Career-related internships or fieldwork, Federal Work-Study, scholarships/grants, and unspecified assistantships available. Support available to part-time students. Financial award application deadline: 3/1. *Faculty research:* Developmental, clinical, and administrative aspects of reading and language arts instruction. *Unit head:* Dr. Helen Abadiano, Chair, 860-832-2175, E-mail: abadiano@ccsu.edu. *Application contact:* Patricia Gardner, Associate Director of Graduate Studies, 860-832-2350, Fax: 860-832-2362.
Website: http://www.ccsu.edu/leece/index.html

Central Michigan University, Central Michigan University Global Campus, Program in Education, Mount Pleasant, MI 48859. Offers college teaching (Graduate Certificate); community college (MA); curriculum and instruction (MA); educational technology (MA, DET); reading and literacy K-12 (MA); school principalship (MA), including charter school leadership; training and development (MA). *Accreditation:* TEAC. *Program availability:* Part-time, evening/weekend. *Entrance requirements:* For master's, minimum GPA of 2.7 in major. Additional exam requirements/recommendations for international students: Required—TOEFL. Electronic applications accepted.

Central Michigan University, College of Graduate Studies, College of Education and Human Services, Department of Teacher Education and Professional Development, Mount Pleasant, MI 48859. Offers educational technology (MA, Graduate Certificate); elementary education (MA), including classroom teaching, early childhood; reading and literacy K-12 (MA); secondary education (MA). *Program availability:* Part-time, evening/weekend. *Degree requirements:* For master's, thesis or alternative. Electronic applications accepted. *Faculty research:* Integrating literacy across the curriculum, science teaching and aesthetic learning in science, diversity education, educational technology, educational psychology and child development.

Central Washington University, School of Graduate Studies and Research, College of Education and Professional Studies, Department of Education, Development, Teaching, and Learning, Ellensburg, WA 98926. Offers literacy (M Ed). *Program availability:* Part-time. *Degree requirements:* For master's, thesis or alternative. *Entrance requirements:* For master's, minimum GPA of 3.0. Additional exam requirements/recommendations for international students: Required—TOEFL (minimum score 550 paper-based; 79 iBT), IELTS (minimum score 6.5). Electronic applications accepted.

Chestnut Hill College, School of Graduate Studies, Department of Education, Program in Reading, Philadelphia, PA 19118-2693. Offers reading specialist (M Ed), including K-12, special education 7-12, special education PreK-8. *Program availability:* Part-time, evening/weekend. *Degree requirements:* For master's, thesis optional. *Entrance requirements:* Additional exam requirements/recommendations for international students: Required—TOEFL (minimum score 500 paper-based) or IELTS (minimum score 6). Electronic applications accepted. *Expenses:* Contact institution. *Faculty research:* Inclusive education, cultural issues in education.

Chicago State University, School of Graduate and Professional Studies, College of Education, Department of Reading, Elementary Education, Library Information and Media Studies, Program in Reading, Chicago, IL 60628. Offers teaching of reading (MS Ed). *Accreditation:* NCATE. *Entrance requirements:* For master's, minimum GPA of 2.75.

The Citadel, The Military College of South Carolina, Citadel Graduate College, Zucker Family School of Education, Charleston, SC 29409. Offers elementary/secondary school administration and supervision (M Ed); elementary/secondary school counseling (M Ed); interdisciplinary STEM education (M Ed); literacy education (M Ed, Graduate Certificate); middle grades (MAT), including English, mathematics, science, social studies; physical education (grades K-12) (MAT); school superintendency (Ed S); secondary education (MAT), including biology, English, mathematics, social studies; student affairs (Graduate Certificate); student affairs and college counseling (M Ed). *Accreditation:* NCATE. *Program availability:* Part-time, evening/weekend, 100% online, blended/hybrid learning. *Degree requirements:* For master's, comprehensive exam (for some programs). *Entrance requirements:* For master's, GRE (minimum combined verbal and quantitative score of 290) or MAT (minimum score 396). Additional exam requirements/recommendations for international students: Required—TOEFL (minimum score 550 paper-based; 79 iBT). Electronic applications accepted. *Expenses:* Tuition, state resident: part-time $595 per credit hour. Tuition, nonresident: part-time $1020 per credit hour. *Required fees:* $90 per term.

City College of the City University of New York, Graduate School, Division of Humanities and the Arts, Department of English, Program in Language and Literacy, New York, NY 10031-9198. Offers MA. *Accreditation:* NCATE. *Entrance requirements:* For master's, 2 writing samples. Additional exam requirements/recommendations for international students: Required—TOEFL (minimum score 600 paper-based; 100 iBT). Electronic applications accepted.

City College of the City University of New York, Graduate School, School of Education, Department of Teaching, Learning and Culture, New York, NY 10031-9198. Offers bilingual education (MS); childhood education (MS); early childhood education (MS); educational theatre (MS); literacy (MS); TESOL (MS). *Accreditation:* NCATE. *Degree requirements:* For master's, thesis. *Entrance requirements:* For master's, Liberal Arts and Sciences Test (LAST), Content Specialty Test (CST). Additional exam requirements/recommendations for international students: Required—TOEFL.

City University of Seattle, Graduate Division, Albright School of Education, Seattle, WA 98121. Offers administrator certification (Certificate); curriculum and instruction (M Ed); elementary education (MIT); guidance and counseling (M Ed); leadership (M Ed); reading and literacy (M Ed); school counseling (M Ed); special education (MIT); superintendent certification (Certificate). *Program availability:* Part-time, evening/weekend, online learning. *Degree requirements:* For master's, comprehensive exam (for some programs), thesis (for some programs). *Entrance requirements:* For master's, baccalaureate degree or equivalent from an accredited or otherwise recognized institution. Additional exam requirements/recommendations for international students: Required—TOEFL (minimum score 567 paper-based; 87 iBT); Recommended—IELTS. Electronic applications accepted. *Expenses:* Contact institution.

Clarion University of Pennsylvania, College of Arts, Education and Sciences, Master of Education Program, Clarion, PA 16214. Offers curriculum and instruction (M Ed); early childhood (M Ed); math education (M Ed); reading (M Ed); science education (M Ed); special education (M Ed); technology (M Ed). *Accreditation:* NCATE. *Program availability:* Part-time, evening/weekend, 100% online, blended/hybrid learning. *Faculty:* 6 full-time (3 women). *Students:* 5 full-time (all women), 85 part-time (73 women); includes 3 minority (2 Black or African American, non-Hispanic/Latino; 1 Two or more races, non-Hispanic/Latino). Average age 30. 57 applicants, 61% accepted, 26 enrolled. In 2018, 51 master's awarded. *Degree requirements:* For master's, comprehensive exam (for some programs), thesis or alternative. *Entrance requirements:* For master's, minimum QPA of 3.0. Additional exam requirements/recommendations for international students: Required—TOEFL (minimum score 550 paper-based; 80 iBT), Or IELTS. Satisfactory completion of a bachelor's degree from an accredited US college or university is also acceptable evidence of English language. *Application deadline:* For fall admission, 8/1 priority date for domestic students, 7/15 priority date for international students; for winter admission, 11/1 priority date for domestic students; for spring admission, 12/1 priority date for domestic students, 11/15 priority date for international students; for summer admission, 4/1 priority date for domestic students. Applications are processed on a rolling basis. Application fee: $40. Electronic applications accepted. *Expenses: Tuition, area resident:* Part-time $516 per credit hour. Tuition, state resident: part-time $516 per credit hour. Tuition, nonresident: part-time $774 per credit hour. *Required fees:* $159 per credit hour. One-time fee: $50 part-time. Tuition and fees vary according to degree level, campus/location and program. *Financial support:* Federal Work-Study, institutionally sponsored loans, and scholarships/grants available. Financial award application deadline: 3/1; financial award applicants required to submit FAFSA. *Unit head:* Dr. John McCullough, Chair, Department of Education, 814-393-2404, Fax: 814-393-2446, E-mail: gradstudies@clarion.edu. *Application contact:* Susan Staub, Graduate Admissions Counselor, 814-393-2337, Fax: 814-393-2722, E-mail: gradstudies@clarion.edu.

Clemson University, Graduate School, College of Education, Department of Education and Human Development, Clemson, SC 29634. Offers counselor education (M Ed, Ed S), including mental health counseling, school counseling, student affairs (M Ed); learning sciences (PhD); literacy (M Ed); literacy, language and culture (PhD); special education (M Ed, MAT, PhD). *Program availability:* Part-time, evening/weekend, 100% online. *Faculty:* 35 full-time (24 women). *Students:* 103 full-time (87 women), 132 part-time (123 women); includes 37 minority (11 Black or African American, non-Hispanic/Latino; 1 American Indian or Alaska Native, non-Hispanic/Latino; 3 Asian, non-Hispanic/Latino; 11 Hispanic/Latino; 11 Two or more races, non-Hispanic/Latino), 5 international. Average age 29. 435 applicants, 67% accepted, 180 enrolled. In 2018, 51 master's, 3 doctorates, 34 other advanced degrees awarded. *Degree requirements:* For master's, thesis (for some programs); for doctorate, comprehensive exam (for some programs), thesis/dissertation. *Entrance requirements:* For master's and doctorate, GRE General Test, unofficial transcripts, letters of recommendation. Additional exam requirements/recommendations for international students: Required—TOEFL (minimum score 80 paper-based; 80 iBT); Recommended—IELTS (minimum score 6.5), TSE (minimum score 54). *Application deadline:* For fall admission, 4/15 priority date for international students; for spring admission, 10/15 priority date for international students. Applications are processed on a rolling basis. Application fee: $80 ($90 for international students). Electronic applications accepted. *Expenses:* $5198 per semester full-time resident, $10123 per semester full-time non-resident, $556 per credit hour part-time resident, $1109 per credit hour part-time non-resident, online $770 per credit hour, $4938 doctoral programs resident, $10405 doctoral programs non-resident, $1144 full-time graduate assistant, other fees may apply per session. *Financial support:* In 2018–19, 78 students received support, including 5 teaching assistantships with full and partial tuition reimbursements available (averaging $8,759 per year); career-related internships or fieldwork and unspecified assistantships also available. *Faculty research:* Literacy, reading recovery, exceptional children, policy development. *Total annual research expenditures:* $1.3 million. *Unit head:* Dr. Debi Switzer, Department Chair, 864-656-5098, E-mail: debi@clemson.edu. *Application contact:* Julie Jones, Student Services Program Coordinator, 864-656-5096, E-mail: jgambre@clemson.edu.
Website: http://www.clemson.edu/education/departments/education-human-development/index.html

Coastal Carolina University, Spadoni College of Education, Conway, SC 29528-6054. Offers education (MAT); educational leadership (M Ed, Ed S); English for speakers of other languages (Certificate); instructional technology (M Ed, Ed S); language, literacy and culture (M Ed); learning and teaching (M Ed); online teaching and training (Certificate); special education (M Ed). *Accreditation:* NCATE. *Program availability:* Part-time, evening/weekend, 100% online, blended/hybrid learning. *Degree requirements:* For master's and other advanced degree, comprehensive exam. *Entrance requirements:* For master's, GRE, GMAT, 2 letters of recommendation, evidence of teacher certification, official transcripts; for other advanced degree, official transcripts, 3 letters of reference, master's degree in related field with minimum overall cumulative GPA of 3.0. Additional exam requirements/recommendations for international students: Required—TOEFL (minimum score 550 paper-based; 79 iBT), IELTS (minimum score 6.5). Electronic applications accepted.

Coker College, Graduate Programs, Hartsville, SC 29550. Offers college athletic administration (MS); criminal and social justice policy (MS); curriculum and instructional technology (M Ed); literacy studies (M Ed); management and leadership (MS). *Program availability:* Part-time, 100% online. *Faculty:* 15 full-time (7 women), 7 part-time/adjunct (3 women). *Students:* 144 full-time (100 women), 6 part-time (2 women); includes 42 minority (33 Black or African American, non-Hispanic/Latino; 1 Asian, non-Hispanic/Latino; 4 Hispanic/Latino; 4 Two or more races, non-Hispanic/Latino). Average age 33. 120 applicants, 61% accepted, 65 enrolled. In 2018, 92 master's awarded. *Entrance requirements:* For master's, 1. Undergraduate overall gpa of 3.0 on 4.0 scale. 2. Official transcripts from all undergraduate institutions. 3. One-page personal statement. 4. Resume. 5. Two professional references. Additionally, for MEd in Literacy Studies - 1 year of teaching in PK-12 and letter of recommendation from principal/assistant principal. *Application deadline:* Applications are processed on a rolling basis. Application fee: $0. Electronic applications accepted. *Financial support:* Unspecified assistantships available. Financial award application deadline: 6/30; financial award applicants required to submit FAFSA. *Unit head:* Dr. Kathryn Flaherty, Dean of Graduate and Professional Programs, 843-857-4227, E-mail: kflaherty@coker.edu. *Application contact:* Lacey Rice-Serafin, Director of Graduate Programs, 843-857-4128, E-mail: lriceserafin@coker.edu.

The College at Brockport, State University of New York, School of Education, Health, and Human Services, Department of Education and Human Development, Brockport, NY 14420-2997. Offers adolescence education (MS Ed), including adolescence biology education, adolescence chemistry education, adolescence English, adolescence mathematics, adolescence physics, adolescence physics education, adolescence social studies education; bilingual education (MS Ed, AGC); childhood curriculum specialist (MS Ed); inclusive generalist education (MS Ed, AGC, Advanced Certificate), including biology (MS Ed, AGC), chemistry (MS Ed), English (MS Ed, Advanced Certificate), mathematics (MS Ed, Advanced Certificate), science (MS Ed, Advanced Certificate), social studies (MS Ed, Advanced Certificate); literacy education B-12 (MS Ed). *Accreditation:* NCATE. *Faculty:* 12 full-time (7 women), 10 part-time/adjunct (6 women). *Students:* 60 full-time (39 women), 227 part-time (157 women); includes 9 minority (1 Asian, non-Hispanic/Latino; 8 Hispanic/Latino). 135 applicants, 71% accepted, 59 enrolled. In 2018, 107 master's, 13 AGCs awarded. *Degree requirements:* For master's, thesis or alternative. *Entrance requirements:* For master's, minimum GPA of 3.0, letters of recommendation, interview (for some programs); statement of objectives, current resume. Additional exam requirements/recommendations for international students: Required—TOEFL (minimum score 550 paper-based; 79 iBT), IELTS (minimum score 6.5). *Application deadline:* For fall admission, 3/15 priority date for domestic and international students; for spring admission, 10/15 priority date for domestic and international students; for summer admission, 3/15 priority date for domestic and international students. Application fee: $80. Electronic applications accepted. *Expenses:* Tuition, state resident: part-time $471 per credit. Tuition, nonresident: part-time $963 per credit. *Financial support:* In 2018–19, 1 fellowship with full tuition reimbursement (averaging $7,500 per year), 1 teaching assistantship with full tuition reimbursement (averaging $6,000 per year) were awarded; Federal Work-Study, scholarships/grants, and unspecified assistantships also available. Support available to part-time students. Financial award application deadline: 3/15; financial award applicants required to submit FAFSA. *Faculty research:* Educational assessment, literacy education, inclusive education, teacher preparation, qualitative methodology. *Unit head:* Dr. Janka Szilagyi, Chairperson, 585-395-5945, Fax: 585-395-2172, E-mail: jszilagy@brockport.edu. *Application contact:* Buffie Edick, Graduate Program Director, 585-395-2326, Fax: 585-395-2172, E-mail: bedick@brockport.edu.
Website: https://www.brockport.edu/academics/education_human_development/department.html

The College of New Jersey, Office of Graduate and Advancing Education, School of Education, Department of Special Education, Language and Literacy, Program in Developmental Reading, Ewing, NJ 08628. Offers M Ed. *Accreditation:* NCATE. *Program availability:* Part-time. *Degree requirements:* For master's, comprehensive exam. *Entrance requirements:* For master's, GRE General Test, minimum GPA of 3.0 in field or 2.75 overall. Additional exam requirements/recommendations for international students: Required—TOEFL. Electronic applications accepted.

The College of New Jersey, Office of Graduate and Advancing Education, School of Education, Department of Special Education, Language and Literacy, Program in Reading Certification, Ewing, NJ 08628. Offers Certificate. *Program availability:* Part-time. *Entrance requirements:* Additional exam requirements/recommendations for international students: Required—TOEFL. Electronic applications accepted.

The College of New Rochelle, Graduate School, Division of Education, Program in Literacy Education, New Rochelle, NY 10805-2308. Offers MS Ed. *Program availability:* Part-time, evening/weekend. *Degree requirements:* For master's, practicum. *Entrance requirements:* For master's, interview, minimum GPA of 3.0 in field, 2.7 overall, early elementary teacher certification.

College of St. Joseph, Graduate Programs, Division of Education, Program in Reading, Rutland, VT 05701-3899. Offers M Ed. *Program availability:* Part-time, evening/weekend. *Degree requirements:* For master's, comprehensive exam. *Entrance requirements:* For master's, PRAXIS I, official college transcripts; 2 letters of reference; minimum GPA of 3.0 (initial licensure) or 2.7 (nonlicensure); interview. Additional exam requirements/recommendations for international students: Required—TOEFL (minimum score 550 paper-based). Electronic applications accepted.

The College of Saint Rose, Graduate Studies, Thelma P. Lally School of Education, Programs in Literacy, Albany, NY 12203-1419. Offers literacy: birth-grade 6 (MS Ed, Advanced Certificate); literacy: grades 5-12 (MS Ed, Advanced Certificate). *Students:* 11 full-time (all women), 14 part-time (13 women); includes 2 minority (both Hispanic/Latino). Average age 25. 15 applicants, 73% accepted, 11 enrolled. In 2018, 16 master's, 2 Advanced Certificates awarded. *Degree requirements:* For master's, field and clinical experiences. *Entrance requirements:* For master's, minimum undergraduate GPA of 3.0, current classroom teaching certification, baccalaureate degree from accredited institution, official transcripts from all colleges/universities attended. Additional exam requirements/recommendations for international students: Required—TOEFL (minimum score 550 paper-based; 80 iBT), IELTS (minimum score 6), PTE (minimum score 56). *Application deadline:* For fall admission, 4/1 priority date for domestic and international students; for spring admission, 10/15 priority date for

domestic and international students. Applications are processed on a rolling basis. Application fee: $40. Electronic applications accepted. *Expenses: Tuition:* Full-time $14,382; part-time $799 per credit hour. *Required fees:* $924; $408 per credit. $286. *Financial support:* Career-related internships or fieldwork, scholarships/grants, tuition waivers (partial), and unspecified assistantships available. Support available to part-time students. Financial award application deadline: 4/15. *Unit head:* Ekaterina Midgette, Co-Chair, 518-485-3797, E-mail: midgette@strose.edu. *Application contact:* Daniel Gallagher, Assistant Vice President for Graduate Recruitment and Enrollment, 518-485-3390, E-mail: grad@strose.edu.
Website: https://www.strose.edu/literacy/

Concordia University, College of Education, Portland, OR 97211-6099. Offers administrative leadership (Ed D); career and technical education (M Ed); curriculum and instruction (M Ed), including adolescent literacy, early childhood education, educational technology leadership, English for speakers of other languages, environmental education, health and physical education, mathematics, methods and curriculum, reading interventionist, science, social studies, STEAM education, teacher leadership, the inclusive classroom, trauma and resilience in educational settings; educational administration (M Ed); educational leadership (M Ed); elementary education (MAT); higher education (Ed D); instructional leadership (Ed D); professional leadership, inquiry, and transformation (Ed D); secondary education (MAT); transformational leadership (Ed D). *Program availability:* Part-time, online learning. *Degree requirements:* For master's, comprehensive exam, work samples/portfolio. *Entrance requirements:* For master's, California Basic Educational Skills Test or PRAXIS I, minimum undergraduate GPA of 2.8, graduate 3.0; 2 letters of recommendation. Additional exam requirements/recommendations for international students: Required—TOEFL (minimum score 525 paper-based). Electronic applications accepted. *Faculty research:* Learner-centered classroom, brain-based learning, future of online learning.

Concordia University Chicago, College of Graduate Studies, Program in Reading Education, River Forest, IL 60305-1499. Offers MA. *Program availability:* Part-time, evening/weekend, online learning. *Degree requirements:* For master's, comprehensive exam, thesis optional. *Entrance requirements:* For master's, minimum GPA of 2.9. Additional exam requirements/recommendations for international students: Required—TOEFL (minimum score 550 paper-based). Electronic applications accepted. *Faculty research:* Early literacy, classroom management and organization in reading, minority students and reading.

Concordia University, Nebraska, Graduate Programs in Education, Program in Reading Education, Seward, NE 68434. Offers M Ed. *Accreditation:* NCATE. *Program availability:* Part-time. *Degree requirements:* For master's, thesis or alternative. *Entrance requirements:* For master's, GRE, MAT, or NTE, minimum GPA of 3.0, BS in education or equivalent.

Concordia University, St. Paul, College of Education, St. Paul, MN 55104-5494. Offers classroom instruction (MA Ed), including K-12 reading; differentiated instruction (MA Ed); early childhood education (MA Ed); education (Ed D); educational leadership (MA Ed); educational technology (MA Ed, Certificate); K-12 principal licensure (Ed S); special education (MA Ed), including autism spectrum disorder, emotional and behavioral disorders, learning disabilities; superintendent (Ed S); teaching (MAT). *Accreditation:* NCATE. *Program availability:* Part-time, evening/weekend, 100% online, blended/hybrid learning. *Faculty:* 13 full-time (9 women), 82 part-time/adjunct (51 women). *Students:* 979 full-time (748 women), 40 part-time (28 women); includes 124 minority (49 Black or African American, non-Hispanic/Latino; 6 American Indian or Alaska Native, non-Hispanic/Latino; 34 Asian, non-Hispanic/Latino; 22 Hispanic/Latino; 1 Native Hawaiian or other Pacific Islander, non-Hispanic/Latino; 12 Two or more races, non-Hispanic/Latino), 11 international. Average age 34. 423 applicants, 99% accepted, 335 enrolled. In 2018, 358 master's, 3 doctorates, 119 other advanced degrees awarded. *Degree requirements:* For master's, thesis (for some programs); for doctorate, thesis/dissertation, capstone projects; for other advanced degree, e-folio review of competencies. *Entrance requirements:* For master's, official transcripts from regionally-accredited institution stating the conferral of a bachelor's degree with minimum cumulative GPA of 3.0; personal statement; professional resume; practitioner in field through work or volunteerism; resume; for doctorate, minimum master's or specialist degree GPA of 3.25; transcript; writing sample; three letters of recommendation; current resume; on-campus interview; for other advanced degree, minimum master's or specialist degree GPA of 3.25; transcript; statement covering employment history and long-term academic and professional goals; two letters of recommendation; interview with program director. Additional exam requirements/recommendations for international students: Recommended—TOEFL (minimum score 547 paper-based; 78 iBT), IELTS (minimum score 6). *Application deadline:* For fall admission, 8/1 for domestic and international students; for spring admission, 12/1 for domestic and international students; for summer admission, 5/1 for domestic and international students. Applications are processed on a rolling basis. Application fee: $0. Electronic applications accepted. *Expenses:* $395 per credit for 30 credits (for MA programs), $440 per credit for 42 credits (for MAT), $415 per credit for 30 credits (for EdS), $615 per credit for 64 credits (for EdD). *Financial support:* In 2018–19, 163 students received support. Federal Work-Study, scholarships/grants, and unspecified assistantships available. Financial award applicants required to submit FAFSA. *Faculty research:* School design for innovative learning practices, equine-assisted instruction, best practices for leadership in early childhood education, mental health needs in K-12 focusing on children of incarcerated parents, competency-based education. *Unit head:* Lonn Maly, Dean, 651-641-8203, E-mail: maly@csp.edu. *Application contact:* Amber Faletti, Director of Enrollment Management, 651-641-8838, Fax: 651-603-6320, E-mail: faletti@csp.edu.

Concordia University Wisconsin, Graduate Programs, School of Education, Program in Literacy, Mequon, WI 53097-2402. Offers MS Ed. *Program availability:* Part-time, evening/weekend, online learning. *Degree requirements:* For master's, comprehensive exam, thesis or alternative. *Entrance requirements:* For master's, minimum GPA of 3.0. Additional exam requirements/recommendations for international students: Required—TOEFL.

Concord University, Graduate Studies, Athens, WV 24712-1000. Offers educational leadership and supervision (M Ed); health promotion (MA); reading specialist (M Ed); social work (MSW); special education (M Ed); teaching (MAT). *Program availability:* Part-time, evening/weekend, 100% online. *Degree requirements:* For master's, thesis (for some programs). *Entrance requirements:* For master's, GRE or MAT, baccalaureate degree with minimum GPA of 2.5 from regionally-accredited institution; teaching license; 2 letters of recommendation; completed disposition assessment form. Electronic applications accepted.

Converse College, Education Specialist Program, Spartanburg, SC 29302. Offers administration and leadership (Ed S); administration and supervision (Ed S); literacy (Ed S). *Accreditation:* AAMFT/COAMFTE. *Program availability:* Part-time. *Entrance requirements:* For degree, GRE or MAT (marriage and family therapy), minimum GPA of 3.0. Electronic applications accepted.

Crandall University, Graduate Programs, Moncton, NB E1C 9L7, Canada. Offers literacy education (M Ed); organizational management (MOM); resource education (M Ed).

Curry College, Graduate Studies, Program in Education, Milton, MA 02186-9984. Offers elementary education (M Ed); foundations (non-license) (M Ed); reading (M Ed, Certificate); special education (M Ed). *Program availability:* Part-time, evening/weekend. *Degree requirements:* For master's, project or thesis. *Entrance requirements:* For master's, interview, recommendations, resume, written statement. Additional exam requirements/recommendations for international students: Required—TOEFL (minimum score 550 paper-based; 80 iBT). *Expenses:* Contact institution. *Faculty research:* Classroom trauma, therapeutic writing, inclusionary practices.

Dallas Baptist University, Dorothy M. Bush College of Education, Program in Reading and English as a Second Language, Dallas, TX 75211-9299. Offers bilingual education (M Ed); reading and English as a second language (M Ed). *Program availability:* Part-time, evening/weekend. *Application deadline:* Applications are processed on a rolling basis. Application fee: $25. Electronic applications accepted. Application fee is waived when completed online. *Expenses: Tuition:* Full-time $17,262; part-time $959 per credit hour. *Required fees:* $1000; $500 per semester. Tuition and fees vary according to course load and degree level. *Unit head:* Dr. Neil Dugger, Dean, 214-333-5202, E-mail: neil@dbu.edu. *Application contact:* Dr. Adelita Baker, Program Director, 214-333-5515, E-mail: adelita@dbu.edu.
Website: https://www.dbu.edu/graduate/degree-programs/med-reading-esl

Delaware State University, Graduate Programs, College of Education, Health and Public Policy, Program in Adult Literacy and Basic Education, Dover, DE 19901-2277. Offers MA. *Entrance requirements:* Additional exam requirements/recommendations for international students: Required—TOEFL (minimum score 550 paper-based). Electronic applications accepted.

DePaul University, College of Education, Chicago, IL 60614. Offers bilingual-bicultural education (M Ed, MA); counseling (M Ed, MA), including clinical mental health counseling, college student development, school counseling; curriculum studies (M Ed, MA, Ed D); early childhood education (M Ed, MA, Ed D); educational leadership (M Ed, MA, Ed D), including Catholic leadership (M Ed, MA), general (M Ed, MA), higher education (M Ed, MA), physical education (M Ed, MA), principal preparation (M Ed), teacher preparation (M Ed); elementary education (M Ed, MA); middle grades education (M Ed); middle school mathematics education (MS); reading specialist (M Ed, MA); secondary education (M Ed, MA); social and cultural foundations in education (M Ed, MA); special education (M Ed); sport, fitness and recreation leadership (MS); value-creating education for global citizenship (M Ed); world languages education (M Ed, MA). *Program availability:* Part-time, evening/weekend, online learning. *Degree requirements:* For doctorate, thesis/dissertation. Electronic applications accepted.

Dickinson State University, Department of Teacher Education, Dickinson, ND 58601-4896. Offers master of arts in teaching (MAT); master of entrepreneurship (ME); middle school education (MAT); reading (MAT). *Program availability:* Part-time, blended/hybrid learning. *Faculty:* 2 full-time (both women). *Students:* 2 full-time (1 woman), 15 part-time (9 women); includes 1 minority (Hispanic/Latino). Average age 36. 8 applicants, 100% accepted, 8 enrolled. *Degree requirements:* For master's, comprehensive exam (for some programs). *Entrance requirements:* For master's, additional admission requirements for the Master of Entrepreneurship Program: complete the SoBE ME Peregrine Entrance Examination, personal statement; transcripts; additional admission requirements for the Master of Entrepreneurship Program: 2 letters of reference in support of their admission to the program. Reference letters should be from prior academic advisors, faculty, professional colleagues, or supervisors. Additional exam requirements/recommendations for international students: Required—TOEFL (minimum score 71 iBT). *Application deadline:* For fall admission, 8/1 for domestic students, 7/1 for international students; for spring admission, 12/1 for domestic students, 11/15 for international students. Applications are processed on a rolling basis. Application fee: $35. Electronic applications accepted. *Expenses: Tuition, area resident:* Full-time $3735; part-time $311 per credit hour. Tuition, state resident: full-time $3735; part-time $311 per credit hour. Tuition, nonresident: full-time $3735; part-time $311 per credit hour. *Required fees:* $138; $138 per credit hour. *Financial support:* Application deadline: 12/1; applicants required to submit FAFSA. *Unit head:* Dr. Deborah Secord, Chair, Department of Teacher Education, 701-483-2178, E-mail: Deborah.Secord@dickinsonstate.edu. *Application contact:* Pamela Krueger, Graduate Studies Coordinator, 701-483-5631, E-mail: Pamela.j.krueger@dickinsonstate.edu.
Website: https://dickinsonstate.edu/academics/fields-of-study/graduate-studies/

Dominican University, School of Education, River Forest, IL 60305-1099. Offers child life studies (MS); early childhood education (MS); education (MAT); elementary education (MA Ed); English as a second language (MA Ed); reading (MA Ed); secondary education (MAT); special education (MS). *Accreditation:* NCATE. *Program availability:* Part-time, evening/weekend, 100% online, blended/hybrid learning. *Entrance requirements:* For master's, Illinois Test of Basic Skills. Additional exam requirements/recommendations for international students: Required—TOEFL (minimum score 550 paper-based; 79 iBT). *Expenses:* Contact institution. *Faculty research:* Governance of private education institutions, reading and language arts, inclusion, organizational planning, leadership and vision.

Drake University, School of Education, Des Moines, IA 50311-4516. Offers applied behavior analysis (MS); counseling (MS); education (PhD); education administration (Ed D); educational leadership (MSE, Ed D); effective teaching (MSE); leadership development (MS); literacy (Ed S); literacy education (MSE); rehabilitation administration (MS); rehabilitation placement (MS); special education (MSE); STEM education (MSE); teacher education (5-12) (MAT); teacher education (K-8) (MST); teacher effectiveness and professional development (MSE). *Program availability:* Part-time, evening/weekend, 100% online, blended/hybrid learning. *Students:* 90 full-time (74 women), 690 part-time (532 women); includes 69 minority (30 Black or African American, non-Hispanic/Latino; 1 American Indian or Alaska Native, non-Hispanic/Latino; 9 Asian, non-Hispanic/Latino; 16 Hispanic/Latino; 13 Two or more races, non-Hispanic/Latino). Average age 34. In 2018, 253 master's, 30 doctorates awarded. *Degree requirements:* For master's and Ed S, comprehensive exam, internships (for some programs); for doctorate, comprehensive exam, thesis/dissertation, internships (for some programs). *Entrance requirements:* For master's, GRE General Test, MAT, or Drake Writing Assessment, resume, 2 letters of recommendation; for doctorate, GRE General Test or MAT, master's degree, 3 letters of recommendation; for Ed S, GRE General Test or MAT. Additional exam requirements/recommendations for international students: Required—TOEFL (minimum score 550 paper-based). *Application deadline:* For fall admission, 7/1 priority date for domestic students, 6/1 priority date for international students; for spring admission, 11/1 priority date for domestic students, 10/1 priority date for international students. Applications are processed on a rolling basis. Application fee: $25. Electronic applications accepted. *Expenses:* Contact institution. *Financial support:* Research assistantships, career-related internships or fieldwork, and unspecified assistantships available. Support available to part-time students. *Faculty research:* Counseling and rehabilitation, behavioral supports, inquiry-based science methods, teacher quality enhancement. *Unit head:* Dr. Janet McMahill, Dean, 515-271-3829, E-mail: janet.mcmahill@drake.edu. *Application contact:* Dr. Janet McMahill, Dean, 515-271-3829, E-mail: janet.mcmahill@drake.edu.
Website: http://www.drake.edu/soe/

Drury University, Master in Education Program, Springfield, MO 65802. Offers curriculum and instruction (M Ed), including elementary education, middle school education, secondary education; instructional leadership (M Ed); instructional technology (M Ed); integrated learning (M Ed); special education (M Ed); special reading (M Ed). *Accreditation:* NCATE. *Program availability:* Part-time, evening/weekend, 100% online, blended/hybrid learning. *Faculty:* 10 full-time (6 women), 8 part-time/adjunct (6 women). *Students:* 167 full-time (133 women). Average age 32. 92 applicants, 92% accepted, 69 enrolled. In 2018, 44 master's awarded. *Entrance requirements:* For master's, bachelor's degree with minimum GPA of 2.75. Additional exam requirements/recommendations for international students: Recommended—TOEFL (minimum score 80 iBT), IELTS (minimum score 6.5). *Application deadline:* For fall admission, 8/4 priority date for domestic and international students; for spring admission, 1/5 priority date for domestic and international students; for summer admission, 5/26 priority date for domestic and international students. Applications are processed on a rolling basis. Application fee: $25. Electronic applications accepted. *Expenses:* Tuition is $366 per credit hour. Fees are $7 per credit hour. Most M.Ed. degrees are 33 credit hours. *Financial support:* In 2018–19, 5 students received support. Career-related internships or fieldwork, scholarships/grants, and unspecified assistantships available. Financial award application deadline: 6/30; financial award applicants required to submit FAFSA. *Faculty research:* Instructional technology, autism, diversity, and social justice. *Unit head:* Dr. Asikaa Cosgrove, Director, Master in Education Program, 417-873-7806, E-mail: acosgrov@drury.edu. *Application contact:* Dr. Asikaa Cosgrove, Director, Master in Education Program, 417-873-7806, E-mail: acosgrov@drury.edu.
Website: http://www.drury.edu/education-masters

Duquesne University, School of Education, Department of Instruction and Leadership, Program in Reading and Literacy, Pittsburgh, PA 15282-0001. Offers MS Ed. *Program availability:* Part-time, evening/weekend. *Faculty:* 2 full-time (both women). *Students:* 5 full-time (all women), 1 (woman) part-time; includes 2 minority (1 Black or African American, non-Hispanic/Latino; 1 Asian, non-Hispanic/Latino). Average age 28. 7 applicants, 86% accepted, 3 enrolled. In 2018, 7 master's awarded. *Entrance requirements:* For master's, bachelor's degree; undergraduate degree with minimum GPA of 3.0 overall or on most recent 48 credits, or minimum overall GPA of 2.8 and PRAXIS I PPST or PAPA exams. Additional exam requirements/recommendations for international students: Required—TOEFL (minimum score 550 paper-based), IELTS (minimum score 7). *Application deadline:* For fall admission, 9/1 for domestic students; for spring admission, 1/2 for domestic students. Applications are processed on a rolling basis. Application fee: $0. Electronic applications accepted. *Expenses: Tuition:* Full-time $23,112; part-time $1284 per credit. Tuition and fees vary according to program. *Financial support:* In 2018–19, 1 student received support, including 1 research assistantship with full tuition reimbursement available (averaging $6,930 per year); Federal Work-Study also available. Support available to part-time students. Financial award applicants required to submit FAFSA. *Faculty research:* Adolescent literacy; multi-modal texts including graphic novels; struggling readers and why they struggle; family engagement and community partnerships; factors that create highly effective teachers;. *Unit head:* Dr. Carla Meyer, Assistant Professor, 412-396.5837, Fax: 412-396-1759, E-mail: meyerc2@duq.edu. *Application contact:* Kelly McGinley, Graduate Admissions Assistant, 412-396-1559, Fax: 412-396-5585, E-mail: mcginleyk@duq.edu.
Website: http://www.duq.edu/academics/schools/education/graduate-programs-education/ms-reading-language-arts

East Carolina University, Graduate School, College of Education, Department of Literacy Studies, English and History Education, Greenville, NC 27858-4353. Offers curriculum and instruction (MA Ed); English education (MAT); history education (MAT); reading education (MA Ed). *Accreditation:* NCATE. *Program availability:* Part-time, evening/weekend, online learning. *Application deadline:* For fall admission, 6/1 priority date for domestic students. *Expenses: Tuition, area resident:* Full-time $4749. Tuition, state resident: full-time $4749. Tuition, nonresident: full-time $17,898. *International tuition:* $17,898 full-time. *Required fees:* $2787. Part-time tuition and fees vary according to course load and program. *Financial support:* Application deadline: 6/1. *Unit head:* Dr. Kristin M Gesmann, Chair, 252-328-5670, E-mail: gaehsmannk18@ecu.edu. *Application contact:* Graduate School Admissions, 252-328-6012, Fax: 252-328-6071, E-mail: gradschool@ecu.edu.
Website: http://www.ecu.edu/cs-educ/libs/index.cfm

Eastern Mennonite University, Program in Teacher Education, Harrisonburg, VA 22802-2462. Offers curriculum and instruction (MA Ed); diverse needs (MA Ed); literacy (MA Ed); restorative justice in education (MA Ed). *Accreditation:* NCATE. *Program availability:* Part-time. *Degree requirements:* For master's, portfolio, research projects. *Entrance requirements:* For master's, 1 year of teaching experience, interview, minimum undergraduate GPA of 2.75. Additional exam requirements/recommendations for international students: Required—TOEFL (minimum score 550 paper-based). Electronic applications accepted. *Expenses:* Contact institution. *Faculty research:* Effective literacy instruction for middle school English language learners, beginning teacher's emotional experiences, constructivist learning environments, restorative discipline.

Eastern Michigan University, Graduate School, College of Education, Department of Teacher Education, Program in Reading, Ypsilanti, MI 48197. Offers MA. *Accreditation:* NCATE. *Program availability:* Part-time, evening/weekend, online learning. *Students:* 2 full-time (both women), 21 part-time (all women); includes 2 minority (1 Black or African American, non-Hispanic/Latino; 1 Two or more races, non-Hispanic/Latino). Average age 31. 7 applicants, 100% accepted, 3 enrolled. In 2018, 6 master's awarded. *Entrance requirements:* For master's, GRE. Additional exam requirements/recommendations for international students: Required—TOEFL. *Application deadline:* Applications are processed on a rolling basis. Application fee: $45. *Financial support:* Fellowships, research assistantships with full tuition reimbursements, teaching assistantships with full tuition reimbursements, career-related internships or fieldwork, Federal Work-Study, institutionally sponsored loans, scholarships/grants, tuition waivers (partial), and unspecified assistantships available. Support available to part-time students. Financial award applicants required to submit FAFSA. *Application contact:* Dr. Linda Lewis-White, Coordinator, 734-487-3260, Fax: 734-487-2101, E-mail: llewiswh@emich.edu.

Eastern Michigan University, Graduate School, College of Education, Department of Teacher Education, Programs in Curriculum and Instruction, Ypsilanti, MI 48197. Offers advanced teaching and learning (MA); early literacy instruction (Graduate Certificate); instructional leadership (MA); learning, motivation and creativity (Graduate Certificate); literacy coaching (Graduate Certificate); online teaching (Certificate); secondary literacy instruction (Graduate Certificate); urban and diversity education (MA). *Students:* 1 (woman) full-time, 28 part-time (21 women); includes 11 minority (3 Black or African American, non-Hispanic/Latino; 1 Asian, non-Hispanic/Latino; 4 Hispanic/Latino; 3 Two or more races, non-Hispanic/Latino). Average age 31. 7 applicants, 71% accepted, 3 enrolled. In 2018, 5 master's awarded. Application fee: $45. *Application contact:* Dr. Virginia Harder, Graduate Coordinator/Advisor, 734-487-2729, Fax: 734-487-2101, E-mail: vharder1@emich.edu.

Eastern Nazarene College, Adult and Graduate Studies, Division of Teacher Education, Quincy, MA 02170. Offers administration (M Ed); early childhood education (M Ed, Certificate); elementary education (M Ed, Certificate); English as a second language (Certificate); instructional enrichment and development (Certificate); middle school education (M Ed, Certificate); moderate special needs education (Certificate); principal (Certificate); program development and supervision (Certificate); secondary education (M Ed, Certificate); special education administrator (Certificate); special needs (M Ed); supervisor (Certificate); teacher of reading (M Ed, Certificate). M Ed also available through weekend program for administration, special needs, and teacher of reading only. *Program availability:* Part-time, evening/weekend. *Entrance requirements:* Additional exam requirements/recommendations for international students: Required—TOEFL (minimum score 550 paper-based).

Eastern New Mexico University, Graduate School, College of Education and Technology, Department of Curriculum and Instruction, Portales, NM 88130. Offers alternative licensure in elementary education (M Ed); bilingual education (M Ed); career and technical education (M Ed); educational technology (M Ed); elementary education (M Ed); English as a second language (M Ed); pedagogy and learning (M Ed); reading/literacy (M Ed). *Program availability:* Part-time, online learning. *Degree requirements:* For master's, comprehensive exam, thesis optional. *Entrance requirements:* For master's, writing assessment, minimum GPA of 3.0, photocopy of teaching license, letter of recommendation. Additional exam requirements/recommendations for international students: Required—TOEFL (minimum score 550 paper-based; 79 iBT), IELTS (minimum score 6). Electronic applications accepted. *Expenses: Tuition, area resident:* Full-time $6776. Tuition, state resident: full-time $6776; part-time $282 per credit hour. Tuition, nonresident: full-time $8986; part-time $374 per credit hour. *Required fees:* $60 per semester. One-time fee: $25.

Eastern University, Graduate Education Programs, St. Davids, PA 19087-3696. Offers ESL program specialist (K-12) (Certificate); general supervisor (PreK-12) (Certificate); health and physical education (K-12) (Certificate); middle level (4-8) (Certificate); multicultural education (M Ed); music (K-12) (Certificate); Pre K-4 (Certificate); Pre K-4 with special education (Certificate); reading (M Ed); reading specialist (K-12) (Certificate); reading supervisor (K-12) (Certificate); school counseling (MA, CAGS); school principalship (preK-12) (Certificate); school psychology (MS, CAGS); secondary biology education (7-12) (Certificate); secondary chemistry education (7-12) (Certificate); secondary communication education (7-12) (Certificate); secondary English education (7-12) (Certificate); secondary math education (7-12) (Certificate); secondary social studies education (7-12) (Certificate); special education (M Ed); special education (7-12) (Certificate); special education (Pre K-8) (Certificate); special education supervisor (K-12) (Certificate); TESOL (M Ed); world language (Certificate), including Spanish. *Program availability:* Part-time, evening/weekend, online learning. *Entrance requirements:* Additional exam requirements/recommendations for international students: Required—TOEFL. Electronic applications accepted. Application fee is waived when completed online. *Expenses:* Contact institution.

Eastern Washington University, Graduate Studies, College of Arts, Letters and Education, Department of Education, Program in Literacy, Cheney, WA 99004-2431. Offers M Ed. *Degree requirements:* For master's, comprehensive exam. *Entrance requirements:* For master's, minimum GPA of 3.0. Additional exam requirements/recommendations for international students: Required—TOEFL (minimum score 580 paper-based; 92 iBT), IELTS (minimum score 7), PTE (minimum score 63). Electronic applications accepted.

East Stroudsburg University of Pennsylvania, Graduate and Extended Studies, College of Education, Department of Reading, East Stroudsburg, PA 18301-2999. Offers M Ed. *Program availability:* Part-time, evening/weekend, online only, 100% online. *Faculty:* 3 full-time (all women). *Students:* 3 full-time (all women), 72 part-time (71 women); includes 3 minority (1 Black or African American, non-Hispanic/Latino; 1 Asian, non-Hispanic/Latino; 1 Hispanic/Latino). Average age 31. 29 applicants, 90% accepted, 18 enrolled. In 2018, 21 master's awarded. *Degree requirements:* For master's, comprehensive exam, research paper, electronic program portfolio. *Entrance requirements:* For master's, PRAXIS/teacher certification, letter of recommendation, Pennsylvania Department of Education requirements. Additional exam requirements/recommendations for international students: Recommended—TOEFL (minimum score 560 paper-based; 83 iBT), IELTS. *Application deadline:* For fall admission, 7/31 priority date for domestic students, 6/30 priority date for international students; for spring admission, 11/30 for domestic students, 10/31 for international students. Applications are processed on a rolling basis. Application fee: $50. Electronic applications accepted. *Expenses: Tuition, area resident:* Full-time $9288; part-time $516 per credit. Tuition, state resident: full-time $9288. Tuition, nonresident: full-time $13,932; part-time $774 per credit. *International tuition:* $13,932 full-time. *Required fees:* $2059; $114 per credit. Tuition and fees vary according to course load and degree level. *Financial support:* Research assistantships with tuition reimbursements, Federal Work-Study, and unspecified assistantships available. Support available to part-time students. Financial award application deadline: 3/1; financial award applicants required to submit FAFSA. *Faculty research:* Portfolio assessment, reading assessment. *Unit head:* Shawn Watkins, Department Chair, 570-422-3416, Fax: 570-422-3920, E-mail: swatkins1@esu.edu. *Application contact:* Kevin Quintero, Associate Director, Graduate and Extended Studies, 570-422-3890, Fax: 570-422-2711, E-mail: kquintero@esu.edu.
Website: https://www.esu.edu/reading/index.cfm

East Tennessee State University, School of Graduate Studies, College of Education, Department of Curriculum and Instruction, Johnson City, TN 37614. Offers advanced studies in teaching and learning (M Ed), including childhood literacy; educational technology (M Ed), including educational communications and technology, school library media; elementary education (M Ed); reading (M Ed, MA), including reading education (MA), storytelling (MA); response to intervention (Post-Master's Certificate); school library professional (Post-Master's Certificate); secondary education (M Ed); STEAM K-12 education (Postbaccalaureate Certificate); storytelling (Postbaccalaureate Certificate); teacher education (MAT), including elementary education K-5, middle grades education 4-8, middle grades education 6-8, secondary education 6-12 and preK-12, secondary education K-12. *Accreditation:* NCATE. *Program availability:* Part-time, evening/weekend, online learning. *Degree requirements:* For master's, comprehensive exam, thesis optional, student teaching, practicum; for other advanced degree, field work (school library); culminating experience (storytelling). *Entrance requirements:* For master's, GRE, SAT, ACT, PRAXIS, minimum GPA of 3.0, interview, 3 letters of recommendation, background check; for other advanced degree, master's degree, TN teaching license. Additional exam requirements/recommendations for international students: Required—TOEFL (minimum score 550 paper-based; 79 iBT). Electronic applications accepted. *Faculty research:* Critical thinking; curriculum development in reading, math, and science education; cultural diversity; cognitive processes; effective teaching strategies.

Edinboro University of Pennsylvania, Department of Early Childhood and Reading, Edinboro, PA 16444. Offers arts infusion (Graduate Certificate); early childhood education (M Ed); reading (M Ed); reading specialist (Graduate Certificate). *Program availability:* Part-time, evening/weekend. *Degree requirements:* For master's, thesis or alternative, competency exam; for Graduate Certificate, thesis or alternative. *Entrance requirements:* For master's and Graduate Certificate, GRE or MAT, minimum QPA of 2.5. Electronic applications accepted.

Elms College, Division of Education, Chicopee, MA 01013-2839. Offers early childhood education (MAT); education (M Ed, CAGS); elementary education (MAT); English as a

second language (MAT); reading (MAT); secondary education (MAT), including biology education, English education, Spanish education; special education (MAT). *Program availability:* Part-time, evening/weekend. *Faculty:* 5 full-time (all women), 6 part-time/adjunct (5 women). *Students:* 3 full-time (all women), 117 part-time (94 women); includes 12 minority (1 Black or African American, non-Hispanic/Latino; 2 Asian, non-Hispanic/Latino; 9 Hispanic/Latino). Average age 34. 27 applicants, 96% accepted, 23 enrolled. In 2018, 34 master's, 3 other advanced degrees awarded. *Degree requirements:* For master's, thesis (for some programs). *Entrance requirements:* For master's, Massachusetts Educators Certification Test, minimum GPA of 3.0; for CAGS, master's degree in education. Additional exam requirements/recommendations for international students: Required—TOEFL. *Application deadline:* For fall admission, 7/1 priority date for domestic students; for spring admission, 11/1 priority date for domestic students. Applications are processed on a rolling basis. Application fee: $30. *Expenses:* Tuition: Full-time $14,328; part-time $796 per credit. *Required fees:* $200. Tuition and fees vary according to degree level and program. *Financial support:* In 2018–19, 2 teaching assistantships with partial tuition reimbursements were awarded. Financial award applicants required to submit FAFSA. *Unit head:* Dr. Mary Janeczek, Chair, Division of Education, 413-594-2761, Fax: 413-592-4871, E-mail: janeczeke@elms.edu. *Application contact:* Nancy Davis, Director, Office of Graduate and Continuing Education Admissions, 413-265-2239, E-mail: davisn@elms.edu.

Emory & Henry College, Graduate Programs, Emory, VA 24327. Offers American history (MA Ed); education professional studies (M Ed); occupational therapy (MOT); organizational leadership (MCOL); physical therapy (DPT); physician assistant studies (MPAS); reading specialist (MA Ed). *Program availability:* Part-time. *Degree requirements:* For master's, thesis optional; for doctorate, thesis/dissertation optional. *Entrance requirements:* For master's, GRE or PRAXIS I, official transcripts from all colleges previously attended, three professional recommendations, essay. Additional exam requirements/recommendations for international students: Recommended—TOEFL, IELTS (minimum score 6). Electronic applications accepted. *Expenses:* Contact institution.

Emporia State University, Program in Instructional Specialist, Emporia, KS 66801-5415. Offers elementary subject matter (MS); reading (MS). *Accreditation:* NCATE. *Program availability:* Part-time. *Degree requirements:* For master's, comprehensive exam or thesis, practicum. *Entrance requirements:* For master's, GRE General Test or MAT, essay exam, appropriate bachelor's degree, letters of recommendation. Additional exam requirements/recommendations for international students: Required—TOEFL (minimum score 520 paper-based; 68 iBT). Electronic applications accepted.

Endicott College, Van Loan School of Graduate and Professional Studies, Program in Reading and Literacy, Beverly, MA 01915-2096. Offers M Ed. *Program availability:* Part-time, evening/weekend, 100% online, blended/hybrid learning. *Degree requirements:* For master's, comprehensive exam, practicum, seminar. *Entrance requirements:* For master's, MAT or GRE, Massachusetts Tests for Educator Licensure (MTEL), Massachusetts teaching certificate, letters of recommendation. Additional exam requirements/recommendations for international students: Required—TOEFL. Electronic applications accepted. *Expenses:* Contact institution.

Evangel University, Department of Education, Springfield, MO 65802. Offers curriculum and instruction (M Ed); educational leadership (M Ed); literacy (M Ed); secondary teaching (M Ed). *Accreditation:* NCATE. *Program availability:* Part-time, evening/weekend, 100% online, blended/hybrid learning. *Entrance requirements:* For master's, PRAXIS II (preferred) or GRE, minimum undergraduate GPA of 3.0. Additional exam requirements/recommendations for international students: Required—TOEFL (minimum score 550 paper-based). Electronic applications accepted. Application fee is waived when completed online.

Fairleigh Dickinson University, Florham Campus, University College: Arts, Sciences, and Professional Studies, Peter Sammartino School of Education, Madison, NJ 07940-1099. Offers education for certified teachers (MA, Certificate); educational leadership (MA); instructional technology (Certificate); literacy/reading (Certificate); teaching (MAT).

Fairleigh Dickinson University, Metropolitan Campus, University College: Arts, Sciences, and Professional Studies, Peter Sammartino School of Education, Teaneck, NJ 07666-1914. Offers dyslexia specialist (Certificate); education for certified teachers (MA); educational leadership (MA); instructional technology (Certificate); learning disabilities (MA); literacy/reading (Certificate); multilingual education (MA); teacher of the handicapped (Certificate); teaching (MAT). *Accreditation:* TEAC. *Program availability:* Part-time. *Degree requirements:* For master's, research project (MAT).

Fairmont State University, Programs in Education, Fairmont, WV 26554. Offers digital media, new literacies and learning (M Ed); education (MAT); exercise science, fitness and wellness (M Ed); professional studies (M Ed); reading (M Ed); special education (M Ed). *Accreditation:* NCATE. *Program availability:* Part-time, evening/weekend, 100% online. *Entrance requirements:* For master's, GRE. Additional exam requirements/recommendations for international students: Required—TOEFL (minimum score 80 iBT), IELTS (minimum score 6.5). Electronic applications accepted.

Fitchburg State University, Division of Graduate and Continuing Education, Program in Interdisciplinary Studies, Fitchburg, MA 01420-2697. Offers applied communications (CAGS); counseling/psychology (CAGS); individualized track (CAGS); reading specialist (CAGS). *Program availability:* Part-time, evening/weekend. *Entrance requirements:* Additional exam requirements/recommendations for international students: Required—TOEFL (minimum score 550 paper-based; 79 iBT). Electronic applications accepted. *Expenses:* Contact institution.

Florida Atlantic University, College of Education, Department of Teaching and Learning, Boca Raton, FL 33431-0991. Offers elementary education (M Ed); environmental education (M Ed); instructional technology (M Ed); reading education (M Ed); secondary education (M Ed). *Accreditation:* NCATE. *Program availability:* Part-time, evening/weekend. *Faculty:* 16 full-time (12 women), 1 part-time/adjunct (0 women). *Students:* 30 full-time (21 women), 45 part-time (36 women); includes 27 minority (14 Black or African American, non-Hispanic/Latino; 3 Asian, non-Hispanic/Latino; 8 Hispanic/Latino; 2 Two or more races, non-Hispanic/Latino), 6 international. Average age 30. 71 applicants, 58% accepted, 28 enrolled. In 2018, 23 master's awarded. *Entrance requirements:* For master's, GRE General Test, minimum GPA of 3.0 in last 2 years of undergraduate course work. Additional exam requirements/recommendations for international students: Required—TOEFL (minimum score 500 paper-based; 61 iBT), IELTS (minimum score 6). *Application deadline:* For fall admission, 7/1 for domestic students, 2/15 for international students; for spring admission, 11/1 for domestic students, 7/15 for international students. Applications are processed on a rolling basis. Application fee: $30. *Expenses: Tuition, area resident:* Full-time $7400; part-time $369.82 per credit. Tuition, state resident: full-time $7400; part-time $369.82 per credit. Tuition, nonresident: full-time $20,496; part-time $1024.81 per credit. *Financial support:* Fellowships with partial tuition reimbursements, research assistantships with partial tuition reimbursements, teaching assistantships with partial tuition reimbursements, career-related internships or fieldwork, scholarships/grants, and unspecified assistantships available. *Faculty research:* Technology, teaching English to speakers of other languages, math teaching, electronic portfolio assessment, global perspectives through social studies. *Unit head:* Dr. Barbara Ridener, Chairperson, 561-

297-3588, E-mail: bridener@fau.edu. *Application contact:* Dr. Debora Shepherd, Associate Dean, 561-296-3570, E-mail: dshep@fau.edu. Website: http://www.coe.fau.edu/academicdepartments/tl/

Florida Gulf Coast University, College of Education, Program in Curriculum and Instruction, Fort Myers, FL 33965-6565. Offers elementary education (M Ed); English education (M Ed); English speakers of other languages endorsement (M Ed); gifted education (M Ed); mathematics education (M Ed); middle school education (M Ed); reading education (M Ed); science education (M Ed); social science education (M Ed); special education (M Ed). *Program availability:* Part-time, evening/weekend, online learning. *Degree requirements:* For master's, final project or portfolio. *Entrance requirements:* For master's, GRE General Test, MAT, minimum undergraduate GPA of 3.0 in last 2 years. Additional exam requirements/recommendations for international students: Required—TOEFL (minimum score 550 paper-based). Electronic applications accepted. *Faculty research:* Internet in schools, technology in pre-service and in-service teacher training.

Florida International University, College of Arts, Sciences, and Education, Department of Teaching and Learning, Miami, FL 33199. Offers art education (MA, MS); curriculum and instruction (MS, Ed D, PhD, Ed S), including curriculum development (MS); elementary education (MS), English education (MS); learning technologies (MS); mathematics education (MS), modern language education (MS), physical education (MS); science education (MS), social studies education (MS), special education (MS); early childhood education (MS); exceptional student education (Ed D); foreign language education (MS), including foreign language education, teaching English to speakers of other languages (TESOL); language, literacy and culture (PhD); mathematics, science, and learning technologies (PhD); physical education (MS), including sport and fitness; reading education (MS). *Program availability:* Part-time, evening/weekend. *Faculty:* 64 full-time (43 women), 104 part-time/adjunct (76 women). *Students:* 169 full-time (144 women), 155 part-time (130 women); includes 260 minority (53 Black or African American, non-Hispanic/Latino; 7 Asian, non-Hispanic/Latino; 193 Hispanic/Latino; 7 Two or more races, non-Hispanic/Latino), 13 international. Average age 33. 184 applicants, 62% accepted, 87 enrolled. In 2018, 153 master's, 10 doctorates awarded. *Degree requirements:* For doctorate, comprehensive exam, thesis/dissertation. *Entrance requirements:* For master's, GRE General Test, Florida General Knowledge Test or Florida College Level Academic Skills Test; for doctorate and Ed S, GRE General Test. Additional exam requirements/recommendations for international students: Required—TOEFL (minimum score 550 paper-based; 80 iBT), IELTS (minimum score 6.3). *Application deadline:* For fall admission, 6/1 priority date for domestic students, 4/1 for international students; for winter admission, 10/1 priority date for domestic students, 9/1 for international students; for spring admission, 3/1 priority date for domestic students, 2/1 for international students. Applications are processed on a rolling basis. Application fee: $30. Electronic applications accepted. *Financial support:* Research assistantships and teaching assistantships available. *Unit head:* Dr. Maria Fernandez, Chair, 305-348-0193, Fax: 305-348-2086, E-mail: Maria.Fernandez9@fiu.edu. *Application contact:* Nanett Rojas, Manager, Admissions Operations, 305-348-7464, Fax: 305-348-7441, E-mail: gradadm@fiu.edu. Website: https://tl.fiu.edu/

Florida Memorial University, School of Education, Miami-Dade, FL 33054. Offers elementary education (MS); exceptional student education (MS); reading (MS). *Degree requirements:* For master's, comprehensive exam or thesis, field and clinical experiences, exit exam. *Entrance requirements:* For master's, GRE, CLAST, PRAXIS I, baccalaureate or graduate degree with minimum GPA of 3.0 in last 60 hours, 3 recommendations. Additional exam requirements/recommendations for international students: Recommended—TOEFL.

Florida State University, The Graduate School, College of Education, School of Teacher Education, Tallahassee, FL 32306. Offers curriculum and instruction (MS, PhD, Ed S), including reading and language arts (Ed S); teaching English to speakers of other languages (Certificate). *Program availability:* Part-time, evening/weekend, 100% online, blended/hybrid learning, asynchronous, minimal on-campus study. *Faculty:* 30 full-time (23 women), 8 part-time/adjunct (7 women). *Students:* 90 full-time (66 women), 66 part-time (51 women); includes 56 minority (12 Black or African American, non-Hispanic/Latino; 19 Asian, non-Hispanic/Latino; 15 Hispanic/Latino; 10 Two or more races, non-Hispanic/Latino), 32 international. Average age 32. 146 applicants, 56% accepted, 52 enrolled. In 2018, 50 master's, 15 doctorates, 2 other advanced degrees awarded. Terminal master's awarded for partial completion of doctoral program. *Degree requirements:* For master's and other advanced degree, comprehensive exam, thesis optional; for doctorate, comprehensive exam, thesis/dissertation, diagnostic exam, preliminary exam, prospectus defense, dissertation defense. *Entrance requirements:* For master's, doctorate, and other advanced degree, GRE General Test, minimum upper-division GPA of 3.0. Additional exam requirements/recommendations for international students: Required—TOEFL (minimum score 550 paper-based, 80 iBT), Michigan English Language Assessment Battery (minimum score 77), IELTS (minimum score 6.5) or PTE (minimum score 55). *Application deadline:* For fall admission, 6/17 for domestic students; for spring admission, 10/18 for domestic students; for summer admission, 2/11 for domestic students. Application fee: $30. Electronic applications accepted. *Expenses:* Tuition, area resident: Part-time $479.32 per credit hour. Tuition and fees vary according to campus/location and program. *Financial support:* Fellowships, research assistantships, teaching assistantships, scholarships/grants, tuition waivers (full and partial), and unspecified assistantships available. Financial award application deadline: 1/15; financial award applicants required to submit FAFSA. *Faculty research:* Identifying effective intervention strategies to improve reading skills; improving literacy teaching and learning through technology; understanding of student sense making, problem solving, the history and structure of STEM disciplines, and teacher education to support the development of ambitious instruction that supports the STEM learning of all students; examining practices of international education; identifying ways to support the professional development of teachers. *Unit head:* Dr. Sherry Southerland, Professor/Department Chair, 850-644-6885, Fax: 850-644-2725, E-mail: ssoutherland@admin.fsu.edu. *Application contact:* Britni DeZerga, Academic Program Specialist, 850-644-2122, Fax: 850-644-7736, E-mail: bpurvis@fsu.edu. Website: http://education.fsu.edu

Fontbonne University, Graduate Programs, St. Louis, MO 63105-3098. Offers accounting (MBA, MS); art (MA); art (K-12) (MAT); business (MBA); computer science (MS); deaf education (MA); early intervention in deaf education (MA); education (MA), including autism spectrum disorders, curriculum and instruction, diverse learners, early childhood education, reading, special education; elementary education (MAT); family and consumer sciences (MA), including multidisciplinary health communication studies; fine arts (MFA); instructional design and technology (MS); management and leadership (MM); middle school education (MAT); secondary education (MAT); special education (MAT); speech-language pathology (MS); supply chain management (MS); theatre (MA). *Accreditation:* ASHA. *Program availability:* Part-time, evening/weekend, online learning. *Degree requirements:* For master's, comprehensive exam (for some programs), thesis (for some programs). *Entrance requirements:* Additional exam requirements/recommendations for international students: Required—TOEFL (minimum score 500 paper-based; 65 iBT). Electronic applications accepted.

Framingham State University, Graduate Studies, Program in Literacy and Language, Framingham, MA 01701-9101. Offers M Ed. *Program availability:* Part-time, evening/weekend. *Entrance requirements:* For master's, MAT.

Fresno Pacific University, Graduate Programs, School of Education, Program in Reading and Language Arts, Fresno, CA 93702-4709. Offers reading (Certificate); reading/English as a second language (MA Ed); reading/language arts (MA Ed). *Program availability:* Part-time, evening/weekend. *Degree requirements:* For master's, thesis or alternative. *Entrance requirements:* For master's, three references. Additional exam requirements/recommendations for international students: Required—TOEFL (minimum score 550 paper-based). Electronic applications accepted. *Expenses:* Contact institution.

Frostburg State University, College of Education, Department of Educational Professions, Program in Reading, Frostburg, MD 21532-1099. Offers M Ed, Ed D. *Accreditation:* NCATE. *Degree requirements:* For master's, thesis or alternative, in-service. *Entrance requirements:* For master's, teaching certificate. Additional exam requirements/recommendations for international students: Required—TOEFL. Electronic applications accepted.

Furman University, Graduate Division, Department of Education, Greenville, SC 29613. Offers curriculum and instruction (MA); early childhood education (MA); educational leadership (Ed S); English as a second language (MA); literacy (MA); school leadership (MA); special education (MA). *Accreditation:* NCATE. *Program availability:* Part-time, online learning. *Degree requirements:* For master's, comprehensive exam (for some programs), thesis or alternative. *Entrance requirements:* For master's, PRAXIS II. *Expenses: Tuition:* Full-time $27,500; part-time $7290 per credit. Tuition and fees vary according to program. *Faculty research:* Literacy, pedagogy and practice, social justice, advanced leadership, achievement in high poverty schools.

Gannon University, School of Graduate Studies, College of Humanities, Education, and Social Sciences, School of Education, Program in Reading, Erie, PA 16541-0001. Offers M Ed. *Program availability:* Part-time, evening/weekend, 100% online. *Degree requirements:* For master's, comprehensive exam, thesis or alternative, portfolio project. *Entrance requirements:* For master's, 3 letters of recommendation, transcript, bachelor's degree from regionally-accredited college or university with minimum GPA of 3.0. Additional exam requirements/recommendations for international students: Required—TOEFL (minimum score 79 iBT). Electronic applications accepted. Application fee is waived when completed online. *Expenses:* Contact institution.

Gannon University, School of Graduate Studies, College of Humanities, Education, and Social Sciences, School of Education, Program in Reading Specialist, Erie, PA 16541-0001. Offers Certificate. *Program availability:* Part-time, evening/weekend, 100% online. *Entrance requirements:* For degree, 3 letters of recommendation, transcript, bachelor's degree from regionally-accredited college or university with minimum GPA of 3.0, valid instructional I or II teaching certificate. Additional exam requirements/recommendations for international students: Required—TOEFL (minimum score 79 iBT). Application fee is waived when completed online.

George Fox University, College of Education, Graduate Teaching and Leading Program, Newberg, OR 97132-2697. Offers administrative leadership (Ed S); continuing administrator license (Certificate); educational leadership (M Ed); educational technology (M Ed); English for speakers of other languages (M Ed); ESOL (Certificate); initial administrator license (Certificate); reading (M Ed, Certificate); special education (M Ed); teaching (MAT). *Accreditation:* NCATE. *Program availability:* Part-time, evening/weekend, online learning. *Degree requirements:* For master's, thesis (for some programs). *Entrance requirements:* For master's, minimum undergraduate GPA of 3.0 during previous 2 years of course work, resume, 3 professional recommendations on university forms, official transcripts. Additional exam requirements/recommendations for international students: Required—TOEFL (minimum score 577 paper-based; 90 iBT). Electronic applications accepted. *Expenses:* Contact institution.

George Mason University, College of Education and Human Development, Programs in Curriculum and Instruction, Fairfax, VA 22030. Offers assistive technology (M Ed); designing digital learning in schools (M Ed); early childhood education (M Ed); early childhood education for diverse learners (M Ed); elementary education (M Ed); English as a second language (M Ed); gifted child education (M Ed); literacy (M Ed), including PK-12 classroom teachers, reading specialist; literacy leadership for diverse schools (M Ed), including K-12 reading; physical education (M Ed); science K-12 (M Ed); secondary education (M Ed), including biology, chemistry, earth science, English, history/social science, math, physics; special education (M Ed); teacher leadership (M Ed); transformative teaching (M Ed). *Program availability:* Part-time, evening/weekend, 100% online, blended/hybrid learning. *Faculty:* 48 full-time (40 women), 28 part-time/adjunct (20 women). *Students:* 165 full-time (147 women), 697 part-time (579 women); includes 243 minority (47 Black or African American, non-Hispanic/Latino; 3 American Indian or Alaska Native, non-Hispanic/Latino; 88 Asian, non-Hispanic/Latino; 85 Hispanic/Latino; 4 Native Hawaiian or other Pacific Islander, non-Hispanic/Latino; 16 Two or more races, non-Hispanic/Latino), 26 international. Average age 34. 450 applicants, 93% accepted, 315 enrolled. In 2018, 421 master's awarded. *Entrance requirements:* For master's, PRAXIS Core (for some programs), 2 letters of recommendation, interview, program goals statement; 9 hours of complete licensure endorsement requirements (for elementary education); minimum GPA of 3.0 in applicant's last 60 hours of undergraduate coursework (for secondary education); at least 1 year of teaching experience (for literacy). Additional exam requirements/recommendations for international students: Required—TOEFL (minimum score 575 paper-based; 88 iBT), IELTS (minimum score 6.5), PTE (minimum score 59). *Application deadline:* For fall admission, 4/2 priority date for domestic and international students; for spring admission, 11/1 for domestic and international students. Application fee: $75 ($80 for international students). Electronic applications accepted. *Financial support:* In 2018–19, 4 students received support, including 1 fellowship, 3 teaching assistantships (averaging $3,745 per year); career-related internships or fieldwork, Federal Work-Study, scholarships/grants, unspecified assistantships, and health care benefits (for full-time research or teaching assistantship recipients) also available. Support available to part-time students. Financial award application deadline: 3/1; financial award applicants required to submit FAFSA. *Faculty research:* Teacher preparation and professional development; adaptive teaching; wonder in science teacher preparation; literacy (digital, adolescent); site based course instruction. *Unit head:* Rebecca Fox, Professor and Academic Program Coordinator, 703-993-4123, E-mail: rfox@gmu.edu. *Application contact:* Rebecca Fox, Professor and Academic Program Coordinator, 703-993-4123, E-mail: rfox@gmu.edu.
Website: http://gse.gmu.edu/programs/gsemasters

Georgetown College, Department of Education, Georgetown, KY 40324-1696. Offers reading and writing (MA Ed); special education (MA Ed); teaching (MA Ed). *Accreditation:* NCATE. *Program availability:* Part-time. *Degree requirements:* For master's, portfolio. *Entrance requirements:* For master's, teaching certificate, minimum GPA of 2.7 or GRE General Test.

Georgia Southern University, Jack N. Averitt College of Graduate Studies, College of Education, Department of Curriculum, Foundations, and Reading, Program in Reading Education, Statesboro, GA 30460. Offers M Ed, Ed S. *Accreditation:* NCATE. *Program availability:* Part-time, evening/weekend. *Degree requirements:* For master's, comprehensive exam, transition point assessments. *Entrance requirements:* For master's, minimum GPA of 2.5. Additional exam requirements/recommendations for international students: Required—TOEFL (minimum score 550 paper-based; 80 iBT), IELTS (minimum score 6). Electronic applications accepted. *Expenses: Tuition, area resident:* Part-time $3324 per semester. Tuition, state resident: full-time $5814; part-time $3324 per semester. Tuition, nonresident: full-time $23,204; part-time $13,260 per semester. *Required fees:* $2092; $2092. Tuition and fees vary according to course load, degree level, campus/location and program. *Faculty research:* Emerging literacy, content literacy, digital literacies, English language learners, literature groups, phonics/whole language, interpreting literacy policy.

Georgia State University, College of Education and Human Development, Department of Middle and Secondary Education, Atlanta, GA 30302-3083. Offers curriculum and instruction (Ed D); English education (MAT); mathematics education (M Ed, MAT); middle level education (MAT); reading, language and literacy education (M Ed, MAT), including reading instruction (M Ed); science education (M Ed, MAT), including biology (MAT), broad field science (MAT), chemistry (MAT), earth science (MAT), physics (MAT); social studies education (M Ed, MAT), including economics (MAT), geography (MAT), history (MAT), political science (MAT); teaching and learning (PhD), including language and literacy, mathematics education, music education, science education, social studies education, teaching and teacher education. *Accreditation:* NCATE. *Program availability:* Part-time, evening/weekend, online learning. *Faculty:* 19 full-time (15 women), 9 part-time/adjunct (7 women). *Students:* 217 full-time (136 women), 203 part-time (140 women); includes 229 minority (156 Black or African American, non-Hispanic/Latino; 23 Asian, non-Hispanic/Latino; 31 Hispanic/Latino; 19 Two or more races, non-Hispanic/Latino), 3 international. Average age 34. 149 applicants, 60% accepted, 70 enrolled. In 2018, 112 master's, 23 doctorates awarded. *Entrance requirements:* For master's, GRE; GACE I (for initial teacher preparation programs), baccalaureate degree or equivalent, resume, goals statement, two letters of recommendation, minimum undergraduate GPA of 2.5; proof of initial teacher certification in the content area (for M Ed); for doctorate, GRE, resume, goals statement, writing sample, two letters of recommendation, minimum graduate GPA of 3.3, interview. *Application deadline:* For fall admission, 1/15 priority date for domestic and international students; for spring admission, 10/1 for domestic and international students. Application fee: $50. Electronic applications accepted. *Expenses: Tuition, area resident:* Full-time $9360; part-time $390 per credit hour. Tuition, state resident: full-time $9360; part-time $390 per credit hour. Tuition, nonresident: full-time $30,024; part-time $1251 per credit hour. *International tuition:* $30,024 full-time. *Required fees:* $2128. *Financial support:* In 2018–19, fellowships with full tuition reimbursements (averaging $19,667 per year), research assistantships with full tuition reimbursements (averaging $5,436 per year), teaching assistantships with full tuition reimbursements (averaging $2,779 per year) were awarded; career-related internships or fieldwork, Federal Work-Study, scholarships/grants, health care benefits, tuition waivers (full and partial), and unspecified assistantships also available. Financial award application deadline: 3/15. *Faculty research:* Teacher education in language and literacy, mathematics, science, and social studies in urban middle and secondary school settings; learning technologies in school, community, and corporate settings; multicultural education and education for social justice; urban education; international education. *Unit head:* Dr. Gertrude Marilyn Tinker Sachs, Chair, 404-413-8384, Fax: 404-413-8063, E-mail: gtinkersachs@gsu.edu. *Application contact:* Shaleen Tibbs, Administrative Specialist, 404-413-8385, Fax: 404-413-8063, E-mail: stibbs@gsu.edu.
Website: http://mse.education.gsu.edu/

Gordon College, Graduate Education Program, Wenham, MA 01984-1899. Offers early childhood (M Ed); educational leadership (M Ed, Ed S); elementary education (M Ed); English as a second language (M Ed, Ed S); math specialist (M Ed); mathematics specialist (Ed S); middle school education (M Ed); moderate disabilities (M Ed); Montessori education (M Ed); reading (M Ed, Ed S); secondary education (M Ed). *Program availability:* Part-time, evening/weekend. *Degree requirements:* For master's, action research or clinical experience (for most programs); for Ed S, action research or clinical experience (for some programs). *Entrance requirements:* For master's, minimum undergraduate GPA of 3.0; 2 official undergraduate transcripts; professional resume; 3 recommendation letters (one professional reference, one academic reference, one personal reference); 500-700 word statement of purpose; for Ed S, minimum master's GPA of 3.3; 2 official transcripts from undergraduate and graduate schools; professional resume; 3 recommendation letters (one professional reference, one academic reference, one personal reference); 500-700 word statement of purpose. Additional exam requirements/recommendations for international students: Required—TOEFL (minimum score 550 paper-based, 80 iBT) or IELTS (minimum score 6.5). *Expenses:* Contact institution. *Faculty research:* Reading, early childhood development, English language learners, universal design for learning.

Goucher College, Graduate Programs in Education, Baltimore, MD 21204-2794. Offers at-risk and diverse learners (M Ed, Certificate); athletic program leadership and administration (M Ed, Certificate); elementary education (MAT); literacy strategies for content learning (M Ed); middle school (M Ed, Certificate); Montessori studies (M Ed); reading instruction (M Ed, Certificate); reducing student, classroom, and school disruption (M Ed); school improvement leadership (M Ed); secondary education (MAT); special education (MAT), including elementary education; special education for certified elementary and secondary teachers (M Ed); teacher as leader in technology (M Ed). *Program availability:* Part-time, evening/weekend. *Degree requirements:* For master's, thesis (M Ed), final presentation (MAT). *Entrance requirements:* For master's, minimum GPA of 3.0. Additional exam requirements/recommendations for international students: Required—TOEFL (minimum score 550 paper-based; 80 iBT), IELTS (minimum score 7). Electronic applications accepted. *Expenses:* Contact institution. *Faculty research:* Urban education, middle school, school improvement, teacher education, at-risk student achievement.

Governors State University, College of Education, Program in Reading, University Park, IL 60484. Offers MA. *Accreditation:* NCATE. *Program availability:* Part-time. *Faculty:* 19 full-time (12 women), 20 part-time/adjunct (13 women). *Students:* 1 (woman) part-time. Average age 33. *Application deadline:* For fall admission, 4/1 for domestic students. Applications are processed on a rolling basis. Application fee: $50. Electronic applications accepted. *Financial support:* Application deadline: 5/1; applicants required to submit FAFSA. *Unit head:* Timothy Harrington, Chair, Division of Education, 708-534-5000 Ext. 4361, E-mail: tharrington2@govst.edu. *Application contact:* Timothy Harrington, Chair, Division of Education, 708-534-5000 Ext. 4361, E-mail: tharrington2@govst.edu.

Graceland University, Gleazer School of Education, Independence, MO 64050. Offers curriculum and instruction: collaborative learning and teaching (M Ed); differentiated instruction (M Ed); instructional leadership (M Ed); literacy instruction (M Ed); management in a quality classroom (M Ed); special education (M Ed); technology integration (M Ed). *Accreditation:* NCATE. *Program availability:* Part-time, 100% online. *Students:* 70 full-time (58 women), 36 part-time (34 women); includes 4 minority (1 Black or African American, non-Hispanic/Latino; 1 Asian, non-Hispanic/Latino; 1 Hispanic/Latino; 1 Two or more races, non-Hispanic/Latino). Average age 34. 29 applicants, 21%

accepted, 1 enrolled. In 2018, 76 master's awarded. *Degree requirements:* For master's, action research capstone. *Entrance requirements:* For master's, minimum GPA of 3.0, teaching certificate, current teaching contract and license, two letters of reference, statement of professional goals, verification of ongoing access to computer technology, including email and Internet. Additional exam requirements/recommendations for international students: Required—TOEFL (minimum score 550 paper-based; 80 iBT). *Application deadline:* For winter admission, 11/1 for domestic students; for spring admission, 2/1 priority date for domestic students; for summer admission, 7/1 for domestic students. Applications are processed on a rolling basis. Application fee: $50. Electronic applications accepted. *Expenses:* Tuition, material fee, university tech fee, program support fee. *Financial support:* Tuition waivers (partial) available. Financial award applicants required to submit FAFSA. *Faculty research:* Literacy, technology, faculty mentoring, adult literacy, e-learning, online teaching. *Unit head:* Dr. Michele Dickey-Kotz, Dean, 641-784-5202, E-mail: dickey@graceland.edu. *Application contact:* Susan Freeze, Admissions Representative, 816-423-4676, Fax: 816-833-2990, E-mail: sfreeze1@graceland.edu.
Website: http://www.graceland.edu/education

Grambling State University, School of Graduate Studies and Research, College of Education, Department of Educational Leadership, Grambling, LA 71245. Offers developmental education (MS, Ed D, PMC), including curriculum and instructional design (Ed D), English (MS), guidance and counseling (MS), higher education administration and management (Ed D), mathematics (MS), reading (MS), science (MS), student development and personnel services (Ed D); educational leadership (M Ed). *Program availability:* Part-time, evening/weekend. *Degree requirements:* For master's, comprehensive exam, thesis (for some programs); for doctorate, comprehensive exam, thesis/dissertation. *Entrance requirements:* For master's, GRE, minimum GPA of 2.5 on last degree; for doctorate, GRE (minimum score 1000, 500 on Verbal), master's degree, minimum GPA of 3.0 on last degree. Additional exam requirements/recommendations for international students: Required—TOEFL (minimum score 500 paper-based; 62 iBT). Electronic applications accepted.

Grand Canyon University, College of Education, Phoenix, AZ 85017-1097. Offers autism spectrum disorders (MA); curriculum and instruction (MA); early childhood education (M Ed); educational administration (M Ed); educational leadership (M Ed); elementary education (M Ed); gifted education (MA); instructional technology (MS); K-12 leadership (Ed S); reading (MA); secondary education (M Ed); secondary humanities education (M Ed); secondary STEM education (M Ed); special education (M Ed); teaching and learning (Ed D); teaching English to speakers of other languages (MA). *Program availability:* Part-time, evening/weekend, online learning. *Degree requirements:* For master's, publishable research paper (M Ed), e-portfolio. *Entrance requirements:* For master's, undergraduate degree from accredited, GCU-approved college, university, or program with minimum GPA 2.8. Additional exam requirements/recommendations for international students: Required—TOEFL (minimum score 550 paper-based; 79 iBT), IELTS (minimum score 6). Electronic applications accepted.

Grand Valley State University, College of Education, Program in Literacy Studies, Allendale, MI 49401-9403. Offers M Ed. *Program availability:* Part-time, evening/weekend. *Students:* 3 full-time (all women), 117 part-time (112 women); includes 9 minority (3 Black or African American, non-Hispanic/Latino; 3 American Indian or Alaska Native, non-Hispanic/Latino; 2 Hispanic/Latino; 1 Two or more races, non-Hispanic/Latino), 3 international. Average age 32. 41 applicants, 100% accepted, 14 enrolled. In 2018, 38 master's awarded. *Entrance requirements:* For master's, minimum GPA of 3.0 or GRE General Test, last 60 credits from regionally-accredited college/university, 3 letters of recommendation. Additional exam requirements/recommendations for international students: Required—TOEFL (minimum iBT score of 80), IELTS (6.5), or Michigan English Language Assessment Battery (77). *Application deadline:* Applications are processed on a rolling basis. Application fee: $30. Electronic applications accepted. *Expenses:* $652 per credit hour, 33 credits. *Financial support:* In 2018–19, 42 students received support, including 41 fellowships, 1 research assistantship; unspecified assistantships also available. *Unit head:* Dr. Elizabeth Stolle, Program Coordinator, 616-331-6241, Fax: 616-331-6515, E-mail: stollee@gvsu.edu. *Application contact:* Annukka Thelen, Director, Student Information and Services Center, 616-331-6205, Fax: 616-331-6217, E-mail: thelenan@gvsu.edu.
Website: http://www.gvsu.edu/grad/literacy/

Grand Valley State University, College of Education, Program in Reading and Language Arts, Allendale, MI 49401-9403. Offers M Ed. *Accreditation:* NCATE. *Program availability:* Part-time, evening/weekend. *Students:* 1 (woman) part-time. Average age 44. *Entrance requirements:* For master's, GRE General Test or minimum GPA of 3.0; last 60 credits from regionally-accredited college/university; 3 letters of recommendation. Additional exam requirements/recommendations for international students: Required—TOEFL (minimum iBT score of 80), IELTS (6.5), or Michigan English Language Assessment Battery (77). *Application deadline:* Applications are processed on a rolling basis. Application fee: $30. Electronic applications accepted. *Expenses:* $677 per credit hour, K-12 Reading and Language Arts Specialist endorsement is 36 credits, Elementary/ Secondary Reading and Language Arts endorsement is 33 credits. *Financial support:* Career-related internships or fieldwork, Federal Work-Study, scholarships/grants, and unspecified assistantships available. *Faculty research:* Culture of literacy, literacy acquisition, assessment, content area literacy, writing pedagogy. *Unit head:* Dr. Elizabeth Stolle, Graduate Program Director, 616-331-6242, Fax: 616-331-6516, E-mail: stollee@gvsu.edu. *Application contact:* Annukka Thelen, Director, Student Information and Services Center, 616-331-6205, Fax: 616-331-6217, E-mail: thelenan@gvsu.edu.

Hamline University, School of Education, St. Paul, MN 55104-1284. Offers education (MA Ed, Ed D); English as a second language (MA); literacy education (MA); natural science and environmental education (MA Ed); teaching (MAT); teaching English to speakers of other languages (MA). *Accreditation:* NCATE (one or more programs are accredited). *Program availability:* Part-time, evening/weekend, 100% online, blended/hybrid learning. *Degree requirements:* For master's, thesis (for some programs), thesis or capstone project; for doctorate, comprehensive exam, thesis/dissertation. *Entrance requirements:* For master's, official transcripts, essay, letters of recommendation, minimum GPA of 3.0 from bachelor's work; resume and/or writing samples (for some programs); for doctorate, personal statement, master's degree with minimum GPA of 3.0, letters of recommendation, writing sample. Additional exam requirements/recommendations for international students: Required—TOEFL (minimum score 550 paper-based; 80 iBT), IELTS (minimum score 6.5). Electronic applications accepted. *Expenses:* Contact institution. *Faculty research:* Adult basic education, service-learning, teacher dispositions, diversity, technology.

Hannibal-LaGrange University, Program in Education, Hannibal, MO 63401-1999. Offers literacy (MS Ed); teaching and learning (MS Ed). *Program availability:* Part-time, evening/weekend. *Degree requirements:* For master's, thesis, portfolio, documenting of program outcomes, public sharing of research. *Entrance requirements:* For master's, copy of current teaching certificate; minimum GPA of 2.75. *Faculty research:* Reading assessment, reading remediation, handwriting instruction, early childhood intervention.

Harding University, Cannon-Clary College of Education, Searcy, AR 72149-0001. Offers advanced studies in teaching and learning (M Ed); art (MSE); behavioral science (MSE); counseling (MS, Ed S); early childhood special education (M Ed, MSE); education (MSE); educational leadership (M Ed, Ed S); elementary education (M Ed); English (MSE); French (MSE); history/social science (MSE); kinesiology (MSE); math (MSE); reading (M Ed); secondary education (M Ed); Spanish (MSE); teaching (MAT); teaching English as a second language (MSE). *Accreditation:* NCATE. *Program availability:* Part-time, evening/weekend. *Degree requirements:* For master's, comprehensive exam (for some programs), thesis optional, portfolio(s); for Ed S, comprehensive exam, portfolio, project. *Entrance requirements:* For master's, GRE, MAT, PRAXIS; for Ed S, MAT or GRE. Additional exam requirements/recommendations for international students: Required—TOEFL (minimum score 550 paper-based; 79 iBT). *Faculty research:* Reading, comprehension, school violence, educational technology, behavior, college choice, differentiated instruction, brain-based teaching.

Hardin-Simmons University, Graduate School, College of Human Sciences and Educational Studies, Department of Educational Studies, Program in Reading Specialist Education, Abilene, TX 79698-0001. Offers reading education (M Ed). *Program availability:* Part-time. *Students:* 5 part-time (all women); includes 1 minority (Hispanic/Latino). Average age 38. 2 applicants, 100% accepted, 2 enrolled. *Degree requirements:* For master's, comprehensive exam. *Entrance requirements:* For master's, minimum undergraduate GPA of 3.0 in major or all upper-level coursework, 2.7 overall. Additional exam requirements/recommendations for international students: Required—TOEFL (minimum score 550 paper-based; 79 iBT). *Application deadline:* For fall admission, 8/15 priority date for domestic students, 4/1 for international students; for spring admission, 1/5 priority date for domestic students, 9/1 for international students. Applications are processed on a rolling basis. Application fee: $50. Electronic applications accepted. *Expenses: Tuition:* Full-time $750; part-time $750 per credit hour. *Required fees:* $1300; $880 per credit. Tuition and fees vary according to degree level and program. *Financial support:* Fellowships and scholarships/grants available. Support available to part-time students. Financial award application deadline: 6/30; financial award applicants required to submit FAFSA. *Faculty research:* Social networking as a gatekeeper, reflective process of teachers, growth of reflective practice in pre-service teachers, multicultural children's literature. *Unit head:* Dr. Emily Dean, Program Director, 325-671-5784, Fax: 325-670-5859, E-mail: emily.o.dean@hsutx.edu. *Application contact:* Dr. Nancy Kucinski, Dean of Graduate Studies, 325-670-1298, Fax: 325-670-1564, E-mail: gradoff@hsutx.edu.
Website: http://www.hsutx.edu/academics/irvin/graduate/readinged

Harvard University, Harvard Graduate School of Education, Master's Programs in Education, Cambridge, MA 02138. Offers arts in education (Ed M); education policy and management (Ed M); higher education (Ed M); human development and psychology (Ed M); international education policy (Ed M); language and literacy (Ed M); learning and teaching (Ed M); mind, brain, and education (Ed M); prevention science and practice (Ed M); school leadership (Ed M); special studies (Ed M); teacher education (Ed M); technology, innovation, and education (Ed M). *Program availability:* Part-time. *Entrance requirements:* For master's, GRE General Test, statement of purpose, 3 letters of recommendation, resume, official transcripts. Additional exam requirements/recommendations for international students: Required—TOEFL (minimum score 613 paper-based; 104 iBT), TWE (minimum score 5). Electronic applications accepted. *Faculty research:* Learning and development, educational leadership and organizations, education policy analysis.

Heritage University, Graduate Programs in Education, Program in Professional Studies, Toppenish, WA 98948-9599. Offers bilingual education/ESL (M Ed); biology (M Ed); English and literature (M Ed); reading/literacy (M Ed); special education (M Ed). *Program availability:* Part-time, evening/weekend. *Degree requirements:* For master's, comprehensive exam (for some programs), thesis (for some programs).

Hofstra University, School of Education, Specialized Programs in Education, Hempstead, NY 11549. Offers applied behavior analysis (Advanced Certificate); childhood special education (MS Ed); early childhood special education (MS Ed, Advanced Certificate); educational and policy leadership (Ed D); educational leadership (Advanced Certificate); educational leadership and policy studies (MS Ed), including K-12; elementary special education (MS Ed); gifted education (Advanced Certificate); health education (MS); health professions pedagogy and leadership (MS); higher education leadership and policy studies (MS Ed); inclusive early childhood special education (MS Ed); inclusive elementary special education (MS Ed); inclusive secondary special education (MS Ed); literacy studies (MA, MS Ed, Ed D, Advanced Certificate); pedagogy for health professions (Advanced Certificate); physical education (MS); school district business leader (Advanced Certificate); secondary education generalist - students with disabilities 7-12 (MS Ed); secondary special education generalist - secondary education (MS Ed); special education (MS Ed, Advanced Certificate); special education assessment and diagnosis (Advanced Certificate); special education early childhood intervention (MS Ed); special education: international perspectives (MS Ed); teaching students with severe or multiple disabilities (Advanced Certificate). *Program availability:* Part-time, evening/weekend, blended/hybrid learning. *Students:* 126 full-time (91 women), 230 part-time (175 women); includes 90 minority (40 Black or African American, non-Hispanic/Latino; 4 American Indian or Alaska Native, non-Hispanic/Latino; 11 Asian, non-Hispanic/Latino; 32 Hispanic/Latino; 3 Two or more races, non-Hispanic/Latino), 4 international. Average age 32. 215 applicants, 90% accepted, 117 enrolled. In 2018, 130 master's, 9 doctorates, 23 other advanced degrees awarded. *Degree requirements:* For master's, one foreign language, comprehensive exam (for some programs), thesis (for some programs), electronic portfolio, capstone course, internship, practicum, student teaching, seminars, minimum GPA of 3.0; for doctorate, one foreign language, comprehensive exam, thesis/dissertation, qualifying hearing. *Entrance requirements:* For master's, GRE, interview, letters of recommendation, portfolio, essay, certification; for doctorate, GRE or MAT, interview, resume, essay, master's degree, 3 letters of recommendation, writing sample; for Advanced Certificate, GRE, interview, letters of recommendation, essay, professional experience, resume, master's degree. Additional exam requirements/recommendations for international students: Required—TOEFL (minimum score 550 paper-based; 80 iBT). *Application deadline:* Applications are processed on a rolling basis. Application fee: $75. Electronic applications accepted. *Financial support:* In 2018–19, 208 students received support, including 105 fellowships with full and partial tuition reimbursements available (averaging $3,948 per year), 12 research assistantships with full and partial tuition reimbursements available (averaging $6,573 per year); career-related internships or fieldwork, Federal Work-Study, institutionally sponsored loans, scholarships/grants, traineeships, tuition waivers (full and partial), unspecified assistantships, and scholarships and endowed scholarships also available. Support available to part-time students. Financial award applicants required to submit FAFSA. *Faculty research:* Water quality and income inequality; girls and stem; new media literacies; applied behavior analysis; k-12 leadership development. *Unit head:* Dr. Alan Flurkey, Chairperson, 516-463-5237, E-mail: alan.d.flurkey@hofstra.edu. *Application contact:* Sunil Samuel, Assistant Vice President of Admissions, 516-463-4723, Fax: 516-463-4664, E-mail: graduateadmission@hofstra.edu.
Website: http://www.hofstra.edu/education/

Holy Family University, Graduate and Professional Programs, School of Education, Master of Education Programs, Philadelphia, PA 19114. Offers early elementary

education (PreK-Grade 4) (M Ed); education leadership (M Ed); general education (M Ed); reading specialist (M Ed); special education (M Ed); TESOL and literacy (M Ed). *Program availability:* Part-time. *Degree requirements:* For master's, thesis optional. Electronic applications accepted.

Hood College, Graduate School, Department of Education, Frederick, MD 21701-8575. Offers curriculum and instruction (MS), including elementary education, elementary science and mathematics education, secondary education, special education; education, multidisciplinary studies (MS); educational leadership (MS, Certificate); reading specialization (MS); STEM education (Certificate). *Accreditation:* NCATE. *Program availability:* Part-time-only, evening/weekend. *Faculty:* 5 full-time (3 women), 32 part-time/adjunct (24 women). *Students:* 3 full-time (all women), 306 part-time (253 women); includes 65 minority (22 Black or African American, non-Hispanic/Latino; 9 Asian, non-Hispanic/Latino; 17 Hispanic/Latino; 17 Two or more races, non-Hispanic/Latino), 3 international. Average age 33. 80 applicants, 99% accepted, 45 enrolled. In 2018, 59 master's, 47 other advanced degrees awarded. *Degree requirements:* For master's, action research project, portfolio (for reading specialization); for Certificate, STEM capstone activity. *Entrance requirements:* For master's, minimum GPA of 2.75, teaching certification, writing sample during interview, letter of recommendation from principal (for educational leadership program only). Additional exam requirements/recommendations for international students: Required—TOEFL (minimum score 575 paper-based; 89 iBT), IELTS (minimum score 6.5). *Application deadline:* For fall admission, 8/15 priority date for domestic students, 8/5 for international students; for spring admission, 12/1 priority date for domestic students, 12/1 for international students; for summer admission, 5/1 priority date for domestic students, 4/15 for international students. Applications are processed on a rolling basis. Application fee: $50 ($100 for international students). Electronic applications accepted. *Expenses: Tuition:* Full-time $17,640; part-time $4410 per semester. *Required fees:* $125 per semester. Tuition and fees vary according to degree level and program. *Financial support:* Tuition waivers (partial) and unspecified assistantships available. Financial award applicants required to submit FAFSA. *Faculty research:* Leadership, action research, brain research, learning styles. *Unit head:* Dr. April M. Boulton, Dean of the Graduate School, 301-696-3612, E-mail: gofurther@hood.edu. *Application contact:* Tanith Fowler Corsi, Assistant Director of Graduate Admissions, 301-696-3603, E-mail: gofurther@hood.edu.
Website: https://www.hood.edu/academics/departments/department-education/programs-offered

Houston Baptist University, College of Education and Behavioral Sciences, Programs in Education, Houston, TX 77074-3298. Offers bilingual education (M Ed); counselor education (M Ed); curriculum and instruction (M Ed); curriculum and instruction (EC-6 bilingual) (M Ed); curriculum and instruction in all-level art, Spanish, music, or physical education (M Ed); curriculum and instruction in EC-6 and special education (EC-12) (M Ed); curriculum and instruction in instructional technology (M Ed); curriculum and instruction in mathematics, science, or social studies (4-8) (M Ed); curriculum and instruction with EC-6 generalist (M Ed); curriculum and instruction with English language arts and reading (4-8) (M Ed); educational administration (M Ed); educational diagnostician (M Ed); executive educational leadership (Ed D); higher education in business management (M Ed); higher education in Christian studies (M Ed); higher education in counseling (M Ed); higher education in educational technology (M Ed); reading (M Ed); special educational leadership (Ed D). *Program availability:* Part-time, evening/weekend, 100% online, blended/hybrid learning. *Degree requirements:* For master's, comprehensive exam; for doctorate, thesis/dissertation. *Entrance requirements:* For master's, minimum GPA of 2.75, two recommendations, resume, bachelor's degree conferred transcript; interview (for non-certified teachers); for doctorate, GRE, 5 letters of recommendation. Additional exam requirements/recommendations for international students: Required—TOEFL (minimum score 80 iBT), IELTS (minimum score 6.5). Electronic applications accepted. Application fee is waived when completed online. *Expenses:* Contact institution. *Faculty research:* Autism and inclusion, integrating technology into instruction, school change and leadership trust.

Idaho State University, Graduate School, College of Education, Department of Teaching and Educational Studies, Pocatello, ID 83209-8059. Offers deaf education (M Ed); elementary education (M Ed); human exceptionality (M Ed); literacy (M Ed); music education (M Ed); secondary education (M Ed). *Program availability:* Part-time. *Degree requirements:* For master's, comprehensive exam, thesis (for some programs), oral thesis defense or written comprehensive exam and oral exam. *Entrance requirements:* For master's, GRE or MAT, minimum undergraduate GPA of 3.0, bachelor's degree, professional experience in an educational context. Additional exam requirements/recommendations for international students: Required—TOEFL (minimum score 550 paper-based; 80 iBT). Electronic applications accepted. *Faculty research:* Literacy, school psychology, special education.

Illinois State University, Graduate School, College of Education, Department of Curriculum and Instruction, Program in Reading, Normal, IL 61790. Offers MS Ed. *Accreditation:* NCATE. *Faculty:* 102 full-time (76 women), 132 part-time/adjunct (107 women). *Students:* 3 part-time (2 women); includes 1 minority (Hispanic/Latino). Average age 35. 7 applicants, 86% accepted, 3 enrolled. In 2018, 17 master's awarded. *Degree requirements:* For master's, practicum. *Entrance requirements:* For master's, GRE General Test, minimum GPA of 3.0 in last 60 hours of course work, course work in reading. *Application deadline:* Applications are processed on a rolling basis. Application fee: $40. *Expenses: Tuition, area resident:* Full-time $7264.62. Tuition, state resident: full-time $9466. Tuition, nonresident: full-time $17,290. *International tuition:* $15,089.40 full-time. *Required fees:* $1481.04. *Financial support:* In 2018–19, 18 research assistantships were awarded; tuition waivers (full) also available. Financial award application deadline: 4/1. *Unit head:* Dr. Alan Bates, Interim Director, 309-438-5425, E-mail: abates@ilstu.edu. *Application contact:* Dr. Alan Bates, Interim Director, 309-438-5425, E-mail: abates@ilstu.edu.
Website: http://www.coe.ilstu.edu/c+idept/grad/rdmast.html/

Indiana University Bloomington, School of Education, Department of Literacy, Culture, and Language Education, Bloomington, IN 47405-7000. Offers MS, Ed D, PhD, Ed S. *Accreditation:* NCATE. *Program availability:* Part-time, evening/weekend, online learning. Terminal master's awarded for partial completion of doctoral program. *Degree requirements:* For doctorate, thesis/dissertation, internship; for Ed S, comprehensive exam or project. *Entrance requirements:* For master's, GRE General Test or minimum GPA of 3.0; for doctorate, GRE General Test, minimum graduate GPA of 3.5; for Ed S, GRE General Test. Additional exam requirements/recommendations for international students: Required—TOEFL. *Faculty research:* Discourse analysis, sociolinguistics, critical literacy, cultural studies.

Indiana University of Pennsylvania, School of Graduate Studies and Research, College of Education and Communications, Department of Professional Studies in Education, Program in Literacy, Indiana, PA 15705. Offers literacy (M Ed); reading (Certificate). *Accreditation:* NCATE. *Program availability:* Part-time. *Faculty:* 11 full-time (8 women), 2 part-time/adjunct (1 woman). *Students:* 17 full-time (16 women), 11 part-time (10 women); includes 2 minority (both Black or African American, non-Hispanic/Latino). Average age 25. 27 applicants, 81% accepted, 19 enrolled. In 2018, 16 master's

awarded. *Degree requirements:* For master's, thesis optional. *Entrance requirements:* For master's, 2 letters of recommendation. Additional exam requirements/recommendations for international students: Required—TOEFL (minimum score 540 paper-based). *Application deadline:* For fall admission, 7/1 for domestic students; for spring admission, 11/1 for domestic students. Applications are processed on a rolling basis. Application fee: $50. Electronic applications accepted. *Expenses:* Tuition, state resident: full-time $12,384; part-time $516 per credit hour. Tuition: nonresident: full-time $18,576; part-time $774 per credit hour. *Required fees:* $4454; $186 per credit hour. $65 per semester. Tuition and fees vary according to program and reciprocity agreements. *Financial support:* In 2018–19, 16 research assistantships with tuition reimbursements (averaging $4,500 per year) were awarded; fellowships, career-related internships or fieldwork, Federal Work-Study, scholarships/grants, and unspecified assistantships also available. Support available to part-time students. Financial award application deadline: 4/15; financial award applicants required to submit FAFSA. *Unit head:* Dr. Julie Ankrum, Graduate Coordinator, 724-357-2416, E-mail: jankrum@iup.edu. *Application contact:* Dr. Julie Ankrum, Graduate Coordinator, 724-357-2416, E-mail: jankrum@iup.edu.
Website: http://www.iup.edu/pse/grad/literacy-med-reading-specialist-certification/default.aspx

Indiana University–Purdue University Indianapolis, School of Education, Indianapolis, IN 46202-5155. Offers curriculum and instruction (MS); early childhood (MS); educational leadership (MS, Certificate); English as a second language (Certificate); kindergarten (Certificate); language education (MS); reading (Certificate); school counseling (MS); special education (MS, Certificate). *Program availability:* Part-time, evening/weekend. Terminal master's awarded for partial completion of doctoral program. *Degree requirements:* For master's, thesis optional. *Entrance requirements:* For master's, GRE General Test, minimum GPA of 2.5; for Certificate, official transcripts. Additional exam requirements/recommendations for international students: Required—TOEFL (minimum score 60 iBT), IELTS (minimum score 5.5). Electronic applications accepted. *Expenses:* Contact institution. *Faculty research:* Educational policies and school leaders' responses to these; issues of intersectionality in the experiences of African American lesbian, gay, and bisexual students attending historically black colleges and universities and those who belong to black Greek-letter organizations; students' experiential knowledge and their evolving disciplinary-specific literacy and understanding; innovative program development; urban ESL teacher preparation; target-based instructional coaching.

Jackson State University, Graduate School, College of Education and Human Development, Department of Elementary and Early Childhood Education, Jackson, MS 39217. Offers early childhood education (MS Ed, Ed D); elementary education (MS Ed, Ed S); reading education (MS Ed). *Accreditation:* NCATE. *Program availability:* Part-time, evening/weekend, 100% online, blended/hybrid learning. Terminal master's awarded for partial completion of doctoral program. *Degree requirements:* For master's, comprehensive exam, thesis or alternative; for doctorate, comprehensive exam, thesis/dissertation. *Entrance requirements:* For master's, GRE General Test; for doctorate, MAT, teaching experience. Additional exam requirements/recommendations for international students: Required—TOEFL (minimum score 520 paper-based; 67 iBT). Electronic applications accepted. *Expenses:* Contact institution.

Jacksonville State University, Graduate Studies, School of Education, Program in Reading Specialist, Jacksonville, AL 36265-1602. Offers MS Ed. *Program availability:* Part-time, evening/weekend. *Degree requirements:* For master's, comprehensive exam, thesis (for some programs). *Entrance requirements:* Additional exam requirements/recommendations for international students: Required—TOEFL (minimum score 500 paper-based; 61 iBT). Electronic applications accepted.

James Madison University, The Graduate School, College of Education, Program in Education, Harrisonburg, VA 22807. Offers early childhood education (preK-3) (MAT); educational leadership (M Ed); educational technology (M Ed); elementary education (MAT); equity and cultural diversity (M Ed); inclusive early childhood education (MAT); K-8 mathematics specialist (M Ed); middle education (MAT); reading education (M Ed); secondary education (MAT); Spanish language and culture for educators (M Ed); TESOL (MAT). *Accreditation:* NCATE. *Program availability:* Part-time, evening/weekend. *Students:* 255 full-time (224 women), 200 part-time (140 women); includes 56 minority (13 Black or African American, non-Hispanic/Latino; 8 Asian, non-Hispanic/Latino; 21 Hispanic/Latino; 14 Two or more races, non-Hispanic/Latino), 1 international. Average age 30. In 2018, 295 master's awarded. Application fee: $60. Electronic applications accepted. *Expenses:* Tuition, state resident: full-time $10,848. Tuition, nonresident: full-time $27,888. *Required fees:* $1128. *Financial support:* In 2018–19, 22 students received support. Teaching assistantships, career-related internships or fieldwork, Federal Work-Study, and assistantships (averaging $7911) available. Financial award application deadline: 3/1; financial award applicants required to submit FAFSA. *Unit head:* Dr. Phillip M. Wishon, Dean, 540-568-6572, E-mail: wishonpm@jmu.edu. *Application contact:* Lynette D. Michael, Director of Graduate Admissions, 540-568-6131 Ext. 6395, Fax: 540-568-7860, E-mail: michaeld@jmu.edu.
Website: http://www.jmu.edu/coe/index.shtml

James Madison University, The Graduate School, College of Education, Program in Reading Education, Harrisonburg, VA 22807. Offers M Ed. *Accreditation:* NCATE. *Program availability:* Part-time. *Entrance requirements:* For master's, GRE General Test. Additional exam requirements/recommendations for international students: Required—TOEFL. *Application deadline:* For fall admission, 5/1 priority date for domestic students; for spring admission, 9/1 priority date for domestic students. Applications are processed on a rolling basis. Electronic applications accepted. *Expenses:* Tuition, state resident: full-time $10,848. Tuition, nonresident: full-time $27,888. *Required fees:* $1128. *Financial support:* Federal Work-Study and unspecified assistantships available. Financial award application deadline: 3/1; financial award applicants required to submit FAFSA. *Unit head:* Dr. Martha Ross, Academic Unit Head, 540-568-6255. *Application contact:* Lynette M. Bible, Director of Graduate Admissions, 540-568-6395, Fax: 540-568-7860, E-mail: biblelm@jmu.edu.

Judson University, Doctor of Education in Literacy Program, Elgin, IL 60123-1498. Offers Ed D. *Faculty:* 5 full-time (3 women), 10 part-time/adjunct (all women). *Students:* 13 full-time (all women), 19 part-time (17 women); includes 1 minority (Hispanic/Latino). Average age 43. 15 applicants, 93% accepted, 14 enrolled. In 2018, 9 doctorates awarded. *Degree requirements:* For doctorate, thesis/dissertation, 4 authentic benchmark assessments. *Entrance requirements:* For doctorate, resume/curriculum vitae; official transcript(s) of all master's work; three letters of recommendation; minimum GPA of 3.35; essay; interview; live writing sample. *Application deadline:* For fall admission, 11/15 for domestic and international students. Application fee: $200. *Expenses:* Estimated per semester tuition and fees: $3,750 tuition, $1,500 living expenses, $500 books and supplies, $300 transportation. *Financial support:* Teaching assistantships available. Financial award application deadline: 11/15; financial award applicants required to submit FAFSA. *Faculty research:* Literacy, social justice, linguistics, communication theory, higher education. *Unit head:* Dr. Brenda Buckley-Hughes, Co-Director, 847-628-1060, E-mail: bbuckley-hughes@judsonu.edu. *Application contact:* Brenda Buckley-Hughes, Co-Director, 847-628-1060, E-mail: bbuckley-hughes@judsonu.edu.
Website: http://www.judsonu.edu/literacydoctor/

Judson University, Master of Education in Literacy Program, Elgin, IL 60123-1498. Offers M Ed. *Faculty:* 4 full-time (2 women), 8 part-time/adjunct (7 women). *Students:* 19 part-time (all women); includes 2 minority (both Hispanic/Latino). Average age 31. 19 applicants, 100% accepted, 19 enrolled. *Degree requirements:* For master's, completion and submission of a feature article to a peer-reviewed journal in the field. *Entrance requirements:* For master's, copy of official teaching certificate; official transcript(s) of all college coursework; bachelor's degree with minimum GPA of 3.0; 2 letters of reference; essay; interview; live writing sample. *Application deadline:* For fall admission, 4/15 for domestic and international students. Applications are processed on a rolling basis. Application fee: $55. *Expenses:* Estimated tuition and fees by semester: Tuition: $5,975, Living Expenses: $2,000, Trans: $500. *Financial support:* Tuition discounts available. Financial award application deadline: 4/15; financial award applicants required to submit FAFSA. *Faculty research:* Affective domain in reading, children's and adolescent literature, cross-curricular writing, critical thinking, administration in higher education, linguistics. *Unit head:* Dr. Kristy Piebenga, Director, 847-628-1086, E-mail: kristy.piebenga@judsonu.edu. *Application contact:* Dr. Kristy Piebenga, Director, 847-628-1086, E-mail: kristy.piebenga@judsonu.edu.

Kansas State University, Graduate School, College of Education, Department of Curriculum and Instruction, Manhattan, KS 66506. Offers curriculum and instruction (Ed D, PhD); digital teaching and learning (MS); educational computing, design and online learning (MS); elementary/middle level curriculum and instruction (MS); online learning (Certificate); reading specialist endorsement (MS); reading/language arts (MS); teacher leader/school improvement (MS); teaching and learning (Certificate). *Accreditation:* NCATE. *Program availability:* Part-time, online learning. *Degree requirements:* For master's, comprehensive exam, portfolio, project, report or thesis; for doctorate, comprehensive exam, thesis/dissertation, preliminary exam; for Certificate, comprehensive exam, portfolio. *Entrance requirements:* For master's, minimum GPA of 3.0, 3 letters of recommendation; for doctorate, GRE, minimum GPA of 3.0, 3 letters of recommendation, evidence of scholarly writing; for Certificate, minimum GPA of 3.0, letters of recommendation. Additional exam requirements/recommendations for international students: Required—TOEFL (minimum score 550 paper-based; 80 iBT) or IELTS. Electronic applications accepted. *Faculty research:* Literacy and technology, critical race theory and diversity, achievement gaps, school improvement, teacher education.

Kennesaw State University, Bagwell College of Education, Program in Reading, Kennesaw, GA 30144. Offers M Ed. *Program availability:* Part-time-only, evening/weekend, online only, 100% online. *Students:* 10 part-time (all women); includes 1 minority (Hispanic/Latino). Average age 29. 6 applicants, 83% accepted, 4 enrolled. In 2018, 4 master's awarded. *Entrance requirements:* For master's, valid teaching certificate, endorsement, degree in early childhood education, or GACE. Additional exam requirements/recommendations for international students: Required—TOEFL (minimum score 80 iBT), IELTS (minimum score 6.5). *Application deadline:* For fall admission, 7/1 for domestic students; for summer admission, 4/1 for domestic students. Applications are processed on a rolling basis. Application fee: $60. Electronic applications accepted. *Expenses: Tuition, area resident:* Full-time $6960; part-time $290 per credit hour. Tuition, state resident: full-time $6960; part-time $290 per credit hour. Tuition, nonresident: full-time $25,080; part-time $1045 per credit hour. *International tuition:* $25,080 full-time. *Required fees:* $2006; $1706 per semester. $853 per semester. *Application contact:* Admission Counselor, 470-578-4377, Fax: 470-578-9172, E-mail: ksugrad@kennesaw.edu.
Website: http://bagwell.kennesaw.edu/departments/smge/programs/med/reading/

Kent State University, College of Education, Health and Human Services, School of Teaching, Learning and Curriculum Studies, Program in Reading Specialization, Kent, OH 44242-0001. Offers M Ed, MA. *Accreditation:* NCATE. *Program availability:* Part-time, evening/weekend. *Faculty:* 7 full-time (5 women), 1 (woman) part-time/adjunct. *Students:* 1 (woman) full-time, 32 part-time (29 women). 15 applicants, 60% accepted. In 2018, 14 master's awarded. *Degree requirements:* For master's, thesis (for some programs). *Entrance requirements:* For master's, 2 letters of reference, goals statement. Additional exam requirements/recommendations for international students: Required—TOEFL (minimum score 550 paper-based; 80 iBT). *Application deadline:* Applications are processed on a rolling basis. Application fee: $45 ($60 for international students). Electronic applications accepted. *Expenses:* Tuition, state resident: full-time $11,766; part-time $536 per credit. Tuition, nonresident: full-time $21,952; part-time $999 per credit. *International tuition:* $21,952 full-time. Tuition and fees vary according to course load. *Financial support:* Research assistantships with full tuition reimbursements, Federal Work-Study, scholarships/grants, and unspecified assistantships available. Financial award application deadline: 4/1; financial award applicants required to submit FAFSA. *Faculty research:* Adolescent literacy, adult and family literacy, school change in literacy education, struggling readers. *Unit head:* Dr. Denise Morgan, Coordinator, 330-672-0663, E-mail: dmorgan2@kent.edu. *Application contact:* Cheryl Slusarczyk, Academic Program Director, Office of Graduate Student Services, 330-672-2576, Fax: 330-672-9162, E-mail: ogs@kent.edu.
Website: http://www.kent.edu/ehhs/le/

Kutztown University of Pennsylvania, College of Education, Program in Reading, Kutztown, PA 19530-0730. Offers M Ed. *Accreditation:* NCATE. *Program availability:* Part-time, evening/weekend. *Students:* 1 (woman) full-time, 62 part-time (57 women); includes 3 minority (1 Asian, non-Hispanic/Latino; 2 Hispanic/Latino). Average age 31. 19 applicants, 89% accepted, 14 enrolled. In 2018, 15 master's awarded. *Degree requirements:* For master's, comprehensive project. *Entrance requirements:* For master's, GRE General Test, PRAXIS II, NTE, or 10 years' experience in elementary or secondary school with appropriate certification, valid PA instructional I or II teaching certificate, 3 graduate evaluation forms from professionals in education. Additional exam requirements/recommendations for international students: Required—TOEFL (minimum score 550 paper-based, 79 iBT), IELTS (minimum score 6.5), or PTE (minimum score 53). *Application deadline:* For fall admission, 8/1 for domestic and international students; for spring admission, 12/1 for domestic and international students. Application fee: $35. Electronic applications accepted. *Expenses:* Tuition, state resident: part-time $516 per credit. Tuition, nonresident: part-time $774 per credit. *Required fees:* $119 per credit. One-time fee: $50 part-time. Tuition and fees vary according to degree level. *Financial support:* Career-related internships or fieldwork, Federal Work-Study, and unspecified assistantships available. Financial award application deadline: 3/1; financial award applicants required to submit FAFSA. *Unit head:* Dr. Catherine McGeehan, Associate Professor, 484-646-4347, E-mail: mcgeehan@kutztown.edu. *Application contact:* Dr. Catherine McGeehan, Associate Professor, 484-646-4347, E-mail: mcgeehan@kutztown.edu.
Website: https://www.kutztown.edu/academics/graduate-programs/reading.htm

La Salle University, School of Arts and Sciences, Program in Education, Philadelphia, PA 19141-1199. Offers autism spectrum disorders (MA, Certificate); bilingual/bicultural studies (MA); classroom management (MA); dual early childhood and special education (MA); dual middle-level science and math and special education (MA); education (MA); English (MA); English as a second language (Certificate); history (MA); instructional coach (Certificate); instructional leadership (MA); reading specialist (MA, Certificate); secondary education (MA); special education (MA, Certificate). *Program availability:* Part-time, evening/weekend. *Degree requirements:* For master's, comprehensive exam. *Entrance requirements:* For master's, MAT or GRE, 2 letters of recommendation; for Certificate, GMAT or GRE, 2 letters of recommendation. Additional exam requirements/recommendations for international students: Required—TOEFL. Electronic applications accepted. Application fee is waived when completed online. *Expenses:* Contact institution.

Lehman College of the City University of New York, School of Education, Department of Counseling, Leadership, Literacy, and Special Education, Program in Literacy Studies, Bronx, NY 10468-1589. Offers MS Ed. *Accreditation:* NCATE. *Program availability:* Evening/weekend. *Entrance requirements:* For master's, interview, minimum GPA of 2.7. *Faculty research:* Emergent literacy, language-based classrooms, primary and secondary social contexts of language and literacy, innovative in-service education models, adult literacy.

Le Moyne College, Department of Education, Syracuse, NY 13214. Offers adolescent education (MS Ed, MST); adolescent education/special education (MS Ed, MST); adolescent English (MST), including grades 7-12; adolescent English/special education (MST), including grades 7-12; adolescent foreign language (MST), including grades 7-12; adolescent history (MST), including grades 7-12; childhood education (MS Ed); childhood education/special education (MS Ed); elementary education (MS Ed); general education (MS Ed); inclusive childhood education (MST); literacy education (MS Ed), including birth to grade 6, grades 5-12; school building leader (MS Ed); school building leadership (CAS); school district business leader (MS Ed, CAS); school district leader (MS Ed); school district leadership (CAS); secondary education (MS Ed); special education (MS Ed); teaching English to speakers of other languages (MS Ed); urban studies (MS Ed). *Accreditation:* TEAC. *Program availability:* Part-time, evening/weekend. *Faculty:* 7 full-time (5 women), 16 part-time/adjunct (11 women). *Students:* 35 full-time (28 women), 119 part-time (84 women); includes 14 minority (5 Black or African American, non-Hispanic/Latino; 1 Asian, non-Hispanic/Latino; 7 Hispanic/Latino; 1 Two or more races, non-Hispanic/Latino), 1 international. Average age 30. 123 applicants, 89% accepted, 96 enrolled. In 2018, 66 master's, 48 CASs awarded. Terminal master's awarded for partial completion of doctoral program. *Degree requirements:* For master's, thesis. *Entrance requirements:* For master's, bachelor's degree with minimum undergraduate GPA of 3.0, 2 letters of recommendation, transcripts. Additional exam requirements/recommendations for international students: Required—TOEFL (minimum score 79 iBT); Recommended—IELTS (minimum score 6.5). *Application deadline:* For fall admission, 4/1 priority date for domestic and international students; for spring admission, 10/1 priority date for domestic and international students; for summer admission, 3/1 priority date for domestic and international students. Applications are processed on a rolling basis. Electronic applications accepted. *Expenses:* $734 per credit hour; wellness fee $70 per semester for full-time graduate students taking 9+ credit hours; technology fee $75 per semester for full-time graduate students taking 9+ credit hours, $25 per semester for part-time students; $1,470 per credit hour (for ED.D.). *Financial support:* In 2018–19, 44 students received support. Career-related internships or fieldwork, scholarships/grants, and health care benefits available. Support available to part-time students. Financial award applicants required to submit FAFSA. *Faculty research:* Minority teachers, special education, multiculturalism, literacy, technology, media literacy learning, autism, school district organization, service-learning, higher level problem solving, teacher leadership. *Unit head:* Dr. Stephen C. Fleury, Chair, Department of Education, 315-445-4376, Fax: 315-445-4744, E-mail: fleurysc@lemoyne.edu. *Application contact:* Jody F Manning, Assistant Director for Graduate Admission, 315-445-5444, Fax: 315-445-6092, E-mail: manninjf@lemoyne.edu.
Website: http://www.lemoyne.edu/education

Lesley University, Graduate School of Education, Cambridge, MA 02138-2790. Offers arts, community, and education (M Ed); autism studies (Certificate); curriculum and instruction (M Ed, CAGS); early childhood education (M Ed); ecological teaching and learning (MS); educational studies (PhD), including adult learning, educational leadership, individually designed; elementary education (M Ed); emergent technologies for educators (Certificate); ESLArts: language learning through the arts (M Ed); high school education (M Ed); individually designed (M Ed); integrated teaching through the arts (M Ed); literacy for K-8 classroom teachers (M Ed); mathematics education (M Ed); middle school education (M Ed); moderate disabilities (M Ed); online learning (Certificate); reading (CAGS); science in education (M Ed); severe disabilities (M Ed); special needs (CAGS); specialist teacher of reading (M Ed); teacher of visual art (M Ed); technology in education (M Ed, CAGS). *Accreditation:* TEAC. *Program availability:* Part-time, evening/weekend, online learning. *Degree requirements:* For master's, practicum; for doctorate, thesis/dissertation. *Entrance requirements:* For master's, Massachusetts Tests for Educator Licensure (MTEL), transcripts, statement of purpose, recommendations; interview (for special education); for doctorate, GRE General Test, transcripts, statement of purpose, recommendations, interview, master's degree, resume; for other advanced degree, interview, master's degree. Additional exam requirements/recommendations for international students: Required—TOEFL (minimum score 550 paper-based; 80 iBT). Electronic applications accepted. *Faculty research:* Assessment in literacy, mathematics and science; autism spectrum disorders; instructional technology and online learning; multicultural education and English language learners.

Lewis University, College of Education, Program in Curriculum and Instruction: Literacy and English Language Learning, Romeoville, IL 60446. Offers M Ed. *Program availability:* Part-time. *Students:* 1 (woman) full-time, 1 part-time (0 women). Average age 31. *Degree requirements:* For master's, comprehensive exam. *Entrance requirements:* For master's, Test of Academic Proficiency/Basic Skills Test/ACT/SAT, bachelor's degree, minimum undergraduate GPA of 2.75, state licensure with teaching endorsement. Additional exam requirements/recommendations for international students: Required—TOEFL (minimum score 550 paper-based; 79 iBT), IELTS (minimum score 6). *Application deadline:* For fall admission, 5/1 priority date for international students; for spring admission, 11/1 for international students. Application fee: $40. Electronic applications accepted. *Financial support:* Federal Work-Study and unspecified assistantships available. Financial award application deadline: 5/1; financial award applicants required to submit FAFSA. *Unit head:* Dr. Christopher Kline, Foundations, Leadership & Literacy Department Chair. *Application contact:* Kathy Lisak, Graduate Admission Counselor, 815-836-5610, E-mail: grad@lewisu.edu.
Website: http://www.lewisu.edu/academics/literacy-ELL/index.htm

Lewis University, College of Education, Programs in Reading and Literacy, Romeoville, IL 60446. Offers M Ed, MA. *Program availability:* Part-time. *Students:* 8 part-time (all women). Average age 31. *Degree requirements:* For master's, comprehensive exam, departmental qualifying exam. *Entrance requirements:* For master's, writing exam, Test of Academic Proficiency/Basic Skills Test/ACT/SAT, bachelor's degree, minimum GPA of 2.75, 2 letters of recommendation, professional educator license. Additional exam requirements/recommendations for international students: Required—TOEFL (minimum score 550 paper-based; 79 iBT), IELTS (minimum score 6). *Application deadline:* For fall admission, 5/1 priority date for international students; for spring admission, 11/15 priority date for international students. Applications are processed on a rolling basis. Application fee: $40. Electronic applications accepted. *Financial support:* Federal Work-Study, scholarships/grants, and

unspecified assistantships available. Financial award application deadline: 5/1; financial award applicants required to submit FAFSA. *Unit head:* Dr. Jung Kim, Program Director. *Application contact:* Kathy Lisak, Graduate Admission Counselor, 815-836-5610, E-mail: grad@lewisu.edu.

Liberty University, School of Education, Lynchburg, VA 24515. Offers reading specialist (M Ed). *Accreditation:* NCATE. *Program availability:* Part-time, online learning. *Students:* 2,922 full-time (2,241 women), 3,559 part-time (2,621 women); includes 1,770 minority (1,342 Black or African American, non-Hispanic/Latino; 38 American Indian or Alaska Native, non-Hispanic/Latino; 68 Asian, non-Hispanic/Latino; 177 Hispanic/Latino; 18 Native Hawaiian or other Pacific Islander, non-Hispanic/Latino; 127 Two or more races, non-Hispanic/Latino), 71 international. Average age 38. 9,077 applicants, 37% accepted, 1886 enrolled. In 2018, 1,020 master's, 173 doctorates, 402 other advanced degrees awarded. *Degree requirements:* For doctorate, comprehensive exam, thesis/dissertation. *Entrance requirements:* For master's, GRE General Test or MAT (if taken in or before 1999), 2 letters of recommendation, minimum undergraduate GPA of 3.0, curriculum vitae; for doctorate and other advanced degree, GRE General Test or MAT (if taken before 1999), minimum master's GPA of 3.0, 3 years of teaching experience. Additional exam requirements/recommendations for international students: Required—TOEFL (minimum score 600 paper-based; 100 iBT). *Application deadline:* For fall admission, 6/1 for domestic students; for spring admission, 11/1 for domestic students. Applications are processed on a rolling basis. Application fee: $50. Electronic applications accepted. *Expenses:* Contact institution. *Financial support:* In 2018–19, 265 students received support. Federal Work-Study and tuition waivers (partial) available. *Faculty research:* Self-determination, character education, bibliotherapy, learning styles, distance education. *Unit head:* Dr. Deanna Keith, Dean, 434-582-2417, E-mail: dkeith@liberty.edu. *Application contact:* Jay Bridge, Director of Graduate Admissions, 800-424-9595, Fax: 800-628-7977, E-mail: gradadmissions@liberty.edu. Website: https://www.liberty.edu/education/

Lipscomb University, College of Education, Nashville, TN 37204-3951. Offers applied behavior analysis (MS, Certificate); coaching for learning (M Ed, Certificate, Ed S); educational leadership (M Ed, Ed S); English language learning (M Ed, Ed S); instructional coaching (M Ed, Certificate, Ed S); instructional practice (M Ed); learning organizations and strategic change (Ed D); literacy coaching (Certificate, Ed S); reading specialty (M Ed, Ed S); school counseling (M Ed, Ed S); special education (M Ed); teaching, learning, and leading (M Ed); technology integration (M Ed, Ed S); technology integration specialist (Certificate). *Accreditation:* NCATE. *Program availability:* Part-time, evening/weekend, 100% online. *Degree requirements:* For master's, comprehensive exam, portfolio, research project and presentation; for doctorate, practical capstone project in experiential setting. *Entrance requirements:* For master's, MAT (minimum score 31) or GRE General Test (minimum score 294), 2 reference letters, goals statement, writing sample, interview; for doctorate, MAT or GRE General Test, 3 reference letters, artifact of demonstrated academic excellence, written personal statements, interview. Additional exam requirements/recommendations for international students: Required—TOEFL (minimum score 570 paper-based; 80 iBT). Electronic applications accepted. *Expenses:* Contact institution. *Faculty research:* Facilitative learning styles, leadership, student assessment, interactive multimedia inclusion, learning organizations and strategic change.

Long Island University–Brentwood Campus, Graduate Programs, Brentwood, NY 11717. Offers childhood education (MS), including grades 1-6; childhood education/literacy B-6 (MS); childhood education/special education (grades 1-6) (MS); clinical mental health counseling (MS, Advanced Certificate); criminal justice (MS); early childhood education (MS); educational leadership (MS Ed); family nurse practitioner (MS, Advanced Certificate); health administration (MPA); library and information science (MS); literacy (B-6) (MS Ed); school counselor (MS, Advanced Certificate); social work (MSW); special education (MS Ed); students with disabilities generalist (grades 7-12) (Advanced Certificate). *Program availability:* Part-time. *Entrance requirements:* For master's and Advanced Certificate, GRE. Additional exam requirements/recommendations for international students: Required—TOEFL or IELTS. Electronic applications accepted.

Long Island University–Hudson, Graduate School, Purchase, NY 10577. Offers autism (Advanced Certificate); bilingual education (Advanced Certificate); childhood education (MS Ed); crisis management (Advanced Certificate); early childhood education (MS Ed); educational leadership (MS Ed); health administration (MPA); literacy (MS Ed); marriage and family therapy (MS); mental health counseling (MS, Advanced Certificate), including credentialed alcoholism and substance abuse counselor (MS); middle childhood and adolescence education (MS Ed); pharmaceutics (MS), including cosmetic science, industrial pharmacy; public administration (MPA); school counseling (MS Ed, Advanced Certificate); school psychology (MS Ed); special education (MS Ed); TESOL (MS Ed); TESOL (all grades) (Advanced Certificate). *Program availability:* Part-time, evening/weekend. *Entrance requirements:* Additional exam requirements/recommendations for international students: Required—TOEFL. Electronic applications accepted. *Expenses:* Contact institution.

Long Island University–LIU Post, College of Education, Information and Technology, Brookville, NY 11548-1300. Offers adolescence education (MS); adolescence education 7-12 (MS); archives and records management (AC); art education (MS); childhood education (MS); childhood education/literacy B-6 (MS); childhood education/special education (MS); clinical mental health counseling (MS, AC); early childhood education (MS); early childhood education/childhood education (MS); educational leadership (AC); educational technology (MS); information studies (PhD); interdisciplinary educational studies (Ed D); middle childhood education (MS); music education (MS); public library administration (AC); school counselor (MS); special education (MS Ed); speech-language pathology (MA); students with disabilities, 7-12 generalist (AC); TESOL (MA). *Accreditation:* ASHA; TEAC. *Program availability:* Part-time, 100% online, blended/hybrid learning. Terminal master's awarded for partial completion of doctoral program. *Degree requirements:* For master's, variable foreign language requirement, comprehensive exam (for some programs), thesis optional; for doctorate, comprehensive exam, thesis/dissertation. *Entrance requirements:* For master's and AC, GRE (for some programs). Additional exam requirements/recommendations for international students: Required—TOEFL (minimum score 550 paper-based, 75 iBT), IELTS, or PTE. Electronic applications accepted. *Faculty research:* Sleep; use of technology to develop executive function by students with disabilities; early childhood literacy development through play; social justice through education; using a structured protocol to discuss Bad News.

Long Island University–Riverhead, Graduate Programs, Riverhead, NY 11901. Offers applied behavior analysis (Advanced Certificate); childhood education (MS), including grades 1-6; cybersecurity policy (Advanced Certificate); homeland security management (MS, Advanced Certificate); literacy education (MS); literacy education B-6 (MS); teaching students with disabilities (MS), including grades 1-6; TESOL (Advanced Certificate). *Accreditation:* TEAC. *Program availability:* Part-time. *Entrance requirements:* Additional exam requirements/recommendations for international students: Required—TOEFL or IELTS. Electronic applications accepted. *Expenses:* Contact institution.

Longwood University, College of Graduate and Professional Studies, College of Education and Human Services, Program in Reading, Literacy and Learning, Farmville, VA 23909. Offers M Ed. *Program availability:* Part-time, evening/weekend. *Degree requirements:* For master's, professional portfolio. *Entrance requirements:* For master's, bachelor's degree from regionally-accredited institution, 2 recommendations, minimum 500-word personal essay, official transcripts, minimum GPA of 2.75, valid teaching license. Additional exam requirements/recommendations for international students: Required—TOEFL (minimum score 570 paper-based; 80 iBT), IELTS (minimum score 6.5). Electronic applications accepted. *Expenses:* Contact institution.

Lourdes University, Graduate School, Sylvania, OH 43560-2898. Offers business (MBA); leadership (M Ed); nurse anesthesia (MSN); nurse educator (MSN); nurse leader (MSN); organizational leadership (MOL); reading (M Ed); teaching and curriculum (M Ed); theology (MA). *Accreditation:* AANA/CANAEP. *Program availability:* Evening/weekend. *Entrance requirements:* Additional exam requirements/recommendations for international students: Required—TOEFL.

Loyola Marymount University, School of Education, Program in Literacy Education, Los Angeles, CA 90045. Offers MA. *Unit head:* Dr. Candace Poindexter, Director, Literacy and Educational Studies, 310-338-7314, E-mail: cpoindex@lmu.edu. *Application contact:* Ammar Dalal, Assistant Vice Provost for Graduate Enrollment, 310-338-2721, Fax: 310-338-6086, E-mail: graduateinfo@lmu.edu. Website: http://soe.lmu.edu

Loyola Marymount University, School of Education, Program in Literacy Instruction for Urban Environments, Los Angeles, CA 90045. Offers MA. *Unit head:* Dr. Candace Poindexter, Director, Literacy and Educational Studies, 310-338-7314, E-mail: cpoindex@lmu.edu. *Application contact:* Ammar Dalal, Assistant Vice Provost for Graduate Enrollment, 310-338-2721, Fax: 310-338-6086, E-mail: graduateinfo@lmu.edu.
Website: http://soe.lmu.edu/academics/literacyinstructionforurbanenvironmentsonline

Loyola Marymount University, School of Education, Program in Literacy/Language Arts, Los Angeles, CA 90045. Offers MA. *Unit head:* Dr. Candace Poindexter, Director, Literacy and Educational Studies, 310-338-7314, E-mail: cpoindex@lmu.edu. *Application contact:* Ammar Dalal, Assistant Vice Provost for Graduate Enrollment, 310-338-2721, Fax: 310-338-6086, E-mail: graduateinfo@lmu.edu.
Website: http://soe.lmu.edu

Loyola Marymount University, School of Education, Program in Reading Instruction, Los Angeles, CA 90045. Offers MA. *Unit head:* Dr. Candace Poindexter, Director, Literacy and Educational Studies, 310-338-7314, E-mail: cpoindex@lmu.edu. *Application contact:* Ammar Dalal, Associate Dean of Graduate Studies, 310-338-2721, Fax: 310-338-6086, E-mail: graduateinfo@lmu.edu.
Website: http://soe.lmu.edu/academics/readinginstruction

Loyola University Maryland, Graduate Programs, School of Education, Program in Literacy/Reading, Baltimore, MD 21210-2699. Offers literacy teacher (M Ed); reading specialist (M Ed). *Accreditation:* NCATE. *Program availability:* Part-time. *Entrance requirements:* For master's, essay, 2 letters of recommendation, resume, transcripts. Additional exam requirements/recommendations for international students: Required—TOEFL (minimum score 550 paper-based), IELTS (minimum score 7). Electronic applications accepted. *Expenses:* Contact institution.

Madonna University, Programs in Education, Livonia, MI 48150-1173. Offers Catholic school leadership (MSA); educational leadership (MSA); learning disabilities (MAT); literacy education (MAT); teaching and learning (MAT). *Accreditation:* NCATE. *Program availability:* Part-time, evening/weekend. *Degree requirements:* For master's, thesis or alternative. Electronic applications accepted. *Expenses: Tuition:* Full-time $15,030; part-time $835 per credit hour. Tuition and fees vary according to degree level and program.

Manhattanville College, School of Education, Program in Literacy Education, Purchase, NY 10577-2132. Offers literacy (birth-grade 6) and special education childhood (grades 1-6) (MPS); literacy 5-12; special education generalist 7-12; special ed specialist 7-12 (MPS); literacy specialist (birth-grade 6) (MPS); literacy specialist (grades 5-12) (MPS); science of reading: multisensory instruction – the rose institute for learning and literacy (Advanced Certificate). *Program availability:* Part-time, evening/weekend. *Faculty:* 3 full-time (all women), 15 part-time/adjunct (14 women). *Students:* 2 full-time (both women), 8 part-time (all women). Average age 26. 6 applicants, 50% accepted, 1 enrolled. In 2018, 8 master's, 11 Advanced Certificates awarded. *Degree requirements:* For master's, comprehensive exam (for some programs), thesis (for some programs), student teaching, research seminars, portfolios, internships, writing assessment; for Advanced Certificate, comprehensive exam (for some programs). *Entrance requirements:* For master's, for programs leading to certification, candidates must submit scores from GRE or MAT(Miller Analogies Test), minimum undergraduate GPA of 3.0, all transcripts from all colleges and universities attended, 2 letters of recommendation, interview, essay (2-3 page personal statement that describes reasons for choosing education as profession and personal philosophy of education), proof of immunization (for those born after 1957). Additional exam requirements/recommendations for international students: Required—TOEFL (minimum score 600 paper-based; 110 iBT); Recommended—IELTS (minimum score 8). *Application deadline:* Applications are processed on a rolling basis. Application fee: $75. Electronic applications accepted. *Expenses:* 935 per credit. *Financial support:* Teaching assistantships, career-related internships or fieldwork, Federal Work-Study, institutionally sponsored loans, scholarships/grants, and unspecified assistantships available. Financial award application deadline: 3/15; financial award applicants required to submit FAFSA. *Faculty research:* Power of story for literacy development, English learners. *Total annual research expenditures:* $800. *Unit head:* Dr. Shelley Wepner, Dean, 914-323-3153, Fax: 914-323-5493, E-mail: Shelley.Wepner@mville.edu. *Application contact:* Alissa Wilson, Director, SOE Graduate Enrollment Management, 914-323-3150, Fax: 914-694-1732, E-mail: edschool@mville.edu.
Website: http://www.mville.edu/programs/literacy-education

Manhattanville College, School of Education, Program in Middle Childhood/Adolescence Education (Grades 5-12), Purchase, NY 10577-2132. Offers biology and special education (MPS); chemistry and special education (MPS); education for sustainability (Advanced Certificate); English and special education (MPS); literacy and special education (MPS); literacy specialist (MPS); math and special education (MPS); mathematics (Advanced Certificate); middle childhood/adolescence ed science (biology or chemistry grades 5-12) or (physics grades 7-12) (MAT); middle childhood/adolescence education (grades 5-12) English (MAT, Advanced Certificate); middle childhood/adolescence education (grades 5-12) mathematics (MAT, Advanced Certificate); middle childhood/adolescence education (grades 5-12) science (biology chemistry, physics, earth science) (Advanced Certificate); middle childhood/adolescence education (grades 5-12) social studies (MAT, Advanced Certificate); physics (MAT, Advanced Certificate); social studies (MAT); social studies and special education (MPS); special education generalist (MPS). *Program availability:* Part-time, evening/weekend. *Faculty:* 3 full-time (2 women), 9 part-time/adjunct (4 women). *Students:* 11 full-time (6 women), 17 part-time (12 women); includes 3 minority (1 Black or African American, non-Hispanic/Latino; 2 Hispanic/Latino). Average age 31. 17 applicants, 71% accepted, 7 enrolled. In 2018, 8 master's, 3 other advanced degrees

awarded. *Degree requirements:* For master's, comprehensive exam (for some programs), thesis (for some programs), student teaching, research seminars, portfolios, internships, writing assessment; for Advanced Certificate, comprehensive exam (for some programs). *Entrance requirements:* For master's, for programs leading to certification, candidates must submit scores from GRE or MAT(Miller Analogies Test), minimum undergraduate GPA of 3.0, all transcripts from all colleges and universities attended, 2 letters of recommendation, interview, essay (2-3 page personal statement that describes reasons for choosing education as profession and personal philosophy of education), proof of immunization (for those born after 1957). Additional exam requirements/recommendations for international students: Required—TOEFL (minimum score 600 paper-based; 110 iBT); Recommended—IELTS (minimum score 8). *Application deadline:* Applications are processed on a rolling basis. Application fee: $75. Electronic applications accepted. *Expenses:* 935 per credit. *Financial support:* Teaching assistantships, career-related internships or fieldwork, Federal Work-Study, institutionally sponsored loans, scholarships/grants, and unspecified assistantships available. Financial award application deadline: 3/15; financial award applicants required to submit FAFSA. *Faculty research:* Education for sustainability. *Unit head:* Dr. Shelley Wepner, Dean, 914-323-3153, Fax: 914-323-5493, E-mail: Shelley.Wepner@mville.edu. *Application contact:* Alissa Wilson, Director, Graduate Admissions, 914-323-3150, Fax: 914-694-1732, E-mail: edschool@mville.edu.
Website: http://www.mville.edu/programs#/search/19

Manhattanville College, School of Education, Program in Special Education, Purchase, NY 10577-2132. Offers childhood education (grades 1-6) and special education: childhood (grades 1-6) (MPS); early childhood (birth-grade 2) and special education: early childhood (birth-grade 2) (MPS); English (5-9 and 7-12); special ed generalist (7-12); se English (7-12) (MPS); literacy (birth-grade 6) and special education childhood (grades 1-6) (MPS); literacy 5-12; special education generalist 7-12; special ed specialist 7-12 (MPS); math (5-9 and 7-12); special ed generalist (7-12); se math (7-12) (MPS); science: biology or chemistry (5-9 and 7-12); special ed generalist (7-12); se science (7-12) (MPS); social studies (5-9 and 7-12); special ed generalist (7-12); se soc.st. (7-12) (MPS); special ed early childhood and childhood (birth-grade 6) (MPS); special education childhood (grades 1-6) (MPS); special education: childhood (grades 1-6) (Certificate); special education: early childhood (birth-grade 2) (MPS, Certificate); special education: early childhood (birth-grade 2) and childhood (grades 1-6) (Certificate); special education: grades 7-12 generalist (MPS, Certificate). *Program availability:* Part-time, evening/weekend. *Faculty:* 5 full-time (3 women), 35 part-time/adjunct (23 women). *Students:* 45 full-time (36 women), 179 part-time (152 women); includes 31 minority (6 Black or African American, non-Hispanic/Latino; 4 Asian, non-Hispanic/Latino; 19 Hispanic/Latino; 2 Native Hawaiian or other Pacific Islander, non-Hispanic/Latino), 1 international. Average age 28. 76 applicants, 68% accepted, 40 enrolled. In 2018, 99 master's, 2 Certificates awarded. *Degree requirements:* For master's, comprehensive exam (for some programs), thesis (for some programs), student teaching, research seminars, portfolios, internships, writing assessment; for Certificate, comprehensive exam (for some programs). *Entrance requirements:* For master's, for programs leading to certification, candidates must submit scores from GRE or MAT(Miller Analogies Test), minimum undergraduate GPA of 3.0, all transcripts from all colleges and universities attended, 2 letters of recommendation, interview, essay (2-3 page personal statement that describes reasons for choosing education as profession and personal philosophy of education), proof of immunization (for those born after 1957). Additional exam requirements/recommendations for international students: Required—TOEFL (minimum score 600 paper-based; 110 iBT); Recommended—IELTS (minimum score 8). *Application deadline:* Applications are processed on a rolling basis. Application fee: $75. Electronic applications accepted. *Expenses:* 935 per credit. *Financial support:* Teaching assistantships, career-related internships or fieldwork, Federal Work-Study, institutionally sponsored loans, scholarships/grants, and unspecified assistantships available. Financial award application deadline: 3/15; financial award applicants required to submit FAFSA. *Faculty research:* Students with emotional difficulties, literacy and adolescents, mindfulness, studying the effects of the environment on special populations, the most difficult cases, students who are presented with multiple challenges: learning, behavioral and ACE experiences who see criminal behavior as a way to cope; working on giving them the tools they need to succeed emotionally and cognitively despite the odds stacked against them. *Unit head:* Dr. Shelley Wepner, Dean, 914-323-3153, Fax: 914-323-5493, E-mail: Shelley.Wepner@mville.edu. *Application contact:* Alissa Wilson, Director, SOE Graduate Enrollment Management, 914-323-3150, Fax: 914-694-1732, E-mail: edschool@mville.edu.
Website: http://www.mville.edu/programs/special-education

Marquette University, Graduate School, College of Education, Department of Educational Policy and Leadership, Milwaukee, WI 53201-1881. Offers college student personnel administration (M Ed); curriculum and instruction (MA); education (MA); educational administration (M Ed); educational policy and foundations (MA); elementary education (Certificate); literacy (MA); principal (Certificate); reading specialist (Certificate); reading teacher (Certificate); secondary education (Certificate); superintendent (Certificate). *Program availability:* Part-time, evening/weekend. Terminal master's awarded for partial completion of doctoral program. *Degree requirements:* For master's, comprehensive exam, thesis (for some programs); for doctorate, thesis/dissertation, qualifying exam. *Entrance requirements:* For master's, GRE General Test or MAT, official transcripts from all current and previous colleges/universities except Marquette, three letters of recommendation, statement of purpose; for doctorate, GRE General Test, MAT, sample of written work, official transcripts from all current and previous colleges/universities except Marquette, three letters of recommendation, statement of purpose, resume/curriculum vitae; for Certificate, GRE General Test or MAT, master's degree. Additional exam requirements/recommendations for international students: Required—TOEFL (minimum score 530 paper-based). *Expenses:* Contact institution. *Faculty research:* Leadership; social justice in education; development of lifelong learners; race, class, and schooling in historical perspective; urban teacher education.

Marshall University, Academic Affairs Division, College of Education and Professional Development, Program in Literacy Education, Huntington, WV 25755. Offers MA. *Accreditation:* NCATE. *Program availability:* Part-time, evening/weekend. *Degree requirements:* For master's, thesis optional, comprehensive or oral assessment, final project. *Entrance requirements:* For master's, GRE General Test or MAT.

Mary Baldwin University, Graduate Studies, Programs in Education, Staunton, VA 24401-3610. Offers applied behavior analysis (MS); autism spectrum disorders (M Ed); elementary education (M Ed, MAT); English as a second language (M Ed); environment-based learning (M Ed); gifted education (M Ed); higher education (MS); leadership (M Ed); middle grades education (MAT); reading education (M Ed); special education (M Ed). *Accreditation:* TEAC.

Marygrove College, Graduate Studies, Detroit, MI 48221-2599. Offers autism spectrum disorders (M Ed, Certificate); curriculum instruction and assessment (MAT); educational leadership (MA); educational technology (M Ed); effective teaching in the 21st century-classroom focus (MAT); effective teaching in the 21st century-technology focus (MAT); human resource management (MA, Certificate); mathematics 6-8 (MAT); mathematics K-5 (MAT); reading and literacy K-6 (MAT); reading specialist (M Ed); school administrator (Certificate); social justice (MA); special education (MAT); special education - learning disabilities (M Ed); teaching - pre-elementary education (M Ed); teaching - pre-secondary education (M Ed). *Program availability:* Part-time, evening/weekend, 100% online, blended/hybrid learning. *Entrance requirements:* For master's, all official bachelor's transcripts. Additional exam requirements/recommendations for international students: Required—TOEFL (minimum score 550 paper-based; 80 iBT). Electronic applications accepted.

Maryville University of Saint Louis, School of Education, St. Louis, MO 63141-7299. Offers early childhood education (MA Ed); educational leadership (Ed D); educational leadership w/principal certification (MA Ed); elementary education (MA Ed); gifted (MA Ed); higher education leadership (Ed D); middle grades education (MA Ed); reading/literacy specialist (MA Ed); teacher as leader (Ed D). *Accreditation:* NCATE. *Program availability:* Part-time, 100% online, blended/hybrid learning. *Faculty:* 16 full-time (8 women), 18 part-time/adjunct (11 women). *Students:* 12 full-time (all women), 311 part-time (234 women); includes 99 minority (84 Black or African American, non-Hispanic/Latino; 2 Asian, non-Hispanic/Latino; 9 Hispanic/Latino; 4 Two or more races, non-Hispanic/Latino), 2 international. Average age 38. In 2018, 25 master's, 100 doctorates awarded. *Degree requirements:* For master's, thesis, project. *Entrance requirements:* For master's, minimum cumulative GPA of 3.0, 3 professional recommendations, essays, interview with program faculty; for doctorate, minimum GPA of 3.0, 3 professional recommendations, essay, interview, on-site writing sample. Additional exam requirements/recommendations for international students: Required—TOEFL (minimum score 550 paper-based; 79 iBT). *Application deadline:* Applications are processed on a rolling basis. Electronic applications accepted. *Expenses:* $449 per credit hour for master's programs; $897 per credit hour for doctoral programs. *Financial support:* Career-related internships or fieldwork, Federal Work-Study, tuition waivers (partial), and professional educator discounts available. Financial award application deadline: 4/1; financial award applicants required to submit FAFSA. *Faculty research:* Collaboration with public schools, pre-service program development, mathematics, diversity, literacy. *Unit head:* Dr. Maschael Schappe, Dean, 314-529-9670, Fax: 314-529-9921, E-mail: mschappe@maryville.edu. *Application contact:* Stacey Ruffin, Director of Clinical Experiences & Partnerships, 314-529-9542, Fax: 314-529-9921, E-mail: sruffin@maryville.edu.
Website: http://www.maryville.edu/ed/graduate-programs/

Marywood University, Academic Affairs, Reap College of Education and Human Development, Department of Education, Program in Reading Education, Scranton, PA 18509-1598. Offers MS. *Accreditation:* NCATE. *Program availability:* Part-time. Electronic applications accepted.

Massachusetts College of Liberal Arts, Graduate Programs, North Adams, MA 01247-4100. Offers business (MBA); educational administration (M Ed); educational leadership (CAGS); instruction and curriculum (M Ed); instructional technology (M Ed); physical education and health (M Ed); reading (M Ed); special education (M Ed). *Program availability:* Part-time, evening/weekend. *Degree requirements:* For master's, thesis. *Entrance requirements:* For master's, writing sample.

McDaniel College, Graduate and Professional Studies, Program for Reading Specialists: Literacy Leadership, Westminster, MD 21157-4390. Offers MS. *Accreditation:* NCATE. *Program availability:* Part-time-only, evening/weekend. *Degree requirements:* For master's, comprehensive exam, thesis optional. *Entrance requirements:* For master's, PRAXIS I, 3 references, teaching certificate. Additional exam requirements/recommendations for international students: Required—TOEFL (minimum score 79 iBT), IELTS (minimum score 6). Electronic applications accepted.

McKendree University, Graduate Programs, Programs in Education, Lebanon, IL 62254-1299. Offers curriculum design and instruction (Ed D, Ed S); educational administration and leadership (MA Ed); educational studies (MA Ed); higher education administrative services (MA Ed); music education (MA Ed); reading (MA Ed); special education (MA Ed); teacher leadership (MA Ed); teaching certification (MA Ed). *Accreditation:* NCATE. *Program availability:* Part-time, evening/weekend, online learning. *Entrance requirements:* For master's, official transcripts from all institutions previously attended, minimum GPA of 3.0, resume, references; for doctorate, GRE (within the past 5 years), master's degree in education and Ed S, or the equivalent, from regionally-accredited institution; official transcripts from all institutions previously attended; curriculum vitae/resume; essay/personal statement; two years of teaching/professional experience; for Ed S, GRE (within the past 5 years), master's degree in education from regionally-accredited institution of higher education; official transcripts from all institutions previously attended; curriculum vitae/resume; essay/personal statement; two years of teaching/professional experience. Additional exam requirements/recommendations for international students: Required—TOEFL. Electronic applications accepted.

McNeese State University, Doré School of Graduate Studies, Burton College of Education, Department of Education Professions, Program in Curriculum and Instruction, Lake Charles, LA 70609. Offers academically gifted education (M Ed); elementary education (M Ed); reading (M Ed); secondary education (M Ed); special education (M Ed). *Program availability:* Evening/weekend. *Entrance requirements:* For master's, GRE, teaching certificate.

Medaille College, Program in Education, Buffalo, NY 14214-2695. Offers adolescent education (MS Ed); curriculum and instruction (MS Ed); education preparation (MS Ed); literacy (MS Ed); special education (MS). *Accreditation:* TEAC. *Program availability:* Part-time, evening/weekend. *Degree requirements:* For master's, comprehensive exam (for some programs), thesis or alternative. *Entrance requirements:* For master's, minimum undergraduate GPA of 2.7. Additional exam requirements/recommendations for international students: Required—TOEFL (minimum score 550 paper-based). Electronic applications accepted. *Faculty research:* Curriculum planning, truancy, tracking minority students, curriculum design, mentoring students.

Mercy College, School of Education, Program in Teaching Literacy, Dobbs Ferry, NY 10522-1189. Offers teaching literacy (Advanced Certificate); teaching literacy, birth-6 (MS); teaching literacy, grades 5-12 (MS). *Program availability:* Part-time, evening/weekend. *Students:* 7 full-time (all women), 27 part-time (24 women); includes 9 minority (2 Black or African American, non-Hispanic/Latino; 7 Hispanic/Latino). Average age 35. 33 applicants, 64% accepted, 17 enrolled. In 2018, 2 master's, 10 other advanced degrees awarded. *Degree requirements:* For master's and Advanced Certificate, Capstone project; clinical practice; for initial New York State certification, passing scores in the following are required: Educating All Students, Content Specialty Test, edTPA. *Entrance requirements:* For master's and Advanced Certificate, GRE or PRAXIS, transcript(s); resume. Additional exam requirements/recommendations for international students: Required—TOEFL (minimum score 600 paper-based; 71 iBT), IELTS (minimum score 8). *Application deadline:* Applications are processed on a rolling basis. Application fee: $40. Electronic applications accepted. *Expenses: Tuition:* Full-time $15,696; part-time $872 per credit. *Required fees:* $642; $161 per term. Tuition and fees vary according to course load, degree level and program. *Financial support:* Career-related internships or fieldwork, Federal Work-Study, scholarships/grants, and unspecified assistantships available. Support available to part-time students. Financial

award applicants required to submit FAFSA. *Unit head:* Dr. Eric Martone, Interim Dean, School of Education, 914-674-7618, Fax: 914-674-7352, E-mail: emartone@mercy.edu. *Application contact:* Allison Gurdineer, Executive Director of Admissions, 877-637-2946, Fax: 914-674-7382, E-mail: admissions@mercy.edu.
Website: https://www.mercy.edu/education/literacy-and-multilingual-studies

Meredith College, School of Education, Health and Human Sciences, Raleigh, NC 27607-5298. Offers academically and intellectually gifted (M Ed); elementary education (M Ed, MAT); English as a second language (M Ed, MAT); health and physical education (MAT); nutrition, health and human performance (MS, Postbaccalaureate Certificate), including dietetic internship (Postbaccalaureate Certificate), nutrition (MS); psychology (MA), including industrial/organizational psychology; reading (M Ed); special education (MAT); special education (general curriculum) (M Ed). *Accreditation:* NCATE. *Program availability:* Part-time, evening/weekend. *Students:* 97 full-time (89 women), 76 part-time (73 women); includes 39 minority (17 Black or African American, non-Hispanic/Latino; 1 American Indian or Alaska Native, non-Hispanic/Latino; 9 Asian, non-Hispanic/Latino; 10 Hispanic/Latino; 2 Two or more races, non-Hispanic/Latino). Average age 28. In 2018, 56 master's, 36 other advanced degrees awarded. *Degree requirements:* For master's, thesis optional. *Entrance requirements:* For master's, GRE General Test or MAT, minimum GPA of 2.5, teaching license, recommendations. Additional exam requirements/recommendations for international students: Required—TOEFL. *Application deadline:* For fall admission, 7/1 priority date for domestic students; for spring admission, 11/1 priority date for domestic students. Applications are processed on a rolling basis. Application fee: $50. Electronic applications accepted. *Expenses:* $575 per credit hour for masters degree in education, $725 (for MS. PSY.IO degree), $20,295 (for pre-health post-baccalaureate certificate), $13,600 (for dietetic internship). *Financial support:* Career-related internships or fieldwork, institutionally sponsored loans, and tuition waivers (partial) available. Support available to part-time students. Financial award application deadline: 2/15; financial award applicants required to submit FAFSA. *Unit head:* Dr. Monica McKinney, Graduate Program Manager, 919-760-8056, Fax: 919-760-2303, E-mail: mckinneym@meredith.edu. *Application contact:* Dr. Monica McKinney, Graduate Program Manager, 919-760-8056, Fax: 919-760-2303, E-mail: mckinneym@meredith.edu.
Website: https://www.meredith.edu/school-of-education-health-and-human-sciences

MGH Institute of Health Professions, School of Health and Rehabilitation Sciences, Department of Communication Sciences and Disorders, Boston, MA 02129. Offers reading (Certificate); speech-language pathology (MS). *Accreditation:* ASHA (one or more programs are accredited). *Program availability:* Part-time. *Degree requirements:* For master's, thesis or alternative, research proposal. *Entrance requirements:* For master's, GRE General Test, bachelor's degree from regionally-accredited college or university. Additional exam requirements/recommendations for international students: Required—TOEFL (minimum score 550 paper-based; 80 iBT). Electronic applications accepted. *Faculty research:* Children's language disorders, reading, speech disorders, voice disorders, augmentative communication, autism.

Michigan State University, The Graduate School, College of Education, Program in Literacy Instruction, East Lansing, MI 48824. Offers MA. *Accreditation:* TEAC. *Program availability:* Part-time. *Degree requirements:* For master's, comprehensive exam (for some programs), final exam or portfolio. *Entrance requirements:* Additional exam requirements/recommendations for international students: Required—TOEFL, Michigan State University ELT (minimum score 85), Michigan English Language Assessment Battery (minimum score 83). Electronic applications accepted.

MidAmerica Nazarene University, Professional and Graduate Studies in Education, Olathe, KS 66062-1899. Offers ESOL (M Ed); reading specialist (M Ed); technology enhanced teaching (M Ed). *Accreditation:* NCATE. *Program availability:* Part-time, evening/weekend, online only, 100% online. *Entrance requirements:* For master's, bachelor's degree from an accredited college or university, minimum undergraduate GPA of 3.0, valid teaching license. Additional exam requirements/recommendations for international students: Required—TOEFL (minimum score 81 iBT), IELTS (minimum score 6). Electronic applications accepted. *Expenses:* Contact institution.

Middle Tennessee State University, College of Graduate Studies, College of Education, Department of Elementary and Special Education, Major in Reading, Murfreesboro, TN 37132. Offers M Ed. *Accreditation:* NCATE. *Program availability:* Part-time, evening/weekend, online learning. *Degree requirements:* For master's, comprehensive exam. *Entrance requirements:* For master's, GRE, MAT or PRAXIS. Additional exam requirements/recommendations for international students: Required—TOEFL (minimum score 525 paper-based; 71 iBT) or IELTS (minimum score 6). Electronic applications accepted.

Middle Tennessee State University, College of Graduate Studies, College of Education, PhD in Literacy Studies Program, Murfreesboro, TN 37132. Offers PhD. *Program availability:* Part-time, evening/weekend, online learning. *Degree requirements:* For doctorate, comprehensive exam, thesis/dissertation. *Entrance requirements:* For doctorate, GRE. Additional exam requirements/recommendations for international students: Required—TOEFL (minimum score 525 paper-based; 71 iBT) or IELTS (minimum score 6).

Middle Tennessee State University, College of Graduate Studies, University College, Murfreesboro, TN 37132. Offers advanced studies in teaching and learning (M Ed); human resources leadership (MPS); nursing administration (MSN); nursing education (MSN); strategic leadership (MPS); training and development (MPS). *Program availability:* Part-time, evening/weekend, online learning. *Entrance requirements:* Additional exam requirements/recommendations for international students: Required—TOEFL (minimum score 525 paper-based; 71 iBT) or IELTS (minimum score 6).

Midwestern State University, Billie Doris McAda Graduate School, West College of Education, Program in Reading, Wichita Falls, TX 76308. Offers M Ed. *Program availability:* Part-time, evening/weekend. *Degree requirements:* For master's, comprehensive exam. *Entrance requirements:* For master's, GRE General Test, MAT or GMAT. Additional exam requirements/recommendations for international students: Required—TOEFL (minimum score 550 paper-based). Electronic applications accepted. *Faculty research:* Collective learning, school culture, early literacy development, family literacy, brain-based learning.

Millersville University of Pennsylvania, College of Graduate Studies and Adult Learning, College of Education and Human Services, Department of Early, Middle, and Exceptional Education, Millersville, PA 17551-0302. Offers early childhood education (M Ed); gifted education (M Ed); language and literacy (M Ed); language and literacy education (M Ed); special education (M Ed); special education: 7-12 (M Ed); special education: PreK-8 (M Ed). *Accreditation:* NCATE. *Program availability:* Part-time, evening/weekend, 100% online, blended/hybrid learning. *Faculty:* 10 full-time (6 women), 13 part-time/adjunct (9 women). *Students:* 9 full-time (6 women), 113 part-time (102 women); includes 11 minority (2 Black or African American, non-Hispanic/Latino; 3 Asian, non-Hispanic/Latino; 5 Hispanic/Latino; 1 Two or more races, non-Hispanic/Latino). Average age 32. 40 applicants, 98% accepted, 28 enrolled. In 2018, 25 master's awarded. *Entrance requirements:* For master's, GRE or MAT, required only if cumulative GPA is lower than 3.0, Teaching Certificate; Interview. Additional exam requirements/recommendations for international students: Required—TOEFL, IELTS (minimum score 6), PTE (minimum score 60). *Application deadline:* Applications are processed on a rolling basis. Application fee: $40. Electronic applications accepted. *Expenses: Tuition, area resident:* Full-time $9288; part-time $516 per credit. Tuition, state resident: full-time $9288; part-time $516 per credit. Tuition, nonresident: full-time $13,932; part-time $774 per credit. *International tuition:* $13,932 full-time. *Required fees:* $2623.50; $145.75 per credit. Tuition and fees vary according to course load, degree level and program. *Financial support:* In 2018–19, 5 students received support. Unspecified assistantships available. Financial award application deadline: 3/15; financial award applicants required to submit FAFSA. *Faculty research:* Co-teaching, needs of new teachers, use of popular culture in education. *Unit head:* Dr. Rich Mehrenberg, Department Chair, 717-871-7343, E-mail: richard.mehrenberg@millersville.edu. *Application contact:* Dr. James A. Delle, Acting Dean of College of Graduate Studies and Adult Learning/Associate Provost, Academic Administration, 717-871-7462, E-mail: James.Delle@millersville.edu.
Website: http://www.millersville.edu/eled/

Misericordia University, College of Health Sciences and Education, Program in Education, Dallas, PA 18612-1098. Offers instructional technology (MS); reading specialist (MS); special education (MS). *Program availability:* Part-time, evening/weekend. *Entrance requirements:* For master's, minimum undergraduate GPA of 3.0. Additional exam requirements/recommendations for international students: Required—TOEFL. Electronic applications accepted.

Mississippi State University, College of Education, Department of Curriculum, Instruction and Special Education, Mississippi State, MS 39762. Offers early childhood education (PhD); elementary education (MS, PhD, Ed S), including early childhood education (MS), general elementary education (MS), middle level education (MS); general curriculum and instruction (PhD); reading education (PhD); secondary education (MAT, MS, PhD, Ed S); special education (MAT, MS, PhD, Ed S). *Accreditation:* NCATE. *Program availability:* Part-time, evening/weekend. *Faculty:* 20 full-time (14 women), 1 (woman) part-time/adjunct. *Students:* 24 full-time (16 women), 151 part-time (109 women); includes 44 minority (38 Black or African American, non-Hispanic/Latino; 3 American Indian or Alaska Native, non-Hispanic/Latino; 1 Hispanic/Latino; 2 Two or more races, non-Hispanic/Latino), 3 international. Average age 32. 65 applicants, 65% accepted, 38 enrolled. In 2018, 57 master's, 3 doctorates, 1 other advanced degree awarded. *Degree requirements:* For master's, comprehensive exam; for doctorate, thesis/dissertation; for Ed S, comprehensive exam, thesis or alternative. *Entrance requirements:* For master's, GRE, minimum GPA of 2.75 in junior and senior year, eligibility for initial teacher certification; for doctorate, GRE, minimum GPA of 3.4 on previous graduate work; for Ed S, GRE, minimum GPA of 3.2 on master's degree. Additional exam requirements/recommendations for international students: Required—TOEFL (minimum score 550 paper-based; 79 iBT); Recommended—IELTS (minimum score 6.5). *Application deadline:* For fall admission, 3/1 priority date for domestic students, 5/1 for international students; for spring admission, 9/1 priority date for domestic students, 9/1 for international students. Applications are processed on a rolling basis. Application fee: $60 ($80 for international students). Electronic applications accepted. *Expenses:* Tuition, state resident: full-time $8450; part-time $360.59 per credit hour. Tuition, nonresident: full-time $23,140; part-time $969.09 per credit hour. *Required fees:* $110. One-time fee: $55 full-time. Part-time tuition and fees vary according to course load, degree level, campus/location and reciprocity agreements. *Financial support:* In 2018–19, 5 research assistantships with partial tuition reimbursements (averaging $11,453 per year), 1 teaching assistantship (averaging $11,700 per year) were awarded; Federal Work-Study, institutionally sponsored loans, scholarships/grants, and unspecified assistantships also available. Financial award application deadline: 4/1; financial award applicants required to submit FAFSA. *Faculty research:* Early childhood education, reading, rural schools, multicultural education, use of technology in instruction. *Unit head:* Dr. Linda Cornelious, Professor and Head, 662-325-3747, Fax: 662-325-7857, E-mail: lcornelious@colled.msstate.edu. *Application contact:* Robbie Salters, Admissions and Enrollment Assistant, 662-325-7400, E-mail: rsalters@grad.msstate.edu.
Website: http://www.cise.msstate.edu/

Mississippi University for Women, Graduate School, College of Education and Human Sciences, Columbus, MS 39701-9998. Offers differentiated instruction (M Ed); educational leadership (M Ed); gifted studies (M Ed); reading/literacy (M Ed); teaching (MAT). *Accreditation:* ASHA; NCATE. *Program availability:* Part-time. *Degree requirements:* For master's, comprehensive exam, thesis optional. *Entrance requirements:* For master's, GRE General Test or NTE (M Ed in gifted education or MS in speech/language pathology), MAT (M Ed in instructional management), minimum QPA of 3.0.

Missouri State University, Graduate College, College of Education, Department of Reading, Foundations, and Technology, Program in Literacy, Springfield, MO 65897. Offers MS Ed, Graduate Certificate. *Program availability:* Part-time, 100% online, blended/hybrid learning. *Faculty:* 6 full-time (all women). *Students:* 2 full-time (both women), 91 part-time (87 women); includes 6 minority (1 Black or African American, non-Hispanic/Latino; 3 Hispanic/Latino; 2 Two or more races, non-Hispanic/Latino). Average age 28. 22 applicants, 77% accepted. In 2018, 24 master's awarded. *Degree requirements:* For master's, comprehensive exam, thesis or alternative. *Entrance requirements:* For master's, GRE or minimum GPA of 3.0, teaching certificate. Additional exam requirements/recommendations for international students: Required—TOEFL (minimum score 550 paper-based; 79 iBT), IELTS (minimum score 6). *Application deadline:* For fall admission, 7/20 priority date for domestic students, 5/1 for international students; for spring admission, 12/20 priority date for domestic students, 9/1 for international students; for summer admission, 5/20 priority date for domestic students. Applications are processed on a rolling basis. Application fee: $55 ($60 for international students). Electronic applications accepted. Tuition and fees vary according to class time, course level, course load, degree level, campus/location, program and student level. *Financial support:* Federal Work-Study, institutionally sponsored loans, scholarships/grants, and unspecified assistantships available. Financial award application deadline: 1/31; financial award applicants required to submit FAFSA. *Unit head:* Dr. Emmett Sawyer, Interim Department Head, 417-836-6769, E-mail: rft@missouristate.edu. *Application contact:* Lakan Drinker, Director, Graduate Enrollment Management, 417-836-5330, Fax: 417-836-6200, E-mail: lakandrinker@missouristate.edu.
Website: http://education.missouristate.edu/rft/

Monmouth University, Graduate Studies, School of Education, West Long Branch, NJ 07764-1898. Offers applied behavior analysis (Certificate); autism (Certificate); director of school counseling services (Post-Master's Certificate); early childhood (M Ed); educational leadership (Ed D); elementary education (MAT), including elementary level, secondary level; English as a second language (M Ed); learning disabilities teacher-consultant (Post-Master's Certificate); literacy (MS Ed); school counseling (MS Ed); special education (MS Ed), including autism, learning disabilities teacher-consultant, teacher of students with disabilities, teaching in inclusive settings; speech-language pathology (MS Ed); student affairs and college counseling (MS Ed); supervisor (Post-Master's Certificate); teaching English to speakers of other languages (Certificate). *Accreditation:* NCATE. *Program availability:* Part-time, evening/weekend, 100% online,

blended/hybrid learning. *Faculty:* 29 full-time (23 women), 32 part-time/adjunct (24 women). *Students:* 214 full-time (187 women), 148 part-time (127 women); includes 60 minority (13 Black or African American, non-Hispanic/Latino; 2 Asian, non-Hispanic/Latino; 40 Hispanic/Latino; 5 Two or more races, non-Hispanic/Latino). Average age 27. In 2018, 108 master's, 9 other advanced degrees awarded. *Entrance requirements:* For master's, GRE taken within last 5 years (for MS Ed in speech-language pathology); SAT (minimum combined score of 1660 in 3 sections), ACT (23), GRE (minimum score of 4.0 on analytical writing section and minimum combined score of 310 on quantitative and verbal sections), or passing scores on 3 parts of Core Academic Skills Educators, minimum GPA of 3.0 in major; 2 letters of recommendation (for some programs); resume, personal statement or essay (depending on program). Additional exam requirements/recommendations for international students: Required—TOEFL (minimum score 550 paper-based; 79 iBT), IELTS (minimum score 6), Michigan English Language Assessment Battery (minimum score 77) or Certificate of Advanced English (minimum score 160). *Application deadline:* For fall admission, 7/15 priority date for domestic students, 7/1 for international students; for spring admission, 12/1 priority date for domestic students, 11/1 for international students; for summer admission, 5/1 for domestic students. Applications are processed on a rolling basis. Application fee: $50. Electronic applications accepted. *Expenses: Tuition:* Part-time $1233 per credit. *Required fees:* $178 per term. *Financial support:* In 2018–19, 290 students received support. Institutionally sponsored loans, scholarships/grants, and unspecified assistantships available. Support available to part-time students. Financial award applicants required to submit FAFSA. *Faculty research:* Multicultural literacy, science and mathematics teaching strategies, teacher as reflective practitioner, children with disabilities. *Unit head:* Dr. John E. Henning, Dean, 732-263-5513, Fax: 732-263-5277, E-mail: kodonnel@monmouth.edu. *Application contact:* Kirsten Sneeringer, Graduate Admission Counselor, 732-571-3452, Fax: 732-263-5123, E-mail: gradadm@monmouth.edu.
Website: http://www.monmouth.edu/academics/schools/education/default.asp

Montana State University Billings, College of Education, Department of Educational Theory and Practice, Option in Reading, Billings, MT 59101. Offers M Ed. *Accreditation:* NCATE. *Program availability:* Part-time. *Degree requirements:* For master's, thesis or professional paper and/or field experience. *Entrance requirements:* For master's, GRE General Test or MAT, minimum GPA of 3.0. Additional exam requirements/recommendations for international students: Required—TOEFL (minimum score 79 iBT), IELTS (minimum score 6.5). Electronic applications accepted.

Montclair State University, The Graduate School, College of Education and Human Services, Program in Reading, Montclair, NJ 07043-1624. Offers MA. *Program availability:* Part-time, evening/weekend. *Entrance requirements:* For master's, GRE General Test, interview, essay, 2 letters of recommendation. Additional exam requirements/recommendations for international students: Required—TOEFL (minimum score 83 iBT), IELTS (minimum score 6.5). Electronic applications accepted.

Morehead State University, Graduate School, College of Education, Department of Foundational and Graduate Studies in Education, Morehead, KY 40351. Offers adult and higher education (MA, Ed S); certified professional counselor (Ed S); counseling P-12 (MA); curriculum and instruction (Ed S); educational technology (MA Ed); instructional leadership (Ed S); school administration (MA); school counseling (Ed S); teacher leader business and marketing content (MA Ed); teacher leader business and marketing technology (MA Ed); teacher leader educational technology (MA Ed); teacher leader English (MA Ed); teacher leader gifted education (MA Ed); teacher leader IECE certification (MA Ed); teacher leader interdisciplinary education P-5 (MA Ed); teacher leader middle grades (MA Ed); teacher leader non IECE certification (MA Ed); teacher leader reading/writing - non-certification (MA Ed); teacher leader reading/writing certification (MA Ed); teacher leader school communication - certification (MA Ed); teacher leader school communication - non-certification (MA Ed); teacher leader social studies (MA Ed); teacher leader special education (MA Ed). *Accreditation:* NCATE. *Program availability:* Part-time, evening/weekend. *Degree requirements:* For master's, thesis optional, oral and/or written comprehensive exams; for Ed S, thesis, oral exam. *Entrance requirements:* For master's, GRE General Test, minimum overall undergraduate GPA of 2.5; for Ed S, GRE General Test, interview, master's degree, minimum GPA of 3.5, work experience. Additional exam requirements/recommendations for international students: Required—TOEFL (minimum score 500 paper-based). Electronic applications accepted. *Faculty research:* Character education, school accountability, computer applications for school administrators.

Mount Mercy University, Program in Education, Cedar Rapids, IA 52402-4797. Offers reading (MA Ed); special education (MA Ed); teacher leadership (MA Ed). *Entrance requirements:* For master's, minimum cumulative GPA of 3.0, 2 letters of recommendation, resume, valid teaching license. Additional exam requirements/recommendations for international students: Required—TOEFL (minimum score 570 paper-based; 88 iBT). Electronic applications accepted.

Mount St. Joseph University, Graduate Education Program, Cincinnati, OH 45233-1670. Offers adolescent to young adult education (MA); dyslexia (Certificate); inclusive early childhood education (MA); middle childhood education (MA); multicultural special education (MA); reading science (MA). *Accreditation:* TEAC. *Program availability:* Part-time, evening/weekend, 100% online, blended/hybrid learning. *Degree requirements:* For master's, comprehensive exam, thesis, research project, student teaching, clinical and field-based experiences. *Entrance requirements:* For master's, GRE (if GPA is below 3.0), letter of intent, 2 referrals, background check, interview, resume, minimum undergraduate GPA of 3.0. Additional exam requirements/recommendations for international students: Required—TOEFL (minimum score 560 paper-based; 83 iBT). Electronic applications accepted. *Expenses:* Contact institution. *Faculty research:* Foreign and second language learning problems/reading disabilities, multicultural/bilingual special education, science education, pedagogical content knowledge, early childhood, response to intervention.

Mount Saint Mary College, Division of Education, Newburgh, NY 12550-3494. Offers adolescence and special education (MS Ed); childhood education (MS Ed); literacy education (MS Ed); middle school (7-9) (MS Ed). *Accreditation:* NCATE. *Program availability:* Part-time, evening/weekend. *Faculty:* 7 full-time (6 women), 7 part-time/adjunct (all women). *Students:* 19 full-time (14 women), 78 part-time (64 women); includes 7 minority (5 Hispanic/Latino; 1 Native Hawaiian or other Pacific Islander, non-Hispanic/Latino; 1 Two or more races, non-Hispanic/Latino). Average age 28. 31 applicants, 61% accepted, 17 enrolled. In 2018, 28 master's awarded. *Entrance requirements:* Additional exam requirements/recommendations for international students: Required—TOEFL (minimum score 80 iBT). *Application deadline:* Applications are processed on a rolling basis. Application fee: $45. Electronic applications accepted. Application fee is waived when completed online. *Expenses: Tuition:* Full-time $14,454; part-time $803 per credit. *Required fees:* $172; $86 per semester. *Financial support:* In 2018–19, 17 students received support. Institutionally sponsored loans, scholarships/grants, and unspecified assistantships available. Financial award application deadline: 4/15; financial award applicants required to submit FAFSA. *Faculty research:* Learning and teaching styles, computers in special education, language development. *Unit head:* Dr. Vicki Caruana, Graduate Coordinator, 845-569-3530, Fax: 845-569-3551, E-mail: Victoria.caruana@msmc.edu. *Application contact:* Eileen Bardney, Director of Admissions, 845-569-3254, Fax: 845-569-3438, E-mail: Eileen.Bardney@msmc.edu.
Website: http://www.msmc.edu/Academics/Graduate_Programs/Master_of_Science_in_Education

Mount Saint Vincent University, Graduate Programs, Faculty of Education, Program in Literacy Education, Halifax, NS B3M 2J6, Canada. Offers M Ed, MA Ed, MA-R. *Program availability:* Part-time, evening/weekend, online learning. *Degree requirements:* For master's, thesis (for some programs). *Entrance requirements:* For master's, minimum B average, 1 year of teaching experience, bachelor's degree in related field. Electronic applications accepted. *Faculty research:* Writing processes and instruction, assessment and evaluation of literacy education, critical literacy, early literacy development, gender and literacy.

National Louis University, National College of Education, Chicago, IL 60603. Offers administration and supervision (M Ed, Ed D, CAS, Ed S); curriculum and instruction (M Ed, MS Ed, CAS); early childhood administration (M Ed, CAS); early childhood education (M Ed, MAT, MS Ed, CAS); education (Ed D); educational psychology/human learning and development (M Ed, MS Ed, CAS, Ed S); elementary education (MAT); interdisciplinary curriculum and instruction (M Ed); mathematics education (M Ed, MS Ed, CAS); middle grades education (MAT); reading and language (M Ed, MS Ed, CAS); school psychology (M Ed, Ed S); science education (M Ed, MS Ed, CAS); secondary education (MAT); special education (M Ed, MAT, CAS); technology in education (M Ed, CAS). *Accreditation:* NCATE. *Program availability:* Part-time, evening/weekend. *Degree requirements:* For doctorate, comprehensive exam, thesis/dissertation. *Entrance requirements:* For master's, MAT or GRE, minimum GPA of 3.0; for doctorate, GRE General Test, minimum GPA of 3.25, interview, resume, writing sample, 4 recommendations. Additional exam requirements/recommendations for international students: Required—TOEFL (minimum score 550 paper-based; 79 iBT).

Nazareth College of Rochester, Graduate Studies, Department of Education, Program in Literacy Education, Rochester, NY 14618. Offers MS Ed. *Accreditation:* TEAC. *Program availability:* Part-time, evening/weekend. *Entrance requirements:* For master's, minimum GPA of 3.0. Additional exam requirements/recommendations for international students: Required—TOEFL or IELTS.

Newman University, Master of Science in Education Program, Wichita, KS 67213-2097. Offers building leadership (MS Ed); curriculum and instruction (MS Ed), including English as a second language, reading specialist; organizational leadership (MS Ed). *Accreditation:* NCATE. *Program availability:* Part-time, evening/weekend, online learning. *Degree requirements:* For master's, thesis optional. *Entrance requirements:* For master's, 3 years' full-time teaching experience, minimum GPA of 3.0, writing sample, 2 letters of recommendation, evidence of teaching certification. Additional exam requirements/recommendations for international students: Required—TOEFL (minimum score 600 paper-based; 100 iBT). Electronic applications accepted. *Expenses:* Contact institution. *Faculty research:* Online course design and deliver, staff engagement, classroom action.

New Mexico State University, College of Education, Department of Curriculum and Instruction, Las Cruces, NM 88003-8001. Offers bilingual education (MA); curriculum and instruction (Ed D, PhD); early childhood education (MA); educational diagnostics (Ed S); language, literacy and culture (MA); learning design and technologies (MA); teaching (MAT); teaching English to speakers of other languages (MA). *Accreditation:* NCATE. *Program availability:* Part-time, evening/weekend, 100% online. *Faculty:* 22 full-time (17 women), 7 part-time/adjunct (5 women). *Students:* 82 full-time (49 women), 186 part-time (134 women); includes 153 minority (13 Black or African American, non-Hispanic/Latino; 2 American Indian or Alaska Native, non-Hispanic/Latino; 3 Asian, non-Hispanic/Latino; 129 Hispanic/Latino; 6 Two or more races, non-Hispanic/Latino), 33 international. Average age 37. 110 applicants, 79% accepted, 60 enrolled. In 2018, 75 master's, 13 doctorates, 16 other advanced degrees awarded. *Degree requirements:* For master's, comprehensive exam, thesis; for doctorate, comprehensive exam, thesis/dissertation. *Entrance requirements:* For master's, minimum cumulative GPA of 3.0; for doctorate, portfolio, minimum cumulative GPA of 3.0. Additional exam requirements/recommendations for international students: Required—TOEFL (minimum score 550 paper-based; 79 iBT), IELTS (minimum score 6.5). *Application deadline:* For fall admission, 12/15 priority date for domestic and international students. Applications are processed on a rolling basis. Application fee: $40 ($50 for international students). Electronic applications accepted. *Expenses: Tuition, area resident:* Full-time $4216.70; part-time $252.70 per credit hour. Tuition, state resident: full-time $4216.70; part-time $252.70 per credit hour. Tuition, nonresident: full-time $12,769; part-time $881.10 per credit hour. *International tuition:* $12,769.30 full-time. *Required fees:* $878.40; $48.80 per credit hour. Full-time tuition and fees vary according to course load and reciprocity agreements. *Financial support:* In 2018–19, 111 students received support, including 2 fellowships (averaging $4,548 per year), 11 research assistantships (averaging $11,673 per year), 10 teaching assistantships (averaging $10,582 per year); career-related internships or fieldwork, Federal Work-Study, scholarships/grants, traineeships, health care benefits, and unspecified assistantships also available. Support available to part-time students. Financial award application deadline: 3/1. *Faculty research:* STEM education, bilingual and English as a second language education, critical pedagogy/multicultural education, learning design and technology, early childhood education. *Total annual research expenditures:* $10,685. *Unit head:* Dr. David Rutledge, Department Head, 575-646-5411, Fax: 575-646-5436, E-mail: rutledge@nmsu.edu. *Application contact:* Dr. David Rutledge, Associate Department Head for Graduate Programs, 575-646-5411, Fax: 575-646-5436, E-mail: rutledge@nmsu.edu.
Website: http://ci.education.nmsu.edu

New York University, Steinhardt School of Culture, Education, and Human Development, Department of Teaching and Learning, Program in Literacy Education, New York, NY 10012-1019. Offers MA. *Accreditation:* TEAC. *Program availability:* Part-time. *Degree requirements:* For master's, thesis (for some programs), fieldwork. *Entrance requirements:* For master's, teacher certification. Additional exam requirements/recommendations for international students: Required—TOEFL (minimum score 100 iBT). Electronic applications accepted. *Faculty research:* Early literacy intervention and development, psycho and sociolinguistics, multicultural education, literacy assessment and instruction.

Niagara University, Graduate Division of Education, Concentration in Literacy Instruction, Niagara University, NY 14109. Offers MS Ed. *Program availability:* Part-time. *Students:* 11 full-time (all women), 19 part-time (17 women); includes 3 minority (2 Black or African American, non-Hispanic/Latino; 1 Hispanic/Latino). Average age 27. In 2018, 15 master's awarded. *Entrance requirements:* For master's, GRE. Additional exam requirements/recommendations for international students: Required—TOEFL (minimum score 550 paper-based; 79 iBT), IELTS (minimum score 6). *Application deadline:* For fall admission, 8/1 for domestic students. Applications are processed on a rolling basis. Electronic applications accepted. *Expenses:* Contact institution. *Financial support:* Research assistantships with tuition reimbursements, teaching assistantships with tuition reimbursements, career-related internships or fieldwork, Federal Work-Study, scholarships/grants, and unspecified assistantships available. Support available to part-time students. Financial award application deadline: 4/15; financial award applicants required to submit FAFSA. *Unit head:* Dr. Robin Erwin, Chair, 716-286-8551, E-mail: rerwin@niagara.edu. *Application contact:* Evan Pierce, Associate Director for Graduate Recruitment, 716-286-8327, Fax: 716-286-8710, E-mail: epierce@niagara.edu.
Website: http://www.niagara.edu/literacy-instruction

North Carolina Agricultural and Technical State University, The Graduate College, College of Education, Department of Administration and Instructional Services, Greensboro, NC 27411. Offers instructional technology (MS); reading education (MA Ed); school administration (MSA). *Accreditation:* NCATE. *Program availability:* Part-time, evening/weekend. *Degree requirements:* For master's, comprehensive exam, qualifying exam. *Entrance requirements:* For master's, GRE General Test, minimum GPA of 3.0.

Northeastern Illinois University, College of Graduate Studies and Research, Daniel L. Goodwin College of Education, Program in Literacy Education, Chicago, IL 60625. Offers MA. *Program availability:* Part-time, evening/weekend. *Degree requirements:* For master's, comprehensive exam, thesis optional. *Entrance requirements:* For master's, previous course work in psychology or tests and measurements, minimum GPA of 2.75. Additional exam requirements/recommendations for international students: Required—TOEFL (minimum score 550 paper-based; 79 iBT). Electronic applications accepted. *Faculty research:* Early literacy, reading disabilities, cognitive processes, multicultural and linguistic diversity, use of literature in the classroom.

Northeastern State University, College of Education, Department of Curriculum and Instruction, Program in Reading, Tahlequah, OK 74464-2399. Offers M Ed. *Program availability:* Part-time, evening/weekend. *Faculty:* 15 full-time (11 women), 3 part-time/adjunct (1 woman). *Students:* 7 full-time (6 women), 47 part-time (46 women); includes 24 minority (3 Black or African American, non-Hispanic/Latino; 4 American Indian or Alaska Native, non-Hispanic/Latino; 5 Hispanic/Latino; 12 Two or more races, non-Hispanic/Latino), 1 international. Average age 36. In 2018, 25 master's awarded. *Degree requirements:* For master's, thesis. *Entrance requirements:* For master's, MAT or GRE, minimum GPA of 2.5. Additional exam requirements/recommendations for international students: Required—TOEFL. *Application deadline:* For fall admission, 6/1 priority date for domestic students. Applications are processed on a rolling basis. Application fee: $25. Electronic applications accepted. *Expenses: Tuition, area resident:* Full-time $4500; part-time $250 per credit hour. Tuition, state resident: full-time $4500; part-time $250 per credit hour. Tuition, nonresident: full-time $9999; part-time $555.50 per credit hour. *International tuition:* $9999 full-time. *Required fees:* $601.20; $33.40 per credit hour. *Financial support:* Teaching assistantships and Federal Work-Study available. Financial award application deadline: 3/1. *Unit head:* Dr. Meagan Moreland, Reading Chair, 918-449-6441, E-mail: morela02@nsuok.edu. *Application contact:* Josh McCollum, Graduate Coordinator, 918-444-2093, E-mail: mccolluj@nsuok.edu.
Website: https://academics.nsuok.edu/education/EducationHome/COEDepartments/CurriculumInstruction.aspx

Northern Michigan University, Office of Graduate Education and Research, College of Health Sciences and Professional Studies, School of Education, Leadership and Public Service, Marquette, MI 49855-5301. Offers administration and supervision (MAE); instruction (MAE); learning disabilities (MAE); postsecondary biology education (MS); reading education (MAE), including reading, reading specialist. *Accreditation:* TEAC. *Program availability:* Part-time, online learning. *Degree requirements:* For master's, thesis (for some programs). *Entrance requirements:* For master's, minimum GPA of 3.0. Additional exam requirements/recommendations for international students: Required—TOEFL (minimum score 550 paper-based; 79 iBT), IELTS (minimum score 6.5). Electronic applications accepted.

Northern Vermont University–Lyndon, Graduate Programs in Education, Department of Education, Lyndonville, VT 05851. Offers curriculum and instruction (M Ed); reading specialist (M Ed); special education (M Ed); teaching and counseling (M Ed). *Program availability:* Part-time, evening/weekend. *Degree requirements:* For master's, exam or major field project. *Entrance requirements:* Additional exam requirements/recommendations for international students: Recommended—TOEFL (minimum score 500 paper-based).

Northwestern Oklahoma State University, School of Professional Studies, Reading Specialist Program, Alva, OK 73717-2799. Offers M Ed. *Accreditation:* NCATE. *Program availability:* Part-time. *Degree requirements:* For master's, thesis optional, portfolio. *Entrance requirements:* For master's, GRE General Test or MAT, minimum GPA of 2.75.

Northwestern State University of Louisiana, Graduate Studies and Research, College of Education and Human Development, Programs in Educational Leadership and Instruction, Natchitoches, LA 71497. Offers counseling (Ed S); educational leadership (M Ed, Ed S); educational technology (Ed S); elementary teaching (Ed S); reading (Ed S); secondary teaching (Ed S); special education (Ed S). *Accreditation:* NASAD. *Degree requirements:* For master's, comprehensive exam, thesis (for some programs). *Entrance requirements:* For master's and Ed S, GRE General Test. Additional exam requirements/recommendations for international students: Required—TOEFL. Electronic applications accepted.

Northwest Missouri State University, Graduate School, School of Education, Maryville, MO 64468-6001. Offers early childhood education (MS Ed); education leadership (MS Ed), including elementary, K-12, secondary; educational leadership (Ed S), including elementary school principalship, secondary school principalship, superintendency; educational leadership and policy analysis (Ed D); elementary education (MS Ed); elementary mathematics (MS Ed); higher education leadership (MS); middle school education (MS Ed); reading (MS Ed); special education (MS Ed); teacher leadership (MS Ed); teaching English language learners (MS Ed). *Accreditation:* NCATE. *Program availability:* Part-time. *Faculty:* 26 full-time (16 women). *Students:* 109 full-time (87 women), 385 part-time (270 women); includes 30 minority (10 Black or African American, non-Hispanic/Latino; 2 American Indian or Alaska Native, non-Hispanic/Latino; 3 Asian, non-Hispanic/Latino; 12 Hispanic/Latino; 1 Native Hawaiian or other Pacific Islander, non-Hispanic/Latino; 2 Two or more races, non-Hispanic/Latino), 1 international. Average age 33. 210 applicants, 72% accepted, 142 enrolled. In 2018, 71 master's, 11 other advanced degrees awarded. *Degree requirements:* For master's, comprehensive exam; for Ed S, comprehensive exam, thesis. *Entrance requirements:* For master's, GRE General Test, writing sample; for Ed S, minimum graduate GPA of 3.25. Additional exam requirements/recommendations for international students: Required—TOEFL (minimum score 550 paper-based). *Application deadline:* For fall admission, 7/1 for domestic and international students; for spring admission, 11/15 for domestic and international students. Applications are processed on a rolling basis. Application fee: $0 ($75 for international students). Electronic applications accepted. *Expenses:* $389.11 in-state and $653.92 out-of-state per credit hour. *Financial support:* Research assistantships with full tuition reimbursements, teaching assistantships with full tuition reimbursements, and unspecified assistantships available. Financial award application deadline: 4/1; financial award applicants required to submit FAFSA. *Unit head:* Dr. Tim Wall, Director, 660-562-1179, E-mail: timwall@nwmissouri.edu. *Application contact:* Dr. Tim Wall, Director, 660-562-1179, E-mail: timwall@nwmissouri.edu.
Website: https://www.nwmissouri.edu/education/index.htm

Notre Dame College, Graduate Programs, South Euclid, OH 44121-4293. Offers mild/moderate needs (M Ed); reading (M Ed); security policy studies (MA, Graduate Certificate); technology (M Ed). *Program availability:* Part-time, evening/weekend. *Degree requirements:* For master's, thesis. *Entrance requirements:* For master's, GRE General Test, MAT, minimum undergraduate GPA of 2.75, valid teaching certificate, bachelor's degree in an education-related field from accredited college or university, official transcripts of most recent college work. *Faculty research:* Cognitive psychology, teaching critical thinking in the classroom.

Oakland University, Graduate Study and Lifelong Learning, School of Education and Human Services, Department of Reading and Language Arts, Rochester, MI 48309-4401. Offers advanced microcomputer applications (Graduate Certificate); digital literacies and learning (Graduate Certificate); microcomputer applications (Graduate Certificate); reading and language arts (MAT); reading education (PhD); reading, language arts and literature (PMC). *Accreditation:* TEAC. *Degree requirements:* For doctorate, thesis/dissertation. *Entrance requirements:* For master's, minimum GPA of 3.0; for doctorate, MAT, minimum GPA of 3.0. Electronic applications accepted.

Ohio University, Graduate College, Gladys W. and David H. Patton College of Education and Human Services, Department of Teacher Education, Athens, OH 45701-2979. Offers adolescent to young adult education (M Ed); curriculum and instruction (M Ed, PhD); early childhood/special education (M Ed); intervention specialist/mild-moderate needs (M Ed); intervention specialist/moderate-intensive needs (M Ed); middle childhood education (M Ed); reading education (M Ed). *Program availability:* Part-time, evening/weekend. *Degree requirements:* For master's, thesis or alternative; for doctorate, comprehensive exam, thesis/dissertation. *Entrance requirements:* For master's, GRE General Test or MAT (if GPA is below 2.9); for doctorate, GRE General Test, minimum GPA of 3.4, work experience. Additional exam requirements/recommendations for international students: Required—TOEFL (minimum score 550 paper-based; 80 iBT) or IELTS (minimum score 6.5). Electronic applications accepted. *Faculty research:* Cognition literacy, character education, teacher's education reform, disabilities.

Old Dominion University, Darden College of Education, Program in Literacy Leadership, Norfolk, VA 23529. Offers PhD. *Program availability:* Part-time, evening/weekend. *Degree requirements:* For doctorate, comprehensive exam, thesis/dissertation. *Entrance requirements:* For doctorate, GRE, minimum GPA of 3.0, MS in reading or related degree, letters of recommendation. Additional exam requirements/recommendations for international students: Required—TOEFL (minimum score 600 paper-based). Electronic applications accepted. *Faculty research:* Literacy for students with special needs, children's reading first instruction, reading in the content area.

Old Dominion University, Darden College of Education, Program in Reading Education, Norfolk, VA 23529. Offers reading specialist (MS Ed). *Accreditation:* NCATE. *Program availability:* Part-time, evening/weekend, 100% online, blended/hybrid learning. *Degree requirements:* For master's, thesis optional, Virginia Reading Specialist Exam. *Entrance requirements:* For master's, minimum GPA of 3.0 in major, 2.8 overall; 5-year renewable teaching certificate; official transcripts; 2 letters of reference; essay. Additional exam requirements/recommendations for international students: Required—TOEFL (minimum score 550 paper-based; 80 iBT). Electronic applications accepted. *Faculty research:* Metacognition and reading, strategies for improving comprehension in reading science, reading in content areas, vocabulary instruction for adolescents, literacy with special needs children, Reading First instruction, reading in the content area, vocabulary, diversity and literacy.

Olivet Nazarene University, Graduate School, Division of Education, Program in Reading Specialist, Bourbonnais, IL 60914. Offers MAE.

Pace University, School of Education, New York, NY 10038. Offers adolescent education (MST), including biology, chemistry, earth science, English, foreign languages, mathematics, physics, social studies; childhood education (MST); early childhood development, learning and intervention (MST); educational technology studies (MS); inclusive adolescent education (MST), including biology, chemistry, earth science, English, foreign languages, mathematics, physics, social studies; integrated instruction for educational technology (Certificate); integrated instruction for literacy and technology (Certificate); literacy (MS Ed); special education (MS Ed). *Accreditation:* NCATE. *Program availability:* Part-time, evening/weekend, 100% online, blended/hybrid learning. *Faculty:* 19 full-time (13 women), 86 part-time/adjunct (49 women). *Students:* 98 full-time (82 women), 542 part-time (391 women); includes 256 minority (116 Black or African American, non-Hispanic/Latino; 2 American Indian or Alaska Native, non-Hispanic/Latino; 45 Asian, non-Hispanic/Latino; 83 Hispanic/Latino; 10 Two or more races, non-Hispanic/Latino), 4 international. Average age 30. 223 applicants, 89% accepted, 130 enrolled. In 2018, 269 master's, 12 other advanced degrees awarded. *Degree requirements:* For master's and Certificate, certification exams. *Entrance requirements:* For master's, GRE (for initial certification programs only), teaching certificate (for MS Ed in literacy and special education programs only). Additional exam requirements/recommendations for international students: Required—TOEFL (minimum score 88 iBT), IELTS or PTE. *Application deadline:* For fall admission, 8/1 priority date for domestic students, 6/1 for international students; for spring admission, 12/1 priority date for domestic students, 10/1 for international students. Applications are processed on a rolling basis. Application fee: $70. Electronic applications accepted. *Expenses:* Contact institution. *Financial support:* In 2018–19, 17 students received support, including 17 research assistantships with partial tuition reimbursements available (averaging $6,020 per year); career-related internships or fieldwork, Federal Work-Study, scholarships/grants, and unspecified assistantships also available. Financial award application deadline: 9/1; financial award applicants required to submit FAFSA. *Faculty research:* STEM education, TESOL, teacher education, special education, language and literary development. *Total annual research expenditures:* $1.4 million. *Unit head:* Dr. Harriet Feldman, Dean, School of Education, 914-773-3829, E-mail: hfeldman@pace.edu. *Application contact:* Susan Ford-Goldschein, Director of Graduate Admissions, 212-346-1531, Fax: 212-346-1585, E-mail: graduateadmission@pace.edu.
Website: http://www.pace.edu/school-of-education

Park University, School of Graduate and Professional Studies, Kansas City, MO 54105. Offers adult education (M Ed); business and government leadership (Graduate Certificate); business, government, and global society (MPA); communication and leadership (MA); creative and life writing (Graduate Certificate); disaster and emergency management (MPA, Graduate Certificate); educational leadership (M Ed); finance (MBA, Graduate Certificate); general business (MBA); global business (Graduate Certificate); healthcare administration (MHA); healthcare services management and leadership (Graduate Certificate); international business (MBA); language and literacy (M Ed), including English for speakers of other languages, special reading teacher/literacy coach; leadership of international healthcare organizations (Graduate Certificate); management information systems (MBA, Graduate Certificate); music performance (ADP, Graduate Certificate), including cello (MM, ADP), piano (MM, ADP), viola (MM, ADP), violin (MM, ADP); nonprofit and community services management (MPA); nonprofit leadership (Graduate Certificate); performance (MM), including cello (MM, ADP), piano (MM, ADP), viola (MM, ADP), violin (MM, ADP); public management (MPA); social work (MSW); teacher leadership (M Ed), including curriculum and assessment, instructional leader. *Program availability:* Part-time, evening/weekend, online learning. *Degree requirements:* For master's, comprehensive exam (for some programs), thesis (for some programs), internship (for some programs); exam (for some programs). *Entrance requirements:* For master's, GRE or GMAT (for some programs), teacher certification (for some M Ed programs), letters of recommendation, essay,

resume (for some programs). Additional exam requirements/recommendations for international students: Required—TOEFL (minimum score 550 paper-based; 79 iBT), IELTS (minimum score 6). Electronic applications accepted.

Penn State Harrisburg, Graduate School, School of Behavioral Sciences and Education, Middletown, PA 17057. Offers adult education in the health and medical professions (Certificate); applied behavior analysis (MA); applied clinical psychology (MA); applied psychological research (MA); community psychology and social change (MA); English as a second language (ESL) program specialist and leadership (Certificate); health education (M Ed); lifelong learning and adult education (M Ed, D Ed); literacy education (M Ed); literacy leadership (Certificate); psychology: applications in clinical psychology (Certificate); psychology: health psychology (Certificate); teaching and curriculum (M Ed); training and development (M Ed, Certificate). *Program availability:* Part-time, evening/weekend.

Providence College, Program in Literacy, Providence, RI 02918. Offers M Ed. *Program availability:* Part-time, evening/weekend. *Degree requirements:* For master's, portfolio. *Entrance requirements:* Additional exam requirements/recommendations for international students: Required—TOEFL (minimum score 577 paper-based; 90 iBT).

Purdue University, Graduate School, College of Education, Department of Curriculum and Instruction, West Lafayette, IN 47907. Offers agricultural and extension education (MS, MS Ed, PhD, Ed S); art education (PhD); career and technical education (MS Ed, PhD, Ed S); curriculum studies (MS Ed, PhD, Ed S); educational technology (MS Ed, PhD, Ed S); elementary education (MS Ed); family and consumer sciences education (MS Ed, PhD, Ed S); foreign language education (MS Ed, PhD, Ed S); industrial technology (PhD, Ed S); language arts (MS Ed, PhD, Ed S); literacy (MS Ed, PhD, Ed S); mathematics education (MS, MS Ed, PhD, Ed S); science education (MS, MS Ed, PhD, Ed S); social studies education (MS Ed, PhD, Ed S). *Accreditation:* NCATE. *Program availability:* Part-time, evening/weekend, online learning. *Faculty:* 34 full-time (24 women), 3 part-time/adjunct (1 woman). *Students:* 75 full-time (52 women), 357 part-time (271 women); includes 83 minority (29 Black or African American, non-Hispanic/Latino; 1 American Indian or Alaska Native, non-Hispanic/Latino; 14 Asian, non-Hispanic/Latino; 29 Hispanic/Latino; 1 Native Hawaiian or other Pacific Islander, non-Hispanic/Latino; 9 Two or more races, non-Hispanic/Latino), 43 international. Average age 36. 169 applicants, 83% accepted, 102 enrolled. In 2018, 141 master's, 15 doctorates awarded. *Degree requirements:* For master's, thesis optional; for doctorate, thesis/dissertation, oral and written exams; for Ed S, oral presentation, project. *Entrance requirements:* For master's, GRE General Test (if undergraduate GPA is below 3.0), minimum undergraduate GPA of 3.0 or equivalent; for doctorate, GRE General Test (minimum combined verbal and quantitative score of 1000, 300 for new scoring), minimum undergraduate GPA of 3.0 or equivalent; master's degree with minimum GPA of 3.0 or equivalent; for Ed S, GRE General Test (minimum combined verbal and quantitative score of 1000, 300 for new scoring), minimum undergraduate GPA of 3.0 or equivalent; master's degree. Additional exam requirements/recommendations for international students: Required—TOEFL (minimum score 550 paper-based; 77 iBT). *Application deadline:* For fall admission, 12/15 for domestic students, 3/1 for international students; for spring admission, 9/15 for domestic students, 8/1 for international students. Application fee: $60 ($75 for international students). Electronic applications accepted. *Financial support:* Fellowships with full tuition reimbursements, research assistantships with full tuition reimbursements, teaching assistantships with full tuition reimbursements, career-related internships or fieldwork, and tuition waivers (full) available. Support available to part-time students. Financial award application deadline: 3/1; financial award applicants required to submit FAFSA. *Faculty research:* Literacy acquisition and development, teacher beliefs and knowledge, recruitment and retention of underrepresented students, economic education, literacy discourse. *Unit head:* Janet M. Alsup, Head, 765-494-9667, E-mail: alsupj@purdue.edu. *Application contact:* Heather Brinkman, Graduate Contact, 765-494-2345, E-mail: hbrinkma@purdue.edu. Website: http://www.edci.purdue.edu/

Purdue University Global, School of Teacher Education, Davenport, IA 52807. Offers education (M Ed); secondary education (M Ed); teaching and learning (MA); teaching literacy and language: grades 6-12 (MA); teaching literacy and language: grades K-6 (MA); teaching mathematics: grades 6-8 (MA); teaching mathematics: grades 9-12 (MA); teaching mathematics: grades K-5 (MA); teaching science: grades 6-12 (MA); teaching science: grades K-6 (MA); teaching students with special needs (MA); teaching with technology (MA). *Program availability:* Part-time, evening/weekend, online learning. *Entrance requirements:* Additional exam requirements/recommendations for international students: Required—TOEFL (minimum score 550 paper-based; 80 iBT).

Queens College of the City University of New York, Division of Education, Department of Elementary and Early Childhood Education, Queens, NY 11367-1597. Offers bilingual education (MAT, MS Ed, AC); childhood education (MAT, MS Ed); early childhood education birth-2 (MAT, MS Ed, AC); literacy education birth-grade 6 (MS Ed, AC). *Program availability:* Part-time, evening/weekend. *Faculty:* 19 full-time (13 women), 35 part-time/adjunct (32 women). *Students:* 117 full-time (102 women), 376 part-time (344 women); includes 264 minority (27 Black or African American, non-Hispanic/Latino; 75 Asian, non-Hispanic/Latino; 154 Hispanic/Latino; 1 Native Hawaiian or other Pacific Islander, non-Hispanic/Latino; 7 Two or more races, non-Hispanic/Latino), 15 international. Average age 30. 351 applicants, 75% accepted, 204 enrolled. In 2018, 156 master's, 48 other advanced degrees awarded. *Degree requirements:* For master's, Research project; for AC, Field-based research project. *Entrance requirements:* For master's, GRE General Test, minimum undergraduate cumulative GPA of 3.00; for AC, GRE General Test (required for all MAT and other graduate programs leading to NYS initial teacher certification), NYS initial teacher certification in the appropriate certification area is required for admission into MSEd programs. Additional exam requirements/recommendations for international students: Required—TOEFL (minimum score 575 paper-based; 90 iBT). *Application deadline:* For fall admission, 4/1 for domestic students. Applications are processed on a rolling basis. Application fee: $125. Electronic applications accepted. *Financial support:* Career-related internships or fieldwork and Federal Work-Study available. Financial award application deadline: 4/1; financial award applicants required to submit FAFSA. *Faculty research:* Biliteracy, computational thinking, social justice education, technology in early childhood education, children from immigrant families. *Unit head:* Daisuke Akiba, Chair, 718-997-5300, E-mail: daisuke.akiba@qc.cuny.edu. *Application contact:* Elizabeth D'Amico-Ramirez, Assistant Director of Graduate Admissions, 718-997-5203, E-mail: elizabeth.damicoramirez@qc.cuny.edu.

Queens College of the City University of New York, Division of Education, Department of Secondary Education and Youth Services, Queens, NY 11367-1597. Offers adolescent biology (MAT); art (MS Ed); biology (MS Ed, AC); chemistry (MS Ed, AC); earth sciences (MS Ed, AC); English (MS Ed, AC); French (MS Ed); Italian (MS Ed, AC); literacy education (MS Ed); mathematics (MS Ed, AC); music (MS Ed, AC); physics (MS Ed, AC); social studies (MS Ed, AC); Spanish (MS Ed, AC). *Program availability:* Part-time, evening/weekend. *Faculty:* 22 full-time (14 women), 35 part-time/adjunct (24 women). *Students:* 33 full-time (19 women), 358 part-time (228 women); includes 182 minority (15 Black or African American, non-Hispanic/Latino; 62 Asian, non-Hispanic/Latino; 91 Hispanic/Latino; 4 Native Hawaiian or other Pacific Islander, non-Hispanic/Latino; 10 Two or more races, non-Hispanic/Latino), 13 international. Average age 29.

216 applicants, 74% accepted, 109 enrolled. In 2018, 108 master's, 35 other advanced degrees awarded. *Degree requirements:* For master's, research project. *Entrance requirements:* For master's, GRE, minimum GPA of 3.0. Additional exam requirements/recommendations for international students: Required—TOEFL, IELTS. *Application deadline:* For fall admission, 4/1 for domestic students; for spring admission, 11/1 for domestic students. Applications are processed on a rolling basis. Application fee: $125. Electronic applications accepted. *Financial support:* Career-related internships or fieldwork available. Financial award application deadline: 4/1; financial award applicants required to submit FAFSA. *Faculty research:* Self regulated learning, teacher learning, assessment and teaching, language diversity, teaching and learning history. *Unit head:* Dr. Eleanor Armour-Thomas, Chairperson, 718-997-5150, E-mail: eleanor.armour-thomas@qc.cuny.edu. *Application contact:* Elizabeth D'Amico-Ramirez, Assistant Director of Graduate Admissions, 718-997-5203, E-mail: elizabeth.damicoramirez@qc.cuny.edu.

Queens University of Charlotte, Wayland H. Cato, Jr. School of Education, Charlotte, NC 28274-0002. Offers educational leadership (MA); K-6 (MAT); literacy K-12 (M Ed). *Accreditation:* NCATE. *Program availability:* Part-time, evening/weekend, online learning. *Degree requirements:* For master's, comprehensive exam. *Entrance requirements:* For master's, GRE General Test. *Expenses:* Contact institution.

Quincy University, Master of Science in Education Programs, Quincy, IL 62301-2699. Offers curriculum and instruction (MS Ed), including bilingual/English as a second language; education studies (MS Ed); leadership (MS Ed); reading education (MS Ed); teacher leader (MS Ed). *Program availability:* Part-time, evening/weekend, online learning. *Degree requirements:* For master's, comprehensive exam (for some programs), thesis optional. *Entrance requirements:* For master's, MAT or GRE, personal resume. Additional exam requirements/recommendations for international students: Required—TOEFL (minimum score 550 paper-based; 79 iBT). Electronic applications accepted. Application fee is waived when completed online.

Radford University, College of Graduate Studies and Research, Program in Literacy Education, Radford, VA 24142. Offers MS. *Accreditation:* NCATE. *Program availability:* Part-time, evening/weekend. *Faculty:* 3 full-time (2 women), 1 (woman) part-time/adjunct. *Students:* 1 (woman) full-time, 13 part-time (all women); includes 2 minority (1 Black or African American, non-Hispanic/Latino; 1 Two or more races, non-Hispanic/Latino). Average age 37. In 2018, 8 master's awarded. *Degree requirements:* For master's, comprehensive exam. *Entrance requirements:* For master's, minimum GPA of 2.75; copy of teaching license; 2 letters of reference; personal essay; resume; official transcripts. Additional exam requirements/recommendations for international students: Required—TOEFL (minimum score 550 paper-based; 79 iBT), IELTS (minimum score 6.5). *Application deadline:* For fall admission, 2/15 priority date for domestic students, 12/1 for international students; for spring admission, 7/1 for international students. Applications are processed on a rolling basis. Application fee: $50. Electronic applications accepted. *Expenses:* Tuition, area resident: Full-time $8915; part-time $371 per credit hour. Tuition, state resident: full-time $8915; part-time $371 per credit hour. Tuition, nonresident: full-time $17,441. *Required fees:* $3288; $138 per credit hour. *Financial support:* In 2018–19, 4 students received support. Career-related internships or fieldwork, scholarships/grants, and unspecified assistantships available. Support available to part-time students. Financial award application deadline: 3/1; financial award applicants required to submit FAFSA. *Unit head:* Dr. Jennifer Jones-Powell, Graduate Program Coordinator, 540-831-5311, E-mail: jjones292@radford.edu. *Application contact:* Dr. Jennifer Jones-Powell, Graduate Program Coordinator, 540-831-5311, E-mail: jjones292@radford.edu. Website: http://www.radford.edu/content/cehd/home/teacher-ed/programs/master-literacy.html

Regent University, Graduate School, School of Education, Virginia Beach, VA 23464-9800. Offers education (M Ed, Ed D, PhD), including adult education (Ed D, PhD, Ed S), advanced educational leadership (Ed D, PhD, Ed S), character education (Ed D, PhD, Ed S), Christian education leadership (Ed D, PhD, Ed S), Christian school administration (M Ed), curriculum and instruction (Ed D, PhD, Ed S), curriculum and instruction - adult education (M Ed), curriculum and instruction - Christian school (M Ed), curriculum and instruction - gifted and talented (M Ed), curriculum and instruction - STEM education (M Ed), curriculum and instruction - teacher leader (M Ed), discipleship for ministry (M Ed), educational leadership (M Ed), educational psychology (Ed D, PhD, Ed S), educational technology and online learning (Ed D, PhD, Ed S), elementary education (M Ed), exceptional education executive leadership (Ed D, PhD, Ed S), higher education (Ed D, PhD, Ed S), higher education leadership and management (Ed D, PhD, Ed S), instructional design and technology (M Ed), K-12 school leadership (Ed D, PhD, Ed S), K-12 special education (M Ed), leadership in mathematics education (M Ed), reading specialist (M Ed), special education (Ed D, PhD, Ed S), student affairs (M Ed), TESOL - adult education (M Ed), TESOL - K-12 (M Ed); educational specialist (Ed S), including adult education (Ed D, PhD, Ed S), advanced educational leadership (Ed D, PhD, Ed S), character education (Ed D, PhD, Ed S), Christian education leadership (Ed D, PhD, Ed S), curriculum and instruction (Ed D, PhD, Ed S), educational psychology (Ed D, PhD, Ed S), educational technology and online learning (Ed D, PhD, Ed S), exceptional education executive leadership (Ed D, PhD, Ed S), higher education (Ed D, PhD, Ed S), higher education leadership and management (Ed D, PhD, Ed S), K-12 school leadership (Ed D, PhD, Ed S), special education (Ed D, PhD, Ed S). *Accreditation:* TEAC. *Program availability:* Part-time, evening/weekend, 100% online, blended/hybrid learning. *Degree requirements:* For master's, thesis or alternative; for doctorate, comprehensive exam, thesis/dissertation. *Entrance requirements:* For master's, Virginia Communication and Literacy Assessment (VCLA), PRAXIS, college transcripts, writing sample, interview; for doctorate, GRE, writing sample, resume, transcripts, interview. Additional exam requirements/recommendations for international students: Required—TOEFL (minimum score 577 paper-based). Electronic applications accepted. *Expenses:* Contact institution. *Faculty research:* Christian school administration, curriculum and instruction, educational technology and online learning, higher education, special education.

Regis University, College of Contemporary Liberal Studies, Denver, CO 80221-1099. Offers creative writing (MFA); criminology (M Sc); curriculum, instruction and assessment (M Ed); education - teacher leadership (M Ed); educational leadership (M Ed); elementary education (M Ed); literacy (Certificate); reading (M Ed); secondary education (M Ed); special education (M Ed); teacher academic leadership (Certificate); teacher leadership (MA); teacher/educational leadership (M Ed); teaching the linguistically diverse (M Ed). *Program availability:* Part-time, evening/weekend, 100% online, blended/hybrid learning. *Degree requirements:* For master's, thesis (for some programs). *Entrance requirements:* For master's, official transcript reflecting baccalaureate degree awarded from regionally-accredited college or university, work experience, resume, letters of recommendation. Additional exam requirements/recommendations for international students: Required—TOEFL (minimum score 550 paper-based; 82 iBT). Electronic applications accepted. *Expenses:* Contact institution.

Rhode Island College, School of Graduate Studies, Feinstein School of Education and Human Development, Department of Elementary Education, Providence, RI 02908-1991. Offers early childhood education (M Ed); elementary education (M Ed, MAT); reading (M Ed). *Accreditation:* NCATE. *Program availability:* Part-time, evening/

weekend. *Faculty:* 7 full-time (all women), 4 part-time/adjunct (2 women). *Students:* 18 full-time (17 women), 20 part-time (17 women); includes 1 minority (Black or African American, non-Hispanic/Latino). Average age 31. In 2018, 21 master's awarded. *Degree requirements:* For master's, comprehensive exam (for some programs), comprehensive assessment. *Entrance requirements:* For master's, GRE General Test or MAT, PRAXIS II (elementary content knowledge), undergraduate transcripts; minimum undergraduate GPA of 3.0; 3 letters of recommendation. Additional exam requirements/recommendations for international students: Required—TOEFL (minimum score 550 paper-based; 80 iBT). *Application deadline:* For fall admission, 3/1 for domestic students; for spring admission, 11/1 for domestic students. Applications are processed on a rolling basis. Application fee: $50. Electronic applications accepted. *Expenses: Tuition, area resident:* Part-time $407 per credit. Tuition, nonresident: part-time $792 per credit. *Required fees:* $29 per credit. $100 per semester. *Financial support:* Teaching assistantships with full tuition reimbursements, Federal Work-Study, scholarships/grants, and health care benefits available. Support available to part-time students. Financial award application deadline: 5/15; financial award applicants required to submit FAFSA. *Unit head:* Dr. Carolyn Obel-Omia, Chair, 401-456-8016. *Application contact:* Dr. Carolyn Obel-Omia, Chair, 401-456-8016. Website: http://www.ric.edu/elementaryeducation/Pages/Graduate-Programs.aspx

Rivier University, School of Graduate Studies, Department of Education, Nashua, NH 03060. Offers curriculum and instruction (M Ed); early childhood education (M Ed); educational administration (M Ed); educational studies (M Ed); elementary education (M Ed); elementary education and general special education (M Ed); emotional and behavioral disorders (M Ed); general social education (M Ed); leadership and learning (Ed D, CAGS); learning disabilities (M Ed); learning disabilities and reading (M Ed); mental health counseling (MA); reading (M Ed); school counseling (M Ed). *Program availability:* Part-time, evening/weekend. *Degree requirements:* For master's, comprehensive exam (for some programs), internships. *Entrance requirements:* For master's, GRE General Test or MAT.

Roberts Wesleyan College, Graduate Teacher Education Programs, Rochester, NY 14624-1997. Offers adolescence and special education (M Ed); childhood and special education (M Ed); literacy education (M Ed); special education (M Ed). *Program availability:* Part-time, evening/weekend. *Degree requirements:* For master's, thesis. Electronic applications accepted.

Rockford University, Graduate Studies, Department of Education, Program in Reading, Rockford, IL 61108-2393. Offers MAT. *Program availability:* Part-time, evening/weekend. *Degree requirements:* For master's, thesis optional. *Entrance requirements:* For master's, GRE General Test, 3 letters of recommendation. Additional exam requirements/recommendations for international students: Required—TOEFL (minimum score 550 paper-based; 79 iBT). Electronic applications accepted.

Roger Williams University, Feinstein School of Humanities, Arts and Education, Bristol, RI 02809. Offers literacy education (MA); middle school certification (Certificate). *Program availability:* Part-time-only, evening/weekend. *Faculty:* 5 full-time (4 women), 5 part-time/adjunct (2 women). *Students:* 7 part-time (all women). Average age 36. 1 applicant, 100% accepted, 1 enrolled. In 2018, 6 master's awarded. *Entrance requirements:* For master's, resume, 2 letters of recommendation, college transcript, letter of intent, verification of active teaching license. Additional exam requirements/recommendations for international students: Required—TOEFL (minimum score 85 iBT), IELTS (minimum score 6.5). *Application deadline:* Applications are processed on a rolling basis. Application fee: $50. Electronic applications accepted. *Expenses:* $593 per credit hour for academic year 2018-2019 (for Master of Arts in Literacy, Middle School Endorsement Certificate), $267 graduation fee for all programs for academic year 2018-2019. *Financial support:* Application deadline: 3/15; applicants required to submit FAFSA. *Unit head:* Dr. Cynthia Scheinberg, Dean, 401-254-3828, E-mail: cscheinberg@rwu.edu. *Application contact:* Marcus Hanscom, Director of Graduate Admissions, 401-254-3345, Fax: 401-254-3557, E-mail: gradadmit@rwu.edu. Website: http://www.rwu.edu/academics/schools-and-colleges/fshae

Roosevelt University, Graduate Division, College of Education, Program in Reading, Chicago, IL 60605. Offers reading teacher education (MA). *Program availability:* Part-time, evening/weekend. Electronic applications accepted.

Rowan University, Graduate School, College of Education, Department of Language, Literacy, and Sociocultural Education, Program in Reading Education, Glassboro, NJ 08028-1701. Offers MA, CGS. Electronic applications accepted.

Rutgers University–New Brunswick, Graduate School of Education, Department of Learning and Teaching, Program in Literacy Education, Piscataway, NJ 08854-8097. Offers Ed M, Ed D. *Program availability:* Part-time. Terminal master's awarded for partial completion of doctoral program. *Degree requirements:* For master's, comprehensive exam; for doctorate, thesis/dissertation, qualifying exam. *Entrance requirements:* For master's, GRE General Test, minimum undergraduate GPA of 3.0; for doctorate, GRE General Test, 2 years of teaching experience, certification, minimum graduate GPA of 3.5. Additional exam requirements/recommendations for international students: Required—TOEFL. Electronic applications accepted. *Faculty research:* Early childhood literacy development, discourse analysis-adult literacy.

Rutgers University–New Brunswick, Graduate School of Education, Department of Learning and Teaching, Program in Reading Education, Piscataway, NJ 08854-8097. Offers Ed M. *Program availability:* Part-time. *Degree requirements:* For master's, comprehensive exam or paper. *Entrance requirements:* For master's, GRE General Test. Electronic applications accepted.

Rutgers University–New Brunswick, Graduate School of Education, Doctoral Program in Education, New Brunswick, NJ 08901. Offers educational policy (PhD); educational psychology (PhD); literacy education (PhD); mathematics education (PhD). *Program availability:* Part-time. *Degree requirements:* For doctorate, thesis/dissertation, qualifying exam. *Entrance requirements:* For doctorate, GRE General Test, GRE Subject Test (mathematics education). Additional exam requirements/recommendations for international students: Required—TOEFL (minimum score 575 paper-based; 83 iBT). Electronic applications accepted. *Faculty research:* Literacy education, math education, educational psychology, educational policy, learning sciences.

Sacred Heart University, Graduate Programs, Isabelle Farrington College of Education, Department of Leadership/Literacy, Fairfield, CT 06825. Offers advanced studies in administration (Professional Certificate); advanced studies in literacy (Professional Certificate). *Program availability:* Part-time, evening/weekend. *Degree requirements:* For Professional Certificate, thesis or alternative. *Entrance requirements:* For degree, CT teacher certification. Electronic applications accepted. *Expenses:* Contact institution.

Sage Graduate School, Esteves School of Education, Program in Childhood Education/Literacy, Troy, NY 12180-4115. Offers MS. *Program availability:* Part-time, evening/weekend. *Faculty:* 2 full-time (both women), 9 part-time/adjunct (5 women). *Students:* 13 full-time (12 women), 2 part-time (both women); includes 2 minority (both Black or African American, non-Hispanic/Latino). Average age 30. 20 applicants, 50% accepted, 6 enrolled. In 2018, 6 master's awarded. *Degree requirements:* For master's, thesis optional. *Entrance requirements:* For master's, GRE (minimum scores: Verbal

Reasoning 145, Quantitative Reasoning 145, Analytical Writing 3.5) or MAT (minimum score: 350), bachelor's degree in a liberal arts or science area, minimum cumulative GPA of 3.0. Additional exam requirements/recommendations for international students: Required—TOEFL (minimum score 550 paper-based). *Application deadline:* Applications are processed on a rolling basis. Application fee: $30. Electronic applications accepted. *Financial support:* Fellowships, research assistantships, scholarships/grants, and unspecified assistantships available. Financial award application deadline: 3/1; financial award applicants required to submit FAFSA. *Unit head:* Dr. John Pelizza, Dean, Esteves School of Education, 518-244-2051, Fax: 518-244-2334, E-mail: pelizj@sage.edu. *Application contact:* Dr. Kathleen Gormley, Chair and Professor of Education, 518-244-2403, Fax: 518-244-2334, E-mail: gormlk@sage.edu.

Sage Graduate School, Esteves School of Education, Program in Literacy, Troy, NY 12180-4115. Offers MS Ed. *Accreditation:* NCATE. *Program availability:* Part-time, evening/weekend. *Faculty:* 2 full-time (both women), 9 part-time/adjunct (5 women). *Students:* 3 full-time (all women), 3 part-time (all women); includes 1 minority (Black or African American, non-Hispanic/Latino). Average age 29. 6 applicants, 83% accepted, 2 enrolled. In 2018, 4 master's awarded. *Entrance requirements:* For master's, minimum GPA of 2.75, resume, 2 letters of recommendation. Additional exam requirements/recommendations for international students: Required—TOEFL (minimum score 550 paper-based). *Application deadline:* Applications are processed on a rolling basis. Application fee: $30. *Financial support:* Fellowships, research assistantships, scholarships/grants, and unspecified assistantships available. Financial award application deadline: 3/1; financial award applicants required to submit FAFSA. *Faculty research:* Literacy development in at-risk children. *Unit head:* Dr. John Pelizza, Dean, Esteves School of Education, 518-244-2051, Fax: 518-244-2334, E-mail: pelizj@sage.edu. *Application contact:* Kathleen Gormley, Chair & Professor of Education, 518-244-2403, Fax: 518-244-2334, E-mail: gormlk@sage.edu.

Sage Graduate School, Esteves School of Education, Program in Literacy/Childhood Special Education, Troy, NY 12180-4115. Offers MS Ed. *Accreditation:* NCATE. *Program availability:* Part-time, evening/weekend. *Faculty:* 2 full-time (both women), 9 part-time/adjunct (5 women). *Students:* 2 part-time (both women). Average age 29. 2 applicants, 50% accepted, 1 enrolled. In 2018, 3 master's awarded. *Entrance requirements:* For master's, MAT (minimum score of 350), GRE (minimum scores: 145 verbal; 145 quantitative; 3.5 analytical writing), application, minimum cumulative GPA of 3.0, current teacher certification, interview with appropriate advisor. Additional exam requirements/recommendations for international students: Required—TOEFL (minimum score 550 paper-based). *Application deadline:* Applications are processed on a rolling basis. Application fee: $30. Electronic applications accepted. *Financial support:* Fellowships, research assistantships, scholarships/grants, and unspecified assistantships available. Financial award application deadline: 3/1; financial award applicants required to submit FAFSA. *Faculty research:* Commonalities in the roles of reading specialists and resource/consultant teachers. *Unit head:* Dr. John Pelizza, Dean, Esteves School of Education, 518-244-2051, Fax: 518-244-2334, E-mail: pelizj@sage.edu. *Application contact:* Kathleen Gormley, Chair and Professor of Education, 518-244-2403, Fax: 518-244-2334, E-mail: gormlk@sage.edu.

Saginaw Valley State University, College of Education, Program in K-12 Literacy Specialist, University Center, MI 48710. Offers MAT. *Program availability:* Part-time, evening/weekend. *Students:* 25 part-time (23 women); includes 2 minority (both Hispanic/Latino). Average age 31. 11 applicants, 91% accepted, 9 enrolled. In 2018, 1 master's awarded. *Degree requirements:* For master's, capstone course. *Entrance requirements:* For master's, minimum GPA of 3.0. Additional exam requirements/recommendations for international students: Required—TOEFL (minimum score 550 paper-based; 79 iBT). *Application deadline:* For fall admission, 7/15 for international students; for winter admission, 11/15 for international students; for spring admission, 4/15 for international students. Applications are processed on a rolling basis. Application fee: $30 ($90 for international students). Electronic applications accepted. *Expenses: Tuition, area resident:* Full-time $6225; part-time $623 per credit hour. Tuition, state resident: full-time $6225; part-time $623 per credit hour. Tuition, nonresident: full-time $14,215; part-time $1185 per credit hour. International tuition: $14,215 full-time. *Required fees:* $263; $14.60 per credit hour. Tuition and fees vary according to degree level. *Financial support:* Federal Work-Study and scholarships/grants available. Support available to part-time students. Financial award applicants required to submit FAFSA. *Unit head:* Dr. Gretchen Owocki, Professor of Teacher Education, 989-964-7393, Fax: 989-964-4563, E-mail: coeconnect@svsu.edu. *Application contact:* Jenna Briggs, Director, Graduate and International Admissions, 989-964-6096, Fax: 989-964-2788, E-mail: gradadm@svsu.edu.

Saginaw Valley State University, College of Education, Program in Reading Education, University Center, MI 48710. Offers MAT. *Accreditation:* NCATE. *Program availability:* Part-time, evening/weekend. *Degree requirements:* For master's, capstone course, practicum. *Entrance requirements:* For master's, minimum GPA of 3.0, teaching certificate. Additional exam requirements/recommendations for international students: Required—TOEFL (minimum score 550 paper-based; 79 iBT). *Application deadline:* For fall admission, 7/15 for international students; for winter admission, 11/15 for international students; for spring admission, 4/15 for international students. Applications are processed on a rolling basis. Application fee: $30 ($90 for international students). Electronic applications accepted. *Expenses: Tuition, area resident:* Full-time $6225; part-time $623 per credit hour. Tuition, state resident: full-time $6225; part-time $623 per credit hour. Tuition, nonresident: full-time $14,215; part-time $1185 per credit hour. International tuition: $14,215 full-time. *Required fees:* $263; $14.60 per credit hour. Tuition and fees vary according to degree level. *Financial support:* Federal Work-Study and scholarships/grants available. Support available to part-time students. Financial award applicants required to submit FAFSA. *Faculty research:* Pre-service, middle school, secondary teacher, literacy education. *Unit head:* Dr. Craig Douglas, Dean, 989-964-4057, Fax: 989-964-4385, E-mail: coeconnect@svsu.edu. *Application contact:* Jenna Briggs, Director, Graduate and International Admissions, 989-964-6096, Fax: 989-964-2788, E-mail: gradadm@svsu.edu.

St. Bonaventure University, School of Graduate School, School of Education, Literacy Programs, St. Bonaventure, NY 14778-2284. Offers adolescent literacy 5-12 (MS Ed); childhood literacy B-6 (MS Ed). *Accreditation:* NCATE. *Program availability:* Part-time, evening/weekend. *Faculty:* 1 (woman) full-time, 1 part-time/adjunct. *Students:* 9 full-time (all women), 2 part-time (1 woman); all minorities (all Black or African American, non-Hispanic/Latino). Average age 22. 10 applicants, 100% accepted. In 2018, 12 master's awarded. *Degree requirements:* For master's, comprehensive exam, thesis optional, minimum cumulative GPA of 3.0, clinical practicum, literacy coaching internship, electronic portfolio. *Entrance requirements:* For master's, GRE or MAT, teaching certificate in matching area in-hand or pending, transcripts from all previous colleges, minimum GPA of 3.0, 2 references, interview, writing sample. Additional exam requirements/recommendations for international students: Required—TOEFL (minimum score 550 paper-based; 80 iBT). *Application deadline:* For fall admission, 3/15 priority date for domestic students, 2/1 for international students; for spring admission, 10/15 priority date for domestic students, 7/1 for international students. Applications are processed on a rolling basis. Application fee: $0. Electronic applications accepted.

Financial support: Scholarships/grants, health care benefits, and unspecified assistantships available. Financial award application deadline: 4/15; financial award applicants required to submit FAFSA. *Unit head:* Dr. Sheri Voss, Director, 716-375-2368, Fax: 716-375-2360, E-mail: svoss@sbu.edu. *Application contact:* Matthew Retchless, Director of Graduate Admissions, 716-375-2021, Fax: 716-375-4015, E-mail: gradsch@sbu.edu.
Website: http://www.sbu.edu/academics/schools/education/graduate-degrees-certificates/msed-in-childhood-literacy

Saint Francis University, Graduate Education Program, Loretto, PA 15940-0600. Offers education (M Ed); leadership (M Ed); reading (M Ed). *Program availability:* Part-time, 100% online, blended/hybrid learning. *Degree requirements:* For master's, comprehensive exam, thesis optional. *Entrance requirements:* For master's, GRE or MAT (if undergraduate GPA less than 3.0). Additional exam requirements/recommendations for international students: Required—TOEFL (minimum score 550 paper-based; 75 iBT), IELTS (minimum score 6.5), International Test of English proficiency (minimum score 4). Electronic applications accepted. *Expenses:* Contact institution.

St. John Fisher College, Ralph C. Wilson Jr. School of Education, Program in Literacy Education, Rochester, NY 14618-3597. Offers literacy birth to grade 6 (MS); literacy grades 5 to 12 (MS). *Program availability:* Part-time, evening/weekend. *Faculty:* 3 full-time (all women). *Students:* 5 full-time (all women), 5 part-time (all women). Average age 24. 4 applicants, 100% accepted. In 2018, 15 master's awarded. *Degree requirements:* For master's, capstone project, practicum. *Entrance requirements:* For master's, teacher certification, 2 letters of recommendation, personal statement, current resume. Additional exam requirements/recommendations for international students: Required—TOEFL (minimum score 575 paper-based; 80 iBT). *Application deadline:* Applications are processed on a rolling basis. Application fee: $30. Electronic applications accepted. *Expenses:* Contact institution. *Financial support:* Scholarships/grants available. Financial award applicants required to submit FAFSA. *Faculty research:* Adolescent use of new literacies (instant messaging), referral practices, at risk early literacy, new literacies (Internet, technology), equity in education. *Unit head:* Dr. Kathleen Broikou, Program Director, 585-385-8112, E-mail: kbroikou@sjfc.edu. *Application contact:* Michelle Gosier, Director of Transfer and Graduate Admissions, 585-385-8064, E-mail: mgosier@sjfc.edu.
Website: https://www.sjfc.edu/graduate-programs/ms-in-literacy-education/

St. John's University, The School of Education, Department of Education Specialties, Program in Literacy, Queens, NY 11439. Offers literacy (PhD); literacy leadership (Adv C); teaching literacy (MS Ed, Adv C); teaching literacy (5-12) and TESOL (K-12) (MS Ed); teaching literacy (B-6) and teaching children with disabilities in childhood education (MS Ed); teaching literacy (B-6) and TESOL (K-12) (MS Ed). *Program availability:* Part-time, evening/weekend, 100% online. *Degree requirements:* For master's, comprehensive exam, practicum completion of 50-hours of field work; for doctorate, comprehensive exam, thesis/dissertation. *Entrance requirements:* For doctorate, GRE, resume, statement of goals, official master's transcripts. Electronic applications accepted. *Faculty research:* Literacy and language; diversity; urban education; reading and writing; digital literacies.

St. Joseph's College, New York, Programs in Education, Field of Literacy and Cognition, Brooklyn, NY 11205-3688. Offers MA. *Program availability:* Part-time, evening/weekend. *Faculty:* 2 full-time (both women), 2 part-time/adjunct (both women). *Students:* 13 part-time (12 women); includes 6 minority (all Hispanic/Latino). Average age 23. 11 applicants, 82% accepted, 7 enrolled. In 2018, 8 master's awarded. *Entrance requirements:* For master's, GRE, PRAXIS or MAT, Application, $25 application fee, official transcripts, two letters of recommendation, current resume, copy of NYS teacher certifications. Additional exam requirements/recommendations for international students: Required—TOEFL (minimum score 80 iBT). *Application deadline:* Applications are processed on a rolling basis. Application fee: $25. Electronic applications accepted. *Expenses: Tuition:* Full-time $18,450; part-time $1025 per credit. *Required fees:* $414. *Financial support:* In 2018–19, 8 students received support. *Unit head:* Esther Berkowitz, Associate Professor/Director of the Literacy and Cognition Program, 718-940-5692, E-mail: eberkowitz@sjcny.edu. *Application contact:* Esther Berkowitz, Associate Professor/Director of the Literacy and Cognition Program, 718-940-5692, E-mail: eberkowitz@sjcny.edu.
Website: http://www.sjcny.edu

Saint Joseph's University, College of Arts and Sciences, Graduate Programs in Education, Philadelphia, PA 19131-1395. Offers curriculum supervisor (Certificate); educational leadership (MS, Ed D); elementary education (MS, Certificate); elementary/middle school education (Certificate); organizational development and leadership (MS); principal (Certificate); professional education (MS); reading specialist (MS, Certificate); reading supervisor (Certificate); secondary education (MS, Certificate); special education (MS); special education 7-12 (Certificate); special education PK-8 (Certificate); superintendent's letter of eligibility (Certificate); supervisor of special education (Certificate); teacher of the deaf and hard of hearing (Certificate). *Program availability:* Part-time, evening/weekend, blended/hybrid learning. *Degree requirements:* For master's, thesis or alternative; for doctorate, comprehensive exam, thesis/dissertation. *Entrance requirements:* For master's, 2 letters of recommendation, minimum GPA of 3.0, official transcripts, personal statement; for doctorate, GRE, master's degree from accredited institution, minimum graduate GPA of 3.5, computer competence, interview with program director. Additional exam requirements/recommendations for international students: Required—TOEFL (minimum score 550 paper-based; 80 iBT), IELTS (minimum score 6.5), PTE (minimum score 60). Electronic applications accepted. *Expenses:* Contact institution. *Faculty research:* Factors predicting early mathematics skills for low income children, early child care and development, preschool quality, parent communication and home-school collaboration issues, education of terminally ill children, preparing literacy teachers for urban schools.

Saint Mary's University of Minnesota, Schools of Graduate and Professional Programs, Graduate School of Education, Literacy Education Program, Winona, MN 55987-1399. Offers K-12 reading teacher (Certificate); literacy education (MA). *Unit head:* Cindy Kronebusch, Assistant Program Director, 507-457-6637, E-mail: ckronebu@smumn.edu. *Application contact:* Laurie Roy, Director of Admission of Schools of Graduate and Professional Programs, 507-457-8606, Fax: 612-728-5121, E-mail: lroy@smumn.edu.
Website: http://www.smumn.edu/graduate-home/areas-of-study/graduate-school-of-education/ma-in-literacy-education

Saint Michael's College, Graduate Programs, Program in Education, Colchester, VT 05439. Offers arts in education (CAGS); literacy (M Ed); school leadership (CAGS); special education (M Ed). *Program availability:* Part-time, evening/weekend. *Degree requirements:* For master's, thesis. *Entrance requirements:* For master's, minimum GPA of 3.0, official transcripts, essay, interview. Electronic applications accepted. *Expenses: Tuition:* Part-time $590 per credit. *Faculty research:* Integrative curriculum, moral and spiritual dimensions of education, learning styles, multiple intelligences, integrating technology into the curriculum.

Saint Peter's University, Graduate Programs in Education, Program in Special Education, Jersey City, NJ 07306-5997. Offers literacy (MA Ed). *Program availability:* Part-time, evening/weekend. *Degree requirements:* For master's, comprehensive exam. *Entrance requirements:* For master's, GRE or MAT. Additional exam requirements/recommendations for international students: Required—TOEFL. Electronic applications accepted.

Saint Peter's University, Graduate Programs in Education, Reading Program, Jersey City, NJ 07306-5997. Offers MA Ed. *Accreditation:* TEAC. *Program availability:* Part-time, evening/weekend. *Degree requirements:* For master's, comprehensive exam. *Entrance requirements:* For master's, GRE or MAT. Additional exam requirements/recommendations for international students: Required—TOEFL. Electronic applications accepted.

St. Thomas Aquinas College, Division of Teacher Education, Sparkill, NY 10976. Offers adolescence education (MST); childhood and special education (MST); childhood education (MST); educational leadership (MS Ed); reading (MS Ed, PMC); special education (MS Ed, PMC); teaching (MS Ed), including elementary education, middle school education, secondary education. *Accreditation:* NCATE. *Program availability:* Part-time, evening/weekend. *Degree requirements:* For master's, comprehensive exam, comprehensive professional portfolio; for PMC, action research project. *Entrance requirements:* For master's, New York State Qualifying Exam, GRE General Test or minimum GPA of 3.0, teaching certificate; for PMC, GRE General Test or minimum GPA of 3.0. Electronic applications accepted. *Faculty research:* Computer applications in education, adolescent special education students, literacy development, inclusive practices for special education students.

St. Thomas University, School of Leadership Studies, Institute for Education, Miami Gardens, FL 33054-6459. Offers earth/space science (Certificate); educational administration (MS, Certificate); educational leadership (Ed D); elementary education (MS); ESOL (Certificate); gifted education (Certificate); instructional technology (MS, Certificate); professional/studies (Certificate); reading (MS, Certificate); special education (MS). *Program availability:* Part-time, evening/weekend. *Degree requirements:* For master's, comprehensive exam; for doctorate, comprehensive exam, thesis/dissertation. *Entrance requirements:* For master's, interview, minimum GPA of 3.0 or GRE; for doctorate, GRE or MAT. Additional exam requirements/recommendations for international students: Required—TOEFL (minimum score 550 paper-based; 79 iBT). Electronic applications accepted.

Saint Xavier University, Graduate Studies, School of Education, Chicago, IL 60655-3105. Offers counseling (MA); curriculum and instruction (MA); early childhood education (MA); educational administration (MA); elementary education (MA); individualized studies (MA), including educational technology, English as a second language (ESL), ISTEM (integrative science, technology, engineering, and math), science education; music education (MA); reading (MA); secondary education (MA); Spanish education (MA); special education (MA); teaching and leadership (MA). *Accreditation:* NCATE. *Program availability:* Part-time, evening/weekend. *Degree requirements:* For master's, thesis or project. *Entrance requirements:* For master's, minimum GPA of 3.0. *Expenses:* Contact institution.

Salem College, Graduate Studies, Winston-Salem, NC 27101. Offers art education (MAT); elementary education (M Ed, MAT); language and literacy (M Ed); middle school education (MAT); organ (MM); piano (MM); school counseling (M Ed); second language studies (MAT); secondary education (MAT); special education (M Ed, MAT). *Accreditation:* NCATE. *Program availability:* Part-time, evening/weekend, online learning. *Degree requirements:* For master's, practicum (MAT), action research project (M Ed). *Entrance requirements:* For master's, minimum GPA of 3.0, two academic/professional recommendations, acceptable criminal background check. Additional exam requirements/recommendations for international students: Recommended—TOEFL. Electronic applications accepted. *Faculty research:* Teacher professional development, adolescent literacy, instructional technology.

Salem State University, School of Graduate Studies, Program in Reading, Salem, MA 01970-5353. Offers M Ed. *Accreditation:* NCATE. *Program availability:* Part-time, evening/weekend. *Entrance requirements:* For master's, GRE or MAT. Additional exam requirements/recommendations for international students: Required—TOEFL (minimum score 550 paper-based; 80 iBT) or IELTS (minimum score 5.5).

Salisbury University, Program in Contemporary Curriculum Theory and Instruction: Literacy, Salisbury, MD 21801-6837. Offers literacy (Ed D). *Program availability:* Part-time, evening/weekend, 100% online, blended/hybrid learning. *Faculty:* 6 full-time (4 women). *Students:* 18 full-time (14 women), 25 part-time (20 women); includes 3 minority (2 Black or African American, non-Hispanic/Latino; 1 Two or more races, non-Hispanic/Latino), 2 international. Average age 40. 19 applicants, 89% accepted, 15 enrolled. *Degree requirements:* For doctorate, comprehensive exam, thesis/dissertation. *Entrance requirements:* For doctorate, GRE General, transcripts from all colleges and universities attended; statement of interest; writing sample; three letters of recommendation. Additional exam requirements/recommendations for international students: Required—TOEFL (minimum score 550 paper-based; 79 iBT), IELTS (minimum score 6.5). *Application deadline:* For fall admission, 3/31 priority date for domestic and international students. Applications are processed on a rolling basis. Application fee: $65. Electronic applications accepted. *Expenses:* Resident - $550 per credit hour; Non-resident - $960 per credit hour; Fees - $108. *Financial support:* In 2018–19, 4 students received support, including 3 teaching assistantships with full tuition reimbursements available (averaging $8,000 per year); career-related internships or fieldwork and scholarships/grants also available. Support available to part-time students. Financial award application deadline: 3/1; financial award applicants required to submit FAFSA. *Faculty research:* Adolescent literacy; eye movement miscue analysis; literacy research; disciplinary literacy. *Unit head:* Dr. Judith Franzak, Graduate Program Director, 410-677-0238, E-mail: jkfranzak@salisbury.edu. *Application contact:* Dr. Judith Franzak, Graduate Program Director, 410-677-0238, E-mail: jkfranzak@salisbury.edu.
Website: https://www.salisbury.edu/explore-academics/programs/graduate-degree-programs/contemporary-curriculum-doctor/

Salisbury University, Program in Reading Specialist, Salisbury, MD 21801-6837. Offers reading specialist (M Ed). *Program availability:* Part-time, evening/weekend. *Faculty:* 2 full-time (1 woman). *Students:* 23 part-time (22 women); includes 2 minority (both Asian, non-Hispanic/Latino). Average age 28. 10 applicants, 80% accepted, 8 enrolled. In 2018, 4 master's awarded. *Entrance requirements:* For master's, transcripts from colleges and universities attended; minimum GPA of 3.0; three letters of recommendation; current teaching certificate. Additional exam requirements/recommendations for international students: Required—TOEFL (minimum score 550 paper-based; 79 iBT), IELTS (minimum score 6.5). *Application deadline:* For fall admission, 3/1 priority date for domestic and international students; for spring admission, 10/1 priority date for domestic and international students; for summer admission, 3/1 priority date for domestic and international students. Applications are processed on a rolling basis. Application fee: $65. Electronic applications accepted. *Expenses:* Resident - $412 per credit hour; Non-resident - $746 per credit hour; Fees - $108. *Financial support:* In 2018–19, 4 students received support. Career-related

internships or fieldwork and scholarships/grants available. Support available to part-time students. Financial award application deadline: 3/1; financial award applicants required to submit FAFSA. *Faculty research:* Emergent literacy; classroom literacy instruction; support for struggling readers; diversity and equity in literacy. *Unit head:* Dr. Joyce Wiencek, Graduate Program Director, 410-543-6288, E-mail: bjwiencek@salisbury.edu. *Application contact:* Dr. Joyce Wiencek, Graduate Program Director, 410-543-6288, E-mail: bjwiencek@salisbury.edu.
Website: https://www.salisbury.edu/explore-academics/programs/graduate-degree-programs/med-programs/reading-specialist-masters/

Sam Houston State University, College of Education, Department of Language, Literacy, and Special Populations, Huntsville, TX 77341. Offers international literacy (M Ed); reading (M Ed); special education (M Ed, MA), including low incidence disabilities and autism. *Program availability:* Part-time, evening/weekend, online learning. *Degree requirements:* For master's, comprehensive exam (for some programs), thesis optional, comprehensive portfolio; for doctorate, comprehensive exam, thesis/dissertation. *Entrance requirements:* For master's, GRE General Test, MAT, writing sample, recommendations; for doctorate, GRE General Test, MAT, master's degree, personal statement, recommendations. Additional exam requirements/recommendations for international students: Required—TOEFL (minimum score 550 paper-based; 79 iBT), IELTS (minimum score 6.5). Electronic applications accepted.

San Diego State University, Graduate and Research Affairs, College of Education, School of Teacher Education, Program in Reading Education, San Diego, CA 92182. Offers MA. *Accreditation:* NCATE. *Program availability:* Part-time. *Entrance requirements:* For master's, GRE General Test, letters of reference. Additional exam requirements/recommendations for international students: Required—TOEFL. Electronic applications accepted. *Faculty research:* Literacy, writing, reading/writing connection, class size reduction in reading, book clubs, evaluation instruments in reading/language arts.

San Francisco State University, Division of Graduate Studies, College of Education, Department of Elementary Education, Program in Language and Literacy Education, San Francisco, CA 94132-1722. Offers language and literacy education (MA); reading (Certificate); reading and literacy leadership (Credential).

San Francisco State University, Division of Graduate Studies, College of Liberal and Creative Arts, Department of English Language and Literature, San Francisco, CA 94132-1722. Offers composition (MA, Certificate); immigrant literacies (Certificate); linguistics (MA); literature (MA); teaching English to speakers of other languages (MA); teaching post-secondary reading (Certificate). *Program availability:* Part-time. *Application deadline:* Applications are processed on a rolling basis. *Unit head:* Dr. Sugie Goen-Salter, Chair, 415-338-7582, Fax: 415-338-6159, E-mail: sgoen@sfsu.edu. *Application contact:* Cynthia Losinsky, Graduate Programs Coordinator, 415-338-2660, Fax: 415-338-6159, E-mail: cynthial@sfsu.edu.
Website: http://english.sfsu.edu/

San Jose State University, Program in Elementary Education, San Jose, CA 95192-0001. Offers curriculum and instruction (MA); reading (Certificate). *Accreditation:* NCATE. *Degree requirements:* For master's, thesis or alternative. Electronic applications accepted.

Seattle Pacific University, Master of Education in Literacy Program, Seattle, WA 98119-1997. Offers M Ed. *Program availability:* Part-time. *Students:* 13 part-time (all women); includes 1 minority (Asian, non-Hispanic/Latino). Average age 30. 2 applicants, 100% accepted, 2 enrolled. In 2018, 6 master's awarded. *Degree requirements:* For master's, comprehensive exam. *Entrance requirements:* For master's, MAT or GRE (unless minimum undergraduate GPA of 3.4 or master's degree from accredited university), copy of teaching certificate, official transcript(s) from each college/university attended, personal statement (1-2 pages), two letters of recommendation, moral and character fitness policy form, resume. *Application deadline:* For fall admission, 8/15 for domestic students; for winter admission, 11/15 for domestic students; for spring admission, 2/15 for domestic students; for summer admission, 5/15 for domestic students. Applications are processed on a rolling basis. Application fee: $50. Electronic applications accepted. *Financial support:* Scholarships/grants available. Financial award applicants required to submit FAFSA. *Unit head:* Dr. Scott F. Beers, Chair, 206-281-2707, E-mail: sbeers@spu.edu. *Application contact:* The Graduate Center, 206-281-2091.
Website: http://spu.edu/academics/school-of-education/graduate-programs/masters-programs/literacy

Shippensburg University of Pennsylvania, School of Graduate Studies, College of Education and Human Services, Department of Teacher Education, Shippensburg, PA 17257-2299. Offers curriculum and instruction (M Ed), including biology, early childhood education, elementary education, geography/earth science, history, mathematics, middle school education, modern languages; reading (M Ed). *Accreditation:* NCATE. *Program availability:* Part-time, evening/weekend, 100% online, blended/hybrid learning. *Faculty:* 12 full-time (9 women), 2 part-time/adjunct (0 women). *Students:* 10 full-time (8 women), 68 part-time (64 women); includes 7 minority (2 Black or African American, non-Hispanic/Latino; 4 Hispanic/Latino; 1 Two or more races, non-Hispanic/Latino). Average age 31. 41 applicants, 73% accepted, 19 enrolled. In 2018, 34 master's awarded. *Degree requirements:* For master's, comprehensive exam (for some programs), thesis optional, practicum or internship; capstone seminar (for some programs). *Entrance requirements:* For master's, MAT or GRE (if GPA less than 2.75), interview, 3 letters of reference, questionnaire of teaching background and future goals, resume. Additional exam requirements/recommendations for international students: Required—TOEFL (minimum score 550 paper-based; 68 iBT), IELTS (minimum score 6), TOEFL (minimum score 550 paper-based, 68 iBT) or IELTS (minimum score 6). *Application deadline:* For fall admission, 4/1 priority date for domestic students, 4/30 for international students; for spring admission, 9/1 priority date for domestic students, 9/30 for international students; for summer admission, 2/1 priority date for domestic students. Applications are processed on a rolling basis. Application fee: $45. Electronic applications accepted. *Expenses:* Tuition, state resident: part-time $516 per credit. Tuition, nonresident: part-time $750 per credit. *Required fees:* $149 per credit. *Financial support:* In 2018–19, 5 students received support. Career-related internships or fieldwork, scholarships/grants, unspecified assistantships, and resident hall director and student payroll positions available. Support available to part-time students. Financial award application deadline: 3/1; financial award applicants required to submit FAFSA. *Unit head:* Dr. Christine A. Royce, Chairperson, 717-477-1688, Fax: 717-477-4046, E-mail: caroyc@ship.edu. *Application contact:* Maya T. Mapp, Director of Admissions, 717-477-1231, Fax: 717-477-4016, E-mail: mtmapp@ship.edu.
Website: http://www.ship.edu/teacher/

Siena Heights University, Graduate College, Adrian, MI 49221-1796. Offers clinical mental health counseling (MA); educational leadership (Specialist); leadership (MA), including health care leadership, organizational leadership; teacher education (MA), including early childhood education, early childhood education: Montessori, education leadership: principal, elementary education: reading K-12, leadership: higher education, secondary education: reading K-12, special education: cognitive impairment, special education: learning disabilities. *Program availability:* Part-time, evening/weekend. *Faculty:* 10 full-time (6 women), 16 part-time/adjunct (6 women). *Students:* 34 full-time (20 women), 183 part-time (126 women); includes 64 minority (38 Black or African American, non-Hispanic/Latino; 2 American Indian or Alaska Native, non-Hispanic/Latino; 4 Asian, non-Hispanic/Latino; 14 Hispanic/Latino; 6 Two or more races, non-Hispanic/Latino). Average age 36. 97 applicants, 41% accepted, 30 enrolled. In 2018, 72 master's awarded. *Degree requirements:* For master's, thesis, Presentation. *Entrance requirements:* For master's, Minimum GPA of 3.0, current resume, essay, all post-secondary transcripts, 3 letters of reference, conviction disclosure form; copy of teaching certificate (for some education programs); for Specialist, Master's degree, minimum GPA of 3.0, current resume, essay, all post-secondary transcripts, 3 letters of reference, conviction disclosure form; copy of teaching certificate (for some education programs). Additional exam requirements/recommendations for international students: Recommended—TOEFL, IELTS, TWE, TSE. *Application deadline:* Applications are processed on a rolling basis. Application fee: $50. Electronic applications accepted. *Expenses: Tuition:* Full-time $11,340; part-time $7560 per year. *Required fees:* $454; $454 per unit. $227 per semester. One-time fee: $100. Tuition and fees vary according to program. *Financial support:* In 2018–19, 55 students received support. Scholarships/grants, tuition waivers (full and partial), unspecified assistantships, and State of Michigan Scholarships/Grants available. Support available to part-time students. Financial award application deadline: 9/1; financial award applicants required to submit FAFSA. *Unit head:* Dr. Cheryl Betz, Dean, College for Professional Studies and Graduate College, 517-264-7234, Fax: 517-264-7714, E-mail: cbetz@sienaheights.edu. *Application contact:* Elizabeth Brooks, Assistant Director, 517-264-7165, Fax: 517-264-7714, E-mail: ebrooks@sienaheights.edu.
Website: http://www.sienaheights.edu

Simon Fraser University, Office of Graduate Studies and Postdoctoral Fellows, Faculty of Education, Program in Languages, Cultures, and Literacies, Burnaby, BC V5A 1S6, Canada. Offers PhD.

Slippery Rock University of Pennsylvania, Graduate Studies (Recruitment), College of Education, Department of Elementary Education and Early Childhood, Slippery Rock, PA 16057-1383. Offers instructional coach (M Ed); K-12 reading (M Ed); K-12 science and math (M Ed); reading specialist (M Ed). *Accreditation:* NCATE. *Program availability:* Part-time, evening/weekend, online only, 100% online. *Faculty:* 5 full-time (all women). *Students:* 6 full-time (all women), 115 part-time (107 women); includes 3 minority (1 Asian, non-Hispanic/Latino; 2 Hispanic/Latino). Average age 29. 106 applicants, 83% accepted, 45 enrolled. In 2018, 73 master's awarded. *Degree requirements:* For master's, comprehensive exam (for some programs), thesis optional. *Entrance requirements:* For master's, minimum GPA of 3.0, resume, teaching certification, transcripts, letters of recommendation (depending on program). Additional exam requirements/recommendations for international students: Required—TOEFL (minimum score 550 paper-based; 80 iBT). *Application deadline:* For fall admission, 3/1 priority date for domestic students, 5/1 priority date for international students; for spring admission, 10/1 priority date for domestic students, 9/1 priority date for international students. Applications are processed on a rolling basis. Application fee: $25 ($30 for international students). Electronic applications accepted. *Expenses:* Contact institution. *Financial support:* Career-related internships or fieldwork, Federal Work-Study, institutionally sponsored loans, scholarships/grants, tuition waivers (partial), and unspecified assistantships available. Support available to part-time students. Financial award application deadline: 5/1; financial award applicants required to submit FAFSA. *Unit head:* Dr. Suzanne Rose, Graduate Coordinator, 724-738-2042, Fax: 724-738-2779, E-mail: suzanne.rose@sru.edu. *Application contact:* Brandi Weber-Mortimer, Director of Graduate Admissions, 724-738-2051, Fax: 724-738-2146, E-mail: graduate.admissions@sru.edu.
Website: http://www.sru.edu/academics/colleges-and-departments/coe/departments/elementary-education-/-early-childhood/graduate-programs

Sonoma State University, School of Education, Rohnert Park, CA 94928-3609. Offers administrative services (Credential); curriculum, teaching, and learning (MA); early childhood education (MA); education specialist (Credential); educational leadership (MA); multiple subject (Credential); reading and literacy (MA, Credential); single subject (Credential); special education (MA). *Accreditation:* NCATE. *Program availability:* Part-time, evening/weekend. *Entrance requirements:* For master's, minimum GPA of 2.5. Additional exam requirements/recommendations for international students: Required—TOEFL (minimum score 500 paper-based).

Southeastern Louisiana University, College of Arts, Humanities and Social Sciences, Department of English, Hammond, LA 70402. Offers creative writing (MA); language and literacy (MA); professional writing (MA); publishing studies (MA). *Program availability:* Part-time. *Faculty:* 18 full-time (8 women). *Students:* 8 full-time (6 women), 16 part-time (14 women); includes 7 minority (2 Black or African American, non-Hispanic/Latino; 1 Hispanic/Latino; 4 Two or more races, non-Hispanic/Latino). Average age 26. 10 applicants, 80% accepted, 6 enrolled. In 2018, 11 master's awarded. *Degree requirements:* For master's, comprehensive exam, thesis optional. *Entrance requirements:* For master's, GRE verbal score of 150 or greater required. Additional exam requirements/recommendations for international students: Required—TOEFL (minimum score 500 paper-based; 61 iBT). *Application deadline:* For fall admission, 7/15 priority date for domestic students, 6/1 priority date for international students; for spring admission, 12/1 priority date for domestic students, 10/1 priority date for international students. Applications are processed on a rolling basis. Application fee: $20 ($30 for international students). Electronic applications accepted. *Expenses: Tuition, area resident:* Full-time $6684. Tuition, state resident: full-time $6684. Tuition, nonresident: full-time $19,162. *Required fees:* $2097. *Financial support:* In 2018–19, 19 students received support, including 8 research assistantships with tuition reimbursements available (averaging $8,494 per year); institutionally sponsored loans, scholarships/grants, and unspecified assistantships also available. Support available to part-time students. Financial award application deadline: 5/1; financial award applicants required to submit FAFSA. *Faculty research:* Digital Humanities, John Donne and Liminality, Film: From Analog to Digital, Animal Studies and Literature, John Ruskin's Juvenalia/Digital Humanities Project. *Total annual research expenditures:* $64,854. *Unit head:* Dr. David Hanson, Department Head, 985-549-2100, Fax: 985-549-5021, E-mail: dhanson@southeastern.edu. *Application contact:* Office of Admissions, 985-549-5637, Fax: 985-549-5632, E-mail: admissions@southeastern.edu.
Website: http://www.southeastern.edu/acad_research/depts/engl

Southeastern Oklahoma State University, School of Education, Durant, OK 74701-0609. Offers math specialist (M Ed); reading specialist (M Ed); school administration (M Ed); school counseling (M Ed). *Accreditation:* NCATE. *Program availability:* Part-time, evening/weekend. *Degree requirements:* For master's, comprehensive exam, thesis optional, portfolio (M Ed). *Entrance requirements:* For master's, GRE General Test (for school counseling), minimum GPA of 3.0 in last 60 hours or 2.75 overall. Additional exam requirements/recommendations for international students: Required—TOEFL (minimum score 550 paper-based; 79 iBT). Electronic applications accepted.

Southeastern University, College of Education, Lakeland, FL 33801-6099. Offers curriculum and instruction (Ed D); educational leadership (M Ed); elementary education (M Ed); exceptional student education (M Ed); exceptional student education/educational therapy (M Ed); kinesiology (M Ed); organizational leadership (Ed D); reading education (M Ed); teaching English to speakers of other languages (M Ed). Electronic applications accepted.

Southern Adventist University, School of Education and Psychology, Collegedale, TN 37315-0370. Offers clinical mental health counseling (MS); instructional leadership (MS Ed); literacy education (MS Ed); outdoor education (MS Ed); professional school counseling (MS). *Accreditation:* NCATE. *Program availability:* Part-time, evening/weekend, 100% online, blended/hybrid learning. *Faculty:* 11 full-time (8 women), 11 part-time/adjunct (5 women). *Students:* 42 full-time (32 women), 40 part-time (29 women). 13 applicants, 38% accepted, 4 enrolled. *Degree requirements:* For master's, comprehensive exam (for some programs), thesis optional, portfolio (MS) portfolio (MS Ed in outdoor education). *Entrance requirements:* For master's, interview (MS); 9 semester hours of upper-division course work in psychology or related field, including 1 course in psychology research or statistics; 9 semester hours of education (MS Ed). Additional exam requirements/recommendations for international students: Required—TOEFL (minimum score 100 iBT). *Application deadline:* For fall admission, 7/1 priority date for domestic students, 6/1 priority date for international students; for winter admission, 11/1 priority date for domestic students, 10/1 priority date for international students; for spring admission, 4/1 priority date for domestic students, 3/1 priority date for international students. Applications are processed on a rolling basis. Application fee: $40. Electronic applications accepted. *Financial support:* Scholarships/grants and unspecified assistantships available. Support available to part-time students. Financial award application deadline: 4/1; financial award applicants required to submit FAFSA. *Faculty research:* Millennials, spiritual self-awareness, parenting styles, attitudes toward student mental health issues, reliance on social media. *Unit head:* Dr. Tammy Overstreet, Dean, 423-236-2444, Fax: 423-236-1765, E-mail: toverstreet@ southern.edu. *Application contact:* Mikhaile Spence, Graduate Program Manager, 423-236-2496, Fax: 423-236-1765, E-mail: maspence@southern.edu.
Website: https://www.southern.edu/academics/edpsych.html

Southern Connecticut State University, School of Graduate Studies, School of Education, Program in Reading, New Haven, CT 06515-1355. Offers MS, Diploma. *Program availability:* Part-time, evening/weekend. *Degree requirements:* For master's, thesis or alternative. *Entrance requirements:* For master's, interview, teaching certificate; for Diploma, master's degree. Electronic applications accepted.

Southern Illinois University Edwardsville, Graduate School, School of Education, Health, and Human Behavior, Department of Curriculum and Instruction, Program in Literacy Education, Edwardsville, IL 62026. Offers MS Ed. *Program availability:* Part-time, evening/weekend. *Degree requirements:* For master's, comprehensive exam, research paper. *Entrance requirements:* Additional exam requirements/ recommendations for international students: Required—TOEFL (minimum score 550 paper-based; 79 iBT), IELTS (minimum score 6.5). Electronic applications accepted.

Southern Illinois University Edwardsville, Graduate School, School of Education, Health, and Human Behavior, Department of Curriculum and Instruction, Program in Literacy Specialist, Edwardsville, IL 62026. Offers Post-Master's Certificate. *Program availability:* Part-time. *Entrance requirements:* Additional exam requirements/ recommendations for international students: Required—TOEFL (minimum score 550 paper-based; 79 iBT), IELTS (minimum score 6.5). Electronic applications accepted.

Southern Methodist University, Simmons School of Education and Human Development, Department of Teaching and Learning, Dallas, TX 75275. Offers bilingual education (MBE); education (M Ed, PhD); English as a second language (M Ed); gifted and talented (M Ed); literacy studies (M Ed); special education (M Ed). *Program availability:* Part-time, evening/weekend. Terminal master's awarded for partial completion of doctoral program. *Degree requirements:* For master's, comprehensive exam, minimum GPA of 3.0; for doctorate, thesis/dissertation, qualifying exams, major area paper, evidence of teaching competency, dissemination of research (e.g., conference presentation), professional portfolio. *Entrance requirements:* For master's, minimum GPA of 3.0 or GRE, 3 letters of recommendation; for doctorate, GRE, minimum GPA of 3.3, 3 years of full-time teaching, 3 letters of recommendation, interview. Additional exam requirements/recommendations for international students: Required—TOEFL. Electronic applications accepted. *Faculty research:* Reading intervention, mathematics intervention, bilingual education, new literacies.

Southern New Hampshire University, School of Education, Manchester, NH 03106-1045. Offers curriculum and instruction (M Ed), including dyslexia studies and language-based learning disabilities, educational leadership, reading, special education, technology integration; dyslexia studies and language-based learning disabilities (Certificate); early childhood and special education (M Ed); educational leadership (M Ed, Ed D); educational studies (M Ed); elementary and special education (M Ed); field based education (M Ed); higher education administration (MS); teaching English as a foreign language (MS). *Program availability:* Part-time, evening/weekend, online learning. *Degree requirements:* For master's, comprehensive exam (for some programs), thesis or alternative. *Entrance requirements:* For master's, PRAXIS I, minimum GPA of 2.75. Additional exam requirements/recommendations for international students: Required—TOEFL (minimum score 550 paper-based). Electronic applications accepted. *Expenses:* Contact institution.

Southern Oregon University, Graduate Studies, School of Education, Ashland, OR 97520. Offers elementary education (MA Ed, MS Ed), including classroom teacher, early childhood, handicapped learner, reading, supervision; secondary education (MA Ed, MS Ed), including classroom teacher, handicapped learner, reading, supervision; teaching (MAT). *Program availability:* Online learning. *Degree requirements:* For master's, thesis optional. *Entrance requirements:* For master's, GRE General Test, minimum cumulative GPA of 3.0 in the last 90 quarter credits (60 semester credits) of undergraduate coursework. Additional exam requirements/recommendations for international students: Required—TOEFL (minimum score 540 paper-based; 76 iBT), IELTS (minimum score 6), ELPT (minimum score 964) or ELS (minimum score 112). Electronic applications accepted.

Southwestern Adventist University, Education Department, Keene, TX 76059. Offers curriculum and instruction with reading emphasis (M Ed); educational leadership (M Ed). *Program availability:* Part-time, evening/weekend. *Degree requirements:* For master's, thesis or alternative, professional paper. *Entrance requirements:* For master's, GRE General Test.

Southwest Minnesota State University, Department of Education, Marshall, MN 56258. Offers ESL (MS); math (MS); reading (MS); special education (MS), including developmental disabilities, early childhood education, emotional behavioral disorders, learning disabilities; teaching, learning and leadership (MS). *Program availability:* Part-time, evening/weekend, online learning. *Entrance requirements:* Additional exam requirements/recommendations for international students: Required—TOEFL or IELTS; Recommended—TOEFL (minimum score 550 paper-based; 80 iBT), IELTS.

Spring Arbor University, School of Education, Spring Arbor, MI 49283-9799. Offers education (MAE); reading (MAR); special education (MSE). *Accreditation:* TEAC. *Program availability:* Part-time, evening/weekend, online learning. *Degree requirements:* For master's, thesis. *Entrance requirements:* For master's, official transcripts from all institutions attended, including evidence of an earned bachelor's degree from regionally-accredited college or university with minimum cumulative GPA of 3.0 for the last two years of the bachelor's degree; two professional letters of recommendation. Additional

exam requirements/recommendations for international students: Required—TOEFL (minimum score 600 paper-based). Electronic applications accepted.

State University of New York at Fredonia, College of Education, Fredonia, NY 14063-1136. Offers curriculum and instruction (MS Ed); literacy education (MS Ed), including birth-grade 12, grades 5-12; music education (M Mus), including k-12; TESOL (MS Ed). *Accreditation:* NCATE. *Program availability:* Part-time. *Faculty:* 16 full-time (14 women), 13 part-time/adjunct (11 women). *Students:* 39 full-time (33 women), 44 part-time (36 women); includes 5 minority (1 Asian, non-Hispanic/Latino; 3 Hispanic/Latino; 1 Two or more races, non-Hispanic/Latino), 4 international. Average age 27. 44 applicants, 89% accepted, 34 enrolled. In 2018, 25 master's awarded. *Degree requirements:* For master's, thesis. *Entrance requirements:* For master's, GRE, minimum undergraduate GPA of 3.0. Additional exam requirements/recommendations for international students: Required—TOEFL (minimum score 79 iBT), IELTS (minimum score 6.5). *Application deadline:* For fall admission, 4/1 priority date for domestic and international students; for spring admission, 11/1 priority date for domestic students, 11/1 for international students. Applications are processed on a rolling basis. Application fee: $75. Electronic applications accepted. *Expenses:* Tuition, state resident: full-time $6870; part-time $462 per credit hour. Tuition, nonresident: full-time $16,650; part-time $944 per credit hour. *International tuition:* $16,650 full-time. *Required fees:* $25; $2 per credit hour. $1 per semester. *Financial support:* In 2018–19, 13 students received support. Unspecified assistantships available. Financial award application deadline: 3/15; financial award applicants required to submit FAFSA. *Faculty research:* Positive behavioral intervention and support (PBIS), place-based science education, peer support for education, primary source material for social studies education, policies and practices in learning English language. *Unit head:* Dr. Christine Givner, Dean, 716-673-3311, E-mail: christine.givner@fredonia.edu. *Application contact:* Wendy S. Dunst, Interim Graduate Recruitment and Admissions Associate, 716-673-3808, Fax: 716-673-3712, E-mail: wendy.dunst@fredonia.edu.
Website: http://www.fredonia.edu/coe/

State University of New York at New Paltz, Graduate and Extended Learning School, School of Education, Program of Educational Administration, Program in Special Education, New Paltz, NY 12561. Offers adolescence special education (7-12) (MS Ed); adolescence special education and literacy (MS Ed); childhood special education (1-6) (MS Ed); childhood special education and literacy (MS Ed); early childhood special education (B-2) (MS Ed). *Accreditation:* NCATE. *Program availability:* Part-time, evening/weekend. *Faculty:* 4 full-time (3 women), 1 (woman) part-time/adjunct. *Students:* 14 full-time (11 women), 34 part-time (26 women); includes 4 minority (all Hispanic/Latino). 26 applicants, 85% accepted, 21 enrolled. In 2018, 15 master's awarded. *Entrance requirements:* For master's, minimum GPA of 3.0 (3.2 for special education and literacy programs), New York state teaching certificate. Additional exam requirements/recommendations for international students: Required—TOEFL (minimum score 550 paper-based; 80 iBT), IELTS (minimum score 6.5). *Application deadline:* For fall admission, 3/15 priority date for domestic students, 3/15 for international students; for spring admission, 11/1 for domestic and international students. Application fee: $50. Electronic applications accepted. *Financial support:* Application deadline: 8/1. *Unit head:* Dr. Jane Sileo, Coordinator, 845-257-2835, E-mail: sileoj@newpaltz.edu. *Application contact:* Vika Shock, Director of Graduate Admissions, 845-257-3286, E-mail: gradstudies@newpaltz.edu.
Website: http://www.newpaltz.edu/schoolofed/department-of-teaching—learning/special_ed.html

State University of New York at Oswego, Graduate Studies, School of Education, Department of Curriculum and Instruction, Oswego, NY 13126. Offers adolescence education (MST); art education (MAT); childhood education (MST); curriculum and instruction (MS Ed); literacy education (MS Ed); special education (MS Ed). *Program availability:* Part-time, evening/weekend. *Degree requirements:* For master's, comprehensive exam (for some programs), thesis optional. *Entrance requirements:* For master's, GRE General Test, minimum GPA of 2.7, provisional teaching certificate. Additional exam requirements/recommendations for international students: Required—TOEFL (minimum score 560 paper-based). *Faculty research:* Classroom applications for microcomputers; classroom questioning, wait-time, and achievement; values clarification and academic achievement.

State University of New York at Plattsburgh, School of Education, Health, and Human Services, Program in Teacher Education: Literacy Education, Plattsburgh, NY 12901-2681. Offers birth-grade 6 (MS Ed); grades 5-12 (MS Ed). *Accreditation:* TEAC. *Program availability:* Part-time, evening/weekend. *Entrance requirements:* For master's, minimum GPA of 2.75. Additional exam requirements/recommendations for international students: Required—TOEFL. *Faculty research:* Reading pedagogy, early childhood literacy, children's literature, integrated language arts.

State University of New York College at Cortland, Graduate Studies, School of Education, Program in Literacy Education, Cortland, NY 13045. Offers MS Ed. *Accreditation:* NCATE. *Program availability:* Part-time, evening/weekend. *Degree requirements:* For master's, one foreign language, comprehensive exam, thesis (for some programs). *Entrance requirements:* Additional exam requirements/ recommendations for international students: Required—TOEFL.

State University of New York College at Geneseo, Graduate Studies, School of Education, Program in Reading and Literacy, Geneseo, NY 14454-1401. Offers reading and literacy B-12 (MS Ed). *Program availability:* Part-time. *Degree requirements:* For master's, thesis optional, two reading clinics (practicum), action research project. *Entrance requirements:* For master's, GRE, MAT, EAS, edTPA, PRAXIS, or another substantially equivalent test, proof of New York State initial certification or equivalent certification from another state. Additional exam requirements/recommendations for international students: Required—TOEFL (minimum score 525 paper-based; 71 iBT), IELTS (minimum score 6.5), PTE, iTEP. Electronic applications accepted. *Expenses:* Contact institution.

State University of New York College at Oneonta, Graduate Programs, Division of Education, Department of Elementary Education and Reading, Oneonta, NY 13820-4015. Offers childhood education (MS Ed); literacy education (MS Ed). *Accreditation:* NCATE. *Program availability:* Part-time, evening/weekend. *Entrance requirements:* For master's, GRE General Test.

State University of New York College at Potsdam, School of Education and Professional Studies, Program in Literacy, Potsdam, NY 13676. Offers literacy educator (MS Ed); literacy specialist (MS Ed), including birth-grade 6, grades 5-12. *Accreditation:* NCATE. *Program availability:* Part-time, online learning. *Entrance requirements:* For master's, minimum GPA of 2.75 in last 60 hours of course work. Additional exam requirements/recommendations for international students: Required—TOEFL (minimum score 550 paper-based; 80 iBT), IELTS (minimum score 6). Electronic applications accepted.

Sul Ross State University, College of Professional Studies, Department of Education, Program in Reading Specialist, Alpine, TX 79832. Offers master reading teacher (Certificate); Texas reading specialist (M Ed). *Program availability:* Part-time, evening/weekend. *Degree requirements:* For master's, thesis optional. *Entrance requirements:* For master's, GMAT or GRE General Test, minimum GPA of 2.5 in last 60 hours of undergraduate work.

Sul Ross State University, Rio Grande College of Sul Ross State University, Alpine, TX 79832. Offers business administration (MBA); teacher education (M Ed), including bilingual education, counseling, educational diagnostics, elementary education, general education, reading, school administration, secondary education. *Program availability:* Part-time, evening/weekend, online learning. *Degree requirements:* For master's, comprehensive exam, thesis optional, minimum GPA of 3.0. *Entrance requirements:* For master's, GMAT or GRE General Test, minimum GPA of 2.5 in last 60 hours of undergraduate work. Additional exam requirements/recommendations for international students: Required—TOEFL.

Syracuse University, School of Education, MS Program in Literacy Education (Birth - Grade 12), Syracuse, NY 13244. Offers MS. *Program availability:* Part-time. *Students:* Average age 24. *Entrance requirements:* For master's, GRE, baccalaureate degree from regionally-accredited college/university, New York State teaching certification, strong writing skills, letters of recommendation, personal statement. Additional exam requirements/recommendations for international students: Required—TOEFL (minimum score 100 iBT). *Application deadline:* For fall admission, 1/15 priority date for domestic and international students. Applications are processed on a rolling basis. Application fee: $75. Electronic applications accepted. *Financial support:* Fellowships with full tuition reimbursements, research assistantships, teaching assistantships, career-related internships or fieldwork, and scholarships/grants available. Financial award application deadline: 1/15. *Faculty research:* Literacy, knowledge modeling, assessment, teaching of literature, writing. *Unit head:* Dr. Marcelle Haddix, Chair of Reading and Language Arts/Associate Professor, 315-443-7642, E-mail: mhaddix@syr.edu. *Application contact:* Speranza Migliore, Graduate Admissions Recruiter, 315-443-2505, E-mail: gradrcrt@syr.edu.
Website: http://soe.syr.edu/academic/reading_language_arts/graduate/masters/literacy_education/default.aspx

Syracuse University, School of Education, PhD Program in Literacy Education, Syracuse, NY 13244. Offers PhD. *Program availability:* Part-time. *Entrance requirements:* For doctorate, GRE, master's degree, three references, personal statement, college/university transcripts. Additional exam requirements/recommendations for international students: Required—TOEFL (minimum score 100 iBT). *Application deadline:* For fall admission, 1/15 priority date for domestic and international students; for spring admission, 10/15 priority date for domestic and international students. Applications are processed on a rolling basis. Application fee: $75. Electronic applications accepted. *Financial support:* Fellowships with full tuition reimbursements, research assistantships, teaching assistantships, career-related internships or fieldwork, and scholarships/grants available. Financial award application deadline: 1/15. *Faculty research:* Social and critical perspectives toward language and literacy development, instruction and teacher education, programs and curriculum development related to childhood or adolescent reading and writing instruction, literacy across the curriculum, multimodal literacies. *Unit head:* Dr. Marcelle Haddix, Chair of Reading and Language Arts/Associate Professor, 315-443-7642, E-mail: mhaddix@syr.edu. *Application contact:* Speranza Migliore, Graduate Admissions Recruiter, 315-443-2505, E-mail: gradrcrt@syr.edu.
Website: http://soe.syr.edu/academic/reading_language_arts/graduate/phd/default.aspx

Teachers College, Columbia University, Department of Curriculum and Teaching, New York, NY 10027-6696. Offers curriculum and teaching (Ed M, MA, Ed D); curriculum and teaching: elementary education (MA); curriculum and teaching: secondary education (MA); early childhood education (MA, Ed D); early childhood education: special education (MA); elementary education-gifted extension (MA); elementary inclusive education (MA); gifted education (MA); literacy specialist (MA); secondary inclusive education (MA); special inclusive elementary education (MA). *Program availability:* Part-time, evening/weekend. *Students:* 88 full-time (77 women), 264 part-time (239 women); includes 129 minority (45 Black or African American, non-Hispanic/Latino; 1 American Indian or Alaska Native, non-Hispanic/Latino; 41 Asian, non-Hispanic/Latino; 28 Hispanic/Latino; 14 Two or more races, non-Hispanic/Latino), 48 international. Average age 30. 460 applicants, 73% accepted, 149 enrolled. Terminal master's awarded for partial completion of doctoral program. *Unit head:* Prof. Daniel Friedrich, Chair, 212-678-3263, E-mail: friedrich@exchange.tc.columbia.edu. *Application contact:* Kelly Sutton-Skinner, Director of Admission & New Student Enrollment, E-mail: kms2237@tc.columbia.edu.

Teachers College, Columbia University, Department of Health and Behavior Studies, New York, NY 10027-6696. Offers applied behavior analysis (MA, PhD); applied educational psychology: school psychology (Ed M, PhD); behavioral nutrition (PhD), including nutrition (Ed D, PhD); community health education (MS); community nutrition education (Ed M), including community nutrition education; education of deaf and hard of hearing (MA, PhD); health education (MA, Ed D); hearing impairment (Ed D); intellectual disability/autism (MA, Ed D, PhD); nursing education (Ed D, Advanced Certificate); nutrition and education (MS); nutrition and exercise physiology (MS); nutrition and public health (MS); nutrition education (Ed D), including nutrition (Ed D, PhD); physical disabilities (Ed D); reading specialist (MA); severe or multiple disabilities (MA); special education (Ed M, MA, Ed D); teaching of sign language (MA). *Program availability:* Part-time, evening/weekend. *Students:* 157 full-time (145 women), 344 part-time (310 women); includes 169 minority (46 Black or African American, non-Hispanic/Latino; 2 American Indian or Alaska Native, non-Hispanic/Latino; 55 Asian, non-Hispanic/Latino; 57 Hispanic/Latino; 9 Two or more races, non-Hispanic/Latino), 64 international. Average age 31. 495 applicants, 64% accepted, 171 enrolled. Terminal master's awarded for partial completion of doctoral program. *Unit head:* Prof. Dolores Perin, Chair, 212-678-3091, E-mail: dp111@tc.columbia.edu. *Application contact:* Kelly Sutton-Skinner, Director of Admission & New Student Enrollment, E-mail: kms2237@tc.columbia.edu.
Website: http://www.tc.columbia.edu/health-and-behavior-studies/

Tennessee Technological University, College of Graduate Studies, College of Education, Department of Curriculum and Instruction, Program in Exceptional Learning, Cookeville, TN 38505. Offers applied behavior analysis (PhD); literacy (PhD); program planning and evaluation (PhD); STEM education (PhD). *Program availability:* Part-time, evening/weekend. *Students:* 14 full-time (8 women), 20 part-time (12 women); includes 2 minority (1 Black or African American, non-Hispanic/Latino; 1 Two or more races, non-Hispanic/Latino), 3 international. 16 applicants, 56% accepted, 2 enrolled. In 2018, 8 doctorates awarded. *Degree requirements:* For doctorate, comprehensive exam, thesis/dissertation. *Entrance requirements:* For doctorate, GRE, minimum GPA of 3.0. Additional exam requirements/recommendations for international students: Required—TOEFL (minimum score 550 paper-based; 79 iBT), IELTS (minimum score 5.5), PTE (minimum score 53), or TOEIC (Test of English as an International Communication). *Application deadline:* For fall admission, 8/1 for domestic students, 5/1 for international students; for spring admission, 12/1 for domestic students, 10/1 for international students; for summer admission, 5/1 for domestic students, 2/1 for international students. Applications are processed on a rolling basis. Application fee: $35 ($40 for international students). Electronic applications accepted. *Financial support:* Fellowships, research assistantships, and teaching assistantships available. Financial award application deadline: 4/1. *Unit head:* Dr. Lisa Zagumny, Dean, College of Education, 931-372-3078, Fax: 931-372-3517, E-mail: lzagumny@tntech.edu. *Application contact:* Shelia K. Kendrick, Coordinator of Graduate Studies, 931-372-3808, Fax: 931-372-3497, E-mail: skendrick@tntech.edu.
Website: https://www.tntech.edu/education/elphd/

Texas A&M University–Commerce, College of Education and Human Services, Commerce, TX 75429. Offers counseling (M Ed, MS, PhD); early childhood education (M Ed, MS); educational administration (M Ed, MS, Ed D); educational psychology (PhD); educational technology leadership (M Ed, MS); educational technology library science (M Ed, MS); elementary education (M Ed); health, kinesiology and sports studies (MS); higher education (MS, Ed D); psychology (MS); reading (M Ed, MS); school psychology (SSP); secondary education (M Ed, MS); social work (MSW); special education (M Ed, MS); supervision, curriculum and instruction-elementary education (Ed D); training and development (MS). *Program availability:* Part-time, evening/weekend, 100% online, blended/hybrid learning. *Faculty:* 95 full-time (59 women), 29 part-time/adjunct (22 women). *Students:* 356 full-time (295 women), 1,262 part-time (992 women); includes 683 minority (349 Black or African American, non-Hispanic/Latino; 9 American Indian or Alaska Native, non-Hispanic/Latino; 30 Asian, non-Hispanic/Latino; 238 Hispanic/Latino; 57 Two or more races, non-Hispanic/Latino), 9 international. Average age 37. 951 applicants, 42% accepted, 304 enrolled. In 2018, 532 master's, 51 doctorates awarded. *Degree requirements:* For master's, comprehensive exam, thesis optional, departmental qualifying exams (for some programs); for doctorate, comprehensive exam, thesis/dissertation, departmental qualifying exam; for SSP, comprehensive exam. *Entrance requirements:* For master's, GRE General Test, official transcripts, letters of recommendation, resume, statement of goals; for doctorate, GRE General Test, letters of recommendation, statement of goals, writing samples, writing sessions, resumes. Additional exam requirements/recommendations for international students: Required—TOEFL (minimum score 550 paper-based; 79 iBT), IELTS (minimum score 6), PTE (minimum score 53). *Application deadline:* For fall admission, 6/1 priority date for international students; for spring admission, 10/15 priority date for international students; for summer admission, 3/15 priority date for international students. Applications are processed on a rolling basis. Application fee: $50 ($75 for international students). Electronic applications accepted. *Expenses: Tuition, area resident:* Full-time $3630. Tuition, state resident: full-time $3630. Tuition, nonresident: full-time $11,100. *International tuition:* $11,100 full-time. *Required fees:* $2794. Tuition and fees vary according to course load, degree level and program. *Financial support:* In 2018–19, 116 students received support, including 94 research assistantships with partial tuition reimbursements available (averaging $3,863 per year), 38 teaching assistantships with partial tuition reimbursements available (averaging $4,728 per year); career-related internships or fieldwork, Federal Work-Study, institutionally sponsored loans, scholarships/grants, health care benefits, and unspecified assistantships also available. Financial award application deadline: 5/1; financial award applicants required to submit FAFSA. *Faculty research:* Cognitive and bilingual education, positive behavioral intervention, literacy, math readiness. *Total annual research expenditures:* $1.1 million. *Unit head:* Dr. Madeline Justice, Interim Dean, 903-886-5181, Fax: 903-886-5905, E-mail: madeline.justice@tamuc.edu. *Application contact:* Vicky Turner, Doctoral Degree and Special Programs Coordinator, 903-886-5167, E-mail: vicky.turner@tamuc.edu.
Website: http://www.tamuc.edu/academics/graduateSchool/programs/education/default.aspx

Texas A&M University–Corpus Christi, College of Graduate Studies, College of Education and Human Development, Corpus Christi, TX 78412. Offers counseling (MS), including counseling; counselor education (PhD); curriculum and instruction (MS, PhD); early childhood education (MS); educational administration (MS); educational leadership (Ed D); elementary education (MS); instructional design and educational technology (MS); kinesiology (MS); reading (MS); secondary education (MS); special education (MS). *Program availability:* Part-time, evening/weekend, blended/hybrid learning. *Degree requirements:* For master's, comprehensive exam, capstone; for doctorate, thesis/dissertation. *Entrance requirements:* For master's, GRE General Test, essay (300 words); for doctorate, GRE, essay, resume, 3-4 reference forms. Electronic applications accepted.

Texas A&M University–Kingsville, College of Graduate Studies, College of Education and Human Performance, Department of Teacher and Bilingual Education, Program in Reading Specialization, Kingsville, TX 78363. Offers MS. *Program availability:* Part-time, evening/weekend. *Degree requirements:* For master's, variable foreign language requirement, comprehensive exam, thesis (for some programs). *Entrance requirements:* For master's, GRE, MAT, GMAT. Additional exam requirements/recommendations for international students: Required—TOEFL (minimum score 550 paper-based; 79 iBT). Electronic applications accepted.

Texas A&M University–San Antonio, Department of Educator and Leadership Preparation, San Antonio, TX 78224. Offers bilingual education (MS); early childhood education (M Ed); educational administration (MA); reading specialization (MS); special education (M Ed), including educational diagnostician. *Program availability:* Part-time, evening/weekend, online learning. *Degree requirements:* For master's, comprehensive exam, thesis or alternative. *Entrance requirements:* For master's, GRE (Quantitative and Verbal) or MAT. Additional exam requirements/recommendations for international students: Required—TOEFL (minimum score 550 paper-based; 79 iBT), IELTS (minimum score 6). Electronic applications accepted. *Faculty research:* Equity in education, biliteracy practices among Latina and immigrants, academic achievement of low socio-economic students, equity practices in instruction and educational leadership in diverse settings, racial identity development and multicultural education.

Texas Christian University, College of Education, Master's Programs in Education, Fort Worth, TX 76129-0002. Offers counseling (M Ed); curriculum and instruction (M Ed), including curriculum studies, language and literacy, math education, science education; education (MAT); educational leadership (M Ed); special education (M Ed). *Program availability:* Part-time, evening/weekend. *Faculty:* 29 full-time (21 women), 3 part-time/adjunct (1 woman). *Students:* 124 full-time (94 women), 14 part-time (12 women); includes 52 minority (14 Black or African American, non-Hispanic/Latino; 2 American Indian or Alaska Native, non-Hispanic/Latino; 3 Asian, non-Hispanic/Latino; 28 Hispanic/Latino; 5 Two or more races, non-Hispanic/Latino), 1 international. Average age 28. 172 applicants, 69% accepted, 86 enrolled. In 2018, 62 master's awarded. *Degree requirements:* For master's, comprehensive exam (for some programs), thesis (for some programs). *Entrance requirements:* For master's, GRE General Test; Pre-Admission Content Test (for MAT). Additional exam requirements/recommendations for international students: Required—TOEFL (minimum score 550 paper-based; 80 iBT), IELTS (minimum score 6.5). *Application deadline:* For fall admission, 3/1 for domestic and international students; for spring admission, 11/16 for domestic and international students; for summer admission, 3/1 for domestic and international students. Application fee: $60. Electronic applications accepted. *Financial support:* In 2018–19, 135 students received support, including 3 research assistantships with full tuition reimbursements available (averaging $15,000 per year), 33 teaching assistantships with full tuition reimbursements available (averaging $15,000 per year); career-related internships or fieldwork, scholarships/grants, health care benefits, and unspecified assistantships also available. Support available to part-time students. Financial award application deadline: 3/1. *Unit head:* Dr. Jan Lacina, Interim Dean, 817-257-6786, Fax: 817-257-7466, E-mail:

j.lacina@tcu.edu. *Application contact:* Lori Kimball, Graduate Studies Coordinator, 817-257-7661, Fax: 817-257-7466, E-mail: l.kimball@tcu.edu.
Website: http://coe.tcu.edu/graduate-overview/

Texas State University, The Graduate College, College of Education, Program in Reading Education, San Marcos, TX 78666. Offers early childhood-12 reading specialist (M Ed). *Program availability:* Part-time, evening/weekend. *Faculty:* 12 full-time (11 women), 1 (woman) part-time/adjunct. *Students:* 1 (woman) full-time, 9 part-time (8 women); includes 5 minority (1 Black or African American, non-Hispanic/Latino; 4 Hispanic/Latino). Average age 36. 5 applicants, 80% accepted, 4 enrolled. In 2018, 9 master's awarded. *Degree requirements:* For master's, comprehensive exam. *Entrance requirements:* For master's, baccalaureate degree from regionally-accredited institution with minimum GPA of 3.0 in last 60 hours of course work, statement of purpose, official teaching certificate. Additional exam requirements/recommendations for international students: Required—TOEFL, IELTS, TOEFL (minimum iBT scores: 22 listening, 22 reading, 24 speaking, 21 writing). *Application deadline:* For fall admission, 2/1 priority date for domestic and international students; for spring admission, 10/15 priority date for domestic students, 10/1 for international students; for summer admission, 4/15 for domestic students, 3/15 for international students. Applications are processed on a rolling basis. Application fee: $55 ($90 for international students). Electronic applications accepted. *Expenses:* Tuition, state resident: full-time $8102; part-time $4051 per semester. Tuition, nonresident: full-time $18,229; part-time $9115 per semester. *International tuition:* $18,229 full-time. *Required fees:* $2116; $120 per credit hour. Tuition and fees vary according to course load. *Financial support:* In 2018–19, 5 students received support. Research assistantships, teaching assistantships, career-related internships or fieldwork, Federal Work-Study, institutionally sponsored loans, scholarships/grants, and unspecified assistantships available. Support available to part-time students. Financial award application deadline: 1/15; financial award applicants required to submit FAFSA. *Faculty research:* Reciprocal Teaching; Instructional design for "long-term English learners; Bilingual students' linguistic experiences and literacy instruction; motivation to read; teacher perceptions of teaching literacy; Oral History methodology; literacies of linguistically and culturally diverse children, families, and communities; developing reading through mentoring. *Total annual research expenditures:* $91,671. *Unit head:* Dr. Jesse Gainer, Graduate Advisor, 512-245-3534, Fax: 512-245-8365, E-mail: jg51@txstate.edu. *Application contact:* Dr. Andrea Golato, Dean of Graduate School, 512-245-2581, Fax: 512-245-8365, E-mail: gradcollege@txstate.edu.
Website: http://www.education.txstate.edu/ci/degrees-certifications/graduate/reading.html

Texas Tech University, Graduate School, College of Education, Department of Curriculum and Instruction, Lubbock, TX 79409-1071. Offers bilingual education (M Ed); curriculum and instruction (M Ed, PhD); elementary education (M Ed); language/literacy education (M Ed); multidisciplinary science (MS); secondary education (M Ed). *Accreditation:* NCATE. *Program availability:* Part-time, evening/weekend, online learning. *Faculty:* 17 full-time (11 women), 1 (woman) part-time/adjunct. *Students:* 48 full-time (41 women), 265 part-time (220 women); includes 103 minority (25 Black or African American, non-Hispanic/Latino; 9 Asian, non-Hispanic/Latino; 64 Hispanic/Latino; 5 Two or more races, non-Hispanic/Latino), 27 international. Average age 40. 101 applicants, 65% accepted, 51 enrolled. In 2018, 26 master's, 21 doctorates awarded. Terminal master's awarded for partial completion of doctoral program. *Degree requirements:* For master's, comprehensive exam (for some programs), thesis optional; for doctorate, comprehensive exam, thesis/dissertation. *Entrance requirements:* For master's, bachelor's degree; resume; letter of intent; academic writing sample; 2 letters of recommendation; for doctorate, GRE, master's degree; resume; letter of intent; academic writing sample; 3 letters of recommendation. Additional exam requirements/recommendations for international students: Required—TOEFL (minimum score 550 paper-based; 79 iBT). *Application deadline:* For fall admission, 6/1 priority date for domestic students, 1/15 priority date for international students; for spring admission, 9/1 priority date for domestic students, 6/15 priority date for international students. Applications are processed on a rolling basis. Application fee: $65. Electronic applications accepted. *Expenses:* Contact institution. *Financial support:* In 2018–19, 142 students received support, including 136 fellowships (averaging $2,895 per year), 28 research assistantships (averaging $12,296 per year), 7 teaching assistantships (averaging $14,175 per year); Federal Work-Study, institutionally sponsored loans, scholarships/grants, health care benefits, and unspecified assistantships also available. Support available to part-time students. Financial award application deadline: 2/1; financial award applicants required to submit FAFSA. *Faculty research:* Teacher education, curriculum studies, bilingual education, science and math education, language and literacy education. *Total annual research expenditures:* $79,025. *Unit head:* Dr. Jerry Dwyer, Professor, Interim Department Chair, 806-834-7399, Fax: 806-742-2179, E-mail: jerry.dwyer@ttu.edu. *Application contact:* Brandi Stephens, Graduate Academic Advisor, 806-834-4554, Fax: 806-742-2179, E-mail: brandi.stephens@ttu.edu.
Website: www.educ.ttu.edu

Texas Woman's University, Graduate School, College of Professional Education, Department of Reading, Denton, TX 76204. Offers reading education (M Ed, MA, PhD); Texas all-level (K-12) reading specialist (Certificate); Texas master reading teacher (Certificate). *Program availability:* Part-time. *Faculty:* 10 full-time (all women), 2 part-time/adjunct (both women). *Students:* 68 part-time (65 women); includes 35 minority (8 Black or African American, non-Hispanic/Latino; 25 Hispanic/Latino; 2 Two or more races, non-Hispanic/Latino). Average age 40. 20 applicants, 85% accepted, 17 enrolled. In 2018, 8 master's, 9 doctorates awarded. *Degree requirements:* For master's, comprehensive exam, thesis (for some programs), thesis or portfolio; for doctorate, comprehensive exam, thesis/dissertation. *Entrance requirements:* For master's, minimum GPA of 3.0 in undergraduate study and all prior graduate work, vita/resume, essay; for doctorate, master's degree, minimum GPA of 3.0, on-site writing sample, curriculum vitae/resume, 1-2 page statement of professional experience and goals. Additional exam requirements/recommendations for international students: Required—TOEFL (minimum score 550 paper-based; 79 iBT); Recommended—IELTS (minimum score 6.5), TSE (minimum score 53). *Application deadline:* Applications are processed on a rolling basis. Application fee: $50 ($75 for international students). Electronic applications accepted. *Expenses: Tuition, area resident:* Full-time $4852; part-time $270 per semester hour. Tuition, state resident: full-time $4852; part-time $270 per semester hour. Tuition, nonresident: full-time $12,322; part-time $685 per semester hour. *International tuition:* $12,322 full-time. *Required fees:* $2714; $113 per semester hour. $296 per semester. Tuition and fees vary according to course level, course load, degree level, campus/location and program. *Financial support:* In 2018–19, 13 students received support, including 1 research assistantship; career-related internships or fieldwork, Federal Work-Study, institutionally sponsored loans, scholarships/grants, traineeships, health care benefits, and unspecified assistantships also available. Support available to part-time students. Financial award application deadline: 3/1; financial award applicants required to submit FAFSA. *Faculty research:* Early literacy intervention, home/school partnerships, literacy language acquisitions, multicultural education, children's literature. *Unit head:* Dr. Connie Briggs, Chair, 940-898-2227, Fax: 940-898-2224, E-mail: reading@twu.edu. *Application contact:* Korie Hawkins, Associate Director of Admissions, Graduate Recruitment, 940-898-3188, Fax: 940-898-3081, E-mail: admissions@twu.edu.
Website: http://www.twu.edu/reading/

Touro College, Graduate School of Education, New York, NY 10010. Offers education and special education (MS); instructional technology (MS); mathematics education (MS); school leadership (MS); teaching English to speakers of other languages (MS); teaching literacy (MS). *Accreditation:* TEAC. *Program availability:* Part-time, evening/weekend, online learning. *Entrance requirements:* Additional exam requirements/recommendations for international students: Required—TOEFL (minimum score 83 iBT), IELTS (minimum score 6.5). *Faculty research:* Equity assistance, language development, scholarly communications, Latin American studies and cultural sensitivity, behavior management techniques and strategies in special education.

Towson University, College of Education, Program in Reading, Towson, MD 21252-0001. Offers reading (M Ed); reading education (CAS). *Accreditation:* NCATE. *Program availability:* Part-time, evening/weekend. *Entrance requirements:* For master's, minimum GPA of 3.0, essay; for CAS, 3 letters of reference, portfolio, master's degree in reading or related field. Electronic applications accepted. *Expenses: Tuition, area resident:* Full-time $9196; part-time $418 per unit. Tuition, state resident: full-time $9196; part-time $418 per unit. Tuition, nonresident: full-time $19,030; part-time $865 per unit. *International tuition:* $19,030 full-time. *Required fees:* $3102; $141 per year. $423 per term. Tuition and fees vary according to campus/location and program.

Trident University International, College of Education, Program in Education, Cypress, CA 90630. Offers adult education (MA Ed); aviation education (MA Ed); children's literacy development (MA Ed); e-learning (MA Ed); early childhood education (MA Ed); enrollment management (MA Ed); higher education (MA Ed); teaching and instruction (MA Ed); training and development (MA Ed). *Program availability:* Part-time, evening/weekend, online learning. *Degree requirements:* For master's, capstone project with integrative paper. *Entrance requirements:* For master's, minimum GPA of 2.5 (students with GPA 3.0 or greater may transfer up to 30% of graduate level credits). Additional exam requirements/recommendations for international students: Required—TOEFL (minimum score 525 paper-based). Electronic applications accepted.

Trinity Washington University, School of Education, Washington, DC 20017-1094. Offers clinical mental health counseling (MA); early childhood education (MAT); educating for change (M Ed); educational administration (MSA); elementary education (MAT); reading (M Ed); school counseling (MA); secondary education (MAT), including English, social studies; special education (MAT). *Accreditation:* NCATE. *Program availability:* Part-time, evening/weekend. *Degree requirements:* For master's, thesis (for some programs), capstone project(s). *Entrance requirements:* For master's, PRAXIS I, minimum GPA of 2.8. Additional exam requirements/recommendations for international students: Required—TOEFL (minimum score 550 paper-based). *Faculty research:* Technology, literacy, special education, organizations, inclusion models.

Union College, Graduate Programs, Department of Education, Barbourville, KY 40906-1499. Offers elementary education (MA); health and physical education (MA); middle grades (MA); music education (MA); principalship (MA); reading specialist (MA); secondary education (MA); special education (MA). *Degree requirements:* For master's, thesis optional. *Entrance requirements:* For master's, GRE General Test, NTE.

University at Albany, State University of New York, School of Education, Department of Literacy Teaching and Learning, Albany, NY 12222-0001. Offers MS, PhD, CAS. *Program availability:* Evening/weekend. *Faculty:* 16 full-time (14 women), 2 part-time/adjunct (1 woman). *Students:* 13 full-time (all women), 124 part-time (119 women); includes 6 minority (1 Black or African American, non-Hispanic/Latino; 2 Asian, non-Hispanic/Latino; 3 Hispanic/Latino), 3 international. Average age 33. 65 applicants, 74% accepted, 44 enrolled. In 2018, 38 master's, 2 doctorates, 2 other advanced degrees awarded. *Degree requirements:* For doctorate, one foreign language, thesis/dissertation. *Entrance requirements:* For doctorate, GRE General Test. Additional exam requirements/recommendations for international students: Required—TOEFL (minimum score 550 paper-based). *Application deadline:* For fall admission, 3/1 for domestic students. Applications are processed on a rolling basis. Application fee: $75. Electronic applications accepted. *Financial support:* Fellowships available. Financial award application deadline: 4/15. *Unit head:* Dr. Virginia Goatley, Chair, 518-442-5104, E-mail: vgoatley@albany.edu. *Application contact:* Dr. Virginia Goatley, Chair, 518-442-5104, E-mail: vgoatley@albany.edu.

University at Buffalo, the State University of New York, Graduate School, Graduate School of Education, Department of Learning and Instruction, Buffalo, NY 14260. Offers biology education (Ed M, Certificate); chemistry education (Ed M, Certificate); childhood education (Ed M); childhood education with bilingual extension (Ed M); college teaching (Advanced Certificate); curriculum, instruction and the science of learning (PhD); early childhood education (Ed M); early childhood education with bilingual extension (Ed M); earth science education (Ed M, Certificate); education and technology (Ed M); education studies (Ed M); educational technology and new literacies (Certificate); educational technology and new literacies (Advanced Certificate); elementary education (Ed D); English education (Ed M, Certificate); English education studies (Ed M); English for speakers of other languages (Ed M); foreign and second language education (PhD); French education (Ed M, Certificate); German education (Ed M, Certificate); gifted education (Certificate); Latin education (Ed M, Certificate); literacy education studies (Ed M); literacy specialist (Ed M); literacy teaching and learning (Certificate); mathematics education (Ed M, Certificate); music education (Ed M, Certificate); music education studies (Ed M); music learning theory (Advanced Certificate); online education (Advanced Certificate); physics education (Ed M, Certificate); science and the public (Ed M); social studies education (Ed M, Certificate); Spanish education (Ed M, Certificate); special education (PhD); teaching English to speakers of other languages (Ed M). *Program availability:* Part-time, evening/weekend, 100% online. *Faculty:* 31 full-time (22 women), 41 part-time/adjunct (27 women). *Students:* 161 full-time (107 women), 369 part-time (260 women); includes 76 minority (26 Black or African American, non-Hispanic/Latino; 3 American Indian or Alaska Native, non-Hispanic/Latino; 30 Asian, non-Hispanic/Latino; 14 Hispanic/Latino; 3 Two or more races, non-Hispanic/Latino), 41 international. Average age 34. 368 applicants, 70% accepted, 179 enrolled. In 2018, 100 master's, 26 doctorates, 19 other advanced degrees awarded. *Degree requirements:* For master's, comprehensive exam; for doctorate, thesis/dissertation, research analysis exam, research experience. *Entrance requirements:* For master's, letters of reference; for doctorate, GRE General Test or MAT, interview, writing sample, letters of recommendation. Additional exam requirements/recommendations for international students: Required—TOEFL (minimum score 600 paper-based; 96 iBT), IELTS (minimum score 6.5), PTE (minimum score 55). *Application deadline:* For fall admission, 2/1 priority date for domestic and international students; for spring admission, 11/15 priority date for domestic students, 10/1 for international students. Applications are processed on a rolling basis. Application fee: $50. Electronic applications accepted. *Financial support:* In 2018–19, 42 fellowships (averaging $5,181 per year), 44 research assistantships with tuition reimbursements (averaging $10,908 per year) were awarded; teaching assistantships, career-related internships or fieldwork, Federal Work-Study, institutionally sponsored loans, scholarships/grants, tuition waivers (full and partial), and unspecified assistantships also available. Financial award application deadline: 2/28; financial award applicants required to submit FAFSA. *Faculty*

research: Science assessment, foreign language teaching and learning, early learning, new literacies, gender and education. *Total annual research expenditures:* $413,233. *Unit head:* Dr. Julie Gorlewski, Department Chair, 716-645-2455, Fax: 716-645-3161, E-mail: jgorlews@buffalo.edu. *Application contact:* Renad Aref, Assistant Director of Admission Recruitment, 716-645-2110, Fax: 716-645-7937, E-mail: gseinfo@buffalo.edu.
Website: http://ed.buffalo.edu/teaching.html

The University of Akron, Graduate School, College of Education, Department of Curricular and Instructional Studies, Program in Elementary Education - Literacy Option, Akron, OH 44325. Offers MA. *Accreditation:* NCATE. *Degree requirements:* For master's, comprehensive exam, thesis optional. *Entrance requirements:* For master's, valid teaching license. Additional exam requirements/recommendations for international students: Required—TOEFL (minimum score 79 iBT), IELTS (minimum score 6.5). Electronic applications accepted.

The University of Alabama at Birmingham, School of Education, Program in Reading, Birmingham, AL 35294. Offers MA Ed. *Program availability:* Online learning. *Entrance requirements:* For master's, two years' teaching experience, teaching certificate. *Expenses: Tuition, area resident:* Full-time $8100; part-time $8100 per year. Tuition, state resident: full-time $8100. Tuition, nonresident: full-time $19,188; part-time $19,188 per year. Tuition and fees vary according to program.

The University of Alabama in Huntsville, School of Graduate Studies, College of Education, Huntsville, AL 35899. Offers autism spectrum disorders (M Ed, Graduate Certificate); biology (MAT); chemistry (MAT); differentiated instruction in elementary education (M Ed); English language arts (MAT); English speakers of other languages (M Ed, MAT); history (MAT); mathematics (MAT); physics (MAT); reading education (M Ed); secondary education (M Ed). *Program availability:* Part-time. *Faculty:* 13 full-time (10 women). *Students:* 38 full-time (30 women), 39 part-time (37 women); includes 17 minority (10 Black or African American, non-Hispanic/Latino; 3 American Indian or Alaska Native, non-Hispanic/Latino; 2 Asian, non-Hispanic/Latino; 2 Two or more races, non-Hispanic/Latino). Average age 33. 47 applicants, 83% accepted, 29 enrolled. In 2018, 31 master's awarded. *Degree requirements:* For master's, comprehensive exam, thesis or alternative, oral and written. *Entrance requirements:* For master's, GRE General Test, minimum GPA of 3.0. Additional exam requirements/recommendations for international students: Required—TOEFL (minimum score 500 paper-based; 80 iBT), IELTS (minimum score 6.5). *Application deadline:* For fall admission, 7/15 priority date for domestic students, 4/1 priority date for international students; for spring admission, 11/30 priority date for domestic students, 9/1 priority date for international students. Applications are processed on a rolling basis. Application fee: $50. Electronic applications accepted. *Expenses: Tuition, area resident:* Full-time $10,632; part-time $412 per credit hour. Tuition, state resident: full-time $10,632. Tuition, nonresident: full-time $23,604; part-time $412 per credit hour. *Required fees:* $582; $582. Tuition and fees vary according to course load and program. *Financial support:* In 2018–19, 2 students received support, including 1 teaching assistantship with full tuition reimbursement available (averaging $4,500 per year); career-related internships or fieldwork, Federal Work-Study, institutionally sponsored loans, scholarships/grants, health care benefits, tuition waivers (full and partial), and unspecified assistantships also available. Support available to part-time students. Financial award application deadline: 4/1; financial award applicants required to submit FAFSA. *Unit head:* Dr. Beth Nason Quick, Dean, 256-824-2325, E-mail: beth.quick@uah.edu. *Application contact:* Kim Gray, Graduate Studies Admissions Coordinator, 256-824-6002, Fax: 256-824-6405, E-mail: deangrad@uah.edu.
Website: http://www.uah.edu/education/

University of Alaska Southeast, Graduate Programs, Program in Education, Juneau, AK 99801. Offers educational leadership (M Ed); elementary education (MAT); learning design and technology (M Ed); mathematics education (M Ed); reading specialist (M Ed); secondary education (MAT); special education (M Ed, MAT). *Accreditation:* NCATE. *Program availability:* Part-time, evening/weekend, online learning. *Degree requirements:* For master's, comprehensive exam or project, portfolio. *Entrance requirements:* For master's, PRAXIS, minimum GPA of 3.0, writing sample, letters of recommendation. Electronic applications accepted. *Faculty research:* Applied classroom research, culturally responsive practices, action research, teaching effectiveness.

The University of Arizona, College of Education, Department of Teaching, Learning and Sociocultural Studies, Program in Language, Reading and Culture, Tucson, AZ 85721. Offers MA, Ed D, PhD, Ed S. *Program availability:* Part-time. *Entrance requirements:* Additional exam requirements/recommendations for international students: Required—TOEFL (minimum score 550 paper-based; 79 iBT); Recommended—IELTS (minimum score 7). Electronic applications accepted. *Faculty research:* Literacy acquisition, sociocultural theory, indigenous education, heritage-language revitalization, the study of households and community settings, children's and adolescent literatures and literacy.

University of Arkansas at Little Rock, Graduate School, College of Education and Health Professions, Department of Teacher Education, Program in Reading Education, Little Rock, AR 72204-1099. Offers M Ed, PhD, Ed S.

University of Bridgeport, School of Education, Department of Education, Bridgeport, CT 06604. Offers education (MS); educational management (Ed D, Diploma), including intermediate administrator or supervisor (Diploma), leadership (Ed D); elementary education (MS, Diploma), including early childhood education, elementary education; middle school education (MS); music education (MS); remedial reading and language arts (Diploma); secondary education (MS, Diploma), including computer specialist (Diploma), international education (Diploma), reading specialist, secondary education. *Program availability:* Part-time, evening/weekend. *Degree requirements:* For master's, final exam, final project, or thesis; for doctorate, comprehensive exam, thesis/dissertation; for Diploma, thesis or alternative, final project. *Entrance requirements:* For master's, minimum undergraduate QPA of 2.67; for doctorate, GRE, MAT; for Diploma, GRE General Test or MAT, minimum graduate QPA of 3.0. Additional exam requirements/recommendations for international students: Recommended—TOEFL (minimum score 550 paper-based; 80 iBT), IELTS (minimum score 6.5). Electronic applications accepted. *Expenses:* Contact institution.

The University of British Columbia, Faculty of Education, Department of Language and Literacy Education, Vancouver, BC V6T 1Z2, Canada. Offers literacy education (M Ed, MA, PhD); modern languages education (M Ed, MA); teaching English as a second language (M Ed, MA, PhD). *Program availability:* Part-time, evening/weekend. *Degree requirements:* For master's, thesis (MA); for doctorate, thesis/dissertation. *Entrance requirements:* For master's and doctorate, minimum B+ average in last 2 years with minimum 2 courses at A standing. Additional exam requirements/recommendations for international students: Required—TOEFL, TWE. Electronic applications accepted. *Expenses:* Contact institution. *Faculty research:* Language and literacy development, second language acquisition, Asia Pacific language curriculum, children's literature, whole language instruction.

University of Central Arkansas, Graduate School, College of Education, Department of Early Childhood and Special Education, Program in Reading Education, Conway, AR 72035-0001. Offers MSE. *Accreditation:* NCATE. *Program availability:* Part-time, evening/weekend, online learning. *Degree requirements:* For master's, comprehensive exam, thesis optional. *Entrance requirements:* For master's, GRE General Test, minimum GPA of 2.7. Additional exam requirements/recommendations for international students: Required—TOEFL (minimum score 550 paper-based; 80 iBT).

University of Central Florida, College of Community Innovation and Education, School of Teacher Education, Program in Reading Education, Orlando, FL 32816. Offers M Ed, Certificate. *Accreditation:* NCATE. *Program availability:* Part-time, evening/weekend. *Students:* 1 (woman) full-time, 15 part-time (13 women); includes 6 minority (2 Black or African American, non-Hispanic/Latino; 1 Asian, non-Hispanic/Latino; 3 Hispanic/Latino). Average age 34. 14 applicants, 64% accepted, 4 enrolled. In 2018, 14 master's awarded. *Degree requirements:* For master's, comprehensive exam, thesis or alternative, portfolio, Reading K-12 Subject Area Exam of the Florida Teacher Certification Examination. *Entrance requirements:* Additional exam requirements/recommendations for international students: Required—TOEFL. *Application deadline:* For fall admission, 7/15 for domestic students; for spring admission, 12/1 for domestic students; for summer admission, 4/15 for domestic students. Application fee: $30. Electronic applications accepted. *Financial support:* Career-related internships or fieldwork, Federal Work-Study, institutionally sponsored loans, tuition waivers (partial), and unspecified assistantships available. Financial award application deadline: 3/1; financial award applicants required to submit FAFSA. *Unit head:* Dr. Karri J. Williams, Program Coordinator, 321-433-7922, E-mail: karri.williams@ucf.edu. *Application contact:* Associate Director, Graduate Admissions, 407-823-2766, Fax: 407-823-6442, E-mail: gradadmissions@ucf.edu.
Website: http://www.education.ucf.edu/readinged/

University of Central Missouri, The Graduate School, Warrensburg, MO 64093. Offers accountancy (MA); accounting (MBA); applied mathematics (MS); aviation safety (MA); biology (MS); business administration (MBA); career and technical education leadership (MS); college student personnel administration (MS); communication (MA); computer science (MS); counseling (MS); criminal justice (MS); educational leadership (Ed D); educational technology (MS); elementary and early childhood education (MSE); English (MA); environmental studies (MA); finance (MBA); history (MA); human services/educational technology (Ed S); human services/learning resources (Ed S); human services/professional counseling (Ed S); industrial hygiene (MS); industrial management (MS); information systems (MBA); information technology (MS); kinesiology (MS); library science and information services (MS); literacy education (MSE); marketing (MBA); mathematics (MS); music (MA); occupational safety management (MS); psychology (MS); rural family nursing (MS); school administration (MSE); social gerontology (MS); sociology (MA); special education (MSE); speech language pathology (MS); superintendency (Ed S); teaching (MAT); teaching English as a second language (MA); technology (MS); technology management (PhD); theatre (MA). *Accreditation:* ASHA. *Program availability:* Part-time, 100% online, blended/hybrid learning. *Degree requirements:* For master's and Ed S, comprehensive exam (for some programs), thesis (for some programs). *Entrance requirements:* Additional exam requirements/recommendations for international students: Required—TOEFL (minimum score 550 paper-based; 79 iBT). Electronic applications accepted.

University of Central Oklahoma, The Jackson College of Graduate Studies, College of Education and Professional Studies, Donna Nigh Department of Advanced Professional and Special Services, Edmond, OK 73034-5209. Offers educational leadership (M Ed); library media education (M Ed); reading (M Ed); school counseling (M Ed); special education (M Ed), including mild/moderate disabilities, severe-profound/multiple disabilities; speech-language pathology (MS). *Accreditation:* ASHA. *Program availability:* Part-time. *Degree requirements:* For master's, comprehensive exam (for some programs), thesis (for some programs). *Entrance requirements:* Additional exam requirements/recommendations for international students: Required—TOEFL (minimum score 550 paper-based; 79 iBT), IELTS (minimum score 6.5). Electronic applications accepted.

University of Cincinnati, Graduate School, College of Education, Criminal Justice, and Human Services, School of Education, Program in Literacy and Second Language Studies, Cincinnati, OH 45221. Offers M Ed, Ed D. *Accreditation:* NCATE. *Program availability:* Part-time. *Degree requirements:* For master's, thesis or alternative; for doctorate, thesis/dissertation. *Entrance requirements:* For master's, GRE General Test. Additional exam requirements/recommendations for international students: Required—TOEFL (minimum score 550 paper-based), TWE (minimum score 4.5), OEPT. Electronic applications accepted.

University of Colorado Denver, School of Education and Human Development, Teacher Education Programs, Denver, CO 80217. Offers elementary linguistically diverse education (MA); elementary math and science education (MA); elementary math education (MA); elementary reading and writing (MA); elementary science education (MA); secondary English education (MA); secondary linguistically diverse education (MA); secondary math education (MA); secondary reading and writing (MA); secondary science education (MA); special education (MA). *Accreditation:* NCATE. *Program availability:* Part-time, evening/weekend. *Degree requirements:* For master's, comprehensive exam. *Entrance requirements:* For master's, GRE or MAT (for those with GPA below 2.75), transcripts, resume, letters of recommendation. Additional exam requirements/recommendations for international students: Required—TOEFL (minimum score 537 paper-based; 75 iBT); Recommended—IELTS (minimum score 6.5). Electronic applications accepted. *Expenses:* Tuition, state resident: full-time $6786; part-time $337 per credit hour. Tuition, nonresident: full-time $22,590; part-time $1255 per credit hour. *Required fees:* $1231; $137 per credit hour. Tuition and fees vary according to program and reciprocity agreements. *Faculty research:* Linguistically diverse education/ESL, elementary reading and writing, elementary teacher education, secondary teacher education, special education.

University of Connecticut, Graduate School, Neag School of Education, Department of Curriculum and Instruction, Program in Reading Education, Storrs, CT 06269. Offers MA, PhD. *Accreditation:* NCATE. Terminal master's awarded for partial completion of doctoral program. *Degree requirements:* For master's, comprehensive exam, thesis or alternative; for doctorate, thesis/dissertation. *Entrance requirements:* For doctorate, GRE General Test. Additional exam requirements/recommendations for international students: Required—TOEFL (minimum score 550 paper-based). Electronic applications accepted.

University of Dayton, Department of Teacher Education, Dayton, OH 45469. Offers adolescence to young adult education (MS Ed); early childhood leadership and advocacy (MS Ed); interdisciplinary education (MS Ed), including visual arts; interdisciplinary education studies (MS Ed); leadership in educational systems (MS Ed); literacy (MS Ed); mathematics education (MS Ed); middle childhood education (MS Ed); multi-age education (MS Ed), including world languages; music education (MS Ed); teacher as leader (MS Ed); teacher education (MS Ed); technology-enhanced learning (MS Ed); trans-disciplinary early childhood education (MS Ed). *Program availability:* Part-time, 100% online. *Degree requirements:* For master's, variable foreign language requirement, thesis or alternative, internship (for teaching licensure or endorsement). *Entrance requirements:* For master's, GRE (minimum score of 149 verbal, 4 on writing) or MAT (minimum score of 396) if undergraduate GPA was under 2.75, minimum GPA of 2.75, 3 letters of recommendation, personal statement or resume, official transcripts.

Additional exam requirements/recommendations for international students: Required—TOEFL (minimum score 550 paper-based; 80 iBT); Recommended—IELTS (minimum score 6.5). Electronic applications accepted. *Expenses:* Contact institution. *Faculty research:* Social emotional learning, culturally responsive teaching, urban teaching, literacy, instructional strategies, pre-service teacher education preparation.

The University of Findlay, Office of Graduate Admissions, Findlay, OH 45840-3653. Offers applied security and analytics (MSAS); athletic training (MAT); business (MBA), including certified management accountant, certified public accountant, health care management, hospitality management; education (MA Ed, Ed D), including children's literature (MA Ed), curriculum and teaching (MA Ed), education (MA Ed), educational administration (MA Ed), human resource development (MA Ed), mathematics (MA Ed), reading (MA Ed), science education (MA Ed), superintendent (Ed D), teaching (Ed D), technology (MA Ed); environmental, safety, and health management (MSEM); health informatics (MS); occupational therapy (MOT); pharmacy (Pharm D); physical therapy (DPT); physician assistant (MPA); rhetoric and writing (MA); teaching English to speakers of other languages (TESOL) and applied linguistics (MA). *Program availability:* Part-time, evening/weekend, 100% online, blended/hybrid learning. *Degree requirements:* For master's, comprehensive exam (for some programs), thesis (for some programs), cumulative project, capstone project; for doctorate, thesis/dissertation (for some programs). *Entrance requirements:* For master's, GRE/GMAT, bachelor's degree from accredited institution, minimum undergraduate GPA of 2.5 in last 64 hours of course work; for doctorate, GRE, MAT, minimum cumulative GPA of 3.0. Additional exam requirements/recommendations for international students: Required—TOEFL (minimum score 79 iBT), IELTS (minimum score 7), PTE (minimum score 61). Electronic applications accepted.

University of Florida, Graduate School, College of Education, School of Teaching and Learning, Gainesville, FL 32611. Offers curriculum and instruction (M Ed, MAE, Ed D, PhD, Ed S); elementary education (M Ed, MAE); English education (M Ed, MAE); mathematics education (M Ed, MAE); reading education (M Ed, MAE); science education (M Ed, MAE); social studies education (M Ed, MAE). *Accreditation:* NCATE. *Program availability:* Part-time, evening/weekend, online learning. Terminal master's awarded for partial completion of doctoral program. *Degree requirements:* For master's, comprehensive exam (for some programs), thesis (for some programs); for doctorate, comprehensive exam (for some programs), thesis/dissertation (for some programs). *Entrance requirements:* For master's and doctorate, GRE General Test, minimum GPA of 3.0; for Ed S, GRE General Test. Additional exam requirements/recommendations for international students: Required—TOEFL (minimum score 550 paper-based; 80 iBT), IELTS (minimum score 6). Electronic applications accepted. *Faculty research:* STEM education; curriculum; teaching and teacher education; languages and literacy; schools, culture, and society; theories and processes of learning.

University of Georgia, College of Education, Department of Language and Literacy Education, Athens, GA 30602. Offers English education (M Ed); language and literacy education (PhD). *Accreditation:* NCATE. *Degree requirements:* For doctorate, variable foreign language requirement. *Entrance requirements:* For master's, GRE General Test or MAT; for doctorate, GRE General Test. Additional exam requirements/recommendations for international students: Required—TOEFL (minimum score 550 paper-based). Electronic applications accepted. *Faculty research:* Comprehension, critical literacy, literacy and technology, vocabulary instruction, content area reading.

University of Guam, Office of Graduate Studies, School of Education, Program in Language and Literacy, Mangilao, GU 96923. Offers M Ed. *Program availability:* Part-time. *Degree requirements:* For master's, comprehensive oral and written exams, special project or thesis. *Entrance requirements:* For master's, GRE General Test. Additional exam requirements/recommendations for international students: Required—TOEFL.

University of Houston–Clear Lake, School of Education, Program in Curriculum and Instruction, Houston, TX 77058-1002. Offers curriculum and instruction (MS); early childhood education (MS); reading (MS); school library and information science (MS). *Program availability:* Part-time, evening/weekend. *Degree requirements:* For master's, thesis (for some programs). *Entrance requirements:* For master's, GRE or minimum GPA of 3.0 in last 60 hours. Additional exam requirements/recommendations for international students: Required—TOEFL (minimum score 550 paper-based). Electronic applications accepted.

University of Houston–Victoria, School of Education, Health Professions and Human Development, Victoria, TX 77901-4450. Offers administration and supervision (M Ed); adult and higher education (M Ed); counselor education (M Ed); curriculum and instruction (M Ed); dyslexia education (Certificate); educational technology (M Ed); special education (M Ed). *Program availability:* Part-time, evening/weekend, online learning. *Degree requirements:* For master's, comprehensive exam, project or thesis. *Entrance requirements:* For master's, GRE General Test. Additional exam requirements/recommendations for international students: Required—TOEFL. Electronic applications accepted. *Expenses: Tuition, area resident:* Full-time $6154; part-time $3077 per semester. *Tuition, state resident:* full-time $6154; part-time $3077 per semester. Tuition, nonresident: full-time $13,624; part-time $6812 per semester. *International tuition:* $13,624 full-time. *Required fees:* $1405; $847 per semester. $423 per semester. Tuition and fees vary according to program. *Faculty research:* Reading and language arts education, evaluation and diagnosis of special children's abilities.

University of Kentucky, Graduate School, College of Education, Program in Curriculum and Instruction, Lexington, KY 40506-0032. Offers curriculum and instruction (Ed D, PhD); elementary education (MA Ed); instructional system design (MS Ed); literacy (MA Ed); middle school education (MA Ed, MS Ed); secondary education (MA Ed, MS Ed). *Accreditation:* NCATE. *Degree requirements:* For master's, comprehensive exam, thesis optional; for doctorate, comprehensive exam, thesis/dissertation. *Entrance requirements:* For master's, GRE General Test, minimum undergraduate GPA of 2.75; for doctorate, GRE General Test, minimum graduate GPA of 3.0. Additional exam requirements/recommendations for international students: Required—TOEFL (minimum score 550 paper-based). Electronic applications accepted. *Faculty research:* Educational reform, multicultural education, classroom instructional practices, performance based assessment, primary school programs.

University of La Verne, LaFetra College of Education, Program in Reading, La Verne, CA 91750-4443. Offers reading (M Ed, Certificate); reading and language arts specialist (Credential). *Entrance requirements:* For master's, MAT, California Basic Educational Skills Test, minimum GPA of 3.0, basic teaching credential, interview, 3 letters of reference. *Expenses:* Contact institution.

University of Lynchburg, Graduate Studies, M Ed Program in Reading, Lynchburg, VA 24501-3199. Offers reading instruction (M Ed); reading specialist (M Ed). *Program availability:* Part-time, evening/weekend. *Degree requirements:* For master's, comprehensive exam (for some programs), practicum; portfolio or state license exam. *Entrance requirements:* For master's, GRE, minimum GPA of 3.0 (preferred), three letters of recommendation, official transcripts (bachelor's, others as relevant), career goals statement. Additional exam requirements/recommendations for international students: Required—TOEFL (minimum score 550 paper-based; 80 iBT), IELTS

(minimum score 6). Electronic applications accepted. Application fee is waived when completed online. *Expenses:* Contact institution.

University of Maine, Graduate School, College of Education and Human Development, School of Learning and Teaching, Orono, ME 04469. Offers counselor education (M Ed, MA, MS, CAS); early childhood teacher (CGS); education (PhD), including counselor education, literacy education, prevention and intervention studies; elementary education (M Ed, CAS); individualized education (M Ed); literacy education (CAS); response to intervention for behavior (CGS); secondary education (M Ed, CAS); social studies education (M Ed); special education (M Ed, CAS). *Program availability:* Part-time. *Faculty:* 21 full-time (12 women), 37 part-time/adjunct (29 women). *Students:* 113 full-time (96 women), 224 part-time (191 women); includes 11 minority (3 Black or African American, non-Hispanic/Latino; 4 American Indian or Alaska Native, non-Hispanic/Latino; 1 Asian, non-Hispanic/Latino; 2 Hispanic/Latino; 1 Two or more races, non-Hispanic/Latino), 3 international. Average age 37. 195 applicants, 99% accepted, 147 enrolled. In 2018, 82 master's, 2 doctorates, 49 other advanced degrees awarded. *Degree requirements:* For master's, thesis (for some programs); for doctorate, comprehensive exam, thesis/dissertation. *Entrance requirements:* For master's, GRE General Test, MAT. Additional exam requirements/recommendations for international students: Required—TOEFL (minimum score 550 paper-based; 80 iBT), IELTS (minimum score 6.5). *Application deadline:* For fall admission, 2/1 priority date for domestic students. Applications are processed on a rolling basis. Application fee: $65. Electronic applications accepted. *Financial support:* In 2018–19, 22 students received support, including 8 teaching assistantships with full tuition reimbursements available (averaging $1,600 per year); Federal Work-Study, scholarships/grants, and unspecified assistantships also available. Financial award application deadline: 3/1. *Faculty research:* Gender and leadership, virtual reality, using writing to improve performance in athletics, digital citizenship, professional development for special and general education. *Total annual research expenditures:* $2.1 million. *Unit head:* Dr. Jim Artesani, Associate Dean of Accreditation and Graduate Affairs, 207-581-4061. *Application contact:* Scott G. Delcourt, Assistant Vice President for Graduate Studies and Senior Associate Dean, 207-581-3291, Fax: 207-581-3232, E-mail: graduate@maine.edu. Website: http://umaine.edu/edhd/

University of Mary, Liffrig Family School of Education and Behavioral Sciences, Department of Education, Bismarck, ND 58504-9652. Offers curriculum, instruction and assessment (M Ed); education (Ed D); elementary administration (M Ed); reading (M Ed); secondary administration (M Ed); special education strategist (M Ed). *Program availability:* Part-time. *Degree requirements:* For master's, portfolio or thesis. *Entrance requirements:* For master's, interview, letters of reference, minimum GPA of 2.5. Additional exam requirements/recommendations for international students: Required—TOEFL (minimum score 500 paper-based; 71 iBT). Electronic applications accepted.

University of Maryland, College Park, Academic Affairs, College of Education, Department of Teaching, Learning, Policy and Leadership, College Park, MD 20742. Offers reading (M Ed, MA, PhD, CAGS); secondary education (M Ed, MA, Ed D, PhD, CAGS); teaching English to speakers of other languages (M Ed). *Accreditation:* NCATE. *Program availability:* Part-time, evening/weekend, online learning. *Degree requirements:* For master's, comprehensive exam, seminar paper; for doctorate, comprehensive exam, thesis/dissertation, published paper, oral exam. *Entrance requirements:* For master's, GRE General Test or MAT, minimum GPA of 3.0, 3 letters of recommendation; for doctorate, GRE General Test or MAT, minimum undergraduate GPA of 3.0, graduate 3.5; 3 letters of recommendation. Electronic applications accepted. *Faculty research:* Teacher preparation, curriculum study, in-service education.

University of Massachusetts Amherst, Graduate School, College of Education, Program in Education, Amherst, MA 01003. Offers bilingual, English as a second language, and multicultural education (M Ed, Ed S); child study and early education (M Ed); children, families and schools (Ed D, Ed S); early childhood and elementary teacher education (M Ed); educational leadership (M Ed); educational policy and leadership (Ed D); higher education (M Ed); international education (M Ed); language, literacy and culture (Ed D); learning, media and technology (M Ed, Ed S); mathematics, science, and learning technologies (Ed D); reading and writing (M Ed); research, educational measurement and psychometrics (Ed D); school counselor education (M Ed, Ed S); school psychology (Ed S); science education (Ed S); secondary teacher education (M Ed); social justice education (M Ed, Ed D, Ed S); special education (M Ed, Ed D, Ed S); teacher education and school improvement (Ed D, Ed S). *Accreditation:* NCATE. *Program availability:* Part-time, online learning. Terminal master's awarded for partial completion of doctoral program. *Degree requirements:* For doctorate, comprehensive exam, thesis/dissertation. *Entrance requirements:* Additional exam requirements/recommendations for international students: Required—TOEFL (minimum score 550 paper-based; 80 iBT), IELTS (minimum score 6.5). Electronic applications accepted.

University of Memphis, Graduate School, College of Education, Department of Instruction and Curriculum Leadership, Memphis, TN 38152. Offers advanced studies in teaching and learning (M Ed); applied behavior analysis (Graduate Certificate); autism studies (Graduate Certificate); early childhood education (MAT, MS, Ed D); elementary education (MAT); instruction and curriculum (MS, Ed D); instruction design and technology (MS, Ed D); instructional design and technology (Graduate Certificate); literacy, leadership, and coaching (Graduate Certificate); reading (MS, Ed D); school library information specialist (Graduate Certificate); secondary education (MAT); special education (MAT, MS, Ed D); STEM teacher leadership (Graduate Certificate); urban education (Graduate Certificate). *Accreditation:* NCATE (one or more programs are accredited). *Program availability:* Part-time. *Students:* 62 full-time (45 women), 412 part-time (326 women); includes 209 minority (179 Black or African American, non-Hispanic/Latino; 1 American Indian or Alaska Native, non-Hispanic/Latino; 5 Asian, non-Hispanic/Latino; 17 Hispanic/Latino; 7 Two or more races, non-Hispanic/Latino), 4 international. Average age 35. 195 applicants, 91% accepted, 143 enrolled. In 2018, 122 master's, 13 doctorates, 29 other advanced degrees awarded. Terminal master's awarded for partial completion of doctoral program. *Degree requirements:* For master's, comprehensive exam, thesis or alternative; for doctorate, comprehensive exam, thesis/dissertation. *Entrance requirements:* For master's, GRE General Test, PRAXIS, minimum GPA of 2.5, letters of reference; for doctorate, GRE General Test, GRE Subject Test, 2 years of teaching experience, letters of reference, statement of purpose, interview. Additional exam requirements/recommendations for international students: Required—TOEFL (minimum score 550 paper-based; 79 iBT). *Application deadline:* For fall admission, 4/1 priority date for domestic students; for spring admission, 10/1 priority date for domestic students; for summer admission, 2/1 priority date for domestic students. Applications are processed on a rolling basis. Application fee: $35 ($60 for international students). Electronic applications accepted. *Expenses: Tuition, area resident:* Full-time $10,240; part-time $503 per credit hour. Tuition, state resident: full-time $10,464. Tuition, nonresident: full-time $20,224; part-time $991 per credit hour. *Required fees:* $850; $106 per credit hour. *Financial support:* Research assistantships with full tuition reimbursements, teaching assistantships with full tuition reimbursements, career-related internships or fieldwork, Federal Work-Study, institutionally sponsored loans, scholarships/grants, traineeships, and unspecified assistantships available. Support available to part-time students. Financial award application deadline: 2/1; financial

award applicants required to submit FAFSA. *Faculty research:* Effective urban teachers, preparation and retention of urban teachers, technology utilization in schools, field-based teacher preparation programs, effective use of online instruction. *Unit head:* Dr. Christian Mueller, Chair, 901-678-2365, E-mail: cemuellr@memphis.edu. *Application contact:* Dr. Lee Allen, Director of Graduate Programs, 901-678-4073, E-mail: allenlee@memphis.edu.
Website: http://www.memphis.edu/icl/

University of Miami, Graduate School, School of Education and Human Development, Department of Teaching and Learning, Program in Teaching and Learning, Coral Gables, FL 33124. Offers language and literacy learning in multilingual settings (PhD); science, technology, engineering and mathematics (stem) (PhD); special education (PhD). *Faculty:* 14 full-time (10 women), 9 part-time/adjunct (all women). *Students:* 18 full-time (12 women); includes 8 minority (2 Black or African American, non-Hispanic/Latino; 1 Asian, non-Hispanic/Latino; 4 Hispanic/Latino; 1 Two or more races, non-Hispanic/Latino), 6 international. Average age 36. 15 applicants, 33% accepted, 3 enrolled. In 2018, 4 doctorates awarded. *Degree requirements:* For doctorate, thesis/dissertation, electronic portfolio. *Entrance requirements:* For doctorate, GRE General Test. Additional exam requirements/recommendations for international students: Required—TOEFL (minimum score 550 paper-based; 80 iBT); Recommended—IELTS (minimum score 6.5). *Application deadline:* For fall admission, 6/30 for domestic students, 10/1 for international students. Application fee: $75. Electronic applications accepted. *Financial support:* Fellowships, research assistantships, teaching assistantships, health care benefits, tuition waivers (full and partial), and unspecified assistantships available. Financial award application deadline: 3/1; financial award applicants required to submit FAFSA. *Faculty research:* Teacher education, multicultural education, special education, second language acquisition, math and science education. *Unit head:* Dr. Matthew Deroo, Assistant Professor and Program Director, 305-284-5217, Fax: 305-284-6998, E-mail: deroomat@miami.edu. *Application contact:* Lois Heffernan, Graduate Admission Coordinator, 305-284-2167, Fax: 305-284-9395, E-mail: lheffernan@miami.edu.
Website: http://www.education.miami.edu

University of Michigan–Flint, School of Education and Human Services, Department of Education, Flint, MI 48502-1950. Offers curriculum and instruction (Ed S); early childhood education (MA); education (Ed D); educational leadership (Ed S); educational technology (MA), including curriculum and instruction, developer; literacy education (MA); secondary education with certification (MA). *Program availability:* Part-time, evening/weekend, online only, 100% online, mixed mode format (for some programs). *Faculty:* 16 full-time (10 women), 28 part-time/adjunct (14 women). *Students:* 31 full-time (23 women), 179 part-time (135 women); includes 54 minority (42 Black or African American, non-Hispanic/Latino; 3 Asian, non-Hispanic/Latino; 4 Hispanic/Latino; 1 Native Hawaiian or other Pacific Islander, non-Hispanic/Latino; 4 Two or more races, non-Hispanic/Latino), 1 international. Average age 39. 133 applicants, 72% accepted, 61 enrolled. In 2018, 60 master's awarded. *Degree requirements:* For master's, thesis optional; for doctorate, thesis/dissertation. *Entrance requirements:* For master's, bachelor's degree from regionally-accredited institution, minimum overall undergraduate GPA of 3.0 on 4.0 scale; for doctorate, completion of Eds minimum overall graduate GPA of 3.3 (6.0 on a 9.0 scale) or equivalent; at least 3 years of work experience in a P-16 educational institution or in an education-related position; for Ed S, MA or MS in education-related field from accredited institution; minimum overall graduate GPA of 3.0 (6.0 on a 9.0 scale) or equivalent; at least 3 years of work experience in an educational setting. Additional exam requirements/recommendations for international students: Required—TOEFL (minimum score 84 iBT), IELTS (minimum score 6.5). *Application deadline:* For fall admission, 8/1 for domestic students, 5/1 for international students; for winter admission, 11/15 for domestic students, 9/15 for international students; for spring admission, 3/15 for domestic students, 1/15 for international students; for summer admission, 5/15 for domestic students. Applications are processed on a rolling basis. Application fee: $55. Electronic applications accepted. *Expenses:* Contact institution. *Financial support:* Federal Work-Study, scholarships/grants, and unspecified assistantships available. Financial award application deadline: 3/1; financial award applicants required to submit FAFSA. *Unit head:* Dr. Mary Jo Finney, Department Chair/Associate Professor, 810-766-6617, E-mail: mjfinney@umflint.edu. *Application contact:* Matt Bohlen, Director of Graduate Admissions, 810-762-3171, Fax: 810-766-6789, E-mail: mbohlen@umflint.edu.
Website: https://www.umflint.edu/education/graduate-programs

University of Minnesota, Twin Cities Campus, Graduate School, College of Education and Human Development, Department of Curriculum and Instruction, Minneapolis, MN 55455-0213. Offers art education (M Ed, MA, PhD); curriculum and instruction (M Ed, MA, PhD); elementary education (MA, PhD); English education (PhD); language and immersion education (Certificate); learning technologies (MA, PhD); literacy education (MA, PhD); second language education (MA, PhD); social studies education (MA, PhD); STEM education (MA, PhD); teaching (M Ed), including mathematics, science, social studies, teaching; teaching English to speakers of other languages (MA); technology enhanced learning (Certificate). *Faculty:* 33 full-time (18 women). *Students:* 414 full-time (293 women), 247 part-time (170 women); includes 129 minority (16 Black or African American, non-Hispanic/Latino; 3 American Indian or Alaska Native, non-Hispanic/Latino; 38 Asian, non-Hispanic/Latino; 47 Hispanic/Latino; 25 Two or more races, non-Hispanic/Latino), 57 international. Average age 31. 610 applicants, 69% accepted, 349 enrolled. In 2018, 338 master's, 21 doctorates, 41 other advanced degrees awarded. Application fee: $75 ($95 for international students). *Financial support:* In 2018–19, 9 fellowships, 35 research assistantships with full tuition reimbursements (averaging $11,380 per year), 85 teaching assistantships with full tuition reimbursements (averaging $11,180 per year) were awarded. *Faculty research:* Teaching and learning; influence of cultural, linguistic, social, political, and technological factors on teaching, learning and educational research; relationship between educational practice and a democratic and just society; urban education; immigrant education, racial justice and education. *Total annual research expenditures:* $3.9 million. *Unit head:* Dr. Mark Vagle, Chair, 612-625-4006, E-mail: mvagle@umn.edu. *Application contact:* Dr. Mark Vagle, Chair, 612-625-4006, E-mail: mvagle@umn.edu.
Website: http://www.cehd.umn.edu/ci

University of Minnesota, Twin Cities Campus, Graduate School, College of Education and Human Development, Department of Organizational Leadership, Policy and Development, Minneapolis, MN 55455-0213. Offers adult literacy (Certificate); comparative and international development education (MA, PhD); disability policy and services (Certificate); education policy and leadership (M Ed, MA, Ed D, PhD), including educational policy and leadership (MA, Ed D, PhD), leadership in education (M Ed); evaluation studies (MA, PhD); higher education (MA, Ed D, PhD), including higher education (MA, PhD), multicultural college teaching and learning (MA); human resource development (M Ed, MA, Ed D, PhD, Certificate); PK-12 administrative licensure (Certificate); private college leadership (Certificate); professional development (Certificate); program evaluation (Certificate); technical education (Certificate); undergraduate multicultural teaching and learning (Certificate). *Faculty:* 33 full-time (16 women). *Students:* 332 full-time (220 women), 194 part-time (139 women); includes 130 minority (46 Black or African American, non-Hispanic/Latino; 5 American Indian or Alaska Native, non-Hispanic/Latino; 37 Asian, non-Hispanic/Latino; 22 Hispanic/Latino; 20 Two or more races, non-Hispanic/Latino), 75 international. Average age 36. 379 applicants, 68% accepted, 187 enrolled. In 2018, 67 master's, 39 doctorates, 64 other advanced degrees awarded. Application fee: $75 ($95 for international students). *Financial support:* In 2018–19, 6 fellowships, 34 research assistantships with full tuition reimbursements (averaging $10,071 per year), 17 teaching assistantships with full tuition reimbursements (averaging $9,608 per year) were awarded; scholarships/grants also available. *Faculty research:* Organizational issues in schools, universities, and other organizations; international education and development; program evaluation and research on applied evaluation methods; international human resource development and change; gender and race/ethnicity in relation to learning and leadership. *Total annual research expenditures:* $732,047. *Unit head:* Dr. Kenneth Bartlett, Chair, 612-625-1006, Fax: 612-624-3377, E-mail: bartlett@umn.edu. *Application contact:* Dr. Jeremy J. Hernandez, Coordinator of Graduate Studies, 612-626-9377, E-mail: olpd@umn.edu.
Website: http://www.cehd.umn.edu/olpd/

University of Mississippi, Graduate School, School of Education, University, MS 38677. Offers counselor education (M Ed, PhD); counselor education - play therapy (Ed S); early childhood (M Ed); educational leadership K-12 (M Ed, Ed D, PhD, Ed S); elementary education (M Ed, Ed D, Ed S); higher education/student personnel (Ed D, PhD); literacy education (M Ed); math education (Ed D); secondary education (M Ed, PhD, Ed S); special education (M Ed, PhD, Ed S); teacher corporations (MA); teacher education (MA). *Accreditation:* NCATE. *Faculty:* 59 full-time (35 women), 34 part-time/adjunct (26 women). *Students:* 169 full-time (137 women), 461 part-time (329 women); includes 199 minority (185 Black or African American, non-Hispanic/Latino; 3 Asian, non-Hispanic/Latino; 7 Hispanic/Latino; 4 Two or more races, non-Hispanic/Latino), 5 international. Average age 33. In 2018, 180 master's, 57 doctorates, 37 other advanced degrees awarded. *Entrance requirements:* For master's, GRE General Test, minimum GPA of 3.0; for doctorate, GRE General Test. Additional exam requirements/recommendations for international students: Required—TOEFL. *Application deadline:* Applications are processed on a rolling basis. Application fee: $50. Electronic applications accepted. *Financial support:* Scholarships/grants available. Financial award application deadline: 3/1; financial award applicants required to submit FAFSA. *Unit head:* Dr. David Rock, Dean, 662-915-7063, Fax: 662-915-7249, E-mail: soe@olemiss.edu. *Application contact:* Temeka Smith, Graduate Activities Specialist for Admissions, 662-915-7474, Fax: 662-915-7577, E-mail: gschool@olemiss.edu.

University of Missouri, Office of Research and Graduate Studies, College of Education, Department of Learning, Teaching and Curriculum, Columbia, MO 65211. Offers agricultural education (M Ed, PhD, Ed S); art education (M Ed, PhD, Ed S); business and office education (M Ed, PhD, Ed S); early childhood education (M Ed, PhD, Ed S); elementary education (M Ed, PhD, Ed S); English education (M Ed, PhD, Ed S); foreign language education (M Ed, PhD, Ed S); health education and promotion (M Ed, PhD); learning and instruction (M Ed); marketing education (M Ed, PhD, Ed S); mathematics education (M Ed, PhD, Ed S); music education (M Ed, PhD, Ed S); reading education (M Ed, PhD, Ed S); science education (M Ed, PhD, Ed S); social studies education (M Ed, PhD, Ed S); vocational education (M Ed, PhD, Ed S). *Program availability:* Part-time. Terminal master's awarded for partial completion of doctoral program. *Entrance requirements:* For master's and Ed S, GRE General Test or MAT, minimum GPA of 3.0; for doctorate, GRE General Test, minimum GPA of 3.0. Additional exam requirements/recommendations for international students: Required—TOEFL.

University of Missouri–Kansas City, School of Education, Kansas City, MO 64110-2499. Offers administration (Ed D); counseling and guidance (MA, Ed S), including mental health counseling (Ed S), school counseling (Ed S); counseling psychology (PhD); curriculum and instruction (MA, Ed S), including language and literacy (Ed S); education (PhD), including higher education administration, PK-12 education administration; educational administration (MA, Ed S), including advanced principal (Ed S), beginning principal (Ed S), district-level administration (Ed S); reading education (MA); special education (MA). PhD in education offered through the School of Graduate Studies. *Accreditation:* NCATE. *Program availability:* Part-time, evening/weekend. *Degree requirements:* For doctorate, thesis/dissertation, internship, practicum. *Entrance requirements:* For master's, GRE, minimum GPA of 2.75, 2 letters of reference, written statement of purpose; for doctorate, GRE, minimum GPA of 3.0; for Ed S, minimum GPA of 3.0. Additional exam requirements/recommendations for international students: Required—TOEFL (minimum score 550 paper-based; 80 iBT). *Faculty research:* Urban education, inquiry-based field study, theories of counseling and psychotherapy, school literacy, educational technology.

University of Missouri–St. Louis, College of Education, Department of Educator Preparation, Innovation and Research, St. Louis, MO 63121. Offers elementary education (M Ed), including early childhood, general, reading; secondary education (M Ed), including curriculum and instruction, general, middle level education, reading, teaching English to speakers of other languages (TESOL); special education (M Ed), including autism and developmental disabilities, early childhood special education. *Program availability:* Part-time, evening/weekend. *Degree requirements:* For master's, comprehensive exam. *Entrance requirements:* Additional exam requirements/recommendations for international students: Recommended—TOEFL (minimum score 550 paper-based; 79 iBT), IELTS (minimum score 6.5). Electronic applications accepted.

University of Nebraska at Kearney, College of Education, Department of Teacher Education, Kearney, NE 68849-0001. Offers curriculum and instruction (MA Ed), including early childhood education, elementary education, English as a second language, instructional effectiveness, reading/special education, secondary education; instructional technology (MS Ed), including information technology, instructional technology, school librarian; reading PK-12 (MA Ed); special education (MA Ed), including advanced practitioner: assistive technology specialist, advanced practitioner: behavioral interventionist, advanced practitioner: inclusive collaboration specialist, gifted, teacher education. *Program availability:* Part-time, evening/weekend, online only, 100% online. *Degree requirements:* For master's, comprehensive exam, thesis optional. *Entrance requirements:* For master's, portfolio or GRE. Additional exam requirements/recommendations for international students: Recommended—TOEFL (minimum score 550 paper-based; 79 iBT), IELTS (minimum score 6.5). Electronic applications accepted. *Expenses:* Contact institution.

University of Nevada, Reno, Graduate School, College of Education, Department of Educational Specialties, Program in Literacy Studies, Reno, NV 89557. Offers M Ed, MA, Ed D, PhD. Terminal master's awarded for partial completion of doctoral program. *Degree requirements:* For master's, thesis optional; for doctorate, thesis/dissertation. *Entrance requirements:* For master's, minimum GPA of 2.75; for doctorate, GRE General Test, minimum GPA of 3.0. Additional exam requirements/recommendations for international students: Required—TOEFL (minimum score 500 paper-based; 61 iBT), IELTS (minimum score 6). Electronic applications accepted. *Faculty research:* Cognitive language process, literacy.

University of New England, College of Graduate and Professional Studies, Portland, ME 04005-9526. Offers advanced educational leadership (CAGS); applied nutrition (MS); career and technical education (MS Ed); curriculum and instruction (MS Ed); education (CAGS, Post-Master's Certificate); educational leadership (MS Ed, Ed D);

generalist (MS Ed); health informatics (MS, Graduate Certificate); inclusion education (MS Ed); literacy K-12 (MS Ed); medical education leadership (MMEL); public health (MPH, Graduate Certificate); reading specialist (MS Ed); social work (MSW). *Program availability:* Part-time, evening/weekend, online only, 100% online. *Faculty:* 109 part-time/adjunct (78 women). *Students:* 1,207 full-time (972 women), 561 part-time (450 women); includes 411 minority (280 Black or African American, non-Hispanic/Latino; 17 American Indian or Alaska Native, non-Hispanic/Latino; 74 Asian, non-Hispanic/Latino; 25 Hispanic/Latino; 9 Native Hawaiian or other Pacific Islander, non-Hispanic/Latino; 6 Two or more races, non-Hispanic/Latino). Average age 36. 740 applicants, 92% accepted, 494 enrolled. In 2018, 586 master's, 44 doctorates, 85 other advanced degrees awarded. *Application deadline:* Applications are processed on a rolling basis. Electronic applications accepted. *Financial support:* Application deadline: 5/1; applicants required to submit FAFSA. *Unit head:* Dr. Martha Wilson, Dean of the College of Graduate and Professional Studies, 207-221-4985, E-mail: mwilson13@une.edu. *Application contact:* Nicole Lindsay, Director of Online Admissions, 207-221-4966, E-mail: nlindsay1@une.edu.
Website: http://online.une.edu

University of New Mexico, Graduate Studies, College of Education, Program in Language, Literacy and Sociocultural Studies, Albuquerque, NM 87131-2039. Offers American Indian education (MA); bilingual education (MA, PhD); educational linguistics (PhD); educational thought and sociocultural studies (MA, PhD); literacy/language arts (MA, PhD); social studies (MA); TESOL (MA, PhD). *Students:* Average age 40. 61 applicants, 38% accepted, 23 enrolled. In 2018, 36 master's, 4 doctorates awarded. *Degree requirements:* For master's, comprehensive exam, thesis optional; for doctorate, comprehensive exam, thesis/dissertation, research skills. *Entrance requirements:* For master's, letter of intent, 3 letters of recommendation, resume, BA/BS, department demographic form, transcripts; for doctorate, writing sample, letter of intent, 3 letters of recommendation, resume, BA/BS, MA, department demographic form, transcripts. Additional exam requirements/recommendations for international students: Required—TOEFL. *Application deadline:* For fall admission, 12/1 for domestic and international students; for spring admission, 9/15 for domestic and international students. Application fee: $50. Electronic applications accepted. *Financial support:* Fellowships, research assistantships, teaching assistantships, career-related internships or fieldwork, institutionally sponsored loans, scholarships/grants, and unspecified assistantships available. Support available to part-time students. Financial award application deadline: 3/1; financial award applicants required to submit FAFSA. *Faculty research:* School reform, professional development, history of education, Native American education, politics of education, feminism and issues of sexual identity, critical race theory, bilingualism, literacy reading, adolescent literature, second language acquisition, critical theory and schooling, indigenous languages. *Unit head:* Dr. Lois M. Meyer, Chair, 505-277-7244, Fax: 505-277-8362, E-mail: lsmeyer@unm.edu. *Application contact:* Debra Schaffer, Administrative Assistant, 505-277-0437, Fax: 505-277-8362, E-mail: schaffer@unm.edu.
Website: http://coe.unm.edu/departments-programs/llss/index.html

The University of North Carolina at Chapel Hill, Graduate School, School of Education, Program in Education, Chapel Hill, NC 27599. Offers culture, curriculum and change (MA, PhD); early childhood, intervention and literacy (MA, PhD); educational psychology, measurement and evaluation (MA, PhD). *Accreditation:* NCATE. *Degree requirements:* For master's, thesis; for doctorate, comprehensive exam, thesis/dissertation. *Entrance requirements:* For master's, GRE General Test, minimum GPA of 3.0 during last 2 years of undergraduates course work; for doctorate, GRE General Test, minimum GPA of 3.0 during last 2 years of undergraduate course work. Additional exam requirements/recommendations for international students: Required—TOEFL (minimum score 550 paper-based). Electronic applications accepted.

The University of North Carolina at Charlotte, Cato College of Education, Department of Reading and Elementary Education, Charlotte, NC 28223-0001. Offers elementary education (M Ed, Graduate Certificate); elementary mathematics education (Graduate Certificate); reading education (M Ed). *Program availability:* Part-time, evening/weekend, 100% online, blended/hybrid learning. *Students:* 58 part-time (all women); includes 15 minority (12 Black or African American, non-Hispanic/Latino; 1 American Indian or Alaska Native, non-Hispanic/Latino; 2 Two or more races, non-Hispanic/Latino). Average age 31. 39 applicants, 95% accepted, 35 enrolled. In 2018, 29 master's, 23 other advanced degrees awarded. *Entrance requirements:* For master's, GRE or MAT, three letters of recommendation, official transcripts, academic and professional goals statement, valid teacher's license, bachelor's degree in elementary education; NC A-level license or its equivalent in another state (for reading education). Additional exam requirements/recommendations for international students: Required—TOEFL (minimum score 523 paper-based; 70 iBT), IELTS (minimum score 6), TOEFL (minimum score 523 paper-based, 70 iBT) or IELTS (6). *Application deadline:* Applications are processed on a rolling basis. Application fee: $75. Electronic applications accepted. Tuition and fees vary according to course load and program. *Financial support:* Research assistantships, career-related internships or fieldwork, institutionally sponsored loans, scholarships/grants, and unspecified assistantships available. Support available to part-time students. Financial award application deadline: 3/1; financial award applicants required to submit FAFSA. *Total annual research expenditures:* $146,699. *Unit head:* Dr. Mike Putman, Chair, 704-687-8019, E-mail: michael.putman@uncc.edu. *Application contact:* Kathy B. Giddings, Director of Graduate Admissions, 704-687-5503, Fax: 704-687-1668, E-mail: gradadm@uncc.edu.
Website: http://reel.uncc.edu/

The University of North Carolina at Greensboro, Graduate School, School of Education, Department of Teacher Education and Higher Education, Greensboro, NC 27412-5001. Offers college teaching and adult learning (Certificate); curriculum and instruction (M Ed), including chemistry education, elementary education, English as a second language, French education, instructional technology, mathematics education, middle grades education, reading education, science education, social studies education, Spanish education; curriculum and teaching (PhD), including higher education, teacher education and development; English as a second language (Certificate); higher education (M Ed); supervision (M Ed). *Accreditation:* NCATE. *Program availability:* Part-time. *Degree requirements:* For doctorate, thesis/dissertation. *Entrance requirements:* For master's and doctorate, GRE General Test. Additional exam requirements/recommendations for international students: Required—TOEFL. Electronic applications accepted. *Faculty research:* Community college literacy program, middle school mathematics/computer mathematics.

The University of North Carolina at Pembroke, The Graduate School, School of Education, Program in Reading Education, Pembroke, NC 28372-1510. Offers MA Ed. *Accreditation:* NCATE. *Program availability:* Part-time, evening/weekend. *Degree requirements:* For master's, comprehensive exam, thesis optional. *Entrance requirements:* For master's, GRE General Test or MAT, minimum GPA of 3.0 in major, 2.5 overall; teaching license; one year of teaching experience; three professional references. Additional exam requirements/recommendations for international students: Required—TOEFL.

The University of North Carolina Wilmington, Watson College of Education, Department of Early Childhood, Elementary, Middle, Literacy and Special Education,

Wilmington, NC 28403-3297. Offers educational leadership, policy, and advocacy (M Ed); elementary education (M Ed, MAT); language and literacy (M Ed); middle grades education (MAT). *Accreditation:* NCATE. *Program availability:* Part-time, blended/hybrid learning. *Degree requirements:* For master's, thesis or alternative, exit portfolio, oral presentation, internship, research project (depending on specialization). *Entrance requirements:* For master's, 3 letters of recommendations, NC Class A teacher license in related field, education statement of interest essay. Additional exam requirements/recommendations for international students: Required—TOEFL (minimum score 550 paper-based; 79 iBT), IELTS (minimum score 6.5). Electronic applications accepted.

University of North Dakota, Graduate School, College of Education and Human Development, Program in Reading Education, Grand Forks, ND 58202. Offers M Ed, MS. *Accreditation:* NCATE. *Program availability:* Part-time, online learning. *Degree requirements:* For master's, comprehensive exam, thesis or alternative. *Entrance requirements:* For master's, minimum GPA of 3.0. Additional exam requirements/recommendations for international students: Required—TOEFL (minimum score 550 paper-based; 79 iBT), IELTS (minimum score 6.5). Electronic applications accepted. *Faculty research:* Whole language, multicultural education, child-focused learning, experiential science, cooperative learning.

University of Northern Colorado, Graduate School, College of Education and Behavioral Sciences, School of Teacher Education, Program in Literacy, Greeley, CO 80639. Offers MA. *Accreditation:* NCATE. *Program availability:* Part-time, evening/weekend, online learning. *Degree requirements:* For master's, comprehensive exam, thesis or alternative. *Entrance requirements:* For master's, GRE General Test (if undergraduate GPA less than 3.0), resume, letters of reference. Electronic applications accepted.

University of Northern Iowa, Graduate College, College of Education, Department of Curriculum and Instruction, MAE Program in Literacy Education, Cedar Falls, IA 50614. Offers MAE. *Program availability:* Part-time, evening/weekend. *Degree requirements:* For master's, comprehensive exam, thesis or alternative. *Entrance requirements:* For master's, writing exam, minimum GPA of 3.0, two recommendations from professional educators. Additional exam requirements/recommendations for international students: Required—TOEFL (minimum score 500 paper-based; 61 iBT). Electronic applications accepted.

University of North Florida, College of Education and Human Services, Department of Childhood Education, Literacy, and TESOL, Jacksonville, FL 32224. Offers literacy (M Ed); professional education (M Ed); TESOL (M Ed). *Accreditation:* NCATE. *Program availability:* Part-time, evening/weekend. *Faculty:* 9 full-time (6 women), 3 part-time/adjunct (2 women). *Students:* 12 full-time (all women), 23 part-time (20 women); includes 15 minority (10 Black or African American, non-Hispanic/Latino; 4 Hispanic/Latino; 1 Two or more races, non-Hispanic/Latino), 2 international. Average age 32. 18 applicants, 67% accepted, 8 enrolled. In 2018, 14 master's awarded. *Entrance requirements:* For master's, GRE General Test, minimum GPA of 3.0 in last 60 hours, 3 letters of recommendation, interview. Additional exam requirements/recommendations for international students: Required—TOEFL (minimum score 500 paper-based). *Application deadline:* For fall admission, 8/1 priority date for domestic students, 5/1 for international students; for spring admission, 12/1 priority date for domestic students, 10/1 for international students; for summer admission, 3/15 priority date for domestic students, 2/1 for international students. Application fee: $30. Electronic applications accepted. *Expenses:* Tuition, area resident: Part-time $408.10 per credit hour. Tuition, state resident: part-time $408.10 per credit hour. Tuition, nonresident: part-time $932.61 per credit hour. *Required fees:* $111.81 per credit hour. Tuition and fees vary according to course load, campus/location and program. *Financial support:* In 2018–19, 2 students received support. Federal Work-Study, tuition waivers (partial), and unspecified assistantships available. Support available to part-time students. Financial award application deadline: 4/1; financial award applicants required to submit FAFSA. *Faculty research:* Social context of and processes in learning, inter-disciplinary instruction, cross-cultural conflict resolution, the Vygotskian perspective on literacy diagnosis and instruction, performance poetry and teaching the language arts through drama. *Total annual research expenditures:* $630. *Unit head:* Dr. Paul Parkison, Chair, 904-620-5352, Fax: 904-620-1025, E-mail: n01230143@unf.edu. *Application contact:* Dr. Amanda Pascale, Director, The Graduate School, 904-620-1360, Fax: 904-620-1362, E-mail: graduateschool@unf.edu.
Website: http://www.unf.edu/coehs/celt/

University of Oklahoma, College of Arts and Sciences, Department of English, Norman, OK 73019. Offers literary and cultural studies (MA, PhD); writing and rhetoric studies (MA, PhD). *Program availability:* Part-time. *Faculty:* 25 full-time (13 women). *Students:* 26 full-time (22 women), 16 part-time (7 women); includes 13 minority (1 Black or African American, non-Hispanic/Latino; 2 American Indian or Alaska Native, non-Hispanic/Latino; 2 Asian, non-Hispanic/Latino; 5 Hispanic/Latino; 3 Two or more races, non-Hispanic/Latino), 2 international. Average age 31. 38 applicants, 45% accepted, 6 enrolled. In 2018, 9 master's, 3 doctorates awarded. *Degree requirements:* For master's, one foreign language, comprehensive exam (for some programs), thesis (for some programs), exam or thesis; for doctorate, one foreign language, comprehensive exam, thesis/dissertation. *Entrance requirements:* For master's, GRE, BA in English or related field; for doctorate, GRE, MA in English or related field. Additional exam requirements/recommendations for international students: Required—TOEFL (minimum score 79 iBT) or IELTS (minimum score 6.5). *Application deadline:* For fall admission, 1/5 priority date for domestic and international students. Application fee: $50 ($100 for international students). Electronic applications accepted. *Expenses:* Tuition, state resident: full-time $5683.20; part-time $236.80 per credit hour. Tuition, nonresident: full-time $20,342; part-time $847.60 per credit hour. International tuition: $20,342.40 full-time. *Required fees:* $2894.20; $110.05 per credit hour. $126.50 per semester. Tuition and fees vary according to course load and program. *Financial support:* In 2018–19, 40 students received support, including 6 research assistantships with full tuition reimbursements available (averaging $14,515 per year), 31 teaching assistantships with full tuition reimbursements available (averaging $12,496 per year); fellowships with full tuition reimbursements available, scholarships/grants, health care benefits, and unspecified assistantships also available. Financial award application deadline: 6/1; financial award applicants required to submit FAFSA. *Faculty research:* American Indian literature and culture; composition and rhetoric; American literature; British literature; postcolonial literature and culture. *Total annual research expenditures:* $101. *Unit head:* Dr. Daniela Garofalo, Professor and Chair, 405-325-4661, Fax: 405-325-0831, E-mail: dg@ou.edu. *Application contact:* Sara Day, Graduate Assistant, 405-325-0489, Fax: 405-325-0831, E-mail: redpanda@ou.edu.
Website: http://cas.ou.edu/english

University of Oklahoma, Jeannine Rainbolt College of Education, Department of Instructional Leadership and Academic Curriculum, Norman, OK 73072. Offers instructional leadership and academic curriculum (M Ed, PhD), including biomedical education (PhD), early childhood education, elementary education, English education, instructional leadership, mathematics education, reading education, science education, social studies education, world languages education (M Ed); reading specialist (M Ed). *Accreditation:* NCATE. *Program availability:* Part-time. *Faculty:* 26 full-time (12 women),

1 part-time/adjunct (0 women). *Students:* 42 full-time (32 women), 113 part-time (85 women); includes 33 minority (9 Black or African American, non-Hispanic/Latino; 5 American Indian or Alaska Native, non-Hispanic/Latino; 6 Asian, non-Hispanic/Latino; 4 Hispanic/Latino; 1 Native Hawaiian or other Pacific Islander, non-Hispanic/Latino; 8 Two or more races, non-Hispanic/Latino), 9 international. Average age 35. 42 applicants, 79% accepted, 21 enrolled. In 2018, 30 master's, 17 doctorates awarded. Terminal master's awarded for partial completion of doctoral program. *Degree requirements:* For master's, comprehensive exam (for some programs), thesis (for some programs); for doctorate, comprehensive exam (for some programs), thesis/dissertation. *Entrance requirements:* For doctorate, GRE. Additional exam requirements/recommendations for international students: Required—TOEFL (minimum score 79 iBT) or IELTS (minimum score 6.5). Application fee: $50 ($100 for international students). Electronic applications accepted. *Expenses:* Tuition, state resident: full-time $5683.20; part-time $236.80 per credit hour. Tuition, nonresident: full-time $20,342; part-time $847.60 per credit hour. *International tuition:* $20,342.40 full-time. *Required fees:* $2894.20; $110.05 per credit hour. $126.50 per semester. Tuition and fees vary according to course load and program. *Financial support:* Fellowships, research assistantships, teaching assistantships, scholarships/grants, and unspecified assistantships available. Financial award application deadline: 6/1; financial award applicants required to submit FAFSA. *Faculty research:* Teacher preparation; instruction; curriculum; learning; constructivist theory. *Unit head:* Dr. Stacy Reeder, Chair, 405-325-1498, Fax: 405-325-4061, E-mail: reeder@ou.edu. *Application contact:* Anna Steele, Graduate Programs Officer, 405-325-4525, E-mail: anna.steele@ou.edu.
Website: http://www.ou.edu/education/ilac

University of Oklahoma Health Sciences Center, Graduate College, College of Allied Health, Department of Communication Sciences and Disorders, Oklahoma City, OK 73190. Offers audiology (MS, Au D, PhD); communication sciences and disorders (Certificate), including reading, speech-language pathology; education of the deaf (MS); speech-language pathology (MS, PhD). *Accreditation:* ASHA (one or more programs are accredited). *Program availability:* Part-time. Terminal master's awarded for partial completion of doctoral program. *Degree requirements:* For master's, comprehensive exam, thesis optional; for doctorate, one foreign language, comprehensive exam, thesis/dissertation. *Entrance requirements:* For master's and doctorate, GRE General Test, 3 letters of recommendation. Additional exam requirements/recommendations for international students: Required—TOEFL (minimum score 550 paper-based). *Faculty research:* Event-related potentials, cleft palate, fluency disorders, language disorders, hearing and speech science.

University of Pennsylvania, Graduate School of Education, Division of Literacy, Culture, and International Education, Program in Language and Literacy, Philadelphia, PA 19104. Offers MS Ed. *Students:* 1 (woman) full-time. 19 applicants, 42% accepted, 1 enrolled. In 2018, 1 master's awarded. Application fee: $80.

University of Phoenix–Online Campus, College of Education, Phoenix, AZ 85034-7209. Offers administration and supervision (MAEd, Certificate); adult education and training (MAEd); curriculum and instruction (MAEd), including computer education, curriculum and instruction, English as a second language, language arts, mathematics, reading; early childhood education (MAEd); educational studies (MAEd); elementary teacher education (MAEd), including early childhood, elementary teacher education, high school middle level, middle level; principal licensure (Certificate); secondary teacher education (MAEd); special education (MAEd, Certificate); teacher education (MAEd), including middle level generalist; teacher education middle level mathematics (MAEd), including middle level mathematics; teacher education middle level science (MAEd), including middle level science; teacher education secondary mathematics (MAEd); teacher education secondary science (MAEd); teacher leadership (MAEd); teachers of English learners (Certificate); transition to teaching (Certificate), including elementary education, secondary education. *Program availability:* Evening/weekend, online learning. *Entrance requirements:* Additional exam requirements/recommendations for international students: Required—TOEFL, TOEIC (Test of English as an International Communication), Berlitz Online English Proficiency Exam, PTE, or IELTS. Electronic applications accepted. *Expenses:* Contact institution.

University of Phoenix–Phoenix Campus, College of Education, Tempe, AZ 85282-2371. Offers administration and supervision (MA Ed); adult education and training (MA Ed); curriculum and instruction reading (MA Ed); early childhood education (MA Ed); education studies (MA Ed); elementary teacher education (MA Ed); secondary teacher education (MA Ed); special education (MA Ed); teacher leadership (MA Ed). *Program availability:* Evening/weekend, online learning. *Entrance requirements:* Additional exam requirements/recommendations for international students: Required—TOEFL, TOEIC (Test of English as an International Communication), Berlitz Online English Proficiency Exam, PTE, or IELTS. Electronic applications accepted. *Expenses:* Contact institution.

University of Pittsburgh, School of Education, Department of Instruction and Learning, Program in Reading Education, Pittsburgh, PA 15260. Offers M Ed, Ed D, PhD. *Degree requirements:* For master's, thesis; for doctorate, thesis/dissertation. *Entrance requirements:* For master's, PRAXIS I; for doctorate, GRE General Test. Additional exam requirements/recommendations for international students: Required—TOEFL.

University of Pittsburgh, School of Education, Department of Instruction and Learning, Program in Secondary Education, Pittsburgh, PA 15260. Offers English and communications education (M Ed, MAT); foreign language education (M Ed, MAT); language, literacy and culture education (Ed D, PhD); mathematics education (M Ed, MAT, Ed D, PhD); science education (M Ed, MAT, Ed D, PhD); secondary education (PhD); social studies education (M Ed, MAT); STEM education (Ed D). *Program availability:* Part-time, evening/weekend. *Degree requirements:* For master's, thesis; for doctorate, thesis/dissertation. *Entrance requirements:* For master's, PRAXIS I; for doctorate, GRE General Test. Additional exam requirements/recommendations for international students: Required—TOEFL. Electronic applications accepted.

University of Portland, School of Education, Portland, OR 97203-5798. Offers education (MA, MAT); educational leadership (M Ed); English for speakers of other languages (M Ed); initial administrator licensure (M Ed); neuroeducation (M Ed, Ed D); organizational leadership and development (Ed D); reading (M Ed); school leadership and development (Ed D); special education (M Ed). *Accreditation:* NCATE. *Program availability:* Part-time, evening/weekend. *Students:* 32 full-time (30 women), 239 part-time (187 women); includes 33 minority (7 Black or African American, non-Hispanic/Latino; 3 American Indian or Alaska Native, non-Hispanic/Latino; 13 Asian, non-Hispanic/Latino; 1 Native Hawaiian or other Pacific Islander, non-Hispanic/Latino; 9 Two or more races, non-Hispanic/Latino). Average age 34. 92 applicants, 60% accepted, 42 enrolled. In 2018, 57 master's, 16 doctorates awarded. *Degree requirements:* For doctorate, thesis/dissertation. *Entrance requirements:* For master's, minimum GPA of 3.0, teaching certificate, letters of recommendation, resume, statement of goals, official transcripts; for doctorate, 2 letters of recommendation, resume, essays, official transcripts. Additional exam requirements/recommendations for international students: Required—TOEFL (minimum score 550 paper-based; 80 iBT), IELTS (minimum score 7). *Application deadline:* For fall admission, 7/15 priority date for domestic and international students; for spring admission, 12/15 priority date for domestic and international students; for summer admission, 4/15 for domestic and international students. Applications are processed on a rolling basis. Electronic applications accepted. *Expenses:* MAT degree - $995/credit hour; EDD and Educational Specialist - $813/credit hour; all other degrees and certificates - $663/credit hour. *Financial support:* Fellowships, Federal Work-Study, and scholarships/grants available. Support available to part-time students. Financial award application deadline: 3/1; financial award applicants required to submit FAFSA. *Faculty research:* Multicultural education, supervision/leadership. *Unit head:* Dr. Bruce Weitzel, Associate Dean, 503-943-7135, E-mail: soed@up.edu. *Application contact:* Caitlin Biddulph, Graduate Programs and Admissions Specialist, 503-943-7107, E-mail: biddulph@up.edu.
Website: http://education.up.edu/default.aspx?cid-4318&pid-5590

University of Rhode Island, Graduate School, Alan Shawn Feinstein College of Education and Professional Studies, School of Education, Kingston, RI 02881. Offers education (PhD); reading (MA); special education (MA). *Accreditation:* NCATE. *Program availability:* Part-time, evening/weekend. *Faculty:* 19 full-time (13 women). *Students:* 53 full-time (35 women), 151 part-time (124 women); includes 28 minority (13 Black or African American, non-Hispanic/Latino; 3 American Indian or Alaska Native, non-Hispanic/Latino; 4 Asian, non-Hispanic/Latino; 5 Hispanic/Latino; 3 Two or more races, non-Hispanic/Latino), 6 international. 79 applicants, 71% accepted, 44 enrolled. In 2018, 54 master's, 6 doctorates awarded. *Entrance requirements:* For master's, 2 letters of recommendation; personal statement; two official transcripts; interview and minimum undergraduate GPA of 3.0 (for special education applicants); for doctorate, GRE, 3 letters of recommendation, resume, personal statement, two copies of official transcripts. Additional exam requirements/recommendations for international students: Required—TOEFL. Application fee: $65. Electronic applications accepted. *Expenses: Tuition, area resident:* Full-time $13,226; part-time $735 per credit. Tuition, state resident: full-time $13,226; part-time $735 per credit. Tuition, nonresident: full-time $25,854; part-time $1436 per credit. *International tuition:* $25,854 full-time. *Required fees:* $1698; $50 per credit. $35 per semester. One-time fee: $165. *Financial support:* In 2018–19, 1 research assistantship with tuition reimbursement (averaging $9,040 per year), 4 teaching assistantships with tuition reimbursements (averaging $15,776 per year) were awarded. Financial award applicants required to submit FAFSA. *Unit head:* Dr. David Byrd, Director, School of Education, 401-874-5484, Fax: 401-874-5471, E-mail: dbyrd@uri.edu. *Application contact:* Dr. David Byrd, Director, School of Education, 401-874-5484, Fax: 401-874-5471, E-mail: dbyrd@uri.edu.
Website: https://web.uri.edu/education/

University of St. Francis, College of Education, Joliet, IL 60435-6169. Offers educational leadership (MS, Ed D); elementary education (M Ed); reading (MS); secondary education (M Ed), including English education, math education, science education, social studies education, visual arts education; special education (M Ed); teaching and learning (MS); TESOL (Certificate). *Accreditation:* NCATE. *Program availability:* Part-time, evening/weekend, 100% online, blended/hybrid learning. *Faculty:* 11 full-time (8 women), 58 part-time/adjunct (38 women). *Students:* 43 full-time (35 women), 453 part-time (354 women); includes 110 minority (48 Black or African American, non-Hispanic/Latino; 7 Asian, non-Hispanic/Latino; 52 Hispanic/Latino; 3 Two or more races, non-Hispanic/Latino), 3 international. Average age 37. 300 applicants, 66% accepted, 164 enrolled. In 2018, 151 master's, 42 doctorates, 4 other advanced degrees awarded. *Degree requirements:* For master's, comprehensive exam; for doctorate, thesis/dissertation. *Entrance requirements:* Additional exam requirements/recommendations for international students: Required—TOEFL (minimum score 550 paper-based; 79 iBT), IELTS (minimum score 6). *Application deadline:* Applications are processed on a rolling basis. Electronic applications accepted. Application fee is waived when completed online. *Expenses:* Contact institution. *Financial support:* In 2018–19, 33 students received support. Scholarships/grants and tuition waivers (partial) available. Support available to part-time students. Financial award applicants required to submit FAFSA. *Unit head:* Dr. John Gambro, Dean, 815-740-3456, E-mail: jgambro@stfrancis.edu. *Application contact:* Sandee Sloka, Director Adult & Graduate Admissions, 800-735-7500, E-mail: ssloka@stfrancis.edu.
Website: https://www.stfrancis.edu/education/

University of Saint Joseph, Department of Education, West Hartford, CT 06117-2700. Offers curriculum and instruction (MA); elementary education (MAT); instructional technology (MA); literacy (MA); secondary education (MAT); TESOL (MA). *Program availability:* Part-time, evening/weekend. *Degree requirements:* For master's, comprehensive exam, thesis or alternative. *Entrance requirements:* For master's, 2 letters of recommendation. Electronic applications accepted. Application fee is waived when completed online.

University of St. Thomas, School of Education and Human Services, Houston, TX 77006-4696. Offers all level education (M Ed); bilingual/dual language (M Ed); Catholic school teaching (M Ed); Catholic/private school leadership (M Ed); counselor education (M Ed); curriculum and instruction (M Ed); education (Ed D); educational leadership (M Ed); elementary teaching (M Ed); English as a second language (M Ed); exceptionality/educational diagnostician (M Ed); exceptionality/special education (M Ed); generalist (M Ed); reading (M Ed); secondary teaching (M Ed); teaching (MAT). *Accreditation:* TEAC. *Program availability:* Part-time, evening/weekend, online learning. *Degree requirements:* For master's, thesis, field experience. *Entrance requirements:* For master's, GRE or MAT if GPA is below 3.0, bachelor's degree; minimum GPA of 2.75 in bachelor's degree or last 60 credit hours; official transcripts from all institutions; goal statement of 250-300 words; 1 reference. Additional exam requirements/recommendations for international students: Required—TOEFL (minimum score 94 iBT), IELTS (minimum score 7), PTE (minimum score 53). Electronic applications accepted. *Expenses:* Contact institution. *Faculty research:* Leadership, diversity, personality traits, second language acquisition.

University of San Diego, School of Leadership and Education Sciences, Department of Learning and Teaching, San Diego, CA 92110-2492. Offers curriculum and instruction (M Ed), including inclusive learning, literacy and digital learning, school leadership, steam (science, technology, engineering, arts, and mathematics); inclusive learning (M Ed); literacy and digital learning (M Ed); school leadership (M Ed); special education (M Ed); STEAM (science, technology, engineering, arts, and mathematics) (M Ed); TESOL, literacy and culture (M Ed). *Program availability:* Part-time, evening/weekend. *Faculty:* 9 full-time (7 women), 34 part-time/adjunct (26 women). *Students:* 136 full-time (102 women), 223 part-time (177 women); includes 130 minority (17 Black or African American, non-Hispanic/Latino; 21 Asian, non-Hispanic/Latino; 74 Hispanic/Latino; 3 Native Hawaiian or other Pacific Islander, non-Hispanic/Latino; 15 Two or more races, non-Hispanic/Latino), 10 international. Average age 33. 391 applicants, 85% accepted, 190 enrolled. In 2018, 201 master's awarded. *Degree requirements:* For master's, thesis (for some programs), international experience. *Entrance requirements:* For master's, California Basic Educational Skills Test, California Subject Examination for Teachers. Additional exam requirements/recommendations for international students: Required—TOEFL (minimum score 580 paper-based; 83 iBT), TWE. *Application deadline:* Applications are processed on a rolling basis. Application fee: $45. Electronic applications accepted. *Financial support:* In 2018–19, 127 students received support. Career-related internships or fieldwork, Federal Work-Study, institutionally sponsored loans, scholarships/grants, and stipends available. Financial award application deadline: 4/1; financial award applicants required to submit FAFSA. *Faculty research:* Action

research methodology, cultural studies, instructional theories and practices, second language acquisition, school reform. *Unit head:* Dr. Reyes Quezada, Chair, 619-260-7655, E-mail: rquezada@sandiego.edu. *Application contact:* Erika Garwood, Associate Director of Graduate Admissions, 619-260-4524, Fax: 619-260-4158, E-mail: grads@sandiego.edu.
Website: http://www.sandiego.edu/soles/learning-and-teaching/

University of San Francisco, School of Education, Department of Learning and Instruction, San Francisco, CA 94117. Offers digital technologies for teaching and learning (MA); learning and instruction (MA, Ed D); special education (MA, Ed D); teaching reading (MA). *Program availability:* Part-time, evening/weekend. *Students:* 34 full-time (25 women), 11 part-time (8 women); includes 12 minority (4 Black or African American, non-Hispanic/Latino; 3 Asian, non-Hispanic/Latino; 5 Hispanic/Latino), 11 international. Average age 40. 24 applicants, 96% accepted, 16 enrolled. In 2018, 9 doctorates awarded. *Degree requirements:* For doctorate, thesis/dissertation. *Entrance requirements:* Additional exam requirements/recommendations for international students: Required—TOEFL, IELTS, PTE. *Application deadline:* For fall admission, 3/1 priority date for domestic and international students; for spring admission, 11/1 priority date for domestic and international students. Applications are processed on a rolling basis. Application fee: $55 ($65 for international students). Electronic applications accepted. *Financial support:* In 2018–19, 13 students received support. Fellowships, research assistantships, and teaching assistantships available. Financial award application deadline: 3/2; financial award applicants required to submit FAFSA. *Unit head:* Dr. Kevin Oh, Chair, 415-422-2099. *Application contact:* Peter Cole, Admission Coordinator, 415-422-5467, E-mail: schoolofeducation@usfca.edu.

University of San Francisco, School of Education, Department of Teacher Education, San Francisco, CA 94117. Offers digital media and learning (MA); teaching (MA); teaching reading (MA); teaching urban education and social justice (MA). *Program availability:* Part-time. *Students:* 377 full-time (280 women), 51 part-time (43 women); includes 228 minority (28 Black or African American, non-Hispanic/Latino; 62 Asian, non-Hispanic/Latino; 121 Hispanic/Latino; 1 Native Hawaiian or other Pacific Islander, non-Hispanic/Latino; 16 Two or more races, non-Hispanic/Latino), 22 international. Average age 29. 536 applicants, 70% accepted, 182 enrolled. In 2018, 212 master's awarded. *Entrance requirements:* Additional exam requirements/recommendations for international students: Required—TOEFL, IELTS, PTE. *Application deadline:* For fall admission, 3/1 priority date for domestic and international students; for spring admission, 10/15 priority date for domestic students, 10/1 for international students. Applications are processed on a rolling basis. Electronic applications accepted. *Financial support:* Applicants required to submit FAFSA. *Unit head:* Dr. Noah Borrero, Chair, 415-422-6481. *Application contact:* Peter Cole, Admission Coordinator, 415-422-5467, E-mail: schoolofeducation@usfca.edu.
Website: https://www.usfca.edu/catalog/graduate/school-of-education/programs-teacher-education

The University of Scranton, Panuska College of Professional Studies, Department of Education, Program in Reading Education, Scranton, PA 18510. Offers MS. *Accreditation:* NCATE. *Program availability:* Part-time, evening/weekend. *Degree requirements:* For master's, comprehensive exam (for some programs), thesis (for some programs), capstone experience. *Entrance requirements:* For master's, minimum GPA of 3.0, three letters of reference. Additional exam requirements/recommendations for international students: Required—TOEFL (minimum score 500 paper-based; 80 iBT), IELTS (minimum score 6.5). Electronic applications accepted.

University of Sioux Falls, Fredrikson School of Education, Sioux Falls, SD 57105-1699. Offers educational administration (Ed S), including principal leadership, superintendent and district leadership; leadership in reading (M Ed); leadership in schools (M Ed); leadership in technology (M Ed); teaching (M Ed). Admission in summer only. *Accreditation:* NCATE. *Program availability:* Part-time, evening/weekend. *Degree requirements:* For master's, comprehensive exam (for some programs), research application project; for Ed S, comprehensive exam, portfolio. *Entrance requirements:* For master's, minimum GPA of 3.0, 1 year of teaching experience; for Ed S, minimum 3 years of teaching experience, minimum cumulative GPA of 3.5, 1 year of administrative experience. Additional exam requirements/recommendations for international students: Required—TOEFL. *Faculty research:* Reading, literacy, leadership.

University of South Alabama, College of Education and Professional Studies, Department of Leadership and Teacher Education, Mobile, AL 36688. Offers art education (M Ed); early childhood education (M Ed); educational leadership (M Ed, Ed D); elementary education (M Ed); reading education (M Ed); science education (M Ed); secondary education (M Ed); special education (M Ed). *Accreditation:* NCATE. *Program availability:* Part-time. *Degree requirements:* For master's, comprehensive exam, thesis (for some programs); for doctorate, comprehensive exam, thesis/dissertation. *Entrance requirements:* For master's, GRE General Test or MAT, minimum GPA of 3.0; for doctorate, GRE, minimum graduate GPA of 3.25, 3 years of experience in field, 3 letters of recommendation, interview, official transcripts. Additional exam requirements/recommendations for international students: Required—TOEFL. Electronic applications accepted.

University of South Carolina, The Graduate School, College of Education, Department of Instruction and Teacher Education, Program in Language and Literacy, Columbia, SC 29208. Offers M Ed, PhD. *Accreditation:* NCATE. *Degree requirements:* For master's, comprehensive exam; for doctorate, one foreign language, comprehensive exam, thesis/dissertation. *Entrance requirements:* For master's, GRE General Test, Miller Analogies Test, teaching certificate, resume, letters of reference, letter of intent; for doctorate, GRE General Test, Miller Analogies Test, resumé, letters of reference, letter of intent, interview. *Faculty research:* Remedial and compensatory education, metacognition and learning, literacy, learning, teacher change.

University of South Dakota, Graduate School, School of Education, Division of Curriculum and Instruction, Program in Elementary Education, Vermillion, SD 57069. Offers elementary education (MA), including early childhood education, English language learning, reading specialist/literacy coach, science, technology and math (STEM). *Accreditation:* NCATE. *Program availability:* Part-time, 100% online, blended/hybrid learning. *Degree requirements:* For master's, comprehensive exam, thesis or alternative. *Entrance requirements:* For master's, GRE General Test, MAT, minimum GPA of 2.7. Additional exam requirements/recommendations for international students: Required—TOEFL (minimum score 550 paper-based; 79 iBT). Electronic applications accepted.

University of Southern Maine, College of Management and Human Service, School of Education and Human Development, Program in Literacy Education, Portland, ME 04103. Offers applied literacy (MS Ed); English as a second language (MS Ed, CAS, CGS); literacy education (MS Ed, CAS, CGS). *Accreditation:* TEAC. *Program availability:* Part-time, evening/weekend. *Degree requirements:* For master's, comprehensive exam, thesis or alternative; for other advanced degree, thesis or alternative. *Entrance requirements:* For master's, teacher certification; for other advanced degree, master's degree. Additional exam requirements/recommendations for international students: Required—TOEFL (minimum score 550 paper-based; 79 iBT). Electronic applications accepted. *Faculty research:* Teacher research in literacy,

multiliteracies, learning to teach culturally and linguistically diverse students, motivation to read.

University of South Florida, College of Education, Department of Teaching and Learning, Tampa, FL 33620-9951. Offers early childhood education (M Ed, MA, PhD); elementary education (MA, MAT, PhD); reading/language arts (MA, PhD, Ed S). *Accreditation:* NCATE. *Faculty:* 36 full-time (27 women). *Students:* 244 full-time (193 women), 283 part-time (204 women); includes 140 minority (62 Black or African American, non-Hispanic/Latino; 2 American Indian or Alaska Native, non-Hispanic/Latino; 10 Asian, non-Hispanic/Latino; 61 Hispanic/Latino; 5 Two or more races, non-Hispanic/Latino), 70 international. Average age 36. 204 applicants, 84% accepted, 131 enrolled. In 2018, 67 master's, 3 doctorates awarded. *Degree requirements:* For master's, comprehensive exam, thesis (for some programs); for doctorate, comprehensive exam, thesis/dissertation (for some programs). *Entrance requirements:* For master's, GRE may be required (varies by major), statement of purpose; letters of recommendation; be eligible for professional certification (if applicable to major); passing GKT (if applicable to major); for doctorate, GRE may be required (varies by major), Master's degree with 3.5 GPA; CV; statement of purpose; letters of recommendation; faculty interview; language proficiency (if applicable). Additional exam requirements/recommendations for international students: Required—TOEFL. Application fee: $30. *Expenses:* Tuition, state resident: full-time $6350. Tuition, nonresident: full-time $19,048. International tuition: $19,048 full-time. *Required fees:* $2079. *Total annual research expenditures:* $2.7 million. *Unit head:* Dr. Denisse Thompson, Chair, 813-974-4110. *Application contact:* Dr. Denisse Thompson, Chair, 813-974-4110.
Website: http://www.coedu.usf.edu/main/departments/ce/ce.html

University of South Florida, St. Petersburg, College of Education, St. Petersburg, FL 33701. Offers educational leadership development (M Ed); elementary education (MA), including math/science; English education (MA); middle grades STEM education (MS); reading education (MA). *Program availability:* Part-time. *Degree requirements:* For master's, comprehensive exam, practicum, internship, comprehensive portfolio. *Entrance requirements:* For master's, State of Florida General Knowledge Test (GKT), Florida Teaching Certificate (for non-initial certification programs), letters of recommendation. Additional exam requirements/recommendations for international students: Required—TOEFL (minimum score 550 paper-based; 79 iBT); Recommended—IELTS. Electronic applications accepted.

The University of Tennessee, Graduate School, College of Education, Health and Human Sciences, Program in Education, Knoxville, TN 37996. Offers art education (MS); counseling education (PhD); cultural studies in education (PhD); curriculum (MS, Ed S); curriculum, educational research and evaluation (Ed D, PhD); early childhood education (PhD); early childhood special education (MS); education of deaf and hard of hearing (MS); educational administration and policy studies (Ed D, PhD); educational administration and supervision (Ed S); educational psychology (Ed D, PhD); elementary education (MS, Ed S); elementary teaching (MS); English education (MS, Ed S); exercise science (PhD); foreign language/ESL education (MS, Ed S); instructional technology (MS, Ed D, PhD, Ed S); literacy, language and ESL education (PhD); literacy, language education, and ESL education (Ed D); mathematics education (MS, Ed S); modified and comprehensive special education (MS); reading education (MS, Ed S); school counseling (Ed S); school psychology (PhD, Ed S); science education (MS, Ed S); secondary teaching (MS); social foundations (MS); social science education (MS, Ed S); socio-cultural foundations of sports and education (PhD); special education (Ed S); teacher education (Ed D, PhD). *Accreditation:* NCATE. *Program availability:* Part-time, evening/weekend. *Degree requirements:* For master's and Ed S, thesis optional; for doctorate, variable foreign language requirement, thesis/dissertation. *Entrance requirements:* For master's, minimum GPA of 2.7; for doctorate and Ed S, GRE General Test, minimum GPA of 2.7. Additional exam requirements/recommendations for international students: Required—TOEFL. Electronic applications accepted.

The University of Texas at Arlington, Graduate School, College of Education, Department of Curriculum and Instruction, Arlington, TX 76019. Offers curriculum and instruction (M Ed), including literacy studies, mathematics education, mind, brain, and education, science education; teaching (with certification) (M Ed T). *Accreditation:* NCATE. *Program availability:* Part-time, evening/weekend, online learning. *Degree requirements:* For master's, comprehensive exam (for some programs), comprehensive activity, research project. *Entrance requirements:* For master's, GRE General Test, minimum undergraduate GPA of 3.0 in last 60 hours of course work, writing sample, 3 letters of recommendation. Additional exam requirements/recommendations for international students: Required—TOEFL (minimum score 550 paper-based). Electronic applications accepted.

The University of Texas at Austin, Graduate School, College of Education, Department of Curriculum and Instruction, Austin, TX 78712-1111. Offers bilingual/bicultural education (M Ed, MA, PhD); cultural studies in education (M Ed, MA, PhD); early childhood education (M Ed, MA, PhD); language and literacy studies (M Ed, PhD); learning technologies (M Ed, MA, PhD); physical education (M Ed, MA, PhD). Terminal master's awarded for partial completion of doctoral program. *Degree requirements:* For doctorate, thesis/dissertation. *Entrance requirements:* For master's and doctorate, GRE General Test. Electronic applications accepted.

The University of Texas at El Paso, Graduate School, College of Education, Department of Teacher Education, El Paso, TX 79968-0001. Offers education (MA); instruction (M Ed); reading education (M Ed); teaching, learning, and culture (PhD). *Program availability:* Part-time, evening/weekend. *Degree requirements:* For master's, thesis optional. *Entrance requirements:* For master's, GRE General Test, minimum GPA of 3.0. Additional exam requirements/recommendations for international students: Required—TOEFL. Electronic applications accepted.

The University of Texas at San Antonio, College of Education and Human Development, Department of Bicultural and Bilingual Studies, San Antonio, TX 78249-0617. Offers bicultural and bilingual studies (MA), including bicultural and bilingual education, bicultural studies; culture, literacy, and language (PhD); teaching English as a second language (MA). *Program availability:* Part-time, evening/weekend. *Degree requirements:* For master's, one foreign language, comprehensive exam, thesis optional; for doctorate, one foreign language, comprehensive exam, thesis/dissertation. *Entrance requirements:* For master's, bachelor's degree with 18 credit hours in field of study or in another appropriate field of study; for doctorate, GRE General Test, resume or curriculum vitae, 3 letters of recommendation, statement of purpose, master's degree. Additional exam requirements/recommendations for international students: Required—TOEFL (minimum score 550 paper-based; 79 iBT), IELTS (minimum score 6.5). Electronic applications accepted. *Expenses:* Contact institution. *Faculty research:* Bilingual and ESL teacher preparation; transnational communities; applied linguistics; cultural studies; bilingualism, biliteracy and second language acquisition.

The University of Texas at San Antonio, College of Education and Human Development, Department of Interdisciplinary Learning and Teaching, San Antonio, TX 78249-0617. Offers education (MA), including curriculum and instruction, early childhood and elementary education, instructional technology, reading and literacy, special education; interdisciplinary learning and teaching (PhD). *Program availability:*

Part-time, evening/weekend. *Degree requirements:* For master's, comprehensive exam, thesis optional, 36 hours of course work without thesis (33 with thesis); for doctorate, comprehensive exam, thesis/dissertation, minimum of 60 semester credit hours. *Entrance requirements:* For master's, bachelor's degree with minimum GPA of 3.0 in last 60 hours of coursework; 18 hours of undergraduate coursework in education or related field; for doctorate, GRE, transcripts from all colleges and universities attended, professional vitae demonstrating experience in work environment where education was primary professional emphasis, 3 letters of recommendation, statement of purpose, minimum GPA of 3.5. Additional exam requirements/recommendations for international students: Required—TOEFL (minimum score 550 paper-based; 79 iBT), IELTS (minimum score 6.5). Electronic applications accepted. *Faculty research:* Explorations of science, learning and teaching, family involvement in early childhood, culturally-responsive literacy instruction in diverse settings, STEM education, autism spectrum disorder.

The University of Texas at Tyler, College of Education and Psychology, School of Education, Tyler, TX 75799-0001. Offers early childhood education (M Ed, MA); reading (M Ed, MA); special education (M Ed, MA). *Program availability:* Part-time, evening/weekend. *Students:* 4 full-time (3 women), 30 part-time (all women); includes 4 minority (3 Black or African American, non-Hispanic/Latino; 1 Hispanic/Latino), 2 international. Average age 37. 13 applicants, 100% accepted, 6 enrolled. In 2018, 14 master's awarded. *Degree requirements:* For master's, comprehensive exam, thesis (for some programs), research project. *Entrance requirements:* For master's, GRE General Test. Additional exam requirements/recommendations for international students: Required—TOEFL. *Application deadline:* For fall admission, 8/17 priority date for domestic students, 7/1 priority date for international students; for spring admission, 12/21 priority date for domestic students, 11/1 priority date for international students. Applications are processed on a rolling basis. Application fee: $25 ($50 for international students). Electronic applications accepted. *Financial support:* In 2018–19, 2 research assistantships (averaging $12,000 per year) were awarded; scholarships/grants also available. Financial award application deadline: 7/1. *Faculty research:* Improving quality in childcare settings, play and creativity, teacher interactions, effects of modeling on early childhood teachers, biofeedback, literacy instruction. *Unit head:* Dr. Wes Hickey, Dean, 903-565-5669, E-mail: whickey@uttyler.edu. *Application contact:* Dr. Wes Hickey, Dean, 903-565-5669, E-mail: whickey@uttyler.edu.
Website: http://www.uttyler.edu/education/

The University of Texas of the Permian Basin, Office of Graduate Studies, School of Education, Program in Reading, Odessa, TX 79762-0001. Offers MA. *Degree requirements:* For master's, comprehensive exam (for some programs), thesis (for some programs). *Entrance requirements:* For master's, GRE General Test. Additional exam requirements/recommendations for international students: Required—TOEFL (minimum score 550 paper-based).

The University of Texas Rio Grande Valley, College of Education and P-16 Integration, Department of Bilingual and Literacy Studies, Edinburg, TX 78539. Offers bilingual education (M Ed), including dual language, ESL; reading and literacy (M Ed), including adolescent literacy, biliteracy, digital literacy, reading specialist. *Program availability:* Part-time, evening/weekend. *Degree requirements:* For master's, comprehensive exam (for some programs), thesis optional. *Entrance requirements:* For master's, minimum GPA of 3.0 in undergraduate coursework. Additional exam requirements/recommendations for international students: Required—TOEFL (minimum score 550 paper-based; 79 iBT), IELTS (minimum score 6.5). Electronic applications accepted. *Expenses: Tuition, area resident:* Full-time $6888. Tuition, state resident: full-time $6888. Tuition, nonresident: full-time $14,484. *International tuition:* $14,484 full-time. *Required fees:* $1468. *Faculty research:* Bilingual education, reading instruction, multicultural education, English as a second language.

University of the Cumberlands, Graduate Programs in Education, Williamsburg, KY 40769-1372. Offers all grades (P-12) (M Ed); business and marketing (MA Ed, MAT); counselor education and supervision (Ed D); director of pupil personnel (Certificate); director of special education (Certificate); educational administration and supervision (Ed S); educational leadership (Ed D); elementary education (MA Ed, MAT); instructional leadership - principalship (MA Ed); instructional leadership - school principal (Certificate); middle school education (MA Ed, MAT); reading and writing (MA Ed); school counseling (MA Ed); school superintendent (Certificate); secondary education (MA Ed, MAT); special education (MAT); supervisor of instruction (Certificate); teacher leader (MA Ed). *Program availability:* Part-time, evening/weekend, online learning. *Degree requirements:* For master's, comprehensive exam. Electronic applications accepted.

University of Utah, Graduate School, College of Education, Department of Educational Psychology, Salt Lake City, UT 84112. Offers clinical mental health counseling (M Ed); counseling psychology (PhD); elementary education (M Ed); instructional design and educational technology (M Ed); instructional design and technology (MS); learning and cognition (MS, PhD); reading and literacy (M Ed, PhD); school counseling (M Ed); school psychology (M Ed, PhD, Ed S); statistics (M Stat). *Accreditation:* APA (one or more programs are accredited. *Faculty:* 20 full-time (12 women), 50 part-time/adjunct (34 women). *Students:* 127 full-time (93 women), 92 part-time (63 women); includes 33 minority (1 Black or African American, non-Hispanic/Latino; 7 Asian, non-Hispanic/Latino; 18 Hispanic/Latino; 1 Native Hawaiian or other Pacific Islander, non-Hispanic/Latino; 6 Two or more races, non-Hispanic/Latino), 5 international. Average age 32. 296 applicants, 27% accepted, 73 enrolled. In 2018, 68 master's, 10 doctorates, 3 other advanced degrees awarded. Terminal master's awarded for partial completion of doctoral program. *Degree requirements:* For master's, thesis (for some programs); for doctorate, thesis/dissertation. *Entrance requirements:* For master's and doctorate, GRE General Test, minimum GPA of 3.0. Additional exam requirements/recommendations for international students: Required—TOEFL (minimum score 80 iBT). *Application deadline:* For fall admission, 12/15 for domestic and international students; for winter admission, 11/1 for domestic and international students; for spring admission, 3/15 for domestic and international students. Application fee: $55 ($65 for international students). Electronic applications accepted. *Expenses:* Contact institution. *Financial support:* In 2018–19, 72 students received support, including 6 fellowships with full and partial tuition reimbursements available (averaging $17,000 per year), 14 research assistantships with full and partial tuition reimbursements available (averaging $15,750 per year), 27 teaching assistantships with full and partial tuition reimbursements available (averaging $15,500 per year); career-related internships or fieldwork, scholarships/grants, traineeships, health care benefits, and unspecified assistantships also available. Financial award application deadline: 4/1; financial award applicants required to submit FAFSA. *Faculty research:* Autism, computer technology and instruction, cognitive behavior, aging, group counseling. *Total annual research expenditures:* $620,935. *Unit head:* Dr. Anne E. Cook, Chair, 801-581-7148, Fax: 801-581-5566, E-mail: anne.cook@utah.edu. *Application contact:* JoLynn N. Yates, Academic Coordinator, 801-581-7148, Fax: 801-581-5566, E-mail: jo.yates@utah.edu.
Website: http://www.ed.utah.edu/edps/

University of Victoria, Faculty of Graduate Studies, Faculty of Education, Department of Curriculum and Instruction, Victoria, BC V8W 2Y2, Canada. Offers art education (M Ed, PhD); curriculum studies (M Ed, MA, PhD); early childhood education (M Ed,

PhD); educational studies (PhD); language and literacy (M Ed, MA, PhD); mathematics (M Ed, MA, PhD); music education (M Ed, MA, PhD); science (M Ed, MA, PhD); social studies (M Ed, MA); social, cultural and foundational studies (MA, PhD); technology and environmental education (PhD). *Program availability:* Part-time. *Degree requirements:* For master's, thesis, project (M Ed); for doctorate, comprehensive exam, thesis/dissertation. *Entrance requirements:* For master's, minimum B average. Additional exam requirements/recommendations for international students: Required—TOEFL (minimum score 575 paper-based), IELTS (minimum score 7). Electronic applications accepted. *Faculty research:* Elementary and secondary English, language arts, curriculum theory and practice, educational media and technology, educational administration and leadership, history and philosophy of education.

University of Virginia, Curry School of Education, Program in Education, Charlottesville, VA 22903. Offers administration and supervision (PhD); applied developmental science (PhD); counselor education (PhD); curriculum and instruction (PhD); early childhood special education (MT); education evaluation (PhD); educational psychology (PhD); educational research (PhD); elementary education (MT); English education (MT, PhD); foreign language education (MT); higher education (PhD); instructional technology (PhD); kinesiology (MT, PhD); math education (PhD); reading education (PhD); research, statistics and evaluation (PhD); school psychology (PhD); science education (PhD); social studies education (MT, PhD); special education (PhD); world languages education (MT). *Degree requirements:* For master's, comprehensive exam (for some programs), field project; for doctorate, comprehensive exam, thesis/dissertation. *Entrance requirements:* For doctorate, GRE General Test. Additional exam requirements/recommendations for international students: Required—TOEFL (minimum score 600 paper-based; 90 iBT), IELTS (minimum score 7). Electronic applications accepted.

University of Washington, Graduate School, College of Education, Seattle, WA 98195. Offers curriculum and instruction (M Ed, Ed D, PhD), including educational technology, general curriculum (Ed D, PhD); language, literacy, and culture, mathematics education, multicultural education, reading and language arts education (Ed D), science education, social studies education, teaching and curriculum (M Ed); educational leadership and policy studies (M Ed, Ed D, PhD), including administration (Ed D), educational policy, organization, and leadership (M Ed, PhD), higher education, leadership for learning (Ed D), social and cultural foundations of education (M Ed, PhD); educational psychology (M Ed, PhD), including educational psychology (PhD), human development and cognition (M Ed), learning sciences, measurement, statistics and research design (M Ed), school psychology (M Ed); instructional leadership (M Ed); intercollegiate athletic leadership (M Ed); special education (M Ed, Ed D, PhD), including early childhood special education (M Ed), emotional and behavioral disabilities (M Ed), learning disabilities (M Ed), low-incidence disabilities (M Ed), severe disabilities (M Ed), special education (Ed D, PhD); teacher education (MIT). *Accreditation:* APA. *Program availability:* Part-time, evening/weekend. *Degree requirements:* For master's, thesis optional; for doctorate, thesis/dissertation. *Entrance requirements:* For master's and doctorate, GRE General Test, minimum GPA of 3.0. Additional exam requirements/recommendations for international students: Required—TOEFL. Electronic applications accepted. *Faculty research:* School restructuring/effective schools, special education interventions, literacy and writing, technology, school partnerships, teacher preparation.

University of West Florida, College of Education and Professional Studies, Department of Teacher Education and Educational Leadership, Program in Reading Education, Pensacola, FL 32514-5750. Offers M Ed. *Program availability:* Part-time, evening/weekend. *Degree requirements:* For master's, portfolio, teacher certification exams (general knowledge, professional, reading subject area). *Entrance requirements:* For master's, GRE (minimum score 450 verbal) or MAT (minimum score 396) if bachelor's GPA less than 3.0, state teaching certification; letter of intent; two professional references. Additional exam requirements/recommendations for international students: Required—TOEFL (minimum score 550 paper-based).

University of West Georgia, College of Education, Carrollton, GA 30118. Offers business education (M Ed); early childhood education (M Ed, Ed S); educational leadership (M Ed, Ed S); media (M Ed, Ed S); professional counseling (M Ed, Ed S); professional counseling and supervision (Ed D); reading instruction (M Ed); school improvement (Ed D); secondary education (M Ed); special education (M Ed, Ed S), including teaching (M Ed); speech language pathology (M Ed); teaching (MAT). *Accreditation:* NCATE. *Program availability:* Part-time, evening/weekend, 100% online, blended/hybrid learning. *Faculty:* 39 full-time (23 women). *Students:* 368 full-time (316 women), 1,140 part-time (960 women); includes 460 minority (376 Black or African American, non-Hispanic/Latino; 1 American Indian or Alaska Native, non-Hispanic/Latino; 11 Asian, non-Hispanic/Latino; 44 Hispanic/Latino; 28 Two or more races, non-Hispanic/Latino), 6 international. Average age 35. 625 applicants, 77% accepted, 401 enrolled. In 2018, 399 master's, 25 doctorates, 273 other advanced degrees awarded. *Entrance requirements:* Additional exam requirements/recommendations for international students: Required—TOEFL (minimum score 523 paper-based; 69 iBT). Recommended—IELTS (minimum score 6.5). *Application deadline:* For fall admission, 7/21 for domestic students, 6/1 for international students; for spring admission, 11/30 for domestic students, 10/15 for international students; for summer admission, 4/15 for domestic students, 3/30 for international students. Applications are processed on a rolling basis. Application fee: $40. Electronic applications accepted. Tuition and fees vary according to course load, degree level, campus/location and program. *Financial support:* Fellowships, research assistantships, teaching assistantships, career-related internships or fieldwork, Federal Work-Study, institutionally sponsored loans, scholarships/grants, and unspecified assistantships available. Support available to part-time students. Financial award application deadline: 4/1; financial award applicants required to submit FAFSA. *Unit head:* Dr. Diane Hoff, Dean, College of Education, 678-839-6570, Fax: 678-839-6098, E-mail: dhoff@westga.edu. *Application contact:* Dr. Toby Ziglar, Assistant Dean of the Graduate School, 678-839-1394, Fax: 678-839-1395, E-mail: graduate@westga.edu.
Website: http://www.westga.edu/education/

University of Wisconsin–Eau Claire, College of Education and Human Sciences, Program in Reading, Eau Claire, WI 54702-4004. Offers MST. *Program availability:* Part-time. *Degree requirements:* For master's, comprehensive exam, portfolio with an oral examination. *Entrance requirements:* For master's, certification to teach. Additional exam requirements/recommendations for international students: Required—TOEFL (minimum score 79 iBT).

University of Wisconsin–La Crosse, School of Education, La Crosse, WI 54601-3742. Offers English language arts elementary (Graduate Certificate); professional development in education (ME-PD); reading (MS Ed); special education (MS Ed). *Program availability:* Part-time, evening/weekend. *Entrance requirements:* For master's, GRE. Additional exam requirements/recommendations for international students: Required—TOEFL (minimum score 550 paper-based; 79 iBT). Electronic applications accepted.

University of Wisconsin–Milwaukee, Graduate School, School of Education, Department of Curriculum and Instruction, Milwaukee, WI 53201-0413. Offers curriculum and instruction (MS), including cross-curricular focus, early childhood education, English education, mathematics education, middle childhood/early

adolescence education, reading education, science education, urban social studies education. *Program availability:* Part-time. *Students:* 19 full-time (15 women), 56 part-time (49 women); includes 15 minority (3 Black or African American, non-Hispanic/Latino; 1 American Indian or Alaska Native, non-Hispanic/Latino; 3 Asian, non-Hispanic/Latino; 1 Hispanic/Latino; 7 Two or more races, non-Hispanic/Latino), 2 international. Average age 33. 27 applicants, 44% accepted, 11 enrolled. In 2018, 20 master's awarded. *Entrance requirements:* Additional exam requirements/recommendations for international students: Required—TOEFL (minimum score 550 paper-based; 79 iBT), IELTS (minimum score 6.5). *Application deadline:* For fall admission, 1/1 priority date for domestic students; for spring admission, 9/1 for domestic students. Application fee: $56 ($96 for international students). Electronic applications accepted. *Financial support:* Fellowships, research assistantships, teaching assistantships, career-related internships or fieldwork, health care benefits, unspecified assistantships, and project assistantships available. Support available to part-time students. Financial award application deadline: 4/15; financial award applicants required to submit FAFSA. *Application contact:* General Information Contact, 414-229-4721, E-mail: soeinfo@uwm.edu.
Website: http://uwm.edu/education/academics/curriculum-instruction-department/

University of Wisconsin–Oshkosh, Graduate Studies, College of Education and Human Services, Department of Reading Education, Oshkosh, WI 54901. Offers MSE. Program offered jointly with University of Wisconsin–Green Bay. *Program availability:* Part-time. *Degree requirements:* For master's, thesis or alternative, reflective journey course. *Entrance requirements:* For master's, interview, teaching certificate, undergraduate degree in teacher education, letters of recommendation. Additional exam requirements/recommendations for international students: Required—TOEFL (minimum score 550 paper-based; 79 iBT). Electronic applications accepted. *Faculty research:* Writing and reading, assessment, learner-centered instruction, multicultural literature, family literacy.

University of Wisconsin–River Falls, Outreach and Graduate Studies, College of Education and Professional Studies, Department of Teacher Education, River Falls, WI 54022. Offers elementary education (MSE); professional development shared inquiry communities (MSE); reading (MSE). *Program availability:* Part-time. *Degree requirements:* For master's, comprehensive exam, thesis or alternative. *Entrance requirements:* For master's, minimum GPA of 2.75. Additional exam requirements/recommendations for international students: Required—TOEFL (minimum score 500 paper-based; 65 iBT), IELTS (minimum score 5.5). Electronic applications accepted.

University of Wisconsin–Stevens Point, College of Professional Studies, School of Education, Program in Education—General/Reading, Stevens Point, WI 54481-3897. Offers MSE. *Program availability:* Part-time. *Degree requirements:* For master's, comprehensive exam, thesis or alternative. *Entrance requirements:* For master's, minimum undergraduate GPA of 3.0, teacher certification, 2 years' teaching experience, letters of recommendation. Additional exam requirements/recommendations for international students: Required—TOEFL (minimum score 523 paper-based). *Faculty research:* Reading strategies in the content areas, gifted education, curriculum and instruction, standards-based education.

University of Wisconsin–Superior, Graduate Division, Department of Teacher Education, Program in Teaching Reading, Superior, WI 54880-4500. Offers MSE. *Program availability:* Part-time, evening/weekend. *Degree requirements:* For master's, comprehensive exam, thesis or alternative, research project. *Entrance requirements:* For master's, minimum GPA of 2.75, teaching certificate. Electronic applications accepted.

Upper Iowa University, Master of Education Program, Fayette, IA 52142-1857. Offers early childhood (M Ed); English as a second language (M Ed); higher education (M Ed); instructional strategist (M Ed); reading (M Ed); teacher leadership (M Ed).

Utah Valley University, Program in Education, Orem, UT 84058-5999. Offers educational technology (M Ed); elementary mathematics (M Ed); elementary STEM (M Ed); English as a second language (M Ed); reading (M Ed); teachers as leaders (M Ed). *Accreditation:* TEAC. *Program availability:* Part-time. *Degree requirements:* For master's, project. *Entrance requirements:* For master's, GRE, 3 letters of recommendation, interview, essay. Additional exam requirements/recommendations for international students: Required—TOEFL (minimum score 83 iBT). Electronic applications accepted. *Expenses:* Contact institution.

Vanderbilt University, Peabody College, Department of Teaching and Learning, Nashville, TN 37240-1001. Offers elementary education (M Ed); English language learners (M Ed); reading education (M Ed); secondary education (M Ed). *Accreditation:* NCATE. *Program availability:* Part-time. *Faculty:* 47 full-time (34 women), 19 part-time/adjunct (16 women). *Students:* 122 full-time (99 women), 37 part-time (27 women); includes 34 minority (22 Black or African American, non-Hispanic/Latino; 2 American Indian or Alaska Native, non-Hispanic/Latino; 4 Asian, non-Hispanic/Latino; 4 Hispanic/Latino; 2 Two or more races, non-Hispanic/Latino), 41 international. Average age 26. 359 applicants, 74% accepted, 106 enrolled. In 2018, 113 master's awarded. *Degree requirements:* For master's, comprehensive exam, thesis optional. *Entrance requirements:* For master's, GRE General Test, MAT. Additional exam requirements/recommendations for international students: Required—TOEFL (minimum score 550 paper-based; 80 iBT). *Application deadline:* For fall admission, 12/31 priority date for domestic and international students; for spring admission, 11/1 priority date for domestic and international students. Applications are processed on a rolling basis. Application fee: $0. Electronic applications accepted. *Expenses: Tuition:* Full-time $47,208; part-time $2026 per credit hour. *Required fees:* $478. *Financial support:* Fellowships with partial tuition reimbursements, research assistantships with partial tuition reimbursements, teaching assistantships with partial tuition reimbursements, Federal Work-Study, institutionally sponsored loans, scholarships/grants, tuition waivers (partial), and unspecified assistantships available. Support available to part-time students. Financial award application deadline: 1/15; financial award applicants required to submit FAFSA. *Faculty research:* Literacy education; science education; math education; learning sciences; diversity studies. *Unit head:* Dr. Deborah Rowe, Chair, 615-322-8100, Fax: 615-322-8999, E-mail: deborah.w.rowe@vanderbilt.edu. *Application contact:* Angela Saylor, Educational Coordinator, 615-322-8092, Fax: 615-322-8999, E-mail: angela.saylor@vanderbilt.edu.

Virginia Commonwealth University, Graduate School, School of Education, Program in Adult Learning, Richmond, VA 23284-9005. Offers adult literacy (M Ed); human resource development (M Ed); teaching and learning with technology (M Ed). *Accreditation:* NCATE. *Program availability:* Part-time. *Entrance requirements:* For master's, GRE General Test or MAT. Additional exam requirements/recommendations for international students: Required—TOEFL (minimum score 600 paper-based; 100 iBT). Electronic applications accepted. *Faculty research:* Adult development and learning, program planning and evaluation.

Virginia Commonwealth University, Graduate School, School of Education, Program in Reading, Richmond, VA 23284-9005. Offers reading (M Ed); reading specialist (Certificate). *Accreditation:* NCATE. *Degree requirements:* For master's, comprehensive exam. *Entrance requirements:* For master's, GRE General Test or MAT. Additional exam requirements/recommendations for international students: Required—TOEFL (minimum score 600 paper-based; 100 iBT). Electronic applications accepted.

Viterbo University, Graduate Programs in Education, La Crosse, WI 54601-4797. Offers cross-categorical special education (Certificate); director of instruction (Certificate); director of special education and pupil services (Certificate); early childhood (Certificate); education (MAE); literacy coaching (Certificate); PreK-12 principal/supervisor of special education (Certificate); principal (Certificate); reading specialist endorsement (Certificate); reading teacher (Certificate); reading teacher 5-12 endorsement (Certificate); reading teacher K-8 endorsement (Certificate); superintendent (Certificate); talented and gifted endorsement (Certificate); Wisconsin school business administrator (Certificate). Weekend courses available in summer. *Accreditation:* NCATE. *Program availability:* Part-time, evening/weekend. *Degree requirements:* For master's, comprehensive exam, thesis, 30 credits of course work. *Entrance requirements:* For master's, BS, transcripts, teaching license, written narrative. Electronic applications accepted. *Expenses:* Contact institution.

Walden University, Graduate Programs, Richard W. Riley College of Education and Leadership, Minneapolis, MN 55401. Offers adult education (Post-Master's Certificate); adult learning (Graduate Certificate); college teaching and learning (Graduate Certificate); community college leadership (Ed D); curriculum, instruction and assessment (Ed D, Ed S, Graduate Certificate); developmental education (Graduate Certificate); early childhood administration, management, and leadership (Graduate Certificate); early childhood education (Ed D, Ed S); early childhood public policy and advocacy (Graduate Certificate); early childhood studies (MS), including administration, management and leadership, early childhood public policy and advocacy, teaching adults in the early childhood field, teaching and diversity in early childhood education; education (MS, PhD), including adolescent literacy and learning (MS), curriculum, instruction, and assessment (grades K-12) (MS), curriculum, instruction, assessment, and evaluation (PhD), early childhood leadership and advocacy (PhD), early childhood special education (PhD), educational leadership (MS), educational leadership and administration (principal preparation) (MS), educational technology and design (PhD), elementary reading and literacy (PreK-6) (MS), elementary reading and mathematics (grades K-6) (MS), global and comparative education (PhD), higher education leadership management and policy (PhD), integrating technology in the classroom (grades K-12) (MS), learning, instruction and innovation (PhD), mathematics (grades 5-8) (MS), mathematics (grades K-6) (MS), mathematics and science (grades K-8) (MS), organizational research, assessment, and evaluation (PhD), reading and literacy with a reading K-12 endorsement (MS), reading literacy assessment and evaluation (PhD), science (grades K-8) (MS), special education (non-licensure) (grades K-12) (MS), teacher leadership (grades K-12) (MS), teaching English language learners (grades K-12) (MS); educational administration and leadership (Ed D); educational leadership and administration (principal preparation) (Ed S); educational technology (Ed D, Ed S, Post Master's Certificate); elementary reading and literacy (Graduate Certificate); engaging culturally diverse learners (Graduate Certificate); enrollment management and institutional marketing (Graduate Certificate); higher education (MS), including adult learning, college teaching and learning, enrollment management and institutional marketing, global higher education, leadership for student success, online and distance learning; higher education and adult learning (Ed D); higher education leadership and management (Ed D); higher education leadership for student success (Graduate Certificate); instructional design and technology (MS, Postbaccalaureate Certificate), including general program (MS), online learning (MS), training and performance improvement (MS); integrating technology in the classroom (Graduate Certificate); mathematics 5-8 (Graduate Certificate); mathematics K-6 (Graduate Certificate); online teaching for adult educators (Graduate Certificate); reading, literacy, and assessment (Ed D, Ed S); science K-8 (Graduate Certificate); special education (Ed D, Ed S, Graduate Certificate); special education (K-age 21) (MAT); teacher leadership (Graduate Certificate); teaching adults English as a second language (Graduate Certificate); teaching adults in the early childhood field (Graduate Certificate); teaching and diversity in early childhood education (Graduate Certificate); teaching English language learners (grades K-12) (Graduate Certificate); teaching K-12 students online (Graduate Certificate). *Accreditation:* NCATE. *Program availability:* Part-time, evening/weekend, online only, 100% online. *Degree requirements:* For doctorate, thesis/dissertation (for some programs), residency; for other advanced degree, residency (for some programs). *Entrance requirements:* For master's, bachelor's degree or higher; minimum GPA of 2.5; official transcripts; goal statement (for some programs); access to computer and Internet; for doctorate, master's degree or higher; three years of related professional or academic experience (preferred); minimum GPA of 3.0; goal statement and current resume (for select programs); official transcripts; access to computer and Internet; for other advanced degree, relevant work experience; access to computer and Internet. Additional exam requirements/recommendations for international students: Required—TOEFL (minimum score 550 paper-based, 79 iBT), IELTS (minimum score 6.5), Michigan English Language Assessment Battery (minimum score 82), or PTE (minimum score 53). Electronic applications accepted.

Walla Walla University, Graduate Studies, School of Education and Psychology, College Place, WA 99324. Offers curriculum and instruction (M Ed, MAT); educational leadership (M Ed, MAT); literacy instruction (M Ed, MAT); special education (M Ed, MAT). *Program availability:* Part-time. *Entrance requirements:* For master's, GRE General Test, minimum GPA of 2.75. Additional exam requirements/recommendations for international students: Required—TOEFL (minimum score 550 paper-based; 79 iBT). Electronic applications accepted. *Faculty research:* Admissions/retention, instructional psychology, moral development, teaching of reading.

Walsh University, Graduate Programs, Program in Education, North Canton, OH 44720-3396. Offers leadership with principal license (MA Ed); reading literacy (MA Ed). *Accreditation:* NCATE. *Program availability:* Part-time, evening/weekend. *Degree requirements:* For master's, comprehensive exam (for some programs), thesis optional, action research project or comprehensive exam. *Entrance requirements:* For master's, MAT (minimum score 396), GRE (minimum scores: verbal 145, quantitative 146, combined 291, writing 3.0), or minimum GPA of 3.0 on the baccalaureate transcript, interview, minimum GPA of 3.0, writing sample, 3 recommendation forms, notarized affidavit of good moral character. Additional exam requirements/recommendations for international students: Required—TOEFL (minimum score 500 paper-based; 61 iBT). Electronic applications accepted. Application fee is waived when completed online. *Expenses:* Contact institution. *Faculty research:* Learning and the brain, primary STEM, effective assessment practices, literacy.

Washburn University, College of Arts and Sciences, Department of Education, Topeka, KS 66621. Offers curriculum and instruction (M Ed); educational leadership (M Ed); reading (M Ed); special education (M Ed). *Accreditation:* NCATE. *Program availability:* Part-time. *Degree requirements:* For master's, comprehensive exam, thesis or alternative, portfolio, comprehensive paper, or action research project. *Entrance requirements:* For master's, department exam, GRE General Test, or MAT, minimum GPA of 3.0 in graduate coursework or last 60 hours of undergraduate coursework. Additional exam requirements/recommendations for international students: Required—TOEFL (minimum score 80 iBT). *Faculty research:* Reading/literature/literacy, foundations, special education, diversity, teaching and technology.

Washington State University, College of Education, Department of Teaching and Learning, Pullman, WA 99164-2132. Offers cultural studies and social thought in education (PhD); curriculum and instruction (Ed M, MA); English language learners (Ed M, MA); language, literacy and technology (PhD); literacy education (Ed M, MA); mathematics education (PhD); special education (Ed M, MA, PhD); teacher leadership (Ed D); teaching (MIT), including elementary education, secondary education. Programs offered at the Pullman, Spokane, Tri-cities, Vancouver and Global (online) campuses. *Program availability:* Part-time, online learning. *Degree requirements:* For master's, comprehensive exam, thesis, oral or written exam; for doctorate, comprehensive exam, thesis/dissertation, oral and written exam. *Entrance requirements:* For master's, GRE General Test, minimum GPA of 3.0, 3 letters of recommendation, letter of intent, transcripts, resume/curriculum vitae; for doctorate, GRE General Test, minimum GPA of 3.0, 3 letters of recommendation, letter of intent, transcripts, writing sample, resume/curriculum vitae. Additional exam requirements/recommendations for international students: Required—TOEFL (minimum score 550 paper-based; 80 iBT). Electronic applications accepted. *Faculty research:* Intersection of gender, youth cultures and schooling; examination of ideology of power in children's literature; early childhood special education; analyzing pre-service and in-service teacher development; second language acquisition.

Wayne State University, College of Education, Division of Teacher Education, Detroit, MI 48202. Offers art education (M Ed); bilingual/bicultural education (Certificate); curriculum and instruction (Ed D, PhD, Ed S), including English as a second language (MAT, Ed D, Ed S), K-12 curriculum (PhD); elementary education (MAT), including bilingual/bicultural education (M Ed, MAT), early childhood education (M Ed, MAT), English as a second language (MAT, Ed D, Ed S), foreign language education, science education (M Ed, MAT), special education (M Ed, MAT); elementary mathematics specialist (Certificate); English as a second language (Certificate); reading (M Ed, Ed S); reading, language and literature (Ed D); secondary education (MAT), including bilingual/bicultural education (M Ed, MAT), early childhood education (M Ed, MAT), English as a second language (MAT, Ed D, Ed S), English education, foreign language education, mathematics education (M Ed, MAT), science education (M Ed, MAT), social studies education (M Ed, MAT); special education (MAT), including career and technical education; teaching and learning (M Ed), including bilingual/bicultural education (M Ed, MAT), early childhood education (M Ed, MAT), elementary education, foreign language, mathematics education (M Ed, MAT), science education (M Ed, MAT), social studies education (M Ed, MAT), special education (M Ed, MAT). *Program availability:* Part-time, evening/weekend. *Faculty:* 20. *Students:* 121 full-time (94 women), 251 part-time (209 women); includes 116 minority (83 Black or African American, non-Hispanic/Latino; 3 American Indian or Alaska Native, non-Hispanic/Latino; 3 Asian, non-Hispanic/Latino; 14 Hispanic/Latino; 13 Two or more races, non-Hispanic/Latino), 11 international. Average age 37. 171 applicants, 23% accepted, 32 enrolled. In 2018, 112 master's, 8 doctorates, 11 other advanced degrees awarded. *Degree requirements:* For master's, thesis (for some programs), essay or project (for some M Ed programs), professional field experience (for MAT programs); for doctorate, comprehensive exam, thesis/dissertation. *Entrance requirements:* For master's, undergraduate degree, verification of participation in group work with children, Michigan State Police criminal background check, negative tb test, personal statement (for MAT programs); for all other master's programs: undergraduate degree, personal statement; for doctorate, minimum undergraduate GPA of 3.0, graduate 3.5; interview; curriculum vitae; references; writing sample; letter of application; master's degree (for most programs); for other advanced degree, education specialist certificate: undergraduate with GPA of 2.5 or better and master's degree with GPA of 2.75 or better; personal statement. Additional exam requirements/recommendations for international students: Required—TOEFL (minimum score 550 paper-based; 79 iBT); Recommended—IELTS (minimum score 6.5), TWE (minimum score 5.5), TSE (minimum score 58). *Application deadline:* Applications are processed on a rolling basis. Application fee: $50. Electronic applications accepted. *Financial support:* In 2018–19, 85 students received support, including 3 fellowships (averaging $14,275 per year); research assistantships with tuition reimbursements available, Federal Work-Study, scholarships/grants, and unspecified assistantships also available. Support available to part-time students. Financial award applicants required to submit FAFSA. *Faculty research:* Improving students' skill achievement in mathematics, improving elementary children's understanding of informational text, teachers' use of their pedagogical and mathematical knowledge in the interactive work of teaching, the intersection of identity construction in teaching and learning, identifying effective methods of literacy instruction and assessments for bilingual students in elementary language arts classrooms. *Unit head:* Dr. Roland Coloma, Assistant Dean for Teacher Education, 313-577-0902, E-mail: rscoloma@wayne.edu. *Application contact:* Dr. Mary L. Waker, Graduate Admissions Officer, 313-577-1601, Fax: 313-577-7904, E-mail: m.waker@wayne.edu.
Website: http://coe.wayne.edu/ted/index.php

Webster University, School of Education, Department of Communication Arts, Reading and Early Childhood, St. Louis, MO 63119-3194. Offers communication arts (MAT); reading (MA). *Entrance requirements:* For master's, minimum GPA of 2.5. Additional exam requirements/recommendations for international students: Required—TOEFL. *Expenses:* Tuition: Full-time $22,500; part-time $750 per credit hour. Tuition and fees vary according to degree level, campus/location and program.

Webster University, School of Education, Department of Multidisciplinary Studies, St. Louis, MO 63119-3194. Offers applied educational psychology (MA, Ed S); communication arts (MA); early childhood education (MA, MAT); education and innovation (MA); educational technology (MET); elementary education (MAT); mathematics for educators (MA); middle school education (MAT); multidisciplinary studies (MAT); multimodal literacy for global impact (MA); reading (MA); secondary school education (MAT); special education (MA, MAT); teaching English as a second language (MA); transformative learning in the global community (Ed S). *Program availability:* Part-time. *Entrance requirements:* For master's, minimum GPA of 2.5. Additional exam requirements/recommendations for international students: Required—TOEFL. *Expenses:* Tuition: Full-time $22,500; part-time $750 per credit hour. Tuition and fees vary according to degree level, campus/location and program.

West Chester University of Pennsylvania, College of Education and Social Work, Department of Literacy, West Chester, PA 19383. Offers literacy (Certificate); literacy coaching (Certificate); reading (M Ed); reading specialist (Teaching Certificate). *Program availability:* Part-time, evening/weekend. *Degree requirements:* For master's, minimum GPA of 3.0, portfolio assessment; for other advanced degree, comprehensive exam. *Entrance requirements:* For master's, GRE or MAT if GPA is below 3.0, minimum GPA of 3.0, teaching certificate, two letters of reference. Additional exam requirements/recommendations for international students: Required—TOEFL or IELTS. Electronic applications accepted. *Faculty research:* Teaching and mentoring pre-service and in-service teachers to teach literacy in urban settings, literacy and technology, children's and young adult literature, literacy and diversity, developmental word knowledge.

Western Connecticut State University, Division of Graduate Studies, School of Professional Studies, Department of Education and Educational Psychology, Danbury, CT 06810-6885. Offers clinical mental health counseling (MS); curriculum (MS); instructional leadership (Ed D); instructional technology (MS); reading (MS); school counseling (MS); special education (MS). *Accreditation:* NCATE. *Program availability:* Part-time. *Students:* 14 full-time (12 women), 255 part-time (208 women). Average age 33. *Degree requirements:* For master's, thesis or alternative, completion of program in 6 years. *Entrance requirements:* For master's, MAT (if GPA is below 2.8), valid teaching certificate, letters of reference; for doctorate, GRE or MAT, resume, three recommendations (one in a supervisory capacity in an educational setting), satisfactory interview with WCSU representatives from the Ed D Admissions Committee. Additional exam requirements/recommendations for international students: Recommended—TOEFL (minimum score 550 paper-based; 79 iBT), IELTS (minimum score 6). *Application deadline:* For fall admission, 8/5 priority date for domestic students; for spring admission, 1/5 for domestic students. Applications are processed on a rolling basis. Application fee: $50. *Expenses:* Contact institution. *Financial support:* Scholarships/grants available. Financial award application deadline: 5/1; financial award applicants required to submit FAFSA. *Faculty research:* Cultural diversity in teacher and counselor education programs, African-American educational leaders, urban education and equity. *Unit head:* Dr. Catherine O'Callaghan, Chairperson, 203-837-3267, Fax: 203-837-8413. *Application contact:* Dr. Chris Shankle, Associate Director of Graduate Studies, 203-837-9005, Fax: 203-837-8326, E-mail: shanklec@wcsu.edu.
Website: http://www.wcsu.edu/education/

Western Illinois University, School of Graduate Studies, College of Education and Human Services, Department of Curriculum and Instruction, Program in Reading, Macomb, IL 61455-1390. Offers MS Ed. *Accreditation:* NCATE. *Program availability:* Part-time. *Students:* 26 part-time (25 women); includes 2 minority (both Hispanic/Latino), 1 international. Average age 34. 3 applicants, 100% accepted, 2 enrolled. In 2018, 12 master's awarded. *Entrance requirements:* For master's, teacher certification. Additional exam requirements/recommendations for international students: Required—TOEFL (minimum score 550 paper-based; 80 iBT). *Application deadline:* Applications are processed on a rolling basis. Application fee: $30. Electronic applications accepted. *Financial support:* Applicants required to submit FAFSA. *Unit head:* Dr. Eric Sheffield, Chairperson, 309-298-1183. *Application contact:* Dr. Mark Mossman, Assistant Director of Graduate Studies, 309-298-1806, Fax: 309-298-2345, E-mail: grad-office@wiu.edu.
Website: http://wiu.edu/curriculum

Western Kentucky University, Graduate School, College of Education and Behavioral Sciences, School of Teacher Education, Bowling Green, KY 42101. Offers elementary education (MAE, Ed S); exceptional education: learning and behavioral disorders (MAE); instructional design (MS); interdisciplinary early childhood education (MAE); library media education (MS); literacy education (MAE); middle grades education (MAE); secondary education (MAE, Ed S); special education: moderate and severe disabilities (MAE). *Program availability:* Part-time, evening/weekend, online learning. *Degree requirements:* For master's, comprehensive exam. *Entrance requirements:* For master's, GRE General Test. Additional exam requirements/recommendations for international students: Required—TOEFL (minimum score 555 paper-based; 79 iBT). *Faculty research:* Teacher preparation in moderate/severe disabilities.

Western Michigan University, Graduate College, College of Education and Human Development, Department of Special Education and Literacy Studies, Kalamazoo, MI 49008. Offers literacy studies (MA); special education (MA, Ed D), including clinical teacher (MA); teaching children with visual impairments (MA).

Western New Mexico University, Graduate Division, School of Education, Silver City, NM 88062-0680. Offers bilingual education (MAT); educational leadership (MA); elementary education (MAT); reading (MAT); secondary education (MAT); special education (MAT); TESOL (teaching English to speakers of other languages) (MAT). *Accreditation:* NCATE. *Program availability:* Part-time, online learning. *Degree requirements:* For master's, comprehensive exam. *Entrance requirements:* For master's, minimum GPA of 3.0 in last 64 hours of undergraduate study. Additional exam requirements/recommendations for international students: Required—TOEFL (minimum score 550 paper-based; 79 iBT). Electronic applications accepted. *Faculty research:* International education, electronic reading assessment, developing STEM teachers.

Western State Colorado University, Graduate Programs in Education, Gunnison, CO 81231. Offers education administrator leadership (MA); reading leadership (MA); teacher leadership (MA). *Program availability:* Online learning. *Degree requirements:* For master's, capstone.

Westfield State University, College of Graduate and Continuing Education, Department of Education, Program in Reading Specialist, Westfield, MA 01086. Offers M Ed. *Accreditation:* NCATE. *Program availability:* Part-time, evening/weekend. *Degree requirements:* For master's, comprehensive exam, practicum. *Entrance requirements:* For master's, GRE General Test or MAT, minimum undergraduate GPA of 2.8. Additional exam requirements/recommendations for international students: Recommended—TOEFL (minimum score 550 paper-based; 79 iBT).

West Liberty University, College of Education and Human Performance, West Liberty, WV 26074. Offers community education research and leadership (MA Ed); innovative instruction (MA Ed); leadership in disability services (MA Ed); leadership studies (MA Ed); multi-categorical special education (MA Ed); reading specialist (MA Ed); sports leadership and coaching (MA Ed). *Accreditation:* NCATE. *Program availability:* Part-time, evening/weekend. *Degree requirements:* For master's, capstone experience. *Entrance requirements:* For master's, minimum GPA of 2.5 or 3.0 (depending on track). Additional exam requirements/recommendations for international students: Required—TOEFL. Electronic applications accepted.

Westminster College, Graduate School, Program in Special Education and Reading Specialist, New Wilmington, PA 16172-0001. Offers M Ed. *Program availability:* Part-time, evening/weekend. *Degree requirements:* For master's, comprehensive exam, portfolio. *Entrance requirements:* For master's, minimum GPA of 3.0.

West Texas A&M University, College of Education and Social Sciences, Department of Education, Program in Reading Education, Canyon, TX 79015. Offers M Ed. *Program availability:* Part-time, evening/weekend. *Degree requirements:* For master's, comprehensive exam. *Entrance requirements:* For master's, GRE General Test, interview with master's committee chairperson, state certification as a reading specialist with 3 years of teaching experience. Electronic applications accepted. *Faculty research:* Multicultural child and adolescent literature, bilingual, dual language, monolingual classrooms.

West Virginia University, College of Education and Human Services, Morgantown, WV 26506. Offers audiology (Au D); autism spectrum disorder (MA); clinical rehabilitation and mental health counseling (MS); communication science and disorders (PhD); counseling (MA); counseling psychology (PhD); curriculum and instruction (Ed D); early childhood education (MA); early intervention/ early childhood special education (MA); education (PhD); educational leadership (MA); educational leadership/ public school administration (Ed D); educational leadership/public school administration (MA); educational psychology (MA, Ed D); elementary education (MA); gifted education (MA); higher education administration (MA, Ed D); higher education curriculum and teaching (MA); institutional design and technology (MA); instructional design and technology (Ed D); literacy education (MA); secondary education (MA); secondary education/ English (MA); special education (Ed D); speech pathology (MS). *Accreditation:* ASHA; NCATE. *Program availability:* Part-time, evening/weekend, online learning. *Students:*

392 full-time (325 women), 337 part-time (285 women); includes 44 minority (16 Black or African American, non-Hispanic/Latino; 16 Hispanic/Latino; 12 Two or more races, non-Hispanic/Latino), 11 international. In 2018, 303 master's, 6 doctorates awarded. *Degree requirements:* For master's, content exams; for doctorate, comprehensive exam, thesis/dissertation. *Entrance requirements:* Additional exam requirements/recommendations for international students: Required—TOEFL (minimum score 500 paper-based; 61 iBT). *Application deadline:* For fall admission, 8/1 for domestic students; for spring admission, 1/1 for domestic students; for summer admission, 5/1 for domestic students. Application fee: $60. Electronic applications accepted. *Financial support:* Fellowships, research assistantships, teaching assistantships, career-related internships or fieldwork, Federal Work-Study, institutionally sponsored loans, health care benefits, tuition waivers (full and partial), and administrative assistantships available. Financial award applicants required to submit FAFSA. *Faculty research:* Internet training and integration for teachers, rural education, teacher preparation, organization of schools, evaluation of personnel. *Unit head:* Dr. Tracy L. Morris, Interim Dean, 304-293-0816, Fax: 304-293-7565, E-mail: Tracy.Morris@mail.wvu.edu. *Application contact:* Dr. Melissa Luna, Associate Dean for Research, 304-293-2174, Fax: 304-293-3802, E-mail: Melissa.Luna@mail.wvu.edu.
Website: http://cehs.wvu.edu/

Widener University, School of Human Service Professions, Center for Education, Chester, PA 19013-5792. Offers adult education (M Ed); counseling in higher education (M Ed); counselor education (M Ed); early childhood education (M Ed); educational foundations (M Ed); educational leadership (Ed D); educational psychology (M Ed); elementary education (M Ed); English and language arts (M Ed); health education (M Ed); higher education leadership (Ed D); home and school visitor (M Ed); human sexuality (M Ed, PhD); mathematics education (M Ed); middle school education (M Ed); principalship (M Ed); reading and language arts (Ed D); reading education (M Ed); school administration (Ed D); science education (M Ed); social studies education (M Ed); special education (M Ed); technology education (M Ed). *Accreditation:* NCATE. *Program availability:* Part-time, evening/weekend. Terminal master's awarded for partial completion of doctoral program. *Degree requirements:* For doctorate, thesis/dissertation. *Entrance requirements:* For master's, minimum GPA of 2.5; for doctorate, GRE or MAT, minimum GPA of 2.0 (undergraduate), 3.5 (graduate). Electronic applications accepted. *Expenses:* Contact institution. *Faculty research:* Reading and cognition, adult education, technology education, educational leadership, special education.

Wilkes University, College of Graduate and Professional Studies, School of Education, Wilkes-Barre, PA 18766-0002. Offers educational development and strategies (MS Ed); educational leadership (MS Ed, Ed D); effective teaching (MS Ed); instructional media (MS Ed); instructional technology (MS Ed); international school leadership (MS Ed); international teaching and learning (MS Ed); literacy (MS Ed); middle level education (MS Ed); online teaching (MS Ed); school business leadership (MS Ed); special education (MS Ed); teaching English to speakers of other languages (MS Ed). *Program availability:* Part-time, evening/weekend, 100% online, blended/hybrid learning. *Students:* 87 full-time (67 women), 1,418 part-time (1,078 women); includes 87 minority (13 Black or African American, non-Hispanic/Latino; 1 American Indian or Alaska Native, non-Hispanic/Latino; 11 Asian, non-Hispanic/Latino; 40 Hispanic/Latino; 22 Two or more races, non-Hispanic/Latino). Average age 35. In 2018, 611 master's, 9 doctorates awarded. *Entrance requirements:* Additional exam requirements/recommendations for international students: Required—TOEFL (minimum score 550 paper-based; 79 iBT). *Application deadline:* Applications are processed on a rolling basis. Application fee: $45 ($65 for international students). Electronic applications accepted. *Expenses:* Contact institution. *Financial support:* Unspecified assistantships available. Financial award application deadline: 3/1; financial award applicants required to submit FAFSA. *Unit head:* Dr. Rhonda Rabbitt, Dean, 570-408-4680, Fax: 570-408-7872, E-mail: rhonda.rabbitt@wilkes.edu. *Application contact:* Stephanie Wasmanski, Associate Director of Graduate Admissions, 570-408-5535, Fax: 570-408-7846, E-mail: stephanie.wasmanski@wilkes.edu.
Website: http://www.wilkes.edu/academics/graduate-programs/masters-programs/graduate-education/index.aspx

William Paterson University of New Jersey, College of Education, Wayne, NJ 07470-8420. Offers curriculum and learning (M Ed); early childhood education (Certificate); educational leadership (M Ed); educational media specialist (Certificate); elementary education (MAT, Certificate); elementary education subject area (Certificate); higher education administration (MA); learning disabilities consultant (Certificate); literacy (M Ed); middle level education (M Ed); middle school education subject area (Certificate); professional counseling (M Ed); reading specialist (Certificate); school library media specialist (Certificate); school principal (Certificate); school supervisor (Certificate); secondary education (MAT); special education (M Ed); teacher of students with disabilities (Certificate). *Accreditation:* NCATE. *Program availability:* Part-time, evening/weekend. *Students:* Average age 35. 347 applicants, 87% accepted, 226 enrolled. In 2018, 136 master's awarded. *Degree requirements:* For master's, comprehensive exam, thesis (for some programs), exit interview (for some programs); practicum/internship; minimum GPA of 3.0 (for some programs); exit portfolio (for some programs). *Entrance requirements:* For master's, GRE/MAT, minimum GPA of 2.75; teaching certificate; essay; interview; 2 letters of recommendation; personal statement. Additional exam requirements/recommendations for international students: Required—TOEFL (minimum score 550 paper-based; 79 iBT), IELTS (minimum score 6). *Application deadline:* For fall admission, 6/1 for domestic students, 3/1 for international students; for spring admission, 11/1 for domestic students, 10/1 for international students. Applications are processed on a rolling basis. Application fee: $50. Electronic applications accepted. *Expenses: Tuition, area resident:* Full-time $14,714; part-time $727 per credit. Tuition, state resident: full-time $14,714; part-time $727 per credit. Tuition, nonresident: full-time $22,952; part-time $727 per credit. *International tuition:* $22,952 full-time. *Required fees:* $4 per semester. Tuition and fees vary according to course load, degree level and program. *Financial support:* In 2018–19, 8,416 students received support. Career-related internships or fieldwork, Federal Work-Study, scholarships/grants, and unspecified assistantships available. Support available to part-time students. Financial award application deadline: 3/15; financial award applicants required to submit FAFSA. *Faculty research:* Code switching and creative writing, language instruction, teacher evaluation, preschools, history of educational theories. *Total annual research expenditures:* $311,226. *Unit head:* Dr. Dorothy Feola, Dean, 973-720-2138, Fax: 973-720-3647, E-mail: feolad@wpunj.edu. *Application contact:* Liana Fornarotto, Director of Education Enrollment and Certification, 973-720-2206, Fax: 973-720-2989, E-mail: fornarottol@wpunj.edu.
Website: http://www.wpunj.edu/coe

Wilmington College, Department of Education, Wilmington, OH 45177. Offers reading (M Ed); special education (M Ed). *Accreditation:* TEAC. *Program availability:* Part-time. *Degree requirements:* For master's, comprehensive exam. *Entrance requirements:* For master's, GRE or MAT, minimum GPA of 3.0, 2 letters of recommendation. Additional exam requirements/recommendations for international students: Required—TOEFL. *Faculty research:* Reading instruction, special education practices, conflict resolution in the schools, models of higher education for teachers.

Wilmington University, College of Education, New Castle, DE 19720-6491. Offers applied technology in education (M Ed); career and technical education (M Ed); educational leadership (Ed D); elementary and secondary school counseling (M Ed); elementary studies (M Ed); ESOL literacy (M Ed); higher education leadership (Ed D); instruction: gifted and talented (M Ed); instruction: teacher of reading (M Ed); instruction: teaching and learning (M Ed); organizational leadership (Ed D); school leadership (M Ed); secondary education (MAT); special education (M Ed). *Accreditation:* NCATE. *Program availability:* Part-time, evening/weekend. *Entrance requirements:* For master's, 2 letters of recommendation, interview. Additional exam requirements/recommendations for international students: Required—TOEFL (minimum score 500 paper-based). Electronic applications accepted.

Worcester State University, Graduate School, Department of Education, Worcester, MA 01602-2597. Offers adult English as a esl (Postbaccalaureate Certificate); curriculum and instruction (Ed S); early childhood education (M Ed); education (M Ed); elementary education (M Ed); English as a second language (M Ed, Postbaccalaureate Certificate); middle school education (M Ed); middle/secondary school education (Postbaccalaureate Certificate); moderate disabilities (M Ed, Postbaccalaureate Certificate); reading (M Ed, Postbaccalaureate Certificate); reading specialist (Postbaccalaureate Certificate); school leadership and education administration (M Ed); school psychology (M Ed, Ed S); secondary education (M Ed, Ed S, Postbaccalaureate Certificate). *Faculty:* 10 full-time (9 women), 23 part-time/adjunct (11 women). *Students:* 38 full-time (33 women), 281 part-time (212 women); includes 30 minority (4 Black or African American, non-Hispanic/Latino; 3 American Indian or Alaska Native, non-Hispanic/Latino; 2 Asian, non-Hispanic/Latino; 16 Hispanic/Latino; 5 Two or more races, non-Hispanic/Latino), 2 international. Average age 41. 102 applicants, 98% accepted, 88 enrolled. In 2018, 132 master's, 52 Ed Ss awarded. *Degree requirements:* For master's, comprehensive exam (for some programs), thesis (for some programs), For a detail list of degree completion requirements please see the graduate catalog at catalog.worcester.edu. *Entrance requirements:* For master's, GRE General Test, MAT or GMAT, teaching certificate. For a detail list of entrance requirements please see the graduate catalog at catalog.worcester.edu. Additional exam requirements/recommendations for international students: Required—TOEFL (minimum score 550 paper-based; 79 iBT), PTE. *Application deadline:* For fall admission, 3/1 for domestic and international students; for spring admission, 11/1 for domestic and international students; for summer admission, 3/1 for domestic and international students. Applications are processed on a rolling basis. Application fee: $50. Electronic applications accepted. *Expenses: Tuition, area resident:* Full-time $3042; part-time $169 per credit hour. Tuition, state resident: full-time $3042; part-time $169 per credit hour. Tuition, nonresident: full-time $3042; part-time $169 per credit hour. *International tuition:* $3042 full-time. *Required fees:* $2754; $153 per credit hour. *Financial support:* Career-related internships or fieldwork, scholarships/grants, and unspecified assistantships available. Support available to part-time students. Financial award application deadline: 3/1; financial award applicants required to submit FAFSA. *Unit head:* Dr. Sara Young, Graduate Program Coordinator, 508-929-8246, Fax: 508-929-8164, E-mail: syoung3@worcester.edu. *Application contact:* Sara Grady, Associate Dean of Graduate and Continuing Education, 508-929-8130, Fax: 508-929-8100, E-mail: sara.grady@worcester.edu.

Xavier University, College of Professional Sciences, School of Education, Department of Childhood Education and Literacy, Cincinnati, OH 45207. Offers children's multicultural literature (M Ed); elementary education (M Ed); Montessori education (M Ed); reading (M Ed). *Program availability:* Part-time. *Degree requirements:* For master's, comprehensive exam, thesis, 30 semester hours. *Entrance requirements:* For master's, GRE, MAT, official transcript; 3 letters of recommendation (for Montessori education); resume; statement of purpose. Additional exam requirements/recommendations for international students: Required—TOEFL (minimum score 550 paper-based; 79 iBT). Electronic applications accepted. Application fee is waived when completed online. *Expenses:* Contact institution. *Faculty research:* Multicultural literacy/fluency, early literacy development, writing/creative and across curriculum, assessment of reading abilities.

York College of Pennsylvania, Graduate Programs in Behavioral Sciences and Education, York, PA 17403-3651. Offers educational leadership (M Ed); educational technology (M Ed); reading specialist (M Ed). *Program availability:* Part-time-only, evening/weekend. *Faculty:* 1 full-time (0 women), 10 part-time/adjunct (8 women). *Students:* 1 full-time (0 women), 107 part-time (77 women); includes 3 minority (1 Hispanic/Latino; 2 Two or more races, non-Hispanic/Latino). Average age 34. 35 applicants, 69% accepted, 23 enrolled. In 2018, 10 master's awarded. *Degree requirements:* For master's, comprehensive exam (for some programs), thesis (for some programs). *Entrance requirements:* For master's, statement of applicant's professional and academic goals, 2 letters of recommendation, letter from current supervisor, official undergraduate and graduate transcript(s), copy of teaching certificate(s), current professional resume, interview. *Application deadline:* For fall admission, 7/15 priority date for domestic students; for spring admission, 11/15 priority date for domestic students; for summer admission, 4/15 priority date for domestic students. Applications are processed on a rolling basis. Application fee: $0. Electronic applications accepted. *Expenses:* $640 per credit; no general fee. *Financial support:* Scholarships/grants available. Financial award applicants required to submit FAFSA. *Faculty research:* Classroom technology, assessment, educational leadership, professional development, literacy. *Unit head:* Dr. Joshua D. DeSantis, Director, Graduate Programs in Behavioral Science and Education, 717-815-1936, E-mail: jdesant1@ycp.edu. *Application contact:* Dr. Joshua D. DeSantis, Director, Graduate Programs in Behavioral Science and Education, 717-815-1936, E-mail: jdesant1@ycp.edu.
Website: https://www.ycp.edu/med

Youngstown State University, College of Graduate Studies, Beeghly College of Education, Department of Teacher Education, Youngstown, OH 44555-0001. Offers content area concentration (MS Ed); curriculum and instruction (MS Ed); literacy (MS Ed); special education (MS Ed), including special education. *Accreditation:* NCATE. *Program availability:* Part-time, evening/weekend. *Degree requirements:* For master's, comprehensive exam. *Entrance requirements:* For master's, GRE, MAT, or teaching certificate; minimum GPA of 2.7. Additional exam requirements/recommendations for international students: Required—TOEFL. *Faculty research:* Multicultural literacy, hands-on mathematics teaching, integrated instruction, reading comprehension, emergent curriculum.

Religious Education

Andrews University, School of Graduate Studies, Seventh-day Adventist Theological Seminary, Program in Religious Education, Berrien Springs, MI 49104. Offers MA, Ed D, PhD, Ed S. *Program availability:* Part-time. Terminal master's awarded for partial completion of doctoral program. *Degree requirements:* For doctorate, thesis/dissertation. *Entrance requirements:* For master's, GRE Subject Test. Additional exam requirements/recommendations for international students: Required—TOEFL (minimum score 550 paper-based). *Faculty research:* Marriage and family, spiritual gifts and temperament.

Asbury Theological Seminary, Graduate and Professional Programs, Wilmore, KY 40390-1199. Offers M Div, MA, MAAS, MACE, MACL, MACM, MACP, MAMFC, MAMHC, MAPC, MASF, MAYM, Th M, D Min, PhD, Certificate. *Accreditation:* ATS. *Program availability:* Part-time, online learning. Terminal master's awarded for partial completion of doctoral program. *Degree requirements:* For master's, thesis (for some programs); for doctorate, thesis/dissertation, qualifying exam. *Entrance requirements:* For master's, minimum GPA of 2.75; for doctorate, minimum GPA of 3.0. Additional exam requirements/recommendations for international students: Required—TOEFL, IELTS. Electronic applications accepted.

Biola University, Talbot School of Theology, La Mirada, CA 90639-0001. Offers adult/family ministry (MACE); Bible exposition (MA, Th M); Biblical and theological studies (Certificate); children's ministry (MACE); Christian education (M Div); cross-cultural education ministry (MACE); educational studies (Ed D, PhD); evangelism and discipleship (M Div); general Christian education (MACE); Messianic Jewish studies (M Div, Certificate); missions and intercultural studies (M Div); New Testament (MA, Th M); Old Testament (MA); Old Testament and Semitics (Th M); pastoral and general ministry (M Div); pastoral care and counseling (M Div, MACML); philosophy (MA); preaching and pastoral ministry (MACML); spiritual formation (M Div, Certificate); spiritual formation and soul care (MA); sports ministry (MACML); theology (MA, Th M, D Min, Certificate); youth ministry (MACE). *Program availability:* Part-time, evening/weekend. *Entrance requirements:* For master's, bachelor's degree from accredited college or university; minimum GPA of 2.6 (for M Div), 3.0 (for MA); for doctorate, M Div or MA. Additional exam requirements/recommendations for international students: Required—TOEFL (minimum score 600 paper-based; 88 iBT). Electronic applications accepted. *Faculty research:* New Testament, Old Testament, spiritual formation, Christian education, theological studies, Christian ministry, preaching and pastoral ministry, language and literature, bible exposition, Christian leadership.

Boston College, Lynch School of Education and Human Development, Department of Teacher Education, Special Education and Curriculum and Instruction, Chestnut Hill, MA 02467-3800. Offers curriculum and instruction (M Ed, PhD, CAES); early childhood education (M Ed); elementary education (M Ed); law and curriculum and instruction (JD/M Ed); reading specialist (M Ed, CAES); religious education (M Ed, CAES); secondary education (M Ed, MAT, MST), including biology (MST), chemistry (MST), English (MAT), French (MAT), geology (MST), history (MAT), Latin and classical humanities (MAT), mathematics (MST), physics (MST), secondary teaching (M Ed), Spanish (MAT); special needs: moderate disabilities (M Ed, CAES); special needs: severe disabilities (M Ed); JD/M Ed. *Program availability:* Part-time, evening/weekend, 100% online. *Faculty:* 19 full-time (11 women). *Students:* 186 full-time (140 women), 92 part-time (74 women); includes 58 minority (20 Black or African American, non-Hispanic/Latino; 4 Asian, non-Hispanic/Latino; 29 Hispanic/Latino; 5 Two or more races, non-Hispanic/Latino), 33 international. Average age 28. In 2018, 132 master's, 13 doctorates awarded. Terminal master's awarded for partial completion of doctoral program. *Degree requirements:* For master's, comprehensive exam; for doctorate, comprehensive exam, thesis/dissertation. *Entrance requirements:* Additional exam requirements/recommendations for international students: Required—TOEFL. Application fee: $75. Electronic applications accepted. *Financial support:* Fellowships with full and partial tuition reimbursements, research assistantships with full and partial tuition reimbursements, teaching assistantships with full and partial tuition reimbursements, career-related internships or fieldwork, Federal Work-Study, institutionally sponsored loans, scholarships/grants, traineeships, health care benefits, tuition waivers (full and partial), and unspecified assistantships available. Support available to part-time students. Financial award applicants required to submit FAFSA. *Faculty research:* Teacher education, education research and policy, bilingual education, science education, disabilities, urban education. *Unit head:* Dr. Susan Bruce, Chairperson, 617-552-4214, Fax: 617-552-0812. *Application contact:* Jessica Rivers, Assistant Dean of Graduate Admission and Financial Aid, 617-552-4214, Fax: 617-552-0398, E-mail: riversja@bc.edu.
Website: http://www.bc.edu/education

Boston College, School of Theology and Ministry, Chestnut Hill, MA 02467-3800. Offers church leadership (MA); divinity (M Div); pastoral ministry (MA), including Hispanic ministry, liturgy and worship, pastoral care and counseling, spirituality; religious education (MA, PhD); sacred theology (STD, STL); social justice/social ministry (MA); spiritual direction (MA); theological studies (MTS); theology (Th M, PhD); youth ministry (MA); MA/MA; MS/MA; MSW/MA. *Accreditation:* TEAC. *Program availability:* Part-time. *Degree requirements:* For doctorate, one foreign language, thesis/dissertation. *Entrance requirements:* For doctorate, GRE. Additional exam requirements/recommendations for international students: Required—TOEFL (minimum score 550 paper-based). Electronic applications accepted. *Faculty research:* Philosophy and practice of religious education, pastoral psychology, liturgical and spiritual theology, spiritual formation for the practice of ministry.

Boston University, School of Theology, Boston, MA 02215. Offers chaplaincy (M Div); choral conducting (MSM); church and the arts (M Div); community and global engagement (M Div); organ (MSM); pastoral ministry (M Div); practical theology (PhD), including church and society, congregation and community, evangelism and missiology, homiletics, leadership and administration, pastoral theology and psychology, religious education, spirituality studies, worship; religion and the academy (M Div); transformational leadership (D Min); M Div/MSM; M Div/MSW; MTS/MSW. PhD in mission studies offered in collaboration with Gordon-Conwell Theological Seminary. *Accreditation:* ACIPE; ATS. *Program availability:* Part-time, blended/hybrid learning. *Faculty:* 39 full-time (17 women), 11 part-time/adjunct (5 women). *Students:* 250 full-time (120 women), 90 part-time (41 women); includes 76 minority (36 Black or African American, non-Hispanic/Latino; 1 American Indian or Alaska Native, non-Hispanic/Latino; 11 Asian, non-Hispanic/Latino; 22 Hispanic/Latino; 6 Two or more races, non-Hispanic/Latino), 61 international. Average age 34. 334 applicants, 69% accepted, 106 enrolled. In 2018, 77 master's, 20 doctorates awarded. *Degree requirements:* For master's, comprehensive exam (for some programs), thesis optional, contextual education; for doctorate, 2 languages, dissertation, and comprehensive exam (for PhD). *Entrance requirements:* For master's, minimum GPA of 3.0; for doctorate, GRE General Test, minimum GPA of 3.3. Additional exam requirements/recommendations for international students: Required—TOEFL (minimum score 570 paper-based; 89 iBT). *Application deadline:* For fall admission, 1/15 priority date for domestic and international students; for spring admission, 10/15 priority date for domestic and international students. Applications are processed on a rolling basis. Application fee: $95. Electronic applications accepted. *Expenses:* Contact institution. *Financial support:* In 2018–19, 236 students received support, including 102 fellowships with full tuition reimbursements available (averaging $7,500 per year), 11 research assistantships with full tuition reimbursements available (averaging $22,000 per year), 12 teaching assistantships with full tuition reimbursements available (averaging $22,000 per year); career-related internships or fieldwork, Federal Work-Study, scholarships/grants, and health care benefits also available. Support available to part-time students. Financial award application deadline: 7/15. *Faculty research:* Practical theology, ethics, environmental theology, religion and conflict transformation, chaplaincy. *Total annual research expenditures:* $2.5 million. *Unit head:* Rev. Dr. Mary Elizabeth Moore, Dean, 617-353-3050, Fax: 617-353-3061, E-mail: memoore@bu.edu. *Application contact:* Rev. Dr. Anastasia Kidd, Director of Enrollment, 617-353-3036, Fax: 617-358-0140, E-mail: sthadmis@bu.edu.
Website: http://www.bu.edu/sth

Brandeis University, Graduate School of Arts and Sciences, Department of Education, Waltham, MA 02454-9110. Offers Jewish day schools (MAT); public elementary education (MAT); secondary education (MAT), including Bible, biology, chemistry, Chinese, English, history, Jewish day schools, math, physics; teacher leadership (Ed M, AGC). *Faculty:* 5 full-time (3 women), 9 part-time/adjunct (all women). *Students:* 17 full-time (13 women), 36 part-time (33 women); includes 9 minority (1 Black or African American, non-Hispanic/Latino; 6 Asian, non-Hispanic/Latino; 1 Hispanic/Latino; 1 Two or more races, non-Hispanic/Latino). Average age 36. 90 applicants, 79% accepted, 50 enrolled. In 2018, 44 master's, 18 other advanced degrees awarded. *Degree requirements:* For master's, thesis or alternative, internship, research project, capstone. *Entrance requirements:* For master's, GRE or MAT, transcripts, letters of recommendation, resume, statement of purpose; for AGC, transcripts, letters of recommendation, resume, statement of purpose, interview. Additional exam requirements/recommendations for international students: Required—TOEFL, IELTS, PTE. *Application deadline:* For fall admission, 3/15 priority date for domestic students. Applications are processed on a rolling basis. Application fee: $75. Electronic applications accepted. *Financial support:* Scholarships/grants available. *Faculty research:* Teacher education, education, teaching, elementary education, secondary education, Jewish education, English, history, biology, chemistry, physics, math, Chinese, Bible/Tanakh. *Unit head:* Danielle Igra, Director of Graduate Study, 781-736-8519, E-mail: digra@brandeis.edu. *Application contact:* Manuel Tuan, Administrator, 781-736-2002, E-mail: tuan@brandeis.edu.
Website: http://www.brandeis.edu/gsas/programs/education.html

Brigham Young University, Graduate Studies, College of Religious Education, Provo, UT 84602. Offers MA. *Degree requirements:* For master's, thesis. *Entrance requirements:* For master's, GRE, minimum GPA of 3.0 in last 60 hours, letter of recommendation. Electronic applications accepted. *Expenses:* Contact institution.

Calvary University, Graduate School and Seminary, Kansas City, MO 64147. Offers Bible and theology (MS); Biblical counseling (MA); education (MS), including administration and leadership, Christian education, curriculum and instruction, elementary education; organizational development (MS); pastoral studies (M Div); worship arts (MS). *Program availability:* Part-time, evening/weekend. *Degree requirements:* For master's, variable foreign language requirement, comprehensive exam, thesis or alternative. *Entrance requirements:* For master's, minimum GPA of 2.5, BA or BS, doctrine agreement. Additional exam requirements/recommendations for international students: Required—TOEFL (minimum score 550 paper-based). Electronic applications accepted. *Expenses:* Contact institution.

Calvin Theological Seminary, Graduate and Professional Programs, Grand Rapids, MI 49546-4387. Offers Bible and theology (MA); divinity (M Div), including ancient near eastern languages and literature, contextual ministry, evangelism and teaching, history of Christianity, new church development, New Testament, Old Testament, pastoral care and leadership, preaching and worship, theological studies, youth and family ministries; educational ministry (MA); historical theology (PhD); missions and evangelism (MA); pastoral care (MA); philosophical and moral theology (PhD); systematic theology (PhD); theological studies (MTS); theology (Th M); worship (MA); youth and family ministries (MA). *Accreditation:* ACIPE; ATS. *Program availability:* Part-time. *Degree requirements:* For master's, variable foreign language requirement, thesis (for some programs); for doctorate, 4 foreign languages, comprehensive exam, thesis/dissertation. *Entrance requirements:* For doctorate, GRE General Test, Hebrew, Greek, and a modern foreign language. Additional exam requirements/recommendations for international students: Required—TOEFL (minimum score 550 paper-based), TWE (minimum score 4). Electronic applications accepted. *Faculty research:* Recent Trinity theory, Christian anthropology, Proverbs, reformed confessions, Paul's view of law.

Capital University, Trinity Lutheran Seminary, Columbus, OH 43209-2394. Offers African American studies (MTS); Biblical studies (MTS, STM); Christian education (MA); Christian spirituality (STM); church in the world (MTS); church music (MA); divinity (M Div); general theological studies (MTS); mission and evangelism (STM); pastoral leadership and practice (STM); youth and family ministry (MA); MSN/MTS; MTS/JD. *Accreditation:* ACIPE; ATS. *Program availability:* Part-time. *Degree requirements:* For master's, variable foreign language requirement, comprehensive exam (for some programs), thesis (for some programs), field experience (for some programs). *Entrance requirements:* For master's, BA or equivalent (for MA, M Div, MTS); M Div, MTS, or equivalent (for STM); audition (for MACM). Additional exam requirements/recommendations for international students: Required—TOEFL. Electronic applications accepted. *Expenses:* Contact institution.

Carolina Christian College, Program in Religious Education, Winston-Salem, NC 27102-0777. Offers Christian education (MRE); pastoral care (MRE). *Entrance requirements:* For master's, bachelor's degree from accredited institution, minimum undergraduate "B" average.

Claremont School of Theology, Graduate and Professional Programs, Program in Religion, Claremont, CA 91711-3199. Offers practical theology (PhD), including religious education and formation, spiritual care and counseling; religion (MA, PhD), including comparative theology and philosophy (PhD), Hebrew Bible and Jewish studies (PhD), New Testament and Christian origins (PhD), process studies (PhD), religion, ethics, and society (PhD). *Accreditation:* ACIPE; ATS. Terminal master's awarded for partial completion of doctoral program. *Degree requirements:* For master's, thesis; for doctorate, 2 foreign languages, thesis/dissertation. *Entrance requirements:* For doctorate, GRE General Test. Additional exam requirements/recommendations for international students: Required—TOEFL. Electronic applications accepted.

Religious Education

Clarks Summit University, Baptist Bible Seminary, South Abington Township, PA 18411. Offers Biblical apologetics (MA); Biblical studies (MA); church education (M Min); church planting (M Div, M Min); communication (D Min); counseling and spiritual development (D Min); global ministry (M Min, D Min); ministry (PhD); missions (M Min); organizational leadership (M Min); outreach pastor (M Min); pastoral counseling (M Min); pastoral leadership (M Div, M Min); pastoral ministry (D Min); theological studies (D Min); theology (Th M); youth pastor (M Min). M Min in missions available only for Association of Baptists for World Evangelism missionary personnel. *Program availability:* Part-time, evening/weekend, online learning. Terminal master's awarded for partial completion of doctoral program. *Degree requirements:* For master's, 2 foreign languages, thesis, oral exam (for M Div); for doctorate, 2 foreign languages, comprehensive exam (for some programs), thesis/dissertation, oral exam. *Entrance requirements:* For doctorate, Greek and Hebrew entrance exams (for PhD). Electronic applications accepted.

Clarks Summit University, Online Master's Programs, South Abington Township, PA 18411. Offers Bible (MA); counseling (MA, MS); curriculum and instruction (M Ed); educational administration (M Ed); literature (MA); organizational leadership (MA). *Program availability:* Part-time, evening/weekend, online learning. *Entrance requirements:* Additional exam requirements/recommendations for international students: Required—TOEFL (minimum score 500 paper-based).

Columbia International University, Columbia Graduate School, Columbia, SC 29203. Offers Bible teaching (MABT); counseling (MACN); early childhood and elementary education (MAT); educational administration (M Ed); educational leadership (PhD); instruction and learning (M Ed); teaching English as a foreign language (Certificate); teaching English as a foreign language and intercultural studies (MATF). *Program availability:* Part-time, evening/weekend, online learning. *Degree requirements:* For master's, internships, professional project. *Entrance requirements:* For master's, MAT; GRE (for some programs), minimum GPA of 2.7. Additional exam requirements/recommendations for international students: Required—TOEFL. Electronic applications accepted.

Concordia University Chicago, College of Graduate Studies, Program in Christian Education, River Forest, IL 60305-1499. Offers MA. *Program availability:* Blended/hybrid learning. *Entrance requirements:* Additional exam requirements/recommendations for international students: Required—TOEFL (minimum score 550 paper-based). Electronic applications accepted.

Concordia University, Nebraska, Graduate Programs in Education, Program in Parish Education, Seward, NE 68434. Offers MPE. *Accreditation:* NCATE. *Program availability:* Part-time, evening/weekend. *Degree requirements:* For master's, thesis or alternative. *Entrance requirements:* For master's, GRE, MAT, or NTE, minimum GPA of 3.0, BS in education or equivalent.

Dallas Baptist University, Graduate School of Ministry, Program in Children's Ministry, Dallas, TX 75211-9299. Offers general (MA); special needs children ministry (MA). *Program availability:* Part-time, evening/weekend, online learning. *Application deadline:* Applications are processed on a rolling basis. Application fee: $25. Electronic applications accepted. Application fee is waived when completed online. *Expenses: Tuition:* Full-time $17,262; part-time $959 per credit hour. *Required fees:* $1000; $500 per semester. Tuition and fees vary according to course load and degree level. *Unit head:* Dr. Robert R. Brooks, Dean, 214-333-5494, Fax: 214-333-5673, E-mail: bobb@dbu.edu. *Application contact:* Dr. Shelly Melia, Program Director, 214-333-5943, E-mail: shelly@dbu.edu.
Website: http://www.dbu.edu/ministry/degree-programs/ma-in-childrens-ministry

Dallas Baptist University, Graduate School of Ministry, Program in Student Ministry, Dallas, TX 75211-9299. Offers MA. *Program availability:* Part-time, evening/weekend, online learning. *Application deadline:* Applications are processed on a rolling basis. Application fee: $25. Electronic applications accepted. Application fee is waived when completed online. *Expenses: Tuition:* Full-time $17,262; part-time $959 per credit hour. *Required fees:* $1000; $500 per semester. Tuition and fees vary according to course load and degree level. *Unit head:* Dr. Robert R. Brooks, Dean, 214-333-5494, Fax: 214-333-5673, E-mail: bobb@dbu.edu. *Application contact:* Dr. Chris Shirley, Program Director, 214-333-5256, Fax: 214-333-5689, E-mail: chrissh@dbu.edu.
Website: http://www.dbu.edu/ministry/degree-programs/m-a-in-student-ministry

Dallas Theological Seminary, Graduate Programs, Dallas, TX 75204-6499. Offers adult education (Th M); apologetics (Th M); Bible backgrounds (Th M); Bible translation (Th M); Biblical and theological studies (Certificate); biblical counseling (MA); biblical exegesis and linguistics (MA); biblical exposition (PhD); biblical studies (MA); Biblical theology (Th M); children's education (Th M); Christian education (MA, D Min); Christian leadership (MA); cross-cultural ministries (MA); educational administration (Th M); educational leadership (Th M); evangelism and discipleship (Th M); exposition of Biblical books (Th M); family life education (Th M); general studies (Th M); Hebrew and cognate studies (Th M); hermeneutics (Th M); historical theology (Th M); homiletics (Th M); intercultural ministries (Th M); Jesus studies (Th M); leadership studies (Th M); media and communication (MA); media arts (Th M); ministry (D Min); ministry with women (Th M); New Testament studies (Th M, PhD); Old Testament studies (Th M, PhD); parachurch ministries (Th M); pastoral care and counseling (Th M); pastoral theology and practice (Th M); philosophy (Th M); sacred theology (STM); spiritual formation (Th M); systematic theology (Th M); teaching in Christian institutions (Th M); theological studies (PhD); urban ministries (Th M); worship studies (Th M); youth education (Th M). *Program availability:* Part-time, online learning. *Degree requirements:* For master's, variable foreign language requirement, thesis (for some programs); for doctorate, 2 foreign languages, thesis/dissertation. *Entrance requirements:* For master's, GRE or MAT (if minimum undergraduate cumulative GPA is below 2.5 or undergraduate degree is unaccredited). Additional exam requirements/recommendations for international students: Required—TOEFL (minimum score 575 paper-based; 85 iBT), TWE. Electronic applications accepted.

Felician University, Program in Religious Education, Lodi, NJ 07644-2117. Offers MA, Certificate. *Accreditation:* TEAC. *Program availability:* Part-time, evening/weekend, online only, 100% online. *Degree requirements:* For master's, thesis, presentation; for Certificate, thesis, capstone project. *Entrance requirements:* For master's, letter of recommendation, interview, reading/writing sample, ministerial discount form, notarized copy of valid passport, graduation from accredited baccalaureate program. Additional exam requirements/recommendations for international students: Required—TOEFL (minimum score 550 paper-based; 79 iBT), IELTS (minimum score 6.5), PTE (minimum score 56). Electronic applications accepted. Application fee is waived when completed online. *Expenses:* Contact institution. *Faculty research:* Catechesis and evangelization, education ministry, religious education, church leadership, faith formation.

Fordham University, Graduate School of Religion and Religious Education, New York, NY 10458. Offers pastoral counseling and spiritual care (MA); pastoral ministry/spirituality/pastoral counseling (D Min); religion and religious education (MA); religious education (MS, PhD, PD); spiritual direction (Certificate). *Program availability:* Part-time. Terminal master's awarded for partial completion of doctoral program. *Degree requirements:* For master's, research paper; for doctorate, comprehensive exam, thesis/dissertation. *Entrance requirements:* For doctorate, MAT. Electronic applications accepted. *Expenses:* Contact institution. *Faculty research:* Spirituality and spiritual direction, pastoral care and counseling, adult family and community, growth and young adult.

Gardner-Webb University, School of Divinity, Boiling Springs, NC 28017. Offers biblical studies (M Div); Christian education and formation (M Div); intercultural studies (M Div); ministry (D Min); missiology (M Div); pastoral care and counseling (M Div); pastoral care and counseling/member care for missionaries (D Min); pastoral studies (M Div); M Div/MA; M Div/MBA. *Accreditation:* ACIPE. *Program availability:* Part-time. *Entrance requirements:* For master's, minimum GPA of 2.6; for doctorate, minimum GPA of 2.75. Additional exam requirements/recommendations for international students: Required—TOEFL (minimum score 500 paper-based; 61 iBT). Electronic applications accepted. *Expenses:* Contact institution. *Faculty research:* Jewish-Christian dialogue, Islam.

Garrett-Evangelical Theological Seminary, Graduate and Professional Programs, Evanston, IL 60201-3298. Offers Bible and culture (PhD); Christian education (MA); Christian education and congregational studies (PhD); contemporary theology and culture (PhD); divinity (M Div); ethics, church, and society (MA); liturgical studies (PhD); ministry (D Min); music ministry (MA); pastoral care and counseling (MA); pastoral theology, personality, and culture (PhD); spiritual formation and evangelism (MA); theological studies (MTS); M Div/MSW. M Div/MSW offered jointly with Loyola University Chicago. *Accreditation:* ACIPE; ATS (one or more programs are accredited). *Program availability:* Part-time. *Degree requirements:* For master's, thesis (for some programs); for doctorate, thesis/dissertation. *Entrance requirements:* For doctorate, GRE (PhD). Additional exam requirements/recommendations for international students: Required—TOEFL (minimum score 560 paper-based). Electronic applications accepted.

Global University, Graduate School of Theology, Springfield, MO 65804. Offers bible and theology (D Min); biblical language (M Div); biblical studies (MA); Christian ministry (M Div, D Min); ministerial studies (MA), including education, leadership, missions, New Testament, Old Testament. *Program availability:* Part-time, evening/weekend, online learning. *Degree requirements:* For master's, thesis (for some programs). *Entrance requirements:* For master's, minimum undergraduate GPA of 3.0. Electronic applications accepted. *Faculty research:* Higher education, cross-cultural missions.

Gratz College, Graduate Programs, Program in Jewish Education, Melrose Park, PA 19027. Offers education leadership (Ed D); Jewish instructional education (MA); MA/MA. *Program availability:* Part-time, evening/weekend, online learning. *Degree requirements:* For master's, one foreign language, internship. *Entrance requirements:* For master's, interview.

Hebrew College, Shoolman Graduate School of Jewish Education, Newton Centre, MA 02459. Offers early childhood Jewish education (Certificate); Jewish day school education (Certificate); Jewish education (MJ Ed); Jewish family education (Certificate); Jewish special education (Certificate); Jewish youth education, informal education and camping (Certificate). *Program availability:* Part-time, evening/weekend, online learning. *Degree requirements:* For master's, one foreign language. *Entrance requirements:* For master's, GRE, interview. Additional exam requirements/recommendations for international students: Required—TOEFL.

Hebrew Union College–Jewish Institute of Religion, School of Education, New York, NY 10012-1186. Offers MARE. *Program availability:* Part-time. *Degree requirements:* For master's, one foreign language, thesis. *Entrance requirements:* For master's, GRE, minimum 2 years of college-level Hebrew.

Houston Baptist University, College of Education and Behavioral Sciences, Programs in Education, Houston, TX 77074-3298. Offers bilingual education (M Ed); counselor education (M Ed); curriculum and instruction (M Ed); curriculum and instruction (EC-6 bilingual) (M Ed); curriculum and instruction in all-level art, Spanish, music, or physical education (M Ed); curriculum and instruction in EC-6 and special education (EC-12) (M Ed); curriculum and instruction in instructional technology (M Ed); curriculum and instruction in mathematics, science, or social studies (4-8) (M Ed); curriculum and instruction with EC-6 generalist (M Ed); curriculum and instruction with English language arts and reading (4-8) (M Ed); educational administration (M Ed); educational diagnostician (M Ed); executive educational leadership (Ed D); higher education in business management (M Ed); higher education in Christian studies (M Ed); higher education in counseling (M Ed); higher education in educational technology (M Ed); reading (M Ed); special educational leadership (Ed D). *Program availability:* Part-time, evening/weekend, 100% online, blended/hybrid learning. *Degree requirements:* For master's, comprehensive exam; for doctorate, thesis/dissertation. *Entrance requirements:* For master's, minimum GPA of 2.75, two recommendations, resume, bachelor's degree conferred transcript; interview (for non-certified teachers); for doctorate, GRE, 5 letters of recommendation. Additional exam requirements/recommendations for international students: Required—TOEFL (minimum score 80 iBT), IELTS (minimum score 6.5). Electronic applications accepted. Application fee is waived when completed online. *Expenses:* Contact institution. *Faculty research:* Autism and inclusion, integrating technology into instruction, school change and leadership trust.

Inter American University of Puerto Rico, Metropolitan Campus, Graduate Programs, Program in Christian Education, San Juan, PR 00919-1293. Offers PhD.

Interdenominational Theological Center, Graduate and Professional Programs, Atlanta, GA 30314-4112. Offers Christian education (MACE); ministry (D Min); pastoral counseling (Th D); theology (M Div); M Div/MACE. D Min and Th D programs offered in collaboration with the Atlanta Theological Association. *Accreditation:* ACIPE; ATS (one or more programs are accredited). *Program availability:* Part-time, evening/weekend, blended/hybrid learning. *Degree requirements:* For doctorate, thesis/dissertation. *Entrance requirements:* For doctorate, master's degree. Electronic applications accepted.

The Jewish Theological Seminary, William Davidson Graduate School of Jewish Education, New York, NY 10027-4649. Offers MA, Ed D. Offered in conjunction with The Rabbinical School; H. L. Miller Cantorial School and College of Jewish Music; Teacher's College, Columbia University; and Union Theological Seminary. *Program availability:* Part-time, online learning. *Degree requirements:* For master's, one foreign language, thesis optional; for doctorate, one foreign language, comprehensive exam, thesis/dissertation. *Entrance requirements:* For master's, GRE or MAT, 3 letters of recommendation; for doctorate, GRE or MAT, writing sample, 3 letters of recommendation. Additional exam requirements/recommendations for international students: Recommended—TOEFL.

Lancaster Theological Seminary, Graduate and Professional Programs, Lancaster, PA 17603-2812. Offers biblical studies (MAR); Christian education (MAR); Christianity and the arts (MAR); church history (MAR); congregational life (MAR); lay leadership (Certificate); theological studies (M Div); theology (D Min); theology and ethics (MAR). *Accreditation:* ACIPE; ATS. *Degree requirements:* For doctorate, thesis/dissertation.

La Sierra University, School of Religion, Riverside, CA 92505. Offers pastoral ministry (M Div); religion (MA); religious education (MA); religious studies (MA). *Program availability:* Part-time. *Degree requirements:* For master's, one foreign language, thesis or alternative. *Entrance requirements:* For master's, GRE General Test, minimum GPA of 3.0.

Liberty University, School of Divinity, Lynchburg, VA 24515. Offers Biblical exposition (MA); Biblical languages (M Div); Biblical studies (M Div, MA, MAR, Th M, D Min); chaplaincy (M Div, D Min); Christian apologetics (M Div, MA, MAR, Th M); Christian leadership and church ministries (M Div); Christian ministries (M Div); Christian ministry (MA); Christian thought (M Div); church history (M Div, MAR, Th M); community chaplaincy (M Div, MAR); discipleship (D Min); discipleship and church ministry (M Div, MAR, MCM); evangelism and church planting (MAR, MCM, D Min); expository preaching (D Min); global ministry (MA); global studies (M Div, MAR, MCM, MGS, Th M); healthcare chaplaincy (M Div); homiletics (M Div, MAR, Th M); leadership (M Div, MAR); marketplace chaplaincy (M Div, MCM); ministry leadership (Ed D); pastoral counseling (M Div, MA, MAR, D Min), including addictions and recovery (MA), crisis response and trauma (MA), discipleship and church ministries (MA), leadership (MA), life coaching (MA), marketplace chaplaincy (MA), marriage and family (MA), military resilience (MA), pastoral counseling (MA); pastoral leadership (D Min); pastoral ministries (M Div, M Serv Soc, MCM); religious education (MRE); sports chaplaincy (MA); theology (M Div, MAR, MTS, Th M); theology and apologetics (D Min, PhD); worship (M Div, MAR, MCM, D Min); youth and family ministries (M Div). *Program availability:* Part-time, online learning. *Students:* 2,414 full-time (700 women), 2,600 part-time (757 women); includes 1,336 minority (965 Black or African American, non-Hispanic/Latino; 29 American Indian or Alaska Native, non-Hispanic/Latino; 88 Asian, non-Hispanic/Latino; 164 Hispanic/Latino; 10 Native Hawaiian or other Pacific Islander, non-Hispanic/Latino; 80 Two or more races, non-Hispanic/Latino), 115 international. Average age 42. 4,358 applicants, 35% accepted, 957 enrolled. In 2018, 1,331 master's, 82 doctorates awarded. *Degree requirements:* For master's, 2 foreign languages, thesis (for some programs); for doctorate, 2 foreign languages, thesis/dissertation. *Entrance requirements:* For master's, minimum undergraduate GPA of 2.0; for doctorate, GRE General Test or MAT, minimum graduate GPA of 3.0. Additional exam requirements/recommendations for international students: Required—TOEFL (minimum score 600 paper-based; 100 iBT). *Application deadline:* For fall admission, 6/1 for domestic students; for spring admission, 11/1 for domestic students. Applications are processed on a rolling basis. Application fee: $50. Electronic applications accepted. *Expenses:* Contact institution. *Financial support:* Teaching assistantships with tuition reimbursements, career-related internships or fieldwork, and Federal Work-Study available. Financial award applicants required to submit FAFSA. *Unit head:* Dr. Ed Hindson, Dean, 434-582-2569, E-mail: divinity@liberty.edu. *Application contact:* Jay Bridge, Director of Graduate Admissions, 800-424-9595, Fax: 800-628-7977, E-mail: gradadmissions@liberty.edu.
Website: https://www.liberty.edu/divinity/

Lincoln Christian Seminary, Graduate and Professional Programs, Lincoln, IL 62656-2167. Offers Bible and theology (MA); Christian ministries (MA); counseling (MA); divinity (M Div); leadership ministry (D Min); religious education (MRE). *Accreditation:* ACIPE; ATS. *Program availability:* Part-time. *Degree requirements:* For master's, 2 foreign languages, thesis; for doctorate, thesis/dissertation. *Entrance requirements:* For master's, minimum GPA of 2.5; for doctorate, M Div or equivalent. Additional exam requirements/recommendations for international students: Required—TOEFL (minimum score 550 paper-based). Electronic applications accepted.

Loyola University Chicago, Institute of Pastoral Studies, Chicago, IL 60611. Offers Christian spirituality (MA), including spiritual direction; church management (Certificate); counseling for ministry (MA); divinity (M Div); health care ministry leadership (Certificate); health care mission leadership (MA); pastoral counseling (MA, Certificate); pastoral studies (MA); religious education (Certificate); social justice (MA, Certificate); spiritual direction (Certificate); M Div/MA; M Div/MSW; MSW/MA. MSW/MA offered with School of Social Work. *Accreditation:* ACIPE. *Program availability:* Part-time, evening/weekend, 100% online, blended/hybrid learning. *Faculty:* 9 full-time (3 women), 20 part-time/adjunct (7 women). *Students:* 80 full-time (51 women), 150 part-time (107 women); includes 58 minority (24 Black or African American, non-Hispanic/Latino; 7 Asian, non-Hispanic/Latino; 27 Hispanic/Latino), 29 international. Average age 45. 128 applicants, 79% accepted, 72 enrolled. In 2018, 53 master's, 5 other advanced degrees awarded. *Degree requirements:* For master's, thesis optional, project. *Entrance requirements:* Additional exam requirements/recommendations for international students: Required—TOEFL (minimum score 550 paper-based; 79 iBT), IELTS (minimum score 6.5). *Application deadline:* Applications are processed on a rolling basis. Application fee: $50. Electronic applications accepted. Application fee is waived when completed online. *Expenses:* 1240.00. *Financial support:* In 2018–19, 111 students received support. Career-related internships or fieldwork, Federal Work-Study, scholarships/grants, and unspecified assistantships available. Support available to part-time students. Financial award application deadline: 3/15. *Faculty research:* Catholic theology, skills of religious ministry, family ministries, spirituality and divorced men. *Unit head:* Dr. Peter L Jones, Interim Dean, 312-915-7400, Fax: 312-915-7504, E-mail: pjones5@luc.edu. *Application contact:* Dr. Peter L Jones, Interim Dean, 312-915-7400, Fax: 312-915-7504, E-mail: pjones5@luc.edu.
Website: http://www.luc.edu/ips/

Maple Springs Baptist Bible College and Seminary, Graduate and Professional Programs, Capitol Heights, MD 20743. Offers biblical studies (MA, Certificate); Christian counseling (MA); church administration (MA); divinity (M Div); ministry (D Min); religious education (MRE).

Midwestern Baptist Theological Seminary, Graduate and Professional Programs, Kansas City, MO 64118-4697. Offers Christian education (MACE); Christian foundations (Graduate Certificate); church music (MCM); counseling (MA); ministry (D Ed Min, D Min); Old or New Testament studies (PhD); theology (M Div). *Accreditation:* ATS. *Program availability:* Part-time, online learning. *Degree requirements:* For doctorate, thesis/dissertation. *Entrance requirements:* For doctorate, MAT. Electronic applications accepted. *Faculty research:* Ministerial studies, Biblical and theological studies, missions, counseling.

Milligan College, Emmanuel Christian Seminary at Milligan College, Milligan College, TN 37682. Offers Christian care and counseling (M Div); Christian education (M Div); Christian ministries (MACM, Graduate Certificate); Christian ministry (M Div); Christian theology (M Div, MAR); church history (MAR); church history/historical theology (M Div); general studies (M Div); ministry (D Min); New Testament (M Div, MAR); Old Testament (M Div, MAR); urban ministry (M Div); world missions (M Div). *Accreditation:* ACIPE; ATS. *Program availability:* Part-time, blended/hybrid learning. *Faculty:* 12 full-time (1 woman), 10 part-time/adjunct (1 woman). *Students:* 70 full-time (29 women), 67 part-time (29 women); includes 15 minority (7 Black or African American, non-Hispanic/Latino; 1 American Indian or Alaska Native, non-Hispanic/Latino; 1 Asian, non-Hispanic/Latino; 5 Hispanic/Latino; 1 Two or more races, non-Hispanic/Latino), 9 international. Average age 37. 61 applicants, 98% accepted, 49 enrolled. In 2018, 13 master's, 2 doctorates awarded. *Degree requirements:* For master's, 2 foreign languages, thesis or alternative, portfolio; for doctorate, thesis/dissertation. *Entrance requirements:* For master's, undergraduate degree and supporting transcripts, essay/personal statement, professional recommendations, interview; for doctorate, M Div or equivalent, essay/personal statement, professional recommendations. Additional exam requirements/recommendations for international students: Required—TOEFL (minimum score 550 paper-based, 79 iBT) or IELTS (6.5). *Application deadline:* For fall admission, 8/1 for domestic students, 6/1 for international students; for spring admission, 12/15 for domestic students, 8/1 for international students. Applications are processed on a rolling basis. Application fee: $30 ($0 for international students). Electronic applications accepted. *Expenses:* $485 per hour; $375 fees per semester; $75 one time records fee. *Financial support:* Scholarships/grants and unspecified assistantships available. Financial award application deadline: 12/1; financial award applicants required to submit FAFSA. *Faculty research:* Theology of Old Testament prophets; performance criticism of New Testament texts; practical theology and spiritual formation for Christian leaders; church history and missions; constructive theology, art and imagination. *Unit head:* Dr. Rollin Ramsaran, Academic Dean, Emmanuel Christian Seminary, 423-461-1524, Fax: 423-926-6198, E-mail: raramsaran@milligan.edu. *Application contact:* Lauren Gullett, Director of Admissions and Recruitment for Emmanuel Christian Seminary, 423-461-1535, Fax: 423-926-6198, E-mail: lwgullett@milligan.edu.
Website: http://ecs.milligan.edu/

Moody Theological Seminary–Michigan, Graduate Programs, Plymouth, MI 48170. Offers Bible (Graduate Certificate); Christian education (MA); counseling psychology (MA); divinity (M Div); theological studies (MA). *Accreditation:* ATS. *Program availability:* Part-time, evening/weekend. *Degree requirements:* For master's, one foreign language, thesis. *Faculty research:* Judaism, cults, world religions.

Newman Theological College, Religious Education Programs, Edmonton, AB T6V 1H3, Canada. Offers MRE, Graduate Certificate. *Program availability:* Part-time, blended/hybrid learning. *Faculty:* 2 full-time (1 woman), 4 part-time/adjunct (1 woman). *Students:* 1 (woman) full-time, 80 part-time (66 women). Average age 40. 20 applicants, 100% accepted, 20 enrolled. In 2018, 15 master's awarded. *Degree requirements:* For master's, Field Education. *Entrance requirements:* For master's, 2 years of teaching experience, graduate diploma in religious education; for Graduate Certificate, bachelor's degree in education, teaching certificate. Additional exam requirements/recommendations for international students: Required—TOEFL (minimum score 560 paper-based; 86 iBT), IELTS (minimum score 6.5), CAEL. *Application deadline:* For fall admission, 8/19 priority date for domestic students, 2/19 priority date for international students; for winter admission, 11/20 priority date for domestic students; for spring admission, 2/19 priority date for domestic students. Applications are processed on a rolling basis. Application fee: $45 ($250 for international students). *Expenses:* $663 per 3-credit course; $207 per field education unit; $35 administrative fee per semester; $10 library fee per course; $30 part-time student association fee per semester. *Financial support:* In 2018–19, 9 students received support. Tuition bursaries available. Support available to part-time students. Financial award application deadline: 5/31. *Unit head:* Sandra Talarico, Director, 780-392-2450 Ext. 2214, Fax: 780-462-4013, E-mail: sandra.talarico@newman.edu. *Application contact:* Maria Saulnier, Registrar, 780-392-2451, Fax: 780-462-4013, E-mail: registrar@newman.edu.
Website: http://www.newman.edu/

New Orleans Baptist Theological Seminary, Graduate and Professional Programs, Division of Christian Education Ministries, New Orleans, LA 70126-4858. Offers Christian education (M Div, MACE, D Min, DEM, PhD). *Program availability:* Evening/weekend, online learning. *Degree requirements:* For master's, 2 foreign languages; for doctorate, 3 foreign languages, comprehensive exam, thesis/dissertation. *Entrance requirements:* For doctorate, GRE General Test.

Oral Roberts University, School of Theology and Missions, Tulsa, OK 74171. Offers biblical literature (MA), including advanced languages, Judaic-Christian studies; church ministries and leadership (D Min); clinical pastoral education (M Div); missions (MA); pastoral care and chaplaincy (M Div, D Min); practical theology (MA), including teaching ministries, urban ministries; professional counseling (MA), including addiction studies, marriage and family therapy; theological/historical studies (MA). *Accreditation:* ATS. *Program availability:* Part-time, online learning. *Degree requirements:* For master's, thesis (for some programs), practicum/internship; for doctorate, thesis/dissertation, applied research project. *Entrance requirements:* For master's, GRE General Test or MAT (waived for those with undergraduate degree from regionally accredited institution and 3.0 or higher GPA), minimum GPA of 2.5 (professional) or 3.0 (academic); for doctorate, M Div, minimum GPA of 3.0, 3 years of full-time ministry experience. Additional exam requirements/recommendations for international students: Recommended—TOEFL (minimum score 550 paper-based; 79 iBT), IELTS (minimum score 7). Electronic applications accepted. Application fee is waived when completed online.

Palm Beach Atlantic University, School of Ministry, West Palm Beach, FL 33416-4708. Offers Christian studies (MA); ministry (M Div). *Program availability:* Part-time. *Faculty:* 12 full-time (3 women), 2 part-time/adjunct (1 woman). *Students:* 22 full-time (6 women), 28 part-time (9 women); includes 16 minority (8 Black or African American, non-Hispanic/Latino; 7 Hispanic/Latino; 1 Two or more races, non-Hispanic/Latino), 2 international. Average age 28. In 2018, 8 master's awarded. *Degree requirements:* For master's, one foreign language, comprehensive exam (for some programs), thesis optional, 8 credits of biblical language (for MDiv). *Entrance requirements:* For master's, minimum GPA of 2.75; writing samples. Additional exam requirements/recommendations for international students: Required—TOEFL (minimum score 550 paper-based; 79 iBT). *Application deadline:* Applications are processed on a rolling basis. Application fee: $50. Electronic applications accepted. *Expenses: Tuition:* Part-time $767 per credit. Tuition and fees vary according to program. *Financial support:* In 2018–19, 47 students received support. Scholarships/grants, unspecified assistantships, and employee education grants available. Financial award application deadline: 5/1; financial award applicants required to submit FAFSA. *Faculty research:* Ethics, apologetics, spiritual formation, theology. *Unit head:* Dr. Justin Hardin, Director of the M Div Program, 561-803-2377. *Application contact:* Graduate Admissions, 888-468-6722, E-mail: grad@pba.edu.
Website: http://learn-well.pba.edu/academics/som-grad/index.html

Pfeiffer University, Program in Practical Theology, Misenheimer, NC 28109-0960. Offers MA. *Program availability:* Part-time, evening/weekend. *Entrance requirements:* For master's, minimum GPA of 2.75.

Phillips Theological Seminary, Programs in Theology, Tulsa, OK 74116. Offers administration of church agencies (M Div); campus ministry (M Div); church-related social work (M Div); college and seminary teaching (M Div); global mission work (M Div); institutional chaplaincy (M Div); ministerial vocations in Christian education (M Div); ministry (D Min), including parish ministry, pastoral counseling, practices of ministry; ministry and culture (MAMC), including Christian education, congregational leadership, history and practice of Christian spirituality, theology, ethics, and culture; ministry of music (M Div); pastoral care and counseling (M Div); pastoral ministry (M Div); theological studies (MTS). *Accreditation:* ATS. *Program availability:* Part-time, online learning. *Degree requirements:* For master's, thesis (for some programs); for doctorate, thesis/dissertation. *Entrance requirements:* For master's, minimum GPA of 2.5; for doctorate, M Div, minimum GPA of 3.0. *Faculty research:* Biblical studies, historical studies, theology and culture, practical theology, theology and film.

Pontifical Catholic University of Puerto Rico, College of Education, Program in Religious Education, Ponce, PR 00717-0777. Offers MRE.

Religious Education

Providence University College & Theological Seminary, Theological Seminary, Otterburne, MB R0A 1G0, Canada. Offers children's ministry (Certificate); Christian studies (MA, Certificate); counseling (MA); cross-cultural discipleship (Certificate); divinity (M Div); educational studies (MA), including counseling psychology, educational ministries, student development, teaching English to speakers of other languages, training teachers of English to speakers of other languages; global studies (MA); lay counseling (Diploma); ministry (D Min); teaching English to speakers of other languages (Certificate); theological studies (MA); training teacher of English to speakers of other languages (Certificate); youth ministry (Certificate). *Accreditation:* ATS. *Program availability:* Part-time. *Degree requirements:* For master's, variable foreign language requirement, thesis (for some programs); for doctorate, thesis/dissertation. *Entrance requirements:* Additional exam requirements/recommendations for international students: Recommended—TOEFL (minimum score 550 paper-based). *Faculty research:* Studies in Isaiah, theology of sin.

Reformed Theological Seminary–Jackson Campus, Graduate and Professional Programs, Jackson, MS 39209-3004. Offers Bible, theology, and missions (Certificate); Biblical exegesis (M Div); biblical studies (MA); Christian education (MA); counseling (M Div); marriage and family therapy (MA); ministry (D Min); missions (M Div, MA, D Min); theological studies (MA). *Accreditation:* AAMFT/COAMFTE (one or more programs are accredited); ATS (one or more programs are accredited). *Degree requirements:* For master's, thesis (for some programs), fieldwork; for doctorate, 2 foreign languages, thesis/dissertation. *Entrance requirements:* For master's, minimum GPA of 2.6; for doctorate, minimum GPA of 3.0. Additional exam requirements/recommendations for international students: Required—TOEFL.

Regent University, Graduate School, School of Divinity, Virginia Beach, VA 23464-9800. Offers Christian spirituality and formation (MA); divinity (M Div), including Biblical studies (M Div, MTS, Th M, PhD), chaplain ministry, Christian theology (M Div, MTS, Th M, PhD), church and ministry (M Div, MA), history of Christianity (M Div, MTS, Th M, PhD), inter-cultural studies (M Div, MA), interdisciplinary studies (M Div, MA, MTS), marketplace ministry (M Div, MA), missional discipleship, practical healing ministry (M Div, MA), worship and media (M Div, MA); leadership and renewal (D Min), including Christian leadership and renewal, clinical pastoral education, community transformation, military ministry, ministry leadership coaching; practical theology (MA), including church and ministry (M Div, MA), cosmogony, inter-cultural studies (M Div, MA), interdisciplinary studies (M Div, MA, MTS), marketplace ministry (M Div, MA), practical healing ministry (M Div, MA), worship and media (M Div, MA); renewal theology (PhD), including Biblical studies (M Div, MTS, Th M, PhD), Christian theology (M Div, MTS, Th M, PhD), history of Christianity (M Div, MTS, Th M, PhD), practical theology; theological studies (MTS), including Biblical studies (M Div, MTS, Th M, PhD), Christian theology (M Div, MTS, Th M, PhD), history of Christianity (M Div, MTS, Th M, PhD), interdisciplinary studies (M Div, MA, MTS); theology (Th M), including Biblical studies (M Div, MTS, Th M, PhD), Christian theology (M Div, MTS, Th M, PhD), history of Christianity (M Div, MTS, Th M, PhD). *Accreditation:* ACIPE; ATS. *Program availability:* Part-time, evening/weekend, 100% online, blended/hybrid learning. *Degree requirements:* For master's, comprehensive exam, thesis or alternative, internship; for doctorate, thesis/dissertation or alternative. *Entrance requirements:* For master's, minimum undergraduate GPA of 2.75, writing sample, personal goal statement, college transcripts; for doctorate, GRE, minimum graduate GPA of 3.5 (PhD), 3.0 (D Min); clergy recommendations; writing sample; transcripts; resume; interview. Additional exam requirements/recommendations for international students: Required—TOEFL (minimum score 577 paper-based). Electronic applications accepted. *Expenses:* Contact institution. *Faculty research:* Greek and Hebrew, theology, spiritual formation, global missions and world Christianity, women in ministry leadership.

Regent University, Graduate School, School of Education, Virginia Beach, VA 23464-9800. Offers education (M Ed, Ed D, PhD), including adult education (Ed D, PhD, Ed S), advanced educational leadership (Ed D, PhD, Ed S), character education (Ed D, PhD, Ed S), Christian education leadership (Ed D, PhD, Ed S), Christian school administration (M Ed), curriculum and instruction (Ed D, PhD, Ed S), curriculum and instruction - adult education (M Ed), curriculum and instruction - Christian school (M Ed), curriculum and instruction - gifted and talented (M Ed), curriculum and instruction - STEM education (M Ed), curriculum and instruction - teacher leader (M Ed), discipleship for ministry (M Ed), educational leadership (M Ed), educational psychology (Ed D, PhD, Ed S), educational technology and online learning (Ed D, PhD, Ed S), elementary education (M Ed), exceptional education executive leadership (Ed D, PhD, Ed S), higher education (Ed D, PhD, Ed S), higher education leadership and management (Ed D, PhD, Ed S), instructional design and technology (M Ed), K-12 school leadership (Ed D, PhD, Ed S), K-12 special education (M Ed), leadership in mathematics education (M Ed), reading specialist (M Ed), special education (Ed D, PhD, Ed S), student affairs (M Ed), TESOL - adult education (M Ed), TESOL - K-12 (M Ed); educational specialist (Ed S), including adult education (Ed D, PhD, Ed S), advanced educational leadership (Ed D, PhD, Ed S), character education (Ed D, PhD, Ed S), Christian education leadership (Ed D, PhD, Ed S), curriculum and instruction (Ed D, PhD, Ed S), educational psychology (Ed D, PhD, Ed S), educational technology and online learning (Ed D, PhD, Ed S), exceptional education executive leadership (Ed D, PhD, Ed S), higher education (Ed D, PhD, Ed S), higher education leadership and management (Ed D, PhD, Ed S), K-12 school leadership (Ed D, PhD, Ed S), special education (Ed D, PhD, Ed S). *Accreditation:* TEAC. *Program availability:* Part-time, evening/weekend, 100% online, blended/hybrid learning. *Degree requirements:* For master's, thesis or alternative; for doctorate, comprehensive exam, thesis/dissertation. *Entrance requirements:* For master's, Virginia Communication and Literacy Assessment (VCLA), PRAXIS, college transcripts, writing sample, interview; for doctorate, GRE, writing sample, resume, transcripts, interview. Additional exam requirements/recommendations for international students: Required—TOEFL (minimum score 577 paper-based). Electronic applications accepted. *Expenses:* Contact institution. *Faculty research:* Christian school administration, curriculum and instruction, educational technology and online learning, higher education, special education.

Rochester College, Center for Missional Leadership, Rochester Hills, MI 48307-2764. Offers MRE.

St. Augustine's Seminary of Toronto, Graduate and Professional Programs, Scarborough, ON M1M 1M3, Canada. Offers divinity (M Div); lay ministry (Diploma); religious education (MRE); theological studies (MTS, Diploma). *Accreditation:* ATS. *Program availability:* Part-time, evening/weekend. *Entrance requirements:* Additional exam requirements/recommendations for international students: Required—TOEFL (minimum score 580 paper-based), TWE (minimum score 5).

Saint Mary's University of Minnesota, Schools of Graduate and Professional Programs, Graduate School of Education, Institute for LaSallian Studies, Winona, MN 55987-1399. Offers LaSallian leadership (MA); LaSallian studies (MA). *Unit head:* Dr. Roxanne Eubank, Director, 612-728-5217, E-mail: reubank@smumn.edu. *Application contact:* Laurie Roy, Director of Admission of Schools of Graduate and Professional Programs, 507-457-8606, Fax: 612-728-5121, E-mail: lroy@smumn.edu.
Website: https://www.smumn.edu/about/institutes-affiliates/institute-for-lasallian-studies

Saints Cyril and Methodius Seminary, Graduate and Professional Programs, Orchard Lake, MI 48324. Offers pastoral ministry (MAPM); religious education (MARE); theology (M Div, MA). *Program availability:* Part-time.

Selma University, Graduate Programs, Selma, AL 36701-5299. Offers Bible and Christian education (MA); Bible and pastoral ministry (MA).

Shasta Bible College, Program in Biblical Counseling, Redding, CA 96002. Offers biblical counseling and Christian family life education (MA). *Program availability:* Part-time. *Degree requirements:* For master's, comprehensive exam (for some programs), thesis or alternative. *Entrance requirements:* For master's, minimum GPA of 2.5. Additional exam requirements/recommendations for international students: Required—TOEFL (minimum score 550 paper-based).

Southeastern Baptist Theological Seminary, Graduate and Professional Programs, Wake Forest, NC 27587. Offers advanced biblical studies (M Div); Christian education (M Div, MACE); Christian ethics (PhD); Christian ministry (M Div); Christian planting (M Div); church music (MACM); counseling (MACO); evangelism (PhD); language (M Div); ministry (D Min); New Testament (PhD); Old Testament (PhD); philosophy (PhD); theology (Th M, PhD); women's studies (M Div). *Accreditation:* ACIPE; ATS (one or more programs are accredited). *Degree requirements:* For master's, thesis (for some programs), oral exam; for doctorate, thesis/dissertation, fieldwork. *Entrance requirements:* For master's, Cooperative English Test, minimum GPA of 2.0, M Div or equivalent (Th M); for doctorate, GRE General Test or MAT, Cooperative English Test, M Div or equivalent, 3 years of professional experience.

Southern Adventist University, School of Religion, Collegedale, TN 37315-0370. Offers evangelism and ministry (M Min); old Testament studies (MA); religious studies (MA). *Program availability:* Part-time. *Faculty:* 11 full-time, 5 part-time/adjunct. *Degree requirements:* For master's, comprehensive exam, thesis (for some programs). *Entrance requirements:* Additional exam requirements/recommendations for international students: Required—TOEFL (minimum score 100 iBT). *Application deadline:* For spring admission, 5/1 priority date for domestic students, 4/30 for international students. Applications are processed on a rolling basis. Application fee: $40. *Financial support:* Tuition waivers (full) and Employee Sponsored available. Support available to part-time students. Financial award application deadline: 8/1; financial award applicants required to submit FAFSA. *Faculty research:* Biblical archaeology. *Unit head:* Dr. Greg A. King, Dean, 423-236-2975, Fax: 423-236-1976, E-mail: gking@southern.edu. *Application contact:* Dr. Alan Parker, Program Coordinator, 423-236-2683, Fax: 423-236-1976, E-mail: parker@southern.edu.
Website: https://www.southern.edu/academics/academic-sites/religion/

Southern Evangelical Seminary, Graduate Programs, Matthews, NC 28105. Offers apologetics (MA, D Min, Certificate); Christian education (MA); church ministry (MA, Certificate); divinity (Certificate), including apologetics (M Div, Certificate); Islamic studies (MA, Certificate); Jewish studies (MA); philosophy (MA); philosophy of religion (PhD); religion (MA); theology (M Div), including apologetics (M Div, Certificate), Biblical studies; youth ministry (MA). *Program availability:* Part-time, evening/weekend, online learning. *Degree requirements:* For master's, thesis (for some programs); for doctorate, 2 foreign languages, comprehensive exam (for some programs), thesis/dissertation. *Entrance requirements:* Additional exam requirements/recommendations for international students: Required—TOEFL (minimum score 600 paper-based).

Southwestern Assemblies of God University, Thomas F. Harrison School of Graduate Studies, Program in Education, Waxahachie, TX 75165-5735. Offers Christian school administration (MS); curriculum development (MS); early education administration (M Ed); middle and secondary education (M Ed). *Degree requirements:* For master's, comprehensive written and oral exams. *Entrance requirements:* For master's, GRE General Test, minimum GPA of 2.5. Electronic applications accepted.

Southwestern Baptist Theological Seminary, Jack D. Terry School of Church and Family Ministries, Fort Worth, TX 76122-0000. Offers MA, MACE, MACSE, DEM, PhD. *Program availability:* Part-time, evening/weekend. Terminal master's awarded for partial completion of doctoral program. *Degree requirements:* For master's, thesis; for doctorate, thesis/dissertation, statistics comprehensive exam. *Entrance requirements:* For doctorate, GRE or MAT, MACE or equivalent, minimum GPA of 3.0. Additional exam requirements/recommendations for international students: Required—TOEFL, TWE. Electronic applications accepted.

Trinity International University, Trinity Evangelical Divinity School, Deerfield, IL 60015-1284. Offers academic ministry (M Div); Biblical and Near Eastern archaeology and languages (MA); chaplaincy and ministry care (MA); Christian studies (Certificate); church and parachurch ministry (M Div); church history (MA, Th M); counseling (Th M); educational ministries (MA); educational ministry (Th M); educational studies (PhD); intercultural studies (MA, PhD); leadership and management (D Min); mental health counseling (MA); military chaplaincy (D Min); ministry (MA); missions (Th M); missions and evangelism (D Min); New Testament (MA, Th M); Old Testament (Th M); Old Testament and Semitic languages (MA); pastoral ministry and care (D Min); pastoral theology (Th M); preaching and teaching (D Min); spiritual formation and education (D Min); systematic theology (MA, Th M); theological studies (MA, PhD); urban ministry (MA). *Program availability:* Part-time, online learning. *Degree requirements:* For master's, comprehensive exam, thesis, fieldwork; for doctorate, comprehensive exam (for some programs), thesis/dissertation; for Certificate, comprehensive exam, integrative papers. *Entrance requirements:* For master's, GRE, MAT, minimum cumulative undergraduate GPA of 3.0; for doctorate, GRE, minimum cumulative graduate GPA of 3.2; for Certificate, GRE, MAT, minimum undergraduate GPA of 2.5. Additional exam requirements/recommendations for international students: Required—TOEFL (minimum score 580 paper-based), TWE (minimum score 4). Electronic applications accepted.

Unification Theological Seminary, Graduate Programs, Barrytown, NY 12507. Offers family and educational ministry (D Min); interfaith peacebuilding (MRE); peace and justice ministry (D Min); religious education (MRE), including interfaith peacebuilding; religious studies (MA); theology (M Div). *Program availability:* Part-time, evening/weekend. *Faculty:* 3 full-time (1 woman), 9 part-time/adjunct (1 woman). *Students:* 48 full-time (16 women), 56 part-time (21 women); includes 49 minority (26 Black or African American, non-Hispanic/Latino; 19 Asian, non-Hispanic/Latino; 2 Hispanic/Latino; 2 Two or more races, non-Hispanic/Latino), 38 international. Average age 46. In 2018, 8 master's, 3 doctorates awarded. *Degree requirements:* For master's, variable foreign language requirement, thesis (for some programs); for doctorate, thesis/dissertation. *Entrance requirements:* For master's, bachelor's degree; for doctorate, M Div or equivalency. Additional exam requirements/recommendations for international students: Required—TOEFL (minimum score 550 paper-based). *Application deadline:* For fall admission, 3/15 priority date for domestic and international students; for spring admission, 9/15 priority date for domestic and international students. Applications are processed on a rolling basis. Application fee: $30. Electronic applications accepted. *Expenses: Tuition:* Full-time $9450; part-time $525 per credit. *Required fees:* $260; $210 per semester. $105 per semester. *Financial support:* In 2018–19, 104 students received support. Scholarships/grants available. Financial award application deadline: 6/15; financial award applicants required to submit FAFSA. *Faculty research:* Church leadership, church history, world religions, ecumenism, interfaith peace building,

service-learning. *Unit head:* Michael Mickler, Vice-President, 845-752-3235, Fax: 845-752-3014, E-mail: mm@uts.edu. *Application contact:* Henry Christopher, Director of Admissions and Financial Aid, 212-563-6647 Ext. 105, Fax: 845-752-3014, E-mail: admissions@uts.edu.
Website: http://www.uts.edu/academics/academic-programs

Union Presbyterian Seminary, Graduate and Professional Programs, Richmond, VA 23227-4597. Offers M Div, MACE, Th M, PhD, M Div/MACE. *Program availability:* Part-time, evening/weekend, online learning. *Degree requirements:* For master's, oral and written exams. *Entrance requirements:* For master's, three references, transcripts, background check; for doctorate, GRE General Test, three references, transcripts, background check, statement of goals, essay. Additional exam requirements/recommendations for international students: Required—TOEFL (minimum score 550 paper-based), TWE (minimum score 4). Electronic applications accepted.

University of Detroit Mercy, College of Liberal Arts and Education, Detroit, MI 48221. Offers addiction counseling (MA); addiction studies (Certificate); clinical mental health counseling (MA); clinical psychology (MA, PhD); computer and information systems (MS); criminal justice (MA); curriculum and instruction (MA); economics (MA); educational administration (MA); financial economics (MA); industrial/organizational psychology (MA); information assurance (MS); intelligence analysis (MA); liberal studies (MALS); religious studies (MA); school counseling (MA, Certificate); school psychology (Spec); security administration (MS); special education: emotionally impaired/behaviorally disordered (MA); special education: learning disabilities (MA). *Program availability:* Part-time, evening/weekend. *Degree requirements:* For doctorate, departmental qualifying exam. *Faculty research:* Psychology of aging, history of technology, Renaissance humanism, U.S. and Japanese economic relations.

University of St. Michael's College, Faculty of Theology, Toronto, ON M5S 1J4, Canada. Offers Catholic leadership (MA); eastern Christian studies (Diploma); religious education (Diploma); theological studies (Diploma); theology (M Div, MA, MRE, MTS, D Min, PhD, Th D); theology and Jewish studies (MA). Th D offered jointly with University of Toronto. *Accreditation:* ATS (one or more programs are accredited). *Program availability:* Part-time. *Degree requirements:* For master's, thesis (for some programs), 1 foreign language (MA), 2 foreign languages (Th M); for doctorate, 3 foreign languages, comprehensive exam, thesis/dissertation; for other advanced degree, thesis optional. *Entrance requirements:* For master's, M Div or BA, course work in an ancient or modern language, minimum GPA of 3.3; for doctorate, MA in theology, Th M, or M Div with thesis, minimum GPA of 3.7; for other advanced degree, minimum GPA of 2.7. Additional exam requirements/recommendations for international students: Required—TOEFL (minimum score 600 paper-based). Electronic applications accepted. *Expenses:* Contact institution. *Faculty research:* Patristics, eastern Christianity, ecology and theology, ecumenism, Jewish Christian studies.

University of St. Thomas, The Saint Paul Seminary School of Divinity, St. Paul, MN 55105. Offers pastoral ministry (MAPM); religious education (MARE); theology (MA). *Accreditation:* ACIPE; ATS. *Program availability:* Part-time, evening/weekend. *Degree requirements:* For master's, one foreign language, comprehensive exam (for some programs), thesis (for some programs). *Entrance requirements:* For master's, GRE, 3 letters of recommendation, interview. Additional exam requirements/recommendations for international students: Required—TOEFL (minimum score 550 paper-based). Electronic applications accepted. *Expenses:* Contact institution. *Faculty research:* Theological education.

University of St. Thomas, School of Education and Human Services, Houston, TX 77006-4696. Offers all level education (M Ed); bilingual/dual language (M Ed); Catholic school teaching (M Ed); Catholic/private school leadership (M Ed); counselor education (M Ed); curriculum and instruction (M Ed); education (Ed D); educational leadership (M Ed); elementary teaching (M Ed); English as a second language (M Ed); exceptionality/educational diagnostician (M Ed); exceptionality/special education (M Ed); generalist (M Ed); reading (M Ed); secondary teaching (M Ed); teaching (MAT). *Accreditation:* TEAC. *Program availability:* Part-time, evening/weekend, online learning. *Degree requirements:* For master's, thesis, field experience. *Entrance requirements:* For master's, GRE or MAT if GPA is below 3.0, bachelor's degree; minimum GPA of 2.75 in bachelor's degree or last 60 credit hours; official transcripts from all institutions; goal statement of 250-300 words; 1 reference. Additional exam requirements/recommendations for international students: Required—TOEFL (minimum score 94 iBT), IELTS (minimum score 7), PTE (minimum score 53). Electronic applications accepted. *Expenses:* Contact institution. *Faculty research:* Leadership, diversity, personality traits, second language acquisition.

University of San Francisco, School of Education, Catholic Educational Leadership Program, San Francisco, CA 94117. Offers Catholic school leadership (Ed D). *Program availability:* Part-time, evening/weekend. *Students:* 14 full-time (5 women), 11 part-time (4 women); includes 8 minority (4 Asian, non-Hispanic/Latino; 2 Hispanic/Latino; 1 Native Hawaiian or other Pacific Islander, non-Hispanic/Latino; 1 Two or more races, non-Hispanic/Latino), 6 international. Average age 38. 14 applicants, 86% accepted, 7 enrolled. In 2018, 16 master's, 5 doctorates awarded. *Degree requirements:* For doctorate, thesis/dissertation. *Entrance requirements:* Additional exam requirements/recommendations for international students: Required—TOEFL, IELTS, PTE. Application fee: $55 ($65 for international students). Electronic applications accepted. *Financial support:* Fellowships, research assistantships, and teaching assistantships available. Financial award application deadline: 3/2; financial award applicants required to submit FAFSA. *Unit head:* Dr. Patricia Mitchell, Chair, 415-422-6226. *Application contact:* Peter Cole, Admission Coordinator, 415-422-5467, E-mail: schoolofeducation@usfca.edu.
Website: https://www.usfca.edu/catalog/graduate/school-of-education/programs-catholic-educational-leadership

Vancouver School of Theology, Graduate and Professional Programs, Vancouver, BC V6T 1Z1, Canada. Offers denominational studies (Diploma); indigenous and inter-religious studies (MA, Diploma); public and pastoral leadership (MA); public and pastoral leadership in spiritual care (MA); theological studies (MATS, Diploma, Graduate Diploma); theology (M Div, Th M). *Accreditation:* ATS. *Program availability:* Part-time, online learning. *Degree requirements:* For master's, comprehensive exam (for some programs), thesis (for some programs); for other advanced degree, one foreign language, thesis. *Entrance requirements:* Additional exam requirements/recommendations for international students: Required—TOEFL (minimum score 80 iBT); Recommended—IELTS (minimum score 6.5). Electronic applications accepted. *Faculty research:* Old Testament studies, pastoral theology, New Testament studies, field education, church history, systematic theology, spirituality.

Vanguard University of Southern California, Graduate Programs in Education, Costa Mesa, CA 92626. Offers Christian education leadership (MA); curriculum and instruction (MA); teacher leadership (MA). *Program availability:* Evening/weekend. *Degree requirements:* For master's, thesis or alternative. *Entrance requirements:* For master's, California Basic Educational Skills Test, California Subject Examinations for Teachers, minimum GPA of 3.0. Additional exam requirements/recommendations for international students: Required—TOEFL (minimum score 550 paper-based; 79 iBT). Electronic applications accepted. *Expenses:* Contact institution. *Faculty research:* Reading, educational administration.

Walsh University, Graduate Programs, Master of Arts in Theology Program, North Canton, OH 44720-3396. Offers parish administration (MA); pastoral ministry (MA); religious education (MA). *Program availability:* Part-time, evening/weekend. *Degree requirements:* For master's, thesis or alternative, culminating assignment. *Entrance requirements:* For master's, MAT or GRE (minimum scores: Verbal 145, Quantitative 146, Combined 291, Writing 3.0), minimum GPA of 3.0. Additional exam requirements/recommendations for international students: Required—TOEFL. Electronic applications accepted. Application fee is waived when completed online. *Expenses:* Contact institution. *Faculty research:* Cardinal Newman, phenomenological method, Flavius Josephus, post-conciliar moral teaching.

Wesley Biblical Seminary, Graduate Programs, Jackson, MS 39206. Offers apologetics (MA); Biblical languages (M Div); Biblical literature (MA); Christian studies (MA); context and mission (M Div); honors research (M Div); interpretation (M Div); ministry (M Div); spiritual formation (M Div); teaching (M Div); theology (MA). *Accreditation:* ATS. *Program availability:* Part-time. *Degree requirements:* For master's, thesis. *Entrance requirements:* Additional exam requirements/recommendations for international students: Required—TOEFL. Electronic applications accepted. *Faculty research:* Patristics, missiology, culture, hermeneutics.

Wheaton College, Graduate School, Christian Formation and Ministry Program, Wheaton, IL 60187-5593. Offers MA. *Program availability:* Part-time. *Faculty:* 3 full-time (1 woman), 1 (woman) part-time/adjunct. *Students:* 16 full-time (9 women), 18 part-time (11 women); includes 6 minority (3 Asian, non-Hispanic/Latino; 1 Hispanic/Latino; 2 Two or more races, non-Hispanic/Latino), 5 international. Average age 27. 30 applicants, 87% accepted, 13 enrolled. In 2018, 14 master's awarded. *Degree requirements:* For master's, thesis or alternative. *Entrance requirements:* For master's, GRE General Test or MAT. Additional exam requirements/recommendations for international students: Required—TOEFL (minimum score 550 paper-based; 80 iBT), IELTS (minimum score 6.5). *Application deadline:* For fall admission, 5/1 for domestic students, 1/1 for international students; for spring admission, 11/1 for domestic students. Applications are processed on a rolling basis. Application fee: $30. Electronic applications accepted. *Expenses: Tuition:* Full-time $20,400; part-time $850 per credit hour. Tuition and fees vary according to degree level and program. *Financial support:* Career-related internships or fieldwork, scholarships/grants, and unspecified assistantships available. Financial award application deadline: 3/1; financial award applicants required to submit FAFSA. *Unit head:* Dr. David Setran, Program Coordinator. *Application contact:* Terrance Campbell, Director of Graduate Admissions, 630-752-5195, Fax: 630-752-7047, E-mail: graduate.admissions@wheaton.edu.
Website: https://www.wheaton.edu/graduate-school/degrees/ma-in-christian-formation-and-ministry/

Xavier University, College of Arts and Sciences, Department of Theology, Cincinnati, OH 45207. Offers health care mission integration (MA); theology (MA), including religious education, social and pastoral ministry, theology. *Program availability:* Part-time, evening/weekend. *Degree requirements:* For master's, final paper (or thesis) and defense or comprehension exam. *Entrance requirements:* For master's, MAT or GRE, 2 letters of recommendation; statement of reasons and goals for enrolling in program (1,000-2,000 words); resume; transcript. Additional exam requirements/recommendations for international students: Required—TOEFL (minimum score 550 paper-based; 79 iBT). Electronic applications accepted. Application fee is waived when completed online. *Expenses:* Contact institution. *Faculty research:* Scripture, ethics, constructive theology, historical theology.

Yeshiva University, Azrieli Graduate School of Jewish Education and Administration, New York, NY 10033-4391. Offers MS, Ed D, Specialist. *Accreditation:* TEAC. *Program availability:* Part-time, evening/weekend. Terminal master's awarded for partial completion of doctoral program. *Degree requirements:* For master's, one foreign language, student teaching experience, comprehensive exam or thesis; for doctorate, one foreign language, comprehensive exam, thesis/dissertation, certifying exams, internship; for Specialist, one foreign language, comprehensive exam, certifying exams, internship. *Entrance requirements:* For master's, GRE General Test, BA in Jewish studies or equivalent; for doctorate and Specialist, GRE General Test, master's degree in Jewish education, 2 years of teaching experience. *Expenses:* Contact institution. *Faculty research:* Social patterns of American and Israeli Jewish population, special education, adult education, technology in education, return to religious values.

Science Education

Adams State University, Office of Graduate Studies, Department of Teacher Education, Alamosa, CO 81101. Offers teacher education (MA), including adaptive leadership, curriculum and instruction, curriculum and instruction-STEM, educational leadership. *Program availability:* Part-time, online learning. *Degree requirements:* For master's, qualifying exam. *Entrance requirements:* For master's, GRE General Test or MAT, minimum undergraduate GPA of 3.0.

Alabama Agricultural and Mechanical University, School of Graduate Studies, College of Education, Humanities, and Behavioral Sciences, Department of Educational Leadership and Secondary Education, Huntsville, AL 35811. Offers biology (M Ed); business/marketing education (M Ed, Ed S); chemistry (M Ed); collaborative teacher secondary education (M Ed, Ed S); education (M Ed, Ed S); English language arts (M Ed); family/consumer science education (M Ed, Ed S); general science (M Ed); general social science (M Ed); mathematics (M Ed, Ed S); physics (M Ed, Ed S); technology education (M Ed). *Accreditation:* NCATE. *Program availability:* Evening/weekend. *Degree requirements:* For master's, comprehensive exam; for Ed S, thesis. *Entrance requirements:* For master's, GRE General Test. Additional exam requirements/recommendations for international students: Required—TOEFL (minimum score 500 paper-based; 61 iBT). Electronic applications accepted. *Faculty research:* World peace through education, computer-assisted instruction.

Science Education

Alabama State University, College of Education, Department of Curriculum and Instruction, Montgomery, AL 36101-0271. Offers early childhood education (Ed S); secondary education (M Ed), including biology education, English language arts education, history education, math education, music education, reading education, social science education. *Program availability:* Part-time, evening/weekend, online only, 100% online. *Faculty:* 7 full-time (4 women), 7 part-time/adjunct (4 women). *Students:* 22 full-time (19 women), 58 part-time (49 women); includes 235 minority (234 Black or African American, non-Hispanic/Latino; 1 Hispanic/Latino), 5 international. Average age 36. 45 applicants, 33% accepted, 6 enrolled. In 2018, 34 master's awarded. *Degree requirements:* For master's, comprehensive exam, thesis optional; for Ed S, comprehensive exam, thesis. *Entrance requirements:* For master's, GRE General Test, MAT, writing competency test; for Ed S, writing competency test, GRE, MAT. Additional exam requirements/recommendations for international students: Required—TOEFL (minimum score 500 paper-based). *Application deadline:* For fall admission, 4/15 for domestic and international students; for spring admission, 11/15 for domestic and international students; for summer admission, 3/15 for domestic and international students. Applications are processed on a rolling basis. Application fee: $25. Electronic applications accepted. *Expenses:* Contact institution. *Financial support:* Fellowships, teaching assistantships, career-related internships or fieldwork, scholarships/grants, tuition waivers (partial), and unspecified assistantships available. Financial award application deadline: 6/30; financial award applicants required to submit FAFSA. *Unit head:* Dr. Joyce Johnson, Acting Chairperson, 334-229-4485, Fax: 334-229-5603, E-mail: jjohnson@alasu.edu. *Application contact:* Dr. Ed Brown, Dean of Graduate Studies, 334-229-4274, Fax: 334-229-4928, E-mail: ebrown@alasu.edu.
Website: http://www.alasu.edu/academics/colleges—departments/college-of-education/curriculum—instruction/index.aspx

Alverno College, School of Professional Studies - Education Division, Milwaukee, WI 53234-3922. Offers adaptive education (MA); administrative leadership (MA); adult education and organizational development (MA); adult educational and instructional design (MA); adult educational and instructional technology (MA); global connections in the humanities (MA); instructional leadership (MA); instructional technology for K-12 settings (MA); professional development (MA); reading education (MA); reading education with adaptive education (MA); science education (MA); special education (MA); teaching in alternative schools (MA). *Accreditation:* NCATE. *Program availability:* Part-time, evening/weekend. *Degree requirements:* For master's, presentation/defense of proposal, conference presentation of inquiry projects. *Entrance requirements:* For master's, bachelor's degree in related field, communication samples from work setting, 3 letters of recommendation. Additional exam requirements/recommendations for international students: Required—TOEFL. Electronic applications accepted. *Expenses:* Contact institution. *Faculty research:* Student self-assessment, self-reflection, integration of curriculum, identifying needs of students in strategic situations and designing appropriate classroom strategies.

American University of Beirut, Graduate Programs, Faculty of Arts and Sciences, Beirut 1107 2020, Lebanon. Offers anthropology (MA); Arab and Middle Eastern history (PhD); Arabic language and literature (MA, PhD); archaeology (MA); art history and curating (MA); biology (MS); cell and molecular biology (PhD); chemistry (MS); clinical psychology (MA); computational sciences (MS); computer science (MS); economics (MA); education (MA), including administration and policy studies, elementary education, mathematics education, psychology school guidance, psychology test and measurements, science education, teaching English as a foreign language; English language (MA); English literature (MA); environmental policy planning (MS); financial economics (MAFE); general psychology (MA); geology (MS); history (MA); Islamic studies (MA); mathematics (MS); media studies (MA); Middle East studies (MA); philosophy (MA); physics (MS); political studies (MA); public administration (MA); public policy and international affairs (MA); sociology (MA); theoretical physics (PhD). *Program availability:* Part-time. *Faculty:* 187 full-time (64 women), 27 part-time/adjunct (15 women). *Students:* 292 full-time (215 women), 216 part-time (148 women). Average age 27. 422 applicants, 64% accepted, 124 enrolled. In 2018, 90 master's, 3 doctorates awarded. *Degree requirements:* For master's, comprehensive exam, thesis (for some programs), project; for doctorate, comprehensive exam, thesis/dissertation (for some programs). *Entrance requirements:* For master's, GRE General Test (for archaeology, clinical psychology, general psychology, economics, financial economics and biology); for doctorate, GRE General Test for all PhD programs, GRE Subject Test for theoretical physics. Additional exam requirements/recommendations for international students: Required—TOEFL (minimum score 583 paper-based; 97 iBT), IELTS (minimum score 7). *Application deadline:* For fall admission, 3/18 for domestic students; for spring admission, 11/5 for domestic students. Application fee: $50. Electronic applications accepted. *Expenses:* MA/MS: Humanities and social sciences=$912/credit. Sciences=$943/credit. Financial economics=$986/credit. Thesis: Humanities/social sciences=$6565 and sciences=$6865. *Financial support:* In 2018–19, 227 fellowships with full tuition reimbursements, 17 research assistantships with full tuition reimbursements, 83 teaching assistantships with full tuition reimbursements were awarded; scholarships/grants, tuition waivers (full and partial), and unspecified assistantships also available. Financial award application deadline: 3/18. *Faculty research:* Sciences: Physics: High energy, Particle, Polymer and Soft Matter, Thermal, Plasma; String Theory, Mathematical physics, Astrophysics (stellar evolution, planet and galaxy formation and evolution, astrophysical dynamics), Solid State physics/thin films, Spintronics, Magnetic properties of materials, Mineralogy, Petrology, and Geochemistry of Hard Rocks, Geochemistry and Petrophysics, Hydrogeology, Micropaleontology, Sedimentology, and Stratigraphy, Structural Geology and Geotectonics, Renewable en. *Total annual research expenditures:* $4.3 million. *Unit head:* Dr. Nadia Maria El Cheikh, Dean, Faculty of Arts and Sciences, 961-1-350000 Ext. 3800, Fax: 961-1-744461, E-mail: nmcheikh@aub.edu.lb. *Application contact:* Adriana Michelle Zanaty, Curriculum and Graduate Studies Officer, 961-1-350000 Ext. 3833, Fax: 961-1-744461, E-mail: az48@aub.edu.lb.
Website: https://www.aub.edu.lb/fas/Pages/default.aspx

American University of Puerto Rico, Program in Education, Bayamon, PR 00960-2037. Offers art education (M Ed); elementary education 4-6 (M Ed); elementary education K-3 (M Ed); general science education (M Ed); physical education (M Ed); special education (M Ed). *Program availability:* Part-time, evening/weekend. *Entrance requirements:* For master's, EXADEP, GRE, or MAT, 2 letters of recommendation, minimum GPA of 2.5.

Andrews University, School of Graduate Studies, College of Arts and Sciences, Department of Biology, Berrien Springs, MI 49104. Offers MAT, MS. *Degree requirements:* For master's, comprehensive exam, thesis. *Entrance requirements:* For master's, GRE Subject Test. Additional exam requirements/recommendations for international students: Required—TOEFL (minimum score 550 paper-based). *Faculty research:* Manatee habitat characterization, seabird habitat dynamics.

Andrews University, School of Graduate Studies, School of Education, Department of Teaching, Learning, and Curriculum, Berrien Springs, MI 49104. Offers curriculum and instruction (MA, Ed D, PhD, Ed S); elementary education (MAT); secondary education (MAT), including biology, education, English, English as a second language, French, history, physics; teacher education (MAT). *Entrance requirements:* For master's, GRE Subject Test. Additional exam requirements/recommendations for international students: Required—TOEFL (minimum score 550 paper-based).

Antioch University New England, Graduate School, Department of Education, Integrated Learning Program, Keene, NH 03431-3552. Offers early childhood education (M Ed); elementary education (M Ed), including arts and humanities, science and environmental education; special education (M Ed). *Degree requirements:* For master's, internship. *Entrance requirements:* For master's, previous course work or work experience in education. Additional exam requirements/recommendations for international students: Required—TOEFL (minimum score 550 paper-based). Electronic applications accepted. *Expenses:* Contact institution. *Faculty research:* Problem-based learning, place-based education, mathematics education, democratic classrooms, art education.

Antioch University New England, Graduate School, Department of Environmental Studies, Science Teacher Certification Program, Keene, NH 03431-3552. Offers MS. *Degree requirements:* For master's, practicum, seminar, student teaching. *Entrance requirements:* Additional exam requirements/recommendations for international students: Required—TOEFL (minimum score 550 paper-based). Electronic applications accepted.

Appalachian State University, Cratis D. Williams School of Graduate Studies, Department of Curriculum and Instruction, Boone, NC 28608. Offers curriculum specialist (MA); educational media (MA); elementary education (MA); middle grades education (MA), including language arts, mathematics, science, social studies. *Accreditation:* NCATE. *Program availability:* Part-time, evening/weekend, online learning. *Degree requirements:* For master's, comprehensive exam, thesis or alternative. *Entrance requirements:* For master's, GRE General Test or MAT, 3 letters of recommendation. Additional exam requirements/recommendations for international students: Required—TOEFL (minimum score 570 paper-based; 79 iBT), IELTS (minimum score 6.5). Electronic applications accepted. *Expenses: Tuition, area resident:* Full-time $4839; part-time $237 per credit hour. Tuition, state resident: full-time $4839; part-time $237 per credit hour. Tuition, nonresident: full-time $18,271; part-time $895.50 per credit hour. *Faculty research:* Media literacy, elementary teaching, curriculum development, online learning environments.

Arcadia University, School of Education, Glenside, PA 19038-3295. Offers art education (M Ed); computer education (CAS); curriculum (CAS); curriculum studies (M Ed); early childhood education (M Ed), including individualized, master teacher, research in child development; educational leadership (M Ed, Ed D, CAS); elementary education (M Ed); English education (MA Ed); environmental education (MA Ed); instructional technology (M Ed); language arts (M Ed); library science (M Ed); mathematics education (M Ed, MA Ed); music education (MA Ed); psychology (MA Ed); reading (M Ed, CAS); science education (M Ed, CAS); secondary education (M Ed, CAS); special education (M Ed, Ed D, CAS); theater arts (MA Ed); written communication (MA Ed). *Accreditation:* NASAD. *Program availability:* Part-time, evening/weekend, online learning. *Faculty:* 14 full-time (10 women). *Students:* 35 full-time (24 women), 299 part-time (243 women); includes 72 minority (49 Black or African American, non-Hispanic/Latino; 1 American Indian or Alaska Native, non-Hispanic/Latino; 12 Asian, non-Hispanic/Latino; 8 Hispanic/Latino; 2 Two or more races, non-Hispanic/Latino), 5 international. In 2018, 152 master's, 8 doctorates awarded. *Entrance requirements:* Additional exam requirements/recommendations for international students: Required—Official results from the TOEFL or IELTS are required. *Application deadline:* Applications are processed on a rolling basis. Application fee: $25. Electronic applications accepted. *Expenses:* Contact institution. *Financial support:* Career-related internships or fieldwork, tuition waivers (partial), and unspecified assistantships available. *Unit head:* Kimberly Dean, Chair, 215-572-8629. *Application contact:* 215-572-2925, Fax: 215-572-2126, E-mail: grad@arcadia.edu.

Arkansas State University, Graduate School, College of Sciences and Mathematics, Department of Biological Sciences, State University, AR 72467. Offers biological sciences (MA); biology (MS); biology education (MSE, SCCT); biotechnology (PSM). *Program availability:* Part-time. *Degree requirements:* For master's, comprehensive exam, thesis (for some programs); for SCCT, comprehensive exam. *Entrance requirements:* For master's, GRE General Test, appropriate bachelor's degree, letters of reference, interview, official transcripts, immunization records, statement of educational objectives and career goals, teaching certificate (for MSE); for SCCT, GRE General Test or MAT, interview, master's degree, letters of reference, official transcript, personal statement, immunization records. Additional exam requirements/recommendations for international students: Required—TOEFL (minimum score 550 paper-based; 79 iBT), IELTS (minimum score 6), PTE (minimum score 56). Electronic applications accepted.

Arkansas State University, Graduate School, College of Sciences and Mathematics, Department of Chemistry and Physics, State University, AR 72467. Offers chemistry (MS); chemistry education (MSE, SCCT). *Program availability:* Part-time. *Degree requirements:* For master's, comprehensive exam, thesis or alternative; for SCCT, comprehensive exam. *Entrance requirements:* For master's, GRE General Test or MAT, appropriate bachelor's degree, official transcript, immunization records, valid teaching certificate (for MSE); for SCCT, GRE General Test or MAT, interview, master's degree, official transcript, immunization records. Additional exam requirements/recommendations for international students: Required—TOEFL (minimum score 550 paper-based; 79 iBT), IELTS (minimum score 6), PTE (minimum score 56). Electronic applications accepted.

Asbury University, School of Graduate and Professional Studies, Wilmore, KY 40390-1198. Offers biology: alternative certificate (MA Ed); chemistry: alternative certificate (MA Ed); English (MA Ed); English as a second language (MA Ed); ESL (MA Ed); French (MA Ed); Latin: alternative certificate (MA Ed); mathematics: alternative certificate (MA Ed); reading/writing endorsement (MA Ed); social studies (MA Ed); social work (MSW), including child and family services; Spanish (MA Ed); special education (MA Ed); special education: alternative certificate (MA Ed); teacher as leader endorsement (MA Ed). *Accreditation:* NCATE. *Program availability:* Part-time. *Degree requirements:* For master's, action research project, portfolio. *Entrance requirements:* For master's, PRAXIS/NTE, minimum GPA of 2.75, letters of recommendation. Additional exam requirements/recommendations for international students: Required—TOEFL (minimum score 550 paper-based). Electronic applications accepted.

Athabasca University, Faculty of Science and Technology, Athabasca, AB T9S 3A3, Canada. Offers architecture (Postgraduate Diploma); information systems (M Sc). *Program availability:* Part-time, online learning. *Degree requirements:* For master's, thesis optional. *Entrance requirements:* For master's, B Sc in computing or other bachelor's degree and IT experience. Electronic applications accepted. *Expenses:* Contact institution. *Faculty research:* Distributed systems multimedia, computer science education, e-services.

Augustana University, MA in Education Program, Sioux Falls, SD 57197. Offers instructional strategies (MA); reading (MA); special populations (MA); STEM (MA); technology (MA). *Accreditation:* NCATE. *Program availability:* Part-time-only, evening/weekend, online only, 100% online. *Degree requirements:* For master's, thesis. *Entrance requirements:* For master's, appropriate bachelor's degree, minimum GPA of 3.0, teaching certificate. Additional exam requirements/recommendations for

international students: Required—TOEFL (minimum score 550 paper-based). Electronic applications accepted. *Expenses:* Contact institution. *Faculty research:* Multicultural education, education of students with autism, well-being in school settings, factors that predict academic hopefulness.

Aurora University, School of Arts and Sciences, Aurora, IL 60506-4892. Offers homeland security (MS); mathematics (MS); mathematics and science education for elementary teachers (MA); mathematics education (MA); science education (MA). *Program availability:* Part-time, evening/weekend, 100% online. *Faculty:* 3 full-time (1 woman), 10 part-time/adjunct (4 women). *Students:* 9 full-time (4 women), 76 part-time (52 women); includes 13 minority (6 Black or African American, non-Hispanic/Latino; 1 Asian, non-Hispanic/Latino; 5 Hispanic/Latino; 1 Two or more races, non-Hispanic/Latino). Average age 36. 54 applicants, 98% accepted, 24 enrolled. In 2018, 6 master's awarded. *Degree requirements:* For master's, research seminars, capstone project. *Entrance requirements:* For master's, bachelor's degree in mathematics or in some other field with extensive course work in mathematics (for MS in mathematics). Additional exam requirements/recommendations for international students: Required—TOEFL (minimum score 550 paper-based; 79 iBT). *Application deadline:* For fall admission, 6/1 for international students; for spring admission, 10/1 for international students. Applications are processed on a rolling basis. Application fee: $0. Electronic applications accepted. *Expenses:* Contact institution. *Financial support:* In 2018–19, 2 students received support. Federal Work-Study, scholarships/grants, and unspecified assistantships available. Financial award applicants required to submit FAFSA. *Unit head:* Dr. Frank Buscher, Vice President for Academic Affairs, 630-844-5252, E-mail: fbuscher@aurora.edu. *Application contact:* Center for Graduate Studies, 630-947-8955, E-mail: AUadmission@aurora.edu.

Austin Peay State University, College of Graduate Studies, College of Science, Technology, Engineering and Mathematics, Clarksville, TN 37044. Offers MS, PSM. *Program availability:* Part-time, online learning. *Faculty:* 29 full-time (5 women), 3 part-time/adjunct (1 woman). *Students:* 54 full-time (14 women), 102 part-time (45 women); includes 26 minority (9 Black or African American, non-Hispanic/Latino; 5 Asian, non-Hispanic/Latino; 7 Hispanic/Latino; 5 Two or more races, non-Hispanic/Latino), 44 international. Average age 31. 102 applicants, 87% accepted, 59 enrolled. In 2018, 28 master's awarded. *Degree requirements:* For master's, comprehensive exam, thesis optional. *Entrance requirements:* For master's, GRE General Test, 3 letters of recommendation, minimum undergraduate GPA of 2.5. Additional exam requirements/recommendations for international students: Required—TOEFL (minimum score 500 paper-based). *Application deadline:* For fall admission, 8/21 priority date for domestic students. Applications are processed on a rolling basis. Application fee: $45 ($55 for international students). Electronic applications accepted. *Expenses:* Tuition, area resident: Part-time $450 per credit hour. Tuition, state resident: full-time $5987; part-time $450 per credit hour. Tuition, nonresident: full-time $8757; part-time $806 per credit hour. *Required fees:* $1583; $79.15 per credit hour. *Financial support:* Research assistantships with full tuition reimbursements, career-related internships or fieldwork, Federal Work-Study, institutionally sponsored loans, scholarships/grants, and unspecified assistantships available. Support available to part-time students. Financial award application deadline: 7/1; financial award applicants required to submit FAFSA. *Unit head:* Dr. Karen Meisch, Interim Dean, 931-221-7780, Fax: 931-221-7984, E-mail: meischk@apsu.edu. *Application contact:* Megan Mitchell, Coordinator of Graduate Admissions, 931-221-6189, Fax: 931-221-7641, E-mail: mitchellm@apsu.edu. Website: http://www.apsu.edu/costem/index.php

Bard College, Master of Arts in Teaching Program, Annandale-on-Hudson, NY 12504. Offers secondary education (MAT), including biology, history, literature, mathematics, Spanish; MS/MAT. *Program availability:* Part-time. *Degree requirements:* For master's, year-long teaching residencies in area middle and high schools. *Entrance requirements:* For master's, GRE General Test, resume, 3 letters of recommendation, personal statement, official transcripts. Additional exam requirements/recommendations for international students: Required—TOEFL. Electronic applications accepted. Application fee is waived when completed online.

Binghamton University, State University of New York, Graduate School, College of Community and Public Affairs, Department of Teaching, Learning and Educational Leadership, Program in Adolescence Education, Binghamton, NY 13902-6000. Offers biology education (MAT, MS Ed); chemistry education (MAT, MS Ed); earth science education (MAT, MS Ed); English education (MAT, MS Ed); French education (MAT, MS Ed); mathematical sciences education (MAT, MS Ed); physics (MAT, MS Ed); social studies (MAT, MS Ed); Spanish education (MAT, MS Ed). *Accreditation:* TEAC. *Program availability:* Part-time, evening/weekend. *Degree requirements:* For master's, portfolio. *Entrance requirements:* For master's, GRE General Test, teaching certification. Additional exam requirements/recommendations for international students: Required—TOEFL (minimum score 550 paper-based; 80 iBT). Electronic applications accepted.

Biola University, School of Arts and Sciences, La Mirada, CA 90639-0001. Offers Christian apologetics (MA, Certificate); science and religion (MA); speech language pathology (MA). *Program availability:* Part-time, evening/weekend, online learning. *Entrance requirements:* For master's, minimum GPA of 3.0, bachelor's degree from accredited college or university (in science-related field for science and religion program). Additional exam requirements/recommendations for international students: Required—TOEFL (minimum score 600 paper-based; 100 iBT). Electronic applications accepted. *Faculty research:* Apologetics, science and religion, intelligent design.

Bloomsburg University of Pennsylvania, School of Graduate Studies, College of Education, Department of Teaching and Learning, Program in Middle Level Education Grades 4-8, Bloomsburg, PA 17815-1301. Offers language arts (M Ed); math (M Ed); science (M Ed); social studies (M Ed). *Accreditation:* NCATE. *Degree requirements:* For master's, thesis optional, practicum, student teaching. *Entrance requirements:* For master's, MAT, GRE, or PRAXIS, minimum QPA of 3.0, teaching certificate, U.S. citizenship, related undergraduate coursework, professional liability insurance, recent TB test. Additional exam requirements/recommendations for international students: Required—TOEFL (minimum score 550 paper-based), IELTS. Electronic applications accepted.

Blue Mountain College, Program in Secondary Education - Biology, Blue Mountain, MS 38610. Offers M Ed. *Program availability:* Part-time, evening/weekend. *Degree requirements:* For master's, comprehensive exam. *Entrance requirements:* For master's, PRAXIS, GRE, or MAT, official transcripts; bachelor's degree in a field of education from an accredited college or university; teaching certificate; three recommendations. Additional exam requirements/recommendations for international students: Required—TOEFL (minimum score 550 paper-based). Electronic applications accepted.

Boston College, Lynch School of Education and Human Development, Department of Teacher Education, Special Education and Curriculum and Instruction, Chestnut Hill, MA 02467-3800. Offers curriculum and instruction (M Ed, PhD, CAES); early childhood education (M Ed); elementary education (M Ed); law and curriculum and instruction (JD/M Ed); reading specialist (M Ed, CAES); religious education (M Ed, CAES); secondary education (M Ed, MAT, MST), including biology (MST), chemistry (MST), English (MAT), French (MAT), geology (MST), history (MAT), Latin and classical humanities (MAT),

mathematics (MST), physics (MST), secondary teaching (M Ed), Spanish (MAT); special needs: moderate disabilities (M Ed, CAES); special needs: severe disabilities (M Ed); JD/M Ed. *Program availability:* Part-time, evening/weekend, 100% online. *Faculty:* 19 full-time (11 women). *Students:* 186 full-time (140 women), 92 part-time (74 women); includes 58 minority (20 Black or African American, non-Hispanic/Latino; 4 Asian, non-Hispanic/Latino; 29 Hispanic/Latino; 5 Two or more races, non-Hispanic/Latino), 33 international. Average age 28. In 2018, 132 master's, 13 doctorates awarded. Terminal master's awarded for partial completion of doctoral program. *Degree requirements:* For master's, comprehensive exam; for doctorate, comprehensive exam, thesis/dissertation. *Entrance requirements:* Additional exam requirements/recommendations for international students: Required—TOEFL. Application fee: $75. Electronic applications accepted. *Financial support:* Fellowships with full and partial tuition reimbursements, research assistantships with full and partial tuition reimbursements, teaching assistantships with full and partial tuition reimbursements, career-related internships or fieldwork, Federal Work-Study, institutionally sponsored loans, scholarships/grants, traineeships, health care benefits, tuition waivers (full and partial), and unspecified assistantships available. Support available to part-time students. Financial award applicants required to submit FAFSA. *Faculty research:* Teacher education, education research and policy, bilingual education, science education, disabilities, urban education. *Unit head:* Dr. Susan Bruce, Chairperson, 617-552-4214, Fax: 617-552-0812. *Application contact:* Jessica Rivers, Assistant Dean of Graduate Admission and Financial Aid, 617-552-4214, Fax: 617-552-0398, E-mail: riversja@bc.edu. Website: http://www.bc.edu/education

Boston College, Morrissey Graduate School of Arts and Sciences, Department of Chemistry, Chestnut Hill, MA 02467-3800. Offers biochemistry (PhD); inorganic chemistry (PhD); organic chemistry (PhD); physical chemistry (PhD); science education (MST). *Degree requirements:* For doctorate, thesis/dissertation, qualifying exam. *Entrance requirements:* For doctorate, GRE General Test, GRE Subject Test. Additional exam requirements/recommendations for international students: Required—TOEFL (minimum score 600 paper-based; 100 iBT), IELTS (minimum score 8). Electronic applications accepted. *Faculty research:* Organic and organometallic chemistry, chemical biology and biochemistry, physical and theoretical chemistry, inorganic chemistry.

Bowling Green State University, Graduate College, College of Arts and Sciences, Department of Physics and Astronomy, Bowling Green, OH 43403. Offers geophysics (MS); physics (MAT, MS). *Degree requirements:* For master's, thesis or alternative. *Entrance requirements:* For master's, GRE General Test. Additional exam requirements/recommendations for international students: Required—TOEFL. Electronic applications accepted. *Faculty research:* Computational physics, solid-state physics, materials science, theoretical physics.

Bridgewater State University, College of Graduate Studies, Bartlett College of Science and Mathematics, Department of Biological Sciences, Bridgewater, MA 02325. Offers biology (MAT). *Program availability:* Part-time, evening/weekend. *Entrance requirements:* For master's, GRE General Test.

Bridgewater State University, College of Graduate Studies, Bartlett College of Science and Mathematics, Department of Physics, Bridgewater, MA 02325. Offers MAT. *Accreditation:* NCATE. *Program availability:* Part-time, evening/weekend. *Entrance requirements:* For master's, GRE General Test.

Bridgewater State University, College of Graduate Studies, College of Humanities and Social Sciences, Program in Physical Sciences, Bridgewater, MA 02325. Offers MAT. *Accreditation:* NCATE. *Program availability:* Part-time, evening/weekend. *Entrance requirements:* For master's, GRE General Test.

Brigham Young University, Graduate Studies, College of Life Sciences, Department of Biology, Provo, UT 84602. Offers biological science education (MS); biology (MS, PhD). *Faculty:* 25 full-time (3 women). *Students:* 34 full-time (13 women); includes 6 minority (4 Hispanic/Latino; 2 Native Hawaiian or other Pacific Islander, non-Hispanic/Latino), 4 international. Average age 30. 24 applicants, 54% accepted, 9 enrolled. In 2018, 7 master's, 4 doctorates awarded. *Degree requirements:* For master's, comprehensive exam, thesis, prospectus, defense of research, defense of thesis; for doctorate, comprehensive exam, thesis/dissertation, prospectus, defense of research, defense of dissertation. *Entrance requirements:* For master's and doctorate, minimum cumulative GPA of 3.0 for undergraduate degree. Additional exam requirements/recommendations for international students: Required—TOEFL (minimum score 580 paper-based; 85 iBT), IELTS (minimum score 7), E3PT, CAE. *Application deadline:* For fall admission, 1/15 for domestic and international students. Application fee: $50. Electronic applications accepted. *Financial support:* In 2018–19, 30 students received support, including 2 fellowships with full tuition reimbursements available (averaging $30,000 per year), 38 research assistantships with full and partial tuition reimbursements available (averaging $5,984 per year), 42 teaching assistantships with full and partial tuition reimbursements available (averaging $6,544 per year); institutionally sponsored loans, scholarships/grants, tuition waivers (full and partial), and unspecified assistantships also available. Financial award application deadline: 3/1; financial award applicants required to submit FAFSA. *Faculty research:* Systematics, bioinformatics, ecology, evolution, biology education. *Total annual research expenditures:* $1.7 million. *Unit head:* Dr. Richard Gill, Chair, 801-422-3856, E-mail: rgill@byu.edu. *Application contact:* Gentri Glaittli, Graduate Program Manager, 801-422-7137, E-mail: biogradmanager@byu.edu. Website: http://biology.byu.edu/

Brooklyn College of the City University of New York, School of Education, Program in Adolescence Science Education and Special Subjects, Brooklyn, NY 11210-2889. Offers adolescence science education (MAT); biology teacher (7-12) (MA); chemistry teacher (7-12) (MA); earth science teacher (7-12) (MAT); English teacher (7-12) (MA); French teacher (7-12) (MA); mathematics teacher (7-12) (MA); music teacher (MA); physics teacher (7-12) (MA); social studies teacher (7-12) (MA); Spanish teacher (7-12) (MA). *Program availability:* Part-time, evening/weekend. *Degree requirements:* For master's, comprehensive exam (for some programs), thesis (for some programs). *Entrance requirements:* For master's, LAST, previous course work in education, resume, 2 letters of recommendation, essay. Additional exam requirements/recommendations for international students: Required—TOEFL (minimum score 500 paper-based; 61 iBT). Electronic applications accepted. *Faculty research:* Interdisciplinary education, semiotics, discourse analysis, autobiography, teacher identity.

Brooklyn College of the City University of New York, School of Education, Program in Childhood Education, Brooklyn, NY 11210-2889. Offers bilingual education (MS Ed); liberal arts (MS Ed); mathematics (MS Ed); science and environmental education (MS Ed). *Program availability:* Part-time, evening/weekend. *Entrance requirements:* For master's, LAST, interview, previous course work in education, writing sample, resume, 2 letters of recommendation. Additional exam requirements/recommendations for international students: Required—TOEFL (minimum score 500 paper-based; 61 iBT). Electronic applications accepted. *Faculty research:* Emotional intelligence, multiculturalism, arts immersion, the Holocaust.

Brooklyn College of the City University of New York, School of Education, Program in Middle Childhood Science Education, Brooklyn, NY 11210-2889. Offers biology (MA);

chemistry (MA); earth science (MA); general science (MA); physics (MA). *Program availability:* Part-time, evening/weekend. *Entrance requirements:* For master's, LAST, interview, previous course work in education and mathematics, resume, 2 letters of recommendation, essay. Additional exam requirements/recommendations for international students: Required—TOEFL (minimum score 500 paper-based; 61 iBT). Electronic applications accepted. *Faculty research:* Geometric thinking, mastery of basic facts, problem-solving strategies, history of mathematics.

Brown University, Graduate School, Department of Education, Program in Teaching, Providence, RI 02912. Offers elementary education (MAT); English (MAT); history/social studies (MAT); science (MAT); secondary education (MAT). *Degree requirements:* For master's, student teaching, portfolio. *Entrance requirements:* For master's, GRE General Test, transcript, personal statement, 3 letters of recommendation, interview, writing sample (English applicants only). Additional exam requirements/recommendations for international students: Required—TOEFL (minimum score 577 paper-based). Electronic applications accepted. *Faculty research:* Literacy, English language learners, diversity, special education, biodiversity.

Buffalo State College, State University of New York, The Graduate School, School of Natural and Social Sciences, Department of Biology, Buffalo, NY 14222-1095. Offers biology (MA); secondary education (MS Ed), including biology. *Program availability:* Evening/weekend. *Degree requirements:* For master's, thesis (for some programs), project. *Entrance requirements:* For master's, minimum GPA of 2.75. Additional exam requirements/recommendations for international students: Required—TOEFL (minimum score 550 paper-based).

Buffalo State College, State University of New York, The Graduate School, School of Natural and Social Sciences, Department of Earth Sciences and Science Education, Buffalo, NY 14222-1095. Offers science education (MS Ed), including science. *Accreditation:* NCATE. *Program availability:* Part-time, evening/weekend. *Degree requirements:* For master's, thesis or alternative, project. *Entrance requirements:* For master's, 36 undergraduate hours in mathematics and science. Additional exam requirements/recommendations for international students: Required—TOEFL (minimum score 550 paper-based).

Buffalo State College, State University of New York, The Graduate School, School of Natural and Social Sciences, Department of Physics, Buffalo, NY 14222-1095. Offers physics education (7-12) (MS Ed). *Degree requirements:* For master's, project. *Entrance requirements:* For master's, minimum GPA of 2.5, New York State teaching certification. Additional exam requirements/recommendations for international students: Required—TOEFL (minimum score 550 paper-based).

California Baptist University, Program in Education, Riverside, CA 92504-3206. Offers educational leadership (MS); educational leadership for faith-based institutions (MS); educational leadership for public institutions (MS); educational technology (MS); instructional computer applications (MS); international education (MS); leadership and adult learning (MS); leadership and organizational studies (MS); online teaching and learning (MS); reading (MS); science education (MA); special education in mild/moderate disabilities (MS); special education in moderate/severe disabilities (MS); teacher leadership (MS); teaching (MS); teaching and learning (MS). *Program availability:* Part-time, evening/weekend, 100% online, blended/hybrid learning. *Faculty:* 26 full-time (13 women), 28 part-time/adjunct (21 women). *Students:* 201 full-time (164 women), 265 part-time (209 women); includes 226 minority (23 Black or African American, non-Hispanic/Latino; 4 American Indian or Alaska Native, non-Hispanic/Latino; 7 Asian, non-Hispanic/Latino; 169 Hispanic/Latino; 6 Native Hawaiian or other Pacific Islander, non-Hispanic/Latino; 17 Two or more races, non-Hispanic/Latino), 2 international. Average age 39. 145 applicants, 97% accepted, 141 enrolled. In 2018, 253 master's awarded. *Degree requirements:* For master's, comprehensive exam, project, or thesis. *Entrance requirements:* For master's, minimum undergraduate GPA of 2.75; 500-word essay; three letters of recommendation; two prerequisite courses completed with minimum C grade. Additional exam requirements/recommendations for international students: Required—TOEFL (minimum score 80 iBT). *Application deadline:* For fall admission, 8/1 priority date for domestic students, 7/1 for international students; for spring admission, 12/1 priority date for domestic students, 11/1 for international students. Applications are processed on a rolling basis. Application fee: $45. Electronic applications accepted. *Expenses:* $634 per unit. *Financial support:* In 2018–19, 312 students received support. Federal Work-Study and scholarships/grants available. Financial award applicants required to submit CSS PROFILE or FAFSA. *Faculty research:* Leadership development, complexity theory, faith and learning, special education, social and philosophical contexts of education. *Unit head:* Dr. Robin Duncan, Dean, School of Education, 951-552-8948, E-mail: rduncan@calbaptist.edu. *Application contact:* Dr. Shari Farris, Program Director, Online MS in Education, 951-343-2455, E-mail: sfarris@calbaptist.edu.
Website: http://www.calbaptist.edu/mastersined/

California State University, Bakersfield, Division of Graduate Studies, School of Natural Sciences, Mathematics, and Engineering, Program in Geological Sciences, Bakersfield, CA 93311. Offers geological sciences (MS); hydrogeology (MS); petroleum geology (MS); science education (MS). *Program availability:* Part-time, evening/weekend. *Faculty:* 4 full-time (0 women). *Students:* 6 full-time (2 women), 17 part-time (7 women); includes 13 minority (1 Black or African American, non-Hispanic/Latino; 1 American Indian or Alaska Native, non-Hispanic/Latino; 10 Hispanic/Latino; 1 Two or more races, non-Hispanic/Latino). Average age 30. 18 applicants, 94% accepted, 15 enrolled. In 2018, 12 master's awarded. *Degree requirements:* For master's, thesis. *Entrance requirements:* For master's, GRE General Test, BS in geology. *Application deadline:* Applications are processed on a rolling basis. Application fee: $55. *Financial support:* In 2018–19, fellowships (averaging $1,850 per year) were awarded; Federal Work-Study, scholarships/grants, and tuition waivers (full and partial) also available. Financial award application deadline: 3/2; financial award applicants required to submit FAFSA. *Unit head:* Dr. William Krugh, Director, 661-654-3126, Fax: 661-654-2040, E-mail: wkrugh@csub.edu. *Application contact:* Martha Manriquez, Graduate Student Center Coordinator, 661-654-2786, Fax: 661-654-2791, E-mail: gsc@csub.edu.
Website: https://www.csub.edu/geology/index.html

California State University, Long Beach, Graduate Studies, College of Natural Sciences and Mathematics, Department of Science Education, Long Beach, CA 90840. Offers MS. *Application deadline:* For fall admission, 6/1 for domestic students. *Expenses: Required fees:* $2628 per term. Tuition and fees vary according to class time, course level, course load, degree level, campus/location and program. *Financial support:* Federal Work-Study, institutionally sponsored loans, and scholarships/grants available. Financial award application deadline: 3/2; financial award applicants required to submit FAFSA. *Unit head:* Laura Henriques, Chair, 562-985-1408, E-mail: laura.henriques@csulb.edu. *Application contact:* Dr. Adam Colburn, Graduate Program Advisor, 562-985-5948, E-mail: alan.colburn@csulb.edu.
Website: www.csulb.edu/scied

California State University, Northridge, Graduate Studies, Michael D. Eisner College of Education, Department of Secondary Education, Northridge, CA 91330. Offers educational technology (MA); English education (MA); mathematics education (MA); secondary science education (MA); teaching and learning (MA). *Accreditation:* NCATE. *Program availability:* Part-time. *Degree requirements:* For master's, thesis optional. *Entrance requirements:* For master's, GRE General Test or minimum GPA of 3.0. Additional exam requirements/recommendations for international students: Required—TOEFL.

California University of Pennsylvania, School of Graduate Studies and Research, College of Education and Human Services, Department of Childhood Education, California, PA 15419-1394. Offers early childhood education (M Ed); elementary education (M Ed); STEM education (M Ed). *Accreditation:* NCATE. *Program availability:* Part-time, evening/weekend. *Degree requirements:* For master's, comprehensive exam, thesis optional. *Entrance requirements:* For master's, MAT, PRAXIS, minimum GPA of 3.0, state police clearances. Additional exam requirements/recommendations for international students: Required—TOEFL (minimum score 550 paper-based; 80 iBT). Electronic applications accepted. *Faculty research:* English as a second language, adult literacy, emerging literacy, diagnosis and remediation, phonemic awareness.

Cambridge College, School of Education, Boston, MA 02129. Offers autism specialist (M Ed); autism/behavior analyst (M Ed); behavior analyst (Post-Master's Certificate); curriculum and instruction (CAGS); early childhood teacher (M Ed); educational leadership (M Ed, Ed D); elementary teacher (M Ed); English as a second language (M Ed, Certificate); general science (M Ed); health education (Post-Master's Certificate); interdisciplinary studies (M Ed); library teacher (M Ed); mathematics education (M Ed); mathematics specialist (Certificate); school administration (M Ed, CAGS); school nurse education (M Ed); teacher of students with moderate disabilities (M Ed); teaching skills and methodologies (M Ed). *Program availability:* Part-time, evening/weekend, online learning. *Degree requirements:* For master's, thesis, internship/practicum (licensure program only); for doctorate, thesis/dissertation; for other advanced degree, thesis. *Entrance requirements:* For master's, interview, resume, documentation of licensure, 2 professional references; for doctorate, official transcripts, interview, resume, written personal statement/essay, portfolio of scholarly and professional work, 2 professional references, health insurance, immunizations form; for other advanced degree, official transcripts, interview, resume, written personal statement/essay, 2 professional references, health insurance, immunizations form. Additional exam requirements/recommendations for international students: Required—TOEFL (minimum score 550 paper-based; 79 iBT), Michigan English Language Assessment Battery (minimum score 85); Recommended—IELTS (minimum score 6). *Application deadline:* Applications are processed on a rolling basis. Application fee: $30. Electronic applications accepted. *Expenses:* Contact institution. *Financial support:* Career-related internships or fieldwork, Federal Work-Study, and scholarships/grants available. Financial award applicants required to submit FAFSA. *Faculty research:* Adult education, accelerated learning, mathematics education, brain compatible learning, special education and law. *Unit head:* Dr. Mary Garrity, Interim Dean, 617-873-0168, E-mail: mary.garrity@cambridgecollege.edu. *Application contact:* Salvadore Liberto, Interim Assistant Vice President of Enrollment, 800-877-4723, E-mail: admissions@cambridgecollege.edu.
Website: https://www.cambridgecollege.edu/school/school-education

Campbellsville University, School of Education, Campbellsville, KY 42718-2799. Offers education (MA); school counseling (MA); school improvement (MA); special education (MASE); special education-teacher leader (MA); teacher leader (MA); teaching (MAT), including middle grades biology, middle grades chemistry, middle grades English. *Accreditation:* NCATE. *Program availability:* Part-time, evening/weekend, 100% online, blended/hybrid learning. *Faculty:* 16 full-time (10 women), 13 part-time/adjunct (7 women). *Students:* 154 full-time (122 women), 44 part-time (36 women); includes 18 minority (16 Black or African American, non-Hispanic/Latino; 1 Hispanic/Latino; 1 Two or more races, non-Hispanic/Latino), 1 international. Average age 34. 280 applicants, 30% accepted, 72 enrolled. In 2018, 66 master's awarded. *Degree requirements:* For master's, comprehensive exam (for some programs), thesis, research paper. *Entrance requirements:* For master's, GRE or PRAXIS, minimum undergraduate GPA of 2.75, teaching certificate, professional growth plan, letters of recommendation, interview. Additional exam requirements/recommendations for international students: Recommended—TOEFL (minimum score 550 paper-based; 79 iBT), IELTS (minimum score 6). *Application deadline:* Applications are processed on a rolling basis. Application fee: $25. Electronic applications accepted. Application fee is waived when completed online. *Expenses:* $299/credit hour. *Financial support:* Unspecified assistantships available. Financial award applicants required to submit FAFSA. *Faculty research:* Professional development, curriculum development, school governance, assessment, special education. *Unit head:* Dr. Lisa Allen, Dean of School of Education, 270-789-5344, Fax: 270-789-5206, E-mail: lsallen@campbellsville.edu. *Application contact:* Monica Bamwine, Director of Graduate Admissions, 270-789-5221, Fax: 270-789-5071, E-mail: mkbamwine@campbellsville.edu.

Caribbean University, Graduate School, Bayamón, PR 00960-0493. Offers administration and supervision (MA Ed); criminal justice (MA); curriculum and instruction (MA Ed, PhD), including elementary education (MA Ed), English education (MA Ed), history education (MA Ed), mathematics education (MA Ed), primary education (MA Ed), science education (MA Ed), Spanish education (MA Ed); educational technology in instructional systems (MA Ed); gerontology (MSN); human resources (MBA); museology, archiving and art history (MA Ed); neonatal pediatrics (MSN); physical education (MA Ed); special education (MA Ed). *Entrance requirements:* For master's, interview, minimum GPA of 2.5.

Carlow University, College of Learning and Innovation, Program in Curriculum and Instruction, Pittsburgh, PA 15213-3165. Offers autism (M Ed); early childhood leadership (M Ed); online learning instructional design (M Ed); STEM (M Ed). *Program availability:* Part-time, evening/weekend. *Entrance requirements:* For master's, personal essay; resume or curriculum vitae; two recommendations; official transcripts; interview; minimum undergraduate GPA of 3.0. Additional exam requirements/recommendations for international students: Required—TOEFL (minimum score 550 paper-based). *Application deadline:* Applications are processed on a rolling basis. Electronic applications accepted. *Expenses: Tuition:* Full-time $13,090; part-time $5100 per semester. *Required fees:* $215; $84. Tuition and fees vary according to course load, degree level and program. *Financial support:* Application deadline: 4/1; applicants required to submit FAFSA. *Unit head:* Dr. Keeley Baronak, Chair, 412-578-6135, Fax: 412-578-6326, E-mail: kobaronak@carlow.edu. *Application contact:* Dr. Keeley Baronak, Chair, 412-578-6135, Fax: 412-578-6326, E-mail: kobaronak@carlow.edu.
Website: http://www.carlow.edu/Curriculum_and_Instruction_MEd.aspx

Carthage College, Division of Teacher Education, Kenosha, WI 53140. Offers classroom guidance and counseling (M Ed); creative arts (M Ed); gifted and talented children (M Ed); language arts (M Ed); modern language (M Ed); natural sciences (M Ed); reading (M Ed, Certificate); social sciences (M Ed); teacher leadership (M Ed). *Program availability:* Part-time, evening/weekend. *Degree requirements:* For master's, thesis optional. *Entrance requirements:* For master's, MAT, minimum B average, letters of reference.

Catawba College, Department of Teacher Education, Salisbury, NC 28144-2488. Offers STEM education (M Ed). *Accreditation:* NCATE. *Program availability:* Part-time-only. *Degree requirements:* For master's, portfolio. *Entrance requirements:* For master's, NTE, PRAXIS II, minimum undergraduate GPA of 3.0, valid teaching license, official transcripts, 3 references, essay, interview, practicing teacher. Electronic applications accepted. *Expenses:* Contact institution.

Central Connecticut State University, School of Graduate Studies, School of Engineering, Science and Technology, Department of Geological Sciences, New Britain, CT 06050-4010. Offers STEM education (MS). *Program availability:* Part-time, evening/weekend. *Students:* 3 applicants, 67% accepted. *Degree requirements:* For master's, thesis or alternative, special project. *Entrance requirements:* For master's, minimum undergraduate GPA of 2.7. Additional exam requirements/recommendations for international students: Required—TOEFL (minimum score 550 paper-based; 79 iBT); Recommended—IELTS (minimum score 6.5). *Application deadline:* For fall admission, 6/1 for domestic students, 5/1 for international students; for spring admission, 11/1 for domestic and international students. Applications are processed on a rolling basis. Application fee: $50. Electronic applications accepted. *Expenses: Tuition, area resident:* Full-time $7027; part-time $388 per credit. Tuition, state resident: full-time $9750; part-time $388 per credit. Tuition, nonresident: full-time $18,102; part-time $388 per credit. *International tuition:* $18,102 full-time. *Required fees:* $266 per semester. *Financial support:* Application deadline: 3/1; applicants required to submit FAFSA. *Unit head:* Dr. Mark Evans, Chair, 860-832-2930, E-mail: evansmaa@ccsu.edu. *Application contact:* Patricia Gardner, Associate Director of Graduate Studies, 860-832-2350, Fax: 860-832-2362.
Website: http://www.ccsu.edu/geolsci/

Central Connecticut State University, School of Graduate Studies, School of Engineering, Science and Technology, Department of Physics and Engineering Physics, New Britain, CT 06050-4010. Offers science education (Certificate). *Program availability:* Part-time, evening/weekend. *Students:* 1 applicant. *Degree requirements:* For Certificate, qualifying exam. *Entrance requirements:* Additional exam requirements/recommendations for international students: Required—TOEFL (minimum score 550 paper-based; 79 iBT); Recommended—IELTS (minimum score 6.5). *Application deadline:* For fall admission, 6/1 for domestic students, 5/1 for international students; for spring admission, 11/1 for domestic and international students. Applications are processed on a rolling basis. Application fee: $50. Electronic applications accepted. *Expenses: Tuition, area resident:* Full-time $7027; part-time $388 per credit. Tuition, state resident: full-time $9750; part-time $388 per credit. Tuition, nonresident: full-time $18,102; part-time $388 per credit. *International tuition:* $18,102 full-time. *Required fees:* $266 per semester. *Financial support:* Application deadline: 3/1. *Faculty research:* Elementary and secondary science education, particle and solid states, weather patterns, planetary studies. *Unit head:* Dr. Peter LeMaire, Chair, 860-832-2930, E-mail: lemaire@ccsu.edu. *Application contact:* Patricia Gardner, Associate Director of Graduate Studies, 860-832-2350, Fax: 860-832-2362, E-mail: graduateadmissions@ccsu.edu.
Website: http://www.ccsu.edu/physics/

Central Michigan University, College of Graduate Studies, College of Science and Engineering, Department of Chemistry, Mount Pleasant, MI 48859. Offers chemistry (MS); teaching chemistry (MA), including teaching college chemistry, teaching high school chemistry. *Program availability:* Part-time. *Degree requirements:* For master's, comprehensive exam, thesis or alternative. *Entrance requirements:* For master's, GRE. Electronic applications accepted. *Faculty research:* Analytical and organic-inorganic chemistry, biochemistry, catalysis, dendrimer and polymer studies, nanotechnology.

Chatham University, Program in Education, Pittsburgh, PA 15232-2826. Offers early childhood education (MAT); elementary education (MAT); environmental education (K-12) (MAT); secondary art (MAT); secondary biology education (MAT); secondary chemistry education (MAT); secondary English education (MAT); secondary math education (MAT); secondary physics education (MAT); secondary social studies education (MAT); special education (MAT). *Degree requirements:* For master's, thesis, teaching experience. *Entrance requirements:* For master's, minimum GPA of 3.0, sample of written work, recommendation letters. Additional exam requirements/recommendations for international students: Required—TOEFL (minimum score 600 paper-based; 100 iBT), IELTS (minimum score 7), TWE. Electronic applications accepted. Application fee is waived when completed online. *Faculty research:* Gifted education, environmental education, technology in education, writing as learning, class size and achievement.

The Citadel, The Military College of South Carolina, Citadel Graduate College, Zucker Family School of Education, Charleston, SC 29409. Offers elementary/secondary school administration and supervision (M Ed); elementary/secondary school counseling (M Ed); interdisciplinary STEM education (M Ed); literacy education (M Ed, Graduate Certificate); middle grades (MAT), including English, mathematics, science, social studies; physical education (grades K-12) (MAT); school superintendency (Ed S); secondary education (MAT), including biology, English, mathematics, social studies; student affairs (Graduate Certificate); student affairs and college counseling (M Ed). *Accreditation:* NCATE. *Program availability:* Part-time, evening/weekend, 100% online, blended/hybrid learning. *Degree requirements:* For master's, comprehensive exam (for some programs). *Entrance requirements:* For master's, GRE (minimum combined verbal and quantitative score of 290) or MAT (minimum score 396). Additional exam requirements/recommendations for international students: Required—TOEFL (minimum score 550 paper-based; 79 iBT). Electronic applications accepted. *Expenses:* Tuition, state resident: part-time $595 per credit hour. Tuition, nonresident: part-time $1020 per credit hour. *Required fees:* $90 per term.

City College of the City University of New York, Graduate School, School of Education, Department of Secondary Education, Program in Science Education, New York, NY 10031-9198. Offers MA. *Accreditation:* NCATE. *Entrance requirements:* For master's, Liberal Arts and Sciences Test (LAST), Content Specialty Test (CST). Additional exam requirements/recommendations for international students: Required—TOEFL.

Clarion University of Pennsylvania, College of Arts, Education and Sciences, Master of Education Program, Clarion, PA 16214. Offers curriculum and instruction (M Ed); early childhood (M Ed); math education (M Ed); reading (M Ed); science education (M Ed); special education (M Ed); technology (M Ed). *Accreditation:* NCATE. *Program availability:* Part-time, evening/weekend, 100% online, blended/hybrid learning. *Faculty:* 6 full-time (3 women). *Students:* 5 full-time (all women), 85 part-time (73 women); includes 3 minority (2 Black or African American, non-Hispanic/Latino; 1 Two or more races, non-Hispanic/Latino). Average age 30. 57 applicants, 61% accepted, 26 enrolled. In 2018, 51 master's awarded. *Degree requirements:* For master's, comprehensive exam (for some programs), thesis or alternative. *Entrance requirements:* For master's, minimum QPA of 3.0. Additional exam requirements/recommendations for international students: Required—TOEFL (minimum score 550 paper-based; 80 iBT), Or IELTS. Satisfactory completion of a bachelor's degree from an accredited US college or university is also acceptable evidence of English language. *Application deadline:* For fall admission, 8/1 priority date for domestic students, 7/15 priority date for international students; for winter admission, 11/1 priority date for domestic students; for spring admission, 12/1 priority date for domestic students, 11/15 priority date for international students; for summer admission, 4/1 priority date for domestic students. Applications are processed on a rolling basis. Application fee: $40. Electronic applications accepted. *Expenses: Tuition, area resident:* Part-time $516 per credit hour. Tuition, state resident: part-time $516 per credit hour. Tuition, nonresident: part-time $774 per credit hour. *Required fees:* $159 per credit hour. One-time fee: $50 part-time. Tuition and fees vary according to degree level, campus/location and program. *Financial support:* Federal Work-Study, institutionally sponsored loans, and scholarships/grants available. Financial award application deadline: 3/1; financial award applicants required to submit FAFSA. *Unit head:* Dr. John McCullough, Chair, Department of Education, 814-393-2404, Fax: 814-393-2446, E-mail: gradstudies@clarion.edu. *Application contact:* Susan Staub, Graduate Admissions Counselor, 814-393-2337, Fax: 814-393-2722, E-mail: gradstudies@clarion.edu.

Clark Atlanta University, School of Education, Department of Curriculum and Instruction, Atlanta, GA 30314. Offers special education general curriculum (MA); teaching math and science (MAT). *Program availability:* Part-time. *Degree requirements:* For master's, one foreign language, comprehensive exam. *Entrance requirements:* For master's, GRE General Test, minimum undergraduate GPA of 2.6. Additional exam requirements/recommendations for international students: Required—TOEFL (minimum score 500 paper-based; 61 iBT).

Clemson University, Graduate School, College of Engineering, Computing and Applied Sciences, Department of Engineering and Science Education, Clemson, SC 29634. Offers PhD, Certificate. *Faculty:* 9 full-time (8 women). *Students:* 12 full-time (9 women), 2 part-time (1 woman); includes 5 minority (1 Black or African American, non-Hispanic/Latino; 3 Asian, non-Hispanic/Latino; 1 Hispanic/Latino). Average age 30. 6 applicants, 50% accepted, 3 enrolled. In 2018, 1 doctorate, 6 other advanced degrees awarded. *Degree requirements:* For doctorate, comprehensive exam, thesis/dissertation, qualifying exam. *Entrance requirements:* For doctorate and Certificate, GRE General Test, unofficial transcripts, letters of recommendation. Additional exam requirements/recommendations for international students: Required—TOEFL (minimum score 80 paper-based; 80 iBT); Recommended—IELTS (minimum score 6.5), TSE (minimum score 54). *Application deadline:* For fall admission, 4/15 for international students; for spring admission, 10/15 for international students. Applications are processed on a rolling basis. Application fee: $80 ($90 for international students). Electronic applications accepted. *Expenses:* $5536 per semester full-time resident, $11003 per semester full-time non-resident, $717 per credit hour part-time resident, $1408 per credit hour part-time non-resident, $1144 full-time graduate assistant, other fees may apply per session. *Financial support:* In 2018–19, 6 students received support, including 1 fellowship with full and partial tuition reimbursement available (averaging $10,667 per year), 4 research assistantships with full and partial tuition reimbursements available (averaging $16,054 per year); career-related internships or fieldwork and unspecified assistantships also available. *Faculty research:* Student success, mathematics education, underserved communities in engineering education, undergraduate research. *Total annual research expenditures:* $568,596. *Unit head:* Dr. Cindy Lee, Department Chair, 864-656-1006, E-mail: lc@clemson.edu. *Application contact:* Dr. Karen High, Program Coordinator, 864-656-4240, E-mail: khigh@clemson.edu.
Website: http://www.clemson.edu/cecas/departments/ese/

Cleveland State University, College of Graduate Studies, College of Education and Human Services, Department of Teacher Education, Cleveland, OH 44115. Offers art education (M Ed); early childhood education (M Ed); foreign language education (M Ed); middle childhood mathematics and science education (M Ed); special education (M Ed), including mild/moderate disabilities, moderate/intensive disabilities; teaching English to speakers of other languages (M Ed). *Program availability:* Part-time, evening/weekend. *Faculty:* 19 full-time (14 women), 32 part-time/adjunct (27 women). *Students:* 56 full-time (40 women), 344 part-time (278 women); includes 104 minority (74 Black or African American, non-Hispanic/Latino; 1 American Indian or Alaska Native, non-Hispanic/Latino; 5 Asian, non-Hispanic/Latino; 9 Hispanic/Latino; 15 Two or more races, non-Hispanic/Latino), 14 international. Average age 34. 177 applicants, 55% accepted, 68 enrolled. In 2018, 117 master's awarded. *Degree requirements:* For master's, comprehensive exam (for some programs), thesis or alternative. *Entrance requirements:* For master's, GRE General Test or MAT, minimum GPA of 2.75. Additional exam requirements/recommendations for international students: Required—TOEFL (minimum score 550 paper-based; 78 iBT), IELTS (minimum score 6). *Application deadline:* For fall admission, 7/1 priority date for domestic students, 5/15 for international students; for spring admission, 11/15 for domestic students, 11/1 for international students; for summer admission, 4/1 for domestic students, 3/15 for international students. Applications are processed on a rolling basis. Application fee: $30. *Expenses:* Tuition, state resident: full-time $7232.55; part-time $6676 per credit hour. Tuition, nonresident: full-time $12,375. *International tuition:* $18,914 full-time. *Required fees:* $80; $80 $40. Tuition and fees vary according to program. *Financial support:* In 2018–19, 13 research assistantships with full tuition reimbursements (averaging $15,845 per year) were awarded; tuition waivers (partial) and unspecified assistantships also available. Financial award application deadline: 2/15; financial award applicants required to submit FAFSA. *Faculty research:* Early childhood education, literacy education, special education: mild/moderate, moderate/intensive, early childhood intervention specialist), teaching English to speakers of other languages (TESOL). *Total annual research expenditures:* $275,907. *Unit head:* Dr. Tachelle Banks, Department Chairperson, 216-687-4600, Fax: 216-687-5379, E-mail: t.i.banks@csuohio.edu. *Application contact:* Rosalyn Adams, Administrative Coordinator, 216-523-7139, Fax: 216-687-5491, E-mail: r.m.adams@csuohio.edu.
Website: http://www.csuohio.edu/cehs/te/te

The College at Brockport, State University of New York, School of Education, Health, and Human Services, Department of Education and Human Development, Brockport, NY 14420-2997. Offers adolescence education (MS Ed), including adolescence biology education, adolescence chemistry education, adolescence English, adolescence mathematics, adolescence physics, adolescence physics education, adolescence social studies education; bilingual education (MS Ed, AGC); childhood curriculum specialist (MS Ed); inclusive generalist education (MS Ed, AGC, Advanced Certificate), including biology (MS Ed, AGC), chemistry (MS Ed), English (MS Ed, Advanced Certificate), mathematics (MS Ed, Advanced Certificate), science (MS Ed, Advanced Certificate), social studies (MS Ed, Advanced Certificate); literacy education B-12 (MS Ed). *Accreditation:* NCATE. *Faculty:* 12 full-time (7 women), 10 part-time/adjunct (6 women). *Students:* 60 full-time (39 women), 227 part-time (157 women); includes 9 minority (1 Asian, non-Hispanic/Latino; 8 Hispanic/Latino). 135 applicants, 71% accepted, 59 enrolled. In 2018, 107 master's, 13 AGCs awarded. *Degree requirements:* For master's, thesis or alternative. *Entrance requirements:* For master's, minimum GPA of 3.0, letters of recommendation, interview (for some programs); statement of objectives, current resume. Additional exam requirements/recommendations for international students: Required—TOEFL (minimum score 550 paper-based; 79 iBT), IELTS (minimum score 6.5). *Application deadline:* For fall admission, 3/15 priority date for domestic and international students; for spring admission, 10/15 priority date for domestic and international students; for summer admission, 3/15 priority date for domestic and international students. Application fee: $80. Electronic applications accepted. *Expenses:* Tuition, state resident: part-time $471 per credit. Tuition, nonresident: part-time $963 per credit. *Financial support:* In 2018–19, 1 fellowship with full tuition reimbursement (averaging $7,500 per year), 1 teaching assistantship with full tuition reimbursement (averaging $6,000 per year) were awarded; Federal Work-Study, scholarships/grants, and unspecified assistantships also available. Support available to part-time students. Financial award application deadline: 3/15; financial award applicants required to submit FAFSA. *Faculty research:* Educational

assessment, literacy education, inclusive education, teacher preparation, qualitative methodology. *Unit head:* Dr. Janka Szilagyi, Chairperson, 585-395-5945, Fax: 585-395-2172, E-mail: jszilagy@brockport.edu. *Application contact:* Buffie Edick, Graduate Program Director, 585-395-2326, Fax: 585-395-2172, E-mail: bedick@brockport.edu. Website: https://www.brockport.edu/academics/education_human_development/department.html

College of Charleston, Graduate School, School of Education, Health, and Human Performance, Program in Science and Mathematics for Teachers, Charleston, SC 29424-0001. Offers M Ed. *Accreditation:* NCATE. *Program availability:* Part-time, evening/weekend. *Degree requirements:* For master's, capstone project. *Entrance requirements:* For master's, GRE or PRAXIS, 2 letters of recommendation, copy of teaching certificate. Additional exam requirements/recommendations for international students: Required—TOEFL (minimum score 81 iBT). Electronic applications accepted.

The Colorado College, Education Department, Experienced Teacher Program, Colorado Springs, CO 80903-3294. Offers arts and humanities (MAT); integrated natural sciences (MAT); liberal arts (MAT); Southwest studies (MAT). Programs offered during summer only. *Program availability:* Part-time. *Degree requirements:* For master's, thesis, oral exam, 50-page paper. *Expenses:* Contact institution.

The Colorado College, Education Department, Program in Secondary Education, Colorado Springs, CO 80903-3294. Offers art teaching (K-12) (MAT); English teaching (MAT); foreign language teaching (MAT); mathematics teaching (MAT); music teaching (MAT); science teaching (MAT); social studies teaching (MAT). *Degree requirements:* For master's, thesis, internship. Electronic applications accepted.

Columbia University, College of Dental Medicine and Graduate School of Arts and Sciences, Programs in Dental Specialties, New York, NY 10027. Offers advanced education in general dentistry (Certificate); biomedical informatics (MA, PhD); endodontics (Certificate); orthodontics (MS, Certificate); periodontics (MS, Certificate); prosthodontics (MS, Certificate); science education (MA). *Degree requirements:* For master's, thesis, presentation of seminar. *Entrance requirements:* For master's, GRE General Test, DDS or equivalent. *Expenses:* Contact institution. *Faculty research:* Analysis of growth/form, pulpal microcirculation, implants, microbiology of oral environment, calcified tissues.

Columbus State University, Graduate Studies, College of Education and Health Professions, Department of Teacher Education, Columbus, GA 31907-5645. Offers curriculum and instruction in accomplished teaching (M Ed); early childhood education (M Ed, MAT, Ed S); middle grades education (M Ed, MAT, Ed S); secondary education (M Ed, MAT, Ed S), including biology (MAT), chemistry (MAT), earth and space science (MAT), English/language arts, general science (M Ed), history (MAT), mathematics, science (Ed S), social science (M Ed, Ed S); special education (M Ed, MAT, Ed S), including general curriculum (M Ed, MAT); teacher leadership (M Ed). *Accreditation:* NCATE. *Program availability:* Part-time, evening/weekend, 100% online, blended/hybrid learning. *Faculty:* 20 full-time (12 women), 20 part-time/adjunct (15 women). *Students:* 110 full-time (84 women), 143 part-time (115 women); includes 105 minority (96 Black or African American, non-Hispanic/Latino; 4 Hispanic/Latino; 5 Two or more races, non-Hispanic/Latino). Average age 33. 147 applicants, 56% accepted, 62 enrolled. In 2018, 112 master's, 11 other advanced degrees awarded. *Degree requirements:* For Ed S, thesis or alternative. *Entrance requirements:* For master's, GRE General Test, minimum undergraduate GPA of 2.75; for Ed S, GRE General Test, minimum undergraduate GPA of 2.75, graduate 3.0. Additional exam requirements/recommendations for international students: Required—TOEFL (minimum score 550 paper-based; 79 iBT). *Application deadline:* For fall admission, 6/30 for domestic students, 5/1 for international students; for spring admission, 11/1 for domestic and international students; for summer admission, 3/1 for domestic and international students. Applications are processed on a rolling basis. Application fee: $50. Electronic applications accepted. *Expenses: Tuition, area resident:* Full-time $4924; part-time $618 per credit hour. Tuition, state resident: full-time $4924; part-time $618 per credit hour. Tuition, nonresident: full-time $19,218; part-time $2403 per credit hour. *International tuition:* $19,218 full-time. *Required fees:* $1870; $802. Tuition and fees vary according to course load, degree level and program. *Financial support:* In 2018–19, 29 students received support, including 7 research assistantships with partial tuition reimbursements available (averaging $3,000 per year); career-related internships or fieldwork, Federal Work-Study, institutionally sponsored loans, scholarships/grants, tuition waivers (partial), and unspecified assistantships also available. Support available to part-time students. Financial award application deadline: 5/1; financial award applicants required to submit FAFSA. *Unit head:* Dr. Jan Burcham, Department Chair, 706-507-8519, Fax: 706-568-3134, E-mail: burcham_jan@columbusstate.edu. *Application contact:* Catrina Smith-Edmond, Assistant Director for Graduate and Global Admission, 706-507-8824, Fax: 706-568-5091, E-mail: smithedmond_catrina@columbusstate.edu.
Website: http://te.columbusstate.edu/

Columbus State University, Graduate Studies, College of Letters and Sciences, Department of Earth and Space Sciences, Columbus, GA 31907-5645. Offers natural sciences (MS), including biology, chemistry, environmental science, geosciences. *Program availability:* Part-time, evening/weekend. *Faculty:* 5 full-time (2 women), 8 part-time/adjunct (0 women). *Students:* 19 full-time (7 women), 10 part-time (5 women); includes 7 minority (4 Black or African American, non-Hispanic/Latino; 2 Hispanic/Latino; 1 Two or more races, non-Hispanic/Latino), 4 international. Average age 27. 21 applicants, 48% accepted, 7 enrolled. In 2018, 6 master's awarded. *Degree requirements:* For master's, thesis. *Entrance requirements:* For master's, GRE General Test, minimum GPA of 3.0. Additional exam requirements/recommendations for international students: Required—TOEFL (minimum score 550 paper-based; 79 iBT). *Application deadline:* For fall admission, 6/30 priority date for domestic students, 5/1 for international students; for spring admission, 11/1 for domestic and international students; for summer admission, 3/1 for domestic and international students. Applications are processed on a rolling basis. Application fee: $50. Electronic applications accepted. *Expenses: Tuition, area resident:* Full-time $4924; part-time $618 per credit hour. Tuition, state resident: full-time $4924; part-time $618 per credit hour. Tuition, nonresident: full-time $19,218; part-time $2403 per credit hour. *International tuition:* $19,218 full-time. *Required fees:* $1870; $802. Tuition and fees vary according to course load, degree level and program. *Financial support:* In 2018–19, 1 student received support, including 15 research assistantships with partial tuition reimbursements available (averaging $3,000 per year); career-related internships or fieldwork, Federal Work-Study, institutionally sponsored loans, scholarships/grants, and unspecified assistantships also available. Support available to part-time students. Financial award application deadline: 5/1; financial award applicants required to submit FAFSA. *Unit head:* Dr. Clint Barineau, Department Chair, 706-569-3026, E-mail: barineau_clinton@columbusstate.edu. *Application contact:* Catrina Smith-Edmond, Assistant Director for Graduate and Global Admission, 706-507-8824, Fax: 706-568-5091, E-mail: smithedmond_catrina@columbusstate.edu.
Website: http://ess.columbusstate.edu/

Concordia University, College of Education, Portland, OR 97211-6099. Offers administrative leadership (Ed D); career and technical education (M Ed); curriculum and instruction (M Ed), including adolescent literacy, early childhood education, educational technology leadership, English for speakers of other languages, environmental education, health and physical education, mathematics, methods and curriculum, reading interventionist, science, social studies, STEAM education, teacher leadership, the inclusive classroom, trauma and resilience in educational settings; educational administration (M Ed); educational leadership (M Ed); elementary education (MAT); higher education (Ed D); instructional leadership (Ed D); professional leadership, inquiry, and transformation (Ed D); secondary education (MAT); transformational leadership (Ed D). *Program availability:* Part-time, online learning. *Degree requirements:* For master's, comprehensive exam, work samples/portfolio. *Entrance requirements:* For master's, California Basic Educational Skills Test or PRAXIS I, minimum undergraduate GPA of 2.8, graduate 3.0; 2 letters of recommendation. Additional exam requirements/recommendations for international students: Required—TOEFL (minimum score 525 paper-based). Electronic applications accepted. *Faculty research:* Learner-centered classroom, brain-based learning, future of online learning.

Converse College, Program in Middle Level Education, Spartanburg, SC 29302. Offers language arts/English (MAT); mathematics (MAT); middle level education (M Ed); science (MAT); social studies (MAT).

Converse College, Program in Secondary Education, Spartanburg, SC 29302. Offers biology (MAT); chemistry (MAT); English (M Ed, MAT); mathematics (M Ed, MAT); natural sciences (M Ed); social sciences (M Ed, MAT). *Program availability:* Part-time. *Degree requirements:* For master's, capstone paper. *Entrance requirements:* For master's, NTE or PRAXIS II (M Ed), minimum GPA of 2.75, 2 recommendations. Electronic applications accepted.

Delaware State University, Graduate Programs, College of Education, Health and Public Policy, Program in Science Education, Dover, DE 19901-2277. Offers MA. *Program availability:* Part-time, evening/weekend. *Degree requirements:* For master's, comprehensive exam, thesis optional. *Entrance requirements:* For master's, GRE General Test, minimum GPA of 3.0 in major, 2.75 overall. Electronic applications accepted. *Faculty research:* Science reform in schools, inquiry science.

Delaware State University, Graduate Programs, Department of Biological Sciences, Program in Biology Education, Dover, DE 19901-2277. Offers MS. *Entrance requirements:* Additional exam requirements/recommendations for international students: Required—TOEFL (minimum score 550 paper-based).

Delaware State University, Graduate Programs, Department of Physics, Dover, DE 19901-2277. Offers applied optics (MS); optics (PhD); physics (MS); physics teaching (MS). *Program availability:* Part-time, evening/weekend. *Entrance requirements:* For master's, minimum GPA of 3.0 in major, 2.75 overall. Additional exam requirements/recommendations for international students: Required—TOEFL. Electronic applications accepted. *Faculty research:* Thermal properties of solids, nuclear physics, radiation damage in solids.

DePaul University, College of Science and Health, Chicago, IL 60604-2287. Offers applied mathematics (MS); applied statistics (MS); biological sciences (MA, MS); chemistry (MS); environmental science (MS); mathematics education (MA); mathematics for teaching (MS); nursing (MS); nursing practice (DNP); physics (MS); polymer and coatings science (MS); psychology (MS); pure mathematics (MS); science education (MS); MA/PhD. *Accreditation:* AACN. Electronic applications accepted.

Drake University, School of Education, Des Moines, IA 50311-4516. Offers applied behavior analysis (MS); counseling (MS); education (PhD); education administration (Ed D); educational leadership (MSE, Ed D); effective teaching (MSE); leadership development (MS); literacy (Ed S); literacy education (MSE); rehabilitation administration (MS); rehabilitation placement (MS); special education (MSE); STEM education (MSE); teacher education (5-12) (MAT); teacher education (K-8) (MST); teacher effectiveness and professional development (MSE). *Program availability:* Part-time, evening/weekend, 100% online, blended/hybrid learning. *Students:* 90 full-time (74 women), 690 part-time (532 women); includes 69 minority (30 Black or African American, non-Hispanic/Latino; 1 American Indian or Alaska Native, non-Hispanic/Latino; 9 Asian, non-Hispanic/Latino; 16 Hispanic/Latino; 13 Two or more races, non-Hispanic/Latino). Average age 34. In 2018, 253 master's, 30 doctorates awarded. *Degree requirements:* For master's and Ed S, comprehensive exam, internships (for some programs); for doctorate, comprehensive exam, thesis/dissertation, internships (for some programs). *Entrance requirements:* For master's, GRE General Test, MAT, or Drake Writing Assessment, resume, 2 letters of recommendation; for doctorate, GRE General Test or MAT, master's degree, 3 letters of recommendation; for Ed S, GRE General Test or MAT. Additional exam requirements/recommendations for international students: Required—TOEFL (minimum score 550 paper-based). *Application deadline:* For fall admission, 7/1 priority date for domestic students, 6/1 priority date for international students; for spring admission, 11/1 priority date for domestic students, 10/1 priority date for international students. Applications are processed on a rolling basis. Application fee: $25. Electronic applications accepted. *Expenses:* Contact institution. *Financial support:* Research assistantships, career-related internships or fieldwork, and unspecified assistantships available. Support available to part-time students. *Faculty research:* Counseling and rehabilitation, behavioral supports, inquiry-based science methods, teacher quality enhancement. *Unit head:* Dr. Janet McMahill, Dean, 515-271-3829, E-mail: janet.mcmahill@drake.edu. *Application contact:* Dr. Janet McMahill, Dean, 515-271-3829, E-mail: janet.mcmahill@drake.edu.
Website: http://www.drake.edu/soe/

Duquesne University, School of Education, Department of Instruction and Leadership, Program in Secondary Education, Pittsburgh, PA 15282-0001. Offers biology (MS Ed); chemistry (MS Ed); English (MS Ed); K-12 education (MS Ed), including Latin; mathematics (MS Ed); physics (MS Ed); social studies (MS Ed). *Program availability:* Part-time, evening/weekend. *Faculty:* 5 full-time (4 women). *Students:* 20 full-time (12 women); includes 3 minority (1 Black or African American, non-Hispanic/Latino; 1 Hispanic/Latino; 1 Two or more races, non-Hispanic/Latino). Average age 24. 20 applicants, 85% accepted, 13 enrolled. In 2018, 14 master's awarded. *Entrance requirements:* For master's, two letters of recommendation, letter of intent, interview, bachelor's degree. Additional exam requirements/recommendations for international students: Required—TOEFL (minimum score 550 paper-based), IELTS (minimum score 7). *Application deadline:* For fall admission, 9/1 for domestic students; for spring admission, 1/2 for domestic students. Applications are processed on a rolling basis. Application fee: $0. Electronic applications accepted. *Expenses: Tuition:* Full-time $23,112; part-time $1284 per credit. Tuition and fees vary according to program. *Financial support:* In 2018–19, 1 student received support, including 1 teaching assistantship with full tuition reimbursement available; Federal Work-Study also available. Support available to part-time students. Financial award applicants required to submit FAFSA. *Faculty research:* Factors that create highly effective teachers; how to best support teachers to support students in reform-oriented environments; urban education; models of teacher leadership; improving instruction in mathematics/science/social studies/English. *Total annual research expenditures:* $120,139. *Unit head:* Dr. Melissa Boston, Associate Dean for Teacher Education/Professor, 412-396.6109, Fax: 412-396-5585, E-mail: bostonm@duq.edu. *Application contact:* Kelly McGinley, Graduate Admissions Assistant, 412-396-1559, Fax: 412-396-5585, E-mail: mcginleyk@duq.edu.
Website: http://www.duq.edu/academics/schools/education/graduate-programs-education/ms-ed-secondary-education

East Carolina University, Graduate School, College of Education, Department of Mathematics, Science, and Instructional Technology Education, Greenville, NC 27858-4353. Offers distance learning and administration (Certificate); elementary mathematics education (Certificate); instructional technology (MA Ed, MS); mathematics education (MA Ed); science education (MA Ed, MAT); special endorsement in computer education (Certificate). *Program availability:* Part-time, evening/weekend. *Application deadline:* For fall admission, 6/1 priority date for domestic students. *Expenses: Tuition, area resident:* Full-time $4749. Tuition, state resident: full-time $4749. Tuition, nonresident: full-time $17,898. *International tuition:* $17,898 full-time. *Required fees:* $2787. Part-time tuition and fees vary according to course load and program. *Financial support:* Application deadline: 6/1. *Unit head:* Dr. Ron Preston, Director of Students, 252-737-9355, E-mail: prestonr@ecu.edu. *Application contact:* Graduate School Admissions, 252-328-6012, Fax: 252-328-6071, E-mail: gradschool@ecu.edu.
Website: http://www.ecu.edu/cs-educ/msite/

Eastern Kentucky University, The Graduate School, College of Education, Department of Curriculum and Instruction, Program in Secondary and Higher Education, Richmond, KY 40475-3102. Offers secondary education (MA Ed), including agricultural education, art education, biological sciences education, business education, English education, geography education, history education, home economics education, industrial education, mathematical sciences education, physical education, school health education. *Accreditation:* NCATE. *Program availability:* Part-time. *Entrance requirements:* For master's, GRE General Test, minimum GPA of 2.5.

Eastern Michigan University, Graduate School, College of Arts and Sciences, Department of Biology, Ypsilanti, MI 48197. Offers community college biology teaching (MS); general biology (MS). *Program availability:* Part-time, evening/weekend, online learning. *Faculty:* 25 full-time (8 women). *Students:* 9 full-time (7 women), 31 part-time (19 women); includes 7 minority (3 Asian, non-Hispanic/Latino; 3 Hispanic/Latino; 1 Two or more races, non-Hispanic/Latino), 2 international. Average age 27. 43 applicants, 65% accepted, 19 enrolled. In 2018, 13 master's awarded. *Entrance requirements:* For master's, GRE General Test, GRE Subject Test. Additional exam requirements/recommendations for international students: Required—TOEFL. *Application deadline:* Applications are processed on a rolling basis. Application fee: $45. *Financial support:* Fellowships, research assistantships with full tuition reimbursements, teaching assistantships with full tuition reimbursements, career-related internships or fieldwork, Federal Work-Study, institutionally sponsored loans, scholarships/grants, tuition waivers (partial), and unspecified assistantships available. Support available to part-time students. Financial award applicants required to submit FAFSA. *Unit head:* Dr. Marianne Laporte, Department Head, 734-487-4242, Fax: 734-487-9235, E-mail: mlaporte@emich.edu. *Application contact:* Dr. Cara Shillilngton, Graduate Coordinator, 734-487-4433, Fax: 734-487-9235, E-mail: cshilling@emich.edu.
Website: http://www.emich.edu/biology

Eastern Michigan University, Graduate School, College of Arts and Sciences, Department of Geography and Geology, Program in Earth Science Education, Ypsilanti, MI 48197. Offers MS. *Students:* 1 (woman) part-time; minority (Hispanic/Latino). Average age 26. Application fee: $45. *Application contact:* Dr. Katherine Ryker, Program Advisor, 734-487-6712, E-mail: kryker@emich.edu.

Eastern University, Graduate Education Programs, St. Davids, PA 19087-3696. Offers ESL program specialist (K-12) (Certificate); general supervisor (PreK-12) (Certificate); health and physical education (K-12) (Certificate); middle level (4-8) (Certificate); multicultural education (M Ed); music (K-12) (Certificate); Pre K-4 (Certificate); Pre K-4 with special education (Certificate); reading (M Ed); reading specialist (K-12) (Certificate); reading supervisor (K-12) (Certificate); school counseling (MA, CAGS); school principalship (preK-12) (Certificate); school psychology (MS, CAGS); secondary biology education (7-12) (Certificate); secondary chemistry education (7-12) (Certificate); secondary communication education (7-12) (Certificate); secondary English education (7-12) (Certificate); secondary math education (7-12) (Certificate); secondary social studies education (7-12) (Certificate); special education (M Ed); special education (7-12) (Certificate); special education (Pre K-8) (Certificate); special education supervisor (K-12) (Certificate); TESOL (M Ed); world language (Certificate), including Spanish. *Program availability:* Part-time, evening/weekend, online learning. *Entrance requirements:* Additional exam requirements/recommendations for international students: Required—TOEFL. Electronic applications accepted. Application fee is waived when completed online. *Expenses:* Contact institution.

Elizabeth City State University, Master of Science in Biology Program, Elizabeth City, NC 27909-7806. Offers biological sciences (MS); biology education (MS). *Program availability:* Part-time, evening/weekend. *Degree requirements:* For master's, thesis. *Entrance requirements:* For master's, GRE, minimum GPA of 3.0, 3 letters of recommendation, 2 official transcripts from all undergraduate/graduate schools attended, typewritten one-page expository description of student educational preparation, research interests and career aspirations. Additional exam requirements/recommendations for international students: Required—TOEFL (minimum score 550 paper-based, 80 iBT) or IELTS (minimum score 6.5). Electronic applications accepted. *Faculty research:* Apoptosis and cancer, plant bioengineering, development of biofuels, microbial degradation, developmental toxicology.

Elms College, Division of Education, Chicopee, MA 01013-2839. Offers early childhood education (MAT); education (M Ed, CAGS); elementary education (MAT); English as a second language (MAT); reading (MAT); secondary education (MAT), including biology education, English education, Spanish education; special education (MAT). *Program availability:* Part-time, evening/weekend. *Faculty:* 5 full-time (all women), 6 part-time/adjunct (5 women). *Students:* 3 full-time (all women), 117 part-time (94 women); includes 12 minority (1 Black or African American, non-Hispanic/Latino; 2 Asian, non-Hispanic/Latino; 9 Hispanic/Latino). Average age 34. 27 applicants, 96% accepted, 23 enrolled. In 2018, 34 master's, 3 other advanced degrees awarded. *Degree requirements:* For master's, thesis (for some programs). *Entrance requirements:* For master's, Massachusetts Educators Certification Test, minimum GPA of 3.0; for CAGS, master's degree in education. Additional exam requirements/recommendations for international students: Required—TOEFL. *Application deadline:* For fall admission, 7/1 priority date for domestic students; for spring admission, 11/1 priority date for domestic students. Applications are processed on a rolling basis. Application fee: $30. *Expenses: Tuition:* Full-time $14,328; part-time $796 per credit. *Required fees:* $200. Tuition and fees vary according to degree level and program. *Financial support:* In 2018–19, 2 teaching assistantships with partial tuition reimbursements were awarded. Financial award applicants required to submit FAFSA. *Unit head:* Dr. Mary Janeczek, Chair, Division of Education, 413-594-2761, Fax: 413-592-4871, E-mail: janeczeke@elms.edu. *Application contact:* Nancy Davis, Director, Office of Graduate and Continuing Education Admissions, 413-265-2239, E-mail: davisn@elms.edu.

Fairleigh Dickinson University, Metropolitan Campus, University College: Arts, Sciences, and Professional Studies, School of Natural Sciences, Program in Science, Teaneck, NJ 07666-1914. Offers MA. *Accreditation:* TEAC.

Fitchburg State University, Division of Graduate and Continuing Education, Program in Middle School Education, Fitchburg, MA 01420-2697. Offers English (M Ed); general science (M Ed); history (M Ed); math (M Ed). *Accreditation:* NCATE. *Program availability:* Part-time, evening/weekend. *Entrance requirements:* Additional exam requirements/recommendations for international students: Required—TOEFL (minimum score 550 paper-based; 79 iBT). Electronic applications accepted. *Expenses:* Contact institution.

Fitchburg State University, Division of Graduate and Continuing Education, Program in Science Education, Fitchburg, MA 01420-2697. Offers M Ed. *Accreditation:* NCATE. *Program availability:* Part-time, evening/weekend. *Entrance requirements:* Additional exam requirements/recommendations for international students: Required—TOEFL (minimum score 550 paper-based; 79 iBT). Electronic applications accepted. *Expenses:* Contact institution.

Fitchburg State University, Division of Graduate and Continuing Education, Programs in Biology and Teaching Biology (Secondary Level), Fitchburg, MA 01420-2697. Offers biology (MA). *Accreditation:* NCATE. *Program availability:* Part-time, evening/weekend. *Entrance requirements:* Additional exam requirements/recommendations for international students: Required—TOEFL (minimum score 550 paper-based; 79 iBT). Electronic applications accepted. *Expenses:* Contact institution.

Florida Agricultural and Mechanical University, Division of Graduate Studies, Research, and Continuing Education, College of Education, Program in Secondary Education and Foundation, Tallahassee, FL 32307-3200. Offers biology (M Ed); chemistry (MS Ed); English (MS Ed); history (MS Ed); math (MS Ed); physics (MS Ed). *Accreditation:* NCATE. *Degree requirements:* For master's, thesis (for some programs). *Entrance requirements:* For master's, GRE General Test, minimum GPA of 3.0. Additional exam requirements/recommendations for international students: Required—TOEFL.

Florida Atlantic University, Charles E. Schmidt College of Science, Department of Biological Sciences, Boca Raton, FL 33431-0991. Offers biology (MS, MST). *Program availability:* Part-time. *Faculty:* 46 full-time (19 women). *Students:* 89 full-time (56 women), 72 part-time (34 women); includes 47 minority (6 Black or African American, non-Hispanic/Latino; 6 Asian, non-Hispanic/Latino; 26 Hispanic/Latino; 9 Two or more races, non-Hispanic/Latino), 16 international. Average age 28. 110 applicants, 40% accepted, 43 enrolled. In 2018, 47 master's awarded. *Entrance requirements:* For master's, GRE General Test, minimum GPA of 3.0. Additional exam requirements/recommendations for international students: Required—TOEFL (minimum score 500 paper-based; 61 iBT), IELTS (minimum score 6). *Application deadline:* For fall admission, 3/15 for domestic and international students; for spring admission, 10/1 for domestic and international students. Application fee: $30. *Expenses: Tuition, area resident:* Full-time $7400; part-time $369.82 per credit. Tuition, state resident: full-time $7400; part-time $369.82 per credit. Tuition, nonresident: full-time $20,496; part-time $1024.81 per credit. *Financial support:* Fellowships, research assistantships, teaching assistantships, career-related internships or fieldwork, and Federal Work-Study available. *Faculty research:* Ecology of the Everglades, molecular biology and biotechnology, marine biology. *Unit head:* Sarah Milton, Interim Chair, 561-297-3327, E-mail: smilton@fau.edu. *Application contact:* Sarah Milton, Interim Chair, 561-297-3327, E-mail: smilton@fau.edu.
Website: http://www.science.fau.edu/biology/

Florida Atlantic University, Charles E. Schmidt College of Science, Department of Physics, Boca Raton, FL 33431-0991. Offers physics (MS, MST, PhD). *Program availability:* Part-time. *Faculty:* 12 full-time (2 women), 4 part-time/adjunct (1 woman). *Students:* 23 full-time (10 women), 26 part-time (6 women); includes 6 minority (1 Asian, non-Hispanic/Latino; 4 Hispanic/Latino; 1 Two or more races, non-Hispanic/Latino), 28 international. Average age 31. 28 applicants, 46% accepted, 13 enrolled. In 2018, 4 master's, 2 doctorates awarded. *Entrance requirements:* For master's, GRE General Test, minimum GPA of 3.0; for doctorate, GRE General Test. Additional exam requirements/recommendations for international students: Required—TOEFL (minimum score 500 paper-based; 61 iBT), IELTS (minimum score 6). *Application deadline:* For fall admission, 7/1 for domestic students, 2/15 for international students; for spring admission, 11/1 for domestic students, 7/15 for international students. Applications are processed on a rolling basis. Application fee: $30. *Expenses: Tuition, area resident:* Full-time $7400; part-time $369.82 per credit. Tuition, state resident: full-time $7400; part-time $369.82 per credit. Tuition, nonresident: full-time $20,496; part-time $1024.81 per credit. *Financial support:* Fellowships, research assistantships, teaching assistantships, Federal Work-Study, and unspecified assistantships available. *Faculty research:* Astrophysics, spectroscopy, mathematical physics, theory of metals, superconductivity. *Unit head:* Luc Wille, Professor/Chair, 561-297-3380, E-mail: willel@fau.edu. *Application contact:* Luc Wille, Professor/Chair, 561-297-3380, E-mail: willel@fau.edu.
Website: http://physics.fau.edu/

Florida Gulf Coast University, College of Education, Program in Curriculum and Instruction, Fort Myers, FL 33965-6565. Offers elementary education (M Ed); English education (M Ed); English speakers of other languages endorsement (M Ed); gifted education (M Ed); mathematics education (M Ed); middle school education (M Ed); reading education (M Ed); science education (M Ed); social science education (M Ed); special education (M Ed). *Program availability:* Part-time, evening/weekend, online learning. *Degree requirements:* For master's, final project or portfolio. *Entrance requirements:* For master's, GRE General Test, MAT, minimum undergraduate GPA of 3.0 in last 2 years. Additional exam requirements/recommendations for international students: Required—TOEFL (minimum score 550 paper-based). Electronic applications accepted. *Faculty research:* Internet in schools, technology in pre-service and in-service teacher training.

Florida International University, College of Arts, Sciences, and Education, Department of Teaching and Learning, Miami, FL 33199. Offers art education (MA, MS); curriculum and instruction (MS, Ed D, PhD, Ed S), including curriculum development (MS), elementary education (MS), English education (MS), learning technologies (MS), mathematics education (MS), modern language education (MS), physical education (MS), science education (MS), social studies education (MS), special education (MS); early childhood education (MS); exceptional student education (Ed D); foreign language education (MS), including foreign language education, teaching English to speakers of other languages (TESOL); language, literacy and culture (PhD); mathematics, science, and learning technologies (PhD); physical education (MS), including sport and fitness; reading education (MS). *Program availability:* Part-time, evening/weekend. *Faculty:* 64 full-time (43 women), 104 part-time/adjunct (76 women). *Students:* 169 full-time (144 women), 155 part-time (130 women); includes 260 minority (53 Black or African American, non-Hispanic/Latino; 7 Asian, non-Hispanic/Latino; 193 Hispanic/Latino; 7 Two or more races, non-Hispanic/Latino), 13 international. Average age 33. 184 applicants, 62% accepted, 87 enrolled. In 2018, 153 master's, 10 doctorates awarded. *Degree requirements:* For doctorate, comprehensive exam, thesis/dissertation. *Entrance requirements:* For master's, GRE General Test, Florida General Knowledge Test or Florida College Level Academic Skills Test; for doctorate and Ed S, GRE General Test. Additional exam requirements/recommendations for international students: Required—TOEFL (minimum score 550 paper-based; 80 iBT), IELTS (minimum score 6.3). *Application deadline:* For fall admission, 6/1 priority date for domestic students, 4/1 for international students; for winter admission, 10/1 priority date for domestic students, 9/1 for international students; for spring admission, 3/1 priority date for domestic students, 2/1 for international students. Applications are processed on

a rolling basis. Application fee: $30. Electronic applications accepted. *Financial support:* Research assistantships and teaching assistantships available. *Unit head:* Dr. Maria Fernandez, Chair, 305-348-0193, Fax: 305-348-2086, E-mail: Maria.Fernandez9@fiu.edu. *Application contact:* Nanett Rojas, Manager, Admissions Operations, 305-348-7464, Fax: 305-348-7441, E-mail: gradadm@fiu.edu. Website: https://tl.fiu.edu/

Florida State University, The Graduate School, Department of Anthropology, Department of Biological Science, Tallahassee, FL 32306-4295. Offers cell and molecular biology (MS, PhD); ecology and evolutionary biology (MS, PhD); science teaching (MST). *Faculty:* 48 full-time (14 women). *Students:* 127 full-time (71 women); includes 15 minority (3 Black or African American, non-Hispanic/Latino; 1 Hispanic/Latino; 11 Two or more races, non-Hispanic/Latino), 30 international. Average age 30. 168 applicants, 36% accepted, 63 enrolled. In 2018, 3 master's, 11 doctorates awarded. Terminal master's awarded for partial completion of doctoral program. *Degree requirements:* For master's, comprehensive exam (for some programs), thesis (for some programs), teaching experience, seminar presentations; for doctorate, comprehensive exam, thesis/dissertation, teaching experience; seminar presentations. *Entrance requirements:* For master's and doctorate, GRE General Test, minimum upper-division GPA of 3.0. Additional exam requirements/recommendations for international students: Required—TOEFL (minimum score 600 paper-based; 92 iBT). *Application deadline:* For fall admission, 12/1 priority date for domestic students, 12/1 for international students. Application fee: $30. Electronic applications accepted. *Expenses: Tuition, area resident:* Part-time $479.32 per credit hour. Tuition and fees vary according to campus/location and program. *Financial support:* In 2018–19, 117 students received support, including 9 fellowships with full tuition reimbursements available (averaging $30,000 per year), 70 teaching assistantships with full tuition reimbursements available (averaging $23,000 per year); scholarships/grants, traineeships, and unspecified assistantships also available. Financial award application deadline: 12/1; financial award applicants required to submit FAFSA. *Faculty research:* Cell and molecular biology and genetics, ecology and evolutionary biology, neuroscience, plant science, structural biology. *Unit head:* Dr. Thomas A. Houpt, Professor and Associate Chair, 850-644-4906, Fax: 850-644-4783, E-mail: houpt@bio.fsu.edu. *Application contact:* Jessica Webber, Graduate Coordinator, 850-644-3023, Fax: 850-644-9829, E-mail: gradinfo@bio.fsu.edu. Website: http://www.bio.fsu.edu/

Fresno Pacific University, Graduate Programs, School of Education, Program in STEM Education, Fresno, CA 93702-4709. Offers MA Ed. *Program availability:* Part-time, evening/weekend. *Degree requirements:* For master's, thesis or alternative. *Entrance requirements:* Additional exam requirements/recommendations for international students: Required—TOEFL (minimum score 550 paper-based). *Expenses:* Contact institution.

George Mason University, College of Education and Human Development, Programs in Curriculum and Instruction, Fairfax, VA 22030. Offers assistive technology (M Ed); designing digital learning in schools (M Ed); early childhood education (M Ed); early childhood education for diverse learners (M Ed); elementary education (M Ed); English as a second language (M Ed); gifted child education (M Ed); literacy (M Ed), including PK-12 classroom teachers, reading specialist; literacy leadership for diverse schools (M Ed), including K-12 reading; physical education (M Ed); science K-12 (M Ed); secondary education (M Ed), including biology, chemistry, earth science, English, history/social science, math, physics; special education (M Ed); teacher leadership (M Ed); transformative teaching (M Ed). *Program availability:* Part-time, evening/weekend, 100% online, blended/hybrid learning. *Faculty:* 48 full-time (40 women), 28 part-time/adjunct (20 women). *Students:* 165 full-time (147 women), 697 part-time (579 women); includes 243 minority (47 Black or African American, non-Hispanic/Latino; 3 American Indian or Alaska Native, non-Hispanic/Latino; 88 Asian, non-Hispanic/Latino; 85 Hispanic/Latino; 4 Native Hawaiian or other Pacific Islander, non-Hispanic/Latino; 16 Two or more races, non-Hispanic/Latino), 26 international. Average age 34. 450 applicants, 93% accepted, 315 enrolled. In 2018, 421 master's awarded. *Entrance requirements:* For master's, PRAXIS Core (for some programs), 2 letters of recommendation, interview, program goals statement; 9 hours of complete licensure endorsement requirements (for elementary education); minimum GPA of 3.0 in applicant's last 60 hours of undergraduate coursework (for secondary education); at least 1 year of teaching experience (for literacy). Additional exam requirements/recommendations for international students: Required—TOEFL (minimum score 575 paper-based; 88 iBT), IELTS (minimum score 6.5), PTE (minimum score 59). *Application deadline:* For fall admission, 4/2 priority date for domestic and international students; for spring admission, 11/1 for domestic and international students. Application fee: $75 ($80 for international students). Electronic applications accepted. *Financial support:* In 2018–19, 4 students received support, including 1 fellowship, 3 teaching assistantships (averaging $3,745 per year); career-related internships or fieldwork, Federal Work-Study, scholarships/grants, unspecified assistantships, and health care benefits (for full-time research or teaching assistantship recipients) also available. Support available to part-time students. Financial award application deadline: 3/1; financial award applicants required to submit FAFSA. *Faculty research:* Teacher preparation and professional development; adaptive teaching; wonder in science teacher preparation; literacy (digital, adolescent); site based course instruction. *Unit head:* Rebecca Fox, Professor and Academic Program Coordinator, 703-993-4123, E-mail: rfox@gmu.edu. *Application contact:* Rebecca Fox, Professor and Academic Program Coordinator, 703-993-4123, E-mail: rfox@gmu.edu. Website: http://gse.gmu.edu/programs/gsemasters

The George Washington University, Graduate School of Education and Human Development, Department of Curriculum and Pedagogy, Program in Secondary Education, Washington, DC 20052. Offers Arabic (M Ed); Italian (M Ed); math (M Ed); physics (M Ed); Russian (M Ed). Programs also offered in Arlington and Ashburn, VA. *Accreditation:* NCATE. *Students:* 7 full-time (3 women), 23 part-time (13 women); includes 10 minority (5 Black or African American, non-Hispanic/Latino; 2 American Indian or Alaska Native, non-Hispanic/Latino; 1 Hispanic/Latino; 1 Native Hawaiian or other Pacific Islander, non-Hispanic/Latino; 1 Two or more races, non-Hispanic/Latino). Average age 33. 55 applicants, 69% accepted, 16 enrolled. In 2018, 17 master's awarded. *Entrance requirements:* For master's, GRE General Test or MAT, interview, minimum GPA of 2.75. *Application deadline:* For fall admission, 1/15 priority date for domestic students; for spring admission, 10/1 for domestic students. Applications are processed on a rolling basis. Application fee: $75. *Financial support:* Fellowships, career-related internships or fieldwork, Federal Work-Study, tuition waivers (full and partial), and stipends available. Financial award application deadline: 1/15; financial award applicants required to submit FAFSA. *Unit head:* Prof. Curtis Pyke, Chair, 202-994-4516, E-mail: cpyke@gwu.edu. *Application contact:* Sarah Lang, Director of Graduate Admissions, 202-994-1447, Fax: 202-994-7207, E-mail: slang@gwu.edu.

Georgia State University, College of Education and Human Development, Department of Middle and Secondary Education, Atlanta, GA 30302-3083. Offers curriculum and instruction (Ed D); English education (MAT); mathematics education (M Ed, MAT); middle level education (MAT); reading, language and literacy education (M Ed, MAT), including reading instruction (M Ed); science education (M Ed, MAT), including biology (MAT), broad field science (MAT), chemistry (MAT), earth science (MAT), physics (MAT); social studies education (M Ed, MAT), including economics (MAT), geography (MAT), history (MAT), political science (MAT); teaching and learning (PhD), including language and literacy, mathematics education, music education, science education, social studies education, teaching and teacher education. *Accreditation:* NCATE. *Program availability:* Part-time, evening/weekend, online learning. *Faculty:* 19 full-time (15 women), 9 part-time/adjunct (7 women). *Students:* 217 full-time (136 women), 203 part-time (140 women); includes 229 minority (156 Black or African American, non-Hispanic/Latino; 23 Asian, non-Hispanic/Latino; 31 Hispanic/Latino; 19 Two or more races, non-Hispanic/Latino), 3 international. Average age 34. 149 applicants, 60% accepted, 70 enrolled. In 2018, 112 master's, 23 doctorates awarded. *Entrance requirements:* For master's, GRE; GACE I (for initial teacher preparation programs), baccalaureate degree or equivalent, resume, goals statement, two letters of recommendation, minimum undergraduate GPA of 2.5; proof of initial teacher certification in the content area (for M Ed); for doctorate, GRE, resume, goals statement, writing sample, two letters of recommendation, minimum graduate GPA of 3.3, interview. *Application deadline:* For fall admission, 1/15 priority date for domestic and international students; for spring admission, 10/1 for domestic and international students. Application fee: $50. Electronic applications accepted. *Expenses: Tuition, area resident:* Full-time $9360; part-time $390 per credit hour. Tuition, state resident: full-time $9360; part-time $390 per credit hour. Tuition, nonresident: full-time $30,024; part-time $1251 per credit hour. *International tuition:* $30,024 full-time. *Required fees:* $2128. *Financial support:* In 2018–19, fellowships with full tuition reimbursements (averaging $19,667 per year), research assistantships with full tuition reimbursements (averaging $5,436 per year), teaching assistantships with full tuition reimbursements (averaging $2,779 per year) were awarded; career-related internships or fieldwork, Federal Work-Study, scholarships/grants, health care benefits, tuition waivers (full and partial), and unspecified assistantships also available. Financial award application deadline: 3/15. *Faculty research:* Teacher education in language and literacy, mathematics, science, and social studies in urban middle and secondary school settings; learning technologies in school, community, and corporate settings; multicultural education and education for social justice; urban education; international education. *Unit head:* Dr. Gertrude Marilyn Tinker Sachs, Chair, 404-413-8384, Fax: 404-413-8063, E-mail: gtinkersachs@gsu.edu. *Application contact:* Shaleen Tibbs, Administrative Specialist, 404-413-8385, Fax: 404-413-8063, E-mail: stibbs@gsu.edu. Website: http://mse.education.gsu.edu/

Grambling State University, School of Graduate Studies and Research, College of Education, Department of Educational Leadership, Grambling, LA 71245. Offers developmental education (MS, Ed D, PMC), including curriculum and instructional design (Ed D), English (MS), guidance and counseling (MS), higher education administration and management (Ed D), mathematics (MS), reading (MS), science (MS), student development and personnel services (Ed D); educational leadership (M Ed). *Program availability:* Part-time, evening/weekend. *Degree requirements:* For master's, comprehensive exam, thesis (for some programs); for doctorate, comprehensive exam, thesis/dissertation. *Entrance requirements:* For master's, GRE, minimum GPA of 2.5 on last degree; for doctorate, GRE (minimum score 1000, 500 on Verbal), master's degree, minimum GPA of 3.0 on last degree. Additional exam requirements/recommendations for international students: Required—TOEFL (minimum score 500 paper-based; 62 iBT). Electronic applications accepted.

Grand Canyon University, College of Education, Phoenix, AZ 85017-1097. Offers autism spectrum disorders (MA); curriculum and instruction (MA); early childhood education (M Ed); educational administration (M Ed); educational leadership (M Ed); elementary education (M Ed); gifted education (MA); instructional technology (MS); K-12 leadership (Ed S); reading (MA); secondary education (M Ed); secondary humanities education (M Ed); secondary STEM education (M Ed); special education (M Ed); teaching and learning (Ed D); teaching English to speakers of other languages (MA). *Program availability:* Part-time, evening/weekend, online learning. *Degree requirements:* For master's, publishable research paper (M Ed), e-portfolio. *Entrance requirements:* For master's, undergraduate degree from accredited, GCU-approved college, university, or program with minimum GPA 2.8. Additional exam requirements/recommendations for international students: Required—TOEFL (minimum score 550 paper-based; 79 iBT), IELTS (minimum score 6). Electronic applications accepted.

Hamline University, School of Education, St. Paul, MN 55104-1284. Offers education (MA Ed, Ed D); English as a second language (MA); literacy education (MA); natural science and environmental education (MA Ed); teaching (MAT); teaching English to speakers of other languages (MA). *Accreditation:* NCATE (one or more programs are accredited). *Program availability:* Part-time, evening/weekend, 100% online, blended/hybrid learning. *Degree requirements:* For master's, thesis (for some programs), thesis or capstone project; for doctorate, comprehensive exam, thesis/dissertation. *Entrance requirements:* For master's, official transcripts, essay, letters of recommendation, minimum GPA of 3.0 from bachelor's work; resume and/or writing samples (for some programs); for doctorate, personal statement, master's degree with minimum GPA of 3.0, letters of recommendation, writing sample. Additional exam requirements/recommendations for international students: Required—TOEFL (minimum score 550 paper-based; 80 iBT), IELTS (minimum score 6.5). Electronic applications accepted. *Expenses:* Contact institution. *Faculty research:* Adult basic education, service-learning, teacher dispositions, diversity, technology.

Harrison Middleton University, Graduate Program, Tempe, AZ 85282. Offers education (MA, Ed D); humanities (MA); imaginative literature (MA); interdisciplinary studies (DA); jurisprudence (MA); natural science (MA); philosophy and religion (MA); social science (MA). *Program availability:* Part-time, evening/weekend, online learning. *Degree requirements:* For master's and doctorate, capstone project. *Entrance requirements:* For master's, interview; for doctorate, 2 academic letters of reference, interview, essay. Additional exam requirements/recommendations for international students: Required—TOEFL (minimum score 550 paper-based; 80 iBT). Electronic applications accepted. *Faculty research:* Japanese animation, educational leadership, war art, John Muir's wilderness.

Heritage University, Graduate Programs in Education, Program in Professional Studies, Toppenish, WA 98948-9599. Offers bilingual education/ESL (M Ed); biology (M Ed); English and literature (M Ed); reading/literacy (M Ed); special education (M Ed). *Program availability:* Part-time, evening/weekend. *Degree requirements:* For master's, comprehensive exam (for some programs), thesis (for some programs).

Hofstra University, School of Education, Programs in Teacher Education, Hempstead, NY 11549. Offers bilingual education (MA); bilingual extension (Advanced Certificate); business education (MS Ed); curriculum studies (MS Ed); early childhood and childhood education (MS Ed); early childhood education (MA, MS Ed); educational technology (Advanced Certificate); elementary education (MA, MS Ed); English education (MS Ed); family and consumer science (MS Ed); fine arts and music education (Advanced Certificate); fine arts education (MS Ed); foreign language and TESOL (MS Ed); foreign language education (MA, MS Ed); languages other than English and teaching English as a second language (MA); learning and teaching (Ed D); mathematics education (MA, MS Ed); middle childhood extension (Advanced Certificate); music education (MA, MS Ed); science education (MA); secondary education (Advanced Certificate); social studies education (MA, MS Ed); teaching languages other than English and TESOL

(MS Ed); technology for learning (MA); TESOL (MS Ed, Advanced Certificate); TESOL with specialization in STEM (MA); work based learning extension (Advanced Certificate). *Program availability:* Part-time, evening/weekend, blended/hybrid learning. *Students:* 138 full-time (94 women), 109 part-time (78 women); includes 66 minority (16 Black or African American, non-Hispanic/Latino; 17 Asian, non-Hispanic/Latino; 31 Hispanic/Latino; 2 Native Hawaiian or other Pacific Islander, non-Hispanic/Latino), 6 international. Average age 29. 217 applicants, 86% accepted, 113 enrolled. In 2018, 105 master's, 11 doctorates, 25 other advanced degrees awarded. *Degree requirements:* For master's, comprehensive exam, thesis (for some programs), exit project, student teaching, fieldwork, electronic portfolio, curriculum project, minimum GPA of 3.0; for doctorate, dissertation; for Advanced Certificate, 3 foreign languages, comprehensive exam (for some programs), thesis project. *Entrance requirements:* For master's, GRE, 2 letters of recommendation, portfolio, teacher certification (MA), interview, essay; for doctorate, GMAT, GRE, LSAT, or MAT; for Advanced Certificate, 2 letters of recommendation, essay, interview and/or portfolio, teaching certificate. Additional exam requirements/recommendations for international students: Required—TOEFL (minimum score 550 paper-based; 80 iBT). *Application deadline:* Applications are processed on a rolling basis. Application fee: $75. Electronic applications accepted. *Financial support:* In 2018–19, 86 students received support, including 51 fellowships with full and partial tuition reimbursements available (averaging $5,080 per year), 2 research assistantships with full and partial tuition reimbursements available (averaging $3,470 per year); career-related internships or fieldwork, Federal Work-Study, institutionally sponsored loans, scholarships/grants, traineeships, tuition waivers (full and partial), unspecified assistantships, and scholarships and endowed scholarships also available. Support available to part-time students. Financial award applicants required to submit FAFSA. *Faculty research:* Impact of memory on learning; brain function, cognitive-development, learning, and achievement; student activism and civic education; using children's literature to promote diversity; 2nd language acquisition. *Unit head:* Dr. Alan Singer, Chairperson, 516-463-5853, Fax: 516-463-6275, E-mail: alan.j.singer@hofstra.edu. *Application contact:* Sunil Samuel, Assistant Vice President of Admissions, 516-463-4723, Fax: 516-463-4664, E-mail: graduateadmission@hofstra.edu.
Website: http://www.hofstra.edu/education/

Hood College, Graduate School, Department of Education, Frederick, MD 21701-8575. Offers curriculum and instruction (MS), including elementary education, elementary science and mathematics education, secondary education, special education; education, multidisciplinary studies (MS); educational leadership (MS, Certificate); reading specialization (MS); STEM education (Certificate). *Accreditation:* NCATE. *Program availability:* Part-time-only, evening/weekend. *Faculty:* 5 full-time (3 women), 32 part-time/adjunct (24 women). *Students:* 3 full-time (all women), 306 part-time (253 women); includes 65 minority (22 Black or African American, non-Hispanic/Latino; 9 Asian, non-Hispanic/Latino; 17 Hispanic/Latino; 17 Two or more races, non-Hispanic/Latino), 3 international. Average age 33. 80 applicants, 99% accepted, 45 enrolled. In 2018, 59 master's, 47 other advanced degrees awarded. *Degree requirements:* For master's, action research project, portfolio (for reading specialization); for Certificate, STEM capstone activity. *Entrance requirements:* For master's, minimum GPA of 2.75, teaching certification, writing sample during interview, letter of recommendation from principal (for educational leadership program only). Additional exam requirements/recommendations for international students: Required—TOEFL (minimum score 575 paper-based; 89 iBT), IELTS (minimum score 6.5). *Application deadline:* For fall admission, 8/15 priority date for domestic students, 8/5 for international students; for spring admission, 12/1 priority date for domestic students, 12/1 for international students; for summer admission, 5/1 priority date for domestic students, 4/15 for international students. Applications are processed on a rolling basis. Application fee: $50 ($100 for international students). Electronic applications accepted. *Expenses: Tuition:* Full-time $17,640; part-time $4410 per semester. *Required fees:* $125 per semester. Tuition and fees vary according to degree level and program. *Financial support:* Tuition waivers (partial) and unspecified assistantships available. Financial award applicants required to submit FAFSA. *Faculty research:* Leadership, action research, brain research, learning styles. *Unit head:* Dr. April M. Boulton, Dean of the Graduate School, 301-696-3612, E-mail: gofurther@hood.edu. *Application contact:* Tanith Fowler Corsi, Assistant Director of Graduate Admissions, 301-696-3603, E-mail: gofurther@hood.edu.
Website: https://www.hood.edu/academics/departments/department-education/programs-offered

Houston Baptist University, College of Education and Behavioral Sciences, Programs in Education, Houston, TX 77074-3298. Offers bilingual education (M Ed); counselor education (M Ed); curriculum and instruction (M Ed); curriculum and instruction (EC-6 bilingual) (M Ed); curriculum and instruction in all-level art, Spanish, music, or physical education (M Ed); curriculum and instruction in EC-6 and special education (EC-12) (M Ed); curriculum and instruction in instructional technology (M Ed); curriculum and instruction in mathematics, science, or social studies (4-8) (M Ed); curriculum and instruction with EC-6 generalist (M Ed); curriculum and instruction with English language arts and reading (4-8) (M Ed); educational administration (M Ed); educational diagnostician (M Ed); executive educational leadership (Ed D); higher education in business management (M Ed); higher education in Christian studies (M Ed); higher education in counseling (M Ed); higher education in educational technology (M Ed); reading (M Ed); special educational leadership (Ed D). *Program availability:* Part-time, evening/weekend, 100% online, blended/hybrid learning. *Degree requirements:* For master's, comprehensive exam; for doctorate, thesis/dissertation. *Entrance requirements:* For master's, minimum GPA of 2.75, two recommendations, resume, bachelor's degree conferred transcript; interview (for non-certified teachers); for doctorate, GRE, 5 letters of recommendation. Additional exam requirements/recommendations for international students: Required—TOEFL (minimum score 80 iBT), IELTS (minimum score 6.5). Electronic applications accepted. Application fee is waived when completed online. *Expenses:* Contact institution. *Faculty research:* Autism and inclusion, integrating technology into instruction, school change and leadership trust.

Hunter College of the City University of New York, Graduate School, School of Education, Programs in Secondary Education, Concentration in Biology Education, New York, NY 10065-5085. Offers MA. *Accreditation:* NCATE. *Degree requirements:* For master's, thesis, professional teaching portfolio, New York State Teacher Certification Exams, research project. *Entrance requirements:* For master's, minimum GPA of 2.8, 2 letters of reference, 21 credits of course work in biology. Additional exam requirements/recommendations for international students: Required—TOEFL, TWE.

Hunter College of the City University of New York, Graduate School, School of Education, Programs in Secondary Education, Concentration in Chemistry Education, New York, NY 10065-5085. Offers MA. *Accreditation:* NCATE. *Degree requirements:* For master's, thesis, professional teaching portfolio, New York State Teacher Certification Exam. *Entrance requirements:* For master's, minimum GPA of 2.8, 2 letters of reference, minimum of 29 credits in science and mathematics.

Illinois Institute of Technology, Graduate College, College of Science, Department of Mathematics and Science Education, Chicago, IL 60616. Offers mathematics education (MAS, PhD); science education (MAS, PhD). *Degree requirements:* For master's, comprehensive exam (for some programs), thesis optional; for doctorate, comprehensive exam, thesis/dissertation. *Entrance requirements:* For master's, GRE General Test (minimum score 900 quantitative and verbal; 2.5 analytical writing), minimum undergraduate GPA of 3.0; two-page professional statement of goals/objectives; curriculum vita; three letters of recommendation; for doctorate, GRE General Test (minimum score 1000 quantitative and verbal; 3.0 analytical writing), minimum GPA of 3.0, 3 years of teaching experience. Additional exam requirements/recommendations for international students: Required—TOEFL (minimum score 600 paper-based; 80 iBT). Electronic applications accepted. *Faculty research:* Informal science/math education, curriculum development, integration of science/math disciplines and across disciplines, instructional methods, students' and teachers' conceptions of scientific/mathematical inquiry and the nature of science/math, instructional models, evaluation, and research design.

Indiana State University, College of Graduate and Professional Studies, College of Arts and Sciences, Department of Biology, Terre Haute, IN 47809. Offers cellular and molecular biology (PhD); ecology, systematics and evolution (PhD); life sciences (MS); physiology (PhD); science education (MS). *Degree requirements:* For master's, thesis optional; for doctorate, comprehensive exam, thesis/dissertation. *Entrance requirements:* For master's and doctorate, GRE General Test. Electronic applications accepted.

Indiana University Bloomington, School of Education, Department of Curriculum and Instruction, Bloomington, IN 47405-7000. Offers art education (MS, Ed D, PhD); curriculum studies (Ed D, PhD); elementary education (MS, Ed D, PhD, Ed S); mathematics education (MS, Ed D, PhD); science education (MS, Ed D, PhD); secondary education (MS, Ed D, PhD); social studies education (MS, PhD); special education (PhD, Ed S). *Accreditation:* NCATE. *Program availability:* Part-time, evening/weekend. Terminal master's awarded for partial completion of doctoral program. *Degree requirements:* For doctorate, thesis/dissertation; for Ed S, comprehensive exam or project. *Entrance requirements:* For master's, doctorate, and Ed S, GRE General Test. Electronic applications accepted.

Indiana University Bloomington, University Graduate School, College of Arts and Sciences, Department of Biology, Bloomington, IN 47405. Offers biology teaching (MAT); biotechnology (MA); evolution, ecology, and behavior (MA, PhD); genetics (PhD); microbiology (MA, PhD); molecular, cellular, and developmental biology (PhD); plant sciences (MA, PhD); zoology (MA, PhD). Terminal master's awarded for partial completion of doctoral program. *Degree requirements:* For master's, thesis, oral defense; for doctorate, thesis/dissertation, oral defense. *Entrance requirements:* For master's and doctorate, GRE General Test. Additional exam requirements/recommendations for international students: Required—TOEFL (minimum score 100 iBT). Electronic applications accepted. *Faculty research:* Evolution, ecology and behavior; microbiology; molecular biology and genetics; plant biology.

Indiana University Bloomington, University Graduate School, College of Arts and Sciences, Department of Chemistry, Bloomington, IN 47405. Offers analytical chemistry (PhD); chemical biology (PhD); chemistry (MAT); inorganic chemistry (PhD); materials chemistry (PhD); organic chemistry (PhD); physical chemistry (PhD); MSES/MS. Terminal master's awarded for partial completion of doctoral program. *Degree requirements:* For master's, thesis; for doctorate, thesis/dissertation. *Entrance requirements:* For master's and doctorate, GRE General Test, GRE Subject Test. Additional exam requirements/recommendations for international students: Required—TOEFL. Electronic applications accepted. *Faculty research:* Synthesis of complex natural products, organic reaction mechanisms, organic electrochemistry, transitive-metal chemistry, solid-state and surface chemistry.

Instituto Tecnológico y de Estudios Superiores de Monterrey, Campus Monterrey, Graduate and Research Division, Program in Natural and Social Sciences, Monterrey, Mexico. Offers biotechnology (MS); chemistry (MS, PhD); communications (MS); education (MA). *Program availability:* Part-time. *Degree requirements:* For master's, one foreign language, thesis; for doctorate, one foreign language, thesis/dissertation. *Entrance requirements:* For master's, EXADEP; for doctorate, EXADEP, master's degree in related field. Additional exam requirements/recommendations for international students: Required—TOEFL. *Faculty research:* Cultural industries, mineral substances, bioremediation, food processing, CQ in industrial chemical processing.

Inter American University of Puerto Rico, Arecibo Campus, Programs in Education, Arecibo, PR 00614-4050. Offers administration and educational supervision (MA Ed); counseling and guidance (MA Ed); curriculum and teaching (MA Ed), including biology education, English as a second language, history education, math education, Spanish; elementary education (MA Ed). *Accreditation:* TEAC. *Degree requirements:* For master's, comprehensive exam, thesis optional. *Entrance requirements:* For master's, GRE, EXADEP, bachelor's degree in education or teaching license (administration and supervision) or courses in education and psychology (counseling and guidance), minimum GPA of 2.5 in last 60 credits.

Inter American University of Puerto Rico, Metropolitan Campus, Graduate Programs, Program in Teaching of Science, San Juan, PR 00919-1293. Offers MA. *Degree requirements:* For master's, comprehensive exam. *Entrance requirements:* For master's, GRE or EXADEP, interview. Electronic applications accepted.

Inter American University of Puerto Rico, Ponce Campus, Graduate School, Mercedita, PR 00715-1602. Offers accounting (MBA); biology (M Ed); chemistry (M Ed); criminal justice (MA); elementary education (M Ed); English as a Second Language (M Ed); finance (MBA); history (M Ed); human resources (MBA); marketing (MBA); mathematics (M Ed); Spanish (M Ed). *Entrance requirements:* For master's, minimum GPA of 2.5.

Inter American University of Puerto Rico, San Germán Campus, Graduate Studies Center, Program in Science Education, San Germán, PR 00683-5008. Offers MA. *Accreditation:* TEAC. *Program availability:* Part-time, evening/weekend. *Degree requirements:* For master's, comprehensive exam. *Entrance requirements:* For master's, GRE General Test or EXADEP, minimum GPA of 3.0. *Expenses: Tuition:* Full-time $212; part-time $212 per credit. *Required fees:* $366 per semester. One-time fee: $31. Tuition and fees vary according to degree level and program.

Iona College, School of Arts and Science, Department of Education, New Rochelle, NY 10801-1890. Offers adolescence education: biology (MS Ed, MST); adolescence education: English (MS Ed); adolescence education: mathematics (MST); adolescence education: social studies (MS Ed, MST); adolescence education: Spanish (MS Ed); adolescence special education 5-12 (MST); childhood and special education (MST); early childhood and childhood (MST); educational leadership (MS Ed). *Accreditation:* NCATE. *Program availability:* Part-time, evening/weekend. *Faculty:* 7 full-time (5 women), 9 part-time/adjunct (5 women). *Students:* 33 full-time (30 women), 26 part-time (20 women); includes 21 minority (6 Black or African American, non-Hispanic/Latino; 1 Asian, non-Hispanic/Latino; 13 Hispanic/Latino; 1 Two or more races, non-Hispanic/Latino). Average age 25. 39 applicants, 87% accepted, 14 enrolled. In 2018, 20 master's awarded. *Degree requirements:* For master's, thesis or alternative. *Entrance requirements:* For master's, minimum GPA of 3.0, NY State teaching certificate and bachelor's degree (for MS Ed). Additional exam requirements/recommendations for international students: Required—TOEFL (minimum score 550 paper-based; 80 iBT),

IELTS (minimum score 6.5). *Application deadline:* For fall admission, 8/1 priority date for domestic students, 5/1 priority date for international students; for spring admission, 1/1 priority date for domestic students, 9/1 priority date for international students. Applications are processed on a rolling basis. Electronic applications accepted. *Expenses: Tuition:* Full-time $14,064; part-time $7032 per credit. *Required fees:* $245 per semester. One-time fee: $250. Tuition and fees vary according to program. *Financial support:* In 2018–19, 2 students received support. Unspecified assistantships available. Support available to part-time students. Financial award application deadline: 4/15; financial award applicants required to submit FAFSA. *Faculty research:* Engaging teacher educators in scientific process, cross-national comparisons of mathematics teaching, questioning strategies in the classroom, research methods, literacy development. *Unit head:* Malissa Scheuring Leipold, EdD, Chair, 914-633-2210, Fax: 914-633-2281, E-mail: mleipold@iona.edu. *Application contact:* Christopher Kash, Assistant Director of Graduate Admissions, 914-633-2403, E-mail: ckash@iona.edu. Website: http://www.iona.edu/Academics/School-of-Arts-Science/Departments/Education/Graduate-Programs.aspx

Iowa State University of Science and Technology, Program in Science Education, Ames, IA 50011. Offers MAT. *Entrance requirements:* For master's, GRE, three letters of recommendation, undergraduate degree in sciences (preferred). Additional exam requirements/recommendations for international students: Required—TOEFL (minimum score 560 paper-based; 83 iBT), IELTS (minimum score 6.5). Electronic applications accepted.

Jackson State University, Graduate School, College of Science, Engineering and Technology, Department of Physics, Atmospheric Sciences, and Geoscience, Jackson, MS 39217. Offers physical science (MS, PhD); science education (MST). *Program availability:* Part-time, evening/weekend. *Degree requirements:* For master's, comprehensive exam. *Entrance requirements:* For master's, GRE General Test. Additional exam requirements/recommendations for international students: Required—TOEFL (minimum score 520 paper-based; 67 iBT).

Kennesaw State University, Bagwell College of Education, MAT Program, Kennesaw, GA 30144. Offers art education (MAT); secondary English (MAT); secondary mathematics (MAT); secondary science (MAT); special education (MAT); teaching English to speakers of other languages (MAT). *Program availability:* Part-time, evening/weekend. *Students:* 44 full-time (36 women), 10 part-time (6 women); includes 15 minority (10 Black or African American, non-Hispanic/Latino; 4 Hispanic/Latino; 1 Two or more races, non-Hispanic/Latino). Average age 32. 3 applicants. In 2018, 32 master's awarded. *Entrance requirements:* For master's, GRE, GACE I (state certificate exam), minimum GPA of 2.75, 2 recommendations, resume. Additional exam requirements/recommendations for international students: Required—TOEFL (minimum score 550 paper-based; 80 iBT), IELTS (minimum score 6.5). *Application deadline:* For fall admission, 6/1 for domestic and international students; for spring admission, 3/1 for domestic and international students; for summer admission, 4/15 for domestic and international students. Applications are processed on a rolling basis. Application fee: $60. Electronic applications accepted. *Expenses: Tuition, area resident:* Full-time $6960; part-time $290 per credit hour. Tuition, state resident: full-time $6960; part-time $290 per credit hour. Tuition, nonresident: full-time $25,080; part-time $1045 per credit hour. *International tuition:* $25,080 full-time. *Required fees:* $2006; $1706 per semester. $853 per semester. *Financial support:* Research assistantships with tuition reimbursements and unspecified assistantships available. Financial award application deadline: 4/1; financial award applicants required to submit FAFSA. *Unit head:* Director, 470-578-3093. *Application contact:* Admissions Counselor, 470-578-4377, Fax: 470-578-9172, E-mail: ksugrad@kennesaw.edu.

Lake Forest College, Master of Arts in Teaching Program, Lake Forest, IL 60045. Offers elementary education (MAT); K-12 French (MAT); K-12 music (MAT); K-12 Spanish (MAT); K-12 visual art (MAT); secondary biology (MAT); secondary chemistry (MAT); secondary English (MAT); secondary history (MAT); secondary mathematics (MAT). *Degree requirements:* For master's, comprehensive exam, portfolio. *Entrance requirements:* For master's, GRE.

Laurentian University, School of Graduate Studies and Research, Programme in Science Communication, Sudbury, ON P3E 2C6, Canada. Offers G Dip.

Lawrence Technological University, College of Arts and Sciences, Southfield, MI 48075-1058. Offers bioinformatics (Graduate Certificate); computer science (MS), including data science, big data, and data mining, intelligent systems; educational technology (MA), including robotics; instructional design, communication, and presentation (Graduate Certificate); integrated science (MA); science education (MA); technical and professional communication (MS, Graduate Certificate); writing for the digital age (Graduate Certificate). *Program availability:* Part-time, evening/weekend. *Degree requirements:* For master's, thesis (for some programs). *Entrance requirements:* Additional exam requirements/recommendations for international students: Required—TOEFL (minimum score 550 paper-based; 79 iBT), IELTS (minimum score 6.5). Electronic applications accepted. *Faculty research:* Computer analysis of music, machine learning of literature and lyrics, customer sentiments and response analysis through social media, peta-scale computing in astronomical databases, early detection of diseases with pattern recognition.

Lebanon Valley College, Program in Science Education, Annville, PA 17003-1400. Offers integrative STEM education (Certificate); STEM education (MSE). *Program availability:* Part-time-only, evening/weekend, 100% online, blended/hybrid learning. *Degree requirements:* For master's, thesis or capstone project. *Entrance requirements:* For master's, baccalaureate degree, minimum GPA of 3.0, teacher certification, 3 letters of recommendation, transcripts, goal statement. Additional exam requirements/recommendations for international students: Required—TOEFL (minimum score 80 iBT). Electronic applications accepted. *Expenses:* Contact institution. *Faculty research:* Teacher quality and student achievement, STEM reform, STEM education, effective teaching.

Lehman College of the City University of New York, School of Education, Department of Middle and High School Education, Program in Science Education, Bronx, NY 10468-1589. Offers MS Ed. *Accreditation:* NCATE.

Lesley University, Graduate School of Education, Cambridge, MA 02138-2790. Offers arts, community, and education (M Ed); autism studies (Certificate); curriculum and instruction (M Ed, CAGS); early childhood education (M Ed); ecological teaching and learning (MS); educational studies (PhD), including adult learning, educational leadership, individually designed; elementary education (M Ed); emergent technologies for educators (Certificate); ESLArts: language learning through the arts (M Ed); high school education (M Ed); individually designed (M Ed); integrated teaching through the arts (M Ed); literacy for K-8 classroom teachers (M Ed); mathematics education (M Ed); middle school education (M Ed); moderate disabilities (M Ed); online learning (Certificate); reading (CAGS); science in education (M Ed); severe disabilities (M Ed); special needs (CAGS); specialist teacher of reading (M Ed); teacher of visual art (M Ed); technology in education (M Ed, CAGS). *Accreditation:* TEAC. *Program availability:* Part-time, evening/weekend, online learning. *Degree requirements:* For master's, practicum; for doctorate, thesis/dissertation. *Entrance requirements:* For master's, Massachusetts Tests for Educator Licensure (MTEL), transcripts, statement of purpose, recommendations; interview (for special education); for doctorate, GRE General Test, transcripts, statement of purpose, recommendations, interview, master's degree, resume; for other advanced degree, interview, master's degree. Additional exam requirements/recommendations for international students: Required—TOEFL (minimum score 550 paper-based; 80 iBT). Electronic applications accepted. *Faculty research:* Assessment in literacy, mathematics and science; autism spectrum disorders; instructional technology and online learning; multicultural education and English language learners.

Lewis University, College of Education, Program in Secondary Education, Romeoville, IL 60446. Offers chemistry (MA); English (MA); history (MA); physics (MA); psychology and social science (MA). *Program availability:* Part-time. *Students:* 24 full-time (9 women), 28 part-time (17 women); includes 16 minority (2 Black or African American, non-Hispanic/Latino; 2 Asian, non-Hispanic/Latino; 10 Hispanic/Latino; 2 Two or more races, non-Hispanic/Latino). Average age 27. *Degree requirements:* For master's, comprehensive exam, departmental qualifying exam. *Entrance requirements:* For master's, writing exam, Test of Academic Proficiency/Basic Skills Test/ACT/SAT, bachelor's degree, minimum GPA of 2.75, 2 letters of recommendation. Additional exam requirements/recommendations for international students: Required—TOEFL (minimum score 550 paper-based; 79 iBT), IELTS (minimum score 6). *Application deadline:* For fall admission, 5/1 priority date for international students; for spring admission, 11/15 priority date for international students. Applications are processed on a rolling basis. Application fee: $40. Electronic applications accepted. *Financial support:* Federal Work-Study, scholarships/grants, and unspecified assistantships available. Financial award application deadline: 5/1; financial award applicants required to submit FAFSA. *Unit head:* Dr. Chris Palmi, Program Director. *Application contact:* Kathy Lisak, Graduate Admission Counselor, 815-836-5610, E-mail: grad@lewisu.edu.

Manhattanville College, School of Education, Jump Start Program, Purchase, NY 10577-2132. Offers childhood education and special education (grades 1-6) (MPS); early childhood education (birth-grade 2) (MAT); education (Advanced Certificate); English and special education (grades 5-12) (MPS); mathematics and special education (grades 5-12) (MPS); science and special education (grades 5-12) (MPS); social studies and special education (grades 5-12) (MPS); Spanish (grades 7-12) (MAT); tesol - teaching English as a second language (all grades) (MPS). *Program availability:* Part-time, evening/weekend. *Faculty:* 11 full-time (7 women), 78 part-time/adjunct (50 women). *Students:* 3 full-time (2 women), 16 part-time (11 women); includes 5 minority (1 Black or African American, non-Hispanic/Latino; 3 Hispanic/Latino; 1 Native Hawaiian or other Pacific Islander, non-Hispanic/Latino). Average age 31. 48 applicants, 54% accepted, 22 enrolled. In 2018, 23 master's, 1 other advanced degree awarded. *Degree requirements:* For master's, comprehensive exam (for some programs), thesis (for some programs), student teaching, research seminars, portfolios, internships, writing assessment; for Advanced Certificate, comprehensive exam (for some programs). *Entrance requirements:* For master's, for programs leading to certification, candidates must submit scores from GRE or MAT(miller analogies test), minimum undergraduate GPA of 3.0, all transcripts from all colleges and universities attended, 2 letters of recommendation, interview, essay (2-3 page personal statement that describes reasons for choosing education as profession and personal philosophy of education), proof of immunization (for those born after 1957). Additional exam requirements/recommendations for international students: Required—TOEFL (minimum score 600 paper-based; 110 iBT); Recommended—IELTS (minimum score 8). *Application deadline:* Applications are processed on a rolling basis. Application fee: $75. Electronic applications accepted. *Expenses:* 935 per credit. *Financial support:* Teaching assistantships, career-related internships or fieldwork, Federal Work-Study, institutionally sponsored loans, scholarships/grants, and unspecified assistantships available. Financial award application deadline: 3/15; financial award applicants required to submit FAFSA. *Faculty research:* Early childhood and technology, professional development schools and community schools, students with emotional difficulties, literacy and adolescents, mindfulness, changing suburbs institute, and community schools, studying the effects of the environment on special populations, the most difficult cases, students who are presented with multiple challenges: learning, behavioral and ACE experiences who see criminal behavior as a way to cope; working on giving them the tools they need to succeed. *Unit head:* Dr. Shelley Wepner, Dean, 914-323-3153, E-mail: Shelly.Wepner@mville.edu. *Application contact:* Alissa Wilson, Director, SOE Graduate Enrollment Management, 914-323-3150, Fax: 914-694-1732, E-mail: edschool@mville.edu.
Website: http://www.mville.edu/programs/jump-start

Manhattanville College, School of Education, Program in Middle Childhood/Adolescence Education (Grades 5-12), Purchase, NY 10577-2132. Offers biology and special education (MPS); chemistry and special education (MPS); education for sustainability (Advanced Certificate); English and special education (MPS); literacy and special education (MPS); literacy specialist (MPS); math and special education (MPS); mathematics (Advanced Certificate); middle childhood/adolescence ed science (biology or chemistry grades 5-12) or (physics grades 7-12) (MAT); middle childhood/adolescence education (grades 5-12) English (MAT, Advanced Certificate); middle childhood/adolescence education (grades 5-12) mathematics (MAT, Advanced Certificate); middle childhood/adolescence education (grades 5-12) science (biology chemistry, physics, earth science) (Advanced Certificate); middle childhood/adolescence education (grades 5-12) social studies (MAT, Advanced Certificate); physics (MAT, Advanced Certificate); social studies (MAT); social studies and special education (MPS); special education generalist (MPS). *Program availability:* Part-time, evening/weekend. *Faculty:* 3 full-time (2 women), 9 part-time/adjunct (4 women). *Students:* 11 full-time (6 women), 17 part-time (12 women); includes 3 minority (1 Black or African American, non-Hispanic/Latino; 2 Hispanic/Latino). Average age 31. 17 applicants, 71% accepted, 7 enrolled. In 2018, 8 master's, 3 other advanced degrees awarded. *Degree requirements:* For master's, comprehensive exam (for some programs), thesis (for some programs), student teaching, research seminars, portfolios, internships, writing assessment; for Advanced Certificate, comprehensive exam (for some programs). *Entrance requirements:* For master's, for programs leading to certification, candidates must submit scores from GRE or MAT(Miller Analogies Test), minimum undergraduate GPA of 3.0, all transcripts from all colleges and universities attended, 2 letters of recommendation, interview, essay (2-3 page personal statement that describes reasons for choosing education as profession and personal philosophy of education), proof of immunization (for those born after 1957). Additional exam requirements/recommendations for international students: Required—TOEFL (minimum score 600 paper-based; 110 iBT); Recommended—IELTS (minimum score 8). *Application deadline:* Applications are processed on a rolling basis. Application fee: $75. Electronic applications accepted. *Expenses:* 935 per credit. *Financial support:* Teaching assistantships, career-related internships or fieldwork, Federal Work-Study, institutionally sponsored loans, scholarships/grants, and unspecified assistantships available. Financial award application deadline: 3/15; financial award applicants required to submit FAFSA. *Faculty research:* Education for sustainability. *Unit head:* Dr. Shelley Wepner, Dean, 914-323-3153, Fax: 914-323-5493, E-mail: Shelley.Wepner@mville.edu. *Application contact:* Alissa Wilson, Director, Graduate Admissions, 914-323-3150, Fax: 914-694-1732, E-mail: edschool@mville.edu.
Website: http://www.mville.edu/programs#/search/19

Manhattanville College, School of Education, Program in Special Education, Purchase, NY 10577-2132. Offers childhood education (grades 1-6) and special education: childhood (grades 1-6) (MPS); early childhood (birth-grade 2) and special education: early childhood (birth-grade 2) (MPS); English (5-9 and 7-12); special ed generalist (7-12); se English (7-12) (MPS); literacy (birth-grade 6) and special education childhood (grades 1-6) (MPS); literacy 5-12; special education generalist 7-12; special ed specialist 7-12 (MPS); math (5-9 and 7-12); special ed generalist (7-12); se math (7-12) (MPS); science: biology or chemistry (5-9 and 7-12); special ed generalist (7-12); se science (7-12) (MPS); social studies (5-9 and 7-12); special ed generalist (7-12); se soc.st. (7-12) (MPS); special ed early childhood and childhood (birth-grade 6) (MPS); special education childhood (grades 1-6) (MPS); special education: childhood (grades 1-6) (Certificate); special education: early childhood (birth-grade 2) (MPS, Certificate); special education: early childhood (birth-grade 2) and childhood (grades 1-6) (Certificate); special education: grades 7-12 generalist (MPS, Certificate). *Program availability:* Part-time, evening/weekend. *Faculty:* 5 full-time (3 women), 35 part-time/adjunct (23 women). *Students:* 45 full-time (36 women), 179 part-time (152 women); includes 31 minority (6 Black or African American, non-Hispanic/Latino; 4 Asian, non-Hispanic/Latino; 19 Hispanic/Latino; 2 Native Hawaiian or other Pacific Islander, non-Hispanic/Latino); 1 international. Average age 28. 76 applicants, 68% accepted, 40 enrolled. In 2018, 99 master's, 2 Certificates awarded. *Degree requirements:* For master's, comprehensive exam (for some programs), thesis (for some programs), student teaching, research seminars, portfolios, internships, writing assessment; for Certificate, comprehensive exam (for some programs). *Entrance requirements:* For master's, for programs leading to certification, candidates must submit scores from GRE or MAT(Miller Analogies Test), minimum undergraduate GPA of 3.0, all transcripts from all colleges and universities attended, 2 letters of recommendation, interview, essay (2-3 page personal statement that describes reasons for choosing education as profession and personal philosophy of education), proof of immunization (for those born after 1957). Additional exam requirements/recommendations for international students: Required—TOEFL (minimum score 600 paper-based; 110 iBT); Recommended—IELTS (minimum score 8). *Application deadline:* Applications are processed on a rolling basis. Application fee: $75. Electronic applications accepted. *Expenses:* 935 per credit. *Financial support:* Teaching assistantships, career-related internships or fieldwork, Federal Work-Study, institutionally sponsored loans, scholarships/grants, and unspecified assistantships available. Financial award application deadline: 3/15; financial award applicants required to submit FAFSA. *Faculty research:* Students with emotional difficulties, literacy and adolescents, mindfulness, studying the effects of the environment on special populations, the most difficult cases, students who are presented with multiple challenges: learning, behavioral and ACE experiences who see criminal behavior as a way to cope; working on giving them the tools they need to succeed emotionally and cognitively despite the odds stacked against them. *Unit head:* Dr. Shelley Wepner, Dean, 914-323-3153, Fax: 914-323-5493, E-mail: Shelley.Wepner@mville.edu. *Application contact:* Alissa Wilson, Director, SOE Graduate Enrollment Management, 914-323-3150, Fax: 914-694-1732, E-mail: edschool@mville.edu.
Website: http://www.mville.edu/programs/special-education

McDaniel College, Graduate and Professional Studies, Program in Elementary and Secondary Education, Westminster, MD 21157-4390. Offers elementary education (MS); elementary STEM instructional leader (Postbaccalaureate Certificate); equity and excellence in education (Postbaccalaureate Certificate); learning technology specialist (Postbaccalaureate Certificate); secondary education (MS). *Accreditation:* NCATE. *Program availability:* Part-time, evening/weekend. *Degree requirements:* For master's, comprehensive exam (for some programs), thesis optional. *Entrance requirements:* For master's, PRAXIS, 2 references. Additional exam requirements/recommendations for international students: Required—TOEFL (minimum score 79 iBT), IELTS (minimum score 6). Electronic applications accepted.

McNeese State University, Doré School of Graduate Studies, Burton College of Education, Department of Education Professions, Program in Middle School Education Grades 4-8, Lake Charles, LA 70609. Offers middle school education grades 4-8 (Postbaccalaureate Certificate), including mathematics, science. *Entrance requirements:* For degree, PRAXIS, 2 letters of recommendation, autobiography.

Mercer University, Graduate Studies, Macon Campus, Tift College of Education (Macon), Macon, GA 31207. Offers curriculum and instruction (PhD); early childhood education (M Ed, Ed S); educational leadership (M Ed, PhD, Ed S), including higher education (PhD), P-12; higher education leadership (M Ed); independent and charter school leadership (M Ed); secondary education (MAT), including STEM; teacher leadership (Ed S). *Accreditation:* NCATE. *Program availability:* Part-time, evening/weekend, 100% online, blended/hybrid learning. *Degree requirements:* For master's, research project report; for doctorate, comprehensive exam, thesis/dissertation. *Entrance requirements:* For master's, GRE or MAT, minimum GPA of 2.75; for doctorate, GRE, minimum GPA of 3.5; interview; writing sample; 3 recommendations; for Ed S, GRE or MAT, minimum GPA of 3.5 (for teacher leadership), 3.0 (for educational leadership). Additional exam requirements/recommendations for international students: Required—TOEFL (minimum score 80 iBT). Electronic applications accepted. *Expenses:* Contact institution. *Faculty research:* Teacher effectiveness, specific learning disabilities, inclusion.

Metropolitan State University, School of Urban Education, St. Paul, MN 55106-5000. Offers curriculum, pedagogy and schooling (MS); English as a second language (MS); secondary education (MS), including English teaching, life sciences teaching, mathematics teaching, social studies teaching; special education (MS).

Michigan Technological University, Graduate School, College of Sciences and Arts, Department of Cognitive and Learning Sciences, Houghton, MI 49931. Offers applied cognitive science and human factors (MS, PhD); applied science education (MS); post-secondary STEM education (Graduate Certificate). *Program availability:* Part-time, blended/hybrid learning. *Faculty:* 21 full-time (9 women), 6 part-time/adjunct. *Students:* 12 full-time (7 women), 22 part-time (16 women); includes 4 minority (3 Black or African American, non-Hispanic/Latino; 1 Two or more races, non-Hispanic/Latino), 5 international. Average age 35. 55 applicants, 38% accepted, 11 enrolled. In 2018, 6 master's, 1 doctorate, 2 other advanced degrees awarded. Terminal master's awarded for partial completion of doctoral program. *Degree requirements:* For master's, comprehensive exam (for some programs), thesis (for some programs); for doctorate, comprehensive exam, thesis/dissertation, applied internship experience. *Entrance requirements:* For master's, GRE (for applied cognitive science and human factors program only), statement of purpose, personal statement, official transcripts, 3 letters of recommendation, resume/curriculum vitae; for doctorate, GRE, statement of purpose, personal statement, official transcripts, 3 letters of recommendation, resume/curriculum vitae. Additional exam requirements/recommendations for international students: Required—TOEFL, TOEFL (recommended minimum score 90 iBT) or IELTS. *Application deadline:* For fall admission, 2/1 priority date for domestic and international students. Applications are processed on a rolling basis. Electronic applications accepted. *Expenses: Tuition, area resident:* Full-time $18,126; part-time $1007 per credit. Tuition, state resident: full-time $18,126; part-time $1007 per credit. Tuition, nonresident: full-time $18,126; part-time $1007 per credit. *International tuition:* $18,126

full-time. *Required fees:* $248; $124 per semester. Tuition and fees vary according to course load and program. *Financial support:* In 2018–19, 20 students received support, including 2 fellowships (averaging $16,590 per year), 3 research assistantships with tuition reimbursements available (averaging $16,590 per year), 5 teaching assistantships (averaging $16,590 per year); career-related internships or fieldwork, scholarships/grants, health care benefits, unspecified assistantships, and adjunct instructor positions also available. Financial award application deadline: 12/15; financial award applicants required to submit FAFSA. *Faculty research:* Human-computer interaction, models of aging in motor movements, cognitive task analyses, decision support technologies, cognitive workload and computational mental modeling. *Total annual research expenditures:* $474,263. *Unit head:* Dr. Susan L. Amato-Henderson, Chair, 906-487-2536, Fax: 906-487-2468, E-mail: slamato@mtu.edu. *Application contact:* Dr. Kelly S. Steelman, Graduate Program Director, 906-487-2792, Fax: 906-487-2468, E-mail: steelman@mtu.edu.
Website: http://www.mtu.edu/cls/

Middle Tennessee State University, College of Graduate Studies, College of Basic and Applied Sciences, Department of Aerospace, Murfreesboro, TN 37132. Offers aerospace education (M Ed); aviation administration (MS). *Program availability:* Part-time, evening/weekend, online learning. *Degree requirements:* For master's, comprehensive exam, thesis optional. *Entrance requirements:* For master's, GRE General Test or MAT. Additional exam requirements/recommendations for international students: Required—TOEFL (minimum score 525 paper-based; 71 iBT) or IELTS (minimum score 6). Electronic applications accepted.

Middle Tennessee State University, College of Graduate Studies, Interdisciplinary Program in Mathematics and Science Education, Murfreesboro, TN 37132. Offers PhD. *Program availability:* Part-time, evening/weekend, online learning. *Entrance requirements:* For doctorate, GRE. Additional exam requirements/recommendations for international students: Required—TOEFL (minimum score 525 paper-based; 71 iBT) or IELTS (minimum score 6). Electronic applications accepted.

Millersville University of Pennsylvania, College of Graduate Studies and Adult Learning, College of Education and Human Services, Department of Educational Foundations, Millersville, PA 17551-0302. Offers assessment, curriculum and teaching - online teaching (M Ed), including online instruction; assessment, curriculum and teaching - stem education (M Ed), including integrative stem education; educational leadership (Ed D); leadership for teaching and learning (M Ed). Doctor of Educational Leadership: Collaborative program with Shippensburg University. *Program availability:* Part-time, evening/weekend, 100% online, blended/hybrid learning. *Faculty:* 10 full-time (9 women), 10 part-time/adjunct (6 women). *Students:* 1 full-time (0 women), 78 part-time (53 women); includes 5 minority (3 Black or African American, non-Hispanic/Latino; 2 Hispanic/Latino). Average age 34. 42 applicants, 98% accepted, 21 enrolled. In 2018, 21 master's, 2 doctorates awarded. *Degree requirements:* For master's, comprehensive exam (for some programs), thesis (for some programs), graded portfolio and portfolio defense; for doctorate, comprehensive exam, thesis/dissertation. *Entrance requirements:* For master's, GRE or MAT, only if undergraduate cumulative GPA is lower than 2.8, Interview (Leadership for Teaching and Learning), Teaching Certificate; for doctorate, teaching certificate, resume, letter of sponsorship, 3-5 years of professional experience as specified by PDE CSPG #96. Additional exam requirements/recommendations for international students: Required—TOEFL, IELTS (minimum score 6), PTE (minimum score 60). *Application deadline:* Applications are processed on a rolling basis. Application fee: $40. Electronic applications accepted. *Expenses: Tuition, area resident:* Full-time $9288; part-time $516 per credit. Tuition, state resident: full-time $9288; part-time $516 per credit. Tuition, nonresident: full-time $13,932; part-time $774 per credit. *International tuition:* $13,932 full-time. *Required fees:* $2623.50; $145.75 per credit. Tuition and fees vary according to course load, degree level and program. *Financial support:* Unspecified assistantships available. Financial award application deadline: 3/15; financial award applicants required to submit FAFSA. *Faculty research:* Instructional technology, poverty research, support for LGBTQ educators and students, diversifying the teaching workforce, inclusive education. *Total annual research expenditures:* $741,634. *Unit head:* Dr. Timothy E. Mahoney, Chair, 717-871-7202, E-mail: timothy.mahoney@millersville.edu. *Application contact:* Dr. James A. Delle, Acting Dean of College of Graduate Studies and Adult Learning/Associate Provost, Academic Administration, 717-871-7462, E-mail: James.Delle@millersville.edu.
Website: http://www.millersville.edu/edfoundations/

Millersville University of Pennsylvania, College of Graduate Studies and Adult Learning, College of Science and Technology, Millersville, PA 17551-0302. Offers family nurse practitioner (MSN); nursing practice (DNP); technology and innovation (MS), including enterprise. *Program availability:* Part-time, 100% online. *Faculty:* 20 full-time (6 women), 17 part-time/adjunct (13 women). *Students:* 26 full-time (9 women), 175 part-time (109 women); includes 31 minority (10 Black or African American, non-Hispanic/Latino; 1 American Indian or Alaska Native, non-Hispanic/Latino; 5 Asian, non-Hispanic/Latino; 11 Hispanic/Latino; 4 Two or more races, non-Hispanic/Latino), 3 international. Average age 36. 121 applicants, 82% accepted, 71 enrolled. In 2018, 62 master's awarded. *Degree requirements:* For master's, comprehensive exam (for some programs), thesis optional, graded portfolio (educational foundations); Field Practicum; internship, applied research or scholarly project; for doctorate, thesis/dissertation optional, scholarly project, clinical hours. *Entrance requirements:* For master's, GRE or MAT (if under specified GPA), Resume; Prerequisite Courses for some programs; Interview for some programs; for doctorate, goal statement, 3-5 page (APA 6th Ed.) Writing Sample Defining a Specific Issue or Problem in Nursing Practices, current resume/CV, verification of MSN Clinical Hours, completed MSN or MPH, with a minimum 3.5 GPA. Additional exam requirements/recommendations for international students: Required—TOEFL, IELTS (minimum score 6), PTE (minimum score 60). *Application deadline:* Applications are processed on a rolling basis. Application fee: $40. Electronic applications accepted. *Expenses: Tuition, area resident:* Full-time $9288; part-time $516 per credit. Tuition, state resident: full-time $9288; part-time $516 per credit. Tuition, nonresident: full-time $13,932; part-time $774 per credit. *International tuition:* $13,932 full-time. *Required fees:* $2623.50; $145.75 per credit. Tuition and fees vary according to course load, degree level and program. *Financial support:* In 2018–19, 15 students received support. Unspecified assistantships available. Financial award application deadline: 3/15; financial award applicants required to submit FAFSA. *Faculty research:* Engineering design, emergency management, continuity of operations, regional planning, disaster law and policy, community preparedness and mitigation efforts, climatology and meteorology, weather derivatives, risk management, environmental economics and policy, business operations analysis, training of secondary mathematics teachers, the use of technology and equity in mathematics, questioning techniques of teacher educators, family nurse practitioner, nurse education, primary care, health promo. *Total annual research expenditures:* $141,856. *Unit head:* Dr. Michael Jackson, Dean, College of Science and Technology, 717-871-4292, E-mail: michael.jackson@millersville.edu. *Application contact:* Dr. James A. Delle, Acting Dean of Graduate Studies and Adult Learning/Associate Provost, Academic Administration, 717-871-7462, E-mail: James.Delle@millersville.edu.
Website: https://www.millersville.edu/scienceandmath/

Science Education

Minnesota State University Mankato, College of Graduate Studies and Research, College of Science, Engineering and Technology, Department of Biological Sciences, Mankato, MN 56001. Offers biology (MS); biology education (MS); environmental sciences (MS). *Program availability:* Part-time. *Degree requirements:* For master's, one foreign language, comprehensive exam, thesis or alternative. *Entrance requirements:* For master's, minimum GPA of 3.0 during previous 2 years of course work. Additional exam requirements/recommendations for international students: Required—TOEFL. Electronic applications accepted.

Minnesota State University Mankato, College of Graduate Studies and Research, College of Science, Engineering and Technology, Department of Physics and Astronomy, Mankato, MN 56001. Offers physics (MS); physics education (MS). *Degree requirements:* For master's, one foreign language, comprehensive exam, thesis or alternative. *Entrance requirements:* For master's, minimum GPA of 2.75, two recommendation letters, one-page personal statement. Additional exam requirements/recommendations for international students: Required—TOEFL (minimum score 530 paper-based; 72 iBT). Electronic applications accepted.

Minot State University, Graduate School, Program in Biological and Agricultural Sciences, Minot, ND 58707-0002. Offers science (MAT). *Degree requirements:* For master's, thesis. *Entrance requirements:* For master's, minimum GPA of 3.0 or GRE General Test, secondary teaching certificate. Additional exam requirements/recommendations for international students: Required—TOEFL (minimum score 79 iBT), IELTS (minimum score 6). *Faculty research:* Science education.

Mississippi College, Graduate School, School of Education, Department of Teacher Education and Leadership, Clinton, MS 39058. Offers art (M Ed); biological science (M Ed); business education (M Ed); computer science (M Ed); dyslexia therapy (M Ed); educational leadership (M Ed, Ed D, Ed S); elementary education (M Ed, Ed S); English (M Ed); higher education administration (MS); mathematics (M Ed); secondary education (M Ed); social studies (history) (M Ed); teaching arts (M Ed). *Program availability:* Part-time, online learning. *Degree requirements:* For master's, comprehensive exam, thesis optional. *Entrance requirements:* For master's, NTE. Additional exam requirements/recommendations for international students: Recommended—TOEFL, IELTS. Electronic applications accepted.

Missouri State University, Graduate College, College of Natural and Applied Sciences, Department of Biology, Springfield, MO 65897. Offers biology (MS); natural and applied science (MNAS), including biology (MNAS, MS Ed); secondary education (MS Ed), including biology (MNAS, MS Ed). *Faculty:* 18 full-time (3 women), 7 part-time/adjunct (2 women). *Students:* 23 full-time (12 women), 21 part-time (13 women); includes 2 minority (1 Black or African American, non-Hispanic/Latino; 1 Two or more races, non-Hispanic/Latino), 8 international. Average age 24. 28 applicants, 46% accepted. In 2018, 17 master's awarded. *Degree requirements:* For master's, comprehensive exam, thesis or alternative. *Entrance requirements:* For master's, GRE (MS, MNAS), 24 hours of course work in biology (MS); minimum GPA of 3.0 (MS, MNAS); 9-12 teacher certification (MS Ed). Additional exam requirements/recommendations for international students: Required—TOEFL (minimum score 550 paper-based; 79 iBT), IELTS (minimum score 6). *Application deadline:* For fall admission, 7/20 priority date for domestic students, 5/1 for international students; for spring admission, 12/20 priority date for domestic students, 9/1 for international students; for summer admission, 5/20 priority date for domestic students. Applications are processed on a rolling basis. Application fee: $55 ($60 for international students). Electronic applications accepted. Tuition and fees vary according to class time, course level, course load, degree level, campus/location, program and student level. *Financial support:* In 2018–19, 2 research assistantships with full tuition reimbursements (averaging $10,672 per year), 26 teaching assistantships with full tuition reimbursements (averaging $9,746 per year) were awarded; Federal Work-Study, institutionally sponsored loans, scholarships/grants, and unspecified assistantships also available. Financial award application deadline: 1/31; financial award applicants required to submit FAFSA. *Faculty research:* Hibernation physiology of bats, behavioral ecology of salamanders, mussel conservation, plant evolution and systematics, cellular/molecular mechanisms involved in migraine pathology. *Unit head:* Dr. S. Alicia Mathis, Department Head, 417-836-5126, Fax: 417-836-6934, E-mail: biology@missouristate.edu. *Application contact:* Lakan Drinker, Director, Graduate Enrollment Management, 417-836-5330, Fax: 417-836-6200, E-mail: lakandrinker@missouristate.edu.
Website: http://biology.missouristate.edu/

Missouri State University, Graduate College, College of Natural and Applied Sciences, Department of Geography, Geology, and Planning, Springfield, MO 65897. Offers geography, geology, and planning (Certificate); natural and applied science (MNAS), including geography, geology and planning; secondary education (MS Ed), including earth science, physical geography. *Program availability:* Part-time, evening/weekend. *Faculty:* 18 full-time (4 women), 1 part-time/adjunct (0 women). *Students:* 24 full-time (10 women), 10 part-time (5 women); includes 2 minority (1 Hispanic/Latino; 1 Two or more races, non-Hispanic/Latino), 5 international. Average age 25. 26 applicants, 50% accepted. In 2018, 8 master's awarded. *Degree requirements:* For master's, comprehensive exam, thesis (for some programs). *Entrance requirements:* For master's, GRE General Test (MS, MNAS), minimum undergraduate GPA of 3.0 (MS, MNAS), 9-12 teacher certification (MS Ed). Additional exam requirements/recommendations for international students: Required—TOEFL (minimum score 550 paper-based; 79 iBT), IELTS (minimum score 6). *Application deadline:* For fall admission, 7/20 priority date for domestic students, 5/1 for international students; for spring admission, 12/20 priority date for domestic students, 9/1 for international students. Applications are processed on a rolling basis. Application fee: $55 ($60 for international students). Electronic applications accepted. Tuition and fees vary according to class time, course level, course load, degree level, campus/location, program and student level. *Financial support:* In 2018–19, 3 research assistantships with full tuition reimbursements (averaging $11,574 per year), 15 teaching assistantships with full tuition reimbursements (averaging $9,365 per year) were awarded; career-related internships or fieldwork, Federal Work-Study, institutionally sponsored loans, scholarships/grants, and unspecified assistantships also available. Financial award application deadline: 1/31; financial award applicants required to submit FAFSA. *Faculty research:* Stratigraphy and ancient meteorite impacts, environmental geochemistry of karst, hyperspectral image processing, water quality, small town planning. *Unit head:* Dr. Toby Dogwiler, Department Head, 417-836-5800, Fax: 417-836-6934, E-mail: tobydogwiler@missouristate.edu. *Application contact:* Lakan Drinker, Director, Graduate Enrollment Management, 417-836-5330, Fax: 417-836-6200, E-mail: lakandrinker@missouristate.edu.
Website: http://geosciences.missouristate.edu/

Missouri State University, Graduate College, College of Natural and Applied Sciences, Department of Physics, Astronomy, and Materials Science, Springfield, MO 65897. Offers materials science (MS); natural and applied science (MNAS), including physics (MNAS, MS Ed); secondary education (MS Ed), including physics (MNAS, MS Ed). *Program availability:* Part-time. *Faculty:* 9 full-time (0 women). *Students:* 11 full-time (1 woman), 4 part-time (1 woman); includes 1 minority (Hispanic/Latino), 13 international. Average age 26. 12 applicants, 92% accepted. In 2018, 9 master's awarded. *Degree requirements:* For master's, comprehensive exam, thesis. *Entrance requirements:* For master's, GRE (MS, MNAS), minimum undergraduate GPA of 3.0 (MS and MNAS), 9-12 teaching certification (MS Ed). Additional exam requirements/recommendations for international students: Required—TOEFL (minimum score 550 paper-based; 79 iBT), IELTS (minimum score 6). *Application deadline:* For fall admission, 7/20 priority date for domestic students, 5/1 for international students; for spring admission, 12/20 priority date for domestic students, 9/1 for international students. Applications are processed on a rolling basis. Application fee: $55 ($60 for international students). Electronic applications accepted. Tuition and fees vary according to class time, course level, course load, degree level, campus/location, program and student level. *Financial support:* In 2018–19, 6 research assistantships with full tuition reimbursements (averaging $10,672 per year), 11 teaching assistantships with full tuition reimbursements (averaging $10,672 per year) were awarded; Federal Work-Study, institutionally sponsored loans, scholarships/grants, and unspecified assistantships also available. Financial award application deadline: 1/31; financial award applicants required to submit FAFSA. *Faculty research:* Nanocomposites, ferroelectricity, infrared focal plane array sensors, biosensors, pulsating stars. *Unit head:* Dr. Robert Mayanovic, Department Head, 417-836-5131, Fax: 417-836-6226, E-mail: physics@missouristate.edu. *Application contact:* Lakan Drinker, Director, Graduate Enrollment Management, 417-836-5330, Fax: 417-836-6200, E-mail: lakandrinker@missouristate.edu.
Website: http://physics.missouristate.edu/

Molloy College, Graduate Education Program, Rockville Centre, NY 11571-5002. Offers adolescent education in biology (MS); adolescent special education (Advanced Certificate); bilingual extension (Advanced Certificate); childhood education (MS); childhood special education (Advanced Certificate); early childhood education (MS); educational technology (MS); English (MS); mathematics (MS); social studies (MS); Spanish (MS); special education on both childhood and adolescent levels (MS); teaching English to speakers of other languages (TESOL) in grades pre-K to 12 (MS); TESOL (Advanced Certificate). *Accreditation:* NCATE. *Program availability:* Part-time, evening/weekend. *Faculty:* 24 full-time (22 women), 26 part-time/adjunct (19 women). *Students:* 106 full-time (78 women), 203 part-time (154 women); includes 65 minority (14 Black or African American, non-Hispanic/Latino; 5 Asian, non-Hispanic/Latino; 41 Hispanic/Latino; 5 Two or more races, non-Hispanic/Latino). Average age 41. 147 applicants, 63% accepted, 79 enrolled. In 2018, 120 master's, 1 other advanced degree awarded. *Entrance requirements:* Additional exam requirements/recommendations for international students: Required—TOEFL (minimum score 550 paper-based; 79 iBT). *Application deadline:* Applications are processed on a rolling basis. Application fee: $60. Electronic applications accepted. *Expenses: Tuition:* Full-time $20,790; part-time $1155 per credit. *Required fees:* $1060; $900. Tuition and fees vary according to course load and degree level. *Financial support:* Application deadline: 3/1; applicants required to submit FAFSA. *Faculty research:* English Language Learners; social emotional needs of students; gifted education; cultural diversity; collaborative teaching methods. *Unit head:* Joanne O'Brien, Dean, 516-323-3116, E-mail: jobrien@molloy.edu. *Application contact:* Faye Hood, Assistant Director for Admissions, 516-323-4009, E-mail: fhood@molloy.edu.

Montclair State University, The Graduate School, College of Education and Human Services, MAT Program in Teaching, Montclair, NJ 07043-1624. Offers art (MAT); biology (MAT); chemistry (MAT); earth science (MAT); English (MAT); French (MAT); health and physical education (MAT); health education (MAT); mathematics (MAT); music (MAT); physical education (MAT); physical science (MAT); social studies (MAT); Spanish (MAT); teacher of English as a second language (MAT). *Degree requirements:* For master's, comprehensive exam, thesis or alternative. *Entrance requirements:* For master's, interview, 2 letters of recommendation. Additional exam requirements/recommendations for international students: Required—TOEFL (minimum score 83 iBT), IELTS (minimum score 6.5). Electronic applications accepted.

Montclair State University, The Graduate School, College of Science and Mathematics, Program in Biology, Montclair, NJ 07043-1624. Offers biological science/education (MS); biology (MS); ecology and evolution (MS); physiology (MS).

Morehead State University, Graduate School, College of Education, Department of Middle Grades and Secondary Education, Morehead, KY 40351. Offers business and marketing education (MAT); English/language arts 5-9 (MAT); French (MAT); health P-12 (MAT); mathematics 5-9 (MAT); physical education P-12 (MAT); science 5-9 (MAT); secondary biology (MAT); secondary chemistry (MAT); secondary earth science (MAT); secondary English (MAT); secondary math (MAT); secondary physics (MAT); secondary social studies (MAT); social studies 5-9 (MAT); Spanish (MAT). *Program availability:* Part-time, evening/weekend. *Degree requirements:* For master's, portfolio. *Entrance requirements:* For master's, GRE or PRAXIS II content exam, minimum overall undergraduate GPA of 2.5. Additional exam requirements/recommendations for international students: Required—TOEFL (minimum score 500 paper-based). Electronic applications accepted.

Morgan State University, School of Graduate Studies, School of Education and Urban Studies, Department of Advanced Studies, Leadership and Policy, Program in Science Education, Baltimore, MD 21251. Offers MS, Ed D. *Entrance requirements:* Additional exam requirements/recommendations for international students: Required—TOEFL (minimum score 550 paper-based).

National Louis University, National College of Education, Chicago, IL 60603. Offers administration and supervision (M Ed, Ed D, CAS, Ed S); curriculum and instruction (M Ed, MS Ed, CAS); early childhood administration (M Ed, CAS); early childhood education (M Ed, MAT, MS Ed, CAS); education (Ed D); educational psychology/human learning and development (M Ed, MS Ed, CAS, Ed S); elementary education (MAT); interdisciplinary curriculum and instruction (M Ed); mathematics education (M Ed, MS Ed, CAS); middle grades education (MAT); reading and language (M Ed, MS Ed, CAS); school psychology (M Ed, Ed S); science education (M Ed, MS Ed, CAS); secondary education (MAT); special education (M Ed, MAT, CAS); technology in education (M Ed, CAS). *Accreditation:* NCATE. *Program availability:* Part-time, evening/weekend. *Degree requirements:* For doctorate, comprehensive exam, thesis/dissertation. *Entrance requirements:* For master's, MAT or GRE, minimum GPA of 3.0; for doctorate, GRE General Test, minimum GPA of 3.25, interview, resume, writing sample, 4 recommendations. Additional exam requirements/recommendations for international students: Required—TOEFL (minimum score 550 paper-based; 79 iBT).

New Mexico Institute of Mining and Technology, Center for Graduate Studies, Department of Management, Socorro, NM 87801. Offers STEM education (MEM). *Program availability:* Part-time.

New Mexico Institute of Mining and Technology, Center for Graduate Studies, Master of Science for Teachers Interdepartmental Program, Socorro, NM 87801. Offers MST. *Degree requirements:* For master's, thesis optional. *Entrance requirements:* For master's, GRE General Test. Additional exam requirements/recommendations for international students: Required—TOEFL (minimum score 540 paper-based). Electronic applications accepted. *Faculty research:* Teaching secondary school science and/or mathematics.

New York Institute of Technology, School of Interdisciplinary Studies and Education, Department of Instructional Technology, Old Westbury, NY 11568-8000. Offers

emerging technologies for trainers (Advanced Certificate); instructional design for global e-learning (Advanced Certificate); instructional technology (MS), including educators, trainers; STEM education (Advanced Certificate). *Program availability:* Part-time, evening/weekend, 100% online, blended/hybrid learning. *Faculty:* 2 full-time (1 woman), 13 part-time/adjunct (5 women). *Students:* 1 full-time (0 women), 80 part-time (51 women); includes 22 minority (8 Black or African American, non-Hispanic/Latino; 5 Asian, non-Hispanic/Latino; 7 Hispanic/Latino; 2 Two or more races, non-Hispanic/Latino). Average age 33. 56 applicants, 63% accepted, 25 enrolled. In 2018, 54 master's, 6 other advanced degrees awarded. *Entrance requirements:* For master's, bachelor's degree; minimum undergraduate GPA of 3.0; demonstrated proficiency in basic uses of instructional technologies; initial/provisional or permanent/professional NY state certification in any teaching area; for Advanced Certificate, BS; minimum undergraduate GPA of 3.0; demonstrated proficiency in basic uses of instructional technologies. Additional exam requirements/recommendations for international students: Required—TOEFL (minimum score 79 iBT), IELTS (minimum score 6), PTE (minimum score 53). *Application deadline:* Applications are processed on a rolling basis. Application fee: $50. Electronic applications accepted. *Expenses:* $1285 per credit plus $215 fees per year (full-time) or $175 fees per year (part-time); $1395 per three-credit education UFT or off-site graduate course. *Financial support:* Career-related internships or fieldwork, scholarships/grants, health care benefits, tuition waivers (full and partial), and unspecified assistantships available. Support available to part-time students. Financial award application deadline: 2/15; financial award applicants required to submit FAFSA. *Faculty research:* Integration of information and communication technologies (ICTs) and media literacy education into learning environments; urban K-12 teachers' effective use of technology to enhance student achievement; instructional design and transdisciplinary curriculum studies for online instruction; STEM and computing partnerships for K-12 teachers; experiential, collaborative, and performance-based approaches to pedagogy and technology integration in the K-12 classroom. *Unit head:* Dr. Melda Yildiz, Department Chair, 516-686-1053, Fax: 516-686-7655, E-mail: myildiz@nyit.edu. *Application contact:* Alice Dolitsky, Director, Graduate Admissions, 516-686-7520, Fax: 516-686-1116, E-mail: admissions@nyit.edu.
Website: http://www.nyit.edu/departments_instructional_technology

New York Institute of Technology, School of Interdisciplinary Studies and Education, Department of Teacher Education, Old Westbury, NY 11568-8000. Offers adolescence education (MS), including math (MAT, MS), science; adolescent education (MAT), including biology, chemistry, English, math (MAT, MS), social studies; childhood education (MS); early childhood (MS). *Program availability:* Part-time, evening/weekend, 100% online, blended/hybrid learning. *Faculty:* 2 full-time (both women), 8 part-time/adjunct (5 women). *Students:* 47 full-time (45 women), 56 part-time (47 women); includes 36 minority (13 Black or African American, non-Hispanic/Latino; 1 American Indian or Alaska Native, non-Hispanic/Latino; 7 Asian, non-Hispanic/Latino; 12 Hispanic/Latino; 1 Native Hawaiian or other Pacific Islander, non-Hispanic/Latino; 2 Two or more races, non-Hispanic/Latino), 3 international. Average age 31. 81 applicants, 53% accepted, 27 enrolled. In 2018, 27 master's awarded. *Entrance requirements:* For master's, GRE or MAT, BS or equivalent; minimum cumulative undergraduate GPA of 3.0; NY state initial certification; BS with major (or minimum 30 credits in a concentration) in biology, chemistry, English, math, physics, or social studies (for MS in childhood, early childhood education, and MAT); interview; personal statement. Additional exam requirements/recommendations for international students: Required—TOEFL (minimum score 79 iBT), IELTS (minimum score 6), PTE (minimum score 53). *Application deadline:* Applications are processed on a rolling basis. Application fee: $50. Electronic applications accepted. *Expenses:* $1285 per credit plus $215 fees per year (full-time) or $175 fees per year (part-time); $1395 per 3-credit education UFT or off-site graduate course. *Financial support:* Career-related internships or fieldwork, Federal Work-Study, scholarships/grants, tuition waivers (full and partial), and unspecified assistantships available. Support available to part-time students. Financial award application deadline: 2/15; financial award applicants required to submit FAFSA. *Faculty research:* Evolving definition of new literacies and its impact on teaching and learning (twenty-first century skills), new literacies practices in teacher education, teachers' professional development, English language and literacy learning through mobile learning, teaching reading to culturally and linguistically diverse children. *Application contact:* Alice Dolitsky, Director, Graduate Admissions, 516-686-7520, Fax: 516-686-1116, E-mail: admissions@nyit.edu.
Website: http://www.nyit.edu/departments/teacher_education

New York University, Steinhardt School of Culture, Education, and Human Development, Department of Teaching and Learning, New York, NY 10012. Offers clinically rich integrated science (MA), including clinically rich integrated science, teaching biology grades 7-12, teaching chemistry 7-12, teaching physics 7-12; early childhood and childhood education (MA), including childhood education, early childhood education, early childhood education/early childhood special education; English education (MA, PhD, Advanced Certificate), including clinically-based English education, grades 7-12 (MA), English education (PhD, Advanced Certificate), English education, grades 7-12 (MA); environmental conservation education (MA); literacy education (MA), including literacy 5-12, literacy B-6; mathematics education (MA), including teachers of mathematics 7-12; multilingual/multicultural studies (MA, PhD, Advanced Certificate), including bilingual education, foreign language education (MA), teaching English to speakers of other languages (MA, PhD), teaching foreign languages, 7-12 (MA), teaching French as a foreign language (MA), teaching Spanish as a foreign language (MA); social studies education (MA), including teaching art/social studies 7-12, teaching social studies 7-12; special education (MA), including childhood, early childhood; teaching and learning (Ed D, PhD). *Program availability:* Part-time. *Entrance requirements:* For doctorate, GRE General Test, interview; for Advanced Certificate, master's degree. Additional exam requirements/recommendations for international students: Required—TOEFL (minimum score 100 iBT). Electronic applications accepted. *Faculty research:* Cultural contexts for literacy learning, school restructuring, parenting and education, teacher learning, language assessment.

North Carolina Agricultural and Technical State University, The Graduate College, College of Science and Technology, Department of Biology, Greensboro, NC 27411. Offers biology (MS); biology education (MAT). *Program availability:* Part-time, evening/weekend. *Degree requirements:* For master's, comprehensive exam, thesis (for some programs), qualifying exam. *Entrance requirements:* For master's, GRE General Test, personal statement. *Faculty research:* Physical ecology, cytochemistry, botany, parasitology, microbiology.

North Carolina State University, Graduate School, College of Education, Department of Science, Technology, Engineering, and Mathematics Education, Program in Science Education, Raleigh, NC 27695. Offers M Ed, MS, PhD. *Accreditation:* NCATE. *Program availability:* Part-time. *Degree requirements:* For master's, thesis (for some programs), oral exam; for doctorate, one foreign language, thesis/dissertation, oral and written exams. *Entrance requirements:* For master's, GRE General Test or MAT, minimum GPA of 3.0; for doctorate, GRE General Test, minimum GPA of 3.0, interview. Electronic applications accepted. *Faculty research:* Teacher development, sociocultural issues in learning, student science misconceptions, technical applications to science teaching.

North Dakota State University, College of Graduate and Interdisciplinary Studies, College of Engineering, Doctoral Program in Engineering, Fargo, ND 58102. Offers environmental and conservation science (PhD); materials and nanotechnology (PhD); natural resource management (PhD); STEM education (PhD); transportation and logistics (PhD). *Degree requirements:* For doctorate, comprehensive exam, thesis/dissertation. *Entrance requirements:* For doctorate, bachelor's degree in engineering, minimum GPA of 3.0. Additional exam requirements/recommendations for international students: Required—TOEFL. Electronic applications accepted. *Expenses:* Contact institution.

North Dakota State University, College of Graduate and Interdisciplinary Studies, Program in STEM Education, Fargo, ND 58102. Offers PhD. Electronic applications accepted.

Northeastern Illinois University, College of Graduate Studies and Research, Daniel L. Goodwin College of Education, MAT Program in Secondary Education, Chicago, IL 60625. Offers English language arts (MAT); mathematics (MAT); science (MAT); social science (MAT).

Northeastern State University, College of Science and Health Professions, Department of Natural Sciences, Program in Science Education, Tahlequah, OK 74464-2399. Offers M Ed. *Program availability:* Part-time, evening/weekend. *Faculty:* 7 full-time (2 women), 1 part-time/adjunct (0 women). *Students:* 1 (woman) full-time, 19 part-time (16 women); includes 5 minority (3 Asian, non-Hispanic/Latino; 2 Hispanic/Latino). Average age 36. In 2018, 13 master's awarded. *Entrance requirements:* For master's, MAT or GRE, minimum GPA of 2.5. *Application deadline:* For fall admission, 6/1 for domestic students. Applications are processed on a rolling basis. Application fee: $25. Electronic applications accepted. *Expenses: Tuition,* area resident: Full-time $4500; part-time $250 per credit hour. Tuition, state resident: full-time $4500; part-time $250 per credit hour. Tuition, nonresident: full-time $9999; part-time $555.50 per credit hour. *International tuition:* $9999 full-time. *Required fees:* $601.20; $33.40 per credit hour. *Unit head:* Dr. Pamela Christol, Program Chair, 918-449-6539, E-mail: christol@nsuok.edu. *Application contact:* Josh McCollum, Graduate Coordinator, 918-444-2093, E-mail: mccolluj@nsuok.edu.
Website: http://academics.nsuok.edu/naturalsciences/Degrees/Graduate/MEdScienceEducation.aspx

Northern Arizona University, College of Environment, Forestry, and Natural Sciences, Center for Science Teaching and Learning, Flagstaff, AZ 86011. Offers science teaching (MA); science with certification (MAT). *Program availability:* Part-time, 100% online, blended/hybrid learning. *Degree requirements:* For master's, variable foreign language requirement, comprehensive exam (for some programs), thesis (for some programs). *Entrance requirements:* Additional exam requirements/recommendations for international students: Required—TOEFL (minimum score 80 iBT), IELTS (minimum score 6.5). Electronic applications accepted.

Northern Michigan University, Office of Graduate Education and Research, College of Health Sciences and Professional Studies, School of Education, Leadership and Public Service, Marquette, MI 49855-5301. Offers administration and supervision (MAE); instruction (MAE); learning disabilities (MAE); postsecondary biology education (MS); reading education (MAE), including reading, reading specialist. *Accreditation:* TEAC. *Program availability:* Part-time, online learning. *Degree requirements:* For master's, thesis (for some programs). *Entrance requirements:* For master's, minimum GPA of 3.0. Additional exam requirements/recommendations for international students: Required—TOEFL (minimum score 550 paper-based; 79 iBT), IELTS (minimum score 6.5). Electronic applications accepted.

Northern Vermont University–Lyndon, Graduate Programs in Education, Department of Natural Sciences, Lyndonville, VT 05851. Offers science education (MST). *Program availability:* Part-time. *Degree requirements:* For master's, exam or major field project. *Entrance requirements:* Additional exam requirements/recommendations for international students: Recommended—TOEFL (minimum score 500 paper-based). *Faculty research:* Fern genetics, comparative butterfly research.

Northwest Missouri State University, Graduate School, College of Arts and Sciences, Maryville, MO 64468-6001. Offers biology (MS); elementary mathematics specialist (MS Ed); English (MA); English education (MS Ed); English pedagogy (MA); geographic information science (MS, Certificate); history (MS Ed); mathematics (MS); mathematics education (MS Ed); teaching: science (MS Ed). *Program availability:* Part-time. *Faculty:* 20 full-time (9 women). *Students:* 15 full-time (9 women), 66 part-time (30 women); includes 6 minority (2 Black or African American, non-Hispanic/Latino; 1 American Indian or Alaska Native, non-Hispanic/Latino; 1 Hispanic/Latino; 2 Two or more races, non-Hispanic/Latino), 2 international. Average age 34. 32 applicants, 66% accepted, 19 enrolled. In 2018, 17 master's awarded. *Degree requirements:* For master's, comprehensive exam. *Entrance requirements:* For master's, GRE General Test, writing sample. Additional exam requirements/recommendations for international students: Required—TOEFL (minimum score 550 paper-based). *Application deadline:* For fall admission, 7/1 for domestic and international students; for spring admission, 11/15 for domestic and international students. Applications are processed on a rolling basis. Application fee: $0 ($75 for international students). Electronic applications accepted. *Expenses: Tuition,* area resident: Full-time $4551; part-time $252.86 per credit hour. Tuition, state resident: full-time $4551; part-time $252.86 per credit hour. Tuition, nonresident: full-time $9103; part-time $505.72 per credit hour. *International tuition:* $9103 full-time. *Required fees:* $2668; $148.20 per credit hour. Tuition and fees vary according to program. *Financial support:* Research assistantships with full tuition reimbursements, teaching assistantships with full tuition reimbursements, and administrative assistantships, tutorial assistantships available. Financial award application deadline: 4/1; financial award applicants required to submit FAFSA. *Unit head:* Dr. Michael Steiner, Dean, 660-562-1197. *Application contact:* Dr. Michael Steiner, Dean, 660-562-1197.
Website: https://www.nwmissouri.edu/academics/undergraduate/majors/liberal-arts-sciences.htm

Oregon State University, College of Education, Program in Education, Corvallis, OR 97331. Offers agricultural education (PhD); language equity and education policy (PhD); mathematics education (MS); science education (MS); science/mathematics education (PhD). *Program availability:* Part-time, 100% online, blended/hybrid learning. Terminal master's awarded for partial completion of doctoral program. *Degree requirements:* For master's, variable foreign language requirement, thesis (for some programs); for doctorate, variable foreign language requirement, thesis/dissertation. *Entrance requirements:* Additional exam requirements/recommendations for international students: Required—TOEFL (minimum score 575 paper-based). *Faculty research:* School administration, educational foundations, research methodology, education policy development, higher education administration.

Oregon State University, College of Education, Program in Teaching, Corvallis, OR 97331. Offers clinically based elementary education (MAT); elementary education (MAT); language arts (MAT); mathematics (MAT); music education (MAT); science (MAT); social studies (MAT). *Program availability:* Part-time, blended/hybrid learning. *Entrance requirements:* For master's, CBEST. Additional exam requirements/recommendations for international students: Required—TOEFL (minimum score 575 paper-based). *Expenses:* Contact institution.

Science Education

Our Lady of the Lake University, College of Professional Studies, Program in Curriculum and Instruction, San Antonio, TX 78207-4689. Offers integrated science teaching (M Ed). *Program availability:* Part-time, evening/weekend. *Faculty:* 1 (woman) full-time, 1 (woman) part-time/adjunct. *Students:* 5 full-time (all women), 7 part-time (4 women); includes 10 minority (all Hispanic/Latino). Average age 34. 9 applicants, 100% accepted, 6 enrolled. In 2018, 1 master's awarded. *Degree requirements:* For master's, comprehensive exam. *Entrance requirements:* For master's, GRE General Test or MAT, official transcripts demonstrating bachelor's degree with minimum cumulative GPA of 2.75, personal statement, 2 references, completed FERPA Consent to Release Education Records and Information form, interview. Additional exam requirements/recommendations for international students: Required—TOEFL. *Application deadline:* For fall admission, 6/15 for domestic and international students; for spring admission, 11/15 for domestic and international students; for summer admission, 4/15 for domestic and international students. Applications are processed on a rolling basis. Application fee: $40 ($50 for international students). Electronic applications accepted. Application fee is waived when completed online. *Expenses: Tuition:* Full-time $16,326; part-time $907 per credit. *Financial support:* In 2018–19, 11 students received support. Federal Work-Study, scholarships/grants, unspecified assistantships, and tuition discounts available. Support available to part-time students. Financial award application deadline: 5/1; financial award applicants required to submit FAFSA. *Faculty research:* Multicultural Issues, technology integration, mentoring teachers, teacher retention. *Unit head:* Dr. Alycia Maurer, Chair, Education Department, 210-434-6711 Ext. 7152, E-mail: admaurer@ollusa.edu. *Application contact:* Office of Graduate Admissions, 210-431-3995, Fax: 210-431-3945, E-mail: gradadm@lake.ollusa.edu.
Website: http://www.ollusa.edu/s/1190/hybrid/default-hybrid-ollu.aspx?sid-1190&gid-1&pgid-7883

Pacific University, College of Education, Forest Grove, OR 97116-1797. Offers early childhood education (MAT); education (MAE); elementary education (MAT); ESOL (MAT); high school education (MAT); middle school education (MAT); special education (MAT); speech-language pathology (MS); STEM education (MAT); talented and gifted (M Ed); visual function in learning (M Ed). *Accreditation:* ASHA; NCATE. *Program availability:* Part-time, evening/weekend. *Degree requirements:* For master's, research project. *Entrance requirements:* For master's, California Basic Educational Skills Test, PRAXIS II, minimum undergraduate GPA of 2.75, 3.0 graduate. Additional exam requirements/recommendations for international students: Required—TOEFL. Electronic applications accepted. *Expenses:* Contact institution. *Faculty research:* Defining a culturally competent classroom, technology in the K-12 classroom, Socratic seminars, social studies education.

Portland State University, Graduate Studies, College of Liberal Arts and Sciences, Department of Geology, Portland, OR 97207-0751. Offers environmental sciences and resources (PhD); geology (MA, MS, Certificate); science/geology (MAT, MST). *Program availability:* Part-time. *Degree requirements:* For master's, comprehensive exam, thesis or alternative, field comprehensive; for doctorate, thesis/dissertation. *Entrance requirements:* For master's, GRE General Test, GRE Subject Test, BA/BS in geology, minimum GPA of 3.0 in geology-related and allied sciences, resume, statement of intent, 2 letters of recommendation. Additional exam requirements/recommendations for international students: Required—TOEFL (minimum score 550 paper-based; 80 iBT). Electronic applications accepted. *Faculty research:* Sediment transport, volcanic environmental geology, coastal and fluvial processes.

Portland State University, Graduate Studies, College of Liberal Arts and Sciences, Interdisciplinary Programs in General Science, General Social Science, and General Arts and Letters, Portland, OR 97207-0751. Offers general arts and letters education (MAT, MST); general science education (MAT, MST); general social science education (MAT, MST). *Program availability:* Part-time, evening/weekend. *Degree requirements:* For master's, variable foreign language requirement, written exam. *Entrance requirements:* For master's, minimum GPA of 3.0 in upper-division course work or 2.75 overall. Additional exam requirements/recommendations for international students: Required—TOEFL (minimum score 550 paper-based; 80 iBT), IELTS (minimum score 6.5).

Purdue University, College of Engineering, School of Engineering Education, West Lafayette, IN 47907. Offers PhD. *Degree requirements:* For doctorate, thesis/dissertation. *Entrance requirements:* For doctorate, GRE General Test, minimum GPA of 3.0. Electronic applications accepted. *Faculty research:* Engineering teaching and learning, learning environments, problem solving, technology, teaming, diversity.

Purdue University, Graduate School, College of Education, Department of Curriculum and Instruction, West Lafayette, IN 47907. Offers agricultural and extension education (MS, MS Ed, PhD, Ed S); art education (PhD); career and technical education (MS Ed, PhD, Ed S); curriculum studies (MS Ed, PhD, Ed S); educational technology (MS Ed, PhD, Ed S); elementary education (MS Ed); family and consumer sciences education (MS Ed, PhD, Ed S); foreign language education (MS Ed, PhD, Ed S); industrial technology (PhD, Ed S); language arts (MS Ed, PhD, Ed S); literacy (MS Ed, PhD, Ed S); mathematics education (MS, MS Ed, PhD, Ed S); science education (MS, MS Ed, PhD, Ed S); social studies education (MS Ed, PhD, Ed S). *Accreditation:* NCATE. *Program availability:* Part-time, evening/weekend, online learning. *Faculty:* 34 full-time (24 women), 3 part-time/adjunct (1 woman). *Students:* 75 full-time (52 women), 357 part-time (271 women); includes 83 minority (29 Black or African American, non-Hispanic/Latino; 1 American Indian or Alaska Native, non-Hispanic/Latino; 14 Asian, non-Hispanic/Latino; 29 Hispanic/Latino; 1 Native Hawaiian or other Pacific Islander, non-Hispanic/Latino; 9 Two or more races, non-Hispanic/Latino), 43 international. Average age 36. 169 applicants, 83% accepted, 102 enrolled. In 2018, 141 master's, 15 doctorates awarded. *Degree requirements:* For master's, thesis optional; for doctorate, thesis/dissertation, oral and written exams; for Ed S, oral presentation, project. *Entrance requirements:* For master's, GRE General Test (if undergraduate GPA is below 3.0), minimum undergraduate GPA of 3.0 or equivalent; for doctorate, GRE General Test (minimum combined verbal and quantitative score of 1000, 300 for new scoring), minimum undergraduate GPA of 3.0 or equivalent; master's degree with minimum GPA of 3.0 or equivalent; for Ed S, GRE General Test (minimum combined verbal and quantitative score of 1000, 300 for new scoring), minimum undergraduate GPA of 3.0 or equivalent; master's degree. Additional exam requirements/recommendations for international students: Required—TOEFL (minimum score 550 paper-based; 77 iBT). *Application deadline:* For fall admission, 12/15 for domestic students, 3/1 for international students; for spring admission, 9/15 for domestic students, 8/1 for international students. Application fee: $60 ($75 for international students). Electronic applications accepted. *Financial support:* Fellowships with full tuition reimbursements, research assistantships with full tuition reimbursements, teaching assistantships with full tuition reimbursements, career-related internships or fieldwork, and tuition waivers (full) available. Support available to part-time students. Financial award application deadline: 3/1; financial award applicants required to submit FAFSA. *Faculty research:* Literacy acquisition and development, teacher beliefs and knowledge, recruitment and retention of underrepresented students, economic education, literacy discourse. *Unit head:* Janet M. Alsup, Head, 765-494-9667, E-mail: alsupj@purdue.edu. *Application contact:* Heather Brinkman, Graduate Contact, 765-494-2345, E-mail: hbrinkma@purdue.edu.
Website: http://www.edci.purdue.edu/

Purdue University, Graduate School, College of Science, Department of Chemistry, West Lafayette, IN 47907. Offers analytical chemistry (PhD); biochemistry (MS, PhD); chemical education (MS, PhD); inorganic chemistry (MS, PhD); organic chemistry (MS, PhD); physical chemistry (PhD). *Faculty:* 47 full-time (13 women), 2 part-time/adjunct (0 women). *Students:* 314 full-time (124 women), 18 part-time (13 women); includes 63 minority (16 Black or African American, non-Hispanic/Latino; 15 Asian, non-Hispanic/Latino; 25 Hispanic/Latino; 7 Two or more races, non-Hispanic/Latino), 146 international. Average age 26. 711 applicants, 27% accepted, 64 enrolled. In 2018, 9 master's, 50 doctorates awarded. Terminal master's awarded for partial completion of doctoral program. *Degree requirements:* For master's, thesis; for doctorate, comprehensive exam, thesis/dissertation. *Entrance requirements:* For master's and doctorate, minimum undergraduate GPA of 3.0. Additional exam requirements/recommendations for international students: Required—TOEFL (minimum score 550 paper-based; 77 iBT); Recommended—TWE. *Application deadline:* For fall admission, 2/15 priority date for domestic students, 1/1 for international students. Applications are processed on a rolling basis. Application fee: $60 ($75 for international students). Electronic applications accepted. *Financial support:* In 2018–19, 2 fellowships with partial tuition reimbursements (averaging $18,000 per year), 55 teaching assistantships with partial tuition reimbursements (averaging $18,000 per year) were awarded; research assistantships with partial tuition reimbursements and tuition waivers (partial) also available. Support available to part-time students. Financial award applicants required to submit FAFSA. *Unit head:* Christine A. Hrycyna, Head, 765-494-5203, E-mail: hrycyna@purdue.edu. *Application contact:* Betty L. Hatfield, Director of Graduate Admissions, 765-494-5208, E-mail: bettyh@purdue.edu.
Website: https://www.chem.purdue.edu/

Purdue University Global, School of Teacher Education, Davenport, IA 52807. Offers education (M Ed); secondary education (M Ed); teaching and learning (MA); teaching literacy and language: grades 6-12 (MA); teaching literacy and language: grades K-6 (MA); teaching mathematics: grades 6-8 (MA); teaching mathematics: grades 9-12 (MA); teaching mathematics: grades K-5 (MA); teaching science: grades 6-12 (MA); teaching science: grades K-6 (MA); teaching students with special needs (MA); teaching with technology (MA). *Program availability:* Part-time, evening/weekend, online learning. *Entrance requirements:* Additional exam requirements/recommendations for international students: Required—TOEFL (minimum score 550 paper-based; 80 iBT).

Purdue University Northwest, Graduate Studies Office, School of Engineering, Mathematics, and Science, Department of Biological Sciences, Hammond, IN 46323-2094. Offers biology (MS); biology teaching (MS); biotechnology (MS). *Entrance requirements:* For master's, GRE. Additional exam requirements/recommendations for international students: Required—TOEFL. Electronic applications accepted. *Faculty research:* Cell biology, molecular biology, genetics, microbiology, neurophysiology.

Queens College of the City University of New York, Division of Education, Department of Secondary Education and Youth Services, Queens, NY 11367-1597. Offers adolescent biology (MAT); art (MS Ed); biology (MS Ed, AC); chemistry (MS Ed, AC); earth sciences (MS Ed, AC); English (MS Ed, AC); French (MS Ed); Italian (MS Ed, AC); literacy education (MS Ed); mathematics (MS Ed, AC); music (MS Ed, AC); physics (MS Ed, AC); social studies (MS Ed, AC); Spanish (MS Ed, AC). *Program availability:* Part-time, evening/weekend. *Faculty:* 22 full-time (14 women), 35 part-time/adjunct (24 women). *Students:* 33 full-time (19 women), 358 part-time (228 women); includes 182 minority (15 Black or African American, non-Hispanic/Latino; 62 Asian, non-Hispanic/Latino; 91 Hispanic/Latino; 4 Native Hawaiian or other Pacific Islander, non-Hispanic/Latino; 10 Two or more races, non-Hispanic/Latino), 13 international. Average age 29. 216 applicants, 74% accepted, 109 enrolled. In 2018, 108 master's, 35 other advanced degrees awarded. *Degree requirements:* For master's, research project. *Entrance requirements:* For master's, GRE, minimum GPA of 3.0. Additional exam requirements/recommendations for international students: Required—TOEFL, IELTS. *Application deadline:* For fall admission, 4/1 for domestic students; for spring admission, 11/1 for domestic students. Applications are processed on a rolling basis. Application fee: $125. Electronic applications accepted. *Financial support:* Career-related internships or fieldwork available. Financial award application deadline: 4/1; financial award applicants required to submit FAFSA. *Faculty research:* Self regulated learning, teacher learning, assessment and teaching, language diversity, teaching and learning history. *Unit head:* Dr. Eleanor Armour-Thomas, Chairperson, 718-997-5150, E-mail: eleanor.armour-thomas@qc.cuny.edu. *Application contact:* Elizabeth D'Amico-Ramirez, Assistant Director of Graduate Admissions, 718-997-5203, E-mail: elizabeth.damicoramirez@qc.cuny.edu.

Quinnipiac University, School of Education, Program in Secondary Education, Hamden, CT 06518-1940. Offers biology (MAT); English (MAT); history (MAT); mathematics (MAT); Spanish (MAT). *Accreditation:* NCATE. *Entrance requirements:* For master's, PRAXIS I or PRAXIS Core Academic Skills Exam, minimum GPA of 3.0, interview. Electronic applications accepted. *Faculty research:* Multicultural and urban education/leadership, challenges of teaching diverse learners, scholarship of teaching and learning, technology and teaching, humor and education.

Regent University, Graduate School, School of Education, Virginia Beach, VA 23464-9800. Offers education (M Ed, Ed D, PhD), including adult education (Ed D, PhD, Ed S), advanced educational leadership (Ed D, PhD, Ed S), character education (Ed D, PhD, Ed S), Christian education leadership (Ed D, PhD, Ed S), Christian school administration (M Ed), curriculum and instruction (Ed D, PhD, Ed S), curriculum and instruction - adult education (M Ed), curriculum and instruction - Christian school (M Ed), curriculum and instruction - gifted and talented (M Ed), curriculum and instruction - STEM education (M Ed), curriculum and instruction - teacher leader (M Ed), discipleship for ministry (M Ed), educational leadership (M Ed), educational psychology (Ed D, PhD, Ed S), educational technology and online learning (Ed D, PhD, Ed S), elementary education (M Ed), exceptional education executive leadership (Ed D, PhD, Ed S), higher education (Ed D, PhD, Ed S), higher education leadership and management (Ed D, PhD, Ed S), instructional design and technology (M Ed), K-12 school leadership (Ed D, PhD, Ed S), K-12 special education (M Ed), leadership in mathematics education (M Ed), reading specialist (M Ed), special education (Ed D, PhD, Ed S), student affairs (M Ed), TESOL - adult education (M Ed), TESOL - K-12 (M Ed); educational specialist (Ed S), including adult education (Ed D, PhD, Ed S), advanced educational leadership (Ed D, PhD, Ed S), character education (Ed D, PhD, Ed S), Christian education leadership (Ed D, PhD, Ed S), curriculum and instruction (Ed D, PhD, Ed S), educational psychology (Ed D, PhD, Ed S), educational technology and online learning (Ed D, PhD, Ed S), exceptional education executive leadership (Ed D, PhD, Ed S), higher education (Ed D, PhD, Ed S), higher education leadership and management (Ed D, PhD, Ed S), K-12 school leadership (Ed D, PhD, Ed S), special education (Ed D, PhD, Ed S). *Accreditation:* TEAC. *Program availability:* Part-time, evening/weekend, 100% online, blended/hybrid learning. *Degree requirements:* For master's, thesis or alternative; for doctorate, comprehensive exam, thesis/dissertation. *Entrance requirements:* For master's, Virginia Communication and Literacy Assessment (VCLA), PRAXIS, college transcripts, writing sample, interview; for doctorate, GRE, writing sample, resume, transcripts, interview. Additional exam requirements/recommendations for international students: Required—TOEFL (minimum score 577 paper-based). Electronic applications accepted. *Expenses:* Contact institution. *Faculty research:* Christian school administration, curriculum and instruction, educational technology and online learning, higher education, special education.

Rice University, Graduate Programs, Wiess School of Natural Sciences, Department of Physics and Astronomy, Houston, TX 77251-1892. Offers nanoscale physics (MS); physics and astronomy (PhD); science teaching (MST). *Program availability:* Part-time. *Degree requirements:* For master's, thesis (for some programs); for doctorate, thesis/dissertation, minimum B average. *Entrance requirements:* For master's, GRE General Test; for doctorate, GRE General Test, GRE Subject Test. Additional exam requirements/recommendations for international students: Required—TOEFL (minimum score 600 paper-based; 90 iBT). Electronic applications accepted. *Faculty research:* Optical physics; ultra cold atoms; membrane electr-statics, peptides, proteins and lipids; solar astrophysics; stellar activity; magnetic fields; young stars.

Rowan University, Graduate School, College of Education, Department of Science, Technology, Engineering, Art and Math Education, Glassboro, NJ 08028-1701. Offers educational technology (CGS); STEM education (MA). *Program availability:* Part-time, evening/weekend. *Degree requirements:* For master's, thesis. *Entrance requirements:* For master's, GRE General Test. Additional exam requirements/recommendations for international students: Required—TOEFL. Electronic applications accepted.

Rutgers University–New Brunswick, Graduate School of Education, Department of Learning and Teaching, Program in Science Education, Piscataway, NJ 08854-8097. Offers Ed M, Ed D. *Program availability:* Part-time. Terminal master's awarded for partial completion of doctoral program. *Degree requirements:* For master's, comprehensive exam (for some programs); for doctorate, thesis/dissertation, qualifying exam. *Entrance requirements:* For master's, GRE General Test, minimum GPA of 3.0; for doctorate, GRE General Test, minimum GPA of 3.5. Additional exam requirements/recommendations for international students: Required—TOEFL. Electronic applications accepted.

St. John Fisher College, School of Arts and Sciences, Program in Applied Data Science, Rochester, NY 14618-3597. Offers MS. *Program availability:* Part-time, evening/weekend. *Faculty:* 2 full-time (0 women). *Students:* 13 part-time (6 women); includes 4 minority (2 Black or African American, non-Hispanic/Latino; 2 Asian, non-Hispanic/Latino). Average age 28. 26 applicants, 100% accepted, 13 enrolled. *Degree requirements:* For master's, directed research project. *Entrance requirements:* For master's, 2 letters of recommendation, personal statement, current resume. Additional exam requirements/recommendations for international students: Required—TOEFL (minimum score 575 paper-based; 80 iBT). Application fee: $30. *Expenses: Tuition:* Full-time $950; part-time $950 per credit hour. *Required fees:* $15; $15 per semester. *Financial support:* Scholarships/grants available. *Unit head:* Dr. Bernard Ricca, Director, 585-899-3866, E-mail: bricca@sjfc.edu. *Application contact:* Michelle Gosier, Director of Transfer and Graduate Admissions, 585-385-8064, E-mail: mgosier@sjfc.edu.
Website: https://www.sjfc.edu/graduate-programs/ms-in-applied-data-science/

St. John's University, The School of Education, Department of Curriculum and Instruction, PhD in Curriculum and Instruction Program, Queens, NY 11439. Offers early childhood (PhD); global education (PhD); STEM education (PhD); teaching, learning, and knowing (PhD). *Program availability:* Part-time-only. *Degree requirements:* For doctorate, comprehensive exam, thesis/dissertation. *Entrance requirements:* For doctorate, teacher certification (or equivalent), at least three years' teaching experience or the equivalent in informal learning environments, master's degree. Additional exam requirements/recommendations for international students: Required—TOEFL. Electronic applications accepted. *Faculty research:* Literacies, early childhood, STEM, school culture, global education.

Saint Xavier University, Graduate Studies, School of Education, Chicago, IL 60655-3105. Offers counseling (MA); curriculum and instruction (MA); early childhood education (MA); educational administration (MA); elementary education (MA); individualized studies (MA), including educational technology, English as a second language (ESL), ISTEM (integrative science, technology, engineering, and math), science education; music education (MA); reading (MA); secondary education (MA); Spanish education (MA); special education (MA); teaching and leadership (MA). *Accreditation:* NCATE. *Program availability:* Part-time, evening/weekend. *Degree requirements:* For master's, thesis or project. *Entrance requirements:* For master's, minimum GPA of 3.0. *Expenses:* Contact institution.

Salem State University, School of Graduate Studies, Program in Chemistry, Salem, MA 01970-5353. Offers MAT. *Program availability:* Part-time, evening/weekend. *Entrance requirements:* For master's, GRE or MAT. Additional exam requirements/recommendations for international students: Required—TOEFL (minimum score 550 paper-based; 80 iBT) or IELTS (minimum score 5.5).

Salem State University, School of Graduate Studies, Program in Middle School General Science, Salem, MA 01970-5353. Offers MAT. *Program availability:* Part-time, evening/weekend. *Entrance requirements:* For master's, GRE or MAT. Additional exam requirements/recommendations for international students: Required—TOEFL (minimum score 550 paper-based; 80 iBT) or IELTS (minimum score 5.5).

San Diego State University, Graduate and Research Affairs, College of Sciences, Department of Mathematics and Statistics, San Diego, CA 92182. Offers applied mathematics (MS); mathematics (MA); mathematics and science education (PhD); statistics (MS). PhD offered jointly wtih University of California, San Diego. *Program availability:* Part-time. *Degree requirements:* For doctorate, thesis/dissertation. *Entrance requirements:* For master's, GRE General Test; for doctorate, GRE, minimum GPA of 3.25 in last 30 undergraduate semester units, minimum graduate GPA of 3.5, MSE recommendation form, 3 letters of recommendation. Additional exam requirements/recommendations for international students: Required—TOEFL. Electronic applications accepted. *Faculty research:* Teacher education in mathematics.

Seattle Pacific University, Program in Teaching Mathematics and Science, Seattle, WA 98119-1997. Offers MTMS. *Students:* 11 full-time (4 women), 2 part-time (both women); includes 2 minority (1 Asian, non-Hispanic/Latino; 1 Two or more races, non-Hispanic/Latino). Average age 33. 38 applicants, 55% accepted, 13 enrolled. In 2018, 15 master's awarded. *Degree requirements:* For master's, internship. *Application deadline:* For fall admission, 8/15 for domestic students; for winter admission, 11/15 for domestic students; for spring admission, 2/15 for domestic students; for summer admission, 5/15 for domestic students. *Unit head:* David W. Dento, Graduate Teacher Education Chair, 206-281-2504, E-mail: dentod@spu.edu. *Application contact:* David W. Dento, Graduate Teacher Education Chair, 206-281-2504, E-mail: dentod@spu.edu.
Website: http://spu.edu/academics/school-of-education/graduate-programs/masters-programs/master-in-teaching-mathematics-and-science

Shippensburg University of Pennsylvania, School of Graduate Studies, College of Education and Human Services, Department of Teacher Education, Shippensburg, PA 17257-2299. Offers curriculum and instruction (M Ed), including biology, early childhood education, elementary education, geography/earth science, history, mathematics, middle school education, modern languages; reading (M Ed). *Accreditation:* NCATE. *Program availability:* Part-time, evening/weekend, 100% online, blended/hybrid learning. *Faculty:* 12 full-time (9 women), 2 part-time/adjunct (0 women). *Students:* 10 full-time (8 women), 68 part-time (64 women); includes 7 minority (2 Black or African American, non-Hispanic/Latino; 4 Hispanic/Latino; 1 Two or more races, non-Hispanic/Latino). Average age 31. 41 applicants, 73% accepted, 19 enrolled. In 2018, 34 master's awarded. *Degree requirements:* For master's, comprehensive exam (for some programs), thesis optional, practicum or internship; capstone seminar (for some programs). *Entrance requirements:* For master's, MAT or GRE (if GPA less than 2.75), interview, 3 letters of reference, questionnaire of teaching background and future goals, resume. Additional exam requirements/recommendations for international students: Required—TOEFL (minimum score 550 paper-based; 68 iBT), IELTS (minimum score 6), TOEFL (minimum score 550 paper-based, 68 iBT) or IELTS (minimum score 6). *Application deadline:* For fall admission, 4/1 priority date for domestic students, 4/30 for international students; for spring admission, 9/1 priority date for domestic students, 9/30 for international students; for summer admission, 2/1 priority date for domestic students. Applications are processed on a rolling basis. Application fee: $45. Electronic applications accepted. *Expenses:* Tuition, state resident: part-time $516 per credit. Tuition, nonresident: part-time $750 per credit. *Required fees:* $149 per credit. *Financial support:* In 2018–19, 5 students received support. Career-related internships or fieldwork, scholarships/grants, unspecified assistantships, and resident hall director and student payroll positions available. Support available to part-time students. Financial award application deadline: 3/1; financial award applicants required to submit FAFSA. *Unit head:* Dr. Christine A. Royce, Chairperson, 717-477-1688, Fax: 717-477-4046, E-mail: caroyc@ship.edu. *Application contact:* Maya T. Mapp, Director of Admissions, 717-477-1231, Fax: 717-477-4016, E-mail: mtmapp@ship.edu.
Website: http://www.ship.edu/teacher/

Shippensburg University of Pennsylvania, School of Graduate Studies, College of Education and Human Services, Master of Arts in Teaching STEM Education Program, Shippensburg, PA 17257-2299. Offers MAT. *Program availability:* Part-time, evening/weekend, blended/hybrid learning. *Students:* 10 full-time (5 women), 5 part-time (3 women). Average age 31. 17 applicants, 82% accepted, 7 enrolled. In 2018, 9 master's awarded. *Degree requirements:* For master's, 12-week student teaching practicum (12 credits), two capstone projects which include professional portfolio and the results of a research project. *Entrance requirements:* For master's, Pre-Service Academic Performance Assessment (PAPA), PRAXIS II Subject Assessment, statement of intent summarizing motivations and goals for entering the teaching profession, two letters of recommendation. Additional exam requirements/recommendations for international students: Required—TOEFL (minimum score 550 paper-based; 68 iBT), IELTS (minimum score 6), TOEFL (minimum score 550 paper-based, 68 iBT) or IELTS (minimum score 6). *Application deadline:* For fall admission, 4/30 for international students; for spring admission, 9/30 for international students. Applications are processed on a rolling basis. Application fee: $45. Electronic applications accepted. *Expenses:* Tuition, state resident: part-time $516 per credit. Tuition, nonresident: part-time $750 per credit. *Required fees:* $149 per credit. *Financial support:* In 2018–19, 1 student received support. Career-related internships or fieldwork and resident hall director and student payroll positions available. Support available to part-time students. Financial award application deadline: 3/1; financial award applicants required to submit FAFSA. *Unit head:* Dr. Joseph W. Shane, Professor and Program Coordinator, 717-477-1572, Fax: 717-477-4048, E-mail: jwshan@ship.edu. *Application contact:* Maya T. Mapp, Director of Admissions, 717-477-1231, Fax: 717-477-4016, E-mail: mtmapp@ship.edu.
Website: http://www.ship.edu/STEM/

Slippery Rock University of Pennsylvania, Graduate Studies (Recruitment), College of Education, Department of Elementary Education and Early Childhood, Slippery Rock, PA 16057-1383. Offers instructional coach (M Ed); K-12 reading (M Ed); K-12 science and math (M Ed); reading specialist (M Ed). *Accreditation:* NCATE. *Program availability:* Part-time, evening/weekend, online only, 100% online. *Faculty:* 5 full-time (all women). *Students:* 6 full-time (all women), 115 part-time (107 women); includes 3 minority (1 Asian, non-Hispanic/Latino; 2 Hispanic/Latino). Average age 29. 106 applicants, 83% accepted, 45 enrolled. In 2018, 73 master's awarded. *Degree requirements:* For master's, comprehensive exam (for some programs), thesis optional. *Entrance requirements:* For master's, minimum GPA of 3.0, resume, teaching certification, transcripts, letters of recommendation (depending on program). Additional exam requirements/recommendations for international students: Required—TOEFL (minimum score 550 paper-based; 80 iBT). *Application deadline:* For fall admission, 3/1 priority date for domestic students, 5/1 priority date for international students; for spring admission, 10/1 priority date for domestic students, 9/1 priority date for international students. Applications are processed on a rolling basis. Application fee: $25 ($30 for international students). Electronic applications accepted. *Expenses:* Contact institution. *Financial support:* Career-related internships or fieldwork, Federal Work-Study, institutionally sponsored loans, scholarships/grants, tuition waivers (partial), and unspecified assistantships available. Support available to part-time students. Financial award application deadline: 5/1; financial award applicants required to submit FAFSA. *Unit head:* Dr. Suzanne Rose, Graduate Coordinator, 724-738-2042, Fax: 724-738-2779, E-mail: suzanne.rose@sru.edu. *Application contact:* Brandi Weber-Mortimer, Director of Graduate Admissions, 724-738-2051, Fax: 724-738-2146, E-mail: graduate.admissions@sru.edu.
Website: http://www.sru.edu/academics/colleges-and-departments/coe/departments/elementary-education-/-early-childhood/graduate-programs

Slippery Rock University of Pennsylvania, Graduate Studies (Recruitment), College of Education, Department of Secondary Education/Foundations of Education, Slippery Rock, PA 16057-1383. Offers secondary education (M Ed), including English, math/science, social studies. *Accreditation:* NCATE. *Program availability:* Part-time, evening/weekend, 100% online. *Faculty:* 9 full-time (4 women), 1 part-time/adjunct (0 women). *Students:* 45 full-time (36 women), 232 part-time (191 women); includes 2 minority (both Black or African American, non-Hispanic/Latino). Average age 28. 58 applicants, 76% accepted, 28 enrolled. In 2018, 34 master's awarded. *Degree requirements:* For master's, comprehensive exam, thesis (for some programs). *Entrance requirements:* For master's, copy of teaching certification and two letters of recommendation (for some programs). Additional exam requirements/recommendations for international students: Required—TOEFL (minimum score 550 paper-based; 80 iBT). *Application deadline:* For fall admission, 3/1 priority date for domestic students, 5/1 priority date for international students; for spring admission, 10/1 priority date for domestic students, 9/1 priority date for international students. Applications are processed on a rolling basis. Application fee: $25 ($30 for international students). Electronic applications accepted. *Expenses:* Contact institution. *Financial support:* In 2018–19, 9 students received support. Career-related internships or fieldwork, Federal Work-Study, institutionally sponsored loans, scholarships/grants, tuition waivers (partial), and unspecified assistantships available. Support available to part-time students. Financial award application deadline: 5/1; financial award applicants required to submit FAFSA. *Unit head:* Dr. Jeffrey Lehman, Graduate Coordinator, 724-738-2311, Fax: 724-738-4987, E-mail: jeffrey.lehman@sru.edu. *Application contact:* Brandi Weber-Mortimer, Director of Graduate Studies, 724-738-2051, Fax: 724-738-2146, E-mail: graduate.admissions@sru.edu.
Website: http://www.sru.edu/academics/colleges-and-departments/coe/departments/secondary-education-/-foundations-of-education

Smith College, Graduate and Special Programs, Department of Education and Child Study, Program in Secondary Education, Northampton, MA 01063. Offers secondary education (MAT), including biological sciences education, chemistry education, English education, geology education, government education, history education, mathematics

education, physics education. *Program availability:* Part-time. *Students:* 8 full-time (all women), 2 part-time (0 women); includes 2 minority (1 Black or African American, non-Hispanic/Latino; 1 Asian, non-Hispanic/Latino), 2 international. Average age 27. 25 applicants, 84% accepted, 10 enrolled. In 2018, 8 master's awarded. *Entrance requirements:* Additional exam requirements/recommendations for international students: Required—TOEFL (minimum score 595 paper-based; 97 iBT), IELTS (minimum score 7.5). *Application deadline:* For fall admission, 4/15 for domestic students, 1/15 priority date for international students; for spring admission, 12/1 for domestic students. Applications are processed on a rolling basis. Application fee: $60. *Expenses:* The total tuition cost to each M.A.T. student (the full program fee, after 'built-in' scholarship award) is $18,500. *Financial support:* In 2018–19, 9 students received support, including 2 fellowships with full tuition reimbursements available; scholarships/grants and human resources employee benefit also available. Support available to part-time students. Financial award application deadline: 4/15; financial award applicants required to submit CSS PROFILE or FAFSA. *Unit head:* Rosetta Cohen, Graduate Student Advisor, 413-585-3266, E-mail: rcohen@smith.edu. *Application contact:* Ruth Morgan, Program Coordinator, 413-585-3050, Fax: 413-585-3054, E-mail: gradstdy@smith.edu.
Website: http://www.smith.edu/educ/

Smith College, Graduate and Special Programs, Department of Physics, Northampton, MA 01063. Offers secondary education (MAT), including physics education. *Program availability:* Part-time. *Students:* 1 part-time (0 women). Average age 38. In 2018, 1 master's awarded. *Entrance requirements:* Additional exam requirements/recommendations for international students: Required—TOEFL (minimum score 595 paper-based; 97 iBT), IELTS. *Application deadline:* For fall admission, 4/15 for domestic students, 1/15 for international students; for spring admission, 12/1 for domestic students. Applications are processed on a rolling basis. Application fee: $60. *Expenses:* The total tuition cost to each M.A.T. student (the full program fee, after 'built-in' scholarship award) is $18,500. *Financial support:* In 2018–19, 1 student received support. Fellowships and scholarships/grants available. Support available to part-time students. Financial award application deadline: 4/15; financial award applicants required to submit CSS PROFILE or FAFSA. *Unit head:* Gary Felder, Graduate Adviser, 413-585-4489, E-mail: gfelder@smith.edu. *Application contact:* Ruth Morgan, Program Coordinator, 413-585-3050, Fax: 413-585-3054, E-mail: gradstdy@smith.edu.

South Carolina State University, College of Graduate and Professional Studies, Department of Education, Orangeburg, SC 29117-0001. Offers early childhood education (MAT); education (M Ed); elementary education (M Ed, MAT); English (MAT); general science/biology (MAT); mathematics (MAT); secondary education (M Ed), including biology education, business education, counselor education, English education, home economics education, industrial education, mathematics education, science education, social studies education; special education (M Ed), including emotionally handicapped, learning disabilities, mentally handicapped. *Accreditation:* NCATE. *Program availability:* Part-time, evening/weekend. *Faculty:* 17 full-time (6 women), 12 part-time/adjunct (5 women). *Students:* 42 full-time (32 women), 93 part-time (64 women); includes 121 minority (119 Black or African American, non-Hispanic/Latino; 2 Asian, non-Hispanic/Latino), 2 international. Average age 40. 50 applicants, 98% accepted, 39 enrolled. In 2018, 9 master's awarded. *Degree requirements:* For master's, thesis optional, departmental qualifying exam. *Entrance requirements:* For master's, GRE General Test, NTE, interview, teaching certificate. *Application deadline:* For fall admission, 6/15 priority date for domestic students, 6/15 for international students; for spring admission, 11/1 for domestic and international students. Application fee: $25. Electronic applications accepted. *Expenses: Tuition, area resident:* Full-time $9928; part-time $552 per credit hour. Tuition, state resident: full-time $9928. Tuition, nonresident: full-time $21,038; part-time $1169 per credit hour. *Required fees:* $1532; $85 per credit hour. *Financial support:* Fellowships, career-related internships or fieldwork, Federal Work-Study, and scholarships/grants available. Financial award application deadline: 6/1. *Unit head:* Dr. Charlie Spell, Chair, Department of Education, 803-536-8963, Fax: 803-516-4568, E-mail: cspell@scsu.edu. *Application contact:* Curtis Foskey, Coordinator of Graduate Studies, 803-536-8419, Fax: 803-536-8812, E-mail: cfoskey@scsu.edu.

Southern Connecticut State University, School of Graduate Studies, School of Arts and Sciences, Department of Environment, Geography and Marine Sciences, New Haven, CT 06515-1355. Offers environmental education (MS); science education (MS, Diploma). *Accreditation:* NCATE. *Program availability:* Part-time, evening/weekend. *Degree requirements:* For master's, thesis or alternative. *Entrance requirements:* For master's, interview; for Diploma, master's degree. Electronic applications accepted.

Southern University and Agricultural and Mechanical College, Graduate School, College of Sciences and Engineering, Department of Science/Mathematics Education, Baton Rouge, LA 70813. Offers PhD. *Accreditation:* NCATE. *Degree requirements:* For doctorate, thesis/dissertation. *Entrance requirements:* For doctorate, GRE General Test. Additional exam requirements/recommendations for international students: Required—TOEFL (minimum score 525 paper-based). *Faculty research:* Performance assessment in science/mathematics education, equity in science/mathematics education, technology and distance learning, science/mathematics concept formation, cognitive themes, problem solving in science/mathematics education.

Southwestern Oklahoma State University, College of Professional and Graduate Studies, School of Behavioral Sciences and Education, Specialization in Natural Sciences, Weatherford, OK 73096-3098. Offers M Ed. *Program availability:* Part-time. *Degree requirements:* For master's, exam. *Entrance requirements:* For master's, GRE General Test or minimum undergraduate GPA of 3.0. Additional exam requirements/recommendations for international students: Required—TOEFL (minimum score 550 paper-based), IELTS (minimum score 6.5).

State University of New York at New Paltz, Graduate and Extended Learning School, School of Education, Department of Teaching and Learning, New Paltz, NY 12561. Offers adolescence education: biology (MAT, MS Ed); adolescence education: chemistry (MAT, MS Ed); adolescence education: earth science (MAT, MS Ed); adolescence education: English (MAT, MS Ed); adolescence education: French (MAT, MS Ed); adolescence education: social studies (MAT, MS Ed); adolescence education: Spanish (MAT, MS Ed); second language education (MS Ed, AC), including second language education (MS Ed), teaching English language learners (AC). *Accreditation:* NCATE. *Program availability:* Part-time, evening/weekend. *Faculty:* 21 full-time (16 women), 15 part-time/adjunct (12 women). *Students:* 127 full-time (91 women), 171 part-time (149 women); includes 48 minority (5 Black or African American, non-Hispanic/Latino; 2 Asian, non-Hispanic/Latino; 37 Hispanic/Latino; 4 Two or more races, non-Hispanic/Latino). 152 applicants, 84% accepted, 104 enrolled. In 2018, 135 master's, 19 other advanced degrees awarded. *Degree requirements:* For master's, comprehensive exam (for some programs), portfolio. *Entrance requirements:* For master's, minimum GPA of 3.0, New York state teaching certificate (MS Ed). Additional exam requirements/recommendations for international students: Required—TOEFL (minimum score 550 paper-based; 80 iBT), IELTS (minimum score 6.5). *Application deadline:* For fall admission, 3/1 priority date for domestic students, 3/1 for international students; for spring admission, 10/1 priority date for domestic students, 10/1 for international students. Application fee: $50. Electronic applications accepted. *Financial support:* Application deadline: 8/1. *Unit head:* Dr. Aaron Isabelle, Associate Dean, 845-257-2837, E-mail: isabella@newpaltz.edu. *Application contact:* Vika Shock, Director of Graduate Admissions, 845-257-3285, Fax: 845-257-3284, E-mail: gradstudies@newpaltz.edu.
Website: http://www.newpaltz.edu/secondaryed/

State University of New York at Plattsburgh, School of Arts and Sciences, Program in Natural Science, Plattsburgh, NY 12901-2681. Offers MS, PSM. *Accreditation:* TEAC. *Program availability:* Part-time. *Entrance requirements:* For master's, GRE General Test (minimum score of 1200), bachelor's degree in science discipline, minimum GPA of 3.0. Additional exam requirements/recommendations for international students: Required—TOEFL.

State University of New York at Plattsburgh, School of Education, Health, and Human Services, Program in Teacher Education: Adolescence Education, Plattsburgh, NY 12901-2681. Offers adolescence education (MST); biology 7-12 (MST); chemistry 7-12 (MST); earth science 7-12 (MST); English 7-12 (MST); French 7-12 (MST); mathematics 7-12 (MST); physics 7-12 (MST); social studies 7-12 (MST); Spanish 7-12 (MST). *Accreditation:* TEAC. *Program availability:* Part-time, evening/weekend. *Entrance requirements:* For master's, minimum GPA of 2.75. Additional exam requirements/recommendations for international students: Required—TOEFL.

State University of New York College at Cortland, Graduate Studies, School of Arts and Sciences, Programs in Adolescence Education, Cortland, NY 13045. Offers biology (MAT); chemistry (MAT); English (MAT, MS Ed); mathematics (MAT); mathematics and physics (MS Ed); physics (MAT, MS Ed). *Accreditation:* NCATE. *Program availability:* Part-time, evening/weekend. *Degree requirements:* For master's, one foreign language, comprehensive exam (for some programs), thesis (for some programs). *Entrance requirements:* For master's, GRE General Test.

State University of New York College at Old Westbury, School of Education, Old Westbury, NY 11568-0210. Offers biology (MAT, MS); chemistry (MAT, MS); English language arts (MAT, MS); math (MAT, MS); social studies (MAT, MS); Spanish (MAT, MS). *Program availability:* Part-time, evening/weekend. *Entrance requirements:* For master's, Liberal Arts and Sciences Test, undergraduate degree with at least 30 semester hours of appropriate coursework as defined by the respective discipline; minimum cumulative undergraduate GPA of 3.0; two letters of recommendation (one from an academic source); essay. Additional exam requirements/recommendations for international students: Required—TOEFL (minimum score 550 paper-based); Recommended—IELTS.

State University of New York College at Potsdam, School of Education and Professional Studies, Program in Secondary Education, Potsdam, NY 13676. Offers English education (MST); mathematics education (MST); science education (MST), including biology, chemistry, earth science, physics; social studies education (MST). *Accreditation:* NCATE. *Degree requirements:* For master's, culminating experience. *Entrance requirements:* For master's, minimum GPA of 2.75 in last 60 hours of course work (3.0 for English program). Additional exam requirements/recommendations for international students: Required—TOEFL (minimum score 550 paper-based; 80 iBT), IELTS (minimum score 6). Electronic applications accepted.

Stevenson University, Master of Arts in Teaching Program, Stevenson, MD 21153. Offers secondary biology (MAT); secondary chemistry (MAT); secondary mathematics (MAT). *Program availability:* Part-time, blended/hybrid learning. *Faculty:* 5 part-time/adjunct (all women). *Students:* 13 part-time (9 women); includes 5 minority (1 Black or African American, non-Hispanic/Latino; 2 Asian, non-Hispanic/Latino; 2 Hispanic/Latino). Average age 31. 8 applicants, 75% accepted, 6 enrolled. *Degree requirements:* For master's, internship, portfolio, action research project. *Entrance requirements:* For master's, PRAXIS, GRE, SAT, or ACT, official transcripts from each college or university attended verifying completion of baccalaureate degree in a science or math discipline from regionally-accredited institution. *Application deadline:* Applications are processed on a rolling basis. Electronic applications accepted. *Expenses:* Contact institution. *Financial support:* Unspecified assistantships available. Financial award applicants required to submit FAFSA. *Unit head:* Dr. Anne P. Davis, Dean, Stevenson University Online. *Application contact:* Amanda Millar, Director, Admissions, 443-352-4243, Fax: 443-352-4440, E-mail: amillar@stevenson.edu.
Website: http://www.stevenson.edu/online/academics/online-graduate-programs/master-arts-teaching/

Stony Brook University, State University of New York, Graduate School, College of Arts and Sciences, Department of Physics and Astronomy, Stony Brook, NY 11794. Offers astronomy (PhD); physics (MA, MAT, MS, PhD), including modern research instrumentation (MS), physics (MA, PhD), physics education (MAT). MAT offered through the School of Professional Development. *Faculty:* 55 full-time (7 women), 3 part-time/adjunct (1 woman). *Students:* 214 full-time (35 women), 5 part-time (0 women); includes 23 minority (2 Black or African American, non-Hispanic/Latino; 14 Asian, non-Hispanic/Latino; 7 Hispanic/Latino), 152 international. Average age 26. 560 applicants, 26% accepted, 66 enrolled. In 2018, 17 master's, 15 doctorates awarded. *Entrance requirements:* For master's, GRE General Test; for doctorate, GRE General Test, GRE Subject Test (physics). Additional exam requirements/recommendations for international students: Required—TOEFL (minimum score 90 iBT). *Application deadline:* For fall admission, 1/15 for domestic students; for spring admission, 10/1 for domestic students. Application fee: $100. Electronic applications accepted. *Expenses:* Contact institution. *Financial support:* In 2018–19, 5 fellowships, 69 research assistantships, 55 teaching assistantships were awarded. *Faculty research:* Astronomy, condensed matter physics, physics, quantum physics, solid state physics. *Total annual research expenditures:* $19.4 million. *Unit head:* Dr. Axel Drees, Chair, 631-632-8114, Fax: 631-632-8176, E-mail: axel.drees@stonybrook.edu. *Application contact:* Donald Sheehan, Coordinator, 631-632-8759, Fax: 631-632-8176, E-mail: donald.j.sheehan@stonybrook.edu.
Website: http://www.physics.sunysb.edu/Physics/

Stony Brook University, State University of New York, Graduate School, College of Arts and Sciences, Institute for STEM Education, Stony Brook, NY 11794. Offers PhD. *Faculty:* 5 full-time (4 women), 4 part-time/adjunct (2 women). *Students:* 1 full-time (0 women), 29 part-time (20 women); includes 2 minority (1 Black or African American, non-Hispanic/Latino; 1 Hispanic/Latino). Average age 35. In 2018, 3 doctorates awarded. *Degree requirements:* For doctorate, comprehensive exam, thesis/dissertation. *Entrance requirements:* For doctorate, GRE, graduate GPA of at least 3.0, 3 letters of recommendation, statement of intent. Additional exam requirements/recommendations for international students: Required—TOEFL (minimum score 550 paper-based; 90 iBT), IELTS (minimum score 6.5), TOEFL with minimum iBT score of 85 (for master's programs). *Application deadline:* For fall admission, 1/15 for domestic students; for spring admission, 10/1 for domestic students. Application fee: $100. *Expenses: Tuition, area resident:* Full-time $11,090; part-time $462 per credit hour. Tuition, state resident: full-time $11,090; part-time $462 per credit hour. Tuition, nonresident: full-time $22,650; part-time $944 per credit hour. *International tuition:* $22,650 full-time. *Required fees:* $1917. *Financial support:* In 2018–19, 1 teaching assistantship was awarded. *Faculty research:* Educational evaluation or assessment, educational improvement, educational psychology. *Unit head:* Dr. Keith Sheppard, Director, 631-632-2989, E-mail: keith.sheppard@stonybrook.edu. *Application contact:* Judith Nimmo, Coordinator, 631-632-9750, E-mail: judith.nimmo@stonybrook.edu.
Website: https://www.stonybrook.edu/istem/

Syracuse University, College of Arts and Sciences, Program in College Science Teaching, Syracuse, NY 13244. Offers PhD. *Program availability:* Part-time. *Entrance requirements:* For doctorate, GRE General Test, three letters of recommendation, personal statement, transcripts, scholarly writing sample. Additional exam requirements/recommendations for international students: Required—TOEFL (minimum score 100 iBT). *Application deadline:* For fall admission, 2/1 priority date for domestic and international students. Applications are processed on a rolling basis. Application fee: $75. Electronic applications accepted. *Financial support:* Fellowships with full tuition reimbursements, research assistantships, teaching assistantships, and scholarships/grants available. Financial award application deadline: 1/15; financial award applicants required to submit FAFSA. *Faculty research:* Philosophy of science, methods of teaching science in higher education, research focused on the problems of college teaching, curriculum development. *Unit head:* Dr. John W. Tillotson, Department Chairperson, 315-443-9137, E-mail: jwtillot@syr.edu. *Application contact:* Heather Thompson, Administrative Assistant, Earth Sciences and Science Teaching, 315-443-2672, E-mail: hethomps@syr.edu.
Website: http://sciteach.syr.edu/academics/program-science-teaching-phd.html

Syracuse University, School of Education, Programs in Science Education, Syracuse, NY 13244. Offers biology (MS); chemistry (MS, PhD). *Program availability:* Part-time. *Students:* Average age 38. In 2018, 4 doctorates awarded. *Degree requirements:* For doctorate, comprehensive exam, thesis/dissertation. *Entrance requirements:* For master's, GRE General Test or MAT, official transcripts from previous academic institutions, 3 letters of recommendation (preferably from faculty), personal statement that makes a clear and compelling argument for why applicant wants to teach secondary science; for doctorate, GRE General Test or MAT, master's degree, interview. Additional exam requirements/recommendations for international students: Required—TOEFL (minimum score 100 iBT). *Application deadline:* For fall admission, 1/15 priority date for domestic and international students; for spring admission, 10/15 priority date for domestic and international students. Applications are processed on a rolling basis. Application fee: $75. Electronic applications accepted. *Financial support:* Fellowships with full tuition reimbursements, research assistantships, teaching assistantships, and scholarships/grants available. Financial award application deadline: 1/15. *Faculty research:* Diverse field experiences and theoretical and practical knowledge in research-based science teaching, biology, chemistry, earth science, and physics. *Unit head:* Dr. Sharon Dotger, Program Coordinator, 315-443-9138, E-mail: sdotger@syr.edu. *Application contact:* Speranza Migliore, Graduate Admissions Recruiter, 315-443-2505, E-mail: gradrcrt@syr.edu.
Website: http://soe.syr.edu/academic/teaching_and_leadership/graduate/masters/science_education/

Teachers College, Columbia University, Department of Mathematics, Science and Technology, New York, NY 10027-6696. Offers biology 7-12 (MA); chemistry 7-12 (MA); communication and education (MA, Ed D); computing in education (MA); earth science 7-12 (MA); instructional technology and media (Ed M, MA, Ed D); mathematics education (Ed M, MA, Ed D, Ed DCT, PhD); physics 7-12 (MA); science and dental education (MA); science education (Ed M, MS, Ed DCT, PhD); supervisor/teacher of science education (MA); technology specialist (MA). *Program availability:* Part-time, evening/weekend, online learning. *Students:* 155 full-time (114 women), 254 part-time (162 women); includes 136 minority (44 Black or African American, non-Hispanic/Latino; 1 American Indian or Alaska Native, non-Hispanic/Latino; 59 Asian, non-Hispanic/Latino; 23 Hispanic/Latino; 9 Two or more races, non-Hispanic/Latino), 140 international. Average age 31. 484 applicants, 60% accepted, 138 enrolled. Terminal master's awarded for partial completion of doctoral program. *Unit head:* Prof. Erica Walker, Chair, 212-678-8246, E-mail: ewalker@tc.columbia.edu. *Application contact:* Kelly Sutton Skinner, Director of Admission & New Student Enrollment, E-mail: kms2237@tc.columbia.edu.
Website: http://www.tc.columbia.edu/mathematics-science-and-technology/

Teachers College of San Joaquin, Master's Program in Education, Stockton, CA 95206. Offers early education (M Ed); educational inquiry (M Ed); educational leadership and school development (M Ed); science, technology, engineering, and mathematics (M Ed); special education (M Ed). *Expenses: Tuition:* Full-time $5520. Tuition and fees vary according to course load and program.

Temple University, College of Education, Department of Teaching and Learning, Philadelphia, PA 19122-6096. Offers career and technical education (Ed M), including business, computing, and information technology, industrial education, marketing education; middle grades education (Ed M), including math and language arts, math and science, science and language arts; secondary education (Ed M), including English, math, social studies; teaching English to speakers of other languages (MS Ed); urban education (Ed M). *Program availability:* Part-time, evening/weekend. *Faculty:* 27 full-time (19 women), 71 part-time/adjunct (51 women). *Students:* 181 full-time (126 women), 128 part-time (78 women); includes 71 minority (25 Black or African American, non-Hispanic/Latino; 1 American Indian or Alaska Native, non-Hispanic/Latino; 20 Asian, non-Hispanic/Latino; 19 Hispanic/Latino; 1 Native Hawaiian or other Pacific Islander, non-Hispanic/Latino; 5 Two or more races, non-Hispanic/Latino), 12 international. 234 applicants, 67% accepted, 103 enrolled. In 2018, 148 master's awarded. *Degree requirements:* For master's, thesis (for some programs). *Entrance requirements:* For master's, statement of goals, 2 letters of recommendation. Additional exam requirements/recommendations for international students: Required—TOEFL (minimum score 79 iBT), IELTS, PTE, one of three is required. Application fee: $60. Electronic applications accepted. *Financial support:* Fellowships, research assistantships, teaching assistantships, career-related internships or fieldwork, Federal Work-Study, scholarships/grants, health care benefits, and unspecified assistantships available. Financial award applicants required to submit FAFSA. *Faculty research:* Career & technical education, early childhood education, middle grades education, secondary education, special education. *Unit head:* Matthew Tincani, Prof. of Applied Behavior Analysis and Dept. Chairperson, 215-204-8073, E-mail: matthew.tincani@temple.edu. *Application contact:* Stacey Sanginette, Academic Coordinator, 215-204-6143, E-mail: stacey.sangtinette@temple.edu.
Website: http://education.temple.edu/tl

Tennessee Technological University, College of Graduate Studies, College of Education, Department of Curriculum and Instruction, Program in STEM Education, Cookeville, TN 38505. Offers MA, Ed S. *Program availability:* Part-time, evening/weekend. *Students:* 2 full-time (both women), 4 part-time (3 women); includes 1 minority (Two or more races, non-Hispanic/Latino). 3 applicants, 100% accepted, 3 enrolled. *Degree requirements:* For master's, comprehensive exam, thesis or alternative. *Entrance requirements:* For master's, GRE, MAT. Additional exam requirements/recommendations for international students: Required—TOEFL (minimum score 527 paper-based; 71 iBT), IELTS (minimum score 5.5) or PTE (48). *Application deadline:* For fall admission, 8/1 for domestic students, 5/1 for international students; for spring admission, 2/1 for domestic students, 10/1 for international students; for summer admission, 5/1 for domestic students, 2/1 for international students. Applications are processed on a rolling basis. Application fee: $35 ($40 for international students). Electronic applications accepted. *Financial support:* Application deadline: 4/1. *Unit head:* Dr. Jeremy Wendt, Chairperson, 931-372-3181, E-mail: jwendt@tntech.edu. *Application contact:* Shelia K. Kendrick, Coordinator of Graduate Studies, 931-372-3808, Fax: 931-372-3497, E-mail: skendrick@tntech.edu.

Texas A&M University–Kingsville, College of Graduate Studies, College of Education and Human Performance, Department of Teacher and Bilingual Education, Program in Science in Education, Kingsville, TX 78363. Offers MS. *Program availability:* Part-time, evening/weekend. *Degree requirements:* For master's, comprehensive exam, thesis or alternative, research report. *Entrance requirements:* For master's, GRE General Test, MAT, minimum GPA of 3.0. *Faculty research:* Professional development/technology, interdisciplinary teaming, educational restructuring.

Texas Christian University, College of Education, Doctoral Programs in Education, Fort Worth, TX 76129-0002. Offers counseling and counselor education (PhD); curriculum studies (PhD); educational leadership (Ed D); higher educational leadership (Ed D); science education (PhD); MBA/Ed D. *Program availability:* Part-time, evening/weekend. *Faculty:* 29 full-time (21 women), 3 part-time/adjunct (1 woman). *Students:* 80 full-time (57 women), 26 part-time (13 women); includes 41 minority (15 Black or African American, non-Hispanic/Latino; 6 Asian, non-Hispanic/Latino; 17 Hispanic/Latino; 3 Two or more races, non-Hispanic/Latino), 6 international. Average age 39. 109 applicants, 50% accepted, 23 enrolled. In 2018, 12 doctorates awarded. *Degree requirements:* For doctorate, comprehensive exam, thesis/dissertation. *Entrance requirements:* For doctorate, GRE General Test. Additional exam requirements/recommendations for international students: Required—TOEFL (minimum score 550 paper-based; 80 iBT), IELTS (minimum score 6.5). *Application deadline:* For fall admission, 2/1 for domestic and international students; for winter admission, 2/1 for domestic and international students; for spring admission, 11/16 for domestic and international students. Application fee: $60. Electronic applications accepted. *Financial support:* In 2018–19, 66 students received support, including 1 fellowship with full tuition reimbursement available (averaging $18,500 per year), 8 research assistantships with full tuition reimbursements available (averaging $18,500 per year), 6 teaching assistantships with full tuition reimbursements available (averaging $18,500 per year); career-related internships or fieldwork, scholarships/grants, health care benefits, and unspecified assistantships also available. Support available to part-time students. Financial award application deadline: 2/1. *Unit head:* Dr. Jan Lacina, Interim Dean, 817-257-6786, Fax: 817-257-7466, E-mail: j.lacina@tcu.edu. *Application contact:* Lori Kimball, Graduate Studies Coordinator, 817-257-7661, Fax: 817-257-7466, E-mail: l.kimball@tcu.edu.
Website: http://coe.tcu.edu/graduate-overview/

Texas Christian University, College of Education, Master's Programs in Education, Fort Worth, TX 76129-0002. Offers counseling (M Ed); curriculum and instruction (M Ed), including curriculum studies, language and literacy, math education, science education; education (MAT); educational leadership (M Ed); special education (M Ed). *Program availability:* Part-time, evening/weekend. *Faculty:* 29 full-time (21 women), 3 part-time/adjunct (1 woman). *Students:* 124 full-time (94 women), 14 part-time (12 women); includes 52 minority (14 Black or African American, non-Hispanic/Latino; 2 American Indian or Alaska Native, non-Hispanic/Latino; 3 Asian, non-Hispanic/Latino; 28 Hispanic/Latino; 5 Two or more races, non-Hispanic/Latino), 1 international. Average age 28. 172 applicants, 69% accepted, 86 enrolled. In 2018, 62 master's awarded. *Degree requirements:* For master's, comprehensive exam (for some programs), thesis (for some programs). *Entrance requirements:* For master's, GRE General Test; Pre-Admission Content Test (for MAT). Additional exam requirements/recommendations for international students: Required—TOEFL (minimum score 550 paper-based; 80 iBT), IELTS (minimum score 6.5). *Application deadline:* For fall admission, 3/1 for domestic and international students; for spring admission, 11/16 for domestic and international students; for summer admission, 3/1 for domestic and international students. Application fee: $60. Electronic applications accepted. *Financial support:* In 2018–19, 135 students received support, including 3 research assistantships with full tuition reimbursements available (averaging $15,000 per year), 33 teaching assistantships with full tuition reimbursements available (averaging $15,000 per year); career-related internships or fieldwork, scholarships/grants, health care benefits, and unspecified assistantships also available. Support available to part-time students. Financial award application deadline: 3/1. *Unit head:* Dr. Jan Lacina, Interim Dean, 817-257-6786, Fax: 817-257-7466, E-mail: j.lacina@tcu.edu. *Application contact:* Lori Kimball, Graduate Studies Coordinator, 817-257-7661, Fax: 817-257-7466, E-mail: l.kimball@tcu.edu.
Website: http://coe.tcu.edu/graduate-overview/

Texas Tech University, Graduate School, College of Education, Department of Curriculum and Instruction, Lubbock, TX 79409-1071. Offers bilingual education (M Ed); curriculum and instruction (M Ed, PhD); elementary education (M Ed); language/literacy education (M Ed); multidisciplinary science (MS); secondary education (M Ed). *Accreditation:* NCATE. *Program availability:* Part-time, evening/weekend, online learning. *Faculty:* 17 full-time (11 women), 1 (woman) part-time/adjunct. *Students:* 48 full-time (41 women), 265 part-time (220 women); includes 103 minority (25 Black or African American, non-Hispanic/Latino; 9 Asian, non-Hispanic/Latino; 64 Hispanic/Latino; 5 Two or more races, non-Hispanic/Latino), 27 international. Average age 40. 101 applicants, 65% accepted, 51 enrolled. In 2018, 26 master's, 21 doctorates awarded. Terminal master's awarded for partial completion of doctoral program. *Degree requirements:* For master's, comprehensive exam (for some programs), thesis optional; for doctorate, comprehensive exam, thesis/dissertation. *Entrance requirements:* For master's, bachelor's degree; resume; letter of intent; academic writing sample; 2 letters of recommendation; for doctorate, GRE, master's degree; resume; letter of intent; academic writing sample; 3 letters of recommendation. Additional exam requirements/recommendations for international students: Required—TOEFL (minimum score 550 paper-based; 79 iBT). *Application deadline:* For fall admission, 6/1 priority date for domestic students, 1/15 priority date for international students; for spring admission, 9/1 priority date for domestic students, 6/15 priority date for international students. Applications are processed on a rolling basis. Application fee: $65. Electronic applications accepted. *Expenses:* Contact institution. *Financial support:* In 2018–19, 142 students received support, including 136 fellowships (averaging $2,895 per year), 28 research assistantships (averaging $12,296 per year), 7 teaching assistantships (averaging $14,175 per year); Federal Work-Study, institutionally sponsored loans, scholarships/grants, health care benefits, and unspecified assistantships also available. Support available to part-time students. Financial award application deadline: 2/1; financial award applicants required to submit FAFSA. *Faculty research:* Teacher education, curriculum studies, bilingual education, science and math education, language and literacy education. *Total annual research expenditures:* $79,025. *Unit head:* Dr. Jerry Dwyer, Professor, Interim Department Chair, 806-834-7399, Fax: 806-742-2179, E-mail: jerry.dwyer@ttu.edu. *Application contact:* Brandi Stephens, Graduate Academic Advisor, 806-834-4554, Fax: 806-742-2179, E-mail: brandi.stephens@ttu.edu.
Website: www.educ.ttu.edu

Tufts University, Graduate School of Arts and Sciences, Department of Education, Program in Education, Medford, MA 02155. Offers educational studies (MA); elementary education (MAT); middle and secondary education (MAT); museum education (MA); secondary education (MA); STEM education (MS, PhD). *Program availability:* Part-time. *Degree requirements:* For master's, thesis optional. *Entrance requirements:* For master's, GRE General Test, portfolio (for art education only); for doctorate, GRE

Science Education

General Test, writing sample. Additional exam requirements/recommendations for international students: Required—TOEFL (minimum score 550 paper-based; 80 iBT), IELTS (minimum score 6.5). Electronic applications accepted. *Expenses:* Contact institution.

Tufts University, Graduate School of Arts and Sciences, Department of Physics and Astronomy, Medford, MA 02155. Offers astrophysics (MS, PhD); chemical physics (PhD); physics (MS, PhD); physics education (PhD). Terminal master's awarded for partial completion of doctoral program. *Degree requirements:* For master's, thesis optional; for doctorate, thesis/dissertation, oral qualifying exam. *Entrance requirements:* For master's and doctorate, GRE General Test. Additional exam requirements/recommendations for international students: Required—TOEFL (minimum score 550 paper-based; 80 iBT), IELTS (minimum score 6.5). Electronic applications accepted. *Expenses:* Contact institution.

Universidad Nacional Pedro Henriquez Urena, Graduate School, Santo Domingo, Dominican Republic. Offers agricultural diversity (MS), including horticultural/fruit production, tropical animal production; conservation of monuments and cultural assets (M Arch); ecology and environment (MS); environmental engineering (MEE); international relations (MA); natural resource management (MS); political science (MA); project optimization (MPM); project feasibility (MPM); project management (MPM); sanitation engineering (ME); science for teachers (MS); tropical Caribbean architecture (M Arch).

University at Buffalo, the State University of New York, Graduate School, Graduate School of Education, Department of Learning and Instruction, Buffalo, NY 14260. Offers biology education (Ed M, Certificate); chemistry education (Ed M, Certificate); childhood education (Ed M); childhood education with bilingual extension (Ed M); college teaching (Advanced Certificate); curriculum, instruction and the science of learning (PhD); early childhood education (Ed M); early childhood education with bilingual extension (Ed M); earth science education (Ed M, Certificate); education and technology (Ed M); education studies (Ed M); educational technology and new literacies (Certificate); educational technology and new literacies (Advanced Certificate); elementary education (Ed D); English education (Ed M, Certificate); English education studies (Ed M); English for speakers of other languages (Ed M); foreign and second language education (PhD); French education (Ed M, Certificate); German education (Ed M, Certificate); gifted education (Certificate); Latin education (Ed M, Certificate); literacy education studies (Ed M); literacy specialist (Ed M); literacy teaching and learning (Certificate); mathematics education (Ed M, Certificate); music education (Ed M, Certificate); music education studies (Ed M); music learning theory (Advanced Certificate); online education (Advanced Certificate); physics education (Ed M, Certificate); science and the public (Ed M); social studies education (Ed M, Certificate); Spanish education (Ed M, Certificate); special education (PhD); teaching English to speakers of other languages (Ed M). *Program availability:* Part-time, evening/weekend, 100% online. *Faculty:* 31 full-time (22 women), 41 part-time/adjunct (27 women). *Students:* 161 full-time (107 women), 369 part-time (260 women); includes 76 minority (26 Black or African American, non-Hispanic/Latino; 3 American Indian or Alaska Native, non-Hispanic/Latino; 30 Asian, non-Hispanic/Latino; 14 Hispanic/Latino; 3 Two or more races, non-Hispanic/Latino), 41 international. Average age 34. 368 applicants, 70% accepted, 179 enrolled. In 2018, 100 master's, 26 doctorates, 19 other advanced degrees awarded. *Degree requirements:* For master's, comprehensive exam; for doctorate, thesis/dissertation, research analysis exam, research experience. *Entrance requirements:* For master's, letters of reference; for doctorate, GRE General Test or MAT, interview, writing sample, letters of recommendation. Additional exam requirements/recommendations for international students: Required—TOEFL (minimum score 600 paper-based; 96 iBT), IELTS (minimum score 6.5), PTE (minimum score 55). *Application deadline:* For fall admission, 2/1 priority date for domestic and international students; for spring admission, 11/15 priority date for domestic students, 10/1 for international students. Applications are processed on a rolling basis. Application fee: $50. Electronic applications accepted. *Financial support:* In 2018–19, 42 fellowships (averaging $5,181 per year), 44 research assistantships with tuition reimbursements (averaging $10,908 per year) were awarded; teaching assistantships, career-related internships or fieldwork, Federal Work-Study, institutionally sponsored loans, scholarships/grants, tuition waivers (full and partial), and unspecified assistantships also available. Financial award application deadline: 2/28; financial award applicants required to submit FAFSA. *Faculty research:* Science assessment, foreign language teaching and learning, early learning, new literacies, gender and education. *Total annual research expenditures:* $413,233. *Unit head:* Dr. Julie Gorlewski, Department Chair, 716-645-2455, Fax: 716-645-3161, E-mail: jgorlews@buffalo.edu. *Application contact:* Renad Aref, Assistant Director of Admission Recruitment, 716-645-2110, Fax: 716-645-7937, E-mail: gseinfo@buffalo.edu.
Website: http://ed.buffalo.edu/teaching.html

The University of Akron, Graduate School, College of Education, Department of Curricular and Instructional Studies, Program in Adolescent to Young Adult Education, Akron, OH 44325. Offers chemistry (MS); chemistry and physics (MS); earth science (MS); earth science and chemistry (MS); earth science and physics (MS); integrated language arts (MS); integrated mathematics (MS); integrated social studies (MS); life science (MS); life science and chemistry (MS); life science and earth science (MS); life science and physics (MS); physics (MS). *Accreditation:* NCATE. *Degree requirements:* For master's, comprehensive exam. *Entrance requirements:* For master's, minimum GPA of 3.0. Additional exam requirements/recommendations for international students: Required—TOEFL (minimum score 79 iBT), IELTS (minimum score 6.5). Electronic applications accepted.

The University of Alabama in Huntsville, School of Graduate Studies, College of Education, Huntsville, AL 35899. Offers autism spectrum disorders (M Ed, Graduate Certificate); biology (MAT); chemistry (MAT); differentiated instruction in elementary education (M Ed); English language arts (MAT); English speakers of other languages (M Ed, MAT); history (MAT); mathematics (MAT); physics (MAT); reading education (M Ed); secondary education (M Ed). *Program availability:* Part-time. *Faculty:* 13 full-time (10 women). *Students:* 38 full-time (30 women), 39 part-time (37 women); includes 17 minority (10 Black or African American, non-Hispanic/Latino; 3 American Indian or Alaska Native, non-Hispanic/Latino; 2 Asian, non-Hispanic/Latino; 2 Two or more races, non-Hispanic/Latino). Average age 33. 47 applicants, 83% accepted, 29 enrolled. In 2018, 31 master's awarded. *Degree requirements:* For master's, comprehensive exam, thesis or alternative, oral and written. *Entrance requirements:* For master's, GRE General Test, minimum GPA of 3.0. Additional exam requirements/recommendations for international students: Required—TOEFL (minimum score 500 paper-based; 80 iBT), IELTS (minimum score 6.5). *Application deadline:* For fall admission, 7/15 priority date for domestic students, 4/1 priority date for international students; for spring admission, 11/30 priority date for domestic students, 9/1 priority date for international students. Applications are processed on a rolling basis. Application fee: $50. Electronic applications accepted. *Expenses: Tuition, area resident:* Full-time $10,632; part-time $412 per credit hour. Tuition, state resident: full-time $10,632. Tuition, nonresident: full-time $23,604; part-time $412 per credit hour. *Required fees:* $582; $582. Tuition and fees vary according to course load and program. *Financial support:* In 2018–19, 2 students received support, including 1 teaching assistantship with full tuition

reimbursement available (averaging $4,500 per year); career-related internships or fieldwork, Federal Work-Study, institutionally sponsored loans, scholarships/grants, health care benefits, tuition waivers (full and partial), and unspecified assistantships also available. Support available to part-time students. Financial award application deadline: 4/1; financial award applicants required to submit FAFSA. *Unit head:* Dr. Beth Nason Quick, Dean, 256-824-2325, E-mail: beth.quick@uah.edu. *Application contact:* Kim Gray, Graduate Studies Admissions Coordinator, 256-824-6002, Fax: 256-824-6405, E-mail: deangrad@uah.edu.
Website: http://www.uah.edu/education/

The University of Alabama in Huntsville, School of Graduate Studies, College of Science, Department of Biological Sciences, Huntsville, AL 35899. Offers biology (MS); biotechnology science and engineering (PhD); education (MS). *Program availability:* Part-time. *Faculty:* 14 full-time (2 women), 3 part-time/adjunct. *Students:* 43 full-time (30 women), 12 part-time (7 women); includes 8 minority (3 Black or African American, non-Hispanic/Latino; 2 Asian, non-Hispanic/Latino; 3 Hispanic/Latino), 11 international. Average age 33. 36 applicants, 64% accepted, 14 enrolled. In 2018, 2 master's, 5 doctorates awarded. *Degree requirements:* For master's, comprehensive exam, thesis or alternative, oral and written exams. *Entrance requirements:* For master's, GRE General Test, previous course work in biochemistry and organic chemistry, minimum GPA of 3.0. Additional exam requirements/recommendations for international students: Required—TOEFL (minimum score 550 paper-based; 80 iBT), IELTS (minimum score 6.5). *Application deadline:* For fall admission, 7/15 priority date for domestic students, 4/1 priority date for international students; for spring admission, 11/30 for domestic students, 9/1 priority date for international students. Applications are processed on a rolling basis. Application fee: $50. Electronic applications accepted. *Expenses: Tuition, area resident:* Full-time $10,632; part-time $412 per credit hour. Tuition, state resident: full-time $10,632. Tuition, nonresident: full-time $23,604; part-time $412 per credit hour. *Required fees:* $582; $582. Tuition and fees vary according to course load and program. *Financial support:* In 2018–19, 11 students received support, including 1 research assistantship with full tuition reimbursement available (averaging $2,500 per year), 10 teaching assistantships with full tuition reimbursements available (averaging $6,000 per year); career-related internships or fieldwork, Federal Work-Study, institutionally sponsored loans, scholarships/grants, health care benefits, tuition waivers (full and partial), and unspecified assistantships also available. Support available to part-time students. Financial award application deadline: 4/1; financial award applicants required to submit FAFSA. *Faculty research:* Physiology, microbiology, genomics and protemics, ecology and evolution, drug discovery. *Unit head:* Dr. Bruce W. Stallsmith, Associate Professor and Interim Chair, 256-824-6260, Fax: 256-824-6305, E-mail: stallsb@uah.edu. *Application contact:* Kim Gray, Graduate Studies Admissions Manager, 256-824-6002, Fax: 256-824-6405, E-mail: deangrad@uah.edu.
Website: http://www.uah.edu/science/departments/biology

The University of Alabama in Huntsville, School of Graduate Studies, College of Science, Department of Chemistry, Huntsville, AL 35899. Offers biotechnology science and engineering (PhD); chemistry (MS); education (MS); materials science (MS, PhD). *Program availability:* Part-time. *Faculty:* 5 full-time (3 women). *Students:* 14 full-time (5 women), 8 part-time (5 women); includes 5 minority (all Black or African American, non-Hispanic/Latino), 4 international. Average age 29. 26 applicants, 77% accepted, 9 enrolled. In 2018, 3 master's awarded. *Degree requirements:* For master's, comprehensive exam, thesis or alternative, oral and written exams. *Entrance requirements:* For master's, GRE General Test, minimum GPA of 3.0. Additional exam requirements/recommendations for international students: Required—TOEFL (minimum score 550 paper-based; 80 iBT), IELTS (minimum score 6.5). *Application deadline:* For fall admission, 7/15 priority date for domestic students, 4/1 priority date for international students; for spring admission, 11/30 priority date for domestic students, 9/1 priority date for international students. Applications are processed on a rolling basis. Application fee: $50. Electronic applications accepted. *Expenses: Tuition, area resident:* Full-time $10,632; part-time $412 per credit hour. Tuition, state resident: full-time $10,632. Tuition, nonresident: full-time $23,604; part-time $412 per credit hour. *Required fees:* $582; $582. Tuition and fees vary according to course load and program. *Financial support:* In 2018–19, 8 students received support, including 1 research assistantship with full tuition reimbursement available (averaging $6,000 per year), 7 teaching assistantships with full tuition reimbursements available (averaging $6,000 per year); career-related internships or fieldwork, Federal Work-Study, institutionally sponsored loans, scholarships/grants, health care benefits, tuition waivers (full and partial), and unspecified assistantships also available. Support available to part-time students. Financial award application deadline: 4/1; financial award applicants required to submit FAFSA. *Faculty research:* Natural products drug discovery, protein biochemistry, macromolecular biophysics, polymer synthesis, surface modification and analysis of materials. *Unit head:* Dr. John Foster, Professor and Chair, 256-824-6253, Fax: 256-824-6349, E-mail: john.foster@uah.edu. *Application contact:* Kim Gray, Graduate Studies Admissions Coordinator, 256-824-6002, Fax: 256-824-6405, E-mail: deangrad@uah.edu.
Website: http://chemistry.uah.edu

The University of Alabama in Huntsville, School of Graduate Studies, College of Science, Department of Physics, Huntsville, AL 35899. Offers education (MS); optics and photonics technology (MS); physics (MS, PhD). *Program availability:* Part-time. *Faculty:* 5 full-time, 2 part-time/adjunct. *Students:* 20 full-time (7 women), 12 part-time (1 woman); includes 2 minority (1 Black or African American, non-Hispanic/Latino; 1 Two or more races, non-Hispanic/Latino), 8 international. Average age 31. 22 applicants, 73% accepted, 6 enrolled. In 2018, 4 master's, 2 doctorates awarded. *Degree requirements:* For master's, comprehensive exam, thesis or alternative, oral and written exams; for doctorate, comprehensive exam, thesis/dissertation, oral and written exams. *Entrance requirements:* For master's and doctorate, GRE General Test, minimum GPA of 3.0. Additional exam requirements/recommendations for international students: Required—TOEFL (minimum score 550 paper-based; 80 iBT), IELTS (minimum score 6.5). *Application deadline:* For fall admission, 7/15 priority date for domestic students, 4/1 priority date for international students; for spring admission, 11/30 priority date for domestic students, 9/1 priority date for international students. Applications are processed on a rolling basis. Application fee: $50. Electronic applications accepted. *Expenses: Tuition, area resident:* Full-time $10,632; part-time $412 per credit hour. Tuition, state resident: full-time $10,632. Tuition, nonresident: full-time $23,604; part-time $412 per credit hour. *Required fees:* $582; $582. Tuition and fees vary according to course load and program. *Financial support:* In 2018–19, 18 students received support, including 7 research assistantships with full tuition reimbursements available (averaging $9,130 per year), 10 teaching assistantships with full tuition reimbursements available (averaging $7,444 per year); career-related internships or fieldwork, Federal Work-Study, institutionally sponsored loans, scholarships/grants, health care benefits, and unspecified assistantships also available. Support available to part-time students. Financial award application deadline: 4/1; financial award applicants required to submit FAFSA. *Faculty research:* Space and solar physics, computational physics, optics, high energy astrophysics. *Unit head:* Dr. James A. Miller, Chair, 256-824-2483, Fax: 256-824-6873, E-mail: millerja@uah.edu. *Application contact:* Kim Gray, Graduate Studies Admissions Coordinator, 256-824-6002, Fax: 256-824-6405, E-mail: deangrad@uah.edu.
Website: http://physics.uah.edu/

University of Arkansas at Pine Bluff, School of Education, Pine Bluff, AR 71601-2799. Offers elementary education (M Ed); secondary education (M Ed), including English education, mathematics education, science education, social studies education; teaching (MAT). *Accreditation:* NCATE. *Program availability:* Part-time, evening/weekend. *Degree requirements:* For master's, comprehensive exam. *Entrance requirements:* For master's, GRE, minimum GPA of 2.75, NTE or Standard Arkansas Teaching Certificate. *Faculty research:* Teacher certification, accreditation, assessment, standards, portfolio development, rehabilitation, technology.

The University of British Columbia, Faculty of Education, Department of Curriculum and Pedagogy, Vancouver, BC V6T 1Z4, Canada. Offers art education (M Ed, MA); curriculum studies (M Ed, MA, PhD); home economics education (M Ed, MA); mathematics education (M Ed, MA); media and technology studies education (M Ed, MA); music education (M Ed, MA); physical education (M Ed, MA); science education (M Ed, MA); social studies education (M Ed, MA). *Program availability:* Part-time, online learning. *Degree requirements:* For master's, thesis (MA); for doctorate, comprehensive exam, thesis/dissertation. *Entrance requirements:* Additional exam requirements/recommendations for international students: Required—TOEFL, IELTS. Electronic applications accepted. *Expenses:* Contact institution. *Faculty research:* School subjects, teaching and learning.

University of California, Berkeley, Graduate Division, School of Education, Group in Science and Mathematics Education, Berkeley, CA 94720. Offers PhD, MA/Credential. Electronic applications accepted.

University of California, Berkeley, Graduate Division, School of Education, Programs in Education, Berkeley, CA 94720. Offers development in mathematics and science (MA); education in mathematics, science, and technology (MA, PhD); human development and education (MA, PhD); leadership education (MA); special education (PhD); teacher education (MA); MA/Credential; PhD/Credential; PhD/MA. Terminal master's awarded for partial completion of doctoral program. *Degree requirements:* For master's, exam or thesis; for doctorate, thesis/dissertation, oral qualifying exam. *Entrance requirements:* For master's and doctorate, GRE General Test, minimum GPA of 3.0 during last 2 years of undergraduate course work. Electronic applications accepted. *Faculty research:* Human development, social and moral educational psychology, developmental teacher preparation.

University of California, San Diego, Graduate Division, Program in Mathematics and Science Education, La Jolla, CA 92093. Offers PhD. Program offered jointly with San Diego State University. *Students:* 1 full-time (0 women), 14 part-time (9 women). In 2018, 4 doctorates awarded. *Degree requirements:* For doctorate, thesis/dissertation, teaching practicum. *Entrance requirements:* For doctorate, GRE General Test, minimum GPA of 3.25. Additional exam requirements/recommendations for international students: Required—TOEFL (minimum score 550 paper-based; 80 iBT), IELTS (minimum score 7). Electronic applications accepted. *Financial support:* Scholarships/grants and stipends available. Financial award applicants required to submit FAFSA. *Faculty research:* Effective teaching of rational numbers, teacher development, development of number sense and estimation. *Unit head:* Gabriele Wienhausen, Chair, 858-534-3105, E-mail: gwienhausen@ucsd.edu. *Application contact:* Sherry Seethaler, Graduate Coordinator, 858-534-4656, E-mail: sseethaler@ucsd.edu. Website: http://sci.sdsu.edu/CRMSE/msed/

University of Central Florida, College of Community Innovation and Education, School of Teacher Education, Program in K-8 Mathematics and Science Education, Orlando, FL 32816. Offers M Ed, Certificate. *Accreditation:* NCATE. *Program availability:* Part-time. *Students:* 1 full-time (0 women), 50 part-time (46 women); includes 19 minority (8 Black or African American, non-Hispanic/Latino; 11 Hispanic/Latino). Average age 36. 2 applicants, 100% accepted, 1 enrolled. In 2018, 7 master's awarded. *Entrance requirements:* Additional exam requirements/recommendations for international students: Required—TOEFL. *Application deadline:* For summer admission, 4/15 for domestic students. Application fee: $30. Electronic applications accepted. *Financial support:* In 2018–19, 1 student received support, including 2 research assistantships with partial tuition reimbursements available (averaging $5,702 per year). Financial award application deadline: 3/1; financial award applicants required to submit FAFSA. *Unit head:* Dr. Malcolm Butler, Program Coordinator, 407-823-3272, E-mail: malcolm.butler@ucf.edu. *Application contact:* Associate Director, Graduate Admissions, 407-823-2766, Fax: 407-823-6442, E-mail: gradadmissions@ucf.edu. Website: http://education.ucf.edu/mathed/

University of Central Florida, College of Community Innovation and Education, School of Teacher Education, Program in Teacher Education, Orlando, FL 32816. Offers MAT. *Accreditation:* NCATE. *Program availability:* Part-time, evening/weekend. *Students:* 130 full-time (94 women), 96 part-time (79 women); includes 64 minority (25 Black or African American, non-Hispanic/Latino; 12 Asian, non-Hispanic/Latino; 23 Hispanic/Latino; 4 Two or more races, non-Hispanic/Latino), 23 international. Average age 33. 214 applicants, 52% accepted, 75 enrolled. In 2018, 41 master's awarded. *Entrance requirements:* For master's, Florida Teacher Certification Examination/General Knowledge Test or GRE General Test. Additional exam requirements/recommendations for international students: Required—TOEFL. *Application deadline:* For spring admission, 12/1 for domestic students; for summer admission, 4/15 for domestic students. Application fee: $30. Electronic applications accepted. *Financial support:* In 2018–19, 80 students received support, including 28 fellowships (averaging $5,518 per year), 41 research assistantships (averaging $8,487 per year), 58 teaching assistantships (averaging $11,573 per year); career-related internships or fieldwork, Federal Work-Study, institutionally sponsored loans, tuition waivers (partial), and unspecified assistantships also available. Financial award application deadline: 3/1; financial award applicants required to submit FAFSA. *Unit head:* Dr. Michael Hynes, Director, 407-823-2005, E-mail: mychael.hynes@ucf.edu. *Application contact:* Associate Director, Graduate Admissions, 407-823-2766, Fax: 407-823-6442, E-mail: gradadmissions@ucf.edu. Website: http://www.graduatecatalog.ucf.edu/programs/program.aspx?id-9727&program-Teacher%20Education%20MAT

University of Chicago, Division of the Social Sciences, Committee on Conceptual and Historical Studies of Science, Chicago, IL 60637. Offers PhD. *Degree requirements:* For doctorate, one foreign language, thesis/dissertation, 2 oral exams. *Entrance requirements:* For doctorate, GRE General Test, 3 letters of recommendation, statement of purpose, transcripts, resume or curriculum vitae, writing sample (dependent on department). Additional exam requirements/recommendations for international students: Required—TOEFL (minimum score 104 iBT), IELTS (minimum score 7). Electronic applications accepted.

University of Colorado Denver, School of Education and Human Development, Program in Educational Leadership and Innovation, Denver, CO 80217. Offers educational studies and research (PhD), including administrative leadership and policy, early childhood special education, math education, research, assessment and evaluation, science education, urban ecologies. *Program availability:* Part-time, evening/weekend. *Degree requirements:* For doctorate, comprehensive exam, thesis/dissertation, 75 credit hours (for PhD). *Entrance requirements:* For doctorate, GRE or equivalent, resume or curriculum vitae, letters of recommendation, master's degree or

equivalent, completion of basic or advanced statistics course with minimum B grade. Additional exam requirements/recommendations for international students: Required—TOEFL (minimum score 537 paper-based; 75 iBT); Recommended—IELTS (minimum score 6.5). Electronic applications accepted. *Expenses:* Tuition, state resident: full-time $6786; part-time $337 per credit hour. Tuition, nonresident: full-time $22,590; part-time $1255 per credit hour. *Required fees:* $1231; $137 per credit hour. Tuition and fees vary according to program and reciprocity agreements. *Faculty research:* Administrative leadership and policy studies, early childhood education, research in diversity, paraprofessionals in education, urban schools lab.

University of Colorado Denver, School of Education and Human Development, Program in Education and Human Development, Denver, CO 80217. Offers administrative leadership and policy (PhD); assessment (MA); early childhood special education/early childhood education (PhD); family science and human development (PhD); human development and family relations (MA); learning (MA); mathematics education (PhD); research and evaluation methods (MA); research, assessment and evaluation (PhD); science education (PhD); urban ecologies (PhD). MA program also offered in partnership with Boulder Journey School, Friends School and Stanley British Primary School. *Program availability:* Part-time, evening/weekend. *Degree requirements:* For master's, comprehensive exam, 9 hours of core courses embedded within a minimum of 36 to 38 hours of relevant coursework, including an educational psychology practicum, independent study project or thesis (recommended). *Entrance requirements:* For master's, GRE if undergraduate GPA below 2.75, resume, three letters of recommendation, transcripts. Additional exam requirements/recommendations for international students: Required—TOEFL (minimum score 537 paper-based; 75 iBT); Recommended—IELTS (minimum score 6.5). Electronic applications accepted. *Expenses:* Contact institution. *Faculty research:* Crisis response and intervention, school violence prevention, immigrant experience, educational environments for English language learners, culturally competent assessment and intervention, child and youth suicide.

University of Colorado Denver, School of Education and Human Development, Teacher Education Programs, Denver, CO 80217. Offers elementary linguistically diverse education (MA); elementary math and science education (MA); elementary math education (MA); elementary reading and writing (MA); elementary science education (MA); secondary English education (MA); secondary linguistically diverse education (MA); secondary math education (MA); secondary reading and writing (MA); secondary science education (MA); special education (MA). *Accreditation:* NCATE. *Program availability:* Part-time, evening/weekend. *Degree requirements:* For master's, comprehensive exam. *Entrance requirements:* For master's, GRE or MAT (for those with GPA below 2.75), transcripts, resume, letters of recommendation. Additional exam requirements/recommendations for international students: Required—TOEFL (minimum score 537 paper-based; 75 iBT); Recommended—IELTS (minimum score 6.5). Electronic applications accepted. *Expenses:* Tuition, state resident: full-time $6786; part-time $337 per credit hour. Tuition, nonresident: full-time $22,590; part-time $1255 per credit hour. *Required fees:* $1231; $137 per credit hour. Tuition and fees vary according to program and reciprocity agreements. *Faculty research:* Linguistically diverse education/ESL, elementary reading and writing, elementary teacher education, secondary teacher education, special education.

University of Connecticut, Graduate School, Neag School of Education, Department of Curriculum and Instruction, Program in Science Education, Storrs, CT 06269. Offers MA, PhD. *Accreditation:* NCATE. Terminal master's awarded for partial completion of doctoral program. *Degree requirements:* For master's, comprehensive exam, thesis or alternative; for doctorate, thesis/dissertation. *Entrance requirements:* For doctorate, GRE General Test. Additional exam requirements/recommendations for international students: Required—TOEFL (minimum score 550 paper-based). Electronic applications accepted.

The University of Findlay, Office of Graduate Admissions, Findlay, OH 45840-3653. Offers applied security and analytics (MSAS); athletic training (MAT); business (MBA), including certified management accountant, certified public accountant, health care management, hospitality management; education (MA Ed, Ed D), including children's literature (MA Ed); curriculum and teaching (MA Ed), education (MA Ed), educational administration (MA Ed), human resource development (MA Ed), mathematics (MA Ed), reading (MA Ed), science education (MA Ed), superintendent (Ed D), teaching (Ed D), technology (MA Ed); environmental, safety, and health management (MSEM); health informatics (MS); occupational therapy (MOT); pharmacy (Pharm D); physical therapy (DPT); physician assistant (MPA); rhetoric and writing (MA); teaching English to speakers of other languages (TESOL) and applied linguistics (MA). *Program availability:* Part-time, evening/weekend, 100% online, blended/hybrid learning. *Degree requirements:* For master's, comprehensive exam (for some programs), thesis (for some programs), cumulative project, capstone project; for doctorate, thesis/dissertation (for some programs). *Entrance requirements:* For master's, GRE/GMAT, bachelor's degree from accredited institution, minimum undergraduate GPA of 2.5 in last 64 hours of course work; for doctorate, GRE, MAT, minimum cumulative GPA of 3.0. Additional exam requirements/recommendations for international students: Required—TOEFL (minimum score 79 iBT), IELTS (minimum score 7), PTE (minimum score 61). Electronic applications accepted.

University of Florida, Graduate School, College of Education, School of Teaching and Learning, Gainesville, FL 32611. Offers curriculum and instruction (M Ed, MAE, Ed D, PhD, Ed S); elementary education (M Ed, MAE); English education (M Ed, MAE); mathematics education (M Ed, MAE); reading education (M Ed, MAE); science education (M Ed, MAE); social studies education (M Ed, MAE). *Accreditation:* NCATE. *Program availability:* Part-time, evening/weekend, online learning. Terminal master's awarded for partial completion of doctoral program. *Degree requirements:* For master's, comprehensive exam (for some programs), thesis (for some programs); for doctorate, comprehensive exam (for some programs), thesis/dissertation (for some programs). *Entrance requirements:* For master's and doctorate, GRE General Test, minimum GPA of 3.0; for Ed S, GRE General Test. Additional exam requirements/recommendations for international students: Required—TOEFL (minimum score 550 paper-based; 80 iBT), IELTS (minimum score 6). Electronic applications accepted. *Faculty research:* STEM education; curriculum; teaching and teacher education; languages and literacy; schools, culture, and society; theories and processes of learning.

University of Georgia, College of Education, Department of Mathematics and Science Education, Athens, GA 30602. Offers mathematics education (M Ed, PhD, Ed S).

University of Illinois at Chicago, Program in Learning Sciences, Chicago, IL 60607-7128. Offers PhD.

University of Illinois at Urbana–Champaign, Graduate College, College of Engineering, Department of Physics, Champaign, IL 61820. Offers physics (MS, PhD); teaching of physics (MS).

University of Illinois at Urbana–Champaign, Graduate College, College of Liberal Arts and Sciences, School of Chemical Sciences, Department of Chemistry, Champaign, IL 61820. Offers astrochemistry (PhD); chemical physics (PhD); chemistry (MA, MS, PhD); teaching of chemistry (MS); MS/JD; MS/MBA.

Science Education

University of Illinois at Urbana–Champaign, Graduate College, College of Liberal Arts and Sciences, School of Earth, Society and Environment, Department of Geology, Champaign, IL 61820. Offers geology (MS, PhD); teaching of earth sciences (MS). Terminal master's awarded for partial completion of doctoral program.

University of Indianapolis, Graduate Programs, School of Education, Indianapolis, IN 46227-3697. Offers art education (MAT); biology (MAT); chemistry (MAT); curriculum and instruction (MA); earth sciences (MAT); education (MA, MAT); educational leadership (MA); elementary education (MA); English (MAT); French (MAT); math (MAT); physical education (MAT); physics (MAT); secondary education (MA), including art education, education, English education, social studies education; social studies (MAT); Spanish (MAT). *Accreditation:* NCATE. *Program availability:* Part-time, evening/weekend. *Entrance requirements:* For master's, GRE Subject Test, PRAXIS I, minimum GPA of 2.5, 3 letters of recommendation, interview. Additional exam requirements/recommendations for international students: Required—TOEFL (minimum score 550 paper-based). *Faculty research:* Assessment of teacher education, perceptions of prospective teachers by parents.

The University of Iowa, Graduate College, College of Education, Department of Teaching and Learning, Program in Education, Iowa City, IA 52242-1316. Offers art education (MA); developmental reading (MA); elementary education (MA); English education (MA, MAT); foreign and second language education (MAT); foreign language education (MA); foreign language/ESL education (PhD); language, literacy and culture (PhD); mathematics education (MA, MAT, PhD); music education (MM, PhD); science education (MA); secondary education (MA); social studies (MA, PhD). *Degree requirements:* For master's, thesis optional, exam; for doctorate, comprehensive exam, thesis/dissertation. *Entrance requirements:* For master's and doctorate, GRE General Test, minimum GPA of 3.0. Additional exam requirements/recommendations for international students: Required—TOEFL (minimum score 550 paper-based; 81 iBT). Electronic applications accepted.

University of Lynchburg, Graduate Studies, M Ed Program in Science Education, Lynchburg, VA 24501-3199. Offers science education (M Ed), including earth science, math. *Program availability:* Part-time, evening/weekend. *Degree requirements:* For master's, comprehensive exam. *Entrance requirements:* For master's, GRE, minimum GPA of 3.0 (preferred), official transcripts (bachelor's, others as relevant), three letters of recommendation, career goals statement. Additional exam requirements/recommendations for international students: Required—TOEFL (minimum score 550 paper-based; 80 iBT), IELTS (minimum score 6). Electronic applications accepted. Application fee is waived when completed online. *Expenses:* Contact institution.

University of Maryland, Baltimore County, The Graduate School, College of Arts, Humanities and Social Sciences, Department of Education, Master of Arts in Education Program, Baltimore, MD 21250. Offers K-8 mathematics instructional leadership (MAE); K-8 science education (MAE); K-8 STEM education (MAE); secondary mathematics education (MAE); secondary science education (MAE); secondary STEM education (MAE). *Program availability:* Part-time-only, evening/weekend, 100% online, blended/hybrid learning. *Degree requirements:* For master's, comprehensive exam (for some programs), thesis (for some programs). Electronic applications accepted. *Expenses:* Contact institution.

University of Maryland, Baltimore County, The Graduate School, College of Arts, Humanities and Social Sciences, Department of Education, Program in Teaching, Baltimore, MD 21250. Offers early childhood education (MAT); elementary education (MAT); teaching (MAT), including art, biology, chemistry, choral music, classical foreign language, dance, earth/space science, English, instrumental music, mathematics, modern foreign language, physical science, physics, social studies, theatre. *Program availability:* Part-time, evening/weekend. *Degree requirements:* For master's, comprehensive exam (for some programs), thesis (for some programs). *Entrance requirements:* For master's, PRAXIS Core Examination or GRE (minimum score of 1000), minimum GPA of 3.0. Additional exam requirements/recommendations for international students: Required—TOEFL. Electronic applications accepted. *Faculty research:* STEM teacher education, culturally sensitive pedagogy, ESOL/bilingual education, early childhood education, language, literacy and culture.

University of Massachusetts Amherst, Graduate School, College of Education, Program in Education, Amherst, MA 01003. Offers bilingual, English as a second language, and multicultural education (M Ed, Ed S); child study and early education (M Ed); children, families and schools (Ed D, Ed S); early childhood and elementary teacher education (M Ed); educational leadership (M Ed); educational policy and leadership (Ed D); higher education (M Ed); international education (M Ed); language, literacy and culture (Ed D); learning, media and technology (M Ed, Ed S); mathematics, science, and learning technologies (Ed D); reading and writing (M Ed); research, educational measurement and psychometrics (Ed D); school counselor education (M Ed, Ed S); school psychology (Ed S); science education (Ed S); secondary teacher education (M Ed); social justice education (M Ed, Ed D, Ed S); special education (M Ed, Ed D, Ed S); teacher education and school improvement (Ed D, Ed S). *Accreditation:* NCATE. *Program availability:* Part-time, online learning. Terminal master's awarded for partial completion of doctoral program. *Degree requirements:* For doctorate, comprehensive exam, thesis/dissertation. *Entrance requirements:* Additional exam requirements/recommendations for international students: Required—TOEFL (minimum score 550 paper-based; 80 iBT), IELTS (minimum score 6.5). Electronic applications accepted.

University of Massachusetts Dartmouth, Graduate School, College of Arts and Sciences, School of Education, Department of STEM Education and Teacher Development, North Dartmouth, MA 02747-2300. Offers English as a second language (Postbaccalaureate Certificate); mathematics education (PhD); middle school education (MAT); secondary school education (MAT). *Program availability:* Part-time. *Faculty:* 9 full-time (6 women), 3 part-time/adjunct (2 women). *Students:* 21 full-time (18 women), 100 part-time (53 women); includes 20 minority (3 Black or African American, non-Hispanic/Latino; 2 Asian, non-Hispanic/Latino; 11 Hispanic/Latino; 4 Two or more races, non-Hispanic/Latino), 3 international. Average age 34. 63 applicants, 90% accepted, 45 enrolled. In 2018, 68 master's, 1 doctorate, 1 other advanced degree awarded. *Degree requirements:* For doctorate, thesis/dissertation. *Entrance requirements:* For master's, Statement of Purpose, Resume, Official Transcripts, copy of MA MTELs, 2 letters of recommendation, Proof of License (for Professional Licensure Program); for doctorate, GRE Score, Statement of Purpose, Resume, Official transcripts, 3 letters of recommendation; for Postbaccalaureate Certificate, Statement of Purpose, Resume, Official Transcripts, 2 letters of recommendation, MTEL Score Report. Additional exam requirements/recommendations for international students: Required—TOEFL (minimum score 550 paper-based; 79 iBT), IELTS (minimum score 6.5). *Application deadline:* For fall admission, 1/15 priority date for domestic students, 12/15 priority date for international students; for spring admission, 12/15 priority date for domestic students, 11/15 priority date for international students. Application fee: $60. Electronic applications accepted. *Financial support:* In 2018–19, 1 fellowship (averaging $18,000 per year), 3 research assistantships (averaging $10,897 per year), 6 teaching assistantships (averaging $8,017 per year) were awarded; tuition waivers (full) and doctoral support also available. Financial award application deadline: 3/1; financial award applicants required to submit FAFSA. *Faculty research:* Mindfulness in education, literacies,

assessment of teacher knowledge, curriculum tools for supporting mathematics learning. *Total annual research expenditures:* $1.8 million. *Unit head:* Traci Almeida, Coordinator of Graduate Admissions and Licensure, 508-999-8098, Fax: 508-910-8183, E-mail: talmeida@umassd.edu. *Application contact:* Scott Webster, Director of Graduate Studies and Admissions, 508-999-8604, Fax: 508-999-8183, E-mail: graduate@umassd.edu.
Website: http://www.umassd.edu/cas/schoolofeducation/departments/stemeducationandteacherdevelopment/

University of Memphis, Graduate School, College of Education, Department of Instruction and Curriculum Leadership, Memphis, TN 38152. Offers advanced studies in teaching and learning (M Ed); applied behavior analysis (Graduate Certificate); autism studies (Graduate Certificate); early childhood education (MAT, MS, Ed D); elementary education (MAT); instruction and curriculum (MS, Ed D); instruction design and technology (MS, Ed D); instructional design and technology (Graduate Certificate); literacy, leadership, and coaching (Graduate Certificate); reading (MS, Ed D); school library information specialist (Graduate Certificate); secondary education (MAT); special education (MAT, MS, Ed D); STEM teacher leadership (Graduate Certificate); urban education (Graduate Certificate). *Accreditation:* NCATE (one or more programs are accredited). *Program availability:* Part-time. *Students:* 62 full-time (45 women), 412 part-time (326 women); includes 209 minority (179 Black or African American, non-Hispanic/Latino; 1 American Indian or Alaska Native, non-Hispanic/Latino; 5 Asian, non-Hispanic/Latino; 17 Hispanic/Latino; 7 Two or more races, non-Hispanic/Latino), 4 international. Average age 35. 195 applicants, 91% accepted, 143 enrolled. In 2018, 122 master's, 13 doctorates, 29 other advanced degrees awarded. Terminal master's awarded for partial completion of doctoral program. *Degree requirements:* For master's, comprehensive exam, thesis or alternative; for doctorate, comprehensive exam, thesis/dissertation. *Entrance requirements:* For master's, GRE General Test, PRAXIS, minimum GPA of 2.5, letters of reference; for doctorate, GRE General Test, GRE Subject Test, 2 years of teaching experience, letters of reference, statement of purpose, interview. Additional exam requirements/recommendations for international students: Required—TOEFL (minimum score 550 paper-based; 79 iBT). *Application deadline:* For fall admission, 4/1 priority date for domestic students; for spring admission, 10/1 priority date for domestic students; for summer admission, 2/1 priority date for domestic students. Applications are processed on a rolling basis. Application fee: $35 ($60 for international students). Electronic applications accepted. *Expenses: Tuition, area resident:* Full-time $10,240; part-time $503 per credit hour. Tuition, state resident: Full-time $10,464. Tuition, nonresident: full-time $20,224; part-time $991 per credit hour. *Required fees:* $850; $106 per credit hour. *Financial support:* Research assistantships with full tuition reimbursements, teaching assistantships with full tuition reimbursements, career-related internships or fieldwork, Federal Work-Study, institutionally sponsored loans, scholarships/grants, traineeships, and unspecified assistantships available. Support available to part-time students. Financial award application deadline: 2/1; financial award applicants required to submit FAFSA. *Faculty research:* Effective urban teachers, preparation and retention of urban teachers, technology utilization in schools, field-based teacher preparation programs, effective use of online instruction. *Unit head:* Dr. Christian Mueller, Chair, 901-678-2365, E-mail: cemuellr@memphis.edu. *Application contact:* Dr. Lee Allen, Director of Graduate Programs, 901-678-4073, E-mail: allenlee@memphis.edu.
Website: http://www.memphis.edu/icl/

University of Miami, Graduate School, School of Education and Human Development, Department of Teaching and Learning, Program in Teaching and Learning, Coral Gables, FL 33124. Offers language and literacy learning in multilingual settings (PhD); science, technology, engineering and mathematics (stem) (PhD); special education (PhD). *Faculty:* 14 full-time (10 women), 9 part-time/adjunct (all women). *Students:* 18 full-time (12 women); includes 8 minority (2 Black or African American, non-Hispanic/Latino; 1 Asian, non-Hispanic/Latino; 4 Hispanic/Latino; 1 Two or more races, non-Hispanic/Latino), 6 international. Average age 36. 15 applicants, 33% accepted, 3 enrolled. In 2018, 4 doctorates awarded. *Degree requirements:* For doctorate, thesis/dissertation, electronic portfolio. *Entrance requirements:* For doctorate, GRE General Test. Additional exam requirements/recommendations for international students: Required—TOEFL (minimum score 550 paper-based; 80 iBT); Recommended—IELTS (minimum score 6.5). *Application deadline:* For fall admission, 6/30 for domestic students, 10/1 for international students. Application fee: $75. Electronic applications accepted. *Financial support:* Fellowships, research assistantships, teaching assistantships, health care benefits, tuition waivers (full and partial), and unspecified assistantships available. Financial award application deadline: 3/1; financial award applicants required to submit FAFSA. *Faculty research:* Teacher education, multicultural education, special education, second language acquisition, math and science education. *Unit head:* Dr. Matthew Deroo, Assistant Professor and Program Director, 305-284-5217, Fax: 305-284-6998, E-mail: deroomat@miami.edu. *Application contact:* Lois Heffernan, Graduate Admission Coordinator, 305-284-2167, Fax: 305-284-9395, E-mail: lheffernan@miami.edu.
Website: http://www.education.miami.edu

University of Minnesota, Twin Cities Campus, Graduate School, College of Education and Human Development, Department of Curriculum and Instruction, Program in Teaching, Minneapolis, MN 55455-0213. Offers teaching (M Ed), including arts in education, elementary education, English education, mathematics, science, second language education, social studies. *Students:* 249 full-time (182 women), 101 part-time (59 women); includes 57 minority (5 Black or African American, non-Hispanic/Latino; 16 Asian, non-Hispanic/Latino; 25 Hispanic/Latino; 11 Two or more races, non-Hispanic/Latino), 12 international. Average age 28. 383 applicants, 79% accepted, 261 enrolled. In 2018, 292 master's awarded. Application fee: $75 ($95 for international students). *Unit head:* Dr. Mark Vagle, Chair, 612-625-4006, Fax: 612-624-8277, E-mail: mvagle@umn.edu. *Application contact:* Dr. Mark Vagle, Chair, 612-625-4006, Fax: 612-624-8277, E-mail: mvagle@umn.edu.
Website: http://www.cehd.umn.edu/ci/

University of Missouri, Office of Research and Graduate Studies, College of Education, Department of Learning, Teaching and Curriculum, Columbia, MO 65211. Offers agricultural education (M Ed, PhD, Ed S); art education (M Ed, PhD, Ed S); business and office education (M Ed, PhD, Ed S); early childhood education (M Ed, PhD, Ed S); elementary education (M Ed, PhD, Ed S); English education (M Ed, PhD, Ed S); foreign language education (M Ed, PhD, Ed S); health education and promotion (M Ed, PhD); learning and instruction (M Ed); marketing education (M Ed, PhD, Ed S); mathematics education (M Ed, PhD, Ed S); music education (M Ed, PhD, Ed S); reading education (M Ed, PhD, Ed S); science education (M Ed, PhD, Ed S); social studies education (M Ed, PhD, Ed S); vocational education (M Ed, PhD, Ed S). *Program availability:* Part-time. Terminal master's awarded for partial completion of doctoral program. *Entrance requirements:* For master's and Ed S, GRE General Test or MAT, minimum GPA of 3.0; for doctorate, GRE General Test, minimum GPA of 3.0. Additional exam requirements/recommendations for international students: Required—TOEFL.

University of Nebraska at Kearney, College of Natural and Social Sciences, Department of Biology, Kearney, NE 68849. Offers biology (MS); science/math education (MA Ed). *Program availability:* Part-time, evening/weekend, 100% online.

Degree requirements: For master's, comprehensive exam, thesis optional. *Entrance requirements:* For master's, GRE (for thesis option and for online program applicants if undergraduate GPA is below 2.75), letter of interest. Additional exam requirements/recommendations for international students: Recommended—TOEFL (minimum score 550 paper-based; 79 iBT), IELTS (minimum score 6.5). Electronic applications accepted. *Expenses:* Contact institution. *Faculty research:* Pollution injury, molecular biology-viral gene expression, prairie range condition modeling, evolution of symbiotic nitrogen fixation, geographic information systems (GIS), molecular genetics of aging.

University of Nebraska at Omaha, Graduate Studies, College of Arts and Sciences, Department of Biology, Omaha, NE 68182. Offers biology (MS); business for bioscientists (Certificate). *Program availability:* Part-time. *Degree requirements:* For master's, comprehensive exam (for some programs), thesis (for some programs). *Entrance requirements:* For master's, GRE General Test, minimum GPA of 3.0, transcripts, 24 undergraduate biology hours, 3 letters of recommendation, statement of purpose. Additional exam requirements/recommendations for international students: Required—TOEFL, IELTS, PTE. Electronic applications accepted.

University of New Hampshire, Graduate School, College of Engineering and Physical Sciences, Department of Chemistry, Durham, NH 03824. Offers chemistry (MS, PhD); chemistry education (PhD). Terminal master's awarded for partial completion of doctoral program. *Entrance requirements:* For master's and doctorate, GRE. Additional exam requirements/recommendations for international students: Required—TOEFL (minimum score 550 paper-based; 80 iBT). Electronic applications accepted.

University of New Mexico, School of Medicine, Program in University Science Teaching, Albuquerque, NM 87131-2039. Offers Certificate.

The University of North Carolina at Chapel Hill, Graduate School, School of Education, Program in Secondary Education, Chapel Hill, NC 27599. Offers English (Grades 9-12) (MAT); English as a second language (MAT); French (Grades K-12) (MAT); German (Grades K-12) (MAT); Japanese (Grades K-12) (MAT); Latin (Grades 9-12) (MAT); mathematics (Grades 9-12) (MAT); music (Grades K-12) (MAT); science (Grades 9-12) (MAT); social studies (Grades 9-12) (MAT); Spanish (Grades K-12) (MAT). *Accreditation:* NCATE. *Degree requirements:* For master's, comprehensive exam. *Entrance requirements:* For master's, GRE General Test, minimum GPA of 3.0 during last 2 years of undergraduate course work. Additional exam requirements/recommendations for international students: Required—TOEFL (minimum score 550 paper-based). Electronic applications accepted.

The University of North Carolina at Greensboro, Graduate School, School of Education, Department of Teacher Education and Higher Education, Greensboro, NC 27412-5001. Offers college teaching and adult learning (Certificate); curriculum and instruction (M Ed), including chemistry education, elementary education, English as a second language, French education, instructional technology, mathematics education, middle grades education, reading education, science education, social studies education, Spanish education; curriculum and teaching (PhD), including higher education, teacher education and development; English as a second language (Certificate); higher education (M Ed); supervision (M Ed). *Accreditation:* NCATE. *Program availability:* Part-time. *Degree requirements:* For doctorate, thesis/dissertation. *Entrance requirements:* For master's and doctorate, GRE General Test. Additional exam requirements/recommendations for international students: Required—TOEFL. Electronic applications accepted. *Faculty research:* Community college literacy program, middle school mathematics/computer mathematics.

The University of North Carolina at Pembroke, The Graduate School, Department of Biology, Pembroke, NC 28372-1510. Offers science education (MA, MAT). *Program availability:* Part-time, evening/weekend. *Entrance requirements:* For master's, GRE or MAT, minimum GPA of 3.0 in major or 2.5 overall.

University of Northern Colorado, Graduate School, College of Natural and Health Sciences, Department of Chemistry and Biochemistry, Greeley, CO 80639. Offers chemical education (MS, PhD); chemistry (MS). *Program availability:* Part-time. *Degree requirements:* For master's, comprehensive exam, thesis or alternative; for doctorate, comprehensive exam, thesis/dissertation. *Entrance requirements:* For master's, 3 letters of reference; for doctorate, GRE General Test, 3 letters of reference. Electronic applications accepted.

University of Northern Colorado, Graduate School, College of Natural and Health Sciences, School of Biology, Program in Biology Education, Greeley, CO 80639. Offers PhD. *Program availability:* Part-time. *Degree requirements:* For doctorate, comprehensive exam, thesis/dissertation. *Entrance requirements:* For doctorate, GRE General Test, 3 letters of recommendation. Electronic applications accepted.

University of Northern Iowa, Graduate College, College of Humanities, Arts and Sciences, MA Program in Science Education, Cedar Falls, IA 50614. Offers earth science education (MA); physics education (MA); science education (MA). *Degree requirements:* For master's, comprehensive exam (for some programs), thesis or alternative. *Entrance requirements:* For master's, minimum GPA of 3.0. Additional exam requirements/recommendations for international students: Required—TOEFL (minimum score 500 paper-based; 61 iBT). Electronic applications accepted.

University of North Georgia, Program in Middle Grades Math and Science, Dahlonega, GA 30597. Offers M Ed. *Program availability:* Part-time, evening/weekend, online only, 100% online. *Degree requirements:* For master's, teaching practicum. *Entrance requirements:* For master's, baccalaureate degree from regionally-accredited, four-year institution with minimum cumulative GPA of 2.75; employment as teacher in middle grades classroom working with students at least 20 hours per week; clear/renewable teaching certificate in middle grades math or science in the state of Georgia or equivalent. Additional exam requirements/recommendations for international students: Required—TOEFL (minimum score 550 paper-based; 79 iBT), IELTS (minimum score 6.5). Electronic applications accepted. *Expenses:* Contact institution.

University of Oklahoma, Jeannine Rainbolt College of Education, Department of Instructional Leadership and Academic Curriculum, Norman, OK 73072. Offers instructional leadership and academic curriculum (M Ed, PhD), including biomedical education (PhD), early childhood education, elementary education, English education, instructional leadership, mathematics education, reading education, science education, social studies education, world languages education (M Ed); reading specialist (M Ed). *Accreditation:* NCATE. *Program availability:* Part-time. *Faculty:* 26 full-time (12 women), 1 part-time/adjunct (0 women). *Students:* 42 full-time (32 women), 113 part-time (85 women); includes 33 minority (9 Black or African American, non-Hispanic/Latino; 5 American Indian or Alaska Native, non-Hispanic/Latino; 6 Asian, non-Hispanic/Latino; 4 Hispanic/Latino; 1 Native Hawaiian or other Pacific Islander, non-Hispanic/Latino; 8 Two or more races, non-Hispanic/Latino), 9 international. Average age 35. 42 applicants, 79% accepted, 21 enrolled. In 2018, 30 master's, 17 doctorates awarded. Terminal master's awarded for partial completion of doctoral program. *Degree requirements:* For master's, comprehensive exam (for some programs), thesis (for some programs); for doctorate, comprehensive exam (for some programs), thesis/dissertation. *Entrance requirements:* For doctorate, GRE. Additional exam requirements/recommendations for international students: Required—TOEFL (minimum score 79 iBT) or IELTS (minimum score 6.5). Application fee: $50 ($100 for international students). Electronic applications

accepted. *Expenses:* Tuition, state resident: full-time $5683.20; part-time $236.80 per credit hour. Tuition, nonresident: full-time $20,342; part-time $847.60 per credit hour. *International tuition:* $20,342.40 full-time. *Required fees:* $2894.20; $110.05 per credit hour. $126.50 per semester. Tuition and fees vary according to course load and program. *Financial support:* Fellowships, research assistantships, teaching assistantships, scholarships/grants, and unspecified assistantships available. Financial award application deadline: 6/1; financial award applicants required to submit FAFSA. *Faculty research:* Teacher preparation; instruction; curriculum; learning; constructivist theory. *Unit head:* Dr. Stacy Reeder, Chair, 405-325-1498, Fax: 405-325-4061, E-mail: reeder@ou.edu. *Application contact:* Anna Steele, Graduate Programs Officer, 405-325-4525, E-mail: anna.steele@ou.edu.
Website: http://www.ou.edu/education/ilac

University of Pennsylvania, Graduate School of Education, Medical Education Program, Philadelphia, PA 19104. Offers MS Ed, Certificate. Program offered jointly with Perelman School of Medicine and The Children's Hospital of Philadelphia. *Program availability:* Evening/weekend. *Students:* 33 full-time (15 women); includes 7 minority (2 Black or African American, non-Hispanic/Latino; 4 Asian, non-Hispanic/Latino; 1 Two or more races, non-Hispanic/Latino). Average age 37. 46 applicants, 74% accepted, 32 enrolled. In 2018, 5 master's awarded. *Entrance requirements:* For master's, bachelor's degree; professional health care experience. Additional exam requirements/recommendations for international students: Required—TOEFL, IELTS. *Application deadline:* Applications are processed on a rolling basis. Application fee: $80. Electronic applications accepted. *Faculty research:* Strategic leadership, workplace learning, evidenced-best decision making, technology in the work place. *Unit head:* Associate Director, 215-573-0591. *Application contact:* Associate Director, 215-573-0591.
Website: http://www.gse.upenn.edu/med-ed/

University of Phoenix–Online Campus, College of Education, Phoenix, AZ 85034-7209. Offers administration and supervision (MAEd, Certificate); adult education and training (MAEd); curriculum and instruction (MAEd), including computer education, curriculum and instruction, English as a second language, language arts, mathematics, reading; early childhood education (MAEd); educational studies (MAEd); elementary teacher education (MAEd), including early childhood, elementary teacher education, high school middle level, middle level; principal licensure (Certificate); secondary teacher education (MAEd); special education (MAEd, Certificate); teacher education (MAEd), including middle level generalist; teacher education middle level mathematics (MAEd), including middle level mathematics; teacher education middle level science (MAEd), including middle level science; teacher education secondary mathematics (MAEd); teacher education secondary science (MAEd); teacher leadership (MAEd); teachers of English learners (Certificate); transition to teaching (Certificate), including elementary education, secondary education. *Program availability:* Evening/weekend, online learning. *Entrance requirements:* Additional exam requirements/recommendations for international students: Required—TOEFL, TOEIC (Test of English as an International Communication), Berlitz Online English Proficiency Exam, PTE, or IELTS. Electronic applications accepted. *Expenses:* Contact institution.

University of Pittsburgh, School of Education, Department of Instruction and Learning, Program in Secondary Education, Pittsburgh, PA 15260. Offers English and communications education (M Ed, MAT); foreign language education (M Ed, MAT); language, literacy and culture education (Ed D, PhD); mathematics education (M Ed, MAT, Ed D, PhD); science education (M Ed, MAT, Ed D, PhD); secondary education (PhD); social studies education (M Ed, MAT); STEM education (Ed D). *Program availability:* Part-time, evening/weekend. *Degree requirements:* For master's, thesis; for doctorate, thesis/dissertation. *Entrance requirements:* For master's, PRAXIS I; for doctorate, GRE General Test. Additional exam requirements/recommendations for international students: Required—TOEFL. Electronic applications accepted.

University of Puerto Rico–Río Piedras, College of Education, Program in Curriculum and Teaching, San Juan, PR 00931-3300. Offers biology education (M Ed); chemistry education (M Ed); curriculum and teaching (Ed D); history education (M Ed); mathematics education (M Ed); physics education (M Ed); Spanish education (M Ed). *Program availability:* Part-time. *Degree requirements:* For master's, thesis; for doctorate, thesis/dissertation, internship. *Entrance requirements:* For master's, PAEG or GRE, minimum GPA of 3.0, letter of recommendation; for doctorate, GRE or PAEG, master's degree, minimum GPA of 3.0, letter of recommendation (2), interview. *Faculty research:* Curriculum, math teaching.

University of St. Francis, College of Education, Joliet, IL 60435-6169. Offers educational leadership (MS, Ed D); elementary education (M Ed); reading (MS); secondary education (M Ed), including English education, math education, science education, social studies education, visual arts education; special education (M Ed); teaching and learning (MS); TESOL (Certificate). *Accreditation:* NCATE. *Program availability:* Part-time, evening/weekend, 100% online, blended/hybrid learning. *Faculty:* 11 full-time (8 women), 58 part-time/adjunct (38 women). *Students:* 43 full-time (35 women), 453 part-time (354 women); includes 110 minority (48 Black or African American, non-Hispanic/Latino; 7 Asian, non-Hispanic/Latino; 52 Hispanic/Latino; 3 Two or more races, non-Hispanic/Latino), 3 international. Average age 37. 300 applicants, 66% accepted, 164 enrolled. In 2018, 151 master's, 42 doctorates, 4 other advanced degrees awarded. *Degree requirements:* For master's, comprehensive exam; for doctorate, thesis/dissertation. *Entrance requirements:* Additional exam requirements/recommendations for international students: Required—TOEFL (minimum score 550 paper-based; 79 iBT), IELTS (minimum score 6). *Application deadline:* Applications are processed on a rolling basis. Electronic applications accepted. Application fee is waived when completed online. *Expenses:* Contact institution. *Financial support:* In 2018–19, 33 students received support. Scholarships/grants and tuition waivers (partial) available. Support available to part-time students. Financial award applicants required to submit FAFSA. *Unit head:* Dr. John Gambro, Dean, 815-740-3456, E-mail: jgambro@stfrancis.edu. *Application contact:* Sandee Sloka, Director Adult & Graduate Admissions, 800-735-7500, E-mail: ssloka@stfrancis.edu.
Website: https://www.stfrancis.edu/education/

University of San Diego, School of Leadership and Education Sciences, Department of Learning and Teaching, San Diego, CA 92110-2492. Offers curriculum and instruction (M Ed), including inclusive learning, literacy and digital learning, school leadership, steam (science, technology, engineering, arts, and mathematics); inclusive learning (M Ed); literacy and digital learning (M Ed); school leadership (M Ed); special education (M Ed); STEAM (science, technology, engineering, arts, and mathematics) (M Ed); TESOL, literacy and culture (M Ed). *Program availability:* Part-time, evening/weekend. *Faculty:* 9 full-time (7 women), 34 part-time/adjunct (26 women). *Students:* 136 full-time (102 women), 223 part-time (177 women); includes 130 minority (17 Black or African American, non-Hispanic/Latino; 21 Asian, non-Hispanic/Latino; 74 Hispanic/Latino; 3 Native Hawaiian or other Pacific Islander, non-Hispanic/Latino; 15 Two or more races, non-Hispanic/Latino), 10 international. Average age 33. 391 applicants, 85% accepted, 190 enrolled. In 2018, 201 master's awarded. *Degree requirements:* For master's, thesis (for some programs), international experience. *Entrance requirements:* For master's, California Basic Educational Skills Test, California Subject Examination for Teachers. Additional exam requirements/recommendations for international students: Required—TOEFL (minimum score 580 paper-based; 83 iBT), TWE. *Application deadline:*

Science Education

Applications are processed on a rolling basis. Application fee: $45. Electronic applications accepted. *Financial support:* In 2018–19, 127 students received support. Career-related internships or fieldwork, Federal Work-Study, institutionally sponsored loans, scholarships/grants, and stipends available. Financial award application deadline: 4/1; financial award applicants required to submit FAFSA. *Faculty research:* Action research methodology, cultural studies, instructional theories and practices, second language acquisition, school reform. *Unit head:* Dr. Reyes Quezada, Chair, 619-260-7655, E-mail: rquezada@sandiego.edu. *Application contact:* Erika Garwood, Associate Director of Graduate Admissions, 619-260-4524, Fax: 619-260-4158, E-mail: grads@sandiego.edu.
Website: http://www.sandiego.edu/soles/learning-and-teaching/

University of South Africa, College of Human Sciences, Pretoria, South Africa. Offers adult education (M Ed); African languages (MA, PhD); African politics (MA, PhD); Afrikaans (MA, PhD); ancient history (MA, PhD); ancient Near Eastern studies (MA, PhD); anthropology (MA, PhD); applied linguistics (MA); Arabic (MA, PhD); archaeology (MA); art history (MA); Biblical archaeology (MA); Biblical studies (M Th, D Th, PhD); Christian spirituality (M Th, D Th); church history (M Th, D Th); classical studies (MA, PhD); clinical psychology (MA); communication (MA, PhD); comparative education (M Ed, Ed D); consulting psychology (D Admin, D Com, PhD); curriculum studies (M Ed, Ed D); development studies (M Admin, MA, D Admin, PhD); didactics (M Ed, Ed D); education (M Tech); education management (M Ed, Ed D); educational psychology (M Ed); English (MA); environmental education (M Ed); French (MA, PhD); German (MA, PhD); Greek (MA); guidance and counseling (M Ed); health studies (MA, PhD), including health sciences education (MA), health services management (MA), medical and surgical nursing science (critical care general) (MA), midwifery and neonatal nursing science (MA), trauma and emergency care (MA); history (MA, PhD); history of education (Ed D); inclusive education (M Ed, Ed D); information and communications technology policy and regulation (MA); information science (MA, MIS, PhD); international politics (MA, PhD); Islamic studies (MA, PhD); Italian (MA, PhD); Judaica (MA, PhD); linguistics (MA, PhD); mathematical education (M Ed); mathematics education (MA); missiology (M Th, D Th); modern Hebrew (MA, PhD); musicology (MA, MMus, D Mus, PhD); natural science education (M Ed); New Testament (M Th, D Th); Old Testament (D Th); pastoral therapy (M Th, D Th); philosophy (MA); philosophy of education (M Ed, Ed D); politics (MA, PhD); Portuguese (MA, PhD); practical theology (M Th, D Th); psychology (MA, MS, PhD); psychology of education (M Ed, Ed D); public health (MA); religious studies (MA, D Th, PhD); Romance languages (MA); Russian (MA, PhD); Semitic languages (MA, PhD); social behavior studies in HIV/AIDS (MA); social science (mental health) (MA); social science in development studies (MA); social science in psychology (MA); social science in social work (MA); social science in sociology (MA); social work (MSW, DSW, PhD); socio-education (M Ed, Ed D); sociolinguistics (MA); sociology (MA, PhD); Spanish (MA, PhD); systematic theology (M Th, D Th); TESOL (teaching English to speakers of other languages) (MA); theological ethics (M Th, D Th); theory of literature (MA, PhD); urban ministries (D Th); urban ministry (M Th).

University of South Africa, Institute for Science and Technology Education, Pretoria, South Africa. Offers mathematics, science and technology education (M Sc, PhD).

University of South Alabama, College of Education and Professional Studies, Department of Leadership and Teacher Education, Mobile, AL 36688. Offers art education (M Ed); early childhood education (M Ed); educational leadership (M Ed, Ed D); elementary education (M Ed); reading education (M Ed); science education (M Ed); secondary education (M Ed); special education (M Ed). *Accreditation:* NCATE. *Program availability:* Part-time. *Degree requirements:* For master's, comprehensive exam, thesis (for some programs); for doctorate, comprehensive exam, thesis/dissertation. *Entrance requirements:* For master's, GRE General Test or MAT, minimum GPA of 3.0; for doctorate, GRE, minimum graduate GPA of 3.25, 3 years of experience in field, 3 letters of recommendation, interview, official transcripts. Additional exam requirements/recommendations for international students: Required—TOEFL. Electronic applications accepted.

University of South Carolina, The Graduate School, College of Arts and Sciences, Department of Biological Sciences, Columbia, SC 29208. Offers biology (MS, PhD); biology education (IMA, MAT); ecology, evolution and organismal biology (MS, PhD); molecular, cellular, and developmental biology (MS, PhD). IMA and MAT offered in cooperation with the College of Education. Terminal master's awarded for partial completion of doctoral program. *Degree requirements:* For master's, one foreign language, thesis (for some programs); for doctorate, one foreign language, thesis/dissertation. *Entrance requirements:* For master's and doctorate, GRE General Test, minimum GPA of 3.0 in science. Electronic applications accepted. *Faculty research:* Marine ecology, population and evolutionary biology, molecular biology and genetics, development.

University of South Carolina, The Graduate School, College of Arts and Sciences, Department of Geography, Columbia, SC 29208. Offers geography (MA, MS, PhD); geography education (IMA). IMA and MAT offered in cooperation with the College of Education. *Program availability:* Part-time. *Degree requirements:* For master's, comprehensive exam, thesis (for some programs); for doctorate, comprehensive exam, thesis/dissertation. *Entrance requirements:* For master's, GRE General Test; for doctorate, GRE General Test, master's degree. Electronic applications accepted. *Faculty research:* Geographic information processing; economic, cultural, physical, and environmental geography.

University of South Carolina, The Graduate School, College of Education, Department of Instruction and Teacher Education, Program in Secondary Education, Columbia, SC 29208. Offers art education (IMA, MAT); business education (IMA, MAT); English (MAT); foreign language (MAT); health education (MAT); mathematics (MAT); science (IMA, MAT); secondary (Ed D); secondary education (MT, PhD); social studies (MAT); theatre and speech (MAT). IMA and MT offered jointly with the subject areas. *Accreditation:* NCATE. *Degree requirements:* For master's, comprehensive exam, thesis (for some programs), foreign language (MA); for doctorate, one foreign language, comprehensive exam, thesis/dissertation. *Entrance requirements:* For master's, GRE General Test or MAT, teaching certificate (IMA, M Ed), interview; for doctorate, GRE General Test or MAT, interview. *Faculty research:* Middle school programs, professional development, school collaboration.

University of South Dakota, Graduate School, School of Education, Division of Curriculum and Instruction, Program in Elementary Education, Vermillion, SD 57069. Offers elementary education (MA), including early childhood education, English language learning, reading specialist/literacy coach, science, technology and math (STEM). *Accreditation:* NCATE. *Program availability:* Part-time, 100% online, blended/hybrid learning. *Degree requirements:* For master's, comprehensive exam, thesis or alternative. *Entrance requirements:* For master's, GRE General Test, MAT, minimum GPA of 2.7. Additional exam requirements/recommendations for international students: Required—TOEFL (minimum score 550 paper-based; 79 iBT). Electronic applications accepted.

University of South Dakota, Graduate School, School of Education, Division of Curriculum and Instruction, Program in Secondary Education, Vermillion, SD 57069. Offers secondary education (MA), including English language learning, science,

technology and math (STEM), secondary education plus certification. *Accreditation:* NCATE. *Program availability:* Part-time, online learning. *Degree requirements:* For master's, comprehensive exam, thesis or alternative. *Entrance requirements:* For master's, GRE General Test, MAT, minimum GPA of 2.7. Additional exam requirements/recommendations for international students: Required—TOEFL (minimum score 550 paper-based; 79 iBT). Electronic applications accepted.

University of South Florida, St. Petersburg, College of Education, St. Petersburg, FL 33701. Offers educational leadership development (M Ed); elementary education (MA), including math/science; English education (MA); middle grades STEM education (MS); reading education (MA). *Program availability:* Part-time. *Degree requirements:* For master's, comprehensive exam, practicum, internship, comprehensive portfolio. *Entrance requirements:* For master's, State of Florida General Knowledge Test (GKT), Florida Teaching Certificate (for non-initial certification programs), letters of recommendation. Additional exam requirements/recommendations for international students: Required—TOEFL (minimum score 550 paper-based; 79 iBT); Recommended—IELTS. Electronic applications accepted.

The University of Tennessee, Graduate School, College of Education, Health and Human Sciences, Program in Education, Knoxville, TN 37996. Offers art education (MS); counseling education (PhD); cultural studies in education (PhD); curriculum (MS, Ed S); curriculum, educational research and evaluation (Ed D, PhD); early childhood education (PhD); early childhood special education (MS); education of deaf and hard of hearing (MS); educational administration and policy studies (Ed D, PhD); educational administration and supervision (Ed S); educational psychology (Ed D, PhD); elementary education (MS, Ed S); elementary teaching (MS); English education (MS, Ed S); exercise science (PhD); foreign language/ESL education (MS, Ed S); instructional technology (MS, Ed D, PhD, Ed S); literacy, language and ESL education (PhD); literacy, language education, and ESL education (Ed D); mathematics education (MS, Ed S); modified and comprehensive special education (MS); reading education (MS, Ed S); school counseling (Ed S); school psychology (PhD, Ed S); science education (MS, Ed S); secondary teaching (MS); social foundations (MS); social science education (MS, Ed S); socio-cultural foundations of sports and education (PhD); special education (Ed S); teacher education (Ed D, PhD). *Accreditation:* NCATE. *Program availability:* Part-time, evening/weekend. *Degree requirements:* For master's and Ed S, thesis optional; for doctorate, variable foreign language requirement, thesis/dissertation. *Entrance requirements:* For master's, minimum GPA of 2.7; for doctorate and Ed S, GRE General Test, minimum GPA of 2.7. Additional exam requirements/recommendations for international students: Required—TOEFL. Electronic applications accepted.

The University of Texas at Arlington, Graduate School, College of Education, Department of Curriculum and Instruction, Arlington, TX 76019. Offers curriculum and instruction (M Ed), including literacy studies, mathematics education, mind, brain, and education, science education; teaching (with certification) (M Ed T). *Accreditation:* NCATE. *Program availability:* Part-time, evening/weekend, online learning. *Degree requirements:* For master's, comprehensive exam (for some programs), comprehensive activity, research project. *Entrance requirements:* For master's, GRE General Test, minimum undergraduate GPA of 3.0 in last 60 hours of course work, writing sample, 3 letters of recommendation. Additional exam requirements/recommendations for international students: Required—TOEFL (minimum score 550 paper-based). Electronic applications accepted.

The University of Texas at Dallas, School of Natural Sciences and Mathematics, Department of Science/Mathematics Education, Richardson, TX 75080. Offers mathematics education (MAT); science education (MAT). *Program availability:* Part-time, evening/weekend, online learning. *Faculty:* 3 full-time (1 woman), 2 part-time/adjunct (1 woman). *Students:* 9 full-time (6 women), 23 part-time (17 women); includes 17 minority (2 Black or African American, non-Hispanic/Latino; 9 Asian, non-Hispanic/Latino; 4 Hispanic/Latino; 2 Two or more races, non-Hispanic/Latino), 3 international. Average age 31. 21 applicants, 57% accepted, 8 enrolled. In 2018, 9 master's awarded. *Degree requirements:* For master's, thesis optional. *Entrance requirements:* For master's, GRE General Test, minimum GPA of 3.0 in upper-level coursework in field. Additional exam requirements/recommendations for international students: Required—TOEFL (minimum score 550 paper-based). *Application deadline:* For fall admission, 7/15 for domestic students, 5/1 priority date for international students; for spring admission, 11/15 for domestic students, 9/1 priority date for international students. Applications are processed on a rolling basis. Application fee: $50 ($100 for international students). Electronic applications accepted. *Expenses: Tuition, area resident:* Full-time $13,458. Tuition, state resident: full-time $13,458. Tuition, nonresident: full-time $26,852. *International tuition:* $26,852 full-time. Tuition and fees vary according to course load. *Financial support:* In 2018–19, 4 students received support, including 1 research assistantship with partial tuition reimbursement available (averaging $22,800 per year), 3 teaching assistantships with partial tuition reimbursements available (averaging $17,100 per year); fellowships, career-related internships or fieldwork, Federal Work-Study, institutionally sponsored loans, scholarships/grants, and unspecified assistantships also available. Support available to part-time students. Financial award application deadline: 4/30; financial award applicants required to submit FAFSA. *Faculty research:* Innovative science/math education programs. *Unit head:* Dr. Mary Urquhart Kelly, Department Head, 972-883-2496, Fax: 972-883-6796, E-mail: scimathed@utdallas.edu. *Application contact:* Dr. Mary Urquhart Kelly, Department Head, 972-883-2496, Fax: 972-883-6796, E-mail: scimathed@utdallas.edu.
Website: http://www.utdallas.edu/sme/

The University of Toledo, College of Graduate Studies, Judith Herb College of Education, Department of Curriculum and Instruction, Toledo, OH 43606-3390. Offers art education (ME); career and technical education (ME, Ed S); curriculum and instruction (ME, PhD, Ed S); early childhood education (Ed S); education and anthropology (MAE); education and biology (MES); education and chemistry (MES); education and classics (MAE); education and economics (MAE); education and English (MAE); education and French (MAE); education and geology (MES); education and German (MAE); education and history (MAE); education and mathematics (MAE, MES); education and physics (MES); education and political science (MAE); education and sociology (MAE); education and Spanish (MAE); educational media (PhD); educational technology (ME); educational technology: virtual educator (Certificate); elementary education (PhD); English as a second language (MAE); gifted and talented education (PhD); middle childhood education (ME); secondary education (ME, PhD); special education (PhD). *Accreditation:* NCATE. *Program availability:* Part-time, evening/weekend. *Degree requirements:* For master's, comprehensive exam, thesis or alternative; for doctorate, comprehensive exam, thesis/dissertation; for other advanced degree, thesis optional. *Entrance requirements:* For master's, doctorate, and other advanced degree, minimum cumulative GPA of 2.7 for all previous academic work, letters of recommendation. Additional exam requirements/recommendations for international students: Required—TOEFL (minimum score 550 paper-based; 80 iBT). Electronic applications accepted.

University of Utah, Graduate School, College of Science, Department of Chemistry, Salt Lake City, UT 84112-0850. Offers chemistry (MS, PhD); science teacher education (MS). *Program availability:* Part-time, online learning. *Faculty:* 29 full-time (9 women), 15

part-time/adjunct (3 women). *Students:* 137 full-time (64 women), 22 part-time (2 women); includes 20 minority (1 American Indian or Alaska Native, non-Hispanic/Latino; 10 Asian, non-Hispanic/Latino; 7 Hispanic/Latino; 2 Two or more races, non-Hispanic/Latino), 38 international. Average age 27. 298 applicants, 34% accepted, 37 enrolled. In 2018, 11 master's, 24 doctorates awarded. Terminal master's awarded for partial completion of doctoral program. *Degree requirements:* For master's, thesis optional, 20 hours of course work, 10 hours of research; for doctorate, thesis/dissertation, 18 hours of course work, 14 hours of research. *Entrance requirements:* For master's and doctorate, GRE General Test, minimum GPA of 3.0. Additional exam requirements/recommendations for international students: Required—TOEFL (minimum score 620 paper-based; 105 iBT). *Application deadline:* For fall admission, 4/1 for domestic students, 2/1 for international students; for spring admission, 11/1 for domestic and international students. Application fee: $55 ($65 for international students). Electronic applications accepted. Application fee is waived when completed online. *Expenses:* Contact institution. *Financial support:* In 2018–19, 175 students received support, including 1 fellowship with full tuition reimbursement available (averaging $25,000 per year), 119 research assistantships with tuition reimbursements available (averaging $25,500 per year), 55 teaching assistantships with tuition reimbursements available (averaging $25,000 per year); scholarships/grants and tuition waivers (full) also available. Financial award application deadline: 4/1; financial award applicants required to submit FAFSA. *Faculty research:* Analytical, biological, inorganic, materials, organic, physical and theoretical chemistry. *Unit head:* Dr. Cynthia J. Burrows, Chair, 801-585-7290, Fax: 801-581-8433, E-mail: chair@chemistry.utah.edu. *Application contact:* Jo Vallejo, Graduate Coordinator, 801-581-4393, E-mail: jvallejo@chem.utah.edu.
Website: http://www.chem.utah.edu/

University of Utah, Graduate School, College of Science, Department of Physics and Astronomy, Salt Lake City, UT 84112. Offers chemical physics (PhD); medical physics (MS, PhD); physics (MA, MS, PhD); physics teaching (PhD). *Program availability:* Part-time. *Faculty:* 37 full-time (4 women), 15 part-time/adjunct (2 women). *Students:* 69 full-time (21 women); includes 3 minority (all Hispanic/Latino), 30 international. Average age 27. In 2018, 3 master's, 17 doctorates awarded. Terminal master's awarded for partial completion of doctoral program. *Degree requirements:* For master's, comprehensive exam, https://gradschool.utah.edu/graduate-catalog/degree-requirements/; for doctorate, comprehensive exam, thesis/dissertation, https://gradschool.utah.edu/graduate-catalog/degree-requirements/. *Entrance requirements:* For master's and doctorate, GRE General Test (Subject Test not required), minimum GPA of 3.0. Additional exam requirements/recommendations for international students: Required—TOEFL (minimum score 550 paper-based; 85 iBT). *Application deadline:* For fall admission, 1/15 for domestic and international students. Application fee: $55 ($65 for international students). Electronic applications accepted. *Expenses:* Https://fbs.admin.utah.edu/income/tuition/. *Financial support:* In 2018–19, 67 students received support, including 66 research assistantships with full tuition reimbursements available (averaging $25,000 per year), 66 teaching assistantships with full tuition reimbursements available (averaging $25,000 per year); scholarships/grants, health care benefits, and unspecified assistantships also available. Financial award application deadline: 2/15; financial award applicants required to submit FAFSA. *Faculty research:* High-energy, cosmic-ray, medical physics, condensed matter, relativity applied physics, biophysics, astronomy and astrophysics. *Total annual research expenditures:* $6 million. *Unit head:* Dr. Christoph Bhoehme, Chair, 801-581-6806, Fax: 801-581-4801, E-mail: bhoeme@physics.utah.edu. *Application contact:* Bryce Nelson, Graduate Coordinator, 801-581-6861, Fax: 801-581-4801, E-mail: bryce@physics.utah.edu.
Website: http://www.physics.utah.edu/

University of Vermont, Graduate College, College of Arts and Sciences, Department of Biology, Burlington, VT 05405. Offers biology (MS, PhD); biology education (MST). *Degree requirements:* For master's, thesis; for doctorate, thesis/dissertation. *Entrance requirements:* For master's and doctorate, GRE General Test. Additional exam requirements/recommendations for international students: Required—TOEFL (minimum score 550 paper-based, 90 iBT) or IELTS (6.5). Electronic applications accepted.

University of Victoria, Faculty of Graduate Studies, Faculty of Education, Department of Curriculum and Instruction, Victoria, BC V8W 2Y2, Canada. Offers art education (M Ed, PhD); curriculum studies (M Ed, MA, PhD); early childhood education (M Ed, PhD); educational studies (PhD); language and literacy (M Ed, MA, PhD); mathematics (M Ed, MA, PhD); music education (M Ed, MA, PhD); science (M Ed, MA, PhD); social studies (M Ed, MA); social, cultural and foundational studies (MA, PhD); technology and environmental education (PhD). *Program availability:* Part-time. *Degree requirements:* For master's, thesis, project (M Ed); for doctorate, comprehensive exam, thesis/dissertation. *Entrance requirements:* For master's, minimum B average. Additional exam requirements/recommendations for international students: Required—TOEFL (minimum score 575 paper-based), IELTS (minimum score 7). Electronic applications accepted. *Faculty research:* Elementary and secondary English, language arts, curriculum theory and practice, educational media and technology, educational administration and leadership, history and philosophy of education.

University of Virginia, College and Graduate School of Arts and Sciences, Department of Physics, Charlottesville, VA 22903. Offers physics (MA, MS, PhD); physics education (MAPE). *Degree requirements:* For master's, thesis (for some programs); for doctorate, comprehensive exam, thesis/dissertation. *Entrance requirements:* For master's and doctorate, GRE General Test, GRE Subject Test, 2 or more letters of recommendation. Additional exam requirements/recommendations for international students: Required—TOEFL (minimum score 600 paper-based; 90 iBT), IELTS. Electronic applications accepted.

University of Virginia, Curry School of Education, Department of Curriculum, Instruction, and Special Education, Program in Curriculum and Instruction, Charlottesville, VA 22903. Offers curriculum and instruction (M Ed, Ed S); elementary education (M Ed, Ed D); English education (M Ed, Ed D); foreign language education (M Ed); mathematics education (M Ed, Ed D); science education (Ed D); social studies education (M Ed); MBA/M Ed. *Program availability:* 100% online. *Degree requirements:* For master's, comprehensive exam (for some programs); for doctorate, comprehensive exam, thesis/dissertation; for Ed S, comprehensive exam. *Entrance requirements:* For master's, doctorate, and Ed S, GRE General Test, 2 letters of recommendation. Additional exam requirements/recommendations for international students: Required—TOEFL (minimum score 600 paper-based; 90 iBT), IELTS (minimum score 7). Electronic applications accepted.

University of Virginia, Curry School of Education, Program in Education, Charlottesville, VA 22903. Offers administration and supervision (PhD); applied developmental science (PhD); counselor education (PhD); curriculum and instruction (PhD); early childhood special education (MT); education evaluation (PhD); educational psychology (PhD); educational research (PhD); elementary education (MT); English education (MT, PhD); foreign language education (MT); higher education (PhD); instructional technology (PhD); kinesiology (MT, PhD); math education (PhD); reading education (PhD); research, statistics and evaluation (PhD); school psychology (PhD); science education (PhD); social studies education (MT, PhD); special education (PhD); world languages education (MT). *Degree requirements:* For master's, comprehensive exam (for some programs), field project; for doctorate, comprehensive exam, thesis/dissertation. *Entrance requirements:* For doctorate, GRE General Test. Additional exam requirements/recommendations for international students: Required—TOEFL (minimum score 600 paper-based; 90 iBT), IELTS (minimum score 7). Electronic applications accepted.

University of Washington, Graduate School, College of Education, Seattle, WA 98195. Offers curriculum and instruction (M Ed, Ed D, PhD), including educational technology, general curriculum (Ed D, PhD), language, literacy, and culture, mathematics education, multicultural education, reading and language arts education (Ed D), science education, social studies education, teaching and curriculum (M Ed); educational leadership and policy studies (M Ed, Ed D, PhD), including administration (Ed D), educational policy, organization, and leadership (M Ed, PhD), higher education, leadership for learning (Ed D), social and cultural foundations of education (M Ed, PhD); educational psychology (M Ed, PhD), including educational psychology (PhD), human development and cognition (M Ed), learning sciences, measurement, statistics and research design (M Ed), school psychology (M Ed); instructional leadership (M Ed); intercollegiate athletic leadership (M Ed); special education (M Ed, Ed D, PhD), including early childhood special education (M Ed), emotional and behavioral disabilities (M Ed), learning disabilities (M Ed), low-incidence disabilities (M Ed), severe disabilities (M Ed), special education (Ed D, PhD); teacher education (MIT). *Accreditation:* APA. *Program availability:* Part-time, evening/weekend. *Degree requirements:* For master's, thesis optional; for doctorate, thesis/dissertation. *Entrance requirements:* For master's and doctorate, GRE General Test, minimum GPA of 3.0. Additional exam requirements/recommendations for international students: Required—TOEFL. Electronic applications accepted. *Faculty research:* School restructuring/effective schools, special education interventions, literacy and writing, technology, school partnerships, teacher preparation.

University of Washington, Graduate School, Interdisciplinary Program in Biology for Teachers, Seattle, WA 98195. Offers MS. *Program availability:* Part-time. *Degree requirements:* For master's, research project and oral exam. *Entrance requirements:* For master's, GRE General Test, minimum GPA of 3.0, teaching certificate or professional teaching experience. Electronic applications accepted.

University of Washington, Tacoma, Graduate Programs, Program in Education, Tacoma, WA 98402-3100. Offers education (M Ed); educational administration (principal or program administrator certification) (M Ed); elementary education teacher certification (M Ed); elementary education/special education teacher certification (M Ed); secondary science or math teacher certification (M Ed). *Program availability:* Part-time, evening/weekend. *Degree requirements:* For master's, culminating project. *Entrance requirements:* For master's, WEST-B, WEST-E (teacher certification programs only), official sealed transcript from every college/university attended, personal goal statement, letters of recommendation, copy of valid teaching certificate. Additional exam requirements/recommendations for international students: Required—TOEFL (minimum score 580 paper-based; 92 iBT). Electronic applications accepted. *Faculty research:* Global learning communities for English/Chinese languages, evaluation of mathematics and reading intervention programs, response to intervention, school-wide behavioral and emotional support, mathematics education and culturally responsive mathematics education.

The University of West Alabama, School of Graduate Studies, College of Education, Program in Secondary Education, Livingston, AL 35470. Offers biology (MAT); English language arts (MAT); high school 6-12 (M Ed); history (MAT); mathematics (MAT); science (MAT); social science (MAT). *Program availability:* Part-time, evening/weekend, 100% online. *Faculty:* 18 full-time (6 women), 8 part-time/adjunct (2 women). *Students:* 232 full-time (165 women), 34 part-time (24 women); includes 53 minority (44 Black or African American, non-Hispanic/Latino; 3 American Indian or Alaska Native, non-Hispanic/Latino; 2 Hispanic/Latino; 4 Two or more races, non-Hispanic/Latino), 3 international. Average age 31. 84 applicants, 93% accepted, 67 enrolled. In 2018, 100 master's awarded. *Degree requirements:* For master's, comprehensive exam, thesis optional. *Entrance requirements:* For master's, GRE, minimum GPA of 2.75, verification of background clearance/fingerprints, valid bachelor's-level Professional Educator Certificate in same teaching field. Additional exam requirements/recommendations for international students: Required—TOEFL (minimum score 500 paper-based; 61 iBT). *Application deadline:* Applications are processed on a rolling basis. Application fee: $40. Electronic applications accepted. *Expenses: Tuition, area resident:* Full-time $9100. Tuition, state resident: full-time $9100. Tuition, nonresident: full-time $19,200. *Required fees:* $1890; $130. *Financial support:* Teaching assistantships, Federal Work-Study, scholarships/grants, and unspecified assistantships available. Support available to part-time students. Financial award application deadline: 3/1; financial award applicants required to submit FAFSA. *Unit head:* Dr. Jodie Winship, Chair of College of Education, 205-652-5415, Fax: 205-652-3706, E-mail: jwinship@uwa.edu. *Application contact:* Dr. B. J. Kimbrough, Dean of Graduate Studies, 205-652-3647, Fax: 205-652-3670, E-mail: bkimbrough@uwa.edu.

University of Wisconsin–Milwaukee, Graduate School, School of Education, Department of Curriculum and Instruction, Milwaukee, WI 53201-0413. Offers curriculum and instruction (MS), including cross-curricular focus, early childhood education, English education, mathematics education, middle childhood/early adolescence education, reading education, science education, urban social studies education. *Program availability:* Part-time. *Students:* 19 full-time (15 women), 56 part-time (49 women); includes 15 minority (3 Black or African American, non-Hispanic/Latino; 1 American Indian or Alaska Native, non-Hispanic/Latino; 3 Asian, non-Hispanic/Latino; 1 Hispanic/Latino; 7 Two or more races, non-Hispanic/Latino), 2 international. Average age 33. 27 applicants, 44% accepted, 11 enrolled. In 2018, 20 master's awarded. *Entrance requirements:* Additional exam requirements/recommendations for international students: Required—TOEFL (minimum score 550 paper-based; 79 iBT), IELTS (minimum score 6.5). *Application deadline:* For fall admission, 1/1 priority date for domestic students; for spring admission, 9/1 for domestic students. Application fee: $56 ($96 for international students). Electronic applications accepted. *Financial support:* Fellowships, research assistantships, teaching assistantships, career-related internships or fieldwork, health care benefits, unspecified assistantships, and project assistantships available. Support available to part-time students. Financial award application deadline: 4/15; financial award applicants required to submit FAFSA. *Application contact:* General Information Contact, 414-229-4721, E-mail: soeinfo@uwm.edu.
Website: http://uwm.edu/education/academics/curriculum-instruction-department/

University of Wisconsin–River Falls, Outreach and Graduate Studies, College of Arts and Science, Program in Science, River Falls, WI 54022. Offers science education (MSE). *Program availability:* Part-time. *Degree requirements:* For master's, comprehensive exam, thesis or alternative. *Entrance requirements:* For master's, minimum GPA of 2.75. Additional exam requirements/recommendations for international students: Required—TOEFL (minimum score 500 paper-based; 65 iBT), IELTS (minimum score 5.5). Electronic applications accepted.

University of Wisconsin–Stevens Point, College of Letters and Science, Department of Biology, Stevens Point, WI 54481-3897. Offers MST. *Degree requirements:* For master's, thesis or alternative. *Entrance requirements:* For master's, minimum undergraduate GPA of 2.75 overall, 3.0 in biology; bachelor's degree; teacher's license.

University of Wyoming, College of Education, Science and Mathematics Teaching Center, Laramie, WY 82071. Offers MS, MST. *Degree requirements:* For master's, thesis. *Entrance requirements:* For master's, GRE General Test, minimum GPA of 3.0, writing sample, 3 letters of recommendation. Electronic applications accepted. *Expenses: Tuition, area resident:* Full-time $6504; part-time $271 per credit hour. Tuition, state resident: full-time $6504; part-time $271 per credit hour. Tuition, nonresident: full-time $19,464; part-time $811 per credit hour. *International tuition:* $19,464 full-time. *Required fees:* $1410.94; $343.82 per semester. $343.82 per semester. Tuition and fees vary according to course load, program and reciprocity agreements.

Wagner College, Division of Graduate Studies, Education Department, Program in Secondary Education/Students with Disabilities, Staten Island, NY 10301-4495. Offers secondary education 7-12 (MS Ed), including language arts, languages other than English, mathematics and technology, science and technology, social studies. *Program availability:* Evening/weekend. *Degree requirements:* For master's, thesis (for some programs), completion of state certification exams before student teaching. *Entrance requirements:* For master's, GRE, minimum GPA of 3.0, interview, recommendations. Additional exam requirements/recommendations for international students: Required—TOEFL (minimum score 550 paper-based; 79 iBT), IELTS (minimum score 6.5). Electronic applications accepted. *Expenses:* Contact institution.

Walden University, Graduate Programs, Richard W. Riley College of Education and Leadership, Minneapolis, MN 55401. Offers adult education (Post-Master's Certificate); adult learning (Graduate Certificate); college teaching and learning (Graduate Certificate); community college leadership (Ed D); curriculum, instruction and assessment (Ed D, Ed S, Graduate Certificate); developmental education (Graduate Certificate); early childhood administration, management, and leadership (Graduate Certificate); early childhood education (Ed D, Ed S); early childhood public policy and advocacy (Graduate Certificate); early childhood studies (MS), including administration, management and leadership, early childhood public policy and advocacy, teaching adults in the early childhood field, teaching and diversity in early childhood education; education (MS, PhD), including adolescent literacy and learning (MS), curriculum, instruction, and assessment (grades K-12) (MS), curriculum, instruction, assessment, and evaluation (PhD), early childhood leadership and advocacy (PhD), early childhood special education (PhD), educational leadership (MS), educational leadership and administration (principal preparation) (MS), educational technology and design (PhD), elementary reading and literacy (PreK-6) (MS), elementary reading and mathematics (grades K-6) (MS), global and comparative education (PhD), higher education leadership management and policy (PhD), integrating technology in the classroom (grades K-12) (MS), learning, instruction and innovation (PhD), mathematics (grades 5-8) (MS), mathematics (grades K-6) (MS), mathematics and science (grades K-8) (MS), organizational research, assessment, and evaluation (PhD), reading and literacy with a reading K-12 endorsement (MS), reading literacy assessment and evaluation (PhD), science (grades K-8) (MS), special education (non-licensure) (grades K-12) (MS), teacher leadership (grades K-12) (MS), teaching English language learners (grades K-12) (MS); educational administration and leadership (Ed D); educational leadership and administration (principal preparation) (Ed S); educational technology (Ed D, Ed S, Post Master's Certificate); elementary reading and literacy (Graduate Certificate); engaging culturally diverse learners (Graduate Certificate); enrollment management and institutional marketing (Graduate Certificate); higher education (MS), including adult learning, college teaching and learning, enrollment management and institutional marketing, global higher education, leadership for student success, online and distance learning; higher education and adult learning (Ed D); higher education leadership and management (Ed D); higher education leadership for student success (Graduate Certificate); instructional design and technology (MS, Postbaccalaureate Certificate), including general program (MS), online learning (MS), training and performance improvement (MS); integrating technology in the classroom (Graduate Certificate); mathematics 5-8 (Graduate Certificate); mathematics K-6 (Graduate Certificate); online teaching for adult educators (Graduate Certificate); reading, literacy, and assessment (Ed D, Ed S); science K-8 (Graduate Certificate); special education (Ed D, Ed S, Graduate Certificate); special education (K-age 21) (MAT); teacher leadership (Graduate Certificate); teaching adults English as a second language (Graduate Certificate); teaching adults in the early childhood field (Graduate Certificate); teaching and diversity in early childhood education (Graduate Certificate); teaching English language learners (grades K-12) (Graduate Certificate); teaching K-12 students online (Graduate Certificate). *Accreditation:* NCATE. *Program availability:* Part-time, evening/weekend, online only, 100% online. *Degree requirements:* For doctorate, thesis/dissertation (for some programs), residency; for other advanced degree, residency (for some programs). *Entrance requirements:* For master's, bachelor's degree or higher; minimum GPA of 2.5; official transcripts; goal statement (for some programs); access to computer and Internet; for doctorate, master's degree or higher; three years of related professional or academic experience (preferred); minimum GPA of 3.0; goal statement and current resume (for select programs); official transcripts; access to computer and Internet; for other advanced degree, relevant work experience; access to computer and Internet. Additional exam requirements/recommendations for international students: Required—TOEFL (minimum score 550 paper-based, 79 iBT), IELTS (minimum score 6.5), Michigan English Language Assessment Battery (minimum score 82), or PTE (minimum score 53). Electronic applications accepted.

Warner University, School of Education, Lake Wales, FL 33859. Offers curriculum and instruction (MAEd); elementary education (MAEd); science, technology, engineering, and mathematics (STEM) (MAEd). *Program availability:* Part-time, evening/weekend, online learning. *Degree requirements:* For master's, thesis, accomplished practices portfolio. *Entrance requirements:* For master's, minimum GPA of 3.0 in last 60 hours of undergraduate coursework; 2 letters of recommendation. Additional exam requirements/recommendations for international students: Required—TOEFL (minimum score 550 paper-based). Electronic applications accepted.

Wayland Baptist University, Graduate Programs, Program in Education, Plainview, TX 79072-6998. Offers education administration (M Ed); education diagnostics (M Ed); education literacy (M Ed); elementary certification (M Ed); English (M Ed); English as a second language (M Ed); higher education administration (M Ed); human resources (M Ed); instructional leadership (M Ed); instructional technology (M Ed); leadership training and development (M Ed); science education (M Ed); secondary certification (M Ed); social studies (M Ed); special education (M Ed); sports administration and management (M Ed). *Program availability:* Part-time, evening/weekend, 100% online. *Degree requirements:* For master's, comprehensive exam, capstone course. *Entrance requirements:* For master's, GRE, GMAT or MAT. Additional exam requirements/recommendations for international students: Required—TOEFL (minimum score 500 paper-based; 61 iBT). Electronic applications accepted.

Wayne State College, School of Education and Counseling, Department of Educational Foundations and Leadership, Program in Curriculum and Instruction, Wayne, NE 68787. Offers alternative education (MSE); business and information technology education (MSE); communication arts education (MSE); early childhood education (MSE); elementary education (MSE); English as a second language (MSE); English education (MSE); family and consumer sciences education (MSE); industrial technology and vocational education (MSE); learning communities (MSE); mathematics education (MSE);

music education (MSE); science education (MSE); social science education (MSE). *Accreditation:* NCATE. *Program availability:* Part-time, evening/weekend. *Degree requirements:* For master's, comprehensive exam, thesis optional. *Entrance requirements:* For master's, GRE General Test. Additional exam requirements/recommendations for international students: Required—TOEFL (minimum score 550 paper-based).

Wayne State University, College of Education, Division of Teacher Education, Detroit, MI 48202. Offers art education (M Ed); bilingual/bicultural education (Certificate); curriculum and instruction (Ed D, PhD, Ed S), including English as a second language (MAT, Ed D, Ed S), K-12 curriculum (PhD); elementary education (MAT), including bilingual/bicultural education (M Ed, MAT), early childhood education (M Ed, MAT), English as a second language (MAT, Ed D, Ed S), foreign language education, science education (M Ed, MAT), special education (M Ed, MAT); elementary mathematics specialist (Certificate); English as a second language (Certificate); reading (M Ed, Ed S); reading, language and literature (Ed D); secondary education (MAT), including bilingual/bicultural education (M Ed, MAT), early childhood education (M Ed, MAT), English as a second language (MAT, Ed D, Ed S), English education, foreign language education, mathematics education (M Ed, MAT), science education (M Ed, MAT), social studies education (M Ed, MAT), special education (MAT), including career and technical education; teaching and learning (M Ed), including bilingual/bicultural education (M Ed, MAT), early childhood education (M Ed, MAT), elementary education, foreign language, mathematics education (M Ed, MAT), science education (M Ed, MAT), social studies education (M Ed, MAT), special education (M Ed, MAT). *Program availability:* Part-time, evening/weekend. *Faculty:* 20. *Students:* 121 full-time (94 women), 251 part-time (209 women); includes 116 minority (83 Black or African American, non-Hispanic/Latino; 3 American Indian or Alaska Native, non-Hispanic/Latino; 3 Asian, non-Hispanic/Latino; 14 Hispanic/Latino; 13 Two or more races, non-Hispanic/Latino), 11 international. Average age 37. 171 applicants, 23% accepted, 32 enrolled. In 2018, 112 master's, 8 doctorates, 11 other advanced degrees awarded. *Degree requirements:* For master's, thesis (for some programs), essay or project (for some M Ed programs), professional field experience (for MAT programs); for doctorate, comprehensive exam, thesis/dissertation. *Entrance requirements:* For master's, undergraduate degree, verification of participation in group work with children, Michigan State Police criminal background check, negative tb test, personal statement (for MAT programs); for all other master's programs: undergraduate degree, personal statement; for doctorate, minimum undergraduate GPA of 3.0, graduate 3.5; interview; curriculum vitae; references; writing sample; letter of application; master's degree (for most programs); for other advanced degree, education specialist certificate: undergraduate with GPA of 2.5 or better and master's degree with GPA of 2.75 or better; personal statement. Additional exam requirements/recommendations for international students: Required—TOEFL (minimum score 550 paper-based; 79 iBT); Recommended—IELTS (minimum score 6.5), TWE (minimum score 5.5), TSE (minimum score 58). *Application deadline:* Applications are processed on a rolling basis. Application fee: $50. Electronic applications accepted. *Financial support:* In 2018–19, 85 students received support, including 3 fellowships (averaging $14,275 per year); research assistantships with tuition reimbursements available, Federal Work-Study, scholarships/grants, and unspecified assistantships also available. Support available to part-time students. Financial award applicants required to submit FAFSA. *Faculty research:* Improving students' skill achievement in mathematics, improving elementary children's understanding of informational text, teachers' use of their pedagogical and mathematical knowledge in the interactive work of teaching, the intersection of identity construction in teaching and learning, identifying effective methods of literacy instruction and assessments for bilingual students in elementary language arts classrooms. *Unit head:* Dr. Roland Coloma, Assistant Dean for Teacher Education, 313-577-0902, E-mail: rscoloma@wayne.edu. *Application contact:* Dr. Mary L. Waker, Graduate Admissions Officer, 313-577-1601, Fax: 313-577-7904, E-mail: m.waker@wayne.edu.
Website: http://coe.wayne.edu/ted/index.php

West Chester University of Pennsylvania, College of the Sciences and Mathematics, Department of Biology, West Chester, PA 19383. Offers MS, Teaching Certificate. *Program availability:* Part-time, evening/weekend. *Degree requirements:* For master's, comprehensive exam (for some programs), thesis (for some programs). *Entrance requirements:* For master's, two letters of reference. Additional exam requirements/recommendations for international students: Required—TOEFL or IELTS. Electronic applications accepted. *Faculty research:* Medical microbiology, molecular genetics and physiology of living systems, mammalian biomechanics, invertebrate and vertebrate animal systems, aquatic and terrestrial ecology.

West Chester University of Pennsylvania, College of the Sciences and Mathematics, Department of Physics, West Chester, PA 19383. Offers Teaching Certificate. *Entrance requirements:* For degree, bachelor's degree or higher, minimum GPA of 3.0. Additional exam requirements/recommendations for international students: Required—TOEFL or IELTS. Electronic applications accepted.

Western Governors University, Teachers College, Salt Lake City, UT 84107. Offers curriculum and instruction (MS); educational leadership (MS); elementary education (MAT, Postbaccalaureate Certificate); English education (5-12) (MAT); English language learning (PreK-12) (MA); instructional design (M Ed); learning and technology (M Ed); mathematics (5-12) (MAT); mathematics (5-9) (MAT); mathematics education (5-12) (MA); mathematics education (5-9) (MA); mathematics education (K-6) (MA); science (5-12) (MAT); science education (5-12) (MA), including biology, chemistry, earth science, physics; science education (5-9) (MA); special education (MS). *Accreditation:* NCATE. *Program availability:* Evening/weekend, online learning. *Degree requirements:* For master's, capstone project. *Entrance requirements:* For master's and Postbaccalaureate Certificate, transcripts. Additional exam requirements/recommendations for international students: Required—TOEFL (minimum score 450 paper-based; 80 iBT). Electronic applications accepted. Application fee is waived when completed online. *Expenses:* Contact institution.

Western Michigan University, Graduate College, College of Arts and Sciences, Department of Interdisciplinary Arts and Sciences, Kalamazoo, MI 49008. Offers science education (MA, PhD), including biological sciences (PhD), chemistry (PhD), geosciences (PhD), physical geography (PhD), physics (PhD), science education (PhD). *Degree requirements:* For doctorate, thesis/dissertation.

Western Oregon University, Graduate Programs, College of Education, Division of Teacher Education, Program in Secondary Education, Monmouth, OR 97361. Offers bilingual education (MS Ed); health (MS Ed); humanities (MAT, MS Ed); initial licensure (MAT); mathematics (MAT, MS Ed); science (MAT, MS Ed); social science (MAT, MS Ed). *Accreditation:* NCATE. *Program availability:* Part-time, evening/weekend. *Degree requirements:* For master's, thesis optional, written exam. *Entrance requirements:* For master's, minimum GPA of 3.0, teaching license. Additional exam requirements/recommendations for international students: Required—TOEFL (minimum score 550 paper-based; 79 iBT), IELTS (minimum score 6.5). *Faculty research:* Literacy, science in primary grades, geography education, retention, teacher burnout.

Western Washington University, Graduate School, College of Sciences and Technology, Program in Natural Science/Science Education, Bellingham, WA 98225-5996. Offers M Ed. Electronic applications accepted. *Faculty research:* Science education reform.

Westfield State University, College of Graduate and Continuing Education, Department of Education, Westfield, MA 01086. Offers early childhood education (M Ed); elementary education (M Ed); reading specialist (M Ed); secondary education (M Ed), including biology teacher education, chemistry teacher education, general science teacher education, history teacher education, mathematics teacher education, physical education teacher education; special education (M Ed), including moderate disabilities, 5-12, moderate disabilities, preK-8; vocational technical education (M Ed). *Accreditation:* NCATE. *Program availability:* Part-time, evening/weekend. *Degree requirements:* For master's, comprehensive exam, practicum. *Entrance requirements:* For master's, GRE General Test or MAT, minimum undergraduate GPA of 2.8. Additional exam requirements/recommendations for international students: Recommended—TOEFL (minimum score 550 paper-based; 79 iBT). *Faculty research:* Collaborative teacher education, developmental early childhood education.

Westfield State University, College of Graduate and Continuing Education, Department of Education, Programs in Secondary Education, Program in Biology Teacher Education, Westfield, MA 01086. Offers secondary education-biology (M Ed). *Program availability:* Part-time, evening/weekend. *Degree requirements:* For master's, comprehensive exam, thesis (for some programs). *Entrance requirements:* For master's, GRE General Test or MAT, minimum undergraduate GPA of 2.8. Additional exam requirements/recommendations for international students: Recommended—TOEFL (minimum score 550 paper-based; 79 iBT).

Widener University, School of Human Service Professions, Center for Education, Chester, PA 19013-5792. Offers adult education (M Ed); counseling in higher education (M Ed); counselor education (M Ed); early childhood education (M Ed); educational foundations (M Ed); educational leadership (M Ed); educational psychology (M Ed); elementary education (M Ed); English and language arts (M Ed); health education (M Ed); higher education leadership (Ed D); home and school visitor (M Ed); human sexuality (M Ed, PhD); mathematics education (M Ed); middle school education (M Ed); principalship (M Ed); reading and language arts (Ed D); reading education (M Ed); school administration (Ed D); science education (M Ed); social studies education (M Ed); special education (M Ed); technology education (M Ed). *Accreditation:* NCATE. *Program availability:* Part-time, evening/weekend. Terminal master's awarded for partial completion of doctoral program. *Degree requirements:* For doctorate, thesis/dissertation. *Entrance requirements:* For master's, minimum GPA of 2.5; for doctorate, GRE or MAT, minimum GPA of 2.0 (undergraduate), 3.5 (graduate). Electronic applications accepted. *Expenses:* Contact institution. *Faculty research:* Reading and cognition, adult education, technology education, educational leadership, special education.

Wisconsin Lutheran College, College of Adult and Graduate Studies, Milwaukee, WI 53226-9942. Offers high performance instruction (MA Ed); instructional technology (MA Ed); leadership and innovation (MA Ed); science instruction (MA Ed).

Wright State University, Graduate School, College of Science and Mathematics, Department of Earth and Environmental Sciences, Program in Earth Science Education, Dayton, OH 45435. Offers MST. *Entrance requirements:* For master's, GRE General Test. Additional exam requirements/recommendations for international students: Required—TOEFL. *Faculty research:* Pedagogy.

Wright State University, Graduate School, College of Science and Mathematics, Interdisciplinary Program in Science and Mathematics, Dayton, OH 45435. Offers PhD.

Youngstown State University, College of Graduate Studies, College of Science, Technology, Engineering and Mathematics, Department of Chemistry, Youngstown, OH 44555-0001. Offers analytical chemistry (MS); biochemistry (MS); chemistry education (MS); inorganic chemistry (MS); organic chemistry (MS); physical chemistry (MS). *Program availability:* Part-time. *Degree requirements:* For master's, thesis. *Entrance requirements:* For master's, bachelor's degree in chemistry, minimum GPA of 2.7. Additional exam requirements/recommendations for international students: Required—TOEFL. *Faculty research:* Analysis of antioxidants, chromatography, defects and disorder in crystalline oxides, hydrogen bonding, novel organic and organometallic materials.

Social Sciences Education

Alabama Agricultural and Mechanical University, School of Graduate Studies, College of Education, Humanities, and Behavioral Sciences, Department of Educational Leadership and Secondary Education, Huntsville, AL 35811. Offers biology (M Ed); business/marketing education (M Ed, Ed S); chemistry (M Ed); collaborative teacher secondary education (M Ed, Ed S); education (M Ed, Ed S); English language arts (M Ed); family/consumer science education (M Ed, Ed S); general science (M Ed); general social science (M Ed); mathematics (M Ed, Ed S); physics (M Ed, Ed S); technology education (M Ed). *Accreditation:* NCATE. *Program availability:* Evening/weekend. *Degree requirements:* For master's, comprehensive exam; for Ed S, thesis. *Entrance requirements:* For master's, GRE General Test. Additional exam requirements/recommendations for international students: Required—TOEFL (minimum score 500 paper-based; 61 iBT). Electronic applications accepted. *Faculty research:* World peace through education, computer-assisted instruction.

Alabama State University, College of Education, Department of Curriculum and Instruction, Montgomery, AL 36101-0271. Offers early childhood education (Ed S); secondary education (M Ed), including biology education, English language arts education, history education, math education, music education, reading education, social science education. *Program availability:* Part-time, evening/weekend, online only, 100% online. *Faculty:* 7 full-time (4 women), 7 part-time/adjunct (4 women). *Students:* 22 full-time (19 women), 58 part-time (49 women); includes 235 minority (234 Black or African American, non-Hispanic/Latino; 1 Hispanic/Latino), 5 international. Average age 36. 45 applicants, 33% accepted, 6 enrolled. In 2018, 34 master's awarded. *Degree requirements:* For master's, comprehensive exam, thesis optional; for Ed S, comprehensive exam, thesis. *Entrance requirements:* For master's, GRE General Test, MAT, writing competency test; for Ed S, writing competency test, GRE, MAT. Additional exam requirements/recommendations for international students: Required—TOEFL (minimum score 500 paper-based). *Application deadline:* For fall admission, 4/15 for domestic and international students; for spring admission, 11/15 for domestic and international students; for summer admission, 3/15 for domestic and international students. Applications are processed on a rolling basis. Application fee: $25. Electronic applications accepted. *Expenses:* Contact institution. *Financial support:* Fellowships, teaching assistantships, career-related internships or fieldwork, scholarships/grants, tuition waivers (partial), and unspecified assistantships available. Financial award application deadline: 6/30; financial award applicants required to submit FAFSA. *Unit head:* Dr. Joyce Johnson, Acting Chairperson, 334-229-4485, Fax: 334-229-5603, E-mail: jjohnson@alasu.edu. *Application contact:* Dr. Ed Brown, Dean of Graduate Studies, 334-229-4274, Fax: 334-229-4928, E-mail: ebrown@alasu.edu.
Website: http://www.alasu.edu/academics/colleges—departments/college-of-education/curriculum—instruction/index.aspx

Andrews University, School of Graduate Studies, School of Education, Department of Teaching, Learning, and Curriculum, Berrien Springs, MI 49104. Offers curriculum and instruction (MA, Ed D, PhD, Ed S); elementary education (MAT); secondary education (MAT), including biology, education, English, English as a second language, French, history, physics; teacher education (MAT). *Entrance requirements:* For master's, GRE Subject Test. Additional exam requirements/recommendations for international students: Required—TOEFL (minimum score 550 paper-based).

Appalachian State University, Cratis D. Williams School of Graduate Studies, Department of Curriculum and Instruction, Boone, NC 28608. Offers curriculum specialist (MA); educational media (MA); elementary education (MA); middle grades education (MA), including language arts, mathematics, science, social studies. *Accreditation:* NCATE. *Program availability:* Part-time, evening/weekend, online learning. *Degree requirements:* For master's, comprehensive exam, thesis or alternative. *Entrance requirements:* For master's, GRE General Test or MAT, 3 letters of recommendation. Additional exam requirements/recommendations for international students: Required—TOEFL (minimum score 570 paper-based; 79 iBT), IELTS (minimum score 6.5). Electronic applications accepted. *Expenses: Tuition, area resident:* Full-time $4839; part-time $237 per credit hour. Tuition, state resident: full-time $4839; part-time $237 per credit hour. Tuition, nonresident: full-time $18,271; part-time $895.50 per credit hour. *Faculty research:* Media literacy, elementary teaching, curriculum development, online learning environments.

Arkansas State University, Graduate School, College of Humanities and Social Sciences, Department of Criminology, Sociology, and Geography, State University, AR 72467. Offers criminal justice (MA); sociology (MA); sociology education (SCCT). *Program availability:* Part-time. *Degree requirements:* For master's, one foreign language, comprehensive exam, thesis or alternative; for SCCT, comprehensive exam. *Entrance requirements:* For master's, GRE General Test or MAT, appropriate bachelor's degree, letters of recommendation, official transcripts, immunization records; for SCCT, GRE General Test or MAT, interview, master's degree, official transcript, immunization records. Additional exam requirements/recommendations for international students: Required—TOEFL (minimum score 550 paper-based; 79 iBT), IELTS (minimum score 6), PTE (minimum score 56). Electronic applications accepted.

Arkansas State University, Graduate School, College of Humanities and Social Sciences, Department of History, State University, AR 72467. Offers history (MA); history education (SCCT); social science education (MSE). *Program availability:* Part-time. *Degree requirements:* For master's, comprehensive exam, thesis or alternative; for SCCT, comprehensive exam. *Entrance requirements:* For master's, GRE General Test or MAT, GMAT, appropriate bachelor's degree, letters of reference, official transcript, valid teaching certificate (for MSE), immunization records; for SCCT, GRE General Test or MAT, interview, master's degree, letters of reference, official transcript, immunization records. Additional exam requirements/recommendations for international students: Required—TOEFL (minimum score 550 paper-based; 79 iBT), IELTS (minimum score 6), PTE (minimum score 56). Electronic applications accepted.

Arkansas State University, Graduate School, College of Humanities and Social Sciences, Department of Political Science, State University, AR 72467. Offers political science (MA); political science education (SCCT); public administration (MPA). *Accreditation:* NASPAA (one or more programs are accredited). *Program availability:* Part-time. *Degree requirements:* For master's, comprehensive exam, thesis or alternative; for SCCT, comprehensive exam. *Entrance requirements:* For master's, GRE General Test or MAT, GMAT, appropriate bachelor's degree, letters of recommendation, official transcripts, immunization records, statement of purpose; for SCCT, GRE General Test or MAT, GMAT, interview, master's degree, official transcript, letters of recommendation, immunization records. Additional exam requirements/recommendations for international students: Required—TOEFL (minimum score 550 paper-based; 79 iBT), IELTS (minimum score 6), PTE (minimum score 56). Electronic applications accepted.

Arkansas State University, Graduate School, College of Humanities and Social Sciences, Heritage Studies Program, State University, AR 72467. Offers heritage studies (MA, PhD). *Program availability:* Part-time. *Degree requirements:* For master's, comprehensive exam, thesis or alternative, portfolio; for doctorate, comprehensive exam, thesis/dissertation, portfolio. *Entrance requirements:* For master's, GRE, MAT or GMAT, appropriate bachelor's degree, letters of reference, official transcript, interview, letter of interest, writing sample, immunization records; for doctorate, GRE, MAT, or GMAT, appropriate bachelor's or master's degree, interview, letters of reference, official transcript, letter of interest, writing sample, immunization records. Additional exam requirements/recommendations for international students: Required—TOEFL (minimum score 550 paper-based; 79 iBT), IELTS (minimum score 6), PTE (minimum score 56). Electronic applications accepted.

Asbury University, School of Graduate and Professional Studies, Wilmore, KY 40390-1198. Offers biology: alternative certificate (MA Ed); chemistry: alternative certificate (MA Ed); English (MA Ed); English as a second language (MA Ed); ESL (MA Ed); French (MA Ed); Latin: alternative certificate (MA Ed); mathematics: alternative certificate (MA Ed); reading/writing endorsement (MA Ed); social studies (MA Ed); social work (MSW), including child and family services; Spanish (MA Ed); special education (MA Ed); special education: alternative certificate (MA Ed); teacher as leader endorsement (MA Ed). *Accreditation:* NCATE. *Program availability:* Part-time. *Degree requirements:* For master's, action research project, portfolio. *Entrance requirements:* For master's, PRAXIS/NTE, minimum GPA of 2.75, letters of recommendation. Additional exam requirements/recommendations for international students: Required—TOEFL (minimum score 550 paper-based). Electronic applications accepted.

Binghamton University, State University of New York, Graduate School, College of Community and Public Affairs, Department of Teaching, Learning and Educational Leadership, Program in Adolescence Education, Binghamton, NY 13902-6000. Offers biology education (MAT, MS Ed); chemistry education (MAT, MS Ed); earth science education (MAT, MS Ed); English education (MAT, MS Ed); French education (MAT, MS Ed); mathematical sciences education (MAT, MS Ed); physics (MAT, MS Ed); social

studies (MAT, MS Ed); Spanish education (MAT, MS Ed). *Accreditation:* TEAC. *Program availability:* Part-time, evening/weekend. *Degree requirements:* For master's, portfolio. *Entrance requirements:* For master's, GRE General Test, teaching certification. Additional exam requirements/recommendations for international students: Required—TOEFL (minimum score 550 paper-based; 80 iBT). Electronic applications accepted.

Bloomsburg University of Pennsylvania, School of Graduate Studies, College of Education, Department of Teaching and Learning, Program in Middle Level Education Grades 4-8, Bloomsburg, PA 17815-1301. Offers language arts (M Ed); math (M Ed); science (M Ed); social studies (M Ed). *Accreditation:* NCATE. *Degree requirements:* For master's, thesis optional, practicum, student teaching. *Entrance requirements:* For master's, MAT, GRE, or PRAXIS, minimum QPA of 3.0, teaching certificate, U.S. citizenship, related undergraduate coursework, professional liability insurance, recent TB test. Additional exam requirements/recommendations for international students: Required—TOEFL (minimum score 550 paper-based), IELTS. Electronic applications accepted.

Bob Jones University, Graduate Programs, Greenville, SC 29614. Offers accountancy (MS); Bible (MA); Bible translation (MA); Biblical studies (Certificate); business administration (MBA); church history (MA, PhD); church ministries (MA); church music (MM); cinema and video production (MA); counseling (MS); curriculum and instruction (Ed D); divinity (M Div); dramatic production (MA); educational leadership (MS, Ed D, Ed S); elementary education (M Ed, MAT); English (M Ed, MA, MAT); fine arts (MA); graphic design (MA); history (M Ed, MA); illustration (MA); interpretative speech (MA); mathematics (M Ed, MAT); medical missions (Certificate); ministry (MM, D Min); multi-categorical special education (M Ed, MAT); music (M Ed); New Testament interpretation (PhD); Old Testament interpretation (PhD); orchestral instrument performance (MM); organ performance (MM); pastoral studies (MA); personnel services (MS, Ed S); piano pedagogy (MM); piano performance (MM); platform arts (MA); rhetoric and public address (MA); secondary education (M Ed); studio art (MA); teaching Bible (MA); theology (MA, PhD); voice performance (MM); youth ministries (MA); M Div/MM.

Boston College, Lynch School of Education and Human Development, Department of Teacher Education, Special Education and Curriculum and Instruction, Chestnut Hill, MA 02467-3800. Offers curriculum and instruction (M Ed, PhD, CAES); early childhood education (M Ed); elementary education (M Ed); law and curriculum and instruction (JD/M Ed); reading specialist (M Ed, CAES); religious education (M Ed, CAES); secondary education (M Ed, MAT, MST), including biology (MST), chemistry (MST), English (MAT), French (MAT), geology (MST), history (MAT), Latin and classical humanities (MAT), mathematics (MST), physics (MST), secondary teaching (M Ed), Spanish (MAT); special needs: moderate disabilities (M Ed, CAES); special needs: severe disabilities (M Ed); JD/M Ed. *Program availability:* Part-time, evening/weekend, 100% online. *Faculty:* 19 full-time (11 women). *Students:* 186 full-time (140 women), 92 part-time (74 women); includes 58 minority (20 Black or African American, non-Hispanic/Latino; 4 Asian, non-Hispanic/Latino; 29 Hispanic/Latino; 5 Two or more races, non-Hispanic/Latino), 33 international. Average age 28. In 2018, 132 master's, 13 doctorates awarded. Terminal master's awarded for partial completion of doctoral program. *Degree requirements:* For master's, comprehensive exam; for doctorate, comprehensive exam, thesis/dissertation. *Entrance requirements:* Additional exam requirements/recommendations for international students: Required—TOEFL. Application fee: $75. Electronic applications accepted. *Financial support:* Fellowships with full and partial tuition reimbursements, research assistantships with full and partial tuition reimbursements, teaching assistantships with full and partial tuition reimbursements, career-related internships or fieldwork, Federal Work-Study, institutionally sponsored loans, scholarships/grants, traineeships, health care benefits, tuition waivers (full and partial), and unspecified assistantships available. Support available to part-time students. Financial award applicants required to submit FAFSA. *Faculty research:* Teacher education, education research and policy, bilingual education, science education, disabilities, urban education. *Unit head:* Dr. Susan Bruce, Chairperson, 617-552-4214, Fax: 617-552-0812. *Application contact:* Jessica Rivers, Assistant Dean of Graduate Admission and Financial Aid, 617-552-4214, Fax: 617-552-0398, E-mail: riversja@bc.edu.
Website: http://www.bc.edu/education

Bridgewater State University, College of Graduate Studies, College of Humanities and Social Sciences, Department of History, Bridgewater, MA 02325. Offers MAT. *Program availability:* Part-time, evening/weekend. *Entrance requirements:* For master's, GRE General Test.

Brooklyn College of the City University of New York, School of Education, Program in Adolescence Science Education and Special Subjects, Brooklyn, NY 11210-2889. Offers adolescence science education (MAT); biology teacher (7-12) (MA); chemistry teacher (7-12) (MA); earth science teacher (7-12) (MAT); English teacher (7-12) (MA); French teacher (7-12) (MA); mathematics teacher (7-12) (MA); music teacher (MA); physics teacher (7-12) (MA); social studies teacher (7-12) (MA); Spanish teacher (7-12) (MA). *Program availability:* Part-time, evening/weekend. *Degree requirements:* For master's, comprehensive exam (for some programs), thesis (for some programs). *Entrance requirements:* For master's, LAST, previous course work in education, resume, 2 letters of recommendation, essay. Additional exam requirements/recommendations for international students: Required—TOEFL (minimum score 500 paper-based; 61 iBT). Electronic applications accepted. *Faculty research:* Interdisciplinary education, semiotics, discourse analysis, autobiography, teacher identity.

Brown University, Graduate School, Department of Education, Program in Teaching, Providence, RI 02912. Offers elementary education (MAT); English (MAT); history/social studies (MAT); science (MAT); secondary education (MAT). *Degree requirements:* For master's, student teaching, portfolio. *Entrance requirements:* For master's, GRE General Test, transcript, personal statement, 3 letters of recommendation, interview, writing sample (English applicants only). Additional exam requirements/recommendations for international students: Required—TOEFL (minimum score 577 paper-based). Electronic applications accepted. *Faculty research:* Literacy, English language learners, diversity, special education, biodiversity.

Buffalo State College, State University of New York, The Graduate School, School of Natural and Social Sciences, Department of History and Social Studies Education, Buffalo, NY 14222-1095. Offers history (MA); museum studies (MA); secondary education (MS Ed), including social studies. *Program availability:* Part-time, evening/weekend. *Degree requirements:* For master's, one foreign language, thesis (for some programs), project (MS Ed). *Entrance requirements:* For master's, minimum GPA of 2.75, 30 hours in history (MA), 36 hours in history or social sciences (MS Ed). Additional exam requirements/recommendations for international students: Required—TOEFL (minimum score 550 paper-based).

California State University, East Bay, Office of Graduate Studies, College of Letters, Arts, and Social Sciences, Department of History, Hayward, CA 94542-3000. Offers history (MA); public history (MA); teaching (MA). *Program availability:* Part-time, evening/weekend. *Degree requirements:* For master's, one foreign language, comprehensive exam, project, thesis, or exam. *Entrance requirements:* For master's, GRE (strongly recommended), minimum GPA of 3.0 in field, 3.3 in history; 2 letters of recommendation; writing sample. Additional exam requirements/recommendations for international students: Required—TOEFL (minimum score 550 paper-based). Electronic applications accepted. *Faculty research:* Digital history, American women, early America, Native Americans, medieval colonial India.

California State University, Fresno, Division of Research and Graduate Studies, College of Social Sciences, Department of History, Fresno, CA 93740-8027. Offers history (MA); history teaching (MA). *Program availability:* Part-time, evening/weekend. *Degree requirements:* For master's, project; thesis or comprehensive examination. *Entrance requirements:* For master's, GRE General Test, minimum GPA of 3.0. Additional exam requirements/recommendations for international students: Required—TOEFL. Electronic applications accepted. *Faculty research:* International education, classical art history, improving teacher quality.

Caribbean University, Graduate School, Bayamón, PR 00960-0493. Offers administration and supervision (MA Ed); criminal justice (MA); curriculum and instruction (MA Ed, PhD), including elementary education (MA Ed), English education (MA Ed), history education (MA Ed), mathematics education (MA Ed), primary education (MA Ed), science education (MA Ed), Spanish education (MA Ed); educational technology in instructional systems (MA Ed); gerontology (MSN); human resources (MBA); museology, archiving and art history (MA Ed); neonatal pediatrics (MSN); physical education (MA Ed); special education (MA Ed). *Entrance requirements:* For master's, interview, minimum GPA of 2.5.

Carthage College, Division of Teacher Education, Kenosha, WI 53140. Offers classroom guidance and counseling (M Ed); creative arts (M Ed); gifted and talented children (M Ed); language arts (M Ed); modern language (M Ed); natural sciences (M Ed); reading (M Ed, Certificate); social sciences (M Ed); teacher leadership (M Ed). *Program availability:* Part-time, evening/weekend. *Degree requirements:* For master's, thesis optional. *Entrance requirements:* For master's, MAT, minimum B average, letters of reference.

Chadron State College, School of Professional and Graduate Studies, Department of Education, Chadron, NE 69337. Offers business (MA Ed); community counseling (MA Ed); educational administration (MS Ed, Sp Ed); elementary education (MS Ed); history (MA Ed); language and literature (MA Ed); secondary administration (MS Ed); secondary education (MS Ed). *Accreditation:* NCATE. *Program availability:* Part-time, evening/weekend, online learning. *Degree requirements:* For master's, thesis optional. *Entrance requirements:* For master's, GRE General Test, GRE Writing Test, minimum GPA of 2.75 or 12 graduate hours at CSC with minimum GPA of 3.25. Additional exam requirements/recommendations for international students: Required—TOEFL. Electronic applications accepted. *Faculty research:* Rural education, technology, mental health.

Chatham University, Program in Education, Pittsburgh, PA 15232-2826. Offers early childhood education (MAT); elementary education (MAT); environmental education (K-12) (MAT); secondary art (MAT); secondary biology education (MAT); secondary chemistry education (MAT); secondary English education (MAT); secondary math education (MAT); secondary physics education (MAT); secondary social studies education (MAT); special education (MAT). *Degree requirements:* For master's, thesis, teaching experience. *Entrance requirements:* For master's, minimum GPA of 3.0, sample of written work, recommendation letters. Additional exam requirements/recommendations for international students: Required—TOEFL (minimum score 600 paper-based; 100 iBT), IELTS (minimum score 7), TWE. Electronic applications accepted. Application fee is waived when completed online. *Faculty research:* Gifted education, environmental education, technology in education, writing as learning, class size and achievement.

The Citadel, The Military College of South Carolina, Citadel Graduate College, Zucker Family School of Education, Charleston, SC 29409. Offers elementary/secondary school administration and supervision (M Ed); elementary/secondary school counseling (M Ed); interdisciplinary STEM education (M Ed); literacy education (M Ed, Graduate Certificate); middle grades (MAT), including English, mathematics, science, social studies; physical education (grades K-12) (MAT); school superintendency (Ed S); secondary education (MAT), including biology, English, mathematics, social studies; student affairs (Graduate Certificate); student affairs and college counseling (M Ed). *Accreditation:* NCATE. *Program availability:* Part-time, evening/weekend, 100% online, blended/hybrid learning. *Degree requirements:* For master's, comprehensive exam (for some programs). *Entrance requirements:* For master's, GRE (minimum combined verbal and quantitative score of 290) or MAT (minimum score 396). Additional exam requirements/recommendations for international students: Required—TOEFL (minimum score 550 paper-based; 79 iBT). Electronic applications accepted. *Expenses:* Tuition, state resident: part-time $595 per credit hour. Tuition, nonresident: part-time $1020 per credit hour. *Required fees:* $90 per term.

City College of the City University of New York, Graduate School, School of Education, Department of Secondary Education, New York, NY 10031-9198. Offers adolescent mathematics education (MA, AC); English education (MA); middle school mathematics education (MS); science education (MA); social studies education (AC). *Accreditation:* NCATE. *Entrance requirements:* For master's, Liberal Arts and Sciences Test (LAST), Content Specialty Test (CST). Additional exam requirements/recommendations for international students: Required—TOEFL.

The College at Brockport, State University of New York, School of Education, Health, and Human Services, Department of Education and Human Development, Brockport, NY 14420-2997. Offers adolescence education (MS Ed), including adolescence biology education, adolescence chemistry education, adolescence English, adolescence mathematics, adolescence physics, adolescence physics education, adolescence social studies education; bilingual education (MS Ed, AGC); childhood curriculum specialist (MS Ed); inclusive generalist education (MS Ed, AGC, Advanced Certificate), including biology (MS Ed, AGC), chemistry (MS Ed), English (MS Ed, Advanced Certificate), mathematics (MS Ed, Advanced Certificate), science (MS Ed, Advanced Certificate), social studies (MS Ed, Advanced Certificate); literacy education B-12 (MS Ed). *Accreditation:* NCATE. *Faculty:* 12 full-time (7 women), 10 part-time/adjunct (6 women). *Students:* 60 full-time (39 women), 227 part-time (157 women); includes 9 minority (1 Asian, non-Hispanic/Latino; 8 Hispanic/Latino). 135 applicants, 71% accepted, 59 enrolled. In 2018, 107 master's, 13 AGCs awarded. *Degree requirements:* For master's, thesis or alternative. *Entrance requirements:* For master's, minimum GPA of 3.0, letters of recommendation, interview (for some programs); statement of objectives, current resume. Additional exam requirements/recommendations for international students: Required—TOEFL (minimum score 550 paper-based; 79 iBT), IELTS (minimum score 6.5). *Application deadline:* For fall admission, 3/15 priority date for domestic and international students; for spring admission, 10/15 priority date for domestic and international students; for summer admission, 3/15 priority date for domestic and international students. Application fee: $80. Electronic applications accepted. *Expenses:* Tuition, state resident: part-time $471 per credit. Tuition, nonresident: part-time $963 per credit. *Financial support:* In 2018–19, 1 fellowship with full tuition reimbursement (averaging $7,500 per year), 1 teaching assistantship with full tuition reimbursement (averaging $6,000 per year) were awarded; Federal Work-Study, scholarships/grants, and unspecified assistantships also available. Support available to part-time students. Financial award application deadline: 3/15;

financial award applicants required to submit FAFSA. *Faculty research:* Educational assessment, literacy education, inclusive education, teacher preparation, qualitative methodology. *Unit head:* Dr. Janka Szilagyi, Chairperson, 585-395-5945, Fax: 585-395-2172, E-mail: jszilagy@brockport.edu. *Application contact:* Buffie Edick, Graduate Program Director, 585-395-2326, Fax: 585-395-2172, E-mail: bedick@brockport.edu.
Website: https://www.brockport.edu/academics/education_human_development/department.html

College of St. Joseph, Graduate Programs, Division of Education, Program in Secondary Education, Rutland, VT 05701-3899. Offers English (M Ed); social studies (M Ed). *Program availability:* Part-time, evening/weekend. *Degree requirements:* For master's, comprehensive exam. *Entrance requirements:* For master's, PRAXIS I, official college transcripts; 2 letters of reference; minimum GPA of 3.0 (initial licensure) or 2.7 (nonlicensure); interview. Additional exam requirements/recommendations for international students: Required—TOEFL (minimum score 550 paper-based). Electronic applications accepted.

The Colorado College, Education Department, Program in Secondary Education, Colorado Springs, CO 80903-3294. Offers art teaching (K-12) (MAT); English teaching (MAT); foreign language teaching (MAT); mathematics teaching (MAT); music teaching (MAT); science teaching (MAT); social studies teaching (MAT). *Degree requirements:* For master's, thesis, internship. Electronic applications accepted.

Columbus State University, Graduate Studies, College of Education and Health Professions, Department of Teacher Education, Columbus, GA 31907-5645. Offers curriculum and instruction in accomplished teaching (M Ed); early childhood education (M Ed, MAT, Ed S); middle grades education (M Ed, MAT, Ed S); secondary education (M Ed, MAT, Ed S), including biology (MAT), chemistry (MAT), earth and space science (MAT), English/language arts, general science (M Ed), history (MAT), mathematics, science (Ed S), social science (M Ed, Ed S); special education (M Ed, MAT, Ed S), including general curriculum (M Ed, MAT); teacher leadership (M Ed). *Accreditation:* NCATE. *Program availability:* Part-time, evening/weekend, 100% online, blended/hybrid learning. *Faculty:* 20 full-time (12 women), 20 part-time/adjunct (15 women). *Students:* 110 full-time (84 women), 143 part-time (115 women); includes 105 minority (96 Black or African American, non-Hispanic/Latino; 4 Hispanic/Latino; 5 Two or more races, non-Hispanic/Latino). Average age 33. 147 applicants, 56% accepted, 62 enrolled. In 2018, 112 master's, 11 other advanced degrees awarded. *Degree requirements:* For Ed S, thesis or alternative. *Entrance requirements:* For master's, GRE General Test, minimum undergraduate GPA of 2.75; for Ed S, GRE General Test, minimum undergraduate GPA of 2.75, graduate 3.0. Additional exam requirements/recommendations for international students: Required—TOEFL (minimum score 550 paper-based; 79 iBT). *Application deadline:* For fall admission, 6/30 for domestic students, 5/1 for international students; for spring admission, 11/1 for domestic and international students; for summer admission, 3/1 for domestic and international students. Applications are processed on a rolling basis. Application fee: $50. Electronic applications accepted. *Expenses: Tuition, area resident:* Full-time $4924; part-time $618 per credit hour. Tuition, state resident: full-time $4924; part-time $618 per credit hour. Tuition, nonresident: full-time $19,218; part-time $2403 per credit hour. *International tuition:* $19,218 full-time. *Required fees:* $1870; $802. Tuition and fees vary according to course load, degree level and program. *Financial support:* In 2018–19, 29 students received support, including 7 research assistantships with partial tuition reimbursements available (averaging $3,000 per year); career-related internships or fieldwork, Federal Work-Study, institutionally sponsored loans, scholarships/grants, tuition waivers (partial), and unspecified assistantships also available. Support available to part-time students. Financial award application deadline: 5/1; financial award applicants required to submit FAFSA. *Unit head:* Dr. Jan Burcham, Department Chair, 706-507-8519, Fax: 706-568-3134, E-mail: burcham_jan@columbusstate.edu. *Application contact:* Catrina Smith-Edmond, Assistant Director for Graduate and Global Admission, 706-507-8824, Fax: 706-568-5091, E-mail: smithedmond_catrina@columbusstate.edu.
Website: http://te.columbusstate.edu/

Concordia University, College of Education, Portland, OR 97211-6099. Offers administrative leadership (Ed D); career and technical education (M Ed); curriculum and instruction (M Ed), including adolescent literacy, early childhood education, educational technology leadership, English for speakers of other languages, environmental education, health and physical education, mathematics, methods and curriculum, reading interventionist, science, social studies, STEAM education, teacher leadership, the inclusive classroom, trauma and resilience in educational settings; educational administration (M Ed); educational leadership (M Ed); elementary education (MAT); higher education (Ed D); instructional leadership (Ed D); professional leadership, inquiry, and transformation (Ed D); secondary education (MAT); transformational leadership (Ed D). *Program availability:* Part-time, online learning. *Degree requirements:* For master's, comprehensive exam, work samples/portfolio. *Entrance requirements:* For master's, California Basic Educational Skills Test or PRAXIS I, minimum undergraduate GPA of 2.8, graduate 3.0; 2 letters of recommendation. Additional exam requirements/recommendations for international students: Required—TOEFL (minimum score 525 paper-based). Electronic applications accepted. *Faculty research:* Learner-centered classroom, brain-based learning, future of online learning.

Converse College, Program in Middle Level Education, Spartanburg, SC 29302. Offers language arts/English (MAT); mathematics (MAT); middle level education (M Ed); science (MAT); social studies (MAT).

Converse College, Program in Secondary Education, Spartanburg, SC 29302. Offers biology (MAT); chemistry (MAT); English (M Ed, MAT); mathematics (M Ed, MAT); natural sciences (M Ed); social sciences (M Ed, MAT). *Program availability:* Part-time. *Degree requirements:* For master's, capstone paper. *Entrance requirements:* For master's, NTE or PRAXIS II (M Ed), minimum GPA of 2.75, 2 recommendations. Electronic applications accepted.

Delta State University, Graduate Programs, College of Arts and Sciences, Division of Social Sciences and History, Cleveland, MS 38733-0001. Offers community development (MS); social justice and criminology (MSJC); social science secondary education (M Ed), including history, social sciences. *Program availability:* Part-time, online learning. *Degree requirements:* For master's, thesis or alternative. *Expenses: Tuition, area resident:* Full-time $7076; part-time $393 per credit hour. Tuition, state resident: full-time $7076; part-time $393 per credit hour. Tuition, nonresident: full-time $7076; part-time $393 per credit hour. *International tuition:* $7076 full-time. *Required fees:* $170; $18.90 per credit hour. $9.45 per semester. Part-time tuition and fees vary according to program.

Duquesne University, School of Education, Department of Instruction and Leadership, Program in Secondary Education, Pittsburgh, PA 15282-0001. Offers biology (MS Ed); chemistry (MS Ed); English (MS Ed); K-12 education (MS Ed), including Latin; mathematics (MS Ed); physics (MS Ed); social studies (MS Ed). *Program availability:* Part-time, evening/weekend. *Faculty:* 5 full-time (4 women). *Students:* 20 full-time (12 women); includes 3 minority (1 Black or African American, non-Hispanic/Latino; 1 Hispanic/Latino; 1 Two or more races, non-Hispanic/Latino). Average age 24. 20 applicants, 85% accepted, 13 enrolled. In 2018, 14 master's awarded. *Entrance requirements:* For master's, two letters of recommendation, letter of intent, interview, bachelor's degree. Additional exam requirements/recommendations for international students: Required—TOEFL (minimum score 550 paper-based), IELTS (minimum score 7). *Application deadline:* For fall admission, 9/1 for domestic students; for spring admission, 1/2 for domestic students. Applications are processed on a rolling basis. Application fee: $0. Electronic applications accepted. *Expenses: Tuition:* Full-time $23,112; part-time $1284 per credit. Tuition and fees vary according to program. *Financial support:* In 2018–19, 1 student received support, including 1 teaching assistantship with full tuition reimbursement available; Federal Work-Study also available. Support available to part-time students. Financial award applicants required to submit FAFSA. *Faculty research:* Factors that create highly effective teachers; how to best support teachers to support students in reform-oriented environments; urban education; models of teacher leadership; improving instruction in mathematics/science/social studies/English. *Total annual research expenditures:* $120,139. *Unit head:* Dr. Melissa Boston, Associate Dean for Teacher Education/Professor, 412-396.6109, Fax: 412-396-5585, E-mail: bostonm@duq.edu. *Application contact:* Kelly McGinley, Graduate Admissions Assistant, 412-396-1559, Fax: 412-396-5585, E-mail: mcginleyk@duq.edu.
Website: http://www.duq.edu/academics/schools/education/graduate-programs-education/ms-ed-secondary-education

East Carolina University, Graduate School, College of Education, Department of Literacy Studies, English and History Education, Greenville, NC 27858-4353. Offers curriculum and instruction (MA Ed); English education (MAT); history education (MAT); reading education (MA Ed). *Accreditation:* NCATE. *Program availability:* Part-time, evening/weekend, online learning. *Application deadline:* For fall admission, 6/1 priority date for domestic students. *Expenses: Tuition, area resident:* Full-time $4749. Tuition, state resident: full-time $4749. Tuition, nonresident: full-time $17,898. *International tuition:* $17,898 full-time. *Required fees:* $2787. Part-time tuition and fees vary according to course load and program. *Financial support:* Application deadline: 6/1. *Unit head:* Dr. Kristin M Gesmann, Chair, 252-328-5670, E-mail: gaehsmannk18@ecu.edu. *Application contact:* Graduate School Admissions, 252-328-6012, Fax: 252-328-6071, E-mail: gradschool@ecu.edu.
Website: http://www.ecu.edu/cs-educ/libs/index.cfm

Eastern Kentucky University, The Graduate School, College of Education, Department of Curriculum and Instruction, Program in Secondary and Higher Education, Richmond, KY 40475-3102. Offers secondary education (MA Ed), including agricultural education, art education, biological sciences education, business education, English education, geography education, history education, home economics education, industrial education, mathematical sciences education, physical education, school health education. *Accreditation:* NCATE. *Program availability:* Part-time. *Entrance requirements:* For master's, GRE General Test, minimum GPA of 2.5.

Eastern University, Graduate Education Programs, St. Davids, PA 19087-3696. Offers ESL program specialist (K-12) (Certificate); general supervisor (PreK-12) (Certificate); health and physical education (K-12) (Certificate); middle level (4-8) (Certificate); multicultural education (M Ed); music (K-12) (Certificate); Pre K-4 (Certificate); Pre K-4 with special education (Certificate); reading (M Ed); reading specialist (K-12) (Certificate); reading supervisor (K-12) (Certificate); school counseling (MA, CAGS); school principalship (preK-12) (Certificate); school psychology (MS, CAGS); secondary biology education (7-12) (Certificate); secondary chemistry education (7-12) (Certificate); secondary communication education (7-12) (Certificate); secondary English education (7-12) (Certificate); secondary math education (7-12) (Certificate); secondary social studies education (7-12) (Certificate); special education (M Ed); special education (7-12) (Certificate); special education (Pre K-8) (Certificate); special education supervisor (K-12) (Certificate); TESOL (M Ed); world language (Certificate), including Spanish. *Program availability:* Part-time, evening/weekend, online learning. *Entrance requirements:* Additional exam requirements/recommendations for international students: Required—TOEFL. Electronic applications accepted. Application fee is waived when completed online. *Expenses:* Contact institution.

Fayetteville State University, Graduate School, Programs in Middle Grades, Secondary, Special and Elementary Education, Fayetteville, NC 28301-4298. Offers middle grades (MA Ed); sociology (MA Ed); special education (MA Ed), including behavioral-emotional handicaps, mentally handicapped, specific training disability. *Accreditation:* NCATE. *Program availability:* Part-time, evening/weekend. *Faculty:* 10 full-time (6 women), 1 (woman) part-time/adjunct. *Students:* 24 full-time (20 women), 31 part-time (29 women); includes 38 minority (35 Black or African American, non-Hispanic/Latino; 2 Hispanic/Latino; 1 Two or more races, non-Hispanic/Latino), 1 international. Average age 35. 8 applicants, 88% accepted, 3 enrolled. In 2018, 7 master's awarded. *Degree requirements:* For master's, comprehensive exam, internship. *Entrance requirements:* Additional exam requirements/recommendations for international students: Required—TOEFL. *Application deadline:* For fall admission, 4/15 for domestic students; for spring admission, 10/15 for domestic students. Applications are processed on a rolling basis. Application fee: $40. Electronic applications accepted. *Financial support:* Application deadline: 3/1; applicants required to submit FAFSA. *Faculty research:* Reading assessment; reading remediation; learning disabilities; parenting; and adolescents with autism spectrum disorders social-communication development. *Unit head:* Dr. Cynthia Shamberger, Chair of Middle Grades, Secondary and Specialized Subjects, 910-672-2464, Fax: 910-672-1941, E-mail: cshamber@uncfsu.edu. *Application contact:* Dr. Cynthia Shamberger, Chair of Middle Grades, Secondary and Specialized Subjects, 910-672-2464, Fax: 910-672-1941, E-mail: cshamber@uncfsu.edu.

Fitchburg State University, Division of Graduate and Continuing Education, Programs in History and Teaching History (Secondary Level), Fitchburg, MA 01420-2697. Offers MA. *Accreditation:* NCATE. *Program availability:* Part-time, evening/weekend. *Entrance requirements:* Additional exam requirements/recommendations for international students: Required—TOEFL (minimum score 550 paper-based; 79 iBT). Electronic applications accepted. *Expenses:* Contact institution.

Florida Agricultural and Mechanical University, Division of Graduate Studies, Research, and Continuing Education, College of Education, Program in Secondary Education and Foundation, Tallahassee, FL 32307-3200. Offers biology (M Ed); chemistry (MS Ed); English (MS Ed); history (MS Ed); math (MS Ed); physics (MS Ed). *Accreditation:* NCATE. *Degree requirements:* For master's, thesis (for some programs). *Entrance requirements:* For master's, GRE General Test, minimum GPA of 3.0. Additional exam requirements/recommendations for international students: Required—TOEFL.

Florida Gulf Coast University, College of Education, Program in Curriculum and Instruction, Fort Myers, FL 33965-6565. Offers elementary education (M Ed); English education (M Ed); English speakers of other languages endorsement (M Ed); gifted education (M Ed); mathematics education (M Ed); middle school education (M Ed); reading education (M Ed); science education (M Ed); social science education (M Ed); special education (M Ed). *Program availability:* Part-time, evening/weekend, online learning. *Degree requirements:* For master's, final project or portfolio. *Entrance requirements:* For master's, GRE General Test, MAT, minimum undergraduate GPA of 3.0 in last 2 years. Additional exam requirements/recommendations for international students: Required—TOEFL (minimum score 550 paper-based). Electronic applications accepted. *Faculty research:* Internet in schools, technology in pre-service and in-service teacher training.

Social Sciences Education

Florida International University, College of Arts, Sciences, and Education, Department of Teaching and Learning, Miami, FL 33199. Offers art education (MA, MS); curriculum and instruction (MS, Ed D, PhD, Ed S), including curriculum development (MS); elementary education (MS); English education (MS); learning technologies (MS); mathematics education (MS); modern language education (MS); physical education (MS); science education (MS); social studies education (MS); special education (MS); early childhood education (MS); exceptional student education (Ed D); foreign language education (MS), including foreign language education, teaching English to speakers of other languages (TESOL); language, literacy and culture (PhD); mathematics, science, and learning technologies (PhD); physical education (MS), including sport and fitness; reading education (MS). *Program availability:* Part-time, evening/weekend. *Faculty:* 64 full-time (43 women), 104 part-time/adjunct (76 women). *Students:* 169 full-time (144 women), 155 part-time (130 women); includes 260 minority (53 Black or African American, non-Hispanic/Latino; 7 Asian, non-Hispanic/Latino; 193 Hispanic/Latino; 7 Two or more races, non-Hispanic/Latino), 13 international. Average age 33. 184 applicants, 62% accepted, 87 enrolled. In 2018, 153 master's, 10 doctorates awarded. *Degree requirements:* For doctorate, comprehensive exam, thesis/dissertation. *Entrance requirements:* For master's, GRE General Test, Florida General Knowledge Test or Florida College Level Academic Skills Test; for doctorate and Ed S, GRE General Test. Additional exam requirements/recommendations for international students: Required—TOEFL (minimum score 550 paper-based; 80 iBT), IELTS (minimum score 6.3). *Application deadline:* For fall admission, 6/1 priority date for domestic students, 4/1 for international students; for winter admission, 10/1 priority date for domestic students, 9/1 for international students; for spring admission, 3/1 priority date for domestic students, 2/1 for international students. Applications are processed on a rolling basis. Application fee: $30. Electronic applications accepted. *Financial support:* Research assistantships and teaching assistantships available. *Unit head:* Dr. Maria Fernandez, Chair, 305-348-0193, Fax: 305-348-2086, E-mail: Maria.Fernandez9@fiu.edu. *Application contact:* Nanett Rojas, Manager, Admissions Operations, 305-348-7464, Fax: 305-348-7441, E-mail: gradadm@fiu.edu.
Website: https://tl.fiu.edu/

George Mason University, College of Education and Human Development, Programs in Curriculum and Instruction, Fairfax, VA 22030. Offers assistive technology (M Ed); designing digital learning in schools (M Ed); early childhood education (M Ed); early childhood education for diverse learners (M Ed); elementary education (M Ed); English as a second language (M Ed); gifted child education (M Ed); literacy (M Ed), including PK-12 classroom teachers, reading specialist; literacy leadership for diverse schools (M Ed), including K-12 reading; physical education (M Ed); science K-12 (M Ed); secondary education (M Ed), including biology, chemistry, earth science, English, history/social science, math, physics; special education (M Ed); teacher leadership (M Ed); transformative teaching (M Ed). *Program availability:* Part-time, evening/weekend, 100% online, blended/hybrid learning. *Faculty:* 48 full-time (40 women), 28 part-time/adjunct (20 women). *Students:* 165 full-time (147 women), 697 part-time (579 women); includes 243 minority (47 Black or African American, non-Hispanic/Latino; 3 American Indian or Alaska Native, non-Hispanic/Latino; 88 Asian, non-Hispanic/Latino; 85 Hispanic/Latino; 4 Native Hawaiian or other Pacific Islander, non-Hispanic/Latino; 16 Two or more races, non-Hispanic/Latino), 26 international. Average age 34. 450 applicants, 93% accepted, 315 enrolled. In 2018, 421 master's awarded. *Entrance requirements:* For master's, PRAXIS Core (for some programs), 2 letters of recommendation, interview, program goals statement; 9 hours of complete licensure endorsement requirements (for elementary education); minimum GPA of 3.0 in applicant's last 60 hours of undergraduate coursework (for secondary education); at least 1 year of teaching experience (for literacy). Additional exam requirements/recommendations for international students: Required—TOEFL (minimum score 575 paper-based; 88 iBT), IELTS (minimum score 6.5), PTE (minimum score 59). *Application deadline:* For fall admission, 4/2 priority date for domestic and international students; for spring admission, 11/1 for domestic and international students. Application fee: $75 ($80 for international students). Electronic applications accepted. *Financial support:* In 2018–19, 4 students received support, including 1 fellowship, 3 teaching assistantships (averaging $3,745 per year); career-related internships or fieldwork, Federal Work-Study, scholarships/grants, unspecified assistantships, and health care benefits (for full-time research or teaching assistantship recipients) also available. Support available to part-time students. Financial award application deadline: 3/1; financial award applicants required to submit FAFSA. *Faculty research:* Teacher preparation and professional development; adaptive teaching; wonder in science teacher preparation; literacy (digital, adolescent); site based course instruction. *Unit head:* Rebecca Fox, Professor and Academic Program Coordinator, 703-993-4123, E-mail: rfox@gmu.edu. *Application contact:* Rebecca Fox, Professor and Academic Program Coordinator, 703-993-4123, E-mail: rfox@gmu.edu.
Website: http://gse.gmu.edu/programs/gsemasters

Georgia State University, College of Education and Human Development, Department of Middle and Secondary Education, Atlanta, GA 30302-3083. Offers curriculum and instruction (Ed D); English education (MAT); mathematics education (M Ed, MAT); middle level education (MAT); reading, language and literacy education (M Ed, MAT), including reading instruction (M Ed); science education (M Ed, MAT), including biology (MAT), broad field science (MAT), chemistry (MAT), earth science (MAT), physics (MAT); social studies education (M Ed, MAT), including economics (MAT), geography (MAT), history (MAT), political science (MAT); teaching and learning (PhD), including language and literacy, mathematics education, music education, science education, social studies education, teaching and teacher education. *Accreditation:* NCATE. *Program availability:* Part-time, evening/weekend, online learning. *Faculty:* 19 full-time (15 women), 9 part-time/adjunct (7 women). *Students:* 217 full-time (136 women), 203 part-time (140 women); includes 229 minority (156 Black or African American, non-Hispanic/Latino; 23 Asian, non-Hispanic/Latino; 31 Hispanic/Latino; 19 Two or more races, non-Hispanic/Latino), 3 international. Average age 34. 149 applicants, 60% accepted, 70 enrolled. In 2018, 112 master's, 23 doctorates awarded. *Entrance requirements:* For master's, GRE; GACE I (for initial teacher preparation programs), baccalaureate degree or equivalent, resume, goals statement, two letters of recommendation, minimum undergraduate GPA of 2.5; proof of initial teacher certification in the content area (for M Ed); for doctorate, GRE, resume, goals statement, writing sample, two letters of recommendation, minimum graduate GPA of 3.3, interview. *Application deadline:* For fall admission, 1/15 priority date for domestic and international students; for spring admission, 10/1 for domestic and international students. Application fee: $50. Electronic applications accepted. *Expenses:* Tuition, area resident: Full-time $9360; part-time $390 per credit hour. Tuition, state resident: full-time $9360; part-time $390 per credit hour. Tuition, nonresident: full-time $30,024; part-time $1251 per credit hour. International tuition: $30,024 full-time. *Required fees:* $2128. *Financial support:* In 2018–19, fellowships with full tuition reimbursements (averaging $19,667 per year), research assistantships with full tuition reimbursements (averaging $5,436 per year), teaching assistantships with full tuition reimbursements (averaging $2,779 per year) were awarded; career-related internships or fieldwork, Federal Work-Study, scholarships/grants, health care benefits, tuition waivers (full and partial), and unspecified assistantships also available. Financial award application deadline: 3/15. *Faculty research:* Teacher education in language and literacy, mathematics, science,

and social studies in urban middle and secondary school settings; learning technologies in school, community, and corporate settings; multicultural education and education for social justice; urban education; international education. *Unit head:* Dr. Gertrude Marilyn Tinker Sachs, Chair, 404-413-8384, Fax: 404-413-8063, E-mail: gtinkersachs@gsu.edu. *Application contact:* Shaleen Tibbs, Administrative Specialist, 404-413-8385, Fax: 404-413-8063, E-mail: stibbs@gsu.edu.
Website: http://mse.education.gsu.edu/

Grambling State University, School of Graduate Studies and Research, College of Arts and Sciences, Department of History and Geography, Grambling, LA 71245. Offers social sciences (MA). *Program availability:* Part-time. *Degree requirements:* For master's, comprehensive exam (for some programs), thesis optional. *Entrance requirements:* For master's, GRE, minimum GPA of 3.0 on last degree. Additional exam requirements/recommendations for international students: Required—TOEFL (minimum score 500 paper-based; 62 iBT). Electronic applications accepted.

Harding University, Cannon-Clary College of Education, Searcy, AR 72149-0001. Offers advanced studies in teaching and learning (M Ed); art (MSE); behavioral science (MSE); counseling (MS, Ed S); early childhood special education (M Ed, MSE); education (MSE); educational leadership (M Ed, Ed S); elementary education (M Ed); English (MSE); French (MSE); history/social science (MSE); kinesiology (MSE); math (MSE); reading (M Ed); secondary education (M Ed); Spanish (MSE); teaching (MAT); teaching English as a second language (MSE). *Accreditation:* NCATE. *Program availability:* Part-time, evening/weekend. *Degree requirements:* For master's, comprehensive exam (for some programs), thesis optional, portfolio(s); for Ed S, comprehensive exam, portfolio, project. *Entrance requirements:* For master's, GRE, MAT, PRAXIS; for Ed S, MAT or GRE. Additional exam requirements/recommendations for international students: Required—TOEFL (minimum score 550 paper-based; 79 iBT). *Faculty research:* Reading, comprehension, school violence, educational technology, behavior, college choice, differentiated instruction, brain-based teaching.

Hofstra University, School of Education, Programs in Teacher Education, Hempstead, NY 11549. Offers bilingual education (MA); bilingual extension (Advanced Certificate); business education (MS Ed); curriculum studies (MS Ed); early childhood and childhood education (MS Ed); early childhood education (MA, MS Ed); educational technology (Advanced Certificate); elementary education (MA, MS Ed); English education (MS Ed); family and consumer science (MS Ed); fine arts and music education (Advanced Certificate); fine arts education (MS Ed); foreign language and TESOL (MS Ed); foreign language education (MA, MS Ed); languages other than English and teaching English as a second language (MA); learning and teaching (Ed D); mathematics education (MA, MS Ed); middle childhood extension (Advanced Certificate); music education (MA, MS Ed); science education (MA); secondary education (Advanced Certificate); social studies education (MA, MS Ed); teaching languages other than English and TESOL (MS Ed); technology for learning (MA); TESOL (MS Ed, Advanced Certificate); TESOL with specialization in STEM (MA); work based learning extension (Advanced Certificate). *Program availability:* Part-time, evening/weekend, blended/hybrid learning. *Students:* 138 full-time (94 women), 109 part-time (78 women); includes 66 minority (16 Black or African American, non-Hispanic/Latino; 17 Asian, non-Hispanic/Latino; 31 Hispanic/Latino; 2 Native Hawaiian or other Pacific Islander, non-Hispanic/Latino), 6 international. Average age 29. 217 applicants, 86% accepted, 113 enrolled. In 2018, 105 master's, 11 doctorates, 25 other advanced degrees awarded. *Degree requirements:* For master's, comprehensive exam, thesis (for some programs), exit project, student teaching, fieldwork, electronic portfolio, curriculum project, minimum GPA of 3.0; for doctorate, dissertation; for Advanced Certificate, 3 foreign languages, comprehensive exam (for some programs), thesis project. *Entrance requirements:* For master's, GRE, 2 letters of recommendation, portfolio, teacher certification (MA), interview, essay; for doctorate, GMAT, GRE, LSAT, or MAT; for Advanced Certificate, 2 letters of recommendation, essay, interview and/or portfolio, teaching certificate. Additional exam requirements/recommendations for international students: Required—TOEFL (minimum score 550 paper-based; 80 iBT). *Application deadline:* Applications are processed on a rolling basis. Application fee: $75. Electronic applications accepted. *Financial support:* In 2018–19, 86 students received support, including 51 fellowships with full and partial tuition reimbursements available (averaging $5,080 per year), 2 research assistantships with full and partial tuition reimbursements available (averaging $3,470 per year); career-related internships or fieldwork, Federal Work-Study, institutionally sponsored loans, scholarships/grants, traineeships, tuition waivers (full and partial), unspecified assistantships, and scholarships and endowed scholarships also available. Support available to part-time students. Financial award applicants required to submit FAFSA. *Faculty research:* Impact of memory on learning; brain function, cognitive-development, learning, and achievement; student activism and civic education; using children's literature to promote diversity; 2nd language acquisition. *Unit head:* Dr. Alan Singer, Chairperson, 516-463-5853, Fax: 516-463-6275, E-mail: alan.j.singer@hofstra.edu. *Application contact:* Sunil Samuel, Assistant Vice President of Admissions, 516-463-4723, Fax: 516-463-4664, E-mail: graduateadmission@hofstra.edu.
Website: http://www.hofstra.edu/education/

Hunter College of the City University of New York, Graduate School, School of Education, Programs in Secondary Education, Concentration in Social Studies Education, New York, NY 10065-5085. Offers MA. *Accreditation:* NCATE. *Degree requirements:* For master's, thesis, professional teaching portfolio, New York State Teacher Certification Exam, research project. *Entrance requirements:* For master's, minimum GPA of 3.0 in history, 2.8 overall; 2 letters of reference; minimum of 30 credits in social studies areas. Additional exam requirements/recommendations for international students: Required—TOEFL, TWE.

Indiana University Bloomington, School of Education, Department of Curriculum and Instruction, Bloomington, IN 47405-7000. Offers art education (MS, Ed D, PhD); curriculum studies (Ed D, PhD); elementary education (MS, Ed D, PhD, Ed S); mathematics education (MS, Ed D, PhD); science education (MS, Ed D, PhD); secondary education (MS, Ed D, PhD); social studies education (MS, PhD); special education (PhD, Ed S). *Accreditation:* NCATE. *Program availability:* Part-time, evening/weekend. Terminal master's awarded for partial completion of doctoral program. *Degree requirements:* For doctorate, thesis/dissertation; for Ed S, comprehensive exam or project. *Entrance requirements:* For master's, doctorate, and Ed S, GRE General Test. Electronic applications accepted.

Instituto Tecnologico de Santo Domingo, Graduate School, Area of Humanities and Social Sciences, Santo Domingo, Dominican Republic. Offers accounting (Certificate); adult education (Certificate); applied linguistics (MA); economics (MA); education (M Ed); educational psychology (MA, Certificate); gender and development (MA, Certificate); humanistic studies (MA); international marketing management (Certificate); international relations in the Caribbean basin (Certificate); intervention systems in family therapy (MA); linguistic and literary communication (Certificate); pedagogical support (MA); social science education (M Ed); sustainable human development (MA); terminal illness and death psychology (Certificate); youth and adult education (M Ed).

Inter American University of Puerto Rico, Arecibo Campus, Programs in Education, Arecibo, PR 00614-4050. Offers administration and educational supervision (MA Ed); counseling and guidance (MA Ed); curriculum and teaching (MA Ed), including biology education, English as a second language, history education, math education, Spanish;

elementary education (MA Ed). *Accreditation:* TEAC. *Degree requirements:* For master's, comprehensive exam, thesis optional. *Entrance requirements:* For master's, GRE, EXADEP, bachelor's degree in education or teaching license (administration and supervision) or courses in education and psychology (counseling and guidance), minimum GPA of 2.5 in last 60 credits.

Inter American University of Puerto Rico, Metropolitan Campus, Graduate Programs, Program in History Education, San Juan, PR 00919-1293. Offers MA.

Inter American University of Puerto Rico, Ponce Campus, Graduate School, Mercedita, PR 00715-1602. Offers accounting (MBA); biology (M Ed); chemistry (M Ed); criminal justice (MA); elementary education (M Ed); English as a Second Language (M Ed); finance (MBA); history (M Ed); human resources (MBA); marketing (MBA); mathematics (M Ed); Spanish (M Ed). *Entrance requirements:* For master's, minimum GPA of 2.5.

Iona College, School of Arts and Science, Department of Education, New Rochelle, NY 10801-1890. Offers adolescence education: biology (MS Ed, MST); adolescence education: English (MS Ed); adolescence education: mathematics (MST); adolescence education: social studies (MS Ed, MST); adolescence education: Spanish (MS Ed); adolescence special education 5-12 (MST); childhood and special education (MST); early childhood and childhood (MST); educational leadership (MS Ed). *Accreditation:* NCATE. *Program availability:* Part-time, evening/weekend. *Faculty:* 7 full-time (5 women), 9 part-time/adjunct (5 women). *Students:* 33 full-time (30 women), 26 part-time (20 women); includes 21 minority (6 Black or African American, non-Hispanic/Latino; 1 Asian, non-Hispanic/Latino; 13 Hispanic/Latino; 1 Two or more races, non-Hispanic/Latino). Average age 25. 39 applicants, 87% accepted, 14 enrolled. In 2018, 20 master's awarded. *Degree requirements:* For master's, thesis or alternative. *Entrance requirements:* For master's, minimum GPA of 3.0, NY State teaching certificate and bachelor's degree (for MS Ed). Additional exam requirements/recommendations for international students: Required—TOEFL (minimum score 550 paper-based; 80 iBT), IELTS (minimum score 6.5). *Application deadline:* For fall admission, 8/1 priority date for domestic students, 5/1 priority date for international students; for spring admission, 1/1 priority date for domestic students, 9/1 priority date for international students. Applications are processed on a rolling basis. Electronic applications accepted. *Expenses: Tuition:* Full-time $14,064; part-time $7032 per credit. *Required fees:* $245 per semester. One-time fee: $250. Tuition and fees vary according to program. *Financial support:* In 2018–19, 2 students received support. Unspecified assistantships available. Support available to part-time students. Financial award application deadline: 4/15; financial award applicants required to submit FAFSA. *Faculty research:* Engaging teacher educators in scientific process, cross-national comparisons of mathematics teaching, questioning strategies in the classroom, research methods, literacy development. *Unit head:* Malissa Scheuring Leipold, EdD, Chair, 914-633-2210, Fax: 914-633-2281, E-mail: mleipold@iona.edu. *Application contact:* Christopher Kash, Assistant Director of Graduate Admissions, 914-633-2403, E-mail: ckash@iona.edu. Website: http://www.iona.edu/Academics/School-of-Arts-Science/Departments/Education/Graduate-Programs.aspx

Kent State University, College of Arts and Sciences, Department of History, Kent, OH 44242-0001. Offers history (MA, PhD), including history (MA), history for teachers (MA). *Program availability:* Part-time. *Faculty:* 8 full-time (4 women). *Students:* 21 full-time (7 women), 5 part-time (2 women); includes 2 minority (both Black or African American, non-Hispanic/Latino), 3 international. Average age 36. 28 applicants, 54% accepted, 7 enrolled. In 2018, 1 master's, 2 doctorates awarded. *Degree requirements:* For master's, one foreign language, thesis (for some programs); for doctorate, one foreign language, comprehensive exam, thesis/dissertation. *Entrance requirements:* For master's, GRE General Test, official transcript(s), statement of purpose describing professional objectives and proposed field of study, significant piece of written work, three letters of recommendation (preferably academic); for doctorate, GRE General Test, official transcript(s), master's degree in history or related discipline, statement of purpose describing professional objectives and proposed field of study, significant piece of written work, three letters of recommendation (preferably academic). Additional exam requirements/recommendations for international students: Required—TOEFL (minimum score 550 paper-based, 79 iBT), Michigan English Language Assessment Battery (minimum score 77), IELTS (minimum score 6.5) or PTE (minimum score 58). *Application deadline:* For fall admission, 2/1 for domestic and international students. Applications are processed on a rolling basis. Application fee: $45 ($70 for international students). Electronic applications accepted. *Expenses:* Tuition, state resident: full-time $11,766; part-time $536 per credit. Tuition, nonresident: full-time $21,952; part-time $999 per credit. *International tuition:* $21,952 full-time. Tuition and fees vary according to course load. *Financial support:* Teaching assistantships with full tuition reimbursements and unspecified assistantships available. Financial award application deadline: 2/1. *Unit head:* Dr. Kevin Adams, Professor and Chair, 330-672-8902, E-mail: kadams9@kent.edu. *Application contact:* Dr. Mary Ann Heiss, Associate Professor and Graduate Coordinator, E-mail: mheiss@kent.edu. Website: https://www.kent.edu/history/

Kutztown University of Pennsylvania, College of Education, Program in Secondary Education, Kutztown, PA 19530-0730. Offers biology (M Ed); curriculum and instruction (M Ed); English (M Ed); mathematics (M Ed); middle level (M Ed); social studies (M Ed); teaching (M Ed); transformational teaching and learning (Ed D). *Accreditation:* NCATE. *Program availability:* Part-time, evening/weekend, 100% online, blended/hybrid learning. *Faculty:* 5 full-time (3 women), 3 part-time/adjunct (0 women). *Students:* 25 full-time (16 women), 80 part-time (51 women); includes 8 minority (1 Black or African American, non-Hispanic/Latino; 5 Hispanic/Latino; 2 Two or more races, non-Hispanic/Latino), 1 international. Average age 32. 86 applicants, 93% accepted, 45 enrolled. In 2018, 3,531 master's awarded. *Degree requirements:* For master's, comprehensive exam, thesis optional; for doctorate, thesis/dissertation. *Entrance requirements:* For master's, GRE General Test, minimum undergraduate major GPA of 3.0, 3 letters of recommendation, copy of PRAXIS II or valid instructional I or II teaching certificate; for doctorate, master's or specialist degree in education or related field from regionally-accredited institution of higher learning with minimum graduate GPA of 3.25, significant educational experience, employment in an education setting (preferred). Additional exam requirements/recommendations for international students: Required—TOEFL (minimum score 550 paper-based, 79 iBT), IELTS (minimum score 6.5), or PTE (minimum score 53). *Application deadline:* For fall admission, 8/1 for domestic and international students; for spring admission, 12/1 for domestic and international students. Application fee: $35. Electronic applications accepted. *Expenses: Tuition,* state resident: part-time $516 per credit. Tuition, nonresident: part-time $774 per credit. *Required fees:* $119 per credit. One-time fee: $50 part-time. Tuition and fees vary according to degree level. *Financial support:* Career-related internships or fieldwork, Federal Work-Study, scholarships/grants, and unspecified assistantships available. Financial award application deadline: 3/1; financial award applicants required to submit FAFSA. *Unit head:* Dr. Georgeos Sirrakos, Department Chair, 610-683-4279, Fax: 610-683-1338, E-mail: sirrakos@kutztown.edu. *Application contact:* Dr. Patricia Walsh Coates, Graduate Coordinator, 610-638-4289, Fax: 610-683-1338, E-mail: coates@kutztown.edu. Website: https://www.kutztown.edu/academcs/graduate-programs/secondary-education.htm

Lake Forest College, Master of Arts in Teaching Program, Lake Forest, IL 60045. Offers elementary education (MAT); K-12 French (MAT); K-12 music (MAT); K-12 Spanish (MAT); K-12 visual art (MAT); secondary biology (MAT); secondary chemistry (MAT); secondary English (MAT); secondary history (MAT); secondary mathematics (MAT). *Degree requirements:* For master's, comprehensive exam, portfolio. *Entrance requirements:* For master's, GRE.

La Salle University, School of Arts and Sciences, Program in Education, Philadelphia, PA 19141-1199. Offers autism spectrum disorders (MA, Certificate); bilingual/bicultural studies (MA); classroom management (MA); dual early childhood and special education (MA); dual middle-level science and math and special education (MA); education (MA); English (MA); English as a second language (Certificate); history (MA); instructional coach (Certificate); instructional leadership (MA); reading specialist (MA, Certificate); secondary education (MA); special education (MA, Certificate). *Program availability:* Part-time, evening/weekend. *Degree requirements:* For master's, comprehensive exam. *Entrance requirements:* For master's, MAT or GRE, 2 letters of recommendation; for Certificate, GMAT or GRE, 2 letters of recommendation. Additional exam requirements/recommendations for international students: Required—TOEFL. Electronic applications accepted. Application fee is waived when completed online. *Expenses:* Contact institution.

La Salle University, School of Arts and Sciences, Program in History, Philadelphia, PA 19141-1199. Offers American history (Certificate); European history (Certificate); history (MA); history for educators (MA); public history (MA); teaching advanced placement history (Certificate); world history (Certificate). *Program availability:* Part-time. *Degree requirements:* For master's, thesis or comprehensive exam. *Entrance requirements:* For master's, GRE or MAT, 18 hours of undergraduate coursework in history or a related discipline with minimum GPA of 3.0; two letters of recommendation; brief personal statement (250 to 500 words); writing sample (preferably from an undergraduate research paper). Additional exam requirements/recommendations for international students: Required—TOEFL. Electronic applications accepted. Application fee is waived when completed online. *Expenses:* Contact institution.

Lebanon Valley College, Program in Science Education, Annville, PA 17003-1400. Offers integrative STEM education (Certificate); STEM education (MSE). *Program availability:* Part-time-only, evening/weekend, 100% online, blended/hybrid learning. *Degree requirements:* For master's, thesis or capstone project. *Entrance requirements:* For master's, baccalaureate degree, minimum GPA of 3.0, teacher certification, 3 letters of recommendation, transcripts, goal statement. Additional exam requirements/recommendations for international students: Required—TOEFL (minimum score 80 iBT). Electronic applications accepted. *Expenses:* Contact institution. *Faculty research:* Teacher quality and student achievement, STEM reform, STEM education, effective teaching.

Lee University, Program in Education, Cleveland, TN 37320-3450. Offers art (MAT); curriculum and instruction (M Ed, Ed S); early childhood (MAT); educational leadership (M Ed, Ed S); elementary education (MAT); English and math (MAT); English and science (MAT); English and social studies (MAT); higher education administration (MS); history (MAT); history and economics (MAT); math and science (MAT); math and social studies (MAT); middle grades (MAT); science and social studies (MASW); secondary education (MAT); Spanish (MAT); special education (M Ed, MAT); TESOL (MAT). *Accreditation:* NCATE. *Program availability:* Part-time. *Faculty:* 13 full-time (5 women), 13 part-time/adjunct (7 women). *Students:* 32 full-time (26 women), 73 part-time (49 women); includes 13 minority (10 Black or African American, non-Hispanic/Latino; 3 Two or more races, non-Hispanic/Latino), 3 international. Average age 30. 56 applicants, 73% accepted, 34 enrolled. In 2018, 60 master's, 3 other advanced degrees awarded. *Degree requirements:* For master's, variable foreign language requirement, thesis optional, internship. *Entrance requirements:* For master's, MAT or GRE General Test, minimum undergraduate GPA of 2.75, 3 letters of recommendation, interview, writing sample, official transcripts, background check; for Ed S, minimum undergraduate and master's GPA of 2.75, official transcripts for undergraduate and master's degrees. Additional exam requirements/recommendations for international students: Required—TOEFL (minimum score 61 iBT). *Application deadline:* For fall admission, 6/1 priority date for domestic and international students; for spring admission, 11/1 priority date for domestic and international students; for summer admission, 4/1 priority date for domestic and international students. Applications are processed on a rolling basis. Application fee: $25. Electronic applications accepted. *Financial support:* In 2018–19, 43 students received support. Career-related internships or fieldwork, Federal Work-Study, institutionally sponsored loans, scholarships/grants, and unspecified assistantships available. Financial award application deadline: 3/1; financial award applicants required to submit FAFSA. *Unit head:* Dr. William Kamm, Director, 423-614-8544, E-mail: wkamm@leeuniversity.edu. *Application contact:* Jeffery McGirt, Director of Graduate Enrollment, 423-614-8691, Fax: 423-614-8317, E-mail: jmcgirt@leeuniversity.edu. Website: http://www.leeuniversity.edu/academics/graduate/education

Lehman College of the City University of New York, School of Education, Department of Middle and High School Education, Program in Social Studies Education, Bronx, NY 10468-1589. Offers MA. *Accreditation:* NCATE. *Entrance requirements:* For master's, minimum GPA of 3.0 in social sciences, 2.7 overall.

Le Moyne College, Department of Education, Syracuse, NY 13214. Offers adolescent education (MS Ed, MST); adolescent education/special education (MS Ed, MST); adolescent English (MST), including grades 7-12; adolescent English/special education (MST), including grades 7-12; adolescent foreign language (MST), including grades 7-12; adolescent history (MST), including grades 7-12; childhood education (MS Ed); childhood education/special education (MS Ed); elementary education (MS Ed); general education (MS Ed); inclusive childhood education (MST); literacy education (MS Ed), including birth to grade 6, grades 5-12; school building leader (MS Ed); school building leadership (CAS); school district business leader (MS Ed, CAS); school district leader (MS Ed); school district leadership (CAS); secondary education (MS Ed); special education (MS Ed); teaching English to speakers of other languages (MS Ed); urban studies (MS Ed). *Accreditation:* TEAC. *Program availability:* Part-time, evening/weekend. *Faculty:* 7 full-time (5 women), 16 part-time/adjunct (11 women). *Students:* 35 full-time (28 women), 119 part-time (84 women); includes 14 minority (5 Black or African American, non-Hispanic/Latino; 1 Asian, non-Hispanic/Latino; 7 Hispanic/Latino; 1 Two or more races, non-Hispanic/Latino), 1 international. Average age 30. 123 applicants, 89% accepted, 96 enrolled. In 2018, 66 master's, 48 CASs awarded. Terminal master's awarded for partial completion of doctoral program. *Degree requirements:* For master's, thesis. *Entrance requirements:* For master's, bachelor's degree with minimum undergraduate GPA of 3.0, 2 letters of recommendation, transcripts. Additional exam requirements/recommendations for international students: Required—TOEFL (minimum score 79 iBT); Recommended—IELTS (minimum score 6.5). *Application deadline:* For fall admission, 4/1 priority date for domestic and international students; for spring admission, 10/1 priority date for domestic and international students; for summer admission, 3/1 priority date for domestic and international students. Applications are processed on a rolling basis. Electronic applications accepted. *Expenses:* $734 per credit hour; wellness fee $70 per semester for full-time graduate students taking 9+ credit hours; technology fee $75 per semester for full-time graduate students taking 9+

credit hours, $25 per semester for part-time students; $1,470 per credit hour (for ED.D.). *Financial support:* In 2018–19, 44 students received support. Career-related internships or fieldwork, scholarships/grants, and health care benefits available. Support available to part-time students. Financial award applicants required to submit FAFSA. *Faculty research:* Minority teachers, special education, multiculturalism, literacy, technology, media literacy learning, autism, school district organization, service-learning, higher level problem solving, teacher leadership. *Unit head:* Dr. Stephen C. Fleury, Chair, Department of Education, 315-445-4376, Fax: 315-445-4744, E-mail: fleurysc@lemoyne.edu. *Application contact:* Jody F Manning, Assistant Director for Graduate Admission, 315-445-5444, Fax: 315-445-6092, E-mail: manninjf@lemoyne.edu.
Website: http://www.lemoyne.edu/education

Lewis University, College of Education, Program in Secondary Education, Romeoville, IL 60446. Offers chemistry (MA); English (MA); history (MA); physics (MA); psychology and social science (MA). *Program availability:* Part-time. *Students:* 24 full-time (9 women), 28 part-time (17 women); includes 16 minority (2 Black or African American, non-Hispanic/Latino; 2 Asian, non-Hispanic/Latino; 10 Hispanic/Latino; 2 Two or more races, non-Hispanic/Latino). Average age 27. *Degree requirements:* For master's, comprehensive exam, departmental qualifying exam. *Entrance requirements:* For master's, writing exam, Test of Academic Proficiency/Basic Skills Test/ACT/SAT, bachelor's degree, minimum GPA of 2.75, 2 letters of recommendation. Additional exam requirements/recommendations for international students: Required—TOEFL (minimum score 550 paper-based; 79 iBT), IELTS (minimum score 6). *Application deadline:* For fall admission, 5/1 priority date for international students; for spring admission, 11/15 priority date for international students. Applications are processed on a rolling basis. Application fee: $40. Electronic applications accepted. *Financial support:* Federal Work-Study, scholarships/grants, and unspecified assistantships available. Financial award application deadline: 5/1; financial award applicants required to submit FAFSA. *Unit head:* Dr. Chris Palmi, Program Director. *Application contact:* Kathy Lisak, Graduate Admission Counselor, 815-836-5610, E-mail: grad@lewisu.edu.

Long Island University–LIU Brooklyn, Richard L. Conolly College of Liberal Arts and Sciences, Brooklyn, NY 11201-8423. Offers biology (MS); chemistry (MS); clinical psychology (PhD); creative writing (MFA); English (MA); media arts (MA, MFA); political science (MA); psychology (MA); social science (MS); United Nations (Advanced Certificate); urban studies (MA); writing and production for television (MFA). *Program availability:* Part-time. Terminal master's awarded for partial completion of doctoral program. *Degree requirements:* For master's, comprehensive exam (for some programs), thesis (for some programs); for doctorate, thesis/dissertation. *Entrance requirements:* For doctorate, GRE. Additional exam requirements/recommendations for international students: Required—TOEFL (minimum score 550 paper-based, 79 iBT) or IELTS. Electronic applications accepted. *Faculty research:* Quantum gravity and astrophysics; string theory; pharmaceutical biotechnology with a focus on molecular details of drug susceptibility/resistance mechanisms; entomology, population and community ecology, agroecology, and biodiversity; psychotherapy process-outcome, particularly therapeutic alliance development, the role of common factors, and the study of treatment failures; personality pathology, borderline personality disorder and pathological narcissism.

Manhattanville College, School of Education, Jump Start Program, Purchase, NY 10577-2132. Offers childhood education and special education (grades 1-6) (MPS); early childhood education (birth-grade 2) (MAT); education (Advanced Certificate); English and special education (grades 5-12) (MPS); mathematics and special education (grades 5-12) (MPS); science and special education (grades 5-12) (MPS); social studies and special education (grades 5-12) (MPS); Spanish (grades 7-12) (MAT); tesol - teaching English as a second language (all grades) (MPS). *Program availability:* Part-time, evening/weekend. *Faculty:* 11 full-time (7 women), 78 part-time/adjunct (50 women). *Students:* 3 full-time (2 women), 16 part-time (11 women); includes 5 minority (1 Black or African American, non-Hispanic/Latino; 3 Hispanic/Latino; 1 Native Hawaiian or other Pacific Islander, non-Hispanic/Latino). Average age 31. 48 applicants, 54% accepted, 22 enrolled. In 2018, 23 master's, 1 other advanced degree awarded. *Degree requirements:* For master's, comprehensive exam (for some programs), thesis (for some programs), student teaching, research seminars, portfolios, internships, writing assessment; for Advanced Certificate, comprehensive exam (for some programs). *Entrance requirements:* For master's, for programs leading to certification, candidates must submit scores from GRE or MAT(miller analogies test), minimum undergraduate GPA of 3.0, all transcripts from all colleges and universities attended, 2 letters of recommendation, interview, essay (2-3 page personal statement that describes reasons for choosing education as profession and personal philosophy of education), proof of immunization (for those born after 1957). Additional exam requirements/recommendations for international students: Required—TOEFL (minimum score 600 paper-based; 110 iBT); Recommended—IELTS (minimum score 8). *Application deadline:* Applications are processed on a rolling basis. Application fee: $75. Electronic applications accepted. *Expenses:* 935 per credit. *Financial support:* Teaching assistantships, career-related internships or fieldwork, Federal Work-Study, institutionally sponsored loans, scholarships/grants, and unspecified assistantships available. Financial award application deadline: 3/15; financial award applicants required to submit FAFSA. *Faculty research:* Early childhood and technology, professional development schools and community schools, students with emotional difficulties, literacy and adolescents, mindfulness, changing suburbs institute, and community schools, studying the effects of the environment on special populations, the most difficult cases, students who are presented with multiple challenges: learning, behavioral and ACE experiences who see criminal behavior as a way to cope; working on giving them the tools they need to succeed. *Unit head:* Dr. Shelley Wepner, Dean, 914-323-3153, E-mail: Shelly.Wepner@mville.edu. *Application contact:* Alissa Wilson, Director, SOE Graduate Enrollment Management, 914-323-3150, Fax: 914-694-1732, E-mail: edschool@mville.edu.
Website: http://www.mville.edu/programs/jump-start

Manhattanville College, School of Education, Program in Middle Childhood/Adolescence Education (Grades 5-12), Purchase, NY 10577-2132. Offers biology and special education (MPS); chemistry and special education (MPS); education for sustainability (Advanced Certificate); English and special education (MPS); literacy and special education (MPS); literacy specialist (MPS); math and special education (MPS); mathematics (Advanced Certificate); middle childhood/adolescence ed science (biology or chemistry grades 5-12) or (physics grades 7-12) (MAT); middle childhood/adolescence education (grades 5-12) English (MAT, Advanced Certificate); middle childhood/adolescence education (grades 5-12) mathematics (MAT, Advanced Certificate); middle childhood/adolescence education (grades 5-12) science (biology chemistry, physics, earth science) (Advanced Certificate); middle childhood/adolescence education (grades 5-12) social studies (MAT, Advanced Certificate); physics (MAT, Advanced Certificate); social studies (MAT); social studies and special education (MPS); special education generalist (MPS). *Program availability:* Part-time, evening/weekend. *Faculty:* 3 full-time (2 women), 9 part-time/adjunct (4 women). *Students:* 11 full-time (6 women), 17 part-time (12 women); includes 3 minority (1 Black or African American, non-Hispanic/Latino; 2 Hispanic/Latino). Average age 31. 17 applicants, 71% accepted, 7 enrolled. In 2018, 8 master's, 3 other advanced degrees awarded. *Degree requirements:* For master's, comprehensive exam (for some programs), thesis (for some programs), student teaching, research seminars, portfolios, internships, writing assessment; for Advanced Certificate, comprehensive exam (for some programs). *Entrance requirements:* For master's, for programs leading to certification, candidates must submit scores from GRE or MAT(Miller Analogies Test), minimum undergraduate GPA of 3.0, all transcripts from all colleges and universities attended, 2 letters of recommendation, interview, essay (2-3 page personal statement that describes reasons for choosing education as profession and personal philosophy of education), proof of immunization (for those born after 1957). Additional exam requirements/recommendations for international students: Required—TOEFL (minimum score 600 paper-based; 110 iBT); Recommended—IELTS (minimum score 8). *Application deadline:* Applications are processed on a rolling basis. Application fee: $75. Electronic applications accepted. *Expenses:* 935 per credit. *Financial support:* Teaching assistantships, career-related internships or fieldwork, Federal Work-Study, institutionally sponsored loans, scholarships/grants, and unspecified assistantships available. Financial award application deadline: 3/15; financial award applicants required to submit FAFSA. *Faculty research:* Education for sustainability. *Unit head:* Dr. Shelley Wepner, Dean, 914-323-3153, Fax: 914-323-5493, E-mail: Shelley.Wepner@mville.edu. *Application contact:* Alissa Wilson, Director, Graduate Admissions, 914-323-3150, Fax: 914-694-1732, E-mail: edschool@mville.edu.
Website: http://www.mville.edu/programs#/search/19

Manhattanville College, School of Education, Program in Special Education, Purchase, NY 10577-2132. Offers childhood education (grades 1-6) and special education: childhood (grades 1-6) (MPS); early childhood (birth-grade 2) and special education: early childhood (birth-grade 2) (MPS); English (5-9 and 7-12); special ed generalist (7-12); se English (7-12) (MPS); literacy (birth-grade 6) and special education childhood (grades 1-6) (MPS); literacy 5-12; special education generalist 7-12; special ed specialist 7-12 (MPS); math (5-9 and 7-12); special ed generalist (7-12); se math (7-12) (MPS); science: biology or chemistry (5-9 and 7-12); special ed generalist (7-12); se science (7-12) (MPS); social studies (5-9 and 7-12); special ed generalist (7-12); se soc.st. (7-12) (MPS); special ed early childhood and childhood (birth-grade 6) (MPS); special education childhood (grades 1-6) (MPS); special education: childhood (grades 1-6) (Certificate); special education: early childhood (birth-grade 2) (MPS, Certificate); special education: early childhood (birth-grade 2) and childhood (grades 1-6) (Certificate); special education: grades 7-12 generalist (MPS, Certificate). *Program availability:* Part-time, evening/weekend. *Faculty:* 5 full-time (3 women), 35 part-time/adjunct (23 women). *Students:* 45 full-time (36 women), 179 part-time (152 women); includes 31 minority (6 Black or African American, non-Hispanic/Latino; 4 Asian, non-Hispanic/Latino; 19 Hispanic/Latino; 2 Native Hawaiian or other Pacific Islander, non-Hispanic/Latino), 1 international. Average age 28. 76 applicants, 68% accepted, 40 enrolled. In 2018, 99 master's, 2 Certificates awarded. *Degree requirements:* For master's, comprehensive exam (for some programs), thesis (for some programs), student teaching, research seminars, portfolios, internships, writing assessment; for Certificate, comprehensive exam (for some programs). *Entrance requirements:* For master's, for programs leading to certification, candidates must submit scores from GRE or MAT(Miller Analogies Test), minimum undergraduate GPA of 3.0, all transcripts from all colleges and universities attended, 2 letters of recommendation, interview, essay (2-3 page personal statement that describes reasons for choosing education as profession and personal philosophy of education), proof of immunization (for those born after 1957). Additional exam requirements/recommendations for international students: Required—TOEFL (minimum score 600 paper-based; 110 iBT); Recommended—IELTS (minimum score 8). *Application deadline:* Applications are processed on a rolling basis. Application fee: $75. Electronic applications accepted. *Expenses:* 935 per credit. *Financial support:* Teaching assistantships, career-related internships or fieldwork, Federal Work-Study, institutionally sponsored loans, scholarships/grants, and unspecified assistantships available. Financial award application deadline: 3/15; financial award applicants required to submit FAFSA. *Faculty research:* Students with emotional difficulties, literacy and adolescents, mindfulness, studying the effects of the environment on special populations, the most difficult cases, students who are presented with multiple challenges: learning, behavioral and ACE experiences who see criminal behavior as a way to cope; working on giving them the tools they need to succeed emotionally and cognitively despite the odds stacked against them. *Unit head:* Dr. Shelley Wepner, Dean, 914-323-3153, Fax: 914-323-5493, E-mail: Shelley.Wepner@mville.edu. *Application contact:* Alissa Wilson, Director, SOE Graduate Enrollment Management, 914-323-3150, Fax: 914-694-1732, E-mail: edschool@mville.edu.
Website: http://www.mville.edu/programs/special-education

Metropolitan State University, School of Urban Education, St. Paul, MN 55106-5000. Offers curriculum, pedagogy and schooling (MS); English as a second language (MS); secondary education (MS), including English teaching, life sciences teaching, mathematics teaching, social studies teaching; special education (MS).

Michigan State University, The Graduate School, College of Social Science, Department of History, East Lansing, MI 48824. Offers history (MA, PhD); history-secondary school teaching (MA). *Entrance requirements:* Additional exam requirements/recommendations for international students: Required—TOEFL. Electronic applications accepted.

Minnesota State University Mankato, College of Graduate Studies and Research, College of Social and Behavioral Sciences, Department of History, Mankato, MN 56001. Offers history (MA, MS); social studies (MAT). *Degree requirements:* For master's, one foreign language, comprehensive exam, thesis or alternative. *Entrance requirements:* For master's, minimum GPA of 3.0, statement of purpose. Additional exam requirements/recommendations for international students: Required—TOEFL (minimum score 600 paper-based). Electronic applications accepted.

Mississippi College, Graduate School, School of Education, Department of Teacher Education and Leadership, Clinton, MS 39058. Offers art (M Ed); biological science (M Ed); business education (M Ed); computer science (M Ed); dyslexia therapy (M Ed); educational leadership (M Ed, Ed D, Ed S); elementary education (M Ed, Ed S); English (M Ed); higher education administration (MS); mathematics (M Ed); secondary education (M Ed); social studies (history) (M Ed); teaching arts (M Ed). *Program availability:* Part-time, online learning. *Degree requirements:* For master's, comprehensive exam, thesis optional. *Entrance requirements:* For master's, NTE. Additional exam requirements/recommendations for international students: Recommended—TOEFL, IELTS. Electronic applications accepted.

Missouri State University, Graduate College, College of Humanities and Public Affairs, Department of History, Springfield, MO 65897. Offers history (MA); history education (MS Ed); history for teachers (Certificate). *Program availability:* Part-time, 100% online, blended/hybrid learning. *Faculty:* 18 full-time (7 women). *Students:* 14 full-time (5 women), 45 part-time (19 women); includes 4 minority (1 Black or African American, non-Hispanic/Latino; 1 Asian, non-Hispanic/Latino; 2 Hispanic/Latino). Average age 26. 31 applicants, 39% accepted. In 2018, 19 master's awarded. *Degree requirements:* For master's, comprehensive exam, thesis or alternative. *Entrance requirements:* For master's, minimum GPA of 2.75, 24 hours of undergraduate course work in history (MA), 9-12 teaching certification (MS Ed). Additional exam requirements/recommendations for international students: Required—TOEFL (minimum score 550 paper-based; 79 iBT),

IELTS (minimum score 6). *Application deadline:* For fall admission, 7/20 priority date for domestic students, 5/1 for international students; for spring admission, 12/20 priority date for domestic students, 9/1 for international students. Applications are processed on a rolling basis. Application fee: $55 ($60 for international students). Electronic applications accepted. Tuition and fees vary according to class time, course level, course load, degree level, campus/location, program and student level. *Financial support:* Federal Work-Study, scholarships/grants, and unspecified assistantships available. Support available to part-time students. Financial award application deadline: 1/31; financial award applicants required to submit FAFSA. *Faculty research:* Early modern France, cultural history of modern Britain, Latin American history, women's history, American Civil War in Missouri. *Unit head:* Dr. Kathleen Kennedy, Department Head, 417-836-5511, Fax: 417-836-5523, E-mail: history@missouristate.edu. *Application contact:* Lakan Drinker, Director, Graduate Enrollment Management, 417-836-5330, Fax: 417-836-6200, E-mail: lakandrinker@missouristate.edu.
Website: http://history.missouristate.edu/

Molloy College, Graduate Education Program, Rockville Centre, NY 11571-5002. Offers adolescent education in biology (MS); adolescent special education (Advanced Certificate); bilingual extension (Advanced Certificate); childhood education (MS); childhood special education (Advanced Certificate); early childhood education (MS); educational technology (MS); English (MS); mathematics (MS); social studies (MS); Spanish (MS); special education on both childhood and adolescent levels (MS); teaching English to speakers of other languages (TESOL) in grades pre-K to 12 (MS); TESOL (Advanced Certificate). *Accreditation:* NCATE. *Program availability:* Part-time, evening/weekend. *Faculty:* 24 full-time (22 women), 26 part-time/adjunct (19 women). *Students:* 106 full-time (78 women), 203 part-time (154 women); includes 65 minority (14 Black or African American, non-Hispanic/Latino; 5 Asian, non-Hispanic/Latino; 41 Hispanic/Latino; 5 Two or more races, non-Hispanic/Latino). Average age 41. 147 applicants, 63% accepted, 79 enrolled. In 2018, 120 master's, 1 other advanced degree awarded. *Entrance requirements:* Additional exam requirements/recommendations for international students: Required—TOEFL (minimum score 550 paper-based; 79 iBT). *Application deadline:* Applications are processed on a rolling basis. Application fee: $60. Electronic applications accepted. *Expenses: Tuition:* Full-time $20,790; part-time $1155 per credit. *Required fees:* $1060; $900. Tuition and fees vary according to course load and degree level. *Financial support:* Application deadline: 3/1; applicants required to submit FAFSA. *Faculty research:* English Language Learners; social emotional needs of students; gifted education; cultural diversity; collaborative teaching methods. *Unit head:* Joanne O'Brien, Dean, 516-323-3116, E-mail: jobrien@molloy.edu. *Application contact:* Faye Hood, Assistant Director for Admissions, 516-323-4009, E-mail: fhood@molloy.edu.

Morehead State University, Graduate School, College of Education, Department of Foundational and Graduate Studies in Education, Morehead, KY 40351. Offers adult and higher education (MA, Ed S); certified professional counselor (Ed S); counseling P-12 (MA); curriculum and instruction (Ed S); educational technology (MA Ed); instructional leadership (Ed S); school administration (MA); school counseling (Ed S); teacher leader business and marketing content (MA Ed); teacher leader business and marketing technology (MA Ed); teacher leader educational technology (MA Ed); teacher leader English (MA Ed); teacher leader gifted education (MA Ed); teacher leader IECE certification (MA Ed); teacher leader interdisciplinary education P-5 (MA Ed); teacher leader middle grades (MA Ed); teacher leader non IECE certification (MA Ed); teacher leader reading/writing - non-certification (MA Ed); teacher leader reading/writing certification (MA Ed); teacher leader school communication - certification (MA Ed); teacher leader school communication - non-certification (MA Ed); teacher leader social studies (MA Ed); teacher leader special education (MA Ed). *Accreditation:* NCATE. *Program availability:* Part-time, evening/weekend. *Degree requirements:* For master's, thesis optional, oral and/or written comprehensive exams; for Ed S, thesis, oral exam. *Entrance requirements:* For master's, GRE General Test, minimum overall undergraduate GPA of 2.5; for Ed S, GRE General Test, interview, master's degree, minimum GPA of 3.5, work experience. Additional exam requirements/recommendations for international students: Required—TOEFL (minimum score 500 paper-based). Electronic applications accepted. *Faculty research:* Character education, school accountability, computer applications for school administrators.

Morehead State University, Graduate School, College of Education, Department of Middle Grades and Secondary Education, Morehead, KY 40351. Offers business and marketing education (MAT); English/language arts 5-9 (MAT); French (MAT); health P-12 (MAT); mathematics 5-9 (MAT); physical education P-12 (MAT); science 5-9 (MAT); secondary biology (MAT); secondary chemistry (MAT); secondary earth science (MAT); secondary English (MAT); secondary math (MAT); secondary physics (MAT); secondary social studies (MAT); social studies 5-9 (MAT); Spanish (MAT). *Program availability:* Part-time, evening/weekend. *Degree requirements:* For master's, portfolio. *Entrance requirements:* For master's, GRE or PRAXIS II content exam, minimum overall undergraduate GPA of 2.5. Additional exam requirements/recommendations for international students: Required—TOEFL (minimum score 500 paper-based). Electronic applications accepted.

New York Institute of Technology, School of Interdisciplinary Studies and Education, Department of Teacher Education, Old Westbury, NY 11568-8000. Offers adolescence education (MS), including math (MAT, MS), science; adolescent education (MAT), including biology, chemistry, English, math (MAT, MS), social studies; childhood education (MS); early childhood (MS). *Program availability:* Part-time, evening/weekend, 100% online, blended/hybrid learning. *Faculty:* 2 full-time (both women), 8 part-time/adjunct (5 women). *Students:* 47 full-time (45 women), 56 part-time (47 women); includes 36 minority (13 Black or African American, non-Hispanic/Latino; 1 American Indian or Alaska Native, non-Hispanic/Latino; 7 Asian, non-Hispanic/Latino; 12 Hispanic/Latino; 1 Native Hawaiian or other Pacific Islander, non-Hispanic/Latino; 2 Two or more races, non-Hispanic/Latino), 3 international. Average age 31. 81 applicants, 53% accepted, 27 enrolled. In 2018, 27 master's awarded. *Entrance requirements:* For master's, GRE or MAT, BS or equivalent; minimum cumulative undergraduate GPA of 3.0; NY state initial certification; BS with major (or minimum 30 credits in a concentration) in biology, chemistry, English, math, physics, or social studies (for MS in childhood, early childhood education, and MAT); interview; personal statement. Additional exam requirements/recommendations for international students: Required—TOEFL (minimum score 79 iBT), IELTS (minimum score 6), PTE (minimum score 53). *Application deadline:* Applications are processed on a rolling basis. Application fee: $50. Electronic applications accepted. *Expenses:* $1285 per credit plus $215 fees per year (full-time) or $175 fees per year (part-time); $1395 per 3-credit education UFT or off-site graduate course. *Financial support:* Career-related internships or fieldwork, Federal Work-Study, scholarships/grants, tuition waivers (full and partial), and unspecified assistantships available. Support available to part-time students. Financial award application deadline: 2/15; financial award applicants required to submit FAFSA. *Faculty research:* Evolving definition of new literacies and its impact on teaching and learning (twenty-first century skills), new literacies practices in teacher education, teachers' professional development, English language and literacy learning through mobile learning, teaching reading to culturally and linguistically diverse children. *Application contact:* Alice Dolitsky, Director, Graduate Admissions, 516-686-7520, Fax: 516-686-1116, E-mail: admissions@nyit.edu.
Website: http://www.nyit.edu/departments/teacher_education

New York University, Steinhardt School of Culture, Education, and Human Development, Department of Art and Art Professions, Program in Art Education, New York, NY 10003-5799. Offers art, education, and community practice (MA); teachers of art, all grades (MA); teaching art/social studies 7-12 (MA), including 5-6 extension. *Accreditation:* TEAC. *Program availability:* Part-time. *Entrance requirements:* For master's, portfolio. Additional exam requirements/recommendations for international students: Required—TOEFL (minimum score 100 iBT). Electronic applications accepted. *Faculty research:* Multicultural aesthetic inquiry, urban art education, feminism, equity and social justice.

New York University, Steinhardt School of Culture, Education, and Human Development, Department of Music and Performing Arts Professions, Program in Educational Theatre, New York, NY 10012. Offers educational theatre and English 7-12 (MA); educational theatre and social studies 7-12 (MA); educational theatre in colleges and communities (MA, Ed D, PhD); educational theatre, all grades (MA). *Program availability:* Part-time. *Entrance requirements:* For master's, audition; for doctorate, GRE General Test, interview. Additional exam requirements/recommendations for international students: Required—TOEFL (minimum score 100 iBT). Electronic applications accepted. *Faculty research:* Theatre for young audiences, drama in education, applied theatre, arts education assessment, reflective praxis.

New York University, Steinhardt School of Culture, Education, and Human Development, Department of Teaching and Learning, Program in Social Studies Education, New York, NY 10012. Offers teaching art/social studies 7-12 (MA), including 5-6 extension; teaching social studies 7-12 (MA). *Accreditation:* TEAC. *Program availability:* Part-time, evening/weekend. *Entrance requirements:* Additional exam requirements/recommendations for international students: Required—TOEFL (minimum score 100 iBT). Electronic applications accepted. *Faculty research:* Social studies education reform, ethnography and oral history, civic education, labor history and social studies curriculum, material culture.

Northeastern Illinois University, College of Graduate Studies and Research, Daniel L. Goodwin College of Education, MAT Program in Secondary Education, Chicago, IL 60625. Offers English language arts (MAT); mathematics (MAT); science (MAT); social science (MAT).

Northwest Missouri State University, Graduate School, College of Arts and Sciences, Maryville, MO 64468-6001. Offers biology (MS); elementary mathematics specialist (MS Ed); English (MA); English education (MS Ed); English pedagogy (MA); geographic information science (MS, Certificate); history (MS Ed); mathematics (MS); mathematics education (MS Ed); teaching: science (MS Ed). *Program availability:* Part-time. *Faculty:* 20 full-time (9 women). *Students:* 15 full-time (9 women), 66 part-time (30 women); includes 6 minority (2 Black or African American, non-Hispanic/Latino; 1 American Indian or Alaska Native, non-Hispanic/Latino; 1 Hispanic/Latino; 2 Two or more races, non-Hispanic/Latino), 2 international. Average age 34. 32 applicants, 66% accepted, 19 enrolled. In 2018, 17 master's awarded. *Degree requirements:* For master's, comprehensive exam. *Entrance requirements:* For master's, GRE General Test, writing sample. Additional exam requirements/recommendations for international students: Required—TOEFL (minimum score 550 paper-based). *Application deadline:* For fall admission, 7/1 for domestic and international students; for spring admission, 11/15 for domestic and international students. Applications are processed on a rolling basis. Application fee: $0 ($75 for international students). Electronic applications accepted. *Expenses: Tuition, area resident:* Full-time $4551; part-time $252.86 per credit hour. Tuition, state resident: full-time $4551; part-time $252.86 per credit hour. Tuition, nonresident: full-time $9103; part-time $505.72 per credit hour. *International tuition:* $9103 full-time. *Required fees:* $2668; $148.20 per credit hour. Tuition and fees vary according to program. *Financial support:* Research assistantships with full tuition reimbursements, teaching assistantships with full tuition reimbursements, and administrative assistantships, tutorial assistantships available. Financial award application deadline: 4/1; financial award applicants required to submit FAFSA. *Unit head:* Dr. Michael Steiner, Dean, 660-562-1197. *Application contact:* Dr. Michael Steiner, Dean, 660-562-1197.
Website: https://www.nwmissouri.edu/academics/undergraduate/majors/liberal-arts-sciences.htm

Oregon State University, College of Education, Program in Teaching, Corvallis, OR 97331. Offers clinically based elementary education (MAT); elementary education (MAT); language arts (MAT); mathematics (MAT); music education (MAT); science (MAT); social studies (MAT). *Program availability:* Part-time, blended/hybrid learning. *Entrance requirements:* For master's, CBEST. Additional exam requirements/recommendations for international students: Required—TOEFL (minimum score 575 paper-based). *Expenses:* Contact institution.

Oregon State University, Interdisciplinary/Institutional Programs, Program in Environmental Sciences, Corvallis, OR 97331. Offers biogeochemistry (MA, MS, PSM, PhD); ecology (MA, MS, PSM, PhD); environmental education (MA, MS, PhD); quantitative analysis (PSM); social science (MA, MS, PSM, PhD); water resources (MA, MS, PhD). *Program availability:* Part-time. *Degree requirements:* For master's, variable foreign language requirement, thesis; for doctorate, thesis/dissertation. *Entrance requirements:* For master's and doctorate, GRE. Additional exam requirements/recommendations for international students: Required—TOEFL (minimum score 80 iBT), IELTS (minimum score 6.5).

Pace University, School of Education, New York, NY 10038. Offers adolescent education (MST), including biology, chemistry, earth science, English, foreign languages, mathematics, physics, social studies; childhood education (MST); early childhood development, learning and intervention (MST); educational technology studies (MS); inclusive adolescent education (MST), including biology, chemistry, earth science, English, foreign languages, mathematics, physics, social studies; integrated instruction for educational technology (Certificate); integrated instruction for literacy and technology (Certificate); literacy (MS Ed); special education (MS Ed). *Accreditation:* NCATE. *Program availability:* Part-time, evening/weekend, 100% online, blended/hybrid learning. *Faculty:* 19 full-time (13 women), 86 part-time/adjunct (49 women). *Students:* 98 full-time (82 women), 542 part-time (391 women); includes 256 minority (116 Black or African American, non-Hispanic/Latino; 2 American Indian or Alaska Native, non-Hispanic/Latino; 45 Asian, non-Hispanic/Latino; 83 Hispanic/Latino; 10 Two or more races, non-Hispanic/Latino), 4 international. Average age 30. 223 applicants, 89% accepted, 130 enrolled. In 2018, 269 master's, 12 other advanced degrees awarded. *Degree requirements:* For master's and Certificate, certification exams. *Entrance requirements:* For master's, GRE (for initial certification programs only), teaching certificate (for MS Ed in literacy and special education programs only). Additional exam requirements/recommendations for international students: Required—TOEFL (minimum score 88 iBT), IELTS or PTE. *Application deadline:* For fall admission, 8/1 priority date for domestic students, 6/1 for international students; for spring admission, 12/1 priority date for domestic students, 10/1 for international students. Applications are processed on a rolling basis. Application fee: $70. Electronic applications accepted. *Expenses:* Contact institution. *Financial support:* In 2018–19, 17 students received support,

including 17 research assistantships with partial tuition reimbursements available (averaging $6,020 per year); career-related internships or fieldwork, Federal Work-Study, scholarships/grants, and unspecified assistantships also available. Financial award application deadline: 9/1; financial award applicants required to submit FAFSA. *Faculty research:* STEM education, TESOL, teacher education, special education, language and literary development. *Total annual research expenditures:* $1.4 million. *Unit head:* Dr. Harriet Feldman, Dean, School of Education, 914-773-3829, E-mail: hfeldman@pace.edu. *Application contact:* Susan Ford-Goldschein, Director of Graduate Admissions, 212-346-1531, Fax: 212-346-1585, E-mail: graduateadmission@pace.edu.
Website: http://www.pace.edu/school-of-education

Plymouth State University, College of Graduate Studies, Graduate Studies in Education, Program in Heritage Studies, Plymouth, NH 03264-1595. Offers M Ed. *Program availability:* Part-time, evening/weekend. *Entrance requirements:* For master's, GRE General Test or MAT, minimum GPA of 3.0, resume.

Portland State University, Graduate Studies, College of Liberal Arts and Sciences, Interdisciplinary Programs in General Science, General Social Science, and General Arts and Letters, Portland, OR 97207-0751. Offers general arts and letters education (MAT, MST); general science education (MAT, MST); general social science education (MAT, MST). *Program availability:* Part-time, evening/weekend. *Degree requirements:* For master's, variable foreign language requirement, written exam. *Entrance requirements:* For master's, minimum GPA of 3.0 in upper-division course work or 2.75 overall. Additional exam requirements/recommendations for international students: Required—TOEFL (minimum score 550 paper-based; 80 iBT), IELTS (minimum score 6.5).

Purdue University, Graduate School, College of Education, Department of Curriculum and Instruction, West Lafayette, IN 47907. Offers agricultural and extension education (MS, MS Ed, PhD, Ed S); art education (PhD); career and technical education (MS Ed, PhD, Ed S); curriculum studies (MS Ed, PhD, Ed S); educational technology (MS Ed, PhD, Ed S); elementary education (MS Ed); family and consumer sciences education (MS Ed, PhD, Ed S); foreign language education (MS Ed, PhD, Ed S); industrial technology (PhD, Ed S); language arts (MS Ed, PhD, Ed S); literacy (MS Ed, PhD, Ed S); mathematics education (MS, MS Ed, PhD, Ed S); science education (MS, MS Ed, PhD, Ed S); social studies education (MS Ed, PhD, Ed S). *Accreditation:* NCATE. *Program availability:* Part-time, evening/weekend, online learning. *Faculty:* 34 full-time (24 women), 3 part-time/adjunct (1 woman). *Students:* 75 full-time (52 women), 357 part-time (271 women); includes 83 minority (29 Black or African American, non-Hispanic/Latino; 1 American Indian or Alaska Native, non-Hispanic/Latino; 14 Asian, non-Hispanic/Latino; 29 Hispanic/Latino; 1 Native Hawaiian or other Pacific Islander, non-Hispanic/Latino; 9 Two or more races, non-Hispanic/Latino), 43 international. Average age 36. 169 applicants, 83% accepted, 102 enrolled. In 2018, 141 master's, 15 doctorates awarded. *Degree requirements:* For master's, thesis optional; for doctorate, thesis/dissertation, oral and written exams; for Ed S, oral presentation, project. *Entrance requirements:* For master's, GRE General Test (if undergraduate GPA is below 3.0), minimum undergraduate GPA of 3.0 or equivalent; for doctorate, GRE General Test (minimum combined verbal and quantitative score of 1000, 300 for new scoring), minimum undergraduate GPA of 3.0 or equivalent; master's degree with minimum GPA of 3.0 or equivalent; for Ed S, GRE General Test (minimum combined verbal and quantitative score of 1000, 300 for new scoring), minimum undergraduate GPA of 3.0 or equivalent; master's degree. Additional exam requirements/recommendations for international students: Required—TOEFL (minimum score 550 paper-based; 77 iBT). *Application deadline:* For fall admission, 12/15 for domestic students, 3/1 for international students; for spring admission, 9/15 for domestic students, 8/1 for international students. Application fee: $60 ($75 for international students). Electronic applications accepted. *Financial support:* Fellowships with full tuition reimbursements, research assistantships with full tuition reimbursements, teaching assistantships with full tuition reimbursements, career-related internships or fieldwork, and tuition waivers (full) available. Support available to part-time students. Financial award application deadline: 3/1; financial award applicants required to submit FAFSA. *Faculty research:* Literacy acquisition and development, teacher beliefs and knowledge, recruitment and retention of underrepresented students, economic education, literacy discourse. *Unit head:* Janet M. Alsup, Head, 765-494-9667, E-mail: alsupj@purdue.edu. *Application contact:* Heather Brinkman, Graduate Contact, 765-494-2345, E-mail: hbrinkma@purdue.edu.
Website: http://www.edci.purdue.edu/

Queens College of the City University of New York, Division of Education, Department of Secondary Education and Youth Services, Queens, NY 11367-1597. Offers adolescent biology (MAT); art (MS Ed); biology (MS Ed, AC); chemistry (MS Ed, AC); earth sciences (MS Ed, AC); English (MS Ed, AC); French (MS Ed); Italian (MS Ed, AC); literacy education (MS Ed); mathematics (MS Ed, AC); music (MS Ed, AC); physics (MS Ed, AC); social studies (MS Ed, AC); Spanish (MS Ed, AC). *Program availability:* Part-time, evening/weekend. *Faculty:* 22 full-time (14 women), 35 part-time/adjunct (24 women). *Students:* 33 full-time (19 women), 358 part-time (228 women); includes 182 minority (15 Black or African American, non-Hispanic/Latino; 62 Asian, non-Hispanic/Latino; 91 Hispanic/Latino; 4 Native Hawaiian or other Pacific Islander, non-Hispanic/Latino; 10 Two or more races, non-Hispanic/Latino), 13 international. Average age 29. 216 applicants, 74% accepted, 109 enrolled. In 2018, 108 master's, 35 other advanced degrees awarded. *Degree requirements:* For master's, research project. *Entrance requirements:* For master's, GRE, minimum GPA of 3.0. Additional exam requirements/recommendations for international students: Required—TOEFL, IELTS. *Application deadline:* For fall admission, 4/1 for domestic students; for spring admission, 11/1 for domestic students. Applications are processed on a rolling basis. Application fee: $125. Electronic applications accepted. *Financial support:* Career-related internships or fieldwork available. Financial award application deadline: 4/1; financial award applicants required to submit FAFSA. *Faculty research:* Self regulated learning, teacher learning, assessment and teaching, language diversity, teaching and learning history. *Unit head:* Dr. Eleanor Armour-Thomas, Chairperson, 718-997-5150, E-mail: eleanor.armour-thomas@qc.cuny.edu. *Application contact:* Elizabeth D'Amico-Ramirez, Assistant Director of Graduate Admissions, 718-997-5203, E-mail: elizabeth.damicoramirez@qc.cuny.edu.

Quinnipiac University, School of Education, Program in Secondary Education, Hamden, CT 06518-1940. Offers biology (MAT); English (MAT); history (MAT); mathematics (MAT); Spanish (MAT). *Accreditation:* NCATE. *Entrance requirements:* For master's, PRAXIS I or PRAXIS Core Academic Skills Exam, minimum GPA of 3.0, interview. Electronic applications accepted. *Faculty research:* Multicultural and urban education/leadership, challenges of teaching diverse learners, scholarship of teaching and learning, technology and teaching, humor and education.

Rhode Island College, School of Graduate Studies, Feinstein School of Education and Human Development, Department of Educational Studies, Providence, RI 02908-1991. Offers advanced studies in teaching and learning (M Ed); English (MAT); French (MAT); history (MAT); math (MAT); secondary education (MAT); Spanish (MAT); teaching English as a second language (M Ed). *Accreditation:* NCATE. *Program availability:* Part-time, evening/weekend. *Faculty:* 12 full-time (9 women), 7 part-time/adjunct (6 women). *Students:* 12 full-time (10 women), 31 part-time (28 women); includes 5 minority (1 Black or African American, non-Hispanic/Latino; 1 Asian, non-Hispanic/Latino; 3 Hispanic/Latino). Average age 33. In 2018, 24 master's awarded. *Degree requirements:* For master's, capstone or comprehensive assessment. *Entrance requirements:* For master's, GRE or MAT (for most programs), minimum undergraduate GPA of 3.0; baccalaureate degree in English, French, history, math or Spanish; 3 letters of recommendation; interview. Additional exam requirements/recommendations for international students: Required—TOEFL (minimum score 550 paper-based; 80 iBT). *Application deadline:* For fall admission, 3/1 for domestic students; for spring admission, 11/1 for domestic students. Applications are processed on a rolling basis. Application fee: $50. Electronic applications accepted. *Expenses: Tuition, area resident:* Part-time $407 per credit. Tuition, nonresident: part-time $792 per credit. *Required fees:* $29 per credit. $100 per semester. *Financial support:* Teaching assistantships, career-related internships or fieldwork, Federal Work-Study, scholarships/grants, health care benefits, and unspecified assistantships available. Support available to part-time students. Financial award application deadline: 5/15; financial award applicants required to submit FAFSA. *Unit head:* Dr. Leslie Bogad, Chair, 401-456-8170. *Application contact:* Dr. Leslie Bogad, Chair, 401-456-8170.
Website: http://www.ric.edu/educationalStudies/Pages/default.aspx

Rivier University, School of Graduate Studies, Department of History, Law and Government, Nashua, NH 03060. Offers social studies education (MAT).

Rutgers University–New Brunswick, Graduate School of Education, Department of Educational Theory, Policy and Administration, Program in Social Studies Education, Piscataway, NJ 08854-8097. Offers Ed M, Ed D. *Program availability:* Part-time, evening/weekend. Terminal master's awarded for partial completion of doctoral program. *Degree requirements:* For master's, comprehensive exam; for doctorate, thesis/dissertation, qualifying exam. *Entrance requirements:* For master's and doctorate, GRE General Test. Additional exam requirements/recommendations for international students: Required—TOEFL. Electronic applications accepted. *Faculty research:* Academic freedom, equal educational opportunity, social studies curricula.

St. John Fisher College, Ralph C. Wilson Jr. School of Education, Program in Adolescence Education and Special Education, Rochester, NY 14618-3597. Offers adolescence education: biology with special education (MS Ed); adolescence education: chemistry with special education (MS Ed); adolescence education: English with special education (MS Ed); adolescence education: French with special education (MS Ed); adolescence education: math with special education (MS Ed); adolescence education: physics with special education (MS Ed); adolescence education: social studies with special education (MS Ed); adolescence education: Spanish with special education (MS Ed). *Program availability:* Part-time, evening/weekend. *Faculty:* 8 full-time (6 women), 2 part-time/adjunct (both women). *Students:* 13 full-time (4 women), 2 part-time (1 woman); includes 2 minority (1 Black or African American, non-Hispanic/Latino; 1 Two or more races, non-Hispanic/Latino). Average age 27. 24 applicants, 58% accepted, 4 enrolled. In 2018, 9 master's awarded. *Degree requirements:* For master's, field experiences, student teaching. *Entrance requirements:* For master's, LAST, 2 letters of recommendation, personal statement, current resume. Additional exam requirements/recommendations for international students: Required—TOEFL (minimum score 575 paper-based; 80 iBT). *Application deadline:* Applications are processed on a rolling basis. Application fee: $30. Electronic applications accepted. *Expenses:* Contact institution. *Financial support:* Scholarships/grants available. Financial award applicants required to submit FAFSA. *Faculty research:* Arts and humanities, urban schools, constructivist learning, at-risk students, mentoring. *Unit head:* Dr. Susan Hildenbrand, Program Director, 585-385-7297, E-mail: shildenbrand@sjfc.edu. *Application contact:* Michelle Gosier, Director of Transfer and Graduate Admissions, 585-385-8064, E-mail: mgosier@sjfc.edu.

Slippery Rock University of Pennsylvania, Graduate Studies (Recruitment), College of Education, Department of Secondary Education/Foundations of Education, Slippery Rock, PA 16057-1383. Offers secondary education (M Ed), including English, math/science, social studies. *Accreditation:* NCATE. *Program availability:* Part-time, evening/weekend, 100% online. *Faculty:* 9 full-time (4 women), 1 part-time/adjunct (0 women). *Students:* 45 full-time (36 women), 232 part-time (191 women); includes 2 minority (both Black or African American, non-Hispanic/Latino). Average age 28. 58 applicants, 76% accepted, 28 enrolled. In 2018, 34 master's awarded. *Degree requirements:* For master's, comprehensive exam, thesis (for some programs). *Entrance requirements:* For master's, copy of teaching certification and two letters of recommendation (for some programs). Additional exam requirements/recommendations for international students: Required—TOEFL (minimum score 550 paper-based; 80 iBT). *Application deadline:* For fall admission, 3/1 priority date for domestic students, 5/1 priority date for international students; for spring admission, 10/1 priority date for domestic students, 9/1 priority date for international students. Applications are processed on a rolling basis. Application fee: $25 ($30 for international students). Electronic applications accepted. *Expenses:* Contact institution. *Financial support:* In 2018–19, 9 students received support. Career-related internships or fieldwork, Federal Work-Study, institutionally sponsored loans, scholarships/grants, tuition waivers (partial), and unspecified assistantships available. Support available to part-time students. Financial award application deadline: 5/1; financial award applicants required to submit FAFSA. *Unit head:* Dr. Jeffrey Lehman, Graduate Coordinator, 724-738-2311, Fax: 724-738-4987, E-mail: jeffrey.lehman@sru.edu. *Application contact:* Brandi Weber-Mortimer, Director of Graduate Studies, 724-738-2051, Fax: 724-738-2146, E-mail: graduate.admissions@sru.edu.
Website: http://www.sru.edu/academics/colleges-and-departments/coe/departments/secondary-education-/-foundations-of-education

Smith College, Graduate and Special Programs, Department of Education and Child Study, Program in Secondary Education, Northampton, MA 01063. Offers secondary education (MAT), including biological sciences education, chemistry education, English education, geology education, government education, history education, mathematics education, physics education. *Program availability:* Part-time. *Students:* 8 full-time (all women), 2 part-time (0 women); includes 2 minority (1 Black or African American, non-Hispanic/Latino; 1 Asian, non-Hispanic/Latino), 2 international. Average age 27. 25 applicants, 84% accepted, 10 enrolled. In 2018, 8 master's awarded. *Entrance requirements:* Additional exam requirements/recommendations for international students: Required—TOEFL (minimum score 595 paper-based; 97 iBT), IELTS (minimum score 7.5). *Application deadline:* For fall admission, 4/15 for domestic students, 1/15 priority date for international students; for spring admission, 12/1 for domestic students. Applications are processed on a rolling basis. Application fee: $60. *Expenses:* The total tuition cost to each M.A.T. student (the full program fee, after 'built-in' scholarship award) is $18,500. *Financial support:* In 2018–19, 9 students received support, including 2 fellowships with full tuition reimbursements available; scholarships/grants and human resources employee benefit also available. Support available to part-time students. Financial award application deadline: 4/15; financial award applicants required to submit CSS PROFILE or FAFSA. *Unit head:* Rosetta Cohen, Graduate Student Advisor, 413-585-3266, E-mail: rcohen@smith.edu. *Application contact:* Ruth Morgan, Program Coordinator, 413-585-3050, Fax: 413-585-3054, E-mail: gradstdy@smith.edu.
Website: http://www.smith.edu/educ/

Smith College, Graduate and Special Programs, Department of Government, Northampton, MA 01063. Offers secondary education (MAT), including government

education. *Program availability:* Part-time. *Students:* 1 (woman) full-time, all international. Average age 30. 2 applicants, 100% accepted, 1 enrolled. *Entrance requirements:* Additional exam requirements/recommendations for international students: Required—TOEFL (minimum score 595 paper-based; 97 iBT), IELTS. *Application deadline:* For fall admission, 4/15 for domestic students, 1/15 for international students; for spring admission, 12/1 for domestic students. Applications are processed on a rolling basis. Application fee: $60. *Expenses:* The total tuition cost to each M.A.T. student (the full program fee, after 'built-in' scholarship award) is $18,500. *Financial support:* In 2018–19, 1 student received support. Fellowships and scholarships/grants available. Support available to part-time students. Financial award application deadline: 4/15; financial award applicants required to submit CSS PROFILE or FAFSA. *Unit head:* Don Baumer, Department Chair / Graduate Adviser, 413-585-3534, E-mail: dbaumer@smith.edu. *Application contact:* Ruth Morgan, Program Coordinator, 413-585-3050, Fax: 413-585-3054, E-mail: gradstdy@smith.edu. Website: http://www.smith.edu/gov/

Smith College, Graduate and Special Programs, Department of History, Northampton, MA 01063. Offers secondary education (MAT), including history education. *Program availability:* Part-time. *Students:* 1 (woman) full-time, 1 part-time (0 women); includes 1 minority (Black or African American, non-Hispanic/Latino). Average age 26. 3 applicants, 67% accepted, 2 enrolled. In 2018, 1 master's awarded. *Entrance requirements:* Additional exam requirements/recommendations for international students: Required—TOEFL (minimum score 595 paper-based; 97 iBT), IELTS. *Application deadline:* For fall admission, 4/15 for domestic students, 1/15 for international students; for spring admission, 12/1 for domestic students. Applications are processed on a rolling basis. Application fee: $60. *Expenses:* The total tuition cost to each M.A.T. student (the full program fee, after 'built-in' scholarship award) is $18,500. *Financial support:* In 2018–19, 2 students received support. Fellowships and scholarships/grants available. Support available to part-time students. Financial award application deadline: 4/15; financial award applicants required to submit CSS PROFILE or FAFSA. *Unit head:* Joshua Birk, Graduate Student Adviser, 413-585-3740, E-mail: jbirk@smith.edu. *Application contact:* Ruth Morgan, Program Coordinator, 413-585-3050, Fax: 413-585-3054, E-mail: gradstdy@smith.edu. Website: http://www.smith.edu/history/

South Carolina State University, College of Graduate and Professional Studies, Department of Education, Orangeburg, SC 29117-0001. Offers early childhood education (MAT); education (M Ed); elementary education (M Ed, MAT); English (MAT); general science/biology (MAT); mathematics (MAT); secondary education (M Ed), including biology education, business education, counselor education, English education, home economics education, industrial education, mathematics education, science education, social studies education; special education (M Ed), including emotionally handicapped, learning disabilities, mentally handicapped. *Accreditation:* NCATE. *Program availability:* Part-time, evening/weekend. *Faculty:* 17 full-time (6 women), 12 part-time/adjunct (5 women). *Students:* 42 full-time (32 women), 93 part-time (64 women); includes 121 minority (119 Black or African American, non-Hispanic/Latino; 2 Asian, non-Hispanic/Latino), 2 international. Average age 40. 50 applicants, 98% accepted, 39 enrolled. In 2018, 9 master's awarded. *Degree requirements:* For master's, thesis optional, departmental qualifying exam. *Entrance requirements:* For master's, GRE General Test, NTE, interview, teaching certificate. *Application deadline:* For fall admission, 6/15 priority date for domestic students, 6/15 for international students; for spring admission, 11/1 for domestic and international students. Application fee: $25. Electronic applications accepted. *Expenses: Tuition, area resident:* Full-time $9928; part-time $552 per credit hour. Tuition, state resident: full-time $9928. Tuition, nonresident: full-time $21,038; part-time $1169 per credit hour. *Required fees:* $1532; $85 per credit hour. *Financial support:* Fellowships, career-related internships or fieldwork, Federal Work-Study, and scholarships/grants available. Financial award application deadline: 6/1. *Unit head:* Dr. Charlie Spell, Chair, Department of Education, 803-536-8963, Fax: 803-516-4568, E-mail: cspell@scsu.edu. *Application contact:* Curtis Foskey, Coordinator of Graduate Studies, 803-536-8419, Fax: 803-536-8812, E-mail: cfoskey@scsu.edu.

Southwestern Oklahoma State University, College of Professional and Graduate Studies, School of Behavioral Sciences and Education, Program in Social Sciences, Weatherford, OK 73096-3098. Offers M Ed. *Degree requirements:* For master's, exam. *Entrance requirements:* For master's, GRE General Test or minimum undergraduate GPA of 3.0. Additional exam requirements/recommendations for international students: Required—TOEFL (minimum score 550 paper-based), IELTS (minimum score 6.5).

State University of New York at New Paltz, Graduate and Extended Learning School, School of Education, Department of Teaching and Learning, New Paltz, NY 12561. Offers adolescence education: biology (MAT, MS Ed); adolescence education: chemistry (MAT, MS Ed); adolescence education: earth science (MAT, MS Ed); adolescence education: English (MAT, MS Ed); adolescence education: French (MAT, MS Ed); adolescence education: social studies (MAT, MS Ed); adolescence education: Spanish (MAT, MS Ed); second language education (MS Ed, AC), including second language education (MS Ed), teaching English language learners (AC). *Accreditation:* NCATE. *Program availability:* Part-time, evening/weekend. *Faculty:* 21 full-time (16 women), 15 part-time/adjunct (12 women). *Students:* 127 full-time (91 women), 171 part-time (149 women); includes 48 minority (5 Black or African American, non-Hispanic/Latino; 2 Asian, non-Hispanic/Latino; 37 Hispanic/Latino; 4 Two or more races, non-Hispanic/Latino). 152 applicants, 84% accepted, 104 enrolled. In 2018, 135 master's, 19 other advanced degrees awarded. *Degree requirements:* For master's, comprehensive exam (for some programs), portfolio. *Entrance requirements:* For master's, minimum GPA of 3.0, New York state teaching certificate (MS Ed). Additional exam requirements/recommendations for international students: Required—TOEFL (minimum score 550 paper-based; 80 iBT), IELTS (minimum score 6.5). *Application deadline:* For fall admission, 3/1 priority date for domestic students, 3/1 for international students; for spring admission, 10/1 priority date for domestic students, 10/1 for international students. Application fee: $50. Electronic applications accepted. *Financial support:* Application deadline: 8/1. *Unit head:* Dr. Aaron Isabelle, Associate Dean, 845-257-2837, E-mail: isabella@newpaltz.edu. *Application contact:* Vika Shock, Director of Graduate Admissions, 845-257-3285, Fax: 845-257-3284, E-mail: gradstudies@newpaltz.edu. Website: http://www.newpaltz.edu/secondaryed/

State University of New York at Plattsburgh, School of Education, Health, and Human Services, Program in Teacher Education: Adolescence Education, Plattsburgh, NY 12901-2681. Offers adolescence education (MST); biology 7-12 (MST); chemistry 7-12 (MST); earth science 7-12 (MST); English 7-12 (MST); French 7-12 (MST); mathematics 7-12 (MST); physics 7-12 (MST); social studies 7-12 (MST); Spanish 7-12 (MST). *Accreditation:* TEAC. *Program availability:* Part-time, evening/weekend. *Entrance requirements:* For master's, minimum GPA of 2.75. Additional exam requirements/recommendations for international students: Required—TOEFL.

State University of New York College at Geneseo, Graduate Studies, School of Education, Program in Adolescence Education, Geneseo, NY 14454-1401. Offers English 7-12 (MS Ed); French 7-12 (MS Ed); social studies 7-12 (MS Ed); Spanish 7-12 (MS Ed). *Program availability:* Part-time, evening/weekend. *Degree requirements:* For master's, 2 foreign languages, comprehensive examination, thesis or research project.

Entrance requirements: For master's, GRE, MAT, EAS, edTPA, PRAXIS, or another substantially equivalent test, proof of New York State initial certification or equivalent certification from another state. Additional exam requirements/recommendations for international students: Required—TOEFL (minimum score 525 paper-based; 71 iBT), IELTS (minimum score 6.5), PTE, iTEP. Electronic applications accepted. *Expenses:* Contact institution.

State University of New York College at Old Westbury, School of Education, Old Westbury, NY 11568-0210. Offers biology (MAT, MS); chemistry (MAT, MS); English language arts (MAT, MS); math (MAT, MS); social studies (MAT, MS); Spanish (MAT, MS). *Program availability:* Part-time, evening/weekend. *Entrance requirements:* For master's, Liberal Arts and Sciences Test, undergraduate degree with at least 30 semester hours of appropriate coursework as defined by the respective discipline; minimum cumulative undergraduate GPA of 3.0; two letters of recommendation (one from an academic source); essay. Additional exam requirements/recommendations for international students: Required—TOEFL (minimum score 550 paper-based); Recommended—IELTS.

State University of New York College at Potsdam, School of Education and Professional Studies, Program in Secondary Education, Potsdam, NY 13676. Offers English education (MST); mathematics education (MST); science education (MST), including biology, chemistry, earth science, physics; social studies education (MST). *Accreditation:* NCATE. *Degree requirements:* For master's, culminating experience. *Entrance requirements:* For master's, minimum GPA of 2.75 in last 60 hours of course work (3.0 for English program). Additional exam requirements/recommendations for international students: Required—TOEFL (minimum score 550 paper-based; 80 iBT), IELTS (minimum score 6). Electronic applications accepted.

Stony Brook University, State University of New York, School of Professional Development, Stony Brook, NY 11794. Offers coaching (Graduate Certificate); environmental management (MPS); German (MAT); higher education administration (MA, Certificate); human resource management (MS, Graduate Certificate); Italian (MAT); liberal studies (MA); mathematics (MAT); school district business leadership (Advanced Certificate); social studies (MAT); Spanish (MAT). *Program availability:* Part-time, evening/weekend, online learning. *Faculty:* 3 full-time (2 women), 94 part-time/adjunct (40 women). *Students:* 214 full-time (138 women), 1,100 part-time (813 women); includes 313 minority (117 Black or African American, non-Hispanic/Latino; 2 American Indian or Alaska Native, non-Hispanic/Latino; 32 Asian, non-Hispanic/Latino; 140 Hispanic/Latino; 3 Native Hawaiian or other Pacific Islander, non-Hispanic/Latino; 19 Two or more races, non-Hispanic/Latino), 7 international. Average age 33. 483 applicants, 89% accepted, 337 enrolled. In 2018, 315 master's, 178 other advanced degrees awarded. *Entrance requirements:* Additional exam requirements/recommendations for international students: Required—TOEFL (minimum score 85 iBT). *Application deadline:* For fall admission, 1/15 for domestic students, 6/1 for international students; for spring admission, 10/1 for domestic and international students. Applications are processed on a rolling basis. Application fee: $100. *Expenses:* Contact institution. *Financial support:* Fellowships, research assistantships, teaching assistantships, and career-related internships or fieldwork available. Support available to part-time students. *Unit head:* Patricia Malone, Associate Vice President for Professional Education and Assistant Provost for Engaged Learning, 631-632-7512, Fax: 631-632-9046, E-mail: patricia.malone@stonybrook.edu. *Application contact:* Melissa Jordan, Assistant Dean, 631-632-7751, E-mail: melissa.jordan@stonybrook.edu. Website: http://www.stonybrook.edu/spd/

Syracuse University, School of Education, MS Program in Social Studies Education Preparation (Grades 7-12), Syracuse, NY 13244. Offers MS. *Program availability:* Part-time. *Students:* Average age 24. *Entrance requirements:* For master's, GRE, baccalaureate degree from regionally-accredited college/university, experience working with young people, personal statement, recommendations. Additional exam requirements/recommendations for international students: Required—TOEFL (minimum score 100 iBT). *Application deadline:* For fall admission, 1/15 priority date for domestic and international students; for spring admission, 10/15 priority date for domestic and international students; for summer admission, 4/15 priority date for domestic and international students. Applications are processed on a rolling basis. Application fee: $75. Electronic applications accepted. *Financial support:* Fellowships with full tuition reimbursements, research assistantships, teaching assistantships, career-related internships or fieldwork, and scholarships/grants available. Financial award application deadline: 1/15; financial award applicants required to submit FAFSA. *Faculty research:* Teaching youth with diverse backgrounds and abilities, issues in educating English language learners, social studies and democracy, assessment and data driven instruction, literacy across the curriculum. *Unit head:* Dr. Jeffery Mangram, Program Coordinator/Associate Professor, 315-443-3293, E-mail: jamangra@syr.edu. *Application contact:* Speranza Migliore, Graduate Admissions Recruiter, 315-443-2505, E-mail: gradrcrt@syr.edu. Website: http://soe.syr.edu/academic/teaching_and_leadership/graduate/masters/social_studies/default.aspx

Teachers College, Columbia University, Department of Arts and Humanities, New York, NY 10027. Offers applied linguistics (MA, Ed D); art and art education (Ed M, MA, Ed D, Ed DCT); arts administration (MA); bilingual and bicultural education (MA); global competence (Certificate); history and education (Ed D, PhD); music and music education (Ed DCT); philosophy and education (MA, Ed D, PhD); social studies education (Ed M, PhD); teaching English to speakers of other languages (Ed M); teaching of English and English education (Ed M, MA, Ed D, PhD), including English education (Ed M, Ed D, PhD), teaching of English (MA); teaching of social studies (MA); TESOL (MA, Ed D). *Program availability:* Part-time, evening/weekend. *Students:* 267 full-time (216 women), 569 part-time (400 women); includes 235 minority (62 Black or African American, non-Hispanic/Latino; 2 American Indian or Alaska Native, non-Hispanic/Latino; 88 Asian, non-Hispanic/Latino; 69 Hispanic/Latino; 14 Two or more races, non-Hispanic/Latino), 229 international. Average age 31. 1,075 applicants, 56% accepted, 342 enrolled. Terminal master's awarded for partial completion of doctoral program. *Financial support:* Fellowships, research assistantships, teaching assistantships, career-related internships or fieldwork, Federal Work-Study, institutionally sponsored loans, tuition waivers (full and partial), and unspecified assistantships available. Support available to part-time students. *Unit head:* Prof. ZhaoHong Han, Department Chair, E-mail: zhh2@tc.columbia.edu. *Application contact:* Kelly Sutton-Skinner, Director of Admissions & New Student Enrollment, E-mail: kms2237@tc.columbia.edu.

Temple University, College of Education, Department of Teaching and Learning, Philadelphia, PA 19122-6096. Offers career and technical education (Ed M), including business, computing, and information technology, industrial education, marketing education; middle grades education (Ed M), including math and language arts, math and science, science and language arts; secondary education (Ed M), including English, math, social studies; teaching English to speakers of other languages (MS Ed); urban education (Ed M). *Program availability:* Part-time, evening/weekend. *Faculty:* 27 full-time (19 women), 71 part-time/adjunct (51 women). *Students:* 181 full-time (126 women), 128 part-time (78 women); includes 71 minority (25 Black or African American,

non-Hispanic/Latino; 1 American Indian or Alaska Native, non-Hispanic/Latino; 20 Asian, non-Hispanic/Latino; 19 Hispanic/Latino; 1 Native Hawaiian or other Pacific Islander, non-Hispanic/Latino; 5 Two or more races, non-Hispanic/Latino), 12 international. 234 applicants, 67% accepted, 103 enrolled. In 2018, 148 master's awarded. *Degree requirements:* For master's, thesis (for some programs). *Entrance requirements:* For master's, statement of goals, 2 letters of recommendation. Additional exam requirements/recommendations for international students: Required—TOEFL (minimum score 79 iBT), IELTS, PTE, one of three is required. Application fee: $60. Electronic applications accepted. *Financial support:* Fellowships, research assistantships, teaching assistantships, career-related internships or fieldwork, Federal Work-Study, scholarships/grants, health care benefits, and unspecified assistantships available. Financial award applicants required to submit FAFSA. *Faculty research:* Career & technical education, early childhood education, middle grades education, secondary education, special education. *Unit head:* Matthew Tincani, Prof. of Applied Behavior Analysis and Dept. Chairperson, 215-204-8073, E-mail: matthew.tincani@temple.edu. *Application contact:* Stacey Sanginette, Academic Coordinator, 215-204-6143, E-mail: stacey.sangtinette@temple.edu.
Website: http://education.temple.edu/tl

Texas Tech University, Graduate School, Interdisciplinary Programs, Lubbock, TX 79409-1030. Offers arid land studies (MS); biotechnology (MS); heritage and museum sciences (MA); interdisciplinary studies (MA, MS); wind science and engineering (PhD); JD/MS. *Program availability:* Part-time, 100% online, blended/hybrid learning. *Faculty:* 10 full-time (5 women). *Students:* 98 full-time (50 women), 82 part-time (52 women); includes 75 minority (33 Black or African American, non-Hispanic/Latino; 1 American Indian or Alaska Native, non-Hispanic/Latino; 7 Asian, non-Hispanic/Latino; 31 Hispanic/Latino; 3 Two or more races, non-Hispanic/Latino), 19 international. Average age 30. 96 applicants, 76% accepted, 55 enrolled. In 2018, 64 master's, 1 doctorate awarded. Terminal master's awarded for partial completion of doctoral program. *Degree requirements:* For master's, comprehensive exam (for some programs), thesis (for some programs); for doctorate, comprehensive exam, thesis/dissertation (for some programs). *Entrance requirements:* Additional exam requirements/recommendations for international students: Required—TOEFL (minimum score 550 paper-based; 79 iBT), IELTS (minimum score 6.5), PTE (minimum score 60), Cambridge Advanced (B), Cambridge Proficiency (C), ELS English for Academic Purposes (Level 112). *Application deadline:* For fall admission, 6/1 priority date for domestic students, 1/15 priority date for international students; for spring admission, 9/1 priority date for domestic students, 6/15 priority date for international students. Applications are processed on a rolling basis. Application fee: $65. Electronic applications accepted. *Expenses:* Tuition, state resident: full-time $7776; part-time $324 per credit hour. Tuition, nonresident: full-time $17,736; part-time $739 per credit hour. *Required fees:* $2504; $53.50 per credit hour. $610 per semester. Tuition and fees vary according to program. *Financial support:* In 2018–19, 124 students received support, including 111 fellowships (averaging $4,942 per year), 27 research assistantships (averaging $17,595 per year), 8 teaching assistantships (averaging $13,758 per year); scholarships/grants and unspecified assistantships also available. Financial award application deadline: 4/15; financial award applicants required to submit FAFSA. *Total annual research expenditures:* $2.3 million. *Unit head:* Dr. Mark A. Sheridan, Vice Provost for Graduate and Postdoctoral Affairs/Dean of the Graduate School, 806-742-2787, Fax: 806-742-1746, E-mail: mark.sheridan@ttu.edu. *Application contact:* David Doerfert, Associate Dean, 806-834-4477, Fax: 806-742-4038, E-mail: david.doerfert@ttu.edu.
Website: www.depts.ttu.edu/gradschool/

Trinity Washington University, School of Education, Washington, DC 20017-1094. Offers clinical mental health counseling (MA); early childhood education (MAT); educating for change (M Ed); educational administration (MSA); elementary education (MAT); reading (M Ed); school counseling (MA); secondary education (MAT), including English, social studies; special education (MAT). *Accreditation:* NCATE. *Program availability:* Part-time, evening/weekend. *Degree requirements:* For master's, thesis (for some programs), capstone project(s). *Entrance requirements:* For master's, PRAXIS I, minimum GPA of 2.8. Additional exam requirements/recommendations for international students: Required—TOEFL (minimum score 550 paper-based). *Faculty research:* Technology, literacy, special education, organizations, inclusion models.

University at Buffalo, the State University of New York, Graduate School, Graduate School of Education, Department of Learning and Instruction, Buffalo, NY 14260. Offers biology education (Ed M, Certificate); chemistry education (Ed M, Certificate); childhood education (Ed M); childhood education with bilingual extension (Ed M); college teaching (Advanced Certificate); curriculum, instruction and the science of learning (PhD); early childhood education (Ed M); early childhood education with bilingual extension (Ed M); earth science education (Ed M, Certificate); education and technology (Ed M); education studies (Ed M); educational technology and new literacies (Certificate); educational technology and new literacies (Advanced Certificate); elementary education (Ed D); English education (Ed M, Certificate); English education studies (Ed M); English for speakers of other languages (Ed M); foreign and second language education (PhD); French education (Ed M, Certificate); German education (Ed M, Certificate); gifted education (Certificate); Latin education (Ed M, Certificate); literacy education studies (Ed M); literacy specialist (Ed M); literacy teaching and learning (Certificate); mathematics education (Ed M, Certificate); music education (Ed M, Certificate); music education studies (Ed M); music learning theory (Advanced Certificate); online education (Advanced Certificate); physics education (Ed M, Certificate); science and the public (Ed M); social studies education (Ed M, Certificate); Spanish education (Ed M, Certificate); special education (PhD); teaching English to speakers of other languages (Ed M). *Program availability:* Part-time, evening/weekend, 100% online. *Faculty:* 31 full-time (22 women), 41 part-time/adjunct (27 women). *Students:* 161 full-time (107 women), 369 part-time (260 women); includes 76 minority (26 Black or African American, non-Hispanic/Latino; 3 American Indian or Alaska Native, non-Hispanic/Latino; 30 Asian, non-Hispanic/Latino; 14 Hispanic/Latino; 3 Two or more races, non-Hispanic/Latino), 41 international. Average age 34. 368 applicants, 70% accepted, 179 enrolled. In 2018, 100 master's, 26 doctorates, 19 other advanced degrees awarded. *Degree requirements:* For master's, comprehensive exam; for doctorate, thesis/dissertation, research analysis exam, research experience. *Entrance requirements:* For master's, letters of reference; for doctorate, GRE General Test or MAT, interview, writing sample, letters of recommendation. Additional exam requirements/recommendations for international students: Required—TOEFL (minimum score 600 paper-based; 96 iBT), IELTS (minimum score 6.5), PTE (minimum score 55). *Application deadline:* For fall admission, 2/1 priority date for domestic and international students; for spring admission, 11/15 priority date for domestic students, 10/1 for international students. Applications are processed on a rolling basis. Application fee: $50. Electronic applications accepted. *Financial support:* In 2018–19, 42 fellowships (averaging $5,181 per year), 44 research assistantships with tuition reimbursements (averaging $10,908 per year) were awarded; teaching assistantships, career-related internships or fieldwork, Federal Work-Study, institutionally sponsored loans, scholarships/grants, tuition waivers (full and partial), and unspecified assistantships also available. Financial award application deadline: 2/28; financial award applicants required to submit FAFSA. *Faculty research:* Science assessment, foreign language teaching and learning, early learning, new literacies, gender and education. *Total annual research expenditures:* $413,233.

Unit head: Dr. Julie Gorlewski, Department Chair, 716-645-2455, Fax: 716-645-3161, E-mail: jgorlews@buffalo.edu. *Application contact:* Renad Aref, Assistant Director of Admission Recruitment, 716-645-2110, Fax: 716-645-7937, E-mail: gseinfo@buffalo.edu.
Website: http://ed.buffalo.edu/teaching.html

The University of Akron, Graduate School, College of Education, Department of Curricular and Instructional Studies, Program in Adolescent to Young Adult Education, Akron, OH 44325. Offers chemistry (MS); chemistry and physics (MS); earth science (MS); earth science and chemistry (MS); earth science and physics (MS); integrated language arts (MS); integrated mathematics (MS); integrated social studies (MS); life science (MS); life science and chemistry (MS); life science and earth science (MS); life science and physics (MS); physics (MS). *Accreditation:* NCATE. *Degree requirements:* For master's, comprehensive exam. *Entrance requirements:* For master's, minimum GPA of 3.0. Additional exam requirements/recommendations for international students: Required—TOEFL (minimum score 79 iBT), IELTS (minimum score 6.5). Electronic applications accepted.

The University of Alabama in Huntsville, School of Graduate Studies, College of Education, Huntsville, AL 35899. Offers autism spectrum disorders (M Ed, Graduate Certificate); biology (MAT); chemistry (MAT); differentiated instruction in elementary education (M Ed); English language arts (MAT); English speakers of other languages (M Ed, MAT); history (MAT); mathematics (MAT); physics (MAT); reading education (M Ed); secondary education (M Ed). *Program availability:* Part-time. *Faculty:* 13 full-time (10 women). *Students:* 38 full-time (30 women), 39 part-time (37 women); includes 17 minority (10 Black or African American, non-Hispanic/Latino; 3 American Indian or Alaska Native, non-Hispanic/Latino; 2 Asian, non-Hispanic/Latino; 2 Two or more races, non-Hispanic/Latino). Average age 33. 47 applicants, 83% accepted, 29 enrolled. In 2018, 31 master's awarded. *Degree requirements:* For master's, comprehensive exam, thesis or alternative, oral and written. *Entrance requirements:* For master's, GRE General Test, minimum GPA of 3.0. Additional exam requirements/recommendations for international students: Required—TOEFL (minimum score 500 paper-based; 80 iBT), IELTS (minimum score 6.5). *Application deadline:* For fall admission, 7/15 priority date for domestic students, 4/1 priority date for international students; for spring admission, 11/30 priority date for domestic students, 9/1 priority date for international students. Applications are processed on a rolling basis. Application fee: $50. Electronic applications accepted. *Expenses: Tuition, area resident:* Full-time $10,632; part-time $412 per credit hour. Tuition, state resident: full-time $10,632. Tuition, nonresident: full-time $23,604; part-time $412 per credit hour. *Required fees:* $582; $582. Tuition and fees vary according to course load and program. *Financial support:* In 2018–19, 2 students received support, including 1 teaching assistantship with full tuition reimbursement available (averaging $4,500 per year); career-related internships or fieldwork, Federal Work-Study, institutionally sponsored loans, scholarships/grants, health care benefits, tuition waivers (full and partial), and unspecified assistantships also available. Support available to part-time students. Financial award application deadline: 4/1; financial award applicants required to submit FAFSA. *Unit head:* Dr. Beth Nason Quick, Dean, 256-824-2325, E-mail: beth.quick@uah.edu. *Application contact:* Kim Gray, Graduate Studies Admissions Coordinator, 256-824-6002, Fax: 256-824-6405, E-mail: deangrad@uah.edu.
Website: http://www.uah.edu/education/

University of Arkansas at Pine Bluff, School of Education, Pine Bluff, AR 71601-2799. Offers elementary education (M Ed); secondary education (M Ed), including English education, mathematics education, science education, social studies education; teaching (MAT). *Accreditation:* NCATE. *Program availability:* Part-time, evening/weekend. *Degree requirements:* For master's, comprehensive exam. *Entrance requirements:* For master's, GRE, minimum GPA of 2.75, NTE or Standard Arkansas Teaching Certificate. *Faculty research:* Teacher certification, accreditation, assessment, standards, portfolio development, rehabilitation, technology.

The University of British Columbia, Faculty of Education, Department of Curriculum and Pedagogy, Vancouver, BC V6T 1Z4, Canada. Offers art education (M Ed, MA); curriculum studies (M Ed, MA, PhD); home economics education (M Ed, MA); mathematics education (M Ed, MA); media and technology studies education (M Ed, MA); music education (M Ed, MA); physical education (M Ed, MA); science education (M Ed, MA); social studies education (M Ed, MA). *Program availability:* Part-time, online learning. *Degree requirements:* For master's, thesis (MA); for doctorate, comprehensive exam, thesis/dissertation. *Entrance requirements:* Additional exam requirements/recommendations for international students: Required—TOEFL, IELTS. Electronic applications accepted. *Expenses:* Contact institution. *Faculty research:* School subjects, teaching and learning.

University of California, Santa Cruz, Division of Graduate Studies, Division of Social Sciences, Program in Social Documentation, Santa Cruz, CA 95064. Offers MA. *Entrance requirements:* For master's, resume or curriculum vitae, sample of documentary production work. Additional exam requirements/recommendations for international students: Required—TOEFL (minimum score 550 paper-based; 83 iBT); Recommended—IELTS (minimum score 8). Electronic applications accepted. *Faculty research:* Documentation of underrepresented areas of community life.

University of Central Florida, College of Community Innovation and Education, School of Teacher Education, Orlando, FL 32816. Offers applied learning and instruction (MA); curriculum and instruction (M Ed); elementary education (M Ed, MA); exceptional student education (M Ed, MA, Certificate), including autism spectrum disorders (Certificate), exceptional student education (M Ed), exceptional student education K-12 (MA), intervention specialist (Certificate), pre-kindergarten disabilities (Certificate), severe or profound disabilities (Certificate), special education (Certificate); K-8 mathematics and science education (M Ed, Certificate); reading education (M Ed, Certificate); teacher education (MAT), including art education, English language, mathematics education, middle school mathematics, middle school science, science education, social science education; world languages education - English for speakers of other languages (ESOL) (Certificate); world languages education - languages other than English (LOTE) (Certificate). *Program availability:* Part-time, evening/weekend. *Degree requirements:* For Certificate, thesis or alternative. *Entrance requirements:* For degree, GRE General Test, minimum GPA of 3.0. Additional exam requirements/recommendations for international students: Required—TOEFL. Electronic applications accepted.

University of Connecticut, Graduate School, Neag School of Education, Department of Curriculum and Instruction, Program in History and Social Sciences Education, Storrs, CT 06269. Offers MA, PhD. *Accreditation:* NCATE. Terminal master's awarded for partial completion of doctoral program. *Degree requirements:* For master's, comprehensive exam, thesis or alternative; for doctorate, thesis/dissertation. *Entrance requirements:* For doctorate, GRE General Test. Additional exam requirements/recommendations for international students: Required—TOEFL (minimum score 550 paper-based). Electronic applications accepted.

University of Florida, Graduate School, College of Education, School of Teaching and Learning, Gainesville, FL 32611. Offers curriculum and instruction (M Ed, MAE, Ed D, PhD, Ed S); elementary education (M Ed, MAE); English education (M Ed, MAE);

mathematics education (M Ed, MAE); reading education (M Ed, MAE); science education (M Ed, MAE); social studies education (M Ed, MAE). *Accreditation:* NCATE. *Program availability:* Part-time, evening/weekend, online learning. Terminal master's awarded for partial completion of doctoral program. *Degree requirements:* For master's, comprehensive exam (for some programs), thesis (for some programs); for doctorate, comprehensive exam (for some programs), thesis/dissertation (for some programs). *Entrance requirements:* For master's and doctorate, GRE General Test, minimum GPA of 3.0; for Ed S, GRE General Test. Additional exam requirements/recommendations for international students: Required—TOEFL (minimum score 550 paper-based; 80 iBT), IELTS (minimum score 6). Electronic applications accepted. *Faculty research:* STEM education; curriculum; teaching and teacher education; languages and literacy; schools, culture, and society; theories and processes of learning.

University of Illinois at Chicago, Program in Learning Sciences, Chicago, IL 60607-7128. Offers PhD.

University of Indianapolis, Graduate Programs, School of Education, Indianapolis, IN 46227-3697. Offers art education (MAT); biology (MAT); chemistry (MAT); curriculum and instruction (MA); earth sciences (MAT); education (MA, MAT); educational leadership (MA); elementary education (MA); English (MAT); French (MAT); math (MAT); physical education (MAT); physics (MAT); secondary education (MA), including art education, education, English education, social studies education; social studies (MAT); Spanish (MAT). *Accreditation:* NCATE. *Program availability:* Part-time, evening/weekend. *Entrance requirements:* For master's, GRE Subject Test, PRAXIS I, minimum GPA of 2.5, 3 letters of recommendation, interview. Additional exam requirements/recommendations for international students: Required—TOEFL (minimum score 550 paper-based). *Faculty research:* Assessment of teacher education, perceptions of prospective teachers by parents.

The University of Iowa, Graduate College, College of Education, Department of Teaching and Learning, Program in Education, Iowa City, IA 52242-1316. Offers art education (MA); developmental reading (MA); elementary education (MA); English education (MA, MAT); foreign and second language education (MAT); foreign language education (MA); foreign language/ESL education (PhD); language, literacy and culture (PhD); mathematics education (MA, MAT, PhD); music education (MM, PhD); science education (MA); secondary education (MA); social studies (MA, PhD). *Degree requirements:* For master's, thesis optional, exam; for doctorate, comprehensive exam, thesis/dissertation. *Entrance requirements:* For master's and doctorate, GRE General Test, minimum GPA of 3.0. Additional exam requirements/recommendations for international students: Required—TOEFL (minimum score 550 paper-based; 81 iBT). Electronic applications accepted.

University of Maine, Graduate School, College of Education and Human Development, School of Learning and Teaching, Orono, ME 04469. Offers counselor education (M Ed, MA, MS, CAS); early childhood teacher (CGS); education (PhD), including counselor education, literacy education, prevention and intervention studies; elementary education (M Ed, CAS); individualized education (M Ed); literacy education (CAS); response to intervention for behavior (CGS); secondary education (M Ed, CAS); social studies education (M Ed); special education (M Ed, CAS). *Program availability:* Part-time. *Faculty:* 21 full-time (12 women), 37 part-time/adjunct (29 women). *Students:* 113 full-time (96 women), 224 part-time (191 women); includes 11 minority (3 Black or African American, non-Hispanic/Latino; 4 American Indian or Alaska Native, non-Hispanic/Latino; 1 Asian, non-Hispanic/Latino; 2 Hispanic/Latino; 1 Two or more races, non-Hispanic/Latino), 3 international. Average age 37. 195 applicants, 99% accepted, 147 enrolled. In 2018, 82 master's, 2 doctorates, 49 other advanced degrees awarded. *Degree requirements:* For master's, thesis (for some programs); for doctorate, comprehensive exam, thesis/dissertation. *Entrance requirements:* For master's, GRE General Test, MAT. Additional exam requirements/recommendations for international students: Required—TOEFL (minimum score 550 paper-based; 80 iBT), IELTS (minimum score 6.5). *Application deadline:* For fall admission, 2/1 priority date for domestic students. Applications are processed on a rolling basis. Application fee: $65. Electronic applications accepted. *Financial support:* In 2018–19, 22 students received support, including 8 teaching assistantships with full tuition reimbursements available (averaging $1,600 per year); Federal Work-Study, scholarships/grants, and unspecified assistantships also available. Financial award application deadline: 3/1. *Faculty research:* Gender and leadership, virtual reality, using writing to improve performance in athletics, digital citizenship, professional development for special and general education. *Total annual research expenditures:* $2.1 million. *Unit head:* Dr. Jim Artesani, Associate Dean of Accreditation and Graduate Affairs, 207-581-4061. *Application contact:* Scott G. Delcourt, Assistant Vice President for Graduate Studies and Senior Associate Dean, 207-581-3291, Fax: 207-581-3232, E-mail: graduate@maine.edu.
Website: http://umaine.edu/edhd/

University of Maryland, Baltimore County, The Graduate School, College of Arts, Humanities and Social Sciences, Department of Education, Program in Teaching, Baltimore, MD 21250. Offers early childhood education (MAT); elementary education (MAT); teaching (MAT), including art, biology, chemistry, choral music, classical foreign language, dance, earth/space science, English, instrumental music, mathematics, modern foreign language, physical science, physics, social studies, theatre. *Program availability:* Part-time, evening/weekend. *Degree requirements:* For master's, comprehensive exam (for some programs), thesis (for some programs). *Entrance requirements:* For master's, PRAXIS Core Examination or GRE (minimum score of 1000), minimum GPA of 3.0. Additional exam requirements/recommendations for international students: Required—TOEFL. Electronic applications accepted. *Faculty research:* STEM teacher education, culturally sensitive pedagogy, ESOL/bilingual education, early childhood education, language, literacy and culture.

University of Minnesota, Twin Cities Campus, Graduate School, College of Education and Human Development, Department of Curriculum and Instruction, Program in Teaching, Minneapolis, MN 55455-0213. Offers teaching (M Ed), including arts in education, elementary education, English education, mathematics, science, second language education, social studies. *Students:* 249 full-time (182 women), 101 part-time (59 women); includes 57 minority (5 Black or African American, non-Hispanic/Latino; 16 Asian, non-Hispanic/Latino; 25 Hispanic/Latino; 11 Two or more races, non-Hispanic/Latino), 12 international. Average age 28. 383 applicants, 79% accepted, 261 enrolled. In 2018, 292 master's awarded. Application fee: $75 ($95 for international students). *Unit head:* Dr. Mark Vagle, Chair, 612-625-4006, Fax: 612-624-8277, E-mail: mvagle@umn.edu. *Application contact:* Dr. Mark Vagle, Chair, 612-625-4006, Fax: 612-624-8277, E-mail: mvagle@umn.edu.
Website: http://www.cehd.umn.edu/ci/

University of Missouri, Office of Research and Graduate Studies, College of Education, Department of Learning, Teaching and Curriculum, Columbia, MO 65211. Offers agricultural education (M Ed, PhD, Ed S); art education (M Ed, PhD, Ed S); business and office education (M Ed, PhD, Ed S); early childhood education (M Ed, PhD, Ed S); elementary education (M Ed, PhD, Ed S); English education (M Ed, PhD, Ed S); foreign language education (M Ed, PhD, Ed S); health education and promotion (M Ed, PhD); learning and instruction (M Ed); marketing education (M Ed, PhD, Ed S); mathematics education (M Ed, PhD, Ed S); music education (M Ed, PhD, Ed S); reading education (M Ed, PhD, Ed S); science education (M Ed, PhD, Ed S); social studies education (M Ed, PhD, Ed S); vocational education (M Ed, PhD, Ed S). *Program availability:* Part-time. Terminal master's awarded for partial completion of doctoral program. *Entrance requirements:* For master's and Ed S, GRE General Test or MAT, minimum GPA of 3.0; for doctorate, GRE General Test, minimum GPA of 3.0. Additional exam requirements/recommendations for international students: Required—TOEFL.

University of Missouri–St. Louis, College of Arts and Sciences, Department of History, St. Louis, MO 63121. Offers history (MA); history education (Certificate); museum studies (MA, Certificate). *Program availability:* Part-time, evening/weekend. *Degree requirements:* For master's, thesis (for some programs). *Entrance requirements:* For master's, writing sample; minimum GPA of 2.75 (for history), 3.2 (for museum studies). Additional exam requirements/recommendations for international students: Required—TOEFL (minimum score 550 paper-based; 79 iBT), IELTS (minimum score 6.5). Electronic applications accepted. *Faculty research:* United States, European, East Asian, Latin American, and African history.

The University of North Carolina at Chapel Hill, Graduate School, School of Education, Program in Secondary Education, Chapel Hill, NC 27599. Offers English (Grades 9-12) (MAT); English as a second language (MAT); French (Grades K-12) (MAT); German (Grades K-12) (MAT); Japanese (Grades K-12) (MAT); Latin (Grades 9-12) (MAT); mathematics (Grades 9-12) (MAT); music (Grades K-12) (MAT); science (Grades 9-12) (MAT); social studies (Grades 9-12) (MAT); Spanish (Grades K-12) (MAT). *Accreditation:* NCATE. *Degree requirements:* For master's, comprehensive exam. *Entrance requirements:* For master's, GRE General Test, minimum GPA of 3.0 during last 2 years of undergraduate course work. Additional exam requirements/recommendations for international students: Required—TOEFL (minimum score 550 paper-based). Electronic applications accepted.

The University of North Carolina at Greensboro, Graduate School, School of Education, Department of Teacher Education and Higher Education, Greensboro, NC 27412-5001. Offers college teaching and adult learning (Certificate); curriculum and instruction (M Ed), including chemistry education, elementary education, English as a second language, French education, instructional technology, mathematics education, middle grades education, reading education, science education, social studies education, Spanish education; curriculum and teaching (PhD), including higher education, teacher education and development; English as a second language (Certificate); higher education (M Ed); supervision (M Ed). *Accreditation:* NCATE. *Program availability:* Part-time. *Degree requirements:* For doctorate, thesis/dissertation. *Entrance requirements:* For master's and doctorate, GRE General Test. Additional exam requirements/recommendations for international students: Required—TOEFL. Electronic applications accepted. *Faculty research:* Community college literacy program, middle school mathematics/computer mathematics.

The University of North Carolina at Pembroke, The Graduate School, Department of History, Pembroke, NC 28372-1510. Offers social studies education (MA, MAT). *Program availability:* Part-time, evening/weekend. *Entrance requirements:* For master's, GRE General Test or MAT, minimum GPA of 3.0 in major, 2.5 overall. Additional exam requirements/recommendations for international students: Required—TOEFL.

University of North Georgia, Master of Arts in Teaching Program, Dahlonega, GA 30597. Offers physical education (MAT); secondary education - English (MAT); secondary education - history (MAT); secondary education - mathematics (MAT); secondary education - middle grades (MAT). *Degree requirements:* For master's, internship, capstone. *Entrance requirements:* For master's, GRE or MAT, GACE I and II, GA pre-service application, lawful presence verification, official transcripts, GA Educator Ethics Program entry assessment. Additional exam requirements/recommendations for international students: Required—TOEFL (minimum score 550 paper-based; 79 iBT), IELTS (minimum score 6.5). Electronic applications accepted. *Expenses:* Contact institution.

University of Oklahoma, Jeannine Rainbolt College of Education, Department of Instructional Leadership and Academic Curriculum, Norman, OK 73072. Offers instructional leadership and academic curriculum (M Ed, PhD), including biomedical education (PhD), early childhood education, elementary education, English education, instructional leadership, mathematics education, reading education, science education, social studies education, world languages education (M Ed); reading specialist (M Ed). *Accreditation:* NCATE. *Program availability:* Part-time. *Faculty:* 26 full-time (12 women), 1 part-time/adjunct (0 women). *Students:* 42 full-time (32 women), 113 part-time (85 women); includes 33 minority (9 Black or African American, non-Hispanic/Latino; 5 American Indian or Alaska Native, non-Hispanic/Latino; 6 Asian, non-Hispanic/Latino; 4 Hispanic/Latino; 1 Native Hawaiian or other Pacific Islander, non-Hispanic/Latino; 8 Two or more races, non-Hispanic/Latino), 9 international. Average age 35. 42 applicants, 79% accepted, 21 enrolled. In 2018, 30 master's, 17 doctorates awarded. Terminal master's awarded for partial completion of doctoral program. *Degree requirements:* For master's, comprehensive exam (for some programs), thesis (for some programs); for doctorate, comprehensive exam (for some programs), thesis/dissertation. *Entrance requirements:* For doctorate, GRE. Additional exam requirements/recommendations for international students: Required—TOEFL (minimum score 79 iBT) or IELTS (minimum score 6.5). Application fee: $50 ($100 for international students). Electronic applications accepted. *Expenses:* Tuition, state resident: full-time $5683.20; part-time $236.80 per credit hour. Tuition, nonresident: full-time $20,342; part-time $847.60 per credit hour. *International tuition:* $20,342.40 full-time. *Required fees:* $2894.20; $110.05 per credit hour. $126.50 per semester. Tuition and fees vary according to course load and program. *Financial support:* Fellowships, research assistantships, teaching assistantships, scholarships/grants, and unspecified assistantships available. Financial award application deadline: 6/1; financial award applicants required to submit FAFSA. *Faculty research:* Teacher preparation; instruction; curriculum; learning; constructivist theory. *Unit head:* Dr. Stacy Reeder, Chair, 405-325-1498, Fax: 405-325-4061, E-mail: reeder@ou.edu. *Application contact:* Anna Steele, Graduate Programs Officer, 405-325-4525, E-mail: anna.steele@ou.edu.
Website: http://www.ou.edu/education/ilac

University of Pittsburgh, School of Education, Department of Instruction and Learning, Program in Secondary Education, Pittsburgh, PA 15260. Offers English and communications education (M Ed, MAT); foreign language education (M Ed, MAT); language, literacy and culture education (Ed D, PhD); mathematics education (M Ed, MAT, Ed D, PhD); science education (M Ed, MAT, Ed D, PhD); secondary education (PhD); social studies education (M Ed, MAT); STEM education (Ed D). *Program availability:* Part-time, evening/weekend. *Degree requirements:* For master's, thesis; for doctorate, thesis/dissertation. *Entrance requirements:* For master's, PRAXIS I; for doctorate, GRE General Test. Additional exam requirements/recommendations for international students: Required—TOEFL. Electronic applications accepted.

University of Puerto Rico–Río Piedras, College of Education, Program in Curriculum and Teaching, San Juan, PR 00931-3300. Offers biology education (M Ed); chemistry education (M Ed); curriculum and teaching (Ed D); history education (M Ed); mathematics education (M Ed); physics education (M Ed); Spanish education (M Ed). *Program availability:* Part-time. *Degree requirements:* For master's, thesis; for doctorate, thesis/dissertation, internship. *Entrance requirements:* For master's, PAEG or GRE, minimum GPA of 3.0, letter of recommendation; for doctorate, GRE or PAEG, master's degree, minimum GPA of 3.0, letter of recommendation (2), interview. *Faculty research:* Curriculum, math teaching.

Social Sciences Education

University of St. Francis, College of Education, Joliet, IL 60435-6169. Offers educational leadership (MS, Ed D); elementary education (M Ed); reading (MS); secondary education (M Ed), including English education, math education, science education, social studies education, visual arts education; special education (M Ed); teaching and learning (MS); TESOL (Certificate). *Accreditation:* NCATE. *Program availability:* Part-time, evening/weekend, 100% online, blended/hybrid learning. *Faculty:* 11 full-time (8 women), 58 part-time/adjunct (38 women). *Students:* 43 full-time (35 women), 453 part-time (354 women); includes 110 minority (48 Black or African American, non-Hispanic/Latino; 7 Asian, non-Hispanic/Latino; 52 Hispanic/Latino; 3 Two or more races, non-Hispanic/Latino), 3 international. Average age 37. 300 applicants, 66% accepted, 164 enrolled. In 2018, 151 master's, 42 doctorates, 4 other advanced degrees awarded. *Degree requirements:* For master's, comprehensive exam; for doctorate, thesis/dissertation. *Entrance requirements:* Additional exam requirements/recommendations for international students: Required—TOEFL (minimum score 550 paper-based; 79 iBT), IELTS (minimum score 6). *Application deadline:* Applications are processed on a rolling basis. Electronic applications accepted. Application fee is waived when completed online. *Expenses:* Contact institution. *Financial support:* In 2018–19, 33 students received support. Scholarships/grants and tuition waivers (partial) available. Support available to part-time students. Financial award applicants required to submit FAFSA. *Unit head:* Dr. John Gambro, Dean, 815-740-3456, E-mail: jgambro@stfrancis.edu. *Application contact:* Sandee Sloka, Director Adult & Graduate Admissions, 800-735-7500, E-mail: ssloka@stfrancis.edu.
Website: https://www.stfrancis.edu/education/

University of South Carolina, The Graduate School, College of Education, Department of Instruction and Teacher Education, Program in Secondary Education, Columbia, SC 29208. Offers art education (IMA, MAT); business education (IMA, MAT); English (MAT); foreign language (MAT); health education (MAT); mathematics (MAT); science (IMA, MAT); secondary (Ed D); secondary education (MT, PhD); social studies (MAT); theatre and speech (MAT). IMA and MT offered jointly with the subject areas. *Accreditation:* NCATE. *Degree requirements:* For master's, comprehensive exam, thesis (for some programs), foreign language (MA); for doctorate, one foreign language, comprehensive exam, thesis/dissertation. *Entrance requirements:* For master's, GRE General Test or MAT, teaching certificate (IMA, M Ed), interview; for doctorate, GRE General Test or MAT, interview. *Faculty research:* Middle school programs, professional development, school collaboration.

University of South Florida, College of Arts and Sciences, Department of Anthropology, Tampa, FL 33620-9951. Offers applied anthropology (MA, PhD), including archaeological and forensic sciences, biocultural medical anthropology, cultural resource management, heritage studies; medical anthropology (Graduate Certificate). *Program availability:* Part-time. *Faculty:* 19 full-time (12 women). *Students:* 61 full-time (38 women), 49 part-time (35 women); includes 29 minority (6 Black or African American, non-Hispanic/Latino; 20 Hispanic/Latino; 3 Two or more races, non-Hispanic/Latino), 7 international. Average age 32. 152 applicants, 23% accepted, 29 enrolled. In 2018, 11 master's, 11 doctorates awarded. *Degree requirements:* For master's, one foreign language, comprehensive exam, thesis; for doctorate, one foreign language, comprehensive exam, thesis/dissertation. *Entrance requirements:* For master's, GRE (no minimum score requirement), minimum GPA of 3.0, 3 letters of recommendation, statement of purpose, signed research ethics statement, resume or curriculum vitae, writing sample (optional), GA Application (optional); for doctorate, GRE required, minimum GPA of 3.0, 3 letters of recommendation, statement of purpose, signed research ethics statement, resume or curriculum vitae, writing sample (optional), GA Application (optional); for Graduate Certificate, bachelor's degree with minimum GPA of 3.0. Additional exam requirements/recommendations for international students: Required—TOEFL, TOEFL (minimum score 550 paper-based; 79 iBT) or IELTS (minimum score 6.5). *Application deadline:* For fall admission, 12/15 priority date for domestic and international students. Application fee: $30. Electronic applications accepted. *Expenses:* Tuition, state resident: full-time $6350. Tuition, nonresident: full-time $19,048. *International tuition:* $19,048 full-time. *Required fees:* $2079. *Financial support:* In 2018–19, 27 students received support, including 14 research assistantships with tuition reimbursements available (averaging $14,475 per year), 52 teaching assistantships with partial tuition reimbursements available (averaging $12,540 per year); scholarships/grants and tuition waivers (partial) also available. Financial award application deadline: 1/15; financial award applicants required to submit FAFSA. *Faculty research:* Biocultural medical anthropology; archaeology and culture resource management in the Americas; community identity and heritage; urban community issues; verbal and nonverbal communications in media and education; global dynamics of sustainable resource management and economic development; social and cultural constructions of race, ethnicity, and gender. *Total annual research expenditures:* $811,312. *Unit head:* Dr. David Himmelgreen, Professor/Chair, 813-974-5455, E-mail: dhimmelg@usf.edu. *Application contact:* Dr. Rebecca Zarger, Associate Professor and Graduate Director, 813-974-0069, E-mail: rzarger@usf.edu.
Website: http://anthropology.usf.edu/graduate/

The University of Tennessee, Graduate School, College of Education, Health and Human Sciences, Program in Education, Knoxville, TN 37996. Offers art education (MS); counseling education (PhD); cultural studies in education (PhD); curriculum (MS, Ed S); curriculum, educational research and evaluation (Ed D, PhD); early childhood education (PhD); early childhood special education (MS); education of deaf and hard of hearing (MS); educational administration and policy studies (Ed D, PhD); educational administration and supervision (Ed S); educational psychology (Ed D, PhD); elementary education (MS, Ed S); elementary teaching (MS); English education (MS, Ed S); exercise science (PhD); foreign language/ESL education (MS, Ed S); instructional technology (MS, Ed D, PhD, Ed S); literacy, language and ESL education (PhD); literacy, language education, and ESL education (Ed D); mathematics education (MS, Ed S); modified and comprehensive special education (MS); reading education (MS, Ed S); school counseling (Ed S); school psychology (PhD, Ed S); science education (MS, Ed S); secondary teaching (MS); social foundations (MS); social science education (MS, Ed S); socio-cultural foundations of sports and education (PhD); special education (Ed S); teacher education (Ed D, PhD). *Accreditation:* NCATE. *Program availability:* Part-time, evening/weekend. *Degree requirements:* For master's and Ed S, thesis optional; for doctorate, variable foreign language requirement, thesis/dissertation. *Entrance requirements:* For master's, minimum GPA of 2.7; for doctorate and Ed S, GRE General Test, minimum GPA of 2.7. Additional exam requirements/recommendations for international students: Required—TOEFL. Electronic applications accepted.

University of the District of Columbia, College of Arts and Sciences, Program in Teaching, Washington, DC 20008-1175. Offers elementary education (MAT); middle school mathematics (MAT); secondary English language arts (MAT); secondary social studies (MAT).

The University of Toledo, College of Graduate Studies, Judith Herb College of Education, Department of Curriculum and Instruction, Toledo, OH 43606-3390. Offers art education (ME); career and technical education (ME, Ed S); curriculum and instruction (ME, PhD, Ed S); early childhood education (Ed S); education and anthropology (MAE); education and biology (MES); education and chemistry (MES); education and classics (MAE); education and economics (MAE); education and English (MAE); education and French (MAE); education and geology (MES); education and German (MAE); education and history (MAE); education and mathematics (MAE, MES); education and physics (MES); education and political science (MAE); education and sociology (MAE); education and Spanish (MAE); educational media (PhD); educational technology (ME); educational technology: virtual educator (Certificate); elementary education (PhD); English as a second language (MAE); gifted and talented education (PhD); middle childhood education (ME); secondary education (ME, PhD); special education (PhD). *Accreditation:* NCATE. *Program availability:* Part-time, evening/weekend. *Degree requirements:* For master's, comprehensive exam, thesis or alternative; for doctorate, comprehensive exam, thesis/dissertation; for other advanced degree, thesis optional. *Entrance requirements:* For master's, doctorate, and other advanced degree, minimum cumulative GPA of 2.7 for all previous academic work, letters of recommendation. Additional exam requirements/recommendations for international students: Required—TOEFL (minimum score 550 paper-based; 80 iBT). Electronic applications accepted.

University of Victoria, Faculty of Graduate Studies, Faculty of Education, Department of Curriculum and Instruction, Victoria, BC V8W 2Y2, Canada. Offers art education (M Ed, PhD); curriculum studies (M Ed, MA, PhD); early childhood education (M Ed, PhD); educational studies (PhD); language and literacy (M Ed, MA, PhD); mathematics (M Ed, MA, PhD); music education (M Ed, MA, PhD); science (M Ed, MA, PhD); social studies (M Ed, MA); social, cultural and foundational studies (MA, PhD); technology and environmental education (PhD). *Program availability:* Part-time. *Degree requirements:* For master's, thesis, project (M Ed); for doctorate, comprehensive exam, thesis/dissertation. *Entrance requirements:* For master's, minimum B average. Additional exam requirements/recommendations for international students: Required—TOEFL (minimum score 575 paper-based), IELTS (minimum score 7). Electronic applications accepted. *Faculty research:* Elementary and secondary English, language arts, curriculum theory and practice, educational media and technology, educational administration and leadership, history and philosophy of education.

University of Virginia, Curry School of Education, Department of Curriculum, Instruction, and Special Education, Program in Curriculum and Instruction, Charlottesville, VA 22903. Offers curriculum and instruction (M Ed, Ed S); elementary education (M Ed, Ed D); English education (M Ed, Ed D); foreign language education (M Ed); mathematics education (M Ed, Ed D); science education (Ed D); social studies education (M Ed); MBA/M Ed. *Program availability:* 100% online. *Degree requirements:* For master's, comprehensive exam (for some programs); for doctorate, comprehensive exam, thesis/dissertation; for Ed S, comprehensive exam. *Entrance requirements:* For master's, doctorate, and Ed S, GRE General Test, 2 letters of recommendation. Additional exam requirements/recommendations for international students: Required—TOEFL (minimum score 600 paper-based; 90 iBT), IELTS (minimum score 7). Electronic applications accepted.

University of Virginia, Curry School of Education, Program in Education, Charlottesville, VA 22903. Offers administration and supervision (PhD); applied developmental science (PhD); counselor education (PhD); curriculum and instruction (PhD); early childhood special education (MT); education evaluation (PhD); educational psychology (PhD); educational research (PhD); elementary education (MT); English education (MT, PhD); foreign language education (MT); higher education (PhD); instructional technology (PhD); kinesiology (MT, PhD); math education (PhD); reading education (PhD); research, statistics and evaluation (PhD); school psychology (PhD); science education (PhD); social studies education (MT, PhD); special education (PhD); world languages education (MT). *Degree requirements:* For master's, comprehensive exam (for some programs), field project; for doctorate, comprehensive exam, thesis/dissertation. *Entrance requirements:* For doctorate, GRE General Test. Additional exam requirements/recommendations for international students: Required—TOEFL (minimum score 600 paper-based; 90 iBT), IELTS (minimum score 7). Electronic applications accepted.

University of Washington, Graduate School, College of Education, Seattle, WA 98195. Offers curriculum and instruction (M Ed, Ed D, PhD), including educational technology, general curriculum (Ed D, PhD), language, literacy, and culture, mathematics education, multicultural education, reading and language arts education (Ed D), science education, social studies education, teaching and curriculum (M Ed); educational leadership and policy studies (M Ed, Ed D, PhD), including administration (Ed D), educational policy, organization, and leadership (M Ed, PhD), higher education, leadership for learning (Ed D), social and cultural foundations of education (M Ed, PhD); educational psychology (M Ed, PhD), including educational psychology (PhD), human development and cognition (M Ed), learning sciences, measurement, statistics and research design (M Ed), school psychology (M Ed); instructional leadership (M Ed); intercollegiate athletic leadership (M Ed); special education (M Ed, Ed D, PhD), including early childhood special education (M Ed), emotional and behavioral disabilities (M Ed), learning disabilities (M Ed), low-incidence disabilities (M Ed), severe disabilities (M Ed), special education (Ed D, PhD); teacher education (MIT). *Accreditation:* APA. *Program availability:* Part-time, evening/weekend. *Degree requirements:* For master's, thesis optional; for doctorate, thesis/dissertation. *Entrance requirements:* For master's and doctorate, GRE General Test, minimum GPA of 3.0. Additional exam requirements/recommendations for international students: Required—TOEFL. Electronic applications accepted. *Faculty research:* School restructuring/effective schools, special education interventions, literacy and writing, technology, school partnerships, teacher preparation.

The University of West Alabama, School of Graduate Studies, College of Education, Program in Secondary Education, Livingston, AL 35470. Offers biology (MAT); English language arts (MAT); high school 6-12 (M Ed); history (MAT); mathematics (MAT); science (MAT); social science (MAT). *Program availability:* Part-time, evening/weekend, 100% online. *Faculty:* 18 full-time (6 women), 8 part-time/adjunct (2 women). *Students:* 232 full-time (165 women), 34 part-time (24 women); includes 53 minority (44 Black or African American, non-Hispanic/Latino; 3 American Indian or Alaska Native, non-Hispanic/Latino; 2 Hispanic/Latino; 4 Two or more races, non-Hispanic/Latino), 3 international. Average age 31. 84 applicants, 93% accepted, 67 enrolled. In 2018, 100 master's awarded. *Degree requirements:* For master's, comprehensive exam, thesis optional. *Entrance requirements:* For master's, GRE, minimum GPA of 2.75, verification of background clearance/fingerprints, valid bachelor's-level Professional Educator Certificate in same teaching field. Additional exam requirements/recommendations for international students: Required—TOEFL (minimum score 500 paper-based; 61 iBT). *Application deadline:* Applications are processed on a rolling basis. Application fee: $40. Electronic applications accepted. *Expenses: Tuition, area resident:* Full-time $9100. Tuition, state resident: full-time $9100. Tuition, nonresident: full-time $19,200. *Required fees:* $1890; $130. *Financial support:* Teaching assistantships, Federal Work-Study, scholarships/grants, and unspecified assistantships available. Support available to part-time students. Financial award application deadline: 3/1; financial award applicants required to submit FAFSA. *Unit head:* Dr. Jodie Winship, Chair of College of Education, 205-652-5415, Fax: 205-652-3706, E-mail: jwinship@uwa.edu. *Application contact:* Dr. B. J. Kimbrough, Dean of Graduate Studies, 205-652-3647, Fax: 205-652-3670, E-mail: bkimbrough@uwa.edu.

University of Wisconsin–Milwaukee, Graduate School, School of Education, Department of Curriculum and Instruction, Milwaukee, WI 53201-0413. Offers curriculum and instruction (MS), including cross-curricular focus, early childhood education, English education, mathematics education, middle childhood/early adolescence education, reading education, science education, urban social studies education. *Program availability:* Part-time. *Students:* 19 full-time (15 women), 56 part-time (49 women); includes 15 minority (3 Black or African American, non-Hispanic/Latino; 1 American Indian or Alaska Native, non-Hispanic/Latino; 3 Asian, non-Hispanic/Latino; 1 Hispanic/Latino; 7 Two or more races, non-Hispanic/Latino), 2 international. Average age 33. 27 applicants, 44% accepted, 11 enrolled. In 2018, 20 master's awarded. *Entrance requirements:* Additional exam requirements/recommendations for international students: Required—TOEFL (minimum score 550 paper-based; 79 iBT), IELTS (minimum score 6.5). *Application deadline:* For fall admission, 1/1 priority date for domestic students; for spring admission, 9/1 for domestic students. Application fee: $56 ($96 for international students). Electronic applications accepted. *Financial support:* Fellowships, research assistantships, teaching assistantships, career-related internships or fieldwork, health care benefits, unspecified assistantships, and project assistantships available. Support available to part-time students. Financial award application deadline: 4/15; financial award applicants required to submit FAFSA. *Application contact:* General Information Contact, 414-229-4721, E-mail: soeinfo@uwm.edu.
Website: http://uwm.edu/education/academics/curriculum-instruction-department/

University of Wisconsin–River Falls, Outreach and Graduate Studies, College of Arts and Science, Department of History and Philosophy, River Falls, WI 54022. Offers social science education (MSE). *Program availability:* Part-time. *Degree requirements:* For master's, thesis (for some programs). *Entrance requirements:* For master's, minimum GPA of 2.75. Additional exam requirements/recommendations for international students: Required—TOEFL (minimum score 500 paper-based; 65 iBT), IELTS (minimum score 5.5). Electronic applications accepted. *Faculty research:* World War II, Hitler, modern China, women's history, immigration history.

University of Wisconsin–Stevens Point, College of Letters and Science, Department of History and International Studies, Stevens Point, WI 54481-3897. Offers history (MST). *Degree requirements:* For master's, thesis or alternative.

Virginia Polytechnic Institute and State University, Graduate School, College of Liberal Arts and Human Sciences, Blacksburg, VA 24061. Offers career and technical education (MS Ed, Ed S); communication (MA); counselor education (MA); creative writing (MFA); curriculum and instruction (MA Ed, Ed S); educational leadership and policy studies (Ed S); educational research and evaluation (PhD); English (MA); social, political, ethical, and cultural thought (PhD); Ed D/PhD. *Faculty:* 420 full-time (221 women), 1 (woman) part-time/adjunct. *Students:* 603 full-time (428 women), 359 part-time (237 women); includes 189 minority (107 Black or African American, non-Hispanic/Latino; 4 American Indian or Alaska Native, non-Hispanic/Latino; 24 Asian, non-Hispanic/Latino; 27 Hispanic/Latino; 2 Native Hawaiian or other Pacific Islander, non-Hispanic/Latino; 25 Two or more races, non-Hispanic/Latino), 84 international. Average age 33. 856 applicants, 48% accepted, 262 enrolled. In 2018, 270 master's, 63 doctorates awarded. *Degree requirements:* For master's, comprehensive exam (for some programs), thesis (for some programs); for doctorate, comprehensive exam (for some programs), thesis/dissertation (for some programs). *Entrance requirements:* For master's and doctorate, GRE/GMAT. Additional exam requirements/recommendations for international students: Required—TOEFL (minimum score 90 iBT). *Application deadline:* For fall admission, 8/1 for domestic students, 4/1 for international students; for spring admission, 1/1 for domestic students, 9/1 for international students. Applications are processed on a rolling basis. Application fee: $75. Electronic applications accepted. *Expenses:* Tuition, state resident: full-time $15,510; part-time $739.50 per credit hour. Tuition, nonresident: full-time $29,629; part-time $1490.25 per credit hour. *Required fees:* $2804; $550 per semester. Tuition and fees vary according to course load, campus/location and program. *Financial support:* In 2018–19, 4 fellowships with full tuition reimbursements (averaging $23,122 per year), 28 research assistantships with full tuition reimbursements (averaging $15,605 per year), 245 teaching assistantships with full tuition reimbursements (averaging $16,046 per year) were awarded; scholarships/grants and unspecified assistantships also available. Financial award application deadline: 3/1; financial award applicants required to submit FAFSA. *Total annual research expenditures:* $7.5 million. *Unit head:* Dr. Laura Belmonte, Dean, 540-231-6779, Fax: 540-231-7157, E-mail: belmonte@vt.edu. *Application contact:* Chelsea Blanchet, Executive Assistant, 540-231-6779, Fax: 540-231-7157, E-mail: bchels1@vt.edu.
Website: http://www.liberalarts.vt.edu/

Wagner College, Division of Graduate Studies, Education Department, Program in Secondary Education/Students with Disabilities, Staten Island, NY 10301-4495. Offers secondary education 7-12 (MS Ed), including language arts, languages other than English, mathematics and technology, science and technology, social studies. *Program availability:* Evening/weekend. *Degree requirements:* For master's, thesis (for some programs), completion of state certification exams before student teaching. *Entrance requirements:* For master's, GRE, minimum GPA of 3.0, interview, recommendations. Additional exam requirements/recommendations for international students: Required—TOEFL (minimum score 550 paper-based; 79 iBT), IELTS (minimum score 6.5). Electronic applications accepted. *Expenses:* Contact institution.

Wayland Baptist University, Graduate Programs, Program in Education, Plainview, TX 79072-6998. Offers education administration (M Ed); education diagnostics (M Ed); education literacy (M Ed); elementary certification (M Ed); English (M Ed); English as a second language (M Ed); higher education administration (M Ed); human resources (M Ed); instructional leadership (M Ed); instructional technology (M Ed); leadership training and development (M Ed); science education (M Ed); secondary certification (M Ed); social studies (M Ed); special education (M Ed); sports administration and management (M Ed). *Program availability:* Part-time, evening/weekend, 100% online. *Degree requirements:* For master's, comprehensive exam, capstone course. *Entrance requirements:* For master's, GRE, GMAT or MAT. Additional exam requirements/recommendations for international students: Required—TOEFL (minimum score 500 paper-based; 61 iBT). Electronic applications accepted.

Wayne State College, School of Education and Counseling, Department of Educational Foundations and Leadership, Program in Curriculum and Instruction, Wayne, NE 68787. Offers alternative education (MSE); business and information technology education (MSE); communication arts education (MSE); early childhood education (MSE); elementary education (MSE); English as a second language (MSE); English education (MSE); family and consumer sciences education (MSE); industrial technology and vocational education (MSE); learning communities (MSE); mathematics education (MSE); music education (MSE); science education (MSE); social science education (MSE). *Accreditation:* NCATE. *Program availability:* Part-time, evening/weekend. *Degree requirements:* For master's, comprehensive exam, thesis optional. *Entrance requirements:* For master's, GRE General Test. Additional exam requirements/recommendations for international students: Required—TOEFL (minimum score 550 paper-based).

Wayne State University, College of Education, Division of Teacher Education, Detroit, MI 48202. Offers art education (M Ed); bilingual/bicultural education (Certificate); curriculum and instruction (Ed D, PhD, Ed S), including English as a second language (MAT, Ed D, Ed S), K-12 curriculum (PhD); elementary education (MAT), including bilingual/bicultural education (M Ed, MAT), early childhood education (M Ed, MAT), English as a second language (MAT, Ed D, Ed S), foreign language education, science education (M Ed, MAT), special education (M Ed, MAT); elementary mathematics specialist (Certificate); English as a second language (Certificate); reading (M Ed, Ed S); reading, language and literature (Ed D); secondary education (MAT), including bilingual/bicultural education (M Ed, MAT), early childhood education (M Ed, MAT), English as a second language (MAT, Ed D, Ed S), English education, foreign language education, mathematics education (M Ed, MAT), science education (M Ed, MAT), social studies education (M Ed, MAT); special education (MAT), including career and technical education; teaching and learning (M Ed), including bilingual/bicultural education (M Ed, MAT), early childhood education (M Ed, MAT), elementary education, foreign language, mathematics education (M Ed, MAT), science education (M Ed, MAT), social studies education (M Ed, MAT), special education (M Ed, MAT). *Program availability:* Part-time, evening/weekend. *Faculty:* 20. *Students:* 121 full-time (94 women), 251 part-time (209 women); includes 116 minority (83 Black or African American, non-Hispanic/Latino; 3 American Indian or Alaska Native, non-Hispanic/Latino; 3 Asian, non-Hispanic/Latino; 14 Hispanic/Latino; 13 Two or more races, non-Hispanic/Latino), 11 international. Average age 37. 171 applicants, 23% accepted, 32 enrolled. In 2018, 112 master's, 8 doctorates, 11 other advanced degrees awarded. *Degree requirements:* For master's, thesis (for some programs), essay or project (for some M Ed programs), professional field experience (for MAT programs); for doctorate, comprehensive exam, thesis/dissertation. *Entrance requirements:* For master's, undergraduate degree, verification of participation in group work with children, Michigan State Police criminal background check, negative tb test, personal statement (for MAT programs); for all other master's programs: undergraduate degree, personal statement; for doctorate, minimum undergraduate GPA of 3.0, graduate 3.5; interview; curriculum vitae; references; writing sample; letter of application; master's degree (for most programs); for other advanced degree, education specialist certificate: undergraduate with GPA of 2.5 or better and master's degree with GPA of 2.75 or better; personal statement. Additional exam requirements/recommendations for international students: Required—TOEFL (minimum score 550 paper-based; 79 iBT); Recommended—IELTS (minimum score 6.5), TWE (minimum score 5.5), TSE (minimum score 58). *Application deadline:* Applications are processed on a rolling basis. Application fee: $50. Electronic applications accepted. *Financial support:* In 2018–19, 85 students received support, including 3 fellowships (averaging $14,275 per year); research assistantships with tuition reimbursements available, Federal Work-Study, scholarships/grants, and unspecified assistantships also available. Support available to part-time students. Financial award applicants required to submit FAFSA. *Faculty research:* Improving students' skill achievement in mathematics, improving elementary children's understanding of informational text, teachers' use of their pedagogical and mathematical knowledge in the interactive work of teaching, the intersection of identity construction in teaching and learning, identifying effective methods of literacy instruction and assessments for bilingual students in elementary language arts classrooms. *Unit head:* Dr. Roland Coloma, Assistant Dean for Teacher Education, 313-577-0902, E-mail: rscoloma@wayne.edu. *Application contact:* Dr. Mary L. Waker, Graduate Admissions Officer, 313-577-1601, Fax: 313-577-7904, E-mail: m.waker@wayne.edu.
Website: http://coe.wayne.edu/ted/index.php

Western Oregon University, Graduate Programs, College of Education, Division of Teacher Education, Program in Secondary Education, Monmouth, OR 97361. Offers bilingual education (MS Ed); health (MS Ed); humanities (MAT, MS Ed); initial licensure (MAT); mathematics (MAT, MS Ed); science (MAT, MS Ed); social science (MAT, MS Ed). *Accreditation:* NCATE. *Program availability:* Part-time, evening/weekend. *Degree requirements:* For master's, thesis optional, written exam. *Entrance requirements:* For master's, minimum GPA of 3.0, teaching license. Additional exam requirements/recommendations for international students: Required—TOEFL (minimum score 550 paper-based; 79 iBT), IELTS (minimum score 6.5). *Faculty research:* Literacy, science in primary grades, geography education, retention, teacher burnout.

Westfield State University, College of Graduate and Continuing Education, Department of Education, Westfield, MA 01086. Offers early childhood education (M Ed); elementary education (M Ed); reading specialist (M Ed); secondary education (M Ed), including biology teacher education, chemistry teacher education, general science teacher education, history teacher education, mathematics teacher education, physical education teacher education; special education (M Ed), including moderate disabilities, 5-12, moderate disabilities, preK-8; vocational technical education (M Ed). *Accreditation:* NCATE. *Program availability:* Part-time, evening/weekend. *Degree requirements:* For master's, comprehensive exam, practicum. *Entrance requirements:* For master's, GRE General Test or MAT, minimum undergraduate GPA of 2.8. Additional exam requirements/recommendations for international students: Recommended—TOEFL (minimum score 550 paper-based; 79 iBT). *Faculty research:* Collaborative teacher education, developmental early childhood education.

Westfield State University, College of Graduate and Continuing Education, Department of Education, Programs in Secondary Education, Program in History Teacher Education, Westfield, MA 01086. Offers secondary education-history (M Ed). *Program availability:* Part-time, evening/weekend. *Degree requirements:* For master's, comprehensive exam, thesis (for some programs). *Entrance requirements:* For master's, GRE General Test or MAT, minimum undergraduate GPA of 2.8. Additional exam requirements/recommendations for international students: Recommended—TOEFL (minimum score 550 paper-based; 79 iBT).

Widener University, School of Human Service Professions, Center for Education, Chester, PA 19013-5792. Offers adult education (M Ed); counseling in higher education (M Ed); counselor education (M Ed); early childhood education (M Ed); educational foundations (M Ed); educational leadership (M Ed); educational psychology (M Ed); elementary education (M Ed); English and language arts (M Ed); health education (M Ed); higher education leadership (Ed D); home and school visitor (M Ed); human sexuality (M Ed, PhD); mathematics education (M Ed); middle school education (M Ed); principalship (M Ed); reading and language arts (Ed D); reading education (M Ed); school administration (Ed D); science education (M Ed); social studies education (M Ed); special education (M Ed); technology education (M Ed). *Accreditation:* NCATE. *Program availability:* Part-time, evening/weekend. Terminal master's awarded for partial completion of doctoral program. *Degree requirements:* For doctorate, thesis/dissertation. *Entrance requirements:* For master's, minimum GPA of 2.5; for doctorate, GRE or MAT, minimum GPA of 2.0 (undergraduate), 3.5 (graduate). Electronic applications accepted. *Expenses:* Contact institution. *Faculty research:* Reading and cognition, adult education, technology education, educational leadership, special education.

William Carey University, School of Education, Hattiesburg, MS 39401. Offers art education (M Ed); art of teaching (M Ed); elementary education (M Ed, Ed S); English education (M Ed); gifted education (M Ed); history and social science (M Ed); mild/moderate disabilities (M Ed); secondary education (M Ed). *Accreditation:* NCATE.

Program availability: Part-time. *Degree requirements:* For master's, comprehensive exam. *Entrance requirements:* For master's, GRE, MAT, minimum GPA of 2.5, Class A teacher's license. Additional exam requirements/recommendations for international students: Required—TOEFL (minimum score 550 paper-based).

Worcester State University, Graduate School, Program in History, Worcester, MA 01602-2597. Offers MA. *Program availability:* Part-time. *Faculty:* 6 full-time (4 women), 2 part-time/adjunct (0 women). *Students:* 5 full-time (1 woman), 13 part-time (6 women); includes 2 minority (1 Black or African American, non-Hispanic/Latino; 1 American Indian or Alaska Native, non-Hispanic/Latino). Average age 40. 6 applicants, 100% accepted, 5 enrolled. In 2018, 6 master's awarded. *Degree requirements:* For master's, comprehensive exam (for some programs), thesis, portfolio. For a detail list in Degree Completion requirements please see the graduate catalog at catalog.worcester.edu. *Entrance requirements:* For master's, GRE General Test or MAT, For a detail list of entrance requirements please see the graduate catalog at catalog.worcester.edu. Additional exam requirements/recommendations for international students: Required—

TOEFL (minimum score 550 paper-based; 79 iBT), IELTS (minimum score 6). *Application deadline:* For fall admission, 3/1 for domestic and international students; for spring admission, 11/1 for domestic and international students; for summer admission, 3/1 for domestic and international students. Applications are processed on a rolling basis. Application fee: $50. Electronic applications accepted. *Expenses: Tuition, area resident:* Full-time $3042; part-time $169 per credit hour. Tuition, state resident: full-time $3042; part-time $169 per credit hour. Tuition, nonresident: full-time $3042; part-time $169 per credit hour. *International tuition:* $3042 full-time. *Required fees:* $2754; $153 per credit hour. *Financial support:* Career-related internships or fieldwork, scholarships/grants, and unspecified assistantships available. Financial award application deadline: 3/1; financial award applicants required to submit FAFSA. *Unit head:* Dr. Tona Hangen, Graduate Coordinator, 508-929-8688, Fax: 508-929-8155, E-mail: thangen@worcester.edu. *Application contact:* Sara Grady, Associate Dean, Graduate Studies and Professional Development, 508-929-8130, Fax: 508-929-8100, E-mail: sara.grady@worcester.edu.

Vocational and Technical Education

Alcorn State University, School of Graduate Studies, School of Agriculture and Applied Sciences, Department of Advanced Technologies, Lorman, MS 39096-7500. Offers workforce education leadership (MS).

Alcorn State University, School of Graduate Studies, School of Education and Psychology, Lorman, MS 39096-7500. Offers agricultural education (MS Ed); elementary education (MAT, MS Ed, Ed S); guidance and counseling (MS Ed); industrial education (MS Ed); secondary education (MAT, MS Ed), including health and physical education (MS Ed), NCAA compliance and academic progress reporting (MS Ed); special education (MS Ed). *Accreditation:* NCATE. *Degree requirements:* For master's, thesis optional.

Appalachian State University, Cratis D. Williams School of Graduate Studies, Department of Sustainable Technology and the Built Environment, Boone, NC 28608. Offers appropriate technology (MS); renewable energy engineering (MS). *Program availability:* Part-time. *Degree requirements:* For master's, comprehensive exam, thesis optional. *Entrance requirements:* For master's, GRE General Test, 3 letters of recommendation. Additional exam requirements/recommendations for international students: Required—TOEFL (minimum score 550 paper-based; 79 iBT), IELTS (minimum score 6.5). Electronic applications accepted. *Expenses: Tuition, area resident:* Full-time $4839; part-time $237 per credit hour. Tuition, state resident: full-time $4839; part-time $237 per credit hour. Tuition, nonresident: full-time $18,271; part-time $895.50 per credit hour. *Faculty research:* Wind power, biofuels, green construction, solar energy production.

Athens State University, Graduate Programs, Athens, AL 35611. Offers career and technical education (M Ed); global logistics and supply chain management (MS); religious studies (MA).

Bowling Green State University, Graduate College, College of Technology, Program in Career and Technology Education, Bowling Green, OH 43403. Offers career and technology education (M Ed), including technology. *Program availability:* Part-time. *Degree requirements:* For master's, thesis or alternative. *Entrance requirements:* For master's, GRE General Test. Additional exam requirements/recommendations for international students: Required—TOEFL. Electronic applications accepted. *Faculty research:* Curriculum in technology education.

Buffalo State College, State University of New York, The Graduate School, School of Education, Department of Career and Technical Education, Buffalo, NY 14222-1095. Offers business and marketing education (MS Ed); career and technical education (MS Ed); technology education (MS Ed). *Accreditation:* NCATE. *Program availability:* Part-time, evening/weekend. *Degree requirements:* For master's, thesis or project. *Entrance requirements:* For master's, minimum GPA of 2.5 in last 60 hours, New York teaching certificate. Additional exam requirements/recommendations for international students: Required—TOEFL (minimum score 550 paper-based).

California Baptist University, Program in Education, Riverside, CA 92504-3206. Offers educational leadership (MS); educational leadership for faith-based institutions (MS); educational leadership for public institutions (MS); educational technology (MS); instructional computer applications (MS); international education (MS); leadership and adult learning (MS); leadership and organizational studies (MS); online teaching and learning (MS); reading (MS); science education (MA); special education in mild/moderate disabilities (MS); special education in moderate/severe disabilities (MS); teacher leadership (MS); teaching (MS); teaching and learning (MS). *Program availability:* Part-time, evening/weekend, 100% online, blended/hybrid learning. *Faculty:* 26 full-time (13 women), 28 part-time/adjunct (21 women). *Students:* 201 full-time (164 women), 265 part-time (209 women); includes 226 minority (23 Black or African American, non-Hispanic/Latino; 4 American Indian or Alaska Native, non-Hispanic/Latino; 7 Asian, non-Hispanic/Latino; 169 Hispanic/Latino; 6 Native Hawaiian or other Pacific Islander, non-Hispanic/Latino; 17 Two or more races, non-Hispanic/Latino), 2 international. Average age 39. 145 applicants, 97% accepted, 141 enrolled. In 2018, 253 master's awarded. *Degree requirements:* For master's, comprehensive exam, project, or thesis. *Entrance requirements:* For master's, minimum undergraduate GPA of 2.75; 500-word essay; three letters of recommendation; two prerequisite courses completed with minimum C grade. Additional exam requirements/recommendations for international students: Required—TOEFL (minimum score 80 iBT). *Application deadline:* For fall admission, 8/1 priority date for domestic students, 7/1 for international students; for spring admission, 12/1 priority date for domestic students, 11/1 for international students. Applications are processed on a rolling basis. Application fee: $45. Electronic applications accepted. *Expenses:* $634 per unit. *Financial support:* In 2018–19, 312 students received support. Federal Work-Study and scholarships/grants available. Financial award applicants required to submit CSS PROFILE or FAFSA. *Faculty research:* Leadership development, complexity theory, faith and learning, special education, social and philosophical contexts of education. *Unit head:* Dr. Robin Duncan, Dean, School of Education, 951-552-8948, E-mail: rduncan@calbaptist.edu. *Application contact:* Dr. Shari Farris, Program Director, Online MS in Education, 951-343-2455, E-mail: sfarris@calbaptist.edu.
Website: http://www.calbaptist.edu/mastersined/

California University of Pennsylvania, School of Graduate Studies and Research, College of Education and Human Services, Program in Technology Education, California, PA 15419-1394. Offers M Ed. *Accreditation:* NCATE. *Program availability:* Part-time, evening/weekend, online only, 100% online. *Degree requirements:* For master's, comprehensive exam, thesis optional. *Entrance requirements:* For master's,

MAT, minimum GPA of 3.0, teaching experience in industrial arts. Additional exam requirements/recommendations for international students: Required—TOEFL (minimum score 550 paper-based; 80 iBT). Electronic applications accepted. *Faculty research:* Curriculum, trends in technology, standards-based assessment.

Capella University, School of Business and Technology, Doctoral Programs in Technology, Minneapolis, MN 55402. Offers general information technology (PhD); global operations and supply chain management (DBA); information assurance and security (PhD); information technology education (PhD); information technology management (DBA, PhD).

Central Connecticut State University, School of Graduate Studies, School of Engineering, Science and Technology, Department of Technology and Engineering Education, New Britain, CT 06050-4010. Offers MS. *Program availability:* Part-time, evening/weekend. *Faculty:* 3 full-time (1 woman), 2 part-time/adjunct (0 women). *Students:* 8 full-time (3 women), 34 part-time (22 women); includes 3 minority (all Hispanic/Latino). Average age 34. 30 applicants, 87% accepted, 18 enrolled. In 2018, 11 master's awarded. *Degree requirements:* For master's, thesis or alternative, special project. *Entrance requirements:* For master's, minimum undergraduate GPA of 2.7. Additional exam requirements/recommendations for international students: Required—TOEFL (minimum score 550 paper-based; 79 iBT); Recommended—IELTS (minimum score 6.5). *Application deadline:* For fall admission, 6/1 for domestic students, 5/1 for international students; for spring admission, 11/1 for domestic and international students. Applications are processed on a rolling basis. Application fee: $50. Electronic applications accepted. *Expenses: Tuition, area resident:* Full-time $7027; part-time $388 per credit. Tuition, state resident: full-time $9750; part-time $388 per credit. Tuition, nonresident: full-time $18,102; part-time $388 per credit. *International tuition:* $18,102 full-time. *Required fees:* $266 per semester. *Financial support:* In 2018–19, 8 students received support. Career-related internships or fieldwork, Federal Work-Study, scholarships/grants, and unspecified assistantships available. Support available to part-time students. Financial award application deadline: 3/1; financial award applicants required to submit FAFSA. *Faculty research:* Instruction, curriculum development, administration, occupational training. *Unit head:* Dr. James DeLaura, Chair, 860-832-1850, E-mail: delaura@ccsu.edu. *Application contact:* Patricia Gardner, Associate Director of Graduate Studies, 860-832-2350, Fax: 860-832-2362.
Website: http://www.ccsu.edu/teched/

Central Washington University, School of Graduate Studies and Research, College of Education and Professional Studies, Department of Family and Consumer Sciences, Ellensburg, WA 98926. Offers career and technical education (MS); family and child life (MS); family and consumer sciences education (MS). *Program availability:* Part-time. *Entrance requirements:* For master's, minimum GPA of 3.0. Additional exam requirements/recommendations for international students: Required—TOEFL (minimum score 550 paper-based; 79 iBT). Electronic applications accepted.

Chicago State University, School of Graduate and Professional Studies, College of Education, Department of Reading, Elementary Education, Library Information and Media Studies, Program in Technology and Performance Improvement Studies, Chicago, IL 60628. Offers MS. *Program availability:* Online learning. *Entrance requirements:* For master's, minimum GPA of 2.75.

Clarion University of Pennsylvania, College of Arts, Education and Sciences, Master of Education Program, Clarion, PA 16214. Offers curriculum and instruction (M Ed); early childhood (M Ed); math education (M Ed); reading (M Ed); science education (M Ed); special education (M Ed); technology (M Ed). *Accreditation:* NCATE. *Program availability:* Part-time, evening/weekend, 100% online, blended/hybrid learning. *Faculty:* 6 full-time (3 women). *Students:* 5 full-time (all women), 85 part-time (73 women); includes 3 minority (2 Black or African American, non-Hispanic/Latino; 1 Two or more races, non-Hispanic/Latino). Average age 30. 57 applicants, 61% accepted, 26 enrolled. In 2018, 51 master's awarded. *Degree requirements:* For master's, comprehensive exam (for some programs), thesis or alternative. *Entrance requirements:* For master's, minimum QPA of 3.0. Additional exam requirements/recommendations for international students: Required—TOEFL (minimum score 550 paper-based; 80 iBT), Or IELTS. Satisfactory completion of a bachelor's degree from an accredited US college or university is also acceptable evidence of English language. *Application deadline:* For fall admission, 8/1 priority date for domestic students, 7/15 priority date for international students; for winter admission, 11/1 priority date for domestic students; for spring admission, 12/1 priority date for domestic students, 11/15 priority date for international students; for summer admission, 4/1 priority date for domestic students. Applications are processed on a rolling basis. Application fee: $40. Electronic applications accepted. *Expenses: Tuition, area resident:* Part-time $516 per credit hour. Tuition, state resident: part-time $516 per credit hour. Tuition, nonresident: part-time $774 per credit hour. *Required fees:* $159 per credit hour. One-time fee: $50 part-time. Tuition and fees vary according to degree level, campus/location and program. *Financial support:* Federal Work-Study, institutionally sponsored loans, and scholarships/grants available. Financial award application deadline: 3/1; financial award applicants required to submit FAFSA. *Unit head:* Dr. John McCullough, Chair, Department of Education, 814-393-2404, Fax: 814-393-2446, E-mail: gradstudies@clarion.edu. *Application contact:* Susan Staub, Graduate Admissions Counselor, 814-393-2337, Fax: 814-393-2722, E-mail: gradstudies@clarion.edu.

Concordia University, College of Education, Portland, OR 97211-6099. Offers administrative leadership (Ed D); career and technical education (M Ed); curriculum and

instruction (M Ed), including adolescent literacy, early childhood education, educational technology leadership, English for speakers of other languages, environmental education, health and physical education, mathematics, methods and curriculum, reading interventionist, science, social studies, STEAM education, teacher leadership, the inclusive classroom, trauma and resilience in educational settings; educational administration (M Ed); educational leadership (M Ed); elementary education (MAT); higher education (Ed D); instructional leadership (Ed D); professional leadership, inquiry, and transformation (Ed D); secondary education (MAT); transformational leadership (Ed D). *Program availability:* Part-time, online learning. *Degree requirements:* For master's, comprehensive exam, work samples/portfolio. *Entrance requirements:* For master's, California Basic Educational Skills Test or PRAXIS I, minimum undergraduate GPA of 2.8, graduate 3.0; 2 letters of recommendation. Additional exam requirements/recommendations for international students: Required—TOEFL (minimum score 525 paper-based). Electronic applications accepted. *Faculty research:* Learner-centered classroom, brain-based learning, future of online learning.

East Carolina University, Graduate School, College of Education, Department of Interdisciplinary Professions, Greenville, NC 27858-4353. Offers adult education (MA Ed); business and marketing education (MA Ed); community college instruction (Certificate); counselor education (MS); education in the healthcare professions (Certificate); library science (MLS); student affairs in higher education (Certificate); vocational education (MS). *Accreditation:* ACA; ALA; NCATE. *Program availability:* Part-time, evening/weekend. *Application deadline:* For fall admission, 5/15 priority date for domestic students. *Expenses: Tuition, area resident:* Full-time $4749. Tuition, state resident: full-time $4749. Tuition, nonresident: full-time $17,898. *International tuition:* $17,898 full-time. *Required fees:* $2787. Part-time tuition and fees vary according to course load and program. *Financial support:* Application deadline: 6/1. *Unit head:* Dr. Scott Glass, Professor, 252-328-5670, E-mail: glassj@ecu.edu. *Application contact:* Graduate School Admissions, 252-328-6012, Fax: 252-328-6071, E-mail: gradschool@ecu.edu.
Website: http://www.ecu.edu/cs-educ/idp/index.cfm

Eastern Kentucky University, The Graduate School, College of Business and Technology, Department of Technology, Program in Industrial Education, Richmond, KY 40475-3102. Offers occupational training and development (MS); technical administration (MS); technology education (MS). *Accreditation:* NCATE. *Program availability:* Part-time. *Entrance requirements:* For master's, GRE General Test, minimum GPA of 2.5.

Eastern Kentucky University, The Graduate School, College of Education, Department of Curriculum and Instruction, Program in Secondary and Higher Education, Richmond, KY 40475-3102. Offers secondary education (MA Ed), including agricultural education, art education, biological sciences education, business education, English education, geography education, history education, home economics education, industrial education, mathematical sciences education, physical education, school health education. *Accreditation:* NCATE. *Program availability:* Part-time. *Entrance requirements:* For master's, GRE General Test, minimum GPA of 2.5.

Eastern New Mexico University, Graduate School, College of Education and Technology, Department of Curriculum and Instruction, Portales, NM 88130. Offers alternative licensure in elementary education (M Ed); bilingual education (M Ed); career and technical education (M Ed); educational technology (M Ed); elementary education (M Ed); English as a second language (M Ed); pedagogy and learning (M Ed); reading/literacy (M Ed). *Program availability:* Part-time, online learning. *Degree requirements:* For master's, comprehensive exam, thesis optional. *Entrance requirements:* For master's, writing assessment, minimum GPA of 3.0, photocopy of teaching license, letter of recommendation. Additional exam requirements/recommendations for international students: Required—TOEFL (minimum score 550 paper-based; 79 iBT), IELTS (minimum score 6). Electronic applications accepted. *Expenses: Tuition, area resident:* Full-time $6776. Tuition, state resident: full-time $6776; part-time $282 per credit hour. Tuition, nonresident: full-time $8986; part-time $374 per credit hour. *Required fees:* $60 per semester. One-time fee: $25.

Fitchburg State University, Division of Graduate and Continuing Education, Program in Occupational Education, Fitchburg, MA 01420-2697. Offers M Ed. *Accreditation:* NCATE. *Program availability:* Part-time, evening/weekend. *Entrance requirements:* Additional exam requirements/recommendations for international students: Required—TOEFL (minimum score 550 paper-based; 79 iBT). Electronic applications accepted. *Expenses:* Contact institution.

Fitchburg State University, Division of Graduate and Continuing Education, Program in Technology Education, Fitchburg, MA 01420-2697. Offers M Ed. *Accreditation:* NCATE. *Program availability:* Part-time, evening/weekend. *Entrance requirements:* Additional exam requirements/recommendations for international students: Required—TOEFL (minimum score 550 paper-based; 79 iBT). Electronic applications accepted.

Florida Agricultural and Mechanical University, Division of Graduate Studies, Research, and Continuing Education, College of Education, Department of Vocational Education, Tallahassee, FL 32307-3200. Offers business education (MBE); industrial education (MS Ed); technology education (M Ed). *Accreditation:* NCATE. *Degree requirements:* For master's, thesis (for some programs). *Entrance requirements:* For master's, GRE General Test, minimum GPA of 3.0. Additional exam requirements/recommendations for international students: Required—TOEFL.

The George Washington University, Graduate School of Education and Human Development, Department of Counseling and Human Development, Program in Job Development and Placement, Washington, DC 20052. Offers Graduate Certificate. *Program availability:* Online learning. *Financial support:* Fellowships available. *Unit head:* Dr. Kenneth C. Hergenrather, Director, 202-994-1334, E-mail: hergenkc@gwu.edu. *Application contact:* Sarah Lang, Director of Graduate Admissions, 202-994-1447, Fax: 202-994-7207, E-mail: slang@gwu.edu.
Website: http://gsehd.gwu.edu/

Indiana State University, College of Graduate and Professional Studies, College of Technology, Department of Human Resource Development and Performance Technologies, Terre Haute, IN 47809. Offers career and technical education (MS); human resource development (MS).

Indiana University of Pennsylvania, School of Graduate Studies and Research, College of Education and Communications, Department of Adult and Community Education, Program in Business/Administrative, Indiana, PA 15705. Offers M Ed. *Program availability:* Part-time. *Faculty:* 2 full-time (both women). *Students:* 3 part-time (2 women). Average age 52. In 2018, 1 master's awarded. *Degree requirements:* For master's, thesis optional. *Entrance requirements:* For master's, GMAT or GRE. Additional exam requirements/recommendations for international students: Required—TOEFL (minimum score 540 paper-based). *Application deadline:* Applications are processed on a rolling basis. Application fee: $50. Electronic applications accepted. *Expenses:* Tuition, state resident: full-time $12,384; part-time $516 per credit hour. Tuition, nonresident: full-time $18,576; part-time $774 per credit hour. *Required fees:* $4454; $186 per credit hour. $65 per semester. Tuition and fees vary according to program and reciprocity agreements. *Financial support:* Career-related internships or fieldwork, Federal Work-Study, scholarships/grants, and unspecified assistantships available. Financial award application deadline: 4/15; financial award applicants required to submit FAFSA. *Unit head:* Prof. Jacqueline McGinty, Coordinator, 724-357-2470, E-mail: jacqueline.mcginty@iup.edu. *Application contact:* Prof. Jacqueline McGinty, Coordinator, 724-357-2470, E-mail: jacqueline.mcginty@iup.edu.
Website: http://www.iup.edu/ace/grad/default.aspx

Inter American University of Puerto Rico, Metropolitan Campus, Graduate Programs, Program in Occupational Education, San Juan, PR 00919-1293. Offers MA. *Degree requirements:* For master's, comprehensive exam. *Entrance requirements:* For master's, GRE or EXADEP, interview. Electronic applications accepted.

Iowa State University of Science and Technology, Program in Industrial Agriculture and Technology, Ames, IA 50011. Offers MS, PhD. *Entrance requirements:* For master's and doctorate, GRE General Test. Additional exam requirements/recommendations for international students: Required—TOEFL (minimum score 550 paper-based; 79 iBT), IELTS (minimum score 6.5). Electronic applications accepted. *Faculty research:* Industrial technology, technology education, training and development, technical education.

Jackson State University, Graduate School, College of Science, Engineering and Technology, Department of Civil and Environmental Engineering and Industrial Systems and Technology, Jackson, MS 39217. Offers civil engineering (MS, PhD); coastal engineering (MS, PhD); environmental engineering (MS, PhD); hazardous materials management (MS); technology education (MS Ed). *Program availability:* Part-time, evening/weekend. *Degree requirements:* For master's, comprehensive exam, thesis or alternative. *Entrance requirements:* For master's, GRE General Test. Additional exam requirements/recommendations for international students: Required—TOEFL (minimum score 520 paper-based; 67 iBT).

James Madison University, The Graduate School, College of Education, Program in Adult Education and Human Resource Development, Harrisonburg, VA 22807. Offers higher education (MS Ed); human resource management (MS Ed); individualized (MS Ed); instructional design (MS Ed); leadership and facilitation (MS Ed); program evaluation and measurement (MS Ed). *Accreditation:* NCATE. *Program availability:* Part-time, evening/weekend. *Students:* 10 full-time (7 women), 11 part-time (8 women); includes 8 minority (5 Black or African American, non-Hispanic/Latino; 1 American Indian or Alaska Native, non-Hispanic/Latino; 1 Hispanic/Latino; 1 Two or more races, non-Hispanic/Latino), 1 international. Average age 30. In 2018, 10 master's awarded. Application fee: $60. Electronic applications accepted. *Expenses:* Tuition, state resident: full-time $10,848. Tuition, nonresident: full-time $27,888. *Required fees:* $1128. *Financial support:* In 2018–19, 8 students received support. Teaching assistantships, Federal Work-Study, and assistantships (averaging $7911) available. Financial award application deadline: 3/1; financial award applicants required to submit FAFSA. *Unit head:* Dr. Jane B. Thall, Department Head, 540-568-5531, E-mail: thalljb@jmu.edu. *Application contact:* Lynette D. Michael, Director of Graduate Admissions, 540-568-6131 Ext. 6395, Fax: 540-568-7860, E-mail: michaeld@jmu.edu.

Kent State University, College of Education, Health and Human Services, School of Teaching, Learning and Curriculum Studies, Program in Career Technical Teacher Education, Kent, OH 44242-0001. Offers M Ed. *Program availability:* Part-time, evening/weekend. *Faculty:* 2 full-time (0 women), 2 part-time/adjunct (1 woman). *Students:* 30 part-time (16 women); includes 1 minority (Black or African American, non-Hispanic/Latino). 7 applicants, 43% accepted. In 2018, 7 master's awarded. *Entrance requirements:* For master's, 2 letters of reference, goals statement. Additional exam requirements/recommendations for international students: Required—TOEFL (minimum score 550 paper-based; 80 iBT). *Application deadline:* Applications are processed on a rolling basis. Application fee: $45 ($60 for international students). Electronic applications accepted. *Expenses:* Tuition, state resident: full-time $11,766; part-time $536 per credit. Tuition, nonresident: full-time $21,952; part-time $999 per credit. *International tuition:* $21,952 full-time. Tuition and fees vary according to course load. *Financial support:* Research assistantships with full tuition reimbursements, Federal Work-Study, scholarships/grants, and unspecified assistantships available. Financial award application deadline: 4/1; financial award applicants required to submit FAFSA. *Faculty research:* Workforce education/development, adult education, training and organizational change. *Unit head:* Dr. Patrick O'Connor, Coordinator, 330-672-0689, E-mail: poconnor@kent.edu. *Application contact:* Cheryl Slusarczyk, Academic Program Director, Office of Graduate Student Services, 330-672-2576, Fax: 330-672-9162, E-mail: ogs@kent.edu.

Louisiana State University and Agricultural & Mechanical College, Graduate School, College of Human Sciences and Education, School of Human Resource Education and Workforce Development, Baton Rouge, LA 70803. Offers agriculture and extension education and youth development (MS, PhD); career and technical education (MS, PhD); comprehensive vocational education (MS, PhD); extension and international education (MS, PhD); human resource and leadership development (MS, PhD); industrial education (MS); vocational agriculture education (MS, PhD); vocational business education (MS); vocational home economics education (MS). *Accreditation:* NCATE.

Middle Tennessee State University, College of Graduate Studies, College of Basic and Applied Sciences, Department of Engineering Technology and Industrial Studies, Murfreesboro, TN 37132. Offers engineering technology (MS). *Program availability:* Part-time, evening/weekend, online learning. *Degree requirements:* For master's, comprehensive exam. *Entrance requirements:* For master's, GRE. Additional exam requirements/recommendations for international students: Required—TOEFL (minimum score 525 paper-based; 71 iBT) or IELTS (minimum score 6). Electronic applications accepted.

Mississippi State University, College of Education, Department of Instructional Systems and Workforce Development, Mississippi State, MS 39762. Offers instructional systems and workforce development (MSIT, PhD); technology (MST, Ed S). *Faculty:* 9 full-time (5 women). *Students:* 11 full-time (5 women), 45 part-time (34 women); includes 32 minority (31 Black or African American, non-Hispanic/Latino; 1 Two or more races, non-Hispanic/Latino). Average age 36. 11 applicants, 36% accepted, 3 enrolled. In 2018, 3 master's, 6 doctorates, 2 other advanced degrees awarded. *Degree requirements:* For master's, thesis optional, comprehensive oral or written exam; for doctorate, thesis/dissertation, comprehensive oral and written exam; for Ed S, thesis, comprehensive written exam. *Entrance requirements:* For master's, GRE, minimum GPA of 2.75 on undergraduate work, 3.0 graduate; for doctorate, GRE, minimum GPA of 3.4 on graduate work; for Ed S, GRE, minimum GPA of 3.2, master's degree. Additional exam requirements/recommendations for international students: Required—TOEFL (minimum score 550 paper-based; 79 iBT); Recommended—IELTS (minimum score 6.5). *Application deadline:* For fall admission, 7/1 for domestic students, 5/1 for international students; for spring admission, 11/1 for domestic students, 9/1 for international students. Applications are processed on a rolling basis. Application fee: $60 ($80 for international students). Electronic applications accepted. *Expenses:* Tuition, state resident: full-time $8450; part-time $360.59 per credit hour. Tuition, nonresident: full-time $23,140; part-time $969.09 per credit hour. *Required fees:* $110. One-time fee: $55 full-time. Part-time tuition and fees vary according to course load, degree level, campus/location and reciprocity agreements. *Financial support:* In 2018–

19, 1 teaching assistantship with full tuition reimbursement (averaging $10,800 per year) was awarded; Federal Work-Study, institutionally sponsored loans, scholarships/grants, and unspecified assistantships also available. Financial award application deadline: 4/1; financial award applicants required to submit FAFSA. *Faculty research:* Computer technology, nontraditional students, interactive video, instructional technology, educational leadership. *Unit head:* Dr. Trey Martindale, Associate Professor and Head, 662-325-7258, Fax: 662-325-7599, E-mail: tmartindale@colled.msstate.edu. *Application contact:* Angie Campbell, Admissions and Enrollment Assistant, 662-325-9514, E-mail: acampbell@grad.msstate.edu.
Website: http://www.iswd.msstate.edu

Mississippi State University, College of Education, Educational Leadership Program, Mississippi State, MS 39762. Offers community college education (MAT); community college leadership (PhD); higher education leadership (PhD); P-12 school leadership (PhD); school administration (MS, Ed S); student affairs and higher education (MS); workforce education leadership (MS). MS in workforce education leadership held jointly with Alcorn State University. *Faculty:* 12 full-time (9 women). *Students:* 74 full-time (43 women), 145 part-time (89 women); includes 86 minority (75 Black or African American, non-Hispanic/Latino; 1 American Indian or Alaska Native, non-Hispanic/Latino; 6 Hispanic/Latino; 4 Two or more races, non-Hispanic/Latino). Average age 35. 83 applicants, 82% accepted, 55 enrolled. In 2018, 48 master's, 12 doctorates, 13 other advanced degrees awarded. *Degree requirements:* For master's and Ed S, comprehensive exam, thesis; for doctorate, comprehensive exam, thesis/dissertation. *Entrance requirements:* For master's, GRE, minimum GPA of 2.75 in junior and senior courses; for doctorate, GRE, minimum GPA of 3.4 on previous graduate work; for Ed S, GRE, minimum GPA of 3.2, master's degree. Additional exam requirements/ recommendations for international students: Required—TOEFL (minimum score 550 paper-based; 79 iBT); Recommended—IELTS (minimum score 6.5). *Application deadline:* For fall admission, 7/1 for domestic students, 5/1 for international students; for spring admission, 11/1 for domestic students, 9/1 for international students. Application fee: $60 ($80 for international students). Electronic applications accepted. *Expenses:* Tuition, state resident: full-time $8450; part-time $360.59 per credit hour. Tuition, nonresident: full-time $23,140; part-time $969.09 per credit hour. *Required fees:* $110. One-time fee: $55 full-time. Part-time tuition and fees vary according to course load, degree level, campus/location and reciprocity agreements. *Financial support:* In 2018–19, 1 research assistantship with full tuition reimbursement (averaging $11,861 per year) was awarded; Federal Work-Study, institutionally sponsored loans, and unspecified assistantships also available. Financial award application deadline: 4/1; financial award applicants required to submit FAFSA. *Unit head:* Dr. Eric Moyen, Associate Professor and Head, 662-325-0969, Fax: 662-325-0975, E-mail: em1621@msstate.edu. *Application contact:* Nathan Drake, Admissions and Enrollment Assistant, 662-325-3804, E-mail: ndrake@grad.msstate.edu.
Website: http://www.educationalleadership.msstate.edu/

Montana State University, The Graduate School, College of Education, Health, and Human Development, Department of Education, Bozeman, MT 59717. Offers adult and higher education (Ed D); curriculum and instruction (M Ed, Ed D), including professional educator (M Ed), technology education (M Ed); education (M Ed), including adult and higher education, educational leadership, school counseling; educational leadership (Ed D, Ed S). *Accreditation:* TEAC. *Program availability:* Part-time, online learning. *Degree requirements:* For master's, comprehensive exam; for doctorate, comprehensive exam, thesis/dissertation. *Entrance requirements:* For master's, GRE, 3 letters of reference, essays, BA transcripts; for doctorate, GRE, MAT, 3 letters of reference, essay, BA and M Ed transcripts; for Ed S, PRAXIS. Additional exam requirements/recommendations for international students: Required—TOEFL (minimum score 550 paper-based). Electronic applications accepted. *Faculty research:* Critical literacy; standards-based education; school Improvement, organizational change, leadership in rural education, leadership in Indian education; student Learning; multicultural/culturally responsive education for social justice Native American indigenous education, community-centered education teacher preparation.

Morehead State University, Graduate School, Elmer R. Smith College of Business and Technology, Department of Engineering and Technology Management, Morehead, KY 40351. Offers career and technical education (MS); computer information systems and analytics (MS); engineering and technology (MS). *Entrance requirements:* For master's, GRE, GMAT. Additional exam requirements/recommendations for international students: Required—TOEFL (minimum score 525 paper-based). Electronic applications accepted.

Murray State University, College of Education and Human Services, Department of Adolescent, Career, and Special Education, Murray, KY 42071. Offers career and technical education (MS); middle school teacher leader (MA Ed); secondary teacher leader (MA Ed); special education (MA Ed), including mild learning and behavior disorders, moderate to severe disabilities (P-12), teacher leader in special education learning and behavior disorders; teacher education and professional development (Ed S). *Accreditation:* NCATE. *Program availability:* Part-time. *Entrance requirements:* For master's and Ed S, GRE or GMAT, minimum university GPA of 2.75. Additional exam requirements/recommendations for international students: Required—TOEFL (minimum score 527 paper-based; 71 iBT). Electronic applications accepted.

North Carolina State University, Graduate School, College of Education, Department of Educational Leadership, Policy, and Human Development, Program in Training and Development, Raleigh, NC 27695. Offers M Ed, Ed D, Certificate. *Program availability:* Online learning. *Degree requirements:* For master's, thesis optional. *Entrance requirements:* For master's, GRE General Test or MAT, minimum GPA of 3.0 in major. Electronic applications accepted.

Northern Arizona University, College of Education, Department of Educational Specialties, Flagstaff, AZ 86011. Offers autism spectrum disorders (Certificate); bilingual/multicultural education (M Ed), including bilingual, ESL; career and technical education (M Ed, Certificate); educational technology (M Ed, Certificate); English as a second language (Certificate); positive behavior support (Certificate); special education (M Ed), including early childhood special education, mild/moderate disabilities. *Program availability:* Part-time, 100% online, blended/hybrid learning. *Degree requirements:* For master's, variable foreign language requirement, comprehensive exam (for some programs), thesis (for some programs); for Certificate, comprehensive exam (for some programs). *Entrance requirements:* Additional exam requirements/recommendations for international students: Required—TOEFL (minimum score 80 iBT), IELTS (minimum score 6.5). Electronic applications accepted.

Old Dominion University, Darden College of Education, Programs in STEM Education and Professional Studies, Norfolk, VA 23529. Offers community college teaching (MS); human resources training (PhD); technology education (PhD). *Accreditation:* NCATE (one or more programs are accredited). *Program availability:* Part-time, evening/ weekend, mix of synchronous and asynchronous study. Terminal master's awarded for partial completion of doctoral program. *Degree requirements:* For master's, comprehensive exam, thesis optional, writing exam, candidacy exam; for doctorate, comprehensive exam, thesis/dissertation, writing exam, candidacy exam. *Entrance requirements:* For master's, GRE General Test or MAT, minimum GPA of 2.8, 2 letters of reference; for doctorate, GRE, minimum GPA of 3.0, 3 letters of reference. Additional exam requirements/recommendations for international students: Required—TOEFL. Electronic applications accepted. *Faculty research:* Training and development, STEM education, visualization, leadership, technology literacy.

Penn State University Park, Graduate School, College of Education, Department of Learning and Performance Systems, University Park, PA 16802. Offers learning, design, and technology (M Ed, MS, PhD, Certificate); lifelong learning and adult education (M Ed, D Ed, PhD, Certificate); workforce education and development (M Ed, MS, PhD).

Pittsburg State University, Graduate School, College of Technology, Department of Technology and Workforce Learning, Pittsburg, KS 66762. Offers career and technical education (MS); human resource development (MS); technology (MS), including automotive technology, construction management, graphic design, graphics management, information technology, innovation in technology, personnel development, technology management, workforce learning; workforce development and education (Ed S). *Program availability:* Part-time, evening/weekend, 100% online, blended/hybrid learning. *Degree requirements:* For master's, thesis or alternative; for Ed S, thesis optional. *Entrance requirements:* Additional exam requirements/recommendations for international students: Required—TOEFL (minimum score 520 paper-based; 68 iBT), IELTS (minimum score 6), PTE (minimum score 47). Electronic applications accepted. *Expenses:* Contact institution.

Purdue University, Graduate School, College of Education, Department of Curriculum and Instruction, West Lafayette, IN 47907. Offers agricultural and extension education (MS, MS Ed, PhD, Ed S); art education (PhD); career and technical education (MS Ed, PhD, Ed S); curriculum studies (MS Ed, PhD, Ed S); educational technology (MS Ed, PhD, Ed S); elementary education (MS Ed); family and consumer sciences education (MS Ed, PhD, Ed S); foreign language education (MS Ed, PhD, Ed S); industrial technology (PhD, Ed S); language arts (MS Ed, PhD, Ed S); literacy (MS Ed, PhD, Ed S); mathematics education (MS, MS Ed, PhD, Ed S); science education (MS, MS Ed, PhD, Ed S); social studies education (MS Ed, PhD, Ed S). *Accreditation:* NCATE. *Program availability:* Part-time, evening/weekend, online learning. *Faculty:* 34 full-time (24 women), 3 part-time/adjunct (1 woman). *Students:* 75 full-time (52 women), 357 part-time (271 women); includes 83 minority (29 Black or African American, non-Hispanic/Latino; 1 American Indian or Alaska Native, non-Hispanic/Latino; 14 Asian, non-Hispanic/Latino; 29 Hispanic/Latino; 1 Native Hawaiian or other Pacific Islander, non-Hispanic/Latino; 9 Two or more races, non-Hispanic/Latino), 43 international. Average age 36. 169 applicants, 83% accepted, 102 enrolled. In 2018, 141 master's, 15 doctorates awarded. *Degree requirements:* For master's, thesis optional; for doctorate, thesis/dissertation, oral and written exams; for Ed S, oral presentation, project. *Entrance requirements:* For master's, GRE General Test (if undergraduate GPA is below 3.0), minimum undergraduate GPA of 3.0 or equivalent; for doctorate, GRE General Test (minimum combined verbal and quantitative score of 1000, 300 for new scoring), minimum undergraduate GPA of 3.0 or equivalent; master's degree with minimum GPA of 3.0 or equivalent; for Ed S, GRE General Test (minimum combined verbal and quantitative score of 1000, 300 for new scoring), minimum undergraduate GPA of 3.0 or equivalent; master's degree. Additional exam requirements/recommendations for international students: Required—TOEFL (minimum score 550 paper-based; 77 iBT). *Application deadline:* For fall admission, 12/15 for domestic students, 3/1 for international students; for spring admission, 9/15 for domestic students, 8/1 for international students. Application fee: $60 ($75 for international students). Electronic applications accepted. *Financial support:* Fellowships with full tuition reimbursements, research assistantships with full tuition reimbursements, teaching assistantships with full tuition reimbursements, career-related internships or fieldwork, and tuition waivers (full) available. Support available to part-time students. Financial award application deadline: 3/1; financial award applicants required to submit FAFSA. *Faculty research:* Literacy acquisition and development, teacher beliefs and knowledge, recruitment and retention of underrepresented students, economic education, literacy discourse. *Unit head:* Janet M. Alsup, Head, 765-494-9667, E-mail: alsupj@purdue.edu. *Application contact:* Heather Brinkman, Graduate Contact, 765-494-2345, E-mail: hbrinkma@purdue.edu.
Website: http://www.edci.purdue.edu/

Rochester Institute of Technology, Graduate Enrollment Services, College of Applied Science and Technology, School of International Hospitality and Service Innovation, Advanced Certificate Program in Workplace Learning and Instruction, Rochester, NY 14623-5603. Offers Advanced Certificate. *Program availability:* Part-time, evening/ weekend, 100% online, blended/hybrid learning. *Entrance requirements:* For degree, minimum GPA of 3.0 (recommended). Additional exam requirements/recommendations for international students: Required—TOEFL (minimum score 570 paper-based; 88 iBT), IELTS (minimum score 6.5), PTE (minimum score 62). *Application deadline:* Applications are processed on a rolling basis. Application fee: $65. Electronic applications accepted. *Expenses:* Contact institution. *Financial support:* Scholarships/ grants available. Support available to part-time students. Financial award applicants required to submit FAFSA. *Faculty research:* Training, instructional design, performance management, employee development, strategic leadership. *Unit head:* Linda Tolan, Senior Associate Dean, 585-475-5078, E-mail: latcad@rit.edu. *Application contact:* Diane Ellison, Senior Associate Vice President, Graduate Enrollment Services, 585-475-2229, Fax: 585-475-7164, E-mail: gradinfo@rit.edu.
Website: https://www.rit.edu/study/workplace-learning-and-instruction-adv-cert

South Carolina State University, College of Graduate and Professional Studies, Department of Education, Orangeburg, SC 29117-0001. Offers early childhood education (MAT); education (M Ed); elementary education (M Ed, MAT); English (MAT); general science/biology (MAT); mathematics (MAT); secondary education (M Ed), including biology education, business education, counselor education, English education, home economics education, industrial education, mathematics education, science education, social studies education; special education (M Ed), including emotionally handicapped, learning disabilities, mentally handicapped. *Accreditation:* NCATE. *Program availability:* Part-time, evening/weekend. *Faculty:* 17 full-time (6 women), 12 part-time/adjunct (5 women). *Students:* 42 full-time (32 women), 93 part-time (64 women); includes 121 minority (119 Black or African American, non-Hispanic/ Latino; 2 Asian, non-Hispanic/Latino), 2 international. Average age 40. 50 applicants, 98% accepted, 39 enrolled. In 2018, 9 master's awarded. *Degree requirements:* For master's, thesis optional, departmental qualifying exam. *Entrance requirements:* For master's, GRE General Test, NTE, interview, teaching certificate. *Application deadline:* For fall admission, 6/15 priority date for domestic students, 6/15 for international students; for spring admission, 11/1 for domestic and international students. Application fee: $25. Electronic applications accepted. *Expenses: Tuition, area resident:* Full-time $9928; part-time $552 per credit hour. Tuition, state resident: full-time $9928. Tuition, nonresident: full-time $21,038; part-time $1169 per credit hour. *Required fees:* $1532; $85 per credit hour. *Financial support:* Fellowships, career-related internships or fieldwork, Federal Work-Study, and scholarships/grants available. Financial award application deadline: 6/1. *Unit head:* Dr. Charlie Spell, Chair, Department of Education, 803-536-8963, Fax: 803-516-4568, E-mail: cspell@scsu.edu. *Application contact:* Curtis Foskey, Coordinator of Graduate Studies, 803-536-8419, Fax: 803-536-8812, E-mail: cfoskey@scsu.edu.

Southern Illinois University Carbondale, Graduate School, College of Education and Human Services, Department of Workforce Education and Development, Carbondale, IL

62901-4701. Offers MS Ed, PhD. *Accreditation:* NCATE. *Program availability:* Part-time. *Degree requirements:* For master's, thesis; for doctorate, thesis/dissertation. *Entrance requirements:* For master's, minimum GPA of 2.7; for doctorate, GRE General Test, minimum GPA of 3.25. Additional exam requirements/recommendations for international students: Required—TOEFL. *Faculty research:* Career education, technical training, curriculum development, competency-based instruction, impact of technology on workplace and workforce.

State University of New York at Oswego, Graduate Studies, School of Education, Department of Technology, Oswego, NY 13126. Offers MS Ed. *Accreditation:* NCATE. *Program availability:* Part-time. *Degree requirements:* For master's, thesis optional, departmental exam. *Entrance requirements:* For master's, provisional teaching certificate in technology education. Additional exam requirements/recommendations for international students: Required—TOEFL (minimum score 560 paper-based). *Faculty research:* Curriculum development, microcomputer applications.

State University of New York at Oswego, Graduate Studies, School of Education, Department of Vocational Teacher Preparation, Oswego, NY 13126. Offers agriculture (MS Ed); business and marketing (MS Ed); family and consumer sciences (MS Ed); health careers (MS Ed); technical education (MS Ed); trade education (MS Ed). *Accreditation:* NCATE. *Program availability:* Part-time, evening/weekend. *Degree requirements:* For master's, comprehensive exam, thesis or alternative. *Entrance requirements:* Additional exam requirements/recommendations for international students: Required—TOEFL (minimum score 560 paper-based).

Temple University, College of Education, Department of Teaching and Learning, Philadelphia, PA 19122-6096. Offers career and technical education (Ed M), including business, computing, and information technology, industrial education, marketing education; middle grades education (Ed M), including math and language arts, math and science, science and language arts; secondary education (Ed M), including English, math, social studies; teaching English to speakers of other languages (MS Ed); urban education (Ed M). *Program availability:* Part-time, evening/weekend. *Faculty:* 27 full-time (19 women), 71 part-time/adjunct (51 women). *Students:* 181 full-time (126 women), 128 part-time (78 women); includes 71 minority (25 Black or African American, non-Hispanic/Latino; 1 American Indian or Alaska Native, non-Hispanic/Latino; 20 Asian, non-Hispanic/Latino; 19 Hispanic/Latino; 1 Native Hawaiian or other Pacific Islander, non-Hispanic/Latino; 5 Two or more races, non-Hispanic/Latino), 12 international. 234 applicants, 67% accepted, 103 enrolled. In 2018, 148 master's awarded. *Degree requirements:* For master's, thesis (for some programs). *Entrance requirements:* For master's, statement of goals, 2 letters of recommendation. Additional exam requirements/recommendations for international students: Required—TOEFL (minimum score 79 iBT), IELTS, PTE, one of three is required. Application fee: $60. Electronic applications accepted. *Financial support:* Fellowships, research assistantships, teaching assistantships, career-related internships or fieldwork, Federal Work-Study, scholarships/grants, health care benefits, and unspecified assistantships available. Financial award applicants required to submit FAFSA. *Faculty research:* Career & technical education, early childhood education, middle grades education, secondary education, special education. *Unit head:* Matthew Tincani, Prof. of Applied Behavior Analysis and Dept. Chairperson, 215-204-8073, E-mail: matthew.tincani@temple.edu. *Application contact:* Stacey Sanginette, Academic Coordinator, 215-204-6143, E-mail: stacey.sangtinette@temple.edu.
Website: http://education.temple.edu/tl

Texas State University, The Graduate College, College of Applied Arts, Interdisciplinary Studies Program in Occupational Education, San Marcos, TX 78666. Offers MAIS, MSIS. *Program availability:* Part-time, evening/weekend, blended/hybrid learning. *Faculty:* 8 full-time (4 women), 3 part-time/adjunct (2 women). *Students:* 27 full-time (18 women), 37 part-time (30 women); includes 28 minority (14 Black or African American, non-Hispanic/Latino; 1 American Indian or Alaska Native, non-Hispanic/Latino; 1 Asian, non-Hispanic/Latino; 10 Hispanic/Latino; 2 Two or more races, non-Hispanic/Latino), 1 international. Average age 35. 21 applicants, 95% accepted, 17 enrolled. In 2018, 18 master's awarded. *Degree requirements:* For master's, comprehensive exam, thesis optional. *Entrance requirements:* For master's, baccalaureate degree from regionally-accredited university; minimum GPA of 2.75 for last 60 hours of undergraduate work or GRE General Test; statement of personal goals. Additional exam requirements/recommendations for international students: Required—TOEFL (minimum score 550 paper-based; 78 iBT), IELTS (minimum score 6.5). *Application deadline:* For fall admission, 2/1 priority date for domestic and international students; for spring admission, 10/15 for domestic students, 10/1 for international students; for summer admission, 4/15 for domestic students, 3/15 for international students. Applications are processed on a rolling basis. Application fee: $55 ($90 for international students). Electronic applications accepted. *Expenses:* Tuition, state resident: full-time $8102; part-time $4051 per semester. Tuition, nonresident: full-time $18,229; part-time $9115 per semester. *International tuition:* $18,229 full-time. *Required fees:* $2116; $120 per credit hour. Tuition and fees vary according to course load. *Financial support:* In 2018–19, 48 students received support, including 1 research assistantship (averaging $13,500 per year); teaching assistantships, Federal Work-Study, institutionally sponsored loans, scholarships/grants, health care benefits, and unspecified assistantships also available. Support available to part-time students. Financial award application deadline: 1/15; financial award applicants required to submit FAFSA. *Faculty research:* Reaching under served rural agricultural Latinos and veterans; College Credit for Heroes; broadening participation of underrepresented minorities in Science, Technology, Engineering, Entrepreneurship, Agriculture, Mathematics, and Computer Science. Adult development and transition in the work place, Competency based education, Prior Learning assessment and survey research, Veterans and PTSD. *Total annual research expenditures:* $236,710. *Unit head:* Dr. Mary Jo Garcia Biggs, Chair of Occupational, Workforce, and Leadership Studies Department, 512-245-1680, E-mail: mb56@txstate.edu. *Application contact:* Dr. Andrea Golato, Dean of Graduate School, 512-245-2581, Fax: 512-245-8365, E-mail: gradcollege@txstate.edu.
Website: http://www.OCED.txstate.edu/

Texas State University, The Graduate College, College of Applied Arts, Program in Management of Technical Education, San Marcos, TX 78666. Offers M Ed. *Program availability:* Part-time, evening/weekend. *Faculty:* 6 full-time (3 women), 4 part-time/adjunct (2 women). *Students:* 3 full-time (0 women), 11 part-time (5 women); includes 8 minority (2 Black or African American, non-Hispanic/Latino; 1 American Indian or Alaska Native, non-Hispanic/Latino; 1 Asian, non-Hispanic/Latino; 4 Hispanic/Latino). Average age 40. 2 applicants. In 2018, 9 master's awarded. *Degree requirements:* For master's, comprehensive exam. *Entrance requirements:* For master's, baccalaureate degree from regionally-accredited university with minimum GPA of 2.75 in last 60 hours of course work or GRE General Test; statement of purpose. Additional exam requirements/recommendations for international students: Required—TOEFL (minimum score 550 paper-based; 78 iBT), IELTS (minimum score 6.5). *Application deadline:* For fall admission, 2/1 priority date for domestic and international students; for spring admission, 10/15 for domestic students, 10/1 for international students; for summer admission, 4/15 for domestic students, 3/15 for international students. Applications are processed on a rolling basis. Application fee: $55 ($90 for international students). Electronic applications accepted. *Expenses:* Tuition, state resident: full-time $8102; part-time $4051 per semester. Tuition, nonresident: full-time $18,229; part-time $9115 per semester. *International tuition:* $18,229 full-time. *Required fees:* $2116; $120 per credit hour. Tuition and fees vary according to course load. *Financial support:* In 2018–19, 5 students received support. Research assistantships, teaching assistantships, career-related internships or fieldwork, Federal Work-Study, institutionally sponsored loans, scholarships/grants, and unspecified assistantships available. Support available to part-time students. Financial award application deadline: 1/15; financial award applicants required to submit FAFSA. *Faculty research:* Veterans and PTSD; Adult development and transition in workplace contexts; Prior Learning Assessment, Leadership, Survey Research; Competency-Based Education. *Total annual research expenditures:* $143,441. *Unit head:* Dr. Shailen Singh, Graduate Advisor, 512-716-4541, E-mail: s_s980@txstate.edu. *Application contact:* Dr. Andrea Golato, Dean of the Graduate College, 512-245-2581, Fax: 512-245-8365, E-mail: gradcollege@txstate.edu.
Website: http://www.gradcollege.txstate.edu/programs/mtech.html

University of Arkansas, Graduate School, College of Education and Health Professions, Department of Rehabilitation, Human Resources and Communication Disorders, Fayetteville, AR 72701. Offers adult and lifelong learning (M Ed, Ed D); communication disorders (MS); counselor education (MS, PhD); educational statistics and research methods (MS, PhD); higher education (M Ed, Ed D, Ed S); human resource and workforce development education (M Ed, Ed D); rehabilitation (MS, PhD). *Program availability:* Part-time. In 2018, 211 master's, 56 doctorates, 10 other advanced degrees awarded. *Application deadline:* For fall admission, 8/1 for domestic students, 4/1 for international students; for spring admission, 12/1 for domestic students, 10/1 for international students; for summer admission, 4/15 for domestic students, 3/1 for international students. Applications are processed on a rolling basis. Application fee: $60. Electronic applications accepted. *Financial support:* In 2018–19, 55 research assistantships, 3 teaching assistantships were awarded; fellowships with tuition reimbursements, career-related internships or fieldwork, and Federal Work-Study also available. Support available to part-time students. Financial award application deadline: 4/1; financial award applicants required to submit FAFSA. *Unit head:* Dr. Michael Hevel, Department Head, 479-575-4924, Fax: 479-575-3319, E-mail: hevel@uark.edu. *Application contact:* Vicki Dieffenderfer, Graduate Program Coordinator, 479-575-5239, Fax: 575-3319, E-mail: vmdieffe@uark.edu.
Website: http://rhrc.uark.edu/

The University of British Columbia, Faculty of Education, Department of Curriculum and Pedagogy, Vancouver, BC V6T 1Z4, Canada. Offers art education (M Ed, MA); curriculum studies (M Ed, MA, PhD); home economics education (M Ed, MA); mathematics education (M Ed, MA); media and technology studies education (M Ed, MA); music education (M Ed, MA); physical education (M Ed, MA); science education (M Ed, MA); social studies education (M Ed, MA). *Program availability:* Part-time, online learning. *Degree requirements:* For master's, thesis (MA); for doctorate, comprehensive exam, thesis/dissertation. *Entrance requirements:* Additional exam requirements/recommendations for international students: Required—TOEFL, IELTS. Electronic applications accepted. *Expenses:* Contact institution. *Faculty research:* School subjects, teaching and learning.

University of Central Florida, College of Community Innovation and Education, Department of Educational Leadership and Higher Education, Orlando, FL 32816. Offers career and technical education (MA); educational leadership (M Ed, MA, Ed S); higher education/college teaching and leadership (MA); higher education/student personnel (MA). *Program availability:* Part-time, evening/weekend. *Degree requirements:* For master's, thesis or alternative; for Ed S, thesis or alternative, final exam. *Entrance requirements:* For master's, GRE General Test; for Ed S, GRE General Test, minimum GPA of 3.0, resume, letters of recommendation. Additional exam requirements/recommendations for international students: Required—TOEFL. Electronic applications accepted.

University of Central Missouri, The Graduate School, Warrensburg, MO 64093. Offers accountancy (MA); accounting (MBA); applied mathematics (MS); aviation safety (MA); biology (MS); business administration (MBA); career and technical education leadership (MS); college student personnel administration (MS); communication (MA); computer science (MS); counseling (MS); criminal justice (MS); educational leadership (Ed D); educational technology (MS); elementary and early childhood education (MSE); English (MA); environmental studies (MA); finance (MBA); history (MA); human services/educational technology (Ed S); human services/learning resources (Ed S); human services/professional counseling (Ed S); industrial hygiene (MS); industrial management (MS); information systems (MBA); information technology (MS); kinesiology (MS); library science and information services (MS); literacy education (MSE); marketing (MBA); mathematics (MS); music (MA); occupational safety management (MS); psychology (MS); rural family nursing (MS); school administration (MSE); social gerontology (MS); sociology (MA); special education (MSE); speech language pathology (MS); superintendency (Ed S); teaching (MAT); teaching English as a second language (MA); technology (MS); technology management (PhD); theatre (MA). *Accreditation:* ASHA. *Program availability:* Part-time, 100% online, blended/hybrid learning. *Degree requirements:* For master's and Ed S, comprehensive exam (for some programs), thesis (for some programs). *Entrance requirements:* Additional exam requirements/recommendations for international students: Required—TOEFL (minimum score 550 paper-based; 79 iBT). Electronic applications accepted.

University of Georgia, College of Education, Department of Career and Information Studies, Athens, GA 30602. Offers learning, design, and technology (M Ed, PhD, Ed S), including instructional design and development (M Ed, Ed S); workforce education (MAT, Ed D), including business education (MAT). *Accreditation:* NCATE. *Entrance requirements:* For master's, GRE General Test, MAT; for doctorate, GRE General Test; for Ed S, GRE General Test or MAT. Electronic applications accepted.

University of Idaho, College of Graduate Studies, College of Education, Health and Human Sciences, Department of Curriculum and Instruction, Moscow, ID 83844-3082. Offers career and technology education (M Ed); curriculum and instruction (M Ed, Ed S); special education (M Ed). *Faculty:* 28 full-time (19 women). *Students:* 30 full-time (24 women), 37 part-time (29 women). Average age 37. In 2018, 32 master's awarded. *Entrance requirements:* For master's, minimum GPA of 3.0. Additional exam requirements/recommendations for international students: Required—TOEFL (minimum score 79 iBT). *Application deadline:* For fall admission, 8/1 for domestic students; for spring admission, 12/15 for domestic students. Applications are processed on a rolling basis. Application fee: $60. Electronic applications accepted. *Expenses:* Tuition, state resident: full-time $7266.44; part-time $474.50 per credit hour. Tuition, nonresident: full-time $24,902; part-time $1453.50 per credit hour. *Required fees:* $2085.56; $45.50 per credit hour. *Financial support:* Research assistantships and teaching assistantships available. Financial award applicants required to submit FAFSA.
Website: http://www.uidaho.edu/ed/ci

University of Maryland Eastern Shore, Graduate Programs, Department of Technology, Princess Anne, MD 21853. Offers career and technology education (M Ed). *Program availability:* Part-time, evening/weekend. *Degree requirements:* For master's, comprehensive exam, seminar paper. *Entrance requirements:* For master's, PRAXIS, writing sample. Additional exam requirements/recommendations for international students: Required—TOEFL (minimum score 80 iBT). Electronic applications accepted. *Faculty research:* Doppler Radar study.

Vocational and Technical Education

University of Minnesota, Twin Cities Campus, Graduate School, College of Education and Human Development, Department of Organizational Leadership, Policy and Development, Minneapolis, MN 55455-0213. Offers adult literacy (Certificate); comparative and international development education (MA, PhD); disability policy and services (Certificate); education policy and leadership (M Ed, MA, Ed D, PhD), including educational policy and leadership (MA, Ed D, PhD), leadership in education (M Ed); evaluation studies (MA, PhD); higher education (MA, Ed D, PhD), including higher education (MA, PhD), multicultural college teaching and learning (MA); human resource development (M Ed, MA, Ed D, PhD, Certificate); PK-12 administrative licensure (Certificate); private college leadership (Certificate); professional development (Certificate); program evaluation (Certificate); technical education (Certificate); undergraduate multicultural teaching and learning (Certificate). *Faculty:* 33 full-time (16 women). *Students:* 332 full-time (220 women), 194 part-time (139 women); includes 130 minority (46 Black or African American, non-Hispanic/Latino; 5 American Indian or Alaska Native, non-Hispanic/Latino; 37 Asian, non-Hispanic/Latino; 22 Hispanic/Latino; 20 Two or more races, non-Hispanic/Latino), 75 international. Average age 36. 379 applicants, 68% accepted, 187 enrolled. In 2018, 67 master's, 39 doctorates, 64 other advanced degrees awarded. Application fee: $75 ($95 for international students). *Financial support:* In 2018–19, 6 fellowships, 34 research assistantships with full tuition reimbursements (averaging $10,071 per year), 17 teaching assistantships with full tuition reimbursements (averaging $9,608 per year) were awarded; scholarships/grants also available. *Faculty research:* Organizational issues in schools, universities, and other organizations; international education and development; program evaluation and research on applied evaluation methods; international human resource development and change; gender and race/ethnicity in relation to learning and leadership. *Total annual research expenditures:* $732,047. *Unit head:* Dr. Kenneth Bartlett, Chair, 612-625-1006, Fax: 612-624-3377, E-mail: bartlett@umn.edu. *Application contact:* Dr. Jeremy J. Hernandez, Coordinator of Graduate Studies, 612-626-9377, E-mail: olpd@umn.edu.
Website: http://www.cehd.umn.edu/olpd/

University of Missouri, Office of Research and Graduate Studies, College of Education, Department of Learning, Teaching and Curriculum, Columbia, MO 65211. Offers agricultural education (M Ed, PhD, Ed S); art education (M Ed, PhD, Ed S); business and office education (M Ed, PhD, Ed S); early childhood education (M Ed, PhD, Ed S); elementary education (M Ed, PhD, Ed S); English education (M Ed, PhD, Ed S); foreign language education (M Ed, PhD, Ed S); health education and promotion (M Ed, PhD); learning and instruction (M Ed); marketing education (M Ed, PhD, Ed S); mathematics education (M Ed, PhD, Ed S); music education (M Ed, PhD, Ed S); reading education (M Ed, PhD, Ed S); science education (M Ed, PhD, Ed S); social studies education (M Ed, PhD, Ed S); vocational education (M Ed, PhD, Ed S). *Program availability:* Part-time. Terminal master's awarded for partial completion of doctoral program. *Entrance requirements:* For master's and Ed S, GRE General Test or MAT, minimum GPA of 3.0; for doctorate, GRE General Test, minimum GPA of 3.0. Additional exam requirements/recommendations for international students: Required—TOEFL.

University of Nebraska–Lincoln, Graduate College, College of Education and Human Sciences, Department of Teaching, Learning and Teacher Education, Lincoln, NE 68588. Offers adult and continuing education (MA); educational studies (Ed D, PhD), including special education (Ed D); teaching, learning and teacher education (M Ed, MA, MST, Ed D, PhD); vocational and adult education (M Ed, MA). *Accreditation:* NCATE. *Degree requirements:* For master's, thesis optional. *Entrance requirements:* Additional exam requirements/recommendations for international students: Required—TOEFL (minimum score 550 paper-based). Electronic applications accepted. *Faculty research:* Teacher education, instructional leadership, literacy education, technology, improvement of school curriculum.

University of New England, College of Graduate and Professional Studies, Portland, ME 04005-9526. Offers advanced educational leadership (CAGS); applied nutrition (MS); career and technical education (MS Ed); curriculum and instruction (MS Ed); education (CAGS, Post-Master's Certificate); educational leadership (MS Ed, Ed D); generalist (MS Ed); health informatics (MS, Graduate Certificate); inclusion education (MS Ed); literacy K-12 (MS Ed); medical education leadership (MMEL); public health (MPH, Graduate Certificate); reading specialist (MS Ed); social work (MSW). *Program availability:* Part-time, evening/weekend, online only, 100% online. *Faculty:* 109 part-time/adjunct (78 women). *Students:* 1,207 full-time (972 women), 561 part-time (450 women); includes 411 minority (280 Black or African American, non-Hispanic/Latino; 17 American Indian or Alaska Native, non-Hispanic/Latino; 74 Asian, non-Hispanic/Latino; 25 Hispanic/Latino; 9 Native Hawaiian or other Pacific Islander, non-Hispanic/Latino; 6 Two or more races, non-Hispanic/Latino). Average age 36. 740 applicants, 92% accepted, 494 enrolled. In 2018, 586 master's, 44 doctorates, 85 other advanced degrees awarded. *Application deadline:* Applications are processed on a rolling basis. Electronic applications accepted. *Financial support:* Application deadline: 5/1; applicants required to submit FAFSA. *Unit head:* Dr. Martha Wilson, Dean of the College of Graduate and Professional Studies, 207-221-4985, E-mail: mwilson13@une.edu. *Application contact:* Nicole Lindsay, Director of Online Admissions, 207-221-4966, E-mail: nlindsay1@une.edu.
Website: http://online.une.edu

University of Northern Iowa, Graduate College, College of Humanities, Arts and Sciences, Department of Technology, Doctor of Industrial Technology Program, Cedar Falls, IA 50614. Offers DIT.

University of Northern Iowa, Graduate College, College of Humanities, Arts and Sciences, Department of Technology, MS Program in Technology, Cedar Falls, IA 50614. Offers MS.

University of North Texas, Toulouse Graduate School, Denton, TX 76203-5459. Offers accounting (MS); applied anthropology (MA, MS); applied behavior analysis (Certificate); applied geography (MA); applied technology and performance improvement (M Ed, MS); art education (MA); art history (MA); arts leadership (Certificate); audiology (Au D); behavior analysis (MS); behavioral science (PhD); biochemistry and molecular biology (MS); biology (MA, MS); biomedical engineering (MS); business analysis (MS); chemistry (MS); clinical health psychology (PhD); communication studies (MA, MS); computer engineering (MS); computer science (MS); counseling (M Ed, MS), including clinical mental health counseling (MS), college and university counseling, elementary school counseling, secondary school counseling; creative writing (MA); criminal justice (MS); curriculum and instruction (M Ed); decision sciences (MBA); design (MA, MFA), including fashion design (MFA), innovation studies, interior design (MFA); early childhood studies (MS); economics (MS); educational leadership (M Ed, Ed D); educational psychology (MS, PhD), including family studies (MS), gifted and talented (MS), human development (MS), learning and cognition (MS), research, measurement and evaluation (MS); electrical engineering (MS); emergency management (MPA); engineering technology (MS); English (MA); English as a second language (MA); environmental science (MS); finance (MBA, MS); financial management (MPA); French (MA); health services management (MBA); higher education (M Ed, Ed D); history (MA, MS); hospitality management (MS); human resources management (MPA); information science (MS); information systems (PhD); information technologies (MBA); interdisciplinary studies (MA, MS); international studies (MA); international sustainable tourism (MS); jazz studies (MM); journalism (MA, MJ, Graduate Certificate), including interactive and virtual digital communication (Graduate Certificate), narrative journalism (Graduate Certificate), public relations (Graduate Certificate); kinesiology (MS); linguistics (MA); local government management (MPA); logistics (PhD); logistics and supply chain management (MBA); long-term care, senior housing, and aging services (MA); management (PhD); marketing (MBA); mathematics (MA, MS); mechanical and energy engineering (MS, PhD); music (MA), including ethnomusicology, music theory, musicology, performance; music composition (PhD); music education (MM Ed, PhD); nonprofit management (MPA); operations and supply chain management (MBA); performance (MM, DMA); philosophy (MA); political science (MA); professional and technical communication (MA); radio, television and film (MA, MFA); rehabilitation counseling (Certificate); sociology (MA); Spanish (MA); special education (M Ed); speech-language pathology (MA); strategic management (MBA); studio art (MFA); teaching (M Ed); MBA/MS. *Program availability:* Part-time, evening/weekend, online learning. Terminal master's awarded for partial completion of doctoral program. *Degree requirements:* For master's, variable foreign language requirement, comprehensive exam (for some programs), thesis (for some programs); for doctorate, variable foreign language requirement, comprehensive exam (for some programs), thesis/dissertation; for other advanced degree, variable foreign language requirement, comprehensive exam (for some programs). *Entrance requirements:* For master's and doctorate, GRE, GMAT. Additional exam requirements/recommendations for international students: Required—TOEFL (minimum score 550 paper-based; 79 iBT). Electronic applications accepted.

University of Phoenix–Phoenix Campus, College of Education, Tempe, AZ 85282-2371. Offers administration and supervision (MA Ed); adult education and training (MA Ed); curriculum and instruction reading (MA Ed); early childhood education (MA Ed); education studies (MA Ed); elementary teacher education (MA Ed); secondary teacher education (MA Ed); special education (MA Ed); teacher leadership (MA Ed). *Program availability:* Evening/weekend, online learning. *Entrance requirements:* Additional exam requirements/recommendations for international students: Required—TOEFL, TOEIC (Test of English as an International Communication), Berlitz Online English Proficiency Exam, PTE, or IELTS. Electronic applications accepted. *Expenses:* Contact institution.

University of South Africa, Institute for Science and Technology Education, Pretoria, South Africa. Offers mathematics, science and technology education (M Sc, PhD).

University of South Florida, College of Education, Department of Leadership, Counseling, Adult, Career and Higher Education, Tampa, FL 33620-9951. Offers adult education (MA, Ed D, PhD, Ed S); career and technical education (MA); career and workforce education (PhD); higher education/community college teaching (MA, Ed D, PhD); vocational education (Ed S). *Faculty:* 19 full-time (11 women). *Students:* 107 full-time (81 women), 275 part-time (185 women); includes 143 minority (67 Black or African American, non-Hispanic/Latino; 2 American Indian or Alaska Native, non-Hispanic/Latino; 10 Asian, non-Hispanic/Latino; 56 Hispanic/Latino; 8 Two or more races, non-Hispanic/Latino), 14 international. Average age 36. 188 applicants, 54% accepted, 73 enrolled. In 2018, 51 master's, 8 doctorates, 3 other advanced degrees awarded. *Entrance requirements:* For master's, GRE may be required, goals statement; letters of recommendation; proof of educational or professional experience; prerequisites, if needed; for doctorate, GRE may be required, letters of recommendation; masters degree in appropriate field; optional interview; evidence of professional experience; personal statement. Additional exam requirements/recommendations for international students: Required—TOEFL. Application fee: $30. *Expenses:* Tuition, state resident: full-time $6350. Tuition, nonresident: full-time $19,048. *International tuition:* $19,048 full-time. *Required fees:* $2079. *Financial support:* In 2018–19, 19 students received support. *Total annual research expenditures:* $40,520. *Unit head:* Dr. Judith Ponticell, Chair, 813-974-4897, Fax: 813-974-5423, E-mail: jponticell@usf.edu. *Application contact:* Dr. Judith Ponticell, Chair, 813-974-4897, Fax: 813-974-5423, E-mail: jponticell@usf.edu.
Website: http://www.coedu.usf.edu/main/departments/ache/ache.html

The University of Toledo, College of Graduate Studies, Judith Herb College of Education, Department of Curriculum and Instruction, Toledo, OH 43606-3390. Offers art education (ME); career and technical education (ME, Ed S); curriculum and instruction (ME, PhD, Ed S); early childhood education (Ed S); education and anthropology (MAE); education and biology (MES); education and chemistry (MES); education and classics (MAE); education and economics (MAE); education and English (MAE); education and French (MAE); education and geology (MES); education and German (MAE); education and history (MAE); education and mathematics (MAE, MES); education and physics (MES); education and political science (MAE); education and sociology (MAE); education and Spanish (MAE); educational media (PhD); educational technology (ME); educational technology: virtual educator (Certificate); elementary education (PhD); English as a second language (MAE); gifted and talented education (PhD); middle childhood education (ME); secondary education (ME, PhD); special education (PhD). *Accreditation:* NCATE. *Program availability:* Part-time, evening/weekend. *Degree requirements:* For master's, comprehensive exam, thesis or alternative; for doctorate, comprehensive exam, thesis/dissertation; for other advanced degree, thesis optional. *Entrance requirements:* For master's, doctorate, and other advanced degree, minimum cumulative GPA of 2.7 for all previous academic work, letters of recommendation. Additional exam requirements/recommendations for international students: Required—TOEFL (minimum score 550 paper-based; 80 iBT). Electronic applications accepted.

University of Victoria, Faculty of Graduate Studies, Faculty of Education, Department of Curriculum and Instruction, Victoria, BC V8W 2Y2, Canada. Offers art education (M Ed, PhD); curriculum studies (M Ed, MA, PhD); early childhood education (M Ed, PhD); educational studies (PhD); language and literacy (M Ed, MA, PhD); mathematics (M Ed, MA, PhD); music education (M Ed, MA, PhD); science (M Ed, MA, PhD); social studies (M Ed, MA); social, cultural and foundational studies (MA, PhD); technology and environmental education (PhD). *Program availability:* Part-time. *Degree requirements:* For master's, thesis, project (M Ed); for doctorate, comprehensive exam, thesis/dissertation. *Entrance requirements:* For master's, minimum B average. Additional exam requirements/recommendations for international students: Required—TOEFL (minimum score 575 paper-based), IELTS (minimum score 7). Electronic applications accepted. *Faculty research:* Elementary and secondary English, language arts, curriculum theory and practice, educational media and technology, educational administration and leadership, history and philosophy of education.

University of Wisconsin–Stout, Graduate School, College of Education, Health and Human Sciences, School of Education, Program in Career and Technical Education, Menomonie, WI 54751. Offers MS, Ed D, Ed S. *Program availability:* Part-time, online learning. *Degree requirements:* For master's and Ed S, thesis. *Entrance requirements:* For master's, minimum GPA of 2.75; for Ed S, minimum GPA of 3.25. Additional exam requirements/recommendations for international students: Required—TOEFL (minimum score 500 paper-based; 61 iBT). Electronic applications accepted. *Faculty research:* Needs assessment, task analysis, instructional development, learning technologies.

Utah State University, School of Graduate Studies, College of Engineering, Department of Engineering Education, Logan, UT 84322. Offers PhD. *Program*

availability: Part-time, evening/weekend. *Entrance requirements:* Additional exam requirements/recommendations for international students: Required—TOEFL. *Faculty research:* Computer-aided design drafting, technology and the public school, materials, electronics, aviation.

Valley City State University, Online Graduate Programs, Valley City, ND 58072. Offers elementary education (M Ed); English education (M Ed); library and information technologies (M Ed); teaching (MAT); teaching and technology (M Ed); teaching English language learners (M Ed); technology education (M Ed). *Accreditation:* NCATE. *Program availability:* Part-time, evening/weekend, online only, 100% online. *Faculty:* 20 full-time (11 women), 13 part-time/adjunct (8 women). *Students:* 5 full-time (2 women), 133 part-time (100 women); includes 8 minority (1 Black or African American, non-Hispanic/Latino; 3 American Indian or Alaska Native, non-Hispanic/Latino; 2 Asian, non-Hispanic/Latino; 2 Hispanic/Latino). Average age 36. 23 applicants, 74% accepted, 12 enrolled. In 2018, 47 master's awarded. *Degree requirements:* For master's, action research report, comprehensive portfolio. *Entrance requirements:* For master's, GRE, MAT, PRAXIS II or National Teaching Board for Professional Standards (if GPA is less than 3.0). Additional exam requirements/recommendations for international students: Required—TOEFL (minimum score 525 paper-based; 71 iBT); Recommended—IELTS (minimum score 5.5). *Application deadline:* For fall admission, 7/26 for domestic and international students; for spring admission, 12/13 for domestic and international students; for summer admission, 5/18 for domestic and international students. Applications are processed on a rolling basis. Application fee: $35. Electronic applications accepted. *Expenses:* $396.39 per credit for all students regardless of residency. *Financial support:* In 2018–19, 16 students received support. Scholarships/grants, tuition waivers (full and partial), and unspecified assistantships available. Financial award applicants required to submit FAFSA. *Faculty research:* Universal accessibility, instructional design and technology, gender communication, STEM education in K-12, English language learners. *Unit head:* Dr. Sheri Okland, Dean, 701-845-7184, E-mail: sheri.l.okland@vcsu.edu. *Application contact:* Misty Lindgren, Graduate Studies, 701-845-7303, Fax: 701-845-7190, E-mail: misty.lindgren@vcsu.edu. Website: http://www.vcsu.edu/graduate

Virginia Polytechnic Institute and State University, Graduate School, College of Liberal Arts and Human Sciences, Blacksburg, VA 24061. Offers career and technical education (MS Ed, Ed S); communication (MA); counselor education (MA); creative writing (MFA); curriculum and instruction (MA Ed, Ed S); educational leadership and policy studies (Ed S); educational research and evaluation (PhD); English (MA); social, political, ethical, and cultural thought (PhD); Ed D/PhD. *Faculty:* 420 full-time (221 women), 1 (woman) part-time/adjunct. *Students:* 603 full-time (428 women), 359 part-time (237 women); includes 189 minority (107 Black or African American, non-Hispanic/Latino; 4 American Indian or Alaska Native, non-Hispanic/Latino; 24 Asian, non-Hispanic/Latino; 27 Hispanic/Latino; 2 Native Hawaiian or other Pacific Islander, non-Hispanic/Latino; 25 Two or more races, non-Hispanic/Latino), 84 international. Average age 33. 856 applicants, 48% accepted, 262 enrolled. In 2018, 270 master's, 63 doctorates awarded. *Degree requirements:* For master's, comprehensive exam (for some programs), thesis (for some programs); for doctorate, comprehensive exam (for some programs), thesis/dissertation (for some programs). *Entrance requirements:* For master's and doctorate, GRE/GMAT. Additional exam requirements/recommendations for international students: Required—TOEFL (minimum score 90 iBT). *Application deadline:* For fall admission, 8/1 for domestic students, 4/1 for international students; for spring admission, 1/1 for domestic students, 9/1 for international students. Applications are processed on a rolling basis. Application fee: $75. Electronic applications accepted. *Expenses:* Tuition, state resident: full-time $15,510; part-time $739.50 per credit hour. Tuition, nonresident: full-time $29,629; part-time $1490.25 per credit hour. *Required fees:* $2804; $550 per semester. Tuition and fees vary according to course load, campus/location and program. *Financial support:* In 2018–19, 4 fellowships with full tuition reimbursements (averaging $23,122 per year), 28 research assistantships with full tuition reimbursements (averaging $15,605 per year), 245 teaching assistantships with full tuition reimbursements (averaging $16,046 per year) were awarded; scholarships/grants and unspecified assistantships also available. Financial award application deadline: 3/1; financial award applicants required to submit FAFSA. *Total annual research expenditures:* $7.5 million. *Unit head:* Dr. Laura Belmonte, Dean, 540-231-6779, Fax: 540-231-7157, E-mail: belmonte@vt.edu. *Application contact:* Chelsea Blanchet, Executive Assistant, 540-231-6779, Fax: 540-231-7157, E-mail: bchels1@vt.edu. Website: http://www.liberalarts.vt.edu/

Virginia Polytechnic Institute and State University, VT Online, Blacksburg, VA 24061. Offers advanced transportation systems (Certificate); aerospace engineering (MS); agricultural and life sciences (MSLFS); business information systems (Graduate Certificate); career and technical education (MS); civil engineering (MS); computer engineering (M Eng, MS); decision support systems (Graduate Certificate); eLearning leadership (MA); electrical engineering (M Eng, MS); engineering administration (MEA); environmental engineering (Certificate); environmental politics and policy (Graduate Certificate); environmental sciences and engineering (MS); foundations of political analysis (Graduate Certificate); health product risk management (Graduate Certificate); industrial and systems engineering (MS); information policy and society (Graduate Certificate); information security (Graduate Certificate); information technology (MIT); instructional technology (MA); integrative STEM education (MA Ed); liberal arts (Graduate Certificate); life sciences: health product risk management (MS); natural resources (MNR, Graduate Certificate); networking (Graduate Certificate); nonprofit and nongovernmental organization management (Graduate Certificate); ocean engineering (MS); political science (MA); security studies (Graduate Certificate); software development (Graduate Certificate). *Expenses:* Tuition, state resident: full-time $15,510; part-time $739.50 per credit hour. Tuition, nonresident: full-time $29,629; part-time $1490.25 per credit hour. *Required fees:* $2804; $550 per semester. Tuition and fees vary according to course load, campus/location and program. *Application contact:* Graduate Admissions and Academic Progress, 540-231-8636, E-mail: grads@vt.edu. Website: http://www.vto.vt.edu/

Washington State University, College of Education, Department of Teaching and Learning, Pullman, WA 99164-2132. Offers cultural studies and social thought in education (PhD); curriculum and instruction (Ed M, MA); English language learners (Ed M, MA); language, literacy and technology (PhD); literacy education (Ed M, MA); mathematics education (PhD); special education (Ed M, MA, PhD); teacher leadership (Ed D); teaching (MIT), including elementary education, secondary education. Programs offered at the Pullman, Spokane, Tri-cities, Vancouver and Global (online) campuses. *Program availability:* Part-time, online learning. *Degree requirements:* For master's, comprehensive exam, thesis, oral or written exam; for doctorate, comprehensive exam, thesis/dissertation, oral and written exam. *Entrance requirements:* For master's, GRE General Test, minimum GPA of 3.0, 3 letters of recommendation, letter of intent, transcripts, resume/curriculum vitae; for doctorate, GRE General Test, minimum GPA of 3.0, 3 letters of recommendation, letter of intent, transcripts, writing sample, resume/curriculum vitae. Additional exam requirements/recommendations for international students: Required—TOEFL (minimum score 550 paper-based; 80 iBT). Electronic applications accepted. *Faculty research:* Intersection of gender, youth cultures and schooling; examination of ideology of power in children's literature; early childhood special education; analyzing pre-service and in-service teacher development; second language acquisition.

Wayne State College, School of Education and Counseling, Department of Educational Foundations and Leadership, Program in Curriculum and Instruction, Wayne, NE 68787. Offers alternative education (MSE); business and information technology education (MSE); communication arts education (MSE); early childhood education (MSE); elementary education (MSE); English as a second language (MSE); English education (MSE); family and consumer sciences education (MSE); industrial technology and vocational education (MSE); learning communities (MSE); mathematics education (MSE); music education (MSE); science education (MSE); social science education (MSE). *Accreditation:* NCATE. *Program availability:* Part-time, evening/weekend. *Degree requirements:* For master's, comprehensive exam, thesis optional. *Entrance requirements:* For master's, GRE General Test. Additional exam requirements/recommendations for international students: Required—TOEFL (minimum score 550 paper-based).

Western Michigan University, Graduate College, College of Education and Human Development, Department of Family and Consumer Sciences, Kalamazoo, MI 49008. Offers career and technical education (MA); family and consumer sciences (MA).

Westfield State University, College of Graduate and Continuing Education, Department of Education, Program in Vocational Technical Education, Westfield, MA 01086. Offers M Ed. *Accreditation:* NCATE. *Program availability:* Part-time, evening/weekend. *Degree requirements:* For master's, comprehensive exam. *Entrance requirements:* For master's, GRE General Test or MAT, minimum undergraduate GPA of 2.8. Additional exam requirements/recommendations for international students: Recommended—TOEFL (minimum score 550 paper-based; 79 iBT).

Wilmington University, College of Education, New Castle, DE 19720-6491. Offers applied technology in education (M Ed); career and technical education (M Ed); educational leadership (Ed D); elementary and secondary school counseling (M Ed); elementary studies (M Ed); ESOL literacy (M Ed); higher education leadership (Ed D); instruction: gifted and talented (M Ed); instruction: teacher of reading (M Ed); instruction: teaching and learning (M Ed); organizational leadership (Ed D); school leadership (M Ed); secondary education (MAT); special education (M Ed). *Accreditation:* NCATE. *Program availability:* Part-time, evening/weekend. *Entrance requirements:* For master's, 2 letters of recommendation, interview. Additional exam requirements/recommendations for international students: Required—TOEFL (minimum score 500 paper-based). Electronic applications accepted.

ACADEMIC AND PROFESSIONAL
PROGRAMS IN LAW

Section 27
Law

This section contains a directory of institutions offering graduate work in law. Additional information about programs listed in the directory may be obtained by writing directly to the dean of a graduate school or chair of a department at the address given in the directory.

For programs offering related work, see also in this book *Business Administration and Management* and *Social Work.* In the other guides in this series:

Graduate Programs in the Humanities, Arts & Social Sciences

See *Criminology and Forensics; Public, Regional, and Industrial Affairs; Economics;* and *Political Science and International Affairs*

Graduate Programs in the Physical Sciences, Mathematics, Agricultural Sciences, the Environment & Natural Resources

See *Environmental Sciences and Management*

Graduate Programs in Engineering & Applied Sciences

See *Management of Engineering and Technology*

CONTENTS

Program Directories

Environmental Law

Chapman University, Dale E. Fowler School of Law, Orange, CA 92866. Offers advocacy and dispute resolution (JD); business law (LL M, JD); criminal law (JD); entertainment and media law (LL M); entertainment law (JD); environmental, land use, and real estate law (JD); international and comparative law (LL M); international law (JD); law (JD); prosecutorial science (LL M); tax law (JD); taxation (LL M); trial advocacy (LL M); JD/MBA; JD/MFA. *Accreditation:* ABA. *Program availability:* Part-time. *Entrance requirements:* For doctorate, LSAT. Additional exam requirements/recommendations for international students: Required—TOEFL (minimum score 600 paper-based; 100 iBT). Electronic applications accepted. *Expenses:* Contact institution.

Florida State University, College of Law, Tallahassee, FL 32306-1601. Offers American law for foreign lawyers (LL M); business law (LL M); environmental law and policy (LL M); financial regulation and compliance (JM); health law compliance (JM); law (JM, JD); legal risk management and HR compliance (JM); JD/MAES; JD/MBA; JD/MPA; JD/MS; JD/MSI; JD/MSP; JD/MSW. *Accreditation:* ABA. *Program availability:* Part-time, 100% online. *Students:* Average age 26. 1,805 applicants, 36% accepted, 225 enrolled. In 2018, 18 master's, 218 doctorates awarded. Terminal master's awarded for partial completion of doctoral program. *Entrance requirements:* For master's, one graduate-level standardized test (for JM), JD or equivalent degree (for LL M); for doctorate, LSAT or GRE (for JD). Additional exam requirements/recommendations for international students: Required—TOEFL (minimum score 600 paper-based; 100 iBT), IELTS (minimum score 7.5). *Application deadline:* For fall admission, 6/30 for domestic and international students; for spring admission, 12/1 for domestic students; for summer admission, 4/15 for domestic students. Applications are processed on a rolling basis. Application fee: $30. Electronic applications accepted. *Expenses:* Contact institution. *Financial support:* In 2018–19, 400 students received support, including 2 fellowships with full tuition reimbursements available (averaging $20,683 per year), 30 research assistantships (averaging $1,205 per year), 10 teaching assistantships (averaging $1,354 per year); career-related internships or fieldwork, scholarships/grants, and unspecified assistantships also available. Financial award application deadline: 3/1; financial award applicants required to submit FAFSA. *Faculty research:* Business law; environmental, energy and land use law; international law; criminal law. *Total annual research expenditures:* $99,375. *Unit head:* Erin O'Hara O'Connor, Dean, 850-644-3400, Fax: 850-644-5487, E-mail: eoconnor@law.fsu.edu. *Application contact:* Jennifer L. Kessinger, Director of Admissions and Records, 850-644-3787, Fax: 850-644-7284, E-mail: jkessing@law.fsu.edu.
Website: http://www.law.fsu.edu/

Georgetown University, Law Center, Washington, DC 20001. Offers environmental law (LL M); global health law (LL M); global health law and international institutions (LL M); individualized study (LL M); international business and economic law (LL M); law (JD, SJD); national security law (LL M); securities and financial regulation (LL M); taxation (LL M); JD/LL M; JD/MA; JD/MBA; JD/MPH; JD/PhD. *Accreditation:* ABA. *Program availability:* Part-time, evening/weekend. *Degree requirements:* For master's, thesis; for doctorate, thesis/dissertation (for some programs). *Entrance requirements:* For master's, JD, LL B, or first law degree earned in country of origin; for doctorate, LSAT (for JD). Additional exam requirements/recommendations for international students: Required—TOEFL. *Expenses:* Contact institution. *Faculty research:* Constitutional law, legal history, jurisprudence.

Golden Gate University, School of Law, San Francisco, CA 94105-2968. Offers environmental law (LL M); estate planning (LL M); intellectual property law (LL M); international legal studies (LL M, SJD); law (JD); taxation law (LL M); U.S. legal studies (LL M); JD/MBA. *Accreditation:* ABA. *Program availability:* Part-time, evening/weekend. *Degree requirements:* For doctorate, thesis/dissertation (for some programs). *Entrance requirements:* For doctorate, LSAT (for JD). Additional exam requirements/recommendations for international students: Required—TOEFL (minimum score 600 paper-based). Electronic applications accepted. *Expenses:* Contact institution. *Faculty research:* International law, intellectual property law, environmental law, real estate, civil rights.

Lehigh University, College of Arts and Sciences, Environmental Policy Program, Bethlehem, PA 18015. Offers environmental health (Graduate Certificate); environmental justice (Graduate Certificate); environmental policy and law (Graduate Certificate); environmental policy design (MA); sustainable development (Graduate Certificate); urban environmental policy (Graduate Certificate). *Faculty:* 7 full-time (3 women). *Students:* 10 full-time (7 women), 3 part-time (2 women); includes 2 minority (1 Asian, non-Hispanic/Latino; 1 Hispanic/Latino), 1 international. Average age 24. 12 applicants, 100% accepted, 9 enrolled. In 2018, 3 master's awarded. *Degree requirements:* For master's, thesis or additional course work. *Entrance requirements:* For master's, GRE, minimum GPA of 2.75, 3.0 for last two undergraduate semesters; essay; 2 letters of recommendation. Additional exam requirements/recommendations for international students: Required—TOEFL (minimum score 85 iBT), IELTS (minimum score 6.5). *Application deadline:* For fall admission, 1/1 for domestic and international students; for spring admission, 12/1 for domestic and international students. Application fee: $75. Tuition and fees vary according to program. *Financial support:* Application deadline: 1/1. *Faculty research:* Environmental policy, environmental law, urban policy, urban politics, urban environmental policy, sustainability, sustainable development, international environmental law, international environmental policy, environmental justice, social justice. *Unit head:* Dr. Karen B. Pooley, Director, 610-758-1238, E-mail: kbp312@lehigh.edu. *Application contact:* Mandy Fraley, Academic Coordinator, 610-758-5837, Fax: 610-758-6232, E-mail: amf518@lehigh.edu.
Website: http://ei.cas2.lehigh.edu/

Lewis & Clark College, Lewis & Clark Law School, Portland, OR 97219. Offers animal law (LL M); environmental, natural resources, and energy law (LL M, MSL); law (JD). *Accreditation:* ABA. *Program availability:* Part-time, evening/weekend. *Entrance requirements:* For doctorate, LSAT. Additional exam requirements/recommendations for international students: Recommended—TOEFL (minimum score 600 paper-based). Electronic applications accepted. Application fee is waived when completed online. *Expenses:* Contact institution.

Montclair State University, The Graduate School, College of Science and Mathematics, Environmental Forensics Certificate Program, Montclair, NJ 07043-1624. Offers Certificate.

Pace University, Elisabeth Haub School of Law, White Plains, NY 10603. Offers comparative legal studies (LL M); environmental law (LL M, SJD), including energy and climate change law (LL M), global environmental law (LL M); law (JD); JD/LL M; JD/MA; JD/MBA; JD/MEM; JD/MPA; JD/MS. JD/MA offered jointly with Sarah Lawrence College; JD/MEM offered jointly with Yale University School of Forestry and Environmental Studies. *Accreditation:* ABA. *Program availability:* Part-time. *Degree requirements:* For doctorate, thesis/dissertation (for some programs), extensive thesis proposal (for SJD). *Entrance requirements:* For master's, writing sample; for doctorate, LSAT (for JD). Additional exam requirements/recommendations for international students: Required—TOEFL (minimum score 100 iBT); Recommended—TWE. Electronic applications accepted. *Expenses:* Contact institution. *Faculty research:* Reform of energy regulations, international law, land use law, prosecutorial misconduct, corporation law.

St. Mary's University, School of Law, Master of Jurisprudence Program, San Antonio, TX 78228. Offers business and entrepreneurship law (MJ); commercial law (MJ); compliance, business law and risk (MJ); criminal justice (MJ); education law (MJ); environmental law (MJ); health law (MJ); healthcare compliance (MJ); international comparative law (MJ); military and national security law (MJ); natural resource law (MJ); tax law (MJ). *Program availability:* Part-time, evening/weekend, 100% online, blended/hybrid learning. *Students:* 14 full-time (10 women), 21 part-time (16 women); includes 17 minority (1 Black or African American, non-Hispanic/Latino; 16 Hispanic/Latino). Average age 41. 37 applicants, 89% accepted, 22 enrolled. In 2018, 9 master's awarded. *Degree requirements:* For master's, 30 credits, minimum GPA of 2.0. *Entrance requirements:* For master's, official transcripts, personal statement, resume, 2 letters of recommendation, proof of four-year undergraduate degree from accredited U.S. college/university or foreign institution approved by government or accrediting authority. Additional exam requirements/recommendations for international students: Required—TOEFL (minimum score 550 paper-based; 80 iBT), IELTS (minimum score 6). *Application deadline:* Applications are processed on a rolling basis. Application fee: $0. Electronic applications accepted. *Expenses:* 36550. *Financial support:* Applicants required to submit FAFSA. *Unit head:* Dean Colin Marks, Assistant Dean of Grad. and Summer Programs, 210-431 Ext. 2248, E-mail: cmarks@stmarytx.edu. *Application contact:* Alyssa Turrieta, Coordinator, 210-436-3829.
Website: https://law.stmarytx.edu/academics/programs/master-of-jurisprudence/

Stanford University, Law School, Stanford, CA 94305-8610. Offers corporate governance and practice (LL M); environmental law and policy (LL M); international economic law, business and policy (LL M); international legal studies (JSM); law (JD, JSD); law, science and technology (LL M); legal studies (MLS); JD/MA; JD/MBA; JD/MPP; JD/MS; JD/PhD. *Accreditation:* ABA. *Expenses: Tuition:* Full-time $50,703; part-time $32,970 per year. *Required fees:* $651. *Unit head:* M. Elizabeth Magill, Dean, 650-723-4455, Fax: 650-725-0253, E-mail: emagill@law.stanford.edu. *Application contact:* Graduate Admissions, 866-432-7472, Fax: 650-723-8371, E-mail: gradadmissions@stanford.edu.
Website: http://www.law.stanford.edu/

University at Buffalo, the State University of New York, Graduate School, School of Law, Buffalo, NY 14260. Offers criminal law (LL M); cross-border legal studies (LL M); environmental law (LL M); general law (LL M); law (JD); JD/MA; JD/MBA; JD/MLS; JD/MSW; JD/MUP; JD/PhD; LL M/LL M. *Accreditation:* ABA. *Faculty:* 56 full-time (29 women), 74 part-time/adjunct (30 women). *Students:* 451 full-time (250 women), 10 part-time (6 women); includes 91 minority (30 Black or African American, non-Hispanic/Latino; 2 American Indian or Alaska Native, non-Hispanic/Latino; 23 Asian, non-Hispanic/Latino; 23 Hispanic/Latino; 13 Two or more races, non-Hispanic/Latino), 18 international. Average age 26. 895 applicants, 60% accepted, 168 enrolled. In 2018, 1 master's, 153 doctorates awarded. *Entrance requirements:* For doctorate, LSAT or GRE (JD only). Additional exam requirements/recommendations for international students: Required—TOEFL (minimum score 90 iBT), IELTS (minimum score 7). *Application deadline:* For fall admission, 3/1 priority date for domestic and international students. Applications are processed on a rolling basis. Application fee: $85. Electronic applications accepted. *Expenses:* $14,037 per semester full-time tuition and fees, $1,275 per credit part-time tuition and fees. *Financial support:* In 2018–19, 350 students received support. Federal Work-Study, institutionally sponsored loans, scholarships/grants, tuition waivers (full and partial), and unspecified assistantships available. Financial award application deadline: 3/1; financial award applicants required to submit FAFSA. *Faculty research:* Criminal law, environmental law, international law and human rights, law and finance, cross-border legal studies. *Total annual research expenditures:* $29,552. *Unit head:* Aviva Abramovsky, Dean, 716-645-2052, E-mail: aabramov@buffalo.edu. *Application contact:* Lindsay Gladney, Vice Dean for Admissions, 716-645-2907, Fax: 716-645-6676, E-mail: law-admissions@buffalo.edu.
Website: http://www.law.buffalo.edu/

University of Calgary, Faculty of Graduate Studies, Faculty of Law, Certificate Program in Natural Resources, Energy and Environmental Law, Calgary, AB T2N 1N4, Canada. Offers LL M, Postbaccalaureate Certificate. *Program availability:* Part-time, evening/weekend. *Degree requirements:* For master's, thesis optional. *Entrance requirements:* For master's, JD or LL B. Additional exam requirements/recommendations for international students: Required—TOEFL (minimum score 100 iBT), IELTS (minimum score 7). Electronic applications accepted. *Faculty research:* Natural resources law and regulations; environmental law, ethics and policies; oil and gas and energy law; water and municipal law; Aboriginal law.

University of Colorado Denver, School of Public Affairs, Program in Public Affairs and Administration, Denver, CO 80127. Offers public administration (MPA), including domestic violence, emergency management and homeland security, environmental policy, management and law, homeland security and defense, local government, nonprofit management, public administration; public affairs (PhD). *Accreditation:* NASPAA. *Program availability:* Part-time, evening/weekend, online learning. *Expenses:* Tuition, state resident: full-time $6786; part-time $337 per credit hour. Tuition, nonresident: full-time $22,590; part-time $1255 per credit hour. *Required fees:* $1231; $137 per credit hour. Tuition and fees vary according to program and reciprocity agreements.

University of Florida, Levin College of Law, Gainesville, FL 32611. Offers comparative law (LL M), including tropical conservation and development; environmental and land use law (LL M); international taxation (LL M); law (JD); taxation (LL M, SJD). *Accreditation:* ABA. *Entrance requirements:* For doctorate, LSAT (for JD). Electronic applications accepted. *Faculty research:* Environmental and land use law, taxation, dispute resolution, family law, Constitutional law.

University of Houston, University of Houston Law Center, Houston, TX 77204-6060. Offers energy, environment, and natural resources (LL M); health law (LL M); intellectual property and information law (LL M); international law (LL M); law (JD); tax law (LL M); U.S. law (LL M). *Accreditation:* ABA. *Program availability:* Part-time, evening/weekend. *Faculty:* 58 full-time (22 women), 148 part-time/adjunct (45 women). *Students:* 606 full-time (303 women), 98 part-time (41 women); includes 260 minority (43 Black or African American, non-Hispanic/Latino; 6 American Indian or Alaska Native, non-Hispanic/Latino; 72 Asian, non-Hispanic/Latino; 137 Hispanic/Latino; 2 Native Hawaiian or other Pacific Islander, non-Hispanic/Latino), 14 international. Average age 26. 2,596

applicants, 33% accepted, 202 enrolled. In 2018, 75 master's awarded. *Degree requirements:* For master's, thesis optional. *Entrance requirements:* For doctorate, LSAT. Additional exam requirements/recommendations for international students: Required—TOEFL (minimum score 600 paper-based; 100 iBT), IELTS (minimum score 7). *Application deadline:* For fall admission, 2/15 for domestic and international students. Applications are processed on a rolling basis. Application fee: $0. Electronic applications accepted. Application fee is waived when completed online. *Expenses:* Texas Resident $31,090/year; Non Texas Resident $45,640/year. *Financial support:* In 2018–19, 573 students received support, including 47 fellowships (averaging $3,768 per year); research assistantships, career-related internships or fieldwork, Federal Work-Study, scholarships/grants, and tuition waivers (full and partial) also available. Support available to part-time students. Financial award application deadline: 3/15; financial award applicants required to submit FAFSA. *Faculty research:* Health law, international law, tax, environmental law/energy, information law/intellectual property. *Total annual research expenditures:* $336,944. *Unit head:* Leonard M. Baynes, Dean and Professor of Law, 713-743-2100, Fax: 713-743-2122, E-mail: lbaynes@central.uh.edu. *Application contact:* Pilar Mensah, Assistant Dean for Admissions, 713-743-2280, Fax: 713-743-2194, E-mail: lpmensah@central.uh.edu.
Website: http://www.law.uh.edu/

University of Pittsburgh, School of Law, Master of Studies in Law Program, Pittsburgh, PA 15260. Offers biomedical and health services research (MSL); business law (MSL), including commercial law, corporate law, general business law, international business, tax law; Constitutional law (MSL); criminal law and justice (MSL); disability law (MSL); elder and estate planning law (MSL); employment and labor law (MSL); energy law (MSL); environmental and real estate law (MSL); family law (MSL); health law (MSL); intellectual property and technology law (MSL); international and human rights law (MSL); jurisprudence (MSL); regulatory law (MSL); self-designed (MSL). *Program availability:* Part-time. *Entrance requirements:* Additional exam requirements/recommendations for international students: Required—TOEFL (minimum score 600 paper-based; 100 iBT), IELTS (minimum score 7). *Faculty research:* Law, health law, business law, contracts, intellectual property, environmental law.

The University of Tulsa, College of Law, Tulsa, OK 74104. Offers American Indian and indigenous law (LL M); American law for foreign lawyers (LL M); energy and natural resources law (LL M); energy law (MJ); health law (Certificate); Indian law (MJ); law (JD); Native American law (Certificate); sustainable energy and resources law (Certificate); JD/MA; JD/MBA; JD/MS. *Accreditation:* ABA. *Program availability:* Part-time. *Faculty:* 27 full-time (15 women), 19 part-time/adjunct (7 women). *Students:* 250 full-time (110 women), 31 part-time (14 women); includes 80 minority (10 Black or African American, non-Hispanic/Latino; 17 American Indian or Alaska Native, non-Hispanic/Latino; 4 Asian, non-Hispanic/Latino; 12 Hispanic/Latino; 37 Two or more races, non-Hispanic/Latino), 5 international. Average age 28. 581 applicants, 42% accepted, 100 enrolled. In 2018, 1 master's, 81 doctorates, 14 Certificates awarded. *Entrance requirements:* For doctorate, LSAT, BS or BA from 4-year regionally-accredited college/university. Additional exam requirements/recommendations for international students: Required—TOEFL (minimum score 570 paper-based; 90 iBT), TOEFL preferred; Recommended—IELTS (minimum score 6.5). *Application deadline:* For fall admission, 7/31 priority date for domestic and international students; for spring admission, 12/1 priority date for domestic students, 12/1 for international students; for summer admission, 4/13 for domestic and international students. Applications are processed on a rolling basis. Application fee: $30. Electronic applications accepted. *Expenses:* $25,254 full-time; $17,490 (8-11 hours); $13,734 (6-7 hours). *Financial support:* In 2018–19, 251 students received support. Scholarships/grants available. Support available to part-time students. Financial award application deadline: 8/1; financial award applicants required to submit FAFSA. *Faculty research:* Criminal law, copyright law, cybersecurity law, energy and natural resources law, international law. *Unit head:* Prof. Lyn Suzanne Entzeroth, Dean, 918-631-2400, Fax: 918-631-3126, E-mail: lyn-entzeroth@utulsa.edu. *Application contact:* April M. Fox, Associate Dean of Admissions and Financial Aid, 918-631-2406, Fax: 918-631-3630, E-mail: april-fox@utulsa.edu.
Website: http://www.utulsa.edu/law/

Vermont Law School, Graduate and Professional Programs, Master's Programs, South Royalton, VT 05068-0096. Offers American legal studies (LL M); energy law (LL M); energy regulation and law (MERL); environmental law (LL M); environmental law and policy (MELP); food and agriculture law (LL M); food and agriculture law and policy (MFALP); JD/MELP; JD/MERL; JD/MFALP. *Program availability:* Part-time, 100% online, blended/hybrid learning. *Entrance requirements:* Additional exam requirements/recommendations for international students: Required—TOEFL. *Faculty research:* Environment and new economy; takings; international environmental law; interaction among science, law, and environmental policy; climate change and the law.

Western Michigan University Thomas M. Cooley Law School, Graduate Programs, Lansing, MI 48901-3038. Offers administrative law (public law) (JD); business transactions (JD); Canadian law practice (JD); corporate law and finance (LL M); environmental law (public law) (JD); general practice (JD), including solo and small firm; general studies (LL M); homeland and national security law (LL M); insurance law (LL M); intellectual property (JD); intellectual property law (LL M); international law (JD); litigation (JD); taxation (LL M); U.S. legal studies for foreign attorneys (LL M); JD/LL M; JD/MBA; JD/MHA; JD/MPA; JD/MSW. *Accreditation:* ABA. *Program availability:* Part-time, evening/weekend, 100% online, blended/hybrid learning. *Degree requirements:* For master's, thesis (for some programs); for doctorate, minimum of 3 credits of clinical experience. *Entrance requirements:* For master's, JD or LL B; for doctorate, LSAT. Additional exam requirements/recommendations for international students: Required—TOEFL (for U.S. legal studies for foreign attorneys LL M program); Recommended—TOEFL. Electronic applications accepted. *Expenses:* Contact institution. *Faculty research:* Wrongful convictions, civil rights, environmental law, litigation techniques, data mining, intellectual property, practical and skills-based legal education.

Health Law

Boston University, School of Public Health, Health Law, Policy and Management Department, Boston, MA 02215. Offers health law, policy and management (MPH); health services and systems research (MS); health services research (PhD). *Accreditation:* CAHME. *Program availability:* Part-time, evening/weekend. *Faculty:* 37 full-time, 31 part-time/adjunct. *Students:* 98 full-time (82 women), 62 part-time (52 women); includes 46 minority (15 Black or African American, non-Hispanic/Latino; 11 Asian, non-Hispanic/Latino; 13 Hispanic/Latino; 7 Two or more races, non-Hispanic/Latino), 9 international. Average age 28. 507 applicants, 44% accepted, 77 enrolled. In 2018, 71 master's, 5 doctorates awarded. *Degree requirements:* For master's, comprehensive exam (for some programs), thesis (for some programs); for doctorate, comprehensive exam, thesis/dissertation. *Entrance requirements:* For master's, GRE, MCAT, GMAT; for doctorate, GRE. Additional exam requirements/recommendations for international students: Required—TOEFL (minimum score 600 paper-based; 100 iBT), IELTS (minimum score 7). *Application deadline:* For fall admission, 12/1 priority date for domestic and international students; for spring admission, 10/15 priority date for domestic students. Applications are processed on a rolling basis. Application fee: $115. Electronic applications accepted. *Financial support:* Career-related internships or fieldwork, Federal Work-Study, institutionally sponsored loans, scholarships/grants, and tuition waivers (partial) available. Support available to part-time students. Financial award application deadline: 3/1; financial award applicants required to submit FAFSA. *Faculty research:* Health policy, health law and ethics, human rights, healthcare management. *Unit head:* Dr. David Rosenbloom, Interim Chair, 617-638-5042. *Application contact:* LePhan Quan, Associate Director of Admissions, 617-638-4640, Fax: 617-638-5299, E-mail: asksph@bu.edu.
Website: http://www.bu.edu/sph/about/departments/health-law-policy-and-management/

Case Western Reserve University, School of Law, Cleveland, OH 44106. Offers financial integrity (MA); health law (SJD); intellectual property law (LL M, ML); international business law (LL M, ML); international criminal law (LL M); law (JD, SJD); patent practice (MA); U.S. and global legal studies (LL M, ML); JD/MA; JD/MBA; JD/MD; JD/MNM; JD/MPH; JD/MS; JD/MSSA. *Accreditation:* ABA. *Faculty:* 47 full-time (16 women), 63 part-time/adjunct (16 women). *Students:* 433 full-time (238 women); includes 91 minority (37 Black or African American, non-Hispanic/Latino; 1 American Indian or Alaska Native, non-Hispanic/Latino; 19 Asian, non-Hispanic/Latino; 26 Hispanic/Latino; 8 Two or more races, non-Hispanic/Latino), 30 international. Average age 24. 1,415 applicants, 50% accepted, 157 enrolled. In 2018, 126 master's awarded. *Entrance requirements:* For doctorate, LSAT, LSDAS. Additional exam requirements/recommendations for international students: Required—TOEFL. *Application deadline:* For fall admission, 4/1 priority date for domestic and international students. Applications are processed on a rolling basis. Application fee: $40. Electronic applications accepted. Application fee is waived when completed online. *Expenses:* Contact institution. *Financial support:* In 2018–19, 394 students received support. Career-related internships or fieldwork, Federal Work-Study, institutionally sponsored loans, and scholarships/grants available. Financial award application deadline: 5/1; financial award applicants required to submit FAFSA. *Unit head:* Jessica Berg, Co-Dean, 216-368-3283. *Application contact:* Kelli Curtis, Associate Dean for Admissions, 216-368-3600, Fax: 216-368-0185, E-mail: lawadmissions@case.edu.
Website: http://law.case.edu/

DePaul University, College of Law, Chicago, IL 60604. Offers business law and taxation (MJ); criminal law (MJ); health and intellectual property law (MJ); health care compliance (MJ); health law (LL M, MJ); intellectual property law (LL M); international and comparative law (MJ); international law (LL M); law (JD); public interest law (MJ); taxation (LL M); U.S. legal studies (LL M); JD/LL M; JD/MA; JD/MBA; JD/MS. *Accreditation:* ABA. *Program availability:* Part-time, evening/weekend. *Entrance requirements:* For doctorate, LSAT, LSAC applicant evaluation/letter of recommendation, personal statement, resume. Additional exam requirements/recommendations for international students: Required—TOEFL (minimum score 577 paper-based; 90 iBT), IELTS (minimum score 6.5). Electronic applications accepted. *Expenses:* Contact institution.

Drexel University, Thomas R. Kline School of Law, Philadelphia, PA 19104-2875. Offers business and entrepreneurship law (JD); criminal law (MLS, JD); cybersecurity and information privacy compliance (MLS); entrepreneurship and law (MLS); financial regulatory compliance (MLS); health care compliance (MLS); health law (JD); higher education compliance (MLS); human resources compliance (MLS); intellectual property law (JD); NCAA compliance and sports law (MLS). *Accreditation:* ABA.

Florida State University, College of Law, Tallahassee, FL 32306-1601. Offers American law for foreign lawyers (LL M); business law (LL M); environmental law and policy (LL M); financial regulation and compliance (JM); health law compliance (JM); law (JM, JD); legal risk management and HR compliance (JM); JD/MAES; JD/MBA; JD/MPA; JD/MS; JD/MSI; JD/MSP; JD/MSW. *Accreditation:* ABA. *Program availability:* Part-time, 100% online. *Students:* Average age 26. 1,805 applicants, 36% accepted, 225 enrolled. In 2018, 18 master's, 218 doctorates awarded. Terminal master's awarded for partial completion of doctoral program. *Entrance requirements:* For master's, one graduate-level standardized test (for JM), JD or equivalent degree (for LL M); for doctorate, LSAT or GRE (for JD). Additional exam requirements/recommendations for international students: Required—TOEFL (minimum score 600 paper-based; 100 iBT), IELTS (minimum score 7.5). *Application deadline:* For fall admission, 6/30 for domestic and international students; for spring admission, 12/1 for domestic students; for summer admission, 4/15 for domestic students. Applications are processed on a rolling basis. Application fee: $30. Electronic applications accepted. *Expenses:* Contact institution. *Financial support:* In 2018–19, 400 students received support, including 2 fellowships with full tuition reimbursements available (averaging $20,683 per year), 30 research assistantships (averaging $1,205 per year), 10 teaching assistantships (averaging $1,354 per year); career-related internships or fieldwork, scholarships/grants, and unspecified assistantships also available. Financial award application deadline: 3/1; financial award applicants required to submit FAFSA. *Faculty research:* Business law; environmental, energy and land use law; international law; criminal law. *Total annual research expenditures:* $99,375. *Unit head:* Erin O'Hara O'Connor, Dean, 850-644-3400, Fax: 850-644-5487, E-mail: eoconnor@law.fsu.edu. *Application contact:* Jennifer L. Kessinger, Director of Admissions and Records, 850-644-3787, Fax: 850-644-7284, E-mail: jkessing@law.fsu.edu.
Website: http://www.law.fsu.edu/

Georgetown University, Law Center, Washington, DC 20001. Offers environmental law (LL M); global health law (LL M); global health law and international institutions (LL M); individualized study (LL M); international business and economic law (LL M); law (JD, SJD); national security law (LL M); securities and financial regulation (LL M); taxation (LL M); JD/LL M; JD/MA; JD/MBA; JD/MPH; JD/PhD. *Accreditation:* ABA. *Program availability:* Part-time, evening/weekend. *Degree requirements:* For master's, thesis; for doctorate, thesis/dissertation (for some programs). *Entrance requirements:* For master's, JD, LL B, or first law degree earned in country of origin; for doctorate,

LSAT (for JD). Additional exam requirements/recommendations for international students: Required—TOEFL. *Expenses:* Contact institution. *Faculty research:* Constitutional law, legal history, jurisprudence.

Hofstra University, Maurice A. Deane School of Law, Hempstead, NY 11549. Offers alternative dispute resolution (JD); American legal studies (LL M); business law honors (JD); clinical bioethics (Certificate); corporate compliance (JD); criminal law and procedure (JD); family law (LL M, JD); health law (JD); health law and policy (LL M, MA); intellectual property law honors (JD); international law honors (JD); JD/MBA; JD/MPH. *Accreditation:* ABA. *Program availability:* Part-time, 100% online. *Faculty:* 41 full-time (21 women), 78 part-time/adjunct (24 women). *Students:* 712 full-time (374 women), 137 part-time (88 women); includes 181 minority (53 Black or African American, non-Hispanic/Latino; 2 American Indian or Alaska Native, non-Hispanic/Latino; 34 Asian, non-Hispanic/Latino; 82 Hispanic/Latino; 7 Native Hawaiian or other Pacific Islander, non-Hispanic/Latino; 3 Two or more races, non-Hispanic/Latino), 13 international. Average age 27. 3,104 applicants, 50% accepted, 301 enrolled. In 2018, 37 master's, 234 doctorates awarded. *Entrance requirements:* For doctorate, LSAT, letter of recommendation, personal statement, undergraduate transcripts; for Certificate, 2 letters of recommendation, JD or LLB, personal statement, law school transcripts. Additional exam requirements/recommendations for international students: Recommended—TOEFL (minimum score 600 paper-based; 100 iBT). *Application deadline:* For fall admission, 4/15 priority date for domestic and international students. Applications are processed on a rolling basis. Application fee: $0. Electronic applications accepted. *Expenses:* $29,607 per term for Full-time (tuition and fees). *Financial support:* In 2018–19, 578 students received support, including 565 fellowships with full and partial tuition reimbursements available (averaging $32,425 per year); research assistantships with full and partial tuition reimbursements available, career-related internships or fieldwork, Federal Work-Study, institutionally sponsored loans, scholarships/grants, tuition waivers (full and partial), unspecified assistantships, and scholarships and endowed scholarships also available. Support available to part-time students. Financial award applicants required to submit FAFSA. *Faculty research:* Family law; international law; constitutional law; legal ethics; health law. *Unit head:* Gail Prudenti, Dean, 516-463-4068, E-mail: gail.prudenti@hofstra.edu. *Application contact:* Sunil Samuel, Assistant Vice President of Admissions, 516-463-4723, Fax: 516-463-4664.
Website: http://law.hofstra.edu/

Indiana University–Purdue University Indianapolis, Robert H. McKinney School of Law, Indianapolis, IN 46202. Offers advocacy skills (Certificate); American law for foreign lawyers (LL M); civil and human rights (Certificate); corporate and commercial law (LL M, Certificate); criminal law (Certificate); environmental and natural resources (Certificate); health law (Certificate); health law, policy and bioethics (LL M); intellectual property law (LL M, Certificate); international and comparative law (LL M, Certificate); international human rights law (LL M); law (MJ, JD, SJD); JD/M Phil; JD/MBA; JD/MD; JD/MHA; JD/MLS; JD/MPA; JD/MPH; JD/MSW. *Accreditation:* ABA. *Program availability:* Part-time. *Entrance requirements:* For doctorate, LSAT. Additional exam requirements/recommendations for international students: Required—TOEFL (minimum score 79 iBT), IELTS (minimum score 6.5). Electronic applications accepted. *Expenses:* Contact institution.

Loyola University Chicago, School of Law, Chicago, IL 60611. Offers advocacy (LL M); business and compliance (MJ); business law (LL M); child and family (LL M); child and family law (MJ, Certificate); global competition (LL M, MJ); health law (LL M, MJ, Certificate); international law (LL M); law (JD); public interest law (Certificate); rule of law for development (LL M, MJ); tax (LL M); tax law (Certificate); transactional law (Certificate); trial advocacy (Certificate); JD/MA; JD/MBA; JD/MPP; JD/MSW; MJ/MSW; MS/MJ. *Accreditation:* ABA. *Program availability:* Part-time, evening/weekend, 100% online, blended/hybrid learning. *Faculty:* 69 full-time (36 women), 306 part-time/adjunct (148 women). *Students:* 870 full-time (530 women), 239 part-time (185 women); includes 380 minority (134 Black or African American, non-Hispanic/Latino; 64 Asian, non-Hispanic/Latino; 142 Hispanic/Latino; 40 Two or more races, non-Hispanic/Latino), 34 international. Average age 31. 2,711 applicants, 46% accepted, 387 enrolled. In 2018, 151 master's, 193 doctorates, 152 Certificates awarded. *Entrance requirements:* For doctorate, LSAT. Additional exam requirements/recommendations for international students: Required—TOEFL (minimum score 100 iBT); Recommended—IELTS (minimum score 7). *Application deadline:* For fall admission, 4/1 for domestic and international students. Applications are processed on a rolling basis. Application fee: $0. Electronic applications accepted. *Expenses:* Contact institution. *Financial support:* In 2018–19, 598 students received support, including 67 fellowships; research assistantships, Federal Work-Study, scholarships/grants, and health care benefits also available. Financial award application deadline: 3/1; financial award applicants required to submit FAFSA. *Faculty research:* Constitutional law including hate speech and supreme court advocacy; early childhood education including law policy and pedagogy; hedonic psychology - legal and social determinants of happiness; racial inequality; intersection of law, science, and technology. *Unit head:* Dr. James Faught, JD, Associate Dean for Administration, Law School, 312-915-7131, Fax: 312-915-6911, E-mail: law-admissions@luc.edu. *Application contact:* Jill Schur, Director, Graduate Enrollment Management, 312-915-8902, E-mail: gradinfo@luc.edu.
Website: http://www.luc.edu/law/

Nova Southeastern University, Shepard Broad College of Law, Fort Lauderdale, FL 33314. Offers education law (MS), including cybersecurity law, education law advocacy, exceptional education; employment law (MS), including cybersecurity law, employee relations law, human resource managerial law; health law (MS, JD), including clinical research law and regulatory compliance (MS), cybersecurity law (MS), health care administrative law (MS), regulatory compliance (MS), risk management (MS); international law (JD); law and policy (MS), including cybersecurity law; JD/DO; JD/M Acc; JD/M Tax; JD/MBA; JD/MPA; JD/MS; JD/PhD. *Accreditation:* ABA. *Program availability:* Part-time, evening/weekend, 100% online, blended/hybrid learning. *Degree requirements:* For master's, thesis optional, capstone research project; for doctorate, rigorous upper-level writing fulfilled through faculty-supervised seminar paper, law journal article, workshop, or other research; 6 credits' experiential learning. *Entrance requirements:* For master's, regionally-accredited undergraduate degree; at least 2 years' experience in related field (for employment law and health law); for doctorate, LSAT. Additional exam requirements/recommendations for international students: Recommended—TOEFL (minimum score 600 paper-based; 100 iBT), IELTS (minimum score 7). Electronic applications accepted. *Expenses:* Contact institution. *Faculty research:* Legal issues in health law, international law, the legal profession, family law, civil rights.

St. Mary's University, School of Law, Master of Jurisprudence Program, San Antonio, TX 78228. Offers business and entrepreneurship law (MJ); commercial law (MJ); compliance, business law and risk (MJ); criminal justice (MJ); education law (MJ); environmental law (MJ); health law (MJ); healthcare compliance (MJ); international comparative law (MJ); military and national security law (MJ); natural resource law (MJ); tax law (MJ). *Program availability:* Part-time, evening/weekend, 100% online, blended/hybrid learning. *Students:* 14 full-time (10 women), 21 part-time (16 women); includes 17 minority (1 Black or African American, non-Hispanic/Latino; 16 Hispanic/Latino). Average age 41. 37 applicants, 89% accepted, 22 enrolled. In 2018, 9 master's awarded. *Degree requirements:* For master's, 30 credits, minimum GPA of 2.0. *Entrance requirements:* For master's, official transcripts, personal statement, resume, 2 letters of recommendation, proof of four-year undergraduate degree from accredited U.S. college/university or foreign institution approved by government or accrediting authority. Additional exam requirements/recommendations for international students: Required—TOEFL (minimum score 550 paper-based; 80 iBT), IELTS (minimum score 6). *Application deadline:* Applications are processed on a rolling basis. Application fee: $0. Electronic applications accepted. *Expenses:* 36550. *Financial support:* Applicants required to submit FAFSA. *Unit head:* Dean Colin Marks, Assistant Dean of Grad. and Summer Programs, 210-431 Ext. 2248, E-mail: cmarks@stmarytx.edu. *Application contact:* Alyssa Turrieta, Coordinator, 210-436-3829.
Website: https://law.stmarytx.edu/academics/programs/master-of-jurisprudence/

Seattle University, School of Law, Seattle, WA 98122-4340. Offers American legal studies (LL M); business development (MLS); elder law (LL M); health law (MLS); innovation and technology (LL M, MLS); tribal law and governance (LL M, MLS); JD/MATL; JD/MBA; JD/MCJ; JD/MIB; JD/MPA; JD/MSAL; JD/MSF; JD/MSL. *Accreditation:* ABA. *Program availability:* Part-time, evening/weekend. *Entrance requirements:* For doctorate, LSAT. Additional exam requirements/recommendations for international students: Required—TOEFL (minimum score 600 paper-based; 100 iBT). Electronic applications accepted. *Expenses:* Contact institution. *Faculty research:* Innovation, technology and cybersecurity; secrecy and democratic decisions; linguistic features of police culture and the coercive impact of police officer swearing in police-citizen interaction; the imprisoned parent: differential power in same-sex families based on legal and cultural understandings of parentage; theology in public reason and legal discourse: a case for the preferential option for the poor.

Seton Hall University, School of Law, Newark, NJ 07102-5210. Offers health law (LL M, JD); intellectual property (LL M, JD); law (MSJ); JD/MADIR; JD/MBA; MD/JD; MD/MSJ. MD/JD, MD/MSJ offered jointly with University of Medicine and Dentistry of New Jersey. *Accreditation:* ABA. *Program availability:* Part-time, evening/weekend. *Degree requirements:* For master's, thesis optional. *Entrance requirements:* For master's, professional experience, letters of recommendation; for doctorate, LSAT, active LSDAS registration, letters of recommendation. Additional exam requirements/recommendations for international students: Recommended—TOEFL. Electronic applications accepted. *Expenses:* Contact institution. *Faculty research:* Health law, intellectual property law, science and the law, international law and employment/labor law.

Southern Illinois University Carbondale, School of Law, Program in Legal Studies, Carbondale, IL 62901-4701. Offers general law (MLS); health law and policy (MLS).

Suffolk University, Law School, Boston, MA 02108. Offers business law and financial services (JD); civil litigation (JD); global law and technology (LL M); health and biomedical law (JD); intellectual property law (JD); international law (JD); JD/MBA; JD/MPA; JD/MSCJ; JD/MSF; JD/MSIE. *Accreditation:* ABA. *Program availability:* Part-time, evening/weekend. *Faculty:* 64 full-time (31 women), 51 part-time/adjunct (19 women). *Students:* 730 full-time (341 women), 363 part-time (192 women); includes 198 minority (42 Black or African American, non-Hispanic/Latino; 48 Asian, non-Hispanic/Latino; 85 Hispanic/Latino; 2 Native Hawaiian or other Pacific Islander, non-Hispanic/Latino; 21 Two or more races, non-Hispanic/Latino), 50 international. Average age 27. 1,971 applicants, 65% accepted, 374 enrolled. In 2018, 18 master's, 290 doctorates awarded. *Degree requirements:* For master's, legal writing. *Entrance requirements:* For master's, 2 letters of recommendation, resume, personal statement; for doctorate, LSAT, LSDAS, dean's certification, recommendation. Additional exam requirements/recommendations for international students: Required—TOEFL (minimum score 600 paper-based; 100 iBT). *Application deadline:* For fall admission, 4/1 for domestic and international students. Applications are processed on a rolling basis. Application fee: $60. Electronic applications accepted. *Expenses:* Contact institution. *Financial support:* In 2018–19, 778 students received support, including 1 fellowship (averaging $31,390 per year); career-related internships or fieldwork, Federal Work-Study, institutionally sponsored loans, and scholarships/grants also available. Support available to part-time students. Financial award application deadline: 3/1; financial award applicants required to submit FAFSA. *Faculty research:* Civil law, international law, health/biomedical law, business and finance, intellectual property. *Unit head:* Andrew Perlman, Dean, 617-573-8144, Fax: 617-994-6838, E-mail: lawadmin@suffolk.edu. *Application contact:* Matthew Gavin, Assistant Dean for Admissions and Financial Aid, 617-573-8144, Fax: 617-994-6838, E-mail: lawadm@suffolk.edu.
Website: http://www.suffolk.edu/law/

Université de Sherbrooke, Faculty of Law, Sherbrooke, QC J1K 2R1, Canada. Offers alternative dispute resolution (LL M, Diploma); business law (Diploma); common law (JD); criminal and penal law (Diploma); health law (LL M, Diploma); international law (LL M); law (LL D); legal management (Diploma); notarial law (Diploma); transnational law (Diploma). *Program availability:* Part-time, evening/weekend. *Degree requirements:* For master's, thesis; for Diploma, one foreign language. *Entrance requirements:* For master's and Diploma, LL B. Electronic applications accepted.

University of California, San Francisco, Graduate Division, Program in Health Policy and Law, San Francisco, CA 94143. Offers MS. Program offered in conjunction with University of California, Hastings College of the Law and University of California, Berkeley. *Program availability:* Part-time, online learning. *Degree requirements:* For master's, capstone project, comprehensive written and oral final examination.

University of Houston, University of Houston Law Center, Houston, TX 77204-6060. Offers energy, environment, and natural resources (LL M); health law (LL M); intellectual property and information law (LL M); international law (LL M); law (JD); tax law (LL M); U.S. law (LL M). *Accreditation:* ABA. *Program availability:* Part-time, evening/weekend. *Faculty:* 58 full-time (22 women), 148 part-time/adjunct (45 women). *Students:* 606 full-time (303 women), 98 part-time (41 women); includes 260 minority (43 Black or African American, non-Hispanic/Latino; 6 American Indian or Alaska Native, non-Hispanic/Latino; 72 Asian, non-Hispanic/Latino; 137 Hispanic/Latino; 2 Native Hawaiian or other Pacific Islander, non-Hispanic/Latino), 14 international. Average age 26. 2,596 applicants, 33% accepted, 202 enrolled. In 2018, 75 master's awarded. *Degree requirements:* For master's, thesis optional. *Entrance requirements:* For doctorate, LSAT. Additional exam requirements/recommendations for international students: Required—TOEFL (minimum score 600 paper-based; 100 iBT), IELTS (minimum score 7). *Application deadline:* For fall admission, 2/15 for domestic and international students. Applications are processed on a rolling basis. Application fee: $0. Electronic applications accepted. Application fee is waived when completed online. *Expenses:* Texas Resident $31,090/year; Non Texas Resident $45,640/year. *Financial support:* In 2018–19, 573 students received support, including 47 fellowships (averaging $3,768 per year); research assistantships, career-related internships or fieldwork, Federal Work-Study, scholarships/grants, and tuition waivers (full and partial) also available. Support available to part-time students. Financial award application deadline: 3/15; financial award applicants required to submit FAFSA. *Faculty research:* Health law, international law, tax, environmental law/energy, information law/intellectual property. *Total annual research expenditures:* $336,944. *Unit head:* Leonard M. Baynes, Dean and Professor of Law, 713-743-2100, Fax: 713-743-2122, E-mail: lbaynes@central.uh.edu. *Application contact:* Pilar Mensah, Assistant Dean for Admissions, 713-743-2280, Fax: 713-743-2194, E-mail: lpmensah@central.uh.edu.
Website: http://www.law.uh.edu/

The University of Manchester, School of Law, Manchester, United Kingdom. Offers bioethics and medical jurisprudence (PhD); criminology (M Phil, PhD); law (M Phil, PhD).

University of Pittsburgh, School of Law, Master of Studies in Law Program, Pittsburgh, PA 15260. Offers biomedical and health services research (MSL); business law (MSL), including commercial law, corporate law, general business law, international business, tax law; Constitutional law (MSL); criminal law and justice (MSL); disability law (MSL); elder and estate planning law (MSL); employment and labor law (MSL); energy law (MSL); environmental and real estate law (MSL); family law (MSL); health law (MSL); intellectual property and technology law (MSL); international and human rights law (MSL); jurisprudence (MSL); regulatory law (MSL); self-designed (MSL). *Program availability:* Part-time. *Entrance requirements:* Additional exam requirements/recommendations for international students: Required—TOEFL (minimum score 600 paper-based; 100 iBT), IELTS (minimum score 7). *Faculty research:* Law, health law, business law, contracts, intellectual property, environmental law.

The University of Tulsa, College of Law, Tulsa, OK 74104. Offers American Indian and indigenous law (LL M); American law for foreign lawyers (LL M); energy and natural resources law (LL M); energy law (MJ); health law (Certificate); Indian law (MJ); law (JD); Native American law (Certificate); sustainable energy and resources law (Certificate); JD/MA; JD/MBA; JD/MS. *Accreditation:* ABA. *Program availability:* Part-time. *Faculty:* 27 full-time (15 women), 19 part-time/adjunct (7 women). *Students:* 250 full-time (110 women), 31 part-time (14 women); includes 80 minority (10 Black or African American, non-Hispanic/Latino; 17 American Indian or Alaska Native, non-Hispanic/Latino; 4 Asian, non-Hispanic/Latino; 12 Hispanic/Latino; 37 Two or more races, non-Hispanic/Latino), 5 international. Average age 28. 581 applicants, 42% accepted, 100 enrolled. In 2018, 1 master's, 81 doctorates, 14 Certificates awarded. *Entrance requirements:* For doctorate, LSAT, BS or BA from 4-year regionally-accredited college/university. Additional exam requirements/recommendations for international students: Required—TOEFL (minimum score 570 paper-based; 90 iBT), TOEFL preferred; Recommended—IELTS (minimum score 6.5). *Application deadline:* For fall admission, 7/31 priority date for domestic and international students; for spring admission, 12/1 priority date for domestic students, 12/1 for international students; for summer admission, 4/13 for domestic and international students. Applications are processed on a rolling basis. Application fee: $30. Electronic applications accepted. *Expenses:* $25,254 full-time; $17,490 (8-11 hours); $13,734 (6-7 hours). *Financial support:* In 2018–19, 251 students received support. Scholarships/grants available. Support available to part-time students. Financial award application deadline: 8/1; financial award applicants required to submit FAFSA. *Faculty research:* Criminal law, copyright law, cybersecurity law, energy and natural resources law, international law. *Unit head:* Prof. Lyn Suzanne Entzeroth, Dean, 918-631-2400, Fax: 918-631-3126, E-mail: lyn-entzeroth@utulsa.edu. *Application contact:* April M. Fox, Associate Dean of Admissions and Financial Aid, 918-631-2406, Fax: 918-631-3630, E-mail: april-fox@utulsa.edu.
Website: http://www.utulsa.edu/law/

Widener University, Delaware Law School, Wilmington, DE 19803-0474. Offers corporate and business law (MJ); corporate law and finance (LL M); health law (LL M, MJ, D Law); higher education compliance (MJ); juridical science (SJD); law (JD). *Accreditation:* ABA. *Program availability:* Part-time, 100% online. *Degree requirements:* For doctorate, thesis/dissertation (for some programs). *Entrance requirements:* For master's, GMAT.

Intellectual Property Law

Case Western Reserve University, School of Law, Cleveland, OH 44106. Offers financial integrity (MA); health law (SJD); intellectual property law (LL M, ML); international business law (LL M, ML); international criminal law (LL M); law (JD, SJD); patent practice (MA); U.S. and global legal studies (LL M, ML); JD/MA; JD/MBA; JD/MD; JD/MNM; JD/MPH; JD/MS; JD/MSSA. *Accreditation:* ABA. *Faculty:* 47 full-time (16 women), 63 part-time/adjunct (16 women). *Students:* 433 full-time (238 women); includes 91 minority (37 Black or African American, non-Hispanic/Latino; 1 American Indian or Alaska Native, non-Hispanic/Latino; 19 Asian, non-Hispanic/Latino; 26 Hispanic/Latino; 8 Two or more races, non-Hispanic/Latino), 30 international. Average age 24. 1,415 applicants, 50% accepted, 157 enrolled. In 2018, 126 master's awarded. *Entrance requirements:* For doctorate, LSAT, LSDAS. Additional exam requirements/recommendations for international students: Required—TOEFL. *Application deadline:* For fall admission, 4/1 priority date for domestic and international students. Applications are processed on a rolling basis. Application fee: $40. Electronic applications accepted. Application fee is waived when completed online. *Expenses:* Contact institution. *Financial support:* In 2018–19, 394 students received support. Career-related internships or fieldwork, Federal Work-Study, institutionally sponsored loans, and scholarships/grants available. Financial award application deadline: 5/1; financial award applicants required to submit FAFSA. *Unit head:* Jessica Berg, Co-Dean, 216-368-3283. *Application contact:* Kelli Curtis, Associate Dean for Admissions, 216-368-3600, Fax: 216-368-0185, E-mail: lawadmissions@case.edu.
Website: http://law.case.edu/

DePaul University, College of Law, Chicago, IL 60604. Offers business law and taxation (MJ); criminal law (MJ); health and intellectual property law (MJ); health care compliance (MJ); health law (LL M, MJ); intellectual property law (LL M); international and comparative law (MJ); international law (LL M); law (JD); public interest law (MJ); taxation (LL M); U.S. legal studies (LL M); JD/LL M; JD/MA; JD/MBA; JD/MS. *Accreditation:* ABA. *Program availability:* Part-time, evening/weekend. *Entrance requirements:* For doctorate, LSAT, LSAC applicant evaluation/letter of recommendation, personal statement, resume. Additional exam requirements/recommendations for international students: Required—TOEFL (minimum score 577 paper-based; 90 iBT), IELTS (minimum score 6.5). Electronic applications accepted. *Expenses:* Contact institution.

Drexel University, Thomas R. Kline School of Law, Philadelphia, PA 19104-2875. Offers business and entrepreneurship law (JD); criminal law (MLS, JD); cybersecurity and information privacy compliance (MLS); entrepreneurship and law (MLS); financial regulatory compliance (MLS); health care compliance (MLS); health law (JD); higher education compliance (MLS); human resources compliance (MLS); intellectual property law (JD); NCAA compliance and sports law (MLS). *Accreditation:* ABA.

Fordham University, School of Law, New York, NY 10023. Offers banking, corporate and finance law (LL M); corporate compliance (MSL); fashion law (MSL); intellectual property and information law (LL M); international business and trade law (LL M); law (JD); JD/MA; JD/MBA; JD/MSW. *Accreditation:* ABA. *Program availability:* Part-time, evening/weekend. *Entrance requirements:* For doctorate, LSAT. Additional exam requirements/recommendations for international students: Required—TOEFL. Electronic applications accepted. *Expenses:* Contact institution. *Faculty research:* Intellectual property, business law, international law.

Golden Gate University, School of Law, San Francisco, CA 94105-2968. Offers environmental law (LL M); estate planning (LL M); intellectual property law (LL M); international legal studies (LL M, SJD); law (JD); taxation law (LL M); U.S. legal studies (LL M); JD/MBA. *Accreditation:* ABA. *Program availability:* Part-time, evening/weekend. *Degree requirements:* For doctorate, thesis/dissertation (for some programs). *Entrance requirements:* For doctorate, LSAT (for JD). Additional exam requirements/recommendations for international students: Required—TOEFL (minimum score 600 paper-based). Electronic applications accepted. *Expenses:* Contact institution. *Faculty research:* International law, intellectual property law, environmental law, real estate, civil rights.

Hofstra University, Maurice A. Deane School of Law, Hempstead, NY 11549. Offers alternative dispute resolution (JD); American legal studies (LL M); business law honors (JD); clinical bioethics (Certificate); corporate compliance (JD); criminal law and procedure (JD); family law (LL M, JD); health law (JD); health law and policy (LL M, MA); intellectual property law honors (JD); international law honors (JD); JD/MBA; JD/MPH. *Accreditation:* ABA. *Program availability:* Part-time, 100% online. *Faculty:* 41 full-time (21 women), 78 part-time/adjunct (24 women). *Students:* 712 full-time (374 women), 137 part-time (88 women); includes 181 minority (53 Black or African American, non-Hispanic/Latino; 2 American Indian or Alaska Native, non-Hispanic/Latino; 34 Asian, non-Hispanic/Latino; 82 Hispanic/Latino; 7 Native Hawaiian or other Pacific Islander, non-Hispanic/Latino; 3 Two or more races, non-Hispanic/Latino), 13 international. Average age 27. 3,104 applicants, 50% accepted, 301 enrolled. In 2018, 37 master's, 234 doctorates awarded. *Entrance requirements:* For doctorate, LSAT, letter of recommendation, personal statement, undergraduate transcripts; for Certificate, 2 letters of recommendation, JD or LLB, personal statement, law school transcripts. Additional exam requirements/recommendations for international students: Recommended—TOEFL (minimum score 600 paper-based; 100 iBT). *Application deadline:* For fall admission, 4/15 priority date for domestic and international students. Applications are processed on a rolling basis. Application fee: $0. Electronic applications accepted. *Expenses:* $29,607 per term for Full-time (tuition and fees). *Financial support:* In 2018–19, 578 students received support, including 565 fellowships with full and partial tuition reimbursements available (averaging $32,425 per year); research assistantships with full and partial tuition reimbursements available, career-related internships or fieldwork, Federal Work-Study, institutionally sponsored loans, scholarships/grants, tuition waivers (full and partial), unspecified assistantships, and scholarships and endowed scholarships also available. Support available to part-time students. Financial award applicants required to submit FAFSA. *Faculty research:* Family law; international law; constitutional law; legal ethics; health law. *Unit head:* Gail Prudenti, Dean, 516-463-4068, E-mail: gail.prudenti@hofstra.edu. *Application contact:* Sunil Samuel, Assistant Vice President of Admissions, 516-463-4723, Fax: 516-463-4664.
Website: http://law.hofstra.edu/

Indiana University–Purdue University Indianapolis, Robert H. McKinney School of Law, Indianapolis, IN 46202. Offers advocacy skills (Certificate); American law for foreign lawyers (LL M); civil and human rights (Certificate); corporate and commercial law (LL M, Certificate); criminal law (Certificate); environmental and natural resources (Certificate); health law (Certificate); health law, policy and bioethics (LL M); intellectual property law (LL M, Certificate); international and comparative law (LL M, Certificate); international human rights law (LL M); law (MJ, JD, SJD); JD/M Phil; JD/MBA; JD/MD; JD/MHA; JD/MLS; JD/MPA; JD/MPH; JD/MSW. *Accreditation:* ABA. *Program availability:* Part-time. *Entrance requirements:* For doctorate, LSAT. Additional exam requirements/recommendations for international students: Required—TOEFL (minimum score 79 iBT), IELTS (minimum score 6.5). Electronic applications accepted. *Expenses:* Contact institution.

Michigan State University College of Law, Graduate and Professional Programs, East Lansing, MI 48824-1300. Offers American legal system (LL M, MJ); global food law (LL M, MJ); intellectual property law (LL M, MJ); law (JD); legal studies (MLS). *Accreditation:* ABA. *Program availability:* Part-time. *Entrance requirements:* For doctorate, LSAT. Additional exam requirements/recommendations for international students: Required—TOEFL (minimum score 600 paper-based), IELTS. Electronic applications accepted. *Expenses: Tuition:* Full-time $44,200. *Required fees:* $37. *Faculty research:* International, constitutional, health, tax and environmental law; intellectual property, trial practice, corporate law.

Montclair State University, The Graduate School, College of Humanities and Social Sciences, MA Program in Law and Governance, Montclair, NJ 07043-1624. Offers conflict management and peace studies (MA); governance, compliance and regulation (MA); intellectual property (MA); law and governance (MA); legal management (MA). *Program availability:* Part-time, evening/weekend. *Degree requirements:* For master's, thesis or comprehensive exam. *Entrance requirements:* For master's, GRE General Test, minimum cumulative GPA of 2.75 for undergraduate work, 2 letters of recommendation, essay. Additional exam requirements/recommendations for international students: Required—TOEFL (minimum score 83 iBT) or IELTS (minimum score 6.5). Electronic applications accepted.

Santa Clara University, School of Law, Santa Clara, CA 95053. Offers high tech law (Certificate); intellectual property (LL M); international and comparative law (LL M); international law (Certificate); law (JD); public interest and social justice law (Certificate); United States law (LL M); JD/MBA; JD/MSIS. *Accreditation:* ABA. *Program availability:* Part-time, online learning. *Faculty:* 47 full-time (23 women), 52 part-time/adjunct (28 women). *Students:* 681 full-time (389 women), 29 part-time (16 women); includes 310 minority (22 Black or African American, non-Hispanic/Latino; 128 Asian, non-Hispanic/Latino; 152 Hispanic/Latino; 4 Native Hawaiian or other Pacific Islander, non-Hispanic/Latino; 4 Two or more races, non-Hispanic/Latino), 38 international. Average age 27. 2,126 applicants, 57% accepted, 246 enrolled. In 2018, 54 master's, 217 doctorates awarded. *Entrance requirements:* For master's, LSAT, JD-CAS, personal statement. Additional exam requirements/recommendations for international students: Required—TOEFL. Application fee: $75 ($0 for international students). Electronic applications accepted. *Financial support:* Fellowships, Federal Work-Study, and scholarships/grants available. Support available to part-time students. Financial award applicants required to submit FAFSA. *Unit head:* Anna Han, Interim Dean, 408-554-4362, Fax: 408-554-5095,

E-mail: lkloppenberg@scu.edu. *Application contact:* Anna Han, Interim Dean, 408-554-4362, Fax: 408-554-5095, E-mail: lkloppenberg@scu.edu.
Website: http://law.scu.edu/

Suffolk University, Law School, Boston, MA 02108. Offers business law and financial services (JD); civil litigation (JD); global law and technology (LL M); health and biomedical law (JD); intellectual property law (JD); international law (JD); JD/MBA; JD/MPA; JD/MSCJ; JD/MSF; JD/MSIE. *Accreditation:* ABA. *Program availability:* Part-time, evening/weekend. *Faculty:* 64 full-time (31 women), 51 part-time/adjunct (19 women). *Students:* 730 full-time (341 women), 363 part-time (192 women); includes 198 minority (42 Black or African American, non-Hispanic/Latino; 48 Asian, non-Hispanic/Latino; 85 Hispanic/Latino; 2 Native Hawaiian or other Pacific Islander, non-Hispanic/Latino; 21 Two or more races, non-Hispanic/Latino), 50 international. Average age 27. 1,971 applicants, 65% accepted, 374 enrolled. In 2018, 18 master's, 290 doctorates awarded. *Degree requirements:* For master's, legal writing. *Entrance requirements:* For master's, 2 letters of recommendation, resume, personal statement; for doctorate, LSAT, LSDAS, dean's certification, recommendation. Additional exam requirements/recommendations for international students: Required—TOEFL (minimum score 600 paper-based; 100 iBT). *Application deadline:* For fall admission, 4/1 for domestic and international students. Applications are processed on a rolling basis. Application fee: $60. Electronic applications accepted. *Expenses:* Contact institution. *Financial support:* In 2018–19, 778 students received support, including 1 fellowship (averaging $31,390 per year); career-related internships or fieldwork, Federal Work-Study, institutionally sponsored loans, and scholarships/grants also available. Support available to part-time students. Financial award application deadline: 3/1; financial award applicants required to submit FAFSA. *Faculty research:* Civil law, international law, health/biomedical law, business and finance, intellectual property. *Unit head:* Andrew Perlman, Dean, 617-573-8144, Fax: 617-994-6838, E-mail: lawadmin@suffolk.edu. *Application contact:* Matthew Gavin, Assistant Dean for Admissions and Financial Aid, 617-573-8144, Fax: 617-994-6838, E-mail: lawadm@suffolk.edu.
Website: http://www.suffolk.edu/law/

Texas A&M University, School of Law, College Station, TX 77843. Offers intellectual property (M Jur); jurisprudence (M Jur); law (JD). *Accreditation:* ABA. *Faculty:* 82. *Students:* 465 full-time (251 women), 112 part-time (39 women); includes 174 minority (38 Black or African American, non-Hispanic/Latino; 5 American Indian or Alaska Native, non-Hispanic/Latino; 14 Asian, non-Hispanic/Latino; 112 Hispanic/Latino; 5 Two or more races, non-Hispanic/Latino), 5 international. Average age 30. 463 applicants, 100% accepted, 233 enrolled. In 2018, 1 master's awarded. *Entrance requirements:* For doctorate, LSAT, personal statement, resume, all post-secondary transcripts, 2-4 letters of recommendation and up to 2 LSAC evaluations, CAS Report. *Application deadline:* For fall admission, 7/1 for domestic students. Applications are processed on a rolling basis. Application fee: $55. *Expenses:* Contact institution. *Financial support:* In 2018–19, 447 students received support, including 4 fellowships with tuition reimbursements available (averaging $20,207 per year); career-related internships or fieldwork, institutionally sponsored loans, scholarships/grants, traineeships, health care benefits, and tuition waivers (full and partial) also available. Support available to part-time students. Financial award applicants required to submit FAFSA. *Unit head:* Dr. Andrew P. Morriss, Dean, 817-212-4139, Fax: 817-212-4139, E-mail: amorriss@law.tamu.edu. *Application contact:* Law School Admissions, 817-212-4040, E-mail: law-admissions@law.tamu.edu.
Website: http://law.tamu.edu/

University of Baltimore, School of Law, Baltimore, MD 21201. Offers business law (JD); criminal practice (JD); estate planning (JD); family law (JD); intellectual property (JD); international law (JD); law (JD); law of the United States (LL M); litigation and advocacy (JD); public service (JD); real estate practice (JD); taxation (LL M); JD/LL M; JD/MBA; JD/MPA; JD/MS; JD/PhD. JD/MS offered jointly with Division of Criminology, Criminal Justice, and Social Policy; JD/PhD with University of Maryland, Baltimore. *Accreditation:* ABA. *Program availability:* Part-time, evening/weekend. *Entrance requirements:* For doctorate, LSAT. Additional exam requirements/recommendations for international students: Required—TOEFL (for LL M in law of the United States). Electronic applications accepted. *Expenses:* Contact institution. *Faculty research:* Plain view doctrine, statute of limitations, bankruptcy, family law, international and comparative law, Constitutional law.

University of Houston, University of Houston Law Center, Houston, TX 77204-6060. Offers energy, environment, and natural resources (LL M); health law (LL M); intellectual property and information law (LL M); international law (LL M); law (JD); tax law (LL M); U.S. law (LL M). *Accreditation:* ABA. *Program availability:* Part-time, evening/weekend. *Faculty:* 58 full-time (22 women), 148 part-time/adjunct (45 women). *Students:* 606 full-time (303 women), 98 part-time (41 women); includes 260 minority (43 Black or African American, non-Hispanic/Latino; 6 American Indian or Alaska Native, non-Hispanic/Latino; 72 Asian, non-Hispanic/Latino; 137 Hispanic/Latino; 2 Native Hawaiian or other Pacific Islander, non-Hispanic/Latino), 14 international. Average age 26. 2,596 applicants, 33% accepted, 202 enrolled. In 2018, 75 master's awarded. *Degree requirements:* For master's, thesis optional. *Entrance requirements:* For doctorate, LSAT. Additional exam requirements/recommendations for international students: Required—TOEFL (minimum score 600 paper-based; 100 iBT), IELTS (minimum score 7). *Application deadline:* For fall admission, 2/15 for domestic and international students. Applications are processed on a rolling basis. Application fee: $0. Electronic applications accepted. Application fee is waived when completed online. *Expenses:* Texas Resident $31,090/year; Non Texas Resident $45,640/year. *Financial support:* In 2018–19, 573 students received support, including 47 fellowships (averaging $3,768 per year); research assistantships, career-related internships or fieldwork, Federal Work-Study, scholarships/grants, and tuition waivers (full and partial) also available. Support available to part-time students. Financial award application deadline: 3/15; financial award applicants required to submit FAFSA. *Faculty research:* Health law, international law, tax, environmental law/energy, information law/intellectual property. *Total annual research expenditures:* $336,944. *Unit head:* Leonard M. Baynes, Dean and Professor of Law, 713-743-2100, Fax: 713-743-2122, E-mail: lbaynes@central.uh.edu. *Application contact:* Pilar Mensah, Assistant Dean for Admissions, 713-743-2280, Fax: 713-743-2194, E-mail: lpmensah@central.uh.edu.
Website: http://www.law.uh.edu/

University of New Hampshire, School of Law, Concord, NH 03301. Offers business law (JD); commerce and technology (LL M, MCT, Diploma); criminal law (JD); intellectual property (LL M, MIP, JD, Diploma), including patent law (JD), trademarks and copyright (JD); international criminal law and justice (LL M, MICLJ); litigation (JD); public interest and social justice (JD); sports and entertainment law (JD); JD/LL M; JD/MBA; JD/MIP; JD/MPP; JD/MSW. *Accreditation:* ABA. *Program availability:* Part-time, 100% online, limited residential. *Degree requirements:* For doctorate, comprehensive exam. *Entrance requirements:* For doctorate, LSAT. Additional exam requirements/recommendations for international students: Required—TOEFL (minimum score 600 paper-based; 100 iBT), minimum TOEFL iBT score of 80 (for master's programs). Electronic applications accepted. *Expenses:* Contact institution. *Faculty research:* Intellectual property, health law and policy, sports and entertainment law, patent law, trademarks and copyright.

University of Pittsburgh, School of Law, Master of Studies in Law Program, Pittsburgh, PA 15260. Offers biomedical and health services research (MSL); business law (MSL), including commercial law, corporate law, general business law, international business, tax law; Constitutional law (MSL); criminal law and justice (MSL); disability law (MSL); elder and estate planning law (MSL); employment and labor law (MSL); energy law (MSL); environmental and real estate law (MSL); family law (MSL); health law (MSL); intellectual property and technology law (MSL); international and human rights law (MSL); jurisprudence (MSL); regulatory law (MSL); self-designed (MSL). *Program availability:* Part-time. *Entrance requirements:* Additional exam requirements/recommendations for international students: Required—TOEFL (minimum score 600 paper-based; 100 iBT), IELTS (minimum score 7). *Faculty research:* Law, health law, business law, contracts, intellectual property, environmental law.

University of San Francisco, School of Law, Master of Law Programs, San Francisco, CA 94117. Offers intellectual property and technology law (LL M); international transactions and comparative law (LL M). *Program availability:* Part-time. *Students:* 11 full-time (5 women), 3 part-time (1 woman); includes 3 minority (2 Hispanic/Latino; 1 Two or more races, non-Hispanic/Latino), 10 international. Average age 32. 60 applicants, 92% accepted, 13 enrolled. In 2018, 14 master's awarded. *Entrance requirements:* For master's, law degree from U.S. or foreign school (intellectual property and technology law); law degree from foreign school (international transactions and comparative law). Additional exam requirements/recommendations for international students: Required—TOEFL (minimum score 90 paper-based; 90 iBT). *Application deadline:* For fall admission, 2/15 for domestic students. Applications are processed on a rolling basis. Application fee: $70. Electronic applications accepted. *Financial support:* In 2018–19, 28 students received support. Scholarships/grants available. Financial award applicants required to submit FAFSA. *Unit head:* Olivera Jovanovic, Director, 415-422-6900. *Application contact:* Margaret Mullane, Assistant Director, 415-422-6658, E-mail: masterlaws@usfca.edu.
Website: http://www.usfca.edu/law/llm/

University of Washington, Graduate School, School of Law, Seattle, WA 98195-3020. Offers Asian law (LL M, PhD); intellectual property law and policy (LL M); law (JD); law of sustainable international development (LL M); taxation (LL M); JD/LL M; JD/MA; JD/MAIS; JD/MBA; JD/MPA; JD/MS; JD/PhD. *Accreditation:* ABA. *Degree requirements:* For master's, thesis; for doctorate, thesis/dissertation (for some programs). *Entrance requirements:* For master's, language proficiency (LL M in Asian law); for doctorate, LSAT (for JD). Additional exam requirements/recommendations for international students: Required—TOEFL. *Expenses:* Contact institution. *Faculty research:* Asian, international and comparative law, intellectual property law, health law, environmental law, taxation.

Western Michigan University Thomas M. Cooley Law School, Graduate Programs, Lansing, MI 48901-3038. Offers administrative law (public law) (JD); business transactions (JD); Canadian law practice (JD); corporate law and finance (LL M); environmental law (public law) (JD); general practice (JD), including solo and small firm; general studies (LL M); homeland and national security law (LL M); insurance law (LL M); intellectual property (JD); intellectual property law (LL M); international law (JD); litigation (JD); taxation (LL M); U.S. legal studies for foreign attorneys (LL M); JD/LL M; JD/MBA; JD/MHA; JD/MPA; JD/MSW. *Accreditation:* ABA. *Program availability:* Part-time, evening/weekend, 100% online, blended/hybrid learning. *Degree requirements:* For master's, thesis (for some programs); for doctorate, minimum of 3 credits of clinical experience. *Entrance requirements:* For master's, JD or LL B; for doctorate, LSAT. Additional exam requirements/recommendations for international students: Required—TOEFL (for U.S. legal studies for foreign attorneys LL M program); Recommended—TOEFL. Electronic applications accepted. *Expenses:* Contact institution. *Faculty research:* Wrongful convictions, civil rights, environmental law, litigation techniques, data mining, intellectual property, practical and skills-based legal education.

Yeshiva University, Benjamin N. Cardozo School of Law, New York, NY 10003-4301. Offers comparative legal thought (LL M); dispute resolution and advocacy (LL M); general studies (LL M); intellectual property law (LL M); law (JD). Joint JD/MSW (Masters in Social Work) with Benjamin N. Cardozo School of Law & the Wurzweiler School of Social Work; joint JD/MBE (Masters in Bioethics) with Benjamin N. Cardozo School of Law and the Albert Einstein College of Medicine. *Accreditation:* ABA. *Program availability:* 100% online. *Faculty:* 61 full-time (25 women), 111 part-time/adjunct (46 women). *Students:* 960 full-time (537 women), 85 part-time (46 women); includes 229 minority (38 Black or African American, non-Hispanic/Latino; 83 Asian, non-Hispanic/Latino; 83 Hispanic/Latino; 25 Two or more races, non-Hispanic/Latino), 86 international. 2,584 applicants, 49% accepted, 365 enrolled. In 2018, 75 master's, 282 doctorates awarded. *Entrance requirements:* For master's, LLM Program requirements: personal statement, one letter of recommendation, English language proficiency score, Curriculum Vitae (CV), and an evaluation of student's transcripts; for doctorate, LSAT, Two letters of recommendation. Additional exam requirements/recommendations for international students: Required—TOEFL (minimum score 100 iBT), Cardozo accepts either a TOEFL or an IELTS score as a part of the English language requirement. Recommended—IELTS (minimum score 7). *Application deadline:* For fall admission, 4/1 priority date for domestic students, 6/15 priority date for international students; for spring admission, 12/1 for domestic students, 12/1 priority date for international students. Applications are processed on a rolling basis. Application fee: $0 ($50 for international students). Electronic applications accepted. *Expenses:* $29,970 per semester full-time; $19,398 per semester part-time; $2,671 per credit (for less than 7 credits per semester). *Financial support:* In 2018–19, 831 students received support, including 114 research assistantships (averaging $1,512 per year); career-related internships or fieldwork, Federal Work-Study, institutionally sponsored loans, scholarships/grants, health care benefits, and tuition waivers (full and partial) also available. Support available to part-time students. Financial award application deadline: 3/1; financial award applicants required to submit FAFSA. *Faculty research:* Corporate and commercial law, intellectual property law, criminal law and litigation, constitutional law, legal theory and jurisprudence. *Unit head:* Dean Melanie Leslie, Dean and Samuel Belkin Professor of Law, 212-790-0310, Fax: 212-790-0203, E-mail: DeansOfficeCardozo@yu.edu. *Application contact:* David G. Martinidez, Dean of Admissions, 212-790-0274, Fax: 212-790-0482, E-mail: lawinfo@yu.edu.
Website: http://www.cardozo.yu.edu/

Law

Abraham Lincoln University, School of Law, Los Angeles, CA 90010. Offers JD.

Albany Law School, Professional Program, Albany, NY 12208-3494. Offers LL M, JD, JD/MBA, JD/MPA, JD/MRP, JD/MS, JD/MSW. JD/MBA offered jointly with The College of Saint Rose, The Sage Colleges, Union Graduate College, and University at Albany, State University of New York; JD/MPA, JD/MRP, and JD/MSW offered jointly with University at Albany, State University of New York. *Accreditation:* ABA. *Program availability:* Part-time. *Entrance requirements:* For master's, GRE or LSAT; for doctorate, LSAT. Additional exam requirements/recommendations for international students: Recommended—TOEFL (minimum score 600 paper-based). *Expenses:* Contact institution. *Faculty research:* Federal tax, Constitutional law, secured transactions, international law, American politics.

Alliant International University–San Francisco, San Francisco Law School, JD Program, San Francisco, CA 94133. Offers JD. *Program availability:* Part-time, evening/weekend. *Entrance requirements:* For doctorate, LSAT, personal statement, interview. Electronic applications accepted.

American University, Washington College of Law, Washington, DC 20016-8181. Offers LL M, JD, SJD, JD/LL M, JD/MA, JD/MBA, JD/MPA, JD/MPP, JD/MS, LL M/MBA, LL M/MIS, LL M/MPA, LL M/MPP. *Accreditation:* ABA. *Program availability:* Part-time, evening/weekend, 100% online, blended/hybrid learning. *Faculty:* 72 full-time (39 women), 112 part-time/adjunct (37 women). *Students:* 1,108 full-time (700 women), 349 part-time (205 women); includes 489 minority (113 Black or African American, non-Hispanic/Latino; 2 American Indian or Alaska Native, non-Hispanic/Latino; 94 Asian, non-Hispanic/Latino; 209 Hispanic/Latino; 1 Native Hawaiian or other Pacific Islander, non-Hispanic/Latino; 70 Two or more races, non-Hispanic/Latino), 109 international. Average age 28. 5,120 applicants, 52% accepted, 561 enrolled. In 2018, 115 master's, 376 doctorates awarded. *Entrance requirements:* For master's, Please visit the website: https://www.wcl.american.edu/academics/degrees/, statement of purpose, 2 letters of recommendation, transcripts, resume; for doctorate, LSAT, transcript, letters of recommendation. Additional exam requirements/recommendations for international students: Required—TOEFL. Application fee: $70. Electronic applications accepted. *Expenses:* Contact institution. *Financial support:* Institutionally sponsored loans and scholarships/grants available. Financial award applicants required to submit FAFSA. *Unit head:* Camille A. Nelson, Dean, 202-274 4000. *Application contact:* Akira Shiroma, Asst. Dean of Admissions, 202-274-4101.
Website: http://www.wcl.american.edu/

The American University in Cairo, School of Global Affairs and Public Policy, Cairo, Egypt. Offers gender and women's studies (MA); global affairs (MGA); international and comparative law (LL M); international human rights law (MA); journalism and mass communication (MA); Middle East studies (MA); migration and refugee studies (MA, Diploma); public administration (MPA); public policy (MPP); television and digital journalism (MA). *Program availability:* Part-time, evening/weekend. *Degree requirements:* For master's, comprehensive exam (for some programs), thesis (for some programs). *Entrance requirements:* Additional exam requirements/recommendations for international students: Required—TOEFL (minimum score 450 paper-based; 45 iBT), IELTS (minimum score 5). Electronic applications accepted. *Expenses:* Contact institution. *Faculty research:* Law, media and journalism; public policy and public administration; gender studies; Middle East Studies; global affairs; refugees studies.

American University of Armenia, Graduate Programs, Yerevan, Armenia. Offers business administration (MBA); computer and information science (MS), including business management, design and manufacturing, energy (ME, MS), industrial engineering and systems management; economics (MS); industrial engineering and systems management (ME), including business, computer aided design/manufacturing, energy (ME, MS), information technology; law (LL M); political science and international affairs (MPSIA); public health (MPH); teaching English as a foreign language (MA). *Program availability:* Part-time, evening/weekend. *Degree requirements:* For master's, thesis (for some programs), capstone/project. *Entrance requirements:* For master's, GRE, GMAT, or LSAT. Additional exam requirements/recommendations for international students: Recommended—TOEFL (minimum score 79 iBT), IELTS (minimum score 6.5). *Faculty research:* Microfinance, finance (rural/development, international, corporate), firm life cycle theory, TESOL, language proficiency testing, public policy, administrative law, economic development, cryptography, artificial intelligence, energy efficiency/renewable energy, computer-aided design/manufacturing, health financing, tuberculosis control, mother/child health, preventive ophthalmology, post-earthquake psychopathological investigations, tobacco control, environmental health risk assessments.

The American University of Paris, Graduate Programs, Paris, France. Offers cross-cultural and sustainable business management (MA); cultural translation (MA); global communications (MA); global communications and civil society (MA); international affairs (MA); international affairs, conflict resolution and civil society development (MA); Middle East and Islamic studies (MA); Middle East and Islamic studies and international affairs (MA); public policy and international affairs (MA); public policy and international law (MA). *Degree requirements:* For master's, thesis (for some programs). *Entrance requirements:* For master's, minimum undergraduate GPA of 3.0. Additional exam requirements/recommendations for international students: Recommended—TOEFL, IELTS. Electronic applications accepted.

Appalachian School of Law, Professional Program in Law, Grundy, VA 24614. Offers JD. *Accreditation:* ABA. *Faculty:* 12 full-time (2 women), 9 part-time/adjunct (4 women). *Students:* 146 full-time (75 women); includes 39 minority (18 Black or African American, non-Hispanic/Latino; 7 American Indian or Alaska Native, non-Hispanic/Latino; 8 Asian, non-Hispanic/Latino; 6 Hispanic/Latino). 409 applicants, 63% accepted, 61 enrolled. In 2018, 34 doctorates awarded. *Entrance requirements:* For doctorate, LSAT, bachelor's degree from accredited institution, personal statement, letters of recommendation. *Application deadline:* For fall admission, 7/25 for domestic students; for winter admission, 12/27 for domestic students. Applications are processed on a rolling basis. Application fee: $0. Electronic applications accepted. Application fee is waived when completed online. *Expenses:* Contact institution. *Financial support:* In 2018–19, 83 students received support. Research assistantships, teaching assistantships, career-related internships or fieldwork, Federal Work-Study, institutionally sponsored loans, scholarships/grants, and tuition waivers (full and partial) available. Financial award application deadline: 7/25; financial award applicants required to submit FAFSA. *Faculty research:* Natural resources, criminal law, Constitutional law, professional ethics, intellectual property. *Unit head:* Sandra Keen McGlothlin, Dean, 276-935-4349 Ext. 1265, Fax: 276-935-8261, E-mail: smcglothlin@asl.edu. *Application contact:* Kelsea Wagner, Director of Admissions, 276-244-1245, Fax: 276-935-8496, E-mail: kwagner@asl.edu.
Website: http://www.asl.edu/jd-curriculum-overview/

Arizona State University at the Tempe campus, Sandra Day O'Connor College of Law, Phoenix, AZ 85287-7906. Offers biotechnology and genomics (LL M); law (JD); legal studies (MLS); patent practice (MLS); sports law and business (MSLB); tribal policy, law and government (LL M); JD/MBA; JD/MD; JD/MSW; JD/PhD. JD/MD offered jointly with Mayo Medical School. *Accreditation:* ABA. *Program availability:* 100% online. *Faculty:* 62 full-time (26 women), 146 part-time/adjunct (40 women). *Students:* 812 full-time (372 women); includes 201 minority (16 Black or African American, non-Hispanic/Latino; 15 American Indian or Alaska Native, non-Hispanic/Latino; 37 Asian, non-Hispanic/Latino; 97 Hispanic/Latino; 3 Native Hawaiian or other Pacific Islander, non-Hispanic/Latino; 33 Two or more races, non-Hispanic/Latino), 16 international. Average age 28. 3,363 applicants, 34% accepted, 271 enrolled. In 2018, 131 master's, 276 doctorates awarded. *Entrance requirements:* For master's, bachelor's degree and JD (for LL M); for doctorate, LSAT, bachelor's degree. Additional exam requirements/recommendations for international students: Required—TOEFL (minimum score 550 paper-based; 80 iBT). *Application deadline:* For fall admission, 3/1 priority date for domestic and international students. Applications are processed on a rolling basis. Application fee: $0. Electronic applications accepted. *Expenses:* $27,584 resident tuition and fees (for JD), $45,940 non-resident tuition and fees (for JD). *Financial support:* In 2018–19, 579 students received support. Institutionally sponsored loans and scholarships/grants available. Financial award application deadline: 3/15; financial award applicants required to submit FAFSA. *Faculty research:* Emerging technologies and the law, Indian law, international law, intellectual property, health law, sports law and business. *Total annual research expenditures:* $2.8 million. *Unit head:* Douglas Sylvester, Dean/Professor, 480-965-6188, Fax: 480-965-6521, E-mail: douglas.sylvester@asu.edu. *Application contact:* Chitra Damania, Director, 480-965-1474, Fax: 480-727-7930, E-mail: law.admissions@asu.edu.
Website: http://www.law.asu.edu/

Atlanta's John Marshall Law School, JD and LL M Programs, Atlanta, GA 30309. Offers American legal studies (LL M); employment law (LL M); law (JD). *Accreditation:* ABA. *Program availability:* Part-time, evening/weekend, online learning. *Entrance requirements:* For master's, JD from accredited law school or bar admission; for doctorate, LSAT, LSDAS report, personal statement, two letters of reference. Additional exam requirements/recommendations for international students: Required—TOEFL. Electronic applications accepted. *Faculty research:* Tort reform, terrorism and the use of the U.S. military, Title VII's referral and deferral scheme, public utilities, eminent domain and land use regulations, recent films and their visions of law in Western society.

Ave Maria School of Law, Professional Program, Naples, FL 34119. Offers law (JD). *Accreditation:* ABA. *Faculty:* 22 full-time (7 women), 18 part-time/adjunct (7 women). *Students:* 241 full-time (132 women); includes 67 minority (13 Black or African American, non-Hispanic/Latino; 1 American Indian or Alaska Native, non-Hispanic/Latino; 1 Asian, non-Hispanic/Latino; 52 Hispanic/Latino), 7 international. Average age 26. 568 applicants, 55% accepted, 97 enrolled. In 2018, 81 doctorates awarded. *Entrance requirements:* For doctorate, LSAT, 2 letters of recommendation, LSDAS, personal statement. Additional exam requirements/recommendations for international students: Required—TOEFL (minimum score 600 paper-based). *Application deadline:* For fall admission, 7/15 priority date for domestic and international students. Applications are processed on a rolling basis. Application fee: $0. Electronic applications accepted. *Expenses:* Tuition: Full-time $39,450. *Required fees:* $2256. *Financial support:* In 2018–19, 182 students received support. Research assistantships, career-related internships or fieldwork, Federal Work-Study, and scholarships/grants available. Financial award application deadline: 6/30; financial award applicants required to submit FAFSA. *Faculty research:* International law, immigration, religious freedom, litigation, military law. *Unit head:* Kevin Cieply, President/Dean, 239-687-5300, E-mail: kcieply@avemarialaw.edu. *Application contact:* Claire T. O'Keefe, Associate Dean of Admissions and Student Engagement, 239-687-5423, Fax: 239-352-2890, E-mail: info@avemarialaw.edu.
Website: http://www.avemarialaw.edu/

Barry University, Dwayne O. Andreas School of Law, Orlando, FL 32807. Offers JD, JD/MS. *Accreditation:* ABA. *Entrance requirements:* For doctorate, LSAT.

Baylor University, School of Law, Waco, TX 76798-7288. Offers JD, JD/M Div, JD/M Tax, JD/MBA, JD/MPPA. *Accreditation:* ABA. *Faculty:* 32 full-time (11 women), 55 part-time/adjunct (14 women). *Students:* 431 full-time (203 women); includes 108 minority (11 Black or African American, non-Hispanic/Latino; 8 American Indian or Alaska Native, non-Hispanic/Latino; 20 Asian, non-Hispanic/Latino; 58 Hispanic/Latino; 1 Native Hawaiian or other Pacific Islander, non-Hispanic/Latino; 10 Two or more races, non-Hispanic/Latino), 3 international. Average age 24. 1,559 applicants, 50% accepted, 86 enrolled. In 2018, 118 doctorates awarded. *Entrance requirements:* For doctorate, LSAT. Additional exam requirements/recommendations for international students: Recommended—TOEFL. *Application deadline:* For fall admission, 3/16 for domestic and international students; for spring admission, 11/15 for domestic and international students; for summer admission, 3/16 for domestic and international students. Applications are processed on a rolling basis. Application fee: $0. Electronic applications accepted. Application fee is waived when completed online. *Expenses:* $60,049.5 per year. *Financial support:* In 2018–19, 325 students received support. Federal Work-Study and scholarships/grants available. Financial award application deadline: 2/1; financial award applicants required to submit FAFSA. *Unit head:* Bradley J. B. Toben, Dean, 254-710-1911, Fax: 254-710-2316. *Application contact:* Jenny Branson, Assistant Dean of Admissions and Financial Aid, 254-710-1911, Fax: 254-710-2316, E-mail: jenny_branson@baylor.edu.
Website: http://www.baylor.edu/law

Belmont University, College of Law, Nashville, TN 37212. Offers JD, JD/Certificate. *Accreditation:* ABA. *Faculty:* 18 full-time (8 women), 9 part-time/adjunct (3 women). *Students:* Average age 26. 760 applicants, 47% accepted, 113 enrolled. In 2018, 82 doctorates awarded. *Entrance requirements:* For doctorate, LSAT. Additional exam requirements/recommendations for international students: Required—TOEFL. *Application deadline:* For fall admission, 7/15 priority date for domestic and international students. Applications are processed on a rolling basis. Application fee: $50. Electronic applications accepted. *Expenses:* Contact institution. *Financial support:* In 2018–19, 180 students received support. Career-related internships or fieldwork and scholarships/grants available. Financial award application deadline: 12/1; financial award applicants required to submit FAFSA. *Unit head:* Judge Alberto R. Gonzales, Dean, 615-460-8259, E-mail: alberto.gonzales@belmont.edu. *Application contact:* Drew Ford, Recruiting Coordinator, 615-460-8250, Fax: 615-460-8250, E-mail: drew.ford@belmont.edu.
Website: http://www.belmont.edu/law/

Boston College, Law School, Newton, MA 02459. Offers JD, JD/MA, JD/MBA, JD/MSW. *Accreditation:* ABA. *Entrance requirements:* For doctorate, LSAT. Additional

exam requirements/recommendations for international students: Required—TOEFL. Electronic applications accepted. *Expenses:* Contact institution. *Faculty research:* Commercial law, labor law, legal history, comparative law, international law, business law, intellectual property law, tax law, environmental law.

Boston University, School of Law, Boston, MA 02215. Offers LL M, JD, JD/LL M, JD/MA, JD/MBA, JD/MPH, JD/MS, MD/JD. MD/JD offered jointly with the School of Medicine. *Accreditation:* ABA. *Program availability:* 100% online, blended/hybrid learning. *Students:* 983 full-time (588 women), 101 part-time (53 women); includes 218 minority (38 Black or African American, non-Hispanic/Latino; 1 American Indian or Alaska Native, non-Hispanic/Latino; 54 Asian, non-Hispanic/Latino; 93 Hispanic/Latino; 1 Native Hawaiian or other Pacific Islander, non-Hispanic/Latino; 31 Two or more races, non-Hispanic/Latino), 252 international. Average age 26. 5,450 applicants, 29% accepted, 233 enrolled. In 2018, 262 master's, 227 doctorates awarded. *Degree requirements:* For master's, thesis (for some programs); for doctorate, thesis/dissertation, research project resulting in a paper. *Entrance requirements:* For master's, JD; for doctorate, LSAT. Additional exam requirements/recommendations for international students: Required—TOEFL (minimum score 100 iBT), IELTS. *Application deadline:* For fall admission, 4/1 for domestic and international students. Applications are processed on a rolling basis. Application fee: $85. Electronic applications accepted. *Expenses:* Contact institution. *Financial support:* In 2018–19, 650 students received support. Career-related internships or fieldwork, Federal Work-Study, institutionally sponsored loans, scholarships/grants, and resident assistantships available. Financial award application deadline: 3/1; financial award applicants required to submit FAFSA. *Faculty research:* Health law, tax, intellectual property, Constitutional law, corporate law, business organizations and financial law, international law, family law. *Total annual research expenditures:* $3.1 million. *Unit head:* Maureen A. O'Rourke, Dean, 617-353-3112, Fax: 617-358-4706, E-mail: lawdean@bu.edu. *Application contact:* Alissa Leonard, Director of Admissions and Financial Aid, 617-353-3100, Fax: 617-353-0578, E-mail: bulawadm@bu.edu.
Website: http://www.bu.edu/law/

Brigham Young University, Graduate Studies, J. Reuben Clark Law School, Provo, UT 84602-8000. Offers LL M, JD, JD/M Ed, JD/MBA, JD/MPA. *Accreditation:* ABA. *Faculty:* 37 full-time (13 women), 35 part-time/adjunct (7 women). *Students:* 356 full-time (144 women); includes 60 minority (3 Black or African American, non-Hispanic/Latino; 2 American Indian or Alaska Native, non-Hispanic/Latino; 5 Asian, non-Hispanic/Latino; 26 Hispanic/Latino; 5 Native Hawaiian or other Pacific Islander, non-Hispanic/Latino; 19 Two or more races, non-Hispanic/Latino), 6 international. Average age 28. 451 applicants, 38% accepted, 104 enrolled. In 2018, 5 master's, 138 doctorates awarded. *Degree requirements:* For doctorate, comprehensive exam. *Entrance requirements:* For doctorate, LSAT or GRE. Additional exam requirements/recommendations for international students: Recommended—TOEFL (minimum score 590 paper-based; 96 iBT), IELTS (minimum score 7). *Application deadline:* For fall admission, 3/1 for domestic and international students. Applications are processed on a rolling basis. Application fee: $0. Electronic applications accepted. Application fee is waived when completed online. *Expenses:* 13060 Latter-day Saint tuition; 26,120 Non- Latter-day Saint tuition (both amounts: annual fixed cost based on full-time enrollment). *Financial support:* In 2018–19, 227 students received support, including 20 fellowships (averaging $40,000 per year); career-related internships or fieldwork, institutionally sponsored loans, scholarships/grants, unspecified assistantships, and Student employment also available. Financial award application deadline: 6/1; financial award applicants required to submit FAFSA. *Faculty research:* Law, innovation, and entrepreneurship; law and disadvantaged peoples; law and corpus linguistics; law and religion; and international law. *Total annual research expenditures:* $554,062. *Unit head:* D. Gordon Smith, Dean, 801-422-6383, Fax: 801-422-0389, E-mail: smithg@law.byu.edu. *Application contact:* Jillyn Comstock, Admissions Coordinator, 801-422-4356, Fax: 801-422-0389, E-mail: comstockj@law.byu.edu.
Website: http://www.law.byu.edu/

Brooklyn Law School, Graduate and Professional Programs, Brooklyn, NY 11201-3798. Offers LL M, JD, JD/MA, JD/MBA, JD/MS, JD/MUP. JD/MBA offered jointly with Bernard M. Baruch College of the City University of New York; JD/MS with Pratt Institute; JD/MUP with Hunter College of the City University of New York; and JD/MA with Brooklyn College of the City University of New York. *Accreditation:* ABA. *Program availability:* Part-time, evening/weekend. *Entrance requirements:* For doctorate, LSAT, dean's certification, 2 faculty letters of evaluation. Additional exam requirements/recommendations for international students: Required—TOEFL and TWE (required for Foreign Trained Lawyers Program); Recommended—TOEFL (minimum score 600 paper-based; 100 iBT), TWE. Electronic applications accepted. *Faculty research:* Civil procedure, securities regulation, family law, corporate finance, international business and law, health law.

California Western School of Law, Graduate and Professional Programs, San Diego, CA 92101-3090. Offers law (JD); Spanish language in trial advocacy (LL M); JD/MBA; JD/MSW; MCL/LL M. JD/MSW and JD/MBA offered jointly with San Diego State University. *Accreditation:* ABA. *Program availability:* Part-time. *Entrance requirements:* For doctorate, LSAT. Additional exam requirements/recommendations for international students: Required—TOEFL. Electronic applications accepted. *Faculty research:* Biotechnology, health law, international law, labor and employment law, business law.

Campbell University, Graduate and Professional Programs, Norman Adrian Wiggins School of Law, Raleigh, NC 27603. Offers JD, JD/MPA. JD/MPA offered in partnership with North Carolina State University. *Accreditation:* ABA. *Entrance requirements:* For doctorate, LSAT, interview. Additional exam requirements/recommendations for international students: Recommended—TOEFL. Electronic applications accepted. *Expenses:* Contact institution. *Faculty research:* Interdisciplinary approaches to legal problems, management and planning for lawyers, church/state constitutional problems, basic research in substantive legal areas.

Capital University, Law School, Columbus, OH 43215-3200. Offers LL M, MT, JD, JD/LL M, JD/MBA, JD/MSA, JD/MSN, JD/MTS. *Accreditation:* ABA. *Program availability:* Part-time, evening/weekend. *Entrance requirements:* For master's, 24 credit hours of business and accounting courses (including a federal taxation course and business law course); 4-year bachelor's degree from regionally-accredited college or university; for doctorate, LSAT, 4-year bachelor's degree from regionally-accredited college or university. Additional exam requirements/recommendations for international students: Required—TOEFL (minimum score 600 paper-based; 100 iBT); Recommended—IELTS (minimum score 7). Electronic applications accepted. *Expenses:* Contact institution.

Case Western Reserve University, School of Law, Cleveland, OH 44106. Offers financial integrity (MA); health law (SJD); intellectual property law (LL M, ML); international business law (LL M, ML); international criminal law (LL M); law (JD, SJD); patent practice (MA); U.S. and global legal studies (LL M, ML); JD/MA; JD/MBA; JD/MD; JD/MNM; JD/MPH; JD/MS; JD/MSSA. *Accreditation:* ABA. *Faculty:* 47 full-time (16 women), 63 part-time/adjunct (16 women). *Students:* 433 full-time (238 women); includes 91 minority (37 Black or African American, non-Hispanic/Latino; 1 American Indian or Alaska Native, non-Hispanic/Latino; 19 Asian, non-Hispanic/Latino; 26 Hispanic/Latino; 8 Two or more races, non-Hispanic/Latino), 30 international. Average age 24. 1,415 applicants, 50% accepted, 157 enrolled. In 2018, 126 master's awarded. *Entrance requirements:* For doctorate, LSAT, LSDAS. Additional exam requirements/recommendations for international students: Required—TOEFL. *Application deadline:* For fall admission, 4/1 priority date for domestic and international students. Applications are processed on a rolling basis. Application fee: $40. Electronic applications accepted. Application fee is waived when completed online. *Expenses:* Contact institution. *Financial support:* In 2018–19, 394 students received support. Career-related internships or fieldwork, Federal Work-Study, institutionally sponsored loans, and scholarships/grants available. Financial award application deadline: 5/1; financial award applicants required to submit FAFSA. *Unit head:* Jessica Berg, Co-Dean, 216-368-3283. *Application contact:* Kelli Curtis, Associate Dean for Admissions, 216-368-3600, Fax: 216-368-0185, E-mail: lawadmissions@case.edu.
Website: http://law.case.edu/

The Catholic University of America, Columbus School of Law, Washington, DC 20064. Offers MLS, JD, JD/JCL, JD/MA, JD/MLS, JD/MSBA, JD/MSW. *Accreditation:* ABA. *Program availability:* Part-time, evening/weekend. *Entrance requirements:* For doctorate, LSAT. Additional exam requirements/recommendations for international students: Required—TOEFL (minimum score 600 paper-based; 100 iBT), IELTS (minimum score 7). Electronic applications accepted. Application fee is waived when completed online. *Expenses:* Contact institution.

Central European University, Department of Legal Studies, Budapest, Hungary. Offers comparative Constitutional law (LL M); human rights (LL M, MA); international business law (LL M); juridical sciences (SJD). Terminal master's awarded for partial completion of doctoral program. *Degree requirements:* For master's, one foreign language, thesis; for doctorate, one foreign language, comprehensive exam, thesis/dissertation. *Entrance requirements:* For master's and doctorate, LSAT. Additional exam requirements/recommendations for international students: Required—TOEFL (minimum score 570 paper-based); Recommended—IELTS (minimum score 6.5). Electronic applications accepted. *Expenses:* Contact institution. *Faculty research:* Institutional, Constitutional and human rights in European Union law; biomedical law and reproductive rights; data protection law; comparative and international business law and the regulation of business environments;.

Champlain College, Graduate Studies, Burlington, VT 05402-0670. Offers business (MBA); digital forensic science (MS); early childhood education (M Ed); emergent media (MFA, MS); executive leadership (MS); health care administration (MS); information security operations (MS); law (MS); mediation and applied conflict studies (MS). MS in emergent media program held in Shanghai. *Program availability:* Part-time, online learning. *Degree requirements:* For master's, capstone project. *Entrance requirements:* Additional exam requirements/recommendations for international students: Required—TOEFL (minimum score 550 paper-based; 80 iBT). Electronic applications accepted.

Chapman University, Dale E. Fowler School of Law, Orange, CA 92866. Offers advocacy and dispute resolution (JD); business law (LL M, JD); criminal law (JD); entertainment and media law (LL M); entertainment law (JD); environmental, land use, and real estate law (JD); international and comparative law (LL M); international law (JD); law (JD); prosecutorial science (LL M); tax law (JD); taxation (LL M); trial advocacy (LL M); JD/MBA; JD/MFA. *Accreditation:* ABA. *Program availability:* Part-time. *Entrance requirements:* For doctorate, LSAT. Additional exam requirements/recommendations for international students: Required—TOEFL (minimum score 600 paper-based; 100 iBT). Electronic applications accepted. *Expenses:* Contact institution.

Charleston School of Law, Graduate and Professional Programs, Charleston, SC 29403. Offers law (JD). *Accreditation:* ABA. *Entrance requirements:* For doctorate, LSAT, two letters of recommendation, personal statement, current resume, official transcripts. Electronic applications accepted. *Expenses: Tuition:* Full-time $40,596; part-time $32,618 per year. *Required fees:* $1034; $1034 per unit. Tuition and fees vary according to student level.

City University of New York School of Law, Professional Program, Long Island City, NY 11101-4356. Offers JD. *Accreditation:* ABA. *Program availability:* Part-time, evening/weekend. *Faculty:* 51 full-time (37 women), 28 part-time/adjunct (14 women). *Students:* 417 full-time (254 women), 161 part-time (94 women); includes 297 minority (68 Black or African American, non-Hispanic/Latino; 54 Asian, non-Hispanic/Latino; 135 Hispanic/Latino; 1 Native Hawaiian or other Pacific Islander, non-Hispanic/Latino; 39 Two or more races, non-Hispanic/Latino), 16 international. Average age 29. 1,606 applicants, 38% accepted, 205 enrolled. In 2018, 165 doctorates awarded. *Entrance requirements:* For doctorate, LSAT, CAS report, bachelor's degree. Additional exam requirements/recommendations for international students: Recommended—TOEFL. *Application deadline:* For fall admission, 5/15 priority date for domestic students. Applications are processed on a rolling basis. Application fee: $60. Electronic applications accepted. *Expenses: Tuition, area resident:* Full-time $15,000; part-time $10,300 per year. Tuition, state resident: full-time $15,000. Tuition, nonresident: full-time $24,900; part-time $17,120 per year. *Required fees:* $562.90; $347.90 per unit. Tuition and fees vary according to program. *Financial support:* In 2018–19, 148 students received support, including 50 fellowships (averaging $15,488 per year), 33 research assistantships (averaging $1,194 per year); Federal Work-Study, scholarships/grants, tuition waivers (full and partial), and unspecified assistantships also available. Support available to part-time students. Financial award application deadline: 7/15; financial award applicants required to submit FAFSA. *Faculty research:* Capital punishment, domestic violence, indigenous land rights, cross cultural lawyering, LGBT issues, aging, ecology, international human rights, pedagogy, environmental justice. *Unit head:* Mary Lu Bilek, Dean/Professor of Law, 718-340-4201, Fax: 718-340-4482. *Application contact:* Degna P. Levister, Assistant Dean of Admissions and Enrollment Management, 718-340-4210, Fax: 718-340-4435, E-mail: admissions@law.cuny.edu.
Website: http://www.law.cuny.edu/

Cleveland State University, Cleveland-Marshall College of Law, Cleveland, OH 44115. Offers LL M, MLS, JD, Certificate, JD/MAES, JD/MBA, JD/MPA, JD/MSES, JD/MUPDD. *Accreditation:* ABA. *Program availability:* Part-time, evening/weekend. *Faculty:* 34 full-time (17 women), 61 part-time/adjunct (16 women). *Students:* 258 full-time (120 women), 132 part-time (77 women); includes 72 minority (44 Black or African American, non-Hispanic/Latino; 10 Asian, non-Hispanic/Latino; 13 Hispanic/Latino; 5 Two or more races, non-Hispanic/Latino), 4 international. Average age 28. 711 applicants, 44% accepted, 118 enrolled. In 2018, 11 master's, 88 doctorates, 2 Certificates awarded. *Entrance requirements:* For master's, JD or LL B (for LL M); bachelor's degree (for MLS); for doctorate, LSAT, bachelor's degree. Additional exam requirements/recommendations for international students: Required—TOEFL (minimum score 550 paper-based; 78 iBT), TOEFL minimum score 600 paper-based, 100 iBT or IELTS minimum score 7 (for LL M). *Application deadline:* For fall admission, 5/1 for domestic and international students. Applications are processed on a rolling basis. Application fee: $0. Electronic applications accepted. *Expenses:* Contact institution. *Financial support:* In 2018–19, 198 students received support, including 17 fellowships (averaging $2,500 per year), 34 research assistantships, 7 teaching assistantships with partial tuition reimbursements available (averaging $6,700 per year); career-related internships or fieldwork, Federal Work-Study, scholarships/grants, and unspecified assistantships also available. Support available to part-time students. Financial award application deadline: 5/1; financial award applicants required to submit FAFSA. *Faculty research:* Health law, international law, Constitutional law, criminal law, business law.

Unit head: Lee Fisher, Dean, 216-687-2300, Fax: 216-687-6881, E-mail: lee.fisher@csuohio.edu. *Application contact:* Christopher Lucak, Assistant Dean for Admission and Financial Aid, 216-687-4692, Fax: 216-687-6881, E-mail: law.admissions@csuohio.edu. Website: http://www.law.csuohio.edu/

The College of William and Mary, William & Mary Law School, Williamsburg, VA 23187-8795. Offers LL M, JD, JD/MA, JD/MBA, JD/MPP. *Accreditation:* ABA. *Faculty:* 44 full-time (19 women), 61 part-time/adjunct (17 women). *Students:* 643 full-time (359 women), 6 part-time (4 women); includes 111 minority (40 Black or African American, non-Hispanic/Latino; 2 American Indian or Alaska Native, non-Hispanic/Latino; 24 Asian, non-Hispanic/Latino; 27 Hispanic/Latino; 18 Two or more races, non-Hispanic/Latino), 50 international. Average age 25. 3,747 applicants, 38% accepted, 224 enrolled. In 2018, 38 master's, 187 doctorates awarded. *Degree requirements:* For doctorate, major paper. *Entrance requirements:* For master's, LL.B., LL.M, or J.M. in a foreign country or completion of the necessary legal education to take the equivalent of the law examination in that country, or qualified to practice law in a foreign country or, possess sufficient legal education or equivalent to satisfactorily complete the LL.M. program; for doctorate, LSAT, baccalaureate degree, references. Additional exam requirements/recommendations for international students: Required—TOEFL, IELTS, TOEFL (minimum iBT score of 90) or IELTS (6). *Application deadline:* For fall admission, 3/1 priority date for domestic and international students. Applications are processed on a rolling basis. Application fee: $0. Electronic applications accepted. Application fee is waived when completed online. *Expenses:* Contact institution. *Financial support:* In 2018–19, 597 students received support, including 15 fellowships with partial tuition reimbursements available (averaging $4,000 per year), 185 research assistantships (averaging $1,854 per year), 41 teaching assistantships (averaging $4,012 per year); career-related internships or fieldwork, scholarships/grants, and tuition waivers also available. Financial award application deadline: 2/15; financial award applicants required to submit FAFSA. *Faculty research:* Constitutional law, criminal law, corporate law, international law, intellectual property law. *Total annual research expenditures:* $388,581. *Unit head:* Davison M. Douglas, Dean/Professor, 757-221-3790, Fax: 757-221-3261, E-mail: dmdoug@wm.edu. *Application contact:* Dexter A. Smith, Associate Dean for Admissions, 757-221-3785, Fax: 757-221-3261, E-mail: dsmith05@wm.edu. Website: http://law.wm.edu/

Columbia University, School of Law, New York, NY 10027. Offers LL M, JD, JSD, JD/M Phil, JD/MA, JD/MBA, JD/MFA, JD/MIA, JD/MPA, JD/MPH, JD/MSW. *Accreditation:* ABA. *Entrance requirements:* For doctorate, LSAT or GRE (for JD). Electronic applications accepted. *Expenses:* Contact institution. *Faculty research:* Human rights, law and philosophy, corporate governance, regulation of the workplace, death penalty.

Concordia University, School of Law, Boise, ID 83702. Offers JD. *Entrance requirements:* For doctorate, LSAT, bachelor's degree, 2 letters of recommendation. Electronic applications accepted. *Expenses:* Contact institution.

Concord Law School, Program in Law, Los Angeles, CA 90024. Offers EJD, JD. *Program availability:* Part-time, evening/weekend, online learning. *Degree requirements:* For doctorate, comprehensive exam. *Entrance requirements:* For doctorate, online admissions test. Additional exam requirements/recommendations for international students: Required—TOEFL (minimum score 520 paper-based). Electronic applications accepted.

Cornell University, Cornell Law School, Ithaca, NY 14853-4901. Offers LL M, JD, JSD, JD/DESS, JD/LL M, JD/MA, JD/MBA, JD/MILR, JD/MLLP, JD/MLP, JD/MPA, JD/MRP, JD/Maitrise en Droit, JD/PhD. JD/MLLP offered jointly with Humboldt University, Berlin; JD/DESS offered jointly with Institut d'etudes Politiques de Paris ("Sciences Po") and Paris I. *Accreditation:* ABA. *Entrance requirements:* For doctorate, LSAT (for JD). Electronic applications accepted. *Expenses:* Contact institution. *Faculty research:* International law, Constitutional law, corporate laws, public interest law, feminist legal theory.

Cornell University, Graduate School, Graduate Field in the Law School, Ithaca, NY 14853. Offers JSD. *Entrance requirements:* For doctorate, JD, LL M, or equivalent; 2 letters of recommendation. Additional exam requirements/recommendations for international students: Required—TOEFL (minimum score 550 paper-based). Electronic applications accepted. *Expenses:* Contact institution. *Faculty research:* International economic integration (World Trade Organization and European Union), international commercial arbitration, feminist jurisprudence, human rights.

Creighton University, School of Law, Omaha, NE 68178-0001. Offers MS, JD, Certificate, JD/MBA, JD/MS. *Accreditation:* ABA. *Program availability:* Part-time. *Entrance requirements:* For doctorate, LSAT, bachelor's degree. Additional exam requirements/recommendations for international students: Recommended—TOEFL. Electronic applications accepted. Application fee is waived when completed online. *Expenses:* Contact institution. *Faculty research:* Conflict of laws, international law, evidence, cyber warfare, Constitutional law.

Dalhousie University, Faculty of Graduate Studies, Schulich School of Law, Halifax, NS B3H 4H9, Canada. Offers LL M, JSD, LL B/MBA, LL B/MLIS, LL B/MPA. *Program availability:* Part-time. *Degree requirements:* For master's, thesis or alternative; for doctorate, thesis/dissertation. *Entrance requirements:* For master's, LL B; for doctorate, LL M. Additional exam requirements/recommendations for international students: Required—1 of 5 approved tests: TOEFL, IELTS, CANTEST, CAEL, Michigan English Language Assessment Battery. Electronic applications accepted. *Expenses:* Contact institution. *Faculty research:* Marine and environmental law, health law, the family law program.

DePaul University, College of Law, Chicago, IL 60604. Offers business law and taxation (MJ); criminal law (MJ); health and intellectual property law (MJ); health care compliance (MJ); health law (LL M, MJ); intellectual property law (LL M); international and comparative law (MJ); international law (LL M); law (JD); public interest law (MJ); taxation (LL M); U.S. legal studies (LL M); JD/LL M; JD/MA; JD/MBA; JD/MS. *Accreditation:* ABA. *Program availability:* Part-time, evening/weekend. *Entrance requirements:* For doctorate, LSAT, LSAC applicant evaluation/letter of recommendation, personal statement, resume. Additional exam requirements/recommendations for international students: Required—TOEFL (minimum score 577 paper-based; 90 iBT), IELTS (minimum score 6.5). Electronic applications accepted. *Expenses:* Contact institution.

Drake University, Law School, Des Moines, IA 50311-4505. Offers LL M, MJ, JD, JD/LL M, JD/MA, JD/MBA, JD/MHA, JD/MPA, JD/MPH, JD/MS, JD/MSW, JD/Pharm D. *Accreditation:* ABA. *Program availability:* Part-time. *Students:* 307 full-time (153 women), 33 part-time (17 women); includes 51 minority (16 Black or African American, non-Hispanic/Latino; 6 Asian, non-Hispanic/Latino; 17 Hispanic/Latino; 12 Two or more races, non-Hispanic/Latino), 5 international. Average age 27. In 2018, 5 master's, 101 doctorates awarded. *Degree requirements:* For doctorate, 2 internships. *Entrance requirements:* For doctorate, LSAT, LSDAS report. Additional exam requirements/recommendations for international students: Required—TOEFL (minimum score 560 paper-based), TWE. *Application deadline:* For fall admission, 4/1 priority date for domestic and international students. Applications are processed on a rolling basis. Application fee: $40. Electronic applications accepted. *Expenses:* Contact institution. *Financial support:* Research assistantships, teaching assistantships, career-related internships or fieldwork, Federal Work-Study, institutionally sponsored loans, scholarships/grants, and tuition waivers (full and partial) available. Support available to part-time students. Financial award application deadline: 3/1; financial award applicants required to submit FAFSA. *Faculty research:* Constitutional law, environmental law, agricultural law, computers and the law, bioethics and health law. *Unit head:* Jerry Anderson, Dean, 515-271-2658, Fax: 515-271-4118, E-mail: jerry.anderson@drake.edu. *Application contact:* Kara Blanchard, Assistant Dean for Admission and Financial Aid, 515-271-2953, Fax: 515-271-2530, E-mail: kara.blanchard@drake.edu. Website: http://www.drake.edu/law

Drexel University, Thomas R. Kline School of Law, Philadelphia, PA 19104-2875. Offers business and entrepreneurship law (JD); criminal law (MLS, JD); cybersecurity and information privacy compliance (MLS); entrepreneurship and law (MLS); financial regulatory compliance (MLS); health care compliance (MLS); health law (JD); higher education compliance (MLS); human resources compliance (MLS); intellectual property law (JD); NCAA compliance and sports law (MLS). *Accreditation:* ABA.

Duke University, School of Law, Durham, NC 27708. Offers American law (LL M); bioethics and science policy (JD/MA); international and comparative law or law and entrepreneurship (JD/LL M); judicial studies (MJS); law (JD, SJD); law and entrepreneurship (LL M); JD/LL M; JD/MA; JD/MBA; JD/MEM; JD/MPP; JD/MTS; JD/PhD; MD/JD. Sanford School of Public Policy, Fuqua School of Business, Nicholas School of the Environment, Duke Divinity School, Institut d'Etudes Politiques de Paris. *Accreditation:* ABA. *Faculty:* 95 full-time (41 women), 86 part-time/adjunct (23 women). *Students:* 682; includes 167 minority (47 Black or African American, non-Hispanic/Latino; 1 American Indian or Alaska Native, non-Hispanic/Latino; 56 Asian, non-Hispanic/Latino; 53 Hispanic/Latino; 10 Two or more races, non-Hispanic/Latino), 52 international. Average age 24. 5,558 applicants, 20% accepted, 230 enrolled. *Degree requirements:* For doctorate, thesis/dissertation (for some programs). *Entrance requirements:* For doctorate, LSAT (for JD). Additional exam requirements/recommendations for international students: Required—TOEFL (minimum score 600 paper-based). *Application deadline:* For fall admission, 2/15 for domestic and international students. Applications are processed on a rolling basis. Application fee: $70. Electronic applications accepted. *Expenses:* $66,000 tuition, $1,358 fees. *Financial support:* Institutionally sponsored loans, scholarships/grants, and unspecified assistantships available. Financial award application deadline: 3/15; financial award applicants required to submit FAFSA. *Faculty research:* International Law; Constitutional and public law; intellectual property law; science and technology law; business, finance, and corporate law. *Unit head:* Kerry Abrams, Dean/Professor of Law, 919-613-7001, Fax: 919-613-7158. *Application contact:* William J. Hoye, Associate Dean for Admissions and Student Affairs, 919-613-7020, Fax: 919-613-7257, E-mail: hoye@law.duke.edu.
Website: http://www.law.duke.edu/

Dunlap-Stone University, Graduate Law Center, Phoenix, AZ 85024. Offers regulatory trade compliance (M Sc); U.S. regulatory trade law (LL M).

Duquesne University, Bayer School of Natural and Environmental Sciences, Program in Forensic Science and Law, Pittsburgh, PA 15282-0001. Offers MS. *Faculty:* 8 full-time (4 women), 14 part-time/adjunct (7 women). *Students:* 18 full-time (12 women); includes 1 minority (Hispanic/Latino). Average age 22. In 2018, 16 master's awarded. *Degree requirements:* For master's, comprehensive exam. *Entrance requirements:* For master's, SAT or ACT, recommendation form; minimum total QPA of 3.0, 2.5 in math and science. *Application deadline:* For fall admission, 7/1 for domestic and international students. Applications are processed on a rolling basis. Application fee: $0. Electronic applications accepted. *Expenses:* $1376 per credit hour. *Financial support:* In 2018–19, 20 students received support. Career-related internships or fieldwork, scholarships/grants, and tuition waivers (full and partial) available. Financial award application deadline: 5/1. *Faculty research:* Extraction protocols, mass spectrometry, synthetic fiber analysis, synthetic polymer characterization, trace analysis, amplification of DNA, methods for labeling DNA, construction of a genetic profile, experiential exploration of mitochondrial DNA, the Y-chromosome, amelogenin. *Unit head:* Dr. Pamela Marshall, Director, 412-396-1703, E-mail: marshallp@duq.edu. *Application contact:* Valerie L. Lijewski, Assistant Director/Academic Advisor, 412-396-1084, E-mail: lijewski@duq.edu. Website: http://www.duq.edu/academics/schools/natural-and-environmental-sciences/academic-programs/forensic-science-and-law

Duquesne University, School of Law, Pittsburgh, PA 15282-0700. Offers American law for foreign lawyers (LL M); law (JD); JD/M Div; JD/MBA; JD/MS; JD/MSEM. JD/M Div offered jointly with Pittsburgh Theological Seminary. *Accreditation:* ABA. *Program availability:* Part-time, evening/weekend. *Faculty:* 30 full-time (16 women), 35 part-time/adjunct (9 women). *Students:* 436 full-time (236 women); includes 41 minority (16 Black or African American, non-Hispanic/Latino; 1 American Indian or Alaska Native, non-Hispanic/Latino; 7 Asian, non-Hispanic/Latino; 14 Hispanic/Latino; 3 Two or more races, non-Hispanic/Latino), 4 international. Average age 26. 759 applicants, 63% accepted, 171 enrolled. In 2018, 1 master's, 119 doctorates awarded. *Entrance requirements:* For doctorate, LSAT. Additional exam requirements/recommendations for international students: Required—TOEFL (minimum score 85 iBT), IELTS (minimum score 6.5). *Application deadline:* For fall admission, 3/1 priority date for domestic and international students. Applications are processed on a rolling basis. Application fee: $0. Electronic applications accepted. *Expenses:* $16,919 part-time per semester (for day and evening law), $22,016 per semester (for day law), $12,712 per semester (for LL M). *Financial support:* In 2018–19, 338 students received support, including 25 research assistantships with partial tuition reimbursements available (averaging $2,500 per year), 20 teaching assistantships with partial tuition reimbursements available (averaging $2,500 per year); career-related internships or fieldwork, scholarships/grants, tuition waivers (partial), and library assistants also available. Support available to part-time students. Financial award application deadline: 5/1; financial award applicants required to submit FAFSA. *Faculty research:* Constitutional law, law and religion, intellectual property and patents, neuroscience and law, civil and criminal law and procedure, feminist perspective on environmental law. *Total annual research expenditures:* $100,000. *Unit head:* Maureen Lally-Green, Dean, 412-396-6280, Fax: 412-396-6283, E-mail: lallygreen@duq.edu. *Application contact:* Office of Admissions, 412-396-6296, Fax: 412-396-6659, E-mail: lawadmissions@duq.edu.
Website: https://www.law.duq.edu/

Elon University, Program in Law, Elon, NC 27244-2010. Offers JD. *Accreditation:* ABA. *Faculty:* 27 full-time (14 women), 12 part-time/adjunct (4 women). *Students:* 360 full-time (211 women); includes 80 minority (56 Black or African American, non-Hispanic/Latino; 5 American Indian or Alaska Native, non-Hispanic/Latino; 18 Hispanic/Latino; 1 Two or more races, non-Hispanic/Latino), 1 international. Average age 25. 1,018 applicants, 36% accepted, 146 enrolled. In 2018, 111 doctorates awarded. *Entrance requirements:* For doctorate, LSAT, LSDAS. Additional exam requirements/recommendations for international students: Required—TOEFL (minimum score 550 paper-based; 79 iBT). *Application deadline:* For fall admission, 7/15 for domestic students. Applications are processed on a rolling basis. Application fee: $0. Electronic applications accepted. *Financial support:* Scholarships/grants available. Financial award applicants required to submit FAFSA. *Faculty research:* Quality of life and job satisfaction, civil procedure, damages, assessment for development of instruments, psychological types. *Unit head:*

Dr. Luke Bierman, Dean, 336-279-9201, E-mail: lbierman@elon.edu. *Application contact:* Alan Woodlief, Associate Dean of School of Law/Director of Law School Admissions, 336-279-9203, E-mail: awoodlief@elon.edu.
Website: https://www.elon.edu/law

Emory University, School of Law, Atlanta, GA 30322-2770. Offers LL M, JD, Certificate, JD/Certificate, JD/LL M, JD/M Div, JD/MA, JD/MBA, JD/MPH, JD/MTS, JD/PhD. *Accreditation:* ABA. *Entrance requirements:* For doctorate, LSAT, 2 letters of recommendation. Additional exam requirements/recommendations for international students: Required—TOEFL (minimum score 600 paper-based). Electronic applications accepted. *Expenses:* Contact institution. *Faculty research:* Law and economics, law and religion, international law, human rights, feminism and legal theory.

Empire College, School of Law, Santa Rosa, CA 95403. Offers MLS, JD.

Faulkner University, Thomas Goode Jones School of Law, Montgomery, AL 36109-3398. Offers JD. *Accreditation:* ABA. *Entrance requirements:* For doctorate, LSAT. Additional exam requirements/recommendations for international students: Recommended—TOEFL. Electronic applications accepted.

Florida Agricultural and Mechanical University, College of Law, Tallahassee, FL 32307-3200. Offers JD. *Accreditation:* ABA. *Program availability:* Part-time, evening/weekend. *Entrance requirements:* For doctorate, LSAT, LSDAS, 2 letters of recommendation. Additional exam requirements/recommendations for international students: Required—TOEFL. *Expenses:* Contact institution.

Florida Coastal School of Law, Professional Program, Jacksonville, FL 32256. Offers JD. *Accreditation:* ABA. *Program availability:* Part-time. *Entrance requirements:* For doctorate, LSAT. Additional exam requirements/recommendations for international students: Recommended—TOEFL (minimum score 600 paper-based). Electronic applications accepted. *Expenses:* Contact institution. *Faculty research:* Law and business, law technology and intellectual property, juvenile justice and family law, constitutional law, labor law.

Florida International University, College of Law, Miami, FL 33199. Offers American law for foreign lawyers (LL M); law (JD); JD/MA; JD/MIB. *Accreditation:* ABA. *Program availability:* Part-time, evening/weekend. *Students:* Average age 27. 1,778 applicants, 32% accepted, 204 enrolled. In 2018, 14 master's, 154 doctorates awarded. *Entrance requirements:* For doctorate, LSAT, 3 letters of recommendation. Additional exam requirements/recommendations for international students: Recommended—TOEFL. *Application deadline:* For fall admission, 5/1 for domestic and international students. Applications are processed on a rolling basis. Application fee: $20. Electronic applications accepted. *Expenses:* Contact institution. *Financial support:* Application deadline: 3/1; applicants required to submit FAFSA. *Unit head:* Tawia B Ansah, Acting Dean, 305-348-1118, Fax: 305-348-1159, E-mail: tawia.ansah@fiu.edu. *Application contact:* Tawia B Ansah, Acting Dean, 305-348-1118, Fax: 305-348-1159, E-mail: tawia.ansah@fiu.edu.
Website: http://law.fiu.edu

Florida State University, College of Law, Tallahassee, FL 32306-1601. Offers American law for foreign lawyers (LL M); business law (LL M); environmental law and policy (LL M); financial regulation and compliance (JM); health law compliance (JM); law (JM, JD); legal risk management and HR compliance (JM); JD/MAES; JD/MBA; JD/MPA; JD/MS; JD/MSI; JD/MSP; JD/MSW. *Accreditation:* ABA. *Program availability:* Part-time, 100% online. *Students:* Average age 26. 1,805 applicants, 36% accepted, 225 enrolled. In 2018, 18 master's, 218 doctorates awarded. Terminal master's awarded for partial completion of doctoral program. *Entrance requirements:* For master's, one graduate-level standardized test (for JM), JD or equivalent degree (for LL M); for doctorate, LSAT or GRE (for JD). Additional exam requirements/recommendations for international students: Required—TOEFL (minimum score 600 paper-based; 100 iBT), IELTS (minimum score 7.5). *Application deadline:* For fall admission, 6/30 for domestic and international students; for spring admission, 12/1 for domestic students; for summer admission, 4/15 for domestic students. Applications are processed on a rolling basis. Application fee: $30. Electronic applications accepted. *Expenses:* Contact institution. *Financial support:* In 2018–19, 400 students received support, including 2 fellowships with full tuition reimbursements available (averaging $20,683 per year), 30 research assistantships (averaging $1,205 per year), 10 teaching assistantships (averaging $1,354 per year); career-related internships or fieldwork, scholarships/grants, and unspecified assistantships also available. Financial award application deadline: 3/1; financial award applicants required to submit FAFSA. *Faculty research:* Business law; environmental, energy and land use law; international law; criminal law. *Total annual research expenditures:* $99,375. *Unit head:* Erin O'Hara O'Connor, Dean, 850-644-3400, Fax: 850-644-5487, E-mail: eoconnor@law.fsu.edu. *Application contact:* Jennifer L. Kessinger, Director of Admissions and Records, 850-644-3787, Fax: 850-644-7284, E-mail: jkessing@law.fsu.edu.
Website: http://www.law.fsu.edu/

Fordham University, School of Law, New York, NY 10023. Offers banking, corporate and finance law (LL M); corporate compliance (MSL); fashion law (MSL); intellectual property and information law (LL M); international business and trade law (LL M); law (JD); JD/MA; JD/MBA; JD/MSW. *Accreditation:* ABA. *Program availability:* Part-time, evening/weekend. *Entrance requirements:* For doctorate, LSAT. Additional exam requirements/recommendations for international students: Required—TOEFL. Electronic applications accepted. *Expenses:* Contact institution. *Faculty research:* Intellectual property, business law, international law.

Friends University, Graduate School, Wichita, KS 67213. Offers family therapy (MSFT); global business administration (MBA), including accounting, business law, change management, health care leadership, management information systems, supply chain management and logistics; health care leadership (MHCL); management information systems (MMIS); professional business administration (MBA), including accounting, business law, change management, health care leadership, management information systems, supply chain management and logistics. *Program availability:* Part-time, evening/weekend, online learning. *Degree requirements:* For master's, research project. *Entrance requirements:* For master's, bachelor's degree from accredited institution, official transcripts, interview with program director, letter(s) of recommendation. Additional exam requirements/recommendations for international students: Required—TOEFL (minimum score 560 paper-based). Electronic applications accepted.

George Mason University, Antonin Scalia Law School, Arlington, VA 22201. Offers global antitrust law and economics (LL M); intellectual property (LL M); law (JD); law and economics (LL M); U.S. law (LL M); JD/MA; JD/MPP; JD/PhD. *Accreditation:* ABA. *Program availability:* Part-time, evening/weekend. *Faculty:* 44 full-time (9 women), 157 part-time/adjunct (41 women). *Students:* 457 full-time (228 women), 141 part-time (57 women); includes 158 minority (18 Black or African American, non-Hispanic/Latino; 1 American Indian or Alaska Native, non-Hispanic/Latino; 61 Asian, non-Hispanic/Latino; 51 Hispanic/Latino; 27 Two or more races, non-Hispanic/Latino), 49 international. Average age 29. 2,452 applicants, 25% accepted, 175 enrolled. In 2018, 169 doctorates awarded. *Entrance requirements:* For master's, JD or international equivalent; for doctorate, LSAT or GRE, baccalaureate degree or international equivalent. Additional exam requirements/recommendations for international students: Required—TOEFL or IELTS (for LL M applicants only). *Application deadline:* For fall admission, 6/15 for domestic and international students. Applications are processed on a rolling basis. Application fee: $0. Electronic applications accepted. *Expenses:* Contact institution. *Financial support:* In 2018–19, 451 students received support, including 2 fellowships with full tuition reimbursements available; research assistantships, career-related internships or fieldwork, scholarships/grants, and tuition waivers (full and partial) also available. Support available to part-time students. Financial award applicants required to submit FAFSA. *Faculty research:* Law and economics; infrastructure protection, including homeland and national security; intellectual property. *Unit head:* Henry N. Butler, Dean, 703-993-8644, Fax: 703-993-8088. *Application contact:* Sabrina A. Huffman, Director of Admissions, 703-993-8010, Fax: 703-993-8088, E-mail: lawadmit@gmu.edu.
Website: http://www.law.gmu.edu/

Georgetown University, Law Center, Washington, DC 20001. Offers environmental law (LL M); global health law (LL M); global health law and international institutions (LL M); individualized study (LL M); international business and economic law (LL M); law (JD, SJD); national security law (LL M); securities and financial regulation (LL M); taxation (LL M); JD/LL M; JD/MA; JD/MBA; JD/MPH; JD/PhD. *Accreditation:* ABA. *Program availability:* Part-time, evening/weekend. *Degree requirements:* For master's, thesis; for doctorate, thesis/dissertation (for some programs). *Entrance requirements:* For master's, JD, LL B, or first law degree earned in country of origin; for doctorate, LSAT (for JD). Additional exam requirements/recommendations for international students: Required—TOEFL. *Expenses:* Contact institution. *Faculty research:* Constitutional law, legal history, jurisprudence.

The George Washington University, Law School, Washington, DC 20052. Offers law (SJD); national security and U.S. foreign relations (LL M). *Accreditation:* ABA. *Program availability:* Part-time, evening/weekend. *Faculty:* 84 full-time (33 women), 233 part-time/adjunct (65 women). *Students:* 1,499 full-time (777 women), 234 part-time (107 women); includes 387 minority (137 Black or African American, non-Hispanic/Latino; 11 American Indian or Alaska Native, non-Hispanic/Latino; 191 Asian, non-Hispanic/Latino; 35 Hispanic/Latino; 4 Native Hawaiian or other Pacific Islander, non-Hispanic/Latino; 9 Two or more races, non-Hispanic/Latino), 173 international. Average age 27. 173 applicants, 100% accepted, 125 enrolled. In 2018, 151 master's, 2 doctorates awarded. *Entrance requirements:* For master's, JD or equivalent; for doctorate, LSAT (for JD), LL M or equivalent (for SJD). *Application deadline:* For fall admission, 3/1 for domestic students. Applications are processed on a rolling basis. Application fee: $75. *Expenses:* Contact institution. *Financial support:* Research assistantships, career-related internships or fieldwork, Federal Work-Study, institutionally sponsored loans, scholarships/grants, and tuition waivers (full and partial) available. Support available to part-time students. Financial award application deadline: 3/1; financial award applicants required to submit CSS PROFILE or FAFSA. *Unit head:* Blake D. Morant, Dean, E-mail: bmorant@law.gwu.edu. *Application contact:* Sophia Sim, Assistant Dean of Admissions and Financial Aid, 202-994-7235, Fax: 202-739-0624, E-mail: ssim@law.gwu.edu.
Website: http://www.law.gwu.edu/

Georgia State University, College of Law, Atlanta, GA 30302-4037. Offers JD, JD/MA, JD/MBA, JD/MCRP, JD/MHA, JD/MPA, JD/MSHA. *Accreditation:* ABA. *Program availability:* Part-time, evening/weekend. *Faculty:* 52 full-time (29 women), 10 part-time/adjunct (3 women). *Students:* 480 full-time (239 women), 159 part-time (85 women); includes 202 minority (88 Black or African American, non-Hispanic/Latino; 2 American Indian or Alaska Native, non-Hispanic/Latino; 42 Asian, non-Hispanic/Latino; 54 Hispanic/Latino; 16 Two or more races, non-Hispanic/Latino), 15 international. Average age 28. 1,478 applicants, 41% accepted, 214 enrolled. In 2018, 179 doctorates awarded. *Entrance requirements:* For doctorate, LSAT. Additional exam requirements/recommendations for international students: Recommended—TOEFL. *Application deadline:* For fall admission, 3/15 for domestic students, 3/15 priority date for international students. Applications are processed on a rolling basis. Application fee: $50. Electronic applications accepted. *Expenses:* Contact institution. *Financial support:* In 2018–19, research assistantships with tuition reimbursements (averaging $2,500 per year), teaching assistantships (averaging $2,500 per year) were awarded; scholarships/grants, tuition waivers, and unspecified assistantships also available. Financial award application deadline: 4/1; financial award applicants required to submit FAFSA. *Faculty research:* Health law; land use, urban planning and environmental law; intellectual property; criminal law and procedure; Constitutional law. *Unit head:* Dr. Leslie E. Wolf, Interim Dean, College of Law, 404-413-9035, Fax: 404-413-9227, E-mail: lwolf@gsu.edu. *Application contact:* Dr. Monique McCarthy, Senior Director of Admissions, 404-413-9004, Fax: 404-413-9203, E-mail: mmccarthy18@gsu.edu.
Website: http://law.gsu.edu/

Golden Gate University, School of Law, San Francisco, CA 94105-2968. Offers environmental law (LL M); estate planning (LL M); intellectual property law (LL M); international legal studies (LL M, SJD); law (JD); taxation law (LL M); U.S. legal studies (LL M); JD/MBA. *Accreditation:* ABA. *Program availability:* Part-time, evening/weekend. *Degree requirements:* For doctorate, thesis/dissertation (for some programs). *Entrance requirements:* For doctorate, LSAT (for JD). Additional exam requirements/recommendations for international students: Required—TOEFL (minimum score 600 paper-based). Electronic applications accepted. *Expenses:* Contact institution. *Faculty research:* International law, intellectual property law, environmental law, real estate, civil rights.

Gonzaga University, School of Law, Spokane, WA 99220-3528. Offers JD. *Accreditation:* ABA. *Program availability:* Part-time. *Degree requirements:* For doctorate, experiential learning, public service. *Entrance requirements:* For doctorate, LSAT, bachelor's degree, all academic transcripts, 2-4 letters of recommendation, resume, personal statement. Electronic applications accepted. *Expenses:* Contact institution. *Faculty research:* Environmental law, business law, public interest law, tax law, international law.

Harvard University, Law School, Graduate Programs in Law, Cambridge, MA 02138. Offers LL M, SJD. *Accreditation:* ABA. *Degree requirements:* For master's, thesis optional; for doctorate, thesis/dissertation. *Entrance requirements:* Additional exam requirements/recommendations for international students: Required—TOEFL. *Faculty research:* Corporation finance, national and international law, legal ethics, family law, criminal law, administrative law, constitutional law.

Harvard University, Law School, Professional Programs in Law, Cambridge, MA 02138. Offers international and comparative law (JD); law and business (JD); law and government (JD); law and social change (JD); law, science and technology (JD); JD/MALD; JD/MBA; JD/MPH; JD/MPP; JD/PhD. *Accreditation:* ABA. *Degree requirements:* For doctorate, 3rd-year paper. *Entrance requirements:* For doctorate, LSAT. *Faculty research:* Constitutional law, voting rights law, cyber law.

Hofstra University, Maurice A. Deane School of Law, Hempstead, NY 11549. Offers alternative dispute resolution (JD); American legal studies (LL M); business law honors (JD); clinical bioethics (Certificate); corporate compliance (JD); criminal law and procedure (JD); family law (LL M, JD); health law (JD); health law and policy (LL M, MA); intellectual property law honors (JD); international law honors (JD); JD/MBA; JD/MPH. *Accreditation:* ABA. *Program availability:* Part-time, 100% online. *Faculty:* 41 full-time

(21 women), 78 part-time/adjunct (24 women). *Students:* 712 full-time (374 women), 137 part-time (88 women); includes 181 minority (53 Black or African American, non-Hispanic/Latino; 2 American Indian or Alaska Native, non-Hispanic/Latino; 34 Asian, non-Hispanic/Latino; 82 Hispanic/Latino; 7 Native Hawaiian or other Pacific Islander, non-Hispanic/Latino; 3 Two or more races, non-Hispanic/Latino), 13 international. Average age 27. 3,104 applicants, 50% accepted, 301 enrolled. In 2018, 37 master's, 234 doctorates awarded. *Entrance requirements:* For doctorate, LSAT, letter of recommendation, personal statement, undergraduate transcripts; for Certificate, 2 letters of recommendation, JD or LLB, personal statement, law school transcripts. Additional exam requirements/recommendations for international students: Recommended—TOEFL (minimum score 600 paper-based; 100 iBT). *Application deadline:* For fall admission, 4/15 priority date for domestic and international students. Applications are processed on a rolling basis. Application fee: $0. Electronic applications accepted. *Expenses:* $29,607 per term for Full-time (tuition and fees). *Financial support:* In 2018–19, 578 students received support, including 565 fellowships with full and partial tuition reimbursements available (averaging $32,425 per year); research assistantships with full and partial tuition reimbursements available, career-related internships or fieldwork, Federal Work-Study, institutionally sponsored loans, scholarships/grants, tuition waivers (full and partial), unspecified assistantships, and scholarships and endowed scholarships also available. Support available to part-time students. Financial award applicants required to submit FAFSA. *Faculty research:* Family law; international law; constitutional law; legal ethics; health law. *Unit head:* Gail Prudenti, Dean, 516-463-4068, E-mail: gail.prudenti@hofstra.edu. *Application contact:* Sunil Samuel, Assistant Vice President of Admissions, 516-463-4723, Fax: 516-463-4664.
Website: http://law.hofstra.edu/

Howard University, School of Law, Washington, DC 20008. Offers LL M, JD, JD/MBA. *Accreditation:* ABA. *Degree requirements:* For master's, one foreign language, thesis; for doctorate, thesis/dissertation (for some programs). *Entrance requirements:* For doctorate, LSAT. Additional exam requirements/recommendations for international students: Required—TOEFL. Electronic applications accepted. *Expenses:* Contact institution. *Faculty research:* Criminal law, family law, telecommunications, religion, antitrust.

Humphreys University, Drivon School of Law, Stockton, CA 95207-3896. Offers JD. *Program availability:* Part-time, evening/weekend. *Entrance requirements:* For doctorate, LSAT, minimum GPA of 2.5. Electronic applications accepted. Application fee is waived when completed online. *Expenses:* Contact institution.

Illinois Institute of Technology, Chicago-Kent College of Law, Chicago, IL 60661-3691. Offers family law (LL M); financial services law (LL M); international intellectual property law (LL M); law (JD); legal studies (JSD); taxation (LL M); U.S., international, and transnational law (LL M); JD/LL M; JD/MBA; JD/MPA; JD/MPH; JD/MS. *Accreditation:* ABA. *Program availability:* Part-time, evening/weekend. Terminal master's awarded for partial completion of doctoral program. *Entrance requirements:* For master's, 1st degree in law or certified license to practice law; for doctorate, LSAT. Additional exam requirements/recommendations for international students: Required—TOEFL (minimum score 600 paper-based; 100 iBT); Recommended—IELTS (minimum score 7). Electronic applications accepted. *Expenses:* Contact institution. *Faculty research:* Constitutional law, bioethics, environmental law, intellectual property.

Indiana University Bloomington, Maurer School of Law, Bloomington, IN 47405-7000. Offers comparative law (MCL); juridical science (SJD); law (LL M, JD); law and social sciences (PhD); legal studies (Certificate); JD/MA; JD/MBA; JD/MLS; JD/MPA; JD/MS; JD/MSES. PhD offered through University Graduate School. *Accreditation:* ABA. *Degree requirements:* For master's, thesis or practicum; for doctorate, thesis/dissertation (for some programs), research seminar (for JD). *Entrance requirements:* For master's, LSAT, 3 letters of recommendation, law degree or license to practice; for doctorate, LSAT. Additional exam requirements/recommendations for international students: Required—TOEFL (minimum score 560 paper-based; 80 iBT). Electronic applications accepted. *Faculty research:* Environmental risk assessment and policy analysis, information privacy and security, judicial independence, accountability, ethics.

Indiana University–Purdue University Indianapolis, Robert H. McKinney School of Law, Indianapolis, IN 46202. Offers advocacy skills (Certificate); American law for foreign lawyers (LL M); civil and human rights (Certificate); corporate and commercial law (LL M, Certificate); criminal law (Certificate); environmental and natural resources (Certificate); health law (Certificate); health law, policy and bioethics (LL M); intellectual property law (LL M, Certificate); international and comparative law (LL M, Certificate); international human rights law (LL M); law (MJ, JD, SJD); JD/M Phil; JD/MBA; JD/MD; JD/MHA; JD/MLS; JD/MPA; JD/MPH; JD/MSW. *Accreditation:* ABA. *Program availability:* Part-time. *Entrance requirements:* For doctorate, LSAT. Additional exam requirements/recommendations for international students: Required—TOEFL (minimum score 79 iBT), IELTS (minimum score 6.5). Electronic applications accepted. *Expenses:* Contact institution.

Instituto Tecnológico y de Estudios Superiores de Monterrey, Campus Ciudad de México, School of Humanities and Social Sciences, Ciudad de Mexico, Mexico. Offers LL B. *Program availability:* Part-time, evening/weekend. *Entrance requirements:* For degree, Instituto entrance exam. Additional exam requirements/recommendations for international students: Required—TOEFL. *Faculty research:* Law; politics; international relations.

Inter American University of Puerto Rico School of Law, Professional Program, San Juan, PR 00936-8351. Offers JD. *Accreditation:* ABA. *Program availability:* Part-time, evening/weekend. *Entrance requirements:* For doctorate, LSAT, PAEG, minimum GPA of 2.5. *Expenses:* Contact institution.

John F. Kennedy University, College of Law, Pleasant Hill, CA 94523-4817. Offers JD. Program also offered on San Jose campus. *Program availability:* Part-time, evening/weekend, blended/hybrid learning. *Entrance requirements:* For doctorate, LSAT, interview. Additional exam requirements/recommendations for international students: Required—TOEFL. *Expenses:* Contact institution.

The John Marshall Law School, Graduate and Professional Programs, Chicago, IL 60604-3968. Offers LL M, MJ, JD, JD/LL M, JD/MA, JD/MBA, JD/MPA. *Accreditation:* ABA. *Program availability:* Part-time, evening/weekend, 100% online, blended/hybrid learning. *Degree requirements:* For master's, 24 credits; for doctorate, 90 credits. *Entrance requirements:* For doctorate, LSAT, GRE. Additional exam requirements/recommendations for international students: Required—TOEFL (minimum score 90 iBT), IELTS (minimum score 7). Electronic applications accepted.

The Judge Advocate General's School, U.S. Army, Graduate Programs, Charlottesville, VA 22903-1781. Offers LL M. Program available only to active duty military lawyers. *Accreditation:* ABA. *Degree requirements:* For master's, thesis optional. *Entrance requirements:* For master's, active duty military lawyer, international military officer, or DOD civilian attorney; JD or LL B. *Faculty research:* Criminal law, administrative and civil law, contract law, international law, legal research and writing.

Lewis & Clark College, Lewis & Clark Law School, Portland, OR 97219. Offers animal law (LL M); environmental, natural resources, and energy law (LL M, MSL); law (JD). *Accreditation:* ABA. *Program availability:* Part-time, evening/weekend. *Entrance requirements:* For doctorate, LSAT. Additional exam requirements/recommendations for international students: Recommended—TOEFL (minimum score 600 paper-based). Electronic applications accepted. Application fee is waived when completed online. *Expenses:* Contact institution.

Liberty University, School of Law, Lynchburg, VA 24515. Offers American legal studies (JM); international legal studies (JM, LL M). *Accreditation:* ABA. *Program availability:* Online learning. *Students:* 258 full-time (131 women), 138 part-time (63 women); includes 97 minority (45 Black or African American, non-Hispanic/Latino; 2 American Indian or Alaska Native, non-Hispanic/Latino; 10 Asian, non-Hispanic/Latino; 20 Hispanic/Latino; 1 Native Hawaiian or other Pacific Islander, non-Hispanic/Latino; 19 Two or more races, non-Hispanic/Latino), 7 international. Average age 33. 387 applicants, 50% accepted, 142 enrolled. *Entrance requirements:* Additional exam requirements/recommendations for international students: Required—TOEFL (minimum score 600 paper-based; 100 iBT). *Application deadline:* For fall admission, 6/1 for domestic students. *Expenses:* Contact institution. *Financial support:* In 2018–19, 208 students received support. Federal Work-Study available. Financial award applicants required to submit FAFSA. *Unit head:* B. Keith Faulkner, Dean, 434-592-5300, Fax: 434-592-5400, E-mail: law@liberty.edu. *Application contact:* Joleen Thaxton, Assistant Director of Admissions, 434-592-5300, Fax: 434-592-5400, E-mail: lawadmissions@liberty.edu.
Website: https://www.liberty.edu/law/

Lincoln Memorial University, Duncan School of Law, Harrogate, TN 37752-1901. Offers JD. *Program availability:* Part-time. *Entrance requirements:* For doctorate, LSAT. Additional exam requirements/recommendations for international students: Required—TOEFL (minimum score 500 paper-based). Electronic applications accepted. *Expenses:* Contact institution.

London Metropolitan University, Graduate Programs, London, United Kingdom. Offers applied psychology (M Sc); architecture (MA); biomedical science (M Sc); blood science (M Sc); cancer pharmacology (M Sc); computer networking and cyber security (M Sc); computing and information systems (M Sc); conference interpreting (MA); counter-terrorism studies (M Sc); creative, digital and professional writing (MA); crime, violence and prevention (M Sc); criminology (M Sc); curating contemporary art (MA); data analytics (M Sc); digital media (MA); early childhood studies (MA); education (MA, Ed D); financial services law, regulation and compliance (LL M); food science (M Sc); forensic psychology (M Sc); health and social care management and policy (M Sc); human nutrition (M Sc); human resource management (MA); human rights and international conflict (MA); information technology (M Sc); intelligence and security studies (M Sc); international oil, gas and energy law (LL M); international relations (MA); interpreting (MA); learning and teaching in higher education (MA); legal practice (LL M); media and entertainment law (LL M); organizational and consumer psychology (M Sc); psychological therapy (M Sc); psychology of mental health (M Sc); public health (M Sc); public policy and management (MPA); security studies (M Sc); social work (M Sc); spatial planning and urban design (MA); sports therapy (M Sc); supporting older children and young people with dyslexia (MA); teaching languages (MA), including Arabic, English; translation (MA); woman and child abuse (MA).

Louisiana State University and Agricultural & Mechanical College, Paul M. Hebert Law Center, Baton Rouge, LA 70803. Offers LL M, JD. *Accreditation:* ABA. *Faculty:* 39 full-time (17 women), 19 part-time/adjunct (1 woman). *Students:* 569 full-time (262 women); includes 114 minority (44 Black or African American, non-Hispanic/Latino; 2 American Indian or Alaska Native, non-Hispanic/Latino; 13 Asian, non-Hispanic/Latino; 42 Hispanic/Latino; 13 Two or more races, non-Hispanic/Latino), 8 international. Average age 26. 899 applicants, 62% accepted, 205 enrolled. In 2018, 8 master's awarded. *Degree requirements:* For master's, thesis optional. *Entrance requirements:* For doctorate, LSAT. Additional exam requirements/recommendations for international students: Required—TOEFL (minimum score 600 paper-based; 100 iBT). *Application deadline:* For fall admission, 3/1 priority date for domestic and international students. Applications are processed on a rolling basis. Application fee: $50. Electronic applications accepted. Application fee is waived when completed online. *Expenses:* Contact institution. *Financial support:* In 2018–19, 528 students received support. Scholarships/grants and tuition waivers (full and partial) available. Financial award application deadline: 7/1; financial award applicants required to submit FAFSA. *Unit head:* Thomas Galligan, Dean, 225-578-8491, Fax: 225-578-8202, E-mail: tgalligan@lsu.edu. *Application contact:* Jake T. Henry, III, Director of Admissions, 225-578-8646, Fax: 225-578-8647, E-mail: jakeh@lsu.edu.
Website: http://www.law.lsu.edu/

Loyola Marymount University, College of Business Administration, MBA/JD Program, Los Angeles, CA 90045-2659. Offers MBA/JD. *Unit head:* William Semos, Interim Associate Dean and Director, MBA Program, 310-338-2848, E-mail: william.semos@lmu.edu. *Application contact:* Ammar Dalal, Assistant Vice Provost for Graduate Enrollment, 310-338-2721, Fax: 310-338-6086, E-mail: graduateinfo@lmu.edu.
Website: http://lls.edu/admissionsaid/degreeprograms/jdprograms/jdmbaprogram

Loyola Marymount University, Loyola Law School Los Angeles, Los Angeles, CA 90015. Offers law (LL M, MLS, JD, JSD); law/business (JD/MBA); law/tax law (JD/LL M); tax law (LL M in Tax, MT); JD/LL M; JD/MBA. *Accreditation:* ABA. *Program availability:* Part-time, evening/weekend. *Faculty:* 65 full-time (33 women), 120 part-time/adjunct (47 women). *Students:* 913 full-time (510 women), 194 part-time (95 women); includes 445 minority (48 Black or African American, non-Hispanic/Latino; 2 American Indian or Alaska Native, non-Hispanic/Latino; 117 Asian, non-Hispanic/Latino; 225 Hispanic/Latino; 1 Native Hawaiian or other Pacific Islander, non-Hispanic/Latino; 52 Two or more races, non-Hispanic/Latino), 80 international. Average age 27. 4,012 applicants, 36% accepted, 309 enrolled. In 2018, 62 master's, 281 doctorates awarded. *Degree requirements:* For master's, comprehensive exam; for doctorate, thesis/dissertation, defense of dissertation (for JSD). *Entrance requirements:* For master's, Master of Science in Legal Studies (MLS): English proficiency score required if applicable; Master of Laws (LLM): English proficiency score required if applicable; Master of Laws in Taxation (Tax LLM): English proficiency score required if applicable; Master of Tax Law (MT): GMAT, GRE, LSAT, SAT or ACT required; for doctorate, LSAT (for JD day program, JD/Tax LLM), LSAT or GRE required (for JD evening program), LSAT and GMAT (for JD/MBA), no exam required for Doctor of Juridical Science (JSD) program. Additional exam requirements/recommendations for international students: Required—TOEFL (minimum score 600 paper-based; 90 iBT), IELTS (minimum score 6.5). For international LLM applicants: TOEFL and IELTS is required; Duolingo is accepted. *Application deadline:* For fall admission, 2/1 priority date for domestic students, 2/1 for international students. Applications are processed on a rolling basis. Application fee: $0. Electronic applications accepted. *Expenses:* Tuition, General Student Fee, Student Bar Association Fee. *Financial support:* In 2018–19, 645 students received support, including 40 research assistantships (averaging $1,823 per year); career-related internships or fieldwork, Federal Work-Study, scholarships/grants, and tuition waivers (partial) also available. Support available to part-time students. Financial award application deadline: 3/15; financial award applicants required to submit FAFSA. *Faculty research:* Business law and innovation, criminal law, entertainment law, litigation and public interest law, international law. *Unit head:* Michael Waterstone, Dean, 213-736-2243, Fax: 213-487-6736, E-mail: michael.waterstone@lls.edu. *Application contact:*

Jannell Lundy Roberts, Senior Assistant Dean, Admissions and Enrollment Services, 213-736-1074, Fax: 213-736-6523, E-mail: admissions@lls.edu.
Website: http://www.lls.edu/

Loyola University Chicago, School of Law, Chicago, IL 60611. Offers advocacy (LL M); business and compliance (MJ); business law (LL M); child and family (LL M); child and family law (MJ, Certificate); global competition (LL M, MJ); health law (LL M, MJ, Certificate); international law (LL M); law (JD); public interest law (Certificate); rule of law for development (LL M, MJ); tax (LL M); tax law (Certificate); transactional law (Certificate); trial advocacy (Certificate); JD/MA; JD/MBA; JD/MPP; JD/MSW; MJ/MSW; MS/MJ. *Accreditation:* ABA. *Program availability:* Part-time, evening/weekend, 100% online, blended/hybrid learning. *Faculty:* 69 full-time (36 women), 306 part-time/adjunct (148 women). *Students:* 870 full-time (530 women), 239 part-time (185 women); includes 380 minority (134 Black or African American, non-Hispanic/Latino; 64 Asian, non-Hispanic/Latino; 142 Hispanic/Latino; 40 Two or more races, non-Hispanic/Latino), 34 international. Average age 31. 2,711 applicants, 46% accepted, 387 enrolled. In 2018, 151 master's, 193 doctorates, 152 Certificates awarded. *Entrance requirements:* For doctorate, LSAT. Additional exam requirements/recommendations for international students: Required—TOEFL (minimum score 100 iBT); Recommended—IELTS (minimum score 7). *Application deadline:* For fall admission, 4/1 for domestic and international students. Applications are processed on a rolling basis. Application fee: $0. Electronic applications accepted. *Expenses:* Contact institution. *Financial support:* In 2018–19, 598 students received support, including 67 fellowships; research assistantships, Federal Work-Study, scholarships/grants, and health care benefits also available. Financial award application deadline: 3/1; financial award applicants required to submit FAFSA. *Faculty research:* Constitutional law including hate speech and supreme court advocacy; early childhood education including law policy and pedagogy; hedonic psychology - legal and social determinants of happiness; racial inequality; intersection of law, science, and technology. *Unit head:* Dr. James Faught, JD, Associate Dean for Administration, Law School, 312-915-7131, Fax: 312-915-6911, E-mail: law-admissions@luc.edu. *Application contact:* Jill Schur, Director, Graduate Enrollment Management, 312-915-8902, E-mail: gradinfo@luc.edu.
Website: http://www.luc.edu/law/

Loyola University New Orleans, College of Law, New Orleans, LA 70118. Offers LL M, JD, JD/MBA, JD/MPA, JD/MURP. *Accreditation:* ABA. *Program availability:* Part-time, online learning. *Faculty:* 42 full-time (21 women), 26 part-time/adjunct (11 women). *Students:* 429 full-time (242 women), 80 part-time (37 women); includes 185 minority (85 Black or African American, non-Hispanic/Latino; 12 American Indian or Alaska Native, non-Hispanic/Latino; 16 Asian, non-Hispanic/Latino; 66 Hispanic/Latino; 6 Two or more races, non-Hispanic/Latino), 6 international. Average age 27. 795 applicants, 61% accepted, 170 enrolled. In 2018, 4 master's, 144 doctorates awarded. *Entrance requirements:* For doctorate, LSAT, 2 letters of recommendation, interview, resume, personal statement, bachelor's degree from accredited college/university. Additional exam requirements/recommendations for international students: Required—TOEFL (minimum score 550 paper-based; 89 iBT). *Application deadline:* For fall admission, 8/1 priority date for domestic and international students. Applications are processed on a rolling basis. Application fee: $0. Electronic applications accepted. *Expenses:* $21,848 per semester full-time, fees: $730; $16,386 per semester part-time, fees: $381. *Financial support:* Fellowships, research assistantships, teaching assistantships, career-related internships or fieldwork, institutionally sponsored loans, scholarships/grants, traineeships, health care benefits, tuition waivers, and unspecified assistantships available. Support available to part-time students. Financial award applicants required to submit FAFSA. *Faculty research:* Louisiana civil code, international law, commercial law, comparative law. *Unit head:* Madeleine Landrieu, Dean, 504-861-5847, Fax: 504-861-5677, E-mail: lmoore@loyno.edu. *Application contact:* Kimberly Jones, Director of Law Admissions, 504-861-5575, Fax: 504-861-5772, E-mail: ladmit@loyno.edu.
Website: http://www.loyno.edu/law/

Marquette University, Law School, Milwaukee, WI 53201-1881. Offers JD, JD/Certificate, JD/MA, JD/MBA. *Accreditation:* ABA. *Program availability:* Part-time, evening/weekend. *Entrance requirements:* For doctorate, LSAT, subscription to LSAC's Credential Assembly Service. Additional exam requirements/recommendations for international students: Required—TOEFL. Electronic applications accepted. *Expenses:* Contact institution. *Faculty research:* Constitutional law, sports law, dispute resolution, intellectual property, legal ethics.

Massachusetts School of Law at Andover, Professional Program, Andover, MA 01810. Offers JD. *Program availability:* Part-time, evening/weekend. *Entrance requirements:* For doctorate, Massachusetts School of Law Aptitude Test (MSLAT), interview. Additional exam requirements/recommendations for international students: Recommended—TOEFL. Electronic applications accepted.

McGill University, Faculty of Graduate and Postdoctoral Studies, Faculty of Law, Department of Law, Montréal, QC H3A 2T5, Canada. Offers LL M, DCL.

McGill University, Faculty of Graduate and Postdoctoral Studies, Faculty of Law, Institute of Air and Space Law, Montréal, QC H3A 2T5, Canada. Offers LL M, DCL, Graduate Certificate.

McGill University, Faculty of Graduate and Postdoctoral Studies, Faculty of Law, Institute of Comparative Law, Montréal, QC H3A 2T5, Canada. Offers LL M, DCL, Graduate Certificate.

Mercer University, Mercer University School of Law, Macon, GA 31207. Offers JD, JD/MBA. JD/MBA offered jointly with Eugene W. Stetson School of Business and Economics. *Accreditation:* ABA. *Entrance requirements:* For doctorate, LSAT. Additional exam requirements/recommendations for international students: Recommended—TOEFL (minimum score 600 paper-based; 100 iBT). Electronic applications accepted. *Expenses:* Contact institution. *Faculty research:* Legal ethics, environmental law, employment discrimination, statutory law, legal writing.

Michigan State University College of Law, Graduate and Professional Programs, East Lansing, MI 48824-1300. Offers American legal system (LL M, MJ); global food law (LL M, MJ); intellectual property law (LL M, MJ); law (JD); legal studies (MLS). *Accreditation:* ABA. *Program availability:* Part-time. *Entrance requirements:* For doctorate, LSAT. Additional exam requirements/recommendations for international students: Required—TOEFL (minimum score 600 paper-based), IELTS. Electronic applications accepted. *Expenses: Tuition:* Full-time $44,200. *Required fees:* $37. *Faculty research:* International, constitutional, health, tax and environmental law; intellectual property, trial practice, corporate law.

Mississippi College, School of Law, Jackson, MS 39201. Offers civil law studies (Certificate); law (JD); JD/MBA. *Accreditation:* ABA. *Degree requirements:* For doctorate, thesis/dissertation. *Entrance requirements:* For doctorate, LSAT, LDAS report. Additional exam requirements/recommendations for international students: Recommended—TOEFL, IELTS. Electronic applications accepted. *Expenses:* Contact institution.

Mitchell Hamline School of Law, Graduate and Professional Programs, Saint Paul, MN 55105-3076. Offers LL M, JD. *Accreditation:* ABA. *Program availability:* Part-time, evening/weekend, blended/hybrid learning. *Entrance requirements:* For master's, any law degree from the U.S. or foreign country; for doctorate, LSAT. Additional exam requirements/recommendations for international students: Required—TOEFL. Electronic applications accepted. *Faculty research:* Child protection, domestic violence, elder law, intellectual property law, preventive detention and post-release civil commitment.

Montclair State University, The Graduate School, College of Humanities and Social Sciences, MA Program in Law and Governance, Montclair, NJ 07043-1624. Offers conflict management and peace studies (MA); governance, compliance and regulation (MA); intellectual property (MA); law and governance (MA); legal management (MA). *Program availability:* Part-time, evening/weekend. *Degree requirements:* For master's, thesis or comprehensive exam. *Entrance requirements:* For master's, GRE General Test, minimum cumulative GPA of 2.75 for undergraduate work, 2 letters of recommendation, essay. Additional exam requirements/recommendations for international students: Required—TOEFL (minimum score 83 iBT) or IELTS (minimum score 6.5). Electronic applications accepted.

New England Law–Boston, Graduate Programs, Boston, MA 02116-5687. Offers American law (LL M); law (JD). *Accreditation:* ABA. *Program availability:* Part-time, evening/weekend. *Entrance requirements:* For doctorate, LSAT, LSDAS. Additional exam requirements/recommendations for international students: Required—TOEFL (minimum score 600 paper-based; 100 iBT). Electronic applications accepted.

New York Law School, Graduate Programs, New York, NY 10013. Offers LL M, JD, JD/MA, JD/MBA. JD/MBA offered jointly with Baruch College of the City University of New York; JD/MA in forensic psychology offered jointly with John Jay College of Criminal Justice of the City University of New York. *Accreditation:* ABA. *Program availability:* Part-time, evening/weekend. *Faculty:* 56 full-time (27 women), 83 part-time/adjunct (26 women). *Students:* 791 full-time (467 women), 251 part-time (136 women); includes 334 minority (61 Black or African American, non-Hispanic/Latino; 74 Asian, non-Hispanic/Latino; 170 Hispanic/Latino; 1 Native Hawaiian or other Pacific Islander, non-Hispanic/Latino; 28 Two or more races, non-Hispanic/Latino), 26 international. Average age 27. 2,837 applicants, 52% accepted, 385 enrolled. In 2018, 13 master's, 272 doctorates awarded. *Entrance requirements:* For master's, JD (for LL M); for doctorate, LSAT, undergraduate degree, letter of recommendation, resume, essay/personal statement. Additional exam requirements/recommendations for international students: Required—TOEFL (minimum score 600 paper-based; 100 iBT). *Application deadline:* For fall admission, 7/1 priority date for domestic and international students. Applications are processed on a rolling basis. Application fee: $0. Electronic applications accepted. *Expenses: Tuition:* Full-time $50,008; part-time $38,536 per year. *Required fees:* $1724; $1224 per unit. Tuition and fees vary according to course load and degree level. *Financial support:* In 2018–19, 698 students received support, including 107 fellowships (averaging $4,110 per year), 22 research assistantships (averaging $4,663 per year), 19 teaching assistantships (averaging $4,661 per year); career-related internships or fieldwork, Federal Work-Study, and scholarships/grants also available. Support available to part-time students. Financial award application deadline: 7/1; financial award applicants required to submit FAFSA. *Faculty research:* Immigration law, intellectual property, civil rights, family law, international law. *Unit head:* Anthony W. Crowell, Dean and President, 212-431-2840, Fax: 212-219-3752, E-mail: anthony.crowell@nyls.edu. *Application contact:* Ella Mae Estrada, Associate Dean for Enrollment Management, Financial Aid and Diversity Initiatives, 212-431-2888, Fax: 212-966-1522, E-mail: admissions@nyls.edu.
Website: http://www.nyls.edu

New York University, School of Law, New York, NY 10012-1019. Offers law (LL M, JD, JSD); law and business (Advanced Certificate); taxation (MSL, Advanced Certificate); JD/LL M; JD/MA; JD/MBA; JD/MPA; JD/MPP; JD/MSW; JD/MUP; JD/PhD. *Accreditation:* ABA. *Program availability:* Part-time, blended/hybrid learning. *Entrance requirements:* For doctorate, LSAT (for JD). Electronic applications accepted. *Expenses:* Contact institution. *Faculty research:* International law, environmental law, corporate law, globalization of law, philosophy of law.

North Carolina Central University, School of Law, Durham, NC 27707. Offers JD, JD/MPA, JD/MPP, MBA/JD. *Accreditation:* ABA. *Program availability:* Part-time, evening/weekend. *Entrance requirements:* For doctorate, LSAT, LSDAS. Additional exam requirements/recommendations for international students: Required—TOEFL. *Expenses:* Contact institution.

Northeastern University, School of Law, Boston, MA 02115-5005. Offers LL M, MLS, JD, JD/MA, JD/MBA, JD/MELP, JD/MPH, JD/MS, JD/MSA/MBA, LL M/MA, LL M/MBA. JD/MPH offered jointly with Tufts University; JD/MSA/MBA with Graduate School of Professional Accounting; JD/MS with Program in Law and Public Policy; JD/MELP with Vermont Law School; and JD/MA with Brandeis University. *Accreditation:* ABA. *Program availability:* Online learning. Electronic applications accepted. *Expenses:* Contact institution. *Faculty research:* Human rights law, health law, criminal law, corporate/finance law, international law.

Northern Illinois University, College of Law, De Kalb, IL 60115-2854. Offers JD. *Accreditation:* ABA. *Program availability:* Part-time. *Faculty:* 22 full-time (11 women). *Students:* 221 full-time (105 women), 39 part-time (15 women); includes 61 minority (27 Black or African American, non-Hispanic/Latino; 8 Asian, non-Hispanic/Latino; 18 Hispanic/Latino; 2 Native Hawaiian or other Pacific Islander, non-Hispanic/Latino; 6 Two or more races, non-Hispanic/Latino), 3 international. Average age 27. 611 applicants, 51% accepted, 92 enrolled. In 2018, 77 doctorates awarded. *Entrance requirements:* For doctorate, LSAT. Additional exam requirements/recommendations for international students: Required—TOEFL. *Application deadline:* For fall admission, 4/1 priority date for domestic and international students. Applications are processed on a rolling basis. Electronic applications accepted. *Expenses:* Contact institution. *Financial support:* In 2018–19, 8 teaching assistantships were awarded; research assistantships, career-related internships or fieldwork, Federal Work-Study, tuition waivers (full and partial), and unspecified assistantships also available. Support available to part-time students. Financial award application deadline: 3/1; financial award applicants required to submit FAFSA. *Faculty research:* Criminal practice, intellectual property, environmental law, taxation. *Unit head:* Laurel Rigertas, Interim Dean, 815-753-5300, Fax: 815-753-8552, E-mail: lrigertas@niu.edu. *Application contact:* Amanda Noascono, Director of Admissions and Financial Aid, 815-753-8595, Fax: 815-753-5680, E-mail: law-admit@niu.edu.
Website: http://law.niu.edu/

Northern Kentucky University, Chase College of Law, Highland Heights, KY 41099. Offers JD, JD/MBA, JD/MBI. *Accreditation:* ABA. *Program availability:* Part-time, evening/weekend. *Faculty:* 25 full-time (8 women), 37 part-time/adjunct (9 women). *Students:* 283 full-time (147 women), 154 part-time (84 women); includes 48 minority (30 Black or African American, non-Hispanic/Latino; 6 Asian, non-Hispanic/Latino; 12 Hispanic/Latino). Average age 27. 542 applicants, 68% accepted, 140 enrolled. In 2018, 93 doctorates awarded. *Entrance requirements:* For doctorate, LSAT, bachelor's degree. Additional exam requirements/recommendations for international students: Required—TOEFL (minimum score 92 iBT), IELTS (minimum score 6.5). *Application deadline:* For fall admission, 4/1 priority date for domestic and international students; for summer admission, 3/15 priority date for domestic students, 3/15 for international

students. Applications are processed on a rolling basis. Application fee: $40. Electronic applications accepted. *Expenses:* Tuition rates for 2018-2019: $10,166 per semester resident full-time, $782 per credit hour resident part-time, $16,445 per semester non-resident full-time, $1,265 per credit hour non-resident part-time. *Financial support:* Fellowships, research assistantships, career-related internships or fieldwork, Federal Work-Study, scholarships/grants, and unspecified assistantships available. Support available to part-time students. Financial award application deadline: 3/1; financial award applicants required to submit FAFSA. *Unit head:* Judith Daar, Dean. *Application contact:* Ashley Siemer, Director of Student Affairs and Enrollment Management, 859-572-5841, E-mail: graya4@nku.edu.
Website: chaselaw.nku.edu

Northwestern University, Pritzker School of Law, Chicago, IL 60611-3069. Offers international human rights (LL M); law (MSL, JD); tax (LL M in Tax); JD/LL M; JD/MBA; JD/PhD; LL M/Certificate. Executive LL M programs offered in Madrid (Spain), Seoul (South Korea), and Tel Aviv (Israel). *Accreditation:* ABA. *Program availability:* Part-time, online learning. *Entrance requirements:* For master's, law degree or equivalent, letter of recommendation, resume; for doctorate, LSAT, 1 letter of recommendation, resume. Additional exam requirements/recommendations for international students: Required—TOEFL. Electronic applications accepted. *Expenses:* Contact institution. *Faculty research:* Constitutional law, corporate law, international law, law and social policy, ethical studies.

Nova Southeastern University, Shepard Broad College of Law, Fort Lauderdale, FL 33314. Offers education law (MS), including cybersecurity law, education law advocacy, exceptional education; employment law (MS), including cybersecurity law, employee relations law, human resource managerial law; health law (MS, JD), including clinical research law and regulatory compliance (MS), cybersecurity law (MS), health care administrative law (MS), regulatory compliance (MS), risk management (MS); international law (JD); law and policy (MS), including cybersecurity law; JD/DO; JD/M Acc; JD/M Tax; JD/MBA; JD/MPA; JD/MS; JD/PhD. *Accreditation:* ABA. *Program availability:* Part-time, evening/weekend, 100% online, blended/hybrid learning. *Degree requirements:* For master's, thesis optional, capstone research project; for doctorate, rigorous upper-level writing fulfilled through faculty-supervised seminar paper, law journal article, workshop, or other research; 6 credits' experiential learning. *Entrance requirements:* For master's, regionally-accredited undergraduate degree; at least 2 years' experience in related field (for employment law and health law); for doctorate, LSAT. Additional exam requirements/recommendations for international students: Recommended—TOEFL (minimum score 600 paper-based; 100 iBT), IELTS (minimum score 7). Electronic applications accepted. *Expenses:* Contact institution. *Faculty research:* Legal issues in health law, international law, the legal profession, family law, civil rights.

Ohio Northern University, Claude W. Pettit College of Law, Ada, OH 45810-1599. Offers LL M, JD. *Accreditation:* ABA. *Entrance requirements:* For doctorate, LSAT. Additional exam requirements/recommendations for international students: Required—TOEFL. Electronic applications accepted. *Expenses:* Contact institution. *Faculty research:* Constitutional law, environmental law, business law and taxation, criminal law, public interest law, death penalty for women and juveniles, international human rights, sports violence.

The Ohio State University, Moritz College of Law, Columbus, OH 43210. Offers LL M, MSL, JD, JD/MA, JD/MBA, JD/MD, JD/MHA, JD/MPH. *Accreditation:* ABA. *Entrance requirements:* Additional exam requirements/recommendations for international students: Required—TOEFL (minimum score 650 paper-based; 100 iBT). Electronic applications accepted. *Expenses:* Contact institution. *Faculty research:* Alternative dispute resolution, law and policy, criminal law, intellectual property, big data and governance.

Oklahoma City University, School of Law, Oklahoma City, OK 73106-1402. Offers LL M, JD, JD/MBA. *Accreditation:* ABA. *Program availability:* Part-time, evening/weekend. *Entrance requirements:* For doctorate, LSAT, bachelor's degree from accredited undergraduate institution (except for OCU students admitted through the Oxford plan). Additional exam requirements/recommendations for international students: Required—TOEFL (minimum score 100 iBT). Electronic applications accepted. *Expenses:* Contact institution. *Faculty research:* Family law, environmental law, consumer law, alternative dispute resolution, criminal law and procedure.

Pace University, Elisabeth Haub School of Law, White Plains, NY 10603. Offers comparative legal studies (LL M); environmental law (LL M, SJD), including energy and climate change law (LL M), global environmental law (LL M); law (JD); JD/LL M; JD/MA; JD/MBA; JD/MEM; JD/MPA; JD/MS. JD/MA offered jointly with Sarah Lawrence College; JD/MEM offered jointly with Yale University School of Forestry and Environmental Studies. *Accreditation:* ABA. *Program availability:* Part-time. *Degree requirements:* For doctorate, thesis/dissertation (for some programs), extensive thesis proposal (for SJD). *Entrance requirements:* For master's, writing sample; for doctorate, LSAT (for JD). Additional exam requirements/recommendations for international students: Required—TOEFL (minimum score 100 iBT); Recommended—TWE. Electronic applications accepted. *Expenses:* Contact institution. *Faculty research:* Reform of energy regulations, international law, land use law, prosecutorial misconduct, corporation law.

Penn State University–Dickinson Law, Graduate and Professional Programs, Carlisle, PA 17013. Offers LL M, JD. *Accreditation:* ABA. *Entrance requirements:* For doctorate, LSAT. Electronic applications accepted.

Penn State University Park, Penn State Law, University Park, PA 16802. Offers LL M, JD, SJD. *Accreditation:* ABA. *Entrance requirements:* For master's, BA or LL B in law; for doctorate, LSAT. Additional exam requirements/recommendations for international students: Required—TOEFL, IELTS. Electronic applications accepted.

Pontifical Catholic University of Puerto Rico, School of Law, Ponce, PR 00717-0777. Offers JD. *Accreditation:* ABA. *Program availability:* Part-time, evening/weekend. *Entrance requirements:* For doctorate, LSAT, PAEG, 3 letters of recommendation.

Pontificia Universidad Catolica Madre y Maestra, Graduate School, Faculty of Social and Administrative Sciences, Santiago, Dominican Republic. Offers business administration (MBA), including business development, finance, international business, management skills (M Mgmt, MBA), marketing, operations, strategic cost management, strategy, tourist destination planning and management; law (LL M), including civil law, corporate business law, criminal law, international relations, real estate law; management (M Mgmt), including higher financial management, insurance program administration, management skills (M Mgmt, MBA); psychology (MA), including clinical child and adolescent psychology, forensic psychology; strategic human resources (EMBA).

Purdue University Global, School of Criminal Justice, Davenport, IA 52807. Offers corrections (MSCJ); global issues in criminal justice (MSCJ); law (MSCJ); leadership and executive management (MSCJ); policing (MSCJ). *Program availability:* Part-time, evening/weekend, online learning. *Entrance requirements:* Additional exam requirements/recommendations for international students: Required—TOEFL (minimum score 550 paper-based; 80 iBT). Electronic applications accepted.

Queen's University at Kingston, Faculty of Law, Kingston, ON K7L 3N6, Canada. Offers LL M, JD, JD/MBA, JD/MIR, JD/MPA. *Program availability:* Part-time. *Degree requirements:* For master's, thesis. *Entrance requirements:* For doctorate, LSAT, minimum 2 years of college. Additional exam requirements/recommendations for international students: Required—TOEFL, TWE. *Faculty research:* Labor relations law, tax law and policy, criminal law and policy, critical legal theories, international legal relations.

Quinnipiac University, School of Law, Hamden, CT 06518-1940. Offers LL M, JD, JD/MBA, JD/MELP. *Accreditation:* ABA. *Program availability:* Part-time, evening/weekend. *Entrance requirements:* For doctorate, LSAT. Additional exam requirements/recommendations for international students: Recommended—TOEFL. Electronic applications accepted. Application fee is waived when completed online. *Expenses:* Contact institution. *Faculty research:* Sentencing, death penalty, public health law, tax law, legal history.

Regent University, Graduate School, Robertson School of Government, Virginia Beach, VA 23464-9800. Offers government (MA), including American government, healthcare policy and ethics (MA, MPA), international relations, law and public policy, national security studies, political communication, political theory, religion and politics; national security studies (MA), including cybersecurity, homeland security, international security, Middle East politics; public administration (MPA), including emergency management and homeland security, federal government, general public administration, healthcare policy and ethics (MA, MPA), law, nonprofit administration and faith-based organizations, public leadership and management, servant leadership. *Program availability:* Part-time, evening/weekend, 100% online, blended/hybrid learning. *Degree requirements:* For master's, thesis optional, internship. *Entrance requirements:* For master's, GRE General Test or LSAT, personal essay, writing sample, resume, college transcripts. Additional exam requirements/recommendations for international students: Required—TOEFL (minimum score 577 paper-based). Electronic applications accepted. *Expenses:* Contact institution. *Faculty research:* International relations and politics, public administration, leadership and ethics, Biblical law, Constitutional law and Supreme Court.

Regent University, Graduate School, School of Law, Virginia Beach, VA 23464-9800. Offers American legal studies (LL M); human rights (LL M); law (MA, JD), including advanced paralegal studies (MA), alternative dispute resolution (MA), business (MA), criminal justice (MA), general legal studies (MA), human resources management (MA), human rights and rule of law (MA), national security (MA), non-profit organizational law (MA), regulatory compliance (MA), wealth management and financial planning (MA); JD/MA; JD/MBA. *Accreditation:* ABA. *Program availability:* Part-time, 100% online, blended/hybrid learning. *Entrance requirements:* For master's, college transcripts, resume, personal statement; for doctorate, LSAT, minimum undergraduate GPA of 3.0, official transcripts, 2 letters of recommendation, resume, personal statement. Additional exam requirements/recommendations for international students: Required—TOEFL (minimum score 600 paper-based). Electronic applications accepted. *Expenses:* Contact institution. *Faculty research:* Family law, Constitutional law, law and culture, evidence and practice, intellectual property.

Roger Williams University, School of Law, Bristol, RI 02809-5171. Offers MSL, JD, JD/MLRHR, JD/MMA, JD/MS, JD/MSCJ. JD/MMA and JD/MLRHR offered jointly with University of Rhode Island. *Accreditation:* ABA. *Program availability:* Part-time. *Faculty:* 27 full-time (16 women), 31 part-time/adjunct (14 women). *Students:* 461 full-time (244 women); includes 125 minority (35 Black or African American, non-Hispanic/Latino; 1 American Indian or Alaska Native, non-Hispanic/Latino; 16 Asian, non-Hispanic/Latino; 54 Hispanic/Latino; 19 Two or more races, non-Hispanic/Latino), 6 international. Average age 27. 849 applicants, 71% accepted, 161 enrolled. In 2018, 4 master's, 129 doctorates awarded. *Entrance requirements:* For master's, GRE, GMAT; for doctorate, LSAT. Additional exam requirements/recommendations for international students: Required—TOEFL (minimum score 600 paper-based; 100 iBT). *Application deadline:* For fall admission, 4/1 priority date for domestic and international students. Applications are processed on a rolling basis. Application fee: $60. Electronic applications accepted. *Financial support:* In 2018–19, 255 students received support, including 9 fellowships (averaging $1,739 per year), 51 research assistantships (averaging $931 per year); Federal Work-Study also available. Financial award application deadline: 3/15; financial award applicants required to submit FAFSA. *Faculty research:* Civil rights, Constitutional law, contract law, intellectual property, conflicts of law, national security, international law. *Unit head:* Michael Yelnosky, Dean, 401-254-4500, Fax: 401-254-3525, E-mail: myelnosky@rwu.edu. *Application contact:* Michael W. Donnelly-Boylen, Assistant Dean of Admissions, 401-254-4555, Fax: 401-254-4516, E-mail: mdonnelly-boylen@rwu.edu.
Website: http://law.rwu.edu

Rutgers University–Camden, School of Law, Camden, NJ 08102. Offers JD, JD/DO, JD/MA, JD/MBA, JD/MCRP, JD/MD, JD/MPA, JD/MPH, JD/MS, JD/MSW. JD/MCRP, JD/MA, JD/MPA, JD/MSW, JD/MS offered jointly with Rutgers, The State University of New Jersey, New Brunswick; JD/MPA, JD/MD, JD/DO with University of Medicine and Dentistry of New Jersey. *Accreditation:* ABA. *Program availability:* Part-time, evening/weekend. *Entrance requirements:* For doctorate, LSAT. Additional exam requirements/recommendations for international students: Recommended—TOEFL. Electronic applications accepted. *Expenses:* Contact institution. *Faculty research:* International law, commercial law, public law, health law, constitutional law, jurisprudence.

Rutgers University–Newark, School of Law, Newark, NJ 07102-3094. Offers JD, JD/MA, JD/MBA, JD/MCRP, JD/MD, JD/MSW, JD/PhD. JD/MCRP, JD/PhD offered jointly with Rutgers, The State University of New Jersey, New Brunswick. *Accreditation:* ABA. *Program availability:* Part-time, evening/weekend. *Entrance requirements:* For doctorate, LSAT. *Expenses:* Contact institution. *Faculty research:* Civil rights and liberties, women and the law, international human rights and world order, corporate law, employment law.

St. John's University, School of Law, Program in Law, Queens, NY 11439. Offers JD, JD/LL M, MA/JD, MBA/JD. *Accreditation:* ABA. *Program availability:* Part-time, evening/weekend. *Entrance requirements:* For doctorate, LSAT or GRE, bachelor's degree, personal statement, CAS report, 2 letters of recommendation. Additional exam requirements/recommendations for international students: Recommended—TOEFL (minimum score 600 paper-based; 100 iBT), IELTS (minimum score 7). Electronic applications accepted. *Expenses:* Contact institution.

Saint Joseph's University, College of Arts and Sciences, Department of Criminal Justice, Philadelphia, PA 19131-1395. Offers behavior analysis (MS, Post-Master's Certificate); behavior management (MS); criminal justice (MS); federal law enforcement (MS); intelligence and crime analysis (MS). *Program availability:* Part-time, evening/weekend, 100% online, blended/hybrid learning. *Degree requirements:* For master's, thesis optional. *Entrance requirements:* For master's, 2 letters of recommendation, personal statement, resume, official transcripts, minimum GPA of 3.0. Additional exam requirements/recommendations for international students: Required—TOEFL (minimum score 550 paper-based; 80 iBT). Electronic applications accepted. *Expenses:* Contact institution. *Faculty research:* Ethics in policing, multiculturalism, behavior analysis.

Saint Louis University, School of Law, St. Louis, MO 63108. Offers LL M, JD. *Accreditation:* ABA. *Program availability:* Part-time, evening/weekend. *Degree*

requirements: For master's, thesis (for some programs). *Entrance requirements:* For master's, JD or equivalent; for doctorate, LSAT, letters of recommendation, resume, personal statement, LSDAS. Additional exam requirements/recommendations for international students: Required—TOEFL (minimum score 590 paper-based). Electronic applications accepted. *Expenses:* Contact institution. *Faculty research:* Health law, employment law, international comparative law, lawyering skills (clinical).

St. Mary's University, School of Law, JD Program, San Antonio, TX 78228. Offers JD. *Accreditation:* ABA. *Program availability:* Part-time, evening/weekend. *Students:* 661 full-time (323 women), 74 part-time (43 women); includes 425 minority (38 Black or African American, non-Hispanic/Latino; 7 American Indian or Alaska Native, non-Hispanic/Latino; 21 Asian, non-Hispanic/Latino; 358 Hispanic/Latino; 1 Native Hawaiian or other Pacific Islander, non-Hispanic/Latino), 3 international. Average age 28. In 2018, 212 doctorates awarded. *Degree requirements:* For doctorate, 90 credit hours, minimum cumulative GPA of 2.0. *Entrance requirements:* For doctorate, LSAT, explanation of affirmative responses to character and fitness questions, personal statement. Additional exam requirements/recommendations for international students: Required—TOEFL (minimum score 550 paper-based; 80 iBT), IELTS (minimum score 6), LSAT. *Application deadline:* For fall admission, 3/1 priority date for domestic students, 3/1 for international students; for spring admission, 3/1 priority date for domestic students. Application fee: $0. Electronic applications accepted. *Expenses:* Contact institution. *Financial support:* Fellowships, research assistantships, teaching assistantships, career-related internships or fieldwork, and scholarships/grants available. Support available to part-time students. Financial award application deadline: 3/1; financial award applicants required to submit FAFSA. *Unit head:* Stephen Sheppard, Dean, 210-436-3684, E-mail: sheppard@stmarytx.edu. *Application contact:* Catherine Casiano, Director of Admissions and Recruitment, 210-436-3525, E-mail: ccasiano@stmarytx.edu.
Website: https://law.stmarytx.edu/academics/jd-programs/

St. Mary's University, School of Law, LL M Program, San Antonio, TX 78228. Offers American legal studies (LL M); international and comparative law (LL M); international criminal law (LL M). *Program availability:* Part-time. *Students:* 12 full-time (6 women), 5 part-time (2 women); includes 9 minority (1 Black or African American, non-Hispanic/Latino; 8 Hispanic/Latino), 5 international. Average age 35. 41 applicants, 95% accepted, 8 enrolled. In 2018, 12 master's awarded. *Degree requirements:* For master's, thesis, 24 hours of academic credit. *Entrance requirements:* For master's, official transcripts, personal statement, resume, 2 letters of recommendation. Additional exam requirements/recommendations for international students: Required—TOEFL (minimum score 550 paper-based; 80 iBT), IELTS (minimum score 6). *Application deadline:* Applications are processed on a rolling basis. Application fee: $0. Electronic applications accepted. *Expenses:* 37320. *Financial support:* Scholarships/grants available. Financial award applicants required to submit FAFSA. *Unit head:* Dean Colin Marks, Assistant Dean of Grad. and Summer Programs, 210-431-2248, E-mail: cmarks@stmarytx.edu. *Application contact:* Lupe Valdez, Legal Secretary, 210-431-6878, E-mail: gvaldez@stmarytx.edu.
Website: https://law.stmarytx.edu/academics/programs/ll-m-degrees/

St. Mary's University, School of Law, Master of Jurisprudence Program, San Antonio, TX 78228. Offers business and entrepreneurship law (MJ); commercial law (MJ); compliance, business law and risk (MJ); criminal justice (MJ); education law (MJ); environmental law (MJ); health law (MJ); healthcare compliance (MJ); international comparative law (MJ); military and national security law (MJ); natural resource law (MJ); tax law (MJ). *Program availability:* Part-time, evening/weekend, 100% online, blended/hybrid learning. *Students:* 14 full-time (10 women), 21 part-time (16 women); includes 17 minority (1 Black or African American, non-Hispanic/Latino; 16 Hispanic/Latino). Average age 41. 37 applicants, 89% accepted, 22 enrolled. In 2018, 9 master's awarded. *Degree requirements:* For master's, 30 credits, minimum GPA of 2.0. *Entrance requirements:* For master's, official transcripts, personal statement, resume, 2 letters of recommendation, proof of four-year undergraduate degree from accredited U.S. college/university or foreign institution approved by government or accrediting authority. Additional exam requirements/recommendations for international students: Required—TOEFL (minimum score 550 paper-based; 80 iBT), IELTS (minimum score 6). *Application deadline:* Applications are processed on a rolling basis. Application fee: $0. Electronic applications accepted. *Expenses:* 36550. *Financial support:* Applicants required to submit FAFSA. *Unit head:* Dean Colin Marks, Assistant Dean of Grad. and Summer Programs, 210-431 Ext. 2248, E-mail: cmarks@stmarytx.edu. *Application contact:* Alyssa Turrieta, Coordinator, 210-436-3829.
Website: https://law.stmarytx.edu/academics/programs/master-of-jurisprudence/

St. Thomas University, School of Law, Miami Gardens, FL 33054-6459. Offers international human rights (LL M); international taxation (LL M); law (JD); JD/MBA; JD/MS. *Accreditation:* ABA. *Program availability:* Online learning. *Degree requirements:* For master's, thesis (international taxation). *Entrance requirements:* For doctorate, LSAT. Electronic applications accepted. *Expenses:* Contact institution.

Samford University, Cumberland School of Law, Birmingham, AL 35229. Offers LL M, MCL, MSL, JD, JD/M Acc, JD/M Div, JD/MATS, JD/MBA, JD/MPA, JD/MPH, JD/MS, JD/MSEM. Samford University, University of Alabama Birmingham. *Accreditation:* ABA. *Program availability:* Part-time, 100% online. *Faculty:* 17 full-time (7 women), 21 part-time/adjunct (8 women). *Students:* 453 full-time (231 women), 11 part-time (4 women); includes 87 minority (55 Black or African American, non-Hispanic/Latino; 5 American Indian or Alaska Native, non-Hispanic/Latino; 6 Asian, non-Hispanic/Latino; 17 Hispanic/Latino; 1 Native Hawaiian or other Pacific Islander, non-Hispanic/Latino; 3 Two or more races, non-Hispanic/Latino), 1 international. Average age 27. 607 applicants, 74% accepted, 170 enrolled. In 2018, 13 master's, 142 doctorates awarded. *Entrance requirements:* For master's, personal statement, professional resume; 1 letter of recommendation; JD or enrolled as JD student and letter of recommendation; for doctorate, LSAT, undergraduate degree. Additional exam requirements/recommendations for international students: Required—TOEFL (minimum score 550 paper-based; 90 iBT). *Application deadline:* For fall admission, 6/1 for domestic students, 6/1 priority date for international students. Electronic applications accepted. *Expenses:* Less than 10 hours JD Law - 1300 per hour 10-16 Hours JD Law - 19,800 per semester Masters of Law - 837 per hour Fees - 275 each semester. *Financial support:* In 2018–19, 374 students received support. Scholarships/grants available. Financial award application deadline: 3/1; financial award applicants required to submit FAFSA. *Faculty research:* Environmental, criminal, constitutional law, evidence, civil procedure. *Unit head:* Henry C. Strickland, Dean and Ethel P. Malugen Professor of Law, 205-726-2704, Fax: 205-726-4457, E-mail: hcstrick@samford.edu. *Application contact:* Whitney Dachelet, Interim Director of Admissions and Student Recruiting, 205-726-2702, Fax: 205-726-2057, E-mail: wdachele@samford.edu.
Website: http://cumberland.samford.edu/

San Joaquin College of Law, Law Program, Clovis, CA 93612-1312. Offers JD. *Program availability:* Part-time, evening/weekend. *Entrance requirements:* For doctorate, LSAT.

The Santa Barbara and Ventura Colleges of Law–Santa Barbara, Graduate and Professional Programs, Santa Barbara, CA 93101. Offers MLS, JD.

The Santa Barbara and Ventura Colleges of Law–Ventura, Graduate and Professional Programs, Ventura, CA 93003. Offers MLS, JD.

Santa Clara University, School of Law, Santa Clara, CA 95053. Offers high tech law (Certificate); intellectual property (LL M); international and comparative law (LL M); international law (Certificate); law (JD); public interest and social justice law (Certificate); United States law (LL M); JD/MBA; JD/MSIS. *Accreditation:* ABA. *Program availability:* Part-time, online learning. *Faculty:* 47 full-time (23 women), 52 part-time/adjunct (28 women). *Students:* 681 full-time (389 women), 29 part-time (16 women); includes 310 minority (22 Black or African American, non-Hispanic/Latino; 128 Asian, non-Hispanic/Latino; 152 Hispanic/Latino; 4 Native Hawaiian or other Pacific Islander, non-Hispanic/Latino; 4 Two or more races, non-Hispanic/Latino), 38 international. Average age 27. 2,126 applicants, 57% accepted, 246 enrolled. In 2018, 54 master's, 217 doctorates awarded. *Entrance requirements:* For master's, LSAT, JD-CAS, personal statement. Additional exam requirements/recommendations for international students: Required—TOEFL. Application fee: $75 ($0 for international students). Electronic applications accepted. *Financial support:* Fellowships, Federal Work-Study, and scholarships/grants available. Support available to part-time students. Financial award applicants required to submit FAFSA. *Unit head:* Anna Han, Interim Dean, 408-554-4362, Fax: 408-554-5095, E-mail: lkloppenberg@scu.edu. *Application contact:* Anna Han, Interim Dean, 408-554-4362, Fax: 408-554-5095, E-mail: lkloppenberg@scu.edu.
Website: http://law.scu.edu/

Seattle University, School of Law, Seattle, WA 98122-4340. Offers American legal studies (LL M); business development (MLS); elder law (LL M); health law (MLS); innovation and technology (LL M, MLS); tribal law and governance (LL M, MLS); JD/MATL; JD/MBA; JD/MCJ; JD/MIB; JD/MPA; JD/MSAL; JD/MSF; JD/MSL. *Accreditation:* ABA. *Program availability:* Part-time, evening/weekend. *Entrance requirements:* For doctorate, LSAT. Additional exam requirements/recommendations for international students: Required—TOEFL (minimum score 600 paper-based; 100 iBT). Electronic applications accepted. *Expenses:* Contact institution. *Faculty research:* Innovation, technology and cybersecurity; secrecy and democratic decisions; linguistic features of police culture and the coercive impact of police officer swearing in police-citizen interaction; the imprisoned parent: differential power in same-sex families based on legal and cultural understandings of parentage; theology in public reason and legal discourse: a case for the preferential option for the poor.

Seton Hall University, School of Law, Newark, NJ 07102-5210. Offers health law (LL M, JD); intellectual property (LL M, JD); law (MSJ); JD/MADIR; JD/MBA; MD/JD; MD/MSJ. MD/JD, MD/MSJ offered jointly with University of Medicine and Dentistry of New Jersey. *Accreditation:* ABA. *Program availability:* Part-time, evening/weekend. *Degree requirements:* For master's, thesis optional. *Entrance requirements:* For master's, professional experience, letters of recommendation; for doctorate, LSAT, active LSDAS registration, letters of recommendation. Additional exam requirements/recommendations for international students: Recommended—TOEFL. Electronic applications accepted. *Expenses:* Contact institution. *Faculty research:* Health law, intellectual property law, science and the law, international law and employment/labor law.

Southern Illinois University Carbondale, School of Law, Carbondale, IL 62901-6804. Offers general law (LL M); health law and policy (LL M); law (JD); legal studies (MLS), including general law, health law and policy; JD/M Acc; JD/MBA; JD/MD; JD/MPA; JD/MSW; JD/PhD. *Accreditation:* ABA. *Program availability:* Part-time. *Entrance requirements:* For doctorate, LSAT. Additional exam requirements/recommendations for international students: Required—TOEFL (minimum score 600 paper-based). Electronic applications accepted. *Expenses:* Contact institution. *Faculty research:* Health care, criminal, environmental, and international law; tort reform.

Southern Methodist University, Dedman College of Humanities and Sciences, Department of Economics, Dallas, TX 75205. Offers applied economics (MA); applied economics and predictive analytics (MS); economics (PhD); law and economics (MA). *Program availability:* Part-time, evening/weekend. Terminal master's awarded for partial completion of doctoral program. *Degree requirements:* For master's, thesis, oral qualifying exam; for doctorate, thesis/dissertation, written exams. *Entrance requirements:* For master's, GRE General Test or GMAT, 12 hours of course work in economics, minimum GPA of 3.0, previous course work in calculus and statistics; for doctorate, GRE General Test, minimum GPA of 3.0; 3 semesters of course work in calculus; 1 semester each of course work in statistics and linear algebra. Additional exam requirements/recommendations for international students: Required—TOEFL (minimum score 550 paper-based). Electronic applications accepted. *Faculty research:* Economic theory, game theory, econometrics, international trade, labor.

Southern Methodist University, Dedman School of Law, Dallas, TX 75275-0110. Offers general law (LL M); international and comparative law (LL M); law (JD, SJD); taxation (LL M); JD/MA; JD/MBA. *Accreditation:* ABA. *Program availability:* Part-time, evening/weekend. *Degree requirements:* For master's, thesis optional; for doctorate, thesis/dissertation (for some programs), 30 hours of public service (for JD). *Entrance requirements:* For master's, JD; for doctorate, LSAT (for JD). Additional exam requirements/recommendations for international students: Required—TOEFL (minimum score 575 paper-based; 91 iBT). Electronic applications accepted. *Expenses:* Contact institution. *Faculty research:* Corporate law, intellectual property, international law, commercial law, dispute resolution.

Southern University and Agricultural and Mechanical College, Southern University Law Center, Baton Rouge, LA 70813. Offers JD. *Accreditation:* ABA; SACS/CC. *Program availability:* Part-time, evening/weekend. *Entrance requirements:* For doctorate, LSAT. Additional exam requirements/recommendations for international students: Recommended—TOEFL. Electronic applications accepted. *Expenses:* Contact institution. *Faculty research:* Civil law, comparative law, constitutional law, civil rights law.

South Texas College of Law Houston, Professional Program, Houston, TX 77002-7000. Offers JD. *Accreditation:* ABA. *Program availability:* Part-time, evening/weekend. *Degree requirements:* For doctorate, completion of 90 hours within 7 years of enrollment. *Entrance requirements:* For doctorate, LSAT (taken within last 4 years), degree from accredited 4-year institution. Electronic applications accepted.

Southwestern Law School, Graduate and Professional Programs, Los Angeles, CA 90010. Offers entertainment and media law (LL M); individualized studies (LL M); law (JD). *Accreditation:* ABA. *Program availability:* Part-time, evening/weekend. *Faculty:* 60 full-time (30 women), 83 part-time/adjunct (37 women). *Students:* 517 full-time (270 women), 200 part-time (129 women); includes 338 minority (43 Black or African American, non-Hispanic/Latino; 58 Asian, non-Hispanic/Latino; 195 Hispanic/Latino; 3 Native Hawaiian or other Pacific Islander, non-Hispanic/Latino; 39 Two or more races, non-Hispanic/Latino), 14 international. Average age 27. 1,752 applicants, 46% accepted, 271 enrolled. In 2018, 7 master's, 182 doctorates awarded. *Degree requirements:* For doctorate, 87 units, minimum cumulative GPA of 2.33. *Entrance requirements:* For doctorate, LSAT, bachelor's degree from accredited U.S. institution or equivalent with transcript evaluation; personal statement; LSAC Credential Assembly Service Registration (CAS); 1 to 3 letters of recommendation. *Application deadline:* For fall admission, 4/1 priority date for domestic and international students. Applications are

processed on a rolling basis. Application fee: $60. Electronic applications accepted. *Expenses:* $54,166 full-time tuition and fees, $36,194 part-time tuition and fees. *Financial support:* In 2018–19, 369 students received support. Federal Work-Study, institutionally sponsored loans, and scholarships/grants available. Support available to part-time students. Financial award application deadline: 6/1; financial award applicants required to submit FAFSA. *Faculty research:* International trade and law, mediation/arbitration, land use and urban planning, antitrust law, entertainment and media law. *Unit head:* Susan Westerberg Prager, Dean, 213-738-6710, Fax: 213-383-1688. *Application contact:* Lisa Gear, Assistant Dean of Admissions, 213-738-6834, Fax: 213-738-6899, E-mail: admissions@swlaw.edu.
Website: http://www.swlaw.edu

Stanford University, Law School, Stanford, CA 94305-8610. Offers corporate governance and practice (LL M); environmental law and policy (LL M); international economic law, business and policy (LL M); international legal studies (JSM); law (JD, JSD); law, science and technology (LL M); legal studies (MLS); JD/MA; JD/MBA; JD/MPP; JD/MS; JD/PhD. *Accreditation:* ABA. *Expenses: Tuition:* Full-time $50,703; part-time $32,970 per year. *Required fees:* $651. *Unit head:* M. Elizabeth Magill, Dean, 650-723-4455, Fax: 650-725-0253, E-mail: emagill@law.stanford.edu. *Application contact:* Graduate Admissions, 866-432-7472, Fax: 650-723-8371, E-mail: gradadmissions@stanford.edu.
Website: http://www.law.stanford.edu/

Stetson University, College of Law, Gulfport, FL 33707-3299. Offers LL M, M Jur, JD, JD/LL M, JD/MBA. *Accreditation:* ABA. *Program availability:* Part-time, evening/weekend, 100% online. *Faculty:* 42 full-time (22 women), 56 part-time/adjunct (24 women). *Students:* 764 full-time (415 women), 130 part-time (67 women); includes 245 minority (67 Black or African American, non-Hispanic/Latino; 3 American Indian or Alaska Native, non-Hispanic/Latino; 19 Asian, non-Hispanic/Latino; 124 Hispanic/Latino; 32 Two or more races, non-Hispanic/Latino), 15 international. Average age 27. 2,029 applicants, 47% accepted, 316 enrolled. In 2018, 27 master's, 247 doctorates awarded. *Entrance requirements:* For doctorate, LSAT. Additional exam requirements/recommendations for international students: Required—PTE, TOEFL or IELTS. *Application deadline:* For fall admission, 5/15 for domestic and international students. Applications are processed on a rolling basis. Application fee: $55. Electronic applications accepted. *Expenses:* $43,880 (for full-time JD); $30,398 (for part-time JD); $43,990 (for LL M in international law); $16,900 (for LL M in elder law); $14,500 (for LL M in advocacy); $13,600 (for MJur in healthcare); $11,800 (for MJur in aging and policy); $43,880 (for MJur in international and comparative law). *Financial support:* In 2018–19, 669 students received support, including 50 research assistantships (averaging $1,370 per year), 53 teaching assistantships (averaging $949 per year); career-related internships or fieldwork, Federal Work-Study, scholarships/grants, unspecified assistantships, and tuition waivers (for staff and dependents) also available. Support available to part-time students. Financial award application deadline: 8/15; financial award applicants required to submit FAFSA. *Faculty research:* Advocacy and legal communication, law and higher education, elder law, international law including biodiversity and Caribbean law, veterans law and policy. *Total annual research expenditures:* $255,400. *Unit head:* Michèle Alexandre, Dean/Professor of Law, 727-562-7809, Fax: 727-562-7800, E-mail: malexandre@law.stetson.edu. *Application contact:* Darren Kettles, Director of Admissions, 727-562-7802, Fax: 727-562-7670, E-mail: lawadmit@law.stetson.edu.
Website: http://www.law.stetson.edu/

Suffolk University, Law School, Boston, MA 02108. Offers business law and financial services (JD); civil litigation (JD); global law and technology (LL M); health and biomedical law (JD); intellectual property law (JD); international law (JD); JD/MBA; JD/MPA; JD/MSCJ; JD/MSF; JD/MSIE. *Accreditation:* ABA. *Program availability:* Part-time, evening/weekend. *Faculty:* 64 full-time (31 women), 51 part-time/adjunct (19 women). *Students:* 730 full-time (341 women), 363 part-time (192 women); includes 198 minority (42 Black or African American, non-Hispanic/Latino; 48 Asian, non-Hispanic/Latino; 85 Hispanic/Latino; 2 Native Hawaiian or other Pacific Islander, non-Hispanic/Latino; 21 Two or more races, non-Hispanic/Latino), 50 international. Average age 27. 1,971 applicants, 65% accepted, 374 enrolled. In 2018, 18 master's, 290 doctorates awarded. *Degree requirements:* For master's, legal writing. *Entrance requirements:* For master's, 2 letters of recommendation, resume, personal statement; for doctorate, LSAT, LSDAS, dean's certification, recommendation. Additional exam requirements/recommendations for international students: Required—TOEFL (minimum score 600 paper-based; 100 iBT). *Application deadline:* For fall admission, 4/1 for domestic and international students. Applications are processed on a rolling basis. Application fee: $60. Electronic applications accepted. *Expenses:* Contact institution. *Financial support:* In 2018–19, 778 students received support, including 1 fellowship (averaging $31,390 per year); career-related internships or fieldwork, Federal Work-Study, institutionally sponsored loans, and scholarships/grants also available. Support available to part-time students. Financial award application deadline: 3/1; financial award applicants required to submit FAFSA. *Faculty research:* Civil law, international law, health/biomedical law, business and finance, intellectual property. *Unit head:* Andrew Perlman, Dean, 617-573-8144, Fax: 617-994-6838, E-mail: lawadmin@suffolk.edu. *Application contact:* Matthew Gavin, Assistant Dean for Admissions and Financial Aid, 617-573-8144, Fax: 617-994-6838, E-mail: lawadm@suffolk.edu.
Website: http://www.suffolk.edu/law/

Syracuse University, College of Law, JD Program, Syracuse, NY 13244. Offers JD. *Accreditation:* ABA. *Entrance requirements:* For doctorate, LSAT, CAS registration, transcripts of all previous college or university study, 2 letters of recommendation. *Application deadline:* For fall admission, 4/1 priority date for domestic students. *Unit head:* Craig M. Boise, Dean and Professor of Law, 315-443-9580, E-mail: cmboise@law.syr.edu. *Application contact:* Steve Budgar, Director of Admissions, 315-443-1962, Fax: 315-443-9568, E-mail: sbudgar@law.syr.edu.
Website: http://law.syr.edu/admissions/jd-admissions

Syracuse University, College of Law, Master of Laws Program in American Law, Syracuse, NY 13244. Offers LL M. *Entrance requirements:* For master's, first degree in law from foreign institution; interview via Skype. Additional exam requirements/recommendations for international students: Recommended—TOEFL (minimum score 90 iBT), IELTS (minimum score 6). *Application deadline:* For fall admission, 5/15 for international students; for spring admission, 12/15 for international students. *Faculty research:* Human rights and comparative disability law, technology commercialization, corporate law. *Unit head:* Craig M. Boise, Dean and Professor of Law, 315-443-9580, E-mail: cmboise@law.syr.edu. *Application contact:* Steve Budgar, Director of Admissions, 315-443-1962, Fax: 315-443-9568, E-mail: sbudgar@law.syr.edu.
Website: http://law.syr.edu/academics/llm-degree

Taft University System, Taft Law School, Denver, CO 80246. Offers American jurisprudence (LL M); law (JD); taxation (LL M).

Temple University, Beasley School of Law, JD Program, Philadelphia, PA 19122-6096. Offers JD. *Accreditation:* ABA.

Temple University, Beasley School of Law, Master's and Certificate Programs, Philadelphia, PA 19122-6096. Offers Asian law (LL M); business law (Certificate); employee benefits (Certificate); estate planning (Certificate); trial advocacy (LL M); trial advocacy and litigation (Certificate).

Texas A&M University, School of Law, College Station, TX 77843. Offers intellectual property (M Jur); jurisprudence (M Jur); law (JD). *Accreditation:* ABA. *Faculty:* 82. *Students:* 465 full-time (251 women), 112 part-time (39 women); includes 174 minority (38 Black or African American, non-Hispanic/Latino; 5 American Indian or Alaska Native, non-Hispanic/Latino; 14 Asian, non-Hispanic/Latino; 112 Hispanic/Latino; 5 Two or more races, non-Hispanic/Latino), 5 international. Average age 30. 463 applicants, 100% accepted, 233 enrolled. In 2018, 1 master's awarded. *Entrance requirements:* For doctorate, LSAT, personal statement, resume, all post-secondary transcripts, 2-4 letters of recommendation and up to 2 LSAC evaluations, CAS Report. *Application deadline:* For fall admission, 7/1 for domestic students. Applications are processed on a rolling basis. Application fee: $55. *Expenses:* Contact institution. *Financial support:* In 2018–19, 447 students received support, including 4 fellowships with tuition reimbursements available (averaging $20,207 per year); career-related internships or fieldwork, institutionally sponsored loans, scholarships/grants, traineeships, health care benefits, and tuition waivers (full and partial) also available. Support available to part-time students. Financial award applicants required to submit FAFSA. *Unit head:* Dr. Andrew P. Morriss, Dean, 817-212-4139, Fax: 817-212-4139, E-mail: amorriss@law.tamu.edu. *Application contact:* Law School Admissions, 817-212-4040, E-mail: law-admissions@law.tamu.edu.
Website: http://law.tamu.edu/

Texas Southern University, Thurgood Marshall School of Law, Houston, TX 77004-4584. Offers JD. *Accreditation:* ABA. *Entrance requirements:* For doctorate, LSAT. Electronic applications accepted. *Expenses:* Contact institution. *Faculty research:* Sports law, civil rights and minors, international economics regulation, contracts principle, standards of judicial review.

Texas Tech University, School of Law, Lubbock, TX 79409-0004. Offers law (JD); United States legal studies (LL M); JD/M Engr; JD/MBA; JD/MD; JD/MPA; JD/MS; JD/MSA. *Accreditation:* ABA. *Faculty:* 33 full-time (14 women), 11 part-time/adjunct (4 women). *Students:* 412 full-time (173 women), 1 (woman) part-time; includes 118 minority (12 Black or African American, non-Hispanic/Latino; 1 American Indian or Alaska Native, non-Hispanic/Latino; 11 Asian, non-Hispanic/Latino; 61 Hispanic/Latino; 33 Two or more races, non-Hispanic/Latino). Average age 25. 1,164 applicants, 44% accepted, 150 enrolled. In 2018, 155 doctorates awarded. *Entrance requirements:* For doctorate, LSAT. Additional exam requirements/recommendations for international students: Required—TOEFL (minimum score 600 paper-based; 100 iBT), IELTS (minimum score 7), TOEFL (minimum score 600 paper-based; 100 iBT) or IELTS (minimum score 7) for LL M. *Application deadline:* For fall admission, 3/1 priority date for domestic and international students. Applications are processed on a rolling basis. Application fee: $0. Electronic applications accepted. *Expenses:* Contact institution. *Financial support:* In 2018–19, 314 students received support. Federal Work-Study, scholarships/grants, and Tutor available. Financial award application deadline: 5/1; financial award applicants required to submit FAFSA. *Faculty research:* Advocacy/practice skills/procedure, criminal Law/constitutional law, business law/tax/estate planning & family law, energy law/natural resources, law and science. *Total annual research expenditures:* $61,878. *Unit head:* Dean Jack Wade Nowlin, Dean and W. Frank Newton Professor of Law, 806-834-1504, Fax: 806-742-1629, E-mail: jack.nowlin@ttu.edu. *Application contact:* Dean Danielle I. Saavedra, Assistant Dean of Admissions, 806-834-7092, Fax: 806-742-1629, E-mail: admissions.law@ttu.edu.
Website: www.law.ttu.edu/

Thomas Jefferson School of Law, Graduate and Professional Programs, San Diego, CA 92110-2905. Offers JD. JD/MBA offered in partnership with San Diego State University. *Accreditation:* ABA. *Program availability:* Part-time, evening/weekend. *Entrance requirements:* For doctorate, LSAT. Additional exam requirements/recommendations for international students: Required—TOEFL. Electronic applications accepted. *Faculty research:* Tenant's rights, fetal rights/medical ethics, bilateral treaties/international law, sexual harassment and gender treatment.

Touro College, Jacob D. Fuchsberg Law Center, Central Islip, NY 11743. Offers general law (LL M); law (JD); U.S. legal studies (LL M); JD/MBA; JD/MPA; JD/MSW. JD/MBA and JD/MPA offered with Long Island University-LIU Post; JD/MSW offered with Stony Brook University, State University of New York. *Accreditation:* ABA. *Program availability:* Part-time, evening/weekend. *Entrance requirements:* For doctorate, LSAT. *Expenses:* Contact institution. *Faculty research:* Business law, civil rights, international law, criminal justice.

Trinity International University, Trinity Law School, Santa Ana, CA 92705. Offers bioethics (MLS); church and ministry management (MLS); general legal studies (MLS); human resources management (MLS); human rights (MLS); law (JD); nonprofit organizations (MLS). *Program availability:* Part-time, evening/weekend. *Entrance requirements:* For doctorate, LSAT. Additional exam requirements/recommendations for international students: Required—TOEFL (minimum score 580 paper-based). *Expenses:* Contact institution.

Tufts University, The Fletcher School of Law and Diplomacy, Medford, MA 02155. Offers economics and public policy (PhD); international affairs (PhD); international business (MIB); international law (LL M); law and diplomacy (MA, MALD); transatlantic affairs (MA); DVM/MA; JD/MALD; MALD/MA; MALD/MBA; MALD/MS; MD/MA. MA in transatlantic affairs offered jointly with The College of Europe; PhD in economics and public policy with Tufts' Graduate School of Arts and Sciences. *Program availability:* Online learning. *Degree requirements:* For master's, one foreign language, thesis; for doctorate, one foreign language, comprehensive exam, thesis/dissertation, dissertation defense. *Entrance requirements:* For master's and doctorate, GMAT or GRE General Test. Additional exam requirements/recommendations for international students: Required—TOEFL (minimum score 600 paper-based; 100 iBT), IELTS (minimum score 7). Electronic applications accepted. *Expenses:* Contact institution. *Faculty research:* Negotiation and conflict resolution, international organizations, international business and economic law, security studies, development economics.

Tulane University, School of Law, New Orleans, LA 70118. Offers American business law (LL M); international development (MS, PhD), including international development; law (JD, SJD). *Accreditation:* ABA. *Degree requirements:* For doctorate, thesis/dissertation (for some programs). *Entrance requirements:* For doctorate, LSAT (for JD). Additional exam requirements/recommendations for international students: Required—TOEFL (minimum score 575 paper-based). Electronic applications accepted. *Expenses:* Contact institution. *Faculty research:* Civil law.

Universidad Autonoma de Guadalajara, Graduate Programs, Guadalajara, Mexico. Offers administrative law and justice (LL M); advertising and corporate communications (MA); architecture (M Arch); business (MBA); computational science (MCC); education (Ed M, Ed D); English-Spanish translation (MA); entrepreneurship and management (MBA); integrated management of digital animation (MA); international business (MIB); international corporate law (LL M); Internet technologies (MS); manufacturing systems (MMS); occupational health (MS); philosophy (MA, PhD); power electronics (MS); quality systems (MQS); renewable energy (MS); social evaluation of projects (MBA); strategic market research (MBA); tax law (MA); teaching mathematics (MA).

Law

Universidad Central del Este, Law School, San Pedro de Macoris, Dominican Republic. Offers JD.

Universidad Iberoamericana, Graduate School, Santo Domingo D.N., Dominican Republic. Offers business administration (MBA, PMBA); constitutional law (LL M); dentistry (DMD); educational management (MA); integrated marketing communication (MA); psychopedagogical intervention (M Ed); real estate law (LL M); strategic management of human talent (MM).

Université de Montréal, Faculty of Law, Montréal, QC H3C 3J7, Canada. Offers business law (DESS); common law (North America) (JD); international law (DESS); law (LL M, LL D, DDN, DESS, LL B); tax law (LL M). *Program availability:* Part-time. *Degree requirements:* For master's, thesis; for doctorate, thesis/dissertation, project; for other advanced degree, thesis (for some programs). Electronic applications accepted. *Faculty research:* Legal theory; constitutional, private, and public law.

Université de Sherbrooke, Faculty of Law, Sherbrooke, QC J1K 2R1, Canada. Offers alternative dispute resolution (LL M, Diploma); business law (Diploma); common law (JD); criminal and penal law (Diploma); health law (LL M, Diploma); international law (LL M); law (LL D); legal management (Diploma); notarial law (Diploma); transnational law (Diploma). *Program availability:* Part-time, evening/weekend. *Degree requirements:* For master's, thesis; for Diploma, one foreign language. *Entrance requirements:* For master's and Diploma, LL B. Electronic applications accepted.

Université du Québec à Montréal, Graduate Programs, Program in Social and Labor Law, Montréal, QC H3C 3P8, Canada. Offers Certificate.

Université Laval, Faculty of Law, Programs in Law, Québec, QC G1K 7P4, Canada. Offers environment, sustainable development and food safety (LL M); international and transnational law (LL M, Diploma); law (LL M, LL D); law of business (LL M, Diploma). *Program availability:* Part-time. Terminal master's awarded for partial completion of doctoral program. *Degree requirements:* For master's, thesis (for some programs); for doctorate, thesis/dissertation. *Entrance requirements:* For master's, doctorate, and Diploma, knowledge of French and English. Electronic applications accepted.

University at Buffalo, the State University of New York, Graduate School, School of Law, Buffalo, NY 14260. Offers criminal law (LL M); cross-border legal studies (LL M); environmental law (LL M); general law (LL M); law (JD); JD/MA; JD/MBA; JD/MLS; JD/MSW; JD/MUP; JD/PhD; LL M/LL M. *Accreditation:* ABA. *Faculty:* 56 full-time (29 women), 74 part-time/adjunct (30 women). *Students:* 451 full-time (250 women), 10 part-time (6 women); includes 91 minority (30 Black or African American, non-Hispanic/Latino; 2 American Indian or Alaska Native, non-Hispanic/Latino; 23 Asian, non-Hispanic/Latino; 23 Hispanic/Latino; 13 Two or more races, non-Hispanic/Latino), 18 international. Average age 26. 895 applicants, 60% accepted, 168 enrolled. In 2018, 1 master's, 153 doctorates awarded. *Entrance requirements:* For doctorate, LSAT or GRE (JD only). Additional exam requirements/recommendations for international students: Required—TOEFL (minimum score 90 iBT), IELTS (minimum score 7). *Application deadline:* For fall admission, 3/1 priority date for domestic and international students. Applications are processed on a rolling basis. Application fee: $85. Electronic applications accepted. *Expenses:* $14,037 per semester full-time tuition and fees, $1,275 per credit part-time tuition and fees. *Financial support:* In 2018–19, 350 students received support. Federal Work-Study, institutionally sponsored loans, scholarships/grants, tuition waivers (full and partial), and unspecified assistantships available. Financial award application deadline: 3/1; financial award applicants required to submit FAFSA. *Faculty research:* Criminal law, environmental law, international law and human rights, law and finance, cross-border legal studies. *Total annual research expenditures:* $29,552. *Unit head:* Aviva Abramovsky, Dean, 716-645-2052, E-mail: aabramov@buffalo.edu. *Application contact:* Lindsay Gladney, Vice Dean for Admissions, 716-645-2907, Fax: 716-645-6676, E-mail: law-admissions@buffalo.edu.
Website: http://www.law.buffalo.edu/

The University of Akron, School of Law, Akron, OH 44325. Offers LL M, JD, JD/LL M, JD/M Tax, JD/MAP, JD/MBA, JD/MPA. *Accreditation:* ABA. *Program availability:* Part-time, evening/weekend. *Entrance requirements:* For doctorate, LSAT, LSDAS. Additional exam requirements/recommendations for international students: Required—TOEFL (minimum score 650 paper-based; 115 iBT). Electronic applications accepted. *Expenses:* Contact institution. *Faculty research:* Intellectual property; law and science; trust and elder law, including taxation and retirement benefits; professional responsibility and judicial ethics; Constitutional law, theory, and process.

The University of Alabama, Hugh F. Culverhouse Jr. School of Law, Tuscaloosa, AL 35487. Offers business transactions (LL M); comparative law (LL M, JSD); law (JD, JSD); taxation (LL M); JD/MBA. *Accreditation:* ABA. *Degree requirements:* For master's, 24 hours, exams; for doctorate, 90 hours, including 6 hours of experiential learning, 1 seminar, and 34 required hours. *Entrance requirements:* For master's, LSAT, JD (for business transactions and taxation); undergraduate degree in law, letters of recommendation, personal statement, resume, and official transcripts (for comparative law); for doctorate, LSAT (for JD), undergraduate degree, letter of recommendation, resume, personal statement, and CAS report (for JD). Additional exam requirements/recommendations for international students: Required—TOEFL, IELTS. Electronic applications accepted. *Expenses:* Contact institution. *Faculty research:* Public interest law, Constitutional law, civil rights, international law, tax law.

University of Alberta, Faculty of Law, Edmonton, AB T6G 2E1, Canada. Offers LL M, PhD. *Program availability:* Part-time. *Degree requirements:* For master's, thesis. *Entrance requirements:* For master's, minimum GPA of 3.0, curriculum vitae, 3 letters of recommendation; for doctorate, LSAT. Additional exam requirements/recommendations for international students: Required—TOEFL (minimum score 600 paper-based). Electronic applications accepted. *Faculty research:* Health law, environmental law, native law issues, constitutional law, human rights.

The University of Arizona, James E. Rogers College of Law, Tucson, AZ 85721-0176. Offers indigenous people's law and policy (LL M); international trade and business law (LL M); law (JD); JD/MA; JD/MBA; JD/MPA; JD/PhD. *Accreditation:* ABA. *Degree requirements:* For doctorate, publishable paper. *Entrance requirements:* For doctorate, LSAT, LSDAS, resume, 2 letters of recommendation. Additional exam requirements/recommendations for international students: Required—TOEFL. Electronic applications accepted. *Expenses:* Contact institution. *Faculty research:* Tax law, employment law, corporate law, torts, trial practice and skills, Constitutional law, Indian law, family law, estates and trusts.

University of Arkansas, School of Law, Fayetteville, AR 72701. Offers agricultural law (LL M); law (JD). *Accreditation:* ABA. In 2018, 5 master's, 119 doctorates awarded. *Entrance requirements:* For doctorate, LSAT. *Application deadline:* For fall admission, 8/1 for domestic students, 4/1 for international students; for spring admission, 12/1 for domestic students, 10/1 for international students; for summer admission, 4/15 for domestic students, 3/1 for international students. Applications are processed on a rolling basis. Application fee: $60. Electronic applications accepted. *Expenses:* Contact institution. *Financial support:* In 2018–19, fellowships with full tuition reimbursements (averaging $6,000 per year), 8 research assistantships (averaging $2,500 per year) were awarded; teaching assistantships, career-related internships or fieldwork, Federal Work-Study, and scholarships/grants also available. Support available to part-time students. Financial award application deadline: 4/1; financial award applicants required to submit FAFSA. *Unit head:* Stacy L. Leeds, Dean, 479-575-3873, E-mail: sleeds@uark.edu. *Application contact:* Stacy L. Leeds, Dean, 479-575-3873, E-mail: sleeds@uark.edu.
Website: https://law.uark.edu/

University of Arkansas at Little Rock, William H. Bowen School of Law, Little Rock, AR 72202-5142. Offers JD, JD/MPS. *Accreditation:* ABA. *Program availability:* Part-time, evening/weekend. *Entrance requirements:* For doctorate, LSAT. Electronic applications accepted. *Expenses:* Contact institution. *Faculty research:* Employment discrimination, uniform commercial code, Arkansas legal history, scientific evidence, mediation.

University of Baltimore, School of Law, Baltimore, MD 21201. Offers business law (JD); criminal practice (JD); estate planning (JD); family law (JD); intellectual property (JD); international law (JD); law (JD); law of the United States (LL M); litigation and advocacy (JD); public service (JD); real estate practice (JD); taxation (LL M); JD/LL M; JD/MBA; JD/MPA; JD/MS; JD/PhD. JD/MS offered jointly with Division of Criminology, Criminal Justice, and Social Policy; JD/PhD with University of Maryland, Baltimore. *Accreditation:* ABA. *Program availability:* Part-time, evening/weekend. *Entrance requirements:* For doctorate, LSAT. Additional exam requirements/recommendations for international students: Required—TOEFL (for LL M in law of the United States). Electronic applications accepted. *Expenses:* Contact institution. *Faculty research:* Plain view doctrine, statute of limitations, bankruptcy, family law, international and comparative law, Constitutional law.

The University of British Columbia, Peter A. Allard School of Law, Vancouver, BC V6T 1Z1, Canada. Offers common law (LL M CL); law (LL M, PhD); taxation (LL M). *Program availability:* Part-time. *Degree requirements:* For master's, variable foreign language requirement, thesis, seminar; for doctorate, variable foreign language requirement, comprehensive exam, thesis/dissertation, seminar. *Entrance requirements:* For master's, LL B or JD, thesis proposal, 3 letters of reference; for doctorate, LL B or JD, LL M, thesis proposal, 3 letters of reference. Additional exam requirements/recommendations for international students: Required—TOEFL, IELTS. Electronic applications accepted. *Expenses:* Contact institution. *Faculty research:* Aboriginal rights/native law, Asian legal studies, criminal law, environmental law, international law, corporate, human rights, intellectual property, dispute resolution, entertainment.

University of Calgary, Faculty of Graduate Studies, Faculty of Law, Calgary, AB T2N 1N4, Canada. Offers LL M, JD, Postbaccalaureate Certificate, JD/MBA. *Entrance requirements:* For doctorate, LSAT. Additional exam requirements/recommendations for international students: Required—TOEFL (minimum score 600 paper-based; 100 iBT). *Expenses:* Contact institution.

University of California, Berkeley, Graduate Division, Haas School of Business and School of Law, Concurrent JD/MBA Program, Berkeley, CA 94720. Offers JD/MBA. *Accreditation:* AACSB; ABA. *Entrance requirements:* Additional exam requirements/recommendations for international students: Required—TOEFL (minimum score 570 paper-based; 90 iBT). Electronic applications accepted. *Expenses:* Contact institution. *Faculty research:* Accounting, business and public policy, economic analysis and public policy, entrepreneurship, finance, management of organizations, marketing, operations and information technology management, real estate.

University of California, Berkeley, School of Law, Berkeley, CA 94720-7200. Offers jurisprudence and social policy (PhD); law (LL M, JD, JSD); JD/MA; JD/MBA; JD/MCP; JD/MJ; JD/MPP; JD/MSW. *Accreditation:* ABA. Terminal master's awarded for partial completion of doctoral program. *Degree requirements:* For master's, thesis; for doctorate, variable foreign language requirement, thesis/dissertation (for some programs). *Entrance requirements:* For master's and doctorate, letters of recommendation. Additional exam requirements/recommendations for international students: Required—TOEFL. *Expenses:* Contact institution. *Faculty research:* Law and technology; social justice; environmental law; business, law and economics; international/comparative law.

University of California, Davis, School of Law, Davis, CA 95616-5201. Offers LL M, JD, JD/MA, JD/MBA. *Accreditation:* ABA. *Degree requirements:* For doctorate, 88 semester units, including skills courses (6 units), Professional Responsibility and upper-division writing requirement. *Entrance requirements:* For doctorate, LSAT. Additional exam requirements/recommendations for international students: Required—TOEFL (minimum score 570 paper-based; 88 iBT). Electronic applications accepted. *Expenses:* Contact institution. *Faculty research:* International law, intellectual property, immigration, environmental law, public interest law.

University of California, Hastings College of the Law, Graduate Programs, San Francisco, CA 94102-4978. Offers LL M, MS, MSL, JD. MSL and MS offered jointly with University of California, San Francisco. *Accreditation:* ABA. *Program availability:* 100% online, blended/hybrid learning. *Faculty:* 70 full-time (36 women), 106 part-time/adjunct (66 women). *Students:* 971 full-time (574 women), 31 part-time (20 women); includes 380 minority (21 Black or African American, non-Hispanic/Latino; 11 American Indian or Alaska Native, non-Hispanic/Latino; 171 Asian, non-Hispanic/Latino; 169 Hispanic/Latino; 2 Native Hawaiian or other Pacific Islander, non-Hispanic/Latino; 6 Two or more races, non-Hispanic/Latino), 60 international. Average age 24. 3,234 applicants, 45% accepted, 303 enrolled. In 2018, 59 master's, 277 doctorates awarded. *Entrance requirements:* For doctorate, LSAT. Additional exam requirements/recommendations for international students: Recommended—TOEFL, IELTS. *Application deadline:* For fall admission, 3/31 for domestic students, 5/1 for international students. Applications are processed on a rolling basis. Application fee: $0. Electronic applications accepted. Application fee is waived when completed online. *Expenses: Tuition, area resident:* Full-time $43,486; part-time $1812 per credit. *Tuition, state resident:* full-time $43,486; part-time $1812 per credit. *Tuition, nonresident:* full-time $49,486; part-time $2062 per credit. *International tuition:* $49,486 full-time. *Required fees:* $840; $840 per unit. *Financial support:* In 2018–19, 844 students received support. Fellowships, research assistantships, teaching assistantships, career-related internships or fieldwork, Federal Work-Study, institutionally sponsored loans, scholarships/grants, traineeships, health care benefits, and unspecified assistantships available. Support available to part-time students. Financial award application deadline: 3/1; financial award applicants required to submit FAFSA. *Unit head:* Bryan Zerbe, Admissions Office, 415-565-4623, Fax: 415-581-8946, E-mail: admiss@uchastings.edu. *Application contact:* Admissions Office, 415-565-4623, Fax: 415-565-4863, E-mail: admiss@uchastings.edu.
Website: http://www.uchastings.edu/

University of California, Irvine, School of Law, Irvine, CA 92617. Offers JD. *Accreditation:* ABA. *Degree requirements:* For doctorate, project. *Entrance requirements:* For doctorate, LSAT, bachelor's degree, official transcripts, two letters of recommendation, personal statement, current resume. Electronic applications accepted. *Expenses:* Contact institution.

University of California, Los Angeles, School of Law, Los Angeles, CA 90095. Offers LL M, JD, SJD, JD/MA, JD/MBA, JD/MPH, JD/MPP, JD/MSW, JD/MURP, JD/PhD. We offer the following formal joint degree programs: Law and African-American Studies; Law and American Indian Studies; Law and Management; Law and Philosophy; Law and Public Health; Law and Public Policy; Law and Social Welfare; Law and Urban

Planning. *Accreditation:* ABA. *Faculty:* 108 full-time (48 women), 113 part-time/adjunct (53 women). *Students:* 1,154 full-time (601 women); includes 319 minority (35 Black or African American, non-Hispanic/Latino; 3 American Indian or Alaska Native, non-Hispanic/Latino; 141 Asian, non-Hispanic/Latino; 101 Hispanic/Latino; 1 Native Hawaiian or other Pacific Islander, non-Hispanic/Latino; 38 Two or more races, non-Hispanic/Latino), 212 international. Average age 24. 6,243 applicants, 23% accepted, 311 enrolled. In 2018, 195 master's, 320 doctorates awarded. *Entrance requirements:* For doctorate, LSAT or GRE (for JD). Additional exam requirements/recommendations for international students: Required—TOEFL for LL M. *Application deadline:* For fall admission, 2/1 for domestic students. Applications are processed on a rolling basis. Application fee: $75. Electronic applications accepted. *Financial support:* In 2018–19, 759 students received support. Career-related internships or fieldwork, scholarships/grants, health care benefits, tuition waivers (full and partial), and unspecified assistantships available. Financial award application deadline: 3/2. *Faculty research:* (1) critical race studies; (2) entertainment, media, technology and intellectual property law (3) environmental law; (4) international and comparative law (5) public interest law and policy. *Unit head:* Jennifer L. Mnookin, Dean/Professor of Law, 310-825-8202. *Application contact:* Admissions Office, 310-825-2080.
Website: http://www.law.ucla.edu/

University of Chicago, The Law School, Chicago, IL 60637. Offers LL M, MCL, DCL, JD, JSD, JD/AM, JD/MBA, JD/MPP. *Accreditation:* ABA. *Entrance requirements:* For doctorate, LSAT (for JD). Additional exam requirements/recommendations for international students: Required—TOEFL (minimum score 104 iBT). Electronic applications accepted. *Expenses:* Contact institution. *Faculty research:* Law.

University of Cincinnati, College of Law, Cincinnati, OH 45221-0040. Offers LL M, JD, JD/MA, JD/MBA, JD/MCP, JD/MWS. *Accreditation:* ABA. *Entrance requirements:* For master's, Credential evaluation report, diploma for law degree, curriculum vitae, personal statement, two letters of recommendation; for doctorate, LSAT. Additional exam requirements/recommendations for international students: Required—TOEFL (minimum iBT score of 85), IELTS (7), or PTE (65). Electronic applications accepted. *Expenses:* Contact institution. *Faculty research:* Constitutional law; business law; international law; employment law; civil procedure.

University of Colorado Boulder, School of Law, Boulder, CO 80309-0401. Offers JD, JD/MBA, JD/MPA, JD/MS, JD/PhD. *Accreditation:* ABA. *Entrance requirements:* For doctorate, LSAT, minimum undergraduate GPA of 2.75. Electronic applications accepted. Application fee is waived when completed online. *Expenses:* Contact institution. *Faculty research:* Law and society; constitutional law; law; business/corporate law; environmental law.

University of Connecticut, School of Law, Hartford, CT 06105. Offers JD, JD/LL M, JD/MBA, JD/MLS, JD/MPA, JD/MPH, JD/MSW. *Accreditation:* ABA. *Program availability:* Part-time. *Degree requirements:* For doctorate, extensive research paper. *Entrance requirements:* For doctorate, LSAT, undergraduate degree. Additional exam requirements/recommendations for international students: Required—TOEFL. Electronic applications accepted. *Expenses:* Contact institution. *Faculty research:* International law, intellectual property, human rights, taxation, energy and environmental law.

University of Dayton, School of Law, Dayton, OH 45469-2772. Offers American and transnational law (LL M); criminal law (JD); government contracting and procurement (MSL); intellectual property and technology (MSL). *Accreditation:* ABA. *Program availability:* Part-time, 100% online. Terminal master's awarded for partial completion of doctoral program. *Degree requirements:* For master's, variable foreign language requirement, comprehensive exam (for some programs), thesis optional; for doctorate, variable foreign language requirement, comprehensive exam, thesis/dissertation optional. *Entrance requirements:* For master's, GMAT, GRE or waiver from director/dean, bachelor's degree (for MSL); transcripts and law degree (for LL M); for doctorate, LSAT, bachelor's degree, transcripts, letter of recommendation, character and fitness personal statement. Additional exam requirements/recommendations for international students: Required—TOEFL (minimum score 600 paper-based; 100 iBT); Recommended—IELTS (minimum score 7). *Expenses:* Contact institution. *Faculty research:* Trademark and unfair competition law, cyber and cybersecurity law, patent law, trade secret law, copyright law.

University of Denver, Sturm College of Law, JD Program, Denver, CO 80208. Offers JD. *Accreditation:* ABA. *Program availability:* Part-time, evening/weekend. *Faculty:* 63 full-time (34 women), 4 part-time/adjunct (1 woman). *Students:* 723 full-time (401 women), 24 part-time (18 women); includes 169 minority (16 Black or African American, non-Hispanic/Latino; 3 American Indian or Alaska Native, non-Hispanic/Latino; 22 Asian, non-Hispanic/Latino; 105 Hispanic/Latino; 23 Two or more races, non-Hispanic/Latino), 4 international. Average age 28. 2,623 applicants, 47% accepted, 259 enrolled. In 2018, 245 doctorates awarded. *Entrance requirements:* For doctorate, LSAT, resume; transcripts; personal statement. Additional exam requirements/recommendations for international students: Required—TOEFL (minimum score 587 paper-based; 95 iBT). *Application deadline:* For fall admission, 3/1 for domestic and international students. Applications are processed on a rolling basis. Application fee: $65. Electronic applications accepted. *Expenses:* Contact institution. *Financial support:* In 2018–19, 475 students received support. Teaching assistantships, career-related internships or fieldwork, Federal Work-Study, institutionally sponsored loans, scholarships/grants, unspecified assistantships, and tutorships available. Support available to part-time students. Financial award application deadline: 2/15; financial award applicants required to submit FAFSA. *Faculty research:* Lawyering skills, international and legal studies, natural resources law (domestic and international), transportation law, public interest law, business and commercial law. *Unit head:* Dr. Bruce Smith, Dean, 303-871-6103. *Application contact:* Yvonne Cherena-Pacheco, Associate Director of Admissions, 303-871-6151, E-mail: admissions@law.du.edu.
Website: http://www.law.du.edu

University of Denver, Sturm College of Law, Programs in Environmental and Natural Resources Law and Policy, Denver, CO 80208. Offers environmental and natural resources law and policy (LL M, MLS); natural resources law and policy (Certificate). *Students:* 3 full-time (1 woman), 7 part-time (3 women); includes 1 minority (Black or African American, non-Hispanic/Latino), 2 international. Average age 33. In 2018, 15 master's awarded. *Degree requirements:* For master's, capstone. *Entrance requirements:* For master's, bachelor's degree (for MRLS), JD (for LLM), transcripts, two letters of recommendation, resume, personal statement. Additional exam requirements/recommendations for international students: Required—TOEFL (minimum score 550 paper-based; 80 iBT). *Application deadline:* For fall admission, 8/5 for domestic and international students; for spring admission, 12/23 for domestic and international students; for summer admission, 5/18 for domestic and international students. Applications are processed on a rolling basis. Application fee: $65. Electronic applications accepted. *Expenses:* $40,700 per year full-time. *Financial support:* In 2018–19, 10 students received support. Federal Work-Study, institutionally sponsored loans, scholarships/grants, and unspecified assistantships available. Support available to part-time students. Financial award application deadline: 2/15; financial award applicants required to submit FAFSA.
Website: http://www.law.du.edu/index.php/graduate-legal-studies/masters-programs/mls-enrlp

University of Detroit Mercy, School of Law, Detroit, MI 48226. Offers JD, JD/MBA. *Accreditation:* ABA. *Program availability:* Part-time. *Entrance requirements:* For doctorate, LSAT. *Expenses:* Contact institution.

University of Florida, Levin College of Law, Gainesville, FL 32611. Offers comparative law (LL M), including tropical conservation and development; environmental and land use law (LL M); international taxation (LL M); law (JD); taxation (LL M, SJD). *Accreditation:* ABA. *Entrance requirements:* For doctorate, LSAT (for JD). Electronic applications accepted. *Faculty research:* Environmental and land use law, taxation, dispute resolution, family law, Constitutional law.

University of Georgia, School of Law, Athens, GA 30602. Offers LL M, MSL, JD. *Accreditation:* ABA. *Degree requirements:* For master's, thesis. *Entrance requirements:* For doctorate, LSAT. Additional exam requirements/recommendations for international students: Required—TOEFL. Electronic applications accepted. *Expenses:* Contact institution.

University of Hawaii at Manoa, William S. Richardson School of Law, Honolulu, HI 96822-2328. Offers LL M, JD, Graduate Certificate, JD/Certificate, JD/MA, JD/MBA, JD/MLI Sc, JD/MS, JD/MURP, JD/PhD. *Accreditation:* ABA. *Degree requirements:* For doctorate, 6 semesters of full-time residency. *Entrance requirements:* For doctorate, LSAT. Additional exam requirements/recommendations for international students: Required—TOEFL. *Expenses:* Contact institution. *Faculty research:* Law of the sea, Asian and Pacific comparative law, native Hawaiian rights, environmental law.

University of Houston, University of Houston Law Center, Houston, TX 77204-6060. Offers energy, environment, and natural resources (LL M); health law (LL M); intellectual property and information law (LL M); international law (LL M); law (JD); tax law (LL M); U.S. law (LL M). *Accreditation:* ABA. *Program availability:* Part-time, evening/weekend. *Faculty:* 58 full-time (22 women), 148 part-time/adjunct (45 women). *Students:* 606 full-time (303 women), 98 part-time (41 women); includes 260 minority (43 Black or African American, non-Hispanic/Latino; 6 American Indian or Alaska Native, non-Hispanic/Latino; 72 Asian, non-Hispanic/Latino; 137 Hispanic/Latino; 2 Native Hawaiian or other Pacific Islander, non-Hispanic/Latino), 14 international. Average age 26. 2,596 applicants, 33% accepted, 202 enrolled. In 2018, 75 master's awarded. *Degree requirements:* For master's, thesis optional. *Entrance requirements:* For doctorate, LSAT. Additional exam requirements/recommendations for international students: Required—TOEFL (minimum score 600 paper-based; 100 iBT), IELTS (minimum score 7). *Application deadline:* For fall admission, 2/15 for domestic and international students. Applications are processed on a rolling basis. Application fee: $0. Electronic applications accepted. Application fee is waived when completed online. *Expenses:* Texas Resident $31,090/year; Non Texas Resident $45,640/year. *Financial support:* In 2018–19, 573 students received support, including 47 fellowships (averaging $3,768 per year); research assistantships, career-related internships or fieldwork, Federal Work-Study, scholarships/grants, and tuition waivers (full and partial) also available. Support available to part-time students. Financial award application deadline: 3/15; financial award applicants required to submit FAFSA. *Faculty research:* Health law, international law, tax, environmental law/energy, information law/intellectual property. *Total annual research expenditures:* $336,944. *Unit head:* Leonard M. Baynes, Dean and Professor of Law, 713-743-2100, Fax: 713-743-2122, E-mail: lbaynes@central.uh.edu. *Application contact:* Pilar Mensah, Assistant Dean for Admissions, 713-743-2280, Fax: 713-743-2194, E-mail: lpmensah@central.uh.edu.
Website: http://www.law.uh.edu/

University of Idaho, College of Law, Moscow, ID 83844-2321. Offers LL M, JD. *Accreditation:* ABA. *Faculty:* 34 full-time, 9 part-time/adjunct. *Students:* 308 full-time, 7 part-time. Average age 29. *Entrance requirements:* For doctorate, LSAT, Law School Admission Council Credential Assembly Service (CAS) Report. Additional exam requirements/recommendations for international students: Required—TOEFL. *Application deadline:* For fall admission, 3/15 priority date for domestic students. Applications are processed on a rolling basis. Electronic applications accepted. *Expenses:* Contact institution. *Financial support:* Career-related internships or fieldwork, Federal Work-Study, and institutionally sponsored loans available. Financial award applicants required to submit FAFSA. *Unit head:* Jerrold Long, Term Dean, 208-885-4977, E-mail: uilaw@uidaho.edu. *Application contact:* Carole Wells, Director of Admissions, 208-885-2300, E-mail: lawadmit@uidaho.edu.
Website: http://www.uidaho.edu/law/

University of Illinois at Urbana–Champaign, College of Law, Champaign, IL 61820. Offers LL M, MCL, JD, JSD, JD/DVM, JD/MBA, JD/MCS, JD/MHRIR, JD/MS, JD/MUP, MAS/JD, MD/JD. *Accreditation:* ABA. *Expenses:* Contact institution.

The University of Iowa, College of Law, Iowa City, IA 52242. Offers LL M, MSL, JD, SJD, JD/MA, JD/MBA, JD/MD, JD/MHA, JD/MPH, JD/MS, JD/PhD. *Accreditation:* ABA. *Faculty:* 49 full-time (22 women), 38 part-time/adjunct (15 women). *Students:* 437 full-time (193 women); includes 93 minority (17 Black or African American, non-Hispanic/Latino; 2 American Indian or Alaska Native, non-Hispanic/Latino; 18 Asian, non-Hispanic/Latino; 39 Hispanic/Latino; 17 Two or more races, non-Hispanic/Latino), 31 international. Average age 24. 1,823 applicants, 46% accepted, 163 enrolled. In 2018, 3 master's, 141 doctorates awarded. *Degree requirements:* For master's, thesis (for some programs); for doctorate, thesis/dissertation. *Entrance requirements:* For doctorate, LSAT. Additional exam requirements/recommendations for international students: Required—TOEFL. *Application deadline:* For fall admission, 5/1 priority date for domestic and international students. Applications are processed on a rolling basis. Application fee: $0. Electronic applications accepted. Application fee is waived when completed online. *Expenses:* JD Resident - 27,343.50, NonResident - 46,823.50; LLM Resident - 24,763.50, NonResident - 29,375.50; SJD Resident - 24,763.50, NonResdent - 29,375.50; MSL Resident - 15,933 NonResident 27,766.50. *Financial support:* In 2018–19, 345 students received support, including 345 fellowships with tuition reimbursements available (averaging $18,769 per year), 127 research assistantships with partial tuition reimbursements available (averaging $2,175 per year); career-related internships or fieldwork, scholarships/grants, and health care benefits also available. Financial award applicants required to submit FAFSA. *Faculty research:* International and comparative law, business law, intellectual property and property law, criminal law, and constitutional law. *Total annual research expenditures:* $937,837. *Unit head:* Kevin Washburn, Dean, 319-335-9034, Fax: 319-335-9019, E-mail: kevin-washburn@uiowa.edu. *Application contact:* Collins Byrd, Assistant Dean of Enrollment Management, 319-335-9095, Fax: 319-335-9646, E-mail: law-admissions@uiowa.edu.
Website: https://law.uiowa.edu/

The University of Kansas, School of Law, Lawrence, KS 66045-7608. Offers law (JD); JD/MA; JD/MBA; JD/MHSA; JD/MPA; JD/MS; JD/MSW; JD/MUP. *Accreditation:* ABA. *Program availability:* Part-time. *Faculty:* 31 full-time (18 women), 20 part-time/adjunct (8 women). *Students:* 317 full-time (152 women), 32 part-time (10 women); includes 62 minority (16 Black or African American, non-Hispanic/Latino; 4 American Indian or Alaska Native, non-Hispanic/Latino; 12 Asian, non-Hispanic/Latino; 24 Hispanic/Latino; 6 Two or more races, non-Hispanic/Latino), 21 international. Average age 24. 731 applicants, 51% accepted, 107 enrolled. In 2018, 102 doctorates awarded. *Entrance*

requirements: For doctorate, LSAT, 2 letters of recommendation, personal statement, resume, official transcripts. Additional exam requirements/recommendations for international students: Required—TOEFL (minimum score 100 iBT), IELTS (minimum score 7). *Application deadline:* For fall admission, 4/1 priority date for domestic students, 4/1 for international students. Applications are processed on a rolling basis. Application fee: $55. Electronic applications accepted. *Expenses:* $744 per credit resident (for JD, LLM, SJD), $1302 per credit non-resident (for JD, LLM, SJD), $966 per year fee for all degrees, $10,000 per year fee (for SJD), $670 per credit (for MS). *Financial support:* In 2018–19, 6 fellowships (averaging $1,310 per year), 70 research assistantships (averaging $1,215 per year), 7 teaching assistantships (averaging $800 per year) were awarded; career-related internships or fieldwork, Federal Work-Study, institutionally sponsored loans, scholarships/grants, and unspecified assistantships also available. Financial award application deadline: 2/15; financial award applicants required to submit FAFSA. *Faculty research:* International law, business law, criminal law, tribal law, law and public policy. *Unit head:* Stephen W. Mazza, Dean, 785-864-4550, Fax: 785-864-5054. *Application contact:* Steven Freedman, Assistant Dean for Admissions, 866-220-3654, E-mail: admitlaw@ku.edu.
Website: http://www.law.ku.edu/

University of Kentucky, College of Law, Lexington, KY 40506-0048. Offers JD, JD/MA, JD/MBA, JD/MPA. *Accreditation:* ABA. *Entrance requirements:* For doctorate, LSAT, LSDAS. Additional exam requirements/recommendations for international students: Required—TOEFL. Electronic applications accepted. *Expenses:* Contact institution. *Faculty research:* Health law, education law, advocacy, business law, white collar crime, international trade law, corporate mergers, taxation of Internet transactions.

University of La Verne, College of Law, Ontario, CA 91764. Offers JD. *Accreditation:* ABA. *Program availability:* Part-time, evening/weekend. *Entrance requirements:* For doctorate, LSAT. Additional exam requirements/recommendations for international students: Recommended—TOEFL. Electronic applications accepted. *Expenses:* Contact institution.

University of Louisville, Louis D. Brandeis School of Law, Louisville, KY 40208. Offers JD, JD/M Div, JD/MAH, JD/MAPS, JD/MBA, JD/MSSW, JD/MUP. *Accreditation:* ABA. *Program availability:* Part-time. *Degree requirements:* For doctorate, 30 work hours of pro bono service. *Entrance requirements:* For doctorate, LSAT. Additional exam requirements/recommendations for international students: Required—TOEFL (minimum score 550 paper-based). Electronic applications accepted. *Expenses:* Contact institution. *Faculty research:* Intellectual property, environmental law, corporate law, taxation, health law, disability law.

University of Maine, University of Maine School of Law, Portland, ME 04102. Offers JD, JD/MBA, JD/MPH, JD/MPPM. JD/MBA offered in conjunction with the University of Maine and University of Southern Maine; JD/MPH and JD/MPPM offered with the Muskie School of Public Service. *Accreditation:* ABA. *Program availability:* Part-time. *Faculty:* 23 full-time (12 women), 52 part-time/adjunct (21 women). *Students:* 241 full-time (135 women), 9 part-time (4 women); includes 25 minority (6 Black or African American, non-Hispanic/Latino; 3 American Indian or Alaska Native, non-Hispanic/Latino; 7 Asian, non-Hispanic/Latino; 9 Hispanic/Latino), 2 international. Average age 27. 592 applicants, 53% accepted, 80 enrolled. In 2018, 77 doctorates awarded. *Degree requirements:* For doctorate, 90 academic credits. *Entrance requirements:* Additional exam requirements/recommendations for international students: Required—TOEFL (minimum score 550 paper-based; 79 iBT), IELTS (minimum score 6.5), TOEFL (minimum score 550 paper-based, 79 iBT) or IELTS (6.5). *Application deadline:* For fall admission, 7/31 for domestic students, 6/1 for international students; for spring admission, 11/15 for international students. Applications are processed on a rolling basis. Application fee: $0. Electronic applications accepted. *Expenses:* $743 per credit hour; $22,290 per year for residents; $1,112 per credit hour; $33,360 per year for non-residents. *Financial support:* In 2018–19, 165 students received support, including 20 fellowships (averaging $5,000 per year), 5 research assistantships (averaging $1,000 per year), 6 teaching assistantships with partial tuition reimbursements available (averaging $2,500 per year); Federal Work-Study, scholarships/grants, and unspecified assistantships also available. Financial award application deadline: 2/15; financial award applicants required to submit FAFSA. *Faculty research:* Commercial and tax law aspects of intellectual property; domestic violence; race, gender, and law; environmental and land use law; bankruptcy and predatory lending; international investment law; community development law; law governing use and development of the arctic. *Unit head:* Dmitry Bam, Dean, 207-780-4344, Fax: 207-780-4239. *Application contact:* Caroline Wilshusen, Associate Dean of Admissions, 207-780-4341, Fax: 207-780-4239, E-mail: lawadmissions@maine.edu.
Website: http://mainelaw.maine.edu/

The University of Manchester, School of Law, Manchester, United Kingdom. Offers bioethics and medical jurisprudence (PhD); criminology (M Phil, PhD); law (M Phil, PhD).

University of Manitoba, Faculty of Graduate Studies, Faculty of Law, Winnipeg, MB R3T 2N2, Canada. Offers LL M. *Degree requirements:* For master's, thesis. *Entrance requirements:* For master's, LL B, minimum GPA of 3.0. Additional exam requirements/recommendations for international students: Required—TOEFL (minimum score 600 paper-based). Electronic applications accepted. *Faculty research:* Constitutional law, alternative dispute resolution, human rights law, international trade law, corporate law.

University of Maryland, Baltimore, Francis King Carey School of Law, Baltimore, MD 21201. Offers LL M, JD, JD/MA, JD/MBA, JD/MCP, JD/MPH, JD/MPM, JD/MPP, JD/MS, JD/MSN, JD/MSW, JD/PhD, JD/Pharm D. *Accreditation:* ABA. *Program availability:* Part-time, evening/weekend, 100% online. *Faculty:* 48 full-time (23 women), 64 part-time/adjunct (22 women). *Students:* 556 full-time (318 women), 200 part-time (116 women); includes 263 minority (123 Black or African American, non-Hispanic/Latino; 1 American Indian or Alaska Native, non-Hispanic/Latino; 60 Asian, non-Hispanic/Latino; 53 Hispanic/Latino; 26 Two or more races, non-Hispanic/Latino), 16 international. Average age 27. 2,323 applicants, 50% accepted, 281 enrolled. In 2018, 68 master's, 192 doctorates awarded. *Degree requirements:* For master's, thesis optional. *Entrance requirements:* For doctorate, LSAT, CAS registration (transcripts, transcript analysis, letters of recommendation). Additional exam requirements/recommendations for international students: Required—TOEFL (minimum score 600 paper-based; 90 iBT), IELTS (minimum score 7). *Application deadline:* For fall admission, 4/1 priority date for domestic and international students. Applications are processed on a rolling basis. Application fee: $70. Electronic applications accepted. *Expenses:* $31,743 flat for year 1 (32 credits); $1,202 per credit year 2-3 (53 credits). *Financial support:* In 2018–19, 536 students received support, including 23 fellowships (averaging $5,000 per year); Federal Work-Study, institutionally sponsored loans, and scholarships/grants also available. Support available to part-time students. Financial award application deadline: 3/1; financial award applicants required to submit FAFSA. *Faculty research:* Environmental regulation, health care policy, information privacy, race and criminal justice, international and comparative law. *Total annual research expenditures:* $4.6 million. *Unit head:* Donald B. Tobin, Dean/Professor, 410-706-7214, Fax: 410-706-4045, E-mail: dtobin@law.umaryland.edu. *Application contact:* Katrin Hussmann Schroll, Assistant Dean for Admissions, 410-706-3492, Fax: 410-706-1793, E-mail: admissions@law.umaryland.edu.
Website: http://www.law.umaryland.edu/

University of Maryland, College Park, Academic Affairs, Robert H. Smith School of Business, Program in Business Management/Law, College Park, MD 20742. Offers JD/MBA. *Accreditation:* AACSB. *Entrance requirements:* Additional exam requirements/recommendations for international students: Required—TOEFL.

University of Maryland, College Park, Academic Affairs, School of Public Policy, Joint Program in Public Policy/Law, College Park, MD 20742. Offers JD/MPM. Electronic applications accepted.

University of Massachusetts Dartmouth, Graduate School, University of Massachusetts School of Law–Dartmouth, Dartmouth, MA 02747-2300. Offers JD. *Accreditation:* ABA. *Program availability:* Part-time, evening/weekend. *Faculty:* 15 full-time (7 women), 11 part-time/adjunct (2 women). *Students:* 169 full-time (91 women), 55 part-time (29 women); includes 69 minority (19 Black or African American, non-Hispanic/Latino; 2 American Indian or Alaska Native, non-Hispanic/Latino; 9 Asian, non-Hispanic/Latino; 28 Hispanic/Latino; 1 Native Hawaiian or other Pacific Islander, non-Hispanic/Latino; 10 Two or more races, non-Hispanic/Latino), 4 international. Average age 30. 958 applicants, 57% accepted, 94 enrolled. In 2018, 49 doctorates awarded. *Degree requirements:* For doctorate, comprehensive exam, bar exam. *Entrance requirements:* For doctorate, LSAT, 2 letters of recommendation, resume, personal statement (minimum 2-3 pages), official transcripts. Additional exam requirements/recommendations for international students: Required—TOEFL. *Application deadline:* For fall admission, 6/30 priority date for domestic students, 5/30 priority date for international students. Application fee: $60. Electronic applications accepted. *Financial support:* Fellowships, research assistantships, teaching assistantships, and tuition waivers available. Financial award application deadline: 3/1; financial award applicants required to submit FAFSA. *Faculty research:* Gender violence, ethics, feminist jurisprudence, legal history, legal philosophy, criminal law, criminal procedure issues, law and inequality, legal education and methodology, liberalism, procedural due process, copyright law, legal writing and rhetoric. *Unit head:* Daniel Fitzpatrick, Assistant Dean, 508-985-1109, Fax: 508-985-1175, E-mail: lawadmissions@umassd.edu. *Application contact:* Nancy Hebert, Assistant Director of Law School Recruiting & Marketing, 508-985-1110, Fax: 508-985-1175, E-mail: lawadmissions@umassd.edu.
Website: http://www.umassd.edu/law

University of Memphis, Cecil C. Humphreys School of Law, Memphis, TN 38103-2189. Offers JD, JD/MA, JD/MBA, JD/MPH. *Accreditation:* ABA. *Program availability:* Part-time. *Faculty:* 27 full-time (13 women), 31 part-time/adjunct (5 women). *Students:* 312 (137 women); includes 79 minority (60 Black or African American, non-Hispanic/Latino; 5 American Indian or Alaska Native, non-Hispanic/Latino; 5 Asian, non-Hispanic/Latino; 9 Hispanic/Latino). Average age 25. 647 applicants, 52% accepted, 107 enrolled. In 2018, 1 doctorate awarded. *Entrance requirements:* For doctorate, LSAT, CAS report, letters of recommendation, or evaluations. Additional exam requirements/recommendations for international students: Required—TOEFL. *Application deadline:* For fall admission, 3/15 priority date for domestic and international students. Applications are processed on a rolling basis. Application fee: $0 ($40 for international students). Electronic applications accepted. *Expenses:* 2018-2019 academic year (fall & spring semesters): $19,197* tuition and fees in-state; $26,402 tuition and fees out-of-state. *Financial support:* In 2018–19, 140 students received support, including 26 fellowships (averaging $12,118 per year), 20 research assistantships (averaging $5,000 per year); teaching assistantships, career-related internships or fieldwork, Federal Work-Study, scholarships/grants, and tuition waivers (partial) also available. Support available to part-time students. Financial award application deadline: 5/1; financial award applicants required to submit FAFSA. *Faculty research:* Tort law, gun violence, mass incarceration, evidence law, employment law. *Total annual research expenditures:* $37,000. *Unit head:* Katharine Traylor Schaffzin, Dean, 901-678-1623, Fax: 901-678-5210, E-mail: ktschffz@memphis.edu. *Application contact:* Dr. Sue Ann McClellan, Assistant Dean for Law Admissions, Recruiting and Scholarships, 901-678-5403, Fax: 901-678-0741, E-mail: smcclell@memphis.edu.
Website: http://www.memphis.edu/law/

University of Miami, Graduate School, University of Miami School of Law, Coral Gables, FL 33124-8087. Offers LL M, JD, JD/LL M, JD/MA, JD/MBA, JD/MBA/LL M, JD/MD, JD/MM, JD/MPA, JD/MPH, JD/MPS, JD/MS Ed, JD/PhD. *Accreditation:* ABA. *Faculty:* 83 full-time (45 women), 93 part-time/adjunct (20 women). *Students:* 1,101 full-time (544 women), 89 part-time (43 women); includes 544 minority (68 Black or African American, non-Hispanic/Latino; 3 American Indian or Alaska Native, non-Hispanic/Latino; 27 Asian, non-Hispanic/Latino; 406 Hispanic/Latino; 40 Two or more races, non-Hispanic/Latino), 102 international. Average age 25. 2,576 applicants, 62% accepted, 360 enrolled. *Entrance requirements:* For doctorate, LSAT, 2 letters of recommendation. Additional exam requirements/recommendations for international students: Required—TOEFL (minimum score 580 paper-based; 92 iBT), IELTS (minimum score 7). *Application deadline:* For fall admission, 7/31 for domestic and international students. Applications are processed on a rolling basis. Application fee: $60. Electronic applications accepted. *Expenses:* Contact institution. *Financial support:* Fellowships, research assistantships, career-related internships or fieldwork, Federal Work-Study, institutionally sponsored loans, scholarships/grants, and unspecified assistantships available. Financial award application deadline: 3/1; financial award applicants required to submit FAFSA. *Faculty research:* Energy/climate change, international finance, Internet law/law of electronic commerce, race/social justice, art law/cultural heritage law. *Unit head:* Michael Goodnight, Associate Dean of Admissions and Enrollment Management, 305-284-2527, Fax: 305-284-3084, E-mail: mgoodnig@law.miami.edu. *Application contact:* Therese Lambert, Director of Student Recruitment, 305-284-6746, Fax: 305-284-3084, E-mail: tlambert@law.miami.edu.
Website: http://www.law.miami.edu/

University of Michigan, Law School, Ann Arbor, MI 48109-1215. Offers comparative law (MCL); international tax (LL M); law (LL M, JD, SJD); JD/MA; JD/MBA; JD/MHSA; JD/MPH; JD/MPP; JD/MS; JD/MSI; JD/MSW; JD/MUP; JD/PhD. *Accreditation:* ABA. *Faculty:* 106 full-time (37 women), 89 part-time/adjunct (23 women). *Students:* 1,012 full-time (490 women); includes 238 minority (45 Black or African American, non-Hispanic/Latino; 6 American Indian or Alaska Native, non-Hispanic/Latino; 77 Asian, non-Hispanic/Latino; 63 Hispanic/Latino; 47 Two or more races, non-Hispanic/Latino), 39 international. 5,698 applicants, 20% accepted, 362 enrolled. In 2018, 37 master's, 291 doctorates awarded. *Entrance requirements:* For doctorate, LSAT. *Application deadline:* For fall admission, 2/15 for domestic students. Applications are processed on a rolling basis. Application fee: $75. Electronic applications accepted. *Expenses:* Contact institution. *Financial support:* In 2018–19, 876 students received support. Career-related internships or fieldwork, Federal Work-Study, institutionally sponsored loans, and scholarships/grants available. Financial award applicants required to submit FAFSA. *Unit head:* Mark D. West, Dean, 734-764-1358. *Application contact:* Sarah C. Zearfoss, Assistant Dean and Director of Admissions, 734-764-0537, Fax: 734-647-3218, E-mail: law.jd.admissions@umich.edu.
Website: http://www.law.umich.edu/

University of Minnesota, Twin Cities Campus, Law School, Minneapolis, MN 55455. Offers LL M, MS, JD, SJD, JD/MA, JD/MBA, JD/MBS, JD/MD, JD/MHA, JD/MPA, JD/MPH, JD/MPP, JD/MS, JD/MSST, JD/MURP, JD/PhD. *Accreditation:* ABA. *Faculty:* 62 full-time (25 women), 138 part-time/adjunct (44 women). *Students:* 590 full-time (299

women); includes 92 minority (5 Black or African American, non-Hispanic/Latino; 6 American Indian or Alaska Native, non-Hispanic/Latino; 33 Asian, non-Hispanic/Latino; 31 Hispanic/Latino; 1 Native Hawaiian or other Pacific Islander, non-Hispanic/Latino; 16 Two or more races, non-Hispanic/Latino), 55 international. 1,966 applicants, 35% accepted, 220 enrolled. In 2018, 193 doctorates awarded. *Entrance requirements:* For doctorate, LSAT. Additional exam requirements/recommendations for international students: Recommended—TOEFL, IELTS. *Application deadline:* For fall admission, 7/15 for domestic students. Applications are processed on a rolling basis. Application fee: $60. Electronic applications accepted. *Expenses:* Contact institution. *Financial support:* In 2018–19, 577 students received support. Fellowships, research assistantships, career-related internships or fieldwork, Federal Work-Study, institutionally sponsored loans, and scholarships/grants available. Financial award application deadline: 7/1; financial award applicants required to submit FAFSA. *Faculty research:* International and comparative law; law, science, and technology; criminal justice; environmental and energy law; business law. *Unit head:* Garry W. Jenkins, Dean, 612-625-4841. *Application contact:* Robin Ingli, Director of Admissions, 612-625-3487, Fax: 612-625-2011, E-mail: jdadmissions@umn.edu.
Website: http://www.law.umn.edu/

University of Mississippi, School of Law, University, MS 38677. Offers LL M, JD, JD/MBA. *Accreditation:* ABA. *Faculty:* 31 full-time (12 women), 10 part-time/adjunct (4 women). *Students:* 363 full-time (162 women), 3 part-time (2 women); includes 94 minority (56 Black or African American, non-Hispanic/Latino; 1 American Indian or Alaska Native, non-Hispanic/Latino; 5 Asian, non-Hispanic/Latino; 24 Hispanic/Latino; 8 Two or more races, non-Hispanic/Latino), 2 international. Average age 25. In 2018, 1 master's, 108 doctorates awarded. *Entrance requirements:* For doctorate, LSAT, LSDAS. Additional exam requirements/recommendations for international students: Required—TOEFL. *Application deadline:* Applications are processed on a rolling basis. Application fee: $50. Electronic applications accepted. *Financial support:* Fellowships, research assistantships, teaching assistantships, career-related internships or fieldwork, Federal Work-Study, institutionally sponsored loans, and scholarships/grants available. Support available to part-time students. Financial award application deadline: 3/1; financial award applicants required to submit FAFSA. *Unit head:* Dr. Susan Duncan, Dean, School of Law, 662-915-7361, Fax: 662-915-6895, E-mail: lawadmin@olemiss.edu. *Application contact:* Temeka Smith, Graduate Activities Specialist for Admissions, 662-915-7474, Fax: 662-915-7577, E-mail: gschool@olemiss.edu.

University of Missouri, School of Law, Columbia, MO 65211. Offers dispute resolution (LL M); law (JD). *Accreditation:* ABA. *Entrance requirements:* For doctorate, LSAT. Additional exam requirements/recommendations for international students: Required—TOEFL (minimum score 600 paper-based; 100 iBT), IELTS (minimum score 7). *Expenses:* Contact institution.

University of Missouri–Kansas City, School of Law, Kansas City, MO 64110-2499. Offers LL M, JD, JD/LL M, JD/MBA, JD/MPA, LL M/MPA. *Accreditation:* ABA. *Program availability:* Part-time. *Degree requirements:* For master's, thesis (for general). *Entrance requirements:* For master's, LSAT, minimum GPA of 3.0 (for general), 2.7 (for taxation); for doctorate, LSAT. Additional exam requirements/recommendations for international students: Required—TOEFL (minimum score 550 paper-based; 80 iBT). Electronic applications accepted. *Expenses:* Contact institution. *Faculty research:* Family and children's issues, litigation, estate planning, urban law, business, tax entrepreneurial law.

University of Montana, Alexander Blewett III School of Law, Missoula, MT 59812. Offers JD, JD/MBA, JD/MPA. *Accreditation:* ABA. *Degree requirements:* For doctorate, oral presentation, paper. *Entrance requirements:* For doctorate, LSAT. *Expenses:* Contact institution. *Faculty research:* Legal education curriculum, business and probate law reform, rules of civil procedure reform, tribal courts, women's issues.

University of Nebraska–Lincoln, College of Law, Lincoln, NE 68583-0902. Offers law (JD); legal studies (MLS); space and telecommunications law (LL M); JD/MA; JD/MBA; JD/MCRP; JD/MPA; JD/PhD. *Accreditation:* ABA. *Entrance requirements:* For doctorate, LSAT. Electronic applications accepted. *Expenses:* Contact institution. *Faculty research:* Law and medicine, constitutional law, criminal procedure, international trade.

University of Nevada, Las Vegas, William S. Boyd School of Law, Las Vegas, NV 89154-1003. Offers gaming law and regulation (LL M); law (JD); JD/MBA; JD/MSW; JD/PhD. *Accreditation:* ABA. *Program availability:* Part-time, evening/weekend. *Faculty:* 43 full-time (27 women), 46 part-time/adjunct (11 women). *Students:* 354 full-time (182 women), 63 part-time (28 women); includes 150 minority (32 Black or African American, non-Hispanic/Latino; 20 Asian, non-Hispanic/Latino; 78 Hispanic/Latino; 20 Two or more races, non-Hispanic/Latino), 1 international. Average age 29. 883 applicants, 31% accepted, 157 enrolled. In 2018, 18 master's, 106 doctorates awarded. *Entrance requirements:* For doctorate, LSAT, Bachelor's degree from an accredited institution. *Application deadline:* For fall admission, 3/15 for domestic and international students. Applications are processed on a rolling basis. Application fee: $50. Electronic applications accepted. *Expenses:* 25900 tuition 1202 fees. *Financial support:* In 2018–19, 331 students received support, including 10 fellowships (averaging $4,750 per year); scholarships/grants also available. Support available to part-time students. Financial award application deadline: 3/15. *Faculty research:* Conflict/dispute resolution, health law, immigration, intellectual property, workplace law. *Total annual research expenditures:* $167,175. *Unit head:* Dr. Daniel W. Hamilton, Dean, 702-895-1876, Fax: 702-895-1095, E-mail: daniel.hamilton@unlv.edu. *Application contact:* Dr. Brain Wall, Assistant Dean for Admissions and Financial Aid, 702-895-1350, Fax: 702-895-2414, E-mail: brian.wall@unlv.edu.
Website: http://law.unlv.edu

University of New Hampshire, School of Law, Concord, NH 03301. Offers business law (JD); commerce and technology (LL M, MCT, Diploma); criminal law (JD); intellectual property (LL M, MIP, JD, Diploma), including patent law (JD), trademarks and copyright (JD); international criminal law and justice (LL M, MICLJ); litigation (JD); public interest and social justice (JD); sports and entertainment law (JD); JD/LL M; JD/MBA; JD/MIP; JD/MPP; JD/MSW. *Accreditation:* ABA. *Program availability:* Part-time, 100% online, limited residential. *Degree requirements:* For doctorate, comprehensive exam. *Entrance requirements:* For doctorate, LSAT. Additional exam requirements/recommendations for international students: Required—TOEFL (minimum score 600 paper-based; 100 iBT), minimum TOEFL iBT score of 80 (for master's programs). Electronic applications accepted. *Expenses:* Contact institution. *Faculty research:* Intellectual property, health law and policy, sports and entertainment law, patent law, trademarks and copyright.

University of New Mexico, School of Law, Albuquerque, NM 87131-0001. Offers JD, JD/M Acct, JD/MA, JD/MBA, JD/MPA. *Accreditation:* ABA. *Degree requirements:* For doctorate, ethics class, 2 writing classes, clinic. *Entrance requirements:* For doctorate, LSAT, bachelor's degree. Additional exam requirements/recommendations for international students: Required—TOEFL (minimum score 600 paper-based; 100 iBT). Electronic applications accepted. *Expenses:* Contact institution. *Faculty research:* Clinical legal education, international law, Indian law, natural resources and environmental law, Constitutional law, business and tax law, legal writing.

University of North Alabama, College of Arts and Sciences, Department of Politics, Justice, and Law, Florence, AL 35632-0001. Offers criminal justice (MSCJ). *Program availability:* Part-time, 100% online. *Degree requirements:* For master's, comprehensive exam (for some programs), thesis optional. *Entrance requirements:* For master's, GRE General Test, MAT, three letters of recommendation; essay. Additional exam requirements/recommendations for international students: Required—TOEFL (minimum score 79 iBT), IELTS (minimum score 6), PTE (minimum score 54). Electronic applications accepted.

The University of North Carolina at Chapel Hill, School of Law, Chapel Hill, NC 27599-3380. Offers LL M, JD, JD/MAMC, JD/MBA, JD/MPA, JD/MPH, JD/MPP, JD/MRP, JD/MSA, JD/MSIS, JD/MSLS, JD/MSW, JD/PhD. *Accreditation:* ABA. *Entrance requirements:* For doctorate, LSAT, bachelor's degree from accredited college or university, two letters of recommendation, essays, resume. Additional exam requirements/recommendations for international students: Required—TOEFL (minimum score 650 paper-based; 100 iBT). Electronic applications accepted. *Expenses:* Contact institution. *Faculty research:* Corporate and banking law, environmental policy, state and U.S. Constitutional law, health law policy, immigration law and civil rights.

University of North Dakota, School of Law, Grand Forks, ND 58202. Offers JD. *Accreditation:* ABA. *Entrance requirements:* For doctorate, LSAT. *Expenses:* Contact institution.

University of North Texas at Dallas, College of Law, Dallas, TX 75241. Offers JD.

University of Notre Dame, The Law School, Notre Dame, IN 46556-0780. Offers human rights (LL M, JSD); international and comparative law (LL M); law (JD). *Accreditation:* ABA. *Degree requirements:* For master's, thesis, 1-year residency; for doctorate, thesis/dissertation, 2-year residency (for JSD). *Entrance requirements:* For doctorate, LSAT (for JD), LL M (for JSD). Additional exam requirements/recommendations for international students: Required—TOEFL. Electronic applications accepted. *Expenses:* Contact institution. *Faculty research:* Constitutional structure; international law (public and private); law and religion; land, energy, and environmental law; intellectual property, including patent, copyright, and trademark law.

University of Oklahoma, College of Law, Norman, OK 73019. Offers LL M, JD, JD/MA, JD/MBA, JD/MPH, JD/MS. *Accreditation:* ABA. *Program availability:* Part-time, 100% online. *Faculty:* 33 full-time (15 women), 10 part-time/adjunct (3 women). *Students:* 608 full-time (302 women), 291 part-time (193 women); includes 307 minority (32 Black or African American, non-Hispanic/Latino; 150 American Indian or Alaska Native, non-Hispanic/Latino; 13 Asian, non-Hispanic/Latino; 66 Hispanic/Latino; 1 Native Hawaiian or other Pacific Islander, non-Hispanic/Latino; 45 Two or more races, non-Hispanic/Latino), 7 international. Average age 32. 896 applicants, 55% accepted, 264 enrolled. In 2018, 182 master's, 178 doctorates awarded. *Entrance requirements:* For master's, JD or equivalent; for doctorate, LSAT. Additional exam requirements/recommendations for international students: Required—TOEFL minimum score 550 paper-based, 79 iBT (for LL M); 600 paper-based, 100 iBT (for JD). *Application deadline:* For fall admission, 3/15 for domestic and international students. Applications are processed on a rolling basis. Application fee: $50. Electronic applications accepted. *Expenses:* $62,709 for residents to complete a degree; $96,864 for non-residents to complete a degree. *Financial support:* In 2018–19, 472 students received support. Career-related internships or fieldwork, Federal Work-Study, scholarships/grants, and tuition waivers (full and partial) available. Financial award application deadline: 6/1; financial award applicants required to submit FAFSA. *Faculty research:* Energy and natural resources; indigenous peoples law; business and commercial; litigation and procedure; tax, pensions and retirement. *Unit head:* Katheleen Guzman, Interim Dean, 405-325-4884, Fax: 405-325-7712, E-mail: kguzman@ou.edu. *Application contact:* Madeline Farris, Assoc. Director of Admissions, 405-325-8521, Fax: 405-325-0502, E-mail: admissions@law.ou.edu.
Website: http://www.law.ou.edu/

University of Oregon, School of Law, Eugene, OR 97403. Offers MA, MS, JD, JD/MBA, JD/MS. *Accreditation:* ABA. *Entrance requirements:* For doctorate, LSAT. *Expenses:* Contact institution.

University of Ottawa, Faculty of Graduate and Postdoctoral Studies, Faculty of Law, Ottawa, ON K1N 6N5, Canada. Offers LL M, LL D. *Program availability:* Part-time, evening/weekend. *Degree requirements:* For master's, thesis or alternative; for doctorate, thesis/dissertation. *Entrance requirements:* For master's, minimum B average, LL B; for doctorate, LL M, minimum B+ average. Electronic applications accepted. *Faculty research:* International law, human rights law, family law.

University of Pennsylvania, Law School, Philadelphia, PA 19104. Offers LL CM, LL M, ML, JD, SJD, JD/DMD, JD/Ed D, JD/LL M, JD/MA, JD/MBA, JD/MBE, JD/MCIT, JD/MCP, JD/MD, JD/MES, JD/MPA, JD/MPH, JD/MS, JD/MS Ed, JD/MSE, JD/MSSP, JD/MSW, JD/PhD. JD/LLM offered jointly with Hong Kong University; JD/MA Global Governance Studies with Sciences Po (Paris); JD/LLM Transnational Arbitration with Sciences Po (Paris). *Accreditation:* ABA. *Faculty:* 87 full-time (34 women), 155 part-time/adjunct (52 women). *Students:* 755 full-time (386 women); includes 226 minority (53 Black or African American, non-Hispanic/Latino; 2 American Indian or Alaska Native, non-Hispanic/Latino; 81 Asian, non-Hispanic/Latino; 51 Hispanic/Latino; 39 Two or more races, non-Hispanic/Latino), 39 international. Average age 27. 6,413 applicants, 15% accepted, 238 enrolled. In 2018, 24 master's, 250 doctorates awarded. *Degree requirements:* For doctorate, thesis/dissertation. *Entrance requirements:* For doctorate, GRE, GMAT, OR LSAT. Additional exam requirements/recommendations for international students: Recommended—TOEFL, IELTS. *Application deadline:* For fall admission, 3/1 for domestic and international students. Applications are processed on a rolling basis. Application fee: $80. Electronic applications accepted. *Expenses:* Contact institution. *Financial support:* In 2018–19, 390 students received support, including 56 research assistantships (averaging $1,166 per year), 13 teaching assistantships (averaging $3,501 per year); fellowships, career-related internships or fieldwork, Federal Work-Study, institutionally sponsored loans, and scholarships/grants also available. Financial award application deadline: 3/1; financial award applicants required to submit CSS PROFILE or FAFSA. *Faculty research:* Administrative law and regulation, business and corporate law, civil procedure, Constitutional law, criminal law, environmental law, health law, intellectual property and technology law, international and comparative law, law and economics, legal history, philosophy, tax law and policy. *Total annual research expenditures:* $955,958. *Unit head:* Theodore W. Ruger, Dean, 215-898-7463, Fax: 215-573-2025, E-mail: deanruger@law.upenn.edu. *Application contact:* Renee Post, Associate Dean of Admissions and Financial Aid, 215-898-7400, Fax: 215-898-9606, E-mail: contactadmissions@law.upenn.edu.
Website: http://www.law.upenn.edu/

University of Pittsburgh, Katz Graduate School of Business, MBA/Juris Doctor Program, Pittsburgh, PA 15260. Offers MBA/JD. *Entrance requirements:* Additional exam requirements/recommendations for international students: Required—TOEFL (minimum score 100 iBT) or IELTS (minimum score 7.0). Electronic applications accepted. *Faculty research:* Accounting systems/financial reporting, corporate finance, shopper marketing/consumer behavior, management information systems, organizational behavior and entrepreneurship.

University of Pittsburgh, School of Law, LL M Program for Foreign-Trained Lawyers, Pittsburgh, PA 15260. Offers LL M. Program offered to international students only.

Accreditation: ABA. *Program availability:* Part-time. *Entrance requirements:* For master's, law degree from foreign university. Additional exam requirements/recommendations for international students: Required—TOEFL (minimum score 577 paper-based; 90 iBT), IELTS (minimum score 6.5). Electronic applications accepted. *Expenses:* Contact institution. *Faculty research:* International arbitration, private international law, Islamic law, environmental criminal and comparative law.

University of Puerto Rico–Río Piedras, School of Law, San Juan, PR 00931-3349. Offers LL M, JD. *Accreditation:* ABA. *Program availability:* Part-time, evening/weekend. *Entrance requirements:* For master's, LSAT, minimum GPA of 3.0, letter of recommendation; for doctorate, GMAT, GRE, LSAT, EXADEP, minimum GPA of 3.0. Additional exam requirements/recommendations for international students: Required—TOEFL. *Faculty research:* Civil code; Puerto Rico constitutional law; professional behavior, rules and regulations; international law; expert testimony.

University of Richmond, School of Law, University of Richmond, VA 23173. Offers JD, JD/MA, JD/MBA, JD/MHA, JD/MPA, JD/MS, JD/MSW, JD/MURP. JD/MSW, JD/MHA, JD/MPA offered jointly with Virginia Commonwealth University; JD/MURP with Virginia Commonwealth University; JD/MA with Department of History; JD/MS with Department of Biology. *Accreditation:* ABA. *Entrance requirements:* For doctorate, LSAT. Electronic applications accepted. *Expenses:* Contact institution.

University of St. Thomas, School of Law, Minneapolis, MN 55403-2015. Offers law (JD); law/business administration (JD/MBA); law/catholic studies (JD/MA); law/organizational ethics and compliance (JD/LL M); law/social work (JD/MSW); organizational ethics and compliance (LL M, MSL); U.S. law (LL M); JD/LL M; JD/MA; JD/MBA; JD/MSW. *Accreditation:* ABA. *Program availability:* 100% online. *Faculty:* 27 full-time (6 women), 70 part-time/adjunct (29 women). *Students:* 434 full-time (228 women); includes 70 minority (24 Black or African American, non-Hispanic/Latino; 1 American Indian or Alaska Native, non-Hispanic/Latino; 12 Asian, non-Hispanic/Latino; 21 Hispanic/Latino; 12 Two or more races, non-Hispanic/Latino), 13 international. Average age 26. 699 applicants, 61% accepted, 149 enrolled. In 2018, 2 master's, 101 doctorates awarded. *Degree requirements:* For doctorate, mentor externship, public service. *Entrance requirements:* For doctorate, LSAT, 2 letters of recommendation, personal statement. Additional exam requirements/recommendations for international students: Recommended—TOEFL (minimum score 80 iBT). *Application deadline:* For fall admission, 8/1 priority date for domestic and international students. Applications are processed on a rolling basis. Application fee: $0. Electronic applications accepted. *Expenses:* $41,442 per academic year. *Financial support:* In 2018–19, 385 students received support. Scholarships/grants available. Financial award application deadline: 7/1; financial award applicants required to submit FAFSA. *Faculty research:* Constitutional law (executive powers and First Amendment); banking, securities, and financial markets; law, religion, and jurisprudence; international law, development and dispute resolution; formation of professional identity, values, and skills. *Unit head:* Robert K. Vischer, Dean, 651-962-4838, Fax: 651-962-4881, E-mail: rkvischer@stthomas.edu. *Application contact:* Cari Haaland, Assistant Dean for Admissions, 651-962-4872, Fax: 651-962-4876, E-mail: lawschool@stthomas.edu.
Website: http://www.stthomas.edu/law/

University of San Diego, School of Law, San Diego, CA 92110. Offers business and corporate law (LL M); comparative law (LL M); general studies (LL M); international law (LL M); law (JD); legal studies (MS); peace and law (JD/MA); taxation (LL M, Diploma); JD/IMBA; JD/MA; JD/MBA. *Accreditation:* ABA. *Program availability:* Part-time, evening/weekend. *Faculty:* 45 full-time (16 women), 72 part-time/adjunct (21 women). *Students:* 661 full-time (363 women), 92 part-time (49 women); includes 244 minority (31 Black or African American, non-Hispanic/Latino; 12 American Indian or Alaska Native, non-Hispanic/Latino; 75 Asian, non-Hispanic/Latino; 110 Hispanic/Latino; 4 Native Hawaiian or other Pacific Islander, non-Hispanic/Latino; 12 Two or more races, non-Hispanic/Latino), 31 international. Average age 27. 3,511 applicants, 240 enrolled. In 2018, 59 master's, 264 doctorates awarded. *Entrance requirements:* For master's, JD, LL B or equivalent from an ABA-accredited law school; for doctorate, LSAT (less than 5 years old), bachelor's degree, registration with the Credential Assemble Service (CAS). Additional exam requirements/recommendations for international students: Required—TOEFL (minimum score 600 paper-based; 100 iBT), IELTS (minimum score 7). *Application deadline:* For fall admission, 2/1 priority date for domestic students. Applications are processed on a rolling basis. Application fee: $0. Electronic applications accepted. *Expenses:* Contact institution. *Financial support:* In 2018–19, 640 students received support. Career-related internships or fieldwork, Federal Work-Study, institutionally sponsored loans, and scholarships/grants available. Support available to part-time students. Financial award application deadline: 3/1; financial award applicants required to submit FAFSA. *Faculty research:* Corporate law, children's advocacy, Constitutional and criminal law, international and comparative law, public interest law, intellectual property and tax law. *Unit head:* Dr. Stephen C. Ferruolo, Dean, 619-260-4527, E-mail: lawdean@sandiego.edu. *Application contact:* Jorge Garcia, Assistant Dean, JD Admissions, 619-260-4528, Fax: 619-260-2218, E-mail: jdinfo@sandiego.edu.
Website: http://www.sandiego.edu/law/

University of San Francisco, School of Law, JD Program, San Francisco, CA 94117. Offers JD. *Accreditation:* ABA. *Program availability:* Part-time, evening/weekend. *Students:* 336 full-time (187 women), 65 part-time (36 women); includes 212 minority (27 Black or African American, non-Hispanic/Latino; 46 Asian, non-Hispanic/Latino; 107 Hispanic/Latino; 3 Native Hawaiian or other Pacific Islander, non-Hispanic/Latino; 29 Two or more races, non-Hispanic/Latino), 13 international. Average age 28. 1,751 applicants, 56% accepted, 146 enrolled. In 2018, 173 doctorates awarded. *Entrance requirements:* Additional exam requirements/recommendations for international students: Required—TOEFL (minimum score 100 paper-based; 100 iBT), IELTS. *Application deadline:* For fall admission, 2/1 for domestic students. Applications are processed on a rolling basis. Application fee: $60. Electronic applications accepted. *Expenses:* 2019-20 FT - $50,690; PT - $1,755 per unit. *Financial support:* Application deadline: 2/15; applicants required to submit FAFSA. *Unit head:* Susan Freiwald, Dean of the School of Law. *Application contact:* Alan P. Guerrero, Director of Admissions, 415-422-2975, E-mail: lawadmissions@usfca.edu.
Website: http://www.usfca.edu/law/academics/jd

University of Saskatchewan, College of Graduate and Postdoctoral Studies, College of Law, Saskatoon, SK S7N 5A2, Canada. Offers LL M, JD. *Program availability:* Part-time. *Degree requirements:* For master's, thesis. *Entrance requirements:* For master's, LL B; for doctorate, LSAT. Additional exam requirements/recommendations for international students: Required—TOEFL. *Faculty research:* Cooperative, native/aboriginal, constitutional, commercial, consumer, and natural resource law; criminal justice; human rights.

University of South Africa, College of Law, Pretoria, South Africa. Offers correctional services management (M Tech); criminology (MA, PhD); law (LL M, LL D); penology (MA, PhD); police science (MA, PhD); policing (M Tech); security risk management (M Tech); social science in criminology (MA).

University of South Carolina, School of Law, Columbia, SC 29208. Offers JD, JD/IMBA, JD/M Acc, JD/MCJ, JD/MEERM, JD/MHA, JD/MHR, JD/MIBS, JD/MPA, JD/MSEL, JD/MSW. *Accreditation:* ABA. *Degree requirements:* For doctorate, thesis/dissertation. *Entrance requirements:* For doctorate, LSAT. *Expenses:* Contact institution.

University of South Dakota, Graduate School, School of Law, Vermillion, SD 57069. Offers JD, JD/MA, JD/MBA, JD/MP Acc, JD/MPA, JD/MS. *Accreditation:* ABA. *Program availability:* Part-time. *Entrance requirements:* For doctorate, LSAT. Additional exam requirements/recommendations for international students: Required—TOEFL (minimum score 600 paper-based). Electronic applications accepted. *Expenses:* Contact institution. *Faculty research:* Indian law, skills training, international law, family law, evidence.

University of Southern California, Graduate School, Gould School of Law, Los Angeles, CA 90089. Offers comparative law for foreign attorneys (MCL); law (JD); law for foreign-educated attorneys (LL M); JD/MA; JD/MBA; JD/MBT; JD/MPA; JD/MPP; JD/MRED; JD/MS; JD/MSW; JD/PhD; JD/Pharm D. *Accreditation:* ABA. *Entrance requirements:* For doctorate, LSAT. Additional exam requirements/recommendations for international students: Required—TOEFL. *Faculty research:* Intellectual property law, tax law, criminal law, law and philosophy, law and history.

The University of Tennessee, College of Law, Knoxville, TN 37996-1810. Offers business transactions (JD); law (JD); trial advocacy and dispute resolution (JD); JD/MA; JD/MBA; JD/MPH; JD/MPPA. *Accreditation:* ABA. *Faculty:* 45 full-time (20 women), 84 part-time/adjunct (31 women). *Students:* 360 full-time (165 women); includes 71 minority (28 Black or African American, non-Hispanic/Latino; 4 American Indian or Alaska Native, non-Hispanic/Latino; 2 Asian, non-Hispanic/Latino; 26 Hispanic/Latino; 11 Two or more races, non-Hispanic/Latino), 2 international. Average age 24. 1,006 applicants, 37% accepted, 124 enrolled. In 2018, 100 doctorates awarded. *Entrance requirements:* For doctorate, LSAT. Additional exam requirements/recommendations for international students: Recommended—TOEFL. *Application deadline:* For fall admission, 3/1 priority date for domestic and international students. Applications are processed on a rolling basis. Application fee: $35. Electronic applications accepted. Application fee is waived when completed online. *Expenses:* $19,674 in-state, $38,348 out-of-state. *Financial support:* In 2018–19, 249 students received support, including 13 research assistantships with full tuition reimbursements available (averaging $27,928 per year); career-related internships or fieldwork, Federal Work-Study, institutionally sponsored loans, scholarships/grants, and unspecified assistantships also available. Support available to part-time students. Financial award application deadline: 3/1; financial award applicants required to submit FAFSA. *Faculty research:* Legal expert systems, medical malpractice remedies, professional ethics, insanity defense. *Unit head:* Sarah Busse, Director, Admissions and Financial Aid, 865-974-4131, Fax: 865-974-1572, E-mail: lawadmit@utk.edu. *Application contact:* Sarah Busse, Director, Admissions and Financial Aid, 865-974-4131, Fax: 865-974-1572, E-mail: lawadmit@utk.edu.
Website: http://www.law.utk.edu/

The University of Texas at Austin, Graduate School, College of Liberal Arts, Teresa Lozano Long Institute of Latin American Studies, Austin, TX 78712-1111. Offers cultural politics of Afro-Latin and indigenous peoples (MA); development studies (MA); environmental studies (MA); human rights (MA); Latin American and international law (LL M); JD/MA; MA/MA; MBA/MA; MP Aff/MA; MSCRP/MA. LL M offered jointly with The University of Texas School of Law. *Entrance requirements:* For master's, GRE General Test.

The University of Texas at Austin, School of Law, Austin, TX 78705-3224. Offers LL M, JD, JD/MA, JD/MBA, JD/MGPS, JD/MP Aff, JD/MSCRP. *Accreditation:* ABA. *Entrance requirements:* For doctorate, LSAT, minimum GPA of 2.2. Electronic applications accepted. *Expenses:* Contact institution. *Faculty research:* Constitutional law, corporate law, environmental law, employment and labor law, intellectual property law.

The University of Texas at Dallas, School of Economic, Political and Policy Sciences, Program in Political Science, Richardson, TX 75080. Offers Constitutional law (MA); legislative studies (MA); political science (MA, PhD). *Program availability:* Part-time, evening/weekend. *Faculty:* 12 full-time (2 women), 1 part-time/adjunct (0 women). *Students:* 25 full-time (8 women), 15 part-time (7 women); includes 8 minority (3 Black or African American, non-Hispanic/Latino; 1 Asian, non-Hispanic/Latino; 2 Hispanic/Latino; 2 Two or more races, non-Hispanic/Latino), 11 international. Average age 35. 35 applicants, 57% accepted, 10 enrolled. In 2018, 6 master's, 3 doctorates awarded. Terminal master's awarded for partial completion of doctoral program. *Degree requirements:* For master's, thesis optional, independent study; for doctorate, thesis/dissertation, practicum research. *Entrance requirements:* For master's, GRE (minimum combined verbal and quantitative score of 1100), minimum undergraduate GPA of 3.0; for doctorate, GRE (minimum combined verbal and quantitative score of 1200, writing 4.5), minimum undergraduate GPA of 3.2. Additional exam requirements/recommendations for international students: Required—TOEFL (minimum score 550 paper-based). *Application deadline:* For fall admission, 7/15 for domestic students, 5/1 priority date for international students; for spring admission, 11/15 for domestic students, 9/1 priority date for international students. Applications are processed on a rolling basis. Application fee: $50 ($100 for international students). Electronic applications accepted. *Expenses: Tuition, area resident:* Full-time $13,458. Tuition, state resident: full-time $13,458. Tuition, nonresident: full-time $26,852. *International tuition:* $26,852 full-time. Tuition and fees vary according to course load. *Financial support:* In 2018–19, 15 students received support, including 2 research assistantships with partial tuition reimbursements available (averaging $18,000 per year), 13 teaching assistantships with partial tuition reimbursements available (averaging $13,500 per year); career-related internships or fieldwork, Federal Work-Study, institutionally sponsored loans, and scholarships/grants also available. Support available to part-time students. Financial award application deadline: 4/30; financial award applicants required to submit FAFSA. *Faculty research:* Terrorism and democratic stability, redistricting and representation, trust and social exchange, how economic ideas impact political thought and public policy. *Unit head:* Dr. Banks Miller, Program Head, 972-883-2930, Fax: 972-883-2735, E-mail: ph.psci@utdallas.edu. *Application contact:* Marjorie McDonald, Graduate Program Administrator, 972-883-6406, Fax: 972-883-2735, E-mail: psci@utdallas.edu.
Website: https://epps.utdallas.edu/about/programs/political-science/

University of the District of Columbia, David A. Clarke School of Law, Washington, DC 20008. Offers clinical teaching and social justice (LL M); law (JD). *Accreditation:* ABA. *Program availability:* Part-time, evening/weekend. *Faculty:* 21 full-time (9 women), 22 part-time/adjunct (12 women). *Students:* 123 full-time (83 women), 133 part-time (80 women); includes 158 minority (100 Black or African American, non-Hispanic/Latino; 1 American Indian or Alaska Native, non-Hispanic/Latino; 25 Asian, non-Hispanic/Latino; 32 Hispanic/Latino), 2 international. Average age 28. 675 applicants, 20% accepted, 94 enrolled. In 2018, 64 doctorates awarded. *Degree requirements:* For doctorate, 90 credits, advanced legal writing. *Entrance requirements:* For doctorate, LSAT. Additional exam requirements/recommendations for international students: Required—TOEFL. *Application deadline:* For fall admission, 3/15 priority date for domestic and international students. Applications are processed on a rolling basis. Application fee: $35. Electronic applications accepted. Application fee is waived when completed online. *Expenses:* $37,548 resident full-time, $38,408 resident part-time, $72,090 non-resident full-time, $72,640 non-resident part-time to complete the degree. *Financial support:* In 2018–19, 172 students received support, including 46 fellowships (averaging $4,250 per year), 4

research assistantships (averaging $3,000 per year), 39 teaching assistantships (averaging $3,000 per year); Federal Work-Study and scholarships/grants also available. Financial award application deadline: 3/15; financial award applicants required to submit FAFSA. *Faculty research:* Civil Rights and Equality, Criminal Law, Family and Juvenile Law, Housing and Community Development Law, and Immigration Law and Human Rights. *Unit head:* Renee M. Hutchins, Dean, 202-274-7346, Fax: 202-274-5583, E-mail: renee.hutchins@udc.edu. *Application contact:* Jino Ray, Associate Dean of Admission, 202-274-7336, Fax: 202-274-5583, E-mail: jino.ray@udc.edu.
Website: http://www.law.udc.edu/

University of the Pacific, McGeorge School of Law, Sacramento, CA 95817. Offers advocacy (JD); international water resources law (JSD); public policy and law (LL M); JD/MBA; JD/MPPA. *Accreditation:* ABA. *Program availability:* Part-time, evening/weekend. *Degree requirements:* For master's, thesis (for some programs); for doctorate, thesis/dissertation (for some programs). *Entrance requirements:* For master's, JD; for doctorate, LSAT (for JD), LL M (for JSD). Additional exam requirements/recommendations for international students: Required—TOEFL (minimum score 600 paper-based; 100 iBT). Electronic applications accepted. *Expenses:* Contact institution. *Faculty research:* International legal studies, public policy and law, advocacy, intellectual property law, taxation, criminal law.

The University of Toledo, College of Law, Toledo, OH 43606. Offers compliance (Certificate); health care compliance (Certificate); higher education compliance (Certificate); law (MLW, JD); JD/MACJ; JD/MBA; JD/MD; JD/MPH; JD/MSE. *Accreditation:* ABA. *Program availability:* Part-time, evening/weekend, 100% online. *Faculty:* 20 full-time (9 women), 11 part-time/adjunct (5 women). *Students:* 231 full-time (119 women), 63 part-time (40 women); includes 49 minority (13 Black or African American, non-Hispanic/Latino; 1 American Indian or Alaska Native, non-Hispanic/Latino; 10 Asian, non-Hispanic/Latino; 19 Hispanic/Latino; 1 Native Hawaiian or other Pacific Islander, non-Hispanic/Latino; 5 Two or more races, non-Hispanic/Latino). Average age 29. 422 applicants, 62% accepted, 97 enrolled. In 2018, 6 master's, 55 doctorates, 3 Certificates awarded. *Degree requirements:* For master's, thesis or alternative, 30 credits (mix of required and elective courses); for doctorate, 89 credits (mix of required and elective courses); for Certificate, 15 credits. *Entrance requirements:* For doctorate, LSAT, bachelor's degree. Additional exam requirements/recommendations for international students: Recommended—TOEFL (minimum score 600 paper-based; 100 iBT). *Application deadline:* For fall admission, 8/1 priority date for domestic students, 7/31 for international students; for winter admission, 11/15 for domestic students. Applications are processed on a rolling basis. Application fee: $0. Electronic applications accepted. *Expenses:* Full time state resident $20,905.20; full time non-state resident $31,873.20; part time state resident $15,678.90; part time non-state resident $23,904.90. *Financial support:* In 2018–19, 226 students received support. Research assistantships, career-related internships or fieldwork, Federal Work-Study, and scholarships/grants available. Support available to part-time students. Financial award application deadline: 8/1; financial award applicants required to submit FAFSA. *Faculty research:* Securities regulation in cyberspace; reconceptualization of the doctrine of willful blindness; white collar crime; employment discrimination; bankruptcy; interlocutory appeals in federal court; trademark dilution; canons of statutory interpretation; theories of corporation; reproductive rights as it relates to disposition of jointly-created frozen embryos. *Total annual research expenditures:* $74,900. *Unit head:* D. Benjamin Barros, Dean, 419-530-2379, Fax: 419-530-4526, E-mail: ben.barros@utoledo.edu. *Application contact:* Jessica Mehl, Assistant Dean of Law Admissions, 419-530-4131, Fax: 419-530-4345, E-mail: law.admissions@utoledo.edu.
Website: http://www.utoledo.edu/law/

University of Toronto, School of Graduate Studies, Faculty of Law and School of Graduate Studies, Graduate Programs in Law, Toronto, ON M5S 1A1, Canada. Offers LL M, MSL, SJD. *Degree requirements:* For master's, thesis (for some programs); for doctorate, thesis/dissertation. *Entrance requirements:* Additional exam requirements/recommendations for international students: Required—TOEFL (minimum score 600 paper-based; 100 iBT), TWE (minimum score 5). Electronic applications accepted.

University of Toronto, School of Graduate Studies, Faculty of Law, Professional Program in Law, Toronto, ON M5S 1A1, Canada. Offers JD, JD/Certificate, JD/MA, JD/MBA, JD/MI, JD/MSW, JD/PhD. *Entrance requirements:* For doctorate, LSAT. *Expenses:* Contact institution.

The University of Tulsa, College of Law, Tulsa, OK 74104. Offers American Indian and indigenous law (LL M); American law for foreign lawyers (LL M); energy and natural resources law (LL M); energy law (MJ); health law (Certificate); Indian law (MJ); law (JD); Native American law (Certificate); sustainable energy and resources law (Certificate); JD/MA; JD/MBA; JD/MS. *Accreditation:* ABA. *Program availability:* Part-time. *Faculty:* 27 full-time (15 women), 19 part-time/adjunct (7 women). *Students:* 250 full-time (110 women), 31 part-time (14 women); includes 80 minority (10 Black or African American, non-Hispanic/Latino; 17 American Indian or Alaska Native, non-Hispanic/Latino; 4 Asian, non-Hispanic/Latino; 12 Hispanic/Latino; 37 Two or more races, non-Hispanic/Latino), 5 international. Average age 28. 581 applicants, 42% accepted, 100 enrolled. In 2018, 1 master's, 81 doctorates, 14 Certificates awarded. *Entrance requirements:* For doctorate, LSAT, BS or BA from 4-year regionally-accredited college/university. Additional exam requirements/recommendations for international students: Required—TOEFL (minimum score 570 paper-based; 90 iBT), TOEFL preferred; Recommended—IELTS (minimum score 6.5). *Application deadline:* For fall admission, 7/31 priority date for domestic and international students; for spring admission, 12/1 priority date for domestic students, 12/1 for international students; for summer admission, 4/13 for domestic and international students. Applications are processed on a rolling basis. Application fee: $30. Electronic applications accepted. *Expenses:* $25,254 full-time; $17,490 (8-11 hours); $13,734 (6-7 hours). *Financial support:* In 2018–19, 251 students received support. Scholarships/grants available. Support available to part-time students. Financial award application deadline: 8/1; financial award applicants required to submit FAFSA. *Faculty research:* Criminal law, copyright law, cybersecurity law, energy and natural resources law, international law. *Unit head:* Prof. Lyn Suzanne Entzeroth, Dean, 918-631-2400, Fax: 918-631-3126, E-mail: lyn-entzeroth@utulsa.edu. *Application contact:* April M. Fox, Associate Dean of Admissions and Financial Aid, 918-631-2406, Fax: 918-631-3630, E-mail: april-fox@utulsa.edu.
Website: http://www.utulsa.edu/law/

University of Utah, S.J. Quinney College of Law, Salt Lake City, UT 84112-0730. Offers LL M, MLS, JD, JD/MBA, JD/MCMP, JD/MPA, JD/MPP, JD/MRED, JD/MSW. *Accreditation:* ABA. *Program availability:* Part-time, evening/weekend. *Faculty:* 25 full-time (11 women), 42 part-time/adjunct (17 women). *Students:* 295 full-time (130 women), 3 part-time (2 women); includes 43 minority (1 Black or African American, non-Hispanic/Latino; 3 American Indian or Alaska Native, non-Hispanic/Latino; 8 Asian, non-Hispanic/Latino; 28 Hispanic/Latino; 1 Native Hawaiian or other Pacific Islander, non-Hispanic/Latino; 2 Two or more races, non-Hispanic/Latino), 3 international. Average age 29. In 2018, 1 master's, 93 doctorates awarded. *Degree requirements:* For doctorate, comprehensive exam. *Entrance requirements:* For doctorate, LSAT, bachelor's degree from college or university whose accreditation is recognized by the U.S. Department of Education. Additional exam requirements/recommendations for international students: Required—TOEFL. *Application deadline:* For fall admission, 1/15 priority date for domestic students, 2/15 priority date for international students. Applications are processed on a rolling basis. Application fee: $60. Electronic applications accepted. *Expenses:* First-year state resident tuition and fees $28354, first-year nonresident tuition and fees $37011. *Financial support:* Fellowships with partial tuition reimbursements, Federal Work-Study, institutionally sponsored loans, scholarships/grants, and tuition waivers (full and partial) available. Financial award application deadline: 2/1; financial award applicants required to submit FAFSA. *Faculty research:* Environmental law, intellectual property, international law, criminal law, business law. *Unit head:* Elizabeth K. Warner, Dean, 801-585-9318, E-mail: elizabeth.warner@law.utah.edu. *Application contact:* Reyes Aquilar, Associate Director for Admission and Financial Aid, 801-581-6563, E-mail: reyes.aguilar@law.utah.edu.
Website: http://www.law.utah.edu

University of Victoria, Faculty of Law, Victoria, BC V8W 2Y2, Canada. Offers LL M, JD, PhD, MBA/JD, MPA/JD. *Program availability:* Part-time. *Degree requirements:* For master's, thesis; for doctorate, thesis/dissertation (for some programs), major research paper (for JD). *Entrance requirements:* For master's, LL B or JD; for doctorate, LSAT (for JD), LL B or JD (for PhD); minimum 3 years of full-time study or part-time equivalent leading toward a bachelor's degree (for JD). Additional exam requirements/recommendations for international students: Required—TOEFL (minimum score 600 paper-based; 100 iBT). Electronic applications accepted. *Expenses:* Contact institution. *Faculty research:* Environmental law and policy, international law, alternative dispute resolution, intellectual property law, Aboriginal law.

University of Virginia, School of Law, Charlottesville, VA 22903-1789. Offers LL M, JD, SJD, JD/MA, JD/MBA, JD/MP, JD/MPH, JD/MS, JD/MUEP. JD/MA in international relations offered jointly with The Johns Hopkins University. *Accreditation:* ABA. *Degree requirements:* For doctorate, thesis/dissertation (for some programs), oral exam (for SJD). *Entrance requirements:* For master's, 2 letters of recommendation; personal statement; for doctorate, LSAT (for JD). Additional exam requirements/recommendations for international students: Required—TOEFL. Electronic applications accepted. *Expenses:* Contact institution.

University of Washington, Graduate School, School of Law, Seattle, WA 98195-3020. Offers Asian law (LL M, PhD); intellectual property law and policy (LL M); law (JD); law of sustainable international development (LL M); taxation (LL M); JD/LL M; JD/MA; JD/MAIS; JD/MBA; JD/MPA; JD/MS; JD/PhD. *Accreditation:* ABA. *Degree requirements:* For master's, thesis; for doctorate, thesis/dissertation (for some programs). *Entrance requirements:* For master's, language proficiency (LL M in Asian law); for doctorate, LSAT (for JD). Additional exam requirements/recommendations for international students: Required—TOEFL. *Expenses:* Contact institution. *Faculty research:* Asian, international and comparative law, intellectual property law, health law, environmental law, taxation.

The University of Western Ontario, Faculty of Law, London, ON N6A 3K7, Canada. Offers LL M, MLS, JD, Diploma. *Entrance requirements:* For master's, B+ average in BA, sample of legal academic writing; for doctorate, LSAT. Additional exam requirements/recommendations for international students: Required—TOEFL. *Expenses:* Contact institution. *Faculty research:* Taxation, administrative law, torts, drug and alcohol law and policy, property.

University of West Los Angeles, School of Law, Inglewood, CA 90301. Offers JD. *Program availability:* Part-time, evening/weekend. *Entrance requirements:* Additional exam requirements/recommendations for international students: Required—TOEFL (minimum score 550 paper-based). Electronic applications accepted.

University of Wisconsin–Madison, Law School, Madison, WI 53706-1399. Offers LL M, JD, SJD. *Accreditation:* ABA. *Program availability:* Part-time, evening/weekend. *Faculty:* 64 full-time (38 women), 56 part-time/adjunct (20 women). *Students:* 617 full-time (294 women), 36 part-time (21 women); includes 124 minority (26 Black or African American, non-Hispanic/Latino; 2 American Indian or Alaska Native, non-Hispanic/Latino; 22 Asian, non-Hispanic/Latino; 53 Hispanic/Latino; 1 Native Hawaiian or other Pacific Islander, non-Hispanic/Latino; 20 Two or more races, non-Hispanic/Latino), 66 international. Average age 26. 1,712 applicants, 46% accepted, 271 enrolled. In 2018, 41 master's, 158 doctorates awarded. *Degree requirements:* For master's, thesis (for some programs); for doctorate, comprehensive exam (for some programs), thesis/dissertation (for some programs). *Entrance requirements:* For doctorate, LSAT (for JD). Additional exam requirements/recommendations for international students: Required—TOEFL. *Application deadline:* For fall admission, 4/1 for domestic and international students. Applications are processed on a rolling basis. Application fee: $60. Electronic applications accepted. *Expenses:* $23,517.44 per year resident full-time; $1,027.56 per credit resident part-time; $42,213.68 per year nonresident full-time; $1,806.57 per credit nonresident part-time. *Financial support:* In 2018–19, 485 students received support. Fellowships, research assistantships, teaching assistantships, career-related internships or fieldwork, Federal Work-Study, scholarships/grants, health care benefits, tuition waivers (full and partial), and unspecified assistantships available. Support available to part-time students. Financial award application deadline: 4/1. *Unit head:* Margaret Raymond, Dean, 608-265-3750, Fax: 608-890-0134. *Application contact:* Rebecca L. Scheller, Assistant Dean for Admissions and Financial Aid, 608-262-5914, Fax: 608-263-3190, E-mail: admissions@law.wisc.edu.
Website: https://www.law.wisc.edu/

University of Wyoming, College of Law, Laramie, WY 82071. Offers JD, JD/MPA. *Accreditation:* ABA. *Entrance requirements:* For doctorate, LSAT. Additional exam requirements/recommendations for international students: Required—TOEFL. Electronic applications accepted. *Expenses:* Contact institution. *Faculty research:* Environmental, public land, constitutional, securities law, criminal law.

Vanderbilt University, Vanderbilt Law School, Nashville, TN 37203. Offers law (LL M, JD); law and economics (PhD); JD/M Div; JD/MA; JD/MBA; JD/MD; JD/MPP; JD/MTS; JD/PhD; LL M/MA. *Accreditation:* ABA. *Degree requirements:* For doctorate, comprehensive exam (for some programs), thesis/dissertation (for some programs), 72 hours of coursework and research (for PhD). *Entrance requirements:* For master's, foreign law degree; for doctorate, GRE (for PhD), LSAT, advanced undergraduate economics (for PhD). Additional exam requirements/recommendations for international students: Required—TOEFL. Electronic applications accepted. *Expenses:* Contact institution.

Vermont Law School, Graduate and Professional Programs, Professional Program, South Royalton, VT 05068-0096. Offers JD, JD/LL M, JD/MELP, JD/MERL, JD/MFALP. *Accreditation:* ABA. *Entrance requirements:* For doctorate, LSAT, LSDAS/registration, resume. Additional exam requirements/recommendations for international students: Required—TOEFL (minimum score 600 paper-based). Electronic applications accepted. *Expenses:* Contact institution. *Faculty research:* Environmental law, energy regulation and law, food and agriculture law, international law, water and justice.

Villanova University, Charles Widger School of Law, Program in Law, Villanova, PA 19085. Offers JD, JD/LL M, JD/MBA. *Accreditation:* ABA. *Entrance requirements:* For doctorate, LSAT. Electronic applications accepted. *Expenses:* Contact institution. *Faculty research:* Business law; international law (public and private); tax law; criminal law, procedure, and sentencing; law and religion.

Law

Wake Forest University, School of Law, Winston-Salem, NC 27109. Offers LL M, MSL, JD, SJD, JD/M Div, JD/MA, JD/MBA. LL M program is designed for foreign law graduates in American law. *Accreditation:* ABA. *Entrance requirements:* For doctorate, LSAT (for JD). Additional exam requirements/recommendations for international students: Required—TOEFL (minimum score 600 paper-based, 100 iBT) or IELTS (minimum score 7). Electronic applications accepted. *Expenses:* Contact institution. *Faculty research:* Constitutional law, family law, land use planning, torts, taxation.

Walden University, Graduate Programs, School of Public Policy and Administration, Minneapolis, MN 55401. Offers criminal justice (MPA, MPP, MS, Graduate Certificate), including emergency management (MS, PhD), general program (MS), global leadership (MS, PhD), homeland security and policy coordination (MS, PhD), law and public policy (MS, PhD), policy analysis (MS, PhD), public management and leadership (MS, PhD), self-designed (MS), terrorism, mediation, and peace (MS, PhD); criminal justice and executive management (MS), including global leadership (MS, PhD); criminal justice leadership and executive management (MS), including emergency management (MS, PhD), general program, homeland security and policy coordination (MS, PhD), law and public policy (MS, PhD), policy analysis (MS, PhD), public management and leadership (MS, PhD), self-designed, terrorism, mediation, and peace (MS, PhD); emergency management (MPA, MPP, MS), including criminal justice (MS, PhD), general program (MS), homeland security (MS), public management and leadership (MS, PhD), terrorism and emergency management (MS); general program (MPA, MPP); global leadership (MPA, MPP); government management (Graduate Certificate); health policy (MPA, MPP); homeland security (Graduate Certificate); homeland security and policy coordination (MPA, MPP); international nongovernmental organizations (MPA, MPP); law and public policy (MPA, MPP); local government management for sustainable communities (MPA, MPP); nonprofit management (Graduate Certificate); nonprofit management and leadership (MPA, MPP, MS), including global leadership (MS, PhD), international nongovernmental organization (MS), local government for sustainable communities (MS), self-designed (MS); online teaching in higher education (Post-Master's Certificate); policy analysis (MPA); public management and leadership (MPA, MPP, Graduate Certificate); public policy (Graduate Certificate); public policy and administration (PhD), including criminal justice (MS, PhD), emergency management (MS, PhD), global leadership (MS, PhD), health policy, homeland security and policy coordination (MS, PhD), international nongovernmental organizations, law and public policy (MS, PhD), local government management for sustainable communities, nonprofit management and leadership, policy analysis (MS, PhD), public management and leadership (MS, PhD), terrorism, mediation, and peace (MS, PhD); strategic planning and public policy (Graduate Certificate); terrorism, mediation, and peace (MPA, MPP). *Program availability:* Part-time, evening/weekend, online only, 100% online. *Degree requirements:* For doctorate, thesis/dissertation, residency. *Entrance requirements:* For master's, bachelor's degree or higher; minimum GPA of 2.5; official transcripts; goal statement (for some programs); access to computer and Internet; for doctorate, master's degree or higher; three years of related professional or academic experience (preferred); minimum GPA of 3.0; goal statement and current resume (for select programs); official transcripts; access to computer and Internet; for other advanced degree, relevant work experience; access to computer and Internet. Additional exam requirements/recommendations for international students: Required—TOEFL (minimum score 550 paper-based, 79 iBT), IELTS (minimum score 6.5), Michigan English Language Assessment Battery (minimum score 82), or PTE (minimum score 53). Electronic applications accepted.

Washburn University, School of Law, Topeka, KS 66621. Offers global legal studies (LL M); law (MSL, JD). *Accreditation:* ABA. *Entrance requirements:* For doctorate, LSAT. Additional exam requirements/recommendations for international students: Recommended—TOEFL (minimum score 550 paper-based). Electronic applications accepted. Application fee is waived when completed online. *Expenses:* Contact institution. *Faculty research:* Constitutional law, family law, energy law, banking and securities law, oil and gas.

Washington and Lee University, School of Law, Lexington, VA 24450. Offers law (JD). *Accreditation:* ABA. *Entrance requirements:* For doctorate, LSAT. Electronic applications accepted. *Expenses:* Contact institution. *Faculty research:* Criminal law, corporate law, experiential education, international and comparative law, public interest law.

Washington University in St. Louis, School of Law, St. Louis, MO 63130-4899. Offers LL M, MJS, JD, JSD, JD/MA, JD/MBA, JD/MHA, JD/MS, JD/MSW, JD/PhD. *Accreditation:* ABA. *Entrance requirements:* For doctorate, LSAT or GRE. Electronic applications accepted. *Expenses:* Contact institution. *Faculty research:* International law, environmental law, employment discrimination, reproductive rights, bankruptcy and white-collar crime.

Wayne State University, Law School, Detroit, MI 48202. Offers corporate and finance law (LL M); labor and employment law (LL M); law (JD); taxation (LL M); United States law (LL M); JD/MA; JD/MADR; JD/MBA; JD/MS. *Accreditation:* ABA. *Program availability:* Part-time, evening/weekend. *Faculty:* 43 full-time (18 women), 17 part-time/adjunct (9 women). *Students:* 406 full-time (198 women), 38 part-time (9 women); includes 51 minority (35 Black or African American, non-Hispanic/Latino; 3 American Indian or Alaska Native, non-Hispanic/Latino; 7 Asian, non-Hispanic/Latino; 1 Hispanic/Latino; 5 Two or more races, non-Hispanic/Latino), 15 international. Average age 26. 859 applicants, 49% accepted, 137 enrolled. In 2018, 6 master's awarded. *Degree requirements:* For master's, thesis (for some programs). *Entrance requirements:* For master's, JD or LL B from ABA-accredited institution and member institution of the AALS; for doctorate, LSAT, LDAS report, bachelor's degree from accredited institution, personal statement, transcripts from all U.S. undergraduate schools attended and an analysis and summary of the transcripts; letter of recommendation (up to two are accepted). Additional exam requirements/recommendations for international students: Required—TOEFL, Michigan English Language Assessment Battery (minimum score 85); Recommended—IELTS. *Application deadline:* For fall admission, 7/1 for domestic students. Applications are processed on a rolling basis. Application fee: $0. Electronic applications accepted. *Expenses:* Resident tuition: $1,055.56 per credit hour, $315.70 per semester registration fee, $54.56 per credit hour student service fee. Non-resident tuition: $1,158 per credit hour, $315.70 per semester registration fee, $54.56 per credit hour student service fee. *Financial support:* In 2018–19, 365 students received support. Fellowships, Federal Work-Study, and scholarships/grants available. Support available to part-time students. Financial award application deadline: 6/30; financial award applicants required to submit FAFSA. *Unit head:* Richard A. Bierschbach, Dean and Professor of Law, 313-577-3933, E-mail: rbierschbach@wayne.edu. *Application contact:* Kathy Fox, Assistant Dean of Admissions, 313-577-3937, Fax: 313-993-8129, E-mail: lawinquire@wayne.edu.
Website: http://law.wayne.edu/

Western Michigan University Thomas M. Cooley Law School, Graduate Programs, Lansing, MI 48901-3038. Offers administrative law (public law) (JD); business transactions (JD); Canadian law practice (JD); corporate law and finance (LL M); environmental law (public law) (JD); general practice (JD), including solo and small firm; general studies (LL M); homeland and national security law (LL M); insurance law (LL M); intellectual property (JD); intellectual property law (LL M); international law (JD); litigation (JD); taxation (LL M); U.S. legal studies for foreign attorneys (LL M); JD/LL M; JD/MBA; JD/MHA; JD/MPA; JD/MSW. *Accreditation:* ABA. *Program availability:* Part-time, evening/weekend, 100% online, blended/hybrid learning. *Degree requirements:* For master's, thesis (for some programs); for doctorate, minimum of 3 credits of clinical experience. *Entrance requirements:* For master's, JD or LL B; for doctorate, LSAT. Additional exam requirements/recommendations for international students: Required—TOEFL (for U.S. legal studies for foreign attorneys LL M program); Recommended—TOEFL. Electronic applications accepted. *Expenses:* Contact institution. *Faculty research:* Wrongful convictions, civil rights, environmental law, litigation techniques, data mining, intellectual property, practical and skills-based legal education.

Western New England University, School of Law, Springfield, MA 01119. Offers LL M, MS, JD, JD/MBA, JD/MRP, JD/MS, JD/MSW. *Accreditation:* ABA. *Program availability:* Part-time, evening/weekend. *Faculty:* 19 full-time (11 women), 18 part-time/adjunct (6 women). *Students:* 184 full-time (102 women), 100 part-time (57 women); includes 67 minority (28 Black or African American, non-Hispanic/Latino; 3 American Indian or Alaska Native, non-Hispanic/Latino; 9 Asian, non-Hispanic/Latino; 27 Hispanic/Latino), 2 international. Average age 30. 638 applicants, 59% accepted, 88 enrolled. In 2018, 2 master's, 79 doctorates awarded. *Entrance requirements:* For master's, MS students require official school transcript, resume; LLM students require official law school transcript, resume; for doctorate, LSAT, two letters of recommendation, personal statement. *Application deadline:* For fall admission, 3/15 priority date for domestic students. Applications are processed on a rolling basis. Application fee: $0. Electronic applications accepted. *Expenses:* Contact institution. *Financial support:* Career-related internships or fieldwork, Federal Work-Study, and scholarships/grants available. Support available to part-time students. Financial award application deadline: 4/15; financial award applicants required to submit FAFSA. *Unit head:* Sudha Setty, Dean and Professor of Law, 413-782-1431, E-mail: sudha.setty@law.wne.edu. *Application contact:* Anthony Orlando, Director of Law Admissions, 413-782-1281, Fax: 413-796-2067, E-mail: admissions@law.wne.edu.
Website: http://www.law.wne.edu/

Western State College of Law at Argosy University, Professional Program, Irvine, CA 92618-3601. Offers JD. *Accreditation:* ABA. *Program availability:* Part-time, evening/weekend. *Entrance requirements:* For doctorate, LSAT, 2 letters of recommendation. Additional exam requirements/recommendations for international students: Required—TOEFL (minimum score 550 paper-based; 80 iBT). Electronic applications accepted. *Faculty research:* Criminal law and practice, entrepreneurship, teaching effectiveness and student success, learning theory and legal education.

West Virginia University, College of Law, Morgantown, WV 26506-6130. Offers energy law and sustainable development (LL M); forensic justice (LL M); law (JD); white collar forensic justice (LL M). *Accreditation:* ABA. *Program availability:* Part-time. *Students:* 324 full-time (146 women), 5 part-time (2 women); includes 40 minority (12 Black or African American, non-Hispanic/Latino; 4 Asian, non-Hispanic/Latino; 10 Hispanic/Latino; 14 Two or more races, non-Hispanic/Latino). In 2018, 4 master's awarded. *Entrance requirements:* For doctorate, LSAT. Additional exam requirements/recommendations for international students: Required—TOEFL (minimum score 600 paper-based; 100 iBT). *Application deadline:* For fall admission, 2/1 for domestic and international students. Applications are processed on a rolling basis. Application fee: $60. Electronic applications accepted. *Expenses:* Contact institution. *Financial support:* Fellowships, research assistantships, teaching assistantships, career-related internships or fieldwork, Federal Work-Study, institutionally sponsored loans, scholarships/grants, health care benefits, tuition waivers (full), unspecified assistantships, and administrative assistantships, resident assistantships available. Support available to part-time students. Financial award application deadline: 3/1; financial award applicants required to submit FAFSA. *Faculty research:* Constitutional law, public interest law, corporate law, environment and natural resources innocence project, professional skills, leadership, intellectual property, entrepreneurship, labor, sustainable development, family law, IR human rights, immigration. *Unit head:* Gregory W. Bowman, Dean, College of Law, 304-293-3199, Fax: 304-293-8102, E-mail: gregory.bowman@mail.wvu.edu. *Application contact:* Gregory W. Bowman, Dean, College of Law, 304-293-3199, Fax: 304-293-8102, E-mail: gregory.bowman@mail.wvu.edu.
Website: https://law.wvu.edu

Widener University, Commonwealth Law School, Harrisburg, PA 17106-9381. Offers JD. *Accreditation:* ABA. *Program availability:* Part-time. *Entrance requirements:* For doctorate, LSAT. Electronic applications accepted. *Expenses:* Contact institution. *Faculty research:* Health law, toxic torts, Constitutional law, intellectual property, corporate law.

Widener University, Delaware Law School, Wilmington, DE 19803-0474. Offers corporate and business law (MJ); corporate law and finance (LL M); health law (LL M, MJ, D Law); higher education compliance (MJ); juridical science (SJD); law (JD). *Accreditation:* ABA. *Program availability:* Part-time, 100% online. *Degree requirements:* For doctorate, thesis/dissertation (for some programs). *Entrance requirements:* For master's, GMAT.

Widener University, School of Human Service Professions, Institute for Graduate Clinical Psychology, Law-Psychology Program, Chester, PA 19013-5792. Offers JD/Psy D. Electronic applications accepted.

Willamette University, College of Law, Salem, OR 97301-3922. Offers dispute resolution (LL M); law (MLS, JD); transnational law (LL M); JD/MBA. *Accreditation:* ABA. *Program availability:* Part-time. *Degree requirements:* For master's, thesis, 25 credit hours (for LL M); 26 credit hours (for MLS); for doctorate, thesis/dissertation, 90 credit hours. *Entrance requirements:* For master's, bachelor's degree (for MLS); domestic or foreign JD (for LL M); for doctorate, LSAT. Additional exam requirements/recommendations for international students: Required—TOEFL (minimum score 480 paper-based; 45 iBT); Recommended—IELTS (minimum score 5). Electronic applications accepted. Application fee is waived when completed online. *Expenses:* Contact institution. *Faculty research:* Dispute resolution, international law, business law, law and government, sustainability.

Yale University, Yale Law School, New Haven, CT 06520-8215. Offers LL M, MSL, JD, JSD, PhD, JD/MA, JD/MAR, JD/MBA, JD/MD, JD/MES, JD/PhD. *Accreditation:* ABA. *Faculty:* 93 full-time, 164 part-time/adjunct. *Students:* 620 full-time (309 women). Average age 25. 3,473 applicants, 7% accepted, 204 enrolled. *Entrance requirements:* For doctorate, LSAT or GRE (for JD). Additional exam requirements/recommendations for international students: Required—TOEFL (minimum score 600 paper-based). *Application deadline:* For fall admission, 2/28 for domestic students. Applications are processed on a rolling basis. Application fee: $85. Electronic applications accepted. *Expenses:* $66,128. *Financial support:* Application deadline: 3/15; applicants required to submit FAFSA. *Unit head:* Heather Gerken, Dean, 203-432-1660. *Application contact:* Craig Janecek, Assistant Dean of Admissions, 203-432-4995, E-mail: admissions.law@yale.edu.
Website: http://www.law.yale.edu/

Yeshiva University, Benjamin N. Cardozo School of Law, New York, NY 10003-4301. Offers comparative legal thought (LL M); dispute resolution and advocacy (LL M);

general studies (LL M); intellectual property law (LL M); law (JD). Joint JD/MSW (Masters in Social Work) with Benjamin N. Cardozo School of Law & the Wurzweiler School of Social Work; joint JD/MBE (Masters in Bioethics) with Benjamin N. Cardozo School of Law and the Albert Einstein College of Medicine. *Accreditation:* ABA. *Program availability:* 100% online. *Faculty:* 61 full-time (25 women), 111 part-time/adjunct (46 women). *Students:* 960 full-time (537 women), 85 part-time (46 women); includes 229 minority (38 Black or African American, non-Hispanic/Latino; 83 Asian, non-Hispanic/Latino; 83 Hispanic/Latino; 25 Two or more races, non-Hispanic/Latino), 86 international. 2,584 applicants, 49% accepted, 365 enrolled. In 2018, 75 master's, 282 doctorates awarded. *Entrance requirements:* For master's, LLM Program requirements: personal statement, one letter of recommendation, English language proficiency score, Curriculum Vitae (CV), and an evaluation of student's transcripts; for doctorate, LSAT, Two letters of recommendation. Additional exam requirements/recommendations for international students: Required—TOEFL (minimum score 100 iBT), Cardozo accepts either a TOEFL or an IELTS score as a part of the English language requirement. Recommended—IELTS (minimum score 7). *Application deadline:* For fall admission, 4/1 priority date for domestic students, 6/15 priority date for international students; for spring admission, 12/1 for domestic students, 12/1 priority date for international students. Applications are processed on a rolling basis. Application fee: $0 ($50 for international students). Electronic applications accepted. *Expenses:* $29,970 per semester full-time; $19,398 per semester part-time; $2,671 per credit (for less than 7 credits per semester).

Financial support: In 2018–19, 831 students received support, including 114 research assistantships (averaging $1,512 per year); career-related internships or fieldwork, Federal Work-Study, institutionally sponsored loans, scholarships/grants, health care benefits, and tuition waivers (full and partial) also available. Support available to part-time students. Financial award application deadline: 3/1; financial award applicants required to submit FAFSA. *Faculty research:* Corporate and commercial law, intellectual property law, criminal law and litigation, constitutional law, legal theory and jurisprudence. *Unit head:* Dean Melanie Leslie, Dean and Samuel Belkin Professor of Law, 212-790-0310, Fax: 212-790-0203, E-mail: DeansOfficeCardozo@yu.edu. *Application contact:* David G. Martinidez, Dean of Admissions, 212-790-0274, Fax: 212-790-0482, E-mail: lawinfo@yu.edu.
Website: http://www.cardozo.yu.edu/

York University, Faculty of Graduate Studies, Faculty of Liberal Arts and Professional Studies, Program in Public Policy, Administration and Law, Toronto, ON M3J 1P3, Canada. Offers MPPAL.

York University, Faculty of Graduate Studies, Osgoode Hall Law School, Toronto, ON M3J 1P3, Canada. Offers LL M, JD, PhD. *Program availability:* Part-time, evening/weekend. *Degree requirements:* For master's, thesis; for doctorate, comprehensive exam, thesis/dissertation. *Entrance requirements:* For doctorate, LSAT. Electronic applications accepted.

Legal and Justice Studies

Arizona State University at the Tempe campus, College of Liberal Arts and Sciences, School of Social Transformation, Tempe, AZ 85287-4902. Offers African studies (Graduate Certificate); gender studies (PhD, Graduate Certificate); justice studies (MS, PhD); social and cultural pedagogy (MA); socio-economic justice (Graduate Certificate); PhD/JD. *Program availability:* Part-time. Terminal master's awarded for partial completion of doctoral program. *Degree requirements:* For master's, thesis or alternative, interactive Program of Study (iPOS) submitted before completing 50 percent of required credit hours; for doctorate, comprehensive exam, thesis/dissertation, interactive Program of Study (iPOS) submitted before completing 50 percent of required credit hours. *Entrance requirements:* For master's, GRE or LSAT, minimum GPA of 3.0 or equivalent in last 2 years of work leading to bachelor's degree; for doctorate, GRE or LSAT (for justice studies program), minimum GPA of 3.0 or equivalent in last 2 years of work leading to bachelor's degree. Additional exam requirements/recommendations for international students: Required—TOEFL, IELTS, or PTE. Electronic applications accepted.

Arizona State University at the Tempe campus, New College of Interdisciplinary Arts and Sciences, Program in Social Justice and Human Rights, Phoenix, AZ 85069-7100. Offers MA. Fall admission only. *Program availability:* Part-time, evening/weekend. *Degree requirements:* For master's, thesis or applied project, interactive Program of Study (iPOS) submitted before completing 50 percent of required credit hours. *Entrance requirements:* For master's, GRE, minimum GPA of 3.0 or equivalent in last 2 years of work leading to bachelor's degree, 2 letters of recommendation, official transcripts, writing sample, personal statement, resume. Additional exam requirements/recommendations for international students: Required—TOEFL, IELTS, or PTE. Electronic applications accepted. *Faculty research:* Social movements, violence against women, globalization, innovative uses of human rights law, environmental ethics, social justice and art, women and international development, slavery, genocide, metropolitan studies, urban culture and social space, fair trade, citizenship; immigration.

Arizona State University at the Tempe campus, Sandra Day O'Connor College of Law, Phoenix, AZ 85287-7906. Offers biotechnology and genomics (LL M); law (JD); legal studies (MLS); patent practice (MLS); sports law and business (MSLB); tribal policy, law and government (LL M); JD/MBA; JD/MD; JD/MSW; JD/PhD. JD/MD offered jointly with Mayo Medical School. *Accreditation:* ABA. *Program availability:* 100% online. *Faculty:* 62 full-time (26 women), 146 part-time/adjunct (40 women). *Students:* 812 full-time (372 women); includes 201 minority (16 Black or African American, non-Hispanic/Latino; 15 American Indian or Alaska Native, non-Hispanic/Latino; 37 Asian, non-Hispanic/Latino; 97 Hispanic/Latino; 3 Native Hawaiian or other Pacific Islander, non-Hispanic/Latino; 33 Two or more races, non-Hispanic/Latino), 16 international. Average age 28. 3,363 applicants, 34% accepted, 271 enrolled. In 2018, 131 master's, 276 doctorates awarded. *Entrance requirements:* For master's, bachelor's degree and JD (for LL M); for doctorate, LSAT, bachelor's degree. Additional exam requirements/recommendations for international students: Required—TOEFL (minimum score 550 paper-based; 80 iBT). *Application deadline:* For fall admission, 3/1 priority date for domestic and international students. Applications are processed on a rolling basis. Application fee: $0. Electronic applications accepted. *Expenses:* $27,584 resident tuition and fees (for JD), $45,940 non-resident tuition and fees (for JD). *Financial support:* In 2018–19, 579 students received support. Institutionally sponsored loans and scholarships/grants available. Financial award application deadline: 3/15; financial award applicants required to submit FAFSA. *Faculty research:* Emerging technologies and the law, Indian law, international law, intellectual property, health law, sports law and business. Total annual research expenditures: $2.8 million. *Unit head:* Douglas Sylvester, Dean/Professor, 480-965-6188, Fax: 480-965-6521, E-mail: douglas.sylvester@asu.edu. *Application contact:* Chitra Damania, Director, 480-965-1474, Fax: 480-727-7930, E-mail: law.admissions@asu.edu.
Website: http://www.law.asu.edu/

Auburn University at Montgomery, College of Public Policy and Justice, Department of Justice and Public Safety, Montgomery, AL 36124-4023. Offers criminal studies (MSJPS). *Program availability:* Part-time, evening/weekend. *Students:* Average age 30. 24 applicants, 75% accepted, 9 enrolled. In 2018, 23 master's awarded. *Degree requirements:* For master's, comprehensive exam, thesis optional. *Entrance requirements:* For master's, GRE General Test or MAT. Additional exam requirements/recommendations for international students: Recommended—TOEFL (minimum score 500 paper-based; 61 iBT), IELTS (minimum score 5.5), TSE (minimum score 44). *Application deadline:* For fall admission, 7/15 for international students; for spring admission, 11/15 for international students; for summer admission, 4/15 for international students. Applications are processed on a rolling basis. Application fee: $25. Electronic applications accepted. *Expenses:* Tuition, area resident: Full-time $7146; part-time $4764 per credit hour. Tuition, state resident: full-time $7146; part-time $4764 per credit hour. Tuition, nonresident: full-time $16,056; part-time $10,704 per credit hour. International tuition: $16,056 full-time. *Required fees:* $766. One-time fee: $25 full-time. *Financial support:* Career-related internships or fieldwork and scholarships/grants available. Support available to part-time students. Financial award application deadline: 3/1; financial award applicants required to submit FAFSA. *Faculty research:* Law

enforcement, corrections, juvenile justice. *Unit head:* Dr. Ralph Ioimo, Head, 334-244-3691, Fax: 334-244-3244, E-mail: rioimo@aum.edu. *Application contact:* Dr. Ralph Ioimo, Head, 334-244-3691, Fax: 334-244-3244, E-mail: rioimo@aum.edu.
Website: http://cppj.aum.edu/departments/justice-and-public-safety

Binghamton University, State University of New York, Graduate School, Harpur College of Arts and Sciences, Program in Social, Political, Ethical and Legal Philosophy, Binghamton, NY 13902-6000. Offers MA, PhD. *Program availability:* Part-time. Terminal master's awarded for partial completion of doctoral program. *Degree requirements:* For master's, comprehensive exam, thesis or alternative; for doctorate, one foreign language, thesis/dissertation. *Entrance requirements:* For master's and doctorate, GRE General Test, writing sample. Additional exam requirements/recommendations for international students: Required—TOEFL (minimum score 550 paper-based; 80 iBT). Electronic applications accepted.

Brock University, Faculty of Graduate Studies, Faculty of Social Sciences, Program in Social Justice and Equity Studies, St. Catharines, ON L2S 3A1, Canada. Offers MA. *Program availability:* Part-time. *Degree requirements:* For master's, thesis optional. *Entrance requirements:* For master's, honors degree. Additional exam requirements/recommendations for international students: Required—TOEFL (minimum score 550 paper-based; 80 iBT), IELTS (minimum score 6.5), TWE (minimum score 4). Electronic applications accepted. *Faculty research:* Social inequality, social movements, gender, racism, environmental justice.

California University of Pennsylvania, School of Graduate Studies and Research, College of Liberal Arts, Department of History, Politics, Society and Law, California, PA 15419-1394. Offers legal studies (MS), including criminal justice, homeland security, law and public policy. *Program availability:* Part-time, evening/weekend, online learning. *Degree requirements:* For master's, thesis optional. *Entrance requirements:* For master's, interview, minimum GPA of 3.0. Additional exam requirements/recommendations for international students: Required—TOEFL (minimum score 550 paper-based; 80 iBT). Electronic applications accepted. *Faculty research:* Ethics in political practice, ethics and law, law and morality, St. Thomas Aquinas and crime, police policy.

Campbellsville University, College of Arts and Sciences, Campbellsville, KY 42718-2799. Offers justice studies (MS); sport management (MA). *Program availability:* Part-time, evening/weekend, 100% online, blended/hybrid learning. *Faculty:* 16 full-time (7 women), 4 part-time/adjunct (2 women). *Students:* 51 full-time (28 women), 10 part-time (6 women); includes 12 minority (11 Black or African American, non-Hispanic/Latino; 1 Asian, non-Hispanic/Latino), 6 international. Average age 30. 65 applicants, 37% accepted, 21 enrolled. In 2018, 26 master's awarded. *Degree requirements:* For master's, comprehensive exam, thesis optional. *Entrance requirements:* For master's, GRE General Test, minimum GPA of 2.9, letters of recommendation, college transcripts. Additional exam requirements/recommendations for international students: Recommended—TOEFL, IELTS. *Application deadline:* Applications are processed on a rolling basis. Application fee: $25. Electronic applications accepted. Application fee is waived when completed online. *Expenses:* MASM = $399/credit hour, MTESL = $399/credit hour; MSJS = $399/credit hour. *Financial support:* Unspecified assistantships available. Financial award application deadline: 6/1; financial award applicants required to submit FAFSA. *Unit head:* Dr. Mike Page, Dean of the College of Arts and Sciences, 270-789-5394. *Application contact:* Monica Bamwine, Director of Graduate Admissions, 270-789-5221, Fax: 270-789-5071, E-mail: mkbamwine@campbellsville.edu.
Website: http://www.campbellsville.edu/

Capital University, School of Nursing, Columbus, OH 43209-2394. Offers administration (MSN); legal studies (MSN); theological studies (MSN); JD/MSN; MBA/MSN; MSN/MTS. *Accreditation:* AACN. *Program availability:* Part-time, evening/weekend. *Degree requirements:* For master's, thesis or alternative. *Entrance requirements:* For master's, BSN, current RN license, minimum GPA of 3.0, undergraduate courses in statistics and research. Additional exam requirements/recommendations for international students: Required—TOEFL (minimum score 550 paper-based). *Expenses:* Contact institution. *Faculty research:* Bereavement, wellness/health promotion, emergency cardiac care, critical thinking, complementary and alternative healthcare.

Carleton University, Faculty of Graduate Studies, Faculty of Public Affairs and Management, Department of Law, Ottawa, ON K1S 5B6, Canada. Offers conflict resolution (Certificate); legal studies (MA). *Degree requirements:* For master's, thesis. *Entrance requirements:* For master's, honors degree. Additional exam requirements/recommendations for international students: Required—TOEFL. *Faculty research:* Legal and social theory; women, law, and gender relations; law, crime, and social order; political economy of law; international law.

Case Western Reserve University, School of Law, Cleveland, OH 44106. Offers financial integrity (MA); health law (SJD); intellectual property law (LL M, ML); international business law (LL M, ML); international criminal law (LL M); law (JD, SJD); patent practice (MA); U.S. and global legal studies (LL M, ML); JD/MA; JD/MBA; JD/MD;

JD/MNM; JD/MPH; JD/MS; JD/MSSA. *Accreditation:* ABA. *Faculty:* 47 full-time (16 women), 63 part-time/adjunct (16 women). *Students:* 433 full-time (238 women); includes 91 minority (37 Black or African American, non-Hispanic/Latino; 1 American Indian or Alaska Native, non-Hispanic/Latino; 19 Asian, non-Hispanic/Latino; 26 Hispanic/Latino; 8 Two or more races, non-Hispanic/Latino), 30 international. Average age 24. 1,415 applicants, 50% accepted, 157 enrolled. In 2018, 126 master's awarded. *Entrance requirements:* For doctorate, LSAT, LSDAS. Additional exam requirements/recommendations for international students: Required—TOEFL. *Application deadline:* For fall admission, 4/1 priority date for domestic and international students. Applications are processed on a rolling basis. Application fee: $40. Electronic applications accepted. Application fee is waived when completed online. *Expenses:* Contact institution. *Financial support:* In 2018–19, 394 students received support. Career-related internships or fieldwork, Federal Work-Study, institutionally sponsored loans, and scholarships/grants available. Financial award application deadline: 5/1; financial award applicants required to submit FAFSA. *Unit head:* Jessica Berg, Co-Dean, 216-368-3283. *Application contact:* Kelli Curtis, Associate Dean for Admissions, 216-368-3600, Fax: 216-368-0185, E-mail: lawadmissions@case.edu.
Website: http://law.case.edu/

The Catholic University of America, School of Canon Law, Washington, DC 20064. Offers Canon law (JCD, JCL); church administration (MCA); JD/JCL. JD/JCL offered jointly with Columbus School of Law. *Program availability:* Part-time. *Faculty:* 6 full-time (1 woman), 1 part-time/adjunct (0 women). *Students:* 30 full-time (6 women), 48 part-time (8 women); includes 12 minority (4 Black or African American, non-Hispanic/Latino; 4 Asian, non-Hispanic/Latino; 2 Hispanic/Latino; 2 Two or more races, non-Hispanic/Latino), 9 international. Average age 38. 46 applicants, 80% accepted, 23 enrolled. In 2018, 13 master's, 2 doctorates awarded. *Degree requirements:* For master's, one foreign language, comprehensive exam, thesis, fluency in canonical Latin; for doctorate, 2 foreign languages, thesis/dissertation, fluency in canonical Latin. *Entrance requirements:* For master's, GRE General Test, statement of purpose, official copies of academic transcripts, two letters of recommendation; for doctorate, GRE General Test, minimum A- average, JCL. Additional exam requirements/recommendations for international students: Required—TOEFL (minimum score 550 paper-based; 80 iBT). *Application deadline:* For fall admission, 7/15 priority date for domestic students, 7/1 for international students; for spring admission, 11/15 priority date for domestic students, 11/1 for international students. Applications are processed on a rolling basis. Application fee: $55. Electronic applications accepted. *Expenses:* Contact institution. *Financial support:* Fellowships, research assistantships, teaching assistantships, Federal Work-Study, scholarships/grants, tuition waivers (full and partial), and unspecified assistantships available. Financial award application deadline: 2/1; financial award applicants required to submit FAFSA. *Faculty research:* Ecclesiology and the Sacrament of Orders, procedural law, temporal goods, matrimonial jurisprudence, sacramental and liturgical law. *Unit head:* Msgr. Ronny Jenkins, Dean, 202-319-5492, Fax: 202-319-4187, E-mail: cua-canonlaw@cua.edu. *Application contact:* Dr. Steven Brown, Director of Graduate Admissions, 202-319-5057, Fax: 202-319-6533, E-mail: cua-admissions@cua.edu.
Website: https://canonlaw.catholic.edu/

Central European University, Department of Legal Studies, Budapest, Hungary. Offers comparative Constitutional law (LL M); human rights (LL M, MA); international business law (LL M); juridical sciences (SJD). Terminal master's awarded for partial completion of doctoral program. *Degree requirements:* For master's, one foreign language, thesis; for doctorate, one foreign language, comprehensive exam, thesis/dissertation. *Entrance requirements:* For master's and doctorate, LSAT. Additional exam requirements/recommendations for international students: Required—TOEFL (minimum score 570 paper-based); Recommended—IELTS (minimum score 6.5). Electronic applications accepted. *Expenses:* Contact institution. *Faculty research:* Institutional, Constitutional and human rights in European Union law; biomedical law and reproductive rights; data protection law; comparative and international business law and the regulation of business environments;.

Columbia University, Graduate School of Arts and Sciences, New York, NY 10027. Offers African-American studies (MA); American studies (MA); anthropology (MA, PhD); art history and archaeology (MA, PhD); astronomy (PhD); biological sciences (PhD); biotechnology (MA); chemical physics (PhD); chemistry (PhD); classical studies (MA, PhD); classics (MA, PhD); climate and society (MA); conservation biology (MA); earth and environmental sciences (PhD); East Asia: regional studies (MA); East Asian languages and cultures (MA, PhD); ecology, evolution and environmental biology (MA), including conservation biology; ecology, evolution, and environmental biology (PhD), including ecology and evolutionary biology, evolutionary primatology; economics (MA, PhD); English and comparative literature (MA, PhD); French and Romance philology (MA, PhD); Germanic languages (MA, PhD); global French studies (MA); global thought (MA); Hispanic cultural studies (MA); history (PhD); history and literature (MA); human rights studies (MA); Islamic studies (MA); Italian (MA, PhD); Japanese pedagogy (MA); Jewish studies (MA); Latin America and the Caribbean: regional studies (MA); Latin American and Iberian cultures (PhD); mathematics (MA, PhD), including finance (MA); medieval and Renaissance studies (MA); Middle Eastern, South Asian, and African studies (MA, PhD); modern art: critical and curatorial studies (MA); modern European studies (MA); museum anthropology (MA); music (DMA, PhD); oral history (MA); philosophical foundations of physics (MA); philosophy (MA, PhD); physics (PhD); political science (MA, PhD); psychology (PhD); quantitative methods in the social sciences (MA); religion (MA, PhD); Russia, Eurasia and East Europe: regional studies (MA); Russian translation (MA); Slavic cultures (MA); Slavic languages (MA, PhD); sociology (MA, PhD); South Asian studies (MA); statistics (MA, PhD); theatre (PhD). Dual-degree programs require admission to both Graduate School of Arts and Sciences and another Columbia school. *Program availability:* Part-time. Terminal master's awarded for partial completion of doctoral program. *Degree requirements:* For master's, variable foreign language requirement, comprehensive exam (for some programs), thesis (for some programs); for doctorate, variable foreign language requirement, comprehensive exam (for some programs), thesis/dissertation. *Entrance requirements:* For master's and doctorate, GRE General Test, GRE Subject Test (for some programs). Additional exam requirements/recommendations for international students: Required—TOEFL, IELTS. Electronic applications accepted.

The George Washington University, College of Professional Studies, Paralegal Studies Programs, Washington, DC 20052. Offers MPS, Graduate Certificate. *Students:* 27 full-time (20 women), 83 part-time (68 women); includes 45 minority (27 Black or African American, non-Hispanic/Latino; 1 American Indian or Alaska Native, non-Hispanic/Latino; 3 Asian, non-Hispanic/Latino; 12 Hispanic/Latino; 2 Two or more races, non-Hispanic/Latino), 1 international. Average age 38. 103 applicants, 81% accepted, 60 enrolled. In 2018, 32 master's, 21 other advanced degrees awarded. *Application deadline:* For fall admission, 7/15 for domestic and international students; for spring admission, 10/1 for domestic and international students. Electronic applications accepted. *Unit head:* Toni Marsh, Director, 202-994-2844, E-mail: marsht01@gwu.edu. *Application contact:* Analisa Encinas, Paralegal Studies Program Representative, 703-248-6011, E-mail: aencinas@gwu.edu.
Website: http://nearyou.gwu.edu/plx/

The George Washington University, College of Professional Studies, Program in Law Firm Management, Washington, DC 20052. Offers MPS, Graduate Certificate. Program offered in partnership with The Hildebrandt Institute and held in Alexandria, VA. *Program availability:* Online learning. *Students:* 23 part-time (16 women); includes 4 minority (1 Black or African American, non-Hispanic/Latino; 2 Hispanic/Latino; 1 Two or more races, non-Hispanic/Latino), 2 international. Average age 42. 14 applicants, 100% accepted, 10 enrolled. In 2018, 13 master's awarded. *Entrance requirements:* For master's, resume, 2 references. Additional exam requirements/recommendations for international students: Required—TOEFL. *Application deadline:* For fall admission, 4/1 for domestic and international students. Electronic applications accepted. *Unit head:* Kathleen M. Burke, Dean, 202-994-9711. *Application contact:* Kristin Williams, Assistant Vice President for Graduate and Special Enrollment Management, 202-994-0467, Fax: 202-994-0371, E-mail: ksw@gwu.edu.
Website: http://nearyou.gwu.edu/lawfirm/

The George Washington University, Columbian College of Arts and Sciences, Department of Political Science, Washington, DC 20052. Offers legal institutions and theory (MA); political science (MA). *Program availability:* Part-time, evening/weekend. *Students:* 46 full-time (20 women), 32 part-time (12 women); includes 8 minority (1 Black or African American, non-Hispanic/Latino; 4 Asian, non-Hispanic/Latino; 3 Hispanic/Latino), 21 international. Average age 29. 320 applicants, 21% accepted, 19 enrolled. In 2018, 9 master's, 11 doctorates awarded. Terminal master's awarded for partial completion of doctoral program. *Degree requirements:* For master's, one foreign language, comprehensive exam, thesis or alternative; for doctorate, 2 foreign languages, thesis/dissertation, general exam. *Entrance requirements:* For master's and doctorate, GRE General Test, minimum GPA of 3.0. Additional exam requirements/recommendations for international students: Required—TOEFL (minimum score 550 paper-based; 80 iBT). *Application deadline:* For fall admission, 1/15 priority date for domestic students; for spring admission, 10/1 priority date for domestic students. Applications are processed on a rolling basis. Application fee: $75. Electronic applications accepted. *Financial support:* In 2018–19, 43 students received support. Fellowships, teaching assistantships, Federal Work-Study, and tuition waivers available. *Unit head:* Christopher J. Deering, Chair, 202-994-6564, E-mail: rocket@gwu.edu. *Application contact:* Christopher J. Deering, Chair, 202-994-6564, E-mail: rocket@gwu.edu.
Website: http://politicalscience.columbian.gwu.edu/

Georgian Court University, School of Arts and Sciences, Lakewood, NJ 08701-2697. Offers applied behavior analysis (MA); autism spectrum disorders (Certificate); clinical mental health counseling (MA); criminal justice and human rights (MS); holistic health studies (MA, Certificate); homeland security (Certificate); instructional technology (CPC); mercy spirituality (Certificate); parish business management (Certificate); professional counselor (Certificate); school psychology (MA, Certificate); theology (MA, Certificate). *Program availability:* Part-time, evening/weekend. *Faculty:* 15 full-time (9 women), 11 part-time/adjunct (9 women). *Students:* 90 full-time (84 women), 99 part-time (67 women); includes 28 minority (9 Black or African American, non-Hispanic/Latino; 1 Asian, non-Hispanic/Latino; 14 Hispanic/Latino; 4 Two or more races, non-Hispanic/Latino), 2 international. Average age 34. 138 applicants, 59% accepted, 60 enrolled. In 2018, 68 master's, 19 other advanced degrees awarded. *Degree requirements:* For master's, comprehensive exam (for some programs), thesis (for some programs). *Entrance requirements:* For master's, GRE, GMAT, or NTE/PRAXIS, 3 letters of recommendation. Additional exam requirements/recommendations for international students: Required—TOEFL (minimum score 550 paper-based; 79 iBT). *Application deadline:* For fall admission, 8/15 for domestic students, 5/1 for international students; for spring admission, 1/15 for domestic students, 10/1 for international students. Applications are processed on a rolling basis. Application fee: $40. Electronic applications accepted. *Expenses: Tuition:* Full-time $856; part-time $856 per credit hour. *Required fees:* $968; $496 per unit. $248 per semester. Tuition and fees vary according to campus/location and program. *Financial support:* Scholarships/grants, health care benefits, and unspecified assistantships available. Financial award application deadline: 4/15; financial award applicants required to submit FAFSA. *Unit head:* Dr. Mary Chinery, Dean, 732-987-2493, Fax: 732-987-2007, E-mail: mchinery@georgian.edu. *Application contact:* Patrick Givens, Director of Graduate and Professional Studies Admissions, 732-987-2736, Fax: 732-987-2000, E-mail: gps@georgian.edu.
Website: https://georgian.edu/academics/school-of-arts-sciences/

Golden Gate University, School of Law, San Francisco, CA 94105-2968. Offers environmental law (LL M); estate planning (LL M); intellectual property law (LL M); international legal studies (LL M, SJD); law (JD); taxation law (LL M); U.S. legal studies (LL M); JD/MBA. *Accreditation:* ABA. *Program availability:* Part-time, evening/weekend. *Degree requirements:* For doctorate, thesis/dissertation (for some programs). *Entrance requirements:* For doctorate, LSAT (for JD). Additional exam requirements/recommendations for international students: Required—TOEFL (minimum score 600 paper-based). Electronic applications accepted. *Expenses:* Contact institution. *Faculty research:* International law, intellectual property law, environmental law, real estate, civil rights.

Governors State University, College of Arts and Sciences, Program in Political and Justice Studies, University Park, IL 60484. Offers MA. *Program availability:* Part-time. *Faculty:* 58 full-time (34 women), 89 part-time/adjunct (43 women). *Students:* 4 full-time (2 women), 21 part-time (12 women); includes 16 minority (14 Black or African American, non-Hispanic/Latino; 2 Hispanic/Latino). Average age 39. In 2018, 4 master's awarded. *Application deadline:* For fall admission, 4/1 for domestic students. Applications are processed on a rolling basis. Application fee: $50. Electronic applications accepted. *Financial support:* Application deadline: 5/1; applicants required to submit FAFSA. *Unit head:* Jason Zingsheim, Chair, Division of Arts and Letters, 708-534-5000 Ext. 7493, E-mail: jzingsheim@govst.edu. *Application contact:* Jason Zingsheim, Chair, Division of Arts and Letters, 708-534-5000 Ext. 7493, E-mail: jzingsheim@govst.edu.

Harrison Middleton University, Graduate Program, Tempe, AZ 85282. Offers education (MA, Ed D); humanities (MA); imaginative literature (MA); interdisciplinary studies (DA); jurisprudence (MA); natural science (MA); philosophy and religion (MA); social science (MA). *Program availability:* Part-time, evening/weekend, online learning. *Degree requirements:* For master's and doctorate, capstone project. *Entrance requirements:* For master's, interview; for doctorate, 2 academic letters of reference, interview, essay. Additional exam requirements/recommendations for international students: Required—TOEFL (minimum score 550 paper-based; 80 iBT). Electronic applications accepted. *Faculty research:* Japanese animation, educational leadership, war art, John Muir's wilderness.

Harvard University, Law School, Professional Programs in Law, Cambridge, MA 02138. Offers international and comparative law (JD); law and business (JD); law and government (JD); law and social change (JD); law, science and technology (JD); JD/MALD; JD/MBA; JD/MPH; JD/MPP; JD/PhD. *Accreditation:* ABA. *Degree requirements:* For doctorate, 3rd-year paper. *Entrance requirements:* For doctorate, LSAT. *Faculty research:* Constitutional law, voting rights law, cyber law.

Hodges University, Graduate Programs, Naples, FL 34119. Offers accounting (M Acc); business administration (MBA); clinical mental health counseling (MS); health services

administration (MS); information systems management (MIS); legal studies (MS); management (MSM). *Program availability:* Part-time, evening/weekend, 100% online, blended/hybrid learning. *Degree requirements:* For master's, comprehensive exam (for some programs), thesis (for some programs). *Entrance requirements:* For master's, essay. Additional exam requirements/recommendations for international students: Recommended—TOEFL. Electronic applications accepted.

Hofstra University, Maurice A. Deane School of Law, Hempstead, NY 11549. Offers alternative dispute resolution (JD); American legal studies (LL M); business law honors (JD); clinical bioethics (Certificate); corporate compliance (JD); criminal law and procedure (JD); family law (LL M, JD); health law (JD); health law and policy (LL M, MA); intellectual property law honors (JD); international law honors (JD); JD/MBA; JD/MPH. *Accreditation:* ABA. *Program availability:* Part-time, 100% online. *Faculty:* 41 full-time (21 women), 78 part-time/adjunct (24 women). *Students:* 712 full-time (374 women), 137 part-time (88 women); includes 181 minority (53 Black or African American, non-Hispanic/Latino; 2 American Indian or Alaska Native, non-Hispanic/Latino; 34 Asian, non-Hispanic/Latino; 82 Hispanic/Latino; 7 Native Hawaiian or other Pacific Islander, non-Hispanic/Latino; 3 Two or more races, non-Hispanic/Latino), 13 international. Average age 27. 3,104 applicants, 50% accepted, 301 enrolled. In 2018, 37 master's, 234 doctorates awarded. *Entrance requirements:* For doctorate, LSAT, letter of recommendation, personal statement, undergraduate transcripts; for Certificate, 2 letters of recommendation, JD or LLB, personal statement, law school transcripts. Additional exam requirements/recommendations for international students: Recommended—TOEFL (minimum score 600 paper-based; 100 iBT). *Application deadline:* For fall admission, 4/15 priority date for domestic and international students. Applications are processed on a rolling basis. Application fee: $0. Electronic applications accepted. *Expenses:* $29,607 per term for Full-time (tuition and fees). *Financial support:* In 2018–19, 578 students received support, including 565 fellowships with full and partial tuition reimbursements available (averaging $32,425 per year); research assistantships with full and partial tuition reimbursements available, career-related internships or fieldwork, Federal Work-Study, institutionally sponsored loans, scholarships/grants, tuition waivers (full and partial), unspecified assistantships, and scholarships and endowed scholarships also available. Support available to part-time students. Financial award applicants required to submit FAFSA. *Faculty research:* Family law; international law; constitutional law; legal ethics; health law. *Unit head:* Gail Prudenti, Dean, 516-463-4068, E-mail: gail.prudenti@hofstra.edu. *Application contact:* Sunil Samuel, Assistant Vice President of Admissions, 516-463-4723, Fax: 516-463-4664.
Website: http://law.hofstra.edu/

Illinois Institute of Technology, Chicago-Kent College of Law, Chicago, IL 60661-3691. Offers family law (LL M); financial services law (LL M); international intellectual property law (LL M); law (JD); legal studies (JSD); taxation (LL M); U.S., international, and transnational law (LL M); JD/LL M; JD/MBA; JD/MPA; JD/MPH; JD/MS. *Accreditation:* ABA. *Program availability:* Part-time, evening/weekend. Terminal master's awarded for partial completion of doctoral program. *Entrance requirements:* For master's, 1st degree in law or certified license to practice law; for doctorate, LSAT. Additional exam requirements/recommendations for international students: Required—TOEFL (minimum score 600 paper-based; 100 iBT); Recommended—IELTS (minimum score 7). Electronic applications accepted. *Expenses:* Contact institution. *Faculty research:* Constitutional law, bioethics, environmental law, intellectual property.

Indiana University South Bend, College of Liberal Arts and Sciences, South Bend, IN 46615. Offers advanced computer programming (Graduate Certificate); applied informatics (Graduate Certificate); applied mathematics and computer science (MS); behavior modification (Graduate Certificate); computer applications (Graduate Certificate); computer programming (Graduate Certificate); correctional management and supervision (Graduate Certificate); English (MA); health systems management (Graduate Certificate); international studies (Graduate Certificate); liberal studies (MLS); nonprofit management (Graduate Certificate); paralegal studies (Graduate Certificate); professional writing (Graduate Certificate); public affairs (MPA); public management (Graduate Certificate); social and cultural diversity (Graduate Certificate); strategic sustainability leadership (Graduate Certificate); technology for administration (Graduate Certificate). *Program availability:* Part-time, evening/weekend. *Degree requirements:* For master's, variable foreign language requirement, thesis (for some programs). *Entrance requirements:* For master's, minimum GPA of 3.0. Additional exam requirements/recommendations for international students: Required—TOEFL (minimum score 550 paper-based; 80 iBT). *Expenses:* Contact institution. *Faculty research:* Artificial intelligence, bioinformatics, English language and literature, creative writing, computer networks.

John Jay College of Criminal Justice of the City University of New York, Graduate Studies, Programs in Criminal Justice, New York, NY 10019. Offers criminal justice (MA, PhD); criminology and deviance (PhD); forensic psychology (PhD); forensic science (PhD); international crime and justice (MA); law and philosophy (PhD); organizational behavior (PhD); public policy (PhD). *Program availability:* Part-time, evening/weekend. Terminal master's awarded for partial completion of doctoral program. *Degree requirements:* For master's, thesis or alternative; for doctorate, one foreign language, thesis/dissertation. *Entrance requirements:* For master's, GRE General Test, minimum B average; for doctorate, GRE General Test. Additional exam requirements/recommendations for international students: Required—TOEFL (minimum score 500 paper-based).

Liberty University, School of Law, Lynchburg, VA 24515. Offers American legal studies (JM); international legal studies (JM, LL M). *Accreditation:* ABA. *Program availability:* Online learning. *Students:* 258 full-time (131 women), 138 part-time (63 women); includes 97 minority (45 Black or African American, non-Hispanic/Latino; 2 American Indian or Alaska Native, non-Hispanic/Latino; 10 Asian, non-Hispanic/Latino; 20 Hispanic/Latino; 1 Native Hawaiian or other Pacific Islander, non-Hispanic/Latino; 19 Two or more races, non-Hispanic/Latino), 7 international. Average age 33. 387 applicants, 50% accepted, 142 enrolled. *Entrance requirements:* Additional exam requirements/recommendations for international students: Required—TOEFL (minimum score 600 paper-based; 100 iBT). *Application deadline:* For fall admission, 6/1 for domestic students. *Expenses:* Contact institution. *Financial support:* In 2018–19, 208 students received support. Federal Work-Study available. Financial award applicants required to submit FAFSA. *Unit head:* B. Keith Faulkner, Dean, 434-592-5300, Fax: 434-592-5400, E-mail: law@liberty.edu. *Application contact:* Joleen Thaxton, Assistant Director of Admissions, 434-592-5300, Fax: 434-592-5400, E-mail: lawadmissions@liberty.edu.
Website: https://www.liberty.edu/law/

Loyola University Chicago, Institute of Pastoral Studies, Chicago, IL 60611. Offers Christian spirituality (MA), including spiritual direction; church management (Certificate); counseling for ministry (MA); divinity (M Div); health care ministry leadership (Certificate); health care mission leadership (MA); pastoral counseling (MA, Certificate); pastoral studies (MA); religious education (Certificate); social justice (MA, Certificate); spiritual direction (Certificate); M Div/MA; M Div/MSW; MSW/MA. MSW/MA offered with School of Social Work. *Accreditation:* ACIPE. *Program availability:* Part-time, evening/weekend, 100% online, blended/hybrid learning. *Faculty:* 9 full-time (3 women), 20 part-time/adjunct (7 women). *Students:* 80 full-time (51 women), 150 part-time (107 women); includes 58 minority (24 Black or African American, non-Hispanic/Latino; 7 Asian, non-Hispanic/Latino; 27 Hispanic/Latino), 29 international. Average age 45. 128 applicants, 79% accepted, 72 enrolled. In 2018, 53 master's, 5 other advanced degrees awarded. *Degree requirements:* For master's, thesis optional, project. *Entrance requirements:* Additional exam requirements/recommendations for international students: Required—TOEFL (minimum score 550 paper-based; 79 iBT), IELTS (minimum score 6.5). *Application deadline:* Applications are processed on a rolling basis. Application fee: $50. Electronic applications accepted. Application fee is waived when completed online. *Expenses:* 1240.00. *Financial support:* In 2018–19, 111 students received support. Career-related internships or fieldwork, Federal Work-Study, scholarships/grants, and unspecified assistantships available. Support available to part-time students. Financial award application deadline: 3/15. *Faculty research:* Catholic theology, skills of religious ministry, family ministries, spirituality and divorced men. *Unit head:* Dr. Peter L Jones, Interim Dean, 312-915-7400, Fax: 312-915-7504, E-mail: pjones5@luc.edu. *Application contact:* Dr. Peter L Jones, Interim Dean, 312-915-7400, Fax: 312-915-7504, E-mail: pjones5@luc.edu.
Website: http://www.luc.edu/ips/

Marlboro College, Graduate and Professional Studies, Program in Teaching for Social Justice, Marlboro, VT 05344. Offers MAT. *Program availability:* Evening/weekend. *Degree requirements:* For master's, 36 credits including teaching internship and portfolio. *Entrance requirements:* For master's, statement of intent, 2 letters of recommendation, transcripts, interview. Additional exam requirements/recommendations for international students: Required—TOEFL (minimum score of 577 paper-based, 90 iBT) or IELTS (minimum score of 7). Electronic applications accepted. *Expenses:* Contact institution.

Marygrove College, Graduate Studies, Detroit, MI 48221-2599. Offers autism spectrum disorders (M Ed, Certificate); curriculum instruction and assessment (MAT); educational leadership (MA); educational technology (M Ed); effective teaching in the 21st century-classroom focus (MAT); effective teaching in the 21st century-technology focus (MAT); human resource management (MA, Certificate); mathematics 6-8 (MAT); mathematics K-5 (MAT); reading and literacy K-6 (MAT); reading specialist (M Ed); school administrator (Certificate); social justice (MA); special education (MAT); special education - learning disabilities (M Ed); teaching - pre-elementary education (M Ed); teaching - pre-secondary education (M Ed). *Program availability:* Part-time, evening/weekend, 100% online, blended/hybrid learning. *Entrance requirements:* For master's, all official bachelor's transcripts. Additional exam requirements/recommendations for international students: Required—TOEFL (minimum score 550 paper-based; 80 iBT). Electronic applications accepted.

Michigan State University College of Law, Graduate and Professional Programs, East Lansing, MI 48824-1300. Offers American legal system (LL M, MJ); global food law (LL M, MJ); intellectual property law (LL M, MJ); law (JD); legal studies (MLS). *Accreditation:* ABA. *Program availability:* Part-time. *Entrance requirements:* For doctorate, LSAT. Additional exam requirements/recommendations for international students: Required—TOEFL (minimum score 600 paper-based), IELTS. Electronic applications accepted. *Expenses:* *Tuition:* Full-time $44,200. *Required fees:* $37. *Faculty research:* International, constitutional, health, tax and environmental law; intellectual property, trial practice, corporate law.

Mississippi College, Graduate School, College of Arts and Sciences, School of Humanities and Social Sciences, Department of History and Political Science, Clinton, MS 39058. Offers administration of justice (MSS); history (M Ed, MA, MSS); paralegal studies (Certificate); political science (MSS); social sciences (M Ed, MSS). *Program availability:* Part-time. *Degree requirements:* For master's, one foreign language, comprehensive exam, thesis (for some programs). *Entrance requirements:* For master's, GRE or NTE, minimum GPA of 2.5. Additional exam requirements/recommendations for international students: Recommended—TOEFL, IELTS. Electronic applications accepted.

Montclair State University, The Graduate School, College of Humanities and Social Sciences, Paralegal Studies Certificate Program, Montclair, NJ 07043-1624. Offers Certificate. *Program availability:* Part-time, evening/weekend. *Entrance requirements:* For degree, 2 letters of recommendation, essay. Additional exam requirements/recommendations for international students: Required—TOEFL (minimum score 83 iBT) or IELTS. Electronic applications accepted.

National Paralegal College, Graduate Programs, Phoenix, AZ 85014. Offers compliance law (MS); legal studies (MS); taxation (MS). *Program availability:* Part-time. Electronic applications accepted.

National University, School of Professional Studies, La Jolla, CA 92037-1011. Offers criminal justice (MCJ); digital cinema production (MFA); digital journalism (MA); homeland security and emergency management (MS); juvenile justice (MS); professional screenwriting (MFA); public administration (MPA), including human resource management, organizational leadership. *Program availability:* Part-time, evening/weekend, 100% online, blended/hybrid learning. *Degree requirements:* For master's, thesis (for some programs). *Entrance requirements:* For master's, interview, minimum GPA of 2.5. Additional exam requirements/recommendations for international students: Required—TOEFL (minimum score 550 paper-based; 79 iBT), IELTS (minimum score 6). Electronic applications accepted. *Expenses:* *Tuition:* Full-time $10,320; part-time $430 per unit. Tuition and fees vary according to degree level.

New York University, Graduate School of Arts and Science and School of Law, Institute for Law and Society, New York, NY 10012-1019. Offers MA, PhD, JD/MA, JD/PhD. In 2018, 1 doctorate awarded. *Degree requirements:* For doctorate, one foreign language, thesis/dissertation. *Entrance requirements:* Additional exam requirements/recommendations for international students: Required—TOEFL. *Financial support:* Fellowships, teaching assistantships, career-related internships or fieldwork, Federal Work-Study, institutionally sponsored loans, scholarships/grants, health care benefits, and unspecified assistantships available. Financial award applicants required to submit FAFSA. *Faculty research:* Politics of law, law and social policy, law in comparative global perspective, rights and social movements. *Unit head:* Jo Dixon, Director of Graduate Studies, 212-998-8040, Fax: 212-995-4557, E-mail: gsas.admissions@nyu.edu. *Application contact:* Carly Vignogna, Graduate Administrator, 212-998-8040, Fax: 212-995-4557, E-mail: gsas.admissions@nyu.edu.

Northeastern University, College of Social Sciences and Humanities, Boston, MA 02115. Offers criminology and criminal justice (MSCJ); criminology and justice policy (PhD); economics (MA, PhD); English (MA, PhD); international affairs (MA); law and public policy (PhD); political science (MA, PhD); public administration (MPA); public policy (MPP); security and resilience studies (MS); sociology (MA, PhD); urban and regional policy (MS); urban informatics (MS); world history (MA, PhD). *Program availability:* Online learning. *Degree requirements:* For doctorate, variable foreign language requirement, comprehensive exam, thesis/dissertation. *Entrance requirements:* For master's and doctorate, GRE. Additional exam requirements/recommendations for international students: Required—TOEFL, IELTS. Electronic applications accepted. *Expenses:* Contact institution.

Nova Southeastern University, Shepard Broad College of Law, Fort Lauderdale, FL 33314. Offers education law (MS), including cybersecurity law, education law advocacy,

exceptional education; employment law (MS), including cybersecurity law, employee relations law, human resource managerial law; health law (MS, JD), including clinical research law and regulatory compliance (MS), cybersecurity law (MS), health care administrative law (MS), regulatory compliance (MS), risk management (MS); international law (JD); law and policy (MS), including cybersecurity law; JD/DO; JD/M Acc; JD/M Tax; JD/MBA; JD/MPA; JD/MS; JD/PhD. *Accreditation:* ABA. *Program availability:* Part-time, evening/weekend, 100% online, blended/hybrid learning. *Degree requirements:* For master's, thesis optional, capstone research project; for doctorate, rigorous upper-level writing fulfilled through faculty-supervised seminar paper, law journal article, workshop, or other research; 6 credits' experiential learning. *Entrance requirements:* For master's, regionally-accredited undergraduate degree; at least 2 years' experience in related field (for employment law and health law); for doctorate, LSAT. Additional exam requirements/recommendations for international students: Recommended—TOEFL (minimum score 600 paper-based; 100 iBT), IELTS (minimum score 7). Electronic applications accepted. *Expenses:* Contact institution. *Faculty research:* Legal issues in health law, international law, the legal profession, family law, civil rights.

Pace University, Elisabeth Haub School of Law, White Plains, NY 10603. Offers comparative legal studies (LL M); environmental law (LL M, SJD), including energy and climate change law (LL M), global environmental law (LL M); law (JD); JD/LL M; JD/MA; JD/MBA; JD/MEM; JD/MPA; JD/MS. JD/MA offered jointly with Sarah Lawrence College; JD/MEM offered jointly with Yale University School of Forestry and Environmental Studies. *Accreditation:* ABA. *Program availability:* Part-time. *Degree requirements:* For doctorate, thesis/dissertation (for some programs), extensive thesis proposal (for SJD). *Entrance requirements:* For master's, writing sample; for doctorate, LSAT (for JD). Additional exam requirements/recommendations for international students: Required—TOEFL (minimum score 100 iBT); Recommended—TWE. Electronic applications accepted. *Expenses:* Contact institution. *Faculty research:* Reform of energy regulations, international law, land use law, prosecutorial misconduct, corporation law.

Prairie View A&M University, College of Juvenile Justice and Psychology, Prairie View, TX 77446. Offers clinical adolescent psychology (PhD); juvenile forensic psychology (MSJFP); juvenile justice (MSJJ, PhD). *Program availability:* Part-time, evening/weekend, online only, 100% online, Master's in Juvenile Justice. *Faculty:* 8 full-time (4 women). *Students:* 19 full-time (13 women), 20 part-time (17 women); includes 35 minority (29 Black or African American, non-Hispanic/Latino; 5 Hispanic/Latino; 1 Two or more races, non-Hispanic/Latino), 3 international. Average age 32. 28 applicants, 32% accepted, 7 enrolled. In 2018, 14 master's, 1 doctorate awarded. *Degree requirements:* For master's, comprehensive exam; for doctorate, thesis/dissertation. *Entrance requirements:* For master's, GRE, minimum GPA of 2.75; for doctorate, GRE, previous course work in clinical adolescent psychology, minimum GPA of 3.5. Additional exam requirements/recommendations for international students: Required—TOEFL (minimum score 550 paper-based; 79 iBT). *Application deadline:* For fall admission, 5/1 priority date for domestic and international students; for spring admission, 10/1 priority date for domestic students, 9/1 priority date for international students; for summer admission, 3/1 priority date for domestic students, 2/1 priority date for international students. Applications are processed on a rolling basis. Application fee: $50. Electronic applications accepted. *Expenses: Tuition, area resident:* Full-time $3172; part-time $317 per credit. Tuition, state resident: full-time $3172; part-time $317 per credit. Tuition, nonresident: full-time $7965; part-time $796 per credit. *Required fees:* $4847; $485 per credit. *Financial support:* In 2018–19, 21 research assistantships with full tuition reimbursements (averaging $22,000 per year), 6 teaching assistantships with full tuition reimbursements (averaging $18,000 per year) were awarded; career-related internships or fieldwork, institutionally sponsored loans, scholarships/grants, health care benefits, tuition waivers (full), and unspecified assistantships also available. Support available to part-time students. Financial award application deadline: 4/1; financial award applicants required to submit FAFSA. *Faculty research:* Cross-over youth(juvenile justice and foster care), juvenile gang involvement, juvenile forensic psychology, correctional staff deviance, cryptocurrencies. *Unit head:* Dr. Camille Gibson, Interim Dean, 936-261-5265 Ext. 5265, Fax: 936-261-5253, E-mail: cbgibson@pvamu.edu. *Application contact:* Pauline Walker, Executive Secretary, Graduate Program, 936-261-3521, Fax: 936-261-3529, E-mail: gradadmissions@pvamu.edu.

Prescott College, Graduate Programs, Program in Arts and Humanities, Prescott, AZ 86301. Offers humanities (MA); social justice and human rights (MA); student-directed independent study (MA). *Program availability:* Part-time, online learning. *Degree requirements:* For master's, thesis, fieldwork or internship, practicum. *Entrance requirements:* For master's, 2 letters of recommendation, resume, essay. Additional exam requirements/recommendations for international students: Required—TOEFL (minimum score 500 paper-based). Electronic applications accepted.

Purdue University Global, School of Legal Studies, Davenport, IA 52807. Offers health care delivery (MS); pathway to paralegal (Postbaccalaureate Certificate); state and local government (MS). *Program availability:* Part-time, evening/weekend, online learning. *Entrance requirements:* Additional exam requirements/recommendations for international students: Required—TOEFL (minimum score 550 paper-based; 80 iBT).

Queen's University at Kingston, School of Graduate Studies, Faculty of Arts and Science, Department of Sociology, Kingston, ON K7L 3N6, Canada. Offers communication and information technology (MA, PhD); feminist sociology (MA, PhD); socio-legal studies (MA, PhD); sociological theory (MA, PhD). *Program availability:* Part-time. *Degree requirements:* For master's, thesis; for doctorate, comprehensive exam, thesis/dissertation. *Entrance requirements:* For master's, honors bachelor's degree in sociology; for doctorate, honors bachelor's degree, master's degree in sociology. Additional exam requirements/recommendations for international students: Required—TOEFL. *Faculty research:* Social change and modernization, social control, deviance and criminology, surveillance.

Regent University, Graduate School, School of Law, Virginia Beach, VA 23464-9800. Offers American legal studies (LL M); human rights (LL M); law (MA, JD), including advanced paralegal studies (MA), alternative dispute resolution (MA), business (MA), criminal justice (MA), general legal studies (MA), human resources management (MA), human rights and rule of law (MA), national security (MA), non-profit organizational law (MA), regulatory compliance (MA), wealth management and financial planning (MA); JD/MA; JD/MBA. *Accreditation:* ABA. *Program availability:* Part-time, 100% online, blended/hybrid learning. *Entrance requirements:* For master's, college transcripts, resume, personal statement; for doctorate, LSAT, minimum undergraduate GPA of 3.0, official transcripts, 2 letters of recommendation, resume, personal statement. Additional exam requirements/recommendations for international students: Required—TOEFL (minimum score 600 paper-based). Electronic applications accepted. *Expenses:* Contact institution. *Faculty research:* Family law, Constitutional law, law and culture, evidence and practice, intellectual property.

Rhode Island College, School of Graduate Studies, Faculty of Arts and Sciences, Department of Sociology, Providence, RI 02908-1991. Offers justice studies (MA). *Program availability:* Part-time. *Faculty:* 1 (woman) full-time. *Students:* 1 full-time (0 women), 1 part-time (0 women). Average age 42. *Degree requirements:* For master's, research based thesis or evaluation project. *Entrance requirements:* For master's, GRE, 3 letters of recommendation. Additional exam requirements/recommendations for international students: Required—TOEFL (minimum score 550 paper-based; 80 iBT). *Application deadline:* Applications are processed on a rolling basis. Application fee: $50. Electronic applications accepted. *Expenses: Tuition, area resident:* Part-time $407 per credit. Tuition, nonresident: part-time $792 per credit. *Required fees:* $29 per credit. $100 per semester. *Financial support:* Research assistantships, scholarships/grants, health care benefits, and unspecified assistantships available. Support available to part-time students. Financial award application deadline: 5/15; financial award applicants required to submit FAFSA. *Unit head:* Dr. Mikaila Arthur, Chair, 401-456-8026, Fax: 401-456-8665. *Application contact:* Dr. Mikaila Arthur, Chair, 401-456-8026, Fax: 401-456-8665.
Website: http://www.ric.edu/sociology/Pages/M.A.-in-Justice-Studies.aspx

Royal Roads University, Graduate Studies, Peace and Conflict Studies Program, Victoria, BC V9B 5Y2, Canada. Offers conflict analysis (G Dip); conflict analysis and management (MA); disaster and emergency management (MA, G Dip); human security and peacebuilding (MA, G Dip); justice studies (G Dip); peace and conflict studies (MAIS). *Program availability:* Blended/hybrid learning. *Degree requirements:* For master's, thesis. *Entrance requirements:* For master's, 5-7 years of related work experience. Additional exam requirements/recommendations for international students: Required—TOEFL (minimum score 570 paper-based) or IELTS (7) recommended. Electronic applications accepted. *Expenses: Tuition, area resident:* Full-time $27,000 Canadian dollars. Tuition, state resident: full-time $27,000 Canadian dollars. Tuition, nonresident: full-time $33,000 Canadian dollars. *Required fees:* $662 Canadian dollars. *Faculty research:* Conflict analysis, ethno-political conflict reconciliation, international relations, displaced persons, resiliency.

Rutgers University–New Brunswick, Graduate School-New Brunswick, Department of Political Science, Piscataway, NJ 08854-8097. Offers American politics (PhD); comparative politics (PhD); international relations (PhD); political theory (PhD); public law (PhD); United Nations and global policy studies (MA); women and politics (PhD). *Degree requirements:* For doctorate, one foreign language, comprehensive exam, thesis/dissertation. *Entrance requirements:* For master's, bachelor's degree from accredited U.S. college or university or a comparable institution in another country; for doctorate, GRE General Test. Additional exam requirements/recommendations for international students: Required—TOEFL.

St. John's University, St. John's College of Liberal Arts and Sciences, Program in Global Development and Social Justice, Queens, NY 11439. Offers MA. *Program availability:* Blended/hybrid learning, Program is 90% Online. *Degree requirements:* For master's, thesis or alternative, capstone research paper. *Entrance requirements:* For master's, letters of recommendation, transcripts, resume, personal statement. Additional exam requirements/recommendations for international students: Required—TOEFL (minimum score 80 iBT), IELTS (minimum score 6.5). Electronic applications accepted. *Faculty research:* Global development; sustainability, social justice, migration, peace-building.

St. John's University, School of Law, Program in Bankruptcy, Queens, NY 11439. Offers LL M. *Program availability:* Part-time, evening/weekend. *Degree requirements:* For master's, 24 credits. *Entrance requirements:* For master's, LSAT, bachelor's degree, two letters of recommendation, personal statement, resume, official transcripts from law school (including class rank) and undergraduate schools attended. Additional exam requirements/recommendations for international students: Recommended—TOEFL (minimum score 600 paper-based; 100 iBT), IELTS (minimum score 7). Electronic applications accepted. *Expenses:* Contact institution. *Faculty research:* Bankruptcy, commercial law and consumer law, international insolvency, creditor's rights, corporate reorganization and insolvency.

St. John's University, School of Law, Program in Transnational Legal Practice, Queens, NY 11439. Offers LL M. *Program availability:* Part-time. *Degree requirements:* For master's, 24 credits. *Entrance requirements:* For master's, LSAT, bachelor's degree, two letters of recommendation, personal statement, resume, official transcripts from law school (including class rank) and undergraduate schools attended. Additional exam requirements/recommendations for international students: Recommended—TOEFL (minimum score 600 paper-based; 100 iBT), IELTS (minimum score 7). Electronic applications accepted. *Expenses:* Contact institution. *Faculty research:* Public and private international law, international human rights law, international security and the resolution of armed conflict, the role and influence of international law in the United States, international finance.

St. John's University, School of Law, Program in U.S. Legal Studies for Foreign Law School Graduates, Queens, NY 11439. Offers LL M. *Program availability:* Part-time. *Degree requirements:* For master's, 24 credits. *Entrance requirements:* For master's, LSAT, law degree from non-U.S. law school, bachelor's degree, two letters of recommendation, personal statement, resume, official transcripts from law school (including class rank) and undergraduate schools attended. Additional exam requirements/recommendations for international students: Recommended—TOEFL (minimum score 600 paper-based; 100 iBT), IELTS (minimum score 7). Electronic applications accepted. *Expenses:* Contact institution.

Saint Leo University, Graduate Studies in Public Safety Administration, Saint Leo, FL 33574-6665. Offers criminal justice (MS, DCJ), including behavioral studies (MS), corrections (MS), criminal investigation (MS), criminal justice (MS), emergency and disaster management (MS), forensic science (MS), legal studies (MS); emergency and disaster management (MS), including emergency and disaster management, fire science. *Program availability:* Part-time, evening/weekend, 100% online, blended/hybrid learning. *Faculty:* 8 full-time (3 women), 29 part-time/adjunct (7 women). *Students:* 3 full-time (1 woman), 800 part-time (492 women); includes 400 minority (281 Black or African American, non-Hispanic/Latino; 3 American Indian or Alaska Native, non-Hispanic/Latino; 8 Asian, non-Hispanic/Latino; 90 Hispanic/Latino; 1 Native Hawaiian or other Pacific Islander, non-Hispanic/Latino; 17 Two or more races, non-Hispanic/Latino), 1 international. Average age 37. 300 applicants, 86% accepted, 195 enrolled. In 2018, 235 master's awarded. *Degree requirements:* For master's, comprehensive project. *Entrance requirements:* For master's, official transcripts, bachelor's degree from regionally-accredited university with minimum GPA of 3.0. Additional exam requirements/recommendations for international students: Required—TOEFL (minimum score 550 paper-based; 78 iBT). *Application deadline:* For fall admission, 7/1 priority date for domestic and international students; for spring admission, 11/1 priority date for domestic and international students. Applications are processed on a rolling basis. Application fee: $80. Electronic applications accepted. *Expenses:* Master's $575 per credit, Doctorate $750 per credit. *Financial support:* In 2018–19, 21 students received support. Scholarships/grants and tuition remission for Saint Leo employees and their dependents available. Financial award application deadline: 3/1; financial award applicants required to submit FAFSA. *Faculty research:* Emergency management, fire science, community policing. *Unit head:* Dr. Robert Diemer, Director of Graduate Studies in Safety Administration, 352-588-8974, Fax: 352-588-8660, E-mail: graduatepublicsafety@saintleo.edu. *Application contact:* Mark Russum, Assistant Vice President, Enrollment, 800-707-8846, Fax: 352-588-7873, E-mail: grad.admissions@saintleo.edu.
Website: https://www.saintleo.edu/criminal-justice-master-degree

St. Mary's University, School of Law, LL M Program, San Antonio, TX 78228. Offers American legal studies (LL M); international and comparative law (LL M); international criminal law (LL M). *Program availability:* Part-time. *Students:* 12 full-time (6 women), 5 part-time (2 women); includes 9 minority (1 Black or African American, non-Hispanic/Latino; 8 Hispanic/Latino), 5 international. Average age 35. 41 applicants, 95% accepted, 8 enrolled. In 2018, 12 master's awarded. *Degree requirements:* For master's, thesis, 24 hours of academic credit. *Entrance requirements:* For master's, official transcripts, personal statement, resume, 2 letters of recommendation. Additional exam requirements/recommendations for international students: Required—TOEFL (minimum score 550 paper-based; 80 iBT), IELTS (minimum score 6). *Application deadline:* Applications are processed on a rolling basis. Application fee: $0. Electronic applications accepted. *Expenses:* 37320. *Financial support:* Scholarships/grants available. Financial award applicants required to submit FAFSA. *Unit head:* Dean Colin Marks, Assistant Dean of Grad. and Summer Programs, 210-431-2248, E-mail: cmarks@stmarytx.edu. *Application contact:* Lupe Valdez, Legal Secretary, 210-431-6878, E-mail: gvaldez@stmarytx.edu.
Website: https://law.stmarytx.edu/academics/programs/ll-m-degrees/

San Francisco State University, Division of Graduate Studies, College of Education, Department of Equity, Leadership Studies, and Instructional Technologies, Program in Equity and Social Justice, San Francisco, CA 94132-1722. Offers MA. *Unit head:* Dr. Doris Flowers, Chair, 415-338-2614, Fax: 415-338-0568, E-mail: dflowers@sfsu.edu. *Application contact:* Dr. Ming Yeh Lee, Graduate Coordinator, 415-338-1061, Fax: 415-338-0568, E-mail: mylee@sfsu.edu.
Website: http://elsit.sfsu.edu/

The Santa Barbara and Ventura Colleges of Law–Santa Barbara, Graduate and Professional Programs, Santa Barbara, CA 93101. Offers MLS, JD.

The Santa Barbara and Ventura Colleges of Law–Ventura, Graduate and Professional Programs, Ventura, CA 93003. Offers MLS, JD.

Simon Fraser University, Office of Graduate Studies and Postdoctoral Fellows, Faculty of Arts and Social Sciences, School of Criminology, Burnaby, BC V5A 1S6, Canada. Offers applied legal studies (MA); criminology (MA, PhD). *Degree requirements:* For master's, thesis or alternative, practicum; for doctorate, thesis/dissertation. *Entrance requirements:* For master's, minimum GPA of 3.0 (on scale of 4.33) or 3.33 based on last 60 credits of undergraduate courses; for doctorate, minimum GPA of 3.5 (on scale of 4.33). Additional exam requirements/recommendations for international students: Recommended—TOEFL (minimum score 580 paper-based; 93 iBT), IELTS (minimum score 7), TWE (minimum score 5). Electronic applications accepted. *Faculty research:* Media and crime, feminist jurisprudence, policy evaluation, forensic entomology, restorative justice.

Southern Illinois University Carbondale, School of Law, Program in Legal Studies, Carbondale, IL 62901-4701. Offers general law (MLS); health law and policy (MLS).

Southern New Hampshire University, School of Business, Manchester, NH 03106-1045. Offers accounting (MBA, Graduate Certificate); accounting finance (MS); accounting/auditing (MS); accounting/forensic accounting (MS); accounting/management accounting (MS); accounting/taxation (MS); applied economics (MS); athletic administration (MBA, Graduate Certificate); business administration (IMBA, Certificate), including business information systems (Certificate), human resource management (Certificate); business analytics (MBA); business intelligence (MBA); communication (MA), including new media and marketing, public relations; community economic development (MBA); criminal justice (MBA); data analytics (MS); economics (MBA); engineering management (MBA); entrepreneurship (MBA); finance (MBA, MS, Graduate Certificate); finance/corporate finance (MS); finance/investments (MS); forensic accounting (MBA); forensic accounting and fraud examination (Graduate Certificate); healthcare informatics (MBA); healthcare management (MBA); human resource management (MS); human resources (MBA); information technology (MS); information technology management (MBA); international business (PhD); Internet marketing (MBA); leadership (MBA); leadership of nonprofit organizations (Graduate Certificate); management (MS); marketing (MBA, MS, Graduate Certificate); music business (MBA); operations and project management (MS); operations and supply chain management (MBA, Graduate Certificate); organizational leadership (MS); project management (MBA, Graduate Certificate); public administration (MBA, Graduate Certificate); quantitative analysis (MBA); Six Sigma (Graduate Certificate); Six Sigma quality (MBA); social media marketing (MBA, Graduate Certificate); sport management (MBA, MS, Graduate Certificate); sustainability and environmental compliance (MBA); MBA/Certificate. *Accreditation:* ACBSP. *Program availability:* Part-time, evening/weekend, online learning. Terminal master's awarded for partial completion of doctoral program. *Degree requirements:* For master's, one foreign language, comprehensive exam (for some programs), thesis or alternative; for doctorate, one foreign language, comprehensive exam, thesis/dissertation. *Entrance requirements:* For master's, minimum GPA of 2.5; for doctorate, GMAT. Additional exam requirements/recommendations for international students: Required—TOEFL (minimum score 500 paper-based). Electronic applications accepted.

Stanford University, Law School, Stanford, CA 94305-8610. Offers corporate governance and practice (LL M); environmental law and policy (LL M); international economic law, business and policy (LL M); international legal studies (JSM); law (JD, JSD); law, science and technology (LL M); legal studies (MLS); JD/MA; JD/MBA; JD/MPP; JD/MS; JD/PhD. *Accreditation:* ABA. *Expenses:* Tuition: Full-time $50,703; part-time $32,970 per year. *Required fees:* $651. *Unit head:* M. Elizabeth Magill, Dean, 650-723-4455, Fax: 650-725-0253, E-mail: emagill@law.stanford.edu. *Application contact:* Graduate Admissions, 866-432-7472, Fax: 650-723-8371, E-mail: gradadmissions@stanford.edu.
Website: http://www.law.stanford.edu/

Taft University System, Taft Law School, Denver, CO 80246. Offers American jurisprudence (LL M); law (JD); taxation (LL M).

Temple University, Beasley School of Law, Philadelphia, PA 19122. Offers Asian law (LL M); law (JD); legal education (SJD); taxation (LL M); transnational law (LL M); trial advocacy (LL M); JD/LL M; JD/MBA; JD/MPH. *Accreditation:* ABA. *Program availability:* Part-time, evening/weekend. *Entrance requirements:* For doctorate, LSAT (for JD). Additional exam requirements/recommendations for international students: Recommended—TOEFL. Electronic applications accepted. *Expenses:* Contact institution. *Faculty research:* Cybersecurity, gender issues, health care law, immigration law, intellectual property law.

Texas State University, The Graduate College, College of Liberal Arts, Program in Legal Studies, San Marcos, TX 78666. Offers MA. *Program availability:* Part-time. *Faculty:* 5 full-time (1 woman), 2 part-time/adjunct (1 woman). *Students:* 44 full-time (32 women), 37 part-time (33 women); includes 44 minority (14 Black or African American, non-Hispanic/Latino; 29 Hispanic/Latino; 1 Two or more races, non-Hispanic/Latino), 1 international. Average age 29. 50 applicants, 80% accepted, 30 enrolled. In 2018, 32 master's awarded. *Degree requirements:* For master's, comprehensive exam. *Entrance requirements:* For master's, baccalaureate degree from regionally-accredited university with minimum GPA of 3.0 on last 60 undergraduate semester hours, interview with legal studies graduate advisor. Additional exam requirements/recommendations for

international students: Required—TOEFL (minimum score 550 paper-based; 78 iBT), IELTS (minimum score 6.5). *Application deadline:* For fall admission, 2/1 priority date for domestic and international students; for spring admission, 10/15 for domestic students, 10/1 for international students; for summer admission, 4/15 for domestic students, 3/15 for international students. Applications are processed on a rolling basis. Application fee: $55 ($90 for international students). Electronic applications accepted. *Expenses:* Tuition, state resident: full-time $8102; part-time $4051 per semester. Tuition, nonresident: full-time $18,229; part-time $9115 per semester. *International tuition:* $18,229 full-time. *Required fees:* $2116; $120 per credit hour. Tuition and fees vary according to course load. *Financial support:* In 2018–19, 45 students received support, including 3 teaching assistantships (averaging $13,226 per year); research assistantships, Federal Work-Study, institutionally sponsored loans, scholarships/grants, health care benefits, and unspecified assistantships also available. Financial award application deadline: 1/15; financial award applicants required to submit FAFSA. *Unit head:* Dr. G. Lynn Crossett, Graduate Advisor, 512-245-2233, Fax: 512-245-7815, E-mail: lc25@txstate.edu. *Application contact:* Dr. Andrea Golato, Dean of Graduate School, 512-245-2581, Fax: 512-245-8365, E-mail: gradcollege@txstate.edu.
Website: http://mals.polisci.txstate.edu/

Texas Tech University, School of Law, Lubbock, TX 79409-0004. Offers law (JD); United States legal studies (LL M); JD/M Engr; JD/MBA; JD/MD; JD/MPA; JD/MS; JD/MSA. *Accreditation:* ABA. *Faculty:* 33 full-time (14 women), 11 part-time/adjunct (4 women). *Students:* 412 full-time (173 women), 1 (woman) part-time; includes 118 minority (12 Black or African American, non-Hispanic/Latino; 1 American Indian or Alaska Native, non-Hispanic/Latino; 11 Asian, non-Hispanic/Latino; 61 Hispanic/Latino; 33 Two or more races, non-Hispanic/Latino). Average age 25. 1,164 applicants, 44% accepted, 150 enrolled. In 2018, 155 doctorates awarded. *Entrance requirements:* For doctorate, LSAT. Additional exam requirements/recommendations for international students: Required—TOEFL (minimum score 600 paper-based; 100 iBT), IELTS (minimum score 7), TOEFL (minimum score 600 paper-based; 100 iBT) or IELTS (minimum score 7) for LL M. *Application deadline:* For fall admission, 3/1 priority date for domestic and international students. Applications are processed on a rolling basis. Application fee: $0. Electronic applications accepted. *Expenses:* Contact institution. *Financial support:* In 2018–19, 314 students received support. Federal Work-Study, scholarships/grants, and Tutor available. Financial award application deadline: 5/1; financial award applicants required to submit FAFSA. *Faculty research:* Advocacy/practice skills/procedure, criminal Law/constitutional law, business law/tax/estate planning & family law, energy law/natural resources, law and science. *Total annual research expenditures:* $61,878. *Unit head:* Dean Jack Wade Nowlin, Dean and W. Frank Newton Professor of Law, 806-834-1504, Fax: 806-742-1629, E-mail: jack.nowlin@ttu.edu. *Application contact:* Dean Danielle I. Saavedra, Assistant Dean of Admissions, 806-834-7092, Fax: 806-742-1629, E-mail: admissions.law@ttu.edu.
Website: www.law.ttu.edu/

Touro College, Jacob D. Fuchsberg Law Center, Central Islip, NY 11743. Offers general law (LL M); law (JD); U.S. legal studies (LL M); JD/MBA; JD/MPA; JD/MSW. JD/MBA and JD/MPA offered with Long Island University-LIU Post; JD/MSW offered with Stony Brook University, State University of New York. *Accreditation:* ABA. *Program availability:* Part-time, evening/weekend. *Entrance requirements:* For doctorate, LSAT. *Expenses:* Contact institution. *Faculty research:* Business law, civil rights, international law, criminal justice.

Trident University International, College of Health Sciences, Program in Health Sciences, Cypress, CA 90630. Offers clinical research administration (MS, Certificate); emergency and disaster management (MS, Certificate); environmental health science (Certificate); health care administration (PhD); health care management (MS), including health informatics; health education (MS, Certificate); health informatics (Certificate); health sciences (PhD); international health (MS); international health: educator or researcher option (PhD); international health: practitioner option (PhD); law and expert witness studies (MS, Certificate); public health (MS); quality assurance (Certificate). *Program availability:* Part-time, evening/weekend, online learning. *Degree requirements:* For doctorate, comprehensive exam, thesis/dissertation, defense of dissertation. *Entrance requirements:* For master's, minimum GPA of 2.5 (students with GPA 3.0 or greater may transfer up to 30% of graduate level credits); for doctorate, minimum GPA of 3.4, curriculum vitae, course work in research methods or statistics. Additional exam requirements/recommendations for international students: Required—TOEFL. Electronic applications accepted.

Universidad Autonoma de Guadalajara, Graduate Programs, Guadalajara, Mexico. Offers administrative law and justice (LL M); advertising and corporate communications (MA); architecture (M Arch); business (MBA); computational science (MCC); education (Ed M, Ed D); English-Spanish translation (MA); entrepreneurship and management (MBA); integrated management of digital animation (MA); international business (MIB); international corporate law (LL M); Internet technologies (MS); manufacturing systems (MMS); occupational health (MS); philosophy (MA, PhD); power electronics (MS); quality systems (MQS); renewable energy (MS); social evaluation of projects (MBA); strategic market research (MBA); tax law (MA); teaching mathematics (MA).

Université Laval, Faculty of Law, Program in Notarial Law, Québec, QC G1K 7P4, Canada. Offers Diploma. *Program availability:* Part-time. *Entrance requirements:* For degree, knowledge of French. Electronic applications accepted.

University at Buffalo, the State University of New York, Graduate School, School of Law, Buffalo, NY 14260. Offers criminal law (LL M); cross-border legal studies (LL M); environmental law (LL M); general law (LL M); law (JD); JD/MA; JD/MBA; JD/MLS; JD/MSW; JD/MUP; JD/PhD; LL M/LL M. *Accreditation:* ABA. *Faculty:* 56 full-time (29 women), 74 part-time/adjunct (30 women). *Students:* 451 full-time (250 women), 10 part-time (6 women); includes 91 minority (30 Black or African American, non-Hispanic/Latino; 2 American Indian or Alaska Native, non-Hispanic/Latino; 23 Asian, non-Hispanic/Latino; 23 Hispanic/Latino; 13 Two or more races, non-Hispanic/Latino), 18 international. Average age 26. 895 applicants, 60% accepted, 168 enrolled. In 2018, 1 master's, 153 doctorates awarded. *Entrance requirements:* For doctorate, LSAT or GRE (JD only). Additional exam requirements/recommendations for international students: Required—TOEFL (minimum score 90 iBT), IELTS (minimum score 7). *Application deadline:* For fall admission, 3/1 priority date for domestic and international students. Applications are processed on a rolling basis. Application fee: $85. Electronic applications accepted. *Expenses:* $14,037 per semester full-time tuition and fees, $1,275 per credit part-time tuition and fees. *Financial support:* In 2018–19, 350 students received support. Federal Work-Study, institutionally sponsored loans, scholarships/grants, tuition waivers (full and partial), and unspecified assistantships available. Financial award application deadline: 3/1; financial award applicants required to submit FAFSA. *Faculty research:* Criminal law, environmental law, international law and human rights, law and finance, cross-border legal studies. *Total annual research expenditures:* $29,552. *Unit head:* Aviva Abramovsky, Dean, 716-645-2052, E-mail: aabramov@buffalo.edu. *Application contact:* Lindsay Gladney, Vice Dean for Admissions, 716-645-2907, Fax: 716-645-6676, E-mail: law-admissions@buffalo.edu.
Website: http://www.law.buffalo.edu/

University of Baltimore, Graduate School, Yale Gordon College of Arts and Sciences, Program in Legal Studies, Baltimore, MD 21201-5779. Offers MA. *Program availability:*

Legal and Justice Studies

Part-time, evening/weekend. *Degree requirements:* For master's, thesis optional. *Entrance requirements:* For master's, minimum GPA of 3.0. Additional exam requirements/recommendations for international students: Required—TOEFL (minimum score 550 paper-based). Electronic applications accepted. *Faculty research:* Morality in law and economics, religion in lawmaking, comparative legal history, law and social change, critical issues in Constitutional law, theories of justice.

University of Calgary, Faculty of Graduate Studies, Faculty of Law, Certificate Program in Natural Resources, Energy and Environmental Law, Calgary, AB T2N 1N4, Canada. Offers LL M, Postbaccalaureate Certificate. *Program availability:* Part-time, evening/ weekend. *Degree requirements:* For master's, thesis optional. *Entrance requirements:* For master's, JD or LL B. Additional exam requirements/recommendations for international students: Required—TOEFL (minimum score 100 iBT), IELTS (minimum score 7). Electronic applications accepted. *Faculty research:* Natural resources law and regulations; environmental law, ethics and policies; oil and gas and energy law; water and municipal law; Aboriginal law.

University of California, Berkeley, School of Law, Program in Jurisprudence and Social Policy, Berkeley, CA 94720. Offers PhD. *Degree requirements:* For doctorate, one foreign language, thesis/dissertation, oral qualifying exam. *Entrance requirements:* For doctorate, GRE General Test, sample of written work, letters of recommendation. Electronic applications accepted. *Expenses:* Contact institution. *Faculty research:* Law and philosophy, legal history, law and economics, law and political science, law and sociology.

University of Charleston, Master of Forensic Accounting Program, Charleston, WV 25304-1099. Offers EMFA. *Program availability:* Part-time, blended/hybrid learning. *Entrance requirements:* Additional exam requirements/recommendations for international students: Required—TOEFL. Electronic applications accepted.

University of Denver, Sturm College of Law, Program in Legal Administration, Denver, CO 80208. Offers MSLA, Certificate. *Program availability:* Part-time, evening/weekend. *Faculty:* 8 full-time (3 women), 2 part-time/adjunct (1 woman). *Students:* 14 part-time (11 women); includes 4 minority (2 Black or African American, non-Hispanic/Latino; 1 Asian, non-Hispanic/Latino; 1 Hispanic/Latino). Average age 35. 10 applicants, 90% accepted, 5 enrolled. In 2018, 9 master's, 1 Certificate awarded. *Entrance requirements:* For master's, GRE General Test, GMAT, or LSAT, transcripts; two letters of recommendation; personal statement; resume. Additional exam requirements/ recommendations for international students: Required—TOEFL (minimum score 600 paper-based; 100 iBT). *Application deadline:* For fall admission, 8/5 for domestic and international students; for spring admission, 12/23 for domestic and international students; for summer admission, 5/18 for domestic and international students. Applications are processed on a rolling basis. Application fee: $65. Electronic applications accepted. *Expenses:* $40,700 per year full-time. *Financial support:* In 2018–19, 11 students received support. Career-related internships or fieldwork, Federal Work-Study, scholarships/grants, and unspecified assistantships available. Support available to part-time students. Financial award application deadline: 2/15; financial award applicants required to submit FAFSA. *Unit head:* Lori Reynolds, Assistant Dean, Graduate Legal Studies, 303-871-6312, E-mail: gradlegalstudies@law.du.edu. *Application contact:* Lori Reynolds, Assistant Dean, Graduate Legal Studies, 303-871-6312, E-mail: gradlegalstudies@law.du.edu.
Website: http://www.law.du.edu/index.php/msla

University of Illinois at Springfield, Graduate Programs, College of Public Affairs and Administration, Program in Legal Studies, Springfield, IL 62703-5407. Offers MA. *Program availability:* Part-time, evening/weekend, 100% online. *Faculty:* 4 full-time (3 women). *Students:* 1 (woman) full-time, 42 part-time (26 women); includes 15 minority (7 Black or African American, non-Hispanic/Latino; 2 Asian, non-Hispanic/Latino; 4 Hispanic/Latino; 2 Two or more races, non-Hispanic/Latino), 2 international. Average age 40. 62 applicants, 31% accepted, 10 enrolled. In 2018, 17 master's awarded. *Degree requirements:* For master's, thesis or seminar. *Entrance requirements:* For master's, minimum undergraduate GPA of 3.0; demonstration of writing ability. Additional exam requirements/recommendations for international students: Required—TOEFL (minimum score 570 paper-based; 100 iBT). *Application deadline:* Applications are processed on a rolling basis. Application fee: $60 ($75 for international students). Electronic applications accepted. *Financial support:* In 2018–19, research assistantships with full tuition reimbursements (averaging $10,384 per year), teaching assistantships with full tuition reimbursements (averaging $10,303 per year) were awarded; fellowships, career-related internships or fieldwork, Federal Work-Study, scholarships/grants, health care benefits, and unspecified assistantships also available. Support available to part-time students. Financial award application deadline: 11/15; financial award applicants required to submit FAFSA. *Unit head:* Dr. Robert Smith, Interim Program Administrator, 217-206-6535, Fax: 217-206-7807, E-mail: les@uis.edu. *Application contact:* Dr. Robert Smith, Interim Program Administrator, 217-206-6535, Fax: 217-206-7807, E-mail: les@uis.edu.
Website: http://www.uis.edu/legalstudies/

University of Massachusetts Lowell, College of Fine Arts, Humanities and Social Sciences, School of Criminology and Justice Studies, Lowell, MA 01854. Offers criminal justice (MA). *Program availability:* Part-time, evening/weekend. *Degree requirements:* For master's, thesis optional. *Entrance requirements:* For master's, GRE General Test or MAT. Electronic applications accepted. *Faculty research:* Family violence, criminal justice management, corrections, policing, delinquency.

University of Montana, Graduate School, College of Humanities and Sciences, Department of Sociology, Missoula, MT 59812. Offers criminology (MA); inequality and social justice (MA); rural and environmental change (MA); sociology (MA). *Entrance requirements:* For master's, GRE General Test. Additional exam requirements/ recommendations for international students: Required—TOEFL. *Faculty research:* Housing, homelessness, hunger, infant mortality, work safety.

University of Nebraska–Lincoln, College of Law, Program in Legal Studies, Lincoln, NE 68588. Offers MLS. *Entrance requirements:* For master's, GRE or LSAT. Additional exam requirements/recommendations for international students: Required—TOEFL (minimum score 600 paper-based). Electronic applications accepted.

University of Nevada, Reno, Graduate School, College of Liberal Arts, School of Social Research and Justice Studies, Program in Judicial Studies, Reno, NV 89557. Offers MJS, PhD. Offered jointly with the National Judicial College and the National Council of Juvenile and Family Court Judges. *Program availability:* Part-time. Terminal master's awarded for partial completion of doctoral program. *Degree requirements:* For master's, thesis; for doctorate, thesis/dissertation. *Entrance requirements:* For master's and doctorate, sitting judge, law degree from an accredited school. Additional exam requirements/recommendations for international students: Required—TOEFL (minimum score 500 paper-based; 61 iBT), IELTS (minimum score 6). Electronic applications accepted. *Expenses:* Contact institution. *Faculty research:* Jury research, capital punishment, expert testimony, environmental law, medical issues.

University of New Hampshire, Graduate School, College of Liberal Arts, Program in Justice Studies, Durham, NH 03824. Offers MA. Program offered in summer only. *Program availability:* Part-time. *Entrance requirements:* For master's, GRE. Additional exam requirements/recommendations for international students: Required—TOEFL (minimum score 550 paper-based; 80 iBT); Recommended—TWE. Electronic applications accepted.

University of New Hampshire, School of Law, Concord, NH 03301. Offers business law (JD); commerce and technology (LL M, MCT, Diploma); criminal law (JD); intellectual property (LL M, MIP, JD, Diploma), including patent law (JD), trademarks and copyright (JD); international criminal law and justice (LL M, MICLJ); litigation (JD); public interest and social justice (JD); sports and entertainment law (JD); JD/LL M; JD/MBA; JD/MIP; JD/MPP; JD/MSW. *Accreditation:* ABA. *Program availability:* Part-time, 100% online, limited residential. *Degree requirements:* For doctorate, comprehensive exam. *Entrance requirements:* For doctorate, LSAT. Additional exam requirements/ recommendations for international students: Required—TOEFL (minimum score 600 paper-based; 100 iBT), minimum TOEFL iBT score of 80 (for master's programs). Electronic applications accepted. *Expenses:* Contact institution. *Faculty research:* Intellectual property, health law and policy, sports and entertainment law, patent law, trademarks and copyright.

University of Pennsylvania, Wharton School, Legal Studies and Business Ethics Department, Philadelphia, PA 19104. Offers MBA, PhD.

University of Pittsburgh, School of Law, Master of Studies in Law Program, Pittsburgh, PA 15260. Offers biomedical and health services research (MSL); business law (MSL), including commercial law, corporate law, general business law, international business, tax law; Constitutional law (MSL); criminal law and justice (MSL); disability law (MSL); elder and estate planning law (MSL); employment and labor law (MSL); energy law (MSL); environmental and real estate law (MSL); family law (MSL); health law (MSL); intellectual property and technology law (MSL); international and human rights law (MSL); jurisprudence (MSL); regulatory law (MSL); self-designed (MSL). *Program availability:* Part-time. *Entrance requirements:* Additional exam requirements/ recommendations for international students: Required—TOEFL (minimum score 600 paper-based; 100 iBT), IELTS (minimum score 7). *Faculty research:* Law, health law, business law, contracts, intellectual property, environmental law.

University of San Diego, School of Law, San Diego, CA 92110. Offers business and corporate law (LL M); comparative law (LL M); general studies (LL M); international law (LL M); law (JD); legal studies (MS); peace and law (JD/MA); taxation (LL M, Diploma); JD/IMBA; JD/MA; JD/MBA. *Accreditation:* ABA. *Program availability:* Part-time, evening/ weekend. *Faculty:* 45 full-time (16 women), 72 part-time/adjunct (21 women). *Students:* 661 full-time (363 women), 92 part-time (49 women); includes 244 minority (31 Black or African American, non-Hispanic/Latino; 12 American Indian or Alaska Native, non-Hispanic/Latino; 75 Asian, non-Hispanic/Latino; 110 Hispanic/Latino; 4 Native Hawaiian or other Pacific Islander, non-Hispanic/Latino; 12 Two or more races, non-Hispanic/ Latino), 31 international. Average age 27. 3,511 applicants, 240 enrolled. In 2018, 59 master's, 264 doctorates awarded. *Entrance requirements:* For master's, JD, LL B or equivalent from an ABA-accredited law school; for doctorate, LSAT (less than 5 years old), bachelor's degree, registration with the Credential Assemble Service (CAS). Additional exam requirements/recommendations for international students: Required—TOEFL (minimum score 600 paper-based; 100 iBT), IELTS (minimum score 7). *Application deadline:* For fall admission, 2/1 priority date for domestic students. Applications are processed on a rolling basis. Application fee: $0. Electronic applications accepted. *Expenses:* Contact institution. *Financial support:* In 2018–19, 640 students received support. Career-related internships or fieldwork, Federal Work-Study, institutionally sponsored loans, and scholarships/grants available. Support available to part-time students. Financial award application deadline: 3/1; financial award applicants required to submit FAFSA. *Faculty research:* Corporate law, children's advocacy, Constitutional and criminal law, international and comparative law, public interest law, intellectual property and tax law. *Unit head:* Dr. Stephen C. Ferruolo, Dean, 619-260-4527, E-mail: lawdean@sandiego.edu. *Application contact:* Jorge Garcia, Assistant Dean, JD Admissions, 619-260-4528, Fax: 619-260-2218, E-mail: jdinfo@sandiego.edu.
Website: http://www.sandiego.edu/law/

University of South Florida, Innovative Education, Tampa, FL 33620-9951. Offers adult, career and higher education (Graduate Certificate), including college teaching, leadership in developing human resources, leadership in higher education; Africana studies (Graduate Certificate), including diasporas and health disparities, genocide and human rights; aging studies (Graduate Certificate), including gerontology; art research (Graduate Certificate), including museum studies; business foundations (Graduate Certificate); chemical and biomedical engineering (Graduate Certificate), including materials science and engineering, water, health and sustainability; child and family studies (Graduate Certificate), including positive behavior support; civil and industrial engineering (Graduate Certificate), including transportation systems analysis; community and family health (Graduate Certificate), including maternal and child health, social marketing and public health, violence and injury: prevention and intervention, women's health; criminology (Graduate Certificate), including criminal justice administration; data science for public administration (Graduate Certificate); digital humanities (Graduate Certificate); educational measurement and research (Graduate Certificate), including evaluation; English (Graduate Certificate), including comparative literary studies, creative writing, professional and technical communication; entrepreneurship (Graduate Certificate); environmental health (Graduate Certificate), including safety management; epidemiology and biostatistics (Graduate Certificate), including applied biostatistics, biostatistics, concepts and tools of epidemiology, epidemiology, epidemiology of infectious diseases; geography, environment and planning (Graduate Certificate), including community development, environmental policy and management, geographical information systems; geology (Graduate Certificate), including hydrogeology; global health (Graduate Certificate), including disaster management, global health and Latin American and Caribbean studies, global health practice, humanitarian assistance, infection control; government and international affairs (Graduate Certificate), including Cuban studies, globalization studies; health policy and management (Graduate Certificate), including health management and leadership, public health policy and programs; hearing specialist: early intervention (Graduate Certificate); industrial and management systems engineering (Graduate Certificate), including systems engineering, technology management; information studies (Graduate Certificate), including school library media specialist; information systems/decision sciences (Graduate Certificate), including analytics and business intelligence; instructional technology (Graduate Certificate), including distance education, Florida digital/virtual educator, instructional design, multimedia design, Web design; internal medicine, bioethics and medical humanities (Graduate Certificate), including biomedical ethics; Latin American and Caribbean studies (Graduate Certificate); leadership for coastal resiliency planning (Graduate Certificate); mass communications (Graduate Certificate), including multimedia journalism; mathematics and statistics (Graduate Certificate), including mathematics; medicine (Graduate Certificate), including aging and neuroscience, bioinformatics, biotechnology, brain fitness and memory management, clinical investigation, hand and upper limb rehabilitation, health informatics, health sciences, integrative weight management, intellectual property, medicine and gender, metabolic and nutritional medicine, metabolic cardiology, pharmacy sciences; national and competitive intelligence (Graduate Certificate); nursing (Graduate Certificate), including simulation based academic fellowship in advanced pain management; psychological and social foundations (Graduate Certificate), including career

counseling, college teaching, diversity in education, mental health counseling, school counseling; public affairs (Graduate Certificate), including nonprofit management, public management, research administration; public health (Graduate Certificate), including assessing chemical toxicity and public health risks, health equity, pharmacoepidemiology, public health generalist, toxicology, translational research in adolescent behavioral health; public health practices (Graduate Certificate), including planning for healthy communities; rehabilitation and mental health counseling (Graduate Certificate), including integrative mental health care, marriage and family therapy, rehabilitation technology; secondary education (Graduate Certificate), including ESOL, foreign language education: culture and content, foreign language education: professional; social work (Graduate Certificate), including geriatric social work/clinical gerontology; special education (Graduate Certificate), including autism spectrum disorder, disabilities education: severe/profound; world languages (Graduate Certificate), including teaching English as a second language (TESL) or foreign language. *Expenses:* Tuition, state resident: full-time $6350. Tuition, nonresident: full-time $19,048. *International tuition:* $19,048 full-time. *Required fees:* $2079. *Unit head:* Dr. Cynthia DeLuca, Associate Vice President and Assistant Vice Provost, 813-974-3077, Fax: 813-974-7061, E-mail: deluca@usf.edu. *Application contact:* Owen Hooper, Director, Summer and Alternative Calendar Programs, 813-974-6917, E-mail: hooper@usf.edu.
Website: http://www.usf.edu/innovative-education/

University of the District of Columbia, David A. Clarke School of Law, Washington, DC 20008. Offers clinical teaching and social justice (LL M); law (JD). *Accreditation:* ABA. *Program availability:* Part-time, evening/weekend. *Faculty:* 21 full-time (9 women), 22 part-time/adjunct (12 women). *Students:* 123 full-time (83 women), 133 part-time (80 women); includes 158 minority (100 Black or African American, non-Hispanic/Latino; 1 American Indian or Alaska Native, non-Hispanic/Latino; 25 Asian, non-Hispanic/Latino; 32 Hispanic/Latino), 2 international. Average age 28. 675 applicants, 20% accepted, 94 enrolled. In 2018, 64 doctorates awarded. *Degree requirements:* For doctorate, 90 credits, advanced legal writing. *Entrance requirements:* For doctorate, LSAT. Additional exam requirements/recommendations for international students: Required—TOEFL. *Application deadline:* For fall admission, 3/15 priority date for domestic and international students. Applications are processed on a rolling basis. Application fee: $35. Electronic applications accepted. Application fee is waived when completed online. *Expenses:* $37,548 resident full-time, $38,408 resident part-time, $72,090 non-resident full-time, $72,640 non-resident part-time to complete the degree. *Financial support:* In 2018–19, 172 students received support, including 46 fellowships (averaging $4,250 per year), 4 research assistantships (averaging $3,000 per year), 39 teaching assistantships (averaging $3,000 per year); Federal Work-Study and scholarships/grants also available. Financial award application deadline: 3/15; financial award applicants required to submit FAFSA. *Faculty research:* Civil Rights and Equality, Criminal Law, Family and Juvenile Law, Housing and Community Development Law, and Immigration Law and Human Rights. *Unit head:* Renee M. Hutchins, Dean, 202-274-7346, Fax: 202-274-5583, E-mail: renee.hutchins@udc.edu. *Application contact:* Jino Ray, Associate Dean of Admission, 202-274-7336, Fax: 202-274-5583, E-mail: jino.ray@udc.edu.
Website: http://www.law.udc.edu/

University of the Sacred Heart, Graduate Programs, Program in Systems of Justice, San Juan, PR 00914-0383. Offers human rights and anti-discriminatory processes (MASJ); mediation and transformation of conflicts (MASJ).

University of Washington, Graduate School, School of Law, Seattle, WA 98195-3020. Offers Asian law (LL M, PhD); intellectual property law and policy (LL M); law (JD); law of sustainable international development (LL M); taxation (LL M); JD/LL M; JD/MA; JD/MAIS; JD/MBA; JD/MPA; JD/MS; JD/PhD. *Accreditation:* ABA. *Degree requirements:* For master's, thesis; for doctorate, thesis/dissertation (for some programs). *Entrance requirements:* For master's, language proficiency (LL M in Asian law); for doctorate, LSAT (for JD). Additional exam requirements/recommendations for international students: Required—TOEFL. *Expenses:* Contact institution. *Faculty research:* Asian, international and comparative law, intellectual property law, health law, environmental law, taxation.

University of Windsor, Faculty of Graduate Studies, Faculty of Arts and Social Sciences, Department of Communication Studies, Windsor, ON N9B 3P4, Canada. Offers communication and social justice (MA). *Degree requirements:* For master's, thesis. *Entrance requirements:* For master's, writing sample/media production or multimedia portfolio. Additional exam requirements/recommendations for international students: Required—TOEFL (minimum score 600 paper-based). Electronic applications accepted. *Faculty research:* Sociology of news, media ownership and control, communication networks and social movements, issues of media representation.

Vermont Law School, Graduate and Professional Programs, Master's Programs, South Royalton, VT 05068-0096. Offers American legal studies (LL M); energy law (LL M); energy regulation and law (MERL); environmental law (LL M); environmental law and policy (MELP); food and agriculture law (LL M); food and agriculture law and policy (MFALP); JD/MELP; JD/MERL; JD/MFALP. *Program availability:* Part-time, 100% online, blended/hybrid learning. *Entrance requirements:* Additional exam requirements/recommendations for international students: Required—TOEFL. *Faculty research:* Environment and new economy; takings; international environmental law; interaction among science, law, and environmental policy; climate change and the law.

Washburn University, School of Law, Topeka, KS 66621. Offers global legal studies (LL M); law (MSL, JD). *Accreditation:* ABA. *Entrance requirements:* For doctorate, LSAT. Additional exam requirements/recommendations for international students: Recommended—TOEFL (minimum score 550 paper-based). Electronic applications accepted. Application fee is waived when completed online. *Expenses:* Contact institution. *Faculty research:* Constitutional law, family law, energy law, banking and securities law, oil and gas.

Weber State University, College of Social and Behavioral Sciences, Program in Criminal Justice, Ogden, UT 84408-1001. Offers MCJ. *Program availability:* Part-time, evening/weekend, 100% online. *Faculty:* 6 full-time (1 woman). *Students:* 5 full-time (4 women), 22 part-time (10 women); includes 5 minority (1 American Indian or Alaska Native, non-Hispanic/Latino; 3 Hispanic/Latino; 1 Native Hawaiian or other Pacific Islander, non-Hispanic/Latino). Average age 34. In 2018, 15 master's awarded. *Entrance requirements:* Additional exam requirements/recommendations for international students: Required—TOEFL (minimum score 550 paper-based). *Application deadline:* For fall admission, 7/29 for domestic students; for spring admission, 12/11 for domestic students; for summer admission, 4/1 for domestic students. Application fee: $60 ($90 for international students). Electronic applications accepted. *Expenses:* 6626.52 per year. *Financial support:* In 2018–19, 4 students received support. Scholarships/grants available. Financial award application deadline: 2/1; financial award applicants required to submit FAFSA. *Unit head:* Dr. Bruce Bayley, Graduate Director/Associate Professor, 801-626-8134, Fax: 801-626-6145, E-mail: bbayley@weber.edu. *Application contact:* Faye Medd, Secretary, 801-626-6146, Fax: 801-626-6146, E-mail: fmedd@weber.edu.
Website: http://www.weber.edu/cj/CJMastersDegree/CJMastersDegree.html

Webster University, College of Arts and Sciences, Department of Legal Studies, St. Louis, MO 63119-3194. Offers MA, Graduate Certificate. *Program availability:* Part-time, evening/weekend. *Degree requirements:* For master's, thesis optional. *Entrance requirements:* Additional exam requirements/recommendations for international students: Required—TOEFL. *Expenses: Tuition:* Full-time $22,500; part-time $750 per credit hour. Tuition and fees vary according to degree level, campus/location and program. *Faculty research:* Intellectual property rights, emerging torts, death penalty, juvenile justice, confidentiality issues in banking.

Western Michigan University Thomas M. Cooley Law School, Graduate Programs, Lansing, MI 48901-3038. Offers administrative law (public law) (JD); business transactions (JD); Canadian law practice (JD); corporate law and finance (LL M); environmental law (public law) (JD); general practice (JD), including solo and small firm; general studies (LL M); homeland and national security law (LL M); insurance law (LL M); intellectual property (JD); intellectual property law (LL M); international law (JD); litigation (JD); taxation (LL M); U.S. legal studies for foreign attorneys (LL M); JD/LL M; JD/MBA; JD/MHA; JD/MPA; JD/MSW. *Accreditation:* ABA. *Program availability:* Part-time, evening/weekend, 100% online, blended/hybrid learning. *Degree requirements:* For master's, thesis (for some programs); for doctorate, minimum of 3 credits of clinical experience. *Entrance requirements:* For master's, JD or LL B; for doctorate, LSAT. Additional exam requirements/recommendations for international students: Required—TOEFL (for U.S. legal studies for foreign attorneys LL M program); Recommended—TOEFL. Electronic applications accepted. *Expenses:* Contact institution. *Faculty research:* Wrongful convictions, civil rights, environmental law, litigation techniques, data mining, intellectual property, practical and skills-based legal education.

West Virginia University, College of Law, Morgantown, WV 26506-6130. Offers energy law and sustainable development (LL M); forensic justice (LL M); law (JD); white collar forensic justice (LL M). *Accreditation:* ABA. *Program availability:* Part-time. *Students:* 324 full-time (146 women), 5 part-time (2 women); includes 40 minority (12 Black or African American, non-Hispanic/Latino; 4 Asian, non-Hispanic/Latino; 10 Hispanic/Latino; 14 Two or more races, non-Hispanic/Latino). In 2018, 4 master's awarded. *Entrance requirements:* For doctorate, LSAT. Additional exam requirements/recommendations for international students: Required—TOEFL (minimum score 600 paper-based; 100 iBT). *Application deadline:* For fall admission, 2/1 for domestic and international students. Applications are processed on a rolling basis. Application fee: $60. Electronic applications accepted. *Expenses:* Contact institution. *Financial support:* Fellowships, research assistantships, teaching assistantships, career-related internships or fieldwork, Federal Work-Study, institutionally sponsored loans, scholarships/grants, health care benefits, tuition waivers (full), unspecified assistantships, and administrative assistantships, resident assistantships available. Support available to part-time students. Financial award application deadline: 3/1; financial award applicants required to submit FAFSA. *Faculty research:* Constitutional law, public interest law, corporate law, environment and natural resources innocence project, professional skills, leadership, intellectual property, entrepreneurship, labor, sustainable development, family law, IR human rights, immigration. *Unit head:* Gregory W. Bowman, Dean, College of Law, 304-293-3199, Fax: 304-293-8102, E-mail: gregory.bowman@mail.wvu.edu. *Application contact:* Gregory W. Bowman, Dean, College of Law, 304-293-3199, Fax: 304-293-8102, E-mail: gregory.bowman@mail.wvu.edu.
Website: https://law.wvu.edu

West Virginia University, Eberly College of Arts and Sciences, Morgantown, WV 26506. Offers biology (MS, PhD); chemistry (MS, PhD); communication studies (MA, PhD); computational statistics (PhD); creative writing (MFA); English (MA, PhD); forensic and investigative science (MS); forensic science (PhD); geography (MA); geology (MA, PhD); history (MA, PhD); legal studies (MLS); mathematics (MS); physics (MS, PhD); political science (MA, PhD); professional writing and editing (MA); psychology (MA); public administration (MPA); social work (MSW); sociology (MA, PhD); statistics (MS). *Program availability:* Part-time, evening/weekend, online learning. *Students:* 803 full-time (434 women), 237 part-time (138 women); includes 99 minority (31 Black or African American, non-Hispanic/Latino; 1 American Indian or Alaska Native, non-Hispanic/Latino; 16 Asian, non-Hispanic/Latino; 25 Hispanic/Latino; 26 Two or more races, non-Hispanic/Latino), 208 international. In 2018, 285 master's, 63 doctorates awarded. Terminal master's awarded for partial completion of doctoral program. *Degree requirements:* For master's, thesis (for some programs); for doctorate, comprehensive exam, thesis/dissertation. *Entrance requirements:* For master's and doctorate, GRE. Additional exam requirements/recommendations for international students: Required—TOEFL (minimum score 600 paper-based); Recommended—TWE. *Application deadline:* For spring admission, 2/15 priority date for domestic and international students. Applications are processed on a rolling basis. Application fee: $45. Electronic applications accepted. *Financial support:* Fellowships with full tuition reimbursements, research assistantships with full tuition reimbursements, teaching assistantships with full tuition reimbursements, career-related internships or fieldwork, Federal Work-Study, institutionally sponsored loans, scholarships/grants, health care benefits, tuition waivers (full and partial), unspecified assistantships, and administrative assistantships available. Financial award application deadline: 2/1; financial award applicants required to submit FAFSA. *Faculty research:* Humanities, social sciences, life science, physical sciences, mathematics. *Unit head:* Dr. Gregory Dunaway, Dean, 304-293-4611, Fax: 304-293-6858, E-mail: gregory.dunaway@mail.wvu.edu. *Application contact:* Dr. Jessica Queener, Director of Graduate Studies, 304-293-7476 Ext. 5205, Fax: 304-293-6858, E-mail: Jessica.queener@mail.wvu.edu.
Website: http://www.as.wvu.edu/

Wilfrid Laurier University, Faculty of Graduate and Postdoctoral Studies, School of International Policy and Governance, Global Governance Program, Waterloo, ON N2L 3C5, Canada. Offers conflict and security (PhD); global environment (PhD); global justice and human rights (PhD); global political economy (PhD); global social governance (PhD); multilateral institutions and diplomacy (PhD). Offered jointly with University of Waterloo. *Degree requirements:* For doctorate, thesis/dissertation. *Entrance requirements:* For doctorate, MA in political science, history, economics, international development studies, international peace studies, globalization studies, environmental studies or related field with minimum A-. Additional exam requirements/recommendations for international students: Required—TOEFL (minimum score 89 iBT). Electronic applications accepted. *Faculty research:* Global political economy, global environment, conflict and security, global justice and human rights, multilateral institutions and diplomacy.

Sports and Entertainment Law

Arizona State University at the Tempe campus, Sandra Day O'Connor College of Law, Phoenix, AZ 85287-7906. Offers biotechnology and genomics (LL M); law (JD); legal studies (MLS); patent practice (MLS); sports law and business (MSLB); tribal policy, law and government (LL M); JD/MBA; JD/MD; JD/MSW; JD/PhD. JD/MD offered jointly with Mayo Medical School. *Accreditation:* ABA. *Program availability:* 100% online. *Faculty:* 62 full-time (26 women), 146 part-time/adjunct (40 women). *Students:* 812 full-time (372 women); includes 201 minority (16 Black or African American, non-Hispanic/Latino; 15 American Indian or Alaska Native, non-Hispanic/Latino; 37 Asian, non-Hispanic/Latino; 97 Hispanic/Latino; 3 Native Hawaiian or other Pacific Islander, non-Hispanic/Latino; 33 Two or more races, non-Hispanic/Latino), 16 international. Average age 28. 3,363 applicants, 34% accepted, 271 enrolled. In 2018, 131 master's, 276 doctorates awarded. *Entrance requirements:* For master's, bachelor's degree and JD (for LL M); for doctorate, LSAT, bachelor's degree. Additional exam requirements/recommendations for international students: Required—TOEFL (minimum score 550 paper-based; 80 iBT). *Application deadline:* For fall admission, 3/1 priority date for domestic and international students. Applications are processed on a rolling basis. Application fee: $0. Electronic applications accepted. *Expenses:* $27,584 resident tuition and fees (for JD), $45,940 non-resident tuition and fees (for JD). *Financial support:* In 2018–19, 579 students received support. Institutionally sponsored loans and scholarships/grants available. Financial award application deadline: 3/15; financial award applicants required to submit FAFSA. *Faculty research:* Emerging technologies and the law, Indian law, international law, intellectual property, health law, sports law and business. *Total annual research expenditures:* $2.8 million. *Unit head:* Douglas Sylvester, Dean/Professor, 480-965-6188, Fax: 480-965-6521, E-mail: douglas.sylvester@asu.edu. *Application contact:* Chitra Damania, Director, 480-965-1474, Fax: 480-727-7930, E-mail: law.admissions@asu.edu.
Website: http://www.law.asu.edu/

Chapman University, Dale E. Fowler School of Law, Orange, CA 92866. Offers advocacy and dispute resolution (JD); business law (LL M, JD); criminal law (JD); entertainment and media law (LL M); entertainment law (JD); environmental, land use, and real estate law (JD); international and comparative law (LL M); international law (JD); law (JD); prosecutorial science (LL M); tax law (JD); taxation (LL M); trial advocacy (LL M); JD/MBA; JD/MFA. *Accreditation:* ABA. *Program availability:* Part-time. *Entrance requirements:* For doctorate, LSAT. Additional exam requirements/recommendations for international students: Required—TOEFL (minimum score 600 paper-based; 100 iBT). Electronic applications accepted. *Expenses:* Contact institution.

Drexel University, Thomas R. Kline School of Law, Philadelphia, PA 19104-2875. Offers business and entrepreneurship law (JD); criminal law (MLS, JD); cybersecurity and information privacy compliance (MLS); entrepreneurship and law (MLS); financial regulatory compliance (MLS); health care compliance (MLS); health law (JD); higher education compliance (MLS); human resources compliance (MLS); intellectual property law (JD); NCAA compliance and sports law (MLS). *Accreditation:* ABA.

London Metropolitan University, Graduate Programs, London, United Kingdom. Offers applied psychology (M Sc); architecture (MA); biomedical science (M Sc); blood science (M Sc); cancer pharmacology (M Sc); computer networking and cyber security (M Sc); computing and information systems (M Sc); conference interpreting (MA); counter-terrorism studies (M Sc); creative, digital and professional writing (MA); crime, violence and prevention (M Sc); criminology (M Sc); curating contemporary art (MA); data analytics (M Sc); digital media (MA); early childhood studies (MA); education (MA, Ed D); financial services law, regulation and compliance (LL M); food science (M Sc); forensic psychology (M Sc); health and social care management and policy (M Sc); human nutrition (M Sc); human resource management (MA); human rights and international conflict (MA); information technology (M Sc); intelligence and security studies (M Sc); international oil, gas and energy law (LL M); international relations (MA); interpreting (MA); learning and teaching in higher education (MA); legal practice (LL M); media and entertainment law (LL M); organizational and consumer psychology (M Sc); psychological therapy (M Sc); psychology of mental health (M Sc); public health (M Sc); public policy and management (MPA); security studies (M Sc); social work (M Sc); spatial planning and urban design (MA); sports therapy (M Sc); supporting older children and young people with dyslexia (MA); teaching languages (MA), including Arabic, English; translation (MA); woman and child abuse (MA).

New York University, School of Professional Studies, Preston Robert Tisch Institute for Global Sport, New York, NY 10012-1019. Offers sports business (MS), including global sports media, professional and collegiate sports operations, sports law, sports marketing and sales. *Program availability:* Part-time, evening/weekend. *Degree requirements:* For master's, thesis. *Entrance requirements:* For master's, GRE or GMAT (only upon request), bachelor's degree, resume with relevant professional work, internship or volunteer experience, two letters of recommendation, statement of purpose. Additional exam requirements/recommendations for international students: Required—TOEFL (minimum score 600 paper-based; 100 iBT), IELTS (minimum score 7). Electronic applications accepted. *Expenses:* Contact institution.

Southwestern Law School, Graduate and Professional Programs, Los Angeles, CA 90010. Offers entertainment and media law (LL M); individualized studies (LL M); law (JD). *Accreditation:* ABA. *Program availability:* Part-time, evening/weekend. *Faculty:* 60 full-time (30 women), 83 part-time/adjunct (37 women). *Students:* 517 full-time (270 women), 200 part-time (129 women); includes 338 minority (43 Black or African American, non-Hispanic/Latino; 58 Asian, non-Hispanic/Latino; 195 Hispanic/Latino; 3 Native Hawaiian or other Pacific Islander, non-Hispanic/Latino; 39 Two or more races, non-Hispanic/Latino), 14 international. Average age 27. 1,752 applicants, 46% accepted, 271 enrolled. In 2018, 7 master's, 182 doctorates awarded. *Degree requirements:* For doctorate, 87 units, minimum cumulative GPA of 2.33. *Entrance requirements:* For doctorate, LSAT, bachelor's degree from accredited U.S. institution or equivalent with transcript evaluation; personal statement; LSAC Credential Assembly Service Registration (CAS); 1 to 3 letters of recommendation. *Application deadline:* For fall admission, 4/1 priority date for domestic and international students. Applications are processed on a rolling basis. Application fee: $60. Electronic applications accepted. *Expenses:* $54,166 full-time tuition and fees, $36,194 part-time tuition and fees. *Financial support:* In 2018–19, 369 students received support. Federal Work-Study, institutionally sponsored loans, and scholarships/grants available. Support available to part-time students. Financial award application deadline: 6/1; financial award applicants required to submit FAFSA. *Faculty research:* International trade and law, mediation/arbitration, land use and urban planning, antitrust law, entertainment and media law. *Unit head:* Susan Westerberg Prager, Dean, 213-738-6710, Fax: 213-383-1688. *Application contact:* Lisa Gear, Assistant Dean of Admissions, 213-738-6834, Fax: 213-738-6899, E-mail: admissions@swlaw.edu.
Website: http://www.swlaw.edu

University of New Hampshire, School of Law, Concord, NH 03301. Offers business law (JD); commerce and technology (LL M, MCT, Diploma); criminal law (JD); intellectual property (LL M, MIP, JD, Diploma), including patent law (JD), trademarks and copyright (JD); international criminal law and justice (LL M, MICLJ); litigation (JD); public interest and social justice (JD); sports and entertainment law (JD); JD/LL M; JD/MBA; JD/MIP; JD/MPP; JD/MSW. *Accreditation:* ABA. *Program availability:* Part-time, 100% online, limited residential. *Degree requirements:* For doctorate, comprehensive exam. *Entrance requirements:* For doctorate, LSAT. Additional exam requirements/recommendations for international students: Required—TOEFL (minimum score 600 paper-based; 100 iBT), minimum TOEFL iBT score of 80 (for master's programs). Electronic applications accepted. *Expenses:* Contact institution. *Faculty research:* Intellectual property, health law and policy, sports and entertainment law, patent law, trademarks and copyright.

ACADEMIC AND PROFESSIONAL PROGRAMS IN LIBRARY AND INFORMATION STUDIES

Section 28
Library and Information Studies

This section contains a directory of institutions offering graduate work in library and information studies, followed by in-depth entries submitted by institutions that chose to prepare detailed program descriptions. Additional information about programs listed in the directory but not augmented by an in-depth entry may be obtained by writing directly to the dean of a graduate school or chair of a department at the address given in the directory.

For programs offering related work, see also in this book *Education*. In another guide in this series:

Graduate Programs in Engineering & Applied Sciences
See *Computer Science and Information Technology*

CONTENTS

Program Directories

Archives/Archival Administration

Claremont Graduate University, Graduate Programs, School of Arts and Humanities, Department of History, Claremont, CA 91711-6160. Offers Africana history (Certificate); American studies and U.S. history (MA, PhD); archival studies (MA); early modern studies (MA, PhD); European studies (MA, PhD); oral history (MA, PhD); MBA/MA; MBA/PhD. Terminal master's awarded for partial completion of doctoral program. *Entrance requirements:* For master's and doctorate, GRE General Test. Additional exam requirements/recommendations for international students: Required—TOEFL (minimum score 75 iBT). Electronic applications accepted. *Faculty research:* Intellectual and social history, cultural studies, gender studies, Western history, Chicano history.

Clayton State University, School of Graduate Studies, College of Information and Mathematical Sciences, Program in Archival Studies, Morrow, GA 30260-0285. Offers MAS. *Program availability:* Online learning. *Entrance requirements:* For master's, GRE, 2 official transcripts; 3 letters of recommendation; statement of purpose; essay. Additional exam requirements/recommendations for international students: Required—TOEFL (minimum score 550 paper-based). Electronic applications accepted. *Expenses: Tuition, area resident:* Full-time $3528; part-time $2352 per year. Tuition, state resident: full-time $3528; part-time $2352 per year. Tuition, nonresident: full-time $13,176; part-time $8784 per year. *International tuition:* $13,176 full-time. *Required fees:* $1474; $1474 per unit. Tuition and fees vary according to campus/location and program.

Columbia University, School of Professional Studies, Program in Information and Archive Management, New York, NY 10027. Offers MS. *Program availability:* Part-time. *Entrance requirements:* For master's, minimum undergraduate GPA of 3.0. Additional exam requirements/recommendations for international students: Required—American Language Program placement test. Electronic applications accepted. *Faculty research:* Library science technology, information systems.

Drexel University, Westphal College of Media Arts and Design, Program in Museum Leadership, Philadelphia, PA 19104-2875. Offers MS. Offered in partnership with the Academy of Natural Sciences of Drexel University. *Program availability:* Part-time, online learning. *Degree requirements:* For master's, practicum.

East Tennessee State University, School of Graduate Studies, School of Continuing Studies and Academic Outreach, Johnson City, TN 37614. Offers archival studies (Postbaccalaureate Certificate); liberal studies (MALS); reinforcing education through artistic learning (Postbaccalaureate Certificate); strategic leadership (MPS); training and development (MPS). *Program availability:* Part-time, online learning. *Degree requirements:* For master's, comprehensive exam, thesis (for some programs), professional project. *Entrance requirements:* For master's, GRE General Test, minimum GPA of 2.75, professional portfolio, three letters of recommendation, interview, writing sample; for Postbaccalaureate Certificate, minimum GPA of 2.5, three letters of recommendation, interview. Additional exam requirements/recommendations for international students: Required—TOEFL (minimum score 550 paper-based; 79 iBT). Electronic applications accepted. *Faculty research:* Appalachian studies, women's and gender studies, interdisciplinary theory, regional and Southern cultures.

Middle Tennessee State University, College of Graduate Studies, College of Liberal Arts, Department of History, Murfreesboro, TN 37132. Offers archival management (Graduate Certificate); history (MA); public history (PhD). *Program availability:* Part-time, evening/weekend, online learning. *Degree requirements:* For master's, one foreign language, comprehensive exam, thesis optional; for doctorate, one foreign language, comprehensive exam, thesis/dissertation. *Entrance requirements:* For master's and doctorate, GRE. Additional exam requirements/recommendations for international students: Required—TOEFL (minimum score 525 paper-based; 71 iBT) or IELTS (minimum score 6). Electronic applications accepted.

Montclair State University, The Graduate School, College of the Arts, Program in Fine Art, Montclair, NJ 07043-1624. Offers museum management (MA); studio (MA). *Accreditation:* NASAD. *Program availability:* Part-time, evening/weekend. *Degree requirements:* For master's, project. *Entrance requirements:* For master's, GRE or MAT, 2 letters of recommendation, essay. Electronic applications accepted.

New York University, Graduate School of Arts and Science, Department of History, New York, NY 10012-1019. Offers African diaspora (PhD); African history (PhD); archival management (Advanced Certificate); Atlantic history (PhD); French studies/ history (PhD); Hebrew and Judaic studies/history (PhD); history (MA, PhD), including Europe (PhD), Latin America and the Caribbean (PhD), United States (PhD), women's history (MA); Middle Eastern history (MA); Middle Eastern studies/history (PhD); public history (Advanced Certificate); world history (MA); JD/MA; MA/Advanced Certificate. *Program availability:* Part-time. *Students:* 117 full-time (64 women), 23 part-time (13 women); includes 31 minority (13 Black or African American, non-Hispanic/Latino; 1 American Indian or Alaska Native, non-Hispanic/Latino; 2 Asian, non-Hispanic/Latino; 10 Hispanic/Latino; 5 Two or more races, non-Hispanic/Latino), 40 international. Average age 28. 301 applicants, 36% accepted, 40 enrolled. In 2018, 12 master's, 14 doctorates, 1 other advanced degree awarded. Terminal master's awarded for partial completion of doctoral program. *Degree requirements:* For master's, seminar paper; for doctorate, one foreign language, thesis/dissertation, oral and written exams; for Advanced Certificate, internship. *Entrance requirements:* For master's, GRE General Test, minimum GPA of 3.0, writing sample; for doctorate, GRE. Additional exam requirements/recommendations for international students: Required—TOEFL. *Application deadline:* For fall admission, 12/18 for domestic and international students. Application fee: $110. *Financial support:* Fellowships, research assistantships, teaching assistantships, career-related internships or fieldwork, Federal Work-Study, institutionally sponsored loans, scholarships/grants, health care benefits, and unspecified assistantships available. Financial award application deadline: 12/18; financial award applicants required to submit FAFSA. *Faculty research:* African, East Asian, medieval, early modern, and modern European history; U.S. history; African and African diaspora; Latin American history; Atlantic world. *Unit head:* Barbara Weinstein, Chair, 212-998-8600, Fax: 212-995-4017, E-mail: history.admissions@nyu.edu. *Application contact:* Stepfanos Geroulanos, Director of Graduate Studies, 212-998-8600, Fax: 212-995-4017, E-mail: history.admissions@nyu.edu.
Website: http://history.as.nyu.edu/

New York University, Tisch School of the Arts and Graduate School of Arts and Science, Department of Cinema Studies, New York, NY 10002. Offers cinema studies (MA, PhD); moving image archiving and preservation (MA). *Faculty:* 18 full-time (9 women), 29 part-time/adjunct (17 women). *Students:* 86 full-time (60 women); includes 49 minority (5 Black or African American, non-Hispanic/Latino; 35 Asian, non-Hispanic/Latino; 8 Hispanic/Latino; 1 Two or more races, non-Hispanic/Latino), 25 international. Average age 29. 203 applicants, 48% accepted, 42 enrolled. In 2018, 43 master's, 8 doctorates awarded. *Degree requirements:* For master's, comprehensive exam; for doctorate, one foreign language, thesis/dissertation, 3 comprehensive exams. *Entrance requirements:* For master's, sample of written work; for doctorate, master's degree,

writing sample. Additional exam requirements/recommendations for international students: Required—TOEFL, IELTS, TOEFL or IELTS. *Application deadline:* For fall admission, 12/1 for domestic and international students. Application fee: $65. Electronic applications accepted. *Expenses:* Per point for MA degree $1850. Fall 2019. Accepted PhD students are fully covered by a 7 year fellowship. *Financial support:* In 2018–19, 72 students received support, including 45 fellowships with full and partial tuition reimbursements available, 4 teaching assistantships with full tuition reimbursements available; Federal Work-Study, scholarships/grants, health care benefits, and tuition waivers (full and partial) also available. Support available to part-time students. Financial award application deadline: 2/15; financial award applicants required to submit FAFSA. *Faculty research:* History and aesthetics of American, European, and Third World cinemas; theory of film and the moving image; cultural studies; gay and lesbian media; new media. *Unit head:* Dr. Anna McCarthy, Chair, 212-998-1600. *Application contact:* Joseph Miserendino, Director of Graduate Admissions, 212-998-1918, Fax: 212-995-4060, E-mail: tisch.gradadmissions@nyu.edu.
Website: http://tisch.nyu.edu/cinema-studies

New York University, Tisch School of the Arts, Program in Moving Image Archiving and Preservation, New York, NY 10012. Offers MA. *Faculty:* 3 full-time (1 woman), 9 part-time/adjunct (7 women). *Students:* 8 full-time (7 women), 1 (woman) part-time; includes 6 minority (2 Black or African American, non-Hispanic/Latino; 2 Asian, non-Hispanic/Latino; 1 Hispanic/Latino; 1 Two or more races, non-Hispanic/Latino), 3 international. Average age 29. 33 applicants, 70% accepted, 8 enrolled. In 2018, 16 master's awarded. *Degree requirements:* For master's, thesis. *Entrance requirements:* Additional exam requirements/recommendations for international students: Required—TOEFL. *Application deadline:* For fall admission, 1/15 for domestic students. Application fee: $60. Electronic applications accepted. *Expenses:* Contact institution. *Financial support:* In 2018–19, 8 students received support, including 8 fellowships (averaging $7,000 per year); Federal Work-Study, institutionally sponsored loans, scholarships/grants, tuition waivers (partial), and unspecified assistantships also available. Financial award application deadline: 1/15; financial award applicants required to submit FAFSA. *Unit head:* Juana Suárez, Director, Associate Arts Professor, 212-998-1618, E-mail: tisch.preservation@nyu.edu. *Application contact:* Jessica Cayer, Academic Program Manager, 212-998-1618, Fax: 212-995-4060, E-mail: tisch.preservation@nyu.edu.
Website: https://tisch.nyu.edu/cinema-studies/miap

Queens College of the City University of New York, Division of Social Sciences, Graduate School of Library and Information Studies, Queens, NY 11367-1597. Offers archives and preservation of cultural materials (AC); children's and young adult services in the public library (AC); librarianship (AC); library science (MLS); school library media specialist (MLS). *Accreditation:* ALA (one or more programs are accredited). *Program availability:* Part-time, evening/weekend. *Faculty:* 9 full-time (5 women), 13 part-time/adjunct (9 women). *Students:* 26 full-time (17 women), 309 part-time (231 women); includes 123 minority (39 Black or African American, non-Hispanic/Latino; 1 American Indian or Alaska Native, non-Hispanic/Latino; 17 Asian, non-Hispanic/Latino; 56 Hispanic/Latino; 1 Native Hawaiian or other Pacific Islander, non-Hispanic/Latino; 9 Two or more races, non-Hispanic/Latino), 4 international. Average age 32. In 2018, 88 master's, 1 other advanced degree awarded. *Degree requirements:* For master's, thesis; for AC, thesis optional. *Entrance requirements:* For master's, minimum GPA of 3.0; for AC, master's degree or equivalent. Additional exam requirements/recommendations for international students: Required—TOEFL, IELTS. *Application deadline:* For fall admission, 4/1 for domestic students; for spring admission, 11/1 for domestic students. Applications are processed on a rolling basis. Application fee: $125. Electronic applications accepted. *Financial support:* Career-related internships or fieldwork and unspecified assistantships available. Financial award application deadline: 4/1; financial award applicants required to submit FAFSA. *Unit head:* Kwong Bor Ng, Director/Chair, 718-997-3790, E-mail: kwongbor.ng@qc.cuny.edu. *Application contact:* Elizabeth D'Amico-Ramirez, Assistant Director of Graduate Admissions, 718-997-5203, E-mail: elizabeth.damicoramirez@qc.cuny.edu.

The University of British Columbia, Faculty of Arts, School of Library, Archival and Information Studies, Master of Archival Studies Program, Vancouver, BC V6T 1Z1, Canada. Offers MAS. *Degree requirements:* For master's, thesis optional. *Entrance requirements:* For master's, minimum B+ average or minimum GPA of 3.3 in undergraduate upper-division courses. Additional exam requirements/recommendations for international students: Required—TOEFL. Electronic applications accepted. *Expenses:* Contact institution. *Faculty research:* Diplomatic, electronic record, appraisal, descriptive standards, preservation.

The University of British Columbia, Faculty of Arts, School of Library, Archival and Information Studies, PhD Program in Library, Archival and Information Studies, Vancouver, BC V6T 1Z1, Canada. Offers PhD. *Degree requirements:* For doctorate, thesis/dissertation. *Entrance requirements:* For doctorate, GRE, minimum GPA of 3.3 in MAS or MLIS. Additional exam requirements/recommendations for international students: Required—TOEFL. Electronic applications accepted. *Expenses:* Contact institution. *Faculty research:* Computer systems/database design; library and archival management; archival description and organization; children's literature and youth services; interactive information retrieval.

University of California, Los Angeles, Graduate Division, Graduate School of Education and Information Studies, Department of Information Studies, Los Angeles, CA 90095-1521. Offers archival studies (MLIS); informatics (MLIS); information studies (PhD); library and information science (Certificate); library studies (MLIS); moving image archive studies (MA); rare books, print and visual culture (MLIS); MBA/MLIS; MLIS/MA. *Accreditation:* ALA (one or more programs are accredited). Terminal master's awarded for partial completion of doctoral program. *Degree requirements:* For master's, thesis or alternative, professional portfolio; for doctorate, thesis/dissertation, oral and written qualifying exams. *Entrance requirements:* For master's, GRE General Test, previous course work in statistics; for doctorate, GRE General Test, previous course work in statistics, 2 samples of research writing in English. Additional exam requirements/recommendations for international students: Required—TOEFL (minimum score 560 paper-based; 87 iBT), IELTS (minimum score 7). Electronic applications accepted. *Faculty research:* Digital libraries, archives and electronic records, interface design, cultural informatics, preservation/conservation, access.

University of California, Los Angeles, Graduate Division, School of Theater, Film and Television, Interdepartmental Program in Moving Image Archive Studies, Los Angeles, CA 90095. Offers MA. *Degree requirements:* For master's, comprehensive exam, thesis. *Entrance requirements:* For master's, bachelor's degree; minimum undergraduate GPA of 3.0 (or its equivalent if letter grade system not used); writing sample. Additional exam requirements/recommendations for international students: Required—TOEFL. Electronic applications accepted.

University of California, Riverside, Graduate Division, Department of History, Riverside, CA 92521-0102. Offers archival management (MA); history (PhD). *Program availability:* Part-time. Terminal master's awarded for partial completion of doctoral program. *Degree requirements:* For master's, one foreign language, comprehensive exam, internship report and oral exams, or thesis; for doctorate, 2 foreign languages, thesis/dissertation, qualifying exams. *Entrance requirements:* For master's and doctorate, GRE General Test, minimum GPA of 3.2. Additional exam requirements/recommendations for international students: Required—TOEFL (minimum score 550 paper-based; 80 iBT). Electronic applications accepted. *Faculty research:* Native American history, United States, public history, Europe, Latin America.

University of Manitoba, Faculty of Graduate Studies, Faculty of Arts, Department of History, Winnipeg, MB R3T 2N2, Canada. Offers archival studies (MA); history (MA, PhD). MA offered jointly with The University of Winnipeg. *Degree requirements:* For master's, thesis; for doctorate, one foreign language, thesis/dissertation.

University of Massachusetts Boston, College of Liberal Arts, Program in History, Boston, MA 02125-3393. Offers archival methods (MA). *Program availability:* Part-time, evening/weekend. *Faculty:* 16 full-time (10 women), 9 part-time/adjunct (5 women). *Students:* 16 full-time (9 women), 65 part-time (36 women); includes 8 minority (3 Black or African American, non-Hispanic/Latino; 1 Asian, non-Hispanic/Latino; 4 Hispanic/Latino), 1 international. Average age 35. 55 applicants, 91% accepted, 29 enrolled. In 2018, 18 master's awarded. *Entrance requirements:* For master's, minimum GPA of 2.75. *Application deadline:* For fall admission, 1/15 for domestic students. Application fee: $60 ($100 for international students). Electronic applications accepted. *Expenses: Tuition, area resident:* Full-time $17,896. Tuition, state resident: full-time $17,896. Tuition, nonresident: full-time $34,932. *International tuition:* $34,932 full-time. *Required fees:* $355. *Financial support:* Research assistantships, teaching assistantships, career-related internships or fieldwork, Federal Work-Study, and unspecified assistantships available. Support available to part-time students. Financial award application deadline: 3/1; financial award applicants required to submit FAFSA. *Faculty research:* European intellectual history, American labor and social history in nineteenth century, colonial American Revolution, Afro-American Cold War. *Unit head:* Dr. Elizabeth McCahill, Associate Professor of History, 617-287.6864, E-mail: Elizabeth.McCahill@umb.edu. *Application contact:* Graduate Admissions Coordinator, 617-287-6400, Fax: 617-287-6236, E-mail: graduate.admissions@umb.edu.

University of Oklahoma, College of Arts and Sciences, School of Library and Information Studies, Norman, OK 73019. Offers archival studies (Graduate Certificate); digital humanities (Graduate Certificate); information studies (PhD); library and information studies (MLIS); M Ed/MLIS; MBA/MLIS. *Accreditation:* ALA (one or more programs are accredited). *Program availability:* Part-time, evening/weekend, 100% online, blended/hybrid learning. *Faculty:* 7 full-time (6 women), 2 part-time/adjunct (1 woman). *Students:* 63 full-time (53 women), 133 part-time (108 women); includes 48 minority (8 Black or African American, non-Hispanic/Latino; 4 American Indian or Alaska Native, non-Hispanic/Latino; 5 Asian, non-Hispanic/Latino; 14 Hispanic/Latino; 1 Native Hawaiian or other Pacific Islander, non-Hispanic/Latino; 16 Two or more races, non-Hispanic/Latino), 2 international. Average age 32. 60 applicants, 93% accepted, 41 enrolled. In 2018, 54 master's, 9 other advanced degrees awarded. Terminal master's awarded for partial completion of doctoral program. *Degree requirements:* For master's, comprehensive exam (for some programs), thesis optional; for doctorate, comprehensive exam, thesis/dissertation. *Entrance requirements:* For master's, three letters of recommendation, personal statement, resume, transcript; for doctorate, GRE, three letters of recommendation, personal statement, resume, writing sample; for Graduate Certificate, transcripts, personal statement (for some certificates), letter of recommendation (for some certificates). Additional exam requirements/recommendations for international students: Required—TOEFL (minimum score 79 iBT) or IELTS (minimum score 6.5). *Application deadline:* Applications are processed on a rolling basis. Application fee: $50 ($100 for international students). Electronic applications accepted. *Expenses:* Tuition, state resident: full-time $5683.20; part-time $236.80 per credit hour. Tuition, nonresident: full-time $20,342; part-time $847.60 per credit hour. *International tuition:* $20,342.40 full-time. *Required fees:* $2894.20; $110.05 per credit hour. $126.50 per semester. Tuition and fees vary according to course load and program. *Financial support:* Research assistantships, teaching assistantships, scholarships/grants, health care benefits, and unspecified assistantships available. Financial award application deadline: 6/1; financial award applicants required to submit FAFSA. *Faculty research:* Family and youth technology in libraries, consumer health information, text mining, big data analytics. *Unit head:* Dr. Susan K. Burke, Director, 405-

325-3921, E-mail: sburke@ou.edu. *Application contact:* Sarah Connelly, Admissions and Student Services Coordinator, 405-325-3921, E-mail: sarahee@ou.edu.
Website: http://slis.ou.edu

University of Rochester, School of Arts and Sciences, Program in Photographic Preservation and Collections Management, Rochester, NY 14627. Offers MA. Program offered jointly with George Eastman Museum. *Students:* 7 full-time (5 women); includes 1 minority (Black or African American, non-Hispanic/Latino), 1 international. Average age 30. 10 applicants, 80% accepted, 4 enrolled. In 2018, 5 master's awarded. *Degree requirements:* For master's, essay (counts as qualifying exam). *Entrance requirements:* For master's, writing sample, transcripts, three letters of recommendation, one- to two-page statement of purpose. Additional exam requirements/recommendations for international students: Required—TOEFL. *Application deadline:* For fall admission, 1/15 for domestic and international students. Application fee: $60. Electronic applications accepted. *Expenses: Tuition:* Full-time $52,974; part-time $1654 per credit hour. *Required fees:* $612. One-time fee: $30 part-time. Tuition and fees vary according to campus/location and program. *Financial support:* Tuition waivers (partial) available. Financial award application deadline: 1/15. *Unit head:* Joan Saab, PPCM Program Co-Director and Associate Professor of Art History, 585-275-7922, E-mail: joan.saab@rochester.edu. *Application contact:* Martin Collier, Administrator, 585-275-7451, E-mail: marty.collier@rochester.edu.
Website: https://www.sas.rochester.edu/ppc/

University of South Carolina, The Graduate School, College of Arts and Sciences, Department of History, Program in Public History, Columbia, SC 29208. Offers archive management (MA); historic preservation (MA); museum administration (MA); museum management (Certificate); MLIS/MA. *Degree requirements:* For master's, one foreign language, thesis, internship. *Entrance requirements:* For master's, GRE General Test, writing sample. Additional exam requirements/recommendations for international students: Required—TOEFL. Electronic applications accepted. *Faculty research:* Museum studies, historic preservation, archives administration.

Wayne State University, School of Information Sciences, Detroit, MI 48202. Offers archival administration (Graduate Certificate); information management (MS, Graduate Certificate); library and information science (MLIS, Graduate Certificate, Spec); public library services to children and young adults (Graduate Certificate); MLIS/MA. WSU History Department. *Accreditation:* ALA (one or more programs are accredited). *Program availability:* Part-time, evening/weekend, 100% online, blended/hybrid learning. *Faculty:* 12 full-time (9 women), 17 part-time/adjunct (12 women). *Students:* 85 full-time (74 women), 316 part-time (258 women); includes 77 minority (42 Black or African American, non-Hispanic/Latino; 2 American Indian or Alaska Native, non-Hispanic/Latino; 3 Asian, non-Hispanic/Latino; 19 Hispanic/Latino; 1 Native Hawaiian or other Pacific Islander, non-Hispanic/Latino; 10 Two or more races, non-Hispanic/Latino), 1 international. Average age 33. 258 applicants, 60% accepted, 100 enrolled. In 2018, 149 master's, 34 other advanced degrees awarded. *Degree requirements:* For master's and other advanced degree, e-portfolio. *Entrance requirements:* For master's, GRE or MAT (if undergraduate GPA is between 2.5 and 2.99), minimum undergraduate GPA of 3.0 or graduate degree, personal statement, resume or curriculum vitae; for other advanced degree, GRE or MAT (if undergraduate GPA is between 2.5 and 2.99), minimum undergraduate GPA of 3.0 or graduate degree, personal statement, resume or curriculum vitae, MLIS (for specialist certificate). Additional exam requirements/recommendations for international students: Required—TOEFL (minimum score 550 paper-based; 79 iBT); Recommended—IELTS (minimum score 6.5), TWE (minimum score 5.5). *Application deadline:* For fall admission, 7/1 for domestic students, 5/1 priority date for international students; for winter admission, 10/1 priority date for domestic students, 9/1 priority date for international students; for spring admission, 2/1 priority date for domestic students, 1/1 priority date for international students. Applications are processed on a rolling basis. Application fee: $50. Electronic applications accepted. *Expenses:* 15,000/year. *Financial support:* In 2018–19, 133 students received support. Fellowships with tuition reimbursements available, scholarships/grants, health care benefits, and unspecified assistantships available. Support available to part-time students. Financial award applicants required to submit FAFSA. *Faculty research:* Library services, information management issues, digital content management, library/community engagement, archives and preservation. *Unit head:* Dr. Jon Cawthorne, Dean, 313-577-4020, E-mail: jon.cawthorne@wayne.edu. *Application contact:* Academic Services Officer II, 313-577-1825, E-mail: asklis@wayne.edu.
Website: http://slis.wayne.edu/

Information Studies

The Catholic University of America, School of Arts and Sciences, Department of Library and Information Science, Washington, DC 20064. Offers MSLS, Certificate, JD/MSLS, MSLS/MA, MSLS/MS. *Accreditation:* ALA (one or more programs are accredited). *Program availability:* Part-time. *Faculty:* 6 full-time (all women), 5 part-time/adjunct (0 women). *Students:* 19 full-time (17 women), 72 part-time (55 women); includes 26 minority (13 Black or African American, non-Hispanic/Latino; 2 Asian, non-Hispanic/Latino; 4 Hispanic/Latino; 7 Two or more races, non-Hispanic/Latino), 1 international. Average age 33. 67 applicants, 90% accepted, 30 enrolled. In 2018, 26 master's awarded. *Degree requirements:* For master's, comprehensive exam. *Entrance requirements:* For master's, statement of purpose, official copies of academic transcripts, three letters of recommendation, interview. Additional exam requirements/recommendations for international students: Required—TOEFL (minimum score 550 paper-based; 80 iBT). *Application deadline:* For fall admission, 7/15 priority date for domestic students, 7/1 for international students; for spring admission, 11/15 priority date for domestic students, 11/1 for international students. Applications are processed on a rolling basis. Application fee: $55. Electronic applications accepted. *Expenses:* Contact institution. *Financial support:* Fellowships, research assistantships, teaching assistantships, Federal Work-Study, scholarships/grants, tuition waivers (full and partial), and unspecified assistantships available. Financial award application deadline: 2/1; financial award applicants required to submit FAFSA. *Faculty research:* Digital collections, library and information science education, information design and architecture, information system design and evaluation. *Unit head:* Dr. Youngok Choi, Chair, 202-319-5877, E-mail: choiy@cua.edu. *Application contact:* Dr. Steven Brown, Director of Graduate Admissions, 202-319-5057, Fax: 202-319-6533, E-mail: cua-admissions@cua.edu.
Website: http://lis.cua.edu/

Central Connecticut State University, School of Graduate Studies, College of Liberal Arts and Social Sciences, Department of Design, New Britain, CT 06050-4010. Offers information design (MA). *Program availability:* Part-time, evening/weekend. *Faculty:* 1

full-time (0 women), 1 (woman) part-time/adjunct. *Students:* 10 full-time (5 women), 6 part-time (5 women); includes 3 minority (1 Black or African American, non-Hispanic/Latino; 1 Asian, non-Hispanic/Latino; 1 Two or more races, non-Hispanic/Latino). Average age 28. 4 applicants, 100% accepted, 2 enrolled. In 2018, 1 master's awarded. *Degree requirements:* For master's, thesis or alternative, research project. *Entrance requirements:* For master's, portfolio, minimum undergraduate GPA of 3.0, essay. Additional exam requirements/recommendations for international students: Required—TOEFL (minimum score 550 paper-based; 79 iBT); Recommended—IELTS (minimum score 6.5). *Application deadline:* For fall admission, 6/1 for domestic students, 5/1 for international students; for spring admission, 11/1 for domestic and international students. Applications are processed on a rolling basis. Application fee: $50. Electronic applications accepted. *Expenses: Tuition, area resident:* Full-time $7027; part-time $388 per credit. Tuition, state resident: full-time $9750; part-time $388 per credit. Tuition, nonresident: full-time $18,102; part-time $388 per credit. *International tuition:* $18,102 full-time. *Required fees:* $266 per semester. *Financial support:* In 2018–19, 4 students received support. Career-related internships or fieldwork, Federal Work-Study, scholarships/grants, and unspecified assistantships available. Support available to part-time students. Financial award application deadline: 3/1; financial award applicants required to submit FAFSA. *Unit head:* Dr. Eleanor Thornton, Chair, 860-832-2564, E-mail: thorntone@ccsu.edu. *Application contact:* Patricia Gardner, Associate Director of Graduate Studies, 860-832-2350, Fax: 860-832-2362.
Website: http://www.design.ccsu.edu/

Columbia University, School of Professional Studies, Program in Information and Archive Management, New York, NY 10027. Offers MS. *Program availability:* Part-time. *Entrance requirements:* For master's, minimum undergraduate GPA of 3.0. Additional exam requirements/recommendations for international students: Required—American Language Program placement test. Electronic applications accepted. *Faculty research:* Library science technology, information systems.

Information Studies

Cornell University, Graduate School, Graduate Fields of Arts and Sciences, Field of Information Science, Ithaca, NY 14853. Offers cognition (PhD); human computer interaction (PhD); information science (PhD); information systems (PhD); social aspects of information (PhD). *Degree requirements:* For doctorate, comprehensive exam, thesis/dissertation. *Entrance requirements:* For doctorate, GRE General Test, 3 letters of recommendation. Additional exam requirements/recommendations for international students: Required—TOEFL (minimum score 550 paper-based; 77 iBT). Electronic applications accepted. *Faculty research:* Digital libraries, game theory, data mining, human-computer interaction, computational linguistics.

Dalhousie University, Faculty of Management, School of Information Management, Halifax, NS B3H 3J5, Canada. Offers MIM, MLIS, LL B/MLIS, MBA/MLIS, MLIS/MPA, MLIS/MREM. *Accreditation:* ALA (one or more programs are accredited). *Program availability:* Part-time. *Degree requirements:* For master's, one foreign language, thesis optional. *Entrance requirements:* For master's, resume, interview. Additional exam requirements/recommendations for international students: Required—TOEFL, IELTS, CANTEST, CAEL, or Michigan English Language Assessment Battery. Electronic applications accepted. *Faculty research:* Information-seeking behavior, electronic text design, browsing in digital environments, information diffusion among scientists.

Dominican University, School of Information Studies, River Forest, IL 60305-1099. Offers information management (MSIM); knowledge management (Certificate); library and information science (MLIS, MPS, PhD); special studies (CSS); MBA/MLIS; MLIS/MA. MLIS/M Div offered jointly with McCormick Theological Seminary, MLIS/MA with Loyola University Chicago, MLIS/MM with Northwestern University. *Accreditation:* ALA (one or more programs are accredited). *Program availability:* Part-time, evening/weekend, 100% online, blended/hybrid learning. *Degree requirements:* For doctorate, thesis/dissertation. *Entrance requirements:* For master's, minimum GPA of 3.0, GRE General Test, or MAT; for doctorate, MLIS or related MA, minimum GPA of 3.0, GRE General Test, or MAT. Additional exam requirements/recommendations for international students: Required—TOEFL. *Expenses:* Contact institution. *Faculty research:* Productivity and the information environment, bibliometrics, library history, subject access, library materials and services for children.

Lock Haven University of Pennsylvania, The Stephen Poorman College of Business, Information Systems, and Human Services, Lock Haven, PA 17745-2390. Offers clinical mental health counseling (MS); sport science (MS). *Program availability:* Online learning. *Degree requirements:* For master's, thesis. *Entrance requirements:* For master's, minimum undergraduate GPA of 3.0. Additional exam requirements/recommendations for international students: Required—TOEFL. Electronic applications accepted.

Louisiana State University and Agricultural & Mechanical College, Graduate School, College of Human Sciences and Education, School of Library and Information Science, Baton Rouge, LA 70803. Offers MLIS. *Accreditation:* ALA.

Mansfield University of Pennsylvania, Graduate Studies, Program in School Library and Information Technologies, Mansfield, PA 16933. Offers library science (M Ed). *Program availability:* Part-time, evening/weekend, online learning. *Degree requirements:* For master's, comprehensive exam, thesis optional. *Entrance requirements:* For master's, minimum GPA of 3.0. Additional exam requirements/recommendations for international students: Required—TOEFL (minimum score 550 paper-based). Electronic applications accepted. *Expenses:* Contact institution.

McGill University, Faculty of Graduate and Postdoctoral Studies, Faculty of Education, School of Information Studies, Montréal, QC H3A 2T5, Canada. Offers MLIS, PhD, Certificate, Diploma. *Accreditation:* ALA (one or more programs are accredited).

Metropolitan State University, College of Management, St. Paul, MN 55106-5000. Offers business administration (MBA, DBA); business analytics (Graduate Certificate); database administration (Graduate Certificate); global supply chain management (Graduate Certificate); information assurance security (Graduate Certificate); management information systems (MMIS); MIS generalist (Graduate Certificate); MIS systems analysis and design (Graduate Certificate); project management (Graduate Certificate). *Program availability:* Part-time, evening/weekend. *Degree requirements:* For master's, thesis optional, computer language (MMIS). *Entrance requirements:* For master's, GMAT (for MBA), resume. Additional exam requirements/recommendations for international students: Required—TOEFL (minimum score 550 paper-based). Electronic applications accepted. *Faculty research:* Yugoslav economic system, workers' cooperatives, participative management and job enrichment, global business systems.

Monmouth University, Graduate Studies, Program in Computer Science, West Long Branch, NJ 07764-1898. Offers MS. *Program availability:* Part-time, evening/weekend. *Faculty:* 3 full-time (0 women), 5 part-time/adjunct (0 women). *Students:* 30 full-time (10 women), 20 part-time (3 women); includes 6 minority (2 Black or African American, non-Hispanic/Latino; 3 Asian, non-Hispanic/Latino; 1 Hispanic/Latino), 22 international. Average age 28. In 2018, 18 master's awarded. *Degree requirements:* For master's, thesis (for some programs), practicum. *Entrance requirements:* For master's, minimum GPA of 3.0 in major, 2.75 overall; two letters of recommendation; calculus I and II with minimum C grade; two semesters of computer programming within past five years with minimum B grade; undergraduate degree in major that requires substantial component of software development and/or business administration. Additional exam requirements/recommendations for international students: Required—TOEFL (minimum score 550 paper-based, 79 iBT), IELTS (minimum score 6), Michigan English Language Assessment Battery (minimum score 77) or Certificate of Advanced English (minimum score 160). *Application deadline:* For fall admission, 7/15 priority date for domestic students, 6/1 for international students; for spring admission, 12/1 priority date for domestic students, 11/1 for international students; for summer admission, 5/1 for domestic students. Applications are processed on a rolling basis. Application fee: $50. Electronic applications accepted. *Expenses: Tuition:* Part-time $1233 per credit. *Required fees:* $178 per term. *Financial support:* In 2018–19, 41 students received support. Institutionally sponsored loans, scholarships/grants, and unspecified assistantships available. Support available to part-time students. Financial award applicants required to submit FAFSA. *Faculty research:* Databases, natural language processing, protocols, performance analysis, communications networks (systems), cybersecurity. *Unit head:* Dr. Jiacun Wang, Program Director, 732-571-7501, Fax: 732-263-5202, E-mail: jwang@monmouth.edu. *Application contact:* Laurie Kuhn, Associate Director of Graduate Admission, 732-571-3452, Fax: 732-263-5123, E-mail: gradadm@monmouth.edu.
Website: https://www.monmouth.edu/graduate/ms-computer-science/

North Carolina Central University, School of Library and Information Sciences, Durham, NC 27707-3129. Offers MIS, MLS. *Accreditation:* ALA (one or more programs are accredited). *Program availability:* Part-time, evening/weekend. *Degree requirements:* For master's, one foreign language, thesis, research paper, or project. *Entrance requirements:* For master's, GRE, 90 hours in liberal arts. Additional exam requirements/recommendations for international students: Required—TOEFL.

Pratt Institute, School of Information, New York, NY 10011. Offers MS, Adv C, JD/MS, MS/MFA. *Accreditation:* ALA. *Program availability:* Part-time. *Faculty:* 10 full-time (8 women), 21 part-time/adjunct (11 women). *Students:* Average age 30. 303 applicants, 75% accepted, 67 enrolled. In 2018, 59 master's, 1 other advanced degree awarded. *Entrance requirements:* For degree, master's degree in library and information science. Additional exam requirements/recommendations for international students: Required—TOEFL (minimum score 600 paper-based; 100 iBT). *Application deadline:* For fall admission, 1/5 for domestic and international students; for spring admission, 10/1 for domestic and international students. Applications are processed on a rolling basis. Application fee: $50 ($90 for international students). Electronic applications accepted. *Expenses:* Contact institution. *Financial support:* Career-related internships or fieldwork, Federal Work-Study, institutionally sponsored loans, scholarships/grants, health care benefits, and unspecified assistantships available. Support available to part-time students. Financial award application deadline: 2/1; financial award applicants required to submit FAFSA. *Faculty research:* Development of urban libraries and information centers, medical and law librarianship, information management. *Unit head:* Anthony Cocciolo, Interim Dean, 212-647-7702, Fax: 212-367-2492, E-mail: acocciol@pratt.edu. *Application contact:* Natalie Capannelli, Director of Graduate Admissions, 718-636-3551, Fax: 718-399-4242, E-mail: ncapanne@pratt.edu.
Website: https://www.pratt.edu/academics/information/

Queens College of the City University of New York, Division of Social Sciences, Graduate School of Library and Information Studies, Queens, NY 11367-1597. Offers archives and preservation of cultural materials (AC); children's and young adult services in the public library (AC); librarianship (AC); library science (MLS); school library media specialist (MLS). *Accreditation:* ALA (one or more programs are accredited). *Program availability:* Part-time, evening/weekend. *Faculty:* 9 full-time (5 women), 13 part-time/adjunct (9 women). *Students:* 26 full-time (17 women), 309 part-time (231 women); includes 123 minority (39 Black or African American, non-Hispanic/Latino; 1 American Indian or Alaska Native, non-Hispanic/Latino; 17 Asian, non-Hispanic/Latino; 56 Hispanic/Latino; 1 Native Hawaiian or other Pacific Islander, non-Hispanic/Latino; 9 Two or more races, non-Hispanic/Latino), 4 international. Average age 32. In 2018, 88 master's, 1 other advanced degree awarded. *Degree requirements:* For master's, thesis; for AC, thesis optional. *Entrance requirements:* For master's, minimum GPA of 3.0; for AC, master's degree or equivalent. Additional exam requirements/recommendations for international students: Required—TOEFL, IELTS. *Application deadline:* For fall admission, 4/1 for domestic students; for spring admission, 11/1 for domestic students. Applications are processed on a rolling basis. Application fee: $125. Electronic applications accepted. *Financial support:* Career-related internships or fieldwork and unspecified assistantships available. Financial award application deadline: 4/1; financial award applicants required to submit FAFSA. *Unit head:* Kwong Bor Ng, Director/Chair, 718-997-3790, E-mail: kwongbor.ng@qc.cuny.edu. *Application contact:* Elizabeth D'Amico-Ramirez, Assistant Director of Graduate Admissions, 718-997-5203, E-mail: elizabeth.damicoramirez@qc.cuny.edu.

Queen's University at Kingston, School of Graduate Studies, Faculty of Arts and Science, Department of Sociology, Kingston, ON K7L 3N6, Canada. Offers communication and information technology (MA, PhD); feminist sociology (MA, PhD); socio-legal studies (MA, PhD); sociological theory (MA, PhD). *Program availability:* Part-time. *Degree requirements:* For master's, thesis; for doctorate, comprehensive exam, thesis/dissertation. *Entrance requirements:* For master's, honors bachelor's degree in sociology; for doctorate, honors bachelor's degree, master's degree in sociology. Additional exam requirements/recommendations for international students: Required—TOEFL. *Faculty research:* Social change and modernization, social control, deviance and criminology, surveillance.

Rutgers University–New Brunswick, School of Communication and Information, Ph.D. program in Communication, Information and Media, New Brunswick, NJ 08901. Offers PhD. *Program availability:* Part-time. *Degree requirements:* For doctorate, comprehensive exam, thesis/dissertation, qualifying exams. *Entrance requirements:* For doctorate, GRE General Test, proficiency in statistics. Additional exam requirements/recommendations for international students: Required—TOEFL (minimum score 600 paper-based). Electronic applications accepted. *Faculty research:* Information science, media studies.

Rutgers University–New Brunswick, School of Communication and Information, Program in Communication and Information Studies, Piscataway, NJ 08854-8097. Offers MCIS. *Program availability:* Part-time. *Faculty:* 23 full-time (12 women). *Students:* 19 full-time (14 women), 20 part-time (12 women); includes 6 minority (2 Black or African American, non-Hispanic/Latino; 3 Asian, non-Hispanic/Latino; 1 Hispanic/Latino), 4 international. Average age 31. 71 applicants, 39% accepted, 16 enrolled. In 2018, 16 master's awarded. *Entrance requirements:* For master's, GRE General Test. Additional exam requirements/recommendations for international students: Required—TOEFL. *Application deadline:* For fall admission, 2/1 priority date for domestic students, 2/1 for international students; for spring admission, 9/15 for domestic and international students. Applications are processed on a rolling basis. Application fee: $50. Electronic applications accepted. *Financial support:* In 2018–19, 8 fellowships with full tuition reimbursements (averaging $19,815 per year) were awarded; career-related internships or fieldwork, Federal Work-Study, and institutionally sponsored loans also available. Support available to part-time students. Financial award application deadline: 2/1; financial award applicants required to submit FAFSA. *Faculty research:* Communication processes and systems, information process and systems, human information and communication behavior. *Unit head:* Dr. Laurie Lewis, Director, 732-932-7500 Ext. 8141, Fax: 732-932-6916, E-mail: lewisl@rci.rutgers.edu. *Application contact:* Linda J. Costa, Director of Graduate Admissions, 732-932-7711, Fax: 732-932-8231, E-mail: smeds@rci.rutgers.edu.

St. Catherine University, Graduate Programs, Program in Library and Information Science, St. Paul, MN 55105. Offers MLIS. *Accreditation:* ALA. *Program availability:* Part-time, evening/weekend. *Degree requirements:* For master's, microcomputer competency. *Entrance requirements:* For master's, GRE or MAT, minimum GPA of 3.2 or GRE. Additional exam requirements/recommendations for international students: Required—Michigan English Language Assessment Battery or TOEFL (minimum score 600 paper-based; 100 iBT). *Expenses:* Contact institution.

St. John's University, St. John's College of Liberal Arts and Sciences, Division of Library and Information Science, Queens, NY 11439. Offers library science (MS); management for information professionals (Adv C); MA/MS. *Accreditation:* ALA (one or more programs are accredited). *Program availability:* Part-time, online only, 100% online. *Degree requirements:* For master's, e-portfolio end-of-program assessment; for Adv C, 15 credits (five courses) including capstone course. *Entrance requirements:* For master's, letters of recommendation, transcripts, resume, personal statement. Additional exam requirements/recommendations for international students: Required—TOEFL (minimum score 80 iBT), IELTS (minimum score 6.5). Electronic applications accepted. *Expenses:* Contact institution. *Faculty research:* Social justice in the information professions, teen spaces in public libraries, information organization, management, marketing and advocacy in information organizations, digital libraries.

Southern Connecticut State University, School of Graduate Studies, School of Education, Department of Information and Library Science, New Haven, CT 06515-1355. Offers information studies (Diploma); library science (MLS). *Program availability:* Part-time, evening/weekend. *Degree requirements:* For master's and Diploma, thesis or alternative. *Entrance requirements:* For master's, GRE General Test, interview, minimum QPA of 2.7, introductory computer science course; for Diploma, master's degree in library science or information science. Electronic applications accepted.

Syracuse University, School of Information Studies, MS Program in Information Management, Syracuse, NY 13244. Offers MS. *Program availability:* Part-time, evening/weekend, online learning. *Entrance requirements:* For master's, GRE General Test, personal statement, two letters of recommendation, resume. Additional exam requirements/recommendations for international students: Required—TOEFL (minimum score 100 iBT). *Application deadline:* For fall admission, 2/1 priority date for domestic and international students; for spring admission, 10/15 priority date for domestic and international students. Applications are processed on a rolling basis. Application fee: $75. Electronic applications accepted. *Financial support:* Fellowships with full tuition reimbursements, research assistantships with partial tuition reimbursements, teaching assistantships with partial tuition reimbursements, and scholarships/grants available. Financial award application deadline: 1/1; financial award applicants required to submit FAFSA. *Faculty research:* Increasing the effectiveness of managers and executives who work with information resources, designing and managing mission-critical information technologies within organizations, developing corporate and government policies to maximize the benefits resulting from the widespread use of these technologies. *Unit head:* Carsten Oesterlund, Program Director, 315-443-2911, Fax: 315-443-6886, E-mail: igrad@syr.edu. *Application contact:* Susan Corieri, Assistant Dean for Enrollment Management, 315-443-2575, E-mail: igrad@syr.edu.
Website: https://ischool.syr.edu/academics/graduate/masters-degrees/ms-in-information-management/

Universidad del Turabo, Graduate Programs, Programs in Education, Program in Library Service and Information Technology, Gurabo, PR 00778-3030. Offers M Ed. *Program availability:* Part-time, evening/weekend. *Entrance requirements:* For master's, GRE, EXADEP, GMAT, interview, official transcript, essay, recommendation letters. Electronic applications accepted.

Université de Montréal, Faculty of Arts and Sciences, School of Library and Information Sciences, Montréal, QC H3C 3J7, Canada. Offers information sciences (MIS, PhD). *Accreditation:* ALA (one or more programs are accredited). *Degree requirements:* For master's, thesis optional. *Entrance requirements:* For master's, interview, master's degree in library and information science or equivalent. Electronic applications accepted.

University at Buffalo, the State University of New York, Graduate School, Graduate School of Education, Department of Information Science, Buffalo, NY 14260. Offers information and library science (MS); library and information studies (Certificate); school librarianship (MS). *Accreditation:* ALA (one or more programs are accredited). *Program availability:* Part-time, 100% online. *Faculty:* 11 full-time (6 women), 6 part-time/adjunct (4 women). *Students:* 75 full-time (58 women), 130 part-time (109 women); includes 14 minority (4 Black or African American, non-Hispanic/Latino; 1 American Indian or Alaska Native, non-Hispanic/Latino; 5 Asian, non-Hispanic/Latino; 2 Hispanic/Latino; 1 Native Hawaiian or other Pacific Islander, non-Hispanic/Latino; 1 Two or more races, non-Hispanic/Latino). Average age 33. 122 applicants, 87% accepted, 72 enrolled. In 2018, 85 master's, 1 other advanced degree awarded. *Degree requirements:* For master's, thesis optional; for Certificate, thesis. *Entrance requirements:* For master's, letters of recommendation. Additional exam requirements/recommendations for international students: Required—TOEFL (minimum score 600 paper-based; 79 iBT), IELTS (minimum score 6.5), PTE (minimum score 55). *Application deadline:* For fall admission, 4/1 priority date for domestic and international students; for spring admission, 10/15 priority date for domestic students, 10/15 for international students. Applications are processed on a rolling basis. Application fee: $50. Electronic applications accepted. *Financial support:* In 2018–19, 16 fellowships (averaging $2,345 per year), 6 research assistantships with tuition reimbursements (averaging $10,222 per year) were awarded; teaching assistantships, Federal Work-Study, scholarships/grants, tuition waivers (full and partial), and unspecified assistantships also available. Support available to part-time students. Financial award application deadline: 2/1; financial award applicants required to submit FAFSA. *Faculty research:* Information-seeking behavior, thesauri, impact of technology, questioning behaviors, educational informatics. *Total annual research expenditures:* $56,553. *Unit head:* Dr. Heidi Julien, Chair, 716-645-1474, Fax: 716-645-3775, E-mail: heidijul@buffalo.edu. *Application contact:* Renad Aref, Assistant Director of Admission Recruitment, 716-645-2110, Fax: 716-645-7937, E-mail: gseinfo@buffalo.edu.
Website: http://www.gse.buffalo.edu/lis/

The University of Alabama, Graduate School, College of Communication and Information Sciences, School of Library and Information Studies, Tuscaloosa, AL 35487. Offers book arts (MFA); library and information studies (MLIS, PhD). *Accreditation:* ALA (one or more programs are accredited). *Program availability:* Part-time, evening/weekend, online learning. *Degree requirements:* For master's, comprehensive exam (for some programs), thesis optional; for doctorate, comprehensive exam, thesis/dissertation. *Entrance requirements:* For master's, GRE General Test or MAT, minimum GPA of 3.0; for doctorate, GRE. Additional exam requirements/recommendations for international students: Required—TOEFL. Electronic applications accepted. *Faculty research:* Library administration, user services, digital libraries, book arts, evaluation.

University of Alberta, Faculty of Graduate Studies and Research, School of Library and Information Studies, Edmonton, AB T6G 2E1, Canada. Offers MLIS. *Accreditation:* ALA. *Entrance requirements:* Additional exam requirements/recommendations for international students: Required—TOEFL, Canadian Academic English Language Assessment. Electronic applications accepted. *Faculty research:* Intellectual freedom, materials for children and young adults, library classification, multi-media literacy.

The University of Arizona, College of Social and Behavioral Sciences, School of Information, Tucson, AZ 85721. Offers MA, PhD. *Accreditation:* ALA (one or more programs are accredited). *Program availability:* Part-time. *Degree requirements:* For master's, proficiency in disk operating system (DOS); for doctorate, thesis/dissertation. *Entrance requirements:* For master's and doctorate, GRE General Test, 3 letters of recommendation, resume. Additional exam requirements/recommendations for international students: Required—TOEFL (minimum score 550 paper-based; 79 iBT). Electronic applications accepted. *Faculty research:* Microcomputer applications; quantitative methods systems; information transfer, planning, evaluation, and technology.

The University of British Columbia, Faculty of Arts, School of Library, Archival and Information Studies, Dual Master of Archival Studies/Master of Library and Information Studies Program, Vancouver, BC V6T 1Z1, Canada. Offers MLIS/MAS. *Entrance requirements:* Additional exam requirements/recommendations for international students: Required—TOEFL. Electronic applications accepted. *Expenses:* Contact institution. *Faculty research:* Computer systems/database design, information-seeking behavior, archives and records management, children's literature and services, digital libraries and archives.

The University of British Columbia, Faculty of Arts, School of Library, Archival and Information Studies, Master of Library and Information Studies Program, Vancouver, BC V6T 1Z1, Canada. Offers MLIS. *Accreditation:* ALA. *Program availability:* Part-time. *Degree requirements:* For master's, thesis optional. *Entrance requirements:* For master's, minimum GPA of 3.3 in undergraduate upper-division courses. Additional exam requirements/recommendations for international students: Required—TOEFL. Electronic applications accepted. *Expenses:* Contact institution. *Faculty research:* Computer systems/database design; digital libraries; metadata/classification; human-computer interaction; children's literature and services.

The University of British Columbia, Faculty of Arts, School of Library, Archival and Information Studies, PhD Program in Library, Archival and Information Studies, Vancouver, BC V6T 1Z1, Canada. Offers PhD. *Degree requirements:* For doctorate, thesis/dissertation. *Entrance requirements:* For doctorate, GRE, minimum GPA of 3.3 in MAS or MLIS. Additional exam requirements/recommendations for international students: Required—TOEFL. Electronic applications accepted. *Expenses:* Contact institution. *Faculty research:* Computer systems/database design; library and archival management; archival description and organization; children's literature and youth services; interactive information retrieval.

University of California, Berkeley, Graduate Division, School of Information, Berkeley, CA 94720. Offers MIDS, MIMS, PhD. *Degree requirements:* For doctorate, thesis/dissertation, qualifying exam. *Entrance requirements:* For master's, GRE General Test, minimum GPA of 3.0, previous course work in java or C programming, 3 letters of recommendation; for doctorate, GRE General Test, minimum GPA of 3.0. Additional exam requirements/recommendations for international students: Required—TOEFL. Electronic applications accepted. *Faculty research:* Information retrieval research, design and evaluation of information systems, work practice-based design of information systems, economics of information, intellectual property law.

University of California, Los Angeles, Graduate Division, Graduate School of Education and Information Studies, Department of Information Studies, Los Angeles, CA 90095-1521. Offers archival studies (MLIS); informatics (MLIS); information studies (PhD); library and information science (Certificate); library studies (MLIS); moving image archive studies (MA); rare books, print and visual culture (MLIS); MBA/MLIS; MLIS/MA. *Accreditation:* ALA (one or more programs are accredited). Terminal master's awarded for partial completion of doctoral program. *Degree requirements:* For master's, thesis or alternative, professional portfolio; for doctorate, thesis/dissertation, oral and written qualifying exams. *Entrance requirements:* For master's, GRE General Test, previous course work in statistics; for doctorate, GRE General Test, previous course work in statistics, 2 samples of research writing in English. Additional exam requirements/recommendations for international students: Required—TOEFL (minimum score 560 paper-based; 87 iBT), IELTS (minimum score 7). Electronic applications accepted. *Faculty research:* Digital libraries, archives and electronic records, interface design, cultural informatics, preservation/conservation, access.

University of Hawaii at Manoa, Office of Graduate Education, College of Natural Sciences, Department of Information and Computer Sciences, Library and Information Science Program, Honolulu, HI 96822-2233. Offers advanced library and information science (Graduate Certificate); library and information science (MLI Sc). *Accreditation:* ALA (one or more programs are accredited). *Program availability:* Part-time. *Degree requirements:* For master's, comprehensive exam, thesis optional. *Entrance requirements:* For master's, GRE General Test. Additional exam requirements/recommendations for international students: Required—TOEFL (minimum score 600 paper-based). Electronic applications accepted. *Faculty research:* Information behavior, evaluation of electronic information sources, online learning, history of libraries, information literacy.

University of Illinois at Urbana–Champaign, Graduate College, School of Information Sciences, Champaign, IL 61820. Offers bioinformatics (MS); digital libraries (CAS); information management (MS); library and information science (MS, PhD, CAS). *Accreditation:* ALA (one or more programs are accredited). *Program availability:* Part-time, online learning. *Entrance requirements:* For degree, master's degree in library and information science or related field with minimum GPA of 3.0.

The University of Iowa, Graduate College, School of Library and Information Science, Iowa City, IA 52242-1316. Offers MA, PhD, MA/Certificate, PhD/Certificate. *Accreditation:* ALA (one or more programs are accredited). *Degree requirements:* For master's, thesis optional, exam, portfolio. *Entrance requirements:* For master's, GRE General Test, minimum GPA of 3.0. Additional exam requirements/recommendations for international students: Required—TOEFL (minimum score 550 paper-based; 81 iBT). Electronic applications accepted.

University of Maryland, College Park, Academic Affairs, College of Information Studies, College Park, MD 20742. Offers MIM, MLS, PhD, MA/MLS. *Accreditation:* ALA (one or more programs are accredited). *Program availability:* Part-time, evening/weekend. Terminal master's awarded for partial completion of doctoral program. *Degree requirements:* For master's, thesis optional; for doctorate, comprehensive exam, thesis/dissertation, 1-year residency. *Entrance requirements:* For master's and doctorate, GRE General Test, minimum GPA of 3.0, 3 letters of recommendation. Additional exam requirements/recommendations for international students: Required—TOEFL. Electronic applications accepted.

University of Michigan, School of Information, Ann Arbor, MI 48109-1285. Offers health informatics (MHI); information (MSI, PhD). *Accreditation:* ALA (one or more programs are accredited). *Program availability:* Part-time. *Students:* 453 full-time (270 women), 32 part-time (20 women); includes 99 minority (16 Black or African American, non-Hispanic/Latino; 49 Asian, non-Hispanic/Latino; 21 Hispanic/Latino; 13 Two or more races, non-Hispanic/Latino), 212 international. Average age 27. 829 applicants, 53% accepted, 199 enrolled. In 2018, 179 master's, 7 doctorates awarded. Terminal master's awarded for partial completion of doctoral program. *Degree requirements:* For master's, thesis optional, internship; for doctorate, thesis/dissertation. *Entrance requirements:* For master's and doctorate, GRE General Test. Additional exam requirements/recommendations for international students: Required—TOEFL (minimum score 100 iBT). *Application deadline:* Applications are processed on a rolling basis. Application fee: $75 ($90 for international students). Electronic applications accepted. *Expenses:* Contact institution. *Financial support:* In 2018–19, 122 students received support, including 2 fellowships (averaging $28,200 per year), 33 research assistantships (averaging $28,200 per year), 41 teaching assistantships (averaging $28,200 per year); scholarships/grants and tuition waivers (full and partial) also available. *Unit head:* Dr. Thomas A. Finholt, Dean, School of Information, 734-647-3576. *Application contact:* School of Information Admissions, 734-763-2285, Fax: 734-615-3587, E-mail: umsi.admissions@umich.edu.
Website: http://www.si.umich.edu/

University of Missouri, Office of Research and Graduate Studies, College of Education, School of Information Science and Learning Technologies, Columbia, MO 65211. Offers information science and learning technology (PhD). *Accreditation:* ALA. *Program availability:* Part-time, evening/weekend. *Entrance requirements:* Additional exam requirements/recommendations for international students: Required—TOEFL. Electronic applications accepted.

The University of North Carolina at Chapel Hill, Graduate School, School of Information and Library Science, Chapel Hill, NC 27599. Offers data curation (PMC); digital curation and management (PSM); information and library science (PhD); information science (MSIS); library science (MSLS). *Accreditation:* ALA (one or more programs are accredited). *Program availability:* Part-time, 100% online, blended/hybrid learning. *Faculty:* 31 full-time (13 women), 46 part-time/adjunct (23 women). *Students:*

255 full-time (188 women), 29 part-time (18 women); includes 34 minority (11 Black or African American, non-Hispanic/Latino; 6 Asian, non-Hispanic/Latino; 8 Hispanic/Latino; 9 Two or more races, non-Hispanic/Latino), 62 international. Average age 28. 303 applicants, 69% accepted, 98 enrolled. In 2018, 125 master's, 17 doctorates, 2 other advanced degrees awarded. Terminal master's awarded for partial completion of doctoral program. *Degree requirements:* For master's, comprehensive exam, paper or project; for doctorate, comprehensive exam, thesis/dissertation. *Entrance requirements:* For master's and doctorate, GRE General Test. Additional exam requirements/ recommendations for international students: Required—TOEFL (minimum score 90 iBT). *Application deadline:* For fall admission, 12/10 priority date for domestic and international students; for spring admission, 10/8 for domestic and international students; for summer admission, 3/10 for domestic and international students. Applications are processed on a rolling basis. Application fee: $90. Electronic applications accepted. *Expenses:* $15,000 in-state per year, $31,250 out-of-state per year (for MSLS/MSIS); $15,000 in-state per year, $30,000 out-of-state per year (for PSM); $16,500 in-state per year, $32,500 out-of-state per year (for PMC). *Financial support:* In 2018–19, 59 fellowships with full tuition reimbursements (averaging $2,565 per year), 46 research assistantships with full tuition reimbursements (averaging $3,528 per year), 7 teaching assistantships with full tuition reimbursements (averaging $22,917 per year) were awarded; career-related internships or fieldwork, Federal Work-Study, scholarships/grants, health care benefits, and unspecified assistantships also available. Financial award application deadline: 12/12. *Faculty research:* Information retrieval and management, digital libraries, management of information resources, archives and records management, health informatics. *Total annual research expenditures:* $3 million. *Unit head:* Dr. Gary Marchionini, Dean, 919-962-8363, Fax: 919-962-8071, E-mail: gary@ils.unc.edu. *Application contact:* Lara Bailey, Student Services Coordinator, 919-962-7601, Fax: 919-962-8071, E-mail: bailey@email.unc.edu.
Website: http://sils.unc.edu

The University of North Carolina at Greensboro, Graduate School, School of Education, Department of Library and Information Studies, Greensboro, NC 27412-5001. Offers MLIS. *Accreditation:* ALA. *Program availability:* Part-time, evening/ weekend, online learning. *Degree requirements:* For master's, portfolio. *Entrance requirements:* For master's, GRE General Test. Additional exam requirements/ recommendations for international students: Required—TOEFL (minimum score 550 paper-based), IELTS (minimum score 6.5). Electronic applications accepted. *Faculty research:* Library history, gender studies, children's literature, web design, homeless, technical services.

University of Oklahoma, College of Arts and Sciences, School of Library and Information Studies, Norman, OK 73019. Offers archival studies (Graduate Certificate); digital humanities (Graduate Certificate); information studies (PhD); library and information studies (MLIS); M Ed/MLIS; MBA/MLIS. *Accreditation:* ALA (one or more programs are accredited). *Program availability:* Part-time, evening/weekend, 100% online, blended/hybrid learning. *Faculty:* 7 full-time (6 women), 2 part-time/adjunct (1 woman). *Students:* 63 full-time (53 women), 133 part-time (108 women); includes 48 minority (8 Black or African American, non-Hispanic/Latino; 4 American Indian or Alaska Native, non-Hispanic/Latino; 5 Asian, non-Hispanic/Latino; 14 Hispanic/Latino; 1 Native Hawaiian or other Pacific Islander, non-Hispanic/Latino; 16 Two or more races, non-Hispanic/Latino), 2 international. Average age 32. 60 applicants, 93% accepted, 41 enrolled. In 2018, 54 master's, 9 other advanced degrees awarded. Terminal master's awarded for partial completion of doctoral program. *Degree requirements:* For master's, comprehensive exam (for some programs), thesis optional; for doctorate, comprehensive exam, thesis/dissertation. *Entrance requirements:* For master's, three letters of recommendation, personal statement, resume, transcript; for doctorate, GRE, three letters of recommendation, personal statement, resume, writing sample; for Graduate Certificate, transcripts, personal statement (for some certificates), letter of recommendation (for some certificates). Additional exam requirements/ recommendations for international students: Required—TOEFL (minimum score 79 iBT) or IELTS (minimum score 6.5). *Application deadline:* Applications are processed on a rolling basis. Application fee: $50 ($100 for international students). Electronic applications accepted. *Expenses:* Tuition, state resident: full-time $5683.20; part-time $236.80 per credit hour. Tuition, nonresident: full-time $20,342; part-time $847.60 per credit hour. *International tuition:* $20,342.40 full-time. *Required fees:* $2894.20; $110.05 per credit hour. $126.50 per semester. Tuition and fees vary according to course load and program. *Financial support:* Research assistantships, teaching assistantships, scholarships/grants, health care benefits, and unspecified assistantships available. Financial award application deadline: 6/1; financial award applicants required to submit FAFSA. *Faculty research:* Family and youth technology in libraries, consumer health information, text mining, big data analytics. *Unit head:* Dr. Susan K. Burke, Director, 405-325-3921, E-mail: sburke@ou.edu. *Application contact:* Sarah Connelly, Admissions and Student Services Coordinator, 405-325-3921, E-mail: sarahee@ou.edu.
Website: http://slis.ou.edu

University of Puerto Rico–Río Piedras, Graduate School of Information Sciences and Technologies, San Juan, PR 00931-3300. Offers administration of academic libraries (PMC); administration of public libraries (PMC); administration of special libraries (PMC); consultant in information services (PMC); documents and files administration (Post-Graduate Certificate); electronic information resources analyst (Post-Graduate Certificate); information science (MIS); librarianship and information services (MLS); school librarian (Post-Graduate Certificate); school librarian distance education mode (Post-Graduate Certificate); specialist in legal information (PMC). *Accreditation:* ALA. *Program availability:* Part-time. *Degree requirements:* For master's, comprehensive exam, thesis, portfolio. *Entrance requirements:* For master's, PAEG, GRE, interview, minimum GPA of 3.0, 3 letters of recommendation; for other advanced degree, PAEG, GRE, minimum GPA of 3.0, IST master's degree. *Faculty research:* Investigating the users needs and preferences for a specialized environmental library.

University of Rhode Island, Graduate School, College of Arts and Sciences, Graduate School of Library and Information Studies, Kingston, RI 02881. Offers libraries, leadership and transforming communities (MLIS); organization of digital media (MLIS); school library media (MLIS); MLIS/MA; MLIS/MPA. *Accreditation:* ALA (one or more programs are accredited). *Program availability:* Part-time. *Faculty:* 4 full-time (all women). *Students:* 24 full-time (14 women), 73 part-time (62 women); includes 8 minority (3 Asian, non-Hispanic/Latino; 1 Hispanic/Latino; 1 Native Hawaiian or other Pacific Islander, non-Hispanic/Latino; 3 Two or more races, non-Hispanic/Latino). 50 applicants, 86% accepted, 27 enrolled. In 2018, 38 master's awarded. *Entrance requirements:* For master's, GRE or MAT if undergraduate GPA below 3.3, 2 letters of recommendation. Additional exam requirements/recommendations for international students: Required—TOEFL. *Application deadline:* For fall admission, 6/15 for domestic students, 2/1 for international students; for spring admission, 10/15 for domestic students, 7/15 for international students; for summer admission, 3/15 for domestic students. Application fee: $65. Electronic applications accepted. *Expenses: Tuition, area resident:* Full-time $13,226; part-time $735 per credit. Tuition, state resident: full-time $13,226; part-time $735 per credit. Tuition, nonresident: full-time $25,854; part-time $1436 per credit. *International tuition:* $25,854 full-time. *Required fees:* $1698; $50 per credit. $35 per semester. One-time fee: $165. *Financial support:* Application deadline: 1/15; applicants required to submit FAFSA. *Unit head:* Dr. Valerie Karno, Director, Graduate School of Library and Information Studies, 401-874-4682, Fax: 401-874-4127, E-mail: karno@uri.edu. *Application contact:* Dr. Valerie Karno, Director, Graduate School of Library and Information Studies, 401-874-4682, Fax: 401-874-4127, E-mail: karno@uri.edu.
Website: http://www.uri.edu/artsci/lsc/

University of South Carolina, The Graduate School, College of Information and Communications, School of Library and Information Science, Columbia, SC 29208. Offers MLIS, PhD, Certificate, Specialist, MLIS/MA. *Accreditation:* ALA (one or more programs are accredited). *Program availability:* Part-time, online learning. *Degree requirements:* For master's, end of program portfolio; for doctorate, comprehensive exam, thesis/dissertation. *Entrance requirements:* For master's and other advanced degree, GRE General Test or MAT; for doctorate, GTE, writing sample. Additional exam requirements/recommendations for international students: Required—TOEFL (minimum score 570 paper-based; 75 iBT). Electronic applications accepted. *Faculty research:* Information technology management, distance education, library services for children and young adults, special libraries.

University of South Florida, College of Arts and Sciences, School of Information, Tampa, FL 33620-9951. Offers intelligence studies (MS), including cyber intelligence, strategic intelligence; library and information science (MA). *Accreditation:* ALA (one or more programs are accredited). *Program availability:* Part-time, evening/weekend, online learning. *Faculty:* 15 full-time (7 women). *Students:* 108 full-time (77 women), 182 part-time (137 women); includes 83 minority (23 Black or African American, non-Hispanic/Latino; 7 Asian, non-Hispanic/Latino; 49 Hispanic/Latino; 4 Two or more races, non-Hispanic/Latino). Average age 32. 141 applicants, 86% accepted, 71 enrolled. In 2018, 128 master's awarded. *Degree requirements:* For master's, comprehensive exam, thesis (for some programs). *Entrance requirements:* For master's, GRE not required for Intelligence Studies; GRE required for Library and Information Science with preferred minimum scores of 734d percentile (156v), 10th percentile (141Q). May be waived under certain criteria, goals statement, resume or CV, some programs need understanding of programming/coding, computational problem solving and operating systems (for Intelligence Studies); GRE, writing sample, 3 letters of recommendation, resume, statement of purpose (for Library and Information Science). Additional exam requirements/recommendations for international students: Required—TOEFL, TOEFL (minimum score 550 paper-based; 79 iBT) or IELTS (minimum score 6.5). *Application deadline:* For fall admission, 6/1 priority date for domestic students, 5/1 for international students; for spring admission, 10/15 priority date for domestic students, 9/15 for international students. Applications are processed on a rolling basis. Application fee: $30. Electronic applications accepted. *Expenses:* Tuition, state resident: full-time $6350. Tuition, nonresident: full-time $19,048. *International tuition:* $19,048 full-time. *Required fees:* $2079. *Financial support:* In 2018–19, 62 students received support. Unspecified assistantships available. Financial award application deadline: 6/30. *Faculty research:* Youth services in libraries, community engagement and libraries, information architecture, biomedical informatics, health informatics. *Total annual research expenditures:* $21,733. *Unit head:* Dr. Jim Andrews, Director and Associate Professor, 813-974-2108, Fax: 813-974-6840, E-mail: jimandrews@usf.edu. *Application contact:* Dr. Randy Borum, Graduate Program Director, 813-974-3520, Fax: 813-974-6840, E-mail: wborum@usf.edu.
Website: http://si.usf.edu/

University of South Florida, Innovative Education, Tampa, FL 33620-9951. Offers adult, career and higher education (Graduate Certificate), including college teaching, leadership in developing human resources, leadership in higher education; Africana studies (Graduate Certificate), including diasporas and health disparities, genocide and human rights; aging studies (Graduate Certificate), including gerontology; art research (Graduate Certificate), including museum studies; business foundations (Graduate Certificate); chemical and biomedical engineering (Graduate Certificate), including materials science and engineering, water, health and sustainability; child and family studies (Graduate Certificate), including positive behavior support; civil and industrial engineering (Graduate Certificate), including transportation systems analysis; community and family health (Graduate Certificate), including maternal and child health, social marketing and public health, violence and injury: prevention and intervention, women's health; criminology (Graduate Certificate), including criminal justice administration; data science for public administration (Graduate Certificate); digital humanities (Graduate Certificate); educational measurement and research (Graduate Certificate), including evaluation; English (Graduate Certificate), including comparative literary studies, creative writing, professional and technical communication; entrepreneurship (Graduate Certificate); environmental health (Graduate Certificate), including safety management; epidemiology and biostatistics (Graduate Certificate), including applied biostatistics, biostatistics, concepts and tools of epidemiology, epidemiology, epidemiology of infectious diseases; geography, environment and planning (Graduate Certificate), including community development, environmental policy and management, geographical information systems; geology (Graduate Certificate), including hydrogeology; global health (Graduate Certificate), including disaster management, global health and Latin American and Caribbean studies, global health practice, humanitarian assistance, infection control; government and international affairs (Graduate Certificate), including Cuban studies, globalization studies; health policy and management (Graduate Certificate), including health management and leadership, public health policy and programs; hearing specialist: early intervention (Graduate Certificate); industrial and management systems engineering (Graduate Certificate), including systems engineering, technology management; information studies (Graduate Certificate), including school library media specialist; information systems/decision sciences (Graduate Certificate), including analytics and business intelligence; instructional technology (Graduate Certificate), including distance education, Florida digital/virtual educator, instructional design, multimedia design, Web design; internal medicine, bioethics and medical humanities (Graduate Certificate), including biomedical ethics; Latin American and Caribbean studies (Graduate Certificate); leadership for coastal resiliency planning (Graduate Certificate); mass communications (Graduate Certificate), including multimedia journalism; mathematics and statistics (Graduate Certificate), including mathematics; medicine (Graduate Certificate), including aging and neuroscience, bioinformatics, biotechnology, brain fitness and memory management, clinical investigation, hand and upper limb rehabilitation, health informatics, health sciences, integrative weight management, intellectual property, medicine and gender, metabolic and nutritional medicine, metabolic cardiology, pharmacy sciences; national and competitive intelligence (Graduate Certificate); nursing (Graduate Certificate), including simulation based academic fellowship in advanced pain management; psychological and social foundations (Graduate Certificate), including career counseling, college teaching, diversity in education, mental health counseling, school counseling; public affairs (Graduate Certificate), including nonprofit management, public management, research administration; public health (Graduate Certificate), including assessing chemical toxicity and public health risks, health equity, pharmacoepidemiology, public health generalist, toxicology, translational research in adolescent behavioral health; public health practices (Graduate Certificate), including planning for healthy communities; rehabilitation and mental health counseling (Graduate Certificate), including integrative mental health care, marriage and family therapy, rehabilitation technology; secondary education (Graduate Certificate), including ESOL,

foreign language education: culture and content, foreign language education: professional; social work (Graduate Certificate), including geriatric social work/clinical gerontology; special education (Graduate Certificate), including autism spectrum disorder, disabilities education: severe/profound; world languages (Graduate Certificate), including teaching English as a second language (TESL) or foreign language. *Expenses:* Tuition, state resident: full-time $6350. Tuition, nonresident: full-time $19,048. *International tuition:* $19,048 full-time. *Required fees:* $2079. *Unit head:* Dr. Cynthia DeLuca, Associate Vice President and Assistant Vice Provost, 813-974-3077, Fax: 813-974-7061, E-mail: deluca@usf.edu. *Application contact:* Owen Hooper, Director, Summer and Alternative Calendar Programs, 813-974-6917, E-mail: hooper@usf.edu.
Website: http://www.usf.edu/innovative-education/

The University of Texas at Austin, Graduate School, School of Information, Austin, TX 78712-1111. Offers identity management and security (MSIMS); information (PhD); information studies (MSIS); MSIS/MA. MSIMS program offered in conjunction with the Center for Identity. *Accreditation:* ALA (one or more programs are accredited). *Program availability:* Part-time. *Degree requirements:* For doctorate, 2 foreign languages, thesis/dissertation. *Entrance requirements:* For master's and doctorate, GRE General Test. Electronic applications accepted. *Faculty research:* Information retrieval and artificial intelligence, library history and administration, classification and cataloguing.

University of Toronto, School of Graduate Studies, Faculty of Information, Toronto, ON M5S 1A1, Canada. Offers information (MI, PhD); museum studies (MM St); JD/MI. *Accreditation:* ALA (one or more programs are accredited). *Program availability:* Part-time. *Degree requirements:* For master's, thesis optional; for doctorate, thesis/dissertation, oral exam/thesis defense. *Entrance requirements:* For master's, 2 letters of reference; for doctorate, 3 letters of reference, minimum B+ average. Additional exam requirements/recommendations for international students: Required—TOEFL (minimum score 600 paper-based; 100 iBT), IELTS (minimum score 8), TWE (minimum score 5.5), or Michigan English Language Assessment Battery (minimum score 95). Electronic applications accepted. *Expenses:* Contact institution.

The University of Western Ontario, School of Graduate and Postdoctoral Studies, Faculty of Information and Media Studies, Programs in Library and Information Science, London, ON N6A 3K7, Canada. Offers MLIS, PhD. Program conducted on a trimester basis. *Accreditation:* ALA (one or more programs are accredited). *Program availability:* Part-time, evening/weekend. *Degree requirements:* For doctorate, comprehensive exam, thesis/dissertation. *Entrance requirements:* For master's, honors degree, minimum B average during previous 2 years of course work; for doctorate, MLIS or equivalent. Additional exam requirements/recommendations for international students: Required—TOEFL (minimum score 625 paper-based), TWE (minimum score 5). Electronic applications accepted. *Faculty research:* Information, individuals, and society; information systems, policy, power, and institutions.

University of Wisconsin–Madison, Graduate School, College of Letters and Science, Information School, Madison, WI 53706-1380. Offers MA, PhD. *Accreditation:* ALA (one or more programs are accredited). *Program availability:* Part-time. *Degree requirements:* For doctorate, comprehensive exam, thesis/dissertation. Electronic applications accepted. *Faculty research:* Intellectual freedom, children's literature, print culture history, information systems design and evaluation, school library media centers.

University of Wisconsin–Milwaukee, Graduate School, School of Information Studies, Milwaukee, WI 53201-0413. Offers MLIS, MS, PhD, CAS. *Accreditation:* ALA (one or more programs are accredited). *Program availability:* Part-time. *Students:* 157 full-time (101 women), 257 part-time (191 women); includes 71 minority (23 Black or African American, non-Hispanic/Latino; 1 American Indian or Alaska Native, non-Hispanic/Latino; 17 Asian, non-Hispanic/Latino; 6 Hispanic/Latino; 1 Native Hawaiian or other Pacific Islander, non-Hispanic/Latino; 23 Two or more races, non-Hispanic/Latino), 16 international. Average age 34. 310 applicants, 64% accepted, 138 enrolled. In 2018, 104 master's, 2 doctorates awarded. *Entrance requirements:* For master's, GRE General Test or MAT; for doctorate, GRE. Additional exam requirements/recommendations for international students: Required—TOEFL (minimum score 550 paper-based), IELTS (minimum score 6.5). *Application deadline:* For fall admission, 1/1 priority date for domestic students; for spring admission, 9/1 for domestic students. Application fee: $56 ($96 for international students). Electronic applications accepted. *Financial support:* Fellowships, research assistantships, teaching assistantships, career-related internships or fieldwork, Federal Work-Study, health care benefits, unspecified assistantships, and project assistantships available. Support available to part-time students. Financial award application deadline: 4/15; financial award applicants required to submit FAFSA. *Unit head:* Tomas A. Lipinski, Dean/Professor, 414-229-4707, E-mail: tlipinsk@uwm.edu. *Application contact:* Linda Barajas, Admissions Coordinator, 414-229-3316, E-mail: barajas@uwm.edu.
Website: http://uwm.edu/informationstudies

Valdosta State University, Program in Library and Information Science, Valdosta, GA 31698. Offers MLIS. *Accreditation:* ALA. *Program availability:* 100% online. *Degree requirements:* For master's, comprehensive exam. *Entrance requirements:* For master's, two essays, resume, three recommendations. Additional exam requirements/recommendations for international students: Required—TOEFL (minimum score 523 paper-based); Recommended—IELTS. *Expenses:* Contact institution.

Wayne State University, School of Information Sciences, Detroit, MI 48202. Offers archival administration (Graduate Certificate); information management (MS, Graduate Certificate); library and information science (MLIS, Graduate Certificate, Spec); public library services to children and young adults (Graduate Certificate); MLIS/MA. WSU History Department. *Accreditation:* ALA (one or more programs are accredited). *Program availability:* Part-time, evening/weekend, 100% online, blended/hybrid learning. *Faculty:* 12 full-time (9 women), 17 part-time/adjunct (12 women). *Students:* 85 full-time (74 women), 316 part-time (258 women); includes 77 minority (42 Black or African American, non-Hispanic/Latino; 2 American Indian or Alaska Native, non-Hispanic/Latino; 3 Asian, non-Hispanic/Latino; 19 Hispanic/Latino; 1 Native Hawaiian or other Pacific Islander, non-Hispanic/Latino; 10 Two or more races, non-Hispanic/Latino), 1 international. Average age 33. 258 applicants, 60% accepted, 100 enrolled. In 2018, 149 master's, 34 other advanced degrees awarded. *Degree requirements:* For master's and other advanced degree, e-portfolio. *Entrance requirements:* For master's, GRE or MAT (if undergraduate GPA is between 2.5 and 2.99), minimum undergraduate GPA of 3.0 or graduate degree, personal statement, resume or curriculum vitae; for other advanced degree, GRE or MAT (if undergraduate GPA is between 2.5 and 2.99), minimum undergraduate GPA of 3.0 or graduate degree, personal statement, resume or curriculum vitae, MLIS (for specialist certificate). Additional exam requirements/recommendations for international students: Required—TOEFL (minimum score 550 paper-based; 79 iBT); Recommended—IELTS (minimum score 6.5), TWE (minimum score 5.5). *Application deadline:* For fall admission, 7/1 for domestic students, 5/1 priority date for international students; for winter admission, 10/1 priority date for domestic students, 9/1 priority date for international students; for spring admission, 2/1 priority date for domestic students, 1/1 priority date for international students. Applications are processed on a rolling basis. Application fee: $50. Electronic applications accepted. *Expenses:* 15,000/year. *Financial support:* In 2018–19, 133 students received support. Fellowships with tuition reimbursements available, scholarships/grants, health care benefits, and unspecified assistantships available. Support available to part-time students. Financial award applicants required to submit FAFSA. *Faculty research:* Library services, information management issues, digital content management, library/community engagement, archives and preservation. *Unit head:* Dr. Jon Cawthorne, Dean, 313-577-4020, E-mail: jon.cawthorne@wayne.edu. *Application contact:* Academic Services Officer II, 313-577-1825, E-mail: asklis@wayne.edu.
Website: http://slis.wayne.edu/

Library Science

Appalachian State University, Cratis D. Williams School of Graduate Studies, Department of Leadership and Educational Studies, Boone, NC 28608. Offers educational administration (Ed S); educational media (MA); higher education (MA, Ed S); library science (MLS); school administration (MSA). *Program availability:* Part-time, evening/weekend, online learning. *Degree requirements:* For master's and Ed S, comprehensive exam, thesis optional. *Entrance requirements:* For master's and Ed S, GRE or MAT, 3 letters of recommendation. Additional exam requirements/recommendations for international students: Required—TOEFL (minimum score 570 paper-based; 79 iBT), IELTS (minimum score 6.5). Electronic applications accepted. *Expenses: Tuition, area resident:* Full-time $4839; part-time $237 per credit hour. Tuition, state resident: full-time $4839; part-time $237 per credit hour. Tuition, nonresident: full-time $18,271; part-time $895.50 per credit hour. *Faculty research:* Brain, learning and meditation; leadership of teaching and learning.

The Catholic University of America, School of Arts and Sciences, Department of Library and Information Science, Washington, DC 20064. Offers MSLS, Certificate, JD/MSLS, MSLS/MA, MSLS/MS. *Accreditation:* ALA (one or more programs are accredited). *Program availability:* Part-time. *Faculty:* 6 full-time (all women), 5 part-time/adjunct (0 women). *Students:* 19 full-time (17 women), 72 part-time (55 women); includes 26 minority (13 Black or African American, non-Hispanic/Latino; 2 Asian, non-Hispanic/Latino; 4 Hispanic/Latino; 7 Two or more races, non-Hispanic/Latino), 1 international. Average age 33. 67 applicants, 90% accepted, 30 enrolled. In 2018, 26 master's awarded. *Degree requirements:* For master's, comprehensive exam. *Entrance requirements:* For master's, statement of purpose, official copies of academic transcripts, three letters of recommendation, interview. Additional exam requirements/recommendations for international students: Required—TOEFL (minimum score 550 paper-based; 80 iBT). *Application deadline:* For fall admission, 7/15 priority date for domestic students, 7/1 for international students; for spring admission, 11/15 priority date for domestic students, 11/1 for international students. Applications are processed on a rolling basis. Application fee: $55. Electronic applications accepted. *Expenses:* Contact institution. *Financial support:* Fellowships, research assistantships, teaching assistantships, Federal Work-Study, scholarships/grants, tuition waivers (full and partial), and unspecified assistantships available. Financial award application deadline: 2/1; financial award applicants required to submit FAFSA. *Faculty research:* Digital collections, library and information science education, information design and architecture, information system design and evaluation. *Unit head:* Dr. Youngok Choi, Chair, 202-319-5877, E-mail: choiy@cua.edu. *Application contact:* Dr. Steven Brown, Director of Graduate Admissions, 202-319-5057, Fax: 202-319-6533, E-mail: cua-admissions@cua.edu.
Website: http://lis.cua.edu/

Chicago State University, School of Graduate and Professional Studies, College of Education, Department of Reading, Elementary Education, Library Information and Media Studies, Program in Library Science, Chicago, IL 60628. Offers MS. *Entrance requirements:* For master's, minimum GPA of 2.75.

Clarion University of Pennsylvania, College of Business Administration and Information Sciences, MSLS Program in Information and Library Science, Clarion, PA 16214. Offers information and library science (MSLS); school library media (MSLS). *Accreditation:* ALA. *Program availability:* Part-time, evening/weekend, online-only, 100% online. *Faculty:* 5 full-time (4 women), 5 part-time/adjunct (3 women). *Students:* 117 full-time (97 women), 247 part-time (206 women); includes 55 minority (23 Black or African American, non-Hispanic/Latino; 7 Asian, non-Hispanic/Latino; 19 Hispanic/Latino; 6 Two or more races, non-Hispanic/Latino), 2 international. Average age 33. 239 applicants, 62% accepted, 139 enrolled. In 2018, 129 master's awarded. *Entrance requirements:* For master's, Overall GPA for the bacc degree of at least 3.00 on a 4.00 scale; Or a 3.00 GPA for the last 60 credits of the bacc degree with an overall QPA of at least 2.75; or a 2.75 to 2.99 overall GPA for the bacc degree with a score of at least 412 on the MAT or score of at least 300 on the GRE; or a graduate degree with at least a GPA of 3.00. Additional exam requirements/recommendations for international students: Required—TOEFL (minimum score 80 iBT), International students are required to achieve a minimum score of 213 computer-based or 80 internet-based on the TOEFL MSLS with Pennsylvania. *Application deadline:* For fall admission, 8/1 priority date for domestic students, 7/15 priority date for international students; for winter admission, 11/1 priority date for domestic students; for spring admission, 12/1 priority date for domestic students, 11/15 priority date for international students; for summer admission, 4/1 priority date for domestic students. Applications are processed on a rolling basis. Application fee: $40. Electronic applications accepted. *Expenses:* $675.60 per credit including fees in state. *Financial support:* Career-related internships or fieldwork, institutionally sponsored loans, scholarships/grants, and unspecified assistantships available. Financial award application deadline: 3/1; financial award applicants required to submit FAFSA. *Unit head:* Dr. Linda Lillard, Department Chair, 814-393-2383, E-mail: llillard@clarion.edu. *Application contact:* Susan Staub, Graduate Admissions Counselor, 814-393-2337, Fax: 814-393-2722, E-mail: gradstudies@clarion.edu.
Website: http://www.clarion.edu/academics/colleges-and-schools/college-of-business-administration-and-information-sciences/library-science/

Library Science

Dalhousie University, Faculty of Management, School of Information Management, Halifax, NS B3H 3J5, Canada. Offers MIM, MLIS, LL B/MLIS, MBA/MLIS, MLIS/MPA, MLIS/MREM. *Accreditation:* ALA (one or more programs are accredited). *Program availability:* Part-time. *Degree requirements:* For master's, one foreign language, thesis optional. *Entrance requirements:* For master's, resume, interview. Additional exam requirements/recommendations for international students: Required—TOEFL, IELTS, CANTEST, CAEL, or Michigan English Language Assessment Battery. Electronic applications accepted. *Faculty research:* Information-seeking behavior, electronic text design, browsing in digital environments, information diffusion among scientists.

Drexel University, College of Computing and Informatics, Philadelphia, PA 19104-2875. Offers MS, PhD, Post-Master's Certificate, Postbaccalaureate Certificate. *Accreditation:* ALA (one or more programs are accredited). *Program availability:* Part-time, evening/weekend, 100% online. *Faculty:* 51 full-time (16 women), 22 part-time/adjunct (9 women). *Students:* 222 full-time (113 women), 296 part-time (160 women); includes 108 minority (33 Black or African American, non-Hispanic/Latino; 32 Asian, non-Hispanic/Latino; 22 Hispanic/Latino; 21 Two or more races, non-Hispanic/Latino), 109 international. Average age 32. 1,012 applicants, 40% accepted, 206 enrolled. In 2018, 187 master's, 15 doctorates, 19 other advanced degrees awarded. *Degree requirements:* For doctorate, thesis/dissertation. *Entrance requirements:* For master's and doctorate, GRE General Test. Additional exam requirements/recommendations for international students: Required—TOEFL (minimum score 90 iBT), IELTS (minimum score 6.5). *Application deadline:* For fall admission, 8/15 for domestic students, 7/15 for international students; for spring admission, 3/1 for domestic students, 2/1 for international students. Applications are processed on a rolling basis. Application fee: $65. Electronic applications accepted. *Financial support:* Fellowships, research assistantships, teaching assistantships, career-related internships or fieldwork, institutionally sponsored loans, scholarships/grants, health care benefits, and tuition waivers (partial) available. Support available to part-time students. Financial award application deadline: 3/1; financial award applicants required to submit FAFSA. *Faculty research:* Computer science: theory of algorithms, graph theory, combinatorial optimization, computer vision; human-centered computing: social computing, human-computer interaction, computer-supported cooperative work, computer-supported collaborative learning, information literacy; systems and software engineering: formal software design modeling and analysis, software economics, software evolution and modularity. *Unit head:* Dr. Yi Deng, Dean/Professor, 215-895-2475, Fax: 215-895-2494, E-mail: yd362@drexel.edu. *Application contact:* Matthew Lechtenberg, Director, Recruitment, 215-895-2474, Fax: 215-895-2303, E-mail: cciinfo@drexel.edu. Website: http://cci.drexel.edu/

East Carolina University, Graduate School, College of Education, Department of Interdisciplinary Professions, Greenville, NC 27858-4353. Offers adult education (MA Ed); business and marketing education (MA Ed); community college instruction (Certificate); counselor education (MS); education in the healthcare professions (Certificate); library science (MLS); student affairs in higher education (Certificate); vocational education (MS). *Accreditation:* ACA; ALA; NCATE. *Program availability:* Part-time, evening/weekend. *Application deadline:* For fall admission, 5/15 priority date for domestic students. *Expenses: Tuition, area resident:* Full-time $4749. *Tuition, state resident:* full-time $4749. *Tuition, nonresident:* full-time $17,898. *International tuition:* $17,898 full-time. *Required fees:* $2787. Part-time tuition and fees vary according to course load and program. *Financial support:* Application deadline: 6/1. *Unit head:* Dr. Scott Glass, Professor, 252-328-5670, E-mail: glassj@ecu.edu. *Application contact:* Graduate School Admissions, 252-328-6012, Fax: 252-328-6071, E-mail: gradschool@ecu.edu. Website: http://www.ecu.edu/cs-educ/idp/index.cfm

Eastern Kentucky University, The Graduate School, College of Education, Department of Curriculum and Instruction, Richmond, KY 40475-3102. Offers elementary education (MA Ed), including early elementary education, reading; library science (MA Ed); music education (MA Ed); secondary and higher education (MA Ed), including secondary education; teaching (MAT). *Accreditation:* NCATE. *Program availability:* Part-time. *Degree requirements:* For master's, portfolio is part of exam. *Entrance requirements:* For master's, GRE General Test, PRAXIS II (KY), minimum GPA of 2.5. *Faculty research:* Technology in education, reading instruction, e-portfolios, induction to teacher education, dispositions of teachers.

East Tennessee State University, School of Graduate Studies, College of Education, Department of Curriculum and Instruction, Johnson City, TN 37614. Offers advanced studies in teaching and learning (M Ed), including childhood literacy; educational technology (M Ed), including educational communications and technology, school library media; elementary education (M Ed); reading (M Ed, MA), including reading education (MA), storytelling (MA); response to intervention (Post-Master's Certificate); school library professional (Post-Master's Certificate); secondary education (M Ed); STEAM K-12 education (Postbaccalaureate Certificate); storytelling (Postbaccalaureate Certificate); teacher education (MAT), including elementary education K-5, middle grades education 4-8, middle grades education 6-8, secondary education 6-12 and preK-12, secondary education K-12. *Accreditation:* NCATE. *Program availability:* Part-time, evening/weekend, online learning. *Degree requirements:* For master's, comprehensive exam, thesis optional, student teaching, practicum; for other advanced degree, field work (school library); culminating experience (storytelling). *Entrance requirements:* For master's, GRE, SAT, ACT, PRAXIS, minimum GPA of 3.0, interview, 3 letters of recommendation, background check; for other advanced degree, master's degree, TN teaching license. Additional exam requirements/recommendations for international students: Required—TOEFL (minimum score 550 paper-based; 79 iBT). Electronic applications accepted. *Faculty research:* Critical thinking; curriculum development in reading, math, and science education; cultural diversity; cognitive processes; effective teaching strategies.

Emporia State University, School of Library and Information Management, Emporia, KS 66801-5415. Offers archives studies (Certificate); information technology and science literacy (Certificate); library and information management (MLS, PhD). *Accreditation:* ALA. *Program availability:* Part-time, evening/weekend, online learning. *Degree requirements:* For master's, comprehensive exam, thesis optional; for doctorate, thesis/dissertation. *Entrance requirements:* For master's, GRE General Test, interview, minimum undergraduate GPA of 3.0, letters of recommendation; for doctorate, GRE General Test, interview, minimum graduate GPA of 3.5. Additional exam requirements/recommendations for international students: Required—TOEFL (minimum score 520 paper-based; 68 iBT). Electronic applications accepted.

Indiana University Bloomington, School of Informatics, Computing, and Engineering, Department of Information and Library Science, Bloomington, IN 47405-3907. Offers information architecture (Graduate Certificate); information science (MIS, PhD); library and information science (Sp LIS); library science (MLS); JD/MLS; MIS/MA; MLS/MA; MPA/MIS; MPA/MLS. *Accreditation:* ALA (one or more programs are accredited). *Program availability:* Part-time. Terminal master's awarded for partial completion of doctoral program. *Degree requirements:* For master's, internship; for doctorate, comprehensive exam, thesis/dissertation. *Entrance requirements:* For master's, GRE General Test (for applicants whose previous undergraduate degree GPA was below 3.0 or previous graduate degree GPA was below 3.2), 3 letters of reference, resume,

personal statement (500 words minimum), transcripts; for doctorate, GRE General Test, resume, personal statement (800-1000 words), writing sample, transcripts, 3 letters of reference. Additional exam requirements/recommendations for international students: Required—TOEFL (minimum score 600 paper-based; 100 iBT), IELTS. Electronic applications accepted. *Expenses:* Contact institution. *Faculty research:* Scholarly communication, interface design, library and management policy, computer-mediated communication, information retrieval, documentation, web analysis, e-business, information architecture, social informatics, virtual groups and online communities, online deviant behaviors, knowledge sharing, indexing, philosophy of information, information policy, resource management, research methods digital humanities, digital libraries, semantic web, digital preservation, natural language processing.

Indiana University–Purdue University Indianapolis, School of Informatics and Computing, Department of Library and Information Science, Indianapolis, IN 46202. Offers MLS. *Accreditation:* ALA. *Program availability:* Part-time, evening/weekend, 100% online. *Entrance requirements:* For master's, GRE General Test. Additional exam requirements/recommendations for international students: Required—TOEFL (minimum score 600 paper-based).

Indiana University–Purdue University Indianapolis, School of Public and Environmental Affairs, Indianapolis, IN 46202. Offers criminal justice and public safety (MS); homeland security and emergency management (Graduate Certificate); library management (Graduate Certificate); nonprofit management (Graduate Certificate); public affairs (MPA); public management (Graduate Certificate); social entrepreneurship: nonprofit and public benefit organizations (Graduate Certificate); JD/MPA; MLS/NMC; MLS/PMC; MPA/MA. *Accreditation:* CAHME (one or more programs are accredited); NASPAA. *Program availability:* Part-time, evening/weekend, online learning. *Entrance requirements:* For master's, GRE General Test, GMAT or LSAT, minimum GPA of 3.0 (preferred). Additional exam requirements/recommendations for international students: Required—TOEFL (minimum score 93 iBT), IELTS (minimum score 6.5). Electronic applications accepted. *Faculty research:* Nonprofit and public management, public policy, urban policy, sustainability policy, disaster preparedness and recovery, vehicular safety, homicide, offender rehabilitation and re-entry.

Instituto Tecnológico y de Estudios Superiores de Monterrey, Campus Irapuato, Graduate Programs, Irapuato, Mexico. Offers administration (MBA); administration of information technology (MAIT); administration of telecommunications (MAT); architecture (M Arch); computer science (MCS); education (M Ed); educational administration (MEA); educational innovation and technology (DEIT); educational technology (MET); electronic commerce (MBA); environmental administration and planning (MEAP); environmental systems (MES); finances (MBA); humanistic studies (MHS); international management for Latin American executives (MIMLAE); library and information science (MLIS); manufacturing quality management (MMQM); marketing research (MBA).

Inter American University of Puerto Rico, Barranquitas Campus, Program in Education, Barranquitas, PR 00794. Offers curriculum and teaching (M Ed), including biology, English as a second language, history, Spanish; educational leadership and management (MA); elementary education (M Ed); information and library service technology (M Ed); special education (MA). *Accreditation:* TEAC. *Program availability:* Part-time, evening/weekend. *Degree requirements:* For master's, 2 foreign languages, comprehensive exam, thesis (for some programs). *Entrance requirements:* For master's, GRE or EXADEP, bachelor's degree or its equivalent from accredited institution, official academic transcript from institution that conferred bachelor's degree, minimum GPA of 2.5, two recommendation letters, interview (for some programs), essay (for some programs). Electronic applications accepted. *Expenses:* Contact institution.

Inter American University of Puerto Rico, San Germán Campus, Graduate Studies Center, Program in Library Sciences, San Germán, PR 00683-5008. Offers MLS. *Program availability:* Part-time, evening/weekend. *Degree requirements:* For master's, comprehensive exam. *Entrance requirements:* For master's, GRE General Test or EXADEP, minimum GPA of 3.0. *Expenses: Tuition:* Full-time $212; part-time $212 per credit. *Required fees:* $366 per semester. One-time fee: $31. Tuition and fees vary according to degree level and program.

Kent State University, College of Communication and Information, School of Information, Kent, OH 44242-0001. Offers health informatics (MS), including health informatics, knowledge management, user experience design; library and information science (MLIS), including K-12 school library media; M Ed/MLIS; MBA/MLIS; MLIS/MS. *Accreditation:* ALA (one or more programs are accredited). *Program availability:* Part-time, 100% online. *Faculty:* 16 full-time (13 women), 10 part-time/adjunct (6 women). *Students:* 114 full-time (91 women), 235 part-time (162 women); includes 52 minority (24 Black or African American, non-Hispanic/Latino; 8 Asian, non-Hispanic/Latino; 15 Hispanic/Latino; 5 Two or more races, non-Hispanic/Latino), 4 international. Average age 32. 212 applicants, 99% accepted, 147 enrolled. In 2018, 308 master's awarded. *Degree requirements:* For master's, portfolio (MLIS); internship, project, paper, or thesis. *Entrance requirements:* For master's, GRE if total GPA is below 3.0 in highest completed degree, minimum GPA of 3.0, statement of purpose, 3 letters of recommendation, curriculum vitae/resume, transcripts, writing sample, personal interview. Additional exam requirements/recommendations for international students: Required—TOEFL (minimum score 587 paper-based, 94 iBT), Michigan English Language Assessment Battery (minimum score 82), IELTS (minimum score 7.0) or PTE (minimum score 65). *Application deadline:* For fall admission, 3/15 priority date for domestic students, 3/15 for international students; for spring admission, 9/15 priority date for domestic students, 9/15 for international students; for summer admission, 1/15 priority date for domestic students, 1/15 for international students. Applications are processed on a rolling basis. Application fee: $45 ($70 for international students). Electronic applications accepted. *Expenses:* Tuition, state resident: full-time $11,766; part-time $536 per credit. Tuition, nonresident: full-time $21,952; part-time $999 per credit. *International tuition:* $21,952 full-time. Tuition and fees vary according to course load. *Financial support:* Fellowships with full tuition reimbursements, research assistantships with full tuition reimbursements, teaching assistantships with full tuition reimbursements, scholarships/grants, and unspecified assistantships available. Financial award application deadline: 3/1. *Unit head:* Dr. Kendra Albright, Director and Professor, 330-672-8535, E-mail: kalbrig7@kent.edu. *Application contact:* Dr. Karen Gracy, Graduate Co-Coordinator/Associate Professor, 330-672-2782, E-mail: kgracy@kent.edu. Website: https://www.kent.edu/iSchool

Kutztown University of Pennsylvania, College of Education, Program in Library Science, Kutztown, PA 19530-0730. Offers MLS. *Program availability:* Part-time, evening/weekend, 100% online, blended/hybrid learning. *Faculty:* 1 (woman) full-time, 2 part-time/adjunct (1 woman). *Students:* 8 full-time (7 women), 26 part-time (22 women); includes 2 minority (1 Black or African American, non-Hispanic/Latino; 1 Hispanic/Latino). Average age 36. 28 applicants, 93% accepted, 12 enrolled. In 2018, 2 master's awarded. *Entrance requirements:* For master's, GRE General Test or valid PA teaching certificate, 3 letters of recommendation. Additional exam requirements/recommendations for international students: Required—TOEFL (minimum score 550 paper-based, 79 iBT), IELTS (minimum score 6.5), or PTE (minimum score 53). *Application deadline:* For fall admission, 8/1 for domestic and international students; for

spring admission, 12/1 for domestic and international students. Application fee: $35. Electronic applications accepted. *Expenses:* Tuition, state resident: part-time $516 per credit. Tuition, nonresident: part-time $774 per credit. *Required fees:* $119 per credit. One-time fee: $50 part-time. Tuition and fees vary according to degree level. *Financial support:* Career-related internships or fieldwork, Federal Work-Study, and unspecified assistantships available. Financial award application deadline: 3/1; financial award applicants required to submit FAFSA. *Unit head:* Dr. Andrea Harmer, Professor, 610-683-4301, Fax: 610-683-1326, E-mail: harmer@kutztown.edu. *Application contact:* Dr. Andrea Harmer, Professor, 610-683-4301, Fax: 610-683-1326, E-mail: harmer@kutztown.edu.
Website: https://www.kutztown.edu/academics/graduate-programs/library-science.htm

Long Island University–Brentwood Campus, Graduate Programs, Brentwood, NY 11717. Offers childhood education (MS), including grades 1-6; childhood education/literacy B-6 (MS); childhood education/special education (grades 1-6) (MS); clinical mental health counseling (MS, Advanced Certificate); criminal justice (MS); early childhood education (MS); educational leadership (MS Ed); family nurse practitioner (MS, Advanced Certificate); health administration (MPA); library and information science (MS); literacy (B-6) (MS Ed); school counselor (MS, Advanced Certificate); social work (MSW); special education (MS Ed); students with disabilities generalist (grades 7-12) (Advanced Certificate). *Program availability:* Part-time. *Entrance requirements:* For master's and Advanced Certificate, GRE. Additional exam requirements/recommendations for international students: Required—TOEFL or IELTS. Electronic applications accepted.

Long Island University–LIU Post, College of Education, Information and Technology, Brookville, NY 11548-1300. Offers adolescence education (MS); adolescence education 7-12 (MS); archives and records management (AC); art education (MS); childhood education (MS); childhood education/literacy B-6 (MS); childhood education/special education (MS); clinical mental health counseling (MS, AC); early childhood education (MS); early childhood education/childhood education (MS); educational leadership (AC); educational technology (MS); information studies (PhD); interdisciplinary educational studies (Ed D); middle childhood education (MS); music education (MS); public library administration (AC); school counselor (MS); special education (MS Ed); speech-language pathology (MA); students with disabilities, 7-12 generalist (AC); TESOL (MA). *Accreditation:* ASHA; TEAC. *Program availability:* Part-time, 100% online, blended/hybrid learning. Terminal master's awarded for partial completion of doctoral program. *Degree requirements:* For master's, variable foreign language requirement, comprehensive exam (for some programs), thesis optional; for doctorate, comprehensive exam, thesis/dissertation. *Entrance requirements:* For master's and AC, GRE (for some programs). Additional exam requirements/recommendations for international students: Required—TOEFL (minimum score 550 paper-based, 75 iBT), IELTS, or PTE. Electronic applications accepted. *Faculty research:* Sleep; use of technology to develop executive function by students with disabilities; early childhood literacy development through play; social justice through education; using a structured protocol to discuss Bad News.

Louisiana State University and Agricultural & Mechanical College, Graduate School, College of Human Sciences and Education, School of Library and Information Science, Baton Rouge, LA 70803. Offers MLIS. *Accreditation:* ALA.

Mansfield University of Pennsylvania, Graduate Studies, Program in School Library and Information Technologies, Mansfield, PA 16933. Offers library science (M Ed). *Program availability:* Part-time, evening/weekend, online learning. *Degree requirements:* For master's, comprehensive exam, thesis optional. *Entrance requirements:* For master's, minimum GPA of 3.0. Additional exam requirements/recommendations for international students: Required—TOEFL (minimum score 550 paper-based). Electronic applications accepted. *Expenses:* Contact institution.

McDaniel College, Graduate and Professional Studies, Program in School Librarianship, Westminster, MD 21157-4390. Offers MS. *Program availability:* Part-time, evening/weekend, online only, 100% online. *Degree requirements:* For master's, comprehensive exam, thesis optional. *Entrance requirements:* For master's, PRAXIS, 3 recommendations, essay. Additional exam requirements/recommendations for international students: Required—TOEFL (minimum score 79 iBT), IELTS (minimum score 6). Electronic applications accepted.

McGill University, Faculty of Graduate and Postdoctoral Studies, Faculty of Education, School of Information Studies, Montréal, QC H3A 2T5, Canada. Offers MLIS, PhD, Certificate, Diploma. *Accreditation:* ALA (one or more programs are accredited).

McNeese State University, Doré School of Graduate Studies, Burton College of Education, Department of Education Professions, Program in School Librarian, Lake Charles, LA 70609. Offers Postbaccalaureate Certificate. *Entrance requirements:* For degree, PRAXIS, 2 letters of recommendation, autobiography.

North Carolina Central University, School of Library and Information Sciences, Durham, NC 27707-3129. Offers MIS, MLS. *Accreditation:* ALA (one or more programs are accredited). *Program availability:* Part-time, evening/weekend. *Degree requirements:* For master's, one foreign language, thesis, research paper, or project. *Entrance requirements:* For master's, GRE, 90 hours in liberal arts. Additional exam requirements/recommendations for international students: Required—TOEFL.

Old Dominion University, Darden College of Education, Program in Elementary/Middle Education, Norfolk, VA 23529. Offers elementary education (Postbaccalaureate Certificate); instructional technology (MS Ed); library science (MS Ed). *Accreditation:* NCATE. *Program availability:* Part-time, evening/weekend, 100% online, blended/hybrid learning. *Degree requirements:* For master's, comprehensive exam. *Entrance requirements:* For master's, GRE General Test or MAT; PRAXIS I, SAT or ACT, minimum GPA of 2.8. Additional exam requirements/recommendations for international students: Required—TOEFL (minimum score 600 paper-based). Electronic applications accepted. *Expenses:* Contact institution. *Faculty research:* Education pre-K to 6, school librarianship, reading, TESOL, literacy.

Olivet Nazarene University, Graduate School, Division of Education, Program in Library Information Specialist, Bourbonnais, IL 60914. Offers MAE.

Pratt Institute, School of Information, New York, NY 10011. Offers MS, Adv C, JD/MS, MS/MFA. *Accreditation:* ALA. *Program availability:* Part-time. *Faculty:* 10 full-time (8 women), 21 part-time/adjunct (11 women). *Students:* Average age 30. 303 applicants, 75% accepted, 67 enrolled. In 2018, 59 master's, 1 other advanced degree awarded. *Entrance requirements:* For degree, master's degree in library and information science. Additional exam requirements/recommendations for international students: Required—TOEFL (minimum score 600 paper-based; 100 iBT). *Application deadline:* For fall admission, 1/5 for domestic and international students; for spring admission, 10/1 for domestic and international students. Applications are processed on a rolling basis. Application fee: $50 ($90 for international students). Electronic applications accepted. *Expenses:* Contact institution. *Financial support:* Career-related internships or fieldwork, Federal Work-Study, institutionally sponsored loans, scholarships/grants, health care benefits, and unspecified assistantships available. Support available to part-time students. Financial award application deadline: 2/1; financial award applicants required to submit FAFSA. *Faculty research:* Development of urban libraries and

information centers, medical and law librarianship, information management. *Unit head:* Anthony Cocciolo, Interim Dean, 212-647-7702, Fax: 212-367-2492, E-mail: acocciol@pratt.edu. *Application contact:* Natalie Capannelli, Director of Graduate Admissions, 718-636-3551, Fax: 718-399-4242, E-mail: ncapanne@pratt.edu.
Website: https://www.pratt.edu/academics/information/

Queens College of the City University of New York, Division of Social Sciences, Graduate School of Library and Information Studies, Queens, NY 11367-1597. Offers archives and preservation of cultural materials (AC); children's and young adult services in the public library (AC); librarianship (AC); library science (MLS); school library media specialist (MLS). *Accreditation:* ALA (one or more programs are accredited). *Program availability:* Part-time, evening/weekend. *Faculty:* 9 full-time (5 women), 13 part-time/adjunct (9 women). *Students:* 26 full-time (17 women), 309 part-time (231 women); includes 123 minority (39 Black or African American, non-Hispanic/Latino; 1 American Indian or Alaska Native, non-Hispanic/Latino; 17 Asian, non-Hispanic/Latino; 56 Hispanic/Latino; 1 Native Hawaiian or other Pacific Islander, non-Hispanic/Latino; 9 Two or more races, non-Hispanic/Latino), 4 international. Average age 32. In 2018, 88 master's, 1 other advanced degree awarded. *Degree requirements:* For master's, thesis; for AC, thesis optional. *Entrance requirements:* For master's, minimum GPA of 3.0; for AC, master's degree or equivalent. Additional exam requirements/recommendations for international students: Required—TOEFL, IELTS. *Application deadline:* For fall admission, 4/1 for domestic students; for spring admission, 11/1 for domestic students. Applications are processed on a rolling basis. Application fee: $125. Electronic applications accepted. *Financial support:* Career-related internships or fieldwork and unspecified assistantships available. Financial award application deadline: 4/1; financial award applicants required to submit FAFSA. *Unit head:* Kwong Bor Ng, Director/Chair, 718-997-3790, E-mail: kwongbor.ng@qc.cuny.edu. *Application contact:* Elizabeth D'Amico-Ramirez, Assistant Director of Graduate Admissions, 718-997-5203, E-mail: elizabeth.damicoramirez@qc.cuny.edu.

Rowan University, Graduate School, College of Education, Department of Educational Services and Leadership, Glassboro, NJ 08028-1701. Offers counseling in educational settings (MA); educational leadership (Ed D, CAGS); higher education administration (MA); principal preparation (CAGS); school administration (MA); school and public librarianship (MA); school nursing (Postbaccalaureate Certificate); school psychology (MA, Ed S); supervisor (CAGS). *Accreditation:* NCATE. *Program availability:* Part-time, evening/weekend. *Degree requirements:* For master's, comprehensive exam, thesis; for other advanced degree, thesis or alternative. *Entrance requirements:* For master's and other advanced degree, GRE General Test. Additional exam requirements/recommendations for international students: Required—TOEFL. Electronic applications accepted.

Rutgers University–New Brunswick, School of Communication and Information, Ph.D. program in Communication, Information and Media, New Brunswick, NJ 08901. Offers PhD. *Program availability:* Part-time. *Degree requirements:* For doctorate, comprehensive exam, thesis/dissertation, qualifying exams. *Entrance requirements:* For doctorate, GRE General Test, proficiency in statistics. Additional exam requirements/recommendations for international students: Required—TOEFL (minimum score 600 paper-based). Electronic applications accepted. *Faculty research:* Information science, media studies.

St. Catherine University, Graduate Programs, Program in Library and Information Science, St. Paul, MN 55105. Offers MLIS. *Accreditation:* ALA. *Program availability:* Part-time, evening/weekend. *Degree requirements:* For master's, microcomputer competency. *Entrance requirements:* For master's, GRE or MAT, minimum GPA of 3.2 or GRE. Additional exam requirements/recommendations for international students: Required—Michigan English Language Assessment Battery or TOEFL (minimum score 600 paper-based; 100 iBT). *Expenses:* Contact institution.

St. John's University, St. John's College of Liberal Arts and Sciences, Department of Government and Politics and Division of Library and Information Science, Program in Government and Library and Information Science, Queens, NY 11439. Offers MA/MS. *Program availability:* Part-time, evening/weekend. *Entrance requirements:* Additional exam requirements/recommendations for international students: Required—TOEFL (minimum score 80 iBT), IELTS (minimum score 6.5). Electronic applications accepted. *Faculty research:* Presidential leadership, morality and politics, U.S. foreign policy, U.S. national security policy, NY state and local government and politics, state building and social policy, public opinion, campaigns and elections, education politics, North African politics, energy and European Union politics.

St. John's University, St. John's College of Liberal Arts and Sciences, Division of Library and Information Science, Queens, NY 11439. Offers library science (MS); management for information professionals (Adv C); MA/MS. *Accreditation:* ALA (one or more programs are accredited). *Program availability:* Part-time, online only, 100% online. *Degree requirements:* For master's, e-portfolio end-of-program assessment; for Adv C, 15 credits (five courses) including capstone course. *Entrance requirements:* For master's, letters of recommendation, transcripts, resume, personal statement. Additional exam requirements/recommendations for international students: Required—TOEFL (minimum score 80 iBT), IELTS (minimum score 6.5). Electronic applications accepted. *Expenses:* Contact institution. *Faculty research:* Social justice in the information professions, teen spaces in public libraries, information organization, management, marketing and advocacy in information organizations, digital libraries.

Sam Houston State University, College of Education, Department of Library Science, Huntsville, TX 77341. Offers MLS. *Program availability:* Part-time, evening/weekend. *Degree requirements:* For master's, portfolio, internship. *Entrance requirements:* For master's, GRE General Test. Additional exam requirements/recommendations for international students: Required—TOEFL (minimum score 550 paper-based; 79 iBT), IELTS (minimum score 6.5). Electronic applications accepted.

Southern Arkansas University–Magnolia, School of Graduate Studies, Magnolia, AR 71753. Offers agriculture (MS); business administration (MBA), including agribusiness, social entrepreneurship, supply chain management; clinical and mental health counseling (MS); computer and information sciences (MS), including cyber security and privacy, data science, information technology; gifted and talented (M Ed), including curriculum and instruction, educational administration and supervision, gifted and talented P-8/7-12, instructional specialist P-4; higher, adult and lifelong education (M Ed); kinesiology (M Ed), including coaching; library media and information specialist (M Ed); public administration (MPA); school counseling K-12 (M Ed); student affairs and college counseling (M Ed); teaching (MAT). *Accreditation:* NCATE. *Program availability:* Part-time, 100% online, blended/hybrid learning. *Faculty:* 36 full-time (21 women), 32 part-time/adjunct (15 women). *Students:* 164 full-time (77 women), 762 part-time (510 women); includes 192 minority (163 Black or African American, non-Hispanic/Latino; 7 American Indian or Alaska Native, non-Hispanic/Latino; 13 Asian, non-Hispanic/Latino; 1 Hispanic/Latino; 8 Two or more races, non-Hispanic/Latino), 213 international. Average age 28. 363 applicants, 100% accepted, 237 enrolled. In 2018, 716 master's awarded. *Degree requirements:* For master's, comprehensive exam (for some programs), thesis optional. *Entrance requirements:* For master's, GRE, MAT or GMAT, minimum GPA of 2.5. Additional exam requirements/recommendations for international students: Required—TOEFL (minimum score 550 paper-based), IELTS (minimum score

6). *Application deadline:* For fall admission, 8/1 for domestic and international students; for spring admission, 12/1 for domestic students, 11/15 for international students; for summer admission, 4/1 for domestic students, 5/10 for international students. Applications are processed on a rolling basis. Application fee: $25 ($90 for international students). Electronic applications accepted. *Expenses: Tuition, area resident:* Full-time $5130; part-time $3420 per year. Tuition, state resident: full-time $5130; part-time $3420 per year. Tuition, nonresident: full-time $7866; part-time $5244 per year. *International tuition:* $7866 full-time. *Required fees:* $1052; $710 per unit. Tuition and fees vary according to course load. *Financial support:* Career-related internships or fieldwork, Federal Work-Study, scholarships/grants, tuition waivers (full), and unspecified assistantships available. Financial award applicants required to submit FAFSA. *Faculty research:* Alternative certification for teachers, supervision of instruction, instructional leadership, counseling. *Unit head:* Dr. Kim Bloss, Dean, School of Graduate Studies, 870-235-4150, Fax: 870-235-5227, E-mail: kkbloss@saumag.edu. *Application contact:* Talia Jett, Admissions Coordinator, 870-2355450, Fax: 870-235-5227, E-mail: taliajett@saumag.edu.
Website: http://www.saumag.edu/graduate

Southern Connecticut State University, School of Graduate Studies, School of Education, Department of Information and Library Science, New Haven, CT 06515-1355. Offers information studies (Diploma); library science (MLS). *Program availability:* Part-time, evening/weekend. *Degree requirements:* For master's and Diploma, thesis or alternative. *Entrance requirements:* For master's, GRE General Test, interview, minimum QPA of 2.7, introductory computer science course; for Diploma, master's degree in library science or information science. Electronic applications accepted.

Syracuse University, School of Information Studies, MS Program in Library and Information Science, Syracuse, NY 13244. Offers MS. *Accreditation:* ALA. *Program availability:* Part-time, evening/weekend, online learning. *Students:* Average age 30. *Entrance requirements:* For master's, GRE General Test, two letters of recommendation, personal statement, resume. Additional exam requirements/recommendations for international students: Required—TOEFL (minimum score 100 iBT). *Application deadline:* For fall admission, 2/1 priority date for domestic and international students; for spring admission, 10/15 priority date for domestic and international students. Applications are processed on a rolling basis. Application fee: $75. Electronic applications accepted. *Financial support:* Fellowships with full tuition reimbursements and teaching assistantships available. Financial award application deadline: 1/1; financial award applicants required to submit FAFSA. *Faculty research:* Information environments, library planning and marketing, management principles, information policy. *Unit head:* Prof. Caroline Haythornthwaite, Program Director, 315-443-2911, E-mail: igrad@syr.edu. *Application contact:* Susan Corieri, Director of Enrollment Management, 315-443-1070, E-mail: ischool@syr.edu.
Website: https://ischool.syr.edu/academics/graduate/masters-degrees/ms-library-and-information-science/

Tennessee Technological University, College of Graduate Studies, College of Education, Department of Curriculum and Instruction, Program in Library Science, Cookeville, TN 38505. Offers MA, Ed S. *Program availability:* Part-time, evening/weekend. *Students:* 4 full-time (all women), 8 part-time (all women). 6 applicants, 100% accepted, 4 enrolled. *Degree requirements:* For master's, comprehensive exam, thesis or alternative. *Entrance requirements:* For master's, MAT or GRE. Additional exam requirements/recommendations for international students: Required—TOEFL (minimum score 527 paper-based; 71 iBT), IELTS (minimum score 5.5), PTE (minimum score 48), or TOEIC (Test of English as an International Communication). *Application deadline:* For fall admission, 8/1 for domestic students, 5/1 for international students; for spring admission, 12/1 for domestic students, 10/1 for international students; for summer admission, 5/1 for domestic students, 2/1 for international students. Applications are processed on a rolling basis. Application fee: $35 ($40 for international students). Electronic applications accepted. *Financial support:* Research assistantships and teaching assistantships available. Financial award application deadline: 4/1. *Unit head:* Dr. Jeremy Wendt, Chairperson, 931-372-3181, Fax: 931-372-6270, E-mail: jwendt@tntech.edu. *Application contact:* Shelia K. Kendrick, Coordinator of Graduate Studies, 931-372-3808, Fax: 931-372-3497, E-mail: skendrick@tntech.edu.

Texas A&M University–Commerce, College of Education and Human Services, Commerce, TX 75429. Offers counseling (M Ed, MS, PhD); early childhood education (M Ed, MS); educational administration (M Ed, MS, Ed D); educational psychology (PhD); educational technology leadership (M Ed, MS); educational technology library science (M Ed, MS); elementary education (M Ed); health, kinesiology and sports studies (MS); higher education (MS, Ed D); psychology (MS); reading (M Ed, MS); school psychology (SSP); secondary education (M Ed, MS); social work (MSW); special education (M Ed, MS); supervision, curriculum and instruction-elementary education (Ed D); training and development (MS). *Program availability:* Part-time, evening/weekend, 100% online, blended/hybrid learning. *Faculty:* 95 full-time (59 women), 29 part-time/adjunct (22 women). *Students:* 356 full-time (295 women), 1,262 part-time (992 women); includes 683 minority (349 Black or African American, non-Hispanic/Latino; 9 American Indian or Alaska Native, non-Hispanic/Latino; 30 Asian, non-Hispanic/Latino; 238 Hispanic/Latino; 57 Two or more races, non-Hispanic/Latino), 9 international. Average age 37. 951 applicants, 42% accepted, 304 enrolled. In 2018, 532 master's, 51 doctorates awarded. *Degree requirements:* For master's, comprehensive exam, thesis optional, departmental qualifying exams (for some programs); for doctorate, comprehensive exam, thesis/dissertation, departmental qualifying exam; for SSP, comprehensive exam. *Entrance requirements:* For master's, GRE General Test, official transcripts, letters of recommendation, resume, statement of goals; for doctorate, GRE General Test, letters of recommendation, statement of goals, writing samples, writing sessions, resumes. Additional exam requirements/recommendations for international students: Required—TOEFL (minimum score 550 paper-based; 79 iBT), IELTS (minimum score 6), PTE (minimum score 53). *Application deadline:* For fall admission, 6/1 priority date for international students; for spring admission, 10/15 priority date for international students; for summer admission, 3/15 priority date for international students. Applications are processed on a rolling basis. Application fee: $50 ($75 for international students). Electronic applications accepted. *Expenses: Tuition, area resident:* Full-time $3630. Tuition, state resident: full-time $3630. Tuition, nonresident: full-time $11,100. *International tuition:* $11,100 full-time. *Required fees:* $2794. Tuition and fees vary according to course load, degree level and program. *Financial support:* In 2018–19, 116 students received support, including 94 research assistantships with partial tuition reimbursements available (averaging $3,863 per year), 38 teaching assistantships with partial tuition reimbursements available (averaging $4,728 per year); career-related internships or fieldwork, Federal Work-Study, institutionally sponsored loans, scholarships/grants, health care benefits, and unspecified assistantships also available. Financial award application deadline: 5/1; financial award applicants required to submit FAFSA. *Faculty research:* Cognitive and bilingual education, positive behavioral intervention, literacy, math readiness. *Total annual research expenditures:* $1.1 million. *Unit head:* Dr. Madeline Justice, Interim Dean, 903-886-5181, Fax: 903-886-5905, E-mail: madeline.justice@tamuc.edu. *Application contact:* Vicky Turner, Doctoral Degree and Special Programs Coordinator, 903-886-5167, E-mail: vicky.turner@tamuc.edu.

Website: http://www.tamuc.edu/academics/graduateSchool/programs/education/default.aspx

Texas Woman's University, Graduate School, College of Professional Education, School of Library and Information Studies, Denton, TX 76204. Offers library science (MA, MLS). *Accreditation:* ALA (one or more programs are accredited). *Program availability:* Part-time, evening/weekend, online only, 100% online. *Faculty:* 13 full-time (10 women), 19 part-time/adjunct (13 women). *Students:* 101 full-time (97 women), 446 part-time (428 women); includes 174 minority (28 Black or African American, non-Hispanic/Latino; 8 Asian, non-Hispanic/Latino; 127 Hispanic/Latino; 11 Two or more races, non-Hispanic/Latino), 1 international. Average age 36. 179 applicants, 80% accepted, 97 enrolled. In 2018, 177 master's awarded. *Degree requirements:* For master's, comprehensive exam, portfolio, practicum (for MLS); thesis (for MA). *Entrance requirements:* For master's, 3 letters of recommendation, 2-page statement of intent, resume. Additional exam requirements/recommendations for international students: Required—TOEFL (minimum score 550 paper-based; 79 iBT); Recommended—IELTS (minimum score 6.5), TSE (minimum score 53). *Application deadline:* For fall admission, 6/1 for domestic and international students; for spring admission, 11/1 for domestic and international students; for summer admission, 4/1 for domestic and international students. Application fee: $50 ($75 for international students). Electronic applications accepted. *Expenses:* $1,502 in-state resident per 3 hour course, $2,768 out-of-state resident per 3 hour course. *Financial support:* In 2018–19, 96 students received support, including 1 research assistantship, 6 teaching assistantships (averaging $7,483 per year); career-related internships or fieldwork, Federal Work-Study, institutionally sponsored loans, scholarships/grants, traineeships, health care benefits, and unspecified assistantships also available. Support available to part-time students. Financial award application deadline: 3/1; financial award applicants required to submit FAFSA. *Faculty research:* Information needs analysis, school library leadership, library management and assessment, informatics, information retrieval. *Unit head:* Dr. Ling Hwey Jeng, Director, 940-898-2602, Fax: 940-898-2611, E-mail: slis@twu.edu. *Application contact:* Korie Hawkins, Associate Director of Admissions, Graduate Recruitment, 940-898-3188, Fax: 940-898-3081, E-mail: admissions@twu.edu.
Website: http://www.twu.edu/slis/

Trevecca Nazarene University, Graduate Education Program, Nashville, TN 37210-2877. Offers accountability and instructional leadership (Ed S); curriculum and instruction for Christian school educators (M Ed); curriculum and instruction K-12 (M Ed); educational leadership (M Ed); English second language (M Ed); library and information science (MLI Sc); special education: visual impairments (M Ed); teaching (MAT), including teaching 6-12, teaching K-5. *Accreditation:* NCATE. *Program availability:* Part-time, evening/weekend, online learning. *Degree requirements:* For master's, comprehensive exam, exit assessment/e-portfolio. *Entrance requirements:* For master's, GRE or MAT; PRAXIS (for MAT), minimum GPA of 3.0, official transcript from regionally-accredited institution, references, interview, writing sample, at least 3 years' successful teaching experience (for M Ed in educational leadership); for Ed S, GRE or MAT, master's degree with minimum GPA of 3.0, official transcript from regionally accredited institution, at least 3 years' successful teaching experience, interview, writing sample, background and fingerprinting check, recommendations. Additional exam requirements/recommendations for international students: Required—TOEFL (minimum score 550 paper-based). Electronic applications accepted. *Expenses:* Contact institution.

Universidad del Turabo, Graduate Programs, Programs in Education, Program in Library Service and Information Technology, Gurabo, PR 00778-3030. Offers M Ed. *Program availability:* Part-time, evening/weekend. *Entrance requirements:* For master's, GRE, EXADEP, GMAT, interview, official transcript, essay, recommendation letters. Electronic applications accepted.

Université de Montréal, Faculty of Arts and Sciences, School of Library and Information Sciences, Montréal, QC H3C 3J7, Canada. Offers information sciences (MIS, PhD). *Accreditation:* ALA (one or more programs are accredited). *Degree requirements:* For master's, thesis optional. *Entrance requirements:* For master's, interview, master's degree in library and information science or equivalent. Electronic applications accepted.

University at Buffalo, the State University of New York, Graduate School, Graduate School of Education, Department of Information Science, Buffalo, NY 14260. Offers information and library science (MS); library and information studies (Certificate); school librarianship (MS). *Accreditation:* ALA (one or more programs are accredited). *Program availability:* Part-time, 100% online. *Faculty:* 11 full-time (6 women), 6 part-time/adjunct (4 women). *Students:* 75 full-time (58 women), 130 part-time (109 women); includes 14 minority (4 Black or African American, non-Hispanic/Latino; 1 American Indian or Alaska Native, non-Hispanic/Latino; 5 Asian, non-Hispanic/Latino; 2 Hispanic/Latino; 1 Native Hawaiian or other Pacific Islander, non-Hispanic/Latino; 1 Two or more races, non-Hispanic/Latino). Average age 33. 122 applicants, 87% accepted, 72 enrolled. In 2018, 85 master's, 1 other advanced degree awarded. *Degree requirements:* For master's, thesis optional; for Certificate, thesis. *Entrance requirements:* For master's, letters of recommendation. Additional exam requirements/recommendations for international students: Required—TOEFL (minimum score 600 paper-based; 79 iBT), IELTS (minimum score 6.5), PTE (minimum score 55). *Application deadline:* For fall admission, 4/1 priority date for domestic and international students; for spring admission, 10/15 priority date for domestic students, 10/15 for international students. Applications are processed on a rolling basis. Application fee: $50. Electronic applications accepted. *Financial support:* In 2018–19, 16 fellowships (averaging $2,345 per year), 6 research assistantships with tuition reimbursements (averaging $10,222 per year) were awarded; teaching assistantships, Federal Work-Study, scholarships/grants, tuition waivers (full and partial), and unspecified assistantships also available. Support available to part-time students. Financial award application deadline: 2/1; financial award applicants required to submit FAFSA. *Faculty research:* Information-seeking behavior, thesauri, impact of technology, questioning behaviors, educational informatics. *Total annual research expenditures:* $56,553. *Unit head:* Dr. Heidi Julien, Chair, 716-645-1474, Fax: 716-645-3775, E-mail: heidijul@buffalo.edu. *Application contact:* Renad Aref, Assistant Director of Admission Recruitment, 716-645-2110, Fax: 716-645-7937, E-mail: gseinfo@buffalo.edu.
Website: http://www.gse.buffalo.edu/lis/

The University of Alabama, Graduate School, College of Communication and Information Sciences, School of Library and Information Studies, Tuscaloosa, AL 35487. Offers book arts (MFA); library and information studies (MLIS, PhD). *Accreditation:* ALA (one or more programs are accredited). *Program availability:* Part-time, evening/weekend, online learning. *Degree requirements:* For master's, comprehensive exam (for some programs), thesis optional; for doctorate, comprehensive exam, thesis/dissertation. *Entrance requirements:* For master's, GRE General Test or MAT, minimum GPA of 3.0; for doctorate, GRE. Additional exam requirements/recommendations for international students: Required—TOEFL. Electronic applications accepted. *Faculty research:* Library administration, user services, digital libraries, book arts, evaluation.

University of Alberta, Faculty of Graduate Studies and Research, School of Library and Information Studies, Edmonton, AB T6G 2E1, Canada. Offers MLIS. *Accreditation:* ALA. *Entrance requirements:* Additional exam requirements/recommendations for

international students: Required—TOEFL, Canadian Academic English Language Assessment. Electronic applications accepted. *Faculty research:* Intellectual freedom, materials for children and young adults, library classification, multi-media literacy.

The University of Arizona, College of Social and Behavioral Sciences, School of Information, Tucson, AZ 85721. Offers MA, PhD. *Accreditation:* ALA (one or more programs are accredited). *Program availability:* Part-time. *Degree requirements:* For master's, proficiency in disk operating system (DOS); for doctorate, thesis/dissertation. *Entrance requirements:* For master's and doctorate, GRE General Test, 3 letters of recommendation, resume. Additional exam requirements/recommendations for international students: Required—TOEFL (minimum score 550 paper-based; 79 iBT). Electronic applications accepted. *Faculty research:* Microcomputer applications; quantitative methods systems; information transfer, planning, evaluation, and technology.

The University of British Columbia, Faculty of Arts, School of Library, Archival and Information Studies, Dual Master of Archival Studies/Master of Library and Information Studies Program, Vancouver, BC V6T 1Z1, Canada. Offers MLIS/MAS. *Entrance requirements:* Additional exam requirements/recommendations for international students: Required—TOEFL. Electronic applications accepted. *Expenses:* Contact institution. *Faculty research:* Computer systems/database design, information-seeking behavior, archives and records management, children's literature and services, digital libraries and archives.

The University of British Columbia, Faculty of Arts, School of Library, Archival and Information Studies, Master of Library and Information Studies Program, Vancouver, BC V6T 1Z1, Canada. Offers MLIS. *Accreditation:* ALA. *Program availability:* Part-time. *Degree requirements:* For master's, thesis optional. *Entrance requirements:* For master's, minimum GPA of 3.3 in undergraduate upper-division courses. Additional exam requirements/recommendations for international students: Required—TOEFL. Electronic applications accepted. *Expenses:* Contact institution. *Faculty research:* Computer systems/database design; digital libraries; metadata/classification; human-computer interaction; children's literature and services.

The University of British Columbia, Faculty of Arts, School of Library, Archival and Information Studies, PhD Program in Library, Archival and Information Studies, Vancouver, BC V6T 1Z1, Canada. Offers PhD. *Degree requirements:* For doctorate, thesis/dissertation. *Entrance requirements:* For doctorate, GRE, minimum GPA of 3.3 in MAS or MLIS. Additional exam requirements/recommendations for international students: Required—TOEFL. Electronic applications accepted. *Expenses:* Contact institution. *Faculty research:* Computer systems/database design; library and archival management; archival description and organization; children's literature and youth services; interactive information retrieval.

University of California, Los Angeles, Graduate Division, Graduate School of Education and Information Studies, Department of Information Studies, Los Angeles, CA 90095-1521. Offers archival studies (MLIS); informatics (MLIS); information studies (PhD); library and information science (Certificate); library studies (MLIS); moving image archive studies (MA); rare books, print and visual culture (MLIS); MBA/MLIS; MLIS/MA. *Accreditation:* ALA (one or more programs are accredited). Terminal master's awarded for partial completion of doctoral program. *Degree requirements:* For master's, thesis or alternative, professional portfolio; for doctorate, thesis/dissertation, oral and written qualifying exams. *Entrance requirements:* For master's, GRE General Test, previous course work in statistics; for doctorate, GRE General Test, previous course work in statistics, 2 samples of research writing in English. Additional exam requirements/recommendations for international students: Required—TOEFL (minimum score 560 paper-based; 87 iBT), IELTS (minimum score 7). Electronic applications accepted. *Faculty research:* Digital libraries, archives and electronic records, interface design, cultural informatics, preservation/conservation, access.

University of Central Arkansas, Graduate School, College of Education, Department of Leadership Studies, Program in Library Media and Information Technology, Conway, AR 72035-0001. Offers MS. *Program availability:* Part-time, evening/weekend, online learning. *Degree requirements:* For master's, comprehensive exam. *Entrance requirements:* For master's, GRE General Test, minimum GPA of 2.7. Additional exam requirements/recommendations for international students: Required—TOEFL (minimum score 550 paper-based). Electronic applications accepted.

University of Central Missouri, The Graduate School, Warrensburg, MO 64093. Offers accountancy (MA); accounting (MBA); applied mathematics (MS); aviation safety (MA); biology (MS); business administration (MBA); career and technical education leadership (MS); college student personnel administration (MS); communication (MA); computer science (MS); counseling (MS); criminal justice (MS); educational leadership (Ed D); educational technology (MS); elementary and early childhood education (MSE); English (MA); environmental studies (MA); finance (MBA); history (MA); human services/educational technology (Ed S); human services/learning resources (Ed S); human services/professional counseling (Ed S); industrial hygiene (MS); industrial management (MS); information systems (MBA); information technology (MS); kinesiology (MS); library science and information services (MS); literacy education (MSE); marketing (MBA); mathematics (MS); music (MA); occupational safety management (MS); psychology (MS); rural family nursing (MS); school administration (MSE); social gerontology (MS); sociology (MA); special education (MSE); speech language pathology (MS); superintendency (Ed S); teaching (MAT); teaching English as a second language (MA); technology (MS); technology management (PhD); theatre (MA). *Accreditation:* ASHA. *Program availability:* Part-time, 100% online, blended/hybrid learning. *Degree requirements:* For master's and Ed S, comprehensive exam (for some programs), thesis (for some programs). *Entrance requirements:* Additional exam requirements/recommendations for international students: Required—TOEFL (minimum score 550 paper-based; 79 iBT). Electronic applications accepted.

University of Central Oklahoma, The Jackson College of Graduate Studies, College of Education and Professional Studies, Donna Nigh Department of Advanced Professional and Special Services, Edmond, OK 73034-5209. Offers educational leadership (M Ed); library media education (M Ed); reading (M Ed); school counseling (M Ed); special education (M Ed), including mild/moderate disabilities, severe-profound/multiple disabilities; speech-language pathology (MS). *Accreditation:* ASHA. *Program availability:* Part-time. *Degree requirements:* For master's, comprehensive exam (for some programs), thesis (for some programs). *Entrance requirements:* Additional exam requirements/recommendations for international students: Required—TOEFL (minimum score 550 paper-based; 79 iBT), IELTS (minimum score 6.5). Electronic applications accepted.

University of Denver, Morgridge College of Education, Denver, CO 80208. Offers child, family and school psychology (MA, PhD, Ed S); counseling psychology (MA, PhD); curriculum and instruction (MA, Ed D, PhD); curriculum instruction and teaching (Certificate); early childhood special education (MA, Certificate); educational leadership and policy studies (MA, Ed D, PhD, Certificate); higher education (Ed D, PhD); library and information science (MLIS); research methods and statistics (MA, PhD). *Accreditation:* ALA; APA (one or more programs are accredited). *Program availability:* Part-time, evening/weekend, online learning. *Faculty:* 49 full-time (35 women), 33 part-time/adjunct (20 women). *Students:* 509 full-time (400 women), 365 part-time (277

women); includes 236 minority (53 Black or African American, non-Hispanic/Latino; 6 American Indian or Alaska Native, non-Hispanic/Latino; 28 Asian, non-Hispanic/Latino; 116 Hispanic/Latino; 33 Two or more races, non-Hispanic/Latino), 56 international. Average age 31. 1,372 applicants, 57% accepted, 382 enrolled. In 2018, 258 master's, 41 doctorates, 162 other advanced degrees awarded. Terminal master's awarded for partial completion of doctoral program. *Degree requirements:* For master's, comprehensive exam (for some programs); for doctorate, comprehensive exam (for some programs), thesis/dissertation. *Entrance requirements:* For master's, GRE General Test or GMAT, bachelors degree; transcripts; two letters of recommendation; personal statement; resume; for doctorate, GRE General Test or GMAT, Masters degree; transcripts; two letters of recommendation; personal statement(s); resume. Additional exam requirements/recommendations for international students: Required—TOEFL (minimum score 550 paper-based; 80 iBT). *Application deadline:* Applications are processed on a rolling basis. Application fee: $65. Electronic applications accepted. *Expenses:* $33,183 per year full-time. *Financial support:* In 2018–19, 690 students received support, including 29 research assistantships with tuition reimbursements available (averaging $11,465 per year), 9 teaching assistantships with tuition reimbursements available (averaging $2,527 per year); career-related internships or fieldwork, Federal Work-Study, institutionally sponsored loans, scholarships/grants, and unspecified assistantships also available. Support available to part-time students. Financial award application deadline: 2/15; financial award applicants required to submit FAFSA. *Faculty research:* Early childhood education, educational leadership, access and opportunity to postsecondary education, marriage and family therapy, data management and archival research. *Total annual research expenditures:* $2.3 million. *Unit head:* Dr. Karen Riley, Dean, 303-871-3665, E-mail: karen.riley@du.edu. *Application contact:* Jodi Dye, Director of Admissions, 303-871-2510, E-mail: jodi.dye@du.edu.
Website: http://morgridge.du.edu

University of Hawaii at Manoa, Office of Graduate Education, College of Natural Sciences, Department of Information and Computer Sciences, Library and Information Science Program, Honolulu, HI 96822-2233. Offers advanced library and information science (Graduate Certificate); library and information science (MLI Sc). *Accreditation:* ALA (one or more programs are accredited). *Program availability:* Part-time. *Degree requirements:* For master's, comprehensive exam, thesis optional. *Entrance requirements:* For master's, GRE General Test. Additional exam requirements/recommendations for international students: Required—TOEFL (minimum score 600 paper-based). Electronic applications accepted. *Faculty research:* Information behavior, evaluation of electronic information sources, online learning, history of libraries, information literacy.

University of Houston–Clear Lake, School of Education, Program in Curriculum and Instruction, Houston, TX 77058-1002. Offers curriculum and instruction (MS); early childhood education (MS); reading (MS); school library and information science (MS). *Program availability:* Part-time, evening/weekend. *Degree requirements:* For master's, thesis (for some programs). *Entrance requirements:* For master's, GRE or minimum GPA of 3.0 in last 60 hours. Additional exam requirements/recommendations for international students: Required—TOEFL (minimum score 550 paper-based). Electronic applications accepted.

University of Illinois at Urbana–Champaign, Graduate College, School of Information Sciences, Champaign, IL 61820. Offers bioinformatics (MS); digital libraries (CAS); information management (MS); library and information science (MS, PhD, CAS). *Accreditation:* ALA (one or more programs are accredited). *Program availability:* Part-time, online learning. *Entrance requirements:* For degree, master's degree in library and information science or related field with minimum GPA of 3.0.

The University of Iowa, Graduate College, School of Library and Information Science, Iowa City, IA 52242-1316. Offers MA, PhD, MA/Certificate, PhD/Certificate. *Accreditation:* ALA (one or more programs are accredited). *Degree requirements:* For master's, thesis optional, exam, portfolio. *Entrance requirements:* For master's, GRE General Test, minimum GPA of 3.0. Additional exam requirements/recommendations for international students: Required—TOEFL (minimum score 550 paper-based; 81 iBT). Electronic applications accepted.

University of Kentucky, Graduate School, College of Communication and Information, Program in Library Science, Lexington, KY 40506-0032. Offers MA, MSLS. *Accreditation:* ALA (one or more programs are accredited). *Program availability:* Part-time. *Degree requirements:* For master's, variable foreign language requirement, comprehensive exam. *Entrance requirements:* For master's, GRE General Test, minimum undergraduate GPA of 2.75. Additional exam requirements/recommendations for international students: Required—TOEFL (minimum score 550 paper-based). *Faculty research:* Information retrieval systems, information-seeking behavior, organizational behavior, computer cataloging, library resource sharing.

University of Maryland, College Park, Academic Affairs, Program in History, Library, and Information Services, College Park, MD 20742. Offers MA/MLS. *Entrance requirements:* Additional exam requirements/recommendations for international students: Required—TOEFL. Electronic applications accepted.

University of Missouri, Office of Research and Graduate Studies, College of Education, School of Information Science and Learning Technologies, Columbia, MO 65211. Offers information science and learning technology (PhD). *Accreditation:* ALA. *Program availability:* Part-time, evening/weekend. *Entrance requirements:* Additional exam requirements/recommendations for international students: Required—TOEFL. Electronic applications accepted.

University of Nebraska at Kearney, College of Education, Department of Teacher Education, Kearney, NE 68849-0001. Offers curriculum and instruction (MA Ed), including early childhood education, elementary education, English as a second language, instructional effectiveness, reading/special education, secondary education; instructional technology (MS Ed), including information technology, instructional technology, school librarian; reading PK-12 (MA Ed); special education (MA Ed), including advanced practitioner: assistive technology specialist, advanced practitioner: behavioral interventionist, advanced practitioner: inclusive collaboration specialist, gifted, teacher education. *Program availability:* Part-time, evening/weekend, online only, 100% online. *Degree requirements:* For master's, comprehensive exam, thesis optional. *Entrance requirements:* For master's, portfolio or GRE. Additional exam requirements/recommendations for international students: Recommended—TOEFL (minimum score 550 paper-based; 79 iBT), IELTS (minimum score 6.5). Electronic applications accepted. *Expenses:* Contact institution.

The University of North Carolina at Chapel Hill, Graduate School, School of Information and Library Science, Chapel Hill, NC 27599. Offers data curation (PMC); digital curation and management (PSM); information and library science (PhD); information science (MSIS); library science (MSLS). *Accreditation:* ALA (one or more programs are accredited). *Program availability:* Part-time, 100% online, blended/hybrid learning. *Faculty:* 31 full-time (13 women), 46 part-time/adjunct (23 women). *Students:* 255 full-time (188 women), 29 part-time (18 women); includes 34 minority (11 Black or African American, non-Hispanic/Latino; 6 Asian, non-Hispanic/Latino; 8 Hispanic/Latino; 9 Two or more races, non-Hispanic/Latino), 62 international. Average age 28. 303

applicants, 69% accepted, 98 enrolled. In 2018, 125 master's, 17 doctorates, 2 other advanced degrees awarded. Terminal master's awarded for partial completion of doctoral program. *Degree requirements:* For master's, comprehensive exam, paper or project; for doctorate, comprehensive exam, thesis/dissertation. *Entrance requirements:* For master's and doctorate, GRE General Test. Additional exam requirements/recommendations for international students: Required—TOEFL (minimum score 90 iBT). *Application deadline:* For fall admission, 12/10 priority date for domestic and international students; for spring admission, 10/8 for domestic and international students; for summer admission, 3/10 for domestic and international students. Applications are processed on a rolling basis. Application fee: $90. Electronic applications accepted. *Expenses:* $15,000 in-state per year, $31,250 out-of-state per year (for MSLS/MSIS); $15,000 in-state per year, $30,000 out-of-state per year (for PSM); $16,500 in-state per year, $32,500 out-of-state per year (for PMC). *Financial support:* In 2018–19, 59 fellowships with full tuition reimbursements (averaging $2,565 per year), 46 research assistantships with full tuition reimbursements (averaging $3,528 per year), 7 teaching assistantships with full tuition reimbursements (averaging $22,917 per year) were awarded; career-related internships or fieldwork, Federal Work-Study, scholarships/grants, health care benefits, and unspecified assistantships also available. Financial award application deadline: 12/12. *Faculty research:* Information retrieval and management, digital libraries, management of information resources, archives and records management, health informatics. *Total annual research expenditures:* $3 million. *Unit head:* Dr. Gary Marchionini, Dean, 919-962-8363, Fax: 919-962-8071, E-mail: gary@ils.unc.edu. *Application contact:* Lara Bailey, Student Services Coordinator, 919-962-7601, Fax: 919-962-8071, E-mail: bailey@email.unc.edu. Website: http://sils.unc.edu

The University of North Carolina at Greensboro, Graduate School, School of Education, Department of Library and Information Studies, Greensboro, NC 27412-5001. Offers MLIS. *Accreditation:* ALA. *Program availability:* Part-time, evening/weekend, online learning. *Degree requirements:* For master's, portfolio. *Entrance requirements:* For master's, GRE General Test. Additional exam requirements/recommendations for international students: Required—TOEFL (minimum score 550 paper-based), IELTS (minimum score 6.5). Electronic applications accepted. *Faculty research:* Library history, gender studies, children's literature, web design, homeless, technical services.

University of Oklahoma, College of Arts and Sciences, School of Library and Information Studies, Norman, OK 73019. Offers archival studies (Graduate Certificate); digital humanities (Graduate Certificate); information studies (PhD); library and information studies (MLIS); M Ed/MLIS; MBA/MLIS. *Accreditation:* ALA (one or more programs are accredited). *Program availability:* Part-time, evening/weekend, 100% online, blended/hybrid learning. *Faculty:* 7 full-time (6 women), 2 part-time/adjunct (1 woman). *Students:* 63 full-time (53 women), 133 part-time (108 women); includes 48 minority (8 Black or African American, non-Hispanic/Latino; 4 American Indian or Alaska Native, non-Hispanic/Latino; 5 Asian, non-Hispanic/Latino; 14 Hispanic/Latino; 1 Native Hawaiian or other Pacific Islander, non-Hispanic/Latino; 16 Two or more races, non-Hispanic/Latino), 2 international. Average age 32. 60 applicants, 93% accepted, 41 enrolled. In 2018, 54 master's, 9 other advanced degrees awarded. Terminal master's awarded for partial completion of doctoral program. *Degree requirements:* For master's, comprehensive exam (for some programs), thesis optional; for doctorate, comprehensive exam, thesis/dissertation. *Entrance requirements:* For master's, three letters of recommendation, personal statement, resume, transcript; for doctorate, GRE, three letters of recommendation, personal statement, resume, writing sample; for Graduate Certificate, transcripts, personal statement (for some certificates), letter of recommendation (for some certificates). Additional exam requirements/recommendations for international students: Required—TOEFL (minimum score 79 iBT) or IELTS (minimum score 6.5). *Application deadline:* Applications are processed on a rolling basis. Application fee: $50 ($100 for international students). Electronic applications accepted. *Expenses:* Tuition, state resident: full-time $5683.20; part-time $236.80 per credit hour. Tuition, nonresident: full-time $20,342; part-time $847.60 per credit hour. *International tuition:* $20,342.40 full-time. *Required fees:* $2894.20; $110.05 per credit hour. $126.50 per semester. Tuition and fees vary according to course load and program. *Financial support:* Research assistantships, teaching assistantships, scholarships/grants, health care benefits, and unspecified assistantships available. Financial award application deadline: 6/1; financial award applicants required to submit FAFSA. *Faculty research:* Family and youth technology in libraries, consumer health information, text mining, big data analytics. *Unit head:* Dr. Susan K. Burke, Director, 405-325-3921, E-mail: sburke@ou.edu. *Application contact:* Sarah Connelly, Admissions and Student Services Coordinator, 405-325-3921, E-mail: sarahee@ou.edu. Website: http://slis.ou.edu

University of Pittsburgh, School of Computing and Information, Department of Information Culture and Data Stewardship, Pittsburgh, PA 15260. Offers library and information science (MLIS, PhD). *Accreditation:* ALA. *Program availability:* Part-time, evening/weekend, 100% online. *Degree requirements:* For master's, thesis optional; for doctorate, comprehensive exam, thesis/dissertation. *Entrance requirements:* For master's, GRE General Test, GMAT, MAT, MCAT, LSAT, bachelor's degree with minimum GPA of 3.0; for doctorate, GRE General Test, GMAT, MAT, MCAT, LSAT, master's degree with minimum GPA of 3.5. Additional exam requirements/recommendations for international students: Required—TOEFL (minimum score 550 paper-based; 80 iBT), IELTS (minimum score 6.5). Electronic applications accepted. *Expenses:* Contact institution. *Faculty research:* Data and information, archives and data preservation, information and society, children and youth services, research data management.

University of Puerto Rico–Río Piedras, Graduate School of Information Sciences and Technologies, San Juan, PR 00931-3300. Offers administration of academic libraries (PMC); administration of public libraries (PMC); administration of special libraries (PMC); consultant in information services (PMC); documents and files administration (Post-Graduate Certificate); electronic information resources analyst (Post-Graduate Certificate); information science (MIS); librarianship and information services (MLS); school librarian (Post-Graduate Certificate); school librarian distance education mode (Post-Graduate Certificate); specialist in legal information (PMC). *Accreditation:* ALA. *Program availability:* Part-time. *Degree requirements:* For master's, comprehensive exam, thesis, portfolio. *Entrance requirements:* For master's, PAEG, GRE, interview, minimum GPA of 3.0, 3 letters of recommendation; for other advanced degree, PAEG, GRE, minimum GPA of 3.0, IST master's degree. *Faculty research:* Investigating the users needs and preferences for a specialized environmental library.

University of Rhode Island, Graduate School, College of Arts and Sciences, Graduate School of Library and Information Studies, Kingston, RI 02881. Offers libraries, leadership and transforming communities (MLIS); organization of digital media (MLIS); school library media (MLIS); MLIS/MA; MLIS/MPA. *Accreditation:* ALA (one or more programs are accredited). *Program availability:* Part-time. *Faculty:* 4 full-time (all women). *Students:* 24 full-time (14 women), 73 part-time (62 women); includes 8 minority (3 Asian, non-Hispanic/Latino; 1 Hispanic/Latino; 1 Native Hawaiian or other Pacific Islander, non-Hispanic/Latino; 3 Two or more races, non-Hispanic/Latino). 50 applicants, 86% accepted, 27 enrolled. In 2018, 38 master's awarded. *Entrance*

requirements: For master's, GRE or MAT if undergraduate GPA below 3.3, 2 letters of recommendation. Additional exam requirements/recommendations for international students: Required—TOEFL. *Application deadline:* For fall admission, 6/15 for domestic students, 2/1 for international students; for spring admission, 10/15 for domestic students, 7/15 for international students; for summer admission, 3/15 for domestic students. Application fee: $65. Electronic applications accepted. *Expenses: Tuition, area resident:* Full-time $13,226; part-time $735 per credit. Tuition, state resident: full-time $13,226; part-time $735 per credit. Tuition, nonresident: full-time $25,854; part-time $1436 per credit. *International tuition:* $25,854 full-time. *Required fees:* $1698; $50 per credit. $35 per semester. One-time fee: $165. *Financial support:* Application deadline: 1/15; applicants required to submit FAFSA. *Unit head:* Dr. Valerie Karno, Director, Graduate School of Library and Information Studies, 401-874-4682, Fax: 401-874-4127, E-mail: karno@uri.edu. *Application contact:* Dr. Valerie Karno, Director, Graduate School of Library and Information Studies, 401-874-4682, Fax: 401-874-4127, E-mail: karno@uri.edu. Website: http://www.uri.edu/artsci/lsc/

University of South Carolina, The Graduate School, College of Information and Communications, School of Library and Information Science, Columbia, SC 29208. Offers MLIS, PhD, Certificate, Specialist, MLIS/MA. *Accreditation:* ALA (one or more programs are accredited). *Program availability:* Part-time, online learning. *Degree requirements:* For master's, end of program portfolio; for doctorate, comprehensive exam, thesis/dissertation. *Entrance requirements:* For master's and other advanced degree, GRE General Test or MAT; for doctorate, GTE, writing sample. Additional exam requirements/recommendations for international students: Required—TOEFL (minimum score 570 paper-based; 75 iBT). Electronic applications accepted. *Faculty research:* Information technology management, distance education, library services for children and young adults, special libraries.

University of Southern Mississippi, College of Education and Human Sciences, School of Library and Information Science, Hattiesburg, MS 39406-0001. Offers library and information science (MLIS); youth services and literature (Graduate Certificate). *Accreditation:* ALA (one or more programs are accredited). *Program availability:* Part-time, evening/weekend, online learning. *Degree requirements:* For master's, comprehensive exam, thesis. *Entrance requirements:* For master's, GRE General Test, minimum GPA of 3.0. Additional exam requirements/recommendations for international students: Required—TOEFL, IELTS. Electronic applications accepted. *Faculty research:* Printing, library history, children's literature, telecommunications, management.

University of South Florida, College of Arts and Sciences, School of Information, Tampa, FL 33620-9951. Offers intelligence studies (MS), including cyber intelligence, strategic intelligence; library and information science (MA). *Accreditation:* ALA (one or more programs are accredited). *Program availability:* Part-time, evening/weekend, online learning. *Faculty:* 15 full-time (7 women). *Students:* 108 full-time (77 women), 182 part-time (137 women); includes 83 minority (23 Black or African American, non-Hispanic/Latino; 7 Asian, non-Hispanic/Latino; 49 Hispanic/Latino; 4 Two or more races, non-Hispanic/Latino). Average age 32. 141 applicants, 86% accepted, 71 enrolled. In 2018, 128 master's awarded. *Degree requirements:* For master's, comprehensive exam, thesis (for some programs). *Entrance requirements:* For master's, GRE not required for Intelligence Studies; GRE required for Library and Information Science with preferred minimum scores of 734d percentile (156v), 10th percentile (141Q). May be waived under certain criteria, goals statement, resume or CV, some programs need understanding of programming/coding, computational problem solving and operating systems (for Intelligence Studies); GRE, writing sample, 3 letters of recommendation, resume, statement of purpose (for Library and Information Science). Additional exam requirements/recommendations for international students: Required—TOEFL, TOEFL (minimum score 550 paper-based; 79 iBT) or IELTS (minimum score 6.5). *Application deadline:* For fall admission, 6/1 priority date for domestic students, 5/1 for international students; for spring admission, 10/15 priority date for domestic students, 9/15 for international students. Applications are processed on a rolling basis. Application fee: $30. Electronic applications accepted. *Expenses:* Tuition, state resident: full-time $6350. Tuition, nonresident: full-time $19,048. *International tuition:* $19,048 full-time. *Required fees:* $2079. *Financial support:* In 2018–19, 62 students received support. Unspecified assistantships available. Financial award application deadline: 6/30. *Faculty research:* Youth services in libraries, community engagement and libraries, information architecture, biomedical informatics, health informatics. *Total annual research expenditures:* $21,733. *Unit head:* Dr. Jim Andrews, Director and Associate Professor, 813-974-2108, Fax: 813-974-6840, E-mail: jimandrews@usf.edu. *Application contact:* Dr. Randy Borum, Graduate Program Director, 813-974-3520, Fax: 813-974-6840, E-mail: wborum@usf.edu. Website: http://si.usf.edu/

University of Washington, Graduate School, Information School, Seattle, WA 98195. Offers information management (MSIM), including business intelligence, data science, information architecture, information consulting, information security, user experience; information science (PhD); library and information science (MLIS). *Accreditation:* ALA (one or more programs are accredited). *Program availability:* Part-time, evening/weekend, 100% online coursework with required attendance at on-campus orientation at start of program. *Faculty:* 51 full-time (23 women), 38 part-time/adjunct (21 women). *Students:* 347 full-time (229 women), 259 part-time (195 women); includes 129 minority (23 Black or African American, non-Hispanic/Latino; 7 American Indian or Alaska Native, non-Hispanic/Latino; 59 Asian, non-Hispanic/Latino; 36 Hispanic/Latino; 4 Native Hawaiian or other Pacific Islander, non-Hispanic/Latino), 160 international. Average age 32. 1,190 applicants, 42% accepted, 264 enrolled. In 2018, 231 master's, 10 doctorates awarded. Terminal master's awarded for partial completion of doctoral program. *Degree requirements:* For master's, comprehensive exam (for some programs), thesis or alternative, capstone or culminating project; for doctorate, comprehensive exam, thesis/dissertation. *Entrance requirements:* For master's, GRE General Test, GMAT; for doctorate, GRE General Test. Additional exam requirements/recommendations for international students: Required—TOEFL (minimum score 590 paper-based; 100 iBT). *Application deadline:* For fall admission, 12/1 priority date for domestic and international students. Application fee: $85. Electronic applications accepted. *Expenses:* MLIS: $825/credit $51,975 approximate tuition without fees; MSIM: $837/credit, $54,405 approximate tuition without fees. *Financial support:* In 2018–19, 73 students received support. Fellowships with full tuition reimbursements available, research assistantships with full tuition reimbursements available, teaching assistantships with full tuition reimbursements available, Federal Work-Study, institutionally sponsored loans, scholarships/grants, health care benefits, tuition waivers (full and partial), and unspecified assistantships available. Support available to part-time students. Financial award application deadline: 10/1; financial award applicants required to submit FAFSA. *Unit head:* Dr. Anind Dey, Dean, E-mail: anind@uw.edu. *Application contact:* Kari Brothers, Admissions Counselor, 206-616-5541, Fax: 206-616-3152, E-mail: kari683@uw.edu. Website: http://ischool.uw.edu/

The University of Western Ontario, School of Graduate and Postdoctoral Studies, Faculty of Information and Media Studies, Programs in Library and Information Science, London, ON N6A 3K7, Canada. Offers MLIS, PhD. Program conducted on a trimester

basis. *Accreditation:* ALA (one or more programs are accredited). *Program availability:* Part-time, evening/weekend. *Degree requirements:* For doctorate, comprehensive exam, thesis/dissertation. *Entrance requirements:* For master's, honors degree, minimum B average during previous 2 years of course work; for doctorate, MLIS or equivalent. Additional exam requirements/recommendations for international students: Required—TOEFL (minimum score 625 paper-based), TWE (minimum score 5). Electronic applications accepted. *Faculty research:* Information, individuals, and society; information systems, policy, power, and institutions.

University of Wisconsin–Eau Claire, College of Education and Human Sciences, Program in Secondary Education, Eau Claire, WI 54702-4004. Offers professional development (ME-PD), including library science, professional development. *Program availability:* Part-time, online learning. *Degree requirements:* For master's, comprehensive exam, thesis, research paper, portfolio or written exam; oral exam. *Entrance requirements:* For master's, certification to teach, minimum GPA of 2.75. Additional exam requirements/recommendations for international students: Required— TOEFL (minimum score 79 iBT).

University of Wisconsin–Madison, Graduate School, College of Letters and Science, Information School, Madison, WI 53706-1380. Offers MA, PhD. *Accreditation:* ALA (one or more programs are accredited). *Program availability:* Part-time. *Degree requirements:* For doctorate, comprehensive exam, thesis/dissertation. Electronic applications accepted. *Faculty research:* Intellectual freedom, children's literature, print culture history, information systems design and evaluation, school library media centers.

University of Wisconsin–Milwaukee, Graduate School, School of Information Studies, Milwaukee, WI 53201-0413. Offers MLIS, MS, PhD, CAS. *Accreditation:* ALA (one or more programs are accredited). *Program availability:* Part-time. *Students:* 157 full-time (101 women), 257 part-time (191 women); includes 71 minority (23 Black or African American, non-Hispanic/Latino; 1 American Indian or Alaska Native, non-Hispanic/ Latino; 17 Asian, non-Hispanic/Latino; 6 Hispanic/Latino; 1 Native Hawaiian or other Pacific Islander, non-Hispanic/Latino; 23 Two or more races, non-Hispanic/Latino), 16 international. Average age 34. 310 applicants, 64% accepted, 138 enrolled. In 2018, 104 master's, 2 doctorates awarded. *Entrance requirements:* For master's, GRE General Test or MAT; for doctorate, GRE. Additional exam requirements/recommendations for international students: Required—TOEFL (minimum score 550 paper-based), IELTS (minimum score 6.5). *Application deadline:* For fall admission, 1/1 priority date for domestic students; for spring admission, 9/1 for domestic students. Application fee: $56 ($96 for international students). Electronic applications accepted. *Financial support:* Fellowships, research assistantships, teaching assistantships, career-related internships or fieldwork, Federal Work-Study, health care benefits, unspecified assistantships, and project assistantships available. Support available to part-time students. Financial award application deadline: 4/15; financial award applicants required to submit FAFSA. *Unit head:* Tomas A. Lipinski, Dean/Professor, 414-229-4707, E-mail: tlipinsk@uwm.edu. *Application contact:* Linda Barajas, Admissions Coordinator, 414-229-3316, E-mail: barajas@uwm.edu.
Website: http://uwm.edu/informationstudies

Valdosta State University, Program in Library and Information Science, Valdosta, GA 31698. Offers MLIS. *Accreditation:* ALA. *Program availability:* 100% online. *Degree requirements:* For master's, comprehensive exam. *Entrance requirements:* For master's, two essays, resume, three recommendations. Additional exam requirements/ recommendations for international students: Required—TOEFL (minimum score 523 paper-based); Recommended—IELTS. *Expenses:* Contact institution.

Valley City State University, Online Graduate Programs, Valley City, ND 58072. Offers elementary education (M Ed); English education (M Ed); library and information technologies (M Ed); teaching (MAT); teaching and technology (M Ed); teaching English language learners (M Ed); technology education (M Ed). *Accreditation:* NCATE. *Program availability:* Part-time, evening/weekend, online only, 100% online. *Faculty:* 20 full-time (11 women), 13 part-time/adjunct (8 women). *Students:* 5 full-time (2 women), 133 part-time (100 women); includes 8 minority (1 Black or African American, non-Hispanic/Latino; 3 American Indian or Alaska Native, non-Hispanic/Latino; 2 Asian, non-Hispanic/Latino; 2 Hispanic/Latino). Average age 36. 23 applicants, 74% accepted, 12 enrolled. In 2018, 47 master's awarded. *Degree requirements:* For master's, action research report, comprehensive portfolio. *Entrance requirements:* For master's, GRE, MAT, PRAXIS II or National Teaching Board for Professional Standards (if GPA is less than 3.0). Additional exam requirements/recommendations for international students: Required—TOEFL (minimum score 525 paper-based; 71 iBT); Recommended—IELTS (minimum score 5.5). *Application deadline:* For fall admission, 7/26 for domestic and international students; for spring admission, 12/13 for domestic and international students; for summer admission, 5/18 for domestic and international students. Applications are processed on a rolling basis. Application fee: $35. Electronic applications accepted. *Expenses:* $396.39 per credit for all students regardless of residency. *Financial support:* In 2018–19, 16 students received support. Scholarships/ grants, tuition waivers (full and partial), and unspecified assistantships available. Financial award applicants required to submit FAFSA. *Faculty research:* Universal accessibility, instructional design and technology, gender communication, STEM education in K-12, English language learners. *Unit head:* Dr. Sheri Okland, Dean, 701-845-7184, E-mail: sheri.l.okland@vcsu.edu. *Application contact:* Misty Lindgren, Graduate Studies, 701-845-7303, Fax: 701-845-7190, E-mail: misty.lindgren@vcsu.edu.
Website: http://www.vcsu.edu/graduate

Wayne State University, School of Information Sciences, Detroit, MI 48202. Offers archival administration (Graduate Certificate); information management (MS, Graduate Certificate); library and information science (MLIS, Graduate Certificate, Spec); public library services to children and young adults (Graduate Certificate); MLIS/MA. WSU History Department. *Accreditation:* ALA (one or more programs are accredited). *Program availability:* Part-time, evening/weekend, 100% online, blended/hybrid learning. *Faculty:* 12 full-time (9 women), 17 part-time/adjunct (12 women). *Students:* 85 full-time (74 women), 316 part-time (258 women); includes 77 minority (42 Black or African American, non-Hispanic/Latino; 2 American Indian or Alaska Native, non-Hispanic/ Latino; 3 Asian, non-Hispanic/Latino; 19 Hispanic/Latino; 1 Native Hawaiian or other Pacific Islander, non-Hispanic/Latino; 10 Two or more races, non-Hispanic/Latino), 1 international. Average age 33. 258 applicants, 60% accepted, 100 enrolled. In 2018, 149 master's, 34 other advanced degrees awarded. *Degree requirements:* For master's and other advanced degree, e-portfolio. *Entrance requirements:* For master's, GRE or MAT (if undergraduate GPA is between 2.5 and 2.99), minimum undergraduate GPA of 3.0 or graduate degree, personal statement, resume or curriculum vitae; for other advanced degree, GRE or MAT (if undergraduate GPA is between 2.5 and 2.99), minimum undergraduate GPA of 3.0 or graduate degree, personal statement, resume or curriculum vitae, MLIS (for specialist certificate). Additional exam requirements/ recommendations for international students: Required—TOEFL (minimum score 550 paper-based; 79 iBT); Recommended—IELTS (minimum score 6.5), TWE (minimum score 5.5). *Application deadline:* For fall admission, 7/1 for domestic students, 5/1 priority date for international students; for winter admission, 10/1 priority date for domestic students, 9/1 priority date for international students; for spring admission, 2/1 priority date for domestic students, 1/1 priority date for international students. Applications are processed on a rolling basis. Application fee: $50. Electronic applications accepted. *Expenses:* 15,000/year. *Financial support:* In 2018–19, 133 students received support. Fellowships with tuition reimbursements available, scholarships/grants, health care benefits, and unspecified assistantships available. Support available to part-time students. Financial award applicants required to submit FAFSA. *Faculty research:* Library services, information management issues, digital content management, library/community engagement, archives and preservation. *Unit head:* Dr. Jon Cawthorne, Dean, 313-577-4020, E-mail: jon.cawthorne@wayne.edu. *Application contact:* Academic Services Officer II, 313-577-1825, E-mail: asklis@ wayne.edu.
Website: http://slis.wayne.edu/

ACADEMIC AND PROFESSIONAL PROGRAMS IN PHYSICAL EDUCATION, SPORTS, AND RECREATION

Section 29
Leisure Studies and Recreation

This section contains a directory of institutions offering graduate work in leisure studies and recreation. Additional information about programs listed in the directory may be obtained by writing directly to the dean of a graduate school or chair of a department at the address given in the directory.

In the other guides in this series:

Graduate Programs in the Humanities, Arts & Social Sciences
See *Performing Arts*

Graduate Programs in the Physical Sciences, Mathematics, Agricultural Sciences, the Environment & Natural Resources

See *Natural Resources*

CONTENTS

Program Directories

Leisure Studies

Bowling Green State University, Graduate College, College of Education and Human Development, School of Human Movement, Sport, and Leisure Studies, Bowling Green, OH 43403. Offers developmental kinesiology (M Ed); recreation and leisure (M Ed); sport administration (M Ed). *Program availability:* Part-time. *Degree requirements:* For master's, thesis or alternative. *Entrance requirements:* For master's, GRE General Test, minimum GPA of 2.7. Additional exam requirements/recommendations for international students: Required—TOEFL. Electronic applications accepted. *Faculty research:* Teacher-learning process, travel and tourism, sport marketing and management, exercise physiology and sport psychology, life-span motor development.

California State University, Long Beach, Graduate Studies, College of Health and Human Services, Department of Recreation and Leisure Studies, Long Beach, CA 90840. Offers recreation administration (MS). *Program availability:* Part-time. *Degree requirements:* For master's, comprehensive exam or thesis. *Entrance requirements:* For master's, GRE General Test. *Application deadline:* For fall admission, 4/1 for domestic students. Applications are processed on a rolling basis. Application fee: $55. Electronic applications accepted. *Expenses: Required fees:* $2628 per term. Tuition and fees vary according to class time, course level, course load, degree level, campus/location and program. *Financial support:* Federal Work-Study, institutionally sponsored loans, and scholarships/grants available. Financial award application deadline: 3/2; financial award applicants required to submit FAFSA. *Unit head:* Terry Robertson, Chair, 562-985-1098, E-mail: Terry.Robertson@csulb.edu. *Application contact:* Heewon Yang, Graduate Advisor, 562-985-1495, E-mail: Heewon.Yang@csulb.edu.
Website: http://web.csulb.edu/colleges/chhs/departments/recreation-and-leisure-studies/

Dalhousie University, Faculty of Health, School of Health and Human Performance, Program in Leisure Studies, Halifax, NS B3H 1T8, Canada. Offers MA. *Program availability:* Part-time. *Degree requirements:* For master's, thesis. *Entrance requirements:* For master's, minimum GPA of 3.3. Additional exam requirements/recommendations for international students: Required—TOEFL, IELTS, CANTEST, CAEL, or Michigan English Language Assessment Battery. Electronic applications accepted. *Faculty research:* Leisure and lifestyles of social groups such as older adults, women, and persons with health problems or disabilities; historical analysis of leisure; sport and leisure administration.

East Carolina University, Graduate School, College of Health and Human Performance, Department of Recreation and Leisure Studies, Greenville, NC 27858-4353. Offers aquatic therapy (Certificate); biofeedback (Certificate); recreation services and interventions (MS), including generalist. *Program availability:* Part-time, evening/weekend, online learning. *Application deadline:* For fall admission, 6/1 priority date for domestic students. *Expenses: Tuition, area resident:* Full-time $4749. Tuition, state resident: full-time $4749. Tuition, nonresident: full-time $17,898. *International tuition:* $17,898 full-time. *Required fees:* $2787. Part-time tuition and fees vary according to course load and program. *Financial support:* Application deadline: 6/1. *Unit head:* Dr. Edwin Gómez, Chair, 252-328-4638, E-mail: gomeze17@ecu.edu. *Application contact:* Graduate Student Admissions, 252-328-6012, Fax: 252-328-6071, E-mail: gradschool@ecu.edu.
Website: https://hhp.ecu.edu/rcls/

Howard University, Graduate School, Department of Health, Human Performance and Leisure Studies, Washington, DC 20059-0002. Offers exercise physiology (MS); health education (MS); sports studies (MS), including sociology of sports, sports management; urban recreation (MS), including leisure studies. *Program availability:* Part-time, evening/weekend. *Degree requirements:* For master's, comprehensive exam, thesis. *Entrance requirements:* For master's, BS in human performance or related field. Additional exam requirements/recommendations for international students: Recommended—TOEFL. Electronic applications accepted. *Faculty research:* Health promotion, cardiovascular hypertension, physical activity, sport and human rights issues.

Indiana University Bloomington, School of Public Health, Department of Recreation, Park, and Tourism Studies, Bloomington, IN 47405-7000. Offers leisure behavior (PhD); outdoor recreation (MS); park and public lands management (MS); recreation administration (MS); recreational sports administration (MS); recreational therapy (MS); tourism management (MS). Terminal master's awarded for partial completion of doctoral program. *Degree requirements:* For master's, thesis optional; for doctorate, comprehensive exam, thesis/dissertation. *Entrance requirements:* For master's, GRE General Test, minimum GPA of 2.8; for doctorate, GRE General Test, minimum GPA of 3.0 (undergraduate), 3.5 (graduate). Additional exam requirements/recommendations for international students: Required—TOEFL (minimum score 550 paper-based; 80 iBT). Electronic applications accepted. *Faculty research:* Leisure counseling, gerontology, special populations, planning and development.

Penn State University Park, Graduate School, College of Health and Human Development, Department of Recreation, Park and Tourism Management, University Park, PA 16802. Offers MS, PhD.

Prescott College, Graduate Programs, Program in Adventure Education, Prescott, AZ 86301. Offers adventure education (MA); adventure-based environmental education (MA); student-directed concentration (MA). *Program availability:* Part-time, online learning. *Degree requirements:* For master's, thesis, fieldwork or internship, practicum. *Entrance requirements:* For master's, 2 letters of recommendation, resume. Additional exam requirements/recommendations for international students: Required—TOEFL (minimum score 500 paper-based). Electronic applications accepted.

San Francisco State University, Division of Graduate Studies, College of Health and Social Sciences, Department of Recreation, Parks, and Tourism, San Francisco, CA 94132-1722. Offers MS. *Program availability:* Part-time. *Application deadline:* Applications are processed on a rolling basis. *Financial support:* Career-related internships or fieldwork available. *Unit head:* Dr. Erik Rosegard, Chair, 415-338-7529, Fax: 415-338-0543, E-mail: rosegard@sfsu.edu. *Application contact:* Dr. Jackson Wilson, Graduate Coordinator, 415-338-1487, Fax: 415-338-0543, E-mail: wilsonj@sfsu.edu.
Website: http://recdept.sfsu.edu/graduate

Southeast Missouri State University, School of Graduate Studies, Kinesiology, Nutrition and Recreation, Cape Girardeau, MO 63701-4799. Offers MS. *Program availability:* Part-time. *Faculty:* 8 full-time (2 women), 2 part-time/adjunct (1 woman). *Students:* 15 full-time (8 women), 12 part-time (11 women); includes 1 minority (Black or African American, non-Hispanic/Latino), 6 international. Average age 26. 31 applicants, 84% accepted, 15 enrolled. In 2018, 7 master's awarded. *Degree requirements:* For master's, comprehensive exam, thesis optional. *Entrance requirements:* For master's, GRE General Test (minimum combined score of 950). Additional exam requirements/

recommendations for international students: Required—TOEFL (minimum score 550 paper-based; 79 iBT), IELTS (minimum score 6), PTE (minimum score 53). *Application deadline:* For fall admission, 8/1 for domestic students, 5/1 for international students; for spring admission, 11/21 for domestic students, 10/1 for international students; for summer admission, 5/15 for domestic students. Applications are processed on a rolling basis. Application fee: $30 ($40 for international students). Electronic applications accepted. *Expenses:* Contact institution. *Financial support:* In 2018–19, 10 students received support, including 7 teaching assistantships with full tuition reimbursements available; career-related internships or fieldwork, Federal Work-Study, scholarships/grants, traineeships, tuition waivers (full), and unspecified assistantships also available. Financial award application deadline: 6/30; financial award applicants required to submit FAFSA. *Faculty research:* Body composition assessment techniques, serum lipid adaptations with physical activity in smokers, professional attitudes of pre-service teachers, high intensity training with clinical populations. *Unit head:* Dr. Joe Pujol, Professor and Chairperson, 573-651-2664, Fax: 573-651-5150, E-mail: jpujol@semo.edu. *Application contact:* Dr. Jeremy Barnes, Professor/Graduate Coordinator, 573-651-2197, Fax: 573-651-5150, E-mail: jbarnes@semo.edu.
Website: http://www.semo.edu/health/

Southern Connecticut State University, School of Graduate Studies, School of Health and Human Services, Department of Recreation and Leisure Studies, New Haven, CT 06515-1355. Offers MS. *Program availability:* Part-time, evening/weekend. *Degree requirements:* For master's, thesis or alternative. *Entrance requirements:* For master's, interview, minimum undergraduate QPA of 3.0 in graduate major field or 2.5 overall. Electronic applications accepted.

Texas State University, The Graduate College, College of Education, Program in Recreation Management, San Marcos, TX 78666. Offers recreation management (MSRLS). *Program availability:* Part-time. *Faculty:* 6 full-time (3 women), 1 (woman) part-time/adjunct. *Students:* 12 full-time (1 woman), 7 part-time (1 woman); includes 9 minority (4 Black or African American, non-Hispanic/Latino; 5 Hispanic/Latino), 1 international. Average age 29. 23 applicants, 61% accepted, 8 enrolled. In 2018, 12 master's awarded. *Degree requirements:* For master's, comprehensive exam, thesis optional. *Entrance requirements:* For master's, baccalaureate degree from regionally-accredited institution with minimum GPA of 2.75 in last 60 hours of course work, background course work in marketing and management, statement of purpose. Additional exam requirements/recommendations for international students: Required—TOEFL (minimum score 550 paper-based; 78 iBT), IELTS (minimum score 6.5). *Application deadline:* For fall admission, 2/1 priority date for domestic students, 2/1 for international students; for spring admission, 10/15 priority date for domestic students, 10/1 for international students; for summer admission, 4/15 for domestic students, 3/15 for international students. Applications are processed on a rolling basis. Application fee: $55 ($90 for international students). Electronic applications accepted. *Expenses:* Tuition, state resident: full-time $8102; part-time $4051 per semester. Tuition, nonresident: full-time $18,229; part-time $9115 per semester. *International tuition:* $18,229 full-time. *Required fees:* $2116; $120 per credit hour. Tuition and fees vary according to course load. *Financial support:* In 2018–19, 14 students received support, including 1 research assistantship (averaging $12,685 per year), 2 teaching assistantships (averaging $13,447 per year); scholarships/grants and unspecified assistantships also available. Financial award application deadline: 1/15; financial award applicants required to submit FAFSA. *Faculty research:* Lasting perceptions of wilderness orientation programming: A longitudinal follow-up study; State of Leisure Studies in Australia and New Zealand; Champions for Health in the Community: Critical Service Learning, Transformative Education, and Community Empowerment. *Total annual research expenditures:* $1,442. *Unit head:* Dr. Jan Hodges, Graduate Advisor, 512-245-7482, Fax: 512-245-8678, E-mail: jh223@txstate.edu. *Application contact:* Dr. Andrea Golato, Dean of the Graduate College, 512-245-2581, Fax: 512-245-8365, E-mail: gradcollege@txstate.edu.
Website: http://www.gradcollege.txstate.edu/programs/msrls-mgmt.html

Universidad Metropolitana, School of Education, Program in Managing Recreation and Sports Services, San Juan, PR 00928-1150. Offers M Ed. *Program availability:* Part-time. *Degree requirements:* For master's, thesis or alternative. *Entrance requirements:* For master's, EXADEP, interview. Electronic applications accepted.

Université du Québec à Trois-Rivières, Graduate Programs, Program in Leisure, Culture and Tourism Sciences, Trois-Rivières, QC G9A 5H7, Canada. Offers MA, DESS. *Program availability:* Part-time. *Degree requirements:* For master's, thesis optional. *Entrance requirements:* For master's, appropriate bachelor's degree, proficiency in French.

University of Illinois at Urbana–Champaign, Graduate College, College of Applied Health Sciences, Department of Recreation, Sport and Tourism, Champaign, IL 61820. Offers MS, PhD. *Program availability:* Part-time, online learning.

The University of Iowa, Graduate College, College of Liberal Arts and Sciences, Department of Health and Human Physiology, Iowa City, IA 52242-1316. Offers athletic training (MS); clinical exercise physiology (MS); health and human physiology (PhD); leisure studies (MA, PhD), including recreational sport management (PhD); therapeutic recreation (MA). *Degree requirements:* For master's, thesis optional, exam; for doctorate, comprehensive exam, thesis/dissertation. *Entrance requirements:* For master's and doctorate, GRE General Test, minimum GPA of 3.0. Additional exam requirements/recommendations for international students: Required—TOEFL (minimum score 600 paper-based; 100 iBT). Electronic applications accepted.

University of Nebraska at Kearney, College of Education, Kinesiology and Sport Sciences Department, Kearney, NE 68849-0001. Offers general physical education (MA Ed), including recreation and leisure, sports administration; physical education exercise science (MA Ed); physical education master teacher (MA Ed), including pedagogy, special populations. *Program availability:* Part-time, evening/weekend, 100% online. *Degree requirements:* For master's, comprehensive exam, thesis optional. *Entrance requirements:* For master's, GRE General Test (for some programs), personal statement. Additional exam requirements/recommendations for international students: Recommended—TOEFL (minimum score 550 paper-based; 79 iBT), IELTS (minimum score 6.5). Electronic applications accepted. *Faculty research:* Ergonomic aids, nutrition, motor development, sports pedagogy, applied behavior analysis, physical activity and wellness, athletic training, therapeutic Interventions, exercise physiology, endocrinology and metabolism.

The University of Tennessee, Graduate School, College of Education, Health and Human Sciences, Department of Exercise, Sport, and Leisure Studies, Knoxville, TN 37996. Offers exercise science (MS, PhD), including biomechanics/sports medicine, exercise physiology; recreation and leisure studies (MS); sport management (MS); sport studies (MS, PhD); therapeutic recreation (MS). *Program availability:* Part-time, evening/

weekend. *Degree requirements:* For master's, thesis optional. *Entrance requirements:* For master's, minimum GPA of 2.7. Additional exam requirements/recommendations for international students: Required—TOEFL. Electronic applications accepted.

The University of Toledo, College of Graduate Studies, College of Health and Human Services, School of Exercise and Rehabilitation Sciences, Toledo, OH 43606-3390. Offers athletic training (MSES); exercise physiology (MSES); exercise science (PhD); occupational therapy (OTD); physical therapy (DPT); recreation and leisure studies (MA), including recreation administration, recreation therapy. *Degree requirements:* For master's, comprehensive exam, thesis; for doctorate, thesis/dissertation or alternative. *Entrance requirements:* For master's, GRE, minimum cumulative GPA of 2.7 for all previous academic work, letters of recommendation; for doctorate, GRE, minimum cumulative GPA of 3.0 for all previous academic work, letters of recommendation; OTCAS or PTCAS application and UT supplemental application (for OTD and DPT). Additional exam requirements/recommendations for international students: Required—TOEFL (minimum score 550 paper-based; 80 iBT). Electronic applications accepted.

University of Utah, Graduate School, College of Health, Department of Health, Kinesiology, and Recreation, Salt Lake City, UT 84112. Offers kinesiology (MS, PhD); parks, recreation, and tourism (MS, PhD). *Program availability:* Part-time. *Faculty:* 21 full-time (9 women), 11 part-time/adjunct (6 women). *Students:* 82 full-time (55 women), 12 part-time (4 women); includes 5 minority (1 Black or African American, non-Hispanic/Latino; 1 American Indian or Alaska Native, non-Hispanic/Latino; 3 Asian, non-Hispanic/Latino), 1 international. Average age 28. 92 applicants, 23% accepted, 16 enrolled. In 2018, 33 master's, 5 doctorates awarded. Terminal master's awarded for partial completion of doctoral program. *Degree requirements:* For master's, comprehensive exam, thesis or alternative; for doctorate, comprehensive exam, thesis/dissertation. *Entrance requirements:* For master's and doctorate, GRE General Test, minimum GPA of 3.0. Additional exam requirements/recommendations for international students: Required—TOEFL (minimum score 500 paper-based). *Application deadline:* For fall admission, 1/15 for domestic and international students. Application fee: $55 ($65 for international students). Electronic applications accepted. *Expenses: Tuition, area resident:* Full-time $7190.66; part-time $2112.48 per year. Tuition, state resident: full-time $7190.66. Tuition, nonresident: full-time $25,195. *Required fees:* $558; $555.04 per unit. Tuition and fees vary according to course level, course load, degree level, program and student level. *Financial support:* In 2018–19, 38 students received support, including 7 research assistantships with full tuition reimbursements available, 31 teaching assistantships with full tuition reimbursements available; career-related internships or fieldwork, scholarships/grants, health care benefits, and unspecified assistantships also available. Financial award application deadline: 1/15; financial award applicants required to submit FAFSA. *Faculty research:* Cognitive and motor neuroscience, physical activity and well being, exercise and disease, healthy communities and environments. *Total annual research expenditures:* $55,000. *Unit head:* Dr. Kelly S. Bricker, Program Director, 801-585-6503, E-mail: kelly.bricker@ health.utah.edu. *Application contact:* Dr. Jim Sibthorp, Director of Graduate Studies, 801-581-5940, Fax: 801-581-4930, E-mail: jim.sibthorp@health.utah.edu. Website: http://www.health.utah.edu/prt/

University of Victoria, Faculty of Graduate Studies, Faculty of Education, School of Exercise Science, Physical, and Health Education, Victoria, BC V8W 2Y2, Canada. Offers coaching studies (co-operative education) (M Ed); kinesiology (M Sc, MA); leisure service administration (MA); physical education (MA). *Program availability:* Part-time. *Degree requirements:* For master's, comprehensive exam (for some programs), thesis (for some programs). *Entrance requirements:* For master's, minimum B average. Additional exam requirements/recommendations for international students: Required—TOEFL (minimum score 575 paper-based), IELTS (minimum score 7). Electronic applications accepted. *Faculty research:* Children and exercise, mental skills in sports, teaching effectiveness, neural control of human movement, physical performance and health.

University of Waterloo, Graduate Studies and Postdoctoral Affairs, Faculty of Applied Health Sciences, Department of Recreation and Leisure Studies, Waterloo, ON N2L 3G1, Canada. Offers MA, PhD. *Program availability:* Part-time. *Degree requirements:* For master's, thesis; for doctorate, comprehensive exam, thesis/dissertation. *Entrance requirements:* For master's, honors degree, minimum B average, writing sample, resume; for doctorate, GRE (recommended), master's degree, minimum B average, writing sample, resume. Additional exam requirements/recommendations for international students: Required—TOEFL, IELTS, PTE. *Application deadline:* For fall admission, 2/1 for domestic and international students. Application fee: $125 Canadian dollars. Electronic applications accepted. *Financial support:* In 2018–19, teaching assistantships (averaging $6,141 per year) were awarded; research assistantships, career-related internships or fieldwork, Federal Work-Study, institutionally sponsored loans, scholarships/grants, and university-sponsored bursaries also available. *Faculty research:* Tourism, leisure behavior, special populations, leisure service management, outdoor resources, aging, health and well-being, work and health. *Application contact:* Tracy Taves, Graduate Studies Coordinator, 519-888-4567 Ext. 36149, Fax: 519-746-6776, E-mail: tltaves@uwaterloo.ca. Website: https://uwaterloo.ca/recreation-and-leisure-studies/

University of West Florida, Usha Kundu, MD College of Health, Department of Exercise Science and Community Health, Pensacola, FL 32514-5750. Offers health promotion (MS); health, leisure, and exercise science (MS), including exercise science, physical education. *Program availability:* Part-time, evening/weekend. *Degree requirements:* For master's, thesis or alternative. *Entrance requirements:* For master's, GRE or MAT, official transcripts; minimum GPA of 3.0; letter of intent; three personal references; work experience as reflected in resume. Additional exam requirements/recommendations for international students: Required—TOEFL (minimum score 550 paper-based).

Recreation and Park Management

Acadia University, Faculty of Professional Studies, School of Recreation Management and Community Development, Wolfville, NS B4P 2R6, Canada. Offers recreation management (MR). *Entrance requirements:* Additional exam requirements/recommendations for international students: Required—TOEFL (minimum score 630 paper-based; 93 iBT), IELTS (minimum score 6.5).

Bowling Green State University, Graduate College, College of Education and Human Development, School of Human Movement, Sport, and Leisure Studies, Bowling Green, OH 43403. Offers developmental kinesiology (M Ed); recreation and leisure (M Ed); sport administration (M Ed). *Program availability:* Part-time. *Degree requirements:* For master's, thesis or alternative. *Entrance requirements:* For master's, GRE General Test, minimum GPA of 2.7. Additional exam requirements/recommendations for international students: Required—TOEFL. Electronic applications accepted. *Faculty research:* Teacher-learning process, travel and tourism, sport marketing and management, exercise physiology and sport psychology, life-span motor development.

California State University, Chico, Office of Graduate Studies, College of Communication and Education, Recreation, Hospitality and Parks Management Department, Chico, CA 95929-0722. Offers recreation, parks, and tourism (MS). *Program availability:* Part-time. *Faculty:* 1 full-time (0 women), 3 part-time/adjunct (all women). *Students:* 2 full-time (0 women), 10 part-time (6 women); includes 3 minority (1 American Indian or Alaska Native, non-Hispanic/Latino; 1 Asian, non-Hispanic/Latino; 1 Hispanic/Latino). 4 applicants, 100% accepted, 4 enrolled. In 2018, 1 master's awarded. *Degree requirements:* For master's, thesis or project. *Entrance requirements:* For master's, GRE General Test, 3 letters of recommendation, statement of purpose, resume. Additional exam requirements/recommendations for international students: Required—TOEFL (minimum score 550 paper-based; 80 iBT), IELTS (minimum score 6.5), PTE. Application fee: $55. Electronic applications accepted. *Expenses: Tuition, area resident:* Full-time $4622; part-time $3116 per unit. Tuition, state resident: full-time $4622; part-time $3116 per unit. Tuition, nonresident: full-time $10,634. *Required fees:* $2160; $1620 per year. Tuition and fees vary according to class time and program. *Financial support:* Fellowships, research assistantships, teaching assistantships, career-related internships or fieldwork, Federal Work-Study, scholarships/grants, traineeships, health care benefits, unspecified assistantships, and stipends available. Support available to part-time students. Financial award application deadline: 3/2; financial award applicants required to submit FAFSA. *Unit head:* Dr. Emilyn Sheffield, Chair, 530-898-6408, Fax: 530-898-6557, E-mail: recr@csuchico.edu. *Application contact:* Micah Lehner, Graduate Admissions Coordinator, 530-898-5416, Fax: 530-898-3342, E-mail: mlehner@csuchico.edu. Website: https://www.csuchico.edu/rhpm/degrees-options/masters.shtml

California State University, East Bay, Office of Graduate Studies, College of Education and Allied Studies, Department of Hospitality, Recreation and Tourism, Hayward, CA 94542-3000. Offers recreation and tourism (MS). *Program availability:* Part-time, evening/weekend, online learning. *Degree requirements:* For master's, thesis optional. *Entrance requirements:* For master's, minimum GPA of 2.75; 2 years' related work experience; 3 letters of recommendation; resume; baccalaureate degree. Additional exam requirements/recommendations for international students: Required—TOEFL (minimum score 550 paper-based). Electronic applications accepted. *Faculty research:* Leisure, online vs. face-to-face (F2F) learning, risk management, leadership, tourism consumer behavior.

California State University, Long Beach, Graduate Studies, College of Health and Human Services, Department of Recreation and Leisure Studies, Long Beach, CA 90840. Offers recreation administration (MS). *Program availability:* Part-time. *Degree requirements:* For master's, comprehensive exam or thesis. *Entrance requirements:* For master's, GRE General Test. *Application deadline:* For fall admission, 4/1 for domestic students. Applications are processed on a rolling basis. Application fee: $55. Electronic applications accepted. *Expenses: Required fees:* $2628 per term. Tuition and fees vary according to class time, course level, course load, degree level, campus/location and program. *Financial support:* Federal Work-Study, institutionally sponsored loans, and scholarships/grants available. Financial award application deadline: 3/2; financial award applicants required to submit FAFSA. *Unit head:* Terry Robertson, Chair, 562-985-1098, E-mail: Terry.Robertson@csulb.edu. *Application contact:* Heewon Yang, Graduate Advisor, 562-985-1495, E-mail: Heewon.Yang@csulb.edu. Website: http://web.csulb.edu/colleges/chhs/departments/recreation-and-leisure-studies/

California State University, Northridge, Graduate Studies, College of Health and Human Development, Department of Recreation and Tourism Management, Northridge, CA 91330. Offers hospitality and tourism (MS); recreational sport management/campus recreation (MS). *Degree requirements:* For master's, thesis (for some programs). *Entrance requirements:* For master's, GRE (if cumulative undergraduate GPA less than 3.0). Additional exam requirements/recommendations for international students: Required—TOEFL.

California State University, Northridge, Graduate Studies, Tseng College, Northridge, CA 91330. Offers business administration (Graduate Certificate); health administration (MPA); health education (MPH); knowledge management (MKM); music industry administration (MA); nonprofit-sector management (Graduate Certificate); public administration (MPA); public sector management and leadership (MPA); social work (MSW); taxation (MS); tourism, hospitality and recreation management (MS). *Entrance requirements:* For master's, GRE (if cumulative undergraduate GPA less than 3.0).

California State University, Sacramento, College of Health and Human Services, Department of Recreation, Parks and Tourism Administration, Sacramento, CA 95819. Offers MS. *Program availability:* Part-time. *Degree requirements:* For master's, thesis or project; writing proficiency exam. *Entrance requirements:* For master's, minimum overall GPA of 2.75, 3.0 in the major. Additional exam requirements/recommendations for international students: Required—TOEFL (minimum score 550 paper-based; 80 iBT); Recommended—IELTS, TSE. Electronic applications accepted. *Expenses:* Contact institution.

Central Michigan University, Central Michigan University Global Campus, Program in Administration, Mount Pleasant, MI 48859. Offers acquisitions administration (MSA, Certificate); engineering management administration (MSA, Certificate); general administration (MSA, Certificate); health services administration (MSA, Certificate); human resources administration (MSA, Certificate); information resource management (MSA); information resource management administration (Certificate); international administration (MSA, Certificate); leadership (MSA, Certificate); philanthropy and fundraising administration (MSA, Certificate); public administration (MSA, Certificate); recreation and park administration (MSA); research administration (MSA, Certificate). *Program availability:* Part-time, evening/weekend, online learning. *Entrance requirements:* For master's, minimum GPA of 2.7 in major. Electronic applications accepted.

Clemson University, Graduate School, College of Behavioral, Social and Health Sciences, Department of Parks, Recreation, and Tourism Management, Clemson, SC 29634-0735. Offers international parks and tourism (Certificate); parks, recreation and tourism management (MS, PhD), including recreational therapy (PhD); public

administration (MPA, Certificate); recreational therapy (MS); youth development leadership (MS, Certificate). *Program availability:* Part-time, evening/weekend, 100% online. *Faculty:* 31 full-time (10 women), 3 part-time/adjunct (0 women). *Students:* 84 full-time (58 women), 227 part-time (140 women); includes 62 minority (45 Black or African American, non-Hispanic/Latino; 1 American Indian or Alaska Native, non-Hispanic/Latino; 1 Asian, non-Hispanic/Latino; 9 Hispanic/Latino; 6 Two or more races, non-Hispanic/Latino), 18 international. Average age 31. 275 applicants, 80% accepted, 135 enrolled. In 2018, 72 master's, 9 doctorates, 26 other advanced degrees awarded. *Degree requirements:* For master's, comprehensive exam (for some programs), thesis (for some programs); for doctorate, comprehensive exam, thesis/dissertation; for Certificate, portfolio. *Entrance requirements:* For master's and doctorate, GRE General Test, unofficial transcripts, letter of intent, letters of reference; for Certificate, letter of recommendation, unofficial transcripts, personal statement, resume. Additional exam requirements/recommendations for international students: Required—TOEFL (minimum score 80 paper-based; 80 iBT); Recommended—IELTS (minimum score 6.5), TSE (minimum score 54). *Application deadline:* For fall admission, 4/15 priority date for international students; for spring admission, 10/15 priority date for international students. Applications are processed on a rolling basis. Application fee: $80 ($90 for international students). Electronic applications accepted. *Expenses: Tuition, area resident:* Full-time $11,270; part-time $8688 per credit hour. Tuition, state resident: full-time $11,796. Tuition, nonresident: full-time $23,802; part-time $17,412 per credit hour. *International tuition:* $23,246 full-time. *Required fees:* $1196; $497 per semester. Tuition and fees vary according to course load, degree level, campus/location and program. *Financial support:* In 2018–19, 59 students received support, including 1 research assistantship with full and partial tuition reimbursement available (averaging $4,324 per year), 55 teaching assistantships with full and partial tuition reimbursements available (averaging $10,318 per year); career-related internships or fieldwork and unspecified assistantships also available. *Faculty research:* Land use, recreational therapy, sustainability, tourism, public administration. *Total annual research expenditures:* $532,593. *Unit head:* Dr. Fran McGuire, Interim Chair, 864-656-3036, E-mail: lefty@clemson.edu. *Application contact:* Dr. Jeff Hallo, Graduate Coordinator, 864-656-3237, E-mail: jhallo@clemson.edu.
Website: http://www.clemson.edu/hehd/departments/prtm/

Colorado State University, Warner College of Natural Resources, Department of Human Dimensions of Natural Resources, Fort Collins, CO 80523-1480. Offers human dimensions of natural resources (MS, PhD); tourism management (MTM). *Program availability:* Part-time, evening/weekend, 100% online. Terminal master's awarded for partial completion of doctoral program. *Degree requirements:* For master's, thesis (for some programs); for doctorate, comprehensive exam, thesis/dissertation. *Entrance requirements:* For master's, GRE General Test, minimum GPA of 3.0, 3 letters of recommendation, statement of interest, official transcripts; for doctorate, GRE General Test, minimum GPA of 3.0, 3 letters of recommendation, copy of master's thesis or professional paper, statement of interest, official transcripts. Electronic applications accepted. *Expenses:* Contact institution. *Faculty research:* Biocultural approaches to conservation; conservation governance; dimensions of wildlife management; marine conservation; park recreation and management.

Delta State University, Graduate Programs, College of Education, Division of Health, Physical Education, and Recreation, Cleveland, MS 38733-0001. Offers health, physical education, and recreation (M Ed); sport and human performance (MS). *Program availability:* Part-time, evening/weekend. *Degree requirements:* For master's, thesis optional. *Entrance requirements:* For master's, GRE General Test or MAT, Class A teaching certificate. *Expenses: Tuition, area resident:* Full-time $7076; part-time $393 per credit hour. Tuition, state resident: full-time $7076; part-time $393 per credit hour. Tuition, nonresident: full-time $7076; part-time $393 per credit hour. *International tuition:* $7076 full-time. *Required fees:* $170; $18.90 per credit hour. $9.45 per semester. Part-time tuition and fees vary according to program. *Faculty research:* Blood pressure, body fat, power and reaction time, learning disorders of athletes, effects of walking.

East Carolina University, Graduate School, College of Health and Human Performance, Department of Recreation and Leisure Studies, Greenville, NC 27858-4353. Offers aquatic therapy (Certificate); biofeedback (Certificate); recreation services and interventions (MS), including generalist. *Program availability:* Part-time, evening/weekend, online learning. *Application deadline:* For fall admission, 6/1 priority date for domestic students. *Expenses: Tuition, area resident:* Full-time $4749. Tuition, state resident: full-time $4749. Tuition, nonresident: full-time $17,898. *International tuition:* $17,898 full-time. *Required fees:* $2787. Part-time tuition and fees vary according to course load and program. *Financial support:* Application deadline: 6/1. *Unit head:* Dr. Edwin Gómez, Chair, 252-328-4638, E-mail: gomeze17@ecu.edu. *Application contact:* Graduate Student Admissions, 252-328-6012, Fax: 252-328-6071, E-mail: gradschool@ecu.edu.
Website: https://hhp.ecu.edu/rcls/

Eastern Kentucky University, The Graduate School, College of Health Sciences, Department of Recreation and Park Administration, Richmond, KY 40475-3102. Offers MS. *Program availability:* Part-time. *Degree requirements:* For master's, comprehensive exam, thesis optional. *Entrance requirements:* For master's, GRE General Test, MAT, minimum GPA of 2.5. *Faculty research:* Marketing, at risk youth, outdoor education, event planning, TR in schools.

Eastern Washington University, Graduate Studies, College of Arts, Letters and Education, Department of Physical Education, Health and Recreation, Cheney, WA 99004-2431. Offers exercise science (MS); sports and recreation administration (MS). *Degree requirements:* For master's, comprehensive exam, thesis or alternative. *Entrance requirements:* For master's, minimum GPA of 3.0. Additional exam requirements/recommendations for international students: Required—TOEFL (minimum score 580 paper-based; 92 iBT), IELTS (minimum score 7), PTE (minimum score 63). Electronic applications accepted.

Florida International University, College of Arts, Sciences, and Education, Department of Leadership and Professional Studies, Miami, FL 33199. Offers adult education and human resource development (MS, Ed D); counseling (MS), including rehabilitation counseling, school counseling; counselor education (MS), including clinical mental health counseling; educational administration and supervision (Ed D); educational leadership (MS, Certificate, Ed S); higher education (Ed D); higher education administration (MS); international and comparative education (MS); recreation and sport management (MS), including recreation and sport management, recreational therapy; school psychology (Ed S); urban education (MS), including instruction in urban settings, learning technologies, multicultural/bilingual, multicultural/TESOL, urban education. *Program availability:* Part-time, evening/weekend. *Faculty:* 64 full-time (43 women), 104 part-time/adjunct (76 women). *Students:* 258 full-time (196 women), 217 part-time (155 women); includes 387 minority (118 Black or African American, non-Hispanic/Latino; 8 Asian, non-Hispanic/Latino; 249 Hispanic/Latino; 12 Two or more races, non-Hispanic/Latino), 11 international. Average age 31. 345 applicants, 57% accepted, 126 enrolled. In 2018, 172 master's, 11 doctorates awarded. *Entrance requirements:* For master's, minimum GPA of 3.0; for doctorate and other advanced degree, GRE General Test. Additional exam requirements/recommendations for international students: Required—TOEFL (minimum score 550 paper-based; 80 iBT), IELTS (minimum score 6.3). *Application deadline:* For fall admission, 6/1 priority date for domestic students, 4/1 for international students; for winter admission, 10/1 priority date for domestic students, 9/1 for international students; for spring admission, 3/1 priority date for domestic students, 2/1 for international students. Applications are processed on a rolling basis. Application fee: $30. Electronic applications accepted. *Financial support:* Fellowships, research assistantships, teaching assistantships, Federal Work-Study, and tuition waivers (full and partial) available. Support available to part-time students. Financial award applicants required to submit FAFSA. *Unit head:* Dr. Benjamin Baez, Chair, 305-348-3214, Fax: 305-348-1515, E-mail: benjamin.baez@fiu.edu. *Application contact:* Nanett Rojas, Manager, Admissions Operations, 305-348-7464, Fax: 305-348-7441, E-mail: gradadm@fiu.edu.
Website: http://education.fiu.edu

Frostburg State University, College of Education, Program in Parks and Recreational Management, Frostburg, MD 21532-1099. Offers MS. *Program availability:* Part-time, evening/weekend. *Faculty:* 3 full-time (0 women), 3 part-time/adjunct (2 women). *Students:* 1 (woman) full-time, 18 part-time (7 women); includes 4 minority (3 Black or African American, non-Hispanic/Latino; 1 Hispanic/Latino). Average age 32. 11 applicants, 100% accepted, 10 enrolled. In 2018, 7 master's awarded. *Degree requirements:* For master's, thesis. *Entrance requirements:* For master's, resume. Additional exam requirements/recommendations for international students: Required—TOEFL. *Application deadline:* For fall admission, 7/15 priority date for domestic students. Applications are processed on a rolling basis. Application fee: $45. Electronic applications accepted. *Financial support:* In 2018–19, 1 research assistantship with full tuition reimbursement (averaging $5,000 per year) was awarded; career-related internships or fieldwork and Federal Work-Study also available. Financial award application deadline: 4/1; financial award applicants required to submit FAFSA. *Unit head:* Dr. Natalia Buta, Coordinator, 301-687-4458, E-mail: nbuta@frostburg.edu. *Application contact:* Vickie Mazer, Director, Graduate Services, 301-687-7053, Fax: 301-687-4597, E-mail: vmmazer@frostburg.edu.

Hardin-Simmons University, Graduate School, College of Human Sciences and Educational Studies, Kinesiology, Sport, and Recreation Program, Abilene, TX 79698-0001. Offers kinesiology, sport, and recreation (M Ed). *Program availability:* Part-time. *Students:* 40 part-time (16 women); includes 17 minority (8 Black or African American, non-Hispanic/Latino; 7 Hispanic/Latino; 2 Two or more races, non-Hispanic/Latino). Average age 25. 20 applicants, 100% accepted, 15 enrolled. In 2018, 17 master's awarded. *Degree requirements:* For master's, comprehensive exam, professional project. *Entrance requirements:* For master's, minimum undergraduate GPA of 3.0 in major, 2.7 overall; writing sample; letters of recommendation; resume; personal interview. Additional exam requirements/recommendations for international students: Required—TOEFL (minimum score 550 paper-based; 79 iBT). *Application deadline:* For fall admission, 8/15 priority date for domestic students, 4/1 for international students; for spring admission, 1/5 priority date for domestic students, 9/1 for international students. Applications are processed on a rolling basis. Application fee: $50. Electronic applications accepted. *Expenses: Tuition:* Full-time $750; part-time $750 per credit hour. *Required fees:* $1300; $880 per credit. Tuition and fees vary according to degree level and program. *Financial support:* Fellowships, career-related internships or fieldwork, scholarships/grants, and unspecified assistantships available. Support available to part-time students. Financial award application deadline: 6/30; financial award applicants required to submit FAFSA. *Unit head:* Dr. Lindsay Edwards, Program Director, 325-670-5893, Fax: 325-670-1572, E-mail: ledwards@hsutx.edu. *Application contact:* Dr. Nancy Kucinski, Dean of Graduate Studies, 325-670-1298, Fax: 325-670-1564, E-mail: gradoff@hsutx.edu.
Website: http://www.hsutx.edu/academics/irvin/graduate/kinesiology

Indiana State University, College of Graduate and Professional Studies, College of Health and Human Services, Department of Kinesiology, Recreation, and Sport, Terre Haute, IN 47809. Offers physical education (MS); recreation and sport management (MS); sport management (PhD). *Degree requirements:* For master's, comprehensive exam (for some programs), thesis (for some programs). *Entrance requirements:* For master's, GRE General Test, undergraduate major in related field. Electronic applications accepted.

Indiana University Bloomington, School of Public Health, Department of Recreation, Park, and Tourism Studies, Bloomington, IN 47405-7000. Offers leisure behavior (PhD); outdoor recreation (MS); park and public lands management (MS); recreation administration (MS); recreational sports administration (MS); recreational therapy (MS); tourism management (MS). Terminal master's awarded for partial completion of doctoral program. *Degree requirements:* For master's, thesis optional; for doctorate, comprehensive exam, thesis/dissertation. *Entrance requirements:* For master's, GRE General Test, minimum GPA of 2.8; for doctorate, GRE General Test, minimum GPA of 3.0 (undergraduate), 3.5 (graduate). Additional exam requirements/recommendations for international students: Required—TOEFL (minimum score 550 paper-based; 80 iBT). Electronic applications accepted. *Faculty research:* Leisure counseling, gerontology, special populations, planning and development.

Iona College, School of Business, Department of Marketing and International Business, New Rochelle, NY 10801-1890. Offers international business (AC, PMC); marketing (MBA); sports and entertainment management (AC). *Program availability:* Part-time, evening/weekend. *Faculty:* 3 full-time (1 woman), 3 part-time/adjunct (1 woman). *Students:* 14 full-time (10 women), 26 part-time (13 women); includes 17 minority (4 Black or African American, non-Hispanic/Latino; 1 Asian, non-Hispanic/Latino; 12 Hispanic/Latino), 3 international. Average age 25. 15 applicants, 93% accepted, 8 enrolled. In 2018, 13 master's, 78 other advanced degrees awarded. *Entrance requirements:* For master's, GMAT, 2 letters of recommendation, minimum GPA of 3.0; for other advanced degree, GMAT, minimum GPA of 3.0. Additional exam requirements/recommendations for international students: Required—TOEFL (minimum score 550 paper-based; 80 iBT), IELTS (minimum score 6.5). *Application deadline:* For fall admission, 8/15 priority date for domestic students, 8/1 priority date for international students; for winter admission, 11/15 priority date for domestic students, 11/1 priority date for international students; for spring admission, 2/15 priority date for domestic students, 2/1 priority date for international students; for summer admission, 5/15 for domestic students, 5/1 priority date for international students. Applications are processed on a rolling basis. Application fee: $50. Electronic applications accepted. *Expenses:* Contact institution. *Financial support:* In 2018–19, 38 students received support. Scholarships/grants, tuition waivers (partial), and unspecified assistantships available. Support available to part-time students. Financial award application deadline: 4/15; financial award applicants required to submit FAFSA. *Faculty research:* Business ethics, international retailing, mega-marketing, consumer behavior and consumer confidence. *Unit head:* Dr. Susan G. Rozensher, Department Chair, 914-637-2748, E-mail: srozensher@iona.edu. *Application contact:* Kimberly Kelly, Director of Graduate Business Admissions, 914-633-2271, Fax: 914-633-2012, E-mail: kkelly@iona.edu.
Website: http://www.iona.edu/Academics/Hagan-School-of-Business/Departments/Marketing/Graduate-Programs.aspx

Kent State University, College of Education, Health and Human Services, School of Foundations, Leadership and Administration, Sports and Recreation Management, Kent, OH 44242-0001. Offers sport and recreation management (MA); sports studies

(MA). *Faculty:* 9 full-time (5 women), 19 part-time/adjunct (9 women). *Students:* 41 full-time (10 women), 14 part-time (6 women); includes 12 minority (9 Black or African American, non-Hispanic/Latino; 1 Asian, non-Hispanic/Latino; 2 Native Hawaiian or other Pacific Islander, non-Hispanic/Latino), 5 international. 61 applicants, 62% accepted. In 2018, 26 master's awarded. *Degree requirements:* For master's, thesis optional. *Entrance requirements:* For master's, GRE if undergraduate GPA below 3.0, goals statement, 2 letters of recommendation. Additional exam requirements/recommendations for international students: Required—TOEFL (minimum score 550 paper-based; 80 iBT). *Application deadline:* Applications are processed on a rolling basis. Application fee: $45 ($60 for international students). Electronic applications accepted. *Expenses:* Tuition, state resident: full-time $11,766; part-time $536 per credit. Tuition, nonresident: full-time $21,952; part-time $999 per credit. *International tuition:* $21,952 full-time. Tuition and fees vary according to course load. *Financial support:* In 2018–19, 7 research assistantships (averaging $8,500 per year) were awarded; teaching assistantships, Federal Work-Study, scholarships/grants, and unspecified assistantships also available. *Unit head:* Aaron Mulrooney, Coordinator, 330-672-0204, E-mail: amulroon@kent.edu. *Application contact:* Cheryl Slusarczyk, Academic Program Director, Office of Graduate Student Services, 330-672-2576, Fax: 330-672-9162, E-mail: ogs@kent.edu.

Lasell College, Graduate and Professional Studies in Sport Management, Newton, MA 02466-2709. Offers athletic administration (MS); parks and recreation (MS); sport leadership (MS, Graduate Certificate); sport tourism and hospitality (MS). *Program availability:* Part-time, evening/weekend, online only, 100% online. *Faculty:* 4 full-time (1 woman), 4 part-time/adjunct (2 women). *Students:* 15 full-time (7 women), 32 part-time (11 women); includes 17 minority (12 Black or African American, non-Hispanic/Latino; 4 Hispanic/Latino; 1 Two or more races, non-Hispanic/Latino). Average age 29. 36 applicants, 39% accepted, 11 enrolled. In 2018, 20 master's awarded. *Degree requirements:* For master's, minimum GPA of 3.0; internship or thesis. *Entrance requirements:* For master's, one-page personal statement, 2 letters of recommendation, resume, bachelor's degree transcript; for Graduate Certificate, bachelor's degree transcript, 2 letters of recommendation, 1-page personal statement, resume. Additional exam requirements/recommendations for international students: Required—TOEFL (minimum score 550 paper-based, 79 iBT) or IELTS (minimum score 6). *Application deadline:* For fall admission, 8/31 priority date for domestic students, 6/30 priority date for international students; for spring admission, 12/31 priority date for domestic students, 10/31 priority date for international students. Applications are processed on a rolling basis. Electronic applications accepted. *Expenses:* Tuition: Part-time $600 per credit. *Required fees:* $40 per course. *Financial support:* Federal Work-Study, scholarships/grants, and tuition discounts available. Support available to part-time students. Financial award application deadline: 8/31; financial award applicants required to submit FAFSA. *Faculty research:* How do fans attribute team failure; investigating cross-cultural difference in attribution; sense of ownership as a key predictor of fan loyalty; fans' normative beliefs about sponsorship and sponsors; investigation of new attitudinal variables in sponsorship. *Unit head:* Eric Turner, Vice President of Graduate and Professional Studies, 617-243-2071, Fax: 617-243-2450, E-mail: gradinfo@lasell.edu. *Application contact:* Adrienne Franciosi, Assistant Vice President of Graduate and Professional Studies, 617-243-2214, Fax: 617-243-2450, E-mail: gradinfo@lasell.edu. Website: http://www.lasell.edu/academics/graduate-and-professional-studies/programs-of-study/master-of-science-in-sport-management.html

Lehman College of the City University of New York, School of Health Sciences, Human Services and Nursing, Department of Health Sciences, Program in Recreation Education, Bronx, NY 10468-1589. Offers recreation education (MS Ed). *Program availability:* Part-time, evening/weekend. *Degree requirements:* For master's, comprehensive exam, thesis or alternative. *Entrance requirements:* For master's, minimum GPA of 2.7. *Faculty research:* Therapeutic recreation philosophy, curriculum, current approaches to treatment, impact of societal trends, ethical issues.

Loyola Marymount University, Bellarmine College of Liberal Arts, Program in Yoga Studies, Los Angeles, CA 90045. Offers MA. *Unit head:* Dr. Khalsa Nirinjan, Director, Master of Arts in Yoga Studies, 310-258-8621, E-mail: Nirinjan.Khalsa@lmu.edu. *Application contact:* Ammar Dalal, Assistant Vice Provost for Graduate Enrollment, 310-338-2721, Fax: 310-338-6086, E-mail: graduateinfo@lmu.edu. Website: http://bellarmine.lmu.edu/yoga/

Michigan State University, The Graduate School, College of Agriculture and Natural Resources, Department of Community Sustainability, East Lansing, MI 48824. Offers MS, PhD. *Entrance requirements:* Additional exam requirements/recommendations for international students: Required—TOEFL. Electronic applications accepted.

Middle Tennessee State University, College of Graduate Studies, College of Behavioral and Health Sciences, Department of Health and Human Performance, Program in Health, Physical Education and Recreation, Murfreesboro, TN 37132. Offers health and human performance (MS); leisure and sport management (MS). *Program availability:* Part-time, evening/weekend, online learning. *Degree requirements:* For master's, comprehensive exam, thesis optional. *Entrance requirements:* For master's, GRE. Additional exam requirements/recommendations for international students: Required—TOEFL (minimum score 525 paper-based; 71 iBT) or IELTS (minimum score 6). *Faculty research:* Kinesiometrics, leisure behavior, health, lifestyles.

Naropa University, Graduate Programs, Program in Clinical Mental Health Counseling, Concentration in Transpersonal Wilderness Therapy, Boulder, CO 80302-6697. Offers MA. *Degree requirements:* For master's, internship, counseling practicum. *Entrance requirements:* For master's, interview; 2 letters of recommendation; transcripts; curriculum vitae/resume with pertinent academic, employment and volunteer activities; statement of interest essay; 10 consecutive days of wilderness experience in the backcountry; wilderness/outdoor skills. Additional exam requirements/recommendations for international students: Required—TOEFL (minimum score 550 paper-based; 80 iBT). Electronic applications accepted. *Expenses:* Contact institution.

New England College, Program in Sports and Recreation Management: Coaching, Henniker, NH 03242-3293. Offers MS. *Entrance requirements:* For master's, resume, 2 letters of reference.

North Carolina Central University, College of Behavioral and Social Sciences, Department of Physical Education and Recreation, Durham, NC 27707-3129. Offers general physical education (MS); recreation administration (MS). *Program availability:* Part-time, evening/weekend. *Degree requirements:* For master's, one foreign language, comprehensive exam, thesis. *Entrance requirements:* For master's, GRE, minimum GPA of 3.0 in major, 2.5 overall. Additional exam requirements/recommendations for international students: Required—TOEFL.

North Carolina State University, Graduate School, College of Natural Resources, Department of Parks, Recreation and Tourism Management, Raleigh, NC 27695. Offers natural resource management (MPRTM, MS); park and recreation management (MPRTM, MS); parks, recreation and tourism management (PhD); recreational sport management (MPRTM, MS); spatial information science (MPRTM, MS); tourism policy and development (MPRTM, MS). *Degree requirements:* For master's, thesis (for some programs); for doctorate, thesis/dissertation. *Entrance requirements:* For master's and doctorate, GRE General Test. Additional exam requirements/recommendations for

international students: Required—TOEFL. Electronic applications accepted. *Faculty research:* Tourism policy and development, spatial information systems, natural resource management, recreational sports management, park and recreation management.

Northern Arizona University, College of Social and Behavioral Sciences, Department of Geography, Planning, and Recreation, Flagstaff, AZ 86011. Offers applied geospatial sciences (MS); community planning (Certificate); geographic information systems (Certificate); parks and recreation management (MS). *Program availability:* Part-time, 100% online, blended/hybrid learning. *Degree requirements:* For master's, variable foreign language requirement, comprehensive exam (for some programs), thesis (for some programs); for Certificate, comprehensive exam (for some programs). *Entrance requirements:* Additional exam requirements/recommendations for international students: Required—TOEFL (minimum score 80 iBT), IELTS (minimum score 6.5). Electronic applications accepted.

Northwest Missouri State University, Graduate School, School of Health Science and Wellness, Maryville, MO 64468-6001. Offers applied health and sport sciences (MS); guidance and counseling (MS Ed); health and physical education (MS Ed); recreation (MS); sport and exercise psychology (MS). *Accreditation:* NCATE. *Program availability:* Part-time. *Faculty:* 15 full-time (7 women). *Students:* 58 full-time (35 women), 27 part-time (17 women); includes 9 minority (7 Black or African American, non-Hispanic/Latino; 1 Hispanic/Latino; 1 Two or more races, non-Hispanic/Latino), 6 international. Average age 26. 50 applicants, 74% accepted, 23 enrolled. In 2018, 54 master's awarded. *Degree requirements:* For master's, comprehensive exam. *Entrance requirements:* For master's, GRE General Test, minimum undergraduate GPA of 2.75, teaching certificate, writing sample. Additional exam requirements/recommendations for international students: Required—TOEFL (minimum score 550 paper-based; 79 iBT). *Application deadline:* For fall admission, 7/1 for domestic and international students; for spring admission, 11/15 for domestic and international students. Applications are processed on a rolling basis. Application fee: $0 ($75 for international students). *Expenses:* Tuition, area resident: Full-time $4551; part-time $252.86 per credit hour. Tuition, state resident: full-time $4551; part-time $252.86 per credit hour. Tuition, nonresident: full-time $9103; part-time $505.72 per credit hour. *International tuition:* $9103 full-time. *Required fees:* $2668; $148.20 per credit hour. Tuition and fees vary according to program. *Financial support:* Teaching assistantships with full tuition reimbursements and unspecified assistantships available. Financial award application deadline: 4/1; financial award applicants required to submit FAFSA. *Unit head:* Dr. Terry Long, Director, School of Health Science and Wellness, 660-562-1706, Fax: 660-562-1483, E-mail: tlong@nwmissouri.edu. *Application contact:* Gina Smith, Office Manager, 660-562-1297, Fax: 660-562-1963, E-mail: smigina@nwmissouri.edu. Website: http://www.nwmissouri.edu/health/

Ohio University, Graduate College, Gladys W. and David H. Patton College of Education and Human Services, Department of Recreation and Sport Pedagogy, Program in Recreation Studies, Athens, OH 45701-2979. Offers MS. *Program availability:* Part-time. *Degree requirements:* For master's, thesis or alternative. *Entrance requirements:* For master's, GRE. Additional exam requirements/recommendations for international students: Required—TOEFL (minimum score 550 paper-based; 80 iBT) or IELTS (minimum score 6.5). Electronic applications accepted. *Faculty research:* Recreation, leisure studies, physical education, national parks.

Old Dominion University, Darden College of Education, Program in Park, Recreation and Tourism Studies, Norfolk, VA 23529. Offers park, recreation and tourism (MS). *Program availability:* Part-time, evening/weekend, blended/hybrid learning. *Degree requirements:* For master's, comprehensive exam, thesis or alternative, research project. *Entrance requirements:* For master's, GRE, minimum GPA of 2.8 overall, 3.0 in major. Additional exam requirements/recommendations for international students: Required—TOEFL (minimum score 500 paper-based). Electronic applications accepted. *Faculty research:* Outdoor recreation and education, recreation programming, sustainable tourism, sense of community and urban parks.

Penn State University Park, Graduate School, College of Health and Human Development, Department of Recreation, Park and Tourism Management, University Park, PA 16802. Offers MS, PhD.

Purdue University, Graduate School, College of Health and Human Sciences, Department of Health and Kinesiology, West Lafayette, IN 47907. Offers athletic training education administration (MS, PhD); biomechanics (MS, PhD); exercise physiology (MS, PhD); health education (MS, PhD); history/philosophy of sport (MS, PhD); motor control and development (MS, PhD); physical education pedagogy (PhD); physical education teacher education (MS); recreation and sport management (MS, PhD); sport and exercise psychology (MS, PhD). *Program availability:* Part-time. *Faculty:* 23 full-time (10 women). *Students:* 29 full-time (13 women), 8 part-time (5 women); includes 3 minority (1 Asian, non-Hispanic/Latino; 1 Hispanic/Latino; 1 Two or more races, non-Hispanic/Latino), 8 international. Average age 26. 61 applicants, 26% accepted, 14 enrolled. In 2018, 14 master's awarded. *Degree requirements:* For master's, thesis optional; for doctorate, comprehensive exam, thesis/dissertation, qualifying examination, preliminary examination. *Entrance requirements:* For master's, GRE General Test (minimum score 1000 combined verbal and quantitative), minimum undergraduate GPA of 3.0 or equivalent; for doctorate, GRE General Test (minimum score 1100 combined verbal and quantitative), minimum undergraduate GPA of 3.0 or equivalent; master's degree with minimum GPA of 3.25 (recommended). Additional exam requirements/recommendations for international students: Required—TOEFL (minimum score 77 iBT); Recommended—TWE. *Application deadline:* For fall admission, 4/30 for domestic and international students; for spring admission, 10/15 for domestic and international students. Applications are processed on a rolling basis. Application fee: $60 ($75 for international students). Electronic applications accepted. *Financial support:* Fellowships with partial tuition reimbursements, research assistantships with partial tuition reimbursements, teaching assistantships with partial tuition reimbursements, and Federal Work-Study available. Support available to part-time students. Financial award applicants required to submit FAFSA. *Faculty research:* Wellness, motivation, teaching effectiveness, learning and development. *Unit head:* Dr. Timothy P. Gavin, Head of the Graduate Program, 765-494-3178, Fax: 765-494-1239, E-mail: gavin1@purdue.edu. *Application contact:* David B. Klenosky, Graduate Contact, 765-494-0865, E-mail: klenosky@purdue.edu. Website: http://www.purdue.edu/hhs/hk/

San Francisco State University, Division of Graduate Studies, College of Health and Social Sciences, Department of Recreation, Parks, and Tourism, San Francisco, CA 94132-1722. Offers MS. *Program availability:* Part-time. *Application deadline:* Applications are processed on a rolling basis. *Financial support:* Career-related internships or fieldwork available. *Unit head:* Dr. Erik Rosegard, Chair, 415-338-7529, Fax: 415-338-0543, E-mail: rosegard@sfsu.edu. *Application contact:* Dr. Jackson Wilson, Graduate Coordinator, 415-338-1487, Fax: 415-338-0543, E-mail: wilsonj@sfsu.edu. Website: http://recdept.sfsu.edu/graduate

Slippery Rock University of Pennsylvania, Graduate Studies (Recruitment), College of Health, Environment, and Science, Department of Parks, Conservation and

Recreation Therapy, Slippery Rock, PA 16057-1383. Offers environmental education (M Ed); park and resource management (MS). *Program availability:* Part-time, evening/weekend, online only, 100% online. *Faculty:* 2 full-time (1 woman), 2 part-time/adjunct (1 woman). *Students:* 4 full-time (3 women), 69 part-time (44 women); includes 5 minority (1 Black or African American, non-Hispanic/Latino; 3 Hispanic/Latino; 1 Two or more races, non-Hispanic/Latino). Average age 33. 44 applicants, 73% accepted, 20 enrolled. In 2018, 34 master's awarded. *Degree requirements:* For master's, comprehensive exam (for some programs), thesis (for some programs), internship. *Entrance requirements:* For master's, official transcripts, minimum GPA of 2.75, personal statement. Additional exam requirements/recommendations for international students: Required—TOEFL (minimum score 550 paper-based; 80 iBT). *Application deadline:* For fall admission, 3/1 priority date for domestic students, 5/1 priority date for international students; for spring admission, 10/1 priority date for domestic students, 9/1 priority date for international students. Applications are processed on a rolling basis. Application fee: $25 ($30 for international students). Electronic applications accepted. *Expenses:* Contact institution. *Financial support:* In 2018–19, 4 students received support. Career-related internships or fieldwork, Federal Work-Study, institutionally sponsored loans, scholarships/grants, tuition waivers (partial), and unspecified assistantships available. Support available to part-time students. Financial award application deadline: 5/1; financial award applicants required to submit FAFSA. *Unit head:* Dr. John Lisco, Graduate Coordinator, 724-738-2596, Fax: 724-738-2938, E-mail: john.lisco@sru.edu. *Application contact:* Brandi Weber-Mortimer, Director of Graduate Admissions, 724-738-2051, Fax: 724-738-2146, E-mail: graduate.admissions@sru.edu.
Website: http://www.sru.edu/academics/colleges-and-departments/ches/departments/parks-and-recreation

South Dakota State University, Graduate School, College of Education and Human Sciences, Department of Health and Nutritional Sciences, Brookings, SD 57007. Offers athletic training (MS); dietetics (MS); nutrition and exercise sciences (MS, PhD); sport and recreation studies (MS). *Program availability:* Part-time. *Degree requirements:* For master's, comprehensive exam (for some programs), thesis (for some programs), oral exam. *Entrance requirements:* Additional exam requirements/recommendations for international students: Required—TOEFL (minimum score 525 paper-based). *Faculty research:* Food chemistry, bone density, functional food, nutrition education, nutrition biochemistry.

Southern Connecticut State University, School of Graduate Studies, School of Health and Human Services, Department of Recreation and Leisure Studies, New Haven, CT 06515-1355. Offers MS. *Program availability:* Part-time, evening/weekend. *Degree requirements:* For master's, thesis or alternative. *Entrance requirements:* For master's, interview, minimum undergraduate QPA of 3.0 in graduate major field or 2.5 overall. Electronic applications accepted.

Southern Illinois University Carbondale, Graduate School, College of Education and Human Services, Department of Health Education and Recreation, Program in Recreation, Carbondale, IL 62901-4701. Offers MS Ed. *Program availability:* Part-time. *Degree requirements:* For master's, thesis. *Entrance requirements:* For master's, minimum GPA of 2.7. Additional exam requirements/recommendations for international students: Required—TOEFL. *Faculty research:* Leisure across the life span, outdoor recreation, recreation therapy, leisure service administration.

Southern University and Agricultural and Mechanical College, College of Nursing and Allied Health, Department of Therapeutic Recreation and Leisure Studies, Baton Rouge, LA 70813. Offers therapeutic recreation (MS). *Degree requirements:* For master's, comprehensive exam, thesis optional. *Entrance requirements:* For master's, GMAT or GRE General Test. Additional exam requirements/recommendations for international students: Required—TOEFL (minimum score 525 paper-based).

Southwestern Oklahoma State University, College of Professional and Graduate Studies, School of Behavioral Sciences and Education, Specialization in Parks and Recreation Management, Weatherford, OK 73096-3098. Offers M Ed. *Entrance requirements:* Additional exam requirements/recommendations for international students: Required—TOEFL (minimum score 550 paper-based), IELTS (minimum score 6.5).

Springfield College, Graduate Programs, Programs in Sport Management and Recreation, Springfield, MA 01109-3797. Offers recreation management (M Ed, MS); sport management (M Ed, MS); therapeutic recreation management (M Ed, MS). *Program availability:* Part-time. *Degree requirements:* For master's, comprehensive exam, research project. *Entrance requirements:* Additional exam requirements/recommendations for international students: Required—TOEFL (minimum score 550 paper-based); Recommended—IELTS (minimum score 7). Electronic applications accepted.

State University of New York College at Cortland, Graduate Studies, School of Professional Studies, Department of Recreation, Parks and Leisure Studies, Cortland, NY 13045. Offers outdoor education (MS, MS Ed); recreation management (MS, MS Ed); therapeutic recreation (MS, MS Ed). *Program availability:* Part-time, evening/weekend. *Degree requirements:* For master's, comprehensive exam, thesis (for some programs). *Entrance requirements:* Additional exam requirements/recommendations for international students: Required—TOEFL.

Temple University, College of Public Health, Department of Health and Rehabilitation Sciences, Philadelphia, PA 19122-6096. Offers occupational therapy (MOT, DOT); recreational therapy (MS), including recreation therapy. *Accreditation:* AOTA. *Program availability:* Part-time, evening/weekend, online learning. *Faculty:* 27 full-time (19 women), 5 part-time/adjunct (3 women). *Students:* 301 full-time (218 women), 19 part-time (15 women); includes 54 minority (6 Black or African American, non-Hispanic/Latino; 19 Asian, non-Hispanic/Latino; 12 Hispanic/Latino; 17 Two or more races, non-Hispanic/Latino), 1 international. 16 applicants, 81% accepted, 9 enrolled. In 2018, 54 master's, 63 doctorates awarded. *Degree requirements:* For doctorate, thesis/dissertation (for some programs), area paper, capstone project, clinical experiences, practice project. *Entrance requirements:* For master's, GRE General Test, letters of recommendation, statement of goals, clearances for clinical/field education; for doctorate, GRE General Test, statement of goals, letters of recommendation. Additional exam requirements/recommendations for international students: Required—TOEFL (minimum score 79 iBT), IELTS, PTE, one of three is required. Application fee: $60. Electronic applications accepted. *Expenses:* Contact institution. *Financial support:* Research assistantships, teaching assistantships, career-related internships or fieldwork, Federal Work-Study, health care benefits, and unspecified assistantships available. Financial award applicants required to submit FAFSA. *Faculty research:* Adolescent health, childhood development, quality of life, community reintegration, mental health. *Unit head:* Scott Burns, Interim Department Chair, 215-204-9016, E-mail: scott.burns@temple.edu. *Application contact:* Tre Grue, Assistant Director of Admissions, 215-204-5806, E-mail: tre@temple.edu.
Website: https://cph.temple.edu/healthrehabsci/home

Texas A&M University, College of Agriculture and Life Sciences, Department of Recreation, Park and Tourism Sciences, College Station, TX 77843. Offers recreation and resources development (MRRD); recreation, park, and tourism science (PhD). *Faculty:* 19. *Students:* 50 full-time (26 women), 20 part-time (7 women); includes 12 minority (4 Black or African American, non-Hispanic/Latino; 2 Asian, non-Hispanic/Latino; 5 Hispanic/Latino; 1 Two or more races, non-Hispanic/Latino), 18 international. Average age 32. 20 applicants, 100% accepted, 16 enrolled. In 2018, 15 master's, 5 doctorates awarded. *Degree requirements:* For master's, thesis (for some programs), internship and professional paper (M Agr); for doctorate, thesis/dissertation. *Entrance requirements:* For master's and doctorate, GRE General Test. Additional exam requirements/recommendations for international students: Required—TOEFL (minimum score 550 paper-based; 80 iBT), IELTS (minimum score 6), PTE (minimum score 53). *Application deadline:* For fall admission, 3/1 for domestic and international students; for spring admission, 8/1 for domestic and international students; for summer admission, 11/1 for domestic and international students. Applications are processed on a rolling basis. Application fee: $50 ($90 for international students). Electronic applications accepted. *Expenses:* Contact institution. *Financial support:* In 2018–19, 57 students received support, including 2 fellowships with tuition reimbursements available (averaging $13,165 per year), 11 research assistantships with tuition reimbursements available (averaging $9,378 per year), 26 teaching assistantships with tuition reimbursements available (averaging $13,223 per year); career-related internships or fieldwork, institutionally sponsored loans, scholarships/grants, traineeships, health care benefits, tuition waivers (full and partial), and unspecified assistantships also available. Support available to part-time students. Financial award application deadline: 3/15; financial award applicants required to submit FAFSA. *Faculty research:* Administration and tourism, outdoor recreation, commercial recreation, environmental law, system planning. *Unit head:* Dr. Gary Ellis, Department Head, 979-845-7324, E-mail: gellis@ag.tamu.edu. *Application contact:* Irina Shatruk, Graduate Program Coordinator, 979-845-5412, E-mail: jshatruk@tamu.edu.
Website: http://rpts.tamu.edu/

Texas State University, The Graduate College, College of Education, Program in Recreation Management, San Marcos, TX 78666. Offers recreation management (MSRLS). *Program availability:* Part-time. *Faculty:* 6 full-time (3 women), 1 (woman) part-time/adjunct. *Students:* 12 full-time (1 woman), 7 part-time (1 woman); includes 9 minority (4 Black or African American, non-Hispanic/Latino; 5 Hispanic/Latino), 1 international. Average age 29. 23 applicants, 61% accepted, 8 enrolled. In 2018, 12 master's awarded. *Degree requirements:* For master's, comprehensive exam, thesis optional. *Entrance requirements:* For master's, baccalaureate degree from regionally-accredited institution with minimum GPA of 2.75 in last 60 hours of course work, background course work in marketing and management, statement of purpose. Additional exam requirements/recommendations for international students: Required—TOEFL (minimum score 550 paper-based; 78 iBT), IELTS (minimum score 6.5). *Application deadline:* For fall admission, 2/1 priority date for domestic students, 2/1 for international students; for spring admission, 10/15 priority date for domestic students, 10/1 for international students; for summer admission, 4/15 for domestic students, 3/15 for international students. Applications are processed on a rolling basis. Application fee: $55 ($90 for international students). Electronic applications accepted. *Expenses:* Tuition, state resident: full-time $8102; part-time $4051 per semester. Tuition, nonresident: full-time $18,229; part-time $9115 per semester. *International tuition:* $18,229 full-time. *Required fees:* $2116; $120 per credit hour. Tuition and fees vary according to course load. *Financial support:* In 2018–19, 14 students received support, including 1 research assistantship (averaging $12,685 per year), 2 teaching assistantships (averaging $13,447 per year); scholarships/grants and unspecified assistantships also available. Financial award application deadline: 1/15; financial award applicants required to submit FAFSA. *Faculty research:* Lasting perceptions of wilderness orientation programming: A longitudinal follow-up study; State of Leisure Studies in Australia and New Zealand; Champions for Health in the Community: Critical Service Learning, Transformative Education, and Community Empowerment. *Total annual research expenditures:* $1,442. *Unit head:* Dr. Jan Hodges, Graduate Advisor, 512-245-7482, Fax: 512-245-8678, E-mail: jh223@txstate.edu. *Application contact:* Dr. Andrea Golato, Dean of the Graduate College, 512-245-2581, Fax: 512-245-8365, E-mail: gradcollege@txstate.edu.
Website: http://www.gradcollege.txstate.edu/programs/msrls-mgmt.html

United States Sports Academy, Graduate Programs, Program in Recreation Management, Daphne, AL 36526-7055. Offers MSS. *Program availability:* Part-time, 100% online. *Degree requirements:* For master's, comprehensive exam, thesis optional. *Entrance requirements:* For master's, GRE General Test, GMAT, or MAT, minimum GPA of 2.5, 3 letters of recommendation, personal statement. Additional exam requirements/recommendations for international students: Required—TOEFL (minimum score 550 paper-based; 79 iBT). Electronic applications accepted. *Expenses:* Contact institution. *Faculty research:* Psychiatric aspects of injury rehabilitation, geriatric exercises and mobility.

Universidad Metropolitana, School of Education, Program in Managing Recreation and Sports Services, San Juan, PR 00928-1150. Offers M Ed. *Program availability:* Part-time. *Degree requirements:* For master's, thesis or alternative. *Entrance requirements:* For master's, EXADEP, interview. Electronic applications accepted.

University of Alberta, Faculty of Kinesiology, Sport, and Recreation, Edmonton, AB T6G 2E1, Canada. Offers physical education (M Sc); recreation and physical education (MA, PhD). *Program availability:* Part-time. Terminal master's awarded for partial completion of doctoral program. *Degree requirements:* For master's, thesis (for some programs); for doctorate, thesis/dissertation. *Entrance requirements:* For master's, bachelor's degree in related field; for doctorate, master's degree in related field with thesis. Additional exam requirements/recommendations for international students: Required—TOEFL. *Faculty research:* Motivation and adherence to physical ability, performance enhancement, adapted physical activity, exercise physiology, sport administration, tourism.

University of Arkansas, Graduate School, College of Education and Health Professions, Department of Health, Human Performance and Recreation, Program in Recreation and Sports Management, Fayetteville, AR 72701. Offers M Ed, Ed D. In 2018, 19 master's, 1 doctorate awarded. *Degree requirements:* For master's, thesis optional; for doctorate, thesis/dissertation. *Entrance requirements:* For doctorate, GRE General Test. *Application deadline:* For fall admission, 8/1 for domestic students, 4/1 for international students; for spring admission, 12/1 for domestic students, 10/1 for international students; for summer admission, 4/15 for domestic students, 3/1 for international students. Applications are processed on a rolling basis. Application fee: $60. Electronic applications accepted. *Financial support:* In 2018–19, 8 research assistantships, 10 teaching assistantships were awarded; fellowships with tuition reimbursements, career-related internships or fieldwork, and Federal Work-Study also available. Support available to part-time students. Financial award application deadline: 4/1; financial award applicants required to submit FAFSA. *Unit head:* Dr. Matthew Ganio, Department Head, 479-575-2956, E-mail: msganio@uark.edu. *Application contact:* Dr. Paul Calleja, Assistant Dept. Head - HHPR, Graduate Coordinator, 479-575-2854, Fax: 479-575-5778, E-mail: pcallej@uark.edu.
Website: https://hhpr.uark.edu

University of Florida, Graduate School, College of Health and Human Performance, Department of Tourism, Recreation and Sport Management, Gainesville, FL 32611. Offers health and human performance (PhD), including historic preservation (MS, PhD);

recreation, parks and tourism (MS, PhD), sport management; recreation, parks and tourism (MS), including historic preservation (MS, PhD), natural resource recreation, recreation, parks and tourism (MS, PhD), therapeutic recreation, tourism, tropical conservation and development; sport management (MS), including historic preservation (MS, PhD), tropical conservation and development; JD/MS; MSM/MS. *Degree requirements:* For master's, comprehensive exam (for some programs), thesis (for some programs); for doctorate, comprehensive exam, thesis/dissertation. *Entrance requirements:* For master's and doctorate, GRE General Test, minimum GPA of 3.0. Additional exam requirements/recommendations for international students: Required—TOEFL (minimum score 550 paper-based; 80 iBT), IELTS (minimum score 6). Electronic applications accepted. *Faculty research:* Hospitality, natural resource management, sport management, tourism.

The University of Iowa, Graduate College, College of Liberal Arts and Sciences, Department of Health and Human Physiology, Iowa City, IA 52242-1316. Offers athletic training (MS); clinical exercise physiology (MS); health and human physiology (PhD); leisure studies (MA, PhD), including recreational sport management (PhD); therapeutic recreation (MA). *Degree requirements:* For master's, thesis optional, exam; for doctorate, comprehensive exam, thesis/dissertation. *Entrance requirements:* For master's and doctorate, GRE General Test, minimum GPA of 3.0. Additional exam requirements/recommendations for international students: Required—TOEFL (minimum score 600 paper-based; 100 iBT). Electronic applications accepted.

University of Louisiana at Monroe, Graduate School, College of Health Sciences, Department of Kinesiology, Monroe, LA 71209-0001. Offers applied exercise science (MS); clinical exercise physiology (MS); sports, fitness and recreation management (MS). *Program availability:* Part-time, evening/weekend, online learning. *Faculty:* 6 full-time (2 women), 1 part-time/adjunct (0 women). *Students:* 39 full-time (17 women), 4 part-time (2 women); includes 16 minority (10 Black or African American, non-Hispanic/Latino; 1 American Indian or Alaska Native, non-Hispanic/Latino; 3 Hispanic/Latino; 2 Two or more races, non-Hispanic/Latino), 2 international. Average age 25. 16 applicants, 88% accepted, 11 enrolled. In 2018, 22 master's awarded. *Degree requirements:* For master's, comprehensive exam, thesis, 6-hour internship. *Entrance requirements:* For master's, GRE General Test. Additional exam requirements/recommendations for international students: Required—TOEFL (minimum score 500 paper-based; 61 iBT). *Application deadline:* For fall admission, 8/24 priority date for domestic students, 7/1 for international students; for winter admission, 12/14 priority date for domestic students; for spring admission, 1/19 for domestic students, 11/1 for international students. Applications are processed on a rolling basis. Application fee: $20 ($30 for international students). Electronic applications accepted. *Financial support:* In 2018–19, 12 students received support. Research assistantships, career-related internships or fieldwork, Federal Work-Study, and unspecified assistantships available. Financial award application deadline: 4/1; financial award applicants required to submit FAFSA. *Faculty research:* Cardiovascular disease risk factors; exercise and immunological system; attitude, exercise, and the aged. *Unit head:* Dr. Ken Alford, Director, 318-342-1306, E-mail: alford@ulm.edu. *Application contact:* Dr. Tommie Church, Director of Graduate Studies, 318-342-1321, E-mail: church@ulm.edu. Website: http://www.ulm.edu/kinesiology/

University of Manitoba, Faculty of Graduate Studies, Faculty of Kinesiology and Recreation Management, Winnipeg, MB R3T 2N2, Canada. Offers kinesiology and recreation (M Sc, MA).

University of Mississippi, Graduate School, School of Applied Sciences, University, MS 38677. Offers communicative disorders (MS); criminal justice (MCJ); exercise science (MS); food and nutrition services (MS); health and kinesiology (PhD); health promotion (MS); nutrition and hospitality management (PhD); park and recreation management (MA); social welfare (PhD); social work (MSW). *Faculty:* 66 full-time (36 women), 27 part-time/adjunct (13 women). *Students:* 192 full-time (148 women), 40 part-time (25 women); includes 50 minority (41 Black or African American, non-Hispanic/Latino; 1 American Indian or Alaska Native, non-Hispanic/Latino; 1 Asian, non-Hispanic/Latino; 5 Hispanic/Latino; 2 Two or more races, non-Hispanic/Latino), 16 international. Average age 26. In 2018, 72 master's, 5 doctorates awarded. *Entrance requirements:* For master's, GRE General Test, minimum GPA of 3.0. Additional exam requirements/recommendations for international students: Required—TOEFL. *Application deadline:* Applications are processed on a rolling basis. Application fee: $50. Electronic applications accepted. *Financial support:* Scholarships/grants available. Financial award application deadline: 3/1; financial award applicants required to submit FAFSA. *Unit head:* Dr. Peter Grandjean, Dean of Applied Sciences, 662-915-7900, Fax: 662-915-7901, E-mail: applsci@olemiss.edu. *Application contact:* Temeka Smith, Graduate Activities Specialist for Admissions, 662-915-7474, Fax: 662-915-7577, E-mail: gschool@olemiss.edu.

University of Montana, Graduate School, College of Forestry and Conservation, Missoula, MT 59812. Offers fish and wildlife biology (PhD); forest and conservation sciences (PhD); forestry (MS); recreation management (MS); resource conservation (MS); systems ecology (MS, PhD); wildlife biology (MS). *Degree requirements:* For doctorate, thesis/dissertation. *Entrance requirements:* For master's and doctorate, GRE General Test. Additional exam requirements/recommendations for international students: Required—TOEFL (minimum score 575 paper-based).

University of Nebraska at Kearney, College of Education, Kinesiology and Sport Sciences Department, Kearney, NE 68849-0001. Offers general physical education (MA Ed), including recreation and leisure, sports administration; physical education exercise science (MA Ed); physical education master teacher (MA Ed), including pedagogy, special populations. *Program availability:* Part-time, evening/weekend, 100% online. *Degree requirements:* For master's, comprehensive exam, thesis optional. *Entrance requirements:* For master's, GRE General Test (for some programs), personal statement. Additional exam requirements/recommendations for international students: Recommended—TOEFL (minimum score 550 paper-based; 79 iBT), IELTS (minimum score 6.5). Electronic applications accepted. *Faculty research:* Ergonomic aids, nutrition, motor development, sports pedagogy, applied behavior analysis, physical activity and wellness, athletic training, therapeutic Interventions, exercise physiology, endocrinology and metabolism.

University of New Brunswick Fredericton, School of Graduate Studies, Faculty of Kinesiology, Fredericton, NB E3B 5A3, Canada. Offers exercise and sport science (M Sc); sport and recreation management (MBA); sport and recreation studies (MA). *Program availability:* Part-time. *Degree requirements:* For master's, thesis (for some programs). *Entrance requirements:* For master's, GMAT (minimum score of 550 for sport and recreation management program), minimum GPA of 3.0, written statement of research goals and interests. Additional exam requirements/recommendations for international students: Required—TOEFL (minimum score 92 iBT), IELTS (minimum score 7). Electronic applications accepted.

University of New Hampshire, Graduate School, College of Health and Human Services, Department of Recreation Management and Policy, Durham, NH 03824. Offers adaptive sports (MS); recreation administration (MS); therapeutic recreation administration (MS). *Program availability:* Part-time. *Entrance requirements:* Additional exam requirements/recommendations for international students: Required—TOEFL

(minimum score 550 paper-based; 80 iBT); Recommended—TWE. Electronic applications accepted.

The University of North Carolina at Greensboro, Graduate School, School of Health and Human Sciences, Department of Community and Therapeutic Recreation, Greensboro, NC 27412-5001. Offers community recreation management (MS); therapeutic recreation (MS). *Degree requirements:* For master's, thesis. *Entrance requirements:* For master's, GRE General Test. Additional exam requirements/recommendations for international students: Required—TOEFL. Electronic applications accepted.

University of Rhode Island, Graduate School, College of Health Sciences, Department of Kinesiology, Kingston, RI 02881. Offers cultural studies of sport and physical culture (MS); exercise science (MS); psychosocial/behavioral aspects of physical activity (MS). *Accreditation:* NCATE. *Program availability:* Part-time. *Faculty:* 16 full-time (11 women). *Students:* 13 full-time (5 women), 2 part-time (1 woman), 1 international. 18 applicants, 100% accepted, 8 enrolled. In 2018, 5 master's awarded. *Entrance requirements:* Additional exam requirements/recommendations for international students: Required—TOEFL. *Application deadline:* For fall admission, 7/15 for domestic students, 2/1 for international students; for spring admission, 11/15 for domestic students, 7/15 for international students. Application fee: $65. Electronic applications accepted. *Expenses:* Tuition, area resident: Full-time $13,226; part-time $735 per credit. Tuition, state resident: full-time $13,226; part-time $735 per credit. Tuition, nonresident: full-time $25,854; part-time $1436 per credit. International tuition: $25,854 full-time. *Required fees:* $1698; $50 per credit. $35 per semester. One-time fee: $165. *Financial support:* In 2018–19, 1 research assistantship (averaging $8,862 per year), 6 teaching assistantships with tuition reimbursements (averaging $16,247 per year) were awarded. Financial award application deadline: 2/1; financial award applicants required to submit FAFSA. *Unit head:* Dr. Disa Hatfield, Interim Chair, 401-874-5183, E-mail: doch@uri.edu. *Application contact:* Dr. Matthew Delmonico, Graduate Program Director, 401-874-5440, E-mail: delmonico@uri.edu.
Website: http://web.uri.edu/kinesiology/

The University of Tennessee, Graduate School, College of Education, Health and Human Sciences, Department of Exercise, Sport, and Leisure Studies, Knoxville, TN 37996. Offers exercise science (MS, PhD), including biomechanics/sports medicine, exercise physiology; recreation and leisure studies (MS); sport management (MS); sport studies (MS, PhD); therapeutic recreation (MS). *Program availability:* Part-time, evening/weekend. *Degree requirements:* For master's, thesis optional. *Entrance requirements:* For master's, minimum GPA of 2.7. Additional exam requirements/recommendations for international students: Required—TOEFL. Electronic applications accepted.

The University of Toledo, College of Graduate Studies, College of Health and Human Services, School of Exercise and Rehabilitation Sciences, Toledo, OH 43606-3390. Offers athletic training (MSES); exercise physiology (MSES); exercise science (PhD); occupational therapy (OTD); physical therapy (DPT); recreation and leisure studies (MA), including recreation administration, recreation therapy. *Degree requirements:* For master's, comprehensive exam, thesis; for doctorate, thesis/dissertation or alternative. *Entrance requirements:* For master's, GRE, minimum cumulative GPA of 2.7 for all previous academic work, letters of recommendation; for doctorate, GRE, minimum cumulative GPA of 3.0 for all previous academic work, letters of recommendation; OTCAS or PTCAS application and UT supplemental application (for OTD and DPT). Additional exam requirements/recommendations for international students: Required—TOEFL (minimum score 550 paper-based; 80 iBT). Electronic applications accepted.

University of Utah, Graduate School, College of Health, Department of Health, Kinesiology, and Recreation, Salt Lake City, UT 84112. Offers kinesiology (MS, PhD); parks, recreation, and tourism (MS, PhD). *Program availability:* Part-time. *Faculty:* 21 full-time (9 women), 11 part-time/adjunct (6 women). *Students:* 82 full-time (55 women), 12 part-time (4 women); includes 5 minority (1 Black or African American, non-Hispanic/Latino; 1 American Indian or Alaska Native, non-Hispanic/Latino; 3 Asian, non-Hispanic/Latino), 1 international. Average age 28. 92 applicants, 23% accepted, 16 enrolled. In 2018, 33 master's, 5 doctorates awarded. Terminal master's awarded for partial completion of doctoral program. *Degree requirements:* For master's, comprehensive exam, thesis or alternative; for doctorate, comprehensive exam, thesis/dissertation. *Entrance requirements:* For master's and doctorate, GRE General Test, minimum GPA of 3.0. Additional exam requirements/recommendations for international students: Required—TOEFL (minimum score 500 paper-based). *Application deadline:* For fall admission, 1/15 for domestic and international students. Application fee: $55 ($65 for international students). Electronic applications accepted. *Expenses:* Tuition, area resident: Full-time $7190.66; part-time $2112.48 per year. Tuition, state resident: full-time $7190.66. Tuition, nonresident: full-time $25,195. *Required fees:* $558; $555.04 per unit. Tuition and fees vary according to course level, course load, degree level, program and student level. *Financial support:* In 2018–19, 38 students received support, including 7 research assistantships with full tuition reimbursements available, 31 teaching assistantships with full tuition reimbursements available; career-related internships or fieldwork, scholarships/grants, health care benefits, and unspecified assistantships also available. Financial award application deadline: 1/15; financial award applicants required to submit FAFSA. *Faculty research:* Cognitive and motor neuroscience, physical activity and well being, exercise and disease, healthy communities and environments. *Total annual research expenditures:* $55,000. *Unit head:* Dr. Kelly S. Bricker, Program Director, 801-585-6503, E-mail: kelly.bricker@health.utah.edu. *Application contact:* Dr. Jim Sibthorp, Director of Graduate Studies, 801-581-5940, Fax: 801-581-4930, E-mail: jim.sibthorp@health.utah.edu.
Website: http://www.health.utah.edu/prt/

University of Utah, Graduate School, College of Health, Department of Occupational and Recreational Therapies, Salt Lake City, UT 84108. Offers MOT, OTD. *Accreditation:* AOTA. *Program availability:* Part-time, evening/weekend, 100% online. *Faculty:* 9 full-time (all women), 4 part-time/adjunct (2 women). *Students:* 102 full-time (79 women), 21 part-time (16 women); includes 24 minority (3 Black or African American, non-Hispanic/Latino; 6 Asian, non-Hispanic/Latino; 10 Hispanic/Latino; 1 Native Hawaiian or other Pacific Islander, non-Hispanic/Latino; 4 Two or more races, non-Hispanic/Latino). Average age 31. 200 applicants, 28% accepted, 36 enrolled. In 2018, 34 master's, 9 doctorates awarded. *Entrance requirements:* For master's, GRE General Test. Additional exam requirements/recommendations for international students: Required—TOEFL (minimum score 575 paper-based). *Application deadline:* For fall admission, 11/15 for domestic and international students. Application fee: $125. Electronic applications accepted. *Expenses:* $68,000 resident tuition to complete MOT, $19,000 tuition to complete OTD. *Financial support:* In 2018–19, 10 students received support. Career-related internships or fieldwork, Federal Work-Study, institutionally sponsored loans, scholarships/grants, and unspecified assistantships available. Financial award application deadline: 2/15; financial award applicants required to submit FAFSA. *Faculty research:* Community-based practice, occupational science, refugees, resilience, executive function, traumatic brain injury, pediatrics. *Total annual research expenditures:* $50,000. *Unit head:* Dr. Lorie Richards, Chairperson, 801-585-1069, Fax: 801-585-1001, E-mail: lorie.richards@hsc.utah.edu. *Application contact:* Kelly C. Brown, Academic Advisor, 801-585-0555, Fax: 801-585-1001, E-mail: kelly.brown@hsc.utah.edu.
Website: http://health.utah.edu/occupational-recreational-therapies/

Recreation and Park Management

University of Waterloo, Graduate Studies and Postdoctoral Affairs, Faculty of Applied Health Sciences, Department of Recreation and Leisure Studies, Waterloo, ON N2L 3G1, Canada. Offers MA, PhD. *Program availability:* Part-time. *Degree requirements:* For master's, thesis; for doctorate, comprehensive exam, thesis/dissertation. *Entrance requirements:* For master's, honors degree, minimum B average, writing sample, resume; for doctorate, GRE (recommended), master's degree, minimum B average, writing sample, resume. Additional exam requirements/recommendations for international students: Required—TOEFL, IELTS, PTE. *Application deadline:* For fall admission, 2/1 for domestic and international students. Application fee: $125 Canadian dollars. Electronic applications accepted. *Financial support:* In 2018–19, teaching assistantships (averaging $6,141 per year) were awarded; research assistantships, career-related internships or fieldwork, Federal Work-Study, institutionally sponsored loans, scholarships/grants, and university-sponsored bursaries also available. *Faculty research:* Tourism, leisure behavior, special populations, leisure service management, outdoor resources, aging, health and well-being, work and health. *Application contact:* Tracy Taves, Graduate Studies Coordinator, 519-888-4567 Ext. 36149, Fax: 519-746-6776, E-mail: tltaves@uwaterloo.ca.
Website: https://uwaterloo.ca/recreation-and-leisure-studies/

University of Wisconsin–La Crosse, College of Science and Health, Department of Recreation Management and Therapeutic Recreation, La Crosse, WI 54601-3742. Offers recreation management (MS); therapeutic recreation (MS). *Program availability:* Part-time. *Degree requirements:* For master's, thesis or alternative, project or internship. *Entrance requirements:* Additional exam requirements/recommendations for international students: Required—TOEFL (minimum score 550 paper-based; 79 iBT). Electronic applications accepted.

University of Wisconsin–Milwaukee, Graduate School, College of Health Sciences, Department of Occupational Science and Technology, Milwaukee, WI 53201-0413. Offers assistive technology and design (MS); disability and occupation (MS); ergonomics (MS); therapeutic recreation (MS). *Accreditation:* AOTA. *Students:* 96 full-time (85 women), 2 part-time (both women); includes 13 minority (4 Asian, non-Hispanic/Latino; 2 Hispanic/Latino; 7 Two or more races, non-Hispanic/Latino), 2 international. Average age 28. 131 applicants, 28% accepted, 33 enrolled. In 2018, 34 master's awarded. *Entrance requirements:* Additional exam requirements/recommendations for international students: Required—TOEFL (minimum score 550 paper-based; 79 iBT), IELTS (minimum score 6.5). *Application deadline:* For fall admission, 1/1 priority date for domestic students; for spring admission, 9/1 for domestic students. Applications are processed on a rolling basis. Application fee: $56 ($75 for international students). *Financial support:* Fellowships, research assistantships, teaching assistantships, and unspecified assistantships available. Support available to part-time students. Financial award application deadline: 4/15. *Unit head:* Jay Kapellusch, PhD, Department Chair, 414-229-5292, Fax: 414-229-2619, E-mail: kap@uwm.edu. *Application contact:* Bhagwant S. Sindhu, PhD, Graduate Program Coordinator, 414-229-1180, Fax: 414-229-5100, E-mail: sindhu@uwm.edu.
Website: http://uwm.edu/healthsciences/academics/occupational-science-technology/

Utah State University, School of Graduate Studies, S.J. and Jessie E. Quinney College of Natural Resources, Department of Environment and Society, Logan, UT 84322. Offers bioregional planning (MS); geography (MA, MS); human dimensions of ecosystem science and management (MS, PhD); recreation resource management (MS, PhD). *Degree requirements:* For master's, comprehensive exam, thesis (for some programs). *Entrance requirements:* For master's and doctorate, GRE General Test, minimum GPA of 3.0. Additional exam requirements/recommendations for international students: Required—TOEFL. Electronic applications accepted. *Faculty research:* Geographic information systems/geographic and environmental education, bioregional planning, natural resource and environmental policy, outdoor recreation and tourism, natural resource and environmental management.

Virginia Commonwealth University, Graduate School, School of Education, Program in Sport Leadership, Richmond, VA 23284-9005. Offers M Ed. *Entrance requirements:* For master's, GRE General Test or MAT. Additional exam requirements/recommendations for international students: Required—TOEFL (minimum score 600 paper-based; 100 iBT). Electronic applications accepted.

Western Illinois University, School of Graduate Studies, College of Education and Human Services, Department of Recreation, Park, and Tourism Administration, Macomb, IL 61455-1390. Offers MS. *Program availability:* Part-time. *Students:* 24 full-time (16 women), 7 part-time (5 women); includes 6 minority (all Black or African American, non-Hispanic/Latino), 3 international. Average age 26. 28 applicants, 93% accepted, 21 enrolled. In 2018, 17 master's awarded. *Entrance requirements:* Additional exam requirements/recommendations for international students: Required—TOEFL (minimum score 550 paper-based; 80 iBT). *Application deadline:* Applications are processed on a rolling basis. Application fee: $30. Electronic applications accepted. *Financial support:* Unspecified assistantships available. Financial award applicants required to submit FAFSA. *Unit head:* Dr. Michael Lukkarinene, Interim Chairperson, 309-298-1967. *Application contact:* Dr. Mark Mossman, Director of Graduate Studies, 309-298-1806, Fax: 309-298-2345, E-mail: grad-office@wiu.edu.
Website: http://www.wiu.edu/rpta

Western Kentucky University, Graduate School, College of Health and Human Services, Department of Kinesiology, Recreation and Sport, Bowling Green, KY 42101. Offers athletic administration and coaching (MS); physical education (MS); recreation and sport administration (MS). *Program availability:* Part-time, evening/weekend, online learning. *Degree requirements:* For master's, comprehensive exam, thesis optional. *Entrance requirements:* For master's, GRE General Test, minimum GPA of 2.75. Additional exam requirements/recommendations for international students: Required—TOEFL (minimum score 555 paper-based; 79 iBT). *Faculty research:* Orthopedic rehabilitation, fitness center coordination, heat acclimation, biomechanical and physiological parameters.

West Virginia University, Davis College of Agriculture, Forestry and Consumer Sciences, Morgantown, WV 26506. Offers agricultural and extension education (MS, PhD); agriculture and resource management (MS); agriculture, natural resources and design (M Agr); agronomy (MS); animal and food science (PhD); animal physiology (MS); applied and environmental microbiology (MS); design and merchandising (MS); entomology (MS); forest resource science (PhD); forestry (MSF); genetics and developmental biology (MS, PhD); horticulture (MS); human and community development (PhD); landscape architecture (MLA); natural resource economics (PhD); nutritional and food science (MS); plant and soil science (PhD); plant pathology (MS); recreation, parks and tourism resources (MS); reproductive physiology (MS, PhD); wildlife and fisheries resources (PhD). *Accreditation:* ASLA. *Program availability:* Part-time. *Students:* 188 full-time (86 women), 47 part-time (30 women); includes 22 minority (5 Black or African American, non-Hispanic/Latino; 5 Asian, non-Hispanic/Latino; 8 Hispanic/Latino; 4 Two or more races, non-Hispanic/Latino), 60 international. In 2018, 56 master's, 14 doctorates awarded. *Degree requirements:* For master's, thesis; for doctorate, thesis/dissertation. *Entrance requirements:* Additional exam requirements/recommendations for international students: Required—TOEFL (minimum score 550 paper-based). *Application deadline:* For fall admission, 6/1 priority date for domestic students, 6/1 for international students; for spring admission, 1/5 for domestic and international students. Applications are processed on a rolling basis. Application fee: $60. Electronic applications accepted. *Financial support:* Fellowships, research assistantships, teaching assistantships, career-related internships or fieldwork, Federal Work-Study, institutionally sponsored loans, tuition waivers (full and partial), and unspecified assistantships available. Financial award application deadline: 2/1; financial award applicants required to submit FAFSA. *Faculty research:* Reproductive physiology, soil and water quality, human nutrition, aquaculture, wildlife management. *Unit head:* Dr. Ken Blemings, Interim Dean, 304-293-2395, Fax: 304-293-3740, E-mail: ken.blemings@mail.wvu.edu. *Application contact:* Dr. J. Todd Petty, Associate Dean, 304-293-2278, Fax: 304-293-3740, E-mail: jtpetty@mail.wvu.edu.
Website: https://www.davis.wvu.edu

Section 30
Physical Education and Kinesiology

This section contains a directory of institutions offering graduate work in physical education and kinesiology. Additional information about programs listed in the directory may be obtained by writing directly to the dean of a graduate school or chair of a department at the address given in the directory.

For programs offering related work, see also in this book *Business Administration and Management, Education,* and *Sports Management.* In another guide in this series:

Graduate Programs in the Humanities, Arts & Social Sciences
See *Performing Arts*

CONTENTS

Program Directories

Athletic Training and Sports Medicine

Adrian College, Graduate Programs, Adrian, MI 49221-2575. Offers accounting (MS); athletic training (MS); criminal justice (MA). *Degree requirements:* For master's, comprehensive exam (for some programs), thesis (for some programs), thesis, internship or practicum with corresponding in-depth paper and/or presentation. *Entrance requirements:* For master's, appropriate undergraduate degree, minimum cumulative and major GPA of 3.0, personal statement.

A.T. Still University, Arizona School of Health Sciences, Mesa, AZ 85206. Offers advanced occupational therapy (MS); advanced physician assistant studies (MS); athletic training (MS, DAT); audiology (Au D); clinical decision making in athletic training (Graduate Certificate); occupational therapy (MS, OTD); orthopedic rehabilitation (Graduate Certificate); physical therapy (DPT); physician assistant studies (MS); post-professional audiology (Au D); post-professional physical therapy (DPT). *Accreditation:* AOTA (one or more programs are accredited); ASHA. *Program availability:* Part-time, 100% online. *Faculty:* 88 full-time (65 women), 215 part-time/adjunct (157 women). *Students:* 627 full-time (429 women), 349 part-time (228 women); includes 302 minority (46 Black or African American, non-Hispanic/Latino; 6 American Indian or Alaska Native, non-Hispanic/Latino; 99 Asian, non-Hispanic/Latino; 108 Hispanic/Latino; 43 Two or more races, non-Hispanic/Latino), 88 international. Average age 32. 5,235 applicants, 13% accepted, 431 enrolled. In 2018, 140 master's, 310 doctorates, 1 other advanced degree awarded. *Degree requirements:* For master's, thesis (for some programs); for doctorate, thesis/dissertation (for some programs). *Entrance requirements:* For master's, GRE General Test; for doctorate, GRE, Physical Therapist Evaluation Tool (for DPT), current state licensure. Additional exam requirements/recommendations for international students: Required—TOEFL (minimum score 80 iBT). *Application deadline:* For fall admission, 7/7 for domestic and international students; for winter admission, 10/3 for domestic and international students; for spring admission, 1/16 for domestic and international students; for summer admission, 4/17 for domestic and international students. Applications are processed on a rolling basis. Application fee: $70. Electronic applications accepted. *Financial support:* In 2018–19, 161 students received support. Federal Work-Study and scholarships/grants available. Financial award application deadline: 6/1; financial award applicants required to submit FAFSA. *Faculty research:* Pediatric sport-related concussion, adolescent athlete health-related quality of life; geriatric and pediatric well-being, pain management for participation, practice-based research network, BMI and dental caries. *Total annual research expenditures:* $104,655. *Unit head:* Dr. Ann Lee Burch, Dean, 480-219-6061, E-mail: aburch@atsu.edu. *Application contact:* Donna Sparks, Director, Admissions Processing, 660-626-2117, Fax: 660-626-2969, E-mail: admissions@atsu.edu.
Website: http://www.atsu.edu/ashs

Azusa Pacific University, School of Behavioral and Applied Sciences, Department of Kinesiology, Azusa, CA 91702-7000. Offers athletic training (MS); physical education (MA, MS).

Barry University, School of Human Performance and Leisure Sciences, Programs in Movement Science, Specialization in Athletic Training, Miami Shores, FL 33161-6695. Offers MS. *Program availability:* Part-time, evening/weekend. *Degree requirements:* For master's, comprehensive exam, project or thesis. *Entrance requirements:* For master's, GRE General Test, minimum GPA of 3.0. Electronic applications accepted. *Faculty research:* Pain management, prevention and injury analysis, low energy static magnetic field therapy, upper extremity biomechanics.

Baylor University, Graduate School, Robbins College of Health and Human Sciences, Department of Health, Human Performance and Recreation, Waco, TX 76798. Offers athletic training (MS); exercise physiology (MS); kinesiology, exercise nutrition, and health promotion (PhD); sport pedagogy (MS). *Accreditation:* NCATE. *Program availability:* Part-time. *Students:* 72 full-time (40 women), 13 part-time (8 women); includes 20 minority (5 Black or African American, non-Hispanic/Latino; 1 American Indian or Alaska Native, non-Hispanic/Latino; 1 Asian, non-Hispanic/Latino; 7 Hispanic/Latino; 6 Two or more races, non-Hispanic/Latino), 5 international. 109 applicants, 59% accepted, 44 enrolled. In 2018, 35 master's, 2 doctorates awarded. *Degree requirements:* For master's, comprehensive exam, thesis optional; for doctorate, comprehensive exam, thesis/dissertation. *Entrance requirements:* For master's and doctorate, GRE General Test. Additional exam requirements/recommendations for international students: Required—TOEFL (minimum score 550 paper-based; 80 iBT). *Application deadline:* For fall admission, 2/1 priority date for domestic students, 2/1 for international students; for spring admission, 10/1 for domestic and international students. Applications are processed on a rolling basis. Application fee: $25. Electronic applications accepted. *Financial support:* In 2018–19, 60 students received support, including 1 research assistantship with full tuition reimbursement available (averaging $12,700 per year), 33 teaching assistantships with full tuition reimbursements available (averaging $7,650 per year); career-related internships or fieldwork, Federal Work-Study, institutionally sponsored loans, scholarships/grants, tuition waivers (full), and unspecified assistantships also available. Financial award application deadline: 2/1. *Faculty research:* Exercise testing, cardio-metabolic health, resistance exercise and training, nutritional intervention, population health, health promotion, global health epidemiology, coaching, natural resource management, stimulant misuse, diet, microbiome and colon cancer etiology. *Total annual research expenditures:* $250,118. *Unit head:* Dr. Jaeho Shim, Graduate Program Director, 254-710-4009, Fax: 254-710-3527, E-mail: joe_shim@baylor.edu. *Application contact:* Deepa Morris, Graduate Program Coordinator, 254-710-3526, Fax: 254-710-3527, E-mail: deepa_morris@baylor.edu.
Website: http://www.baylor.edu/HHPR/

Bellarmine University, College of Health Professions, School of Movement and Rehabilitation Sciences, Louisville, KY 40205. Offers athletic training (MSAT); physical therapy (DPT). *Program availability:* Part-time. *Faculty:* 20 full-time (14 women), 30 part-time/adjunct (17 women). *Students:* 213 full-time (136 women), 1 (woman) part-time; includes 17 minority (3 Black or African American, non-Hispanic/Latino; 3 Asian, non-Hispanic/Latino; 3 Hispanic/Latino; 8 Two or more races, non-Hispanic/Latino), 1 international. Average age 24. 663 applicants, 18% accepted, 81 enrolled. In 2018, 76 doctorates awarded. *Degree requirements:* For master's and doctorate, comprehensive exam. *Entrance requirements:* For master's, minimum undergraduate GPA of 2.75 or GRE, 3.0 in prerequisite courses; grade of C or better in all prerequisites; for doctorate, GRE, minimum undergraduate GPA of 2.75, 3.0 in prerequisite courses; grade of C or better in all prerequisites; documented work/volunteer hours in PT setting; physical ability to perform tasks required of a physical therapist. Additional exam requirements/recommendations for international students: Required—TOEFL (minimum iBT score of 83, 26 on speaking test), IELTS (minimum score 7, speaking band score of 8). *Application deadline:* Applications are processed on a rolling basis. Application fee: $40. Electronic applications accepted. Tuition and fees vary according to class time, degree level and program. *Financial support:* Applicants required to submit FAFSA. *Unit head:* Dr. Tony Brosky, Dean, 502-272-8375, E-mail: jbrosky@bellarmine.edu. *Application contact:* Dr. Sara Pettingill, Dean of Graduate Admission, 502-272-8401, Fax: 502-272-8002, E-mail: spettingill@bellarmine.edu.
Website: https://www.bellarmine.edu/movement/

Bloomsburg University of Pennsylvania, School of Graduate Studies, College of Science and Technology, Department of Exercise Science and Athletics, Bloomsburg, PA 17815-1301. Offers clinical athletic training (MS); exercise science (MS). *Degree requirements:* For master's, thesis optional, practical clinical experience. *Entrance requirements:* For master's, GRE, minimum QPA of 3.0, related undergraduate coursework, interview. Additional exam requirements/recommendations for international students: Required—TOEFL (minimum score 550 paper-based; 79 iBT), IELTS. Electronic applications accepted.

Boston University, College of Health and Rehabilitation Sciences: Sargent College, Department of Physical Therapy and Athletic Training, Boston, MA 02215. Offers athletic training (MS); physical therapy (DPT); rehabilitation sciences (PhD). *Accreditation:* APTA (one or more programs are accredited). *Faculty:* 16 full-time (13 women), 6 part-time/adjunct (4 women). *Students:* 186 full-time (129 women); includes 36 minority (2 Black or African American, non-Hispanic/Latino; 20 Asian, non-Hispanic/Latino; 10 Hispanic/Latino; 4 Two or more races, non-Hispanic/Latino), 11 international. Average age 25. 778 applicants, 19% accepted, 53 enrolled. In 2018, 3 master's, 70 doctorates awarded. *Degree requirements:* For doctorate, comprehensive exam and thesis (for PhD). *Entrance requirements:* For master's, GRE General Test, bachelor's degree; for doctorate, GRE General Test, bachelor's degree (for DPT), master's degree (for PhD). Additional exam requirements/recommendations for international students: Required—TOEFL (minimum score 550 paper-based; 84 iBT). *Application deadline:* For fall admission, 12/15 priority date for domestic and international students. Applications are processed on a rolling basis. Application fee: $145. Electronic applications accepted. *Financial support:* In 2018–19, 120 students received support, including 16 research assistantships with full tuition reimbursements available (averaging $22,000 per year), 6 teaching assistantships (averaging $2,500 per year); fellowships, career-related internships or fieldwork, Federal Work-Study, institutionally sponsored loans, scholarships/grants, and tuition waivers (full and partial) also available. Financial award application deadline: 12/15; financial award applicants required to submit FAFSA. *Faculty research:* Gait, balance, motor control, dynamic systems analysis, muscle function. *Total annual research expenditures:* $1.5 million. *Unit head:* Dr. Theresa Ellis, Department Chair, 617-353-7571, E-mail: pt@bu.edu. *Application contact:* Sharon Sankey, Assistant Dean, Student Services, 617-353-2713, Fax: 617-353-7500, E-mail: ssankey@bu.edu.

Bridgewater College, Program in Athletic Training, Bridgewater, VA 22812-1599. Offers MS. Electronic applications accepted.

Brigham Young University, Graduate Studies, College of Life Sciences, Department of Exercise Sciences, Provo, UT 84602. Offers athletic training (MS); exercise physiology (MS, PhD); exercise sciences (MS); health promotion (MS, PhD); physical medicine and rehabilitation (PhD). *Faculty:* 19 full-time (2 women). *Students:* 11 full-time (3 women), 7 part-time (3 women); includes 3 minority (all Asian, non-Hispanic/Latino). Average age 30. 16 applicants, 75% accepted, 10 enrolled. In 2018, 13 master's, 6 doctorates awarded. *Degree requirements:* For master's, thesis, oral defense; for doctorate, comprehensive exam, thesis/dissertation, oral defense, oral and written exams. *Entrance requirements:* For master's, GRE General Test (minimum score of 300, 4.0 on analytic writing portion), minimum GPA of 3.2 in last 60 hours of course work; for doctorate, GRE General Test (minimum score of 300, 4.0 on analytic writing portion), minimum GPA of 3.5 in last 60 hours of course work. Additional exam requirements/recommendations for international students: Required—TOEFL (minimum score 580 paper-based; 85 iBT), IELTS (minimum score 7). *Application deadline:* For fall admission, 2/1 for domestic and international students. Application fee: $50. Electronic applications accepted. *Financial support:* In 2018–19, 20 students received support, including 52 research assistantships (averaging $5,800 per year), 32 teaching assistantships (averaging $4,400 per year); scholarships/grants, unspecified assistantships, and 5 PhD full-tuition scholarships also available. Financial award application deadline: 4/15. *Faculty research:* Injury prevention and rehabilitation, human skeletal muscle adaptation, cardiovascular health and fitness, lifestyle modification and health promotion. *Total annual research expenditures:* $126,101. *Unit head:* Dr. Allen Parcell, Chair, 801-422-4450, Fax: 801-422-0555, E-mail: allenparcell@gmail.com. *Application contact:* Dr. J. Ty Hopkins, Graduate Coordinator, 801-422-1573, Fax: 801-422-0555, E-mail: tyhopkins@byu.edu.
Website: http://exsc.byu.edu/

California Baptist University, Program in Athletic Training, Riverside, CA 92504-3206. Offers MS. *Program availability:* Part-time. *Faculty:* 5 full-time (3 women). *Students:* 43 full-time (23 women); includes 31 minority (4 Black or African American, non-Hispanic/Latino; 6 Asian, non-Hispanic/Latino; 20 Hispanic/Latino; 1 Two or more races, non-Hispanic/Latino). Average age 27. 1 applicant. In 2018, 18 master's awarded. *Degree requirements:* For master's, thesis, 53-56 units of core courses; at least 900 cumulative hours of athletic training clinical education courses. *Entrance requirements:* For master's, minimum GPA of 2.75; three recommendations; comprehensive essay; current resume; CPR Professional Rescuer Certification; 150 hours of clinical observation; interview. Additional exam requirements/recommendations for international students: Required—TOEFL (minimum score 80 iBT). *Application deadline:* For fall admission, 8/1 priority date for domestic students, 7/1 for international students; for spring admission, 12/1 priority date for domestic students, 11/1 for international students. Applications are processed on a rolling basis. Application fee: $45. Electronic applications accepted. *Expenses:* $665 per unit. *Financial support:* In 2018–19, 1 student received support. Federal Work-Study, scholarships/grants, and unspecified assistantships available. Financial award applicants required to submit CSS PROFILE or FAFSA. *Faculty research:* Nutrition, weight management, public health, stress, athletic training. *Unit head:* Dr. David Pearson, Dean of the College of Health Science, 951-343-4298, E-mail: dpearson@calbaptist.edu. *Application contact:* Dr. Nicole MacDonald, Director, Athletic Training Program, 951-343-4379, E-mail: nmacdona@calbaptist.edu.
Website: http://www.calbaptist.edu/at/

California State University, Long Beach, Graduate Studies, College of Health and Human Services, Department of Kinesiology, Long Beach, CA 90840. Offers adapted physical education (MA); coaching and student athlete development (MA); exercise physiology and nutrition (MS); exercise science (MS); individualized studies (MA); kinesiology (MA); pedagogical studies (MA); sport and exercise psychology (MS); sport management (MA); sports medicine and injury studies (MS). *Program availability:* Part-time. *Degree requirements:* For master's, oral and written comprehensive exams or thesis. *Entrance requirements:* For master's, GRE General Test, minimum GPA of 2.75

during previous 2 years of course work. *Application deadline:* Applications are processed on a rolling basis. Application fee: $55. Electronic applications accepted. *Expenses: Required fees:* $2628 per term. Tuition and fees vary according to class time, course level, course load, degree level, campus/location and program. *Financial support:* Federal Work-Study, institutionally sponsored loans, and scholarships/grants available. Financial award application deadline: 3/2; financial award applicants required to submit FAFSA. *Faculty research:* Pulmonary functioning, feedback and practice structure, strength training, history and politics of sports, special population research issues. *Unit head:* Tiffanye Vargas, Chair, 562-985-4051, E-mail: tiffanye.vargas@csulb.edu. *Application contact:* Tiffanye Vargas, Chair, 562-985-4051, E-mail: tiffanye.vargas@csulb.edu.
Website: https://fullerton-csm.symplicity.com/

California University of Pennsylvania, School of Graduate Studies and Research, College of Education and Human Services, Department of Health Science, California, PA 15419-1394. Offers athletic training (MS). *Degree requirements:* For master's, comprehensive exam, thesis. *Entrance requirements:* For master's, minimum GPA of 3.0. Additional exam requirements/recommendations for international students: Required—TOEFL (minimum score 550 paper-based; 80 iBT). *Faculty research:* Exercise physiology, pedagogy, athletic training, biomechanical engineering, case studies in injury and athletic medicine.

Campbell University, Graduate and Professional Programs, College of Pharmacy and Health Sciences, Buies Creek, NC 27506. Offers athletic training (MAT); clinical research (MS); pharmaceutical sciences (MS); pharmacy (Pharm D); physical therapy (DPT); physician assistant (MPAP); public health (MS). *Accreditation:* ACPE; CEPH. *Program availability:* Part-time, evening/weekend. *Entrance requirements:* For master's, MCAT, PCAT, GRE, bachelor's degree in health sciences or related field; for doctorate, PCAT. Additional exam requirements/recommendations for international students: Required—TOEFL (minimum score 550 paper-based; 79 iBT). Electronic applications accepted. *Expenses:* Contact institution. *Faculty research:* Immunology, medicinal chemistry, pharmaceutics, applied pharmacology.

The College of St. Scholastica, Graduate Studies, Department of Athletic Training, Duluth, MN 55811-4199. Offers MS. *Program availability:* Part-time, online learning. *Entrance requirements:* Additional exam requirements/recommendations for international students: Required—TOEFL. Electronic applications accepted.

Drake University, College of Pharmacy and Health Sciences, Des Moines, IA 50311-4516. Offers athletic training (MAT); occupational therapy (OTD); pharmacy (Pharm D); Pharm D/JD; Pharm D/MBA; Pharm D/MPA. *Accreditation:* ACPE. *Students:* 486 full-time (351 women), 2 part-time (0 women); includes 75 minority (2 Black or African American, non-Hispanic/Latino; 51 Asian, non-Hispanic/Latino; 16 Hispanic/Latino; 6 Two or more races, non-Hispanic/Latino), 5 international. Average age 23. In 2018, 104 doctorates awarded. *Degree requirements:* For doctorate, rotations. *Entrance requirements:* For doctorate, PCAT, interview. Additional exam requirements/recommendations for international students: Required—TOEFL. *Application deadline:* For fall admission, 2/1 priority date for domestic students. Application fee: $135. Electronic applications accepted. *Expenses:* Contact institution. *Financial support:* Teaching assistantships, career-related internships or fieldwork, Federal Work-Study, institutionally sponsored loans, and scholarships/grants available. Support available to part-time students. Financial award application deadline: 3/1; financial award applicants required to submit FAFSA. *Faculty research:* Cost-benefit and cost-analysis of pharmaceutical products and services, patient satisfaction, community health planning and development, nutrition, ambulatory care. *Unit head:* Dr. Renae Chesnut, Dean, 515-271-3018, Fax: 515-271-4171, E-mail: renae.chesnut@drake.edu. *Application contact:* Dr. Renae Chesnut, Dean, 515-271-3018, Fax: 515-271-4171, E-mail: renae.chesnut@drake.edu.
Website: http://www.drake.edu/cphs/

Eastern Michigan University, Graduate School, College of Health and Human Services, School of Health Promotion and Human Performance, Programs in Exercise Physiology, Ypsilanti, MI 48197. Offers exercise physiology (MS); sports medicine-biomechanics (MS); sports medicine-corporate adult fitness (MS); sports medicine-exercise physiology (MS). *Program availability:* Part-time, evening/weekend. *Students:* 13 full-time (4 women), 11 part-time (4 women); includes 5 minority (1 Black or African American, non-Hispanic/Latino; 1 Asian, non-Hispanic/Latino; 2 Hispanic/Latino; 1 Two or more races, non-Hispanic/Latino), 2 international. Average age 29. 40 applicants, 63% accepted, 10 enrolled. In 2018, 15 master's awarded. *Degree requirements:* For master's, comprehensive exam, thesis or 450-hour internship. *Entrance requirements:* Additional exam requirements/recommendations for international students: Required—TOEFL. *Application deadline:* For fall admission, 8/1 for domestic students, 5/1 for international students; for winter admission, 12/1 for domestic students, 10/1 for international students; for spring admission, 3/15 for domestic students, 3/1 for international students. Application fee: $45. *Application contact:* Dr. Becca Moore, Program Coordinator, 734-487-2824, Fax: 734-487-2024, E-mail: rmoore41@emich.edu.

Eastern Michigan University, Graduate School, College of Health and Human Services, School of Health Promotion and Human Performance, Programs in Orthotics and Prosthetics, Ypsilanti, MI 48197. Offers MS, Graduate Certificate. *Students:* 44 full-time (26 women); includes 3 minority (1 Asian, non-Hispanic/Latino; 2 Two or more races, non-Hispanic/Latino), 1 international. Average age 25. 110 applicants, 43% accepted, 22 enrolled. In 2018, 20 master's awarded. *Degree requirements:* For master's, comprehensive exam, thesis or project, 500 hours of clinicals. *Entrance requirements:* For master's, MAT. Additional exam requirements/recommendations for international students: Required—TOEFL. *Application deadline:* For fall admission, 5/1 for domestic students. Applications are processed on a rolling basis. Application fee: $45. *Financial support:* Fellowships, research assistantships with full tuition reimbursements, teaching assistantships with full tuition reimbursements, career-related internships or fieldwork, Federal Work-Study, institutionally sponsored loans, scholarships/grants, tuition waivers (partial), and unspecified assistantships available. Support available to part-time students. Financial award applicants required to submit FAFSA. *Application contact:* Wendy Beattie, Clinical and Program Director, 734-487-2814, Fax: 734-487-2024, E-mail: wbeattie@emich.edu.

East Stroudsburg University of Pennsylvania, Graduate and Extended Studies, College of Health Sciences, Department of Athletic Training, East Stroudsburg, PA 18301-2999. Offers MS. *Program availability:* Part-time, evening/weekend, online learning. *Faculty:* 5 full-time (2 women). *Students:* 41 full-time (17 women), 2 part-time (0 women); includes 10 minority (1 Black or African American, non-Hispanic/Latino; 2 Asian, non-Hispanic/Latino; 6 Hispanic/Latino; 1 Two or more races, non-Hispanic/Latino), 2 international. Average age 25. 34 applicants, 50% accepted. In 2018, 38 master's awarded. *Entrance requirements:* For master's, GRE. Additional exam requirements/recommendations for international students: Recommended—TOEFL (minimum score 560 paper-based; 83 iBT), IELTS. *Application deadline:* For fall admission, 7/31 for domestic students, 6/30 for international students; for spring admission, 10/30 for domestic students, 10/31 for international students. Applications are processed on a rolling basis. Application fee: $50. Electronic applications accepted. *Expenses: Tuition, area resident:* Full-time $9288; part-time $516 per credit. Tuition,

state resident: full-time $9288. Tuition, nonresident: full-time $13,932; part-time $774 per credit. *International tuition:* $13,932 full-time. *Required fees:* $2059; $114 per credit. Tuition and fees vary according to course load and degree level. *Financial support:* Research assistantships with tuition reimbursements, career-related internships or fieldwork, Federal Work-Study, and unspecified assistantships available. Support available to part-time students. Financial award application deadline: 3/1; financial award applicants required to submit FAFSA. *Unit head:* Gerard Rozea, Coordinator Advanced Clinical Practice, 570-4223231, Fax: 570-4223616, E-mail: grozea@esu.edu. *Application contact:* Kevin Quintero, Associate Director, Graduate and Extended Studies, 570-422-3890, Fax: 570-422-2711, E-mail: kquintero@esu.edu.
Website: https://www.esu.edu/athletic_training/graduate_programs/index.cfm

Florida International University, Nicole Wertheim College of Nursing and Health Sciences, Department of Athletic Training, Miami, FL 33199. Offers MS. *Faculty:* 5 full-time (3 women), 5 part-time/adjunct (2 women). *Students:* 36 full-time (24 women); includes 26 minority (6 Black or African American, non-Hispanic/Latino; 18 Hispanic/Latino; 2 Two or more races, non-Hispanic/Latino), 1 international. Average age 24. 12 applicants, 50% accepted, 6 enrolled. In 2018, 21 master's awarded. *Entrance requirements:* For master's, bachelor's degree from accredited institution; minimum GPA of 3.0 overall and in last 60 credits of upper-division courses of the bachelor's degree; three letters of recommendation; resume; personal statement of professional/educational goals. Additional exam requirements/recommendations for international students: Required—TOEFL (minimum score 550 paper-based; 80 iBT). *Application deadline:* For fall admission, 2/15 for domestic and international students. Application fee: $30. Electronic applications accepted. *Expenses:* Contact institution. *Financial support:* Institutionally sponsored loans and scholarships/grants available. Financial award application deadline: 3/1; financial award applicants required to submit FAFSA. *Faculty research:* Continuing professional education, leadership styles and outcomes, professionalism and professional image. *Unit head:* Dr. MIchelle Odai, Interim Chair, 305-348-6335, Fax: 305-348-2125, E-mail: Michelle.Odai@fiu.edu. *Application contact:* Nanett Rojas, Manager, Admissions Operations, 305-348-7464, Fax: 305-348-7441, E-mail: gradadm@fiu.edu.

Franklin College, Program in Athletic Training, Franklin, IN 46131. Offers MSAT.

Gannon University, School of Graduate Studies, Morosky College of Health Professions and Sciences, School of Health Professions, Program in Athletic Training, Erie, PA 16541-0001. Offers MAT. *Program availability:* Part-time, evening/weekend. *Entrance requirements:* For master's, undergraduate degree in exercise science, kinesiology, human performance, sports medicine or related field; minimum GPA of 2.75; 3 letters of recommendation. Additional exam requirements/recommendations for international students: Required—TOEFL (minimum score 79 iBT). Electronic applications accepted. Application fee is waived when completed online.

George Mason University, College of Education and Human Development, School of Recreation, Health and Tourism, Manassas, VA 20110. Offers athletic training (MS); exercise, fitness, and health promotion (MS), including advanced practitioner, wellness practitioner; international sport management (Certificate); recreation, health and tourism (Certificate); sport management (MS), including sport and recreation studies. *Program availability:* Part-time, evening/weekend. *Faculty:* 33 full-time (15 women), 84 part-time/adjunct (44 women). *Students:* 76 full-time (33 women), 21 part-time (5 women); includes 32 minority (25 Black or African American, non-Hispanic/Latino; 1 American Indian or Alaska Native, non-Hispanic/Latino; 1 Asian, non-Hispanic/Latino; 3 Hispanic/Latino; 1 Native Hawaiian or other Pacific Islander, non-Hispanic/Latino; 1 Two or more races, non-Hispanic/Latino), 17 international. Average age 26. 77 applicants, 88% accepted, 41 enrolled. In 2018, 26 master's, 1 other advanced degree awarded. *Entrance requirements:* For master's, 3 letters of recommendation; official transcripts; expanded goals statement; undergraduate course in statistics and minimum GPA of 3.0 in last 60 credit hours and overall (for MS in sport and recreation studies); baccalaureate degree related to kinesiology, exercise science or athletic training (for MS in exercise, fitness and health promotion). Additional exam requirements/recommendations for international students: Required—TOEFL (minimum score 575 paper-based; 88 iBT), IELTS (minimum score 6.5), PTE (minimum score 59). *Application deadline:* For fall admission, 4/2 priority date for domestic and international students; for spring admission, 11/1 for domestic and international students. Application fee: $75 ($80 for international students). Electronic applications accepted. *Financial support:* In 2018–19, 6 students received support, including 6 research assistantships with tuition reimbursements available (averaging $7,242 per year); career-related internships or fieldwork, Federal Work-Study, scholarships/grants, unspecified assistantships, and health care benefits (for full-time research or teaching assistantship recipients) also available. Support available to part-time students. Financial award application deadline: 3/1; financial award applicants required to submit FAFSA. *Faculty research:* Sport for development and peace, sport analytics, leadership and coaching, diversity and inclusion in sport, sport communication. *Total annual research expenditures:* $826,386. *Unit head:* Martin Ford, Senior Associate Dean, 703-993-2004, E-mail: mford@gmu.edu. *Application contact:* Lindsey Olson, Office Assistant, 703-993-2098, Fax: 703-993-2025, E-mail: lolson7@gmu.edu.
Website: http://rht.gmu.edu/

Georgia Southern University, Jack N. Averitt College of Graduate Studies, Waters College of Health Professions, Department of Health Sciences and Kinesiology, Statesboro, GA 30460. Offers dietetics (Certificate), including school nutrition; health administration (MHA); kinesiology (MS); sport management (MS); sports medicine (MSSM, Certificate), including sports medicine (MSSM), strength and conditioning (Certificate). *Program availability:* Part-time, evening/weekend, blended/hybrid learning. *Faculty:* 38 full-time (16 women). *Students:* 68 full-time (36 women), 84 part-time (38 women); includes 42 minority (28 Black or African American, non-Hispanic/Latino; 3 Asian, non-Hispanic/Latino; 7 Hispanic/Latino; 4 Two or more races, non-Hispanic/Latino), 5 international. Average age 25. 159 applicants, 43% accepted, 55 enrolled. In 2018, 75 master's awarded. *Degree requirements:* For master's, comprehensive exam (for some programs), thesis (for some programs). *Entrance requirements:* For master's, Most programs require the GRE, but the MS in Kinesiology - Coaching, MS in Kinesiology - Exercise Science, and Gerontology certificate programs do not., Some programs have a minimum GPA of 2.5, others 2.75, and others 3.0. Most programs also require a resume and letters of reference. Additional exam requirements/recommendations for international students: Required—TOEFL (minimum score 550 paper-based; 80 iBT), IELTS (minimum score 6). *Application deadline:* For fall admission, 2/1 priority date for domestic and international students; for spring admission, 10/1 priority date for domestic students, 10/1 for international students. Applications are processed on a rolling basis. Application fee: $50. Electronic applications accepted. *Expenses: Tuition, area resident:* Part-time $3324 per semester. Tuition, state resident: full-time $5814; part-time $3324 per semester. Tuition, nonresident: full-time $23,204; part-time $13,260 per semester. *Required fees:* $2092; $2092. Tuition and fees vary according to course load, degree level, campus/location and program. *Financial support:* In 2018–19, 85 students received support, including 1 fellowship with full tuition reimbursement available (averaging $7,750 per year), 4 research assistantships with full tuition reimbursements available (averaging $7,750 per year), 35 teaching assistantships with full tuition reimbursements available (averaging

$7,750 per year); tuition waivers (full) and unspecified assistantships also available. Financial award application deadline: 4/15; financial award applicants required to submit FAFSA. *Faculty research:* Concussions and postural control, overtraining in athletes, sport supplements and performance, mental training and performance, exercise and health psychology interventions, positive psychology in sports, psychological impact of youth sports, parental influence in sport, ethics in sport, psychology of injury, spirituality in sport, physical activity interventions for chronic diseases, autonomy supportive coaching, motivation in sport, obesity bias in allied health professions, health/pharmaceuti. *Total annual research expenditures:* $99,590. *Unit head:* Dr. John Dobson, Interim Chair, 912-478-0200, Fax: 912-478-0381, E-mail: jdobson@georgiasouthern.edu.
Website: https://chp.georgiasouthern.edu/hk/

Georgia State University, College of Education and Human Development, Department of Kinesiology and Health, Program in Sports Medicine, Atlanta, GA 30302-3083. Offers MS. *Entrance requirements:* For master's, GRE General Test, minimum GPA of 2.5. Application fee: $50. *Expenses: Tuition, area resident:* Full-time $9360; part-time $390 per credit hour. Tuition, state resident: full-time $9360; part-time $390 per credit hour. Tuition, nonresident: full-time $30,024; part-time $1251 per credit hour. *International tuition:* $30,024 full-time. *Required fees:* $2128. *Financial support:* Research assistantships available. *Faculty research:* Athletic training. *Unit head:* Dr. Jacalyn Lea Lund, Chair, 404-413-8051, E-mail: jlund@gsu.edu. *Application contact:* Dr. Jacalyn Lea Lund, Chair, 404-413-8051, E-mail: jlund@gsu.edu.
Website: https://education.gsu.edu/kh/

Grand View University, Graduate Studies, Des Moines, IA 50316-1599. Offers athletic training (MS); clinical nurse leader (MSN, Post Master's Certificate); nursing education (MSN, Post Master's Certificate); organizational leadership (MS); sport management (MS); teacher leadership (M Ed); urban education (M Ed). *Program availability:* Part-time, evening/weekend. *Degree requirements:* For master's, completion of all required coursework in common core and selected track with minimum cumulative GPA of 3.0 and no more than two grades of C. *Entrance requirements:* For master's, GRE, GMAT, or essay, minimum undergraduate GPA of 3.0, professional resume, 3 letters of recommendation, interview. Additional exam requirements/recommendations for international students: Required—TOEFL (minimum score 550 paper-based). Electronic applications accepted.

High Point University, Norcross Graduate School, High Point, NC 27268. Offers athletic training (MSAT); business administration (MBA); educational leadership (M Ed, Ed D); elementary education (M Ed, MAT); pharmacy (Pharm D); physical therapy (DPT); physician assistant studies (MPAS); secondary mathematics (M Ed, MAT); special education (M Ed); strategic communication (MA). *Accreditation:* NCATE. *Program availability:* Part-time, evening/weekend. *Degree requirements:* For master's, comprehensive exam (for some programs), thesis (for some programs). *Entrance requirements:* For master's, GMAT (MBA), GRE, MAT, minimum GPA of 3.0. Additional exam requirements/recommendations for international students: Required—TOEFL (minimum score 550 paper-based). Electronic applications accepted.

Idaho State University, Graduate School, College of Education, Department of Sport Science and Physical Education, Pocatello, ID 83209-8105. Offers athletic administration (MPE); athletic training (MSAT). *Program availability:* Part-time. *Degree requirements:* For master's, comprehensive exam (for some programs), thesis optional, internship, oral defense of dissertation, or written exams. *Entrance requirements:* For master's, MAT or GRE General Test, minimum GPA of 3.0 in upper division classes. Additional exam requirements/recommendations for international students: Required—TOEFL (minimum score 550 paper-based; 80 iBT). Electronic applications accepted. *Faculty research:* Gender and diversity; concussion awareness/sports medicine; legal aspects of athletic health care; sports psychology; exercise physiology; sports management and leadership; adapted activities; fitness, wellness, and nutrition; coaching perspectives; critical features of athletic activities.

Indiana State University, College of Graduate and Professional Studies, College of Health and Human Services, Department of Applied Medicine and Rehabilitation, Terre Haute, IN 47809. Offers athletic training (MS, DAT); occupational therapy (MS); physical therapy (DPT); physician assistant (MS). *Accreditation:* AOTA. *Degree requirements:* For master's, thesis or alternative. *Entrance requirements:* For master's, GRE General Test. Electronic applications accepted.

Indiana University Bloomington, School of Public Health, Department of Kinesiology, Bloomington, IN 47405. Offers applied sport science (MS); athletic administration/sport management (MS); athletic training (MS); biomechanics (MS); ergonomics (MS); exercise physiology (MS); human performance (PhD), including biomechanics, exercise physiology, motor learning/control, sport management; motor learning/control (MS); physical activity (MPH); physical activity, fitness and wellness (MS). *Program availability:* Part-time. Terminal master's awarded for partial completion of doctoral program. *Degree requirements:* For master's, thesis optional; for doctorate, variable foreign language requirement, comprehensive exam, thesis/dissertation. *Entrance requirements:* For master's, GRE General Test, minimum GPA of 2.8; for doctorate, GRE General Test, minimum graduate GPA of 3.5, undergraduate 3.0. Additional exam requirements/recommendations for international students: Required—TOEFL (minimum score 80 iBT). *Faculty research:* Exercise physiology and biochemistry, sports biomechanics, human motor control, adaptation of fitness and exercise to special populations.

Indiana Wesleyan University, Graduate School, School of Health Sciences, Marion, IN 46953-4974. Offers athletic training (MS); occupational therapy (OTD); public health (MPH).

Inter American University of Puerto Rico, Metropolitan Campus, Graduate Programs, Program in Physical Education, San Juan, PR 00919-1293. Offers teaching of physical education (MA); training and sport performance (MA). *Degree requirements:* For master's, comprehensive exam. *Entrance requirements:* For master's, GRE or EXADEP, interview. Electronic applications accepted.

Kent State University, College of Education, Health and Human Services, School of Health Sciences, Program in Exercise Physiology, Kent, OH 44242-0001. Offers athletic training (MS); exercise physiology (PhD). *Faculty:* 11 full-time (6 women). *Students:* 38 full-time (21 women), 17 part-time (12 women); includes 5 minority (4 Asian, non-Hispanic/Latino; 1 Native Hawaiian or other Pacific Islander, non-Hispanic/Latino), 2 international. 47 applicants, 60% accepted. In 2018, 11 master's, 4 doctorates awarded. *Degree requirements:* For doctorate, comprehensive exam, thesis/dissertation. *Entrance requirements:* For master's, GRE, 2 letters of reference, goals statement; for doctorate, GRE, 2 letters of reference, goals statement, minimum master's-level GPA of 3.0. Additional exam requirements/recommendations for international students: Required—TOEFL (minimum score 550 paper-based; 80 iBT). *Application deadline:* Applications are processed on a rolling basis. Application fee: $45 ($60 for international students). Electronic applications accepted. *Expenses:* Tuition, state resident: full-time $11,766; part-time $536 per credit. Tuition, nonresident: full-time $21,952; part-time $999 per credit. *International tuition:* $21,952 full-time. Tuition and fees vary according to course load. *Financial support:* In 2018–19, 8 research assistantships (averaging $11,125 per year), 5 teaching assistantships (averaging $9,900 per year) were awarded; Federal Work-Study, scholarships/grants, and unspecified assistantships also available. *Unit head:* Angela Ridgel, Coordinator, 330-672-7495, E-mail: aridgel@kent.edu. *Application contact:* Cheryl Slusarczyk, Academic Program Director, Office of Graduate Student Services, 330-672-2576, Fax: 330-672-9162, E-mail: ogs@kent.edu.

Lebanon Valley College, Program in Athletic Training, Annville, PA 17003-1400. Offers MAT. *Degree requirements:* For master's, research project. *Entrance requirements:* For master's, GRE, BS. Additional exam requirements/recommendations for international students: Required—TOEFL (minimum score 80 iBT). Electronic applications accepted. *Expenses:* Contact institution. *Faculty research:* Epidemiology, clinical education, clinical decision making.

Lenoir-Rhyne University, Graduate Programs, School of Health, Exercise and Sport Science, Program in Athletic Training, Hickory, NC 28601. Offers MS. *Program availability:* Part-time. *Entrance requirements:* For master's, GRE or MAT, official transcripts, 75 observational hours with certififed athletic trainer, essay, resume. Additional exam requirements/recommendations for international students: Required—TOEFL (minimum score 600 paper-based). Electronic applications accepted. *Expenses:* Contact institution.

Life University, College of Graduate and Undergraduate Studies, Marietta, GA 30060-2903. Offers athletic training (MAT); chiropractic sport science (MS); nutrition and sport science (MS), including chiropractic sport science; positive psychology (MS), including life coaching psychology; sport coaching (MS), including exercise sport science; sport injury management (MS), including nutrition and sport science; sports health science (MS), including sports injury management. *Program availability:* Part-time, 100% online, blended/hybrid learning. *Degree requirements:* For master's, comprehensive exam (for some programs), thesis optional. *Entrance requirements:* For master's, GRE General Test, minimum GPA of 3.0, 3 letters of recommendation, curriculum vitae. Additional exam requirements/recommendations for international students: Required—TOEFL (minimum score 500 paper-based). Electronic applications accepted. *Expenses:* Contact institution. *Faculty research:* Nutrient metabolism, organizational effectiveness, injury prevention, athlete development, recovery modalities and treatment, sport nutrition, functional neurology, peace and conflict studies.

Lock Haven University of Pennsylvania, College of Natural, Behavioral and Health Sciences, Lock Haven, PA 17745-2390. Offers actuarial science (PSM); athletic training (MS); health promotion/education (MHS); healthcare management (MHS); physician assistant (MHS). Program also offered at the Clearfield, Coudersport, and Harrisburg campuses. *Accreditation:* ARC-PA. *Entrance requirements:* For master's, minimum undergraduate GPA of 3.0. Additional exam requirements/recommendations for international students: Required—TOEFL. Electronic applications accepted.

London Metropolitan University, Graduate Programs, London, United Kingdom. Offers applied psychology (M Sc); architecture (MA); biomedical science (M Sc); blood science (M Sc); cancer pharmacology (M Sc); computer networking and cyber security (M Sc); computing and information systems (M Sc); conference interpreting (MA); counter-terrorism studies (M Sc); creative, digital and professional writing (MA); crime, violence and prevention (M Sc); criminology (M Sc); curating contemporary art (MA); data analytics (M Sc); digital media (MA); early childhood studies (MA); education (MA, Ed D); financial services law, regulation and compliance (LL M); food science (M Sc); forensic psychology (M Sc); health and social care management and policy (M Sc); human nutrition (M Sc); human resource management (MA); human rights and international conflict (MA); information technology (M Sc); intelligence and security studies (M Sc); international oil, gas and energy law (LL M); international relations (MA); interpreting (MA); learning and teaching in higher education (MA); legal practice (LL M); media and entertainment law (LL M); organizational and consumer psychology (M Sc); psychological therapy (M Sc); psychology of mental health (M Sc); public health (M Sc); public policy and management (MPA); security studies (M Sc); social work (M Sc); spatial planning and urban design (MA); sports therapy (M Sc); supporting older children and young people with dyslexia (MA); teaching languages (MA), including Arabic, English; translation (MA); woman and child abuse (MA).

Long Island University–LIU Brooklyn, School of Health Professions, Brooklyn, NY 11201-8423. Offers athletic training and sport sciences (MS); community health (MS Ed); exercise science (MS); forensic social work (Advanced Certificate); occupational therapy (MS); physical therapy (DPT); physician assistant (MS); public health (MPH); social work (MSW); speech-language pathology (MS). *Accreditation:* AOTA; CEPH. *Degree requirements:* For master's, comprehensive exam (for some programs), thesis (for some programs); for doctorate, comprehensive exam (for some programs). *Entrance requirements:* For master's and doctorate, GRE. Additional exam requirements/recommendations for international students: Required—TOEFL (minimum score 550 paper-based; 79 iBT). Electronic applications accepted. *Faculty research:* Pediatric physical therapy, complementary and alternative medicine, global health and human rights, sport leadership and entrepreneurship, feminist sport psychology.

Manchester University, Master of Athletic Training Program, North Manchester, IN 46962-1225. Offers MAT. *Faculty:* 3 full-time, 3 part-time/adjunct (2 women). *Students:* 3 full-time (2 women); includes 1 minority (Hispanic/Latino). Average age 24. 18 applicants, 72% accepted, 2 enrolled. In 2018, 12 master's awarded. *Degree requirements:* For master's, 51 semester hours; minimum cumulative GPA of 3.0, 2.0 in each required course; completion of all required didactic and clinical courses. *Entrance requirements:* For master's, baccalaureate degree from regionally-accredited institution; minimum cumulative undergraduate GPA of 3.0; certification in first aid and CPR; letters of recommendation. Additional exam requirements/recommendations for international students: Required—TOEFL (minimum score 550 paper-based; 79 iBT). *Application deadline:* For fall admission, 1/1 priority date for domestic students. Applications are processed on a rolling basis. Application fee: $60. Electronic applications accepted. *Expenses:* 39,960. *Financial support:* Fellowships and fellowships are in form of tuition discounts available. Financial award application deadline: 5/1; financial award applicants required to submit FAFSA. *Unit head:* Mark Huntington, Program Director, Graduate Athletic Training Education, 260-982-5033, E-mail: mwhuntington@manchester.edu. *Application contact:* Mark Huntington, Program Director, Graduate Athletic Training Education, 260-982-5033, E-mail: mwhuntington@manchester.edu.
Website: https://www.manchester.edu/academics/colleges/college-of-pharmacy-natural-health-sciences/academic-programs/exercise-science-athletic-training/exercis

Marshall University, Academic Affairs Division, College of Health Professions, School of Kinesiology, Program in Athletic Training, Huntington, WV 25755. Offers MS. *Entrance requirements:* For master's, GRE.

Mercer University, Graduate Studies, Cecil B. Day Campus, College of Health Professions, Atlanta, GA 30341. Offers athletic training (MAT); clinical medical psychology (Psy D); physical therapy (DPT); physician assistant studies (MM Sc); public health (MPH); DPT/MBA; DPT/MPH; MM Sc/MPH; Pharm D/MPH. *Accreditation:* CEPH. *Faculty:* 26 full-time (16 women), 12 part-time/adjunct (7 women). *Students:* 369 full-time (280 women), 67 part-time (56 women); includes 173 minority (110 Black or African American, non-Hispanic/Latino; 35 Asian, non-Hispanic/Latino; 26 Hispanic/Latino; 2 Two or more races, non-Hispanic/Latino), 6 international. Average age 26. In 2018, 141 master's, 51 doctorates awarded. *Expenses:* Contact institution. *Financial support:* Federal Work-Study, traineeships, and unspecified assistantships available.

Faculty research: Scholarship of teaching and learning, health disparities, clinical outcomes, health promotion. *Unit head:* Dr. Lisa Lundquist, Dean/Clinical Professor, 678-547-6308, E-mail: lundquist_lm@mercer.edu. *Application contact:* Laura Ellison, Director of Admissions and Student Affairs, 678-547-6391, E-mail: ellison_la@mercer.edu.
Website: http://chp.mercer.edu/

Merrimack College, School of Health Sciences, North Andover, MA 01845-5800. Offers athletic training (MS); community health education (MS); exercise and sport science (MS); health and wellness management (MS). *Program availability:* Part-time, evening/weekend. *Faculty:* 11 full-time (10 women), 2 part-time/adjunct (both women). *Students:* 93 full-time (62 women), 12 part-time (10 women); includes 3 minority (all Black or African American, non-Hispanic/Latino), 4 international. Average age 26. 163 applicants, 92% accepted, 82 enrolled. In 2018, 71 master's awarded. *Degree requirements:* For master's, capstone (for community health education, exercise and sport science, and health and wellness management). *Entrance requirements:* For master's, resume, official college transcripts, personal statement, 2 recommendations. Additional exam requirements/recommendations for international students: Required—TOEFL (minimum score 84 iBT), IELTS (minimum score 6.5), PTE (minimum score 56). *Application deadline:* For fall admission, 8/24 for domestic students, 7/30 for international students; for summer admission, 5/10 for domestic students, 4/10 for international students. Applications are processed on a rolling basis. Application fee: $0. Electronic applications accepted. Application fee is waived when completed online. *Expenses:* School of Health Sciences (all programs except Athletic Training) $28,420; M.S. in Athletic Training $32,980. *Financial support:* Fellowships with partial tuition reimbursements, career-related internships or fieldwork, scholarships/grants, and health care benefits available. Support available to part-time students. Financial award application deadline: 5/1; financial award applicants required to submit FAFSA. *Unit head:* Dr. Janet Blum, Dean, 978-837-5396, E-mail: blumj@merrimack.edu. *Application contact:* Allison Pena, Office of Graduate Studies, 978-837-3563, E-mail: graduate@merrimack.edu.
Website: http://www.merrimack.edu/academics/health-sciences/

Missouri State University, Graduate College, College of Health and Human Services, Department of Sports Medicine and Athletic Training, Springfield, MO 65897. Offers athletic training (MS); occupational therapy (MOT). *Program availability:* Part-time. *Faculty:* 7 full-time (4 women), 5 part-time/adjunct (3 women). *Students:* 78 full-time (64 women), 28 part-time (23 women); includes 9 minority (2 Black or African American, non-Hispanic/Latino; 1 American Indian or Alaska Native, non-Hispanic/Latino; 4 Hispanic/Latino; 2 Two or more races, non-Hispanic/Latino), 3 international. Average age 24. 54 applicants, 70% accepted. In 2018, 31 master's awarded. *Degree requirements:* For master's, comprehensive exam, thesis or alternative. *Entrance requirements:* For master's, GRE, current Professional Rescuer and AED certification, BOC certification, licensure as an athletic trainer, minimum undergraduate GPA of 3.0 (for MS); OTCAS application (for MOT). Additional exam requirements/recommendations for international students: Required—TOEFL (minimum score 550 paper-based; 79 iBT), IELTS (minimum score 6). *Application deadline:* For fall admission, 1/15 for domestic and international students. Application fee: $55 ($60 for international students). Electronic applications accepted. Tuition and fees vary according to class time, course level, course load, degree level, campus/location, program and student level. *Financial support:* In 2018–19, 5 teaching assistantships with partial tuition reimbursements (averaging $8,772 per year) were awarded; Federal Work-Study, institutionally sponsored loans, and unspecified assistantships also available. Financial award application deadline: 1/31; financial award applicants required to submit FAFSA. *Unit head:* Dr. Tona Hetzler, Department Head, 417-836-8924, Fax: 417-836-8554, E-mail: tonahetzler@missouristate.edu. *Application contact:* Lakan Drinker, Director, Graduate Enrollment Management, 417-836-5330, Fax: 417-836-6200, E-mail: lakandrinker@missouristate.edu.
Website: http://sportsmed.missouristate.edu/

Montana State University Billings, College of Allied Health Professions, Program in Athletic Training, Billings, MT 59101. Offers MS. *Program availability:* Part-time. *Degree requirements:* For master's, thesis optional. *Entrance requirements:* For master's, GRE, minimum GPA of 3.0, letters of recommendation, letter of intent. Additional exam requirements/recommendations for international students: Required—TOEFL (minimum score 79 iBT), IELTS (minimum score 6.5). Electronic applications accepted.

Moravian College, Graduate and Continuing Studies, Rehabilitation Science Programs, Bethlehem, PA 18018-6650. Offers athletic training (MS, DAT); speech-language pathology (MS). *Program availability:* 100% online. *Faculty:* 5 full-time (2 women), 4 part-time/adjunct (3 women). *Students:* 35 full-time (21 women); includes 4 minority (1 Black or African American, non-Hispanic/Latino; 1 Asian, non-Hispanic/Latino; 2 Hispanic/Latino). Average age 27. 224 applicants, 58% accepted, 84 enrolled. In 2018, 7 master's awarded. *Degree requirements:* For master's, completion of clinical rotation. *Entrance requirements:* For master's, official transcripts, bachelor's degree from accredited institution, minimum undergraduate GPA of 3.0, documentation of clinical observation with supervision of certified/licensed athletic trainer, interview, essay; for doctorate, current ATC credentials in good standing, current AT State License if applicable, currently practicing, 5 years of full-time practice preferred. *Application deadline:* For summer admission, 5/1 priority date for domestic and international students. Applications are processed on a rolling basis. Electronic applications accepted. *Financial support:* Applicants required to submit FAFSA. *Faculty research:* Shortwave diathermy, cryotherapy, iontophoresis, immersion clinical education, sacroiliac joint. *Unit head:* Dr. James Scifers, Chair, 610-625-7210, E-mail: scifersj@moravian.edu. *Application contact:* Kristina Sullivan, Director of Student Recruitment Operations, 610-861-1400, Fax: 610-861-1466, E-mail: graduate@moravian.edu.
Website: https://www.moravian.edu/graduate/programs/rehabilitation-sciences#/

North Dakota State University, College of Graduate and Interdisciplinary Studies, College of Human Development and Education, Department of Health, Nutrition, and Exercise Sciences, Fargo, ND 58102. Offers advanced athletic training (MS); athletic training (MAT); dietetics (MS); exercise science and nutrition (PhD); health, nutrition and exercise science (MS). *Program availability:* Part-time, evening/weekend, online learning. *Entrance requirements:* For master's, minimum GPA of 3.0. Additional exam requirements/recommendations for international students: Required—TOEFL (minimum score 525 paper-based; 71 iBT). Electronic applications accepted. *Faculty research:* Biomechanics, sport specialization, recreation, nutrition, athletic training.

Northern Arizona University, College of Health and Human Services, Department of Athletic Training, Flagstaff, AZ 86011. Offers exercise science (MS); physical education (MS). *Program availability:* Part-time. *Degree requirements:* For master's, thesis optional. *Entrance requirements:* For master's, GRE General Test, minimum GPA of 3.0. *Faculty research:* Muscle fiber type conversions, small animal locomotive study, electromyographic patterns.

Ohio University, Graduate College, College of Health Sciences and Professions, School of Applied Health Sciences and Wellness, Program in Athletic Training, Athens, OH 45701-2979. Offers MS. *Entrance requirements:* For master's, GRE. Additional exam requirements/recommendations for international students: Required—TOEFL (minimum score 550 paper-based; 80 iBT) or IELTS (minimum score 7.5). *Faculty research:* Athletic training, heart, injuries, health, muscles, exercise, sport.

Old Dominion University, College of Health Sciences, School of Physical Therapy and Athletic Training, Program in Athletic Training, Norfolk, VA 23529. Offers MSAT. *Degree requirements:* For master's, variable foreign language requirement, comprehensive exam, thesis or alternative. *Entrance requirements:* For master's, GRE, bachelor's degree, minimum undergraduate GPA of 3.0 overall and in all science/athletic training prerequisite course work, three letters of recommendation, two-page statement of career goals, current copy of resume, transcripts. Additional exam requirements/recommendations for international students: Required—TOEFL (minimum score 550 paper-based; 79 iBT). Electronic applications accepted. *Expenses:* Contact institution. *Faculty research:* Patient outcomes, chronic ankle instability, standardized patients, student learning outcomes, lower extremity injuries.

Oregon State University, College of Public Health and Human Sciences, Program in Athletic Training, Corvallis, OR 97331. Offers MATRN. *Entrance requirements:* For master's, GRE, baccalaureate degree; two letters of recommendation; personal statement; minimum of 50 hours of work, volunteering and/or observation under a certified athletic trainer. Electronic applications accepted.

Pacific University, School of Physical Therapy, Forest Grove, OR 97116-1797. Offers athletic training (MSAT); physical therapy (DPT). *Accreditation:* APTA. *Degree requirements:* For doctorate, evidence-based capstone project thesis. *Entrance requirements:* For doctorate, 100 hours of volunteer/observational hours, minimum cumulative GPA of 3.0, prerequisite courses with a C grade or better, minimum GPA of 2.5 in science/statistics. Additional exam requirements/recommendations for international students: Required—TOEFL (minimum score 600 paper-based). Electronic applications accepted. *Expenses:* Contact institution. *Faculty research:* Balance disorders, geriatrics, orthopedic treatment outcomes, obesity, women's health.

Plymouth State University, College of Graduate Studies, Graduate Studies in Education, Program in Athletic Training, Plymouth, NH 03264-1595. Offers MS. *Program availability:* Part-time, evening/weekend. *Entrance requirements:* For master's, MAT, GRE General Test.

Saint Louis University, Graduate Programs, Doisy College of Health Sciences, Department of Physical Therapy, St. Louis, MO 63103. Offers athletic training (MAT); physical therapy (DPT). *Accreditation:* APTA. *Program availability:* Part-time. *Entrance requirements:* Additional exam requirements/recommendations for international students: Required—TOEFL (minimum score 525 paper-based; 55 iBT). Electronic applications accepted. *Faculty research:* Patellofemoral pain and associated risk factors; prevalence of disordered eating in physical therapy students; effects of selected interventions for children with cerebral palsy on gait and posture: hippotherapy, ankle strengthening, supported treadmill training, spirituality in physical therapy/patient care, risk factors for exercise-related leg pain in running athletes.

Salisbury University, Program in Athletic Training, Salisbury, MD 21801-6837. Offers MSAT. *Faculty:* 2 full-time (both women). *Students:* 10 full-time (7 women), 3 part-time (1 woman); includes 3 minority (2 Black or African American, non-Hispanic/Latino; 1 Two or more races, non-Hispanic/Latino). Average age 24. 17 applicants, 82% accepted, 10 enrolled. In 2018, 3 master's awarded. *Degree requirements:* For master's, thesis project. *Entrance requirements:* For master's, official transcripts from all colleges and universities attended; minimum GPA of 3.0; two letters of recommendation; essay. Additional exam requirements/recommendations for international students: Required—TOEFL (minimum score 550 paper-based; 79 iBT), IELTS (minimum score 6.5). *Application deadline:* For summer admission, 1/15 priority date for domestic and international students. Applications are processed on a rolling basis. Application fee: $65. Electronic applications accepted. *Expenses:* $615 per credit hour resident; $765 per credit hour non-resident; $108 fees. *Financial support:* In 2018–19, 1 student received support. Career-related internships or fieldwork and scholarships/grants available. Support available to part-time students. Financial award application deadline: 3/1; financial award applicants required to submit FAFSA. *Faculty research:* Assessing student learning styles and disposition; concussion management protocols; interprofessional education; nutrition; wellness promotion. *Unit head:* Dr. Laura Marinaro, Graduate Program Director, 410-548-3529, E-mail: lmmarinaro@salisbury.edu. *Application contact:* Dr. Laura Marinaro, Graduate Program Director, 410-548-3529, E-mail: lmmarinaro@salisbury.edu.
Website: https://www.salisbury.edu/explore-academics/programs/graduate-degree-programs/athletic-training-master/

Samford University, School of Health Professions, Birmingham, AL 35229. Offers athletic training (MAT); physical therapy (DPT); respiratory care (MS); speech language pathology (MS). *Faculty:* 24 full-time (13 women), 1 (woman) part-time/adjunct. *Students:* 152 full-time (120 women); includes 16 minority (5 Black or African American, non-Hispanic/Latino; 1 American Indian or Alaska Native, non-Hispanic/Latino; 4 Hispanic/Latino; 6 Two or more races, non-Hispanic/Latino). Average age 24. 645 applicants, 32% accepted, 9 enrolled. In 2018, 50 master's awarded. *Degree requirements:* For master's and doctorate, capstone course. *Entrance requirements:* For master's and doctorate, GRE, recommendations, resume, on-campus interview, personal statement, shadowing hours, transcripts. Additional exam requirements/recommendations for international students: Required—TOEFL (minimum score 575 paper-based; 90 iBT), IELTS (minimum score 6.5). *Application deadline:* For fall admission, 8/1 for domestic students; for spring admission, 12/1 for domestic students; for summer admission, 1/1 for domestic students. Application fee: $120. Electronic applications accepted. *Expenses:* $862 per credit hour tuition. *Financial support:* In 2018–19, 5 students received support. Scholarships/grants available. Financial award application deadline: 5/1; financial award applicants required to submit FAFSA. *Faculty research:* Physical disabilities related to Parkinson's disease, neurogenic communication disorders, skeletal muscle physiology, spinal cord injuries, medical ventilation and tobacco treatment and prevention. *Unit head:* Dr. Alan Jung, Ph.D., Dean of the School of Health Professions, 205-726-2716, E-mail: apjung@samford.edu. *Application contact:* Dr. Marian Carter, Ed.D., Assistant Dean of Enrollment Management and Student Services, 205-726-2611, E-mail: mwcarter@samford.edu.
Website: http://www.samford.edu/healthprofessions

Seton Hall University, School of Health and Medical Sciences, Program in Athletic Training, South Orange, NJ 07079-2697. Offers MS. *Degree requirements:* For master's, research project. *Entrance requirements:* Additional exam requirements/recommendations for international students: Required—TOEFL. Electronic applications accepted. *Faculty research:* Electrotherapy.

Shenandoah University, School of Health Professions, Winchester, VA 22602. Offers athletic training (MSAT); occupational therapy (MS); performing arts medicine (Certificate); physical therapy (DPT); physician assistant studies (MS); public health (MPH, Certificate). *Program availability:* Part-time, all online except for two on-site weekend sessions (for DPT). *Faculty:* 39 full-time (31 women), 24 part-time/adjunct (14 women). *Students:* 471 full-time (371 women), 149 part-time (128 women); includes 61 minority (9 Black or African American, non-Hispanic/Latino; 2 American Indian or Alaska Native, non-Hispanic/Latino; 17 Asian, non-Hispanic/Latino; 20 Hispanic/Latino; 13 Two or more races, non-Hispanic/Latino), 23 international. Average age 28. 1,124 applicants, 33% accepted, 226 enrolled. In 2018, 104 master's, 88 doctorates, 6 other advanced degrees awarded. *Degree requirements:* For master's, PT has a capstone research

project but isn't a full thesis/dissertation.; for Certificate, Capstone research project but isn't a full thesis/dissertation. *Entrance requirements:* For master's, GRE, athletic training: interview required; for specific requirements of health professions program: https://www.su.edu/admissions/graduate-students/; for doctorate, GRE, minimum cumulative and prerequisite GPA of 2.8. Additional exam requirements/recommendations for international students: Required—TOEFL (minimum score 558 paper-based; 83 iBT). *Application deadline:* For fall admission, 10/1 for domestic and international students; for spring admission, 12/1 for domestic and international students; for summer admission, 10/1 for domestic and international students. Application fee: $30. Electronic applications accepted. *Expenses:* $875 per credit hour, $160 student services fee, $170 technology fee, $255 online resource fee. *Financial support:* In 2018–19, 21 students received support. Scholarships/grants and unspecified assistantships available. Financial award application deadline: 1/15; financial award applicants required to submit FAFSA. *Faculty research:* 3D motion analysis of running mechanics; quality improvement in clinical practice; functional movement screen to predict injury in professional athletes and dancers; sensory integration for children with autism; chronic ankle instability. *Total annual research expenditures:* $15,000. *Unit head:* Karen Elizabeth Abraham-Justice, Ph.D., Dean of Health Professions, 540-542.6209, Fax: 540-665.5530, E-mail: kabraham@su.edu. *Application contact:* Katie Olivo, Associate Director of Graduate and International Admissions, 540-665.4581, Fax: 540-665.4627, E-mail: kolivo@su.edu.
Website: http://www.health.su.edu

South Dakota State University, Graduate School, College of Education and Human Sciences, Department of Health and Nutritional Sciences, Brookings, SD 57007. Offers athletic training (MS); dietetics (MS); nutrition and exercise sciences (MS, PhD); sport and recreation studies (MS). *Program availability:* Part-time. *Degree requirements:* For master's, comprehensive exam (for some programs), thesis (for some programs), oral exam. *Entrance requirements:* Additional exam requirements/recommendations for international students: Required—TOEFL (minimum score 525 paper-based). *Faculty research:* Food chemistry, bone density, functional food, nutrition education, nutrition biochemistry.

Spalding University, Graduate Studies, Kosair College of Health and Natural Sciences, Program in Athletic Training, Louisville, KY 40203-2188. Offers MS. *Entrance requirements:* For master's, transcripts, letter of recommendation, 20 observation hours, interview, writing sample. Additional exam requirements/recommendations for international students: Required—TOEFL (minimum score 535 paper-based). Application fee is waived when completed online.

Springfield College, Graduate Programs, Programs in Exercise Science and Sport Studies, Springfield, MA 01109-3797. Offers athletic training (MS); clinical exercise physiology (MS); exercise physiology (MS); sport and exercise psychology (MS); strength and conditioning (MS). *Program availability:* Part-time. Terminal master's awarded for partial completion of doctoral program. *Degree requirements:* For master's, comprehensive exam, research project or thesis. *Entrance requirements:* For master's, GRE General Test. Additional exam requirements/recommendations for international students: Required—TOEFL (minimum score 550 paper-based); Recommended—IELTS (minimum score 7). Electronic applications accepted.

Stephen F. Austin State University, Graduate School, James I. Perkins College of Education, Department of Kinesiology and Health Science, Nacogdoches, TX 75962. Offers athletic training (MS); kinesiology (MS). *Degree requirements:* For master's, comprehensive exam. *Entrance requirements:* For master's, GRE General Test. Additional exam requirements/recommendations for international students: Required—TOEFL.

Tarleton State University, College of Graduate Studies, College of Education, School of Kinesiology, Stephenville, TX 76402. Offers athletic training (MS); kinesiology (MS). *Program availability:* Part-time, evening/weekend. *Faculty:* 6 full-time (2 women), 1 (woman) part-time/adjunct. *Students:* 25 full-time (17 women), 48 part-time (25 women). Average age 24. 35 applicants, 83% accepted, 25 enrolled. In 2018, 50 master's awarded. *Degree requirements:* For master's, comprehensive exam, thesis optional. *Entrance requirements:* For master's, GRE General Test, minimum GPA of 3.0. Additional exam requirements/recommendations for international students: Required—TOEFL (minimum score 520 paper-based; 69 iBT); Recommended—IELTS (minimum score 6), TSE (minimum score 50). *Application deadline:* For fall admission, 8/15 priority date for domestic students; for spring admission, 1/7 for domestic students. Applications are processed on a rolling basis. Application fee: $50 ($130 for international students). Electronic applications accepted. *Expenses:* Contact institution. *Financial support:* Research assistantships, teaching assistantships with partial tuition reimbursements, career-related internships or fieldwork, Federal Work-Study, and institutionally sponsored loans available. Support available to part-time students. Financial award application deadline: 5/1; financial award applicants required to submit FAFSA. *Unit head:* Dr. Kayla Peak, Associate Dean, 254-968-9824, E-mail: peak@tarleton.edu. *Application contact:* Information Contact, 254-968-9104, Fax: 254-968-9670, E-mail: gradoffice@tarleton.edu.
Website: http://www.tarleton.edu/kinesiology/

Temple University, College of Public Health, Department of Kinesiology, Philadelphia, PA 19122. Offers athletic training (MSAT, DAT); kinesiology (MS, PhD); neuromotor science (MS, PhD). *Faculty:* 19 full-time (8 women), 5 part-time/adjunct (2 women). *Students:* 56 full-time (36 women), 39 part-time (20 women); includes 26 minority (13 Black or African American, non-Hispanic/Latino; 2 Asian, non-Hispanic/Latino; 6 Hispanic/Latino; 5 Two or more races, non-Hispanic/Latino), 3 international. 78 applicants, 74% accepted, 37 enrolled. In 2018, 15 master's awarded. *Degree requirements:* For master's, thesis optional, research project; for doctorate, thesis/dissertation, preliminary examination. *Entrance requirements:* For master's, GRE/MAT, letters of reference, statement of goals, interview, resume; for doctorate, GRE/MAT, minimum undergraduate GPA of 3.25, 3 letters of reference, statement of goals, writing sample, interview, resume. Additional exam requirements/recommendations for international students: Required—TOEFL (minimum score 79 iBT), IELTS (minimum score 6.5), PTE (minimum score 53), one of three is required. *Application deadline:* For fall admission, 3/1 for domestic students. Applications are processed on a rolling basis. Application fee: $60. Electronic applications accepted. *Expenses:* Contact institution. *Financial support:* Fellowships, research assistantships, teaching assistantships, career-related internships or fieldwork, Federal Work-Study, health care benefits, and unspecified assistantships available. Financial award applicants required to submit FAFSA. *Faculty research:* Integrative exercise physiology, athletic training, evaluation of clinical evidence, osteoarthritis. *Unit head:* Jeffrey S Gehris, Interim Department Chair, 214-204-1954, E-mail: jgehris@temple.edu. *Application contact:* Amy Costik, Assistant Director of Admissions, 215-204-5229, E-mail: amy.costik@temple.edu.
Website: http://cph.temple.edu/kinesiology/home

Texas A&M University, College of Education and Human Development, Department of Health and Kinesiology, College Station, TX 77843. Offers athletic training (MS); health education (MS, PhD); kinesiology (MS, PhD); sports management (MS). *Program availability:* Part-time. *Faculty:* 56. *Students:* 211 full-time (117 women), 80 part-time (41 women); includes 94 minority (35 Black or African American, non-Hispanic/Latino; 3 American Indian or Alaska Native, non-Hispanic/Latino; 5 Asian, non-Hispanic/Latino; 44 Hispanic/Latino; 7 Two or more races, non-Hispanic/Latino), 24 international. Average age 28. 95 applicants, 88% accepted, 60 enrolled. In 2018, 112 master's, 14 doctorates awarded. *Degree requirements:* For master's, thesis (for some programs); for doctorate, comprehensive exam, thesis/dissertation. *Entrance requirements:* For master's and doctorate, GRE General Test. Additional exam requirements/recommendations for international students: Required—TOEFL (minimum score 550 paper-based; 80 iBT), IELTS (minimum score 6), PTE (minimum score 53). *Application deadline:* For fall admission, 1/15 for domestic students; for spring admission, 10/1 for domestic students. Applications are processed on a rolling basis. Application fee: $50 ($90 for international students). Electronic applications accepted. *Expenses:* Contact institution. *Financial support:* In 2018–19, 109 students received support, including 2 fellowships with tuition reimbursements available (averaging $24,073 per year), 41 research assistantships with tuition reimbursements available (averaging $13,093 per year), 68 teaching assistantships with tuition reimbursements available (averaging $11,596 per year); career-related internships or fieldwork, institutionally sponsored loans, scholarships/grants, traineeships, health care benefits, tuition waivers (full and partial), and unspecified assistantships also available. Support available to part-time students. Financial award application deadline: 3/15; financial award applicants required to submit FAFSA. *Unit head:* Dr. Richard Kreider, Head, 979-845-1333, Fax: 979-847-8987, E-mail: rkreider@hlkn.tamu.edu. *Application contact:* Jenny Bilski, Academic Advisor, 979-862-4052, E-mail: jenny.bilski@tamu.edu.
Website: http://hlknweb.tamu.edu/

Texas State University, The Graduate College, College of Education, Program in Athletic Training, San Marcos, TX 78666. Offers MS. *Faculty:* 5 full-time (3 women). *Students:* 32 full-time (20 women); includes 12 minority (5 Black or African American, non-Hispanic/Latino; 3 Asian, non-Hispanic/Latino; 4 Hispanic/Latino). Average age 24. 126 applicants, 34% accepted, 15 enrolled. In 2018, 18 master's awarded. *Degree requirements:* For master's, comprehensive exam, thesis optional. *Entrance requirements:* For master's, baccalaureate degree from regionally-accredited institution with minimum GPA of 3.0 in last 60 hours of undergraduate work, statement of purpose, resume, Athletic Trainer Certification or eligible to sit for the exam, 3 recommendation forms. Additional exam requirements/recommendations for international students: Required—TOEFL (minimum score 550 paper-based; 78 iBT), IELTS (minimum score 6.5). *Application deadline:* For fall admission, 1/15 priority date for domestic and international students. Applications are processed on a rolling basis. Application fee: $55 ($90 for international students). Electronic applications accepted. *Expenses:* Tuition, state resident: full-time $8102; part-time $4051 per semester. Tuition, nonresident: full-time $18,229; part-time $9115 per semester. *International tuition:* $18,229 full-time. *Required fees:* $2116; $120 per credit hour. Tuition and fees vary according to course load. *Financial support:* In 2018–19, 30 students received support, including 9 teaching assistantships (averaging $13,645 per year); research assistantships, Federal Work-Study, scholarships/grants, and unspecified assistantships also available. Financial award application deadline: 1/15; financial award applicants required to submit FAFSA. *Faculty research:* Biomechanics and Sports Medicine; measurement issues in health and human performance, patient-reported outcomes, and concussion assessment; developing a mentoring framework through the examination of mentoring paradigms in a teacher residency program; clinical management of overhead athletes with the goal of improving performance while controlling injury risk. *Total annual research expenditures:* $175,086. *Unit head:* Dr. Natalie Myers, Graduate Advisor, 512-245-2948, E-mail: nlm73@txstate.edu. *Application contact:* Dr. Andrea Golato, Dean of the Graduate College, 512-245-2581, Fax: 512-245-8365, E-mail: gradcollege@txstate.edu.
Website: http://www.gradcollege.txstate.edu/programs/athletic-training.html

Texas Tech University Health Sciences Center, School of Health Professions, Program in Athletic Training, Lubbock, TX 79430. Offers MAT. *Faculty:* 4 full-time (1 woman), 1 (woman) part-time/adjunct. *Students:* 39 full-time (25 women), 2 part-time (both women); includes 24 minority (6 Black or African American, non-Hispanic/Latino; 1 American Indian or Alaska Native, non-Hispanic/Latino; 6 Asian, non-Hispanic/Latino; 11 Hispanic/Latino). Average age 24. 71 applicants, 24% accepted, 27 enrolled. In 2018, 21 master's awarded. *Entrance requirements:* Additional exam requirements/recommendations for international students: Required—TOEFL (minimum score 550 paper-based; 79 iBT). *Application deadline:* For summer admission, 2/1 for domestic students. Applications are processed on a rolling basis. Application fee: $75. Electronic applications accepted. *Financial support:* In 2018–19, 34 students received support. Career-related internships or fieldwork, institutionally sponsored loans, and scholarships/grants available. Financial award application deadline: 9/1; financial award applicants required to submit FAFSA. *Unit head:* Dr. LesLee Taylor, Program Director, 806-743-1032, Fax: 806-743-2189, E-mail: leslee.taylor@ttuhsc.edu. *Application contact:* Lindsay Johnson, Associate Dean for Admissions and Student Affairs, 806-743-3220, Fax: 806-743-2994, E-mail: health.professions@ttuhsc.edu.
Website: http://www.ttuhsc.edu/health-professions/master-athletic-training/

Thomas Jefferson University, Jefferson College of Rehabilitation Sciences, Program in Athletic Training, Philadelphia, PA 19107. Offers MS.

Trinity International University, Trinity Graduate School, Deerfield, IL 60015-1284. Offers athletic training (MA); bioethics (MA); counseling psychology (MA); diverse learning (M Ed); leadership (MA); teaching (MA). *Program availability:* Part-time, evening/weekend, online learning. *Degree requirements:* For master's, comprehensive exam. *Entrance requirements:* For master's, GRE General Test or MAT, minimum undergraduate GPA of 3.0. Additional exam requirements/recommendations for international students: Required—TOEFL (minimum score 580 paper-based), TWE (minimum score 4). Electronic applications accepted.

Universidad del Turabo, Graduate Programs, Programs in Education, Program in Athletic Therapeutic, Gurabo, PR 00778-3030. Offers MPHE. *Program availability:* Part-time, evening/weekend. *Entrance requirements:* For master's, GRE, EXADEP, GMAT, interview, official transcript, essay, recommendation letters. Electronic applications accepted.

University of Arkansas, Graduate School, College of Education and Health Professions, Department of Health, Human Performance and Recreation, Program in Athletic Training, Fayetteville, AR 72701. Offers MAT. In 2018, 20 master's awarded. *Application deadline:* For fall admission, 8/1 for domestic students, 4/1 for international students; for spring admission, 12/1 for domestic students, 10/1 for international students; for summer admission, 4/15 for domestic students, 3/1 for international students. Applications are processed on a rolling basis. Application fee: $60. Electronic applications accepted. *Financial support:* In 2018–19, 2 research assistantships were awarded; teaching assistantships also available. *Unit head:* Dr. Matt Ganio, Department Head, 479-575-2858, E-mail: msganio@uark.edu. *Application contact:* Paul Calleja, Clinical Professor, Kinesiology - Teacher Education, 479-575-2854, E-mail: pcallej@uark.edu.
Website: https://atep.uark.edu/

University of Central Florida, College of Health Professions and Sciences, Program in Athletic Training, Orlando, FL 32816. Offers MAT. *Unit head:* Kristen Couper Schellhase, Director, 407-823-3463, E-mail: kristen.schellhase@ucf.edu. *Application contact:* Associate Director, Graduate Admissions, 407-823-2766, Fax: 407-823-6442, E-mail: gradadmissions@ucf.edu.
Website: https://healthprofessions.ucf.edu/kpt/athletic-training-program/

University of Central Oklahoma, The Jackson College of Graduate Studies, College of Education and Professional Studies, Department of Kinesiology and Health Studies, Edmond, OK 73034-5209. Offers athletic training (MS); wellness management (MS), including exercise science, health promotion. *Degree requirements:* For master's, comprehensive exam (for some programs), thesis (for some programs). *Entrance requirements:* Additional exam requirements/recommendations for international students: Required—TOEFL (minimum score 550 paper-based; 79 iBT), IELTS (minimum score 6.5). Electronic applications accepted.

University of Evansville, College of Education and Health Sciences, School of Health Sciences, Evansville, IN 47722. Offers athletic training (MSAT); health policy (MPH); health services administration (MS). *Program availability:* Part-time, evening/weekend. *Entrance requirements:* Additional exam requirements/recommendations for international students: Required—TOEFL, IELTS (minimum score 6.5). *Expenses:* Contact institution.

The University of Findlay, Office of Graduate Admissions, Findlay, OH 45840-3653. Offers applied security and analytics (MSAS); athletic training (MAT); business (MBA), including certified management accountant, certified public accountant, health care management, hospitality management; education (MA Ed, Ed D), including children's literature (MA Ed), curriculum and teaching (MA Ed), education (MA Ed), educational administration (MA Ed), human resource development (MA Ed), mathematics (MA Ed), reading (MA Ed), science education (MA Ed), superintendent (Ed D), teaching (Ed D), technology (MA Ed); environmental, safety, and health management (MSEM); health informatics (MS); occupational therapy (MOT); pharmacy (Pharm D); physical therapy (DPT); physician assistant (MPA); rhetoric and writing (MA); teaching English to speakers of other languages (TESOL) and applied linguistics (MA). *Program availability:* Part-time, evening/weekend, 100% online, blended/hybrid learning. *Degree requirements:* For master's, comprehensive exam (for some programs), thesis (for some programs), cumulative project, capstone project; for doctorate, thesis/dissertation (for some programs). *Entrance requirements:* For master's, GRE/GMAT, bachelor's degree from accredited institution, minimum undergraduate GPA of 2.5 in last 64 hours of course work; for doctorate, GRE, MAT, minimum cumulative GPA of 3.0. Additional exam requirements/recommendations for international students: Required—TOEFL (minimum score 79 iBT), IELTS (minimum score 7), PTE (minimum score 61). Electronic applications accepted.

University of Florida, Graduate School, College of Health and Human Performance, Department of Applied Physiology and Kinesiology, Gainesville, FL 32611. Offers applied physiology and kinesiology (MS); athletic training/sports medicine (MS); biobehavioral science (MS); clinical exercise physiology (MS); exercise physiology (MS); health and human performance (PhD), including applied physiology and kinesiology, biobehavioral science, exercise physiology; human performance (MS). *Degree requirements:* For master's, comprehensive exam, thesis (for some programs); for doctorate, comprehensive exam, thesis/dissertation. *Entrance requirements:* For master's and doctorate, GRE General Test, minimum GPA of 3.0. Additional exam requirements/recommendations for international students: Required—TOEFL (minimum score 550 paper-based; 80 iBT), IELTS (minimum score 6). Electronic applications accepted. *Faculty research:* Cardiovascular disease; basic mechanisms that underlie exercise-induced changes in the body at the organ, tissue, cellular and molecular level; development of rehabilitation techniques for regaining motor control after stroke or as a consequence of Parkinson's disease; maintaining optimal health and delaying age-related declines in physiological function; psychomotor mechanisms impacting health and performance across the life span.

University of Idaho, College of Graduate Studies, College of Education, Health and Human Sciences, Department of Movement Sciences, Moscow, ID 83844-2401. Offers athletic training (MSAT, DAT); exercise science and health (MS); physical education teacher education (M Ed, MS); recreation, sport, and tourism management (MS). *Faculty:* 19. *Students:* 89 full-time, 9 part-time. Average age 26. In 2018, 43 master's awarded. *Degree requirements:* For doctorate, thesis/dissertation. *Entrance requirements:* For master's and doctorate, minimum GPA of 3.0. Additional exam requirements/recommendations for international students: Required—TOEFL. *Application deadline:* For fall admission, 8/1 for domestic students; for spring admission, 12/15 for domestic students. Applications are processed on a rolling basis. Application fee: $60. Electronic applications accepted. *Expenses:* Tuition, state resident: full-time $7266.44; part-time $474.50 per credit hour. Tuition, nonresident: full-time $24,902; part-time $1453.50 per credit hour. *Required fees:* $2085.56; $45.50 per credit hour. *Financial support:* Research assistantships and teaching assistantships available. Financial award applicants required to submit FAFSA. *Unit head:* Dr. Philip W. Scruggs, Chair, 208-885-7921, E-mail: movementsciences@uidaho.edu. *Application contact:* Dr. Philip W. Scruggs, Chair, 208-885-7921, E-mail: movementsciences@uidaho.edu. Website: https://www.uidaho.edu/ed/mvsc

The University of Iowa, Graduate College, College of Liberal Arts and Sciences, Department of Health and Human Physiology, Iowa City, IA 52242-1316. Offers athletic training (MS); clinical exercise physiology (MS); health and human physiology (PhD); leisure studies (MA, PhD), including recreational sport management (PhD), therapeutic recreation (MA). *Degree requirements:* For master's, thesis optional, exam; for doctorate, comprehensive exam, thesis/dissertation. *Entrance requirements:* For master's and doctorate, GRE General Test, minimum GPA of 3.0. Additional exam requirements/recommendations for international students: Required—TOEFL (minimum score 600 paper-based; 100 iBT). Electronic applications accepted.

University of Kentucky, Graduate School, College of Health Sciences, Division of Athletic Training, Lexington, KY 40506-0032. Offers MS.

University of Lynchburg, Graduate Studies, MS Program in Athletic Training, Lynchburg, VA 24501-3199. Offers MS. *Degree requirements:* For master's, thesis. *Entrance requirements:* Additional exam requirements/recommendations for international students: Required—TOEFL (minimum score 550 paper-based), IELTS (minimum score 6). Electronic applications accepted. Application fee is waived when completed online. *Expenses:* Contact institution.

University of Miami, Graduate School, School of Education and Human Development, Department of Kinesiology and Sport Sciences, Program in Exercise Physiology, Coral Gables, FL 33124. Offers exercise physiology (MS Ed, PhD); strength and conditioning (MS Ed). *Program availability:* Part-time, evening/weekend. *Faculty:* 4 full-time (1 woman). *Students:* 38 full-time (13 women), 4 part-time (0 women); includes 13 minority (2 Black or African American, non-Hispanic/Latino; 1 Asian, non-Hispanic/Latino; 9 Hispanic/Latino; 1 Two or more races, non-Hispanic/Latino), 6 international. Average age 28. 59 applicants, 61% accepted, 17 enrolled. In 2018, 20 master's, 2 doctorates awarded. Terminal master's awarded for partial completion of doctoral program. *Degree requirements:* For master's, comprehensive exam (for some programs), special project; for doctorate, thesis/dissertation, qualifying exam. *Entrance requirements:* For master's and doctorate, GRE General Test. Additional exam requirements/recommendations for international students: Required—TOEFL (minimum score 550 paper-based; 80 iBT); Recommended—IELTS (minimum score 6.5). *Application deadline:* For fall admission, 10/1 for international students; for spring admission, 10/1 for international students. Applications are processed on a rolling basis. Application fee: $75. Electronic

applications accepted. *Financial support:* Fellowships, research assistantships, teaching assistantships, scholarships/grants, health care benefits, tuition waivers (full and partial), and unspecified assistantships available. Support available to part-time students. Financial award application deadline: 3/1; financial award applicants required to submit FAFSA. *Faculty research:* Women's health, cardiovascular health, aging, metabolism, obesity. *Unit head:* Dr. Kevin Jacobs, Associate Professor and Program Director, 305-284-5873, E-mail: k.jacobs@miami.edu. *Application contact:* Lois Heffernan, Graduate Admissions Coordinator, 305-284-2167, Fax: 305-284-9395, E-mail: lheffernan@miami.edu.
Website: http://www.education.miami.edu

University of Nebraska at Omaha, Graduate Studies, College of Education, School of Health and Kinesiology, Omaha, NE 68182. Offers athletic training (MA); exercise science (PhD); health, physical education, and recreation (MA, MS). *Program availability:* Part-time, evening/weekend. *Degree requirements:* For master's, comprehensive exam, thesis (for some programs). *Entrance requirements:* For master's, GRE; entrance exam, minimum GPA of 3.0, official transcripts, statement of purpose, 2 letters of recommendation; for doctorate, GRE, minimum GPA of 3.2, official transcripts, statement of purpose, 3 letters of recommendation, resume, writing sample. Additional exam requirements/recommendations for international students: Required—TOEFL, IELTS, PTE. Electronic applications accepted.

The University of North Carolina at Chapel Hill, Graduate School, College of Arts and Sciences, Department of Exercise and Sport Science, Chapel Hill, NC 27599. Offers athletic training (MA); exercise physiology (MA); sport administration (MA). *Degree requirements:* For master's, comprehensive exam, thesis. *Entrance requirements:* For master's, GRE General Test, minimum GPA of 3.0. Additional exam requirements/recommendations for international students: Required—TOEFL (minimum score 550 paper-based). Electronic applications accepted. *Faculty research:* Mild head injury in sport, endocrine system's response to exercise, obesity and children, effect of aerobic exercise on cerebral bloodflow in elderly population.

The University of North Carolina at Greensboro, Graduate School, School of Health and Human Sciences, Department of Kinesiology, Greensboro, NC 27412-5001. Offers athletic training (MSAT); kinesiology (MS, Ed D, PhD). *Program availability:* Online learning. *Degree requirements:* For master's, thesis (for some programs); for doctorate, thesis/dissertation. *Entrance requirements:* For master's and doctorate, GRE General Test. Additional exam requirements/recommendations for international students: Required—TOEFL. Electronic applications accepted.

University of Northern Iowa, Graduate College, College of Education, School of Kinesiology, Allied Health and Human Services, MS Program in Athletic Training, Cedar Falls, IA 50614. Offers MS. *Program availability:* Part-time, evening/weekend. *Degree requirements:* For master's, comprehensive exam. *Entrance requirements:* Additional exam requirements/recommendations for international students: Required—TOEFL (minimum score 550 paper-based; 79 iBT). Electronic applications accepted.

University of North Georgia, Program in Athletic Training, Dahlonega, GA 30597. Offers MS. *Degree requirements:* For master's, seminar, capstone experience. *Entrance requirements:* For master's, GRE General Test (minimum combined score of 280 on verbal and quantitative sections taken on or after August 1, 2011, 3.5 on analytical writing section), letter of intent, resume, 2 letters of recommendation, proof of minimum of 50 observation hours with a certified athletic trainer, proof of CPR certification, background check, physical and immunization forms, technical standards form signed by a physician, prerequisite courses with minimum grade of C. Additional exam requirements/recommendations for international students: Required—TOEFL (minimum score 550 paper-based; 79 iBT), IELTS (minimum score 6.5). Electronic applications accepted. *Expenses:* Contact institution.

University of Pittsburgh, School of Health and Rehabilitation Sciences, Department of Sports Medicine and Nutrition, Pittsburgh, PA 15260. Offers health and rehabilitation sciences (MS), including sports medicine, wellness and human performance; nutrition and dietetics (MS). *Program availability:* Online learning. *Degree requirements:* For master's, comprehensive exam (for some programs). *Entrance requirements:* Additional exam requirements/recommendations for international students: Required—TOEFL (minimum score 550 paper-based; 80 iBT), IELTS (minimum score 6.5). Electronic applications accepted. *Faculty research:* Nutrition and fitness; movement science; injury prevention and human performance; molecular transducers of physical activity; characterization of psychological resilience and readiness.

University of St. Augustine for Health Sciences, Graduate Programs, Master of Health Science Program, San Marcos, CA 92069. Offers athletic training (MHS); executive leadership (MHS); informatics (MHS); teaching and learning (MHS). *Program availability:* Online learning. *Degree requirements:* For master's, comprehensive project.

University of South Florida, Morsani College of Medicine and College of Graduate Studies, Graduate Programs in Medical Sciences, Tampa, FL 33620-9951. Offers advanced athletic training (MS); athletic training (MS); bioinformatics and computational biology (MSBCB); biotechnology (MSB); health informatics (MSHI); medical sciences (MSMS, PhD), including aging and neuroscience (MSMS), allergy, immunology and infectious disease (PhD), anatomy, biochemistry and molecular biology, clinical and translational research, health science (MSMS), interdisciplinary medical sciences (MSMS), medical microbiology and immunology (MSMS), metabolic and nutritional medicine (MSMS), microbiology and immunology (PhD), molecular medicine, molecular pharmacology and physiology (PhD), neuroscience (PhD), pathology and cell biology (PhD), women's health (MSMS). *Faculty:* 1 (woman) full-time. *Students:* 355 full-time (207 women), 229 part-time (145 women); includes 283 minority (71 Black or African American, non-Hispanic/Latino; 2 American Indian or Alaska Native, non-Hispanic/Latino; 89 Asian, non-Hispanic/Latino; 103 Hispanic/Latino; 2 Native Hawaiian or other Pacific Islander, non-Hispanic/Latino; 16 Two or more races, non-Hispanic/Latino), 48 international. Average age 28. 898 applicants, 57% accepted, 323 enrolled. In 2018, 227 master's, 13 doctorates awarded. Terminal master's awarded for partial completion of doctoral program. *Degree requirements:* For master's, comprehensive exam, thesis; for doctorate, comprehensive exam, thesis/dissertation. *Entrance requirements:* For master's, GRE General Test or GMAT, bachelor's degree or equivalent from regionally-accredited university with minimum GPA of 3.0 in upper-division sciences coursework; prerequisites in general biology, general chemistry, general physics, organic chemistry, quantitative analysis, and integral and differential calculus; for doctorate, GRE General Test, bachelor's degree from regionally-accredited university with minimum GPA of 3.0 in upper-division sciences coursework; 3 letters of recommendation; personal interview; 1-2 page personal statement; prerequisites in biology, chemistry, physics, organic chemistry, quantitative analysis, and integral/differential calculus. Additional exam requirements/recommendations for international students: Required—TOEFL (minimum score 550 paper-based; 79 iBT) or IELTS (minimum score 6.5). *Application deadline:* For fall admission, 2/1 priority date for domestic students, 2/1 for international students. Application fee: $30. Electronic applications accepted. *Expenses:* Contact institution. *Financial support:* In 2018–19, 106 students received support. *Faculty research:* Anatomy, biochemistry, cancer biology, cardiovascular disease, cell biology, immunology, microbiology, molecular biology, neuroscience, pharmacology, physiology. *Total annual research expenditures:* $50.9 million. *Unit head:* Dr. Michael Barber,

Professor/Associate Dean for Graduate and Postdoctoral Affairs, 813-974-9908, Fax: 813-974-4317, E-mail: mbarber@health.usf.edu. *Application contact:* Dr. Eric Bennett, Graduate Director, PhD Program in Medical Sciences, 813-974-1545, Fax: 813-974-4317, E-mail: esbennet@health.usf.edu.
Website: http://health.usf.edu/nocms/medicine/graduatestudies/

The University of Tennessee, Graduate School, College of Education, Health and Human Sciences, Department of Exercise, Sport, and Leisure Studies, Program in Exercise Science, Knoxville, TN 37996. Offers biomechanics/sports medicine (MS, PhD); exercise physiology (MS, PhD). *Accreditation:* CEPH (one or more programs are accredited). *Program availability:* Part-time. *Degree requirements:* For master's, thesis optional. *Entrance requirements:* For master's, minimum GPA of 2.7. Additional exam requirements/recommendations for international students: Required—TOEFL. Electronic applications accepted.

The University of Tennessee at Chattanooga, Department of Health and Human Performance, Chattanooga, TN 37403. Offers athletic training (MSAT); health and human performance (MS). *Degree requirements:* For master's, thesis or alternative, clinical rotations. *Entrance requirements:* For master's, GRE General Test, minimum GPA of 2.75 overall or 3.0 in last 60 hours; CPR and First Aid certification. Additional exam requirements/recommendations for international students: Required—TOEFL (minimum score 550 paper-based; 79 iBT), IELTS (minimum score 6). Electronic applications accepted. *Expenses:* Contact institution. *Faculty research:* Therapeutic exercise, lumbar spine biomechanics, physical activity epidemiology, functional rehabilitation outcomes, metabolic health.

The University of Texas at Arlington, Graduate School, College of Nursing and Health Innovation, Arlington, TX 76019. Offers athletic training (MS); exercise science (MS); kinesiology (PhD); nurse practitioner (MSN); nursing (PhD); nursing administration (MSN); nursing education (MSN); nursing practice (DNP). *Accreditation:* AACN. *Program availability:* Part-time, evening/weekend, online learning. *Degree requirements:* For master's, practicum course; for doctorate, comprehensive exam (for some programs), thesis/dissertation (for some programs), proposal defense dissertation (for PhD); scholarship project (for DNP). *Entrance requirements:* For master's, GRE General Test if GPA less than 3.0, minimum GPA of 3.0, Texas nursing license, minimum C grade in undergraduate statistics course; for doctorate, GRE General Test (waived for MSN-to-PhD applicants), minimum undergraduate, graduate and statistics GPA of 3.0; Texas RN license; interview; written statement of goals. Additional exam requirements/recommendations for international students: Required—TOEFL (minimum score 550 paper-based), IELTS (minimum score 7). *Faculty research:* Simulation in clinical education and practice, cultural diversity, vulnerable populations, substance abuse.

The University of Toledo, College of Graduate Studies, College of Health and Human Services, School of Exercise and Rehabilitation Sciences, Toledo, OH 43606-3390. Offers athletic training (MSES); exercise physiology (MSES); exercise science (PhD); occupational therapy (OTD); physical therapy (DPT); recreation and leisure studies (MA), including recreation administration, recreation therapy. *Degree requirements:* For master's, comprehensive exam, thesis; for doctorate, thesis/dissertation or alternative. *Entrance requirements:* For master's, GRE, minimum cumulative GPA of 2.7 for all previous academic work, letters of recommendation; for doctorate, GRE, minimum cumulative GPA of 3.0 for all previous academic work, letters of recommendation; OTCAS or PTCAS application and UT supplemental application (for OTD and DPT). Additional exam requirements/recommendations for international students: Required—TOEFL (minimum score 550 paper-based; 80 iBT). Electronic applications accepted.

University of Wisconsin–La Crosse, College of Science and Health, Department of Exercise and Sport Science, Program in Human Performance, La Crosse, WI 54601-3742. Offers exercise sport science: human performance (MS), including applied sport science, strength and conditioning. *Program availability:* Part-time. *Degree requirements:* For master's, comprehensive exam (for some programs), thesis optional. *Entrance requirements:* For master's, GRE, course work in anatomy, physiology, biomechanics, and exercise physiology. Additional exam requirements/recommendations for international students: Required—TOEFL (minimum score 550 paper-based; 79 iBT). Electronic applications accepted. *Faculty research:* Anaerobic metabolism, power development, strength training, biomechanics, athletic performance.

University of Wisconsin–Milwaukee, Graduate School, College of Health Sciences, Department of Kinesiology, Milwaukee, WI 53201-0413. Offers athletic training (MS); kinesiology (MS, PhD), including exercise and nutrition in health and disease (MS), integrative human performance (MS), neuromechanics (MS); physical therapy (DPT). *Program availability:* Part-time. *Students:* 108 full-time (59 women), 6 part-time (3 women); includes 11 minority (1 American Indian or Alaska Native, non-Hispanic/Latino; 1 Asian, non-Hispanic/Latino; 3 Hispanic/Latino; 6 Two or more races, non-Hispanic/Latino), 5 international. Average age 28. 47 applicants, 38% accepted, 16 enrolled. In 2018, 9 master's, 21 doctorates awarded. *Degree requirements:* For master's, comprehensive exam, thesis optional. *Entrance requirements:* For master's, GRE General Test. Additional exam requirements/recommendations for international students: Required—TOEFL (minimum score 550 paper-based; 79 iBT), IELTS (minimum score 6.5). *Application deadline:* For fall admission, 1/1 priority date for domestic students; for spring admission, 9/1 for domestic students. Applications are processed on a rolling basis. Application fee: $56 ($96 for international students). *Financial support:* Fellowships, research assistantships, teaching assistantships, career-related internships or fieldwork, unspecified assistantships, and project assistantships available. Support available to part-time students. Financial award application deadline: 4/15. *Unit head:* Dr. Kyle T. Ebersole, Department Chair, 414-229-6717, Fax: 414-229-3366, E-mail: ebersole@uwm.edu. *Application contact:* Stephen C. Cobb, Graduate Program Coordinator, 414-229-3369, Fax: 414-229-3366, E-mail: cobbsc@uwm.edu.
Website: http://uwm.edu/healthsciences/academics/kinesiology/

University of Wisconsin–Stevens Point, College of Professional Studies, School of Health Care Professions, Stevens Point, WI 54481-3897. Offers athletic training (MS).

Wayne State University, College of Education, Division of Kinesiology, Health and Sports Studies, Detroit, MI 48202. Offers athletic training (MSAT); health education (M Ed); kinesiology (M Ed, PhD), including exercise and sport science (PhD), physical education and physical activity leadership (PhD); sports administration (MA). *Program availability:* Part-time, evening/weekend. *Faculty:* 9. *Students:* 76 full-time (47 women), 110 part-time (56 women); includes 73 minority (53 Black or African American, non-Hispanic/Latino; 4 Asian, non-Hispanic/Latino; 8 Hispanic/Latino; 8 Two or more races, non-Hispanic/Latino), 9 international. Average age 30. 163 applicants, 60% accepted, 69 enrolled. In 2018, 70 master's, 4 doctorates awarded. *Degree requirements:* For master's, thesis (for some programs); for doctorate, comprehensive exam, thesis/dissertation. *Entrance requirements:* For master's, minimum undergraduate GPA of 3.0; undergraduate degree directly relating to the field of specialization being applied for or one accompanied by extensive educational background in closely-related field; teaching certificates in specific areas (for some programs); for doctorate, minimum undergraduate GPA of 3.0; undergraduate degree directly relating to the field of specialization being applied for or one accompanied by extensive educational background in closely-related field. Additional exam requirements/recommendations for international students: Required—TOEFL (minimum score 550 paper-based; 79 iBT); Recommended—IELTS (minimum score 6.5), TWE (minimum score 5.5), TSE (minimum score 58). *Application deadline:* Applications are processed on a rolling basis. Application fee: $50. Electronic applications accepted. *Financial support:* In 2018–19, 51 students received support. Fellowships with tuition reimbursements available, research assistantships with tuition reimbursements available, teaching assistantships with tuition reimbursements available, scholarships/grants, health care benefits, and unspecified assistantships available. Support available to part-time students. Financial award applicants required to submit FAFSA. *Faculty research:* Exercise and sport science, nutrition and physical activity interventions, school and community health, obesity prevention. *Unit head:* Dr. Nate McCaughtry, Assistant Dean, Division of Kinesiology, Health and Sport Studies/Director, Center for School Health, 313-577-0014, Fax: 313-577-5002, E-mail: aj4391@wayne.edu. *Application contact:* Heather Ladanyi, Manager, 313-577-1191, E-mail: eb3703@wayne.edu.
Website: http://coe.wayne.edu/kinesiology/index.php

Weber State University, Jerry and Vickie Moyes College of Education, Program in Athletic Training, Ogden, UT 84408-1001. Offers MSAT. *Program availability:* Part-time. *Faculty:* 18 full-time (11 women). *Students:* 28 full-time (19 women), 1 part-time (0 women); includes 13 minority (8 Black or African American, non-Hispanic/Latino; 2 American Indian or Alaska Native, non-Hispanic/Latino; 2 Asian, non-Hispanic/Latino; 1 Hispanic/Latino), 4 international. Average age 25. In 2018, 18 master's awarded. *Degree requirements:* For master's, thesis. *Entrance requirements:* For master's, GRE (if GPA less than 3.0), physical, immunizations. Additional exam requirements/recommendations for international students: Required—TOEFL (minimum score 525 paper-based). *Application deadline:* For fall admission, 1/15 priority date for domestic and international students. Application fee: $60 ($90 for international students). Electronic applications accepted. *Financial support:* In 2018–19, 22 students received support. Scholarships/grants available. Financial award application deadline: 4/1; financial award applicants required to submit FAFSA. *Unit head:* Dr. Valerie W. Herzog, Program Director, 801-626-7675, Fax: 801-626-6228, E-mail: valerieherzog@weber.edu. *Application contact:* Dr. Valerie W. Herzog, Program Director, 801-626-7675, Fax: 801-626-6228, E-mail: valerieherzog@weber.edu.
Website: http://www.weber.edu/athletictraining/graduateprograms.html

West Chester University of Pennsylvania, College of Health Sciences, Department of Kinesiology, West Chester, PA 19383. Offers adapted physical education (Certificate); exercise and sport physiology (MS), including athletic training; sport management and athletics (MPA), including administration. *Program availability:* Part-time, evening/weekend, blended/hybrid learning. *Degree requirements:* For master's, thesis or research report (for MS); two internships and capstone course that includes a research project or thesis (for MPA); for Certificate, six courses of study. *Entrance requirements:* For master's, GRE (for MS), 2 letters of recommendation, statement of professional goals; transcripts (for MS); two letters of reference, career goals, resume (for MPA); for Certificate, two letters of recommendation, transcript. Additional exam requirements/recommendations for international students: Required—TOEFL or IELTS. Electronic applications accepted. *Faculty research:* Metabolism during exercise, biomechanics, rating of perceived exertion, motor learning, environmental physiology.

West Chester University of Pennsylvania, College of Health Sciences, Department of Sports Medicine, West Chester, PA 19383. Offers athletic training (MS). *Entrance requirements:* For master's, ATCAS application, personal statement, three letters of reference, official transcripts, CPR certification. Additional exam requirements/recommendations for international students: Required—TOEFL or IELTS. Electronic applications accepted. *Faculty research:* Heat illness, osteoarthritis, patient centered care, mental health, clinical education, manual therapy.

Western Michigan University, Graduate College, College of Education and Human Development, Department of Health, Physical Education and Recreation, Kalamazoo, MI 49008. Offers athletic training (MS), including exercise physiology; sport management (MA), including pedagogy, special physical education.

West Virginia University, College of Physical Activity and Sport Sciences, Morgantown, WV 26506. Offers athletic training (MS); coaching and sport education (MS); coaching and teaching studies (Ed D, PhD), including curriculum and instruction (PhD); physical education/teacher education (MS); sport coaching (MS); sport management (MS); sport, exercise & performance psychology (MS). *Students:* 98 full-time (40 women), 122 part-time (42 women); includes 38 minority (18 Black or African American, non-Hispanic/Latino; 4 Asian, non-Hispanic/Latino; 10 Hispanic/Latino; 6 Two or more races, non-Hispanic/Latino), 13 international. In 2018, 74 master's, 5 doctorates awarded. *Degree requirements:* For doctorate, comprehensive exam, thesis/dissertation, oral exam. *Entrance requirements:* For master's, GRE or MAT, minimum GPA of 3.0; for doctorate, GRE General Test or MAT, minimum GPA of 3.5. Additional exam requirements/recommendations for international students: Required—TOEFL (minimum score 550 paper-based). *Application deadline:* For fall admission, 12/15 for domestic students, 10/1 for international students. Application fee: $60. Electronic applications accepted. *Financial support:* Research assistantships, teaching assistantships, career-related internships or fieldwork, Federal Work-Study, institutionally sponsored loans, health care benefits, tuition waivers (full and partial), and administrative assistantships available. Support available to part-time students. Financial award application deadline: 2/1; financial award applicants required to submit FAFSA. *Faculty research:* Sport psych sociology, teacher education, exercise psychology, counseling. *Unit head:* Sean Bulger, Online Program Coordinator, 304-293-0845, Fax: 304-293-4641, E-mail: sean.bulger@mail.wvu.edu. *Application contact:* Sean Bulger, Online Program Coordinator, 304-293-0845, Fax: 304-293-4641, E-mail: sean.bulger@mail.wvu.edu.
Website: http://www.cpass.wvu.edu

West Virginia Wesleyan College, School of Exercise Science and Athletic Training, Buckhannon, WV 26201. Offers athletic training (MS).

Xavier University, College of Professional Sciences, Department of Sports Studies, Cincinnati, OH 45207. Offers coaching education and athlete development (M Ed); sport administration (M Ed). *Program availability:* Part-time, evening/weekend, online learning. *Degree requirements:* For master's, thesis optional, internship or research project. *Entrance requirements:* For master's, GRE or MAT, official transcript; resume; one-page statement of career goals; 2 letters of recommendation. Additional exam requirements/recommendations for international students: Required—TOEFL (minimum score 550 paper-based; 79 iBT). Electronic applications accepted. Application fee is waived when completed online. *Expenses:* Contact institution. *Faculty research:* Coaching education, brand equity, strategic management, economic impact, place marketing.

Youngstown State University, College of Graduate Studies, Bitonte College of Health and Human Services, Department of Kinesiology and Sport Science, Youngstown, OH 44555-0001. Offers athletic training (MAT).

Exercise and Sports Science

Adams State University, Office of Graduate Studies, Department of Human Performance and Physical Education, Alamosa, CO 81101. Offers human performance and physical education (MA, MS), including applied sport psychology, coaching (MA), exercise science (MA), sport management (MA). *Program availability:* Part-time. *Entrance requirements:* For master's, GRE General Test or MAT, minimum undergraduate GPA of 2.75.

American International College, School of Health Sciences, Springfield, MA 01109-3189. Offers exercise science (MS); family nurse practitioner (MSN, Post-Master's Certificate); nursing administrator (MSN); nursing educator (MSN); occupational therapy (MSOT, OTD); physical therapy (DPT). *Accreditation:* AOTA. *Program availability:* Part-time, 100% online. *Degree requirements:* For master's, practicum; for doctorate, thesis/dissertation, practicum. *Entrance requirements:* For master's, 3 letters of recommendation, personal goal statement; minimum GPA of 3.2, interview, BS or BA, and 2 clinical PT observations (for DPT); minimum GPA of 3.0, MSOT, OT licensen, and 2 clinical OT observations (for OTD); for doctorate, personal goal statement, 2 letters of recommendation; minimum GPA of 3.0, BS or BA, 2 clinical OT observations (for MSOT); RN license and minimum GPA of 3.0 (for MSN). Additional exam requirements/recommendations for international students: Required—TOEFL (minimum score 577 paper-based; 91 iBT). Electronic applications accepted. *Expenses:* Contact institution. *Faculty research:* Teaching simulation, ergonomics, orthopedics, use of social media in health care.

Appalachian State University, Cratis D. Williams School of Graduate Studies, Department of Health and Exercise Science, Boone, NC 28608. Offers exercise science (MS), including clinical exercise physiology, strength and conditioning. *Degree requirements:* For master's, comprehensive exam, thesis optional. *Entrance requirements:* For master's, GRE General Test, 3 letters of recommendation. Additional exam requirements/recommendations for international students: Required—TOEFL (minimum score 570 paper-based; 79 iBT), IELTS (minimum score 6.5). Electronic applications accepted. *Expenses: Tuition, area resident:* Full-time $4839; part-time $237 per credit hour. Tuition, state resident: full-time $4839; part-time $237 per credit hour. Tuition, nonresident: full-time $18,271; part-time $895.50 per credit hour. *Faculty research:* Exercise immunology, biomechanics, exercise and chronic disease, muscle damage, strength and conditioning.

Arizona State University at the Tempe campus, College of Health Solutions, School of Nutrition and Health Promotion, Tempe, AZ 85287. Offers clinical exercise physiology (MS); exercise and wellness (MS); nutrition (MS), including dietetics, human nutrition; obesity prevention and management (MS); physical activity, nutrition and wellness (PhD).

Arkansas State University, Graduate School, College of Education and Behavioral Science, Department of Health, Physical Education, and Sport Sciences, State University, AR 72467. Offers exercise science (MS); physical education (MSE, SCCT); sports administration (MS). *Program availability:* Part-time. *Degree requirements:* For master's, comprehensive exam, thesis or alternative; for SCCT, comprehensive exam. *Entrance requirements:* For master's, GRE General Test or MAT, appropriate bachelor's degree, official transcripts, immunization records, statement of goals, letters of recommendation; for SCCT, GRE General Test or MAT, interview, master's degree, official transcript, immunization records. Additional exam requirements/recommendations for international students: Required—TOEFL (minimum score 550 paper-based; 79 iBT), IELTS (minimum score 6), PTE (minimum score 56). Electronic applications accepted.

Ashland University, Dwight Schar College of Nursing and Health Sciences, Department of Health Sciences, Ashland, OH 44805-3702. Offers applied exercise science (MS). *Program availability:* Part-time. *Degree requirements:* For master's, practicum, inquiry seminar, thesis, or internship. *Entrance requirements:* For master's, teaching certificate or license, bachelor's degree, minimum cumulative GPA of 2.75. Additional exam requirements/recommendations for international students: Recommended—TOEFL, IELTS, TSE. Electronic applications accepted. *Expenses: Tuition:* Full-time $6660; part-time $3330 per credit hour. *Required fees:* $360; $180 per credit hour. Tuition and fees vary according to program. *Faculty research:* Coaching, legal issues, strength and conditioning, sport management rating of perceived exertion, youth fitness, geriatric exercise science.

Auburn University, Graduate School, College of Education, School of Kinesiology, Auburn University, AL 36849. Offers exercise science (M Ed). *Accreditation:* NCATE. *Program availability:* Part-time. *Degree requirements:* For master's, thesis (for some programs); for doctorate, thesis/dissertation; for Ed S, exam, field project. *Entrance requirements:* For master's, GRE General Test; for doctorate and Ed S, GRE General Test, interview, master's degree. Electronic applications accepted. *Expenses:* Tuition, state resident: full-time $11,282; part-time $535 per credit hour. Tuition, nonresident: full-time $30,542; part-time $1605 per credit hour. *Required fees:* $826 per semester. Tuition and fees vary according to degree level and program. *Faculty research:* Biomechanics, exercise physiology, motor skill learning, school health, curriculum development.

Auburn University at Montgomery, College of Education, Department of Kinesiology, Montgomery, AL 36124-4023. Offers exercise science (M Ed); physical education (Ed S); sport management (M Ed). *Program availability:* Online learning. *Students:* Average age 29. 23 applicants, 74% accepted, 10 enrolled. In 2018, 18 master's awarded. *Entrance requirements:* For master's, GRE or MAT. Additional exam requirements/recommendations for international students: Recommended—TOEFL (minimum score 500 paper-based; 61 iBT), IELTS (minimum score 5.5), TSE (minimum score 44). *Application deadline:* For fall admission, 7/15 for international students; for spring admission, 11/15 for international students; for summer admission, 4/15 for international students. Applications are processed on a rolling basis. Application fee: $25. Electronic applications accepted. *Expenses: Tuition, area resident:* Full-time $7146; part-time $4764 per credit hour. Tuition, state resident: full-time $7146; part-time $4764 per credit hour. Tuition, nonresident: full-time $16,056; part-time $10,704 per credit hour. *International tuition:* $16,056 full-time. *Required fees:* $766. One-time fee: $25 full-time. *Financial support:* Teaching assistantships available. Financial award application deadline: 3/1; financial award applicants required to submit FAFSA. *Unit head:* Dr. George Schaefer, Head, 334-244-3887, Fax: 334-244-3835, E-mail: gschaefe@aum.edu. *Application contact:* Janis Bigelow, Graduate Advisor, 334-244-3135, E-mail: jbigelo1@aum.edu.
Website: http://www.education.aum.edu/academic-programs/academic-programs/kinesiology

Austin Peay State University, College of Graduate Studies, College of Behavioral and Health Sciences, Department of Health and Human Performance, Clarksville, TN 37044. Offers public health education (MS); sports and wellness leadership (MS). *Program availability:* Part-time, evening/weekend, online learning. *Faculty:* 8 full-time (4 women), 1 (woman) part-time/adjunct. *Students:* 18 full-time (8 women), 55 part-time (33 women); includes 21 minority (13 Black or African American, non-Hispanic/Latino; 1 Asian, non-Hispanic/Latino; 2 Hispanic/Latino; 5 Two or more races, non-Hispanic/Latino), 2 international. Average age 30. 81 applicants, 84% accepted, 54 enrolled. In 2018, 35 master's awarded. *Degree requirements:* For master's, comprehensive exam, thesis optional. *Entrance requirements:* For master's, GRE General Test, 3 letters of recommendation, minimum undergraduate GPA of 2.5. Additional exam requirements/recommendations for international students: Required—TOEFL (minimum score 500 paper-based). *Application deadline:* For fall admission, 8/21 priority date for domestic students. Applications are processed on a rolling basis. Application fee: $45 ($55 for international students). Electronic applications accepted. *Expenses: Tuition, area resident:* Part-time $450 per credit hour. Tuition, state resident: full-time $5987; part-time $450 per credit hour. Tuition, nonresident: full-time $8757; part-time $806 per credit hour. *Required fees:* $1583; $79.15 per credit hour. *Financial support:* Research assistantships with full tuition reimbursements, career-related internships or fieldwork, Federal Work-Study, institutionally sponsored loans, scholarships/grants, and unspecified assistantships available. Support available to part-time students. Financial award application deadline: 7/1; financial award applicants required to submit FAFSA. *Unit head:* Dr. Marcy Maurer, Chair, 931-221-6105, Fax: 931-221-7040, E-mail: maurerm@apsu.edu. *Application contact:* Megan Mitchell, Coordinator of Graduate Admissions, 931-221-6189, Fax: 931-221-7641, E-mail: mitchellm@apsu.edu.
Website: http://www.apsu.edu/hhp/index.php

Ball State University, Graduate School, College of Health, School of Kinesiology, Program in Exercise Science, Muncie, IN 47306. Offers exercise science (MA, MS), including biomechanics (MS), clinical exercise physiology, exercise physiology (MS), sports performance. *Program availability:* Part-time. *Entrance requirements:* For master's, GRE General Test, minimum baccalaureate GPA of 2.75 or 3.0 in latter half of baccalaureate, curriculum vitae, three letters of recommendation, transcripts of all prior course work; campus visit to meet faculty and see facilities (strongly encouraged). Additional exam requirements/recommendations for international students: Required—TOEFL (minimum score 550 paper-based; 79 iBT), IELTS (minimum score 6.5). Electronic applications accepted.

Ball State University, Graduate School, College of Health, School of Kinesiology, Program in Human Bioenergetics, Muncie, IN 47306. Offers PhD. *Program availability:* Part-time. *Degree requirements:* For doctorate, comprehensive exam, thesis/dissertation. *Entrance requirements:* For doctorate, GRE General Test, curriculum vitae, three letters of recommendation, electronic transcripts of all prior college work, minimum graduate GPA of 3.2, approval of Human Performance Lab selection committee; campus visit to meet faculty and see facilities (strongly encouraged). Additional exam requirements/recommendations for international students: Required—TOEFL (minimum score 550 paper-based; 79 iBT), IELTS (minimum score 6.5). Electronic applications accepted.

Barry University, School of Human Performance and Leisure Sciences, Programs in Movement Science, Specialization in Exercise Science, Miami Shores, FL 33161-6695. Offers MS. *Degree requirements:* For master's, comprehensive exam, thesis. *Entrance requirements:* For master's, GRE, minimum GPA of 3.0. Electronic applications accepted. *Faculty research:* Physiological adaptations to exercise.

Baylor University, Graduate School, Robbins College of Health and Human Sciences, Department of Health, Human Performance and Recreation, Waco, TX 76798. Offers athletic training (MS); exercise physiology (MS); kinesiology, exercise nutrition, and health promotion (PhD); sport pedagogy (MS). *Accreditation:* NCATE. *Program availability:* Part-time. *Students:* 72 full-time (40 women), 13 part-time (8 women); includes 20 minority (5 Black or African American, non-Hispanic/Latino; 1 American Indian or Alaska Native, non-Hispanic/Latino; 1 Asian, non-Hispanic/Latino; 7 Hispanic/Latino; 6 Two or more races, non-Hispanic/Latino), 5 international. 109 applicants, 59% accepted, 44 enrolled. In 2018, 35 master's, 2 doctorates awarded. *Degree requirements:* For master's, comprehensive exam, thesis optional; for doctorate, comprehensive exam, thesis/dissertation. *Entrance requirements:* For master's and doctorate, GRE General Test. Additional exam requirements/recommendations for international students: Required—TOEFL (minimum score 550 paper-based; 80 iBT). *Application deadline:* For fall admission, 2/1 priority date for domestic students, 2/1 for international students; for spring admission, 10/1 for domestic and international students. Applications are processed on a rolling basis. Application fee: $25. Electronic applications accepted. *Financial support:* In 2018–19, 60 students received support, including 1 research assistantship with full tuition reimbursement available (averaging $12,700 per year), 33 teaching assistantships with full tuition reimbursements available (averaging $7,650 per year); career-related internships or fieldwork, Federal Work-Study, institutionally sponsored loans, scholarships/grants, tuition waivers (full), and unspecified assistantships also available. Financial award application deadline: 2/1. *Faculty research:* Exercise testing, cardio-metabolic health, resistance exercise and training, nutritional intervention, population health, health promotion, global health epidemiology, coaching, natural resource management, stimulant misuse, diet, microbiome and colon cancer etiology. *Total annual research expenditures:* $250,118. *Unit head:* Dr. Jaeho Shim, Graduate Program Director, 254-710-4009, Fax: 254-710-3527, E-mail: joe_shim@baylor.edu. *Application contact:* Deepa Morris, Graduate Program Coordinator, 254-710-3526, Fax: 254-710-3527, E-mail: deepa_morris@baylor.edu.
Website: http://www.baylor.edu/HHPR/

Benedictine University, Graduate Programs, Program in Clinical Exercise Physiology, Lisle, IL 60532. Offers MS. *Program availability:* Part-time. *Faculty:* 4 part-time/adjunct (3 women). *Students:* 11 full-time (6 women), 6 part-time (3 women); includes 4 minority (1 Black or African American, non-Hispanic/Latino; 3 Hispanic/Latino). Average age 25. 6 applicants, 33% accepted. In 2018, 8 master's awarded. *Degree requirements:* For master's, comprehensive exam. *Entrance requirements:* For master's, Essay discussing your education addressing prior exercise physiology and/or exercise testing coursework and career goals; a personal or phone interview; two letters of recommendation: one that can address your academic potential (from a science instructor) and one that can address your interpersonal skills and work ethic (from an employer). Additional exam requirements/recommendations for international students: Required—TOEFL (minimum score 550 paper-based; 79 iBT), IELTS (minimum score 6.5). *Application deadline:* Applications are processed on a rolling basis. Application fee: $40. Electronic applications accepted. *Unit head:* Dr. Regina Schurman, Administrative Program Director, 630-829-2171, E-mail: rschurman@ben.edu. *Application contact:* Dr. Regina Schurman, Administrative Program Director, 630-829-2171, E-mail: rschurman@ben.edu.

Exercise and Sports Science

Bloomsburg University of Pennsylvania, School of Graduate Studies, College of Science and Technology, Department of Exercise Science and Athletics, Bloomsburg, PA 17815-1301. Offers clinical athletic training (MS); exercise science (MS). *Degree requirements:* For master's, thesis optional, practical clinical experience. *Entrance requirements:* For master's, GRE, minimum QPA of 3.0, related undergraduate coursework, interview. Additional exam requirements/recommendations for international students: Required—TOEFL (minimum score 550 paper-based; 79 iBT), IELTS. Electronic applications accepted.

Brigham Young University, Graduate Studies, College of Life Sciences, Department of Exercise Sciences, Provo, UT 84602. Offers athletic training (MS); exercise physiology (MS, PhD); exercise sciences (MS); health promotion (MS, PhD); physical medicine and rehabilitation (PhD). *Faculty:* 19 full-time (2 women). *Students:* 11 full-time (3 women), 7 part-time (3 women); includes 3 minority (all Asian, non-Hispanic/Latino). Average age 30. 16 applicants, 75% accepted, 10 enrolled. In 2018, 13 master's, 6 doctorates awarded. *Degree requirements:* For master's, thesis, oral defense; for doctorate, comprehensive exam, thesis/dissertation, oral defense, oral and written exams. *Entrance requirements:* For master's, GRE General Test (minimum score of 300, 4.0 on analytic writing portion), minimum GPA of 3.2 in last 60 hours of course work; for doctorate, GRE General Test (minimum score of 300, 4.0 on analytic writing portion), minimum GPA of 3.5 in last 60 hours of course work. Additional exam requirements/recommendations for international students: Required—TOEFL (minimum score 580 paper-based; 85 iBT), IELTS (minimum score 7). *Application deadline:* For fall admission, 2/1 for domestic and international students. Application fee: $50. Electronic applications accepted. *Financial support:* In 2018–19, 20 students received support, including 52 research assistantships (averaging $5,800 per year), 32 teaching assistantships (averaging $4,400 per year); scholarships/grants, unspecified assistantships, and 5 PhD full-tuition scholarships also available. Financial award application deadline: 4/15. *Faculty research:* Injury prevention and rehabilitation, human skeletal muscle adaptation, cardiovascular health and fitness, lifestyle modification and health promotion. *Total annual research expenditures:* $126,101. *Unit head:* Dr. Allen Parcell, Chair, 801-422-4450, Fax: 801-422-0555, E-mail: allenparcell@gmail.com. *Application contact:* Dr. J. Ty Hopkins, Graduate Coordinator, 801-422-1573, Fax: 801-422-0555, E-mail: tyhopkins@byu.edu.
Website: http://exsc.byu.edu/

Brooklyn College of the City University of New York, School of Natural and Behavioral Sciences, Department of Kinesiology, Brooklyn, NY 11210-2889. Offers exercise and sports science (MS); physical education teacher (MS); sport management (MS). *Program availability:* Part-time. *Degree requirements:* For master's, comprehensive exam or thesis. *Entrance requirements:* For master's, previous course work in physical education and education, minimum GPA of 3.0, 2 letters of recommendation, essay. Additional exam requirements/recommendations for international students: Required—TOEFL (minimum score 500 paper-based; 61 iBT). Electronic applications accepted. *Faculty research:* Exercise physiology, motor learning, sports psychology, women in athletics.

California Baptist University, Program in Kinesiology, Riverside, CA 92504-3206. Offers exercise science (MS); physical education (MS); sport management (MS). *Program availability:* Part-time, evening/weekend, 100% online, blended/hybrid learning. *Faculty:* 13 full-time (3 women), 5 part-time/adjunct (1 woman). *Students:* 75 full-time (40 women), 77 part-time (37 women); includes 79 minority (10 Black or African American, non-Hispanic/Latino; 1 American Indian or Alaska Native, non-Hispanic/Latino; 6 Asian, non-Hispanic/Latino; 50 Hispanic/Latino; 2 Native Hawaiian or other Pacific Islander, non-Hispanic/Latino; 10 Two or more races, non-Hispanic/Latino), 13 international. Average age 35. 71 applicants, 79% accepted, 56 enrolled. In 2018, 77 master's awarded. *Degree requirements:* For master's, comprehensive exam or research thesis. *Entrance requirements:* For master's, minimum undergraduate GPA of 2.75; completion of course prerequisites with minimum C grade; three recommendations; 500-word essay; resume; interview. Additional exam requirements/recommendations for international students: Required—TOEFL (minimum score 80 iBT). *Application deadline:* For fall admission, 8/1 priority date for domestic students, 7/1 for international students; for spring admission, 12/1 priority date for domestic students, 11/1 for international students. Applications are processed on a rolling basis. Application fee: $45. Electronic applications accepted. *Expenses:* $580 per unit. *Financial support:* In 2018–19, 21 students received support. Federal Work-Study, scholarships/grants, and unspecified assistantships available. Financial award applicants required to submit CSS PROFILE or FAFSA. *Faculty research:* Physical education pedagogy, exercise management and prevention of cardiovascular and metabolic diseases, sport management, immune function, carbohydrate oxidation. *Unit head:* Dr. David Pearson, Dean, College of Health Science, 951-343-4298, E-mail: dpearson@calbaptist.edu. *Application contact:* Dr. Dominick Sturz, Assistant, Health and Human Services, 951-343-2192, E-mail: dsturz@calbaptist.edu.
Website: http://www.calbaptist.edu/mskin/

California State University, Fresno, Division of Research and Graduate Studies, College of Health and Human Services, Department of Kinesiology, Fresno, CA 93740-8027. Offers exercise science (MA); general kinesiology (MA); sport administration (MA); sport psychology (MA). *Program availability:* Part-time, evening/weekend. *Degree requirements:* For master's, thesis or alternative. *Entrance requirements:* For master's, GRE General Test, minimum GPA of 2.7. Additional exam requirements/recommendations for international students: Required—TOEFL. Electronic applications accepted. *Faculty research:* Refugee education, homeless, geriatrics, fitness.

California State University, Long Beach, Graduate Studies, College of Health and Human Services, Department of Kinesiology, Long Beach, CA 90840. Offers adapted physical education (MA); coaching and student athlete development (MA); exercise physiology and nutrition (MS); exercise science (MS); individualized studies (MA); kinesiology (MA); pedagogical studies (MA); sport and exercise psychology (MS); sport management (MA); sports medicine and injury studies (MS). *Program availability:* Part-time. *Degree requirements:* For master's, oral and written comprehensive exams or thesis. *Entrance requirements:* For master's, GRE General Test, minimum GPA of 2.75 during previous 2 years of course work. *Application deadline:* Applications are processed on a rolling basis. Application fee: $55. Electronic applications accepted. *Expenses: Required fees:* $2628 per term. Tuition and fees vary according to class time, course level, course load, degree level, campus/location and program. *Financial support:* Federal Work-Study, institutionally sponsored loans, and scholarships/grants available. Financial award application deadline: 3/2; financial award applicants required to submit FAFSA. *Faculty research:* Pulmonary functioning, feedback and practice structure, strength training, history and politics of sports, special population research issues. *Unit head:* Tiffanye Vargas, Chair, 562-985-4051, E-mail: tiffanye.vargas@csulb.edu. *Application contact:* Tiffanye Vargas, Chair, 562-985-4051, E-mail: tiffanye.vargas@csulb.edu.
Website: https://fullerton-csm.symplicity.com/

California State University, Sacramento, College of Health and Human Services, Department of Kinesiology and Health Science, Sacramento, CA 95819. Offers exercise science (MS); movement studies (MS). *Accreditation:* APTA. *Program availability:* Part-time, evening/weekend. *Degree requirements:* For master's, thesis or project; writing proficiency exam. *Entrance requirements:* For master's, minimum overall GPA of 2.8, 3.0 in last 60 semester units; upper-division statistics course. Additional exam requirements/recommendations for international students: Required—TOEFL (minimum score 550 paper-based; 80 iBT); Recommended—IELTS, TSE. Electronic applications accepted. *Expenses:* Contact institution.

California University of Pennsylvania, School of Graduate Studies and Research, College of Education and Human Services, Department of Exercise Science and Sport Studies, California, PA 15419-1394. Offers applied sport science (MS); exercise science (MS), including group fitness leadership, nutrition, performance enhancement and injury prevention, rehabilitation science; group fitness leadership (MS); nutrition (MS); wellness coaching (MS). *Program availability:* Part-time, evening/weekend, online learning. *Degree requirements:* For master's, comprehensive exam, thesis optional. *Entrance requirements:* For master's, minimum GPA of 3.0. Additional exam requirements/recommendations for international students: Required—TOEFL (minimum score 550 paper-based; 80 iBT). Electronic applications accepted. *Expenses:* Contact institution. *Faculty research:* Reducing obesity in children, sport performance, creating unique biomechanical assessment techniques, web-based training for fitness professionals, Webcams.

Carroll University, Program in Exercise Physiology, Waukesha, WI 53186-5593. Offers MS.

Central Connecticut State University, School of Graduate Studies, School of Education and Professional Studies, Department of Physical Education and Human Performance, New Britain, CT 06050-4010. Offers physical education (MS). *Program availability:* Part-time, evening/weekend. *Faculty:* 8 full-time (3 women). *Students:* 14 full-time (7 women), 23 part-time (10 women); includes 6 minority (1 Black or African American, non-Hispanic/Latino; 1 Asian, non-Hispanic/Latino; 3 Hispanic/Latino; 1 Two or more races, non-Hispanic/Latino). Average age 28. 21 applicants, 62% accepted, 4 enrolled. In 2018, 20 master's, 3 other advanced degrees awarded. *Degree requirements:* For master's, comprehensive exam, thesis or alternative; for Certificate, qualifying exam. *Entrance requirements:* For master's, minimum GPA of 2.7, bachelor's degree in physical education (preferred), essay, interview, letters of recommendation. Additional exam requirements/recommendations for international students: Required—TOEFL (minimum score 550 paper-based; 79 iBT); Recommended—IELTS (minimum score 6.5). *Application deadline:* For fall admission, 6/1 for domestic students, 5/1 for international students; for spring admission, 11/1 for domestic and international students; for summer admission, 5/1 for domestic and international students. Applications are processed on a rolling basis. Application fee: $50. Electronic applications accepted. *Expenses: Tuition, area resident:* Full-time $7027; part-time $388 per credit. Tuition, state resident: full-time $9750; part-time $388 per credit. Tuition, nonresident: full-time $18,102; part-time $388 per credit. *International tuition:* $18,102 full-time. *Required fees:* $266 per semester. *Financial support:* In 2018–19, 10 students received support. Career-related internships or fieldwork, Federal Work-Study, scholarships/grants, and unspecified assistantships available. Support available to part-time students. Financial award application deadline: 3/1; financial award applicants required to submit FAFSA. *Faculty research:* Exercise science, athletic training, preparation of physical education for schools. *Unit head:* Dr. Jason Melnyk, Acting Chair, 860-832-2177, E-mail: melnykjaa@ccsu.edu. *Application contact:* Patricia Gardner, Associate Director of Graduate Studies, 860-832-2350, Fax: 860-832-2362. Website: http://www.ccsu.edu/pehp/

Central Michigan University, College of Graduate Studies, The Herbert H. and Grace A. Dow College of Health Professions, School of Health Sciences, Mount Pleasant, MI 48859. Offers exercise science (MA); health administration (DHA). *Program availability:* Part-time, evening/weekend, online learning. *Degree requirements:* For doctorate, comprehensive exam, thesis/dissertation. *Entrance requirements:* For doctorate, accredited master's or doctoral degree, 5 years of related work experience. Electronic applications accepted. *Faculty research:* Exercise science.

The Citadel, The Military College of South Carolina, Citadel Graduate College, School of Science and Mathematics, Department of Health, Exercise, and Sport Science, Charleston, SC 29409. Offers health, exercise, and sport science (MS); sport management (MA, Graduate Certificate). *Accreditation:* NCATE. *Program availability:* Part-time, evening/weekend. *Degree requirements:* For master's, comprehensive exam (for some programs), internship and professional portfolio (for some programs). *Entrance requirements:* For master's, GRE (minimum combined verbal and quantitative score 290) or MAT (minimum score 396), official transcript reflecting highest degree earned from regionally-accredited college or university, minimum undergraduate GPA of 2.5, 3 letters of recommendation, resume detailing previous work experience. Additional exam requirements/recommendations for international students: Required—TOEFL (minimum score 550 paper-based; 79 iBT). Electronic applications accepted. *Expenses:* Tuition, state resident: part-time $595 per credit hour. Tuition, nonresident: part-time $1020 per credit hour. *Required fees:* $90 per term.

The College of St. Scholastica, Graduate Studies, Department of Exercise Physiology, Duluth, MN 55811-4199. Offers MA. *Program availability:* Part-time. *Degree requirements:* For master's, thesis (for some programs). *Entrance requirements:* Additional exam requirements/recommendations for international students: Required—TOEFL (minimum score 550 paper-based; 79 iBT). Electronic applications accepted. *Faculty research:* Cardiovascular and metabolic responses, cardiorespiratory effects, orthostatic intolerance, lower extremity asymmetry.

Colorado State University, College of Health and Human Sciences, Department of Food Science and Human Nutrition, Fort Collins, CO 80523-1571. Offers dietetics (MS); food science and human nutrition (PhD); food science and nutrition (MS); nutrition and exercise science (MS). *Accreditation:* AND. *Program availability:* Part-time, 100% online, blended/hybrid learning. Terminal master's awarded for partial completion of doctoral program. *Degree requirements:* For master's, thesis; for doctorate, thesis/dissertation. *Entrance requirements:* For master's and doctorate, GRE (minimum 50th percentile), minimum GPA of 3.0; statement of purpose; resume; letters of recommendation; transcript. Additional exam requirements/recommendations for international students: Required—TOEFL (minimum score 550 paper-based; 80 iBT), IELTS (minimum score 6.5). Electronic applications accepted. *Expenses:* Contact institution. *Faculty research:* Community-based interventions on public health outcomes; consumer food handling behavior; adult learning and assessment; food and culture issues; role of microbes in ecosystem functioning.

Colorado State University, College of Health and Human Sciences, Department of Health and Exercise Science, Fort Collins, CO 80523-1582. Offers exercise science and nutrition (MS); human bioenergetics (PhD). Terminal master's awarded for partial completion of doctoral program. *Degree requirements:* For master's, thesis or alternative; for doctorate, comprehensive exam, thesis/dissertation. *Entrance requirements:* For master's, minimum GPA of 3.0; personal statement; identification of faculty mentor; for doctorate, minimum GPA of 3.0; personal statement; funding plan with PhD mentor for all 4 years; bachelor's or master's degree. Additional exam requirements/recommendations for international students: Recommended—TOEFL. Electronic applications accepted. *Expenses:* Tuition, state resident: full-time $10,520; part-time $4675 per credit hour. Tuition, nonresident: full-time $25,791; part-time

$11,462 per credit hour. *International tuition:* $25,791 full-time. *Required fees:* $2392; $576 $288. Tuition and fees vary according to course level, course load, degree level, program and student level. *Faculty research:* Age-related disease and disability, cardiovascular physiology, rehabilitation, neurophysiology, human performance.

Columbus State University, Graduate Studies, College of Education and Health Professions, Kinesiology & Health Sciences, Columbus, GA 31907-5645. Offers exercise science (MS); health and physical education (M Ed, MAT). *Program availability:* Part-time, evening/weekend. *Faculty:* 5 full-time (3 women). *Students:* 17 full-time (7 women), 14 part-time (8 women); includes 13 minority (8 Black or African American, non-Hispanic/Latino; 1 Asian, non-Hispanic/Latino; 3 Hispanic/Latino; 1 Two or more races, non-Hispanic/Latino). Average age 28. 23 applicants, 65% accepted, 12 enrolled. In 2018, 12 master's awarded. *Degree requirements:* For master's, thesis optional. *Entrance requirements:* For master's, GRE, minimum undergraduate GPA of 2.75. Additional exam requirements/recommendations for international students: Required—TOEFL (minimum score 550 paper-based; 79 iBT). *Application deadline:* For fall admission, 5/1 for domestic students, 4/1 for international students; for spring admission, 11/1 for domestic and international students; for summer admission, 2/1 for domestic students, 3/1 for international students. Applications are processed on a rolling basis. Application fee: $50. Electronic applications accepted. *Expenses: Tuition, area resident:* Full-time $4924; part-time $618 per credit hour. Tuition, state resident: full-time $4924; part-time $618 per credit hour. Tuition, nonresident: full-time $19,218; part-time $2403 per credit hour. *International tuition:* $19,218 full-time. *Required fees:* $1870; $802. Tuition and fees vary according to course load, degree level and program. *Financial support:* In 2018–19, 4 students received support, including 7 research assistantships (averaging $3,000 per year). Financial award application deadline: 5/15; financial award applicants required to submit FAFSA. *Unit head:* Dr. Clay Nicks, Chair, 706-507-8293, E-mail: nicks_clayton@columbusstate.edu. *Application contact:* Catrina Smith-Edmond, Assistant Director for Graduate and Global Admission, 706-507-8824, Fax: 706-568-5091, E-mail: smithedmond_catrina@columbusstate.edu. Website: http://hpex.columbusstate.edu/

Concordia University, School of Graduate Studies, Faculty of Arts and Science, Department of Exercise Science, Montréal, QC H3G 1M8, Canada. Offers M Sc.

Concordia University Chicago, College of Graduate Studies, Program in Human Services, River Forest, IL 60305-1499. Offers human services (MA), including administration, exercise science. *Program availability:* Part-time, evening/weekend, 100% online. *Degree requirements:* For master's, comprehensive exam, thesis. *Entrance requirements:* For master's, minimum GPA of 2.9. Additional exam requirements/recommendations for international students: Required—TOEFL (minimum score 550 paper-based). Electronic applications accepted.

Concordia University, St. Paul, College of Health and Science, St. Paul, MN 55104-5494. Offers exercise science (MS); orthotics and prosthetics (MS); physical therapy (DPT); sports management (MA). *Program availability:* Part-time, evening/weekend, 100% online, blended/hybrid learning. *Faculty:* 16 full-time (9 women), 15 part-time/adjunct (8 women). *Students:* 247 full-time (132 women), 27 part-time (9 women); includes 43 minority (18 Black or African American, non-Hispanic/Latino; 1 American Indian or Alaska Native, non-Hispanic/Latino; 4 Asian, non-Hispanic/Latino; 12 Hispanic/Latino; 8 Two or more races, non-Hispanic/Latino), 5 international. Average age 28. 241 applicants, 47% accepted, 86 enrolled. In 2018, 79 master's, 26 doctorates awarded. *Degree requirements:* For master's, comprehensive exam (for some programs), thesis (for some programs); for doctorate, at least one 8-12 week clinical rotation outside the St. Paul area. *Entrance requirements:* For master's, official transcripts from regionally-accredited institution stating the conferral of a bachelor's degree with minimum cumulative GPA of 3.0; personal statement; resume; for doctorate, GRE, official transcript from regionally-accredited institution showing bachelor's degree and minimum coursework GPA of 3.0; 100 physical therapy observation hours; two letters of professional recommendation. Additional exam requirements/recommendations for international students: Recommended—TOEFL (minimum score 547 paper-based; 78 iBT), IELTS (minimum score 6), TSE (minimum score 52). *Application deadline:* For fall admission, 4/1 for domestic students. Applications are processed on a rolling basis. Application fee: $0. Electronic applications accepted. *Expenses:* $475 per credit for 33 credits (for MS), $515 a credit for 36 credits (for MS in Orthotics and Prosthetics), $499 per credit for 36 credits (for MS in Nursing), $850 per credit for 111 credits (for DPT). *Financial support:* In 2018–19, 74 students received support. Federal Work-Study, scholarships/grants, and unspecified assistantships available. Financial award applicants required to submit FAFSA. *Faculty research:* Balance and vestibular function, shoulder kinematics, blood pressure, virtual training and performance, early childhood developmental screening. *Unit head:* Dr. Katie Fischer, Dean, 651-641-8735, E-mail: fischer@csp.edu. *Application contact:* Amber Faletti, Director of Enrollment Management, 651-641-8838, Fax: 651-603-6320, E-mail: faletti@csp.edu.

Delaware State University, Graduate Programs, College of Education, Health and Public Policy, Department of Sport Sciences, Dover, DE 19901-2277. Offers sport administration (MS). *Entrance requirements:* Additional exam requirements/recommendations for international students: Required—TOEFL (minimum score 550 paper-based). Electronic applications accepted.

Delta State University, Graduate Programs, College of Education, Division of Health, Physical Education, and Recreation, Cleveland, MS 38733-0001. Offers health, physical education, and recreation (M Ed); sport and human performance (MS). *Program availability:* Part-time, evening/weekend. *Degree requirements:* For master's, thesis optional. *Entrance requirements:* For master's, GRE General Test or MAT, Class A teaching certificate. *Expenses: Tuition, area resident:* Full-time $7076; part-time $393 per credit hour. Tuition, state resident: full-time $7076; part-time $393 per credit hour. Tuition, nonresident: full-time $7076; part-time $393 per credit hour. *International tuition:* $7076 full-time. *Required fees:* $170; $18.90 per credit hour. $9.45 per semester. Part-time tuition and fees vary according to program. *Faculty research:* Blood pressure, body fat, power and reaction time, learning disorders of athletes, effects of walking.

East Carolina University, Graduate School, College of Health and Human Performance, Department of Kinesiology, Greenville, NC 27858-4353. Offers adapted physical education (MS); bioenergetics and exercise science (PhD); biomechanics and motor control (MS); exercise physiology (MS); physical activity promotion (MS); physical education (MA Ed, MAT); physical education clinical supervision (Certificate); physical education pedagogy (MS); sport and exercise psychology (MS); sport management (MS, Certificate). *Application deadline:* For fall admission, 2/1 priority date for domestic students, 2/1 for international students. *Expenses: Tuition, area resident:* Full-time $4749. Tuition, state resident: full-time $4749. Tuition, nonresident: full-time $17,898. *International tuition:* $17,898 full-time. *Required fees:* $2787. Part-time tuition and fees vary according to course load and program. *Financial support:* Application deadline: 2/1. *Unit head:* Dr. Stacey Altman, Chair, 252-328-4632, E-mail: altmans@ecu.edu. *Application contact:* Graduate School Admissions, 252-328-6012, Fax: 252-328-6071, E-mail: gradschool@ecu.edu. Website: https://hhp.ecu.edu/kine/

Eastern Kentucky University, The Graduate School, College of Health Sciences, Department of Exercise and Sport Science, Richmond, KY 40475-3102. Offers exercise and sport science (MS); exercise and wellness (MS); sports administration (MS). *Program availability:* Part-time. *Entrance requirements:* For master's, GRE General Test (minimum score 700 verbal and quantitative), minimum GPA of 2.5 (for most), minimum GPA of 3.0 (analytical writing). *Faculty research:* Nutrition and exercise.

Eastern Michigan University, Graduate School, College of Health and Human Services, School of Health Promotion and Human Performance, Programs in Exercise Physiology, Ypsilanti, MI 48197. Offers exercise physiology (MS); sports medicine-biomechanics (MS); sports medicine-corporate adult fitness (MS); sports medicine-exercise physiology (MS). *Program availability:* Part-time, evening/weekend. *Students:* 13 full-time (4 women), 11 part-time (4 women); includes 5 minority (1 Black or African American, non-Hispanic/Latino; 1 Asian, non-Hispanic/Latino; 2 Hispanic/Latino; 1 Two or more races, non-Hispanic/Latino), 2 international. Average age 29. 40 applicants, 63% accepted, 10 enrolled. In 2018, 15 master's awarded. *Degree requirements:* For master's, comprehensive exam, thesis or 450-hour internship. *Entrance requirements:* Additional exam requirements/recommendations for international students: Required—TOEFL. *Application deadline:* For fall admission, 8/1 for domestic students, 5/1 for international students; for winter admission, 12/1 for domestic students, 10/1 for international students; for spring admission, 3/15 for domestic students, 3/1 for international students. Application fee: $45. *Application contact:* Dr. Becca Moore, Program Coordinator, 734-487-2824, Fax: 734-487-2024, E-mail: rmoore41@emich.edu.

Eastern New Mexico University, Graduate School, College of Education and Technology, Department of Health and Physical Education, Portales, NM 88130. Offers sport administration (MS), including coaching, sport science. *Program availability:* Part-time. *Degree requirements:* For master's, comprehensive exam, thesis optional. *Entrance requirements:* For master's, minimum GPA of 3.0, 15 hours of leveling courses without bachelor's degree in physical education, two references. Additional exam requirements/recommendations for international students: Required—TOEFL (minimum score 550 paper-based; 79 iBT), IELTS (minimum score 6). Electronic applications accepted. *Expenses: Tuition, area resident:* Full-time $6776. Tuition, state resident: full-time $6776; part-time $282 per credit hour. Tuition, nonresident: full-time $8986; part-time $374 per credit hour. *Required fees:* $60 per semester. One-time fee: $25.

Eastern Washington University, Graduate Studies, College of Arts, Letters and Education, Department of Physical Education, Health and Recreation, Cheney, WA 99004-2431. Offers exercise science (MS); sports and recreation administration (MS). *Degree requirements:* For master's, comprehensive exam, thesis or alternative. *Entrance requirements:* For master's, minimum GPA of 3.0. Additional exam requirements/recommendations for international students: Required—TOEFL (minimum score 580 paper-based; 92 iBT), IELTS (minimum score 7), PTE (minimum score 63). Electronic applications accepted.

East Tennessee State University, School of Graduate Studies, College of Education, Department of Sport, Exercise, Recreation, and Kinesiology, Johnson City, TN 37614-1701. Offers sport management (MA); sport physiology and performance (PhD), including sport performance, sport physiology; sport science and coach education (MS), including applied sport science, strength and conditioning. *Program availability:* Part-time, evening/weekend. Terminal master's awarded for partial completion of doctoral program. *Degree requirements:* For master's, comprehensive exam, thesis or internship; for doctorate, comprehensive exam, thesis/dissertation, 2-semester residency. *Entrance requirements:* For master's, GRE General Test or GMAT, undergraduate degree in related field; minimum GPA of 3.0; resume; three references; essay explaining goals and reasons for pursuing degree; for doctorate, GRE, resume; 4 letters of recommendation; master's or bachelor's degree in related field; minimum GPA of 3.4 overall with master's, 3.0 with bachelor's; interview. Additional exam requirements/recommendations for international students: Required—TOEFL (minimum score 550 paper-based; 79 iBT). Electronic applications accepted. *Faculty research:* Methods of training for individual and team sports, enhancing acute sport performance, fatigue management in athletes, risk management, facilities management, motorsport.

Fairmont State University, Programs in Education, Fairmont, WV 26554. Offers digital media, new literacies and learning (M Ed); education (MAT); exercise science, fitness and wellness (M Ed); professional studies (M Ed); reading (M Ed); special education (M Ed). *Accreditation:* NCATE. *Program availability:* Part-time, evening/weekend, 100% online. *Entrance requirements:* For master's, GRE. Additional exam requirements/recommendations for international students: Required—TOEFL (minimum score 80 iBT), IELTS (minimum score 6.5). Electronic applications accepted.

Florida Atlantic University, Charles E. Schmidt College of Science, Department of Exercise Science and Health Promotion, Boca Raton, FL 33431-0991. Offers MS. *Program availability:* Part-time, evening/weekend. *Faculty:* 7 full-time (2 women). *Students:* 34 full-time (14 women), 14 part-time (10 women); includes 14 minority (5 Black or African American, non-Hispanic/Latino; 7 Hispanic/Latino; 2 Two or more races, non-Hispanic/Latino), 3 international. Average age 29. 65 applicants, 65% accepted, 23 enrolled. In 2018, 29 master's awarded. *Degree requirements:* For master's, comprehensive exam, thesis optional. *Entrance requirements:* For master's, GRE General Test, minimum GPA of 3.0 during last 60 hours of course work. Additional exam requirements/recommendations for international students: Required—TOEFL (minimum score 500 paper-based; 61 iBT), IELTS (minimum score 6). *Application deadline:* For fall admission, 7/1 priority date for domestic students, 2/15 for international students; for spring admission, 11/1 priority date for domestic students, 7/15 for international students. Applications are processed on a rolling basis. Application fee: $30. *Expenses: Tuition, area resident:* Full-time $7400; part-time $369.82 per credit. Tuition, state resident: full-time $7400; part-time $369.82 per credit. Tuition, nonresident: full-time $20,496; part-time $1024.81 per credit. *Financial support:* Research assistantships with partial tuition reimbursements, teaching assistantships with partial tuition reimbursements, and career-related internships or fieldwork available. *Faculty research:* Pulmonary limitations during exercise, metabolism regulation, determinants of performance, age-related change in functional mobility and geriatric exercise, behavioral change aimed at promoting active lifestyles. *Unit head:* Dr. Michael Whitehurst, 561-297-2317, E-mail: eshpinfo@fau.edu. *Application contact:* Dr. Michael Whitehurst, 561-297-2317, E-mail: eshpinfo@fau.edu. Website: http://www.coe.fau.edu/academicdepartments/eshp/

Florida State University, The Graduate School, College of Human Sciences, Department of Nutrition, Food and Exercise Sciences, Tallahassee, FL 32306-1493. Offers exercise physiology (MS, PhD); nutrition and food science (MS, PhD), including nutrition education and health promotion (MS); sports nutrition (MS); sports sciences (MS). *Program availability:* Part-time. *Faculty:* 26 full-time (12 women). *Students:* 71 full-time (49 women), 15 part-time (7 women); includes 15 minority (1 Black or African American, non-Hispanic/Latino; 2 Asian, non-Hispanic/Latino; 1 Hispanic/Latino; 11 Two or more races, non-Hispanic/Latino), 12 international. 177 applicants, 37% accepted, 31 enrolled. In 2018, 24 master's, 6 doctorates awarded. *Degree requirements:* For master's, thesis optional; for doctorate, thesis/dissertation, preliminary examination, minimum of 24 credit hours dissertation, dissertation defense. *Entrance requirements:* For master's, GRE General Test, minimum upper-division GPA of 3.0; for doctorate, GRE General Test, minimum upper-division GPA of 3.0 or awarded master's degree. Additional exam requirements/recommendations for international students: Required—

TOEFL (minimum score 550 paper-based; 80 iBT). *Application deadline:* For fall admission, 4/1 for domestic and international students; for spring admission, 10/1 for domestic and international students. Applications are processed on a rolling basis. Application fee: $30. Electronic applications accepted. *Expenses: Tuition, area resident:* Part-time $479.32 per credit hour. Tuition and fees vary according to campus/location and program. *Financial support:* In 2018–19, 45 students received support, including 12 research assistantships with full tuition reimbursements available (averaging $25,000 per year), 30 teaching assistantships with full tuition reimbursements available (averaging $25,000 per year); career-related internships or fieldwork, Federal Work-Study, institutionally sponsored loans, scholarships/grants, and unspecified assistantships also available. Financial award application deadline: 2/1; financial award applicants required to submit FAFSA. *Faculty research:* Nutrition and health, sports nutrition, energy and human performance, strength training, functional performance, cardiovascular physiology, sarcopenia, chronic disease and aging, functional food, food safety, food allergy, and food safety/quality detection methods. *Total annual research expenditures:* $1.1 million. *Unit head:* Dr. Chester Ray, Department Chair, 850-644-1850, Fax: 850-645-5000, E-mail: caray@fsu.edu. *Application contact:* Mary-Sue McLemore, Academic Support Assistant, 850-644-1117, E-mail: mmclemore@fsu.edu.
Website: https://humansciences.fsu.edu/nutrition-food-exercise-sciences/students/graduate-programs/

Gannon University, School of Graduate Studies, Morosky College of Health Professions and Sciences, School of Health Professions, Program in Sport and Exercise Science, Erie, PA 16541-0001. Offers human performance (MS). *Program availability:* Part-time, evening/weekend. *Degree requirements:* For master's, thesis (for some programs), internship (for some programs). *Entrance requirements:* For master's, undergraduate degree in exercise science, kinesiology, human performance, sports medicine, or related field with minimum GPA of 2.75; 3 letters of recommendation. Additional exam requirements/recommendations for international students: Required—TOEFL (minimum score 79 iBT). Electronic applications accepted. Application fee is waived when completed online.

Gardner-Webb University, Graduate School, Department of Physical Education, Wellness, and Sport Studies, Boiling Springs, NC 28017. Offers sport science and pedagogy (MA). *Program availability:* Part-time, evening/weekend. *Degree requirements:* For master's, comprehensive exam. *Entrance requirements:* For master's, GRE General Test or NTE, PRAXIS, minimum GPA of 2.5. Electronic applications accepted. *Expenses:* Contact institution.

George Mason University, College of Education and Human Development, School of Recreation, Health and Tourism, Manassas, VA 20110. Offers athletic training (MS); exercise, fitness, and health promotion (MS), including advanced practitioner, wellness practitioner; international sport management (Certificate); recreation, health and tourism (Certificate); sport management (MS), including sport and recreation studies. *Program availability:* Part-time, evening/weekend. *Faculty:* 33 full-time (15 women), 84 part-time/adjunct (44 women). *Students:* 76 full-time (33 women), 21 part-time (5 women); includes 32 minority (25 Black or African American, non-Hispanic/Latino; 1 American Indian or Alaska Native, non-Hispanic/Latino; 1 Asian, non-Hispanic/Latino; 3 Hispanic/Latino; 1 Native Hawaiian or other Pacific Islander, non-Hispanic/Latino; 1 Two or more races, non-Hispanic/Latino), 17 international. Average age 26. 77 applicants, 88% accepted, 41 enrolled. In 2018, 26 master's, 1 other advanced degree awarded. *Entrance requirements:* For master's, 3 letters of recommendation; official transcripts; expanded goals statement; undergraduate course in statistics and minimum GPA of 3.0 in last 60 credit hours and overall (for MS in sport and recreation studies); baccalaureate degree related to kinesiology, exercise science or athletic training (for MS in exercise, fitness and health promotion). Additional exam requirements/recommendations for international students: Required—TOEFL (minimum score 575 paper-based; 88 iBT), IELTS (minimum score 6.5), PTE (minimum score 59). *Application deadline:* For fall admission, 4/2 priority date for domestic and international students; for spring admission, 11/1 for domestic and international students. Application fee: $75 ($80 for international students). Electronic applications accepted. *Financial support:* In 2018–19, 6 students received support, including 6 research assistantships with tuition reimbursements available (averaging $7,242 per year); career-related internships or fieldwork, Federal Work-Study, scholarships/grants, unspecified assistantships, and health care benefits (for full-time research or teaching assistantship recipients) also available. Support available to part-time students. Financial award application deadline: 3/1; financial award applicants required to submit FAFSA. *Faculty research:* Sport for development and peace, sport analytics, leadership and coaching, diversity and inclusion in sport, sport communication. *Total annual research expenditures:* $826,386. *Unit head:* Martin Ford, Senior Associate Dean, 703-993-2004, E-mail: mford@gmu.edu. *Application contact:* Lindsey Olson, Office Assistant, 703-993-2098, Fax: 703-993-2025, E-mail: lolson7@gmu.edu.
Website: http://rht.gmu.edu/

The George Washington University, Milken Institute School of Public Health, Department of Exercise and Nutrition Sciences, Washington, DC 20052. Offers MS. *Students:* 33 full-time (21 women), 13 part-time (8 women); includes 15 minority (6 Black or African American, non-Hispanic/Latino; 1 American Indian or Alaska Native, non-Hispanic/Latino; 3 Asian, non-Hispanic/Latino; 1 Hispanic/Latino; 1 Native Hawaiian or other Pacific Islander, non-Hispanic/Latino; 3 Two or more races, non-Hispanic/Latino). Average age 28. 95 applicants, 72% accepted, 19 enrolled. In 2018, 21 master's awarded. *Degree requirements:* For master's, comprehensive exam, thesis. *Entrance requirements:* For master's, GRE General Test or MAT. Additional exam requirements/recommendations for international students: Required—TOEFL. *Application deadline:* For fall admission, 4/15 priority date for domestic students, 4/15 for international students; for spring admission, 11/1 for domestic and international students. Applications are processed on a rolling basis. Application fee: $75. *Financial support:* In 2018–19, 12 students received support. Tuition waivers available. Financial award application deadline: 2/15. *Faculty research:* Fitness and cardiac rehabilitation, exercise testing, women in exercise. *Unit head:* Dr. Loretta DiPietro, Chair, 202-994-4910, Fax: 202-994-1420, E-mail: ldp1@gwu.edu. *Application contact:* Jane Smith, Director of Admissions, 202-994-0248, Fax: 202-994-1860, E-mail: sphhsinfo@gwumc.edu.

Georgia College & State University, Graduate School, College of Health Sciences, School of Health and Human Performance, Milledgeville, GA 31061. Offers health and human performance (MS), including health performance, health promotion; kinesiology/health education (MAT). *Accreditation:* NCATE (one or more programs are accredited). *Program availability:* Part-time, 100% online. *Degree requirements:* For master's, thesis (for some programs), completed in 6 years with minimum GPA of 3.0 (for MS); minimum GPA of 3.0 and electronic teaching portfolio (for MAT). *Entrance requirements:* For master's, GRE with minimum score of 297 or MAT with minimum score of 385 (for MS); GRE with minimum score of 297, MAT 385, SAT 1000, ACT 43, or GACE with 250 on each section (for MAT), resume, 3 professional references; minimum GPA of 2.75 in upper-level undergraduate courses and undergraduate statistics course (for MS); minimum GPA of 2.75 on upper-division major courses (for MAT). Electronic applications accepted. *Expenses:* Contact institution.

Georgia State University, College of Education and Human Development, Department of Kinesiology and Health, Program in Exercise Science, Atlanta, GA 30302-3083. Offers MS. *Entrance requirements:* For master's, GRE General Test, minimum GPA of 2.5. Application fee: $50. *Expenses: Tuition, area resident:* Full-time $9360; part-time $390 per credit hour. Tuition, state resident: full-time $9360; part-time $390 per credit hour. Tuition, nonresident: full-time $30,024; part-time $1251 per credit hour. *International tuition:* $30,024 full-time. *Required fees:* $2128. *Financial support:* Research assistantships available. *Faculty research:* Aging, exercise metabolism, biomechanics and ergonomics, blood pressure regulation, exercise performance. *Unit head:* Dr. Jacalyn Lea Lund, Chair, 404-413-8051, E-mail: jlund@gsu.edu. *Application contact:* Dr. Rebecca Ellis, Program Coordinator, 404-413-8370, E-mail: rellis@gsu.edu.
Website: https://education.gsu.edu/kh/

Hofstra University, School of Health Professions and Human Services, Programs in Health, Hempstead, NY 11549. Offers foundations of public health (Advanced Certificate); health administration (MHA); health informatics (MS); occupational therapy (MS); public health (MPH); security and privacy in health information systems (Advanced Certificate); sports science (MS); teacher of students with speech-language disabilities (Advanced Certificate). *Program availability:* Part-time, evening/weekend. *Students:* 307 full-time (231 women), 101 part-time (72 women); includes 207 minority (76 Black or African American, non-Hispanic/Latino; 1 American Indian or Alaska Native, non-Hispanic/Latino; 69 Asian, non-Hispanic/Latino; 48 Hispanic/Latino; 9 Native Hawaiian or other Pacific Islander, non-Hispanic/Latino; 4 Two or more races, non-Hispanic/Latino), 21 international. Average age 28. 756 applicants, 46% accepted, 151 enrolled. In 2018, 132 master's, 1 other advanced degree awarded. *Degree requirements:* For master's, internship, minimum GPA of 3.0. *Entrance requirements:* For master's, interview, 2 letters of recommendation, essay, resume. Additional exam requirements/recommendations for international students: Required—TOEFL (minimum score 550 paper-based; 80 iBT). *Application deadline:* Applications are processed on a rolling basis. Application fee: $75. Electronic applications accepted. *Financial support:* In 2018–19, 151 students received support, including 113 fellowships with full and partial tuition reimbursements available (averaging $2,868 per year), 6 research assistantships with full and partial tuition reimbursements available (averaging $4,575 per year); career-related internships or fieldwork, Federal Work-Study, institutionally sponsored loans, scholarships/grants, traineeships, tuition waivers (full and partial), unspecified assistantships, and scholarships and endowed scholarships also available. Support available to part-time students. Financial award applicants required to submit FAFSA. *Faculty research:* Health economics, policy and long-term care; palliative care, neurorehabilitation, neurovision; public health and health inequities, particularly in the american suburbs and minority communities; exercise and nutritional strategies; hiv, sti, sexual health. *Unit head:* Dr. Corinne Kyriacou, Chairperson, 516-463-4553, E-mail: corinne.m.kyriacou@hofstra.edu. *Application contact:* Sunil Samuel, Assistant Vice President of Admissions, 516-463-4723, Fax: 516-463-4664, E-mail: graduateadmission@hofstra.edu.
Website: http://www.hofstra.edu/academics/colleges/healthscienceshumanservices/

Howard University, Graduate School, Department of Health, Human Performance and Leisure Studies, Washington, DC 20059-0002. Offers exercise physiology (MS); health education (MS); sports studies (MS), including sociology of sports, sports management; urban recreation (MS), including leisure studies. *Program availability:* Part-time, evening/weekend. *Degree requirements:* For master's, comprehensive exam, thesis. *Entrance requirements:* For master's, BS in human performance or related field. Additional exam requirements/recommendations for international students: Recommended—TOEFL. Electronic applications accepted. *Faculty research:* Health promotion, cardiovascular hypertension, physical activity, sport and human rights issues.

Indiana University Bloomington, School of Public Health, Department of Kinesiology, Bloomington, IN 47405. Offers applied sport science (MS); athletic administration/sport management (MS); athletic training (MS); biomechanics (MS); ergonomics (MS); exercise physiology (MS); human performance (PhD), including biomechanics, exercise physiology, motor learning/control, sport management; motor learning/control (MS); physical activity (MPH); physical activity, fitness and wellness (MS). *Program availability:* Part-time. Terminal master's awarded for partial completion of doctoral program. *Degree requirements:* For master's, thesis optional; for doctorate, variable foreign language requirement, comprehensive exam, thesis/dissertation. *Entrance requirements:* For master's, GRE General Test, minimum GPA of 2.8; for doctorate, GRE General Test, minimum graduate GPA of 3.5, undergraduate 3.0. Additional exam requirements/recommendations for international students: Required—TOEFL (minimum score 80 iBT). *Faculty research:* Exercise physiology and biochemistry, sports biomechanics, human motor control, adaptation of fitness and exercise to special populations.

Indiana University of Pennsylvania, School of Graduate Studies and Research, College of Health and Human Services, Department of Kinesiology, Health, and Sport Science, MS Program in Sport Science/Exercise Science, Indiana, PA 15705. Offers MS. *Program availability:* Part-time. *Faculty:* 11 full-time (3 women). *Students:* 17 full-time (7 women), 1 (woman) part-time; includes 2 minority (1 Hispanic/Latino; 1 Two or more races, non-Hispanic/Latino). Average age 24. 35 applicants, 86% accepted, 15 enrolled. In 2018, 20 master's awarded. *Degree requirements:* For master's, thesis optional. *Entrance requirements:* For master's, 2 letters of recommendation. Additional exam requirements/recommendations for international students: Required—TOEFL (minimum score 540 paper-based). *Application deadline:* Applications are processed on a rolling basis. Application fee: $50. Electronic applications accepted. *Expenses:* Tuition, state resident: full-time $12,384; part-time $516 per credit hour. Tuition, nonresident: full-time $18,576; part-time $774 per credit hour. *Required fees:* $4454; $186 per credit hour. $65 per semester. Tuition and fees vary according to program and reciprocity agreements. *Financial support:* In 2018–19, 18 research assistantships with tuition reimbursements (averaging $3,202 per year) were awarded; fellowships with partial tuition reimbursements, career-related internships or fieldwork, scholarships/grants, and unspecified assistantships also available. Support available to part-time students. Financial award application deadline: 4/15; financial award applicants required to submit FAFSA. *Unit head:* Dr. Madeline Bayles, Coordinator, 724-357-7835, E-mail: mpbayles@iup.edu. *Application contact:* Dr. Madeline Bayles, Coordinator, 724-357-7835, E-mail: mpbayles@iup.edu.
Website: http://www.iup.edu/kines/grad/sport-science-exercise-science-ms/default.aspx

Indiana University of Pennsylvania, School of Graduate Studies and Research, College of Health and Human Services, Department of Kinesiology, Health, and Sport Science, Program in Sport Science/Sport Studies, Indiana, PA 15705. Offers MS. *Program availability:* Part-time. *Faculty:* 11 full-time (3 women). *Students:* 1 (woman) full-time, 3 part-time (1 woman), 1 international. Average age 30. 5 applicants, 60% accepted, 1 enrolled. In 2018, 4 master's awarded. *Degree requirements:* For master's, thesis optional. *Entrance requirements:* Additional exam requirements/recommendations for international students: Required—TOEFL (minimum score 540 paper-based). *Application deadline:* Applications are processed on a rolling basis. Application fee: $50. Electronic applications accepted. *Expenses:* Contact institution. *Financial support:* Research assistantships with tuition reimbursements, career-related internships or fieldwork, Federal Work-Study, scholarships/grants, and unspecified assistantships available. Support available to part-time students. Financial award

application deadline: 4/15; financial award applicants required to submit FAFSA. *Unit head:* Dr. Richard Hsiao, Graduate Coordinator, 724-357-0123, E-mail: hsiao@iup.edu. *Application contact:* Dr. Richard Hsiao, Graduate Coordinator, 724-357-0123, E-mail: hsiao@iup.edu.
Website: http://www.iup.edu/grad/sportscience/default.aspx

Inter American University of Puerto Rico, Metropolitan Campus, Graduate Programs, Program in Physical Education, San Juan, PR 00919-1293. Offers teaching of physical education (MA); training and sport performance (MA). *Degree requirements:* For master's, comprehensive exam. *Entrance requirements:* For master's, GRE or EXADEP, interview. Electronic applications accepted.

Iowa State University of Science and Technology, Program in Diet and Exercise, Ames, IA 50011. Offers MS. *Entrance requirements:* For master's, GRE, minimum GPA of 3.5, 3 letters of recommendation. Additional exam requirements/recommendations for international students: Required—TOEFL (minimum score 550 paper-based; 79 iBT), IELTS (minimum score 6.5). Electronic applications accepted.

Ithaca College, School of Health Sciences and Human Performance, Program in Exercise and Sport Sciences, Ithaca, NY 14850. Offers MS. *Program availability:* Part-time. *Faculty:* 13 full-time (4 women). *Students:* 25 full-time (14 women), 19 part-time (12 women); includes 6 minority (4 Black or African American, non-Hispanic/Latino; 1 Hispanic/Latino; 1 Two or more races, non-Hispanic/Latino), 1 international. Average age 23. 104 applicants, 61% accepted, 21 enrolled. In 2018, 19 master's awarded. *Degree requirements:* For master's, thesis optional. *Entrance requirements:* For master's, GRE General Test. Additional exam requirements/recommendations for international students: Required—TOEFL (minimum score 550 paper-based; 80 iBT). *Application deadline:* For fall admission, 3/1 for domestic and international students. Applications are processed on a rolling basis. Application fee: $40. Electronic applications accepted. *Expenses:* Contact institution. *Financial support:* In 2018–19, 28 students received support, including 28 research assistantships (averaging $14,880 per year); career-related internships or fieldwork, Federal Work-Study, and scholarships/grants also available. Support available to part-time students. Financial award application deadline: 3/1; financial award applicants required to submit FAFSA. *Unit head:* Dr. Deborah King, Chair, 607-274-1479, Fax: 607-274-1263, E-mail: dking@ithaca.edu. *Application contact:* Nicole Eversley Bradwell, Director, Office of Admission, 800-429-4274, Fax: 607-274-1263, E-mail: admission@ithaca.edu.
Website: http://www.ithaca.edu/gradprograms/ess

James Madison University, The Graduate School, College of Health and Behavioral Studies, Program in Kinesiology, Harrisonburg, VA 22807. Offers clinical exercise physiology (MS); exercise physiology (MS); kinesiology (MAT, MS); nutrition and exercise (MS); physical and health education (MAT); sport and recreation leadership (MS). *Program availability:* Part-time, evening/weekend. *Students:* 33 full-time (11 women); includes 3 minority (2 Black or African American, non-Hispanic/Latino; 1 Hispanic/Latino). Average age 30. In 2018, 18 master's awarded. Electronic applications accepted. *Expenses:* Tuition, state resident: full-time $10,848. Tuition, nonresident: full-time $27,888. *Required fees:* $1128. *Financial support:* In 2018–19, 20 students received support, including teaching assistantships with full tuition reimbursements available (averaging $8,837 per year); Federal Work-Study and assistantships (averaging $7911), athletic assistantships (averaging $9284) also available. Financial award application deadline: 3/1; financial award applicants required to submit FAFSA. *Unit head:* Dr. Christopher J. Womack, Department Head, 540-568-6145, E-mail: womackcx@jmu.edu. *Application contact:* Lynette D. Michael, Director of Graduate Admissions, 540-568-6131 Ext. 6395, Fax: 540-568-7860, E-mail: michaeld@jmu.edu.
Website: http://www.jmu.edu/kinesiology/

Kean University, College of Education, Program in Exercise Science, Union, NJ 07083. Offers MS. *Program availability:* Part-time. *Faculty:* 24 full-time (14 women). *Students:* 14 full-time (8 women), 13 part-time (2 women); includes 12 minority (5 Black or African American, non-Hispanic/Latino; 6 Hispanic/Latino; 1 Two or more races, non-Hispanic/Latino). Average age 27. 19 applicants, 100% accepted, 14 enrolled. In 2018, 11 master's awarded. *Degree requirements:* For master's, comprehensive exam, thesis, research component. *Entrance requirements:* For master's, GRE General Test, minimum B average in undergraduate prerequisites; minimum cumulative GPA of 3.0; official transcripts from all institutions attended; two letters of recommendation; personal statement; professional resume/curriculum vitae. Additional exam requirements/recommendations for international students: Required—TOEFL (minimum score 550 paper-based; 79 iBT), IELTS (minimum score 6.5). *Application deadline:* For fall admission, 6/30 for domestic and international students; for spring admission, 12/1 for domestic and international students. Applications are processed on a rolling basis. Application fee: $75. Electronic applications accepted. *Expenses:* Tuition, state resident: full-time $15,025; part-time $733.50 per credit. Tuition, nonresident: full-time $19,890; part-time $884.50 per credit. *Required fees:* $2107.50; $89.50 per credit. Tuition and fees vary according to course level, course load, degree level and program. *Financial support:* Scholarships/grants and unspecified assistantships available. Financial award applicants required to submit FAFSA. *Unit head:* Dr. Walter D. Andzel, Program Coordinator, 908-737-0662, E-mail: wandzel@kean.edu. *Application contact:* Brittany Gerstenhaber, Admissions Counselor, 908-737-7100, E-mail: GradAdmissions@kean.edu.
Website: http://grad.kean.edu/masters-programs/exercise-science

Kennesaw State University, WellStar College of Health and Human Services, Program in Applied Exercise and Health Science, Kennesaw, GA 30144. Offers exercise physiology (MS); sport management (MS). *Program availability:* Part-time, evening/weekend. *Students:* 41 full-time (20 women), 10 part-time (4 women); includes 22 minority (9 Black or African American, non-Hispanic/Latino; 1 Asian, non-Hispanic/Latino; 7 Hispanic/Latino; 5 Two or more races, non-Hispanic/Latino), 2 international. Average age 26. 37 applicants, 73% accepted, 22 enrolled. In 2018, 19 master's awarded. *Entrance requirements:* For master's, GRE, resume. Additional exam requirements/recommendations for international students: Required—TOEFL (minimum score 550 paper-based; 80 iBT), IELTS (minimum score 6.5). *Application deadline:* For fall admission, 6/1 for domestic and international students; for spring admission, 11/1 for domestic and international students; for summer admission, 4/1 for domestic and international students. Applications are processed on a rolling basis. Application fee: $60. Electronic applications accepted. *Expenses: Tuition, area resident:* Full-time $6960; part-time $290 per credit hour. Tuition, state resident: full-time $6960; part-time $290 per credit hour. Tuition, nonresident: full-time $25,080; part-time $1045 per credit hour. *International tuition:* $25,080 full-time. *Required fees:* $2006; $1706 per semester. $853 per semester. *Financial support:* Research assistantships available. Financial award applicants required to submit FAFSA. *Unit head:* Dr. Cherilyn McLester, Program Director, 470-578-2651, E-mail: cmclest1@kennesaw.edu. *Application contact:* Admissions Counselor, 470-578-4377, E-mail: ksugrad@kennesaw.edu.
Website: http://wellstarcollege.kennesaw.edu/essm/applied-exercise-health-science/index.php

Kent State University, College of Education, Health and Human Services, School of Foundations, Leadership and Administration, Sports and Recreation Management, Kent, OH 44242-0001. Offers sport and recreation management (MA); sports studies (MA). *Faculty:* 9 full-time (5 women), 19 part-time/adjunct (9 women). *Students:* 41 full-time (10 women), 14 part-time (6 women); includes 12 minority (9 Black or African American, non-Hispanic/Latino; 1 Asian, non-Hispanic/Latino; 2 Native Hawaiian or other Pacific Islander, non-Hispanic/Latino), 5 international. 61 applicants, 62% accepted. In 2018, 26 master's awarded. *Degree requirements:* For master's, thesis optional. *Entrance requirements:* For master's, GRE if undergraduate GPA below 3.0, goals statement, 2 letters of recommendation. Additional exam requirements/recommendations for international students: Required—TOEFL (minimum score 550 paper-based; 80 iBT). *Application deadline:* Applications are processed on a rolling basis. Application fee: $45 ($60 for international students). Electronic applications accepted. *Expenses:* Tuition, state resident: full-time $11,766; part-time $536 per credit. Tuition, nonresident: full-time $21,952; part-time $999 per credit. *International tuition:* $21,952 full-time. Tuition and fees vary according to course load. *Financial support:* In 2018–19, 7 research assistantships (averaging $8,500 per year) were awarded; teaching assistantships, Federal Work-Study, scholarships/grants, and unspecified assistantships also available. *Unit head:* Aaron Mulrooney, Coordinator, 330-672-0204, E-mail: amulroon@kent.edu. *Application contact:* Cheryl Slusarczyk, Academic Program Director, Office of Graduate Student Services, 330-672-2576, Fax: 330-672-9162, E-mail: ogs@kent.edu.

Kent State University, College of Education, Health and Human Services, School of Health Sciences, Program in Exercise Physiology, Kent, OH 44242-0001. Offers athletic training (MS); exercise physiology (PhD). *Faculty:* 11 full-time (6 women). *Students:* 38 full-time (21 women), 17 part-time (12 women); includes 5 minority (4 Asian, non-Hispanic/Latino; 1 Native Hawaiian or other Pacific Islander, non-Hispanic/Latino), 2 international. 47 applicants, 60% accepted. In 2018, 11 master's, 4 doctorates awarded. *Degree requirements:* For doctorate, comprehensive exam, thesis/dissertation. *Entrance requirements:* For master's, GRE, 2 letters of reference, goals statement; for doctorate, GRE, 2 letters of reference, goals statement, minimum master's-level GPA of 3.0. Additional exam requirements/recommendations for international students: Required—TOEFL (minimum score 550 paper-based; 80 iBT). *Application deadline:* Applications are processed on a rolling basis. Application fee: $45 ($60 for international students). Electronic applications accepted. *Expenses:* Tuition, state resident: full-time $11,766; part-time $536 per credit. Tuition, nonresident: full-time $21,952; part-time $999 per credit. *International tuition:* $21,952 full-time. Tuition and fees vary according to course load. *Financial support:* In 2018–19, 8 research assistantships (averaging $11,125 per year), 5 teaching assistantships (averaging $9,900 per year) were awarded; Federal Work-Study, scholarships/grants, and unspecified assistantships also available. *Unit head:* Angela Ridgel, Coordinator, 330-672-7495, E-mail: aridgel@kent.edu. *Application contact:* Cheryl Slusarczyk, Academic Program Director, Office of Graduate Student Services, 330-672-2576, Fax: 330-672-9162, E-mail: ogs@kent.edu.

Lakehead University, Graduate Studies, School of Kinesiology, Thunder Bay, ON P7B 5E1, Canada. Offers kinesiology (M Sc); kinesiology and gerontology (M Sc). *Program availability:* Part-time. *Degree requirements:* For master's, thesis. *Entrance requirements:* For master's, minimum B average. Additional exam requirements/recommendations for international students: Required—TOEFL. *Faculty research:* Social psychology and physical education, sport history, sports medicine, exercise physiology, gerontology.

Liberty University, School of Health Sciences, Lynchburg, VA 24515. Offers anatomy and cell biology (PhD); biomedical sciences (MS); epidemiology (MPH); exercise science (MS), including clinical, community physical activity, human performance, nutrition; global health (MPH); health promotion (MPH); medical sciences (MA), including biopsychology, business management, health informatics, molecular medicine, public health; nutrition (MPH). *Program availability:* Part-time, online learning. *Students:* 729 full-time (530 women), 760 part-time (555 women); includes 505 minority (327 Black or African American, non-Hispanic/Latino; 9 American Indian or Alaska Native, non-Hispanic/Latino; 38 Asian, non-Hispanic/Latino; 80 Hispanic/Latino; 4 Native Hawaiian or other Pacific Islander, non-Hispanic/Latino; 47 Two or more races, non-Hispanic/Latino), 71 international. Average age 31. 3,363 applicants, 32% accepted, 522 enrolled. In 2018, 373 master's awarded. *Degree requirements:* For master's, thesis (for some programs); for doctorate, thesis/dissertation. *Entrance requirements:* For doctorate, MAT or GRE, minimum GPA of 3.25 in master's program, 2-3 recommendations, writing samples (for some programs), letter of intent, professional vitae. Additional exam requirements/recommendations for international students: Required—TOEFL (minimum score 600 paper-based; 100 iBT). Application fee: $50. *Expenses: Tuition:* Full-time $10,851; part-time $562 per credit hour. *Financial support:* In 2018–19, 918 students received support. Federal Work-Study available. Financial award applicants required to submit FAFSA. *Unit head:* Dr. Ralph Linstra, Dean. *Application contact:* Jay Bridge, Director of Admissions, 800-424-9595, Fax: 800-628-7977, E-mail: gradadmissions@liberty.edu.
Website: https://www.liberty.edu/health-sciences/

Life University, College of Graduate and Undergraduate Studies, Marietta, GA 30060-2903. Offers athletic training (MAT); chiropractic sport science (MS); nutrition and sport science (MS), including chiropractic sport science; positive psychology (MS), including life coaching psychology; sport coaching (MS), including exercise sport science; sport injury management (MS), including nutrition and sport science; sports health science (MS), including sports injury management. *Program availability:* Part-time, 100% online, blended/hybrid learning. *Degree requirements:* For master's, comprehensive exam (for some programs), thesis optional. *Entrance requirements:* For master's, GRE General Test, minimum GPA of 3.0, 3 letters of recommendation, curriculum vitae. Additional exam requirements/recommendations for international students: Required—TOEFL (minimum score 500 paper-based). Electronic applications accepted. *Expenses:* Contact institution. *Faculty research:* Nutrient metabolism, organizational effectiveness, injury prevention, athlete development, recovery modalities and treatment, sport nutrition, functional neurology, peace and conflict studies.

Lipscomb University, Program in Exercise and Nutrition Science, Nashville, TN 37204-3951. Offers MS. *Program availability:* Part-time, evening/weekend. *Degree requirements:* For master's, comprehensive exam (for some programs), thesis optional. *Entrance requirements:* For master's, GRE (minimum score of 800), minimum GPA of 2.75 on all undergraduate work; 2 letters of recommendation; resume. Additional exam requirements/recommendations for international students: Required—TOEFL (minimum score 570 paper-based; 80 iBT). Electronic applications accepted. *Expenses:* Contact institution.

Logan University, College of Health Sciences, Chesterfield, MO 63017. Offers health informatics (MS); health professions education (DHPE); nutrition and human performance (MS); sports science and rehabilitation (MS). *Program availability:* Part-time, online only, 100% online. *Entrance requirements:* For master's, minimum GPA of 2.5; 6 hours of biology and physical science; bachelor's degree and 9 hours of business health administration (for health informatics). Additional exam requirements/recommendations for international students: Required—TOEFL (minimum score 500 paper-based; 79 iBT); Recommended—IELTS (minimum score 6.5). Electronic applications accepted. *Expenses:* Contact institution. *Faculty research:* Ankle injury prevention in high school athletes, low back pain in college football players, short arc banding and low back pain, the effects of enzymes on inflammatory blood markers, gait analysis in high school and college athletes.

Exercise and Sports Science

Long Island University–LIU Brooklyn, School of Health Professions, Brooklyn, NY 11201-8423. Offers athletic training and sport sciences (MS); community health (MS Ed); exercise science (MS); forensic social work (Advanced Certificate); occupational therapy (MS); physical therapy (DPT); physician assistant (MS); public health (MPH); social work (MSW); speech-language pathology (MS). *Accreditation:* AOTA; CEPH. *Degree requirements:* For master's, comprehensive exam (for some programs), thesis (for some programs); for doctorate, comprehensive exam (for some programs). *Entrance requirements:* For master's and doctorate, GRE. Additional exam requirements/recommendations for international students: Required—TOEFL (minimum score 550 paper-based; 79 iBT). Electronic applications accepted. *Faculty research:* Pediatric physical therapy, complementary and alternative medicine, global health and human rights, sport leadership and entrepreneurship, feminist sport psychology.

Manhattanville College, School of Education, Program in Physical Education and Sports Pedagogy, Purchase, NY 10577-2132. Offers health and wellness specialist (Advanced Certificate); physical education and sport pedagogy (MAT). *Program availability:* Part-time, evening/weekend. *Faculty:* 3 full-time (2 women), 10 part-time/adjunct (4 women). *Students:* 44 full-time (12 women), 51 part-time (14 women); includes 17 minority (10 Black or African American, non-Hispanic/Latino; 1 American Indian or Alaska Native, non-Hispanic/Latino; 1 Asian, non-Hispanic/Latino; 5 Hispanic/Latino). Average age 30. 31 applicants, 68% accepted, 18 enrolled. In 2018, 32 master's awarded. *Degree requirements:* For master's, comprehensive exam (for some programs), student teaching, research seminars, portfolios, internships, writing assessment; for Advanced Certificate, comprehensive exam (for some programs). *Entrance requirements:* For master's, for programs leading to certification, candidates must submit scores from GRE or MAT(Miller Analogies Test), minimum undergraduate GPA of 3.0, all transcripts from all colleges and universities attended, 2 letters of recommendation, interview, essay (2-3 page personal statement that describes reasons for choosing education as profession and personal philosophy of education), proof of immunization (for those born after 1957). Additional exam requirements/recommendations for international students: Required—TOEFL (minimum score 600 paper-based; 110 iBT); Recommended—IELTS (minimum score 8). *Application deadline:* Applications are processed on a rolling basis. Application fee: $75. Electronic applications accepted. *Expenses:* 935 per credit. *Financial support:* Teaching assistantships, career-related internships or fieldwork, Federal Work-Study, institutionally sponsored loans, scholarships/grants, and unspecified assistantships available. Financial award application deadline: 3/15; financial award applicants required to submit FAFSA. *Faculty research:* Early childhood and physical education. *Unit head:* Dr. Shelley Wepner, Dean, 914-323-3153, Fax: 914-323-5493, E-mail: Shelley.Wepner@mville.edu. *Application contact:* Alissa Wilson, Director, SOE Graduate Enrollment Management, 914-323-3150, Fax: 914-694-1732, E-mail: edschool@mville.edu.
Website: http://www.mville.edu/programs/physical-education-and-sports-pedagogy

Marshall University, Academic Affairs Division, College of Health Professions, School of Kinesiology, Program in Biomechanics, Huntington, WV 25755. Offers MS.

Marshall University, Academic Affairs Division, College of Health Professions, School of Kinesiology, Program in Exercise Science, Huntington, WV 25755. Offers MS. *Degree requirements:* For master's, thesis optional, comprehensive assessment. *Entrance requirements:* For master's, GRE General Test.

Marywood University, Academic Affairs, College of Health and Human Services, Department of Nutrition and Dietetics, Program in Sports Nutrition and Exercise Science, Scranton, PA 18509-1598. Offers MS. *Program availability:* Part-time. Electronic applications accepted.

McNeese State University, Doré School of Graduate Studies, Burton College of Education, Department of Health and Human Performance, Lake Charles, LA 70609. Offers exercise physiology (MS); health promotion (MS); nutrition and wellness (MS). *Accreditation:* NCATE. *Program availability:* Evening/weekend. *Entrance requirements:* For master's, GRE, undergraduate major or minor in health and human performance or related field of study.

Memorial University of Newfoundland, School of Graduate Studies, School of Human Kinetics and Recreation, St. John's, NL A1C 5S7, Canada. Offers administration, curriculum and supervision (MPE); biomechanics/ergonomics (MS Kin); exercise and work physiology (MS Kin); psychology of sport, exercise and recreation (MS Kin); sociocultural studies of physical activity and health (MS Kin). *Program availability:* Part-time. *Degree requirements:* For master's, thesis optional, seminars, thesis presentations. *Entrance requirements:* For master's, bachelor's degree in a related field, minimum B average. Electronic applications accepted. *Faculty research:* Administration, sociology of sports, kinesiology, physiology/recreation.

Merrimack College, School of Health Sciences, North Andover, MA 01845-5800. Offers athletic training (MS); community health education (MS); exercise and sport science (MS); health and wellness management (MS). *Program availability:* Part-time, evening/weekend. *Faculty:* 11 full-time (10 women), 2 part-time/adjunct (both women). *Students:* 93 full-time (62 women), 12 part-time (10 women); includes 3 minority (all Black or African American, non-Hispanic/Latino), 4 international. Average age 26. 163 applicants, 92% accepted, 82 enrolled. In 2018, 71 master's awarded. *Degree requirements:* For master's, capstone (for community health education, exercise and sport science, and health and wellness management). *Entrance requirements:* For master's, resume, official college transcripts, personal statement, 2 recommendations. Additional exam requirements/recommendations for international students: Required—TOEFL (minimum score 84 iBT), IELTS (minimum score 6.5), PTE (minimum score 56). *Application deadline:* For fall admission, 8/24 for domestic students, 7/30 for international students; for summer admission, 5/10 for domestic students, 4/10 for international students. Applications are processed on a rolling basis. Application fee: $0. Electronic applications accepted. Application fee is waived when completed online. *Expenses:* School of Health Sciences (all programs except Athletic Training) $28,420; M.S. in Athletic Training $32,980. *Financial support:* Fellowships with partial tuition reimbursements, career-related internships or fieldwork, scholarships/grants, and health care benefits available. Support available to part-time students. Financial award application deadline: 5/1; financial award applicants required to submit FAFSA. *Unit head:* Dr. Janet Blum, Dean, 978-837-5396, E-mail: blumj@merrimack.edu. *Application contact:* Allison Pena, Office of Graduate Studies, 978-837-3563, E-mail: graduate@merrimack.edu.
Website: http://www.merrimack.edu/academics/health-sciences/

Miami University, College of Education, Health and Society, Department of Kinesiology and Health, Oxford, OH 45056. Offers MS. *Faculty:* 28 full-time (12 women). *Students:* 66 full-time (37 women), 11 part-time (5 women); includes 15 minority (5 Black or African American, non-Hispanic/Latino; 1 Asian, non-Hispanic/Latino; 4 Hispanic/Latino; 5 Two or more races, non-Hispanic/Latino), 7 international. Average age 23. In 2018, 63 master's awarded. *Unit head:* Dr. Helaine Alessio, Professor and Chair, 513-529-2700, E-mail: alessih@miamioh.edu. *Application contact:* Dr. Helaine Alessio, Professor and Chair, 513-529-2700, E-mail: alessih@miamioh.edu.
Website: http://www.MiamiOH.edu/KNH

Middle Tennessee State University, College of Graduate Studies, College of Behavioral and Health Sciences, Department of Health and Human Performance, Program in Exercise Science, Murfreesboro, TN 37132. Offers MS. *Program availability:* Part-time, evening/weekend, online learning. *Degree requirements:* For master's, comprehensive exam, thesis optional. *Entrance requirements:* For master's, GRE. Additional exam requirements/recommendations for international students: Required—TOEFL (minimum score 525 paper-based; 71 iBT) or IELTS (minimum score 6). *Faculty research:* Kinesiometrics, leisure behavior, health, lifestyles.

Middle Tennessee State University, College of Graduate Studies, College of Behavioral and Health Sciences, Department of Health and Human Performance, Program in Human Performance, Murfreesboro, TN 37132. Offers PhD. *Program availability:* Part-time, evening/weekend, online learning. *Degree requirements:* For doctorate, comprehensive exam, thesis/dissertation. *Entrance requirements:* For doctorate, GRE. Additional exam requirements/recommendations for international students: Required—TOEFL (minimum score 525 paper-based; 71 iBT) or IELTS (minimum score 6). *Faculty research:* Kinesiometrics, leisure behavior, health/lifestyles.

Midwestern State University, Billie Doris McAda Graduate School, Robert D. and Carol Gunn College of Health Sciences and Human Services, Department of Athletic Training and Exercise Physiology, Wichita Falls, TX 76308. Offers exercise physiology (MS). *Program availability:* Part-time. *Degree requirements:* For master's, comprehensive exam, thesis optional. *Entrance requirements:* For master's, GRE General Test or MAT. Additional exam requirements/recommendations for international students: Required—TOEFL (minimum score 550 paper-based). Electronic applications accepted. *Faculty research:* Exercise adherence, muscular tissue remodeling during hypertrophy, student engagement and success, operational paradigms of the exercise sciences.

Mississippi State University, College of Education, Department of Kinesiology, Mississippi State, MS 39762. Offers disability studies (MS); exercise physiology (MS); exercise science (PhD); sport administration (MS); sport pedagogy (MS); sport studies (PhD). *Program availability:* Part-time, blended/hybrid learning. *Faculty:* 15 full-time (3 women). *Students:* 49 full-time (25 women), 16 part-time (3 women); includes 14 minority (5 Black or African American, non-Hispanic/Latino; 1 American Indian or Alaska Native, non-Hispanic/Latino; 2 Asian, non-Hispanic/Latino; 3 Hispanic/Latino; 3 Two or more races, non-Hispanic/Latino), 10 international. Average age 26. 67 applicants, 60% accepted, 23 enrolled. In 2018, 27 master's, 2 doctorates awarded. *Degree requirements:* For master's, comprehensive exam, thesis optional; for doctorate, comprehensive exam. *Entrance requirements:* For master's, GRE General Test, minimum GPA of 2.75 on undergraduate work from four-year accredited institution, 3.0 graduate; for doctorate, GRE, minimum GPA of 3.4 on previous graduate degree(s) earned from accredited institutions. Additional exam requirements/recommendations for international students: Required—TOEFL (minimum score 550 paper-based; 79 iBT); Recommended—IELTS (minimum score 6.5). *Application deadline:* For fall admission, 7/1 for domestic students, 5/1 for international students; for spring admission, 11/1 for domestic students, 9/1 for international students. Applications are processed on a rolling basis. Application fee: $60 ($80 for international students). Electronic applications accepted. *Expenses:* Tuition, state resident: full-time $8450; part-time $360.59 per credit hour. Tuition, nonresident: full-time $23,140; part-time $969.09 per credit hour. *Required fees:* $110. One-time fee: $55 full-time. Part-time tuition and fees vary according to course load, degree level, campus/location and reciprocity agreements. *Financial support:* In 2018–19, 14 teaching assistantships with partial tuition reimbursements (averaging $10,386 per year) were awarded; career-related internships or fieldwork, Federal Work-Study, institutionally sponsored loans, and unspecified assistantships also available. Financial award application deadline: 4/1; financial award applicants required to submit FAFSA. *Faculty research:* Static balance and stepping performance of older adults, organizational justice, public health, strength training and recovery drinks, high risk drinking perceptions and behaviors. *Unit head:* Dr. Stanley P. Brown, Professor and Head, 662-325-7229, Fax: 662-325-4525, E-mail: spb107@msstate.edu. *Application contact:* Ryan King, Admissions and Enrollment Assistant, 662-325-8951, E-mail: rjk101@grad.msstate.edu.
Website: http://www.kinesiology.msstate.edu/

Montclair State University, The Graduate School, College of Education and Human Services, Nutrition and Exercise Science Certificate Program, Montclair, NJ 07043-1624. Offers Certificate. Electronic applications accepted.

Montclair State University, The Graduate School, College of Education and Human Services, Program in Exercise Science and Physical Education, Montclair, NJ 07043-1624. Offers exercise science (MA); sports administration and coaching (MA); teaching and supervision in physical education (MA). *Program availability:* Part-time, evening/weekend. *Degree requirements:* For master's, comprehensive exam, thesis or alternative. *Entrance requirements:* For master's, GRE General Test, essay, 2 letters of recommendation. Additional exam requirements/recommendations for international students: Required—TOEFL (minimum score 83 iBT), IELTS (minimum score 6.5). Electronic applications accepted.

New Mexico Highlands University, Graduate Studies, College of Arts and Sciences, Department of Exercise and Sport Sciences, Las Vegas, NM 87701. Offers human performance and sport (MA), including human performance and sport sciences, sports administration, teacher education. *Program availability:* Part-time. *Degree requirements:* For master's, comprehensive exam, thesis or alternative. *Entrance requirements:* For master's, minimum undergraduate GPA of 3.0. Additional exam requirements/recommendations for international students: Required—TOEFL (minimum score 540 paper-based). *Faculty research:* Child obesity and physical inactivity, body composition and fitness assessment, motor development, sport marketing, sport finance.

North Dakota State University, College of Graduate and Interdisciplinary Studies, College of Human Development and Education, Department of Health, Nutrition, and Exercise Sciences, Fargo, ND 58102. Offers advanced athletic training (MS); athletic training (MAT); dietetics (MS); exercise science and nutrition (PhD); health, nutrition and exercise science (MS). *Program availability:* Part-time, evening/weekend, online learning. *Entrance requirements:* For master's, minimum GPA of 3.0. Additional exam requirements/recommendations for international students: Required—TOEFL (minimum score 525 paper-based; 71 iBT). Electronic applications accepted. *Faculty research:* Biomechanics, sport specialization, recreation, nutrition, athletic training.

Northeastern Illinois University, College of Graduate Studies and Research, Daniel L. Goodwin College of Education, Program in Exercise Science, Chicago, IL 60625. Offers MS. *Degree requirements:* For master's, thesis optional, internship. *Entrance requirements:* For master's, 21 hours of undergraduate course work in science, minimum GPA of 2.75.

Northeastern University, Bouvé College of Health Sciences, Boston, MA 02115-5096. Offers applied behavior analysis (MS); audiology (Au D); counseling psychology (MS, PhD, CAGS); exercise science (MS); nursing (MS, PhD, CAGS), including administration (MS), adult-gerontology acute care nurse practitioner (MS, CAGS), adult-gerontology primary care nurse practitioner (MS, CAGS), anesthesia (MS), family nurse practitioner (MS, CAGS), neonatal nurse practitioner (MS, CAGS), pediatric nurse practitioner (MS, CAGS), psychiatric mental health nurse practitioner (MS, CAGS); nursing practice (DNP); pharmaceutical sciences (MS, PhD), including interdisciplinary concentration, pharmaceutics and drug delivery systems; pharmacology (MS);

pharmacy (Pharm D); school psychology (PhD); speech-language pathology (MS); urban health (MPH); MS/MBA. *Accreditation:* AANA/CANAEP; ACPE (one or more programs are accredited); ASHA; CEPH. *Program availability:* Part-time, evening/weekend, online learning. *Degree requirements:* For doctorate, thesis/dissertation (for some programs); for CAGS, comprehensive exam. Electronic applications accepted. *Expenses:* Contact institution.

Northern Michigan University, Office of Graduate Education and Research, College of Health Sciences and Professional Studies, School of Health and Human Performance, Marquette, MI 49855-5301. Offers exercise science (MS). *Program availability:* Part-time. *Degree requirements:* For master's, thesis (for some programs), two scholarly papers or thesis. *Entrance requirements:* For master's, minimum GPA of 3.0 plus relevant major or 9 semester hours of course work in human anatomy/physiology, exercise physiology, physics, biomechanics, kinesiology. Additional exam requirements/recommendations for international students: Required—TOEFL (minimum score 550 paper-based; 79 iBT), IELTS (minimum score 6.6). Electronic applications accepted. *Faculty research:* Physiology of rock climbing and cross country ski racing, physical activity behaviors of children, exercise training and cancer treatment, normobaric hypoxia, concussion.

Northwest Missouri State University, Graduate School, School of Health Science and Wellness, Maryville, MO 64468-6001. Offers applied health and sport sciences (MS); guidance and counseling (MS Ed); health and physical education (MS Ed); recreation (MS); sport and exercise psychology (MS). *Accreditation:* NCATE. *Program availability:* Part-time. *Faculty:* 15 full-time (7 women). *Students:* 58 full-time (35 women), 27 part-time (17 women); includes 9 minority (7 Black or African American, non-Hispanic/Latino; 1 Hispanic/Latino; 1 Two or more races, non-Hispanic/Latino), 6 international. Average age 26. 50 applicants, 74% accepted, 23 enrolled. In 2018, 54 master's awarded. *Degree requirements:* For master's, comprehensive exam. *Entrance requirements:* For master's, GRE General Test, minimum undergraduate GPA of 2.75, teaching certificate, writing sample. Additional exam requirements/recommendations for international students: Required—TOEFL (minimum score 550 paper-based; 79 iBT). *Application deadline:* For fall admission, 7/1 for domestic and international students; for spring admission, 11/15 for domestic and international students. Applications are processed on a rolling basis. Application fee: $0 ($75 for international students). *Expenses: Tuition, area resident:* Full-time $4551; part-time $252.86 per credit hour. Tuition, state resident: full-time $4551; part-time $252.86 per credit hour. Tuition, nonresident: full-time $9103; part-time $505.72 per credit hour. *International tuition:* $9103 full-time. *Required fees:* $2668; $148.20 per credit hour. Tuition and fees vary according to program. *Financial support:* Teaching assistantships with full tuition reimbursements and unspecified assistantships available. Financial award application deadline: 4/1; financial award applicants required to submit FAFSA. *Unit head:* Dr. Terry Long, Director, School of Health Science and Wellness, 660-562-1706, Fax: 660-562-1483, E-mail: tlong@nwmissouri.edu. *Application contact:* Gina Smith, Office Manager, 660-562-1297, Fax: 660-562-1963, E-mail: smigina@nwmissouri.edu.
Website: http://www.nwmissouri.edu/health/

Oakland University, Graduate Study and Lifelong Learning, School of Health Sciences, Program in Exercise Science, Rochester, MI 48309-4401. Offers MS, Graduate Certificate. *Degree requirements:* For master's, thesis (for some programs). *Entrance requirements:* For master's, minimum GPA of 3.0. Additional exam requirements/recommendations for international students: Required—TOEFL (minimum score 550 paper-based). Electronic applications accepted. *Expenses:* Contact institution.

Oakland University, Graduate Study and Lifelong Learning, School of Health Sciences, Program in Physical Therapy, Rochester, MI 48309-4401. Offers clinical exercise science (Dr Sc PT); complementary medicine and wellness (Dr Sc PT); corporate worksite wellness (Dr Sc PT); exercise science (Dr Sc PT); neurological rehabilitation (Dr Sc PT, TDPT); orthopedic manual physical therapy (Dr Sc PT, TDPT, Graduate Certificate); orthopedic physical therapy (Graduate Certificate); orthopedics (Dr Sc PT, TDPT); pediatric rehabilitation (Dr Sc PT, TDPT); physical therapy (DPT); teaching and learning for rehabilitation professionals (Dr Sc PT, TDPT). *Accreditation:* APTA. *Entrance requirements:* For doctorate, GRE General Test. Additional exam requirements/recommendations for international students: Required—TOEFL (minimum score 550 paper-based). *Expenses:* Contact institution.

Ohio University, Graduate College, College of Arts and Sciences, Department of Biological Sciences, Athens, OH 45701-2979. Offers biological sciences (MS, PhD); cell biology and physiology (MS, PhD); ecology and evolutionary biology (MS, PhD); exercise physiology and muscle biology (MS, PhD); microbiology (MS, PhD); neuroscience (MS, PhD). Terminal master's awarded for partial completion of doctoral program. *Degree requirements:* For master's, comprehensive exam, thesis, 1 quarter of teaching experience; for doctorate, comprehensive exam, thesis/dissertation, 2 quarters of teaching experience. *Entrance requirements:* For master's, GRE General Test, names of three faculty members whose research interests most closely match the applicant's interest; for doctorate, GRE General Test, essay concerning prior training, research interest and career goals, plus names of three faculty members whose research interests most closely match the applicant's interest. Additional exam requirements/recommendations for international students: Required—TOEFL (minimum score 620 paper-based; 105 iBT) or IELTS (minimum score 7.5). Electronic applications accepted. *Faculty research:* Ecology and evolutionary biology, exercise physiology and muscle biology, neurobiology, cell biology, physiology.

Ohio University, Graduate College, College of Health Sciences and Professions, School of Applied Health Sciences and Wellness, Program in Physiology of Exercise, Athens, OH 45701-2979. Offers MS. *Degree requirements:* For master's, thesis or alternative. *Entrance requirements:* For master's, GRE, minimum GPA of 3.0. Additional exam requirements/recommendations for international students: Required—TOEFL (minimum score 550 paper-based; 80 iBT) or IELTS (minimum score 6.5). Electronic applications accepted. *Faculty research:* Blood pressure, heart rate, health skeleton, muscles, training.

Old Dominion University, Darden College of Education, Program in Physical Education, Exercise Science and Wellness Emphasis, Norfolk, VA 23529. Offers physical education (MS Ed), including exercise science and wellness. *Program availability:* Part-time, evening/weekend. *Degree requirements:* For master's, comprehensive exam, thesis or alternative, internship, research project. *Entrance requirements:* For master's, GRE (minimum score of 291 for combined verbal and quantitative), minimum GPA of 2.8 overall, 3.0 in major. Additional exam requirements/recommendations for international students: Required—TOEFL (minimum score 550 paper-based; 79 iBT). Electronic applications accepted. *Faculty research:* Cardiovascular response to exercise, exercise prescription, nutrition, lower extremity biomechanics, metabolic responses in special populations.

Pittsburg State University, Graduate School, College of Education, Department of Health, Physical Education and Recreation, Pittsburg, KS 66762. Offers health, human performance, and recreation (MS), including human performance and wellness, sport and leisure service management. *Program availability:* Part-time, online only, 100% online. *Degree requirements:* For master's, thesis or alternative. *Entrance requirements:* For master's, letter of intent. Additional exam requirements/recommendations for international students: Required—TOEFL (minimum score 520 paper-based; 68 iBT), IELTS (minimum score 6), PTE (minimum score 47). Electronic applications accepted. *Expenses:* Contact institution. *Faculty research:* Personality of athletes, fitness activities for children, aerobic conditioning, fitness evaluation.

Point Loma Nazarene University, Department of Kinesiology, San Diego, CA 92106-2899. Offers exercise science (MS); sport performance (MS), including exercise science, sport management, sport performance. *Program availability:* Part-time, online learning. *Entrance requirements:* For master's, baccalaureate degree, minimum undergraduate cumulative GPA of 3.0. *Expenses:* Contact institution.

Purdue University, Graduate School, College of Health and Human Sciences, Department of Health and Kinesiology, West Lafayette, IN 47907. Offers athletic training education administration (MS, PhD); biomechanics (MS, PhD); exercise physiology (MS, PhD); health education (MS, PhD); history/philosophy of sport (MS, PhD); motor control and development (MS, PhD); physical education pedagogy (PhD); physical education teacher education (MS); recreation and sport management (MS, PhD); sport and exercise psychology (MS, PhD). *Program availability:* Part-time. *Faculty:* 23 full-time (10 women). *Students:* 29 full-time (13 women), 8 part-time (5 women); includes 3 minority (1 Asian, non-Hispanic/Latino; 1 Hispanic/Latino; 1 Two or more races, non-Hispanic/Latino), 8 international. Average age 26. 61 applicants, 26% accepted, 14 enrolled. In 2018, 14 master's awarded. *Degree requirements:* For master's, thesis optional; for doctorate, comprehensive exam, thesis/dissertation, qualifying examination, preliminary examination. *Entrance requirements:* For master's, GRE General Test (minimum score 1000 combined verbal and quantitative), minimum undergraduate GPA of 3.0 or equivalent; for doctorate, GRE General Test (minimum score 1100 combined verbal and quantitative), minimum undergraduate GPA of 3.0 or equivalent; master's degree with minimum GPA of 3.25 (recommended). Additional exam requirements/recommendations for international students: Required—TOEFL (minimum score 77 iBT); Recommended—TWE. *Application deadline:* For fall admission, 4/30 for domestic and international students; for spring admission, 10/15 for domestic and international students. Applications are processed on a rolling basis. Application fee: $60 ($75 for international students). Electronic applications accepted. *Financial support:* Fellowships with partial tuition reimbursements, research assistantships with partial tuition reimbursements, teaching assistantships with partial tuition reimbursements, and Federal Work-Study available. Support available to part-time students. Financial award applicants required to submit FAFSA. *Faculty research:* Wellness, motivation, teaching effectiveness, learning and development. *Unit head:* Dr. Timothy P. Gavin, Head of the Graduate Program, 765-494-3178, Fax: 765-494-1239, E-mail: gavin1@purdue.edu. *Application contact:* David B. Klenosky, Graduate Contact, 765-494-0865, E-mail: klenosky@purdue.edu.
Website: http://www.purdue.edu/hhs/hk/

Queens College of the City University of New York, Mathematics and Natural Sciences Division, Department of Family, Nutrition and Exercise Sciences, Queens, NY 11367-1597. Offers exercise science specialist (MS); family and consumer science (K-12) (AC); family and consumer science/teaching curriculum (K-12) (MS Ed); nutrition and exercise science (MS); nutrition specialist (MS); physical education (K-12) (AC); physical education/teaching curriculum (pre K-12) (MS Ed). *Program availability:* Part-time, evening/weekend. *Faculty:* 18 full-time (15 women), 59 part-time/adjunct (41 women). *Students:* 18 full-time (6 women), 111 part-time (66 women); includes 62 minority (13 Black or African American, non-Hispanic/Latino; 12 Asian, non-Hispanic/Latino; 37 Hispanic/Latino), 3 international. Average age 29. 95 applicants, 76% accepted, 45 enrolled. In 2018, 41 master's, 16 other advanced degrees awarded. *Degree requirements:* For master's, research project or comprehensive examination. *Entrance requirements:* For master's, minimum GPA of 3.0. Additional exam requirements/recommendations for international students: Required—TOEFL (minimum paper-based score of 600) or IELTS=7 (for program in nutrition). *Application deadline:* For fall admission, 4/1 for domestic students; for spring admission, 11/1 for domestic students. Applications are processed on a rolling basis. Application fee: $125. Electronic applications accepted. *Financial support:* Career-related internships or fieldwork and unspecified assistantships available. Financial award application deadline: 4/1; financial award applicants required to submit FAFSA. *Faculty research:* Eating patterns and health; health disparities; correlates of taste acuity; structuring and implementation of competition and competitive activities in physical education; exercise and metabolic risk in people living with HIV/AIDS; biomechanics, motor learning and motor control; exercise interventions to improve physical function in the elderly. *Unit head:* Dr. Ashima K. Kant, Chair, 718-997-4156 Ext. 4475, Fax: 718-997-4163, E-mail: ashima.kant@qc.cuny.edu. *Application contact:* Elizabeth D'Amico-Ramirez, Assistant Director of Graduate Admissions, 718-997-5203, E-mail: elizabeth.damicoramirez@qc.cuny.edu.

Queen's University at Kingston, School of Graduate Studies, School of Kinesiology and Health Studies, Kingston, ON K7L 3N6, Canada. Offers biomechanics and ergonomics (M Sc, PhD); exercise physiology (M Sc, PhD); health promotion (M Sc, PhD); physical activity epidemiology (M Sc, PhD); sociocultural studies of sport, health and the body (MA, PhD); sport psychology (M Sc, PhD). *Program availability:* Part-time. *Degree requirements:* For master's, thesis (for some programs); for doctorate, comprehensive exam, thesis/dissertation. *Entrance requirements:* For master's and doctorate, minimum B+ average. Additional exam requirements/recommendations for international students: Required—TOEFL. Electronic applications accepted. *Faculty research:* Expert performance ergonomics, obesity research, pregnancy and exercise, gender and sport participation.

Rowan University, Graduate School, School of Biomedical Science and Health Professions, Department of Health and Exercise Science, Glassboro, NJ 08028-1701. Offers wellness and lifestyle management (MA). *Degree requirements:* For master's, comprehensive exam, thesis. *Entrance requirements:* For master's, GRE General Test, GRE Subject Test, interview, minimum GPA of 2.8. Additional exam requirements/recommendations for international students: Required—TOEFL. Electronic applications accepted.

Sacred Heart University, Graduate Programs, College of Health Professions, Department of Exercise Science, Fairfield, CT 06825. Offers exercise science and nutrition (MS). *Program availability:* Part-time, evening/weekend. *Degree requirements:* For master's, thesis. *Entrance requirements:* For master's, bachelor's degree in related major, minimum GPA of 3.0, anatomy and physiology (with labs), exercise physiology, nutrition, statistics or health/exercise-specific research methods course, kinesiology (preferred). Additional exam requirements/recommendations for international students: Required—TOEFL (minimum score 570 paper-based, 80 iBT), TWE, or IELTS (6.5). Electronic applications accepted. *Expenses:* Contact institution.

St. Ambrose University, College of Health and Human Services, Program in Exercise Physiology, Davenport, IA 52803-2898. Offers MS.

Saint Mary's College of California, School of Liberal Arts, Department of Kinesiology, Moraga, CA 94575. Offers fitness management (MA); sport management (MA); sport studies (MA). *Program availability:* Part-time. *Degree requirements:* For master's, thesis or special project. *Entrance requirements:* For master's, minimum GPA of 2.75, BA in physical education or related field, or professional experience. Electronic applications accepted. *Expenses:* Contact institution. *Faculty research:* Moral development in sport, applied motor learning, achievement motivation, sport history.

Exercise and Sports Science

San Diego State University, Graduate and Research Affairs, College of Health and Human Services, School of Exercise and Nutritional Sciences, Program in Exercise Physiology, San Diego, CA 92182. Offers MS, MS/MS. *Degree requirements:* For master's, thesis. *Entrance requirements:* For master's, GRE General Test, 2 letters of reference. Additional exam requirements/recommendations for international students: Required—TOEFL. Electronic applications accepted.

Smith College, Graduate and Special Programs, Department of Exercise and Sport Studies, Northampton, MA 01063. Offers MS. *Program availability:* Part-time. *Students:* 27 full-time (18 women), 2 part-time (both women); includes 4 minority (2 Black or African American, non-Hispanic/Latino; 2 Hispanic/Latino). Average age 25. 49 applicants, 37% accepted, 13 enrolled. In 2018, 16 master's awarded. *Entrance requirements:* Additional exam requirements/recommendations for international students: Required—TOEFL (minimum score 595 paper-based; 97 iBT), IELTS (minimum score 7.5). *Application deadline:* For fall admission, 1/15 for domestic and international students; for spring admission, 12/1 for domestic students. Application fee: $60. *Expenses:* Tuition: Full-time $39,120; part-time $1630 per credit. Tuition and fees vary according to course load and program. *Financial support:* In 2018–19, 28 students received support. Scholarships/grants, tuition waivers (full and partial), unspecified assistantships, and human resources employee benefit available. Support available to part-time students. Financial award application deadline: 1/15; financial award applicants required to submit CSS PROFILE or FAFSA. *Faculty research:* Women in sport, perceived exertion, motor programming, race in sport, stress management. *Unit head:* Lynn Oberbillig, Graduate Student Adviser, 413-585-2701, E-mail: loberbil@smith.edu. *Application contact:* Ruth Morgan, Program Coordinator, 413-585-3050, Fax: 413-585-3054, E-mail: rmorgan@smith.edu.
Website: http://www.smith.edu/ess/

Sonoma State University, School of Science and Technology, Department of Kinesiology, Rohnert Park, CA 94928. Offers exercise science/pre-physical therapy (MA); interdisciplinary (MA); interdisciplinary pre-occupational therapy (MA); lifetime physical activity (MA), including coach education, fitness and wellness. *Program availability:* Part-time. *Degree requirements:* For master's, thesis, oral exam. *Entrance requirements:* For master's, minimum GPA of 2.8. Additional exam requirements/recommendations for international students: Required—TOEFL (minimum score 500 paper-based).

South Dakota State University, Graduate School, College of Education and Human Sciences, Department of Health and Nutritional Sciences, Brookings, SD 57007. Offers athletic training (MS); dietetics (MS); nutrition and exercise sciences (MS, PhD); sport and recreation studies (MS). *Program availability:* Part-time. *Degree requirements:* For master's, comprehensive exam (for some programs), thesis (for some programs), oral exam. *Entrance requirements:* Additional exam requirements/recommendations for international students: Required—TOEFL (minimum score 525 paper-based). *Faculty research:* Food chemistry, bone density, functional food, nutrition education, nutrition biochemistry.

Southeast Missouri State University, School of Graduate Studies, Kinesiology, Nutrition and Recreation, Cape Girardeau, MO 63701-4799. Offers MS. *Program availability:* Part-time. *Faculty:* 8 full-time (2 women), 2 part-time/adjunct (1 woman). *Students:* 15 full-time (8 women), 12 part-time (11 women); includes 1 minority (Black or African American, non-Hispanic/Latino), 6 international. Average age 26. 31 applicants, 84% accepted, 15 enrolled. In 2018, 7 master's awarded. *Degree requirements:* For master's, comprehensive exam, thesis optional. *Entrance requirements:* For master's, GRE General Test (minimum combined score of 950). Additional exam requirements/recommendations for international students: Required—TOEFL (minimum score 550 paper-based; 79 iBT), IELTS (minimum score 6), PTE (minimum score 53). *Application deadline:* For fall admission, 8/1 for domestic students, 5/1 for international students; for spring admission, 11/21 for domestic students, 10/1 for international students; for summer admission, 5/15 for domestic students. Applications are processed on a rolling basis. Application fee: $30 ($40 for international students). Electronic applications accepted. *Expenses:* Contact institution. *Financial support:* In 2018–19, 10 students received support, including 7 teaching assistantships with full tuition reimbursements available; career-related internships or fieldwork, Federal Work-Study, scholarships/grants, traineeships, tuition waivers (full), and unspecified assistantships also available. Financial award application deadline: 6/30; financial award applicants required to submit FAFSA. *Faculty research:* Body composition assessment techniques, serum lipid adaptations with physical activity in smokers, professional attitudes of pre-service teachers, high intensity training with clinical populations. *Unit head:* Dr. Joe Pujol, Professor and Chairperson, 573-651-2664, Fax: 573-651-5150, E-mail: jpujol@semo.edu. *Application contact:* Dr. Jeremy Barnes, Professor/Graduate Coordinator, 573-651-2197, Fax: 573-651-5150, E-mail: jbarnes@semo.edu.
Website: http://www.semo.edu/health/

Southern Connecticut State University, School of Graduate Studies, School of Health and Human Services, Department of Exercise Science, New Haven, CT 06515-1355. Offers human performance (MS); physical education (MS); school health education (MS). *Program availability:* Part-time, evening/weekend. *Degree requirements:* For master's, thesis or alternative. *Entrance requirements:* For master's, interview. Electronic applications accepted.

Southern Illinois University Edwardsville, Graduate School, School of Education, Health, and Human Behavior, Department of Kinesiology and Health Education, Program in Exercise Physiology, Edwardsville, IL 62026. Offers MS. *Program availability:* Part-time, evening/weekend. *Degree requirements:* For master's, thesis (for some programs), internship. *Entrance requirements:* Additional exam requirements/recommendations for international students: Required—TOEFL (minimum score 550 paper-based, 79 iBT), IELTS (minimum score 6.5), Michigan Test of English Language Proficiency or PTE. Electronic applications accepted.

Southern Utah University, Program in Sports Conditioning and Performance, Cedar City, UT 84720-2498. Offers MS. *Program availability:* Part-time, online only, three intensive summer courses/clinical workshops on campus for 1-2 weeks. *Faculty:* 8 full-time (4 women). *Students:* 13 full-time (5 women), 56 part-time (21 women); includes 10 minority (1 Black or African American, non-Hispanic/Latino; 1 American Indian or Alaska Native, non-Hispanic/Latino; 3 Asian, non-Hispanic/Latino; 3 Hispanic/Latino; 2 Native Hawaiian or other Pacific Islander, non-Hispanic/Latino). Average age 29. 19 applicants, 89% accepted, 9 enrolled. In 2018, 7 master's awarded. *Entrance requirements:* For master's, GRE or Miller's Analogies required if GPA is lower than 3.25. Additional exam requirements/recommendations for international students: Required—TOEFL (minimum score 550 paper-based; 79 iBT), IELTS (minimum score 6). *Application deadline:* For fall admission, 7/15 for domestic and international students; for spring admission, 10/15 for domestic and international students; for summer admission, 2/15 for domestic and international students. Applications are processed on a rolling basis. Application fee: $60 ($65 for international students). Electronic applications accepted. *Expenses:* Contact institution. *Financial support:* Available to part-time students. *Unit head:* Dr. Camille Thomas, Department Chair, 435-586-7815, Fax: 435-865-8057, E-mail: camillethomas1@suu.edu. *Application contact:* Joan Anderson, Administrative Assistant, 435-586-7816, Fax: 435-865-8057, E-mail: anderson_j@suu.edu.
Website: https://www.suu.edu/ed/kor/master.html

Springfield College, Graduate Programs, Programs in Exercise Science and Sport Studies, Springfield, MA 01109-3797. Offers athletic training (MS); clinical exercise physiology (MS); exercise physiology (MS); sport and exercise psychology (MS); strength and conditioning (MS). *Program availability:* Part-time. Terminal master's awarded for partial completion of doctoral program. *Degree requirements:* For master's, comprehensive exam, research project or thesis. *Entrance requirements:* For master's, GRE General Test. Additional exam requirements/recommendations for international students: Required—TOEFL (minimum score 550 paper-based); Recommended—IELTS (minimum score 7). Electronic applications accepted.

Springfield College, Graduate Programs, Programs in Physical Education, Springfield, MA 01109-3797. Offers adapted physical education (MS); advanced-level coaching (M Ed); athletic administration (MS); exercise physiology (PhD); health promotion and disease prevention (MS); physical education initial licensure (CAGS); sport and exercise psychology (PhD); teaching and administration (PhD). *Program availability:* Part-time. *Degree requirements:* For master's, comprehensive exam, thesis (for some programs). *Entrance requirements:* For master's and doctorate, GRE General Test. Additional exam requirements/recommendations for international students: Required—TOEFL (minimum score 550 paper-based); Recommended—IELTS (minimum score 7). Electronic applications accepted.

Syracuse University, School of Education, MS Program in Exercise Science, Syracuse, NY 13244. Offers MS. *Program availability:* Part-time. *Entrance requirements:* For master's, GRE, baccalaureate degree from regionally-accredited college/university; 8 hours each in general biology and human anatomy and physiology; 6 hours of exercise science (including physiology of exercise and general science); three letters of recommendation; personal statement; resume; transcripts. Additional exam requirements/recommendations for international students: Required—TOEFL. *Application deadline:* For fall admission, 1/15 priority date for domestic and international students; for spring admission, 10/15 priority date for domestic and international students; for summer admission, 1/15 priority date for domestic and international students. Applications are processed on a rolling basis. Application fee: $75. Electronic applications accepted. *Financial support:* Fellowships, research assistantships, teaching assistantships, career-related internships or fieldwork, and scholarships/grants available. Financial award application deadline: 1/15. *Faculty research:* Bone density, obesity in females, cardiovascular functioning, attitudes toward physical education, sports management and psychology. *Unit head:* Dr. Tom Brutsaert, Chair, 315-443-9697, E-mail: tdbrutsa@syr.edu. *Application contact:* Speranza Migliore, Graduate Admissions Recruiter, 315-443-2505, E-mail: gradrcrt@syr.edu.
Website: http://soe.syr.edu/academic/exercise_science/graduate/masters/default.aspx

Tennessee State University, The School of Graduate Studies and Research, College of Health Sciences, Department of Human Performance and Sports Sciences, Nashville, TN 37209-1561. Offers exercise science (MA Ed); sports administration (MA Ed). *Degree requirements:* For master's, thesis optional. *Entrance requirements:* For master's, GRE General Test or MAT.

Texas A&M University–Commerce, College of Education and Human Services, Commerce, TX 75429. Offers counseling (M Ed, MS, PhD); early childhood education (M Ed, MS); educational administration (M Ed, MS, Ed D); educational psychology (PhD); educational technology leadership (M Ed, MS); educational technology library science (M Ed, MS); elementary education (M Ed); health, kinesiology and sports studies (MS); higher education (MS, Ed D); psychology (MS); reading (M Ed, MS); school psychology (SSP); secondary education (M Ed, MS); social work (MSW); special education (M Ed, MS); supervision, curriculum and instruction-elementary education (Ed D); training and development (MS). *Program availability:* Part-time, evening/weekend, 100% online, blended/hybrid learning. *Faculty:* 95 full-time (59 women), 29 part-time/adjunct (22 women). *Students:* 356 full-time (295 women), 1,262 part-time (992 women); includes 683 minority (349 Black or African American, non-Hispanic/Latino; 9 American Indian or Alaska Native, non-Hispanic/Latino; 30 Asian, non-Hispanic/Latino; 238 Hispanic/Latino; 57 Two or more races, non-Hispanic/Latino), 9 international. Average age 37. 951 applicants, 42% accepted, 304 enrolled. In 2018, 532 master's, 51 doctorates awarded. *Degree requirements:* For master's, comprehensive exam, thesis optional, departmental qualifying exams (for some programs); for doctorate, comprehensive exam, thesis/dissertation, departmental qualifying exam; for SSP, comprehensive exam. *Entrance requirements:* For master's, GRE General Test, official transcripts, letters of recommendation, resume, statement of goals; for doctorate, GRE General Test, letters of recommendation, statement of goals, writing samples, writing sessions, resumes. Additional exam requirements/recommendations for international students: Required—TOEFL (minimum score 550 paper-based; 79 iBT), IELTS (minimum score 6), PTE (minimum score 53). *Application deadline:* For fall admission, 6/1 priority date for international students; for spring admission, 10/15 priority date for international students; for summer admission, 3/15 priority date for international students. Applications are processed on a rolling basis. Application fee: $50 ($75 for international students). Electronic applications accepted. *Expenses:* Tuition, area resident: Full-time $3630. Tuition, state resident: full-time $3630. Tuition, nonresident: full-time $11,100. *International tuition:* $11,100 full-time. *Required fees:* $2794. Tuition and fees vary according to course load, degree level and program. *Financial support:* In 2018–19, 116 students received support, including 94 research assistantships with partial tuition reimbursements available (averaging $3,863 per year), 38 teaching assistantships with partial tuition reimbursements available (averaging $4,728 per year); career-related internships or fieldwork, Federal Work-Study, institutionally sponsored loans, scholarships/grants, health care benefits, and unspecified assistantships also available. Financial award application deadline: 5/1; financial award applicants required to submit FAFSA. *Faculty research:* Cognitive and bilingual education, positive behavioral intervention, literacy, math readiness. *Total annual research expenditures:* $1.1 million. *Unit head:* Dr. Madeline Justice, Interim Dean, 903-886-5181, Fax: 903-886-5905, E-mail: madeline.justice@tamuc.edu. *Application contact:* Vicky Turner, Doctoral Degree and Special Programs Coordinator, 903-886-5167, E-mail: vicky.turner@tamuc.edu.
Website: http://www.tamuc.edu/academics/graduateSchool/programs/education/default.aspx

Texas Tech University, Graduate School, College of Arts and Sciences, Department of Kinesiology and Sport Management, Lubbock, TX 79409-3011. Offers kinesiology (MS); sport management (MS). *Program availability:* Part-time. *Faculty:* 28 full-time (13 women), 6 part-time/adjunct (4 women). *Students:* 62 full-time (30 women), 9 part-time (3 women); includes 30 minority (4 Black or African American, non-Hispanic/Latino; 2 Asian, non-Hispanic/Latino; 21 Hispanic/Latino; 3 Two or more races, non-Hispanic/Latino), 7 international. Average age 24. 80 applicants, 64% accepted, 29 enrolled. In 2018, 31 master's awarded. *Degree requirements:* For master's, comprehensive exam (for some programs), thesis (for some programs). *Entrance requirements:* For master's, GRE (only for the M.S. in Kinesiology whose GPA on the last 60 hours of undergraduate coursework is 3.49 and lower), letter of intent, 3 letters of recommendation (preferably from academic professors), minimum GPA of 2.8 in the last 60 hours. Additional exam requirements/recommendations for international students: Required—TOEFL (minimum score 550 paper-based; 79 iBT). *Application deadline:* For fall admission, 6/1 priority date for domestic students, 1/15 priority date for international students; for spring

admission, 9/1 priority date for domestic students, 6/15 priority date for international students. Applications are processed on a rolling basis. Application fee: $65. Electronic applications accepted. *Expenses:* Contact institution. *Financial support:* In 2018–19, 70 students received support, including 70 fellowships (averaging $3,597 per year), 5 research assistantships (averaging $14,098 per year), 41 teaching assistantships (averaging $10,734 per year); career-related internships or fieldwork, scholarships/grants, health care benefits, and unspecified assistantships also available. Financial award application deadline: 8/1; financial award applicants required to submit FAFSA. *Faculty research:* Sport management, exercise physiology, human performance, motor behavior, exercise and sport psychology. *Total annual research expenditures:* $205,282. *Unit head:* Dr. Angela Lumpkin, Professor & Department Chair, 806-834-6935, Fax: 806-742-1688, E-mail: angela.lumpkin@ttu.edu. *Application contact:* Donna Torres, Graduate Admissions Coordinator, 806-834-7968, Fax: 806-742-1688, E-mail: donna.torres@ttu.edu.
Website: www.depts.ttu.edu/ksm/

Texas Woman's University, Graduate School, College of Health Sciences, Department of Nutrition and Food Sciences, Denton, TX 76204. Offers exercise and sports nutrition (MS); food science and flavor chemistry (MS); food systems administration (MS); nutrition (MS, PhD). *Program availability:* Part-time, evening/weekend, 100% online. *Faculty:* 14 full-time (9 women), 3 part-time/adjunct (all women). *Students:* 84 full-time (72 women), 80 part-time (75 women); includes 52 minority (7 Black or African American, non-Hispanic/Latino; 13 Asian, non-Hispanic/Latino; 25 Hispanic/Latino; 7 Two or more races, non-Hispanic/Latino), 10 international. Average age 28. 76 applicants, 82% accepted, 44 enrolled. In 2018, 77 master's, 3 doctorates awarded. *Degree requirements:* For master's, thesis or alternative, thesis (for food and flavor chemistry); thesis or coursework (for exercise and sports nutrition, nutrition), capstone; for doctorate, comprehensive exam, thesis/dissertation, qualifying exam, 50% of all required hours must be earned at TWU. *Entrance requirements:* For master's, GRE General Test (preferred minimum score 143 [350 old version] Verbal, 141 [450 old version] Quantitative), minimum GPA of 3.25 for last 60 undergraduate hours, resume, personal statement of interest (food science and flavor chemistry only); for doctorate, GRE General Test (preferred minimum score 153 [450 old version] Verbal, 146 [550 old version] Quantitative), minimum GPA of 3.5 on last 60 undergraduate hours and graduate course work, 2 letters of reference, resume, statement of purpose. Additional exam requirements/recommendations for international students: Required—TOEFL (minimum score 79 iBT); Recommended—IELTS (minimum score 6.5), TSE (minimum score 53). *Application deadline:* For fall admission, 6/15 for domestic students, 3/1 priority date for international students; for spring admission, 10/1 for domestic students, 7/1 priority date for international students; for summer admission, 4/1 for domestic students, 2/1 priority date for international students. Application fee: $50 ($75 for international students). Electronic applications accepted. *Expenses:* Contact institution. *Financial support:* In 2018–19, 60 students received support, including 1 research assistantship, 18 teaching assistantships (averaging $6,858 per year); career-related internships or fieldwork, Federal Work-Study, institutionally sponsored loans, scholarships/grants, traineeships, health care benefits, and unspecified assistantships also available. Support available to part-time students. Financial award application deadline: 3/1; financial award applicants required to submit FAFSA. *Faculty research:* Bio-active food components and cancer, functional foods in diabetes, obesity and bone health, flavor chemistry, obesity prevention in children. *Unit head:* Dr. K. Shane Broughton, Chair, 940-898-2636, Fax: 940-898-2634, E-mail: nutrfdsci@twu.edu. *Application contact:* Korie Hawkins, Associate Director of Admissions, Graduate Recruitment, 940-898-3188, Fax: 940-898-3081, E-mail: admissions@twu.edu.
Website: http://www.twu.edu/nutrition-food-sciences/

United States Sports Academy, Graduate Programs, Program in Sports Health and Fitness, Daphne, AL 36526-7055. Offers MSS. *Program availability:* Part-time, 100% online. *Degree requirements:* For master's, comprehensive exam, thesis optional. *Entrance requirements:* For master's, GRE General Test, GMAT, or MAT, minimum GPA of 2.5, 3 letters of recommendation, personal statement. Additional exam requirements/recommendations for international students: Required—TOEFL (minimum score 550 paper-based; 79 iBT). Electronic applications accepted. *Expenses:* Contact institution. *Faculty research:* Exercise physiology, conditioning.

United States Sports Academy, Graduate Programs, Program in Sports Studies, Daphne, AL 36526-7055. Offers MSS. *Program availability:* Part-time, 100% online. *Degree requirements:* For master's, comprehensive exam, thesis optional. *Entrance requirements:* For master's, GRE General Test, GMAT, or MAT, minimum GPA of 2.5, 3 letters of recommendation, personal statement. Additional exam requirements/recommendations for international students: Required—TOEFL (minimum score 550 paper-based; 79 iBT). Electronic applications accepted. *Expenses:* Contact institution.

University at Buffalo, the State University of New York, Graduate School, School of Public Health and Health Professions, Department of Exercise and Nutrition Sciences, Buffalo, NY 14260. Offers exercise science (MS, PhD); nutrition (MS, Advanced Certificate). *Program availability:* Part-time. *Entrance requirements:* For master's, doctorate, and Advanced Certificate, GRE General Test, minimum GPA of 3.0. Additional exam requirements/recommendations for international students: Required—TOEFL (minimum score 550 paper-based; 79 iBT), IELTS (minimum score 6.5). Electronic applications accepted. *Faculty research:* Cardiovascular disease-diet and exercise, respiratory control and muscle function, plasticity of connective and neural tissue, exercise nutrition, diet and cancer.

The University of Akron, Graduate School, College of Health Professions, School of Sport Science and Wellness Education, Program in Exercise Physiology/Adult Fitness, Akron, OH 44325. Offers MA, MS. *Degree requirements:* For master's, comprehensive exam, thesis optional. *Entrance requirements:* For master's, minimum GPA of 2.75, three letters of recommendation, statement of purpose. Additional exam requirements/recommendations for international students: Required—TOEFL (minimum score 79 iBT), IELTS (minimum score 6.5). Electronic applications accepted.

The University of Akron, Graduate School, College of Health Professions, School of Sport Science and Wellness Education, Program in Sport Science/Coaching, Akron, OH 44325. Offers MA, MS. *Degree requirements:* For master's, comprehensive exam, thesis optional. *Entrance requirements:* For master's, minimum GPA of 2.75, three letters of recommendation, statement of purpose. Additional exam requirements/recommendations for international students: Required—TOEFL (minimum score 79 iBT), IELTS (minimum score 6.5). Electronic applications accepted.

The University of Alabama, Graduate School, College of Education, Department of Kinesiology, Tuscaloosa, AL 35487. Offers alternative sport pedagogy (MA); exercise science (PhD). *Program availability:* Part-time. *Degree requirements:* For master's, comprehensive exam, thesis optional; for doctorate, comprehensive exam, thesis/dissertation. *Entrance requirements:* For master's and doctorate, GRE, minimum GPA of 3.0. Additional exam requirements/recommendations for international students: Required—TOEFL. Electronic applications accepted.

University of Alberta, Faculty of Kinesiology, Sport, and Recreation, Edmonton, AB T6G 2E1, Canada. Offers physical education (M Sc); recreation and physical education (MA, PhD). *Program availability:* Part-time. Terminal master's awarded for partial

completion of doctoral program. *Degree requirements:* For master's, thesis (for some programs); for doctorate, thesis/dissertation. *Entrance requirements:* For master's, bachelor's degree in related field; for doctorate, master's degree in related field with thesis. Additional exam requirements/recommendations for international students: Required—TOEFL. *Faculty research:* Motivation and adherence to physical ability, performance enhancement, adapted physical activity, exercise physiology, sport administration, tourism.

University of Arkansas at Little Rock, Graduate School, College of Education and Health Professions, Department of Health, Human Performance and Sport Management, Little Rock, AR 72204-1099. Offers exercise science (MS); health education and promotion (MS); sport management (MS). *Program availability:* Part-time, evening/weekend. *Degree requirements:* For master's, directed study or residency. *Entrance requirements:* For master's, GRE General Test, minimum GPA of 3.0, 3 reference letters.

University of California, Davis, Graduate Studies, Graduate Group in Exercise Science, Davis, CA 95616. Offers MS. *Degree requirements:* For master's, thesis. *Entrance requirements:* For master's, GRE, minimum GPA of 3.25. Additional exam requirements/recommendations for international students: Required—TOEFL (minimum score 550 paper-based). Electronic applications accepted.

University of Central Florida, College of Community Innovation and Education, Education Doctoral Programs, Orlando, FL 32816. Offers applied learning and instruction (MA); curriculum and instruction (M Ed); instructional design and technology (MA, Certificate), including e-learning (Certificate), educational technology (Certificate), instructional design (Certificate), instructional design and technology (MA), instructional design for simulations (Certificate); sport and exercise science (MS), including applied exercise physiology. *Program availability:* Part-time, evening/weekend. *Students:* 6 full-time (3 women), 3 part-time (all women); includes 2 minority (both Black or African American, non-Hispanic/Latino). Average age 42. *Entrance requirements:* Additional exam requirements/recommendations for international students: Required—TOEFL. Application fee: $30. Electronic applications accepted. *Financial support:* Scholarships/grants, health care benefits, and unspecified assistantships available. Financial award application deadline: 3/1; financial award applicants required to submit FAFSA. *Unit head:* Dr. Jeffrey Stout, Chair, 407-823-0211, E-mail: jeffrey.stout@ucf.edu. *Application contact:* Associate Director, Graduate Admissions, 407-823-2766, Fax: 407-823-6442, E-mail: gradadmissions@ucf.edu.
Website: https://ccie.ucf.edu/lser/

University of Central Oklahoma, The Jackson College of Graduate Studies, College of Education and Professional Studies, Department of Kinesiology and Health Studies, Edmond, OK 73034-5209. Offers athletic training (MS); wellness management (MS), including exercise science, health promotion. *Degree requirements:* For master's, comprehensive exam (for some programs), thesis (for some programs). *Entrance requirements:* Additional exam requirements/recommendations for international students: Required—TOEFL (minimum score 550 paper-based; 79 iBT), IELTS (minimum score 6.5). Electronic applications accepted.

University of Connecticut, Graduate School, College of Agriculture, Health and Natural Resources, Department of Kinesiology, Program in Exercise Science, Storrs, CT 06269. Offers MS, PhD. Terminal master's awarded for partial completion of doctoral program. *Degree requirements:* For master's, comprehensive exam, thesis or alternative; for doctorate, thesis/dissertation. *Entrance requirements:* For doctorate, GRE General Test. Additional exam requirements/recommendations for international students: Required—TOEFL (minimum score 550 paper-based). Electronic applications accepted.

University of Dayton, Department of Health and Sport Science, Dayton, OH 45469. Offers exercise science (MS Ed). *Program availability:* Part-time, 100% online. *Degree requirements:* For master's, thesis. *Entrance requirements:* For master's, GRE General Test or MAT if undergraduate GPA was 2.75 or below, minimum GPA of 2.75; official academic records of all previously-attended colleges or universities; three letters of recommendation from professors or employers; personal statement or resume. Additional exam requirements/recommendations for international students: Required—TOEFL (minimum score 550 paper-based; 80 iBT). Electronic applications accepted. *Expenses:* Contact institution. *Faculty research:* Exercise science, physiology, nutrition, sport management.

University of Florida, Graduate School, College of Health and Human Performance, Department of Applied Physiology and Kinesiology, Gainesville, FL 32611. Offers applied physiology and kinesiology (MS); athletic training/sports medicine (MS); biobehavioral science (MS); clinical exercise physiology (MS); exercise physiology (MS); health and human performance (PhD), including applied physiology and kinesiology, biobehavioral science, exercise physiology; human performance (MS). *Degree requirements:* For master's, comprehensive exam, thesis (for some programs); for doctorate, comprehensive exam, thesis/dissertation. *Entrance requirements:* For master's and doctorate, GRE General Test, minimum GPA of 3.0. Additional exam requirements/recommendations for international students: Required—TOEFL (minimum score 550 paper-based; 80 iBT), IELTS (minimum score 6). Electronic applications accepted. *Faculty research:* Cardiovascular disease; basic mechanisms that underlie exercise-induced changes in the body at the organ, tissue, cellular and molecular level; development of rehabilitation techniques for regaining motor control after stroke or as a consequence of Parkinson's disease; maintaining optimal health and delaying age-related declines in physiological function; psychomotor mechanisms impacting health and performance across the life span.

University of Houston, College of Liberal Arts and Social Sciences, Department of Health and Human Performance, Houston, TX 77204. Offers exercise science (MS); human nutrition (MS); human space exploration sciences (MS); kinesiology (PhD); physical education (M Ed). *Accreditation:* NCATE (one or more programs are accredited). *Program availability:* Part-time, evening/weekend. *Degree requirements:* For master's, comprehensive exam (for some programs), thesis (for some programs); for doctorate, comprehensive exam, thesis/dissertation, qualifying exam, candidacy paper. *Entrance requirements:* For master's, GRE (minimum 35th percentile on each section), minimum cumulative GPA of 3.0; for doctorate, GRE (minimum 35th percentile on each section), minimum cumulative GPA of 3.3. Additional exam requirements/recommendations for international students: Required—TOEFL (minimum score 550 paper-based; 79 iBT). Electronic applications accepted. *Faculty research:* Biomechanics, exercise physiology, obesity, nutrition, space exploration science.

University of Houston–Clear Lake, School of Human Sciences and Humanities, Programs in Human Sciences, Houston, TX 77058-1002. Offers behavioral sciences (MA), including criminology, cross cultural studies, general psychology, sociology; clinical psychology (MA); criminology (MA); cross cultural studies (MA); family therapy (MA); fitness and human performance (MA); school psychology (MA). *Accreditation:* AAMFT/COAMFTE. *Program availability:* Part-time, evening/weekend, online learning. *Degree requirements:* For master's, thesis or alternative. *Entrance requirements:* For master's, GRE General Test. Additional exam requirements/recommendations for international students: Required—TOEFL (minimum score 550 paper-based). Electronic

applications accepted. *Faculty research:* Smoking cessation, adolescent sexuality, white collar crime, serial murder, human factors/human computer interaction.

University of Idaho, College of Graduate Studies, College of Education, Health and Human Sciences, Department of Movement Sciences, Moscow, ID 83844-2401. Offers athletic training (MSAT, DAT); exercise science and health (MS); physical education teacher education (M Ed, MS); recreation, sport, and tourism management (MS). *Faculty:* 19. *Students:* 89 full-time, 9 part-time. Average age 26. In 2018, 43 master's awarded. *Degree requirements:* For doctorate, thesis/dissertation. *Entrance requirements:* For master's and doctorate, minimum GPA of 3.0. Additional exam requirements/recommendations for international students: Required—TOEFL. *Application deadline:* For fall admission, 8/1 for domestic students; for spring admission, 12/15 for domestic students. Applications are processed on a rolling basis. Application fee: $60. Electronic applications accepted. *Expenses:* Tuition, state resident: full-time $7266.44; part-time $474.50 per credit hour. Tuition, nonresident: full-time $24,902; part-time $1453.50 per credit hour. *Required fees:* $2085.56; $45.50 per credit hour. *Financial support:* Research assistantships and teaching assistantships available. Financial award applicants required to submit FAFSA. *Unit head:* Dr. Philip W. Scruggs, Chair, 208-885-7921, E-mail: movementsciences@uidaho.edu. *Application contact:* Dr. Philip W. Scruggs, Chair, 208-885-7921, E-mail: movementsciences@uidaho.edu.
Website: https://www.uidaho.edu/ed/mvsc

The University of Iowa, Graduate College, College of Liberal Arts and Sciences, Department of Health and Human Physiology, Iowa City, IA 52242-1316. Offers athletic training (MS); clinical exercise physiology (MS); health and human physiology (PhD); leisure studies (MA, PhD), including recreational sport management (PhD), therapeutic recreation (MA). *Degree requirements:* For master's, thesis optional, exam; for doctorate, comprehensive exam, thesis/dissertation. *Entrance requirements:* For master's and doctorate, GRE General Test, minimum GPA of 3.0. Additional exam requirements/recommendations for international students: Required—TOEFL (minimum score 600 paper-based; 100 iBT). Electronic applications accepted.

The University of Kansas, Graduate Studies, School of Education, Department of Health, Sport, and Exercise Sciences, Lawrence, KS 66045. Offers exercise science (MS Ed); health, sport, and exercise sciences (PhD); sport management (MS Ed). *Accreditation:* NCATE. *Program availability:* Part-time, evening/weekend. *Students:* 67 full-time (26 women), 34 part-time (15 women); includes 19 minority (6 Black or African American, non-Hispanic/Latino; 2 American Indian or Alaska Native, non-Hispanic/Latino; 9 Hispanic/Latino; 2 Two or more races, non-Hispanic/Latino), 9 international. Average age 27. 113 applicants, 73% accepted, 53 enrolled. In 2018, 17 master's, 3 doctorates awarded. *Entrance requirements:* For master's, GRE General Test (minimum score 1000, 450 verbal, 450 quantitative, 4.0 analytical), minimum GPA of 3.0, three letters of recommendation, personal statement, resume, writing sample; for doctorate, GRE General Test (minimum score 1100, verbal 500, quantitative 500, analytical 4.5), minimum graduate GPA of 3.5, undergraduate 3.0; three letters of recommendation; personal statement; resume; writing sample; interview with an advisor. Additional exam requirements/recommendations for international students: Required—TOEFL, IELTS. *Application deadline:* For fall admission, 3/15 for domestic and international students; for spring admission, 10/1 for domestic and international students; for summer admission, 3/15 for domestic and international students. Application fee: $65 ($85 for international students). Electronic applications accepted. *Financial support:* Research assistantships, teaching assistantships, Federal Work-Study, scholarships/grants, and unspecified assistantships available. Financial award application deadline: 2/21. *Faculty research:* Exercise and sport psychology, obesity prevention, sexuality health, sport ethics, skeletal muscle cell signaling and performance. *Unit head:* Dr. Joseph Weir, Chair, 785-864-0784, E-mail: joseph.weir@ku.edu. *Application contact:* Robin Bass, Graduate Admissions Coordinator, 785-864-6138, E-mail: rbass@ku.edu.
Website: http://hses.soe.ku.edu/

University of Kentucky, Graduate School, College of Education, Program in Kinesiology and Health Promotion, Lexington, KY 40506-0032. Offers biomechanics (MS); exercise physiology (MS, PhD); exercise science (PhD); health promotion (MS, Ed D); physical education training (Ed D); sport leadership (MS); teaching and coaching (MS). Terminal master's awarded for partial completion of doctoral program. *Degree requirements:* For master's, comprehensive exam, thesis optional; for doctorate, comprehensive exam, thesis/dissertation. *Entrance requirements:* For master's, GRE General Test, minimum undergraduate GPA of 2.75; for doctorate, GRE General Test, minimum graduate GPA of 3.0. Additional exam requirements/recommendations for international students: Required—TOEFL (minimum score 550 paper-based). Electronic applications accepted.

University of Lethbridge, School of Graduate Studies, Lethbridge, AB T1K 3M4, Canada. Offers addictions counseling (M Sc); agricultural biotechnology (M Sc); agricultural studies (M Sc, MA); anthropology (MA); archaeology (M Sc, MA); art (MA, MFA); biochemistry (M Sc); biological sciences (M Sc); biomolecular science (PhD); biosystems and biodiversity (PhD); Canadian studies (MA); chemistry (M Sc); computer science (M Sc); computer science and geographical information science (M Sc); counseling (MC); counseling psychology (M Ed); dramatic arts (MA); earth, space, and physical science (PhD); economics (MA); education (MA, PhD); educational leadership (M Ed); English (MA); environmental science (M Sc); evolution and behavior (PhD); exercise science (M Sc); French (MA); French/German (MA); French/Spanish (MA); general education (M Ed); geography (M Sc, MA); German (MA); health sciences (M Sc); individualized multidisciplinary (M Sc, MA); kinesiology (M Sc, MA); management (M Sc), including accounting, finance, human resource management and labor relations, information systems, international management, marketing, policy and strategy; mathematics (M Sc); music (M Mus, MA); Native American studies (MA); neuroscience (M Sc, PhD); new media (MA, MFA); nursing (M Sc, MN); philosophy (MA); physics (M Sc); political science (MA); psychology (M Sc, MA); religious studies (MA); sociology (MA); theatre and dramatic arts (MFA); theoretical and computational science (PhD); urban and regional studies (MA); women and gender studies (MA). *Program availability:* Part-time, evening/weekend. *Degree requirements:* For master's, thesis (for some programs); for doctorate, comprehensive exam, thesis/dissertation. *Entrance requirements:* For master's, GMAT (for M Sc in management), bachelor's degree in related field, minimum GPA of 3.0 during previous 20 graded semester courses, 2 years' teaching or related experience (M Ed); for doctorate, master's degree, minimum graduate GPA of 3.5. Additional exam requirements/recommendations for international students: Required—TOEFL (minimum score 580 paper-based; 93 iBT). Electronic applications accepted. *Faculty research:* Movement and brain plasticity, gibberellin physiology, photosynthesis, carbon cycling, molecular properties of main-group ring components.

University of Louisiana at Monroe, Graduate School, College of Health Sciences, Department of Kinesiology, Monroe, LA 71209-0001. Offers applied exercise science (MS); clinical exercise physiology (MS); sports, fitness and recreation management (MS). *Program availability:* Part-time, evening/weekend, online learning. *Faculty:* 6 full-time (2 women), 1 part-time/adjunct (0 women). *Students:* 39 full-time (17 women), 4 part-time (2 women); includes 16 minority (10 Black or African American, non-Hispanic/Latino; 1 American Indian or Alaska Native, non-Hispanic/Latino; 3 Hispanic/Latino; 2 Two or more races, non-Hispanic/Latino), 2 international. Average age 25. 16 applicants, 88% accepted, 11 enrolled. In 2018, 22 master's awarded. *Degree requirements:* For master's, comprehensive exam, thesis, 6-hour internship. *Entrance requirements:* For master's, GRE General Test. Additional exam requirements/recommendations for international students: Required—TOEFL (minimum score 500 paper-based; 61 iBT). *Application deadline:* For fall admission, 8/24 priority date for domestic students, 7/1 for international students; for winter admission, 12/14 priority date for domestic students; for spring admission, 1/19 for domestic students, 11/1 for international students. Applications are processed on a rolling basis. Application fee: $20 ($30 for international students). Electronic applications accepted. *Financial support:* In 2018–19, 12 students received support. Research assistantships, career-related internships or fieldwork, Federal Work-Study, and unspecified assistantships available. Financial award application deadline: 4/1; financial award applicants required to submit FAFSA. *Faculty research:* Cardiovascular disease risk factors; exercise and immunological system; attitude, exercise, and the aged. *Unit head:* Dr. Ken Alford, Director, 318-342-1306, E-mail: alford@ulm.edu. *Application contact:* Dr. Tommie Church, Director of Graduate Studies, 318-342-1321, E-mail: church@ulm.edu.
Website: http://www.ulm.edu/kinesiology/

University of Louisville, Graduate School, College of Education and Human Development, Department of Health and Sport Sciences, Louisville, KY 40292-0001. Offers community health education (M Ed); exercise physiology (MS), including health and sport sciences, strength and conditioning; health and physical education (MAT); sport administration (MS). *Program availability:* Part-time, evening/weekend, 100% online, blended/hybrid learning. *Students:* 32 full-time (10 women), 5 part-time (3 women); includes 9 minority (7 Black or African American, non-Hispanic/Latino; 2 Two or more races, non-Hispanic/Latino). Average age 28. 41 applicants, 66% accepted, 21 enrolled. In 2018, 21 master's awarded. Terminal master's awarded for partial completion of doctoral program. *Degree requirements:* For master's, comprehensive exam (for some programs), thesis optional. *Entrance requirements:* For master's, GRE (for most programs), PRAXIS (for educator preparation programs), professional statement, recommendation letters, resume, transcripts. Additional exam requirements/recommendations for international students: Required—TOEFL (minimum score 550 paper-based; 79 iBT); Recommended—IELTS (minimum score 6.5). *Application deadline:* For fall admission, 6/1 priority date for domestic students, 5/1 priority date for international students; for spring admission, 10/1 priority date for domestic students, 11/1 priority date for international students; for summer admission, 3/1 priority date for domestic students, 4/1 priority date for international students. Application fee: $65. *Expenses: Tuition, area resident:* Full-time $6500; part-time $723 per credit hour. Tuition, state resident: full-time $6500. Tuition, nonresident: full-time $13,557; part-time $1507 per credit hour. Tuition and fees vary according to course load and program. *Financial support:* In 2018–19, 15 students received support, including fellowships with full tuition reimbursements available (averaging $21,024 per year), research assistantships (averaging $21,024 per year); teaching assistantships with full tuition reimbursements available, Federal Work-Study, scholarships/grants, health care benefits, tuition waivers (full), and unspecified assistantships also available. Financial award application deadline: 3/1; financial award applicants required to submit FAFSA. *Faculty research:* Sport administration, exercise science, exercise physiology, physical and health education, youth sport development. *Unit head:* Dr. Dylan Naeger, Interim Chair, 502-852-6645, E-mail: hss@louisville.edu. *Application contact:* Dr. Margaret Pentecost, Director of Grad Assistant Dean for Graduate Student Success Graduate Student Services, 502-852-6437, Fax: 502-852-1465, E-mail: gedadm@louisville.edu.
Website: http://www.louisville.edu/education/departments/hss

University of Louisville, Graduate School, College of Education and Human Development, Departments of Early Childhood and Elementary Education, Middle and Secondary Education, and Special Education, Louisville, KY 40292-0001. Offers art education (MAT); autism and applied behavior analysis (Certificate); curriculum and instruction (PhD); early elementary education (MAT); exercise physiology (MS); health and physical education (MAT); health professions education (Certificate); higher education (MA); human resources and organization development (MS); instructional technology (M Ed); interdisciplinary early childhood education (MAT); middle school education (MAT); music education (MAT); secondary education (MAT); special education (MAT); sport administration (MS); teacher leadership (M Ed). *Program availability:* Part-time, evening/weekend, 100% online, blended/hybrid learning. *Faculty:* 97 full-time (64 women), 131 part-time/adjunct (86 women). *Students:* 109 full-time (72 women), 139 part-time (87 women); includes 43 minority (18 Black or African American, non-Hispanic/Latino; 6 Asian, non-Hispanic/Latino; 10 Hispanic/Latino; 9 Two or more races, non-Hispanic/Latino), 9 international. Average age 29. 108 applicants, 75% accepted, 59 enrolled. In 2018, 64 master's awarded. Terminal master's awarded for partial completion of doctoral program. *Degree requirements:* For master's, comprehensive exam (for some programs), thesis optional; for doctorate, comprehensive exam (for some programs), thesis/dissertation. *Entrance requirements:* For master's, GRE (for most programs), PRAXIS (for educator preparation programs), professional statement, recommendation letters, resume, transcripts; for doctorate and Certificate, GRE, professional statement, recommendation letters, resume, transcripts. Additional exam requirements/recommendations for international students: Required—TOEFL (minimum score 550 paper-based; 79 iBT); Recommended—IELTS (minimum score 6.5). *Application deadline:* For fall admission, 6/1 priority date for domestic students, 5/1 priority date for international students; for spring admission, 10/1 for domestic students, 11/1 priority date for international students; for summer admission, 3/1 priority date for domestic students, 4/1 priority date for international students. Application fee: $65. *Expenses: Tuition, area resident:* Full-time $6500; part-time $723 per credit hour. Tuition, state resident: full-time $6500. Tuition, nonresident: full-time $13,557; part-time $1507 per credit hour. Tuition and fees vary according to course load and program. *Financial support:* In 2018–19, 144 students received support, including fellowships with full tuition reimbursements available (averaging $21,024 per year), research assistantships with full tuition reimbursements available (averaging $21,024 per year), teaching assistantships with full tuition reimbursements available (averaging $21,024 per year); Federal Work-Study, scholarships/grants, health care benefits, tuition waivers (full), and unspecified assistantships also available. Financial award application deadline: 3/1; financial award applicants required to submit FAFSA. *Faculty research:* Children's early reading and writing development, crelevance of basic facts in elementary mathematics instruction, clinical model of teacher education, cultural and linguistic context of diverse learners, and STEM-integrated curriculum design and development. STEM teaching and learning, content literacy for English language learners, social justice in teacher education, adolescent literacy, mathematics teacher development. Classroom and behavior management; moderate/severe disabilities, autism. *Unit head:* Dr. Amy Lingo, Interim Dean, 502-852-3235, Fax: 502-852-1464, E-mail: cehdinfo@louisville.edu. *Application contact:* Dr. Margaret Pentecost, Assistant Dean for Graduate Student Success, 502-852-6437, Fax: 502-852-1417, E-mail: gedadm@louisville.edu.
Website: http://louisville.edu/delphi

University of Maine, Graduate School, College of Education and Human Development, School of Kinesiology, Physical Education and Athletic Training, Orono, ME 04469. Offers classroom technology integrationist (CGS); education data specialist (CGS); educational technology coordinator (CGS); kinesiology and physical education (M Ed,

MS); science education (M Ed, MS); STEM education (PhD). *Program availability:* Part-time, evening/weekend. *Faculty:* 3 full-time (0 women). *Students:* 9 full-time (5 women), 2 part-time (0 women); includes 2 minority (1 Black or African American, non-Hispanic/Latino; 1 Asian, non-Hispanic/Latino). Average age 24. 8 applicants, 75% accepted, 3 enrolled. In 2018, 3 master's awarded. *Degree requirements:* For master's, thesis (for some programs); for doctorate, comprehensive exam, thesis/dissertation. *Entrance requirements:* For master's, GRE General Test, MAT; for doctorate, GRE General Test. Additional exam requirements/recommendations for international students: Required—TOEFL. *Application deadline:* For fall admission, 1/15 for domestic students. Applications are processed on a rolling basis. Application fee: $65. Electronic applications accepted. *Financial support:* In 2018–19, 7 students received support, including 6 teaching assistantships with full tuition reimbursements available (averaging $15,600 per year); Federal Work-Study, scholarships/grants, and unspecified assistantships also available. Financial award application deadline: 3/1. *Faculty research:* Geriatric equilibrium, physical activity and technology, muscle cell metabolism, hormonal response to exercise. *Unit head:* Dr. Jim Artesani, Associate Dean of Accreditation and Graduate Affairs, 207-581-4061, Fax: 207-581-2423. *Application contact:* Scott G. Delcourt, Assistant Vice President for Graduate Studies and Senior Associate Dean, 207-581-3291, Fax: 207-581-3232, E-mail: graduate@maine.edu.
Website: http://umaine.edu/edhd/

University of Mary, School of Health Sciences, Program in Clinical Exercise Physiology, Bismarck, ND 58504-9652. Offers MS. *Program availability:* Online learning.

University of Mary Hardin-Baylor, Graduate Studies in Exercise Physiology, Belton, TX 76513. Offers exercise physiology (MS Ed); sport administration (MS Ed). *Program availability:* Part-time, 100% online. *Degree requirements:* For master's, comprehensive exam, thesis optional. *Entrance requirements:* For master's, bachelor's degree in exercise science or related field; minimum GPA of 3.0; interview with program director. Additional exam requirements/recommendations for international students: Required—TOEFL (minimum score 60 iBT), IELTS (minimum score 4.5). Electronic applications accepted. *Faculty research:* Evaluation of the efficacy and safety of Fenugreek extract ingestion on markers of muscle damage and inflammation on healthy non-resistance trained subjects; genetic influences on sport performance and athlete health; examination of biomarkers of sub-concussive impacts in men and women's Division III soccer players; The Acute Response of nutritive vs. non-nutritive sweeteners in soft drinks of blood glucose and insulin in regular soft drink consumers.

University of Massachusetts Boston, College of Nursing and Health Sciences, Program in Exercise and Health Sciences, Boston, MA 02125-3393. Offers MS, PhD. *Faculty:* 15 full-time (9 women), 4 part-time/adjunct (2 women). *Students:* 18 full-time (9 women), 8 part-time (6 women); includes 5 minority (2 Black or African American, non-Hispanic/Latino; 1 Asian, non-Hispanic/Latino; 2 Two or more races, non-Hispanic/Latino), 2 international. Average age 29. 71 applicants, 94% accepted, 31 enrolled. In 2018, 5 master's, 2 doctorates awarded. *Expenses: Tuition, area resident:* Full-time $17,896. Tuition, state resident: full-time $17,896. Tuition, nonresident: full-time $34,932. *International tuition:* $34,932 full-time. *Required fees:* $355. *Unit head:* Dr. Tongjian You, Graduate Program Director, 617-287.5934, E-mail: Tongjian.You@umb.edu. *Application contact:* Graduate Admissions Coordinator, 617-287-6400, Fax: 617-287-6236, E-mail: graduate.admissions@umb.edu.

University of Memphis, Graduate School, School of Health Studies, Memphis, TN 38152. Offers faith and health (Graduate Certificate); health studies (MS), including exercise, sport and movement sciences, health promotion, physical education teacher education; nutrition (MS), including clinical nutrition, environmental nutrition, nutrition science; sport nutrition and dietary supplementation (Graduate Certificate). *Program availability:* 100% online. *Faculty:* 20 full-time (11 women), 3 part-time/adjunct (all women). *Students:* 55 full-time (41 women), 49 part-time (33 women); includes 40 minority (34 Black or African American, non-Hispanic/Latino; 1 Asian, non-Hispanic/Latino; 4 Hispanic/Latino; 1 Two or more races, non-Hispanic/Latino), 6 international. Average age 31. 74 applicants, 64% accepted, 42 enrolled. In 2018, 38 master's, 2 other advanced degrees awarded. *Degree requirements:* For master's, comprehensive exam, thesis or alternative, culminating experience; for Graduate Certificate, practicum. *Entrance requirements:* For master's, GRE or PRAXIS II, letters of recommendation, statement of goals, minimum undergraduate GPA of 2.5; for Graduate Certificate, minimum undergraduate GPA of 2.5. Additional exam requirements/recommendations for international students: Required—TOEFL (minimum score 550 paper-based; 79 iBT). *Application deadline:* For fall admission, 4/15 priority date for domestic students; for spring admission, 10/15 priority date for domestic students; for summer admission, 4/15 priority date for domestic students. Application fee: $35 ($60 for international students). *Expenses: Tuition, area resident:* Full-time $10,240; part-time $503 per credit hour. Tuition, state resident: full-time $10,464. Tuition, nonresident: full-time $20,224; part-time $991 per credit hour. *Required fees:* $850; $106 per credit hour. *Financial support:* Research assistantships, teaching assistantships, career-related internships or fieldwork, Federal Work-Study, scholarships/grants, and unspecified assistantships available. Financial award application deadline: 2/1; financial award applicants required to submit FAFSA. *Unit head:* Dr. Richard Bloomer, Dean, 901-678-4316, Fax: 901-678-3591, E-mail: rbloomer@memphis.edu. *Application contact:* Dr. Richard Bloomer, Dean, 901-678-4316, Fax: 901-678-3591, E-mail: rbloomer@memphis.edu.
Website: http://www.memphis.edu/shs/

University of Miami, Graduate School, School of Education and Human Development, Department of Kinesiology and Sport Sciences, Program in Exercise Physiology, Coral Gables, FL 33124. Offers exercise physiology (MS Ed, PhD); strength and conditioning (MS Ed). *Program availability:* Part-time, evening/weekend. *Faculty:* 4 full-time (1 woman). *Students:* 38 full-time (13 women), 4 part-time (0 women); includes 13 minority (2 Black or African American, non-Hispanic/Latino; 1 Asian, non-Hispanic/Latino; 9 Hispanic/Latino; 1 Two or more races, non-Hispanic/Latino), 6 international. Average age 28. 59 applicants, 61% accepted, 17 enrolled. In 2018, 20 master's, 2 doctorates awarded. Terminal master's awarded for partial completion of doctoral program. *Degree requirements:* For master's, comprehensive exam (for some programs), special project; for doctorate, thesis/dissertation, qualifying exam. *Entrance requirements:* For master's and doctorate, GRE General Test. Additional exam requirements/recommendations for international students: Required—TOEFL (minimum score 550 paper-based; 80 iBT); Recommended—IELTS (minimum score 6.5). *Application deadline:* For fall admission, 10/1 for international students; for spring admission, 10/1 for international students. Applications are processed on a rolling basis. Application fee: $75. Electronic applications accepted. *Financial support:* Fellowships, research assistantships, teaching assistantships, scholarships/grants, health care benefits, tuition waivers (full and partial), and unspecified assistantships available. Support available to part-time students. Financial award application deadline: 3/1; financial award applicants required to submit FAFSA. *Faculty research:* Women's health, cardiovascular health, aging, metabolism, obesity. *Unit head:* Dr. Kevin Jacobs, Associate Professor and Program Director, 305-284-5873, E-mail: k.jacobs@miami.edu. *Application contact:* Lois Heffernan, Graduate Admissions Coordinator, 305-284-2167, Fax: 305-284-9395, E-mail: lheffernan@miami.edu.
Website: http://www.education.miami.edu

University of Minnesota, Twin Cities Campus, Graduate School, College of Education and Human Development, School of Kinesiology, Minneapolis, MN 55455-0213. Offers kinesiology (MS, PhD), including behavioral aspects of physical activity, biomechanics and neuromotor control, exercise physiology, perceptual-motor control and learning, sport and exercise psychology, sport management (PhD), sport sociology; sport and exercise science (M Ed); sport management (M Ed, MA). *Program availability:* Part-time. *Faculty:* 15 full-time (7 women). *Students:* 117 full-time (58 women), 21 part-time (8 women); includes 21 minority (5 Black or African American, non-Hispanic/Latino; 3 Asian, non-Hispanic/Latino; 9 Hispanic/Latino; 4 Two or more races, non-Hispanic/Latino), 23 international. Average age 26. 175 applicants, 62% accepted, 69 enrolled. In 2018, 47 master's, 9 doctorates awarded. Terminal master's awarded for partial completion of doctoral program. *Degree requirements:* For master's, final oral exam; for doctorate, thesis/dissertation, preliminary written/oral exam, final oral exam. *Entrance requirements:* For master's, GRE or MAT, minimum GPA of 3.0; for doctorate, GRE or MAT, minimum GPA of 3.0, writing sample. Application fee: $75 ($95 for international students). *Financial support:* In 2018–19, 3 fellowships, 8 research assistantships with full tuition reimbursements (averaging $8,544 per year), 37 teaching assistantships with full tuition reimbursements (averaging $14,093 per year) were awarded; career-related internships or fieldwork, Federal Work-Study, institutionally sponsored loans, and tuition waivers (full and partial) also available. Support available to part-time students. *Faculty research:* Role of physical activity in preventing health related problems; mechanism of age-related disorders, diseases and mental problems, and the ways to ameliorate them; role of sports in society and social justice; sports among populations with low income and racial diversity; fundamental functions of the body and the mechanism controlling the mechanisms; psychological issues related to physical activity and sports. *Total annual research expenditures:* $525,150. *Unit head:* Dr. Beth Lewis, Director, 612-625-5300, E-mail: blewis@umn.edu. *Application contact:* Nina Wang, 612-625-4380, E-mail: nwang@umn.edu.
Website: http://www.cehd.umn.edu/kin/

University of Mississippi, Graduate School, School of Applied Sciences, University, MS 38677. Offers communicative disorders (MS); criminal justice (MCJ); exercise science (MS); food and nutrition services (MS); health and kinesiology (PhD); health promotion (MS); nutrition and hospitality management (PhD); park and recreation management (MA); social welfare (PhD); social work (MSW). *Faculty:* 66 full-time (36 women), 27 part-time/adjunct (13 women). *Students:* 192 full-time (148 women), 40 part-time (25 women); includes 50 minority (41 Black or African American, non-Hispanic/Latino; 1 American Indian or Alaska Native, non-Hispanic/Latino; 1 Asian, non-Hispanic/Latino; 5 Hispanic/Latino; 2 Two or more races, non-Hispanic/Latino), 16 international. Average age 26. In 2018, 72 master's, 5 doctorates awarded. *Entrance requirements:* For master's, GRE General Test, minimum GPA of 3.0. Additional exam requirements/recommendations for international students: Required—TOEFL. *Application deadline:* Applications are processed on a rolling basis. Application fee: $50. Electronic applications accepted. *Financial support:* Scholarships/grants available. Financial award application deadline: 3/1; financial award applicants required to submit FAFSA. *Unit head:* Dr. Peter Grandjean, Dean of Applied Sciences, 662-915-7900, Fax: 662-915-7901, E-mail: applsci@olemiss.edu. *Application contact:* Temeka Smith, Graduate Activities Specialist for Admissions, 662-915-7474, Fax: 662-915-7577, E-mail: gschool@olemiss.edu.

University of Montana, Graduate School, Phyllis J. Washington College of Education and Human Sciences, Department of Health and Human Performance, Missoula, MT 59812. Offers community health (MS); exercise science (MS); health and human performance generalist (MS). *Program availability:* Part-time. *Entrance requirements:* For master's, GRE General Test. Additional exam requirements/recommendations for international students: Required—TOEFL. *Faculty research:* Exercise physiology, performance psychology, nutrition, pre-employment physical screening, program evaluation.

University of Nebraska at Kearney, College of Education, Kinesiology and Sport Sciences Department, Kearney, NE 68849-0001. Offers general physical education (MA Ed), including recreation and leisure, sports administration; physical education exercise science (MA Ed); physical education master teacher (MA Ed), including pedagogy, special populations. *Program availability:* Part-time, evening/weekend, 100% online. *Degree requirements:* For master's, comprehensive exam, thesis optional. *Entrance requirements:* For master's, GRE General Test (for some programs), personal statement. Additional exam requirements/recommendations for international students: Recommended—TOEFL (minimum score 550 paper-based; 79 iBT), IELTS (minimum score 6.5). Electronic applications accepted. *Faculty research:* Ergonomic aids, nutrition, motor development, sports pedagogy, applied behavior analysis, physical activity and wellness, athletic training, therapeutic Interventions, exercise physiology, endocrinology and metabolism.

University of Nebraska at Omaha, Graduate Studies, College of Education, School of Health and Kinesiology, Omaha, NE 68182. Offers athletic training (MA); exercise science (PhD); health, physical education, and recreation (MA, MS). *Program availability:* Part-time, evening/weekend. *Degree requirements:* For master's, comprehensive exam, thesis (for some programs). *Entrance requirements:* For master's, GRE; entrance exam, minimum GPA of 3.0, official transcripts, statement of purpose, 2 letters of recommendation; for doctorate, GRE, minimum GPA of 3.2, official transcripts, statement of purpose, 3 letters of recommendation, resume, writing sample. Additional exam requirements/recommendations for international students: Required—TOEFL, IELTS, PTE. Electronic applications accepted.

University of Nebraska–Lincoln, Graduate College, College of Education and Human Sciences, Department of Nutrition and Health Sciences, Lincoln, NE 68588. Offers community nutrition and health promotion (MS); nutrition (MS, PhD); nutrition and exercise (MS); nutrition and health sciences (MS, PhD). *Degree requirements:* For master's, thesis optional. *Entrance requirements:* For master's, GRE General Test. Additional exam requirements/recommendations for international students: Required—TOEFL (minimum score 550 paper-based). Electronic applications accepted. *Faculty research:* Foods/food service administration, community nutrition science, diet-health relationships.

University of Nevada, Las Vegas, Graduate College, School of Integrated Health Sciences, Department of Kinesiology and Nutrition Sciences, Las Vegas, NV 89154-3034. Offers exercise kinesiology (MS); kinesiology (PhD); nutrition sciences (MS). *Program availability:* Part-time. *Faculty:* 12 full-time (6 women), 1 (woman) part-time/adjunct. *Students:* 32 full-time (17 women), 12 part-time (8 women); includes 15 minority (3 Black or African American, non-Hispanic/Latino; 1 American Indian or Alaska Native, non-Hispanic/Latino; 3 Asian, non-Hispanic/Latino; 8 Hispanic/Latino), 1 international. Average age 28. 64 applicants, 36% accepted, 15 enrolled. In 2018, 13 master's, 4 doctorates awarded. *Degree requirements:* For master's, thesis (for some programs), professional paper; for doctorate, comprehensive exam, thesis/dissertation. *Entrance requirements:* For master's, GRE General Test, bachelor's degree; statement of purpose; 2 letters of recommendation; for doctorate, GRE General Test (minimum 70th percentile on the Verbal section), master's degree/bachelor's degree with minimum GPA of 3.25; 3 letters of recommendation; statement of purpose; personal interview. Additional exam requirements/recommendations for international students: Required—

TOEFL (minimum score 550 paper-based; 80 iBT), IELTS (minimum score 7). Application fee: $60 ($95 for international students). Electronic applications accepted. *Expenses:* Contact institution. *Financial support:* In 2018–19, 22 students received support, including 12 research assistantships with full tuition reimbursements available (averaging $12,250 per year), 10 teaching assistantships with full tuition reimbursements available (averaging $12,350 per year); institutionally sponsored loans, scholarships/grants, health care benefits, and unspecified assistantships also available. Financial award application deadline: 3/15; financial award applicants required to submit FAFSA. *Faculty research:* Biomechanics of gait, factors in motor skill acquisition and performance, nutritional supplements and performance, lipoprotein biochemistry, transcranial direct current stimulation. *Total annual research expenditures:* $248,520. *Unit head:* Dr. John Mercer, Professor/Acting Chair, 702-895-4672, Fax: 702-895-1356, E-mail: kns.chair@unlv.edu. *Application contact:* Dr. James Navalta, Graduate Coordinator, 702-895-2344, E-mail: kinesiology.gradcoord@unlv.edu.

University of New Brunswick Fredericton, School of Graduate Studies, Faculty of Kinesiology, Fredericton, NB E3B 5A3, Canada. Offers exercise and sport science (M Sc); sport and recreation management (MBA); sport and recreation studies (MA). *Program availability:* Part-time. *Degree requirements:* For master's, thesis (for some programs). *Entrance requirements:* For master's, GMAT (minimum score of 550 for sport and recreation management program), minimum GPA of 3.0, written statement of research goals and interests. Additional exam requirements/recommendations for international students: Required—TOEFL (minimum score 92 iBT), IELTS (minimum score 7). Electronic applications accepted.

University of New Mexico, Graduate Studies, College of Education, Program in Physical Education, Sports and Exercise Science, Albuquerque, NM 87131-2039. Offers curriculum and instruction (PhD); exercise science (PhD); sports administration (PhD). *Program availability:* Part-time. *Students:* Average age 30. 67 applicants, 75% accepted, 35 enrolled. In 2018, 13 doctorates awarded. *Degree requirements:* For doctorate, comprehensive exam, thesis/dissertation, inquiry skills, 24 credits in supporting area. *Entrance requirements:* For doctorate, GRE, letter of intent, 3 letters of reference, minimum cumulative GPA of 3.0 in last 2 years of bachelor's degree. Additional exam requirements/recommendations for international students: Required—TOEFL (minimum score 550 paper-based). *Application deadline:* For fall admission, 3/1 priority date for domestic students; for spring admission, 11/1 priority date for domestic students. Application fee: $50. Electronic applications accepted. *Financial support:* Fellowships, teaching assistantships with full tuition reimbursements, career-related internships or fieldwork, Federal Work-Study, institutionally sponsored loans, scholarships/grants, health care benefits, tuition waivers, and unspecified assistantships available. Financial award application deadline: 3/1; financial award applicants required to submit FAFSA. *Faculty research:* Facility risk management, physical education pedagogy practices, physiological adaptations to exercise, physiological adaptations to heat, sport leadership. *Unit head:* Dr. Todd Seidler, Chair, 505-277-2783, Fax: 505-277-6227, E-mail: tseidler@unm.edu. *Application contact:* Monica Lopez, Program Office, 505-277-5151, Fax: 505-277-6227, E-mail: mllopez@unm.edu.
Website: https://coe.unm.edu/departments-programs/hess/physical-education/physical-education-phd/index.html

University of North Alabama, College of Education, Department of Health, Physical Education, and Recreation, Florence, AL 35632-0001. Offers health and human performance (MS), including exercise science, kinesiology, wellness and health promotion. *Program availability:* Part-time. *Degree requirements:* For master's, comprehensive exam (for some programs), thesis optional. *Entrance requirements:* For master's, MAT or GRE, 3 letters of recommendation, essay. Additional exam requirements/recommendations for international students: Required—TOEFL (minimum score 79 iBT), IELTS (minimum score 6), PTE (minimum score 54). Electronic applications accepted.

The University of North Carolina at Chapel Hill, Graduate School, College of Arts and Sciences, Department of Exercise and Sport Science, Chapel Hill, NC 27599. Offers athletic training (MA); exercise physiology (MA); sport administration (MA). *Degree requirements:* For master's, comprehensive exam, thesis. *Entrance requirements:* For master's, GRE General Test, minimum GPA of 3.0. Additional exam requirements/recommendations for international students: Required—TOEFL (minimum score 550 paper-based). Electronic applications accepted. *Faculty research:* Mild head injury in sport, endocrine system's response to exercise, obesity and children, effect of aerobic exercise on cerebral bloodflow in elderly population.

The University of North Carolina at Pembroke, The Graduate School, School of Education, Department of Health and Human Performance, Pembroke, NC 28372-1510. Offers health/physical education (MAT); physical education (MA), including exercise/sports administration, physical education advanced licensure. *Program availability:* Part-time, evening/weekend. *Degree requirements:* For master's, comprehensive exam, thesis optional. *Entrance requirements:* For master's, MAT or GRE, minimum GPA of 3.0 in major, 2.5 overall. Additional exam requirements/recommendations for international students: Required—TOEFL.

University of Northern Colorado, Graduate School, College of Natural and Health Sciences, School of Sport and Exercise Science, Greeley, CO 80639. Offers exercise science (MS, PhD); physical education and physical activity leadership (MAT); sport administration (MS, PhD); sport pedagogy (MS, PhD); sports coaching (MA). *Program availability:* Part-time, evening/weekend. *Degree requirements:* For master's, comprehensive exam; for doctorate, comprehensive exam, thesis/dissertation. *Entrance requirements:* For master's, 2 letters of recommendation, resume; for doctorate, GRE General Test, 3 letters of recommendation, resume. Electronic applications accepted.

University of North Florida, Brooks College of Health, Department of Clinical and Applied Movement Sciences, Jacksonville, FL 32224. Offers MSH, DPT. *Accreditation:* APTA. *Program availability:* Part-time, evening/weekend. *Faculty:* 15 full-time (9 women), 7 part-time/adjunct (4 women). *Students:* 123 full-time (74 women), 3 part-time (1 woman); includes 25 minority (2 Black or African American, non-Hispanic/Latino; 1 American Indian or Alaska Native, non-Hispanic/Latino; 5 Asian, non-Hispanic/Latino; 11 Hispanic/Latino; 6 Two or more races, non-Hispanic/Latino), 2 international. Average age 26. 465 applicants, 15% accepted, 47 enrolled. In 2018, 19 master's, 26 doctorates awarded. *Entrance requirements:* For master's, GRE General Test, minimum GPA of 3.0 in last 60 hours, volunteer/observation experience. Additional exam requirements/recommendations for international students: Required—TOEFL (minimum score 500 paper-based). *Application deadline:* For fall admission, 7/15 for domestic students, 1/15 for international students. Application fee: $30. Electronic applications accepted. *Expenses:* Contact institution. *Financial support:* In 2018–19, 18 students received support, including 14 research assistantships (averaging $2,454 per year), 1 teaching assistantship (averaging $2,250 per year); career-related internships or fieldwork, Federal Work-Study, scholarships/grants, and tuition waivers (partial) also available. Support available to part-time students. Financial award application deadline: 4/1; financial award applicants required to submit FAFSA. *Faculty research:* Clinical outcomes related to orthopedic physical therapy interventions, instructional multimedia in physical therapy education, effect of functional electrical stimulation orthostatic hypotension in acute complete spinal cord injury individuals. *Total annual research expenditures:* $4,528. *Unit head:* Dr. Joel Beam, Chair, 904-620-2841, E-mail: jbeam@unf.edu. *Application contact:* Amanda Lovins, Assistant Director, 904-620-2841, E-mail: ptadmissions@unf.edu.
Website: http://www.unf.edu/brooks/movement_science/

University of Oklahoma, College of Arts and Sciences, Department of Health and Exercise Science, Norman, OK 73019. Offers exercise physiology (MS, PhD); health and exercise science (MS); health promotion (MS, PhD). *Faculty:* 14 full-time (6 women), 1 part-time/adjunct (0 women). *Students:* 27 full-time (13 women), 14 part-time (7 women); includes 9 minority (2 Black or African American, non-Hispanic/Latino; 1 Asian, non-Hispanic/Latino; 2 Hispanic/Latino; 4 Two or more races, non-Hispanic/Latino), 6 international. Average age 25. 40 applicants, 43% accepted, 15 enrolled. In 2018, 6 master's, 2 doctorates awarded. *Degree requirements:* For master's, comprehensive exam (for some programs), thesis; for doctorate, comprehensive exam, thesis/dissertation. *Entrance requirements:* For master's and doctorate, GRE. Additional exam requirements/recommendations for international students: Required—TOEFL (minimum score 79 iBT) or IELTS (minimum score 6.5). *Application deadline:* For fall admission, 2/1 priority date for domestic and international students. Applications are processed on a rolling basis. Application fee: $50 ($100 for international students). Electronic applications accepted. *Expenses:* Tuition, state resident: full-time $5683.20; part-time $236.80 per credit hour. Tuition, nonresident: full-time $20,342; part-time $847.60 per credit hour. *International tuition:* $20,342.40 full-time. *Required fees:* $2894.20; $110.05 per credit hour. $126.50 per semester. Tuition and fees vary according to course load and program. *Financial support:* Teaching assistantships, health care benefits, tuition waivers, and unspecified assistantships available. Financial award application deadline: 6/1; financial award applicants required to submit FAFSA. *Faculty research:* Health promotion&—behavioral science; exercise physiology&—neuromuscular, aging, endocrine and bone metabolism, cardiovascular. *Unit head:* Dr. Michael G. Bemben, Professor/Chair, 405-325-2717, Fax: 405-325-0594, E-mail: mgbemben@ou.edu. *Application contact:* Dr. Marshall Cheney, Associate Professor and Graduate Liaison, 405-325-6322, Fax: 405-325-0594, E-mail: marshall@ou.edu.
Website: http://www.ou.edu/cas/hes

University of Pittsburgh, School of Education, Department of Health and Physical Activity, Program in Developmental Movement, Pittsburgh, PA 15260. Offers MS. *Degree requirements:* For master's, thesis. *Entrance requirements:* Additional exam requirements/recommendations for international students: Required—TOEFL. Electronic applications accepted.

University of Pittsburgh, School of Education, Department of Health and Physical Activity, Program in Exercise Physiology, Pittsburgh, PA 15260. Offers MS, PhD. *Entrance requirements:* Additional exam requirements/recommendations for international students: Required—TOEFL (minimum score 550 paper-based; 80 iBT). Electronic applications accepted.

University of Puerto Rico–Mayagüez, Graduate Studies, College of Arts and Sciences, Department of Kinesiology, Mayagüez, PR 00681-9000. Offers kinesiology (MA), including biomechanics, education, exercise physiology, sports training. *Program availability:* Part-time. *Degree requirements:* For master's, thesis. *Entrance requirements:* For master's, EXADEP or GRE, minimum GPA of 2.5. Electronic applications accepted.

University of Puerto Rico–Río Piedras, College of Education, Program in Exercise Sciences, San Juan, PR 00931-3300. Offers MS. *Entrance requirements:* For master's, PAEG or GRE, minimum GPA of 3.0.

University of Rhode Island, Graduate School, College of Health Sciences, Department of Kinesiology, Kingston, RI 02881. Offers cultural studies of sport and physical culture (MS); exercise science (MS); psychosocial/behavioral aspects of physical activity (MS). *Accreditation:* NCATE. *Program availability:* Part-time. *Faculty:* 16 full-time (11 women). *Students:* 13 full-time (5 women), 2 part-time (1 woman), 1 international. 18 applicants, 100% accepted, 8 enrolled. In 2018, 5 master's awarded. *Entrance requirements:* Additional exam requirements/recommendations for international students: Required—TOEFL. *Application deadline:* For fall admission, 7/15 for domestic students, 2/1 for international students; for spring admission, 11/15 for domestic students, 7/15 for international students. Application fee: $65. Electronic applications accepted. *Expenses: Tuition, area resident:* Full-time $13,226; part-time $735 per credit. Tuition, state resident: full-time $13,226; part-time $735 per credit. Tuition, nonresident: full-time $25,854; part-time $1436 per credit. *International tuition:* $25,854 full-time. *Required fees:* $1698; $50 per credit. $35 per semester. One-time fee: $165. *Financial support:* In 2018–19, 1 research assistantship (averaging $8,862 per year), 6 teaching assistantships with tuition reimbursements (averaging $16,247 per year) were awarded. Financial award application deadline: 2/1; financial award applicants required to submit FAFSA. *Unit head:* Dr. Disa Hatfield, Interim Chair, 401-874-5183, E-mail: doch@uri.edu. *Application contact:* Dr. Matthew Delmonico, Graduate Program Director, 401-874-5440, E-mail: delmonico@uri.edu.
Website: http://web.uri.edu/kinesiology/

University of South Alabama, College of Education and Professional Studies, Department of Health, Kinesiology, and Sport, Mobile, AL 36688. Offers exercise science (MS); health education (M Ed, MS); physical education (M Ed); sport management (MS). *Accreditation:* NCATE (one or more programs are accredited). *Program availability:* Part-time. *Degree requirements:* For master's, comprehensive exam, thesis optional. *Entrance requirements:* For master's, GRE General Test or MAT, Alabama Class B certificate or the equivalent (for students seeking the master's-level/Class A certification). Additional exam requirements/recommendations for international students: Required—TOEFL. Electronic applications accepted.

University of South Carolina, The Graduate School, Arnold School of Public Health, Department of Exercise Science, Columbia, SC 29208. Offers MS, DPT, PhD. *Program availability:* Part-time. *Degree requirements:* For master's, comprehensive exam, thesis (for some programs), project; for doctorate, comprehensive exam, thesis/dissertation. *Entrance requirements:* For master's and doctorate, GRE General Test. Additional exam requirements/recommendations for international students: Required—TOEFL (minimum score 570 paper-based). Electronic applications accepted. *Faculty research:* Effects of acute and chronic exercise on human function and health, motor control.

University of South Dakota, Graduate School, School of Education, Division of Kinesiology and Sport Management, Vermillion, SD 57069. Offers exercise science (MA); sport management (MA). *Accreditation:* NCATE. *Program availability:* Part-time. *Degree requirements:* For master's, comprehensive exam, thesis or alternative. *Entrance requirements:* For master's, GRE General Test, MAT, minimum GPA of 3.0. Additional exam requirements/recommendations for international students: Required—TOEFL (minimum score 550 paper-based; 79 iBT). Electronic applications accepted.

The University of Tampa, Program in Exercise and Nutrition Science, Tampa, FL 33606-1490. Offers MS. *Program availability:* Part-time, evening/weekend. *Faculty:* 10 part-time/adjunct (2 women). *Students:* 46 full-time (18 women), 10 part-time (7 women); includes 12 minority (6 Black or African American, non-Hispanic/Latino; 1 American Indian or Alaska Native, non-Hispanic/Latino; 3 Hispanic/Latino; 2 Two or more races, non-Hispanic/Latino), 3 international. Average age 25. 165 applicants, 57% accepted, 56 enrolled. In 2018, 39 master's awarded. *Degree requirements:* For master's, comprehensive exam, practicum. *Entrance requirements:* For master's, GMAT or GRE,

official transcripts from all colleges and/or universities previously attended, resume, personal statement, letters of recommendation, bachelor's degree in related field. Additional exam requirements/recommendations for international students: Required—TOEFL (minimum score 577 paper-based; 90 iBT), IELTS (minimum score 7.5). *Application deadline:* Applications are processed on a rolling basis. Application fee: $40. Electronic applications accepted. *Expenses:* Contact institution. *Financial support:* In 2018–19, 6 students received support. Career-related internships or fieldwork, scholarships/grants, and unspecified assistantships available. Financial award applicants required to submit FAFSA. *Unit head:* Dr. Ronda C. Sturgill, Associate Professor, Health Sciences and Human Performance, 813-257-3445, E-mail: rsturgill@ut.edu. *Application contact:* Ashley Russell, Staff Assistant, Admissions for Graduate and Continuing Studies, 813-253-6249, E-mail: arussell@ut.edu.
Website: http://www.ut.edu/msexercisenutrition/

The University of Tennessee, Graduate School, College of Education, Health and Human Sciences, Department of Exercise, Sport, and Leisure Studies, Program in Exercise Science, Knoxville, TN 37996. Offers biomechanics/sports medicine (MS, PhD); exercise physiology (MS, PhD). *Accreditation:* CEPH (one or more programs are accredited). *Program availability:* Part-time. *Degree requirements:* For master's, thesis optional. *Entrance requirements:* For master's, minimum GPA of 2.7. Additional exam requirements/recommendations for international students: Required—TOEFL. Electronic applications accepted.

The University of Tennessee, Graduate School, College of Education, Health and Human Sciences, Program in Education, Knoxville, TN 37996. Offers art education (MS); counseling education (PhD); cultural studies in education (PhD); curriculum (MS, Ed S); curriculum, educational research and evaluation (Ed D, PhD); early childhood education (PhD); early childhood special education (MS); education of deaf and hard of hearing (MS); educational administration and policy studies (Ed D, PhD); educational administration and supervision (Ed S); educational psychology (Ed D, PhD); elementary education (MS, Ed S); elementary teaching (MS); English education (MS, Ed S); exercise science (PhD); foreign language/ESL education (MS, Ed S); instructional technology (MS, Ed D, PhD, Ed S); literacy, language and ESL education (PhD); literacy, language education, and ESL education (Ed D); mathematics education (MS, Ed S); modified and comprehensive special education (MS); reading education (MS, Ed S); school counseling (Ed S); school psychology (PhD, Ed S); science education (MS, Ed S); secondary teaching (MS); social foundations (MS); social science education (MS, Ed S); socio-cultural foundations of sports and education (PhD); special education (Ed S); teacher education (Ed D, PhD). *Accreditation:* NCATE. *Program availability:* Part-time, evening/weekend. *Degree requirements:* For master's and Ed S, thesis optional; for doctorate, variable foreign language requirement, thesis/dissertation. *Entrance requirements:* For master's, minimum GPA of 2.7; for doctorate and Ed S, GRE General Test, minimum GPA of 2.7. Additional exam requirements/recommendations for international students: Required—TOEFL. Electronic applications accepted.

The University of Texas at Arlington, Graduate School, College of Nursing and Health Innovation, Arlington, TX 76019. Offers athletic training (MS); exercise science (MS); kinesiology (PhD); nurse practitioner (MSN); nursing (PhD); nursing administration (MSN); nursing education (MSN); nursing practice (DNP). *Accreditation:* AACN. *Program availability:* Part-time, evening/weekend, online learning. *Degree requirements:* For master's, practicum course; for doctorate, comprehensive exam (for some programs), thesis/dissertation (for some programs), proposal defense dissertation (for PhD); scholarship project (for DNP). *Entrance requirements:* For master's, GRE General Test if GPA less than 3.0, minimum GPA of 3.0, Texas nursing license, minimum C grade in undergraduate statistics course; for doctorate, GRE General Test (waived for MSN-to-PhD applicants), minimum undergraduate, graduate and statistics GPA of 3.0; Texas RN license; interview; written statement of goals. Additional exam requirements/recommendations for international students: Required—TOEFL (minimum score 550 paper-based), IELTS (minimum score 7). *Faculty research:* Simulation in clinical education and practice, cultural diversity, vulnerable populations, substance abuse.

The University of Texas at Austin, Graduate School, College of Education, Department of Kinesiology and Health Education, Austin, TX 78712-1111. Offers behavioral health (PhD); exercise and sport psychology (M Ed, MA); exercise science (M Ed, MS, PhD); health education (M Ed, MS, Ed D, PhD). *Program availability:* Part-time. Terminal master's awarded for partial completion of doctoral program. *Degree requirements:* For master's, thesis (for some programs); for doctorate, thesis/dissertation. *Entrance requirements:* For master's and doctorate, GRE General Test. Additional exam requirements/recommendations for international students: Required—TOEFL. Electronic applications accepted. *Faculty research:* Health promotion, human performance and exercise biochemistry, motor behavior and biomechanics, sport management, aging and pediatric development.

The University of Texas Rio Grande Valley, College of Health Affairs, Department of Health and Human Performance, Edinburg, TX 78539. Offers exercise science (MS); kinesiology (MS). *Program availability:* Part-time-only, evening/weekend, 100% online. *Faculty:* 13 full-time (5 women), 2 part-time/adjunct (0 women). *Students:* 8 full-time (4 women), 31 part-time (8 women); includes 31 minority (1 Black or African American, non-Hispanic/Latino; 30 Hispanic/Latino). Average age 28. 27 applicants, 96% accepted, 25 enrolled. In 2018, 18 master's awarded. *Degree requirements:* For master's, comprehensive exam, thesis optional. *Entrance requirements:* For master's, GRE, minimum GPA of 3.0 in last 60 hours. Additional exam requirements/recommendations for international students: Required—TOEFL (minimum score 550 paper-based; 79 iBT), IELTS (minimum score 6.5). *Application deadline:* For fall admission, 7/17 for domestic students; for spring admission, 11/16 for domestic students. Applications are processed on a rolling basis. Application fee: $50. Electronic applications accepted. *Expenses: Tuition, area resident:* Full-time $6888. Tuition, state resident: full-time $6888. Tuition, nonresident: full-time $14,484. *International tuition:* $14,484 full-time. *Required fees:* $1468. *Financial support:* In 2018–19, 8 students received support, including 9 research assistantships (averaging $5,000 per year); unspecified assistantships also available. Financial award application deadline: 4/15; financial award applicants required to submit FAFSA. *Faculty research:* Physiology of exercise, fitness levels, Mexican American children, nutrition, diabetes prevention. *Unit head:* Dr. Zelma D. Mata, Chair, 956-665-3501, Fax: 956-665-3502, E-mail: zelma.mata@utrgv.edu. *Application contact:* Dr. Murat Karabulut, Associate Professor and Graduate Program Coordinator, 956-882-8290, E-mail: murat.karabulut@utrgv.edu.
Website: http://www.utrgv.edu/hhp/

University of the Pacific, College of the Pacific, Department of Health, Exercise and Sport Science, Stockton, CA 95211-0197. Offers MA. *Degree requirements:* For master's, comprehensive exam (for some programs), thesis (for some programs). *Entrance requirements:* For master's, GRE General Test. Additional exam requirements/recommendations for international students: Required—TOEFL.

The University of Toledo, College of Graduate Studies, College of Health and Human Services, School of Exercise and Rehabilitation Sciences, Toledo, OH 43606-3390. Offers athletic training (MSES); exercise physiology (MSES); exercise science (PhD); occupational therapy (OTD); physical therapy (DPT); recreation and leisure studies (MA), including recreation administration, recreation therapy. *Degree requirements:* For master's, comprehensive exam, thesis; for doctorate, thesis/dissertation or alternative. *Entrance requirements:* For master's, GRE, minimum cumulative GPA of 2.7 for all previous academic work, letters of recommendation; for doctorate, GRE, minimum cumulative GPA of 3.0 for all previous academic work, letters of recommendation; OTCAS or PTCAS application and UT supplemental application (for OTD and DPT). Additional exam requirements/recommendations for international students: Required—TOEFL (minimum score 550 paper-based; 80 iBT). Electronic applications accepted.

University of West Florida, Usha Kundu, MD College of Health, Department of Exercise Science and Community Health, Pensacola, FL 32514-5750. Offers health promotion (MS); health, leisure, and exercise science (MS), including exercise science, physical education. *Program availability:* Part-time, evening/weekend. *Degree requirements:* For master's, thesis or alternative. *Entrance requirements:* For master's, GRE or MAT, official transcripts; minimum GPA of 3.0; letter of intent; three personal references; work experience as reflected in resume. Additional exam requirements/recommendations for international students: Required—TOEFL (minimum score 550 paper-based).

University of Wisconsin–La Crosse, College of Science and Health, Department of Exercise and Sport Science, Program in Clinical Exercise Physiology, La Crosse, WI 54601-3742. Offers MS. *Degree requirements:* For master's, thesis optional. *Entrance requirements:* Additional exam requirements/recommendations for international students: Required—TOEFL (minimum score 550 paper-based; 79 iBT). Electronic applications accepted.

University of Wisconsin–La Crosse, College of Science and Health, Department of Exercise and Sport Science, Program in Human Performance, La Crosse, WI 54601-3742. Offers exercise sport science: human performance (MS), including applied sport science, strength and conditioning. *Program availability:* Part-time. *Degree requirements:* For master's, comprehensive exam (for some programs), thesis optional. *Entrance requirements:* For master's, GRE, course work in anatomy, physiology, biomechanics, and exercise physiology. Additional exam requirements/recommendations for international students: Required—TOEFL (minimum score 550 paper-based; 79 iBT). Electronic applications accepted. *Faculty research:* Anaerobic metabolism, power development, strength training, biomechanics, athletic performance.

University of Wisconsin–Milwaukee, Graduate School, College of Health Sciences, Department of Kinesiology, Milwaukee, WI 53201-0413. Offers athletic training (MS); kinesiology (MS, PhD), including exercise and nutrition in health and disease (MS), integrative human performance (MS), neuromechanics (MS); physical therapy (DPT). *Program availability:* Part-time. *Students:* 108 full-time (59 women), 6 part-time (3 women); includes 11 minority (1 American Indian or Alaska Native, non-Hispanic/Latino; 1 Asian, non-Hispanic/Latino; 3 Hispanic/Latino; 6 Two or more races, non-Hispanic/Latino), 5 international. Average age 28. 47 applicants, 38% accepted, 16 enrolled. In 2018, 9 master's, 21 doctorates awarded. *Degree requirements:* For master's, comprehensive exam, thesis optional. *Entrance requirements:* For master's, GRE General Test. Additional exam requirements/recommendations for international students: Required—TOEFL (minimum score 550 paper-based; 79 iBT), IELTS (minimum score 6.5). *Application deadline:* For fall admission, 1/1 priority date for domestic students; for spring admission, 9/1 for domestic students. Applications are processed on a rolling basis. Application fee: $56 ($96 for international students). *Financial support:* Fellowships, research assistantships, teaching assistantships, career-related internships or fieldwork, unspecified assistantships, and project assistantships available. Support available to part-time students. Financial award application deadline: 4/15. *Unit head:* Dr. Kyle T. Ebersole, Department Chair, 414-229-6717, Fax: 414-229-3366, E-mail: ebersole@uwm.edu. *Application contact:* Stephen C. Cobb, Graduate Program Coordinator, 414-229-3369, Fax: 414-229-3366, E-mail: cobbsc@uwm.edu.
Website: http://uwm.edu/healthsciences/academics/kinesiology/

University of Wyoming, College of Health Sciences, Division of Kinesiology and Health, Laramie, WY 82071. Offers MS. *Accreditation:* NCATE. *Program availability:* Part-time, online learning. *Degree requirements:* For master's, comprehensive exam (for some programs), thesis (for some programs). *Entrance requirements:* For master's, GRE General Test, minimum GPA of 3.0. Additional exam requirements/recommendations for international students: Required—TOEFL. Electronic applications accepted. *Expenses: Tuition, area resident:* Full-time $6504; part-time $271 per credit hour. Tuition, state resident: full-time $6504; part-time $271 per credit hour. Tuition, nonresident: full-time $19,464; part-time $811 per credit hour. *International tuition:* $19,464 full-time. *Required fees:* $1410.94; $343.82 per semester. $343.82 per semester. Tuition and fees vary according to course load, program and reciprocity agreements. *Faculty research:* Teacher effectiveness, effects of exercising on heart function, physiological responses of overtraining, psychological benefits of physical activity, health behavior.

Valdosta State University, College of Nursing and Health Sciences, Valdosta, GA 31698. Offers adult gerontology nurse practitioner (MSN); exercise physiology (MS); family nurse practitioner (MSN); family psychiatric mental health nurse practitioner (MSN). *Accreditation:* AACN. *Program availability:* Part-time, online learning. *Degree requirements:* For master's, thesis (for some programs), comprehensive written and/or oral exams. *Entrance requirements:* For master's, minimum GPA of 2.8. Additional exam requirements/recommendations for international students: Required—TOEFL (minimum score 523 paper-based). Electronic applications accepted. *Faculty research:* Nutrition, children's health beliefs, alternative treatment modalities, job satisfaction, leadership.

Virginia Commonwealth University, Graduate School, College of Humanities and Sciences, Department of Kinesiology and Health Sciences, Program in Health and Movement Sciences, Richmond, VA 23284-9005. Offers MS. *Entrance requirements:* For master's, GRE or MAT. Additional exam requirements/recommendations for international students: Required—TOEFL (minimum score 600 paper-based; 100 iBT). Electronic applications accepted.

Virginia Polytechnic Institute and State University, Graduate School, College of Agriculture and Life Sciences, Blacksburg, VA 24061. Offers agricultural and applied economics (MS, PhD); agricultural and life sciences (MS); agriculture, leadership, and community education (MS, PhD); animal and poultry science (MS, PhD); biochemistry (MS, PhD); crop and soil environmental sciences (MS, PhD); dairy science (MS, PhD); entomology (MS, PhD); food science and technology (MS, PhD); horticulture (PhD); human nutrition, foods and exercise (MS, PhD); plant pathology, physiology, and weed science (MS, PhD). *Faculty:* 244 full-time (79 women), 1 (woman) part-time/adjunct. *Students:* 360 full-time (195 women), 110 part-time (73 women); includes 70 minority (24 Black or African American, non-Hispanic/Latino; 1 American Indian or Alaska Native, non-Hispanic/Latino; 15 Asian, non-Hispanic/Latino; 12 Hispanic/Latino; 18 Two or more races, non-Hispanic/Latino), 110 international. Average age 28. 296 applicants, 54% accepted, 105 enrolled. In 2018, 92 master's, 59 doctorates awarded. *Degree requirements:* For master's, comprehensive exam (for some programs), thesis (for some programs); for doctorate, comprehensive exam (for some programs), thesis/dissertation (for some programs). *Entrance requirements:* For master's and doctorate, GRE/GMAT. Additional exam requirements/recommendations for international students: Required—TOEFL (minimum score 90 iBT). *Application deadline:* For fall admission, 8/1 for

domestic students, 4/1 for international students; for spring admission, 1/1 for domestic students, 9/1 for international students. Applications are processed on a rolling basis. Application fee: $75. Electronic applications accepted. *Expenses:* Tuition, state resident: full-time $15,510; part-time $739.50 per credit hour. Tuition, nonresident: full-time $29,629; part-time $1490.25 per credit hour. *Required fees:* $2804; $550 per semester. Tuition and fees vary according to course load, campus/location and program. *Financial support:* In 2018–19, 3 fellowships with full tuition reimbursements (averaging $25,731 per year), 249 research assistantships with full tuition reimbursements (averaging $19,826 per year), 105 teaching assistantships with full tuition reimbursements (averaging $19,277 per year) were awarded; scholarships/grants and unspecified assistantships also available. Financial award application deadline: 3/1; financial award applicants required to submit FAFSA. *Total annual research expenditures:* $42.4 million. *Unit head:* Dr. Alan L. Grant, Dean, 540-231-4152, Fax: 540-231-4163, E-mail: algrant@vt.edu. *Application contact:* Crystal Tawney, Administrative Assistant, 540-231-4152, Fax: 540-231-4163, E-mail: cdtawney@vt.edu. Website: http://www.cals.vt.edu/

Wake Forest University, Graduate School of Arts and Sciences, Department of Health and Exercise Science, Winston-Salem, NC 27109. Offers MS. *Degree requirements:* For master's, one foreign language, thesis. *Entrance requirements:* For master's, GRE General Test, resume. Additional exam requirements/recommendations for international students: Required—TOEFL (minimum score 79 iBT). Electronic applications accepted. *Faculty research:* Cardiac rehabilitation, biomechanics, health psychology, exercise physiology.

Washington State University, College of Pharmacy and Pharmaceutical Sciences, Nutrition and Exercise Physiology Program, Pullman, WA 99164. Offers MS. Programs offered at the Spokane campus. *Degree requirements:* For master's, internship. *Entrance requirements:* For master's, BS in nutrition and exercise physiology, exercise science, human nutrition, or related degree; interview.

Wayne State College, Department of Health, Human Performance and Sport, Wayne, NE 68787. Offers exercise science (MSE); organizational management (MS), including sport management. *Program availability:* Part-time, evening/weekend. *Degree requirements:* For master's, comprehensive exam, thesis optional. *Entrance requirements:* For master's, GRE General Test, minimum GPA of 3.0. Additional exam requirements/recommendations for international students: Required—TOEFL (minimum score 550 paper-based). Electronic applications accepted.

Wayne State University, College of Education, Division of Kinesiology, Health and Sports Studies, Detroit, MI 48202. Offers athletic training (MSAT); health education (M Ed); kinesiology (M Ed, PhD), including exercise and sport science (PhD), physical education and physical activity leadership (PhD); sports administration (MA). *Program availability:* Part-time, evening/weekend. *Faculty:* 9. *Students:* 76 full-time (47 women), 110 part-time (56 women); includes 73 minority (53 Black or African American, non-Hispanic/Latino; 4 Asian, non-Hispanic/Latino; 8 Hispanic/Latino; 8 Two or more races, non-Hispanic/Latino), 9 international. Average age 30. 163 applicants, 60% accepted, 69 enrolled. In 2018, 70 master's, 4 doctorates awarded. *Degree requirements:* For master's, thesis (for some programs); for doctorate, comprehensive exam, thesis/dissertation. *Entrance requirements:* For master's, minimum undergraduate GPA of 3.0; undergraduate degree directly relating to the field of specialization being applied for or one accompanied by extensive educational background in closely-related field; teaching certificates in specific areas (for some programs); for doctorate, minimum undergraduate GPA of 3.0; undergraduate degree directly relating to the field of specialization being applied for or one accompanied by extensive educational background in closely-related field. Additional exam requirements/recommendations for international students: Required—TOEFL (minimum score 550 paper-based; 79 iBT); Recommended—IELTS (minimum score 6.5), TWE (minimum score 5.5), TSE (minimum score 58). *Application deadline:* Applications are processed on a rolling basis. Application fee: $50. Electronic applications accepted. *Financial support:* In 2018–19, 51 students received support. Fellowships with tuition reimbursements available, research assistantships with tuition reimbursements available, teaching assistantships with tuition reimbursements available, scholarships/grants, health care benefits, and unspecified assistantships available. Support available to part-time students. Financial award applicants required to submit FAFSA. *Faculty research:* Exercise and sport science, nutrition and physical activity interventions, school and community health, obesity prevention. *Unit head:* Dr. Nate McCaughtry, Assistant Dean, Division of Kinesiology, Health and Sport Studies/Director, Center for School Health, 313-577-0014, Fax: 313-577-5002, E-mail: aj4391@wayne.edu. *Application contact:* Heather Ladanyi, Manager, 313-577-1191, E-mail: eb3703@wayne.edu. Website: http://coe.wayne.edu/kinesiology/index.php

West Chester University of Pennsylvania, College of Health Sciences, Department of Kinesiology, West Chester, PA 19383. Offers adapted physical education (Certificate); exercise and sport physiology (MS), including athletic training; sport management and athletics (MPA), including administration. *Program availability:* Part-time, evening/weekend, blended/hybrid learning. *Degree requirements:* For master's, thesis or research report (for MS); two internships and capstone course that includes a research project or thesis (for MPA); for Certificate, six courses of study. *Entrance requirements:* For master's, GRE (for MS), 2 letters of recommendation, statement of professional goals; transcripts (for MS); two letters of reference, career goals, resume (for MPA); for Certificate, two letters of recommendation, transcript. Additional exam requirements/recommendations for international students: Required—TOEFL or IELTS. Electronic applications accepted. *Faculty research:* Metabolism during exercise, biomechanics, rating of perceived exertion, motor learning, environmental physiology.

Western Michigan University, Graduate College, College of Education and Human Development, Department of Health, Physical Education and Recreation, Kalamazoo, MI 49008. Offers athletic training (MS), including exercise physiology; sport management (MA), including pedagogy, special physical education.

Western Washington University, Graduate School, College of Humanities and Social Sciences, Department of Physical Education, Health, and Recreation, Bellingham, WA 98225-5996. Offers exercise science (MS); sport psychology (MS). *Program availability:* Part-time. *Degree requirements:* For master's, thesis. *Entrance requirements:* For master's, GRE General Test, minimum GPA of 3.0 in last 60 semester hours or last 90 quarter hours. Additional exam requirements/recommendations for international students: Required—TOEFL (minimum score 567 paper-based). Electronic applications accepted. *Faculty research:* Spinal motor control, biomechanics/kinesiology, biomechanics of aging, mobility of older adults, fall prevention, exercise interventions and function, magnesium and inspiratory muscle training (IMT).

West Texas A&M University, College of Nursing and Health Sciences, Department of Sports and Exercise Sciences, Canyon, TX 79015. Offers sport management (MS); sports and exercise sciences (MS). *Program availability:* Part-time, evening/weekend. *Degree requirements:* For master's, comprehensive exam, thesis optional. *Entrance requirements:* For master's, GRE General Test. Additional exam requirements/recommendations for international students: Required—TOEFL. Electronic applications accepted.

West Virginia University, School of Medicine, Morgantown, WV 26506. Offers biochemistry and molecular biology (PhD); biomedical science (MS); cancer cell biology (PhD); cellular and integrative physiology (PhD); exercise physiology (MS, PhD); health sciences (MS); immunology (PhD); medicine (MD); occupational therapy (MOT); pathologists assistant' (MHS); physical therapy (DPT). *Accreditation:* AOTA; LCME/AMA. *Program availability:* Part-time, evening/weekend. *Students:* 798 full-time (440 women), 24 part-time (13 women); includes 141 minority (15 Black or African American, non-Hispanic/Latino; 1 American Indian or Alaska Native, non-Hispanic/Latino; 64 Asian, non-Hispanic/Latino; 40 Hispanic/Latino; 1 Native Hawaiian or other Pacific Islander, non-Hispanic/Latino; 20 Two or more races, non-Hispanic/Latino), 36 international. In 2018, 93 master's, 11 doctorates awarded. *Entrance requirements:* Additional exam requirements/recommendations for international students: Required—TOEFL. *Application deadline:* Applications are processed on a rolling basis. Application fee: $60. Electronic applications accepted. *Expenses:* Contact institution. *Financial support:* Fellowships, research assistantships, teaching assistantships, career-related internships or fieldwork, Federal Work-Study, institutionally sponsored loans, health care benefits, tuition waivers (full and partial), and administrative assistantships available. Financial award applicants required to submit FAFSA. *Unit head:* Dr. Clay Marsh, Executive Dean, 304-293-6607, Fax: 304-293-6627, E-mail: clay.marsh@hsc.wvu.edu. *Application contact:* Lisa M. Salati, Assistant Vice President, Graduate Education, 304-293-7759, Fax: 304-293-3080, E-mail: lsalati@hsc.wvu.edu. Website: https://medicine.hsc.wvu.edu

Wichita State University, Graduate School, College of Applied Studies, Department of Human Performance Studies, Wichita, KS 67260. Offers exercise science (M Ed). *Program availability:* Part-time. *Unit head:* Dr. Rich Bomgardner, Chairperson, 316-978-3340, Fax: 316-978-3302, E-mail: rich.bomgardner@wichita.edu. *Application contact:* Jordan Oleson, Admissions Coordinator, 316-978-3095, Fax: 316-978-3253, E-mail: jordan.oleson@wichita.edu. Website: http://www.wichita.edu/hps

William Paterson University of New Jersey, College of Science and Health, Wayne, NJ 07470-8420. Offers adult gerontology nurse practitioner (Certificate); adult nurse practitioner (Certificate); biology (MS); biotechnology (MS); communication disorders (MS); exercise and sport studies (MS); materials chemistry (MS); nursing (MSN); nursing education (Certificate); nursing practice (DNP); school nurse instructional (Certificate). *Accreditation:* ASHA. *Program availability:* Part-time. *Faculty:* 34 full-time (20 women), 24 part-time/adjunct (19 women). *Students:* 62 full-time (49 women), 236 part-time (203 women); includes 135 minority (22 Black or African American, non-Hispanic/Latino; 48 Asian, non-Hispanic/Latino; 57 Hispanic/Latino; 8 Two or more races, non-Hispanic/Latino), 4 international. Average age 33. 546 applicants, 47% accepted, 151 enrolled. In 2018, 75 master's, 8 doctorates awarded. *Degree requirements:* For master's, Programs Differ see: https://academiccatalog.wpunj.edu/content.php?catoid=1&navoid=68. *Entrance requirements:* For master's, program details: https://www.wpunj.edu/admissions/graduate/admission-deadlines-and-requirements/. Additional exam requirements/recommendations for international students: Required—TOEFL (minimum score 550 paper-based; 79 iBT), IELTS (minimum score 6). *Application deadline:* For fall admission, 6/1 for domestic students, 3/1 for international students; for spring admission, 11/1 for domestic students, 10/1 for international students. Applications are processed on a rolling basis. Application fee: $50. Electronic applications accepted. *Expenses: Tuition, area resident:* Full-time $14,714; part-time $727 per credit. Tuition, state resident: full-time $14,714; part-time $727 per credit. Tuition, nonresident: full-time $22,952; part-time $727 per credit. *International tuition:* $22,952 full-time. *Required fees:* $4 per semester. Tuition and fees vary according to course load, degree level and program. *Financial support:* In 2018–19, 18 students received support. Career-related internships or fieldwork, Federal Work-Study, scholarships/grants, tuition waivers, and unspecified assistantships available. Support available to part-time students. Financial award application deadline: 3/15; financial award applicants required to submit FAFSA. *Faculty research:* Behaviors of American long-eared bats, postpartum fatigue, methodologies for coating carbon nanotubes, paleo climatology, prelinguistic gestures in children with language disorders. *Total annual research expenditures:* $248,283. *Unit head:* Dr. Venkat Sharma, Dean, 973-720-2194, Fax: 973-720-3414, E-mail: sharmav@wpunj.edu. *Application contact:* Christina Aiello, Assistant Director, Graduate Admissions, 973-720-2506, Fax: 973-720-2035, E-mail: aielloc@wpunj.edu. Website: http://www.wpunj.edu/cosh

Kinesiology and Movement Studies

Alabama Agricultural and Mechanical University, School of Graduate Studies, College of Education, Humanities, and Behavioral Sciences, Department of Health Sciences, Human Performance, and Communicative Disorders, Huntsville, AL 35811. Offers kinesiology (MS); physical education (MS); speech-language pathology (MS). *Program availability:* Part-time, evening/weekend. *Degree requirements:* For master's, comprehensive exam. *Entrance requirements:* For master's, GRE General Test. Additional exam requirements/recommendations for international students: Required—TOEFL (minimum score 500 paper-based; 61 iBT). Electronic applications accepted. *Faculty research:* Cardiorespiratory assessment.

A.T. Still University, College of Graduate Health Studies, Kirksville, MO 63501. Offers dental public health (MPH); exercise and sport psychology (Certificate); fundamentals of education (Certificate); geriatric exercise science (Certificate); global health (Certificate); health administration (MHA, DHA); health professions (Ed D); health sciences (DH Sc); kinesiology (MS); leadership and organizational behavior (Certificate); public health (MPH); sports conditioning (Certificate). *Accreditation:* CEPH. *Program availability:* Part-time, evening/weekend, online only, 100% online, blended/hybrid learning. *Faculty:* 50 full-time (38 women), 95 part-time/adjunct (57 women). *Students:* 600 full-time (388 women), 512 part-time (306 women); includes 448 minority (185 Black or African American, non-Hispanic/Latino; 14 American Indian or Alaska Native, non-Hispanic/

Latino; 108 Asian, non-Hispanic/Latino; 111 Hispanic/Latino; 1 Native Hawaiian or other Pacific Islander, non-Hispanic/Latino; 29 Two or more races, non-Hispanic/Latino), 31 international. Average age 35. 386 applicants, 82% accepted, 279 enrolled. In 2018, 141 master's, 111 doctorates, 112 other advanced degrees awarded. *Degree requirements:* For master's, thesis, integrated terminal project, practicum; for doctorate, thesis/dissertation. *Entrance requirements:* For master's, minimum GPA of 2.5, bachelor's degree or equivalent, essay, resume, English proficiency; for doctorate, minimum GPA of 2.5, master's or terminal degree, essay, past experience in relevant field, resume, English proficiency. Additional exam requirements/recommendations for international students: Required—TOEFL (minimum score 550 paper-based; 80 iBT). *Application deadline:* For fall admission, 6/25 for domestic and international students; for winter admission, 9/10 for domestic and international students; for spring admission, 12/10 for domestic and international students; for summer admission, 3/4 for domestic and international students. Applications are processed on a rolling basis. Application fee: $70. Electronic applications accepted. *Financial support:* In 2018–19, 8 students received support. Scholarships/grants available. Financial award applicants required to submit FAFSA. *Faculty research:* Public health: influence of availability of comprehensive wellness, resources online, student wellness, oral health care needs assessment of community, oral health knowledge and behaviors of Medicaid-eligible pregnant women and mothers of young children in relations to early childhood caries and tooth decay, alcohol use and alcohol related problems among college students. *Unit head:* Dr. Donald Altman, Dean, 480-219-6008, Fax: 660-626-2826, E-mail: daltman@atsu.edu. *Application contact:* Amie Waldemer, Associate Director, Online Admissions, 480-219-6146, E-mail: awaldemer@atsu.edu.
Website: http://www.atsu.edu/college-of-graduate-health-studies

Azusa Pacific University, School of Behavioral and Applied Sciences, Department of Kinesiology, Azusa, CA 91702-7000. Offers athletic training (MS); physical education (MA, MS).

Ball State University, Graduate School, College of Health, School of Kinesiology, Muncie, IN 47306. Offers athletic coaching education (Certificate); exercise science (MA, MS), including exercise science; human bioenergetics (PhD), including human bioenergetics; physical education (MS); physical education and sport (MA, MS), including physical education and sport; wellness management (MA, MS). *Program availability:* Part-time, 100% online. *Degree requirements:* For doctorate, thesis/dissertation. *Entrance requirements:* For master's, minimum baccalaureate GPA of 2.75 or 3.0 in latter half of baccalaureate; for doctorate, GRE General Test, minimum graduate GPA of 3.2. Additional exam requirements/recommendations for international students: Required—TOEFL (minimum score 550 paper-based; 79 iBT), IELTS (minimum score 6.5). Electronic applications accepted.

Barry University, School of Human Performance and Leisure Sciences, Programs in Movement Science, General Movement Science Program, Miami Shores, FL 33161-6695. Offers MS.

Barry University, School of Human Performance and Leisure Sciences, Programs in Movement Science, Specialization in Biomechanics, Miami Shores, FL 33161-6695. Offers MS. *Entrance requirements:* For master's, GRE General Test, minimum GPA of 3.0. Electronic applications accepted. *Faculty research:* Upper extremity biomechanics, orthopedic biomechanics.

Baylor University, Graduate School, Robbins College of Health and Human Sciences, Department of Health, Human Performance and Recreation, Waco, TX 76798. Offers athletic training (MS); exercise physiology (MS); kinesiology, exercise nutrition, and health promotion (PhD); sport pedagogy (MS). *Accreditation:* NCATE. *Program availability:* Part-time. *Students:* 72 full-time (40 women), 13 part-time (8 women); includes 20 minority (5 Black or African American, non-Hispanic/Latino; 1 American Indian or Alaska Native, non-Hispanic/Latino; 1 Asian, non-Hispanic/Latino; 7 Hispanic/Latino; 6 Two or more races, non-Hispanic/Latino), 5 international. 109 applicants, 59% accepted, 44 enrolled. In 2018, 35 master's, 2 doctorates awarded. *Degree requirements:* For master's, comprehensive exam, thesis optional; for doctorate, comprehensive exam, thesis/dissertation. *Entrance requirements:* For master's and doctorate, GRE General Test. Additional exam requirements/recommendations for international students: Required—TOEFL (minimum score 550 paper-based; 80 iBT). *Application deadline:* For fall admission, 2/1 priority date for domestic students, 2/1 for international students; for spring admission, 10/1 for domestic and international students. Applications are processed on a rolling basis. Application fee: $25. Electronic applications accepted. *Financial support:* In 2018–19, 60 students received support, including 1 research assistantship with full tuition reimbursement available (averaging $12,700 per year), 33 teaching assistantships with full tuition reimbursements available (averaging $7,650 per year); career-related internships or fieldwork, Federal Work-Study, institutionally sponsored loans, scholarships/grants, tuition waivers (full), and unspecified assistantships also available. Financial award application deadline: 2/1. *Faculty research:* Exercise testing, cardio-metabolic health, resistance exercise and training, nutritional intervention, population health, health promotion, global health epidemiology, coaching, natural resource management, stimulant misuse, diet, microbiome and colon cancer etiology. *Total annual research expenditures:* $250,118. *Unit head:* Dr. Jaeho Shim, Graduate Program Director, 254-710-4009, Fax: 254-710-3527, E-mail: joe_shim@baylor.edu. *Application contact:* Deepa Morris, Graduate Program Coordinator, 254-710-3526, Fax: 254-710-3527, E-mail: deepa_morris@baylor.edu.
Website: http://www.baylor.edu/HHPR/

Boise State University, College of Health Sciences, Department of Kinesiology, Boise, ID 83725-0399. Offers athletic leadership (MAL); kinesiology (MK, MS). *Program availability:* Part-time. *Degree requirements:* For master's, thesis (for some programs). *Entrance requirements:* For master's, minimum GPA of 3.0. Additional exam requirements/recommendations for international students: Required—TOEFL (minimum score 550 paper-based; 80 iBT), IELTS (minimum score 6). Electronic applications accepted.

Bowling Green State University, Graduate College, College of Education and Human Development, School of Human Movement, Sport, and Leisure Studies, Bowling Green, OH 43403. Offers developmental kinesiology (M Ed); recreation and leisure (M Ed); sport administration (M Ed). *Program availability:* Part-time. *Degree requirements:* For master's, thesis or alternative. *Entrance requirements:* For master's, GRE General Test, minimum GPA of 2.7. Additional exam requirements/recommendations for international students: Required—TOEFL. Electronic applications accepted. *Faculty research:* Teacher-learning process, travel and tourism, sport marketing and management, exercise physiology and sport psychology, life-span motor development.

Brooklyn College of the City University of New York, School of Natural and Behavioral Sciences, Department of Kinesiology, Brooklyn, NY 11210-2889. Offers exercise and sports science (MS); physical education teacher (MS); sport management (MS). *Program availability:* Part-time. *Degree requirements:* For master's, comprehensive exam or thesis. *Entrance requirements:* For master's, previous course work in physical education and education, minimum GPA of 3.0, 2 letters of recommendation, essay. Additional exam requirements/recommendations for international students: Required—TOEFL (minimum score 500 paper-based; 61 iBT). Electronic applications accepted. *Faculty research:* Exercise physiology, motor learning, sports psychology, women in athletics.

California State Polytechnic University, Pomona, Program in Kinesiology, Pomona, CA 91768-2557. Offers kinesiology (MS). *Program availability:* Part-time, evening/weekend. *Students:* 8 full-time (4 women), 4 part-time (3 women); includes 4 minority (1 Asian, non-Hispanic/Latino; 2 Hispanic/Latino; 1 Two or more races, non-Hispanic/Latino), 1 international. Average age 25. 21 applicants, 43% accepted, 6 enrolled. In 2018, 7 master's awarded. *Degree requirements:* For master's, thesis or alternative. *Entrance requirements:* Additional exam requirements/recommendations for international students: Required—TOEFL (minimum score 550 paper-based). *Application deadline:* Applications are processed on a rolling basis. Application fee: $55. Electronic applications accepted. *Expenses:* Contact institution. *Financial support:* Application deadline: 3/2; applicants required to submit FAFSA. *Unit head:* Dr. Ken Hansen, Professor/Graduate Coordinator, 909-869-4638, Fax: 909-869-4797, E-mail: kahansen@cpp.edu. *Application contact:* Dr. Ken Hansen, Professor/Graduate Coordinator, 909-869-4638, Fax: 909-869-4797, E-mail: kahansen@cpp.edu.
Website: http://www.cpp.edu/~sci/kinesiology-health-promotion/academic-programs/graduate-program.shtml

California State University, Chico, Office of Graduate Studies, College of Communication and Education, Department of Kinesiology, Chico, CA 95929-0722. Offers MA. *Program availability:* Part-time. *Faculty:* 7 full-time (4 women), 2 part-time/adjunct (0 women). *Students:* 22 full-time (9 women), 6 part-time (3 women); includes 11 minority (2 Asian, non-Hispanic/Latino; 7 Hispanic/Latino; 2 Two or more races, non-Hispanic/Latino). 29 applicants, 76% accepted, 18 enrolled. In 2018, 11 master's awarded. *Degree requirements:* For master's, thesis, project, or comprehensive examination. *Entrance requirements:* For master's, GRE General Test, 2 letters of recommendation, statement of purpose. Additional exam requirements/recommendations for international students: Required—TOEFL (minimum score 550 paper-based; 80 iBT), IELTS (minimum score 6.5), PTE (minimum score 59). *Application deadline:* For fall admission, 4/1 priority date for domestic and international students; for spring admission, 10/1 priority date for domestic and international students. Application fee: $55. Electronic applications accepted. *Expenses: Tuition, area resident:* Full-time $4622; part-time $3116 per unit. Tuition, state resident: full-time $4622; part-time $3116 per unit. Tuition, nonresident: full-time $10,634. *Required fees:* $2160; $1620 per year. Tuition and fees vary according to class time and program. *Financial support:* Fellowships, research assistantships, teaching assistantships, career-related internships or fieldwork, Federal Work-Study, scholarships/grants, traineeships, health care benefits, unspecified assistantships, and stipends available. Support available to part-time students. Financial award application deadline: 3/2; financial award applicants required to submit FAFSA. *Unit head:* Dr. Josh Trout, Chair, 530-898-6373, Fax: 530-898-4932, E-mail: kinestudent@csuchico.edu. *Application contact:* Judy L. Morrice, Graduate Admissions Coordinator, 530-898-5416, Fax: 530-898-3342, E-mail: jlmorris@csuchico.edu.
Website: http://www.csuchico.edu/kine/

California State University, Fresno, Division of Research and Graduate Studies, College of Health and Human Services, Department of Kinesiology, Fresno, CA 93740-8027. Offers exercise science (MA); general kinesiology (MA); sport administration (MA); sport psychology (MA). *Program availability:* Part-time, evening/weekend. *Degree requirements:* For master's, thesis or alternative. *Entrance requirements:* For master's, GRE General Test, minimum GPA of 2.7. Additional exam requirements/recommendations for international students: Required—TOEFL. Electronic applications accepted. *Faculty research:* Refugee education, homeless, geriatrics, fitness.

California State University, Long Beach, Graduate Studies, College of Health and Human Services, Department of Kinesiology, Long Beach, CA 90840. Offers adapted physical education (MA); coaching and student athlete development (MA); exercise physiology and nutrition (MS); exercise science (MS); individualized studies (MA); kinesiology (MA); pedagogical studies (MA); sport and exercise psychology (MS); sport management (MA); sports medicine and injury studies (MS). *Program availability:* Part-time. *Degree requirements:* For master's, oral and written comprehensive exams or thesis. *Entrance requirements:* For master's, GRE General Test, minimum GPA of 2.75 during previous 2 years of course work. *Application deadline:* Applications are processed on a rolling basis. Application fee: $55. Electronic applications accepted. *Expenses: Required fees:* $2628 per term. Tuition and fees vary according to class time, course level, course load, degree level, campus/location and program. *Financial support:* Federal Work-Study, institutionally sponsored loans, and scholarships/grants available. Financial award application deadline: 3/2; financial award applicants required to submit FAFSA. *Faculty research:* Pulmonary functioning, feedback and practice structure, strength training, history and politics of sports, special population research issues. *Unit head:* Tiffanye Vargas, Chair, 562-985-4051, E-mail: tiffanye.vargas@csulb.edu. *Application contact:* Tiffanye Vargas, Chair, 562-985-4051, E-mail: tiffanye.vargas@csulb.edu.
Website: https://fullerton-csm.symplicity.com/

California State University, Los Angeles, Graduate Studies, College of Health and Human Services, Department of Kinesiology and Nutritional Sciences, Los Angeles, CA 90032-8530. Offers nutritional science (MS); physical education and kinesiology (MA). *Accreditation:* AND. *Program availability:* Part-time, evening/weekend. *Degree requirements:* For master's, comprehensive exam, project or thesis. *Entrance requirements:* For master's, minimum GPA of 2.75. Additional exam requirements/recommendations for international students: Required—TOEFL (minimum score 500 paper-based).

California State University, Northridge, Graduate Studies, College of Health and Human Development, Department of Kinesiology, Northridge, CA 91330. Offers MS. *Program availability:* Part-time, evening/weekend. *Degree requirements:* For master's, thesis or alternative. *Entrance requirements:* For master's, GRE General Test or minimum GPA of 3.0, 3 letters of recommendation. Additional exam requirements/recommendations for international students: Required—TOEFL.

Canisius College, Graduate Division, School of Education and Human Services, Department of Kinesiology, Buffalo, NY 14208-1098. Offers physical education (MS Ed); physical education birth - 12 (MS Ed). *Program availability:* Part-time, evening/weekend, 100% online, blended/hybrid learning. *Faculty:* 14 full-time (0 women), 17 part-time/adjunct (3 women). *Students:* 40 full-time (14 women), 37 part-time (10 women); includes 13 minority (8 Black or African American, non-Hispanic/Latino; 4 Hispanic/Latino; 1 Two or more races, non-Hispanic/Latino), 1 international. Average age 29. 79 applicants, 96% accepted, 46 enrolled. In 2018, 91 master's awarded. *Degree requirements:* For master's, research project or internship. *Entrance requirements:* For master's, official college and/or university transcript(s) showing completion of bachelor's degree from accredited institution; two letters of recommendation; minimum cumulative undergraduate GPA of 2.7. Additional exam requirements/recommendations for international students: Required—TOEFL (minimum score 550 paper-based, 79 iBT), IELTS (minimum score 6.5), or CAEL (minimum score 70). *Application deadline:* Applications are processed on a rolling basis. Application fee: $0. Electronic applications accepted. *Expenses:* Contact institution. *Financial support:* In 2018–19, 154 students received support. Career-related internships or fieldwork, Federal Work-Study,

scholarships/grants, tuition waivers (partial), and unspecified assistantships available. Support available to part-time students. Financial award application deadline: 4/30; financial award applicants required to submit FAFSA. *Faculty research:* Culturally congruent pedagogy in physical education, information processing and perceptual styles of athletes, qualities of effective coaches. *Unit head:* Dr. Nicolas Lorgnier, Chair/Professor of Kinesiology, 716-888-3733, Fax: 716-888-8445, E-mail: lorgnien@canisius.edu. *Application contact:* Dr. Nicolas Lorgnier, Chair/Professor of Kinesiology, 716-888-3733, Fax: 716-888-8445, E-mail: lorgnien@canisius.edu.
Website: http://www.canisius.edu/graduate/

Columbia University, College of Physicians and Surgeons, Programs in Occupational Therapy, New York, NY 10032. Offers movement science (Ed D), including occupational therapy; occupational therapy (MS); occupational therapy and cognition (OTD); MPH/MS. EdD offered in tandem with Teachers College, Columbia University. *Accreditation:* AOTA. *Degree requirements:* For master's, project, 6 months of fieldwork, thesis (for post-professional students); for doctorate, comprehensive exam, thesis/dissertation. *Entrance requirements:* For master's, undergraduate course work in anatomy, physiology, statistics, psychology, social sciences, humanities, and English composition; for doctorate, master's degree in occupational therapy (for OTD). Additional exam requirements/recommendations for international students: Required—TOEFL (minimum score 100 iBT) or IELTS (minimum score 8). Electronic applications accepted. *Expenses:* Contact institution. *Faculty research:* Community mental health, motor learning, cognition, literacy, LGBTQ.

Dalhousie University, Faculty of Health, School of Health and Human Performance, Program, in Kinesiology, Halifax, NS B3H 3J5, Canada. Offers M Sc. *Program availability:* Part-time. *Degree requirements:* For master's, thesis. *Entrance requirements:* Additional exam requirements/recommendations for international students: Required—TOEFL, IELTS, CANTEST, CAEL, or Michigan English Language Assessment Battery. Electronic applications accepted. *Faculty research:* Sport science, fitness, neuromuscular physiology, biomechanics, ergonomics, sport psychology.

Dallas Baptist University, Dorothy M. Bush College of Education, Program in Kinesiology, Dallas, TX 75211-9299. Offers M Ed. *Program availability:* Part-time, evening/weekend. *Application deadline:* Applications are processed on a rolling basis. Application fee: $25. Electronic applications accepted. Application fee is waived when completed online. *Expenses: Tuition:* Full-time $17,262; part-time $959 per credit hour. *Required fees:* $1000; $500 per semester. Tuition and fees vary according to course load and degree level. *Unit head:* Dr. Neil Dugger, Dean, 214-333-5202, E-mail: neil@dbu.edu. *Application contact:* Dr. Ray Galloway, Program Director, 214-333-5253, E-mail: rayg@dbu.edu.
Website: https://www.dbu.edu/graduate/degree-programs/med-kinesiology

East Carolina University, Graduate School, College of Health and Human Performance, Department of Kinesiology, Greenville, NC 27858-4353. Offers adapted physical education (MS); bioenergetics and exercise science (PhD); biomechanics and motor control (MS); exercise physiology (MS); physical activity promotion (MS); physical education (MA Ed, MAT); physical education clinical supervision (Certificate); physical education pedagogy (MS); sport and exercise psychology (MS); sport management (MS, Certificate). *Application deadline:* For fall admission, 2/1 priority date for domestic students, 2/1 for international students. *Expenses: Tuition, area resident:* Full-time $4749. Tuition, state resident: full-time $4749. Tuition, nonresident: full-time $17,898. *International tuition:* $17,898 full-time. *Required fees:* $2787. Part-time tuition and fees vary according to course load and program. *Financial support:* Application deadline: 2/1. *Unit head:* Dr. Stacey Altman, Chair, 252-328-4632, E-mail: altmans@ecu.edu. *Application contact:* Graduate School Admissions, 252-328-6012, Fax: 252-328-6071, E-mail: gradschool@ecu.edu.
Website: https://hhp.ecu.edu/kine/

Eastern Michigan University, Graduate School, College of Health and Human Services, School of Health Promotion and Human Performance, Programs in Exercise Physiology, Ypsilanti, MI 48197. Offers exercise physiology (MS); sports medicine-biomechanics (MS); sports medicine-corporate adult fitness (MS); sports medicine-exercise physiology (MS). *Program availability:* Part-time, evening/weekend. *Students:* 13 full-time (4 women), 11 part-time (4 women); includes 5 minority (1 Black or African American, non-Hispanic/Latino; 1 Asian, non-Hispanic/Latino; 2 Hispanic/Latino; 1 Two or more races, non-Hispanic/Latino), 2 international. Average age 29. 40 applicants, 63% accepted, 10 enrolled. In 2018, 15 master's awarded. *Degree requirements:* For master's, comprehensive exam, thesis or 450-hour internship. *Entrance requirements:* Additional exam requirements/recommendations for international students: Required—TOEFL. *Application deadline:* For fall admission, 8/1 for domestic students, 5/1 for international students; for winter admission, 12/1 for domestic students, 10/1 for international students; for spring admission, 3/15 for domestic students, 3/1 for international students. Application fee: $45. *Application contact:* Dr. Becca Moore, Program Coordinator, 734-487-2824, Fax: 734-487-2024, E-mail: rmoore41@emich.edu.

East Tennessee State University, School of Graduate Studies, College of Education, Department of Sport, Exercise, Recreation, and Kinesiology, Johnson City, TN 37614-1701. Offers sport management (MA); sport physiology and performance (PhD), including sport performance, sport physiology; sport science and coach education (MS), including applied sport science, strength and conditioning. *Program availability:* Part-time, evening/weekend. Terminal master's awarded for partial completion of doctoral program. *Degree requirements:* For master's, comprehensive exam, thesis or internship; for doctorate, comprehensive exam, thesis/dissertation, 2-semester residency. *Entrance requirements:* For master's, GRE General Test or GMAT, undergraduate degree in related field; minimum GPA of 3.0; resume; three references; essay explaining goals and reasons for pursuing degree; for doctorate, GRE, resume; 4 letters of recommendation; master's or bachelor's degree in related field; minimum GPA of 3.4 overall with master's, 3.0 with bachelor's; interview. Additional exam requirements/recommendations for international students: Required—TOEFL (minimum score 550 paper-based; 79 iBT). Electronic applications accepted. *Faculty research:* Methods of training for individual and team sports, enhancing acute sport performance, fatigue management in athletes, risk management, facilities management, motorsport.

East Texas Baptist University, Master of Science in Kinesiology Program, Marshall, TX 75670-1498. Offers MS. *Program availability:* Part-time, evening/weekend. *Faculty:* 2 full-time (0 women). *Students:* 11 part-time (4 women); includes 1 minority (Black or African American, non-Hispanic/Latino). Average age 23. 14 applicants, 50% accepted, 7 enrolled. In 2018, 6 master's awarded. *Entrance requirements:* Additional exam requirements/recommendations for international students: Recommended—TOEFL (minimum score 550 paper-based; 79 iBT). *Application deadline:* For fall admission, 8/15 for domestic students; for spring admission, 1/2 for domestic students; for summer admission, 5/11 for domestic students. Applications are processed on a rolling basis. Application fee: $50. Electronic applications accepted. *Expenses:* $700 per credit hour tuition; $150 per semester fees (6 or more hours enrolled); $75 per semester fees (1-5 hours enrolled). *Financial support:* In 2018–19, 10 students received support. Federal Work-Study, scholarships/grants, unspecified assistantships, and staff grants available. Financial award applicants required to submit FAFSA. *Unit head:* Dr. Joseph D. Brown, Dean, Frank S. Groner School of Professional Studies, 903-923-2270, Fax: 903-935-4318, E-mail: jbrown@etbu.edu. *Application contact:* Den Murley, Director of Graduate Admissions, 903-923-2079, Fax: 903-934-8115, E-mail: gradadmissions@etbu.edu.
Website: https://www.etbu.edu/academics/academic-schools/frank-s-groner-school-professional-studies/department-kinesiology/programs

Fresno Pacific University, Graduate Programs, Program in Kinesiology, Fresno, CA 93702-4709. Offers MA. *Entrance requirements:* Additional exam requirements/recommendations for international students: Required—TOEFL (minimum score 550 paper-based).

Georgia College & State University, Graduate School, College of Health Sciences, School of Health and Human Performance, Milledgeville, GA 31061. Offers health and human performance (MS), including health performance, health promotion; kinesiology/health education (MAT). *Accreditation:* NCATE (one or more programs are accredited). *Program availability:* Part-time, 100% online. *Degree requirements:* For master's, thesis (for some programs), completed in 6 years with minimum GPA of 3.0 (for MS); minimum GPA of 3.0 and electronic teaching portfolio (for MAT). *Entrance requirements:* For master's, GRE with minimum score of 297 or MAT with minimum score of 385 (for MS); GRE with minimum score of 297, MAT 385, SAT 1000, ACT 43, or GACE with 250 on each section (for MAT), resume, 3 professional references; minimum GPA of 2.75 in upper-level undergraduate courses and undergraduate statistics course (for MS); minimum GPA of 2.75 on upper-division major courses (for MAT). Electronic applications accepted. *Expenses:* Contact institution.

Georgia Southern University, Jack N. Averitt College of Graduate Studies, Waters College of Health Professions, Department of Health Sciences and Kinesiology, Program in Kinesiology, Statesboro, GA 30458. Offers MS. *Program availability:* Part-time. *Entrance requirements:* For master's, minimum GPA of 2.75. Additional exam requirements/recommendations for international students: Required—TOEFL (minimum score 550 paper-based; 80 iBT), IELTS (minimum score 6). Electronic applications accepted. *Expenses:* Contact institution. *Faculty research:* Athletic training, coaching, exercise science, nutrition and food science, sport psychology, sport management, physical education.

Georgia State University, College of Education and Human Development, Department of Kinesiology and Health, Program in Kinesiology, Atlanta, GA 30302-3083. Offers PhD. *Entrance requirements:* For doctorate, GRE General Test or MAT, minimum GPA of 3.3. Application fee: $50. *Expenses: Tuition, area resident:* Full-time $9360; part-time $390 per credit hour. Tuition, state resident: full-time $9360; part-time $390 per credit hour. Tuition, nonresident: full-time $30,024; part-time $1251 per credit hour. *International tuition:* $30,024 full-time. *Required fees:* $2128. *Financial support:* Research assistantships and teaching assistantships available. *Faculty research:* Aging, exercise metabolism, biomechanics and ergonomics, blood pressure regulation, exercise performance. *Unit head:* Dr. Jacalyn Lea Lund, Chair, 404-413-8051, E-mail: jlund@gsu.edu. *Application contact:* Dr. Rebecca Ellis, Program Coordinator, 404-413-8370, E-mail: rellis@gsu.edu.
Website: https://education.gsu.edu/kh/

Hardin-Simmons University, Graduate School, College of Human Sciences and Educational Studies, Kinesiology, Sport, and Recreation Program, Abilene, TX 79698-0001. Offers kinesiology, sport, and recreation (M Ed). *Program availability:* Part-time. *Students:* 40 part-time (16 women); includes 17 minority (8 Black or African American, non-Hispanic/Latino; 7 Hispanic/Latino; 2 Two or more races, non-Hispanic/Latino). Average age 25. 20 applicants, 100% accepted, 15 enrolled. In 2018, 17 master's awarded. *Degree requirements:* For master's, comprehensive exam, professional project. *Entrance requirements:* For master's, minimum undergraduate GPA of 3.0 in major, 2.7 overall; writing sample; letters of recommendation; resume; personal interview. Additional exam requirements/recommendations for international students: Required—TOEFL (minimum score 550 paper-based; 79 iBT). *Application deadline:* For fall admission, 8/15 priority date for domestic students, 4/1 for international students; for spring admission, 1/5 priority date for domestic students, 9/1 for international students. Applications are processed on a rolling basis. Application fee: $50. Electronic applications accepted. *Expenses: Tuition:* Full-time $750; part-time $750 per credit hour. *Required fees:* $1300; $880 per credit. Tuition and fees vary according to degree level and program. *Financial support:* Fellowships, career-related internships or fieldwork, scholarships/grants, and unspecified assistantships available. Support available to part-time students. Financial award application deadline: 6/30; financial award applicants required to submit FAFSA. *Unit head:* Dr. Lindsay Edwards, Program Director, 325-670-5893, Fax: 325-670-1572, E-mail: ledwards@hsutx.edu. *Application contact:* Dr. Nancy Kucinski, Dean of Graduate Studies, 325-670-1298, Fax: 325-670-1564, E-mail: gradoff@hsutx.edu.
Website: http://www.hsutx.edu/academics/irvin/graduate/kinesiology

Houston Baptist University, School of Nursing and Allied Health, Program in Kinesiology - Sport Management, Houston, TX 77074-3298. Offers sport management (MSK). *Program availability:* Online only, 100% online. *Degree requirements:* For master's, internship or thesis. *Entrance requirements:* For master's, GRE, bachelor's degree conferred transcript, personal statement/essay, resume. Additional exam requirements/recommendations for international students: Required—TOEFL (minimum score 80 iBT), IELTS (minimum score 6.5). Electronic applications accepted. Application fee is waived when completed online. *Expenses:* Contact institution.

Humboldt State University, Academic Programs, College of Professional Studies, Department of Kinesiology and Recreation Administration, Arcata, CA 95521-8299. Offers kinesiology (MS). *Faculty:* 10 full-time (7 women), 14 part-time/adjunct (8 women). *Students:* 22 full-time (9 women), 16 part-time (9 women); includes 15 minority (1 Black or African American, non-Hispanic/Latino; 1 Asian, non-Hispanic/Latino; 9 Hispanic/Latino; 4 Two or more races, non-Hispanic/Latino). Average age 28. 20 applicants, 65% accepted, 10 enrolled. In 2018, 37 master's awarded. *Degree requirements:* For master's, thesis or alternative. *Entrance requirements:* For master's, GMAT, minimum GPA of 2.5. Additional exam requirements/recommendations for international students: Required—TOEFL. *Application deadline:* For fall admission, 6/1 for domestic students; for spring admission, 12/2 for domestic students. Applications are processed on a rolling basis. Application fee: $55. *Expenses: Tuition:* Part-time $4649 per semester. *Required fees:* $2121; $1673. Tuition and fees vary according to program. *Financial support:* Teaching assistantships, career-related internships or fieldwork, Federal Work-Study, and institutionally sponsored loans available. Financial award application deadline: 3/1; financial award applicants required to submit FAFSA. *Faculty research:* Human performance, adapted physical education, physical therapy. *Unit head:* Dr. Taylor Bloedon, Graduate Program Coordinator, 707-826-5967, E-mail: kinsgrad@humboldt.edu. *Application contact:* Dr. Taylor Bloedon, Graduate Program Coordinator, 707-826-5967, E-mail: kinsgrad@humboldt.edu.
Website: http://www.humboldt.edu/kra/

Indiana University Bloomington, School of Public Health, Department of Kinesiology, Bloomington, IN 47405. Offers applied sport science (MS); athletic administration/sport management (MS); athletic training (MS); biomechanics (MS); ergonomics (MS); exercise physiology (MS); human performance (PhD), including biomechanics, exercise physiology, motor learning/control, sport management; motor learning/control (MS); physical activity (MPH); physical activity, fitness and wellness (MS). *Program*

availability: Part-time. Terminal master's awarded for partial completion of doctoral program. *Degree requirements:* For master's, thesis optional; for doctorate, variable foreign language requirement, comprehensive exam, thesis/dissertation. *Entrance requirements:* For master's, GRE General Test, minimum GPA of 2.8; for doctorate, GRE General Test, minimum graduate GPA of 3.5, undergraduate 3.0. Additional exam requirements/recommendations for international students: Required—TOEFL (minimum score 80 iBT). *Faculty research:* Exercise physiology and biochemistry, sports biomechanics, human motor control, adaptation of fitness and exercise to special populations.

Indiana University–Purdue University Indianapolis, School of Physical Education and Tourism Management, Indianapolis, IN 46202-5193. Offers event tourism (MS), including sport event tourism; kinesiology (MS), including clinical exercise science; public health (Graduate Certificate). *Degree requirements:* For master's, comprehensive exam (for some programs), thesis (for some programs). *Entrance requirements:* For master's, GRE. Additional exam requirements/recommendations for international students: Required—TOEFL. Electronic applications accepted. *Expenses:* Contact institution. *Faculty research:* Physical activity, exercise and diseases; human movement science; sport performance; sport event tourism; destination marketing and event management.

Inter American University of Puerto Rico, San Germán Campus, Graduate Studies Center, Program in Health and Physical Education, San Germán, PR 00683-5008. Offers MA. *Program availability:* Part-time, evening/weekend. *Degree requirements:* For master's, comprehensive exam. *Entrance requirements:* For master's, GRE General Test or EXADEP, minimum GPA of 3.0. *Expenses: Tuition:* Full-time $212; part-time $212 per credit. *Required fees:* $366 per semester. One-time fee: $31. Tuition and fees vary according to degree level and program.

Iowa State University of Science and Technology, Department of Kinesiology, Ames, IA 50011. Offers MS, PhD. *Entrance requirements:* For master's and doctorate, GRE General Test. Additional exam requirements/recommendations for international students: Required—TOEFL (minimum score 560 paper-based; 79 iBT), IELTS (minimum score 6.5). Electronic applications accepted.

Jacksonville University, Brooks Rehabilitation College of Healthcare Sciences, School of Applied Health Sciences, Program in Kinesiological Sciences, Jacksonville, FL 32211. Offers MS. *Program availability:* Part-time, blended/hybrid learning. *Degree requirements:* For master's, thesis, internship. *Entrance requirements:* For master's, GRE (priority given to students who achieve minimum combined score of 300 on current scale (1080 prior scale) for verbal and quantitative sections), baccalaureate degree from accredited college or university with minimum GPA of 3.0; official transcripts; essay on personal professional goals (minimum 1000 words); resume (education, work experience); 3 letters of recommendation; interview; prerequisites in anatomy, physiology, chemistry, physics, psychology, and statistics. Additional exam requirements/recommendations for international students: Required—TOEFL (minimum score 650 paper-based; 114 iBT), IELTS (minimum score 8). Electronic applications accepted. *Expenses:* Contact institution.

James Madison University, The Graduate School, College of Health and Behavioral Studies, Program in Health Sciences, Harrisonburg, VA 22807. Offers nutrition and physical activity (MS). *Program availability:* Part-time. *Students:* 4 full-time (3 women), 2 part-time (1 woman); includes 1 minority (Black or African American, non-Hispanic/Latino), 1 international. Average age 30. In 2018, 2 master's awarded. Electronic applications accepted. *Expenses:* Tuition, state resident: full-time $10,848. Tuition, nonresident: full-time $27,888. *Required fees:* $1128. *Financial support:* In 2018–19, 4 students received support. Federal Work-Study and assistantships (averaging $7911) available. Financial award application deadline: 3/1; financial award applicants required to submit FAFSA. *Unit head:* Dr. Allen Lewis, Department Head, 540-568-6510, E-mail: amatohk@jmu.edu. *Application contact:* Lynette D. Michael, Director of Graduate Admissions and Student Records, 540-568-6131 Ext. 6395, Fax: 540-568-7860, E-mail: michaeld@jmu.edu.
Website: http://www.healthsci.jmu.edu/index.html

James Madison University, The Graduate School, College of Health and Behavioral Studies, Program in Kinesiology, Harrisonburg, VA 22807. Offers clinical exercise physiology (MS); exercise physiology (MS); kinesiology (MAT, MS); nutrition and exercise (MS); physical and health education (MAT); sport and recreation leadership (MS). *Program availability:* Part-time, evening/weekend. *Students:* 33 full-time (11 women); includes 3 minority (2 Black or African American, non-Hispanic/Latino; 1 Hispanic/Latino). Average age 30. In 2018, 18 master's awarded. Electronic applications accepted. *Expenses:* Tuition, state resident: full-time $10,848. Tuition, nonresident: full-time $27,888. *Required fees:* $1128. *Financial support:* In 2018–19, 20 students received support, including teaching assistantships with full tuition reimbursements available (averaging $8,837 per year); Federal Work-Study and assistantships (averaging $7911), athletic assistantships (averaging $9284) also available. Financial award application deadline: 3/1; financial award applicants required to submit FAFSA. *Unit head:* Dr. Christopher J. Womack, Department Head, 540-568-6145, E-mail: womackcx@jmu.edu. *Application contact:* Lynette D. Michael, Director of Graduate Admissions, 540-568-6131 Ext. 6395, Fax: 540-568-7860, E-mail: michaeld@jmu.edu.
Website: http://www.jmu.edu/kinesiology/

Kansas State University, Graduate School, College of Human Ecology, Department of Food, Nutrition, Dietetics and Health, Manhattan, KS 66506. Offers dietetics (MS); human nutrition (PhD); nutrition, dietetics and sensory sciences (MS); nutritional sciences (PhD); public health nutrition (PhD); public health physical activity (PhD); sensory analysis and consumer behavior (PhD). *Program availability:* Part-time. *Degree requirements:* For master's, thesis or alternative, residency; for doctorate, thesis/dissertation, residency. *Entrance requirements:* For master's, GRE General Test, minimum undergraduate GPA of 3.0; for doctorate, GRE General Test, minimum graduate GPA of 3.0. Additional exam requirements/recommendations for international students: Required—TOEFL (minimum score 550 paper-based; 79 iBT), IELTS (minimum score 6.5). Electronic applications accepted. *Faculty research:* Cancer and immunology, obesity, sensory analysis and consumer behavior, nutrient metabolism, clinical and community interventions.

Kansas State University, Graduate School, College of Human Ecology, Department of Kinesiology, Manhattan, KS 66506. Offers MS, PhD. *Program availability:* Part-time. *Degree requirements:* For master's, thesis or final comprehensive exam; for doctorate, comprehensive exam, thesis/dissertation. *Entrance requirements:* For master's, GRE General Test, bachelor's degree in kinesiology or exercise science, minimum GPA of 3.0; for doctorate, GRE General Test. Additional exam requirements/recommendations for international students: Required—TOEFL. Electronic applications accepted. *Expenses:* Contact institution. *Faculty research:* Exercise physiology, vascular function, cardiorespiratory disease, microgravity, cancer, physical inactivity, exercise adherence and compliance, public health/physical activity.

Kansas State University, Graduate School, College of Human Ecology, Doctorate in Human Ecology Program, Manhattan, KS 66506-1407. Offers apparel and textiles (PhD); applied family sciences (PhD); couple and family therapy (PhD); hospitality administration (PhD); kinesiology (PhD); life-span human development (PhD). *Program availability:* Part-time. *Degree requirements:* For doctorate, thesis/dissertation. *Entrance requirements:* Additional exam requirements/recommendations for international students: Required—TOEFL. Electronic applications accepted.

Lakehead University, Graduate Studies, School of Kinesiology, Thunder Bay, ON P7B 5E1, Canada. Offers kinesiology (M Sc); kinesiology and gerontology (M Sc). *Program availability:* Part-time. *Degree requirements:* For master's, thesis. *Entrance requirements:* For master's, minimum B average. Additional exam requirements/recommendations for international students: Required—TOEFL. *Faculty research:* Social psychology and physical education, sport history, sports medicine, exercise physiology, gerontology.

Lamar University, College of Graduate Studies, College of Education and Human Development, Department of Health and Kinesiology, Beaumont, TX 77710. Offers MS. *Faculty:* 15 full-time (7 women), 4 part-time/adjunct (3 women). *Students:* 22 full-time (16 women), 40 part-time (30 women); includes 30 minority (24 Black or African American, non-Hispanic/Latino; 1 Asian, non-Hispanic/Latino; 1 Hispanic/Latino; 4 Two or more races, non-Hispanic/Latino), 7 international. Average age 29. 46 applicants, 96% accepted, 16 enrolled. In 2018, 23 master's awarded. *Degree requirements:* For master's, comprehensive exam (for some programs), thesis optional. *Entrance requirements:* For master's, GRE General Test, minimum GPA of 2.5. Additional exam requirements/recommendations for international students: Required—TOEFL (minimum score 550 paper-based; 79 iBT), IELTS (minimum score 6.5). *Application deadline:* Applications are processed on a rolling basis. Application fee: $25. Electronic applications accepted. *Expenses:* Tuition, state resident: full-time $6234; part-time $346 per credit hour. Tuition, nonresident: full-time $6852; part-time $761 per credit hour. *International tuition:* $6852 full-time. *Required fees:* $1940; $327 per credit hour. Tuition and fees vary according to course load, campus/location, program and reciprocity agreements. *Financial support:* In 2018–19, 23 students received support, including 4 teaching assistantships (averaging $7,500 per year). Financial award applicants required to submit FAFSA. *Faculty research:* Motor learning, exercise physiology, pedagogy. *Unit head:* Dr. Daniel Chilek, Department Chair, 409-880-8724, Fax: 409-880-1761. *Application contact:* Celeste Contreas, Director, Admissions and Academic Services, 409-880-8888, Fax: 409-880-7419, E-mail: gradmissions@lamar.edu.
Website: http://education.lamar.edu/health-and-kinesiology

Louisiana State University and Agricultural & Mechanical College, Graduate School, College of Human Sciences and Education, Department of Kinesiology, Baton Rouge, LA 70803. Offers MS, PhD.

Louisiana Tech University, Graduate School, College of Education, Ruston, LA 71272. Offers counseling and guidance (MA), including clinical mental health counseling, human services, orientation and mobility; counseling psychology (PhD); curriculum and instruction (M Ed); cyber education (Graduate Certificate); dynamics of domestic and family violence (Graduate Certificate); early childhood education - PreK-3 (MAT); educational leadership (M Ed, Ed D); elementary education and special education mild/moderate grades 1-5 (MAT); higher education administration (Graduate Certificate); industrial/organizational psychology (MA, PhD); kinesiology (MS); middle school education (MAT), including mathematics; orientation and mobility (Graduate Certificate); rehabilitation teaching for the blind (Graduate Certificate); secondary education (MAT), including agriculture, biology, business, chemistry, English; special education: visually impaired (MAT); teacher leader education (Graduate Certificate); visual impairments - blind education (Graduate Certificate). *Accreditation:* NCATE. *Program availability:* Part-time. *Degree requirements:* For master's, thesis; for doctorate, thesis/dissertation. *Entrance requirements:* For master's and doctorate, GRE General Test. Additional exam requirements/recommendations for international students: Required—TOEFL (minimum score 550 paper-based; 80 iBT), IELTS (minimum score 6.5). Electronic applications accepted. *Faculty research:* Blindness and the best methods for increasing independence for individuals who are blind or visually impaired; educating and investigating factors contributing to improvements in human performance across the lifespan and a reduction in injury rates during training.

McDaniel College, Graduate and Professional Studies, Program in Kinesiology, Westminster, MD 21157-4390. Offers MS. *Program availability:* Part-time, evening/weekend. *Degree requirements:* For master's, comprehensive exam, thesis optional. *Entrance requirements:* For master's, 3 references. Additional exam requirements/recommendations for international students: Required—TOEFL (minimum score 79 iBT), IELTS (minimum score 6). Electronic applications accepted.

McGill University, Faculty of Graduate and Postdoctoral Studies, Faculty of Education, Department of Kinesiology and Physical Education, Montréal, QC H3A 2T5, Canada. Offers M Sc, MA, PhD, Certificate, Diploma.

McMaster University, School of Graduate Studies, Faculty of Social Sciences, Department of Kinesiology, Hamilton, ON L8S 4M2, Canada. Offers human biodynamics (M Sc, PhD). *Degree requirements:* For master's, thesis. *Entrance requirements:* For master's, minimum B+ average in undergraduate course work. Additional exam requirements/recommendations for international students: Required—TOEFL (minimum score 580 paper-based). *Faculty research:* Motor learning and control, neuromuscular physiology, exercise rehabilitation, cellular responses to exercise, management.

Memorial University of Newfoundland, School of Graduate Studies, School of Human Kinetics and Recreation, St. John's, NL A1C 5S7, Canada. Offers administration, curriculum and supervision (MPE); biomechanics/ergonomics (MS Kin); exercise and work physiology (MS Kin); psychology of sport, exercise and recreation (MS Kin); socio-cultural studies of physical activity and health (MS Kin). *Program availability:* Part-time. *Degree requirements:* For master's, thesis optional, seminars, thesis presentations. *Entrance requirements:* For master's, bachelor's degree in a related field, minimum B average. Electronic applications accepted. *Faculty research:* Administration, sociology of sports, kinesiology, physiology/recreation.

Michigan State University, The Graduate School, College of Education, Department of Kinesiology, East Lansing, MI 48824. Offers MS, PhD. *Entrance requirements:* Additional exam requirements/recommendations for international students: Required—TOEFL. Electronic applications accepted.

Michigan Technological University, Graduate School, College of Sciences and Arts, Department of Kinesiology and Integrative Physiology, Houghton, MI 49931. Offers integrative physiology (PhD); kinesiology (MS). *Program availability:* Part-time. *Faculty:* 9 full-time, 2 part-time/adjunct. *Students:* 12 full-time, 4 part-time. Average age 25. 21 applicants, 48% accepted, 9 enrolled. In 2018, 4 master's awarded. *Degree requirements:* For master's, thesis (for some programs). *Entrance requirements:* For master's, GRE (Michigan Tech students with a GPA of 3.5 or above exempt), statement of purpose, personal statement, official transcripts, 2-3 letters of recommendation, resume/curriculum vitae. Additional exam requirements/recommendations for international students: Required—TOEFL (recommended minimum score 85 iBT) or IELTS (minimum score 6.5). *Application deadline:* Applications are processed on a rolling basis. Electronic applications accepted. *Expenses: Tuition, area resident:* Full-time $18,126; part-time $1007 per credit. Tuition, state resident: full-time $18,126; part-time $1007 per credit. Tuition, nonresident: full-time $18,126; part-time $1007 per credit. *International tuition:* $18,126 full-time. *Required fees:* $248; $124 per semester. Tuition and fees vary according to course load and program. *Financial support:* In

2018–19, 12 students received support, including 3 fellowships with tuition reimbursements available (averaging $16,590 per year), 3 research assistantships with tuition reimbursements available (averaging $16,590 per year), 3 teaching assistantships with tuition reimbursements available (averaging $16,590 per year); career-related internships or fieldwork, Federal Work-Study, health care benefits, and unspecified assistantships also available. Financial award applicants required to submit FAFSA. *Faculty research:* Electrophysiology and hypertension, neural control of circulation, molecular physiology and hypertension, human biomechanics, musculoskeletal control of movement, nitric oxide production and physiological response, public health interventions. *Total annual research expenditures:* $577,000. *Unit head:* Dr. Megan C. Frost, Chair, 906-487-2715, Fax: 906-487-0985, E-mail: mcfrost@mtu.edu. *Application contact:* Carol T. Wingerson, Administrative Aide, 906-487-2328, Fax: 906-487-2284, E-mail: gradadms@mtu.edu.
Website: http://www.mtu.edu/kip/

Mississippi College, Graduate School, School of Education, Department of Kinesiology, Clinton, MS 39058. Offers athletic administration (MS). *Degree requirements:* For master's, comprehensive exam, thesis optional. *Entrance requirements:* For master's, GRE, GMAT, or PRAXIS, minimum GPA of 2.5. Additional exam requirements/recommendations for international students: Recommended—TOEFL, IELTS. Electronic applications accepted.

Mississippi State University, College of Education, Department of Kinesiology, Mississippi State, MS 39762. Offers disability studies (MS); exercise physiology (MS); exercise science (PhD); sport administration (MS); sport pedagogy (MS); sport studies (PhD). *Program availability:* Part-time, blended/hybrid learning. *Faculty:* 15 full-time (3 women). *Students:* 49 full-time (25 women), 16 part-time (3 women); includes 14 minority (5 Black or African American, non-Hispanic/Latino; 1 American Indian or Alaska Native, non-Hispanic/Latino; 2 Asian, non-Hispanic/Latino; 3 Hispanic/Latino; 3 Two or more races, non-Hispanic/Latino), 10 international. Average age 26. 67 applicants, 60% accepted, 23 enrolled. In 2018, 27 master's, 2 doctorates awarded. *Degree requirements:* For master's, comprehensive exam, thesis optional; for doctorate, comprehensive exam. *Entrance requirements:* For master's, GRE General Test, minimum GPA of 2.75 on undergraduate work from four-year accredited institution, 3.0 graduate; for doctorate, GRE, minimum GPA of 3.4 on previous graduate degree(s) earned from accredited institutions. Additional exam requirements/recommendations for international students: Required—TOEFL (minimum score 550 paper-based; 79 iBT); Recommended—IELTS (minimum score 6.5). *Application deadline:* For fall admission, 7/1 for domestic students, 5/1 for international students; for spring admission, 11/1 for domestic students, 9/1 for international students. Applications are processed on a rolling basis. Application fee: $60 ($80 for international students). Electronic applications accepted. *Expenses:* Tuition, state resident: full-time $8450; part-time $360.59 per credit hour. Tuition, nonresident: full-time $23,140; part-time $969.09 per credit hour. *Required fees:* $110. One-time fee: $55 full-time. Part-time tuition and fees vary according to course load, degree level, campus/location and reciprocity agreements. *Financial support:* In 2018–19, 14 teaching assistantships with partial tuition reimbursements (averaging $10,386 per year) were awarded; career-related internships or fieldwork, Federal Work-Study, institutionally sponsored loans, and unspecified assistantships also available. Financial award application deadline: 4/1; financial award applicants required to submit FAFSA. *Faculty research:* Static balance and stepping performance of older adults, organizational justice, public health, strength training and recovery drinks, high risk drinking perceptions and behaviors. *Unit head:* Dr. Stanley P. Brown, Professor and Head, 662-325-7229, Fax: 662-325-4525, E-mail: spb107@msstate.edu. *Application contact:* Ryan King, Admissions and Enrollment Assistant, 662-325-8951, E-mail: rjk101@grad.msstate.edu.
Website: http://www.kinesiology.msstate.edu/

Missouri State University, Graduate College, College of Health and Human Services, Department of Kinesiology, Springfield, MO 65897. Offers health promotion and wellness management (MS); secondary education (MS Ed), including physical education. *Program availability:* Part-time. *Faculty:* 14 full-time (6 women). *Students:* 14 full-time (5 women), 16 part-time (10 women); includes 2 minority (both Black or African American, non-Hispanic/Latino), 2 international. Average age 23. 23 applicants, 48% accepted. In 2018, 16 master's awarded. *Degree requirements:* For master's, comprehensive exam, thesis or alternative. *Entrance requirements:* For master's, GRE (for MS), minimum GPA of 2.8 (MS); 9-12 teaching certification (MS Ed). Additional exam requirements/recommendations for international students: Required—TOEFL (minimum score 550 paper-based; 79 iBT), IELTS (minimum score 6). *Application deadline:* For fall admission, 7/20 priority date for domestic students, 5/1 for international students; for spring admission, 12/20 priority date for domestic students, 9/1 for international students. Applications are processed on a rolling basis. Application fee: $55 ($60 for international students). Electronic applications accepted. Tuition and fees vary according to class time, course level, course load, degree level, campus/location, program and student level. *Financial support:* In 2018–19, 7 teaching assistantships with partial tuition reimbursements (averaging $8,772 per year) were awarded; Federal Work-Study, institutionally sponsored loans, scholarships/grants, and unspecified assistantships also available. Financial award application deadline: 1/31; financial award applicants required to submit FAFSA. *Unit head:* Dr. Sarah McCallister, Department Head, 417-836-6582, Fax: 417-836-5371, E-mail: sarahmccallister@missouristate.edu. *Application contact:* Lakan Drinker, Director, Graduate Enrollment Management, 417-836-5330, Fax: 417-836-6200, E-mail: lakandrinker@missouristate.edu.
Website: http://www.missouristate.edu/kinesiology/

New York University, Steinhardt School of Culture, Education, and Human Development, Department of Physical Therapy, New York, NY 10010-5615. Offers orthopedic physical therapy (Advanced Certificate); physical therapy (MA, DPT, PhD), including pathokinesiology (MA). *Accreditation:* APTA (one or more programs are accredited). *Program availability:* Part-time. *Entrance requirements:* For master's, physical therapy certificate; for doctorate, GRE General Test, interview, physical therapy certificate. Additional exam requirements/recommendations for international students: Required—TOEFL (minimum score 100 iBT). Electronic applications accepted. *Faculty research:* Motor learning and control, neuromuscular disorders, biomechanics and ergonomics, movement analysis, pathomechanics.

Northeastern State University, College of Education, Department of Health and Kinesiology, Tahlequah, OK 74464-2399. Offers MS. *Program availability:* Part-time, evening/weekend. *Faculty:* 15 full-time (10 women), 2 part-time/adjunct (0 women). *Students:* 12 full-time (7 women), 18 part-time (9 women); includes 14 minority (3 Black or African American, non-Hispanic/Latino; 3 American Indian or Alaska Native, non-Hispanic/Latino; 2 Hispanic/Latino; 6 Two or more races, non-Hispanic/Latino), 2 international. Average age 27. In 2018, 18 master's awarded. *Entrance requirements:* For master's, MAT or GRE, minimum GPA of 2.5. Additional exam requirements/recommendations for international students: Required—TOEFL. *Application deadline:* For fall admission, 6/1 for domestic and international students; for winter admission, 11/1 for domestic and international students; for spring admission, 3/1 for domestic students, 2/1 for international students. Applications are processed on a rolling basis. Application fee: $25. Electronic applications accepted. *Expenses: Tuition, area resident:* Full-time $4500; part-time $250 per credit hour. Tuition, state resident: full-time $4500; part-time $250 per credit hour. Tuition, nonresident: full-time $9999; part-time $555.50 per credit hour. *International tuition:* $9999 full-time. *Required fees:* $601.20; $33.40 per credit hour. *Unit head:* Dee Gerlach, Department Chair, 918-444-3929, E-mail: gerlach@nsuok.edu. *Application contact:* Josh McCollum, Graduate Coordinator, 918-444-2093, E-mail: mccolluj@nsuok.edu.
Website: http://academics.nsuok.edu/education/DegreePrograms/GraduatePrograms/HealthandKinesiology.aspx

Northwestern University, Feinberg School of Medicine, Department of Physical Therapy and Human Movement Sciences, Chicago, IL 60611-2814. Offers neuroscience (PhD), including movement and rehabilitation science; physical therapy (DPT); DPT/MPH; DPT/PhD. *Accreditation:* APTA. *Degree requirements:* For doctorate, research project. *Entrance requirements:* For doctorate, GRE General Test (for DPT), baccalaureate degree with minimum GPA of 3.0 in required course work (DPT). Additional exam requirements/recommendations for international students: Required—TOEFL (minimum score 100 iBT). Electronic applications accepted. *Expenses:* Contact institution.

The Ohio State University, Graduate School, College of Education and Human Ecology, Department of Human Sciences, Columbus, OH 43210. Offers consumer sciences (MS, PhD); human development and family science (PhD); human nutrition (MS, PhD); kinesiology (MA, Ed D, PhD). *Program availability:* Part-time. *Faculty:* 53. *Students:* 119 full-time (68 women), 14 part-time (8 women). Average age 27. In 2018, 46 master's, 17 doctorates awarded. *Degree requirements:* For master's, thesis optional; for doctorate, thesis/dissertation. *Entrance requirements:* For master's and doctorate, GRE. Additional exam requirements/recommendations for international students: Required—TOEFL (minimum score 550 paper-based; 79 iBT), Michigan English Language Assessment Battery (minimum score 82); Recommended—IELTS (minimum score 7). *Application deadline:* For fall admission, 12/1 priority date for domestic and international students. Applications are processed on a rolling basis. Application fee: $60 ($70 for international students). Electronic applications accepted. *Financial support:* Fellowships with tuition reimbursements, research assistantships with tuition reimbursements, teaching assistantships with tuition reimbursements, Federal Work-Study, and institutionally sponsored loans available. Support available to part-time students. *Unit head:* Dr. Erik Porfeli, Chair, E-mail: porfeli.1@osu.edu. *Application contact:* Graduate and Professional Admissions, 614-292-9444, Fax: 614-292-3895, E-mail: gpadmissions@osu.edu.
Website: http://ehe.osu.edu/human-sciences/

Old Dominion University, College of Health Sciences, School of Physical Therapy and Athletic Training, Doctor of Kinesiology and Rehabilitation Program, Norfolk, VA 23529. Offers PhD. *Degree requirements:* For doctorate, comprehensive exam, thesis/dissertation. *Entrance requirements:* For doctorate, master's degree or higher in an associated area of basic science, such as kinesiology, exercise science, or biomechanics, or in a health profession such as athletic training, nursing, occupational therapy, physical therapy, or speech/language pathology. Additional exam requirements/recommendations for international students: Recommended—TOEFL (minimum score 550 paper-based; 79 iBT), IELTS (minimum score 6.5). Electronic applications accepted. *Expenses:* Contact institution. *Faculty research:* Balance and falls, gait, perceptual information in action and virtual reality, sensorimotor compromise following joint injury, evidence-based practice and patient-centered care.

Old Dominion University, Darden College of Education, Program in Human Movement Science, Norfolk, VA 23529. Offers PhD. *Degree requirements:* For doctorate, comprehensive exam, thesis/dissertation. *Entrance requirements:* For doctorate, GRE (minimum combined score for verbal and quantitative of 297, 4.5 for analytical writing), minimum GPA of 3.5. Additional exam requirements/recommendations for international students: Required—TOEFL (minimum score 550 paper-based; 79 iBT). Electronic applications accepted. *Faculty research:* Exercise science, sport management, recreation management, health and physical education.

Old Dominion University, Darden College of Education, Program in Physical Education, Curriculum and Instruction Emphasis, Norfolk, VA 23529. Offers human movement sciences (PhD), including health and sport pedagogy; physical education (MS Ed), including adapted physical education, coaching education, curriculum and instruction. *Program availability:* Part-time, evening/weekend. *Degree requirements:* For master's, comprehensive exam (for some programs), thesis or alternative, internship, research project. *Entrance requirements:* For master's, GRE, PRAXIS tests (for licensure only), minimum GPA of 2.8 overall, 3.0 in major. Additional exam requirements/recommendations for international students: Required—TOEFL (minimum score 500 paper-based; 97 iBT). Electronic applications accepted. *Faculty research:* Motor development, physical activity and fitness, motivation and learning in physical education, curriculum and instruction, adapted physical education.

Oregon State University, College of Public Health and Human Sciences, Program in Kinesiology, Corvallis, OR 97331. Offers biophysical kinesiology (MS, PhD); psychosocial kinesiology (MS, PhD). *Program availability:* Part-time. Terminal master's awarded for partial completion of doctoral program. *Entrance requirements:* For master's and doctorate, GRE, minimum GPA of 3.0 in last 90 hours. Additional exam requirements/recommendations for international students: Required—TOEFL (minimum score 80 iBT), IELTS (minimum score 6.5). Electronic applications accepted. *Faculty research:* Motor control, sports medicine, exercise physiology, sport psychology, biomechanics.

Penn State University Park, Graduate School, College of Health and Human Development, Department of Kinesiology, University Park, PA 16802. Offers MS, PhD, Certificate.

Point Loma Nazarene University, Department of Kinesiology, San Diego, CA 92106-2899. Offers exercise science (MS); sport performance (MS), including exercise science, sport management, sport performance. *Program availability:* Part-time, online learning. *Entrance requirements:* For master's, baccalaureate degree, minimum undergraduate cumulative GPA of 3.0. *Expenses:* Contact institution.

Prairie View A&M University, College of Education, Department of Health and Kinesiology, Prairie View, TX 77446. Offers M Ed, MS. *Accreditation:* NCATE. *Program availability:* Part-time, evening/weekend. *Faculty:* 4 full-time (all women). *Students:* 31 full-time (19 women), 7 part-time (2 women); all minorities (35 Black or African American, non-Hispanic/Latino; 2 Hispanic/Latino; 1 Two or more races, non-Hispanic/Latino). Average age 27. 23 applicants, 87% accepted, 18 enrolled. In 2018, 10 master's awarded. *Degree requirements:* For master's, thesis. *Entrance requirements:* For master's, GRE General Test. Additional exam requirements/recommendations for international students: Required—TOEFL (minimum score 550 paper-based; 79 iBT). *Application deadline:* For fall admission, 5/1 priority date for domestic and international students; for spring admission, 10/1 priority date for domestic students, 9/1 priority date for international students; for summer admission, 3/1 priority date for domestic students, 2/1 priority date for international students. Applications are processed on a rolling basis. Application fee: $50. Electronic applications accepted. *Expenses: Tuition, area resident:* Full-time $3172; part-time $317 per credit. Tuition, state resident: full-time $3172; part-time $317 per credit. Tuition, nonresident: full-time $7965; part-time $796 per credit. *Required fees:* $4847; $485 per credit. *Financial support:* Career-related internships or

fieldwork available. Support available to part-time students. Financial award application deadline: 4/1; financial award applicants required to submit FAFSA. *Unit head:* Dr. Angela Branch-Vital, Department Head, 936-261-3900, Fax: 936-261-3905, E-mail: abranch-vital@pvamu.edu. *Application contact:* Pauline Walker, Administrative Assistant II, Research and Graduate Studies, 936-261-3521, Fax: 936-261-3529, E-mail: gradadmissions@pvamu.edu.

Purdue University, Graduate School, College of Health and Human Sciences, Department of Health and Kinesiology, West Lafayette, IN 47907. Offers athletic training education administration (MS, PhD); biomechanics (MS, PhD); exercise physiology (MS, PhD); health education (MS, PhD); history/philosophy of sport (MS, PhD); motor control and development (MS, PhD); physical education pedagogy (PhD); physical education teacher education (MS); recreation and sport management (MS, PhD); sport and exercise psychology (MS, PhD). *Program availability:* Part-time. *Faculty:* 23 full-time (10 women). *Students:* 29 full-time (13 women), 8 part-time (5 women); includes 3 minority (1 Asian, non-Hispanic/Latino; 1 Hispanic/Latino; 1 Two or more races, non-Hispanic/Latino), 8 international. Average age 26. 61 applicants, 26% accepted, 14 enrolled. In 2018, 14 master's awarded. *Degree requirements:* For master's, thesis optional; for doctorate, comprehensive exam, thesis/dissertation, qualifying examination, preliminary examination. *Entrance requirements:* For master's, GRE General Test (minimum score 1000 combined verbal and quantitative), minimum undergraduate GPA of 3.0 or equivalent; for doctorate, GRE General Test (minimum score 1100 combined verbal and quantitative), minimum undergraduate GPA of 3.0 or equivalent; master's degree with minimum GPA of 3.25 (recommended). Additional exam requirements/recommendations for international students: Required—TOEFL (minimum score 77 iBT); Recommended—TWE. *Application deadline:* For fall admission, 4/30 for domestic and international students; for spring admission, 10/15 for domestic and international students. Applications are processed on a rolling basis. Application fee: $60 ($75 for international students). Electronic applications accepted. *Financial support:* Fellowships with partial tuition reimbursements, research assistantships with partial tuition reimbursements, teaching assistantships with partial tuition reimbursements, and Federal Work-Study available. Support available to part-time students. Financial award applicants required to submit FAFSA. *Faculty research:* Wellness, motivation, teaching effectiveness, learning and development. *Unit head:* Dr. Timothy P. Gavin, Head of the Graduate Program, 765-494-3178, Fax: 765-494-1239, E-mail: gavin1@purdue.edu. *Application contact:* David B. Klenosky, Graduate Contact, 765-494-0865, E-mail: klenosky@purdue.edu.
Website: http://www.purdue.edu/hhs/hk/

Saint Mary's College of California, School of Liberal Arts, Department of Kinesiology, Moraga, CA 94575. Offers fitness management (MA); sport management (MA); sport studies (MA). *Program availability:* Part-time. *Degree requirements:* For master's, thesis or special project. *Entrance requirements:* For master's, minimum GPA of 2.75, BA in physical education or related field, or professional experience. Electronic applications accepted. *Expenses:* Contact institution. *Faculty research:* Moral development in sport, applied motor learning, achievement motivation, sport history.

Sam Houston State University, College of Health Sciences, Department of Kinesiology, Huntsville, TX 77341. Offers sport and human performance (MA); sport management (MA). *Program availability:* Part-time. *Degree requirements:* For master's, comprehensive exam, thesis optional. *Entrance requirements:* For master's, GRE, letters of recommendation, statement of interest/intent. Additional exam requirements/recommendations for international students: Required—TOEFL (minimum score 550 paper-based; 79 iBT), IELTS (minimum score 6.5). Electronic applications accepted.

San Diego State University, Graduate and Research Affairs, College of Health and Human Services, School of Exercise and Nutritional Sciences, Program in Kinesiology, San Diego, CA 92182. Offers MA. *Degree requirements:* For master's, thesis. *Entrance requirements:* For master's, GRE General Test, 2 letters of reference. Additional exam requirements/recommendations for international students: Required—TOEFL. Electronic applications accepted.

San Francisco State University, Division of Graduate Studies, College of Health and Social Sciences, Department of Kinesiology, San Francisco, CA 94132-1722. Offers MS. *Application deadline:* Applications are processed on a rolling basis. *Unit head:* Dr. Matthew Lee, Chair, 415-338-2244, Fax: 415-338-7566, E-mail: cmlee@sfsu.edu. *Application contact:* Prof. Maria Veri, Graduate Coordinator, 415-338-1746, Fax: 415-338-7566, E-mail: mjveri@sfsu.edu.
Website: http://kin.sfsu.edu/

San Jose State University, Program in Kinesiology, San Jose, CA 95192-0001. Offers MA. *Degree requirements:* For master's, comprehensive exam. *Entrance requirements:* For master's, bachelor's degree in physical education. Electronic applications accepted.

Sarah Lawrence College, Graduate Studies, Program in Dance/Movement Therapy, Bronxville, NY 10708-5999. Offers MS. *Degree requirements:* For master's, thesis, practicum.

Simon Fraser University, Office of Graduate Studies and Postdoctoral Fellows, Faculty of Science, Department of Biomedical Physiology and Kinesiology, Burnaby, BC V5A 1S6, Canada. Offers M Sc, PhD. *Degree requirements:* For master's, thesis, thesis proposal; for doctorate, comprehensive exam, thesis/dissertation, dissertation proposal, seminar presentations. *Entrance requirements:* For master's, minimum GPA of 3.0 (on scale of 4.33) or 3.33 based on last 60 credits of undergraduate courses; for doctorate, minimum GPA of 3.5 (on scale of 4.33). Additional exam requirements/recommendations for international students: Recommended—TOEFL (minimum score 580 paper-based; 93 iBT), IELTS (minimum score 7), TWE (minimum score 5). Electronic applications accepted. *Faculty research:* Cardiovascular physiology, chronic disease, environmental physiology, neuromechanics, neuroscience.

Sonoma State University, School of Science and Technology, Department of Kinesiology, Rohnert Park, CA 94928. Offers exercise science/pre-physical therapy (MA); interdisciplinary (MA); interdisciplinary pre-occupational therapy (MA); lifetime physical activity (MA), including coach education, fitness and wellness. *Program availability:* Part-time. *Degree requirements:* For master's, thesis, oral exam. *Entrance requirements:* For master's, minimum GPA of 2.8. Additional exam requirements/recommendations for international students: Required—TOEFL (minimum score 500 paper-based).

Southeastern Louisiana University, College of Nursing and Health Sciences, Department of Kinesiology and Health Studies, Hammond, LA 70402. Offers health and kinesiology (MS). *Accreditation:* NCATE. *Program availability:* Part-time, evening/weekend. *Faculty:* 9 full-time (3 women). *Students:* 28 full-time (18 women), 20 part-time (14 women); includes 23 minority (14 Black or African American, non-Hispanic/Latino; 2 American Indian or Alaska Native, non-Hispanic/Latino; 4 Hispanic/Latino; 1 Native Hawaiian or other Pacific Islander, non-Hispanic/Latino; 2 Two or more races, non-Hispanic/Latino), 2 international. Average age 26. 35 applicants, 51% accepted, 17 enrolled. In 2018, 16 master's awarded. *Degree requirements:* For master's, comprehensive exam (for some programs), thesis optional. *Entrance requirements:* For master's, GRE (minimum combined Verbal and Quantitative score of 286), 4 hours of human anatomy and physiology. Additional exam requirements/recommendations for international students: Required—TOEFL (minimum score 500 paper-based; 61 iBT).

Application deadline: For fall admission, 7/15 priority date for domestic students, 6/1 priority date for international students; for spring admission, 12/1 priority date for domestic students, 10/1 priority date for international students. Applications are processed on a rolling basis. Application fee: $20 ($30 for international students). Electronic applications accepted. *Expenses: Tuition, area resident:* Full-time $6684. Tuition, state resident: full-time $6684. Tuition, nonresident: full-time $19,162. *Required fees:* $2097. *Financial support:* In 2018–19, 25 students received support, including 8 research assistantships with tuition reimbursements available (averaging $8,489 per year), 4 teaching assistantships with tuition reimbursements available (averaging $21,249 per year); career-related internships or fieldwork, Federal Work-Study, institutionally sponsored loans, scholarships/grants, and unspecified assistantships also available. Support available to part-time students. Financial award application deadline: 5/1; financial award applicants required to submit FAFSA. *Faculty research:* Exercise physiology, motor learning, sport and exercise psychology, sport management, health promotion. *Total annual research expenditures:* $9,465. *Unit head:* Dr. Bovorn Sirikul, Interim Department Head, 985-549-2129, Fax: 985-549-5119, E-mail: bsirikul@southeastern.edu. *Application contact:* Office of Admissions, 985-549-5637, Fax: 985-549-5632, E-mail: admissions@southeastern.edu.
Website: http://www.southeastern.edu/acad_research/depts/kin_hs/index.html

Southeastern University, College of Education, Lakeland, FL 33801-6099. Offers curriculum and instruction (Ed D); educational leadership (M Ed); elementary education (M Ed); exceptional student education (M Ed); exceptional student education/educational therapy (M Ed); kinesiology (M Ed); organizational leadership (Ed D); reading education (M Ed); teaching English to speakers of other languages (M Ed). Electronic applications accepted.

Southern Arkansas University–Magnolia, School of Graduate Studies, Magnolia, AR 71753. Offers agriculture (MS); business administration (MBA), including agribusiness, social entrepreneurship, supply chain management; clinical and mental health counseling (MS); computer and information sciences (MS), including cyber security and privacy, data science, information technology; gifted and talented (M Ed), including curriculum and instruction, educational administration and supervision, gifted and talented P-8/7-12, instructional specialist P-4; higher, adult and lifelong education (M Ed); kinesiology (M Ed), including coaching; library media and information specialist (M Ed); public administration (MPA); school counseling K-12 (M Ed); student affairs and college counseling (M Ed); teaching (MAT). *Accreditation:* NCATE. *Program availability:* Part-time, 100% online, blended/hybrid learning. *Faculty:* 36 full-time (21 women), 32 part-time/adjunct (15 women). *Students:* 164 full-time (77 women), 762 part-time (510 women); includes 192 minority (163 Black or African American, non-Hispanic/Latino; 7 American Indian or Alaska Native, non-Hispanic/Latino; 13 Asian, non-Hispanic/Latino; 1 Hispanic/Latino; 8 Two or more races, non-Hispanic/Latino), 213 international. Average age 28. 363 applicants, 100% accepted, 237 enrolled. In 2018, 716 master's awarded. *Degree requirements:* For master's, comprehensive exam (for some programs), thesis optional. *Entrance requirements:* For master's, GRE, MAT or GMAT, minimum GPA of 2.5. Additional exam requirements/recommendations for international students: Required—TOEFL (minimum score 550 paper-based), IELTS (minimum score 6). *Application deadline:* For fall admission, 8/1 for domestic and international students; for spring admission, 12/1 for domestic students, 11/15 for international students; for summer admission, 4/1 for domestic students, 5/10 for international students. Applications are processed on a rolling basis. Application fee: $25 ($90 for international students). Electronic applications accepted. *Expenses: Tuition, area resident:* Full-time $5130; part-time $3420 per year. Tuition, state resident: full-time $5130; part-time $3420 per year. Tuition, nonresident: full-time $7866; part-time $5244 per year. *International tuition:* $7866 full-time. *Required fees:* $1052; $710 per unit. Tuition and fees vary according to course load. *Financial support:* Career-related internships or fieldwork, Federal Work-Study, scholarships/grants, tuition waivers (full), and unspecified assistantships available. Financial award applicants required to submit FAFSA. *Faculty research:* Alternative certification for teachers, supervision of instruction, instructional leadership, counseling. *Unit head:* Dr. Kim Bloss, Dean, School of Graduate Studies, 870-235-4150, Fax: 870-235-5227, E-mail: kkbloss@saumag.edu. *Application contact:* Talia Jett, Admissions Coordinator, 870-2355450, Fax: 870-235-5227, E-mail: taliajett@saumag.edu.
Website: http://www.saumag.edu/graduate

Southern Illinois University Carbondale, Graduate School, College of Education and Human Services, Department of Kinesiology, Carbondale, IL 62901-4701. Offers MS Ed. *Program availability:* Part-time. *Degree requirements:* For master's, thesis. *Entrance requirements:* For master's, GRE, minimum GPA of 2.7. Additional exam requirements/recommendations for international students: Required—TOEFL. *Faculty research:* Caffeine and exercise effects, ground reaction forces in walking and running, social psychology of sports.

Southern Illinois University Edwardsville, Graduate School, School of Education, Health, and Human Behavior, Department of Kinesiology and Health Education, Program in Physical Education and Coaching Pedagogy, Edwardsville, IL 62026. Offers MS Ed. *Program availability:* Part-time, evening/weekend. *Degree requirements:* For master's, comprehensive exam (for some programs), thesis (for some programs). *Entrance requirements:* Additional exam requirements/recommendations for international students: Required—TOEFL (minimum score 550 paper-based, 79 iBT), IELTS (minimum score 6.5), Michigan Test of English Language Proficiency or PTE. Electronic applications accepted.

Southwestern Oklahoma State University, College of Professional and Graduate Studies, School of Behavioral Sciences and Education, Specialization in Kinesiology, Weatherford, OK 73096-3098. Offers health and physical education (M Ed); sports management (M Ed). *Program availability:* Part-time. *Degree requirements:* For master's, exam. *Entrance requirements:* For master's, GRE General Test or minimum undergraduate GPA of 3.0. Additional exam requirements/recommendations for international students: Required—TOEFL (minimum score 550 paper-based), IELTS (minimum score 6.5).

Stephen F. Austin State University, Graduate School, James I. Perkins College of Education, Department of Kinesiology and Health Science, Nacogdoches, TX 75962. Offers athletic training (MS); kinesiology (MS). *Degree requirements:* For master's, comprehensive exam. *Entrance requirements:* For master's, GRE General Test. Additional exam requirements/recommendations for international students: Required—TOEFL.

Syracuse University, David B. Falk College of Sport and Human Dynamics, Syracuse, NY 13244. Offers MA, MS, MSW, PhD, CAS, MSW/MA. *Accreditation:* AAMFT/COAMFTE (one or more programs are accredited). *Program availability:* Part-time, evening/weekend. *Faculty:* 74 full-time (43 women), 22 part-time/adjunct (13 women). *Students:* 200 full-time (172 women), 102 part-time (86 women); includes 66 minority (30 Black or African American, non-Hispanic/Latino; 2 American Indian or Alaska Native, non-Hispanic/Latino; 7 Asian, non-Hispanic/Latino; 20 Hispanic/Latino; 7 Two or more races, non-Hispanic/Latino), 25 international. Average age 29. 366 applicants, 76% accepted, 139 enrolled. In 2018, 124 master's, 5 doctorates, 38 other advanced degrees awarded. *Degree requirements:* For master's, comprehensive exam (for some programs), thesis (for some programs); for doctorate, comprehensive exam, thesis/

dissertation. *Entrance requirements:* For master's, GRE (for most programs), resume, official transcripts, personal statement, three letters of recommendation; for doctorate, GRE, resume, official transcripts, personal statement, three letters of recommendation. Additional exam requirements/recommendations for international students: Required—TOEFL. *Application deadline:* For fall admission, 2/15 priority date for domestic and international students; for spring admission, 11/15 priority date for domestic students, 11/15 for international students; for summer admission, 3/15 priority date for domestic students, 3/15 for international students. Applications are processed on a rolling basis. Application fee: $75. Electronic applications accepted. *Financial support:* Fellowships with full tuition reimbursements, research assistantships, teaching assistantships, and tuition waivers available. Financial award application deadline: 1/1; financial award applicants required to submit FAFSA. *Faculty research:* Child and family studies, marriage and family therapy, public health, food studies and nutrition, social work, sport management. *Unit head:* Dr. Diane Lyden Murphy, Dean, 315-443-5582, Fax: 315-443-2562. *Application contact:* Felicia Otero, Director of College Admissions, 315-443-5555, Fax: 315-443-2562, E-mail: falk@syr.edu.
Website: http://falk.syr.edu/

Tarleton State University, College of Graduate Studies, College of Education, School of Kinesiology, Stephenville, TX 76402. Offers athletic training (MS); kinesiology (MS). *Program availability:* Part-time, evening/weekend. *Faculty:* 6 full-time (2 women), 1 (woman) part-time/adjunct. *Students:* 25 full-time (17 women), 48 part-time (25 women). Average age 24. 35 applicants, 83% accepted, 25 enrolled. In 2018, 50 master's awarded. *Degree requirements:* For master's, comprehensive exam, thesis optional. *Entrance requirements:* For master's, GRE General Test, minimum GPA of 3.0. Additional exam requirements/recommendations for international students: Required—TOEFL (minimum score 520 paper-based; 69 iBT); Recommended—IELTS (minimum score 6), TSE (minimum score 50). *Application deadline:* For fall admission, 8/15 priority date for domestic students; for spring admission, 1/7 for domestic students. Applications are processed on a rolling basis. Application fee: $50 ($130 for international students). Electronic applications accepted. *Expenses:* Contact institution. *Financial support:* Research assistantships, teaching assistantships with partial tuition reimbursements, career-related internships or fieldwork, Federal Work-Study, and institutionally sponsored loans available. Support available to part-time students. Financial award application deadline: 5/1; financial award applicants required to submit FAFSA. *Unit head:* Dr. Kayla Peak, Associate Dean, 254-968-9824, E-mail: peak@tarleton.edu. *Application contact:* Information Contact, 254-968-9104, Fax: 254-968-9670, E-mail: gradoffice@tarleton.edu.
Website: http://www.tarleton.edu/kinesiology/

Teachers College, Columbia University, Department of Biobehavioral Sciences, New York, NY 10027-6696. Offers applied exercise physiology (Ed M, MA, Ed D); communication sciences and disorders (MS, Ed D, PhD); kinesiology (PhD); motor learning and control (Ed M, MA); motor learning/movement science (Ed D); neuroscience and education (MS); physical education (MA, Ed D). *Accreditation:* ASHA. *Program availability:* Part-time, evening/weekend. *Students:* 126 full-time (111 women), 203 part-time (162 women); includes 137 minority (24 Black or African American, non-Hispanic/Latino; 42 Asian, non-Hispanic/Latino; 62 Hispanic/Latino; 9 Two or more races, non-Hispanic/Latino), 36 international. Average age 28. 643 applicants, 51% accepted, 150 enrolled. *Unit head:* Prof. Carol Garber, Chair, 212-678-3891, E-mail: garber@tc.columbia.edu. *Application contact:* Kelly Sutton Skinner, Director of Admission & New Student Enrollment, 212-678-3305, E-mail: kms2237@tc.columbia.edu.
Website: http://www.tc.columbia.edu/biobehavioral-sciences/

Temple University, College of Public Health, Department of Kinesiology, Philadelphia, PA 19122. Offers athletic training (MSAT, DAT); kinesiology (MS, PhD); neuromotor science (MS, PhD). *Faculty:* 19 full-time (8 women), 5 part-time/adjunct (2 women). *Students:* 56 full-time (36 women), 39 part-time (20 women); includes 26 minority (13 Black or African American, non-Hispanic/Latino; 2 Asian, non-Hispanic/Latino; 6 Hispanic/Latino; 5 Two or more races, non-Hispanic/Latino), 3 international. 78 applicants, 74% accepted, 37 enrolled. In 2018, 15 master's awarded. *Degree requirements:* For master's, thesis optional, research project; for doctorate, thesis/dissertation, preliminary examination. *Entrance requirements:* For master's, GRE/MAT, letters of reference, statement of goals, interview, resume; for doctorate, GRE/MAT, minimum undergraduate GPA of 3.25, 3 letters of reference, statement of goals, writing sample, interview, resume. Additional exam requirements/recommendations for international students: Required—TOEFL (minimum score 79 iBT), IELTS (minimum score 6.5), PTE (minimum score 53), one of three is required. *Application deadline:* For fall admission, 3/1 for domestic students. Applications are processed on a rolling basis. Application fee: $60. Electronic applications accepted. *Expenses:* Contact institution. *Financial support:* Fellowships, research assistantships, teaching assistantships, career-related internships or fieldwork, Federal Work-Study, health care benefits, and unspecified assistantships available. Financial award applicants required to submit FAFSA. *Faculty research:* Integrative exercise physiology, athletic training, evaluation of clinical evidence, osteoarthritis. *Unit head:* Jeffrey S Gehris, Interim Department Chair, 214-204-1954, E-mail: jgehris@temple.edu. *Application contact:* Amy Costik, Assistant Director of Admissions, 215-204-5229, E-mail: amy.costik@temple.edu.
Website: http://cph.temple.edu/kinesiology/home

Tennessee Technological University, College of Graduate Studies, College of Education, Department of Exercise Science, Physical Education and Wellness, Cookeville, TN 38505. Offers adapted physical education (MA); elementary/middle school physical education (MA); lifetime wellness (MA); sport management (MA). *Accreditation:* NCATE. *Program availability:* Part-time, online learning. *Faculty:* 7 full-time (0 women). *Students:* 12 full-time (10 women), 45 part-time (22 women); includes 8 minority (3 Black or African American, non-Hispanic/Latino; 1 Asian, non-Hispanic/Latino; 2 Hispanic/Latino; 2 Two or more races, non-Hispanic/Latino), 1 international. 43 applicants, 67% accepted, 22 enrolled. In 2018, 17 master's awarded. *Degree requirements:* For master's, comprehensive exam, thesis or alternative. *Entrance requirements:* For master's, MAT or GRE. Additional exam requirements/recommendations for international students: Required—TOEFL (minimum score 527 paper-based; 71 iBT), IELTS (minimum score 5.5), PTE (minimum score 48), or TOEIC (Test of English as an International Communication). *Application deadline:* For fall admission, 8/1 for domestic students, 5/1 for international students; for spring admission, 12/1 for domestic students, 10/1 for international students; for summer admission, 5/1 for domestic students, 2/1 for international students. Applications are processed on a rolling basis. Application fee: $35 ($40 for international students). Electronic applications accepted. *Financial support:* Fellowships, research assistantships, teaching assistantships, and career-related internships or fieldwork available. Financial award application deadline: 4/1. *Unit head:* Dr. Christy Killman, Chairperson, 931-372-3467, Fax: 931-372-6319, E-mail: ckillman@tntech.edu. *Application contact:* Shelia K. Kendrick, Coordinator of Graduate Studies, 931-372-3808, Fax: 931-372-3497, E-mail: skendrick@tntech.edu.

Texas A&M University, College of Education and Human Development, Department of Health and Kinesiology, College Station, TX 77843. Offers athletic training (MS); health education (MS, PhD); kinesiology (MS, PhD); sports management (MS). *Program availability:* Part-time. *Faculty:* 56. *Students:* 211 full-time (117 women), 80 part-time (41 women); includes 94 minority (35 Black or African American, non-Hispanic/Latino; 3 American Indian or Alaska Native, non-Hispanic/Latino; 5 Asian, non-Hispanic/Latino; 44 Hispanic/Latino; 7 Two or more races, non-Hispanic/Latino), 24 international. Average age 28. 95 applicants, 88% accepted, 60 enrolled. In 2018, 112 master's, 14 doctorates awarded. *Degree requirements:* For master's, thesis (for some programs); for doctorate, comprehensive exam, thesis/dissertation. *Entrance requirements:* For master's and doctorate, GRE General Test. Additional exam requirements/recommendations for international students: Required—TOEFL (minimum score 550 paper-based; 80 iBT), IELTS (minimum score 6), PTE (minimum score 53). *Application deadline:* For fall admission, 1/15 for domestic students; for spring admission, 10/1 for domestic students. Applications are processed on a rolling basis. Application fee: $50 ($90 for international students). Electronic applications accepted. *Expenses:* Contact institution. *Financial support:* In 2018–19, 109 students received support, including 2 fellowships with tuition reimbursements available (averaging $24,073 per year), 41 research assistantships with tuition reimbursements available (averaging $13,093 per year), 68 teaching assistantships with tuition reimbursements available (averaging $11,596 per year); career-related internships or fieldwork, institutionally sponsored loans, scholarships/grants, traineeships, health care benefits, tuition waivers (full and partial), and unspecified assistantships also available. Support available to part-time students. Financial award application deadline: 3/15; financial award applicants required to submit FAFSA. *Unit head:* Dr. Richard Kreider, Head, 979-845-1333, Fax: 979-847-8987, E-mail: rkreider@hlkn.tamu.edu. *Application contact:* Jenny Bilski, Academic Advisor, 979-862-4052, E-mail: jenny.bilski@tamu.edu.
Website: http://hlknweb.tamu.edu/

Texas A&M University–Commerce, College of Education and Human Services, Commerce, TX 75429. Offers counseling (M Ed, MS, PhD); early childhood education (M Ed, MS); educational administration (M Ed, MS, Ed D); educational psychology (PhD); educational technology leadership (M Ed, MS); educational technology library science (M Ed, MS); elementary education (M Ed); health, kinesiology and sports studies (MS); higher education (MS, Ed D); psychology (MS); reading (M Ed, MS); school psychology (SSP); secondary education (M Ed, MS); social work (MSW); special education (M Ed, MS); supervision, curriculum and instruction-elementary education (Ed D); training and development (MS). *Program availability:* Part-time, evening/weekend, 100% online, blended/hybrid learning. *Faculty:* 95 full-time (59 women), 29 part-time/adjunct (22 women). *Students:* 356 full-time (295 women), 1,262 part-time (992 women); includes 683 minority (349 Black or African American, non-Hispanic/Latino; 9 American Indian or Alaska Native, non-Hispanic/Latino; 30 Asian, non-Hispanic/Latino; 238 Hispanic/Latino; 57 Two or more races, non-Hispanic/Latino), 9 international. Average age 37. 951 applicants, 42% accepted, 304 enrolled. In 2018, 532 master's, 51 doctorates awarded. *Degree requirements:* For master's, comprehensive exam, thesis optional, departmental qualifying exams (for some programs); for doctorate, comprehensive exam, thesis/dissertation, departmental qualifying exam; for SSP, comprehensive exam. *Entrance requirements:* For master's, GRE General Test, official transcripts, letters of recommendation, resume, statement of goals; for doctorate, GRE General Test, letters of recommendation, statement of goals, writing samples, writing sessions, resumes. Additional exam requirements/recommendations for international students: Required—TOEFL (minimum score 550 paper-based; 79 iBT), IELTS (minimum score 6), PTE (minimum score 53). *Application deadline:* For fall admission, 6/1 priority date for international students; for spring admission, 10/15 priority date for international students; for summer admission, 3/15 priority date for international students. Applications are processed on a rolling basis. Application fee: $50 ($75 for international students). Electronic applications accepted. *Expenses: Tuition, area resident:* Full-time $3630. Tuition, state resident: full-time $3630. Tuition, nonresident: full-time $11,100. *International tuition:* $11,100 full-time. *Required fees:* $2794. Tuition and fees vary according to course load, degree level and program. *Financial support:* In 2018–19, 116 students received support, including 94 research assistantships with partial tuition reimbursements available (averaging $3,863 per year), 38 teaching assistantships with partial tuition reimbursements available (averaging $4,728 per year); career-related internships or fieldwork, Federal Work-Study, institutionally sponsored loans, scholarships/grants, health care benefits, and unspecified assistantships also available. Financial award application deadline: 5/1; financial award applicants required to submit FAFSA. *Faculty research:* Cognitive and bilingual education, positive behavioral intervention, literacy, math readiness. *Total annual research expenditures:* $1.1 million. *Unit head:* Dr. Madeline Justice, Interim Dean, 903-886-5181, Fax: 903-886-5905, E-mail: madeline.justice@tamuc.edu. *Application contact:* Vicky Turner, Doctoral Degree and Special Programs Coordinator, 903-886-5167, E-mail: vicky.turner@tamuc.edu.
Website: http://www.tamuc.edu/academics/graduateSchool/programs/education/default.aspx

Texas A&M University–Corpus Christi, College of Graduate Studies, College of Education and Human Development, Corpus Christi, TX 78412. Offers counseling (MS), including counseling; counselor education (PhD); curriculum and instruction (MS, PhD); early childhood education (MS); educational administration (MS); educational leadership (Ed D); elementary education (MS); instructional design and educational technology (MS); kinesiology (MS); reading (MS); secondary education (MS); special education (MS). *Program availability:* Part-time, evening/weekend, blended/hybrid learning. *Degree requirements:* For master's, comprehensive exam, capstone; for doctorate, thesis/dissertation. *Entrance requirements:* For master's, GRE General Test, essay (300 words); for doctorate, GRE, essay, resume, 3-4 reference forms. Electronic applications accepted.

Texas A&M University–Kingsville, College of Graduate Studies, College of Education and Human Performance, Department of Health and Kinesiology, Kingsville, TX 78363. Offers MA, MS. *Degree requirements:* For master's, variable foreign language requirement, comprehensive exam, thesis (for some programs). *Entrance requirements:* For master's, GRE, MAT, GMAT, essay. Additional exam requirements/recommendations for international students: Required—TOEFL (minimum score 550 paper-based; 79 iBT). Electronic applications accepted.

Texas A&M University–San Antonio, Department of Counseling, Health and Kinesiology, San Antonio, TX 78224. Offers clinical mental health counseling (MA); counseling and guidance (MA); kinesiology (MS); marriage and family counseling (MA). *Program availability:* Part-time, evening/weekend, online learning. *Degree requirements:* For master's, comprehensive exam, thesis or alternative. *Entrance requirements:* For master's, MAT or GRE (composite quantitative and verbal). Additional exam requirements/recommendations for international students: Required—TOEFL (minimum score 550 paper-based; 79 iBT), IELTS (minimum score 6). Electronic applications accepted.

Texas Christian University, Harris College of Nursing and Health Sciences, Department of Kinesiology, Fort Worth, TX 76129-0002. Offers MS. *Program availability:* Part-time. *Faculty:* 5 full-time (4 women). *Students:* 23 full-time (17 women); includes 5 minority (1 Asian, non-Hispanic/Latino; 4 Hispanic/Latino), 2 international. Average age 24. 39 applicants, 46% accepted, 11 enrolled. In 2018, 8 master's awarded. *Degree requirements:* For master's, thesis. *Entrance requirements:* For master's, GRE General

Test. Additional exam requirements/recommendations for international students: Recommended—TOEFL (minimum score 600 paper-based; 100 iBT). *Application deadline:* For fall admission, 3/1 for domestic and international students; for spring admission, 12/1 for domestic and international students. Applications are processed on a rolling basis. Application fee: $50. Electronic applications accepted. *Financial support:* In 2018–19, 16 students received support, including 16 research assistantships with full and partial tuition reimbursements available (averaging $6,300 per year); tuition waivers (full and partial) also available. Financial award application deadline: 3/1. *Faculty research:* Effect of diet or exercise interventions on cardiovascular risk factors. Effect of recess on behavior and academic performance in elementary school children. Improvement of motor skill performance and learning through the development of novel training paradigms. Enhancement of performance through cognitive and behavior skills training. *Total annual research expenditures:* $150,000. *Unit head:* Dr. Meena Shah, Professor/Chair, 817-257-6871, Fax: 817-257-7702, E-mail: m.shah@tcu.edu. *Application contact:* Meena Shah, PhD, Graduate Program Director and Interim Chair, 817-257-6871, Fax: 817-257-7702, E-mail: m.shah@tcu.edu.
Website: http://www.kinesiology.tcu.edu

Texas Tech University, Graduate School, College of Arts and Sciences, Department of Kinesiology and Sport Management, Lubbock, TX 79409-3011. Offers kinesiology (MS); sport management (MS). *Program availability:* Part-time. *Faculty:* 28 full-time (13 women), 6 part-time/adjunct (4 women). *Students:* 62 full-time (30 women), 9 part-time (3 women); includes 30 minority (4 Black or African American, non-Hispanic/Latino; 2 Asian, non-Hispanic/Latino; 21 Hispanic/Latino; 3 Two or more races, non-Hispanic/Latino), 7 international. Average age 24. 80 applicants, 64% accepted, 29 enrolled. In 2018, 31 master's awarded. *Degree requirements:* For master's, comprehensive exam (for some programs), thesis (for some programs). *Entrance requirements:* For master's, GRE (only for the M.S. in Kinesiology whose GPA on the last 60 hours of undergraduate coursework is 3.49 and lower), letter of intent, 3 letters of recommendation (preferably from academic professors), minimum GPA of 2.8 in the last 60 hours. Additional exam requirements/recommendations for international students: Required—TOEFL (minimum score 550 paper-based; 79 iBT). *Application deadline:* For fall admission, 6/1 priority date for domestic students, 1/15 priority date for international students; for spring admission, 9/1 priority date for domestic students, 6/15 priority date for international students. Applications are processed on a rolling basis. Application fee: $65. Electronic applications accepted. *Expenses:* Contact institution. *Financial support:* In 2018–19, 70 students received support, including 70 fellowships (averaging $3,597 per year), 5 research assistantships (averaging $14,098 per year), 41 teaching assistantships (averaging $10,734 per year); career-related internships or fieldwork, scholarships/grants, health care benefits, and unspecified assistantships also available. Financial award application deadline: 8/1; financial award applicants required to submit FAFSA. *Faculty research:* Sport management, exercise physiology, human performance, motor behavior, exercise and sport psychology. *Total annual research expenditures:* $205,282. *Unit head:* Dr. Angela Lumpkin, Professor & Department Chair, 806-834-6935, Fax: 806-742-1688, E-mail: angela.lumpkin@ttu.edu. *Application contact:* Donna Torres, Graduate Admissions Coordinator, 806-834-7968, Fax: 806-742-1688, E-mail: donna.torres@ttu.edu.
Website: www.depts.ttu.edu/ksm/

Université de Montréal, Department of Kinesiology, Montréal, QC H3C 3J7, Canada. Offers kinesiology (M Sc, DESS); physical activity (M Sc, PhD). *Degree requirements:* For master's, one foreign language, thesis (for some programs); for doctorate, one foreign language, thesis/dissertation, general exam. Electronic applications accepted. *Faculty research:* Physiology of exercise, psychology of sports, biomechanics, dance, sociology of sports.

Université de Sherbrooke, Faculty of Physical Education and Sports, Program in Physical Education, Sherbrooke, QC J1K 2R1, Canada. Offers kinanthropology (M Sc); physical activity (Diploma). *Degree requirements:* For master's, thesis. *Entrance requirements:* For master's, minimum GPA of 2.7; for Diploma, bachelor's degree in physical education. *Faculty research:* Physical fitness, nutrition, human factors, sociology, teaching.

Université du Québec à Montréal, Graduate Programs, Program in Human Movement Studies, Montréal, QC H3C 3P8, Canada. Offers M Sc. *Program availability:* Part-time. *Degree requirements:* For master's, thesis optional. *Entrance requirements:* For master's, appropriate bachelor's degree or equivalent and proficiency in French.

Université Laval, Faculty of Medicine, Graduate Programs in Medicine, Programs in Kinesiology, Québec, QC G1K 7P4, Canada. Offers M Sc, PhD. Terminal master's awarded for partial completion of doctoral program. *Degree requirements:* For master's, thesis; for doctorate, comprehensive exam, thesis/dissertation. *Entrance requirements:* For master's and doctorate, French exam, knowledge of French, comprehension of written English. Electronic applications accepted.

The University of Alabama, Graduate School, College of Education, Department of Kinesiology, Tuscaloosa, AL 35487. Offers alternative sport pedagogy (MA); exercise science (PhD). *Program availability:* Part-time. *Degree requirements:* For master's, comprehensive exam, thesis optional; for doctorate, comprehensive exam, thesis/dissertation. *Entrance requirements:* For master's and doctorate, GRE, minimum GPA of 3.0. Additional exam requirements/recommendations for international students: Required—TOEFL. Electronic applications accepted.

University of Alberta, Faculty of Kinesiology, Sport, and Recreation, Edmonton, AB T6G 2E1, Canada. Offers physical education (M Sc); recreation and physical education (MA, PhD). *Program availability:* Part-time. Terminal master's awarded for partial completion of doctoral program. *Degree requirements:* For master's, thesis (for some programs); for doctorate, thesis/dissertation. *Entrance requirements:* For master's, bachelor's degree in related field; for doctorate, master's degree in related field with thesis. Additional exam requirements/recommendations for international students: Required—TOEFL. *Faculty research:* Motivation and adherence to physical ability, performance enhancement, adapted physical activity, exercise physiology, sport administration, tourism.

University of Arkansas, Graduate School, College of Education and Health Professions, Department of Health, Human Performance and Recreation, Program in Kinesiology, Fayetteville, AR 72701. Offers MS, PhD. In 2018, 18 master's, 4 doctorates awarded. *Entrance requirements:* For doctorate, GRE General Test. *Application deadline:* For fall admission, 8/1 for domestic students, 4/1 for international students; for spring admission, 12/1 for domestic students, 10/1 for international students; for summer admission, 4/15 for domestic students, 3/1 for international students. Applications are processed on a rolling basis. Application fee: $60. Electronic applications accepted. *Financial support:* Fellowships with tuition reimbursements, research assistantships, teaching assistantships, career-related internships or fieldwork, and Federal Work-Study available. Support available to part-time students. Financial award application deadline: 4/1; financial award applicants required to submit FAFSA. *Unit head:* Dr. Matthew Ganio, Department Head, 479-575-2956, E-mail: msganio@uark.edu. *Application contact:* Dr. Paul Calleja, Assistant Dept. Head - HHPR, Graduate Coordinator, 479-575-2854, Fax: 479-5778, E-mail: pcallej@uark.edu.
Website: https://kins.uark.edu/

The University of British Columbia, Faculty of Education, School of Kinesiology, Vancouver, BC V6T 1Z1, Canada. Offers high performance coaching and technical leadership (MHPCTL); kinesiology (M Kin, M Sc, MA, PhD). *Program availability:* Part-time. *Degree requirements:* For master's, thesis (for some programs); for doctorate, comprehensive exam, thesis/dissertation. *Entrance requirements:* For doctorate, thesis-based master's degree. Additional exam requirements/recommendations for international students: Required—TOEFL, IELTS. Electronic applications accepted. *Expenses:* Contact institution. *Faculty research:* Exercise physiology, biomechanics, motor learning, natural sciences, socio-managerial.

University of Calgary, Faculty of Graduate Studies, Faculty of Kinesiology, Calgary, AB T2N 1N4, Canada. Offers M Kin, M Sc, PhD. *Degree requirements:* For master's, thesis (M Sc); for doctorate, thesis/dissertation. *Entrance requirements:* Additional exam requirements/recommendations for international students: Required—TOEFL. Electronic applications accepted. *Faculty research:* Load acting on the human body, muscle mechanics and physiology, optimizing high performance athlete performance, eye movement in sports, analysis of body composition.

University of Central Arkansas, Graduate School, College of Health and Behavioral Sciences, Department of Kinesiology, Conway, AR 72035-0001. Offers MS. *Program availability:* Part-time. *Degree requirements:* For master's, comprehensive exam, thesis optional. *Entrance requirements:* For master's, GRE General Test, minimum GPA of 2.7. Additional exam requirements/recommendations for international students: Required—TOEFL (minimum score 550 paper-based; 80 iBT). Electronic applications accepted.

University of Central Florida, College of Health Professions and Sciences, Program in Kinesiology, Orlando, FL 32816. Offers MS. *Unit head:* David Fukuda, Director, 407-823-0442, E-mail: david.fukuda@ucf.edu. *Application contact:* Associate Director, Graduate Admissions, 407-823-2766, Fax: 407-823-6442, E-mail: gradadmissions@ucf.edu.
Website: https://healthprofessions.ucf.edu/kpt/kinesiology/

University of Central Missouri, The Graduate School, Warrensburg, MO 64093. Offers accountancy (MA); accounting (MBA); applied mathematics (MS); aviation safety (MA); biology (MS); business administration (MBA); career and technical education leadership (MS); college student personnel administration (MS); communication (MA); computer science (MS); counseling (MS); criminal justice (MS); educational leadership (Ed D); educational technology (MS); elementary and early childhood education (MSE); English (MA); environmental studies (MA); finance (MBA); history (MA); human services/educational technology (Ed S); human services/learning resources (Ed S); human services/professional counseling (Ed S); industrial hygiene (MS); industrial management (MS); information systems (MBA); information technology (MS); kinesiology (MS); library science and information services (MS); literacy education (MSE); marketing (MBA); mathematics (MS); music (MA); occupational safety management (MS); psychology (MS); rural family nursing (MS); school administration (MSE); social gerontology (MS); sociology (MA); special education (MSE); speech language pathology (MS); superintendency (Ed S); teaching (MAT); teaching English as a second language (MA); technology (MS); technology management (PhD); theatre (MA). *Accreditation:* ASHA. *Program availability:* Part-time, 100% online, blended/hybrid learning. *Degree requirements:* For master's and Ed S, comprehensive exam (for some programs), thesis (for some programs). *Entrance requirements:* Additional exam requirements/recommendations for international students: Required—TOEFL (minimum score 550 paper-based; 79 iBT). Electronic applications accepted.

University of Colorado Boulder, Graduate School, College of Arts and Sciences, Department of Integrative Physiology, Boulder, CO 80309. Offers MS, PhD. Terminal master's awarded for partial completion of doctoral program. *Degree requirements:* For master's, comprehensive exam, thesis or alternative; for doctorate, thesis/dissertation. *Entrance requirements:* For master's, GRE General Test, minimum undergraduate GPA of 2.75. Electronic applications accepted. Application fee is waived when completed online. *Faculty research:* Aging/gerontology; nervous system; neurophysiology; neuroscience; physiological controls and systems.

University of Delaware, College of Arts and Sciences, Interdisciplinary Program in Biomechanics and Movement Science, Newark, DE 19716. Offers MS, PhD. *Program availability:* Part-time. Terminal master's awarded for partial completion of doctoral program. *Degree requirements:* For master's, thesis; for doctorate, thesis/dissertation. *Entrance requirements:* For master's and doctorate, GRE General Test, minimum undergraduate GPA of 3.0. Additional exam requirements/recommendations for international students: Required—TOEFL (minimum score 550 paper-based). Electronic applications accepted. *Faculty research:* Muscle modeling, gait, motor control, human movement.

University of Delaware, College of Health Sciences, Department of Kinesiology and Applied Physiology, Newark, DE 19716. Offers MS, PhD.

University of Florida, Graduate School, College of Health and Human Performance, Department of Applied Physiology and Kinesiology, Gainesville, FL 32611. Offers applied physiology and kinesiology (MS); athletic training/sports medicine (MS); biobehavioral science (MS); clinical exercise physiology (MS); exercise physiology (MS); health and human performance (PhD), including applied physiology and kinesiology, biobehavioral science, exercise physiology; human performance (MS). *Degree requirements:* For master's, comprehensive exam, thesis (for some programs); for doctorate, comprehensive exam, thesis/dissertation. *Entrance requirements:* For master's and doctorate, GRE General Test, minimum GPA of 3.0. Additional exam requirements/recommendations for international students: Required—TOEFL (minimum score 550 paper-based; 80 iBT), IELTS (minimum score 6). Electronic applications accepted. *Faculty research:* Cardiovascular disease; basic mechanisms that underlie exercise-induced changes in the body at the organ, tissue, cellular and molecular level; development of rehabilitation techniques for regaining motor control after stroke or as a consequence of Parkinson's disease; maintaining optimal health and delaying age-related declines in physiological function; psychomotor mechanisms impacting health and performance across the life span.

University of Georgia, College of Education, Department of Kinesiology, Athens, GA 30602. Offers MS, PhD. *Entrance requirements:* For master's, GRE General Test or MAT; for doctorate, GRE General Test. Additional exam requirements/recommendations for international students: Required—TOEFL. Electronic applications accepted.

University of Hawaii at Manoa, Office of Graduate Education, College of Education, Department of Kinesiology and Rehabilitation Science, Honolulu, HI 96822. Offers kinesiology (MS). *Program availability:* Part-time. *Degree requirements:* For master's, thesis optional. *Entrance requirements:* For master's, GRE General Test. Additional exam requirements/recommendations for international students: Required—TOEFL (minimum score 540 paper-based; 76 iBT), IELTS (minimum score 5).

University of Hawaii at Manoa, Office of Graduate Education, College of Education, PhD in Education Program, Honolulu, HI 96822. Offers curriculum and instruction (PhD); educational administration (PhD); educational foundations (PhD); educational policy studies (PhD); educational psychology (PhD); exceptionalities (PhD); kinesiology (PhD); learning design and technology (PhD). *Program availability:* Part-time, evening/

weekend. *Degree requirements:* For doctorate, thesis/dissertation. *Entrance requirements:* For doctorate, GRE General Test, sample of written work. Additional exam requirements/recommendations for international students: Required—TOEFL (minimum score 600 paper-based; 100 iBT), IELTS (minimum score 7).

University of Houston, College of Liberal Arts and Social Sciences, Department of Health and Human Performance, Houston, TX 77204. Offers exercise science (MS); human nutrition (MS); human space exploration sciences (MS); kinesiology (PhD); physical education (M Ed). *Accreditation:* NCATE (one or more programs are accredited). *Program availability:* Part-time, evening/weekend. *Degree requirements:* For master's, comprehensive exam (for some programs), thesis (for some programs); for doctorate, comprehensive exam, thesis/dissertation, qualifying exam, candidacy paper. *Entrance requirements:* For master's, GRE (minimum 35th percentile on each section), minimum cumulative GPA of 3.0; for doctorate, GRE (minimum 35th percentile on each section), minimum cumulative GPA of 3.3. Additional exam requirements/recommendations for international students: Required—TOEFL (minimum score 550 paper-based; 79 iBT). Electronic applications accepted. *Faculty research:* Biomechanics, exercise physiology, obesity, nutrition, space exploration science.

University of Idaho, College of Graduate Studies, College of Education, Health and Human Sciences, Department of Movement Sciences, Moscow, ID 83844-2401. Offers athletic training (MSAT, DAT); exercise science and health (MS); physical education teacher education (M Ed, MS); recreation, sport, and tourism management (MS). *Faculty:* 19. *Students:* 89 full-time, 9 part-time. Average age 26. In 2018, 43 master's awarded. *Degree requirements:* For doctorate, thesis/dissertation. *Entrance requirements:* For master's and doctorate, minimum GPA of 3.0. Additional exam requirements/recommendations for international students: Required—TOEFL. *Application deadline:* For fall admission, 8/1 for domestic students; for spring admission, 12/15 for domestic students. Applications are processed on a rolling basis. Application fee: $60. Electronic applications accepted. *Expenses:* Tuition, state resident: full-time $7266.44; part-time $474.50 per credit hour. Tuition, nonresident: full-time $24,902; part-time $1453.50 per credit hour. *Required fees:* $2085.56; $45.50 per credit hour. *Financial support:* Research assistantships and teaching assistantships available. Financial award applicants required to submit FAFSA. *Unit head:* Dr. Philip W. Scruggs, Chair, 208-885-7921, E-mail: movementsciences@uidaho.edu. *Application contact:* Dr. Philip W. Scruggs, Chair, 208-885-7921, E-mail: movementsciences@uidaho.edu.
Website: https://www.uidaho.edu/ed/mvsc

University of Illinois at Chicago, College of Applied Health Sciences, Program in Kinesiology, Chicago, IL 60607-7128. Offers MS, PhD. *Program availability:* Part-time. *Degree requirements:* For master's, thesis. *Entrance requirements:* For master's, GRE General Test, minimum GPA of 2.75. Additional exam requirements/recommendations for international students: Required—TOEFL. Electronic applications accepted. *Expenses:* Contact institution. *Faculty research:* Mitochondrial biogenesis, glucocorticoid lipid metabolism, at-risk youth, motor control.

University of Illinois at Urbana–Champaign, Graduate College, College of Applied Health Sciences, Department of Kinesiology and Community Health, Champaign, IL 61820. Offers community health (MS, MSPH, PhD); kinesiology (MS, PhD); public health (MPH); rehabilitation (MS); PhD/MPH.

University of Kentucky, Graduate School, College of Education, Program in Kinesiology and Health Promotion, Lexington, KY 40506-0032. Offers biomechanics (MS); exercise physiology (MS, PhD); exercise science (PhD); health promotion (MS, Ed D); physical education training (Ed D); sport leadership (MS); teaching and coaching (MS). Terminal master's awarded for partial completion of doctoral program. *Degree requirements:* For master's, comprehensive exam, thesis optional; for doctorate, comprehensive exam, thesis/dissertation. *Entrance requirements:* For master's, GRE General Test, minimum undergraduate GPA of 2.75; for doctorate, GRE General Test, minimum graduate GPA of 3.0. Additional exam requirements/recommendations for international students: Required—TOEFL (minimum score 550 paper-based). Electronic applications accepted.

University of Lethbridge, School of Graduate Studies, Lethbridge, AB T1K 3M4, Canada. Offers addictions counseling (M Sc); agricultural biotechnology (M Sc); agricultural studies (M Sc, MA); anthropology (MA); archaeology (M Sc, MA); art (MA, MFA); biochemistry (M Sc); biological sciences (M Sc); biomolecular science (PhD); biosystems and biodiversity (PhD); Canadian studies (MA); chemistry (M Sc); computer science (M Sc); computer science and geographical information science (M Sc); counseling (MC); counseling psychology (M Ed); dramatic arts (MA); earth, space, and physical science (PhD); economics (MA); education (MA, PhD); educational leadership (M Ed); English (MA); environmental science (M Sc); evolution and behavior (PhD); exercise science (M Sc); French (MA); French/German (MA); French/Spanish (MA); general education (M Ed); geography (M Sc, MA); German (MA); health sciences (M Sc); individualized multidisciplinary (M Sc, MA); kinesiology (M Sc, MA); management (M Sc), including accounting, finance, human resource management and labor relations, information systems, international management, marketing, policy and strategy; mathematics (M Sc); music (M Mus, MA); Native American studies (MA); neuroscience (M Sc, PhD); new media (MA, MFA); nursing (M Sc, MN); philosophy (MA); physics (M Sc); political science (MA); psychology (M Sc, MA); religious studies (MA); sociology (MA); theatre and dramatic arts (MFA); theoretical and computational science (PhD); urban and regional studies (MA); women and gender studies (MA). *Program availability:* Part-time, evening/weekend. *Degree requirements:* For master's, thesis (for some programs); for doctorate, comprehensive exam, thesis/dissertation. *Entrance requirements:* For master's, GMAT (for M Sc in management), bachelor's degree in related field, minimum GPA of 3.0 during previous 20 graded semester courses, 2 years' teaching or related experience (M Ed); for doctorate, master's degree, minimum graduate GPA of 3.5. Additional exam requirements/recommendations for international students: Required—TOEFL (minimum score 580 paper-based; 93 iBT). Electronic applications accepted. *Faculty research:* Movement and brain plasticity, gibberellin physiology, photosynthesis, carbon cycling, molecular properties of main-group ring components.

University of Maine, Graduate School, College of Education and Human Development, School of Kinesiology, Physical Education and Athletic Training, Orono, ME 04469. Offers classroom technology integrationist (CGS); education data specialist (CGS); educational technology coordinator (CGS); kinesiology and physical education (M Ed, MS); science education (M Ed, MS); STEM education (PhD). *Program availability:* Part-time, evening/weekend. *Faculty:* 3 full-time (0 women). *Students:* 9 full-time (5 women), 2 part-time (0 women); includes 2 minority (1 Black or African American, non-Hispanic/Latino; 1 Asian, non-Hispanic/Latino). Average age 24. 8 applicants, 75% accepted, 3 enrolled. In 2018, 3 master's awarded. *Degree requirements:* For master's, thesis (for some programs); for doctorate, comprehensive exam, thesis/dissertation. *Entrance requirements:* For master's, GRE General Test, MAT; for doctorate, GRE General Test. Additional exam requirements/recommendations for international students: Required—TOEFL. *Application deadline:* For fall admission, 1/15 for domestic students. Applications are processed on a rolling basis. Application fee: $65. Electronic applications accepted. *Financial support:* In 2018–19, 7 students received support, including 6 teaching assistantships with full tuition reimbursements available (averaging $15,600 per year); Federal Work-Study, scholarships/grants, and unspecified assistantships also available. Financial award application deadline: 3/1. *Faculty research:* Geriatric equilibrium, physical activity and technology, muscle cell metabolism, hormonal response to exercise. *Unit head:* Dr. Jim Artesani, Associate Dean of Accreditation and Graduate Affairs, 207-581-4061, Fax: 207-581-2423. *Application contact:* Scott G. Delcourt, Assistant Vice President for Graduate Studies and Senior Associate Dean, 207-581-3291, Fax: 207-581-3232, E-mail: graduate@maine.edu.
Website: http://umaine.edu/edhd/

University of Manitoba, Faculty of Graduate Studies, Faculty of Kinesiology and Recreation Management, Winnipeg, MB R3T 2N2, Canada. Offers kinesiology and recreation (M Sc, MA).

University of Mary, School of Health Sciences, Program in Kinesiology, Bismarck, ND 58504-9652. Offers MS. *Program availability:* Part-time, online learning.

University of Maryland, College Park, Academic Affairs, School of Public Health, Department of Kinesiology, College Park, MD 20742. Offers MA, PhD. *Program availability:* Part-time, evening/weekend. *Degree requirements:* For master's, thesis optional; for doctorate, thesis/dissertation. *Entrance requirements:* For master's, GRE General Test, minimum GPA of 3.0, 3 letters of recommendation; for doctorate, GRE General Test, minimum GPA of 3.5, 3 letters of recommendation. Electronic applications accepted. *Faculty research:* Sports, biophysical and professional studies, cognitive motor behavior, exercise physiology.

University of Massachusetts Amherst, Graduate School, School of Public Health and Health Sciences, Department of Kinesiology, Amherst, MA 01003. Offers MS, PhD. *Program availability:* Part-time. Terminal master's awarded for partial completion of doctoral program. *Degree requirements:* For master's, comprehensive exam (for some programs), thesis optional; for doctorate, comprehensive exam, thesis/dissertation. *Entrance requirements:* For master's and doctorate, GRE General Test. Additional exam requirements/recommendations for international students: Required—TOEFL (minimum score 550 paper-based; 80 iBT), IELTS (minimum score 6.5). Electronic applications accepted.

University of Michigan, Rackham Graduate School, School of Kinesiology, Ann Arbor, MI 48109. Offers movement science (MS, PhD); sport management (MS, PhD). *Faculty:* 30 full-time (15 women). *Students:* 115 full-time (56 women); includes 31 minority (13 Black or African American, non-Hispanic/Latino; 4 Asian, non-Hispanic/Latino; 11 Hispanic/Latino; 3 Two or more races, non-Hispanic/Latino). Average age 26. 223 applicants, 51% accepted, 64 enrolled. In 2018, 47 master's, 4 doctorates awarded. Terminal master's awarded for partial completion of doctoral program. *Degree requirements:* For master's, thesis optional; for doctorate, comprehensive exam, thesis/dissertation, oral defense of dissertation. *Entrance requirements:* For master's and doctorate, GRE General Test. Additional exam requirements/recommendations for international students: Required—TOEFL (minimum score 84 iBT). *Application deadline:* For fall admission, 12/1 priority date for domestic students, 12/1 for international students. Applications are processed on a rolling basis. Application fee: $75 ($90 for international students). Electronic applications accepted. *Financial support:* In 2018–19, 34 students received support, including 13 fellowships with full tuition reimbursements available, 9 research assistantships with full tuition reimbursements available, 14 teaching assistantships with full tuition reimbursements available; Federal Work-Study, scholarships/grants, traineeships, health care benefits, and unspecified assistantships also available. Financial award application deadline: 12/1. *Faculty research:* Motor development, exercise physiology, biomechanics, sport medicine, sport management. *Unit head:* Dr. Ketra L. Armstrong, Associate Dean for Graduate Affairs, 734-647-3027, Fax: 734-647-2808, E-mail: ketra@umich.edu. *Application contact:* Charlene F. Ruloff, Graduate Program Coordinator, 734-764-1343, Fax: 734-647-2808, E-mail: cruloff@umich.edu.
Website: http://www.kines.umich.edu/

University of Minnesota, Twin Cities Campus, Graduate School, College of Education and Human Development, School of Kinesiology, Minneapolis, MN 55455-0213. Offers kinesiology (MS, PhD), including behavioral aspects of physical activity, biomechanics and neuromotor control, exercise physiology, perceptual-motor control and learning, sport and exercise psychology, sport management (PhD), sport sociology; sport and exercise science (M Ed); sport management (M Ed, MA). *Program availability:* Part-time. *Faculty:* 15 full-time (7 women). *Students:* 117 full-time (58 women), 21 part-time (8 women); includes 21 minority (5 Black or African American, non-Hispanic/Latino; 3 Asian, non-Hispanic/Latino; 9 Hispanic/Latino; 4 Two or more races, non-Hispanic/Latino), 23 international. Average age 26. 175 applicants, 62% accepted, 69 enrolled. In 2018, 47 master's, 9 doctorates awarded. Terminal master's awarded for partial completion of doctoral program. *Degree requirements:* For master's, final oral exam; for doctorate, thesis/dissertation, preliminary written/oral exam, final oral exam. *Entrance requirements:* For master's, GRE or MAT, minimum GPA of 3.0; for doctorate, GRE or MAT, minimum GPA of 3.0, writing sample. Application fee: $75 ($95 for international students). *Financial support:* In 2018–19, 3 fellowships, 8 research assistantships with full tuition reimbursements (averaging $8,544 per year), 37 teaching assistantships with full tuition reimbursements (averaging $14,093 per year) were awarded; career-related internships or fieldwork, Federal Work-Study, institutionally sponsored loans, and tuition waivers (full and partial) also available. Support available to part-time students. *Faculty research:* Role of physical activity in preventing health related problems; mechanism of age-related disorders, diseases and mental problems, and the ways to ameliorate them; role of sports in society and social justice; sports among populations with low income and racial diversity; fundamental functions of the body and the mechanism controlling the mechanisms; psychological issues related to physical activity and sports. *Total annual research expenditures:* $525,150. *Unit head:* Dr. Beth Lewis, Director, 612-625-5300, E-mail: blewis@umn.edu. *Application contact:* Nina Wang, 612-625-4380, E-mail: nwang@umn.edu.
Website: http://www.cehd.umn.edu/kin/

University of Mississippi, Graduate School, School of Applied Sciences, University, MS 38677. Offers communicative disorders (MS); criminal justice (MCJ); exercise science (MS); food and nutrition services (MS); health and kinesiology (PhD); health promotion (MS); nutrition and hospitality management (PhD); park and recreation management (MA); social welfare (PhD); social work (MSW). *Faculty:* 66 full-time (36 women), 27 part-time/adjunct (13 women). *Students:* 192 full-time (148 women), 40 part-time (25 women); includes 50 minority (41 Black or African American, non-Hispanic/Latino; 1 American Indian or Alaska Native, non-Hispanic/Latino; 1 Asian, non-Hispanic/Latino; 5 Hispanic/Latino; 2 Two or more races, non-Hispanic/Latino), 16 international. Average age 26. In 2018, 72 master's, 5 doctorates awarded. *Entrance requirements:* For master's, GRE General Test, minimum GPA of 3.0. Additional exam requirements/recommendations for international students: Required—TOEFL. *Application deadline:* Applications are processed on a rolling basis. Application fee: $50. Electronic applications accepted. *Financial support:* Scholarships/grants available. Financial award application deadline: 3/1; financial award applicants required to submit FAFSA. *Unit head:* Dr. Peter Grandjean, Dean of Applied Sciences, 662-915-7900, Fax: 662-915-7901, E-mail: applsci@olemiss.edu. *Application contact:* Temeka Smith, Graduate Activities Specialist for Admissions, 662-915-7474, Fax: 662-915-7577, E-mail: gschool@olemiss.edu.

University of Nebraska at Omaha, Graduate Studies, College of Education, School of Health and Kinesiology, Omaha, NE 68182. Offers athletic training (MA); exercise science (PhD); health, physical education, and recreation (MA, MS). *Program availability:* Part-time, evening/weekend. *Degree requirements:* For master's, comprehensive exam, thesis (for some programs). *Entrance requirements:* For master's, GRE; entrance exam, minimum GPA of 3.0, official transcripts, statement of purpose, 2 letters of recommendation; for doctorate, GRE, minimum GPA of 3.2, official transcripts, statement of purpose, 3 letters of recommendation, resume, writing sample. Additional exam requirements/recommendations for international students: Required—TOEFL, IELTS, PTE. Electronic applications accepted.

University of Nevada, Las Vegas, Graduate College, School of Integrated Health Sciences, Department of Kinesiology and Nutrition Sciences, Las Vegas, NV 89154-3034. Offers exercise kinesiology (MS); kinesiology (PhD); nutrition sciences (MS). *Program availability:* Part-time. *Faculty:* 12 full-time (6 women), 1 (woman) part-time/adjunct. *Students:* 32 full-time (17 women), 12 part-time (8 women); includes 15 minority (3 Black or African American, non-Hispanic/Latino; 1 American Indian or Alaska Native, non-Hispanic/Latino; 3 Asian, non-Hispanic/Latino; 8 Hispanic/Latino), 1 international. Average age 28. 64 applicants, 36% accepted, 15 enrolled. In 2018, 13 master's, 4 doctorates awarded. *Degree requirements:* For master's, thesis (for some programs), professional paper; for doctorate, comprehensive exam, thesis/dissertation. *Entrance requirements:* For master's, GRE General Test, bachelor's degree; statement of purpose; 2 letters of recommendation; for doctorate, GRE General Test (minimum 70th percentile on the Verbal section), master's degree/bachelor's degree with minimum GPA of 3.25; 3 letters of recommendation; statement of purpose; personal interview. Additional exam requirements/recommendations for international students: Required—TOEFL (minimum score 550 paper-based; 80 iBT), IELTS (minimum score 7). Application fee: $60 ($95 for international students). Electronic applications accepted. *Expenses:* Contact institution. *Financial support:* In 2018–19, 22 students received support, including 12 research assistantships with full tuition reimbursements available (averaging $12,250 per year), 10 teaching assistantships with full tuition reimbursements available (averaging $12,350 per year); institutionally sponsored loans, scholarships/grants, health care benefits, and unspecified assistantships also available. Financial award application deadline: 3/15; financial award applicants required to submit FAFSA. *Faculty research:* Biomechanics of gait, factors in motor skill acquisition and performance, nutritional supplements and performance, lipoprotein biochemistry, transcranial direct current stimulation. *Total annual research expenditures:* $248,520. *Unit head:* Dr. John Mercer, Professor/Acting Chair, 702-895-4672, Fax: 702-895-1356, E-mail: kns.chair@unlv.edu. *Application contact:* Dr. James Navalta, Graduate Coordinator, 702-895-2344, E-mail: kinesiology.gradcoord@unlv.edu.

University of New Hampshire, Graduate School, College of Health and Human Services, Department of Kinesiology, Durham, NH 03824. Offers adapted physical education (Postbaccalaureate Certificate); kinesiology (MS); kinesiology and social work (MS). *Program availability:* Part-time. *Entrance requirements:* For master's, GRE General Test. Additional exam requirements/recommendations for international students: Required—TOEFL (minimum score 550 paper-based; 80 iBT). Electronic applications accepted.

University of North Alabama, College of Education, Department of Health, Physical Education, and Recreation, Florence, AL 35632-0001. Offers health and human performance (MS), including exercise science, kinesiology, wellness and health promotion. *Program availability:* Part-time. *Degree requirements:* For master's, comprehensive exam (for some programs), thesis optional. *Entrance requirements:* For master's, MAT or GRE, 3 letters of recommendation, essay. Additional exam requirements/recommendations for international students: Required—TOEFL (minimum score 79 iBT), IELTS (minimum score 6), PTE (minimum score 54). Electronic applications accepted.

The University of North Carolina at Chapel Hill, School of Medicine and Graduate School, Graduate Programs in Medicine, Department of Allied Health Sciences, Program in Human Movement Science, Chapel Hill, NC 27599. Offers PhD. *Entrance requirements:* Additional exam requirements/recommendations for international students: Required—TOEFL (minimum score 550 paper-based). Electronic applications accepted.

The University of North Carolina at Charlotte, College of Health and Human Services, Department of Kinesiology, Charlotte, NC 28223-0001. Offers kinesiology (MS); respiratory care (MS). *Program availability:* Part-time. *Students:* 20 full-time (14 women), 42 part-time (26 women); includes 18 minority (12 Black or African American, non-Hispanic/Latino; 1 Asian, non-Hispanic/Latino; 4 Hispanic/Latino; 1 Two or more races, non-Hispanic/Latino). Average age 34. 46 applicants, 80% accepted, 28 enrolled. In 2018, 15 master's awarded. *Entrance requirements:* For master's, GRE, minimum overall cumulative GPA of 3.0 in all college coursework, upper-division 3.25; demonstrated evidence of sufficient interest, ability, and preparation to adequately profit from graduate study. Additional exam requirements/recommendations for international students: Required—TOEFL (minimum score 523 paper-based; 70 iBT), IELTS (minimum score 6), TOEFL (minimum score 523 paper-based, 70 iBT) or IELTS (6). *Application deadline:* Applications are processed on a rolling basis. Application fee: $75. Electronic applications accepted. Tuition and fees vary according to course load and program. *Financial support:* Research assistantships, teaching assistantships, career-related internships or fieldwork, institutionally sponsored loans, scholarships/grants, traineeships, and unspecified assistantships available. Support available to part-time students. Financial award application deadline: 3/1; financial award applicants required to submit FAFSA. *Total annual research expenditures:* $233,474. *Unit head:* Dr. Vivian B. Lord, Interim Chair, 704-687-0752, E-mail: vblord@uncc.edu. *Application contact:* Kathy B. Giddings, Director of Graduate Admissions, 704-687-5503, Fax: 704-687-1668, E-mail: gradadm@uncc.edu.
Website: http://kinesiology.uncc.edu/

The University of North Carolina at Greensboro, Graduate School, School of Health and Human Sciences, Department of Kinesiology, Greensboro, NC 27412-5001. Offers athletic training (MSAT); kinesiology (MS, Ed D, PhD). *Program availability:* Online learning. *Degree requirements:* For master's, thesis (for some programs); for doctorate, thesis/dissertation. *Entrance requirements:* For master's and doctorate, GRE General Test. Additional exam requirements/recommendations for international students: Required—TOEFL. Electronic applications accepted.

University of North Dakota, Graduate School, College of Education and Human Development, Department of Kinesiology and Public Health Education, Grand Forks, ND 58202. Offers kinesiology (MS). *Program availability:* Part-time. *Degree requirements:* For master's, thesis or alternative, final or comprehensive examination. *Entrance requirements:* For master's, GRE General Test, minimum GPA of 3.0. Additional exam requirements/recommendations for international students: Required—TOEFL (minimum score 550 paper-based; 79 iBT), IELTS (minimum score 6.5). Electronic applications accepted. *Faculty research:* Exercise physiology, exercise biomechanics, anatomy and physiology, exercise psychology.

University of Northern Iowa, Graduate College, College of Education, School of Kinesiology, Allied Health and Human Services, MA Program in Physical Education,

Cedar Falls, IA 50614. Offers kinesiology (MA); teaching/coaching (MA). *Program availability:* Part-time, evening/weekend. *Degree requirements:* For master's, comprehensive exam, thesis or alternative. *Entrance requirements:* For master's, minimum GPA of 3.0. Additional exam requirements/recommendations for international students: Required—TOEFL (minimum score 500 paper-based; 61 iBT). Electronic applications accepted.

University of North Georgia, Program in Kinesiology, Dahlonega, GA 30597. Offers MS. *Program availability:* Part-time, evening/weekend, online only, 100% online. *Degree requirements:* For master's, capstone course. *Entrance requirements:* For master's, GRE (minimum score of 301) or MAT (minimum score of 391), minimum baccalaureate GPA of 2.75, official transcripts, verification of lawful presence. Additional exam requirements/recommendations for international students: Required—TOEFL (minimum score 550 paper-based; 79 iBT), IELTS (minimum score 6.5). Electronic applications accepted. *Expenses:* Contact institution.

University of North Texas, Toulouse Graduate School, Denton, TX 76203-5459. Offers accounting (MS); applied anthropology (MA, MS); applied behavior analysis (Certificate); applied geography (MA); applied technology and performance improvement (M Ed, MS); art education (MA); art history (MA); arts leadership (Certificate); audiology (Au D); behavior analysis (MS); behavioral science (PhD); biochemistry and molecular biology (MS); biology (MA, MS); biomedical engineering (MS); business analysis (MS); chemistry (MS); clinical health psychology (PhD); communication studies (MA, MS); computer engineering (MS); computer science (MS); counseling (M Ed, MS), including clinical mental health counseling (MS), college and university counseling, elementary school counseling, secondary school counseling; creative writing (MA); criminal justice (MS); curriculum and instruction (M Ed); decision sciences (MBA); design (MA, MFA), including fashion design (MFA), innovation studies, interior design (MFA); early childhood studies (MS); economics (MS); educational leadership (M Ed, Ed D); educational psychology (MS, PhD), including family studies (MS), gifted and talented (MS), human development (MS), learning and cognition (MS), research, measurement and evaluation (MS); electrical engineering (MS); emergency management (MPA); engineering technology (MS); English (MA); English as a second language (MA); environmental science (MS); finance (MBA, MS); financial management (MPA); French (MA); health services management (MBA); higher education (M Ed, Ed D); history (MA, MS); hospitality management (MS); human resources management (MPA); information science (MS); information systems (PhD); information technologies (MBA); interdisciplinary studies (MA, MS); international studies (MA); international sustainable tourism (MS); jazz studies (MM); journalism (MA, MJ, Graduate Certificate), including interactive and virtual digital communication (Graduate Certificate), narrative journalism (Graduate Certificate), public relations (Graduate Certificate); kinesiology (MS); linguistics (MA); local government management (MPA); logistics (PhD); logistics and supply chain management (MBA); long-term care, senior housing, and aging services (MA); management (PhD); marketing (MBA); mathematics (MA, MS); mechanical and energy engineering (MS, PhD); music (MA), including ethnomusicology, music theory, musicology, performance; music composition (PhD); music education (MM Ed, PhD); nonprofit management (MPA); operations and supply chain management (MBA); performance (MM, DMA); philosophy (MA); political science (MA); professional and technical communication (MA); radio, television and film (MA, MFA); rehabilitation counseling (Certificate); sociology (MA); Spanish (MA); special education (M Ed); speech-language pathology (MA); strategic management (MBA); studio art (MFA); teaching (M Ed); MBA/MS. *Program availability:* Part-time, evening/weekend, online learning. Terminal master's awarded for partial completion of doctoral program. *Degree requirements:* For master's, variable foreign language requirement, comprehensive exam (for some programs), thesis (for some programs); for doctorate, variable foreign language requirement, comprehensive exam (for some programs), thesis/dissertation; for other advanced degree, variable foreign language requirement, comprehensive exam (for some programs). *Entrance requirements:* For master's and doctorate, GRE, GMAT. Additional exam requirements/recommendations for international students: Required—TOEFL (minimum score 550 paper-based; 79 iBT). Electronic applications accepted.

University of Ottawa, Faculty of Graduate and Postdoctoral Studies, Faculty of Health Sciences, School of Human Kinetics, Ottawa, ON K1N 6N5, Canada. Offers MA. *Degree requirements:* For master's, thesis or alternative. *Entrance requirements:* For master's, honors degree or equivalent, minimum B average. Electronic applications accepted. *Faculty research:* Psychosocial sciences, physical and health administration of sport and physical activity, intervention and consultation in sport, physical activity and health.

University of Puerto Rico—Mayagüez, Graduate Studies, College of Arts and Sciences, Department of Kinesiology, Mayagüez, PR 00681-9000. Offers kinesiology (MA), including biomechanics, education, exercise physiology, sports training. *Program availability:* Part-time. *Degree requirements:* For master's, thesis. *Entrance requirements:* For master's, EXADEP or GRE, minimum GPA of 2.5. Electronic applications accepted.

University of Regina, Faculty of Graduate Studies and Research, Faculty of Kinesiology and Health Studies, Regina, SK S4S 0A2, Canada. Offers M Sc, PhD. *Program availability:* Part-time. *Faculty:* 18 full-time (9 women), 24 part-time/adjunct (10 women). *Students:* 24 full-time (9 women), 14 part-time (7 women). Average age 30. 14 applicants, 36% accepted, 3 enrolled. In 2018, 3 master's, 1 doctorate awarded. *Degree requirements:* For master's, thesis; for doctorate, thesis/dissertation. *Entrance requirements:* For master's, rationale for pursuing graduate studies, description of the specific area/topic thesis research will likely focus on, post secondary transcripts, 2 letters of recommendation; for doctorate, statement of research interest along with a summary of proposed research program; completion of a thesis-based master's program, or non-thesis based master's program with relevant research experience in a field that is relevant to the area of study in the desired PhD program with a minimum graduating average of 70 percent. Additional exam requirements/recommendations for international students: Required—TOEFL (minimum score 580 paper-based; 80 iBT), IELTS (minimum score 6.5), PTE (minimum score 59), other options are CAEL, MELAB, Cantest and U of R ESL. *Application deadline:* Applications are processed on a rolling basis. Application fee: $100 Canadian dollars. Electronic applications accepted. Tuition and fees vary according to course level, course load, degree level and program. *Financial support:* In 2018–19, 31 students received support, including 12 fellowships, 9 teaching assistantships (averaging $2,552 per year); research assistantships, career-related internships or fieldwork, scholarships/grants, unspecified assistantships, and Travel Award and Graduate Scholarship Base funds also available. Support available to part-time students. Financial award application deadline: 9/30. *Faculty research:* Social psychology of physical activity and health, social science of physical activity and recreation, recreation and leisure, sport management, exercise science. *Unit head:* Dr. Harold Riemer, Dean, 306-585-4535, Fax: 306-585-4854, E-mail: khs.dean@uregina.ca. *Application contact:* Dr. Darren Candow, Associate Dean, Graduate Studies and Research, 306-585-4906, Fax: 306-585-4854, E-mail: darren.candow@uregina.ca. Website: http://www.uregina.ca/kinesiology/

University of Saskatchewan, College of Graduate and Postdoctoral Studies, College of Kinesiology, Saskatoon, SK S7N 5A2, Canada. Offers M Sc, PhD. *Degree requirements:* For master's, thesis; for doctorate, thesis/dissertation. *Entrance requirements:* Additional exam requirements/recommendations for international students: Required—TOEFL.

Kinesiology and Movement Studies

University of South Alabama, College of Education and Professional Studies, Department of Health, Kinesiology, and Sport, Mobile, AL 36688. Offers exercise science (MS); health education (M Ed, MS); physical education (M Ed); sport management (MS). *Accreditation:* NCATE (one or more programs are accredited). *Program availability:* Part-time. *Degree requirements:* For master's, comprehensive exam, thesis optional. *Entrance requirements:* For master's, GRE General Test or MAT, Alabama Class B certificate or the equivalent (for students seeking the master's-level/Class A certification). Additional exam requirements/recommendations for international students: Required—TOEFL. Electronic applications accepted.

University of South Dakota, Graduate School, School of Education, Division of Kinesiology and Sport Management, Vermillion, SD 57069. Offers exercise science (MA); sport management (MA). *Accreditation:* NCATE. *Program availability:* Part-time. *Degree requirements:* For master's, comprehensive exam, thesis or alternative. *Entrance requirements:* For master's, GRE General Test, MAT, minimum GPA of 3.0. Additional exam requirements/recommendations for international students: Required—TOEFL (minimum score 550 paper-based; 79 iBT). Electronic applications accepted.

University of Southern California, Graduate School, Herman Ostrow School of Dentistry, Division of Biokinesiology and Physical Therapy, Los Angeles, CA 90089. Offers biokinesiology (MS, PhD); physical therapy (DPT). *Accreditation:* APTA (one or more programs are accredited). *Degree requirements:* For master's, comprehensive exam; for doctorate, thesis/dissertation. *Entrance requirements:* For master's and doctorate, GRE (minimum combined score 1200, verbal 600, quantitative 600). Additional exam requirements/recommendations for international students: Required—TOEFL. Electronic applications accepted. *Expenses:* Contact institution. *Faculty research:* Exercise and aging biomechanics, musculoskeletal biomechanics, exercise and hormones related to muscle wasting, computational neurorehabilitation, motor behavior and neurorehabilitation, motor development, infant motor performance.

The University of Tennessee, Graduate School, College of Education, Health and Human Sciences, Department of Exercise, Sport, and Leisure Studies, Program in Exercise Science, Knoxville, TN 37996. Offers biomechanics/sports medicine (MS, PhD); exercise physiology (MS, PhD). *Accreditation:* CEPH (one or more programs are accredited). *Program availability:* Part-time. *Degree requirements:* For master's, thesis optional. *Entrance requirements:* For master's, minimum GPA of 2.7. Additional exam requirements/recommendations for international students: Required—TOEFL. Electronic applications accepted.

The University of Texas at Arlington, Graduate School, College of Nursing and Health Innovation, Arlington, TX 76019. Offers athletic training (MS); exercise science (MS); kinesiology (PhD); nurse practitioner (MSN); nursing (PhD); nursing administration (MSN); nursing education (MSN); nursing practice (DNP). *Accreditation:* AACN. *Program availability:* Part-time, evening/weekend, online learning. *Degree requirements:* For master's, practicum course; for doctorate, comprehensive exam (for some programs), thesis/dissertation (for some programs), proposal defense dissertation (for PhD); scholarship project (for DNP). *Entrance requirements:* For master's, GRE General Test if GPA less than 3.0, minimum GPA of 3.0, Texas nursing license, minimum C grade in undergraduate statistics course; for doctorate, GRE General Test (waived for MSN-to-PhD applicants), minimum undergraduate, graduate and statistics GPA of 3.0; Texas RN license; interview; written statement of goals. Additional exam requirements/recommendations for international students: Required—TOEFL (minimum score 550 paper-based), IELTS (minimum score 7). *Faculty research:* Simulation in clinical education and practice, cultural diversity, vulnerable populations, substance abuse.

The University of Texas at Austin, Graduate School, College of Education, Department of Kinesiology and Health Education, Austin, TX 78712-1111. Offers behavioral health (PhD); exercise and sport psychology (M Ed, MA); exercise science (M Ed, MS, PhD); health education (M Ed, MS, Ed D, PhD). *Program availability:* Part-time. Terminal master's awarded for partial completion of doctoral program. *Degree requirements:* For master's, thesis (for some programs); for doctorate, thesis/dissertation. *Entrance requirements:* For master's and doctorate, GRE General Test. Additional exam requirements/recommendations for international students: Required—TOEFL. Electronic applications accepted. *Faculty research:* Health promotion, human performance and exercise biochemistry, motor behavior and biomechanics, sport management, aging and pediatric development.

The University of Texas at El Paso, Graduate School, College of Health Sciences, Department of Kinesiology, El Paso, TX 79968-0001. Offers MS. *Program availability:* Part-time, evening/weekend, online learning. *Degree requirements:* For master's, thesis optional. *Entrance requirements:* For master's, GRE. Additional exam requirements/recommendations for international students: Required—TOEFL; Recommended—IELTS. Electronic applications accepted.

The University of Texas at San Antonio, College of Education and Human Development, Department of Kinesiology, Health, and Nutrition, San Antonio, TX 78249-0617. Offers health and kinesiology (MS). *Program availability:* Part-time, evening/weekend. *Degree requirements:* For master's, comprehensive exam, thesis optional. *Entrance requirements:* For master's, bachelor's degree with minimum GPA of 3.0 in last 60 hours of coursework; resume; statement of purpose; two letters of recommendation. Additional exam requirements/recommendations for international students: Required—TOEFL (minimum score 550 paper-based; 79 iBT), IELTS (minimum score 6.5). Electronic applications accepted. *Expenses:* Contact institution. *Faculty research:* Childhood obesity, health disparities, community health, exercise physiology, sport psychology.

The University of Texas at Tyler, College of Nursing and Health Sciences, Department of Health and Kinesiology, Tyler, TX 75799-0001. Offers health and kinesiology (M Ed, MA); health sciences (MS); kinesiology (MS). *Accreditation:* TEAC. *Program availability:* Part-time, online learning. *Students:* Average age 29. 44 applicants, 100% accepted, 27 enrolled. In 2018, 13 master's awarded. *Degree requirements:* For master's, comprehensive exam (for some programs), thesis (for some programs). *Entrance requirements:* Additional exam requirements/recommendations for international students: Required—TOEFL. *Application deadline:* For fall admission, 8/17 priority date for domestic students, 7/1 priority date for international students; for spring admission, 12/21 priority date for domestic students, 11/1 priority date for international students. Applications are processed on a rolling basis. Application fee: $25 ($50 for international students). Electronic applications accepted. *Financial support:* In 2018–19, 2 teaching assistantships (averaging $6,000 per year) were awarded; research assistantships, Federal Work-Study, and scholarships/grants also available. Financial award application deadline: 7/1. *Faculty research:* Osteoporosis, muscle soreness, economy of locomotion, adoption of rehabilitation programs, effect of inactivity and aging on muscle blood vessels, territoriality. *Unit head:* Dr. David Criswell, Chair, 903-566-7178, E-mail: dcriswell@uttyler.edu. *Application contact:* Dr. David Criswell, Chair, 903-566-7178, E-mail: dcriswell@uttyler.edu.
Website: https://www.uttyler.edu/hkdept/

The University of Texas of the Permian Basin, Office of Graduate Studies, College of Arts and Sciences, Department of Kinesiology, Odessa, TX 79762-0001. Offers MS. *Program availability:* Part-time, evening/weekend, online learning. *Degree requirements:* For master's, comprehensive exam (for some programs), thesis (for some programs).

Entrance requirements: For master's, GRE General Test, minimum GPA of 2.5. Additional exam requirements/recommendations for international students: Required—TOEFL (minimum score 550 paper-based).

The University of Texas Rio Grande Valley, College of Health Affairs, Department of Health and Human Performance, Edinburg, TX 78539. Offers exercise science (MS); kinesiology (MS). *Program availability:* Part-time-only, evening/weekend, 100% online. *Faculty:* 13 full-time (5 women), 2 part-time/adjunct (0 women). *Students:* 8 full-time (4 women), 31 part-time (8 women); includes 31 minority (1 Black or African American, non-Hispanic/Latino; 30 Hispanic/Latino). Average age 28. 27 applicants, 96% accepted, 25 enrolled. In 2018, 18 master's awarded. *Degree requirements:* For master's, comprehensive exam, thesis optional. *Entrance requirements:* For master's, GRE, minimum GPA of 3.0 in last 60 hours. Additional exam requirements/recommendations for international students: Required—TOEFL (minimum score 550 paper-based; 79 iBT), IELTS (minimum score 6.5). *Application deadline:* For fall admission, 7/17 for domestic students; for spring admission, 11/16 for domestic students. Applications are processed on a rolling basis. Application fee: $50. Electronic applications accepted. *Expenses: Tuition, area resident:* Full-time $6888. Tuition, state resident: full-time $6888. Tuition, nonresident: full-time $14,484. *International tuition:* $14,484 full-time. *Required fees:* $1468. *Financial support:* In 2018–19, 8 students received support, including 9 research assistantships (averaging $5,000 per year); unspecified assistantships also available. Financial award application deadline: 4/15; financial award applicants required to submit FAFSA. *Faculty research:* Physiology of exercise, fitness levels, Mexican American children, nutrition, diabetes prevention. *Unit head:* Dr. Zelma D. Mata, Chair, 956-665-3501, Fax: 956-665-3502, E-mail: zelma.mata@utrgv.edu. *Application contact:* Dr. Murat Karabulut, Associate Professor and Graduate Program Coordinator, 956-882-8290, E-mail: murat.karabulut@utrgv.edu.
Website: http://www.utrgv.edu/hhp/

University of the Incarnate Word, Ila Faye Miller School of Nursing and Health Professions, San Antonio, TX 78209-6397. Offers kinesiology (MS); nursing (MSN, DNP); sport management (MS). *Program availability:* Part-time, evening/weekend. *Faculty:* 15 full-time (10 women). *Students:* 106 full-time (74 women), 13 part-time (11 women); includes 80 minority (26 Black or African American, non-Hispanic/Latino; 1 American Indian or Alaska Native, non-Hispanic/Latino; 3 Asian, non-Hispanic/Latino; 47 Hispanic/Latino; 3 Two or more races, non-Hispanic/Latino), 3 international. 43 applicants, 95% accepted, 28 enrolled. In 2018, 26 master's, 19 doctorates awarded. *Degree requirements:* For master's, comprehensive exam (for some programs), thesis or alternative, capstone. *Entrance requirements:* For master's, GRE General Test, MAT, baccalaureate degree in ACEN- or CCNE-accredited nursing program with health assessment and statistics; minimum cumulative GPA of 2.5 (3.0 in upper-division courses); three professional references; Texas State license or multi-state compact. Additional exam requirements/recommendations for international students: Required—TOEFL (minimum score 560 paper-based; 83 iBT). *Application deadline:* Applications are processed on a rolling basis. Application fee: $20. Electronic applications accepted. *Expenses:* $935 per credit hour (for DNP); $250-500 matriculation fee (one time). *Financial support:* Research assistantships, Federal Work-Study, scholarships/grants, tuition waivers (partial), and unspecified assistantships available. Financial award applicants required to submit FAFSA. *Faculty research:* Pediatric oncology, military pregnancy and the family, diabetes prevention, substance abuse and addictions, nursing of vulnerable populations. *Unit head:* Dr. Mary Hoke, Dean, 210-829-3982, Fax: 210-829-3174, E-mail: mhoke@uiwtx.edu. *Application contact:* Jessica Delarosa, Associate Director of Admissions, 210-8296005, Fax: 210-829-3921, E-mail: admis@uiwtx.edu.
Website: https://nursing-and-health-professions.uiw.edu/

University of Toronto, School of Graduate Studies, Faculty of Kinesiology and Physical Education, Toronto, ON M5S 1A1, Canada. Offers M Sc, PhD. *Degree requirements:* For master's, thesis, oral defense of thesis; for doctorate, comprehensive exam, defense of thesis. *Entrance requirements:* For master's, background in physical education and health, minimum B+ average in final year of undergraduate study, 2 letters of reference, resume, 2 writing samples; for doctorate, master's degree with successful defense of thesis, background in exercise sciences, minimum A- average, 2 letters of reference. Additional exam requirements/recommendations for international students: Required—TOEFL (minimum score 580 paper-based; 93 iBT), TWE (minimum score 5). Electronic applications accepted.

The University of Tulsa, Graduate School, Oxley College of Health Sciences, Department of Kinesiology and Rehabilitative Sciences, Tulsa, OK 74104-3189. Offers MAT. Summer enrollment only. *Faculty:* 10 full-time (4 women), 7 part-time/adjunct (2 women). *Students:* 9 full-time (5 women), 3 part-time (2 women); includes 2 minority (1 Black or African American, non-Hispanic/Latino; 1 American Indian or Alaska Native, non-Hispanic/Latino), 2 international. Average age 24. 17 applicants, 71% accepted, 8 enrolled. In 2018, 2 master's awarded. *Entrance requirements:* For master's, GRE General Test. Additional exam requirements/recommendations for international students: Required—TOEFL (minimum score 577 paper-based; 90 iBT), IELTS (minimum score 6.5). Application fee: $55. *Expenses:* Contact institution. *Financial support:* In 2018–19, 1 student received support, including 1 teaching assistantship with full tuition reimbursement available (averaging $17,880 per year). Financial award applicants required to submit FAFSA. *Unit head:* Robin Ploeger, Interim Dean, 918-631-3170, E-mail: robin-ploeger@utulsa.edu. *Application contact:* Dr. Rachel Hildebrand, Program Advisor, 918-631-3204, Fax: 918-631-2156, E-mail: rachel-hildebrand@utulsa.edu.
Website: https://healthsciences.utulsa.edu/departments-schools/athletic-training/graduate-program/

University of Utah, Graduate School, College of Health, Department of Health, Kinesiology, and Recreation, Salt Lake City, UT 84112. Offers kinesiology (MS, PhD); parks, recreation, and tourism (MS, PhD). *Program availability:* Part-time. *Faculty:* 21 full-time (9 women), 11 part-time/adjunct (6 women). *Students:* 82 full-time (55 women), 12 part-time (4 women); includes 5 minority (1 Black or African American, non-Hispanic/Latino; 1 American Indian or Alaska Native, non-Hispanic/Latino; 3 Asian, non-Hispanic/Latino), 1 international. Average age 28. 92 applicants, 23% accepted, 16 enrolled. In 2018, 33 master's, 5 doctorates awarded. Terminal master's awarded for partial completion of doctoral program. *Degree requirements:* For master's, comprehensive exam, thesis or alternative; for doctorate, comprehensive exam, thesis/dissertation. *Entrance requirements:* For master's and doctorate, GRE General Test, minimum GPA of 3.0. Additional exam requirements/recommendations for international students: Required—TOEFL (minimum score 500 paper-based). *Application deadline:* For fall admission, 1/15 for domestic and international students. Application fee: $55 ($65 for international students). Electronic applications accepted. *Expenses: Tuition, area resident:* Full-time $7190.66; part-time $2112.48 per year. Tuition, state resident: full-time $7190.66. Tuition, nonresident: full-time $25,195. *Required fees:* $558; $555.04 per unit. Tuition and fees vary according to course level, course load, degree level, program and student level. *Financial support:* In 2018–19, 38 students received support, including 7 research assistantships with full tuition reimbursements available, 31 teaching assistantships with full tuition reimbursements available; career-related internships or fieldwork, scholarships/grants, health care benefits, and unspecified

assistantships also available. Financial award application deadline: 1/15; financial award applicants required to submit FAFSA. *Faculty research:* Cognitive and motor neuroscience, physical activity and well being, exercise and disease, healthy communities and environments. *Total annual research expenditures:* $55,000. *Unit head:* Dr. Kelly S. Bricker, Program Director, 801-585-6503, E-mail: kelly.bricker@health.utah.edu. *Application contact:* Dr. Jim Sibthorp, Director of Graduate Studies, 801-581-5940, Fax: 801-581-4930, E-mail: jim.sibthorp@health.utah.edu. Website: http://www.health.utah.edu/prt/

University of Victoria, Faculty of Graduate Studies, Faculty of Education, School of Exercise Science, Physical, and Health Education, Victoria, BC V8W 2Y2, Canada. Offers coaching studies (co-operative education) (M Ed); kinesiology (M Sc, MA); leisure service administration (MA); physical education (MA). *Program availability:* Part-time. *Degree requirements:* For master's, comprehensive exam (for some programs), thesis (for some programs). *Entrance requirements:* For master's, minimum B average. Additional exam requirements/recommendations for international students: Required—TOEFL (minimum score 575 paper-based), IELTS (minimum score 7). Electronic applications accepted. *Faculty research:* Children and exercise, mental skills in sports, teaching effectiveness, neural control of human movement, physical performance and health.

University of Virginia, Curry School of Education, Department of Kinesiology, Charlottesville, VA 22903. Offers M Ed, MS, PhD. *Entrance requirements:* For master's and doctorate, GRE General Test, 2 letters of recommendation. Additional exam requirements/recommendations for international students: Required—TOEFL (minimum score 600 paper-based; 90 iBT), IELTS (minimum score 7). Electronic applications accepted.

University of Virginia, Curry School of Education, Program in Education, Charlottesville, VA 22903. Offers administration and supervision (PhD); applied developmental science (PhD); counselor education (PhD); curriculum and instruction (PhD); early childhood special education (MT); education evaluation (PhD); educational psychology (PhD); educational research (PhD); elementary education (MT); English education (MT, PhD); foreign language education (MT); higher education (PhD); instructional technology (PhD); kinesiology (MT, PhD); math education (PhD); reading education (PhD); research, statistics and evaluation (PhD); school psychology (PhD); science education (PhD); social studies education (MT, PhD); special education (PhD); world languages education (MT). *Degree requirements:* For master's, comprehensive exam (for some programs), field project; for doctorate, comprehensive exam, thesis/dissertation. *Entrance requirements:* For doctorate, GRE General Test. Additional exam requirements/recommendations for international students: Required—TOEFL (minimum score 600 paper-based; 90 iBT), IELTS (minimum score 7). Electronic applications accepted.

University of Waterloo, Graduate Studies and Postdoctoral Affairs, Faculty of Applied Health Sciences, Department of Kinesiology, Waterloo, ON N2L 3G1, Canada. Offers M Sc, PhD. *Program availability:* Part-time. *Degree requirements:* For master's, thesis; for doctorate, comprehensive exam, thesis/dissertation. *Entrance requirements:* For master's, honors degree, minimum B average, writing sample; for doctorate, GRE (recommended), master's degree, minimum B average, writing sample. Additional exam requirements/recommendations for international students: Required—TOEFL, IELTS, PTE. Application fee: $125 Canadian dollars. Electronic applications accepted. *Financial support:* In 2018–19, 17 research assistantships were awarded; teaching assistantships, institutionally sponsored loans, scholarships/grants, and university-sponsored bursaries also available. *Faculty research:* Work physiology, biomechanics and neural control of human movement, psychomotor learning and performance, aging, health and well-being, work and health. Website: https://uwaterloo.ca/kinesiology/

The University of Western Ontario, School of Graduate and Postdoctoral Studies, Faculty of Health Sciences, School of Kinesiology, London, ON N6A 3K7, Canada. Offers M Sc, MA, PhD. *Degree requirements:* For master's, thesis optional; for doctorate, comprehensive exam, thesis/dissertation. *Entrance requirements:* For doctorate, MA in physical education or kinesiology. Additional exam requirements/recommendations for international students: Required—Michigan English Language Assessment Battery, TOEFL or IELTS. *Faculty research:* Exercise physiology/biochemistry, sports injuries, sport psychology, sport history, sport philosophy.

University of Windsor, Faculty of Graduate Studies, Faculty of Human Kinetics, Windsor, ON N9B 3P4, Canada. Offers MHK. *Program availability:* Part-time. *Degree requirements:* For master's, thesis optional. *Entrance requirements:* For master's, minimum B average. Additional exam requirements/recommendations for international students: Required—TOEFL (minimum score 600 paper-based). Electronic applications accepted. *Faculty research:* Movement sciences, sport and lifestyle management, historical and sociological studies of sport.

University of Wisconsin–Madison, Graduate School, School of Education, Department of Kinesiology, Madison, WI 53706-1380. Offers kinesiology (MS, PhD); occupational therapy (MS, PhD). *Accreditation:* AOTA. *Degree requirements:* For doctorate, thesis/dissertation. *Entrance requirements:* For master's and doctorate, GRE General Test. Electronic applications accepted.

University of Wisconsin–Milwaukee, Graduate School, College of Health Sciences, Department of Kinesiology, Milwaukee, WI 53201-0413. Offers athletic training (MS); kinesiology (MS, PhD), including exercise and nutrition in health and disease (MS), integrative human performance (MS), neuromechanics (MS); physical therapy (DPT). *Program availability:* Part-time. *Students:* 108 full-time (59 women), 6 part-time (3 women); includes 11 minority (1 American Indian or Alaska Native, non-Hispanic/Latino; 1 Asian, non-Hispanic/Latino; 3 Hispanic/Latino; 6 Two or more races, non-Hispanic/Latino), 5 international. Average age 28. 47 applicants, 38% accepted, 16 enrolled. In 2018, 9 master's, 21 doctorates awarded. *Degree requirements:* For master's, comprehensive exam, thesis optional. *Entrance requirements:* For master's, GRE General Test. Additional exam requirements/recommendations for international students: Required—TOEFL (minimum score 550 paper-based; 79 iBT), IELTS (minimum score 6.5). *Application deadline:* For fall admission, 1/1 priority date for domestic students; for spring admission, 9/1 for domestic students. Applications are processed on a rolling basis. Application fee: $56 ($96 for international students). *Financial support:* Fellowships, research assistantships, teaching assistantships, career-related internships or fieldwork, unspecified assistantships, and project assistantships available. Support available to part-time students. Financial award application deadline: 4/15. *Unit head:* Dr. Kyle T. Ebersole, Department Chair, 414-229-6717, Fax: 414-229-3366, E-mail: ebersole@uwm.edu. *Application contact:* Stephen C. Cobb, Graduate Program Coordinator, 414-229-3369, Fax: 414-229-3366, E-mail: cobbsc@uwm.edu. Website: http://uwm.edu/healthsciences/academics/kinesiology/

University of Wisconsin–Milwaukee, Graduate School, College of Health Sciences, Program in Health Sciences, Milwaukee, WI 53201-0413. Offers health sciences (PhD), including diagnostic and biomedical sciences, disability and rehabilitation, health administration and policy, human movement sciences, population health. *Students:* 23 full-time (14 women), 7 part-time (5 women); includes 6 minority (1 Black or African

American, non-Hispanic/Latino; 3 Asian, non-Hispanic/Latino; 2 Two or more races, non-Hispanic/Latino), 10 international. Average age 33. 15 applicants, 60% accepted, 8 enrolled. In 2018, 2 doctorates awarded. *Degree requirements:* For doctorate, comprehensive exam, thesis/dissertation. *Entrance requirements:* For doctorate, GRE. Additional exam requirements/recommendations for international students: Required—TOEFL (minimum score 600 paper-based), IELTS (minimum score 6.5). Application fee: $56 ($96 for international students). *Financial support:* Fellowships, research assistantships, teaching assistantships, and project assistantships available. *Application contact:* Susan Cashin, PhD, Assistant Dean, 414-229-3303, E-mail: scashin@uwm.edu. Website: http://uwm.edu/healthsciences/academics/phd-health-sciences/

University of Wyoming, College of Health Sciences, Division of Kinesiology and Health, Laramie, WY 82071. Offers MS. *Accreditation:* NCATE. *Program availability:* Part-time, online learning. *Degree requirements:* For master's, comprehensive exam (for some programs), thesis (for some programs). *Entrance requirements:* For master's, GRE General Test, minimum GPA of 3.0. Additional exam requirements/recommendations for international students: Required—TOEFL. Electronic applications accepted. *Expenses: Tuition, area resident:* Full-time $6504; part-time $271 per credit hour. Tuition, state resident: full-time $6504; part-time $271 per credit hour. Tuition, nonresident: full-time $19,464; part-time $811 per credit hour. *International tuition:* $19,464 full-time. *Required fees:* $1410.94; $343.82 per semester. $343.82 per semester. Tuition and fees vary according to course load, program and reciprocity agreements. *Faculty research:* Teacher effectiveness, effects of exercising on heart function, physiological responses of overtraining, psychological benefits of physical activity, health behavior.

Utah State University, School of Graduate Studies, Emma Eccles Jones College of Education and Human Services, Department of Kinesiology and Health Science, Logan, UT 84322. Offers fitness promotion (MS); health and human movement (MS); pathokinesiology (PhD); physical and sport education (M Ed); public health (MPH). *Program availability:* Part-time, evening/weekend, online learning. *Degree requirements:* For master's, thesis (for some programs). *Entrance requirements:* For master's, GRE General Test or MAT, minimum GPA of 3.0. Additional exam requirements/recommendations for international students: Required—TOEFL. *Faculty research:* Sport psychology intervention, motor learning biomechanics, pedagogy, physiology.

Washington University in St. Louis, School of Medicine, Interdisciplinary Program in Movement Science, St. Louis, MO 63130-4899. Offers PhD. *Degree requirements:* For doctorate, thesis/dissertation. *Entrance requirements:* For doctorate, GRE General Test. Electronic applications accepted.

Wayne State University, College of Education, Division of Kinesiology, Health and Sports Studies, Detroit, MI 48202. Offers athletic training (MSAT); health education (M Ed); kinesiology (M Ed, PhD), including exercise and sport science (PhD), physical education and physical activity leadership (PhD); sports administration (MA). *Program availability:* Part-time, evening/weekend. *Faculty:* 9. *Students:* 76 full-time (47 women), 110 part-time (56 women); includes 73 minority (53 Black or African American, non-Hispanic/Latino; 4 Asian, non-Hispanic/Latino; 8 Hispanic/Latino; 8 Two or more races, non-Hispanic/Latino), 9 international. Average age 30. 163 applicants, 60% accepted, 69 enrolled. In 2018, 70 master's, 4 doctorates awarded. *Degree requirements:* For master's, thesis (for some programs); for doctorate, comprehensive exam, thesis/dissertation. *Entrance requirements:* For master's, minimum undergraduate GPA of 3.0; undergraduate degree directly relating to the field of specialization being applied for or one accompanied by extensive educational background in closely-related field; teaching certificates in specific areas (for some programs); for doctorate, minimum undergraduate GPA of 3.0; undergraduate degree directly relating to the field of specialization being applied for or one accompanied by extensive educational background in closely-related field. Additional exam requirements/recommendations for international students: Required—TOEFL (minimum score 550 paper-based; 79 iBT); Recommended—IELTS (minimum score 6.5), TWE (minimum score 5.5), TSE (minimum score 58). *Application deadline:* Applications are processed on a rolling basis. Application fee: $50. Electronic applications accepted. *Financial support:* In 2018–19, 51 students received support. Fellowships with tuition reimbursements available, research assistantships with tuition reimbursements available, teaching assistantships with tuition reimbursements available, scholarships/grants, health care benefits, and unspecified assistantships available. Support available to part-time students. Financial award applicants required to submit FAFSA. *Faculty research:* Exercise and sport science, nutrition and physical activity interventions, school and community health, obesity prevention. *Unit head:* Dr. Nate McCaughtry, Assistant Dean, Division of Kinesiology, Health and Sport Studies/Director, Center for School Health, 313-577-0014, Fax: 313-577-5002, E-mail: aj4391@wayne.edu. *Application contact:* Heather Ladanyi, Manager, 313-577-1191, E-mail: eb3703@wayne.edu. Website: http://coe.wayne.edu/kinesiology/index.php

West Chester University of Pennsylvania, College of Health Sciences, Department of Kinesiology, West Chester, PA 19383. Offers adapted physical education (Certificate); exercise and sport physiology (MS), including athletic training; sport management and athletics (MPA), including administration. *Program availability:* Part-time, evening/weekend, blended/hybrid learning. *Degree requirements:* For master's, thesis or research report (for MS); two internships and capstone course that includes a research project or thesis (for MPA); for Certificate, six courses of study. *Entrance requirements:* For master's, GRE (for MS), 2 letters of recommendation, statement of professional goals; transcripts (for MS); two letters of reference, career goals, resume (for MPA); for Certificate, two letters of recommendation, transcript. Additional exam requirements/recommendations for international students: Required—TOEFL or IELTS. Electronic applications accepted. *Faculty research:* Metabolism during exercise, biomechanics, rating of perceived exertion, motor learning, environmental physiology.

Western Illinois University, School of Graduate Studies, College of Education and Human Services, Department of Kinesiology, Program in Kinesiology, Macomb, IL 61455-1390. Offers MS. *Program availability:* Part-time. *Students:* 34 full-time (15 women), 16 part-time (7 women); includes 9 minority (5 Black or African American, non-Hispanic/Latino; 1 Asian, non-Hispanic/Latino; 3 Hispanic/Latino), 5 international. Average age 25. 38 applicants, 74% accepted, 20 enrolled. In 2018, 19 master's awarded. *Entrance requirements:* For master's, minimum GPA of 3.0. Additional exam requirements/recommendations for international students: Required—TOEFL (minimum score 550 paper-based; 80 iBT). *Application deadline:* Applications are processed on a rolling basis. Application fee: $30. Electronic applications accepted. *Financial support:* Teaching assistantships with full tuition reimbursements and unspecified assistantships available. Financial award applicants required to submit FAFSA. *Unit head:* Renee Polubinsky, Department Chair, 309-298-2050, E-mail: rl-polubinsky@wiu.edu. *Application contact:* Dr. Mark Mossman, Associate Provost and Director of Graduate Studies, 309-298-1806, Fax: 309-298-2345, E-mail: grad-office@wiu.edu. Website: http://www.wiu.edu/coehs/kinesiology/graduate_programs/kin/

Wilfrid Laurier University, Faculty of Graduate and Postdoctoral Studies, Faculty of Science, Department of Kinesiology and Physical Education, Waterloo, ON N2L 3C5, Canada. Offers physical activity and health (M Sc). *Degree requirements:* For master's, thesis. *Entrance requirements:* For master's, honours degree in kinesiology, health,

physical education with a minimum B+ in kinesiology and health-related courses. Additional exam requirements/recommendations for international students: Required—TOEFL (minimum score 89 iBT). Electronic applications accepted. *Faculty research:* Biomechanics, health, exercise physiology, motor control, sport psychology.

York University, Faculty of Graduate Studies, Faculty of Health, Program in Kinesiology and Health Science, Toronto, ON M3J 1P3, Canada. Offers M Sc, MA, PhD. *Program availability:* Part-time. *Degree requirements:* For master's, thesis or alternative; for doctorate, comprehensive exam, thesis/dissertation. Electronic applications accepted.

Physical Education

Adams State University, Office of Graduate Studies, Department of Human Performance and Physical Education, Alamosa, CO 81101. Offers human performance and physical education (MA, MS), including applied sport psychology, coaching (MA), exercise science (MA), sport management (MA). *Program availability:* Part-time. *Entrance requirements:* For master's, GRE General Test or MAT, minimum undergraduate GPA of 2.75.

Adelphi University, College of Education & Health Sciences, College of Educaation & Health Sciences, Garden City, NY 11530-0701. Offers aging (Certificate); physical/educational human performance science (MA). *Program availability:* Part-time, evening/weekend. *Students:* 101 full-time (55 women), 78 part-time (52 women); includes 49 minority (19 Black or African American, non-Hispanic/Latino; 1 American Indian or Alaska Native, non-Hispanic/Latino; 2 Asian, non-Hispanic/Latino; 23 Hispanic/Latino; 1 Native Hawaiian or other Pacific Islander, non-Hispanic/Latino; 3 Two or more races, non-Hispanic/Latino), 17 international. Average age 27. 194 applicants, 68% accepted, 77 enrolled. In 2018, 58 master's awarded. *Degree requirements:* For master's, internship. *Entrance requirements:* For master's, GRE, 2 letters of recommendation, resume, essay, bachelor's degree, transcripts from all universities attended. Additional exam requirements/recommendations for international students: Required—TOEFL (minimum score 550 paper-based; 80 iBT), IELTS (minimum score 6.5). *Application deadline:* Applications are processed on a rolling basis. Application fee: $50. Electronic applications accepted. *Expenses:* Contact institution. *Financial support:* Research assistantships, teaching assistantships, career-related internships or fieldwork, institutionally sponsored loans, scholarships/grants, traineeships, and unspecified assistantships available. Support available to part-time students. Financial award application deadline: 1/1; financial award applicants required to submit FAFSA. *Faculty research:* Physical education for the handicapped, sport sociology, sport pedagogy. *Unit head:* Dr. Emilia Zarco, Chair, 516-877-4261, E-mail: zarco@adelphi.edu. *Application contact:* Dr. Emilia Zarco, Chair, 516-877-4261, E-mail: zarco@adelphi.edu.

Alabama Agricultural and Mechanical University, School of Graduate Studies, College of Education, Humanities, and Behavioral Sciences, Department of Health Sciences, Human Performance, and Communicative Disorders, Huntsville, AL 35811. Offers kinesiology (MS); physical education (MS); speech-language pathology (MS). *Program availability:* Part-time, evening/weekend. *Degree requirements:* For master's, comprehensive exam. *Entrance requirements:* For master's, GRE General Test. Additional exam requirements/recommendations for international students: Required—TOEFL (minimum score 500 paper-based; 61 iBT). Electronic applications accepted. *Faculty research:* Cardiorespiratory assessment.

Alabama State University, College of Education, Department of Health, Physical Education, and Recreation, Montgomery, AL 36101-0271. Offers health education (M Ed); physical education (M Ed). *Program availability:* Part-time, evening/weekend. *Faculty:* 3 full-time (2 women), 2 part-time/adjunct (1 woman). *Students:* 5 full-time (2 women), 4 part-time (2 women); includes 7 minority (all Black or African American, non-Hispanic/Latino), 1 international. Average age 29. 4 applicants, 75% accepted. In 2018, 3 master's awarded. *Degree requirements:* For master's, comprehensive exam. *Entrance requirements:* For master's, GRE General Test, MAT, writing competency test, bachelor's degree or its equivalent from accredited college or university with minimum GPA of 2.5. Additional exam requirements/recommendations for international students: Required—TOEFL (minimum score 500 paper-based). *Application deadline:* For fall admission, 4/15 for domestic and international students; for spring admission, 11/15 for domestic and international students; for summer admission, 3/15 for domestic and international students. Applications are processed on a rolling basis. Application fee: $25. Electronic applications accepted. *Expenses:* Contact institution. *Financial support:* Fellowships, teaching assistantships, career-related internships or fieldwork, scholarships/grants, tuition waivers (partial), and unspecified assistantships available. Financial award application deadline: 6/30; financial award applicants required to submit FAFSA. *Faculty research:* Risk factors for heart disease in the college-age population, cardiovascular reactivity for the Cold Pressor Test. *Unit head:* Dr. Charlie Gibbons, Chair, Associate Professor of Health Education, 334-229-4504, Fax: 334-229-4928, E-mail: cgibbons@alasu.edu. *Application contact:* Dr. Ed Brown, Dean of Graduate Studies, 334-229-4274, Fax: 334-229-4928, E-mail: ebrown@alasu.edu. Website: http://www.alasu.edu/academics/colleges—departments/college-of-education/health-physical-education—recreation/index.aspx

Albany State University, College of Education, Albany, GA 31705-2717. Offers early childhood education (M Ed); educational leadership (Ed S); health and physical education (M Ed); middle grades education (M Ed); school counseling (M Ed); special education (M Ed). *Accreditation:* NCATE. *Program availability:* Part-time, evening/weekend, online learning. *Degree requirements:* For master's, comprehensive exam, internship, GACE Content Exam. *Entrance requirements:* For master's, GRE or MAT. Electronic applications accepted. *Faculty research:* GACE preparation, STEM (science, technology, engineering, and mathematics), technology education, special education, professional teacher development, health implications liberation philosophy, NET-Q, learning community, disabled or at-risk students.

Alcorn State University, School of Graduate Studies, School of Education and Psychology, Lorman, MS 39096-7500. Offers agricultural education (MS Ed); elementary education (MAT, MS Ed, Ed S); guidance and counseling (MS Ed); industrial education (MS Ed); secondary education (MAT, MS Ed), including health and physical education (MS Ed), NCAA compliance and academic progress reporting (MS Ed); special education (MS Ed). *Accreditation:* NCATE. *Degree requirements:* For master's, thesis optional.

American University of Puerto Rico, Program in Education, Bayamon, PR 00960-2037. Offers art education (M Ed); elementary education 4-6 (M Ed); elementary education K-3 (M Ed); general science education (M Ed); physical education (M Ed); special education (M Ed). *Program availability:* Part-time, evening/weekend. *Entrance requirements:* For master's, EXADEP, GRE, or MAT, 2 letters of recommendation, minimum GPA of 2.5.

Arizona State University at the Tempe campus, Mary Lou Fulton Teachers College, Program in Curriculum and Instruction, Phoenix, AZ 85069. Offers curriculum and instruction (M Ed, MA); elementary education (M Ed); physical education (MPE); secondary education (M Ed). *Program availability:* Part-time, evening/weekend, online learning. Terminal master's awarded for partial completion of doctoral program. *Degree requirements:* For master's, thesis or alternative, applied project, interactive Program of Study (iPOS) submitted before completing 50 percent of required credit hours. *Entrance requirements:* For master's, GRE or GMAT (for some programs), minimum GPA of 3.0 or equivalent in last 2 years of work leading to bachelor's degree, 3 letters of recommendation, personal statement describing research and career goals, curriculum vitae or resume, IVP fingerprint clearance card (for those seeking Arizona certification). Additional exam requirements/recommendations for international students: Required—TOEFL, IELTS, or PTE. Electronic applications accepted. *Expenses:* Contact institution. *Faculty research:* Early childhood, media and computers, elementary education, secondary education, English education, bilingual education, language and literacy, science education, engineering education, exercise and wellness education.

Arkansas State University, Graduate School, College of Education and Behavioral Science, Department of Health, Physical Education, and Sport Sciences, State University, AR 72467. Offers exercise science (MS); physical education (MSE, SCCT); sports administration (MS). *Program availability:* Part-time. *Degree requirements:* For master's, comprehensive exam, thesis or alternative; for SCCT, comprehensive exam. *Entrance requirements:* For master's, GRE General Test or MAT, appropriate bachelor's degree, official transcripts, immunization records, statement of goals, letters of recommendation; for SCCT, GRE General Test or MAT, interview, master's degree, official transcript, immunization records. Additional exam requirements/recommendations for international students: Required—TOEFL (minimum score 550 paper-based; 79 iBT), IELTS (minimum score 6), PTE (minimum score 56). Electronic applications accepted.

Auburn University, Graduate School, College of Education, School of Kinesiology, Auburn University, AL 36849. Offers exercise science (M Ed). *Accreditation:* NCATE. *Program availability:* Part-time. *Degree requirements:* For master's, thesis (for some programs); for doctorate, thesis/dissertation; for Ed S, exam, field project. *Entrance requirements:* For master's, GRE General Test; for doctorate and Ed S, GRE General Test, interview, master's degree. Electronic applications accepted. *Expenses:* Tuition, state resident: full-time $11,282; part-time $535 per credit hour. Tuition, nonresident: full-time $30,542; part-time $1605 per credit hour. *Required fees:* $826 per semester. Tuition and fees vary according to degree level and program. *Faculty research:* Biomechanics, exercise physiology, motor skill learning, school health, curriculum development.

Auburn University at Montgomery, College of Education, Department of Kinesiology, Montgomery, AL 36124-4023. Offers exercise science (M Ed); physical education (Ed S); sport management (M Ed). *Program availability:* Online learning. *Students:* Average age 29. 23 applicants, 74% accepted, 10 enrolled. In 2018, 18 master's awarded. *Entrance requirements:* For master's, GRE or MAT. Additional exam requirements/recommendations for international students: Recommended—TOEFL (minimum score 500 paper-based; 61 iBT), IELTS (minimum score 5.5), TSE (minimum score 44). *Application deadline:* For fall admission, 7/15 for international students; for spring admission, 11/15 for international students; for summer admission, 4/15 for international students. Applications are processed on a rolling basis. Application fee: $25. Electronic applications accepted. *Expenses: Tuition, area resident:* Full-time $7146; part-time $4764 per credit hour. Tuition, state resident: full-time $7146; part-time $4764 per credit hour. Tuition, nonresident: full-time $16,056; part-time $10,704 per credit hour. *International tuition:* $16,056 full-time. *Required fees:* $766. One-time fee: $25 full-time. *Financial support:* Teaching assistantships available. Financial award application deadline: 3/1; financial award applicants required to submit FAFSA. *Unit head:* Dr. George Schaefer, Head, 334-244-3887, Fax: 334-244-3835, E-mail: gschaefe@aum.edu. *Application contact:* Janis Bigelow, Graduate Advisor, 334-244-3135, E-mail: jbigelo1@aum.edu. Website: http://www.education.aum.edu/academic-programs/academic-programs/kinesiology

Avila University, School of Education, Kansas City, MO 64145-1698. Offers advanced classroom management (MA); elementary education (Teaching Certificate); English language learners (Advanced Certificate); middle school (Teaching Certificate); physical education K-12 (Teaching Certificate); secondary education (Teaching Certificate). *Program availability:* Part-time, evening/weekend, online learning. *Faculty:* 6 full-time (5 women), 9 part-time/adjunct (8 women). *Students:* 83 full-time (71 women), 84 part-time (69 women); includes 13 minority (6 Black or African American, non-Hispanic/Latino; 2 Asian, non-Hispanic/Latino; 4 Hispanic/Latino; 1 Two or more races, non-Hispanic/Latino), 2 international. Average age 40. 92 applicants, 62% accepted, 40 enrolled. In 2018, 21 master's awarded. *Entrance requirements:* For master's, minimum GPA of 3.0, writing sample, recommendation, interview; for other advanced degree, foreign language. Additional exam requirements/recommendations for international students: Required—TOEFL (minimum score 580 paper-based; 92 iBT). *Application deadline:* Applications are processed on a rolling basis. Electronic applications accepted. *Expenses:* Contact institution. *Financial support:* In 2018–19, 12 students received support. Unspecified assistantships available. Financial award applicants required to submit FAFSA. *Unit head:* Dr. Stacy Keith, Director of Graduate Education, 816-501-2446, Fax: 816-501-2915, E-mail: stacy.keith@avila.edu. *Application contact:* Cory Roup, Graduate Education Enrollment and Academic Advisor, 816-501-2464, E-mail: cory.roup@avila.edu. Website: https://www.avila.edu/academics/graduate-studies/grad-education

Ball State University, Graduate School, College of Health, School of Kinesiology, Program in Physical Education and Sport, Muncie, IN 47306. Offers physical education and sport (MA, MS), including athletic coaching education, sport administration, sport and exercise psychology. *Program availability:* Part-time, 100% online. *Entrance requirements:* For master's, GRE General Test, minimum baccalaureate GPA of 2.75 or 3.0 in latter half of baccalaureate, curriculum vitae, three letters of recommendation; campus visit to meet faculty and see facilities (strongly encouraged). Additional exam requirements/recommendations for international students: Required—TOEFL (minimum score 550 paper-based; 79 iBT), IELTS (minimum score 6.5). Electronic applications accepted.

Baylor University, Graduate School, Robbins College of Health and Human Sciences, Department of Health, Human Performance and Recreation, Waco, TX 76798. Offers athletic training (MS); exercise physiology (MS); kinesiology, exercise nutrition, and health promotion (PhD); sport pedagogy (MS). *Accreditation:* NCATE. *Program availability:* Part-time. *Students:* 72 full-time (40 women), 13 part-time (8 women); includes 20 minority (5 Black or African American, non-Hispanic/Latino; 1 American Indian or Alaska Native, non-Hispanic/Latino; 1 Asian, non-Hispanic/Latino; 7 Hispanic/Latino; 6 Two or more races, non-Hispanic/Latino), 5 international. 109 applicants, 59% accepted, 44 enrolled. In 2018, 35 master's, 2 doctorates awarded. *Degree requirements:* For master's, comprehensive exam, thesis optional; for doctorate, comprehensive exam, thesis/dissertation. *Entrance requirements:* For master's and doctorate, GRE General Test. Additional exam requirements/recommendations for international students: Required—TOEFL (minimum score 550 paper-based; 80 iBT). *Application deadline:* For fall admission, 2/1 priority date for domestic students, 2/1 for international students; for spring admission, 10/1 for domestic and international students. Applications are processed on a rolling basis. Application fee: $25. Electronic applications accepted. *Financial support:* In 2018–19, 60 students received support, including 1 research assistantship with full tuition reimbursement available (averaging $12,700 per year), 33 teaching assistantships with full tuition reimbursements available (averaging $7,650 per year); career-related internships or fieldwork, Federal Work-Study, institutionally sponsored loans, scholarships/grants, tuition waivers (full), and unspecified assistantships also available. Financial award application deadline: 2/1. *Faculty research:* Exercise testing, cardio-metabolic health, resistance exercise and training, nutritional intervention, population health, health promotion, global health epidemiology, coaching, natural resource management, stimulant misuse, diet, microbiome and colon cancer etiology. *Total annual research expenditures:* $250,118. *Unit head:* Dr. Jaeho Shim, Graduate Program Director, 254-710-4009, Fax: 254-710-3527, E-mail: joe_shim@baylor.edu. *Application contact:* Deepa Morris, Graduate Program Coordinator, 254-710-3526, Fax: 254-710-3527, E-mail: deepa_morris@baylor.edu.
Website: http://www.baylor.edu/HHPR/

Bridgewater State University, College of Graduate Studies, College of Education and Allied Studies, Department of Movement Arts, Health Promotion, and Leisure Studies, Program in Physical Education, Bridgewater, MA 02325. Offers MS. *Program availability:* Part-time, evening/weekend. *Degree requirements:* For master's, thesis or alternative. *Entrance requirements:* For master's, GRE General Test.

Brooklyn College of the City University of New York, School of Natural and Behavioral Sciences, Department of Kinesiology, Brooklyn, NY 11210-2889. Offers exercise and sports science (MS); physical education teacher (MS); sport management (MS). *Program availability:* Part-time. *Degree requirements:* For master's, comprehensive exam or thesis. *Entrance requirements:* For master's, previous course work in physical education and education, minimum GPA of 3.0, 2 letters of recommendation, essay. Additional exam requirements/recommendations for international students: Required—TOEFL (minimum score 500 paper-based; 61 iBT). Electronic applications accepted. *Faculty research:* Exercise physiology, motor learning, sports psychology, women in athletics.

California Baptist University, Program in Kinesiology, Riverside, CA 92504-3206. Offers exercise science (MS); physical education (MS); sport management (MS). *Program availability:* Part-time, evening/weekend, 100% online, blended/hybrid learning. *Faculty:* 13 full-time (3 women), 5 part-time/adjunct (1 woman). *Students:* 75 full-time (40 women), 77 part-time (37 women); includes 79 minority (10 Black or African American, non-Hispanic/Latino; 1 American Indian or Alaska Native, non-Hispanic/Latino; 6 Asian, non-Hispanic/Latino; 50 Hispanic/Latino; 2 Native Hawaiian or other Pacific Islander, non-Hispanic/Latino; 10 Two or more races, non-Hispanic/Latino), 13 international. Average age 35. 71 applicants, 79% accepted, 56 enrolled. In 2018, 77 master's awarded. *Degree requirements:* For master's, comprehensive exam or research thesis. *Entrance requirements:* For master's, minimum undergraduate GPA of 2.75; completion of course prerequisites with minimum C grade; three recommendations; 500-word essay; resume; interview. Additional exam requirements/recommendations for international students: Required—TOEFL (minimum score 80 iBT). *Application deadline:* For fall admission, 8/1 priority date for domestic students, 7/1 for international students; for spring admission, 12/1 priority date for domestic students, 11/1 for international students. Applications are processed on a rolling basis. Application fee: $45. Electronic applications accepted. *Expenses:* $580 per unit. *Financial support:* In 2018–19, 21 students received support. Federal Work-Study, scholarships/grants, and unspecified assistantships available. Financial award applicants required to submit CSS PROFILE or FAFSA. *Faculty research:* Physical education pedagogy, exercise management and prevention of cardiovascular and metabolic diseases, sport management, immune function, carbohydrate oxidation. *Unit head:* Dr. David Pearson, Dean, College of Health Science, 951-343-4298, E-mail: dpearson@calbaptist.edu. *Application contact:* Dr. Dominick Sturz, Assistant, Health and Human Services, 951-343-2192, E-mail: dsturz@calbaptist.edu.
Website: http://www.calbaptist.edu/mskin/

California State University, East Bay, Office of Graduate Studies, College of Education and Allied Studies, Department of Kinesiology, Hayward, CA 94542-3000. Offers MS. *Degree requirements:* For master's, exam or thesis. *Entrance requirements:* For master's, BA in kinesiology or related discipline, minimum major course work GPA of 3.0. Additional exam requirements/recommendations for international students: Required—TOEFL (minimum score 550 paper-based). Electronic applications accepted. *Faculty research:* Physiology, psychology of sport/movement, skill acquisition, cultural influence on physical activity.

California State University, Fullerton, Graduate Studies, College of Health and Human Development, Department of Kinesiology, Fullerton, CA 92831-3599. Offers MS. *Program availability:* Part-time. *Entrance requirements:* For master's, minimum GPA of 3.0 in field, 2.5 overall.

California State University, Long Beach, Graduate Studies, College of Health and Human Services, Department of Kinesiology, Long Beach, CA 90840. Offers adapted physical education (MA); coaching and student athlete development (MA); exercise physiology and nutrition (MS); exercise science (MS); individualized studies (MA); kinesiology (MA); pedagogical studies (MA); sport and exercise psychology (MS); sport management (MA); sports medicine and injury studies (MS). *Program availability:* Part-time. *Degree requirements:* For master's, oral and written comprehensive exams or thesis. *Entrance requirements:* For master's, GRE General Test, minimum GPA of 2.75 during previous 2 years of course work. *Application deadline:* Applications are processed on a rolling basis. Application fee: $55. Electronic applications accepted. *Expenses: Required fees:* $2628 per term. Tuition and fees vary according to class time, course level, course load, degree level, campus/location and program. *Financial support:* Federal Work-Study, institutionally sponsored loans, and scholarships/grants available. Financial award application deadline: 3/2; financial award applicants required to submit FAFSA. *Faculty research:* Pulmonary functioning, feedback and practice structure, strength training, history and politics of sports, special population research issues. *Unit head:* Tiffanye Vargas, Chair, 562-985-4051, E-mail: tiffanye.vargas@csulb.edu. *Application contact:* Tiffanye Vargas, Chair, 562-985-4051, E-mail: tiffanye.vargas@csulb.edu.
Website: https://fullerton-csm.symplicity.com/

California State University, Los Angeles, Graduate Studies, College of Health and Human Services, Department of Kinesiology and Nutritional Sciences, Los Angeles, CA 90032-8530. Offers nutritional science (MS); physical education and kinesiology (MA). *Accreditation:* AND. *Program availability:* Part-time, evening/weekend. *Degree requirements:* For master's, comprehensive exam, project or thesis. *Entrance requirements:* For master's, minimum GPA of 2.75. Additional exam requirements/recommendations for international students: Required—TOEFL (minimum score 500 paper-based).

California State University, Sacramento, College of Health and Human Services, Department of Kinesiology and Health Science, Sacramento, CA 95819. Offers exercise science (MS); movement studies (MS). *Accreditation:* APTA. *Program availability:* Part-time, evening/weekend. *Degree requirements:* For master's, thesis or project; writing proficiency exam. *Entrance requirements:* For master's, minimum overall GPA of 2.8, 3.0 in last 60 semester units; upper-division statistics course. Additional exam requirements/recommendations for international students: Required—TOEFL (minimum score 550 paper-based; 80 iBT); Recommended—IELTS, TSE. Electronic applications accepted. *Expenses:* Contact institution.

California State University, Stanislaus, College of Education, Kinesiology and Social Work, MA Program in Education, Turlock, CA 95382. Offers curriculum and instruction (MA), including education technology, elementary education, multilingual education, physical education, reading, secondary education, special education; school administration (MA); school counseling (MA). *Program availability:* Part-time, evening/weekend. *Degree requirements:* For master's, comprehensive exam (for some programs), thesis (for some programs). *Entrance requirements:* For master's, MAT, GRE, or CBEST (varies by concentration), 3 letters of recommendation, personal statement. Additional exam requirements/recommendations for international students: Required—TOEFL (minimum score 550 paper-based). Electronic applications accepted. *Faculty research:* Children's perspectives on historical events, method elementary schools dual language education, K-12 reading programs.

Campbell University, Graduate and Professional Programs, School of Education, Buies Creek, NC 27506. Offers elementary education (M Ed); interdisciplinary studies (M Ed); middle grades education (M Ed); physical education (M Ed); school administration (MSA); school counseling (M Ed); secondary education (M Ed). *Accreditation:* NCATE. *Program availability:* Part-time, evening/weekend. *Degree requirements:* For master's, comprehensive exam. *Entrance requirements:* For master's, GRE General Test, minimum GPA of 2.7. *Faculty research:* Spiritual values and wellness issues in counseling, stress and professional burnout among counselors, thinking strategies, leadership, adaptive technology.

Canisius College, Graduate Division, School of Education and Human Services, Department of Kinesiology, Buffalo, NY 14208-1098. Offers physical education (MS Ed); physical education birth - 12 (MS Ed). *Program availability:* Part-time, evening/weekend, 100% online, blended/hybrid learning. *Faculty:* 14 full-time (0 women), 17 part-time/adjunct (3 women). *Students:* 40 full-time (14 women), 37 part-time (10 women); includes 13 minority (8 Black or African American, non-Hispanic/Latino; 4 Hispanic/Latino; 1 Two or more races, non-Hispanic/Latino), 1 international. Average age 29. 79 applicants, 96% accepted, 46 enrolled. In 2018, 91 master's awarded. *Degree requirements:* For master's, research project or internship. *Entrance requirements:* For master's, official college and/or university transcript(s) showing completion of bachelor's degree from accredited institution; two letters of recommendation; minimum cumulative undergraduate GPA of 2.7. Additional exam requirements/recommendations for international students: Required—TOEFL (minimum score 550 paper-based, 79 iBT), IELTS (minimum score 6.5), or CAEL (minimum score 70). *Application deadline:* Applications are processed on a rolling basis. Application fee: $0. Electronic applications accepted. *Expenses:* Contact institution. *Financial support:* In 2018–19, 154 students received support. Career-related internships or fieldwork, Federal Work-Study, scholarships/grants, tuition waivers (partial), and unspecified assistantships available. Support available to part-time students. Financial award application deadline: 4/30; financial award applicants required to submit FAFSA. *Faculty research:* Culturally congruent pedagogy in physical education, information processing and perceptual styles of athletes, qualities of effective coaches. *Unit head:* Dr. Nicolas Lorgnier, Chair/Professor of Kinesiology, 716-888-3733, Fax: 716-888-8445, E-mail: lorgnien@canisius.edu. *Application contact:* Dr. Nicolas Lorgnier, Chair/Professor of Kinesiology, 716-888-3733, Fax: 716-888-8445, E-mail: lorgnien@canisius.edu.
Website: http://www.canisius.edu/graduate/

Caribbean University, Graduate School, Bayamón, PR 00960-0493. Offers administration and supervision (MA Ed); criminal justice (MA); curriculum and instruction (MA Ed, PhD), including elementary education (MA Ed), English education (MA Ed), history education (MA Ed), mathematics education (MA Ed), primary education (MA Ed), science education (MA Ed), Spanish education (MA Ed); educational technology in instructional systems (MA Ed); gerontology (MSN); human resources (MBA); museology, archiving and art history (MA Ed); neonatal pediatrics (MSN); physical education (MA Ed); special education (MA Ed). *Entrance requirements:* For master's, interview, minimum GPA of 2.5.

Central Connecticut State University, School of Graduate Studies, School of Education and Professional Studies, Department of Physical Education and Human Performance, New Britain, CT 06050-4010. Offers physical education (MS). *Program availability:* Part-time, evening/weekend. *Faculty:* 8 full-time (3 women). *Students:* 14 full-time (7 women), 23 part-time (10 women); includes 6 minority (1 Black or African American, non-Hispanic/Latino; 1 Asian, non-Hispanic/Latino; 3 Hispanic/Latino; 1 Two or more races, non-Hispanic/Latino). Average age 28. 21 applicants, 62% accepted, 4 enrolled. In 2018, 20 master's, 3 other advanced degrees awarded. *Degree requirements:* For master's, comprehensive exam, thesis or alternative; for Certificate, qualifying exam. *Entrance requirements:* For master's, minimum GPA of 2.7, bachelor's degree in physical education (preferred), essay, interview, letters of recommendation. Additional exam requirements/recommendations for international students: Required—TOEFL (minimum score 550 paper-based; 79 iBT); Recommended—IELTS (minimum score 6.5). *Application deadline:* For fall admission, 6/1 for domestic students, 5/1 for international students; for spring admission, 11/1 for domestic and international students; for summer admission, 5/1 for domestic and international students. Applications are processed on a rolling basis. Application fee: $50. Electronic applications accepted. *Expenses: Tuition, area resident:* Full-time $7027; part-time $388 per credit. Tuition, state resident: full-time $9750; part-time $388 per credit. Tuition, nonresident: full-time $18,102; part-time $388 per credit. *International tuition:* $18,102 full-time. *Required fees:* $266 per semester. *Financial support:* In 2018–19, 10 students received support. Career-related internships or fieldwork, Federal Work-Study, scholarships/grants, and unspecified assistantships available. Support available to part-time students. Financial award application deadline: 3/1; financial award applicants required to submit FAFSA. *Faculty research:* Exercise science, athletic training, preparation of physical education for schools. *Unit head:* Dr. Jason Melnyk, Acting Chair, 860-832-2177, E-mail: melnykjaa@ccsu.edu. *Application contact:* Patricia Gardner, Associate Director of Graduate Studies, 860-832-2350, Fax: 860-832-2362.
Website: http://www.ccsu.edu/pehp/

Physical Education

Central Washington University, School of Graduate Studies and Research, College of Education and Professional Studies, Department of Physical Education, School Health and Movement Studies, Ellensburg, WA 98926. Offers athletic administration (MS); health and physical education (MS). *Program availability:* Part-time. *Degree requirements:* For master's, comprehensive exam, thesis or alternative. *Entrance requirements:* For master's, minimum GPA of 3.0. Additional exam requirements/recommendations for international students: Required—TOEFL (minimum score 550 paper-based; 79 iBT), IELTS. Electronic applications accepted.

Chicago State University, School of Graduate and Professional Studies, College of Education, Department of Health, Physical Education and Recreation, Chicago, IL 60628. Offers physical education (MS Ed). *Program availability:* Part-time, evening/weekend, online learning. *Entrance requirements:* For master's, minimum GPA of 2.75. *Faculty research:* Sports psychology, recreation and leisure studies administration.

The Citadel, The Military College of South Carolina, Citadel Graduate College, School of Science and Mathematics, Department of Health, Exercise, and Sport Science, Charleston, SC 29409. Offers health, exercise, and sport science (MS); sport management (MA, Graduate Certificate). *Accreditation:* NCATE. *Program availability:* Part-time, evening/weekend. *Degree requirements:* For master's, comprehensive exam (for some programs), internship and professional portfolio (for some programs). *Entrance requirements:* For master's, GRE (minimum combined verbal and quantitative score 290) or MAT (minimum score 396), official transcript reflecting highest degree earned from regionally-accredited college or university, minimum undergraduate GPA of 2.5, 3 letters of recommendation, resume detailing previous work experience. Additional exam requirements/recommendations for international students: Required—TOEFL (minimum score 550 paper-based; 79 iBT). Electronic applications accepted. *Expenses:* Tuition, state resident: part-time $595 per credit hour. Tuition, nonresident: part-time $1020 per credit hour. *Required fees:* $90 per term.

The Citadel, The Military College of South Carolina, Citadel Graduate College, Zucker Family School of Education, Charleston, SC 29409. Offers elementary/secondary school administration and supervision (M Ed); elementary/secondary school counseling (M Ed); interdisciplinary STEM education (M Ed); literacy education (M Ed, Graduate Certificate); middle grades (MAT), including English, mathematics, science, social studies; physical education (grades K-12) (MAT); school superintendency (Ed S); secondary education (MAT), including biology, English, mathematics, social studies; student affairs (Graduate Certificate); student affairs and college counseling (M Ed). *Accreditation:* NCATE. *Program availability:* Part-time, evening/weekend, 100% online, blended/hybrid learning. *Degree requirements:* For master's, comprehensive exam (for some programs). *Entrance requirements:* For master's, GRE (minimum combined verbal and quantitative score of 290) or MAT (minimum score 396). Additional exam requirements/recommendations for international students: Required—TOEFL (minimum score 550 paper-based; 79 iBT). Electronic applications accepted. *Expenses:* Tuition, state resident: part-time $595 per credit hour. Tuition, nonresident: part-time $1020 per credit hour. *Required fees:* $90 per term.

Cleveland State University, College of Graduate Studies, College of Education and Human Services, Department of Health and Human Performance, Cleveland, OH 44115. Offers physical education pedagogy (M Ed); public health (MPH). *Program availability:* Part-time. *Faculty:* 7 full-time (4 women), 3 part-time/adjunct (2 women). *Students:* 29 full-time (17 women), 50 part-time (28 women); includes 31 minority (23 Black or African American, non-Hispanic/Latino; 1 Asian, non-Hispanic/Latino; 1 Hispanic/Latino; 6 Two or more races, non-Hispanic/Latino), 2 international. Average age 29. 103 applicants, 72% accepted, 43 enrolled. In 2018, 30 master's awarded. *Degree requirements:* For master's, comprehensive exam, thesis optional. *Entrance requirements:* For master's, GRE General Test or MAT (if undergraduate GPA less than 2.75), minimum undergraduate GPA of 2.75. Additional exam requirements/recommendations for international students: Required—TOEFL (minimum score 550 paper-based; 78 iBT), IELTS (minimum score 6). *Application deadline:* For fall admission, 7/15 priority date for domestic students; for spring admission, 12/15 priority date for domestic students. Applications are processed on a rolling basis. Application fee: $30. Electronic applications accepted. *Expenses:* Tuition, state resident: full-time $7232.55; part-time $6676 per credit hour. Tuition, nonresident: full-time $12,375. *International tuition:* $18,914 full-time. *Required fees:* $80; $80 $40. Tuition and fees vary according to program. *Financial support:* In 2018–19, 6 research assistantships with tuition reimbursements (averaging $3,480 per year), 1 teaching assistantship with tuition reimbursement (averaging $3,480 per year) were awarded; career-related internships or fieldwork, tuition waivers (full), and unspecified assistantships also available. Financial award application deadline: 3/15; financial award applicants required to submit FAFSA. *Faculty research:* Bone density, marketing fitness centers, motor development of disabled, online learning and survey research. *Unit head:* Dr. Mike Loovis, Associate Professor/Department Chairperson, 216-687-3665, Fax: 216-687-5410, E-mail: e.loovis@csuohio.edu. *Application contact:* David Easler, Director, Graduate Recruitment, 216-687-5047, Fax: 216-687-5400, E-mail: d.easler@csuohio.edu.
Website: http://www.csuohio.edu/cehs/departments/HPERD/hperd_dept.html

The College at Brockport, State University of New York, School of Education, Health, and Human Services, Department of Kinesiology, Sports Studies and Physical Education, Brockport, NY 14420-2997. Offers adapted physical education (AGC); physical education (MS Ed), including adapted physical education, athletic administration, physical education/pedagogy. *Program availability:* Part-time. *Faculty:* 9 full-time (5 women), 1 part-time/adjunct (0 women). *Students:* 28 full-time (9 women), 62 part-time (23 women); includes 7 minority (3 Black or African American, non-Hispanic/Latino; 2 Asian, non-Hispanic/Latino; 2 Hispanic/Latino). 49 applicants, 84% accepted, 32 enrolled. In 2018, 50 master's awarded. *Degree requirements:* For master's, thesis or alternative. *Entrance requirements:* For master's, minimum GPA of 3.0; statement of objectives. Additional exam requirements/recommendations for international students: Required—TOEFL (minimum score 550 paper-based; 79 iBT), IELTS (minimum score 6.5). *Application deadline:* For fall admission, 4/15 priority date for domestic and international students; for spring admission, 11/15 priority date for domestic and international students; for summer admission, 4/15 priority date for domestic students, 4/15 for international students. Application fee: $80. Electronic applications accepted. *Expenses:* Tuition, state resident: part-time $471 per credit. Tuition, nonresident: part-time $963 per credit. *Financial support:* In 2018–19, 11 teaching assistantships with full tuition reimbursements (averaging $7,000 per year) were awarded; Federal Work-Study, scholarships/grants, and unspecified assistantships also available. Support available to part-time students. Financial award application deadline: 3/15; financial award applicants required to submit FAFSA. *Faculty research:* Athletic administration, adapted physical education, physical education curriculum, physical education teaching/coaching, children's physical activity. *Unit head:* Dr. Cathy Houston-Wilson, Chairperson, 585-395-5352, Fax: 585-395-2771, E-mail: chouston@brockport.edu. *Application contact:* Dr. Melanie Perreault, Graduate Program Director, 585-395-5299, Fax: 585-395-2771, E-mail: mperreault@brockport.edu.
Website: https://www.brockport.edu/academics/kinesiology/

Colorado State University–Pueblo, College of Education, Engineering and Professional Studies, Education Program, Pueblo, CO 81001-4901. Offers art education (M Ed); foreign language education (M Ed); health and physical education (M Ed); instructional technology (M Ed); linguistically diverse education (M Ed); music education

(M Ed); special education (M Ed). *Accreditation:* TEAC. *Program availability:* Part-time. *Degree requirements:* For master's, portfolio. *Entrance requirements:* For master's, 3 recommendations, teaching license. Additional exam requirements/recommendations for international students: Required—TOEFL (minimum score 500 paper-based). Electronic applications accepted. *Faculty research:* Portfolio assessment, math education, science education.

Columbus State University, Graduate Studies, College of Education and Health Professions, Kinesiology & Health Sciences, Columbus, GA 31907-5645. Offers exercise science (MS); health and physical education (M Ed, MAT). *Program availability:* Part-time, evening/weekend. *Faculty:* 5 full-time (3 women). *Students:* 17 full-time (7 women), 14 part-time (8 women); includes 13 minority (8 Black or African American, non-Hispanic/Latino; 1 Asian, non-Hispanic/Latino; 3 Hispanic/Latino; 1 Two or more races, non-Hispanic/Latino). Average age 28. 23 applicants, 65% accepted, 12 enrolled. In 2018, 12 master's awarded. *Degree requirements:* For master's, thesis optional. *Entrance requirements:* For master's, GRE, minimum undergraduate GPA of 2.75. Additional exam requirements/recommendations for international students: Required—TOEFL (minimum score 550 paper-based; 79 iBT). *Application deadline:* For fall admission, 5/1 for domestic students, 4/1 for international students; for spring admission, 11/1 for domestic and international students; for summer admission, 2/1 for domestic students, 3/1 for international students. Applications are processed on a rolling basis. Application fee: $50. Electronic applications accepted. *Expenses:* Tuition, area resident: Full-time $4924; part-time $618 per credit hour. Tuition, state resident: full-time $4924; part-time $618 per credit hour. Tuition, nonresident: full-time $19,218; part-time $2403 per credit hour. *International tuition:* $19,218 full-time. *Required fees:* $1870; $802. Tuition and fees vary according to course load, degree level and program. *Financial support:* In 2018–19, 4 students received support, including 7 research assistantships (averaging $3,000 per year). Financial award application deadline: 5/15; financial award applicants required to submit FAFSA. *Unit head:* Dr. Clay Nicks, Chair, 706-507-8293, E-mail: nicks_clayton@columbusstate.edu. *Application contact:* Catrina Smith-Edmond, Assistant Director for Graduate and Global Admission, 706-507-8824, Fax: 706-568-5091, E-mail: smithedmond_catrina@columbusstate.edu. Website: http://hpex.columbusstate.edu/

Concordia University, College of Education, Portland, OR 97211-6099. Offers administrative leadership (Ed D); career and technical education (M Ed); curriculum and instruction (M Ed), including adolescent literacy, early childhood education, educational technology leadership, English for speakers of other languages, environmental education, health and physical education, mathematics, methods and curriculum, reading interventionist, science, social studies, STEAM education, teacher leadership, the inclusive classroom, trauma and resilience in educational settings; educational administration (M Ed); educational leadership (M Ed); elementary education (MAT); higher education (Ed D); instructional leadership (Ed D); professional leadership, inquiry, and transformation (Ed D); secondary education (MAT); transformational leadership (Ed D). *Program availability:* Part-time, online learning. *Degree requirements:* For master's, comprehensive exam, work samples/portfolio. *Entrance requirements:* For master's, California Basic Educational Skills Test or PRAXIS I, minimum undergraduate GPA of 2.8, graduate 3.0; 2 letters of recommendation. Additional exam requirements/recommendations for international students: Required—TOEFL (minimum score 525 paper-based). Electronic applications accepted. *Faculty research:* Learner-centered classroom, brain-based learning, future of online learning.

Concordia University Irvine, School of Arts and Sciences, Irvine, CA 92612-3299. Offers coaching and athletic administration (MA). *Program availability:* Part-time, evening/weekend, online learning. *Degree requirements:* For master's, culminating project. *Entrance requirements:* For master's, official college/university transcript(s); signed statement of intent. Additional exam requirements/recommendations for international students: Required—TOEFL (minimum score 550 paper-based; 79 iBT). Electronic applications accepted. *Expenses:* Contact institution.

Delta State University, Graduate Programs, College of Education, Division of Health, Physical Education, and Recreation, Cleveland, MS 38733-0001. Offers health, physical education, and recreation (M Ed); sport and human performance (MS). *Program availability:* Part-time, evening/weekend. *Degree requirements:* For master's, thesis optional. *Entrance requirements:* For master's, GRE General Test or MAT, Class A teaching certificate. *Expenses:* Tuition, area resident: Full-time $7076; part-time $393 per credit hour. Tuition, state resident: full-time $7076; part-time $393 per credit hour. Tuition, nonresident: full-time $7076; part-time $393 per credit hour. *International tuition:* $7076 full-time. *Required fees:* $170; $18.90 per credit hour. $9.45 per semester. Part-time tuition and fees vary according to program. *Faculty research:* Blood pressure, body fat, power and reaction time, learning disorders of athletes, effects of walking.

DePaul University, College of Education, Chicago, IL 60614. Offers bilingual-bicultural education (M Ed, MA); counseling (M Ed, MA), including clinical mental health counseling, college student development, school counseling; curriculum studies (M Ed, MA, Ed D); early childhood education (M Ed, MA, Ed D); educational leadership (M Ed, MA, Ed D), including Catholic leadership (M Ed, MA), general (M Ed, MA), higher education (M Ed, MA), physical education (M Ed, MA), principal preparation (M Ed); teacher preparation (M Ed); elementary education (M Ed, MA); middle grades education (M Ed); middle school mathematics education (MS); reading specialist (M Ed, MA); secondary education (M Ed, MA); social and cultural foundations in education (M Ed, MA); special education (M Ed); sport, fitness and recreation leadership (MS); value-creating education for global citizenship (M Ed); world languages education (M Ed, MA). *Program availability:* Part-time, evening/weekend, online learning. *Degree requirements:* For doctorate, thesis/dissertation. Electronic applications accepted.

East Carolina University, Graduate School, College of Health and Human Performance, Department of Kinesiology, Greenville, NC 27858-4353. Offers adapted physical education (MS); bioenergetics and exercise science (PhD); biomechanics and motor control (MS); exercise physiology (MS); physical activity promotion (MS); physical education (MA Ed, MAT); physical education clinical supervision (Certificate); physical education pedagogy (MS); sport and exercise psychology (MS); sport management (MS, Certificate). *Application deadline:* For fall admission, 2/1 priority date for domestic students, 2/1 for international students. *Expenses:* Tuition, area resident: Full-time $4749. Tuition, state resident: full-time $4749. Tuition, nonresident: full-time $17,898. *International tuition:* $17,898 full-time. *Required fees:* $2787. Part-time tuition and fees vary according to course load and program. *Financial support:* Application deadline: 2/1. *Unit head:* Dr. Stacey Altman, Chair, 252-328-4632, E-mail: altmans@ecu.edu. *Application contact:* Graduate School Admissions, 252-328-6012, Fax: 252-328-6071, E-mail: gradschool@ecu.edu.
Website: https://hhp.ecu.edu/kine/

Eastern Kentucky University, The Graduate School, College of Education, Department of Curriculum and Instruction, Program in Secondary and Higher Education, Richmond, KY 40475-3102. Offers secondary education (MA Ed), including agricultural education, art education, biological sciences education, business education, English education, geography education, history education, home economics education, industrial education, mathematical sciences education, physical education, school health education. *Accreditation:* NCATE. *Program availability:* Part-time. *Entrance requirements:* For master's, GRE General Test, minimum GPA of 2.5.

Eastern Michigan University, Graduate School, College of Health and Human Services, School of Health Promotion and Human Performance, Programs in Physical Education Pedagogy, Ypsilanti, MI 48197. Offers adapted physical education (MS); physical education pedagogy (MS). *Program availability:* Part-time, evening/weekend, online learning. *Students:* 1 applicant. In 2018, 1 master's awarded. *Entrance requirements:* Additional exam requirements/recommendations for international students: Required—TOEFL. *Application deadline:* For fall admission, 8/1 for domestic students, 5/1 for international students; for winter admission, 12/1 for domestic students, 10/1 for international students; for spring admission, 4/15 for domestic students, 3/1 for international students. Applications are processed on a rolling basis. Application fee: $45. *Financial support:* Fellowships, research assistantships with full tuition reimbursements, teaching assistantships with full tuition reimbursements, career-related internships or fieldwork, Federal Work-Study, institutionally sponsored loans, scholarships/grants, tuition waivers (partial), and unspecified assistantships available. Support available to part-time students. Financial award applicants required to submit FAFSA. *Application contact:* Dr. Roberta Faust, Program Coordinator, 734-487-7120 Ext. 2745, Fax: 734-487-2024, E-mail: rfaust@emich.edu.

Eastern New Mexico University, Graduate School, College of Education and Technology, Department of Health and Physical Education, Portales, NM 88130. Offers sport administration (MS), including coaching, sport science. *Program availability:* Part-time. *Degree requirements:* For master's, comprehensive exam, thesis optional. *Entrance requirements:* For master's, minimum GPA of 3.0, 15 hours of leveling courses without bachelor's degree in physical education, two references. Additional exam requirements/recommendations for international students: Required—TOEFL (minimum score 550 paper-based; 79 iBT), IELTS (minimum score 6). Electronic applications accepted. *Expenses: Tuition, area resident:* Full-time $6776. Tuition, state resident: full-time $6776; part-time $282 per credit hour. Tuition, nonresident: full-time $8986; part-time $374 per credit hour. *Required fees:* $60 per semester. One-time fee: $25.

Eastern University, Graduate Education Programs, St. Davids, PA 19087-3696. Offers ESL program specialist (K-12) (Certificate); general supervisor (PreK-12) (Certificate); health and physical education (K-12) (Certificate); middle level (4-8) (Certificate); multicultural education (M Ed); music (K-12) (Certificate); Pre K-4 (Certificate); Pre K-4 with special education (Certificate); reading (M Ed); reading specialist (K-12) (Certificate); reading supervisor (K-12) (Certificate); school counseling (MA, CAGS); school principalship (preK-12) (Certificate); school psychology (MS, CAGS); secondary biology education (7-12) (Certificate); secondary chemistry education (7-12) (Certificate); secondary communication education (7-12) (Certificate); secondary English education (7-12) (Certificate); secondary math education (7-12) (Certificate); secondary social studies education (7-12) (Certificate); special education (M Ed); special education (7-12) (Certificate); special education (Pre K-8) (Certificate); special education supervisor (K-12) (Certificate); TESOL (M Ed); world language (Certificate), including Spanish. *Program availability:* Part-time, evening/weekend, online learning. *Entrance requirements:* Additional exam requirements/recommendations for international students: Required—TOEFL. Electronic applications accepted. Application fee is waived when completed online. *Expenses:* Contact institution.

Eastern Washington University, Graduate Studies, College of Arts, Letters and Education, Department of Physical Education, Health and Recreation, Cheney, WA 99004-2431. Offers exercise science (MS); sports and recreation administration (MS). *Degree requirements:* For master's, comprehensive exam, thesis or alternative. *Entrance requirements:* For master's, minimum GPA of 3.0. Additional exam requirements/recommendations for international students: Required—TOEFL (minimum score 580 paper-based; 92 iBT), IELTS (minimum score 7), PTE (minimum score 63). Electronic applications accepted.

East Stroudsburg University of Pennsylvania, Graduate and Extended Studies, College of Health Sciences, Department of Exercise Science, East Stroudsburg, PA 18301-2999. Offers MS. *Program availability:* Part-time, evening/weekend, online learning. *Faculty:* 9 full-time (2 women). *Students:* 53 full-time (20 women), 1 part-time (0 women); includes 3 minority (1 Black or African American, non-Hispanic/Latino; 1 Asian, non-Hispanic/Latino; 1 Native Hawaiian or other Pacific Islander, non-Hispanic/Latino). Average age 23. 21 applicants, 52% accepted. In 2018, 51 master's awarded. *Degree requirements:* For master's, comprehensive exam, thesis or alternative, computer literacy. *Entrance requirements:* For master's, letters of recommendation, resume, professional goals statement. Additional exam requirements/recommendations for international students: Recommended—TOEFL (minimum score 560 paper-based; 83 iBT), IELTS. *Application deadline:* For fall admission, 3/1 priority date for domestic and international students; for spring admission, 11/30 for domestic students, 10/31 for international students. Applications are processed on a rolling basis. Application fee: $50. Electronic applications accepted. *Expenses: Tuition, area resident:* Full-time $9288; part-time $516 per credit. Tuition, state resident: full-time $9288. Tuition, nonresident: full-time $13,932; part-time $774 per credit. *International tuition:* $13,932 full-time. *Required fees:* $2059; $114 per credit. Tuition and fees vary according to course load and degree level. *Financial support:* Research assistantships with tuition reimbursements, Federal Work-Study, and unspecified assistantships available. Support available to part-time students. Financial award application deadline: 3/1; financial award applicants required to submit FAFSA. *Unit head:* Dr. Chad Witmer, Graduate Coordinator, 570-422-3362, E-mail: cwitmer@esu.edu. *Application contact:* Kevin Quintero, Associate Director, Graduate and Extended Studies, 570-422-3890, Fax: 570-422-2711, E-mail: kquintero@esu.edu.
Website: https://www.esu.edu/exercise_science/graduate_programs/exercise_science.cfm

Emporia State University, Department of Health, Physical Education and Recreation, Emporia, KS 66801-5415. Offers MS. *Program availability:* Part-time, 100% online. *Degree requirements:* For master's, comprehensive exam or thesis. *Entrance requirements:* For master's, bachelor's degree in physical education, health, and recreation; letters of recommendation. Additional exam requirements/recommendations for international students: Required—TOEFL (minimum score 520 paper-based; 68 iBT). Electronic applications accepted.

Florida Agricultural and Mechanical University, Division of Graduate Studies, Research, and Continuing Education, College of Education, Department of Health, Physical Education, and Recreation, Tallahassee, FL 32307-3200. Offers sport management (MS). *Accreditation:* NCATE. *Program availability:* Part-time, evening/weekend. *Degree requirements:* For master's, thesis optional. *Entrance requirements:* For master's, GRE General Test, minimum GPA of 3.0. Additional exam requirements/recommendations for international students: Required—TOEFL. *Faculty research:* Administration/curriculum, work behavior, psychology.

Florida International University, College of Arts, Sciences, and Education, Department of Teaching and Learning, Miami, FL 33199. Offers art education (MA, MS); curriculum and instruction (MS, Ed D, PhD, Ed S), including curriculum development (MS), elementary education (MS), English education (MS), learning technologies (MS), mathematics education (MS), modern language education (MS), physical education (MS), science education (MS), social studies education (MS), special education (MS); early childhood education (MS); exceptional student education (Ed D); foreign language education (MS), including foreign language education, teaching English to speakers of other languages (TESOL); language, literacy and culture (PhD); mathematics, science, and learning technologies (PhD); physical education (MS), including sport and fitness; reading education (MS). *Program availability:* Part-time, evening/weekend. *Faculty:* 64 full-time (43 women), 104 part-time/adjunct (76 women). *Students:* 169 full-time (144 women), 155 part-time (130 women); includes 260 minority (53 Black or African American, non-Hispanic/Latino; 7 Asian, non-Hispanic/Latino; 193 Hispanic/Latino; 7 Two or more races, non-Hispanic/Latino), 13 international. Average age 33. 184 applicants, 62% accepted, 87 enrolled. In 2018, 153 master's, 10 doctorates awarded. *Degree requirements:* For doctorate, comprehensive exam, thesis/dissertation. *Entrance requirements:* For master's, GRE General Test, Florida General Knowledge Test or Florida College Level Academic Skills Test; for doctorate and Ed S, GRE General Test. Additional exam requirements/recommendations for international students: Required—TOEFL (minimum score 550 paper-based; 80 iBT), IELTS (minimum score 6.3). *Application deadline:* For fall admission, 6/1 priority date for domestic students, 4/1 for international students; for winter admission, 10/1 priority date for domestic students, 9/1 for international students; for spring admission, 3/1 priority date for domestic students, 2/1 for international students. Applications are processed on a rolling basis. Application fee: $30. Electronic applications accepted. *Financial support:* Research assistantships and teaching assistantships available. *Unit head:* Dr. Maria Fernandez, Chair, 305-348-0193, Fax: 305-348-2086, E-mail: Maria.Fernandez9@fiu.edu. *Application contact:* Nanett Rojas, Manager, Admissions Operations, 305-348-7464, Fax: 305-348-7441, E-mail: gradadm@fiu.edu.
Website: https://tl.fiu.edu/

Fort Hays State University, Graduate School, College of Health and Behavioral Sciences, Department of Health and Human Performance, Hays, KS 67601-4099. Offers MS. *Program availability:* Part-time. *Degree requirements:* For master's, comprehensive exam, thesis optional. *Entrance requirements:* For master's, GRE General Test or MAT. Additional exam requirements/recommendations for international students: Required—TOEFL (minimum score 550 paper-based). Electronic applications accepted. *Faculty research:* Isoproterenol hydrochloride and exercise, dehydrogenase and high-density lipoprotein levels in athletics, venous blood parameters to adipose fat.

Gardner-Webb University, Graduate School, Department of Physical Education, Wellness, and Sport Studies, Boiling Springs, NC 28017. Offers sport science and pedagogy (MA). *Program availability:* Part-time, evening/weekend. *Degree requirements:* For master's, comprehensive exam. *Entrance requirements:* For master's, GRE General Test or NTE, PRAXIS, minimum GPA of 2.5. Electronic applications accepted. *Expenses:* Contact institution.

George Mason University, College of Education and Human Development, Programs in Curriculum and Instruction, Fairfax, VA 22030. Offers assistive technology (M Ed); designing digital learning in schools (M Ed); early childhood education (M Ed); early childhood education for diverse learners (M Ed); elementary education (M Ed); English as a second language (M Ed); gifted child education (M Ed); literacy (M Ed), including PK-12 classroom teachers, reading specialist; literacy leadership for diverse schools (M Ed), including K-12 reading; physical education (M Ed); science K-12 (M Ed); secondary education (M Ed), including biology, chemistry, earth science, English, history/social science, math, physics; special education (M Ed); teacher leadership (M Ed); transformative teaching (M Ed). *Program availability:* Part-time, evening/weekend, 100% online, blended/hybrid learning. *Faculty:* 48 full-time (40 women), 28 part-time/adjunct (20 women). *Students:* 165 full-time (147 women), 697 part-time (579 women); includes 243 minority (47 Black or African American, non-Hispanic/Latino; 3 American Indian or Alaska Native, non-Hispanic/Latino; 88 Asian, non-Hispanic/Latino; 85 Hispanic/Latino; 4 Native Hawaiian or other Pacific Islander, non-Hispanic/Latino; 16 Two or more races, non-Hispanic/Latino), 26 international. Average age 34. 450 applicants, 93% accepted, 315 enrolled. In 2018, 421 master's awarded. *Entrance requirements:* For master's, PRAXIS Core (for some programs), 2 letters of recommendation, interview, program goals statement; 9 hours of complete licensure endorsement requirements (for elementary education); minimum GPA of 3.0 in applicant's last 60 hours of undergraduate coursework (for secondary education); at least 1 year of teaching experience (for literacy). Additional exam requirements/recommendations for international students: Required—TOEFL (minimum score 575 paper-based; 88 iBT), IELTS (minimum score 6.5), PTE (minimum score 59). *Application deadline:* For fall admission, 4/2 priority date for domestic and international students; for spring admission, 11/1 for domestic and international students. Application fee: $75 ($80 for international students). Electronic applications accepted. *Financial support:* In 2018–19, 4 students received support, including 1 fellowship, 3 teaching assistantships (averaging $3,745 per year); career-related internships or fieldwork, Federal Work-Study, scholarships/grants, unspecified assistantships, and health care benefits (for full-time research or teaching assistantship recipients) also available. Support available to part-time students. Financial award application deadline: 3/1; financial award applicants required to submit FAFSA. *Faculty research:* Teacher preparation and professional development; adaptive teaching; wonder in science teacher preparation; literacy (digital, adolescent); site based course instruction. *Unit head:* Rebecca Fox, Professor and Academic Program Coordinator, 703-993-4123, E-mail: rfox@gmu.edu. *Application contact:* Rebecca Fox, Professor and Academic Program Coordinator, 703-993-4123, E-mail: rfox@gmu.edu.
Website: http://gse.gmu.edu/programs/gsemasters

Georgia College & State University, Graduate School, College of Health Sciences, School of Health and Human Performance, Milledgeville, GA 31061. Offers health and human performance (MS), including health performance, health promotion; kinesiology/health education (MAT). *Accreditation:* NCATE (one or more programs are accredited). *Program availability:* Part-time, 100% online. *Degree requirements:* For master's, thesis (for some programs), completed in 6 years with minimum GPA of 3.0 (for MS); minimum GPA of 3.0 and electronic teaching portfolio (for MAT). *Entrance requirements:* For master's, GRE with minimum score of 297 or MAT with minimum score of 385 (for MS); GRE with minimum score of 297, MAT 385, SAT 1000, ACT 43, or GACE with 250 on each section (for MAT), resume, 3 professional references; minimum GPA of 2.75 in upper-level undergraduate courses and undergraduate statistics course (for MS); minimum GPA of 2.75 on upper-division major courses (for MAT). Electronic applications accepted. *Expenses:* Contact institution.

Georgia State University, College of Education and Human Development, Department of Kinesiology and Health, Program in Health and Physical Education, Atlanta, GA 30302-3083. Offers M Ed. *Program availability:* Part-time, evening/weekend. *Entrance requirements:* For master's, GRE General Test, minimum GPA of 2.5. Application fee: $50. *Expenses: Tuition, area resident:* Full-time $9360; part-time $390 per credit hour. Tuition, state resident: full-time $9360; part-time $390 per credit hour. Tuition, nonresident: full-time $30,024; part-time $1251 per credit hour. *International tuition:* $30,024 full-time. *Required fees:* $2128. *Financial support:* Teaching assistantships and career-related internships or fieldwork available. *Faculty research:* Exercise science, teacher behavior. *Unit head:* Dr. Jacalyn Lea Lund, Chair, 404-413-8051, E-mail: jlund@gsu.edu. *Application contact:* Dr. Rachel Gurvitch, Program Coordinator, 404-413-8374, Fax: 404-413-8053, E-mail: rgurvitch@gsu.edu.
Website: https://education.gsu.edu/kh/

Physical Education

Goucher College, Graduate Programs in Education, Baltimore, MD 21204-2794. Offers at-risk and diverse learners (M Ed, Certificate); athletic program leadership and administration (M Ed, Certificate); elementary education (MAT); literacy strategies for content learning (M Ed); middle school (M Ed, Certificate); Montessori studies (M Ed); reading instruction (M Ed, Certificate); reducing student, classroom, and school disruption (M Ed); school improvement leadership (M Ed); secondary education (MAT); special education (MAT), including elementary education; special education for certified elementary and secondary teachers (M Ed); teacher as leader in technology (M Ed). *Program availability:* Part-time, evening/weekend. *Degree requirements:* For master's, thesis (M Ed), final presentation (MAT). *Entrance requirements:* For master's, minimum GPA of 3.0. Additional exam requirements/recommendations for international students: Required—TOEFL (minimum score 550 paper-based; 80 iBT), IELTS (minimum score 7). Electronic applications accepted. *Expenses:* Contact institution. *Faculty research:* Urban education, middle school, school improvement, teacher education, at-risk student achievement.

Henderson State University, Graduate Studies, Teachers College, Department of Health, Physical Education, Recreation and Athletic Training, Arkadelphia, AR 71999-0001. Offers sports administration (MS). *Program availability:* Part-time. *Entrance requirements:* For master's, GRE General Test or MAT, minimum GPA of 2.7 as an undergraduate student. Additional exam requirements/recommendations for international students: Required—TOEFL (minimum score 600 paper-based); Recommended—IELTS (minimum score 6.5).

Hofstra University, School of Education, Specialized Programs in Education, Hempstead, NY 11549. Offers applied behavior analysis (Advanced Certificate); childhood special education (MS Ed); early childhood special education (MS Ed, Advanced Certificate); educational and policy leadership (Ed D); educational leadership (Advanced Certificate); educational leadership and policy studies (MS Ed), including K-12; elementary special education (MS Ed); gifted education (Advanced Certificate); health education (MS); health professions pedagogy and leadership (MS); higher education leadership and policy studies (MS Ed); inclusive early childhood special education (MS Ed); inclusive elementary special education (MS Ed); inclusive secondary special education (MS Ed); literacy studies (MA, MS Ed, Ed D, Advanced Certificate); pedagogy for health professions (Advanced Certificate); physical education (MS); school district business leader (Advanced Certificate); secondary education generalist - students with disabilities 7-12 (MS Ed); secondary special education generalist - secondary education (MS Ed); special education (MS Ed, Advanced Certificate); special education assessment and diagnosis (Advanced Certificate); special education early childhood intervention (MS Ed); special education: international perspectives (MS Ed); teaching students with severe or multiple disabilities (Advanced Certificate). *Program availability:* Part-time, evening/weekend, blended/hybrid learning. *Students:* 126 full-time (91 women), 230 part-time (175 women); includes 90 minority (40 Black or African American, non-Hispanic/Latino; 4 American Indian or Alaska Native, non-Hispanic/Latino; 11 Asian, non-Hispanic/Latino; 32 Hispanic/Latino; 3 Two or more races, non-Hispanic/Latino), 4 international. Average age 32. 215 applicants, 90% accepted, 117 enrolled. In 2018, 130 master's, 9 doctorates, 23 other advanced degrees awarded. *Degree requirements:* For master's, one foreign language, comprehensive exam (for some programs), thesis (for some programs), electronic portfolio, capstone course, internship, practicum, student teaching, seminars, minimum GPA of 3.0; for doctorate, one foreign language, comprehensive exam, thesis/dissertation, qualifying hearing. *Entrance requirements:* For master's, GRE, interview, letters of recommendation, portfolio, essay, certification; for doctorate, GRE or MAT, interview, resume, essay, master's degree, 3 letters of recommendation, writing sample; for Advanced Certificate, GRE, interview, letters of recommendation, essay, professional experience, resume, master's degree. Additional exam requirements/recommendations for international students: Required—TOEFL (minimum score 550 paper-based; 80 iBT). *Application deadline:* Applications are processed on a rolling basis. Application fee: $75. Electronic applications accepted. *Financial support:* In 2018–19, 208 students received support, including 105 fellowships with full and partial tuition reimbursements available (averaging $3,948 per year); 12 research assistantships with full and partial tuition reimbursements available (averaging $6,573 per year); career-related internships or fieldwork, Federal Work-Study, institutionally sponsored loans, scholarships/grants, traineeships, tuition waivers (full and partial), unspecified assistantships, and scholarships and endowed scholarships also available. Support available to part-time students. Financial award applicants required to submit FAFSA. *Faculty research:* Water quality and income inequality; girls and stem; new media literacies; applied behavior analysis; k-12 leadership development. *Unit head:* Dr. Alan Flurkey, Chairperson, 516-463-5237, E-mail: alan.d.flurkey@hofstra.edu. *Application contact:* Sunil Samuel, Assistant Vice President of Admissions, 516-463-4723, Fax: 516-463-4664, E-mail: graduateadmission@hofstra.edu.
Website: http://www.hofstra.edu/education/

Howard University, Graduate School, Department of Health, Human Performance and Leisure Studies, Washington, DC 20059-0002. Offers exercise physiology (MS); health education (MS); sports studies (MS), including sociology of sports, sports management; urban recreation (MS), including leisure studies. *Program availability:* Part-time, evening/weekend. *Degree requirements:* For master's, comprehensive exam, thesis. *Entrance requirements:* For master's, BS in human performance or related field. Additional exam requirements/recommendations for international students: Recommended—TOEFL. Electronic applications accepted. *Faculty research:* Health promotion, cardiovascular hypertension, physical activity, sport and human rights issues.

Idaho State University, Graduate School, College of Education, Department of Sport Science and Physical Education, Pocatello, ID 83209-8105. Offers athletic administration (MPE); athletic training (MSAT). *Program availability:* Part-time. *Degree requirements:* For master's, comprehensive exam (for some programs), thesis optional, internship, oral defense of dissertation, or written exams. *Entrance requirements:* For master's, MAT or GRE General Test, minimum GPA of 3.0 in upper division classes. Additional exam requirements/recommendations for international students: Required—TOEFL (minimum score 550 paper-based; 80 iBT). Electronic applications accepted. *Faculty research:* Gender and diversity; concussion awareness/sports medicine; legal aspects of athletic health care; sports psychology; exercise physiology; sports management and leadership; adapted activities; fitness, wellness, and nutrition; coaching perspectives; critical features of athletic activities.

Illinois State University, Graduate School, College of Applied Science and Technology, School of Kinesiology and Recreation, Normal, IL 61790. Offers health education (MS). *Faculty:* 35 full-time (20 women), 16 part-time/adjunct (10 women). *Students:* 114 full-time (58 women), 22 part-time (9 women); includes 23 minority (7 Black or African American, non-Hispanic/Latino; 2 Asian, non-Hispanic/Latino; 12 Hispanic/Latino; 2 Two or more races, non-Hispanic/Latino), 10 international. Average age 25. 166 applicants, 54% accepted, 68 enrolled. In 2018, 68 master's awarded. *Degree requirements:* For master's, thesis or alternative. *Entrance requirements:* For master's, GRE General Test, minimum GPA of 2.6 in last 60 hours of course work. *Application deadline:* Applications are processed on a rolling basis. Application fee: $40. *Expenses:* Tuition, area resident: Full-time $7264.62. Tuition, state resident: full-time

$9466. Tuition, nonresident: full-time $17,290. *International tuition:* $15,089.40 full-time. *Required fees:* $1481.04. *Financial support:* In 2018–19, 5 research assistantships, 24 teaching assistantships were awarded; career-related internships or fieldwork, Federal Work-Study, tuition waivers (full and partial), and unspecified assistantships also available. Financial award application deadline: 4/1. *Faculty research:* Influences on positive youth development through sport, country-wide health fitness project, graduate practicum in athletic training, perceived exertion and self-selected intensity during resistance exercise in younger and older. *Unit head:* Dr. Dan Elkins, 309-438-8661, E-mail: delkins@IllinoisState.edu. *Application contact:* Dr. Dan Elkins, 309-438-8661, E-mail: delkins@IllinoisState.edu.
Website: http://www.kinrec.ilstu.edu/

Indiana State University, College of Graduate and Professional Studies, College of Health and Human Services, Department of Kinesiology, Recreation, and Sport, Terre Haute, IN 47809. Offers physical education (MS); recreation and sport management (MS); sport management (PhD). *Degree requirements:* For master's, comprehensive exam (for some programs), thesis (for some programs). *Entrance requirements:* For master's, GRE General Test, undergraduate major in related field. Electronic applications accepted.

Indiana University Bloomington, School of Public Health, Department of Kinesiology, Bloomington, IN 47405. Offers applied sport science (MS); athletic administration/sport management (MS); athletic training (MS); biomechanics (MS); ergonomics (MS); exercise physiology (MS); human performance (PhD), including biomechanics, exercise physiology, motor learning/control, sport management; motor learning/control (MS); physical activity (MPH); physical activity, fitness and wellness (MS). *Program availability:* Part-time. Terminal master's awarded for partial completion of doctoral program. *Degree requirements:* For master's, thesis optional; for doctorate, variable foreign language requirement, comprehensive exam, thesis/dissertation. *Entrance requirements:* For master's, GRE General Test, minimum GPA of 2.8; for doctorate, GRE General Test, minimum graduate GPA of 3.5, undergraduate 3.0. Additional exam requirements/recommendations for international students: Required—TOEFL (minimum score 80 iBT). *Faculty research:* Exercise physiology and biochemistry, sports biomechanics, human motor control, adaptation of fitness and exercise to special populations.

Indiana University of Pennsylvania, School of Graduate Studies and Research, College of Health and Human Services, Department of Kinesiology, Health, and Sport Science, Program in Health and Physical Education, Indiana, PA 15705. Offers M Ed. *Program availability:* Part-time. *Faculty:* 44 full-time (27 women), 18 part-time/adjunct (12 women). *Students:* 44 full-time (27 women), 18 part-time (12 women); includes 2 minority (both Black or African American, non-Hispanic/Latino). Average age 25. 54 applicants, 81% accepted, 34 enrolled. In 2018, 24 master's awarded. *Entrance requirements:* Additional exam requirements/recommendations for international students: Required—TOEFL (minimum score 540 paper-based). *Application deadline:* Applications are processed on a rolling basis. Application fee: $50. Electronic applications accepted. *Expenses:* Tuition, state resident: full-time $12,384; part-time $516 per credit hour. Tuition, nonresident: full-time $18,576; part-time $774 per credit hour. *Required fees:* $4454; $186 per credit hour. $65 per semester. Tuition and fees vary according to program and reciprocity agreements. *Financial support:* In 2018–19, 6 research assistantships with tuition reimbursements (averaging $3,083 per year) were awarded; career-related internships or fieldwork, Federal Work-Study, scholarships/grants, and unspecified assistantships also available. Support available to part-time students. Financial award application deadline: 4/15; financial award applicants required to submit FAFSA. *Unit head:* Dr. David Wachob, Coordinator, 724-357-3194, E-mail: d.wachob@iup.edu. *Application contact:* Dr. David Wachob, Coordinator, 724-357-3194, E-mail: d.wachob@iup.edu.
Website: http://www.iup.edu/grad/healthphysed/default.aspx

Indiana University–Purdue University Indianapolis, School of Physical Education and Tourism Management, Indianapolis, IN 46202-5193. Offers event tourism (MS), including sport event tourism; kinesiology (MS), including clinical exercise science; public health (Graduate Certificate). *Degree requirements:* For master's, comprehensive exam (for some programs), thesis (for some programs). *Entrance requirements:* For master's, GRE. Additional exam requirements/recommendations for international students: Required—TOEFL. Electronic applications accepted. *Expenses:* Contact institution. *Faculty research:* Physical activity, exercise and diseases; human movement science; sport performance; sport event tourism; destination marketing and event management.

Inter American University of Puerto Rico, Metropolitan Campus, Graduate Programs, Program in Physical Education, San Juan, PR 00919-1293. Offers teaching of physical education (MA); training and sport performance (MA). *Degree requirements:* For master's, comprehensive exam. *Entrance requirements:* For master's, GRE or EXADEP, interview. Electronic applications accepted.

Inter American University of Puerto Rico, San Germán Campus, Graduate Studies Center, Program in Health and Physical Education, San Germán, PR 00683-5008. Offers MA. *Program availability:* Part-time, evening/weekend. *Degree requirements:* For master's, comprehensive exam. *Entrance requirements:* For master's, GRE General Test or EXADEP, minimum GPA of 3.0. *Expenses:* Tuition: Full-time $212; part-time $212 per credit. *Required fees:* $366 per semester. One-time fee: $31. Tuition and fees vary according to degree level and program.

Ithaca College, School of Health Sciences and Human Performance, Program in Physical Education, Ithaca, NY 14850. Offers MS. In 2018, 1 master's awarded. *Unit head:* Dr. Stewart Auyash, Chair, 607-274-1312, E-mail: auyash@ithaca.edu. *Application contact:* Nicole Eversley Bradwell, Director, Office of Admission, 800-429-4274, Fax: 607-274-1263, E-mail: admission@ithaca.edu.
Website: http://www.ithaca.edu/gradprograms/hppe/programs/physed

Jackson State University, Graduate School, College of Education and Human Development, Department of Health, Physical Education and Recreation, Jackson, MS 39217. Offers physical education (MS Ed); sport science (MS). *Accreditation:* NCATE. *Program availability:* Part-time, evening/weekend, 100% online, blended/hybrid learning. *Degree requirements:* For master's, comprehensive exam, thesis or alternative. *Entrance requirements:* For master's, GRE General Test. Additional exam requirements/recommendations for international students: Required—TOEFL (minimum score 520 paper-based; 67 iBT). Electronic applications accepted. *Expenses:* Contact institution.

Jacksonville State University, Graduate Studies, School of Education, Program in Physical Education, Jacksonville, AL 36265-1602. Offers MS Ed, Ed S. *Accreditation:* NCATE. *Program availability:* Part-time, evening/weekend. *Degree requirements:* For master's, comprehensive exam, thesis (for some programs). *Entrance requirements:* For master's, GRE General Test or MAT. Additional exam requirements/recommendations for international students: Required—TOEFL (minimum score 500 paper-based; 61 iBT). Electronic applications accepted.

James Madison University, The Graduate School, College of Health and Behavioral Studies, Program in Kinesiology, Harrisonburg, VA 22807. Offers clinical exercise physiology (MS); exercise physiology (MS); kinesiology (MAT, MS); nutrition and exercise (MS); physical and health education (MAT); sport and recreation leadership

(MS). *Program availability:* Part-time, evening/weekend. *Students:* 33 full-time (11 women); includes 3 minority (2 Black or African American, non-Hispanic/Latino; 1 Hispanic/Latino). Average age 30. In 2018, 18 master's awarded. Electronic applications accepted. *Expenses:* Tuition, state resident: full-time $10,848. Tuition, nonresident: full-time $27,888. *Required fees:* $1128. *Financial support:* In 2018–19, 20 students received support, including teaching assistantships with full tuition reimbursements available (averaging $8,837 per year); Federal Work-Study and assistantships (averaging $7911), athletic assistantships (averaging $9284) also available. Financial award application deadline: 3/1; financial award applicants required to submit FAFSA. *Unit head:* Dr. Christopher J. Womack, Department Head, 540-568-6145, E-mail: womackcx@jmu.edu. *Application contact:* Lynette D. Michael, Director of Graduate Admissions, 540-568-6131 Ext. 6395, Fax: 540-568-7860, E-mail: michaeld@jmu.edu.
Website: http://www.jmu.edu/kinesiology/

Longwood University, College of Graduate and Professional Studies, College of Education and Human Services, Farmville, VA 23909. Offers education (MS), including algebra and middle school mathematics, counselor education, elementary and middle school mathematics, elementary education, elementary education initial licensure, health and physical education, special education general curriculum, special education initial licensure; reading, literacy and learning (M Ed); school librarianship (M Ed); social work and communication sciences and disorders (MS), including communication sciences and disorders. *Accreditation:* NCATE. *Program availability:* Part-time, evening/weekend. *Degree requirements:* For master's, comprehensive exam (for some programs), thesis optional, professional portfolio, internship, clinical experience, or practicum. *Entrance requirements:* For master's, PRAXIS I (for initial teaching licensure programs); GRE (for some programs), bachelor's degree from regionally-accredited institution, 2 recommendations (3 for some programs), minimum 500-word personal essay, official transcripts, minimum GPA of 2.75, valid teaching license (for some programs). Additional exam requirements/recommendations for international students: Required—TOEFL (minimum score 570 paper-based), IELTS (minimum score 6.5). Electronic applications accepted. *Expenses:* Contact institution.

Massachusetts College of Liberal Arts, Graduate Programs, North Adams, MA 01247-4100. Offers business (MBA); educational administration (M Ed); educational leadership (CAGS); instruction and curriculum (M Ed); instructional technology (M Ed); physical education and health (M Ed); reading (M Ed); special education (M Ed). *Program availability:* Part-time, evening/weekend. *Degree requirements:* For master's, thesis. *Entrance requirements:* For master's, writing sample.

McGill University, Faculty of Graduate and Postdoctoral Studies, Faculty of Education, Department of Kinesiology and Physical Education, Montréal, QC H3A 2T5, Canada. Offers M Sc, MA, PhD, Certificate, Diploma.

McNeese State University, Doré School of Graduate Studies, Burton College of Education, Department of Education Professions, Program in Multiple Levels Grades K-12, Lake Charles, LA 70609. Offers multiple levels grades K-12 (Postbaccalaureate Certificate), including art, health and physical education, music - instrumental, music - vocal. *Entrance requirements:* For degree, PRAXIS, 2 letters of recommendation, autobiography.

Memorial University of Newfoundland, School of Graduate Studies, School of Human Kinetics and Recreation, St. John's, NL A1C 5S7, Canada. Offers administration, curriculum and supervision (MPE); biomechanics/ergonomics (MS Kin); exercise and work physiology (MS Kin); psychology of sport, exercise and recreation (MS Kin); socio-cultural studies of physical activity and health (MS Kin). *Program availability:* Part-time. *Degree requirements:* For master's, thesis optional, seminars, thesis presentations. *Entrance requirements:* For master's, bachelor's degree in a related field, minimum B average. Electronic applications accepted. *Faculty research:* Administration, sociology of sports, kinesiology, physiology/recreation.

Meredith College, School of Education, Health and Human Sciences, Raleigh, NC 27607-5298. Offers academically and intellectually gifted (M Ed); elementary education (M Ed, MAT); English as a second language (M Ed, MAT); health and physical education (MAT); nutrition, health and human performance (MS, Postbaccalaureate Certificate), including dietetic internship (Postbaccalaureate Certificate), nutrition (MS); psychology (MA), including industrial/organizational psychology; reading (M Ed); special education (MAT); special education (general curriculum) (M Ed). *Accreditation:* NCATE. *Program availability:* Part-time, evening/weekend. *Students:* 97 full-time (89 women), 76 part-time (73 women); includes 39 minority (17 Black or African American, non-Hispanic/Latino; 1 American Indian or Alaska Native, non-Hispanic/Latino; 9 Asian, non-Hispanic/Latino; 10 Hispanic/Latino; 2 Two or more races, non-Hispanic/Latino). Average age 28. In 2018, 56 master's, 36 other advanced degrees awarded. *Degree requirements:* For master's, thesis optional. *Entrance requirements:* For master's, GRE General Test or MAT, minimum GPA of 2.5, teaching license, recommendations. Additional exam requirements/recommendations for international students: Required—TOEFL. *Application deadline:* For fall admission, 7/1 priority date for domestic students; for spring admission, 11/1 priority date for domestic students. Applications are processed on a rolling basis. Application fee: $50. Electronic applications accepted. *Expenses:* $575 per credit hour for masters degree in education, $725 (for MS. PSY.IO degree), $20,295 (for pre-health post-baccalaureate certificate), $13,600 (for dietetic internship). *Financial support:* Career-related internships or fieldwork, institutionally sponsored loans, and tuition waivers (partial) available. Support available to part-time students. Financial award application deadline: 2/15; financial award applicants required to submit FAFSA. *Unit head:* Dr. Monica McKinney, Graduate Program Manager, 919-760-8056, Fax: 919-760-2303, E-mail: mckinneym@meredith.edu. *Application contact:* Dr. Monica McKinney, Graduate Program Manager, 919-760-8056, Fax: 919-760-2303, E-mail: mckinneym@meredith.edu.
Website: https://www.meredith.edu/school-of-education-health-and-human-sciences

Middle Tennessee State University, College of Graduate Studies, College of Behavioral and Health Sciences, Department of Health and Human Performance, Program in Health, Physical Education and Recreation, Murfreesboro, TN 37132. Offers health and human performance (MS); leisure and sport management (MS). *Program availability:* Part-time, evening/weekend, online learning. *Degree requirements:* For master's, comprehensive exam, thesis optional. *Entrance requirements:* For master's, GRE. Additional exam requirements/recommendations for international students: Required—TOEFL (minimum score 525 paper-based; 71 iBT) or IELTS (minimum score 6). *Faculty research:* Kinesiometrics, leisure behavior, health, lifestyles.

Millersville University of Pennsylvania, College of Graduate Studies and Adult Learning, College of Education and Human Services, Department of Wellness and Sport Sciences, Millersville, PA 17551-0302. Offers sport management (M Ed); sport management: athletic coaching (Post-Master's Certificate). *Program availability:* Part-time. *Faculty:* 5 full-time (3 women). *Students:* 1 full-time (0 women), 29 part-time (15 women); includes 10 minority (5 Black or African American, non-Hispanic/Latino; 1 Asian, non-Hispanic/Latino; 2 Hispanic/Latino; 2 Two or more races, non-Hispanic/Latino). Average age 27. 11 applicants, 91% accepted, 7 enrolled. In 2018, 15 master's awarded. *Degree requirements:* For master's, thesis optional, internship. *Entrance requirements:* For master's, GRE/MAT/GMAT exam or complete an interview with writing assignment, required only if cumulative GPA is lower than 3.0, all transfer transcripts (even if MU grad), at least 1 academic reference (not from MU Sport Management Dept.), and sport management goal statement. Additional exam requirements/recommendations for international students: Required—TOEFL, IELTS (minimum score 6), PTE (minimum score 60). *Application deadline:* Applications are processed on a rolling basis. Application fee: $40. Electronic applications accepted. *Expenses: Tuition, area resident:* Full-time $9288; part-time $516 per credit. Tuition, state resident: full-time $9288; part-time $516 per credit. Tuition, nonresident: full-time $13,932; part-time $774 per credit. *International tuition:* $13,932 full-time. *Required fees:* $2623.50; $145.75 per credit. Tuition and fees vary according to course load, degree level and program. *Financial support:* In 2018–19, 13 students received support. Unspecified assistantships available. Financial award application deadline: 3/15; financial award applicants required to submit FAFSA. *Faculty research:* Applied sport management; leadership and sport; marketing and sport; gender and sport; leadership development; ADR, restorative justice and hazing; legal issues applied to sport management; women and fitness/sport; childhood health and wellness issues; using technology for monitoring physical activity; college health assessments; Sport Organization's Athlete's Resiliency & Emergency and Critical Incident Management & Response; Sport safety and Title IX. *Unit head:* Dr. Daniel J. Keefer, Chair, 717-871-4218, Fax: 717-871-7987, E-mail: daniel.keefer@millersville.edu. *Application contact:* Dr. James A. Delle, Acting Dean of College of Graduate Studies and Adult Learning/Associate Provost, Academic Administration, 717-871-7462, E-mail: James.Delle@millersville.edu.
Website: http://www.millersville.edu/wssd/

Minnesota State University Mankato, College of Graduate Studies and Research, College of Allied Health and Nursing, Department of Human Performance, Mankato, MN 56001. Offers physical education (MA, MS). *Program availability:* Part-time. *Degree requirements:* For master's, comprehensive exam, thesis. *Entrance requirements:* For master's, minimum GPA of 3.0 during previous 2 years. Additional exam requirements/recommendations for international students: Required—TOEFL.

Mississippi State University, College of Education, Department of Kinesiology, Mississippi State, MS 39762. Offers disability studies (MS); exercise physiology (MS); exercise science (PhD); sport administration (MS); sport pedagogy (MS); sport studies (PhD). *Program availability:* Part-time, blended/hybrid learning. *Faculty:* 15 full-time (3 women). *Students:* 49 full-time (25 women), 16 part-time (3 women); includes 14 minority (5 Black or African American, non-Hispanic/Latino; 1 American Indian or Alaska Native, non-Hispanic/Latino; 2 Asian, non-Hispanic/Latino; 3 Hispanic/Latino; 3 Two or more races, non-Hispanic/Latino), 10 international. Average age 26. 67 applicants, 60% accepted, 23 enrolled. In 2018, 27 master's, 2 doctorates awarded. *Degree requirements:* For master's, comprehensive exam, thesis optional; for doctorate, comprehensive exam. *Entrance requirements:* For master's, GRE General Test, minimum GPA of 2.75 on undergraduate work from four-year accredited institution, 3.0 graduate; for doctorate, GRE, minimum GPA of 3.4 on previous graduate degree(s) earned from accredited institutions. Additional exam requirements/recommendations for international students: Required—TOEFL (minimum score 550 paper-based; 79 iBT); Recommended—IELTS (minimum score 6.5). *Application deadline:* For fall admission, 7/1 for domestic students, 5/1 for international students; for spring admission, 11/1 for domestic students, 9/1 for international students. Applications are processed on a rolling basis. Application fee: $60 ($80 for international students). Electronic applications accepted. *Expenses:* Tuition, state resident: full-time $8450; part-time $360.59 per credit hour. Tuition, nonresident: full-time $23,140; part-time $969.09 per credit hour. *Required fees:* $110. One-time fee: $55 full-time. Part-time tuition and fees vary according to course load, degree level, campus/location and reciprocity agreements. *Financial support:* In 2018–19, 14 teaching assistantships with partial tuition reimbursements (averaging $10,386 per year) were awarded; career-related internships or fieldwork, Federal Work-Study, institutionally sponsored loans, and unspecified assistantships also available. Financial award application deadline: 4/1; financial award applicants required to submit FAFSA. *Faculty research:* Static balance and stepping performance of older adults, organizational justice, public health, strength training and recovery drinks, high risk drinking perceptions and behaviors. *Unit head:* Dr. Stanley P. Brown, Professor and Head, 662-325-7229, Fax: 662-325-4525, E-mail: spb107@msstate.edu. *Application contact:* Ryan King, Admissions and Enrollment Assistant, 662-325-8951, E-mail: rjk101@grad.msstate.edu.
Website: http://www.kinesiology.msstate.edu/

Missouri State University, Graduate College, College of Health and Human Services, Department of Kinesiology, Springfield, MO 65897. Offers health promotion and wellness management (MS); secondary education (MS Ed), including physical education. *Program availability:* Part-time. *Faculty:* 14 full-time (6 women). *Students:* 14 full-time (5 women), 16 part-time (10 women); includes 2 minority (both Black or African American, non-Hispanic/Latino), 2 international. Average age 23. 23 applicants, 48% accepted. In 2018, 16 master's awarded. *Degree requirements:* For master's, comprehensive exam, thesis or alternative. *Entrance requirements:* For master's, GRE (for MS), minimum GPA of 2.8 (MS); 9-12 teaching certification (MS Ed). Additional exam requirements/recommendations for international students: Required—TOEFL (minimum score 550 paper-based; 79 iBT), IELTS (minimum score 6). *Application deadline:* For fall admission, 7/20 priority date for domestic students, 5/1 for international students; for spring admission, 12/20 priority date for domestic students, 9/1 for international students. Applications are processed on a rolling basis. Application fee: $55 ($60 for international students). Electronic applications accepted. Tuition and fees vary according to class time, course level, course load, degree level, campus/location, program and student level. *Financial support:* In 2018–19, 7 teaching assistantships with partial tuition reimbursements (averaging $8,772 per year) were awarded; Federal Work-Study, institutionally sponsored loans, scholarships/grants, and unspecified assistantships also available. Financial award application deadline: 1/31; financial award applicants required to submit FAFSA. *Unit head:* Dr. Sarah McCallister, Department Head, 417-836-6582, Fax: 417-836-5371, E-mail: sarahmccallister@missouristate.edu. *Application contact:* Lakan Drinker, Director, Graduate Enrollment Management, 417-836-5330, Fax: 417-836-6200, E-mail: lakandrinker@missouristate.edu.
Website: http://www.missouristate.edu/kinesiology/

Montclair State University, The Graduate School, College of Education and Human Services, MAT Program in Teaching, Montclair, NJ 07043-1624. Offers art (MAT); biology (MAT); chemistry (MAT); earth science (MAT); English (MAT); French (MAT); health and physical education (MAT); health education (MAT); mathematics (MAT); music (MAT); physical education (MAT); physical science (MAT); social studies (MAT); Spanish (MAT); teacher of English as a second language (MAT). *Degree requirements:* For master's, comprehensive exam, thesis or alternative. *Entrance requirements:* For master's, interview, 2 letters of recommendation. Additional exam requirements/recommendations for international students: Required—TOEFL (minimum score 83 iBT), IELTS (minimum score 6.5). Electronic applications accepted.

Montclair State University, The Graduate School, College of Education and Human Services, Program in Exercise Science and Physical Education, Montclair, NJ 07043-1624. Offers exercise science (MA); sports administration and coaching (MA); teaching and supervision in physical education (MA). *Program availability:* Part-time, evening/weekend. *Degree requirements:* For master's, comprehensive exam, thesis or

alternative. *Entrance requirements:* For master's, GRE General Test, essay, 2 letters of recommendation. Additional exam requirements/recommendations for international students: Required—TOEFL (minimum score 83 iBT), IELTS (minimum score 6.5). Electronic applications accepted.

Montclair State University, The Graduate School, College of Science and Mathematics, Program in Teaching Physical Education, Montclair, NJ 07043-1624. Offers MAT. *Degree requirements:* For master's, comprehensive exam. *Entrance requirements:* For master's, GRE General Test, interview, 2 letters of recommendation, essay. Additional exam requirements/recommendations for international students: Required—TOEFL (minimum score 83 iBT), IELTS (minimum score 6.5). Electronic applications accepted. *Faculty research:* Teaching physics.

Morehead State University, Graduate School, College of Education, Department of Middle Grades and Secondary Education, Morehead, KY 40351. Offers business and marketing education (MAT); English/language arts 5-9 (MAT); French (MAT); health P-12 (MAT); mathematics 5-9 (MAT); physical education P-12 (MAT); science 5-9 (MAT); secondary biology (MAT); secondary chemistry (MAT); secondary earth science (MAT); secondary English (MAT); secondary math (MAT); secondary physics (MAT); secondary social studies (MAT); social studies 5-9 (MAT); Spanish (MAT). *Program availability:* Part-time, evening/weekend. *Degree requirements:* For master's, portfolio. *Entrance requirements:* For master's, GRE or PRAXIS II content exam, minimum overall undergraduate GPA of 2.5. Additional exam requirements/recommendations for international students: Required—TOEFL (minimum score 500 paper-based). Electronic applications accepted.

North Carolina Central University, College of Behavioral and Social Sciences, Department of Physical Education and Recreation, Durham, NC 27707-3129. Offers general physical education (MS); recreation administration (MS). *Program availability:* Part-time, evening/weekend. *Degree requirements:* For master's, one foreign language, comprehensive exam, thesis. *Entrance requirements:* For master's, GRE, minimum GPA of 3.0 in major, 2.5 overall. Additional exam requirements/recommendations for international students: Required—TOEFL.

Northern Illinois University, Graduate School, College of Education, Department of Kinesiology and Physical Education, De Kalb, IL 60115-2854. Offers MS, MS Ed. *Program availability:* Part-time, evening/weekend. *Faculty:* 21 full-time (12 women). *Students:* 81 full-time (30 women), 48 part-time (20 women); includes 29 minority (16 Black or African American, non-Hispanic/Latino; 2 Asian, non-Hispanic/Latino; 4 Hispanic/Latino; 7 Two or more races, non-Hispanic/Latino), 6 international. Average age 26. 90 applicants, 92% accepted, 43 enrolled. In 2018, 60 master's awarded. *Degree requirements:* For master's, comprehensive exam, thesis optional. *Entrance requirements:* For master's, GRE General Test, minimum GPA of 2.75, undergraduate major in related area. Additional exam requirements/recommendations for international students: Required—TOEFL (minimum score 550 paper-based). *Application deadline:* For fall admission, 6/1 for domestic students, 5/1 for international students; for spring admission, 11/1 for domestic students, 10/1 for international students. Applications are processed on a rolling basis. Application fee: $40. Electronic applications accepted. *Financial support:* In 2018–19, 2 research assistantships with full tuition reimbursements, 31 teaching assistantships with full tuition reimbursements were awarded; fellowships with full tuition reimbursements, career-related internships or fieldwork, Federal Work-Study, scholarships/grants, tuition waivers (full), and unspecified assistantships also available. Support available to part-time students. Financial award applicants required to submit FAFSA. *Faculty research:* Leadership in athletic training, motor development, dance education, gait analysis, fat phobia. *Unit head:* Dr. Chad D. McEvoy, Chair, 815-753-8284, Fax: 815-753-1413, E-mail: knpe@niu.edu. *Application contact:* Dr. Chad D. McEvoy, Chair, 815-753-8284, Fax: 815-753-1413, E-mail: knpe@niu.edu.
Website: http://cedu.niu.edu/knpe/

Northwest Missouri State University, Graduate School, School of Health Science and Wellness, Maryville, MO 64468-6001. Offers applied health and sport sciences (MS); guidance and counseling (MS Ed); health and physical education (MS Ed); recreation (MS); sport and exercise psychology (MS). *Accreditation:* NCATE. *Program availability:* Part-time. *Faculty:* 15 full-time (7 women). *Students:* 58 full-time (35 women), 27 part-time (17 women); includes 9 minority (7 Black or African American, non-Hispanic/Latino; 1 Hispanic/Latino; 1 Two or more races, non-Hispanic/Latino), 6 international. Average age 26. 50 applicants, 74% accepted, 23 enrolled. In 2018, 54 master's awarded. *Degree requirements:* For master's, comprehensive exam. *Entrance requirements:* For master's, GRE General Test, minimum undergraduate GPA of 2.75, teaching certificate, writing sample. Additional exam requirements/recommendations for international students: Required—TOEFL (minimum score 550 paper-based; 79 iBT). *Application deadline:* For fall admission, 7/1 for domestic and international students; for spring admission, 11/15 for domestic and international students. Applications are processed on a rolling basis. Application fee: $0 ($75 for international students). *Expenses: Tuition, area resident:* Full-time $4551; part-time $252.86 per credit hour. Tuition, state resident: full-time $4551; part-time $252.86 per credit hour. Tuition, nonresident: full-time $9103; part-time $505.72 per credit hour. *International tuition:* $9103 full-time. *Required fees:* $2668; $148.20 per credit hour. Tuition and fees vary according to program. *Financial support:* Teaching assistantships with full tuition reimbursements and unspecified assistantships available. Financial award application deadline: 4/1; financial award applicants required to submit FAFSA. *Unit head:* Dr. Terry Long, Director, School of Health Science and Wellness, 660-562-1706, Fax: 660-562-1483, E-mail: tlong@nwmissouri.edu. *Application contact:* Gina Smith, Office Manager, 660-562-1297, Fax: 660-562-1963, E-mail: smigina@nwmissouri.edu.
Website: http://www.nwmissouri.edu/health/

The Ohio State University, Graduate School, College of Education and Human Ecology, Department of Human Sciences, Columbus, OH 43210. Offers consumer sciences (MS, PhD); human development and family science (PhD); human nutrition (MS, PhD); kinesiology (MA, Ed D, PhD). *Program availability:* Part-time. *Faculty:* 53. *Students:* 119 full-time (68 women), 14 part-time (8 women). Average age 27. In 2018, 46 master's, 17 doctorates awarded. *Degree requirements:* For master's, thesis optional; for doctorate, thesis/dissertation. *Entrance requirements:* For master's and doctorate, GRE. Additional exam requirements/recommendations for international students: Required—TOEFL (minimum score 550 paper-based; 79 iBT), Michigan English Language Assessment Battery (minimum score 82); Recommended—IELTS (minimum score 7). *Application deadline:* For fall admission, 12/1 priority date for domestic and international students. Applications are processed on a rolling basis. Application fee: $60 ($70 for international students). Electronic applications accepted. *Financial support:* Fellowships with tuition reimbursements, research assistantships with tuition reimbursements, teaching assistantships with tuition reimbursements, Federal Work-Study, and institutionally sponsored loans available. Support available to part-time students. *Unit head:* Dr. Erik Porfeli, Chair, E-mail: porfeli.1@osu.edu. *Application contact:* Graduate and Professional Admissions, 614-292-9444, Fax: 614-292-3895, E-mail: gpadmissions@osu.edu.
Website: http://ehe.osu.edu/human-sciences/

Ohio University, Graduate College, Gladys W. and David H. Patton College of Education and Human Services, Department of Recreation and Sport Pedagogy, Program in Coaching Education, Athens, OH 45701-2979. Offers MS. *Entrance requirements:* For master's, GRE. Additional exam requirements/recommendations for international students: Required—TOEFL (minimum score 550 paper-based; 80 iBT) or IELTS (minimum score 6.5). Electronic applications accepted. *Faculty research:* Sports, physical activity, athletes.

Old Dominion University, Darden College of Education, Program in Physical Education, Adapted Physical Education Emphasis, Norfolk, VA 23529. Offers MS Ed. *Program availability:* Part-time. *Degree requirements:* For master's, comprehensive exam (for some programs), thesis (for some programs). *Entrance requirements:* Additional exam requirements/recommendations for international students: Required—TOEFL (minimum score 550 paper-based; 79 iBT). Electronic applications accepted. *Faculty research:* Adapted physical education/activity, inclusion, individuals with disabilities, assessment and evaluation.

Old Dominion University, Darden College of Education, Program in Physical Education, Coaching Education Emphasis, Norfolk, VA 23529. Offers MS Ed. *Program availability:* Part-time. *Degree requirements:* For master's, comprehensive exam, internship, research project, or thesis. *Entrance requirements:* For master's, GRE, bachelor's degree with minimum cumulative undergraduate GPA of 2.8, 3.0 in undergraduate major courses. Additional exam requirements/recommendations for international students: Required—TOEFL (minimum score 550 paper-based; 79 iBT). Electronic applications accepted. *Faculty research:* Curriculum development, learning and coaching theory, planning and administration in physical education and sports, adapted physical education.

Old Dominion University, Darden College of Education, Program in Physical Education, Curriculum and Instruction Emphasis, Norfolk, VA 23529. Offers human movement sciences (PhD), including health and sport pedagogy; physical education (MS Ed), including adapted physical education, coaching education, curriculum and instruction. *Program availability:* Part-time, evening/weekend. *Degree requirements:* For master's, comprehensive exam (for some programs), thesis or alternative, internship, research project. *Entrance requirements:* For master's, GRE, PRAXIS tests (for licensure only), minimum GPA of 2.8 overall, 3.0 in major. Additional exam requirements/recommendations for international students: Required—TOEFL (minimum score 500 paper-based; 97 iBT). Electronic applications accepted. *Faculty research:* Motor development, physical activity and fitness, motivation and learning in physical education, curriculum and instruction, adapted physical education.

Old Dominion University, Darden College of Education, Program in Physical Education, Exercise Science and Wellness Emphasis, Norfolk, VA 23529. Offers physical education (MS Ed), including exercise science and wellness. *Program availability:* Part-time, evening/weekend. *Degree requirements:* For master's, comprehensive exam, thesis or alternative, internship, research project. *Entrance requirements:* For master's, GRE (minimum score of 291 for combined verbal and quantitative), minimum GPA of 2.8 overall, 3.0 in major. Additional exam requirements/recommendations for international students: Required—TOEFL (minimum score 550 paper-based; 79 iBT). Electronic applications accepted. *Faculty research:* Cardiovascular response to exercise, exercise prescription, nutrition, lower extremity biomechanics, metabolic responses in special populations.

Pittsburg State University, Graduate School, College of Education, Department of Health, Physical Education and Recreation, Pittsburg, KS 66762. Offers health, human performance, and recreation (MS), including human performance and wellness, sport and leisure service management. *Program availability:* Part-time, online only, 100% online. *Degree requirements:* For master's, thesis or alternative. *Entrance requirements:* For master's, letter of intent. Additional exam requirements/recommendations for international students: Required—TOEFL (minimum score 520 paper-based; 68 iBT), IELTS (minimum score 6), PTE (minimum score 47). Electronic applications accepted. *Expenses:* Contact institution. *Faculty research:* Personality of athletes, fitness activities for children, aerobic conditioning, fitness evaluation.

Purdue University, Graduate School, College of Health and Human Sciences, Department of Health and Kinesiology, West Lafayette, IN 47907. Offers athletic training education administration (MS, PhD); biomechanics (MS, PhD); exercise physiology (MS, PhD); health education (MS, PhD); history/philosophy of sport (MS, PhD); motor control and development (MS, PhD); physical education pedagogy (PhD); physical education teacher education (MS); recreation and sport management (MS, PhD); sport and exercise psychology (MS, PhD). *Program availability:* Part-time. *Faculty:* 23 full-time (10 women). *Students:* 29 full-time (13 women), 8 part-time (5 women); includes 3 minority (1 Asian, non-Hispanic/Latino; 1 Hispanic/Latino; 1 Two or more races, non-Hispanic/Latino), 8 international. Average age 26. 61 applicants, 26% accepted, 14 enrolled. In 2018, 14 master's awarded. *Degree requirements:* For master's, thesis optional; for doctorate, comprehensive exam, thesis/dissertation, qualifying examination, preliminary examination. *Entrance requirements:* For master's, GRE General Test (minimum score 1000 combined verbal and quantitative), minimum undergraduate GPA of 3.0 or equivalent; for doctorate, GRE General Test (minimum score 1100 combined verbal and quantitative), minimum undergraduate GPA of 3.0 or equivalent; master's degree with minimum GPA of 3.25 (recommended). Additional exam requirements/recommendations for international students: Required—TOEFL (minimum score 77 iBT); Recommended—TWE. *Application deadline:* For fall admission, 4/30 for domestic and international students; for spring admission, 10/15 for domestic and international students. Applications are processed on a rolling basis. Application fee: $60 ($75 for international students). Electronic applications accepted. *Financial support:* Fellowships with partial tuition reimbursements, research assistantships with partial tuition reimbursements, teaching assistantships with partial tuition reimbursements, and Federal Work-Study available. Support available to part-time students. Financial award applicants required to submit FAFSA. *Faculty research:* Wellness, motivation, teaching effectiveness, learning and development. *Unit head:* Dr. Timothy P. Gavin, Head of the Graduate Program, 765-494-3178, Fax: 765-494-1239, E-mail: gavin1@purdue.edu. *Application contact:* David B. Klenosky, Graduate Contact, 765-494-0865, E-mail: klenosky@purdue.edu.
Website: http://www.purdue.edu/hhs/hk/

Queens College of the City University of New York, Mathematics and Natural Sciences Division, Department of Family, Nutrition and Exercise Sciences, Queens, NY 11367-1597. Offers exercise science specialist (MS); family and consumer science (K-12) (AC); family and consumer science/teaching curriculum (K-12) (MS Ed); nutrition and exercise science (MS); nutrition specialist (MS); physical education (K-12) (AC); physical education/teaching curriculum (pre K-12) (MS Ed). *Program availability:* Part-time, evening/weekend. *Faculty:* 18 full-time (15 women), 59 part-time/adjunct (41 women). *Students:* 18 full-time (6 women), 111 part-time (66 women); includes 62 minority (13 Black or African American, non-Hispanic/Latino; 12 Asian, non-Hispanic/Latino; 37 Hispanic/Latino), 3 international. Average age 29. 95 applicants, 76% accepted, 45 enrolled. In 2018, 41 master's, 16 other advanced degrees awarded. *Degree requirements:* For master's, research project or comprehensive examination. *Entrance requirements:* For master's, minimum GPA of 3.0. Additional exam requirements/recommendations for international students: Required—TOEFL (minimum paper-based score of 600) or IELTS=7 (for program in nutrition). *Application deadline:* For fall admission, 4/1 for domestic students; for spring admission, 11/1 for domestic

students. Applications are processed on a rolling basis. Application fee: $125. Electronic applications accepted. *Financial support:* Career-related internships or fieldwork and unspecified assistantships available. Financial award application deadline: 4/1; financial award applicants required to submit FAFSA. *Faculty research:* Eating patterns and health; health disparities; correlates of taste acuity; structuring and implementation of competition and competitive activities in physical education; exercise and metabolic risk in people living with HIV/AIDS; biomechanics, motor learning and motor control; exercise interventions to improve physical function in the elderly. *Unit head:* Dr. Ashima K. Kant, Chair, 718-997-4156 Ext. 4475, Fax: 718-997-4163, E-mail: ashima.kant@qc.cuny.edu. *Application contact:* Elizabeth D'Amico-Ramirez, Assistant Director of Graduate Admissions, 718-997-5203, E-mail: elizabeth.damicoramirez@qc.cuny.edu.

Rhode Island College, School of Graduate Studies, Feinstein School of Education and Human Development, Department of Health and Physical Education, Providence, RI 02908-1991. Offers health education (M Ed); physical education (CGS). *Accreditation:* NCATE. *Program availability:* Part-time, evening/weekend. *Faculty:* 1 full-time (0 women), 2 part-time/adjunct (0 women). *Students:* 3 part-time (2 women); includes 1 minority (Hispanic/Latino). Average age 35. In 2018, 1 master's awarded. *Degree requirements:* For master's, comprehensive assessment. *Entrance requirements:* For master's, GRE General Test or MAT, undergraduate transcripts; minimum undergraduate GPA of 3.0; 3 letters of recommendation; for CGS, GRE or MAT (for most programs), undergraduate transcripts; minimum undergraduate GPA of 3.0; 3 letters of recommendation. Additional exam requirements/recommendations for international students: Required—TOEFL (minimum score 550 paper-based; 80 iBT). *Application deadline:* For fall admission, 3/1 for domestic students; for spring admission, 11/1 for domestic students. Applications are processed on a rolling basis. Application fee: $50. Electronic applications accepted. *Expenses: Tuition, area resident:* Part-time $407 per credit. Tuition, nonresident: part-time $792 per credit. *Required fees:* $29 per credit. $100 per semester. *Financial support:* Teaching assistantships, Federal Work-Study, scholarships/grants, health care benefits, and unspecified assistantships available. Support available to part-time students. Financial award application deadline: 5/15; financial award applicants required to submit FAFSA. *Unit head:* Dr. Carol Cummings, Chair, 401-456-8046. *Application contact:* Dr. Carol Cummings, Chair, 401-456-8046.
Website: http://www.ric.edu/healthphysicaleducation/Pages/default.aspx

Salem State University, School of Graduate Studies, Program in Physical Education, Salem, MA 01970-5353. Offers M Ed. *Program availability:* Part-time, evening/weekend. *Entrance requirements:* For master's, GRE or MAT. Additional exam requirements/recommendations for international students: Required—TOEFL (minimum score 550 paper-based; 80 iBT) or IELTS (minimum score 5.5).

Slippery Rock University of Pennsylvania, Graduate Studies (Recruitment), College of Education, Department of Physical and Health Education, Slippery Rock, PA 16057-1383. Offers adapted physical activity (MS). *Faculty:* 4 full-time (2 women). *Students:* 12 full-time (8 women), 1 (woman) part-time; includes 1 minority (Black or African American, non-Hispanic/Latino), 2 international. Average age 23. 23 applicants, 70% accepted, 10 enrolled. In 2018, 7 master's awarded. *Degree requirements:* For master's, internship. *Entrance requirements:* For master's, official transcripts, minimum GPA of 2.75, two letters of recommendation, essay. Additional exam requirements/recommendations for international students: Required—TOEFL (minimum score 550 paper-based; 80 iBT). *Application deadline:* For fall admission, 3/1 priority date for domestic students, 5/1 priority date for international students; for spring admission, 10/1 priority date for domestic students. Applications are processed on a rolling basis. Application fee: $25 ($30 for international students). Electronic applications accepted. *Expenses:* Contact institution. *Financial support:* In 2018–19, 8 students received support. Career-related internships or fieldwork, Federal Work-Study, institutionally sponsored loans, scholarships/grants, tuition waivers (partial), and unspecified assistantships available. Support available to part-time students. Financial award application deadline: 5/1; financial award applicants required to submit FAFSA. *Unit head:* Dr. Randall Nichols, Graduate Coordinator, 724-738-2818, Fax: 724-738-2921, E-mail: randall.nichols@sru.edu. *Application contact:* Brandi Weber-Mortimer, Director of Graduate Admissions, 724-738-2051, Fax: 724-738-2146, E-mail: graduate.admissions@sru.edu.
Website: http://www.sru.edu/academics/colleges-and-departments/coe/departments/physical-and-health-education

Southern Connecticut State University, School of Graduate Studies, School of Health and Human Services, Department of Exercise Science, New Haven, CT 06515-1355. Offers human performance (MS); physical education (MS); school health education (MS). *Program availability:* Part-time, evening/weekend. *Degree requirements:* For master's, thesis or alternative. *Entrance requirements:* For master's, interview. Electronic applications accepted.

Southern Illinois University Carbondale, Graduate School, College of Education and Human Services, Department of Kinesiology, Carbondale, IL 62901-4701. Offers MS Ed. *Program availability:* Part-time. *Degree requirements:* For master's, thesis. *Entrance requirements:* For master's, GRE, minimum GPA of 2.7. Additional exam requirements/recommendations for international students: Required—TOEFL. *Faculty research:* Caffeine and exercise effects, ground reaction forces in walking and running, social psychology of sports.

Southern Illinois University Edwardsville, Graduate School, School of Education, Health, and Human Behavior, Department of Kinesiology and Health Education, Program in Physical Education and Coaching Pedagogy, Edwardsville, IL 62026. Offers MS Ed. *Program availability:* Part-time, evening/weekend. *Degree requirements:* For master's, comprehensive exam (for some programs), thesis (for some programs). *Entrance requirements:* Additional exam requirements/recommendations for international students: Required—TOEFL (minimum score 550 paper-based, 79 iBT), IELTS (minimum score 6.5), Michigan Test of English Language Proficiency or PTE. Electronic applications accepted.

Southwestern Oklahoma State University, College of Professional and Graduate Studies, School of Behavioral Sciences and Education, Specialization in Kinesiology, Weatherford, OK 73096-3098. Offers health and physical education (M Ed); sports management (M Ed). *Program availability:* Part-time. *Degree requirements:* For master's, exam. *Entrance requirements:* For master's, GRE General Test or minimum undergraduate GPA of 3.0. Additional exam requirements/recommendations for international students: Required—TOEFL (minimum score 550 paper-based), IELTS (minimum score 6.5).

Springfield College, Graduate Programs, Programs in Physical Education, Springfield, MA 01109-3797. Offers adapted physical education (MS); advanced-level coaching (M Ed); athletic administration (MS); exercise physiology (PhD); health promotion and disease prevention (MS); physical education initial licensure (CAGS); sport and exercise psychology (PhD); teaching and administration (PhD). *Program availability:* Part-time. *Degree requirements:* For master's, comprehensive exam, thesis (for some programs). *Entrance requirements:* For master's and doctorate, GRE General Test. Additional exam requirements/recommendations for international students: Required—TOEFL (minimum score 550 paper-based); Recommended—IELTS (minimum score 7). Electronic applications accepted.

State University of New York College at Cortland, Graduate Studies, School of Professional Studies, Department of Physical Education, Cortland, NY 13045. Offers adapted physical education (MS Ed); coaching pedagogy (MS Ed); physical education leadership (MS Ed). *Program availability:* Part-time, evening/weekend. *Entrance requirements:* Additional exam requirements/recommendations for international students: Required—TOEFL.

Stony Brook University, State University of New York, School of Professional Development, Stony Brook, NY 11794. Offers coaching (Graduate Certificate); environmental management (MPS); German (MAT); higher education administration (MA, Certificate); human resource management (MS, Graduate Certificate); Italian (MAT); liberal studies (MA); mathematics (MAT); school district business leadership (Advanced Certificate); social studies (MAT); Spanish (MAT). *Program availability:* Part-time, evening/weekend, online learning. *Faculty:* 3 full-time (2 women), 94 part-time/adjunct (40 women). *Students:* 214 full-time (138 women), 1,100 part-time (813 women); includes 313 minority (117 Black or African American, non-Hispanic/Latino; 2 American Indian or Alaska Native, non-Hispanic/Latino; 32 Asian, non-Hispanic/Latino; 140 Hispanic/Latino; 3 Native Hawaiian or other Pacific Islander, non-Hispanic/Latino; 19 Two or more races, non-Hispanic/Latino), 7 international. Average age 33. 483 applicants, 89% accepted, 337 enrolled. In 2018, 315 master's, 178 other advanced degrees awarded. *Entrance requirements:* Additional exam requirements/recommendations for international students: Required—TOEFL (minimum score 85 iBT). *Application deadline:* For fall admission, 1/15 for domestic students, 6/1 for international students; for spring admission, 10/1 for domestic and international students. Applications are processed on a rolling basis. Application fee: $100. *Expenses:* Contact institution. *Financial support:* Fellowships, research assistantships, teaching assistantships, and career-related internships or fieldwork available. Support available to part-time students. *Unit head:* Patricia Malone, Associate Vice President for Professional Education and Assistant Provost for Engaged Learning, 631-632-7512, Fax: 631-632-9046, E-mail: patricia.malone@stonybrook.edu. *Application contact:* Melissa Jordan, Assistant Dean, 631-632-7751, E-mail: melissa.jordan@stonybrook.edu.
Website: http://www.stonybrook.edu/spd/

Sul Ross State University, College of Professional Studies, Department of Physical Education, Alpine, TX 79832. Offers M Ed. *Program availability:* Part-time. *Entrance requirements:* For master's, GMAT or GRE General Test, minimum GPA of 2.5 in last 60 hours of undergraduate work.

Teachers College, Columbia University, Department of Biobehavioral Sciences, New York, NY 10027-6696. Offers applied exercise physiology (Ed M, MA, Ed D); communication sciences and disorders (MS, Ed D, PhD); kinesiology (PhD); motor learning and control (Ed M, MA); motor learning/movement science (Ed D); neuroscience and education (MS); physical education (MA, Ed D). *Accreditation:* ASHA. *Program availability:* Part-time, evening/weekend. *Students:* 126 full-time (111 women), 203 part-time (162 women); includes 137 minority (24 Black or African American, non-Hispanic/Latino; 42 Asian, non-Hispanic/Latino; 62 Hispanic/Latino; 9 Two or more races, non-Hispanic/Latino), 36 international. Average age 28. 643 applicants, 51% accepted, 150 enrolled. *Unit head:* Prof. Carol Garber, Chair, 212-678-3891, E-mail: garber@tc.columbia.edu. *Application contact:* Kelly Sutton Skinner, Director of Admission & New Student Enrollment, 212-678-3305, E-mail: kms2237@tc.columbia.edu.
Website: http://www.tc.columbia.edu/biobehavioral-sciences/

Temple University, College of Public Health, Department of Kinesiology, Philadelphia, PA 19122. Offers athletic training (MSAT, DAT); kinesiology (MS, PhD); neuromotor science (MS, PhD). *Faculty:* 19 full-time (8 women), 5 part-time/adjunct (2 women). *Students:* 56 full-time (36 women), 39 part-time (20 women); includes 26 minority (13 Black or African American, non-Hispanic/Latino; 2 Asian, non-Hispanic/Latino; 6 Hispanic/Latino; 5 Two or more races, non-Hispanic/Latino), 3 international. 78 applicants, 74% accepted, 37 enrolled. In 2018, 15 master's awarded. *Degree requirements:* For master's, thesis optional, research project; for doctorate, thesis/dissertation, preliminary examination. *Entrance requirements:* For master's, GRE/MAT, letters of reference, statement of goals, interview, resume; for doctorate, GRE/MAT, minimum undergraduate GPA of 3.25, 3 letters of reference, statement of goals, writing sample, interview, resume. Additional exam requirements/recommendations for international students: Required—TOEFL (minimum score 79 iBT), IELTS (minimum score 6.5), PTE (minimum score 53), one of three is required. *Application deadline:* For fall admission, 3/1 for domestic students. Applications are processed on a rolling basis. Application fee: $60. Electronic applications accepted. *Expenses:* Contact institution. *Financial support:* Fellowships, research assistantships, teaching assistantships, career-related internships or fieldwork, Federal Work-Study, health care benefits, and unspecified assistantships available. Financial award applicants required to submit FAFSA. *Faculty research:* Integrative exercise physiology, athletic training, evaluation of clinical evidence, osteoarthritis. *Unit head:* Jeffrey S Gehris, Interim Department Chair, 214-204-1954, E-mail: jgehris@temple.edu. *Application contact:* Amy Costik, Assistant Director of Admissions, 215-204-5229, E-mail: amy.costik@temple.edu.
Website: http://cph.temple.edu/kinesiology/home

Tennessee State University, The School of Graduate Studies and Research, College of Health Sciences, Department of Human Performance and Sports Sciences, Nashville, TN 37209-1561. Offers exercise science (MA Ed); sports administration (MA Ed). *Degree requirements:* For master's, thesis optional. *Entrance requirements:* For master's, GRE General Test or MAT.

Tennessee Technological University, College of Graduate Studies, College of Education, Department of Exercise Science, Physical Education and Wellness, Cookeville, TN 38505. Offers adapted physical education (MA); elementary/middle school physical education (MA); lifetime wellness (MA); sport management (MA). *Accreditation:* NCATE. *Program availability:* Part-time, online learning. *Faculty:* 7 full-time (0 women). *Students:* 12 full-time (10 women), 45 part-time (22 women); includes 8 minority (3 Black or African American, non-Hispanic/Latino; 1 Asian, non-Hispanic/Latino; 2 Hispanic/Latino; 2 Two or more races, non-Hispanic/Latino), 1 international. 43 applicants, 67% accepted, 22 enrolled. In 2018, 17 master's awarded. *Degree requirements:* For master's, comprehensive exam, thesis or alternative. *Entrance requirements:* For master's, MAT or GRE. Additional exam requirements/recommendations for international students: Required—TOEFL (minimum score 527 paper-based; 71 iBT), IELTS (minimum score 5.5), PTE (minimum score 48), or TOEIC (Test of English as an International Communication). *Application deadline:* For fall admission, 8/1 for domestic students, 5/1 for international students; for spring admission, 12/1 for domestic students, 10/1 for international students; for summer admission, 5/1 for domestic students, 2/1 for international students. Applications are processed on a rolling basis. Application fee: $35 ($40 for international students). Electronic applications accepted. *Financial support:* Fellowships, research assistantships, teaching assistantships, and career-related internships or fieldwork available. Financial award application deadline: 4/1. *Unit head:* Dr. Christy Killman, Chairperson, 931-372-3467, Fax: 931-372-6319, E-mail: ckillman@tntech.edu. *Application contact:* Shelia K. Kendrick, Coordinator of Graduate Studies, 931-372-3808, Fax: 931-372-3497, E-mail: skendrick@tntech.edu.

Physical Education

Texas Southern University, College of Education, Department of Health and Kinesiology, Houston, TX 77004-4584. Offers health education (MS); human performance (MS). *Program availability:* Part-time, evening/weekend. *Degree requirements:* For master's, comprehensive exam, thesis optional. *Entrance requirements:* For master's, GRE General Test, minimum GPA of 2.5. Additional exam requirements/recommendations for international students: Required—TOEFL. Electronic applications accepted.

Union College, Graduate Programs, Department of Education, Barbourville, KY 40906-1499. Offers elementary education (MA); health and physical education (MA); middle grades (MA); music education (MA); principalship (MA); reading specialist (MA); secondary education (MA); special education (MA). *Degree requirements:* For master's, thesis optional. *Entrance requirements:* For master's, GRE General Test, NTE.

United States Sports Academy, Graduate Programs, Program in Sports Coaching, Daphne, AL 36526-7055. Offers MSS. *Program availability:* Part-time, 100% online. *Degree requirements:* For master's, comprehensive exam, thesis optional. *Entrance requirements:* For master's, GRE General Test, GMAT, or MAT, minimum GPA of 2.5, 3 letters of recommendation, personal statement. Additional exam requirements/recommendations for international students: Required—TOEFL (minimum score 550 paper-based; 79 iBT). Electronic applications accepted. *Expenses:* Contact institution. *Faculty research:* Effect of attentional skill on sports performance, survey of coaching qualifications, coaching certification.

Universidad del Turabo, Graduate Programs, Programs in Education, Program in Coaching, Gurabo, PR 00778-3030. Offers MPHE. *Entrance requirements:* For master's, GRE, EXADEP, GMAT, interview, official transcript, essay, recommendation letters. Electronic applications accepted.

Universidad Metropolitana, School of Education, Program in Teaching of Physical Education, San Juan, PR 00928-1150. Offers teaching of adult physical education (M Ed); teaching of elementary physical education (M Ed); teaching of secondary physical education (M Ed). *Degree requirements:* For master's, thesis or alternative. *Entrance requirements:* For master's, EXADEP, interview. Electronic applications accepted.

Université de Montréal, Department of Kinesiology, Montréal, QC H3C 3J7, Canada. Offers kinesiology (M Sc, DESS); physical activity (M Sc, PhD). *Degree requirements:* For master's, one foreign language, thesis (for some programs); for doctorate, one foreign language, thesis/dissertation, general exam. Electronic applications accepted. *Faculty research:* Physiology of exercise, psychology of sports, biomechanics, dance, sociology of sports.

Université de Sherbrooke, Faculty of Physical Education and Sports, Program in Physical Education, Sherbrooke, QC J1K 2R1, Canada. Offers kinanthropology (M Sc); physical activity (Diploma). *Degree requirements:* For master's, thesis. *Entrance requirements:* For master's, minimum GPA of 2.7; for Diploma, bachelor's degree in physical education. *Faculty research:* Physical fitness, nutrition, human factors, sociology, teaching.

Université du Québec à Trois-Rivières, Graduate Programs, Program in Physical Education, Trois-Rivières, QC G9A 5H7, Canada. Offers M Sc. *Program availability:* Part-time. *Degree requirements:* For master's, thesis. *Entrance requirements:* For master's, appropriate bachelor's degree, proficiency in French.

The University of Akron, Graduate School, College of Health Professions, School of Sport Science and Wellness Education, Program in Sport Science/Coaching, Akron, OH 44325. Offers MA, MS. *Degree requirements:* For master's, comprehensive exam, thesis optional. *Entrance requirements:* For master's, minimum GPA of 2.75, three letters of recommendation, statement of purpose. Additional exam requirements/recommendations for international students: Required—TOEFL (minimum score 79 iBT), IELTS (minimum score 6.5). Electronic applications accepted.

The University of Alabama, Graduate School, College of Education, Department of Kinesiology, Tuscaloosa, AL 35487. Offers alternative sport pedagogy (MA); exercise science (PhD). *Program availability:* Part-time. *Degree requirements:* For master's, comprehensive exam, thesis optional; for doctorate, comprehensive exam, thesis/dissertation. *Entrance requirements:* For master's and doctorate, GRE, minimum GPA of 3.0. Additional exam requirements/recommendations for international students: Required—TOEFL. Electronic applications accepted.

University of Alberta, Faculty of Kinesiology, Sport, and Recreation, Edmonton, AB T6G 2E1, Canada. Offers physical education (M Sc); recreation and physical education (MA, PhD). *Program availability:* Part-time. Terminal master's awarded for partial completion of doctoral program. *Degree requirements:* For master's, thesis (for some programs); for doctorate, thesis/dissertation. *Entrance requirements:* For master's, bachelor's degree in related field; for doctorate, master's degree in related field with thesis. Additional exam requirements/recommendations for international students: Required—TOEFL. *Faculty research:* Motivation and adherence to physical ability, performance enhancement, adapted physical activity, exercise physiology, sport administration, tourism.

University of Arkansas, Graduate School, College of Education and Health Professions, Department of Health, Human Performance and Recreation, Program in Physical Education, Fayetteville, AR 72701. Offers M Ed, MAT. In 2018, 15 master's awarded. *Application deadline:* For fall admission, 8/1 for domestic students, 4/1 for international students; for spring admission, 12/1 for domestic students, 10/1 for international students; for summer admission, 4/15 for domestic students, 3/1 for international students. Applications are processed on a rolling basis. Application fee: $60. Electronic applications accepted. *Financial support:* Fellowships with tuition reimbursements, research assistantships, teaching assistantships, career-related internships or fieldwork, and Federal Work-Study available. Support available to part-time students. Financial award application deadline: 4/1; financial award applicants required to submit FAFSA. *Unit head:* Dr. Matthew Ganio, Department Chairperson, 479-575-2956, E-mail: msganio@uark.edu. *Application contact:* Dr. Paul Calleja, Assistant Dept. Head - HHPR, Graduate Coordinator, 479-575-2854, Fax: 479-575-5778, E-mail: pcallej@uark.edu.
Website: https://kins.uark.edu/degrees/med-physical-education/index.php

The University of British Columbia, Faculty of Education, Department of Curriculum and Pedagogy, Vancouver, BC V6T 1Z4, Canada. Offers art education (M Ed, MA); curriculum studies (M Ed, MA, PhD); home economics education (M Ed, MA); mathematics education (M Ed, MA); media and technology studies education (M Ed, MA); music education (M Ed, MA); physical education (M Ed, MA); science education (M Ed, MA); social studies education (M Ed, MA). *Program availability:* Part-time, online learning. *Degree requirements:* For master's, thesis (MA); for doctorate, comprehensive exam, thesis/dissertation. *Entrance requirements:* Additional exam requirements/recommendations for international students: Required—TOEFL, IELTS. Electronic applications accepted. *Expenses:* Contact institution. *Faculty research:* School subjects, teaching and learning.

University of Dayton, Department of Health and Sport Science, Dayton, OH 45469. Offers exercise science (MS Ed). *Program availability:* Part-time, 100% online. *Degree requirements:* For master's, thesis. *Entrance requirements:* For master's, GRE General

Test or MAT if undergraduate GPA was 2.75 or below, minimum GPA of 2.75; official academic records of all previously-attended colleges or universities; three letters of recommendation from professors or employers; personal statement or resume. Additional exam requirements/recommendations for international students: Required—TOEFL (minimum score 550 paper-based; 80 iBT). Electronic applications accepted. *Expenses:* Contact institution. *Faculty research:* Exercise science, physiology, nutrition, sport management.

University of Florida, Graduate School, College of Health and Human Performance, Department of Applied Physiology and Kinesiology, Gainesville, FL 32611. Offers applied physiology and kinesiology (MS); athletic training/sports medicine (MS); biobehavioral science (MS); clinical exercise physiology (MS); exercise physiology (MS); health and human performance (PhD), including applied physiology and kinesiology, biobehavioral science, exercise physiology; human performance (MS). *Degree requirements:* For master's, comprehensive exam, thesis (for some programs); for doctorate, comprehensive exam, thesis/dissertation. *Entrance requirements:* For master's and doctorate, GRE General Test, minimum GPA of 3.0. Additional exam requirements/recommendations for international students: Required—TOEFL (minimum score 550 paper-based; 80 iBT), IELTS (minimum score 6). Electronic applications accepted. *Faculty research:* Cardiovascular disease; basic mechanisms that underlie exercise-induced changes in the body at the organ, tissue, cellular and molecular level; development of rehabilitation techniques for regaining motor control after stroke or as a consequence of Parkinson's disease; maintaining optimal health and delaying age-related declines in physiological function; psychomotor mechanisms impacting health and performance across the life span.

University of Georgia, College of Education, Department of Kinesiology, Athens, GA 30602. Offers MS, PhD. *Entrance requirements:* For master's, GRE General Test or MAT; for doctorate, GRE General Test. Additional exam requirements/recommendations for international students: Required—TOEFL. Electronic applications accepted.

University of Houston, College of Liberal Arts and Social Sciences, Department of Health and Human Performance, Houston, TX 77204. Offers exercise science (MS); human nutrition (MS); human space exploration sciences (MS); kinesiology (PhD); physical education (M Ed). *Accreditation:* NCATE (one or more programs are accredited). *Program availability:* Part-time, evening/weekend. *Degree requirements:* For master's, comprehensive exam (for some programs), thesis (for some programs); for doctorate, comprehensive exam, thesis/dissertation, qualifying exam, candidacy paper. *Entrance requirements:* For master's, GRE (minimum 35th percentile on each section), minimum cumulative GPA of 3.0; for doctorate, GRE (minimum 35th percentile on each section), minimum cumulative GPA of 3.3. Additional exam requirements/recommendations for international students: Required—TOEFL (minimum score 550 paper-based; 79 iBT). Electronic applications accepted. *Faculty research:* Biomechanics, exercise physiology, obesity, nutrition, space exploration science.

University of Idaho, College of Graduate Studies, College of Education, Health and Human Sciences, Department of Movement Sciences, Moscow, ID 83844-2401. Offers athletic training (MSAT, DAT); exercise science and health (MS); physical education teacher education (M Ed, MS); recreation, sport, and tourism management (MS). *Faculty:* 19. *Students:* 89 full-time, 9 part-time. Average age 26. In 2018, 43 master's awarded. *Degree requirements:* For doctorate, thesis/dissertation. *Entrance requirements:* For master's and doctorate, minimum GPA of 3.0. Additional exam requirements/recommendations for international students: Required—TOEFL. *Application deadline:* For fall admission, 8/1 for domestic students; for spring admission, 12/15 for domestic students. Applications are processed on a rolling basis. Application fee: $60. Electronic applications accepted. *Expenses:* Tuition, state resident: full-time $7266.44; part-time $474.50 per credit hour. Tuition, nonresident: full-time $24,902; part-time $1453.50 per credit hour. *Required fees:* $2085.56; $45.50 per credit hour. *Financial support:* Research assistantships and teaching assistantships available. Financial award applicants required to submit FAFSA. *Unit head:* Dr. Philip W. Scruggs, Chair, 208-885-7921, E-mail: movementsciences@uidaho.edu. *Application contact:* Dr. Philip W. Scruggs, Chair, 208-885-7921, E-mail: movementsciences@uidaho.edu. Website: https://www.uidaho.edu/ed/mvsc

University of Indianapolis, Graduate Programs, School of Education, Indianapolis, IN 46227-3697. Offers art education (MAT); biology (MAT); chemistry (MAT); curriculum and instruction (MA); earth sciences (MAT); education (MA, MAT); educational leadership (MA); elementary education (MA); English (MAT); French (MAT); math (MAT); physical education (MAT); physics (MAT); secondary education (MA), including art education, education, English education, social studies education; social studies (MAT); Spanish (MAT). *Accreditation:* NCATE. *Program availability:* Part-time, evening/weekend. *Entrance requirements:* For master's, GRE Subject Test, PRAXIS I, minimum GPA of 2.5, 3 letters of recommendation, interview. Additional exam requirements/recommendations for international students: Required—TOEFL (minimum score 550 paper-based). *Faculty research:* Assessment of teacher education, perceptions of prospective teachers by parents.

The University of Kansas, Graduate Studies, School of Education, Department of Health, Sport, and Exercise Sciences, Lawrence, KS 66045. Offers exercise science (MS Ed); health, sport, and exercise sciences (PhD); sport management (MS Ed). *Accreditation:* NCATE. *Program availability:* Part-time, evening/weekend. *Students:* 67 full-time (26 women), 34 part-time (15 women); includes 19 minority (6 Black or African American, non-Hispanic/Latino; 2 American Indian or Alaska Native, non-Hispanic/Latino; 9 Hispanic/Latino; 2 Two or more races, non-Hispanic/Latino), 9 international. Average age 27. 113 applicants, 73% accepted, 53 enrolled. In 2018, 17 master's, 3 doctorates awarded. *Entrance requirements:* For master's, GRE General Test (minimum score 1000, 450 verbal, 450 quantitative, 4.0 analytical), minimum GPA of 3.0, three letters of recommendation, personal statement, resume, writing sample; for doctorate, GRE General Test (minimum score 1100, verbal 500, quantitative 500, analytical 4.5), minimum graduate GPA of 3.5, undergraduate 3.0; three letters of recommendation; personal statement; resume; writing sample; interview with an advisor. Additional exam requirements/recommendations for international students: Required—TOEFL, IELTS. *Application deadline:* For fall admission, 3/15 for domestic and international students; for spring admission, 10/1 for domestic and international students; for summer admission, 3/15 for domestic and international students. Application fee: $65 ($85 for international students). Electronic applications accepted. *Financial support:* Research assistantships, teaching assistantships, Federal Work-Study, scholarships/grants, and unspecified assistantships available. Financial award application deadline: 2/21. *Faculty research:* Exercise and sport psychology, obesity prevention, sexuality health, sport ethics, skeletal muscle cell signaling and performance. *Unit head:* Dr. Joseph Weir, Chair, 785-864-0784, E-mail: joseph.weir@ku.edu. *Application contact:* Robin Bass, Graduate Admissions Coordinator, 785-864-6138, E-mail: rbass@ku.edu. Website: http://hses.soe.ku.edu/

University of Kentucky, Graduate School, College of Education, Program in Kinesiology and Health Promotion, Lexington, KY 40506-0032. Offers biomechanics (MS); exercise physiology (MS, PhD); exercise science (PhD); health promotion (MS, Ed D); physical education training (Ed D); sport leadership (MS); teaching and coaching (MS). Terminal master's awarded for partial completion of doctoral program. *Degree*

requirements: For master's, comprehensive exam, thesis optional; for doctorate, comprehensive exam, thesis/dissertation. *Entrance requirements:* For master's, GRE General Test, minimum undergraduate GPA of 2.75; for doctorate, GRE General Test, minimum graduate GPA of 3.0. Additional exam requirements/recommendations for international students: Required—TOEFL (minimum score 550 paper-based). Electronic applications accepted.

University of Louisville, Graduate School, College of Education and Human Development, Department of Health and Sport Sciences, Louisville, KY 40292-0001. Offers community health education (M Ed); exercise physiology (MS), including health and sport sciences, strength and conditioning; health and physical education (MAT); sport administration (MS). *Program availability:* Part-time, evening/weekend, 100% online, blended/hybrid learning. *Students:* 32 full-time (10 women), 5 part-time (3 women); includes 9 minority (7 Black or African American, non-Hispanic/Latino; 2 Two or more races, non-Hispanic/Latino). Average age 28. 41 applicants, 66% accepted, 21 enrolled. In 2018, 21 master's awarded. Terminal master's awarded for partial completion of doctoral program. *Degree requirements:* For master's, comprehensive exam (for some programs), thesis optional. *Entrance requirements:* For master's, GRE (for most programs), PRAXIS (for educator preparation programs), professional statement, recommendation letters, resume, transcripts. Additional exam requirements/recommendations for international students: Required—TOEFL (minimum score 550 paper-based; 79 iBT); Recommended—IELTS (minimum score 6.5). *Application deadline:* For fall admission, 6/1 priority date for domestic students, 5/1 priority date for international students; for spring admission, 10/1 priority date for domestic students, 11/1 priority date for international students; for summer admission, 3/1 priority date for domestic students, 4/1 priority date for international students. Application fee: $65. *Expenses: Tuition, area resident:* Full-time $6500; part-time $723 per credit hour. Tuition, state resident: full-time $6500. Tuition, nonresident: full-time $13,557; part-time $1507 per credit hour. Tuition and fees vary according to course load and program. *Financial support:* In 2018–19, 15 students received support, including fellowships with full tuition reimbursements available (averaging $21,024 per year), research assistantships (averaging $21,024 per year); teaching assistantships with full tuition reimbursements available, Federal Work-Study, scholarships/grants, health care benefits, tuition waivers (full), and unspecified assistantships also available. Financial award application deadline: 3/1; financial award applicants required to submit FAFSA. *Faculty research:* Sport administration, exercise science, exercise physiology, physical and health education, youth sport development. *Unit head:* Dr. Dylan Naeger, Interim Chair, 502-852-6645, E-mail: hss@louisville.edu. *Application contact:* Dr. Margaret Pentecost, Director of Grad Assistant Dean for Graduate Student Success Graduate Student Services, 502-852-6437, Fax: 502-852-1465, E-mail: gedadm@louisville.edu. Website: http://www.louisville.edu/education/departments/hss

University of Louisville, Graduate School, College of Education and Human Development, Departments of Early Childhood and Elementary Education, Middle and Secondary Education, and Special Education, Louisville, KY 40292-0001. Offers art education (MAT); autism and applied behavior analysis (Certificate); curriculum and instruction (PhD); early elementary education (MAT); exercise physiology (MS); health and physical education (MAT); health professions education (Certificate); higher education (MA); human resources and organization development (MS); instructional technology (M Ed); interdisciplinary early childhood education (MAT); middle school education (MAT); music education (MAT); secondary education (MAT); special education (MAT); sport administration (MS); teacher leadership (M Ed). *Program availability:* Part-time, evening/weekend, 100% online, blended/hybrid learning. *Faculty:* 97 full-time (64 women), 131 part-time/adjunct (86 women). *Students:* 109 full-time (72 women), 139 part-time (87 women); includes 43 minority (18 Black or African American, non-Hispanic/Latino; 6 Asian, non-Hispanic/Latino; 10 Hispanic/Latino; 9 Two or more races, non-Hispanic/Latino), 9 international. Average age 29. 108 applicants, 75% accepted, 59 enrolled. In 2018, 64 master's awarded. Terminal master's awarded for partial completion of doctoral program. *Degree requirements:* For master's, comprehensive exam (for some programs), thesis optional; for doctorate, comprehensive exam (for some programs), thesis/dissertation. *Entrance requirements:* For master's, GRE (for most programs), PRAXIS (for educator preparation programs), professional statement, recommendation letters, resume, transcripts; for doctorate and Certificate, GRE, professional statement, recommendation letters, resume, transcripts. Additional exam requirements/recommendations for international students: Required—TOEFL (minimum score 550 paper-based; 79 iBT); Recommended—IELTS (minimum score 6.5). *Application deadline:* For fall admission, 6/1 priority date for domestic students, 5/1 priority date for international students; for spring admission, 10/1 for domestic students, 11/1 priority date for international students; for summer admission, 3/1 priority date for domestic students, 4/1 priority date for international students. Application fee: $65. *Expenses: Tuition, area resident:* Full-time $6500; part-time $723 per credit hour. Tuition, state resident: full-time $6500. Tuition, nonresident: full-time $13,557; part-time $1507 per credit hour. Tuition and fees vary according to course load and program. *Financial support:* In 2018–19, 144 students received support, including fellowships with full tuition reimbursements available (averaging $21,024 per year), research assistantships with full tuition reimbursements available (averaging $21,024 per year), teaching assistantships with full tuition reimbursements available (averaging $21,024 per year); Federal Work-Study, scholarships/grants, health care benefits, tuition waivers (full), and unspecified assistantships also available. Financial award application deadline: 3/1; financial award applicants required to submit FAFSA. *Faculty research:* Children's early reading and writing development, crelevance of basic facts in elementary mathematics instruction, clinical model of teacher education, cultural and linguistic context of diverse learners, and STEM-integrated curriculum design and development. STEM teaching and learning, content literacy for English language learners, social justice in teacher education, adolescent literacy, mathematics teacher development. Classroom and behavior management; moderate/severe disabilities, autism. *Unit head:* Dr. Amy Lingo, Interim Dean, 502-852-3235, Fax: 502-852-1464, E-mail: cehdinfo@louisville.edu. *Application contact:* Dr. Margaret Pentecost, Assistant Dean for Graduate Student Success, 502-852-6437, Fax: 502-852-1417, E-mail: gedadm@louisville.edu. Website: http://louisville.edu/delphi

University of Maine, Graduate School, College of Education and Human Development, School of Kinesiology, Physical Education and Athletic Training, Orono, ME 04469. Offers classroom technology integrationist (CGS); education data specialist (CGS); educational technology coordinator (CGS); kinesiology and physical education (M Ed, MS); science education (M Ed, MS); STEM education (PhD). *Program availability:* Part-time, evening/weekend. *Faculty:* 3 full-time (0 women). *Students:* 9 full-time (5 women), 2 part-time (0 women); includes 2 minority (1 Black or African American, non-Hispanic/Latino; 1 Asian, non-Hispanic/Latino). Average age 24. 8 applicants, 75% accepted, 3 enrolled. In 2018, 3 master's awarded. *Degree requirements:* For master's, thesis (for some programs); for doctorate, comprehensive exam, thesis/dissertation. *Entrance requirements:* For master's, GRE General Test, MAT; for doctorate, GRE General Test. Additional exam requirements/recommendations for international students: Required—TOEFL. *Application deadline:* For fall admission, 1/15 for domestic students. Applications are processed on a rolling basis. Application fee: $65. Electronic applications accepted. *Financial support:* In 2018–19, 7 students received support,

including 6 teaching assistantships with full tuition reimbursements available (averaging $15,600 per year); Federal Work-Study, scholarships/grants, and unspecified assistantships also available. Financial award application deadline: 3/1. *Faculty research:* Geriatric equilibrium, physical activity and technology, muscle cell metabolism, hormonal response to exercise. *Unit head:* Dr. Jim Artesani, Associate Dean of Accreditation and Graduate Affairs, 207-581-4061, Fax: 207-581-2423. *Application contact:* Scott G. Delcourt, Assistant Vice President for Graduate Studies and Senior Associate Dean, 207-581-3291, Fax: 207-581-3232, E-mail: graduate@maine.edu. Website: http://umaine.edu/edhd/

University of Manitoba, Faculty of Graduate Studies, Faculty of Kinesiology and Recreation Management, Winnipeg, MB R3T 2N2, Canada. Offers kinesiology and recreation (M Sc, MA).

University of Mary, School of Health Sciences, Program in Sports and Physical Education Administration, Bismarck, ND 58504-9652. Offers MS. *Program availability:* Online learning. *Entrance requirements:* For master's, bachelor's degree in athletic training, exercise science, physical education, or a related field; minimum undergraduate GPA of 2.5.

University of Memphis, Graduate School, School of Health Studies, Memphis, TN 38152. Offers faith and health (Graduate Certificate); health studies (MS), including exercise, sport and movement sciences, health promotion, physical education teacher education; nutrition (MS), including clinical nutrition, environmental nutrition, nutrition science; sport nutrition and dietary supplementation (Graduate Certificate). *Program availability:* 100% online. *Faculty:* 20 full-time (11 women), 3 part-time/adjunct (all women). *Students:* 55 full-time (41 women), 49 part-time (33 women); includes 40 minority (34 Black or African American, non-Hispanic/Latino; 1 Asian, non-Hispanic/Latino; 4 Hispanic/Latino; 1 Two or more races, non-Hispanic/Latino), 6 international. Average age 31. 74 applicants, 64% accepted, 42 enrolled. In 2018, 38 master's, 2 other advanced degrees awarded. *Degree requirements:* For master's, comprehensive exam, thesis or alternative, culminating experience; for Graduate Certificate, practicum. *Entrance requirements:* For master's, GRE or PRAXIS II, letters of recommendation, statement of goals, minimum undergraduate GPA of 2.5; for Graduate Certificate, minimum undergraduate GPA of 2.5. Additional exam requirements/recommendations for international students: Required—TOEFL (minimum score 550 paper-based; 79 iBT). *Application deadline:* For fall admission, 4/15 priority date for domestic students; for spring admission, 10/15 priority date for domestic students; for summer admission, 4/15 priority date for domestic students. Application fee: $35 ($60 for international students). *Expenses: Tuition, area resident:* Full-time $10,240; part-time $503 per credit hour. Tuition, state resident: full-time $10,464. Tuition, nonresident: full-time $20,224; part-time $991 per credit hour. *Required fees:* $850; $106 per credit hour. *Financial support:* Research assistantships, teaching assistantships, career-related internships or fieldwork, Federal Work-Study, scholarships/grants, and unspecified assistantships available. Financial award application deadline: 2/1; financial award applicants required to submit FAFSA. *Unit head:* Dr. Richard Bloomer, Dean, 901-678-4316, Fax: 901-678-3591, E-mail: rbloomer@memphis.edu. *Application contact:* Dr. Richard Bloomer, Dean, 901-678-4316, Fax: 901-678-3591, E-mail: rbloomer@memphis.edu. Website: http://www.memphis.edu/shs/

University of Montana, Graduate School, Phyllis J. Washington College of Education and Human Sciences, Department of Health and Human Performance, Missoula, MT 59812. Offers community health (MS); exercise science (MS); health and human performance generalist (MS). *Program availability:* Part-time. *Entrance requirements:* For master's, GRE General Test. Additional exam requirements/recommendations for international students: Required—TOEFL. *Faculty research:* Exercise physiology, performance psychology, nutrition, pre-employment physical screening, program evaluation.

University of Nebraska at Kearney, College of Education, Kinesiology and Sport Sciences Department, Kearney, NE 68849-0001. Offers general physical education (MA Ed), including recreation and leisure, sports administration; physical education exercise science (MA Ed); physical education master teacher (MA Ed), including pedagogy, special populations. *Program availability:* Part-time, evening/weekend, 100% online. *Degree requirements:* For master's, comprehensive exam, thesis optional. *Entrance requirements:* For master's, GRE General Test (for some programs), personal statement. Additional exam requirements/recommendations for international students: Recommended—TOEFL (minimum score 550 paper-based; 79 iBT), IELTS (minimum score 6.5). Electronic applications accepted. *Faculty research:* Ergonomic aids, nutrition, motor development, sports pedagogy, applied behavior analysis, physical activity and wellness, athletic training, therapeutic Interventions, exercise physiology, endocrinology and metabolism.

University of New Brunswick Fredericton, School of Graduate Studies, Faculty of Kinesiology, Fredericton, NB E3B 5A3, Canada. Offers exercise and sport science (M Sc); sport and recreation management (MBA); sport and recreation studies (MA). *Program availability:* Part-time. *Degree requirements:* For master's, thesis (for some programs). *Entrance requirements:* For master's, GMAT (minimum score of 550 for sport and recreation management program), minimum GPA of 3.0, written statement of research goals and interests. Additional exam requirements/recommendations for international students: Required—TOEFL (minimum score 92 iBT), IELTS (minimum score 7). Electronic applications accepted.

University of New Hampshire, Graduate School, College of Health and Human Services, Department of Kinesiology, Durham, NH 03824. Offers adapted physical education (Postbaccalaureate Certificate); kinesiology (MS); kinesiology and social work (MS). *Program availability:* Part-time. *Entrance requirements:* For master's, GRE General Test. Additional exam requirements/recommendations for international students: Required—TOEFL (minimum score 550 paper-based; 80 iBT). Electronic applications accepted.

University of New Mexico, Graduate Studies, College of Education, Program in Physical Education, Sports and Exercise Science, Albuquerque, NM 87131-2039. Offers curriculum and instruction (PhD); exercise science (PhD); sports administration (PhD). *Program availability:* Part-time. *Students:* Average age 30. 67 applicants, 75% accepted, 35 enrolled. In 2018, 13 doctorates awarded. *Degree requirements:* For doctorate, comprehensive exam, thesis/dissertation, inquiry skills, 24 credits in supporting area. *Entrance requirements:* For doctorate, GRE, letter of intent, 3 letters of reference, minimum cumulative GPA of 3.0 in last 2 years of bachelor's degree. Additional exam requirements/recommendations for international students: Required—TOEFL (minimum score 550 paper-based). *Application deadline:* For fall admission, 3/1 priority date for domestic students; for spring admission, 11/1 priority date for domestic students. Application fee: $50. Electronic applications accepted. *Financial support:* Fellowships, teaching assistantships with full tuition reimbursements, career-related internships or fieldwork, Federal Work-Study, institutionally sponsored loans, scholarships/grants, health care benefits, tuition waivers, and unspecified assistantships available. Financial award application deadline: 3/1; financial award applicants required to submit FAFSA. *Faculty research:* Facility risk management, physical education pedagogy practices, physiological adaptations to exercise, physiological adaptations to heat, sport leadership. *Unit head:* Dr. Todd Seidler, Chair, 505-277-2783, Fax: 505-277-6227,

E-mail: tseidler@unm.edu. *Application contact:* Monica Lopez, Program Office, 505-277-5151, Fax: 505-277-6227, E-mail: mllopez@unm.edu.
Website: https://coe.unm.edu/departments-programs/hess/physical-education/physical-education-phd/index.html

University of North Alabama, College of Education, Department of Health, Physical Education, and Recreation, Florence, AL 35632-0001. Offers health and human performance (MS), including exercise science, kinesiology, wellness and health promotion. *Program availability:* Part-time. *Degree requirements:* For master's, comprehensive exam (for some programs), thesis optional. *Entrance requirements:* For master's, MAT or GRE, 3 letters of recommendation, essay. Additional exam requirements/recommendations for international students: Required—TOEFL (minimum score 79 iBT), IELTS (minimum score 6), PTE (minimum score 54). Electronic applications accepted.

The University of North Carolina at Chapel Hill, Graduate School, College of Arts and Sciences, Department of Exercise and Sport Science, Chapel Hill, NC 27599. Offers athletic training (MA); exercise physiology (MA); sport administration (MA). *Degree requirements:* For master's, comprehensive exam, thesis. *Entrance requirements:* For master's, GRE General Test, minimum GPA of 3.0. Additional exam requirements/recommendations for international students: Required—TOEFL (minimum score 550 paper-based). Electronic applications accepted. *Faculty research:* Mild head injury in sport, endocrine system's response to exercise, obesity and children, effect of aerobic exercise on cerebral bloodflow in elderly population.

The University of North Carolina at Pembroke, The Graduate School, School of Education, Department of Health and Human Performance, Pembroke, NC 28372-1510. Offers health/physical education (MAT); physical education (MA), including exercise/sports administration, physical education advanced licensure. *Program availability:* Part-time, evening/weekend. *Degree requirements:* For master's, comprehensive exam, thesis optional. *Entrance requirements:* For master's, MAT or GRE, minimum GPA of 3.0 in major, 2.5 overall. Additional exam requirements/recommendations for international students: Required—TOEFL.

University of Northern Colorado, Graduate School, College of Natural and Health Sciences, School of Sport and Exercise Science, Greeley, CO 80639. Offers exercise science (MS, PhD); physical education and physical activity leadership (MAT); sport administration (MS, PhD); sport pedagogy (MS, PhD); sports coaching (MA). *Program availability:* Part-time, evening/weekend. *Degree requirements:* For master's, comprehensive exam; for doctorate, comprehensive exam, thesis/dissertation. *Entrance requirements:* For master's, 2 letters of recommendation, resume; for doctorate, GRE General Test, 3 letters of recommendation, resume. Electronic applications accepted.

University of Northern Iowa, Graduate College, College of Education, School of Kinesiology, Allied Health and Human Services, MA Program in Physical Education, Cedar Falls, IA 50614. Offers kinesiology (MA); teaching/coaching (MA). *Program availability:* Part-time, evening/weekend. *Degree requirements:* For master's, comprehensive exam, thesis or alternative. *Entrance requirements:* For master's, minimum GPA of 3.0. Additional exam requirements/recommendations for international students: Required—TOEFL (minimum score 500 paper-based; 61 iBT). Electronic applications accepted.

University of North Georgia, Master of Arts in Teaching Program, Dahlonega, GA 30597. Offers physical education (MAT); secondary education - English (MAT); secondary education - history (MAT); secondary education - mathematics (MAT); secondary education - middle grades (MAT). *Degree requirements:* For master's, internship, capstone. *Entrance requirements:* For master's, GRE or MAT, GACE I and II, GA pre-service application, lawful presence verification, official transcripts, GA Educator Ethics Program entry assessment. Additional exam requirements/recommendations for international students: Required—TOEFL (minimum score 550 paper-based; 79 iBT), IELTS (minimum score 6.5). Electronic applications accepted. *Expenses:* Contact institution.

University of Rhode Island, Graduate School, College of Health Sciences, Department of Kinesiology, Kingston, RI 02881. Offers cultural studies of sport and physical culture (MS); exercise science (MS); psychosocial/behavioral aspects of physical activity (MS). *Accreditation:* NCATE. *Program availability:* Part-time. *Faculty:* 16 full-time (11 women). *Students:* 13 full-time (5 women), 2 part-time (1 woman), 1 international. 18 applicants, 100% accepted, 8 enrolled. In 2018, 5 master's awarded. *Entrance requirements:* Additional exam requirements/recommendations for international students: Required—TOEFL. *Application deadline:* For fall admission, 7/15 for domestic students, 2/1 for international students; for spring admission, 11/15 for domestic students, 7/15 for international students. Application fee: $65. Electronic applications accepted. *Expenses: Tuition, area resident:* Full-time $13,226; part-time $735 per credit. Tuition, state resident: full-time $13,226; part-time $735 per credit. Tuition, nonresident: full-time $25,854; part-time $1436 per credit. *International tuition:* $25,854 full-time. *Required fees:* $1698; $50 per credit. $35 per semester. One-time fee: $165. *Financial support:* In 2018–19, 1 research assistantship (averaging $8,862 per year), 6 teaching assistantships with tuition reimbursements (averaging $16,247 per year) were awarded. Financial award application deadline: 2/1; financial award applicants required to submit FAFSA. *Unit head:* Dr. Disa Hatfield, Interim Chair, 401-874-5183, E-mail: doch@uri.edu. *Application contact:* Dr. Matthew Delmonico, Graduate Program Director, 401-874-5440, E-mail: delmonico@uri.edu.
Website: http://web.uri.edu/kinesiology/

University of Rio Grande, Graduate School, Rio Grande, OH 45674. Offers athletic coaching leadership (M Ed); educational leadership (M Ed); integrated arts (M Ed); intervention specialist in early childhood (M Ed); intervention specialist in mild/moderate (M Ed). *Accreditation:* NCATE. *Program availability:* Part-time. *Degree requirements:* For master's, final research project, portfolio. *Entrance requirements:* For master's, minimum GPA of 2.7 in major, 2.5 overall. Additional exam requirements/recommendations for international students: Required—TOEFL. *Faculty research:* Interagency collaboration, reading and mathematics, learning styles, college access, literacy.

University of South Alabama, College of Education and Professional Studies, Department of Health, Kinesiology, and Sport, Mobile, AL 36688. Offers exercise science (MS); health education (M Ed, MS); physical education (M Ed); sport management (MS). *Accreditation:* NCATE (one or more programs are accredited). *Program availability:* Part-time. *Degree requirements:* For master's, comprehensive exam, thesis optional. *Entrance requirements:* For master's, GRE General Test or MAT, Alabama Class B certificate or the equivalent (for students seeking the master's-level/Class A certification). Additional exam requirements/recommendations for international students: Required—TOEFL. Electronic applications accepted.

University of South Carolina, The Graduate School, College of Education, Department of Physical Education, Columbia, SC 29208. Offers IMA, MAT, MS, PhD. *Program availability:* Part-time. *Degree requirements:* For master's, comprehensive exam, thesis (for some programs); for doctorate, comprehensive exam, thesis/dissertation. *Entrance requirements:* For master's, GRE General Test, or Miller Analogies Test, writing sample, letter of intent, letters of recommendation; for doctorate, GRE General Test or Miller Analogies Test, writing sample, interview, letter of intent, letters of recommendation. *Faculty research:* Teaching/learning processes, anthropometric measurement, growth and development, motor development.

University of Southern Mississippi, College of Education and Human Sciences, School of Kinesiology, Hattiesburg, MS 39406-0001. Offers MS, PhD. *Program availability:* Part-time, evening/weekend. *Degree requirements:* For master's, comprehensive exam, thesis optional; for doctorate, comprehensive exam, thesis/dissertation. *Entrance requirements:* For master's, GRE General Test, minimum GPA of 2.75 in last 60 hours; for doctorate, GRE General Test, minimum GPA of 3.5. Additional exam requirements/recommendations for international students: Required—TOEFL, IELTS. Electronic applications accepted. *Faculty research:* Exercise physiology, health behaviors, resource management, activity interaction, site development.

The University of Tennessee at Chattanooga, Department of Health and Human Performance, Chattanooga, TN 37403. Offers athletic training (MSAT); health and human performance (MS). *Degree requirements:* For master's, thesis or alternative, clinical rotations. *Entrance requirements:* For master's, GRE General Test, minimum GPA of 2.75 overall or 3.0 in last 60 hours; CPR and First Aid certification. Additional exam requirements/recommendations for international students: Required—TOEFL (minimum score 550 paper-based; 79 iBT), IELTS (minimum score 6). Electronic applications accepted. *Expenses:* Contact institution. *Faculty research:* Therapeutic exercise, lumbar spine biomechanics, physical activity epidemiology, functional rehabilitation outcomes, metabolic health.

The University of Tennessee at Martin, Graduate Programs, College of Education, Health and Behavioral Sciences, Program in Teaching, Martin, TN 38238. Offers curriculum and instruction (MS Ed), including 7-12, K-6; initial licensure (MS Ed), including elementary education, secondary education; initial licensure k-8 (MS Ed), including library service, special education; interdisciplinary (MS Ed). *Program availability:* Part-time, online only, 100% online. *Students:* 24 full-time (20 women), 126 part-time (90 women); includes 19 minority (11 Black or African American, non-Hispanic/Latino; 3 Hispanic/Latino; 5 Two or more races, non-Hispanic/Latino). Average age 34. 69 applicants, 58% accepted, 21 enrolled. In 2018, 28 master's awarded. *Degree requirements:* For master's, comprehensive exam. *Entrance requirements:* For master's, GRE General Test, minimum GPA of 2.5, teaching license. Additional exam requirements/recommendations for international students: Required—TOEFL (minimum score 525 paper-based; 71 iBT). *Application deadline:* For fall admission, 7/27 for domestic and international students; for spring admission, 12/17 for domestic and international students; for summer admission, 5/10 for domestic and international students. Applications are processed on a rolling basis. Application fee: $30 ($130 for international students). Electronic applications accepted. *Expenses: Tuition, area resident:* Full-time $8918; part-time $495 per credit hour. Tuition, state resident: full-time $8918; part-time $485 per credit hour. Tuition, nonresident: full-time $14,958; part-time $831 per credit hour. *International tuition:* $22,862 full-time. *Required fees:* $1446; $81 per credit hour. Part-time tuition and fees vary according to course load. *Financial support:* In 2018–19, 26 students received support, including 1 research assistantship with full tuition reimbursement available (averaging $6,283 per year), 5 teaching assistantships with full tuition reimbursements available (averaging $7,464 per year); scholarships/grants and tuition waivers also available. Financial award application deadline: 2/1; financial award applicants required to submit FAFSA. *Faculty research:* Special education, science/math/technology, school reform, reading. *Unit head:* Cynthia West, Dean, 731-881-7125, Fax: 731-881-7975, E-mail: cwest@utm.edu. *Application contact:* Jolene L. Cunningham, Student Services Specialist, 731-881-7012, Fax: 731-881-7499, E-mail: jcunningham@utm.edu.

The University of Texas at Austin, Graduate School, College of Education, Department of Curriculum and Instruction, Austin, TX 78712-1111. Offers bilingual/bicultural education (M Ed, MA, PhD); cultural studies in education (M Ed, MA, PhD); early childhood education (M Ed, MA, PhD); language and literacy studies (M Ed, PhD); learning technologies (M Ed, MA, PhD); physical education (M Ed, MA, PhD). Terminal master's awarded for partial completion of doctoral program. *Degree requirements:* For doctorate, thesis/dissertation. *Entrance requirements:* For master's and doctorate, GRE General Test. Electronic applications accepted.

The University of Toledo, College of Graduate Studies, Judith Herb College of Education, Department of Early Childhood, Physical and Special Education, Toledo, OH 43606-3390. Offers early childhood education (ME); physical education (ME); special education (ME). *Program availability:* Part-time. *Degree requirements:* For master's, thesis. *Entrance requirements:* For master's, minimum cumulative GPA of 2.7 for all previous academic work, letters of recommendation. Additional exam requirements/recommendations for international students: Required—TOEFL (minimum score 550 paper-based; 80 iBT). Electronic applications accepted.

University of Toronto, School of Graduate Studies, Faculty of Kinesiology and Physical Education, Toronto, ON M5S 1A1, Canada. Offers M Sc, PhD. *Degree requirements:* For master's, thesis, oral defense of thesis; for doctorate, comprehensive exam, defense of thesis. *Entrance requirements:* For master's, background in physical education and health, minimum B+ average in final year of undergraduate study, 2 letters of reference, resume, 2 writing samples; for doctorate, master's degree with successful defense of thesis, background in exercise sciences, minimum A- average, 2 letters of reference. Additional exam requirements/recommendations for international students: Required—TOEFL (minimum score 580 paper-based; 93 iBT), TWE (minimum score 5). Electronic applications accepted.

University of Victoria, Faculty of Graduate Studies, Faculty of Education, School of Exercise Science, Physical, and Health Education, Victoria, BC V8W 2Y2, Canada. Offers coaching studies (co-operative education) (M Ed); kinesiology (M Sc, MA); leisure service administration (MA); physical education (MA). *Program availability:* Part-time. *Degree requirements:* For master's, comprehensive exam (for some programs), thesis (for some programs). *Entrance requirements:* For master's, minimum B average. Additional exam requirements/recommendations for international students: Required—TOEFL (minimum score 575 paper-based), IELTS (minimum score 7). Electronic applications accepted. *Faculty research:* Children and exercise, mental skills in sports, teaching effectiveness, neural control of human movement, physical performance and health.

University of Virginia, Curry School of Education, Department of Kinesiology, Charlottesville, VA 22903. Offers M Ed, MS, PhD. *Entrance requirements:* For master's and doctorate, GRE General Test, 2 letters of recommendation. Additional exam requirements/recommendations for international students: Required—TOEFL (minimum score 600 paper-based; 90 iBT), IELTS (minimum score 7). Electronic applications accepted.

University of Washington, Graduate School, College of Education, Seattle, WA 98195. Offers curriculum and instruction (M Ed, Ed D, PhD), including educational technology, general curriculum (Ed D, PhD), language, literacy, and culture, mathematics education, multicultural education, reading and language arts education (Ed D), science education, social studies education, teaching and curriculum (M Ed); educational leadership and policy studies (M Ed, Ed D, PhD), including administration (Ed D), educational policy, organization, and leadership (M Ed, PhD), higher education, leadership for learning (Ed D), social and cultural foundations of education (M Ed, PhD); educational

psychology (M Ed, PhD), including educational psychology (PhD), human development and cognition (M Ed), learning sciences, measurement, statistics and research design (M Ed), school psychology (M Ed); instructional leadership (M Ed); intercollegiate athletic leadership (M Ed); special education (M Ed, Ed D, PhD), including early childhood special education (M Ed), emotional and behavioral disabilities (M Ed), learning disabilities (M Ed), low-incidence disabilities (M Ed), severe disabilities (M Ed), special education (Ed D, PhD); teacher education (MIT). *Accreditation:* APA. *Program availability:* Part-time, evening/weekend. *Degree requirements:* For master's, thesis optional; for doctorate, thesis/dissertation. *Entrance requirements:* For master's and doctorate, GRE General Test, minimum GPA of 3.0. Additional exam requirements/recommendations for international students: Required—TOEFL. Electronic applications accepted. *Faculty research:* School restructuring/effective schools, special education interventions, literacy and writing, technology, school partnerships, teacher preparation.

The University of West Alabama, School of Graduate Studies, College of Natural Sciences and Mathematics, Program in Physical Education, Livingston, AL 35470. Offers M Ed, MAT, MS. *Program availability:* Part-time, evening/weekend, 100% online. *Faculty:* 4 full-time (1 woman), 2 part-time/adjunct (0 women). *Students:* 112 full-time (39 women), 12 part-time (2 women); includes 45 minority (42 Black or African American, non-Hispanic/Latino; 1 American Indian or Alaska Native, non-Hispanic/Latino; 1 Hispanic/Latino; 1 Two or more races, non-Hispanic/Latino), 3 international. Average age 30. 36 applicants, 92% accepted, 29 enrolled. In 2018, 42 master's awarded. *Degree requirements:* For master's, comprehensive exam, thesis optional, field experience, internship. *Entrance requirements:* For master's, GRE, minimum GPA of 2.75. Additional exam requirements/recommendations for international students: Required—TOEFL (minimum score 500 paper-based; 61 iBT). *Application deadline:* Applications are processed on a rolling basis. Application fee: $40. Electronic applications accepted. *Expenses:* Tuition, area resident: Full-time $9100. Tuition, state resident: full-time $9100. Tuition, nonresident: full-time $19,200. *Required fees:* $1890; $130. *Financial support:* In 2018–19, 3 teaching assistantships (averaging $7,344 per year) were awarded; Federal Work-Study, scholarships/grants, and unspecified assistantships also available. Support available to part-time students. Financial award application deadline: 3/1; financial award applicants required to submit FAFSA. *Unit head:* Dr. R. T. Floyd, Assistant Dean of College of Natural Sciences and Mathematics, 205-652-3714, E-mail: rtf@uwa.edu. *Application contact:* Dr. John McCall, Dean of College of Natural Sciences and Mathematics, 205-652-3414, Fax: 205-652-3831, E-mail: jmccall@uwa.edu.
Website: http://www.uwa.edu/academics/collegeofnaturalsciencesandmathematics

University of West Florida, College of Education and Professional Studies, Ed D Programs, Specialization in Physical Education and Health, Pensacola, FL 32514-5750. Offers Ed D. *Program availability:* Part-time, evening/weekend. *Degree requirements:* For doctorate, comprehensive exam, thesis/dissertation. *Entrance requirements:* For doctorate, GRE, MAT, or GMAT, letter of intent; writing sample; three letters of recommendation; two completed disposition assessment forms; written statement of goals; interview with admissions committee. Additional exam requirements/recommendations for international students: Required—TOEFL (minimum score 550 paper-based).

University of West Florida, Usha Kundu, MD College of Health, Department of Exercise Science and Community Health, Pensacola, FL 32514-5750. Offers health promotion (MS); health, leisure, and exercise science (MS), including exercise science, physical education. *Program availability:* Part-time, evening/weekend. *Degree requirements:* For master's, thesis or alternative. *Entrance requirements:* For master's, GRE or MAT, official transcripts; minimum GPA of 3.0; letter of intent; three personal references; work experience as reflected in resume. Additional exam requirements/recommendations for international students: Required—TOEFL (minimum score 550 paper-based).

University of Wisconsin–La Crosse, College of Science and Health, Department of Exercise and Sport Science, Program in Physical Education Teaching, La Crosse, WI 54601-3742. Offers exercise sport science: physical education teaching (MS), including adapted physical education, adventure education. *Program availability:* Part-time, evening/weekend. *Degree requirements:* For master's, thesis optional. *Entrance requirements:* For master's, minimum GPA of 3.0 during previous 2 years, 2.85 overall; BA in physical education. Additional exam requirements/recommendations for international students: Required—TOEFL (minimum score 550 paper-based; 79 iBT). Electronic applications accepted.

University of Wyoming, College of Health Sciences, Division of Kinesiology and Health, Laramie, WY 82071. Offers MS. *Accreditation:* NCATE. *Program availability:* Part-time, online learning. *Degree requirements:* For master's, comprehensive exam (for some programs), thesis (for some programs). *Entrance requirements:* For master's, GRE General Test, minimum GPA of 3.0. Additional exam requirements/recommendations for international students: Required—TOEFL. Electronic applications accepted. *Expenses: Tuition,* area resident: Full-time $6504; part-time $271 per credit hour. Tuition, state resident: full-time $6504; part-time $271 per credit hour. Tuition, nonresident: full-time $19,464; part-time $811 per credit hour. *International tuition:* $19,464 full-time. *Required fees:* $1410.94; $343.82 per semester. $343.82 per semester. Tuition and fees vary according to course load, program and reciprocity agreements. *Faculty research:* Teacher effectiveness, effects of exercising on heart function, physiological responses of overtraining, psychological benefits of physical activity, health behavior.

Utah State University, School of Graduate Studies, Emma Eccles Jones College of Education and Human Services, Department of Kinesiology and Health Science, Logan, UT 84322. Offers fitness promotion (MS); health and human movement (MS); pathokinesiology (PhD); physical and sport education (M Ed); public health (MPH). *Program availability:* Part-time, evening/weekend, online learning. *Degree requirements:* For master's, thesis (for some programs). *Entrance requirements:* For master's, GRE General Test or MAT, minimum GPA of 3.0. Additional exam requirements/recommendations for international students: Required—TOEFL. *Faculty research:* Sport psychology intervention, motor learning biomechanics, pedagogy, physiology.

Wayne State College, Department of Health, Human Performance and Sport, Wayne, NE 68787. Offers exercise science (MSE); organizational management (MS), including sport management. *Program availability:* Part-time, evening/weekend. *Degree requirements:* For master's, comprehensive exam, thesis optional. *Entrance requirements:* For master's, GRE General Test, minimum GPA of 3.0. Additional exam requirements/recommendations for international students: Required—TOEFL (minimum score 550 paper-based). Electronic applications accepted.

Wayne State University, College of Education, Division of Kinesiology, Health and Sports Studies, Detroit, MI 48202. Offers athletic training (MSAT); health education (M Ed); kinesiology (M Ed, PhD), including exercise and sport science (PhD), physical education and physical activity leadership (PhD); sports administration (MA). *Program availability:* Part-time, evening/weekend. *Faculty:* 9. *Students:* 76 full-time (47 women), 110 part-time (56 women); includes 73 minority (53 Black or African American, non-Hispanic/Latino; 4 Asian, non-Hispanic/Latino; 8 Hispanic/Latino; 8 Two or more races, non-Hispanic/Latino), 9 international. Average age 30. 163 applicants, 60% accepted,

69 enrolled. In 2018, 70 master's, 4 doctorates awarded. *Degree requirements:* For master's, thesis (for some programs); for doctorate, comprehensive exam, thesis/dissertation. *Entrance requirements:* For master's, minimum undergraduate GPA of 3.0; undergraduate degree directly relating to the field of specialization being applied for or one accompanied by extensive educational background in closely-related field; teaching certificates in specific areas (for some programs); for doctorate, minimum undergraduate GPA of 3.0; undergraduate degree directly relating to the field of specialization being applied for or one accompanied by extensive educational background in closely-related field. Additional exam requirements/recommendations for international students: Required—TOEFL (minimum score 550 paper-based; 79 iBT); Recommended—IELTS (minimum score 6.5), TWE (minimum score 5.5), TSE (minimum score 58). *Application deadline:* Applications are processed on a rolling basis. Application fee: $50. Electronic applications accepted. *Financial support:* In 2018–19, 51 students received support. Fellowships with tuition reimbursements available, research assistantships with tuition reimbursements available, teaching assistantships with tuition reimbursements available, scholarships/grants, health care benefits, and unspecified assistantships available. Support available to part-time students. Financial award applicants required to submit FAFSA. *Faculty research:* Exercise and sport science, nutrition and physical activity interventions, school and community health, obesity prevention. *Unit head:* Dr. Nate McCaughtry, Assistant Dean, Division of Kinesiology, Health and Sport Studies/Director, Center for School Health, 313-577-0014, Fax: 313-577-5002, E-mail: aj4391@wayne.edu. *Application contact:* Heather Ladanyi, Manager, 313-577-1191, E-mail: eb3703@wayne.edu.
Website: http://coe.wayne.edu/kinesiology/index.php

West Chester University of Pennsylvania, College of Health Sciences, Department of Kinesiology, West Chester, PA 19383. Offers adapted physical education (Certificate); exercise and sport physiology (MS), including athletic training; sport management and athletics (MPA), including administration. *Program availability:* Part-time, evening/weekend, blended/hybrid learning. *Degree requirements:* For master's, thesis or research report (for MS); two internships and capstone course that includes a research project or thesis (for MPA); for Certificate, six courses of study. *Entrance requirements:* For master's, GRE (for MS), 2 letters of recommendation, statement of professional goals; transcripts (for MS); two letters of reference, career goals, resume (for MPA); for Certificate, two letters of recommendation, transcript. Additional exam requirements/recommendations for international students: Required—TOEFL or IELTS. Electronic applications accepted. *Faculty research:* Metabolism during exercise, biomechanics, rating of perceived exertion, motor learning, environmental physiology.

Western Kentucky University, Graduate School, College of Health and Human Services, Department of Kinesiology, Recreation and Sport, Bowling Green, KY 42101. Offers athletic administration and coaching (MS); physical education (MS); recreation and sport administration (MS). *Program availability:* Part-time, evening/weekend, online learning. *Degree requirements:* For master's, comprehensive exam, thesis optional. *Entrance requirements:* For master's, GRE General Test, minimum GPA of 2.75. Additional exam requirements/recommendations for international students: Required—TOEFL (minimum score 555 paper-based; 79 iBT). *Faculty research:* Orthopedic rehabilitation, fitness center coordination, heat acclimation, biomechanical and physiological parameters.

Western Michigan University, Graduate College, College of Education and Human Development, Department of Health, Physical Education and Recreation, Kalamazoo, MI 49008. Offers athletic training (MS), including exercise physiology; sport management (MA), including pedagogy, special physical education.

Western Washington University, Graduate School, College of Humanities and Social Sciences, Department of Physical Education, Health, and Recreation, Bellingham, WA 98225-5996. Offers exercise science (MS); sport psychology (MS). *Program availability:* Part-time. *Degree requirements:* For master's, thesis. *Entrance requirements:* For master's, GRE General Test, minimum GPA of 3.0 in last 60 semester hours or last 90 quarter hours. Additional exam requirements/recommendations for international students: Required—TOEFL (minimum score 567 paper-based). Electronic applications accepted. *Faculty research:* Spinal motor control, biomechanics/kinesiology, biomechanics of aging, mobility of older adults, fall prevention, exercise interventions and function, magnesium and inspiratory muscle training (IMT).

Westfield State University, College of Graduate and Continuing Education, Department of Education, Westfield, MA 01086. Offers early childhood education (M Ed); elementary education (M Ed); reading specialist (M Ed); secondary education (M Ed), including biology teacher education, chemistry teacher education, general science teacher education, history teacher education, mathematics teacher education, physical education teacher education; special education (M Ed), including moderate disabilities, 5-12, moderate disabilities, preK-8; vocational technical education (M Ed). *Accreditation:* NCATE. *Program availability:* Part-time, evening/weekend. *Degree requirements:* For master's, comprehensive exam, practicum. *Entrance requirements:* For master's, GRE General Test or MAT, minimum undergraduate GPA of 2.8. Additional exam requirements/recommendations for international students: Recommended—TOEFL (minimum score 550 paper-based; 79 iBT). *Faculty research:* Collaborative teacher education, developmental early childhood education.

Westfield State University, College of Graduate and Continuing Education, Department of Education, Programs in Secondary Education, Program in Physical Education Teacher Education, Westfield, MA 01086. Offers secondary education-physical education (M Ed). *Program availability:* Part-time, evening/weekend. *Degree requirements:* For master's, comprehensive exam, thesis (for some programs). *Entrance requirements:* For master's, GRE General Test or MAT, minimum undergraduate GPA of 2.8. Additional exam requirements/recommendations for international students: Recommended—TOEFL (minimum score 550 paper-based; 79 iBT).

West Liberty University, College of Education and Human Performance, West Liberty, WV 26074. Offers community education research and leadership (MA Ed); innovative instruction (MA Ed); leadership in disability services (MA Ed); leadership studies (MA Ed); multi-categorical special education (MA Ed); reading specialist (MA Ed); sports leadership and coaching (MA Ed). *Accreditation:* NCATE. *Program availability:* Part-time, evening/weekend. *Degree requirements:* For master's, capstone experience. *Entrance requirements:* For master's, minimum GPA of 2.5 or 3.0 (depending on track). Additional exam requirements/recommendations for international students: Required—TOEFL. Electronic applications accepted.

West Virginia University, College of Physical Activity and Sport Sciences, Morgantown, WV 26506. Offers athletic training (MS); coaching and sport education (MS); coaching and teaching studies (Ed D, PhD), including curriculum and instruction (PhD); physical education/teacher education (MS); sport coaching (MS); sport management (MS); sport, exercise & performance psychology (MS). *Students:* 98 full-time (40 women), 122 part-time (42 women); includes 38 minority (18 Black or African American, non-Hispanic/Latino; 4 Asian, non-Hispanic/Latino; 10 Hispanic/Latino; 6 Two or more races, non-Hispanic/Latino), 13 international. In 2018, 74 master's, 5 doctorates awarded. *Degree requirements:* For doctorate, comprehensive exam, thesis/dissertation, oral exam. *Entrance requirements:* For master's, GRE or MAT, minimum GPA of 3.0; for doctorate, GRE General Test or MAT, minimum GPA of 3.5. Additional

Physical Education

exam requirements/recommendations for international students: Required—TOEFL (minimum score 550 paper-based). *Application deadline:* For fall admission, 12/15 for domestic students, 10/1 for international students. Application fee: $60. Electronic applications accepted. *Financial support:* Research assistantships, teaching assistantships, career-related internships or fieldwork, Federal Work-Study, institutionally sponsored loans, health care benefits, tuition waivers (full and partial), and administrative assistantships available. Support available to part-time students. Financial award application deadline: 2/1; financial award applicants required to submit FAFSA. *Faculty research:* Sport psych sociology, teacher education, exercise psychology, counseling. *Unit head:* Sean Bulger, Online Program Coordinator, 304-293-0845, Fax: 304-293-4641, E-mail: sean.bulger@mail.wvu.edu. *Application contact:* Sean Bulger, Online Program Coordinator, 304-293-0845, Fax: 304-293-4641, E-mail: sean.bulger@mail.wvu.edu.
Website: http://www.cpass.wvu.edu

Wilfrid Laurier University, Faculty of Graduate and Postdoctoral Studies, Faculty of Science, Department of Kinesiology and Physical Education, Waterloo, ON N2L 3C5, Canada. Offers physical activity and health (M Sc). *Degree requirements:* For master's, thesis. *Entrance requirements:* For master's, honours degree in kinesiology, health, physical education with a minimum B+ in kinesiology and health-related courses. Additional exam requirements/recommendations for international students: Required—TOEFL (minimum score 89 iBT). Electronic applications accepted. *Faculty research:* Biomechanics, health, exercise physiology, motor control, sport psychology.

William Woods University, Graduate and Adult Studies, Fulton, MO 65251-1098. Offers administration (M Ed, Ed S); athletic/activities administration (M Ed); curriculum and instruction (M Ed, Ed S); educational leadership (Ed D); equestrian education (M Ed); health management (MBA); human resources (MBA); leadership (MBA); marketing, advertising, and public relations (MBA); teaching and technology (M Ed). *Program availability:* Part-time, evening/weekend. *Degree requirements:* For master's, capstone course (MBA), action research (M Ed); for Ed S, field experience. *Entrance requirements:* Additional exam requirements/recommendations for international students: Required—TOEFL (minimum score 550 paper-based). Electronic applications accepted. *Expenses:* Contact institution.

Winthrop University, College of Education, Program in Physical Education, Rock Hill, SC 29733. Offers MAT. *Program availability:* Part-time. *Students:* 24 full-time (12 women), 3 part-time (0 women); includes 9 minority (all Black or African American, non-Hispanic/Latino). Average age 25. In 2018, 14 master's awarded. *Degree requirements:* For master's, comprehensive exam, thesis optional. *Entrance requirements:* For master's, GRE General Test or PRAXIS. Additional exam requirements/recommendations for international students: Required—TOEFL (minimum score 550 paper-based; 79 iBT), IELTS (minimum score 6). *Application deadline:* For fall admission, 7/15 priority date for domestic students; for spring admission, 12/1 for domestic students. Applications are processed on a rolling basis. Application fee: $50. Electronic applications accepted. *Expenses:* Tuition, state resident: full-time $15,166; part-time $635 per credit hour. Tuition, nonresident: full-time $29,214. *Required fees:* $500; $180 per semester. *Financial support:* Research assistantships with full tuition reimbursements, career-related internships or fieldwork, Federal Work-Study, scholarships/grants, and unspecified assistantships available. Support available to part-time students. Financial award application deadline: 2/1; financial award applicants required to submit FAFSA. *Unit head:* Dan Drane, Graduate Program Advisor, 803-323-2588, E-mail: draned@winthrop.edu. *Application contact:* 800-411-7041, Fax: 803-323-2292, E-mail: graduatestu@winthrop.edu.
Website: http://www.winthrop.edu/graduateschool

Section 31
Sports Management

This section contains a directory of institutions offering graduate work in sports management. Additional information about programs listed in the directory may be obtained by writing directly to the dean of a graduate school or chair of a department at the address given in the directory.

For programs offering related work, see also in this book *Business Administration and Management, Education,* and *Physical Education and Kinesiology.*

CONTENTS

Sports Management

Adams State University, Office of Graduate Studies, Department of Human Performance and Physical Education, Alamosa, CO 81101. Offers human performance and physical education (MA, MS), including applied sport psychology, coaching (MA), exercise science (MA), sport management (MA). *Program availability:* Part-time. *Entrance requirements:* For master's, GRE General Test or MAT, minimum undergraduate GPA of 2.75.

Adelphi University, Robert B. Willumstad School of Business, MBA Program, Garden City, NY 11530-0701. Offers accounting (MBA); finance (MBA); health services administration (MBA); human resource management (MBA); management (MBA); management information systems (MBA); marketing (MBA); sport management (MBA). *Accreditation:* AACSB. *Program availability:* Part-time, evening/weekend. *Students:* 343 full-time (132 women), 101 part-time (56 women); includes 75 minority (22 Black or African American, non-Hispanic/Latino; 2 American Indian or Alaska Native, non-Hispanic/Latino; 20 Asian, non-Hispanic/Latino; 23 Hispanic/Latino; 1 Native Hawaiian or other Pacific Islander, non-Hispanic/Latino; 7 Two or more races, non-Hispanic/Latino), 275 international. Average age 29. 389 applicants, 59% accepted, 187 enrolled. In 2018, 171 master's awarded. *Entrance requirements:* For master's, GMAT, official transcripts, bachelor's degree, 500 word essay, 2 letters of recommendation, resume. Additional exam requirements/recommendations for international students: Required—TOEFL (minimum score 550 paper-based; 80 iBT), IELTS (minimum score 6.5). *Application deadline:* For fall admission, 4/1 for international students; for spring admission, 11/1 for international students. Applications are processed on a rolling basis. Application fee: $50. Electronic applications accepted. *Financial support:* Research assistantships with partial tuition reimbursements, career-related internships or fieldwork, Federal Work-Study, institutionally sponsored loans, scholarships/grants, tuition waivers (partial), and unspecified assistantships available. Financial award application deadline: 3/1; financial award applicants required to submit FAFSA. *Faculty research:* Supply chain management, distribution channels, productivity benchmark analysis, data envelopment analysis, financial portfolio analysis. *Unit head:* Britt'ny Brown, Director of Graduate Programs, 516-877-4605. *Application contact:* Britt'ny Brown, Director of Graduate Programs, 516-877-4605.
Website: https://business.adelphi.edu/

Alcorn State University, School of Graduate Studies, School of Education and Psychology, Lorman, MS 39096-7500. Offers agricultural education (MS Ed); elementary education (MAT, MS Ed, Ed S); guidance and counseling (MS Ed); industrial education (MS Ed); secondary education (MAT, MS Ed), including health and physical education (MS Ed), NCAA compliance and academic progress reporting (MS Ed); special education (MS Ed). *Accreditation:* NCATE. *Degree requirements:* For master's, thesis optional.

American Public University System, AMU/APU Graduate Programs, Charles Town, WV 25414. Offers accounting (MS); applied business analytics (MS); business administration (MBA); criminal justice (MA); cybersecurity studies (MS); educational leadership (M Ed); environmental policy and management (MS); global security (DGS); health information management (MS); history (MA), including American military history, American Revolution, civil war, war since 1945, World War II; information technology (MS); international relations and conflict resolution (MA), including American politics and government, comparative government and development, general, international relations, public policy; national security studies (MA); nursing (MSN); political science (MA); public policy (MPP); reverse logistics management (MA), including comparative and security issues, conflict resolution, international and transnational security issues, peacekeeping; space studies (MS); sports management (MS); strategic intelligence (DSI); teaching (M Ed), including secondary social studies; transportation and logistics management (MA). *Program availability:* Part-time, evening/weekend, online only, 100% online. *Students:* 406 full-time (180 women), 7,826 part-time (3,329 women); includes 2,781 minority (1,438 Black or African American, non-Hispanic/Latino; 44 American Indian or Alaska Native, non-Hispanic/Latino; 193 Asian, non-Hispanic/Latino; 747 Hispanic/Latino; 53 Native Hawaiian or other Pacific Islander, non-Hispanic/Latino; 306 Two or more races, non-Hispanic/Latino), 121 international. Average age 38. In 2018, 2,717 master's awarded. *Degree requirements:* For master's, comprehensive exam or practicum; for doctorate, practicum. *Entrance requirements:* For master's, official transcript showing earned bachelor's degree from institution accredited by recognized accrediting body. Additional exam requirements/recommendations for international students: Required—TOEFL (minimum score 550 paper-based), IELTS (minimum score 6.5). *Application deadline:* Applications are processed on a rolling basis. Application fee: $0. Electronic applications accepted. *Financial support:* Scholarships/grants available. Financial award applicants required to submit FAFSA. *Unit head:* Dr. Wallace Boston, President, 877-468-6268, Fax: 304-728-2348, E-mail: president@apus.edu. *Application contact:* Yoci Deal, Associate Vice President, Graduate and International Admissions, 877-468-6268, Fax: 304-724-3764, E-mail: info@apus.edu.
Website: http://www.apus.edu

American University, School of Professional and Extended Studies, Washington, DC 20016. Offers agile project management (MS); healthcare management (MS, Graduate Certificate); human resource analytics and management (MS, Graduate Certificate); instructional design and learning analytics (MS); measurement and evaluation (MS); project monitoring and evaluation (Graduate Certificate); sports analytics and management (MS, Graduate Certificate). *Program availability:* Part-time, evening/weekend, 100% online, blended/hybrid learning. *Faculty:* 27 full-time (14 women), 33 part-time/adjunct (20 women). *Students:* 2 full-time (both women), 113 part-time (68 women); includes 6 minority (4 Black or African American, non-Hispanic/Latino; 1 Asian, non-Hispanic/Latino; 1 Hispanic/Latino). Average age 31. 156 applicants, 93% accepted, 66 enrolled. In 2018, 1 master's, 6 other advanced degrees awarded. *Entrance requirements:* For master's, Please visit website: https://www.american.edu/spexs/, official transcript(s), resume. Additional exam requirements/recommendations for international students: Required—TOEFL. *Application deadline:* Applications are processed on a rolling basis. Application fee: $55. Electronic applications accepted. *Expenses:* Contact institution. *Financial support:* Applicants required to submit FAFSA. *Unit head:* Jill Klein, Dean, 202-895-4900, E-mail: spexs@american.edu. *Application contact:* Emily Emily, Assistant Director for Recruitment and Admission, 202-885-4910, E-mail: aronoff@american.edu.
Website: http://www.american.edu/spexs

Angelo State University, College of Graduate Studies and Research, Archer College of Health and Human Services, Department of Kinesiology, San Angelo, TX 76909. Offers M Ed. *Program availability:* Part-time, evening/weekend. *Students:* 15 full-time (8 women), 35 part-time (19 women); includes 17 minority (5 Black or African American, non-Hispanic/Latino; 1 Asian, non-Hispanic/Latino; 11 Hispanic/Latino), 5 international. Average age 25. *Entrance requirements:* Additional exam requirements/recommendations for international students: Required—TOEFL or IELTS. *Application*

deadline: For fall admission, 7/15 priority date for domestic students, 6/10 for international students; for spring admission, 12/1 priority date for domestic students, 11/1 for international students. Applications are processed on a rolling basis. Application fee: $40 ($50 for international students). Electronic applications accepted. *Expenses: Tuition, area resident:* Full-time $3964; part-time $220 per credit hour. Tuition, state resident: full-time $3964; part-time $220 per credit hour. Tuition, nonresident: full-time $11,434; part-time $635 per credit hour. *International tuition:* $11,434 full-time. *Financial support:* Career-related internships or fieldwork, Federal Work-Study, scholarships/grants, and unspecified assistantships available. Support available to part-time students. Financial award application deadline: 3/1; financial award applicants required to submit FAFSA. *Unit head:* Dr. Steven Snowden, Chair, 325-486-2173, Fax: 325-942-2129, E-mail: steven.snowden@angelo.edu. *Application contact:* Dr. Warren Simpson, Graduate Advisor, 325-942-2173 Ext. 224, Fax: 325-942-2129, E-mail: warren.simpson@angelo.edu.
Website: http://www.angelo.edu/dept/kinesiology/

Arkansas State University, Graduate School, College of Education and Behavioral Science, Department of Health, Physical Education, and Sport Sciences, State University, AR 72467. Offers exercise science (MS); physical education (MSE, SCCT); sports administration (MS). *Program availability:* Part-time. *Degree requirements:* For master's, comprehensive exam, thesis or alternative; for SCCT, comprehensive exam. *Entrance requirements:* For master's, GRE General Test or MAT, appropriate bachelor's degree, official transcripts, immunization records, statement of goals, letters of recommendation; for SCCT, GRE General Test or MAT, interview, master's degree, official transcript, immunization records. Additional exam requirements/recommendations for international students: Required—TOEFL (minimum score 550 paper-based; 79 iBT), IELTS (minimum score 6), PTE (minimum score 56). Electronic applications accepted.

Ashland University, Dauch College of Business and Economics, Ashland, OH 44805-3702. Offers accounting (MBA); business analytics (MBA); entrepreneurship (MBA); financial management (MBA); global management (MBA); health care management and leadership (MBA); human resource management (MBA); human resources (MBA); management information systems (MBA); project management (MBA); sport management (MBA); supply chain management (MBA). *Accreditation:* ACBSP. *Program availability:* Part-time, evening/weekend, 100% online, blended/hybrid learning. Terminal master's awarded for partial completion of doctoral program. *Degree requirements:* For master's, thesis optional, capstone course. *Entrance requirements:* For master's, 2 years of full-time work experience. Additional exam requirements/recommendations for international students: Required—TOEFL (minimum score 550 paper-based; 78 iBT). Electronic applications accepted. *Expenses:* Contact institution. *Faculty research:* Relationship marketing strategy, executive compensation and company performance, online marketplaces in electronic commerce, diversity training in campus recreation departments, entrepreneurship in developing and emerging economies.

Auburn University at Montgomery, College of Education, Department of Kinesiology, Montgomery, AL 36124-4023. Offers exercise science (M Ed); physical education (Ed S); sport management (M Ed). *Program availability:* Online learning. *Students:* Average age 29. 23 applicants, 74% accepted, 10 enrolled. In 2018, 18 master's awarded. *Entrance requirements:* For master's, GRE or MAT. Additional exam requirements/recommendations for international students: Recommended—TOEFL (minimum score 500 paper-based; 61 iBT), IELTS (minimum score 5.5), TSE (minimum score 44). *Application deadline:* For fall admission, 7/15 for international students; for spring admission, 11/15 for international students; for summer admission, 4/15 for international students. Applications are processed on a rolling basis. Application fee: $25. Electronic applications accepted. *Expenses: Tuition, area resident:* Full-time $7146; part-time $4764 per credit hour. Tuition, state resident: full-time $7146; part-time $4764 per credit hour. Tuition, nonresident: full-time $16,056; part-time $10,704 per credit hour. *International tuition:* $16,056 full-time. *Required fees:* $766. One-time fee: $25 full-time. *Financial support:* Teaching assistantships available. Financial award application deadline: 3/1; financial award applicants required to submit FAFSA. *Unit head:* Dr. George Schaefer, Head, 334-244-3887, Fax: 334-244-3835, E-mail: gschaefe@aum.edu. *Application contact:* Janis Bigelow, Graduate Advisor, 334-244-3135, E-mail: jbigelo1@aum.edu.
Website: http://www.education.aum.edu/academic-programs/academic-programs/kinesiology

Augustana University, Sports Administration and Leadership Program, Sioux Falls, SD 57197. Offers MA. *Program availability:* Part-time. *Degree requirements:* For master's, thesis or alternative. *Entrance requirements:* For master's, GMAT or GRE, minimum cumulative undergraduate GPA of 3.0 for last 60 semester hours; appropriate bachelor's degree; 2-3 page essay discussing academic interests, education goals, and plans for graduate study. Additional exam requirements/recommendations for international students: Required—TOEFL (minimum score 550 paper-based). Electronic applications accepted. *Expenses:* Contact institution.

Austin Peay State University, College of Graduate Studies, College of Behavioral and Health Sciences, Department of Health and Human Performance, Clarksville, TN 37044. Offers public health education (MS); sports and wellness leadership (MS). *Program availability:* Part-time, evening/weekend, online learning. *Faculty:* 8 full-time (4 women), 1 (woman) part-time/adjunct. *Students:* 18 full-time (8 women), 55 part-time (33 women); includes 21 minority (13 Black or African American, non-Hispanic/Latino; 1 Asian, non-Hispanic/Latino; 2 Hispanic/Latino; 5 Two or more races, non-Hispanic/Latino), 2 international. Average age 30. 81 applicants, 84% accepted, 54 enrolled. In 2018, 35 master's awarded. *Degree requirements:* For master's, comprehensive exam, thesis optional. *Entrance requirements:* For master's, GRE General Test, 3 letters of recommendation, minimum undergraduate GPA of 2.5. Additional exam requirements/recommendations for international students: Required—TOEFL (minimum score 500 paper-based). *Application deadline:* For fall admission, 8/21 priority date for domestic students. Applications are processed on a rolling basis. Application fee: $45 ($55 for international students). Electronic applications accepted. *Expenses: Tuition, area resident:* Part-time $450 per credit hour. Tuition, state resident: full-time $5987; part-time $450 per credit hour. Tuition, nonresident: full-time $8757; part-time $806 per credit hour. *Required fees:* $1583; $79.15 per credit hour. *Financial support:* Research assistantships with full tuition reimbursements, career-related internships or fieldwork, Federal Work-Study, institutionally sponsored loans, scholarships/grants, and unspecified assistantships available. Support available to part-time students. Financial award application deadline: 7/1; financial award applicants required to submit FAFSA. *Unit head:* Dr. Marcy Maurer, Chair, 931-221-6105, Fax: 931-221-7040, E-mail: maurerm@apsu.edu. *Application contact:* Megan Mitchell, Coordinator of Graduate Admissions, 931-221-6189, Fax: 931-221-7641, E-mail: mitchellm@apsu.edu.
Website: http://www.apsu.edu/hhp/index.php

Azusa Pacific University, School of Behavioral and Applied Sciences, Department of Leadership and Organizational Psychology, Program in Leadership, Azusa, CA 91702-7000. Offers executive leadership (MA); leadership development (MA); leadership studies (MA); sport management (MA). *Expenses:* Contact institution.

Azusa Pacific University, School of Business and Management, Azusa, CA 91702-7000. Offers accounting (MBA); business administration (MBA); entrepreneurship (MBA); finance (MBA); international business (MBA); marketing (MBA); organizational science (MBA); professional accountancy (M Acc); sport management (MBA). *Program availability:* Part-time, evening/weekend. *Degree requirements:* For master's, thesis (for some programs), final project. *Entrance requirements:* For master's, GMAT, minimum GPA of 3.0. Additional exam requirements/recommendations for international students: Required—TOEFL (minimum score 600 paper-based). *Expenses:* Contact institution. *Faculty research:* Gender issues, financial risk, leadership and ethics, marketing strategy.

Ball State University, Graduate School, College of Health, School of Kinesiology, Program in Physical Education and Sport, Muncie, IN 47306. Offers physical education and sport (MA, MS), including athletic coaching education, sport administration, sport and exercise psychology. *Program availability:* Part-time, 100% online. *Entrance requirements:* For master's, GRE General Test, minimum baccalaureate GPA of 2.75 or 3.0 in latter half of baccalaureate, curriculum vitae, three letters of recommendation; campus visit to meet faculty and see facilities (strongly encouraged). Additional exam requirements/recommendations for international students: Required—TOEFL (minimum score 550 paper-based; 79 iBT), IELTS (minimum score 6.5). Electronic applications accepted.

Barry University, School of Human Performance and Leisure Sciences, Program in Sport Management, Miami Shores, FL 33161-6695. Offers MS. *Program availability:* Part-time, evening/weekend. *Degree requirements:* For master's, comprehensive exam, project or thesis. *Entrance requirements:* For master's, GMAT or GRE General Test, minimum GPA of 3.0. Electronic applications accepted. *Faculty research:* Economic impact of professional sports, sport marketing.

Barry University, School of Human Performance and Leisure Sciences and Andreas School of Business, Program in Sport Management and Business Administration, Miami Shores, FL 33161-6695. Offers MS/MBA. *Program availability:* Part-time, evening/weekend. Electronic applications accepted. *Faculty research:* Economic impact of professional sports, sport marketing.

Belhaven University, School of Business, Jackson, MS 39202-1789. Offers business administration (MBA); health administration (MBA, MHA); human resources (MBA, MSL); leadership (MBA); public administration (MPA); sports administration (MBA, MSA). *Program availability:* Part-time, evening/weekend, 100% online. *Students:* Average age 35. 574 applicants, 75% accepted, 306 enrolled. In 2018, 326 master's awarded. *Degree requirements:* For master's, comprehensive exam (for some programs), thesis or alternative. *Entrance requirements:* For master's, minimum GPA of 2.8 (for MBA and MHA), 2.5 (for MSL, MPA and MSA). *Application deadline:* Applications are processed on a rolling basis. Application fee: $25. Electronic applications accepted. *Expenses:* Contact institution. *Financial support:* Applicants required to submit FAFSA. *Unit head:* Dr. Ralph Mason, Dean, 601-968-8949, Fax: 601-968-8951, E-mail: cmason@belhaven.edu. *Application contact:* Dr. Audrey Kelleher, Vice President of Adult and Graduate Marketing and Development, 407-804-1424, Fax: 407-620-5210, E-mail: akelleher@belhaven.edu.
Website: http://www.belhaven.edu/campuses/index.htm

Boise State University, College of Health Sciences, Department of Kinesiology, Boise, ID 83725-0399. Offers athletic leadership (MAL); kinesiology (MK, MS). *Program availability:* Part-time. *Degree requirements:* For master's, thesis (for some programs). *Entrance requirements:* For master's, minimum GPA of 3.0. Additional exam requirements/recommendations for international students: Required—TOEFL (minimum score 550 paper-based; 80 iBT), IELTS (minimum score 6). Electronic applications accepted.

Bowling Green State University, Graduate College, College of Education and Human Development, School of Human Movement, Sport, and Leisure Studies, Bowling Green, OH 43403. Offers developmental kinesiology (M Ed); recreation and leisure (M Ed); sport administration (M Ed). *Program availability:* Part-time. *Degree requirements:* For master's, thesis or alternative. *Entrance requirements:* For master's, GRE General Test, minimum GPA of 2.7. Additional exam requirements/recommendations for international students: Required—TOEFL. Electronic applications accepted. *Faculty research:* Teacher-learning process, travel and tourism, sport marketing and management, exercise physiology and sport psychology, life-span motor development.

Brooklyn College of the City University of New York, School of Natural and Behavioral Sciences, Department of Kinesiology, Brooklyn, NY 11210-2889. Offers exercise and sports science (MS); physical education teacher (MS); sport management (MS). *Program availability:* Part-time. *Degree requirements:* For master's, comprehensive exam or thesis. *Entrance requirements:* For master's, previous course work in physical education and education, minimum GPA of 3.0, 2 letters of recommendation, essay. Additional exam requirements/recommendations for international students: Required—TOEFL (minimum score 500 paper-based; 61 iBT). Electronic applications accepted. *Faculty research:* Exercise physiology, motor learning, sports psychology, women in athletics.

Bryan College, MBA Program, Dayton, TN 37321. Offers business administration (MBA); healthcare administration (MBA); human resources (MBA); marketing (MBA); ministry (MBA); sports management (MBA). *Program availability:* Online only, 100% online. *Entrance requirements:* For master's, resume, 2 letters of recommendation. Additional exam requirements/recommendations for international students: Required—TOEFL. Electronic applications accepted. *Expenses:* Contact institution.

California Baptist University, Program in Kinesiology, Riverside, CA 92504-3206. Offers exercise science (MS); physical education (MS); sport management (MS). *Program availability:* Part-time, evening/weekend, 100% online, blended/hybrid learning. *Faculty:* 13 full-time (3 women), 5 part-time/adjunct (1 woman). *Students:* 75 full-time (40 women), 77 part-time (37 women); includes 79 minority (10 Black or African American, non-Hispanic/Latino; 1 American Indian or Alaska Native, non-Hispanic/Latino; 6 Asian, non-Hispanic/Latino; 50 Hispanic/Latino; 2 Native Hawaiian or other Pacific Islander, non-Hispanic/Latino; 10 Two or more races, non-Hispanic/Latino), 13 international. Average age 35. 71 applicants, 79% accepted, 56 enrolled. In 2018, 77 master's awarded. *Degree requirements:* For master's, comprehensive exam or research thesis. *Entrance requirements:* For master's, minimum undergraduate GPA of 2.75; completion of course prerequisites with minimum C grade; three recommendations; 500-word essay; resume; interview. Additional exam requirements/recommendations for international students: Required—TOEFL (minimum score 80 iBT). *Application deadline:* For fall admission, 8/1 priority date for domestic students, 7/1 for international students; for spring admission, 12/1 priority date for domestic students, 11/1 for international students. Applications are processed on a rolling basis. Application fee: $45. Electronic applications accepted. *Expenses:* $580 per unit. *Financial support:* In 2018–19, 21 students received support. Federal Work-Study, scholarships/grants, and unspecified assistantships available. Financial award applicants required to submit

CSS PROFILE or FAFSA. *Faculty research:* Physical education pedagogy, exercise management and prevention of cardiovascular and metabolic diseases, sport management, immune function, carbohydrate oxidation. *Unit head:* Dr. David Pearson, Dean, College of Health Science, 951-343-4298, E-mail: dpearson@calbaptist.edu. *Application contact:* Dr. Dominick Sturz, Assistant, Health and Human Services, 951-343-2192, E-mail: dsturz@calbaptist.edu.
Website: http://www.calbaptist.edu/mskin/

California State University, Fresno, Division of Research and Graduate Studies, College of Health and Human Services, Department of Kinesiology, Fresno, CA 93740-8027. Offers exercise science (MA); general kinesiology (MA); sport administration (MA); sport psychology (MA). *Program availability:* Part-time, evening/weekend. *Degree requirements:* For master's, thesis or alternative. *Entrance requirements:* For master's, GRE General Test, minimum GPA of 2.7. Additional exam requirements/recommendations for international students: Required—TOEFL. Electronic applications accepted. *Faculty research:* Refugee education, homeless, geriatrics, fitness.

California State University, Long Beach, Graduate Studies, College of Health and Human Services, Department of Kinesiology, Long Beach, CA 90840. Offers adapted physical education (MA); coaching and student athlete development (MA); exercise physiology and nutrition (MS); exercise science (MS); individualized studies (MA); kinesiology (MA); pedagogical studies (MA); sport and exercise psychology (MS); sport management (MA); sports medicine and injury studies (MS). *Program availability:* Part-time. *Degree requirements:* For master's, oral and written comprehensive exams or thesis. *Entrance requirements:* For master's, GRE General Test, minimum GPA of 2.75 during previous 2 years of course work. *Application deadline:* Applications are processed on a rolling basis. Application fee: $55. Electronic applications accepted. *Expenses:* Required fees: $2628 per term. Tuition and fees vary according to class time, course level, course load, degree level, campus/location and program. *Financial support:* Federal Work-Study, institutionally sponsored loans, and scholarships/grants available. Financial award application deadline: 3/2; financial award applicants required to submit FAFSA. *Faculty research:* Pulmonary functioning, feedback and practice structure, strength training, history and politics of sports, special population research issues. *Unit head:* Tiffanye Vargas, Chair, 562-985-4051, E-mail: tiffanye.vargas@csulb.edu. *Application contact:* Tiffanye Vargas, Chair, 562-985-4051, E-mail: tiffanye.vargas@csulb.edu.
Website: https://fullerton-csm.symplicity.com/

California University of Management and Sciences, Graduate Programs, Anaheim, CA 92801. Offers business administration (MBA, DBA); computer information systems (MS); economics (MS); international business (MS); sports management (MS).

California University of Pennsylvania, School of Graduate Studies and Research, College of Education and Human Services, Program in Sport Management Studies, California, PA 15419-1394. Offers sport management studies (MS), including intercollegiate athletic administration, sport management; strategic sport analysis (MS). *Program availability:* Part-time, 100% online.

Campbellsville University, College of Arts and Sciences, Campbellsville, KY 42718-2799. Offers justice studies (MS); sport management (MA). *Program availability:* Part-time, evening/weekend, 100% online, blended/hybrid learning. *Faculty:* 16 full-time (7 women), 4 part-time/adjunct (2 women). *Students:* 51 full-time (28 women), 10 part-time (6 women); includes 12 minority (11 Black or African American, non-Hispanic/Latino; 1 Asian, non-Hispanic/Latino), 6 international. Average age 30. 65 applicants, 37% accepted, 21 enrolled. In 2018, 26 master's awarded. *Degree requirements:* For master's, comprehensive exam, thesis optional. *Entrance requirements:* For master's, GRE General Test, minimum GPA of 2.9, letters of recommendation, college transcripts. Additional exam requirements/recommendations for international students: Recommended—TOEFL, IELTS. *Application deadline:* Applications are processed on a rolling basis. Application fee: $25. Electronic applications accepted. Application fee is waived when completed online. *Expenses:* MASM = $399/credit hour; MTESL = $399/credit hour; MSJS = $399/credit hour. *Financial support:* Unspecified assistantships available. Financial award application deadline: 6/1; financial award applicants required to submit FAFSA. *Unit head:* Dr. Mike Page, Dean of the College of Arts and Sciences, 270-789-5394. *Application contact:* Monica Bamwine, Director of Graduate Admissions, 270-789-5221, Fax: 270-789-5071, E-mail: mkbamwine@campbellsville.edu.
Website: http://www.campbellsville.edu/

Canisius College, Graduate Division, School of Education and Human Services, Program in Sport Administration, Buffalo, NY 14208-1098. Offers MSA. *Program availability:* Part-time, evening/weekend, 100% online. *Students:* Average age 28. 70 applicants, 93% accepted, 40 enrolled. In 2018, 65 master's awarded. *Entrance requirements:* For master's, transcripts, essay, minimum GPA of 2.7, resume, BA. Additional exam requirements/recommendations for international students: Required—TOEFL (minimum score 550 paper-based, 79 iBT), IELTS (minimum score 6.5), or CAEL (minimum score 70). *Application deadline:* Applications are processed on a rolling basis. Application fee: $0. Electronic applications accepted. *Expenses:* Tuition: Part-time $820 per credit hour. *Required fees:* $25 per semester. One-time fee: $65 part-time. Tuition and fees vary according to program. *Financial support:* Career-related internships or fieldwork, Federal Work-Study, scholarships/grants, tuition waivers (partial), and unspecified assistantships available. Support available to part-time students. Financial award application deadline: 4/30; financial award applicants required to submit FAFSA. *Unit head:* Dr. Shawn O'Rourke, Associate Dean, 716-888-3179, E-mail: orourke1@canisius.edu. *Application contact:* Dr. Shawn O'Rourke, Associate Dean, 716-888-3179, E-mail: orourke1@canisius.edu.
Website: http://www.canisius.edu/graduate/

Cardinal Stritch University, College of Arts and Sciences, Department of Sport Science and Management, Milwaukee, WI 53217-3985. Offers sport management (MS). *Program availability:* Part-time, evening/weekend. *Entrance requirements:* Additional exam requirements/recommendations for international students: Required—TOEFL (minimum score 79 iBT), IELTS (minimum score 6.5). Electronic applications accepted. *Expenses:* Contact institution.

Central Michigan University, College of Graduate Studies, The Herbert H. and Grace A. Dow College of Health Professions, Department of Physical Education and Sport, Mount Pleasant, MI 48859. Offers sport administration (MA). *Program availability:* Part-time, evening/weekend. *Degree requirements:* For master's, thesis or alternative. *Entrance requirements:* For master's, GRE (recommended). Electronic applications accepted. *Faculty research:* Athletic administration and sport management, performance enhancing substance use in sport, computer applications for sport managers, mental skill development for ultimate performance, teaching methods.

Central Michigan University, College of Graduate Studies, Interdisciplinary Administration Programs, Mount Pleasant, MI 48859. Offers acquisitions administration (MSA, Graduate Certificate); general administration (MSA, Graduate Certificate); health services administration (MSA, Graduate Certificate); human resource administration (Graduate Certificate); human resources administration (MSA); information resource management (MSA, Graduate Certificate); international administration (MSA, Graduate Certificate); leadership (MSA, Graduate Certificate); public administration (MSA, Graduate Certificate); research administration (Graduate Certificate); sport

administration (MSA). *Accreditation:* AACSB. *Program availability:* Part-time, evening/weekend, online learning. *Degree requirements:* For master's, thesis or alternative. *Entrance requirements:* For master's, bachelor's degree with minimum GPA of 2.7. Electronic applications accepted. *Faculty research:* Interdisciplinary studies in acquisitions administration, health services administration, sport administration, recreation and park administration, and international administration.

Central Washington University, School of Graduate Studies and Research, College of Education and Professional Studies, Department of Physical Education, School Health and Movement Studies, Ellensburg, WA 98926. Offers athletic administration (MS); health and physical education (MS). *Program availability:* Part-time. *Degree requirements:* For master's, comprehensive exam, thesis or alternative. *Entrance requirements:* For master's, minimum GPA of 3.0. Additional exam requirements/recommendations for international students: Required—TOEFL (minimum score 550 paper-based; 79 iBT), IELTS. Electronic applications accepted.

The Citadel, The Military College of South Carolina, Citadel Graduate College, School of Science and Mathematics, Department of Health, Exercise, and Sport Science, Charleston, SC 29409. Offers health, exercise, and sport science (MS); sport management (MA, Graduate Certificate). *Accreditation:* NCATE. *Program availability:* Part-time, evening/weekend. *Degree requirements:* For master's, comprehensive exam (for some programs), internship and professional portfolio (for some programs). *Entrance requirements:* For master's, GRE (minimum combined verbal and quantitative score 290) or MAT (minimum score 396), official transcript reflecting highest degree earned from regionally-accredited college or university, minimum undergraduate GPA of 2.5, 3 letters of recommendation, resume detailing previous work experience. Additional exam requirements/recommendations for international students: Required—TOEFL (minimum score 550 paper-based; 79 iBT). Electronic applications accepted. *Expenses:* Tuition, state resident: part-time $595 per credit hour. Tuition, nonresident: part-time $1020 per credit hour. *Required fees:* $90 per term.

Clayton State University, School of Graduate Studies, College of Business, Program in Business Administration, Morrow, GA 30260-0285. Offers accounting (MBA); human resource leadership (MBA); international business (MBA); sports and entertainment management (MBA); supply chain management (MBA). *Accreditation:* AACSB. *Program availability:* Part-time, evening/weekend. *Degree requirements:* For master's, thesis. *Entrance requirements:* For master's, GMAT, 3 letters of recommendation; statement of purpose; 2 official transcripts. Additional exam requirements/recommendations for international students: Required—TOEFL (minimum score 550 paper-based; 80 iBT). Electronic applications accepted. *Expenses:* Contact institution.

Clemson University, Graduate School, College of Education, Department of Educational and Organizational Leadership Development, Clemson, SC 29634. Offers administration and supervision (M Ed, Ed S); athletic leadership (MS, Certificate); education systems improvement science (Ed D); educational leadership (PhD), including higher education, P-12; human resource development (MHRD), including human resource development; leadership (Certificate); student affairs (M Ed). *Program availability:* Part-time, evening/weekend, 100% online. *Faculty:* 17 full-time (11 women). *Students:* 105 full-time (64 women), 265 part-time (170 women); includes 76 minority (61 Black or African American, non-Hispanic/Latino; 1 American Indian or Alaska Native, non-Hispanic/Latino; 3 Asian, non-Hispanic/Latino; 5 Hispanic/Latino; 6 Two or more races, non-Hispanic/Latino). Average age 32. 204 applicants, 83% accepted, 123 enrolled. In 2018, 93 master's, 17 doctorates, 28 other advanced degrees awarded. *Degree requirements:* For master's, thesis (for some programs); for doctorate, comprehensive exam, thesis/dissertation. *Entrance requirements:* For master's, doctorate, and other advanced degree, GRE General Test, unofficial transcripts, letters of recommendation. Additional exam requirements/recommendations for international students: Required—TOEFL (minimum score 80 paper-based; 80 iBT); Recommended—IELTS (minimum score 6.5), TSE (minimum score 54). *Application deadline:* For fall admission, 4/15 priority date for international students; for spring admission, 10/15 priority date for international students. Applications are processed on a rolling basis. Application fee: $80 ($90 for international students). Electronic applications accepted. *Expenses:* $5198 per semester full-time resident, $10123 per semester full-time non-resident, $556 per credit hour part-time resident, $1109 per credit hour part-time non-resident, online $770 per credit hour, $4938 doctoral programs resident, $10405 doctoral programs non-resident, $1144 full-time graduate assistant, other fees may apply per session. *Financial support:* In 2018–19, 30 students received support, including 8 fellowships with full and partial tuition reimbursements available (averaging $4,525 per year), 3 research assistantships with full and partial tuition reimbursements available (averaging $7,500 per year); career-related internships or fieldwork and unspecified assistantships also available. *Faculty research:* Leadership, ethics, policy development, performance improvement. *Total annual research expenditures:* $79,638. *Unit head:* Dr. Roy Jones, Interim Department Chair, 864-656-7915, E-mail: royj@clemson.edu. *Application contact:* Alison Search, Student Services Program Coordinator, 864-250-8880, E-mail: alisonp@clemson.edu.
Website: http://www.clemson.edu/education/departments/educational-organizational-leadership-development/index.html

Coastal Carolina University, College of Science, Conway, SC 29528-6054. Offers applied computing and information systems (Certificate); coastal marine and wetland studies (MS); information systems technology (MS); marine science (PhD); sports management (MS). *Program availability:* Part-time, evening/weekend, 100% online. *Degree requirements:* For master's, thesis or internship; for doctorate, comprehensive exam, thesis/dissertation. *Entrance requirements:* For master's, GRE, 3 letters of recommendation, resume, official transcripts, written statement of educational and career goals, baccalaureate degree; for doctorate, GRE, official transcripts; baccalaureate or master's degree; minimum GPA of 3.0 for all collegiate coursework; successful completion of at least two semesters of college-level calculus, physics, and chemistry; 3 letters of recommendation; written statement of educational and career goals; resume; for Certificate, 2 letters of reference, official transcripts, minimum GPA of 3.0 in all computing and information systems courses, documentation of graduation from accredited four-year college or university. Additional exam requirements/recommendations for international students: Required—TOEFL (minimum score 550 paper-based; 79 iBT), IELTS (minimum score 6.5). Electronic applications accepted.

Coker College, Graduate Programs, Hartsville, SC 29550. Offers college athletic administration (MS); criminal and social justice policy (MS); curriculum and instructional technology (M Ed); literacy studies (M Ed); management and leadership (MS). *Program availability:* Part-time, 100% online. *Faculty:* 15 full-time (7 women), 7 part-time/adjunct (3 women). *Students:* 144 full-time (100 women), 6 part-time (2 women); includes 42 minority (33 Black or African American, non-Hispanic/Latino; 1 Asian, non-Hispanic/Latino; 4 Hispanic/Latino; 4 Two or more races, non-Hispanic/Latino). Average age 33. 120 applicants, 61% accepted, 65 enrolled. In 2018, 92 master's awarded. *Entrance requirements:* For master's, 1. Undergraduate overall gpa of 3.0 on 4.0 scale. 2. Official transcripts from all undergraduate institutions. 3. One-page personal statement. 4. Resume. 5. Two professional references. Additionally, for MEd in Literacy Studies - 1 year of teaching in PK-12 and letter of recommendation from principal/assistant principal. *Application deadline:* Applications are processed on a rolling basis. Application fee: $0. Electronic applications accepted. *Financial support:* Unspecified assistantships available. Financial award application deadline: 6/30; financial award applicants required to submit FAFSA. *Unit head:* Dr. Kathryn Flaherty, Dean of Graduate and Professional Programs, 843-857-4227, E-mail: kflaherty@coker.edu. *Application contact:* Lacey Rice-Serafin, Director of Graduate Programs, 843-857-4128, E-mail: lriceserafin@coker.edu.

The College at Brockport, State University of New York, School of Education, Health, and Human Services, Department of Kinesiology, Sports Studies and Physical Education, Brockport, NY 14420-2997. Offers adapted physical education (AGC); physical education (MS Ed), including adapted physical education, athletic administration, physical education/pedagogy. *Program availability:* Part-time. *Faculty:* 9 full-time (5 women), 1 part-time/adjunct (0 women). *Students:* 28 full-time (9 women), 62 part-time (23 women); includes 7 minority (3 Black or African American, non-Hispanic/Latino; 2 Asian, non-Hispanic/Latino; 2 Hispanic/Latino). 49 applicants, 84% accepted, 32 enrolled. In 2018, 50 master's awarded. *Degree requirements:* For master's, thesis or alternative. *Entrance requirements:* For master's, minimum GPA of 3.0; statement of objectives. Additional exam requirements/recommendations for international students: Required—TOEFL (minimum score 550 paper-based; 79 iBT), IELTS (minimum score 6.5). *Application deadline:* For fall admission, 4/15 priority date for domestic and international students; for spring admission, 11/15 priority date for domestic and international students; for summer admission, 4/15 priority date for domestic students, 4/15 for international students. Application fee: $80. Electronic applications accepted. *Expenses:* Tuition, state resident: part-time $471 per credit. Tuition, nonresident: part-time $963 per credit. *Financial support:* In 2018–19, 11 teaching assistantships with full tuition reimbursements (averaging $7,000 per year) were awarded; Federal Work-Study, scholarships/grants, and unspecified assistantships also available. Support available to part-time students. Financial award application deadline: 3/15; financial award applicants required to submit FAFSA. *Faculty research:* Athletic administration, adapted physical education, physical education curriculum, physical education teaching/coaching, children's physical activity. *Unit head:* Dr. Cathy Houston-Wilson, Chairperson, 585-395-5352, Fax: 585-395-2771, E-mail: chouston@brockport.edu. *Application contact:* Dr. Melanie Perreault, Graduate Program Director, 585-395-5299, Fax: 585-395-2771, E-mail: mperreault@brockport.edu.
Website: https://www.brockport.edu/academics/kinesiology/

Columbia University, School of Professional Studies, Program in Global Sports Law and Sports Management, New York, NY 10027. Offers MS/MGSL. Program offered in collaboration with Instituto Superior de Derecho y Economia (ISDE) in Madrid.

Columbia University, School of Professional Studies, Program in Sports Management, New York, NY 10027. Offers MS. *Program availability:* Part-time. *Entrance requirements:* For master's, minimum GPA of 3.0, 2 letters of recommendation, professional resume. Electronic applications accepted.

Concordia University Irvine, School of Arts and Sciences, Irvine, CA 92612-3299. Offers coaching and athletic administration (MA). *Program availability:* Part-time, evening/weekend, online learning. *Degree requirements:* For master's, culminating project. *Entrance requirements:* For master's, official college/university transcript(s); signed statement of intent. Additional exam requirements/recommendations for international students: Required—TOEFL (minimum score 550 paper-based; 79 iBT). Electronic applications accepted. *Expenses:* Contact institution.

Concordia University, St. Paul, College of Health and Science, St. Paul, MN 55104-5494. Offers exercise science (MS); orthotics and prosthetics (MS); physical therapy (DPT); sports management (MA). *Program availability:* Part-time, evening/weekend, 100% online, blended/hybrid learning. *Faculty:* 16 full-time (9 women), 15 part-time/adjunct (8 women). *Students:* 247 full-time (132 women), 27 part-time (9 women); includes 43 minority (18 Black or African American, non-Hispanic/Latino; 1 American Indian or Alaska Native, non-Hispanic/Latino; 4 Asian, non-Hispanic/Latino; 12 Hispanic/Latino; 8 Two or more races, non-Hispanic/Latino), 5 international. Average age 28. 241 applicants, 47% accepted, 86 enrolled. In 2018, 79 master's, 26 doctorates awarded. *Degree requirements:* For master's, comprehensive exam (for some programs), thesis (for some programs); for doctorate, at least one 8-12 week clinical rotation outside the St. Paul area. *Entrance requirements:* For master's, official transcripts from regionally-accredited institution stating the conferral of a bachelor's degree with minimum cumulative GPA of 3.0; personal statement; resume; for doctorate, GRE, official transcript from regionally-accredited institution showing bachelor's degree and minimum coursework GPA of 3.0; 100 physical therapy observation hours; two letters of professional recommendation. Additional exam requirements/recommendations for international students: Recommended—TOEFL (minimum score 547 paper-based; 78 iBT), IELTS (minimum score 6), TSE (minimum score 52). *Application deadline:* For fall admission, 4/1 for domestic students. Applications are processed on a rolling basis. Application fee: $0. Electronic applications accepted. *Expenses:* $475 per credit for 33 credits (for MS), $515 a credit for 36 credits (for MS in Orthotics and Prosthetics), $499 per credit for 36 credits (for MS in Nursing), $850 per credit for 111 credits (for DPT). *Financial support:* In 2018–19, 74 students received support. Federal Work-Study, scholarships/grants, and unspecified assistantships available. Financial award applicants required to submit FAFSA. *Faculty research:* Balance and vestibular function,shoulder kinematics, blood pressure, virtual training and performance, early childhood developmental screening. *Unit head:* Dr. Katie Fischer, Dean, 651-641-8735, E-mail: fischer@csp.edu. *Application contact:* Amber Faletti, Director of Enrollment Management, 651-641-8838, Fax: 651-603-6320, E-mail: faletti@csp.edu.

Dallas Baptist University, Dorothy M. Bush College of Education, Sport Management Program, Dallas, TX 75211-9299. Offers MA. *Program availability:* Part-time, evening/weekend. *Application deadline:* Applications are processed on a rolling basis. Application fee: $25. Electronic applications accepted. Application fee is waived when completed online. *Expenses: Tuition:* Full-time $17,262; part-time $959 per credit hour. *Required fees:* $1000; $500 per semester. Tuition and fees vary according to course load and degree level. *Unit head:* Dr. Neil Dugger, Dean, 214-333-5202, E-mail: neil@dbu.edu. *Application contact:* Dr. Jim Tennison, Program Director, 214-333-5643, E-mail: jimt@dbu.edu.
Website: https://www.dbu.edu/graduate/degree-programs/ma-sport-management

Drexel University, Goodwin College of Professional Studies, School of Technology and Professional Studies, Philadelphia, PA 19104-2875. Offers construction management (MS); creativity and innovation (MS); engineering technology (MS); food science (MS); hospitality management (MS); professional studies: creativity studies (MS); professional studies: e-learning leadership (MS); professional studies: homeland security management (MS); project management (MS); property management (MS); sport management (MS). *Program availability:* Part-time, evening/weekend. *Entrance requirements:* Additional exam requirements/recommendations for international students: Required—TOEFL, IELTS. Electronic applications accepted. Application fee is waived when completed online.

Duquesne University, Palumbo-Donahue School of Business, Pittsburgh, PA 15282-0001. Offers accounting (M Acc); finance (MBA); information systems management (MSISM); management (MBA, MS); marketing (MBA); sports business (MS); supply chain management (MS); sustainability (MBA); JD/MBA; MBA/M Acc; MBA/MA; MBA/MES; MBA/MHMS; MSISM/MBA; Pharm D/MBA. *Accreditation:* AACSB. *Program availability:* Part-time, evening/weekend, 100% online, blended/hybrid learning. *Faculty:*

59 full-time (23 women), 25 part-time/adjunct (6 women). *Students:* 214 full-time (74 women), 42 part-time (20 women); includes 39 minority (12 Black or African American, non-Hispanic/Latino; 13 Asian, non-Hispanic/Latino; 8 Hispanic/Latino; 6 Two or more races, non-Hispanic/Latino), 23 international. Average age 29. 228 applicants, 88% accepted, 118 enrolled. In 2018, 149 master's awarded. *Entrance requirements:* For master's, GMAT or GRE, all official transcripts, two letters of recommendation, current resume, essays. Additional exam requirements/recommendations for international students: Required—TOEFL (minimum score 90 iBT), IELTS (minimum score 7). *Application deadline:* For fall admission, 7/1 priority date for domestic and international students; for spring admission, 12/1 for domestic and international students; for summer admission, 4/1 for domestic and international students. Applications are processed on a rolling basis. Application fee: $0. Electronic applications accepted. *Expenses:* $1,284/credit hour (business), $953/credit hour (management). *Financial support:* In 2018–19, 174 students received support, including 6 fellowships with partial tuition reimbursements available (averaging $24,750 per year); career-related internships or fieldwork, scholarships/grants, and unspecified assistantships also available. Support available to part-time students. Financial award application deadline: 7/1; financial award applicants required to submit FAFSA. *Faculty research:* Investment management, business ethics, technology management, supply chain management, entrepreneurship. *Unit head:* Dr. Karen Donovan, Associate Dean of Graduate Programs and Executive Education, 412-396-5788, Fax: 412-396-1726, E-mail: donovan6@duq.edu. *Application contact:* Chris Rouhier, Director of Graduate Admissions, 412-396-6244, Fax: 412-396-1726, E-mail: rouhierc@duq.edu.
Website: http://www.duq.edu/business/grad

East Carolina University, Graduate School, College of Health and Human Performance, Department of Kinesiology, Greenville, NC 27858-4353. Offers adapted physical education (MS); bioenergetics and exercise science (PhD); biomechanics and motor control (MS); exercise physiology (MS); physical activity promotion (MS); physical education (MA Ed, MAT); physical education clinical supervision (Certificate); physical education pedagogy (MS); sport and exercise psychology (MS); sport management (MS, Certificate). *Application deadline:* For fall admission, 2/1 priority date for domestic students, 2/1 for international students. *Expenses: Tuition, area resident:* Full-time $4749. Tuition, state resident: full-time $4749. Tuition, nonresident: full-time $17,898. *International tuition:* $17,898 full-time. *Required fees:* $2787. Part-time tuition and fees vary according to course load and program. *Financial support:* Application deadline: 2/1. *Unit head:* Dr. Stacey Altman, Chair, 252-328-4632, E-mail: altmans@ecu.edu. *Application contact:* Graduate School Admissions, 252-328-6012, Fax: 252-328-6071, E-mail: gradschool@ecu.edu.
Website: https://hhp.ecu.edu/kine/

Eastern Kentucky University, The Graduate School, College of Health Sciences, Department of Exercise and Sport Science, Richmond, KY 40475-3102. Offers exercise and sport science (MS); exercise and wellness (MS); sports administration (MS). *Program availability:* Part-time. *Entrance requirements:* For master's, GRE General Test (minimum score 700 verbal and quantitative), minimum GPA of 2.5 (for most), minimum GPA of 3.0 (analytical writing). *Faculty research:* Nutrition and exercise.

Eastern Michigan University, Graduate School, College of Health and Human Services, School of Health Promotion and Human Performance, Program in Sports Management, Ypsilanti, MI 48197. Offers MS. *Program availability:* Part-time, evening/weekend. *Students:* 16 full-time (8 women), 19 part-time (11 women); includes 7 minority (1 Black or African American, non-Hispanic/Latino; 1 Asian, non-Hispanic/Latino; 3 Hispanic/Latino; 2 Two or more races, non-Hispanic/Latino), 2 international. Average age 25. 40 applicants, 75% accepted, 14 enrolled. In 2018, 18 master's awarded. *Entrance requirements:* For master's, minimum GPA of 2.75. Additional exam requirements/recommendations for international students: Required—TOEFL. *Application deadline:* For fall admission, 8/1 for domestic students, 5/1 for international students; for winter admission, 12/1 for domestic students, 10/1 for international students; for spring admission, 4/15 for domestic students, 3/1 for international students. Applications are processed on a rolling basis. Application fee: $45. *Financial support:* Fellowships, research assistantships with full tuition reimbursements, teaching assistantships with full tuition reimbursements, career-related internships or fieldwork, Federal Work-Study, institutionally sponsored loans, scholarships/grants, tuition waivers (partial), and unspecified assistantships available. Support available to part-time students. Financial award applicants required to submit FAFSA. *Application contact:* Dr. Brenda Riemer, Advisor, 734-487-0090 Ext. 2745, Fax: 734-487-2024, E-mail: briemer@emich.edu.

Eastern New Mexico University, Graduate School, College of Education and Technology, Department of Health and Physical Education, Portales, NM 88130. Offers sport administration (MS), including coaching, sport science. *Program availability:* Part-time. *Degree requirements:* For master's, comprehensive exam, thesis optional. *Entrance requirements:* For master's, minimum GPA of 3.0, 15 hours of leveling courses without bachelor's degree in physical education, two references. Additional exam requirements/recommendations for international students: Required—TOEFL (minimum score 550 paper-based; 79 iBT), IELTS (minimum score 6). Electronic applications accepted. *Expenses: Tuition, area resident:* Full-time $6776. Tuition, state resident: full-time $6776; part-time $282 per credit hour. Tuition, nonresident: full-time $8986; part-time $374 per credit hour. *Required fees:* $60 per semester. One-time fee: $25.

Eastern Washington University, Graduate Studies, College of Arts, Letters and Education, Department of Physical Education, Health and Recreation, Cheney, WA 99004-2431. Offers exercise science (MS); sports and recreation administration (MS). *Degree requirements:* For master's, comprehensive exam, thesis or alternative. *Entrance requirements:* For master's, minimum GPA of 3.0. Additional exam requirements/recommendations for international students: Required—TOEFL (minimum score 580 paper-based; 92 iBT), IELTS (minimum score 7), PTE (minimum score 63). Electronic applications accepted.

East Stroudsburg University of Pennsylvania, Graduate and Extended Studies, College of Business and Management, Department of Sport Management, East Stroudsburg, PA 18301-2999. Offers MS. *Program availability:* Part-time, evening/weekend, online learning. *Faculty:* 4 full-time (2 women). *Students:* 15 full-time (9 women), 2 part-time (1 woman); includes 1 minority (Black or African American, non-Hispanic/Latino), 3 international. Average age 27. 23 applicants, 83% accepted, 9 enrolled. In 2018, 17 master's awarded. *Degree requirements:* For master's, comprehensive exam. *Entrance requirements:* For master's, GRE and/or GMAT, letters of recommendation, goals statement. Additional exam requirements/recommendations for international students: Recommended—TOEFL (minimum score 560 paper-based; 83 iBT), IELTS. *Application deadline:* For fall admission, 7/31 priority date for domestic students, 6/30 priority date for international students; for spring admission, 11/30 for domestic students, 10/31 for international students. Applications are processed on a rolling basis. Application fee: $50. Electronic applications accepted. *Expenses: Tuition, area resident:* Full-time $9288; part-time $516 per credit. Tuition, state resident: full-time $9288. Tuition, nonresident: full-time $13,932; part-time $774 per credit. *International tuition:* $13,932 full-time. *Required fees:* $2059; $114 per credit. Tuition and fees vary according to course load and degree level. *Financial support:* Research assistantships with tuition reimbursements, Federal Work-Study, and unspecified

assistantships available. Support available to part-time students. Financial award application deadline: 3/1; financial award applicants required to submit FAFSA. *Unit head:* Dr. Jaedock Lee, Chair, 570-422-3340, Fax: 570-422-3824, E-mail: jaedeock@esu.edu. *Application contact:* Kevin Quintero, Associate Director, Graduate and Extended Studies, 570-422-3890, Fax: 570-422-2711, E-mail: kquintero@esu.edu.

East Tennessee State University, School of Graduate Studies, College of Education, Department of Sport, Exercise, Recreation, and Kinesiology, Johnson City, TN 37614-1701. Offers sport management (MA); sport physiology and performance (PhD), including sport performance, sport physiology; sport science and coach education (MS), including applied sport science, strength and conditioning. *Program availability:* Part-time, evening/weekend. Terminal master's awarded for partial completion of doctoral program. *Degree requirements:* For master's, comprehensive exam, thesis or internship; for doctorate, comprehensive exam, thesis/dissertation, 2-semester residency. *Entrance requirements:* For master's, GRE General Test or GMAT, undergraduate degree in related field; minimum GPA of 3.0; resume; three references; essay explaining goals and reasons for pursuing degree; for doctorate, GRE, resume; 4 letters of recommendation; master's or bachelor's degree in related field; minimum GPA of 3.4 overall with master's, 3.0 with bachelor's; interview. Additional exam requirements/recommendations for international students: Required—TOEFL (minimum score 550 paper-based; 79 iBT). Electronic applications accepted. *Faculty research:* Methods of training for individual and team sports, enhancing acute sport performance, fatigue management in athletes, risk management, facilities management, motorsport.

East Tennessee State University, School of Graduate Studies, Program in Global Sport Leadership, Johnson City, TN 37614. Offers Ed D.

Endicott College, Van Loan School of Graduate and Professional Studies, Program in Athletic Administration, Beverly, MA 01915-2096. Offers M Ed. *Program availability:* Part-time, evening/weekend. *Degree requirements:* For master's, thesis, practicum. *Entrance requirements:* For master's, GRE or MAT, undergraduate transcript, personal statement, interview, two letters of recommendation. Additional exam requirements/recommendations for international students: Required—TOEFL. Electronic applications accepted. *Expenses:* Contact institution.

Fairleigh Dickinson University, Florham Campus, Anthony J. Petrocelli College of Continuing Studies, Program in Sports Administration, Madison, NJ 07940-1099. Offers MSA.

Fairleigh Dickinson University, Metropolitan Campus, Anthony J. Petrocelli College of Continuing Studies, Department of Sports Administration, Program in Sports Administration, Teaneck, NJ 07666-1914. Offers MSA.

Florida Agricultural and Mechanical University, Division of Graduate Studies, Research, and Continuing Education, College of Education, Department of Health, Physical Education, and Recreation, Tallahassee, FL 32307-3200. Offers sport management (MS). *Accreditation:* NCATE. *Program availability:* Part-time, evening/weekend. *Degree requirements:* For master's, thesis optional. *Entrance requirements:* For master's, GRE General Test, minimum GPA of 3.0. Additional exam requirements/recommendations for international students: Required—TOEFL. *Faculty research:* Administration/curriculum, work behavior, psychology.

Florida Atlantic University, College of Business, Department of Management, Boca Raton, FL 33431-0991. Offers business administration (MBA); entrepreneurship (MBA); health administration (MBA); international business (MBA); sport management (MBA). *Faculty:* 8 full-time (3 women). *Students:* 109 full-time (81 women), 82 part-time (58 women); includes 106 minority (52 Black or African American, non-Hispanic/Latino; 8 Asian, non-Hispanic/Latino; 40 Hispanic/Latino; 6 Two or more races, non-Hispanic/Latino), 1 international. Average age 35. 113 applicants, 85% accepted, 72 enrolled. In 2018, 120 master's awarded. *Entrance requirements:* For master's, GMAT or GRE General Test, minimum GPA of 3.0 in last 60 hours of course work. Additional exam requirements/recommendations for international students: Required—TOEFL (minimum score 600 paper-based; 61 iBT), IELTS (minimum score 6). *Application deadline:* For fall admission, 7/25 for domestic students, 2/15 for international students; for spring admission, 12/10 for domestic students, 7/15 for international students. Applications are processed on a rolling basis. Application fee: $30. Electronic applications accepted. *Expenses: Tuition, area resident:* Full-time $7400; part-time $369.82 per credit. Tuition, state resident: full-time $7400; part-time $369.82 per credit. Tuition, nonresident: full-time $20,496; part-time $1024.81 per credit. *Financial support:* Research assistantships with full tuition reimbursements, career-related internships or fieldwork, tuition waivers (partial), and unspecified assistantships available. *Faculty research:* Sports administration, healthcare, policy, finance, real estate, senior living. *Unit head:* Dr. Roland Kidwell, Chair, 561-297-4507, E-mail: kidwellr@fau.edu. *Application contact:* Dr. Roland Kidwell, Chair, 561-297-4507, E-mail: kidwellr@fau.edu.
Website: http://business.fau.edu/departments/management/index.aspx

Florida International University, College of Arts, Sciences, and Education, Department of Leadership and Professional Studies, Miami, FL 33199. Offers adult education and human resource development (MS, Ed D); counseling (MS), including rehabilitation counseling; school counseling; counselor education (MS), including clinical mental health counseling; educational administration and supervision (Ed D); educational leadership (MS, Certificate, Ed S); higher education (Ed D); higher education administration (MS); international and comparative education (MS); recreation and sport management (MS), including recreation and sport management, recreational therapy; school psychology (Ed S); urban education (MS), including instruction in urban settings, learning technologies, multicultural/bilingual, multicultural/TESOL, urban education. *Program availability:* Part-time, evening/weekend. *Faculty:* 64 full-time (43 women), 104 part-time/adjunct (76 women). *Students:* 258 full-time (196 women), 217 part-time (155 women); includes 387 minority (118 Black or African American, non-Hispanic/Latino; 8 Asian, non-Hispanic/Latino; 249 Hispanic/Latino; 12 Two or more races, non-Hispanic/Latino), 11 international. Average age 31. 345 applicants, 57% accepted, 126 enrolled. In 2018, 172 master's, 11 doctorates awarded. *Entrance requirements:* For master's, minimum GPA of 3.0; for doctorate and other advanced degree, GRE General Test. Additional exam requirements/recommendations for international students: Required—TOEFL (minimum score 550 paper-based; 80 iBT), IELTS (minimum score 6.3). *Application deadline:* For fall admission, 6/1 priority date for domestic students, 4/1 for international students; for winter admission, 10/1 priority date for domestic students, 9/1 for international students; for spring admission, 3/1 priority date for domestic students, 2/1 for international students. Applications are processed on a rolling basis. Application fee: $30. Electronic applications accepted. *Financial support:* Fellowships, research assistantships, teaching assistantships, Federal Work-Study, and tuition waivers (full and partial) available. Support available to part-time students. Financial award applicants required to submit FAFSA. *Unit head:* Dr. Benjamin Baez, Chair, 305-348-3214, Fax: 305-348-1515, E-mail: benjamin.baez@fiu.edu. *Application contact:* Nanett Rojas, Manager, Admissions Operations, 305-348-7464, Fax: 305-348-7441, E-mail: gradadm@fiu.edu.
Website: http://education.fiu.edu

Florida State University, The Graduate School, College of Education, Department of Sport Management, Tallahassee, FL 32306. Offers MS, PhD. *Program availability:* Part-time, evening/weekend, 100% online, blended/hybrid learning, asynchronous, minimal

on-campus study. *Faculty:* 9 full-time (4 women), 1 part-time/adjunct (0 women). *Students:* 95 full-time (40 women), 16 part-time (5 women); includes 52 minority (16 Black or African American, non-Hispanic/Latino; 14 Asian, non-Hispanic/Latino; 14 Hispanic/Latino; 8 Two or more races, non-Hispanic/Latino), 23 international. Average age 26. 143 applicants, 45% accepted, 38 enrolled. In 2018, 49 master's, 3 doctorates awarded. Terminal master's awarded for partial completion of doctoral program. *Degree requirements:* For master's, comprehensive exam, thesis optional; for doctorate, comprehensive exam, thesis/dissertation, diagnostic exam, preliminary exam, prospectus defense, dissertation defense. *Entrance requirements:* For master's and doctorate, GRE General Test, minimum upper-division GPA of 3.0. Additional exam requirements/recommendations for international students: Required—TOEFL (minimum score 550 paper-based, 80 iBT), IELTS (minimum score 6.5), Michigan English Language Assessment Battery (minimum score 77), or PTE (minimum score 55). Application fee: $30. Electronic applications accepted. *Expenses: Tuition, area resident:* Part-time $479.32 per credit hour. Tuition and fees vary according to campus/location and program. *Financial support:* In 2018–19, 100 teaching assistantships (averaging $13,269 per year) were awarded; fellowships, research assistantships, scholarships/grants, tuition waivers (full and partial), and unspecified assistantships also available. Financial award application deadline: 1/15; financial award applicants required to submit FAFSA. *Faculty research:* Sociology of sport; media and culture studies in sport; sport marketing and sport consumer behavior; legal and policy studies in sport; sports gambling; sport management; social network analysis. *Unit head:* Dr. Jeffrey D. James, Professor/Department Chair, 850-644-6885, Fax: 850-644-2725, E-mail: jdjames@fsu.edu. *Application contact:* Jeffrey Hoh, Academic Program Specialist, 850-644-0577, Fax: 850-644-7903, E-mail: jhoh@admin.fsu.edu.

Franklin Pierce University, Graduate and Professional Studies, Rindge, NH 03461-0060. Offers curriculum and instruction (M Ed); elementary education (MS Ed); emerging network technologies (Graduate Certificate); energy and sustainability studies (MBA, Graduate Certificate); health administration (MBA, Graduate Certificate); human resource management (MBA, Graduate Certificate); information technology (MBA); leadership (MBA); nursing education (MS); nursing leadership (MS); physical therapy (DPT); physician assistant studies (MPAS); special education (M Ed); sports management (MBA). *Accreditation:* APTA. *Program availability:* Part-time, 100% online, blended/hybrid learning. *Degree requirements:* For master's, concentrated original research projects; student teaching; fieldwork and/or internship; leadership project; PRAXIS I and II (for M Ed); for doctorate, concentrated original research projects, clinical fieldwork and/or internship, leadership project. *Entrance requirements:* For master's, minimum GPA of 2.5, 3 letters of recommendation; competencies in accounting, economics, statistics, and computer skills through life experience or undergraduate coursework (for MBA); certification/e-portfolio, minimum C grade in all education courses (for M Ed); license to practice as RN (for MS); for doctorate, GRE, 80 hours of observation/work in PT settings; completion of anatomy, chemistry, physics, and statistics; minimum GPA of 3.0. Additional exam requirements/recommendations for international students: Required—TOEFL (minimum score 550 paper-based; 61 iBT). Electronic applications accepted. *Faculty research:* Evidence-based practice in sports physical therapy, human resource management in economic crisis, leadership in nursing, innovation in sports facility management, differentiated learning and understanding by design.

George Mason University, College of Education and Human Development, School of Recreation, Health and Tourism, Manassas, VA 20110. Offers athletic training (MS); exercise, fitness, and health promotion (MS), including advanced practitioner, wellness practitioner; international sport management (Certificate); recreation, health and tourism (Certificate); sport management (MS), including sport and recreation studies. *Program availability:* Part-time, evening/weekend. *Faculty:* 33 full-time (15 women), 84 part-time/adjunct (44 women). *Students:* 76 full-time (33 women), 21 part-time (5 women); includes 32 minority (25 Black or African American, non-Hispanic/Latino; 1 American Indian or Alaska Native, non-Hispanic/Latino; 1 Asian, non-Hispanic/Latino; 3 Hispanic/Latino; 1 Native Hawaiian or other Pacific Islander, non-Hispanic/Latino; 1 Two or more races, non-Hispanic/Latino), 17 international. Average age 26. 77 applicants, 88% accepted, 41 enrolled. In 2018, 26 master's, 1 other advanced degree awarded. *Entrance requirements:* For master's, 3 letters of recommendation; official transcripts; expanded goals statement; undergraduate course in statistics and minimum GPA of 3.0 in last 60 credit hours and overall (for MS in sport and recreation studies); baccalaureate degree related to kinesiology, exercise science or athletic training (for MS in exercise, fitness and health promotion). Additional exam requirements/recommendations for international students: Required—TOEFL (minimum score 575 paper-based; 88 iBT), IELTS (minimum score 6.5), PTE (minimum score 59). *Application deadline:* For fall admission, 4/2 priority date for domestic and international students; for spring admission, 11/1 for domestic and international students. Application fee: $75 ($80 for international students). Electronic applications accepted. *Financial support:* In 2018–19, 6 students received support, including 6 research assistantships with tuition reimbursements available (averaging $7,242 per year); career-related internships or fieldwork, Federal Work-Study, scholarships/grants, unspecified assistantships, and health care benefits (for full-time research or teaching assistantship recipients) also available. Support available to part-time students. Financial award application deadline: 3/1; financial award applicants required to submit FAFSA. *Faculty research:* Sport for development and peace, sport analytics, leadership and coaching, diversity and inclusion in sport, sport communication. *Total annual research expenditures:* $826,386. *Unit head:* Martin Ford, Senior Associate Dean, 703-993-2004, E-mail: mford@gmu.edu. *Application contact:* Lindsey Olson, Office Assistant, 703-993-2098, Fax: 703-993-2025, E-mail: lolson7@gmu.edu.
Website: http://rht.gmu.edu/

Georgetown University, Graduate School of Arts and Sciences, School of Continuing Studies, Washington, DC 20057. Offers American studies (MALS); applied intelligence (MPS); Catholic studies (MALS); classical civilizations (MALS); emergency and disaster management (MPS); ethics and the professions (MALS); global strategic communications (MPS); hospitality management (MPS); human resources management (MPS); humanities (MALS); individualized study (MALS); integrated marketing communications (MPS); international affairs (MALS); Islam and Muslim-Christian relations (MALS); journalism (MPS); liberal studies (DLS); literature and society (MALS); medieval and early modern European studies (MALS); public relations and corporate communications (MPS); real estate (MPS); religious studies (MALS); social and public policy (MALS); sports industry management (MPS); systems engineering management (MPS); technology management (MPS); the theory and practice of American democracy (MALS); urban and regional planning (MPS); visual culture (MALS). MPS in systems engineering management offered jointly with Stevens Institute of Technology. *Entrance requirements:* Additional exam requirements/recommendations for international students: Required—TOEFL.

The George Washington University, School of Business, Department of Tourism and Hospitality Management, Washington, DC 20052. Offers destination management (Professional Certificate); event and meeting management (MTA); event management (Professional Certificate); hospitality management (MTA); individualized studies (MTA); sport management (MTA); sustainable tourism destination management (MTA); tourism and hospitality management (MBA). *Program availability:* Part-time, online learning. *Students:* 79 full-time (46 women), 35 part-time (28 women); includes 37 minority (21 Black or African American, non-Hispanic/Latino; 5 Asian, non-Hispanic/Latino; 9 Hispanic/Latino; 2 Two or more races, non-Hispanic/Latino), 40 international. Average age 28. 161 applicants, 76% accepted, 47 enrolled. In 2018, 50 master's awarded. *Degree requirements:* For master's, comprehensive exam, thesis. *Entrance requirements:* For master's, GRE General Test. Additional exam requirements/recommendations for international students: Required—TOEFL. *Application deadline:* For fall admission, 4/1 priority date for domestic students; for spring admission, 10/1 for domestic students. Applications are processed on a rolling basis. Application fee: $75. *Financial support:* In 2018–19, 32 students received support. Fellowships, teaching assistantships, career-related internships or fieldwork, Federal Work-Study, institutionally sponsored loans, and tuition waivers (partial) available. Financial award application deadline: 4/1. *Faculty research:* Tourism policy, tourism impact forecasting, geotourism. *Unit head:* Prof. Lisa Delpy Neirotti, Faculty Director, 202-994-6623, E-mail: delpy@gwu.edu. *Application contact:* Christopher Storer, Executive Director, Graduate Admissions, 202-994-1212, E-mail: gwmba@gwu.edu.
Website: http://business.gwu.edu/tourism/

Georgia Southern University, Jack N. Averitt College of Graduate Studies, Waters College of Health Professions, Department of Health Sciences and Kinesiology, Program in Sport Management, Statesboro, GA 30460. Offers MS. *Program availability:* Part-time, 100% online. *Faculty:* 5 full-time (2 women). *Students:* 9 full-time (1 woman), 24 part-time (12 women); includes 10 minority (8 Black or African American, non-Hispanic/Latino; 1 Hispanic/Latino; 1 Two or more races, non-Hispanic/Latino), 1 international. Average age 26. 36 applicants, 67% accepted, 16 enrolled. In 2018, 12 master's awarded. *Degree requirements:* For master's, terminal exam. *Entrance requirements:* For master's, resume, statement of purpose, interview video. Additional exam requirements/recommendations for international students: Required—TOEFL (minimum score 550 paper-based; 80 iBT), IELTS (minimum score 6). *Application deadline:* For fall admission, 3/1 priority date for domestic and international students. Applications are processed on a rolling basis. Application fee: $50. Electronic applications accepted. *Expenses: Tuition, area resident:* Part-time $3324 per semester. Tuition, state resident: full-time $5814; part-time $3324 per semester. Tuition, nonresident: full-time $23,204; part-time $13,260 per semester. *Required fees:* $2092; $2092. Tuition and fees vary according to course load, degree level, campus/location and program. *Financial support:* In 2018–19, 12 students received support, including 1 research assistantship with full tuition reimbursement available (averaging $7,750 per year), 1 teaching assistantship with full tuition reimbursement available (averaging $7,750 per year); scholarships/grants and unspecified assistantships also available. Financial award application deadline: 7/1; financial award applicants required to submit FAFSA. *Faculty research:* Fan/consumer behavior, participant experiences in sport and fitness, sport law, impact of sport and fitness on underresearched populations, sport marketing. *Total annual research expenditures:* $3,000. *Unit head:* Dr. Christina Gipson, Assistant Professor, 912-478-1101, Fax: 912-478-0381, E-mail: Cgipson@georgiasouthern.edu. *Application contact:* Dr. Christina Gipson, 912-4781101, E-mail: cgipson@georgiasouthern.edu.

Georgia State University, College of Education and Human Development, Department of Kinesiology and Health, Program in Sports Administration, Atlanta, GA 30302-3083. Offers MS. *Entrance requirements:* For master's, GRE General Test, minimum GPA of 2.5. Application fee: $50. *Expenses: Tuition, area resident:* Full-time $9360; part-time $390 per credit hour. Tuition, state resident: full-time $9360; part-time $390 per credit hour. Tuition, nonresident: full-time $30,024; part-time $1251 per credit hour. *International tuition:* $30,024 full-time. *Required fees:* $2128. *Financial support:* Research assistantships available. *Faculty research:* Sports marketing. *Unit head:* Dr. Jacalyn Lea Lund, Chair, 404-413-8051, E-mail: jlund@gsu.edu. *Application contact:* Dr. Jacalyn Lea Lund, Chair, 404-413-8051, E-mail: jlund@gsu.edu.
Website: https://education.gsu.edu/kh/

Gonzaga University, School of Education, Spokane, WA 99258. Offers clinical mental health counseling (MA); educational leadership (M Ed, Ed D); elementary education (MIT); marriage and family counseling (MA); school counseling (MA); secondary education (MIT); special education (M Ed, MIT); sport and athletic administration (MA). *Accreditation:* NCATE. *Program availability:* Part-time, evening/weekend, 100% online, blended/hybrid learning. *Degree requirements:* For master's, comprehensive exam. *Entrance requirements:* For master's, GRE, MAT, and/or Washington Educator Skills Test-Basic (WEST-B), Washington Educator Skills Test-Endorsements (WEST-E), official transcripts from all colleges or universities attended, interview, two letters of recommendation, resume, essay, minimum GPA of 3.0. Additional exam requirements/recommendations for international students: Required—TOEFL (minimum score 580 paper-based, 88 iBT) or IELTS (minimum score 6.5). Electronic applications accepted. *Expenses:* Contact institution.

Grambling State University, School of Graduate Studies and Research, College of Education, Department of Kinesiology, Sport and Leisure Studies, Grambling, LA 71245. Offers sports administration (MS). *Program availability:* Part-time. *Degree requirements:* For master's, comprehensive exam. *Entrance requirements:* For master's, GRE General Test, minimum GPA of 2.5 on last degree. Additional exam requirements/recommendations for international students: Required—TOEFL (minimum score 500 paper-based; 62 iBT). Electronic applications accepted. *Faculty research:* Administrative relations and organization, measuring human performance, sport history from ancient times through current date, learning dynamics of personality and sports selection.

Grand Canyon University, Colangelo College of Business, Phoenix, AZ 85017-1097. Offers accounting (MBA, MS); business analytics (MS); disaster preparedness and executive fire service leadership (MS); finance (MBA); general management (MBA); health systems management (MBA); information technology management (MS); leadership (MBA, MS); marketing (MBA); organizational leadership and entrepreneurship (MS); project management (MBA); sports business (MBA); strategic human resource management (MBA). *Accreditation:* ACBSP. *Program availability:* Part-time, evening/weekend, online learning. *Entrance requirements:* For master's, equivalent of two years' full-time professional work experience. Additional exam requirements/recommendations for international students: Required—TOEFL (minimum score 575 paper-based; 90 iBT), IELTS (minimum score 7). Electronic applications accepted.

Grand View University, Graduate Studies, Des Moines, IA 50316-1599. Offers athletic training (MS); clinical nurse leader (MSN, Post Master's Certificate); nursing education (MSN, Post Master's Certificate); organizational leadership (MS); sport management (MS); teacher leadership (M Ed); urban education (M Ed). *Program availability:* Part-time, evening/weekend. *Degree requirements:* For master's, completion of all required coursework in common core and selected track with minimum cumulative GPA of 3.0 and no more than two grades of C. *Entrance requirements:* For master's, GRE, GMAT, or essay, minimum undergraduate GPA of 3.0, professional resume, 3 letters of recommendation, interview. Additional exam requirements/recommendations for international students: Required—TOEFL (minimum score 550 paper-based). Electronic applications accepted.

Hampton University, School of Liberal Arts and Education, Program in Sport Administration, Hampton, VA 23668. Offers intercollegiate athletics (MS); international

sports (MS); organizational behavior and sport business leadership (MS). *Program availability:* Part-time, evening/weekend. *Students:* 32 full-time (12 women), 3 part-time (1 woman); all minorities (all Black or African American, non-Hispanic/Latino). Average age 25. 20 applicants, 90% accepted, 12 enrolled. In 2018, 17 master's awarded. *Degree requirements:* For master's, thesis (for some programs). *Entrance requirements:* For master's, GRE. Additional exam requirements/recommendations for international students: Required—TOEFL (minimum score 525 paper-based) or IELTS (6.5). *Application deadline:* For fall admission, 6/1 priority date for domestic students, 4/1 priority date for international students; for spring admission, 11/1 priority date for domestic students, 9/1 priority date for international students; for summer admission, 4/1 priority date for domestic students, 2/1 priority date for international students. Applications are processed on a rolling basis. Application fee: $35. Electronic applications accepted. *Expenses:* Contact institution. *Financial support:* Fellowships, research assistantships, teaching assistantships, and career-related internships or fieldwork available. Financial award application deadline: 6/30; financial award applicants required to submit FAFSA. *Faculty research:* International sport, intercollegiate sport, sport leadership, professional sport, event management. *Unit head:* Dr. Aaron Livingston, Program Coordinator, 757-637-2278, E-mail: aaron.livingston@hamptonu.edu. *Application contact:* Dr. Aaron Livingston, Program Coordinator, 757-637-2278, E-mail: aaron.livingston@hamptonu.edu.

Hardin-Simmons University, Graduate School, Kelley College of Business, Abilene, TX 79698-0001. Offers business administration (MBA); information science (MS); sports management (MBA). *Accreditation:* ACBSP. *Program availability:* Part-time. *Faculty:* 10 full-time (3 women). *Students:* 32 full-time (6 women), 55 part-time (23 women); includes 16 minority (5 Black or African American, non-Hispanic/Latino; 11 Hispanic/Latino), 2 international. Average age 29. 48 applicants, 96% accepted, 41 enrolled. In 2018, 27 master's awarded. *Degree requirements:* For master's, thesis or alternative. *Entrance requirements:* For master's, GMAT, minimum GPA of 3.0 in upper-level course work, resume, interview. Additional exam requirements/recommendations for international students: Required—TOEFL (minimum score 550 paper-based; 79 iBT). *Application deadline:* For fall admission, 8/15 priority date for domestic students, 4/1 for international students; for spring admission, 1/5 priority date for domestic students, 9/1 for international students. Applications are processed on a rolling basis. Application fee: $50. Electronic applications accepted. *Expenses: Tuition:* Full-time $750; part-time $750 per credit hour. *Required fees:* $1300; $880 per credit. Tuition and fees vary according to degree level and program. *Financial support:* Fellowships and scholarships/grants available. Support available to part-time students. Financial award application deadline: 6/30; financial award applicants required to submit FAFSA. *Unit head:* Dr. Jennifer Plantier, Program Director, 325-671-2166, Fax: 325-670-1523, E-mail: jplantier@hsutx.edu. *Application contact:* Dr. Nancy Kucinski, Dean of Graduate Studies, 325-670-1298, Fax: 325-670-1564, E-mail: gradoff@hsutx.edu.
Website: http://www.hsutx.edu/academics/kelley/graduate/

Henderson State University, Graduate Studies, Teachers College, Department of Health, Physical Education, Recreation and Athletic Training, Arkadelphia, AR 71999-0001. Offers sports administration (MS). *Program availability:* Part-time. *Entrance requirements:* For master's, GRE General Test or MAT, minimum GPA of 2.7 as an undergraduate student. Additional exam requirements/recommendations for international students: Required—TOEFL (minimum score 600 paper-based); Recommended—IELTS (minimum score 6.5).

Hofstra University, Frank G. Zarb School of Business, Programs in Management and General Business, Hempstead, NY 11549. Offers business administration (MBA), including health services management, management, sports and entertainment management, strategic business management, strategic healthcare management; general management (Advanced Certificate); human resource management (MS, Advanced Certificate). *Program availability:* Part-time, evening/weekend, blended/hybrid learning. *Students:* 121 full-time (48 women), 112 part-time (52 women); includes 96 minority (18 Black or African American, non-Hispanic/Latino; 1 American Indian or Alaska Native, non-Hispanic/Latino; 34 Asian, non-Hispanic/Latino; 38 Hispanic/Latino; 5 Two or more races, non-Hispanic/Latino), 16 international. Average age 33. 290 applicants, 75% accepted, 89 enrolled. In 2018, 110 master's awarded. *Degree requirements:* For master's, thesis optional, capstone course (for MBA), thesis (for MS), minimum GPA of 3.0. *Entrance requirements:* For master's, GMAT/GRE, 2 letters of recommendation, resume, essay. Additional exam requirements/recommendations for international students: Required—TOEFL (minimum score 550 paper-based; 80 iBT); Recommended—IELTS (minimum score 6). *Application deadline:* Applications are processed on a rolling basis. Application fee: $75. Electronic applications accepted. *Expenses:* $1,375 per credit plus fees. *Financial support:* In 2018–19, 91 students received support, including 84 fellowships with full and partial tuition reimbursements available (averaging $4,279 per year), 1 research assistantship with full and partial tuition reimbursement available (averaging $9,179 per year); career-related internships or fieldwork, Federal Work-Study, institutionally sponsored loans, scholarships/grants, tuition waivers (full and partial), unspecified assistantships, and scholarships and endowed scholarships also available. Support available to part-time students. Financial award applicants required to submit FAFSA. *Faculty research:* Organizational behavior; sustainability; entrepreneurial spawning; family business; global supply chain strategies. *Unit head:* Dr. Kaushik Sengupta, Chairperson, 516-463-7825, Fax: 516-463-4834, E-mail: kaushik.sengupta@hofstra.edu. *Application contact:* Sunil Samuel, Assistant Vice President of Admissions, 516-463-4723, Fax: 516-463-4664, E-mail: graduateadmission@hofstra.edu.
Website: http://www.hofstra.edu/business/

Houston Baptist University, School of Nursing and Allied Health, Program in Kinesiology - Sport Management, Houston, TX 77074-3298. Offers sport management (MSK). *Program availability:* Online only, 100% online. *Degree requirements:* For master's, internship or thesis. *Entrance requirements:* For master's, GRE, bachelor's degree conferred transcript, personal statement/essay, resume. Additional exam requirements/recommendations for international students: Required—TOEFL (minimum score 80 iBT), IELTS (minimum score 6.5). Electronic applications accepted. Application fee is waived when completed online. *Expenses:* Contact institution.

Howard Payne University, Program in Sport and Wellness Leadership, Brownwood, TX 76801-2715. Offers M Ed. *Program availability:* Part-time. *Entrance requirements:* For master's, baccalaureate degree and major or minor in exercise and sport science, kinesiology, sport administration, wellness or a related field; minimum undergraduate GPA of 3.0; official transcripts; 500-word statement of professional goals; two letters of recommendation. Additional exam requirements/recommendations for international students: Required—TOEFL. Electronic applications accepted.

Howard University, Graduate School, Department of Health, Human Performance and Leisure Studies, Washington, DC 20059-0002. Offers exercise physiology (MS); health education (MS); sports studies (MS), including sociology of sports, sports management; urban recreation (MS), including leisure studies. *Program availability:* Part-time, evening/weekend. *Degree requirements:* For master's, comprehensive exam, thesis. *Entrance requirements:* For master's, BS in human performance or related field. Additional exam requirements/recommendations for international students: Recommended—TOEFL. Electronic applications accepted. *Faculty research:* Health

promotion, cardiovascular hypertension, physical activity, sport and human rights issues.

Husson University, Master of Business Administration Program, Bangor, ME 04401-2999. Offers athletic administration (MBA); biotechnology and innovation (MBA); general business administration (MBA); healthcare management (MBA); hospitality and tourism management (MBA); organizational management (MBA); risk management (MBA). *Program availability:* Part-time, evening/weekend, 100% online, blended/hybrid learning. *Degree requirements:* For master's, comprehensive exam (for some programs), thesis optional. *Entrance requirements:* For master's, minimum GPA of 3.0, letter of recommendation. Additional exam requirements/recommendations for international students: Required—TOEFL (minimum score 550 paper-based; 80 iBT), IELTS (minimum score 6.5). Electronic applications accepted. *Expenses:* Contact institution.

Idaho State University, Graduate School, College of Education, Department of Sport Science and Physical Education, Pocatello, ID 83209-8105. Offers athletic administration (MPE); athletic training (MSAT). *Program availability:* Part-time. *Degree requirements:* For master's, comprehensive exam (for some programs), thesis optional, internship, oral defense of dissertation, or written exams. *Entrance requirements:* For master's, MAT or GRE General Test, minimum GPA of 3.0 in upper division classes. Additional exam requirements/recommendations for international students: Required—TOEFL (minimum score 550 paper-based; 80 iBT). Electronic applications accepted. *Faculty research:* Gender and diversity; concussion awareness/sports medicine; legal aspects of athletic health care; sports psychology; exercise physiology; sports management and leadership; adapted activities; fitness, wellness, and nutrition; coaching perspectives; critical features of athletic activities.

Indiana State University, College of Graduate and Professional Studies, College of Health and Human Services, Department of Kinesiology, Recreation, and Sport, Terre Haute, IN 47809. Offers physical education (MS); recreation and sport management (MS); sport management (PhD). *Degree requirements:* For master's, comprehensive exam (for some programs), thesis (for some programs). *Entrance requirements:* For master's, GRE General Test, undergraduate major in related field. Electronic applications accepted.

Indiana University Bloomington, School of Public Health, Department of Kinesiology, Bloomington, IN 47405. Offers applied sport science (MS); athletic administration/sport management (MS); athletic training (MS); biomechanics (MS); ergonomics (MS); exercise physiology (MS); human performance (PhD), including biomechanics, exercise physiology, motor learning/control, sport management; motor learning/control (MS); physical activity (MPH); physical activity, fitness and wellness (MS). *Program availability:* Part-time. Terminal master's awarded for partial completion of doctoral program. *Degree requirements:* For master's, thesis optional; for doctorate, variable foreign language requirement, comprehensive exam, thesis/dissertation. *Entrance requirements:* For master's, GRE General Test, minimum GPA of 2.8; for doctorate, GRE General Test, minimum graduate GPA of 3.5, undergraduate 3.0. Additional exam requirements/recommendations for international students: Required—TOEFL (minimum score 80 iBT). *Faculty research:* Exercise physiology and biochemistry, sports biomechanics, human motor control, adaptation of fitness and exercise to special populations.

Indiana University Bloomington, School of Public Health, Department of Recreation, Park, and Tourism Studies, Bloomington, IN 47405-7000. Offers leisure behavior (PhD); outdoor recreation (MS); park and public lands management (MS); recreation administration (MS); recreational sports administration (MS); recreational therapy (MS); tourism management (MS). Terminal master's awarded for partial completion of doctoral program. *Degree requirements:* For master's, thesis optional; for doctorate, comprehensive exam, thesis/dissertation. *Entrance requirements:* For master's, GRE General Test, minimum GPA of 2.8; for doctorate, GRE General Test, minimum GPA of 3.0 (undergraduate), 3.5 (graduate). Additional exam requirements/recommendations for international students: Required—TOEFL (minimum score 550 paper-based; 80 iBT). Electronic applications accepted. *Faculty research:* Leisure counseling, gerontology, special populations, planning and development.

Indiana University of Pennsylvania, School of Graduate Studies and Research, College of Health and Human Services, Department of Kinesiology, Health, and Sport Science, Program in Sport Science/Sport Management, Indiana, PA 15705. Offers MS. *Faculty:* 11 full-time (3 women). *Students:* 15 full-time (4 women), 7 part-time (1 woman); includes 6 minority (all Black or African American, non-Hispanic/Latino), 1 international. Average age 25. 20 applicants, 80% accepted, 12 enrolled. In 2018, 12 master's awarded. *Degree requirements:* For master's, thesis or internship. *Entrance requirements:* Additional exam requirements/recommendations for international students: Required—TOEFL (minimum score 540 paper-based). Application fee: $50. *Expenses:* Contact institution. *Financial support:* In 2018–19, 4 research assistantships with tuition reimbursements (averaging $4,136 per year) were awarded. Financial award application deadline: 4/15; financial award applicants required to submit FAFSA. *Unit head:* Dr. Richard Hsaio, Graduate Coordinator, 724-357-0123, E-mail: hsaio@iup.edu. *Application contact:* Dr. Richard Hsaio, Graduate Coordinator, 724-357-0123, E-mail: hsaio@iup.edu.
Website: http://www.iup.edu/grad/sportscience/default.aspx

Iona College, School of Business, Department of Marketing and International Business, New Rochelle, NY 10801-1890. Offers international business (AC, PMC); marketing (MBA); sports and entertainment management (AC). *Program availability:* Part-time, evening/weekend. *Faculty:* 3 full-time (1 woman), 3 part-time/adjunct (1 woman). *Students:* 14 full-time (10 women), 26 part-time (13 women); includes 17 minority (4 Black or African American, non-Hispanic/Latino; 1 Asian, non-Hispanic/Latino; 12 Hispanic/Latino), 3 international. Average age 25. 15 applicants, 93% accepted, 8 enrolled. In 2018, 13 master's, 78 other advanced degrees awarded. *Entrance requirements:* For master's, GMAT, 2 letters of recommendation, minimum GPA of 3.0; for other advanced degree, GMAT, minimum GPA of 3.0. Additional exam requirements/recommendations for international students: Required—TOEFL (minimum score 550 paper-based; 80 iBT), IELTS (minimum score 6.5). *Application deadline:* For fall admission, 8/15 priority date for domestic students, 8/1 priority date for international students; for winter admission, 11/15 priority date for domestic students, 11/1 priority date for international students; for spring admission, 2/15 priority date for domestic students, 2/1 priority date for international students; for summer admission, 5/15 for domestic students, 5/1 priority date for international students. Applications are processed on a rolling basis. Application fee: $50. Electronic applications accepted. *Expenses:* Contact institution. *Financial support:* In 2018–19, 38 students received support. Scholarships/grants, tuition waivers (partial), and unspecified assistantships available. Support available to part-time students. Financial award application deadline: 4/15; financial award applicants required to submit FAFSA. *Faculty research:* Business ethics, international retailing, mega-marketing, consumer behavior and consumer confidence. *Unit head:* Dr. Susan G. Rozensher, Department Chair, 914-637-2748, E-mail: srozensher@iona.edu. *Application contact:* Kimberly Kelly, Director of Graduate Business Admissions, 914-633-2271, Fax: 914-633-2012, E-mail: kkelly@iona.edu.
Website: http://www.iona.edu/Academics/Hagan-School-of-Business/Departments/Marketing/Graduate-Programs.aspx

Sports Management

Ithaca College, School of Business, Program in Business Administration, Ithaca, NY 14850. Offers sport management (MBA). *Accreditation:* AACSB. *Program availability:* Part-time. *Faculty:* 7 full-time (2 women). *Students:* 8 full-time (5 women), 4 part-time (3 women); includes 3 minority (1 Asian, non-Hispanic/Latino; 2 Hispanic/Latino), 1 international. Average age 27. 13 applicants, 77% accepted, 8 enrolled. In 2018, 6 master's awarded. *Entrance requirements:* For master's, GMAT. Additional exam requirements/recommendations for international students: Required—TOEFL (minimum score 550 paper-based; 80 iBT). *Application deadline:* For fall admission, 5/15 for domestic and international students; for spring admission, 11/1 for domestic and international students. Applications are processed on a rolling basis. Application fee: $40. Electronic applications accepted. *Expenses:* Contact institution. *Financial support:* In 2018–19, 9 students received support, including 7 fellowships (averaging $7,857 per year); career-related internships or fieldwork, Federal Work-Study, and scholarships/grants also available. Support available to part-time students. Financial award application deadline: 3/1; financial award applicants required to submit FAFSA. *Unit head:* Dr. Rasoul Rezvanian, Associate Dean and Director, MBA Programs, 607-274-1762, Fax: 607-274-1263, E-mail: rrezvanian@ithaca.edu. *Application contact:* Nicole Eversley Bradwell, Director, Office of Admission, 607-800-429-4274, Fax: 607-274-1263, E-mail: admission@ithaca.edu.
Website: http://www.ithaca.edu/business/programs/

Jackson State University, Graduate School, College of Education and Human Development, Department of Health, Physical Education and Recreation, Jackson, MS 39217. Offers physical education (MS Ed); sport science (MS). *Accreditation:* NCATE. *Program availability:* Part-time, evening/weekend, 100% online, blended/hybrid learning. *Degree requirements:* For master's, comprehensive exam, thesis or alternative. *Entrance requirements:* For master's, GRE General Test. Additional exam requirements/recommendations for international students: Required—TOEFL (minimum score 520 paper-based; 67 iBT). Electronic applications accepted. *Expenses:* Contact institution.

Jacksonville University, Brooks Rehabilitation College of Healthcare Sciences, School of Applied Health Sciences, Program in Sport Management, Jacksonville, FL 32211. Offers MS. Program offered in conjunction with the Davis College of Business. *Program availability:* Part-time, online only, 100% online. *Entrance requirements:* For master's, GRE (minimum total score of 290), baccalaureate degree from accredited college or university with minimum GPA of 3.0; official transcripts; essay on personal professional goals (minimum 1000 words); resume (education, work experience); 3 letters of recommendation; interview. Additional exam requirements/recommendations for international students: Required—TOEFL (minimum score 650 paper-based; 114 iBT), IELTS (minimum score 8). Electronic applications accepted. *Expenses:* Contact institution.

Johnson & Wales University, Graduate Studies, MBA Program, Providence, RI 02903-3703. Offers accounting (MBA); business administration (MBA); finance (MBA); global fashion merchandising and management (MBA); hospitality (MBA); human resource management (MBA); information security/assurance (MBA); information technology (MBA); nonprofit management (MBA); operations and supply chain management (MBA); organizational leadership (MBA); organizational psychology (MBA); sport leadership (MBA). Program also offered on Denver campus. *Program availability:* Part-time, online learning. *Entrance requirements:* For master's, minimum GPA of 2.75. Additional exam requirements/recommendations for international students: Required—TOEFL (minimum score 550 paper-based); Recommended—IELTS, TWE. *Faculty research:* International banking, global economy, international trade, cultural differences.

Johnson & Wales University, Graduate Studies, MS Program in Sport Leadership, Providence, RI 02903-3703. Offers MS.

Kansas Wesleyan University, Program in Business Administration, Salina, KS 67401-6196. Offers business administration (MBA); sports management (MBA). *Program availability:* Part-time, evening/weekend. *Entrance requirements:* For master's, GMAT, minimum graduate GPA of 3.0 or undergraduate GPA of 3.25.

Kennesaw State University, WellStar College of Health and Human Services, Program in Applied Exercise and Health Science, Kennesaw, GA 30144. Offers exercise physiology (MS); sport management (MS). *Program availability:* Part-time, evening/weekend. *Students:* 41 full-time (20 women), 10 part-time (4 women); includes 22 minority (9 Black or African American, non-Hispanic/Latino; 1 Asian, non-Hispanic/Latino; 7 Hispanic/Latino; 5 Two or more races, non-Hispanic/Latino), 2 international. Average age 26. 37 applicants, 73% accepted, 22 enrolled. In 2018, 19 master's awarded. *Entrance requirements:* For master's, GRE, resume. Additional exam requirements/recommendations for international students: Required—TOEFL (minimum score 550 paper-based; 80 iBT), IELTS (minimum score 6.5). *Application deadline:* For fall admission, 6/1 for domestic and international students; for spring admission, 11/1 for domestic and international students; for summer admission, 4/1 for domestic and international students. Applications are processed on a rolling basis. Application fee: $60. Electronic applications accepted. *Expenses: Tuition, area resident:* Full-time $6960; part-time $290 per credit hour. Tuition, state resident: full-time $6960; part-time $290 per credit hour. Tuition, nonresident: full-time $25,080; part-time $1045 per credit hour. *International tuition:* $25,080 full-time. *Required fees:* $2006; $1706 per semester. $853 per semester. *Financial support:* Research assistantships available. Financial award applicants required to submit FAFSA. *Unit head:* Dr. Cherilyn McLester, Program Director, 470-578-2651, E-mail: cmclest1@kennesaw.edu. *Application contact:* Admissions Counselor, 470-578-4377, E-mail: ksugrad@kennesaw.edu.
Website: http://wellstarcollege.kennesaw.edu/essm/applied-exercise-health-science/index.php

Kent State University, College of Education, Health and Human Services, School of Foundations, Leadership and Administration, Sports and Recreation Management, Kent, OH 44242-0001. Offers sport and recreation management (MA); sports studies (MA). *Faculty:* 9 full-time (5 women), 19 part-time/adjunct (9 women). *Students:* 41 full-time (10 women), 14 part-time (6 women); includes 12 minority (9 Black or African American, non-Hispanic/Latino; 1 Asian, non-Hispanic/Latino; 2 Native Hawaiian or other Pacific Islander, non-Hispanic/Latino), 5 international. 61 applicants, 62% accepted. In 2018, 26 master's awarded. *Degree requirements:* For master's, thesis optional. *Entrance requirements:* For master's, GRE if undergraduate GPA below 3.0, goals statement, 2 letters of recommendation. Additional exam requirements/recommendations for international students: Required—TOEFL (minimum score 550 paper-based; 80 iBT). *Application deadline:* Applications are processed on a rolling basis. Application fee: $45 ($60 for international students). Electronic applications accepted. *Expenses:* Tuition, state resident: full-time $11,766; part-time $536 per credit. Tuition, nonresident: full-time $21,952; part-time $999 per credit. *International tuition:* $21,952 full-time. Tuition and fees vary according to course load. *Financial support:* In 2018–19, 7 research assistantships (averaging $8,500 per year) were awarded; teaching assistantships, Federal Work-Study, scholarships/grants, and unspecified assistantships also available. *Unit head:* Aaron Mulrooney, Coordinator, 330-672-0204, E-mail: amulroon@kent.edu. *Application contact:* Cheryl Slusarczyk, Academic Program Director, Office of Graduate Student Services, 330-672-2576, Fax: 330-672-9162, E-mail: ogs@kent.edu.

Lasell College, Graduate and Professional Studies in Sport Management, Newton, MA 02466-2709. Offers athletic administration (MS); parks and recreation (MS); sport leadership (MS, Graduate Certificate); sport tourism and hospitality (MS). *Program availability:* Part-time, evening/weekend, online only, 100% online. *Faculty:* 4 full-time (1 woman), 4 part-time/adjunct (2 women). *Students:* 15 full-time (7 women), 32 part-time (11 women); includes 17 minority (12 Black or African American, non-Hispanic/Latino; 4 Hispanic/Latino; 1 Two or more races, non-Hispanic/Latino). Average age 29. 36 applicants, 39% accepted, 11 enrolled. In 2018, 20 master's awarded. *Degree requirements:* For master's, minimum GPA of 3.0; internship or thesis. *Entrance requirements:* For master's, one-page personal statement, 2 letters of recommendation, resume, bachelor's degree transcript; for Graduate Certificate, bachelor's degree transcript, 2 letters of recommendation, 1-page personal statement, resume. Additional exam requirements/recommendations for international students: Required—TOEFL (minimum score 550 paper-based, 79 iBT) or IELTS (minimum score 6). *Application deadline:* For fall admission, 8/31 priority date for domestic students, 6/30 priority date for international students; for spring admission, 12/31 priority date for domestic students, 10/31 priority date for international students. Applications are processed on a rolling basis. Electronic applications accepted. *Expenses: Tuition:* Part-time $600 per credit. *Required fees:* $40 per course. *Financial support:* Federal Work-Study, scholarships/grants, and tuition discounts available. Support available to part-time students. Financial award application deadline: 8/31; financial award applicants required to submit FAFSA. *Faculty research:* How do fans attribute team failure; investigating cross-cultural difference in attribution; sense of ownership as a key predictor of fan loyalty; fans' normative beliefs about sponsorship and sponsors; investigation of new attitudinal variables in sponsorship. *Unit head:* Eric Turner, Vice President of Graduate and Professional Studies, 617-243-2071, Fax: 617-243-2450, E-mail: gradinfo@lasell.edu. *Application contact:* Adrienne Franciosi, Assistant Vice President of Graduate and Professional Studies, 617-243-2214, Fax: 617-243-2450, E-mail: gradinfo@lasell.edu.
Website: http://www.lasell.edu/academics/graduate-and-professional-studies/programs-of-study/master-of-science-in-sport-management.html

Lewis University, College of Arts and Sciences, Program in Organizational Leadership, Romeoville, IL 60446. Offers higher education/student services (MA); organizational and leadership coaching (MA); training and development (MA). *Program availability:* Part-time, evening/weekend, 100% online, blended/hybrid learning. *Students:* 13 full-time (9 women), 150 part-time (115 women); includes 45 minority (28 Black or African American, non-Hispanic/Latino; 3 Asian, non-Hispanic/Latino; 10 Hispanic/Latino; 4 Two or more races, non-Hispanic/Latino), 2 international. Average age 38. *Entrance requirements:* For master's, bachelor's degree, personal statement, minimum GPA of 3.0, letters of recommendation. Additional exam requirements/recommendations for international students: Required—TOEFL (minimum score 550 paper-based; 79 iBT), IELTS (minimum score 6). *Application deadline:* For fall admission, 5/1 priority date for international students; for spring admission, 11/15 priority date for international students. Applications are processed on a rolling basis. Application fee: $40. Electronic applications accepted. *Financial support:* Federal Work-Study, tuition waivers, and unspecified assistantships available. Financial award application deadline: 5/1; financial award applicants required to submit FAFSA. *Unit head:* Dr. Lesley Page, Chair, Organizational Leadership. *Application contact:* Kathy Lisak, Graduate Admission Counselor, 815-836-5610, E-mail: grad@lewisu.edu.

Lock Haven University of Pennsylvania, The Stephen Poorman College of Business, Information Systems, and Human Services, Lock Haven, PA 17745-2390. Offers clinical mental health counseling (MS); sport science (MS). *Program availability:* Online learning. *Degree requirements:* For master's, thesis. *Entrance requirements:* For master's, minimum undergraduate GPA of 3.0. Additional exam requirements/recommendations for international students: Required—TOEFL. Electronic applications accepted.

Marquette University, Graduate School of Management, Executive MBA Program, Milwaukee, WI 53201-1881. Offers economics (MBA); finance (MBA); human resources (MBA); international business (MBA); management information systems (MBA); marketing (MBA); operations and supply chain management (MBA); sports business (MBA). *Accreditation:* AACSB. *Degree requirements:* For master's, international trip. *Entrance requirements:* For master's, GMAT or GRE, two letters of recommendation, official transcripts from current and previous colleges/universities. Additional exam requirements/recommendations for international students: Required—TOEFL (minimum score 550 paper-based; 88 iBT), IELTS (minimum score 6.5), PTE. Electronic applications accepted. *Expenses:* Contact institution. *Faculty research:* International trade and finance, customer relationship management, consumer satisfaction, customer service.

Marquette University, Graduate School of Management, Program in Business Administration, Milwaukee, WI 53201-1881. Offers business administration (MBA); economics (MBA); entrepreneurship (Certificate); finance (MBA); human resources (MBA); international business (MBA); management information systems (MBA); marketing (MBA); operations and supply chain management (MBA); sports business (MBA); JD/MBA; MBA/MA; MBA/MSN. *Accreditation:* AACSB. *Program availability:* Part-time, evening/weekend. *Degree requirements:* For Certificate, business plan. *Entrance requirements:* For master's, GMAT or GRE, letters of recommendation. Additional exam requirements/recommendations for international students: Required—TOEFL (minimum score 550 paper-based; 88 iBT), IELTS (minimum score 6.5), PTE. Electronic applications accepted. *Faculty research:* Ethics in the professions, services marketing, technology impact on decision-making, mentoring.

Marshall University, Academic Affairs Division, College of Health Professions, School of Kinesiology, Program in Sport Administration, Huntington, WV 25755. Offers MS. *Degree requirements:* For master's, thesis optional, comprehensive assessment. *Entrance requirements:* For master's, GRE General Test.

Maryville University of Saint Louis, The John E. Simon School of Business, St. Louis, MO 63141-7299. Offers accounting (MBA, MS, Certificate); business studies (Certificate); cybersecurity (MBA, MS, Certificate); financial services (MBA, Certificate); health administration (MBA); healthcare administration (Certificate); human resource management (MBA); human resources management (Certificate); information technology (MBA); information technology management (Certificate); management (MBA, Certificate); management and leadership (MA); marketing (MBA, Certificate); project management (MBA, Certificate); sport business management (MBA); supply chain management (Certificate); supply chain management/logistics (MBA). *Accreditation:* ACBSP. *Program availability:* Part-time, 100% online, blended/hybrid learning. *Faculty:* 5 full-time (1 woman), 77 part-time/adjunct (19 women). *Students:* 338 full-time (166 women), 739 part-time (356 women); includes 310 minority (161 Black or African American, non-Hispanic/Latino; 6 American Indian or Alaska Native, non-Hispanic/Latino; 59 Asian, non-Hispanic/Latino; 57 Hispanic/Latino; 27 Two or more races, non-Hispanic/Latino), 30 international. Average age 33. In 2018, 143 master's awarded. *Degree requirements:* For master's, capstone course (for MBA). *Entrance requirements:* Additional exam requirements/recommendations for international students: Required—TOEFL (minimum score 563 paper-based; 85 iBT). *Application deadline:* Applications are processed on a rolling basis. Electronic applications accepted. *Expenses:* Tuition varies by program. *Financial support:* Career-related

internships or fieldwork, Federal Work-Study, tuition waivers (partial), and campus employment available. Financial award application deadline: 4/1; financial award applicants required to submit FAFSA. *Unit head:* Tammy Gocial, Interim Dean, 314-529-9401, Fax: 314-529-9975, E-mail: tgocial@maryville.edu. *Application contact:* Chris Gourdine, Assistant Dean Business Administration, 314-529-6861, Fax: 314-529-9975, E-mail: cgourdine@maryville.edu.
Website: http://www.maryville.edu/bu/business-administration-masters/

Mercyhurst University, Graduate Studies, Program in Organizational Leadership, Erie, PA 16546. Offers accounting (MS); higher education administration (MS); human resources (MS); organizational leadership (MS, Certificate); sports leadership (MS); strategy and innovation (MS). *Program availability:* Part-time, evening/weekend. *Degree requirements:* For master's, thesis. *Entrance requirements:* For master's, GRE General Test or MAT, interview, resume, essay, three professional references, transcripts. Additional exam requirements/recommendations for international students: Required—TOEFL (minimum score 80 iBT), IELTS (minimum score 6.5). Electronic applications accepted. *Faculty research:* Leadership training, organizational communication, leadership pedagogy.

Messiah College, Program in Higher Education, Mechanicsburg, PA 17055. Offers college athletics management (MA); self-designed concentration (MA); student affairs (MA). *Program availability:* Part-time. Electronic applications accepted. *Faculty research:* College athletics management, assessment and student learning outcomes, the life and legacy of Ernest L. Boyer, common learning, student affairs practice.

Midwestern State University, Billie Doris McAda Graduate School, West College of Education, Program in Sport Administration, Wichita Falls, TX 76308. Offers M Ed.

Millersville University of Pennsylvania, College of Graduate Studies and Adult Learning, College of Education and Human Services, Department of Wellness and Sport Sciences, Millersville, PA 17551-0302. Offers sport management (M Ed); sport management: athletic coaching (Post-Master's Certificate). *Program availability:* Part-time. *Faculty:* 5 full-time (3 women). *Students:* 1 full-time (0 women), 29 part-time (15 women); includes 10 minority (5 Black or African American, non-Hispanic/Latino; 1 Asian, non-Hispanic/Latino; 2 Hispanic/Latino; 2 Two or more races, non-Hispanic/Latino). Average age 27. 11 applicants, 91% accepted, 7 enrolled. In 2018, 15 master's awarded. *Degree requirements:* For master's, thesis optional, internship. *Entrance requirements:* For master's, GRE/MAT/GMAT exam or complete an interview with writing assignment, required only if cumulative GPA is lower than 3.0, all transfer transcripts (even if MU grad), at least 1 academic reference (not from MU Sport Management Dept.), and sport management goal statement. Additional exam requirements/recommendations for international students: Required—TOEFL, IELTS (minimum score 6), PTE (minimum score 60). *Application deadline:* Applications are processed on a rolling basis. Application fee: $40. Electronic applications accepted. *Expenses: Tuition, area resident:* Full-time $9288; part-time $516 per credit. Tuition, state resident: full-time $9288; part-time $516 per credit. Tuition, nonresident: full-time $13,932; part-time $774 per credit. *International tuition:* $13,932 full-time. *Required fees:* $2623.50; $145.75 per credit. Tuition and fees vary according to course load, degree level and program. *Financial support:* In 2018–19, 13 students received support. Unspecified assistantships available. Financial award application deadline: 3/15; financial award applicants required to submit FAFSA. *Faculty research:* Applied sport management; leadership and sport; marketing and sport; gender and sport; leadership development; ADR, restorative justice and hazing; legal issues applied to sport management; women and fitness/sport; childhood health and wellness issues; using technology for monitoring physical activity; college health assessments; Sport Organization's Athlete's Resiliency & Emergency and Critical Incident Management & Response; Sport safety and Title IX. *Unit head:* Dr. Daniel J. Keefer, Chair, 717-871-4218, Fax: 717-871-7987, E-mail: daniel.keefer@millersville.edu. *Application contact:* Dr. James A. Delle, Acting Dean of College of Graduate Studies and Adult Learning/ Associate Provost, Academic Administration, 717-871-7462, E-mail: James.Delle@millersville.edu.
Website: http://www.millersville.edu/wssd/

Misericordia University, College of Business, Master of Business Administration Program, Dallas, PA 18612-1098. Offers accounting (MBA); healthcare management (MBA); human resource management (MBA); management (MBA); sport management (MBA). *Program availability:* Part-time, evening/weekend, online learning. *Entrance requirements:* For master's, GMAT, MAT, GRE (50th percentile or higher), or minimum undergraduate GPA of 3.0, interview. Additional exam requirements/recommendations for international students: Required—TOEFL. Electronic applications accepted. Application fee is waived when completed online. *Expenses:* Contact institution.

Mississippi State University, College of Education, Department of Kinesiology, Mississippi State, MS 39762. Offers disability studies (MS); exercise physiology (MS); exercise science (PhD); sport administration (MS); sport pedagogy (MS); sport studies (PhD). *Program availability:* Part-time, blended/hybrid learning. *Faculty:* 15 full-time (3 women). *Students:* 49 full-time (25 women), 16 part-time (3 women); includes 14 minority (5 Black or African American, non-Hispanic/Latino; 1 American Indian or Alaska Native, non-Hispanic/Latino; 2 Asian, non-Hispanic/Latino; 3 Hispanic/Latino; 3 Two or more races, non-Hispanic/Latino), 10 international. Average age 26. 67 applicants, 60% accepted, 23 enrolled. In 2018, 27 master's, 2 doctorates awarded. *Degree requirements:* For master's, comprehensive exam, thesis optional; for doctorate, comprehensive exam. *Entrance requirements:* For master's, GRE General Test, minimum GPA of 2.75 on undergraduate work from four-year accredited institution, 3.0 graduate; for doctorate, GRE, minimum GPA of 3.4 on previous graduate degree(s) earned from accredited institutions. Additional exam requirements/recommendations for international students: Required—TOEFL (minimum score 550 paper-based; 79 iBT); Recommended—IELTS (minimum score 6.5). *Application deadline:* For fall admission, 7/1 for domestic students, 5/1 for international students; for spring admission, 11/1 for domestic students, 9/1 for international students. Applications are processed on a rolling basis. Application fee: $60 ($80 for international students). Electronic applications accepted. *Expenses:* Tuition, state resident: full-time $8450; part-time $360.59 per credit hour. Tuition, nonresident: full-time $23,140; part-time $969.09 per credit hour. *Required fees:* $110. One-time fee: $55 full-time. Part-time tuition and fees vary according to course load, degree level, campus/location and reciprocity agreements. *Financial support:* In 2018–19, 14 teaching assistantships with partial tuition reimbursements (averaging $10,386 per year) were awarded; career-related internships or fieldwork, Federal Work-Study, institutionally sponsored loans, and unspecified assistantships also available. Financial award application deadline: 4/1; financial award applicants required to submit FAFSA. *Faculty research:* Static balance and stepping performance of older adults, organizational justice, public health, strength training and recovery drinks, high risk drinking perceptions and behaviors. *Unit head:* Dr. Stanley P. Brown, Professor and Head, 662-325-7229, Fax: 662-325-4525, E-mail: spb107@msstate.edu. *Application contact:* Ryan King, Admissions and Enrollment Assistant, 662-325-8951, E-mail: rjk101@grad.msstate.edu.
Website: http://www.kinesiology.msstate.edu/

Missouri State University, Graduate College, Interdisciplinary Program in Professional Studies, Springfield, MO 65897. Offers administrative studies (Certificate); applied communication (MS); criminal justice (MS); environmental management (MS); homeland security (MS); individualized (MS); professional studies (MS); screenwriting and producing (MS); sports management (MS). *Program availability:* Part-time, evening/weekend, 100% online, blended/hybrid learning. *Students:* 94 full-time (61 women), 81 part-time (44 women); includes 17 minority (7 Black or African American, non-Hispanic/Latino; 1 American Indian or Alaska Native, non-Hispanic/Latino; 1 Asian, non-Hispanic/Latino; 5 Hispanic/Latino; 3 Two or more races, non-Hispanic/Latino), 62 international. Average age 24. 71 applicants, 63% accepted. In 2018, 62 master's awarded. *Degree requirements:* For master's, comprehensive exam, thesis or alternative. *Entrance requirements:* For master's, GRE, GMAT (if GPA less than 3.0). Additional exam requirements/recommendations for international students: Required—TOEFL (minimum score 550 paper-based; 79 iBT), IELTS (minimum score 6). *Application deadline:* For fall admission, 7/15 priority date for domestic students; for spring admission, 12/1 priority date for domestic students; for summer admission, 5/1 for domestic students. Applications are processed on a rolling basis. Application fee: $55 ($60 for international students). Electronic applications accepted. Tuition and fees vary according to class time, course level, course load, degree level, campus/location, program and student level. *Financial support:* Career-related internships or fieldwork, Federal Work-Study, institutionally sponsored loans, scholarships/grants, and unspecified assistantships available. Support available to part-time students. Financial award application deadline: 1/31; financial award applicants required to submit FAFSA. *Unit head:* Dr. Gerald Masterson, Program Director, 417-836-5251, Fax: 417-836-6888, E-mail: mps@missouristate.edu. *Application contact:* Lakan Drinker, Director, Graduate Enrollment Management, 417-836-5330, Fax: 417-836-6200, E-mail: lakandrinker@missouristate.edu.
Website: https://gip.missouristate.edu/mps/

Missouri Western State University, Program in Applied Science, St. Joseph, MO 64507-2294. Offers chemistry (MAS); engineering technology management (MAS); industrial life science (MAS); sport and fitness management (MAS). *Accreditation:* AACSB. *Program availability:* Part-time. *Students:* 35 full-time (11 women), 14 part-time (5 women); includes 4 minority (1 Black or African American, non-Hispanic/Latino; 1 Asian, non-Hispanic/Latino; 1 Hispanic/Latino; 1 Two or more races, non-Hispanic/Latino), 10 international. Average age 25. 31 applicants, 94% accepted, 20 enrolled. In 2018, 18 master's awarded. *Entrance requirements:* Additional exam requirements/recommendations for international students: Recommended—TOEFL (minimum score 79 iBT), IELTS (minimum score 6). *Application deadline:* For fall admission, 7/15 for domestic and international students; for spring admission, 11/1 for domestic and international students; for summer admission, 4/29 for domestic and international students. Applications are processed on a rolling basis. Application fee: $45 ($50 for international students). Electronic applications accepted. *Expenses: Tuition, area resident:* Part-time $359.39 per credit hour. Tuition, state resident: part-time $359.39 per credit hour. Tuition, nonresident: part-time $643.39 per credit hour. Tuition and fees vary according to program. *Financial support:* Scholarships/grants and unspecified assistantships available. Support available to part-time students. *Unit head:* Dr. Susan Bashinski, Dean of the Graduate School, 816-271-4394, Fax: 816-271-4525, E-mail: graduate@missouriwestern.edu. *Application contact:* Dr. Susan Bashinski, Dean of the Graduate School, 816-271-4394, Fax: 816-271-4525, E-mail: graduate@missouriwestern.edu.

Montclair State University, The Graduate School, College of Education and Human Services, Program in Exercise Science and Physical Education, Montclair, NJ 07043-1624. Offers exercise science (MA); sports administration and coaching (MA); teaching and supervision in physical education (MA). *Program availability:* Part-time, evening/weekend. *Degree requirements:* For master's, comprehensive exam, thesis or alternative. *Entrance requirements:* For master's, GRE General Test, essay, 2 letters of recommendation. Additional exam requirements/recommendations for international students: Required—TOEFL (minimum score 83 iBT), IELTS (minimum score 6.5). Electronic applications accepted.

Mount St. Mary's University, Program in Sport Management, Emmitsburg, MD 21727-7799. Offers MS. *Program availability:* Part-time, evening/weekend. *Degree requirements:* For master's, project or internship. *Entrance requirements:* For master's, personal essay; baccalaureate degree; minimum undergraduate GPA of 2.75, two full years of relevant work experience with resume, or GMAT. Additional exam requirements/recommendations for international students: Required—TOEFL (minimum score 550 paper-based; 83 iBT). Electronic applications accepted. *Expenses:* Contact institution.

Neumann University, Graduate Programs in Business and Information Management, Aston, PA 19014-1298. Offers accounting (MS), including forensic and fraud detection; sport business (MS). *Program availability:* Part-time, evening/weekend. *Degree requirements:* For master's, thesis (for some programs). *Entrance requirements:* For master's, official transcripts from all institutions attended, resume, letter of intent, 2-3 letters of recommendation. Additional exam requirements/recommendations for international students: Required—TOEFL (minimum score 70 iBT). Electronic applications accepted. *Expenses:* Contact institution.

New England College, Program in Sports and Recreation Management: Coaching, Henniker, NH 03242-3293. Offers MS. *Entrance requirements:* For master's, resume, 2 letters of reference.

New Mexico Highlands University, Graduate Studies, College of Arts and Sciences, Department of Exercise and Sport Sciences, Las Vegas, NM 87701. Offers human performance and sport (MA), including human performance and sport sciences, sports administration, teacher education. *Program availability:* Part-time. *Degree requirements:* For master's, comprehensive exam, thesis or alternative. *Entrance requirements:* For master's, minimum undergraduate GPA of 3.0. Additional exam requirements/recommendations for international students: Required—TOEFL (minimum score 540 paper-based). *Faculty research:* Child obesity and physical inactivity, body composition and fitness assessment, motor development, sport marketing, sport finance.

North Carolina State University, Graduate School, College of Natural Resources, Department of Parks, Recreation and Tourism Management, Raleigh, NC 27695. Offers natural resource management (MPRTM, MS); park and recreation management (MPRTM, MS); parks, recreation and tourism management (PhD); recreational sport management (MPRTM, MS); spatial information science (MPRTM, MS); tourism policy and development (MPRTM, MS). *Degree requirements:* For master's, thesis (for some programs); for doctorate, thesis/dissertation. *Entrance requirements:* For master's and doctorate, GRE General Test. Additional exam requirements/recommendations for international students: Required—TOEFL. Electronic applications accepted. *Faculty research:* Tourism policy and development, spatial information systems, natural resource management, recreational sports management, park and recreation management.

Northeastern University, College of Professional Studies, Boston, MA 02115-5096. Offers applied nutrition (MS); college athletics administration (MSL); commerce and economic development (MS); corporate and organizational communication (MS); criminal justice (MS); digital media (MPS); elearning and instructional design (M Ed); elementary education (MAT); geographic information technology (MPS); global studies and international relations (MS); higher education administration (M Ed); homeland

security (MA); human services (MS); informatics (MPS); leadership (MS); learning analytics (M Ed); learning and instruction (M Ed); nonprofit management (MS); professional sports administration (MSL); project management (MS); regulatory affairs for drugs, biologics, and medical devices (MS); respiratory care leadership (MS); special education (M Ed); technical communication (MS). *Program availability:* Part-time, evening/weekend, 100% online, blended/hybrid learning. Electronic applications accepted. *Expenses:* Contact institution.

Northern State University, MS Ed Program in Sport Performance and Leadership, Aberdeen, SD 57401-7198. Offers MS Ed. *Program availability:* Part-time. *Degree requirements:* For master's, comprehensive exam, thesis optional. *Entrance requirements:* For master's, minimum GPA of 2.75. Additional exam requirements/recommendations for international students: Required—TOEFL (minimum score 550 paper-based; 78 iBT), IELTS (minimum score 6). Electronic applications accepted.

Northwestern University, School of Professional Studies, Program in Sports Administration, Evanston, IL 60208. Offers MA. *Program availability:* Part-time, evening/weekend.

Ohio Dominican University, Division of Business, Program in Business Administration, Columbus, OH 43219-2099. Offers accounting (MBA); data analytics (MBA); finance (MBA); leadership (MBA); risk management (MBA); sport management (MBA). *Program availability:* Part-time, evening/weekend, 100% online, blended/hybrid learning. *Faculty:* 10 full-time (4 women), 12 part-time/adjunct (1 woman). *Students:* 42 full-time (17 women), 88 part-time (43 women); includes 29 minority (16 Black or African American, non-Hispanic/Latino; 1 American Indian or Alaska Native, non-Hispanic/Latino; 3 Asian, non-Hispanic/Latino; 5 Hispanic/Latino; 4 Two or more races, non-Hispanic/Latino), 14 international. Average age 31. 97 applicants, 44% accepted, 26 enrolled. In 2018, 56 master's awarded. *Entrance requirements:* For master's, minimum overall GPA of 3.0 in undergraduate degree from regionally-accredited institution or 2.75 in last 60 semester hours of bachelor's degree. Additional exam requirements/recommendations for international students: Required—TOEFL (minimum score 550 paper-based), IELTS (minimum score 6.5). *Application deadline:* For fall admission, 8/15 for domestic students, 6/10 for international students; for spring admission, 1/4 for domestic students, 11/2 for international students; for summer admission, 5/30 for domestic students. Applications are processed on a rolling basis. Application fee: $25. Electronic applications accepted. *Expenses: Tuition:* Full-time $10,800; part-time $600 per credit hour. *Required fees:* $450; $225 per semester. Tuition and fees vary according to program. *Financial support:* Applicants required to submit FAFSA. *Unit head:* Dr. Thomas Eveland, Director of Graduate Programs in Business, 614-251-4569, E-mail: evelandt@ohiodominican.edu. *Application contact:* John W. Naughton, Vice President for Enrollment and Student Success, 614-251-4721, Fax: 614-251-6654, E-mail: grad@ohiodominican.edu.
Website: http://www.ohiodominican.edu/academics/graduate/mba

Ohio Dominican University, Division of Business, Program in Sport Management, Columbus, OH 43219-2099. Offers MS. *Program availability:* Part-time, evening/weekend, online only, 100% online. *Faculty:* 1 full-time (0 women), 4 part-time/adjunct (1 woman). *Students:* 8 full-time (1 woman), 1 part-time (0 women); includes 2 minority (both Black or African American, non-Hispanic/Latino). Average age 25. 18 applicants, 28% accepted, 2 enrolled. In 2018, 3 master's awarded. *Degree requirements:* For master's, thesis or alternative. *Entrance requirements:* For master's, GRE, bachelor's degree from regionally-accredited institution; minimum undergraduate cumulative GPA of 3.0. Additional exam requirements/recommendations for international students: Required—TOEFL (minimum score 550 paper-based), IELTS (minimum score 6.5). *Application deadline:* For fall admission, 8/15 for domestic students, 6/10 for international students; for spring admission, 1/4 for domestic students, 11/2 for international students; for summer admission, 5/30 for domestic students. Applications are processed on a rolling basis. Application fee: $25. Electronic applications accepted. *Expenses: Tuition:* Full-time $10,800; part-time $600 per credit hour. *Required fees:* $450; $225 per semester. Tuition and fees vary according to program. *Financial support:* Applicants required to submit FAFSA. *Unit head:* Dr. Thomas Eveland, Director of Graduate Programs in Business, 614-251-4569, E-mail: evelandt@ohiodominican.edu. *Application contact:* John W. Naughton, Vice President for Enrollment and Student Success, 614-251-4721, Fax: 614-251-6654, E-mail: grad@ohiodominican.edu.
Website: http://www.ohiodominican.edu/academics/graduate/mssm

Ohio University, Graduate College, College of Business, Department of Sports Administration, Athens, OH 45701-2979. Offers athletic administration (MS). *Program availability:* Part-time, evening/weekend, online learning. *Degree requirements:* For master's, 11-week internship. *Entrance requirements:* For master's, interview. Additional exam requirements/recommendations for international students: Required—TOEFL (minimum score 600 paper-based; 100 iBT) or IELTS (minimum score 7.5). Electronic applications accepted. *Faculty research:* Sport management, sport marketing, sports and technology, career development.

Old Dominion University, Darden College of Education, Program in Sport Management, Norfolk, VA 23529. Offers MS. *Program availability:* Part-time, evening/weekend, 100% online, blended/hybrid learning. *Degree requirements:* For master's, comprehensive exam, thesis or alternative, internship, research project. *Entrance requirements:* For master's, GRE, GMAT or MAT, minimum GPA of 2.8 overall, 3.0 in major. Additional exam requirements/recommendations for international students: Required—TOEFL (minimum score 550 paper-based; 79 iBT); Recommended—IELTS (minimum score 6.5). Electronic applications accepted. *Faculty research:* Leadership, consumer behavior in sport, sport finance, sport marketing, sport involvement.

Pittsburg State University, Graduate School, College of Education, Department of Health, Physical Education and Recreation, Pittsburg, KS 66762. Offers health, human performance, and recreation (MS), including human performance and wellness, sport and leisure service management. *Program availability:* Part-time, online only, 100% online. *Degree requirements:* For master's, thesis or alternative. *Entrance requirements:* For master's, letter of intent. Additional exam requirements/recommendations for international students: Required—TOEFL (minimum score 520 paper-based; 68 iBT), IELTS (minimum score 6), PTE (minimum score 47). Electronic applications accepted. *Expenses:* Contact institution. *Faculty research:* Personality of athletes, fitness activities for children, aerobic conditioning, fitness evaluation.

Point Loma Nazarene University, Department of Kinesiology, San Diego, CA 92106-2899. Offers exercise science (MS); sport performance (MS), including exercise science, sport management, sport performance. *Program availability:* Part-time, online learning. *Entrance requirements:* For master's, baccalaureate degree, minimum undergraduate cumulative GPA of 3.0. *Expenses:* Contact institution.

Point Park University, Rowland School of Business, Program in Business Administration, Pittsburgh, PA 15222-1984. Offers business analytics (MBA); global management and administration (MBA); health systems management (MBA); international business (MBA); management (MBA); management information systems (MBA); sports, arts and entertainment management (MBA). *Program availability:* Evening/weekend, 100% online.

Purdue University, Graduate School, College of Health and Human Sciences, Department of Health and Kinesiology, West Lafayette, IN 47907. Offers athletic training education administration (MS, PhD); biomechanics (MS, PhD); exercise physiology (MS, PhD); health education (MS, PhD); history/philosophy of sport (MS, PhD); motor control and development (MS, PhD); physical education pedagogy (PhD); physical education teacher education (MS); recreation and sport management (MS, PhD); sport and exercise psychology (MS, PhD). *Program availability:* Part-time. *Faculty:* 23 full-time (10 women). *Students:* 29 full-time (13 women), 8 part-time (5 women); includes 3 minority (1 Asian, non-Hispanic/Latino; 1 Hispanic/Latino; 1 Two or more races, non-Hispanic/Latino), 8 international. Average age 26. 61 applicants, 26% accepted, 14 enrolled. In 2018, 14 master's awarded. *Degree requirements:* For master's, thesis optional; for doctorate, comprehensive exam, thesis/dissertation, qualifying examination, preliminary examination. *Entrance requirements:* For master's, GRE General Test (minimum score 1000 combined verbal and quantitative), minimum undergraduate GPA of 3.0 or equivalent; for doctorate, GRE General Test (minimum score 1100 combined verbal and quantitative), minimum undergraduate GPA of 3.0 or equivalent; master's degree with minimum GPA of 3.25 (recommended). Additional exam requirements/recommendations for international students: Required—TOEFL (minimum score 77 iBT); Recommended—TWE. *Application deadline:* For fall admission, 4/30 for domestic and international students; for spring admission, 10/15 for domestic and international students. Applications are processed on a rolling basis. Application fee: $60 ($75 for international students). Electronic applications accepted. *Financial support:* Fellowships with partial tuition reimbursements, research assistantships with partial tuition reimbursements, teaching assistantships with partial tuition reimbursements, and Federal Work-Study available. Support available to part-time students. Financial award applicants required to submit FAFSA. *Faculty research:* Wellness, motivation, teaching effectiveness, learning and development. *Unit head:* Dr. Timothy P. Gavin, Head of the Graduate Program, 765-494-3178, Fax: 765-494-1239, E-mail: gavin1@purdue.edu. *Application contact:* David B. Klenosky, Graduate Contact, 765-494-0865, E-mail: klenosky@purdue.edu.
Website: http://www.purdue.edu/hhs/hk/

Robert Morris University Illinois, Morris Graduate School of Management, Chicago, IL 60605. Offers accounting (MBA); accounting/finance (MBA); business analytics (MIS); health care administration (MM); higher education administration (MM); human performance (MS); human resource management (MBA); information security (MIS); information systems management (MIS); law enforcement administration (MM); management (MBA); management/finance (MBA); management/human resource management (MBA); sports administration (MM). *Program availability:* Part-time, evening/weekend. *Entrance requirements:* For master's, official transcripts and letters of recommendation (for some programs); written personal statement. Additional exam requirements/recommendations for international students: Required—TOEFL (minimum score 550 paper-based). Electronic applications accepted.

St. John's University, College of Professional Studies, Department of Sport Management, Queens, NY 11439. Offers MPS. *Entrance requirements:* For master's, letters of recommendation, transcripts, resume, personal statement. Additional exam requirements/recommendations for international students: Required—TOEFL (minimum score 90 iBT), IELTS (minimum score 7). Electronic applications accepted.

Saint Mary's College of California, School of Liberal Arts, Department of Kinesiology, Moraga, CA 94575. Offers fitness management (MA); sport management (MA); sport studies (MA). *Program availability:* Part-time. *Degree requirements:* For master's, thesis or special project. *Entrance requirements:* For master's, minimum GPA of 2.75, BA in physical education or related field, or professional experience. Electronic applications accepted. *Expenses:* Contact institution. *Faculty research:* Moral development in sport, applied motor learning, achievement motivation, sport history.

St. Thomas University, School of Business, Department of Management, Miami Gardens, FL 33054-6459. Offers accounting (MBA); general management (MSM, Certificate); health management (MBA, MSM, Certificate); human resource management (MBA, MSM, Certificate); international business (MBA, MIB, MSM, Certificate); justice administration (MSM, Certificate); management accounting (MSM, Certificate); public management (MSM, Certificate); sports administration (MS). *Program availability:* Part-time, evening/weekend. *Degree requirements:* For master's, comprehensive exam. *Entrance requirements:* For master's, interview, minimum GPA of 3.0 or GMAT. Additional exam requirements/recommendations for international students: Required—TOEFL (minimum score 550 paper-based; 79 iBT). Electronic applications accepted.

Sam Houston State University, College of Health Sciences, Department of Kinesiology, Huntsville, TX 77341. Offers sport and human performance (MA); sport management (MA). *Program availability:* Part-time. *Degree requirements:* For master's, comprehensive exam, thesis optional. *Entrance requirements:* For master's, GRE, letters of recommendation, statement of interest/intent. Additional exam requirements/recommendations for international students: Required—TOEFL (minimum score 550 paper-based; 79 iBT), IELTS (minimum score 6.5). Electronic applications accepted.

San Diego State University, Graduate and Research Affairs, Fowler College of Business, Sports Business Management Program, San Diego, CA 92182. Offers MBA.

Seattle University, College of Arts and Sciences, Center for the Study of Sport and Exercise, Seattle, WA 98122-1090. Offers MSAL, JD/MSAL. *Program availability:* Part-time, evening/weekend. *Faculty:* 3 full-time (1 woman). *Students:* 8 full-time (2 women), 31 part-time (11 women); includes 6 minority (1 Black or African American, non-Hispanic/Latino; 5 Asian, non-Hispanic/Latino), 5 international. Average age 26. 1 applicant, 100% accepted, 1 enrolled. In 2018, 22 master's awarded. *Entrance requirements:* For master's, GRE (Verbal, Quantitative, and Analytical), minimum GPA of 3.0, three letters of recommendation, essay, resume. Additional exam requirements/recommendations for international students: Required—TOEFL, IELTS. *Application deadline:* For fall admission, 2/15 for domestic and international students. Application fee: $55. Electronic applications accepted. *Financial support:* In 2018–19, 20 students received support. Research assistantships and scholarships/grants available. Financial award applicants required to submit FAFSA. *Faculty research:* Sport consumer behavior, strategic management of sport organizations, leadership in sport, organizational behavior, lifestyle sports. *Unit head:* Dr. Dan Tripps, Director, 206-398-4605, E-mail: trippsd@seattleu.edu. *Application contact:* Janet Shandley, Associate Dean of Graduate Admissions, 206-296-5900, Fax: 206-298-5656, E-mail: grad_admissions@seattleu.edu.
Website: https://www.seattleu.edu/artsci/departments/sport-exercise/

Seton Hall University, Stillman School of Business, Programs in Business Administration, South Orange, NJ 07079-2697. Offers accounting (MBA); entrepreneurial studies (Certificate); finance (MBA); financial decision making (Certificate); information technology management (MBA); international business (MBA); management (MBA); marketing (MBA); sport management (MBA); supply chain management (MBA, Certificate). *Program availability:* Part-time, evening/weekend. *Faculty:* 27 full-time (5 women), 18 part-time/adjunct (2 women). *Students:* 85 full-time (40 women), 363 part-time (147 women); includes 78 minority (22 Black or African American, non-Hispanic/Latino; 4 Asian, non-Hispanic/Latino; 18 Hispanic/Latino; 29 Native Hawaiian or other Pacific Islander, non-Hispanic/Latino; 5 Two or more races, non-Hispanic/Latino), 282 international. Average age 34. 483 applicants, 85% accepted,

302 enrolled. In 2018, 96 master's awarded. *Degree requirements:* For master's, 20 hours of community service (Social Responsibility Project). *Entrance requirements:* For master's, GMAT or CPA, GRE (waived based on work experience or advanced degree from AACSB institution), MS in business discipline, professional degree or designation (MD, JD, PhD, DVM, DDS, CPA, etc.), minimum undergraduate GPA of 3.0. Additional exam requirements/recommendations for international students: Required—TOEFL (minimum score 607 paper-based; 80 iBT), IELTS (minimum score 6), PTE. *Application deadline:* For fall admission, 5/31 priority date for domestic students, 4/30 priority date for international students; for spring admission, 10/31 priority date for domestic students, 9/30 priority date for international students; for summer admission, 3/31 priority date for domestic students. Applications are processed on a rolling basis. Application fee: $75. Electronic applications accepted. Application fee is waived when completed online. *Expenses:* Tuition is $1,305 per credit hour and the overall MBA is a 40 credit hour program. University fees are $115 per semester. The university also has a technology that is $125 per semester. *Financial support:* In 2018–19, 44 students received support, including 25 research assistantships with partial tuition reimbursements available (averaging $3,644 per year); career-related internships or fieldwork, scholarships/grants, and unspecified assistantships also available. Financial award application deadline: 6/30; financial award applicants required to submit FAFSA. *Faculty research:* Sport, hedge funds, executive compensation, social media, legal studies. *Unit head:* Dr. Joyce Strawser, Dean, 973-761-9013, Fax: 973-761-9217, E-mail: joyce.strawser@shu.edu. *Application contact:* Alfred Ayoub, Director of Graduate Admissions, 973-761-9262, Fax: 973-761-9208, E-mail: alfred.ayoub@shu.edu.
Website: http://www.shu.edu/business/mba-programs.cfm

Sonoma State University, School of Science and Technology, Department of Kinesiology, Rohnert Park, CA 94928. Offers exercise science/pre-physical therapy (MA); interdisciplinary (MA); interdisciplinary pre-occupational therapy (MA); lifetime physical activity (MA), including coach education, fitness and wellness. *Program availability:* Part-time. *Degree requirements:* For master's, thesis, oral exam. *Entrance requirements:* For master's, minimum GPA of 2.8. Additional exam requirements/recommendations for international students: Required—TOEFL (minimum score 500 paper-based).

Southeastern University, Jannetides College of Business and Entrepreneurial Leadership, Lakeland, FL 33801-6099. Offers executive leadership (MBA); global business administration (MBA); healthcare administration (MBA); missional leadership (MBA); organizational leadership (PhD); sport management (MBA); strategic leadership (DSL). *Accreditation:* ACBSP. *Program availability:* Evening/weekend, online learning. *Entrance requirements:* For master's, GMAT, minimum cumulative GPA of 3.0, writing sample. Electronic applications accepted.

Southeast Missouri State University, School of Graduate Studies, Harrison College of Business and Computing, Cape Girardeau, MO 63701-4799. Offers accounting (MBA); entrepreneurship (MBA); financial management (MBA); sport management (MBA). *Accreditation:* AACSB. *Program availability:* Part-time, evening/weekend, 100% online. *Faculty:* 27 full-time (7 women), 1 (woman) part-time/adjunct. *Students:* 94 full-time (50 women), 88 part-time (39 women); includes 18 minority (9 Black or African American, non-Hispanic/Latino; 4 Asian, non-Hispanic/Latino; 5 Hispanic/Latino), 79 international. Average age 29. 80 applicants, 100% accepted, 80 enrolled. In 2018, 62 master's awarded. *Degree requirements:* For master's, variable foreign language requirement, comprehensive exam (for some programs), thesis or alternative. *Entrance requirements:* For master's, GMAT or GRE, minimum undergraduate GPA of 2.5, minimum grade of C in prerequisite courses. Additional exam requirements/recommendations for international students: Required—TOEFL (minimum score 550 paper-based; 79 iBT), IELTS (minimum score 6), PTE (minimum score 53). *Application deadline:* For fall admission, 8/1 for domestic students, 6/1 for international students; for spring admission, 11/21 for domestic students, 10/1 for international students; for summer admission, 5/15 for domestic students. Applications are processed on a rolling basis. Application fee: $30 ($40 for international students). Electronic applications accepted. *Expenses:* Contact institution. *Financial support:* In 2018–19, 16 students received support. Career-related internships or fieldwork, Federal Work-Study, scholarships/grants, traineeships, tuition waivers (full), and unspecified assistantships available. Financial award application deadline: 6/30; financial award applicants required to submit FAFSA. *Faculty research:* Organizational justice, ethics, leadership, corporate finance, generational differences. *Unit head:* Dr. Alberto Davila, Dean, 573-651-2112, E-mail: adavila@semo.edu. *Application contact:* Dr. Alberto Davila, Dean, 573-651-2112, E-mail: adavila@semo.edu.
Website: http://www.semo.edu/mba

Southern Methodist University, Simmons School of Education and Human Development, Department of Allied Physiology and Wellness, Dallas, TX 75275. Offers applied physiology (PhD); health promotion management (MS); sport management (MS). Program offered jointly with Cox School of Business. *Entrance requirements:* For master's, GMAT, resume, essays, transcripts from all colleges and universities attended, two references. Additional exam requirements/recommendations for international students: Required—TOEFL or PTE.

Southern Nazarene University, College of Professional and Graduate Studies, School of Kinesiology, Bethany, OK 73008. Offers sports management and administration (MA). *Entrance requirements:* For master's, baccalaureate degree from regionally-accredited college or university, official transcripts from each institution attended, three letters of recommendation, essay.

Southern New Hampshire University, School of Business, Manchester, NH 03106-1045. Offers accounting (MBA, Graduate Certificate); accounting finance (MS); accounting/auditing (MS); accounting/forensic accounting (MS); accounting/management accounting (MS); accounting/taxation (MS); applied economics (MS); athletic administration (MBA, Graduate Certificate); business administration (IMBA, Certificate), including business information systems (Certificate), human resource management (Certificate); business analytics (MBA); business intelligence (MBA); communication (MA), including new media and marketing, public relations; community economic development (MBA); criminal justice (MBA); data analytics (MS); economics (MBA); engineering management (MBA); entrepreneurship (MBA); finance (MBA, MS, Graduate Certificate); finance/corporate finance (MS); finance/investments (MS); forensic accounting (MBA); forensic accounting and fraud examination (Graduate Certificate); healthcare informatics (MBA); healthcare management (MBA); human resource management (MS); human resources (MBA); information technology (MS); information technology management (MBA); international business (PhD); Internet marketing (MBA); leadership (MBA); leadership of nonprofit organizations (Graduate Certificate); management (MS); marketing (MBA, MS, Graduate Certificate); music business (MBA); operations and project management (MS); operations and supply chain management (MBA, Graduate Certificate); organizational leadership (MS); project management (MBA, Graduate Certificate); public administration (MBA, Graduate Certificate); quantitative analysis (MBA); Six Sigma (Graduate Certificate); Six Sigma quality (MBA); social media marketing (MBA, Graduate Certificate); sport management (MBA, MS, Graduate Certificate); sustainability and environmental compliance (MBA); MBA/Certificate. *Accreditation:* ACBSP. *Program availability:* Part-time, evening/weekend, online learning. Terminal master's awarded for partial completion of doctoral program. *Degree requirements:* For master's, one foreign language, comprehensive exam (for some programs), thesis or alternative; for doctorate, one foreign language, comprehensive exam, thesis/dissertation. *Entrance requirements:* For master's, minimum GPA of 2.5; for doctorate, GMAT. Additional exam requirements/recommendations for international students: Required—TOEFL (minimum score 500 paper-based). Electronic applications accepted.

Southwestern Oklahoma State University, College of Professional and Graduate Studies, School of Behavioral Sciences and Education, Specialization in Kinesiology, Weatherford, OK 73096-3098. Offers health and physical education (M Ed); sports management (M Ed). *Program availability:* Part-time. *Degree requirements:* For master's, exam. *Entrance requirements:* For master's, GRE General Test or minimum undergraduate GPA of 3.0. Additional exam requirements/recommendations for international students: Required—TOEFL (minimum score 550 paper-based), IELTS (minimum score 6.5).

Springfield College, Graduate Programs, Programs in Physical Education, Springfield, MA 01109-3797. Offers adapted physical education (MS); advanced-level coaching (M Ed); athletic administration (MS); exercise physiology (PhD); health promotion and disease prevention (MS); physical education initial licensure (CAGS); sport and exercise psychology (PhD); teaching and administration (PhD). *Program availability:* Part-time. *Degree requirements:* For master's, comprehensive exam, thesis (for some programs). *Entrance requirements:* For master's and doctorate, GRE General Test. Additional exam requirements/recommendations for international students: Required—TOEFL (minimum score 550 paper-based); Recommended—IELTS (minimum score 7). Electronic applications accepted.

Springfield College, Graduate Programs, Programs in Sport Management and Recreation, Springfield, MA 01109-3797. Offers recreation management (M Ed, MS); sport management (M Ed, MS); therapeutic recreation management (M Ed, MS). *Program availability:* Part-time. *Degree requirements:* For master's, comprehensive exam, research project. *Entrance requirements:* Additional exam requirements/recommendations for international students: Required—TOEFL (minimum score 550 paper-based); Recommended—IELTS (minimum score 7). Electronic applications accepted.

State University of New York College at Cortland, Graduate Studies, School of Professional Studies, Department of Sport Management, Cortland, NY 13045. Offers international sport management (MS); sport management (MS). *Entrance requirements:* For master's, GMAT or GRE, 2 letters of recommendation.

Syracuse University, David B. Falk College of Sport and Human Dynamics, MS Program in Sport Venue and Event Management, Syracuse, NY 13244. Offers MS. *Entrance requirements:* For master's, GRE, undergraduate transcripts, three recommendations, resume, personal statement. Additional exam requirements/recommendations for international students: Required—TOEFL (minimum score 100 iBT). *Application deadline:* For fall admission, 2/15 for domestic students; for spring admission, 11/1 priority date for domestic and international students. Application fee: $75. Electronic applications accepted. *Financial support:* Fellowships, research assistantships, teaching assistantships, and career-related internships or fieldwork available. Financial award application deadline: 1/1; financial award applicants required to submit FAFSA. *Faculty research:* Managing and operating sport and entertainment facilities and events, sociology of sport, psychological and social issues in sport. *Unit head:* Jeff Pauline, Graduate Program Director, 315-443-0364, Fax: 315-443-9811, E-mail: jspaulin@syr.edu. *Application contact:* Felicia Otero, Director of Admissions, 315-443-5555, E-mail: falk@syr.edu.
Website: https://falk.syr.edu/sport-management/academic-programs/#mssvem

Temple University, Fox School of Business, Doctoral Programs in Business, Philadelphia, PA 19122-6096. Offers accounting (PhD); entrepreneurship (PhD); finance (PhD); international business (PhD); management information systems (PhD); marketing (PhD); risk management and insurance (PhD); statistics (PhD); strategic management (PhD); tourism and sport (PhD). *Accreditation:* AACSB. *Degree requirements:* For doctorate, thesis/dissertation. *Entrance requirements:* For doctorate, GRE General Test, GMAT, minimum GPA of 3.0, master's degree. Additional exam requirements/recommendations for international students: Required—TOEFL (minimum score 600 paper-based; 100 iBT), IELTS (minimum score 7.5). Electronic applications accepted.

Temple University, School of Sport, Tourism and Hospitality Management, Philadelphia, PA 19122-6096. Offers sport business (MS); tourism and hospitality management (MTHM); tourism and sport (PhD); travel and tourism (MS). *Program availability:* Part-time, evening/weekend, online learning. *Faculty:* 24 full-time (9 women), 11 part-time/adjunct (4 women). *Students:* 153 full-time (70 women), 56 part-time (25 women); includes 48 minority (28 Black or African American, non-Hispanic/Latino; 5 Asian, non-Hispanic/Latino; 10 Hispanic/Latino; 5 Two or more races, non-Hispanic/Latino), 33 international. 215 applicants, 76% accepted, 107 enrolled. In 2018, 71 master's awarded. *Entrance requirements:* For master's, GMAT or GRE, 500-word statement of goals, 2 letters of recommendation, resume. Additional exam requirements/recommendations for international students: Required—TOEFL, IELTS, PTE, one of three is required. *Application deadline:* For fall admission, 12/15 priority date for domestic students, 3/1 for international students; for spring admission, 11/1 for domestic students, 8/1 for international students. Applications are processed on a rolling basis. Application fee: $60. Electronic applications accepted. *Expenses:* Contact institution. *Financial support:* Scholarships/grants, health care benefits, and unspecified assistantships available. Financial award application deadline: 3/1; financial award applicants required to submit FAFSA. *Unit head:* Ronald C. Anderson, Dean, 215-204-8701, E-mail: sthm@temple.edu. *Application contact:* Michelle Rosar, Assistant Director of Graduate Enrollment, 215-204-3315, E-mail: michelle.rosar@temple.edu.
Website: http://sthm.temple.edu/

Tennessee State University, The School of Graduate Studies and Research, College of Health Sciences, Department of Human Performance and Sports Sciences, Nashville, TN 37209-1561. Offers exercise science (MA Ed); sports administration (MA Ed). *Degree requirements:* For master's, thesis optional. *Entrance requirements:* For master's, GRE General Test or MAT.

Tennessee Technological University, College of Graduate Studies, College of Education, Department of Exercise Science, Physical Education and Wellness, Cookeville, TN 38505. Offers adapted physical education (MA); elementary/middle school physical education (MA); lifetime wellness (MA); sport management (MA). *Accreditation:* NCATE. *Program availability:* Part-time, online learning. *Faculty:* 7 full-time (0 women). *Students:* 12 full-time (10 women), 45 part-time (22 women); includes 8 minority (3 Black or African American, non-Hispanic/Latino; 1 Asian, non-Hispanic/Latino; 2 Hispanic/Latino; 2 Two or more races, non-Hispanic/Latino), 1 international. 43 applicants, 67% accepted, 22 enrolled. In 2018, 17 master's awarded. *Degree requirements:* For master's, comprehensive exam, thesis or alternative. *Entrance requirements:* For master's, MAT or GRE. Additional exam requirements/recommendations for international students: Required—TOEFL (minimum score 527 paper-based; 71 iBT), IELTS (minimum score 5.5), PTE (minimum score 48), or TOEIC (Test of English as an International Communication). *Application deadline:* For fall

admission, 8/1 for domestic students, 5/1 for international students; for spring admission, 12/1 for domestic students, 10/1 for international students; for summer admission, 5/1 for domestic students, 2/1 for international students. Applications are processed on a rolling basis. Application fee: $35 ($40 for international students). Electronic applications accepted. *Financial support:* Fellowships, research assistantships, teaching assistantships, and career-related internships or fieldwork available. Financial award application deadline: 4/1. *Unit head:* Dr. Christy Killman, Chairperson, 931-372-3467, Fax: 931-372-6319, E-mail: ckillman@tntech.edu. *Application contact:* Shelia K. Kendrick, Coordinator of Graduate Studies, 931-372-3808, Fax: 931-372-3497, E-mail: skendrick@tntech.edu.

Texas A&M University, College of Education and Human Development, Department of Health and Kinesiology, College Station, TX 77843. Offers athletic training (MS); health education (MS, PhD); kinesiology (MS, PhD); sports management (MS). *Program availability:* Part-time. *Faculty:* 56. *Students:* 211 full-time (117 women), 80 part-time (41 women); includes 94 minority (35 Black or African American, non-Hispanic/Latino; 3 American Indian or Alaska Native, non-Hispanic/Latino; 5 Asian, non-Hispanic/Latino; 44 Hispanic/Latino; 7 Two or more races, non-Hispanic/Latino), 24 international. Average age 28. 95 applicants, 88% accepted, 60 enrolled. In 2018, 112 master's, 14 doctorates awarded. *Degree requirements:* For master's, thesis (for some programs); for doctorate, comprehensive exam, thesis/dissertation. *Entrance requirements:* For master's and doctorate, GRE General Test. Additional exam requirements/recommendations for international students: Required—TOEFL (minimum score 550 paper-based; 80 iBT), IELTS (minimum score 6), PTE (minimum score 53). *Application deadline:* For fall admission, 1/15 for domestic students; for spring admission, 10/1 for domestic students. Applications are processed on a rolling basis. Application fee: $50 ($90 for international students). Electronic applications accepted. *Expenses:* Contact institution. *Financial support:* In 2018–19, 109 students received support, including 2 fellowships with tuition reimbursements available (averaging $24,073 per year), 41 research assistantships with tuition reimbursements available (averaging $13,093 per year), 68 teaching assistantships with tuition reimbursements available (averaging $11,596 per year); career-related internships or fieldwork, institutionally sponsored loans, scholarships/grants, traineeships, health care benefits, tuition waivers (full and partial), and unspecified assistantships also available. Support available to part-time students. Financial award application deadline: 3/15; financial award applicants required to submit FAFSA. *Unit head:* Dr. Richard Kreider, Head, 979-845-1333, Fax: 979-847-8987, E-mail: rkreider@hlkn.tamu.edu. *Application contact:* Jenny Bilski, Academic Advisor, 979-862-4052, E-mail: jenny.bilski@tamu.edu.
Website: http://hlknweb.tamu.edu/

Texas Tech University, Graduate School, College of Arts and Sciences, Department of Kinesiology and Sport Management, Lubbock, TX 79409-3011. Offers kinesiology (MS); sport management (MS). *Program availability:* Part-time. *Faculty:* 28 full-time (13 women), 6 part-time/adjunct (4 women). *Students:* 62 full-time (30 women), 9 part-time (3 women); includes 30 minority (4 Black or African American, non-Hispanic/Latino; 2 Asian, non-Hispanic/Latino; 21 Hispanic/Latino; 3 Two or more races, non-Hispanic/Latino), 7 international. Average age 24. 80 applicants, 64% accepted, 29 enrolled. In 2018, 31 master's awarded. *Degree requirements:* For master's, comprehensive exam (for some programs), thesis (for some programs). *Entrance requirements:* For master's, GRE (only for the M.S. in Kinesiology whose GPA on the last 60 hours of undergraduate coursework is 3.49 and lower), letter of intent, 3 letters of recommendation (preferably from academic professors), minimum GPA of 2.8 in the last 60 hours. Additional exam requirements/recommendations for international students: Required—TOEFL (minimum score 550 paper-based; 79 iBT). *Application deadline:* For fall admission, 6/1 priority date for domestic students, 1/15 priority date for international students; for spring admission, 9/1 priority date for domestic students, 6/15 priority date for international students. Applications are processed on a rolling basis. Application fee: $65. Electronic applications accepted. *Expenses:* Contact institution. *Financial support:* In 2018–19, 70 students received support, including 70 fellowships (averaging $3,597 per year), 5 research assistantships (averaging $14,098 per year), 41 teaching assistantships (averaging $10,734 per year); career-related internships or fieldwork, scholarships/grants, health care benefits, and unspecified assistantships also available. Financial award application deadline: 8/1; financial award applicants required to submit FAFSA. *Faculty research:* Sport management, exercise physiology, human performance, motor behavior, exercise and sport psychology. *Total annual research expenditures:* $205,282. *Unit head:* Dr. Angela Lumpkin, Professor & Department Chair, 806-834-6935, Fax: 806-742-1688, E-mail: angela.lumpkin@ttu.edu. *Application contact:* Donna Torres, Graduate Admissions Coordinator, 806-834-7968, Fax: 806-742-1688, E-mail: donna.torres@ttu.edu.
Website: www.depts.ttu.edu/ksm/

Tiffin University, Program in Business Administration, Tiffin, OH 44883-2161. Offers finance (MBA); general management (MBA); healthcare administration (MBA); human resource management (MBA); international business (MBA); leadership (MBA); marketing (MBA); non-profit management (MBA); sports management (MBA). *Accreditation:* ACBSP. *Program availability:* Part-time, evening/weekend, online learning. *Entrance requirements:* For master's, minimum undergraduate GPA of 2.5, work experience. Additional exam requirements/recommendations for international students: Required—TOEFL (minimum score 550 paper-based; 79 iBT), IELTS. Electronic applications accepted. Application fee is waived when completed online. *Faculty research:* Small business, executive development operations, research and statistical analysis, market research, management information systems.

Troy University, Graduate School, College of Health and Human Services, Program in Sport and Fitness Management, Troy, AL 36082. Offers MS, DPH. *Program availability:* Part-time, evening/weekend. *Faculty:* 13 full-time (3 women), 2 part-time/adjunct (0 women). *Students:* 54 full-time (23 women), 95 part-time (42 women); includes 28 minority (24 Black or African American, non-Hispanic/Latino; 1 Hispanic/Latino; 3 Two or more races, non-Hispanic/Latino), 16 international. Average age 30. 113 applicants, 74% accepted, 51 enrolled. In 2018, 38 master's awarded. *Degree requirements:* For master's, comprehensive exam, minimum GPA of 3.0, candidacy, research course. *Entrance requirements:* For master's, GRE (minimum score of 850 on old exam or 290 on new exam), GMAT (minimum score of 380), or MAT (minimum score of 385), bachelor's degree; minimum undergraduate GPA of 2.5 or 3.0 on last 30 semester hours, letter of recommendation; for doctorate, GRE (minimum score 1000 on old exam or 297 on new exam), bachelor's or master's degree, minimum GPA of 3.0, 2 letters of recommendation. Additional exam requirements/recommendations for international students: Required—TOEFL (minimum score 523 paper-based; 70 iBT), IELTS (minimum score 6). *Application deadline:* Applications are processed on a rolling basis. Application fee: $50. Electronic applications accepted. *Expenses: Tuition, area resident:* Full-time $425; part-time $425 per credit hour. Tuition, state resident: full-time $425; part-time $425 per credit hour. Tuition, nonresident: full-time $850; part-time $850 per credit hour. *International tuition:* $850 full-time. *Required fees:* $50 per semester. Tuition and fees vary according to campus/location and program. *Financial support:* Fellowships, career-related internships or fieldwork, scholarships/grants, and unspecified assistantships available. Support available to part-time students. *Faculty research:* Sport marketing, fitness, sport law. *Unit head:* Dr. Gi-Yon Koo, Professor, Phd Program Coordinator, 334-670-5763, Fax: 334-670-3743, E-mail: wkoo@troy.edu. *Application contact:* Jessica A. Kimbro, Assistant Director of Graduate Programs, 334-670-3189, E-mail: jacord@troy.edu.
Website: https://www.troy.edu/academics/academic-programs/college-health-human-services-programs.php

United States Sports Academy, Graduate Programs, Program in Sports Management, Daphne, AL 36526-7055. Offers MSS, Ed D. *Program availability:* Part-time, 100% online. *Degree requirements:* For master's, comprehensive exam, thesis optional; for doctorate, comprehensive exam, thesis/dissertation. *Entrance requirements:* For master's, GRE General Test, GMAT, or MAT, minimum GPA of 2.5, 3 letters of recommendation, resume; for doctorate, GRE General Test, GMAT, or MAT, master's degree, 3 letters of recommendation, resume. Additional exam requirements/recommendations for international students: Required—TOEFL (minimum score 500 paper-based). Electronic applications accepted. *Expenses:* Contact institution. *Faculty research:* Sport law, leadership behavior, personnel evaluation.

The University of Alabama, Graduate School, College of Human Environmental Sciences, Program in Human Environmental Science, Tuscaloosa, AL 35487. Offers interactive technology (MS); quality management (MS); restaurant and meeting management (MS); rural community health (MS); sport management (MS). *Program availability:* Part-time, evening/weekend, online learning. *Degree requirements:* For master's, comprehensive exam. *Entrance requirements:* For master's, GRE (for some specializations), minimum GPA of 3.0. Additional exam requirements/recommendations for international students: Required—TOEFL. Electronic applications accepted. *Faculty research:* Rural health, hospitality management, sport management, interactive technology, consumer quality management, environmental health and safety.

University of Alberta, Faculty of Graduate Studies and Research, Program in Business Administration, Edmonton, AB T6G 2E1, Canada. Offers international business (MBA); leisure and sport management (MBA); natural resources and energy (MBA); technology commercialization (MBA); MBA/LL B; MBA/M Ag; MBA/M Eng; MBA/MF; MBA/PhD. *Accreditation:* AACSB. *Program availability:* Part-time, evening/weekend. *Degree requirements:* For master's, thesis or alternative. *Entrance requirements:* For master's, GMAT. Additional exam requirements/recommendations for international students: Required—TOEFL (minimum score 600 paper-based). Electronic applications accepted. *Faculty research:* Natural resources and energy/management and policy/family enterprise/international business/healthcare research management.

University of Arkansas, Graduate School, College of Education and Health Professions, Department of Health, Human Performance and Recreation, Program in Recreation and Sports Management, Fayetteville, AR 72701. Offers M Ed, Ed D. In 2018, 19 master's, 1 doctorate awarded. *Degree requirements:* For master's, thesis optional; for doctorate, thesis/dissertation. *Entrance requirements:* For doctorate, GRE General Test. *Application deadline:* For fall admission, 8/1 for domestic students, 4/1 for international students; for spring admission, 12/1 for domestic students, 10/1 for international students; for summer admission, 4/15 for domestic students, 3/1 for international students. Applications are processed on a rolling basis. Application fee: $60. Electronic applications accepted. *Financial support:* In 2018–19, 8 research assistantships, 10 teaching assistantships were awarded; fellowships with tuition reimbursements, career-related internships or fieldwork, and Federal Work-Study also available. Support available to part-time students. Financial award application deadline: 4/1; financial award applicants required to submit FAFSA. *Unit head:* Dr. Matthew Ganio, Department Head, 479-575-2956, E-mail: msganio@uark.edu. *Application contact:* Dr. Paul Calleja, Assistant Dept. Head - HHPR, Graduate Coordinator, 479-575-2854, Fax: 479-575-5778, E-mail: pcallej@uark.edu.
Website: https://hhpr.uark.edu

University of Arkansas at Little Rock, Graduate School, College of Education and Health Professions, Department of Health, Human Performance and Sport Management, Little Rock, AR 72204-1099. Offers exercise science (MS); health education and promotion (MS); sport management (MS). *Program availability:* Part-time, evening/weekend. *Degree requirements:* For master's, directed study or residency. *Entrance requirements:* For master's, GRE General Test, minimum GPA of 3.0, 3 reference letters.

University of Central Florida, College of Business Administration, DeVos Sport Business Management Program, Orlando, FL 32816. Offers MSBM. *Students:* 57 full-time (28 women), 1 part-time (0 women); includes 21 minority (15 Black or African American, non-Hispanic/Latino; 5 Hispanic/Latino; 1 Two or more races, non-Hispanic/Latino), 6 international. Average age 26. 64 applicants, 47% accepted, 25 enrolled. In 2018, 25 master's awarded. *Degree requirements:* For master's, thesis or alternative, internship. *Entrance requirements:* For master's, GMAT, minimum GPA of 3.0, letters of recommendation, essay, resume. Additional exam requirements/recommendations for international students: Required—TOEFL. *Application deadline:* For fall admission, 1/15 for domestic students. Application fee: $30. Electronic applications accepted. *Financial support:* In 2018–19, 43 students received support, including 43 research assistantships with partial tuition reimbursements available (averaging $8,304 per year), 1 teaching assistantship with partial tuition reimbursement available (averaging $9,994 per year). Financial award application deadline: 11/1; financial award applicants required to submit FAFSA. *Unit head:* Dr. Richard Lapchick, Director and Chair, 407-823-4886, E-mail: rlapchick@ucf.edu. *Application contact:* Associate Director, Graduate Admissions, 407-823-2766, Fax: 407-823-6442, E-mail: gradadmissions@ucf.edu.
Website: http://business.ucf.edu/devos/

University of Cincinnati, Graduate School, College of Education, Criminal Justice, and Human Services, School of Human Services, Program in Sport Administration, Cincinnati, OH 45221. Offers MS. *Program availability:* 100% online. *Degree requirements:* For master's, thesis or alternative, capstone internship. *Entrance requirements:* Additional exam requirements/recommendations for international students: Required—TOEFL. Electronic applications accepted.

University of Colorado Denver, Business School, Program in Management and Organization, Denver, CO 80217. Offers business strategy (MS); change and innovation (MS); enterprise technology management (MS); entrepreneurship and innovation (MS); global management (MS); leadership (MS); managing for sustainability (MS); managing human resources (MS); sports and entertainment (MS); strategic management (MS). *Accreditation:* AACSB. *Program availability:* Part-time, evening/weekend, online learning. *Degree requirements:* For master's, 30 semester hours (12 of required courses, 12 of management electives, and 6 of free electives). *Entrance requirements:* For master's, GMAT, resume, two letters of recommendation, essay, financial statements (for international applicants). Additional exam requirements/recommendations for international students: Required—TOEFL (minimum score 525 paper-based; 71 iBT); Recommended—IELTS (minimum score 6.5). Electronic applications accepted. *Expenses:* Contact institution. *Faculty research:* Human resource management, management of catastrophe, turnaround strategies.

University of Colorado Denver, Business School, Program in Marketing, Denver, CO 80217. Offers advanced market analytics in a big data world (MS); brand communication in the digital era (MS); global marketing (MS); high-tech and entrepreneurial marketing (MS); marketing and global sustainability (MS); marketing intelligence and strategy in the 21st century (MS); sports and entertainment business (MS). *Program availability:*

Part-time, evening/weekend. *Degree requirements:* For master's, 30 semester hours (21 of marketing core courses, 9 of marketing electives). *Entrance requirements:* For master's, GMAT, resume, essay, two letters of recommendation, financial statements (for international applicants). Additional exam requirements/recommendations for international students: Required—TOEFL (minimum score 525 paper-based; 71 iBT); Recommended—IELTS (minimum score 6.5). Electronic applications accepted. *Expenses:* Contact institution. *Faculty research:* Marketing issues in the Chinese environment, impact of individual difference and contextual factors on the risk-taking behaviors of managers making new-business creation decisions, attribution theory perspective of conflict between marketers and engineers, organizational identity and identification, international market entry strategies.

University of Connecticut, Graduate School, College of Agriculture, Health and Natural Resources, Department of Kinesiology, Sport Management Program, Storrs, CT 06269. Offers MS. Terminal master's awarded for partial completion of doctoral program. *Degree requirements:* For master's, comprehensive exam, thesis or alternative. *Entrance requirements:* Additional exam requirements/recommendations for international students: Required—TOEFL (minimum score 550 paper-based). Electronic applications accepted.

University of Dallas, Satish and Yasmin Gupta College of Business, Irving, TX 75062. Offers accounting (MBA, MS); business administration (DBA); business analytics (MS); business management (MBA); corporate finance (MBA); cybersecurity (MS); finance (MS); financial services (MBA); global business (MBA, MS); health services management (MBA); human resource management (MBA); information and technology management (MS); information assurance (MBA); information technology (MBA); information technology service management (MBA); marketing management (MBA); organization development (MBA); project management (MBA); sports and entertainment management (MBA); strategic leadership (MBA); supply chain management (MBA). *Accreditation:* AACSB. *Program availability:* Part-time, evening/weekend, 100% online. *Students:* 147 full-time (56 women), 584 part-time (232 women); includes 402 minority (204 Black or African American, non-Hispanic/Latino; 95 Asian, non-Hispanic/Latino; 92 Hispanic/Latino; 2 Native Hawaiian or other Pacific Islander, non-Hispanic/Latino; 9 Two or more races, non-Hispanic/Latino), 113 international. Average age 34. 992 applicants, 30% accepted, 157 enrolled. In 2018, 336 master's, 5 doctorates awarded. *Degree requirements:* For doctorate, thesis/dissertation. *Entrance requirements:* For master's and doctorate, U.S. bachelor's degree with a minimum cumulative GPA of 2.0 from a regionally accredited college or university (or comparable foreign degree); minimum 3.0 GPA in any graduate-level coursework completed; good academic standing with all colleges attended. Additional exam requirements/recommendations for international students: Required—TOEFL (minimum score 80 iBT), IELTS (minimum score 6.5), PTE (minimum score 67). *Application deadline:* Applications are processed on a rolling basis. Application fee: $50. Electronic applications accepted. *Expenses:* $1250 per credit hour. *Financial support:* In 2018–19, 291 students received support. Research assistantships, teaching assistantships, scholarships/grants, and unspecified assistantships available. Support available to part-time students. Financial award application deadline: 2/15; financial award applicants required to submit FAFSA. *Unit head:* Brett J.L. Landry, Dean, 972-721-5356, E-mail: blandry@udallas.edu. *Application contact:* Breonna Collins, Director, Graduate Admissions, 972-7215304, E-mail: bcollins@udallas.edu. Website: http://www.udallas.edu/cob/

University of Florida, Graduate School, College of Health and Human Performance, Department of Tourism, Recreation and Sport Management, Gainesville, FL 32611. Offers health and human performance (PhD), including historic preservation (MS, PhD), recreation, parks and tourism (MS, PhD), sport management; recreation, parks and tourism (MS), including historic preservation (MS, PhD), natural resource recreation, recreation, parks and tourism (MS, PhD), therapeutic recreation, tourism, tropical conservation and development; sport management (MS), including historic preservation (MS, PhD), tropical conservation and development; JD/MS; MSM/MS. *Degree requirements:* For master's, comprehensive exam (for some programs), thesis (for some programs); for doctorate, comprehensive exam, thesis/dissertation. *Entrance requirements:* For master's and doctorate, GRE General Test, minimum GPA of 3.0. Additional exam requirements/recommendations for international students: Required—TOEFL (minimum score 550 paper-based; 80 iBT), IELTS (minimum score 6). Electronic applications accepted. *Faculty research:* Hospitality, natural resource management, sport management, tourism.

University of Idaho, College of Graduate Studies, College of Education, Health and Human Sciences, Department of Movement Sciences, Moscow, ID 83844-2401. Offers athletic training (MSAT, DAT); exercise science and health (MS); physical education teacher education (M Ed, MS); recreation, sport, and tourism management (MS). *Faculty:* 19. *Students:* 89 full-time, 9 part-time. Average age 26. In 2018, 43 master's awarded. *Degree requirements:* For doctorate, thesis/dissertation. *Entrance requirements:* For master's and doctorate, minimum GPA of 3.0. Additional exam requirements/recommendations for international students: Required—TOEFL. *Application deadline:* For fall admission, 8/1 for domestic students; for spring admission, 12/15 for domestic students. Applications are processed on a rolling basis. Application fee: $60. Electronic applications accepted. *Expenses:* Tuition, state resident: full-time $7266.44; part-time $474.50 per credit hour. Tuition, nonresident: full-time $24,902; part-time $1453.50 per credit hour. *Required fees:* $2085.56; $45.50 per credit hour. *Financial support:* Research assistantships and teaching assistantships available. Financial award applicants required to submit FAFSA. *Unit head:* Dr. Philip W. Scruggs, Chair, 208-885-7921, E-mail: movementsciences@uidaho.edu. *Application contact:* Dr. Philip W. Scruggs, Chair, 208-885-7921, E-mail: movementsciences@uidaho.edu. Website: https://www.uidaho.edu/ed/mvsc

University of Indianapolis, Graduate Programs, College of Health Sciences, Department of Kinesiology, Indianapolis, IN 46227-3697. Offers sport management (MS). *Program availability:* Evening/weekend.

The University of Iowa, Graduate College, College of Liberal Arts and Sciences, Department of Health and Human Physiology, Iowa City, IA 52242-1316. Offers athletic training (MS); clinical exercise physiology (MS); health and human physiology (PhD); leisure studies (MA, PhD), including recreational sport management (PhD), therapeutic recreation (MA). *Degree requirements:* For master's, thesis optional, exam; for doctorate, comprehensive exam, thesis/dissertation. *Entrance requirements:* For master's and doctorate, GRE General Test, minimum GPA of 3.0. Additional exam requirements/recommendations for international students: Required—TOEFL (minimum score 600 paper-based; 100 iBT). Electronic applications accepted.

The University of Kansas, Graduate Studies, School of Education, Department of Health, Sport, and Exercise Sciences, Lawrence, KS 66045. Offers exercise science (MS Ed); health, sport, and exercise sciences (PhD); sport management (MS Ed). *Accreditation:* NCATE. *Program availability:* Part-time, evening/weekend. *Students:* 67 full-time (26 women), 34 part-time (15 women); includes 19 minority (6 Black or African American, non-Hispanic/Latino; 2 American Indian or Alaska Native, non-Hispanic/Latino; 9 Hispanic/Latino; 2 Two or more races, non-Hispanic/Latino), 9 international. Average age 27. 113 applicants, 73% accepted, 53 enrolled. In 2018, 17 master's, 3 doctorates awarded. *Entrance requirements:* For master's, GRE General Test (minimum score 1000, 450 verbal, 450 quantitative, 4.0 analytical), minimum GPA of 3.0, three letters of recommendation, personal statement, resume, writing sample; for doctorate, GRE General Test (minimum score 1100, verbal 500, quantitative 500, analytical 4.5), minimum graduate GPA of 3.5, undergraduate 3.0; three letters of recommendation; personal statement; resume; writing sample; interview with an advisor. Additional exam requirements/recommendations for international students: Required—TOEFL, IELTS. *Application deadline:* For fall admission, 3/15 for domestic and international students; for spring admission, 10/1 for domestic and international students; for summer admission, 3/15 for domestic and international students. Application fee: $65 ($85 for international students). Electronic applications accepted. *Financial support:* Research assistantships, teaching assistantships, Federal Work-Study, scholarships/grants, and unspecified assistantships available. Financial award application deadline: 2/21. *Faculty research:* Exercise and sport psychology, obesity prevention, sexuality health, sport ethics, skeletal muscle cell signaling and performance. *Unit head:* Dr. Joseph Weir, Chair, 785-864-0784, E-mail: joseph.weir@ku.edu. *Application contact:* Robin Bass, Graduate Admissions Coordinator, 785-864-6138, E-mail: rbass@ku.edu. Website: http://hses.soe.ku.edu/

University of Louisiana at Monroe, Graduate School, College of Health Sciences, Department of Kinesiology, Monroe, LA 71209-0001. Offers applied exercise science (MS); clinical exercise physiology (MS); sports, fitness and recreation management (MS). *Program availability:* Part-time, evening/weekend, online learning. *Faculty:* 6 full-time (2 women), 1 part-time/adjunct (0 women). *Students:* 39 full-time (17 women), 4 part-time (2 women); includes 16 minority (10 Black or African American, non-Hispanic/Latino; 1 American Indian or Alaska Native, non-Hispanic/Latino; 3 Hispanic/Latino; 2 Two or more races, non-Hispanic/Latino), 2 international. Average age 25. 16 applicants, 88% accepted, 11 enrolled. In 2018, 22 master's awarded. *Degree requirements:* For master's, comprehensive exam, thesis, 6-hour internship. *Entrance requirements:* For master's, GRE General Test. Additional exam requirements/recommendations for international students: Required—TOEFL (minimum score 500 paper-based; 61 iBT). *Application deadline:* For fall admission, 8/24 priority date for domestic students, 7/1 for international students; for winter admission, 12/14 priority date for domestic students; for spring admission, 1/19 for domestic students, 11/1 for international students. Applications are processed on a rolling basis. Application fee: $20 ($30 for international students). Electronic applications accepted. *Financial support:* In 2018–19, 12 students received support. Research assistantships, career-related internships or fieldwork, Federal Work-Study, and unspecified assistantships available. Financial award application deadline: 4/1; financial award applicants required to submit FAFSA. *Faculty research:* Cardiovascular disease risk factors; exercise and immunological system; attitude, exercise, and the aged. *Unit head:* Dr. Ken Alford, Director, 318-342-1306, E-mail: alford@ulm.edu. *Application contact:* Dr. Tommie Church, Director of Graduate Studies, 318-342-1321, E-mail: church@ulm.edu. Website: http://www.ulm.edu/kinesiology/

University of Louisville, Graduate School, College of Education and Human Development, Department of Health and Sport Sciences, Louisville, KY 40292-0001. Offers community health education (M Ed); exercise physiology (MS), including health and sport sciences, strength and conditioning; health and physical education (MAT); sport administration (MS). *Program availability:* Part-time, evening/weekend, 100% online, blended/hybrid learning. *Students:* 32 full-time (10 women), 5 part-time (3 women); includes 9 minority (7 Black or African American, non-Hispanic/Latino; 2 Two or more races, non-Hispanic/Latino). Average age 28. 41 applicants, 66% accepted, 21 enrolled. In 2018, 21 master's awarded. Terminal master's awarded for partial completion of doctoral program. *Degree requirements:* For master's, comprehensive exam (for some programs), thesis optional. *Entrance requirements:* For master's, GRE (for most programs), PRAXIS (for educator preparation programs), professional statement, recommendation letters, resume, transcripts. Additional exam requirements/recommendations for international students: Required—TOEFL (minimum score 550 paper-based; 79 iBT); Recommended—IELTS (minimum score 6.5). *Application deadline:* For fall admission, 6/1 priority date for domestic students, 5/1 priority date for international students; for spring admission, 10/1 priority date for domestic students, 11/1 priority date for international students; for summer admission, 3/1 priority date for domestic students, 4/1 priority date for international students. Application fee: $65. *Expenses: Tuition, area resident:* Full-time $6500; part-time $723 per credit hour. Tuition, state resident: full-time $6500. Tuition, nonresident: full-time $13,557; part-time $1507 per credit hour. Tuition and fees vary according to course load and program. *Financial support:* In 2018–19, 15 students received support, including fellowships with full tuition reimbursements available (averaging $21,024 per year), research assistantships (averaging $21,024 per year); teaching assistantships with full tuition reimbursements available, Federal Work-Study, scholarships/grants, health care benefits, tuition waivers (full), and unspecified assistantships also available. Financial award application deadline: 3/1; financial award applicants required to submit FAFSA. *Faculty research:* Sport administration, exercise science, exercise physiology, physical and health education, youth sport development. *Unit head:* Dr. Dylan Naeger, Interim Chair, 502-852-6645, E-mail: hss@louisville.edu. *Application contact:* Dr. Margaret Pentecost, Director of Grad Assistant Dean for Graduate Student Success Graduate Student Services, 502-852-6437, Fax: 502-852-1465, E-mail: gedadm@louisville.edu. Website: http://www.louisville.edu/education/departments/hss

University of Louisville, Graduate School, College of Education and Human Development, Departments of Early Childhood and Elementary Education, Middle and Secondary Education, and Special Education, Louisville, KY 40292-0001. Offers art education (MAT); autism and applied behavior analysis (Certificate); curriculum and instruction (PhD); early elementary education (MAT); exercise physiology (MS); health and physical education (MAT); health professions education (Certificate); higher education (MA); human resources and organization development (MS); instructional technology (M Ed); interdisciplinary early childhood education (MAT); middle school education (MAT); music education (MAT); secondary education (MAT); special education (MAT); sport administration (MS); teacher leadership (M Ed). *Program availability:* Part-time, evening/weekend, 100% online, blended/hybrid learning. *Faculty:* 97 full-time (64 women), 131 part-time/adjunct (86 women). *Students:* 109 full-time (72 women), 139 part-time (87 women); includes 43 minority (18 Black or African American, non-Hispanic/Latino; 6 Asian, non-Hispanic/Latino; 10 Hispanic/Latino; 9 Two or more races, non-Hispanic/Latino), 9 international. Average age 29. 108 applicants, 75% accepted, 59 enrolled. In 2018, 64 master's awarded. Terminal master's awarded for partial completion of doctoral program. *Degree requirements:* For master's, comprehensive exam (for some programs), thesis optional; for doctorate, comprehensive exam (for some programs), thesis/dissertation. *Entrance requirements:* For master's, GRE (for most programs), PRAXIS (for educator preparation programs), professional statement, recommendation letters, resume, transcripts; for doctorate and Certificate, GRE, professional statement, recommendation letters, resume, transcripts. Additional exam requirements/recommendations for international students: Required—TOEFL (minimum score 550 paper-based; 79 iBT); Recommended—IELTS (minimum score 6.5). *Application deadline:* For fall admission, 6/1 priority date for domestic students, 5/1 priority date for international students; for spring admission, 10/1 for domestic students, 11/1 priority date for international students; for summer admission, 3/1 priority date for domestic students, 4/1 priority date for international students. Application fee: $65. *Expenses: Tuition, area resident:* Full-time $6500; part-time $723

per credit hour. Tuition, state resident: full-time $6500. Tuition, nonresident: full-time $13,557; part-time $1507 per credit hour. Tuition and fees vary according to course load and program. *Financial support:* In 2018–19, 144 students received support, including fellowships with full tuition reimbursements available (averaging $21,024 per year), research assistantships with full tuition reimbursements available (averaging $21,024 per year), teaching assistantships with full tuition reimbursements available (averaging $21,024 per year); Federal Work-Study, scholarships/grants, health care benefits, tuition waivers (full), and unspecified assistantships also available. Financial award application deadline: 3/1; financial award applicants required to submit FAFSA. *Faculty research:* Children's early reading and writing development, crelevance of basic facts in elementary mathematics instruction, clinical model of teacher education, cultural and linguistic context of diverse learners, and STEM-integrated curriculum design and development. STEM teaching and learning, content literacy for English language learners, social justice in teacher education, adolescent literacy, mathematics teacher development. Classroom and behavior management; moderate/severe disabilities, autism. *Unit head:* Dr. Amy Lingo, Interim Dean, 502-852-3235, Fax: 502-852-1464, E-mail: cehdinfo@louisville.edu. *Application contact:* Dr. Margaret Pentecost, Assistant Dean for Graduate Student Success, 502-852-6437, Fax: 502-852-1417, E-mail: gedadm@louisville.edu.
Website: http://louisville.edu/delphi

University of Mary, School of Health Sciences, Program in Sports and Physical Education Administration, Bismarck, ND 58504-9652. Offers MS. *Program availability:* Online learning. *Entrance requirements:* For master's, bachelor's degree in athletic training, exercise science, physical education, or a related field; minimum undergraduate GPA of 2.5.

University of Mary Hardin-Baylor, Graduate Studies in Exercise Physiology, Belton, TX 76513. Offers exercise physiology (MS Ed); sport administration (MS Ed). *Program availability:* Part-time, 100% online. *Degree requirements:* For master's, comprehensive exam, thesis optional. *Entrance requirements:* For master's, bachelor's degree in exercise science or related field; minimum GPA of 3.0; interview with program director. Additional exam requirements/recommendations for international students: Required—TOEFL (minimum score 60 iBT), IELTS (minimum score 4.5). Electronic applications accepted. *Faculty research:* Evaluation of the efficacy and safety of Fenugreek extract ingestion on markers of muscle damage and inflammation on healthy non-resistance trained subjects; genetic influences on sport performance and athlete health; examination of biomarkers of sub-concussive impacts in men and women's Division III soccer players; The Acute Response of nutritive vs. non-nutritive sweeteners in soft drinks of blood glucose and insulin in regular soft drink consumers.

University of Massachusetts Amherst, Graduate School, Interdisciplinary Programs, Dual Degree Program in Management and Sport Management, Amherst, MA 01003. Offers MBA/MS. *Program availability:* Part-time. *Entrance requirements:* Additional exam requirements/recommendations for international students: Required—TOEFL (minimum score 600 paper-based; 100 iBT), IELTS (minimum score 7). Electronic applications accepted.

University of Massachusetts Amherst, Graduate School, Isenberg School of Management, Department of Sport Management, Amherst, MA 01003. Offers MBA, MS, MBA/MS. *Program availability:* Part-time. Terminal master's awarded for partial completion of doctoral program. *Degree requirements:* For master's, thesis or alternative. *Entrance requirements:* For master's, GMAT or GRE General Test. Additional exam requirements/recommendations for international students: Required—TOEFL (minimum score 550 paper-based; 80 iBT), IELTS (minimum score 6.5). Electronic applications accepted.

University of Massachusetts Amherst, Graduate School, Isenberg School of Management, Program in Management, Amherst, MA 01003. Offers accounting (PhD); business administration (MBA); entrepreneurship (MBA); finance (MBA, PhD); healthcare administration (MBA); hospitality and tourism management (PhD); management science (PhD); marketing (MBA, PhD); organization studies (PhD); sport management (PhD); strategic management (PhD); MBA/MS. *Accreditation:* AACSB. *Program availability:* Part-time, evening/weekend, online learning. Terminal master's awarded for partial completion of doctoral program. *Degree requirements:* For doctorate, comprehensive exam, thesis/dissertation. *Entrance requirements:* For master's and doctorate, GMAT or GRE General Test. Additional exam requirements/recommendations for international students: Required—TOEFL (minimum score 550 paper-based; 80 iBT), IELTS (minimum score 6.5). Electronic applications accepted.

University of Miami, Graduate School, School of Education and Human Development, Department of Kinesiology and Sport Sciences, Program in Sport Administration, Coral Gables, FL 33124. Offers MS Ed. *Program availability:* Part-time, evening/weekend, 100% online. *Faculty:* 7 full-time (4 women). *Students:* 127 full-time (38 women), 13 part-time (5 women); includes 73 minority (43 Black or African American, non-Hispanic/Latino; 2 American Indian or Alaska Native, non-Hispanic/Latino; 3 Asian, non-Hispanic/Latino; 15 Hispanic/Latino; 10 Two or more races, non-Hispanic/Latino), 4 international. Average age 29. 172 applicants, 52% accepted, 44 enrolled. In 2018, 79 master's awarded. *Degree requirements:* For master's, special project. *Entrance requirements:* For master's, GRE General Test. Additional exam requirements/recommendations for international students: Required—TOEFL (minimum score 550 paper-based; 80 iBT); Recommended—IELTS (minimum score 6.5). *Application deadline:* For fall admission, 10/1 for international students; for spring admission, 10/1 for international students. Applications are processed on a rolling basis. Application fee: $75. Electronic applications accepted. *Financial support:* Institutionally sponsored loans and scholarships/grants available. Financial award application deadline: 3/1; financial award applicants required to submit FAFSA. *Faculty research:* Constitutional procedural due process, legal liability, tort law, moral development in sports administration, ethics intervention. *Unit head:* Dr. Windy Dees, Associate Professor and Program Director, 305-284-8345, E-mail: wdees@miami.edu. *Application contact:* Lois Heffernan, Graduate Admissions Coordinator, 305-284-2167, Fax: 305-284-9395, E-mail: lheffernan@miami.edu.
Website: http://www.education.miami.edu

University of Michigan, Rackham Graduate School, School of Kinesiology, Ann Arbor, MI 48109. Offers movement science (MS, PhD); sport management (MS, PhD). *Faculty:* 30 full-time (15 women). *Students:* 115 full-time (56 women); includes 31 minority (13 Black or African American, non-Hispanic/Latino; 4 Asian, non-Hispanic/Latino; 11 Hispanic/Latino; 3 Two or more races, non-Hispanic/Latino). Average age 26. 223 applicants, 51% accepted, 64 enrolled. In 2018, 47 master's, 4 doctorates awarded. Terminal master's awarded for partial completion of doctoral program. *Degree requirements:* For master's, thesis optional; for doctorate, comprehensive exam, thesis/dissertation, oral defense of dissertation. *Entrance requirements:* For master's and doctorate, GRE General Test. Additional exam requirements/recommendations for international students: Required—TOEFL (minimum score 84 iBT). *Application deadline:* For fall admission, 12/1 priority date for domestic students, 12/1 for international students. Applications are processed on a rolling basis. Application fee: $75 ($90 for international students). Electronic applications accepted. *Financial support:* In 2018–19, 34 students received support, including 13 fellowships with full tuition reimbursements available, 9 research assistantships with full tuition reimbursements available, 14 teaching assistantships with full tuition reimbursements available; Federal Work-Study, scholarships/grants, traineeships, health care benefits, and unspecified assistantships also available. Financial award application deadline: 12/1. *Faculty research:* Motor development, exercise physiology, biomechanics, sport medicine, sport management. *Unit head:* Dr. Ketra L. Armstrong, Associate Dean for Graduate Affairs, 734-647-3027, Fax: 734-647-2808, E-mail: ketra@umich.edu. *Application contact:* Charlene F. Ruloff, Graduate Program Coordinator, 734-764-1343, Fax: 734-647-2808, E-mail: cruloff@umich.edu.
Website: http://www.kines.umich.edu/

University of Minnesota, Twin Cities Campus, Graduate School, College of Education and Human Development, School of Kinesiology, Minneapolis, MN 55455-0213. Offers kinesiology (MS, PhD), including behavioral aspects of physical activity, biomechanics and neuromotor control, exercise physiology, perceptual-motor control and learning, sport and exercise psychology, sport management (PhD), sport sociology; sport and exercise science (M Ed); sport management (M Ed, MA). *Program availability:* Part-time. *Faculty:* 15 full-time (7 women). *Students:* 117 full-time (58 women), 21 part-time (8 women); includes 21 minority (5 Black or African American, non-Hispanic/Latino; 3 Asian, non-Hispanic/Latino; 9 Hispanic/Latino; 4 Two or more races, non-Hispanic/Latino), 23 international. Average age 26. 175 applicants, 62% accepted, 69 enrolled. In 2018, 47 master's, 9 doctorates awarded. Terminal master's awarded for partial completion of doctoral program. *Degree requirements:* For master's, final oral exam; for doctorate, thesis/dissertation, preliminary written/oral exam, final oral exam. *Entrance requirements:* For master's, GRE or MAT, minimum GPA of 3.0; for doctorate, GRE or MAT, minimum GPA of 3.0, writing sample. Application fee: $75 ($95 for international students). *Financial support:* In 2018–19, 3 fellowships, 8 research assistantships with full tuition reimbursements (averaging $8,544 per year), 37 teaching assistantships with full tuition reimbursements (averaging $14,093 per year) were awarded; career-related internships or fieldwork, Federal Work-Study, institutionally sponsored loans, and tuition waivers (full and partial) also available. Support available to part-time students. *Faculty research:* Role of physical activity in preventing health related problems; mechanism of age-related disorders, diseases and mental problems, and the ways to ameliorate them; role of sports in society and social justice; sports among populations with low income and racial diversity; fundamental functions of the body and the mechanism controlling the mechanisms; psychological issues related to physical activity and sports. *Total annual research expenditures:* $525,150. *Unit head:* Dr. Beth Lewis, Director, 612-625-5300, E-mail: blewis@umn.edu. *Application contact:* Nina Wang, 612-625-4380, E-mail: nwang@umn.edu.
Website: http://www.cehd.umn.edu/kin/

University of Nebraska at Kearney, College of Education, Kinesiology and Sport Sciences Department, Kearney, NE 68849-0001. Offers general physical education (MA Ed), including recreation and leisure, sports administration; physical education exercise science (MA Ed); physical education master teacher (MA Ed), including pedagogy, special populations. *Program availability:* Part-time, evening/weekend, 100% online. *Degree requirements:* For master's, comprehensive exam, thesis optional. *Entrance requirements:* For master's, GRE General Test (for some programs), personal statement. Additional exam requirements/recommendations for international students: Recommended—TOEFL (minimum score 550 paper-based; 79 iBT), IELTS (minimum score 6.5). Electronic applications accepted. *Faculty research:* Ergonomic aids, nutrition, motor development, sports pedagogy, applied behavior analysis, physical activity and wellness, athletic training, therapeutic Interventions, exercise physiology, endocrinology and metabolism.

University of New Brunswick Fredericton, School of Graduate Studies, Faculty of Business Administration, Fredericton, NB E3B 5A3, Canada. Offers business administration (MBA); engineering management (MBA); entrepreneurship (MBA); sports and recreation management (MBA); MBA/LL B. *Program availability:* Part-time. *Degree requirements:* For master's, thesis optional. *Entrance requirements:* For master's, GMAT (minimum score 550), minimum GPA of 3.0; 3-5 years of work experience; 3 letters of reference with at least one academic reference. Additional exam requirements/recommendations for international students: Required—TOEFL (minimum score 580 paper-based; 92 iBT) or IELTS (minimum score 7). Electronic applications accepted. *Faculty research:* Entrepreneurship, finance, law, sport and recreation management, engineering management.

University of New Brunswick Fredericton, School of Graduate Studies, Faculty of Kinesiology, Fredericton, NB E3B 5A3, Canada. Offers exercise and sport science (M Sc); sport and recreation management (MBA); sport and recreation studies (MA). *Program availability:* Part-time. *Degree requirements:* For master's, thesis (for some programs). *Entrance requirements:* For master's, GMAT (minimum score of 550 for sport and recreation management program), minimum GPA of 3.0, written statement of research goals and interests. Additional exam requirements/recommendations for international students: Required—TOEFL (minimum score 92 iBT), IELTS (minimum score 7). Electronic applications accepted.

University of New Haven, Graduate School, College of Business, Program in Business Administration, West Haven, CT 06516. Offers accounting (MBA); business administration (MBA); business intelligence (MBA); business policy and strategic leadership (MBA); finance (MBA), including chartered financial analyst; global marketing (MBA); human resources management (MBA); sport management (MBA). *Accreditation:* AACSB. *Program availability:* Part-time, evening/weekend. *Students:* 151 full-time (73 women), 70 part-time (30 women); includes 51 minority (23 Black or African American, non-Hispanic/Latino; 13 Asian, non-Hispanic/Latino; 14 Hispanic/Latino; 1 Two or more races, non-Hispanic/Latino), 74 international. Average age 28. 197 applicants, 91% accepted, 82 enrolled. In 2018, 70 master's awarded. *Entrance requirements:* For master's, GMAT. Additional exam requirements/recommendations for international students: Required—TOEFL (minimum score 80 iBT), IELTS, PTE. *Application deadline:* Applications are processed on a rolling basis. Application fee: $50. Electronic applications accepted. Application fee is waived when completed online. *Expenses: Tuition:* Full-time $16,470; part-time $915 per credit hour. *Required fees:* $230; $95 per term. *Financial support:* Research assistantships with partial tuition reimbursements, teaching assistantships with partial tuition reimbursements, career-related internships or fieldwork, Federal Work-Study, scholarships/grants, and unspecified assistantships available. Support available to part-time students. Financial award applicants required to submit FAFSA. *Unit head:* Darell Singleterry, Director, 203-932-7386, E-mail: dsingleterry@newhaven.edu. *Application contact:* Selina O'Toole, Senior Associate Director of Graduate Admissions, 203-932-7337, E-mail: SOToole@newhaven.edu.
Website: http://www.newhaven.edu/business/graduate-programs/mba/index.php

University of New Haven, Graduate School, College of Business, Program in Sport Management, West Haven, CT 06516. Offers collegiate athletic administration (MS); facility management (MS); sport analytics (MS); sport management (Graduate Certificate). *Program availability:* Part-time, evening/weekend. *Students:* 24 full-time (12 women), 3 part-time (0 women); includes 3 minority (1 Black or African American, non-Hispanic/Latino; 1 American Indian or Alaska Native, non-Hispanic/Latino; 1 Hispanic/Latino), 5 international. Average age 25. 41 applicants, 98% accepted, 23 enrolled. In 2018, 14 master's awarded. *Entrance requirements:* For master's, GMAT. Additional exam requirements/recommendations for international students: Required—TOEFL

(minimum score 80 iBT), IELTS, PTE. *Application deadline:* Applications are processed on a rolling basis. Application fee: $50. Electronic applications accepted. Application fee is waived when completed online. *Expenses: Tuition:* Full-time $16,470; part-time $915 per credit hour. *Required fees:* $230; $95 per term. *Financial support:* Research assistantships with partial tuition reimbursements, teaching assistantships with partial tuition reimbursements, Federal Work-Study, scholarships/grants, and unspecified assistantships available. Support available to part-time students. Financial award applicants required to submit FAFSA. *Unit head:* Gil B. Fried, Professor, 203-932-7081, E-mail: gfried@newhaven.edu. *Application contact:* Selina O'Toole, Senior Associate Director of Graduate Admissions, 203-932-7337, E-mail: SOToole@newhaven.edu.
Website: https://www.newhaven.edu/business/graduate-programs/sport-management/

University of New Mexico, Graduate Studies, College of Education, Program in Physical Education, Sports and Exercise Science, Albuquerque, NM 87131-2039. Offers curriculum and instruction (PhD); exercise science (PhD); sports administration (PhD). *Program availability:* Part-time. *Students:* Average age 30. 67 applicants, 75% accepted, 35 enrolled. In 2018, 13 doctorates awarded. *Degree requirements:* For doctorate, comprehensive exam, thesis/dissertation, inquiry skills, 24 credits in supporting area. *Entrance requirements:* For doctorate, GRE, letter of intent, 3 letters of reference, minimum cumulative GPA of 3.0 in last 2 years of bachelor's degree. Additional exam requirements/recommendations for international students: Required—TOEFL (minimum score 550 paper-based). *Application deadline:* For fall admission, 3/1 priority date for domestic students; for spring admission, 11/1 priority date for domestic students. Application fee: $50. Electronic applications accepted. *Financial support:* Fellowships, teaching assistantships with full tuition reimbursements, career-related internships or fieldwork, Federal Work-Study, institutionally sponsored loans, scholarships/grants, health care benefits, tuition waivers, and unspecified assistantships available. Financial award application deadline: 3/1; financial award applicants required to submit FAFSA. *Faculty research:* Facility risk management, physical education pedagogy practices, physiological adaptations to exercise, physiological adaptations to heat, sport leadership. *Unit head:* Dr. Todd Seidler, Chair, 505-277-2783, Fax: 505-277-6227, E-mail: tseidler@unm.edu. *Application contact:* Monica Lopez, Program Office, 505-277-5151, Fax: 505-277-6227, E-mail: mllopez@unm.edu.
Website: https://coe.unm.edu/departments-programs/hess/physical-education/physical-education-phd/index.html

The University of North Carolina at Chapel Hill, Graduate School, College of Arts and Sciences, Department of Exercise and Sport Science, Chapel Hill, NC 27599. Offers athletic training (MA); exercise physiology (MA); sport administration (MA). *Degree requirements:* For master's, comprehensive exam, thesis. *Entrance requirements:* For master's, GRE General Test, minimum GPA of 3.0. Additional exam requirements/recommendations for international students: Required—TOEFL (minimum score 550 paper-based). Electronic applications accepted. *Faculty research:* Mild head injury in sport, endocrine system's response to exercise, obesity and children, effect of aerobic exercise on cerebral bloodflow in elderly population.

The University of North Carolina at Pembroke, The Graduate School, School of Education, Department of Health and Human Performance, Pembroke, NC 28372-1510. Offers health/physical education (MAT); physical education (MA), including exercise/sports administration, physical education advanced licensure. *Program availability:* Part-time, evening/weekend. *Degree requirements:* For master's, comprehensive exam, thesis optional. *Entrance requirements:* For master's, MAT or GRE, minimum GPA of 3.0 in major, 2.5 overall. Additional exam requirements/recommendations for international students: Required—TOEFL.

University of Northern Colorado, Graduate School, College of Natural and Health Sciences, School of Sport and Exercise Science, Greeley, CO 80639. Offers exercise science (MS, PhD); physical education and physical activity leadership (MAT); sport administration (MS, PhD); sport pedagogy (MS, PhD); sports coaching (MA). *Program availability:* Part-time, evening/weekend. *Degree requirements:* For master's, comprehensive exam; for doctorate, comprehensive exam, thesis/dissertation. *Entrance requirements:* For master's, 2 letters of recommendation, resume; for doctorate, GRE General Test, 3 letters of recommendation, resume. Electronic applications accepted.

University of Northern Iowa, Graduate College, College of Education, School of Kinesiology, Allied Health and Human Services, MA Program in Physical Education, Cedar Falls, IA 50614. Offers kinesiology (MA); teaching/coaching (MA). *Program availability:* Part-time, evening/weekend. *Degree requirements:* For master's, comprehensive exam, thesis or alternative. *Entrance requirements:* For master's, minimum GPA of 3.0. Additional exam requirements/recommendations for international students: Required—TOEFL (minimum score 500 paper-based; 61 iBT). Electronic applications accepted.

University of North Florida, College of Education and Human Services, Department of Leadership, School Counseling and Sport Management, Jacksonville, FL 32224. Offers counselor education (M Ed), including school counseling; educational leadership (M Ed, Ed D), including athletic administration (M Ed), educational leadership, educational technology (M Ed), instructional leadership (M Ed). *Program availability:* Part-time, evening/weekend. *Faculty:* 19 full-time (13 women), 3 part-time/adjunct (1 woman). *Students:* 73 full-time (58 women), 228 part-time (179 women); includes 111 minority (66 Black or African American, non-Hispanic/Latino; 7 Asian, non-Hispanic/Latino; 26 Hispanic/Latino; 1 Native Hawaiian or other Pacific Islander, non-Hispanic/Latino; 11 Two or more races, non-Hispanic/Latino), 8 international. Average age 38. 184 applicants, 58% accepted, 74 enrolled. In 2018, 77 master's, 20 doctorates awarded. *Degree requirements:* For doctorate, thesis/dissertation. *Entrance requirements:* For master's, GRE General Test, minimum GPA of 3.0 in last 60 hours, interview, 3 letters of recommendation; for doctorate, GRE General Test, master's degree, interview, 3 letters of recommendation, writing sample. Additional exam requirements/recommendations for international students: Required—TOEFL (minimum score 500 paper-based). *Application deadline:* For fall admission, 5/1 priority date for domestic students, 5/1 for international students. Application fee: $30. Electronic applications accepted. *Expenses: Tuition, area resident:* Part-time $408.10 per credit hour. Tuition, state resident: part-time $408.10 per credit hour. Tuition, nonresident: part-time $932.61 per credit hour. *Required fees:* $111.81 per credit hour. Tuition and fees vary according to course load, campus/location and program. *Financial support:* In 2018–19, 42 students received support, including 1 research assistantship (averaging $8,096 per year), 1 teaching assistantship (averaging $5,824 per year); career-related internships or fieldwork, Federal Work-Study, scholarships/grants, tuition waivers (partial), and unspecified assistantships also available. Support available to part-time students. Financial award application deadline: 4/1; financial award applicants required to submit FAFSA. *Faculty research:* Counseling: ethics; lesbian, bisexual and transgender issues; educational leadership: school culture and climate; educational assessment and accountability; school safety and student discipline. *Total annual research expenditures:* $12,024. *Unit head:* Dr. Liz Gregg, Chair, 904-620-5199, E-mail: liz.gregg@unf.edu. *Application contact:* Dr. Amanda Pascale, Director, The Graduate School, 904-620-1360, Fax: 904-620-1362, E-mail: graduateschool@unf.edu.
Website: http://www.unf.edu/coehs/lscsm/

University of Oregon, Graduate School, Charles H. Lundquist College of Business, Program in Sports Product Management, Portland, OR 97209. Offers MS.

University of San Francisco, College of Arts and Sciences, Sport Management Program, San Francisco, CA 94117. Offers MA. *Program availability:* Evening/weekend. *Students:* 188 full-time (68 women), 16 part-time (8 women); includes 87 minority (22 Black or African American, non-Hispanic/Latino; 17 Asian, non-Hispanic/Latino; 36 Hispanic/Latino; 2 Native Hawaiian or other Pacific Islander, non-Hispanic/Latino; 10 Two or more races, non-Hispanic/Latino), 24 international. Average age 25. 209 applicants, 60% accepted, 72 enrolled. In 2018, 95 master's awarded. *Degree requirements:* For master's, thesis or alternative. *Entrance requirements:* For master's, interview, minimum GPA of 2.75. Additional exam requirements/recommendations for international students: Required—TOEFL (minimum score 79 iBT), IELTS (minimum score 6.5), PTE (minimum score 53). *Application deadline:* For spring admission, 9/1 for domestic and international students; for summer admission, 2/1 for domestic and international students. Applications are processed on a rolling basis. Application fee: $55. Electronic applications accepted. *Financial support:* Career-related internships or fieldwork, Federal Work-Study, institutionally sponsored loans, and scholarships/grants available. Financial award applicants required to submit FAFSA. *Faculty research:* Media and sports, sports marketing, sports law, management and organization, leadership and critical thinking, sport economics and finance, quantitative analysis in sports, strategic management, human resources in sports, accounting, branding, strategic communication, sports and culture, marketing sports, event management in sports. *Unit head:* Brent von Forstmeyer, Graduate Director, 415-422-2678, E-mail: sminfo@usfca.edu. *Application contact:* Brent von Forstmeyer, Graduate Director, 415-422-2678, E-mail: sminfo@usfca.edu.
Website: https://www.usfca.edu/arts-sciences/graduate-programs/sport-management

University of South Alabama, College of Education and Professional Studies, Department of Health, Kinesiology, and Sport, Mobile, AL 36688. Offers exercise science (MS); health education (M Ed, MS); physical education (M Ed); sport management (MS). *Accreditation:* NCATE (one or more programs are accredited). *Program availability:* Part-time. *Degree requirements:* For master's, comprehensive exam, thesis optional. *Entrance requirements:* For master's, GRE General Test or MAT, Alabama Class B certificate or the equivalent (for students seeking the master's-level/Class A certification). Additional exam requirements/recommendations for international students: Required—TOEFL. Electronic applications accepted.

University of South Carolina, The Graduate School, College of Hospitality, Retail, and Sport Management, Department of Sport and Entertainment Management, Columbia, SC 29208. Offers live sport and entertainment events (MS); public assembly facilities management (MS). *Program availability:* Part-time. *Degree requirements:* For master's, comprehensive exam, thesis optional. *Entrance requirements:* For master's, GRE General Test or GMAT (preferred), minimum GPA of 3.0. Additional exam requirements/recommendations for international students: Required—TOEFL (minimum score 570 paper-based; 70 iBT). Electronic applications accepted. *Expenses:* Contact institution. *Faculty research:* Public assembly marketing, operations, box office, booking and scheduling, law/economic impacts.

University of Southern Indiana, Graduate Studies, Pott College of Science, Engineering, and Education, Program in Sport Management, Evansville, IN 47712-3590. Offers MSSM. *Program availability:* Part-time, evening/weekend. *Entrance requirements:* For master's, personal statement, three letters of recommendation. Additional exam requirements/recommendations for international students: Required—TOEFL (minimum score 550 paper-based; 79 iBT), IELTS (minimum score 6). Electronic applications accepted.

University of Southern Mississippi, College of Business and Economic Development, School of Marketing, Hattiesburg, MS 39406-0001. Offers sport management (MS). *Program availability:* Part-time, evening/weekend. *Degree requirements:* For master's, comprehensive exam, thesis optional, internships. *Entrance requirements:* For master's, GMAT or GRE General Test, minimum GPA of 2.75 in last 60 hours. Additional exam requirements/recommendations for international students: Required—TOEFL, IELTS. Electronic applications accepted. *Faculty research:* Economic development, international studies, geography.

University of South Florida, Muma College of Business, Department of Marketing, Tampa, FL 33620-9951. Offers business administration (PhD), including marketing; marketing (MSM); sport and entertainment management (MS). *Program availability:* Part-time, evening/weekend. *Faculty:* 16 full-time (4 women). *Students:* 44 full-time (24 women), 29 part-time (18 women); includes 12 minority (3 Black or African American, non-Hispanic/Latino; 8 Hispanic/Latino; 1 Two or more races, non-Hispanic/Latino), 39 international. Average age 26. 99 applicants, 63% accepted, 33 enrolled. In 2018, 35 master's awarded. Terminal master's awarded for partial completion of doctoral program. *Degree requirements:* For master's, comprehensive exam, thesis (for some programs); for doctorate, comprehensive exam, thesis/dissertation. *Entrance requirements:* For master's, GMAT (preferred) or GRE; MCAT or LSAT may be substituted, minimum GPA of 3.0; letters of recommendation; letter of interest; statement of purpose. Entrepreneurship: Demonstrated competence in Statistics, Accounting, and Finance. Marketing: resume; relevant professional work experience. Sport Mgmt: interview; admission to MBA with Conc in Sport Business; for doctorate, GMAT or GRE, personal statement, recommendations, interview. Additional exam requirements/recommendations for international students: Required—TOEFL, TOEFL (minimum score 550 paper-based; 79 iBT) or IELTS (minimum score 6.5). *Application deadline:* For fall admission, 1/2 for domestic and international students; for spring admission, 10/15 for domestic students, 7/1 for international students. Applications are processed on a rolling basis. Application fee: $30. Electronic applications accepted. *Expenses:* Tuition, state resident: full-time $6350. Tuition, nonresident: full-time $19,048. *International tuition:* $19,048 full-time. *Required fees:* $2079. *Financial support:* In 2018–19, 12 students received support, including 5 research assistantships (averaging $14,943 per year), 6 teaching assistantships (averaging $11,972 per year); health care benefits and unspecified assistantships also available. *Faculty research:* Branding; consumer behavior; marketing communications' effectiveness; customer satisfaction; customer delight; consumer reactions to new technology, products and services; consumer emotions; brand strategies; communications; advertising effectiveness; green alliances; strategic marketing; international business; international marketing; consumer research; customer service branding; focus group research; market surveys; market research; promotion; services marketing; strategic planning. *Total annual research expenditures:* $24,235. *Unit head:* Dr. Doug Hughes, Chair, Professor, 813-974-6215, Fax: 813-974-6175, E-mail: dehughes1@usf.edu. *Application contact:* Stacee Bender, Academic Services Administrator, 813-974-4516, Fax: 813-974-6175, E-mail: staceebender@usf.edu.
Website: http://business.usf.edu/departments/marketing/

The University of Tennessee, Graduate School, College of Education, Health and Human Sciences, Department of Exercise, Sport, and Leisure Studies, Knoxville, TN 37996. Offers exercise science (MS, PhD), including biomechanics/sports medicine, exercise physiology; recreation and leisure studies (MS); sport management (MS); sport studies (MS, PhD); therapeutic recreation (MS). *Program availability:* Part-time, evening/weekend. *Degree requirements:* For master's, thesis optional. *Entrance requirements:* For master's, minimum GPA of 2.7. Additional exam requirements/recommendations for international students: Required—TOEFL. Electronic applications accepted.

Sports Management

University of the Incarnate Word, Ila Faye Miller School of Nursing and Health Professions, San Antonio, TX 78209-6397. Offers kinesiology (MS); nursing (MSN, DNP); sport management (MS). *Program availability:* Part-time, evening/weekend. *Faculty:* 15 full-time (10 women). *Students:* 106 full-time (74 women), 13 part-time (11 women); includes 80 minority (26 Black or African American, non-Hispanic/Latino; 1 American Indian or Alaska Native, non-Hispanic/Latino; 3 Asian, non-Hispanic/Latino; 47 Hispanic/Latino; 3 Two or more races, non-Hispanic/Latino), 3 international. 43 applicants, 95% accepted, 28 enrolled. In 2018, 26 master's, 19 doctorates awarded. *Degree requirements:* For master's, comprehensive exam (for some programs), thesis or alternative, capstone. *Entrance requirements:* For master's, GRE General Test, MAT, baccalaureate degree in ACEN- or CCNE-accredited nursing program with health assessment and statistics; minimum cumulative GPA of 2.5 (3.0 in upper-division courses); three professional references; Texas State license or multi-state compact. Additional exam requirements/recommendations for international students: Required—TOEFL (minimum score 560 paper-based; 83 iBT). *Application deadline:* Applications are processed on a rolling basis. Application fee: $20. Electronic applications accepted. *Expenses:* $935 per credit hour (for DNP); $250-500 matriculation fee (one time). *Financial support:* Research assistantships, Federal Work-Study, scholarships/grants, tuition waivers (partial), and unspecified assistantships available. Financial award applicants required to submit FAFSA. *Faculty research:* Pediatric oncology, military pregnancy and the family, diabetes prevention, substance abuse and addictions, nursing of vulnerable populations. *Unit head:* Dr. Mary Hoke, Dean, 210-829-3982, Fax: 210-829-3174, E-mail: mhoke@uiwtx.edu. *Application contact:* Jessica Delarosa, Associate Director of Admissions, 210-8296005, Fax: 210-829-3921, E-mail: admis@uiwtx.edu.
Website: https://nursing-and-health-professions.uiw.edu/

University of the Southwest, Graduate Programs, Hobbs, NM 88240-9129. Offers business administration (MBA); curriculum and instruction (MSE); curriculum and instruction: bilingual (MSE); curriculum and instruction: TESOL (MSE); early childhood education (MSE); educational administration (MSE); mental health counseling (MSE); school counseling (MSE); special education (MSE); sports management (MBA). *Program availability:* Part-time, evening/weekend, online learning. *Degree requirements:* For master's, comprehensive exam, thesis (for some programs). *Entrance requirements:* Additional exam requirements/recommendations for international students: Recommended—TOEFL. Electronic applications accepted.

University of Wisconsin–Parkside, College of Natural and Health Sciences, Program in Sport Management, Kenosha, WI 53141-2000. Offers MS. *Degree requirements:* For master's, thesis optional. *Entrance requirements:* For master's, official transcripts, at least three letters of recommendation. Additional exam requirements/recommendations for international students: Required—TOEFL (minimum score 525 paper-based; 71 iBT). Electronic applications accepted.

Upper Iowa University, Online Master's Programs, Fayette, IA 52142-1857. Offers accounting (MBA); corporate financial management (MBA); emergency management and homeland security (MPA); general management (MBA); general studies (MPA); government administration (MPA); health and human services (MPA); human resources management (MBA); nonprofit organizational management (MPA); organizational development (MBA); public management (MPA); sport administration (MSA). MBA also available at Madison, WI campus. *Program availability:* Part-time, online learning. *Degree requirements:* For master's, research project. *Entrance requirements:* For master's, GMAT, GRE, or minimum GPA of 2.7 during last 60 hours. Additional exam requirements/recommendations for international students: Required—TOEFL (minimum score 570 paper-based). Electronic applications accepted. *Faculty research:* Total quality management, teams, organization culture and climate, management.

Valparaiso University, Graduate School and Continuing Education, Program in Sports Administration, Valparaiso, IN 46383. Offers MS, JD/MS. *Program availability:* Part-time, evening/weekend. *Entrance requirements:* For master's, minimum GPA of 3.0. Additional exam requirements/recommendations for international students: Required—TOEFL (minimum score 550 paper-based; 80 iBT), IELTS (minimum score 6). Electronic applications accepted.

Waldorf University, Program in Organizational Leadership, Forest City, IA 50436. Offers criminal justice leadership (MA); emergency management leadership (MA); fire/rescue executive leadership (MA); human resource development (MA); public administration (MA); sport management (MA); teacher leader (MA).

Washington State University, College of Education, Department of Educational Leadership, Sports Studies, and Educational/Counseling Psychology, Pullman, WA 99164-2136. Offers counseling psychology (PhD); educational leadership (Ed M, MA, Ed D, PhD); educational psychology (MA, PhD); sport management (MA). Programs also offered at the Spokane, Tri-Cities, Vancouver and Global (online) campuses. *Program availability:* Part-time, online learning. *Degree requirements:* For master's, comprehensive exam (for some programs), thesis (for some programs), oral or written exam; for doctorate, comprehensive exam, thesis/dissertation, oral and written exam, internship. *Entrance requirements:* For master's and doctorate, GRE General Test, minimum GPA of 3.0, 3 letters of recommendation, transcripts showing all college or university course work, statement of professional objectives, current curriculum vitae/resume. Additional exam requirements/recommendations for international students: Required—TOEFL (minimum score 550 paper-based; 80 iBT). Electronic applications accepted. *Faculty research:* Multicultural counseling and career development, educational and psychological measurement issues, business decision-making process and power relationships, leadership practices and processes as suffused with and constituted by emotion work.

Wayland Baptist University, Graduate Programs, Program in Education, Plainview, TX 79072-6998. Offers education administration (M Ed); education diagnostics (M Ed); education literacy (M Ed); elementary certification (M Ed); English (M Ed); English as a second language (M Ed); higher education administration (M Ed); human resources (M Ed); instructional leadership (M Ed); instructional technology (M Ed); leadership training and development (M Ed); science education (M Ed); secondary certification (M Ed); social studies (M Ed); special education (M Ed); sports administration and management (M Ed). *Program availability:* Part-time, evening/weekend, 100% online. *Degree requirements:* For master's, comprehensive exam, capstone course. *Entrance requirements:* For master's, GRE, GMAT or MAT. Additional exam requirements/recommendations for international students: Required—TOEFL (minimum score 500 paper-based; 61 iBT). Electronic applications accepted.

Wayne State College, Department of Health, Human Performance and Sport, Wayne, NE 68787. Offers exercise science (MSE); organizational management (MS), including sport management. *Program availability:* Part-time, evening/weekend. *Degree requirements:* For master's, comprehensive exam, thesis optional. *Entrance requirements:* For master's, GRE General Test, minimum GPA of 3.0. Additional exam requirements/recommendations for international students: Required—TOEFL (minimum score 550 paper-based). Electronic applications accepted.

Wayne State University, College of Education, Division of Kinesiology, Health and Sports Studies, Detroit, MI 48202. Offers athletic training (MSAT); health education (M Ed); kinesiology (M Ed, PhD), including exercise and sport science (PhD), physical education and physical activity leadership (PhD); sports administration (MA). *Program availability:* Part-time, evening/weekend. *Faculty:* 9. *Students:* 76 full-time (47 women), 110 part-time (56 women); includes 73 minority (53 Black or African American, non-Hispanic/Latino; 4 Asian, non-Hispanic/Latino; 8 Hispanic/Latino; 8 Two or more races, non-Hispanic/Latino), 9 international. Average age 30. 163 applicants, 60% accepted, 69 enrolled. In 2018, 70 master's, 4 doctorates awarded. *Degree requirements:* For master's, thesis (for some programs); for doctorate, comprehensive exam, thesis/dissertation. *Entrance requirements:* For master's, minimum undergraduate GPA of 3.0; undergraduate degree directly relating to the field of specialization being applied for or one accompanied by extensive educational background in closely-related field; teaching certificates in specific areas (for some programs); for doctorate, minimum undergraduate GPA of 3.0; undergraduate degree directly relating to the field of specialization being applied for or one accompanied by extensive educational background in closely-related field. Additional exam requirements/recommendations for international students: Required—TOEFL (minimum score 550 paper-based; 79 iBT); Recommended—IELTS (minimum score 6.5), TWE (minimum score 5.5), TSE (minimum score 58). *Application deadline:* Applications are processed on a rolling basis. Application fee: $50. Electronic applications accepted. *Financial support:* In 2018–19, 51 students received support. Fellowships with tuition reimbursements available, research assistantships with tuition reimbursements available, teaching assistantships with tuition reimbursements available, scholarships/grants, health care benefits, and unspecified assistantships available. Support available to part-time students. Financial award applicants required to submit FAFSA. *Faculty research:* Exercise and sport science, nutrition and physical activity interventions, school and community health, obesity prevention. *Unit head:* Dr. Nate McCaughtry, Assistant Dean, Division of Kinesiology, Health and Sport Studies/Director, Center for School Health, 313-577-0014, Fax: 313-577-5002, E-mail: aj4391@wayne.edu. *Application contact:* Heather Ladanyi, Manager, 313-577-1191, E-mail: eb3703@wayne.edu.
Website: http://coe.wayne.edu/kinesiology/index.php

Webber International University, Graduate School of Business, Babson Park, FL 33827. Offers accounting (MBA); business (MBA); criminal justice management (MBA); international business (MBA); sport business management (MBA). *Program availability:* Part-time, evening/weekend, 100% online, blended/hybrid learning. *Faculty:* 11 full-time (5 women), 1 part-time/adjunct (0 women). *Students:* 69 full-time (34 women), 11 part-time (5 women); includes 26 minority (17 Black or African American, non-Hispanic/Latino; 1 Asian, non-Hispanic/Latino; 8 Hispanic/Latino), 10 international. Average age 24. 64 applicants, 61% accepted, 32 enrolled. In 2018, 17 master's awarded. *Degree requirements:* For master's, International Learning Experience required for the master in International Business, other majors have a practicum project. *Entrance requirements:* For master's, three recommendation letters, resume, essay, official transcripts from all colleges and universities attended. Additional exam requirements/recommendations for international students: Recommended—TOEFL (minimum score 500 paper-based; 61 iBT), IELTS (minimum score 6). *Application deadline:* For fall admission, 8/1 for domestic students, 6/1 for international students; for spring admission, 1/1 for domestic students. Applications are processed on a rolling basis. Application fee: $0. Electronic applications accepted. *Financial support:* In 2018–19, 11 students received support. Scholarships/grants and unspecified assistantships available. Financial award application deadline: 8/1; financial award applicants required to submit FAFSA. *Unit head:* Dr. Nikos Orphanoudakis, Dean, 863-638-2910, Fax: 863-638-1591, E-mail: orphanoudakisn@webber.edu. *Application contact:* Lacy Edwards, Admissions Counselor and MBA Coordinator, 863-638-2910, Fax: 863-638-1591, E-mail: admissions@webber.edu.
Website: www.webber.edu

West Chester University of Pennsylvania, College of Health Sciences, Department of Kinesiology, West Chester, PA 19383. Offers adapted physical education (Certificate); exercise and sport physiology (MS), including athletic training; sport management and athletics (MPA), including administration. *Program availability:* Part-time, evening/weekend, blended/hybrid learning. *Degree requirements:* For master's, thesis or research report (for MS); two internships and capstone course that includes a research project or thesis (for MPA); for Certificate, six courses of study. *Entrance requirements:* For master's, GRE (for MS), 2 letters of recommendation, statement of professional goals; transcripts (for MS); two letters of reference, career goals, resume (for MPA); for Certificate, two letters of recommendation, transcript. Additional exam requirements/recommendations for international students: Required—TOEFL or IELTS. Electronic applications accepted. *Faculty research:* Metabolism during exercise, biomechanics, rating of perceived exertion, motor learning, environmental physiology.

Western Illinois University, School of Graduate Studies, College of Education and Human Services, Department of Kinesiology, Program in Sport Management, Macomb, IL 61455-1390. Offers MS. *Program availability:* Part-time. *Students:* 45 full-time (9 women), 4 part-time (2 women); includes 21 minority (16 Black or African American, non-Hispanic/Latino; 2 Hispanic/Latino; 3 Two or more races, non-Hispanic/Latino), 1 international. Average age 25. 25 applicants, 96% accepted, 17 enrolled. In 2018, 23 master's awarded. *Entrance requirements:* For master's, minimum GPA of 3.0. Additional exam requirements/recommendations for international students: Required—TOEFL (minimum score 550 paper-based; 80 iBT). *Application deadline:* Applications are processed on a rolling basis. Application fee: $30. Electronic applications accepted. *Financial support:* Unspecified assistantships available. *Unit head:* Renee Polubinsky, Department Chair, 309-298-2050, E-mail: rl-polubinsky@wiu.edu. *Application contact:* Dr. Mark Mossman, Associate Provost and Director of Graduate Studies, 309-298-1806, Fax: 309-298-2345, E-mail: grad-office@wiu.edu.
Website: http://www.wiu.edu/coehs/kinesiology/graduate_programs/sm/

Western Kentucky University, Graduate School, College of Health and Human Services, Department of Kinesiology, Recreation and Sport, Bowling Green, KY 42101. Offers athletic administration and coaching (MS); physical education (MS); recreation and sport administration (MS). *Program availability:* Part-time, evening/weekend, online learning. *Degree requirements:* For master's, comprehensive exam, thesis optional. *Entrance requirements:* For master's, GRE General Test, minimum GPA of 2.75. Additional exam requirements/recommendations for international students: Required—TOEFL (minimum score 555 paper-based; 79 iBT). *Faculty research:* Orthopedic rehabilitation, fitness center coordination, heat acclimation, biomechanical and physiological parameters.

Western Michigan University, Graduate College, College of Education and Human Development, Department of Health, Physical Education and Recreation, Kalamazoo, MI 49008. Offers athletic training (MS), including exercise physiology; sport management (MA), including pedagogy, special physical education.

Western New England University, College of Business, Program in Sport Leadership and Coaching, Springfield, MA 01119. Offers MS. *Faculty:* 5 full-time (1 woman). *Students:* 6 part-time (1 woman), 1 international. Average age 25. 7 applicants, 100% accepted, 7 enrolled. *Entrance requirements:* For master's, GMAT or GRE, official transcript, two recommendations, personal statement, resume or curriculum vitae. Additional exam requirements/recommendations for international students: Required—TOEFL (minimum score 79 iBT). *Application deadline:* Applications are processed on a rolling basis. Application fee: $30. Electronic applications accepted. *Expenses:* Contact

institution. *Financial support:* Application deadline: 4/15; applicants required to submit FAFSA. *Unit head:* Dr. Sharianne Walker, Dean, 413-782-1389, Fax: 413-796-2068, E-mail: swalker@wne.edu. *Application contact:* Matthew Fox, Executive Director of Graduate Admissions, 413-782-1410, Fax: 413-782-1777, E-mail: study@wne.edu. Website: http://www1.wne.edu/academics/graduate/ms-sport.cfm

West Liberty University, College of Education and Human Performance, West Liberty, WV 26074. Offers community education research and leadership (MA Ed); innovative instruction (MA Ed); leadership in disability services (MA Ed); leadership studies (MA Ed); multi-categorical special education (MA Ed); reading specialist (MA Ed); sports leadership and coaching (MA Ed). *Accreditation:* NCATE. *Program availability:* Part-time, evening/weekend. *Degree requirements:* For master's, capstone experience. *Entrance requirements:* For master's, minimum GPA of 2.5 or 3.0 (depending on track). Additional exam requirements/recommendations for international students: Required—TOEFL. Electronic applications accepted.

West Texas A&M University, College of Nursing and Health Sciences, Department of Sports and Exercise Sciences, Canyon, TX 79015. Offers sport management (MS); sports and exercise sciences (MS). *Program availability:* Part-time, evening/weekend. *Degree requirements:* For master's, comprehensive exam, thesis optional. *Entrance requirements:* For master's, GRE General Test. Additional exam requirements/recommendations for international students: Required—TOEFL. Electronic applications accepted.

West Virginia University, College of Physical Activity and Sport Sciences, Morgantown, WV 26506. Offers athletic training (MS); coaching and sport education (MS); coaching and teaching studies (Ed D, PhD), including curriculum and instruction (PhD); physical education/teacher education (MS); sport coaching (MS); sport management (MS); sport, exercise & performance psychology (MS). *Students:* 98 full-time (40 women), 122 part-time (42 women); includes 38 minority (18 Black or African American, non-Hispanic/Latino; 4 Asian, non-Hispanic/Latino; 10 Hispanic/Latino; 6 Two or more races, non-Hispanic/Latino), 13 international. In 2018, 74 master's, 5 doctorates awarded. *Degree requirements:* For doctorate, comprehensive exam, thesis/dissertation, oral exam. *Entrance requirements:* For master's, GRE or MAT, minimum GPA of 3.0; for doctorate, GRE General Test or MAT, minimum GPA of 3.5. Additional exam requirements/recommendations for international students: Required—TOEFL (minimum score 550 paper-based). *Application deadline:* For fall admission, 12/15 for domestic students, 10/1 for international students. Application fee: $60. Electronic applications accepted. *Financial support:* Research assistantships, teaching assistantships, career-related internships or fieldwork, Federal Work-Study, institutionally sponsored loans, health care benefits, tuition waivers (full and partial), and administrative assistantships available. Support available to part-time students. Financial award application deadline: 2/1; financial award applicants required to submit FAFSA. *Faculty research:* Sport psych sociology, teacher education, exercise psychology, counseling. *Unit head:* Sean Bulger, Online Program Coordinator, 304-293-0845, Fax: 304-293-4641, E-mail: sean.bulger@mail.wvu.edu. *Application contact:* Sean Bulger, Online Program Coordinator, 304-293-0845, Fax: 304-293-4641, E-mail: sean.bulger@mail.wvu.edu. Website: http://www.cpass.wvu.edu

Wichita State University, Graduate School, College of Applied Studies, Department of Sport Management, Wichita, KS 67260. Offers M Ed. *Unit head:* Dr. Mark Vermillion, Chair, 316-978-5444, Fax: 316-978-5451, E-mail: mark.vermillion@wichita.edu. *Application contact:* Jordan Oleson, Admissions Coordinator, 316-978-3095, Fax: 316-978-3253, E-mail: jordan.oleson@wichita.edu. Website: http://www.wichita.edu/sportmanagement

Wingate University, School of Sport Sciences, Wingate, NC 28174. Offers sport management (MA). *Entrance requirements:* For master's, MAT, GRE, or GMAT, bachelor's degree, minimum GPA of 2.75, two recommendation forms, official transcripts. Electronic applications accepted.

Winona State University, College of Education, Department of Leadership Education, Winona, MN 55987. Offers education leadership (MS, Ed S), including k-12 principal (Ed S), superintendent (Ed S); organizational leadership (MS); professional leadership (MS); sport management (MS). MS in sport management offered in cooperation with Department of Physical Education and Sport Science. *Accreditation:* NCATE. *Program availability:* Part-time, evening/weekend. *Degree requirements:* For master's, comprehensive exam, thesis optional; for Ed S, thesis optional.

Xavier University, College of Professional Sciences, Department of Sports Studies, Cincinnati, OH 45207. Offers coaching education and athlete development (M Ed); sport administration (M Ed). *Program availability:* Part-time, evening/weekend, online learning. *Degree requirements:* For master's, thesis optional, internship or research project. *Entrance requirements:* For master's, GRE or MAT, official transcript; resume; one-page statement of career goals; 2 letters of recommendation. Additional exam requirements/recommendations for international students: Required—TOEFL (minimum score 550 paper-based; 79 iBT). Electronic applications accepted. Application fee is waived when completed online. *Expenses:* Contact institution. *Faculty research:* Coaching education, brand equity, strategic management, economic impact, place marketing.

ACADEMIC AND PROFESSIONAL PROGRAMS IN SOCIAL WORK

Section 32
Social Work

This section contains a directory of institutions offering graduate work in social work, followed by in-depth entries submitted by institutions that chose to prepare detailed program descriptions. Additional information about programs listed in the directory but not augmented by an in-depth entry may be obtained by writing directly to the dean of a graduate school or chair of a department at the address given in the directory.

For programs offering related work, see also in this book *Allied Health* and *Education.* In another guide in this series:

Graduate Programs in the Humanities, Arts & Social Sciences
See *Criminology and Forensics, Family and Consumer Sciences, Psychology and Counseling,* and *Sociology, Anthropology, and Archaeology*

CONTENTS
Program Directories

Human Services

Abilene Christian University, Graduate Programs, College of Education and Human Services, Abilene, TX 79699. Offers M Ed, MS, MSSW, Certificate. *Accreditation:* TEAC. *Faculty:* 5 full-time (4 women), 36 part-time/adjunct (27 women). *Students:* 198 full-time (192 women), 46 part-time (37 women); includes 61 minority (12 Black or African American, non-Hispanic/Latino; 1 American Indian or Alaska Native, non-Hispanic/Latino; 5 Asian, non-Hispanic/Latino; 33 Hispanic/Latino; 1 Native Hawaiian or other Pacific Islander, non-Hispanic/Latino; 9 Two or more races, non-Hispanic/Latino), 3 international. 639 applicants, 45% accepted, 146 enrolled. In 2018, 92 master's, 12 other advanced degrees awarded. *Degree requirements:* For master's, comprehensive exam (for some programs), thesis (for some programs), practicum. *Entrance requirements:* For master's, GRE. Additional exam requirements/recommendations for international students: Required—TOEFL (minimum score 80 iBT), IELTS (minimum score 6), PTE. *Application deadline:* For fall admission, 8/15 priority date for domestic students; for winter admission, 10/1 priority date for domestic students; for spring admission, 12/15 priority date for domestic students; for summer admission, 4/15 for domestic students. Applications are processed on a rolling basis. Application fee: $65. Electronic applications accepted. *Expenses:* Contact institution. *Financial support:* In 2018–19, 118 students received support. Career-related internships or fieldwork, Federal Work-Study, institutionally sponsored loans, and scholarships/grants available. Support available to part-time students. Financial award application deadline: 4/1; financial award applicants required to submit FAFSA. *Unit head:* Dr. Jennifer Shewmaker, Dean, 325-674-2700, Fax: 325-674-3707, E-mail: cehs@acu.edu. *Application contact:* Graduate Admission, 325-674-6911, E-mail: gradinfo@acu.edu. Website: http://www.acu.edu/graduate/academics/education-and-human-services.html

Albertus Magnus College, Master of Science in Human Services Program, New Haven, CT 06511-1189. Offers MS. *Program availability:* Part-time, evening/weekend, blended/hybrid learning. *Degree requirements:* For master's, thesis, internship, capstone thesis, minimum GPA of 3.0. *Entrance requirements:* For master's, minimum GPA of 2.8; 2 letters of recommendation; official transcripts; minimum of 15 credits in psychology, human services, and/or social work. Additional exam requirements/recommendations for international students: Required—TOEFL (minimum score 550 paper-based; 80 iBT). Electronic applications accepted. *Expenses:* Contact institution.

Albizu University, Miami Campus, Graduate Programs, Miami, FL 33172-2209. Offers clinical psychology (PhD, Psy D); entrepreneurship (MBA); exceptional student education (MS); human services (PhD); industrial/organizational psychology (MS); marriage and family therapy (MS); mental health counseling (MS); nonprofit management (MBA); organizational management (MBA); school counseling (MS); speech and language pathology (MS); teaching English for speakers of other languages (MS). *Accreditation:* APA. *Program availability:* Part-time, evening/weekend, 100% online, blended/hybrid learning. *Faculty:* 32 full-time (24 women), 27 part-time/adjunct (15 women). *Students:* 479 full-time (410 women), 146 part-time (126 women); includes 539 minority (42 Black or African American, non-Hispanic/Latino; 2 Asian, non-Hispanic/Latino; 490 Hispanic/Latino; 5 Two or more races, non-Hispanic/Latino), 22 international. Average age 33. 314 applicants, 45% accepted, 92 enrolled. In 2018, 101 master's, 64 doctorates awarded. Terminal master's awarded for partial completion of doctoral program. *Degree requirements:* For master's, comprehensive exam (for some programs), integrative project (for MBA); research project (for exceptional student education, teaching English as a second language); for doctorate, comprehensive exam, thesis/dissertation, comprehensive examinations, internship, project/dissertation. *Entrance requirements:* For master's, GRE/EXADEP, bachelor's degree from accredited institution, minimum GPA of 3.0, 3 letters of recommendation, interview, resume, statement of purpose, official transcripts; for doctorate, GRE (for Psy D), 3 letters of recommendation, resume, interview, statement of purpose, official transcripts; bachelor's degree and minimum GPA of 3.25 (for Psy D); master's degree and minimum GPA of 3.0 (for PhD). Additional exam requirements/recommendations for international students: Required—Michigan Test of English Language Proficiency. *Application deadline:* For fall admission, 4/1 priority date for domestic students, 5/1 priority date for international students; for spring admission, 11/1 priority date for domestic students, 9/1 priority date for international students. Applications are processed on a rolling basis. Application fee: $50. Electronic applications accepted. Application fee is waived when completed online. *Expenses:* Contact institution. *Financial support:* In 2018–19, 141 students received support. Federal Work-Study, scholarships/grants, unspecified assistantships, and tuition discounts available. Financial award application deadline: 6/1; financial award applicants required to submit FAFSA. *Faculty research:* Psychotherapy, forensic psychology, neuropsychology, special education, speech-language pathology, criminal justice, human services. *Unit head:* Dr. Jose Pons-Madera, PhD, President, 305-593-1223 Ext. 3120, Fax: 305-477-8983, E-mail: jpons@albizu.edu. *Application contact:* Nancy Alvarez, Director of Enrollment Management, 305-593-1223 Ext. 3136, Fax: 305-593-1854, E-mail: nalvarez@albizu.edu.

Amridge University, Graduate and Professional Programs, Montgomery, AL 36117. Offers Biblical studies (MA, PhD); Christian ministry (MS); family therapy (D Min); human services (MS); leadership and management (MS); marriage and family therapy (M Div, MA, PhD); ministerial leadership (M Div, MS); New Testament studies (MA); Old Testament studies (MA); professional counseling (M Div, MA, PhD); theology (M Div, D Min). *Program availability:* Part-time, evening/weekend, online learning. *Degree requirements:* For master's, one foreign language, comprehensive exam (for some programs), thesis (for some programs); for doctorate, one foreign language, comprehensive exam (for some programs), thesis/dissertation (for some programs). *Entrance requirements:* For master's, official transcript showing an earned 4-year BA or BS from regionally- or nationally-accredited institution; for doctorate, official transcript showing earned graduate degree from regionally- or nationally-accredited institution; writing sample (e.g. career monograph, published journal article, term paper from master's degree or doctoral dissertation); interview. Additional exam requirements/recommendations for international students: Required—TOEFL (minimum score 79 iBT). Electronic applications accepted. *Faculty research:* Technology and mental healthcare, resilience in black families, theology and congregational ministry.

Bellevue University, Graduate School, College of Arts and Sciences, Bellevue, NE 68005-3098. Offers clinical counseling (MS); healthcare administration (MHA); human services (MA); international security and intelligence studies (MS); managerial communication (MA). *Program availability:* Online learning.

Boricua College, Program in Human Services, New York, NY 10032-1560. Offers MS. Program offered in Brooklyn Campus and Bronx Campus. *Program availability:* Evening/weekend. *Faculty:* 2 full-time (1 woman), 2 part-time/adjunct (both women). *Students:* 33 full-time (26 women); includes 31 minority (5 Black or African American, non-Hispanic/Latino; 26 Hispanic/Latino). Average age 39. 73 applicants, 75% accepted, 33 enrolled. In 2018, 33 master's awarded. *Degree requirements:* For master's, thesis. *Entrance requirements:* For master's, interview by the faculty. *Application deadline:* Applications

are processed on a rolling basis. Application fee: $100 ($500 for international students). *Expenses: Tuition:* Full-time $15,000. One-time fee: $100 full-time. *Financial support:* Career-related internships or fieldwork and Federal Work-Study available. Financial award applicants required to submit FAFSA. *Unit head:* Esteban Galvan, Chairperson, 347-964-8600 Ext. 419, E-mail: egalvan@boricuacollege.edu. *Application contact:* Teofilo Santiago, Director of Admissions, 347-964-8600 Ext. 364, E-mail: tsantiago@boricuacollege.edu.

Brandeis University, The Heller School for Social Policy and Management, Program in Nonprofit Management, Waltham, MA 02454-9110. Offers child, youth, and family management (MBA); health care management (MBA); social impact management (MBA); social policy and management (MBA); sustainable development (MBA); MBA/MA; MBA/MD. MBA/MD program offered in conjunction with Tufts University School of Medicine. *Accreditation:* AACSB. *Program availability:* Part-time. *Degree requirements:* For master's, team consulting project. *Entrance requirements:* For master's, GMAT (preferred) or GRE, 2 letters of recommendation, problem statement analysis, 3-5 years of professional experience. Additional exam requirements/recommendations for international students: Required—TOEFL (minimum score 600 paper-based; 100 iBT). Electronic applications accepted. *Expenses:* Contact institution. *Faculty research:* Health care; children and families; elder and disabled services; social impact management; organizations in the non-profit, for-profit, or public sector.

California State University, Sacramento, College of Health and Human Services, Division of Social Work, Sacramento, CA 95819. Offers family and children's services (MSW). *Accreditation:* CSWE. *Program availability:* Part-time, evening/weekend. *Degree requirements:* For master's, thesis, project; writing proficiency exam. *Entrance requirements:* For master's, GRE, minimum GPA of 2.8 during previous 2 years of course work. Additional exam requirements/recommendations for international students: Required—TOEFL (minimum score 550 paper-based; 80 iBT); Recommended—IELTS, TSE. Electronic applications accepted. *Expenses:* Contact institution.

Capella University, School of Public Service Leadership, Doctoral Programs in Healthcare, Minneapolis, MN 55402. Offers criminal justice (PhD); emergency management (PhD); epidemiology (Dr PH); general health administration (DHA); general public administration (DPA); health advocacy and leadership (Dr PH); health care administration (PhD); health care leadership (DHA); health policy advocacy (DHA); multidisciplinary human services (PhD); nonprofit management and leadership (PhD); public safety leadership (PhD); social and community services (PhD).

Capella University, School of Public Service Leadership, Master's Programs in Healthcare, Minneapolis, MN 55402. Offers criminal justice (MS); emergency management (MS); general public health (MPH); gerontology (MS); health administration (MHA); health care operations (MHA); health management policy (MPH); health policy (MHA); homeland security (MS); multidisciplinary human services (MS); public administration (MPA); public safety leadership (MS); social and community services (MS); social behavioral sciences (MPH); MS/MPA.

Chestnut Hill College, School of Graduate Studies, Program in Administration of Human Services, Philadelphia, PA 19118-2693. Offers administration of human services (MS, CAS), including adult and aging services (CAS), leadership development (CAS). *Program availability:* Part-time, evening/weekend. *Degree requirements:* For master's, special projects or internship. *Entrance requirements:* For master's, GRE General Test or MAT, 100 volunteer hours or 1 year of work-related human services experience, statement of professional goals, writing sample, letters of recommendation. Additional exam requirements/recommendations for international students: Required—TOEFL (minimum score 500 paper-based), IELTS (minimum score 6.0), or TWE (minimum score 22). Electronic applications accepted. *Expenses:* Contact institution. *Faculty research:* Best practices and trends in adult education degree programs, middle and late adulthood development, quality of living issues for older persons.

Concordia University Chicago, College of Graduate Studies, Program in Human Services, River Forest, IL 60305-1499. Offers human services (MA), including administration, exercise science. *Program availability:* Part-time, evening/weekend, 100% online. *Degree requirements:* For master's, comprehensive exam, thesis. *Entrance requirements:* For master's, minimum GPA of 2.9. Additional exam requirements/recommendations for international students: Required—TOEFL (minimum score 550 paper-based). Electronic applications accepted.

Concordia University, St. Paul, College of Humanities and Social Sciences, St. Paul, MN 55104-5494. Offers creative writing (MFA); criminal justice leadership (MA); family science (MA); human services (MA), including forensic behavioral health. *Accreditation:* NCATE. *Program availability:* Part-time, evening/weekend, 100% online, blended/hybrid learning. *Faculty:* 8 full-time (5 women), 19 part-time/adjunct (10 women). *Students:* 159 full-time (126 women), 14 part-time (7 women); includes 56 minority (27 Black or African American, non-Hispanic/Latino; 2 American Indian or Alaska Native, non-Hispanic/Latino; 10 Asian, non-Hispanic/Latino; 8 Hispanic/Latino; 9 Two or more races, non-Hispanic/Latino), 1 international. Average age 35. 82 applicants, 95% accepted, 64 enrolled. In 2018, 36 master's awarded. *Degree requirements:* For master's, thesis (for some programs), capstone project. *Entrance requirements:* For master's, official transcripts stating the conferral of a Bachelor's degree with a minimum cumulative GPA of 3.0 based on a 4.0 system; personal statement; writing sample in fiction or non-fiction (MFA students only); resume (MA students only). Additional exam requirements/recommendations for international students: Required—TOEFL (minimum score 547 paper-based; 78 iBT), IELTS (minimum score 6), PTE (minimum score 78). *Application deadline:* For fall admission, 8/1 for domestic students, 7/1 for international students; for spring admission, 12/1 for domestic students, 11/1 for international students. Applications are processed on a rolling basis. Application fee: $0. Electronic applications accepted. *Expenses:* $525 per credit for 36 credits (for MFA); $395-$475 per credit, depending on major, for a 36 credit program (for MA). *Financial support:* In 2018–19, 83 students received support. Federal Work-Study and scholarships/grants available. Financial award applicants required to submit FAFSA. *Faculty research:* Clinical treatment study for forensic populations, neurobiology of trauma and addiction, perceptions of fetal alcohol spectrum disorder in the midwest, sex offender treatment protocols survey. *Unit head:* Dr. Paul Hillmer, Dean, 651-641-8215, E-mail: hillmer@csp.edu. *Application contact:* Amber Faletti, Director of Enrollment Management, 651-641-8838, Fax: 651-603-6320, E-mail: faletti@csp.edu.

Coppin State University, School of Graduate Studies, College of Behavioral and Social Sciences, Program in Human Services Administration, Baltimore, MD 21216-3698. Offers MS. *Program availability:* Part-time, evening/weekend. *Entrance requirements:* For master's, resume, references, interview.

Eastern Michigan University, Graduate School, College of Health and Human Services, Interdisciplinary Program in Health and Human Services, Ypsilanti, MI 48197.

Offers Graduate Certificate. *Program availability:* Part-time, evening/weekend. *Students:* 1 applicant, 100% accepted. *Entrance requirements:* Additional exam requirements/recommendations for international students: Required—TOEFL. Application fee: $45. *Unit head:* Dr. Marcia Bombyk, Program Coordinator, 734-487-0393, Fax: 734-487-8536, E-mail: mbombyk@emich.edu. *Application contact:* Graduate Admissions, 734-487-2400, Fax: 734-487-6559, E-mail: graduate.admissions@emich.edu.

East Tennessee State University, School of Graduate Studies, College of Education, Department of Counseling and Human Services, Johnson City, TN 37614. Offers clinical mental health counseling (MA); college counseling/student affairs higher education (MA); couples and family therapy (MA); human services (MS); school counseling (MA). *Accreditation:* ACA; NCATE. *Program availability:* Part-time. *Degree requirements:* For master's, comprehensive exam, thesis optional, internship, student teaching, culminating experience. *Entrance requirements:* For master's, GRE General Test, minimum GPA of 3.0, three letters of recommendation, interview, 2-3 page essay detailing experiences that have shaped pursuit of degree, resume. Additional exam requirements/recommendations for international students: Required—TOEFL (minimum score 550 paper-based; 79 iBT). Electronic applications accepted. *Faculty research:* Intervention and assistance with at-risk and under-served youth and high conflict families; service and social justice; women and girls' issues in counseling; counseling competence with LGBTQ individuals; counselor education and supervision.

Ferris State University, College of Education and Human Services, Big Rapids, MI 49307. Offers M Ed, MS, MSCJ, MSCTE. *Program availability:* Part-time, evening/weekend, blended/hybrid learning. *Faculty:* 15 full-time (6 women), 1 (woman) part-time/adjunct. *Students:* 10 full-time (7 women), 78 part-time (45 women); includes 20 minority (12 Black or African American, non-Hispanic/Latino; 5 Hispanic/Latino; 3 Two or more races, non-Hispanic/Latino), 2 international. Average age 35. 35 applicants, 97% accepted, 25 enrolled. In 2018, 37 master's awarded. *Degree requirements:* For master's, capstone project, comprehensive exam or thesis/dissertation, research paper or project. *Entrance requirements:* For master's, minimum GPA of 3.0, bachelor's degre in Criminal Justice or related field. Additional exam requirements/recommendations for international students: Required—TOEFL (minimum score 500 paper-based; 79 iBT), IELTS (minimum score 6.5), TOEFL (minimum score 500 paper-based, 79 iBT) or IELTS (minimum score 6.5). *Application deadline:* For fall admission, 7/1 priority date for domestic and international students; for winter admission, 12/15 priority date for domestic and international students; for spring admission, 11/1 priority date for domestic and international students; for summer admission, 3/1 priority date for domestic and international students. Applications are processed on a rolling basis. Application fee: $0 ($30 for international students). Electronic applications accepted. Application fee is waived when completed online. *Financial support:* In 2018–19, 9 students received support, including 2 research assistantships (averaging $5,490 per year); career-related internships or fieldwork, Federal Work-Study, scholarships/grants, and unspecified assistantships also available. Support available to part-time students. Financial award applicants required to submit FAFSA. *Faculty research:* Competency testing, teaching methodologies, assessment of teaching effectiveness, suicide prevention, women in education, special needs. *Unit head:* Leonard Johnson, Interim Dean, 231-591-3648, Fax: 231-592-3792, E-mail: LeonardJohnson@ferris.edu. *Application contact:* Dr. Kristen Salomonson, Dean, Enrollment Services/Director, Admissions and Records, 231-591-2100, Fax: 231-591-3944, E-mail: admissions@ferris.edu.

Georgia State University, Andrew Young School of Policy Studies, School of Social Work, Atlanta, GA 30294. Offers child welfare leadership (Certificate); community partnerships (MSW); forensic social work (Certificate). *Accreditation:* CSWE. *Program availability:* Part-time. *Faculty:* 13 full-time (9 women), 1 part-time/adjunct (0 women). *Students:* 108 full-time (101 women), 19 part-time (18 women); includes 84 minority (68 Black or African American, non-Hispanic/Latino; 2 Asian, non-Hispanic/Latino; 7 Hispanic/Latino; 7 Two or more races, non-Hispanic/Latino). Average age 31. 168 applicants, 50% accepted, 44 enrolled. In 2018, 61 master's awarded. *Entrance requirements:* For master's and Certificate, GRE. Additional exam requirements/recommendations for international students: Required—TOEFL (minimum score 550 paper-based; 100 iBT) or IELTS (minimum score 7). *Application deadline:* For fall admission, 2/1 priority date for domestic and international students. Application fee: $50. Electronic applications accepted. *Expenses: Tuition, area resident:* Full-time $9360; part-time $390 per credit hour. Tuition, state resident: full-time $9360; part-time $390 per credit hour. Tuition, nonresident: full-time $30,024; part-time $1251 per credit hour. *International tuition:* $30,024 full-time. *Required fees:* $2128. *Financial support:* In 2018–19, research assistantships with tuition reimbursements (averaging $4,000 per year), teaching assistantships with tuition reimbursements (averaging $4,000 per year) were awarded; career-related internships or fieldwork, institutionally sponsored loans, scholarships/grants, tuition waivers, and unspecified assistantships also available. Financial award application deadline: 2/1; financial award applicants required to submit FAFSA. *Faculty research:* Community partnership, non-profit organizations, child welfare practice and policy, gerontological practice and policy, restorative justice. *Unit head:* Brian Bride, Director of School of Social Work, 404-413-1052, Fax: 404-413-1075, E-mail: bbride@gsu.edu. *Application contact:* Brian Bride, Director of School of Social Work, 404-413-1052, Fax: 404-413-1075, E-mail: bbride@gsu.edu.
Website: http://aysps.gsu.edu/socialwork

Governors State University, College of Health and Human Services, University Park, IL 60484. Offers MHA, MHS, MOT, MSN, MSW, DPT. *Accreditation:* CAHME; CSWE. *Program availability:* Part-time. *Faculty:* 56 full-time (48 women), 85 part-time/adjunct (61 women). *Students:* 344 full-time (263 women), 351 part-time (303 women); includes 348 minority (237 Black or African American, non-Hispanic/Latino; 25 Asian, non-Hispanic/Latino; 74 Hispanic/Latino; 12 Two or more races, non-Hispanic/Latino), 11 international. Average age 34. 516 applicants, 28% accepted, 105 enrolled. In 2018, 203 master's, 38 doctorates awarded. *Entrance requirements:* For master's, GMAT/GRE. Additional exam requirements/recommendations for international students: Required—TOEFL (minimum score 550 paper-based; 80 iBT), IELTS. *Application deadline:* For fall admission, 4/1 for domestic students. Applications are processed on a rolling basis. Application fee: $50. Electronic applications accepted. *Expenses:* $797/credit hour; $9,564 in tuition/term; $10,694 in tuition and fees/term; $21,388/year. *Financial support:* Federal Work-Study and unspecified assistantships available. Financial award application deadline: 5/1; financial award applicants required to submit FAFSA. *Unit head:* Catherine Balthazar, Dean, College of Health and Human Services, 708-534-5000 Ext. 4592, E-mail: cbalthazar@govst.edu. *Application contact:* Paul McGuinness, Assistant Vice President, Enrollment Management/Director, Admission, 708-534-5000 Ext. 7308, E-mail: pmcguinness@govst.edu.
Website: https://www.govst.edu/chhs/

Judson University, Master of Arts in Human Services Administration, Elgin, IL 60123-1498. Offers MA. *Program availability:* Evening/weekend. *Faculty:* 7 full-time (6 women). *Students:* 11 full-time (8 women), 3 part-time (all women); includes 3 minority (2 Black or African American, non-Hispanic/Latino; 1 Hispanic/Latino). Average age 39. 9 applicants, 67% accepted, 4 enrolled. In 2018, 18 master's awarded. *Entrance requirements:* For master's, Bachelor's degree; two years of work experience; professional resume; minimum GPA of 2.5; official transcripts of all college and graduate work; two letters of reference; essay. *Application deadline:* Applications are processed on a rolling basis. Application fee: $35. Electronic applications accepted. *Expenses: Required fees:* $250. One-time fee: $125 full-time. Tuition and fees vary according to program. *Financial support:* Unspecified assistantships available. *Faculty research:* Dementia and community services, Spirituality and counseling, International mentoring for graduate students, International Leadership Development for graduate students. *Unit head:* Dr. Teri Stein, 847-628-1524, E-mail: tstein@judsonu.edu. *Application contact:* Kim Surin, Enrollment Manager, 847-628-5033, E-mail: kim.surin@info.judsonu.edu.

Kansas State University, Graduate School, College of Human Ecology, School of Family Studies and Human Services, Manhattan, KS 66506-1403. Offers applied family sciences (MS); communication sciences and disorders (MS); conflict resolution (Graduate Certificate); couple and family therapy (MS); early childhood education (MS); family and community service (MS); life-span human development (MS); personal financial planning (MS, PhD, Graduate Certificate); youth development (MS, Graduate Certificate). *Accreditation:* AAMFT/COAMFTE; ASHA. *Program availability:* Part-time, online learning. *Degree requirements:* For master's, comprehensive exam (for some programs), thesis optional. *Entrance requirements:* For master's, GRE, minimum GPA of 3.0 in last 2 years (60 semester hours) of undergraduate study; for doctorate, GRE. Additional exam requirements/recommendations for international students: Required—TOEFL (minimum score 600 paper-based). Electronic applications accepted. *Faculty research:* Health and security of military families, training in and evaluation of professional human services (marriage and couple therapy, family life education, treatment of speech and swallowing disorders, financial therapy), disorders of communication and swallowing, family and relationship development and health, financial decision-making.

Kent State University, College of Education, Health and Human Services, Kent, OH 44242-0001. Offers M Ed, MA, MAT, MS, Au D, PhD, Ed S. *Accreditation:* NCATE. *Program availability:* Part-time, evening/weekend, online learning. *Faculty:* 188 full-time (116 women), 130 part-time/adjunct (87 women). *Students:* 865 full-time (619 women), 559 part-time (425 women); includes 199 minority (103 Black or African American, non-Hispanic/Latino; 9 American Indian or Alaska Native, non-Hispanic/Latino; 42 Asian, non-Hispanic/Latino; 15 Hispanic/Latino; 27 Native Hawaiian or other Pacific Islander, non-Hispanic/Latino; 3 Two or more races, non-Hispanic/Latino), 91 international. In 2018, 401 master's, 27 doctorates, 62 other advanced degrees awarded. *Degree requirements:* For master's, thesis (for some programs); for doctorate, comprehensive exam, thesis/dissertation. *Entrance requirements:* For doctorate and Ed S, GRE General Test. Additional exam requirements/recommendations for international students: Required—TOEFL (minimum score 550 paper-based; 80 iBT). *Application deadline:* Applications are processed on a rolling basis. Application fee: $45 ($60 for international students). Electronic applications accepted. *Expenses:* Tuition, state resident: full-time $11,766; part-time $536 per credit. Tuition, nonresident: full-time $21,952; part-time $999 per credit. *International tuition:* $21,952 full-time. Tuition and fees vary according to course load. *Financial support:* In 2018–19, 112 research assistantships with full tuition reimbursements (averaging $10,564 per year), 28 teaching assistantships (averaging $11,938 per year) were awarded; scholarships/grants, health care benefits, unspecified assistantships, and 30 administrative assistantships (averaging $10,406 per year) also available. Financial award application deadline: 4/1; financial award applicants required to submit FAFSA. *Unit head:* Dr. James Hannon, Dean, 330-672-0566, Fax: 330-672-3407, E-mail: jhannon5@kent.edu. *Application contact:* Cheryl Slusarczyk, Academic Program Director, Office of Graduate Student Services, 330-672-2576, Fax: 330-672-9162, E-mail: cslusarc@kent.edu.
Website: http://www.kent.edu/ehhs/

Lehigh University, College of Education, Program in Counseling Psychology, Bethlehem, PA 18015. Offers counseling and human services (M Ed); counseling psychology (PhD); international counseling (M Ed, Certificate); school counseling (M Ed). *Accreditation:* APA (one or more programs are accredited). *Program availability:* Part-time. *Faculty:* 8 full-time (5 women), 12 part-time/adjunct (9 women). *Students:* 61 full-time (55 women), 33 part-time (27 women); includes 18 minority (3 Black or African American, non-Hispanic/Latino; 5 Asian, non-Hispanic/Latino; 10 Hispanic/Latino), 18 international. Average age 29. 155 applicants, 39% accepted, 32 enrolled. In 2018, 42 master's, 5 doctorates awarded. *Degree requirements:* For master's, thesis (for some programs); for doctorate, comprehensive exam, thesis/dissertation. *Entrance requirements:* For master's, minimum GPA of 3.0, 2 letters of recommendation, essay, transcript; for doctorate, GRE General Test, 2 letters of recommendation, transcript, essay, GRE; for Certificate, minimum GPA of 3.0 (undergraduate), 3.5 (graduate). Additional exam requirements/recommendations for international students: Required—TOEFL (minimum score 600 paper-based; 93 iBT), Either TOEFL or IELTS is required of international students for whom English is not their main language; Recommended—IELTS. *Application deadline:* For fall admission, 2/1 for domestic and international students. Application fee: $65. Electronic applications accepted. Application fee is waived when completed online. *Expenses:* $565 per credit hour. *Financial support:* In 2018–19, 28 students received support, including 2 fellowships (averaging $22,250 per year), 6 research assistantships with full and partial tuition reimbursements available (averaging $16,059 per year); scholarships/grants and unspecified assistantships also available. Financial award application deadline: 2/15; financial award applicants required to submit FAFSA. *Faculty research:* Maternal/infant attachment, multicultural training and counseling, career development and health interventions, intersection of identities, community based participatory research, trauma informed schools, gerontology, multicultural competence, south Asian-Asian American concerns, sexual assault prevention, LGBTQ, intimate partner violence, feminist theory and therapy, sexual and reproductive health, women's health, culture and health, prevention, minority student development, educational access. *Total annual research expenditures:* $419,624. *Unit head:* Dr. Grace Caskie, Director, 610-758-6094, Fax: 610-758-3227, E-mail: caskie@lehigh.edu. *Application contact:* Dominique Jones, Coordinator, Counseling Psychology, 610-758-3250, Fax: 610-758-6223, E-mail: dvj218@lehigh.edu.
Website: https://ed.lehigh.edu/academics/programs/counseling-psychology

Lenoir-Rhyne University, Graduate Programs, School of Counseling and Human Services, Hickory, NC 28601. Offers MA. *Program availability:* Part-time, evening/weekend. *Degree requirements:* For master's, comprehensive exam, thesis optional. *Entrance requirements:* Additional exam requirements/recommendations for international students: Required—TOEFL. Electronic applications accepted. *Expenses:* Contact institution.

Lenoir-Rhyne University, Graduate Programs, School of Education, Program in Human Services, Hickory, NC 28601. Offers management (MA); substance abuse (MA); vocational strategies (MA). *Program availability:* Part-time, online only, 100% online. *Degree requirements:* For master's, comprehensive exam. *Entrance requirements:* For master's, GRE General Test or MAT, essay; minimum GPA of 2.7 undergraduate, 3.0 graduate. Additional exam requirements/recommendations for international students: Required—TOEFL (minimum score 600 paper-based). Electronic applications accepted. *Expenses:* Contact institution.

Liberty University, School of Behavioral Sciences, Lynchburg, VA 24515. Offers applied psychology (MA), including developmental psychology (MA, MS), industrial/organizational psychology (MA, MS); clinical mental health counseling (MA); community care and counseling (Ed D), including marriage and family counseling, pastoral care and

counseling, traumatology; counselor education and supervision (PhD); human services counseling (MA), including addictions and recovery, business, child and family law, Christian ministries, criminal justice, crisis response and trauma, executive leadership, health and wellness, life coaching, marriage and family, military resilience; marriage and family counseling (MA); marriage and family therapy (MA); military resilience (Certificate); pastoral counseling (MA), including addictions and recovery, community chaplaincy, crisis response and trauma, discipleship and church ministry, leadership, life coaching, marriage and family, marriage and family studies, military resilience, parenting and child/adolescent, pastoral counseling, theology; professional counseling (MA); psychology (MS), including developmental psychology (MA, MS), industrial/organizational psychology (MA, MS); school counseling (M Ed). *Program availability:* Part-time, online learning. *Students:* 3,163 full-time (2,537 women), 4,813 part-time (3,790 women); includes 2,399 minority (1,847 Black or African American, non-Hispanic/Latino; 39 American Indian or Alaska Native, non-Hispanic/Latino; 77 Asian, non-Hispanic/Latino; 244 Hispanic/Latino; 13 Native Hawaiian or other Pacific Islander, non-Hispanic/Latino; 179 Two or more races, non-Hispanic/Latino), 129 international. Average age 39. 8,226 applicants, 38% accepted, 1752 enrolled. In 2018, 2,420 master's, 21 doctorates, 79 other advanced degrees awarded. *Application deadline:* Applications are processed on a rolling basis. Application fee: $50. Electronic applications accepted. *Expenses: Tuition:* Full-time $10,851; part-time $562 per credit hour. *Financial support:* In 2018–19, 1,003 students received support. Teaching assistantships and Federal Work-Study available. Financial award applicants required to submit FAFSA. *Unit head:* Dr. Ronald Hawkins, Founding Dean, School of Behavioral Sciences, E-mail: provost@liberty.edu. *Application contact:* Jay Bridge, Director of Admissions, 800-424-9595, Fax: 800-628-7977, E-mail: gradadmissions@liberty.edu. Website: https://www.liberty.edu/behavioral-sciences/

Lincoln University, The School of Adult & Continuing Education, Philadelphia, PA 19104. Offers counseling (MSC); early childhood education (M Ed), including PreK-4; early childhood education and special education (M Ed); educational leadership (M Ed), including principal certification; finance (MBA); human resources management (MBA); human services delivery (MAHS). *Program availability:* Part-time, evening/weekend. *Faculty:* 8 full-time (3 women), 22 part-time/adjunct (12 women). *Students:* 192 full-time (154 women), 62 part-time (40 women); includes 230 minority (218 Black or African American, non-Hispanic/Latino; 9 Hispanic/Latino; 3 Two or more races, non-Hispanic/Latino), 3 international. Average age 33. 278 applicants, 58% accepted, 94 enrolled. In 2018, 105 master's awarded. *Degree requirements:* For master's, comprehensive exam, thesis or alternative, capstone, grant proposal. *Entrance requirements:* For master's, GRE/GMAT (Optional), Official academic transcript(s), letters of recommendation, personal statement, resume, supervisor's evaluation form, Application fee. Additional exam requirements/recommendations for international students: Required—TOEFL (minimum score 500 paper-based; 71 iBT); Recommended—IELTS (minimum score 6.5). *Application deadline:* For fall admission, 8/19 for domestic and international students; for spring admission, 12/30 for domestic and international students. Applications are processed on a rolling basis. Application fee: $50. Electronic applications accepted. *Financial support:* Scholarships/grants available. Financial award application deadline: 4/1; financial award applicants required to submit FAFSA. *Unit head:* Dr. Patricia Joseph, Dean of Faculty, 484-365-7659, E-mail: joseph@lincoln.edu. *Application contact:* Jernice Lea, Director, Student Services and Admissions, 215-590-8231, Fax: 215-387-3859, E-mail: jlea@lincoln.edu. Website: http://www.lincoln.edu/admissions/graduate-admissions

Lock Haven University of Pennsylvania, The Stephen Poorman College of Business, Information Systems, and Human Services, Lock Haven, PA 17745-2390. Offers clinical mental health counseling (MS); sport science (MS). *Program availability:* Online learning. *Degree requirements:* For master's, thesis. *Entrance requirements:* For master's, minimum undergraduate GPA of 3.0. Additional exam requirements/recommendations for international students: Required—TOEFL. Electronic applications accepted.

Louisiana Tech University, Graduate School, College of Education, Ruston, LA 71272. Offers counseling and guidance (MA), including clinical mental health counseling, human services, orientation and mobility; counseling psychology (PhD); curriculum and instruction (M Ed); cyber education (Graduate Certificate); dynamics of domestic and family violence (Graduate Certificate); early childhood education - PreK-3 (MAT); educational leadership (M Ed, Ed D); elementary education and special education mild/moderate grades 1-5 (MAT); higher education administration (Graduate Certificate); industrial/organizational psychology (MA, PhD); kinesiology (MS); middle school education (MAT), including mathematics; orientation and mobility (Graduate Certificate); rehabilitation teaching for the blind (Graduate Certificate); secondary education (MAT), including agriculture, biology, business, chemistry, English; special education: visually impaired (MAT); teacher leader education (Graduate Certificate); visual impairments - blind education (Graduate Certificate). *Accreditation:* NCATE. *Program availability:* Part-time. *Degree requirements:* For master's, thesis; for doctorate, thesis/dissertation. *Entrance requirements:* For master's and doctorate, GRE General Test. Additional exam requirements/recommendations for international students: Required—TOEFL (minimum score 550 paper-based; 80 iBT), IELTS (minimum score 6.5). Electronic applications accepted. *Faculty research:* Blindness and the best methods for increasing independence for individuals who are blind or visually impaired; educating and investigating factors contributing to improvements in human performance across the lifespan and a reduction in injury rates during training.

McDaniel College, Graduate and Professional Studies, Program in Human Services Management, Westminster, MD 21157-4390. Offers MS. *Accreditation:* NCATE. *Program availability:* Evening/weekend. *Degree requirements:* For master's, internship. *Entrance requirements:* For master's, 3 recommendations; successful employment interview with Target Community and Educational Services, Inc. Additional exam requirements/recommendations for international students: Required—TOEFL (minimum score 79 iBT), IELTS (minimum score 6). Electronic applications accepted.

Mercer University, Graduate Studies, Cecil B. Day Campus, Penfield College, Atlanta, GA 30341. Offers certified rehabilitation counseling (MS); clinical mental health (MS); counselor education and supervision (PhD); criminal justice and public safety leadership (MS); health informatics (MS); human services (MS), including child and adolescent services, gerontology services; organizational leadership (MS), including leadership for the health care professional, leadership for the nonprofit organization, organizational development and change; school counseling (MS). *Program availability:* Part-time, evening/weekend, 100% online, blended/hybrid learning. *Degree requirements:* For master's, comprehensive exam (for some programs), thesis (for some programs); for doctorate, thesis/dissertation. *Entrance requirements:* For master's, GRE or MAT, Georgia Professional Standards Commission (GPSC) Certification at the SC-5 level; for doctorate, GRE or MAT. Additional exam requirements/recommendations for international students: Recommended—TOEFL (minimum score 550 paper-based; 80 iBT), IELTS (minimum score 6.5). Electronic applications accepted. Application fee is waived when completed online. *Expenses:* Contact institution. *Faculty research:* Marriage and families issues, leadership and ethics, cyber-bullying, trauma, narrative counseling and theory.

Minnesota State University Mankato, College of Graduate Studies and Research, College of Social and Behavioral Sciences, Department of Sociology and Corrections, Mankato, MN 56001. Offers sociology (MA); sociology: college teaching (MA); sociology: corrections (MS); sociology: human services planning and administration (MS). *Program availability:* Part-time. *Degree requirements:* For master's, comprehensive exam, thesis or alternative. *Entrance requirements:* For master's, minimum GPA of 3.0 during previous 2 years, 3 letters of reference, resume. Additional exam requirements/recommendations for international students: Required—TOEFL. Electronic applications accepted.

Murray State University, College of Education and Human Services, Department of Educational Studies, Leadership and Counseling, Murray, KY 42071. Offers college advising (Certificate); education administration (MA Ed); human development and leadership (MS, Certificate); library media (MA Ed); middle school teacher leader (MA Ed); P-20 and community leadership (Ed D); postsecondary education administration (MA Ed); school counseling (MA Ed); school guidance and counseling (Ed S); secondary teacher leader (MA Ed). *Program availability:* Part-time, evening/weekend, 100% online, blended/hybrid learning. *Entrance requirements:* For master's and other advanced degree, GRE or GMAT, minimum university GPA of 2.75. Additional exam requirements/recommendations for international students: Required—TOEFL (minimum score 527 paper-based; 71 iBT). Electronic applications accepted.

National Louis University, College of Arts and Sciences, Chicago, IL 60603. Offers adult education (Ed D); counseling and human services (MS); language and academic development (M Ed, Certificate); psychology (MA, PhD, Certificate); public policy (MA); written communication (MS, Certificate). *Program availability:* Part-time, evening/weekend, online learning. *Degree requirements:* For master's and Certificate, comprehensive exam (for some programs), thesis (for some programs); for doctorate, thesis/dissertation. *Entrance requirements:* For master's, MAT or GRE, 3 professional or academic references, interview, minimum GPA of 3.0; for doctorate, GRE General Test, MAT, or Watson-Glaser Critical Thinking Appraisal, three professional or academic references, statement of academic and professional goals, 3 years of experience in field, interview, master's degree, resume, writing sample; for Certificate, GRE, MAT, or Watson-Glaser Critical Thinking Appraisal, three professional or academic references, statement of academic and professional goals, interview, minimum GPA of 3.0. Additional exam requirements/recommendations for international students: Required—Department of Language Studies Assessment or TOEFL (minimum score 550 paper-based; 79 iBT). Electronic applications accepted.

National University, School of Health and Human Services, La Jolla, CA 92037-1011. Offers clinical affairs (MS); clinical regulatory affairs (MS); complementary and integrative healthcare (MS); family nurse practitioner (MSN); health and life science analytics (MS); health informatics (MS, Certificate); healthcare administration (MHA); nurse anesthesia (MSNA); nursing administration (MSN); nursing informatics (MSN); psychiatric-mental health nurse practitioner (MSN); public health (MPH), including health promotion, healthcare administration, mental health. *Accreditation:* CEPH. *Program availability:* Part-time, evening/weekend, 100% online, blended/hybrid learning. *Degree requirements:* For master's, thesis (for some programs). *Entrance requirements:* For master's, interview, minimum GPA of 2.5. Additional exam requirements/recommendations for international students: Required—TOEFL (minimum score 550 paper-based; 79 iBT), IELTS (minimum score 6). Electronic applications accepted. *Expenses: Tuition:* Full-time $10,320; part-time $430 per unit. Tuition and fees vary according to degree level. *Faculty research:* Nursing education, obesity prevention, workforce diversity.

New England College, Program in Community Mental Health Counseling, Henniker, NH 03242-3293. Offers human services (MS); mental health counseling (MS). *Program availability:* Part-time, evening/weekend. *Degree requirements:* For master's, internship.

Northeastern University, College of Professional Studies, Boston, MA 02115-5096. Offers applied nutrition (MS); college athletics administration (MSL); commerce and economic development (MS); corporate and organizational communication (MS); criminal justice (MS); digital media (MPS); elearning and instructional design (M Ed); elementary education (MAT); geographic information technology (MPS); global studies and international relations (MS); higher education administration (M Ed); homeland security (MA); human services (MS); informatics (MPS); leadership (MS); learning analytics (M Ed); learning and instruction (M Ed); nonprofit management (MS); professional sports administration (MSL); project management (MS); regulatory affairs for drugs, biologics, and medical devices (MS); respiratory care leadership (MS); special education (M Ed); technical communication (MS). *Program availability:* Part-time, evening/weekend, 100% online, blended/hybrid learning. Electronic applications accepted. *Expenses:* Contact institution.

Pontifical Catholic University of Puerto Rico, College of Graduate Studies in Behavioral Science and Community Affairs, Ponce, PR 00717-0777. Offers clinical psychology (PhD, Psy D); clinical social work (MSW); criminology (MA); industrial psychology (PhD); psychology (PhD); public administration (MSS); rehabilitation counseling (MA). *Program availability:* Part-time, evening/weekend. *Degree requirements:* For master's, thesis; for doctorate, comprehensive exam, thesis/dissertation. *Entrance requirements:* For master's, EXADEP, GRE General Test, 3 letters of recommendation, interview, minimum GPA of 2.75.

Post University, Program in Counseling and Human Services, Waterbury, CT 06723-2540. Offers counseling and human services (MS); counseling and human services/alcohol and drug counseling (MS); counseling and human services/clinical mental health counseling (MS); counseling and human services/forensic mental health counseling (MS); counseling and human services/non-profit management (MS). *Program availability:* Part-time, evening/weekend, online learning. *Entrance requirements:* For master's, resume. *Expenses: Tuition:* Full-time $8300; part-time $570 per credit. *Required fees:* $140 per term. Tuition and fees vary according to course level, campus/location and program.

Purdue University Northwest, Graduate Studies Office, School of Education, Program in Counseling, Hammond, IN 46323-2094. Offers human services (MS Ed); mental health counseling (MS Ed); school counseling (MS Ed). *Accreditation:* ACA. *Entrance requirements:* Additional exam requirements/recommendations for international students: Required—TOEFL.

Regent University, Graduate School, School of Psychology and Counseling, Virginia Beach, VA 23464-9800. Offers clinical mental health counseling (MA); clinical psychology (Psy D); counseling and psychological studies - clinical (PhD); counseling and psychological studies - research (PhD); counseling studies (CAGS); counselor education and supervision (PhD); general psychology (MS); human services (MA), including addictions counseling, Biblical counseling, Christian counseling, conflict and mediation ministry, criminal justice and ministry, grief counseling, human services counseling, human services for student affairs, life coaching, marriage and family ministry, trauma and crisis counseling; marriage, couple, and family counseling (MA); pastoral counseling (MA); school counseling (MA); M Div/MA; M Ed/MA; MBA/MA. *Accreditation:* ACA; APA (one or more programs are accredited). *Program availability:* Part-time, evening/weekend, 100% online, blended/hybrid learning. *Degree requirements:* For master's, thesis or alternative, internship, practicum, written

competency exam; for doctorate, thesis/dissertation or alternative. *Entrance requirements:* For master's, GRE General Test (including writing exam) or MAT, minimum undergraduate GPA of 3.0, resume, transcripts, writing sample, personal goals statement; for doctorate, GRE General Test (including writing exam), minimum undergraduate GPA of 3.0, graduate 3.5; writing sample; 3 recommendations; resume; college transcripts; personal goals statement. Additional exam requirements/recommendations for international students: Required—TOEFL (minimum score 577 paper-based). Electronic applications accepted. *Expenses:* Contact institution. *Faculty research:* Marriage enrichment, clinical psychology, troubled youth, faith and learning, trauma.

Roberts Wesleyan College, Department of Social Work, Rochester, NY 14624-1997. Offers child and family practice (MSW); mental health practice (MSW). *Accreditation:* CSWE. *Entrance requirements:* For master's, minimum GPA of 2.75. *Faculty research:* Religion and social work, family studies, values and ethics.

Rosemont College, Schools of Graduate and Professional Studies, Counseling Psychology Program, Rosemont, PA 19010-1699. Offers human services (MA); school counseling (MA). *Program availability:* Part-time, evening/weekend. *Degree requirements:* For master's, thesis or alternative, practicum. *Entrance requirements:* For master's, minimum undergraduate GPA of 3.0, 3 letters of recommendation. Additional exam requirements/recommendations for international students: Required—TOEFL. Electronic applications accepted. Application fee is waived when completed online. *Expenses:* Contact institution. *Faculty research:* Addictions counseling.

St. Cloud State University, School of Graduate Studies, School of Education, Program in Social Responsibility, St. Cloud, MN 56301-4498. Offers MS. *Degree requirements:* For master's, thesis or alternative. *Entrance requirements:* For master's, GRE General Test, minimum GPA of 2.75. Additional exam requirements/recommendations for international students: Required—Michigan English Language Assessment Battery; Recommended—TOEFL (minimum score 550 paper-based), IELTS (minimum score 6.5). Electronic applications accepted.

St. Joseph's College, Long Island Campus, Programs in Management, Field in Human Services Leadership, Patchogue, NY 11772-2399. Offers MS. *Program availability:* Part-time, evening/weekend, 100% online, blended/hybrid learning. *Faculty:* 13 full-time (5 women), 23 part-time/adjunct (8 women). *Students:* 3 full-time (2 women), 36 part-time (28 women); includes 18 minority (11 Black or African American, non-Hispanic/Latino; 1 Asian, non-Hispanic/Latino; 4 Hispanic/Latino; 2 Two or more races, non-Hispanic/Latino). Average age 38. 42 applicants, 71% accepted, 21 enrolled. In 2018, 10 master's awarded. *Entrance requirements:* For master's, Application, $25 application fee, official transcripts, two letters of recommendation, current resume, 250 word written statement. Additional exam requirements/recommendations for international students: Required—TOEFL (minimum score 80 iBT). *Application deadline:* Applications are processed on a rolling basis. Application fee: $25. Electronic applications accepted. *Expenses: Tuition:* Full-time $18,450; part-time $1025 per credit. *Required fees:* $414. *Financial support:* In 2018–19, 10 students received support. *Unit head:* Dr. Jo Anne Durovich, Director of MS in Human Service Leadership, Assistant Professor, Chairperson, 631-687-5193, E-mail: jdurovich@sjcny.edu. *Application contact:* Dr. Jo Anne Durovich, Director of MS in Human Service Leadership, Assistant Professor, Chairperson, 631-687-5193, E-mail: jdurovich@sjcny.edu.

St. Joseph's College, New York, Programs in Management, Field in Human Services Management and Leadership, Brooklyn, NY 11205-3688. Offers MS. *Program availability:* Part-time, evening/weekend, 100% online, blended/hybrid learning. *Faculty:* 5 part-time/adjunct (4 women). *Students:* 2 full-time (both women), 13 part-time (10 women); includes 11 minority (6 Black or African American, non-Hispanic/Latino; 2 Asian, non-Hispanic/Latino; 3 Hispanic/Latino). Average age 42. 11 applicants, 82% accepted, 5 enrolled. In 2018, 5 master's awarded. *Entrance requirements:* For master's, Application, $25 application fee, two letters of recommendation, current resume, 250 word essay, official transcripts. Additional exam requirements/recommendations for international students: Required—TOEFL (minimum score 80 iBT). *Application deadline:* Applications are processed on a rolling basis. Application fee: $25. Electronic applications accepted. *Expenses: Tuition:* Full-time $18,450; part-time $1025 per credit. *Required fees:* $414. *Financial support:* In 2018–19, 5 students received support. *Unit head:* Sharon Didier, Assistant Chair/Co-Director of Graduate Management Studies/Associate Professor, 718-940-5790, E-mail: sdidier@sjcny.edu. *Application contact:* Sharon Didier, Assistant Chair/Co-Director of Graduate Management Studies/Associate Professor, 718-940-5790, E-mail: sdidier@sjcny.edu.
Website: http://www.sjcny.edu

Saint Leo University, Graduate Studies in Human Services, Saint Leo, FL 33574-6665. Offers MS. *Program availability:* Part-time, evening/weekend, 100% online. *Students:* Average age 40. 77 applicants, 65% accepted, 47 enrolled. In 2018, 44 master's awarded. *Entrance requirements:* For master's, official transcripts, bachelor's degree from regionally-accredited university with minimum GPA of 3.0, current resume, 3 professional recommendations, statement of professional goals. Additional exam requirements/recommendations for international students: Required—TOEFL (minimum score 550 paper-based; 78 iBT). *Application deadline:* For fall admission, 7/1 for domestic and international students; for spring admission, 11/1 for domestic and international students. Applications are processed on a rolling basis. Application fee: $80. Electronic applications accepted. *Expenses:* Contact institution. *Financial support:* In 2018–19, 4 students received support. Career-related internships or fieldwork, scholarships/grants, health care benefits, and tuition remission for Saint Leo employees and their dependents available. Financial award application deadline: 3/1; financial award applicants required to submit FAFSA. *Faculty research:* Grantsmanship, animal-assisted therapy, interdisciplinary education, leadership, creation of human services agencies, child welfare services. *Unit head:* Dr. Susan Kinsella, Dean, School of Education and Social Services, 352-588-8272, Fax: 352-588-8289, E-mail: susan.kinsella@saintleo.edu. *Application contact:* Mary Martinez-Drovie, Graduate Enrollment Counselor, 352-588-5802, Fax: 352-588-8289, E-mail: mary.martinez-drovie@saintleo.edu.
Website: https://www.saintleo.edu/human-services-administration-master-degree

South Carolina State University, College of Graduate and Professional Studies, Department of Human Services, Orangeburg, SC 29117-0001. Offers counselor education (M Ed); rehabilitation counseling (MA). *Accreditation:* CORE. *Program availability:* Part-time, evening/weekend. *Faculty:* 8 full-time (6 women), 7 part-time/adjunct (6 women). *Students:* 88 full-time (70 women), 23 part-time (18 women); includes 104 minority (all Black or African American, non-Hispanic/Latino). Average age 32. 31 applicants, 90% accepted, 28 enrolled. In 2018, 31 master's awarded. *Degree requirements:* For master's, comprehensive exam (for some programs), departmental qualifying exam, internship. *Entrance requirements:* For master's, GRE, MAT, minimum GPA of 2.7. *Application deadline:* For fall admission, 6/15 priority date for domestic students, 6/15 for international students; for spring admission, 11/1 for domestic and international students. Application fee: $25. Electronic applications accepted. *Expenses: Tuition, area resident:* Full-time $9928; part-time $552 per credit hour. Tuition, state resident: full-time $9928. Tuition, nonresident: full-time $21,038; part-time $1169 per credit hour. *Required fees:* $1532; $85 per credit hour. *Financial support:* Fellowships, career-related internships or fieldwork, scholarships/grants, and unspecified assistantships available. Financial award application deadline: 6/1. *Unit head:* Dr. Michelle Maultsby-Priester, Interim Chair, Department of Human Services, 803-536-7075, Fax: 803-533-3636, E-mail: mmaultsb@scsu.edu. *Application contact:* Curtis Foskey, Coordinator of Graduate Admissions, 803-536-8419, Fax: 803-536-8812, E-mail: cfoskey@scsu.edu.

Southeastern University, College of Behavioral and Social Sciences, Lakeland, FL 33801-6099. Offers human services (MA); international community development (MA); marriage and family counseling (MS); professional counseling (MS); school counseling (MS); social work (MSW). *Program availability:* Evening/weekend. Electronic applications accepted.

Springfield College, Graduate Programs, Program in Human Services, Springfield, MA 01109-3797. Offers mental health counseling (MS); organizational management and leadership (MS). *Program availability:* Part-time, evening/weekend, blended/hybrid learning. *Degree requirements:* For master's, comprehensive exam, thesis (for some programs), Community Action Research Project. *Entrance requirements:* Additional exam requirements/recommendations for international students: Required—TOEFL (minimum score 550 paper-based). Electronic applications accepted. *Expenses:* Contact institution.

Texas Southern University, College of Liberal Arts and Behavioral Sciences, Department of Human Services and Consumer Sciences, Houston, TX 77004-4584. Offers MS. *Program availability:* Part-time, evening/weekend. *Degree requirements:* For master's, comprehensive exam, thesis (for some programs). *Entrance requirements:* For master's, GRE General Test, minimum GPA of 2.5. Additional exam requirements/recommendations for international students: Required—TOEFL. Electronic applications accepted. *Faculty research:* Food radiation/food for space travel, adolescent parenting, gerontology/grandparenting.

Thomas University, Department of Human Services, Thomasville, GA 31792-7499. Offers community counseling (MSCC); rehabilitation counseling (MRC). *Accreditation:* CORE. *Program availability:* Part-time. *Entrance requirements:* For master's, resume, 3 academic/professional references. Additional exam requirements/recommendations for international students: Required—TOEFL (minimum score 600 paper-based). Electronic applications accepted.

Universidad del Turabo, Graduate Programs, School of Social Sciences and Humanities, Programs in Public Affairs, Program in Human Services Administration, Gurabo, PR 00778-3030. Offers MPA. *Entrance requirements:* For master's, GRE, EXADEP or GMAT, interview, essay, official transcript, recommendation letters. Electronic applications accepted.

Université de Montréal, Faculty of Arts and Sciences, Programs in Applied Human Sciences, Montréal, QC H3C 3J7, Canada. Offers PhD. *Degree requirements:* For doctorate, thesis/dissertation, general exam. Electronic applications accepted.

University of Baltimore, Graduate School, College of Public Affairs, Program in Human Services Administration, Baltimore, MD 21201-5779. Offers MS. *Program availability:* Part-time, evening/weekend. *Entrance requirements:* For master's, interview. Additional exam requirements/recommendations for international students: Required—TOEFL (minimum score 550 paper-based). Electronic applications accepted.

University of Bridgeport, School of Arts and Sciences, Department of Counseling, Bridgeport, CT 06604. Offers clinical mental health counseling (MS); college student personnel (MS); community counseling (MS); human resource development (MS); human service (MS). *Program availability:* Part-time, evening/weekend. *Degree requirements:* For master's, thesis, project. *Entrance requirements:* Additional exam requirements/recommendations for international students: Recommended—TOEFL (minimum score 550 paper-based; 80 iBT), IELTS (minimum score 6.5). Electronic applications accepted. *Expenses:* Contact institution.

University of Central Missouri, The Graduate School, Warrensburg, MO 64093. Offers accountancy (MA); accounting (MBA); applied mathematics (MS); aviation safety (MA); biology (MS); business administration (MBA); career and technical education leadership (MS); college student personnel administration (MS); communication (MA); computer science (MS); counseling (MS); criminal justice (MS); educational leadership (Ed D); educational technology (MS); elementary and early childhood education (MSE); English (MA); environmental studies (MA); finance (MBA); history (MA); human services/educational technology (Ed S); human services/learning resources (Ed S); human services/professional counseling (Ed S); industrial hygiene (MS); industrial management (MS); information systems (MBA); information technology (MS); kinesiology (MS); library science and information services (MS); literacy education (MSE); marketing (MBA); mathematics (MS); music (MA); occupational safety management (MS); psychology (MS); rural family nursing (MS); school administration (MSE); social gerontology (MS); sociology (MA); special education (MSE); speech language pathology (MS); superintendency (Ed S); teaching (MAT); teaching English as a second language (MA); technology (MS); technology management (PhD); theatre (MA). *Accreditation:* ASHA. *Program availability:* Part-time, 100% online, blended/hybrid learning. *Degree requirements:* For master's and Ed S, comprehensive exam (for some programs), thesis (for some programs). *Entrance requirements:* Additional exam requirements/recommendations for international students: Required—TOEFL (minimum score 550 paper-based; 79 iBT). Electronic applications accepted.

University of Colorado Colorado Springs, College of Education, Colorado Springs, CO 80918. Offers counseling and human services (MA); curriculum and instruction (MA); educational leadership (MA); educational leadership, research and policy (PhD); special education (MA); teaching English to speakers of other languages (MA). *Accreditation:* ACA; NCATE. *Program availability:* Part-time, evening/weekend, 100% online, blended/hybrid learning. *Faculty:* 31 full-time (22 women), 61 part-time/adjunct (47 women). *Students:* 208 full-time (149 women), 351 part-time (256 women); includes 136 minority (30 Black or African American, non-Hispanic/Latino; 1 American Indian or Alaska Native, non-Hispanic/Latino; 12 Asian, non-Hispanic/Latino; 64 Hispanic/Latino; 29 Two or more races, non-Hispanic/Latino), 8 international. Average age 36. 230 applicants, 80% accepted, 101 enrolled. In 2018, 186 master's, 9 doctorates awarded. *Degree requirements:* For master's, comprehensive exam, thesis or alternative, microcomputer proficiency; for doctorate, comprehensive exam, thesis/dissertation, research lab. *Entrance requirements:* For master's, GRE General Test (recommended but not required), career goal statement, professional references; for doctorate, GRE General Test. Additional exam requirements/recommendations for international students: Recommended—TOEFL (minimum score 90 iBT), IELTS (minimum score 6.5). *Application deadline:* For fall admission, 1/28 priority date for domestic and international students; for spring admission, 11/1 priority date for domestic and international students. Applications are processed on a rolling basis. Application fee: $60 ($100 for international students). Electronic applications accepted. *Expenses:* Tuition and fees vary by program, course load, and residency type. Please visit the University of Colorado Colorado Springs Student Financial Services website to estimate current program costs: https://www.uccs.edu/bursar/index.php/estimate-your-bill. *Financial support:* In 2018–19, 15 students received support. Career-related internships or fieldwork, Federal Work-Study, scholarships/grants, and unspecified assistantships available. Support available to part-time students. Financial award application deadline: 3/1; financial award applicants required to submit FAFSA. *Faculty research:*

Linguistically diverse education (LDE), educational policy, evidence-based reading and writing instruction, relational and social aggression, positive behavior supports, inclusive schooling, K-12 education policy. *Total annual research expenditures:* $607,967. *Unit head:* Dr. Valerie Martin Conley, Dean, 719-255-4133, E-mail: vmconley@uccs.edu. *Application contact:* The College of Education Student Resource Office, 719-255-4996, E-mail: education@uccs.edu.
Website: https://www.uccs.edu/coe/

University of Idaho, College of Graduate Studies, College of Education, Health and Human Sciences, Department of Leadership and Counseling, Boise, ID 83702. Offers adult/organizational learning and leadership (Ed S); educational leadership (Ed S); rehabilitation counseling and human services (M Ed); school counseling (M Ed, MS). *Faculty:* 14. *Students:* 32 full-time (19 women), 123 part-time (68 women). Average age 37. In 2018, 53 master's, 22 other advanced degrees awarded. *Entrance requirements:* For master's, minimum GPA of 3.0, writing sample. Additional exam requirements/recommendations for international students: Required—TOEFL (minimum score 79 iBT). *Application deadline:* Applications are processed on a rolling basis. Application fee: $60. Electronic applications accepted. *Expenses:* Tuition, state resident: full-time $7266.44; part-time $474.50 per credit hour. Tuition, nonresident: full-time $24,902; part-time $1453.50 per credit hour. *Required fees:* $2085.56; $45.50 per credit hour. *Financial support:* Applicants required to submit FAFSA. *Unit head:* Dr. Kathy Canfield-Davis, Chair, 208-364-4047, E-mail: lead@uidaho.edu. *Application contact:* Dr. Kathy Canfield-Davis, Chair, 208-364-4047, E-mail: lead@uidaho.edu.
Website: https://www.uidaho.edu/ed/lc

University of Illinois at Springfield, Graduate Programs, College of Education and Human Services, Program in Human Services, Springfield, IL 62703-5407. Offers alcohol and substance abuse (Graduate Certificate); alcoholism and substance abuse (MA); child and family studies (MA); gerontology (MA); social services administration (MA). *Program availability:* Part-time, evening/weekend, 100% online, blended/hybrid learning. *Faculty:* 4 full-time (all women), 1 part-time/adjunct (0 women). *Students:* 7 full-time (6 women), 66 part-time (62 women); includes 36 minority (25 Black or African American, non-Hispanic/Latino; 8 Hispanic/Latino; 3 Two or more races, non-Hispanic/Latino). Average age 32. 45 applicants, 42% accepted, 14 enrolled. In 2018, 25 master's awarded. *Degree requirements:* For master's, internship; capstone project. *Entrance requirements:* For master's, minimum undergraduate GPA of 3.0, 2 letters of recommendation from professional or academic sources, statement of intent, interview. Additional exam requirements/recommendations for international students: Required—TOEFL (minimum score 500 paper-based; 61 iBT). *Application deadline:* Applications are processed on a rolling basis. Application fee: $60 ($75 for international students). Electronic applications accepted. *Financial support:* In 2018–19, research assistantships with full tuition reimbursements (averaging $10,384 per year), teaching assistantships with full tuition reimbursements (averaging $10,303 per year) were awarded; fellowships, career-related internships or fieldwork, Federal Work-Study, scholarships/grants, health care benefits, and unspecified assistantships also available. Support available to part-time students. Financial award application deadline: 11/15; financial award applicants required to submit FAFSA. *Unit head:* Dr. Carolyn Peck, Program Administrator, 217-206-7577, Fax: 217-206-6775, E-mail: peck.carolyn@uis.edu. *Application contact:* Dr. Carolyn Peck, Program Administrator, 217-206-7577, Fax: 217-206-6775, E-mail: peck.carolyn@uis.edu.
Website: http://www.uis.edu/humanservices

University of Illinois at Urbana–Champaign, Graduate College, School of Social Work, Champaign, IL 61820. Offers advocacy, leadership, and social change (MSW); children, youth and family services (MSW); health care (MSW); mental health (MSW); school social work (MSW); social work (PhD). *Accreditation:* CSWE (one or more programs are accredited). *Entrance requirements:* For master's and doctorate, minimum GPA of 3.0.

University of Maryland, Baltimore County, The Graduate School, College of Arts, Humanities and Social Sciences, Department of Psychology, Program in Human Services Psychology, Baltimore, MD 21250. Offers applied behavioral analysis (MA); human services psychology (PhD), including behavioral medicine, clinical psychology, community psychology. *Degree requirements:* For master's, thesis; for doctorate, comprehensive exam, thesis/dissertation. *Entrance requirements:* For master's, GRE General Test, minimum GPA of 3.0; for doctorate, GRE General Test, GRE Subject Test, minimum GPA of 3.0. Additional exam requirements/recommendations for international students: Required—TOEFL. Electronic applications accepted. *Expenses:* Contact institution. *Faculty research:* Addictive behaviors, cardiovascular and cerebrovascular disease, family violence, pediatric psychology, community prevention.

University of Massachusetts Boston, College of Public and Community Service, Program in Human Services, Boston, MA 02125-3393. Offers MS. *Program availability:* Part-time, evening/weekend. *Students:* 2 full-time (both women), 9 part-time (6 women); includes 7 minority (2 Black or African American, non-Hispanic/Latino; 1 Asian, non-Hispanic/Latino; 3 Hispanic/Latino; 1 Two or more races, non-Hispanic/Latino). Average age 37. 14 applicants, 79% accepted. In 2018, 13 master's awarded. *Entrance requirements:* For master's, MAT, GRE, minimum GPA of 2.75. Additional exam requirements/recommendations for international students: Recommended—TOEFL. *Expenses: Tuition, area resident:* Full-time $17,896. Tuition, state resident: full-time $17,896. Tuition, nonresident: full-time $34,932. *International tuition:* $34,932 full-time. *Required fees:* $355. *Financial support:* Research assistantships, teaching assistantships, career-related internships or fieldwork, Federal Work-Study, and unspecified assistantships available. Support available to part-time students. Financial award application deadline: 3/1; financial award applicants required to submit FAFSA. *Faculty research:* Institutional and policy context of human services, ethics and social policy, public law and human services, social welfare, politics and human services. *Unit head:* Dr. Adenrele Awotona, Director, 617-287.7112, E-mail: Adenrele.Awotona@umb.edu. *Application contact:* Graduate Admissions Coordinator, 617-287-6400, Fax: 617-287-6236, E-mail: graduate.admissions@umb.edu.

University of Nebraska at Kearney, College of Business and Technology, Department of Business, Kearney, NE 68849-0001. Offers accounting (MBA); generalist (MBA); human resources (MBA); human services (MBA); marketing (MBA). *Accreditation:* AACSB. *Program availability:* Part-time, evening/weekend. *Degree requirements:* For master's, thesis optional, capstone course. *Entrance requirements:* For master's, GRE or GMAT (if no significant managerial experience), letters of recommendation, essay, resume. Additional exam requirements/recommendations for international students: Recommended—TOEFL (minimum score 550 paper-based; 79 iBT), IELTS (minimum score 6.5). Electronic applications accepted. *Faculty research:* Small business financial management, employment law, expert systems, international trade and marketing, environmental economics.

University of Northern Iowa, Graduate College, College of Education, School of Kinesiology, Allied Health and Human Services, MA Program in Leisure, Youth and Human Services, Cedar Falls, IA 50614. Offers MA. *Degree requirements:* For master's, comprehensive exam, thesis or alternative. *Entrance requirements:* For master's, minimum GPA of 3.0. Additional exam requirements/recommendations for international students: Required—TOEFL (minimum score 500 paper-based; 61 iBT). Electronic applications accepted.

University of North Georgia, Program in Human Services and Delivery Administration, Dahlonega, GA 30597. Offers MS. *Program availability:* Evening/weekend. *Degree requirements:* For master's, service learning. *Entrance requirements:* For master's, GRE or MAT, written statement of goals, 3 UNG recommendation forms, professional resume. Additional exam requirements/recommendations for international students: Required—TOEFL (minimum score 550 paper-based; 79 iBT), IELTS (minimum score 6.5). Electronic applications accepted. *Expenses:* Contact institution.

University of Northwestern–St. Paul, Master of Arts in Human Services Program, St. Paul, MN 55113-1598. Offers MAHS. *Program availability:* Part-time, evening/weekend, online learning. Electronic applications accepted.

University of Oklahoma, College of Arts and Sciences, Department of Human Relations, Norman, OK 73019-0390. Offers clinical mental health (MHR); helping skills in human relations (Graduate Certificate); human relations (MHR); human resource diversity and development (Graduate Certificate); human resources (MHR); licensed professional counselor (MHR). *Program availability:* Part-time, evening/weekend. *Faculty:* 18 full-time (10 women), 8 part-time/adjunct (4 women). *Students:* 256 full-time (178 women), 317 part-time (205 women); includes 268 minority (121 Black or African American, non-Hispanic/Latino; 23 American Indian or Alaska Native, non-Hispanic/Latino; 20 Asian, non-Hispanic/Latino; 58 Hispanic/Latino; 3 Native Hawaiian or other Pacific Islander, non-Hispanic/Latino; 43 Two or more races, non-Hispanic/Latino), 12 international. Average age 35. 130 applicants, 91% accepted, 84 enrolled. In 2018, 222 master's, 99 other advanced degrees awarded. *Entrance requirements:* For degree, minimum GPA of 3.0. Additional exam requirements/recommendations for international students: Required—TOEFL (minimum score 79 iBT) or IELTS (minimum score 6.5). *Application deadline:* For fall admission, 8/21 for domestic and international students; for spring admission, 1/23 for domestic and international students; for summer admission, 6/5 for domestic and international students. Application fee: $50 ($100 for international students). Electronic applications accepted. *Expenses:* Tuition, state resident: full-time $5683.20; part-time $236.80 per credit hour. Tuition, nonresident: full-time $20,342; part-time $847.60 per credit hour. *International tuition:* $20,342.40 full-time. *Required fees:* $2894.20; $110.05 per credit hour. $126.50 per semester. Tuition and fees vary according to course load and program. *Financial support:* In 2018–19, 101 students received support, including 6 research assistantships with full tuition reimbursements available (averaging $11,124 per year), 4 teaching assistantships with full tuition reimbursements available (averaging $12,468 per year); scholarships/grants also available. Financial award application deadline: 6/1; financial award applicants required to submit FAFSA. *Faculty research:* At-risk youth, strength model, women's health, adolescent addiction and recovery, group psychotherapy. *Unit head:* Dr. Wesley Long, Chair of Department of Human Relations, 405-325-1756, Fax: 405-325-4402, E-mail: wlong@ou.edu. *Application contact:* Lawana Miller, Admissions Coordinator, 405-325-1756, Fax: 405-325-4402, E-mail: lmiller@ou.edu.
Website: http://www.ou.edu/cas/humanrelations

University of Oklahoma, College of Professional and Continuing Studies, Norman, OK 73019. Offers administrative leadership (MA, Graduate Certificate), including government and military leadership (MA), organizational leadership (MA), volunteer and non-profit leadership (MA); corrections management (Graduate Certificate); criminal justice (MS); integrated studies (MA), including human and health services administration, integrated studies; museum studies (MA); prevention science (MPS); restorative justice administration (Graduate Certificate). *Program availability:* Part-time, 100% online, blended/hybrid learning. *Degree requirements:* For master's, comprehensive exam, thesis optional, 33 credit hours; project/internship (for museum studies program only); for Graduate Certificate, 12 graduate credit hours (for Graduate Certificate). *Entrance requirements:* For master's and Graduate Certificate, minimum GPA of 3.0 in last 60 undergraduate hours; statement of goals; resume. Additional exam requirements/recommendations for international students: Required—TOEFL (minimum score 79 iBT) or IELTS (minimum score 6.5). Electronic applications accepted. *Expenses:* Tuition, state resident: full-time $5683.20; part-time $236.80 per credit hour. Tuition, nonresident: full-time $20,342; part-time $847.60 per credit hour. *International tuition:* $20,342.40 full-time. *Required fees:* $2894.20; $110.05 per credit hour. $126.50 per semester. Tuition and fees vary according to course load and program. *Faculty research:* Change management and leadership; policing and corrections management; neuro-psychology of addiction; disproportionate minority contact; ethnic identity and nationalism.

University of Providence, Graduate Studies, Program in Organization Management, Great Falls, MT 59405. Offers human development (MSM); management (MSM). *Program availability:* Part-time, evening/weekend, online learning. *Degree requirements:* For master's, thesis optional. *Entrance requirements:* For master's, GRE General Test or MAT, 3 letters of recommendation. Additional exam requirements/recommendations for international students: Required—TOEFL (minimum score 500 paper-based). Electronic applications accepted.

Upper Iowa University, Online Master's Programs, Fayette, IA 52142-1857. Offers accounting (MBA); corporate financial management (MBA); emergency management and homeland security (MPA); general management (MBA); general studies (MPA); government administration (MPA); health and human services (MPA); human resources management (MBA); nonprofit organizational management (MPA); organizational development (MBA); public management (MPA); sport administration (MSA). MBA also available at Madison, WI campus. *Program availability:* Part-time, online learning. *Degree requirements:* For master's, research project. *Entrance requirements:* For master's, GMAT, GRE, or minimum GPA of 2.7 during last 60 hours. Additional exam requirements/recommendations for international students: Required—TOEFL (minimum score 570 paper-based). Electronic applications accepted. *Faculty research:* Total quality management, teams, organization culture and climate, management.

Walden University, Graduate Programs, School of Social Work and Human Services, Minneapolis, MN 55401. Offers addictions and social work (DSW); advanced clinical practice (MSW); clinical expertise (DSW); criminal justice (DSW); disaster, crisis, and intervention (DSW); family studies and interventions (DSW); human and social services (PhD), including advanced research, community and social services, community intervention and leadership, conflict management, criminal justice, disaster crisis and intervention, family studies and intervention, gerontology, global social services, higher education, human services and nonprofit administration, mental health facilitation; medical social work (DSW); military social work (MSW); policy practice (DSW); social work (PhD), including addictions and social work, clinical expertise, criminal justice, disaster, crisis and intervention, family studies and interventions, medical social work, policy practice, social work administration; social work administration (DSW); social work in healthcare (MSW); social work with children and families (MSW). *Accreditation:* CSWE. *Program availability:* Part-time, evening/weekend, online only, 100% online. *Degree requirements:* For master's, residency (for some programs); for doctorate, thesis/dissertation, residency. *Entrance requirements:* For master's, bachelor's degree or higher; minimum GPA of 2.5; official transcripts; goal statement (for some programs); access to computer and Internet; for doctorate, master's degree or higher; three years of related professional or academic experience (preferred); minimum GPA of 3.0; goal statement and current resume (for select programs); official transcripts; access to computer and Internet. Additional exam requirements/recommendations for international

students: Required—TOEFL (minimum score 550 paper-based, 79 iBT), IELTS (minimum score 6.5), Michigan English Language Assessment Battery (minimum score 82), or PTE (minimum score 53). Electronic applications accepted.

Warner Pacific University, Graduate Programs, Portland, OR 97215-4099. Offers human services (MA); not-for-profit leadership (MS); organizational leadership (MS); teaching (MAT). *Program availability:* Part-time, evening/weekend. *Degree requirements:* For master's, thesis or alternative, presentation of defense. *Entrance requirements:* For master's, interview, minimum GPA of 2.5, letters of recommendation. *Faculty research:* New Testament studies, nineteenth-century Wesleyan theology, preaching and church growth, Christian ethics.

Washburn University, School of Applied Studies, Department of Human Services, Topeka, KS 66621. Offers addiction counseling (MA). *Program availability:* Evening/weekend. *Entrance requirements:* For master's, minimum GPA of 3.0 in last 60 hours of coursework. Additional exam requirements/recommendations for international students: Required—TOEFL (minimum score 80 iBT). *Faculty research:* Professional identity development in students, expressive therapeutic writing, prevention, community mental health, agency professional development, behavioral analysis, group living among the elderly, ethical identity development, higher education pedagogy, Morita therapy/anxiety disorders, ecological/contextual healing, post-trauma.

Webster University, College of Arts and Sciences, Department of Anthropology and Sociology, St. Louis, MO 63119-3194. Offers human services (MA). *Expenses: Tuition:* Full-time $22,500; part-time $750 per credit hour. Tuition and fees vary according to degree level, campus/location and program.

Western Michigan University, Graduate College, College of Health and Human Services, Department of Interdisciplinary Health and Human Services, Kalamazoo, MI 49008. Offers interdisciplinary health services (PhD).

West Virginia University, College of Education and Human Services, Morgantown, WV 26506. Offers audiology (Au D); autism spectrum disorder (MA); clinical rehabilitation and mental health counseling (MS); communication science and disorders (PhD); counseling (MA); counseling psychology (PhD); curriculum and instruction (Ed D); early childhood education (MA); early intervention/ early childhood special education (MA); education (PhD); educational leadership (MA); educational leadership/ public school administration (Ed D); educational leadership/public school administration (MA); educational psychology (MA, Ed D); elementary education (MA); gifted education (MA); higher education administration (MA, Ed D); higher education curriculum and teaching (MA); institutional design and technology (MA); instructional design and technology (Ed D); literacy education (MA); secondary education (MA); secondary education/ English (MA); special education (Ed D); speech pathology (MS). *Accreditation:* ASHA; NCATE. *Program availability:* Part-time, evening/weekend, online learning. *Students:* 392 full-time (325 women), 337 part-time (285 women); includes 44 minority (16 Black or African American, non-Hispanic/Latino; 16 Hispanic/Latino; 12 Two or more races, non-Hispanic/Latino), 11 international. In 2018, 303 master's, 6 doctorates awarded. *Degree requirements:* For master's, content exams; for doctorate, comprehensive exam, thesis/dissertation. *Entrance requirements:* Additional exam requirements/recommendations for international students: Required—TOEFL (minimum score 500 paper-based; 61 iBT). *Application deadline:* For fall admission, 8/1 for domestic students; for spring admission, 1/1 for domestic students; for summer admission, 5/1 for domestic students. Application fee: $60. Electronic applications accepted. *Financial support:* Fellowships, research

assistantships, teaching assistantships, career-related internships or fieldwork, Federal Work-Study, institutionally sponsored loans, health care benefits, tuition waivers (full and partial), and administrative assistantships available. Financial award applicants required to submit FAFSA. *Faculty research:* Internet training and integration for teachers, rural education, teacher preparation, organization of schools, evaluation of personnel. *Unit head:* Dr. Tracy L. Morris, Interim Dean, 304-293-0816, Fax: 304-293-7565, E-mail: Tracy.Morris@mail.wvu.edu. *Application contact:* Dr. Melissa Luna, Associate Dean for Research, 304-293-2174, Fax: 304-293-3802, E-mail: Melissa.Luna@mail.wvu.edu.
Website: http://cehs.wvu.edu/

West Virginia University, Eberly College of Arts and Sciences, School of Social Work, Morgantown, WV 26506. Offers aging and health care (MSW); children and families (MSW); community mental health (MSW); community organization and social administration (MSW); direct (clinical) social work practice (MSW). *Program availability:* Part-time. *Degree requirements:* For master's, fieldwork. *Entrance requirements:* For master's, GRE, minimum GPA of 2.75, 2 letters of reference. Additional exam requirements/recommendations for international students: Required—TOEFL. *Faculty research:* Rural and small town social work practice, gerontology, health and mental health, welfare reform, child welfare.

Wichita State University, Graduate School, Fairmount College of Liberal Arts and Sciences, School of Community Affairs, Wichita, KS 67260. Offers criminal justice (MA). *Program availability:* Part-time, 100% online, blended/hybrid learning. *Unit head:* Dr. Andra Bannister, Director, 316-978-7200, Fax: 316-978-3626, E-mail: andra.bannister@wichita.edu. *Application contact:* Jordan Oleson, Admissions Coordinator, 316-978-3095, Fax: 316-978-3253, E-mail: jordan.oleson@wichita.edu.
Website: http://www.wichita.edu/cj

Wilmington University, College of Social and Behavioral Sciences, New Castle, DE 19720-6491. Offers administration of human services (MS); administration of justice (MS); clinical mental health counseling (MS); homeland security (MS). *Accreditation:* ACA. *Program availability:* Part-time, evening/weekend. *Entrance requirements:* Additional exam requirements/recommendations for international students: Required—TOEFL (minimum score 500 paper-based). Electronic applications accepted.

Winona State University, College of Education, Department of Counselor Education, Winona, MN 55987. Offers addiction counseling (Certificate); clinical mental health counseling (MS); human services (MS); school counseling (MS). *Accreditation:* ACA (one or more programs are accredited); NCATE. *Program availability:* Part-time, evening/weekend. *Degree requirements:* For master's, thesis or alternative. *Entrance requirements:* For master's, letters of reference, interview, group activity, on-site writing. Electronic applications accepted.

Youngstown State University, College of Graduate Studies, Bitonte College of Health and Human Services, Department of Health Professions, Youngstown, OH 44555-0001. Offers health and human services (MHHS); public health (MPH). *Accreditation:* NAACLS. *Program availability:* Part-time, evening/weekend. *Degree requirements:* For master's, thesis optional. *Entrance requirements:* For master's, GRE General Test, minimum GPA of 3.0. Additional exam requirements/recommendations for international students: Required—TOEFL. *Faculty research:* Drug prevention, multiskilling in health care, organizational behavior, health care management, health behaviors, research management.

Social Work

Abilene Christian University, Graduate Programs, College of Education and Human Services, School of Social Work, Abilene, TX 79699. Offers MSSW. *Accreditation:* CSWE. *Program availability:* Part-time. *Faculty:* 8 part-time/adjunct (3 women). *Students:* 19 full-time (17 women), 9 part-time (7 women); includes 8 minority (4 Black or African American, non-Hispanic/Latino; 4 Hispanic/Latino), 2 international. 43 applicants, 58% accepted, 13 enrolled. In 2018, 16 master's awarded. *Degree requirements:* For master's, thesis. *Entrance requirements:* For master's, GRE (if undergraduate GPA less than 3.0) or MAT. Additional exam requirements/recommendations for international students: Required—TOEFL (minimum score 80 iBT), IELTS (minimum score 6), PTE. *Application deadline:* For fall admission, 2/16 priority date for domestic students. Applications are processed on a rolling basis. Application fee: $65. Electronic applications accepted. *Financial support:* In 2018–19, 19 students received support, including 9 research assistantships with partial tuition reimbursements available; career-related internships or fieldwork, Federal Work-Study, scholarships/grants, and tuition waivers (partial) also available. Financial award application deadline: 4/1; financial award applicants required to submit FAFSA. *Unit head:* Dr. Thomas Winter, Director, 325-674-2072, Fax: 325-674-6525, E-mail: socialwork@acu.edu. *Application contact:* Graduate Admissions, 325-674-6911, E-mail: gradinfo@acu.edu.
Website: http://www.acu.edu/undergraduate/academics/education-and-human-services/social-work.html

Adelphi University, School of Social Work, MSW Program, Garden City, NY 11530-0701. Offers MSW. *Accreditation:* CSWE. *Program availability:* Part-time. *Students:* 320 full-time (284 women), 174 part-time (149 women); includes 272 minority (138 Black or African American, non-Hispanic/Latino; 2 American Indian or Alaska Native, non-Hispanic/Latino; 16 Asian, non-Hispanic/Latino; 105 Hispanic/Latino; 11 Two or more races, non-Hispanic/Latino), 3 international. Average age 32. 650 applicants, 57% accepted, 180 enrolled. In 2018, 263 master's awarded. *Entrance requirements:* For master's, baccalaureate degree, minimum undergraduate cumulative GPA of 3.0, paid or volunteer experience in human services (preferred), interview, two reference letters, official transcripts, personal statement. Additional exam requirements/recommendations for international students: Required—TOEFL (minimum score 585 paper-based; 80 iBT), IELTS (minimum score 6.5). *Application deadline:* Applications are processed on a rolling basis. Application fee: $50. *Financial support:* Research assistantships, teaching assistantships, career-related internships or fieldwork, institutionally sponsored loans, scholarships/grants, traineeships, and unspecified assistantships available. Support available to part-time students. *Unit head:* Dr. Godfrey Gregg, Director of MSW Programs, 516-877-4439, E-mail: gregg@adelphi.edu. *Application contact:* Dr. Godfrey Gregg, Director of MSW Programs, 516-877-4439, E-mail: gregg@adelphi.edu.

Adelphi University, School of Social Work, PhD in Social Work Program, Garden City, NY 11530-0701. Offers PhD. *Program availability:* Part-time. *Students:* 2 full-time (1 woman), 62 part-time (46 women); includes 35 minority (15 Black or African American, non-Hispanic/Latino; 5 Asian, non-Hispanic/Latino; 11 Hispanic/Latino; 4 Two or more races, non-Hispanic/Latino), 1 international. Average age 42. 49 applicants, 47%

accepted, 12 enrolled. In 2018, 3 doctorates awarded. *Degree requirements:* For doctorate, thesis/dissertation. *Entrance requirements:* For doctorate, four-page essay or personal statement, three letters of recommendation, curriculum vitae, writing sample, official transcripts. Additional exam requirements/recommendations for international students: Required—TOEFL (minimum iBT score of 80) or IELTS (minimum score of 6.5). *Application deadline:* For fall admission, 4/15 for domestic students. Application fee: $50. *Unit head:* Dr. Subadra Panchanadeswaran, Director, 516-877-4310, Fax: 516-877-4392. *Application contact:* Tracy A. Nilsen, Director of Admissions, 516-877-3050, Fax: 516-877-3039, E-mail: graduateadmissions@adelphi.edu.
Website: http://socialwork.adelphi.edu/academics/ph-d-program/

Alabama Agricultural and Mechanical University, School of Graduate Studies, College of Education, Humanities, and Behavioral Sciences, Department of Social Work, Psychology and Counseling, Huntsville, AL 35811. Offers psychology and counseling (MS, Ed S), including clinical psychology (MS), counseling psychology (MS), guidance and counseling, rehabilitation counseling (MS), school counseling (MS), school psychology (MS), school psychometry (MS); social work (MSW). *Accreditation:* CORE; NCATE. *Program availability:* Part-time, evening/weekend. *Degree requirements:* For master's, comprehensive exam. *Entrance requirements:* For master's, GRE General Test. Additional exam requirements/recommendations for international students: Required—TOEFL (minimum score 500 paper-based; 61 iBT). *Faculty research:* Increasing numbers of minorities in special education and speech-language pathology.

Albany State University, College of Arts and Humanities, Albany, GA 31705-2717. Offers criminal justice (MS); English education (M Ed); public administration (MPA), including community and economic development, criminal justice administration, health administration and policy, human resources management, public management, public policy, water resources management and policy; social work (MSW). *Accreditation:* NASPAA. *Program availability:* Part-time. *Degree requirements:* For master's, comprehensive exam, professional portfolio (for MPA), internship, capstone report. *Entrance requirements:* For master's, GRE, MAT, minimum GPA of 3.0, official transcript, pre-medical record/certificate of immunization, letters of reference. Electronic applications accepted. *Faculty research:* HIV prevention for minority students.

American Jewish University, Graduate School of Nonprofit Management, Program in Jewish Communal Studies, Bel Air, CA 90077-1599. Offers MAJCS. *Degree requirements:* For master's, thesis. *Entrance requirements:* For master's, GMAT or GRE General Test, interview.

Andrews University, School of Graduate Studies, College of Arts and Sciences, Department of Social Work, Berrien Springs, MI 49104. Offers MSW. *Accreditation:* CSWE. *Entrance requirements:* For master's, GRE. Additional exam requirements/recommendations for international students: Required—TOEFL (minimum score 550 paper-based).

Anna Maria College, Graduate Division, Program in Social Work, Paxton, MA 01612. Offers MSW. *Program availability:* Part-time.

Social Work

Appalachian State University, Cratis D. Williams School of Graduate Studies, Department of Social Work, Boone, NC 28608. Offers MSW. *Accreditation:* CSWE. *Program availability:* Part-time, evening/weekend, online learning. *Degree requirements:* For master's, comprehensive exam. *Entrance requirements:* For master's, GRE General Test, 3 letters of recommendation. Additional exam requirements/recommendations for international students: Required—TOEFL (minimum score 550 paper-based; 79 iBT), IELTS (minimum score 6.5). Electronic applications accepted. *Expenses: Tuition, area resident:* Full-time $4839; part-time $237 per credit hour. Tuition, state resident: full-time $4839; part-time $237 per credit hour. Tuition, nonresident: full-time $18,271; part-time $895.50 per credit hour. *Faculty research:* Community and organizational practice, individual and family.

Arizona State University at the Tempe campus, College of Public Programs, School of Social Work, Phoenix, AZ 85004-0689. Offers advanced direct practice (MSW); assessment of integrative health modalities (Graduate Certificate); gerontology (Graduate Certificate); Latino cultural competency (Graduate Certificate); planning, administration and community practice (MSW); social work (PhD); trauma and bereavement (Graduate Certificate); MPA/MSW. *Accreditation:* CSWE (one or more programs are accredited). *Program availability:* Part-time. Terminal master's awarded for partial completion of doctoral program. *Degree requirements:* For master's, thesis or alternative, capstone project, interactive Program of Study (iPOS) submitted before completing 50 percent of required credit hours; for doctorate, comprehensive exam, thesis/dissertation, interactive Program of Study (iPOS) submitted before completing 50 percent of required credit hours. *Entrance requirements:* For master's, GRE or MAT, minimum GPA of 3.2 or equivalent in last 2 years of work leading to bachelor's degree; for doctorate, GRE, minimum GPA of 3.0 or equivalent in last 2 years of work leading to bachelor's degree, 3 letters of recommendation, resume, samples of professional writing, personal statement. Additional exam requirements/recommendations for international students: Required—TOEFL, IELTS, or PTE. Electronic applications accepted. *Expenses:* Contact institution.

Arkansas State University, Graduate School, College of Nursing and Health Professions, Department of Social Work, State University, AR 72467. Offers addiction studies (Graduate Certificate); social work (MSW). *Accreditation:* CSWE. *Program availability:* Part-time. *Degree requirements:* For master's and Graduate Certificate, comprehensive exam, thesis (for some programs). *Entrance requirements:* For master's and Graduate Certificate, GRE or MAT, appropriate bachelor's degree, letters of reference, personal statement, resume, official transcript, immunization records. Additional exam requirements/recommendations for international students: Required—TOEFL (minimum score 550 paper-based; 79 iBT), IELTS (minimum score 6), PTE (minimum score 56). Electronic applications accepted. *Expenses:* Contact institution.

Asbury University, School of Graduate and Professional Studies, Master of Social Work Program, Wilmore, KY 40390-1198. Offers child and family services (MSW). *Accreditation:* CSWE. *Degree requirements:* For master's, comprehensive exam, 954 practicum hours completed in agency. *Entrance requirements:* For master's, prerequisite courses in psychology, sociology, and statistics. Additional exam requirements/recommendations for international students: Required—TOEFL. Electronic applications accepted. *Expenses:* Contact institution. *Faculty research:* Integration of faith and practice, survivors of family violence, program evaluation, cross-cultural counseling.

Auburn University, Graduate School, College of Liberal Arts, Department of Sociology, Anthropology, and Social Work, Auburn University, AL 36849. Offers social work (MSW). *Expenses:* Tuition, state resident: full-time $11,282; part-time $535 per credit hour. Tuition, nonresident: full-time $30,542; part-time $1605 per credit hour. *Required fees:* $826 per semester. Tuition and fees vary according to degree level and program.

Augsburg University, Program in Social Work, Minneapolis, MN 55454-1351. Offers MSW. *Accreditation:* CSWE. *Program availability:* Part-time, evening/weekend. *Degree requirements:* For master's, thesis optional. *Entrance requirements:* For master's, previous course work in human biology and statistics.

Aurora University, School of Social Work, Aurora, IL 60506-4892. Offers MSW, DSW. *Accreditation:* CSWE. *Program availability:* Part-time, evening/weekend, 100% online, blended/hybrid learning. *Faculty:* 13 full-time (8 women), 100 part-time/adjunct (95 women). *Students:* 640 full-time (566 women), 360 part-time (311 women); includes 325 minority (149 Black or African American, non-Hispanic/Latino; 1 American Indian or Alaska Native, non-Hispanic/Latino; 19 Asian, non-Hispanic/Latino; 135 Hispanic/Latino; 21 Two or more races, non-Hispanic/Latino). Average age 31. 652 applicants, 98% accepted, 421 enrolled. In 2018, 414 master's, 6 doctorates awarded. *Degree requirements:* For master's, thesis optional, field instruction; for doctorate, comprehensive exam, thesis/dissertation. *Entrance requirements:* For master's, minimum GPA of 3.0; for doctorate, MSW from CSWE-accredited school; minimum GPA of 3.0; at least 3 years of post-MSW social work experience; 3 letters of recommendation; writing sample in the area of clinical social work; personal interview. Additional exam requirements/recommendations for international students: Required—TOEFL (minimum score 550 paper-based; 79 iBT). *Application deadline:* For fall admission, 6/1 for international students; for spring admission, 10/1 for international students. Applications are processed on a rolling basis. Application fee: $0. Electronic applications accepted. *Expenses:* $48,720 (for Doctor of Social Work); $50,535 (for MBA/MSW, MPA/MSW). *Financial support:* In 2018–19, 432 students received support. Federal Work-Study, scholarships/grants, and unspecified assistantships available. Financial award applicants required to submit FAFSA. *Unit head:* Dr. Brenda Barnwell, Dean, School of Social Work, 630-947-8933, E-mail: bbarnwel@aurora.edu. *Application contact:* Center for Graduate Studies, 630-947-8955, E-mail: AUadmission@aurora.edu.
Website: http://aurora.edu/socialwork

Austin Peay State University, College of Graduate Studies, College of Behavioral and Health Sciences, Department of Social Work, Clarksville, TN 37044. Offers MSW. *Program availability:* Part-time, evening/weekend. *Faculty:* 5 full-time (3 women), 1 (woman) part-time/adjunct. *Students:* 30 full-time (25 women), 17 part-time (15 women); includes 23 minority (16 Black or African American, non-Hispanic/Latino; 1 Asian, non-Hispanic/Latino; 4 Hispanic/Latino; 2 Two or more races, non-Hispanic/Latino). Average age 32. 48 applicants, 88% accepted, 33 enrolled. In 2018, 22 master's awarded. *Degree requirements:* For master's, internship of 400-500 hours. *Entrance requirements:* For master's, GRE General Test, 3 letters of recommendation, minimum GPA of 2.75. Additional exam requirements/recommendations for international students: Required—TOEFL (minimum score 500 paper-based). *Application deadline:* For fall admission, 8/21 priority date for domestic students. Applications are processed on a rolling basis. Application fee: $45 ($55 for international students). Electronic applications accepted. *Expenses: Tuition, area resident:* Part-time $450 per credit hour. Tuition, state resident: full-time $5987; part-time $450 per credit hour. Tuition, nonresident: full-time $8757; part-time $806 per credit hour. *Required fees:* $1583; $79.15 per credit hour. *Financial support:* Research assistantships with full tuition reimbursements, career-related internships or fieldwork, Federal Work-Study, institutionally sponsored loans, scholarships/grants, and unspecified assistantships available. Support available to part-time students. Financial award application deadline: 7/1; financial award applicants required to submit FAFSA. *Unit head:* Matthew Kenney, Interim Chair, 931-221-6398, E-mail: kenneym@apsu.edu. *Application contact:* Megan Mitchell, Coordinator of Graduate Admissions, 800-859-4723, Fax: 931-221-7641, E-mail: gradadmissions@apsu.edu.
Website: http://www.apsu.edu/socialwork/

Azusa Pacific University, School of Behavioral and Applied Sciences, Department of Social Work, Azusa, CA 91702-7000. Offers MSW. *Accreditation:* CSWE.

Barry University, Ellen Whiteside McDonnell School of Social Work, Doctoral Program in Social Work, Miami Shores, FL 33161-6695. Offers PhD. *Program availability:* Part-time, evening/weekend. *Degree requirements:* For doctorate, thesis/dissertation. *Entrance requirements:* For doctorate, GRE, MSW from an accredited school of social work, 2 years of professional experience. Electronic applications accepted. *Faculty research:* Family and children services, homelessness, gerontology, school social work.

Barry University, Ellen Whiteside McDonnell School of Social Work, Master's Program in Social Work, Miami Shores, FL 33161-6695. Offers MSW. *Accreditation:* CSWE. *Program availability:* Part-time, evening/weekend. *Degree requirements:* For master's, fieldwork. *Entrance requirements:* For master's, minimum GPA of 3.0, minimum of 30 liberal arts credits. Additional exam requirements/recommendations for international students: Required—TOEFL (minimum score 550 paper-based). Electronic applications accepted. *Faculty research:* Family and children services, homelessness, gerontology, school social work.

Baylor University, Diana R. Garland School of Social Work, Waco, TX 76798-7320. Offers MSW, PhD, M Div/MSW, MSW/MBA, MTS/MSW. *Accreditation:* CSWE. *Program availability:* Part-time, blended/hybrid learning. *Faculty:* 11 full-time (5 women), 13 part-time/adjunct (7 women). *Students:* 123 full-time (115 women), 11 part-time (10 women); includes 46 minority (19 Black or African American, non-Hispanic/Latino; 1 American Indian or Alaska Native, non-Hispanic/Latino; 4 Asian, non-Hispanic/Latino; 16 Hispanic/Latino; 6 Two or more races, non-Hispanic/Latino), 6 international. Average age 27. 190 applicants, 72% accepted, 71 enrolled. In 2018, 69 master's awarded. *Degree requirements:* For master's, research project; for doctorate, comprehensive exam, thesis/dissertation. *Entrance requirements:* For master's, writing sample; for doctorate, GRE, writing sample. Additional exam requirements/recommendations for international students: Required—TOEFL (minimum score 550 paper-based; 80 iBT), IELTS (minimum score 6.5). *Application deadline:* For spring admission, 3/15 for domestic and international students. Applications are processed on a rolling basis. Application fee: $45. Electronic applications accepted. *Financial support:* In 2018–19, 138 students received support, including 12 research assistantships with tuition reimbursements available (averaging $6,800 per year); career-related internships or fieldwork, Federal Work-Study, institutionally sponsored loans, scholarships/grants, traineeships, tuition waivers (full and partial), and unspecified assistantships also available. Support available to part-time students. Financial award application deadline: 2/15; financial award applicants required to submit FAFSA. *Faculty research:* Healthy marriage, family literacy, Alzheimer's and grief, spirituality, congregational community service, clergy sexual abuse, older volunteers, military family support. *Total annual research expenditures:* $533,412. *Unit head:* Melody Zuniga, Associate Dean for Academic Affairs, 254-710-3702, Fax: 254-710-7412, E-mail: melody_zuniga@baylor.edu. *Application contact:* Dr. Crystal Diaz-Espinoza, Director of Recruitment and Career Services, 254-710-4479, Fax: 254-710-6455, E-mail: crystal_diaz-espinoza@baylor.edu.
Website: http://www.baylor.edu/social_work/?_buref-661-48570

Binghamton University, State University of New York, Graduate School, College of Community and Public Affairs, Department of Social Work, Binghamton, NY 13902-6000. Offers MSW. *Accreditation:* CSWE. *Program availability:* Part-time. *Degree requirements:* For master's, thesis. *Entrance requirements:* Additional exam requirements/recommendations for international students: Required—TOEFL (minimum score 550 paper-based; 80 iBT). Electronic applications accepted. *Expenses:* Contact institution.

Boise State University, College of Health Sciences, School of Social Work, Boise, ID 83725-0399. Offers MSW. *Accreditation:* CSWE. *Program availability:* Part-time, 100% online. *Entrance requirements:* For master's, GRE General Test, minimum GPA of 3.0. Additional exam requirements/recommendations for international students: Required—TOEFL (minimum score 550 paper-based; 80 iBT), IELTS (minimum score 6). Electronic applications accepted.

Boston College, School of Social Work, Chestnut Hill, MA 02467-3800. Offers MSW, PhD, JD/MSW, MSW/MA, MSW/MBA. *Accreditation:* CSWE (one or more programs are accredited). *Program availability:* Part-time. *Degree requirements:* For master's, 2 internships; for doctorate, comprehensive exam, thesis/dissertation. *Entrance requirements:* For doctorate, GRE, master's degree. Additional exam requirements/recommendations for international students: Required—TOEFL (minimum score 550 paper-based; 80 iBT). Electronic applications accepted. *Expenses:* Contact institution. *Faculty research:* Well-being of children and families, health and mental health issues, aging and work, consumer-directed services, international social work practice.

Boston University, School of Social Work, Boston, MA 02215. Offers MSW, PhD, D Min/MSW, M Div/MSW, MSW/Ed D, MSW/Ed M, MSW/MPH, MSW/MTS. *Accreditation:* CSWE (one or more programs are accredited). *Program availability:* Part-time, evening/weekend, 100% online. *Faculty:* 33 full-time (23 women), 42 part-time/adjunct (33 women). *Students:* 241 full-time (216 women), 695 part-time (624 women); includes 256 minority (72 Black or African American, non-Hispanic/Latino; 1 American Indian or Alaska Native, non-Hispanic/Latino; 46 Asian, non-Hispanic/Latino; 113 Hispanic/Latino; 2 Native Hawaiian or other Pacific Islander, non-Hispanic/Latino; 22 Two or more races, non-Hispanic/Latino), 13 international. Average age 30. 985 applicants, 74% accepted, 248 enrolled. In 2018, 229 master's, 2 doctorates awarded. *Degree requirements:* For doctorate, one foreign language, thesis/dissertation, critical essay. *Entrance requirements:* For doctorate, GRE General Test or MAT, writing sample. Additional exam requirements/recommendations for international students: Required—TOEFL (minimum score 577 paper-based; 100 iBT), IELTS (minimum score 7). *Application deadline:* For fall admission, 2/10 for domestic students, 1/10 for international students. Application fee: $95. Electronic applications accepted. *Expenses:* 34,278. *Financial support:* In 2018–19, 183 students received support. Career-related internships or fieldwork, Federal Work-Study, scholarships/grants, and stipends available. Support available to part-time students. Financial award application deadline: 3/1; financial award applicants required to submit FAFSA. *Faculty research:* Aging, children and families, substance abuse and HIV, trauma and mental health, public health social work. *Total annual research expenditures:* $6.2 million. *Unit head:* Dr. Jorge Delva, Dean, 617-353-3760, Fax: 617-353-5612. *Application contact:* Julie Billings, Graduate Admissions Specialist, 617-353-1212, Fax: 617-353-5612, E-mail: jbilling@bu.edu.
Website: http://www.bu.edu/ssw/

Bowling Green State University, Graduate College, College of Health and Human Services, Program in Social Work, Bowling Green, OH 43403. Offers MSW.

Brandman University, School of Arts and Sciences, Irvine, CA 92618. Offers psychology (MA), including counseling, marriage and family therapy, professional clinical counseling; social work (MSW).

Brescia University, Program in Social Work, Owensboro, KY 42301-3023. Offers MSW. *Program availability:* Online learning. *Entrance requirements:* For master's, bachelor's degree, minimum GPA of 3.0 for last 60 hours earned, personal statement. Electronic applications accepted.

Bridgewater State University, College of Graduate Studies, College of Humanities and Social Sciences, School of Social Work, Bridgewater, MA 02325. Offers MSW. *Accreditation:* CSWE.

Brigham Young University, Graduate Studies, College of Family, Home, and Social Sciences, School of Social Work, Provo, UT 84602. Offers social work (MSW), including clinical practice, research. *Accreditation:* CSWE. *Degree requirements:* For master's, thesis optional. *Entrance requirements:* For master's, minimum prerequisite courses grade of B- within past 7 years. Additional exam requirements/recommendations for international students: Required—TOEFL (minimum score 580 paper-based; 85 iBT), IELTS (minimum score 7). Electronic applications accepted. *Expenses:* Contact institution. *Faculty research:* Poverty, adoptions, depression, spirituality, child welfare, marriage and family, American Indian child welfare, health care, mental health, mood disorders, substance abuse, refugees, military.

Bryn Mawr College, Graduate School of Social Work and Social Research, Bryn Mawr, PA 19010. Offers MSS, PhD. *Accreditation:* CSWE (one or more programs are accredited). *Program availability:* Part-time, evening/weekend. *Degree requirements:* For master's, fieldwork; for doctorate, comprehensive exam, thesis/dissertation. *Entrance requirements:* For master's, bachelor's degree, personal statement, 3 letters of recommendation, official transcripts, interview; for doctorate, GRE General Test (minimum scores 500 on the verbal and quantitative sections and 5.0 on analytic writing test), master's degree; minimum undergraduate GPA of 3.0, graduate 3.5; 2 years of post-MSW work experience (recommended); personal statement; 3 letters of recommendation (2 from academic references); official transcripts. Electronic applications accepted. *Expenses:* Contact institution.

California Baptist University, Program in Social Work, Riverside, CA 92504-3206. Offers clinical social work (MSW); community social work practice (MSW). *Program availability:* Part-time. *Faculty:* 11 full-time (9 women), 7 part-time/adjunct (6 women). *Students:* 158 full-time (141 women); includes 126 minority (28 Black or African American, non-Hispanic/Latino; 1 Asian, non-Hispanic/Latino; 87 Hispanic/Latino; 10 Two or more races, non-Hispanic/Latino), 1 international. Average age 37. 92 applicants, 100% accepted, 92 enrolled. In 2018, 76 master's awarded. *Entrance requirements:* For master's, bachelor's degree, minimum GPA of 2.75, official transcripts, three recommendations, statistics, essay, interview. Additional exam requirements/recommendations for international students: Required—TOEFL (minimum score 80 iBT). *Application deadline:* For fall admission, 8/1 priority date for domestic students, 7/1 for international students; for spring admission, 12/1 priority date for domestic students, 11/1 for international students. Applications are processed on a rolling basis. Application fee: $45. Electronic applications accepted. *Expenses:* $660 per unit. *Financial support:* In 2018–19, 64 students received support. Federal Work-Study and scholarships/grants available. *Faculty research:* Urban/marginalized communities, healthy marriages and families, community organization/engagement, health disparities, global social work. *Unit head:* Dr. Jacqueline Gustafson, Dean, College of Behavioral and Social Sciences, 951-552-8372, E-mail: jgustafson@calbaptist.edu. *Application contact:* Dr. Charles Lee-Johnson, Program Director, Social Work, 951-552-8081, E-mail: cleejohnson@calbaptist.edu.

California State University, Bakersfield, Division of Graduate Studies, School of Social Sciences and Education, Program in Social Work, Bakersfield, CA 93311. Offers MSW. *Accreditation:* CSWE. *Faculty:* 10 full-time (4 women), 4 part-time/adjunct (3 women). *Students:* 164 full-time (140 women), 6 part-time (all women); includes 153 minority (19 Black or African American, non-Hispanic/Latino; 1 American Indian or Alaska Native, non-Hispanic/Latino; 9 Asian, non-Hispanic/Latino; 119 Hispanic/Latino; 5 Two or more races, non-Hispanic/Latino). Average age 31. 152 applicants, 67% accepted, 76 enrolled. In 2018, 72 master's awarded. *Application deadline:* For fall admission, 2/1 for domestic students. Applications are processed on a rolling basis. Application fee: $55. *Financial support:* In 2018–19, fellowships (averaging $1,850 per year) were awarded; Federal Work-Study, scholarships/grants, and tuition waivers (full and partial) also available. Financial award application deadline: 3/2; financial award applicants required to submit FAFSA. *Unit head:* Dr. Jong Choi, Director, 661-654-2308, Fax: 661-654-6928, E-mail: jchoi6@csub.edu. *Application contact:* Martha Manriquez, Graduate Student Center Coordinator, 661-654-2786, Fax: 661-654-2791, E-mail: gsc@csub.edu.
Website: https://www.csub.edu/socialwork/index.html

California State University, Chico, Office of Graduate Studies, College of Behavioral and Social Sciences, School of Social Work, Chico, CA 95929-0722. Offers MSW. *Accreditation:* CSWE. *Program availability:* Evening/weekend. *Faculty:* 1 (woman) full-time, 18 part-time/adjunct (17 women). *Students:* 58 full-time (49 women), 38 part-time (32 women); includes 47 minority (2 Black or African American, non-Hispanic/Latino; 2 American Indian or Alaska Native, non-Hispanic/Latino; 5 Asian, non-Hispanic/Latino; 30 Hispanic/Latino; 8 Two or more races, non-Hispanic/Latino). 117 applicants, 65% accepted, 59 enrolled. In 2018, 81 master's awarded. *Degree requirements:* For master's, thesis, project, or comprehensive exam. *Entrance requirements:* For master's, GRE General Test (not required for admission into MSW programs, high GRE score will count favorably for applicants who may have a low undergraduate GPA), fall admission only; deadline is January 5th; 3 letters of recommendation on departmental form, statement of purpose, strongly recommend 1 academic reference, strongly recommend 1 professional work experience reference, prerequisites/liberal arts worksheet. Additional exam requirements/recommendations for international students: Required—TOEFL (minimum score 550 paper-based; 80 iBT), IELTS (minimum score 6.5), PTE (minimum score 59). *Application deadline:* For fall admission, 1/5 priority date for domestic and international students. Application fee: $55. Electronic applications accepted. *Expenses:* Tuition, area resident: Full-time $4622; part-time $3116 per unit. Tuition, state resident: full-time $4622; part-time $3116 per unit. Tuition, nonresident: full-time $10,634. *Required fees:* $2160; $1620 per year. Tuition and fees vary according to class time and program. *Financial support:* Fellowships, research assistantships, teaching assistantships, career-related internships or fieldwork, Federal Work-Study, scholarships/grants, traineeships, health care benefits, unspecified assistantships, and stipends available. Support available to part-time students. Financial award application deadline: 3/2; financial award applicants required to submit FAFSA. *Unit head:* Sue Steiner, MSW Director, 530-898-3066, Fax: 530-898-5574, E-mail: sjsteiner@csuchico.edu. *Application contact:* Micah Lehner, Graduate Admissions Coordinator, 530-898-5416, Fax: 530-898-3342, E-mail: jlmorris@csuchico.edu. Website: http://www.csuchico.edu/swrk/

California State University, Dominguez Hills, College of Health, Human Services and Nursing, Program in Social Work, Carson, CA 90747-0001. Offers MSW. *Accreditation:* CSWE. *Program availability:* Part-time, evening/weekend. *Degree requirements:* For master's, thesis. *Entrance requirements:* For master's, minimum GPA of 2.75 in last 60 units; 3 courses in behavioral science, 2 in humanities, 1 each in English composition, elementary statistics, and human biology. *Faculty research:* HIV/AIDS, community capacity, program evaluation.

California State University, East Bay, Office of Graduate Studies, College of Letters, Arts, and Social Sciences, Department of Social Work, Hayward, CA 94542-3000. Offers children, youth, and family services (MSW); community mental health services (MSW). *Accreditation:* CSWE. *Degree requirements:* For master's, comprehensive exam. *Entrance requirements:* For master's, minimum GPA of 2.8; courses in statistics and either human biology, physiology, or anatomy; liberal arts or social science baccalaureate degree; 3 letters of recommendation; personal statement; criminal background check; student professional liability insurance. Additional exam requirements/recommendations for international students: Required—TOEFL (minimum score 550 paper-based). Electronic applications accepted.

California State University, Fresno, Division of Research and Graduate Studies, College of Health and Human Services, Department of Social Work Education, Fresno, CA 93740-8027. Offers MSW. *Accreditation:* CSWE. *Program availability:* Part-time, evening/weekend. *Degree requirements:* For master's, thesis or alternative. *Entrance requirements:* For master's, GRE General Test, minimum GPA of 2.5. Additional exam requirements/recommendations for international students: Required—TOEFL. Electronic applications accepted. *Faculty research:* Children at risk, international cooperation, child welfare training, nutrition.

California State University, Fullerton, Graduate Studies, College of Health and Human Development, Department of Social Work, Fullerton, CA 92831-3599. Offers aging (MSW); child welfare (MSW); community mental health (MSW). *Accreditation:* CSWE. *Program availability:* Part-time. *Entrance requirements:* For master's, minimum GPA of 3.0 for last 60 semester or 90 quarter units.

California State University, Long Beach, Graduate Studies, College of Health and Human Services, School of Social Work, Long Beach, CA 90840. Offers MSW. *Accreditation:* CSWE. *Program availability:* Part-time, evening/weekend, online learning. *Degree requirements:* For master's, thesis. *Application deadline:* For fall admission, 1/15 for domestic students. Applications are processed on a rolling basis. Application fee: $55. Electronic applications accepted. *Expenses: Required fees:* $2628 per term. Tuition and fees vary according to class time, course level, course load, degree level, campus/location and program. *Financial support:* Federal Work-Study, institutionally sponsored loans, and scholarships/grants available. Financial award application deadline: 3/2; financial award applicants required to submit FAFSA. *Unit head:* Nancy Meyer-Adams, Director, 562-985-7774, E-mail: nancy.meyer-adams@csulb.edu. *Application contact:* Molly Ranney, Graduate Advisor, 562-985-5655, Fax: 562-985-5514, E-mail: molly.raney@csulb.edu.
Website: http://web.csulb.edu/colleges/chhs/departments/social-work/

California State University, Los Angeles, Graduate Studies, College of Health and Human Services, School of Social Work, Los Angeles, CA 90032-8530. Offers MSW. *Accreditation:* CSWE. *Entrance requirements:* Additional exam requirements/recommendations for international students: Required—TOEFL (minimum score 500 paper-based).

California State University, Monterey Bay, College of Health Sciences and Human Services, Seaside, CA 93955-8001. Offers social work (MSW). *Accreditation:* CSWE. *Program availability:* Part-time. *Degree requirements:* For master's, internship. *Entrance requirements:* For master's, GRE, curriculum vitae, recommendations. Additional exam requirements/recommendations for international students: Required—TOEFL (minimum score 525 paper-based; 71 iBT). Electronic applications accepted. *Faculty research:* Social policy, health policy, politics and government.

California State University, Northridge, Graduate Studies, College of Social and Behavioral Sciences, Department of Social Work, Northridge, CA 91330. Offers MSW. *Accreditation:* CSWE.

California State University, Northridge, Graduate Studies, Tseng College, Northridge, CA 91330. Offers business administration (Graduate Certificate); health administration (MPA); health education (MPH); knowledge management (MKM); music industry administration (MA); nonprofit-sector management (Graduate Certificate); public administration (MPA); public sector management and leadership (MPA); social work (MSW); taxation (MS); tourism, hospitality and recreation management (MS). *Entrance requirements:* For master's, GRE (if cumulative undergraduate GPA less than 3.0).

California State University, Sacramento, College of Health and Human Services, Division of Social Work, Sacramento, CA 95819. Offers family and children's services (MSW). *Accreditation:* CSWE. *Program availability:* Part-time, evening/weekend. *Degree requirements:* For master's, thesis, project; writing proficiency exam. *Entrance requirements:* For master's, GRE, minimum GPA of 2.8 during previous 2 years of course work. Additional exam requirements/recommendations for international students: Required—TOEFL (minimum score 550 paper-based; 80 iBT); Recommended—IELTS, TSE. Electronic applications accepted. *Expenses:* Contact institution.

California State University, San Bernardino, Graduate Studies, College of Social and Behavioral Sciences, Program in Social Work, San Bernardino, CA 92407. Offers MSW. *Accreditation:* CSWE. *Program availability:* Part-time, evening/weekend. *Faculty:* 7 full-time (3 women), 17 part-time/adjunct (15 women). *Students:* 147 full-time (125 women), 31 part-time (27 women); includes 141 minority (16 Black or African American, non-Hispanic/Latino; 3 Asian, non-Hispanic/Latino; 117 Hispanic/Latino; 5 Two or more races, non-Hispanic/Latino), 1 international. Average age 30. 299 applicants, 36% accepted, 75 enrolled. In 2018, 108 master's awarded. *Entrance requirements:* Additional exam requirements/recommendations for international students: Required—TOEFL. *Application deadline:* For fall admission, 7/16 for domestic students. Application fee: $55. *Financial support:* Institutionally sponsored loans available. Financial award application deadline: 5/1. *Faculty research:* Addiction, computers in social work practice, minority issues, gerontology. *Unit head:* Laurie Smith, Director/Associate Professor/Graduate Coordinator, 909-537-3837, Fax: 909-537-7029, E-mail: lasmith@csusb.edu. *Application contact:* Dr. Dorota Huizinga, Dean of Graduate Studies, 909-537-3064, E-mail: dorota.huizinga@csusb.edu.

California State University, Stanislaus, College of Education, Kinesiology and Social Work, Master of Social Work Program, Turlock, CA 95382. Offers MSW. *Accreditation:* CSWE. *Degree requirements:* For master's, thesis. *Entrance requirements:* For master's, minimum GPA of 3.0, 3 letters of reference, personal statement. Electronic applications accepted. *Faculty research:* Mental health supervision, health issues on adulthood and aging, geriatric social work, effects of violence on children, rural mental health.

California University of Pennsylvania, School of Graduate Studies and Research, College of Education and Human Services, Department of Social Work, California, PA 15419-1394. Offers MSW. *Accreditation:* CSWE. *Program availability:* Part-time. *Degree requirements:* For master's, comprehensive exam. *Entrance requirements:* For master's, GRE, letters of reference. Additional exam requirements/recommendations for international students: Required—TOEFL. Electronic applications accepted. *Faculty research:* Social welfare and policy, housing and community development, health and mental health, Black Appalachian, aging.

Campbellsville University, Carver School of Social Work, Campbellsville, KY 42718-2799. Offers foundation or advanced tracks (MSW). *Accreditation:* CSWE. *Program availability:* Part-time, evening/weekend, 100% online, blended/hybrid learning. *Faculty:*

15 full-time (13 women), 34 part-time/adjunct (32 women). *Students:* 390 full-time (355 women), 56 part-time (49 women); includes 91 minority (83 Black or African American, non-Hispanic/Latino; 6 Hispanic/Latino; 1 Native Hawaiian or other Pacific Islander, non-Hispanic/Latino; 1 Two or more races, non-Hispanic/Latino), 1 international. Average age 33. 380 applicants, 60% accepted, 154 enrolled. In 2018, 129 master's awarded. *Degree requirements:* For master's, variable foreign language requirement, comprehensive exam, thesis (for some programs). *Entrance requirements:* For master's, GRE, college transcripts, 3 letters of recommendation. Additional exam requirements/recommendations for international students: Recommended—TOEFL (minimum score 550 paper-based; 79 iBT), IELTS (minimum score 6). *Application deadline:* Applications are processed on a rolling basis. Application fee: $25. Electronic applications accepted. Application fee is waived when completed online. *Expenses:* $559 per credit hour (60 credit hour program). *Financial support:* Unspecified assistantships available. Financial award applicants required to submit FAFSA. *Unit head:* Dr. Helen K. Mudd, Dean of the Carver School of Social Work, 270-789-5045, Fax: 270-789-5542, E-mail: hkmudd@campbellsville.edu. *Application contact:* Monica Bamwine, Director of Graduate Admissions, 270-789-5221, Fax: 270-789-5071, E-mail: mkbamwine@campbellsville.edu.
Website: http://www.campbellsville.edu/carver-school

Capella University, Harold Abel School of Social and Behavioral Science, Doctoral Programs in Counseling, Minneapolis, MN 55402. Offers general counselor education and supervision (PhD); general social work (DSW). *Accreditation:* ACA.

Carleton University, Faculty of Graduate Studies, Faculty of Public Affairs and Management, School of Social Work, Ottawa, ON K1S 5B6, Canada. Offers MSW. *Program availability:* Part-time. *Degree requirements:* For master's, thesis optional. *Entrance requirements:* For master's, basic research methods course. Additional exam requirements/recommendations for international students: Required—TOEFL. *Faculty research:* Social administration, program evaluation, history of Canadian social welfare, women's issues, education in social work.

Carlow University, College of Leadership and Social Change, Program in Social Work, Pittsburgh, PA 15213-3165. Offers MSW. *Program availability:* Part-time, evening/weekend. *Students:* 11 full-time (9 women); includes 7 minority (all Black or African American, non-Hispanic/Latino). Average age 40. 13 applicants, 100% accepted, 11 enrolled. *Entrance requirements:* For master's, personal essay; resume or curriculum vitae; three recommendations; official transcripts; interview; minimum undergraduate GPA of 3.0. Additional exam requirements/recommendations for international students: Required—TOEFL (minimum score 550 paper-based). *Application deadline:* Applications are processed on a rolling basis. Electronic applications accepted. *Expenses: Tuition:* Full-time $13,090; part-time $5100 per semester. *Required fees:* $215; $84. Tuition and fees vary according to course load, degree level and program. *Financial support:* Application deadline: 4/1; applicants required to submit FAFSA. *Unit head:* Sheila G Roth, Program Director, 412-578-6025, E-mail: sgroth@carlow.edu. *Application contact:* Sheila G Roth, Program Director, 412-578-6025, E-mail: sgroth@carlow.edu.
Website: http://www.carlow.edu/masters_of_social_work.aspx

Case Western Reserve University, Jack, Joseph and Morton Mandel School of Applied Social Sciences, Cleveland, OH 44087. Offers nonprofit management (MNO); social welfare (PhD); social work (MSSA); JD/MSSA; MSSA/MA; MSSA/MBA; MSSA/MNO. *Accreditation:* CSWE (one or more programs are accredited). *Program availability:* Part-time, evening/weekend, 100% online. *Degree requirements:* For master's, fieldwork; for doctorate, thesis/dissertation. *Entrance requirements:* For master's, minimum undergraduate GPA of 2.7 or GRE/MAT; for doctorate, GRE General Test. Additional exam requirements/recommendations for international students: Required—TOEFL (minimum score 557 paper-based, 90 iBT) or IELTS (minimum score 7). Electronic applications accepted. *Expenses:* Contact institution. *Faculty research:* Urban poverty, community social development, substance abuse, health, child welfare, aging, mental health, behavioral health, policy, mixed income communities, trauma, school social work, adoption.

The Catholic University of America, National Catholic School of Social Service, Washington, DC 20064. Offers clinical (MSW), including clinical health care, clinical military, veterans, and families; combined (clinical and social change) (MSW), including clinical and macro practice; social change (MSW); social work (PhD); MSW/JD. MSW/JD offered with Columbus School of Law. *Accreditation:* CSWE (one or more programs are accredited). *Program availability:* Part-time, 100% online. *Faculty:* 15 full-time (13 women), 36 part-time/adjunct (31 women). *Students:* 141 full-time (118 women), 346 part-time (296 women); includes 250 minority (153 Black or African American, non-Hispanic/Latino; 11 Asian, non-Hispanic/Latino; 49 Hispanic/Latino; 1 Native Hawaiian or other Pacific Islander, non-Hispanic/Latino; 36 Two or more races, non-Hispanic/Latino), 8 international. Average age 35. 272 applicants, 81% accepted, 123 enrolled. In 2018, 166 master's, 5 doctorates awarded. *Degree requirements:* For master's, thesis; for doctorate, comprehensive exam, thesis/dissertation, minimum GPA of 3.0. *Entrance requirements:* For master's, GRE or MAT (if undergraduate GPA less than 3.0), statement of purpose, official copies of academic transcripts, three letters of recommendation, resume; for doctorate, GRE General Test, statement of purpose, official copies of academic transcripts, three letters of recommendation, resume, writing sample. Additional exam requirements/recommendations for international students: Required—TOEFL (minimum score 600 paper-based; 92 iBT). *Application deadline:* For fall admission, 7/15 priority date for domestic students, 7/1 for international students; for spring admission, 11/15 priority date for domestic students, 11/1 for international students. Applications are processed on a rolling basis. Application fee: $60. Electronic applications accepted. *Expenses:* Contact institution. *Financial support:* Fellowships, research assistantships, teaching assistantships, Federal Work-Study, scholarships/grants, tuition waivers (full and partial), and unspecified assistantships available. Financial award application deadline: 3/15; financial award applicants required to submit FAFSA. *Faculty research:* International social development; advancement of children, youth, and families; global aging; community development and social justice; promotion of health and mental health well-being. *Total annual research expenditures:* $388,329. *Unit head:* Dr. Marie Raber, Dean, 202-319-5472, Fax: 202-319-5093, E-mail: raber@cua.edu. *Application contact:* Dr. Steven Brown, Director of Graduate Admissions, 202-319-5057, Fax: 202-319-6533, E-mail: cua-admissions@cua.edu.
Website: https://ncsss.catholic.edu/

Chicago State University, School of Graduate and Professional Studies, College of Arts and Sciences, Program in Social Work, Chicago, IL 60628. Offers MSW. *Accreditation:* CSWE. Electronic applications accepted.

Clark Atlanta University, School of Social Work, Atlanta, GA 30314. Offers MSW, PhD. *Accreditation:* CSWE (one or more programs are accredited). *Program availability:* Part-time. Terminal master's awarded for partial completion of doctoral program. *Degree requirements:* For master's, one foreign language; for doctorate, one foreign language, comprehensive exam, thesis/dissertation. *Entrance requirements:* For master's, GRE General Test, minimum undergraduate GPA of 3.0; for doctorate, GRE General Test. Additional exam requirements/recommendations for international students: Required—TOEFL (minimum score 500 paper-based; 61 iBT). Electronic applications accepted.

Clarke University, Department of Social Work, Dubuque, IA 52001-3198. Offers MSW. *Accreditation:* CSWE. *Program availability:* Part-time, evening/weekend. *Entrance requirements:* For master's, prerequisite courses in statistics, biology, psychology, and sociology; minimum major GPA of 3.0; interview. Additional exam requirements/recommendations for international students: Required—TOEFL (minimum score 550 paper-based; 80 iBT), IELTS (minimum score 6.5). Electronic applications accepted. *Expenses:* Contact institution.

Cleveland State University, College of Graduate Studies, College of Liberal Arts and Social Sciences, School of Social Work, Cleveland, OH 44115. Offers MSW. Program offered jointly with The University of Akron. *Accreditation:* CSWE. *Program availability:* Part-time, evening/weekend, online learning. *Faculty:* 10 full-time (2 women), 8 part-time/adjunct (5 women). *Students:* 139 full-time (124 women), 48 part-time (40 women); includes 77 minority (61 Black or African American, non-Hispanic/Latino; 1 Asian, non-Hispanic/Latino; 10 Hispanic/Latino; 5 Two or more races, non-Hispanic/Latino), 2 international. Average age 34. 82 applicants, 78% accepted, 63 enrolled. In 2018, 64 master's awarded. *Entrance requirements:* For master's, 3 letters of reference. Additional exam requirements/recommendations for international students: Required—TOEFL (minimum score 550 paper-based; 78 iBT); Recommended—IELTS (minimum score 6). Application fee: $40. Electronic applications accepted. *Expenses:* Contact institution. *Financial support:* In 2018–19, 15 students received support. Research assistantships and tuition waivers (full) available. Financial award applicants required to submit FAFSA. *Faculty research:* Mental health, aging. *Total annual research expenditures:* $1.2 million. *Unit head:* Dr. Maggie Jackson, Director, 216-687-4599, Fax: 216-687-5590, E-mail: m.jackson@csuohio.edu. *Application contact:* Deborah L. Brown, Interim Assistant Director, Graduate Admissions, 216-523-7572, Fax: 216-687-5400, E-mail: d.l.brown@csuohio.edu.
Website: http://www.csuohio.edu/class/social-work/social-work

The College at Brockport, State University of New York, School of Education, Health, and Human Services, Department of Social Work, Brockport, NY 14420-2997. Offers family and community practice (MSW); gerontology (AGC); interdisciplinary health practice (MSW). *Accreditation:* CSWE. *Program availability:* Part-time. *Faculty:* 7 full-time (6 women), 6 part-time/adjunct (4 women). *Students:* 42 full-time (35 women), 256 part-time (215 women); includes 20 minority (15 Black or African American, non-Hispanic/Latino; 2 Asian, non-Hispanic/Latino; 3 Hispanic/Latino). 174 applicants, 72% accepted, 75 enrolled. In 2018, 149 master's awarded. *Degree requirements:* For master's, thesis or alternative. *Entrance requirements:* For master's, minimum GPA of 3.0, letters of recommendation, statement of objectives. Additional exam requirements/recommendations for international students: Required—TOEFL (minimum score 550 paper-based; 79 iBT), IELTS (minimum score 6.5). *Application deadline:* For fall admission, 1/15 priority date for domestic and international students; for summer admission, 1/15 priority date for domestic and international students. Application fee: $50. Electronic applications accepted. *Expenses:* Tuition, state resident: part-time $471 per credit. Tuition, nonresident: part-time $963 per credit. *Financial support:* Federal Work-Study, scholarships/grants, and unspecified assistantships available. Support available to part-time students. Financial award application deadline: 3/15; financial award applicants required to submit FAFSA. *Faculty research:* Care giving, child welfare, gerontological social work, home-school-community partnerships, domestic violence. *Unit head:* Debra Fromm Faria, Co-Director, 585-395-8455, Fax: 585-395-8603, E-mail: grcmsw@brockport.edu. *Application contact:* Brad Snyder, Coordinator of Admissions, 585-395-3845, Fax: 585-395-8603, E-mail: bsynder@brockport.edu.
Website: https://www.brockport.edu/academics/social_work/graduate/masters.html

The College of Saint Rose, Graduate Studies, School of Mathematics and Sciences, Program in Social Work, Albany, NY 12203-1419. Offers MSSW. *Program availability:* Part-time, evening/weekend. *Students:* 30 full-time (all women), 9 part-time (all women); includes 10 minority (7 Black or African American, non-Hispanic/Latino; 1 Hispanic/Latino; 2 Two or more races, non-Hispanic/Latino). Average age 28. 53 applicants, 75% accepted, 20 enrolled. In 2018, 7 master's awarded. *Entrance requirements:* Additional exam requirements/recommendations for international students: Required—TOEFL (minimum score 550 paper-based; 80 iBT), IELTS (minimum score 6), PTE (minimum score 56). *Application deadline:* For fall admission, 4/1 priority date for domestic and international students; for spring admission, 10/15 priority date for domestic and international students; for summer admission, 3/15 priority date for domestic and international students. Applications are processed on a rolling basis. Application fee: $40. Electronic applications accepted. *Expenses: Tuition:* Full-time $14,382; part-time $799 per credit hour. *Required fees:* $924; $408 per credit. $286. *Financial support:* Career-related internships or fieldwork, scholarships/grants, tuition waivers (partial), and unspecified assistantships available. Support available to part-time students. Financial award application deadline: 4/15. *Unit head:* Maureen Rotondi, Department Chair, 518-454-2003, E-mail: rotondim@strose.edu. *Application contact:* Daniel Gallagher, Assistant Vice President for Graduate Recruitment and Enrollment, 518-485-3390, Fax: 518-458-5479, E-mail: grad@strose.edu.

The College of St. Scholastica, Graduate Studies, Department of Social Work, Duluth, MN 55811-4199. Offers MSW. *Accreditation:* CSWE. *Program availability:* Part-time.

College of Staten Island of the City University of New York, Graduate Programs, School of Health Sciences, Program in Social Work, Staten Island, NY 10314-6600. Offers MSW. *Accreditation:* CSWE. *Program availability:* Part-time, evening/weekend. *Faculty:* 13. *Students:* 80. 148 applicants, 53% accepted, 45 enrolled. In 2018, 29 master's awarded. *Degree requirements:* For master's, 16 required courses, 4 internships, 3 integrative seminars, and 1 social work elective. *Entrance requirements:* For master's, bachelor's degree from regionally-accredited college, statistics course, 3 letters of recommendation, personal statement, resume. Additional exam requirements/recommendations for international students: Required—TOEFL (minimum score 600 paper-based; 100 iBT), IELTS (minimum score 7). *Application deadline:* For fall admission, 2/15 priority date for domestic and international students. Applications are processed on a rolling basis. Application fee: $75. Electronic applications accepted. *Expenses:* $14,210 (full time per year NY resident); $600 per equated credit (part-time NY State resident); $970 (full/part- time per equated credit non-NY resident). *Faculty research:* Children and adults with disabilities and their Parents/Caregivers, Social Work Practice with Older Adults, Alcohol and Drug Problems, Community Alternatives to Incarceration and Critical Multiculturalism, International Disability Justice and Poverty Issues. *Unit head:* Dr. Barbra Teater, Program Director, 718-982-2166, E-mail: barbra.teater@csi.cuny.edu. *Application contact:* Sasha Spence, Associate Director for Graduate Admissions, 718-982-2019, Fax: 718-982-2500, E-mail: sasha.spence@csi.cuny.edu.
Website: http://www.csi.cuny.edu/departments/socialwork/MSW_welcome.html

Colorado State University, College of Health and Human Sciences, School of Social Work, Fort Collins, CO 80523-1586. Offers MSW, PhD, MSW/MPH. *Accreditation:* CSWE. *Program availability:* Part-time, evening/weekend, 100% online, blended/hybrid learning. *Degree requirements:* For master's, thesis (for some programs), thesis or program evaluation; for doctorate, comprehensive exam, thesis/dissertation. *Entrance requirements:* For master's, minimum GPA of 3.0; statement of purpose; experience summary; references; degree from accredited university; 400 hours' human service/volunteer work; three letters of recommendation; transcripts; for doctorate, letter of

intent; resume; transcripts; 3 letters of recommendation; personal statement; interview; MSW. Additional exam requirements/recommendations for international students: Required—TOEFL (minimum score 550 paper-based), IELTS (minimum score 6.5). Electronic applications accepted. *Expenses:* Contact institution. *Faculty research:* Aging and palliative care, alternative treatment to psychopharmacology for mental health issues, healthy cognitive aging and worker engagement, harm reduction for cannabis use among older adolescents, child welfare intervention science.

Columbia University, Columbia School of Social Work, New York, NY 10027. Offers advanced clinical practice (MSSW); advanced generalist practice and programming (MSSW); policy practice (MSSW); social enterprise administration (MSSW); JD/MS; MBA/MS; MPA/MS; MPH/MS; MS/M Div; MS/MA; MS/MS; MS/MS Ed. *Accreditation:* CSWE (one or more programs are accredited). *Program availability:* 100% online, blended/hybrid learning. *Entrance requirements:* Additional exam requirements/recommendations for international students: Required—TOEFL (minimum score 98 iBT); Recommended—IELTS (minimum score 7). Electronic applications accepted. *Faculty research:* Addiction; HIV; gender-based violence and migration in the U.S. and globally; low-income children and families in NYC, the U.S. and other developed countries; dialectical behavior therapy (DBT); bereavement and complicated grief and trauma; responsible fatherhood; social determinants of health and mental health care; racism and health disparities; community violence and social media.

Concordia University Wisconsin, Graduate Programs, School of Health Professions, Program in Social Work, Mequon, WI 53097-2402. Offers MSW.

Concord University, Graduate Studies, Athens, WV 24712-1000. Offers educational leadership and supervision (M Ed); health promotion (MA); reading specialist (M Ed); social work (MSW); special education (M Ed); teaching (MAT). *Program availability:* Part-time, evening/weekend, 100% online. *Degree requirements:* For master's, thesis (for some programs). *Entrance requirements:* For master's, GRE or MAT, baccalaureate degree with minimum GPA of 2.5 from regionally-accredited institution; teaching license; 2 letters of recommendation; completed disposition assessment form. Electronic applications accepted.

Cornell University, Graduate School, Graduate Fields of Human Ecology, Field of Policy Analysis and Management, Ithaca, NY 14853. Offers consumer policy (PhD); family and social welfare policy (PhD); health administration (MHA); health management and policy (PhD); public policy (PhD). *Degree requirements:* For master's, thesis; for doctorate, thesis/dissertation. *Entrance requirements:* For master's, GRE General Test or GMAT, 2 letters of recommendation; for doctorate, GRE General Test, 2 letters of recommendation. Additional exam requirements/recommendations for international students: Required—TOEFL (minimum score 550 paper-based; 77 iBT). Electronic applications accepted. *Faculty research:* Health policy, family policy, social welfare policy, program evaluation, consumer policy.

Daemen College, Social Work Programs, Amherst, NY 14226-3592. Offers MSW. *Accreditation:* CSWE. *Program availability:* Part-time, 100% online, blended/hybrid learning. *Faculty:* 6 full-time (4 women). *Students:* 46 full-time (40 women), 2 part-time (1 woman); includes 11 minority (7 Black or African American, non-Hispanic/Latino; 3 Hispanic/Latino; 1 Two or more races, non-Hispanic/Latino). Average age 28. 68 applicants, 69% accepted, 36 enrolled. In 2018, 12 master's awarded. *Degree requirements:* For master's, Minimum grade point average (GPA) of 3.00. *Entrance requirements:* For master's, Students must complete GRE (285 or higher) or the Miller Analogy Test. Scores cannot be older than 5 years, bachelor's degree; official transcripts; personal statement: 3-4 pages; resume; 3 letters of recommendation; GPA 2.7 or higher; complete Human Biology and Stats: C or better. Additional exam requirements/recommendations for international students: Required—TOEFL (minimum score 77 paper-based), IELTS (minimum score 6.5). *Application deadline:* Applications are processed on a rolling basis. Application fee: $25. Electronic applications accepted. Application fee is waived when completed online. *Expenses: Tuition:* Part-time $977 per credit hour. *Required fees:* $125; $14 per credit hour. *Financial support:* Scholarships/grants and unspecified assistantships available. Support available to part-time students. Financial award applicants required to submit FAFSA. *Unit head:* Dr. Diane Bessel-Matteson, MSW Program Director, 716-566-7876, E-mail: dbessel@daemen.edu. *Application contact:* Megan Beardi, Senior Assistant Director of Graduate Admissions, 716-566-7861, Fax: 716-839-8229, E-mail: mbeardi@daemen.edu. Website: https://www.daemen.edu/academics/areas-study/social-work

Dalhousie University, Faculty of Health, School of Social Work, Halifax, NS B3H3J5, Canada. Offers MSW. *Program availability:* Part-time, online learning. *Degree requirements:* For master's, thesis optional, field placement. *Entrance requirements:* For master's, bachelor's degree in social work, 2 years work experience in social work, minimum GPA of 3.0. Additional exam requirements/recommendations for international students: Required—TOEFL, IELTS, CANTEST, CAEL, or Michigan English Language Assessment Battery. Electronic applications accepted. *Expenses:* Contact institution. *Faculty research:* Family and child welfare, physical and mental health, public policy, elder abuse, violence against women, community practice.

Delaware State University, Graduate Programs, College of Education, Health and Public Policy, Department of Social Work, Program in Social Work, Dover, DE 19901-2277. Offers MSW. *Accreditation:* CSWE. *Program availability:* Evening/weekend. *Entrance requirements:* For master's, GRE, minimum GPA of 3.0 in major, 2.75 overall. Additional exam requirements/recommendations for international students: Required—TOEFL. Electronic applications accepted. *Faculty research:* Gerontology, human behavior, corrections, child welfare, adolescent behavior policy.

DePaul University, College of Liberal Arts and Social Sciences, Chicago, IL 60614. Offers Arabic (MA); Chinese (MA); critical ethnic studies (MA); English (MA); French (MA); German (MA); history (MA); interdisciplinary studies (MA, MS); international public service (MS); international studies (MA); Italian (MA); Japanese (MA); liberal studies (MA); nonprofit management (MNM); public administration (MPA); public health (MPH); public policy (MPP); public service management (MS); refugee and forced migration studies (MS); social work (MSW); sociology (MA); Spanish (MA); sustainable urban development (MA); women's and gender studies (MA); writing and publishing (MA); writing, rhetoric and discourse (MA); MA/PhD. *Accreditation:* CEPH. *Program availability:* Part-time, evening/weekend, online learning. Terminal master's awarded for partial completion of doctoral program. *Degree requirements:* For master's, variable foreign language requirement, comprehensive exam (for some programs), thesis (for some programs). Electronic applications accepted.

Dominican University, School of Social Work, River Forest, IL 60305. Offers MSW, MSW/MBA. *Accreditation:* CSWE. *Program availability:* Part-time. *Entrance requirements:* For master's, minimum GPA of 2.75. Additional exam requirements/recommendations for international students: Required—TOEFL (minimum score 83 iBT); Recommended—IELTS (minimum score 7). Electronic applications accepted. *Expenses:* Contact institution. *Faculty research:* Human trafficking, domestic violence, gerontology, school social work, child welfare.

East Carolina University, Graduate School, College of Health and Human Performance, School of Social Work, Greenville, NC 27858-4353. Offers gerontology (Certificate); social work (MSW); substance abuse (Certificate). *Accreditation:* CSWE. *Program availability:* Online learning. *Application deadline:* For fall admission, 2/1 priority date for domestic and international students. *Expenses: Tuition, area resident:* Full-time $4749. Tuition, state resident: full-time $4749. Tuition, nonresident: full-time $17,898. *International tuition:* $17,898 full-time. *Required fees:* $2787. Part-time tuition and fees vary according to course load and program. *Financial support:* Application deadline: 6/1. *Faculty research:* R. *Unit head:* Dr. Shelia Bunch, Director, 252-328-4202, E-mail: bunchs@ecu.edu. *Application contact:* Graduate School Admissions, 252-328-6012, Fax: 252-328-6071, E-mail: gradschool@ecu.edu. Website: https://hhp.ecu.edu/socw/

Eastern Michigan University, Graduate School, College of Health and Human Services, School of Social Work, Ypsilanti, MI 48197. Offers MSW. *Accreditation:* CSWE. *Program availability:* Part-time, evening/weekend. *Faculty:* 27 full-time (24 women). *Students:* 15 full-time (13 women), 177 part-time (144 women); includes 78 minority (53 Black or African American, non-Hispanic/Latino; 2 American Indian or Alaska Native, non-Hispanic/Latino; 2 Asian, non-Hispanic/Latino; 16 Hispanic/Latino; 1 Native Hawaiian or other Pacific Islander, non-Hispanic/Latino; 4 Two or more races, non-Hispanic/Latino). Average age 32. 180 applicants, 56% accepted, 71 enrolled. In 2018, 78 master's awarded. *Entrance requirements:* Additional exam requirements/recommendations for international students: Required—TOEFL. *Application deadline:* For fall admission, 1/15 priority date for domestic students. Applications are processed on a rolling basis. Application fee: $45. *Financial support:* Fellowships, research assistantships with full tuition reimbursements, teaching assistantships with full tuition reimbursements, career-related internships or fieldwork, Federal Work-Study, institutionally sponsored loans, scholarships/grants, tuition waivers (partial), and unspecified assistantships available. Support available to part-time students. Financial award applicants required to submit FAFSA. *Unit head:* Dr. Jennifer Kellman-Fritz, Interim Director, 734-487-0393, Fax: 734-487-6832, E-mail: jkellman@emich.edu. *Application contact:* Julie Harkema, Admissions Coordinator, 734-487-0393, Fax: 734-487-6832, E-mail: jharkema@emich.edu. Website: http://www.emich.edu/sw

Eastern Washington University, Graduate Studies, College of Social Sciences, School of Social Work, Cheney, WA 99004-2431. Offers MSW, MPA/MSW. *Accreditation:* CSWE. *Program availability:* Part-time. *Degree requirements:* For master's, comprehensive exam. *Entrance requirements:* For master's, minimum GPA of 3.0. Additional exam requirements/recommendations for international students: Required—TOEFL (minimum score 580 paper-based), IELTS (minimum score 7), PTE (minimum score 63). Electronic applications accepted.

East Tennessee State University, School of Graduate Studies, College of Clinical and Rehabilitative Health Sciences, Department of Social Work, Johnson City, TN 37614. Offers MSW. *Accreditation:* CSWE. *Degree requirements:* For master's, comprehensive exam, field practicum. *Entrance requirements:* For master's, bachelor's degree; minimum GPA of 2.75, 3.0 for last 60 hours; three letters of recommendation; resume; autobiographical statement. Additional exam requirements/recommendations for international students: Required—TOEFL (minimum score 550 paper-based; 79 iBT). Electronic applications accepted. *Faculty research:* Social work education, domestic violence, factors that contribute to a quality therapeutic relationship, mental illness stigma.

Edinboro University of Pennsylvania, Department of Social Work, Edinboro, PA 16444. Offers MSW. *Accreditation:* CSWE. *Program availability:* Evening/weekend. *Degree requirements:* For master's, competency exam. Electronic applications accepted.

Erikson Institute, Academic Programs, Program in Social Work, Chicago, IL 60654. Offers MSW.

Fayetteville State University, Graduate School, Program in Social Work, Fayetteville, NC 28301-4298. Offers MSW. *Accreditation:* CSWE. *Program availability:* Part-time, evening/weekend. *Faculty:* 8 full-time (4 women), 7 part-time/adjunct (6 women). *Students:* 88 full-time (77 women), 4 part-time (all women); includes 78 minority (66 Black or African American, non-Hispanic/Latino; 1 American Indian or Alaska Native, non-Hispanic/Latino; 1 Asian, non-Hispanic/Latino; 9 Hispanic/Latino; 1 Two or more races, non-Hispanic/Latino). Average age 35. 73 applicants, 90% accepted, 54 enrolled. In 2018, 64 master's awarded. *Entrance requirements:* For master's, GRE. Additional exam requirements/recommendations for international students: Required—TOEFL. *Application deadline:* For fall admission, 1/15 for domestic students. Application fee: $40. *Financial support:* Application deadline: 3/1; applicants required to submit FAFSA. *Faculty research:* Cultural diversity; child welfare; development and utilization of evidence-based modalities for use with severely traumatized African American adolescents and families; culturally-sensitive pedagogy; and technology and social work education. *Unit head:* Dr. Sharon Williams, Interim Dean of School of Social Work, 910-672-1853, Fax: 910-672-1755, E-mail: swill113@uncfsu.edu. *Application contact:* Dr. Dennis Corbin, Assistant Department Chair and Graduate Coordinator, 910-672-1737, Fax: 910-672-1755, E-mail: dcorbin3@uncfsu.edu.

Ferris State University, College of Arts and Sciences, Big Rapids, MI 49307. Offers social work (MSW). *Program availability:* Part-time, evening/weekend. *Faculty:* 7 full-time (all women), 5 part-time/adjunct (4 women). *Students:* 36 full-time (30 women), 40 part-time (36 women); includes 11 minority (5 Black or African American, non-Hispanic/Latino; 5 Hispanic/Latino; 1 Two or more races, non-Hispanic/Latino). Average age 31. 71 applicants, 86% accepted, 47 enrolled. In 2018, 37 master's awarded. *Degree requirements:* For master's, capstone project. *Entrance requirements:* For master's, minimum GPA of 3.0. *Application deadline:* For fall admission, 10/1 for domestic students. Application fee: $0 ($30 for international students). Electronic applications accepted. *Expenses:* Contact institution. *Financial support:* In 2018–19, 10 students received support. Federal Work-Study available. Financial award applicants required to submit FAFSA. *Unit head:* Dr. Wendy Samuels, Director of Social Work Program, 231-591-5896, E-mail: wendysamuels@ferris.edu. *Application contact:* Dr. Janet Vizina-Roubal, MSW Coordinator, 231-357-2816, E-mail: janetvizinaroubal@ferris.edu. Website: https://ferris.edu/arts-sciences/index.htm

Florida Agricultural and Mechanical University, Division of Graduate Studies, Research, and Continuing Education, College of Social Sciences, Arts and Humanities, Department of History and Political Science, Program in Social Work, Tallahassee, FL 32307-3200. Offers MSW. *Accreditation:* CSWE. *Entrance requirements:* For master's, GRE General Test, minimum GPA of 3.0, 3 letters of recommendation. Additional exam requirements/recommendations for international students: Required—TOEFL.

Florida Atlantic University, College for Design and Social Inquiry, Phyllis and Harvey Sandler School of Social Work, Boca Raton, FL 33431-0991. Offers MSW, DSW. *Accreditation:* CSWE. *Program availability:* Part-time, evening/weekend. *Faculty:* 12 full-time (7 women), 1 (woman) part-time/adjunct. *Students:* 154 full-time (133 women), 120 part-time (103 women); includes 129 minority (61 Black or African American, non-Hispanic/Latino; 1 American Indian or Alaska Native, non-Hispanic/Latino; 5 Asian, non-Hispanic/Latino; 50 Hispanic/Latino; 12 Two or more races, non-Hispanic/Latino), 2 international. Average age 31. 349 applicants, 47% accepted, 145 enrolled. In 2018, 110 master's awarded. *Entrance requirements:* Additional exam requirements/recommendations for international students: Required—TOEFL (minimum score 500 paper-based; 61 iBT), IELTS (minimum score 6). *Application deadline:* For fall

admission, 5/1 priority date for domestic students, 2/15 for international students. Applications are processed on a rolling basis. Application fee: $30. *Expenses: Tuition, area resident:* Full-time $7400; part-time $369.82 per credit. Tuition, state resident: full-time $7400; part-time $369.82 per credit. Tuition, nonresident: full-time $20,496; part-time $1024.81 per credit. *Financial support:* Fellowships, research assistantships, career-related internships or fieldwork, Federal Work-Study, institutionally sponsored loans, and tuition waivers (partial) available. Financial award application deadline: 4/1. *Faculty research:* Child welfare, social work education. *Unit head:* Joy McClellan, Program Coordinator, 561-297-3234, E-mail: jmcclel2@fau.edu. *Application contact:* Joy McClellan, Program Coordinator, 561-297-3234, E-mail: jmcclel2@fau.edu.
Website: http://cdsi.fau.edu/ssw/

Florida Gulf Coast University, Elaine Nicpon Marieb College of Health and Human Services, Program in Social Work, Fort Myers, FL 33965-6565. Offers MSW. *Accreditation:* CSWE. *Program availability:* Part-time, evening/weekend. *Entrance requirements:* For master's, GRE General Test, MAT, minimum GPA of 3.0. Additional exam requirements/recommendations for international students: Required—TOEFL (minimum score 550 paper-based). Electronic applications accepted. *Faculty research:* Gerontology, clinical case management, domestic violence, homelessness, migrant workers.

Florida International University, Robert Stempel College of Public Health and Social Work, School of Social Work, Miami, FL 33199. Offers social welfare (PhD); social work (MSW). *Accreditation:* CSWE (one or more programs are accredited). *Program availability:* Part-time, evening/weekend. *Faculty:* 17 full-time (11 women), 14 part-time/adjunct (10 women). *Students:* 142 full-time (117 women), 44 part-time (40 women); includes 155 minority (44 Black or African American, non-Hispanic/Latino; 2 Asian, non-Hispanic/Latino; 102 Hispanic/Latino; 7 Two or more races, non-Hispanic/Latino), 3 international. Average age 30. 123 applicants, 44% accepted, 45 enrolled. In 2018, 85 master's, 6 doctorates awarded. *Degree requirements:* For doctorate, comprehensive exam, thesis/dissertation. *Entrance requirements:* For master's, minimum undergraduate GPA of 3.0 in upper-level coursework; letters of recommendation; undergraduate courses in biology (including human biology), statistics, and social/behavioral science (12 credits); BSW from accredited program; for doctorate, GRE, minimum graduate GPA of 3.5, 3 letters of recommendation, resume, writing samples, 2 examples of scholarly work. Additional exam requirements/recommendations for international students: Required—TOEFL (minimum score 550 paper-based; 80 iBT). *Application deadline:* For fall admission, 6/1 for domestic students, 4/1 for international students; for spring admission, 10/1 for domestic students, 9/1 for international students. Applications are processed on a rolling basis. Application fee: $30. Electronic applications accepted. *Financial support:* Institutionally sponsored loans and scholarships/grants available. Financial award application deadline: 3/1; financial award applicants required to submit FAFSA. *Unit head:* Dr. Shann Burke, Director, 305-348-7462, E-mail: shanna.burke@fiu.edu. *Application contact:* Nanett Rojas, Manager, Admissions Operations, 305-348-7464, Fax: 305-348-7441, E-mail: gradadm@fiu.edu.

Florida State University, The Graduate School, College of Social Work, Tallahassee, FL 32306-2570. Offers clinical social work (MSW); criminology (MS/MSW); social leadership (MSW); social work (PhD); JD/MSW; MPA/MSW; MS/MSW; MSW/MBA. *Accreditation:* CSWE (one or more programs are accredited). *Program availability:* Part-time, 100% online coursework with face to face internship requirements. *Faculty:* 34 full-time (24 women), 8 part-time/adjunct (4 women). *Students:* 198 full-time (160 women), 447 part-time (404 women); includes 252 minority (139 Black or African American, non-Hispanic/Latino; 1 American Indian or Alaska Native, non-Hispanic/Latino; 7 Asian, non-Hispanic/Latino; 77 Hispanic/Latino; 1 Native Hawaiian or other Pacific Islander, non-Hispanic/Latino; 27 Two or more races, non-Hispanic/Latino), 1 international. Average age 31. 324 applicants, 70% accepted, 197 enrolled. In 2018, 215 master's, 3 doctorates awarded. *Degree requirements:* For master's, thesis optional; for doctorate, comprehensive exam, thesis/dissertation. *Entrance requirements:* For master's, GRE General Test (waiver may be requested for students who meet certain criteria specified on the college's website., minimum upper-division GPA of 3.0; for doctorate, GRE General Test (waiver may be requested for students who meet certain criteria specified on the college's website), minimum upper-division GPA of 3.0. Additional exam requirements/recommendations for international students: Required—TOEFL (minimum score 80 iBT). *Application deadline:* For fall admission, 5/1 for domestic and international students; for spring admission, 10/1 for domestic and international students; for summer admission, 3/1 for domestic and international students. Applications are processed on a rolling basis. Application fee: $30. Electronic applications accepted. *Expenses:* Contact institution. *Financial support:* In 2018–19, 82 students received support, including 28 research assistantships with full tuition reimbursements available, 6 teaching assistantships with full tuition reimbursements available; fellowships with full tuition reimbursements available, career-related internships or fieldwork, scholarships/grants, health care benefits, tuition waivers (full and partial), and unspecified assistantships also available. Financial award application deadline: 5/1; financial award applicants required to submit FAFSA. *Faculty research:* Family violence, AIDS/HIV, aging, family therapy, child welfare, criminal justice, mental health, suicide prevention. *Unit head:* Dr. James Clark, Dean, 850-644-4752, Fax: 850-644-9750, E-mail: jclark5@fsu.edu. *Application contact:* Dana DeBoer, Coordinator of MSW Admissions, 800-378-9550, Fax: 850-644-9591, E-mail: ddeboer2@admin.fsu.edu.
Website: http://csw.fsu.edu/

Fordham University, Graduate School of Social Service, New York, NY 10023. Offers nonprofit leadership (MS); social work (MSW, PhD); JD/MSW; MSW/MPH. MS program jointly sponsored with Graduate School of Business and conducted through the Fordham Center for Nonprofit Leaders; MSW/MPH offered with Ichan School of Public Health at Mount Sinai. *Accreditation:* CSWE (one or more programs are accredited). *Program availability:* Part-time, evening/weekend, 100% online, blended/hybrid learning. *Degree requirements:* For master's, 1200 hours of field placement; for doctorate, comprehensive exam, thesis/dissertation. *Entrance requirements:* For master's, BA in liberal arts; for doctorate, GRE, master's degree in social work or related field. Additional exam requirements/recommendations for international students: Required—TOEFL (minimum score 600 paper-based; 100 iBT), IELTS. Electronic applications accepted. *Expenses:* Contact institution. *Faculty research:* Aging, children and family, healthcare, domestic violence, substance abuse.

Gallaudet University, The Graduate School, Washington, DC 20002-3625. Offers American Sign Language/English bilingual early childhood deaf education: birth to 5 (Certificate); audiology (Au D); clinical psychology (PhD); deaf and hard of hearing infants, toddlers, and their families (Certificate); deaf education (MA, Ed S); deaf history (Certificate); deaf studies (Certificate); educating deaf students with disabilities (Certificate); education: teacher preparation (MA), including deaf education, early childhood education and deaf education, elementary education and deaf education, secondary education and deaf education; educational neuroscience (PhD); hearing, speech and language sciences (MS, PhD); international development (MA); interpretation (MA, PhD), including combined interpreting practice and research (MA), interpreting research (MA); linguistics (MA, PhD); mental health counseling (MA); peer mentoring (Certificate); public administration (MPA); school counseling (MA); school psychology (Psy S); sign language teaching (MA); social work (MSW); speech-language pathology (MS). *Program availability:* Part-time. Terminal master's awarded for partial completion of doctoral program. *Degree requirements:* For master's, comprehensive exam (for some programs), thesis optional; for doctorate, comprehensive exam, thesis/dissertation. *Entrance requirements:* For master's and doctorate, GRE General Test or MAT, letters of recommendation, interviews, goals statement, American Sign Language proficiency interview, written English competency. Additional exam requirements/recommendations for international students: Required—TOEFL. Electronic applications accepted. *Faculty research:* Signing math dictionaries, telecommunications access, cancer genetics, linguistics, visual language and visual learning, integrated quantum materials, deaf legal discourse, advance recruitment and retention in geosciences.

George Fox University, School of Social Work, Newberg, OR 97132-2697. Offers MSW. *Accreditation:* CSWE.

George Mason University, College of Health and Human Services, Department of Social Work, Fairfax, VA 22030. Offers MSW. *Accreditation:* CSWE. *Program availability:* Part-time. *Faculty:* 14 full-time (9 women), 34 part-time/adjunct (28 women). *Students:* 164 full-time (146 women), 43 part-time (37 women); includes 92 minority (39 Black or African American, non-Hispanic/Latino; 12 Asian, non-Hispanic/Latino; 38 Hispanic/Latino; 3 Two or more races, non-Hispanic/Latino), 1 international. Average age 30. 238 applicants, 84% accepted, 89 enrolled. In 2018, 83 master's awarded. *Entrance requirements:* For master's, minimum GPA of 3.0; personal statement; resume; references/recommendations; experience in human services; prerequisites in statistics, history/government, social sciences, and English composition. Additional exam requirements/recommendations for international students: Required—TOEFL (minimum score 570 paper-based; 88 iBT), IELTS (minimum score 6.5), PTE (minimum score 59). *Application deadline:* For fall admission, 1/15 for domestic and international students. Application fee: $75 ($80 for international students). Electronic applications accepted. *Expenses:* $564 per credit in-state, $1,421.75 per credit out-of-state. *Financial support:* In 2018–19, 16 students received support, including 15 research assistantships with tuition reimbursements available (averaging $9,100 per year), 1 teaching assistantship; career-related internships or fieldwork, Federal Work-Study, scholarships/grants, unspecified assistantships, and health care benefits (for full-time research or teaching assistantship recipients) also available. Financial award application deadline: 3/1; financial award applicants required to submit FAFSA. *Faculty research:* Behavioral health; older adults/gerontology; child welfare; immigration; human rights. *Total annual research expenditures:* $104,084. *Unit head:* Michael Wolf-Branigin, Chair, 703-993-4229, Fax: 703-994-2193, E-mail: mwolfbra@gmu.edu. *Application contact:* Vannary Khov, Administrative Program Specialist, 703-993-2030, Fax: 703-993-2193, E-mail: vkhov@gmu.edu.
Website: http://chhs.gmu.edu/socialwork/

Georgia State University, Andrew Young School of Policy Studies, School of Social Work, Atlanta, GA 30294. Offers child welfare leadership (Certificate); community partnerships (MSW); forensic social work (Certificate). *Accreditation:* CSWE. *Program availability:* Part-time. *Faculty:* 13 full-time (9 women), 1 part-time/adjunct (0 women). *Students:* 108 full-time (101 women), 19 part-time (18 women); includes 84 minority (68 Black or African American, non-Hispanic/Latino; 2 Asian, non-Hispanic/Latino; 7 Hispanic/Latino; 7 Two or more races, non-Hispanic/Latino). Average age 31. 168 applicants, 50% accepted, 44 enrolled. In 2018, 61 master's awarded. *Entrance requirements:* For master's and Certificate, GRE. Additional exam requirements/recommendations for international students: Required—TOEFL (minimum score 550 paper-based; 100 iBT) or IELTS (minimum score 7). *Application deadline:* For fall admission, 2/1 priority date for domestic and international students. Application fee: $50. Electronic applications accepted. *Expenses: Tuition, area resident:* Full-time $9360; part-time $390 per credit hour. Tuition, state resident: full-time $9360; part-time $390 per credit hour. Tuition, nonresident: full-time $30,024; part-time $1251 per credit hour. *International tuition:* $30,024 full-time. *Required fees:* $2128. *Financial support:* In 2018–19, research assistantships with tuition reimbursements (averaging $4,000 per year), teaching assistantships with tuition reimbursements (averaging $4,000 per year) were awarded; career-related internships or fieldwork, institutionally sponsored loans, scholarships/grants, tuition waivers, and unspecified assistantships also available. Financial award application deadline: 2/1; financial award applicants required to submit FAFSA. *Faculty research:* Community partnership, non-profit organizations, child welfare practice and policy, gerontological practice and policy, restorative justice. *Unit head:* Brian Bride, Director of School of Social Work, 404-413-1052, Fax: 404-413-1075, E-mail: bbride@gsu.edu. *Application contact:* Brian Bride, Director of School of Social Work, 404-413-1052, Fax: 404-413-1075, E-mail: bbride@gsu.edu.
Website: http://aysps.gsu.edu/socialwork

Governors State University, College of Health and Human Services, Program in Social Work, University Park, IL 60484. Offers MSW. *Accreditation:* CSWE. *Program availability:* Part-time. *Faculty:* 11 full-time (all women), 12 part-time/adjunct (9 women). *Students:* 75 full-time (64 women), 51 part-time (47 women); includes 76 minority (61 Black or African American, non-Hispanic/Latino; 12 Hispanic/Latino; 3 Two or more races, non-Hispanic/Latino). Average age 33. 117 applicants, 44% accepted, 44 enrolled. In 2018, 56 master's awarded. *Application deadline:* For fall admission, 4/1 for domestic students. Applications are processed on a rolling basis. Application fee: $50. Electronic applications accepted. *Financial support:* Application deadline: 5/1; applicants required to submit FAFSA. *Unit head:* Gerri Outlaw, Chair, Department of Social Work, 708-534-5000 Ext. 2178, E-mail: goutlaw@govst.edu. *Application contact:* Gerri Outlaw, Chair, Department of Social Work, 708-534-5000 Ext. 2178, E-mail: goutlaw@govst.edu.

The Graduate Center, City University of New York, Graduate Studies, Program in Social Welfare, New York, NY 10016-4039. Offers DSW, PhD. *Degree requirements:* For doctorate, thesis/dissertation, project, qualifying exam. *Entrance requirements:* For doctorate, MSW or equivalent, 3 years of post-master's work experience. Additional exam requirements/recommendations for international students: Required—TOEFL. Electronic applications accepted.

Grambling State University, School of Graduate Studies and Research, College of Professional Studies, School of Social Work, Grambling, LA 71245. Offers MSW. *Accreditation:* CSWE. *Program availability:* Part-time. *Degree requirements:* For master's, comprehensive exam, research project or thesis. *Entrance requirements:* For master's, GRE, minimum GPA of 3.0 on last degree, 36 hours in liberal arts, autobiography, interview. Additional exam requirements/recommendations for international students: Required—TOEFL (minimum score 500 paper-based; 62 iBT). Electronic applications accepted.

Grand Valley State University, College of Community and Public Service, School of Social Work, Allendale, MI 49401-9403. Offers MSW. *Accreditation:* CSWE. *Program availability:* Part-time. *Faculty:* 12 full-time (7 women), 18 part-time/adjunct (11 women). *Students:* 196 full-time (177 women), 110 part-time (97 women); includes 62 minority (29 Black or African American, non-Hispanic/Latino; 4 American Indian or Alaska Native, non-Hispanic/Latino; 4 Asian, non-Hispanic/Latino; 19 Hispanic/Latino; 6 Two or more races, non-Hispanic/Latino), 1 international. Average age 28. 191 applicants, 93% accepted, 101 enrolled. In 2018, 151 master's awarded. *Degree requirements:* For master's, field education. *Entrance requirements:* For master's, three letters of

recommendation, current resume, 2- to 3-page essay about life experiences that have led to interest in administrative practice in social agency, 2-page essay on how pursuing MSW will help achieve educational and professional career goals. Additional exam requirements/recommendations for international students: Required—TOEFL (minimum iBT score of 80), IELTS (6.5), or Michigan English Language Assessment Battery (77). *Application deadline:* For fall admission, 5/1 priority date for domestic students; for winter admission, 10/1 priority date for domestic students; for spring admission, 3/15 priority date for domestic students. Applications are processed on a rolling basis. Application fee: $30. Electronic applications accepted. *Expenses:* $651 per credit hour, 60 credit hours. *Financial support:* In 2018–19, 45 students received support, including 27 fellowships, 23 research assistantships with full and partial tuition reimbursements available (averaging $4,000 per year); career-related internships or fieldwork, Federal Work-Study, institutionally sponsored loans, and unspecified assistantships also available. *Faculty research:* Drug addiction, aging, management, effectiveness of therapy. *Unit head:* Dr. Scott Berlin, Chair, 616-331-6556, Fax: 616-331-6570, E-mail: berlins@gvsu.edu. *Application contact:* Dr. Cray Mulder, Graduate Program Director/Recruiting Contact, 616-331-6596, Fax: 616-331-6570, E-mail: muldercra@gvsu.edu.

Gratz College, Graduate Programs, Program in Jewish Communal Service, Melrose Park, PA 19027. Offers MA, Certificate, MA/MSW. MA/MSW offered jointly with University of Pennsylvania. *Program availability:* Part-time, evening/weekend, online learning. *Degree requirements:* For master's, one foreign language, internship.

Hawai`i Pacific University, College of Health and Society, Program in Social Work, Honolulu, HI 96813. Offers MSW. *Accreditation:* CSWE. *Program availability:* Part-time, evening/weekend. *Entrance requirements:* Additional exam requirements/recommendations for international students: Recommended—TOEFL (minimum score 550 paper-based; 80 iBT), IELTS (minimum score 6), TWE (minimum score 5). Electronic applications accepted.

Howard University, School of Social Work, Washington, DC 20059. Offers MSW, PhD. *Accreditation:* CSWE (one or more programs are accredited). *Program availability:* Part-time. *Degree requirements:* For doctorate, comprehensive exam, thesis/dissertation, qualifying exam. *Entrance requirements:* For master's, minimum GPA of 2.5; for doctorate, GRE General Test, minimum GPA of 3.3, MSW or master's in related field. Additional exam requirements/recommendations for international students: Required—TOEFL. Electronic applications accepted. *Faculty research:* Infant mortality, child and family services, displaced populations, social work practice, domestic violence, Black males, mental health.

Humboldt State University, Academic Programs, College of Professional Studies, Department of Social Work, Arcata, CA 95521-8299. Offers MSW. *Accreditation:* CSWE. *Faculty:* 7 full-time (5 women), 13 part-time/adjunct (12 women). *Students:* 58 full-time (48 women), 55 part-time (50 women); includes 40 minority (2 Black or African American, non-Hispanic/Latino; 7 American Indian or Alaska Native, non-Hispanic/Latino; 2 Asian, non-Hispanic/Latino; 22 Hispanic/Latino; 7 Two or more races, non-Hispanic/Latino). Average age 36. 80 applicants, 51% accepted, 36 enrolled. In 2018, 52 master's awarded. *Entrance requirements:* For master's, 3 letters of recommendation. Additional exam requirements/recommendations for international students: Required—TOEFL (minimum score 500 paper-based). *Application deadline:* For fall admission, 3/15 for domestic and international students. Applications are processed on a rolling basis. Application fee: $55. *Expenses: Tuition:* Part-time $4649 per semester. *Required fees:* $2121; $1673. Tuition and fees vary according to program. *Financial support:* Application deadline: 3/1; applicants required to submit FAFSA. *Unit head:* Geneva Shaw, Graduate Program Coordinator, 707-826-5340, E-mail: socialwork@humboldt.edu. *Application contact:* Geneva Shaw, Graduate Program Coordinator, 707-826-5340, E-mail: socialwork@humboldt.edu.
Website: http://www.humboldt.edu/~swp/mswhomepage.shtml

Hunter College of the City University of New York, Graduate School, Silberman School of Social Work, New York, NY 10065-5085. Offers MSW. *Accreditation:* CSWE. *Degree requirements:* For master's, major paper. *Entrance requirements:* Additional exam requirements/recommendations for international students: Required—TOEFL. *Faculty research:* Child welfare, AIDS, homeless, aging, mental health.

Illinois State University, Graduate School, College of Arts and Sciences, School of Social Work, Normal, IL 61790. Offers MSW. *Accreditation:* CSWE. *Faculty:* 12 full-time (9 women), 9 part-time/adjunct (8 women). *Students:* 38 full-time (30 women), 27 part-time (22 women); includes 19 minority (11 Black or African American, non-Hispanic/Latino; 5 Hispanic/Latino; 3 Two or more races, non-Hispanic/Latino), 1 international. Average age 27. 55 applicants, 56% accepted, 24 enrolled. In 2018, 24 master's awarded. *Degree requirements:* For master's, practicum. Application fee: $40. *Expenses: Tuition, area resident:* Full-time $7264.62. Tuition, state resident: full-time $9466. Tuition, nonresident: full-time $17,290. *International tuition:* $15,089.40 full-time. *Required fees:* $1481.04. *Financial support:* In 2018–19, 3 research assistantships were awarded. Financial award application deadline: 4/1. *Faculty research:* Developing professional careers in child welfare, research and policy work for the Evan B. Donaldson Adoption Institute, evidence-based practice training pilot evaluation. *Unit head:* Dr. Doris Houston, Director of the School of Social Work, 309-438-8075, E-mail: dmhous2@IllinoisState.edu. *Application contact:* Tuwana Wingfield, Graduate Coordinator, 309-438-5005, E-mail: twingfi@ilstu.edu.
Website: http://www.socialwork.ilstu.edu/

Indiana State University, College of Graduate and Professional Studies, College of Health and Human Services, Department of Social Work, Terre Haute, IN 47809. Offers MSW. *Accreditation:* CSWE.

Indiana University East, School of Social Work, Richmond, IN 47374-1289. Offers MSW.

Indiana University Northwest, School of Social Work, Gary, IN 46408-1197. Offers health (MSW); mental health and addictions (MSW). *Program availability:* Part-time, evening/weekend. *Degree requirements:* For master's, practicum. *Entrance requirements:* For master's, minimum GPA of 3.0; bachelor's degree from accredited university including the successful completion of 6 courses in social or behavioral sciences and 1 course in statistics; 3 professional references. Electronic applications accepted. *Expenses:* Contact institution. *Faculty research:* Educational outcomes, generalist practice, homelessness.

Indiana University–Purdue University Indianapolis, School of Social Work, Indianapolis, IN 46202. Offers MSW, PhD, Certificate. *Accreditation:* CSWE (one or more programs are accredited). *Program availability:* Part-time, evening/weekend. Terminal master's awarded for partial completion of doctoral program. *Degree requirements:* For master's, field practicum; for doctorate, thesis/dissertation, residential internship. *Entrance requirements:* For master's, minimum GPA of 2.5; course work in social behavior, statistics, research methodology, and human biology; for doctorate, GRE General Test. Additional exam requirements/recommendations for international students: Required—TOEFL. *Expenses:* Contact institution. *Faculty research:* Social justice, institutional child welfare, mental health, aging, AIDS/HIV.

Indiana University South Bend, School of Social Work, South Bend, IN 46615. Offers MSW. *Program availability:* Part-time, evening/weekend. *Expenses:* Contact institution.

Institute for Clinical Social Work, Graduate Programs, Chicago, IL 60601. Offers PhD. *Program availability:* Part-time. *Degree requirements:* For doctorate, thesis/dissertation, supervised practicum. *Entrance requirements:* For doctorate, 2 years of experience. *Faculty research:* Impact of AIDS on partners, effects of learning disabilities on children and families, clinical social work issues.

Inter American University of Puerto Rico, Metropolitan Campus, Graduate Programs, Program in Social Work, San Juan, PR 00919-1293. Offers advanced clinical services (MSW); advanced social work administration (MSW); clinical services (MSW); social work administration (MSW). *Program availability:* Evening/weekend. *Degree requirements:* For master's, comprehensive exam. *Entrance requirements:* For master's, GRE or EXADEP, interview. Electronic applications accepted.

Jackson State University, Graduate School, College of Public Service, School of Social Work, Jackson, MS 39217. Offers MSW, PhD. *Accreditation:* CSWE (one or more programs are accredited). *Program availability:* Evening/weekend. *Degree requirements:* For master's, comprehensive exam; for doctorate, comprehensive exam, thesis/dissertation. *Entrance requirements:* For master's, GRE General Test; for doctorate, MAT. Additional exam requirements/recommendations for international students: Required—TOEFL (minimum score 520 paper-based; 67 iBT).

Jacksonville State University, Graduate Studies, School of Human Services and Social Sciences, Department of Sociology and Social Work, Jacksonville, AL 36265-1602. Offers social work (MSW).

Johnson C. Smith University, Program in Social Work, Charlotte, NC 28216. Offers MSW. *Accreditation:* CSWE. *Program availability:* Part-time, evening/weekend. *Faculty:* 6 full-time (2 women), 4 part-time/adjunct (all women). *Students:* 72 full-time (66 women), 13 part-time (12 women); includes 79 minority (78 Black or African American, non-Hispanic/Latino; 1 American Indian or Alaska Native, non-Hispanic/Latino). Average age 32. In 2018, 37 master's awarded. *Degree requirements:* For master's, 60 credit hours (39 for advanced standing) and 900 clock hours of field (500 for advanced standing). *Entrance requirements:* For master's, official transcripts for all colleges attended; 3 references on forms provided; personal statement. Additional exam requirements/recommendations for international students: Required—TOEFL. *Application deadline:* Applications are processed on a rolling basis. Application fee: $40. Electronic applications accepted. *Expenses: Tuition:* Full-time $8640. *Financial support:* Federal Work-Study, scholarships/grants, and unspecified assistantships available. Financial award applicants required to submit FAFSA. *Unit head:* Dr. Melvin Herring, Director of MSW Program, 704-371-6754, E-mail: mherring@jcsu.edu. *Application contact:* Vory Billups, Director of Admissions, 704-3781081, E-mail: vbillups@jcsu.edu.
Website: http://www.jcsu.edu/academics/master-of-social-work/

Kean University, Nathan Weiss Graduate College, Program in Social Work, Union, NJ 07083. Offers MSW. *Accreditation:* CSWE. *Program availability:* Part-time. *Faculty:* 8 full-time (4 women). *Students:* 209 full-time (175 women), 5 part-time (4 women); includes 160 minority (93 Black or African American, non-Hispanic/Latino; 2 Asian, non-Hispanic/Latino; 61 Hispanic/Latino; 4 Two or more races, non-Hispanic/Latino). Average age 31. 232 applicants, 84% accepted, 111 enrolled. In 2018, 60 master's awarded. *Degree requirements:* For master's, field work. *Entrance requirements:* For master's, baccalaureate degree, official transcripts, three letters of recommendation, professional resume/curriculum vitae, personal statement. Additional exam requirements/recommendations for international students: Required—TOEFL (minimum score 550 paper-based; 79 iBT), IELTS (minimum score 6.5). *Application deadline:* For fall admission, 3/1 priority date for domestic and international students. Applications are processed on a rolling basis. Application fee: $75. Electronic applications accepted. *Expenses:* Contact institution. *Financial support:* Scholarships/grants and unspecified assistantships available. Financial award applicants required to submit FAFSA. *Application contact:* Brittany Gerstenhaber, Admissions Counselor, 908-737-7100, E-mail: gradadmissions@kean.edu.
Website: http://grad.kean.edu/msw

Kennesaw State University, WellStar College of Health and Human Services, Program in Social Work, Kennesaw, GA 30144. Offers MSW. *Accreditation:* CSWE. *Students:* 97 full-time (88 women); includes 37 minority (27 Black or African American, non-Hispanic/Latino; 5 Asian, non-Hispanic/Latino; 4 Hispanic/Latino; 1 Two or more races, non-Hispanic/Latino), 1 international. Average age 29. 96 applicants, 81% accepted, 47 enrolled. In 2018, 34 master's awarded. *Entrance requirements:* For master's, GRE, criminal history check, minimum GPA of 2.75, 3 letters of recommendation, resume. Additional exam requirements/recommendations for international students: Required—TOEFL (minimum score 550 paper-based; 80 iBT), IELTS (minimum score 6.5). *Application deadline:* For fall admission, 3/1 for domestic and international students. Application fee: $60. Electronic applications accepted. *Expenses: Tuition, area resident:* Full-time $6960; part-time $290 per credit hour. Tuition, state resident: full-time $6960; part-time $290 per credit hour. Tuition, nonresident: full-time $25,080; part-time $1045 per credit hour. *International tuition:* $25,080 full-time. *Required fees:* $2006; $1706 per semester. $853 per semester. *Financial support:* Research assistantships and unspecified assistantships available. Financial award applicants required to submit FAFSA. *Unit head:* Bernard Goldfine, Interim Department Chair, 470-578-2165, E-mail: bgoldfin@kennesaw.edu. *Application contact:* Admissions Counselor, 470-578-4377, E-mail: ksugrad@kennesaw.edu.
Website: http://wellstarcollege.kennesaw.edu/swhs/social-work/index.php

Keuka College, Program in Social Work, Keuka Park, NY 14478. Offers MSW. *Accreditation:* CSWE. *Degree requirements:* For master's, field practicum. *Entrance requirements:* For master's, BS in social work. Additional exam requirements/recommendations for international students: Required—TOEFL (minimum score 550 paper-based). Electronic applications accepted. *Expenses:* Contact institution. *Faculty research:* Foster care; maternal health; trauma; family.

Kutztown University of Pennsylvania, College of Liberal Arts and Sciences, Program in Social Work, Kutztown, PA 19530-0730. Offers MSW, DSW. *Accreditation:* CSWE. *Program availability:* Part-time, evening/weekend. *Faculty:* 17 full-time (11 women). *Students:* 42 full-time (35 women), 56 part-time (51 women); includes 29 minority (14 Black or African American, non-Hispanic/Latino; 1 American Indian or Alaska Native, non-Hispanic/Latino; 9 Hispanic/Latino; 1 Native Hawaiian or other Pacific Islander, non-Hispanic/Latino; 4 Two or more races, non-Hispanic/Latino), 1 international. Average age 31. 105 applicants, 83% accepted, 47 enrolled. In 2018, 39 master's, 6 doctorates awarded. *Degree requirements:* For master's, comprehensive exam; for doctorate, thesis/dissertation. *Entrance requirements:* For master's, GRE (except for BSW and other master's degree holders), 3 letters of recommendation, personal and social issues essay (waived for Kutztown University BSW holders); for doctorate, MSW from CSWE-accredited program, 3 letters of recommendation, knowledge statement, personal statement. Additional exam requirements/recommendations for international students: Required—TOEFL (minimum score 550 paper-based, 79 iBT), IELTS (minimum score 6.5), or PTE (minimum score 53). *Application deadline:* For fall admission, 8/1 for domestic and international students; for spring admission, 12/1 for domestic and international students. Application fee: $35. Electronic applications accepted. *Expenses:* Tuition, state resident: part-time $516 per credit. Tuition, nonresident: part-time $774 per credit. *Required fees:* $119 per credit. One-time fee: $50 part-time. Tuition and fees

vary according to degree level. *Financial support:* Career-related internships or fieldwork, Federal Work-Study, and unspecified assistantships available. Financial award application deadline: 3/1; financial award applicants required to submit FAFSA. *Unit head:* Dr. John Vafeas, Department Chair, 610-683-4235, E-mail: vafeas@kutztown.edu. *Application contact:* Andrea Snyder, Academic Department Secretary, 610-683-4235, E-mail: asnyder@kutztown.edu.
Website: https://www.kutztown.edu/socialwork

Lakehead University, Graduate Studies, Gerontology Collaborative Program-Northern Educational Center for Aging and Health, Thunder Bay, ON P7B 5E1, Canada. Offers gerontology (M Ed, M Sc, MA, MSW). *Program availability:* Part-time. *Degree requirements:* For master's, thesis (for some programs). *Entrance requirements:* Additional exam requirements/recommendations for international students: Required—TOEFL. *Faculty research:* Integrated health information systems.

Lakehead University, Graduate Studies, School of Social Work, Thunder Bay, ON P7B 5E1, Canada. Offers gerontology (MSW); social work (MSW); women's studies (MSW). *Program availability:* Part-time. *Degree requirements:* For master's, thesis or project. *Entrance requirements:* For master's, minimum B average. Additional exam requirements/recommendations for international students: Required—TOEFL. *Faculty research:* Clinical psychology, social work and practice theory, long-term care, health care for frail elderly, women's studies.

Laurentian University, School of Graduate Studies and Research, School of Social Work, Sudbury, ON P3E 2C6, Canada. Offers MSW. Open only to French-speaking students. *Program availability:* Part-time. *Degree requirements:* For master's, thesis. *Faculty research:* Income security, poverty, violence against women, child poverty, effects of economic crisis on families.

Lehman College of the City University of New York, School of Health Sciences, Human Services and Nursing, Department of Social Work, Bronx, NY 10468-1589. Offers MSW.

Lewis University, College of Arts and Sciences, Program in Social Work, Romeoville, IL 60446. Offers MSW. *Program availability:* Part-time. *Students:* Average age 29. *Entrance requirements:* For master's, bachelor's degree, minimum undergraduate GPA of 3.0, two letters of recommendation, personal statement. Additional exam requirements/recommendations for international students: Required—TOEFL (minimum score 550 paper-based; 79 iBT), IELTS (minimum score 6). *Application deadline:* For fall admission, 5/1 priority date for international students; for spring admission, 11/15 priority date for international students. Application fee: $40. Electronic applications accepted. *Financial support:* Federal Work-Study, health care benefits, and unspecified assistantships available. Financial award application deadline: 5/1; financial award applicants required to submit FAFSA. *Unit head:* Dr. Ellen Thursby, Program Director. *Application contact:* Linda Campbell, Graduate Admissions Counselor, 815-836-5610, E-mail: grad@lewisu.edu.
Website: http://www.lewisu.edu/academics/mssocialwork/index.htm

Loma Linda University, School of Behavioral Health, Department of Social Work and Social Ecology, Loma Linda, CA 92350. Offers criminal justice (MS); gerontology (MS); social policy and social research (PhD); social work (MSW). *Accreditation:* CSWE. *Degree requirements:* For master's, comprehensive exam, thesis optional; for doctorate, comprehensive exam, thesis/dissertation. *Entrance requirements:* For master's and doctorate, GRE General Test. Additional exam requirements/recommendations for international students: Required—TOEFL, Michigan English Language Assessment Battery. Electronic applications accepted.

London Metropolitan University, Graduate Programs, London, United Kingdom. Offers applied psychology (M Sc); architecture (MA); biomedical science (M Sc); blood science (M Sc); cancer pharmacology (M Sc); computer networking and cyber security (M Sc); computing and information systems (M Sc); conference interpreting (MA); counter-terrorism studies (M Sc); creative, digital and professional writing (MA); crime, violence and prevention (M Sc); criminology (M Sc); curating contemporary art (MA); data analytics (M Sc); digital media (MA); early childhood studies (MA); education (MA, Ed D); financial services law, regulation and compliance (LL M); food science (M Sc); forensic psychology (M Sc); health and social care management and policy (M Sc); human nutrition (M Sc); human resource management (MA); human rights and international conflict (MA); information technology (M Sc); intelligence and security studies (M Sc); international oil, gas and energy law (LL M); international relations (MA); interpreting (MA); learning and teaching in higher education (MA); legal practice (LL M); media and entertainment law (LL M); organizational and consumer psychology (M Sc); psychological therapy (M Sc); psychology of mental health (M Sc); public health (M Sc); public policy and management (MPA); security studies (M Sc); social work (M Sc); spatial planning and urban design (MA); sports therapy (M Sc); supporting older children and young people with dyslexia (MA); teaching languages (MA), including Arabic, English; translation (MA); woman and child abuse (MA).

Long Island University–Brentwood Campus, Graduate Programs, Brentwood, NY 11717. Offers childhood education (MS), including grades 1-6; childhood education/literacy B-6 (MS); childhood education/special education (grades 1-6) (MS); clinical mental health counseling (MS, Advanced Certificate); criminal justice (MS); early childhood education (MS); educational leadership (MS Ed); family nurse practitioner (MS, Advanced Certificate); health administration (MPA); library and information science (MS); literacy (B-6) (MS Ed); school counselor (MS, Advanced Certificate); social work (MSW); special education (MS Ed); students with disabilities generalist (grades 7-12) (Advanced Certificate). *Program availability:* Part-time. *Entrance requirements:* For master's and Advanced Certificate, GRE. Additional exam requirements/recommendations for international students: Required—TOEFL or IELTS. Electronic applications accepted.

Long Island University–LIU Brooklyn, School of Health Professions, Brooklyn, NY 11201-8423. Offers athletic training and sport sciences (MS); community health (MS Ed); exercise science (MS); forensic social work (Advanced Certificate); occupational therapy (MS); physical therapy (DPT); physician assistant (MS); public health (MPH); social work (MSW); speech-language pathology (MS). *Accreditation:* AOTA; CEPH. *Degree requirements:* For master's, comprehensive exam (for some programs), thesis (for some programs); for doctorate, comprehensive exam (for some programs). *Entrance requirements:* For master's and doctorate, GRE. Additional exam requirements/recommendations for international students: Required—TOEFL (minimum score 550 paper-based; 79 iBT). Electronic applications accepted. *Faculty research:* Pediatric physical therapy, complementary and alternative medicine, global health and human rights, sport leadership and entrepreneurship, feminist sport psychology.

Long Island University–LIU Post, School of Health Professions and Nursing, Brookville, NY 11548-1300. Offers biomedical science (MS); cardiovascular perfusion (MS); clinical lab sciences (MS); clinical laboratory management (MS); dietetic internship (Advanced Certificate); family nurse practitioner (MS, Advanced Certificate); forensic social work (Advanced Certificate); gerontology (Advanced Certificate); health administration (MPA); non-profit management (Advanced Certificate); nursing education (MS); nutrition (MS); public administration (MPA); social work (MSW). *Program availability:* Part-time, blended/hybrid learning. *Degree requirements:* For master's, comprehensive exam (for some programs), thesis (for some programs). *Entrance requirements:* Additional exam requirements/recommendations for international students: Required—TOEFL (minimum score 85 iBT) or IELTS (7.5). Electronic applications accepted. *Faculty research:* Antibiotic resistance, evidence-based practice, family care, interprofessional learning, simulation learning.

Louisiana College, Graduate Programs, Pineville, LA 71359-0001. Offers clinical nurse leadership (MSN); educational leadership (M Ed); social work (MSW); teaching (MAT).

Louisiana State University and Agricultural & Mechanical College, Graduate School, College of Human Sciences and Education, School of Social Work, Baton Rouge, LA 70803. Offers MSW, PhD. *Accreditation:* CSWE (one or more programs are accredited).

Loyola University Chicago, School of Social Work, Chicago, IL 60660. Offers MSW, PhD, PGC, JD/MSW, M Div/MSW, MJ/MSW, MSW/MA. *Accreditation:* CSWE (one or more programs are accredited). *Program availability:* Part-time. *Degree requirements:* For doctorate, comprehensive exam, thesis/dissertation. *Entrance requirements:* For master's, GRE; for doctorate, GRE or MAT. Additional exam requirements/recommendations for international students: Required—TOEFL (minimum score 550 paper-based; 79 iBT). *Expenses: Tuition:* Full-time $1033; part-time $788 per credit hour. *Required fees:* $700; $400 per credit hour. $400. One-time fee: $100. Tuition and fees vary according to course level, course load, degree level, program and student level. *Faculty research:* Aging, trauma, migration, poverty, substance abuse.

Madonna University, Program in Social Work, Livonia, MI 48150-1173. Offers MSW. *Expenses: Tuition:* Full-time $15,030; part-time $835 per credit hour. Tuition and fees vary according to degree level and program.

Marshall University, Academic Affairs Division, College of Health Professions, Department of Social Work, Huntington, WV 25755. Offers MSW. *Program availability:* Part-time, online learning.

Marywood University, Academic Affairs, Center for Interdisciplinary Studies, Scranton, PA 18509-1598. Offers human development (PhD), including educational administration, health promotion, higher education administration, instructional leadership, social work. *Program availability:* Part-time. Electronic applications accepted. *Expenses:* Contact institution.

Marywood University, Academic Affairs, College of Health and Human Services, School of Social Work, Program in Social Work, Scranton, PA 18509-1598. Offers MSW. *Accreditation:* CSWE. *Program availability:* Part-time. *Entrance requirements:* For master's, minimum GPA of 3.0. Electronic applications accepted.

McGill University, Faculty of Graduate and Postdoctoral Studies, Faculty of Arts, School of Social Work, Montréal, QC H3A 2T5, Canada. Offers MSW, PhD, Diploma, MSW/LL B. PhD offered jointly with Université de Montréal.

McMaster University, School of Graduate Studies, Faculty of Social Sciences, School of Social Work, Hamilton, ON L8S 4M2, Canada. Offers analysis of social welfare policy (MSW); analysis of social work practice (MSW). *Program availability:* Part-time. *Entrance requirements:* For master's, minimum B+ average in final year, BSW from accredited program, half course each in introductory statistics and introductory social research methods. Additional exam requirements/recommendations for international students: Required—TOEFL (minimum score 580 paper-based). *Faculty research:* Health policy, income maintenance, child welfare, native issues, immigration policies, racism.

Memorial University of Newfoundland, School of Graduate Studies, School of Social Work, St. John's, NL A1C 5S7, Canada. Offers MSW, PhD. *Degree requirements:* For master's, thesis optional, internship; for doctorate, comprehensive exam, thesis/dissertation, internship, oral thesis defense. *Entrance requirements:* For master's, BSW with a minimum of 2nd-class standing or equivalent; for doctorate, MSW or equivalent, 3 years of post-BSW practice experience. Electronic applications accepted. *Faculty research:* Violence, child abuse, sexual abuse, social policy, gerontology.

Metropolitan State University of Denver, College of Letters, Arts and Sciences, Denver, CO 80204. Offers individual and families (MSW); macro practice (MSW); social work (MSW). *Accreditation:* CSWE. *Degree requirements:* For master's, field work. *Expenses:* Contact institution.

Michigan State University, The Graduate School, College of Social Science, School of Social Work, East Lansing, MI 48824. Offers clinical social work (MSW); organizational and community practice (MSW); social work (PhD). *Accreditation:* CSWE. *Program availability:* Part-time, online learning. *Entrance requirements:* Additional exam requirements/recommendations for international students: Required—TOEFL. Electronic applications accepted.

Middle Tennessee State University, College of Graduate Studies, College of Behavioral and Health Sciences, Department of Social Work, Murfreesboro, TN 37132. Offers MSW. *Accreditation:* CSWE. *Entrance requirements:* Additional exam requirements/recommendations for international students: Required—TOEFL (minimum score 525 paper-based; 71 iBT), IELTS (minimum score 6). Electronic applications accepted.

Millersville University of Pennsylvania, College of Graduate Studies and Adult Learning, College of Education and Human Services, School of Social Work, Millersville, PA 17551-0302. Offers social work (MSW, DSW). Doctor of Social Work: Collaborative program with Kutztown University; Master of Social Work: Collaborative program with Shippensburg University. *Accreditation:* CSWE. *Program availability:* Part-time, evening/weekend, 100% online, blended/hybrid learning. *Faculty:* 10 full-time (8 women), 5 part-time/adjunct (all women). *Students:* 64 full-time (53 women), 90 part-time (79 women); includes 34 minority (15 Black or African American, non-Hispanic/Latino; 1 American Indian or Alaska Native, non-Hispanic/Latino; 1 Asian, non-Hispanic/Latino; 16 Hispanic/Latino; 1 Two or more races, non-Hispanic/Latino). Average age 32. 104 applicants, 93% accepted, 71 enrolled. In 2018, 69 master's, 7 doctorates awarded. *Degree requirements:* For doctorate, comprehensive exam, MSW. *Entrance requirements:* For master's, GRE or MAT, required only if cumulative GPA from ALL coursework is lower than 2.8, All Transfer transcripts (even if MU grad), 3 references (at least 1 academic and 1 supervisory reference), Resume, 4-5 page goal statement; for doctorate, Resume, writing sample, clearances, completed MSW. Additional exam requirements/recommendations for international students: Required—TOEFL, IELTS (minimum score 6), PTE (minimum score 60). Application fee: $40. Electronic applications accepted. *Expenses: Tuition, area resident:* Full-time $9288; part-time $516 per credit. Tuition, state resident: full-time $9288; part-time $516 per credit. Tuition, nonresident: full-time $13,932; part-time $774 per credit. *International tuition:* $13,932 full-time. *Required fees:* $2623.50; $145.75 per credit. Tuition and fees vary according to course load, degree level and program. *Financial support:* In 2018–19, 17 students received support. Unspecified assistantships available. Financial award application deadline: 3/15; financial award applicants required to submit FAFSA. *Faculty research:* Food and housing insecurity and overall well-being of college students; enhancing compassion and social justice advocacy through intergroup dialogue; bridging the gap through social empathy skills; enhancing students' policy advocacy; LGBTQ+ rights. *Unit head:* Dr. Karen M. Rice, Chair, 717-871-5297, Fax: 717-871-7941, E-mail: karen.rice@millersville.edu. *Application contact:* Dr. James A. Delle, Acting Dean of College of

Graduate Studies and Adult Learning/Associate Provost, Academic Administration, 717-871-7462, E-mail: James.Delle@millersville.edu.
Website: http://www.millersville.edu/socialwork/

Minnesota State University Mankato, College of Graduate Studies and Research, College of Social and Behavioral Sciences, Department of Social Work, Mankato, MN 56001. Offers MSW. *Accreditation:* CSWE. *Entrance requirements:* Additional exam requirements/recommendations for international students: Required—TOEFL.

Missouri State University, Graduate College, College of Health and Human Services, School of Social Work, Springfield, MO 65897. Offers MSW. *Accreditation:* CSWE. *Program availability:* Part-time. *Faculty:* 10 full-time (9 women), 10 part-time/adjunct (7 women). *Students:* 31 full-time (26 women), 32 part-time (27 women); includes 4 minority (2 Black or African American, non-Hispanic/Latino; 1 Hispanic/Latino; 1 Two or more races, non-Hispanic/Latino). Average age 23. 54 applicants, 37% accepted. In 2018, 26 master's awarded. *Degree requirements:* For master's, comprehensive exam, thesis or alternative. *Entrance requirements:* For master's, GRE, minimum GPA of 3.0. Additional exam requirements/recommendations for international students: Required—TOEFL (minimum score 550 paper-based; 79 iBT), IELTS (minimum score 6). *Application deadline:* For fall admission, 1/31 priority date for domestic and international students. Application fee: $55 ($60 for international students). Electronic applications accepted. Tuition and fees vary according to class time, course level, course load, degree level, campus/location, program and student level. *Financial support:* Federal Work-Study, institutionally sponsored loans, scholarships/grants, and unspecified assistantships available. Financial award application deadline: 1/31; financial award applicants required to submit FAFSA. *Faculty research:* Child and family therapy, rural social work, adolescent social issues, domestic violence. *Unit head:* Dr. Michele Day, Department Head, 417-836-6967, Fax: 417-836-7688, E-mail: swk@missouristate.edu. *Application contact:* Lakan Drinker, Director, Graduate Enrollment Management, 417-836-5330, Fax: 417-836-6200, E-mail: lakandrinker@missouristate.edu.
Website: http://www.missouristate.edu/swk/

Monmouth University, Graduate Studies, School of Social Work, West Long Branch, NJ 07764-1898. Offers clinical practice with families and children (MSW); international and community development (MSW); play therapy (Certificate). *Accreditation:* CSWE. *Program availability:* Part-time, evening/weekend. *Faculty:* 12 full-time (7 women), 14 part-time/adjunct (12 women). *Students:* 102 full-time (97 women), 100 part-time (77 women); includes 73 minority (34 Black or African American, non-Hispanic/Latino; 1 American Indian or Alaska Native, non-Hispanic/Latino; 3 Asian, non-Hispanic/Latino; 28 Hispanic/Latino; 7 Two or more races, non-Hispanic/Latino). Average age 30. In 2018, 91 master's, 2 other advanced degrees awarded. *Degree requirements:* For master's, thesis, internship. *Entrance requirements:* For master's, minimum GPA of 3.0 in major, 2.75 overall with college course each in English, math, biology, and psychology (preferred additional work in history, sociology, political science, anthropology, and economics); three recommendation forms; autobiographical statement form; for Certificate, master's degree in medical or mental health discipline and eligibility for licensure in that discipline. Additional exam requirements/recommendations for international students: Required—TOEFL (minimum score 550 paper-based, 79 iBT), IELTS (minimum score 6), Michigan English Language Assessment Battery (minimum score 77) or Certificate of Advanced English (minimum score 160). *Application deadline:* For fall admission, 3/15 for domestic and international students. Applications are processed on a rolling basis. Application fee: $50. Electronic applications accepted. *Expenses: Tuition:* Part-time $1233 per credit. *Required fees:* $178 per term. *Financial support:* In 2018–19, 122 students received support. Institutionally sponsored loans, scholarships/grants, and unspecified assistantships available. Support available to part-time students. Financial award applicants required to submit FAFSA. *Faculty research:* Child welfare citizen participation, cultural diversity, diversity issues, employee help. *Unit head:* Dr. Carolyn Bradley, Program Director, 732-263-5477, Fax: 732-263-5217, E-mail: cbradley@monmouth.edu. *Application contact:* Lucia Fedele, Graduate Admission Counselor, 732-571-3452, Fax: 732-263-5123, E-mail: gradm@monmouth.edu.
Website: https://www.monmouth.edu/graduate/msw-social-work/

Morgan State University, School of Graduate Studies, School of Social Work, Baltimore, MD 21251. Offers MSW. *Accreditation:* CSWE.

Nazareth College of Rochester, Graduate Studies, Department of Social Work, Rochester, NY 14618. Offers MSW. Program offered jointly with The College at Brockport, State University of New York. *Program availability:* Part-time, evening/weekend. *Entrance requirements:* For master's, minimum GPA of 3.0. Additional exam requirements/recommendations for international students: Required—TOEFL (minimum score 550 paper-based, 79 iBT) or IELTS (6.5). Electronic applications accepted. *Expenses:* Contact institution.

Newman University, School of Social Work, Wichita, KS 67213-2097. Offers MSW. *Accreditation:* CSWE. *Program availability:* Online learning. *Degree requirements:* For master's, comprehensive exam (for some programs), thesis optional, fieldwork. *Entrance requirements:* For master's, minimum GPA of 3.0, 3 letters of reference. Additional exam requirements/recommendations for international students: Required—TOEFL (minimum score 600 paper-based; 100 iBT). *Expenses:* Contact institution.

New Mexico Highlands University, Graduate Studies, Facundo Valdez School of Social Work, Las Vegas, NM 87701. Offers bilingual/bicultural clinical practice (MSW); clinical practice (MSW). *Accreditation:* CSWE. *Program availability:* Part-time. *Degree requirements:* For master's, comprehensive exam, thesis or alternative. *Entrance requirements:* For master's, minimum undergraduate GPA of 3.0. Additional exam requirements/recommendations for international students: Required—TOEFL (minimum score 540 paper-based). *Faculty research:* Treatment attrition among domestic violence batterers, children's health and mental health, Dejando Huellas: meeting the bilingual/bicultural needs of the Latino mental health patient, impact of culture on the therapeutic process, effects of generational gang involvement on adolescents' future.

New York University, Silver School of Social Work, New York, NY 10003. Offers MSW, PhD, MSW/JD, MSW/MA, MSW/MPA, MSW/MPH. Sarah Lawrence College offers the MA in Child Development. All other dual degrees are offered within graduate professional schools at New York University. *Accreditation:* CSWE (one or more programs are accredited). *Program availability:* Part-time, evening/weekend. *Faculty:* 34 full-time (26 women), 133 part-time/adjunct (99 women). *Students:* 780 full-time (682 women), 324 part-time (283 women); includes 415 minority (117 Black or African American, non-Hispanic/Latino; 1 American Indian or Alaska Native, non-Hispanic/Latino; 44 Asian, non-Hispanic/Latino; 195 Hispanic/Latino; 58 Two or more races, non-Hispanic/Latino), 76 international. Average age 29. 1,550 applicants, 82% accepted, 554 enrolled. In 2018, 557 master's, 28 doctorates awarded. *Degree requirements:* For doctorate, comprehensive exam, thesis/dissertation. *Entrance requirements:* For master's, Bachelor's degree; for doctorate, GRE, MSW. Additional exam requirements/recommendations for international students: Required—TOEFL (minimum score 580 paper-based; 92 iBT), IELTS (minimum score 7), TWE. *Application deadline:* For fall admission, 1/10 priority date for domestic and international students; for spring admission, 10/4 priority date for domestic and international students; for summer admission, 3/20 priority date for domestic students. Applications are processed on a

rolling basis. Application fee: $60. Electronic applications accepted. *Expenses:* $1,450 per avg credit. *Financial support:* In 2018–19, 1,004 students received support, including 6 fellowships (averaging $22,000 per year), 3 teaching assistantships with full and partial tuition reimbursements available (averaging $28,145 per year); career-related internships or fieldwork, Federal Work-Study, scholarships/grants, health care benefits, tuition waivers (full and partial), and unspecified assistantships also available. Support available to part-time students. Financial award application deadline: 2/15; financial award applicants required to submit FAFSA. *Faculty research:* Health care and social policy, social/behavioral intervention methods, substance use, mental health, healthy aging. *Total annual research expenditures:* $9.9 million. *Unit head:* Dr. Neil B. Guterman, Dean and Paulette Goddard Professor of Social Work, 212-998-5959, Fax: 212-995-4172. *Application contact:* Robert W. Sommo, Jr., Assistant Dean for Enrollment Services, 212-998-5910, Fax: 212-995-4171, E-mail: silver.admissions@nyu.edu.
Website: socialwork.nyu.edu

Norfolk State University, School of Graduate Studies, Ethelyn R. Strong School of Social Work, Norfolk, VA 23504. Offers MSW, PhD. *Accreditation:* CSWE (one or more programs are accredited). *Program availability:* Part-time. *Degree requirements:* For doctorate, thesis/dissertation. *Entrance requirements:* For master's, minimum GPA of 2.7. Additional exam requirements/recommendations for international students: Required—TOEFL.

North Carolina Agricultural and Technical State University, The Graduate College, College of Health and Human Sciences, Department of Social Work and Sociology, Greensboro, NC 27411. Offers social work (MSW). Joint program with The University of North Carolina at Greensboro. *Accreditation:* CSWE. *Program availability:* Part-time, evening/weekend. *Degree requirements:* For master's, comprehensive exam, qualifying exam. *Entrance requirements:* For master's, GRE General Test.

North Carolina Central University, College of Behavioral and Social Sciences, Department of Social Work, Durham, NC 27707-3129. Offers MSW.

North Carolina State University, Graduate School, College of Humanities and Social Sciences, Department of Social Work, Raleigh, NC 27695. Offers MSW. *Accreditation:* CSWE.

Northeastern Illinois University, College of Graduate Studies and Research, College of Arts and Sciences, Program in Social Work, Chicago, IL 60625-4699. Offers MSW.

Northern Kentucky University, Office of Graduate Programs, College of Education and Human Services, Program in Social Work, Highland Heights, KY 41099. Offers MSW. *Accreditation:* CSWE. *Program availability:* Part-time, evening/weekend. *Entrance requirements:* For master's, GRE (minimum score of 1000), minimum GPA of 3.0; undergraduate courses in psychology, sociology, and statistics with minimum C average; 3 letters of recommendation; essay; letter of intent; resume; interview. Additional exam requirements/recommendations for international students: Required—TOEFL (minimum score 79 iBT); Recommended—IELTS (minimum score 6.5). Electronic applications accepted. *Faculty research:* Children and families experiencing homelessness, team-based learning and diversity, impact of mentoring, photovoice and barriers to college, family directed structural therapy.

Northwest Nazarene University, Program in Social Work, Nampa, ID 83686-5897. Offers clinical mental health and addictions practice (MSW). *Accreditation:* CSWE. *Program availability:* Part-time-only, evening/weekend. *Degree requirements:* For master's, comprehensive exam, thesis or alternative. *Entrance requirements:* For master's, interview, letters of reference, degree from regionally-accredited college/university, written personal statement. Electronic applications accepted. *Expenses: Tuition:* Full-time $6744; part-time $3372 per credit. *Required fees:* $190; $190 per unit. $95 per semester. Tuition and fees vary according to course load, degree level and program. *Faculty research:* Test anxiety, trauma, statistics.

Nyack College, School of Social Work, Nyack, NY 10960. Offers clinical social work practice (MSW); leadership in organizations and communities (MSW). *Accreditation:* CSWE. *Program availability:* Part-time, evening/weekend. *Students:* 50 full-time (42 women), 38 part-time (30 women); includes 78 minority (48 Black or African American, non-Hispanic/Latino; 5 Asian, non-Hispanic/Latino; 25 Hispanic/Latino), 2 international. Average age 35. In 2018, 26 master's awarded. *Degree requirements:* For master's, field work. *Entrance requirements:* For master's, official transcripts, academic and professional references, personal statement, essay or case reflection. Additional exam requirements/recommendations for international students: Required—TOEFL (minimum score 550 paper-based; 80 iBT). *Application deadline:* Applications are processed on a rolling basis. Application fee: $45. Electronic applications accepted. *Expenses:* $800/credit. *Financial support:* Scholarships/grants available. Financial award applicants required to submit FAFSA. *Unit head:* Dr. Janet Furness, Director of MSW Program, 646-378-6169. *Application contact:* Dr. Janet Furness, Director of MSW Program, 646-378-6169.
Website: https://www.nyack.edu/msw

The Ohio State University, Graduate School, College of Social Work, Columbus, OH 43210. Offers MSW, PhD. *Accreditation:* CSWE (one or more programs are accredited). *Program availability:* Part-time. *Faculty:* 31. *Students:* 595 full-time (507 women), 110 part-time (88 women). Average age 29. In 2018, 266 master's, 8 doctorates awarded. *Degree requirements:* For master's, thesis optional; for doctorate, thesis/dissertation. *Entrance requirements:* For master's and doctorate, GRE. Additional exam requirements/recommendations for international students: Required—TOEFL (minimum score 550 paper-based; 79 iBT), Michigan English Language Assessment Battery (minimum score 82); Recommended—IELTS (minimum score 7). *Application deadline:* For fall admission, 12/13 priority date for domestic students, 11/30 priority date for international students; for summer admission, 4/1 for domestic students, 3/1 for international students. Applications are processed on a rolling basis. Application fee: $60 ($70 for international students). Electronic applications accepted. *Financial support:* Fellowships, research assistantships, teaching assistantships, Federal Work-Study, institutionally sponsored loans, and unspecified assistantships available. Support available to part-time students. *Unit head:* Dr. Tom Gregoire, Dean, 614-292-9426, E-mail: gregoire.5@osu.edu. *Application contact:* Graduate and Professional Admissions, 614-292-6031, Fax: 614-292-3656, E-mail: gpadmissions@osu.edu.
Website: http://csw.osu.edu/

The Ohio State University at Lima, Graduate Programs, Lima, OH 45804. Offers social work (MSW). *Program availability:* Part-time. Terminal master's awarded for partial completion of doctoral program. *Degree requirements:* For master's, comprehensive exam (for some programs), thesis (for some programs). *Entrance requirements:* For master's, GRE (in some cases), minimum GPA of 3.0. Additional exam requirements/recommendations for international students: Required—TOEFL (minimum score 550 paper-based, 79 iBT), IELTS (minimum score 7), or Michigan English Language Assessment Battery (minimum score 82). Electronic applications accepted.

The Ohio State University at Mansfield, Graduate Programs, Mansfield, OH 44906-1599. Offers education (MA); social work (MSW). *Program availability:* Part-time. *Students:* 2. *Degree requirements:* For master's, comprehensive exam (for some

Social Work

programs), thesis (for some programs). *Entrance requirements:* For master's, GRE, minimum GPA of 3.0. Additional exam requirements/recommendations for international students: Required—TOEFL (minimum 550 paper-based, 79 iBT), IELTS (minimum score 7) or Michigan English Language Assessment Battery (minimum score 82). *Application deadline:* For fall admission, 4/1 for domestic students, 3/1 for international students; for spring admission, 10/15 for domestic and international students. Applications are processed on a rolling basis. Application fee: $60 ($70 for international students). Electronic applications accepted. *Financial support:* Teaching assistantships with full tuition reimbursements, Federal Work-Study, and scholarships/grants available. Support available to part-time students. Financial award application deadline: 2/15; financial award applicants required to submit FAFSA. *Unit head:* Dr. Norman W. Jones, Dean and Director, 419-755-4222, E-mail: jones.2376@osu.edu. *Application contact:* Graduate and Professional Admissions, 614-292-9444, Fax: 614-292-3895, E-mail: gpadmissions@osu.edu.

The Ohio State University at Newark, Graduate Programs, Newark, OH 43055-1797. Offers education - teaching and learning (MA); social work (MSW). *Program availability:* Part-time. *Faculty:* 49. *Students:* 8 (5 women). Average age 37. Terminal master's awarded for partial completion of doctoral program. *Degree requirements:* For master's, comprehensive exam (for some programs), thesis (for some programs). *Entrance requirements:* For master's, GRE, minimum GPA of 3.0. Additional exam requirements/recommendations for international students: Required—TOEFL (minimum score 550 paper-based; 79 iBT), IELTS (minimum score 7), or Michigan English Language Assessment Battery (minimum score 82). *Application deadline:* For fall admission, 3/1 for domestic and international students. Applications are processed on a rolling basis. Application fee: $60 ($70 for international students). Electronic applications accepted. *Financial support:* Application deadline: 2/15. *Unit head:* Dr. William L. MacDonald, Dean and Director, 740-366-9333 Ext. 330, E-mail: macdonald.24@osu.edu. *Application contact:* Graduate and Professional Admissions, 614-292-9444, Fax: 614-292-3985, E-mail: gpadmissions@osu.edu.

Ohio University, Graduate College, College of Health Sciences and Professions, Department of Social and Public Health, Program in Social Work, Athens, OH 45701-2979. Offers MSW. *Accreditation:* CSWE. *Program availability:* Part-time. *Degree requirements:* For master's, fieldwork. *Entrance requirements:* For master's, GRE General Test or minimum GPA of 3.0, liberal arts background with coursework in human biology, statistics, and three social science areas; paid or volunteer work in human services. Additional exam requirements/recommendations for international students: Required—TOEFL (minimum score 620 paper-based; 105 iBT) or IELTS (minimum score 7.5). Electronic applications accepted. *Faculty research:* Violence, families, rural life.

Our Lady of the Lake University, Worden School of Social Service, San Antonio, TX 78207-4689. Offers social work (MSW, PhD). *Accreditation:* CSWE. *Program availability:* Part-time, evening/weekend, 100% online, blended/hybrid learning. *Faculty:* 11 full-time (8 women), 63 part-time/adjunct (49 women). *Students:* 787 full-time (724 women), 100 part-time (88 women); includes 567 minority (241 Black or African American, non-Hispanic/Latino; 7 American Indian or Alaska Native, non-Hispanic/Latino; 6 Asian, non-Hispanic/Latino; 291 Hispanic/Latino; 2 Native Hawaiian or other Pacific Islander, non-Hispanic/Latino; 20 Two or more races, non-Hispanic/Latino). Average age 35. 190 applicants, 90% accepted, 124 enrolled. In 2018, 335 master's awarded. *Entrance requirements:* For master's, official transcripts demonstrating minimum cumulative GPA of 2.5, 3 letters of recommendation, personal statement, current resume. Additional exam requirements/recommendations for international students: Required—TOEFL. *Application deadline:* For fall admission, 6/15 for domestic and international students; for spring admission, 11/15 for domestic and international students; for summer admission, 4/15 for domestic and international students. Applications are processed on a rolling basis. Application fee: $40 ($50 for international students). Electronic applications accepted. *Expenses: Tuition:* Full-time $16,326; part-time $907 per credit. *Financial support:* In 2018–19, 29 students received support, including 1 research assistantship (averaging $15,300 per year); teaching assistantships, Federal Work-Study, scholarships/grants, unspecified assistantships, and tuition discounts also available. Support available to part-time students. Financial award application deadline: 5/1; financial award applicants required to submit FAFSA. *Faculty research:* Acculturation, mindfulness, pedagogy, spirituality, child welfare. *Unit head:* Rebecca Gomez, Program Director, 210-434-6711 Ext. 5578, E-mail: rjgomez@ollusa.edu. *Application contact:* Office of Graduate Admissions, 210-431-3995, Fax: 210-431-3945, E-mail: gradadm@lake.ollusa.edu.
Website: http://www.ollusa.edu/s/1190/hybrid/default-hybrid-ollu.aspx?sid-1190&amp;gid-1&amp;pgid-7916

Pacific University, Program in Social Work, Forest Grove, OR 97116-1797. Offers MSW. *Accreditation:* CSWE.

Park University, School of Graduate and Professional Studies, Kansas City, MO 54105. Offers adult education (M Ed); business and government leadership (Graduate Certificate); business, government, and global society (MPA); communication and leadership (MA); creative and life writing (Graduate Certificate); disaster and emergency management (MPA, Graduate Certificate); educational leadership (M Ed); finance (MBA, Graduate Certificate); general business (MBA); global business (Graduate Certificate); healthcare administration (MHA); healthcare services management and leadership (Graduate Certificate); international business (MBA); language and literacy (M Ed), including English for speakers of other languages, special reading teacher/literacy coach; leadership of international healthcare organizations (Graduate Certificate); management information systems (MBA, Graduate Certificate); music performance (ADP, Graduate Certificate), including cello (MM, ADP), piano (MM, ADP), viola (MM, ADP), violin (MM, ADP); nonprofit and community services management (MPA); nonprofit leadership (Graduate Certificate); performance (MM), including cello (MM, ADP), piano (MM, ADP), viola (MM, ADP), violin (MM, ADP); public management (MPA); social work (MSW); teacher leadership (M Ed), including curriculum and assessment, instructional leader. *Program availability:* Part-time, evening/weekend, online learning. *Degree requirements:* For master's, comprehensive exam (for some programs), thesis (for some programs), internship (for some programs); exam (for some programs). *Entrance requirements:* For master's, GRE or GMAT (for some programs), teacher certification (for some M Ed programs), letters of recommendation, essay, resume (for some programs). Additional exam requirements/recommendations for international students: Required—TOEFL (minimum score 550 paper-based; 79 iBT), IELTS (minimum score 6). Electronic applications accepted.

Phillips Theological Seminary, Programs in Theology, Tulsa, OK 74116. Offers administration of church agencies (M Div); campus ministry (M Div); church-related social work (M Div); college and seminary teaching (M Div); global mission work (M Div); institutional chaplaincy (M Div); ministerial vocations in Christian education (M Div); ministry (D Min), including parish ministry, pastoral counseling, practices of ministry; ministry and culture (MAMC), including Christian education, congregational leadership, history and practice of Christian spirituality, theology, ethics, and culture; ministry of music (M Div); pastoral care and counseling (M Div); pastoral ministry (M Div); theological studies (MTS). *Accreditation:* ATS. *Program availability:* Part-time, online learning. *Degree requirements:* For master's, thesis (for some programs); for doctorate, thesis/dissertation. *Entrance requirements:* For master's, minimum GPA of 2.5; for

doctorate, M Div, minimum GPA of 3.0. *Faculty research:* Biblical studies, historical studies, theology and culture, practical theology, theology and film.

Pontifical Catholic University of Puerto Rico, College of Graduate Studies in Behavioral Science and Community Affairs, Program in Clinical Social Work, Ponce, PR 00717-0777. Offers MSW. *Accreditation:* CSWE. *Program availability:* Part-time, evening/weekend. *Entrance requirements:* For master's, EXADEP, 3 letters of recommendation, interview, minimum GPA of 2.75.

Portland State University, Graduate Studies, School of Social Work, Portland, OR 97207-0751. Offers social work (MSW); social work and social research (PhD). *Accreditation:* CSWE (one or more programs are accredited). *Program availability:* Part-time. *Degree requirements:* For master's, two 500-hour field placements; for doctorate, comprehensive exam, thesis/dissertation, residency. *Entrance requirements:* For master's, minimum GPA of 3.0 in upper-division course work or 2.75 overall, resume, 3 letters of reference, 3-4 page statement of purpose; for doctorate, GRE General Test, 4 references. Additional exam requirements/recommendations for international students: Required—TOEFL (minimum score 550 paper-based; 80 iBT). *Expenses:* Contact institution. *Faculty research:* Child welfare; child mental health; social welfare policies and services; work, family, and dependent care; adult mental health.

Quinnipiac University, School of Health Sciences, Program in Social Work, Hamden, CT 06518-1940. Offers MSW. *Accreditation:* CSWE. *Entrance requirements:* For master's, bachelor's degree with at least 20 semester credits in liberal arts and a course in statistics with minimum C grade; minimum GPA of 3.0. Electronic applications accepted. *Faculty research:* Older adult sexuality, social work practice in health settings, gerontology and social work, adolescent sexuality, prevention programs in social work practice, international social work, evidence-based treatments for children and families, organizational practice, inter-professional education, curriculum development in social work education and inter-professional practice, stress reduction approaches in clinical practice and professional education.

Radford University, College of Graduate Studies and Research, Program in Social Work, Radford, VA 24142. Offers MSW. *Accreditation:* CSWE. *Program availability:* Part-time. *Faculty:* 7 full-time (5 women), 12 part-time/adjunct (10 women). *Students:* 52 full-time (43 women), 60 part-time (55 women); includes 33 minority (26 Black or African American, non-Hispanic/Latino; 1 Asian, non-Hispanic/Latino; 2 Hispanic/Latino; 4 Two or more races, non-Hispanic/Latino). Average age 29. 70 applicants, 77% accepted, 41 enrolled. In 2018, 42 master's awarded. *Degree requirements:* For master's, comprehensive exam. *Entrance requirements:* For master's, minimum GPA of 2.75, 3.0 in last 60 hours of upper-division coursework; 3 letters of reference; personal essay; case study; previous experience in the field of human services; legal/military history form; resume; official transcripts. Additional exam requirements/recommendations for international students: Required—TOEFL (minimum score 550 paper-based; 79 iBT), IELTS (minimum score 6.5). *Application deadline:* For fall admission, 2/15 priority date for domestic students, 12/1 for international students; for spring admission, 7/1 for international students. Applications are processed on a rolling basis. Application fee: $50. Electronic applications accepted. *Expenses: Tuition, area resident:* Full-time $8915; part-time $371 per credit hour. Tuition, state resident: full-time $8915; part-time $371 per credit hour. Tuition, nonresident: full-time $17,441. *Required fees:* $3288; $138 per credit hour. *Financial support:* In 2018–19, 10 students received support, including 1 research assistantship (averaging $7,500 per year), 3 teaching assistantships (averaging $7,000 per year); career-related internships or fieldwork, scholarships/grants, and unspecified assistantships also available. Support available to part-time students. Financial award application deadline: 3/1; financial award applicants required to submit FAFSA. *Unit head:* Deneen Evans, MSW Program Coordinator, 540-831-7681, E-mail: devans18@radford.edu. *Application contact:* Deneen Evans, MSW Program Coordinator, 540-831-7681, E-mail: devans18@radford.edu.
Website: http://www.radford.edu/content/grad/home/academics/graduate-programs/msw.html

Ramapo College of New Jersey, Master of Social Work Program, Mahwah, NJ 07430-1680. Offers MSW. *Accreditation:* CSWE. *Program availability:* Part-time. *Faculty:* 4 full-time (2 women), 11 part-time/adjunct (all women). *Students:* 86 full-time (74 women), 24 part-time (20 women); includes 34 minority (12 Black or African American, non-Hispanic/Latino; 4 Asian, non-Hispanic/Latino; 18 Hispanic/Latino). Average age 30. 224 applicants, 61% accepted, 74 enrolled. In 2018, 56 master's awarded. *Degree requirements:* For master's, The Foundation Year is offered in the Fall requiring 32 credits and 600 field hours for completion. The Second Year requires 32 credits and 600 field hours for completion. Course requirements include 9 credits of electives, including a cluster that prepares you for the License in Clinical Alcohol and Drug Counseling (LCADC) in the State of NJ. *Entrance requirements:* For master's, official transcript of baccalaureate degree from accredited institution with minimum recommended GPA of 3.0; personal statement; 2 letters of recommendation; resume; 3-5 page narrative highlighting personal and professional accomplishments, values, and strengths. Additional exam requirements/recommendations for international students: Required—TOEFL (minimum score 550 paper-based; 79 iBT); Recommended—IELTS (minimum score 6). *Application deadline:* For fall admission, 3/1 for domestic and international students. Applications are processed on a rolling basis. Application fee: $65. Electronic applications accepted. *Expenses:* Tuition, state resident: part-time $706.15 per credit. Tuition, nonresident: part-time $706.15 per credit. *Required fees:* $57.50 per credit. *Financial support:* In 2018–19, 4 students received support. Scholarships/grants available. Financial award application deadline: 3/1; financial award applicants required to submit FAFSA. *Faculty research:* Substance abuse, narrative therapy, military families, child welfare. *Unit head:* Dr. Kathleen Ray, Director of the Master of Social Work program, 201-684-7814, Fax: 201-684-7257, E-mail: kray1@ramapo.edu. *Application contact:* Joyce Wilson, Master of Social Work Coordinator, 201-684-7721, Fax: 201-684-7257, E-mail: jwilson@ramapo.edu.
Website: http://www.ramapo.edu/msw/

Rhode Island College, School of Graduate Studies, School of Social Work, Providence, RI 02908-1991. Offers MSW. *Accreditation:* CSWE. *Program availability:* Part-time. *Faculty:* 15 full-time (9 women), 22 part-time/adjunct (21 women). *Students:* 126 full-time (105 women), 135 part-time (108 women); includes 85 minority (28 Black or African American, non-Hispanic/Latino; 1 American Indian or Alaska Native, non-Hispanic/Latino; 4 Asian, non-Hispanic/Latino; 50 Hispanic/Latino; 2 Two or more races, non-Hispanic/Latino). Average age 31. In 2018, 97 master's awarded. *Entrance requirements:* For master's, official transcripts, personal statement, 3 letters of recommendation. Additional exam requirements/recommendations for international students: Required—TOEFL (minimum score 550 paper-based; 80 iBT). *Application deadline:* For fall admission, 2/1 for domestic students. Applications are processed on a rolling basis. Application fee: $50. Electronic applications accepted. *Expenses:* Contact institution. *Financial support:* Career-related internships or fieldwork, Federal Work-Study, scholarships/grants, health care benefits, and unspecified assistantships available. Support available to part-time students. Financial award application deadline: 5/15; financial award applicants required to submit FAFSA. *Unit head:* Dr. Jayashree Nimmagadda, Interim Dean, 401-456-8042, E-mail: jnimmagadda@ric.edu. *Application contact:* Dr. Jayashree Nimmagadda, Interim Dean, 401-456-8042, E-mail: jnimmagadda@ric.edu.
Website: http://www.ric.edu/socialWork/Pages/default.aspx

Roberts Wesleyan College, Department of Social Work, Rochester, NY 14624-1997. Offers child and family practice (MSW); mental health practice (MSW). *Accreditation:* CSWE. *Entrance requirements:* For master's, minimum GPA of 2.75. *Faculty research:* Religion and social work, family studies, values and ethics.

Rutgers University–New Brunswick, School of Social Work, New Brunswick, NJ 08901. Offers MSW, PhD, JD/MSW, M Div/MSW. *Accreditation:* CSWE (one or more programs are accredited). *Program availability:* Part-time. *Degree requirements:* For doctorate, comprehensive exam, thesis/dissertation. *Entrance requirements:* For doctorate, GRE General Test. Additional exam requirements/recommendations for international students: Required—TOEFL. Electronic applications accepted. *Faculty research:* Family theory, adolescent development, child and adolescent mental health delivery systems, poverty and employment policy.

Sacred Heart University, Graduate Programs, College of Arts and Sciences, Department of Social Work, Fairfield, CT 06825. Offers MSW. *Entrance requirements:* Additional exam requirements/recommendations for international students: Required—TOEFL (minimum iBT score of 80), TWE, or IELTS (6.5).

Saginaw Valley State University, College of Health and Human Services, Program in Social Work, University Center, MI 48710. Offers MSW. *Program availability:* Part-time. *Students:* 69 full-time (55 women), 15 part-time (14 women); includes 14 minority (7 Black or African American, non-Hispanic/Latino; 1 Asian, non-Hispanic/Latino; 4 Hispanic/Latino; 2 Two or more races, non-Hispanic/Latino). Average age 29. 38 applicants, 92% accepted, 21 enrolled. *Entrance requirements:* For master's, minimum preferred GPA of 3.0 in most recent 60 credits. Additional exam requirements/recommendations for international students: Required—TOEFL (minimum score 79 iBT), IELTS (minimum score 6.5). *Application deadline:* For fall admission, 7/1 for international students; for winter admission, 11/1 for international students. Applications are processed on a rolling basis. Application fee: $30 ($90 for international students). Electronic applications accepted. *Expenses: Tuition, area resident:* Full-time $6225; part-time $623 per credit hour. Tuition, state resident: full-time $6225; part-time $623 per credit hour. Tuition, nonresident: full-time $14,215; part-time $1185 per credit hour. *International tuition:* $14,215 full-time. *Required fees:* $263; $14.60 per credit hour. Tuition and fees vary according to degree level. *Financial support:* Career-related internships or fieldwork, Federal Work-Study, and scholarships/grants available. Support available to part-time students. Financial award application deadline: 4/1; financial award applicants required to submit FAFSA. *Unit head:* Lucy Mercier, Director, 989-964-4077, E-mail: mercier@svsu.edu. *Application contact:* Jenna Briggs, Director, Graduate and International Admissions, 989-964-6096, Fax: 989-964-2788, E-mail: gradadm@svsu.edu.
Website: http://svsu.edu/socialworkmsw/

St. Ambrose University, College of Health and Human Services, Program in Social Work, Davenport, IA 52803-2898. Offers MSW. *Accreditation:* CSWE. *Program availability:* Part-time, evening/weekend. *Degree requirements:* For master's, comprehensive exam (for some programs), thesis or alternative, integration projects. *Entrance requirements:* For master's, minimum GPA of 3.0, course work in statistics, bachelor's degree in liberal arts. Additional exam requirements/recommendations for international students: Required—TOEFL. Electronic applications accepted. *Faculty research:* Social work practice, cults/sects, family therapy, developmental disabilities.

St. Catherine University, Graduate Programs, Program in Social Work, St. Paul, MN 55105. Offers MSW, DSW. Program offered jointly with University of St. Thomas. *Accreditation:* CSWE. *Program availability:* Part-time, evening/weekend. *Degree requirements:* For master's, clinical research paper. *Entrance requirements:* For master's, minimum GPA of 3.0. Additional exam requirements/recommendations for international students: Required—Michigan English Language Assessment Battery or TOEFL (minimum score 600 paper-based; 100 iBT). *Expenses:* Contact institution.

St. Cloud State University, School of Graduate Studies, School of Health and Human Services, Department of Social Work, St. Cloud, MN 56301-4498. Offers MSW. *Accreditation:* CSWE. *Program availability:* Part-time. *Entrance requirements:* For master's, minimum GPA of 3.0.

Saint Leo University, Graduate Studies in Social Work, Saint Leo, FL 33574-6665. Offers advanced clinical practice (MSW). *Accreditation:* CSWE. *Program availability:* Online only, blended/hybrid learning. *Faculty:* 9 full-time (7 women), 14 part-time/adjunct (13 women). *Students:* 71 full-time (63 women), 205 part-time (174 women); includes 126 minority (91 Black or African American, non-Hispanic/Latino; 33 Hispanic/Latino; 2 Two or more races, non-Hispanic/Latino). Average age 36. 201 applicants, 64% accepted, 100 enrolled. In 2018, 77 master's awarded. *Entrance requirements:* For master's, official transcripts, current resume, 3 professional recommendations, personal statement. Additional exam requirements/recommendations for international students: Required—TOEFL (minimum score 550 paper-based; 78 iBT). *Application deadline:* For fall admission, 6/1 for domestic and international students. Application fee: $80. Electronic applications accepted. *Expenses:* Master's $495 per credit. *Financial support:* In 2018–19, 4 students received support. Scholarships/grants, unspecified assistantships, and tuition remission for Saint Leo employees and their dependents available. Financial award application deadline: 3/1. *Faculty research:* Juvenile crime and violence, trauma, distance education, animal-assisted therapy, sibling caregivers of families with persons with developmental disabilities, trauma informed care, animal assisted therapy, art therapy, veterans services, aging services. *Unit head:* Dr. Courtney Wiest, Director of Graduate Studies in Social Work, 352-588-8015, Fax: 352-588-8289. *Application contact:* Mark Russum, Assistant Vice President, Enrollment, 800-707-8846, Fax: 352-588-7873, E-mail: grad.admissions@saintleo.edu.
Website: https://www.saintleo.edu/social-work-master-three-year-program-degree

Saint Louis University, Graduate Programs, College for Public Health and Social Justice, School of Social Work, St. Louis, MO 63103. Offers applied behavior analysis (MS); social work (MSW, PhD). *Accreditation:* CSWE. *Program availability:* Part-time. *Entrance requirements:* For master's, minimum GPA of 3.0, letters of recommendation. Additional exam requirements/recommendations for international students: Required—TOEFL (minimum score 550 paper-based). *Expenses:* Contact institution. *Faculty research:* Gerontology, mental health issues, child welfare (especially abuse and neglect), social justice, and peace making, homelessness.

Salem State University, School of Graduate Studies, Program in Social Work, Salem, MA 01970-5353. Offers MSW. *Accreditation:* CSWE. *Program availability:* Part-time, evening/weekend. *Entrance requirements:* For master's, GRE, MAT. Additional exam requirements/recommendations for international students: Required—TOEFL (minimum score 550 paper-based; 80 iBT) or IELTS (minimum score 5.5).

Salisbury University, Department of Social Work, Salisbury, MD 21801-6837. Offers MSW. *Accreditation:* CSWE. *Program availability:* Part-time, evening/weekend, 100% online, blended/hybrid learning. *Faculty:* 24 full-time (20 women), 42 part-time/adjunct (33 women). *Students:* 309 full-time (280 women), 61 part-time (56 women); includes 95 minority (70 Black or African American, non-Hispanic/Latino; 1 American Indian or Alaska Native, non-Hispanic/Latino; 2 Asian, non-Hispanic/Latino; 9 Hispanic/Latino; 2 Native Hawaiian or other Pacific Islander, non-Hispanic/Latino; 11 Two or more races, non-Hispanic/Latino), 1 international. Average age 32. 337 applicants, 71% accepted, 169 enrolled. In 2018, 169 master's awarded. *Entrance requirements:* For master's, transcripts from colleges and universities attended; resume; detailed statement; letters of recommendation. Additional exam requirements/recommendations for international students: Required—TOEFL (minimum score 550 paper-based; 79 iBT), IELTS (minimum score 6.5). *Application deadline:* For fall admission, 1/15 priority date for domestic and international students; for summer admission, 1/15 priority date for domestic and international students. Applications are processed on a rolling basis. Application fee: $65. Electronic applications accepted. *Expenses:* Resident - $412 per credit hour; Non-resident - $746 per credit hour; Fees - $108; Online - $765 per credit hour and no fees. *Financial support:* In 2018–19, 22 students received support, including 2 research assistantships with full tuition reimbursements available (averaging $2,000 per year), 2 teaching assistantships with full tuition reimbursements available (averaging $8,000 per year); career-related internships or fieldwork and scholarships/grants also available. Support available to part-time students. Financial award application deadline: 3/1; financial award applicants required to submit FAFSA. *Faculty research:* Technology and social work; immigration and formulation of national identity; sexuality social justice; unaccompanied refugee minors; homelessness in rural communities. *Unit head:* Dr. Mary Hylton, Graduate Program Director, 410-677-5346, E-mail: mehylton@salisbury.edu. *Application contact:* Lindsey Shockley, Admissions Program Specialist, 410-677-5363, E-mail: lrshockley@salisbury.edu.
Website: https://www.salisbury.edu/explore-academics/programs/graduate-degree-programs/social-work-master/

Samford University, School of Public Health, Birmingham, AL 35229. Offers health informatics (MSHI); healthcare administration (MHA); nutrition (MS); public health (MPH); social work (MSW). *Accreditation:* CSWE. *Program availability:* Part-time, online only, 100% online. *Faculty:* 18 full-time (11 women), 1 (woman) part-time/adjunct. *Students:* 86 full-time (79 women), 6 part-time (all women); includes 18 minority (15 Black or African American, non-Hispanic/Latino; 1 Hispanic/Latino; 2 Two or more races, non-Hispanic/Latino). Average age 28. 93 applicants, 73% accepted, 30 enrolled. In 2018, 59 master's awarded. *Degree requirements:* For master's, capstone course. *Entrance requirements:* For master's, GRE, MAT, recommendations, resume, personal statement, transcripts, application. Additional exam requirements/recommendations for international students: Required—TOEFL (minimum score 590 paper-based; 90 iBT), IELTS (minimum score 6.5). *Application deadline:* For fall admission, 10/1 for domestic students; for winter admission, 12/1 for domestic students; for spring admission, 5/1 for domestic students. Applications are processed on a rolling basis. Application fee: $75. Electronic applications accepted. *Expenses:* $862 per credit hour. *Financial support:* In 2018–19, 39 students received support. Scholarships/grants available. Financial award application deadline: 5/1; financial award applicants required to submit FAFSA. *Faculty research:* Chronic kidney disease, disasters and vulnerable populations, children's health, obesity, metabolism and diabetes, health policy and health care delivery. *Unit head:* Dr. Keith Elder, Ph.D., Dean, School of Public Health, 205-726-4655, E-mail: kelder@samford.edu. *Application contact:* Dr. Marian Carter, Ed.D, Assistant Dean of Enrollment Management and Student Services, 205-726-2611, E-mail: mwcarter@samford.edu.
Website: http://www.samford.edu/publichealth

San Diego State University, Graduate and Research Affairs, College of Health and Human Services, School of Social Work, San Diego, CA 92182. Offers MSW, JD/MSW, MSW/MPH. JD/MSW offered jointly with California Western School of Law. *Accreditation:* CSWE. *Program availability:* Part-time. *Degree requirements:* For master's, comprehensive exam, thesis optional. *Entrance requirements:* For master's, GRE General Test. Additional exam requirements/recommendations for international students: Required—TOEFL. Electronic applications accepted. *Faculty research:* Child maltreatment, substance abuse, neighborhood studies, child welfare.

San Francisco State University, Division of Graduate Studies, College of Health and Social Sciences, School of Social Work, San Francisco, CA 94132-1722. Offers MSW. *Accreditation:* CSWE. *Program availability:* Part-time. *Application deadline:* Applications are processed on a rolling basis. *Financial support:* Career-related internships or fieldwork and Federal Work-Study available. *Unit head:* Dr. Jerald Shapiro, Director, 415-338-2716, Fax: 415-338-0591, E-mail: jshap@sfsu.edu. *Application contact:* Dr. Jerald Shapiro, Director, 415-338-2716, Fax: 415-338-0591, E-mail: jshap@sfsu.edu.
Website: http://socwork.sfsu.edu/

Savannah State University, Master of Social Work Program, Savannah, GA 31404. Offers MSW. *Accreditation:* CSWE. *Degree requirements:* For master's, 1000-hour field practicum, seminar course for each semester in field placement. *Entrance requirements:* For master's, GRE General Test (minimum score of 3.0 in analytical writing portion), minimum GPA of 2.8, degree from accredited institution with liberal arts courses, official transcripts, directed essay, 3 letters of recommendation. Additional exam requirements/recommendations for international students: Required—TOEFL. *Expenses:* Contact institution. *Faculty research:* Clinical and administrative social work.

Seattle University, College of Arts and Sciences, Program in Social Work, Seattle, WA 98122-1090. Offers MSW. *Faculty:* 9 full-time (6 women), 5 part-time/adjunct (4 women). *Students:* 42 full-time (35 women); includes 9 minority (3 Black or African American, non-Hispanic/Latino; 1 American Indian or Alaska Native, non-Hispanic/Latino; 4 Asian, non-Hispanic/Latino; 1 Hispanic/Latino). Average age 28. 72 applicants, 61% accepted, 14 enrolled. In 2018, 26 master's awarded. *Application deadline:* For fall admission, 1/20 priority date for domestic students. *Financial support:* In 2018–19, 30 students received support. *Unit head:* Dr. Hye-Kyung Kang, Director, 206-296-5558, E-mail: kangh@seattleu.edu. *Application contact:* Janet Shandley, Director of Graduate Admissions, 206-296-5900, Fax: 206-298-5656, E-mail: grad_admissions@seattleu.edu.
Website: http://www.seattleu.edu/artsci/msw/

Seton Hall University, College of Arts and Sciences, Department of Sociology, Anthropology and Social Work, South Orange, NJ 07079-2697. Offers social work (MSW). *Accreditation:* CSWE.

Shippensburg University of Pennsylvania, School of Graduate Studies, College of Education and Human Services, Department of Social Work and Gerontology, Shippensburg, PA 17257-2299. Offers social work (MSW). *Program availability:* Part-time, evening/weekend, blended/hybrid learning. *Faculty:* 7 full-time (1 woman), 4 part-time/adjunct (2 women). *Students:* 35 full-time (31 women), 36 part-time (31 women); includes 13 minority (6 Black or African American, non-Hispanic/Latino; 4 Hispanic/Latino; 3 Two or more races, non-Hispanic/Latino), 1 international. Average age 30. 93 applicants, 62% accepted, 42 enrolled. In 2018, 27 master's awarded. *Degree requirements:* For master's, thesis, field practicum. *Entrance requirements:* For master's, GRE or MAT (if GPA is below 2.8), 3 professional references with minimum of one from faculty and one from current or recent agency employer or supervisor; current resume; written personal statement; course work in human biology, economics, government/political science, psychology, sociology/anthropology and statistics. Additional exam requirements/recommendations for international students: Required—TOEFL (minimum score 550 paper-based; 68 iBT), IELTS (minimum score 6), TOEFL (minimum score 550 paper-based, 68 iBT) or IELTS (minimum score 6). *Application deadline:* For fall admission, 4/30 for international students; for spring admission, 9/30 for international students. Applications are processed on a rolling basis. Application fee: $45. Electronic applications accepted. *Expenses:* Tuition, state resident: part-time $516 per credit. Tuition, nonresident: part-time $750 per credit. *Required fees:* $149 per

credit. *Financial support:* In 2018–19, 14 students received support. Career-related internships or fieldwork, scholarships/grants, unspecified assistantships, and resident hall director and student payroll positions available. Support available to part-time students. Financial award application deadline: 3/1; financial award applicants required to submit FAFSA. *Unit head:* Dr. Marita N. Flagler, Co-Director, MU-SU Master of Social Work Program, 717-477-1276, Fax: 717-477-4051, E-mail: mnflagler@ship.edu. *Application contact:* Maya T. Mapp, Director of Admissions, 717-477-1231, Fax: 717-477-4016, E-mail: mtmapp@ship.edu.
Website: http://www.ship.edu/social_work/

Simmons University, College of Social Sciences, Policy, and Practice, Boston, MA 02115. Offers MSW, PhD, MSW/MBA. *Accreditation:* CSWE (one or more programs are accredited). *Program availability:* Part-time, 100% online, blended/hybrid learning. *Faculty:* 50 full-time (40 women), 246 part-time/adjunct (218 women). *Students:* 805 full-time (689 women), 663 part-time (566 women); includes 412 minority (205 Black or African American, non-Hispanic/Latino; 1 American Indian or Alaska Native, non-Hispanic/Latino; 40 Asian, non-Hispanic/Latino; 125 Hispanic/Latino; 2 Native Hawaiian or other Pacific Islander, non-Hispanic/Latino; 39 Two or more races, non-Hispanic/Latino), 6 international. Average age 31. 1,382 applicants, 71% accepted, 457 enrolled. In 2018, 597 master's, 4 doctorates awarded. Terminal master's awarded for partial completion of doctoral program. *Degree requirements:* For master's, thesis (for some programs); for doctorate, comprehensive exam (for some programs), thesis/dissertation (for some programs). *Entrance requirements:* For master's, GRE, MAT, Massachusetts Tests for Education Licensure (for different programs), minimum grade of B in introductory statistics course within five years prior to entering program, resume, transcripts, three letters of recommendation, personal statement; for doctorate, GRE, BCBA Analyst Exam. Additional exam requirements/recommendations for international students: Required—TOEFL (minimum score 600 paper-based; 100 iBT). *Application deadline:* For fall admission, 8/1 for domestic students; for spring admission, 12/15 for domestic students; for summer admission, 5/1 for domestic students. Applications are processed on a rolling basis. Application fee: $35. Electronic applications accepted. *Expenses:* $68,900 (for social work), $65,025 (for public health), $39,060 (for public policy). *Financial support:* In 2018–19, 14 students received support, including 12 fellowships (averaging $2,400 per year), 2 teaching assistantships (averaging $2,000 per year); scholarships/grants also available. Support available to part-time students. Financial award applicants required to submit FAFSA. *Faculty research:* Social work, public health, education, public policy. *Unit head:* Dr. Stephanie Berzin, Dean, 617-521-2759, E-mail: stephanie.berzin@simmons.edu. *Application contact:* Carlos D. Frontado, Director of Admissions, 617-521-3920, Fax: 617-521-3980, E-mail: ssw@simmons.edu.
Website: https://www.simmons.edu/academics/colleges-schools-departments/csspp

Smith College, School for Social Work, Northampton, MA 01063. Offers clinical social work (MSW, PhD). *Accreditation:* CSWE (one or more programs are accredited). *Faculty:* 15 full-time (11 women), 94 part-time/adjunct (68 women). *Students:* 273 full-time (245 women), 50 part-time (41 women); includes 97 minority (31 Black or African American, non-Hispanic/Latino; 2 American Indian or Alaska Native, non-Hispanic/Latino; 22 Asian, non-Hispanic/Latino; 27 Hispanic/Latino; 15 Two or more races, non-Hispanic/Latino), 8 international. Average age 33. 398 applicants, 53% accepted, 114 enrolled. In 2018, 132 master's, 6 doctorates awarded. *Degree requirements:* For doctorate, thesis/dissertation. *Entrance requirements:* For doctorate, MAT or GRE. Additional exam requirements/recommendations for international students: Required—TOEFL (minimum score 94 IBT) or IELTS (7.0). *Application deadline:* For fall admission, 2/21 for domestic students, 2/15 for international students. Applications are processed on a rolling basis. Application fee: $60. Electronic applications accepted. *Expenses:* $30,460 (for MSW), $32,275 (for PhD). *Financial support:* In 2018–19, 265 students received support. Research assistantships, career-related internships or fieldwork, and scholarships/grants available. Financial award application deadline: 3/1; financial award applicants required to submit FAFSA. *Faculty research:* Social work practice, social work research, prevention and intervention for communities experiencing trauma, human behavior in the social environment, increasing resilient contexts. *Unit head:* Dr. Marianne Yoshioka, Dean/Professor, 413-585-7977, E-mail: myoshioka@smith.edu. *Application contact:* Irene Rodriguez Martin, Associate Dean, Graduate Enrollment and Student Services, 413-585-7960, Fax: 413-585-7994, E-mail: imartin@smith.edu.
Website: http://www.smith.edu/ssw/

Southeastern University, College of Behavioral and Social Sciences, Lakeland, FL 33801-6099. Offers human services (MA); international community development (MA); marriage and family counseling (MS); professional counseling (MS); school counseling (MS); social work (MSW). *Program availability:* Evening/weekend. Electronic applications accepted.

Southern Adventist University, School of Social Work, Collegedale, TN 37315-0370. Offers mental health practice in social work (MSW). *Accreditation:* CSWE. *Program availability:* Part-time, evening/weekend. *Faculty:* 8 full-time (7 women). *Students:* 53 full-time (46 women), 23 part-time (18 women); includes 34 minority (21 Black or African American, non-Hispanic/Latino; 1 Asian, non-Hispanic/Latino; 11 Hispanic/Latino; 1 Two or more races, non-Hispanic/Latino). Average age 37. 60 applicants, 60% accepted, 31 enrolled. In 2018, 34 master's awarded. *Degree requirements:* For master's, defend portfolio capstone. *Entrance requirements:* Additional exam requirements/recommendations for international students: Required—TOEFL (minimum score 100 iBT). *Application deadline:* For fall admission, 7/1 for domestic students, 5/1 for international students; for winter admission, 11/1 for domestic students, 9/1 for international students. Applications are processed on a rolling basis. Application fee: $40. Electronic applications accepted. *Financial support:* Unspecified assistantships and Employee Sponsored available. Financial award application deadline: 8/1; financial award applicants required to submit FAFSA. *Faculty research:* Trauma, intersectionality of poverty, racism and sexism, and adverse childhood experiences, and international and domestic community development. *Total annual research expenditures:* $30,000. *Unit head:* Kristie Wilder, JD, Dean, 423-236-2206, E-mail: kwilder@southern.edu. *Application contact:* Tricia Foster, Program Manager, 423-236-2629, Fax: 423-236-1768, E-mail: gradstudies@southern.edu.
Website: https://www.southern.edu/academics/socialwork.html

Southern Connecticut State University, School of Graduate Studies, School of Health and Human Services, Department of Social Work, New Haven, CT 06515-1355. Offers MSW. *Accreditation:* CSWE. *Program availability:* Part-time, evening/weekend. *Degree requirements:* For master's, thesis. *Entrance requirements:* For master's, minimum undergraduate QPA of 3.0 in graduate major field, interview. Electronic applications accepted. *Faculty research:* Social work practice; social service development; services for women, the aging, children, and families in educational and health care systems.

Southern Illinois University Carbondale, Graduate School, College of Education and Human Services, School of Social Work, Carbondale, IL 62901-4701. Offers MSW, JD/MSW. *Accreditation:* CSWE. *Entrance requirements:* For master's, GRE General Test, minimum GPA of 2.7. Additional exam requirements/recommendations for international students: Required—TOEFL. *Faculty research:* Service delivery systems, comparative race relations, advocacy research, gerontology, child welfare and health.

Southern Illinois University Edwardsville, Graduate School, College of Arts and Sciences, Department of Social Work, Edwardsville, IL 62026. Offers school social work (MSW); social work (MSW). *Accreditation:* CSWE. *Program availability:* Part-time, evening/weekend. *Degree requirements:* For master's, final exam, capstone course. *Entrance requirements:* Additional exam requirements/recommendations for international students: Required—TOEFL (minimum score 550 paper-based; 79 iBT), IELTS (minimum score 6.5). Electronic applications accepted.

Southern University at New Orleans, School of Graduate Studies, New Orleans, LA 70126-1009. Offers criminal justice (MA); management information systems (MS); museum studies (MA); social work (MSW). *Accreditation:* CSWE. *Program availability:* Part-time, evening/weekend. *Degree requirements:* For master's, thesis. *Entrance requirements:* For master's, GRE/GMAT. Additional exam requirements/recommendations for international students: Required—TOEFL.

Spalding University, Graduate Studies, Kosair College of Health and Natural Sciences, School of Social Work, Louisville, KY 40203-2188. Offers MSW. *Accreditation:* CSWE. *Program availability:* Evening/weekend. *Degree requirements:* For master's, thesis or alternative. *Entrance requirements:* For master's, transcripts, letters of recommendation, personal essay, personal interview. Additional exam requirements/recommendations for international students: Required—TOEFL (minimum score 535 paper-based). Electronic applications accepted. *Faculty research:* Addictions, spirituality, feminist studies, mental retardation, action research.

Spring Arbor University, School of Human Services, Spring Arbor, MI 49283-9799. Offers counseling (MAC); family studies (MAFS); nursing (MSN); social work (MSW). *Program availability:* Part-time, evening/weekend, online learning. *Entrance requirements:* For master's, bachelor's degree from regionally-accredited college or university, minimum GPA of 3.0 for at least the last two years of the bachelor's degree, at least two recommendations from professional/academic individuals. Additional exam requirements/recommendations for international students: Required—TOEFL (minimum score 600 paper-based). Electronic applications accepted.

Springfield College, Graduate Programs, School of Social Work, Springfield, MA 01108. Offers advanced practice with children and adolescents (Post-Master's Certificate); social work (MSW); JD/MSW. *Accreditation:* CSWE. *Program availability:* Part-time, evening/weekend. *Degree requirements:* For master's, comprehensive exam. *Entrance requirements:* Additional exam requirements/recommendations for international students: Required—TOEFL (minimum score 550 paper-based); Recommended—IELTS (minimum score 7). Electronic applications accepted. *Faculty research:* Children and families, health and mental health, school social work, gerontology, international social work.

Stephen F. Austin State University, Graduate School, College of Liberal and Applied Arts, School of Social Work, Nacogdoches, TX 75962. Offers MSW. *Accreditation:* CSWE. *Degree requirements:* For master's, comprehensive exam, thesis optional. *Entrance requirements:* For master's, GRE General Test, interview. Additional exam requirements/recommendations for international students: Required—TOEFL (minimum score 550 paper-based).

Stockton University, Office of Graduate Studies, Program in Social Work, Galloway, NJ 08205-9441. Offers MSW. *Accreditation:* CSWE. *Program availability:* Evening/weekend. *Faculty:* 7 full-time (5 women), 1 (woman) part-time/adjunct. *Students:* 83 full-time (72 women), 10 part-time (8 women); includes 45 minority (22 Black or African American, non-Hispanic/Latino; 2 Asian, non-Hispanic/Latino; 21 Hispanic/Latino). Average age 32. 138 applicants, 75% accepted, 65 enrolled. In 2018, 52 master's awarded. *Entrance requirements:* Additional exam requirements/recommendations for international students: Required—TOEFL. *Application deadline:* For fall admission, 2/1 for domestic and international students. Applications are processed on a rolling basis. Application fee: $50. Electronic applications accepted. *Expenses:* Contact institution. *Financial support:* Fellowships, research assistantships, career-related internships or fieldwork, Federal Work-Study, scholarships/grants, and unspecified assistantships available. Financial award application deadline: 3/1; financial award applicants required to submit FAFSA. *Unit head:* Dr. Diane Falk, Program Director, 609-626-3640, E-mail: gradschool@stockton.edu. *Application contact:* Tara Williams, Assistant Director of Graduate Enrollment Management, 609-626-3640, Fax: 609-626-6050, E-mail: gradschool@stockton.edu.
Website: http://www.stockton.edu/grad

Stony Brook University, State University of New York, Stony Brook Medicine, School of Social Welfare, Doctoral Program in Social Welfare, Stony Brook, NY 11794. Offers PhD. *Faculty:* 17 full-time (11 women), 45 part-time/adjunct (33 women). *Students:* 9 full-time (7 women), 9 part-time (7 women); includes 4 minority (3 Black or African American, non-Hispanic/Latino; 1 Asian, non-Hispanic/Latino), 1 international. Average age 30. In 2018, 4 doctorates awarded. *Entrance requirements:* For doctorate, GRE, three letters of reference, personal statement, writing sample. Additional exam requirements/recommendations for international students: Required—TOEFL. *Application deadline:* For fall admission, 1/15 for domestic students; for spring admission, 10/1 for domestic students. Application fee: $100. *Expenses:* Contact institution. *Financial support:* Fellowships and teaching assistantships available. Financial award application deadline: 2/1. *Faculty research:* Social welfare, social work, rape or sexual abuse, child welfare, social justice. *Unit head:* Dr. Jacqueline B. Mondros, Dean and Assistant Vice President for Social Determinants of Health, 631-444-2139, E-mail: jacqueline.mondros@stonybrook.edu. *Application contact:* Jamie Weissbach, Staff Assistant, 631-444-3146, Fax: 631-444-7565, E-mail: jamie.weissbach@stonybrook.edu.
Website: http://socialwelfare.stonybrookmedicine.edu/

Stony Brook University, State University of New York, Stony Brook Medicine, School of Social Welfare, Master's Program in Social Work, Stony Brook, NY 11794. Offers MSW. *Accreditation:* CSWE. *Faculty:* 17 full-time (11 women), 45 part-time/adjunct (33 women). *Students:* 437 full-time (366 women), 66 part-time (55 women); includes 204 minority (74 Black or African American, non-Hispanic/Latino; 15 Asian, non-Hispanic/Latino; 106 Hispanic/Latino; 1 Native Hawaiian or other Pacific Islander, non-Hispanic/Latino; 8 Two or more races, non-Hispanic/Latino), 1 international. Average age 30. 420 applicants, 92% accepted, 267 enrolled. In 2018, 238 master's awarded. *Entrance requirements:* For master's, interview, minimum cumulative GPA of 2.5. Additional exam requirements/recommendations for international students: Required—TOEFL. *Application deadline:* For fall admission, 3/1 priority date for domestic students. Application fee: $100. *Expenses:* Contact institution. *Financial support:* Teaching assistantships available. Financial award application deadline: 3/1. *Faculty research:* Social welfare, social work, rape or sexual abuse, child welfare, social justice. *Unit head:* Dr. Jacqueline B. Mondros, Dean and Assistant Vice President for Social Determinants of Health, 631-444-2139, E-mail: jacqueline.mondros@stonybrook.edu. *Application contact:* Dr. Sunday F. Coward, Assistant Dean for Academic Services, 631-444-3154, Fax: 631-444-7565, E-mail: sunday.coward@stonybrook.edu.
Website: http://socialwelfare.stonybrookmedicine.edu/

Syracuse University, David B. Falk College of Sport and Human Dynamics, Dual Master's Program in Social Work and Marriage and Family Therapy (MSW/MA), Syracuse, NY 13244. Offers MSW/MA. *Accreditation:* AAMFT/COAMFTE. *Entrance requirements:* Additional exam requirements/recommendations for international students: Required—TOEFL or IELTS. *Application deadline:* For fall admission, 2/15

priority date for domestic and international students; for summer admission, 1/15 priority date for domestic students, 1/15 for international students. Application fee: $75. Electronic applications accepted. *Financial support:* Fellowships, research assistantships, teaching assistantships, career-related internships or fieldwork, and scholarships/grants available. Financial award application deadline: 1/1. *Faculty research:* Human diversity in social context, foundations of social work practice, policy and services in child welfare, child and family policy, social welfare policy and services. *Unit head:* Prof. Keith Alford, Director, School of Social Work, 315-443-5562, Fax: 315-443-2562, E-mail: kalford@syr.edu. *Application contact:* Felicia Otero, Director of College Admissions, 315-443-5555, Fax: 315-443-2562, E-mail: falk@syr.edu.
Website: https://falk.syr.edu/marriage-family-therapy/academic-programs/#mswmft

Syracuse University, David B. Falk College of Sport and Human Dynamics, MSW Program in Social Work, Syracuse, NY 13244. Offers MSW. *Accreditation:* CSWE. *Program availability:* Part-time, evening/weekend. *Degree requirements:* For master's, thesis or alternative, field placement. *Entrance requirements:* For master's, personal statement, official transcripts, three letters of recommendation, resume. Additional exam requirements/recommendations for international students: Required—TOEFL (minimum score 100 iBT). *Application deadline:* For fall admission, 2/15 priority date for domestic and international students; for spring admission, 11/1 for domestic students, 11/1 priority date for international students. Applications are processed on a rolling basis. Application fee: $75. Electronic applications accepted. *Financial support:* Fellowships with full tuition reimbursements, research assistantships, teaching assistantships, career-related internships or fieldwork, and tuition waivers available. Financial award application deadline: 1/1; financial award applicants required to submit FAFSA. *Faculty research:* Child welfare, substance abuse counseling, health care, public policy, industry and business, school social work, gerontology, mental health services. *Unit head:* Prof. Keith Alford, Director, School of Social Work, 315-443-5562, E-mail: kalford@syr.edu. *Application contact:* Felicia Otero, Director of College Admissions, 315-443-5555, E-mail: falk@syr.edu.
Website: http://falk.syr.edu/SocialWork/Default.aspx

Tarleton State University, College of Graduate Studies, College of Health Sciences and Human Services, Department of Social Work, Stephenville, TX 76402. Offers MSW. *Program availability:* Part-time, evening/weekend. *Faculty:* 7 full-time (all women), 1 (woman) part-time/adjunct. *Students:* 69 full-time (61 women), 22 part-time (20 women). Average age 33. 98 applicants, 89% accepted, 66 enrolled. In 2018, 19 master's awarded. *Degree requirements:* For master's, comprehensive exam, thesis (for some programs). *Entrance requirements:* For master's, GRE, minimum GPA of 3.0. Additional exam requirements/recommendations for international students: Required—TOEFL (minimum score 520 paper-based; 69 iBT); Recommended—IELTS (minimum score 6), TSE (minimum score 50). *Application deadline:* For fall admission, 8/15 for domestic students; for spring admission, 1/5 for domestic students. Applications are processed on a rolling basis. Application fee: $50 ($130 for international students). Electronic applications accepted. *Expenses:* Contact institution. *Financial support:* Applicants required to submit FAFSA. *Unit head:* Dr. Melody Loya, Department Head, 254-968-9276, E-mail: loya@tarleton.edu. *Application contact:* Information Contact, 254-968-9104, Fax: 254-968-9670, E-mail: gradoffice@tarleton.edu.

Temple University, College of Public Health, School of Social Work, Philadelphia, PA 19122-6096. Offers MSW. *Accreditation:* CSWE. *Program availability:* Part-time, evening/weekend, online learning. *Faculty:* 21 full-time (12 women), 11 part-time/adjunct (8 women). *Students:* 224 full-time (197 women), 89 part-time (80 women); includes 136 minority (90 Black or African American, non-Hispanic/Latino; 2 American Indian or Alaska Native, non-Hispanic/Latino; 6 Asian, non-Hispanic/Latino; 26 Hispanic/Latino; 12 Two or more races, non-Hispanic/Latino). 239 applicants, 80% accepted, 82 enrolled. In 2018, 154 master's awarded. *Degree requirements:* For master's, internship/field practicum. *Entrance requirements:* For master's, statement of goals, clearances to complete clinical/field education experiences, resume. Additional exam requirements/recommendations for international students: Required—TOEFL (minimum score 79 iBT), IELTS (minimum score 6.5), PTE (minimum score 53), one of three is required. *Application deadline:* For fall admission, 1/15 priority date for domestic students; for spring admission, 11/1 for domestic students; for summer admission, 1/15 priority date for domestic students. Applications are processed on a rolling basis. Application fee: $60. Electronic applications accepted. *Expenses:* Contact institution. *Financial support:* Career-related internships or fieldwork, Federal Work-Study, and scholarships/grants available. Financial award application deadline: 1/15; financial award applicants required to submit FAFSA. *Faculty research:* Adolescent health, risk behavior, substance abuse, trauma, restorative justice. *Unit head:* Philip McCallion, Director of the School of Social Work, 215-204-8137, E-mail: philip.mccallion@temple.edu. *Application contact:* Tre Grue, Assistant Director of Admissions, 215-204-5806, E-mail: tre@temple.edu.
Website: https://cph.temple.edu/ssa

Tennessee State University, The School of Graduate Studies and Research, College of Public Service, Nashville, TN 37209-1561. Offers human resource management (MPS); public administration (MPA, PhD); social work (MSW); strategic leadership (MPS); training and development (MPS). *Accreditation:* NASPAA (one or more programs are accredited). *Program availability:* Part-time, evening/weekend. *Degree requirements:* For master's, comprehensive exam, thesis optional; for doctorate, comprehensive exam, thesis/dissertation. *Entrance requirements:* For master's, GRE General Test, minimum GPA of 2.5, writing sample; for doctorate, GRE General Test, minimum GPA of 3.25, writing sample. *Faculty research:* Total quality management and process improvement, national health care policy and administration, starting non-profit ventures, public service ethics, state education financing across the U.S. public.

Texas A&M University–Commerce, College of Education and Human Services, Commerce, TX 75429. Offers counseling (M Ed, MS, PhD); early childhood education (M Ed, MS); educational administration (M Ed, MS, Ed D); educational psychology (PhD); educational technology leadership (M Ed, MS); educational technology library science (M Ed, MS); elementary education (M Ed); health, kinesiology and sports studies (MS); higher education (MS, Ed D); psychology (MS); reading (M Ed, MS); school psychology (SSP); secondary education (M Ed, MS); social work (MSW); special education (M Ed, MS); supervision, curriculum and instruction-elementary education (Ed D); training and development (MS). *Program availability:* Part-time, evening/weekend, 100% online, blended/hybrid learning. *Faculty:* 95 full-time (59 women), 29 part-time/adjunct (22 women). *Students:* 356 full-time (295 women), 1,262 part-time (992 women); includes 683 minority (349 Black or African American, non-Hispanic/Latino; 9 American Indian or Alaska Native, non-Hispanic/Latino; 30 Asian, non-Hispanic/Latino; 238 Hispanic/Latino; 57 Two or more races, non-Hispanic/Latino), 9 international. Average age 37. 951 applicants, 42% accepted, 304 enrolled. In 2018, 532 master's, 51 doctorates awarded. *Degree requirements:* For master's, comprehensive exam, thesis optional, departmental qualifying exams (for some programs); for doctorate, comprehensive exam, thesis/dissertation, departmental qualifying exam; for SSP, comprehensive exam. *Entrance requirements:* For master's, GRE General Test, official transcripts, letters of recommendation, resume, statement of goals; for doctorate, GRE General Test, letters of recommendation, statement of goals, writing samples, writing sessions, resumes. Additional exam requirements/recommendations for international students: Required—TOEFL (minimum score 550 paper-based; 79 iBT), IELTS (minimum score 6), PTE (minimum score 53). *Application deadline:* For fall admission, 6/1 priority date for international students; for spring admission, 10/15 priority date for international students; for summer admission, 3/15 priority date for international students. Applications are processed on a rolling basis. Application fee: $50 ($75 for international students). Electronic applications accepted. *Expenses: Tuition, area resident:* Full-time $3630. Tuition, state resident: full-time $3630. Tuition, nonresident: full-time $11,100. *International tuition:* $11,100 full-time. *Required fees:* $2794. Tuition and fees vary according to course load, degree level and program. *Financial support:* In 2018–19, 116 students received support, including 94 research assistantships with partial tuition reimbursements available (averaging $3,863 per year), 38 teaching assistantships with partial tuition reimbursements available (averaging $4,728 per year); career-related internships or fieldwork, Federal Work-Study, institutionally sponsored loans, scholarships/grants, health care benefits, and unspecified assistantships also available. Financial award application deadline: 5/1; financial award applicants required to submit FAFSA. *Faculty research:* Cognitive and bilingual education, positive behavioral intervention, literacy, math readiness. *Total annual research expenditures:* $1.1 million. *Unit head:* Dr. Madeline Justice, Interim Dean, 903-886-5181, Fax: 903-886-5905, E-mail: madeline.justice@tamuc.edu. *Application contact:* Vicky Turner, Doctoral Degree and Special Programs Coordinator, 903-886-5167, E-mail: vicky.turner@tamuc.edu.
Website: http://www.tamuc.edu/academics/graduateSchool/programs/education/default.aspx

Texas A&M University–Kingsville, College of Graduate Studies, College of Arts and Sciences, Program in Social Work, Kingsville, TX 78363. Offers MSW.

Texas Christian University, Harris College of Nursing and Health Sciences, Department of Social Work, Fort Worth, TX 76129-0002. Offers advanced generalist (MSW). Brite MSW/MDiv. *Accreditation:* CSWE. *Program availability:* Part-time. *Faculty:* 5 full-time (3 women), 3 part-time/adjunct (1 woman). *Students:* 32 full-time (29 women); includes 13 minority (6 Black or African American, non-Hispanic/Latino; 2 Asian, non-Hispanic/Latino; 3 Hispanic/Latino; 2 Two or more races, non-Hispanic/Latino), 3 international. Average age 27. 40 applicants, 78% accepted, 22 enrolled. In 2018, 27 master's awarded. *Degree requirements:* For master's, research project in field agency. *Entrance requirements:* Additional exam requirements/recommendations for international students: Recommended—TOEFL (minimum score 550 paper-based; 80 iBT), IELTS (minimum score 6.5). *Application deadline:* For fall admission, 4/2 for domestic and international students. Application fee: $60. Electronic applications accepted. *Expenses:* $29,340 for 30 hour program; $58,680 for 60 hour program. *Financial support:* In 2018–19, 26 students received support. Tuition waivers (partial) available. Financial award application deadline: 4/2. *Faculty research:* Homelessness, sexual violence prevention, developmental disabilities, gendered organizations, social identity transitioning. *Total annual research expenditures:* $25,000. *Unit head:* Dr. James Petrovich, Chair, 817-257-6157, Fax: 817-257-7665, E-mail: j.petrovich@tcu.edu. *Application contact:* Victoria Barth, Academic Program Specialist, 817-257-7612, Fax: 817-257-5784, E-mail: v.barth@tcu.edu.
Website: https://harriscollege.tcu.edu/social-work/

Texas State University, The Graduate College, College of Applied Arts, Program in Social Work, San Marcos, TX 78666. Offers MSW. *Accreditation:* CSWE. *Program availability:* Part-time, evening/weekend, 100% online, blended/hybrid learning. *Faculty:* 30 full-time (19 women), 7 part-time/adjunct (all women). *Students:* 192 full-time (170 women), 166 part-time (149 women); includes 190 minority (54 Black or African American, non-Hispanic/Latino; 6 Asian, non-Hispanic/Latino; 119 Hispanic/Latino; 11 Two or more races, non-Hispanic/Latino). Average age 31. 326 applicants, 31% accepted, 81 enrolled. In 2018, 124 master's awarded. *Degree requirements:* For master's, comprehensive exam, field practicum/internship under the supervision of a licensed master social worker within a social service agency. *Entrance requirements:* For master's, baccalaureate degree from regionally-accredited institution with minimum GPA of 3.0 in last 60 hours of course work, in last two full academic years, and in all undergraduate social work courses; resume; statement of purpose. Additional exam requirements/recommendations for international students: Required—TOEFL (minimum score 550 paper-based; 78 iBT), IELTS (minimum score 6.5). *Application deadline:* For fall admission, 3/15 for domestic and international students. Applications are processed on a rolling basis. Application fee: $55 ($90 for international students). Electronic applications accepted. *Expenses:* Tuition, state resident: full-time $8102; part-time $4051 per semester. Tuition, nonresident: full-time $18,229; part-time $9115 per semester. *International tuition:* $18,229 full-time. *Required fees:* $2116; $120 per credit hour. Tuition and fees vary according to course load. *Financial support:* In 2018–19, 175 students received support, including 9 research assistantships (averaging $12,168 per year), 3 teaching assistantships (averaging $13,003 per year); career-related internships or fieldwork, Federal Work-Study, institutionally sponsored loans, scholarships/grants, and unspecified assistantships also available. Support available to part-time students. Financial award application deadline: 1/15; financial award applicants required to submit FAFSA. *Faculty research:* Treating PTSD through Behavioral Health Workforce Education and Training; Child Adversity and out-of-home placement; intergenerational exercise buddy program for successful aging; conducting a summative and formative evaluation of child welfare services and outcomes. *Total annual research expenditures:* $532,801. *Unit head:* Dr. Angela Ausbrooks, Graduate Advisor, 512-245-9067, E-mail: aa16@txstate.edu. *Application contact:* Dr. Andrea Golato, Dean of the Graduate College, 512-245-2581, Fax: 512-245-8365, E-mail: gradcollege@txstate.edu.
Website: http://www.gradcollege.txstate.edu/programs/msw.html

Texas Tech University, Graduate School, College of Arts and Sciences, Department of Sociology, Anthropology and Social Work, Lubbock, TX 79409-1012. Offers anthropology (MA); social work (MSW); sociology (MA). *Accreditation:* CSWE. *Program availability:* Part-time. *Faculty:* 29 full-time (18 women), 4 part-time/adjunct (2 women). *Students:* 54 full-time (39 women), 8 part-time (6 women); includes 19 minority (4 Black or African American, non-Hispanic/Latino; 1 Asian, non-Hispanic/Latino; 12 Hispanic/Latino; 2 Two or more races, non-Hispanic/Latino), 5 international. Average age 29. 55 applicants, 75% accepted, 34 enrolled. In 2018, 25 master's awarded. *Degree requirements:* For master's, one foreign language, comprehensive exam (for some programs), thesis (for some programs). *Entrance requirements:* For master's, GRE (for MA in anthropology), two letters of recommendation, statement of purpose, writing sample, curriculum vitae; minimum GPA of 3.0 and coursework in sociology or closely-related fields (for MA in sociology); coursework in anthropology (for MA in anthropology). Additional exam requirements/recommendations for international students: Required—TOEFL (minimum score 550 paper-based; 79 iBT). *Application deadline:* For fall admission, 6/1 priority date for domestic students, 1/15 priority date for international students; for spring admission, 9/1 priority date for domestic students, 6/15 priority date for international students. Applications are processed on a rolling basis. Application fee: $65. Electronic applications accepted. *Expenses:* Contact institution. *Financial support:* In 2018–19, 48 students received support, including 41 fellowships (averaging $4,715 per year), 27 teaching assistantships (averaging $13,342 per year); research assistantships, Federal Work-Study, scholarships/grants, tuition waivers (partial), and unspecified assistantships also available. Financial award application deadline: 2/1; financial award applicants required to submit FAFSA. *Faculty research:* Sociology of

criminology/deviance, population/migration, forensic anthropology, archaeology, social work (advanced generalist). *Total annual research expenditures:* $195,903. *Unit head:* Dr. Cristina Bradatan, Associate Professor and Chair, 806-834-1796, Fax: 806-742-1088, E-mail: cristina.bradatan@ttu.edu. *Application contact:* Dr. Martha Smithey, Associate Professor/Sociology Graduate Program Director, 806-834-1995, E-mail: martha.smithey@ttu.edu.
Website: www.depts.ttu.edu/sasw/

Thompson Rivers University, Program in Social Work, Kamloops, BC V2C 0C8, Canada. Offers MSW.

Touro College, Graduate School of Social Work, New York, NY 10010. Offers MSW. *Accreditation:* CSWE. *Entrance requirements:* Additional exam requirements/recommendations for international students: Required—TOEFL (minimum score 83 iBT), IELTS (minimum score 6.5), PTE (minimum score 58).

Troy University, Graduate School, College of Health and Human Services, Program in Social Work, Troy, AL 36082. Offers MSW. *Accreditation:* CSWE. *Program availability:* Part-time, evening/weekend. *Faculty:* 12 full-time (10 women), 6 part-time/adjunct (4 women). *Students:* 191 full-time (178 women), 16 part-time (all women); includes 105 minority (98 Black or African American, non-Hispanic/Latino; 4 Hispanic/Latino; 3 Two or more races, non-Hispanic/Latino), 1 international. Average age 33. 175 applicants, 99% accepted, 144 enrolled. In 2018, 86 master's awarded. *Degree requirements:* For master's, practicum. *Entrance requirements:* For master's, GRE (minimum score of 850 on old exam or 290 on new exam), GMAT (minimum score of 380) or MAT (minimum score of 385), minimum GPA of 2.5 on last 30 semester hours taken, criminal background check. Additional exam requirements/recommendations for international students: Required—TOEFL (minimum score 523 paper-based; 70 iBT), IELTS (minimum score 6). *Application deadline:* Applications are processed on a rolling basis. Application fee: $50. Electronic applications accepted. *Expenses: Tuition, area resident:* Full-time $425; part-time $425 per credit hour. Tuition, state resident: full-time $425; part-time $425 per credit hour. Tuition, nonresident: full-time $850; part-time $850 per credit hour. *International tuition:* $850 full-time. *Required fees:* $50 per semester. Tuition and fees vary according to campus/location and program. *Financial support:* Fellowships, career-related internships or fieldwork, and scholarships/grants available. Support available to part-time students. *Unit head:* Dr. Samantha Ellis, Lecturer, Director, 334-670-5767, E-mail: smellis@troy.edu. *Application contact:* Jessica A. Kimbro, Assistant Director of Graduate Admissions, 334-670-3189, Fax: 334-670-3733, E-mail: jacord@troy.edu.
Website: https://www.troy.edu/academics/academic-programs/college-health-human-services-programs.php

Tulane University, School of Social Work, New Orleans, LA 70118-5669. Offers city, culture and community (PhD); disaster resilience leadership (MS); social work (MSW, DSW). *Accreditation:* CSWE (one or more programs are accredited). *Program availability:* Part-time. *Degree requirements:* For master's, thesis. *Entrance requirements:* Additional exam requirements/recommendations for international students: Required—TOEFL. Electronic applications accepted. *Expenses: Tuition:* Full-time $52,856; part-time $2937 per credit hour. *Required fees:* $2040; $44.50 per credit hour. $580 per term. Tuition and fees vary according to course load, degree level and program.

Union University, School of Social Work, Jackson, TN 38305-3697. Offers MSW. *Accreditation:* CSWE.

Universidad del Este, Graduate School, Carolina, PR 00984. Offers accounting (MBA); adult education (M Ed); agribusiness (MBA); criminal justice and criminology (MA); curriculum and instruction - early education (M Ed); curriculum and instruction - elementary (M Ed); curriculum and instruction - English (M Ed); curriculum and instruction - Spanish (M Ed); human resources (MBA); information security management (MBA); information technology and Web business development (MBA); management (MBA); public policy (MPA); social work (MA), including clinical social work; special education (M Ed); strategic leadership (MBA).

Université de Moncton, Faculty of Arts and Social Sciences, School of Social Work, Moncton, NB E1A 3E9, Canada. Offers MSW. *Degree requirements:* For master's, one foreign language, major paper. *Entrance requirements:* For master's, minimum GPA of 3.0. *Faculty research:* Burnout and education, mental health (institutionalization), unemployment's effect on youth, women and health services.

Université de Montréal, Faculty of Arts and Sciences, School of Social Service, Program in Social Administration, Montréal, QC H3C 3J7, Canada. Offers DESS. Electronic applications accepted.

Université de Sherbrooke, Faculty of Letters and Human Sciences, Department of Social Service, Sherbrooke, QC J1K 2R1, Canada. Offers MSS.

Université du Québec à Montréal, Graduate Programs, Program in Social Intervention, Montréal, QC H3C 3P8, Canada. Offers MA. *Program availability:* Part-time. *Degree requirements:* For master's, thesis. *Entrance requirements:* For master's, appropriate bachelor's degree or equivalent, proficiency in French.

Université du Québec en Abitibi-Témiscamingue, Graduate Programs, Program in Social Work, Rouyn-Noranda, QC J9X 5E4, Canada. Offers MSW.

Université du Québec en Outaouais, Graduate Programs, Program in Social Work, Gatineau, QC J8X 3X7, Canada. Offers MA. *Degree requirements:* For master's, thesis (for some programs).

Université Laval, Faculty of Social Sciences, School of Social Work, Programs in Social Work, Québec, QC G1K 7P4, Canada. Offers M Serv Soc, PhD. Terminal master's awarded for partial completion of doctoral program. *Degree requirements:* For master's, thesis (for some programs); for doctorate, comprehensive exam, thesis/dissertation. *Entrance requirements:* For master's and doctorate, knowledge of French, comprehension of written English. Electronic applications accepted.

University at Albany, State University of New York, School of Social Welfare, Albany, NY 12222-0001. Offers MSW, PhD, MSW/MA. *Accreditation:* CSWE (one or more programs are accredited). *Program availability:* Part-time, evening/weekend. *Faculty:* 28 full-time (23 women), 14 part-time/adjunct (8 women). *Students:* 274 full-time (236 women), 114 part-time (89 women); includes 115 minority (54 Black or African American, non-Hispanic/Latino; 8 Asian, non-Hispanic/Latino; 37 Hispanic/Latino; 16 Two or more races, non-Hispanic/Latino), 15 international. 435 applicants, 63% accepted, 192 enrolled. In 2018, 144 master's, 7 doctorates awarded. *Degree requirements:* For doctorate, thesis/dissertation. *Entrance requirements:* For doctorate, GRE General Test. Additional exam requirements/recommendations for international students: Required—TOEFL (minimum score 550 paper-based). *Application deadline:* For fall admission, 2/15 for domestic and international students. Application fee: $75. Electronic applications accepted. *Expenses:* Contact institution. *Financial support:* Fellowships, career-related internships or fieldwork, and Federal Work-Study available. Financial award application deadline: 2/15. *Faculty research:* Welfare reform, homelessness, children and families, mental health, substance abuse. *Unit head:* Lynn Warner, Dean, 518-442-5324, E-mail: lwarner@albany.edu. *Application contact:* Lynn Warner, Dean, 518-442-5324, E-mail: lwarner@albany.edu.

University at Buffalo, the State University of New York, Graduate School, School of Social Work, Buffalo, NY 14260. Offers social welfare (PhD); social work (MSW); JD/MSW; MBA/MSW; MPH/MSW; MSW/PhD. *Accreditation:* CSWE (one or more programs are accredited). *Program availability:* Part-time, blended/hybrid learning, Coursework Online & Field Education in Agency. *Faculty:* 33 full-time (24 women), 52 part-time/adjunct (41 women). *Students:* 290 full-time (238 women), 277 part-time (241 women); includes 100 minority (59 Black or African American, non-Hispanic/Latino; 5 American Indian or Alaska Native, non-Hispanic/Latino; 17 Asian, non-Hispanic/Latino; 19 Hispanic/Latino). Average age 30. 504 applicants, 66% accepted, 229 enrolled. In 2018, 207 master's, 6 doctorates awarded. *Degree requirements:* For master's, 900 hours of field work; for doctorate, comprehensive exam, thesis/dissertation. *Entrance requirements:* For master's, 24 credits of course work in liberal arts; for doctorate, GRE General Test, MSW or equivalent. Additional exam requirements/recommendations for international students: Required—TOEFL (minimum score 577 paper-based; 90 iBT). *Application deadline:* For fall admission, 3/1 priority date for domestic and international students; for spring admission, 9/15 for domestic and international students; for summer admission, 2/1 for domestic and international students. Application fee: $75. Electronic applications accepted. *Expenses:* Contact institution. *Financial support:* In 2018–19, 10 fellowships with full tuition reimbursements (averaging $9,400 per year), 2 research assistantships with full tuition reimbursements (averaging $17,300 per year), 8 teaching assistantships with full tuition reimbursements (averaging $5,000 per year) were awarded; Federal Work-Study, scholarships/grants, health care benefits, tuition waivers (full and partial), unspecified assistantships, and instructorships and research grants (for PhD students) also available. Financial award application deadline: 4/30; financial award applicants required to submit FAFSA. *Faculty research:* Violence and victimization; trauma and trauma-informed care; health, behavioral health and addictions; children and adolescents; aging. *Total annual research expenditures:* $1 million. *Unit head:* Dr. Nancy J. Smyth, Dean, 716-645-3381, Fax: 716-645-3883, E-mail: sw-dean@buffalo.edu. *Application contact:* Maria Carey, Admissions Processor, 716-645-3381, Fax: 716-645-3456, E-mail: sw-info@buffalo.edu.
Website: http://www.socialwork.buffalo.edu

The University of Akron, Graduate School, College of Health Professions, School of Social Work, Akron, OH 44325. Offers MSW. *Accreditation:* CSWE. *Entrance requirements:* For master's, undergraduate major in social work or related field, three letters of recommendation, essay, resume. Additional exam requirements/recommendations for international students: Required—TOEFL (minimum score 79 iBT), IELTS (minimum score 6.5). Electronic applications accepted. *Faculty research:* Spirituality and alternative healing, child welfare education and training, ethics and social work practice, evidence-based social work practice, social work continuing education.

The University of Alabama, Graduate School, School of Social Work, Tuscaloosa, AL 35487-0314. Offers MSW, PhD. *Accreditation:* CSWE (one or more programs are accredited). *Program availability:* Part-time, blended/hybrid learning. *Degree requirements:* For master's, professional internship; for doctorate, comprehensive exam, thesis/dissertation. *Entrance requirements:* For master's, GRE or MAT (if GPA less than 3.0), minimum GPA of 2.5; for doctorate, GRE, minimum GPA of 3.0. Additional exam requirements/recommendations for international students: Required—TOEFL (minimum score 79 iBT), IELTS, PTE. Electronic applications accepted. *Faculty research:* Children and adolescents at risk, trauma, gerontology, child welfare policy, health.

The University of Alabama at Birmingham, College of Arts and Sciences, Program in Social Work, Birmingham, AL 35294. Offers MSW. *Expenses: Tuition, area resident:* Full-time $8100; part-time $8100 per year. Tuition, state resident: full-time $8100. Tuition, nonresident: full-time $19,188; part-time $19,188 per year. Tuition and fees vary according to program.

University of Alaska Anchorage, College of Health, School of Social Work, Anchorage, AK 99508. Offers children's mental health (Graduate Certificate); social work (MSW); MSW/MPH. *Accreditation:* CSWE. *Program availability:* Part-time, evening/weekend, online learning. *Degree requirements:* For master's, comprehensive exam (for some programs), thesis or alternative, research project. *Entrance requirements:* For master's, GRE General Test, writing sample. Additional exam requirements/recommendations for international students: Required—TOEFL (minimum score 550 paper-based). Electronic applications accepted. *Expenses:* Contact institution.

University of Arkansas, Graduate School, J. William Fulbright College of Arts and Sciences, School of Social Work, Fayetteville, AR 72701. Offers MSW. *Accreditation:* CSWE. In 2018, 17 master's awarded. *Entrance requirements:* For master's, GRE General Test. *Application deadline:* For fall admission, 8/1 for domestic students, 4/1 for international students; for spring admission, 12/1 for domestic students, 10/1 for international students; for summer admission, 4/15 for domestic students, 3/1 for international students. Applications are processed on a rolling basis. Application fee: $60. Electronic applications accepted. *Financial support:* In 2018–19, 4 research assistantships were awarded; fellowships with tuition reimbursements and teaching assistantships also available. *Unit head:* Dr. Alishia Ferguson, Director, 479-575-3796, E-mail: ajfergus@uark.edu. *Application contact:* Sara Collie, Professor, 479-575-4510, E-mail: sjcollie@uark.edu.
Website: https://fulbright.uark.edu/departments/social-work/

University of Arkansas at Little Rock, Graduate School, College of Education and Health Professions, School of Social Work, Program in Social Work, Little Rock, AR 72204-1099. Offers clinical social work (MSW); management and community practice (MSW). *Accreditation:* CSWE. *Entrance requirements:* For master's, GRE General Test or MAT, three letters of reference.

The University of British Columbia, Faculty of Arts, School of Social Work, Vancouver, BC V6T 1Z2, Canada. Offers MSW, PhD. *Degree requirements:* For master's, thesis or essay; for doctorate, comprehensive exam, thesis/dissertation. *Entrance requirements:* For master's, BSW; for doctorate, MSW. Additional exam requirements/recommendations for international students: Required—TOEFL. Electronic applications accepted. *Expenses:* Contact institution. *Faculty research:* Gerontology, family resources, diversity, social inequality.

University of Calgary, Faculty of Graduate Studies, Faculty of Social Work, Calgary, AB T2N 1N4, Canada. Offers MSW, PhD, Postgraduate Diploma. *Degree requirements:* For master's, thesis (for some programs); for doctorate, thesis/dissertation, candidacy exam. *Entrance requirements:* For master's, BSW, minimum undergraduate GPA of 3.4 (1 year program), minimum GPA of 3.5 (2 year program); for doctorate, minimum graduate GPA of 3.5, MSW (preferred); for Postgraduate Diploma, MSW, minimum graduate GPA of 3.5. Additional exam requirements/recommendations for international students: Required—TOEFL (paper-based 550) or IELTS (7). Electronic applications accepted. *Faculty research:* Family violence, direct practice, gerontology, child welfare, community development.

University of California, Berkeley, Graduate Division, School of Social Welfare, Berkeley, CA 94720. Offers MSW, PhD, MSW/PhD. *Accreditation:* CSWE (one or more programs are accredited). Terminal master's awarded for partial completion of doctoral program. *Degree requirements:* For master's, thesis optional; for doctorate, thesis/dissertation, qualifying exam. *Entrance requirements:* For master's and doctorate, GRE

General Test, minimum GPA of 3.0, 3 letters of recommendation. Additional exam requirements/recommendations for international students: Required—TOEFL (minimum score 570 paper-based; 90 iBT), TWE. Electronic applications accepted. *Faculty research:* Child welfare, law and social welfare, minority mental health, social welfare policy analysis, health services.

University of California, Los Angeles, Graduate Division, Luskin School of Public Affairs, Program in Social Welfare, Los Angeles, CA 90095. Offers MSW, PhD, JD/MSW. *Accreditation:* CSWE (one or more programs are accredited). *Degree requirements:* For master's, comprehensive exam, research project; for doctorate, thesis/dissertation, oral and written qualifying exams. *Entrance requirements:* For master's, GRE General Test, minimum GPA of 3.0; for doctorate, GRE General Test, minimum undergraduate GPA of 3.0. Additional exam requirements/recommendations for international students: Required—TOEFL. Electronic applications accepted.

University of Central Florida, College of Health Professions and Sciences, School of Social Work, Orlando, FL 32816. Offers military social work (Certificate); social work (MSW). *Accreditation:* CSWE. *Program availability:* Part-time, evening/weekend. *Students:* 177 full-time (157 women), 298 part-time (267 women); includes 204 minority (87 Black or African American, non-Hispanic/Latino; 2 American Indian or Alaska Native, non-Hispanic/Latino; 11 Asian, non-Hispanic/Latino; 94 Hispanic/Latino; 1 Native Hawaiian or other Pacific Islander, non-Hispanic/Latino; 9 Two or more races, non-Hispanic/Latino). Average age 31. 359 applicants, 55% accepted, 128 enrolled. In 2018, 143 master's, 8 other advanced degrees awarded. *Degree requirements:* For master's, thesis or alternative, field education. *Entrance requirements:* For master's, letters of recommendation, resume, professional statement, academic writing sample. Additional exam requirements/recommendations for international students: Required—TOEFL. *Application deadline:* For fall admission, 4/1 for domestic students. Application fee: $30. Electronic applications accepted. *Financial support:* In 2018–19, 1 student received support, including 1 fellowship (averaging $10,000 per year); career-related internships or fieldwork, institutionally sponsored loans, and unspecified assistantships also available. Financial award application deadline: 3/1; financial award applicants required to submit FAFSA. *Unit head:* Dr. Bonnie Yegidis, Director, 407-823-2114, E-mail: bonnie.yegidis@ucf.edu. *Application contact:* Associate Director, Graduate Admissions, 407-823-2766, Fax: 407-823-6442, E-mail: gradadmissions@ucf.edu.
Website: https://www.cohpa.ucf.edu/socialwork/

University of Chicago, School of Social Service Administration, Doctoral Program, Chicago, IL 60637. Offers PhD, AM/PhD. *Degree requirements:* For doctorate, comprehensive exam, thesis/dissertation. *Entrance requirements:* For doctorate, GRE General Test, prior master's degree in social work; 4 letters of recommendation; transcripts; curriculum vitae or resume; writing sample. Additional exam requirements/recommendations for international students: Required—TOEFL (minimum score 600 paper-based; 104 iBT), IELTS (minimum score 7). Electronic applications accepted. *Faculty research:* Health administration, youth violence prevention, family well-being, social policy, crime, college success, urban education.

University of Chicago, School of Social Service Administration, Master's Program, Chicago, IL 60637. Offers MA, AM/M Div, MBA/AM, MPP/AM. *Accreditation:* CSWE. *Program availability:* Part-time, evening/weekend. *Degree requirements:* For master's, field education. *Entrance requirements:* For master's, transcripts, statement of purpose, 3 letters of recommendation. Additional exam requirements/recommendations for international students: Required—TOEFL (minimum score 600 paper-based; 104 iBT), IELTS (minimum score 7). Electronic applications accepted.

University of Cincinnati, Graduate School, College of Allied Health Sciences, School of Social Work, Cincinnati, OH 45221. Offers children and families, health and aging, mental health (MSW). *Accreditation:* CSWE. *Program availability:* Part-time. *Faculty:* 15 full-time (13 women), 21 part-time/adjunct (12 women). *Students:* 122 full-time (102 women), 34 part-time (29 women); includes 56 minority (32 Black or African American, non-Hispanic/Latino; 1 American Indian or Alaska Native, non-Hispanic/Latino; 1 Asian, non-Hispanic/Latino; 14 Hispanic/Latino; 8 Two or more races, non-Hispanic/Latino). Average age 28. 147 applicants, 99% accepted, 88 enrolled. In 2018, 71 master's awarded. *Entrance requirements:* Additional exam requirements/recommendations for international students: Required—TOEFL (minimum score 95 paper-based). *Application deadline:* For fall admission, 1/14 priority date for domestic students. Application fee: $65. Electronic applications accepted. *Financial support:* In 2018–19, 72 students received support, including 3 research assistantships with full tuition reimbursements available (averaging $17,346 per year); fellowships, career-related internships or fieldwork, tuition waivers (partial), and unspecified assistantships also available. Financial award application deadline: 4/1; financial award applicants required to submit FAFSA. *Faculty research:* Fatherhood, mediation, mental illness, child welfare, elderly. *Unit head:* Dr. Ruth Anne Van Loon, Director, 513-556-4628, E-mail: vanloora@ucmail.uc.edu. *Application contact:* Johnny Arguedas, Program Coordinator, 513-556-4637, Fax: 513-556-2077, E-mail: socialworkweb@uc.edu.
Website: http://www.cahs.uc.edu/SocialWork

University of Connecticut, Graduate School, School of Social Work, Storrs, CT 06269. Offers MSW, PhD. *Accreditation:* CSWE. *Degree requirements:* For master's, comprehensive exam; for doctorate, thesis/dissertation. *Entrance requirements:* Additional exam requirements/recommendations for international students: Required—TOEFL (minimum score 550 paper-based). Electronic applications accepted.

University of Denver, Graduate School of Social Work, Denver, CO 80208. Offers animal-assisted social work (Certificate); couples and family therapy (Certificate); social work (MSW, PhD); social work with Latinos/as (Certificate). *Accreditation:* CSWE (one or more programs are accredited). *Program availability:* Part-time, evening/weekend, online learning. *Faculty:* 41 full-time (28 women), 85 part-time/adjunct (74 women). *Students:* 687 full-time (619 women), 165 part-time (152 women); includes 209 minority (28 Black or African American, non-Hispanic/Latino; 6 American Indian or Alaska Native, non-Hispanic/Latino; 20 Asian, non-Hispanic/Latino; 133 Hispanic/Latino; 1 Native Hawaiian or other Pacific Islander, non-Hispanic/Latino; 21 Two or more races, non-Hispanic/Latino), 5 international. Average age 29. 1,332 applicants, 88% accepted, 523 enrolled. In 2018, 280 master's, 5 doctorates, 62 other advanced degrees awarded. *Degree requirements:* For doctorate, comprehensive exam, thesis/dissertation, research methods and statistics qualifying exam. *Entrance requirements:* For master's, 20 semester hours or 30 quarter hours in undergraduate course work in the arts and humanities, social/behavioral sciences, and biological sciences; completed at least one course in English composition or present evidence of testing out of the English composition requirement; transcripts; two letters of recommendation; essays; resume; for doctorate, GRE, master's degree in social work or in one of the social sciences with substantial professional experience in the social work field; basic proficiency in descriptive and inferential statistics; two years of post-master's practice experience (preferred); transcripts; three letters of recommendation; personal statement; resume; writing sample. Additional exam requirements/recommendations for international students: Required—TOEFL (minimum score 587 paper-based; 95 iBT). *Application deadline:* For fall admission, 1/15 priority date for domestic and international students. Applications are processed on a rolling basis. Application fee: $65. Electronic applications accepted. *Expenses:* $33,183 per year full-time. *Financial support:* In 2018–19, 518 students received support, including 1 research assistantship (averaging

$6,000 per year); teaching assistantships, scholarships/grants, and unspecified assistantships also available. Support available to part-time students. Financial award application deadline: 2/15; financial award applicants required to submit FAFSA. *Faculty research:* Substance abuse, homelessness, fatherhood, paid-leave, multiple systemic therapy. *Total annual research expenditures:* $9.9 million. *Unit head:* Dr. Amanda Moore McBride, Dean, 303-871-2203, E-mail: gssw.communications@du.edu. *Application contact:* Roberto Garcia, Executive Director, Enrollment, 303-871-2602, E-mail: gsswadmission@du.edu.
Website: https://socialwork.du.edu/

University of Georgia, School of Social Work, Athens, GA 30602. Offers MA, MSW, PhD, Certificate, MSW/JD. *Accreditation:* CSWE (one or more programs are accredited). *Program availability:* Part-time, evening/weekend. *Degree requirements:* For master's, thesis or alternative; for doctorate, one foreign language, thesis/dissertation. *Entrance requirements:* For master's and doctorate, GRE General Test. Electronic applications accepted. *Faculty research:* Juvenile justice, substance abuse, civil rights and social justice, gerontology, social policy.

University of Guam, Office of Graduate Studies, College of Natural and Applied Sciences, Program in Social Work, Mangilao, GU 96923. Offers MSW.

University of Hawaii at Manoa, Office of Graduate Education, School of Social Work, Honolulu, HI 96822. Offers social welfare (PhD); social work (MSW). *Accreditation:* CSWE (one or more programs are accredited). *Program availability:* Part-time. *Degree requirements:* For doctorate, comprehensive exam, thesis/dissertation. *Entrance requirements:* For doctorate, master's degree (MSW preferred), minimum GPA of 3.0. Additional exam requirements/recommendations for international students: Required—TOEFL (minimum score 560 paper-based; 83 iBT), IELTS (minimum score 5). *Faculty research:* Health, mental health, AIDS, substance abuse, rural health, community-based research, social policy.

University of Houston, Graduate College of Social Work, Houston, TX 77204. Offers MSW, PhD. *Accreditation:* CSWE (one or more programs are accredited). *Program availability:* Part-time. *Degree requirements:* For master's, 900 clock hours of field experience, integrative paper. *Entrance requirements:* For master's, GRE, minimum GPA of 3.0 in last 60 hours, bachelor's degree. Additional exam requirements/recommendations for international students: Required—TOEFL (minimum score 550 paper-based; 79 iBT). *Faculty research:* Health care, gerontology, political social work, mental health, children and families.

University of Houston–Downtown, College of Public Service, Department of Criminal Justice and Social Work, Houston, TX 77002. Offers MS. *Program availability:* Part-time, evening/weekend, 100% online. *Degree requirements:* For master's, thesis or project. *Entrance requirements:* For master's, personal statement, 3 letters of recommendation, minimum GPA of 3.0 on last 60 hours. Additional exam requirements/recommendations for international students: Required—TOEFL (minimum score 550 paper-based; 50 iBT). Electronic applications accepted. *Expenses:* Contact institution. *Faculty research:* Policing issues, issues in security, community supervision, legal and other issues in prisons, juvenile justice.

University of Illinois at Chicago, Jane Addams College of Social Work, Chicago, IL 60607-7128. Offers MSW, PhD, Certificate. *Accreditation:* CSWE (one or more programs are accredited). *Program availability:* Part-time. Terminal master's awarded for partial completion of doctoral program. *Degree requirements:* For doctorate, thesis/dissertation. *Entrance requirements:* For master's, GMAT, minimum GPA of 2.75; for doctorate, GRE General Test or MAT, minimum GPA of 2.75. Additional exam requirements/recommendations for international students: Required—TOEFL. Electronic applications accepted. *Expenses:* Contact institution. *Faculty research:* Children, youth, and family; criminal justice; health; gerontology; international.

University of Illinois at Urbana–Champaign, Graduate College, School of Social Work, Champaign, IL 61820. Offers advocacy, leadership, and social change (MSW); children, youth and family services (MSW); health care (MSW); mental health (MSW); school social work (MSW); social work (PhD). *Accreditation:* CSWE (one or more programs are accredited). *Entrance requirements:* For master's and doctorate, minimum GPA of 3.0.

University of Indianapolis, Graduate Programs, College of Applied Behavioral Sciences, Indianapolis, IN 46227-3697. Offers addictions counseling (MA); clinical psychology (Psy D); mental health counseling (MA); psychology (MA); social work (MSW). *Accreditation:* APA. *Degree requirements:* For master's, practicum; for doctorate, comprehensive exam, thesis/dissertation, 1200 hours of clinical practicum, 2000-hour internship. *Entrance requirements:* For master's, GRE, 3 letters of recommendation; for doctorate, GRE, minimum GPA of 3.0, 18 hours of course work in psychology, 3 letters of recommendation. Additional exam requirements/recommendations for international students: Required—TOEFL (minimum score 550 paper-based).

The University of Iowa, Graduate College, College of Liberal Arts and Sciences, School of Social Work, Iowa City, IA 52242-1316. Offers MSW, PhD, JD/MSW, MSW/MA, MSW/MS, MSW/PhD. *Accreditation:* CSWE. *Degree requirements:* For master's, thesis optional; for doctorate, comprehensive exam, thesis/dissertation. *Entrance requirements:* For master's, minimum GPA of 3.0; for doctorate, GRE General Test, minimum GPA of 3.0. Additional exam requirements/recommendations for international students: Required—TOEFL (minimum score 600 paper-based; 100 iBT). Electronic applications accepted.

The University of Kansas, Graduate Studies, School of Social Welfare, Lawrence, KS 66045. Offers MSW, PhD, JD/MSW. *Accreditation:* CSWE (one or more programs are accredited). *Program availability:* Part-time, online learning. *Students:* 301 full-time (262 women), 45 part-time (41 women); includes 87 minority (25 Black or African American, non-Hispanic/Latino; 6 American Indian or Alaska Native, non-Hispanic/Latino; 7 Asian, non-Hispanic/Latino; 34 Hispanic/Latino; 15 Two or more races, non-Hispanic/Latino), 4 international. Average age 30. 279 applicants, 92% accepted, 190 enrolled. In 2018, 204 master's, 3 doctorates awarded. *Entrance requirements:* For master's, minimum GPA of 3.0, social work related experience, 3 letters of recommendation, student-issued transcripts from all previously attended schools regardless of degree status; for doctorate, GRE (Quantitative and Verbal), master's degree in social work or related field, minimum GPA of 3.5, personal statement, 3 letters of recommendation, completion of a statistics course with minimum B grade. Additional exam requirements/recommendations for international students: Required—TOEFL, IELTS. *Application deadline:* For fall admission, 1/15 for domestic and international students. Application fee: $65 ($85 for international students). Electronic applications accepted. *Financial support:* Fellowships, research assistantships, teaching assistantships, Federal Work-Study, scholarships/grants, and tuition waivers (partial) available. Support available to part-time students. Financial award application deadline: 1/17; financial award applicants required to submit FAFSA. *Faculty research:* Poverty, child welfare, children's mental health, aging and long-term care, families and connections. *Unit head:* Michelle Carney, Dean, 785-864-5975, E-mail: mmcarney@ku.edu. *Application contact:* Georgiana Spear, Graduate Admissions Contact, 785-864-0115, E-mail: gspear@ku.edu.
Website: http://socwel.ku.edu/

Social Work

University of Kentucky, Graduate School, College of Social Work, Lexington, KY 40506-0032. Offers MSW, PhD. *Accreditation:* CSWE. *Degree requirements:* For master's, comprehensive exam; for doctorate, comprehensive exam, thesis/dissertation. *Entrance requirements:* For master's, GRE General Test, minimum undergraduate GPA of 2.75; for doctorate, GRE General Test, minimum undergraduate GPA of 3.0. Additional exam requirements/recommendations for international students: Required—TOEFL (minimum score 550 paper-based). Electronic applications accepted.

University of Louisville, Graduate School, Kent School of Social Work, Louisville, KY 40292-0001. Offers marriage and family therapy (PMC), including mental health; social work (MSSW, PhD), including alcohol and drug counseling (MSSW), gerontology (MSSW), marriage and family (PhD), school social work (MSSW). *Accreditation:* AAMFT/ COAMFTE; CSWE (one or more programs are accredited). *Program availability:* Part-time, evening/weekend, 100% online, blended/hybrid learning. *Faculty:* 33 full-time (22 women), 63 part-time/adjunct (49 women). *Students:* 413 full-time (369 women), 107 part-time (85 women); includes 149 minority (83 Black or African American, non-Hispanic/Latino; 1 American Indian or Alaska Native, non-Hispanic/Latino; 9 Asian, non-Hispanic/Latino; 26 Hispanic/Latino; 1 Native Hawaiian or other Pacific Islander, non-Hispanic/Latino; 29 Two or more races, non-Hispanic/Latino), 7 international. Average age 31. 406 applicants, 69% accepted, 184 enrolled. In 2018, 175 master's, 2 doctorates awarded. *Degree requirements:* For doctorate, comprehensive exam, thesis/dissertation. *Entrance requirements:* For doctorate, GRE, Transcripts, three letters of recommendation, resume, example of scholarly writing, personal statement. Additional exam requirements/recommendations for international students: Required—TOEFL (minimum score 550 paper-based; 79 iBT), IELTS (minimum score 6.5). *Application deadline:* For fall admission, 5/30 for domestic and international students; for spring admission, 9/30 for domestic and international students; for summer admission, 2/28 for domestic and international students. Applications are processed on a rolling basis. Application fee: $65. Electronic applications accepted. *Expenses:* Contact institution. *Financial support:* In 2018–19, 99 students received support, including 1 fellowship (averaging $19,000 per year), 8 research assistantships with full tuition reimbursements available (averaging $21,500 per year), teaching assistantships with full tuition reimbursements available (averaging $19,000 per year); scholarships/grants, health care benefits, and unspecified assistantships also available. Financial award application deadline: 2/15; financial award applicants required to submit FAFSA. *Faculty research:* Equipping young children with skills, assisting abused or neglected children, illuminating the contributions that men and women make to their families, managing chronic conditions, enhance trauma-informed services, address social and health issues of older adults, palliative and end-of-life care, populations affected by the criminal justice system, human trafficking, issues related to HIV/AIDS, substance use. *Total annual research expenditures:* $9 million. *Unit head:* Dr. David Jenkins, Dean, 502-852-3944, Fax: 502-852-0422, E-mail: d.jenkins@louisville.edu. *Application contact:* Misty Kupka, Program Manager for Admissions and Recruitment, 502-852-0414, Fax: 502-852-0422, E-mail: misty.kupka@louisville.edu. Website: http://www.louisville.edu/kent

University of Maine, Graduate School, College of Natural Sciences, Forestry, and Agriculture, School of Social Work, Orono, ME 04469. Offers MSW, CGS. *Accreditation:* CSWE. *Program availability:* Part-time, evening/weekend. *Faculty:* 12 full-time (10 women), 16 part-time/adjunct (10 women). *Students:* 124 full-time (107 women), 9 part-time (all women); includes 12 minority (2 Black or African American, non-Hispanic/Latino; 3 American Indian or Alaska Native, non-Hispanic/Latino; 2 Hispanic/Latino; 5 Two or more races, non-Hispanic/Latino). Average age 34. 126 applicants, 77% accepted, 62 enrolled. In 2018, 36 master's, 5 other advanced degrees awarded. *Entrance requirements:* For master's, GRE General Test, MAT. Additional exam requirements/recommendations for international students: Required—TOEFL (minimum score 577 paper-based; 77 iBT), IELTS (minimum score 6). *Application deadline:* For fall admission, 2/1 priority date for domestic and international students; for summer admission, 2/1 for domestic and international students. Applications are processed on a rolling basis. Application fee: $65. Electronic applications accepted. *Financial support:* In 2018–19, 22 students received support. Federal Work-Study, scholarships/grants, health care benefits, and unspecified assistantships available. Financial award application deadline: 3/1. *Faculty research:* Intimate partner violence; substance abuse; long-term care workforce; aging and isolation; services and design in assistive technologies. *Total annual research expenditures:* $673,774. *Unit head:* Dr. Gail Werrbach, Director, 207-581-2397, Fax: 207-581-2396. *Application contact:* Scott G. Delcourt, Assistant Vice President for Graduate Studies and Senior Associate Dean, 207-581-3291, Fax: 207-581-3232, E-mail: graduate@maine.edu. Website: https://www.umaine.edu/socialwork/

The University of Manchester, School of Nursing, Midwifery and Social Work, Manchester, United Kingdom. Offers nursing (M Phil, PhD); social work (M Phil, PhD).

University of Manitoba, Faculty of Graduate Studies, Faculty of Social Work, Winnipeg, MB R3T 2N2, Canada. Offers MSW, PhD. *Degree requirements:* For master's, thesis or alternative.

University of Maryland, Baltimore, Graduate School, School of Social Work, Doctoral Program in Social Work, Baltimore, MD 21201. Offers PhD. *Program availability:* Part-time. *Degree requirements:* For doctorate, thesis/dissertation. *Entrance requirements:* For doctorate, GRE General Test, minimum GPA of 3.5, MSW. *Faculty research:* Social work research, social work teaching.

University of Maryland, Baltimore, Graduate School, School of Social Work, Master's Program in Social Work, Baltimore, MD 21201. Offers MSW, MBA/MSW, MSW/JD, MSW/MA, MSW/MPH. MSW/MA offered jointly with Baltimore Hebrew University; MBA/MSU with University of Maryland, College Park; MSW/MPH with The Johns Hopkins University. *Accreditation:* CSWE. *Entrance requirements:* For master's, minimum GPA of 3.0. Additional exam requirements/recommendations for international students: Required—TOEFL. Electronic applications accepted. *Faculty research:* Aging, families and children, health, mental health, social action and community development.

University of Maryland, College Park, Academic Affairs, Robert H. Smith School of Business, Combined MSW/MBA Program, College Park, MD 20742. Offers MSW/MBA. *Accreditation:* AACSB. *Entrance requirements:* Additional exam requirements/ recommendations for international students: Required—TOEFL.

University of Memphis, Graduate School, College of Arts and Sciences, School of Social Work, Memphis, TN 38152. Offers adults and families (MSW); children, youth, and families (MSW). *Accreditation:* CSWE. *Program availability:* Part-time, online learning. *Students:* 103 full-time (91 women), 39 part-time (38 women); includes 94 minority (88 Black or African American, non-Hispanic/Latino; 1 Asian, non-Hispanic/Latino; 1 Hispanic/Latino; 4 Two or more races, non-Hispanic/Latino), 1 international. Average age 32. 67 applicants, 90% accepted, 31 enrolled. In 2018, 62 master's awarded. *Expenses: Tuition, area resident:* Full-time $10,240; part-time $503 per credit hour. *Tuition, state resident:* full-time $10,464. *Tuition, nonresident:* full-time $20,224; part-time $991 per credit hour. *Required fees:* $850; $106 per credit hour. *Financial support:* Research assistantships available. *Unit head:* Dr. Susan Neely-Barnes, Chair, 901-678-3438, Fax: 901-678-2981, E-mail: snlybrns@memphis.edu. *Application contact:* Maggie Landry, Admissions Coordinator, 901-678-3156, E-mail: malandry@memphis.edu. Website: http://www.memphis.edu/socialwork/

University of Michigan, School of Social Work, Master of Social Work Program, Ann Arbor, MI 48109. Offers MSW, MSW/JD, MSW/MBA, MSW/MPH, MSW/MPP, MSW/MSI, MSW/MUP. PhD offered through the Rackham Graduate School. *Accreditation:* CSWE. *Faculty:* 60 full-time (40 women), 73 part-time/adjunct (56 women). *Students:* 765 full-time (642 women); includes 236 minority (88 Black or African American, non-Hispanic/Latino; 2 American Indian or Alaska Native, non-Hispanic/Latino; 49 Asian, non-Hispanic/Latino; 70 Hispanic/Latino; 27 Two or more races, non-Hispanic/Latino), 28 international. Average age 26. 1,249 applicants, 73% accepted, 429 enrolled. In 2018, 424 master's awarded. *Entrance requirements:* For master's, minimum of 20 academic semester credits total in at least three of the following disciplines: psychology, sociology, anthropology, economics, history, political science, government, and/or languages. Additional exam requirements/recommendations for international students: Required—TOEFL (minimum score 600 paper-based; 100 iBT), IELTS (minimum score 7), Michigan English Language Assessment Battery (minimum score 85). *Application deadline:* For fall admission, 3/1 priority date for domestic students, 2/1 priority date for international students. Applications are processed on a rolling basis. Application fee: $75. Electronic applications accepted. *Expenses:* $14,038 MI resident full-time per semester, $22,388 non-resident full-time per semester. *Financial support:* In 2018–19, 646 students received support. Career-related internships or fieldwork, Federal Work-Study, scholarships/grants, traineeships, and unspecified assistantships available. Financial award application deadline: 3/15; financial award applicants required to submit FAFSA. *Faculty research:* Children and families, aging, community organization, health and mental health, policy and evaluation. *Total annual research expenditures:* $4.7 million. *Unit head:* Lynn Videka, Dean, 734-764-5347, Fax: 734-615-5403, E-mail: lvideka@umich.edu. *Application contact:* Timothy Colenback, Assistant Dean for Student Services, 734-936-0961, Fax: 734-936-1961, E-mail: timot@umich.edu. Website: https://ssw.umich.edu/programs/msw

University of Minnesota, Duluth, Graduate School, College of Education and Human Service Professions, Department of Social Work, Duluth, MN 55812-2496. Offers MSW. *Accreditation:* CSWE. *Program availability:* Part-time, evening/weekend, online learning. *Entrance requirements:* For master's, minimum GPA of 3.0. Additional exam requirements/recommendations for international students: Required—TOEFL (minimum score 550 paper-based). *Faculty research:* Domestic abuse, substance abuse, minority health, child welfare, gerontology.

University of Minnesota, Twin Cities Campus, Graduate School, College of Education and Human Development, School of Social Work, Minneapolis, MN 55455-0213. Offers social work (MSW, PhD); youth development leadership (M Ed). *Accreditation:* CSWE (one or more programs are accredited). *Program availability:* Part-time, evening/weekend, online learning. *Faculty:* 21 full-time (13 women). *Students:* 247 full-time (207 women), 39 part-time (25 women); includes 104 minority (36 Black or African American, non-Hispanic/Latino; 4 American Indian or Alaska Native, non-Hispanic/Latino; 24 Asian, non-Hispanic/Latino; 16 Hispanic/Latino; 24 Two or more races, non-Hispanic/Latino), 8 international. Average age 29. 396 applicants, 49% accepted, 153 enrolled. In 2018, 161 master's, 7 doctorates awarded. *Degree requirements:* For doctorate, thesis/dissertation. *Entrance requirements:* For master's, minimum GPA of 3.0, 1 year of work experience; for doctorate, GRE, minimum GPA of 3.0, MSW. *Application deadline:* For fall admission, 1/15 for domestic students. Application fee: $75 ($95 for international students). *Financial support:* In 2018–19, 142 students received support, including 5 fellowships, 30 research assistantships (averaging $13,178 per year), 1 teaching assistantship (averaging $11,310 per year); career-related internships or fieldwork, Federal Work-Study, institutionally sponsored loans, and tuition waivers (full and partial) also available. Support available to part-time students. Financial award applicants required to submit FAFSA. *Faculty research:* Behavioral health, clinical mental health, aging and disability, work with youth, family and community violence prevention, new American and immigrant populations, child welfare, youth leadership, community engagement, mediation and restitution, social justice. *Total annual research expenditures:* $4 million. *Unit head:* Dr. John Bricout, Director, 612-624-3673, E-mail: jbricout@umn.edu. *Application contact:* Dr. Joseph Merighi, Director of Graduate Studies, 612-625-1220, E-mail: jmerighi@umn.edu. Website: http://www.cehd.umn.edu/ssw/

University of Mississippi, Graduate School, School of Applied Sciences, University, MS 38677. Offers communicative disorders (MS); criminal justice (MCJ); exercise science (MS); food and nutrition services (MS); health and kinesiology (PhD); health promotion (MS); nutrition and hospitality management (PhD); park and recreation management (MA); social welfare (PhD); social work (MSW). *Faculty:* 66 full-time (36 women), 27 part-time/adjunct (13 women). *Students:* 192 full-time (148 women), 40 part-time (25 women); includes 50 minority (41 Black or African American, non-Hispanic/Latino; 1 American Indian or Alaska Native, non-Hispanic/Latino; 1 Asian, non-Hispanic/Latino; 5 Hispanic/Latino; 2 Two or more races, non-Hispanic/Latino), 16 international. Average age 26. In 2018, 72 master's, 5 doctorates awarded. *Entrance requirements:* For master's, GRE General Test, minimum GPA of 3.0. Additional exam requirements/recommendations for international students: Required—TOEFL. *Application deadline:* Applications are processed on a rolling basis. Application fee: $50. Electronic applications accepted. *Financial support:* Scholarships/grants available. Financial award application deadline: 3/1; financial award applicants required to submit FAFSA. *Unit head:* Dr. Peter Grandjean, Dean of Applied Sciences, 662-915-7900, Fax: 662-915-7901, E-mail: applsci@olemiss.edu. *Application contact:* Temeka Smith, Graduate Activities Specialist for Admissions, 662-915-7474, Fax: 662-915-7577, E-mail: gschool@olemiss.edu.

University of Missouri, Office of Research and Graduate Studies, School of Social Work, Columbia, MO 65211. Offers gerontological social work (Graduate Certificate); social work (MSW, PhD); MSW/MPH; MSW/PhD. *Accreditation:* CSWE. *Program availability:* Part-time. *Entrance requirements:* For master's, GRE General Test, minimum GPA of 3.0. Additional exam requirements/recommendations for international students: Required—TOEFL (minimum score 90 iBT), IELTS (minimum score 7). Electronic applications accepted.

University of Missouri–Kansas City, College of Arts and Sciences, School of Social Work, Kansas City, MO 64110-2499. Offers MSW. *Accreditation:* CSWE. *Program availability:* Part-time, evening/weekend. *Entrance requirements:* For master's, minimum GPA of 3.0, 3 letters of reference. Additional exam requirements/recommendations for international students: Recommended—TOEFL (minimum score 550 paper-based; 80 iBT). *Faculty research:* Social justice, LGBT issues, deinstitutionalization, community collaboration and partnerships, evaluation of strengths model with addiction model.

University of Missouri–St. Louis, School of Social Work, St. Louis, MO 63121. Offers MSW. *Accreditation:* CSWE. *Program availability:* Part-time. *Entrance requirements:* For master's, 3 letters of recommendation, minimum GPA of 2.75. Additional exam requirements/recommendations for international students: Required—TOEFL (minimum score 550 paper-based; 79 iBT), IELTS (minimum score 6.5). Electronic applications accepted. *Faculty research:* Family violence, child abuse/neglect, immigration, community economic development.

University of Montana, Graduate School, College of Health Professions and Biomedical Sciences, School of Social Work, Missoula, MT 59812. Offers MSW. *Accreditation:* CSWE.

University of Nebraska at Omaha, Graduate Studies, College of Public Affairs and Community Service, Grace Abbott School of Social Work, Omaha, NE 68182. Offers social work (MSW). *Accreditation:* CSWE. *Degree requirements:* For master's, comprehensive exam, thesis (for some programs). *Entrance requirements:* For master's, minimum GPA of 3.0, 3 letters of recommendation, resume, statement of purpose. Additional exam requirements/recommendations for international students: Required—TOEFL (minimum score 550 paper-based; 61 iBT), IELTS (minimum score 5.5), PTE (minimum score 44). Electronic applications accepted.

University of Nevada, Las Vegas, Graduate College, Greenspun College of Urban Affairs, School of Social Work, Las Vegas, NV 89154-5032. Offers social work/law (MSW/JD); MSW/JD. *Accreditation:* CSWE. *Faculty:* 9 full-time (7 women), 8 part-time/adjunct (6 women). *Students:* 136 full-time (113 women), 56 part-time (42 women); includes 121 minority (37 Black or African American, non-Hispanic/Latino; 1 American Indian or Alaska Native, non-Hispanic/Latino; 13 Asian, non-Hispanic/Latino; 56 Hispanic/Latino; 14 Two or more races, non-Hispanic/Latino), 1 international. Average age 32. 135 applicants, 75% accepted, 73 enrolled. In 2018, 78 master's awarded. *Degree requirements:* For master's, thesis (for some programs). *Entrance requirements:* For master's, bachelor's degree with minimum GPA 2.75; 3 letters of recommendation; completion of some liberal arts courses. Additional exam requirements/recommendations for international students: Required—TOEFL (minimum score 550 paper-based; 80 iBT), IELTS (minimum score 7). Application fee: $60 ($95 for international students). Electronic applications accepted. *Expenses:* Contact institution. *Financial support:* In 2018–19, 19 students received support, including 8 research assistantships with full tuition reimbursements available (averaging $11,250 per year), 11 teaching assistantships with full tuition reimbursements available (averaging $11,250 per year); institutionally sponsored loans, scholarships/grants, health care benefits, and unspecified assistantships also available. Financial award application deadline: 3/15; financial award applicants required to submit FAFSA. *Faculty research:* Child welfare and juvenile justice, health and mental health, poverty and social justice, substance abuse, public policy. *Total annual research expenditures:* $1.3 million. *Unit head:* Dr. Carlton Craig, Director/Professor, 702-895-0521, Fax: 702-895-4079, E-mail: socialwork.chair@unlv.edu. *Application contact:* Dr. Maryann Overcamp-Martini, Graduate Coordinator, 702-895-4603, Fax: 702-895-4079, E-mail: socialwork.gradcoord@unlv.edu.
Website: http://socialwork.unlv.edu/

University of Nevada, Reno, Graduate School, Division of Health Sciences, School of Social Work, Reno, NV 89557. Offers MSW. *Accreditation:* CSWE. *Degree requirements:* For master's, thesis optional. *Entrance requirements:* For master's, GRE General Test, minimum GPA of 2.75, statistics course. Additional exam requirements/recommendations for international students: Required—TOEFL (minimum score 500 paper-based; 61 iBT), IELTS (minimum score 6). Electronic applications accepted. *Faculty research:* Policy practice, poverty, women's issues, race and diversity, vulnerable family, social justice, social change, diversity.

University of New England, College of Graduate and Professional Studies, Portland, ME 04005-9526. Offers advanced educational leadership (CAGS); applied nutrition (MS); career and technical education (MS Ed); curriculum and instruction (MS Ed); education (CAGS, Post-Master's Certificate); educational leadership (MS Ed, Ed D); generalist (MS Ed); health informatics (MS, Graduate Certificate); inclusion education (MS Ed); literacy K-12 (MS Ed); medical education leadership (MMEL); public health (MPH, Graduate Certificate); reading specialist (MS Ed); social work (MSW). *Program availability:* Part-time, evening/weekend, online only, 100% online. *Faculty:* 109 part-time/adjunct (78 women). *Students:* 1,207 full-time (972 women), 561 part-time (450 women); includes 411 minority (280 Black or African American, non-Hispanic/Latino; 17 American Indian or Alaska Native, non-Hispanic/Latino; 74 Asian, non-Hispanic/Latino; 25 Hispanic/Latino; 9 Native Hawaiian or other Pacific Islander, non-Hispanic/Latino; 6 Two or more races, non-Hispanic/Latino). Average age 36. 740 applicants, 92% accepted, 494 enrolled. In 2018, 586 master's, 44 doctorates, 85 other advanced degrees awarded. *Application deadline:* Applications are processed on a rolling basis. Electronic applications accepted. *Financial support:* Application deadline: 5/1; applicants required to submit FAFSA. *Unit head:* Dr. Martha Wilson, Dean of the College of Graduate and Professional Studies, 207-221-4985, E-mail: mwilson13@une.edu. *Application contact:* Nicole Lindsay, Director of Online Admissions, 207-221-4966, E-mail: nlindsay1@une.edu.
Website: http://online.une.edu

University of New England, Westbrook College of Health Professions, Biddeford, ME 04005-9526. Offers nurse anesthesia (MSNA); occupational therapy (MS); physical therapy (DPT); physician assistant (MS); social work (MSW). *Accreditation:* AANA/CANAEP; AOTA. *Program availability:* Part-time. *Faculty:* 37 full-time (26 women), 23 part-time/adjunct (15 women). *Students:* 500 full-time (360 women), 5 part-time (all women); includes 52 minority (3 Black or African American, non-Hispanic/Latino; 30 Asian, non-Hispanic/Latino; 10 Hispanic/Latino; 2 Native Hawaiian or other Pacific Islander, non-Hispanic/Latino; 7 Two or more races, non-Hispanic/Latino), 1 international. Average age 27. 2,512 applicants, 18% accepted, 227 enrolled. In 2018, 176 master's, 63 doctorates awarded. *Application deadline:* Applications are processed on a rolling basis. Electronic applications accepted. *Financial support:* Application deadline: 5/1; applicants required to submit FAFSA. *Unit head:* Dr. Karen T. Pardue, Dean, Westbrook College of Health Professions, 207-221-4361, E-mail: kpardue@une.edu. *Application contact:* Scott Steinberg, Vice President of University Admissions, 207-221-4225, Fax: 207-523-1925, E-mail: ssteinberg@une.edu.
Website: http://www.une.edu/wchp/index.cfm

University of New Hampshire, Graduate School, College of Health and Human Services, Department of Kinesiology, Durham, NH 03824. Offers adapted physical education (Postbaccalaureate Certificate); kinesiology (MS); kinesiology and social work (MS). *Program availability:* Part-time. *Entrance requirements:* For master's, GRE General Test. Additional exam requirements/recommendations for international students: Required—TOEFL (minimum score 550 paper-based; 80 iBT). Electronic applications accepted.

University of New Hampshire, Graduate School, College of Health and Human Services, Department of Social Work, Durham, NH 03824. Offers child welfare (Postbaccalaureate Certificate); intellectual and development disabilities (Postbaccalaureate Certificate); social work (MSW); substance use disorders (Postbaccalaureate Certificate); MSW/JD; MSW/MS. *Accreditation:* CSWE. *Program availability:* Part-time, online learning. *Entrance requirements:* Additional exam requirements/recommendations for international students: Required—TOEFL (minimum score 550 paper-based; 80 iBT). Electronic applications accepted.

University of New Hampshire, Graduate School Manchester Campus, Manchester, NH 03101. Offers business administration (MBA); cybersecurity policy and risk management (MS); educational administration and supervision (Ed S); educational studies (M Ed); elementary education (M Ed); information technology (MS); public administration (MPA); public health (MPH, Certificate); secondary education (M Ed, MAT); social work (MSW); substance use disorders (Certificate). *Program availability:* Part-time, evening/weekend. *Entrance requirements:* Additional exam requirements/

recommendations for international students: Required—TOEFL (minimum score 550 paper-based; 80 iBT). Electronic applications accepted.

The University of North Carolina at Chapel Hill, Graduate School, School of Social Work, Chapel Hill, NC 27599. Offers MSW, PhD, JD/MSW, MHA/MCRP, MPA/MSW, MSPH/MSW. *Accreditation:* CSWE (one or more programs are accredited). *Program availability:* Part-time. Terminal master's awarded for partial completion of doctoral program. *Degree requirements:* For doctorate, thesis/dissertation, qualifying exam. *Entrance requirements:* For master's and doctorate, GRE General Test, minimum GPA of 3.0. Electronic applications accepted. *Faculty research:* School success, risk and resiliency, welfare reform, aging, substance abuse.

The University of North Carolina at Charlotte, College of Health and Human Services, School of Social Work, Charlotte, NC 28223-0001. Offers MSW. *Accreditation:* CSWE. *Program availability:* Part-time. *Students:* 166 full-time (151 women), 15 part-time (14 women); includes 98 minority (56 Black or African American, non-Hispanic/Latino; 11 Asian, non-Hispanic/Latino; 26 Hispanic/Latino; 5 Two or more races, non-Hispanic/Latino), 3 international. Average age 29. 299 applicants, 47% accepted, 94 enrolled. In 2018, 79 master's awarded. *Entrance requirements:* For master's, GRE, minimum GPA of 3.0, statement of purpose, liberal arts foundation, resume, 3 letters of recommendation, interview, relevant volunteer and/or paid experience. Additional exam requirements/recommendations for international students: Required—TOEFL (minimum score 523 paper-based; 70 iBT), IELTS (minimum score 6), TOEFL (minimum score 523 paper-based, 70 iBT) or IELTS (6). *Application deadline:* Applications are processed on a rolling basis. Application fee: $75. Electronic applications accepted. Tuition and fees vary according to course load and program. *Financial support:* Research assistantships, career-related internships or fieldwork, Federal Work-Study, institutionally sponsored loans, scholarships/grants, unspecified assistantships, and administrative assistantship available. Support available to part-time students. Financial award application deadline: 3/1; financial award applicants required to submit FAFSA. *Total annual research expenditures:* $1.2 million. *Unit head:* Dr. Diana Rowan, Associate Professor and MSW Director, 704-687-7934, E-mail: drowan@uncc.edu. *Application contact:* Kathy B. Giddings, Director of Graduate Admissions, 704-687-5503, Fax: 704-687-1668, E-mail: gradadm@uncc.edu.
Website: http://socialwork.uncc.edu/

The University of North Carolina at Greensboro, Graduate School, School of Health and Human Sciences, Department of Social Work, Greensboro, NC 27412-5001. Offers MSW. Program offered jointly with North Carolina Agricultural and Technical State University. *Entrance requirements:* For master's, GRE General Test. Additional exam requirements/recommendations for international students: Required—TOEFL. Electronic applications accepted.

The University of North Carolina at Pembroke, The Graduate School, Department of Social Work, Pembroke, NC 28372-1510. Offers MSW. *Accreditation:* CSWE. *Program availability:* Part-time.

The University of North Carolina Wilmington, School of Social Work, Wilmington, NC 28403-3297. Offers MSW. *Accreditation:* CSWE. *Program availability:* Part-time. *Degree requirements:* For master's, comprehensive exam, thesis or alternative, field experience. *Entrance requirements:* For master's, GRE General Test, 3 letters of recommendation; resume; statement of interest; completion of introduction to sociology, introduction to psychology, basic statistics and either human biology or human development courses at the undergraduate level. Additional exam requirements/recommendations for international students: Required—TOEFL (minimum score 550 paper-based; 79 iBT), IELTS (minimum score 6.5). Electronic applications accepted.

University of North Dakota, Graduate School, College of Nursing and Professional Disciplines, Department of Social Work, Grand Forks, ND 58202. Offers MSW. *Accreditation:* CSWE. *Degree requirements:* For master's, comprehensive exam, thesis or alternative. *Entrance requirements:* For master's, minimum GPA of 3.0. Additional exam requirements/recommendations for international students: Required—TOEFL (minimum score 550 paper-based; 79 iBT), IELTS (minimum score 6.5). Electronic applications accepted. *Faculty research:* Mental health, gerontology, chemical abuse, children and families.

University of Northern British Columbia, Office of Graduate Studies, Prince George, BC V2N 4Z9, Canada. Offers business administration (Diploma); community health science (M Sc); disability management (MA); education (M Ed); first nations studies (MA); gender studies (MA); history (MA); interdisciplinary studies (MA); international studies (MA); mathematical, computer and physical sciences (M Sc); natural resources and environmental studies (M Sc, MA, MNRES, PhD); political science (MA); psychology (M Sc, PhD); social work (MSW). *Program availability:* Part-time, evening/weekend, online learning. *Degree requirements:* For master's, thesis; for doctorate, thesis/dissertation. *Entrance requirements:* For master's, GRE, minimum B average in undergraduate course work; for doctorate, candidacy exam, minimum A average in graduate course work.

University of Northern Iowa, Graduate College, College of Social and Behavioral Sciences, Department of Social Work, Cedar Falls, IA 50614. Offers MSW. *Accreditation:* CSWE. *Entrance requirements:* For master's, minimum GPA of 3.0; 3 letters of recommendation; personal autobiographical statement. Additional exam requirements/recommendations for international students: Required—TOEFL (minimum score 500 paper-based; 61 iBT). Electronic applications accepted.

University of North Florida, College of Arts and Sciences, Department of Sociology, Anthropology and Social Work, Jacksonville, FL 32224. Offers social work (MSW). *Program availability:* Part-time, evening/weekend. *Faculty:* 19 full-time (11 women), 1 part-time/adjunct (0 women). *Students:* 31 full-time (26 women); includes 11 minority (all Black or African American, non-Hispanic/Latino). Average age 30. 62 applicants, 37% accepted, 17 enrolled. In 2018, 12 master's awarded. *Degree requirements:* For master's, thesis or alternative. *Entrance requirements:* For master's, GRE General Test, minimum GPA of 3.0 in last 60 hours, letters of recommendation. Additional exam requirements/recommendations for international students: Required—TOEFL (minimum score 500 paper-based). *Application deadline:* Applications are processed on a rolling basis. Application fee: $30. Electronic applications accepted. *Expenses: Tuition, area resident:* Part-time $408.10 per credit hour. Tuition, state resident: part-time $408.10 per credit hour. Tuition, nonresident: part-time $932.61 per credit hour. *Required fees:* $111.81 per credit hour. Tuition and fees vary according to course load, campus/location and program. *Financial support:* In 2018–19, 4 students received support, including 2 research assistantships (averaging $1,273 per year); career-related internships or fieldwork, Federal Work-Study, and tuition waivers (partial) also available. Support available to part-time students. Financial award application deadline: 4/1; financial award applicants required to submit FAFSA. *Faculty research:* Telemarketing fraud, tax evasion practices of small business owners, jury knowledge and education, race and punishment in local schools, urban power structure. *Total annual research expenditures:* $186,862. *Unit head:* Dr. Adam Shapiro, Chair, 904-620-2850, Fax: 904-620-2540, E-mail: ashapiro@unf.edu. *Application contact:* Dr. Krista Paulsen, Graduate Coordinator, 904-620-2850, Fax: 904-620-2540, E-mail: kpaulsen@unf.edu.
Website: http://www.unf.edu/coas/sasw/

Social Work

University of Oklahoma, College of Arts and Sciences, Anne and Henry Zarrow School of Social Work, Norman, OK 73019. Offers direct practice (MSW), including administrative and community practice. *Accreditation:* CSWE. *Program availability:* Part-time, evening/weekend. *Faculty:* 27 full-time (19 women), 4 part-time/adjunct (2 women). *Students:* 220 full-time (188 women), 202 part-time (166 women); includes 183 minority (53 Black or African American, non-Hispanic/Latino; 38 American Indian or Alaska Native, non-Hispanic/Latino; 8 Asian, non-Hispanic/Latino; 38 Hispanic/Latino; 46 Two or more races, non-Hispanic/Latino), 3 international. Average age 32. 181 applicants, 86% accepted, 124 enrolled. In 2018, 170 master's awarded. *Degree requirements:* For master's, comprehensive exam, thesis or alternative. *Entrance requirements:* Additional exam requirements/recommendations for international students: Required—TOEFL (minimum score 79 iBT) or IELTS (minimum score 6.5). *Application deadline:* For fall admission, 2/1 priority date for domestic and international students; for summer admission, 2/1 priority date for domestic and international students. Application fee: $50 ($100 for international students). Electronic applications accepted. *Expenses:* Tuition, state resident: full-time $5683.20; part-time $236.80 per credit hour. Tuition, nonresident: full-time $20,342; part-time $847.60 per credit hour. *International tuition:* $20,342.40 full-time. *Required fees:* $2894.20; $110.05 per credit hour. $126.50 per semester. Tuition and fees vary according to course load and program. *Financial support:* Research assistantships, teaching assistantships, career-related internships or fieldwork, scholarships/grants, traineeships, health care benefits, tuition waivers, and unspecified assistantships available. Support available to part-time students. Financial award application deadline: 6/1; financial award applicants required to submit FAFSA. *Faculty research:* Poverty, health, child welfare, mental health, interpersonal violence, community development. *Unit head:* Dr. Julie Miller-Cribbs, Director, 918-660-3378, Fax: 918-660-3383, E-mail: jmcribbs@ou.edu. *Application contact:* Amy Ann Arnold, Admissions and Enrollment Coordinator, 918-660-3385, Fax: 918-660-3383, E-mail: aarnold@ou.edu.
Website: http://socialwork.ou.edu

University of Ottawa, Faculty of Graduate and Postdoctoral Studies, Faculty of Social Sciences, School of Social Work, Ottawa, ON K1N 6N5, Canada. Offers MSS. Program offered in French. *Degree requirements:* For master's, thesis or alternative. *Entrance requirements:* For master's, honors bachelor's degree or equivalent, minimum B average. Electronic applications accepted. *Faculty research:* Family-children, health.

University of Pennsylvania, School of Social Policy and Practice, Graduate Group on Social Welfare, Philadelphia, PA 19104. Offers PhD. *Degree requirements:* For doctorate, thesis/dissertation. *Entrance requirements:* For doctorate, GRE General Test, MSW or master's degree in related field. Additional exam requirements/recommendations for international students: Required—TOEFL (minimum score 600 paper-based; 100 iBT). Electronic applications accepted. *Faculty research:* Mental health, child welfare, organizational behavior, urban poverty, comparative social welfare.

University of Pennsylvania, School of Social Policy and Practice, Program in Social Work, Philadelphia, PA 19104. Offers MNPL, MSSP, MSW, DSW, JD/MSW, MSW/Certificate, MSW/MBA, MSW/MBE, MSW/MCP, MSW/MGA, MSW/MPH, MSW/MS Ed, MSW/MSC, MSW/PhD. *Accreditation:* CSWE. *Program availability:* Part-time. Terminal master's awarded for partial completion of doctoral program. *Degree requirements:* For master's, fieldwork; for doctorate, thesis/dissertation. *Entrance requirements:* For master's, GRE, GMAT, or LSAT (for MSSP or MNPL); for doctorate, GRE, MSW or master's degree in related field. Additional exam requirements/recommendations for international students: Required—TOEFL (minimum score 600 paper-based; 100 iBT). Electronic applications accepted. *Faculty research:* Homelessness, juvenile justice, mental health/children's mental health, child welfare, domestic and family violence.

University of Pittsburgh, School of Social Work, Pittsburgh, PA 15260. Offers MSW, PhD, Certificate, M Div/MSW, MPA/MSW, MPH/PhD, MPIA/MSW, MSW/JD, MSW/MBA, MSW/MPH. *Accreditation:* CSWE (one or more programs are accredited). *Program availability:* Part-time. *Degree requirements:* For master's, practicum; for doctorate, comprehensive exam, thesis/dissertation. *Entrance requirements:* For master's, minimum GPA of 3.0, course work in statistics; for doctorate, GRE, MSW or related degree, course work in statistics. Additional exam requirements/recommendations for international students: Required—TOEFL (minimum score 600 paper-based; 100 iBT). Electronic applications accepted. *Expenses:* Contact institution. *Faculty research:* Mental health services research, child abuse and neglect, geriatrics, criminal justice, race issues.

University of Puerto Rico–Río Piedras, College of Social Sciences, Graduate School of Social Work, San Juan, PR 00931-3300. Offers MSW, PhD. *Accreditation:* CSWE. *Program availability:* Part-time. *Degree requirements:* For master's, comprehensive exam, thesis; for doctorate, comprehensive exam, thesis/dissertation. *Entrance requirements:* For master's, PAEG or GRE, interview, minimum GPA of 3.0, letter of recommendation; for doctorate, PAEG or GRE, interview, minimum GPA of 3.0, 3 letters of recommendation, social work experience. *Faculty research:* Social work in Puerto Rico, Cuba, and the Dominican Republic; migration; poverty in Puerto Rico.

University of Regina, Faculty of Graduate Studies and Research, Faculty of Social Work, Regina, SK S4S 0A2, Canada. Offers indigenous social work (MISW); social work (MSW, PhD). PhD offered as a special case program. *Program availability:* Part-time. *Faculty:* 25 full-time (17 women), 8 part-time/adjunct (3 women). *Students:* 10 full-time (all women), 1 (woman) part-time. Average age 30. 76 applicants, 25% accepted, 17 enrolled. In 2018, 20 master's awarded. *Degree requirements:* For master's, thesis (for some programs), internship (for MISW); thesis, research practicum, or field practicum (for MSW); for doctorate, thesis/dissertation. *Entrance requirements:* For master's, 4 years of BSW; at least 2 years employment in a social work position following BSW degree; post secondary transcripts and 2 letters of recommendation; supplemental admissions form. Additional exam requirements/recommendations for international students: Required—TOEFL (minimum score 580 paper-based; 80 iBT), IELTS (minimum score 6.5), PTE (minimum score 59), could be any of test listed above. Other option are CANTEST, MELAB, CAEL or UR ESL. *Application deadline:* For fall admission, 1/31 for domestic and international students. Application fee: $100. Electronic applications accepted. *Expenses:* Estimated tuition and fees for one academic year is 6,702.90 for master's. The fee will vary base on your choice program. International students will pay additional 1,191.75 for international surcharge per semester. *Financial support:* In 2018–19, 38 students received support, including 32 fellowships, 6 teaching assistantships (averaging $2,552 per year); research assistantships, career-related internships or fieldwork, Federal Work-Study, scholarships/grants, unspecified assistantships, and travel award and Graduate Scholarship base funds also available. Support available to part-time students. Financial award application deadline: 9/30. *Faculty research:* Social policy analysis; social justice, human rights, and social work; family and child policies and programs; aging, society, and human service work; work, welfare, and social justice. *Unit head:* Dr. Judy White, Dean, 306-585-4037, Fax: 306-585-5691, E-mail: sw.dean@uregina.ca. *Application contact:* Dr. Nuelle Novik, Graduate Program Coordinator, 306-585-4573, Fax: 306-585-4872, E-mail: nuelle.novik@uregina.ca.
Website: http://www.uregina.ca/socialwork/

University of St. Francis, College of Arts and Sciences, Joliet, IL 60435-6169. Offers forensic social work (Post-Master's Certificate); physician assistant practice (MS); social work (MSW). *Program availability:* Part-time. *Faculty:* 12 full-time (10 women), 3 part-time/adjunct (2 women). *Students:* 119 full-time (95 women), 20 part-time (19 women); includes 46 minority (12 Black or African American, non-Hispanic/Latino; 1 American Indian or Alaska Native, non-Hispanic/Latino; 6 Asian, non-Hispanic/Latino; 21 Hispanic/Latino; 1 Native Hawaiian or other Pacific Islander, non-Hispanic/Latino; 5 Two or more races, non-Hispanic/Latino), 6 international. Average age 37. 60 applicants, 42% accepted, 17 enrolled. In 2018, 48 master's awarded. *Entrance requirements:* For master's, GRE (for MS). Additional exam requirements/recommendations for international students: Required—TOEFL (minimum score 550 paper-based; 79 iBT), IELTS (minimum score 6). *Application deadline:* Applications are processed on a rolling basis. Electronic applications accepted. Application fee is waived when completed online. *Expenses:* Contact institution. *Financial support:* In 2018–19, 13 students received support. Scholarships/grants and tuition waivers (partial) available. Support available to part-time students. Financial award applicants required to submit FAFSA. *Unit head:* Dr. Elizabeth Davies, Dean, 815-740-3819, E-mail: edavies@stfrancis.edu. *Application contact:* Sandee Sloka, Director Adult & Graduate Admissions, 800-735-7500, E-mail: ssloka@stfrancis.edu.
Website: https://www.stfrancis.edu/arts-sciences/

University of Saint Joseph, Program in Social Work, West Hartford, CT 06117-2700. Offers MSW.

University of St. Thomas, School of Social Work, St. Paul, MN 55105-1096. Offers MSW. *Accreditation:* CSWE. *Program availability:* Part-time, evening/weekend, 100% online, blended/hybrid learning. *Faculty:* 19 full-time, 42 part-time/adjunct. *Students:* 180 full-time, 188 part-time; includes 69 minority (28 Black or African American, non-Hispanic/Latino; 1 American Indian or Alaska Native, non-Hispanic/Latino; 11 Asian, non-Hispanic/Latino; 19 Hispanic/Latino; 10 Two or more races, non-Hispanic/Latino), 3 international. Average age 36. In 2018, 118 master's awarded. *Degree requirements:* For master's, thesis optional, fieldwork. *Entrance requirements:* For master's, previous undergraduate course work in lifespan developmental psychology, human biology, and statistics or research methods. Additional exam requirements/recommendations for international students: Required—TOEFL (minimum score 80 iBT). *Application deadline:* For fall admission, 1/10 for domestic and international students. Application fee: $0. Electronic applications accepted. *Expenses:* $799.50 per credit (for MSW), $1,131 per credit (for DSW). *Financial support:* In 2018–19, 8 research assistantships with partial tuition reimbursements (averaging $1,425 per year) were awarded; career-related internships or fieldwork, Federal Work-Study, scholarships/grants, and unspecified assistantships also available. Financial award application deadline: 7/1; financial award applicants required to submit FAFSA. *Faculty research:* Clinical supervision and practice, group work, child welfare and social work. *Unit head:* Dr. Corrine Carvalho, Interim Dean and Professor, 651-962-6031, Fax: 651-962-6031, E-mail: clcarvalho@stthomas.edu. *Application contact:* Dr. Corrine Carvalho, Interim Dean and Professor, 651-962-6031, Fax: 651-962-6031, E-mail: clcarvalho@stthomas.edu.
Website: http://www.stthomas.edu/socialwork/

University of South Africa, College of Human Sciences, Pretoria, South Africa. Offers adult education (M Ed); African languages (MA, PhD); African politics (MA, PhD); Afrikaans (MA, PhD); ancient history (MA, PhD); ancient Near Eastern studies (MA, PhD); anthropology (MA, PhD); applied linguistics (MA); Arabic (MA, PhD); archaeology (MA); art history (MA); Biblical archaeology (MA); Biblical studies (M Th, D Th, PhD); Christian spirituality (M Th, D Th); church history (M Th, D Th); classical studies (MA, PhD); clinical psychology (MA); communication (MA, PhD); comparative education (M Ed, Ed D); consulting psychology (D Admin, D Com, PhD); curriculum studies (M Ed, Ed D); development studies (M Admin, MA, D Admin, PhD); didactics (M Ed, Ed D); education (M Tech); education management (M Ed, Ed D); educational psychology (M Ed); English (MA); environmental education (M Ed); French (MA, PhD); German (MA, PhD); Greek (MA); guidance and counseling (M Ed); health studies (MA, PhD), including health sciences education (MA), health services management (MA), medical and surgical nursing science (critical care general) (MA), midwifery and neonatal nursing science (MA), trauma and emergency care (MA); history (MA, PhD); history of education (Ed D); inclusive education (M Ed, Ed D); information and communications technology policy and regulation (MA); information science (MA, MIS, PhD); international politics (MA, PhD); Islamic studies (MA, PhD); Italian (MA, PhD); Judaica (MA, PhD); linguistics (MA, PhD); mathematical education (M Ed); mathematics education (MA); missiology (M Th, D Th); modern Hebrew (MA, PhD); musicology (MA, MMus, D Mus, PhD); natural science education (M Ed); New Testament (M Th, D Th); Old Testament (D Th); pastoral therapy (M Th, D Th); philosophy (MA); philosophy of education (M Ed, Ed D); politics (MA, PhD); Portuguese (MA, PhD); practical theology (M Th, D Th); psychology (MA, MS, PhD); psychology of education (M Ed, Ed D); public health (MA); religious studies (MA, D Th, PhD); Romance languages (MA); Russian (MA, PhD); Semitic languages (MA, PhD); social behavior studies in HIV/AIDS (MA); social science (mental health) (MA); social science in development studies (MA); social science in psychology (MA); social science in social work (MA); social science in sociology (MA); social work (MSW, DSW, PhD); socio-education (M Ed, Ed D); sociolinguistics (MA); sociology (MA, PhD); Spanish (MA, PhD); systematic theology (M Th, D Th); TESOL (teaching English to speakers of other languages) (MA); theological ethics (M Th, D Th); theory of literature (MA, PhD); urban ministries (D Th); urban ministry (M Th).

University of South Carolina, The Graduate School, College of Social Work, Columbia, SC 29208. Offers MSW, PhD, JD/MSW, MSW/MPA, MSW/MPH. *Accreditation:* CSWE (one or more programs are accredited). *Program availability:* Part-time. *Degree requirements:* For master's, comprehensive exam; for doctorate, thesis/dissertation. *Entrance requirements:* For master's, GRE (minimum combined score 800), minimum undergraduate GPA of 3.0. Additional exam requirements/recommendations for international students: Required—TOEFL (minimum score 570 paper-based). Electronic applications accepted. *Expenses:* Contact institution. *Faculty research:* Victimization, child abuse and neglect, families.

University of South Dakota, Graduate School, School of Health Sciences, Department of Social Work, Vermillion, SD 57069. Offers MSW. *Accreditation:* CSWE. *Program availability:* Part-time, 100% online. *Entrance requirements:* For master's, baccalaureate degree, minimum cumulative undergraduate GPA of 3.0. Additional exam requirements/recommendations for international students: Required—TOEFL (minimum score 550 paper-based; 79 iBT), IELTS (minimum score 6).

University of Southern California, Graduate School, Suzanne Dworak-Peck School of Social Work, Los Angeles, CA 90089. Offers community organization, planning and administration (MSW); families and children (MSW); health (MSW); mental health (MSW); Military Social Work and Veterans Services (MSW); older adults (MSW); public child welfare (MSW); school settings (MSW); social work (MSW, PhD); systems of mental illness recovery (MSW); work and life (MSW); JD/MSW; M Pl/MSW; MPA/MSW; MSW/MBA; MSW/MJCS; MSW/MS. *Accreditation:* CSWE (one or more programs are accredited). *Degree requirements:* For doctorate, comprehensive exam, thesis/dissertation, qualifying exam/publishable paper. *Entrance requirements:* For doctorate, GRE General Test. Additional exam requirements/recommendations for international students: Required—TOEFL (minimum score 600 paper-based; 100 iBT), ESL exam. Electronic applications accepted. *Faculty research:* Department of Defense Educational Activity, detection/treatment of depression among older adults, health/aging, psychosocial adaptation to extreme environments/man made disasters; mental health needs of older adults.

University of Southern Indiana, Graduate Studies, College of Liberal Arts, Program in Social Work, Evansville, IN 47712-3590. Offers MSW. *Accreditation:* CSWE. *Entrance requirements:* For master's, minimum GPA of 3.0, evidence of writing skills, personal interview or video, minimum of 24 hours of social/behavioral science. Additional exam requirements/recommendations for international students: Required—TOEFL (minimum score 550 paper-based; 79 iBT), IELTS (minimum score 6). Electronic applications accepted.

University of Southern Maine, College of Management and Human Service, School of Social Work, Portland, ME 04103. Offers MSW. *Accreditation:* CSWE. *Program availability:* Part-time, evening/weekend. *Entrance requirements:* For master's, GRE or MAT. Electronic applications accepted. *Faculty research:* Poverty and discrimination, aging, interpersonal violence, evaluation of interventions and effectiveness, child and adult mental health, social welfare history, diversity issues.

University of Southern Mississippi, College of Education and Human Sciences, School of Social Work, Hattiesburg, MS 39406-0001. Offers MSW. *Accreditation:* CSWE. *Program availability:* Part-time. *Degree requirements:* For master's, comprehensive exam, thesis or alternative, practicum. *Entrance requirements:* For master's, GRE General Test, minimum GPA of 2.75 in last 60 hours. Additional exam requirements/recommendations for international students: Required—TOEFL, IELTS. Electronic applications accepted. *Faculty research:* Delinquency prevention, risk and resiliency in youth, successful aging, women in social service management, social work and the law.

University of South Florida, College of Behavioral and Community Sciences, School of Social Work, Tampa, FL 33620. Offers MSW, PhD, MSW/MPH. *Accreditation:* CSWE. *Program availability:* Part-time, evening/weekend. *Faculty:* 14 full-time (13 women). *Students:* 143 full-time (132 women), 79 part-time (69 women); includes 86 minority (42 Black or African American, non-Hispanic/Latino; 1 American Indian or Alaska Native, non-Hispanic/Latino; 7 Asian, non-Hispanic/Latino; 34 Hispanic/Latino; 2 Two or more races, non-Hispanic/Latino), 3 international. Average age 30. 184 applicants, 42% accepted, 48 enrolled. In 2018, 138 master's awarded. *Degree requirements:* For master's, comprehensive exam, thesis optional; for doctorate, comprehensive exam, thesis/dissertation. *Entrance requirements:* For master's, GRE scores are not required. However, applicants can submit GRE scores for consideration. Quantitative 144 (17%) or higher and Verbal 153 (61%) or higher, SOW application; 3 letters of recommendation; personal statement and essay; prerequisites required; interview may be required; experience in the field preferred; for doctorate, Graduate Record Examination (GRE) with preferred scores of at least 30th percentile in the quantitative section and at least 50th percentile in the verbal section, Master's degree with 3.5 GPA; 2 letters of recommendation; applicant statement; writing sample; interview may be required. Additional exam requirements/recommendations for international students: Required—TOEFL (minimum score 550 paper-based; 79 iBT). *Application deadline:* For fall admission, 2/15 priority date for domestic students, 2/15 for international students; for spring admission, 10/15 for domestic students, 9/15 for international students; for summer admission, 2/15 for domestic students, 1/15 for international students. Applications are processed on a rolling basis. Application fee: $30. Electronic applications accepted. *Expenses:* Tuition, state resident: full-time $6350. Tuition, nonresident: full-time $19,048. *International tuition:* $19,048 full-time. *Required fees:* $2079. *Financial support:* In 2018–19, 53 students received support, including 1 research assistantship with tuition reimbursement available (averaging $9,001 per year); unspecified assistantships also available. Financial award application deadline: 3/15; financial award applicants required to submit FAFSA. *Faculty research:* Kinship care, child trauma, juvenile delinquency, end-of-life issues, aging issues, child welfare, health and mental health disparities among various populations, HIV/AIDS and sexual violence in Haiti, integrated behavioral health care, international social work practice. *Total annual research expenditures:* $719,256. *Unit head:* Dr. Riaan van Zyl, Professor and Director, 813-974-4194, Fax: 813-974-4675, E-mail: nanpark@usf.edu. *Application contact:* Dr. Chris Simmons, MSW Chair and Instructor, 813-974-4306, E-mail: csimmon4@usf.edu.
Website: http://www.cas.usf.edu/social_work/

University of South Florida, Innovative Education, Tampa, FL 33620-9951. Offers adult, career and higher education (Graduate Certificate), including college teaching, leadership in developing human resources, leadership in higher education; Africana studies (Graduate Certificate), including diasporas and health disparities, genocide and human rights; aging studies (Graduate Certificate), including gerontology; art research (Graduate Certificate), including museum studies; business foundations (Graduate Certificate); chemical and biomedical engineering (Graduate Certificate), including materials science and engineering, water, health and sustainability; child and family studies (Graduate Certificate), including positive behavior support; civil and industrial engineering (Graduate Certificate), including transportation systems analysis; community and family health (Graduate Certificate), including maternal and child health, social marketing and public health, violence and injury: prevention and intervention, women's health; criminology (Graduate Certificate), including criminal justice administration; data science for public administration (Graduate Certificate); digital humanities (Graduate Certificate); educational measurement and research (Graduate Certificate), including evaluation; English (Graduate Certificate), including comparative literary studies, creative writing, professional and technical communication; entrepreneurship (Graduate Certificate); environmental health (Graduate Certificate), including safety management; epidemiology and biostatistics (Graduate Certificate), including applied biostatistics, biostatistics, concepts and tools of epidemiology, epidemiology, epidemiology of infectious diseases; geography, environment and planning (Graduate Certificate), including community development, environmental policy and management, geographical information systems; geology (Graduate Certificate), including hydrogeology; global health (Graduate Certificate), including disaster management, global health and Latin American and Caribbean studies, global health practice, humanitarian assistance, infection control; government and international affairs (Graduate Certificate), including Cuban studies, globalization studies; health policy and management (Graduate Certificate), including health management and leadership, public health policy and programs; hearing specialist: early intervention (Graduate Certificate); industrial and management systems engineering (Graduate Certificate), including systems engineering, technology management; information studies (Graduate Certificate), including school library media specialist; information systems/decision sciences (Graduate Certificate), including analytics and business intelligence; instructional technology (Graduate Certificate), including distance education, Florida digital/virtual educator, instructional design, multimedia design, Web design; internal medicine, bioethics and medical humanities (Graduate Certificate), including biomedical ethics; Latin American and Caribbean studies (Graduate Certificate); leadership for coastal resiliency planning (Graduate Certificate); mass communications (Graduate Certificate), including multimedia journalism; mathematics and statistics (Graduate Certificate), including mathematics; medicine (Graduate Certificate), including aging and neuroscience, bioinformatics, biotechnology, brain fitness and memory management, clinical investigation, hand and upper limb rehabilitation, health informatics, health sciences, integrative weight management, intellectual property, medicine and gender, metabolic and nutritional medicine, metabolic cardiology, pharmacy sciences; national and competitive intelligence (Graduate Certificate); nursing (Graduate Certificate),

including simulation based academic fellowship in advanced pain management; psychological and social foundations (Graduate Certificate), including career counseling, college teaching, diversity in education, mental health counseling, school counseling; public affairs (Graduate Certificate), including nonprofit management, public management, research administration; public health (Graduate Certificate), including assessing chemical toxicity and public health risks, health equity, pharmacoepidemiology, public health generalist, toxicology, translational research in adolescent behavioral health; public health practices (Graduate Certificate), including planning for healthy communities; rehabilitation and mental health counseling (Graduate Certificate), including integrative mental health care, marriage and family therapy, rehabilitation technology; secondary education (Graduate Certificate), including ESOL, foreign language education: culture and content, foreign language education: professional; social work (Graduate Certificate), including geriatric social work/clinical gerontology; special education (Graduate Certificate), including autism spectrum disorder, disabilities education: severe/profound; world languages (Graduate Certificate), including teaching English as a second language (TESL) or foreign language. *Expenses:* Tuition, state resident: full-time $6350. Tuition, nonresident: full-time $19,048. *International tuition:* $19,048 full-time. *Required fees:* $2079. *Unit head:* Dr. Cynthia DeLuca, Associate Vice President and Assistant Vice Provost, 813-974-3077, Fax: 813-974-7061, E-mail: deluca@usf.edu. *Application contact:* Owen Hooper, Director, Summer and Alternative Calendar Programs, 813-974-6917, E-mail: hooper@usf.edu.
Website: http://www.usf.edu/innovative-education/

University of South Florida Sarasota-Manatee, College of Liberal Arts and Social Sciences, Sarasota, FL 34243. Offers criminal justice (MA); education (MA); educational leadership (M Ed), including curriculum leadership, K-12 public school leadership, non-public/charter school leadership; elementary education (MAT); English education (MA); social work (MSW). *Program availability:* Part-time, 100% online, blended/hybrid learning. *Faculty:* 14 full-time (9 women), 6 part-time/adjunct (5 women). *Students:* 10 full-time (8 women), 46 part-time (40 women); includes 17 minority (6 Black or African American, non-Hispanic/Latino; 7 Hispanic/Latino; 4 Two or more races, non-Hispanic/Latino). Average age 33. 57 applicants, 46% accepted, 24 enrolled. In 2018, 12 master's awarded. *Degree requirements:* For master's, comprehensive exam (for some programs). *Entrance requirements:* For master's, GRE. Additional exam requirements/recommendations for international students: Required—TOEFL (minimum score 550 paper-based; 79 iBT), IELTS (minimum score 6.5). *Application deadline:* For fall admission, 3/1 priority date for domestic students, 3/1 for international students; for spring admission, 10/1 priority date for domestic students, 10/1 for international students. Applications are processed on a rolling basis. Application fee: $30. Electronic applications accepted. *Expenses:* Tuition, area resident: Full-time $8350; part-time $348 per credit hour. Tuition, state resident: full-time $8350; part-time $348 per credit hour. Tuition, nonresident: full-time $19,048; part-time $794 per credit hour. *Required fees:* $1689; $70 per credit hour. $5 per semester. Tuition and fees vary according to program. *Financial support:* Career-related internships or fieldwork, institutionally sponsored loans, scholarships/grants, health care benefits, and unspecified assistantships available. Support available to part-time students. Financial award application deadline: 6/30; financial award applicants required to submit FAFSA. *Faculty research:* Educational leadership, secondary education, elementary education, and criminal justice. *Total annual research expenditures:* $97,764. *Unit head:* Dr. Jane Rose, Dean, 941-359-4469, Fax: 941-359-4778, E-mail: jane.rose@sar.usf.edu. *Application contact:* Brandon Avery, Assistant Director, Admissions, 941-359-4331, E-mail: bavery@sar.usf.edu.

The University of Tennessee, Graduate School, College of Social Work, Doctor of Social Work Program, Knoxville, TN 37996. Offers clinical practice and leadership (DSW).

The University of Tennessee, Graduate School, College of Social Work, Master of Science in Social Work Program, Knoxville, TN 37996. Offers evidenced-based interpersonal practice (MSSW); management leadership and community practice (MSSW). *Accreditation:* CSWE. *Program availability:* Part-time, online learning.

The University of Tennessee, Graduate School, College of Social Work, PhD in Social Work Program, Knoxville, TN 37996. Offers PhD.

The University of Tennessee at Chattanooga, Program in Social Work, Chattanooga, TN 37403. Offers MSW. *Degree requirements:* For master's, portfolio, field practicum. *Entrance requirements:* For master's, GRE, 2 letters of reference, criminal background check. Additional exam requirements/recommendations for international students: Required—TOEFL (minimum score 550 paper-based; 79 iBT), IELTS (minimum score 6). Electronic applications accepted. *Faculty research:* Dementia care, foster parenting, juvenile justice system.

The University of Texas at Arlington, Graduate School, School of Social Work, Arlington, TX 76019. Offers MSW, PhD. *Accreditation:* CSWE (one or more programs are accredited). *Program availability:* Part-time, evening/weekend, online learning. *Degree requirements:* For master's, thesis optional; for doctorate, comprehensive exam, thesis/dissertation. *Entrance requirements:* For master's, GRE General Test (if GPA less than 3.0), 3 letters of recommendation; for doctorate, GRE General Test (if GPA is below 3.4), minimum graduate GPA of 3.4. Additional exam requirements/recommendations for international students: Required—TOEFL (minimum score 550 paper-based). Electronic applications accepted. *Faculty research:* Community practice, administrative practice, mental health and children and families.

The University of Texas at Austin, Graduate School, Steve Hicks School of Social Work, Austin, TX 78712-1111. Offers MSSW, PhD. *Accreditation:* CSWE (one or more programs are accredited). *Program availability:* Part-time. *Degree requirements:* For doctorate, thesis/dissertation. *Entrance requirements:* For master's and doctorate, GRE General Test. Additional exam requirements/recommendations for international students: Required—TOEFL. *Faculty research:* Substance abuse, child welfare, gerontology, mental health, public policy.

The University of Texas at El Paso, Graduate School, College of Health Sciences, Social Work Program, El Paso, TX 79968-0001. Offers social work in the border region (MSW). *Accreditation:* CSWE. *Program availability:* Part-time. *Entrance requirements:* For master's, statistics and biology, undergraduate degree from accredited university. Additional exam requirements/recommendations for international students: Required—TOEFL (minimum score 550 paper-based; 80 iBT). Electronic applications accepted. *Faculty research:* Immigration, trauma, health, farm workers, child welfare, mental health.

The University of Texas at San Antonio, College of Public Policy, Department of Social Work, San Antonio, TX 78249-0617. Offers MSW. *Accreditation:* CSWE. *Entrance requirements:* For master's, GRE, bachelor's degree, three letters of recommendation, statement of purpose. Additional exam requirements/recommendations for international students: Required—TOEFL (minimum score 550 paper-based; 79 iBT), IELTS (minimum score 6.5). Electronic applications accepted.

University of the Fraser Valley, Graduate Studies, Abbotsford, BC V2S 7M8, Canada. Offers criminal justice (MA); social work (MSW). *Program availability:* Evening/weekend. *Faculty:* 23 full-time (13 women). *Students:* 46 full-time (32 women), 38 part-time (27

women); includes 26 minority (all American Indian or Alaska Native, non-Hispanic/ Latino). Average age 40. 65 applicants, 89% accepted, 58 enrolled. In 2018, 27 master's awarded. *Degree requirements:* For master's, thesis optional, major research paper. *Entrance requirements:* For master's, bachelor's degree, work experience in related field. Additional exam requirements/recommendations for international students: Recommended—TOEFL (minimum score 570 paper-based; 88 iBT), IELTS (minimum score 6.5), TWE (minimum score 4.5), TSE (minimum score 61). *Application deadline:* For fall admission, 1/31 priority date for domestic students, 4/1 priority date for international students; for winter admission, 8/31 priority date for domestic students; for spring admission, 12/31 priority date for domestic students. Application fee: $75 ($250 for international students). Electronic applications accepted. *Expenses:* 7890 tuition; 508 fees. *Financial support:* Research assistantships, scholarships/grants, health care benefits, and bursaries available. Financial award application deadline: 5/10. *Faculty research:* Criminal justice, criminology, social work, child welfare. *Unit head:* Dr. Garry Fehr, Associate Vice President for Research, Engagement and Graduate Studies, 604-504-4074, Fax: 778-880-0356, E-mail: Garry.Fehr@ufv.ca. *Application contact:* Educational Advisors, 604-854-4528, Fax: 604-855-7614, E-mail: advising@ufv.ca.
Website: http://www.ufv.ca/Graduate_Studies.htm

The University of Toledo, College of Graduate Studies, College of Health and Human Services, School of Social Justice, Toledo, OH 43606-3390. Offers criminal justice (MA); social work (MSW).

The University of Toledo, College of Graduate Studies, College of Social Justice and Human Service, Department of Criminal Justice and Social Work, Toledo, OH 43606-3390. Offers child advocacy (Certificate); criminal justice (MA); elder law (Certificate); juvenile justice (Certificate); patient advocacy (Certificate); social work (MSW); JD/MA. *Accreditation:* CSWE. *Program availability:* Part-time. *Degree requirements:* For master's, comprehensive exam, thesis. *Entrance requirements:* For master's and Certificate, minimum cumulative GPA of 2.7 for all previous academic work, letters of recommendation. Additional exam requirements/recommendations for international students: Required—TOEFL (minimum score 550 paper-based; 80 iBT). Electronic applications accepted.

University of Toronto, School of Graduate Studies, Faculty of Social Work, Toronto, ON M5S 1A1, Canada. Offers MSW, PhD, MH Sc/MSW. *Program availability:* Part-time. *Degree requirements:* For doctorate, thesis/dissertation, oral exam/thesis defense. *Entrance requirements:* For master's, minimum mid-B average in final year of full-time study, 3 full courses in social sciences, experience in social services (recommended), 3 letters of reference, resume; for doctorate, MSW or equivalent, minimum B+ average, competency in basic statistical methods. Additional exam requirements/ recommendations for international students: Required—TOEFL (minimum score 580 paper-based; 93 iBT), IELTS (minimum score 7), TWE (minimum score 5), or Michigan English Language Assessment Battery (minimum score 85). Electronic applications accepted. *Expenses:* Contact institution.

University of Utah, Graduate School, College of Social Work, Salt Lake City, UT 84112. Offers MSW, PhD, MSW/JD, MSW/MPA, MSW/MPH. *Accreditation:* CSWE (one or more programs are accredited). *Program availability:* Part-time, evening/weekend. *Faculty:* 17 full-time (8 women), 52 part-time/adjunct (35 women). *Students:* 299 full-time (238 women), 26 part-time (22 women); includes 84 minority (12 Black or African American, non-Hispanic/Latino; 5 American Indian or Alaska Native, non-Hispanic/ Latino; 10 Asian, non-Hispanic/Latino; 41 Hispanic/Latino; 2 Native Hawaiian or other Pacific Islander, non-Hispanic/Latino; 14 Two or more races, non-Hispanic/Latino), 2 international. Average age 32. In 2018, 164 master's, 5 doctorates awarded. *Degree requirements:* For master's, comprehensive exam (for some programs), thesis (for some programs); for doctorate, comprehensive exam (for some programs), thesis/dissertation (for some programs). *Entrance requirements:* For master's, minimum GPA of 3.0; for doctorate, GRE, minimum GPA of 3.0. Additional exam requirements/recommendations for international students: Required—TOEFL (minimum score 80 iBT). Electronic applications accepted. *Expenses:* Contact institution. *Financial support:* Federal Work-Study, institutionally sponsored loans, and scholarships/grants available. Financial award application deadline: 4/30; financial award applicants required to submit FAFSA. *Faculty research:* Criminal justice program, housing support and stability, sobriety, outpatient treatment. *Unit head:* Dr. Martell L. Teasley, Dean, 801-581-6194, E-mail: martell.teasley@utah.edu. *Application contact:* Elizabeth Perez, Director of Academic Advising, 801-585-1596, E-mail: elizabeth.perez@utah.edu.
Website: https://socialwork.utah.edu/

University of Vermont, Graduate College, College of Education and Social Services, Department of Social Work, Burlington, VT 05405. Offers MSW. *Accreditation:* CSWE. *Entrance requirements:* For master's, resume. Additional exam requirements/ recommendations for international students: Required—TOEFL (minimum score 550 paper-based, 90 iBT) or IELTS (6.5). Electronic applications accepted.

University of Victoria, Faculty of Graduate Studies, Faculty of Human and Social Development, School of Social Work, Victoria, BC V8W 2Y2, Canada. Offers MSW. *Entrance requirements:* For master's, BSW. Additional exam requirements/ recommendations for international students: Required—TOEFL (minimum score 575 paper-based), IELTS (minimum score 7). Electronic applications accepted. *Faculty research:* Women's issues, public policy formation and implementation, child welfare, First Nations, community development.

University of Victoria, Faculty of Graduate Studies, Faculty of Human and Social Development, Studies in Policy and Practice Program, Victoria, BC V8W 2Y2, Canada. Offers MA. *Program availability:* Part-time. *Degree requirements:* For master's, thesis. *Entrance requirements:* For master's, resume. Additional exam requirements/ recommendations for international students: Required—TOEFL (minimum score 575 paper-based), IELTS (minimum score 7). Electronic applications accepted. *Faculty research:* Women's issues, public policy formation and implementation, health promotion and education, children, youth and families.

University of Washington, Graduate School, School of Social Work, Seattle, WA 98195. Offers MSW, PhD, MPH/MSW. *Accreditation:* CSWE (one or more programs are accredited). *Program availability:* Evening/weekend, online learning. *Degree requirements:* For master's, thesis optional; for doctorate, thesis/dissertation. *Entrance requirements:* For master's, GRE General Test, minimum GPA of 3.0; for doctorate, master's degree, sample of scholarly work, minimum GPA of 3.0. Additional exam requirements/recommendations for international students: Required—TOEFL. *Faculty research:* Health and mental health; children, youth, and families; multicultural issues; reducing risk and enhancing protective factors in children; etrology of substance use.

University of Washington, Tacoma, Graduate Programs, Program in Social Work, Tacoma, WA 98402-3100. Offers advanced integrative practice (MSW); social work (MSW). *Program availability:* Part-time, evening/weekend. *Degree requirements:* For master's, completion of all 75 required credits with minimum cumulative GPA of 3.0, 2.7 in each course; degree completion within 6 years. *Entrance requirements:* For master's, baccalaureate degree from regionally-accredited institution, minimum GPA of 3.0 on most recent 90 quarter credit hours or 60 semester hours, resume, social service experience form, two essay question responses, criminal/conviction history and background check clearance, three letters of reference. Additional exam requirements/ recommendations for international students: Required—TOEFL (minimum score 580 paper-based; 70 iBT). Electronic applications accepted. *Faculty research:* Domestic violence and prevention, LGBT issues, gerontological social work, transnational social work, child welfare-mental health.

University of West Florida, College of Education and Professional Studies, Department of Social Work, Pensacola, FL 32514-5750. Offers MSW. *Accreditation:* CSWE. *Program availability:* Part-time, evening/weekend. *Entrance requirements:* For master's, GRE or MAT, official transcripts; minimum undergraduate cumulative GPA of 3.0; academic preparation as demonstrated by quality and relevance of undergraduate degree major; letter of intent; 3 letters of recommendation; work experience as documented on the Social Work Supplemental Application. Additional exam requirements/recommendations for international students: Required—TOEFL (minimum score 550 paper-based). Electronic applications accepted.

University of Windsor, Faculty of Graduate Studies, Faculty of Arts and Social Sciences, School of Social Work, Windsor, ON N9B 3P4, Canada. Offers MSW. *Program availability:* Part-time. *Degree requirements:* For master's, thesis or alternative. *Entrance requirements:* For master's, minimum B+ average in last year of undergraduate study. Additional exam requirements/recommendations for international students: Required—TOEFL (minimum score 600 paper-based). Electronic applications accepted. *Faculty research:* Addiction, social policy analysis, gerontology and health care.

University of Wisconsin–Green Bay, Graduate Studies, Program in Social Work, Green Bay, WI 54311-7001. Offers MSW. *Accreditation:* CSWE. *Program availability:* Part-time. *Degree requirements:* For master's, thesis or alternative. *Entrance requirements:* For master's, GRE, minimum GPA of 2.75. Electronic applications accepted. *Faculty research:* Child welfare.

University of Wisconsin–Madison, Graduate School, College of Letters and Science, School of Social Work, Madison, WI 53706-1380. Offers social welfare (PhD); social work (MSW). *Accreditation:* CSWE (one or more programs are accredited). Terminal master's awarded for partial completion of doctoral program. *Degree requirements:* For doctorate, thesis/dissertation. *Entrance requirements:* For master's, minimum GPA of 3.0 on last 60 credits; for doctorate, GRE General Test, minimum GPA of 3.0 on last 60 credits. Electronic applications accepted. *Expenses:* Contact institution. *Faculty research:* Poverty, caregiving, child welfare, developmental disabilities, mental health, severe mental illnesses, adolescence, family, social policy, child support.

University of Wisconsin–Milwaukee, Graduate School, Helen Bader School of Social Welfare, Department of Social Work, Milwaukee, WI 53201-0413. Offers applied gerontology (Graduate Certificate); nonprofit management (Graduate Certificate); social welfare (PhD); social work (MSW, PhD). *Program availability:* Part-time. *Students:* 224 full-time (196 women), 92 part-time (82 women); includes 101 minority (47 Black or African American, non-Hispanic/Latino; 5 American Indian or Alaska Native, non-Hispanic/Latino; 12 Asian, non-Hispanic/Latino; 2 Hispanic/Latino; 35 Two or more races, non-Hispanic/Latino), 3 international. Average age 31. 387 applicants, 59% accepted, 180 enrolled. In 2018, 86 master's, 1 other advanced degree awarded. *Entrance requirements:* For doctorate, GRE, bachelor's degree. Additional exam requirements/recommendations for international students: Required—TOEFL (minimum score 550 paper-based; 79 iBT), IELTS (minimum score 6.5). *Application deadline:* For fall admission, 1/1 priority date for domestic students; for spring admission, 9/1 for domestic students. Application fee: $56 ($96 for international students). Electronic applications accepted. *Financial support:* Fellowships, research assistantships, teaching assistantships, career-related internships or fieldwork, health care benefits, unspecified assistantships, and project assistantships available. Support available to part-time students. Financial award application deadline: 4/15; financial award applicants required to submit FAFSA. *Application contact:* Deb Padgett, Associate Professor, Social Work, 414-229-6452, E-mail: dpadgett@uwm.edu.
Website: http://uwm.edu/socialwelfare/academics/

University of Wisconsin–Oshkosh, Graduate Studies, Department of Social Work, Oshkosh, WI 54901. Offers MSW. Program offered jointly with University of Wisconsin–Green Bay. *Accreditation:* CSWE. *Program availability:* Part-time. *Entrance requirements:* For master's, GRE, letters of recommendation, previous courses in statistics and human biology, work experience. Additional exam requirements/ recommendations for international students: Required—TOEFL (minimum score 550 paper-based; 79 iBT).

University of Wyoming, College of Health Sciences, Division of Social Work, Laramie, WY 82071. Offers MSW. *Accreditation:* CSWE. *Degree requirements:* For master's, comprehensive exam, thesis or alternative. *Entrance requirements:* For master's, minimum GPA of 3.0. Additional exam requirements/recommendations for international students: Required—TOEFL. *Expenses:* Contact institution. *Faculty research:* Social work education, child welfare, mental health, diversity, school social work.

Utah State University, School of Graduate Studies, College of Humanities and Social Sciences, Department of Sociology, Social Work, and Anthropology, Logan, UT 84322. Offers anthropology (MS); social work (MSW); sociology (MS, PhD). *Accreditation:* CSWE. *Degree requirements:* For master's, thesis; for doctorate, comprehensive exam, thesis/dissertation. *Entrance requirements:* For master's, GRE General Test, minimum GPA of 3.0, recommendation letters; for doctorate, GRE General Test, minimum GPA of 3.0, recommendation letters, transcripts, personal statement, MS degree. Additional exam requirements/recommendations for international students: Required—TOEFL; Recommended—TWE. *Faculty research:* Demography, environmental/natural resource sociology, rural community change, international development, health studies.

Utah Valley University, Program in Social Work, Orem, UT 84058-5999. Offers MSW. *Expenses: Tuition, area resident:* Full-time $7932. Tuition, state resident: full-time $7932. Tuition, nonresident: full-time $19,781. *International tuition:* $19,781 full-time. *Required fees:* $700. Tuition and fees vary according to course load and program.

Valdosta State University, Department of Social Work, Valdosta, GA 31698. Offers MSW. *Accreditation:* CSWE. *Program availability:* Part-time, evening/weekend, online learning. *Degree requirements:* For master's, comprehensive exam, 5 practica. *Entrance requirements:* For master's, GRE General Test, MAT, minimum GPA of 3.0 in last 2 years of course work. Additional exam requirements/recommendations for international students: Required—TOEFL (minimum score 523 paper-based); Recommended—IELTS. *Expenses:* Contact institution.

Virginia Commonwealth University, Graduate School, School of Social Work, Doctoral Program in Social Work, Richmond, VA 23284-9005. Offers PhD. *Degree requirements:* For doctorate, comprehensive exam, thesis/dissertation. *Entrance requirements:* For doctorate, GRE General Test, MSW or related degree. Additional exam requirements/recommendations for international students: Required—TOEFL (minimum score 600 paper-based; 100 iBT). Electronic applications accepted.

Virginia Commonwealth University, Graduate School, School of Social Work, Master's Program in Social Work, Richmond, VA 23284-9005. Offers MSW, JD/MSW, MSW/M Div, MSW/MPH. *Accreditation:* CSWE. *Entrance requirements:* Additional exam requirements/recommendations for international students: Required—TOEFL (minimum score 600 paper-based; 100 iBT). Electronic applications accepted.

Walden University, Graduate Programs, School of Social Work and Human Services, Minneapolis, MN 55401. Offers addictions and social work (DSW); advanced clinical practice (MSW); clinical expertise (DSW); criminal justice (DSW); disaster, crisis, and intervention (DSW); family studies and interventions (DSW); human and social services (PhD), including advanced research, community and social services, community intervention and leadership, conflict management, criminal justice, disaster crisis and intervention, family studies and intervention, gerontology, global social services, higher education, human services and nonprofit administration, mental health facilitation; medical social work (DSW); military social work (MSW); policy practice (DSW); social work (PhD), including addictions and social work, clinical expertise, criminal justice, disaster, crisis and intervention, family studies and interventions, medical social work, policy practice, social work administration; social work administration (DSW); social work in healthcare (MSW); social work with children and families (MSW). *Accreditation:* CSWE. *Program availability:* Part-time, evening/weekend, online only, 100% online. *Degree requirements:* For master's, residency (for some programs); for doctorate, thesis/dissertation, residency. *Entrance requirements:* For master's, bachelor's degree or higher; minimum GPA of 2.5; official transcripts; goal statement (for some programs); access to computer and Internet; for doctorate, master's degree or higher; three years of related professional or academic experience (preferred); minimum GPA of 3.0; goal statement and current resume (for select programs); official transcripts; access to computer and Internet. Additional exam requirements/recommendations for international students: Required—TOEFL (minimum score 550 paper-based, 79 iBT), IELTS (minimum score 6.5), Michigan English Language Assessment Battery (minimum score 82), or PTE (minimum score 53). Electronic applications accepted.

Walla Walla University, Graduate Studies, Wilma Hepker School of Social Work and Sociology, College Place, WA 99324. Offers social work (MSW). *Accreditation:* CSWE. *Program availability:* Part-time. *Entrance requirements:* For master's, minimum GPA of 2.75, essay. Additional exam requirements/recommendations for international students: Required—TOEFL (minimum score 550 paper-based; 79 iBT). Electronic applications accepted.

Washburn University, School of Applied Studies, Department of Social Work, Topeka, KS 66621. Offers clinical social work (MSW); JD/MSW. *Accreditation:* CSWE. *Program availability:* Part-time, evening/weekend. *Degree requirements:* For master's, practicum. *Entrance requirements:* For master's, coursework in human biology and cultural anthropology, multiculturalism, or human diversity. Additional exam requirements/recommendations for international students: Required—TOEFL (minimum score 80 iBT). *Faculty research:* Trauma, multicultural issues, school social work, emotional intelligence, animal-assisted therapy.

Washington University in St. Louis, Brown School, St. Louis, MO 63110. Offers American Indian/Alaska native (MSW); children, youth and families (MSW); epidemiology/biostatistics (MPH); generalist (MPH); global health (MPH); health (MSW); health policy analysis (MPH); individualized (MSW), including health; mental health (MSW); older adults and aging societies (MSW); public health sciences (PhD); social and economic development (MSW), including domestic, international; social work (PhD); urban design (MPH); violence and injury prevention (MSW); JD/MSW; M Arch/MSW; MPH/MBA; MSW/M Div; MSW/M Ed; MSW/MAPS; MSW/MBA; MSW/MPH; MUD/MSW. MSW/M Div and MSW/MAPS offered in partnership with Eden Theological Seminary. *Accreditation:* CEPH; CSWE (one or more programs are accredited). *Degree requirements:* For master's, 60 credit hours (for MSW); 52 credit hours (for MPH); practicum; for doctorate, comprehensive exam, thesis/dissertation. *Entrance requirements:* For master's, GRE (preferred), GMAT, LSAT, MCAT, PCAT, or United States Medical Licensing Exam (for MPH); for doctorate, GRE. Additional exam requirements/recommendations for international students: Required—TOEFL (minimum score 100 iBT), IELTS (minimum score 7). Electronic applications accepted. *Expenses:* Contact institution. *Faculty research:* Mental health, social policy, health policy, epidemiology, social and economic development.

Wayne State University, College of Liberal Arts and Sciences, Department of Anthropology, Detroit, MI 48202. Offers anthropology (MA, PhD); social work (PhD). Doctoral program admits for fall only. *Program availability:* Part-time. *Faculty:* 14. *Students:* 28 full-time (21 women), 9 part-time (6 women); includes 6 minority (2 Black or African American, non-Hispanic/Latino; 1 Asian, non-Hispanic/Latino; 2 Hispanic/Latino; 1 Two or more races, non-Hispanic/Latino). Average age 33. 33 applicants, 42% accepted, 4 enrolled. In 2018, 23 master's, 3 doctorates awarded. *Degree requirements:* For master's, thesis (for some programs); for doctorate, one foreign language, thesis/dissertation. *Entrance requirements:* For master's, three letters of recommendation, completion of introduction to anthropology, letter of intent, writing sample, minimum undergraduate GPA of 3.2; for doctorate, GRE, bachelor's degree in anthropology or a related field, three letters of recommendation, completion of introduction to anthropology, letter of intent, writing sample, minimum undergraduate GPA of 3.2. Additional exam requirements/recommendations for international students: Required—TOEFL (minimum score 550 paper-based; 79 iBT), TWE (minimum score 5.5), Michigan English Language Assessment Battery (minimum score 85); Recommended—IELTS (minimum score 6.5). *Application deadline:* For fall admission, 1/10 for domestic and international students; for winter admission, 10/1 for domestic and international students. Application fee: $50. Electronic applications accepted. *Financial support:* In 2018–19, 25 students received support, including 3 fellowships with tuition reimbursements available (averaging $29,333 per year), 2 research assistantships with tuition reimbursements available (averaging $21,286 per year), 5 teaching assistantships with tuition reimbursements available (averaging $19,267 per year); scholarships/grants and unspecified assistantships also available. Financial award applicants required to submit FAFSA. *Faculty research:* Anthropology of Detroit, archaeology, business and organizational anthropology, linguistic anthropology, cultural anthropology, medical anthropology, biological anthropology. *Unit head:* Dr. Andrea Sankar, Professor and Chair, 313-577-6961, E-mail: asankar@wayne.edu. *Application contact:* Dr. Stephen Chrisomalis, Director of Graduate Studies, 313-577-9922, E-mail: chrisomalis@wayne.edu.
Website: http://clas.wayne.edu/anthropology/

Wayne State University, School of Social Work, Detroit, MI 48202. Offers gerontology (Certificate); social work (MSW, PhD). Application deadlines: April 1 for MSW, December 19 for PhD. *Accreditation:* CSWE (one or more programs are accredited). *Program availability:* Part-time, evening/weekend. *Students:* 484 full-time, 162 part-time. 708 applicants, 41% accepted. Terminal master's awarded for partial completion of doctoral program. *Degree requirements:* For master's, field work; for doctorate, comprehensive exam, thesis/dissertation. *Entrance requirements:* For master's, personal interest statement, resume, 3 references; for doctorate, GRE (minimum combined score of 1000 on Verbal and Quantitative components), minimum undergraduate GPA of 3.5, MSW from CSWE-accredited institution (or working towards one), resume, three letters of reference, personal statement, summary of relevant research and professional experience, writing sample, interview; for Certificate, MSW or actively enrolled in advanced portion of MSW program. Additional exam requirements/recommendations for international students: Required—TOEFL (minimum score 550 paper-based; 79 iBT), TWE (minimum score 5.5), Michigan English Language Assessment Battery (minimum score 85); Recommended—IELTS (minimum score 6.5). *Application deadline:* For spring admission, 4/1 for domestic students. Applications are processed on a rolling basis. Application fee: $50. Electronic applications accepted. *Financial support:* Fellowships with tuition reimbursements, research assistantships with tuition reimbursements, teaching assistantships with tuition reimbursements, scholarships/grants, and unspecified assistantships available. Financial award applicants required to submit FAFSA. *Faculty research:* Aging, child welfare, health and behavioral health, interpersonal violence, community development, policy and program development. *Unit head:* Sheryl Kubiak, Dean and Professor, 313-577-4409, E-mail: spk@wayne.edu. *Application contact:* Anwar Najor-Durack, Assistant Dean for Student Affairs, 313-577-4409, E-mail: ac1724@wayne.edu.
Website: http://socialwork.wayne.edu/

West Chester University of Pennsylvania, College of Education and Social Work, Department of Social Work, West Chester, PA 19383. Offers gerontology (Certificate); social work (MSW). *Accreditation:* CSWE. *Program availability:* Part-time, evening/weekend. *Degree requirements:* For master's, completion of foundation courses and field practicums. *Entrance requirements:* For master's, minimum GPA of 3.0, personal statement of 3 to 5 pages clearly articulating professional goals, two letters of recommendation. Additional exam requirements/recommendations for international students: Required—TOEFL or IELTS. Electronic applications accepted. *Faculty research:* Recovery in mental health and substance abuse disorders, integrated health and interprofessional education, trauma and disaster intervention, multicultural resources, human rights including LGBTQA rights.

Western Carolina University, Graduate School, College of Health and Human Sciences, Department of Social Work, Cullowhee, NC 28723. Offers MSW. *Accreditation:* CSWE. *Program availability:* Part-time. *Entrance requirements:* For master's, appropriate undergraduate major with minimum GPA of 3.0, 3 recommendations, resume. Additional exam requirements/recommendations for international students: Required—TOEFL (minimum score 550 paper-based; 79 iBT). *Expenses: Tuition, area resident:* Full-time $4435. Tuition, state resident: full-time $4435. Tuition, nonresident: full-time $14,842. *International tuition:* $14,842 full-time. *Required fees:* $2979. Part-time tuition and fees vary according to course load, degree level and program.

Western Illinois University, School of Graduate Studies, College of Education and Human Services, Department of Health Sciences and Social Work, Macomb, IL 61455-1390. Offers health sciences (MS), including public health, school health. *Accreditation:* NCATE. *Program availability:* Part-time. *Students:* 37 full-time (25 women), 18 part-time (14 women); includes 17 minority (11 Black or African American, non-Hispanic/Latino; 6 Hispanic/Latino), 20 international. Average age 31. 38 applicants, 82% accepted, 12 enrolled. In 2018, 12 master's awarded. *Degree requirements:* For master's, comprehensive exam, thesis or alternative. *Entrance requirements:* Additional exam requirements/recommendations for international students: Required—TOEFL (minimum score 550 paper-based; 80 iBT). *Application deadline:* Applications are processed on a rolling basis. Application fee: $30. Electronic applications accepted. *Financial support:* Unspecified assistantships available. Financial award applicants required to submit FAFSA. *Unit head:* Dr. Lorette Oden, Chairperson, 309-298-1076. *Application contact:* Dr. Mark Mossman, Associate Provost and Director of Graduate Studies, 309-298-1806, Fax: 309-298-2345, E-mail: grad-office@wiu.edu.
Website: http://www.wiu.edu/coehs/health_sciences/

Western Kentucky University, Graduate School, College of Health and Human Services, Department of Social Work, Bowling Green, KY 42101. Offers MSW. *Accreditation:* CSWE. *Entrance requirements:* Additional exam requirements/recommendations for international students: Required—TOEFL (minimum score 555 paper-based; 79 iBT).

Western Michigan University, Graduate College, College of Health and Human Services, School of Social Work, Kalamazoo, MI 49008. Offers MSW. *Accreditation:* CSWE. *Program availability:* Part-time.

Western New Mexico University, Graduate Division, Department of Social Work, Silver City, NM 88062-0680. Offers MSW. *Accreditation:* CSWE. *Program availability:* Part-time, evening/weekend, online learning. Electronic applications accepted.

Westfield State University, College of Graduate and Continuing Education, Department of Social Work, Westfield, MA 01086. Offers MSW. *Accreditation:* CSWE. *Program availability:* Part-time, evening/weekend. *Degree requirements:* For master's, comprehensive exam, thesis (for some programs). *Entrance requirements:* For master's, GRE General Test or MAT, minimum undergraduate GPA of 2.8. Additional exam requirements/recommendations for international students: Recommended—TOEFL (minimum score 550 paper-based; 79 iBT). *Expenses:* Contact institution.

West Texas A&M University, College of Education and Social Sciences, Department of Psychology, Sociology and Social Work, Canyon, TX 79015. Offers psychology (MA); social work (MS). *Accreditation:* CSWE. *Program availability:* Part-time, evening/weekend. *Degree requirements:* For master's, comprehensive exam, thesis optional. *Entrance requirements:* For master's, GRE General Test, 3 letters of recommendation; interview; minimum GPA of 3.25 in psychology, 3.0 overall. Additional exam requirements/recommendations for international students: Required—TOEFL. Electronic applications accepted.

West Virginia University, Eberly College of Arts and Sciences, School of Social Work, Morgantown, WV 26506. Offers aging and health care (MSW); children and families (MSW); community mental health (MSW); community organization and social administration (MSW); direct (clinical) social work practice (MSW). *Program availability:* Part-time. *Degree requirements:* For master's, fieldwork. *Entrance requirements:* For master's, GRE, minimum GPA of 2.75, 2 letters of reference. Additional exam requirements/recommendations for international students: Required—TOEFL. *Faculty research:* Rural and small town social work practice, gerontology, health and mental health, welfare reform, child welfare.

Wichita State University, Graduate School, Fairmount College of Liberal Arts and Sciences, School of Social Work, Wichita, KS 67260. Offers MSW. *Accreditation:* CSWE. *Unit head:* Dr. Kyoung Lee, Director, 316-978-7250, Fax: 316-978-3328, E-mail: kyoung.lee@wichita.edu. *Application contact:* Jordan Oleson, Admissions Coordinator, 316-978-3095, Fax: 316-978-3253, E-mail: jordan.oleson@wichita.edu.
Website: http://www.wichita.edu/sw

Widener University, School of Human Service Professions, Center for Social Work Education, Chester, PA 19013-5792. Offers MSW, PhD. *Accreditation:* CSWE.

Wilfrid Laurier University, Faculty of Graduate and Postdoctoral Studies, Lyle S. Hallman Faculty of Social Work, Waterloo, ON N2L 3C5, Canada. Offers Aboriginal studies (MSW); community, policy, planning and organizations (MSW); critical social policy and organizational studies (PhD); individuals, families and groups (MSW); social work practice (individuals, families, groups and communities) (PhD); social work practice: individuals, families, groups and communities (PhD). *Program availability:* Part-time. *Degree requirements:* For master's, thesis optional; for doctorate, thesis/dissertation. *Entrance requirements:* For master's, course work in social science, research methodology, and statistics; honors BA with a minimum B average; for doctorate, master's degree in social work, minimum A- average. Additional exam

Social Work

requirements/recommendations for international students: Required—TOEFL (minimum score 89 iBT). Electronic applications accepted. *Expenses:* Contact institution.

Winthrop University, College of Arts and Sciences, Program in Social Work, Rock Hill, SC 29733. Offers MSW. *Accreditation:* CSWE. *Students:* 45 full-time (39 women), 94 part-time (85 women); includes 68 minority (60 Black or African American, non-Hispanic/Latino; 2 American Indian or Alaska Native, non-Hispanic/Latino; 1 Asian, non-Hispanic/Latino; 4 Hispanic/Latino; 1 Two or more races, non-Hispanic/Latino), 1 international. Average age 30. In 2018, 53 master's awarded. *Entrance requirements:* For master's, GRE or MAT, minimum GPA of 3.0, 3 letters of recommendation, resume. Additional exam requirements/recommendations for international students: Required—TOEFL (minimum score 550 paper-based; 79 iBT), IELTS (minimum score 6). *Application deadline:* For fall admission, 7/15 priority date for domestic students; for spring admission, 12/1 for domestic students. Applications are processed on a rolling basis. Application fee: $50. Electronic applications accepted. *Expenses:* Tuition, state resident: full-time $15,166; part-time $635 per credit hour. Tuition, nonresident: full-time $29,214. *Required fees:* $500; $180 per semester. *Financial support:* Research assistantships with full tuition reimbursements available. *Faculty research:* Field study placement opportunities. *Unit head:* Dr. Anthony Hill, Graduate Program Director, 803-323-2168, E-mail: hilla@winthrop.edu. *Application contact:* 800-411-7041, Fax: 803-323-2292, E-mail: gradschool@winthrop.edu. Website: http://www.winthrop.edu/cas/socialwork/msw

Yeshiva University, Wurzweiler School of Social Work, New York, NY 10033-3201. Offers MSW, PhD, MSW/Certificate. *Accreditation:* CSWE (one or more programs are accredited). *Program availability:* Part-time, evening/weekend. Terminal master's awarded for partial completion of doctoral program. *Degree requirements:* For master's, thesis, integrative essay; for doctorate, comprehensive exam, thesis/dissertation. *Entrance requirements:* For master's, interview, minimum GPA of 3.0, letters of reference; for doctorate, GRE, interview, letters of reference, writing sample, MSW, minimum of 2 years of professional social work experience. Additional exam requirements/recommendations for international students: Required—TOEFL (minimum score 577 paper-based). *Expenses:* Contact institution. *Faculty research:* Child abuse, AIDS, day care, non profits, gerontology.

York University, Faculty of Graduate Studies, Faculty of Liberal Arts and Professional Studies, Program in Social Work, Toronto, ON M3J 1P3, Canada. Offers MSW, PhD. *Program availability:* Part-time, evening/weekend. *Degree requirements:* For master's, thesis or alternative. Electronic applications accepted.

Youngstown State University, College of Graduate Studies, Bitonte College of Health and Human Services, Program in Social Work, Youngstown, OH 44555-0001. Offers MSW.

APPENDIXES

Institutional Changes
Since the 2019 Edition

Following is an alphabetical listing of institutions that have recently closed, merged with other institutions, or changed their names or status. In the case of a name change, the former name appears first, followed by the new name.

Argosy University, Dallas (Farmers Branch, TX): *closed.*

Argosy University, Denver (Denver, CO): *closed.*

Argosy University, Inland Empire (Ontario, CA): *closed.*

Argosy University, Nashville (Nashville, TN): *closed.*

Argosy University, Salt Lake City (Draper, UT): *closed.*

Argosy University, San Diego (San Diego, CA): *closed.*

Argosy University, San Francisco Bay Area (Alameda, CA): *closed.*

Argosy University, Sarasota (Sarasota, FL): *closed.*

Argosy University, Schaumburg (Schaumburg, IL): *closed.*

Arlington Baptist College (Arlington, TX): *name changed to Arlington Baptist University.*

Armstrong State University (Savannah, GA): *name changed to Georgia Southern University–Armstrong Campus.*

Art Center College of Design (Pasadena, CA): *name changed to ArtCenter College of Design.*

The Art Institute of California–San Francisco, a campus of Argosy University (San Francisco, CA): *closed.*

Augsburg College (Minneapolis, MN): *name changed to Augsburg University.*

Bristol University (Anaheim, CA): *closed.*

Claremont McKenna College (Claremont, CA): *merged into The Claremont Colleges (Claremont, CA).*

Coleman University (San Diego, CA): *closed.*

Digital Media Arts College (Boca Raton, FL): *closed.*

Everest University (Tampa, FL): *no longer offers graduate degrees.*

Fairleigh Dickinson University, College at Florham (Madison, NJ): *name changed to Fairleigh Dickinson University, Florham Campus.*

Faith Evangelical College & Seminary (Tacoma, WA): *name changed to Faith International University.*

Frank Lloyd Wright School of Architecture (Scottsdale, AZ): *name changed to School of Architecture at Taliesin.*

Future Generations Graduate School (Franklin, WV): *name changed to Future Generations University.*

Grace University (Omaha, NE): *closed.*

Greenville College (Greenville, IL): *name changed to Greenville University.*

Hazelden Graduate School of Addiction Studies (Center City, MN): *name changed to Hazelden Betty Ford Graduate School of Addiction.*

Henley-Putnam University (San Jose, CA): *name changed to Henley-Putnam School of Strategic Security.*

Huntington College of Health Sciences (Knoxville, TN): *name changed to Huntington University of Health Sciences.*

The Institute for the Psychological Sciences (Arlington, VA): *name changed to Divine Mercy University.*

International College of the Cayman Islands (Newlands, Cayman Islands): *not accredited by an agency recognized by USDE or CHEA at the time of publication.*

Johnson State College (Johnson, VT): *name changed to Northern Vermont University–Johnson.*

John Wesley University (High Point, NC): *closed.*

Kaplan University, Davenport Campus (Davenport, IA): *name changed to Purdue University Global.*

Knowledge Systems Institute (Skokie, IL): no longer degree granting.

Long Island University–Hudson at Westchester (Purchase, NY): *name changed to Long Island University–Hudson.*

Lutheran Theological Seminary at Gettysburg (Gettysburg, PA): *name changed to United Lutheran Seminary.*

Lynchburg College (Lynchburg, VA): *name changed to University of Lynchburg.*

Lyndon State College (Lyndonville, VT): *name changed to Northern Vermont University–Lyndon.*

Marylhurst University (Marylhurst, OR): *closed.*

McNally Smith College of Music (Saint Paul, MN): *closed.*

Memphis College of Art (Memphis, TN): *closed.*

Mirrer Yeshiva (Brooklyn, NY): *name changed to Mirrer Yeshiva Central Institute.*

Moody Theological Seminary–Michigan (Plymouth, MI): *name changed to Moody Theological Seminary Michigan.*

Mount Ida College (Newton, MA): *closed.*

National American University (Rapid City, SD): no longer offers graduate degrees.

The Ohio State University–Mansfield Campus (Mansfield, OH): *name changed to The Ohio State University at Mansfield.*

The Ohio State University–Newark Campus (Newark, OH): *name changed to The Ohio State University at Newark.*

Our Lady of the Lake College (Baton Rouge, LA): *name changed to Franciscan Missionaries of Our Lady University.*

Philadelphia University (Philadelphia, PA): *closed.*

Rudolf Steiner College (Fair Oaks, CA): *not accredited by an agency recognized by USDE or CHEA at the time of publication.*

Sacred Heart School of Theology (Hales Corners, WI): *name changed to Sacred Heart Seminary and School of Theology.*

Sewanee: The University of the South (Sewanee, TN): *name changed to The University of the South.*

Shepherd University (Los Angeles, CA): *closed.*

Silicon Valley University (San Jose, CA): *closed.*

South University (Novi, MI): *closed.*

South University (High Point, NC): *closed.*

South University (Cleveland, OH): *closed.*

University of Great Falls (Great Falls, MT): *name changed to University of Providence.*

University of Phoenix–Atlanta Campus (Sandy Springs, GA): *closed.*

University of Phoenix–Augusta Campus (Augusta, GA): *closed.*

University of Phoenix–Central Florida Campus (Orlando, FL): *closed.*

University of Phoenix–Charlotte Campus (Charlotte, NC): *closed.*

University of Phoenix–Colorado Campus (Lone Tree, CO): *closed.*

University of Phoenix–Colorado Springs Downtown Campus (Colorado Springs, CO): *closed.*

University of Phoenix–Columbus Georgia Campus (Columbus, GA): *closed.*

University of Phoenix–Jersey City Campus (Jersey City, NJ): *closed.*

University of Phoenix–New Mexico Campus (Albuquerque, NM): *closed.*

University of Phoenix–North Florida Campus (Jacksonville, FL): *closed.*

University of Phoenix–Southern Arizona Campus (Tucson, AZ): *closed.*

University of Phoenix–Southern California Campus (Costa Mesa, CA): *closed.*

University of Phoenix–South Florida Campus (Miramar, FL): *closed.*

University of Phoenix–Utah Campus (Salt Lake City, UT): *closed.*

University of Phoenix–Washington D.C. Campus (Washington, DC): *closed.*

University of Phoenix–Western Washington Campus (Tukwila, WA): *closed.*

University of Puerto Rico, Mayagüez Campus (Mayagüez, PR): *name changed to University of Puerto Rico–Mayagüez.*

University of Puerto Rico, Medical Sciences Campus (San Juan, PR): *name changed to University of Puerto Rico–Medical Sciences Campus.*

University of Puerto Rico, Río Piedras Campus (San Juan, PR): *name changed to University of Puerto Rico–Río Piedras.*

The University of South Dakota (Vermillion, SD): *name changed to University of South Dakota.*

Urbana University (Urbana, OH): *name changed to Urbana University–A Branch Campus of Franklin University.*

Virginia College in Birmingham (Birmingham, AL): *closed.*

Warner Pacific College (Portland, OR): *name changed to Warner Pacific University.*

Wheelock College (Boston, MA): *merged into Boston University (Boston, MA).*

Wright Institute (Berkeley, CA): *name changed to The Wright Institute.*

Yeshiva Karlin Stolin Rabbinical Institute (Brooklyn, NY): *name changed to Yeshiva Karlin Stolin.*

Abbreviations Used in the Guides

The following list includes abbreviations of degree names used in the profiles in the 2020 edition of the guides. Because some degrees (e.g., Doctor of Education) can be abbreviated in more than one way (e.g., D.Ed. or Ed.D.), and because the abbreviations used in the guides reflect the preferences of the individual colleges and universities, the list may include two or more abbreviations for a single degree.

DEGREES

A Mus D	Doctor of Musical Arts
AC	Advanced Certificate
AD	Artist's Diploma
	Doctor of Arts
ADP	Artist's Diploma
Adv C	Advanced Certificate
AGC	Advanced Graduate Certificate
AGSC	Advanced Graduate Specialist Certificate
ALM	Master of Liberal Arts
AM	Master of Arts
AMBA	Accelerated Master of Business Administration
APC	Advanced Professional Certificate
APMPH	Advanced Professional Master of Public Health
App Sc	Applied Scientist
App Sc D	Doctor of Applied Science
AstE	Astronautical Engineer
ATC	Advanced Training Certificate
Au D	Doctor of Audiology
B Th	Bachelor of Theology
CAES	Certificate of Advanced Educational Specialization
CAGS	Certificate of Advanced Graduate Studies
CAL	Certificate in Applied Linguistics
CAPS	Certificate of Advanced Professional Studies
CAS	Certificate of Advanced Studies
CATS	Certificate of Achievement in Theological Studies
CE	Civil Engineer
CEM	Certificate of Environmental Management
CET	Certificate in Educational Technologies
CGS	Certificate of Graduate Studies
Ch E	Chemical Engineer
Clin Sc D	Doctor of Clinical Science
CM	Certificate in Management
CMH	Certificate in Medical Humanities
CMM	Master of Church Ministries
CMS	Certificate in Ministerial Studies
CNM	Certificate in Nonprofit Management
CPC	Certificate in Publication and Communication
CPH	Certificate in Public Health
CPS	Certificate of Professional Studies
CScD	Doctor of Clinical Science
CSD	Certificate in Spiritual Direction
CSS	Certificate of Special Studies
CTS	Certificate of Theological Studies
D Ac	Doctor of Acupuncture
D Admin	Doctor of Administration
D Arch	Doctor of Architecture
D Be	Doctor in Bioethics
D Com	Doctor of Commerce
D Couns	Doctor of Counseling
D Des	Doctorate of Design
D Div	Doctor of Divinity
D Ed	Doctor of Education
D Ed Min	Doctor of Educational Ministry
D Eng	Doctor of Engineering
D Engr	Doctor of Engineering
D Ent	Doctor of Enterprise
D Env	Doctor of Environment
D Law	Doctor of Law
D Litt	Doctor of Letters
D Med Sc	Doctor of Medical Science
D Mgt	Doctor of Management
D Min	Doctor of Ministry
D Miss	Doctor of Missiology
D Mus	Doctor of Music
D Mus A	Doctor of Musical Arts
D Phil	Doctor of Philosophy
D Prof	Doctor of Professional Studies
D Ps	Doctor of Psychology
D Sc	Doctor of Science
D Sc D	Doctor of Science in Dentistry
D Sc IS	Doctor of Science in Information Systems
D Sc PA	Doctor of Science in Physician Assistant Studies
D Th	Doctor of Theology
D Th P	Doctor of Practical Theology
DA	Doctor of Accounting
	Doctor of Arts
DACM	Doctor of Acupuncture and Chinese Medicine
DAIS	Doctor of Applied Intercultural Studies
DAOM	Doctorate in Acupuncture and Oriental Medicine
DAT	Doctorate of Athletic Training
	Professional Doctor of Art Therapy
DBA	Doctor of Business Administration
DBH	Doctor of Behavioral Health
DBL	Doctor of Business Leadership
DC	Doctor of Chiropractic
DCC	Doctor of Computer Science
DCD	Doctor of Communications Design
DCE	Doctor of Computer Engineering
DCJ	Doctor of Criminal Justice
DCL	Doctor of Civil Law
	Doctor of Comparative Law
DCM	Doctor of Church Music
DCN	Doctor of Clinical Nutrition
DCS	Doctor of Computer Science
DDN	Diplôme du Droit Notarial
DDS	Doctor of Dental Surgery
DE	Doctor of Education
	Doctor of Engineering
DED	Doctor of Economic Development
DEIT	Doctor of Educational Innovation and Technology
DEL	Doctor of Executive Leadership
DEM	Doctor of Educational Ministry
DEPD	Diplôme Études Spécialisées
DES	Doctor of Engineering Science
DESS	Diplôme Études Supérieures Spécialisées
DET	Doctor of Educational Technology
DFA	Doctor of Fine Arts
DGP	Diploma in Graduate and Professional Studies
DGS	Doctor of Global Security
DH Sc	Doctor of Health Sciences
DHA	Doctor of Health Administration
DHCE	Doctor of Health Care Ethics
DHL	Doctor of Hebrew Letters
DHPE	Doctorate of Health Professionals Education
DHS	Doctor of Health Science
DHSc	Doctor of Health Science
DIT	Doctor of Industrial Technology

	Doctor of Information Technology
DJS	Doctor of Jewish Studies
DLS	Doctor of Liberal Studies
DM	Doctor of Management
	Doctor of Music
DMA	Doctor of Musical Arts
DMD	Doctor of Dental Medicine
DME	Doctor of Manufacturing Management
	Doctor of Music Education
DMFT	Doctor of Marital and Family Therapy
DMH	Doctor of Medical Humanities
DML	Doctor of Modern Languages
DMP	Doctorate in Medical Physics
DMPNA	Doctor of Management Practice in Nurse Anesthesia
DN Sc	Doctor of Nursing Science
DNAP	Doctor of Nurse Anesthesia Practice
DNP	Doctor of Nursing Practice
DNP-A	Doctor of Nursing Practice - Anesthesia
DNS	Doctor of Nursing Science
DO	Doctor of Osteopathy
DOL	Doctorate of Organizational Leadership
DOM	Doctor of Oriental Medicine
DOT	Doctor of Occupational Therapy
DPA	Diploma in Public Administration
	Doctor of Public Administration
DPDS	Doctor of Planning and Development Studies
DPH	Doctor of Public Health
DPM	Doctor of Plant Medicine
	Doctor of Podiatric Medicine
DPPD	Doctor of Policy, Planning, and Development
DPS	Doctor of Professional Studies
DPT	Doctor of Physical Therapy
DPTSc	Doctor of Physical Therapy Science
Dr DES	Doctor of Design
Dr NP	Doctor of Nursing Practice
Dr OT	Doctor of Occupational Therapy
Dr PH	Doctor of Public Health
Dr Sc PT	Doctor of Science in Physical Therapy
DRSc	Doctor of Regulatory Science
DS	Doctor of Science
DS Sc	Doctor of Social Science
DScPT	Doctor of Science in Physical Therapy
DSI	Doctor of Strategic Intelligence
DSJS	Doctor of Science in Jewish Studies
DSL	Doctor of Strategic Leadership
DSNS	Doctorate of Statecraft and National Security
DSS	Doctor of Strategic Security
DSW	Doctor of Social Work
DTL	Doctor of Talmudic Law
	Doctor of Transformational Leadership
DV Sc	Doctor of Veterinary Science
DVM	Doctor of Veterinary Medicine
DWS	Doctor of Worship Studies
EAA	Engineer in Aeronautics and Astronautics
EASPh D	Engineering and Applied Science Doctor of Philosophy
ECS	Engineer in Computer Science
Ed D	Doctor of Education
Ed DCT	Doctor of Education in College Teaching
Ed L D	Doctor of Education Leadership
Ed M	Master of Education
Ed S	Specialist in Education
Ed Sp	Specialist in Education
EDB	Executive Doctorate in Business
EDM	Executive Doctorate in Management
EE	Electrical Engineer
EJD	Executive Juris Doctor
EMBA	Executive Master of Business Administration

EMFA	Executive Master of Forensic Accounting
EMHA	Executive Master of Health Administration
EMHCL	Executive Master in Healthcare Leadership
EMIB	Executive Master of International Business
EMIR	Executive Master in International Relations
EML	Executive Master of Leadership
EMPA	Executive Master of Public Administration
EMPL	Executive Master in Policy Leadership
	Executive Master in Public Leadership
EMS	Executive Master of Science
EMTM	Executive Master of Technology Management
Eng	Engineer
Eng Sc D	Doctor of Engineering Science
Engr	Engineer
Exec MHA	Executive Master of Health Administration
Exec Ed D	Executive Doctor of Education
Exec MBA	Executive Master of Business Administration
Exec MPA	Executive Master of Public Administration
Exec MPH	Executive Master of Public Health
Exec MS	Executive Master of Science
Executive MA	Executive Master of Arts
G Dip	Graduate Diploma
GBC	Graduate Business Certificate
GDM	Graduate Diploma in Management
GDPA	Graduate Diploma in Public Administration
GEMBA	Global Executive Master of Business Administration
GM Acc	Graduate Master of Accountancy
GMBA	Global Master of Business Administration
GP LL M	Global Professional Master of Laws
GPD	Graduate Performance Diploma
GSS	Graduate Special Certificate for Students in Special Situations
IEMBA	International Executive Master of Business Administration
IMA	Interdisciplinary Master of Arts
IMBA	International Master of Business Administration
IMES	International Master's in Environmental Studies
Ingeniero	Engineer
JCD	Doctor of Canon Law
JCL	Licentiate in Canon Law
JD	Juris Doctor
JM	Juris Master
JSD	Doctor of Juridical Science
	Doctor of Jurisprudence
	Doctor of the Science of Law
JSM	Master of the Science of Law
L Th	Licentiate in Theology
LL B	Bachelor of Laws
LL CM	Master of Comparative Law
LL D	Doctor of Laws
LL M	Master of Laws
LL M in Tax	Master of Laws in Taxation
LL M CL	Master of Laws in Common Law
M Ac	Master of Accountancy
	Master of Accounting
	Master of Acupuncture
M Ac OM	Master of Acupuncture and Oriental Medicine
M Acc	Master of Accountancy
	Master of Accounting
M Acct	Master of Accountancy
	Master of Accounting
M Accy	Master of Accountancy
M Actg	Master of Accounting
M Acy	Master of Accountancy
M Ad	Master of Administration
M Ad Ed	Master of Adult Education
M Adm	Master of Administration

M Adm Mgt	Master of Administrative Management
M Admin	Master of Administration
M ADU	Master of Architectural Design and Urbanism
M Adv	Master of Advertising
M Ag	Master of Agriculture
M Ag Ed	Master of Agricultural Education
M Agr	Master of Agriculture
M App Comp Sc	Master of Applied Computer Science
M App St	Master of Applied Statistics
M Appl Stat	Master of Applied Statistics
M Aq	Master of Aquaculture
M Ar	Master of Architecture
M Arch	Master of Architecture
M Arch I	Master of Architecture I
M Arch II	Master of Architecture II
M Arch E	Master of Architectural Engineering
M Arch H	Master of Architectural History
M Bioethics	Master in Bioethics
M Cat	Master of Catechesis
M Ch E	Master of Chemical Engineering
M Cl D	Master of Clinical Dentistry
M Cl Sc	Master of Clinical Science
M Comm	Master of Communication
M Comp	Master of Computing
M Comp Sc	Master of Computer Science
M Coun	Master of Counseling
M Dent	Master of Dentistry
M Dent Sc	Master of Dental Sciences
M Des	Master of Design
M Des S	Master of Design Studies
M Div	Master of Divinity
M E Sci	Master of Earth Science
M Ec	Master of Economics
M Econ	Master of Economics
M Ed	Master of Education
M Ed T	Master of Education in Teaching
M En	Master of Engineering
M En S	Master of Environmental Sciences
M Eng	Master of Engineering
M Eng Mgt	Master of Engineering Management
M Engr	Master of Engineering
M Ent	Master of Enterprise
M Env	Master of Environment
M Env Des	Master of Environmental Design
M Env E	Master of Environmental Engineering
M Env Sc	Master of Environmental Science
M Ext Ed	Master of Extension Education
M Fin	Master of Finance
M Geo E	Master of Geological Engineering
M Geoenv E	Master of Geoenvironmental Engineering
M Geog	Master of Geography
M Hum	Master of Humanities
M IDST	Master's in Interdisciplinary Studies
M Jur	Master of Jurisprudence
M Kin	Master of Kinesiology
M Land Arch	Master of Landscape Architecture
M Litt	Master of Letters
M Mark	Master of Marketing
M Mat SE	Master of Material Science and Engineering
M Math	Master of Mathematics
M Mech E	Master of Mechanical Engineering
M Med Sc	Master of Medical Science
M Mgmt	Master of Management
M Mgt	Master of Management
M Min	Master of Ministries
M Mtl E	Master of Materials Engineering
M Mu	Master of Music
M Mus	Master of Music
M Mus Ed	Master of Music Education
M Music	Master of Music
M Pet E	Master of Petroleum Engineering
M Pharm	Master of Pharmacy
M Phil	Master of Philosophy
M Phil F	Master of Philosophical Foundations
M Pl	Master of Planning
M Plan	Master of Planning
M Pol	Master of Political Science
M Pr Met	Master of Professional Meteorology
M Prob S	Master of Probability and Statistics
M Psych	Master of Psychology
M Pub	Master of Publishing
M Rel	Master of Religion
M Sc	Master of Science
M Sc A	Master of Science (Applied)
M Sc AC	Master of Science in Applied Computing
M Sc AHN	Master of Science in Applied Human Nutrition
M Sc BMC	Master of Science in Biomedical Communications
M Sc CS	Master of Science in Computer Science
M Sc E	Master of Science in Engineering
M Sc Eng	Master of Science in Engineering
M Sc Engr	Master of Science in Engineering
M Sc F	Master of Science in Forestry
M Sc FE	Master of Science in Forest Engineering
M Sc Geogr	Master of Science in Geography
M Sc N	Master of Science in Nursing
M Sc OT	Master of Science in Occupational Therapy
M Sc P	Master of Science in Planning
M Sc Pl	Master of Science in Planning
M Sc PT	Master of Science in Physical Therapy
M Sc T	Master of Science in Teaching
M SEM	Master of Sustainable Environmental Management
M Serv Soc	Master of Social Service
M Soc	Master of Sociology
M Sp Ed	Master of Special Education
M Stat	Master of Statistics
M Sys E	Master of Systems Engineering
M Sys Sc	Master of Systems Science
M Tax	Master of Taxation
M Tech	Master of Technology
M Th	Master of Theology
M Trans E	Master of Transportation Engineering
M U Ed	Master of Urban Education
M Urb	Master of Urban Planning
M Vet Sc	Master of Veterinary Science
MA	Master of Accounting
	Master of Administration
	Master of Arts
MA Comm	Master of Arts in Communication
MA Ed	Master of Arts in Education
MA Ed/HD	Master of Arts in Education and Human Development
MA Islamic	Master of Arts in Islamic Studies
MA Min	Master of Arts in Ministry
MA Miss	Master of Arts in Missiology
MA Past St	Master of Arts in Pastoral Studies
MA Ph	Master of Arts in Philosophy
MA Psych	Master of Arts in Psychology
MA Sc	Master of Applied Science
MA Sp	Master of Arts (Spirituality)
MA Th	Master of Arts in Theology
MA-R	Master of Arts (Research)
MAA	Master of Applied Anthropology
	Master of Applied Arts
	Master of Arts in Administration
MAAA	Master of Arts in Arts Administration

MAAD	Master of Advanced Architectural Design
MAAE	Master of Arts in Art Education
MAAPPS	Master of Arts in Asia Pacific Policy Studies
MAAS	Master of Arts in Aging and Spirituality
MAASJ	Master of Arts in Applied Social Justice
MAAT	Master of Arts in Applied Theology
MAB	Master of Agribusiness
	Master of Applied Bioengineering
	Master of Arts in Business
MABA	Master's in Applied Behavior Analysis
MABC	Master of Arts in Biblical Counseling
MABE	Master of Arts in Bible Exposition
MABL	Master of Arts in Biblical Languages
MABM	Master of Agribusiness Management
MABS	Master of Arts in Biblical Studies
MABT	Master of Arts in Bible Teaching
MAC	Master of Accountancy
	Master of Accounting
	Master of Arts in Communication
	Master of Arts in Counseling
MACC	Master of Arts in Christian Counseling
MACCT	Master of Accounting
MACD	Master of Arts in Christian Doctrine
MACE	Master of Arts in Christian Education
MACH	Master of Arts in Church History
MACI	Master of Arts in Curriculum and Instruction
MACIS	Master of Accounting and Information Systems
MACJ	Master of Arts in Criminal Justice
MACL	Master of Arts in Christian Leadership
	Master of Arts in Community Leadership
MACM	Master of Arts in Christian Ministries
	Master of Arts in Christian Ministry
	Master of Arts in Church Music
	Master of Arts in Counseling Ministries
MACML	Master of Arts in Christian Ministry and Leadership
MACN	Master of Arts in Counseling
MACO	Master of Arts in Counseling
MAcOM	Master of Acupuncture and Oriental Medicine
MACP	Master of Arts in Christian Practice
	Master of Arts in Church Planting
	Master of Arts in Counseling Psychology
MACS	Master of Applied Computer Science
	Master of Arts in Catholic Studies
	Master of Arts in Christian Studies
MACSE	Master of Arts in Christian School Education
MACT	Master of Arts in Communications and Technology
MAD	Master in Educational Institution Administration
	Master of Art and Design
MADR	Master of Arts in Dispute Resolution
MADS	Master of Applied Disability Studies
MAE	Master of Aerospace Engineering
	Master of Agricultural Economics
	Master of Agricultural Education
	Master of Applied Economics
	Master of Architectural Engineering
	Master of Art Education
	Master of Arts in Education
	Master of Arts in English
MAEd	Master of Arts Education
MAEE	Master of Agricultural and Extension Education
MAEL	Master of Arts in Educational Leadership
MAEM	Master of Arts in Educational Ministries
MAEP	Master of Arts in Economic Policy
	Master of Arts in Educational Psychology
MAES	Master of Arts in Environmental Sciences
MAET	Master of Arts in English Teaching

MAF	Master of Arts in Finance
MAFE	Master of Arts in Financial Economics
MAFM	Master of Accounting and Financial Management
MAFS	Master of Arts in Family Studies
MAG	Master of Applied Geography
MAGU	Master of Urban Analysis and Management
MAH	Master of Arts in Humanities
MAHA	Master of Arts in Humanitarian Assistance
MAHCM	Master of Arts in Health Care Mission
MAHG	Master of American History and Government
MAHL	Master of Arts in Hebrew Letters
MAHN	Master of Applied Human Nutrition
MAHR	Master of Applied Historical Research
MAHS	Master of Arts in Human Services
MAHSR	Master in Applied Health Services Research
MAIA	Master of Arts in International Administration
	Master of Arts in International Affairs
MAICS	Master of Arts in Intercultural Studies
MAIDM	Master of Arts in Interior Design and Merchandising
MAIH	Master of Arts in Interdisciplinary Humanities
MAIOP	Master of Applied Industrial/Organizational Psychology
MAIS	Master of Arts in Intercultural Studies
	Master of Arts in Interdisciplinary Studies
	Master of Arts in International Studies
MAIT	Master of Administration in Information Technology
MAJ	Master of Arts in Journalism
MAJCS	Master of Arts in Jewish Communal Service
MAJPS	Master of Arts in Jewish Professional Studies
MAJS	Master of Arts in Jewish Studies
MAL	Master of Athletic Leadership
MALA	Master of Arts in Liberal Arts
MALCM	Master in Arts Leadership and Cultural Management
MALD	Master of Arts in Law and Diplomacy
MALER	Master of Arts in Labor and Employment Relations
MALL	Master of Arts in Language Learning
MALLT	Master of Arts in Language, Literature, and Translation
MALP	Master of Arts in Language Pedagogy
MALS	Master of Arts in Liberal Studies
MAM	Master of Acquisition Management
	Master of Agriculture and Management
	Master of Applied Mathematics
	Master of Arts in Management
	Master of Arts in Ministry
	Master of Arts Management
	Master of Aviation Management
MAMC	Master of Arts in Mass Communication
	Master of Arts in Ministry and Culture
	Master of Arts in Ministry for a Multicultural Church
MAME	Master of Arts in Missions/Evangelism
MAMFC	Master of Arts in Marriage and Family Counseling
MAMFT	Master of Arts in Marriage and Family Therapy
MAMHC	Master of Arts in Mental Health Counseling
MAMS	Master of Applied Mathematical Sciences
	Master of Arts in Ministerial Studies
	Master of Arts in Ministry and Spirituality
MAMT	Master of Arts in Mathematics Teaching
MAN	Master of Applied Nutrition
MANT	Master of Arts in New Testament
MAOL	Master of Arts in Organizational Leadership
MAOM	Master of Acupuncture and Oriental Medicine
	Master of Arts in Organizational Management

MAOT	Master of Arts in Old Testament
MAP	Master of Applied Politics
	Master of Applied Psychology
	Master of Arts in Planning
	Master of Psychology
	Master of Public Administration
MAP Min	Master of Arts in Pastoral Ministry
MAPA	Master of Arts in Public Administration
MAPC	Master of Arts in Pastoral Counseling
MAPE	Master of Arts in Physics Education
MAPM	Master of Arts in Pastoral Ministry
	Master of Arts in Pastoral Music
	Master of Arts in Practical Ministry
MAPP	Master of Arts in Public Policy
MAPS	Master of Applied Psychological Sciences
	Master of Arts in Pastoral Studies
	Master of Arts in Public Service
MAPW	Master of Arts in Professional Writing
MAQRM	Master's of Actuarial and Quantitative Risk Management
MAR	Master of Arts in Reading
	Master of Arts in Religion
Mar Eng	Marine Engineer
MARC	Master of Arts in Rehabilitation Counseling
MARE	Master of Arts in Religious Education
MARL	Master of Arts in Religious Leadership
MARS	Master of Arts in Religious Studies
MAS	Master of Accounting Science
	Master of Actuarial Science
	Master of Administrative Science
	Master of Advanced Study
	Master of American Studies
	Master of Animal Science
	Master of Applied Science
	Master of Applied Statistics
	Master of Archival Studies
MASA	Master of Advanced Studies in Architecture
MASC	Master of Arts in School Counseling
MASD	Master of Arts in Spiritual Direction
MASE	Master of Arts in Special Education
MASF	Master of Arts in Spiritual Formation
MASJ	Master of Arts in Systems of Justice
MASLA	Master of Advanced Studies in Landscape Architecture
MASM	Master of Aging Services Management
	Master of Arts in Specialized Ministries
MASS	Master of Applied Social Science
MASW	Master of Aboriginal Social Work
MAT	Master of Arts in Teaching
	Master of Arts in Theology
	Master of Athletic Training
	Master's in Administration of Telecommunications
Mat E	Materials Engineer
MATCM	Master of Acupuncture and Traditional Chinese Medicine
MATDE	Master of Arts in Theology, Development, and Evangelism
MATDR	Master of Territorial Management and Regional Development
MATE	Master of Arts for the Teaching of English
MATESL	Master of Arts in Teaching English as a Second Language
MATESOL	Master of Arts in Teaching English to Speakers of Other Languages
MATF	Master of Arts in Teaching English as a Foreign Language/Intercultural Studies
MATFL	Master of Arts in Teaching Foreign Language
MATH	Master of Arts in Therapy

MATI	Master of Administration of Information Technology
MATL	Master of Arts in Teaching of Languages
	Master of Arts in Transformational Leadership
MATM	Master of Arts in Teaching of Mathematics
MATRN	Master of Athletic Training
MATS	Master of Arts in Theological Studies
	Master of Arts in Transforming Spirituality
MAUA	Master of Arts in Urban Affairs
MAUD	Master of Arts in Urban Design
MAURP	Master of Arts in Urban and Regional Planning
MAW	Master of Arts in Worship
MAWSHP	Master of Arts in Worship
MAYM	Master of Arts in Youth Ministry
MB	Master of Bioinformatics
MBA	Master of Business Administration
MBA-AM	Master of Business Administration in Aviation Management
MBA-EP	Master of Business Administration–Experienced Professionals
MBAA	Master of Business Administration in Aviation
MBAE	Master of Biological and Agricultural Engineering
	Master of Biosystems and Agricultural Engineering
MBAH	Master of Business Administration in Health
MBAi	Master of Business Administration–International
MBAICT	Master of Business Administration in Information and Communication Technology
MBC	Master of Building Construction
MBE	Master of Bilingual Education
	Master of Bioengineering
	Master of Bioethics
	Master of Biomedical Engineering
	Master of Business Economics
	Master of Business Education
MBEE	Master in Biotechnology Enterprise and Entrepreneurship
MBET	Master of Business, Entrepreneurship and Technology
MBI	Master in Business Informatics
MBIOT	Master of Biotechnology
MBiotech	Master of Biotechnology
MBL	Master of Business Leadership
MBLE	Master in Business Logistics Engineering
MBME	Master's in Biomedical Engineering
MBMSE	Master of Business Management and Software Engineering
MBOE	Master of Business Operational Excellence
MBS	Master of Biblical Studies
	Master of Biological Science
	Master of Biomedical Sciences
	Master of Bioscience
	Master of Building Science
	Master of Business and Science
	Master of Business Statistics
MBST	Master of Biostatistics
MBT	Master of Biomedical Technology
	Master of Biotechnology
	Master of Business Taxation
MBV	Master of Business for Veterans
MC	Master of Classics
	Master of Communication
	Master of Counseling
MC Ed	Master of Continuing Education
MC Sc	Master of Computer Science
MCA	Master of Commercial Aviation
	Master of Communication Arts
	Master of Criminology (Applied)

MCAM	Master of Computational and Applied Mathematics
MCC	Master of Computer Science
MCD	Master of Communications Disorders
	Master of Community Development
MCE	Master in Electronic Commerce
	Master of Chemistry Education
	Master of Christian Education
	Master of Civil Engineering
	Master of Control Engineering
MCEM	Master of Construction Engineering Management
MCEPA	Master of Chinese Economic and Political Affairs
MCHE	Master of Chemical Engineering
MCIS	Master of Communication and Information Studies
	Master of Computer and Information Science
	Master of Computer Information Systems
MCIT	Master of Computer and Information Technology
MCJ	Master of Criminal Justice
MCL	Master in Communication Leadership
	Master of Canon Law
	Master of Christian Leadership
	Master of Comparative Law
MCM	Master of Christian Ministry
	Master of Church Music
	Master of Communication Management
	Master of Community Medicine
	Master of Construction Management
	Master of Contract Management
MCMin	Master of Christian Ministry
MCMM	Master in Communications and Media Management
MCMP	Master of City and Metropolitan Planning
MCMS	Master of Clinical Medical Science
MCN	Master of Clinical Nutrition
MCOL	Master of Arts in Community and Organizational Leadership
MCP	Master of City Planning
	Master of Community Planning
	Master of Counseling Psychology
	Master of Cytopathology Practice
	Master of Science in Quality Systems and Productivity
MCPD	Master of Community Planning and Development
MCR	Master in Clinical Research
MCRP	Master of City and Regional Planning
	Master of Community and Regional Planning
MCRS	Master of City and Regional Studies
MCS	Master of Chemical Sciences
	Master of Christian Studies
	Master of Clinical Science
	Master of Combined Sciences
	Master of Communication Studies
	Master of Computer Science
	Master of Consumer Science
MCSE	Master of Computer Science and Engineering
MCSL	Master of Catholic School Leadership
MCSM	Master of Construction Science and Management
MCT	Master of Commerce and Technology
MCTM	Master of Clinical Translation Management
MCTP	Master of Communication Technology and Policy
MCTS	Master of Clinical and Translational Science
MCVS	Master of Cardiovascular Science
MD	Doctor of Medicine

MDA	Master of Dietetic Administration
MDB	Master of Design-Build
MDE	Master in Design Engineering
	Master of Developmental Economics
	Master of Distance Education
	Master of the Education of the Deaf
MDH	Master of Dental Hygiene
MDI	Master of Disruptive Innovation
MDM	Master of Design Methods
	Master of Digital Media
MDP	Master in Sustainable Development Practice
	Master of Development Practice
MDR	Master of Dispute Resolution
MDS	Master in Data Science
	Master of Dental Surgery
	Master of Design Studies
	Master of Digital Sciences
MDSPP	Master in Data Science for Public Policy
ME	Master of Education
	Master of Engineering
	Master of Entrepreneurship
ME Sc	Master of Engineering Science
ME-PD	Master of Education–Professional Development
MEA	Master of Educational Administration
	Master of Engineering Administration
MEAE	Master of Entertainment Arts and Engineering
MEAP	Master of Environmental Administration and Planning
MEB	Master of Energy Business
MEBD	Master in Environmental Building Design
MEBT	Master in Electronic Business Technologies
MEC	Master of Electronic Commerce
Mech E	Mechanical Engineer
MEDS	Master of Environmental Design Studies
MEE	Master in Education
	Master of Electrical Engineering
	Master of Energy Engineering
	Master of Environmental Engineering
MEECON	Master of Energy Economics
MEEM	Master of Environmental Engineering and Management
MEENE	Master of Engineering in Environmental Engineering
MEEP	Master of Environmental and Energy Policy
MEERM	Master of Earth and Environmental Resource Management
MEH	Master in Humanistic Studies
	Master of Environmental Health
	Master of Environmental Horticulture
MEHS	Master of Environmental Health and Safety
MEIM	Master of Entertainment Industry Management
	Master of Equine Industry Management
MEL	Master of Educational Leadership
	Master of Engineering Leadership
	Master of English Literature
MELP	Master of Environmental Law and Policy
MEM	Master of Engineering Management
	Master of Environmental Management
	Master of Marketing
MEME	Master of Engineering in Manufacturing Engineering
	Master of Engineering in Mechanical Engineering
MENR	Master of Environment and Natural Resources
MENVEGR	Master of Environmental Engineering
MEP	Master of Engineering Physics
MEPC	Master of Environmental Pollution Control
MEPD	Master of Environmental Planning and Design
MER	Master of Employment Relations

MERE	Master of Entrepreneurial Real Estate	
MERL	Master of Energy Regulation and Law	
MES	Master of Education and Science	
	Master of Engineering Science	
	Master of Environment and Sustainability	
	Master of Environmental Science	
	Master of Environmental Studies	
	Master of Environmental Systems	
MESM	Master of Environmental Science and Management	
MET	Master of Educational Technology	
	Master of Engineering Technology	
	Master of Entertainment Technology	
	Master of Environmental Toxicology	
METM	Master of Engineering and Technology Management	
MEVE	Master of Environmental Engineering	
MF	Master of Finance	
	Master of Forestry	
MFA	Master of Financial Administration	
	Master of Fine Arts	
MFALP	Master of Food and Agriculture Law and Policy	
MFAS	Master of Fisheries and Aquatic Science	
MFC	Master of Forest Conservation	
MFCS	Master of Family and Consumer Sciences	
MFE	Master of Financial Economics	
	Master of Financial Engineering	
	Master of Forest Engineering	
MFES	Master of Fire and Emergency Services	
MFG	Master of Functional Genomics	
MFHD	Master of Family and Human Development	
MFM	Master of Financial Management	
	Master of Financial Mathematics	
MFPE	Master of Food Process Engineering	
MFR	Master of Forest Resources	
MFRC	Master of Forest Resources and Conservation	
MFRE	Master of Food and Resource Economics	
MFS	Master of Food Science	
	Master of Forensic Sciences	
	Master of Forest Science	
	Master of Forest Studies	
	Master of French Studies	
MFST	Master of Food Safety and Technology	
MFT	Master of Family Therapy	
MFWCB	Master of Fish, Wildlife and Conservation Biology	
MFYCS	Master of Family, Youth and Community Sciences	
MGA	Master of Global Affairs	
	Master of Government Administration	
	Master of Governmental Administration	
MGBA	Master of Global Business Administration	
MGC	Master of Genetic Counseling	
MGCS	Master of Genetic Counselor Studies	
MGD	Master of Graphic Design	
MGE	Master of Geotechnical Engineering	
MGEM	Master of Geomatics for Environmental Management	
	Master of Global Entrepreneurship and Management	
MGIS	Master of Geographic Information Science	
	Master of Geographic Information Systems	
MGM	Master of Global Management	
MGMA	Master of Greenhouse Gas Management and Accounting	
MGP	Master of Gestion de Projet	
MGPS	Master of Global Policy Studies	
MGREM	Master of Global Real Estate Management	
MGS	Master of Gender Studies	
	Master of Gerontological Studies	

	Master of Global Studies
MH	Master of Humanities
MH Sc	Master of Health Sciences
MHA	Master of Health Administration
	Master of Healthcare Administration
	Master of Hospital Administration
	Master of Hospitality Administration
MHB	Master of Human Behavior
MHC	Master of Mental Health Counseling
MHCA	Master of Health Care Administration
MHCD	Master of Health Care Design
MHCI	Master of Human-Computer Interaction
MHCL	Master of Health Care Leadership
MHCM	Master of Health Care Management
MHE	Master of Health Education
	Master of Higher Education
	Master of Human Ecology
MHE Ed	Master of Home Economics Education
MHEA	Master of Higher Education Administration
MHHS	Master of Health and Human Services
MHI	Master of Health Informatics
	Master of Healthcare Innovation
MHID	Master of Healthcare Interior Design
MHIHIM	Master of Health Informatics and Health Information Management
MHIIM	Master of Health Informatics and Information Management
MHK	Master of Human Kinetics
MHM	Master of Healthcare Management
MHMS	Master of Health Management Systems
MHP	Master of Health Physics
	Master of Heritage Preservation
	Master of Historic Preservation
MHPA	Master of Heath Policy and Administration
MHPCTL	Master of High Performance Coaching and Technical Leadership
MHPE	Master of Health Professions Education
MHR	Master of Human Resources
MHRD	Master in Human Resource Development
MHRIR	Master of Human Resources and Industrial Relations
MHRLR	Master of Human Resources and Labor Relations
MHRM	Master of Human Resources Management
MHS	Master of Health Science
	Master of Health Sciences
	Master of Health Studies
	Master of Hispanic Studies
	Master of Human Services
	Master of Humanistic Studies
MHSA	Master of Health Services Administration
MHSM	Master of Health Systems Management
MI	Master of Information
	Master of Instruction
MI Arch	Master of Interior Architecture
MIA	Master of Interior Architecture
	Master of International Affairs
MIAA	Master of International Affairs and Administration
MIAM	Master of International Agribusiness Management
MIAPD	Master of Interior Architecture and Product Design
MIB	Master of International Business
MIBS	Master of International Business Studies
MICLJ	Master of International Criminal Law and Justice
MICM	Master of International Construction Management
MID	Master of Industrial Design

	Master of Industrial Distribution		Master of Judicial Studies
	Master of Innovation Design		Master of Juridical Studies
	Master of Interior Design	MK	Master of Kinesiology
	Master of International Development	MKM	Master of Knowledge Management
MIDA	Master of International Development Administration	ML	Master of Latin
			Master of Law
MIDP	Master of International Development Policy	ML Arch	Master of Landscape Architecture
MIDS	Master of Information and Data Science	MLA	Master of Landscape Architecture
MIE	Master of Industrial Engineering		Master of Liberal Arts
MIF	Master of International Forestry		Master of Laboratory Animal Science
MIHTM	Master of International Hospitality and Tourism Management	MLAS	Master of Liberal Arts and Sciences
MIJ	Master of International Journalism	MLAUD	Master of Landscape Architecture in Urban Development
MILR	Master of Industrial and Labor Relations	MLD	Master of Leadership Development
MIM	Master in Ministry		Master of Leadership Studies
	Master of Information Management	MLE	Master of Applied Linguistics and Exegesis
	Master of International Management	MLER	Master of Labor and Employment Relations
	Master of International Marketing	MLI Sc	Master of Library and Information Science
MIMFA	Master of Investment Management and Financial Analysis	MLIS	Master of Library and Information Science
MIMLAE	Master of International Management for Latin American Executives		Master of Library and Information Studies
		MLM	Master of Leadership in Ministry
MIMS	Master of Information Management and Systems	MLPD	Master of Land and Property Development
		MLRHR	Master of Labor Relations and Human Resources
	Master of Integrated Manufacturing Systems	MLS	Master of Leadership Studies
MIP	Master of Infrastructure Planning		Master of Legal Studies
	Master of Intellectual Property		Master of Liberal Studies
	Master of International Policy		Master of Library Science
MIPA	Master of International Public Affairs		Master of Life Sciences
MIPD	Master of Integrated Product Design		Master of Medical Laboratory Sciences
MIPER	Master of International Political Economy of Resources	MLSCM	Master of Logistics and Supply Chain Management
MIPM	Master of International Policy Management	MLT	Master of Language Technologies
MIPP	Master of International Policy and Practice	MLTCA	Master of Long Term Care Administration
	Master of International Public Policy	MLW	Master of Studies in Law
MIPS	Master of International Planning Studies	MLWS	Master of Land and Water Systems
MIR	Master of Industrial Relations	MM	Master of Management
	Master of International Relations		Master of Mediation
MIRD	Master of International Relations and Diplomacy		Master of Ministry
			Master of Music
MIRHR	Master of Industrial Relations and Human Resources	MM Ed	Master of Music Education
		MM Sc	Master of Medical Science
MIS	Master of Imaging Science	MM St	Master of Museum Studies
	Master of Industrial Statistics	MMA	Master of Marine Affairs
	Master of Information Science		Master of Media Arts
	Master of Information Systems		Master of Musical Arts
	Master of Integrated Science	MMAL	Master of Maritime Administration and Logistics
	Master of Interdisciplinary Studies		
	Master of International Service	MMAS	Master of Military Art and Science
	Master of International Studies	MMB	Master of Microbial Biotechnology
MISE	Master of Industrial and Systems Engineering	MMC	Master of Manufacturing Competitiveness
MISKM	Master of Information Sciences and Knowledge Management		Master of Mass Communications
		MMCM	Master of Music in Church Music
MISM	Master of Information Systems Management	MMCSS	Master of Mathematical Computational and Statistical Sciences
MISW	Master of Indigenous Social Work		
MIT	Master in Teaching	MME	Master of Management in Energy
	Master of Industrial Technology		Master of Manufacturing Engineering
	Master of Information Technology		Master of Mathematics Education
	Master of Initial Teaching		Master of Mathematics for Educators
	Master of International Trade		Master of Mechanical Engineering
MITA	Master of Information Technology Administration		Master of Mining Engineering
			Master of Music Education
MITM	Master of Information Technology and Management	MMEL	Master's in Medical Education Leadership
		MMF	Master of Mathematical Finance
MJ	Master of Journalism	MMFC/T	Master of Marriage and Family Counseling/Therapy
	Master of Jurisprudence		
MJ Ed	Master of Jewish Education	MMFT	Master of Marriage and Family Therapy
MJA	Master of Justice Administration	MMG	Master of Management
MJM	Master of Justice Management	MMH	Master of Management in Hospitality
MJS	Master of Judaic Studies		

	Master of Medical Humanities		Master of Planning
MMI	Master of Management of Innovation	MP Ac	Master of Professional Accountancy
MMIS	Master of Management Information Systems	MP Acc	Master of Professional Accountancy
MML	Master of Managerial Logistics		Master of Professional Accounting
MMM	Master of Manufacturing Management		Master of Public Accounting
	Master of Marine Management	MP Aff	Master of Public Affairs
	Master of Medical Management	MP Th	Master of Pastoral Theology
MMP	Master of Marine Policy	MPA	Master of Performing Arts
	Master of Medical Physics		Master of Physician Assistant
	Master of Music Performance		Master of Professional Accountancy
MMPA	Master of Management and Professional Accounting		Master of Professional Accounting
			Master of Public Administration
MMQM	Master of Manufacturing Quality Management		Master of Public Affairs
MMR	Master of Marketing Research	MPAC	Master of Professional Accounting
MMRM	Master of Marine Resources Management	MPAID	Master of Public Administration and International Development
MMS	Master in Migration Studies		
	Master of Management Science	MPAP	Master of Physician Assistant Practice
	Master of Management Studies		Master of Public Administration and Policy
	Master of Manufacturing Systems		Master of Public Affairs and Politics
	Master of Marine Studies	MPAS	Master of Physician Assistant Science
	Master of Materials Science		Master of Physician Assistant Studies
	Master of Mathematical Sciences	MPC	Master of Professional Communication
	Master of Medical Science	MPD	Master of Product Development
	Master of Medieval Studies		Master of Public Diplomacy
MMSE	Master of Manufacturing Systems Engineering	MPDS	Master of Planning and Development Studies
MMSM	Master of Music in Sacred Music	MPE	Master of Physical Education
MMT	Master in Marketing	MPEM	Master of Project Engineering and Management
	Master of Math for Teaching		
	Master of Music Therapy	MPFM	Master of Public Financial Management
	Master's in Marketing Technology	MPH	Master of Public Health
MMus	Master of Music	MPHE	Master of Public Health Education
MN	Master of Nursing	MPHM	Master in Plant Health Management
	Master of Nutrition	MPHS	Master of Population Health Sciences
MN NP	Master of Nursing in Nurse Practitioner	MPHTM	Master of Public Health and Tropical Medicine
MNA	Master of Nonprofit Administration	MPI	Master of Public Informatics
	Master of Nurse Anesthesia	MPIA	Master of Public and International Affairs
MNAE	Master of Nanoengineering	MPL	Master of Pastoral Leadership
MNAL	Master of Nonprofit Administration and Leadership	MPM	Master of Pastoral Ministry
			Master of Pest Management
MNAS	Master of Natural and Applied Science		Master of Policy Management
MNCL	Master of Nonprofit and Civic Leadership		Master of Practical Ministries
MNCM	Master of Network and Communications Management		Master of Professional Management
			Master of Project Management
MNE	Master of Nuclear Engineering		Master of Public Management
MNL	Master in International Business for Latin America	MPNA	Master of Public and Nonprofit Administration
		MPNL	Master of Philanthropy and Nonprofit Leadership
MNM	Master of Nonprofit Management		
MNO	Master of Nonprofit Organization	MPO	Master of Prosthetics and Orthotics
MNPL	Master of Not-for-Profit Leadership	MPOD	Master of Positive Organizational Development
MNpS	Master of Nonprofit Studies	MPP	Master of Public Policy
MNR	Master of Natural Resources	MPPA	Master of Public Policy Administration
MNRD	Master of Natural Resources Development		Master of Public Policy and Administration
MNRES	Master of Natural Resources and Environmental Studies	MPPAL	Master of Public Policy, Administration and Law
		MPPGA	Master of Public Policy and Global Affairs
MNRM	Master of Natural Resource Management	MPPM	Master of Public Policy and Management
MNRMG	Master of Natural Resource Management and Geography	MPR	Master of Public Relations
		MPRTM	Master of Parks, Recreation, and Tourism Management
MNRS	Master of Natural Resource Stewardship		
MNS	Master of Natural Science	MPS	Master of Pastoral Studies
MNSE	Master of Natural Sciences Education		Master of Perfusion Science
MO	Master of Oceanography		Master of Planning Studies
MOD	Master of Organizational Development		Master of Political Science
MOGS	Master of Oil and Gas Studies		Master of Preservation Studies
MOL	Master of Organizational Leadership		Master of Prevention Science
MOM	Master of Organizational Management		Master of Professional Studies
	Master of Oriental Medicine		Master of Public Service
MOR	Master of Operations Research	MPSA	Master of Public Service Administration
MOT	Master of Occupational Therapy		
MP	Master of Physiology	MPSG	Master of Population and Social Gerontology

MPSIA	Master of Political Science and International Affairs	MS Sp Ed	Master of Science in Special Education
MPSL	Master of Public Safety Leadership	MS Stat	Master of Science in Statistics
MPT	Master of Pastoral Theology	MS Surg	Master of Science in Surgery
	Master of Physical Therapy	MS Tax	Master of Science in Taxation
	Master of Practical Theology	MS Tc E	Master of Science in Telecommunications Engineering
MPVM	Master of Preventive Veterinary Medicine	MS-R	Master of Science (Research)
MPW	Master of Professional Writing	MSA	Master of School Administration
	Master of Public Works		Master of Science in Accountancy
MQF	Master of Quantitative Finance		Master of Science in Accounting
MQM	Master of Quality Management		Master of Science in Administration
	Master of Quantitative Management		Master of Science in Aeronautics
MQS	Master of Quality Systems		Master of Science in Agriculture
MR	Master of Recreation		Master of Science in Analytics
	Master of Retailing		Master of Science in Anesthesia
MRA	Master in Research Administration		Master of Science in Architecture
	Master of Regulatory Affairs		Master of Science in Aviation
MRC	Master of Rehabilitation Counseling		Master of Sports Administration
MRCP	Master of Regional and City Planning		Master of Surgical Assisting
	Master of Regional and Community Planning	MSAA	Master of Science in Astronautics and Aeronautics
MRD	Master of Rural Development	MSABE	Master of Science in Agricultural and Biological Engineering
MRE	Master of Real Estate		
	Master of Religious Education	MSAC	Master of Science in Acupuncture
MRED	Master of Real Estate Development	MSACC	Master of Science in Accounting
MREM	Master of Resource and Environmental Management	MSACS	Master of Science in Applied Computer Science
		MSAE	Master of Science in Aeronautical Engineering
MRLS	Master of Resources Law Studies		Master of Science in Aerospace Engineering
MRM	Master of Resources Management		Master of Science in Applied Economics
MRP	Master of Regional Planning		Master of Science in Applied Engineering
MRRD	Master in Recreation Resource Development		Master of Science in Architectural Engineering
MRS	Master of Religious Studies	MSAEM	Master of Science in Aerospace Engineering and Mechanics
MRSc	Master of Rehabilitation Science		
MRUD	Master of Resilient Design	MSAF	Master of Science in Aviation Finance
MS	Master of Science	MSAG	Master of Science in Applied Geosciences
MS Cmp E	Master of Science in Computer Engineering	MSAH	Master of Science in Allied Health
MS Kin	Master of Science in Kinesiology	MSAL	Master of Sport Administration and Leadership
MS Acct	Master of Science in Accounting	MSAM	Master of Science in Applied Mathematics
MS Accy	Master of Science in Accountancy	MSANR	Master of Science in Agriculture and Natural Resources
MS Aero E	Master of Science in Aerospace Engineering		
MS Ag	Master of Science in Agriculture	MSAS	Master of Science in Administrative Studies
MS Arch	Master of Science in Architecture		Master of Science in Applied Statistics
MS Arch St	Master of Science in Architectural Studies		Master of Science in Architectural Studies
MS Bio E	Master of Science in Bioengineering	MSAT	Master of Science in Accounting and Taxation
MS Bm E	Master of Science in Biomedical Engineering		Master of Science in Advanced Technology
MS Ch E	Master of Science in Chemical Engineering		Master of Science in Athletic Training
MS Cp E	Master of Science in Computer Engineering	MSB	Master of Science in Biotechnology
MS Eco	Master of Science in Economics	MSBA	Master of Science in Business Administration
MS Econ	Master of Science in Economics		Master of Science in Business Analysis
MS Ed	Master of Science in Education	MSBAE	Master of Science in Biological and Agricultural Engineering
MS Ed Admin	Master of Science in Educational Administration		
			Master of Science in Biosystems and Agricultural Engineering
MS El	Master of Science in Educational Leadership and Administration	MSBCB	Master's in Bioinformatics and Computational Biology
MS En E	Master of Science in Environmental Engineering		
		MSBE	Master of Science in Biological Engineering
MS Eng	Master of Science in Engineering		Master of Science in Biomedical Engineering
MS Engr	Master of Science in Engineering	MSBENG	Master of Science in Bioengineering
MS Env E	Master of Science in Environmental Engineering	MSBH	Master of Science in Behavioral Health
MS Exp Surg	Master of Science in Experimental Surgery	MSBM	Master of Sport Business Management
MS Mat SE	Master of Science in Material Science and Engineering	MSBME	Master of Science in Biomedical Engineering
		MSBMS	Master of Science in Basic Medical Science
MS Met E	Master of Science in Metallurgical Engineering	MSBS	Master of Science in Biomedical Sciences
MS Mgt	Master of Science in Management	MSBTM	Master of Science in Biotechnology and Management
MS Min	Master of Science in Mining		
MS Min E	Master of Science in Mining Engineering	MSC	Master of Science in Commerce
MS Mt E	Master of Science in Materials Engineering		Master of Science in Communication
MS Otol	Master of Science in Otolaryngology		Master of Science in Counseling
MS Pet E	Master of Science in Petroleum Engineering		Master of Science in Criminology
MS Sc	Master of Social Science		Master of Strategic Communication

MSCC	Master of Science in Community Counseling		MSECE	Master of Science in Electrical and Computer Engineering
MSCD	Master of Science in Communication Disorders		MSED	Master of Sustainable Economic Development
	Master of Science in Community Development		MSEE	Master of Science in Electrical Engineering
MSCE	Master of Science in Chemistry Education			Master of Science in Environmental Engineering
	Master of Science in Civil Engineering		MSEH	Master of Science in Environmental Health
	Master of Science in Clinical Epidemiology		MSEL	Master of Science in Educational Leadership
	Master of Science in Computer Engineering		MSEM	Master of Science in Engineering and Management
	Master of Science in Continuing Education			Master of Science in Engineering Management
MSCEE	Master of Science in Civil and Environmental Engineering			Master of Science in Engineering Mechanics
MSCF	Master of Science in Computational Finance			Master of Science in Environmental Management
MSCH	Master of Science in Chemical Engineering		MSENE	Master of Science in Environmental Engineering
MSChE	Master of Science in Chemical Engineering		MSEO	Master of Science in Electro-Optics
MSCI	Master of Science in Clinical Investigation		MSES	Master of Science in Embedded Software Engineering
MSCID	Master of Science in Community and International Development			Master of Science in Engineering Science
MSCIS	Master of Science in Computer and Information Science			Master of Science in Environmental Science
	Master of Science in Computer and Information Systems			Master of Science in Environmental Studies
	Master of Science in Computer Information Science			Master of Science in Exercise Science
	Master of Science in Computer Information Systems		MSESE	Master of Science in Energy Systems Engineering
MSCIT	Master of Science in Computer Information Technology		MSET	Master of Science in Educational Technology
MSCJ	Master of Science in Criminal Justice			Master of Science in Engineering Technology
MSCJA	Master of Science in Criminal Justice Administration		MSEV	Master of Science in Environmental Engineering
MSCJS	Master of Science in Crime and Justice Studies		MSF	Master of Science in Finance
MSCLS	Master of Science in Clinical Laboratory Studies			Master of Science in Forestry
MSCM	Master of Science in Church Management		MSFA	Master of Science in Financial Analysis
	Master of Science in Conflict Management		MSFCS	Master of Science in Family and Consumer Science
	Master of Science in Construction Management		MSFE	Master of Science in Financial Engineering
	Master of Supply Chain Management		MSFM	Master of Sustainable Forest Management
MSCMP	Master of Science in Cybersecurity Management and Policy		MSFOR	Master of Science in Forestry
MSCNU	Master of Science in Clinical Nutrition		MSFP	Master of Science in Financial Planning
MSCP	Master of Science in Clinical Psychology		MSFS	Master of Science in Financial Sciences
	Master of Science in Community Psychology			Master of Science in Forensic Science
	Master of Science in Computer Engineering		MSFSB	Master of Science in Financial Services and Banking
	Master of Science in Counseling Psychology		MSFT	Master of Science in Family Therapy
MSCPE	Master of Science in Computer Engineering		MSGC	Master of Science in Genetic Counseling
MSCPharm	Master of Science in Pharmacy		MSH	Master of Science in Health
MSCR	Master of Science in Clinical Research			Master of Science in Hospice
MSCRP	Master of Science in City and Regional Planning		MSHA	Master of Science in Health Administration
	Master of Science in Community and Regional Planning		MSHCA	Master of Science in Health Care Administration
MSCS	Master of Science in Clinical Science		MSHCPM	Master of Science in Health Care Policy and Management
	Master of Science in Computer Science		MSHE	Master of Science in Health Education
	Master of Science in Cyber Security		MSHES	Master of Science in Human Environmental Sciences
MSCSD	Master of Science in Communication Sciences and Disorders		MSHFID	Master of Science in Human Factors in Information Design
MSCSE	Master of Science in Computer Science and Engineering		MSHFS	Master of Science in Human Factors and Systems
MSCTE	Master of Science in Career and Technical Education		MSHI	Master of Science in Health Informatics
MSD	Master of Science in Dentistry		MSHP	Master of Science in Health Professions
	Master of Science in Design		MSHR	Master of Science in Human Resources
	Master of Science in Dietetics		MSHRL	Master of Science in Human Resource Leadership
MSDM	Master of Security and Disaster Management		MSHRM	Master of Science in Human Resource Management
MSE	Master of Science Education		MSHROD	Master of Science in Human Resources and Organizational Development
	Master of Science in Economics		MSHS	Master of Science in Health Science
	Master of Science in Education			Master of Science in Health Services
	Master of Science in Engineering			Master of Science in Homeland Security
	Master of Science in Engineering Management		MSHSR	Master of Science in Human Security and Resilience
	Master of Software Engineering			
	Master of Special Education			
	Master of Structural Engineering			

MSI	Master of Science in Information	MSME	Master of Science in Mathematics Education
	Master of Science in Instruction		Master of Science in Mechanical Engineering
	Master of System Integration		Master of Science in Medical Ethics
MSIA	Master of Science in Industrial Administration	MSMHC	Master of Science in Mental Health Counseling
	Master of Science in Information Assurance	MSMIT	Master of Science in Management and Information Technology
MSIDM	Master of Science in Interior Design and Merchandising	MSMLS	Master of Science in Medical Laboratory Science
MSIE	Master of Science in Industrial Engineering		
MSIEM	Master of Science in Information Engineering and Management	MSMOT	Master of Science in Management of Technology
MSIM	Master of Science in Industrial Management	MSMP	Master of Science in Medical Physics
	Master of Science in Information Management		Master of Science in Molecular Pathology
	Master of Science in International Management	MSMS	Master of Science in Management Science
MSIMC	Master of Science in Integrated Marketing Communications		Master of Science in Marine Science
			Master of Science in Medical Sciences
MSIMS	Master of Science in Identity Management and Security	MSMSE	Master of Science in Manufacturing Systems Engineering
MSIS	Master of Science in Information Science		Master of Science in Material Science and Engineering
	Master of Science in Information Studies		Master of Science in Material Science Engineering
	Master of Science in Information Systems		
	Master of Science in Interdisciplinary Studies		Master of Science in Mathematics and Science Education
MSISE	Master of Science in Infrastructure Systems Engineering		
MSISM	Master of Science in Information Systems Management	MSMus	Master of Sacred Music
		MSN	Master of Science in Nursing
MSISPM	Master of Science in Information Security Policy and Management	MSNA	Master of Science in Nurse Anesthesia
		MSNE	Master of Science in Nuclear Engineering
MSIST	Master of Science in Information Systems Technology	MSNS	Master of Science in Natural Science
			Master of Science in Nutritional Science
MSIT	Master of Science in Industrial Technology	MSOD	Master of Science in Organization Development
	Master of Science in Information Technology		
	Master of Science in Instructional Technology		Master of Science in Organizational Development
MSITM	Master of Science in Information Technology Management	MSOEE	Master of Science in Outdoor and Environmental Education
MSJ	Master of Science in Journalism		
	Master of Science in Jurisprudence	MSOES	Master of Science in Occupational Ergonomics and Safety
MSJC	Master of Social Justice and Criminology	MSOH	Master of Science in Occupational Health
MSJFP	Master of Science in Juvenile Forensic Psychology	MSOL	Master of Science in Organizational Leadership
		MSOM	Master of Science in Oriental Medicine
MSJJ	Master of Science in Juvenile Justice	MSOR	Master of Science in Operations Research
MSJPS	Master of Science in Justice and Public Safety	MSOT	Master of Science in Occupational Technology
MSK	Master of Science in Kinesiology		Master of Science in Occupational Therapy
MSL	Master in the Study of Law	MSP	Master of Science in Pharmacy
	Master of School Leadership		Master of Science in Planning
	Master of Science in Leadership		Master of Speech Pathology
	Master of Science in Limnology		Master of Sustainable Peacebuilding
	Master of Sports Leadership	MSPA	Master of Science in Physician Assistant
	Master of Strategic Leadership	MSPAS	Master of Science in Physician Assistant Studies
	Master of Studies in Law	MSPC	Master of Science in Professional Communications
MSLA	Master of Science in Legal Administration		
MSLB	Master of Sports Law and Business	MSPE	Master of Science in Petroleum Engineering
MSLFS	Master of Science in Life Sciences	MSPH	Master of Science in Public Health
MSLP	Master of Speech-Language Pathology	MSPHR	Master of Science in Pharmacy
MSLS	Master of Science in Library Science	MSPM	Master of Science in Professional Management
MSLSCM	Master of Science in Logistics and Supply Chain Management		Master of Science in Project Management
MSLT	Master of Second Language Teaching	MSPNGE	Master of Science in Petroleum and Natural Gas Engineering
MSM	Master of Sacred Ministry		
	Master of Sacred Music	MSPPM	Master of Science in Public Policy and Management
	Master of School Mathematics		
	Master of Science in Management	MSPS	Master of Science in Pharmaceutical Science
	Master of Science in Medicine		Master of Science in Political Science
	Master of Science in Organization Management		Master of Science in Psychological Services
	Master of Security Management	MSPT	Master of Science in Physical Therapy
	Master of Strategic Ministry	MSRA	Master of Science in Recreation Administration
	Master of Supply Management	MSRE	Master of Science in Real Estate
MSMA	Master of Science in Marketing Analysis		Master of Science in Religious Education
MSMAE	Master of Science in Materials Engineering	MSRED	Master of Science in Real Estate Development
MSMC	Master of Science in Management and Communications		Master of Sustainable Real Estate Development
	Master of Science in Mass Communications	MSRLS	Master of Science in Recreation and Leisure Studies

MSRM	Master of Science in Risk Management	MTCM	Master of Traditional Chinese Medicine
MSRMP	Master of Science in Radiological Medical Physics	MTD	Master of Training and Development
		MTE	Master in Educational Technology
MSRS	Master of Science in Radiological Sciences		Master of Technological Entrepreneurship
	Master of Science in Rehabilitation Science	MTESOL	Master in Teaching English to Speakers of Other Languages
MSS	Master of Security Studies		
	Master of Social Science	MTHM	Master of Tourism and Hospitality Management
	Master of Social Services	MTI	Master of Information Technology
	Master of Sports Science	MTID	Master of Tangible Interaction Design
	Master of Strategic Studies	MTL	Master of Talmudic Law
	Master's in Statistical Science	MTM	Master of Technology Management
MSSA	Master of Science in Social Administration		Master of Telecommunications Management
MSSCM	Master of Science in Supply Chain Management		Master of the Teaching of Mathematics
MSSD	Master of Arts in Software Driven Systems Design		Master of Transformative Ministry
			Master of Translational Medicine
	Master of Science in Sustainable Design	MTMH	Master of Tropical Medicine and Hygiene
MSSE	Master of Science in Software Engineering	MTMS	Master in Teaching Mathematics and Science
	Master of Science in Special Education	MTOM	Master of Traditional Oriental Medicine
MSSEM	Master of Science in Systems and Engineering Management	MTPC	Master of Technical and Professional Communication
MSSI	Master of Science in Security Informatics	MTR	Master of Translational Research
	Master of Science in Strategic Intelligence	MTS	Master of Theatre Studies
MSSIS	Master of Science in Security and Intelligence Studies		Master of Theological Studies
		MTW	Master of Teaching Writing
MSSL	Master of Science in School Leadership	MTWM	Master of Trust and Wealth Management
MSSLP	Master of Science in Speech-Language Pathology	MUA	Master of Urban Affairs
		MUAP	Master's of Urban Affairs and Policy
MSSM	Master of Science in Sports Medicine	MUCD	Master of Urban and Community Design
	Master of Science in Systems Management	MUD	Master of Urban Design
MSSP	Master of Science in Social Policy	MUDS	Master of Urban Design Studies
MSSS	Master of Science in Safety Science	MUEP	Master of Urban and Environmental Planning
	Master of Science in Systems Science	MUP	Master of Urban Planning
MSST	Master of Science in Security Technologies	MUPD	Master of Urban Planning and Development
MSSW	Master of Science in Social Work	MUPP	Master of Urban Planning and Policy
MSSWE	Master of Science in Software Engineering	MUPRED	Master of Urban Planning and Real Estate Development
MST	Master of Science and Technology		
	Master of Science in Taxation	MURP	Master of Urban and Regional Planning
	Master of Science in Teaching		Master of Urban and Rural Planning
	Master of Science in Technology	MURPL	Master of Urban and Regional Planning
	Master of Science in Telecommunications	MUS	Master of Urban Studies
	Master of Science Teaching	Mus M	Master of Music
MSTC	Master of Science in Technical Communication	MUSA	Master of Urban Spatial Analytics
	Master of Science in Telecommunications	MVP	Master of Voice Pedagogy
MSTCM	Master of Science in Traditional Chinese Medicine	MVS	Master of Visual Studies
		MWBS	Master of Won Buddhist Studies
MSTE	Master of Science in Telecommunications Engineering	MWC	Master of Wildlife Conservation
		MWR	Master of Water Resources
	Master of Science in Transportation Engineering	MWS	Master of Women's Studies
			Master of Worship Studies
MSTL	Master of Science in Teacher Leadership	MWSc	Master of Wildlife Science
MSTM	Master of Science in Technology Management	Nav Arch	Naval Architecture
	Master of Science in Transfusion Medicine	Naval E	Naval Engineer
MSTOM	Master of Science in Traditional Oriental Medicine	ND	Doctor of Naturopathic Medicine
			Doctor of Nursing
MSUASE	Master of Science in Unmanned and Autonomous Systems Engineering	NE	Nuclear Engineer
		Nuc E	Nuclear Engineer
MSUD	Master of Science in Urban Design	OD	Doctor of Optometry
MSUS	Master of Science in Urban Studies	OTD	Doctor of Occupational Therapy
MSW	Master of Social Work	PBME	Professional Master of Biomedical Engineering
MSWE	Master of Software Engineering	PC	Performer's Certificate
MSWREE	Master of Science in Water Resources and Environmental Engineering	PD	Professional Diploma
		PGC	Post-Graduate Certificate
MT	Master of Taxation	PGD	Postgraduate Diploma
	Master of Teaching	Ph L	Licentiate of Philosophy
	Master of Technology	Pharm D	Doctor of Pharmacy
	Master of Textiles	PhD	Doctor of Philosophy
MTA	Master of Tax Accounting	PhD Otol	Doctor of Philosophy in Otolaryngology
	Master of Teaching Arts	PhD Surg	Doctor of Philosophy in Surgery
	Master of Tourism Administration	PhDEE	Doctor of Philosophy in Electrical Engineering
MTC	Master of Technical Communications		

PMBA	Professional Master of Business Administration
PMC	Post Master Certificate
PMD	Post-Master's Diploma
PMS	Professional Master of Science
	Professional Master's
Post-Doctoral MS	Post-Doctoral Master of Science
Post-MSN Certificate	Post-Master of Science in Nursing Certificate
PPDPT	Postprofessional Doctor of Physical Therapy
Pro-MS	Professional Science Master's
Professional MA	Professional Master of Arts
Professional MBA	Professional Master of Business Administration
Professional MS	Professional Master of Science
PSM	Professional Master of Science
	Professional Science Master's
Psy D	Doctor of Psychology
Psy M	Master of Psychology
Psy S	Specialist in Psychology
Psya D	Doctor of Psychoanalysis
S Psy S	Specialist in Psychological Services
Sc D	Doctor of Science
Sc M	Master of Science
SCCT	Specialist in Community College Teaching
ScDPT	Doctor of Physical Therapy Science
SD	Specialist Degree
SJD	Doctor of Juridical Sciences
SLPD	Doctor of Speech-Language Pathology

SM	Master of Science
SM Arch S	Master of Science in Architectural Studies
SMACT	Master of Science in Art, Culture and Technology
SMBT	Master of Science in Building Technology
SP	Specialist Degree
Sp Ed	Specialist in Education
Sp LIS	Specialist in Library and Information Science
SPA	Specialist in Arts
Spec	Specialist's Certificate
Spec M	Specialist in Music
Spt	Specialist Degree
SSP	Specialist in School Psychology
STB	Bachelor of Sacred Theology
STD	Doctor of Sacred Theology
STL	Licentiate of Sacred Theology
STM	Master of Sacred Theology
tDACM	Transitional Doctor of Acupuncture and Chinese Medicine
TDPT	Transitional Doctor of Physical Therapy
Th D	Doctor of Theology
Th M	Master of Theology
TOTD	Transitional Doctor of Occupational Therapy
VMD	Doctor of Veterinary Medicine
WEMBA	Weekend Executive Master of Business Administration
XMA	Executive Master of Arts

INDEXES

Displays and Close-Ups

Directories and Subject Areas

Following is an alphabetical listing of directories and subject areas. Also listed are cross-references for subject area names not used in the directory structure of the guides, for example, "City and Regional Planning (see Urban and Regional Planning)"

Graduate Programs in the Humanities, Arts & Social Sciences

Addictions/Substance Abuse Counseling
Administration (see Arts Administration; Public Administration)
African-American Studies
African Languages and Literatures (see African Studies)
African Studies
Agribusiness (see Agricultural Economics and Agribusiness)
Agricultural Economics and Agribusiness
Alcohol Abuse Counseling (see Addictions/Substance Abuse Counseling)
American Indian/Native American Studies
American Studies
Anthropology
Applied Arts and Design—General
Applied Behavior Analysis
Applied Economics
Applied History (see Public History)
Applied Psychology
Applied Social Research
Arabic (see Near and Middle Eastern Languages)
Arab Studies (see Near and Middle Eastern Studies)
Archaeology
Architectural History
Architecture
Archives Administration (see Public History)
Area and Cultural Studies (see African-American Studies; African Studies; American Indian/Native American Studies; American Studies; Asian-American Studies; Asian Studies; Canadian Studies; Cultural Studies; East European and Russian Studies; Ethnic Studies; Folklore; Gender Studies; Hispanic Studies; Holocaust Studies; Jewish Studies; Latin American Studies; Near and Middle Eastern Studies; Northern Studies; Pacific Area/Pacific Rim Studies; Western European Studies; Women's Studies)
Art/Fine Arts
Art History
Arts Administration
Arts Journalism
Art Therapy
Asian-American Studies
Asian Languages
Asian Studies
Behavioral Sciences (see Psychology)
Bible Studies (see Religion; Theology)
Biological Anthropology
Black Studies (see African-American Studies)
Broadcasting (see Communication; Film, Television, and Video Production)
Broadcast Journalism
Building Science
Canadian Studies
Celtic Languages
Ceramics (see Art/Fine Arts)
Child and Family Studies
Child Development
Chinese
Chinese Studies (see Asian Languages; Asian Studies)
Christian Studies (see Missions and Missiology; Religion; Theology)
Cinema (see Film, Television, and Video Production)
City and Regional Planning (see Urban and Regional Planning)
Classical Languages and Literatures (see Classics)

Classics
Clinical Psychology
Clothing and Textiles
Cognitive Psychology (see Psychology—General; Cognitive Sciences)
Cognitive Sciences
Communication—General
Community Affairs (see Urban and Regional Planning; Urban Studies)
Community Planning (see Architecture; Environmental Design; Urban and Regional Planning; Urban Design; Urban Studies)
Community Psychology (see Social Psychology)
Comparative and Interdisciplinary Arts
Comparative Literature
Composition (see Music)
Computer Art and Design
Conflict Resolution and Mediation/Peace Studies
Consumer Economics
Corporate and Organizational Communication
Corrections (see Criminal Justice and Criminology)
Counseling (see Counseling Psychology; Pastoral Ministry and Counseling)
Counseling Psychology
Crafts (see Art/Fine Arts)
Creative Arts Therapies (see Art Therapy; Therapies—Dance, Drama, and Music)
Criminal Justice and Criminology
Cultural Anthropology
Cultural Studies
Dance
Decorative Arts
Demography and Population Studies
Design (see Applied Arts and Design; Architecture; Art/Fine Arts; Environmental Design; Graphic Design; Industrial Design; Interior Design; Textile Design; Urban Design)
Developmental Psychology
Diplomacy (see International Affairs)
Disability Studies
Drama Therapy (see Therapies—Dance, Drama, and Music)
Dramatic Arts (see Theater)
Drawing (see Art/Fine Arts)
Drug Abuse Counseling (see Addictions/Substance Abuse Counseling)
Drug and Alcohol Abuse Counseling (see Addictions/Substance Abuse Counseling)
East Asian Studies (see Asian Studies)
East European and Russian Studies
Economic Development
Economics
Educational Theater (see Theater; Therapies—Dance, Drama, and Music)
Emergency Management
English
Environmental Design
Ethics
Ethnic Studies
Ethnomusicology (see Music)
Experimental Psychology
Family and Consumer Sciences—General
Family Studies (see Child and Family Studies)
Family Therapy (see Child and Family Studies; Clinical Psychology; Counseling Psychology; Marriage and Family Therapy)
Filmmaking (see Film, Television, and Video Production)
Film Studies (see Film, Television, and Video Production)
Film, Television, and Video Production
Film, Television, and Video Theory and Criticism
Fine Arts (see Art/Fine Arts)
Folklore
Foreign Languages (see specific language)
Foreign Service (see International Affairs; International Development)
Forensic Psychology
Forensic Sciences
Forensics (see Speech and Interpersonal Communication)

French
Gender Studies
General Studies (*see* Liberal Studies)
Genetic Counseling
Geographic Information Systems
Geography
German
Gerontology
Graphic Design
Greek (*see* Classics)
Health Communication
Health Psychology
Hebrew (*see* Near and Middle Eastern Languages)
Hebrew Studies (*see* Jewish Studies)
Hispanic and Latin American Languages
Hispanic Studies
Historic Preservation
History
History of Art (*see* Art History)
History of Medicine
History of Science and Technology
Holocaust and Genocide Studies
Home Economics (*see* Family and Consumer Sciences—General)
Homeland Security
Household Economics, Sciences, and Management (*see* Family and Consumer Sciences—General)
Human Development
Humanities
Illustration
Industrial and Labor Relations
Industrial and Organizational Psychology
Industrial Design
Interdisciplinary Studies
Interior Design
International Affairs
International Development
International Economics
International Service (*see* International Affairs; International Development)
International Trade Policy
Internet and Interactive Multimedia
Interpersonal Communication (*see* Speech and Interpersonal Communication)
Interpretation (*see* Translation and Interpretation)
Islamic Studies (*see* Near and Middle Eastern Studies; Religion)
Italian
Japanese
Japanese Studies (*see* Asian Languages; Asian Studies; Japanese)
Jewelry (*see* Art/Fine Arts)
Jewish Studies
Journalism
Judaic Studies (*see* Jewish Studies; Religion)
Labor Relations (*see* Industrial and Labor Relations)
Landscape Architecture
Latin American Studies
Latin (*see* Classics)
Law Enforcement (*see* Criminal Justice and Criminology)
Liberal Studies
Lighting Design
Linguistics
Literature (*see* Classics; Comparative Literature; specific language)
Marriage and Family Therapy
Mass Communication
Media Studies
Medical Illustration
Medieval and Renaissance Studies
Metalsmithing (*see* Art/Fine Arts)
Middle Eastern Studies (*see* Near and Middle Eastern Studies)
Military and Defense Studies
Mineral Economics
Ministry (*see* Pastoral Ministry and Counseling; Theology)
Missions and Missiology
Motion Pictures (*see* Film, Television, and Video Production)
Museum Studies
Music
Musicology (*see* Music)

Music Therapy (*see* Therapies—Dance, Drama, and Music)
National Security
Native American Studies (*see* American Indian/Native American Studies)
Near and Middle Eastern Languages
Near and Middle Eastern Studies
Northern Studies
Organizational Psychology (*see* Industrial and Organizational Psychology)
Oriental Languages (*see* Asian Languages)
Oriental Studies (*see* Asian Studies)
Pacific Area/Pacific Rim Studies
Painting (*see* Art/Fine Arts)
Pastoral Ministry and Counseling
Philanthropic Studies
Philosophy
Photography
Playwriting (*see* Theater; Writing)
Policy Studies (*see* Public Policy)
Political Science
Population Studies (*see* Demography and Population Studies)
Portuguese
Printmaking (*see* Art/Fine Arts)
Product Design (*see* Industrial Design)
Psychoanalysis and Psychotherapy
Psychology—General
Public Administration
Public Affairs
Public History
Public Policy
Public Speaking (*see* Mass Communication; Rhetoric; Speech and Interpersonal Communication)
Publishing
Regional Planning (*see* Architecture; Urban and Regional Planning; Urban Design; Urban Studies)
Rehabilitation Counseling
Religion
Renaissance Studies (*see* Medieval and Renaissance Studies)
Rhetoric
Romance Languages
Romance Literatures (*see* Romance Languages)
Rural Planning and Studies
Rural Sociology
Russian
Scandinavian Languages
School Psychology
Sculpture (*see* Art/Fine Arts)
Security Administration (*see* Criminal Justice and Criminology)
Slavic Languages
Slavic Studies (*see* East European and Russian Studies; Slavic Languages)
Social Psychology
Social Sciences
Sociology
Southeast Asian Studies (*see* Asian Studies)
Soviet Studies (*see* East European and Russian Studies; Russian)
Spanish
Speech and Interpersonal Communication
Sport Psychology
Studio Art (*see* Art/Fine Arts)
Substance Abuse Counseling (*see* Addictions/Substance Abuse Counseling)
Survey Methodology
Sustainable Development
Technical Communication
Technical Writing
Telecommunications (*see* Film, Television, and Video Production)
Television (*see* Film, Television, and Video Production)
Textile Design
Textiles (*see* Clothing and Textiles; Textile Design)
Thanatology
Theater
Theater Arts (*see* Theater)
Theology
Therapies—Dance, Drama, and Music
Translation and Interpretation

Transpersonal and Humanistic Psychology
Urban and Regional Planning
Urban Design
Urban Planning (*see* Architecture; Urban and Regional Planning;
    Urban Design; Urban Studies)
Urban Studies
Video (*see* Film, Television, and Video Production)
Visual Arts (*see* Applied Arts and Design; Art/Fine Arts; Film,
    Television, and Video Production; Graphic Design; Illustration;
    Photography)
Western European Studies
Women's Studies
World Wide Web (*see* Internet and Interactive Multimedia)
Writing

Graduate Programs in the Biological/ Biomedical Sciences & Health-Related Medical Professions

Acupuncture and Oriental Medicine
Acute Care/Critical Care Nursing Administration (*see* Health Services
    Management and Hospital Administration; Nursing and Healthcare
    Administration; Pharmaceutical Administration)
Adult Nursing
Advanced Practice Nursing (*see* Family Nurse Practitioner Studies)
Allied Health—General
Allied Health Professions (*see* Clinical Laboratory Sciences/Medical
    Technology; Clinical Research; Communication Disorders; Dental
    Hygiene; Emergency Medical Services; Occupational Therapy;
    Physical Therapy; Physician Assistant Studies; Rehabilitation
    Sciences)
Allopathic Medicine
Anatomy
Anesthesiologist Assistant Studies
Animal Behavior
Bacteriology
Behavioral Sciences (*see* Biopsychology; Neuroscience; Zoology)
Biochemistry
Bioethics
Biological and Biomedical Sciences—General Biological Chemistry
    (*see* Biochemistry)
Biological Oceanography (*see* Marine Biology)
Biophysics
Biopsychology
Botany
Breeding (*see* Botany; Plant Biology; Genetics)
Cancer Biology/Oncology
Cardiovascular Sciences
Cell Biology
Cellular Physiology (*see* Cell Biology; Physiology)
Child-Care Nursing (*see* Maternal and Child/Neonatal Nursing)
Chiropractic
Clinical Laboratory Sciences/Medical Technology
Clinical Research
Community Health
Community Health Nursing
Computational Biology
Conservation (*see* Conservation Biology; Environmental Biology)
Conservation Biology
Crop Sciences (*see* Botany; Plant Biology)
Cytology (*see* Cell Biology)
Dental and Oral Surgery (*see* Oral and Dental Sciences)
Dental Assistant Studies (*see* Dental Hygiene)
Dental Hygiene
Dental Services (*see* Dental Hygiene)
Dentistry
Developmental Biology Dietetics (*see* Nutrition)
Ecology
Embryology (*see* Developmental Biology)
Emergency Medical Services
Endocrinology (*see* Physiology)
Entomology

Environmental Biology
Environmental and Occupational Health
Epidemiology
Evolutionary Biology
Family Nurse Practitioner Studies
Foods (*see* Nutrition)
Forensic Nursing
Genetics
Genomic Sciences
Gerontological Nursing
Health Physics/Radiological Health
Health Promotion
Health-Related Professions (*see* individual allied health professions)
Health Services Management and Hospital Administration
Health Services Research
Histology (*see* Anatomy; Cell Biology)
HIV/AIDS Nursing
Hospice Nursing
Hospital Administration (*see* Health Services Management and
    Hospital Administration)
Human Genetics
Immunology
Industrial Hygiene
Infectious Diseases
International Health
Laboratory Medicine (*see* Clinical Laboratory Sciences/Medical
    Technology; Immunology; Microbiology; Pathology)
Life Sciences (*see* Biological and Biomedical Sciences)
Marine Biology
Maternal and Child Health
Maternal and Child/Neonatal Nursing
Medical Imaging
Medical Microbiology
Medical Nursing (*see* Medical/Surgical Nursing)
Medical Physics
Medical/Surgical Nursing
Medical Technology (*see* Clinical Laboratory Sciences/Medical
    Technology)
Medical Sciences (*see* Biological and Biomedical Sciences)
Medical Science Training Programs (*see* Biological and Biomedical
    Sciences)
Medicinal and Pharmaceutical Chemistry
Medicinal Chemistry (*see* Medicinal and Pharmaceutical Chemistry)
Medicine (*see* Allopathic Medicine; Naturopathic Medicine;
    Osteopathic Medicine; Podiatric Medicine)
Microbiology
Midwifery (*see* Nurse Midwifery)
Molecular Biology
Molecular Biophysics
Molecular Genetics
Molecular Medicine
Molecular Pathogenesis
Molecular Pathology
Molecular Pharmacology
Molecular Physiology
Molecular Toxicology
Naturopathic Medicine
Neural Sciences (*see* Biopsychology; Neurobiology; Neuroscience)
Neurobiology
Neuroendocrinology (*see* Biopsychology; Neurobiology; Neuroscience;
    Physiology)
Neuropharmacology (*see* Biopsychology; Neurobiology; Neuroscience;
    Pharmacology)
Neurophysiology (*see* Biopsychology; Neurobiology; Neuroscience;
    Physiology)
Neuroscience
Nuclear Medical Technology (*see* Clinical Laboratory Sciences/
    Medical Technology)
Nurse Anesthesia
Nurse Midwifery
Nurse Practitioner Studies (*see* Family Nurse Practitioner Studies)
Nursing Administration (*see* Nursing and Healthcare Administration)
Nursing and Healthcare Administration
Nursing Education
Nursing—General
Nursing Informatics

Nutrition

Occupational Health (*see* Environmental and Occupational Health; Occupational Health Nursing)

Occupational Health Nursing

Occupational Therapy

Oncology (*see* Cancer Biology/Oncology)

Oncology Nursing

Optometry

Oral and Dental Sciences

Oral Biology (*see* Oral and Dental Sciences)

Oral Pathology (*see* Oral and Dental Sciences)

Organismal Biology (*see* Biological and Biomedical Sciences; Zoology)

Oriental Medicine and Acupuncture (*see* Acupuncture and Oriental Medicine)

Orthodontics (*see* Oral and Dental Sciences)

Osteopathic Medicine

Parasitology

Pathobiology

Pathology

Pediatric Nursing

Pedontics (*see* Oral and Dental Sciences)

Perfusion

Pharmaceutical Administration

Pharmaceutical Chemistry (*see* Medicinal and Pharmaceutical Chemistry)

Pharmaceutical Sciences

Pharmacology

Pharmacy

Photobiology of Cells and Organelles (*see* Botany; Cell Biology; Plant Biology)

Physical Therapy

Physician Assistant Studies

Physiological Optics (*see* Vision Sciences)

Podiatric Medicine

Preventive Medicine (*see* Community Health and Public Health)

Physiological Optics (*see* Physiology)

Physiology

Plant Biology

Plant Molecular Biology

Plant Pathology

Plant Physiology

Pomology (*see* Botany; Plant Biology)

Psychiatric Nursing

Public Health—General

Public Health Nursing (*see* Community Health Nursing)

Psychiatric Nursing

Psychobiology (*see* Biopsychology)

Psychopharmacology (*see* Biopsychology; Neuroscience; Pharmacology)

Radiation Biology

Radiological Health (*see* Health Physics/Radiological Health)

Rehabilitation Nursing

Rehabilitation Sciences

Rehabilitation Therapy (*see* Physical Therapy)

Reproductive Biology

School Nursing

Sociobiology (*see* Evolutionary Biology)

Structural Biology

Surgical Nursing (*see* Medical/Surgical Nursing)

Systems Biology

Teratology

Therapeutics

Theoretical Biology (*see* Biological and Biomedical Sciences)

Therapeutics (*see* Pharmaceutical Sciences; Pharmacology; Pharmacy)

Toxicology

Transcultural Nursing

Translational Biology

Tropical Medicine (*see* Parasitology)

Veterinary Medicine

Veterinary Sciences

Virology

Vision Sciences

Wildlife Biology (*see* Zoology)

Women's Health Nursing

Zoology

Graduate Programs in the Physical Sciences, Mathematics, Agricultural Sciences, the Environment & Natural Resources

Acoustics

Agricultural Sciences

Agronomy and Soil Sciences

Analytical Chemistry

Animal Sciences

Applied Mathematics

Applied Physics

Applied Statistics

Aquaculture

Astronomy

Astrophysical Sciences (*see* Astrophysics; Atmospheric Sciences; Meteorology; Planetary and Space Sciences)

Astrophysics

Atmospheric Sciences

Biological Oceanography (*see* Marine Affairs; Marine Sciences; Oceanography)

Biomathematics

Biometry

Biostatistics

Chemical Physics

Chemistry

Computational Sciences

Condensed Matter Physics

Dairy Science (*see* Animal Sciences)

Earth Sciences (*see* Geosciences)

Environmental Management and Policy

Environmental Sciences

Environmental Studies (*see* Environmental Management and Policy)

Experimental Statistics (*see* Statistics)

Fish, Game, and Wildlife Management

Food Science and Technology

Forestry

General Science (*see* specific topics)

Geochemistry

Geodetic Sciences

Geological Engineering (*see* Geology)

Geological Sciences (*see* Geology)

Geology

Geophysical Fluid Dynamics (*see* Geophysics)

Geophysics

Geosciences

Horticulture

Hydrogeology

Hydrology

Inorganic Chemistry

Limnology

Marine Affairs

Marine Geology

Marine Sciences

Marine Studies (*see* Marine Affairs; Marine Geology; Marine Sciences; Oceanography)

Mathematical and Computational Finance

Mathematical Physics

Mathematical Statistics (*see* Applied Statistics; Statistics)

Mathematics

Meteorology

Mineralogy

Natural Resource Management (*see* Environmental Management and Policy; Natural Resources)

Natural Resources

Nuclear Physics (*see* Physics)

Ocean Engineering (*see* Marine Affairs; Marine Geology; Marine Sciences; Oceanography)

Oceanography

Optical Sciences

Optical Technologies (*see* Optical Sciences)

Optics (*see* Applied Physics; Optical Sciences; Physics)

Organic Chemistry

Paleontology
Paper Chemistry (*see* Chemistry)
Photonics
Physical Chemistry
Physics
Planetary and Space Sciences
Plant Sciences
Plasma Physics
Poultry Science (*see* Animal Sciences)
Radiological Physics (*see* Physics)
Range Management (*see* Range Science)
Range Science
Resource Management (*see* Environmental Management and Policy; Natural Resources)
Solid-Earth Sciences (*see* Geosciences)
Space Sciences (*see* Planetary and Space Sciences)
Statistics
Theoretical Chemistry
Theoretical Physics
Viticulture and Enology
Water Resources

Graduate Programs in Engineering & Applied Sciences

Aeronautical Engineering (*see* Aerospace/Aeronautical Engineering)
Aerospace/Aeronautical Engineering
Aerospace Studies (*see* Aerospace/Aeronautical Engineering)
Agricultural Engineering
Applied Mechanics (*see* Mechanics)
Applied Science and Technology
Architectural Engineering
Artificial Intelligence/Robotics
Astronautical Engineering (*see* Aerospace/Aeronautical Engineering)
Automotive Engineering
Aviation
Biochemical Engineering
Bioengineering
Bioinformatics
Biological Engineering (*see* Bioengineering)
Biomedical Engineering
Biosystems Engineering
Biotechnology
Ceramic Engineering (*see* Ceramic Sciences and Engineering)
Ceramic Sciences and Engineering
Ceramics (*see* Ceramic Sciences and Engineering)
Chemical Engineering
Civil Engineering
Computer and Information Systems Security
Computer Engineering
Computer Science
Computing Technology (*see* Computer Science)
Construction Engineering
Construction Management
Database Systems
Electrical Engineering
Electronic Materials
Electronics Engineering (*see* Electrical Engineering)
Energy and Power Engineering
Energy Management and Policy
Engineering and Applied Sciences
Engineering and Public Affairs (*see* Technology and Public Policy)
Engineering and Public Policy (*see* Energy Management and Policy; Technology and Public Policy)
Engineering Design
Engineering Management
Engineering Mechanics (*see* Mechanics)
Engineering Metallurgy (*see* Metallurgical Engineering and Metallurgy)
Engineering Physics
Environmental Design (*see* Environmental Engineering)
Environmental Engineering
Ergonomics and Human Factors
Financial Engineering

Fire Protection Engineering
Food Engineering (*see* Agricultural Engineering)
Game Design and Development
Gas Engineering (*see* Petroleum Engineering)
Geological Engineering
Geophysics Engineering (*see* Geological Engineering)
Geotechnical Engineering
Hazardous Materials Management
Health Informatics
Health Systems (*see* Safety Engineering; Systems Engineering)
Highway Engineering (*see* Transportation and Highway Engineering)
Human-Computer Interaction
Human Factors (*see* Ergonomics and Human Factors)
Hydraulics
Hydrology (*see* Water Resources Engineering)
Industrial Engineering (*see* Industrial/Management Engineering)
Industrial/Management Engineering
Information Science
Internet Engineering
Macromolecular Science (*see* Polymer Science and Engineering)
Management Engineering (*see* Engineering Management; Industrial/Management Engineering)
Management of Technology
Manufacturing Engineering
Marine Engineering (*see* Civil Engineering)
Materials Engineering
Materials Sciences
Mechanical Engineering
Mechanics
Medical Informatics
Metallurgical Engineering and Metallurgy
Metallurgy (*see* Metallurgical Engineering and Metallurgy)
Mineral/Mining Engineering
Modeling and Simulation
Nanotechnology
Nuclear Engineering
Ocean Engineering
Operations Research
Paper and Pulp Engineering
Petroleum Engineering
Pharmaceutical Engineering
Plastics Engineering (*see* Polymer Science and Engineering)
Polymer Science and Engineering
Public Policy (*see* Energy Management and Policy; Technology and Public Policy)
Reliability Engineering
Robotics (*see* Artificial Intelligence/Robotics)
Safety Engineering
Software Engineering
Solid-State Sciences (*see* Materials Sciences)
Structural Engineering
Surveying Science and Engineering
Systems Analysis (*see* Systems Engineering)
Systems Engineering
Systems Science
Technology and Public Policy
Telecommunications
Telecommunications Management
Textile Sciences and Engineering
Textiles (*see* Textile Sciences and Engineering)
Transportation and Highway Engineering
Urban Systems Engineering (*see* Systems Engineering)
Waste Management (*see* Hazardous Materials Management)
Water Resources Engineering

Graduate Programs in Business, Education, Information Studies, Law & Social Work

Accounting
Actuarial Science
Adult Education
Advertising and Public Relations
Agricultural Education
Alcohol Abuse Counseling (see Counselor Education)
Archival Management and Studies
Art Education
Athletics Administration (see Kinesiology and Movement Studies)
Athletic Training and Sports Medicine
Audiology (see Communication Disorders)
Aviation Management
Banking (see Finance and Banking)
Business Administration and Management—General
Business Education
Communication Disorders
Community College Education
Computer Education
Continuing Education (see Adult Education)
Counseling (see Counselor Education)
Counselor Education
Curriculum and Instruction
Developmental Education
Distance Education Development
Drug Abuse Counseling (see Counselor Education)
Early Childhood Education
Educational Leadership and Administration
Educational Measurement and Evaluation
Educational Media/Instructional Technology
Educational Policy
Educational Psychology
Education—General
Education of the Blind (see Special Education)
Education of the Deaf (see Special Education)
Education of the Gifted
Education of the Hearing Impaired (see Special Education)
Education of the Learning Disabled (see Special Education)
Education of the Mentally Retarded (see Special Education)
Education of the Physically Handicapped (see Special Education)
Education of Students with Severe/Multiple Disabilities
Education of the Visually Handicapped (see Special Education)
Electronic Commerce
Elementary Education
English as a Second Language
English Education
Entertainment Management
Entrepreneurship
Environmental Education
Environmental Law
Exercise and Sports Science
Exercise Physiology (see Kinesiology and Movement Studies)
Facilities and Entertainment Management
Finance and Banking
Food Services Management (see Hospitality Management)
Foreign Languages Education
Foundations and Philosophy of Education
Guidance and Counseling (see Counselor Education)
Health Education
Health Law
Hearing Sciences (see Communication Disorders)
Higher Education
Home Economics Education
Hospitality Management
Hotel Management (see Travel and Tourism)
Human Resources Development
Human Resources Management
Human Services
Industrial Administration (see Industrial and Manufacturing Management)
Industrial and Manufacturing Management

Industrial Education (see Vocational and Technical Education)
Information Studies
Instructional Technology (see Educational Media/Instructional Technology)
Insurance
Intellectual Property Law
International and Comparative Education
International Business
International Commerce (see International Business)
International Economics (see International Business)
International Trade (see International Business)
Investment and Securities (see Business Administration and Management; Finance and Banking; Investment Management)
Investment Management
Junior College Education (see Community College Education)
Kinesiology and Movement Studies
Law
Legal and Justice Studies
Leisure Services (see Recreation and Park Management)
Leisure Studies
Library Science
Logistics
Management (see Business Administration and Management)
Management Information Systems
Management Strategy and Policy
Marketing
Marketing Research
Mathematics Education
Middle School Education
Movement Studies (see Kinesiology and Movement Studies)
Multilingual and Multicultural Education
Museum Education
Music Education
Nonprofit Management
Nursery School Education (see Early Childhood Education)
Occupational Education (see Vocational and Technical Education)
Organizational Behavior
Organizational Management
Parks Administration (see Recreation and Park Management)
Personnel (see Human Resources Development; Human Resources Management; Organizational Behavior; Organizational Management; Student Affairs)
Philosophy of Education (see Foundations and Philosophy of Education)
Physical Education
Project Management
Public Relations (see Advertising and Public Relations)
Quality Management
Quantitative Analysis
Reading Education
Real Estate
Recreation and Park Management
Recreation Therapy (see Recreation and Park Management)
Religious Education
Remedial Education (see Special Education)
Restaurant Administration (see Hospitality Management)
Science Education
Secondary Education
Social Sciences Education
Social Studies Education (see Social Sciences Education)
Social Work
Special Education
Speech-Language Pathology and Audiology (see Communication Disorders)
Sports Management
Sports Medicine (see Athletic Training and Sports Medicine)
Sports Psychology and Sociology (see Kinesiology and Movement Studies)
Student Affairs
Substance Abuse Counseling (see Counselor Education)
Supply Chain Management
Sustainability Management
Systems Management (see Management Information Systems)
Taxation
Teacher Education (see specific subject areas)

Teaching English as a Second Language (*see* English as a Second Language)
Technical Education (*see* Vocational and Technical Education)
Transportation Management
Travel and Tourism
Urban Education
Vocational and Technical Education
Vocational Counseling (*see* Counselor Education)

Directories and Subject Areas in This Book

NOTES

NOTES